U.S. Army register (Volume II) Re Jaunary 1968

Unknown

Alpha Editions

This edition published in 2020

ISBN: 9789354029011

Design and Setting By
Alpha Editions
email - alphaedis@gmail.com

90th Congress, 2d Session - - - - - - - - - - - - House Document No. 235

DEPARTMENT OF THE ARMY

WASHINGTON, D.C.

U.S. ARMY REGISTER

VOLUME III

RETIRED LISTS

1 January 1968

Published by order of the SECRETARY OF THE ARMY

U.S. GOVERNMENT PRINTING OFFICE
WASHINGTON : 1968

For sale by the Superintendent of Documents, U.S. Government Printing Office
Washington, D.C. 20402 - Price $2.50

Distribution:

Active Army:

DCSLOG (2)
VCofS (2)
USASA (8)
ACSI (2)
DCSPER (2)
OPO (140)
CORC (5)
TJAG (2)
TIG (2)
CNGB (2)
CAR (2)
COA (2)
CMH (3)
CofCh (2)
TPMG (2)
CINFO (2)
CRD (2)
TSG (3)
CofEngrs (2)
Dir of Trans (2)
ACSC-E (2)
CofSptS (12)
TAG (2)
USCONARC (2)
USACDC (24)
USAMC (5)
USAECOM (13)
ARADCOM (1)
ARADCOM Rgn (1)
OS Maj Comd (2) except
  USARHAW (3)
  USARPAC (12)
MDW (2)
Armies (2) except
  1st USA (4)
  4th USA (3)
  6th USA (4)
Corps (2)
Div (1)
Bde (1)
500th MI Gp (1)
Ft Hood (1)
Ft Riley (1)
Ft Bliss (1)
Ft Leavenworth (1)
Ft Sheridan (1)
Ft McClellan (1)
Ft Wolters (1)
Ft Lewis (1)
Ft Carson (1)
Ft MacArthur (1)
Ft Douglas (1)
Ft Gordon (1)
Ft Lee (1)
Ft Hamilton (1)
Ft Niagara (1)
Ft Meade (1)
Ft Sam Houston (1)
Ft Leonard Wood (1)
Ft Slocum (1)
Ft Devens (1)
Ft Wadsworth (1)
Ft Williams (1)
Presidio of San Francisco (1)
AHS (1)
CAMSTA (1)
Boston Army Base (1)
Vint Hill Farms (1)
Army Tml (1)
CAMTMTS (1)
EAMTMTS (1)
WAMTMTS (1)
POE (1)
Arsenals (1)
Lab (1)
GENDEP (OS) (1)
Sup Sec GENDEP (OS) (1)
Army Dep (1)
Dep (OS) (1)
PG (1)
GH (1)
Army Hosp (1)
Centers (1)
DCA (5)
USACGSC (1)
USMA (5)
USAWC (19)
Br Svc Sch (1)
Specialist Sch (1)
Joint Sch (1)
FAOUSA (1)
USAC (1) except
  XVI USAC (12)
TIOH, USA (1)
JBUSMC (1)
MAAG (1)
Mil Msn (1)
Units organized under following TOE's: 12-510 (1)
EACH GENERAL OFFICER ON THE REGULAR ARMY RETIRED LIST (1)

NG: State AG (1).
USAR: None.
For explanation of abbreviations used, see AR 320-50.

TABLE OF CONTENTS

EXPLANATORY NOTES

SOURCE OF DATA: All data is as of 31 December 1967 and was extracted from Retired Personnel Master Tape Record maintained by U.S. Army Data Support Command, Department of the Army, Washington, D.C. 20310.

NAMES: Names appearing in the Register are limited to twenty spaces Due to these space limitations, names appear in truncated form as entered on the Retired Personnel Master Tape Record rather than reduced to abbreviations or initials.

RETIREMENT LISTINGS: Upon Retirement from the Army, members are placed on one of the following Retired Lists. An explanation of the composition of these lists is included in the section divider page prefacing the appropriate retirement listing.

United States Army Retired List
Army of the United States Retired List
Temporary Disability Retired List
Emergency Officers Retired List

PREPARATION OF IDENTIFICATION CARDS: Detailed instructions for the preparation of DD Form 2A (Ret) (gray) (Identification Card) for retired members are contained in section IV, AR 606-5.

ERRORS AND OMISSIONS: Errors in and/or omissions from the Retired Lists will be reported to The Adjutant General, ATTN: AGPF-FC, Department of the Army, Washington, D.C. 20310.

RETIREMENT CODES

CODE	EXPLANATION
1	Retired or granted retired pay for any reason, except those retired for, or granted retired pay for disability and those granted retired pay under title 10, USC, Section 1331 (formerly Title III Act of 29 June 1948).
2	Retired for, or granted retired pay for permanent disability.
3	Granted retired pay under Title 10, USC, Section 1331 (formerly Title III, Act of 29 June 1948).

SECTION 1

UNITED STATES ARMY RETIRED LIST

The United States Army Retired List is composed of Regular Army commissioned officers and warrant officers retired under any provision of law for service, age or permanent disability.

UNITED STATES ARMY RETIRED LIST

NAME	GRADE	SVC NO	DATE RET MO YR	RET CODE
AABEL BERNARD	COL	0-0029239	0662	1
AARON ALTON E	CW4	W-0902686	0762	1
AARON MARGARET E	LTC	N-0000505	0450	1
ABBOTT DONALD I	CPT	0-0060517	1162	1
ABBOTT ELENOR P	LTC	L-0000315	0355	1
ABBOTT LYSLE I	COL	0-0034559	0862	1
ABBOTT OSCAR B	B G	0-0005748	1050	1
ABBOTT STANLEY B	LTC	0-0091730	1065	1
ABBOTT WILLIAM L	LTC	0-0038881	1061	1
ABELL JULIAN D	COL	0-0018666	0862	1
ABER JOHN E	COL	0-0023097	0363	1
ABERCROMBIE JAY A	COL	0-0020604	0859	1
ABERT GEORGE C	COL	0-0021337	0966	2
ABRAMOSKA HELEN M	LTC	N-0001878	0961	1
ABRAMS BERNARD H	CPT	0-0050736	1052	1
ABRAMS GEORGE E	LTC	0-0006962	0841	1
ABSTON AARON A	LTC	0-0071391	1058	1
ABT ALAN B	COL	0-0060323	1167	1
ACHORN ERIK	1LT	0-0014396	1019	2
ACKERMAN STEPHEN W	COL	0-0015708	0752	1
ACKERSON DUANE H	COL	0-0045068	0666	1
ACKERT THOMAS W	COL	0-0032005	0764	1
ACKLEY CHARLES M	LTC	0-0039397	0661	1
ACKRIDGE LENORE W	CPT	L-0000616	0450	2
ACTON LLOYD P	COL	0-0042467	1264	1
ADAIR ALEXANDRIA	COL	0-0007308	0552	1
ADAIR GEORGE T	COL	0-0051901	0767	1
ADAIR HUGH C	COL	0-0007452	0551	1
ADAIR PHINEAS H	2LT	0-0014588	0133	2
ADAMS ALICE I	MAJ	L-0000352	0266	2
ADAMS ANDREW J	M G	0-0018579	0667	1
ADAMS ARVEL T	CW4	W-0902690	0661	1
ADAMS BILLY J	COL	0-0059933	0865	1
ADAMS BURTON R	CW4	W-0902691	0363	1
ADAMS CARL R	COL	0-0005703	0848	1
ADAMS CRUEE L	CW4	W-0902692	0765	1
ADAMS DALE W	CW4	W-0902693	1065	1
ADAMS DEXTER W	LTC	0-0062247	0467	1
ADAMS DONALD L	COL	0-0031339	1066	1
ADAMS DUVAL S	COL	0-0042997	0864	1
ADAMS EDWARD F	COL	0-0015326	0954	1
ADAMS EDWARD P	CW4	W-0902694	1054	1
ADAMS EMORY S	M G	0-0001731	0242	1
ADAMS ERNEST C	COL	0-0020933	0466	2
ADAMS FRANK	COL	0-0051184	1060	1
ADAMS FREDERICK	COL	0-0007964	0848	1
ADAMS GEORGE E	LTC	0-0019412	0758	1
ADAMS GERARD C	COL	0-0044819	0866	1
ADAMS GILBERT N	COL	0-0018737	1062	1
ADAMS HAROLD D	LTC	0-0037281	0667	1
ADAMS HARRY J	COL	0-0043191	0866	1
ADAMS HELEN	CPT	N-0000049	1048	1
ADAMS HOBERT D	LTC	0-0079723	0466	1
ADAMS JAMES A	CW3	W-0904077	0963	1
ADAMS JAMES F	COL	0-0029968	0763	1
ADAMS JAMES Y	COL	0-0019755	0563	1
ADAMS JOHN F	COL	0-0028985	0758	1
ADAMS JOSEPH T	LTC	0-0027529	1066	1
ADAMS JR CHARLES M	COL	0-0012789	0954	1
ADAMS JR EMORY S	COL	0-0023235	0864	1
ADAMS JR JONATHAN E	LTC	0-0023833	0162	1
ADAMS L DOW	COL	0-0021203	0653	1
ADAMS LAWRENCE W	COL	0-0038608	0856	1
ADAMS LESLIE I	CW4	W-0906595	1059	1
ADAMS LUDLOW C	COL	0-0029337	0957	2
ADAMS MARCUS W	COL	0-0040025	0666	1
ADAMS NYAL	COL	0-0007471	0249	2
ADAMS PAUL D	GEN	0-0017306	1166	1
ADAMS PERCY	CPT	0-0007744	0934	1
ADAMS RAY	COL	0-0051010	1158	1
ADAMS RELLIE W	COL	0-0042663	1165	1
ADAMS ROBERT H	M G	0-0019474	0766	2
ADAMS ROWLAND C	LTC	0-0076783	0664	1
ADAMS SAMUEL J	COL	0-0012583	0354	1
ADAMS WILLIAM	LTC	0-0042631	0963	1

NAME	GRADE	SVC NO	DATE RET MO YR	RET CODE
ADAMSON DAVID V	LTC	0-0019096	0653	1
ADAMSON KEITH F	COL	0-0003640	0544	1
ADAMSON KENNETH F	COL	0-0083575	1066	1
ADDINGTON FRANK T	COL	0-0008081	0447	1
ADDISON HATTILU W	LTC	L-0000025	0958	1
ADDISON JOHN K	COL	0-0064547	1265	1
ADDISON WILLIAM A	COL	0-0060111	0864	1
ADKINS ERNEST C	COL	0-0008212	1052	1
ADKINS JR JOHN F	COL	0-0015273	0851	1
ADLER CARL J	COL	0-0003429	1141	1
ADLER CHARLES S	LTC	0-0027179	0866	1
ADLER EUGENE T	LTC	0-0029549	0754	1
ADLER GEORGE	LTC	0-0081939	0466	1
AEBISCHER LOUIS J	LTC	0-0032384	0867	1
AGERS ROBERT D	LTC	0-0040905	0566	1
AGNEW PIERRE A	LTC	0-0009320	1042	2
AGNEW RICHARD H	COL	0-0019958	0544	2
AGOA JOHN J	COL	0-0042205	0763	1
AGRESTA FRANCIS J	CW3	RW-0902696	0163	1
AGUGLIA JOHN R	LTC	0-0033477	0757	1
AHALT HENRY C	COL	0-0028886	1056	1
AHEARN WALTER E	LTC	0-0018249	0557	1
AHEE JOE	COL	0-0022215	0365	1
AHERN JOHN R	LTC	0-0059918	0466	1
AHERN JOSEPH R	COL	0-0023881	0862	1
AHERN LEO J	B G	0-0002587	0946	1
AHLGREN FREDERIC F	LTC	0-0033566	0561	1
AHNFELDT ARNOLD L	COL	0-0021018	0567	1
AHRENS AMBELTIN M	LTC	0-0030026	1061	2
AIKEN ANDREW M	MAJ	L-0000328	0263	1
AIN MILTON	1LT	0-0068858	0159	2
AINES ANDREW A	COL	0-0043463	0467	1
AKANS JAMES E	LTC	0-0039893	0462	1
AKERMAN AMOS T	COL	0-0014060	0655	1
AKERS ELWYN A	LTC	0-0024379	0557	2
AKERS JR RUSSELL F	COL	0-0019243	0461	2
AKERS NORMAN L	COL	0-0051673	1265	1
AKIN SPENCER B	M G	0-0002916	0351	1
AKINS THOMAS W	COL	0-0040076	0167	1
ALBA BIENVENIDO	LTC	0-0016939	0855	2
ALBAN PAUL F	LTC	0-0023500	0661	1
ALBAUGH CORNELIUS	COL	0-0040268	1262	1
ALBERGOTTI JULIAN S	COL	0-0039601	0159	1
ALBERGOTTI WILLIAM M	COL	0-0028883	1056	1
ALBERT BROOKE	CPT	0-0027944	0853	1
ALBERT JOSEPH L	COL	0-0040344	1161	1
ALBERT PAUL W	COL	0-0042507	0165	1
ALBERTIE EDWARD J	LTC	0-0040007	1263	1
ALBIN JOHN R	COL	0-0051296	0262	1
ALBRECHT ALBERT W	LTC	0-0031558	0460	2
ALBRECHT FRANK M	M G	0-0015131	0660	1
ALBRECHT JR EDWIN F	MAJ	0-0067631	0967	1
ALBRECHT LAWRENCE S	COL	0-0049537	0767	1
ALBRIGHT ARNOLD A	COL	0-0018273	0954	1
ALBRIGHT JOHN J	COL	0-0007305	0748	2
ALBRIGHT ROY L	CW4	RW-0902158	0661	1
ALBRIGHT SHANNON D	LTC	0-0040787	0863	1
ALBRO JOHN N	LTC	0-0040217	0763	1
ALBRO ROBERT D	COL	0-0031360	1166	1
ALCORN JAMES P	COL	0-0044844	0666	1
ALDENDERFER JR E W	CPT	0-0069581	0258	2
ALDRICH EDWIN N	CPT	0-0026890	0248	2
ALDRICH HARRY S	COL	0-0014847	0948	2
ALDRICH MYRTLE	MAJ	R-0010003	0754	1
ALDRIDGE THOMAS C	MAJ	0-0058807	0864	1
ALDRUP EARL W	COL	0-0015972	0854	2
ALENIUS ESKIL M J	COL	0-0041452	0357	1
ALEXANDER BERTIE C	MAJ	N-0002395	0662	1
ALEXANDER BOWAN P	COL	0-0042975	0367	1
ALEXANDER DANA S	COL	0-0018114	1046	2
ALEXANDER DAVID B	LTC	0-0059556	1065	1
ALEXANDER DONALD O	LTC	0-0028789	0753	1
ALEXANDER DOUGLAS G	LTC	0-0032927	1065	1
ALEXANDER FRANK O	COL	0-0019607	0763	1
ALEXANDER FREDRICK B	COL	0-0041949	1061	2

NAME	GRADE	SVC NO	DATE RET MO YR	RET CODE
ALEXANDER GEORGE W	LTC	0-0034143	0962	1
ALEXANDER HENRY B	COL	0-0030565	1163	1
ALEXANDER HENRY M	CPT	0-0011185	0335	2
ALEXANDER JOSEPH B	COL	0-0050959	0957	1
ALEXANDER JR DAVID C	COL	0-0039901	0564	1
ALEXANDER JR L G	COL	0-0031058	0759	1
ALEXANDER LAWRENCE H	LTC	0-0051731	0264	1
ALEXANDER MOSES	COL	0-0011821	1146	1
ALEXANDER RALPH H	LTC	0-0050373	1066	1
ALEXANDER ROBERT F	COL	0-0041912	0961	1
ALEXANDER ROBERT W	LTC	0-0040280	1058	1
ALEXANDER SAMUEL H	COL	0-0017830	0859	1
ALEXANDER WILLIAM	COL	0-0004632	1052	1
ALFANO CHARLES F	COL	0-0025640	1266	1
ALFONTE DALLAS P	COL	0-0005441	0146	2
ALFONTE JAMES M	LTC	0-0027562	0966	1
ALFORD JOHN C	LTC	0-0018838	0664	2
ALFORD TRUMAN	LTC	0-0030765	0160	1
ALFRED LEE L	COL	0-0029068	0161	1
ALFREY JOHN	COL	0-0019859	0965	1
ALLAN CHARLES C	COL	0-0017671	0759	1
ALLARD HENRY W	LTC	0-0029747	0950	1
ALLBEE ROGER H	COL	0-0019299	0157	1
ALLBRIGHT JAMES L	MAJ	0-0005744	0-34	2
ALLBRIGHT MARION C	LTC	0-0063678	0166	1
ALLCORN FORD E	COL	0-0081544	0761	1
ALLEBACH CORA L	MAJ	N-0002175	0664	1
ALLEN BEN F	COL	0-0032103	1167	1
ALLEN CHARLES A	COL	0-0018677	0862	1
ALLEN CHESTER F	COL	0-0030060	1262	1
ALLEN GERTRUDE F	MAJ	N-0000251	0560	1
ALLEN GLENN L	COL	0-0005614	0849	1
ALLEN HARLOW E	COL	0-0039922	0964	1
ALLEN HARRY B	COL	0-0006465	0842	1
ALLEN HENRY T	COL	0-0008015	0446	2
ALLEN HUGH E	LTC	0-0043348	1065	1
ALLEN IRVIN L	B G	0-0029810	0265	1
ALLEN JAMES F	COL	0-0029024	0359	1
ALLEN JAMES F	LTC	0-0049955	1166	1
ALLEN JOHN K	MAJ	0-0020978	0345	2
ALLEN JOHN U	COL	0-0020889	0861	1
ALLEN JR ARTHUR W	COL	0-0022034	1063	2
ALLEN JR FRANK A	M G	0-0007415	1156	1
ALLEN JR GILBERT W	MAJ	0-0016912	0348	1
ALLEN JR GLENN L	LTC	0-0084593	0967	1
ALLEN JR ROBERT L	COL	0-0010846	0753	1
ALLEN JR WILLIAM H	COL	0-0018053	0660	1
ALLEN JR WILLIAM J	COL	0-0029725	0961	1
ALLEN LEVEN C	M G	0-0004760	1051	1
ALLEN MARTHA D	MAJ	L-0000235	1159	1
ALLEN MEREDITH E	LTC	0-0021408	0263	1
ALLEN OLLIE J	LTC	0-0032085	0660	1
ALLEN RICHARD H	LTC	0-0050603	0967	1
ALLEN RODERICK R	M G	0-0004652	0554	1
ALLEN TERRY DE L	M G	0-0003481	0846	2
ALLEN THOMAS H	COL	0-0015865	0754	1
ALLEN VIRGIL G	COL	0-0011126	0350	1
ALLEN WILLIAM M	LTC	0-0080369	0967	1
ALLERTON WILLIAM S	LTC	0-0059713	1067	1
ALLEY EDWARD C	COL	0-0005966	0947	2
ALLEY STUART M	COL	0-0030268	1162	1
ALLGAIR JOHN A	LTC	0-0020947	0958	1
ALLGEIER ROBERT M	COL	0-0042822	1255	1
ALLISON AARON F	COL	0-0031016	1167	2
ALLISON DANIEL W	COL	0-0029071	0559	2
ALLISON HASKELL	COL	0-0007529	1046	2
ALLISON PHILIP W	COL	0-0010434	0446	1
ALLISON WALLACE M	COL	0-0010467	0848	1
ALLISON WENDELL G	CPT	0-0026657	0747	2
ALLISON WILLIAM A	LTC	0-0060176	0864	1
ALLMENDINGER VIVIAN	MAJ	N-0000052	0349	1
ALLRED WAYNE	LTC	0-0084584	0967	1
ALLRED WILLIAM H	LTC	0-0058809	0766	1
ALM NINA	MAJ	N-0002227	0459	1
ALMAN CASPER	1LT	0-0011564	1022	2

NAME	GRADE	SVC NO	DATE RET MO YR	RET CODE
ALMOND EDWARD M	LTG	0-0004666	0153	1
ALMOND HUGH H	LTC	0-0081943	0667	1
ALOE ROBERT C	B G	0-0016916	0657	1
ALPHIN HORACE E	COL	0-0043324	0967	1
ALSPACH RUSSELL X	B G	0-0050879	0365	1
ALSPAUGH RALPH	COL	0-0019159	0863	1
ALTEEN LEE F	CW2	W-0901477	0847	1
ALTENHOFEN MATTHEW J	LTC	0-0021054	0858	1
ALTFATHER ELLIS M	COL	0-0017816	0759	1
ALTFILISH ROMAINE S	CW4	W-0906595	0567	1
ALTHAUS KENNETH G	B G	0-0006208	0346	2
ALVAREZ THEODORE P	CPT	0-0060787	1061	1
ALVEY THOMAS W	LTC	0-0032698	0261	1
AMAZEEN CHARLES P	COL	0-0012817	0553	1
AMBRON TYRUS R	LTC	0-0032215	0467	1
AMBROSE DON C	CPT	0-0062179	0462	1
AMBROSE FORREST E	COL	0-0007974	1146	2
AMBROSE JOSEPH P	CW4	RW-0902672	0462	1
AMEND REBECCA V	MAJ	N-0002417	0464	1
AMES JOHN R	LTC	0-0001505	1022	1
AMES KENNETH L	COL	0-0030864	0765	1
AMICK ELLIOTT H	COL	0-0021153	0647	2
AMIS GILBERT H	MAJ	0-0038394	0761	1
AMIS LEWIS W	LTC	0-0005212	0342	2
AMIZICH AMELIA D	LTC	M-0010029	1265	1
AMLONG RANSOM G	COL	0-0015094	0753	1
AMMENWERTH BENJAMIN	LTC	0-0061963	0766	1
AMMERMAN JAMES F	B G	0-0018165	0760	1
AMMON JOHN R	CW4	W-0902708	0863	1
AMMONS BENJAMIN T	COL	0-0038652	0661	1
AMOROSE ARNOLD D	COL	0-0010777	0753	1
AMOROSE LEONARD	COL	0-0030076	0164	1
AMORY HAROLD I	COL	0-0019319	1054	2
AMOS ARTHUR K	COL	0-0020822	0665	1
ANCKER CLINTON J	CPT	0-0011145	0934	2
ANCRUM JAMES N	COL	0-0011061	0250	1
ANDERSEN ELDON B	LTC	0-0035991	1264	1
ANDERSEN HAL P	COL	0-0039920	0964	1
ANDERSEN HERMAN S	LTC	0-0031265	0866	1
ANDERSEN JR ANDREW M	LTC	0-0081945	0467	1
ANDERSEN TOWNSEND C	COL	0-0030195	0664	1
ANDERSLAND LOUISE S	MAJ	J-0000061	0563	1
ANDERSON ALFRED G	MAJ	0-0011153	0627	2
ANDERSON ALFRED H	COL	0-0028805	0555	1
ANDERSON ANNA G	LTC	N-0000498	0548	1
ANDERSON ARTHUR J	COL	0-0033741	0162	1
ANDERSON B CONN	COL	0-0007828	0945	2
ANDERSON BERRY K	COL	0-0030384	0465	1
ANDERSON BLAINE E	COL	0-0038976	0366	2
ANDERSON BRUCE C	CW4	W-0902709	0457	1
ANDERSON CARL A	MAJ	0-0050386	1061	1
ANDERSON CARL E	COL	0-0015395	0251	1
ANDERSON CHARLES H	COL	0-0021072	1066	1
ANDERSON CHESTER H	COL	0-0030096	0164	1
ANDERSON CLARENCE L	LTC	0-0061069	0866	1
ANDERSON DAGNY V J	MAJ	N-0001948	0558	1
ANDERSON DAVID L	COL	0-0025223	0167	1
ANDERSON DAVID M	LTC	0-0080538	0263	1
ANDERSON DELMER P	COL	0-0029965	0763	1
ANDERSON ELSIE	MAJ	N-0001943	0558	1
ANDERSON ETHEL M	MAJ	N-0000548	0954	1
ANDERSON FRANCIS W	COL	0-0030354	0165	1
ANDERSON FREE G	LTC	0-0038473	0966	1
ANDERSON GEORGE B	COL	0-0014620	0753	1
ANDERSON GEORGE K	LTC	0-0036057	0764	1
ANDERSON GEORGE L	LTC	0-0031762	0163	1
ANDERSON GEORGE N	COL	0-0051329	0263	1
ANDERSON GLEN H	COL	0-0008632	0946	2
ANDERSON GORDON V	LTC	0-0047345	1164	1
ANDERSON GRANGER	COL	0-0014931	1051	1
ANDERSON GUSTAV A V	COL	0-0005685	0651	1
ANDERSON JAMES P	COL	0-000500-	0247	2
ANDERSON JOHN B	M G	0-0003686	0646	2
ANDERSON JOHN H	COL	0-0019398	0155	1
ANDERSON JONATHAN W	M G	0-0003196	0650	1

NAME	GRADE	SVC NO	DATE RET MO YR	RET CODE
ANDERSON JOSEPH C	COL	O-0019884	0962	1
ANDERSON KENNETH S	COL	O-0008365	0854	2
ANDERSON LEWIS W	COL	O-0050904	0855	1
ANDERSON MILDRED J	LTC	M-0010026	0966	1
ANDERSON NORMAN A	COL	O-0031483	0861	1
ANDERSON ORVIE P	COL	O-0042727	0766	2
ANDERSON RALPH C	LTC	O-0054269	0864	1
ANDERSON RICHARD E	COL	O-0003361	0831	2
ANDERSON RICHARD F	LTC	O-0083576	0767	1
ANDERSON ROBERT I	LTC	O-0056990	0665	1
ANDERSON ROBERT N	COL	O-0021436	0666	2
ANDERSON ROBERT V	LTC	O-0067548	0767	1
ANDERSON TRUETT C	COL	O-0038804	1164	1
ANDERSON VIRGINIA W	LTC	N-0000372	0366	1
ANDERSON WEBSTER	M G	O-0017101	0765	1
ANDERSON WILBER K	COL	O-0043126	0866	1
ANDERSON WILLIAM H	COL	O-0056864	0164	1
ANDERSON WOODROW W	COL	O-0040220	0661	1
ANDERSSON KINGSLEY	COL	O-0015450	0954	2
ANDERTON EDWARD C	LTC	O-0061094	1167	1
ANDING JAMES G	COL	O-0015677	0654	1
ANDINO EDUARDO	COL	O-0009820	1049	1
ANDINO JOSE A	COL	O-0024575	0766	1
ANDRAE HERBERT H	COL	O-0019546	0860	1
ANDRESON PAUL S	COL	O-0030962	0761	1
ANDREWS CHARLES L	COL	O-0019363	0863	1
ANDREWS FRANK W	LTC	O-0020843	1144	2
ANDREWS JOHN A	COL	O-0007621	0651	1
ANDREWS JR JAMES D	COL	O-0007884	0546	2
ANDREWS OMAR K	LTC	O-0019702	1150	1
ANDREWS REXFORD W	MAJ	O-0017756	0246	1
ANDREWS ROBERT J	LTC	O-0063759	0767	1
ANDRICK EDWIN L	COL	O-0042134	0263	1
ANDRUS BURTON C	COL	O-0006991	0452	1
ANDRUS CLIFT	M G	O-0003268	1052	1
ANDRUSS MALCOLM P	COL	O-0001726	0735	2
ANGEN WILLARD F	COL	O-0023596	0263	2
ANGERS DALE A	MAJ	L-0000101	1163	1
ANGLIN WILLIAM F	LTC	O-0031464	0861	1
ANGLUIN DAVID X	COL	O-0017717	0146	2
ANGSTER ROBERT C	COL	O-0032124	0266	1
ANKROM URA M	MAJ	L-0000207	0155	1
ANNIN ROBERT D	COL	O-0003623	0650	1
ANSEL STURE A	COL	O-0030554	1065	1
ANSLOW RALPH O	LTC	O-0031093	0861	1
ANSON PAUL A	COL	O-0031400	0765	1
ANTHONY ALVIN C	COL	O-0008752	1146	2
ANTLEY HAMPTON L	LTC	O-0031107	0756	1
ANTRIM HAROLD F	LTC	O-0033793	0767	1
ANTRIM JR RALPH C	LTC	O-0065170	0867	1
APGAR THEODORE B	COL	O-0005556	1146	2
APPEL EDWARD J	CPT	O-0060846	1264	1
APPLEGATE EDWARD C	MAJ	O-0014631	0938	2
APPLEGATE REX	LTC	O-0024589	0945	2
ARACK GEORGE	LTC	O-0023588	0746	2
ARCHER HARVEY E	COL	O-0031170	0862	1
ARCHER THEODORE W	COL	O-0048383	0367	1
ARCHIBALD HAROLD G	COL	O-0007561	0847	1
ARCHIBALD HERBERT P	COL	O-0029776	0762	1
ARDREY JOHN E	COL	O-0003579	0149	1
ARENAN JOHN F	COL	O-0042802	1163	1
ARIMA JAMES K	LTC	O-0080280	0166	1
ARLEN EDWARD L	CW4	W-0902719	1057	2
ARMES HERBERT R	CW3	W-0902716	1162	1
ARMITAGE JOHN D	COL	O-0019014	0259	1
ARMOGIDA SALVATORE	COL	O-0019741	0865	1
ARMOR JR MARSHALL H	LTC	O-0045590	0662	1
ARMS JR THOMAS S	LTC	O-0024996	0863	1
ARMS THOMAS S	B G	O-0004729	0946	2
ARMSTRONG ARMOUR S	COL	O-0044372	1166	1
ARMSTRONG CHARLES A	COL	O-0021375	0358	1
ARMSTRONG CHARLES R	1LT	O-0061601	0256	2
ARMSTRONG CLARE H	B G	O-0005318	0353	1
ARMSTRONG DEVERE P	COL	O-0017533	0759	1
ARMSTRONG DONALD	B G	O-0002967	1046	1
ARMSTRONG DONALD K	COL	O-0018578	1058	1
ARMSTRONG EDWARD B	LTC	O-0032267	0864	1
ARMSTRONG ELBERT	LTC	O-0051677	1163	1
ARMSTRONG ELMER J	COL	O-0006869	0-37	1
ARMSTRONG FRANCIS T	COL	O-0003444	1046	1
ARMSTRONG FRANK H	LTC	O-0060273	0766	1
ARMSTRONG FREDERICK	COL	O-0002690	0344	1
ARMSTRONG GEORGE F	M G	O-0016548	0755	1
ARMSTRONG JOHN L	LTC	O-0028469	1167	1
ARMSTRONG JOHN R	LTC	O-0065159	0765	1
ARMSTRONG LESTER K	CW2	W-0906601	0655	1
ARMSTRONG LEWIS R	CPT	O-0011558	0934	2
ARMSTRONG MARVIL G	COL	O-0005313	0753	1
ARMSTRONG NEMESIO A	LTC	O-0059898	1262	1
ARN ROBERT F	COL	O-0023470	0664	1
ARN ROBERT M	LTC	O-0048366	0661	1
ARNEMAN GEORGE F	COL	O-0003271	0-45	2
ARNEST RICHARD T	COL	O-0006551	1047	1
ARNETT THOMAS M	LTC	O-0020566	1047	1
ARNETT VERN R	MAJ	O-0060369	0865	1
ARNOLD ALTON V	COL	O-0041858	0361	1
ARNOLD ARCHIBALD	M G	O-0003395	0548	2
ARNOLD B D	CW3	W-0902718	0562	1
ARNOLD BERTHA G	MAJ	N-0001492	0567	1
ARNOLD BRYAN C	LTC	O-0020801	0758	1
ARNOLD EDGAR L	COL	O-0031902	0267	1
ARNOLD LESLIE A	COL	O-0030819	1066	2
ARNOLD LUTHER D	LTC	O-0022946	0964	1
ARNOLD RHODES F	COL	O-0005160	0753	2
ARNOLD RICHARD J	LTC	O-0058816	0166	1
ARNOLD ROBERT E	MAJ	O-0028313	0563	2
ARNOLD WILLIAM H	LTG	O-0015559	0261	2
ARONSON ROLAND S	COL	O-0025206	0661	1
ARP DAVID H	COL	O-0031445	0267	1
ARROWSMITH JOHN C	B G	O-0011373	0553	1
ARSENAULT HUBERT J	LTC	O-0044917	0262	1
ARTHUR FRANK M	COL	O-0032290	1163	1
ARTHUR JOHN E	COL	O-0032461	0366	1
ARTHUR JOSEPH N	MAJ	O-0009759	0622	2
ARTHUR JR JOHN F	COL	O-0024457	0767	1
ARTHUR ROBERT	COL	O-0002226	0246	2
ARTHUR ROBERT F	LTC	O-0040968	1164	1
ARTISS KENNETH L	LTC	O-0657944	0864	1
ARTMAN ETHEL M	MAJ	N-0002244	0456	2
ARTMAN RALPH T	COL	O-0021023	0558	1
ARTZ CURTIS R	LTC	O-0057825	0856	2
ARTZ ELIZABETH	MAJ	N-0000264	0762	1
ARVIN CHARLES R	LTC	O-0083577	0666	1
ARVIN PAUL D	COL	O-0080360	0867	1
ARZOLA ASDRUBAL	LTC	O-0067785	1164	1
ASCHOFF JR JOHN F	LTC	O-0037856	0467	1
ASELTINE THOMAS H	MAJ	O-0088326	0166	2
ASH ALVIN	LTC	O-0028539	0165	1
ASH JAMES E	COL	O-0004037	0247	2
ASH LAURENCE W	LTC	O-0054165	0464	1
ASHBRIDGE DONALD M	COL	O-0002555	0934	2
ASHBY DE GRAY H	B G	O-0003276	0147	2
ASHBY JR CLAUDE T	MAJ	O-0084846	0867	1
ASHBY JR RAYMOND C	COL	O-0043320	1067	1
ASHCRAFT JAMES H	LTC	O-0051658	1063	1
ASHENFELDER WILLIAM	COL	O-0040008	0764	1
ASHER OWEN S	CW4	W-0902721	1162	1
ASHFORD ALEXANDER	LTC	O-0061183	1265	1
ASHLEY MERLE W	MAJ	O-0080036	0863	1
ASHMAN ALFRED	COL	O-0019846	0764	1
ASHTON DONALD M	COL	O-0014825	0753	1
ASHWORTH EDWARD T	COL	O-0019052	0763	2
ASKINS CHARLES	COL	O-0029852	0163	1
ASLESON ELEANOR R	LTC	N-0000056	1157	1
ASTOR RAYMOND J	LTC	O-005011	0266	1
ASTRELLA THEODORE F	COL	O-0042656	0266	1
ASTROSKY ANNA B	MAJ	N-0002501	0967	1
ATCHISON FRANK E	LTC	O-0058817	0766	1
ATHAN BYRON D	LTC	O-0053237	0764	1
ATKINS EDWIN L	COL	O-0030809	0862	2
ATKINS JAMES L	LTC	O-0039409	1064	1
ATKINS JR HERBERT R	CW4	W-0902722	1067	1
ATKINS JR NEILL S	LTC	O-0042815	0764	1
ATKINSON CHARLES F	COL	O-0006737	0246	2
ATKINSON EDWARD C	COL	O-0010131	0547	2
ATKINSON FREDERICK	B G	O-0018169	0760	1
ATKINSON JAMES W	CW4	W-0902723	0464	1
ATKINSON POLK J	COL	O-0010259	0753	1
ATLAS REYNOLD A	MAJ	O-0031894	0458	1
ATTAWAY ELMER J	COL	O-0040321	1262	1
ATWELL CLYDE L	WO1	W-0800724	1036	1
ATWELL RICHARD N	COL	O-0007293	0246	1
ATWOOD DOROTHY M	MAJ	N-0002144	0861	1
ATWOOD FRANK J	COL	O-0004686	0346	2
ATWOOD GEORGE L	COL	O-0039750	0261	2
ATWOOD JR WILL G	LTC	O-0025067	0961	1
AUBREY GEORGE A	COL	O-0023110	1265	1
AUDERER SAM	CW4	W-0902725	0561	1
AUDET CHARLES W	LTC	O-0052899	0861	1
AUERBACH ALVIN R	LTC	O-0020547	0758	1
AUGSBURGER RUSSELL H	COL	O-0024376	1066	1
AUGUR WAYLAND B	B G	O-0006659	0753	1
AUGUSTIN GEORGE A	CW4	W-0906606	1262	1
AUKBURGH RUTH O	1LT	M-0002024	0247	1
AURAND HENRY S	LTG	O-0003784	0852	1
AUSMUS DELBERT	COL	O-0007898	0846	1
AUSTIN CHARLES F	COL	O-0045239	0866	1
AUSTIN EDWARD A	COL	O-0007999	0-44	2
AUSTIN EDWARD G	COL	O-0071046	0862	1
AUSTIN EDWARD L	COL	O-0038805	0863	1
AUSTIN EDWARD W	COL	O-0051789	0866	1
AUSTIN JR FRANK J	LTC	O-0040207	1062	1
AUSTIN WALLACE	LTC	O-0032191	0367	1
AVARY HUGH C	COL	O-0030838	0864	1
AVENT HUGH P	LTC	O-0003871	1022	2
AVERA WRAY B	COL	O-0012861	0553	1
AVERY BERTREM A	CW4	W-0902726	0257	1
AVERY HENRY H	CW4	W-0906607	0664	1
AVERY IRVING C	COL	O-0004830	0351	1
AVERY LILLIAN V	MAJ	N-0001037	1058	2
AVERY SAMUEL D	COL	O-0006825	0848	2
AVERY WILLIAM B	COL	O-0045706	0865	1
AVERYT CLYDE R	CW3	W-0902727	0565	1
AVNER SAUL L	COL	O-0041701	0157	1
AVRETT MARION E	LTC	O-0080281	0364	1
AX CLARENCE F	LTC	O-0032198	0764	1
AXMANN MARY C	MAJ	N-0000478	0166	1
AXUP ROY W	COL	O-0016894	0757	1
AYCOCK ALBERT L	CW4	W-0904080	0465	1
AYCOCK ROBERT C	COL	O-0046664	0966	1
AYCOCK WILLIAM B	MAJ	O-0035051	0961	1
AYER ERNEST C	LTC	O-0006147	0242	1
AYER FRANKLIN A	LTC	O-0034199	0762	1
AYER WESLEY F	COL	O-0003156	0946	2
AYERS LOREN A	COL	O-0018561	0761	1
AYLOR JAMES L	MAJ	O-0037768	0965	1
AYNES EDITH A	MAJ	N-0000094	0456	1
AYOTTE JOHN U	COL	O-0005570	0553	1
AYRES JR LAURENCE T	COL	O-0043715	0764	2
BABBITT RICHARD C	COL	O-0012178	0946	2
BABCOCK C STANTON	M G	O-0016104	0661	1
BABCOCK FRANKLIN	B G	O-0002968	0846	2
BABCOCK JR LESLIE E	1LT	O-0026914	0452	2
BABER BEN L	LTC	O-0025567	0763	1
BABER BURL B	LTC	O-0051048	0757	2
BACCHIERI LUCILE B	MAJ	N-0000032	1047	1
BACHARACH THEODORE	LTC	O-0057987	0864	1
BACHE CLAUDE V	LTC	O-0061100	0966	1
BACHELOR DONALD M	LTC	O-0043723	0264	1
BACHELOR WILLIAM E	LTC	O-0094040	0666	1
BACHER ROBERT M	COL	O-0051045	0859	1
BACHMAN GEORGE A	LTC	O-0051186	1057	1
BACHMAN JOHN P	COL	O-0016970	0556	1
BACHMAN ROGER M	COL	O-0022226	0765	1
BACIOR AGNES	MAJ	N-0001530	0863	1
BACK GEORGE T	M G	O-0010267	0655	2
BACKHAUS III GUS	MAJ	O-0060714	0864	1
BACKMAN STANLEY G	COL	O-0007833	1145	2
BACKMANN CAROLINE M	MAJ	N-0002241	0960	1
BACON LEONARD A	MAJ	O-0085113	1166	2
BACON WILLIAM J	COL	O-0004081	0846	1
BADGER GEORGE M	B G	O-0012139	0649	1
BADGER THOMAS J	COL	O-0039981	0865	1
BADGLEY THEODORE M	LTC	O-0062975	0767	1
BAER CHARLES M	B G	O-0018718	0762	1
BAER HELENE N	LTC	L-0000003	0156	1
BAETCKE BERND G	COL	O-0029497	1060	1
BAGBY CARROLL A	COL	O-0003093	0450	1
BAGGETT ELLA L	MAJ	N-0002376	1160	1
BAGLEY CHARLES T	MAJ	O-0021424	1144	2
BAGLEY JAMES C	COL	O-0080547	0867	1
BAGLEY RAY M	COL	O-0042902	1166	1
BAGNULO ALDO H	COL	O-0020550	0765	1
BAHE GORDON A	LTC	O-0023616	0246	2
BAHR ROBERT C	COL	O-0019470	1160	2
BAIE JOHN J	LTC	O-0085127	0866	1
BAILEY CLARK N	COL	O-0015839	0555	1
BAILEY DONALD J	COL	O-0016174	0755	2
BAILEY GORDON W	LTC	O-0076848	0567	1
BAILEY JACK L	COL	O-0035552	1167	1
BAILEY JAMES M	COL	O-0031223	1065	1
BAILEY JAMES S	CPT	O-0014236	0620	2
BAILEY JOHN H	CW2	W-0902202	0646	2
BAILEY JOSEPH M	CW2	W-0901259	0544	2
BAILEY JR GEORGE W	COL	O-0012820	0337	2
BAILEY JR HARLE G	LTC	O-0032167	1158	1
BAILEY JR IRWIN C	MAJ	O-0043141	0859	1
BAILEY JR JOHN A	LTC	O-0040602	0962	1
BAILEY JR KINCHEON H	LTC	O-0027531	0966	1
BAILEY KINCHEON H	COL	O-0015489	0253	1
BAILEY SAM P	CW4	W-0906611	1158	1
BAILEY WILLIAM A	COL	O-0019264	0759	1
BAILEY WILLIAM W	COL	O-0020681	0567	1
BAIN BENJAMIN B	COL	O-0007477	0847	1
BAIN JAMES G	COL	O-0017246	0758	1
BAIN JOE A	COL	O-0019306	0660	1
BAIN JR JAMES	LTC	O-0068322	1266	1
BAIR CECILE E	MAJ	N-0002232	0360	1
BAIRD ARTHUR R	COL	O-0009942	0346	2
BAIRD ELWOOD F	CPT	O-0021030	1041	2
BAIRD HARRY H	B G	O-0005789	0350	1
BAIRD JR OLIN J	CPT	O-0068079	0166	1
BAIRD RAYMOND C	COL	O-0002503	0138	1
BAIRD WILLET J	COL	O-0016499	0756	1
BAISH CHARLES F	COL	O-0009309	0354	1
BAKER ARTHUR L	COL	O-0039809	0163	1
BAKER BARTON O	COL	O-0044222	0865	1
BAKER BILLY R	CW3	W-0902739	0560	1
BAKER DAVID A	LTC	O-0039971	0861	1
BAKER DENZIL L	COL	O-0043052	0567	2
BAKER DONALD A	LTC	O-1179281	0367	1
BAKER ELVERSON F	COL	O-0030183	0564	1
BAKER FORREST P	CPT	O-0005425	0622	2
BAKER FRANCIS J	LTC	O-0085467	0165	2
BAKER HAROLD P	LTC	O-0040895	1162	1
BAKER HARRY T	COL	O-0029618	1061	1
BAKER JACK B	COL	O-0030239	0661	1
BAKER JAMES E	COL	O-0042714	0864	1
BAKER JOSEPH K	COL	O-0012168	0854	1
BAKER JR WILLIAM C	M G	O-0016371	0664	1
BAKER LEE R	CW3	W-0902738	0452	1
BAKER MESCAL	MAJ	N-0000109	0159	1
BAKER NINA M	LTC	N-0000594	0463	1
BAKER PAUL T	COL	O-0007490	0244	2
BAKER PHILLIP H	LTC	O-0024442	0462	2
BAKER ROBERT G	COL	O-0019427	0864	1
BAKER ROBERT L	CW2	W-0902012	0751	1
BAKER ROY C	COL	O-0029975	0863	1
BAKER RUSSELL A	COL	O-0015745	0954	1
BAKER SAMUEL E	COL	O-0042395	0764	1

UNITED STATES ARMY RETIRED LIST

NAME	GRADE	SVC NO	DATE RET MO YR	RET CODE
BAKER THOMAS E	COL	0-0031244	0266	1
BAKER THOMAS O	COL	0-0005381	0642	2
BAKER VAN R	LTC	0-0028083	0767	1
BALAS PAUL S	LTC	0-0040234	0860	1
BALCAR PAUL G	COL	0-0010060	0146	2
BALCER CHARLES E	LTC	0-0036519	0764	1
BALDINGER ORA M	COL	0-0003510	0624	2
BALDRY GEORGE A	COL	0-0030615	0664	1
BALDWIN CHARLES P	COL	0-0018624	0859	1
BALDWIN COY W	LTC	0-0031924	0264	2
BALDWIN ORVAL J	COL	0-0039790	0962	1
BALDWIN PERRY L	COL	0-0005137	0351	1
BALDWIN RICHARD T	COL	0-0029113	0859	1
BALDWIN ROSS O	COL	0-0005132	1146	2
BALESTRA JOSEPHINE	LTC	N-0000522	1052	1
BALIKOV BERNARD	MAJ	0-0056775	0665	1
BALKE FRANK T	COL	0-0038592	0355	1
BALKMAN AUSTIN F	LTC	0-0032285	0663	1
BALL ARTHUR C	LTC	0-0032070	1266	1
BALL CLINTON W	COL	0-0006294	0245	2
BALL HORACE G	MAJ	0-0013950	0720	2
BALL RURA O	LTC	0-0028905	0455	1
BALL SPENCER F	CW4	W-0902743	0263	1
BALL WILLIAM E	COL	0-0041586	0459	1
BALLACH ROBERT S	LTC	0-0030009	0961	1
BALLANTYNE JOHN L	COL	0-0015005	0946	2
BALLARD DEWITT	COL	0-0015425	1153	1
BALLARD JAMES L	LTC	0-0006149	1041	2
BALLARD JAMES M	CW3	W-0902745	0763	1
BALLARD JOHN A	COL	0-0007060	1042	1
BALLARD RICHARD W	CW4	W-0902746	0864	1
BALLARD ZORA M	LTC	N-0000495	1148	1
BALLENTINE JOHN F	COL	0-0039983	0865	1
BALLINGER ELDON L	LTC	0-0061202	0367	1
BALLUFF JAMES G	COL	0-0019955	0847	2
BALMER JESMOND D	B G	0-0011389	0153	2
BALS WILSON T	COL	0-0004743	1147	1
BALSAM ALFRED S	COL	0-0003864	1146	2
BALTZER NYLES W	COL	0-0051581	0165	1
BAMBACE FELIX S	COL	0-0056797	0957	1
BANDLEY MARION X	LTC	0-0045222	0962	1
BANE JOHN C	COL	0-0021897	0765	1
BANE JR PAULL A	LTC	0-0032596	1059	1
BANE JR W FREDERIC	CPT	0-0088001	0366	2
BANGS ROBERT R	MAJ	0-0078710	0961	1
BANIGAN CALVIN B	LTC	0-0030376	0263	1
BANK AARON	COL	0-0028959	0258	1
BANK CARL C	B G	0-0003818	0947	1
BANKE HENRY H	LTC	0-0051832	0164	1
BANKS CLYDE G	COL	0-0011646	0747	1
BANKS CURTIS M	LTC	0-0030143	0362	2
BANKS JAMES C	CW3	W-0902748	0760	1
BANKS KEITH B	COL	0-0079695	0661	1
BANKS RETHA H	CPT	N-0002683	0264	2
BANKUS JOHN T	COL	0-0042799	0562	1
BANNER CHARLES V	CW2	W-0901567	0148	1
BANNING EDWARD A	COL	0-0014716	0248	1
BANNISTER RAY K	COL	0-0029784	1062	1
BANTON HUSTON J	COL	0-0016975	0946	2
BANVILLE JAMES H	B G	0-0028921	0657	1
BARAN JR STANLEY	CPT	0-0060519	0863	1
BARBATO LEWIS	MAJ	0-0018636	0733	2
BARBER CHARLES N	MAJ	0-0052568	1050	1
BARBER DOROTHY J	MAJ	N-0002029	1058	1
BARBER HOMER G	COL	0-0022130	0666	1
BARBER JAMES T	LTC	0-0017551	0554	1
BARBER KEITH M	COL	0-0039606	0359	1
BARBER PAULINE A	MAJ	N-0000128	0361	1
BARBER REGINALD C	COL	0-0042560	0563	2
BARBER WILFRED F	LTC	0-0031683	0864	1
BARBERIE FREDERICK	LTC	0-0051050	0957	1
BARBOUR FRED A	CW4	W-0902751	1045	1
BARBOUR THOMAS E P	COL	0-0016469	0754	1
BARCLAY GORDON L	COL	0-0029691	0462	1
BARCLAY JOHN A	M G	0-0018420	0661	1

NAME	GRADE	SVC NO	DATE RET MO YR	RET CODE
BARCO JR ERNEST T	COL	0-0033938	0263	2
BARD C ROBERT	COL	0-0018435	1158	1
BARD LILA	MAJ	L-0000227	0158	1
BARDEN ALBERT	COL	0-0012266	0753	1
BARDSLEY GEORGE H	COL	0-0011868	1044	2
BARE GEORGE H	COL	0-0012957	0354	1
BARE GEORGE S	LTC	0-0032488	1167	1
BARE JR WALTER E	COL	0-0019944	0865	2
BAREFIELD WILLIAM C	COL	0-0042763	0263	1
BARISKI NICK	CW4	RW-9043759	0863	1
BARKALEW RUSSELL G	COL	0-0005957	0751	1
BARKER ERNEST S	COL	0-0009996	0648	1
BARKER GEORGE	COL	0-0004972	0753	1
BARKER GEORGE M	COL	0-0030708	0660	1
BARKER II JAMES W	LTC	0-0030001	0358	2
BARKER LEONARD C	LTC	0-0040213	0764	1
BARKER MARY R	MAJ	N-0002282	0761	1
BARKER MAURICE F	COL	0-0006779	0848	1
BARKER RAY W	M G	0-0003611	0247	2
BARKER STOCKBRIDG	COL	0-0038949	0566	1
BARKER TROY A	LTC	0-0042394	0762	1
BARKER WALTER E	COL	0-0022717	0166	1
BARKER WAYNE L	COL	0-0019379	1153	1
BARKIN ALBERT	COL	0-0051809	0966	1
BARKMAN WILLIAM E	LTC	0-0038899	1164	1
BARKSDALE BATTLE M	COL	0-0020719	0957	1
BARKSDALE WILLIAM E	B G	0-0029478	0157	1
BARLOW BOWMAN C	MAJ	0-0080039	0860	1
BARLOW EVERETT W	COL	0-0018724	0746	2
BARLOW JOHN E	COL	0-0020224	0759	1
BARLOW RAYMOND C	COL	0-0012379	0354	1
BARLOW RUDOLPH	COL	0-0031835	0964	1
BARNABY ADOLPH	COL	0-0039758	0262	1
BARNABY JR KENNETH T	COL	0-0044385	0866	1
BARNARD JOHN M	LTC	0-0056483	1166	1
BARNARD THOMAS W	CPT	0-0007735	0934	2
BARNER THOMAS R	LTC	0-0041820	1158	1
BARNES DEAN W	LTC	0-0040745	1162	1
BARNES ELMER E	COL	0-0012054	0854	1
BARNES FRANCIS H	COL	0-0041601	0859	1
BARNES GEORGE L	COL	0-0029078	0359	1
BARNES GEORGE T	COL	0-0010615	0753	1
BARNES JR WILLIAM P	COL	0-0021048	0263	2
BARNES LYNN C	COL	0-0039641	0360	1
BARNES PAUL I	CW4	W-0902756	0662	1
BARNES THEODORE	COL	0-0003626	0540	2
BARNES VALENTINE	COL	0-0051434	0863	1
BARNES VEROI B	LTC	0-0017198	0565	1
BARNES WALLACE H	B G	0-0016426	0756	1
BARNES WILLIAM W	COL	0-0024425	0466	1
BARNETT ALLISON J	M G	0-0005364	1047	2
BARNETT DAVID F	COL	0-0008239	0850	1
BARNETT FRANK L	COL	0-0030485	0861	1
BARNETT HERBERT C	LTC	0-0056236	0962	1
BARNETT JAMES D	COL	0-0016234	0155	1
BARNETT JAMES W	B G	0-0004604	0649	1
BARNETT JR WILLIAM H	LTC	0-0046540	1065	1
BARNETT KEFF D	1LT	0-0014633	0426	2
BARNETT LACY C	MAJ	0-0094714	0467	1
BARNETT NORMAN P	COL	0-0038784	0461	1
BARNETT WILLIAM H	LTC	0-0022104	0759	1
BARNETTE ELLIOTT J	COL	0-0028847	0256	1
BARNEY JR JAMES P	COL	0-0012796	0152	1
BARNEY KEITH R	M G	0-0016377	0462	1
BARNEY LEONARD C	LTC	0-0037487	0862	1
BARNEY PHYLLIS W	MAJ	N-0001019	0264	1
BARNHART FRANK H	COL	0-0005498	0549	2
BARNHIZER HARRY J	MAJ	0-0080555	0762	1
BARNUM CHARLES V	CPT	0-0011632	0-35	2
BARNUM JOHN M	COL	0-0051780	0461	1
BARNUM RICHARD V	LTC	0-0036167	0763	1
BARNWELL JOHN D	COL	0-0008787	0747	2
BARNWELL JR C H	B G	0-0005571	0652	1
BARON ALBERT S	COL	0-0016674	1054	1
BARON EDWIN W	COL	0-0042012	0567	2

NAME	GRADE	SVC NO	DATE RET MO YR	RET CODE
BARONE SANDRO A	LTC	0-0080556	0567	1
BARR CHRISTINE	MAJ	N-0001642	1064	1
BARR DAVID C	M G	0-0010313	0252	1
BARR DWIGHT P	CW4	W-0902758	1057	1
BARR EARL L	COL	0-0019792	0647	2
BARR EDWARD H	COL	0-0014634	0151	1
BARR WILLIAM H	LTC	0-0059470	0963	1
BARRATT TOM H	COL	0-0024343	0264	1
BARRELL FRANK M	COL	0-0009893	0744	2
BARRETT CARRIE E	COL	N-0000124	0466	1
BARRETT DAVID D	COL	0-0009726	0852	1
BARRETT FRANCES M	MAJ	N-0000730	0364	1
BARRETT JOHN H	CW4	W-0904081	0159	1
BARRETT JOHN T	COL	0-0042015	0462	1
BARRETT JOHN W	LTC	0-0024448	0946	2
BARRETT LAURENCE O	LTC	0-0036652	1166	1
BARRETT LEONARD L	COL	0-0013951	0720	2
BARRETT REX M	LTC	0-0084723	0967	1
BARRETT ROSS P	CPT	0-0058824	0663	1
BARRETT RUTH	MAJ	N-0001884	1159	1
BARRETT WALTER D S	MAJ	0-0043152	0958	2
BARRETT WILLIAM P	LTC	0-0067551	0965	1
BARRICK CARROL C	COL	0-0019330	0959	1
BARRICK HARRY W	COL	0-0012345	1146	1
BARRICKLOW WILLIAM R	COL	0-0056816	0862	1
BARRIGER WILLIAM L	M G	0-0011220	0257	1
BARRIOS WILLIE W J	LTC	0-0036748	0865	1
BARROLL JR MORRIS K	COL	0-0005241	0550	1
BARROW LLEWELLYN	LTC	0-0018949	0244	2
BARROWS RALPH G	COL	0-0004431	0846	1
BARRY ARTHUR R	COL	0-0023160	1165	1
BARRY GEORGE W	COL	0-0039916	1064	1
BARRY JAMES P	LTC	0-0025283	0766	1
BARRY JR CHARLES J	COL	0-0038713	0462	1
BARRY JR ROBERT R	COL	0-0022674	0667	1
BARRY KEVIN C	LTC	0-0063478	1166	1
BARRY MARY S	MAJ	N-0000053	0751	1
BARRY WILLIAM E	LTC	0-0019682	0360	1
BARSCHDORF MILTON P	COL	0-0021085	0859	1
BART WAYNE L	LTC	0-0024707	0759	1
BARTEL THOMAS R	COL	0-0022019	0746	2
BARTELMEZ THEODORE L	MAJ	0-0052051	0453	1
BARTELT ROBERT H	LTC	0-0081888	0766	1
BARTH BERLE I	MAJ	0-0051749	0567	2
BARTH GEORGE R	M G	0-0011241	1057	2
BARTH LUTHER R	COL	0-0043418	1264	1
BARTH ROBERT A	LTC	0-0005996	0636	1
BARTHLE ROBERT C	COL	0-0024246	0566	1
BARTHOLET JOHN C	COL	0-0043845	0164	1
BARTHOLF JOHN C P	B G	0-0003503	1045	2
BARTHOLOMEW HOWARD L	COL	0-0043524	0666	1
BARTHOLOMEW HOWARD W	CW2	W-0904359	0960	1
BARTHOLOMEW JAMES W	CW4	RW-0907121	1066	1
BARTHOLOW WALTER M	CW4	W-0906615	0261	2
BARTLETT FRANK E	LTC	0-0041614	0957	1
BARTLETT HARRY M	LTC	0-0039457	0765	1
BARTLETT LAURENCE W	COL	0-0012707	0749	1
BARTLETT ROY W	COL	0-0041600	0857	1
BARTLETT THOMAS R	MAJ	0-0006452	0-37	2
BARTLETT WILLIAM G	COL	0-0019047	0859	2
BARTLETT WILLIAM H	COL	0-0012695	0854	1
BARTLETT WILLIAM T	LTC	0-0042468	1162	1
BARTLEY JAMES T	LTC	0-0026649	0567	1
BARTLING CARL W	COL	0-0043091	0264	1
BARTON CHESTER T	COL	0-0029529	0261	1
BARTON DEFOREST A	LTC	0-0080558	1067	1
BARTON DOUGLAS C	COL	0-0038829	0466	2
BARTON RAYMOND M	COL	0-0016185	0655	1
BARTOSIK MATTHEW J	COL	0-0052145	0762	1
BARTOW CHARLES P	LTC	0-0052310	1062	1
BARTZ RALPH F	COL	0-0016332	0244	2
BARY ROBERT S	LTC	0-0032296	0762	1
BARZYNSKI JOSEPH E	B G	0-0002082	0744	1
BASBAS JAMES G	COL	0-0042354	0859	1
BASGALL JULIAN F	LTC	0-0087471	0666	1

NAME	GRADE	SVC NO	DATE RET MO YR	RET CODE
BASH JAMES H	LTC	0-0079696	0764	1
BASILE DANIEL	COL	0-0040900	0667	1
BASS ARTHUR C	COL	0-0030292	0562	1
BASS JR ROY W	LTC	0-0039125	0966	1
BASSETT RALPH H	COL	0-0012432	1050	1
BASSITT KASSIER G	COL	0-0019931	0865	1
BASTILLE JOSEPH A	CW4	W-0902762	0656	1
BASTICK JOSEPH E	B G	0-0002805	0247	2
BASTICK JR JOSEPH E	M G	0-0019162	0866	1
BATCH JOSEPH W	COL	0-0020864	0867	2
BATCHELDER HAROLD W	1LT	0-0014439	0920	2
BATCHELDOR GEORGE O	COL	0-0038852	0166	1
BATCHELOR VANCE W	COL	0-0008521	1049	1
BATES GILBERT S	CW4	W-0906617	0762	1
BATES JAMES C	COL	0-0007394	0848	1
BATES JOHN F	LTC	0-0056633	0863	1
BATES JR WILLIAM E	LTC	0-0059939	0767	1
BATES PAUL L	COL	0-0029929	0563	1
BATES WILLIAM H	LTC	0-0039806	1060	1
BATHURST CHARLES R	COL	0-0012060	0554	1
BATLIN ALEXANDER	COL	0-0043927	0162	1
BATSON CURTIS C	LTC	0-0037152	1161	1
BATSON ROSCOE C	COL	0-0003104	0346	2
BATTLEY JOSEPH F	B G	0-0011288	0747	1
BATY JAMES R	LTC	0-0029141	1147	2
BAUCHSPIES ROLLIN L	COL	0-0017819	0959	1
BAUER FRANK L	COL	0-0026430	0663	1
BAUER RICHARD M	LTC	0-0019804	1146	2
BAUGH IRA E	CW4	W-0902764	0665	1
BAUGHN WILMOT I	COL	0-0040155	0761	1
BAUKNIGHT RALPH M	COL	0-0051091	0660	1
BAUM FREDERICK	LTC	0-0023385	0764	1
BAUM INEZ I	MAJ	M-0010084	0255	1
BAUMANN JULIAN H	COL	0-0016326	1155	2
BAUMER DONALD H	MAJ	0-0022987	0150	1
BAUMGARTNER OSWALD R	CW4	W-0902765	0455	1
BAXLEY JAMES W	LTC	0-0078714	1163	1
BAXTER JAMES O	MAJ	0-0060478	0263	1
BAXTER SAMUEL F	LTC	0-0075734	0464	1
BAYA GEORGE E	COL	0-0029817	0560	1
BAYER WILLIAM L	B G	0-0016372	0756	2
BAYERLE JR GEORGE J	COL	0-0023192	0664	1
BAYLESS HARRY H	COL	0-0029104	1157	2
BAYLIES ALFRED L	COL	0-0005874	0747	1
BAYLIS JAMES E	B G	0-0003310	1047	2
BAYLISS MILWARD W	COL	0-0041743	0763	1
BAYNE JOSEPH K	COL	0-0030913	0960	1
BAYNE ROBERT H	COL	0-0019207	0957	1
BAYOT J M	WO1	W-0800601	0733	2
BAYS HAROLD L	COL	0-0018433	0761	1
BAZE MILES J	COL	0-0041378	0155	1
BEACH BENJAMIN D	COL	0-0029505	1060	1
BEACH JOHN R	LTC	0-0025978	0864	1
BEADLE FRANK L	COL	0-0014996	0548	1
BEAGLE NADINE N	MAJ	N-0001711	0863	1
BEALKE JR JACOB W	COL	0-0031365	0865	1
BEALL EDWIN S	CPT	0-0006608	0828	2
BEALL JR CLAUDIUS A	COL	0-0039931	0564	1
BEALS FRANK L	MAJ	0-0014107	0508	2
BEAN EMMETT J	M G	0-0012381	0657	1
BEANE WOODROW H	CW2	W-0902371	1163	1
BEARCE HERRICK F	COL	0-0030498	0765	1
BEARD J H	LTC	0-0084450	1262	1
BEARD ROBERT S	COL	0-0009412	1042	1
BEARD WILLIAM N	COL	0-0020154	0966	1
BEARSS ERNEST H	COL	0-0032020	0165	1
BEASLEY CHARLES H	COL	0-0016542	0147	2
BEASLEY LOUIS J	LTC	0-0022710	0567	1
BEASLEY OSCAR R	COL	0-0018045	0859	1
BEASLEY THOMAS A	LTC	0-0065074	0566	2
BEATTIE HUNTER S	CW4	W-0902769	0462	1
BEATTIE JAMES	CW2	W-0901917	0352	1
BEATTY GEORGE L	COL	0-0019318	1057	1
BEATTY GEORGE S	COL	0-0010070	0250	1
BEATTY JOHN C	COL	0-0013952	0720	2

NAME	GRADE	SVC NO	DATE RET MO YR	RET CODE	NAME	GRADE	SVC NO	DATE RET MO YR	RET CODE	NAME	GRADE	SVC NO	DATE RET MO YR	RET CODE	NAME	GRADE	SVC NO	DATE RET MO YR	RET CODE
BEATY EDWARD R	LTC	0-0080562	1163	1	BELL CLARENCE D	COL	0-0010780	0247	2	BENNETT JR WILLIAM C	COL	0-0012087	0750	1	BESBECK LOUIS B	LTC	0-0042142	0461	1
BEATY WILLIAM F	LTC	0-0022672	0460	1	BELL CLYDE H	CW4	RW-0904082	0661	1	BENNETT PHILIP C	2LT	0-0017593	0533	2	BESS EDWARD J	CW4	W-0902788	0359	1
BEAUCHAMP CHARLES F	M G	0-0018238	0566	1	BELL DOVER	COL	0-0006851	0246	2	BENNETT VERDE W	LTC	0-0034157	0261	1	BESS WALTER B	B G	0-0020151	1166	1
BEAUCHAMP ROBERT J	COL	0-0044907	0667	2	BELL EARL W	LTC	0-0027743	0765	1	BENNETT WILLIAM E	LTC	0-0031754	0168	1	BESSE EDWARD H	COL	0-0006312	0542	1
BEAUCOND CHARLES A	COL	0-0008374	0948	2	BELL ELIZABETH	MAJ	L-0000015	0654	1	BENNETT WILLIAM J	COL	0-0023331	0764	1	BESSE WARREN E	COL	0-0039988	1165	1
BEAUDET BERTRAND N	COL	0-0040119	1264	1	BELL GILBERT F	LTC	0-0020817	0746	2	BENNETT WILMER G	COL	0-0016141	0655	1	BESSELL JR WILLIAM W	B G	0-0012611	0665	2
BEAUMONT LEE ROY H	LTC	0-0055170	0763	1	BELL GILMER M	COL	0-0005472	1046	2	BENNINGER MARION L	LTC	N-0001885	1262	1	BESSER WILLIAM J	LTC	0-0044039	1167	1
BEAVER FRANCIS L	COL	0-0042057	0261	1	BELL GLYNDON D	CW4	RW-0904287	0864	1	BENOIT JOSEPH E	LTC	0-0051070	0455	2	BESSMER EARL S	COL	0-0039824	0363	1
BEAVER ROBERT T	LTC	0-0022188	0645	2	BELL III WILLIAM	LTC	0-0026934	0766	1	BENSER ERNEST A	COL	0-0042360	0664	1	BESSON ROBERT	COL	0-0020771	0967	2
BEAZLEY CHARLES G	CW3	W-0902772	0661	1	BELL JAMES A	LTC	0-0026452	0164	1	BENSON JENEVIEVE	MAJ	N-0002239	0860	1	BEST CHARLES E	LTC	0-0058831	0667	1
BEAZLEY LEWIS K	CPT	0-0019397	0942	2	BELL JAMES F	COL	0-0001687	0130	1	BENSON JOSEPH W	COL	0-0025601	0563	1	BEST CLIFFORD A	COL	0-0016544	0156	1
BECH ALBERT R	COL	0-0042585	0860	1	BELL JAMES K	COL	0-0029912	0261	1	BENSON JR HENRY K	M G	0-0020331	0867	1	BETANCES-RAMIRE CAR	LTC	0-0030524	0163	1
BECK DONALD C	COL	0-0031329	1066	1	BELL JESSE D	COL	0-0029441	0760	1	BENSON ROBERT C	LTC	0-0080569	0762	1	BETCHER ALFRED J	COL	0-0003082	0539	1
BECK HARRY V	LTC	0-0024210	0760	1	BELL JOE D	LTC	0-0063458	0765	1	BENT JR JOSEPH G	COL	0-0029797	1162	1	BETHEA JAMES A	M G	0-0004076	1049	1
BECK HELEN I	MAJ	N-0002271	0563	1	BELL JOHN A	LTC	0-0033577	0764	1	BENT WILLIAM R	LTC	0-0008063	0844	1	BETHEL JOHN M	COL	0-0011203	1146	2
BECK JOHN N	COL	0-0040258	0866	1	BELL JOSEPH	CW4	W-0906622	0862	1	BENTON EDWARD E	LTC	0-0033761	0160	1	BETHUNE PHILIP H	B G	0-0018449	0661	1
BECK JR ROBERT M	M G	0-0001337	0-39	1	BELL JR EUGENE J	LTC	0-0063676	1167	1	BENTON ROBERT G	CW4	W-0902782	0359	1	BETHUNE SAMUEL A	LTC	0-0031502	1162	1
BECK THEODOR J	CPT	0-0018622	0242	1	BELL LEIGH	COL	0-0005114	1147	2	BENTON ROBERT J	CW2	W-0902157	1147	1	BETIT JOSEPH W	LTC	0-0080580	0967	1
BECK THOMAS H	B G	0-0019164	0663	1	BELL MARCUS B	B G	0-0006616	1051	1	BENZ HERBERT T	COL	0-0015603	0646	2	BETTIER RICHARD L	LTC	0-0042528	0666	1
BECK THOMAS R	CW4	W-0902773	0764	1	BELL MATTIE A	MAJ	N-0000694	0365	1	BEPLAT JAMES A	LTC	0-0043694	0866	1	BETTS ROBERT H	LTC	0-0050956	0449	2
BECK TRAVIS A	2LT	0-0019287	0934	2	BELL OLIN L	COL	0-0023119	0765	1	BERARDINELLI STEPHEN	LTC	0-0019669	1062	1	BETTS THOMAS J	B G	0-0007328	0753	1
BECK VANCEL R	COL	0-0030233	0764	1	BELL RAYMOND E	M G	0-0016897	0663	2	BERBERT HENRY	COL	0-0011357	0753	1	BETZOLD CURTIS W	COL	0-0019641	0164	1
BECKER DANIEL	MAJ	0-0006073	0436	2	BELL THOMAS P	MAJ	0-0021392	0147	2	BERENDT HERBERT W	LTC	0-0031861	0466	1	BEUHLER RALPH H	1LT	0-0050729	1150	1
BECKER HENRY C	LTC	0-0031944	0565	1	BELL URCEL L	LTC	0-0031731	1064	1	BERG FREDERICK	COL	0-0018412	0761	1	BEURKET RAYMOND T	COL	0-0015543	0854	2
BECKER HENRY C	LTC	0-0063389	1168	1	BELL VERNE R	MAJ	0-0002189	1022	1	BERG JACOB J	LTC	0-0080571	0367	1	BEVERIDGE THEODORE M	LTC	0-0081957	0666	1
BECKER JANE T	MAJ	N-0002051	0960	1	BELLAMY PAUL E	COL	0-0030220	0862	1	BERG JR JOSEPH P	LTC	0-0027211	0465	1	BEVINGTON HOLMES H	LTC	0-0042133	1060	1
BECKER OLIVER G	MAJ	0-0026874	1058	2	BELLAND WALTER T	COL	0-0043450	0367	1	BERGE TRYGVE O	COL	0-0030980	1164	1	BEVINS LORETTA M	MAJ	N-0001280	0166	1
BECKER WALTER H	COL	0-0051141	0960	1	BELLAVANCE ARMAND L	LTC	0-0040484	0164	1	BERGER MORRIS R	CW4	W-0902387	0966	2	BEYER DONALD S	LTC	0-0028673	0766	1
BECKER WARD I	COL	0-0009802	0553	1	BELLICAN CHARLES R	COL	0-0019285	1054	1	BERGER RAYFIELD R	LTC	0-0080572	1066	1	BEYETTE HUBERT W	B G	0-0008146	1046	2
BECKER WILFRED C	LTC	0-0034839	0364	1	BELLINGER JOHN B	COL	0-0008626	0846	2	BERGIN GERALD A	COL	0-0051722	0366	1	BEYNON JAMES L	COL	0-0017605	0557	1
BECKETT ROBERT C	MAJ	0-0011671	0231	2	BELLONBY EMERY E	COL	0-0024441	0765	1	BERGIN WILLIAM E	M G	0-0007127	0554	2	BIANCHI ELIZABETH	LTC	L-0000042	0261	1
BECKETT THOMAS J	LTC	0-0084724	1066	1	BELMORE RALPH W	CW3	W-0904280	0763	1	BERGLUND HAROLD K	CW4	W-0902783	1263	1	BIASINI ISABELLE	MAJ	L-0000530	0867	1
BECKHAM JOHN B	LTC	0-0032747	0566	1	BELON RALPH G	COL	0-0043746	0261	2	BERGMAN ALFRED N	1LT	0-0012149	0523	2	BIBB JOSEPH R	COL	0-0007454	1047	1
BECKJORD PHILIP R	COL	0-0031051	0960	1	BELOTE BYRON G	COL	0-0042851	0564	1	BERGMANN JOHN A	COL	0-0042300	0164	1	BIBBY WILLIAM L	LTC	0-0026276	1264	1
BECKNER JOHN D	COL	0-0030512	0754	2	BELSER JR WILLIAM G	COL	0-0042897	0963	1	BERGMANN RAY A	CW4	W-0902785	0166	1	BIDDLE WILLIAM S	M G	0-0015180	1060	1
BEDDOW JAMES H	COL	0-0021446	0866	1	BENCH GERALD N	COL	0-0051092	0860	1	BERGQUIST EARL C	M G	0-0016958	0859	1	BIDGOOD CLARENCE	COL	0-0019777	1163	1
BEDELL EDWIN A	COL	0-0039722	0661	1	BENDER CATHERINE	MAJ	M-0010024	0965	1	BERILLA JR GEORGE P	LTC	0-0016147	0952	1	BIDWELL BRUCE W	COL	0-0015552	0954	1
BEDFORD WILLIAM H	COL	0-0043926	0267	1	BENDER GEORGE E	COL	0-0016914	0857	1	BERKEBILE ALMA J	MAJ	N-0002470	0866	1	BIDWELL JAMES W	COL	0-0029508	0459	2
BEDINGER SAMUEL D	COL	0-0005603	1047	2	BENDER PAUL C	COL	0-004770[illegible]	1065	1	BERLINER SYLVAN	COL	0-0015917	0346	2	BIEHL PHILIP F	COL	0-0006539	0650	1
BEE THOMAS J	LTC	0-0044437	0661	1	BENDER THOMAS W	COL	0-0030162	0660	1	BERMAN HARRY L	COL	0-0022697	0860	1	BIENVENU THOMAS F	COL	0-0030401	0363	1
BEEBE JOHN L	COL	0-0039970	0765	1	BENDFELT HARRIETT C	MAJ	L-0000083	0262	1	BERNARD JOSEPH T	COL	0-0045997	1263	1	BIERER BENJAMIN R	COL	0-0033722	0866	1
BEEDLE DORIS I	MAJ	N-0002235	0560	1	BENEDICT ARTHUR L	CPT	0-0009955	1032	2	BERNARD LYLE W	COL	0-0019195	0863	1	BIERI ALFRED C	LTC	0-0033055	1163	1
BEELER DONALD T	COL	0-0015437	1153	2	BENEDICT HAROLD B	COL	0-0031566	0767	1	BERNARD ROBERT J	LTC	0-0058830	1165	1	BIERMAN DONALD L	COL	0-0023175	1064	1
BEELMAN GLENN T	COL	0-0022235	0861	1	BENEDICT MAUDE B	LTC	N-0000197	0760	1	BERNAUER FLOYD V	CW4	W-0902786	0363	1	BIERWIRTH WILLIAM R	1LT	0-0062245	1051	1
BEEMAN AARON W	B G	0-0029063	0259	1	BENEKE ARTHUR R	LTC	0-0084542	0266	1	BERNER BENT E	CPT	0-0060611	0964	1	BIGBY WALTER A	COL	0-0010294	0153	1
BEER WARREN G	LTC	0-0059966	1165	1	BENENSON ABRAM S	COL	0-0024295	0762	1	BERNHARD ALEXANDER	LTC	0-0063419	0966	1	BIGELOW HORACE F	M G	0-0018775	0167	1
BEERE DONALD C	COL	0-0021893	0959	1	BENFORD JAMES A	COL	0-0051676	1265	1	BERNIER DONALD W	COL	0-0019911	0765	1	BIGELOW MAURICE C	COL	0-0005129	0551	1
BEERE DONALD M	COL	0-0002588	0546	2	BENGEL LAWRENCE W	COL	0-0034423	0765	1	BERNIER JOSEPH L	M G	0-0020093	1167	2	BIGGER CHESTER H	LTC	0-0024212	0962	1
BEESON JOHN P	LTC	0-0024686	0767	1	BENGTSON THORE F	LTC	0-0018670	0650	1	BERNINGER ALTA	LTC	N-0000504	0452	1	BIGGS BRADLEY	LTC	0-0036892	0861	1
BEESON WALTER L	COL	0-0031143	1263	1	BENHAM CLAUDE G	CPT	0-0005743	1128	1	BERNUCCI ROBERT J	LTC	0-0063148	0363	1	BIGGS RICHARD C	COL	0-0045688	0166	1
BEETH HOWARD D	LTC	0-0042489	1262	1	BENINATE NICHOLAS A	COL	0-0059464	0567	1	BEROL ALEXANDER	MAJ	0-0033000	0961	1	BIGGS THOMAS R	LTC	0-0063104	0666	1
BEETS WALTER D	COL	0-0029707	0562	1	BENION HARRY G	LTC	0-0020872	0565	1	BERRIEN CLINTON S	COL	0-0011730	1048	2	BILBO JR THEODORE G	COL	0-0019477	0864	1
BEEZLEY ORVA E	COL	0-0004398	1044	2	BENITEZ ENRIQUE M	COL	0-0004841	0451	1	BERRIGAN DONALD B	LTC	0-0028960	0955	2	BILES GEORGE W F	COL	0-0039590	1058	1
BEGANIE HENRY P	LTC	0-0088566	0967	2	BENITEZ ROBERTO E	LTC	0-0058706	1264	1	BERRIGAN PAUL D	B G	0-0016741	0757	1	BILHARZ DWIGHT L	LTC	0-0065952	0764	1
BEGGS EDWIN G	COL	0-0020297	0763	1	BENJAMIN DEN C	LTC	0-0043070	0864	1	BERRIS JR MICHAEL T	LTC	0-0080577	0966	1	BILL ARTHUR T	LTC	0-0030112	0162	1
BEGGS RAYMOND W	COL	0-0039802	0363	1	BENJAMIN ROBERT E	COL	0-0028887	1056	1	BERRY ARY C	CPT	0-0006996	0233	2	BILL DOROTHY A	MAJ	N-0002251	0961	1
BEHNKEN JR B T	LTC	0-0044052	0959	1	BENJAMIN ROY F	LTC	0-0032062	0762	1	BERRY COBURN L	COL	0-0006306	0844	2	BILLING DAVID D	LTC	0-0042820	1160	1
BEHRENS HENRY R	COL	0-0004970	0747	1	BENKOSKY STEPHEN W	COL	0-0028852	0656	1	BERRY DANIEL J	COL	0-0017806	0353	1	BILLINGS EDWARD R	COL	0-0039945	1163	1
BEIDERLINDEN W A	M G	0-0010303	0655	1	BENNER JAMES D	LTC	0-0079697	0960	1	BERRY EDWARD S	COL	0-0018119	0660	1	BILLINGS WILLIAM H	COL	0-0030098	0859	1
BEIDLE GEORGIA V	MAJ	N-0001282	0661	1	BENNER JOHN A	LTC	0-0024203	0162	1	BERRY FLOYD L	COL	0-0038866	1166	1	BILLINGSLEY CLAUDE A	LTC	0-0016620	0754	1
BEIDLEMAN LAURENCE E	CW4	W-0906621	1264	1	BENNER JOHN G	COL	0-0019571	0357	1	BERRY FRANK E	COL	0-0084342	1067	1	BILLINGSLEY ROBERTS	COL	0-0030608	0166	1
BEIGHTLER ROBERT S	M G	0-0038583	0753	1	BENNET ALEXANDER	COL	0-0012257	1146	1	BERRY FRED P	LTC	0-0080578	1064	1	BILLINGSLEY WALTER L	CW4	W-0906625	1163	1
BEIMFOHR CASPER V	COL	0-0081858	0168	1	BENNETT A RECINA	LTC	N-0002407	0166	1	BERRY HARRY W	COL	0-0042480	1264	1	BINDEMAN WILLIAM W	LTC	0-0058713	1067	1
BEISER JOHN J	COL	0-0023025	1161	2	BENNETT ADAM J	LTC	0-0007514	0-34	2	BERRY JOHN A	B G	0-0018473	0661	1	BINDER ROBERT T	LTC	0-0089415	0967	1
BEISHLINE JOHN R	B G	0-0018523	0655	1	BENNETT AUSTIN W	COL	0-0022288	0147	2	BERRY JOHN L	CW4	W-0906624	1065	1	BINFORD THOMAS E	COL	0-0015595	0346	2
BEITER DEAN S	COL	0-0019692	0265	1	BENNETT CLARENCE W	COL	0-0015618	0754	1	BERRY JR JOHN F	MAJ	0-0031707	0552	1	BING JAMES E	CW3	RW-0902795	1165	1
BEITZ JAMES E	CPT	0-0057394	1066	2	BENNETT CLETUS D	COL	0-0028966	0358	1	BERRY LOGAN C	COL	0-0015752	0954	1	BING RALPH C	COL	0-0015255	0854	1
BELANGER GERARD A	COL	0-0019333	1159	1	BENNETT CURTIS H	COL	0-0041821	0758	1	BERRY LUCIEN S S	COL	0-0004461	0253	1	BINGHAM BERNARD A	2LT	0-0014469	0919	2
BELANGER RENALDO G	COL	0-0040109	0762	2	BENNETT EATON W	COL	0-0019604	0656	1	BERRY MORGAN C	COL	0-0006886	1147	2	BINGHAM EMIL S	CW2	W-0901459	1044	2
BELCHER JAYNIE E	CPT	N-0000051	0351	1	BENNETT ELI E	COL	0-0002557	0-43	1	BERRY WILBUR C	COL	0-0020410	0765	1	BINGHAM JR EDWARD C	LTC	0-0040471	0765	1
BELDEN ARTHUR W	LTC	0-0050950	0555	1	BENNETT EUGENE G	COL	0-0041665	0460	1	BERTRAM ROGER A	LTC	0-0025508	0863	1	BINGHAM LEONARD L	COL	0-0015534	0754	1
BELDEN HUGH	COL	0-0028819	0955	1	BENNETT GEORGE W	COL	0-0021434	0255	2	BERTRAND ALOYSIUS F	LTC	0-0067552	0866	1	BINNING MARCEL	LTC	N-0010011	0865	1
BELFLOWER EVA K	CPT	N-0002362	1057	2	BENNETT IVAN L	M G	0-0011936	0454	2	BERTRANG RODNEY H	CW4	W-0502787	0859	1	BINNS JOHN J	M G	0-0015207	1159	2
BELIEU KENNETH E	COL	0-0032223	1055	2	BENNETT JAMES G	LTC	0-0040400	0967	1	BERTSCH JR WILLIAM H	COL	0-0015759	0754	1	BIRCH HORACE M	CW4	W-0902796	0355	1
BELIN HEDWIG C	LTC	L-0000136	0266	1	BENNETT JOHN G	LTC	0-0029387	0758	2	BERWALD HERBERT T	COL	0-0017831	0457	1	BIRCH WILSON H	LTC	0-0042816	0764	1

NAME	GRADE	SVC NO	DATE RET MO YR	RET CODE
BIRO JOHN F	B G	0-0016179	0656	1
BIRO RAFAEL	MAJ	C-0014359	0218	2
BIRO ROBERT J	LTC	0-0032343	0664	1
BIRO VIRON F	LTC	0-0024568	1160	1
BIROSEYE JR M B	LTC	0-0023807	0760	2
BIRKMEYER LOUIS R	CPT	0-0063576	1065	2
BIRKS HAMMOND D	B G	0-0007184	1146	2
BIRMINGHAM RICHARD C	COL	0-0004480	1045	2
BISANT JR OSCAR H	COL	0-0051387	0363	1
BISBING JOHN	COL	0-0031665	1163	1
BISBORT HAROLD E	COL	0-0029934	0862	1
BISHOP CLARENCE F	LTC	0-0080583	0667	1
BISHOP CLIFFORD D	CPT	0-0019611	0242	2
BISHOP EUGENE H	LTC	0-0041167	0865	1
BISHOP HARRY A	COL	0-0010565	0848	1
BISHOP JR NOEL S	COL	0-0009322	0954	2
BISHOP LOREN E	COL	0-0040091	0567	1
BISHOP MARGARET N	LTC	N-0000186	0962	1
BISSELL EDWARD B	COL	0-0021360	0367	1
BISSELL HARRY H	LTC	0-0001986	1128	2
BISSELL JOHN T B	B G	0-0008624	0246	1
BISSELL LEET W	1LT	0-0014364	0419	2
BISSELL PAUL V	COL	0-0041941	0162	1
BISSETT DAVID A	LTC	0-0008456	0934	2
BISSON ROGER R	CPT	0-0069861	0559	2
BITALA JOSEPH A	CW4	W-0907137	1157	1
BITNER LELAND M	LTC	0-0059570	0965	1
BITNER ROBERT F	COL	0-0017371	0254	2
BITROS MINNIE L	MAJ	N-0000691	0752	1
BITTNER JOHN H F	COL	0-0028870	0756	1
BITZEL MARGARET M	MAJ	N-0000531	1054	1
BIVENS ARTHUR L	COL	0-0042105	0163	1
BIXBY HAROLD D	COL	0-0014739	0946	1
BIXBY JR LAWRENCE H	CPT	0-0025440	0648	2
BIXBY LAWRENCE B	COL	0-0012102	0850	1
BIXBY WALLACE W	CW2	W-0902800	0861	1
BIXBY WILLIS W	LTC	0-0035104	0863	1
BIXEL CHARLES P	B G	0-0015808	0757	1
BIZZELL LEE C	COL	0-0010250	0753	1
BJORK DELBERT L	COL	0-0032399	1163	1
BLACK ARTHUR H	COL	0-0038718	0662	1
BLACK ASA C	COL	0-0038894	1066	1
BLACK CLAUDE A	COL	0-0016235	0950	1
BLACK DANIEL N	COL	0-0052309	1263	1
BLACK FLORENCE S	MAJ	N-0000934	0264	1
BLACK FREDERICK	B G	0-0009719	0650	1
BLACK GEORGE W	COL	0-0032192	1255	1
BLACK HAROLD	COL	0-0040373	0565	1
BLACK HENRY M	B G	0-0008598	1053	1
BLACK IRA W	COL	0-0010113	0451	1
BLACK JAMES A	CW2	W-0900607	0446	2
BLACK JAMES G	COL	0-0039833	0363	1
BLACK JOHN W	LTC	0-0018136	0644	2
BLACK JOSEPH E	LTC	0-0039268	0966	1
BLACK JR FREDERICK	LTC	0-0026796	0764	1
BLACK JR GARLAND C	LTC	0-0026106	0165	2
BLACK PAUL J	COL	0-0016500	0755	1
BLACK PERCY G	COL	0-0005264	0340	2
BLACK PETER T L	LTC	0-0031900	1061	2
BLACK ROBERT L	COL	0-0017375	0355	1
BLACK WILLIAM E	LTC	0-0080047	0467	2
BLACKBURN WILLIAM H	LTC	0-0034244	0267	1
BLACKER KEMUEL K	COL	0-0044956	1065	1
BLACKFORD CLIFTON O	COL	0-0018205	0760	1
BLACKFORD JAMES C	MAJ	0-0058836	0563	1
BLACKLOCK WARD T	COL	0-0032899	0965	1
BLACKMARR WILLIAM H	COL	0-0042836	0966	1
BLACKMON ROY F	COL	0-0051569	0165	1
BLACKMORE PHILIP G	B G	0-0003201	0150	1
BLACKSHEAR JOHN P	LTC	0-0019984	0655	1
BLACKWELL HERBERT H	COL	0-0008151	1047	1
BLACKWELL JAMES M	LTC	0-0079647	0765	1
BLACKWELL JOHN R	LTC	0-0053789	0763	1
BLACKWELL LOTUS B	LTC	0-0080375	0965	1
BLADES JACK	COL	0-0033082	0660	1

NAME	GRADE	SVC NO	DATE RET MO YR	RET CODE
BLAIN ARTHUR C	COL	0-0010644	0447	2
BLAIR ARNOLD O	LTC	0-0051477	0457	1
BLAIR EDGAR A	COL	0-0056803	0258	1
BLAIR GEORGE	COL	0-0002954	0642	1
BLAIR III JOHN H	LTC	0-0044388	0864	1
BLAIR JOHN D	COL	0-0041736	0761	2
BLAIR MELVIN R	LTC	0-0032150	1154	1
BLAIR RICHARD A	COL	0-0042858	0167	2
BLAIR ROBERT K	COL	0-0051526	1262	2
BLAIR RUSSELL	MAJ	0-0017220	0150	1
BLAIR VICTOR R	MAJ	0-0037926	1062	1
BLAIR WILLIAM R	COL	0-0012111	1146	1
BLAIR 3RD JOHN S	COL	0-0029340	1159	1
BLAKE ALLEN J	COL	0-0029229	0263	1
BLAKE DONALD G	COL	0-0051875	0565	2
BLAKE ELLIS B	COL	0-0043027	0467	1
BLAKE HOMER C	COL	0-0042955	0165	1
BLAKE HU A	COL	0-0058708	0966	1
BLAKE JR CHARLES J	COL	0-0021122	0762	2
BLAKE MARY S	LTC	L-0000078	0465	1
BLAKE STEWART P	LTC	0-0038221	0764	1
BLAKE WILLIAM R	LTC	0-0036162	0666	1
BLAKELOCK DAVID H	B G	0-0004853	0650	1
BLAKELY CARL P	COL	0-0032870	0765	1
BLAKELY CHARLES S	B G	0-0001909	0838	2
BLAKELY WILLIAM R	COL	0-0015398	1153	1
BLAKENEY CRESWELL G	COL	0-0014764	0854	1
BLAKENEY JAMES P	COL	0-0010000	1046	2
BLAKISTONE JOHN F	LTC	0-0042586	0863	1
BLANCETT ROLLIE N	COL	0-0021416	0764	1
BLANCHARD CHARLES C	B G	0-0011200	0854	2
BLANCHARD ROBERT M	B G	0-0019282	0861	1
BLANCHARD WENDELL	COL	0-0015528	0754	1
BLANCHARD WESTON L	COL	0-0029925	0763	1
BLANCHETT JR LEO M	LTC	[illegible]	0366	1
BLANCHFIELD F A	COL	N-0000001	[illegible]	1
BLANDFORD JR JAMES T	LTC	[illegible]	0866	1
BLANDFORD WILLIAM O	B G	0-0018990	0653	1
BLANEY GEORGE	COL	0-0006337	1046	1
BLANEY KERMIT B	COL	0-0035501	1265	1
BLANK LESLIE H	1LT	0-0014405	0120	2
BLANKENSHIP FRANCIS	COL	0-0042330	0159	1
BLANKENSHIP GEORGE H	MAJ	0-0004509	1021	2
BLANKENSHIP JACOB A	COL	0-0005975	0642	1
BLANTON EARNEST W	CW4	W-0907805	0260	1
BLANTON FRANKLIN S	LTC	0-0038634	0156	1
BLANTON WILLIAM L	COL	0-0007048	0553	1
BLASER EUGENE V	COL	0-0042364	0765	1
BLASINGAME FLOYD	COL	0-0051175	0165	1
BLASINGAME RUBY J	MAJ	N-0001064	1262	1
BLATT JOHN R	COL	0-0018935	1159	2
BLATT MARGARET E	LTC	N-0000593	0862	1
BLATT RAYMOND C	LTC	0-0006397	0939	1
BLATT RAYMOND C	LTC	0-0026186	0664	1
BLAUVELT CHARLES W	LTC	0-0020861	0353	2
BLAUVELT XAVIER F	COL	0-0003021	0-41	1
BLAZEFIC GLADYS M	MAJ	N-0002064	0262	1
BLECH JEANETTE	LTC	N-0000501	1153	1
BLEDSOE CARL E	COL	0-0031592	0767	2
BLEDSOE WILLIAM R	B G	0-0008184	0646	2
BLENCOE GUY W	COL	0-0030245	0853	1
BLIGHT EDWARD H	COL	0-0040191	1067	2
BLISS ARTHUR	COL	0-0018134	0250	1
BLISS CHARLES J	LTC	0-0055423	0366	1
BLISS HAROLD B	COL	0-0008494	0248	2
BLITCH CLIFFORD G	COL	0-0019302	0255	1
BLIZZARD JR JOHN C	COL	0-0007581	0149	1
BLODGETT WILLIAM S	COL	0-0031438	0164	1
BLOM ARTHUR R	COL	0-0079744	0966	1
BLOMFELT OLLE G P	CW4	W-0902034	0955	1
BLOOD KENNETH T	M G	0-0003219	0248	1
BLOOD WILLIAM C	LTC	0-0078721	1068	1
BLOOM FRED H	CW2	W-0901599	1049	1
BLOOMQUIST GEORGE F	COL	0-0006140	0246	2
BLOSS ARNOLD W	LTC	0-0045424	0262	1

NAME	GRADE	SVC NO	DATE RET MO YR	RET CODE
BLOSS JACOB H	COL	0-0041416	0556	1
BLOSSMAN INEZ H	MAJ	N-0001273	0761	1
BLOUNT CHARLES E	LTC	0-0045217	1163	1
BLOUNT ROY E	B G	0-0005176	1047	2
BLOW RALPH C	CW2	W-0907453	0953	1
BLUE ARTHUR C	CW3	W-0902808	1058	1
BLUE DANIEL L	LTC	0-0031997	0861	1
BLUE JR FRANK L	LTC	0-0017496	0955	1
BLUEMEL CLIFFORD	B G	0-0002642	1047	2
BLUM CLYDE F	CW2	W-0902381	0954	1
BLUM MILTON R	COL	0-0031695	0160	2
BLUM VERNON N	MAJ	0-0039729	0651	1
BLUMENFELD CHARLES H	COL	0-0029763	0962	1
BLUMENSAADT PAUL F	LTC	0-0032727	0866	1
BLUMENTHAL RALPH H	LTC	0-0029318	0662	1
BLUST RAYMOND L	LTC	0-0030671	0266	2
BLYTHE WILLIAM J	COL	0-0051308	0562	1
BOARDMAN CHARLES H	LTC	0-0057695	1066	1
BOARDMAN THOMAS G	LTC	0-0038665	0459	1
BOATNER HAYDON L	M G	0-0015661	1060	1
BOATNER JR MARK M	COL	0-0012050	1047	1
BOATSMAN ALFORD C	COL	0-0029588	0961	2
BOBO JR CARL E	LTC	0-0033144	1061	1
BOCHNOWSKI JOSEPH S	COL	0-0051498	0564	1
BOCK FRANK C	LTC	0-0017265	0150	1
BOCKOVEN FREDERICK E	LTC	0-0037354	0766	1
BOCKSEL ARNOLD A	CW2	W-0901770	0649	2
BODE DONALD D	COL	0-0029651	0562	1
BODE JOHN T	CPT	0-0045794	0646	2
BODEAU EDWARD	COL	0-0019008	0254	1
BODINE DONALD [illegible]	COL	0-0020236	0956	1
BODINE JR ROY [illegible]	COL	0-0020489	0451	[illegible]
BODINE ROBERT N	COL	0-0003375	0244	1
BODINE ROY L	MAJ	0-0008709	1047	1
BODIS JEANNETTE	MAJ	N-000[illegible]	1165	1
BOEHMER VIC [illegible]	LTC	0-0051551	1062	1
BOEHMER WILLIAM [illegible]	COL	0-0051353	0451	1
[illegible]	CW4	W-0902282	0264	2
[illegible]	COL	0-0019670	0760	1
[illegible]	COL	0-0003027	1141	1
BOGAN [illegible]	COL	0-0005105	0247	2
BOGART JAMES H	LTC	0-0060847	0235	2
BOGART THEODORE F	M G	0-0018245	0665	1
BOGER MARTHA H	MAJ	N-0010062	1265	1
BOGGAN EDGAR W	LTC	0-0059828	1265	1
BOGINSKI FRANK J	CW4	W-0906626	1066	1
BOGLE JAMES C	COL	0-0052662	0262	1
BOGNER CHARLES	COL	0-0033892	0665	1
BOGNER HOWARD E	COL	0-0051370	0163	1
BOGUE JOY R	COL	0-0029990	0554	1
BOGUE WILLIAM [illegible]	LTC	0-0030470	0663	1
BOHERTY PHILLIP A	LTC	0-0083595	0866	1
BOHLENDER JOHN F	M G	0-0017814	1161	1
BOHN GORDON A	COL	0-0031075	0865	[illegible]
BOHN JOHN J	B G	0-0004582	0245	[illegible]
BOHNER JOHN F	CW4	W-0902489	0555	1
BOINEAU LEON C	COL	0-0011249	0764	1
BOLAN HARRY W	COL	0-0008101	1050	1
BOLDING JR A P	MAJ	0-0046764	0657	2
BOLDUC LUCIEN F	COL	0-0016137	0755	1
BOLES CATHERINE	MAJ	N-0000365	0261	1
BOLEYN JOHN C	LTC	0-0027492	0664	1
BOLEYN PAUL A	COL	0-0020903	0561	1
BOLIBAUGH ORAL R	COL	0-0004170	0450	1
BOLICH JAMES O	LTC	0-0036920	0266	1
BOLING JEAN H	COL	0-0031817	1262	1
BOLKE FRANCIS G	LTC	0-0080591	0766	1
BOLL ARTHUR C	LTC	0-0016142	0346	2
BOLLAND GERHARD L	LTC	0-0019565	0551	1
BOLLENBECK JOSEPH W	CPT	0-0006627	0335	1
BOLLERO ANGELO D	COL	0-0039853	1061	1
BOLT JAMES L	COL	0-0011673	0753	1
BOLTE CHARLES L	GEN	0-0006908	0455	1
BOLTEN RICHARD S	MAJ	0-0021735	0743	2
BOLTWOOD ELIZABETH	MAJ	L-0000026	1155	1

NAME	GRADE	SVC NO	DATE RET MO YR	RET CODE
BOLTZ DELTON N	CW3	W-0906628	0456	2
BOMAR ERNEST C	COL	0-0006733	0352	1
BONO AUBREY F	COL	0-0008876	0349	2
BOND JOHN R F	LTC	0-0036986	0964	1
BOND THOMAS G	LTC	0-0004887	1138	1
BOND VIRGIL W	LTC	0-0042878	1059	1
BONDSHU LOWELL T	COL	0-0051670	0864	1
BONDY EDWARD W	COL	0-0005085	0247	1
BONE HOWARD C	LTC	0-0035792	0161	1
BONHAM DWIGHT D	LTC	0-0033949	0262	1
BONHAM ROSCOE	COL	0-0010767	0750	1
BONIFAY LEWIS A	COL	0-0029040	0159	1
BONNELL JR OEW L	LTC	0-0040098	0863	1
BONNELYCKE CARL	CW4	W-0904401	1054	1
BONNER MARTHA M	LTC	L-0000097	0766	1
BONNEY FRANK F	COL	0-0007441	0644	1
BONNIWELL ALFRED E	COL	0-0042931	0267	1
BONSTEEL FRANCIS T	COL	0-0005480	0650	1
BONTA JAMES C	LTC	0-0034731	0967	1
BOOKER PHILLIP W	COL	0-0002208	0144	1
BOOKOUT HAL H	COL	0-0068179	1167	1
BOOMER EUGENE F	LTC	0-0045846	0861	1
BOON JR STEPHEN	COL	0-0006782	0646	2
BOON WALTER W	COL	0-0007632	1052	1
BOONE ABBOTT	COL	0-0002259	0-43	1
BOONE EDWARD A	COL	0-0010179	0366	2
BOONE JOSEPH W	COL	0-0015341	1150	1
BOONE MILTON C	B G	0-0008127	0548	1
BOOS FRANCIS H	COL	0-0017291	0251	1
BOOTH BENJAMIN N	COL	0-0002204	0430	2
BOOTH DONALD P	LTC	[illegible]	0262	1
BOOTH GEORGE W	CPT	0-0014265	0720	2
BOOTH JAMES W	COL	[illegible]	0866	1
BOOTH MERRITT H	COL	0-0012378	0646	2
BOOTH RIVES C	LTC	0-0019947	0544	2
BOOTH ROBERT H	M G	0-0018093	0365	1
BOOTH ROBERT M	COL	0-0019964	0965	1
BOOTHE JR JOHN E	LTC	0-0052934	0762	1
BORDEN JACK	LTC	0-0023306	0661	1
BORG HELGA C C	LTC	N-0000619	0249	1
BORGFELDT RICHARD N	LTC	0-0042015	1058	1
BORIN GORDON F	LTC	0-0042621	0863	1
BORK LESTER S	B G	[illegible]	0762	1
BORLEIS JOHN H A	COL	0-0018652	0859	1
BORNS CHARLES R	LTC	0-0034245	0264	1
BOROM THOMAS L	LTC	0-0050518	0454	1
BORUP PAUL C	COL	0-0018445	0657	1
BORUSKI ERNEST F	COL	0-0008292	1149	1
BOSBYSHELL JOHN H	COL	0-0010598	0163	1
BOSCO SALVATORE	CW4	W-0906611	1161	2
BOSGIETER ERNEST W	COL	0-0041591	0559	1
BOSS PHILIPPE R	COL	0-0039980	0565	1
BOSWELL JACK	LTC	0-0026080	0763	1
BOSWELL JAMES O	M G	0-0019188	1061	1
BOSWORTH LEROY F	CW4	W-0902914	0451	1
BOTHWELL JR F C	COL	0-0020235	1045	2
BOTHWELL LYMAN C	COL	0-0051046	0859	1
BOTTCHLY JR R V	COL	0-0034071	0167	1
BOTTS JOSEPH H	COL	0-0031514	0567	1
BOTTS LUTHER H	LTC	0-0036752	0864	1
BOUCHER FRANCIS H	COL	0-0006578	0750	1
BOUCHER JEFF W	COL	0-0024123	0964	1
BOUDREAU NAPOLEON	COL	0-0005934	0548	1
BOUDREAUX RAYMOND	COL	0-0023344	0760	1
BOUFFIER HELEN H	LTC	L-0000032	0359	1
BOUGHTON LLOYD L	1LT	0-0014408	0120	2
BOURBON ROLLO R	COL	0-0008909	1047	1
BOURDEAU STEPHEN F	CW4	W-0906632	0664	1
BOURGEOIS EMILINE A	MAJ	N-0002390	0162	1
BOURQUARDEZ CHARLES	MAJ	0-0060337	1063	1
BOUSH JAMES F	COL	0-0010525	1050	1
BOUTELL HORTENSE M	LTC	L-0000094	0566	1
BOUTELLE MAURICE H	LTC	0-0062126	0167	1
BOUTON ARTHUR G	LTC	0-0031304	0862	1
BOUTON IRMA V	LTC	L-0000195	0767	1

UNITED STATES ARMY RETIRED LIST

NAME	GRADE	SVC NO	DATE RET MO YR	RET CODE
BOWDEN EDWIN T	COL	O-0007164	C348	1
BOWDEN MARION P	LTC	O-0033104	0948	2
BOWDEN RICHARD W	COL	C-0042640	0965	1
BOWEN ARTHUR F	LTC	C-0007778	0144	2
BOWEN FRANCIS C	COL	O-0039682	0760	1
BOWEN GENEVA N	LTC	N-0001966	1263	1
BOWEN JOHN W	CPT	C-0014558	C-19	2
BOWEN JR CLAUDE L	COL	O-0019244	0863	1
BOWEN JR FRANK S	M G	O-0016434	1162	1
BOWEN JR JAMES F	COL	O-0015302	0452	1
BOWEN JR WILLARD G	COL	O-0030536	1065	1
BOWEN JR WILLIAM C	LTC	C-0061201	0766	1
BOWEN ROBERT B	CPT	O-0028147	C557	2
BOWEN WILLIAM S	COL	O-0001648	0642	1
BOWER HARVEY	COL	C-0019912	0965	1
BOWER JAMES C	LTC	O-0018934	0651	1
BOWER JAMES R	LTC	O-0042768	0564	1
BOWER JR ROLAND C	COL	C-0018721	0862	1
BOWER LAURENCE P	COL	O-0016019	0952	1
BOWER RALPH E	COL	O-0006610	1045	2
BOWERS ALVIN T	COL	C-0016107	0755	1
BOWERS BERNA T	COL	O-0016300	0454	1
BOWERS GERALD V	1LT	O-0037602	0550	1
BOWERS MERVIN C	COL	C-0042319	0264	1
BOWERS WARNER F	COL	C-0029197	C361	1
BOWERS WILLIAM H	COL	O-0029264	C661	1
BOWERS WILLIAM S	COL	C-0038973	1262	2
BOWLBY LAWRENCE	COL	O-0045718	0766	1
BOWLER LOUIS J	COL	O-0006335	C346	2
BOWLES OTIS R	CW4	W-0902357	0958	1
BOWLING PAULINE J	LTC	N-0000578	1164	1
BOWMAN ALFRED C	COL	C-0056777	C360	1
BOWMAN CLIFFORD A	COL	O-0030728	0664	1
BOWMAN DAVID H	LTC	O-0039711	0359	1
BOWMAN FRANK O	M G	O-0012090	0656	1
BOWMAN HOMER H	COL	C-0031700	0965	1
BOWMAN JAMES C	LTC	O-0085487	0866	2
BOWMAN JAMES E	LTC	O-0088580	C167	2
BOWMAN JAMES W	COL	O-0038813	1265	1
BOWMAN JOHN F	COL	O-0033211	0263	1
BOWMAN LESLIE E	MAJ	C-0008433	1137	2
BOWMAN ORLEY O	COL	C-0010974	0146	2
BOWMAN PRESTON	CW4	W-0904400	C955	1
BOWSKY MERLE C	COL	O-0029386	C260	1
BOWYER OSCAR R	COL	C-0019934	C762	1
BOYCE JOHN E	LTC	O-0042402	0762	1
BOYCE JR ROBERT A	COL	O-0019329	0858	1
BOYCE WILLIAM M	COL	O-0079753	1165	1
BOYD CHARLES W	CW3	W-0902817	0661	1
BOYD DONN T	LTC	C-0062181	0563	1
BOYD HARRY R	COL	O-0018102	0760	1
BOYD JOSEPH L	COL	O-0008783	0347	2
BOYD JR ALLAN S	COL	O-0003278	0342	2
BOYD JR GEORGE W	CW3	W-0907108	C666	1
BOYD JR ROBERT P	COL	C-0040068	0966	1
BOYD LAWRENCE L	COL	C-0030180	1263	1
BOYD LEONARD R	B G	O-0004811	1151	1
BOYD LOGAN W	COL	C-0010387	1052	1
BOYD MARZELLE F	COL	O-0039921	C964	1
BOYD RICHARD K	COL	O-0018548	0761	1
BOYD WILLIAM E	LTC	O-0080598	1265	1
BOYE FREDERIC W	B G	O-0003895	C950	1
BOYER EMILE J	CPT	O-0007275	C933	2
BOYER GEORGE S	LTC	O-0022297	C546	2
BOYER JOSEPH C	COL	C-0029461	0960	1
BOYER RAY Y	LTC	O-0080599	0862	1
BOYER RICHARD J	LTC	O-0037202	0966	1
BOYKIN JESS G	COL	C-0008401	C245	2
BOYKIN RICHARD P	COL	O-0009247	C642	1
BOYLAN PAUL C	COL	O-0008370	C944	2
BOYLAN RUFUS	COL	C-0008045	1145	2
BOYLAN VINCENT L	COL	O-0022162	1065	1
BOYLE CONRAD L	COL	O-0015951	0954	2
BOYLE FRANK F	MAJ	C-0025326	0446	2
BOYLE GEORGE L	COL	O-0014862	1150	1

NAME	GRADE	SVC NO	DATE RET MO YR	RET CODE
BOYLE GUY F	CW4	W-0902820	1159	1
BOYLE JOSEPH E	LTC	O-0040188	0865	1
BOYLE MARVIN	COL	O-0004539	1049	1
BOYLE ROBERT W	CW4	RW-0905714	0166	1
BOYLE RUSSELL T	COL	O-0028900	0457	1
BOYLE THADDEUS A	LTC	O-0035791	1163	1
BOYLE WILLIAM A	COL	O-0006423	0747	1
BOYLE WILLIAM J	COL	O-0021953	0867	1
BOYLES FRANCIS R	COL	C-0029803	1262	1
BOYLES SAMUEL J	COL	O-0032168	0466	1
BOZE WILBURN H	LTC	O-0065320	1067	1
BRAASCH LORAINE J	MAJ	N-0001955	0659	1
BRABSON FAY W	COL	O-0001600	0642	2
BRABSON JR WILLIAM H	LTC	O-0026069	1262	1
BRACHER ALLEN N	COL	O-0015706	0955	1
BRACKEBUSCH CARL O	LTC	O-0059561	0766	1
BRACKETT MORRIS E	COL	O-0025162	0862	2
BRADEN JESSIE M	LTC	N-0000002	0947	1
BRADFORD AUBREY L	COL	O-0017817	0861	1
BRADFORD DAVID E	COL	O-0016273	0637	2
BRADFORD KARL S	B G	O-0003083	1046	2
BRADFORD WILLIAM S	WO1	W-0901144	1035	1
BRADISH ROBERT F	COL	O-0014955	1047	1
BRADLEY ALFORD V	LTC	O-0029259	0261	2
BRADLEY BEN W	LTC	O-0049713	1162	1
BRADLEY EARL M	LTC	O-0058279	0765	1
BRADLEY FRANCIS X	COL	O-0022740	C859	1
BRADLEY GLENN M	LTC	O-0051768	0564	1
BRADLEY JOHN A	COL	O-0039836	0763	1
BRADLEY JR JOHN M	COL	O-0042318	0758	1
BRADLEY ROBERT W	LTC	O-0080600	0767	1
BRADLEY RUBY G	COL	N-0000087	0463	1
BRADLEY RUTH W	MAJ	M-0010021	0963	1
BRADLEY WILLIAM J	B G	O-0015967	0854	2
BRADLEY WILLIAM R	COL	O-0011752	0749	1
BRADSHAW JR AARON	M G	O-0005290	0153	1
BRADSHER MARIE E	MAJ	N-0000164	1059	2
BRADY BROOKNER W	COL	O-0016519	0656	2
BRADY EILEEN W	COL	N-0000091	1263	1
BRADY JOHN W	COL	O-0018627	0258	1
BRADY LAWRENCE W	COL	O-0030703	0666	1
BRADY ROBERT W	LTC	O-0080601	0966	1
BRADY WILLIAM I	COL	O-0012689	0151	1
BRAGALONE ALFRED A	LTC	O-0036080	0863	1
BRAGAN ONTO R	COL	O-0015754	0653	1
BRAGDON KERLIN J	COL	O-0042766	0766	1
BRAGG CLARENCE H	COL	O-0008316	0753	1
BRAID ROBERT B	COL	O-0032950	0766	2
BRALY WILLIAM C	COL	O-0007972	0147	2
BRAMBLE PHILIP H	COL	O-0033341	0767	1
BRAME WAYNE W	COL	O-0035765	0462	1
BRAMLETT HUBERT B	COL	O-0010689	0753	1
BRANCH GOODMAN S	COL	O-0051014	0259	1
BRANCH JAMES C	COL	O-0042279	0761	1
BRAND CLARENCE E	COL	O-0008432	0449	1
BRAND TOM S	COL	O-0007123	1052	1
BRANDEWIE ROBERT A	LTC	O-0060373	0267	1
BRANDHORST HENRY W	COL	O-0011619	0548	2
BRANDIGER FREIDA A V	CPT	N-0000537	0348	1
BRANDNER CARL S	COL	O-0029442	0760	1
BRANDON THURMAN M	MAJ	O-0024754	0562	1
BRANDSTADT WAYNE G	COL	O-0018318	0853	1
BRANDT BERNICE O	MAJ	N-0002124	0360	1
BRANDT JEROME N	LTC	O-0031245	1159	1
BRANDT MARGARET M	MAJ	N-0000543	1057	1
BRANDYBERRY MARCELLA	MAJ	N-0000618	0263	1
BRANHAM CHARLES N	COL	O-0014920	0150	1
BRANIGIN JAMES E	COL	O-0053419	1265	1
BRANN HERBERT P	LTC	O-0030686	0464	1
BRANNAN FRANCIS M	COL	O-0003721	0648	1
BRANNAN JOHN E	COL	O-0007170	0337	2
BRANNON ERNEST M	M G	O-0012292	1054	1
BRANNON MARGARET N	MAJ	N-0000103	0460	2
BRANSON CHARLES E	MAJ	O-0030805	1057	1
BRANSON DON P	CPT	O-0007739	0934	2

NAME	GRADE	SVC NO	DATE RET MO YR	RET CODE
BRANT ESTHER F	MAJ	N-0002288	0865	1
BRANT PHILIP O	COL	O-0020804	0865	1
BRANTLEY JOSEPH W	LTC	O-0030440	0563	1
BRANTON HAROLD M	LTC	O-0037345	1066	1
BRASCHER THOMAS J	COL	C-0039749	0760	1
BRASEL DONALD E	CW3	W-0902823	0961	1
BRASHEAR MARION G	CW2	W-0901554	0849	1
BRASSEL ALFRED L	LTC	O-0023420	0661	1
BRASTED FRED	COL	O-0041854	0361	1
BRATTON DANIEL	COL	O-0006370	0248	1
BRAUD EDITH A	MAJ	N-0000724	0565	1
BRAUDE MEYER A	COL	O-0018802	C862	1
BRAUN EUGENE J	LTC	O-0037790	0966	1
BRAUN PAUL	WO1	W-0901112	0425	1
BRAUN WALTER R	LTC	O-0060509	0564	1
BRAUNECKER MARY P	MAJ	N-0002066	0459	1
BRAUNING EDNA R	CPT	N-0000818	0459	1
BRAV ERNEST A	COL	O-0056995	C564	1
BRAVEMAN MILTON	LTC	O-0065501	0767	1
BRAYSHAW HORACE A	COL	O-0029307	C762	1
BRAZEAL LUCY P	MAJ	N-0000842	0864	2
BRAZEALE EVERETT L	CW4	W-0902824	0164	1
BRAZIER KELLY L	COL	O-0039674	0555	1
BREAKEFIELD DURWARD	B G	O-0019781	1265	1
BREAKS ROBERT W	COL	O-0020273	C866	1
BREAZEALE MARY	MAJ	R-0010117	1160	1
BRECKENRIDGE JAMES O	COL	O-0039897	0464	1
BRECKINRIDGE WILLIAM	M G	O-0017210	0662	1
BREDEN JOHN P	COL	C-0017135	0758	1
BREEN EDITH R	MAJ	N-0000376	0860	1
BREEN FRANCES R	MAJ	N-0002443	C767	1
BREEN JOHN J	COL	O-0012165	C349	1
BREITENBERG EUGENE M	CPT	O-0062819	1263	1
BREITUNG ELIZABETH	LTC	N-0001902	1064	1
BREMER ERNEST K	COL	O-0076835	0164	1
BREMKAMP LOUIS F	COL	O-0079755	C667	1
BRENEMAN RUTH F	MAJ	N-0001328	C763	1
BRENN CHARLES F	COL	O-0006263	1147	2
BRENNAN BEATRICE R	MAJ	L-0000009	1153	1
BRENNAN JAMES T	COL	O-0031183	0766	1
BRENNAN JOHN J	COL	C-0031150	0962	1
BRENNAN MARK F	COL	O-0021279	0767	1
BRENNAN PATRICK J	MAJ	C-0043756	C359	1
BRENNEMAN GARLAND E	LTC	O-0042576	0663	1
BRENNEMAN IVAN L	COL	O-0039627	C959	1
BRENNEMAN LOYD W	COL	O-0029676	0262	1
BRENNER CARL F	LTC	O-0051969	0463	1
BRENNER MATILDA R	1LT	R-0000115	1146	1
BRESLIN JOHN F	COL	O-0057525	C566	1
BRESNAHAN THOMAS F	B G	O-0007378	0348	1
BRESSLER DEAN M	LTC	O-0026809	0665	1
BRETON MARGARITA	LTC	N-0002080	1067	1
BRETT JAMES Q	2LT	O-0018115	0834	2
BRETTELL JR JAMES A	LTC	O-0069600	C967	1
BREWER CARLOS	M G	O-0003539	1050	1
BREWER DWIGHT C	LTC	O-0079756	0761	1
BREWER JAMES N	COL	O-0042220	0863	1
BREWER JOHN E	LTC	O-0052741	0162	1
BREWER KENNETH A	COL	O-0018634	0861	1
BREWER MYRON L	LTC	O-0032495	1065	1
BREWER ROBERT M	COL	C-0022975	C866	1
BREWERTON HENRY R	LTC	O-0023311	0246	2
BREWSTER JR EDWIN S	COL	O-0010620	1146	1
BREWSTER MARGARET F	LTC	L-0000088	1265	1
BREWSTER NATHAN	WO1	W-0901570	0242	2
BREY WILLIAM G	COL	O-0006499	C848	1
BRIAN ADRAIN B	CPT	O-0059332	1057	2
BRIAN ADRIAN P	COL	O-0007332	0750	1
BRICE LAWRENCE S	CPT	O-0060867	C959	2
BRICE MAURICE R	LTC	O-0032557	0361	2
BRICKER L MONROE	COL	O-0007245	0649	1
BRICKLES FRANKLIN R	COL	O-0030278	1064	1
BRICKMAN GEORGE A	1LT	O-0017216	0834	2
BRIDGE CARL J	CPT	O-0073949	C859	2
BRIDGER KILIE E	LTC	N-0000084	1060	1

NAME	GRADE	SVC NO	DATE RET MO YR	RET CODE
BRIDGERS GEORGE A	COL	O-0029395	0560	2
BRIDGES BURLIN C	COL	O-0009488	0645	2
BRIDGES WILLIAM C	COL	O-0016597	0756	1
BRIDGMAN J ALLINGTO	LTC	O-0081965	1062	1
BRIDGMAN RICHARD H	COL	O-0016335	0133	2
BRIEN JR JAMES N	LTC	O-0057538	0256	2
BRIER WILLIAM W	COL	C-0011062	0250	1
BRIGGS EDWIN J	COL	C-0043363	0363	1
BRIGGS GORDON H	LTC	O-0062940	0766	1
BRIGGS JOHN L	LTC	O-0058840	0866	1
BRIGGS RACHEL V	MAJ	N-0002120	0558	1
BRIGGS RICHARD F	LTC	O-0036032	1162	1
BRIGGS RUTH M	LTC	L-0000339	1264	1
BRIGGS WILLIAM A	LTC	O-0042315	0162	1
BRIGGS WINIFRED M	MAJ	N-0000992	0164	1
BRIGHAM CLAUDE E	M G	O-0001356	0937	1
BRIGHTMAN JOHN Y	LTC	O-0031366	0463	2
BRILL ALBERT	MAJ	O-0010884	0337	1
BRILL HEBER C	LTC	O-0026162	0265	1
BRIMMER HOWARD W	COL	O-0012221	0753	1
BRINCKERHOFF JR G G	COL	O-0041686	0560	1
BRINDLE HARRY C	COL	O-0051380	0263	1
BRINDLEY JOHN R	COL	O-0019087	1058	1
BRINGHAM ROBERT A	CPT	O-0014398	1019	2
BRINK JOHNNIE C	COL	O-0034658	0164	1
BRINKLEY JR JOSEPH S	COL	O-0031444	1163	1
BRINSON NOAH M	COL	O-0015883	1147	2
BRINSON ROBERT H	CPT	O-0024352	1044	2
BRISACH RAYMOND C	COL	O-0018202	0559	1
BRISACK FLOYD R	COL	O-0014740	0947	1
BRISCOE WILLIAM T	LTC	O-0054688	1165	1
BRISTER JANE G	LTC	L-0000289	0765	1
BRISTOL MATT C	COL	O-0001559	0737	1
BRISTOE JOHN O	COL	O-0019710	0859	1
BRITELL CLAUDE C	COL	O-0029183	0760	1
BRITT HENRY C	COL	O-0018891	0962	2
BRITT JAMES A	MAJ	O-0084592	0264	1
BRITT JR ALBERT S	COL	O-0042237	0962	1
BRITT JR ROY E	CW4	W-0902826	0961	1
BRITT ROBERT C	LTC	O-0054425	0664	1
BRITTAIN COURTLAND	COL	O-0042341	0163	1
BRITTAIN HOMER E	CW4	W-0902827	0965	1
BRITTEN ROLAND L	LTC	O-0080609	1163	1
BRITTINGHAM JAMES F	B G	O-0005746	0654	2
BRITTINGHAM JR A D	LTC	O-0039577	0356	1
BRITTON FRANK H	M G	O-0018703	0867	1
BRITTON FRANK K	COL	O-0030532	0960	1
BRITTON GEORGE T	COL	O-0062778	0867	2
BRITTON MATTIE E	MAJ	N-0000845	0454	2
BRIZIUS SR CHARLES A	LTC	O-0058841	0667	1
BROADHURST HUGH H	COL	O-0002066	0740	1
BROADHURST ROBERT C	1LT	O-0016418	0734	2
BROBERG RICHARD A	COL	O-0021272	0766	1
BROBERG WALDEMAR S	COL	O-0012330	0854	1
BROCK JOHN A	LTC	O-0042914	1165	1
BROCK KIRK P	COL	O-0041650	0260	1
BROCK LEON A	COL	O-0041508	0858	1
BROCK MILTON F	CW3	W-0906639	1059	1
BROCKETT CHARLES K	LTC	O-0060199	0866	1
BROCKETT RAYMOND C	CW4	W-0907135	0966	2
BROCKHAUSEN FRED C	CW2	W-0901779	0646	2
BROCKMAN ERNEST F	LTC	O-0022147	0867	1
BROCKMAN SIDNEY C	COL	O-0031212	0964	1
BROCKWAY EDGAR K	CPT	O-0007814	0334	2
BRODERICK MERL L	COL	O-0008449	0753	1
BRODEOLCH RUDOLPH W	COL	O-0011161	0849	1
BROGAN WILLIAM T	COL	O-0030194	0664	1
BROIDA DONALD	MAJ	O-0060641	0265	2
BROMLEY JR CHARLES V	M G	O-0015239	0356	1
BRONDSTATTER WALLACE	LTC	O-0085300	0764	1
BRONN CARL H	COL	O-0031748	0166	1
BROCK SR HOWARD F	LTC	O-0042907	1164	1
BROOKE JR JAMES F	COL	O-0017600	0250	1
BROOKENS TREVA B	MAJ	N-0002130	0360	1
BROOKES WYTHE P	LTC	O-0045447	0266	1

NAME	GRADE	SVC NO	DATE RET MO YR	RET CODE
BROOKHART HAROLD C	COL	0-0019562	0864	1
BROOKRESON WADE Y	LTC	0-0035588	0765	1
BROOKS ALBERT G	LTC	0-0026516	0865	1
BROOKS CECIL	MAJ	0-0018313	0934	2
BROOKS DWIGHT M	LTC	0-0050004	0765	1
BROOKS EDWARD H	LTG	0-0006657	0453	1
BROOKS HAROLD F	COL	0-0018152	0760	1
BROOKS IRVING W	COL	0-0039783	0962	1
BROOKS JAMES M	LTC	0-0029736	0860	2
BROOKS JOHN A	COL	0-0003679	0946	1
BROOKS JOHN M	COL	0-0053449	0866	1
BROOKS JR WILLIAM P	COL	0-0031654	0463	1
BROOKS ROLAND ST	LTC	0-0060336	0167	1
BROOKS WILLIAM A	MAJ	0-0069601	1166	1
BROOM THAD A	B G	0-0018246	0660	1
BROPHY FRANCIS J	COL	0-0039723	0761	1
BROSSARD LOUIS F	LTC	0-0028965	1156	2
BROTHERTON RICHARD W	LTC	0-0052658	1263	1
BROTT WILLIAM F	LTC	0-0042966	0265	1
BROUN FLORENCE T	MAJ	N-0000695	0565	1
BROUN PAUL C	LTC	0-0025286	0746	2
BROWDER JEWEL R	LTC	0-0045583	0264	1
BROWER GEORGE W	COL	0-0009433	0646	2
BROWER WESLEY H	MAJ	0-0058320	0965	1
BROWN ALBERT F	M G	0-0003409	0649	1
BROWN ALLAN G	1LT	0-0059326	0353	2
BROWN ARTHUR E	COL	0-0008797	1044	1
BROWN BENJAMIN C	LTC	0-0028493	0966	1
BROWN BOYD L	COL	0-0033215	0466	1
BROWN BRISBANE H	COL	0-0008279	0753	1
BROWN BYRON W	LTC	0-0039340	0763	1
BROWN CAROLUS A	COL	0-0021364	0857	1
BROWN CHARLES C	B G	0-0008042	0347	2
BROWN CHARLES E	COL	0-0019552	0661	1
BROWN CHARLES T	LTC	0-0057375	0355	2
BROWN DALE E	LTC	0-0080284	0767	1
BROWN DAVID F	COL	0-0017540	0859	1
BROWN DAVID H	LTC	0-0020320	0656	1
BROWN DREW F	CW4	W-0902835	0161	1
BROWN EARL J	COL	0-0039031	0767	1
BROWN EARL V	COL	0-0024044	0967	1
BROWN ELI F	COL	0-0008486	0145	2
BROWN ELMER G	COL	0-0039521	0157	1
BROWN ERNEST F	LTC	0-0051928	1165	1
BROWN ERNEST L	LTC	0-0033987	0753	1
BROWN EVERETT E	B G	0-0006303	1049	1
BROWN GARRY M	LTC	0-0084826	0567	1
BROWN GEORGE H	LTC	0-0048840	0864	1
BROWN GERALD F	COL	0-0019806	0861	1
BROWN GREG J	COL	0-0031783	1266	1
BROWN GUY W	LTC	0-0080612	0766	1
BROWN HALCON D	MAJ	0-0062136	0263	1
BROWN HANDY V	COL	0-0010954	1049	1
BROWN HAROLD C	COL	0-0022888	0766	1
BROWN HAROLD M	B G	0-0020832	0267	1
BROWN HAROLD M	COL	0-0030777	0764	1
BROWN HELEN F	LTC	N-0002558	0867	1
BROWN HERBERT E	COL	0-0021437	1064	1
BROWN HUGH C	COL	0-0042539	0355	1
BROWN J TRIMBLE	COL	0-0016666	0356	1
BROWN JAMES A	COL	0-0011166	0846	1
BROWN JOHN K	COL	0-0002371	0845	2
BROWN JOHN M	LTC	0-0018453	0651	1
BROWN JOSEPH T	COL	0-0023969	0764	1
BROWN JR AUBREY K	COL	0-0049959	0466	1
BROWN JR CHARLES F	M G	0-0025845	0867	2
BROWN JR CHARLES P	COL	0-0038922	0965	1
BROWN JR EDWARD A	B G	0-0019355	0861	2
BROWN JR GEORGE K	LTC	0-0058842	1066	2
BROWN JR HARRY F	COL	0-0039900	0564	1
BROWN JR HARVEY L	COL	0-0021253	0847	2
BROWN JR JOHN M	LTC	0-0031897	1163	1
BROWN JR PERCY D	LTC	0-0037255	0658	1
BROWN JR PERCY H	COL	0-0018117	0760	1
BROWN JR ROBERT D	COL	0-0023832	0363	2

NAME	GRADE	SVC NO	DATE RET MO YR	RET CODE
BROWN JR SIDNEY G	COL	0-0018393	0760	1
BROWN KATHRYN J	MAJ	N-0001370	0163	1
BROWN LAURENCE C	COL	0-0020876	0767	1
BROWN LEE R	MAJ	0-0039459	0664	1
BROWN LEROY C	MAJ	0-0033782	1061	1
BROWN LLOYD K	CW4	W-0906641	0160	1
BROWN MARION M	COL	0-0029806	0962	2
BROWN MASKELL E	LTC	0-0039914	1055	1
BROWN MILLS	MAJ	0-0033487	0451	1
BROWN OLIVER B	COL	0-0041418	0656	1
BROWN PAUL H	COL	0-0005324	0549	1
BROWN PERCIVAL S	COL	0-0019487	0660	1
BROWN PHILIP F	COL	0-0007073	1245	2
BROWN RICHARD K	LTC	0-0032333	0767	1
BROWN RICHARD M	MAJ	0-0061086	0367	1
BROWN RICHARD O	LTC	0-0035751	1159	1
BROWN ROBERT O	COL	0-0003608	1046	1
BROWN ROBERT F	COL	0-0052098	1163	1
BROWN ROBERT G	B G	0-0018520	0761	1
BROWN ROLAND C	COL	0-0017080	0258	1
BROWN ROTHWELL H	B G	0-0016604	1056	1
BROWN ROY F	COL	0-0006374	0747	1
BROWN SHANNON O	COL	0-0052247	0866	1
BROWN STAUNTON L	COL	0-0019356	0358	1
BROWN THOMAS J	CW4	W-0904087	0755	1
BROWN TRAVIS T	B G	0-0019574	0864	1
BROWN VALLIE A	1LT	M-0000475	0844	2
BROWN VIVIAN Z	COL	0-0012034	0653	1
BROWN WALTER S	CPT	0-0014117	0809	2
BROWN WILLIAM A	LTC	0-0060815	0865	1
BROWN WILLIAM D	LTC	0-0060426	0765	1
BROWN WILLIAM E	CW4	W-0904088	1059	2
BROWN WILLIAM H	COL	0-0041552	1053	1
BROWN WILLIAM J	LTC	0-0024315	0961	1
BROWN WILLIAM L	LTC	0-0006489	0-36	2
BROWN WILLIAM M	COL	0-0031583	1167	1
BROWN WILLIAM R	MAJ	0-0065603	0367	1
BROWN WYBURN D	B G	0-0012260	0651	1
BROWNE ALLAN R	COL	0-0028831	0156	1
BROWNE BEVERLY F	B G	0-0001339	0528	1
BROWNE HARRISON C	COL	0-0002759	1146	2
BROWNE HARVEY M	LTC	0-0080051	0966	2
BROWNE III HARVEY S	COL	0-0038992	0762	1
BROWNE JOHN T	LTC	0-0040692	1062	2
BROWNE LAURENCE S	COL	0-0047086	0966	1
BROWNE ROLAND A	COL	0-0016126	1047	1
BROWNELL JAMES R	COL	0-0011764	0135	2
BROWNFIELD PAGE H	COL	0-0040395	0564	1
BROWNING HAROLD W	COL	0-0019545	0961	1
BROWNING JOHN W	COL	0-0020767	0657	1
BROWNING NEWTON F	LTC	0-0046964	0661	1
BROWNING PHILIP Y	COL	0-0021142	0565	1
BROWNING SAMUEL R	M G	0-0017081	0758	1
BROWNLEE LAURANCE H	COL	0-0017583	0859	1
BROWNSON HAROLD N	COL	0-0043109	0862	1
BROYLES HARMON F	COL	0-0029038	1156	1
BROYLES NED R	COL	0-0020285	0864	1
BRUBAKER ELDRIDGE L	COL	0-0051445	0861	1
BRUBAKER JACK H	COL	0-0083580	0766	1
BRUBAKER WILLIAM F	COL	0-0032497	0966	1
BRUBECK DAVID L	LTC	0-0080616	0165	1
BRUCE ANDREW D	LTG	0-0005857	0854	1
BRUCE BURTON B	COL	0-0019360	0660	1
BRUCE CHARLES D	COL	0-0020542	0559	1
BRUCE JR THOMAS R	COL	0-0032423	0766	1
BRUCE WALTER F	CW2	W-0902839	1161	1
BRUCH RAY K	LTC	0-0031688	1165	1
BRUCKER JOHN C	LTC	0-0030997	0266	1
BRUCKER WALLACE H	B G	0-0018793	0862	1
BRUGGEE VERNON W	LTC	0-0039966	0359	1
BRUSH JR ROBERT G	COL	0-0025009	0163	1
BRUMBAUGH JOHN O	CPT	0-0017351	0331	2
BRUMBY SEWELL M	COL	0-0018846	0360	1
BRUMFIEL OSCAR M	LTC	0-0023534	0760	1
BRUMMITT LEROY D	COL	0-0044087	0365	1

NAME	GRADE	SVC NO	DATE RET MO YR	RET CODE
BRUNEAU ALFRED W	LTC	0-0023404	0660	1
BRUNI ALBERT V	COL	0-0032195	0467	1
BRUNKE WILLIAM H	COL	0-0016692	1056	1
BRUNNER CLARENCE O	COL	0-0029456	0960	1
BRUNO ANGEL F	COL	0-0039632	1059	1
BRUNS STOCKTON D	LTC	0-0032292	0863	1
BRUNSON MARK V	COL	0-0006231	0353	1
BRUNSON RICHARD W	LTC	0-0028615	0966	1
BRUNSVOLD RUDOLPH K	COL	0-0024201	0860	1
BRUNT WILLIAM R	CW4	W-0902675	0862	1
BRUSHER HAROLD A	COL	0-0016381	0951	1
BRUTON OGDEN C	COL	0-0029283	0661	1
BRYAN BLACKSHEAR	LTG	0-0015004	0260	1
BRYAN FREDERIC G	COL	0-0039670	0356	1
BRYAN HELEN D	MAJ	N-0001222	0467	1
BRYAN JAMES L	LTC	0-0042883	1064	1
BRYAN JUDY	MAJ	L-0000258	1159	2
BRYAN MARY C	LTC	N-0002094	0566	2
BRYAN ROBERT L	LTC	0-0041125	0165	1
BRYAN WILLIAM C	LTC	0-0034150	0161	1
BRYANT BURNELL V	COL	0-0038629	0659	1
BRYANT HAROLD F	LTC	0-0036886	0764	1
BRYANT RANDALL H	COL	0-0031805	0565	1
BRYANT ROBERT A	LTC	0-0030875	0758	2
BRYANT ROBERT L	LTC	0-0058164	0967	1
BRYANT RUBY F	COL	N-0000079	0661	1
BRYANT WILLIAM H	CW2	W-0907099	0960	1
BRYDE WALTER J	COL	0-0019825	0664	1
BRYDEN WILLIAM	M G	0-0001900	0244	1
BRYER PAUL J	COL	0-0019947	0863	1
BUCHA PAUL A	COL	0-0031996	1064	1
BUCHAK KIRK	COL	0-0029864	0661	1
BUCHANAN DALE E	COL	0-0024759	0763	1
BUCHANAN DAVID H	M G	0-0017746	0163	1
BUCHANAN DAVID P	LTC	0-0059563	0866	1
BUCHANAN DEE C	LTC	0-0037509	1064	1
BUCHANAN EARL W	LTC	0-0036352	0767	1
BUCHANAN EVERTS R	LTC	0-0059842	1066	1
BUCHANAN JOHN K	1LT	0-0012190	0329	2
BUCHANAN JOHN O	LTC	0-0058846	1066	1
BUCHANAN MILO V	COL	0-0007219	0854	1
BUCHANAN RICHARD S	LTC	0-0071322	0167	2
BUCHANAN RUSSELL B	LTC	0-0037291	0867	1
BUCHER JOHN C	COL	0-0051494	0464	1
BUCHHOLZ GEORGE H	WO1	W-0900939	0139	1
BUCHLY WALTER E	COL	0-0004617	0951	1
BUCHWALD DONALD F	COL	0-0018599	0761	1
BUCK CARROLL D	COL	0-0001424	0640	2
BUCK CHARLES T	CW4	W-0902844	0455	1
BUCK DONALD G	LTC	0-0030745	0664	1
BUCK JAMES H	LTC	0-0062845	0767	1
BUCK JR CHAMPLIN F	COL	0-0018352	0661	1
BUCK KATHRYN V	LTC	R-0010130	0667	1
BUCK LAURENCE N	COL	0-0017657	1048	2
BUCK WALTER A	COL	0-0015665	0653	1
BUCKALEW JR LOUIS W	LTC	0-0043462	0366	1
BUCKINGHAM JAMES S	LTC	0-0080619	0966	1
BUCKINS ALTHEA V	MAJ	N-0000055	0651	1
BUCKLAND DANIEL R	COL	0-0012447	0753	1
BUCKLER JOHN G	CW4	W-0902845	0756	1
BUCKLER PHILLIP J	LTC	0-0037564	0166	1
BUCKLES RONALD J	LTC	0-0080620	0964	1
BUCKLEY GORDON D	LTC	0-0084347	0464	1
BUCKLEY JOHN L	MAJ	0-0065288	0966	1
BUCKLEY JR MICHAEL	COL	0-0015196	0954	1
BUCKLEY THOMAS	COL	0-0052429	1165	1
BUCY ROY T	COL	0-0051188	0161	1
BUDD JR OTHO W	CPT	0-0007938	1130	1
BUDDEE RUDOLPH S	LTC	0-0088019	0967	1
BUDGE CLARE T	B G	0-0021050	0367	1
BUDGE VERNON M	COL	0-0042017	0562	2
BUDNEY CLIFFORD J	CPT	0-0059776	0663	1
BUDZ JR ANDREW D	LTC	0-0023253	0264	1
BUECHLER THEODORE E	B G	0-0008566	0753	1
BUEHLER JOHN P	COL	0-0019374	0255	1

NAME	GRADE	SVC NO	DATE RET MO YR	RET CODE
BUEHLER VIDA L	CPT	M-0010056	0955	1
BUELL JR GEORGE B	COL	0-0038599	1153	1
BUESS JOHN E	LTC	0-0065436	1266	1
BUFFINGTON ROLAND M	LTC	0-0041429	0551	1
BUGHER WILLIAM A	CPT	0-0015578	1139	2
BUIE WALTER O	COL	0-0012863	0854	1
BULDAIN FRANK J	COL	0-0043495	0566	1
BULL HAROLD R	LTG	0-0003707	0752	1
BULL HENRY T	COL	0-0001608	0934	1
BULL ROBERT H	COL	0-0023424	1165	1
BULLARD ABRAHAM L	COL	0-0010027	0547	1
BULLARD III ROBERT L	MAJ	0-0025774	0564	1
BULLARD MURRAY N	CPT	0-0062020	1057	2
BULLARD PETER C	COL	0-0003664	1152	1
BULLARD WINIFRED W	CPT	M-0000560	0447	1
BULLIS STANLOY W	COL	0-0025182	0855	1
BULLOCK EDMUND T	COL	0-0029367	1059	1
BULLOCK RICHARD B	LTC	0-0024198	1062	1
BULLOCK WILLIAM C	M G	0-0017635	0466	1
BUMEN LOUIS G	COL	0-0029350	1059	1
BUMGARNER CHARLES H	CW4	W-0902846	1055	1
BUNCH EDD	CW3	W-0902848	0157	1
BUNCH HERBERT	WO1	W-0901090	0425	1
BUNDY HAZEL P	MAJ	L-0000075	1060	1
BUNDY JAMES A	LTC	0-0080053	0366	1
BUNGE HERWART A	CW4	W-0902849	1156	1
BUNKER RAYMOND T	COL	0-0028864	0556	1
BUNN RALPH W	COL	0-0041762	0463	1
BUNTING GEOFFREY C	COL	0-0010357	0851	1
BUNTING LOYD C	COL	0-0011120	0551	1
BUNTZ HOWARD E	CW3	W-0902850	0862	2
BURBACH CLAUDE F	B G	0-0016184	0556	1
BURBANK WILLIAM L	COL	0-0016186	0755	1
BURBIDGE LESTER J	COL	0-0050938	0357	1
BURCH CHARLES H	COL	0-0041914	0961	1
BURCH CHARLES T	LTC	0-0063060	0767	1
BURCH CLAUDE O	COL	0-0010365	0550	1
BURCH GEORGE O	COL	0-0042013	0462	2
BURCH JACK P	LTC	0-0045948	0765	1
BURCHAM CLYDE A	LTC	0-0015064	0847	1
BURCHER HARRY E	COL	0-0039645	0258	1
BURCKES MARTIN H	LTC	0-0015491	0852	1
BURD BESSIE C	MAJ	N-0000622	0660	1
BURD HOWARD H	COL	0-0042434	0762	1
BURDGE JR JOHN M	COL	0-0016803	0757	1
BURDICK CHARLES W	CW4	W-0907130	0760	1
BURDD DOROTHY P	MAJ	N-0001651	0666	1
BURGASSER FRANCIS X	LTC	0-0037061	0462	1
BURGER VONNA F	B G	0-0015667	0360	1
BURGESS FRANCIS T	CPT	0-0025353	0345	2
BURGESS GEORGE R	COL	0-0012311	0854	2
BURGESS JR ALBERT F	COL	0-0035280	0767	1
BURGESS JR CHARLES A	LTC	0-0053513	1060	1
BURGESS ROBERT C	LTC	0-0027551	0965	1
BURGESS THOMAS B	COL	0-0005139	0451	1
BURGHEIM JOSEPH H	COL	0-0009114	0753	1
BURGIO JOSEPH C	MAJ	0-0085105	0161	1
BURKE ALVIN L	COL	0-0021148	0764	1
BURKE CARL V	COL	0-0038790	0265	1
BURKE DAVID C	COL	0-0039667	0164	1
BURKE EDWARD J	COL	0-0018857	0953	1
BURKE JAMES F	LTC	0-0080626	0967	1
BURKE MICHAEL J	LTC	0-0050375	0763	1
BURKE THOMAS W	COL	0-0031508	0567	1
BURKE WILLIAM J	COL	0-0009794	1134	2
BURKE WILLIAM J	CW3	W-0904089	0463	1
BURKETT LYMAN O	LTC	0-0030428	0160	2
BURKETT RAYMOND W	COL	0-0030603	0564	1
BURKHART ESHER C	COL	0-0012779	0554	1
BURLESON DERWOOD F	MAJ	0-0037566	0662	1
BURLINGHAM CHARLES F	CW4	W-0902274	0962	1
BURN RICHARD C	COL	0-0034426	0865	1
BURNELL RAY L	B G	0-0004954	0248	2
BURNELL 2ND N A	M G	0-0012337	0857	2
BURNETT BURGH S	COL	0-0004162	1047	1

NAME	GRADE	SVC NO	DATE RET MO YR	RET CODE
BURNETT EDWIN M	COL	0-0010306	0866	2
BURNETT HENRY H	MAJ	C-0026906	0964	1
BURNETT JOHN R	COL	0-0015204	0945	2
BURNETT JOHN W	COL	0-0042578	0761	2
BURNETT ROBERT M	COL	0-0020187	0358	1
BURNHAM MARY C	MAJ	R-0010064	0760	1
BURNS DONALD E	COL	0-0079763	0767	1
BURNS DONALD S	COL	0-0012672	0854	1
BURNS EDWARD J	LTC	0-0041709	1057	2
BURNS ELMER M	COL	0-0029499	1060	1
BURNS HELEN F	MAJ	N-0002355	0558	1
BURNS JAMES H	M G	0-0002332	1044	2
BURNS JOHN J	B G	0-0012299	0553	1
BURNS JOHN R	B G	0-0016509	C656	2
BURNS KENNETH F	LTC	0-0031210	0762	1
BURNS KENNETH P	COL	0-0025194	C767	1
BURNS PAUL	COL	0-0038733	0163	1
BURNS RICHARD F	MAJ	C-0058121	0666	1
BURNS ROBERT E	COL	0-0016172	C848	1
BURNS ROBERT J	LTC	0-0065258	1165	1
BURNS ROBERT W	LTC	0-0052887	C164	1
BURNS SAMUEL E	COL	0-0030394	0963	1
BURNS WILLIAM H	LTC	0-0014813	0934	2
BURNSIDE WALTER	COL	0-0015208	0653	1
BURR DONALD F	1LT	C-0060824	1051	1
BURR II EDWARD	COL	0-0026009	0267	1
BURR LYNN S	LTC	0-0053788	1265	1
BURR RALPH R	COL	0-0039769	0762	2
BURRELL WALTER F	LTC	0-0024492	C262	1
BURRER JOHN D	LTC	0-0061208	0966	1
BURRESS WITHERS A	LTG	0-0004812	1154	1
BURRIS LAYTON D	LTC	0-0037413	1066	1
BURRITT GEORGE E	COL	0-0014863	0854	1
BURROWS JOHN E	COL	0-0023621	C867	1
BURROWS JR ROBERT E	LTC	0-0025918	C866	1
BURROWS MARY L	LTC	N-0002152	0365	1
BURT ERNEST H	B G	0-0004916	1046	2
BURT FARLOW	COL	0-0009752	1146	2
BURT JR REYNOLDS J	COL	0-0012710	0548	1
BURT REYNOLDS J	B G	0-0000520	1037	2
BURT ROBERT F	LTC	0-0063053	1165	1
BURT WALTER L	COL	0-0043093	0966	1
BURT WILKIE C	COL	0-0006609	0753	1
BURT WILLIAM G	MAJ	0-0009008	0240	2
BURTCHAELL JOHN W	COL	0-0023764	C766	1
BURTIS THOMAS R	CW4	W-0902854	0163	1
BURTON ALBERT H	COL	0-0016067	0347	1
BURTON ETHEL	MAJ	N-0000207	0961	1
BURTON JR EMMETTE Y	COL	0-0020672	0867	1
BURTON LLOYD P	LTC	C-0080379	0665	1
BURTS MARJORIE K	MAJ	N-0002196	1263	1
BUSBEE CHARLES M	B G	0-0003794	C753	1
BUSBEY GEORGE W	COL	0-0015639	0854	1
BUSCEMI MICHAEL D	COL	0-0073025	C161	1
BUSCH EVERETT	B G	0-0007260	0852	1
BUSER OSCAR C	COL	0-0042246	0963	1
BUSH BENJAMIN R	COL	0-0040166	0567	1
BUSH CHESTER K	COL	0-0079643	0765	1
BUSH ERNEST L	COL	0-0029843	1262	1
BUSH FRANK O	LTC	0-0047101	0261	1
BUSH GEORGE E	M G	0-0017634	0864	1
BUSH GEORGE P	COL	C-0005376	0844	2
BUSH HAL C	LTC	0-0011072	0142	1
BUSH HARRY R	COL	0-0053342	0563	2
BUSH HOWARD C	COL	0-0030205	C263	1
BUSH JAMES E	COL	0-0010332	C854	1
BUSH JOSEPH K	COL	0-0014710	0651	1
BUSH JR HUGH W	LTC	0-0060626	0466	1
BUSH KENNETH B	M G	0-0006650	0553	1
BUSH NEWTON G	COL	C-0009666	0753	1
BUSH STERLING C	COL	0-0043914	1162	1
BUSHNELL THEODORE L	MAJ	0-0080240	1065	2
BUSK JOSEPH R	1LT	0-0014388	1119	2
BUTCHART JOHN N	LTC	0-0044664	0661	1
BUTCHERS RALPH J	M G	C-0017242	C764	1
BUTH WILLIAM H	LTC	0-0054312	1163	1
BUTKUS WALTER A	LTC	0-0023659	0656	2
BUTLER ALLEN S	COL	0-0030422	0565	1
BUTLER BRAXTON D	COL	0-0011422	0844	2
BUTLER DONALD A	MAJ	0-0059909	0164	1
BUTLER EARLE R	COL	0-0043106	0463	1
BUTLER ERNEST C	LTC	0-0035578	0865	1
BUTLER FREDERIC B	B G	0-0012047	0453	1
BUTLER GEORGE F	COL	0-0007080	0252	1
BUTLER JAMES F	COL	0-0007292	0547	2
BUTLER JAMES J	COL	0-0030068	1263	1
BUTLER JOHN L	LTC	0-0040980	0664	1
BUTLER JR BRADFORD	COL	0-0031425	0766	1
BUTLER MIRIAM L	LTC	L-0000111	0165	1
BUTLER ROBERT G	M G	0-0017191	0759	1
BUTLER ROSE A	MAJ	N-0000590	0762	1
BUTLER SR FARLEY P	LTC	0-0039321	0861	1
BUTLER STANLEY F	LTC	0-0037609	1164	1
BUTLER WARREN A	MAJ	0-0008947	1033	1
BUTNER JR JOHN C	COL	0-0007129	1151	1
BUTSCHER WINSTON	COL	0-0030599	0166	1
BUTTERFIELD JOHN L	LTC	0-0026194	0763	1
BUTTERMORE CHARLES W	COL	0-0029147	0958	1
BUTTERWORTH VIRGINIA	MAJ	N-0002278	0664	1
BUTTNER LOUIS	COL	0-0042100	1162	1
BUTTOLPH LOREN D	COL	0-0042053	0867	1
BUTTS ROBERT E	LTC	0-0032286	0364	1
BUTTS SARA C	MAJ	N-0000257	0959	1
BUYNOSKI ADAM S	COL	0-0020169	0966	1
BUYS JOSEPH H	COL	0-0029689	0462	1
BUZZETTI HELEN J	MAJ	L-0000337	0267	1
BYARS DAVID C	MAJ	0-0013932	0620	2
BYARS JR DAVID O	B G	0-0021273	0167	1
BYERS CLOVIS E	LTG	0-0012769	0659	2
BYERS LEX J	LTC	0-0063366	0666	1
BYERS RUFUS A	COL	0-0009119	0244	1
BYKERK NORMAN H	COL	0-0033038	0765	1
BYNUM PIERRE D	MAJ	0-0078747	0966	1
BYORUM HENRY M	COL	0-0080380	0666	1
BYRD EDWIN L	CW4	W-0902797	0261	1
BYRD JR WILLIAM H	COL	0-0052267	0365	1
BYRD NELNA M	MAJ	N-0001051	0166	1
BYRNE BERNARD A	COL	0-0012404	0854	1
BYRNE JEROME S	LTC	0-0021404	C757	1
BYRNE JOHN D	COL	0-0021837	0465	1
BYRNE JR ROBERT J	LTC	0-0083581	0763	1
BYRNE MALCOLM	COL	0-0006390	0753	1
BYRNE MICHAEL J	CPT	0-0009160	0429	1
BYRNE PAUL P	LTC	0-0051433	0761	1
BYRNE ROBERT E	LTC	0-0043281	0363	1
BYRNS ROBERT E	LTC	0-0051606	0463	1
CABELL HENRY B	LTC	0-0058800	0767	1
CABREY HAZEL S	MAJ	N-0002155	0562	1
CAFARELLI ROOSEVELT	COL	0-0022265	0367	1
CAFFEE MAHLON W	LTC	0-0021769	0644	2
CAFFEY JR BENJAMIN F	B G	0-0004929	0350	1
CAGE LEE E	COL	0-0024909	0567	1
CAHILL EDWIN K	COL	0-0019141	0863	1
CAHILL HOWARD F K	COL	0-0007978	1139	2
CAHILL JR GEORGE T	LTC	0-0076854	0966	1
CAHILL VIRGINIA F	MAJ	N-0000711	0662	1
CAIN CHARLES A	COL	0-0029988	0863	1
CAIN HALL	COL	0-0021984	0647	2
CAIN LAMBERT B	COL	0-0012375	0547	2
CAIN ROBERT C	MAJ	0-0089752	1062	1
CAIN ROBERT S	COL	0-0042210	0863	1
CAIN WALTER J	LTC	0-0027696	0765	1
CAKE JAMES M	LTC	0-0025372	0762	1
CALDWELL ALBIN N	COL	0-0011625	1048	1
CALDWELL DAVID D	1LT	0-0011719	0632	2
CALDWELL GEORGE L	COL	0-0009549	0253	2
CALDWELL JACK R	COL	0-0022316	0962	1
CALDWELL JAMES A	LTC	0-0025315	0763	1
CALDWELL JOHN M	COL	0-0019313	0755	1
CALDWELL R BEVERLY	COL	0-0051185	1060	1
CALDWELL ROSS R	COL	0-0051111	1160	1
CALDWELL WILLIAM R	COL	0-0008754	0448	1
CALDWELL WILLIAM G	COL	0-0017312	0758	1
CALE FRANCES C	MAJ	N-0002033	0760	1
CALENBERG HARRY D	LTC	C-0076855	1265	1
CALHOUN WILLIAM L	B G	0-0042664	0164	1
CALHOUN WILLIAM R	M G	0-0019256	1067	1
CALL WILLIAM A	COL	0-0018719	0559	1
CALLAHAN DEWEY H	CW3	W-0090286	0559	1
CALLAHAN DONALD M	COL	0-0034055	0265	1
CALLAHAN JAMES W	COL	C-0005435	1045	2
CALLENDER GEORGE R	B G	0-0003521	1146	2
CALLICUTT JAMES M	COL	0-0014834	0854	2
CALLISON ROBERT L	COL	0-0019648	1064	1
CALLOWAY CHARLES G	M G	0-0017690	0861	1
CALMES PAUL M	LTC	0-0084827	1167	1
CALUYA PIO Q	LTC	0-0014883	0753	1
CALVERT GEORGE I	LTC	C-0030521	1063	2
CALVERT GEORGE M	COL	0-0036061	0767	1
CALVERT GEORGE N	COL	0-0043053	0966	1
CALVERT PARKER	COL	0-0020794	C948	2
CALVIN CHAUNCEY F	WO1	W-0902864	0850	1
CALVIN HARRY L	LTC	0-0011352	1043	2
CALYER PETER D	COL	0-0017116	0958	2
CAMBRE JEROME D	COL	0-0012185	C648	1
CAMERON ARCHIE D	COL	0-0009628	0846	1
CAMERON DONALD N	LTC	0-0024408	C962	1
CAMERON HENRY H	COL	0-0008206	0847	1
CAMERON RICHARD R	COL	0-0021717	0858	1
CAMERON ROBERT C	1LT	0-0015771	0934	2
CAMERON ROBERT C	COL	0-0023178	C762	1
CAMERON THOMAS J	COL	0-0042804	0766	1
CAMM FRANK	B G	0-0009902	0854	1
CAMP ELWOOD W	COL	0-0043173	0560	1
CAMP HOWARD E	COL	0-0007226	0753	1
CAMP PIERCE H	COL	C-0010208	0845	1
CAMP THOMAS J	B G	0-0016033	1046	2
CAMPANA VICTOR W	LTC	0-0023975	0761	1
CAMPBELL ALEXANDER	COL	0-0005310	0452	1
CAMPBELL BONIFACE	M G	0-0009788	1056	1
CAMPBELL CAREY E	CPT	0-0008311	1134	1
CAMPBELL CHARLES H	LTC	0-0032031	0962	1
CAMPBELL CHARLES T	COL	C-0032180	C867	2
CAMPBELL CLARENCE S	LTC	0-0040163	0565	1
CAMPBELL CLARK S	1LT	0-0027126	1151	1
CAMPBELL EARL A	CW4	W-0902867	0467	2
CAMPBELL ERNEST R	1LT	0-0014419	0270	2
CAMPBELL FRANK P	COL	0-0051129	1151	1
CAMPBELL GEORGE E	COL	0-0041437	C856	1
CAMPBELL HARRY L	COL	0-0007143	0452	1
CAMPBELL JACK P	COL	0-0038610	0557	1
CAMPBELL JAMES B	LTC	0-0026690	C764	1
CAMPBELL JAMES T	COL	0-0006758	0346	1
CAMPBELL JOHN E	LTC	0-0079766	0665	1
CAMPBELL JOHN L	LTC	0-0038863	1160	1
CAMPBELL JR GEORGE T	LTC	0-0026084	0165	2
CAMPBELL JR JAMES R	1LT	0-0014376	0919	2
CAMPBELL JR LEVIN H	LTG	0-0003194	0546	1
CAMPBELL KERMIT W	LTC	0-0030690	0464	1
CAMPBELL NORMAN A	COL	0-0042861	0764	1
CAMPBELL OTIS C	CW3	W-0902869	0161	1
CAMPBELL ROBERT H	LTC	0-0026074	0864	1
CAMPBELL ROSS W	CPT	0-0027508	1051	1
CAMPBELL THOMAS E	LTC	0-0008071	0841	2
CAMPBELL VERGIL J	CW4	W-0902870	0565	1
CAMPBELL WILLIAM A	B G	0-0006493	0248	1
CAMPBELL WILLIAM M	COL	0-0042337	0364	1
CAMPBELL WILLIAM P	B G	0-0014886	0653	1
CANADA CHARLES C	COL	0-0029257	C662	1
CANAN HOWARD V	COL	0-0012098	0754	1
CANARY JESSE F	COL	0-0011971	0447	1
CANBY CLARENCE P	B G	0-0017904	0662	1
CANDEE GEORGE	CW4	W-0902872	0366	1
CANDLER HARRY W	LTC	C-0018562	0651	1
CANDON MARIAN W	MAJ	N-0002381	C561	1
CANINE RALPH J	LTG	0-0007154	0457	2
CANLETT FRANKLIN H	COL	0-0011991	1048	1
CANNING JR AUSTIN J	LTC	0-0026277	0364	1
CANNOLES MARGARET H	LTC	N-0001211		1
CANNON ALFRED R	COL	0-0041725	0861	1
CANNON JOSEPH F	COL	0-0020952	0746	2
CANNON JR CLINTON C	LTC	0-0080636	0765	1
CANNON JR JOSEPH M	LTC	0-0024930	C863	1
CANNON JR LINDEN K	COL	0-0032509	0867	1
CANNON MARGARET R	MAJ	N-0002207	0365	1
CANNON ROBERT M	LTG	0-0016163	0961	2
CANON JACK Y	LTC	0-0043830	0361	1
CANSLER LOUIS	COL	0-0006580	0245	2
CANTAREL RAYMOND H	LTC	0-0080637	0467	1
CANTEY JAMES	COL	0-0030019	1063	1
CANTRELL FRED H	COL	0-0025295	0663	1
CANTY DANIEL J	CPT	0-0005999	0-29	2
CANTY WILLIAM F	CW3	W-0907075	0357	1
CAPERTON JAMES N	COL	0-0004496	1146	1
CAPERTON ROY J	COL	0-0011548	0647	1
CAPITO CHARLES E	COL	0-0029568	C661	1
CARABALLO RAYMOND F	COL	C-0031862	0866	1
CARAWAY FORREST	B G	0-0019466	0761	1
CARAWAY PAUL W	LTG	0-0017659	0864	2
CARBERRY EDMUND J	LTC	0-0025565	0864	1
CARBERRY FRANCIS P	COL	0-0038789	0263	1
CARBONELL ARTHUR J	COL	0-0024626	0466	1
CARDELL ROBERT L	COL	0-0018505	0661	1
CARDINELL ROBERT H	LTC	0-0056158	0367	1
CARDULLO EVERETT P	CW4	RW-0902874	0167	1
CARDWELL EUGENE F	M G	0-0038662	0862	1
CAREW THOMAS E	LTC	0-0087487	1064	1
CAREY FAY F J	COL	C-0038814	0661	1
CAREY GEORGE R	COL	0-0017587	0357	1
CAREY MERLE L	COL	0-0025586	0863	1
CARHART RICHARD B	LTC	0-0018497	1141	2
CARHARTT FORREST A	1LT	0-0027605	0347	2
CARIANO SAMUEL P	LTC	0-0084350	0564	1
CARILLIA THOMAS A	COL	0-0040115	0666	1
CARLAN ULYSSES G	COL	0-0076836	0967	1
CARLAN WILBUR C	MAJ	0-0005479	0934	2
CARLE VERNON K	CW4	W-0902172	0655	1
CARLETON DON E	B G	0-0015415	0854	1
CARLISLE CARSHALL C	LTC	0-0028273	0866	1
CARLISLE JAMES H	1LT	0-0018618	0539	2
CARLL WALTER T	LTC	0-0020106	0456	1
CARLOCK WILLARD B	COL	0-0016790	0657	1
CARLOSS ELIZABETH	LTC	R-0010065	1060	1
CARLOZZO BENEDICT A	CW3	W-0906651	1058	1
CARLQUIST PHILIP R	COL	0-0031011	0665	2
CARLSEN RICARD T	CW2	W-0901082	1146	1
CARLSON CARSTEN D	LTC	0-0080638	1163	1
CARLSON GUNNAR C	M G	0-0018515	0862	1
CARLSON GUNNARD W	COL	0-0018347	1058	1
CARLSON LEO G	COL	0-0022246	0266	1
CARLSON LUTHER M	CW3	W-0907110	1059	2
CARLSON ROLAND P	COL	0-0031456	0860	1
CARLSON VINCENT P	COL	C-0023694	0764	1
CARLSON WILLIAM R	COL	0-0009060	1047	2
CARLSTEN CHESTER A	COL	0-0014794	0949	2
CARLTON DONALD C	LTC	0-0067903	0967	1
CARLTON MORTON B	CPT	0-0059718	0754	2
CARMACK JOSEPH	COL	0-0018322	1046	2
CARMICHAEL JR R L	COL	0-0018176	0760	1
CARMODY JOHN J	COL	0-0051659	0865	1
CARMODY ROBERT E	COL	0-0003620	0740	1
CARN ROBERT M	LTC	0-0083564	0765	1
CARNAHAN GEORGE D	COL	0-0023007	0166	1
CARNE WILLIAM J	LTC	0-0016128	0644	2
CARNES HUGHES A	LTC	0-0043674	0863	1
CARNES JAMES J	COL	0-0015340	0854	2
CARNES NORMAN D	COL	0-0030666	0860	1
CARNES RICHARD C	LTC	0-0027321	0766	1
CARNEY JR TAYLOR E	COL	0-0040264	0966	1
CARNS EDWIN H J	M G	0-0017560	0765	1

UNITED STATES ARMY RETIRED LIST

NAME	GRADE	SVC NO	DATE RET MO YR	RET CODE
CAROTHERS GLENN E	LTC	O-0010125	1041	1
CAROW THEODORE W	COL	O-0020527	0761	2
CARREL RICHARD D	CW4	W-0906653	0565	1
CARPENTER FRANK	COL	O-0015870	0944	1
CARPENTER GEORGE R	COL	O-0051147	0461	1
CARPENTER GILES R	COL	O-0014915	0854	1
CARPENTER JACK R	LTC	O-0053460	0754	1
CARPENTER JAMES S	COL	O-0042622	0862	1
CARPENTER STONEY C	COL	O-0080381	1166	1
CARPENTER STANLEY J	COL	O-0041712	0460	1
CARR FRANK L	COL	O-0008608	1046	2
CARR III JOHN F	LTC	O-0066141	1266	1
CARR LOUIS F	CW4	W-0902879	0165	1
CARR MINNIE L	MAJ	N-0000143	0658	1
CARR ROBERT A	COL	O-0081878	1265	1
CARR THOMAS W	CPT	O-0061918	1057	2
CARR WILLIAM O	MAJ	O-0060420	0364	1
CARR WILLIAM L	LTC	O-0014756	1145	1
CARRAHER RAYMOND W	COL	O-0045292	0966	1
CARRAWAY WILLIAM F	B G	O-0015144	1155	1
CARRAWAY WILLIAM R	CPT	O-0059844	0663	1
CARRELL CHARLES A	MAJ	O-0018886	0747	1
CARRIE JR HECTOR	LTC	O-0073043	0366	1
CARRIG STEPHEN J	CPT	O-0060378	0454	1
CARRIGAN SR JOHN A	COL	O-0028874	0956	1
CARRIKER JOHN H	COL	O-0005490	1049	1
CARRINGTON GEORGE E	1LT	O-0015081	0934	2
CARRITHERS FRED H	MAJ	O-0002873	0622	2
CARRITHERS TRUMAN W	CPT	O-0018079	0-42	2
CARROLL FRANCIS L	COL	O-0066615	0864	1
CARROLL JAMES B	COL	O-0015272	0954	1
CARROLL JAMES H	LTC	O-0023722	0661	1
CARROLL JAMES V	COL	O-0012119	0455	2
CARROLL JOHN E	COL	O-0041877	0851	1
CARROLL JR WALTER D	LTC	O-0079768	0755	1
CARROLL LORNE J	CW4	W-0902880	1054	1
CARROLL MURRAY L	LTC	O-0057462	0867	1
CARROLL NICHOLAS V	LTC	O-0065192	0466	1
CARROLL PAUL L	COL	O-0016502	0754	1
CARROLL PERCY J	B G	O-0004183	0946	2
CARRUTH JOHN H	COL	O-0003672	0250	1
CARSON EUGENE J	COL	O-0051446	1263	2
CARSON JAMES M	COL	O-0051626	0551	1
CARSON LANETTA I	MAJ	N-0002238	0760	1
CARSON MARION	COL	O-0008610	0853	1
CARTER ARTHUR P	COL	O-0029580	0861	1
CARTER CARL	CW4	W-0902881	0162	1
CARTER CLOUD G	LTC	O-0058857	1062	1
CARTER DANIEL W	LTC	O-0031406	0165	1
CARTER GEORGE E	LTC	O-0040430	0767	1
CARTER GEORGE F	COL	O-0023431	0766	1
CARTER HENRY P	COL	O-0003038	0245	2
CARTER JACK H	MAJ	O-0052445	0261	1
CARTER JACK W	CW4	W-0902882	0565	1
CARTER JAMES C	COL	O-0015352	0852	1
CARTER JAMES D	COL	O-0008494	0147	2
CARTER JOSEPH M	CW4	W-0902883	0155	1
CARTER JR GEORGE W	LTC	O-0032349	0767	1
CARTER JR HAMLET R	LTC	O-0026134	0965	1
CARTER JR JACK A	MAJ	O-0038302	1066	1
CARTER LESLIE D	M G	O-0010863	1056	1
CARTER MAYNARD H	COL	O-0015077	0753	1
CARTER PAUL D	COL	O-0008416	1151	1
CARTER PHILIP R	COL	O-0029159	0559	1
CARTER ROBERT F	COL	O-0012364	1146	2
CARTER ROBERT P	MAJ	O-0063396	0367	1
CARTER SAM	LTC	O-0038955	0165	1
CARTER SR JAMES H	CW4	W-0904090	0562	2
CARTER WILEY V	COL	O-0012204	1146	2
CARTER WILLIAM A	M G	O-0019023	0162	1
CARTER WILLIAM V	B G	O-0001928	0842	1
CARTTER PAUL H	CPT	O-0008905	0125	2
CARTWRIGHT LESLIE J	COL	O-0009193	0949	1
CARUSONE JOHN J	COL	O-0021295	0866	1
CARVER GEORGE A	M G	O-0019122	0766	1
CARVER RICHARD K	COL	O-0040039	0866	1
CARVILLE ELIZABETH	MAJ	N-0002368	0860	1
CARY HUGH F	COL	O-0018845	0862	1
CARY MILO G	COL	O-0014608	0949	1
CARY RANDOLPH J	LTC	O-0026905	0664	1
CASE CHARLES E	LTC	O-0051260	1159	1
CASE HOMER	B G	O-0007090	0854	1
CASE RICHARD	CPT	O-0019701	0442	2
CASE ROBERT A	COL	O-0009758	1147	2
CASE ROY	CW4	W-0902884	0257	1
CASEY CHARLES W	COL	O-0032356	0867	1
CASEY EDGAR L	LTC	O-0036324	1060	1
CASEY GLEN T	CW4	W-0902885	1163	1
CASEY HUGH J	M G	O-0009298	1049	1
CASEY ROBERT F	CW4	W-0904092	0964	2
CASH ALBERT W	CW4	W-0902886	0861	1
CASH II JAMES H	B G	O-0039628	1062	1
CASHMAN CHARLES J	COL	O-0019653	0157	1
CASPER RICHARD F	MAJ	O-0058331	0465	1
CASS PHIL	1LT	O-0011979	0930	2
CASSADAY GEORGE C	COL	O-0032658	1166	1
CASSEDY WILLIAM P	LTC	O-0025044	0465	1
CASSELL DONALD R	CW4	W-0902888	1164	1
CASSELL HAROLD A	LTC	O-0029556	0661	1
CASSERLY EDWARD A	MAJ	O-0011685	0334	2
CASSEVANT ALBERT F	M G	O-0018456	0160	1
CASSIBRY ROBERT C	B G	O-0023058	0867	1
CASSIDY JOHN F	B G	O-0012718	0954	1
CASSIDY ROBERT F	COL	O-0021783	0865	1
CASSILL GEORGE F	LTC	O-0030464	0763	2
CASTERLINE JAMES I	LTC	O-0043628	0865	1
CASTLE SHIRLEY W	COL	O-0051850	0667	2
CASTO CARL S	COL	O-0032007	0464	1
CATALAN NEMESIO	CPT	O-0014884	0539	2
CATERER HORACE J	MAJ	O-0012911	0131	2
CATES TRAVIS N	CW4	W-0906655	0266	1
CATHCART WILLIAM T	COL	O-0041521	0758	1
CATHER LEO H	COL	O-0018510	0761	1
CATHRAE WILLIAM F	COL	O-00242[illegible]	0766	1
CATO RAYMOND L	COL	O-0020195	0866	1
CATRON 2ND THOMAS B	B G	O-0002597	0336	1
CATT RICHARD H	CW4	W-0902891	0867	1
CATTE JOSEPH P	MAJ	O-0015033	0941	2
CAUFIELD FRANK J	B G	O-0019515	0864	2
CAUGHRON JAMES W	COL	O-0051513	0664	2
CAUGHRON JR SAMUEL J	CW3	RW-0902676	0764	1
CAULDER LEROY W	LTC	O-0065122	0664	1
CAULKINS RALPH N	LTC	O-0005794	0142	1
CAUM NORMAN F	COL	O-0011803	0854	1
CAUSEY LUTHER G	COL	O-0016336	0655	2
CAUTHEN WILLIAM A	COL	O-0051257	1061	1
CAVANAGH JR JOHN P	LTC	O-0051810	0964	1
CAVE EDMUND H	MAJ	O-0059411	0262	2
CAVE JOHN W	B G	O-0018388	1060	1
CAVE RICHARD L	COL	O-0004396	1143	2
CAVELLI JR CHARLES	COL	O-0016165	0755	1
CAVENAUGH ROBERT L	COL	O-0020090	1006	1
CAVENDER CHARLES C	COL	O-0015307	0953	2
CAVENDER SAVING W	COL	O-0031005	0567	2
CAWLFIELD PAUL A	COL	O-0030378	0862	2
CAWTHORNE TED H	LTC	O-0006559	0244	2
CAYCE BRYCE T	CPT	O-0065185	0765	1
CAYGILL HARRY W	LTC	O-0007205	1141	1
CAYWOOD LINDSAY P	COL	O-0050898	0555	1
CAZAURANG JULIAN J	CW3	RW-0902894	1061	1
CECIL THOMAS J	MAJ	O-0002669	0927	2
CELLA ANDREW	COL	O-0052269	0962	2
CELMER THEODORE H	MAJ	O-0024066	0761	1
CEPEDA EMMANUEL S	LTC	O-0019297	0761	1
CERMACK FRANK P	CW2	W-0901122	0425	1
CERWIN STEVEN S	COL	O-0029526	0561	1
CHABOT JOSEPH L	COL	O-0020721	0966	1
CHACE EDGAR A	MAJ	O-0018701	0-44	2
CHADBOURNE ERNEST O	LTC	O-0069879	0564	2
CHADWICK BENJAMIN F	LTC	O-0012076	0443	2
CHADWICK HAZEL C	MAJ	N-0001289	0261	1
CHADWICK MAURICE P	COL	O-0012286	0150	2
CHAFFEE ELMER F	COL	O-0052057	0966	1
CHAFFEE FREDERIC H	COL	O-0017524	0859	1
CHAFFIN JR ANDREW D	COL	O-0020153	0466	1
CHALLICE JR CHARLES	CPT	O-0008235	0724	2
CHAMBERLAIN HAZEL A	MAJ	N-0000554	0760	1
CHAMBERLAIN JR F R	COL	O-0010785	1146	1
CHAMBERLAIN JR J L	COL	O-0016117	0755	1
CHAMBERLAIN THOMAS C	COL	O-0023145	0766	1
CHAMBERLIN E S	MAJ	N-0002032	1158	1
CHAMBERLIN STEPHEN J	LTG	O-0003397	1051	1
CHAMBERS ARTHUR K	LTC	O-0009095	0342	1
CHAMBERS BEATRICE	MAJ	N-0000107	0560	1
CHAMBERS JOHN H	LTC	O-0021323	0662	1
CHAMBERS JR JOHN S	COL	O-0025357	0967	1
CHAMBERS LAUREL L	LTC	O-0039547	0155	1
CHAMALISS JOHN D	COL	O-0007551	1046	2
CHAMPENY ARTHUR S	B G	O-0008264	0753	1
CHAMPLIN HERBERT H	COL	O-0030661	0467	2
CHANCE ROBERT H	COL	O-0005618	0847	1
CHANCEY GILBERT E	CW3	W-0902896	0961	1
CHANDLER CYRIL C	COL	O-0008327	1046	2
CHANDLER FITZHUGH H	COL	O-0042328	1262	1
CHANDLER HENRY	CW4	W-0902897	0560	1
CHANDLER LEROY L	CW4	W-0901667	0364	1
CHANDLER LEWELL F	CW4	W-0906656	1059	1
CHANDLER MARTIN R	COL	O-0023189	0461	2
CHANDLER MELBOURNE	LTC	O-0037488	0763	1
CHANDLER ROBERT F	COL	O-0017559	0859	1
CHANDLER ROBERT J	MAJ	O-0021386	0547	2
CHANDLER WILLIAM E	COL	O-0018431	0661	1
CHANDLER WILLIAM L	CW3	W-0904094	1058	1
CHAPDELAINE ALBERT J	LTC	O-0051956	1163	1
CHAPLIN ROBERT T	COL	O-0009745	0753	1
CHAPMAN CARLETON G	LTC	O-0002630	1122	1
CHAPMAN CLIFFORD P	COL	O-0010191	0852	1
CHAPMAN GERALD	COL	O-0019035	0361	1
CHAPMAN GRACIE L	LTC	N-0002115	0360	1
CHAPMAN JACK W	COL	O-0020616	0152	1
CHAPMAN LORIN P	LTC	O-0058860	0766	1
CHAPMAN OREN D	LTC	O-0040328	0464	1
CHAPMAN RAYMOND T	COL	O-0029860	0263	1
CHAPMAN RUBERT D	COL	O-0042367	1163	1
CHAPMAN WILLIAM G	CW4	W-0904095	0561	1
CHAPMAN WILLIAM MC	COL	O-0008630	0546	2
CHAPPELEAR LOUIS S	CPT	O-0020310	0841	2
CHAPPELL PAUL E	COL	O-0041968	1061	1
CHAPPUIS STEVE A	B G	O-0020899	0967	1
CHARLEBOIS GEORGE J	MAJ	O-0060767	0951	2
CHARLES JR ROLAND K	COL	O-0017988	0560	1
CHARLES ORMAN G	B G	O-0029954	0763	1
CHARLTON JR JESSE M	COL	O-0024543	0964	1
CHASE EARL R	COL	O-0028811	0855	1
CHASE EDWARD D	COL	O-0030936	1264	1
CHASE JACK P	MAJ	O-0080649	1265	1
CHASE JOHN A	COL	O-0007966	0848	1
CHASE LAWRENCE R	LTC	O-0081972	0463	2
CHASE RICHARD	LTC	O-0016999	1154	1
CHASE STEPHENS F	CW4	W-0902900	0766	2
CHASE WALTER E	COL	O-0016937	0555	1
CHASE WILLIAM	COL	O-0020856	0763	1
CHASE WILLIAM C	M G	O-0004739	0255	1
CHASTAINE BEN-HUR	COL	O-0005113	1249	1
CHATFIELD MILES P	COL	O-0019404	1158	1
CHATHAM ARTHUR R	LTC	O-0031480	0465	1
CHAUFTY JOSEPH V	LTC	O-0025969	0766	1
CHAVERS MILTON	CW4	W-0906657	0864	1
CHAVEZ HELEN A	MAJ	N-0001903	1061	1
CHAVIN RAPHAEL S	B G	O-0004958	1052	1
CHAVIS NEHEMIAH	CW4	W-0902901	0159	1
CHAZAL EDWARD A	COL	O-0015791	0954	1
CHEAR ROBERT M	LTC	O-0018613	0152	1
CHEATHAM RICHARD B	COL	O-0040124	1062	1
CHECK GILBERT J	COL	O-0051936	1167	1
CHEEK ANDREW R	COL	O-0032306	1265	1
CHEEVER CHARLES E	COL	O-0014712	0448	1
CHELL PEARCE R	CW4	RW-0902405	0163	1
CHENOWETH WILLIAM C	LTC	O-0020621	1046	2
CHERNOSKY RAYMOND M	CW4	W-0902903	0862	1
CHERUBIN STANLEY J	COL	O-0020700	0967	1
CHESEL WALTER	CW3	W-0907111	1059	1
CHESLEY JR JOHN W	COL	O-0053264	1166	1
CHESNUT JAMES W	LTC	O-0065046	0566	1
CHESTER GEORGE A	COL	O-0016345	0155	1
CHESTER JOHN E	COL	O-0016971	1146	2
CHESTER ROBERT S	MAJ	O-0022041	1043	2
CHESTON ELLIOTT B	COL	O-0031976	0467	1
CHESTON III DANIEL M	COL	O-0019507	0763	1
CHEVES GILBERT X	M G	O-0007053	0647	1
CHEWNING CLAUDIUS D	LTC	O-0069881	1167	1
CHEYNE ARTHUR C	COL	O-0029512	0161	1
CHILD FRANK W	COL	O-0005516	1049	1
CHILD PROCTOR L	LTC	O-0067905	0767	1
CHILDERS ERNEST	LTC	O-0048416	0965	1
CHILDERS ERNEST W	CW4	W-0902904	0259	1
CHILDERS GEORGE H	CPT	O-0027035	0947	2
CHILDRESS ALBERT W	LTC	O-0027749	0766	1
CHILDRESS CLEMENT J	CW4	W-0902298	0561	1
CHILDRESS ELLERY O	CW3	W-0902905	1159	1
CHILDRESS JOHN F	CW2	W-0902906	0151	1
CHILDRESS WILLIAM G	CW4	W-0902361	0657	1
CHILDS BOB	LTC	O-0011124	0246	1
CHILDS GEORGE W	COL	O-0020294	0755	1
CHILDS STANLEY A	CW3	W-0902907	0258	1
CHILSON LEE C	LTC	O-0039871	0661	1
CHILTON ALEXANDER	COL	O-0002236	0934	2
CHIMENT JOHN A	LTC	O-0027048	0664	1
CHIPMAN ALBERT D	COL	O-0004721	0846	2
CHIPMAN GUY W	COL	O-0002872	0845	2
CHIRAFISI DONALD	MAJ	O-0061405	0366	1
CHIRICO CARL F	COL	O-0029506	1060	1
CHISHOLM JAMES H	CPT	O-0060343	0762	1
CHITTENDEN ALBERT O	LTC	O-0031574	0663	1
CHLOUPEK LAURENCE E	COL	O-0044094	1166	1
CHOQUETTE LOUIS T	CW4	W-0902388	1053	1
CHORPENING CLAUDE H	M G	O-0012088	0656	1
CHORPENNING FRANK W	LTC	O-0038882	0561	1
CHRIETZBERG WILLIAM	LTC	O-0080361	0365	1
CHRISMAN HAROLD F	COL	O-0015961	0750	1
CHRISTENSEN ANCHER E	LTC	O-0045271	0762	1
CHRISTENSEN ARTHUR G	COL	O-0020871	0160	1
CHRISTENSEN JOHN M	COL	O-0023856	0564	1
CHRISTENSEN NELS F	COL	O-0040100	0762	1
CHRISTIAN AVERILL L	LTC	O-0080652	1066	1
CHRISTIAN JR W H	COL	O-0018333	1046	2
CHRISTIAN OTTO	MAJ	O-0005174	0135	2
CHRISTIAN ROBERT L	COL	O-0004609	0346	1
CHRISTIANSEN JAMES G	M G	O-0012075	0954	1
CHRISTIANSON CHARLES	LTC	O-0043913	0163	1
CHRISTIANSON DANA F	CW4	W-0902912	0360	1
CHRISTIE ALBERT F	COL	O-0004913	0248	1
CHRISTIE PAUL F	CW3	W-0906660	0963	1
CHRISTMAN ARTHUR F	CW2	W-0901535	0247	1
CHRISTMAN LOUISE D	MAJ	M-0010007	0357	1
CHRISTMAS THOMAS W F	COL	O-0016965	0157	2
CHRISTOFK ROBERT R	LTC	O-0022212	0959	1
CHRISTY JAMES V	LTC	O-0025909	0865	1
CHRISTY JOSEPH T	CW3	W-0906661	0361	1
CHRONISTER EARL C	CW4	W-0906662	0664	1
CHUBBUCK JAMES A	LTC	O-0021058	0860	1
CHUCK HARRY C	COL	O-0051032	0559	1
CHURCH CORNEILLE	MAJ	O-0069615	1167	1
CHURCH JR MITCHELL E	CW4	W-0902913	0966	1
CHURCHILL GEORGE A	LTC	O-0027362	0966	1
CHURCHILL JAMES H	COL	O-0001854	0642	2
CHURCHILL JR JAMES M	COL	O-0018907	0459	2
CHURCHWELL WILLIAM H	COL	O-0041806	1160	1
CHURNEY OTTO L	COL	O-0018334	0655	1
CHUTTER ROBERT W	LTC	O-0028755	0753	1

NAME	GRADE	SVC NO	DATE RET MO YR	RET CODE
CHYNOWETH BRADFORD G	B G	0-0003499	1047	2
CIANCHINI LUIS F	COL	0-0005553	1052	1
CIBOSKY WILLIAM	CPT	0-0083164	1066	2
CIROTTI JR PHILIP R	LTC	0-0023309	0867	1
CIRLOT JOSEPH S	COL	0-0019311	1057	1
CISTON MICHAEL F	CW4	W-0902914	0464	1
CIZON MAX N	COL	0-0050989	0157	2
CLAFFEE ROBERT A	COL	0-0030810	0964	1
CLAGETT CHARLES T	LTC	0-0020799	0360	1
CLAINOS PETER D	COL	0-0019269	1263	2
CLAIR CHARLIE L	CW4	W-0902915	1054	1
CLANTON HENRY M	COL	0-0030771	1160	1
CLAPP JR EDWIN G	COL	0-0024914	0666	1
CLAPP MARSHALL W	LTC	0-0069882	1167	1
CLAPPER CHARLES L	CW4	W-0902916	0854	1
CLAPPER GERALD M	CW4	W-0902107	1064	1
CLAPPER JR JOHN	COL	0-0042835	0562	1
CLAPS LUIGI F	COL	0-0039855	0759	2
CLARK ALFRED K	COL	0-0032608	0862	1
CLARK ALICE R	LTC	N-0001870	0960	2
CLARK ANNA F W	1LT	N-0000629	1047	1
CLARK CAREY A	LTC	0-0051315	0660	1
CLARK CARL V	LTC	0-0040393	1167	1
CLARK CHARLES T	COL	0-0040070	0667	2
CLARK CHESTER W	M G	0-0041908	0665	1
CLARK FELIE W	MAJ	M-0010002	1154	1
CLARK FRANK S	B G	0-0002551	1145	2
CLARK GERALD H	CPT	0-0047206	0950	1
CLARK HAROLD F	COL	0-0030040	1063	1
CLARK HARRY A	COL	0-0006141	0848	1
CLARK II CHESTER M	LTC	0-0069620	0766	1
CLARK JACK A	COL	0-0031496	0964	1
CLARK JAMES B	LTC	0-0031723	0563	1
CLARK JAMES C	COL	0-0043161	1066	1
CLARK JAMES L	COL	0-0058743	0759	1
CLARK JAMES R	LTC	0-0040342	0660	1
CLARK JAMES T	LTC	0-0033773	1065	1
CLARK JOHN F	LTC	0-0081974	0467	1
CLARK JR ALLEN F	B G	0-0018669	0161	1
CLARK JR CHARLES P	LTC	0-0024423	0859	1
CLARK JR CUYLER L	B G	0-0022947	0966	2
CLARK JR ERNEST C	LTC	0-0042834	0864	1
CLARK JR JULIUS E	LTC	0-0060841	0767	1
CLARK JR PAUL	COL	0-0018118	0760	1
CLARK JR ROBERT H	LTC	0-0003091	1122	1
CLARK LESTER H	LTC	0-0062945	1164	1
CLARK MARK W	GEN	0-0005309	1053	1
CLARK MAURICE N	COL	0-0042690	1263	1
CLARK MELVIN D	COL	0-0023550	1266	1
CLARK MILTON H	COL	0-0070638	0767	1
CLARK ORVILL C	CW3	W-0902918	0859	1
CLARK RAYMOND L	LTC	0-0027300	0765	1
CLARK ROBERT E	COL	0-0023911	0867	1
CLARK ROBERT L	LTC	0-0050575	0865	1
CLARK ROBERT W	LTC	0-0026032	0764	2
CLARK STANLEY A	MAJ	0-0012932	0934	2
CLARK THEODORE S	COL	0-0039998	1265	1
CLARK THOMAS A	COL	0-0002207	0642	2
CLARK THOMAS L	COL	0-0006008	1143	1
CLARK THOMAS R	CW3	W-0902921	0261	1
CLARK WILLIAM D	MAJ	0-0027448	0455	2
CLARK WILLIAM H	CPT	0-0014281	0920	2
CLARK WILLIAM J	LTC	0-0079773	0763	1
CLARK WILLIAM R	COL	0-0031506	0961	1
CLARK WILLIAM S	LTC	0-0021937	0347	2
CLARKE BRUCE C	GEN	0-0016068	0562	1
CLARKE CARTER W	B G	0-0011682	0854	1
CLARKE CHRISTIAN	M G	0-0018213	0163	1
CLARKE ERNEST M	COL	0-0019183	0863	1
CLARKE FRANKLIN W	COL	0-0029792	0662	1
CLARKE GEORGE S	COL	0-0004613	0846	1
CLARKE JOHN	CW2	W-0901359	0343	1
CLARKE JR HOWARD P	LTC	0-0036505	0863	1
CLARKE LOGAN	COL	0-0017713	0859	1
CLARKE TILLIE C	MAJ	N-0002354	0360	1
CLARKE WILLIAM E	CW3	W-0904097	0263	2
CLARKIN THOMAS R	COL	0-0015983	0462	1
CLARKSON HERBERT S	B G	0-0003605	0546	2
CLASSEN GERTRUDE M	MAJ	N-0002038	0360	1
CLATERBOS HENRY L	LTC	0-0089751	0764	1
CLAUSSEN ESTER	LTC	N-0002217	1159	1
CLAUSSEN GEORGE C	CPT	0-0015624	1039	2
CLAUSSEN JOHN S	CPT	0-0006878	0934	2
CLAUTICE EDWARD W	LTC	0-0079774	0964	1
CLAY CARMON L	COL	0-0032673	0267	1
CLAY JAMES D	COL	0-0042666	1163	1
CLAY LUCIUS DUB	GEN	0-0009318	0549	1
CLAY ROBERT R	COL	0-0016212	0755	1
CLAY ROY U	COL	0-0043072	0967	1
CLAY WILLIAM L	COL	0-0023059	0966	1
CLAYMAN DONALD C	B G	0-0020866	0765	1
CLAYPOOL CHARLES R	COL	0-0043693	1166	1
CLAYTON LAWRENCE L	COL	0-0009679	0753	1
CLAYTON REX P	COL	0-0029296	1263	1
CLEAR WARREN J	COL	0-0009753	1135	2
CLEARY EDWARD R	COL	0-0026304	1067	1
CLEARY LOUIS X	LTC	0-0054965	0663	1
CLEAVER RICHARD	CW4	W-0902923	0166	2
CLEAVES HASKELL H	COL	0-0016253	0755	1
CLEER CLYDE E	CW4	W-0906666	0756	1
CLEGG JR WILLIAM J	COL	0-0037542	0867	1
CLEGHORN RUFUS J	MAJ	0-0052767	0861	1
CLELAND JOSEPH P	M G	0-0016239	0655	1
CLELAND RALPH R	COL	0-0029178	0360	1
CLEM REGMAN E	COL	0-0051457	1163	1
CLEMA JOE A	COL	0-0043020	0367	1
CLEMENS CHESTER C	CW4	W-0902924	0565	2
CLEMENSON WENDELL L	COL	0-0006975	0-45	2
CLEMENT JOHN K	COL	0-0002992	0642	2
CLEMENTS THOMAS H	COL	0-0031735	1161	2
CLENDENEN CLARENCE C	COL	0-0012725	0354	1
CLEVE EDWARD A	COL	0-0020510	0857	1
CLEVELAND ALBERT C	CPT	0-0007312	0934	2
CLEVELAND JOHN G	LTC	0-0026559	0467	1
CLEVELAND JOHN H	LTC	0-0059468	1165	1
CLEVELAND JR JOHN A	COL	0-0019136	0657	1
CLEVELAND KATHRYN D	MAJ	L-0000061	0959	1
CLEVELAND ROBERT E	LTC	0-0036664	0764	1
CLEVERLY RICHARD O	COL	0-0021862	0866	1
CLEWELL EDGAR L	B G	0-0007081	1146	2
CLIFFE ROBERT A	COL	0-0029515	0161	1
CLIFFORD CARLETON M	COL	0-0018199	0760	1
CLIFFORD CHARLES L	COL	0-0003749	0747	1
CLIFFORD RICHARD W	LTC	0-0036761	0161	1
CLIFT MILDRED A	MAJ	N-0001832	0365	1
CLIFTON JOHN R	COL	0-0030148	0464	1
CLIFTON JR CHESTER V	M G	0-0020246	0865	1
CLINE EGBERT C	LTC	0-0080659	0766	1
CLINE JESSE T	CW4	W-0902926	0657	1
CLINEBELL GLENN L	COL	0-0030109	0264	1
CLOCK RAYMOND M	COL	0-0022920	0965	1
CLORE DUNCAN D	LTC	0-0026642	0865	1
CLOUGH JR CASPER	COL	0-0021979	0767	1
CLOVIS ERNEST R	MAJ	0-0068022	0967	1
CLOW JAMES M	COL	0-0029364	1157	1
CLOW KELSO G	COL	0-0019784	0865	1
CLUME FRANCIS J	COL	0-0010756	0851	1
CLYDE GORDON F	LTC	0-0047271	1163	1
CLYMER BARBARA A	MAJ	N-0000409	0366	1
COAN BERNARD F	MAJ	0-0078765	0664	1
COAN JACK L	COL	0-0020908	0157	2
COARD LOUISE M	MAJ	N-0001577	0964	1
COATES CHARLES F	COL	0-0030433	0662	1
COATES CHARLES H	COL	0-0015710	0249	2
COATES DONALD L	COL	0-0031912	0666	1
COATES HARRY L	LTC	0-0010651	1041	1
COATES JR CHARLES E	LTC	0-0021746	0867	1
COATES JR EDWARD A	COL	0-0004074	0149	2
COATES THEODORE P	COL	0-0041480	1057	1
COATNEY LOREN C	MAJ	0-0058340	0766	1
COATS JAMES G	COL	0-0031240	1265	1
COBALIS VINCENT J	CW3	W-0906667	0965	1
COBB ARTHUR L	LTC	0-0016845	0755	1
COBB LAWRENCE L	COL	0-0010300	0848	1
COBB ROBERT B	COL	0-0033025	0865	1
COBBS NICHOLAS H	B G	0-0008237	0846	2
COBLE FRANCES J	LTC	N-0002253	1064	1
COBURN GEORGE C	LTC	0-0031025	1163	1
COBURN WILLIAM T	CPT	0-0050279	0263	1
COCANOUGHER EUGENE H	COL	0-0038673	0960	1
COCHEU STEPHEN D	LTC	0-0019925	0655	1
COCHICK MADELEINE	CPT	N-0000371	0948	2
COCHRAN AVERY M	COL	0-0018834	0962	2
COCHRAN JAMES M	COL	0-0021945	0564	1
COCHRAN JOHN H	COL	0-0003814	1046	1
COCHRAN JR JAMES W	COL	0-0089326	1266	1
COCHRAN LORIS R	B G	0-0018889	0862	1
COCKE ALEXANDER	MAJ	0-0014214	0-19	2
COCKE JAMES W	LTC	0-0035168	0561	1
COCKE JOSEPH G	COL	0-0019658	0661	1
COCKRELL JR JAMES W	LTC	0-0024805	0864	1
COCKRILL JOHN C	LTC	0-0024730	0862	1
COCKRILL MCFARLAND	COL	0-0004938	1046	2
CODDINGTON HARVEY W	COL	0-0029316	0664	1
CODE JR JAMES A	M G	0-0005274	0346	1
CODER HAROLD E	COL	0-0018302	0655	1
CODY THOMAS J	COL	0-0017190	0355	2
COE EDWARD H	COL	0-0014759	0854	1
COE MERTON S	LTC	0-0052876	0660	1
COE WILLIAM C	1LT	0-0012637	1026	2
COELING ETHEL W	LTC	M-0010106	0267	1
COEYMAN WILLIAM M	LTC	0-0051316	0660	1
COFFEY JOSEPH I	COL	0-0021904	0960	1
COFFEY PHILIP T	CPT	0-0008121	0527	2
COFFEY ROBERT E	COL	0-0028974	0358	1
COFFEY WILLIAM W	LTC	0-0080663	0763	2
COFFIN FRANK P	COL	0-0007981	0847	1
COFFIN JR EDWARD C	COL	0-0051259	1061	1
COFFIN RALPH R	COL	0-0038895	0964	1
COFFIN SANFORD	LTC	0-0080386	0966	1
COFFMAN JR GEORGE W	COL	0-0042293	1263	1
COFFMAN ROY F	CW4	W-0902930	0367	1
COGSWELL WILLIAM N	COL	0-0041945	1061	1
COHEN BELLE K	MAJ	M-0010059	0165	1
COHEN EPHRAIM B	LTC	0-0022781	0746	2
COHOLAN PHILIP F	COL	0-0010592	0445	2
COINER BEVERLY H	COL	0-0004720	0149	1
COKER DAVID W	CW2	W-0901666	1150	1
COKER SEARS Y	COL	0-0023697	1167	1
COLACICCO FRANK	LTC	0-0023174	1047	2
COLBY ELBRIDGE	COL	0-0008150	0848	1
COLBY JOSEPH M	B G	0-0017562	0959	1
COLE ALBERT S	CW4	W-0902931	0463	1
COLE CLIFFORD B	COL	0-0007601	0951	1
COLE EVERETT B	CW2	W-0902932	1160	1
COLE FRANK L	B G	0-0004114	0650	1
COLE GEORGE M	LTC	0-0017107	0150	1
COLE GEORGE R	LTC	0-0020842	0758	1
COLE GLENN	COL	0-0019917	0865	1
COLE HUBERT M	COL	0-0016144	0655	2
COLE JAMES P	MAJ	0-0014215	1019	2
COLE JOHN D	B G	0-0019749	0164	1
COLE JOHN S	LTC	0-0079700	0367	1
COLE JOHN T	B G	0-0005256	0553	1
COLE JR JOHN L	CPT	0-0036092	0349	2
COLE JR ROY W	COL	0-0020277	1263	1
COLE LOREN F	CPT	0-0018416	0242	2
COLE LYDON B	COL	0-0029848	0163	1
COLE NORMAN E	LTC	0-0032484	0964	1
COLE PAUL W	COL	0-0012956	0554	2
COLE RICHARD A	CPT	0-0065080	0355	2
COLE ROBERT H	COL	0-0029798	0562	1
COLE SAMUEL J	MAJ	0-0014428	0520	2
COLE THELMA L	MAJ	N-0000553	0455	1
COLEMAN BRUCE S	LTC	0-0058862	0664	1
COLEMAN BYERS H	LTC	0-0043342	1065	1
COLEMAN CHARLIE C	COL	0-0024987	0365	1
COLEMAN CARRELL O	CPT	0-5225151	0866	1
COLEMAN EUNICE S	MAJ	N-0002218	0558	1
COLEMAN HOWARD	COL	0-0029457	0858	1
COLEMAN HUBERT P	LTC	0-0042336	0462	1
COLEMAN HUGHE D	COL	0-0039848	0960	1
COLEMAN JAMES M	COL	0-0041582	0459	1
COLEMAN JOSEPH L	LTC	0-0024527	0960	1
COLEMAN JR JAMES C	COL	0-0030053	1163	1
COLEMAN JR RENNIE C	LTC	0-0069886	1066	1
COLEMAN OTTO I	CW4	W-0902373	0263	1
COLEMAN WALTER L	COL	0-0038738	0463	1
COLEMAN WILLIAM D	1LT	0-0014406	0120	2
COLEMAN 3RD F W	B G	0-0019216	0858	1
COLHOUN DANIEL W	MAJ	0-0005949	0226	2
COLHOUN ROSALIE D	LTC	N-0000029	0855	1
COLLADAY EDGAR B	B G	0-0002902	0846	2
COLLEY HENNING F	COL	0-0014007	0-20	1
COLLEY MARTIN H	COL	0-0038582	0466	2
COLLIER CLAY O	COL	0-0042928	0561	1
COLLIER H R	CW4	W-0902933	1062	2
COLLIER JAMES R	CPT	0-0062972	0652	2
COLLIER JAMES V	COL	0-0015474	0753	1
COLLIER JOHN H	LTG	0-0012388	0958	1
COLLIER ROBERT P	CW4	W-0902934	0160	1
COLLIER WILLIAM A	B G	0-0007598	0854	1
COLLINGS KENT J	LTC	0-0080387	0567	1
COLLINS CARTER	COL	0-0006959	0846	2
COLLINS CLAUDE D	LTC	0-0014807	0442	2
COLLINS ESTHER R	MAJ	N-0000570	0561	1
COLLINS GERALD J	COL	0-0029221	0961	1
COLLINS HORACE R	LTC	0-0030845	1060	1
COLLINS HUBERT W	COL	0-0008877	1047	1
COLLINS J LAWTON	GEN	0-0005247	0356	1
COLLINS JAMES F	GEN	0-0016815	0364	1
COLLINS JOHN E	LTC	0-0023116	0761	1
COLLINS JOHN S	CW4	W-0902935	0967	1
COLLINS JR ARTHUR H	LTC	0-0065500	0767	1
COLLINS JR CHARLES E	COL	0-0084043	0863	1
COLLINS JR MATTHEW R	COL	0-0033550	0962	1
COLLINS LAWRENCE C	LTC	0-0011862	0-36	2
COLLINS LEROY P	B G	0-0002203	0345	2
COLLINS PHILIP P	LTC	0-0080666	0767	1
COLLINS RICHARD	M G	0-0029375	1264	1
COLLINS SAMUEL P	B G	0-0016444	0756	1
COLLINS WILLIAM F	LTC	0-0019698	0263	1
COLLISON CORA E	MAJ	N-0000517	0350	1
COLLISON TOM D	LTC	0-0023868	0661	1
COLMAN CHARLES D	COL	0-0041645	0260	2
COLONNA JOHN O	COL	0-0015099	0954	1
COLQUITT RAWLINS M	COL	0-0024189	1066	2
COLSON CHARLES F	B G	0-0012173	0753	1
COLT JOHN R	LTC	0-0080667	0865	2
COLTON ROGER B	M G	0-0002975	0146	2
COLVIN GEORGE T	COL	0-0030474	0565	1
COLVIN LLOYD O	LTC	0-0032853	0161	1
COLVIN REED N	LTC	0-0051190	0159	1
COLWELL LEONARD F	COL	0-0031358	0966	1
COLWELL RUSSELL M	LTC	0-0038839	1157	1
COLYER BETTY L	LTC	N-0001206	0463	1
COMELLA MARTIN S	COL	0-0031084	0161	1
COMERFORD RICHARD W	CW4	W-0902938	1265	1
COMFORT FREDERIC D	COL	0-0014714	0753	1
COMINA MARIE A	MAJ	N-0002406	1267	1
COMPER JOHN B	CW4	W-0902939	0565	1
COMPTON EARL D	COL	0-0021703	0862	1
COMPTON LOUIS	COL	0-0007419	1051	1
COMPTON MARTIN A	COL	0-0021038	0758	1
COMPTON THOMAS C	COL	0-0020692	1057	1
COMSTOCK RICHARD H	COL	0-0051206	0361	1
CONABLE MORRIS E	COL	0-0007989	1046	1
CONANT PERRY E	COL	0-0021357	0865	2
CONANT RALPH E	COL	0-0065408	0367	1
CONARD ARTHUR R	COL	0-0003094	1045	1

NAME	GRADE	SVC NO	DATE RET MO YR	RET CODE
CONDON JOHN F	LTC	0-0039972	C460	2
CONDON MARGARET W	MAJ	L-C000079	C461	1
CONDY WILLIAM	COL	0-002522C	0267	1
CONE JOHN O	COL	0-0017683	0859	1
CONE MONTIE F	COL	0-0029695	C462	1
CONE SIDNEY L	COL	0-0040362	C561	2
CONER CHARLES F	LTC	0-0078643	C864	2
CONFER RODNEY R	LTC	0-0058865	1166	1
CONGDON NORMAN A	LTC	0-0017602	0246	2
CONINE JAMES C	COL	0-0030203	0666	1
CONK ROBERT H	COL	0-0029909	C463	1
CONKLIN ALVIN R	LTC	0-0084352	0661	1
CONKLIN JOHN F	B G	0-0003777	0451	1
CONLEY JR EDGAR T	B G	0-0017665	0859	2
CONLEY SAMUEL G	B G	0-0015707	1155	1
CONLEY WILLIAM H	COL	0-0030823	0967	1
CONLIN PAUL A	LTC	0-0042111	1060	1
CONLON MARCELLA A	MAJ	M-0010035	C360	1
CONN ARTHUR E	COL	0-0029868	C563	2
CONN CHARLES	COL	0-0032550	0966	1
CONN JR ARCHIE F	LTC	0-0063307	C763	1
CONNALLY WILLIAM P	COL	0-0017567	0859	1
CONNATSER WILLIAM T	LTC	0-0005354	C834	2
CONNELL FLORENCE T	MAJ	N-0000337	C464	1
CONNELL JOHN F	COL	0-0011535	1046	2
CONNELL MARY B	LTC	N-0000122	0757	2
CONNELLY JOHN R	MAJ	0-0065135	0865	1
CONNELLY MARY F	MAJ	L-0000230	0758	1
CONNER GEORGE F	COL	0-0017772	C859	2
CONNER HASKETT L	COL	0-0004181	C848	1
CONNER JR STEVEN L	LTC	0-0028432	C766	1
CONNER KARL	COL	0-0031686	1167	1
CONNER LEO R	COL	0-0008617	0448	1
CONNER RAY C	COL	0-0024162	0447	2
CONNER STEVEN L	COL	0-0015122	0354	2
CONNERAT WILLIAM H	COL	0-003073C	C763	1
CONNERS JOHN J	LTC	0-0030034	0961	1
CONNIFF MICHEAL J	CW2	W-0904241	0949	1
CONNOLLY DONALD H	M G	0-0002831	0248	1
CONNOLLY FRANCIS J	CW3	W-0902943	0867	1
CONNOLLY HAVILAND A	COL	0-0031575	C765	1
CONNOLLY PHILIP B	LTC	0-0003296	0834	2
CONNOLLY THOMAS W	LTC	0-0056008	1165	1
CONNOR EDWARD H	COL	0-0009837	C854	1
CONNOR ELINOR J	MAJ	L-0000323	0964	1
CONNOR GEORGE R	COL	0-0011177	1152	1
CONNOR JAMES W	COL	0-0029479	1060	1
CONNOR JOHN R	COL	C-002086C	C867	1
CONNOR MARGARET E	MAJ	N-0000387	1065	1
CONNOR MARY E A	2LT	R-000101C	C845	1
CONNOR ROBERT T	COL	0-0038622	0157	1
CONNOR VORIS H	COL	0-0015405	0152	2
CONNOR WILLIAM M	B G	0-0020137	0866	1
CONNORS AMY I	MAJ	N-0000809	0766	1
CONNORS WILLIAM J	LTC	0-0081977	0965	1
CONQUEST WARD W	COL	0-0041630	1159	1
CONRAD G BRYAN	B G	0-0012226	1046	1
CONRAD HAROLD A	COL	0-0039654	0362	2
CONRAC VINCENT J	COL	0-0012153	C753	2
CONRAN RICHARD J	COL	0-0029820	1262	1
CONROY EDWARD T	1LT	0-0064594	1154	2
CONROY JR ROBERT J	LTC	0-0031321	0161	1
CONSTANCE PHILIP W	LTC	0-0024118	1062	1
CONSTANT SAMUEL V	COL	0-0004738	1046	2
CONWAY HAROLD J	COL	0-0014609	0854	1
CONWAY LEO J	COL	0-0041903	0961	1
CONWAY LEWIS W	COL	0-0037021	1067	1
CONWAY WALTER E	LTC	0-0081978	C865	1
CODEY ARCHIE W	1LT	0-0012461	1134	1
COOGAN HENRY C	CW3	W-0902944	0763	1
COOK BRAINARD S	COL	0-0018144	0160	2
COOK CHARLES H	LTC	0-0034201	0863	1
COOK CHARLES W	MAJ	0-0065968	1266	1
COOK CHARLES W	CW2	W-0901572	0647	1
COOK DAVE J	COL	0-0030051	0761	1

NAME	GRADE	SVC NO	DATE RET MO YR	RET CODE
COOK DONALD L	COL	C-0022255	0163	1
COOK EARLE F	M G	0-0018450	0763	1
COOK EUGENE	COL	0-0030736	0664	1
COOK EVERETT L	COL	0-0008798	1146	2
COOK FREDRIC C	COL	0-0019484	0864	1
COOK GEORGE G	LTC	0-0041090	0864	1
COOK GEORGE L	LTC	0-003545C	0367	1
COOK JAMES M	CW2	W-0905135	0760	1
COOK JAMES W	CW3	W-0902945	0261	1
COOK JOHN C	COL	0-0009091	1045	2
COOK JR JOHN S	CPT	0-0025064	0444	2
COOK JR JOSEPH E	LTC	0-0037876	0661	1
COOK JR WALTER H	LTC	0-0025466	0964	1
COOK JR WILLIAM B	LTC	0-0076861	1163	1
COOK LLOYD H	COL	0-000469C	0846	2
COOK MAXWELL A	LTC	0-0059846	0763	1
COOK RICHARD H	COL	0-0079779	0966	1
COOK ROBERT L	B G	0-0017675	C958	1
COOK ROBERT W	MAJ	C-CC88032	0460	2
COOK TRUMAN F	COL	0-0044727	0467	1
COOK WALTER R	COL	0-0020112	1050	1
COOK WILLIS E	CW3	W-0906674	0660	1
COOKE FREDERICK	COL	0-0029853	0961	1
COOKE JR LANE B	LTC	0-0056257	0663	2
COOKE SAMUEL L	COL	0-0018301	0559	1
COOKE THOMAS J	LTC	0-0045047	0262	1
COOKE WILLOUGHBY	CPT	0-0009722	0521	2
COOKSEY RICHARD W	COL	0-0003908	0547	2
COOKSON GEORGE M	COL	0-0032021	0164	1
COOLEY EDWIN R	COL	0-005177C	0766	2
COOLEY HERBERT W	LTC	0-0039773	0157	1
COOLEY JOHN R	COL	0-0014603	1048	1
COOLEY LAVELL I	COL	0-0028858	1050	1
COOLIDGE GEORGE W	B G	0-0017599	0859	1
COOLIDGE JOSEPH B	COL	0-0018570	0661	1
COOMBS RAYMOND H	COL	0-0015561	0649	1
COONEY JAMES P	M G	0-0017338	0860	1
COONLY WILLIAM J	MAJ	0-0036724	0261	1
COONTZ JOHN R	LTC	0-0023315	C759	1
COOPER AIDEL B	COL	0-0017595	0859	2
COOPER CHARLES F	COL	0-0008040	1049	2
COOPER CHARLES G	COL	0-003343C	1057	2
COOPER EARL M	COL	0-0034191	1160	1
COOPER EDGAR G	MAJ	0-0007723	0-28	2
COOPER EUGENE G	COL	0-0019644	0964	1
COOPER FRANKLIN R	COL	0-0067804	1065	2
COOPER GEORGE J	CW4	W-0902949	1158	1
COOPER GEORGE T	COL	0-0035983	0567	2
COOPER HARRY W	COL	0-0042261	0157	1
COOPER JAMES G	COL	0-0010167	0849	2
COOPER JR AVERY J	COL	0-0019107	0758	1
COOPER JR HARRY B	COL	0-0018469	C761	1
COOPER MARCUS F	COL	0-0051327	0862	1
COOPER OSBORN	LTC	0-0044135	0561	1
COOPER PAUL	COL	0-0015748	0954	2
COOPER RALPH C	M G	0-0017741	1063	1
COOPER RANDOLPH G	LTC	0-0084353	0765	1
COOPER RUSSELL P	LTC	0-0028938	1055	1
COOPER WIBB E	COL	0-0002819	0946	2
COOPER WILLIAM L	COL	0-0020100	0164	1
COOPER WILLIAM L	MAJ	0-0050866	1055	2
COOPER WILLIAM R	LTC	0-0080673	0867	2
COOPERIDER HOWARD V	LTC	0-0022035	0166	1
COOTE JOHN F	LTC	0-0031596	0765	1
COOTEY JOHN L	CPT	0-0014230	0120	2
COOTS FREDERICK	LTC	0-0050995	0856	1
COPE JESSE O	LTC	0-0008948	0136	1
COPELAND EDWARD A	LTC	0-0076862	0866	1
COPELAND JOHN E	B G	0-0004775	0446	2
COPELAND ROBERT M	COL	0-0008059	0547	1
COPLEY JR WILLIAM M	LTC	0-0039114	0962	1
COPTHORNE WILLIAM A	COL	0-0003544	1049	1
CORBETT ADELBERT F	CW4	W-0902952	0858	1
CORBETT JAMES R	COL	0-0018423	0761	1
CORBETT SEWELL M	COL	0-0004081	0845	2

NAME	GRADE	SVC NO	DATE RET MO YR	RET CODE
CORBETT STANLEY B	CW4	W-0902124	C663	1
CORBETT WILLIAM H	COL	0-002115C	C961	1
CORBIN FRANCIS J	COL	C-0033359	1262	1
CORBIN FREDERICK	COL	0-0020972	1059	1
CORDELL BEN E	COL	0-0015455	1153	1
CORDERMAN W PRESTON	M G	0-0016387	0958	2
CORDERO MARIO	COL	0-0007527	1045	1
CORDERO VIRGIL N	COL	0-0007472	0653	1
CORDES JR CLIFFORD F	COL	C-00201F6	C864	1
COREY HAROLD L	COL	0-0056814	0264	1
COREY JR JOHN B	COL	0-0021415	C662	2
COREY KENNETH S	CW4	W-0902953	0664	1
CORGAN FRANCIS H	LTC	0-0042885	1064	1
CORKILL WILLIAM E	COL	0-0007055	0147	2
CORLETT CHARLES H	M G	0-0003746	0546	2
CORLEY JOHN T	B G	0-0021325	1066	1
CORLIES EARL L	CW2	W-0902954	0858	1
CORMIER EVERETT L	COL	0-0032923	0764	1
CORNELL BERNICE R	MAJ	N-0002303	0465	1
CORNELL GORDON D	COL	0-0051531	0867	1
CORNELL JAMES D	CW4	W-0902955	0851	1
CORNELL KENNETH W	CW4	W-0902224	1265	1
CORNELL ROBERT W	LTC	0-0080676	C565	1
CORNELL THEODORE M	COL	C-0007279	0950	1
CORNELSON ARTHUR J	COL	0-0051567	0765	1
CORNETT JACK C	COL	0-0032972	0767	1
CORNISH GEORGE R F	COL	0-0004611	1033	2
CORR JAMES	COL	0-0051082	0360	2
CORRELL LOUIS W	COL	C-0030582	C564	1
CORRELL WALTER D	LTC	0-0040122	0666	2
CORRIDON JOHN H	COL	0-0010063	0846	2
CORT HUGH	B G	0-0011592	0854	1
CORTESI SILVIA	MAJ	L-0000336	0857	1
CORTEZ JAMES J	LTC	0-0053277	C566	2
CORUM DABNEY R	COL	0-0019001	0655	1
CORWIN CHARLES C	LTC	0-0038834	C664	1
COSBY IRA W	COL	0-0019025	C859	1
COSBY J C	CW4	W-0902956	0956	1
COSBY WARREN G	LTC	0-0065710	0667	1
COSGROVE EDWARD J	CW3	W-0902957	0760	1
COSGROVE JAMES J	COL	0-0020768	C157	2
COSGROVE SHERMAN E	COL	0-003899C	0667	1
COSNER JR RICHARD E	MAJ	0-0035933	C448	2
COSTELLO DANIEL J	LTC	0-0057579	0664	1
COSTELLO DARREL G	COL	0-0023449	0566	1
COSTELLO NORMAND A	M G	0-0017764	C864	1
COSTIGAN CHARLES F	LTC	0-0033336	C665	1
COTA NORMAN D	M G	0-0005284	0646	2
COTHRAN FRANCIS E	CPT	0-0014999	1039	2
COTTER ANASTATIA	MAJ	R-0010171	0266	2
COTTER ARTHUR E	COL	0-0079780	0662	1
COTTER CLARENCE E	COL	0-0004974	C854	1
COTTER EDWARD J	COL	0-0018346	0644	2
COTTINGHAM LEVIN R	LTC	0-0042955	C961	1
COTTON JOHN W	COL	0-0004856	0747	1
COTULLA LOUIS F	M G	0-0029069	0359	2
COUCH BUFORD J	LTC	0-0052969	0467	1
COUCH JOSEPH R	COL	0-0023039	1147	2
COUGHLIN JOHN G	COL	0-0018898	0754	1
COUGHLIN JOSEPH V	COL	0-0006351	C444	2
COUGHLIN ROBERT F	COL	0-0012027	C753	1
COUGHLIN WILLIAM L	COL	0-0015776	0754	1
COUGILL JOHN C	COL	0-0080391	0866	1
COUK HAROLD O	CW3	W-0906676	1060	1
COULTER CHARLES S	MAJ	F-0006750	0934	2
COULTER HALVOR G	MAJ	0-0014242	0420	2
COULTER JAMES F	LTC	0-0033386	C761	1
COULTER JOHN A	MAJ	0-0024454	C660	2
COULTER JOHN A	COL	0-0033541	0766	1
COULTER JOHN B	LTC	0-0003488	0152	1
COULTER JR HERBERT W	LTC	0-0084355	1263	1
COUNCIL FRANCIS E	COL	0-0016965	0357	2
COUNIHAN THOMAS J	COL	0-0017183	0758	1
COUPE LAURA C	MAJ	L-0000266	0266	1
COURSER MALCOLM W	COL	0-0042211	0761	2

NAME	GRADE	SVC NO	DATE RET MO YR	RET CODE
COURSEY RICHARD W	COL	0-0012454	0449	1
COURSON JR EVERETT P	LTC	0-0039943	0757	2
COURTNEY RALPH H	MAJ	0-0035196	0862	1
COURVOISIE THOMAS N	LTC	0-0024549	0261	1
COUTTS JAMES W	B G	0-0018875	0762	1
COVELL WILLIAM E	M G	0-0003768	0540	1
COVERDALE GARRISON B	M G	0-0017148	0863	1
COVEY WILLIAM T	LTC	0-0031100	1164	1
COVINGTON CARROLL M	COL	0-0040083	1266	1
COWAN EGBERT W V	B G	0-0011744	0554	1
COWAN GERARD C	COL	0-0018807	0862	1
COWARD RAYMOND	COL	0-0051495	1163	1
COWART BYRON E	LTC	0-0052415	0464	1
COWELL EVELYN M	LTC	N-0000339	0263	1
COHEN EDWARD T	COL	0-0051042	0859	1
COWGILL CHARLES J	COL	0-0037457	1167	1
COWLES CHARLES W	COL	0-0015231	0753	1
COWLES DAVID H	COL	0-0003111	0944	2
COWLES EUGENE R	COL	0-0010476	1051	1
COWLES HARPER B	COL	0-0051515	0764	1
COWLES MILES A	B G	0-0008577	0753	1
COWLES STUART L	COL	0-0015289	0753	1
COWLEY ARCHIBALD	COL	0-0003127	0-44	1
COX CARLISLE B	COL	0-0005798	0151	1
COX CHARLES T	LTC	0-0034699	0367	1
COX CLAUDE F	COL	0-0012921	1146	2
COX EARLE F	LTC	0-0012581	0631	2
COX EDNA L	MAJ	L-0000334	0959	2
COX HERBERT M	MAJ	0-0016017	0142	1
COX JAMES A	CW4	W-0902962	1057	1
COX JOHN F	COL	0-0041534	0758	1
COX JR EMMETT H	LTC	0-0037200	0464	1
COX JR WILLIAM S	LTC	0-0031720	0548	2
COX LAVONNE F	COL	0-0020934	0661	1
COX NOEL M	COL	0-0019883	1057	2
COX RALPH L	COL	0-0029153	0359	1
COX ROBERT W	CW4	W-0907090	0465	1
COX WALTON W	COL	0-0007442	0145	1
COX WELDON W	COL	0-0051453	1163	1
COYKENDALL FREDERICK	LTC	0-0033694	1062	1
COYLE MARVIN J	COL	0-0018602	0461	2
COYNE CHRISTOPHE	COL	0-0021879	1064	1
COYNE FREDERICK	COL	0-0010941	1047	1
COZART CLARENCE A	COL	0-0020152	0864	1
CRABB FREDERICK	COL	0-0018172	1060	1
CRABB LEONARD F	CW4	W-0902964	0355	1
CRABILL EDWIN B	COL	0-0006769	0753	1
CRADDOCK WILLIAM P	LTC	0-0037952	0565	1
CRAFT JOHN B	CW4	W-0902188	0557	1
CRAFT SETH O	COL	0-0016036	0555	2
CRAGIN JOHN W	LTC	0-0062412	0867	1
CRAGUN DRESDEN J	COL	0-0015390	0849	2
CRAIG ALLAN A	COL	0-0019621	0756	1
CRAIG ALMA G	CPT	N-0001076	0353	1
CRAIG CHARLES F	B G	0-0007231	0955	2
CRAIG CLAYTON C	LTC	0-0025262	0262	1
CRAIG C MARGUERI	MAJ	N-0001898	0161	1
CRAIG DAN E	COL	0-0031879	1265	1
CRAIG DAVID W	COL	0-0004786	0153	1
CRAIG FREDERICK	CPT	0-0017795	1033	2
CRAIG HARRY W	LTC	0-0080063	0867	1
CRAIG JAMES L	COL	0-0006942	0747	1
CRAIG JAMES T	COL	0-0021248	0766	1
CRAIG JOHN S	CPT	0-0058868	0962	1
CRAIG JR MALIN	COL	0-0015908	0854	1
CRAIG LOUIS A	M G	0-0003575	0552	1
CRAIG MALCOLM E	COL	0-0008123	0451	1
CRAIG ROBERT J	LTC	0-0081981	1066	1
CRAIG WILLIAM A	LTC	0-0043905	0860	2
CRAIG WILLIAM C	MAJ	0-0023002	0744	2
CRAIG WILLIAM H	COL	0-0007242	0854	2
CRAIN JAMES K	M G	0-0001915	0642	2
CRAIN JOY P	MAJ	N-000195-	0659	1
CRALLE MAURY S	COL	0-0017279	0758	1
CRAMER CHARLES	LTC	0-0006090	0438	2

NAME	GRADE	SVC NO	DATE RET MO YR	RET CODE
CRAMER FREDERIC M	LTC	O-0052273	0564	1
CRAMER MYRON C	M G	O-0003010	1145	1
CRANDALL FRANCIS N	COL	O-0084822	0766	2
CRANDALL HARRY W	M G	O-0016238	0858	1
CRANDALL MURRAY R	LTC	O-0015630	1147	1
CRANDALL ROBERT G	COL	O-0017652	0859	1
CRANDALL WALTER M	COL	O-0005648	0745	1
CRANE DOUGLAS LE	COL	O-0007064	1046	2
CRANE FRANCIS S	COL	O-0039664	0762	1
CRANE FRANK A	LTC	O-0011840	1039	2
CRANE GEORGE E	COL	O-0042377	0764	2
CRANE GLENN	COL	O-0046186	0366	1
CRANE JR HAL R	MAJ	O-0054794	0562	1
CRANE RICHARD Z	COL	O-0009760	0854	1
CRANE WARREN E	COL	O-0042608	0765	1
CRANE WILLIAM C	B G	O-0003538	0247	1
CRANK JAMES R	COL	O-0051346	0859	1
CRANSTON JOSEPH A	B G	O-0012465	0748	1
CRANSTON JR ROBERT W	LTC	O-0063826	1165	1
CRARY FRANCES E	2LT	M-0001208	0945	2
CRARY FRANCIS W	COL	O-0014606	0651	1
CRATCH SAMUEL C	COL	O-0008145	1144	2
CRATE GRACE A	MAJ	N-0001113	0965	1
CRAVEN VIRGIL E	COL	O-0034824	0966	1
CRAVEN WILLIAM O	LTC	O-0053969	0163	1
CRAWFORD CLAUDE L	COL	O-0020266	0164	1
CRAWFORD DONALD A	LTC	O-0037881	0665	1
CRAWFORD HAROLD M	COL	O-0021840	0767	1
CRAWFORD JAMES B	B G	O-0003088	0646	2
CRAWFORD JAMES R	COL	O-0030906	0566	1
CRAWFORD JOHN L	B G	O-0019343	1163	2
CRAWFORD JOSEPH R	B G	O-0019215	0360	2
CRAWFORD JR GROVER L	COL	O-0079784	0766	1
CRAWFORD PAUL M	COL	O-0004093	0950	1
CRAWFORD ROBERT J	LTC	O-0038315	0762	2
CRAWFORD ROBERT N	COL	O-0035353	0767	1
CRAWFORD ROBERT W	M G	O-0003667	1048	1
CRAWFORD ROSCOE C	M G	O-0003345	1149	1
CRAWFORD THOMAS M	COL	O-0012317	0854	1
CRAWLEY JR JOHN L	COL	O-0053963	0866	1
CRAZE JAMES H	LTC	O-0053279	0266	1
CREAMER JOSEPH K	COL	O-0010120	0245	2
CREAMER RAYMOND J	LTC	O-0037472	1263	1
CREASY WILLIAM M	M G	O-0016397	0858	1
CRECELIUS HERBERT F	LTC	O-0025187	0859	1
CREEK ROY E	COL	O-0039099	0867	1
CREEL BUCKNER M	LTC	O-0008460	0832	2
CREHAN JOHN R	COL	O-0009736	0844	2
CREIGHTON ROBERT R	COL	O-0042161	0762	2
CRESSMAN FREDERIC E	LTC	O-0019635	0146	2
CREUSERE MELVILLE S	COL	O-0009065	1146	2
CREWS JR HARRY C	CPT	O-0061871	0759	2
CREWS LEONARD R	COL	O-0007357	0251	1
CRIBB JR WILLIAM J	LTC	O-0060695	0265	1
CRICHLOW JR R W	M G	O-0012430	0254	2
CRIGGER HERMAN J	COL	O-0011070	0152	1
CRIGLER ELLEN G	MAJ	N-0000246	0161	1
CRIM CHARLES H	MAJ	O-0014775	0940	2
CRIM STERLING M	COL	O-0010150	1046	1
CRINKLEY FRANCIS C	MAJ	O-0029669	1051	1
CRIST WILLIAM E	B G	O-0012828	1155	2
CRISTO ANTHONY B	LTC	O-0062849	1066	1
CRISWELL HOWARD D	COL	O-0015899	0551	1
CRITTENBERGER W D	LTG	O-0003548	1052	1
CRITTENDEN EDNA E	MAJ	N-0002411	0563	1
CROCKETT CLEMENT W	LTC	O-0020168	0346	2
CROCKETT CRESTON W	CPT	O-0060462	0563	1
CROCKETT GILMAN K	COL	O-0007381	0550	1
CROCKETT JOHN J	LTC	O-0059848	0864	1
CROFT LUCIAN C	LTC	O-0032189	0964	1
CROMBEZ MARCEL G	B G	O-0016198	0156	1
CROMELIN JOHN M	LTC	O-0020597	0758	1
CROMWELL JACK D	COL	O-0042346	0464	1
CROMWELL SAMUEL M	LTC	O-0032176	0766	1
CRON JR ROBERT E	COL	O-0018127	0857	1
CRON LUCIUS A	COL	O-0018411	0858	1
CRONIN PATRICK M	LTC	O-0040786	0863	1
CRONINGER CARL R	LTC	O-0024507	0166	1
CRONK JEFFERSON	COL	O-0030461	0663	1
CRONRATH CLETUS	CW3	W-0502968	1060	1
CROOK GERARD B	COL	O-0039713	0461	1
CROSBY CHARLES P	COL	O-0029435	0955	2
CROSBY GEORGE O	COL	O-0015512	0954	1
CROSBY GEORGE D	LTC	O-0056157	0467	1
CROSBY HENRY A	COL	O-0043102	1163	1
CROSBY JR WILLIAM H	COL	O-0024639	0965	2
CROSBY PAUL M	LTC	O-0060837	0966	1
CROSBY RALPH O	COL	O-0033981	0766	2
CROSBY ROGER M	COL	O-0051299	0562	1
CROSNO GLADYS M	MAJ	N-0002056	1160	1
CROSS CLIFFORD E	LTC	O-0051733	0464	1
CROSS JACK	LTC	O-0065892	1167	1
CROSS KENNETH W	LTC	O-0035852	0864	1
CROSS WILLIAM O	CW4	W-0904242	0664	1
CROSSEN FLORA C	MAJ	N-0002397	0662	1
CROSSETT FREDERICK	LTC	O-0039963	0263	1
CROSSMAN EDWARD B	COL	O-0042428	0964	1
CROSSMAN RAYMOND S	COL	O-0032583	0566	1
CROSSON JR WILLIAM H	COL	O-0024880	0667	2
CROSSWHITE CLYDE C	LTC	O-0040750	0765	1
CROSWELL MYRTLE A	MAJ	N-0002053	1160	1
CROTEAU LIONEL J	CW2	W-0501704	0954	1
CROTTY MELVIN W	LTC	O-0026985	0965	1
CROUCHER MELVILLE F	CW4	W-0906680	0767	1
CROUGH JAMES A	CPT	O-0058872	1162	1
CROW CARROLL S	CW4	W-0906682	0461	1
CROWDER JAMES H	CW4	W-0506683	0859	1
CROWELL ALBERT H	LTC	O-0052319	0167	1
CROWELL EVANS R	B G	O-0007387	0854	1
CROWELL HAROLD B	COL	O-0008201	0752	1
CROWELL THELMA	CPT	N-0000121	0459	1
CROWLEY ROBERT W	LTC	O-0050171	0865	1
CROWN FRANCIS J	COL	O-0023071	0766	1
CROWNOVER ROBERT L	COL	O-0042968	0764	1
CRUIKSHANK RALPH H	LTC	O-0060803	0566	1
CRUISE EDWARD E	LTC	O-0017738	0656	2
CRUM MAGDALEN I	MAJ	L-0000010	1053	1
CRUMP FREDERIC M	LTC	O-0065530	0165	1
CRUMP IRA A	COL	O-0005250	0352	1
CRUMP JR WILLIAM F	LTC	O-0031983	0356	2
CRUMP WILLUS W	CW4	W-0902970	0666	1
CRUSE CHARLES F	COL	O-0056802	0655	1
CRUSE RALPH E	COL	O-0009307	0453	1
CRUZAN WINSTON V	COL	O-0030981	1167	1
CRYSTAL THOMAS L	COL	O-0001946	0-42	1
CUBBISON DONALD C	M G	O-0001931	0246	2
CUBBISON GORDON R	LTC	O-0060234	0265	1
CUBBISON JR DONALD C	COL	O-0019204	0759	1
CUBRIA MERCEDES O	MAJ	L-0000006	0753	1
CUDE JR HAROLD E	LTC	O-0080394	0665	1
CUDLIPP RALPH L	COL	O-0008817	0346	1
CULBERTSON PAUL W	COL	O-0042263	1163	1
CULBRETH OLIVER C	COL	O-0030429	0665	1
CULIN JR FRANK L	M G	O-0004717	1146	2
CULLEN MARY P	MAJ	N-0002367	1059	1
CULLEN ROBERT E	COL	O-0015700	1047	2
CULLETON JOHN R	COL	O-0012653	0652	2
CULLEY FRANK J	COL	O-0030117	1163	1
CULLINGWORTH WILLIAM	CW3	W-0902973	0963	1
CULLISON GEORGE R	LTC	O-0025193	0865	1
CULLY IRENE E	LTC	N-0000614	0861	1
CULMAN IONE M	CPT	N-0002280	0557	2
CULP CLARENCE M	COL	O-0004953	0852	1
CULP JAMES L	LTC	O-0045508	0866	1
CULP WILLIAM W	COL	O-0018821	0762	2
CULPEPPER GENEVA H	MAJ	N-0002121	1059	1
CULPEPPER JOSEPH T	CPT	O-0065972	0165	1
CULTON A Y	COL	O-0010164	0348	2
CULTON HUGH G	COL	O-0010325	0151	1
CUMBIE THOMAS A	LTC	O-0040542	0566	1
CUMINGS JR CHARLES S	COL	O-0025120	0667	1
CUMMING WILLIAM F	COL	O-0079701	0467	1
CUMMINGS ALEXANDER	COL	O-0008190	0651	1
CUMMINGS ANN	MAJ	L-0000322	0964	1
CUMMINGS EDWIN A	COL	O-0017222	0758	1
CUMMINGS EMERSON L	LTG	O-0015500	0462	1
CUMMINGS HAROLD L	LTC	O-0031194	0556	1
CUMMINGS JR S FRED	COL	O-0019796	0865	2
CUMMINGS KENNETH M	CPT	O-0060526	0963	1
CUMMINGS LAWRENCE E	COL	O-0029392	0462	2
CUMMINGS RALPH B	LTC	O-0039527	1053	1
CUMPSON MERVIN	CW4	W-0902977	0866	1
CUNDIFF ELLSWORTH	LTC	O-0034847	0866	1
CUNDIFF HELEN F	MAJ	N-0001670	0763	1
CUNDIFF ISAAC W	LTC	O-0043096	0865	1
CUNDIFF VIRGINIA F	MAJ	N-0000850	0862	1
CUNDY ELSIE M	MAJ	N-0002718	1167	1
CUNIN KENNETH A	COL	O-0019481	0759	1
CUNKLE AUSTIN C	COL	O-0015303	0954	1
CUNNINGHAM ELEANOR R	MAJ	N-0002408	0763	2
CUNNINGHAM ELMO F	LTC	O-0028618	0567	1
CUNNINGHAM FRANK J	COL	O-0012145	0646	2
CUNNINGHAM HAROLD D	LTC	O-0065973	0767	1
CUNNINGHAM JOHN H	COL	O-0051325	0862	1
CUNNINGHAM JULIAN W	M G	O-0004922	0552	1
CUNNINGHAM MARTIN	COL	O-0040059	0863	1
CUNNINGHAM MELVIN F	MAJ	O-0041146	1062	1
CUNNINGHAM THOMAS J	COL	O-0079787	0667	1
CUNNINGHAM WILLIAM A	COL	O-0007863	0746	1
CUNNINGHAM WILLIAM A	M G	O-0019579	0466	1
CUNNINGHAM WORTHY M	LTC	O-0045258	0262	1
CUNNINGTON EARL C	LTC	O-2047608	1167	1
CUNY CLIFFORD D	COL	O-0006437	0746	2
CUPELLO ALBERT R	COL	O-0038822	0466	1
CUPHAVER CARL A	COL	O-0043296	0864	1
CUPPY MARY K	LTC	N-0000141	0461	1
CURCURU EDMOND H	CPT	O-0026229	0746	2
CURLES CECIL M	LTC	O-0063298	0667	1
CURLEY EDWARD M	COL	O-0009477	0847	1
CURLEY RYTA M	MAJ	N-0002385	0162	1
CURLEY THOMAS W	LTC	O-0023904	0262	1
CURLL EDWIN W L	LTC	O-0049874	1264	1
CURRAN CHARLES D	1LT	O-0017091	0-35	2
CURRAN CORNELIUS	MAJ	O-0019332	1047	1
CURRAN ISABELLE R	LTC	N-0001984	0267	1
CURRAN ROBERT E	LTC	O-0020338	0859	1
CURREN JR WILLIAM F	COL	O-0038749	0963	1
CURRENS RONALD B	COL	O-0041816	1060	2
CURREY WALLACE H	LTC	O-0062212	0767	1
CURRIE WILLIAM R	B G	O-0017115	0758	1
CURRIER CHARLES R	COL	O-0050901	0555	1
CURRIER DON D	LTC	O-0040318	0466	1
CURRIER ROGER M	COL	O-0030522	1165	1
CURRY DONALD A	MAJ	O-0046211	0863	1
CURRY JAMES A	LTC	O-0054865	1065	1
CURTIN EDWIN P	COL	O-0030231	0864	1
CURTIN PAUL J	LTC	O-0026361	0863	1
CURTIN RAYMOND G	COL	O-0038627	0460	1
CURTIS COY L	COL	O-0020737	0867	1
CURTIS DONALD M	COL	O-0038837	0666	1
CURTIS FRANK H	COL	O-0011956	1046	1
CURTIS JAMES W	B G	O-0007973	1048	2
CURTIS JR JAMES O	B G	O-0018108	1060	2
CURTIS KENNETH I	B G	O-0019790	0865	1
CURTIS WILLARD S	COL	O-0010642	0352	1
CURTIS RAYMOND W	M G	O-0016784	0661	1
CURTIS ROBERT T	LTC	O-0050634	0867	1
CURTIS SARAH R	MAJ	N-0002361	0259	1
CUSACK GORDON K	COL	O-0018414	0161	1
CUSHING CHRISTOPHE	LTC	O-0031836	0865	1
CUSHMAN HORACE O	B G	O-0006916	0153	1
CUSTIS ARTHUR B	COL	O-0008618	0852	1
CUSTIS HARRY N	LTC	O-0065027	0866	1
CUTLER STUART	B G	O-0006926	1146	2
CUTTER JAMES F	LTC	O-0079789	0865	1
CUTTING THOMAS E	COL	O-0031397	1064	1
CYGON JOSEPH R	MAJ	O-0003144	0133	2
CYPERT LONNETT H	CW4	W-0902581	0660	2
CYR ARTHUR R	COL	O-0019119	0861	1
CZAJA RUDOLPH P	COL	O-0031267	0966	1
DA COSTC STEPHEN	2LT	O-0014560	1016	2
DABNEY JOHN A	LTG	O-0016602	0961	1
DACQUISTO MICHAEL P	LTC	O-0063785	0267	1
DAEHLER RAYMOND E	COL	O-0042304	0164	1
DAGER HOLMES E	M G	O-0005013	1047	2
DAGUE ROBERT V	LTC	O-0080684	1165	1
DAHL IRWIN A	LTC	O-0043356	0965	1
DAHL LEONARD M	LTC	O-0042935	0164	1
DAHL NIELS H	LTC	O-0024466	0962	1
DAHLQUIST JOHN E	GEN	O-0007120	0256	1
DAHNKE HENRY	LTC	O-0015874	0347	1
DAHRINGER JOHN F	1LT	O-0014464	0419	2
DAILEY GERALD A	COL	O-0025249	0163	1
DAILEY JEREMIAH A	LTC	O-0058242	0159	1
DAILEY RAYMOND	COL	O-0010534	0547	1
DAILY WILLIAM O	MAJ	O-0059915	0963	1
DAINE HENRY W	COL	O-0017804	0159	1
DAKIN MYRON H	LTC	O-0025733	0764	1
DALBY ALBERT S	LTC	O-0024036	0362	1
DALE JOHN R	COL	O-0039857	0960	2
DALE SR JOHN H	LTC	O-0076863	0866	2
DALE THOMAS W	LTC	O-0058874	0367	1
DALESSANDRO JOHN	COL	O-0042510	0165	2
DALEY EDMUND L	B G	O-0002118	0942	1
DALEY ROY M	CW4	W-0902983	0763	1
DALFERES ROY L	COL	O-0010279	0753	1
DALRYMPLE ROBERT W	COL	O-0025329	0765	1
DALTO JOSEPH J	CW3	RW-0902584	0364	1
DALTON HELEN C	MAJ	N-0001886	0360	1
DALTON JAMES J	LTC	O-0040171	0366	2
DALTON JOHN J	COL	O-0042219	0763	1
DALY CORNELIUS	B G	O-0004761	1146	1
DALY EDWARD G	COL	O-0016736	0757	1
DALY JOHN C	COL	O-0004911	0151	1
DALY JOHN H	B G	O-0020284	0764	2
DALY JOHN K	COL	O-0042011	0562	1
DALZELL ROBERT C	LTC	O-0060183	0862	1
DAMAN ELI E	COL	O-0019703	1164	1
DAME HARTLEY F	COL	O-0051487	0464	1
DAMELIO GEORGE L	LTC	O-0044627	0762	1
DAMMER HERMAN W	COL	O-0030634	0166	1
DAMON JOHN F	COL	O-0021208	0759	1
DAMON JR WILLIAM F	COL	O-0019179	0662	1
DAMRON JAMES C	COL	O-0041793	0954	1
DANCAUSE PHILIP T	1LT	O-0068974	0258	2
DANEK RICHARD R	COL	O-0018617	0357	1
DANFORD ROBERT M	M G	O-0001913	0242	1
DANFORTH CARROLL F	LTC	O-0023997	0862	1
DANIEL CHARLES D	COL	O-0015668	0754	1
DANIEL DERRILL M	M G	O-0029500	0563	1
DANIEL JR ROBERT S	LTC	O-0028455	1066	1
DANIEL MAURICE W	B G	O-0012766	0854	1
DANIEL RICHARD L	COL	O-0018329	0245	2
DANIEL WILLIAM J	COL	O-0019019	0660	1
DANIELS EDWARD M	COL	O-0007589	0847	1
DANIELS HENRY F	LTC	O-0023295	0661	1
DANIELS LEONARD R	COL	O-0029550	0461	1
DANIELS LINCOLN F	COL	O-0005260	0246	1
DANIELS MADISON A	COL	O-0051019	0357	1
DANIELS ROBERT W	B G	O-0004648	0753	1
DANIELSON IDA W	LTC	N-0000010	0351	1
DANIELSON OLE W	COL	O-0021130	1047	2
DANIS JOHN J	COL	O-0018959	0248	2
DANNACHER WILLIAM H	CPT	O-0025817	1046	2
DANNEMILLER EDWARD M	LTC	O-0021822	0266	1
DANNENBERG DONALD D	LTC	O-0040798	0863	1
DANNER JAMES C	LTC	O-0053384	0764	1
DANSBY CECIL G	LTC	O-0039452	0566	1
DANSBY JOHN W	COL	O-0016162	0846	2
DANTZER LAURENCE L	LTC	O-0055602	0865	1

NAME	GRADE	SVC NO	DATE RET MO YR	RET CODE
DANTZKER MORRIS	COL	O-0043992	0467	1
DAOUST JR GEORGE A	LTC	O-0027416	0767	1
DAPPRICH ANDREW C	LTC	O-0021080	0947	2
DARCY JR THOMAS F	CPT	O-0020471	1045	1
DARDEN JACK M	LTC	O-0060595	0466	1
DARDEN JR WILLIAM A	COL	O-0042599	0765	1
DARK JOSEPH L	COL	O-0016979	1157	1
DARK ROBERT F	COL	O-0005786	0546	1
DARLING CLARENCE K	COL	O-0015645	0754	1
DARMODY WILLIAM J	COL	O-0028904	0752	1
DARMS JR JOHN L	LTC	O-0079791	0767	1
DARNALL JOSEPH R	COL	O-0011426	1053	2
DARRAGH MATTISON A	COL	O-0042174	0463	1
DARRAH JAMES T	COL	O-0018124	0660	1
DARRAH JR JOHN W	COL	O-0019473	0463	2
DARRAH RAYMOND W	COL	O-0030029	1063	1
DARROW HOWARD W	COL	O-0031488	0866	1
DART RAYMOND O	B G	O-0008922	0750	1
DARWIN GEORGE H	COL	O-0033779	0766	1
DASCHE JAY A	COL	O-0039810	0662	1
DASHER CHARLES L	M G	O-0015634	0760	1
DASHIELL JR GEORGE R	COL	O-0065529	0863	2
DAUBIN JR FREELAND A	MAJ	O-0043709	0751	1
DAUER MAXWELL	LTC	O-0031217	0161	1
DAUGHERITY RICHARD D	COL	O-0005680	0650	1
DAUGHERTY FRANCIS	COL	O-0052222	1065	1
DAUGHERTY GLEN E	LTC	O-0038980	0359	1
DAUGHERTY JOSEPH B	COL	O-0016252	0755	1
DAUGHERTY LESTER A	B G	O-0005559	0951	1
DAUGHERTY WILLIAM A	LTC	O-0027491	0866	1
DAUGHTRY BARNEY A	COL	O-0016902	0160	1
DAUGHYTRY GRACE H	MAJ	N-0000545	0152	1
DAUTRICH HELEN A	MAJ	R-0010002	0355	1
DAVALL HAROLD C	COL	O-0019425	0264	1
DAVENPORT FRANK M	COL	O-0051029	0459	1
DAVENPORT HAROLD A	COL	O-0029385	0360	1
DAVENPORT MERRILL C	COL	O-0021479	0660	2
DAVENPORT WILLIAM W	COL	O-0043077	0760	1
DAVEY JR RALPH H	COL	O-0018689	0247	2
DAVIDOFF JAMES E	COL	O-0033460	0967	1
DAVIDS HOWARD G	COL	O-0000938	0934	2
DAVIDS JOHN L	COL	O-0034783	1264	1
DAVIDSON CECIL M	COL	O-0031560	0764	2
DAVIDSON DONALD M	1LT	O-0017369	1028	2
DAVIDSON GARRISON H	LTG	O-0016755	0564	1
DAVIDSON JR ALFRED H	COL	O-0039808	0762	1
DAVIDSON JR HENRY E	COL	O-0032295	1165	1
DAVIDSON LEWIS C	COL	O-0003821	1049	1
DAVIDSON MAURICE C	COL	O-0020108	0855	1
DAVIDSON ORION L	COL	O-0010358	0854	2
DAVIDSON PAUL W	LTC	O-0054119	0864	1
DAVIDSON RICHARD C	COL	O-0033262	1064	1
DAVIDSON RICHARD P	COL	O-0042785	0666	1
DAVIDSON SHIRLEY	LTC	O-0037122	0663	1
DAVIDSON WILLIAM G	COL	O-0018862	0961	2
DAVIE ROBERT C	COL	O-0040050	1058	2
DAVIES ALBERT C	COL	O-0034916	0767	1
DAVIES ELIZABETH	LTC	M-0010102	0966	1
DAVIES ROBERTINE	MAJ	N-0001263	0865	1
DAVIS ADDISON D	B G	O-0002651	0946	2
DAVIS ANNA L	MAJ	N-0000732	0962	1
DAVIS BENJAMIN M	COL	O-0030282	1164	1
DAVIS BENJAMIN O	B G	O-0001217	0741	1
DAVIS CAROLINE	MAJ	N-0000161	1060	1
DAVIS CHARLES T	COL	O-0042658	1065	1
DAVIS CHARLES J	LTC	O-0026491	0765	1
DAVIS CHARLES W	CW4	W-0904101	0263	1
DAVIS CHESTER E	COL	O-0007163	0949	2
DAVIS CORBIN J	CPT	O-0028570	1052	1
DAVIS DON	COL	O-0045687	1066	1
DAVIS DONALD M	COL	O-0052410	0766	1
DAVIS DOUGLAS C	COL	O-0018985	0550	1
DAVIS EDWARD M	LTC	O-0081947	0767	1
DAVIS ELLIS D	COL	O-0019387	0661	1
DAVIS ELLSWORTH	M G	O-0018658	1066	1
DAVIS FANNIE L	MAJ	L-0000200	0666	1
DAVIS GEORGE A	B G	O-0007078	0246	1
DAVIS GEORGE W	COL	O-0014719	0649	1
DAVIS HARRY C	MAJ	O-0003635	0722	2
DAVIS HARRY R	COL	O-0041894	0859	1
DAVIS HAWTHORNE	COL	O-0051013	0259	1
DAVIS HAZEL D	MAJ	N-0001013	0662	2
DAVIS HELEN M	LTC	R-0010004	0760	1
DAVIS HOWARD H	COL	O-0006537	0753	1
DAVIS III THOMAS W	COL	O-0022059	0367	1
DAVIS JAMES P	COL	O-0028895	0257	1
DAVIS JOHN	COL	O-0043012	0667	1
DAVIS JOHN F	B G	O-0003853	0552	1
DAVIS JOHN H	COL	O-0040036	0766	1
DAVIS JOHN J	COL	O-0019935	0264	2
DAVIS JOHN K	COL	O-0020408	0754	2
DAVIS JOHN M	LTC	O-0031761	0762	1
DAVIS JOHN N	COL	O-0022070	0761	1
DAVIS JOHN N	COL	O-0032808	1065	1
DAVIS JOHN W	COL	O-0016223	0755	1
DAVIS JR CLAIBORNE	LTC	O-0037001	0764	1
DAVIS JR CLARENCE E	COL	O-0053041	0267	1
DAVIS JR EDWARD L	LTC	O-0034079	0761	2
DAVIS JR HOMER L	COL	O-0029869	0363	1
DAVIS JR HOY D	COL	O-0018982	0563	1
DAVIS JR MANLEY E	LTC	O-0058802	0466	1
DAVIS JR PAUL A	LTC	O-0036887	0266	1
DAVIS JR RICHARD W	LTC	O-0027595	0866	1
DAVIS KELTON S	COL	O-0020786	0465	1
DAVIS KERMIT L	M G	O-0019386	1167	1
DAVIS LEE J	COL	O-0029623	1061	1
DAVIS LEONARD L	B G	O-0009829	1048	1
DAVIS LOREN E	LTC	O-0039444	0965	1
DAVIS MAHLON S	MAJ	O-0018095	0146	2
DAVIS MERLE H	B G	O-0009832	0753	1
DAVIS MIKE B	LTC	O-0026188	0761	1
DAVIS ORVILLE E	COL	O-0011066	0947	1
DAVIS PAUL C	COL	O-0021141	0661	1
DAVIS PAUL C	LTC	O-0025218	0861	1
DAVIS ROBERT E	LTC	O-0038307	0166	1
DAVIS ROBERT G	COL	O-0051394	0463	1
DAVIS ROBERT J	COL	O-0033886	1062	1
DAVIS ROBERT L	LTC	O-0025661	0864	1
DAVIS SCOTT H	MAJ	O-0037432	1155	1
DAVIS SR OTTIS A	LTC	O-0040553	0955	1
DAVIS STUART W	COL	O-0041593	0559	1
DAVIS THEODORE W	COL	O-0023259	0861	2
DAVIS THOMAS C	COL	O-0041981	0162	1
DAVIS THOMAS F	COL	O-0009227	1051	1
DAVIS THOMAS R	COL	O-0020380	0864	1
DAVIS VICTOR A	LTC	O-0040453	0561	1
DAVIS WALTER R	CW4	W-0902991	0964	1
DAVIS WALTER W	COL	O-0020878	0567	1
DAVIS WILLIAM	CW4	W-0906686	0764	1
DAVIS WILLIAM A	COL	O-0020198	0664	1
DAVIS WILLIAM A	LTC	O-0055935	0864	1
DAVIS WILLIAM E	LTC	O-0049241	0965	1
DAVIS WILLIAM V	COL	O-0016595	0246	2
DAVIS WILLIS H	LTC	O-0034325	0867	1
DAVISON F MCKENZIE	CPT	O-0014368	0819	2
DAVISON FRANCES M	MAJ	M-0010030	0865	1
DAVISON PAUL R	COL	O-0003660	1145	2
DAVISSON HENRY L	COL	O-0029612	0861	1
DAVITT JAMES H	LTC	O-0043490	0861	1
DAW WILLIAM J	COL	O-0012497	0946	2
DAWLEY ERNEST J	M G	O-0002843	0947	2
DAWLEY JAY P	COL	O-0021750	0866	2
DAWSON ALVIN M	CW4	W-0902992	1164	1
DAWSON CLIFFORD H	LTC	O-0039023	0266	1
DAWSON CYRIL A W	COL	O-0003496	0941	2
DAWSON DALLAS O	LTC	O-0049338	1065	1
DAWSON GORDON E	COL	O-0029587	0761	1
DAWSON HENRY B	LTC	O-0006562	0142	1
DAWSON JAMES T	COL	O-0016346	0146	2
DAWSON JR GEORGE P	LTC	O-0038998	0566	1
DAWSON JR WALLACE H	COL	O-0039712	0757	1
DAWSON MILES H	B G	O-0016079	0456	1
DAY CHARLES H	COL	O-0011712	0146	2
DAY FRANCIS M	M G	O-0015614	0659	1
DAY FRANK R	LTC	O-0018325	0259	1
DAY FREDERICK	COL	O-0016760	0857	1
DAY JAMES M	COL	O-0007033	0753	1
DAY JOHN B	LTC	O-0005619	0730	2
DAY JR JOHN F	COL	O-0051502	0960	1
DAY PARKER S	COL	O-0029573	0661	2
DAY PHILIP S	LTC	O-0008571	0622	2
DAY WILLIAM H	COL	O-0020957	0759	1
DAYHUFF JR CHARLES H	COL	O-0038709	0861	1
DAYKIN ALBERT	COL	O-0042767	0566	1
DAYTON HARRY C	COL	O-0014722	0838	2
DAYTON JOHN B	LTC	O-0028049	0766	1
DE ANGELIS ANTHONY J	COL	O-0039252	0566	1
DE ARMOND GEORGE W	COL	O-0002142	1143	2
DE BARDELEBEN DANIEL	CPT	O-0015164	0637	2
DE BELLIS ANTHONY C	LTC	O-0060862	0866	1
DE BERG DAK E	LTC	O-0042974	0664	1
DE BILL WALTER C	COL	O-0020626	0960	1
DE BRUIN CORNELIUS	CW4	W-0902230	0958	1
DE CAMARA DONALD R	LTC	O-0061108	0966	1
DE CAMARA RICHARD R	COL	O-0034399	0962	1
DE CAMP JR JOHN T	LTC	O-0026040	0765	1
DE CARLO MICHAEL R	COL	O-0042445	1164	1
DE CARD FREDERICK	CPT	O-0007915	0728	2
DE CHOW GEORGE H	COL	O-0024553	0764	1
DE COURSEY ELBERT	M G	O-0017813	0959	1
DE FRATES JAMES J	LTC	O-0084734	0667	1
DE FREES LINDSAY J	COL	O-0083565	0161	1
DE GAVRE CHESTER B	B G	O-0019262	0863	1
DE GON KENNETH C	COL	O-0023676	0563	1
DE GRAFF B R	COL	O-0007594	0850	1
DE HAAS PAUL L	COL	O-0030284	1064	1
DE HAVEN GRACE I B	MAJ	N-0000317	0562	1
DE JARNETTE JAMES T	COL	O-0042344	0464	1
DE JUSSEWICZ LOUIS	LTC	O-0006123	1038	2
DE LA VERGNE JAM	COL	O-0018956	0646	2
DE LANGE WALTER H	COL	O-0015096	1047	2
DE LESDERNIER L F	LTC	O-0020275	0859	1
DE LINE ALMA E	LTC	N-0000167	1262	1
DE LOACH WILBUR V	COL	O-0030449	0565	1
DE LONG JAMES C	CPT	O-0007159	0-32	2
DE LORENZO JOSEPH J	CW4	W-0902997	0461	1
DE LORIMIER ALFRED J	COL	O-0007259	0353	1
DE LORIMIER CHARLES	LTC	O-0078785	0667	1
DE MAIO MARIO	COL	O-0030399	0263	1
DE MARR JAMES O	COL	O-0042273	1163	1
DE MARS EDWARD J	COL	O-0029128	0457	1
DE MARTINO VINCENT	CW4	W-0906690	0862	1
DE MELKER BERT	COL	O-0030679	0466	1
DE MERS ROBERT J	LTC	O-0033159	0661	1
DE METROPOLIS HARRY	MAJ	O-0022021	0355	1
DE NOYA LOUIS L	COL	O-0053352	1265	1
DE PASS MORRIS B	COL	O-0010333	0854	1
DE POLLO HELEN M	MAJ	N-0002447	0267	1
DE RIEMER LOUIS M	COL	O-0017640	0859	1
DE ROHAN FREDERICK	COL	O-0004558	0453	1
DE RUSHA RICHARD A	LTC	O-0063416	1166	1
DE RUSSY JR RENE E	LTC	O-0040164	0864	1
DE SANCTIS JOHN N	LTC	O-0080069	1162	1
DE SAUSSURE EDWARD H	COL	O-0010217	0446	2
DE SHAZO THOMAS E	M G	O-0016479	0960	2
DE SILVA RUDOLPH H	LTC	O-0071339	0766	1
DE VANCEY CARL N	COL	O-0038770	0960	1
DE VEAUX JOHN A	COL	O-0021470	0859	2
DE VECCHIO ROY G	COL	O-0042584	0565	1
DE WARE WILLIAM C	COL	O-0007451	0247	2
DE WEESE JR ROBERT E	LTC	O-0078790	0767	1
DE WEESE WILLIAM R	LTC	O-0084359	0966	1
DE WITT FLORENCE M	MAJ	N-0001887	1059	1
DE WITT JR CALVIN	B G	O-0004459	0854	2
DE WITT JR JOHN L	LTC	O-0029109	0557	1
DE YOUNG DANIEL	LTC	O-0038203	0363	1
DE YOUNG EDWARD M	COL	O-0020076	0661	1
DEAGLE EDWIN A	COL	O-0030237	0509	1
DEAHL JR CHARLES J	COL	O-0008578	0147	1
DEAKINS JOHN A	MAJ	O-0058788	0264	1
DEAN CLARENCE	1LT	O-0014989	0627	2
DEAN TERRANCE W	CW4	W-0903001	0561	1
DEAN WILLIAM A	COL	O-0046007	0267	1
DEAN WILLIAM F	M G	O-0015453	1055	1
DEANE DON L	COL	O-0020492	0357	1
DEANE HAROLD M	LTC	O-0022887	0960	1
DEANE JOHN B	COL	O-0024040	0765	1
DEANE JOHN R	M G	O-0009759	0946	1
DEAR RICHARD H	LTC	O-0022279	1164	1
DEAS ALSTON	COL	O-0008635	1146	1
DEASON CHARLES A	COL	O-0030601	0166	1
DEBOW DUANE L	LTC	O-0040970	0864	1
DECHANT WILSON B	LTC	O-0029173	0158	1
DECKER ARTHUR O	LTC	O-0030583	1263	1
DECKER CHARLES L	M G	O-0018549	1263	1
DECKER ELMER E	CW4	W-0902364	1058	1
DECKER GEORGE H	GEN	O-0015950	1062	1
DECKER JOSEPH F	COL	O-0029999	0863	1
DECKER KENNETH N	COL	O-0015789	0654	2
DECKER NELSON I	COL	O-0030105	0164	1
DECKER SILAS E	COL	O-0020104	0765	1
DEEKLE JR WILLIAM C	LTC	O-0026310	0961	1
DEERY HUGH A	LTC	O-0080648	0765	1
DEERY JAMES J	COL	O-0016123	0455	2
DEGENHARDT JACOB R	LTC	O-0030391	0163	1
DEGUIRE MERLIN L	B G	O-0019446	0163	1
DEHNE EDWARD J	COL	O-0051565	0566	1
DEHNE ERNST	COL	O-0056790	1065	2
DEHNER VERNON E	LTC	O-0037147	0765	2
DEIBER HARRY M	COL	O-0003916	0348	1
DEIHERT RALPH C	COL	O-0012532	0845	2
DEISHER FRANCIS	LTC	O-0018852	0859	1
DEITRICK CARROLL H	M G	O-0014796	0458	1
DEL CAMPO VINCENT A	CW3	W-0903004	0765	2
DEL MAR ROLAND H	M G	O-0029917	1066	1
DEL ZOPPO ROGER A	LTC	O-0039243	0762	1
DELACCRUZ NICOMEDES	CW3	W-0907079	1059	1
DELANEY GRACE	MAJ	N-0000454	1062	1
DELANEY RICHARD	LTC	O-0023711	1162	1
DELANEY WILLIAM M	COL	O-0029590	0861	1
DELAPLANE OSCAR M	CW3	W-0903005	0661	1
DELCAMPO ANGELO R	COL	O-0018361	0456	1
DELEHANTY RUDOLPH D	CPT	O-0008605	0833	2
DELMONICO LOUIS R	COL	O-0017287	0858	1
DELMORE FRED J	B G	O-0029440	0565	1
DELOSUA RAMON F	COL	O-0043713	1066	1
DELP MIRIAM A	MAJ	N-0001944	0558	1
DELUCA ARTHUR J	COL	O-0024400	0965	1
DELUCA FRANK R	MAJ	O-0058066	0854	2
DEMITZ ROBERT S	COL	O-0021255	0657	1
DEMOREST ELSIE M	MAJ	N-0000630	0762	1
DEMPSEY ALBERT	LTC	O-0081894	0463	1
DEMPSEY FREDERICK	LTC	O-0063097	0168	1
DEMPSEY JACK H	COL	O-0031766	0564	1
DEMPSTER ROBERT N	LTC	O-0080700	0767	1
DEMUTH HENRY C	COL	O-0008653	1152	1
DENCHFIELD ROBERT D	LTC	O-0035886	0863	1
DENHAM CHESTER	MAJ	O-0004021	1033	2
DENHAM RUSSELL R	LTC	O-0053714	0867	1
DENISEVICH PETER	LTC	O-0023416	0859	1
DENISON WALCOTT	COL	O-0004035	1049	1
DENIT GUY B	M G	O-0008675	0953	2
DENNEY EARNEST J	CW4	W-0904104	0763	1
DENNIS ALBERT E	COL	O-0018052	0157	1
DENNIS ANNA K	LTC	N-0001965	1163	1
DENNIS DOMINICK C	LTC	O-0044953	0262	1
DENNIS EDWARD R	COL	O-0002973	0742	2
DENNISTON ALFRED B	M G	O-0017315	0562	1
DENNISTON ROBERT N	COL	O-0043552	0767	1
DENNO BRYCE F	COL	O-0023161	1265	2

UNITED STATES ARMY RETIRED LIST

NAME	GRADE	SVC NO	DATE RET MO YR	RET CODE
DENNY CHARLES S	COL	O-0010102	1146	2
DENSON ELEY P	B G	O-0002619	0846	2
DENSON LEE A	COL	O-0012658	0954	1
DENSON PIERRE B	COL	O-0016278	0755	1
DENTREMONT ULYSSES R	CW4	W-0903008	1054	1
DERAGISCH WILLIAM J	MAJ	O-0031202	0658	1
DERBY GEORGE T	COL	O-0016744	0456	1
DERDEN JOHN B	CW4	W-0903010	1065	1
DEROSIER GERALD A	LTC	O-0079797	0965	1
DERRICK HORACE F	MAJ	O-0028626	0367	1
DERRICK JESSE D	COL	O-0008952	1047	2
DERRICK JOHN H	COL	O-0041443	1056	1
DERRYBERRY JEWELL	LTC	N-0000214	0466	1
DERSHIMER ALEXANDER	LTC	O-0009248	0142	1
DERZIS PETER N	COL	O-0081879	0866	1
DES ISLETS ROBERT E	COL	O-0016405	0953	2
DES PLAND JR LEON A	CPT	O-0006709	0934	2
DESCHENEAUX GEORGE	COL	O-0018902	0846	2
DESHON GEORGE F	LTC	O-0021362	0559	1
DESMOND ISABELLE M	MAJ	M-0010010	0862	1
DESOBRY ELMER C	COL	O-0002385	0245	2
DESPINOSA WILLIAM J	COL	O-0015156	0753	1
DESPOSITO JOHN V	LTC	O-0024095	0761	1
DESSERT ROLLAND A	MAJ	O-0028388	0567	1
DETCHEMENDY EDWARD B	LTC	O-0045117	0865	1
DETLIE HARRY C	COL	O-0039996	1265	1
DETTREY GLENN W	LTC	O-0028546	0664	2
DEUTERMANN GEORGE J	COL	O-0016150	0847	2
DEVENBECK FLOYD F	COL	O-0015469	1253	1
DEVENDORF DONALD A	CW3	W-0903014	0457	1
DEVENS W GEORGE	LTC	O-0028008	0766	1
DEVER BERNARD A	LTC	O-0040827	0258	1
DEVEREAUX ALFRED R	COL	O-0016138	0755	1
DEVERS JACOB L	GEN	O-0002599	0949	1
DEVINE JAMES G	B G	O-0006540	0854	2
DEVINE JOHN M	M G	O-0005232	0752	1
DEVINE PATRICK H	B G	O-0031975	0766	1
DEVLIN EDWARD T	LTC	O-0051680	0164	2
DEVORE GERALD B	COL	O-0010329	0753	1
DEVORE JR LELAND S	COL	O-0032404	0965	1
DEWALT EDGAR A	CW3	W-0904244	0953	2
DEWEY GEORGE L	LTC	O-0015188	0449	1
DEWEY HOBART E	LTC	O-0039479	0666	1
DEWEY LAWRENCE R	M G	O-0015575	0361	1
DEWING ELISABETH	CW4	V-0904323	0365	1
DEWITT WILMAR W	COL	O-0014814	0153	1
DEWS OMER S	B G	O-0040079	1166	1
DEXHEIMER ROBERT	LTC	O-0032749	0165	1
DEY JOHN R	COL	O-0029347	1059	1
DEYO JR WILLIAM J	B G	O-0016449	0756	1
DEYO TRUMAN E	LTC	O-0024037	0262	1
DEYOE ALDEN W	CW4	W-0902175	1056	1
DI GIACOMO JOSEPH	LTC	O-0040111	0763	1
DIAL RICHARD J	COL	O-0051230	0761	1
DIALS RALPH P	CW4	W-0903018	0867	1
DIAMOND IRWIN M	COL	O-0039730	0961	1
DIAZ VINCENT N	COL	O-0004842	1145	2
DICE ROBERT I	LTC	O-0022952	0660	1
DICHTENMUELLER HERBE	COL	O-0051706	0765	1
DICKEN KEITH D	COL	O-0043327	0562	2
DICKENSON GLENN G	COL	O-0050954	0757	1
DICKER HERMAN	LTC	O-0043154	0567	1
DICKERSON ALBERT F	COL	O-0016838	0454	1
DICKERSON JOHN D	LTC	O-0022071	0867	1
DICKERSON ROBERT B	COL	O-0040103	0766	1
DICKERSON WILLIAM R	LTC	O-0080704	0663	1
DICKEY CALVIN A L	COL	O-0028961	0158	1
DICKEY III CHARLES H	LTC	O-0044001	1067	1
DICKIE MARGARET P	MAJ	N-0001643	0666	1
DICKIE RALPH L	COL	O-0031493	0164	1
DICKINSON CHARLES W	LTC	O-0026033	0364	1
DICKINSON JR W D	LTC	O-0018038	0432	2
DICKINSON OLIVER A	COL	O-0002336	0142	1
DICKS JAMES H	LTC	O-0030043	1061	1
DICKS JOHN P	COL	O-0029982	0461	1

NAME	GRADE	SVC NO	DATE RET MO YR	RET CODE
DICKSEN DONALD C	COL	O-0032531	1167	1
DICKSON GROVA-NELL	MAJ	N-0000484	0267	1
DICKSON JEAN H	LTC	O-0036606	0465	1
DICKSON MARSHALL W	LTC	O-0042930	1062	1
DICKSON SAMUEL A	COL	O-0016219	1149	1
DIEFENDORF JOHN E	LTC	O-0040009	1163	1
DIEHL FORREST V	LTC	O-0051361	1160	1
DIEKROEGER LUELLA E	LTC	N-0001861	0466	1
DIERCKS FREDERICK	COL	O-0020599	0667	1
DIERDORFF H BEECHER	COL	O-0019347	0263	2
DIERSING MARIE B	MAJ	N-0002236	1064	1
DIES FREDERICK	LTC	O-0051067	1057	1
DIESSNER WARREN H	COL	O-0020519	1055	1
DIESTEL CHESTER J	COL	O-0018448	0761	1
DIETERICH WILLIAM H	LTC	O-0031218	1060	1
DIETRICH JOHN P	1LT	O-0012096	0825	2
DIETRICH STERRETT E	COL	O-0058681	0964	1
DIETSCHE HELEN F	MAJ	N-0000665	0763	1
DIETZ CHARLES W	COL	O-0009642	0441	2
DIETZ GEORGE E	LTC	O-0018500	0859	1
DIGGS JACK F	COL	O-0076868	1066	2
DILDINE SETH C	COL	O-0010405	1046	1
DILL MACEY L	COL	O-0006352	0551	1
DILLARD DAVID S	COL	O-0022175	0367	1
DILLARD EVERETT R	CW3	W-0903021	0457	1
DILLE RICHARD T	MAJ	O-0058882	0564	1
DILLEMUTH RACHEL E	MAJ	N-0001576	0964	1
DILLER LEGRANDE A	B G	O-0015078	0954	2
DILLEY JOHN H	COL	O-0019861	0264	1
DILLEY MARION E	CW4	W-0903023	0764	2
DILLINGER W D	COL	O-0050902	0655	1
DILLON EDWARD H	COL	O-0020552	0465	1
DILLON JOHN R	MAJ	O-0079256	0666	1
DILLON LEO J	COL	O-0008141	0651	1
DILLON WILLIAM H	LTC	O-0058883	0265	1
DILTS PETER K	MAJ	O-0023955	0262	1
DILWORTH JOEL J	COL	O-0024790	0963	1
DILWORTH JOHN R	CW4	W-0903024	0363	1
DIMOND JOHN W	CW4	W-0901221	0552	1
DINGEMAN RAY E	COL	O-0011870	0552	1
DINGLEY NELSON 3D	COL	O-0005025	0851	1
DINGWALL JR ALLAN G	MAJ	O-0037245	0764	1
DIRKSEN LYNN C	COL	O-0029146	0858	1
DISCH FRANK A	COL	O-0029186	0860	1
DISHMAN ADDISON V	COL	O-0018471	0761	1
DISHMAN SILAS P	COL	O-0029052	0163	1
DISMUKES JACKSON B	COL	O-0029144	0858	2
DISSINGER CHARLES E	B G	O-0007374	0853	1
DITMORE HARRY B	1LT	O-0018311	1132	2
DIVINE ROBERT E	LTC	O-0045523	0165	1
DIXON DALE O	COL	O-0038788	1163	1
DIXON FRANK H	COL	O-0003764	0150	1
DIXON FRED	COL	O-0028892	0157	1
DIXON HOLSTON T	LTC	O-0051766	0364	2
DIXON JOBIE J	COL	O-0031744	0864	1
DIXON JOHN H	COL	O-0042733	0266	2
DIXON JR ONESS H	COL	O-0009610	1051	1
DIXON OLIVER O	COL	O-0030494	0762	1
DIXON RUSSELL H	COL	O-0005775	0747	1
DIXON THOMAS V	LTC	O-0051277	0160	1
DLUGENSKY EDMUND L	COL	O-0039727	0357	1
DOAN DONALD P	CPT	O-0014435	0620	2
DOAN HOWARD W	M G	O-0020057	0964	1
DOANE IRVIN F	COL	O-0005200	0949	2
DOANE LESLIE C	LTC	O-0033493	0664	1
DOBAK ALEXANDER	COL	O-0016203	0555	1
DOBBS OSCAR T	CW4	RW-0903027	1163	1
DOBLE JEAN	WO1	W-0800173	1129	2
DOBRINIC MATT P	LTC	O-0042985	0258	2
DOBSON JOHN W	B G	O-0021851	0867	1
DOBYNS THOMAS G	COL	O-0004789	0854	2
DOCKERY ALBERT B	COL	O-0001705	1138	1
DOCKLER CARL J	COL	O-0007505	0820	1
DOCKUM WILBUR G	COL	O-0005692	1146	2
DODD FRANCIS T	COL	O-0015306	0753	1

NAME	GRADE	SVC NO	DATE RET MO YR	RET CODE
DODD WILLIAM R	LTC	O-0080709	0666	1
DODDRIDGE PHILIP	COL	O-0009051	0447	1
DODDS WILLIAM A	COL	O-0020815	0964	1
DODENHOFF DAVID I	COL	O-0029611	0961	1
DODENHOFF HARRY C	COL	O-0030407	0661	1
DODGE CHARLES G	LTG	O-0018072	0466	1
DODGE FLOYD	WO1	W-0901305	0838	1
DODGE FREDERICK	COL	O-0012402	0451	1
DODGE HARLAND L	LTC	O-0080398	0162	1
DODGE HOWARD D	LTC	O-0051550	1159	1
DODGE SARA F	MAJ	L-0000044	0558	1
DODGE WILLIAM I	CW4	W-0903028	0661	1
DODSON MINOT B	COL	O-0032660	1166	1
DOE JENS A	M G	O-0003743	0249	1
DOE ROBERT E	COL	O-0042066	0761	1
DOERFLINGER OSCAR M	COL	O-0031972	0666	1
DOERING SAM F	LTC	O-0053058	0265	1
DOERR PAUL L	COL	O-0039726	0761	1
DOGAN ADAM E	LTC	O-0030413	0463	1
DOGGETT DAVID S	COL	O-0005756	1046	2
DOHERTY DANIEL E	COL	O-0028916	0557	2
DOHERTY HAROLD A	COL	O-0014642	1052	1
DOIDGE JOHN P	LTC	O-0017235	0150	1
DOLAN JR BERNARD J	LTC	O-0063321	0267	1
DOLAN PATRICIA F	LTC	N-0000573	0861	1
DOLAN PHILIP J	LTC	O-0027092	0767	1
DOLL FREDERICK	CW4	W-0903030	0357	1
DOLLAR FRED W	LTC	O-0039385	0865	1
DOLLARD EDMUND J	COL	O-0047369	1167	1
DOLLE WALTER C	COL	O-0021813	0260	1
DOLPH 3RD CYRUS A	M G	O-0019170	1059	2
DOMBROWSKI CHESTER	LTC	O-0031353	1064	1
DOMKE DELMAR E	COL	O-0022788	0264	1
DONAHUE DOROTHY M	LTC	N-0000621	0864	1
DONAHUE EDWARD T	COL	O-0039650	0559	1
DONAHUE FRANCIS G	LTC	O-0029001	0253	1
DONAHUE JAMES H	COL	O-0008455	0148	2
DONAHUE JOSEPH R	LTC	O-0043294	1062	1
DONAHUE JR JAMES J	COL	O-0076870	0966	1
DONAHUE PATRICK H	LTC	O-0034885	0666	1
DONAHUE THOMAS F	COL	O-0041435	0956	1
DONALD SAMUEL E	MAJ	O-0022750	1147	2
DONALDSON WILLIAM R	COL	O-0022198	1167	1
DONEGAN WILLIAM E	COL	O-0011784	0149	1
DONEY CARL S	COL	O-0004456	0646	2
DONLON JR JAMES O	LTC	O-0032039	0459	1
DONNEDY MADELYN F	MAJ	N-0001220	0467	1
DONNELL THOMAS W	COL	O-0030663	0665	2
DONNELLY AUGUSTINE	COL	O-0023681	0866	1
DONNELLY EILEEN E	LTC	N-0000175	0758	1
DONNELLY HOWARD	COL	O-0003868	0347	2
DONNELLY JR W J	LTC	O-0034359	0350	2
DONOGHUE ROSE A	LTC	N-0000877	0866	1
DONOHUE JAMES M	COL	O-0019798	0863	1
DONOHUE JOSEPH R	LTC	O-0023045	1046	2
DONOVAN JAMES F	LTC	O-0057546	0864	1
DONOVAN MARY L	MAJ	N-0002612	0365	1
DONOVAN WILLIAM N	COL	O-0021042	1163	1
DOODY KATHRYN M	MAJ	N-0003383	0666	1
DOOLEY HELEN A	MAJ	N-0002237	0660	1
DOOLEY JAMES F	LTC	O-0010342	1141	1
DOOLING HENRY C	B G	O-0004170	0747	2
DOOLITTLE GEORGE L	MAJ	O-0012723	1022	2
DOOLITTLE HOPE K	CPT	M-0000498	0747	1
DORAN CHARLES R	B G	O-0005891	0548	1
DORAN ROY E	COL	O-0038892	0966	2
DORENKEMPER DOROTHY	MAJ	N-0000577	1061	1
DORIE ARTHUR F	MAJ	O-0056572	1060	2
DORLAND GILBERT M	COL	O-0020132	0656	1
DORMAN PRESTON L	CW4	W-0906699	0267	1
DORN CAMILLE JO	CPT	R-0001107	0947	1
DORN FRANK	B G	O-0015278	1153	1
DORN GEORGE W	COL	O-0041979	0660	1
DORNBLASER JOSEPH H	COL	O-0009588	0748	1
DORNEY JR JOHN F	CW2	W-0800773	1043	2

NAME	GRADE	SVC NO	DATE RET MO YR	RET CODE
DORSET ANNIE M	MAJ	N-0000225	0763	1
DORSEY JOHN R	CW4	W-0904106	1058	1
DORSEY ROBERT E	COL	O-0030100	0264	1
DORSEY WOODROW A	CW3	W-0903034	0857	1
DORST JAMES A	COL	O-0003534	0147	1
DOTY JR DAVID B	MAJ	O-0007565	1022	2
DOTY JR HORACE W	LTC	O-0057379	0860	1
DOTY KIE	COL	O-0010629	0847	1
DOTY OTIS J	LTC	O-0062265	0867	1
DOTY RALPH F	COL	O-0016905	0157	1
DOUD HAROLD	COL	O-0016423	0754	1
DOUGAN RAMON C	COL	O-0030566	1163	1
DOUGERY EDWARD F	MAJ	O-0022711	0944	2
DOUGHERTY CLARENCE A	COL	O-0001564	0440	2
DOUGHERTY GEORGE R	COL	O-0051055	1059	1
DOUGHERTY GERALD A	CW2	W-0907131	0961	1
DOUGHERTY JACK O	LTC	O-0065476	0565	1
DOUGHERTY JOHN H	LTC	O-0031582	0765	1
DOUGHERTY JOSEPH S	COL	O-0008309	0753	1
DOUGLAS GELLERT A	MAJ	O-0017311	1136	2
DOUGLAS HARRY V	LTC	O-0042786	0564	1
DOUGLAS MARION C	LTC	R-0010076	0464	1
DOUGLAS ROBERT H	COL	O-0019212	0863	1
DOUGLASS FRANCIS L	LTC	O-0024254	0963	1
DOUGLASS GEORGE A	COL	O-0030296	1264	1
DOUTHITT TED E	LTC	O-0031626	1262	1
DOVELL CHAUNCEY F	COL	O-0008810	0850	1
DOVERSPIKE JAY W	LTC	O-0042229	0761	1
DOW ARDEN W	COL	O-0024591	0863	1
DOW DONALD G	COL	O-0042389	0964	1
DOWD JR THOMAS F	LTC	O-0027160	0765	1
DOWDEN RICHARD L	LTC	O-0080716	0566	1
DOWDS PETER M	MAJ	O-0086082	0466	1
DOWDY JAMES H	CW4	W-0903035	0762	1
DOWELL RICHARD W	LTC	O-0039225	0562	2
DOWLING PAUL J	COL	O-0004867	1147	1
DOWNER JOHN W	COL	O-0001995	0642	1
DOWNER WILLIAM W	LTC	O-0034854	0861	1
DOWNING EDWARD J	LTC	O-0042655	1163	1
DOWNING ELLSWORTH	COL	O-0018986	0263	1
DOWNING GEORGE J	MAJ	O-0005550	0240	2
DOWNING JR WALTER A	COL	O-0018991	0863	1
DOWNING LELAND A	CW3	W-0903036	0857	1
DOWNING LESLIE B	LTC	O-0012688	1047	1
DOXEY JR THOMAS A	COL	O-0015978	0348	1
DOYEL ERNEST G	COL	O-0041453	0456	2
DOYLE ARTHUR L	LTC	O-0027684	0466	1
DOYLE JOHN F	COL	O-0040127	0765	1
DOYLE JOHN J S	LTC	O-0042617	0863	1
DOYLE JR PIERCE A	LTC	O-0024891	0664	1
DOYLE PHILIP V	LTC	O-0018712	0949	2
DOZIER LINWOOD G	CW4	W-0904370	0456	1
DOZIER SLATER M	COL	O-0058184	0866	1
DRAGOIU VICTORIA R	MAJ	N-0002156	0362	1
DRAHEIM JOHN H	LTC	O-0060034	0866	1
DRAIN JESSE C	B G	O-0002235	0945	1
DRAKE ALBERT F	MAJ	O-0003003	0927	2
DRAKE CHARLES C	B G	O-0003415	1046	2
DRAKE FRANK M	COL	O-0041887	0761	1
DRAKE JAMES H	COL	O-0010635	1052	1
DRAKE LELAND R	COL	O-0043894	0263	1
DRAKE MYRTIE	MAJ	N-0000837	0661	1
DRAKE THOMAS D	COL	O-0015384	0447	2
DRAKE WARREN W	LTC	O-0027727	0966	1
DRAKE WILLIAM O	COL	O-0032158	0862	2
DRAKULICH GEORGIA F	MAJ	N-0002046	0360	1
DRAPER JAMES L	COL	O-0079801	0965	1
DRAPER JR PHILIP H	M G	O-0017543	1162	1
DRAPER ROBERT E	1LT	O-0050857	0652	1
DRAPER STUART I	COL	O-0023599	1065	2
DRAPER WILLIAM B	COL	O-0029176	0460	1
DRAVO EDWARD J	CPT	O-0026937	0647	2
DRAZEN LEONARD	COL	O-0040336	0766	1
DREISBACH ALBERT R	COL	O-0018938	1062	1
DREISS EDWARD	COL	O-0035589	0766	1

NAME	GRADE	SVC NO	DATE RET MO YR	RET CODE
DRENNEN WILLIAM L	COL	O-0031890	0367	1
DRENNON CLARENCE B	COL	O-0083566	0767	1
DRESSELL FLORENCE A	MAJ	N-0000541	0549	1
DRESSER PAUL A	COL	O-0030037	1163	1
DRESSLER JESSE F	CPT	O-0016931	0142	1
DREWES CARL E	COL	O-0024122	0567	1
DREWRY FLAG A	CPT	O-0011170	0433	2
DREWRY GUY H	B G	O-0004950	0846	1
DREYFUS JAMES	M G	O-0029117	0661	1
DRIGGERS CARL E	LTC	O-0005708	0-39	1
DRISCOLL ARTHUR F	LTC	O-0079802	1065	1
DRISCOLL CHARLES L	LTC	O-0017036	0450	1
DRISCOLL DANIEL M	LTC	O-0041773	0363	1
DRISCOLL MAURICE L	COL	O-0030525	1163	1
DRISKILL AUBREY C	CW3	W-0906703	0759	1
DRISKILL JOHN O	CW4	W-0903038	0860	1
DRISSEL HELEN B	LTC	L-0000507	1165	1
DRISSEL VIRGIL H	COL	O-0040010	0266	1
DRIVER COLEMAN F	CPT	O-0007612	1129	2
DROBEK THADDEUS W	LTC	O-0042453	1062	1
DROZD MAGDALENE	MAJ	N-0000257	0561	1
DRULEY EDWIN H	COL	O-0029876	0263	1
DRUM HEISTER H	MAJ	O-0023923	0347	2
DRUM JAMES H	COL	O-0020818	0846	2
DRUM VERNON B	LTC	O-0039318	0764	1
DRUMM BURNETT C	CPT	N-0000048	0550	1
DRUMM JUDITH M	MAJ	N-0002467	0162	2
DRUMMOND BURLEIGH B	COL	O-0051771	0766	1
DRURY FREDERICK	COL	O-0012333	0753	1
DRYE CLARENCE W	COL	O-0052413	1067	1
DU BOSE JR BURNS B	CW4	W-0905205	0658	1
DU HAMEL NOTLEY Y	LTC	O-0004422	0342	2
DU MOND PAUL A	COL	O-0037607	0461	2
DU MOULIN ALFRED W	COL	O-0019943	0865	1
DU RANT ROBERT N	LTC	O-0063803	0467	1
DU VAL CAMILLE H	COL	O-0041440	1056	1
DUBBELDE JOHN	COL	O-0015086	0954	1
DUBIA GILBERT P	COL	O-0039872	0164	1
DUBOIS BIRD S	COL	O-0003392	1047	2
DUBOIS HARRIS A	CPT	O-0065215	0156	2
DUBUC JOSEPH M	CW4	W-0906706	0860	1
DUBUY CARL T	COL	O-0023650	0661	1
DUCKSTAD ERIC E	MAJ	O-0023465	0445	2
DUCKWALL BERTRAM F	COL	O-0004031	0649	1
DUCKWALL RICHARD L	LTC	O-0039053	0564	1
DUCKWORTH BENTON R	LTC	O-0021934	0867	1
DUCOTE WARREN S	LTC	O-0060926	0964	1
DUDDERAR JR SAM K	LTC	O-0031764	0166	1
DUDLEY EDWARD F	LTC	O-0040374	0765	1
DUDLEY HOWARD H	MAJ	O-0018541	0946	1
DUDLEY JOHN H	B G	O-0018049	0760	1
DUDLEY ROBERT E	LTC	O-0033746	0765	1
DUDLEY WILLIAM R	COL	O-0045497	0358	2
DUDLEY WOLCOTT A	COL	O-0015799	0954	1
DUE KENNETH D	CPT	O-0024099	0445	2
DUE WILLIAM F	COL	O-0019268	1163	2
DUEHRING GEORGE C	COL	O-0018070	0460	1
DUEKER FRED E	COL	O-0032051	1060	1
DUELL CLIFFORD C	COL	O-0014645	0553	1
DUEMMEL WARREN G	LTC	O-0045004	1061	1
DUER PAMELA F	MAJ	N-0010105	1063	1
DUERR GEORGE A	COL	O-0078944	1157	1
DUERSON SAMUEL H	LTC	O-0030084	1061	1
DUFF CHARLES R	LTC	O-0018438	0866	1
DUFF FORREST W	COL	O-0043391	0462	2
DUFF ROBINSON F	M G	O-0007388	0153	1
DUFF RUSSELL G	COL	O-0014646	0555	1
DUFFILL HARRISON W	MAJ	O-0005367	0438	2
DUFFNER CARL F	COL	O-0012801	0753	1
DUFFY CATHERINE	MAJ	N-0000567	0561	2
DUFFY JACK W	LTC	O-0037349	0664	1
DUFFY JOHN J	COL	O-0019738	0865	1
DUFRESNE GEORGE R	LTC	O-0062812	0865	1
DUFRESNE ROLAND J	CW4	W-0901591	0957	1
DUGAN AUGUSTINE	COL	O-0015610	0754	1
DUGGAN ROY H	LTC	O-0066147	0866	1
DUGGAN WALTER	LTC	O-0050053	0767	1
DUGGINS GEORGE J	MAJ	O-0058896	0663	1
DUGGINS PERCY F	COL	O-0004144	0548	2
DUHON SIMON J	CW4	W-0903039	1154	1
DUIN GERALD H	COL	O-0020148	0559	1
DUKE HENRY B	COL	O-0079803	0966	1
DUKE JACK W	LTC	O-0033662	0966	2
DUKE JAMES O	LTC	O-0060502	0867	2
DUKE JAMES T	B G	O-0006654	0653	1
DUKE RAYMOND E	COL	O-0020110	0465	1
DUKE STRATFORD	CW4	RW-0903040	0561	1
DUKES ERNEST F	COL	O-0008029	1047	1
DUKES JR DAN K	COL	O-0034283	0964	1
DUKES LENZIE J	LTC	O-0058887	0367	1
DUL PETER A	LTC	O-0080720	0765	1
DULANEY JACK F	CPT	O-0025812	0847	2
DULANEY ROBERT L	M G	O-0015351	0154	1
DULAY PEDRO D	COL	O-0003236	1033	2
DULLUM DELL F	COL	O-0021011	0758	1
DUMAS ALBERT H	COL	O-0007488	0749	2
DUMAS MAMIE	MAJ	N-0000286	0160	1
DUMOND KENNETH S	LTC	O-0030748	0764	1
DUMONT FERNAND G	COL	O-0011954	1149	1
DUMPERT PAUL J	CW3	W-0903041	0859	1
DUNAWAY FINIS E	COL	O-0016085	1046	2
DUNBAR CHARLES H	CW4	W-0906706	0163	1
DUNBAR ELLEN V	MAJ	L-0000138	0764	1
DUNBAR LEE R	COL	O-0002648	0245	2
DUNBAR OLIVER C	LTC	O-0043408	0166	1
DUNCAN GEORGE T	M G	O-0018878	0867	1
DUNCAN HARRY N	LTC	O-0080400	1265	1
DUNCAN III JOSEPH G	COL	O-0021227	0262	1
DUNCAN JAMES W	COL	O-0020834	0766	1
DUNCAN MARGARET E	LTC	N-0000329	0763	1
DUNCAN WILLIAM D	COL	O-0031466	0966	1
DUNCKEL WILLIAM C	M G	O-0006676	0-45	2
DUNFORD DONALD	B G	O-0016267	1155	1
DUNHAM CHARLES E	LTC	O-0014801	0755	1
DUNHAM JR LEE E	COL	O-0022897	0761	1
DUNHAM JR WILLIAM H	COL	O-0012411	0546	2
DUNKELBERG WILBUR E	B G	O-0012206	1155	1
DUNKLE DONALD R	COL	O-0007161	0447	2
DUNLAP CLARENCE R	COL	O-0029975	0965	2
DUNLAP KNOX	COL	O-0019667	0663	2
DUNLOP ROBERT H	B G	O-0002885	0346	1
DUNLOY DEANE A	COL	O-0038825	0466	1
DUNN BEVERLY C	B G	O-0002830	0748	2
DUNN CHARLES G	B G	O-0018996	0863	2
DUNN FLOYD E	COL	O-0016261	0655	1
DUNN JERRY F	COL	O-0034342	0867	1
DUNN JOHN A	COL	O-0022798	0666	2
DUNN JOHN J	COL	O-0031385	0860	1
DUNN JOHN L	COL	O-0004591	1149	1
DUNN MAURICE W	LTC	O-0040985	1066	1
DUNN PHILIP F	LTC	O-0050379	0962	1
DUNN SIDNEY F	COL	O-0005458	0452	1
DUNN STEPHANIE	CPT	N-0002311	0357	2
DUNN THOMAS W	LTG	O-0018157	0767	2
DUNN WELLINGTON	LTC	O-0063287	0866	1
DUNN WILLIAM P	LTC	O-0051413	0461	1
DUNNE DAVID M	COL	O-0015130	0854	1
DUNNE JOSEPH A	MAJ	O-0043200	0753	1
DUNNING MILO P	LTC	O-0009431	0538	1
DUNSTAN HENRY V	LTC	O-0040953	1165	1
DUPONT LEO E	LTC	O-0055889	0565	1
DUPREE JAMES E	COL	O-0040044	0962	1
DUPUY HENRY H	CW3	W-0903046	1058	1
DUPUY RICHARD E	COL	O-0006186	0546	1
DUPUY TREVOR N	COL	O-0021098	0758	1
DURAND PAUL	CW4	W-0903047	0666	1
DURANT BENJAMIN R	CW4	W-0903048	0963	1
DURAY JOSEPH B	LTC	O-0065257	0667	1
DURBIN BELLIS B	COL	O-0021244	0866	1
DURBIN WILLIAM F	COL	O-0051748	0361	1
DURDEN LEWIS M	LTC	O-0030935	1264	1
DURFEE DONALD L	COL	O-0019538	0862	1
DURFEE LOYD V	LTC	O-0008620	0841	2
DURGAN RAYMOND C	COL	O-0023527	1166	2
DURGIN CHESLEY F	COL	O-0032363	0265	2
DURHAM ERNEST E	COL	O-0035709	0962	1
DURHAM FANNY	MAJ	N-0002074	1163	1
DURHAM HOWARD W	LTC	O-0059902	0565	1
DURHAM JAMES R	CW2	W-0903050	1060	1
DURING FRED	COL	O-0005660	0944	1
DURNFORD JAMES A	COL	O-0011418	0250	2
DURR JOHN C	LTC	O-0028345	0966	2
DURST RICHARD H	LTC	O-0080402	0665	1
DURST ROBERT D	COL	O-0028837	0656	1
DURYEA LYMAN C	COL	O-0057522	0158	1
DUSENBURY CARLISLE C	COL	O-0011672	0950	1
DUSENBURY RALPH W	COL	O-0002280	0445	1
DUTCHAK EUGENE M	LTC	O-0057458	0467	1
DUTTON CARL R	COL	O-0016048	0954	1
DUTTON DONALD L	COL	O-0005547	0251	1
DUTTWEILER CHARLES H	LTC	O-0079805	0464	1
DUVAL HELEN G	MAJ	N-0000348	0260	1
DUVALL ANDREW R	COL	O-0010925	1146	2
DUVALL CLIFFORD P	LTC	O-0039270	0764	1
DUVALL EDWARD	COL	O-0041921	1061	1
DUVALL WARD E	COL	O-0003592	0546	2
DWINELL JOHN S	COL	O-0041467	0960	2
DWYER JOHN R	COL	O-0042138	0463	1
DWYER PHILIP R	COL	O-0015171	0554	1
DWYRE DOUGLAS G	COL	O-0017535	0859	1
DYE HAROLD A	COL	O-0076871	0967	1
DYEKMAN IVAN J	COL	O-0030455	0862	2
DYER ARMEL	COL	O-0042674	0862	2
DYER HAROLD F	COL	O-0043328	1164	1
DYER JAMES M	1LT	O-0069001	1156	2
DYER KENNETH R	COL	O-0040065	1264	1
DYKE JR HAROLD H	LTC	O-0053334	0165	1
DYKE LESTER M	COL	O-0016943	0946	1
DYKES CLIFFORD E	LTC	O-0051781	0764	1
DZIUBAN STANLEY W	COL	O-0021738	0864	1
DZURKO ANNA	MAJ	N-0002200	1067	1
EAGAN WARREN C	LTC	O-0069638	0267	1
EAGER BLANCHE H	MAJ	N-0000038	0349	1
EAGER HOWARD	COL	O-0003502	1046	1
EAGER JR GEORGE	LTC	O-0036766	0965	1
EAGLE ALEXANDER	COL	O-0029910	0463	1
EAGLER VERONICA I	MAJ	N-0002265	1162	1
EAGLES WILLIAM W	M G	O-0005270	0153	1
EAKEN ANDREW J	COL	O-0040090	0467	1
EAKER ALAN R	COL	O-0043146	0667	1
EAKER FRED L	COL	O-0042223	0862	1
EAKER JOHN P	CW3	W-0903054	0461	1
EAKIN ALDEAN A	COL	O-0041794	0462	1
EALES JOHN I H	COL	O-0038751	1063	1
EALY RALPH E	CW4	W-0902150	1159	1
EANES EDWARD W	LTC	O-0029249	0860	1
EANES RICHARD H	COL	O-0009453	0949	2
EARL EDWIN C	COL	O-0029097	0457	1
EARLE HIRAM W	LTC	O-0028958	1055	1
EARLE JR JOHN J	1LT	O-0017127	0834	2
EARLES CARL T	LTC	O-0058890	1166	1
EARNEST HERBERT L	M G	O-0007282	0947	1
EASLEY BRUCE	M G	O-0017735	0562	2
EASLEY JR CLAUDIUS M	LTC	O-0035056	0564	1
EASON JAMES F	COL	O-0030435	0665	1
EASON JOHN D	COL	O-0011993	1146	1
EASON RODERICK D	COL	O-0052420	0367	1
EASON SIDNEY S	LTC	O-0080403	0560	1
EAST RALPH D	CW4	W-0903055	0257	1
EASTBURN CHARLEY P	COL	O-0018203	0559	1
EASTERBROOK CHARLES	COL	O-0006130	0144	2
EASTERBROOK ERNEST F	M G	O-0018537	0667	1
EASTMOND THEODORE I	COL	O-0040013	0164	1
EASTON HARRY D	COL	O-0051822	1164	1
EASTON WILLIAM G	COL	O-0020656	0767	2
EASTWOOD HAROLD E	B G	O-0008202	0752	1
EATMAN GEORGE L	COL	O-0019548	0862	1
EATON GAIL A	LTC	O-0042268	1061	1
EATON GALEN R	COL	O-0021940	1046	2
EATON RALPH P	B G	O-0015871	0854	1
EBBERT THEODORE H	LTC	O-0029885	0161	1
EBBS RICHARD F	COL	O-0039579	0558	1
EBEL HENRY W	COL	O-0019434	0862	2
EBERHARD FRANKLIN K	COL	O-0040161	0161	1
EBERHART CLAUDE M	COL	O-0051967	0366	1
EBERLE GEORGE L	M G	O-0006613	0754	2
EBERLE SIDNEY S	COL	O-0004784	0849	1
EBERLIN RALPH	COL	O-0014222	1019	2
EBEY FRANK W	CPT	O-0018905	1047	1
EBLEN GEORGE C	LTC	O-0061195	0666	1
ECHOLS ESTELA B	CPT	N-0000047	0749	1
ECHOLS LEONARD E	COL	O-0042265	0161	1
ECHOLS MARION P	COL	O-0012324	0653	1
ECK DOROTHY J	MAJ	N-0002502	1264	1
ECKERT KENNETH P	COL	O-0039196	0967	1
ECKERT NORMAN J	COL	O-0011591	0854	2
ECKHARDT RICHARD H	COL	O-0019712	0863	1
ECKLAND KENNETH F	COL	O-0032334	0765	1
ECKLES WILLIAM E	COL	O-0029450	0960	1
ECKLON LELAND C	LTC	O-0080732	0867	1
ECKMAN GEORGE R	COL	O-0051005	1054	1
ECKOLS TRUMAN D	COL	O-0043078	0464	1
ECKSTEIN PAUL A	COL	O-0040331	0266	1
EDDINS GRACE T	LTC	N-0002373	0963	1
EDDLEMAN CLYDE D	GEN	O-0015842	0462	2
EDDY ELWIN H	LTC	O-0018354	0154	1
EDDY GEORGE C	B G	O-0012108	0754	2
EDDY KENNETH A	COL	O-0029014	0958	1
EDDY ROBERT A	LTC	O-0022730	0764	1
EDELEN LARUE M	COL	O-0029445	0661	2
EDENFIELD RUTH	LTC	N-0002061	0764	1
EDENS JR ALLEN C	LTC	O-0067567	0767	1
EDENS WALTER A	COL	O-0023543	0862	1
EDGAR JAMES D	COL	O-0030635	0162	1
EDGAR THOMAS I	COL	O-0018083	0157	1
EDGE JR WILMER A	LTC	O-0038747	0553	1
EDGERLY JOHN H	LTC	O-0051684	1160	1
EDGERLY JOHN R	COL	O-0003139	0936	2
EDGERTON ERIC P	LTC	O-0043850	0667	1
EDGERTON GLEN E	M G	O-0002324	0447	2
EDINGTON JAMES F	LTC	O-0050734	0765	1
EDMAN WINIFRED L	CPT	N-0002677	1163	2
EDMOND NEIL S	COL	O-0006806	1043	1
EDMONSON EDWARD M	COL	O-0012683	0950	1
EDMONSTON RAPHAEL A	LTC	O-0019666	0245	2
EDMUNDS ARTHUR E	MAJ	O-0014431	0630	2
EDMUNDS JAMES A	COL	O-0010848	0653	1
EDMUNDS JOHN O	COL	O-0030323	0165	1
EDMUNDS KINZIE R	COL	O-0001936	0642	1
EDNIE ALFRED V	COL	O-0008157	0-45	2
EDRINGTON JR BETHELL	LTC	O-0026329	0965	1
EDSON FRANK T	COL	O-0029527	1262	1
EDSON HALLETT D	B G	O-0019541	0864	1
EDWARDS CORWIN V	LTC	O-0085159	0967	1
EDWARDS DAVID L	COL	O-0020359	0466	1
EDWARDS EARL L	COL	O-0031647	1067	1
EDWARDS EARL W	COL	O-0023502	0862	1
EDWARDS EDMUND R	COL	O-0004927	0254	1
EDWARDS ELMER F	LTC	O-0080405	0667	1
EDWARDS GEORGE H	COL	O-0002771	1143	1
EDWARDS JAMES W	COL	O-0030274	1064	1
EDWARDS JOHN E	LTC	O-0056945	1265	1
EDWARDS JOHN W	LTC	O-0054229	0967	1
EDWARDS JR HENRY R	LTC	O-0058130	0767	1
EDWARDS JR JULIAN R	1LT	O-0070695	0159	2
EDWARDS JR MEYER A	COL	O-0020702	0863	1
EDWARDS JR SPENCER P	COL	O-0033990	0862	1
EDWARDS LEMUEL E	COL	O-0011284	1146	1
EDWARDS MORRIS C	B G	O-0019041	0763	1
EDWARDS PARMER W	M G	O-0016775	0760	1

UNITED STATES ARMY RETIRED LIST

NAME	GRADE	SVC NO	DATE RET MO YR	RET CODE
EDWARDS PAUL S	COL	O-0008955	0347	2
EDWARDS PERRY	LTC	O-0030309	1162	1
EDWARDS RAYMOND F	COL	O-0006778	0548	1
EDWARDS RICHARD T	LTC	O-0005422	1041	1
EDWARDS ROBERT	MAJ	O-0012760	0442	1
EDWARDS ROBERT O	MAJ	O-0017366	1028	1
EDWARDS SAM A	COL	O-0037466	0467	1
EDWARDS SHEFFIELD	COL	O-0015203	1053	1
EDWARDS WALTON M	COL	O-0024377	1163	1
EDWARDS WILLIAM H	COL	O-0042267	0158	1
EFNOR JR SAM	COL	O-0034054	0661	1
EGAN JOHN A	COL	O-0019320	0348	2
EGAN JOHN B	COL	O-0043003	1064	1
EGAN MARGARET M	LTC	N-0002058	0164	1
EGAN ROLAND O	CW4	W-0903057	0255	1
EGAN WILLIAM J	COL	O-0007568	0-45	2
EGBERT JR FRANCIS J	CW4	W-0902380	0667	1
EGE CHARLES C	COL	O-0029102	0559	1
EGGER FLOYD C	COL	O-0052065	0167	1
EGGLESTON HOWARD W	B G	O-0030271	0166	1
EGOZCUE EDWARD J	MAJ	O-0070330	0166	1
EHLEN EDWARD S	B G	O-0019286	0864	1
EHLERS CHRISTINE	MAJ	M-0010036	1058	1
EHRLICH KARL F	COL	O-0030858	0565	1
EICHORN FREDERIC N	COL	O-0039636	0160	1
EICKHOFF ALBERT P	LTC	O-0059853	0862	1
EILER KEITH E	LTC	O-0026533	0565	1
EILTS ALLIE M	MAJ	N-0000589	0460	2
EISENDORFF GRACE I	1LT	R-0000126	1045	2
EISENSCHMIDT CLYDE R	LTC	O-0003844	0640	2
EITT HERBERT F	COL	O-0032477	0966	1
EKLUND KARL F	COL	O-0020557	0467	1
EKMAN CARL N	COL	O-0022293	0561	1
ELA WILLIAM E	COL	O-0041483	1057	2
ELARTH HAROLD H	LTC	O-0009032	1039	2
ELCANO MICHAEL P	LTC	O-0044142	0966	1
ELDER CHARLES J	CW3	W-0903061	0958	1
ELDER EUGENE V	B G	O-0011681	0452	1
ELDER FRANK L	COL	O-0019203	0863	2
ELDER HARTWELL M	COL	O-0012576	0751	1
ELDER JAMES W	CPT	O-0019349	1141	2
ELDRED NORA P	MAJ	N-0000071	0550	1
ELDRIDGE MARY J B	MAJ	L-0000144	1066	1
ELDRIDGE WILLIAM G	COL	O-0029070	0359	1
ELEGAR AUGUSTUS G	B G	O-0018625	0560	1
ELEY WILLIAM S	COL	O-0005325	0353	1
ELGES JR CARL H	COL	O-0030511	0965	1
ELIAN ARTHUR J	LTC	O-0060946	0867	1
ELIAS PAUL	COL	O-0017546	0656	1
ELIOT AMORY V	COL	O-0000336	0753	1
ELKEY JAMES H	LTC	O-0027370	0167	1
ELKINS EDGAR A	CPT	O-0006145	1022	2
ELKINS HARRY W	COL	O-0020766	0765	1
ELKINS JR HORACE N	LTC	O-0039770	0557	1
ELKINS STEPHEN B	B G	O-0010913	0954	1
ELKINTON EDWARD	CW4	W-0903063	0657	1
ELLENBERG JULIAN S	LTC	O-0041756	0556	2
ELLERS CONWAY L	LTC	O-0039051	1064	1
ELLERSON GEOFFREY D	COL	O-0019759	0865	1
ELLERT ROBERT R	LTC	O-0059836	0166	1
ELLERY FREDERICK	B G	O-0018725	0461	1
ELLIGET DONALD A	COL	O-0019719	0963	1
ELLINGER RUTH W	MAJ	M-0001025	0163	1
ELLIOTT ALENE V	LTC	R-0010068	0461	1
ELLIOTT CROSBY N	COL	O-0005513	0846	1
ELLIOTT DABNEY O	B G	O-0003669	0950	1
ELLIOTT DOROTHY V	LTC	N-0002245	0464	1
ELLIOTT EDWIN E	CPT	O-0004979	0928	2
ELLIOTT ESCALUS E	COL	O-0012834	0753	1
ELLIOTT HAROLD S	LTC	O-0064983	1266	1
ELLIOTT HOWARD M	COL	O-0051072	0357	2
ELLIOTT IVAN W	COL	O-0031863	0364	1
ELLIOTT JAMES N	LTC	O-0050051	1163	1
ELLIOTT JESSE D	COL	O-0001848	1039	1
ELLIOTT JOHN T	LTC	O-0026896	0865	1

NAME	GRADE	SVC NO	DATE RET MO YR	RET CODE
ELLIOTT JR CHARLES B	COL	O-0019490	0764	1
ELLIOTT JR EUGENE M	COL	O-0051340	0962	1
ELLIOTT JR WALLACE P	COL	O-0040837	0165	1
ELLIOTT LOWELL A	COL	O-0010712	0449	1
ELLIOTT PHILIP L	COL	O-0022945	0661	1
ELLIOTT RALPH H	COL	O-0030744	1164	1
ELLIOTT RICHARD B	LTC	O-0050442	0765	1
ELLIOTT RICHARD H	CPT	O-0014420	0320	2
ELLIOTT ROBERT H	COL	O-0009324	1052	1
ELLIOTT ROBIN	LTC	L-0000064	1262	1
ELLIS ARTHUR M	LTC	O-0004489	1042	2
ELLIS BURTON F	COL	O-0029033	1158	1
ELLIS DAVID J	COL	O-0063154	0966	1
ELLIS F DETREVIL	COL	O-0003831	0350	1
ELLIS EDWARD H	LTC	O-0050129	0766	1
ELLIS HAROLD B	LTC	O-0025338	0862	1
ELLIS HARRY H	COL	O-0023958	0866	1
ELLIS HARRY V	COL	O-0011945	1048	1
ELLIS HARVIE R	COL	O-0017791	0457	2
ELLIS HERBERT E	MAJ	O-0003216	0132	1
ELLIS JEAN	MAJ	L-0000331	0666	1
ELLIS JR ARTHUR P	LTC	O-0036150	0165	1
ELLIS JR THOMAS G	LTC	O-0065106	0567	1
ELLIS LINDLEY C	LTC	O-0026849	0765	1
ELLIS MURRAY H	COL	O-0006730	0450	1
ELLIS PEARL T	LTC	N-0000016	1047	1
ELLIS WALTER C	COL	O-0008192	0550	1
ELLIS WALTER F	COL	O-0018378	0761	1
ELLIS WILBER R	COL	O-0014652	0848	1
ELLISON HENRY B	COL	O-0011652	1047	1
ELLISON MARVIN C	COL	O-0041494	0358	1
ELLISON MILTON H	COL	O-0080739	0762	1
ELLSWORTH ROBERT A	COL	O-0015780	0146	2
ELLYETT JR JAMES W	CW3	W-0903068	0661	1
ELMES CHESTER H	COL	O-0011365	0753	1
ELMORE JOHN A	B G	O-0015823	0156	2
ELMORE ORVILLE N	CW3	W-0904246	0759	1
ELMS GEORGE G	COL	O-0012391	0854	1
ELOWER CHARLES F	CW4	W-0903070	0957	1
ELSBERRY ROBERT V	LTC	O-0023783	0761	1
ELSER FRED J	COL	O-0029557	0559	1
ELSER MAX A	COL	O-0002163	0743	1
ELTERICH JOHN A	COL	O-0029696	0462	1
ELWARD NYE K	LTC	O-0015827	0445	2
ELWOOD ERNEST A	LTC	O-0011986	1039	2
ELY JR ROBERT L	COL	O-0060211	0367	1
ELY LOUIS B	COL	O-0012270	1053	1
ELY WILLIAM J	LTG	O-0018974	0866	1
EMANUEL EMMETT H	LTC	O-0015435	1035	2
EMBRY JOHN	COL	O-0041798	0860	1
EMERSON GENEVIEVE	MAJ	M-0010073	0859	1
EMERSON GOUVERNEUR	B G	O-0004048	0149	2
EMERSON JR EARL E	LTC	O-0057642	0867	1
EMERSON KARY C	COL	O-0033991	1166	1
EMERSON MAXWELL	COL	O-0041514	0558	1
EMERY HAROLD R	COL	O-0012471	0854	1
EMERY JACK R	COL	O-0040276	0667	1
EMERY JOHN R	LTC	O-0059992	1266	1
EMERY JR FRANK E	COL	O-0003837	0347	1
EMERY JR GUY C	LTC	O-0052481	0261	1
EMIG NICKOLAUS	LTC	O-0040005	0264	1
EMMANUELLI LOUIS S	MAJ	O-0014000	0720	2
EMMONS DAVID R	COL	O-0039979	0765	1
EMOND WILFRED A	COL	O-0019642	1053	2
ENDERTON HERBERT B	COL	O-0015149	0754	2
ENEBOE EDWARD S	LTC	O-0027488	0767	1
ENEY JOHN K	COL	O-0036514	1065	1
ENGDAHL FRANCIS A	CW4	W-0903074	0856	1
ENGELHARDT EDWARD C	1LT	O-0014761	0-30	1
ENGELHART E CARL	COL	O-0012773	0850	1
ENGELLAND LLOYD W	LTC	O-0032551	1159	2
ENGEMAN LEONARD E	COL	O-0029641	1161	1
ENGER EDGAR E	COL	O-0017284	0758	1
ENGERUD HAROLD	COL	O-0011716	0449	1
ENGLAND SANFORD P	COL	O-0023129	0862	1

NAME	GRADE	SVC NO	DATE RET MO YR	RET CODE
ENGLEHARDT JOSEPH F	LTC	O-0033143	0461	2
ENGLEHART FRANCIS A	B G	O-0003542	0846	2
ENGLISH BURT	COL	O-0003971	0-35	1
ENGLISH JR ROBERT O	COL	O-0031371	1266	1
ENGSTROM GUSTAF A	COL	O-0030124	0464	1
ENNIS CHARLES	COL	O-0010338	0753	1
ENNIS JR WILLIAM P	LTG	O-0016436	0962	1
ENNIS ROSA E	MAJ	L-0000214	0456	1
ENNIS WILLIAM P	B G	O-0001331	0841	2
ENOS WILLIAM F	LTC	O-0026819	0865	1
ENQUIST VERA A	MAJ	N-0002043	0360	1
ENSLOW PHILIP H	COL	O-0015241	0754	1
ENSRUD JOSEPH O	COL	O-0017493	0248	2
ENTWHISTLE RICHARD R	COL	O-0040198	1163	1
EPES WILLIAM J	COL	O-0012112	0854	1
EPLEY GERALD G	COL	O-0018770	0762	1
EPLING FENTON G	COL	O-0006574	0145	1
EPPERLY JAMES M	M G	O-0016288	0860	2
EPPERSON ELBERT P	CPT	O-0025807	0546	2
EPPS FREDERICK	CW2	W-0901309	0345	2
EPPS GRADY C	COL	O-0014855	0744	2
EPPS LONNETTE L	MAJ	N-0000636	0161	1
EPSTEIN GERALD S	CPT	O-0028105	1054	2
ERDMAN BENJAMIN K	COL	O-0010354	0753	1
ERGAS LOUISE M	LTC	N-0002114	0857	1
ERICKSON ERIC A	COL	O-0010148	1051	1
ERICKSON JOSEPH L	LTC	O-0010573	0644	2
ERICKSON ROBERT C	COL	O-0052177	0766	1
ERICKSON SIDNEY	B G	O-0003636	1046	2
ERICSON RICHARD A	COL	O-0012117	0854	1
ERION KENNETH W	CW4	W-0903077	0264	1
ERKENBECK VERNON J	COL	O-0019304	1157	1
ERLENKOTTER DAVID	LTC	O-0027350	0765	1
ERLENKOTTER ROBERT	COL	O-0019354	0760	2
ERNST ESTELLE T	MAJ	N-0000314	1059	1
ERNST JACK M	COL	O-0042371	0562	1
ERNST KENNETH F	COL	O-0018639	1159	1
ERSKINE DAVID G	COL	O-0015766	0954	1
ERSKINE JASPER N	LTC	O-0036768	0864	1
ERSPANER FLORIAN J	LTC	O-0023242	0761	1
ERWIN LEWIS D	LTC	O-0028780	0753	1
ESCHBACH ALFRED L	COL	O-0021419	0958	1
ESCUE HODGES S	LTC	O-0063375	0867	1
ESCOORN WALTER H	COL	O-0018337	0445	2
ESPOSITO ALDA G	MAJ	L-0000296	0760	1
ESS EARL O	LTC	O-0069915	0364	2
ESSMAN GRAYDON C	B G	O-0019242	0861	1
ESTABROOK MARCIA E	CW4	V-0904318	1164	1
ESTES CLIFFORD H	LTC	O-0065987	0867	1
ESTES GEORGE H	B G	O-0000456	1036	2
ESTES HOWELL M	COL	O-0003119	1046	2
ESTES WILLIAM B	COL	O-0051126	0158	1
ETHERTON LOUIS M	COL	O-0039940	0862	1
ETKA DALE L	COL	O-0043898	1166	1
ETZLER CHARLES R	COL	O-0020895	0466	1
EUBANK PERRY H	COL	O-0020630	0863	1
EUBANKS C A HOLMES	COL	O-0042014	0462	1
EUBANKS JR FRANK C	MAJ	O-0062838	0567	1
EUBANKS MILDRED	MAJ	N-0022793	0264	1
EVANS ALBERT R	COL	O-0030215	0764	1
EVANS ALBERT L	COL	O-0010669	0143	1
EVANS ANDREW J	COL	O-0014856	1151	1
EVANS BILL A	LTC	O-0030714	0464	2
EVANS BRYAN	COL	O-0012133	0854	1
EVANS GRAHAM R	COL	O-0030656	0366	1
EVANS HOUSTON V	COL	O-0029011	0957	1
EVANS JAMES B	COL	O-0017523	0859	1
EVANS JOHN P	COL	O-0015363	0954	1
EVANS JOHN T	COL	O-0032142	0966	1
EVANS JOSEPH K	COL	O-0010413	1146	1
EVANS JR BELMONT S	LTC	O-0021811	0360	1
EVANS JR BRYAN	MAJ	O-0058897	1265	1
EVANS JR JOHN D	COL	O-0040056	1166	1
EVANS JR ROY T	M G	O-0019140	0363	1
EVANS LEON G	LTC	O-0052521	0465	1

NAME	GRADE	SVC NO	DATE RET MO YR	RET CODE
EVANS RICHARD B	COL	O-0015217	1046	2
EVANS RICHARD L	CPT	O-0025474	0346	2
EVANS ROBERT F	COL	O-0042662	0965	1
EVANS ROBERT H	LTC	O-0031628	0965	1
EVANS ROBERT N	MAJ	O-0028630	0862	2
EVANS ROY C	LTC	O-0042233	0160	1
EVANS SYLVIA M	LTC	N-0000536	0555	2
EVANS THOMAS B	M G	O-0019174	0964	1
EVANS THOMAS N	CW3	W-0902051	0555	1
EVANS VERNON	M G	O-0003818	0153	1
EVANS WILL H	CPT	O-0007878	0229	2
EVANS WILLIAM A	COL	O-0042060	0862	2
EVANS WILLIAM E	LTC	O-0081896	0966	1
EVANS WILLIAM R	CPT	O-0091820	1066	2
EVANS WILLIAM R	CW3	W-0904247	0263	1
EVANS WILLIAM S	COL	O-0005384	0948	2
EVELAND WARREN C	COL	O-0029167	1059	1
EVENS RODLEY C	COL	O-0039924	0161	2
EVENSON DOROTHY M	MAJ	N-0001390	1167	1
EVERETT JR HUGH	COL	O-0039573	0358	1
EVERETT WARREN S	COL	O-0019739	1263	1
EVERITT JR EDWARD A	COL	O-0006558	0450	1
EVERS CLARENCE P	COL	O-0004505	0651	1
EVERSOLE MAC C	LTC	O-0056634	0865	1
EWART JAMES A	LTC	O-0065449	0966	1
EWBANK JR ERNEST W	COL	O-0030474	1065	1
EWBANK KEITH H	COL	O-0018082	0760	1
EWELL GEORGE W	LTC	O-0001766	0-33	2
EWING CHARLES B	COL	O-0016900	0657	1
EWING FRANCIS	MAJ	N-0000069	0554	1
EWING JOHN T	COL	O-0021326	0660	1
EWING PAUL P	MAJ	O-0087511	1266	1
EWING THOMAS P	LTC	O-0033284	1060	1
EWING WALTER R	LTC	O-0042362	0862	1
EYERLY WILLIAM J	COL	O-0015628	0754	1
EYERMAN MELVIN F	COL	O-0021026	0861	1
EYLER GORDON M	COL	O-0019191	0746	2
EYSTER CHARLES H	CW3	W-0906716	1264	1
EZEKIEL RAPHAEL B	CPT	O-0017084	0242	1
FABIAN KEITH P	COL	O-0024151	0764	1
FABRITIUS WILLIAM J	LTC	O-0040021	0464	1
FAGIN RUSSELL D	COL	O-0042145	0363	1
FAHEY PAUL V	COL	O-0033054	0766	1
FAHRINGER EUGENE P	COL	O-0041930	0961	1
FAHY DONALD C	LTC	O-0061064	0766	1
FAIKS WALTER A	COL	O-0020129	0164	1
FAILING FRANK W	LTC	O-0031298	0264	1
FAILS EULA R	MAJ	N-0000812	0254	2
FAINE SYRIL E	COL	O-0012343	1053	1
FAINTER FRANCIS F	COL	O-0006360	0753	2
FAIR CECIL G	CW4	W-0903081	0165	1
FAIRBANKS EMILY	MAJ	M-0000580	0862	1
FAIRBANKS RUSSELL N	LTC	O-0040747	0662	1
FAIRBROTHER HERMAN W	COL	O-0015067	0854	1
FAIRCHILD CLARENCE G	COL	O-0040396	0563	2
FAIRCHILD JAMES M	COL	O-0030844	0165	1
FAIRCHILD JAMES R	CW3	W-0908004	0867	1
FAIRLEY ANNA E	MAJ	N-0001304	0163	1
FAISON THOMAS G	COL	O-0029254	1162	1
FAKE CHARLES W	LTC	O-0010225	0841	2
FALES CLARKE K	COL	O-0005330	1047	1
FALK BYRON A	COL	O-0010091	0950	1
FALK DAVID B	COL	O-0003569	0650	1
FALK JR BYRON A	MAJ	O-0065171	0266	1
FALKE DAVID R	LTC	O-0051542	0962	1
FALKS JACK B	LTC	O-0025266	1164	1
FALLEN ARTHUR J	COL	O-0079705	0865	1
FALLIS REGINALD J	COL	O-0022256	0762	1
FALLON RUDOLPH A	LTC	O-0062225	0266	1
FANCHER PAUL S	B G	O-0018637	0658	1
FANNING CHARLES A	LTC	O-0029939	0561	1
FANNING WILLIAM F	LTC	O-0080293	1066	1
FARBER CHARLES M	B G	O-002047[illegible]	1165	1
FARBER LEO J	LTC	O-0079805	0766	1
FARGO LYNN D	COL	O-0032242	0166	2

NAME	GRADE	SVC NO	DATE RET MO YR	RET CODE
FARIBAULT BEN W	LTC	O-0030801	0965	1
FARINACCI CHARLES J	COL	O-0020518	0960	2
FARIS JR CHARLES A	MAJ	O-0069643	1265	1
FARLEY JULIUS R	LTC	O-0040226	0166	1
FARMAN JR ELBERT E	COL	O-0002595	0824	2
FARMER CLARENCE R	LTC	O-0011483	1138	1
FARMER GARLAND R	LTC	O-0068342	0266	1
FARMER HERBERT F	COL	O-0039704	0660	1
FARMER JACK M	WO1	W-0969750	0759	1
FARMER ROBERT D	LTC	O-0056280	0665	1
FARMER WESLEY E	COL	O-0051398	0453	1
FARMER WILLIAM C	COL	O-0030691	0358	1
FARNER HARRY J	COL	O-0008134	0748	1
FARNHAM KENNETH N	LTC	O-0080751	0667	1
FARNSWORTH EDWARD F	COL	O-0018683	0862	1
FARNSWORTH JOHN A	MAJ	O-0065612	0164	1
FARNSWORTH LOUIS D	COL	O-0019904	0863	1
FARNSWORTH THOMAS H	LTC	O-0025800	0963	1
FARNUM CHARLES W	LTC	O-0042743	0662	2
FARNUM FRANCIS	MAJ	O-0001814	1022	2
FARR EDWARD H	COL	O-0039501	0954	1
FARR RICHARD	COL	O-0033737	0663	1
FARRA JR JOHN F	COL	O-0017294	0545	2
FARRAND EDWARD	M G	O-0016788	0661	1
FARRAR FRED J	LTC	O-0058936	0467	2
FARRAR WILLIAM	COL	O-0034053	0767	1
FARRELL CARL Y	COL	O-0030628	0550	1
FARRELL FRANCIS W	LTC	O-0012794	0640	1
FARRELL RAYMOND J	CPT	O-0014261	0620	2
FARRELL RICHARD J	COL	O-0025168	0866	1
FARREN JAMES H	COL	O-0032670	1067	1
FARRIS GLENN A	COL	O-0018494	0761	1
FARRIS PHILIP A	LTC	O-0028627	0966	1
FARRIS STEPHEN C	LTC	O-0022022	0764	1
FARWICK AUGUST W	COL	O-0016276	0755	1
FATE ROBERT J	COL	O-0023010	0463	1
FAUBLE PHYLLIS H	MAJ	M-0010087	0366	1
FAULCONER JR JOHN W	LTC	O-0004679	0342	2
FAULDS JACK M	COL	O-0042581	0665	1
FAULKNER LYMAN S	COL	O-0023870	0763	1
FAUST LACY W	CW1	W-0906720	1046	1
FAUST ROBERT J	COL	O-0040641	0965	1
FAVORITE JR FRANK C	LTC	O-0065985	0864	1
FAW JOSEPH N	COL	O-0051164	0962	1
FAY JOHN A	WO1	W-0800737	0641	1
FAY JOHN E	LTC	O-0081995	0266	1
FAYLE ORIN A	LTC	O-0088260	0163	1
FEAGANS NELLIE J	LTC	N-0001547	0564	1
FEAGIN CLAUDE W	COL	O-0010820	1046	2
FEAMSTER ROBERT	MAJ	O-0026943	0147	2
FEATHER EDWIN	CPT	O-0016447	0239	2
FEATHERSTON IONE	MAJ	N-0000526	0148	1
FEATHERSTON WALTER C	LTC	O-0044075	1053	1
FEBIGER PAUL C	COL	O-0009761	0644	2
FECHNER WALTER W	COL	O-0031013	1167	1
FEDOR ERNEST J	COL	O-0038657	0766	1
FEEHAN JOHN R	COL	O-0030647	0366	1
FEGAN OSCAR G	COL	O-0010468	1047	1
FEHRS JOHN W	LTC	O-0027086	0865	1
FEIDT GERALD E	COL	O-0031513	0565	1
FEIGHNY ROBERT E	LTC	O-0067564	0767	1
FEIL FREDERICK	COL	O-0030379	0265	1
FEINBERG PHILIP	COL	O-0018591	0155	1
FEIND EMORY F	COL	O-0028787	1051	1
FEINDEL JR WILLIAM H	COL	O-0030177	0962	1
FEJER ALBERT	CW4	W-0903084	1058	1
FELBER JOSEPH G	COL	O-0016984	1157	1
FELDMAN HERMAN	M G	O-0005724	0851	1
FELIX RUSSELL E	LTC	O-0060475	0566	1
FELIZ JAMES F	LTC	O-0043752	0764	1
FELKER LUTHER	MAJ	O-0014151	0116	2
FELL CHARLES F	COL	O-0019369	0757	1
FELLENZ LLOYD E	M G	O-0019485	0867	1
FELLENZ WALTER J	COL	O-0023055	0462	2
FELLERMAN ERWIN A	LTC	O-0080294	0961	1

NAME	GRADE	SVC NO	DATE RET MO YR	RET CODE
FELLERS BONNER F	B G	O-0012134	1146	1
FELLOWS FRANCIS E	COL	O-0017620	0658	1
FELLOWS HAROLD C	COL	O-0004745	1051	1
FELS DOROTHY B	MAJ	N-0000169	0560	2
FELT MARION E	COL	O-0042810	0866	1
FELTON DONALD E	LTC	O-0039058	0761	1
FENN CLARENCE C	B G	O-0008049	0250	1
FENNELL MARTIN A	COL	O-0012431	0947	1
FENNON ISABEL	MAJ	N-0002371	0460	1
FENTON BERNARD J	COL	O-0041755	0667	1
FENTON BRYAN E T	B G	O-0020086	0464	1
FERCHAK MICHAEL P	CW4	W-0906721	0465	1
FERENBAUGH CLAUDE B	LTG	O-0012479	0955	2
FERGASON SYDNEY C	COL	O-0006210	0753	1
FERGUSON HARLEY B	M G	O-0000540	0839	1
FERGUSON JAMES L	COL	O-0030046	1162	1
FERGUSON KENNETH H	CW4	W-0903087	0463	1
FERGUSON LAWRENCE J	COL	O-0010154	0547	2
FERGUSON SAMUEL C	1LT	O-0032590	0659	2
FERGUSON WILLIAM W	LTC	O-0042665	0762	1
FERINGA PETER A	M G	O-0014744	0553	1
FERN VINCENT P	CPT	O-0071491	0663	2
FERNANDEZ CLAUDE T	COL	O-0030454	1164	1
FERNSTROM CARL H	COL	O-0018055	0758	1
FERONY LOUIS T	COL	O-0050979	0458	1
FERREE FLOYD W	COL	O-0007872	0937	2
FERRIN CHARLES S	B G	O-0004580	1152	1
FERRIS BENJAMIN G	B G	O-0003857	0951	1
FERRIS EDWIN H	COL	O-0019962	0649	2
FERRIS JOHN W	COL	O-0019097	0863	2
FERTIG WENDELL W	COL	O-0041406	0156	1
FETTERMAN LELAND L	LTC	O-0056858	0862	1
FICKETT EDWARD M	COL	O-0007216	0854	1
FICKLING RYAN W	CW2	W-0906724	0452	1
FIEDLER ARTHUR G	LTC	O-0034719	0560	1
FIEHN CHARLES W	CW4	W-0903091	0465	1
FIELD DAVID D	LTC	O-0080754	1162	1
FIELD JR HARRY L	LTC	O-0040890	0953	2
FIELD KENNETH S	LTC	O-0036932	0863	2
FIELD LONNIE C	COL	O-0010965	0640	1
FIELD LOUIS M	COL	O-0006436	1047	2
FIELD RAYMOND F	COL	O-0042794	0866	1
FIELD REX C	CW3	W-0903092	0863	1
FIELD WILLIAM	2LT	O-0050832	0648	2
FIELD WINSTON L	COL	O-0039869	0859	1
FIELDER JESSE W	LTC	O-0033842	0863	1
FIELDER KENDALL J	B G	O-0007450	0751	1
FIELDS ALBERT	COL	O-0011505	0447	2
FIELDS BASIL V	CPT	O-0008348	0829	1
FIELDS JESSE A	LTC	O-0028731	0966	1
FIELDS JR HARRY E	COL	O-0043597	0767	1
FIELDS KENNETH E	B G	O-0018957	0455	1
FIELDS WILLIAM R	COL	O-0051288	0162	1
FIGUERAS JAIME J	COL	O-0010864	0946	2
FILES MAYNARD W	LTC	O-0079811	0764	2
FILES VERNON	LTC	O-0037086	1167	1
FILIPPI FRANK A	COL	O-0030701	0566	1
FILLBRANDT ARTHUR C	LTC	O-0030520	0767	1
FILLMORE ROBERT R	COL	O-0030254	0964	1
FINAN BERNARD J	COL	O-0007890	0147	2
FINBERG IRVING W	COL	O-0042716	0863	1
FINCH HENRY A	COL	O-0002119	0642	1
FINCH JOHN E	LTC	O-0031797	0266	1
FINCH JR CHARLES S	LTC	O-0061169	1163	2
FINCH RALPH	MAJ	O-0016324	0947	1
FINCHER JOE E	COL	O-0030145	1059	2
FINGARSON GEORGE C	COL	O-0007041	0854	1
FINK DONALD R	MAJ	O-0062236	0764	1
FINK JAMES L	LTC	O-0037604	1162	1
FINKE JOHN G W	LTC	O-0040037	0854	1
FINKEL JOSHUA A	COL	O-0070253	0856	1
FINKENAUR ROBERT S	COL	O-0015441	0859	1
FINKS JACK F	COL	O-0039625	0159	1
FINLAYSON HARRISON H	COL	O-0042493	0662	1
FINLEY GEORGE A	COL	O-0020138	1064	1

NAME	GRADE	SVC NO	DATE RET MO YR	RET CODE
FINLEY GLENN S	COL	O-0007177	0854	2
FINLEY THOMAS D	M G	O-0004419	0946	2
FINN CALVIN F	LTC	O-0043413	1064	1
FINN JOHN W	COL	O-0030257	0964	1
FINN RUSSELL T	B G	O-0016237	0656	1
FINNEGAN JOHN F	COL	O-0020971	1059	1
FINNEGAN WALTER E	COL	O-0017219	0758	1
FINNEY JOHN R	MAJ	O-0024655	0453	2
FIORE CAESAR F	COL	O-0019897	0157	1
FIREHOCK RAYMOND B	COL	O-0019812	0165	1
FIRNSTAHL NORMAN P	MAJ	O-0080082	1163	1
FISCHER HARRY D	COL	O-0029901	0562	1
FISCHER HARVEY H	LTC	O-0018832	0857	1
FISH FREDERICK	LTC	O-0080758	1066	2
FISH GROSVENOR	LTC	O-0042932	1264	1
FISH HAMILTON W	COL	O-0020592	0867	1
FISH JAMES H	COL	O-0028928	0957	1
FISHBACK JOE	COL	O-0042492	0163	1
FISHER AARON R	CW2	W-0901196	1047	2
FISHER AUSTIN G	COL	O-0020324	0656	1
FISHER CARLETON C	COL	O-0031952	0764	1
FISHER EARL E	COL	O-0029175	0260	1
FISHER HENRY G	COL	O-0015357	0454	1
FISHER JR HENRY A	LTC	O-0063274	0866	1
FISHER MERLE L	COL	O-0018550	0761	1
FISHER SAMUEL H	COL	O-0015835	0754	1
FISHER VINCENT J	1LT	O-0064899	0853	2
FISHER YOEMAN C	CW4	W-0903094	0961	1
FISHKIN LEON J	COL	O-0052215	1164	1
FISICHELLA MELBA A	MAJ	N-0001424	1263	2
FISK ROBERT B	LTC	O-0024614	1066	1
FISK S WALLACE	COL	O-0028045	1157	2
FISK WILLIAM	MAJ	O-0006875	0637	1
FISKE JOHN F	COL	O-0016623	1056	1
FISKE NORMAN E	COL	O-0004741	0753	1
FISKEN ARCHIBALD	COL	O-0006930	0948	1
FITCH ALVA R	LTG	O-0018113	0666	2
FITCH BURDETTE M	B G	O-0010718	0753	1
FITCH ELIZABETH	LTC	N-0000030	0156	1
FITCH HENRY R	COL	O-0030851	0365	1
FITE II WILLIAM C	COL	O-0021331	0155	1
FITTS JR WILLIAM T	B G	O-0011917	0754	1
FITZGERALD DOUGLAS I	COL	O-0078832	1266	1
FITZGERALD EDWARD D	LTC	O-0029870	0161	1
FITZGERALD EDWARD W	COL	O-0030495	1160	1
FITZGERALD EILEEN	LTC	N-0000575	1059	1
FITZGERALD GERALD W	COL	O-0009460	0953	2
FITZGERALD HERBERT M	COL	O-0029022	0956	1
FITZGERALD HUGH J	COL	O-0006719	0751	1
FITZGERALD MAURICE J	COL	O-0028861	0256	1
FITZGERALD ROBERT H	CPT	O-0020676	0348	1
FITZGIBBONS JAMES J	MAJ	O-0017752	0648	1
FITZPATRICK EDWARD O	COL	O-0023288	0167	1
FITZPATRICK JOHN W	LTC	O-0060911	1153	1
FIX FLOYD S	COL	O-0050990	1152	1
FLACHSLAND NORMA K	LTC	L-0000037	0760	1
FLAGER GEORGE W	LTC	O-0053081	0867	1
FLAGG JAMES T	CW3	W-0906725	0960	1
FLAGGERT JR JAMES J	LTC	O-0063345	1266	1
FLAHAVEN WILLIAM J	MAJ	O-0040497	1161	1
FLAIG JOHN W	CW4	W-0903099	0366	1
FLAMM LEWIS	COL	O-0042384	0864	1
FLANAGAN ELIZABETH	MAJ	N-0001042	0766	1
FLANAGAN LUIS J	MAJ	O-0024967	0846	2
FLANDERS CHARLES	COL	O-0024006	1167	1
FLANDERS EDWARD A	COL	O-0022912	0865	1
FLANIGAN EDA J	MAJ	L-0000070	0460	1
FLANIGAN JOSEPH T	CW4	W-0906731	0759	1
FLANIGAN WALTER J	LTC	O-0044422	0966	1
FLANIGEN BARRINGTON	COL	O-0004504	0446	1
FLATTER FINDLAY F	LTC	O-0049941	0751	1
FLAVELLE ELIZABETH	LTC	N-0001896	1263	1
FLECKENSTEIN W A	LTC	O-0019175	0655	1
FLEET GEORGE T	CPT	O-0014297	0421	2
FLEGEL EARL C	COL	O-0006800	0247	2

NAME	GRADE	SVC NO	DATE RET MO YR	RET CODE
FLEIG RAYMOND E	LTC	O-0047197	0862	1
FLEISCHMAN GORDON K	LTC	O-0059477	0967	1
FLEMING DAVID D	LTC	O-0032042	1164	1
FLEMING HERMAN R	COL	O-0028903	0557	1
FLEMING JANET M	MAJ	N-0002055	1060	1
FLEMING JR ROBERT J	M G	O-0017095	0267	1
FLEMING JR ROBERT W	LTC	O-0056737	0965	1
FLEMING JR WILLIAM	LTC	O-0080761	0265	1
FLEMING MARGARET C	CPT	N-0002468	0954	2
FLEMING ROBERT N	LTC	O-0050014	1265	1
FLEMING SAM F	LTC	O-0042863	1062	1
FLEMING WILLIAM O	COL	O-0010834	0249	1
FLEMING WILLIAM J	COL	O-0028910	0657	1
FLEMMING DAMON R	CW4	RW-0906424	1262	1
FLESCH JOSEPH M	COL	O-0031800	0767	1
FLETCHER ALLEN	COL	O-0002957	0642	1
FLETCHER DON S	LTC	O-0050476	0767	1
FLETCHER GEORGE F	COL	O-0018517	1061	1
FLETCHER LESLIE S	COL	O-0015591	0747	2
FLETCHER MAURICE J	COL	O-0041727	0961	1
FLETCHER ROBERT H	COL	O-0002376	0337	2
FLETCHER WILLIAM T	COL	O-0010640	0750	1
FLETTE FRED J	LTC	O-0030594	1263	1
FLETTER RANDOLPH W	COL	O-0019148	0862	1
FLETTERER FLORENCE L	MAJ	N-0002428	1159	2
FLEURY VERNON G	LTC	O-0048245	0864	1
FLEWELLING JOHN O	LTC	O-0038818	0263	1
FLINCHBAUGH RALPH W	COL	O-0051071	0966	1
FLING WILLIAM J	MAJ	O-0022144	0859	1
FLINIAU FRANKLIN M	COL	O-0030263	0767	1
FLINT CHARLES W	COL	O-0043656	0965	1
FLINT GEORGE	LTC	O-0044970	0856	1
FLINT LEWIS M	COL	O-0042615	0265	1
FLINT ROBERT P	LTC	O-0040921	0664	1
FLINT WALKER H	CPT	O-0090802	0665	2
FLINT WILLARD	LTC	O-0041077	0965	1
FLINTER MARCUS H	COL	O-0061168	0264	1
FLINTJER JOHN D	LTC	O-0056920	0766	2
FLOOD CHARLES C	CPT	O-0026970	0246	2
FLOOD CLAIR V	CW4	RW-0906728	0564	1
FLOOK MARGARET H	MAJ	N-0000702	0762	1
FLORA MARVIN W	LTC	O-0034083	0565	1
FLORY LESTER D	B G	O-0017320	0640	1
FLORYAN THADDEUS R	COL	O-0023249	0966	1
FLOURNOY JR ROBERT W	LTC	O-0078834	0567	1
FLOWER III JAMES T	CW3	RW-0903102	0963	1
FLOWERS MARY M	MAJ	N-0000180	0662	1
FLOYD ARTHUR	LTC	O-0017859	1141	1
FLOYD MAX R	LTC	O-0049342	0865	1
FLOYD RAY R	COL	O-0015058	0753	1
FLOYD WILLIAM T	CW2	W-0900160	1144	2
FLYNN EDMUND P	COL	O-0033350	0766	1
FLYNN HENRY L	COL	O-0003387	0947	1
FLYNN JOHN W	LTC	O-0026841	0166	1
FLYNN JOSEPH V	LTC	O-0080762	0765	1
FLYNN WILLIAM J	COL	O-0041563	0154	1
FOGARTY MAXWELL R	COL	O-0042193	0663	1
FOOLE FRED W	COL	O-0005450	0250	1
FOLEN CLIFFORD	COL	O-0040255	1263	1
FOLEY RICHARD	LTC	O-0080765	0866	1
FOLEY WILLIAM	COL	O-0042474	1264	1
FOLK FRANK T	COL	O-0018195	0465	1
FOLKES JOHN C	COL	O-0051057	0959	1
FOLLANSBEE CONRAD	COL	O-0015572	0154	1
FOLLETT JR CHARLES V	MAJ	O-0062003	0966	1
FOLLEY GEORGE W	LTC	O-0051541	0962	1
FOLLING BJARNE	LTC	O-0052068	0464	1
FOLTS RUDOLF H	COL	O-0040784	0767	1
FOLTZ CHRISTIAN	COL	O-0005285	1047	1
FOLTZ GILBERT H	LTC	O-0050316	1066	1
FOLWELL MARY A	MAJ	N-0002014	0867	2
FONTAINE ARCHILLE J	CW2	W-0900746	1144	1
FONTAINE RUSSELL R	COL	O-0039548	0257	1
FONVIELLE JOHN H	COL	O-0012155	0954	1
FOOKS HERBERT C	MAJ	O-0013963	0720	2

UNITED STATES ARMY RETIRED LIST

NAME	GRADE	SVC NO	DATE RET MO YR	RET CODE
FOOKS NELSON I	COL	0-0016919	0657	1
FODR VIRGINIA F	MAJ	N-0000735	0467	1
FOOTE DONALE C	COL	0-0038584	C753	1
FOOTE GEORGE B	COL	0-0022320	C859	1
FOOTE LOUIS H	B G	0-0017010	1157	1
FOOTE SENECA W	COL	0-0019833	C863	1
FOOTE THOMAS C	COL	0-0019488	0864	1
FORAME PETER R	LTC	0-0042866	0964	1
FORBES LAWRENCE G	COL	0-0022903	0167	1
FORBES MERWIN B	COL	0-0030097	1061	1
FORBES WILLIAM A	LTC	0-0058900	0766	1
FORCUM FORREST H	LTC	0-0051464	C562	2
FORD ARTHUR W	COL	0-0003141	0648	1
FORD BLAIR A	COL	0-0018547	0761	1
FORD ELBERT L	M G	0-0005251	1053	1
FORD HOWARD G	COL	0-0038775	1262	1
FORD JAMES S	CW4	W-0906729	0957	1
FORD JOHN A	COL	0-0024497	C965	1
FORD ROBERT L	COL	0-0038767	C858	1
FORD WILLIAM W	B G	0-0012667	0854	1
FORDE HAROLD MC	COL	0-0016409	0656	1
FORDHAM EMORY H	LTC	0-0030340	0658	2
FORDYCE ROBERT C	COL	0-0053996	0264	1
FORE LILLIAN	MAJ	N-0002054	1060	1
FOREMAN ADELE F	MAJ	N-0002164	1162	1
FOREMAN ALLEN H	COL	0-0019913	0865	1
FOREMAN HELEN K	MAJ	L-0000093	0463	1
FOREMAN TAYLOR W	COL	0-0007862	0140	1
FORGIONE ANTHONY W	CW4	W-0903106	0861	1
FORMAN OVID T	COL	0-0015590	0854	1
FORMICA CONRAD F	CW4	W-0903107	0257	1
FORNEY DONALD M	COL	0-0038607	1150	1
FORNEY LESLIE R	COL	0-0C08006	0649	1
FORREST CHARLES R	CPT	0-0010488	0328	1
FORREST FRANK G	COL	0-0022101	0364	1
FORSE WILLIAM B	COL	0-0015470	1153	1
FORSELL JR GEORGE T	LTC	0-0027376	0765	1
FORSTER GEORGE J	B G	0-0010114	0451	1
FORSTER HORACE W	COL	0-0006744	C753	1
FORSYTH ANDREW E	COL	0-0010312	0654	1
FORSYTHE JOHN D	COL	0-0006636	0851	1
FORSYTHE LOIS M	COL	R-0010039	0766	1
FORT ALVIN E	LTC	0-0062163	0667	1
FORT JOHN G	COL	0-0031437	C764	1
FORTIER LOUIS J	B G	0-0006621	1050	1
FORTIN THOMAS L	COL	0-0042605	0665	1
FORTNEY JR CAMDEN P	COL	C-0032949	0863	1
FORTRESS EDWARD	COL	0-0041632	0951	1
FOSS ELMER T	COL	0-0006184	1046	1
FOSS ERLING J	COL	0-0039127	0866	1
FOSS RUSS C	LTC	0-0046767	0867	1
FOSSUM ADOLPH C	LTC	0-0050317	0764	1
FOSTER ALBERT D	COL	0-00C6964	0447	2
FOSTER ANNE R	MAJ	N-0000655	1262	1
FOSTER CORA M	LTC	L-0000033	0459	1
FOSTER EUGENE M	M G	0-0006228	0551	1
FOSTER HARRY	COL	0-0006060	1049	1
FOSTER HARRY G	COL	0-0030291	0860	1
FOSTER HELEN K	MAJ	N-0001993	1167	1
FOSTER IVAN M	LTC	0-0031215	1059	1
FOSTER JAMES F	COL	0-0030256	0964	1
FOSTER JAMES W	LTC	0-0039965	0258	1
FOSTER JR ANDREW P	LTC	0-0015807	0753	1
FOSTER JR JAMES K	LTC	0-0063161	0167	1
FOSTER JR ROBERT W	LTC	0-0025360	1265	1
FOSTER JR RUFUS C	CW3	W-0906730	1058	1
FOSTER KENNETH W	COL	0-0029376	1059	1
FOSTER MARVIN E	CW4	W-0903108	0559	1
FOSTER ROBERT J	COL	0-0003972	0944	2
FOSTER ROBERT T	COL	0-0011258	0451	1
FOSTER ROBERT T	LTC	0-0031279	1047	2
FOSTER ROY M	COL	C-0015375	0751	1
FOSTER VALENTINE	COL	0-0006185	0147	2
FOSTER WILLIAM B	COL	0-0008953	0353	1
FOSTER WILLIAM F	COL	0-0051016	0559	1

NAME	GRADE	SVC NO	DATE RET MO YR	RET CODE
FOSTER WILLIAM W	COL	0-0052802	1065	2
FOUCH WILLIAM R	2LT	0-0063855	0252	1
FOUNTAIN JOHN R	COL	0-0007926	0248	1
FOUNTAIN LEE S	COL	0-0004003	0242	1
FOURT HERBERT J	LTC	0-0080769	0367	1
FOUSHEE LILLIAN F	LTC	L-0000043	0461	1
FOUST CLARENCE T	COL	0-0041860	0561	1
FOWLER CARL C	CW4	W-0901892	0955	1
FOWLER CLAYTON F	COL	0-0041553	0159	1
FOWLER DAVID M	COL	0-0015002	0554	1
FOWLER HANES M	LTC	0-0022696	0646	2
FOWLER IRA H	COL	0-0030531	0763	1
FOWLER JOSEPH G	COL	0-0053218	0965	1
FOWLER LUCILLE I	MAJ	N-0000633	1060	1
FOWLER THOMAS G	LTC	0-0030867	0649	2
FOWLIE GLADYS O	MAJ	N-0002059	0161	1
FOWLKES JR B C	COL	0-0016087	0655	1
FOX ALONZO P	LTG	0-0008434	0757	1
FOX CHARLES K	LTC	0-0041545	0953	1
FOX JR JULIAN P	LTC	0-0051823	0164	1
FOX JR LAWRENCE J	LTC	0-0027859	0865	1
FOX RICHARD A	LTC	0-0083582	0863	1
FOX ROY E	COL	0-0004C63	0949	1
FOX VICTOR B	LTC	0-0029896	0261	1
FOX VINCENT W	LTC	0-0051871	0661	1
FOX WILBUR J	COL	0-0009041	0746	2
FOXWORTH EDWARD M	COL	0-0042598	0665	1
FOXX JAMES E	LTC	0-0040418	1059	1
FOY LEVIE W	COL	0-0007580	0753	1
FRAILE RENE E	COL	0-0005665	0946	2
FRALISH JOHN C	COL	0-0032668	0966	1
FRAME MARSHALL W	COL	0-0C19103	0863	2
FRAMPTON SIDNEY D	COL	0-0042176	0663	1
FRANASZEK JOSEPH J	LTC	0-0C55447	0864	1
FRANCE GERALD D	COL	0-0004115	1045	1
FRANCIS ERNEST H	LTC	0-0040758	0866	1
FRANCIS HARRISON S	LTC	0-0052233	0266	1
FRANCIS HENRY M	LTC	0-0026715	0765	1
FRANCIS JOHN P	COL	0-0005664	1046	2
FRANCIS JR GARNET P	COL	0-0030876	1065	1
FRANCIS ROBERT	COL	0-0062122	0864	1
FRANCIS WILLIAM H	COL	0-0017693	0859	1
FRANDRUP BERNADINE	MAJ	N-0002364	0360	1
FRANK ALVA B	LTC	0-0065951	0865	1
FRANK CHARLES B	COL	0-0031153	1167	1
FRANK CLARENCE A	COL	0-0012401	1050	1
FRANK FRANCIS B	CW4	W-0903112	0563	2
FRANK FRED J	LTC	0-0054078	0867	1
FRANK HENRI F	COL	0-0046187	0465	1
FRANK JACOB	MAJ	0-000250C	0728	2
FRANK KARL C	COL	0-0015063	0753	1
FRANK SELBY H	B G	0-0003546	0851	1
FRANK SELBY H	COL	0-0032620	1161	1
FRANKE JR GUSTAV H	LTC	0-0052959	0764	1
FRANKEL HENRY	COL	0-0040178	0967	1
FRANKENBERGER SAMUEL	COL	0-000169C	0822	2
FRANKENSTEIN LEONARD	LTC	0-0054172	0662	1
FRANKLIN CHARLES C	COL	0-0047521	0766	1
FRANKLIN DANIEL	COL	0-0006270	0546	2
FRANKLIN EDWARD C	COL	0-0016354	0746	1
FRANKLIN ERSKINE A	COL	0-0005852	1046	1
FRANKLIN GEORGE H	LTC	0-0035175	0262	1
FRANKLIN HORACE A	LTC	0-0041618	0957	1
FRANKLIN JOHN F	COL	0-0001837	0642	1
FRANKLIN JOHN H	COL	0-0039864	1263	1
FRANKLIN JOSEPH B	COL	0-0C43304	0967	1
FRANKLIN JR ALBERT G	B G	0-0016642	1056	1
FRANKLIN LOYCE I	MAJ	N-0002264	1162	1
FRANKLIN ROBERT B	COL	0-0019046	0863	1
FRANKLIN VICTOR A	LTC	0-0025658	0364	1
FRANKS ROBERT B	COL	0-0040041	0763	1
FRANSCH JR PAUL D	COL	0-0039065	1059	1
FRASE ROBERT C	LTC	0-0038561	0867	1
FRASER FRANK C	COL	0-001609C	0655	1
FRASER HARVEY R	B G	0-0021747	C765	1

NAME	GRADE	SVC NO	DATE RET MO YR	RET CODE
FRASER JAMES W	COL	0-0C38602	0155	1
FRASER JOSEPH J	COL	C-0008444	C650	1
FRASER JR JOSEPH J	COL	0-0053292	1167	1
FRASER MILDRED L	LTC	N-0000624	1167	1
FRASER POWELL A	COL	0-0034889	0764	1
FRASER RICHARD H	LTC	0-0023080	0949	2
FRASER RICHARD S	COL	0-0023595	0960	1
FRASER WILLIAM B	COL	0-0018692	0959	2
FRASOR GEORGE M	COL	0-0031594	0967	1
FRAZIER LEROY E	COL	0-0030678	1062	1
FRAZIER ROBERT L	LTC	0-0084611	0166	1
FREAKLEY EDWIN M	LTC	0-0039440	0966	1
FREAMAN JAY H	COL	C-0041458	0557	1
FREAR SETH R	MAJ	C-0026166	1046	2
FREDENDALL JR L R	LTC	0-0019235	0157	1
FREDERICK HORACE B	COL	0-0042891	0763	1
FREDERICK JOHN D	COL	0-0012453	0554	1
FREDERICK ROBERT T	M G	0-0017196	0352	1
FREDERICKS JOHN L	MAJ	C-0047721	1060	1
FREDERICKS WILLIAM	CPT	0-0012889	1022	2
FREDERICKSON ERWIN C	LTC	0-0032347	0165	1
FREDIN CATHERINE	MAJ	J-0000005	C967	1
FREDRIKSON GRAYDON F	LTC	0-0035700	0867	1
FREEDLAND SUMNER	LTC	0-0047401	0964	1
FREEMAN ALLEN	CW4	W-0901713	1154	2
FREEMAN DELBERT B	COL	0-0028973	0358	1
FREEMAN EDWARD V	COL	C-0011800	0749	1
FREEMAN EUGENE M	LTC	0-0040503	1161	1
FREEMAN GEORGE C	LTC	0-0044214	0762	1
FREEMAN HENRY M	COL	0-0051926	1167	1
FREEMAN JAMES W	COL	0-0012202	0554	1
FREEMAN JR GEORGE D	COL	0-0000827	0740	1
FREEMAN JR PAUL L	GEN	C-0017704	C767	1
FREEMAN MONROE E	COL	0-0056826	0861	1
FREEMAN NORA G	LTC	N-0000500	0748	1
FREEMAN RICHARD G	LTC	0-0033450	C362	2
FREER BEULAH B	2LT	R-0000569	0545	1
FREESTONE JAMES E	MAJ	0-0036937	0663	1
FREIDINGER HENRY M	COL	0-0042983	0265	1
FRENCH CHARLES A	B G	0-0003250	0248	1
FRENCH DANIEL L	LTC	0-0063850	0667	1
FRENCH EDWARD F	COL	0-0008935	0551	1
FRENCH IRMA J	MAJ	N-0001009	0162	1
FRENCH JR JULES K	COL	0-0028760	1053	1
FRENCH PAUL H	COL	C-0004783	1149	1
FRENCH SEWARD F	MAJ	0-0065994	0966	1
FRENCH STANLEY H	LTC	0-0037418	C661	1
FRENCH 3RD SANFORD W	COL	0-0023603	0760	1
FRENCK ARTHUR G	CW4	W-0903115	0762	1
FRENTZEL WILLIAM Y	B G	0-0019026	0863	1
FRESHOUR JAMES E	CW4	RW-0906733	0163	1
FRESHWATER HAROLD L	COL	0-0051739	0366	1
FREY IRENE	MAJ	N-0000603	0163	1
FRICK JOHN E	COL	0-0042303	0164	1
FRIEDMAN WILLIAM	LTC	0-0024540	0761	1
FRIEND HAROLD C	LTC	0-0028087	1165	1
FRIEND WILLIAM A	CW4	W-0904113	1167	1
FRIERSON ANDREW A	COL	C-0015587	0949	2
FRIES JOSEPHINE	MAJ	N-0001894	0660	1
FRIES STUART G	COL	0-0019827	C865	1
FRINK JAMES L	M G	0-0014587	0846	2
FRISBIE GILBERT A	LTC	0-0063116	0766	1
FRISBY JAMES L	CW4	W-0903116	0467	1
FRISBY VINCENT C	LTC	0-0020543	0555	1
FRISSELL DUNCAN P	COL	C-0014768	1046	2
FRITH ROBERT E	LTC	0-0019881	0863	1
FRITSVOLD MELFORD P	LTC	0-0043473	0566	1
FRITZ EDWIN G	COL	0-0051063	1059	1
FRITZ JOHN E	LTC	0-0025021	0859	1
FRITZ WILLIAM G	COL	0-0019069	0863	1
FRIZ BARBARA M	LTC	M-0010006	1262	1
FRIZZELL CHARLES F	MAJ	0-0014383	0-19	2
FRIZZELL LAWRENCE C	COL	0-0004949	1046	1
FROEHLE BLAIRE A	LTC	0-0042392	C662	1
FROELICH JAMES H	LTC	0-0084365	0967	1

NAME	GRADE	SVC NO	DATE RET MO YR	RET CODE
FROLICH ALEXANDER	COL	0-0021059	0859	1
FROMER PAUL S	LTC	0-0032141	C463	1
FROMME ROBERT J	LTC	0-0039246	0767	1
FROST HUGH W	CW4	W-0903119	1164	1
FROST VIRGINIA L	MAJ	M-0010022	0966	1
FROST WILLIAM R	COL	0-0008162	0846	2
FRY CLAYTON T	LTC	0-0043904	0466	2
FRY EDMUND M	COL	0-0021431	0666	1
FRY JAMES C	M G	0-0015023	1057	1
FRYE JOHN A	COL	0-0030509	0965	1
FRYE JR ARTHUR H	B G	0-0019716	0665	1
FRYE WILLIAM J	WO1	W-0902421	1052	1
FUDGE RUSSELL O	COL	0-0030652	0762	1
FUEG JOHN W	LTC	0-0040289	1065	1
FUERST ALBERT A	CPT	0-006965C	0460	2
FUGELSO ERLING S	COL	0-0020980	0564	1
FUGER ALBERT S	COL	0-0001374	1022	1
FUGITT WILLIAM K	MAJ	0-0039346	0559	1
FULLER ANNE L	LTC	N-0000587	0565	1
FULLER CARL W	LTC	0-0031689	1165	1
FULLER CECIL H	COL	0-0040158	0366	1
FULLER HARRY S	COL	0-0010504	0-40	2
FULLER HURLEY E	COL	0-0005518	1050	1
FULLER JACK G	COL	0-0014893	0650	1
FULLER JR ARTHUR L	COL	0-0018C94	0960	2
FULLER LIDNEL R	LTC	0-0025380	C347	2
FULLER ROBERT G	CPT	0-0014292	1120	2
FULLER WILLIAM C	LTC	0-0028055	C666	1
FULLER WILLIAM H	COL	0-0019190	0863	1
FULLER 3RD ROBERT W	LTC	0-0019422	0246	2
FULLERTON JEANNE T	MAJ	N-0000674	0264	1
FULMER RICHARD P	LTC	0-0039130	0566	1
FULTON ALAN L	COL	0-0012822	0854	1
FULTON HAROLD A	COL	0-0042225	0863	1
FULTON JAMES H	COL	0-0029984	0563	1
FULTON KENNETH P	COL	0-0016938	0857	2
FULTZ ALTON L	CW4	W-0903121	0561	2
FULTZ WILLIAM S	COL	0-0031439	0267	2
FULWOOD MARTHA	MAJ	N-0000044	0150	1
FUNCHESS LINWOOD E	COL	0-0020875	0757	1
FUNK ARNOLD J	B G	0-0005580	0552	1
FUNK CARL	CW4	W-0901686	1054	1
FUNK MYRON A	COL	0-0030798	0866	1
FUNK RUSSELL D	COL	0-0042067	1062	1
FUQUA JR STEPHEN O	B G	0-0C19109	0863	1
FUREY HARRY D	COL	0-0008287	0448	1
FUREY LAWRENCE M	LTC	0-0051674	1163	1
FURMAN HEZEKIAH W	LTC	0-0C39464	0265	1
FURMAN MURRAY	MAJ	0-0084738	0766	1
FURPHEY ROBERT F	CW4	W-0903122	0961	1
FURPHY FOSTER L	COL	0-0020163	1163	1
FURR WILLIAM C	CPT	0-0016025	1127	2
FURRELL ALFRED H	COL	0-0042894	1266	1
FUSI BRUNA G	MAJ	N-0002182	0865	1
FUTCH THEODORE L	B G	0-0008572	0854	1
FUTRAL ALLEN A	COL	0-0042948	0165	2
FUTRELL ALVIN F	LTC	0-0028720	0766	1
FYE JOHN H	COL	0-0005733	0753	1
FYFE JR ROBERT J M	MAJ	0-0024432	0346	2
GABARCY ROBERT L	LTC	0-0058902	0963	1
GABY JR WALTER E	LTC	0-0034656	0667	1
GADDIS JOHN W	COL	0-0C1620C	0755	1
GADDIS SHELTON	COL	0-0079818	0966	1
GAFFE WILTON C	LTC	0-0030179	0162	1
GAERTNER JOHN F	COL	0-0022799	0465	1
GAFFNEY WENDELL W	LTC	0-0044235	0664	1
GAFFNEY WILLIAM F	LTC	0-0051345	0960	1
GAGE GEORGE W	COL	0-004159C	0659	1
GAGE HAROLD C	CW4	W-0902123	0657	1
GAGE JOHN N	COL	0-0005359	0533	2
GAGE JR FREEMAN F	LTC	0-0032055	1057	1
GAGE JR PHILIP S	LTC	0-0020337	0-45	2
GAGE PHILIP S	B G	0-0002623	0447	2
GAGNE JR JAMES V	LTC	0-003945C	0867	1
GAGNON MILDRED S	MAJ	L-0000299	0860	1

NAME	GRADE	SVC NO	DATE RET MO YR	RET CODE
GAHAN JOHN J	COL	0-0010857	0545	2
GAHAN THEODORE R	COL	0-0038686	0461	1
GAIGE JR WILBER M	COL	0-0041538	0858	1
GAILLARD FRED E	COL	0-0010295	0653	1
GAILLARD JEANNE M	MAJ	N-0001970	0361	1
GAINES ARTHUR R	M G	0-0006261	0552	1
GAINES HAROLD W	LTC	0-0032559	0965	1
GAINES JAMES S	MAJ	0-0060655	0266	2
GAINES THOMAS L	COL	0-0041439	0956	1
GAITHER LOREN E	COL	0-0042109	1055	1
GAITHER RIDGELY	LTG	0-0015970	0562	1
GALANTI PHILIP J	COL	0-0030684	0764	1
GALBRAITH JR JOHN M	LTC	0-0033957	0261	2
GALBRAITH NICOLL F	COL	0-0011588	0450	1
GALBREAITH ROBERT B	LTC	0-0033549	0262	1
GALE CARROLL M	LTC	0-0005045	0642	1
GALL JAMES A	COL	0-0030563	0166	2
GALLAGHER FERDINAND	COL	0-0004503	0751	1
GALLAGHER JOHN L	COL	0-0017370	0246	2
GALLAGHER LEONARD A	COL	0-0007646	0947	1
GALLAGHER PHILIP E	M G	0-0011249	0257	2
GALLEZ DOUGLAS W	LTC	0-0026594	0864	1
GALLI MARY F	LTC	N-0000011	1047	1
GALLIER ROBERT H	CPT	0-0006766	0934	2
GALLIETT HAROLD H	COL	0-0005089	0248	1
GALLION SCOTT	WO1	W-0901290	1137	1
GALLOGLY LESTER H	COL	0-0029420	0760	1
GALLOWAY DONALD H	COL	0-0015161	0754	1
GALLOWAY GERALD E	M G	0-0016043	0562	1
GALLOWAY MARIE S	LTC	N-0000511	1159	1
GALLOWAY NEAL C	LTC	0-0034158	0262	1
GALLUP WALTER E	COL	0-0018513	0861	2
GALT EDWARD A	LTC	0-0043743	0563	1
GALUSHA MORRIS E	COL	0-0043345	0261	1
GALVIN JR JAMES O	COL	0-0029263	0363	1
GALVIN MABEL	MAJ	N-0000266	0464	1
GALWEY GEOFFREY	COL	0-0005753	0146	1
GAMBLE ANDREW S	COL	0-0015801	0854	1
GAMBLE CLAUDE L	COL	0-0011282	0946	2
GAMBRILL ROBERT E	COL	0-0039716	0160	2
GAMMON JAMES P	COL	0-0006987	0552	1
GANDIA AMAURY M	COL	0-0019205	0260	1
GAND FRANK W	COL	0-0005598	0947	1
GANSCHOW ALFRED K	LTC	0-0050352	0865	1
GANT ROBERT M	COL	0-0039767	0462	2
GANTT HARRY B	COL	0-0006619	0648	2
GANTT HENRY P	COL	0-0008638	0753	1
GANZ JR EDWARD C	LTC	0-0050570	1264	1
GARANFLO ALICE F	MAJ	N-0001868	0558	1
GARAY STEPHEN L	COL	0-0045416	0266	1
GARCIA JOSEPH G	CW2	W-0900969	0945	2
GARCIN FREDERICK	COL	0-0002905	1046	2
GARD HAROLD R	COL	0-0015585	0754	1
GARD ROBERT G	M G	0-0012247	1159	1
GARDEN FRANK E	LTC	0-0031742	0862	1
GARDES GEORGE W	B G	0-0028840	0756	1
GARDINER HAROLD L	MAJ	0-0002513	1022	1
GARDNER F SEDON	COL	0-0016833	0657	1
GARDNER JAMES C	CW3	W-0904114	0844	1
GARDNER LEON L	COL	0-0016016	0549	2
GARDNER PAUL E	LTC	0-0038951	0563	2
GARDNER RALPH B	CW4	W-0903127	0764	1
GARDNER RICHARD M	COL	0-0076877	0867	1
GARDNER ROBIN R	LTC	0-0038777	0560	1
GARDNER WAYNE B	COL	0-0041366	0735	1
GAREN ELEANOR M	MAJ	N-0001879	0559	1
GARGES PHILIP R	COL	0-0015509	0754	1
GARLAND JR PETER W	COL	0-0020288	0758	1
GARN PHIL R	LTC	0-0050395	1165	1
GARNER HUGH M	LTC	0-0060218	0865	1
GARNER LLOYD M	COL	0-0009650	0653	1
GARNER ROBERT S	LTC	0-0029640	0950	1
GARNER VERNON H	CW4	W-0903129	1160	1
GARNHART GEORGE H	LTC	0-0025267	0766	1
GAROFALO RAPHAEL F	CW4	W-0901731	0163	1
GAROFALE WILLIAM F	LTC	0-0063409	0767	1
GARR ARTHUR S	LTC	0-0080782	0665	1
GARRABRANT EVELYN D	MAJ	L-0000205	1153	1
GARRAHY JOHN	CW2	W-0903130	0562	1
GARRARD CELZENA E	LTC	N-0001890	0263	1
GARRECHT JR F A	COL	0-0015277	1146	1
GARRETSON RALPH B	COL	0-0039835	0657	1
GARRETT JOHN K	LTC	0-0060684	0866	1
GARRETT JOSEPH B	CPT	0-0056512	0860	1
GARRETT JR JAMES M	COL	0-0004920	0947	2
GARRETT PHYLLIS D	MAJ	N-0001741	0766	1
GARRETT ROBERT E	B G	0-0002539	0646	2
GARRETT ROBERT W	COL	0-0023971	0667	1
GARRETT SHIRLEY D	CPT	0-0060687	0962	1
GARRIS HERBERT L	LTC	0-0033872	0267	1
GARRISON ALIDA J	LTC	N-0000012	0348	1
GARRISON CHARLES T	MAJ	0-0063246	0867	1
GARRISON LLOYD R	COL	0-0011580	1052	1
GARRISON RITCHIE	LTC	0-0030696	0464	1
GARTON EDWARD R	LTC	0-0032945	0561	1
GARTON GEORGE G	COL	0-0018138	0760	1
GARVEY DALE M	COL	0-0043910	0759	2
GARVEY DANIEL J	CPT	0-0058506	1155	2
GARVIN CRUMP	M G	0-0012746	1058	1
GARY CEPHAS W	COL	0-0020427	0158	1
GARZA CARLOS M	LTC	0-0096971	0967	1
GASIOR EUGENE J	MAJ	0-0027802	0561	2
GASKILL ROBERT C	COL	0-0019275	0855	2
GASKINS JR STEVE P	COL	0-0026392	0628	1
GASPERINI SILVIO E	LTC	0-0023203	1066	2
GASSETT SILAS	COL	0-0031481	0267	1
GASSMAN FRED L	CW4	W-0907133	0658	2
GASTON FRANK W	CW3	W-0906739	0964	1
GASTON FREDERICK	COL	0-0020276	0866	1
GATCHELL WADE C	COL	0-0007066	1046	2
GATES ELIZABETH	MAJ	N-0002350	0558	1
GATES JOHN L	LTC	0-0040535	0962	2
GATES VINCENT I	COL	0-0079820	0167	1
GAUDETTE DOMINIQUE	CW4	W-09020[illegible]	1154	1
GAURNIER PAUL L	LTC	0-0061337	0967	1
GAVAN PAUL A	M G	0-0017169	0863	1
GAVIN JAMES M	LTG	0-0017676	0358	1
GAVIN JOHN A	COL	0-0018788	0960	1
GAVIN ROBERT J	LTC	0-0033807	0662	2
GAWARECKI JULIA F	LTC	N-0002273	0762	1
GAY HOBART R	LTG	0-0007323	0855	2
GAYDASH GEORGE C	COL	0-0041588	0459	1
GAYLE JR LESTER T	LTC	0-0014219	1119	2
GAYLE JR SETH	COL	0-0017342	0757	1
GAYLE MARY H	MAJ	N-0002034	0360	1
GAYLE RICHARD B	LTC	0-0009740	0840	2
GAYLORD TYYNE N	MAJ	N-0001964	0960	1
GAYNOR CLEMENT J	COL	0-0008743	0248	1
GAYNOR JAMES K	COL	0-0043754	0867	2
GAYNOR JR WAYNE J	LTC	0-0035222	0463	1
GAZELLE ISA P	LTC	N-0000089	0655	1
GAZIANO SAM F	MAJ	0-0059807	0364	1
GEALTA CECIL G	COL	0-0038744	0663	1
GEAN KIRBY A	LTC	0-0025588	0966	1
GEARIN HELEN R	MAJ	R-0010000	0855	1
GEARY JOHN A	LTC	0-0017742	0-44	2
GEBBIE EARL J	LTC	0-0031361	1064	1
GEBHARDT EARL G	COL	0-0011836	1052	1
GEDDES JOHN A	COL	0-0031512	0567	1
GEE CLOUGH F	COL	0-0010263	0846	2
GEELAN WILLIAM A	LTC	0-0040963	0864	1
GEER JOSEPH W	LTC	0-0004696	0-38	1
GEEVER ERVING F	CPT	0-0020404	0739	2
GEHMAN LESTER	MAJ	0-0014015	1020	2
GEHRING FREDERICK	LTC	0-0036462	0664	1
GEIGER EDWARD H	LTC	0-0046621	0867	1
GEIGES JR ELMER A	MAJ	0-0085211	0767	1
GEISE GERALD E	COL	0-0043167	0467	1
GELDERMANN EDWARD L	COL	0-0027803	0661	1
GEMPEL EUGENE P H	COL	0-0006706	0838	2
GENERO PETER P	LTC	0-0063063	0966	1
GENETTI EMIL J	COL	0-0026965	1161	2
GENT ANDREW J	CW4	W-0903138	1164	1
GENTLE MARGARET M	MAJ	L-0000178	0163	1
GENUARIO LOUIS V	LTC	0-0062696	1066	2
GEORGE ALEXANDER	COL	0-0012781	0946	2
GEORGE ANNE	MAJ	N-0001908	1062	1
GEORGE DONALD B	LTC	0-0097906	0467	1
GEORGE JOHN D	LTC	0-0030122	0162	1
GEORGE JR CLAUDE D	COL	0-0031788	0266	1
GEORGE JR HORACE W	1LT	0-0067681	0554	2
GEORGE JULIAN H	COL	0-0008421	0753	1
GEORGE MAX S	COL	0-0020740	1059	1
GEORGE PAUL W	MAJ	0-0011225	0639	1
GEORGE ROBERT D	LTC	0-0043815	0164	1
GEORGE URBAN F	COL	0-0028845	0656	1
GEORGE WILLIAM S	COL	0-0018304	0956	1
GEORGES MICHAEL P	COL	0-0042242	0963	1
GERBERT LEO J	COL	0-0026406	0664	1
GERAGHTY MICHAEL J	COL	0-0016263	1054	1
GERARD PAUL T	COL	0-0030445	1065	2
GERBER AUSTIN J	LTC	0-0063175	1065	1
GERBER FRED F	COL	0-0032023	1166	1
GERDES HENRY G	COL	0-0039513	1051	1
GERE GILES H	COL	0-0051707	0366	2
GERFEN FREDERICK	LTC	0-0053165	0865	1
GERFEN ROYE R	COL	0-0007951	0846	1
GERHARDT CHARLES H	M G	0-0005259	0952	1
GERHARDT JACOB J	COL	0-0003875	1050	1
GERHARDT WILLIAM R	COL	0-0008565	0249	1
GERHART GEORGE H	COL	0-0019569	0762	1
GERIG JR FRANK A	LTC	0-0023701	0661	1
GERKEN WALTER W	COL	0-0042113	0261	1
GERLACH ALBERT G	WO1	W-0901816	0146	1
GERLACH SHIRL L	LTC	0-0063049	0263	1
GEROT JOSEPH O	COL	0-0030818	0864	1
GEROW LEE S	B G	0-0004681	0749	2
GEROW LEONARD T	GEN	0-0003151	0750	1
GERSHENOW LOUIS	COL	0-0031577	0767	1
GERSONI CHARLES S	COL	0-0056185	0365	2
GERSTNER JOHN F	COL	0-0055315	0667	1
GETCHELL WILMAH M	LTC	0-0040737	0762	1
GETTYS CHARLES W	COL	0-0015178	0954	1
GETZ AUSTIN T	COL	0-0018309	1046	2
GEWINNER MARCUS N	LTC	0-0080786	0965	1
GHORMLEY WILLIAM K	M G	0-0017674	1162	1
GIBB FREDERICK	M G	0-0019222	0661	2
GIBBONS DONALD F	COL	0-0038724	0962	1
GIBBONS GILBERT P	COL	0-0039804	0163	1
GIBBS CHARLES H	LTC	0-0043764	0366	1
GIBBS COLEMAN T	CW3	W-0906741	0558	1
GIBBS CYRUS L	MAJ	0-0080788	0863	1
GIBBS DAVID P	M G	0-0019189	0766	1
GIBBS FREDERICK	COL	0-0029129	0557	1
GIBBS GEORGE W	COL	0-0018178	0660	1
GIBBS GERALD G	COL	0-0015637	0754	1
GIBBS JAMES J	LTC	0-0062934	0767	1
GIBNEY JESSE L	COL	0-0012216	0853	1
GIBNEY LOUIS G	COL	0-0005755	0753	1
GIBSON ADELNO	COL	0-0002046	0642	1
GIBSON COMET	LTC	0-0030497	0260	1
GIBSON EDWARD S	COL	0-0014913	0144	2
GIBSON ELMER P	LTC	0-0029145	0157	1
GIBSON EMERY W	LTC	0-0041604	0757	1
GIBSON ERVIN O	COL	0-0029899	0262	1
GIBSON HERBERT D	B G	0-0007152	0946	2
GIBSON HORACE C	COL	0-0020568	0657	1
GIBSON HORACE N	CPT	0-0011079	0435	2
GIBSON HOWLAND A	COL	0-0015496	0751	1
GIBSON JOHN H	COL	0-0029923	0563	1
GIBSON JR THOMAS A	LTC	0-0035478	0962	1
GIBSON LOUIS J	CW4	W-0906742	0657	1
GIBSON RICHMOND T	COL	0-0003841	1047	1
GIBSON ROY S	COL	0-0006520	0647	2
GIBSON SAMUEL A	COL	0-0003586	0951	1
GIBSON WILMOT L	LTC	0-0037562	0367	1
GIDDENS MITCHELL A	LTC	0-0016256	0548	2
GIDENS FLOYD E	COL	0-0030543	1265	2
GIERLAK MICHAEL P	LTC	0-0040363	0165	2
GIES HAROLD W	CW2	W-0902009	0647	2
GIFFORD GERALD K	COL	0-0051539	0964	1
GIGGEY FREDERICK	MAJ	0-0060532	0363	1
GILBERT CHARLES L	COL	0-0029148	1158	2
GILBERT CHARLES M	COL	0-0023457	0766	1
GILBERT CLARENCE L	MAJ	0-0003244	1022	2
GILBERT DOUGLAS G	COL	0-0019202	0181	1
GILBERT HAROLD N	M G	0-0007596	1046	2
GILBERT HORACE C	CW4	W-0903148	0157	1
GILBERT JAMES R	COL	0-0051689	0962	1
GILBERT JAMES T	COL	0-0044348	0765	1
GILBERT LEONARD J	CPT	0-0027066	1050	1
GILBERT WILLIAM A	CW4	W-0903149	0962	1
GILBREATH FREDERICK	M G	0-0003086	0846	2
GILBREATH WILLIAM O	LTC	0-0059454	0464	1
GILBRETH JOSEPH H	COL	0-0007560	0546	1
GILCHRIST MALCOLM F	COL	0-0022077	0762	1
GILDART CHARLES R	COL	0-0012127	0351	1
GILDART ROBERT C	B G	0-0020703	0767	1
GILES JR TEMPY H	LTC	0-0052120	0166	1
GILL ARLO R	LTC	0-0044983	1159	1
GILL BURGO D	LTC	0-0016347	1045	1
GILL CHARLES C	COL	0-0017840	0547	2
GILL EVERT R	CW4	W-0903150	0161	1
GILL GORDON C	COL	0-0042495	0265	1
GILL JR ISAAC	COL	0-0003739	1146	2
GILL MARIE A	MAJ	N-0001971	0461	1
GILL MARK J	LTC	0-0045784	1162	2
GILL ROBERT F	LTC	0-0009969	1041	1
GILL WILLIAM H	M G	0-0003287	0546	2
GILLAND MORRIS W	B G	0-0012066	0948	2
GILLARD MARJORIE G	MAJ	N-0000991	1263	1
GILLASPEY BRUCE N	LTC	0-0059654	1262	1
GILLEM JR ALVAN C	LTG	0-0003030	0850	1
GILLEN JOSEPH K	LTC	0-0079825	0965	1
GILLENTINE LUNCEFORD	LTC	0-0082009	1265	1
GILLENWATERS HENRY L	LTC	0-0041702	0257	1
GILLESPIE ERNEST R	COL	0-0041956	1161	1
GILLESPIE EUGENE R	COL	0-0025320	0764	1
GILLESPIE FLOYD T	COL	0-0011071	0952	1
GILLESPIE FRANCIS J	COL	0-0012215	0854	1
GILLESPIE HAROLD S	MAJ	0-0069934	0465	1
GILLESPIE JAMES O	M G	0-0016711	0357	1
GILLESPIE JOHN J	LTC	0-0032143	0267	1
GILLESPIE JOSEPHINE	MAJ	N-0002256	0262	1
GILLESPIE JR JOHN W	LTC	0-0028577	1166	2
GILLESPIE KENNETH W	COL	0-0030273	0662	2
GILLET BRUNETTA K	MAJ	M-0010019	0558	1
GILLET NORMAN C	COL	0-0011667	0854	1
GILLETTE A WARD	COL	0-0018883	0862	1
GILLETTE CHAUNCEY A	COL	0-0010039	0847	1
GILLETTE DOUGLAS H	COL	0-0003781	0253	1
GILLETTE FRANCIS E	COL	0-0015693	0754	1
GILLETTE GEORGE W	COL	0-0005101	0148	1
GILLETTE JR EDWARD C	B G	0-0012697	0864	1
GILLETTE SHELBY L	COL	0-0030727	0666	1
GILLFILLAN JAY E	COL	0-0004634	1048	2
GILLIAM ARNOLD C	COL	0-0031570	0157	1
GILLIGAN RAMONA A	MAJ	N-0001907	0962	1
GILLIS JOHN R	COL	0-0060313	1066	1
GILLIS MARCEL A	COL	0-0006810	0446	2
GILLIS NEVA G	CPT	L-0000172	0251	1
GILLIS THOMAS D	COL	0-0019864	0865	1
GILLMAN LEONARD	CW4	W-0903151	0362	2
GILLMORE WILLIAM K	LTC	0-0023432	0161	1
GILLMORE WILLIAM N	M G	0-0016196	0562	1
GILLON PAUL N	COL	0-0019048	0756	1
GILLY CLARENCE C	COL	0-0039681	0760	2
GILMAN SEYMOUR I	COL	0-0019377	0160	1
GILMAN SHELDON M	COL	0-0029624	0961	1
GILMAN TURNER W	COL	0-0031831	0661	1

NAME	GRADE	SVC NO	DATE RET MO YR	RET CODE
GILMARTIN AUSTIN F	LTC	0-0015024	0750	1
GILMER DAN	COL	0-0018876	0862	2
GILMOR ALBERT	COL	0-0001835	0841	2
GILMORE JR HUGH M	COL	0-0016555	0656	1
GILMORE ROBERT P	CW4	W-0903152	1262	1
GILSON SHIRLEY M	MAJ	N-0001824	0266	1
GINDER PHILIP D	M G	0-0016904	0559	2
GINGRAS ROLAND A	CW3	W-0903154	1165	1
GINGRICH HAROLD W	LTC	0-0026076	0765	1
GINN EDYTHE L	LTC	N-0001977	0861	1
GINN JR L HOLMES	B G	0-0017341	1058	2
GINN MELVIN R	MAJ	0-0005340	0622	2
GIRARD PAULINE H	LTC	N-0000218	0264	1
GIRARDE LILLIAN C	MAJ	N-0000172	0861	2
GIROUX ROSAIRE	CW4	W-0904117	0354	1
GIRTMAN JR JOHN C	COL	0-0044951	0764	1
GIST EMORY H	COL	0-0006159	0848	1
GIST HARVEY M	CW4	W-0903155	0355	1
GIST JULIAN H	COL	0-0007914	0847	1
GIVEN WILLIAM J	COL	0-0019105	0157	1
GIVIDEN JR GEORGE M	CPT	0-0064146	0860	2
GJELSTEEN EINAR B	M G	0-0015143	0957	1
GLAB JOHN E	LTC	0-0026556	0867	1
GLACE JR FRANK E	MAJ	0-0021755	0939	2
GLADE KENNETH	LTC	0-0021181	0658	1
GLADISH ISAAC O	COL	0-0009126	0947	1
GLAFKA ALVIN R	COL	0-0041559	0259	1
GLASCOCK CAMBELL H	COL	0-0009141	0248	2
GLASCOCK JR HAROLD W	COL	0-0030854	0861	1
GLASEBROOK ARTHUR J	LTC	0-0045192	0667	1
GLASGOW JOSEPH M	COL	0-0012232	0550	1
GLASGOW RALPH I	B G	0-0015576	1055	1
GLASS ABRAHAM M	MAJ	0-0026780	0964	1
GLASS ALBERT J	COL	0-0029247	1163	1
GLASS GEORGE F	LTC	0-0041790	0258	1
GLASS ROY E	MAJ	0-0014529	0120	1
GLASSBURN ROBERT P	COL	0-0002221	0444	2
GLASSEN CHESTER E	COL	0-0033932	1163	1
GLASSER ANTHONY P	LTC	0-0059810	1066	1
GLATTERER MILTON S	COL	0-0018843	0862	1
GLAVIN EDWARD J F	COL	0-0016815	0455	1
GLEASON CHARLES C	LTC	0-0044245	0957	1
GLEASON THOMAS R	LTC	0-0027432	0966	1
GLEISER CHESTER A	COL	0-0031289	0965	1
GLEN GEORGE R	COL	0-0030049	1163	1
GLENDENING JAMES K	LTC	0-0026176	0164	1
GLENN CARL E	LTC	0-0050369	0765	1
GLENN DONALD W	LTC	0-0033931	0962	1
GLEW JR DONALD H	LTC	0-0059550	1065	1
GLICK ARTHUR A	LTC	0-0041444	1054	1
GLICKSON SOLOMON P	LTC	0-0054079	0464	1
GLIDDEN DOROTHY I	MAJ	M-0040155	0465	1
GLITHERO JOHN C	CPT	0-0007248	0227	2
GLORE JAMES	B G	0-0028758	0356	1
GLORIOD JOHN A	COL	0-0019793	0464	1
GLOVER BOB H	COL	0-0030680	0466	1
GLOVER ROBERT L	CW4	W-0904118	0264	2
GLOVER WILLIAM C	COL	0-0034122	0867	1
GLUCKMAN ARCADI	COL	0-0006980	1150	1
GLYNN JOSEPH E	CW4	W-0906746	0266	1
GNAU WILLIAM D	COL	0-0043828	1163	2
GOATLEY FRANCIS J	COL	0-0051256	1161	2
GOCKER LEO L	COL	0-0007338	0446	2
GODBEY PAUL	COL	0-0030281	1164	1
GODBY GARLAND D	LTC	0-0036189	0560	1
GODFREY CARL F	LTC	0-0058410	1066	1
GODLOVE RONALD L	CW4	W-0903160	0157	1
GODSEY DALE R	MAJ	0-0063284	0861	1
GODSHALL MELVIN W	LTC	0-0040184	0865	1
GODWIN JAMES E	COL	0-0018768	0862	1
GODWIN NORMAN A	LTC	0-0046291	0766	1
GODWIN RENA M	MAJ	N-0000244	1163	1
GOE WILLIAM E	COL	0-0007433	1148	1
GOEBEL JR HERMAN P	COL	0-0041475	1057	1
GOEBERT ELMER C	COL	0-0006399	0746	1

NAME	GRADE	SVC NO	DATE RET MO YR	RET CODE
GOERS WILLIAM C	LTC	0-0023487	0761	2
GOERZ PETER P	COL	0-0012095	0349	1
GOETH FREDERICK	LTC	0-0027640	0866	1
GOETHALS GEORGE R	COL	0-0013622	0819	1
GOETZ CARL	LTC	0-0031239	0367	1
GOETZ JOHN B M	COL	0-0043696	0165	1
GOETZ JR HUGO G	LTC	0-0039894	0662	2
GOFF JOHN L	COL	0-0012681	0753	1
GOFF ROBERT F	LTC	0-0081901	0761	1
GOLD WILLIAM M	COL	0-0040179	0762	2
GOLDBERG SEYMOUR L	COL	0-0079829	0966	1
GOLDBRANSON CARL E	CPT	0-0060451	0962	1
GOLDEN JOE E	COL	0-0018872	0862	1
GOLDEN WILLIAM C	COL	0-0039605	0557	1
GOLDMAN ALFRED M	MAJ	0-0005851	1039	1
GOLDRICK ROBERT N	LTC	0-0080796	0967	1
GOLDSMITH HOWARD F	LTC	0-0031946	0866	1
GOLDSMITH ROGER W	COL	0-0017163	0758	1
GOLDSTEIN MARCEL N	LTC	0-0029711	0360	1
GOLDTHWAITE RALPH H	B G	0-0002562	0546	2
GOLEY BYRON H	LTC	0-0080797	0766	2
GOLLADAY EDWARD M	CW4	W-0903164	0157	1
GOLLADAY WILLIAM C	COL	0-0040897	0567	1
GOLSTON JR JOE R	LTC	0-0040657	0262	1
GOMEZ MARY L	LTC	N-0002036	0559	1
GOMELL DAVID R	CW4	W-0906748	0364	1
GONSETH JR JULES F	COL	0-0040211	1064	1
GONTRUM RALPH W	COL	0-0051596	0862	1
GONYE AFTON M	MAJ	N-0002254	1061	1
GONZALEZ JUNE P	LTC	L-0000274	0165	1
GONZALEZ MIGUEL A	CW3	W-0906750	1056	1
GONZALEZ-RODRIG J	LTC	0-0058014	0662	1
GOOCH STACY W	COL	0-0019455	0764	1
GOOD JOHN C	1LT	0-0025346	0545	2
GOOD LARA P	CPT	0-0004977	1022	2
GOOD OTTO S	MAJ	0-0037442	0957	1
GOOD ROBERT E	MAJ	0-0059995	0164	1
GOODALL LESLIE D	COL	0-0030411	0965	2
GOODE ROY F	COL	0-0029921	0563	1
GOODELL FRANK D	COL	0-0017147	0758	1
GOODELL KENNETH J	CW3	W-0906751	0459	1
GOODIN GEORGE W	CW4	W-0906752	0564	1
GOODINE CLARENCE E	COL	0-0020258	0365	1
GOODLEY JOHN E	COL	0-0029566	0661	1
GOODMAN JR JOHN F	COL	0-0062997	0766	1
GOODMAN SANFORD J	COL	0-0015635	0754	1
GOODMAN THELMA B	MAJ	N-0001957	0859	1
GOODMAN WILLIAM P	LTC	0-0062007	0866	1
GOODNOW JAMES L	COL	0-0031363	1266	1
GOODRICH DURWARD V	CW4	W-0903166	0864	1
GOODRICH FLORA E	MAJ	N-0002365	0760	1
GOODRICH GUINN B	COL	0-0042680	1265	1
GOODRICH MAX E	CW3	W-0906753	0964	1
GOODRICH MERLE L	LTC	0-0032693	1062	1
GOODRICH RAYMOND H	COL	0-0022911	1164	1
GOODRICH WALKER R	COL	0-0018815	0261	1
GOODRICH WALTER R	COL	0-0010172	1046	1
GOODRICK DOROTHY S	MAJ	N-0002376	0960	1
GOODRUM JACK T	CW2	W-0900380	0347	2
GOODSELL LEONARD J	COL	0-0024472	0365	1
GOODSON MELROSE C	MAJ	N-0000703	1165	1
GOODSPEED GEORGE F	MAJ	0-0060272	0165	1
GOODWIN ALBERT J	LTC	0-0042588	0663	1
GOODWIN JAMES B	COL	0-0030573	1065	2
GOODWIN JAMES E	COL	0-0020158	0866	1
GOODWIN JAMES E	CW2	W-0901479	0345	1
GOODWIN JAMES M	COL	0-0080799	0862	1
GOODWIN JOYCE	MAJ	N-0001284	0164	1
GOODWIN JR ARTHUR C	COL	0-0018179	0360	1
GOODWIN WALTER P	COL	0-0018733	0862	1
GOODWYN ALLEN A	COL	0-0011825	0653	1
GOOLER MAX H	COL	0-0015082	0754	2
GORBY ALVIN L	M G	0-0016546	0161	1
GORDANIER ROBERT S	LTC	0-0065256	0867	1
GORDER ALEXANDER	B G	0-0007213	0548	1

NAME	GRADE	SVC NO	DATE RET MO YR	RET CODE
GORDON JAMES H	COL	0-0029227	0461	1
GORDON JAMES L	LTC	0-0039213	0767	1
GORDON LYNELL F	COL	0-0028769	0954	1
GORDON PRESTON O	LTC	0-0035828	0364	1
GORDON RANDOLPH	COL	0-0005204	0746	1
GORDON RICHARD A	COL	0-0005915	0854	1
GORDON THOMAS F	LTC	0-0023112	0761	1
GORDON WILL H	COL	0-0005827	1047	1
GORDON WILLIAM M	MAJ	0-0037430	0861	1
GORE THOMAS L	LTC	0-0004079	0-39	1
GORE WILLIAM F	LTC	0-0058911	0966	2
GORHAM FRANK W	LTC	0-0042461	1162	1
GORIUP OTHMAR F	COL	0-0029187	0960	1
GORLINSKI JOSEPH S	COL	0-0012092	0350	1
GORMAN ADAM R	CW4	RW-0903168	0764	1
GORMAN CHARLES L	COL	0-0015031	0148	1
GORMAN EMILY	COL	L-0000055	0866	1
GORMAN FRANK E	CW4	W-0907094	0660	1
GORMAN HARRY W	COL	0-0042062	0862	1
GORN JOHN W	COL	0-0022200	0764	2
GORRELL CHARLES J	LTC	0-0049942	0465	1
GORSKI JOSEPH	LTC	0-0079679	0766	1
GORSUCH EDWARD C	COL	0-0029740	0762	1
GORTON RUTH R	LTC	L-0000100	1063	1
GORTON WALTER T	COL	0-0008188	0847	1
GOSE ELLIOTT B	LTC	0-0016259	0944	2
GOSIGER FRED J	COL	0-0029867	0263	1
GOSS GORDON A	LTC	0-0042688	1162	1
GOSS THOMAS G	CW3	W-0906754	0962	1
GOSSETT HENRY M	LTC	0-0036941	1264	1
GOTT WILLIAM E	LTC	0-0037405	0767	1
GOTTESBUREN ROBERT E	CW3	W-0903170	0260	1
GOTTSCHALK TELESPHOR	COL	0-0002338	1144	2
GOUGH A DEANE	COL	0-0018413	0761	1
GOUGH WESLEY R	LTC	0-0043474	0566	2
GOULD GEORGE A	COL	0-0028968	0358	1
GOULD HAROLD A	COL	0-0080802	0965	1
GOULD HOWARD J	LTC	0-0087760	1066	1
GOULD KARL T	COL	0-0019544	0864	1
GOVERN FRANK W	COL	0-0021031	1065	1
GOWER ARTHUR W	COL	0-0006999	1148	1
GOWER WILFORD O	COL	0-0035699	1263	1
GOYETTE EDWIN M	COL	0-0020530	0257	1
GRABAN BENJAMIN H	COL	0-0010381	0750	1
GRABB ROBERT F	COL	0-0061969	0765	1
GRABER CHARLES D	LTC	0-0037555	1062	1
GRABLE CURNIA L	WO1	W-0902090	0147	2
GRABOVE MAXWELL	COL	0-0059771	0366	1
GRACE CHARLES O	COL	0-0009476	0753	1
GRACE JOHN O	CW4	W-0903172	0157	1
GRACE JR ARTHUR H	LTC	0-0025498	0663	1
GRACE JR WILLIAM P	COL	0-0016619	0657	2
GRADY HENRY W	COL	0-0004143	0846	2
GRAEVES RAYMOND B	COL	0-0032563	0867	1
GRAF RUSSELL E	LTC	0-0059685	0266	1
GRAFTON FRANK L	CPT	0-0026390	0545	2
GRAHAM CLARENCE D	COL	0-0041463	0557	1
GRAHAM ELLIS C	CW4	RW-0905504	1066	1
GRAHAM EUGENE S	COL	0-0041661	0360	1
GRAHAM GROVER C	COL	0-0006034	0947	2
GRAHAM JAMES E	B G	0-0019622	0663	1
GRAHAM JAMES M	COL	0-0000665	0240	2
GRAHAM JAMES W	COL	0-0024064	0767	1
GRAHAM JESSE E	COL	0-0012182	0854	2
GRAHAM JR EPHRAIM F	B G	0-0020838	0867	1
GRAHAM JR THOMAS A	COL	0-0032231	0963	1
GRAHAM RALPH W	LTC	0-0045995	0863	1
GRAHAM RAYMOND E	LTC	0-0070353	1163	1
GRAHAM ROBERT M	COL	0-0008616	1146	2
GRAHAM ROY C L	M G	0-0004971	0952	1
GRAHAM WALTER R	COL	0-0005020	0751	1
GRAHAM WILLIAM D	M G	0-0020067	1165	1
GRAHAM WILLIS B	CPT	0-0061873	0661	2
GRALING FRANCIS	COL	0-0015826	0754	1
GRAMZOW JOHN G	B G	0-0030735	0666	1

NAME	GRADE	SVC NO	DATE RET MO YR	RET CODE
GRANDE IRA W	COL	0-0029503	1060	1
GRANT ANDREW R	LTC	0-0025045	0367	1
GRANT ARTHUR E	LTC	0-0064960	0667	1
GRANT CARL F	COL	0-0031653	0565	1
GRANT CHAPMAN	MAJ	0-0003646	1034	2
GRANT EDWARD J	COL	0-0038743	0761	1
GRANT GEORGE R	MAJ	0-0024980	1046	2
GRANT GILVARY P	LTC	0-0051775	0663	1
GRANT HELEN E	MAJ	N-0001835	0765	1
GRANT JOATHAN M	LTC	0-0036083	0167	1
GRANT JOSEPH A	COL	0-0004487	0651	1
GRANT LOIS K	MAJ	N-0000829	0863	1
GRANT MELVILLE F	COL	0-0014977	0854	2
GRANT PATRICIA E	LTC	L-0000181	0265	1
GRANT RUSSELL P	COL	0-0042646	0965	1
GRANT WALTER M	COL	0-0022093	0666	1
GRANT 3RD ULYSSES S	M G	0-0001790	0745	2
GRASS BARBARA A	MAJ	N-0000369	0165	1
GRAUER FRANKLIN H	COL	0-0057524	0962	1
GRAVER HERBERT A	LTC	0-0078958	1266	1
GRAVES ABIGAIL B	MAJ	N-0000019	0248	1
GRAVES HAROLD K	LTC	0-0059855	0964	1
GRAVES JOHN L	COL	0-0015036	0846	1
GRAVES RUPERT D	COL	0-0015754	0754	1
GRAY CLIFFORD A	CPT	0-0006088	0934	2
GRAY CLIFFORD A	COL	0-0016554	0155	2
GRAY DELL S	COL	0-0008765	0749	2
GRAY GORDON D	COL	0-0040596	0763	1
GRAY HARVEY W	LTC	0-0060582	0267	1
GRAY IRVING	COL	0-0058738	0464	1
GRAY JOHN T	LTC	0-0037480	1162	1
GRAY JR EUGENE W	COL	0-0051183	1065	1
GRAY JR PAUL	COL	0-0023935	0967	1
GRAY LEE F	1LT	0-0012195	0934	2
GRAY MILLARD G	COL	0-0032137	1166	1
GRAY MILO J	COL	0-0041598	0559	1
GRAY ROBERT M	COL	0-0024644	0362	1
GRAYBEAL CARL S	COL	0-0016875	0755	1
GRAYEB GEORGE A	COL	0-0016152	0655	1
GREAVES FIELDING L	LTC	0-0026656	1065	1
GREBE ALFRED A	COL	0-0020502	0655	1
GRECO EMILE J	1LT	0-0019160	0242	1
GRECO JOHN F	COL	0-0018133	1059	1
GREEAR WILLIAM H	COL	0-0017607	0859	1
GREELEY BRENDAN M	COL	0-0017740	0859	1
GREELEY LEONARD J	B G	0-0015449	0959	1
GREEN ALICE F	MAJ	N-0000876	0767	1
GREEN CARL E	COL	0-0018460	0761	1
GREEN CHARLES E	MAJ	0-0058125	1264	1
GREEN CHARLES R	COL	0-0065413	0166	1
GREEN DOROTHY E	CW4	V-0915361	0663	1
GREEN III JAMES O	COL	0-0023850	0865	1
GREEN JAMES P	COL	0-0023423	0966	1
GREEN JAMES C	LTC	0-0022182	0866	1
GREEN JAMES L	COL	0-0017074	0755	1
GREEN JESSE P	COL	0-0005626	1050	1
GREEN JOHN H	COL	0-0033085	0865	1
GREEN JOHN N	COL	0-0028871	0756	1
GREEN JOSEPHINE	LTC	N-0002400	0765	1
GREEN JR DUFF	COL	0-0042235	0763	1
GREEN JR JAMES W	B G	0-0016774	0857	1
GREEN KIRBY	COL	0-0009687	1146	1
GREEN L D	MAJ	0-0079310	0167	2
GREEN LYNELL W	COL	0-0052665	1162	1
GREEN MACK M	B G	0-0016539	0656	1
GREEN MARTIN L	COL	0-0020720	0666	1
GREEN PHILIP P	COL	0-0005400	0451	1
GREEN THOMAS C	COL	0-0050944	0457	1
GREEN THOMAS H	M G	0-0006895	1149	1
GREEN WARRNE J	LTC	0-0042898	1262	1
GREEN WINIFRED C	COL	0-0007076	1150	1
GREENBERG SAMUEL	COL	0-0041692	0656	1
GREENE ALPHONSE A	COL	0-0018400	0859	1
GREENE FRANCIS M	COL	0-0028803	0555	1
GREENE FRED W	COL	0-0038737	0656	1

NAME	GRADE	SVC NO	DATE RET MO YR	RET CODE
GREENE HAROLD F	1LT	0-0011982	0131	1
GREENE JOHN N	CPT	0-0009585	0934	2
GREENE JOHN S	MAJ	0-0040514	0652	1
GREENE PHILIP S	COL	0-0020314	0157	1
CREENE RICHARDSON	COL	0-0007607	0746	1
GREENE WILLIAM H	COL	0-0042130	1262	1
GREENFIFLO LOUIS	COL	0-0041926	1061	1
GREENING ORLANDO L	COL	0-0043906	0761	1
GREENLEAF HENRY M	COL	0-0020983	0858	1
GREENLEE HALFORD R	COL	0-0019801	0365	1
GREENWALD KARL C	COL	0-0003359	0240	1
GREENWELL SAMUEL A	COL	0-0007752	0143	2
GREER FIELOER P	COL	0-0018430	0761	1
GREER FRANK R	LTC	0-0033447	0262	1
GREER HARRY A	COL	0-0043685	0765	1
GREER HARRY J	CW4	W-0903177	0661	1
GREER HERMAN E	LTC	0-0080806	0965	1
GREER RICHARD S	LTC	0-0039343	0761	1
GREEVE GERALD J	COL	0-0029576	0861	1
GREGG CAVID H	COL	0-0019713	0758	1
GREGOIRE WILLIAM N	MAJ	0-0079311	1265	1
GREGORY CLYDE	LTC	0-0043044	0565	1
GREGORY JAMES B	COL	0-0051737	0762	1
GREGORY JR FRANCIS G	COL	0-0031828	0267	1
GREINER EDWIN C	COL	0-0015012	0954	1
GREINER ROBERT E	LTC	0-0038925	0562	1
GRENATA MICHAEL C	COL	0-0009304	0653	1
GRENOON ALEXANDER	COL	0-0039506	1054	1
GRENELLE EDWIN W	COL	0-0038757	0154	1
GRENIER WILLIAM T	COL	0-0030167	0464	1
GRENON JEANNETTE	LTC	N-0001002	0567	2
GRESHAM JR HONSEY T	LTC	0-0045076	0664	1
GRESHAM WENIFORD F	CW4	W-0903180	0160	1
GRETSER GEORGE R	COL	0-0019126	0863	1
GREUBEL ARVEL A	CW3	RW-0904427	1164	1
GREVERT HARRY C	LTC	0-0056077	0966	1
GRICE LETCHER O	B G	0-0008273	0753	1
GRICE THORPE C	LTC	0-0026326	0266	1
GRIDER EDGAR L	COL	0-0042112	1262	1
GRIDLEY JACK P	1LT	0-0066951	0254	2
GRIEGER ALLEN J	LTC	0-0061088	0867	1
GRIESBECK WILSON A	LTC	0-0040604	0766	1
GRIEVES JR LOREN C	MAJ	0-0022143	0148	2
GRIEVES WILLIAM P	COL	0-0019742	0865	1
GRIFFIN CAVID T	COL	0-0020600	0865	1
GRIFFIN JOSEPH	CW4	W-0901662	0660	1
GRIFFIN JR LINWOOD	COL	0-0043074	0767	1
GRIFFIN MARCUS S	COL	0-0019954	0865	1
GRIFFIN ROBERT J	LTC	0-0043005	0465	1
GRIFFIN THOMAS N	M G	0-0017775	0762	1
GRIFFIN WILLIAM E	COL	0-0011894	1050	1
GRIFFING LEWIS S	M G	0-0016413	0464	2
GRIFFITH EDWIN G	LTC	0-0017579	0345	2
GRIFFITH FREDERICK	COL	0-0001704	0642	2
GRIFFITH GEORGE W	1LT	0-0028338	0350	1
GRIFFITH GIRVAN H	MAJ	0-0060591	0963	1
GRIFFITH HENRY V	LTC	0-0069938	1067	1
GRIFFITH JACK H	COL	0-0016915	0857	2
GRIFFITH JR HAROLD S	LTC	0-0023403	0559	1
GRIFFITH RABUN W	LTC	0-0027326	0765	1
GRIFFITH ROBERT E	LTC	0-0080811	1066	1
GRIFFITH WILLIAM H	LTC	0-0044403	0661	1
GRIGG MARTIN C	LTC	0-0030711	0464	1
GRIGGS JOHN R	CW3	W-0906763	1060	1
GRIGGS OSCAR R	COL	0-0029315	0764	1
GRIGSBY ROBERT W	CW3	W-0903181	0862	1
GRILEY JOSEPH F	WO1	W-0901318	0138	2
GRILL HENRY S	MAJ	0-0067686	1265	1
GRIMES ALSTON	COL	0-0019252	0863	1
GRIMES ROBERT A	LTC	0-0042869	1064	1
GRIMME WALTER R	CW4	W-0902148	0364	1
GRIMMER EDWIN W	LTC	0-0005544	0342	2
GRIMSHAW CHARLES W	COL	0-0024872	0167	1
GRIMSLEY CARL E	LTC	0-0042568	0663	2
GRINER JR GEORGE W	M G	0-0007063	0846	1

NAME	GRADE	SVC NO	DATE RET MO YR	RET CODE
GRINSTEAD JOHN B	COL	0-0017134	0858	2
GRIPPER PAUL C	COL	0-0009715	0351	1
GRISCTI WALTER E	COL	0-0034666	0967	1
GRISSOM WILLIE M	MAJ	N-0001987	1164	1
GRISWOLD GEORGE M	COL	0-0031660	1067	1
GRISWOLD STANLEY F	COL	0-0007371	0854	2
GRIZZARD HARRY M	COL	0-0016521	0756	1
GROFF IRENE E	MAJ	L-0000316	0563	1
GROGAN GERARD J	LTC	0-0040429	1054	1
GROGAN JOHN F	COL	0-0042637	1065	1
GROGAN STANLEY J	COL	0-0007354	0951	1
GROH HORTENSE S	MAJ	N-0000256	0359	1
GROH MARY T	MAJ	N-0002008	0764	1
GRONBECK CHRISTIAN	COL	0-0026470	0663	1
GRONDONA RICHARD J	COL	0-0042439	1264	1
GROSE JOHN E	COL	0-0007540	0846	2
GROSECLOSE TOM S	LTC	0-0063108	1266	1
GROSJEAN DOLAS M	MAJ	L-0000027	1055	1
GROSS CHARLES A	COL	0-0030528	0364	1
GROSS CHARLES P	M G	0-0003662	1145	1
GROSS DONALD E	LTC	0-0027805	1065	1
GROSS FELIX E	COL	0-0003125	0546	2
GROSS GARDNER R	COL	0-0029859	1153	2
GROSSMAN HARRY J	COL	0-0022786	1066	2
GROSSMAN LELAND F	2LT	0-0066405	1053	2
GROTE ROBERT W	COL	0-0031717	1165	1
GROTHAUS DONALD G	B G	0-0020221	0466	1
GROTTE HELMER M	COL	0-0031622	1167	1
GROVE EDWARD A	COL	0-0020200	0363	2
GROVE JR WILLIAM R	COL	0-0015185	1052	1
GROVES JASPER M	COL	0-0008305	0646	2
GROVES JOSEPH R	COL	0-0020869	1064	1
GROVES LESLIE R	LTG	0-0012043	0248	1
GROVES WILLICE E	COL	0-0030075	0760	2
GROW ROBERT W	M G	0-0004621	0153	1
GROWDCK JOHN S	LTC	0-0019731	0655	1
GRUBBS ELMER W	COL	0-0020291	0866	1
GRUBBS HAYDON Y	COL	0-0016154	0755	1
GRUBBS WILLIAM E	COL	0-0019146	0760	1
GRUBE GEORGE	CW4	W-0903184	1163	1
GRUBER WILLIAM R	B G	0-0003465	0846	2
GRUBIN EDWARD L	CPT	0-0037635	1047	2
GRUENTHER ALFRED M	GEN	0-0012242	1056	2
GRUHLKEY EMORY M	CW3	W-0903185	1056	1
GRUHN ERNEST W	COL	0-0011192	0753	1
GRUNERT GEORGE	LTG	0-0001534	0745	2
GRUNERT GEORGE R	COL	0-0018859	1050	1
GRUVER GEORGE A	LTC	0-0031207	1060	1
GRZESICW THOMAS H	CPT	0-0070355	0961	1
GUEHRING RAYMOND R	COL	0-0051723	0264	2
GUENTHER AUGUSTUS J	COL	0-0031067	0666	1
GUEST LEROY A	CPT	0-0027013	1046	2
GUEST MARION I	LTC	0-0060856	0366	1
GUEST REVELL A	MAJ	N-0000195	0163	1
GUEST WESLEY T	B G	0-0014654	0859	1
GUEVARA SANTIAGO G	LTC	0-0015334	0753	1
GUICE BILLY W	LTC	0-0080815	0363	1
GUILD DONALD F	LTC	0-0080816	1165	1
GUILD EUGENE R	CPT	0-0014816	1138	2
GUIMOND JOSEPH A	COL	0-0026379	0167	1
GUINEY JR PATRICK W	COL	0-0019066	0756	1
GUION JAMES	COL	0-0005234	0753	1
GUIRAUD RENE J A	MAJ	0-0037942	0552	2
GUISLEMAN GEORGE V	LTC	0-0039793	1060	1
GUITERAS GEORGE G	MAJ	0-0019321	0344	1
GULETSKY WALTER N	LTC	0-0021309	0761	1
GULLATT DOSWELL	COL	0-0012100	0846	2
GULLION MAURICE B	COL	0-0042826	0364	1
GUNDERSON CLARENCE H	LTC	0-0018041	0758	1
GUNLOGSON ALICE	MAJ	N-0002194	0565	1
GUNN CLAUD T	COL	0-0014595	1042	1
GUNN CLEM C	COL	0-0014598	0447	2
GUNN DAMON M	COL	0-0015174	0753	1
GUNN FRANCIS C	LTC	N-0000095	0662	1
GUNNER EDWIN	COL	0-0001869	0642	1

NAME	GRADE	SVC NO	DATE RET MO YR	RET CODE
GUNNER MATTHEW J	B G	0-0003257	1046	1
GUNSTER WALTER E	COL	0-0022928	0467	1
GUNTHER CARL F	COL	0-0029193	0261	2
GURTILL COLIN K	CPT	0-0088265	0967	1
GURFEIN JOSEPH I	COL	0-0023734	0767	1
GURLEY FRANKLIN Y	LTC	0-0015244	0847	1
GURNEE JR WILLIAM H	COL	0-0023974	0863	1
GURSKY ALEX P	LTC	0-0080817	0364	1
GUSHURST CLARENCE F	LTC	0-0022998	0862	1
GUSTAFSON ARTHUR W	COL	0-0051404	0163	1
GUSTIN HARRY W	CW4	W-0903188	1054	2
GUTHRIDGE JOHN R	CW3	W-0903189	1066	1
GUTHRIE AARON S	COL	0-0050894	0555	1
GUTHRIE JAMES D	LTC	0-0031470	0958	1
GUTHRIE JOHN S	M G	0-0018228	0661	1
GUTHRIE PAUL G	COL	0-0030050	0165	1
GUTHRIE PAUL R	COL	0-0008027	1049	1
GUTHRIE RALPH R	LTC	0-0006462	0642	1
GUTHRIE RICHARD F	LTC	0-0049822	0763	1
GWALTNEY HELEN L	MAJ	N-0000210	0563	1
HAAG LUCILE M	MAJ	R-0010110	0963	1
HAAKENSEN NOBLE T	COL	0-0016589	1050	1
HAAS HARRY F	COL	0-0041385	0555	1
HABERER JR WALTER J	COL	0-0052278	1265	1
HABERMAN HOWARD F	COL	0-0040193	0154	1
HABIGER CHARLES F	CW4	W-0903190	0164	1
HACKER JOSEPH F	CW4	W-0903191	0558	1
HACKETT CHARLES J	COL	0-0021954	0867	1
HACKETT EDWARD J	LTC	0-0082019	0866	1
HACKETT PERRY R	LTC	0-0021443	0661	1
HACKETT WALLACE J	LTC	0-0023179	0561	1
HADFIELD WILLIAM A	COL	0-0029727	0662	1
HADFIELD WILLIAM A	COL	0-0029737	0662	1
HADLEY CLEO V	COL	0-0044086	1162	2
HADLEY LEO L	LTC	0-0042481	1262	1
HAEFELE JOSEPH L	COL	0-0080270	0567	1
HAEGELE IDA L	MAJ	N-0002640	0865	1
HAENISCH KATE E	MAJ	N-0000609	0663	1
HAESSLY BURDETT E	COL	0-0023016	0461	2
HAFF ALEXANDER	COL	0-0018260	1054	2
HAFF ROBERT A	CW4	W-0903192	0567	1
HAFFA ROBERT P	COL	0-0021809	0560	1
HAGAN JOHN F	COL	0-0042438	0964	2
HAGE GUNNAR H	COL	0-0029313	0464	1
HAGEDON GEORGE G	LTC	0-0027898	0966	1
HAGEN BERNARD E	COL	0-0029733	0762	1
HAGEN ROBERT P	COL	0-0021373	0966	1
HAGEN THOMAS J	COL	0-0020967	0565	2
HAGENS JOHN M	MAJ	0-0007988	1030	2
HAGERMAN CALVIN G	COL	0-0022252	1265	1
HAGERSTRAND MARTIN A	COL	0-0042957	1060	1
HAGERTY HARRY F	COL	0-0030685	0762	1
HAGERTY JR JAMES J	LTC	0-0082020	0667	1
HAGERTY WILLIAM A	COL	0-0041883	0661	1
HAGGARD EDWIN C	MAJ	0-0023081	0750	1
HAGGART ALEXANDER	COL	0-0010140	0550	1
HAGINS WILLIAM	B G	0-0004050	0448	2
HAGLER ETHEL I	MAJ	N-0002007	0864	1
HAGLER THOMAS	LTC	0-0027052	0863	1
HAGMAN CHARLES M	CW4	W-0903196	0263	1
HAGMAN FRANK C	COL	0-0041697	0459	1
HAGMAN JR CHARLES A	LTC	0-0063291	0766	1
HAGOOD JR JOHNSON	COL	0-0018452	1046	2
HAGUE JAMES F	CW4	W-0903197	0862	1
HAHN CORNMAN L	COL	0-0012063	0753	1
HAHN ERIC L	LTC	0-0065075	0165	1
HAHN LAWSON E	COL	0-0029650	0262	2
HAHN RUSSELL S	COL	0-0056815	0964	1
HAHN THOMAS H	COL	0-0038609	1056	1
HAHNEY EVERETT G	COL	0-0020185	0866	1
HAIG CHESTER R	COL	0-0003303	0247	1
HAIL CLFBERT L	COL	0-0017779	0859	1
HAILE WILLIAM G	LTC	0-0080097	0567	1
HAIN ROBERT W	COL	0-0019072	0863	1
HAINES AUBREY M	LTC	0-0087525	0866	1

NAME	GRADE	SVC NO	DATE RET MO YR	RET CODE
HAINES HAROLD H	LTC	0-0039868	1161	1
HAINES OLIVER L	B G	0-0004670	0951	1
HAINES RALPH E	B G	0-0002991	0845	1
HAINES ROBERT G	COL	0-0029460	0960	1
HAINES ROBERT L	COL	0-0039994	1265	1
HAINES WILLIAM F	CW4	W-0503198	0457	1
HAINS III PETER C	M G	0-0015657	0561	1
HAISLEY CHESTER D	COL	0-0010175	0652	1
HAISLIP WADE H	GEN	0-0003374	0751	1
HAKALA EDWIN W	COL	0-0021456	0758	1
HAKANSON VALERIUS	COL	0-0041371	0155	2
HALADA ROLAND J	COL	0-0042635	0662	2
HALBERT EDWARD C	COL	0-0003615	0444	1
HALDEMAN WILLIAM T	COL	0-0004992	0-45	2
HALE HARRY R	COL	0-0019828	0863	1
HALE MAURICE W	COL	0-0017323	1056	1
HALE MILTON B	COL	0-0041681	1059	1
HALE RALPH N	COL	0-0043968	0863	1
HALE ROBERT A	COL	0-0004174	0744	2
HALE THURMAN A	LTC	0-0030275	0163	2
HALE WILLIAM A	LTC	0-0008238	0935	2
HALE WILLIAM C	LTC	0-0036124	0767	1
HALE WILLIAM H	COL	0-0022184	0265	1
HALEY JOHN J	COL	0-0079835	0167	1
HALEY THEODORE E	COL	0-0006637	1047	1
HALEY 3RD CHARLES L	COL	0-0021226	0859	1
HALL ALLEN K	MAJ	0-0058421	0167	1
HALL ALPHUS W	LTC	0-0054490	1165	1
HALL AUGUSTUS A	COL	0-0051127	0258	1
HALL CARL C	COL	0-0030722	0763	1
HALL CLAUDE H	LTC	0-0047794	0966	1
HALL DEWITT A	COL	0-0022083	0462	1
HALL EARL H	COL	0-0038658	0961	1
HALL FENA F	MAJ	N-0002286	1264	1
HALL ETHEL E L	MAJ	N-0002399	0962	1
HALL FRANCIS G	COL	0-0018794	0262	1
HALL GEORGE P	LTC	0-0080826	0364	1
HALL HARRELL G	COL	0-0051580	0163	1
HALL HARRY A	COL	0-0051819	0861	1
HALL HARRY H	LTC	0-0058913	0766	1
HALL HERBERT A	B G	0-0041631	1159	1
HALL JAMES D	CW3	W-0906767	0467	2
HALL JAMES W	LTC	0-0040692	0867	1
HALL JOHN	LTC	0-0009884	0-40	1
HALL JOSEPH S	LTC	0-0096629	0763	1
HALL JR CHESTER A	COL	0-0048018	1167	2
HALL JR FREDERICK	COL	0-0019747	0761	1
HALL JR JOHN R	COL	0-0023576	0364	1
HALL JR RICHARD E	COL	0-0032330	0765	1
HALL JR TURNER P	LTC	0-0060738	1167	1
HALL JR WILLIAM W	LTC	0-0028005	1167	1
HALL LEWIS A	COL	0-0040085	0766	1
HALL RALPH	COL	0-0005488	0-44	1
HALL ROBERT J	COL	0-0031882	0765	1
HALL ROBERT W	LTC	0-0070358	1067	1
HALL ROBERT S	COL	0-0029174	0258	1
HALL ROY F	CPT	0-0007783	0629	1
HALL SAMUEL L	COL	0-0051584	0960	1
HALL SYLVESTER	COL	0-0040057	1062	1
HALL WILBUR T	LTC	0-0042909	1253	1
HALL WILLIAM C	B G	0-0018391	0463	1
HALLA CARL	COL	0-0004393	0742	1
HALLAM CLYDE W	COL	0-0011587	0554	1
HALLAREN MARY A	COL	L-0000001	0760	1
HALLDEN CHARLES H	LTC	0-0030360	0163	1
HALLINGER ELMER E	LTC	0-0021212	0656	1
HALLINGER JR EARL S	COL	0-0069497	1067	1
HALLMAN LAURA L	MAJ	N-0001636	0864	2
HALLMEYER LAWRENCE O	CW4	W-0904414	1053	1
HALLOCK DUNCAN	B G	0-0018960	0863	1
HALLOCK HOUGHTON V	COL	0-0020612	0657	1
HALLOCK RICHARD R	COL	0-0037767	0667	1
HALLOCK ROBERT F	COL	0-0015113	0854	2
HALLORAN MICHAEL E	COL	0-0007502	0854	1
HALLOWAY HARRY A	CW4	W-0902058	0656	2

NAME	GRADE	SVC NO	DATE RET MO YR	RET CODE
HALLOWAY KENNETH E	CW4	W-0902114	0558	1
HALLOWELL MARGARET O	MAJ	L-0000233	0961	2
HALLUMS JAMES R	LTC	O-0032564	1263	1
HALONEN ALICE S	MAJ	N-0001001	0664	1
HALPIN DANIEL E	COL	O-0024957	1066	1
HALSEY FRANK W	COL	O-0009686	0446	2
HALSEY MILTON R	M G	O-0005305	0153	1
HALSTEAD FRANK	COL	O-0000698	0-26	2
HALSTEAD LESLIE H	LTC	O-0026848	0164	1
HALSTEAD WILLIAM H	COL	O-0005203	0146	2
HALTER BRYAN S	COL	O-0012493	0450	1
HALTERMAN HARRY W	LTC	O-0017209	0549	1
HALTOM JOHN D	LTC	O-0020788	0445	2
HALVERSON HERMAN C	MAJ	O-0007971	1035	2
HALVORSON JOHN A	MAJ	O-0081450	0966	1
HAMBERG WILLIAM A	COL	O-0030741	0661	2
HAMBLEN ARCHELAUS	B G	O-0004731	0754	1
HAMBLIN JAMES M	LTC	O-0025127	0963	1
HAMELE LOUIS F	COL	O-0032610	0965	1
HAMERSLEY DWIGHT T	COL	O-0042159	0363	1
HAMES SARRATT T	COL	O-0015845	0953	2
HAMILL JAMES P	COL	O-0025324	0461	1
HAMILTON AONA C	COL	O-0012480	0454	1
HAMILTON ALLAN C	COL	O-0042456	1163	1
HAMILTON ANDREW W	COL	O-0029767	0962	1
HAMILTON CHARLES S	COL	O-0001759	0239	1
HAMILTON EARL M	COL	O-0030398	0363	1
HAMILTON EDWARD S	LTC	O-0022165	0546	2
HAMILTON FRANK O	LTC	O-0024532	0661	1
HAMILTON FRED L	COL	O-0012716	1147	2
HAMILTON GLADEN R	COL	O-0020089	1152	1
HAMILTON HOMER G	COL	O-0039781	0657	1
HAMILTON J ARTHUR	COL	O-0042294	0661	1
HAMILTON JAMES R	COL	O-0014627	0854	1
HAMILTON JOHN H	COL	O-0010268	0753	1
HAMILTON JR PURLEY W	CW4	W-0906770	0166	2
HAMILTON JR STUART A	LTC	O-0036152	0864	1
HAMILTON LAVERSA M	1LT	M-0000434	0446	1
HAMILTON PAUL	COL	O-0016455	0656	1
HAMILTON RAYMOND C	COL	O-0008303	0753	1
HAMILTON STEPHEN S	COL	O-0015934	0754	1
HAMILTON WILBUR A	LTC	O-0052352	0862	1
HAMILTON WILLIAM L	LTC	O-0010031	0842	2
HAMILTON WILLIAM T	COL	O-0005777	0854	1
HAMLIN GUY A	LTC	O-0063740	0967	1
HAMLIN JOHN A	CW3	W-0903203	0858	2
HAMLIN WILLIAM D	M G	O-0017619	1062	2
HAMM ISSAC B	CW4	W-0902272	0865	1
HAMMACK LOUIS A	COL	O-0017696	0859	1
HAMMARLUND MABEL	LTC	N-0002057	0164	1
HAMMER JAMES E	COL	O-0024599	0967	1
HAMMER WALTER D	LTC	O-0060769	1065	1
HAMMERNESS OSCAR T	LTC	O-0039752	1059	1
HAMMERSBERG ROBERT F	COL	O-0018933	1062	1
HAMMON BERNARD C	COL	O-0020922	0266	1
HAMMOND CLAUDE G	COL	O-0005193	0646	2
HAMMOND DAVID G	COL	O-0020868	0764	1
HAMMOND ELTON F	B G	O-0012291	0854	1
HAMMOND JOHN W	COL	O-0017656	1058	1
HAMMOND JR THOMAS W	COL	O-0017622	0859	1
HAMMOND JR WILLIAM H	LTC	O-0044213	0261	1
HAMMONDS VERNON	COL	O-0051486	1061	2
HAMNER MERLE E	LTC	O-0052805	0262	1
HAMPTON MABEL E	MAJ	J-0000001	0764	1
HAMPTON MCLEAN	LTC	O-0032239	1065	1
HAMPTON WADE F	LTC	O-0043190	0666	2
HAMPTON WILLIAM A	COL	O-0018482	0761	1
HAMRICK ERASTUS N	CW4	W-0903206	0766	1
HANBURGER CHRISTIAN	COL	O-0020554	0866	1
HANCHETT JR FRED P	1LT	O-0009815	0622	2
HANCOCK DANIEL W	COL	O-0035281	0966	1
HANCOCK WILLIAM F	LTC	O-0045013	0762	1
HAND CHARLES M	COL	O-0051669	1265	1
HAND CLIFTON E	LTC	O-0080832	0966	1
HAND HARRY V	LTC	O-0005710	0342	2

NAME	GRADE	SVC NO	DATE RET MO YR	RET CODE
HAND JAMES D	COL	O-0030328	1264	1
HAND ROBERT	LTC	O-0036415	0766	1
HAND ROBERT C	LTC	O-0032294	0765	1
HANDLEY ARTHUR L	WO1	W-0800232	1135	2
HANDLEY JR ARTHUR L	LTC	O-0026884	0865	'
HANDY THOMAS T	GEN	O-0004665	0354	1
HANEY HAROLD	B G	O-0006807	0753	1
HANEY LEE W	COL	O-0014628	1146	2
HANFORD EDWARD C	COL	O-0003317	0742	2
HANFORD THOMAS R	COL	O-0029660	1061	1
HANGER JOHN W	COL	O-0039975	0465	1
HANKEL HALLAND W	LTC	O-0044045	0862	1
HANKINSON JR FRANK E	COL	O-0028884	1056	1
HANKS JAMES K	LTC	O-0042473	1162	1
HANKS LESTER	LTC	O-0030339	0163	1
HANLE WILLIAM D	CPT	O-0060348	0762	1
HANLEY JAMES F	COL	O-0039591	1058	1
HANLEY JAMES M	COL	O-0041688	0660	1
HANLEY JAMES M	CW4	W-0903209	0961	1
HANLEY JOHN F	MAJ	O-0006838	0639	2
HANLON JOHN B	1LT	O-0099740	0366	2
HANMER STEPHEN R	M G	O-0018348	0664	1
HANNA EDWARD J	MAJ	O-0037610	0762	1
HANNA ELIZABETH	LTC	N-0002026	0760	1
HANNA FRED S	COL	O-0038612	1057	1
HANNA GEORGE T	COL	O-0052758	0764	1
HANNA HOMER H	MAJ	O-0069499	1264	1
HANNA LLOYD M	COL	O-0009789	0148	2
HANNA LOYD G	LTC	O-0035843	0564	1
HANNA THOMAS G	COL	O-0080834	0965	1
HANNAH LAUREN F	COL	O-0051358	1162	1
HANNAH THOMAS R	COL	O-0018899	0862	1
HANNIGAN JAMES P	B G	O-0017531	0859	1
HANNIGAN KATHRYN O	LTC	N-0000150	0358	2
HANNIS HENRY E	COL	O-0012618	0750	1
HANNON ALBERT J	COL	O-0042175	0763	1
HANNUM ROBERT C	LTC	O-0056048	0966	1
HANSBOROUGH JOHN W	COL	O-0018376	0761	1
HANSELL HAYWOOD S	COL	O-0001453	0639	1
HANSEN EVERETT A	COL	O-0023528	0760	1
HANSEN FLOYD A	M G	O-0019767	0667	2
HANSEN GEORGE K	LTC	O-0058916	0867	1
HANSEN GEORGE R	LTC	O-0052571	0164	1
HANSEN HARRY F	COL	O-0042618	1161	2
HANSEN HERBERT C	COL	O-0079842	1065	1
HANSEN HOWARD M	LTC	O-0024554	0547	2
HANSEN IRVING S	CW4	W-0901152	0252	1
HANSON AFELLCN F	LTC	O-0025301	0461	1
HANSON CHARLES C	COL	O-0039873	0660	1
HANSON JACK R	1LT	O-0062628	0153	1
HANSON JR THOMAS G	COL	O-0005572	0445	2
HANSON PAUL P	2LT	O-0015336	0927	2
HANSON RUSSELL H	LTC	O-0052615	0961	1
HANSON WALTER S	LTC	O-0079845	0965	1
HANST JR KENNETH F	MAJ	O-0024733	0348	2
HARANT LOUIS J	LTC	O-0010961	0924	2
HARBACK HERBERT O	LTC	O-0044880	0766	1
HARBER WILLIAM V	COL	O-0039578	0658	1
HARDAGE JOHN M	LTC	O-0069500	0967	1
HARDAGE QUENTIN R	LTC	O-0035276	0848	2
HARDAWAY EADS G	B G	O-0020855	0766	1
HARDAWAY FRANCIS R	B G	O-0002671	0449	1
HARDAWAY ROBERT M	B G	O-0003307	0848	2
HARDEE DAVID L	COL	O-0011903	1049	1
HARDEN JR HARRISON B	COL	O-0019818	1064	1
HARDENBERGH ELMER P	B G	O-0028940	1060	2
HARDENBERGH HAL	COL	O-0032740	0766	1
HARDESTY LAWRENCE R	LTC	O-0030996	0757	2
HARDICK WILLIAM L	B G	O-0018558	0661	1
HARDIMAN RALPH S	COL	O-0030492	0765	1
HARDIN DONALD C	COL	O-0012435	0147	2
HARDIN GAEDA N	LTC	N-0000838	0264	1
HARDIN JOHN R	M G	O-0012283	0657	1
HARDIN TOLBERT F	MAJ	O-0002906	0921	2
HARDIN WILLIAM R	COL	O-0030581	0164	1

NAME	GRADE	SVC NO	DATE RET MO YR	RET CODE
HARDING EDWIN F	M G	O-0002628	1046	1
HARDING FLOYD C	COL	O-0007404	0851	1
HARDING HENRY J P	COL	O-0015179	0954	1
HARDING HORACE	B G	O-0009530	0653	1
HARDING STANLEY L	B G	O-0032134	0666	2
HARDMAN MABEL O	MAJ	N-0000853	0163	2
HARDMAN TRACY J	LTC	O-0033007	0165	1
HARDMAN WAYNE	COL	O-0030072	1061	1
HARDWICK ARTHUR R	CW4	W-0901707	0160	1
HARDY CLARENCE W	COL	O-0017835	1153	2
HARDY CONRAD R	COL	O-0011360	1052	1
HARDY EARL C	LTC	O-0027582	0766	1
HARDY HARRY B	LTC	O-0041238	0866	1
HARDY JR DAVID E	MAJ	O-0069665	1064	1
HARE RAY M	B G	O-0006943	0753	1
HARGIS JR THOMAS B	COL	O-0023076	1048	2
HARGRAVE WARREN M	LTC	O-0032071	1058	1
HARGROVE BYRON E	LTC	O-0051202	0259	1
HARGROVE EDNA	MAJ	N-0001880	0360	1
HARGUS LOWELL U	COL	O-0030315	0265	2
HARING ELLIS F	COL	O-0008122	0548	1
HARING LAURA MS	LTC	L-0000022	0658	1
HARKINS ANNA O	MAJ	N-0001416	1264	2
HARKINS BASIL A	COL	O-0051015	0359	1
HARKINS DONALD E	LTC	O-0065217	0767	1
HARKINS PAUL D	GEN	O-0017625	0864	1
HARKLERODD CANA L	LTC	O-0051598	0463	1
HARKNESS LAWRENCE R	LTC	O-0040066	0663	1
HARLAN EDWIN F	LTC	O-0025343	0867	1
HARLAN JOHN F	COL	O-0050949	0557	1
HARLAN ROBERT D	LTC	O-0035861	0861	1
HARLLEE FRANCES E	LTC	L-0000532	0866	1
HARLLEE ROBERT L	LTC	O-0044146	0166	1
HARLOE BARTLEY M	COL	O-0008561	1049	1
HARLOW MARGARET H	MAJ	L-0000309	0462	1
HARMAN THELMA A	LTC	R-0010092	1167	1
HARMELING HENRY	COL	O-0007875	0846	2
HARMELING JR HENRY	LTC	O-0024843	0962	1
HARMON CLYDE G	CW4	W-0902409	0655	1
HARMON ERNEST N	M G	O-0005282	0248	1
HARMON WILLIAM J	CW4	W-0904122	1058	1
HARMONSON LOUIS H	CW2	W-0901911	1146	1
HARMONY JOHN W	M G	O-0015240	1059	2
HARNAR ALLEN H	COL	O-0042470	0265	1
HARNED BEN G	CW3	W-0903216	0556	1
HARNESS LESLIE J	COL	O-0023415	1166	2
HARNETT HELEN	MAJ	N-0002151	0362	1
HARNETT JOHN S	COL	O-0023094	1160	1
HARNEY JR CHARLES J	CPT	O-0049704	1147	2
HARNSTROM EDMUND V	LTC	O-0032414	0165	1
HAROUFF DONALD L	MAJ	O-0065165	0765	1
HARP CLIFFORD E	MAJ	O-0063800	0664	2
HARPER ADAM W	LTC	O-0060395	0266	1
HARPER ARTHUR MCK	M G	O-0005288	1053	2
HARPER JAMES C	LTC	O-0063379	0866	1
HARPER JAMES E	COL	O-0042404	0564	1
HARPER JOSEPH H	M G	O-0015083	1159	1
HARPER JR PHILIP V	1LT	OF-0104774	1067	2
HARPER MARGARET	COL	N-0000147	1163	1
HARPER NEAL A	B G	O-0004025	0852	2
HARPER NEAL W	COL	O-0030262	0860	1
HARPOLD HARLEY O	COL	O-0041831	0459	2
HARPOLE HUGH S	COL	O-0012528	0347	1
HARPOLE RUSSELL C	COL	O-0029023	1058	1
HARR EMMA T	MAJ	M-0010004	0658	2
HARRE ELMER C	LTC	O-0051577	0352	1
HARRELL CLYDE V	CW4	W-0902140	0455	1
HARRELL JAMES L	LTC	O-0085178	0867	1
HARRELL JOE	COL	O-0018929	0256	1
HARRELSON ELMER H	COL	O-0042350	0464	1
HARRELSON JOSEPH S	COL	O-0062119	0667	1
HARRIGAN THOMAS L	LTC	O-0043538	0964	1
HARRINGTON EDWIN J	COL	O-0041587	0457	1
HARRINGTON JAMES B	LTC	O-0027455	0865	1
HARRINGTON JAMES L	LTC	O-0065221	0867	1

NAME	GRADE	SVC NO	DATE RET MO YR	RET CODE
HARRINGTON JOHN H	COL	O-0006359	0753	1
HARRINGTON PATRICK W	COL	O-0033372	1167	1
HARRINGTON ROBERT H	LTC	O-0056543	0566	1
HARRIOTT DONALD B	B G	O-0029631	0958	2
HARRIS AARON E	COL	O-0019712	0656	1
HARRIS ALAN W	CW4	W-0903219	0462	2
HARRIS ARTHUR R	B G	O-0003676	0448	2
HARRIS BENJAMIN T	B G	O-0019166	0863	1
HARRIS CECIL F	CW3	W-0903220	1060	1
HARRIS CHARLES E	COL	O-0046675	0463	1
HARRIS CHARLES K	LTC	O-0023848	0767	1
HARRIS CHARLES S	B G	O-0007284	0753	1
HARRIS EDWARD E	CW4	W-0903221	0157	1
HARRIS EDWARD M	COL	O-0019819	0961	1
HARRIS FRANKIE D	MAJ	N-0000579	1161	1
HARRIS FREDERICK	B G	O-0012750	0854	1
HARRIS HARRY B	LTC	O-0062165	0766	1
HARRIS HERBERT H	COL	O-0011817	0854	1
HARRIS HERBERT K	LTC	O-0040600	0262	1
HARRIS HUGH P	GEN	O-0018518	0365	1
HARRIS JACK R	COL	O-0044544	0963	1
HARRIS JESSE T	COL	O-0011920	0249	1
HARRIS JOHN F	COL	O-0058751	0865	1
HARRIS JOHN P	COL	O-0009115	0852	1
HARRIS JOSEPH	COL	O-0012703	0451	1
HARRIS JUNE O	MAJ	N-0001182	1265	1
HARRIS KATHLEEN R	LTC	L-0000145	0263	1
HARRIS LEE V	COL	O-0010823	0854	1
HARRIS LEON M	COL	O-0080840	0866	1
HARRIS LEONARD H	MAJ	O-0063127	0467	1
HARRIS MARGOT L	MAJ	L-0000243	0962	1
HARRIS MURRAY D	COL	O-0029048	1058	1
HARRIS PAUL A	COL	O-0014624	1153	2
HARRIS ROBERT C	COL	O-0030529	1165	1
HARRIS RONALD V	MAJ	O-0069670	0166	1
HARRIS RUSSEL D	COL	O-0039671	0460	1
HARRIS WILLIAM A	M G	O-0018976	1166	2
HARRIS WILLIAM H	B G	O-0018155	0565	1
HARRIS WILLIAM W	B G	O-0018170	0460	1
HARRISON CHARLES E	LTC	O-0022953	0862	1
HARRISON DENNIS J	LTC	O-0058921	0667	1
HARRISON EDWIN H	COL	O-0015573	0854	1
HARRISON EUGENE L	B G	O-0015265	1053	1
HARRISON FRANCIS B	COL	O-0021147	0866	1
HARRISON FRANK R	COL	O-0020858	0662	1
HARRISON GEORGE P	CPT	O-0016353	1041	1
HARRISON HAROLD E	COL	O-0020078	0764	2
HARRISON JAMES J	LTC	O-0080844	0867	1
HARRISON JOHN H	LTC	O-0040121	1161	1
HARRISON JOSEPH H	COL	O-0031396	0865	1
HARRISON JR GEORGE R	LTC	O-0022152	0659	1
HARRISON JR W K	LTG	O-0005279	0257	1
HARRISON MATTHEW C	COL	O-0023875	0764	1
HARRISON REGINALD W	CW4	W-0903223	0557	1
HARRISON RICHARD H	B G	O-0018409	0661	1
HARRISON ROGER B	COL	O-0003723	0446	1
HARRISON WILLIAM C	LTC	O-0020091	0546	2
HARRISON WILLIAM F	COL	O-0029991	0963	1
HARROLD THOMAS L	LTG	O-0016051	0661	1
HARRON JAMES A	LTC	O-0041615	0857	1
HARROP JOHN W	LTC	O-0038136	1065	2
HARRY JOHN	COL	O-0014750	0753	1
HARSTAD LEROY O	MAJ	O-0060453	0663	1
HART ALACIN J	COL	O-0012758	0650	1
HART CATHERINE	MAJ	L-0000065	1059	1
HART CHARLES E	LTG	O-0015788	0760	1
HART HARRY L	LTC	O-0030241	0862	1
HART IRA W	LTC	O-0029808	1060	1
HART JOHN J	LTC	O-0051618	0463	1
HART JOHN L	MAJ	O-0062261	0167	1
HART JOHN M	COL	O-0034665	0867	1
HART JOHN S	CW4	W-0902363	0557	1
HART RICHARD V	COL	O-0038732	1262	1
HART ROSEMARY	MAJ	L-0000311	0962	1
HART WALTER	CPT	O-0005828	0132	1

NAME	GRADE	SVC NO	DATE RET MO YR	RET CODE
HARTEL FREDERICK	B G	0-0019254	1066	2
HARTFORD ELLIS W	CPT	0-0008112	1122	2
HARTFORD THOMAS J	M G	0-0018330	C961	1
HARTGERING JAMES B	COL	0-0049931	0664	1
HARTH JOHN F	LTC	0-0036997	0764	1
HARTLEY GLENN E	LTC	0-0084367	1067	1
HARTLEY LEROY P	COL	0-0005958	1151	2
HARTLEY MARY E	LTC	N-0001375	C467	1
HARTMAN ALLISON R	COL	0-0017204	1053	2
HARTMAN CARL W	LTC	0-0062171	C166	1
HARTMAN DURELL B	LTC	0-0039466	C666	1
HARTMAN GEORGE E	B G	0-0006538	0454	2
HARTMAN HENRY M	COL	0-0044177	0766	1
HARTMAN JACOB L	B G	0-0009551	0654	1
HARTMAN LINTON Y	LTC	0-0010008	1041	1
HARTMAN LULU J	MAJ	N-0001724	0964	1
HARTMAN NORMAN E	COL	0-0010269	0753	1
HARTMAN ROLAND F	COL	0-0041872	0561	1
HARTNESS HARLAN N	M G	0-0012269	1054	1
HARTON THOMAS G	COL	C-0042385	C364	1
HARTRIDGE THEODORE L	LTC	0-0022763	0959	1
HARTSHORN JR EDWIN S	B G	0-0018716	0862	1
HARTSOCK RAYMOND J	CW3	W-0906776	0163	1
HARTUNG HERBERT W	LTC	0-0044261	1066	1
HARVEY CLYDE E	CW3	RW-0903226	0463	1
HARVEY DWIGHT	LTC	0-0016220	0753	1
HARVEY JAMES V	MAJ	0-0068012	0866	2
HARVEY JOHN B	LTC	0-0047778	0760	2
HARVEY JOHN J	LTC	0-0006241	0741	1
HARVEY MAXINE F	MAJ	N-0001425	0463	1
HARVEY MURRAY L	LTC	0-0038833	C661	1
HARVEY OLIVER C	M G	0-0038776	0866	1
HARVEY RAYMOND J	B G	C-0020116	C866	1
HARVEY ROBERT C	CPT	0-0023492	0743	2
HARVEY THOMAS H	COL	0-0018817	C862	1
HARVEY WILLIAM T	COL	0-0080846	0967	1
HARVIE CHESTER T	LTC	0-0025138	C962	1
HARWELL MACLOLM H	COL	0-001646C	0756	1
HARWOOD EDWARD C	COL	0-0012615	0137	1
HASBROUCK ROBERT W	M G	0-0008588	0947	2
HASBROUCK SHERMAN V	B G	0-0012744	0855	1
HASELMIRE NORA C	MAJ	N-0000643	0463	1
HASEMAN LEONARD L	COL	0-0022925	C366	2
HASH WILLIAM A	LTC	0-0036625	0566	1
HASKELL HAROLD G	COL	0-0030588	0862	2
HASKELL JAMES B	COL	0-0003708	C846	1
HASKELL JOSEPH F	COL	0-0018197	1146	1
HASKELL LOUIS W	COL	0-0015226	0854	1
HASKELL ROBERT K	COL	0-0015097	0454	1
HASKIN JAY R	MAJ	0-0011044	0934	2
HASLAM JAMES I	MAJ	C-0033C79	0162	1
HASLEY CLARENCE F	CW3	W-0907144	C264	1
HASS MARTIN F	B G	0-0015889	C754	1
HASSELBACK FREDERICK	COL	0-0022673	C865	1
HASSENFELT HAROLD E	COL	0-0022195	C760	1
HASSLOCK LOUIS W	COL	0-0005017	0348	1
HASSMAN PHILLIP E	LTC	0-0059972	0866	1
HASSON JOHN P	COL	C-0001190	0442	1
HASTING HOWARD F	COL	0-0039676	0460	1
HASTINGS ALBERT J	COL	0-0011721	1046	1
HASTINGS HENRY S	LTC	0-0032830	0561	1
HASTINGS KESTER L	M G	0-0012219	0357	1
HASTINGS WILLIAM C	COL	0-0031248	C867	1
HASTINGS WILLIAM P	LTC	C-C050054	1066	1
HASWELL CLAUDE E	COL	0-0012731	0137	1
HATCH CARL H	COL	0-0029341	C764	1
HATCH FRANK E	CW4	W-0903227	C557	1
HATCH HOWARD G	CW4	W-0903228	0760	1
HATCH JOHN F	COL	0-C003073	0946	1
HATCH MCCLACHLIN	COL	0-0025578	C966	1
HATCH MELTON A	COL	0-0012136	C854	1
HATFIELD MILLS C	COL	0-C023741	C864	2
HATFIELD RALPH H	COL	0-0039755	C362	2
HATHAWAY GAYNOR W	LTC	0-0025124	0262	1
HATHAWAY JAMES L	COL	C-0017215	0758	1
HATHAWAY LEANDER R	COL	0-0004752	0151	1
HATHAWAY PAUL	MAJ	0-0004567	0934	2
HATTAN ROY E	COL	0-0017563	0859	1
HATTOX JAMES G	COL	0-0030253	1263	1
HAUCK JR CLARENCE J	M G	0-0018260	0160	1
HAUGHEY JOHN E	COL	0-0029142	0558	1
HAUSCHULTZ EARL H	COL	0-0042789	0566	2
HAUSE MABEL E	MAJ	N-0000045	1050	1
HAUSEMAN DAVID N	B G	0-0010511	0946	1
HAUSER JOHN N	COL	C-0003358	0549	1
HAUSER JOHN R	LTC	0-0037946	0866	1
HAUSER ROBERT L	CW4	W-0906778	0163	2
HAUSMAN WILLIAM	COL	0-0058273	1066	1
HAVEN SAMUEL R	COL	0-001797C	0360	1
HAVEY SYLVESTER	CW2	W-0901211	0945	2
HAW JOSEPH C	COL	0-0003826	0353	1
HAWES BENJAMIN W	COL	0-0019929	0347	2
HAWES GLENN A	COL	0-0042077	0861	1
HAWES HAROLD V	LTC	0-0052711	0166	1
HAWHEE GUY E	CW4	W-090323C	0258	1
HAWKINS ARTHUR C	CPT	0-0007171	0822	2
HAWKINS ARTHUR O	CPT	C-0015495	0132	2
HAWKINS JEAN M	MAJ	R-001C093	0963	1
HAWKINS JONATHAN O	COL	0-0016629	1154	1
HAWKINS JR JAMES J	LTC	0-0045759	0763	1
HAWKINS RUSSELL L	COL	0-001996C	0865	1
HAWKINS SAMUEL F	COL	0-0003221	0142	1
HAWKINSON CARROLL G	LTC	0-0C22318	0859	1
HAWKSWORTH F W	LTC	0-0043619	1160	2
HAWLEY HARVEY O	LTC	0-0C50402	0964	1
HAWLEY ROBERT C	CPT	0-0028254	0658	2
HAWORTH VIOLET	MAJ	N-0002430	0965	1
HAWTHORNE WILLIAM B	COL	0-0016512	0756	1
HAXTHAUSEN HALLEENE	MAJ	M-0010110	0567	1
HAYCOCK CHESTER P	COL	0-0007877	1146	2
HAYCOCK WILLIAM M	COL	C-0031712	1166	1
HAYCRAFT KENNETH C	COL	C-0C29704	0861	1
HAYDEL JUANITA F	MAJ	N-000190C	0761	1
HAYDEN EVERETT C	LTC	0-0017744	0749	1
HAYDEN FREDERIC L	B G	0-0012627	0955	2
HAYDEN HERBERT B	LTC	0-0013936	0620	2
HAYDEN JAMES L	COL	C-0005254	0740	2
HAYDEN OAKES M	LTC	0-006C327	0866	1
HAYDEN RAY R	MAJ	C-0065131	0164	1
HAYDEN ROBERT F	CW4	W-0903233	1263	1
HAYDEN ROBERT H	COL	0-0042356	1262	1
HAYDON PERCY S	COL	0-0006767	0948	1
HAYENGA VIRGINIA P	MAJ	N-0001976	0462	1
HAYES EDWARD S	LTC	0-0014232	0220	2
HAYES JAMES H	COL	0-0024646	0765	1
HAYES JAMES L	CW4	W-0903234	0857	1
HAYES JOHN G	1LT	0-0059331	1051	2
HAYES JOHNNIE M	CW4	W-0903235	1158	1
HAYES KATHERINE	LTC	N-0000688	0462	1
HAYES LEO V	LTC	0-0026213	0965	1
HAYES LINCOLN R	LTC	0-008C851	0566	1
HAYES PAUL	COL	0-0017809	0559	1
HAYES PAUL W	COL	0-0030903	0361	1
HAYES ROBERT L	LTC	0-0041016	0263	1
HAYES SALLY C	LTC	N-0001241	0767	1
HAYES TAYLOR C T	LTC	0-0043542	0364	1
HAYES THOMAS F	COL	0-0034738	0867	1
HAYES WAYNE A	COL	0-0020486	0167	1
HAYES WILLIAM P	COL	0-0011655	0763	1
HAYFORD BERTRAM F	M G	0-0012272	1155	1
HAYFORD 3RD WARREN	COL	0-001C347	C854	1
HAYMAN GEORGE R	COL	0-0007225	0851	1
HAYMAN JR GEORGE R	LTC	0-0026576	0865	1
HAYNE FRANK B	COL	0-0006446	1147	2
HAYNE JR PAUL	LTC	0-0039619	0657	1
HAYNES ALLEN F	COL	0-001260C	0954	1
HAYNES ASHTON H	COL	0-0018545	0761	1
HAYNES CHARLEY W	LTC	C-0043715	0764	1
HAYNES CHESTER H	LTC	0-0080854	C767	1
HAYNES EDITH S	LTC	N-0000090	0157	1
HAYNES HAROLD M	MAJ	C-0011556	0934	2
HAYNES INEZ	COL	N-0000088	C859	1
HAYNES JAMES R	1LT	0-0014360	C518	2
HAYNES LOYAL M	B G	0-0008379	0754	2
HAYNES RETURN C	MAJ	C-0063102	0964	1
HAYNES THOMAS E	COL	C-0076883	C766	1
HAYS GEORGE P	LTG	0-0007149	0453	1
HAYWARD CECELIA L	MAJ	N-0001062	C662	1
HAYWARD HAROLD S	LTC	0-0051213	C459	2
HAYWORTH HELEN G	MAJ	N-0002128	C360	1
HAZEL CHARLES E	LTC	C-0039260	0363	1
HAZLEHURST MAX W	COL	C-0038723	C862	1
HAZLETT HOWARD	COL	C-0038621	1058	1
HAZLETT ROBERT T	COL	0-0039792	0461	1
HEA JAMES J	COL	0-0008661	0753	1
HEAD HAROLD S	LTC	0-0026272	C766	1
HEAD NELSON L	COL	0-0018814	0158	1
HEALEY MICHAEL V	1LT	0-0015041	0927	2
HEALTON CURTIS E	LTC	0-0032275	0764	1
HEALY JOHN H	MAJ	0-0010129	C235	2
HEALY JOHN J	LTC	0-0039707	C259	1
HEALY JR DANIEL F	COL	0-0015742	C954	2
HEALY JR REMEYN J	COL	0-0020918	C357	1
HEALY PATRICK J	LTC	0-0030657	0364	1
HEANEY JR GEORGE F	COL	0-0015181	0753	1
HEARD JACK W	M G	0-0002867	C946	2
HEARD OLGA S	MAJ	R-0010095	C562	1
HEARD R TOWNSEND	B G	0-0004639	1146	2
HEARD WILLIAM C	LTC	0-0069672	0767	1
HEARD WILLIAM R	COL	0-0039811	0263	1
HEARING VINCENT J	LTC	0-0050126	0466	1
HEARN ROBERT J	COL	0-0051131	0557	1
HEARN THOMAS G	M G	C-0003859	C846	2
HEARNES WARREN E	1LT	0-0028379	1049	1
HEARON VIRGIL R	CW4	W-0903236	0357	2
HEASTY JR CHARLES F	COL	0-0022665	C166	1
HEATH ALBERT	CW4	W-0906780	0760	1
HEATH BERNICE I	MAJ	N-0001385	1164	1
HEATH CALVIN A	COL	0-0024431	C66C	1
HEATH LOUIS T	M G	0-001806C	C862	1
HEATH RALPH M	LTC	C-0066013	1266	1
HEATHCOTE EARL W	B G	0-0028900	0355	1
HEAVEY WILLIAM F	B G	0-0005223	C148	1
HEBERT KENNETH	CW2	W-0900978	C744	1
HECK DONALD	LTC	0-0024157	C561	1
HECK GEORGE	COL	0-0051469	1163	1
HECKEMEYER BENJAMIN	COL	0-0019930	0165	1
HECTOR JOHN R	COL	0-0030717	C666	1
HEDDEN WILLIS A	COL	0-0006534	0345	2
HEDGE GEORGE R	COL	C-0006458	0642	2
HEDGES LOVEAIRE A	COL	C-0029786	1062	1
HEEN MYLO L	LTC	0-0022208	0958	1
HEEP JR MATTHEW S	MAJ	0-0056981	0762	1
HEFFELFINGER HUGO W	COL	0-0046143	0966	1
HEFFERNON GEORGE A	COL	0-0029273	1159	1
HEFFNER JR PETE T	COL	C-0010319	C753	1
HEFLEBOWER ROY C	B G	0-00C2770	0846	2
HEM GERARD F	CW4	W-0903238	C762	1
HEIBERG HARRISON H	COL	0-0012306	C854	1
HEIDE MARGITH H	MAJ	N-0001293	0467	1
HEIDENREICH ELLSWORT	MAJ	C-0060214	0865	1
HEIDLAND ERNEST F	COL	0-0017688	0655	1
HEIDNER ALVIN A	COL	C-0041635	1159	1
HEIDT JR GEORGE F	LTC	C-0041076	C465	1
HEIL GEORGE J	LTC	0-0039109	C262	1
HEIL JR JOHN H	COL	C-0029400	C360	1
HEILFRON MILTON	COL	0-0007506	0753	1
HEIMSTEAD MERTEN K	COL	0-002088C	C266	1
HEIN FREDERICK	COL	C-0014956	0753	1
HEIN NEIL F	COL	0-0051467	C563	1
HEINE WALTER F	LTC	0-0017355	C943	2
HEINEL WALTER C	COL	0-0050947	0958	2
HEINLEIN JR REX I	COL	0-0016991	1033	2
HEINRICH CHARLES T	COL	C-0C39014	1167	1
HEINRICH HELEN M	MAJ	N-0000203	0661	1
HEINZ HELEN O	MAJ	N-0002065	C662	1
HEINZEL CHESTER H	CW4	W-0903239	0765	1
HEISER BENJAMIN P	B G	0-0C16450	0756	1
HEISS CLARENCE L	MAJ	0-0066992	0866	1
HEISS GERSON K	B G	0-0015092	0954	2
HEISS GUSTAVE M	COL	0-0018594	1146	2
HEISS JONAS S	COL	C-0051262	1061	1
HEITMAN JR CHARLES E	COL	C-0018059	0760	1
HEJNA JOHN J	LTC	0-0045033	0167	1
HELBER GEORGE Z	LTC	C-0045094	0861	1
HELD BURT	LTC	0-0C19605	0245	2
HELFERS MELVIN C	LTC	C-0021359	C546	2
HELFERT PETER A	LTC	0-0032385	0962	1
HELFRICH JESSE B	LTC	0-0017792	0144	2
HELGESTAD JAMES E	COL	0-0040003	0764	1
HELIKER SHERBURNE	COL	C-0C29528	C562	1
HELLER THEODORE P	LTC	0-0052389	0664	1
HELLIER EDWARD G	COL	0-0041892	0761	1
HELM MARGARET C	MAJ	N-0002401	0762	1
HELMICK CHARLES G	M G	0-0C03606	0752	1
HELMICK GEORGE R	2LT	0-CC16303	0229	2
HELMICK GLENN R	MAJ	0-0059856	1162	1
HELMS KENNETH R	LTC	0-0037023	0465	2
HELMUTH OLIVER J	COL	0-0032395	0765	2
HELSLEY LLEWELLYN	LTC	0-0C36900	1166	1
HELTON BURRELL W	LTC	0-0C21808	0845	2
HELTON JOHN W	LTC	0-0023337	C354	2
HELTZEL WILLIAM F	COL	0-0029891	C463	1
HEMBREE TOM P	COL	0-0029789	1062	1
HEMION ROGER H	COL	0-0040075	0964	1
HEMLER DAVID W	CW2	W-080C355	1045	1
HEMPEL JOHN H	COL	0-0042457	1160	1
HEMPERLY CECIL W	LTC	0-0C80301	0865	1
HEMPLING LEONARD J	COL	C-0C59784	C767	1
HENCHEY FRANCES C	LTC	N-0000023	0451	1
HENDERLY HAROLD B	LTC	0-0036065	1163	1
HENDERSON ALFRED D	COL	0-0041647	0160	1
HENDERSON BASIL W	COL	0-0046671	0966	1
HENDERSON BENEDICT A	COL	0-0038653	0463	1
HENDERSON BLAIR E	COL	C-0039813	0263	1
HENDERSON CARROLL B	COL	0-0C29421	0660	1
HENDERSON DONALD H	LTC	0-0027293	0866	1
HENDERSON FRED R	COL	0-004154C	1058	2
HENDERSON GLENN H	LTC	0-0069674	C867	1
HENDERSON HARRY MC C	COL	0-0005168	0545	2
HENDERSON IVAN W	CW4	W-0906783	0959	2
HENDERSON JAMES A	CW4	W-0904314	0966	1
HENDERSON JR HARRY W	LTC	0-0057409	1065	1
HENDERSON JR JOHN M	B G	0-0029410	C560	1
HENDERSON PHILIP J	LTC	0-0016584	1043	2
HENDERSON ROLAND S	COL	0-0011665	0753	1
HENDERSON THOMAS J	COL	0-0C42203	0963	1
HENDERSON WILBURN H	MAJ	C-0004423	1022	2
HENDERSON WILLIAM G	LTC	0-0C37707	0961	1
HENDERSON WILLIAM W	LTC	0-0049834	0965	1
HENDLEY ROBERT C	LTC	0-0014869	1144	2
HENDRICKS CLARENCE P	LTC	0-0C42302	0362	2
HENDRICKS LELIA M	LTC	M-0C00605	0163	1
HENDRICKSON HARVEY F	COL	0-0017339	C446	2
HENDRICKSON W H	LTC	0-0020345	C246	2
HENDRIX MARGUERITE	MAJ	N-000055C	0756	2
HENDRIX RALEIGH R	M G	C-0015897	0961	1
HENDRIX THOMAS L	LTC	0-0C59206	0665	1
HENDRY CHARLES R	CW4	W-0904126	0762	1
HENDRY EARL	CPT	0-0C09804	C231	1
HENINGER GRANT	COL	0-001135C	0246	1
HENION KARL F	COL	0-0007236	0856	1
HENKLE HARRY L	COL	0-0008090	1050	1
HENLEY CHARLES W	COL	0-0020897	0746	2
HENLEY JACK J	LTC	0-0033959	0863	1
HENLINE CLAIR G	LTC	0-0045087	0262	1
HENN EDWIN A	COL	0-0005847	1051	1
HENNE CHARLES A	COL	0-0046253	0767	1
HENNEBERGER JOSIAH B	LTC	0-0004C92	0-42	2
HENNESSEE JOE D	LTC	0-0024897	0663	1

NAME	GRADE	SVC NO	DATE RET MO YR	RET CODE
HENNESSEY JAMES T	COL	0-0032274	0565	1
HENNESSY HAROLD P	COL	0-0010292	0754	1
HENNESSY JAMES T	COL	0-0023148	0264	1
HENNESSY RICHARD L	COL	0-0024690	0764	1
HENNIES ELMA F	LTC	N-0000401	1065	1
HENNIG WILLIAM H	M G	0-0017122	0764	2
HENNING JR FRANK A	B G	0-0012648	0754	1
HENRY ALBERT C	LTC	0-0034497	0563	1
HENRY CHARLES H	COL	0-0007193	0844	2
HENRY CHARLES O	LTC	0-0080860	1066	1
HENRY FRANK S	B G	0-0018989	0863	2
HENRY GUY V	M G	0-0000605	0139	1
HENRY HAROLD P	COL	0-0012589	0653	1
HENRY ISABELLA M	MAJ	L-0000302	1060	1
HENRY JAMES E	LTC	0-0088732	0965	1
HENRY JR LEE S	LTC	0-0063337	1167	1
HENRY JR STEPHEN G	CPT	0-0028446	0152	2
HENRY LYLE K	COL	0-0041605	0859	1
HENRY STEPHEN G	M G	0-0005164	1046	2
HENRY THOMAS	LTC	0-0009092	0641	1
HENRY WALTER F	WO1	W-0902152	1046	2
HENRY WILLIAM J	COL	0-0007830	0-45	2
HENRY WILLIAM J	COL	0-0021928	0767	2
HENSEL MAX G	MAJ	0-0024238	0846	2
HENSEL RAYMOND G	LTC	0-0066016	0667	1
HENSEL WILLIAM E	COL	0-0025531	0164	1
HENSEY JR WALTER R	COL	0-0014950	0854	2
HENSHAW JAMES L	LTC	0-0027357	0866	1
HENSLEY EMERY M	LTC	0-0035720	0266	1
HENSON IRA C	MAJ	0-0036423	0761	1
HENTGES ELSIE M	MAJ	N-0000350	0662	1
HEPNER JOHN F	COL	0-0006638	1046	2
HERALD FRANCIS R	CPT	0-0019957	1042	2
HERB EDWARD G	COL	0-0018973	0655	1
HERBER DAVID	COL	0-0032689	1067	1
HERBERT GEORGE F	COL	0-0010253	0753	1
HERBERT JAMES K	B G	0-0018027	0746	1
HERBERT JR FRANK	CPT	0-0064993	1162	1
HERBERT WILLIAM D	COL	0-0003514	0440	2
HERBERTH JR FRANK W	COL	0-0029829	1262	1
HERCZ ARTHUR R	COL	0-0018566	0757	1
HERENDEEN EDWARD	COL	0-0014623	0351	1
HERGERT IONE F	MAJ	N-0002363	0360	1
HERMAN CHARLES G	COL	0-0018885	1058	2
HERMAN DEAN A	COL	0-0018563	0761	1
HERMAN FREDERICK	COL	0-0003671	0846	1
HERMAN JOHN B	COL	0-0019301	0562	2
HERMANN JOHN R	COL	0-0004876	1144	2
HERMES ELMER R	LTC	0-0069680	0867	1
HERNDON LOWE H	COL	0-0051223	0259	2
HERNDON ROBERT B	LTC	0-0051984	0366	1
HERON GORDON J F	COL	0-0004728	0751	1
HERPEL FREDERICK	LTC	0-0004153	1022	2
HERR FREDERICK	COL	0-0003735	0448	1
HERREN THOMAS W	LTG	0-0007430	0757	1
HERRES HARRY L	LTC	0-0041049	0764	1
HERRICK CURTIS J	M G	0-0018538	0667	2
HERRICK HUGH N	B G	0-0007370	0144	2
HERRICK PARK B	LTC	0-0012775	1045	2
HERRIN HERBERT T	CPT	0-0062810	1158	2
HERRINGTON RUSSELL M	COL	0-0005436	1147	1
HERRMANN CHARLES R	COL	0-0039779	0661	1
HERRMANN WALTER J	CW3	W-0903248	1264	1
HERROD JOHN T	COL	0-0029577	0660	1
HERRON CHARLES D	M G	0-0000777	1046	1
HERRON DONALD B	COL	0-0012696	0851	1
HERRON THOMAS M R	MAJ	0-0002293	0722	2
HERSHEY JACOB R	LTC	0-0030286	0762	1
HERSHEY JR CHARLES G	LTC	0-0037364	1165	1
HERSHEY LEWIS B	LTG	0-0006530	1046	2
HERSHEY LYLE E	COL	0-0052502	0666	1
HERSPERGER WEBB S	MAJ	0-0088099	0865	2
HERT PAUL	COL	0-0039952	0365	1
HERTE ROY J	COL	0-0016516	0756	1
HERTFORD KENNER F	M G	0-0015120	0755	1

NAME	GRADE	SVC NO	DATE RET MO YR	RET CODE
HERVEY RAY F	CW4	W-0906788	0463	1
HERVEY STEWART D	COL	0-0007263	0547	2
HERWIG LEOPOLD J	CPT	0-0014209	0-19	2
HERZER ARNO P	COL	0-0081905	1066	1
HESKETH WILLIAM	B G	0-0007516	0648	1
HESKETT MARCUS W	COL	0-0042218	0763	1
HESS ALFRED W	LTC	0-0020303	0946	2
HESS BLIE	COL	0-0042375	0961	2
HESS CLARENCE L	CW4	W-0902123	0655	1
HESS GLENN C	LTC	0-0051753	0862	1
HESS GUSTIN A	LTC	0-0040180	0762	1
HESS JR WALTER W	B G	0-0003850	0352	1
HESS MILTON C	CW4	W-0903250	0864	1
HESS OLIVER A	COL	0-0004764	0452	1
HESSELBACHER GEORGE	COL	0-0024651	1266	1
HESSIN ARTHUR L	LTC	0-0041757	1061	1
HESTER HENRY R	LTC	0-0019419	1155	1
HESTER HUGH B	B G	0-0008405	0851	1
HESTER JOHN H	M G	0-0002382	0246	2
HESTER SUE I	MAJ	N-0000442	1065	1
HESTON JOHN T	LTC	0-0052371	0665	1
HEUBERGER NEWTON J	COL	0-0035476	0566	1
HEUER HERMAN H	COL	0-0030895	0466	1
HEVENER JAMES W	MAJ	0-0037121	0459	1
HEWETT JR ROBERT F	LTC	0-0028528	0866	1
HEWETTE JAMES B	LTC	0-0044430	0761	1
HEWITT CLARENCE B	COL	0-0049926	0764	1
HEWITT HARRY	COL	0-0030558	0464	2
HEWITT MERRITT L	LTC	0-0023934	0561	1
HEWITT ROBERT A	M G	0-0018713	0867	1
HEWITT WILBUR J	MAJ	0-0063123	1266	1
HEWLETT THOMAS H	COL	0-0057932	0964	1
HEYDUCK LAWRENCE E	COL	0-0011583	1149	1
HEYER HERBERT R	COL	0-0040042	0764	1
HEYMONT IRVING	COL	0-0025040	0864	1
HEYNE DANIEL H	COL	0-0019493	0864	1
HEYWOOD FRANK A	COL	0-0005201	0553	1
HIATT WRIGHT	COL	0-0020139	0657	1
HIBBERD CLEMMIE L	CPT	N-0000C[illegible]	0748	1
HIBBS LOUIS F	M G	0-0004426	0147	2
HIBLER CLYDE J	1LT	0-0019247	0639	2
HICKEY ALBERT N	COL	0-0017000	0457	1
HICKEY JOHN C	CW2	W-0901573	0747	1
HICKEY JR DANIEL W	B G	0-0007544	0654	1
HICKEY RALPH W	CPT	0-0014269	0720	2
HICKEY TERRENCE R	COL	0-0018567	0761	1
HICKEY THOMAS F	LTG	0-0010362	0458	2
HICKISCH FRANK L	LTC	0-0039686	0858	1
HICKLIN ALLEN B	COL	0-0010222	0445	2
HICKMAN CARROLL P	LTC	0-0042564	0463	1
HICKMAN EDWIN G	LTC	0-0019575	0859	1
HICKMAN JR GEORGE W	M G	0-0016420	1060	1
HICKS JR GRACY L	LTC	0-0038006	1167	1
HICKS LAWRENCE S	CW4	W-0903254	0165	1
HIDDLESTON EUGENE W	COL	0-0018480	0761	2
HIEBERT SAMUEL L	LTC	0-0029321	0662	1
HIESTER DAVID W	B G	0-0020191	0467	1
HIGDON ROBERT S	COL	0-0021459	1163	1
HIGGINS CHARLES C	COL	0-0015348	0853	1
HIGGINS CHARLES W	COL	0-0007369	1052	1
HIGGINS ELMER R	COL	0-0038755	1162	1
HIGGINS GERALD J	M G	0-0019530	0855	1
HIGGINS HAROLD O	LTC	0-0023554	0660	1
HIGGINS JAMES L	COL	0-0036306	1167	1
HIGGINS JOHN G	LTC	0-0057706	0766	1
HIGGINS JOSEPH P	LTC	0-0048665	1167	1
HIGGINS JR JAMES W	COL	0-0029542	0461	1
HIGGINS MAURICE C	COL	0-0039630	1059	1
HIGGINS ROGER E	COL	0-0039867	1263	1
HIGGINS STANTON	COL	0-0009894	0546	1
HIGGINS WALTER A	LTC	0-0026112	0962	1
HIGGINS WARREN J	LTC	0-0049460	1265	2
HIGGINS WAYNE G	COL	0-0079851	0765	1
HIGGINS WILSON R	COL	0-0012624	0948	2
HIGHTOWER DAN	LTC	0-0063222	1166	1

NAME	GRADE	SVC NO	DATE RET MO YR	RET CODE
HIGLEY HOWARD C	COL	0-0038821	0266	1
HILDEBRAND HARRY B	COL	0-0005016	0746	1
HILDEBRANT CONARD	COL	0-0029902	0363	1
HILDITCH NORMAN	CPT	0-0040617	0353	1
HILDRETH RAYMOND C	COL	0-00091[illegible]4	0248	1
HILL ALTON A	COL	0-0029384	0160	1
HILL BENJAMIN I	COL	0-0024791	0767	1
HILL BERNICE M	MAJ	N-0000075	1060	1
HILL CARL R	COL	0-0042101	0861	1
HILL CHARLES W	COL	0-0019430	0960	1
HILL CLIFFORD B	LTC	0-0040055	0663	1
HILL CYRIL C	COL	0-0028792	0555	1
HILL DONALD C	COL	0-0015504	0654	1
HILL EDWARD M	LTC	0-0036185	1163	1
HILL FRANCIS	B G	0-0019058	0863	1
HILL GUY C	COL	0-0029272	0663	1
HILL HAROLD E	LTC	0-0041142	0364	1
HILL HARRY G	LTC	0-0034106	0760	1
HILL HELEN R	MAJ	N-0000564	0361	1
HILL IRA B	COL	0-0004860	0946	2
HILL JESSE N	COL	0-0030702	0866	2
HILL JOHN F	CPT	0-0006400	0934	2
HILL JOHN G	B G	0-0015797	0854	1
HILL JOSEPH A	LTC	0-0061965	1065	1
HILL JOSEPH C	LTC	0-0027838	0167	1
HILL JR GEORGE P	COL	0-0019972	0865	2
HILL JR JAMES W	LTC	0-0080107	0264	1
HILL JR ROBERT J	COL	0-0021933	0566	2
HILL JR WILLIAM H	COL	0-0031348	1066	1
HILL KENNETH R	LTC	0-0031898	0365	1
HILL LEROY C	LTC	0-0031874	1165	1
HILL LEVENIA E	MAJ	N-0002062	0761	2
HILL MILTON A	B G	0-0010177	1046	2
HILL PHILIP H	LTC	0-0042805	0864	1
HILL RAY C	COL	0-0002284	0839	1
HILL RAYMOND L	COL	0-0017495	1058	1
HILL RICHARD F	COL	0-0042973	0367	1
HILL ROBERT B	B G	0-0004046	1150	1
HILL SAMUEL T	COL	0-0041680	0560	1
HILL VERNE C	COL	0-0016297	0147	1
HILL WILLIAM	COL	0-0012642	0754	1
HILL WILLIAM B	LTC	0-0058167	0767	1
HILL WILLIAM V	COL	0-0020482	1166	2
HILLBERG LAURI J	COL	0-0018710	1058	1
HILLDRING JOHN H	M G	0-0007420	0746	2
HILLEBRAND ALVIN R	COL	0-0030586	0166	1
HILLIARD LEE F	LTC	0-0033246	0461	1
HILLIARD LEONARD L	LTC	0-0015046	0444	2
HILLMAN BURLEIGH F	COL	0-0028907	0457	1
HILLMAN CHARLES C	B G	0-0003517	0147	1
HILLS J HUNTINGT	COL	0-0004769	0752	1
HILLYARD HARRY L	M G	0-0019524	1167	2
HILPERT ROBERT C	MAJ	0-0023446	1046	2
HILSABECK CARTER L	LTC	0-0031389	0459	1
HILSMAN EDWARD H	COL	0-0043021	0667	1
HILSMAN ROGER	COL	0-0005012	0848	2
HILTON JR CORSON L	COL	0-0024438	1167	1
HILTON KATHLYN C	MAJ	L-0000308	0462	1
HIMES CECIL	COL	0-0020731	0967	1
HIMES DONALD S	COL	0-0030224	0864	1
HIMES WILLIAM J	COL	0-0019365	0762	1
HINCHIE JOHN C	LTC	0-0031537	0861	1
HINCKE JOHN T	COL	0-0015539	0854	1
HINCKLEY LOIS S	LTC	L-0000301	1263	1
HINDLE CLIFFORD O	COL	0-0006693	1050	1
HINDMAN JOHN T	CW3	W-0906792	0460	1
HINDMAN THOMAS O	LTC	0-0084842	1266	1
HINDS JOHN H	M G	0-0012106	0356	1
HINDS SIDNEY R	B G	0-0012851	0247	2
HINE DANIEL L	COL	0-0019134	0762	2
HINE JR HENRY C	COL	0-0012738	0654	1
HINES CHARLES B	COL	0-0020585	0864	1
HINES CLIFFORD C	COL	0-0042289	0164	1
HINES JOHN B	COL	0-0020606	0966	1
HINES JOHN L	GEN	0-0000023	0532	1

NAME	GRADE	SVC NO	DATE RET MO YR	RET CODE
HINES JR JOHN L	COL	0-0016749	0552	2
HINES MARY L	MAJ	N-0001974	1061	1
HINGES NORMAN P	LTC	0-0060652	0767	1
HINMAN ELMER C	COL	0-0038633	0757	2
HINRICHS HERBERT H	LTC	0-0079665	0867	1
HINRICHS JOHN H	LTG	0-0017174	0662	1
HINSHAW FREDERICK	COL	0-0018867	0560	1
HINSON CLAUDE R	LTC	0-0051922	0964	1
HINTON ALFRED E	CW4	W-0903259	0858	2
HINTON JOE A	COL	0-0011654	1147	1
HIRSCH GEORGE W	COL	0-0008580	0854	1
HIRSCH OLIVER M	COL	0-0040060	1163	1
HIRSCHFELDER CHESTER	COL	0-0006124	0749	2
HIRSCHMANN LLOYD E	COL	0-0043433	0167	1
HIRSHSON B J L	B G	0-0051762	0566	1
HISGEN KARL W	COL	0-0014604	0452	1
HISLE ROBERT F	LTC	0-0051476	0162	1
HITCHCOCK LOUIS M	MAJ	0-0006376	0722	2
HITCHING JOHN L	LTC	0-0015737	0348	1
HITCHINGS DONALD L	COL	0-0052081	1067	1
HITE MERLE L	LTC	0-0038036	1165	1
HITT PARKER	COL	0-0000963	1128	1
HITTLE LESLIE L	COL	0-0015430	0954	1
HIXON CHARLES E	COL	0-0012131	1052	2
HIXSON GROVER G	CW4	W-0903260	1263	1
HJERTBERG F M I	MAJ	0-0037266	0655	2
HJORT JR SAMUEL C	CW2	W-0906794	1060	1
HLOPKO JOHN J	LTC	0-0030841	1162	1
HOAAS OLE G	COL	0-0012005	0843	2
HOAG ROBERT E	COL	0-0084370	1066	1
HOAGLAND CHARLES E	LTC	0-0034645	0961	1
HOAGLAND DALE M	COL	0-0006981	0753	1
HOAGLAND ROBERT J	COL	0-0020516	0267	1
HOARD JR MAURICE A	LTC	0-0043725	0964	1
HOBBINS ELIZABETH	MAJ	N-0000569	0561	1
HOBBS EDWARD C	2LT	0-0020823	0339	2
HOBBS JR ARTHUR A	MAJ	0-0012605	0934	2
HOBBS MORRIS F	LTC	0-0031416	0163	1
HOBSON EDITH M	MAJ	R-0010042	0265	1
HOBSON HOWARD M	B G	0-0029673	0262	1
HOBSON JR VICTOR W	B G	0-0023038	1065	2
HOCHELLA MICHAEL F	LTC	0-0036480	0663	2
HOCKER RICHARD W	COL	0-0005028	1048	1
HOCKER WOODSON F	COL	0-0016879	0757	1
HODGE ROBERT O	LTC	0-0039563	1055	1
HODGES ARTHUR W	COL	0-0024437	1066	1
HODGES JOHN W	CW2	W-0901839	0849	1
HODGES JR JOSEPH H	COL	0-0020733	0766	1
HODGES JR WILLARD J	COL	0-0021401	0866	1
HODGSON JOHN A	COL	0-0083584	1167	1
HODNETTE LOVIC P	COL	0-0008263	0342	2
HODSON FREMONT B	B G	0-0011158	0952	1
HOEBEKE ADRIAN I	COL	0-0019334	1163	1
HOEBEKE ARNOLD J	LTC	0-0023930	0861	1
HOEFFER HENRY J	B G	0-0016765	0757	1
HOEFLING ADAM F	CPT	0-0067579	0166	1
HOEHNE ERVIN O K	COL	0-0039878	0164	1
HOEMAN ARTHUR J	LTC	0-0042485	0163	1
HOEY WILLIAM R	MAJ	0-0081457	0866	1
HOFF JR ERNEST R	CPT	0-0063686	0466	1
HOFF RAYMOND L	LTC	0-0025140	1062	1
HOFF STUART S	M G	0-0038766	0863	1
HOFFER EUGENE	CW3	W-0903261	0761	1
HOFFMAN ALDON H	COL	0-0042975	1065	1
HOFFMAN EDWIN H	CW4	W-0901810	1054	1
HOFFMAN JACK N	LTC	0-0027459	0966	1
HOFFMAN JR C W	LTC	0-0058243	0660	1
HOFFMAN JR JOHN G	COL	0-0031856	0163	1
HOFFMAN PAUL O	COL	0-0030517	0765	1
HOFFMAN RALPH W	LTC	0-0036786	0564	1
HOFFMAN RAYMOND E	CPT	0-0008329	0722	2
HOFFMAN RAYMOND F	LTC	0-0044240	0264	1
HOFFMAN ROBERT J	COL	0-0008646	0547	2
HOFFMAN ROY A	LTC	0-0026726	0866	1
HOFFMAN THEODORE F	COL	0-0019403	0864	1

NAME	GRADE	SVC NO	DATE RET MO YR	RET CODE
HOFFMAN WILLIAM C	COL	0-0039719	0955	1
HOFFMANN KENNETH L	LTC	0-0078649	0467	1
HOFINGER LEOPOLD F	LTC	0-0044368	C165	1
HOFTO GLEN E	COL	0-0041585	C459	1
HOGAN ARTHUR H	COL	C-0018551	0159	1
HOGAN GERTRUDE F	MAJ	N-0002225	C360	1
HOGAN M LEON	LTC	0-0008762	0927	2
HOGAN JAMES H	LTC	0-0037144	0764	1
HOGAN JULIAN L	LTC	C-0032178	C367	1
HOGAN MARY I	LTC	N-0002117	1160	1
HOGE BENJAMIN F	COL	0-0003734	C151	1
HOGE JR WILLIAM M	LTC	0-0023894	1166	1
HOGE KENNETH O	CW3	W-0906795	0563	1
HOGE KENNETH G	COL	0-0012753	0646	2
HOGE WILLIAM C	MAJ	C-0037742	1061	2
HOGE WILLIAM M	GEN	0-0004437	0155	2
HOGLE JAMES C	COL	C-0042901	1266	1
HOHERZ MELVIN A	COL	C-0042819	0259	1
HOIN ELSIE K	MAJ	N-0002230	0559	1
HOKE WILLIAM M	COL	0-0015441	1153	1
HOKENSON CHARLES K	MAJ	C-0035615	0763	1
HOLBROOK FRANK C	M G	0-0016654	1055	1
HOLBROCK JOHN	LTC	0-0051646	0963	1
HOLBROOK JR W A	B G	0-0012177	1146	1
HOLCOMB CARL W	COL	C-0016082	0755	1
HOLCOMB CORNELIUS	COL	C-0C29610	0961	1
HOLCOMB JAMES F	LTC	0-0027219	C866	1
HOLCOMB JOEL P	COL	C-0046829	1265	1
HOLCOMB WILLIAM L	LTC	0-0053160	C164	1
HOLCCMBE FRANK S	COL	0-0024218	C463	1
HOLCOMBE JAMES H	LTC	0-0045349	0867	1
HOLCOMBE WILLIAM H	B G	0-0003661	1046	1
HOLDEN ANNA S	LTC	N-0000507	0349	1
HOLDEN MAURICE C	COL	C-0024534	C765	1
HOLDEN OLIVER	MAJ	C-0014221	1119	2
HOLDER WILLIAM G	COL	0-0012685	0753	1
HOLDERNESS STEPHEN W	COL	0-0020157	C766	1
HOLDRIDGE HERBERT C	B G	0-0005263	0244	2
HOLDRIDGE WALTER H	COL	0-0051895	1167	1
HOLLADAY NORMAN C	MAJ	C-0038540	0865	1
HOLLAND ALICE E	MAJ	N-0002048	C460	1
HOLLAND DIXON B	COL	0-0020539	C656	1
HOLLAND DONALD B	LTC	0-0083842	1067	1
HOLLAND JEREMIAH P	B G	0-0016812	0757	2
HOLLAND JR JAMES C	COL	0-0024573	0967	1
HOLLAND JR WILLIAM E	COL	C-0048873	0167	1
HOLLAND TEMPLE G	COL	C-0015321	0554	2
HOLLANDER BENNET N	LTC	0-0050693	0867	1
HOLLE CHARLES G	M G	0-0012612	1058	1
HOLLENBACH ALBERT M	COL	0-0029240	0762	1
HOLLER WALKER W	COL	0-0015905	0854	1
HOLLEY JAMES E	COL	C-0017185	0758	1
HOLLEY JR JOSHUA L	LTC	0-0040612	0266	1
HOLLEY WILLIAM C	COL	0-0021433	C759	1
HOLLIDAY MILTON G	COL	0-0001572	0-38	1
HOLLIFIELD WILLIAM C	LTC	0-0059671	0867	1
HOLLINGER JOHN C	COL	0-0030448	C663	1
HOLLINGER MARGARET A	LTC	N-0001962	C863	1
HOLLINGSWORTH CHARLE	LTC	0-0058075	C264	2
HOLLINGSWORTH FRANK	COL	C-0006889	C145	2
HOLLINGSWORTH P R	COL	0-0057526	0560	1
HOLLIS CHARLES E	LTC	0-0079857	0361	1
HOLLIS DWIGHT S	COL	C-0030975	C558	1
HOLLIS JEFF F	COL	0-0031528	0664	1
HOLLIS ROBERT P	M G	C-0015079	1057	1
HOLLISTER FRED M	CW4	W-0903269	C263	1
HOLLISTER PAUL G	B G	0-0029547	C461	1
HOLLOWAY KENNETH H	MAJ	C-0058441	0867	1
HOLLOWELL HARRY H	CW4	W-0902118	C964	1
HOLLY JOSEPH A	B G	0-0012360	0151	1
HOLLY LEO V	COL	C-0042420	0864	1
HOLLY ULMONT W	COL	0-0010262	1147	2
HOLM CLIFFORD P	LTC	0-0038630	0757	1
HOLM WILLIAM N	COL	0-0023282	0966	1
HOLMAN JONATHAN L	M G	0-0011226	0656	2

NAME	GRADE	SVC NO	DATE RET MO YR	RET CODE
HCLMAN RCBERT E	COL	0-0038815	0465	1
HOLMBERG DCNALD W	COL	0-0038937	1164	1
HOLMBERG GERALD W	LTC	0-0029328	0854	1
HOLMES CARL C	CPT	0-0009926	0837	2
HOLMES CLAUDE O	COL	0-0C04217	0944	1
HOLMES DON N	COL	0-0008271	1047	2
HOLMES ERNEST V	B G	0-0016100	0755	2
HOLMES HARRY C	COL	0-0029286	1163	1
HOLMES JOEL G	B G	0-0005272	0852	1
HOLMES JR HENRY B	B G	0-0004656	0847	1
HOLMES JR WILLIAM F	COL	0-0020525	0746	2
HOLMES ROBERT H	COL	C-0085572	0866	1
HOLMES ROBERT M	LTC	0-0026110	0863	1
HOLMES THOMAS R	COL	0-0009702	0947	1
HOLMES WILLIAM W	COL	0-0032247	C464	1
HOLMSTROM HELMER A	COL	0-0030382	0962	1
HOLOCHWOST GEORGE G	LTC	0-0C81906	0667	1
HCLPER AMBROSE C	LTC	0-0078885	C866	1
HOLSINGER GEORGE L	COL	C-0015989	0854	1
HOLSINGER JAMES W	B G	0-0029432	0760	1
HOLST JCHN J	COL	0-0016872	0757	1
HOLT ARTHUR E	COL	0-0032326	0464	1
HOLT FRANK T	COL	0-0021908	0759	1
HOLT HAROLD G	COL	C-0006783	0151	1
HOLT HENRY W	COL	0-0011202	0854	1
HOLT JCHN H	LTC	0-0037814	1163	1
HOLT JCHN W	LTC	0-0041154	0561	1
HOLT OLIN P	COL	0-0043298	0961	1
HOLT RCGER H	COL	0-0029574	0661	1
HOLT RUFUS L	COL	0-0008714	0150	2
HCLT WILLIAM O	CW4	W-0903271	0657	1
HOLTER PAUL W	COL	0-0020483	1166	1
HOLTERMAN GORDON H	COL	0-0020135	0866	1
HOLTON EARL F	COL	0-0020241	0966	1
HOLTON JR RUSSELL G	LTC	0-0080421	0865	1
HOLTZ WERNER	LTC	0-0C32209	0661	1
HOLTZCLAW EVERST A	CW4	W-0902434	1056	1
HOLTZWORTH BERTRAM A	M G	0-0016804	0863	1
HOLYCROSS FORREST L	COL	0-0009483	1047	1
HOLZBACH JR HENRY E	LTC	0-0046861	0763	1
HOMAN SAMMIE N	COL	0-0034279	0665	1
HCMBURG JR ALBERT H	LTC	0-0035159	0166	2
HOMEWOOD JOHN W	COL	0-0015472	0151	1
HCMS JCSE M	LTC	0-0031249	0467	1
HONNEN GEORGE	M G	0-0012816	1157	1
HOOD JCHN O	COL	0-0005332	0946	1
HOOD JCHN H	COL	0-0002786	0746	1
HOOD LUND F	COL	C-0039892	0364	1
HOOD PATRICK W	MAJ	0-0031308	0458	1
HOOD RALPH E	COL	0-0032443	0260	2
HOOK GLADYS T	MAJ	R-0010017	0961	1
HOOKER HOWARD C	LTC	0-0043717	0467	1
HOOPER ETHEL M	MAJ	L-0000253	0564	2
HOOPES JOSEPH V	CW4	W-0906797	0163	1
HOORN FREDERICK	COL	C-0007411	0746	1
HCOVER CHRIS C	COL	0-0037408	0764	1
HCOVER GERALD B	LTC	0-0094863	0267	1
HOOVER HALLIE E	CPT	N-000C398	1160	1
HOOVER HCLMAN O	COL	0-0030305	1264	1
HOOVER HUBERT O	M G	0-0007924	0248	1
HCOVER THOMAS H	LTC	0-0037565	0664	1
HCOVER WARREN H	COL	0-0018418	0761	1
HOPE FRANCIS M	LTC	0-0030541	0559	2
HOPKINS ARMAND	COL	0-0016083	0755	1
HOPKINS EDWARD C	COL	0-0012395	0854	1
HOPKINS GEORGE E	CW2	W-0904389	1059	1
HOPKINS JOHN	MAJ	C-0007976	0436	1
HOPKINS JR JCHN W	LTC	0-0040504	0261	1
HCPKINS JR WALTER G	COL	0-0033551	0366	1
HOPKINS MALCOLM J	MAJ	0-0032512	0148	2
HOPPENSTEIN ISAAC	COL	0-0032373	0967	1
HOPPER BRISTOW S	LTC	0-0032815	1060	1
HOPPER HAROLD W	COL	0-0080880	1166	1
HOPPOCK ELEANOR M	MAJ	N-0002377	1060	1
HOPSON BRANNON J	LTC	0-0029223	1059	1

NAME	GRADE	SVC NO	DATE RET MO YR	RET CODE
HORAN EARL C	COL	0-000761C	0749	1
HORAN JOHN P	COL	0-0005520	0448	2
HORAN LEONA E	MAJ	N-0002431	0665	1
HORGER CHARLES A	COL	0-0007359	1046	1
HORKAN GEORGE A	M G	0-0007201	0154	2
HORLOCK FRED H	LTC	0-0080422	1065	1
HORMEL HAROLD P	CW3	W-0903275	0560	1
HORN WILEY H	LTC	C-0031078	C862	2
HORNADAY RALPH J	LTC	0-0030423	C463	1
HORNE ELIZABETH	LTC	N-0001277	0767	2
HORNE JAMES C	COL	0-0011156	0348	1
HORNECKER HARRY E	COL	0-0029082	C459	1
HORNER ALBERT A	COL	C-0016254	0555	1
HORNER HAROLD J	CW2	W-0903276	1053	2
HORNER II SAMUEL W	COL	C-0018711	C862	1
HORNISH WILLIAM N	COL	0-0041457	C457	1
HORNISHER CHARLES J	COL	0-0026461	1163	1
HORNISHER JOSEPH J	COL	0-0017989	0158	2
HORNOR JR JOHN L	COL	C-0017726	1055	1
HOROWICZ LEO S	COL	0-0080423	0565	1
HORRIDGE JOSEPH	B G	0-0017555	C456	1
HORSFALL GEORGE	COL	0-0017827	0959	2
HORSTMAN SANFORD W	COL	0-0019783	0865	1
HORSTMANN JOHN W	LTC	0-0042566	0463	1
HORTON JAMES C	CW3	W-0906798	0159	1
HORTON JOHN B	B G	0-0015150	1060	1
HORTON JOHN P	LTC	0-0042259	1061	1
HORTON PAUL J	LTC	C-0002223	0934	2
HORTON ROBERT L	CW3	W-0902068	C556	1
HORTCN ROY W	COL	0-0030626	0164	1
HORTON RUSSELL H	COL	C-0030125	1060	1
HORTON WILLIAM F	LTC	C-0023118	C761	1
HOSEA SILAS W	LTC	C-0015651	C753	1
HOSEMANN JOSEPH F	LTC	0-0080881	0865	1
HOSHAL QUENTIN S	LTC	0-0082029	0265	1
HOSKA JR LUKAS E	COL	0-0020717	C867	1
HOSKINS JR HARRY D	COL	0-0043846	0763	1
HOSKINS OLIVE L	WO1	W-0800013	0937	1
HOSKOT NATHANIEL	COL	C-0031379	C963	1
HOSPITAL RALPH	B G	0-0003625	C151	1
HOSS CHARLES A	COL	0-0008255	C653	1
HOSTERMAN FRANK M	COL	0-0038631	C859	1
HOSTETLER JEROME K	COL	0-0088744	1065	1
HOTALING ROBERT P	LTC	C-0062177	C863	1
HOUCK JOSEPH F	COL	0-0029162	0659	1
HOUCK ROSE E	MAJ	N-0002141	C761	1
HOUGH CHESTER C	COL	0-0011359	C854	1
HOUGH LLOYD W	LTC	0-0023251	0464	2
HOUGHTON FRANCIS E	COL	0-0039742	1061	1
HOUGHTON RUSSELL T	COL	0-0030430	0665	2
HOUGHTON WILLIAM C	MAJ	C-0003674	C534	2
HOULE GEORGE E	LTC	0-0013629	C-19	1
HOULSON KEITH H	LTC	0-0052229	1264	1
HOULT CHARLES S	COL	0-0042047	1161	2
HOUSE BARBARA M	LTC	R-0010074	C166	1
HOUSE JR JOHN M	COL	0-0029729	C762	1
HOUSE WILLIAM E	B G	0-0C16406	0656	1
HOUSEMAN EVAN M	M G	0-0017307	C961	1
HOUSER JACK	COL	0-0031263	C867	1
HOUSER JR HOUSTON P	COL	0-0018615	0159	1
HOUSMAN WALTER S	LTC	0-0053308	C961	1
HOUSTON EMMA F	LTC	N-00C1960	0463	1
HOUSTON EVA D	LTC	N-00C1950	1061	1
HOUSTON JR B Z	MAJ	C-0031979	1155	1
HOUSTON PAULINE V	LTC	L-0000054	C662	1
HOUTZ JCHN W	LTC	0-0063326	0166	1
HOVELL BERGEN B	COL	0-0023450	C662	1
HOWARD ALBERT N	CW2	W-0800264	0148	1
HOWARD CHARLES E	COL	C-0018521	0761	2
HOWARD CHARLES E	LTC	0-0030605	C164	1
HOWARD CHARLES F	COL	0-0017270	1047	2
HOWARD CHARLES R	LTC	0-0080109	1065	1
HOWARD CHARLES W	LTC	0-0059785	C766	1
HOWARD CLAUDE M	COL	0-0019464	0158	1
HOWARD EDWIN B	B G	0-0015361	C954	1

NAME	GRADE	SVC NO	DATE RET MO YR	RET CODE
HOWARD FRANCIS F	B G	0-0016776	C756	2
HOWARD HARMON	LTC	0-0062180	0966	1
HOWARD HAROLD F	LTC	0-0030643	0264	1
HOWARD HERBERT H	LTC	0-0046959	1062	1
HOWARD JAMES W	COL	0-0019601	1064	2
HOWARD JOHN E	COL	0-0038695	0855	1
HOWARD JOHN G	COL	0-0012704	0954	1
HOWARD JR ROBERT A	COL	0-0017182	0758	1
HOWARD KENNETH G	LTC	0-0037550	1262	1
HOWARD LULA J	MAJ	N-0002378	0261	1
HOWARD MARTIN L	CPT	0-000747C	0722	2
HOWARD ROBERT C	COL	0-0053368	0867	1
HOWARD THEODORE O	CW4	W-0903280	1156	1
HOWARD THOMAS J	LTC	0-0C33508	0660	1
HOWARD WARD C	COL	C-0042515	0265	2
HOWARD WILLIAM R	LTC	0-0051629	0860	1
HOWARD WILLIAM R	LTC	C-0067828	0467	1
HOWARTH ALBERT E R	COL	0-0018837	0862	1
HOWE CHARLES P	COL	0-0045555	0463	1
HOWE JEROME W	MAJ	0-0003464	0424	2
HOWE PAUL C	LTC	0-0014836	0438	2
HOWELL ALVIS M	LTC	0-0032797	0361	1
HOWELL ANN E	MAJ	N-0000985	C561	1
HOWELL CLIFFORD W	COL	0-0031462	0367	1
HOWELL EDWIN N	COL	0-0021194	0165	1
HOWELL GEORGE P	B G	0-0015291	1045	2
HOWELL HAROLD K	COL	0-0021421	1160	2
HOWELL JOHN N	COL	0-0019840	0865	1
HOWELL JR ALBERT S	2LT	0-001487C	0-25	2
HOWELL JR HARRY R	COL	C-0046248	0267	1
HOWELL JR WILLIAM C	COL	0-0030085	0661	1
HOWELL LENORE P	LTC	L-0000177	1264	1
HOWELL LYLBURNE M	COL	0-0C29C42	1058	1
HOWELL MAURICE M	MAJ	C-0035883	0763	1
HOWELL WALTER F	MAJ	C-0039149	1035	1
HOWLAND CHAUNCEY E	COL	0-0041671	0460	1
HOWLAND WILLIAM A	COL	0-0005102	1047	2
HOWZE HAMILTON H	GEN	0-0018088	0765	1
HOWZE JR ROBERT L	M G	0-0016055	C562	1
HOWZE MARION W	COL	0-0001797	0642	1
HOY CHARLES E	M G	0-0018556	0359	2
HOY CHARLES J	COL	0-0019905	1046	2
HOYLE LOUIS R	CW2	W-0901619	0451	1
HOYLE RENE DE R	M G	0-0002157	0845	2
HOYNE JOHN T	LTC	0-0029739	0860	1
HOYNE RAYMOND E	COL	0-0028804	0655	1
HUBARD RANDOLPH B	LTC	0-0017714	0150	1
HUBBARD ANNA K	MAJ	L-0000057	0659	1
HUBBARD DANIEL W	LTC	0-0060775	0967	1
HUBBARD EDMUND J	CW3	W-0904249	1162	2
HUBBARD FRANK G	LTC	0-0052430	0562	1
HUBBARD HARRY J	COL	0-0019459	0758	1
HUBBARD JACK A	LTC	0-007137C	0867	1
HUBBARD JEROME	COL	0-0041814	1060	1
HUBBARD JOHN R	COL	C-0009677	0942	1
HUBBARD JR FRANK R	LTC	0-0030165	1061	1
HUBBARD WILLIS W	MAJ	0-0014370	0819	2
HUBBART CLARENCE G	COL	0-0C29718	0662	1
HUBBELL REGINALD W	LTC	0-0012194	1041	1
HUBER DALE E	1LT	0-0019573	0241	2
HUBER WILLIAM R	COL	0-0018797	C862	1
HUBERT ENRIQUE J	LTC	0-0036518	0261	1
HUCHTHAUSEN W A	COL	0-0039665	0560	2
HUCKINS JOHN H	LTC	0-005129C	0360	1
HUDDLESTON JAMES M	LTC	0-0025554	0866	1
HUDDON ALBERT T	CW4	W-0903284	0158	1
HUDELSON MCCLURE	LTC	0-0043371	0660	2
HUDIBURG HOWARD B	COL	0-0031741	0562	1
HUDNALL JAMES R	COL	0-0005823	0448	2
HUDSON CARROLL O	COL	0-0028785	0954	1
HUDSON CHARLES C	CW4	W-0903285	0165	1
HUDSON GEORGE B	COL	0-0011233	0753	1
HUDSON GEORGE E	COL	C-0044410	0867	1
HUDSON HEBER S	LTC	0-0065446	1167	1
HUDSON JACK F	COL	C-0042184	0463	1

NAME	GRADE	SVC NO	DATE RET MO YR	RET CODE
HUOSON JAMES A	COL	0-0052137	C766	1
HUDSON KENNETH E	COL	0-0022278	C267	1
HUBSON LOIS E	MAJ	L-0000241	0262	1
HUDSON MAUDE A	MAJ	N-0000233	0963	1
HUDSON PAUL R	LTC	0-0005482	0841	2
HUEBNER CLARENCE R	LTG	0-0004552	1150	1
HUEBNER OTTO W	LTC	0-0050346	0966	1
HUETTER JOHN J	LTC	0-0063316	C962	1
HUFCUT VIRA B	MAJ	N-0002243	C261	1
HUFF JOHN S	LTC	0-0059859	0864	1
HUFF ROY P	COL	0-0014637	C347	2
HUFF RUFUS O	COL	0-0029311	1264	2
HUFF TOM	LTC	0-0058929	1162	1
HUFFMAN LESSIE P	MAJ	N-0002228	C360	1
HUFFORD GLENN D	LTC	0-0005477	1041	1
HUFFSMITH VICTOR C	COL	C-0019539	0646	2
HUGGINS GEORGE H	CW4	W-0906801	0665	1
HUGGINS ROSCOE C	COL	0-0018851	0162	1
HUGHES BERNICE G	LTC	L-0000208	C158	1
HUGHES CLYDE E	LTC	0-0048881	0764	1
HUGHES DWIGHT	COL	0-0006594	0444	2
HUGHES FREDRICK K	LTC	0-0024471	0762	1
HUGHES GEORGE F	COL	0-0030733	C666	1
HUGHES HAROLD L	LTC	0-0080888	C263	1
HUGHES J P	LTC	0-0042745	C364	1
HUGHES JAMES E	LTC	0-0058444	C766	1
HUGHES JAMES R	COL	0-0020343	1057	1
HUGHES JOHN B	COL	0-0012101	1148	1
HUGHES JR HENRY J	LTC	0-0027831	1165	1
HUGHES JR JAMES F	COL	0-0033956	1067	1
HUGHES JR ROBERT I	LTC	C-0091876	0867	1
HUGHES JR THOMAS W L	MAJ	0-0062577	C765	2
HUGHES JR WALTER P	MAJ	0-0062816	0866	1
HUGHES JR WILLIAM N	COL	0-0012962	1122	1
HUGHES OLIVER W	B G	0-0014974	0854	1
HUGHES ROBERT P	COL	0-0022769	0858	1
HUGHES THOMAS K	COL	C-0024449	1167	1
HUHNER MYRTLE C	MAJ	N-0000042	C650	1
HULING JR JOHN	COL	0-0007587	C446	2
HULKA SR JOHN P	CW4	W-0903288	1065	1
HULL DONALD F	COL	0-0022067	C262	1
HULL JAMES M	LTC	0-0065733	0767	1
HULL JOHN B	MAJ	C-0026308	C947	2
HULL JOHN E	GEN	0-0007377	C455	1
HULL KEITH M	LTC	0-0021885	1061	1
HULPA CHARLES A	CW3	W-0906803	0859	1
HULSE ALLEN O	B G	0-0021238	0863	1
HUMBERD QUENTIN L	LTC	0-0059897	C867	1
HUME HOWARD	COL	C-0004327	C646	1
HUME WAYNE S	COL	0-0059422	0263	1
HUMMEL JOHN F	COL	0-0042712	C266	1
HUMPHREY BEN K	MAJ	C-0023475	C546	2
HUMPHREY CHARLES F	B G	0-0000668	0340	2
HUMPHREY CHARLES V	LTC	0-0040945	C764	1
HUMPHREY CLARENCE L	LTC	0-0031609	0954	1
HUMPHREY LEON B	COL	0-0029073	0359	1
HUMPHREYS LEONARD A	LTC	0-0027467	C765	1
HUMPHREYS RUSSELL W	COL	0-0031910	0566	1
HUMPHREYS WILLIAM A	LTC	0-0028348	C766	1
HUMPHRIES F M	COL	C-0019012	0656	1
HUMPHRIES TROY T	CW4	W-0903289	0760	1
HUNDLEY DANIEL H	COL	C-0015862	0654	2
HUNEYCUTT ROBERT E	COL	0-0029946	C664	1
HUNGATE JR JAMES W	LTC	0-0039951	0263	1
HUNN CLIFFORD I	COL	0-0011363	0348	2
HUNNICUTT LEE V	COL	0-0008217	0546	1
HUNT CLIFTON T	COL	0-0011909	0950	1
HUNT GEORGE A	COL	C-0007117	0546	1
HUNT GEORGE M	COL	C-0030782	0962	1
HUNT GEORGE T	MAJ	0-0036777	0161	1
HUNT HAROLD H	MAJ	C-0016978	0648	1
HUNT JR HERMAN T	LTC	0-0026053	C865	1
HUNT JR JOHN M	COL	0-0031089	1266	1
HUNT LEWIS A	COL	C-0039889	0364	1
HUNT ORA E	B G	C-0000450	C923	1

NAME	GRADE	SVC NO	DATE RET MO YR	RET CODE
HUNT RICHARD J	COL	0-0018752	0862	1
HUNTER CHARLES N	COL	0-001771C	0859	1
HUNTER FLOYD W	COL	C-0004517	1146	1
HUNTER HOWARD W	COL	0-0018387	0946	2
HUNTER ROBERT C	LTC	0-0040045	0461	1
HUNTER THOMAS R	COL	0-0038791	1163	1
HUNTER W HAMILTON	COL	0-0016772	0757	1
HUNTER 3RD GEORGE W	COL	C-0029126	0355	1
HUNTINGTON ROBERT E	CW4	W-0903291	0758	1
HUNTZINGER HARVEY W	LTC	0-0070287	0867	1
HUPALO WILLIAM	COL	0-0040265	1164	1
HUPPERT JR GEORGE H	COL	0-0032277	0565	1
HURDIS CHARLES E	M G	0-0005229	1146	2
HURLESS BERNARD F	COL	0-0007417	0854	1
HURLEY EMERSON F	LTC	0-0031533	0856	2
HURLEY FREDERICK	COL	0-0046434	0364	1
HURLEY JOHN F	CW4	W-0903293	0658	1
HURLEY WESLEY C	LTC	0-0043319	1065	1
HURSH LAURENCE W	COL	0-0025146	0761	1
HURST JR CAM J	LTC	0-0065491	0767	1
HURST KENNETH M	COL	0-0041947	1161	1
HURST RAY H	LTC	0-004572C	0660	2
HURST RICHARD M	B G	0-0030191	1062	1
HURT HUGH A	MAJ	0-0044210	1054	2
HURT SHIRLEY R	COL	0-0011155	0447	2
HURT WILLIAM J	COL	0-0056811	1165	1
HUSE RALPH N	COL	C-0030819	1066	1
HUSMAN DONALD L	COL	C-0032431	0766	1
HUSSEY WILLIAM J	COL	0-0022205	0466	1
HUSTEAD GEORGE L T	LTC	0-0079863	0165	1
HUSTEAD JR CHARLES L	LTC	0-0043711	1062	2
HUSTEAD 2ND JAMES M	LTC	0-0024175	0660	1
HUSTON FRED R	LTC	C-0043612	0766	1
HUSTON WILBURN N	B G	C-0030612	0865	1
HUSTON ROBERT M	LTC	0-0038943	0361	1
HUTCHESON JOHN C	LTC	0-0007768	0242	1
HUTCHIN WALTER J	LTC	0-0025916	0865	1
HUTCHINS CARROLL R	COL	0-0011531	0947	1
HUTCHINS CHARLES W	LTC	0-0029714	0654	1
HUTCHINS ROBERT B	COL	0-0012407	1146	2
HUTCHINSON ARTHUR G	COL	C-0007615	C849	1
HUTCHINSON CARY B	COL	0-0015644	0954	1
HUTCHINSON D R	COL	0-0028822	0949	2
HUTCHINSON GEORGE W	LTC	0-0029744	0560	1
HUTCHINSON JR J W	1LT	0-0064117	1053	2
HUTCHINSON MELVILLE	MAJ	C-0037445	0861	1
HUTCHINSON PHILIP A	COL	0-0033200	0267	1
HUTCHINSON WILLIAM S	COL	C-0032611	0366	1
HUTCHISON CHARLES R	M G	0-0016795	0363	1
HUTCHISON JAMES H	MAJ	0-0060282	1163	1
HUTCHISON JOHN G	CW4	W-0903295	0462	1
HUTCHISON MORTIMER J	LTC	C-0034727	1061	1
HUTCHISON RUSSELL J	LTC	C-0052921	0667	1
HUTCHISON WARREN S	LTC	0-0084373	0367	1
HUTSINPILLER HERSC	LTC	0-0035487	0763	1
HUTSON JAMES C	COL	0-0004645	0845	2
HUTSON RICHARD K	COL	0-0032212	0766	1
HUTSON WILLIAM W	COL	0-0006918	1047	2
HYDE EARL A	LTC	0-0007883	1141	1
HYDE JR JAMES F C	MAJ	0-0624766	0447	2
HYLAND ANN T	MAJ	N-0000469	0465	1
HYLDEN MAURICE W	LTC	0-002698C	C863	1
HYMAN MARY F	MAJ	N-0001953	0859	1
HYNDMAN FLOYD M	LTC	0-0006822	0239	2
HYSSONG CLYDE L	M G	C-0008386	0749	1
HYZER PETER C	B G	C-0020589	0367	1
ICKLER JULIUS F	LTC	0-0050667	0767	1
IGERSHEIMER MILO	LTC	0-0037678	0761	1
IGO CLARENCE C	MAJ	0-0069692	0665	1
ILLIG JAMES M	B G	0-002033C	0765	1
IMHOFF JOSEPH J	COL	C-0051009	1156	1
IMMEL JOSEPH P	WO1	W-0901421	0342	1
IMRIE MATTHEW H	COL	0-0029181	0560	1
INFOSINO LUCY M	MAJ	N-0000861	0165	1
INGE ANDREW V	COL	0-0021448	0766	1

NAME	GRADE	SVC NO	DATE RET MO YR	RET CODE
INGEMAN MILTON J	COL	0-0042124	1262	1
INGHAM HENRY L	COL	0-0014792	1148	1
INGLES HARRY C	M G	0-0003689	0347	1
INGLES EDWARD	LTC	0-0031964	0562	1
INGOLD JOHN G	LTC	0-0003301	0837	2
INGRAHAM GORDON D	COL	0-0028848	C256	1
INGRAM ALBERTA T	MAJ	N-0000391	0961	1
INGRAM FORNEY H	COL	0-0029698	C756	1
INGRAM JERRY S	1LT	0-0064219	0453	2
INGRAM LIONEL R	COL	C-0029096	0459	1
INGRAM LOUIS L	COL	C-0019492	0766	2
INGRAM RUPERT	COL	C-0051103	C960	1
INGRAM SALLIE H	MAJ	N-0001302	C666	1
INGRUM LESLIE E	CW4	W-0903299	1057	1
INMAN JAMES G	COL	0-0041734	0163	1
INMON ERNER H	LTC	0-0008843	C540	2
INMON ERNEST G	CW3	W-0906806	C463	1
INMON THOMAS W	COL	0-0056254	C965	1
INNES JEAN W	MAJ	N-0002402	C862	1
INWOOD EUGENE R	COL	0-0020993	C654	2
IPPOLITO CHARLES J	LTC	0-0037208	1063	1
IRBY FRED B	LTC	C-0042683	1263	2
IRBY VERNON C	LTC	0-0025251	0266	2
IRBY WILLIAM B	COL	C-0031035	C866	1
IRELAND ARTHUR P	COL	0-0051543	0964	1
IRELAND THOMAS R	COL	0-0051004	1058	1
IREY NELSON S	COL	0-0030928	1165	1
IRICK JR EDWARD F	LTC	0-0060791	0667	1
IRISH RALPH G	LTC	0-0080897	C664	1
IRISH WYNOT R	COL	C-0011227	0354	1
IRONS ARTHUR L	B G	0-0016526	C857	1
IRVIN JR RICHARD	COL	0-0025118	C666	1
IRVIN ROY D	COL	0-0042104	1162	1
IRVINE ELROY S J	COL	0-0004420	1047	1
IRVINE MICHAEL M	COL	0-0018404	0761	1
IRVINE RICHARD H	LTC	0-0036705	C165	1
IRVINE WILLARD W	M G	0-0005838	C452	1
IRVING CHARLES R	CPT	0-0014223	1019	2
IRVING FREDERICK	M G	0-0005261	0854	1
IRVING HAROLD W	CW3	W-0903300	0455	1
IRVING JR JOHN H	LTC	0-0027004	C864	1
IRVING VERNIE M	MAJ	N-0001906	C862	1
IRWIN CONSTANT L	B G	0-0004757	0344	2
IRWIN GORDON C	COL	0-0005729	C847	2
IRWIN SAMUEL L	LTC	0-0031346	1064	1
ISAAC LEE	LTC	0-0080112	C866	1
ISAACSON DONALD F	LTC	0-0031965	0262	1
ISAACSON HAROLD S	COL	0-0016836	0757	1
ISACCS GEORGE	COL	0-0015959	0754	1
ISBELL HENRY W	COL	0-0009978	C947	1
ISELEY CHARLES M	COL	0-0018828	C862	1
ISEMAN JOSEPH D	COL	0-0033798	C865	1
ISENBERG CONLEY G	LTC	0-0040104	1262	2
ISH GEORGE D	LTC	0-0036102	0861	1
ISHAM CARL T	COL	0-0019856	0965	1
ISHIDA GEORGE S	MAJ	0-0078895	C265	1
ISHOY VICTOR A	COL	0-0031640	1164	1
ISKER ROHLAND A	COL	0-0007355	0546	1
ISNER ALVIS E	LTC	0-0046626	0863	1
ISON FRANK S	COL	0-0039819	0263	1
ISRAELSON JOHN A	COL	0-0080898	0765	1
ISRAELSON NATHANIEL	LTC	C-0080113	C866	1
ISRIN MICHAEL D	LTC	0-0030756	0664	1
ITSCHNER EMERSON C	LTG	0-0015516	0461	1
IULTUCCI THOMAS P	COL	0-0024848	0963	1
IVERSON VERNON L	MAJ	0-0078896	0765	1
IVES ALBERT R	COL	C-0004863	0147	2
IVES H DUDLEY	M G	0-0029509	1265	1
IVES WASHINGTON	COL	0-0015698	0954	1
IVEY RICHARD G	MAJ	0-0021116	1046	2
IVINS CHARLES F	COL	0-0012862	0554	1
JACCARD PAUL A	COL	0-0016694	1054	1
JACKMAN ALBERT H	COL	0-0051402	0562	2
JACKS GORDON L	LTC	0-0049357	C266	1
JACKS SAMUEL T	COL	0-0079707	1066	1

NAME	GRADE	SVC NO	DATE RET MO YR	RET CODE
JACKSON ALBERT M	COL	C-0005854	1146	1
JACKSON ASBURY H	LTC	0-0029629	C961	2
JACKSON FRED C	COL	C-0047577	0867	1
JACKSON GAIL M	CW4	W-0903305	0466	1
JACKSON GEORGE D	LTC	0-0027821	0865	1
JACKSON GORDON E	LTC	0-004695C	0267	1
JACKSON HAROLD R	B G	0-0005237	0653	1
JACKSON JAMES H	LTC	0-0031580	0560	1
JACKSON JOSEPH C	COL	0-0029089	0359	1
JACKSON JR HAL G	LTC	0-0088753	0966	1
JACKSON JR LANGDON A	COL	0-0020251	0864	1
JACKSON JR W F	COL	0-0028820	1055	2
JACKSON JR ROBERT J	LTC	0-0038586	0761	1
JACKSON KINGSBURY	LTC	C-0080428	0965	1
JACKSON LOUIS W	COL	0-0029474	1060	1
JACKSON MARGARET E	MAJ	N-0000918	1167	1
JACKSON MARION H	COL	0-0031629	0263	1
JACKSON NEWTON L P	CW3	W-0907123	0860	1
JACKSON NORTON	LTC	0-0040054	0862	2
JACKSON PAGE S	CPT	0-0026042	0350	1
JACKSON RALPH B	CW4	W-0906808	0563	1
JACKSON THOMAS M	CW4	W-0903307	0757	1
JACKSON WENDELL T	COL	0-0057897	0966	2
JACKSON WILLIAM D	COL	0-0039628	1059	1
JACKSON WILLIAM F	COL	0-0051529	0464	1
JACO JR CHARLES M	LTC	0-0028203	0866	1
JACOBS BEN R	COL	C-0011641	0453	1
JACOBS EUGENE C	COL	0-0020499	0665	1
JACOBS FRED A	LTC	0-0041935	1059	1
JACOBS GERALD O	COL	0-0031548	1066	1
JACOBS JAMES R	MAJ	0-0003259	1022	2
JACOBS JR RICHARD C	COL	C-0010908	0548	1
JACOBS LAWRENCE P	B G	0-0031556	0466	1
JACOBS MARVIN L	COL	0-0022915	0862	1
JACOBS STANLEY E	COL	0-0052256	1064	1
JACOBSON LUCY E	LTC	N-0001873	1160	1
JACOBSON SIMON	COL	0-0009577	0747	1
JACOBSON WALTER A	MAJ	C-0050473	C762	1
JACOBY ARTHUR M	COL	0-0020125	0765	1
JACOBY LESLIE E	COL	0-001230C	0753	1
JACOBY PHILIP R	LTC	0-0076262	0167	2
JACQUES DONALD M	COL	0-0050934	0157	1
JACULA PETER M	LTC	0-0028716	0767	1
JACUNSKI EDWARD W	LTC	0-0021334	1141	2
JADWIN CORNELIUS	COL	0-0011213	0948	1
JAEGER VERNON P	COL	0-0018954	0163	1
JAGGAR JOSEPH L	COL	0-0051071	0160	1
JAGIELLO WALTER A	MAJ	0-0027584	0866	1
JAHNKE JR EDWARD J	COL	0-0059591	0967	1
JAKUBIAK ALICE P	1LT	M-0000799	0545	1
JAMES EDWARD B	COL	0-0041545	0459	1
JAMES GEORGE W	COL	0-0030146	0364	1
JAMES GLENN A	CW4	W-0903310	0762	1
JAMES III CHARLES A	CPT	0-0060000	0766	1
JAMES JR JOSEPH E	COL	0-0018237	0658	1
JAMES JR STANLEY L	LTC	0-0025833	0864	1
JAMES LEE B	COL	C-0025619	1163	1
JAMES OTTIS E	COL	0-0029192	1160	1
JAMES WILLARD W	LTC	0-0031167	0666	1
JAMESON ROY A	COL	0-0032072	1062	1
JAMULA CECILIA P	LTC	N-0000485	C367	1
JANAIRO MAXIMIANO	COL	0-0018098	0860	2
JANDA EARL J	LTC	C-0066027	0867	1
JANES CLINTON W	COL	C-0038730	1160	1
JANES ERNEST L	COL	0-0031587	0767	1
JANK ARTHUR W	LTC	0-0027926	0567	1
JANKOVIAK ANGELINE P	LTC	N-0000996	0767	1
JANKOWSKI HENORINA	MAJ	N-0002385	0961	1
JANOF THEODORE	COL	0-0020382	0864	1
JANOUSEK NEAL F	LTC	0-0036127	0662	2
JANSEN JOSEPH F	LTC	0-0084057	1166	1
JANZ DONALD H	LTC	0-0024217	0762	1
JAPINGA ROBERT M	MAJ	0-0065142	1167	1
JARBOE JESSE J	COL	0-0030921	1265	1
JARK CARL H	LTG	0-0017556	0864	2

NAME	GRADE	SVC NO	DATE RET MO YR	RET CODE
JARRELL JULIUS B	CW4	W-0903312	0860	1
JARRELL SHAFFER F	COL	O-0051112	1160	2
JARRETT DONALD L	LTC	O-0041845	0358	1
JARRETT JOHN A	LTC	O-0065016	0661	2
JARROLD MILTON	LTC	O-0043699	0861	1
JARVIS JOSEPH W	LTC	O-0031530	0252	1
JARVIS 3RD GEORGE M	COL	O-0050975	1057	1
JASTREMSKI BRUNO	COL	O-0020526	0258	1
JAUERNIG RUSSELL P	LTC	O-0058019	0867	1
JAY HENRY D	B G	O-0004952	0948	1
JAYCOX JOHN W	MAJ	O-0022078	0658	1
JAYNE HARRIET J	MAJ	N-0000708	0261	1
JAYNES LAWRENCE C	M G	O-0010540	0853	1
JEFFCOTT GEORGE F	COL	O-0020077	0960	1
JEFFER KAZMIERA A	CPT	N-0000313	0350	1
JEFFERDS JEROME S	COL	O-0052283	0964	1
JEFFERIS TOMAS C	COL	O-0031137	0467	1
JEFFERS RICHARD F	COL	O-0040165	0662	1
JEFFERS ULIE H	CW2	W-0800230	0450	1
JEFFERSON LESLIE W	COL	O-0009767	0751	1
JEFFERSON MARIAN Y	LTC	N-0000081	0354	1
JEFFERSON WAYNE D	COL	O-0029766	0962	1
JEFFERSON WILLIAM T	CW4	W-0903314	0164	1
JEFFERY ARTHUR B	COL	O-0030201	0664	1
JEFFERES JAMES F	LTC	O-0007206	0941	2
JEFFRESS VINNIE H	COL	O-0018638	0355	2
JEFFREY ALTA R	CPT	N-0001443	0954	2
JEFFREY JACK C	COL	O-0030763	0863	1
JEFFREYS ALICE C	MAJ	N-0001229	0460	1
JEFFRIES CHARLES E	LTC	O-0040208	0361	1
JEFFUS CHARLES J	COL	O-0019730	0954	1
JELLETT DAVID T	LTC	O-0019273	1054	1
JENICEK JOHN A	COL	O-0057989	0967	1
JENKINS CHARLES A	COL	O-0031369	1166	1
JENKINS DONALD L	COL	O-0045935	0365	1
JENKINS JAMES R	LTC	O-0035054	1058	1
JENKINS JESSE S	CW3	W-0904130	0556	1
JENKINS JR JOHN M	COL	O-0004716	1050	1
JENKINS PARK T	COL	O-0032218	0467	1
JENKINS PAUL H	COL	O-0015663	1046	2
JENKINS REUBEN E	LTG	O-0011658	0254	2
JENKINS THOMAS G	COL	O-0005760	0452	1
JENKINS WALTER E	COL	O-0005155	0753	1
JENKINS WILBUR G	COL	O-0008528	1146	2
JENKS HAROLD F	COL	O-0031691	0167	1
JENKS LOREN T	COL	O-0024356	0561	2
JENNA RUSSELL W	COL	O-0019564	0661	1
JENNA WILLIAM W	COL	O-0008642	0954	1
JENNERSON HORACE L	LTC	O-0039620	0657	1
JENNINGS CATHERINE	MAJ	N-0002125	1159	1
JENNINGS CLARENCE M	COL	O-0041643	0457	1
JENNINGS MAURICE E	COL	O-0011320	1048	1
JENNINGS RAYMOND J	LTC	O-0034120	0561	2
JENNINGS THOMAS A	COL	O-0015793	0654	1
JENNINGS WALTER F	COL	O-0014728	0854	1
JENNINGS WILLIAM [illegible]	COL	O-0019640	0961	1
JENNINGS WILLIAM [illegible]	COL	O-0039964	0962	2
JENSEN ALLEN	COL	O-0023692	0765	1
JENSEN DORIS F	MAJ	N-0001963	0860	1
JENSEN DOVRE C	LTC	O-0052166	0666	1
JENSEN HUBERT J	MAJ	O-0058452	0766	1
JENSEN MELVIN N	LTC	O-0045771	0863	1
JENSEN NAOMI J	LTC	N-0000080	0459	1
JENSEN OSWALD R	COL	O-0021461	0957	1
JENSEN ROLAND F	LTC	O-0053300	0763	1
JENSEN WALTER A	M G	O-0019006	0567	1
JENSEN WANDA	MAJ	N-0002123	1159	1
JENSON LLOYD K	COL	O-0059788	0265	2
JEPSON HANS C	COL	O-0029966	0963	1
JERBI FRANK C	COL	O-0052027	0965	1
JERVEY JOHN P	LTC	O-0049219	0865	1
JERVEY JR JAMES P	LTC	O-0012091	0825	2
JERVEY THOMAS M	COL	O-0007977	1148	2
JESPERSEN HANS C	COL	O-0010801	0546	1
JESSE WILLIAM C	COL	O-0042446	1056	2

NAME	GRADE	SVC NO	DATE RET MO YR	RET CODE
JESSEN RAYMOND F	LTC	O-0051590	0263	1
JESURUN HAROLD M	COL	O-0026439	0767	1
JETER JOHN R	COL	O-0016342	1055	1
JETT RICHARD C	LTC	O-0027856	0367	1
JEWELL KENNETH T	CW4	W-0903317	0664	1
JEWETT JOHN J	LTC	O-0039890	0262	1
JEWETT LEONARD G	COL	O-0022236	0867	1
JEWETT RAYMOND F	CW4	W-0903318	0960	1
JEWETT RICHARD L	B G	O-0018339	0761	1
JOERNS FREDERICK	LTC	O-0069695	0765	1
JOFFRAY EUGENE A	CW4	W-0903319	0461	1
JOGL JOSEPH W	COL	O-0030330	1262	1
JOHANNES HENRY C	COL	O-0006364	0945	2
JOHANSEN RAYMOND R	CPT	O-0019628	0239	2
JOHANSSON ADRIAN	LTC	O-0051710	1155	1
JOHN ERNEST	COL	O-0005792	0446	2
JOHN HOWARD J	COL	O-0015802	0854	1
JOHNS CAROL A	CPT	O-0063061	0363	1
JOHNS DWIGHT F	B G	O-0004417	1249	1
JOHNS JR GLOVER S	COL	O-0031501	0467	1
JOHNS CRAS L	COL	O-0029323	0864	1
JOHNS WALTER E	COL	O-0017142	0946	2
JOHNSON ALBERT M	COL	O-0039858	1263	1
JOHNSON ALBERT W	COL	O-0012174	0147	1
JOHNSON ALCORN B	COL	O-0041636	1059	1
JOHNSON ALFRED B	COL	O-0003550	0548	1
JOHNSON ALICE J	MAJ	N-0000518	1149	1
JOHNSON AMOS G	LTC	O-0021363	0665	1
JOHNSON ANDREW L	LTC	O-0030934	1264	1
JOHNSON BERTIL A	LTC	O-0023086	1264	1
JOHNSON BERTRAM H	LTC	O-0051503	0562	1
JOHNSON BRIARD P	M G	O-0029293	1163	2
JOHNSON BRUCE H	LTC	O-0030042	1060	1
JOHNSON BURCHARD M	LTC	O-0029051	1056	1
JOHNSON CHARLES E	M G	O-0019534	1167	1
JOHNSON CHARLES F	COL	O-0008019	0849	2
JOHNSON CHARLES S	COL	O-0007191	0753	1
JOHNSON CHARLES W	COL	O-0036315	0764	1
JOHNSON CLARENCE F	LTC	O-0041747	1161	1
JOHNSON CLAYTON E	LTC	O-0062244	0867	1
JOHNSON DAVID F	LTC	O-0063164	0967	1
JOHNSON DAVID T	COL	O-0012067	0753	1
JOHNSON DOUGLAS V	M G	O-0015072	0360	1
JOHNSON DWIGHT B	M G	O-0018722	0867	1
JOHNSON DWIGHT F	LTC	O-0039932	1162	2
JOHNSON EARLE A	COL	O-0008240	0353	1
JOHNSON EDNA L	MAJ	N-0001909	1062	1
JOHNSON EDWARD C	LTC	O-0030753	0664	1
JOHNSON EDWARD C	CW4	W-0904132	0564	1
JOHNSON EDWARD M	WO1	W-0800147	0137	2
JOHNSON EDWARD T	COL	O-0029856	0361	1
JOHNSON EDWIN H	COL	O-0005434	0753	1
JOHNSON EDWIN L	B G	O-0016158	0656	1
JOHNSON ELIZABETH	MAJ	N-0000083	0954	1
JOHNSON EWINC C	LTC	O-0019851	1050	1
JOHNSON FINIS G	COL	O-0040067	1066	1
JOHNSON FOLKEY L	LTC	O-0029431	0758	1
JOHNSON FRANK M S	COL	O-0005566	0549	2
JOHNSON GEORGE B	CW2	W-0901675	0647	1
JOHNSON GEORGE V	COL	O-0039871	0963	2
JOHNSON GORDON M	COL	O-0029406	0361	1
JOHNSON HAROLD P	COL	O-0029352	0558	1
JOHNSON HARRY W	M G	O-0016351	0161	1
JOHNSON HARRY W	LTC	O-0042821	0762	1
JOHNSON HARVEY A	COL	O-0041462	0757	1
JOHNSON HELEN V	LTC	N-0000031	0948	1
JOHNSON HORACE W	1LT	O-0016625	0233	2
JOHNSON HUGH C	COL	O-0015345	0954	1
JOHNSON IRVIN A	COL	O-0040464	0864	1
JOHNSON JAMES A	MAJ	O-0089343	0367	1
JOHNSON JAMES E	COL	O-0043704	0667	1
JOHNSON JAMES M	COL	O-0054002	0367	2
JOHNSON JAMES R	COL	O-0020256	0867	1
JOHNSON JAMES W	LTC	O-0033307	0761	1
JOHNSON JESSE H	COL	O-0051797	0966	1

NAME	GRADE	SVC NO	DATE RET MO YR	RET CODE
JOHNSON JOHN E	COL	O-0039828	0463	1
JOHNSON JOHN F	LTC	O-0025538	0260	1
JOHNSON JOHN G	COL	O-0021929	0864	1
JOHNSON JOHN J	COL	O-0011865	0943	2
JOHNSON JOHN P	COL	O-0043677	0765	2
JOHNSON JOHNNIE D	CW4	W-0903322	0757	1
JOHNSON JOSEPH L	1LT	O-0019358	0142	1
JOHNSON JR CHARLES R	COL	O-0008299	0647	1
JOHNSON JR CHARLES W	LTC	O-0080115	1265	1
JOHNSON JR EDWARD D	1LT	O-0086328	0163	2
JOHNSON JR ELMER	LTC	O-0038799	0663	1
JOHNSON JR HERBERT A	LTC	O-0033140	0257	2
JOHNSON JR JOHN A	CW3	W-0906812	0167	1
JOHNSON JR JOHN N	LTC	O-0007854	1041	1
JOHNSON JR LEHMAN H	LTC	O-0044831	0262	1
JOHNSON JR VICTOR L	COL	O-0022013	1146	2
JOHNSON JR WILLIAM H	COL	O-0029908	0863	2
JOHNSON KENNETH C	COL	O-0044090	0467	1
JOHNSON KENNETH L	COL	O-0015416	1153	1
JOHNSON LAURENCE A	LTC	O-0033361	0361	1
JOHNSON LEONARD H	LTC	O-0040227	0561	1
JOHNSON LEONARD L	COL	O-0035441	0666	1
JOHNSON LEONARD M	COL	O-0015921	0754	1
JOHNSON LEONARD M	COL	O-0042329	0364	1
JOHNSON LOUIS H	LTC	O-0046097	0762	1
JOHNSON LUTHER F	LTC	O-0030535	0761	1
JOHNSON MARGARET R	LTC	L-0000086	0263	1
JOHNSON MAX	M G	O-0016745	0259	1
JOHNSON MILTON L	LTC	O-0042284	1061	1
JOHNSON NANCY A	MAJ	N-0000705	0161	1
JOHNSON NEAL C	B G	O-0005023	0152	1
JOHNSON RAGNAR F	COL	O-0028813	0755	1
JOHNSON RALPH K	COL	O-0042213	0763	1
JOHNSON RALPH R	LTC	O-0068018	0867	1
JOHNSON RICHARD A	LTC	O-0028145	0167	1
JOHNSON RICHARD P	COL	O-0018940	0856	1
JOHNSON ROBERT E	LTC	O-0051309	0560	1
JOHNSON ROBERT M	LTC	O-0024498	1160	1
JOHNSON ROBERT P	COL	O-0023926	0867	1
JOHNSON ROY E	CW4	W-0906815	0359	1
JOHNSON SEWALL H F	LTC	O-0028712	0768	1
JOHNSON STANLEY T	COL	O-0019743	0865	1
JOHNSON SUSIE G	MAJ	N-0002330	1264	1
JOHNSON THOMAS J	COL	O-0002374	1039	2
JOHNSON TILLMAN O	LTC	O-0022301	0459	1
JOHNSON VERNON R	COL	O-0039584	0658	1
JOHNSON WALTER M	B G	O-0016835	0657	2
JOHNSON WALTER R	CW2	W-0901644	0748	1
JOHNSON WARREN R	COL	O-0043697	0466	1
JOHNSON WENDELL G	COL	O-0019312	0954	1
JOHNSON WESLEY L	CW4	W-0903325	0856	1
JOHNSON WILBUR M	COL	O-0030577	1265	1
JOHNSON WILHELM R	M G	O-0017229	0762	2
JOHNSON WILLIAM A	COL	O-0021228	0858	2
JOHNSON WILLIAM P	COL	O-0008447	0746	2
JOHNSON WILLIAM G	COL	O-0038756	0454	1
JOHNSON WILLIAM L	COL	O-0015657	1146	2
JOHNSON WILLIAM O	MAJ	O-0009691	0131	1
JOHNSON WILLIAM [illegible]	COL	O-0011111	0247	1
JOHNSON WRIGHT H	CPT	O-0007399	0926	2
JOHNSTON CARL R	LTC	O-0087538	0565	2
JOHNSTON EDWARD S	COL	O-0004906	0744	2
JOHNSTON EUGENE [illegible]	COL	O-0012727	0954	1
JOHNSTON HAROLD L	CW3	W-0906814	0361	1
JOHNSTON JOSEPH E	COL	O-0030424	0565	1
JOHNSTON JOSEPH W	B G	O-0030462	1065	1
JOHNSTON JR DANA W	COL	O-0019506	0864	1
JOHNSTON JR MONT S	COL	O-0053169	0463	1
JOHNSTON KELBOURNE	COL	O-0017252	0650	1
JOHNSTON MARVIN V	COL	O-0043313	0962	1
JOHNSTON OSCAR P	COL	O-0012771	1051	1
JOHNSTON PAULINE V	LTC	N-0002140	0264	1
JOHNSTON ROBERT B	COL	O-0014843	0751	1
JOHNSTON ROBERT D	COL	O-0018498	0661	1
JOHNSTON ROBERT L	CW3	W-0906816	0756	1

NAME	GRADE	SVC NO	DATE RET MO YR	RET CODE
JOHNSTON SR ROBERT G	COL	O-0051033	0559	2
JOHNSTONE JOHN C	LTC	O-0044702	1162	1
JOHNSTONE ROBERT R	WO1	W-0800032	0938	2
JOINER PHILLIP M	CW4	W-0903327	0263	1
JOINER TALLEY D	COL	O-0007569	0446	2
JOINER WILLIAM H	COL	O-0005464	0542	1
JOLLEY PAUL L	COL	O-0030764	0364	2
JOLLIFFE KATHARINE	LTC	N-0000077	1058	1
JONES ALAN W	M G	O-0005886	0-45	2
JONES ARGYLE P	LTC	O-0039842	0158	1
JONES ARTHUR T	LTC	O-0021678	0758	1
JONES BEVERLY D	COL	O-0019081	0863	1
JONES BRUCE D	COL	O-0034238	0866	1
JONES CATESBYAPC	COL	O-0006936	1146	1
JONES CHARLES P	COL	O-0012262	0946	2
JONES CHARLES R	COL	O-0005615	0946	2
JONES CHESLEY H	LTC	O-0078901	1065	2
JONES CLIFFORD	COL	O-0001805	0642	2
JONES CLIFFORD R	COL	O-0003833	0251	1
JONES CLYDE L	COL	O-0019074	0863	1
JONES DANIEL R	LTC	O-0037937	1163	1
JONES DAVID W	COL	O-0043631	1265	1
JONES DE WITT C	COL	O-0002021	0642	1
JONES DEAN H	LTC	O-0030724	0664	1
JONES EDWIN W	LTC	O-0040530	1162	2
JONES ELIZABETH	LTC	M-0010114	0662	1
JONES EMMETT G	LTC	O-0051170	0762	1
JONES ERNEST E	LTC	O-0080122	1166	1
JONES ERWIN A	COL	O-0041528	0758	2
JONES ERWIN P	COL	O-0036168	0667	1
JONES FRANK A	COL	O-0005187	0450	1
JONES FRED E	LTC	O-0027232	0765	1
JONES GEORGE A A	COL	O-0014845	0854	1
JONES GEORGE W	LTC	O-0031521	0867	1
JONES GILBERT C	LTC	O-0064598	1064	1
JONES GORDON A	LTC	O-0031090	0263	1
JONES H CRAMPTON	COL	O-0004441	0753	1
JONES HAROLD C	COL	O-0028772	0354	1
JONES HAROLD L	LTC	O-0043337	0965	1
JONES HARRIS	B G	O-0005222	0756	2
JONES HAZEL M	MAJ	N-0000944	1165	1
JONES HENRY C	COL	O-0014745	0251	1
JONES HENRY L C	M G	O-0003168	0246	2
JONES HERBERT M	M G	O-0012251	1058	1
JONES HOMER W	COL	O-0012529	0747	1
JONES JENNER G	COL	O-0019603	0657	1
JONES JOHN T	LTC	O-0030687	1060	1
JONES JR CHARLES A	MAJ	O-0024533	0860	1
JONES JR CHARLES M	LTC	O-0025590	0765	1
JONES JR HERMAN A	COL	O-0031212	1066	1
JONES JR JOHN P	COL	O-0030807	0866	1
JONES JR LLOYD F	LTC	O-0025396	0963	1
JONES JR RICHARD W	LTC	O-0051090	1058	2
JONES JR WAYLAND	COL	O-0035763	0967	1
JONES KENNETH C	COL	O-0042115	0657	1
JONES KENNETH P	COL	O-0024720	1058	1
JONES LAURENCE W	COL	O-0045646	0765	1
JONES LAWRENCE M	COL	O-0009578	0537	1
JONES LEE G	LTC	O-0024757	0962	1
JONES LOUIS V	COL	O-0010153	0549	1
JONES MALCOLM D	COL	O-0016435	0656	1
JONES MARCUS E	COL	O-0010291	0753	1
JONES NELSON H	LTC	O-0059703	0367	1
JONES OPAL M	MAJ	N-0002404	1262	1
JONES PEGGY C	LTC	N-0000363	1160	1
JONES RALPH E	COL	O-0002659	0939	2
JONES REMUS J	LTC	O-0406029	0763	1
JONES RICHARD A	COL	O-0007638	0353	1
JONES RICHARD T	COL	O-0030410	0463	1
JONES ROBERT D	COL	O-0080918	1166	1
JONES ROBERT E	COL	O-0007766	0546	1
JONES ROBERT J	COL	O-0028970	0357	1
JONES SHERBERT H	LTC	O-0047988	0265	1
JONES STANLEY H	M G	O-0017747	0365	2
JONES THOMAS B	COL	O-0042915	1166	1

UNITED STATES ARMY RETIRED LIST

NAME	GRADE	SVC NO	DATE RET MO YR	RET CODE
JONES THOMAS C	LTC	0-0020065	C757	1
JONES THOMAS R	LTC	0-0019331	C153	1
JONES THOMAS S	COL	0-0052403	C962	1
JONES THORNTON E	COL	0-0030214	C764	1
JONES VIRLYN Y	LTC	0-0030739	0664	1
JONES WALTER E	CW2	W-0901295	C244	2
JONES WERNER E	COL	0-002885C	0356	1
JONES WILLIAM H	COL	C-0003578	C949	2
JONES WILLIAM M	LTC	0-0037209	0665	1
JONES WILLIAM P	CW2	W-0901337	C946	1
JONES WILLIAM S	LTC	0-0029402	C458	1
JONES WILLIE H H	COL	0-0039626	1059	1
JONES WINSTON A	LTC	0-0032602	0460	2
JONES WINSTON I	COL	0-0051954	1167	1
JONES WOODFIN G	COL	0-0003712	0547	2
JONES 3RD WILLIAM C	1LT	0-C026916	0246	2
JONSON WAYNE H	LTC	0-0037484	0160	2
JORDAHN ERIK W	COL	0-0044060	1065	1
JORDAN EDGAR J	LTC	0-0021943	1047	2
JORDAN EDWARD E	LTC	0-0054028	C866	1
JORDAN FRANK B	COL	0-0003617	0651	1
JORDAN HAROLD R	LTC	0-0011771	0836	1
JORDAN HERBERT A	COL	0-0038795	C660	2
JORDAN HERBERT S	COL	C-0015389	1148	1
JORDAN HOWELL H	COL	C-0016906	0157	1
JORDAN LEWIS R	COL	C-0011988	C854	1
JORDAN MARY C	LTC	N-0000987	0965	1
JORDAN RICHARD H	B G	0-0001647	0740	1
JORDAN WALTER E	COL	0-0041910	1061	1
JORDAN WILLIAM H	COL	0-0020249	1047	2
JORDAN WOODROW W	LTC	C-0080431	0565	1
JORGENSON ARTHUR L	LTC	0-0032436	0859	1
JORGENSON GEORGE H	CW2	W-0902156	C149	2
JOSEPH DONALD J	COL	0-0060027	1067	1
JOSEPH EDWIN M	LTC	0-0028522	C567	1
JOSEPH HENRY B	COL	0-0029054	C159	1
JOSEPH JOHN T	COL	0-0033756	0966	1
JOSEPH ROBERT E	COL	0-0028836	0154	1
JOSEPHSON STANTON W	COL	0-0024745	C867	1
JOSEY CLAUDE K	CPT	0-0027433	1058	2
JOSLIN WILL D	COL	0-0031816	0464	1
JOSLYN CLYDE A	LTC	0-0049893	0264	1
JOYCE JR CLAUDE P	COL	0-0042426	0862	1
JOYCE MAHLEN A	COL	0-0003644	0935	2
JOYCE THOMAS F	COL	0-0010204	1052	1
JOYCE WILLIAM A	LTC	C-0020386	0-44	2
JOYNER CHARLES A	MAJ	C-0038560	0766	1
JOYNER RALPH L	LTC	0-0005586	0934	2
JUDSON PHILIP M	LTC	0-0030516	0963	1
JUDSON ROBERT R	COL	C-0039794	0961	1
JUDSON WILLIAM J	LTC	0-0031769	C562	1
JUDY JACKSON K	COL	0-0039825	C361	1
JULIAN LEONARD J	LTC	0-0051814	1164	1
JUNGE EDWIN B	LTC	0-0059964	0866	1
JURASH HELEN J	LTC	N-0000528	0456	1
JURDEN DELBERT A	LTC	0-0062241	0765	1
JURGENS KENNETH E	COL	0-0043496	0864	1
JUSKALIAN GEORGE	COL	0-0032371	C567	1
JUSTICE LONZO O	MAJ	0-0038565	0165	1
JUZEK HARRY J	COL	C-0009467	C651	1
KABRICH CHARLES E	COL	0-0039856	1063	1
KACHMAN EVELYN A	MAJ	N-0000343	0463	1
KADROVACH DAN G	LTC	0-0037613	C163	1
KAESER WILLIAM G	LTC	0-0042685	1263	1
KAESSER HERMAN H	COL	0-0019057	C155	1
KAHN WILBUR L	LTC	0-0026631	C764	1
KAIGLER JOHNATHON	COL	0-0029721	C662	1
KAISER CLIFFORD	COL	C-0028801	0355	1
KAISER CLIFFORD F	LTC	C-002912C	C957	2
KAISER EMMA S	MAJ	N-0000224	0260	1
KAISER MAURICE E	COL	0-0019165	C863	1
KAISER ROSALYN J	LTC	L-0000053	0459	1
KAIT HARRY C	COL	0-0029532	C361	1
KALE LESTER W	COL	C-0029815	1162	1
KALEY WILLIAM E	COL	C-0041818	1160	1

NAME	GRADE	SVC NO	DATE RET MO YR	RET CODE
KALISTA CLIFFORD J	MAJ	0-0027038	0859	2
KALLIS STEPHEN A	LTC	0-0038687	0559	2
KAMARAS JOHN G	LTC	0-0028100	1166	1
KAMINSKIE ALEX	LTC	0-0051116	1058	2
KAMINSKY AARON L	LTC	C-0023593	1150	1
KAMISH ROBERT J	COL	0-0029295	0964	1
KAMMERAAD ANGIE C	LTC	N-0001529	0566	1
KAMMERER MALCOLM R	COL	0-0016403	C656	1
KAMP JR ANTHONY M	LTC	0-0033482	0467	2
KAMY HARRY O	COL	0-0042321	0364	1
KANAGA CLARENCE J	COL	0-0C12302	0-36	2
KANE ANDREW D	COL	0-0042073	1162	2
KANE GEORGE W	LTC	0-0055446	0863	1
KANE HARLAND M	CW4	W-0903334	C360	1
KANE JOHN H	COL	0-0016492	0445	2
KANE JR FRANK R	LTC	C-0079874	0966	1
KANE JR MICHAEL	COL	0-0031476	0467	1
KANE LEO M	LTC	0-0024569	0965	1
KANE O NEILL K	COL	0-0018150	0654	2
KANE STEPHEN W	COL	0-0041754	1061	1
KANTAK GREGORY H	CW4	W-0903335	0360	1
KARNS ROBERT H	MAJ	0-0080125	0463	1
KARPEN RAYMOND J	COL	C-0041764	0764	1
KARR JR GUY A	LTC	0-0080922	1166	1
KARRER ROBERT J	COL	0-0051195	0659	2
KARRICK SAMUEL N	COL	0-0009256	0749	1
KASDORF WALTER W	LTC	0-0080923	0966	1
KASPER ROBERT J	COL	0-0021084	0264	1
KASPER WILLIAM M	COL	0-002321C	0465	1
KASSE CARL M	CW4	W-0903337	0665	1
KASTNER ALFRED E	B G	0-0014932	0954	1
KATES ROBERT C	LTC	0-0024787	0167	1
KATHERMAN ELLIOTT T	COL	0-0053023	0567	1
KATIN JOSEPH G	COL	0-0043758	0761	1
KATSARSKY SLAFTCHO	COL	0-0039832	0563	2
KATZ HENRY J	COL	0-0020138	0766	1
KATZ PHILLIP R	LTC	0-0059957	0467	2
KATZ SIDNEY	LTC	0-0026327	0763	1
KAUFFMAN KATHREN L	MAJ	N-0002127	0360	1
KAUFFMAN MILDRED B	MAJ	N-0002274	1063	1
KAUFFMAN ROY K	COL	0-0018598	0561	1
KAUFMAN LEE S	COL	0-0032388	0266	1
KAUFMAN PHILLIP	LTC	0-0063092	1166	2
KAWAMURA NORMAN I	1LT	0-0092596	1263	2
KAY HELEN F	MAJ	N-0002063	0162	1
KAY PAUL J	MAJ	0-0060126	0962	1
KAYLOR JOHN P	COL	0-0016905	0757	1
KAYLOR ROY	COL	C-0016462	0656	1
KAYSER HAROLD P	COL	0-000454C	0749	1
KEAGY ROBERT B	COL	0-0024072	0963	1
KEAN WILLIAM S	LTG	0-0012470	0954	1
KEANE SYLVESTER	CPT	0-0015172	0139	1
KEANE WALTER J	MAJ	0-0069961	1164	1
KEANE WILLIAM M	COL	0-0C38702	0260	1
KEARNEY CHARLES F	COL	0-0017771	0659	2
KEARNEY LESTER A	LTC	0-0033010	0861	1
KEARNS JR EDWIN B	B G	0-0016224	0655	1
KEASEY CHARLES R	LTC	0-0038736	0261	1
KEASLER JAMES L	COL	0-0012234	0753	1
KEATING FRANK A	M G	0-000536C	0850	1
KEATING FRANK W	LTC	0-0038929	1058	1
KEATING JOHN G	2LT	0-0024167	0142	2
KEATING JOHN W	B G	0-0018897	0862	2
KEATING JOSEPH W	COL	0-0019800	0465	1
KEATING MARIE A	MAJ	N-0000671	1166	1
KEATINGE JOHN H	COL	0-0007194	1149	1
KEATLEY EDWIN F	COL	0-0007019	1150	1
KEAYS DOROTHY B	MAJ	N-0002352	0558	2
KEDERICH CHARLES H	LTC	0-0043556	1062	1
KEEBAUCH DONALD R	LTC	0-0C83096	0667	2
KEEFE JAMES H	LTC	0-0043634	1166	1
KEEFE JOHN L	COL	0-0C29080	0359	1
KEEGAN JR THOMAS F	LTC	0-0060676	0665	1
KEEHN KENT	LTC	0-0028336	0867	1
KEELEY JOHN T	COL	0-0012437	1148	1

NAME	GRADE	SVC NO	DATE RET MO YR	RET CODE
KEEN HUGH B	COL	0-0003509	C846	2
KEENAN JOHN W	CW2	W-0901630	1043	2
KEENER ERMA D	MAJ	L-0000303	1060	1
KEENER ERVIN L	COL	0-0029572	0161	1
KEENEY PAUL A	COL	0-0029143	1055	2
KEESEY CHARLES R	CW4	W-090334C	C157	1
KEETH EUGENE L	LTC	0-0034687	C464	1
KEFAUVER LLOYD A	COL	0-0003058	0946	2
KEGERREIS JOHN B	COL	0-0031242	0764	2
KEHM HAROLD D	COL	0-0015138	0854	1
KEHOE CECILIA F	CPT	N-0000046	0949	2
KEHOE EMMETT L	COL	0-0019613	1163	1
KEHOE FRANK M	LTC	0-0043380	C764	1
KEIFER FREDERICK	LTC	0-0026927	C865	1
KEIFFER JR PIERRE V	COL	0-0020122	C264	1
KEILER REEVE D	LTC	0-0015857	C346	2
KEISER LAURENCE B	M G	0-0005316	0153	2
KEISH WILLIAM J	COL	C-0041885	1159	1
KEISLER DAVID S	COL	C-0032657	C465	1
KEITH CATHERINE	MAJ	N-0000662	0461	1
KEITH HUBERT W	COL	C-0009954	1046	1
KEITH JAMES E	LTC	0-0080930	0567	1
KEITHLY THOMAS G	COL	C-0041657	0260	1
KELEHER REYNOLDS R	LTC	C-0023941	C162	1
KELL JR ELMER A	COL	0-0038699	1061	1
KELLAM PAUL	COL	0-0011553	0854	1
KELLEHER GERALD C	B G	0-0038750	1063	1
KELLEHER JAMES E	COL	0-0025611	0767	1
KELLER ANDREW K	LTC	0-0026474	0765	1
KELLER EDWARD B	1LT	C-0C17117	0234	2
KELLER HENRY A	COL	0-0039637	C560	1
KELLER KENNETH A	LTC	0-0033248	C762	1
KELLER PAUL E	COL	0-0018923	0762	2
KELLER ROBERT S	1LT	0-0061665	1153	2
KELLER WILLIAM S	LTC	C-0011957	C348	2
KELLERS FRANK	COL	C-0051432	0762	1
KELLEY DONALD C	LTC	C-0020387	1057	1
KELLEY JOSEPH J	CW4	W-0904138	C263	1
KELLEY LAURA C	MAJ	N-0000078	1055	1
KELLEY MARTIN L	CPT	0-0006028	0934	2
KELLEY PAUL A	LTC	0-0028688	1066	1
KELLEY ROBERT R	COL	C-0020984	1060	1
KELLEY SAMUEL P	LTC	0-0018187	0650	1
KELLEY THOMAS W	LTC	0-006124C	C965	1
KELLNER FRED W	LTC	0-0032358	0767	1
KELLOGG DOUGLAS S	COL	0-0016287	C455	2
KELLOGG JAMES P	LTC	0-0084048	1066	1
KELLY BURNIS M	COL	0-0019950	0955	1
KELLY CHARLEE L	LTC	L-0000024	0256	2
KELLY CLYDE	LTC	0-0007970	1033	2
KELLY DAVID C	COL	0-0006887	1048	1
KELLY EDMONDE B	COL	0-0020544	C266	1
KELLY ELBERT	MAJ	0-0015028	0336	2
KELLY ELLSWORTH	COL	0-0020488	0661	1
KELLY HENRY E	COL	C-0010286	0654	1
KELLY HENRY J	COL	0-0041974	0162	1
KELLY JAMES C	LTC	0-0044863	0765	1
KELLY JAMES H	CW4	W-0903343	C465	1
KELLY JOHN D	COL	0-0003407	C847	2
KELLY JOHN J	COL	0-0022185	0759	1
KELLY JOHN R A	LTC	C-0022154	C458	1
KELLY JOHN S	COL	C-0019647	C557	1
KELLY JOSEPH E	1LT	0-0012002	1030	2
KELLY JOSEPH M	LTC	0-0058012	0763	1
KELLY JR EVANDER F	COL	0-0051377	C263	1
KELLY JR HAROLD L	COL	0-0052292	0761	1
KELLY JR JOHN J	LTC	0-0025869	C764	1
KELLY LEM M	COL	0-0032378	0867	2
KELLY LEO F	COL	0-0050895	0255	1
KELLY MARY E	LTC	L-0000341	0867	1
KELLY PATRICK	COL	C-0008724	C644	2
KELLY PAUL B	B G	0-0012121	0551	1
KELLY PAUL C	COL	0-0012825	0934	2
KELLY PETER K	COL	0-0004703	0652	1
KELLY RALPH W	CW4	W-0903344	C466	1

NAME	GRADE	SVC NO	DATE RET MO YR	RET CODE
KELLY ROBERT M	LTC	0-0038267	0866	1
KELLY SAMUEL G	LTC	0-0038664	0458	1
KELLY THOMAS D	LTC	0-0065420	1066	1
KELLY THOMAS J	CW2	W-0901627	0847	1
KELSEY PHILIP R	LTC	0-0080932	0165	1
KELTNER EDGAR H	COL	0-0008241	0253	1
KELTON EDWIN C	COL	0-0003786	0244	2
KEMBLE JOHN W	LTC	0-0020398	0756	1
KEMBLE JR FRANKLIN	COL	0-0019418	0762	1
KEMM ROBERT R	LTC	0-0052139	0366	1
KEMMAN LAWRENCE H	COL	0-0038616	0556	1
KEMP DONALD C	CPT	0-0010020	0135	2
KEMP HERBERT E	LTC	0-0025742	0263	1
KEMP JAMES B	COL	0-0C43282	0963	1
KEMP LEILA	MAJ	N-0000379	0261	1
KEMP ROBERT B	LTC	0-004004C	0862	1
KEMP ROBERT K	LTC	0-0031364	C762	1
KEMPHER LARRY W	CW4	W-0904140	0155	2
KENDALL CHARLES B	COL	0-0004101	0152	1
KENDALL FREDERICK	B G	0-0051236	0761	1
KENDALL JR VICTOR S	MAJ	0-0032521	1159	2
KENDALL PAUL G	COL	0-0015415	0953	2
KENDALL PAUL W	LTG	0-0012199	0855	2
KENDALL QUENTIN L	COL	0-0029745	0762	1
KENDALL REX S	COL	0-0043123	0464	1
KENDALL WILLIAM H	COL	0-0015714	0954	2
KENDERGINE JOHN M	B G	0-0043446	1167	1
KENDRICK DOUGLAS B	M G	0-0020511	0567	1
KENGLE JR LANSFORD F	LTC	0-0025975	0764	1
KENNA GEORGE W	COL	0-0084376	0666	1
KENNEDY AGNES M	MAJ	L-0000171	0264	1
KENNEDY BERNARD R	CPT	0-0014380	0-19	2
KENNEDY CHESTER F	COL	0-0024242	0264	1
KENNEDY ELMER B	COL	0-0020900	0965	1
KENNEDY GRAFTON L	COL	0-0006675	0346	1
KENNEDY GREGORY R	COL	0-0030847	0265	1
KENNEDY HAROLD R	COL	0-0046534	0767	1
KENNEDY HARRY V	CW2	W-0901353	0448	2
KENNEDY JOHN T	B G	0-0002360	0146	2
KENNEDY JOSEPH	COL	0-0005463	0246	1
KENNEDY JULIEN C	LTC	0-0057382	0264	1
KENNEDY JUSTUS C	LTC	0-0043856	0767	1
KENNEDY MARGARET K	MAJ	N-0001661	0463	1
KENNEDY NEAL D	CPT	0-0058463	0764	1
KENNEDY PAUL R	LTC	0-0035563	0664	1
KENNEDY ROBERT J	LTC	0-005061C	1166	1
KENNEDY ROBERT N	CW3	W-0906826	0358	1
KENNEDY ROBERT S	COL	0-0020780	0967	1
KENNEDY STANLEY Y	LTC	C-0005898	0142	2
KENNETT WALTER H	COL	0-0016352	1153	1
KENNEY MAX W	CW4	W-0903345	0657	1
KENNINGTON ROBERT E	LTC	C-0023623	1161	1
KENNON BLAISDELL	COL	0-0008191	0152	1
KENNY EUGENE A	COL	0-0018193	0760	1
KENT EDWARD F	COL	0-0020909	0263	1
KENT HAROLD R	COL	0-0034103	0767	1
KENT HENRY T	COL	0-0009053	0747	2
KENT ISABEL M	MAJ	N-0001973	1061	1
KENT MOSE	COL	C-0006568	0251	1
KEOGH WILLIAM T	LTC	0-0033742	0861	1
KER HOWARD	M G	0-0015518	0562	1
KERANEN CHARLES M	LTC	0-0051578	0163	1
KERBER CHARLES J	CW3	W-0906828	1060	1
KERCHER FERRIS A	LTC	0-0033456	0661	1
KERIG CHAN V	LTC	0-0066172	0967	1
KERKERING JOHN H	COL	0-0020120	0765	1
KERLIN HENRY C	COL	0-0029463	1060	1
KERN THOMAS F	COL	0-0009306	0753	1
KERN TRUMAN H	COL	0-0042305	1163	1
KERN WILLIAM B	COL	0-0C19566	0864	2
KERNAN MELVIN M	COL	C-0040236	0863	1
KERNAN WILLIAM F	COL	0-0006688	0844	2
KERNAN WILLIAM H	COL	0-0012891	1045	2
KERNKAMP MELVIN W	COL	0-0042923	1060	1
KERR DAVID R	COL	C-00C4780	0151	1

NAME	GRADE	SVC NO	DATE RET MO YR	RET CODE
KERR EDWIN R	MAJ	0-0027796	0759	2
KERR GEORGE M	LTC	0-0029319	0662	1
KERR JAMES W	LTC	0-0025417	0264	1
KERR JOHN H	CW4	W-0904143	0366	1
KERR JR GERALD L	LTC	0-0041033	0364	1
KERR MAURICE S	COL	0-0010973	0853	1
KERSEY SIDNEY P	LTC	0-0079877	0865	1
KERSH HENRY L	COL	0-0011579	0852	2
KERSHAW CLIFFORD C	COL	0-0010106	0148	1
KESSINGER HOWARD E	B G	0-0015692	0854	1
KESSLER ROBERT H	COL	0-0020178	0466	1
KESTHELY LOUIS J	CW4	W-0906829	0464	1
KETCHAM JR EDWARD P	COL	0-0038963	1167	1
KETTLETY RAYMOND F	CW4	W-0903352	0463	1
KEUKER CHRISTOPHE	CPT	0-0096007	1067	2
KEVIN HUGH H	COL	0-0041583	0559	1
KEY GENIE	CPT	N-0000843	1157	2
KEY JOHN O	LTC	0-0006484	0539	1
KEY JR HERBERT L	LTC	0-0054858	0764	1
KEY MARY J	MAJ	L-0000004	0753	1
KEY ROBERT C	MAJ	0-0028072	0162	2
KEY WILMA H	MAJ	L-0000019	1054	1
KEYES GEORGE W	LTC	0-0065619	0667	1
KEYES LEWIS H	COL	0-0038765	0464	1
KEYES RICHARD W	COL	0-0031467	0267	1
KEYES SR ROY V	1LT	0-0017643	0638	2
KEYS EDNA M	MAJ	N-0001690	0965	1
KEYSER GEORGE V	B G	0-0012089	0354	1
KEYSER ROBERT W	LTC	0-0033355	0361	1
KIBLER GEORGE N	COL	0-0029490	0161	2
KIBLER JR EDGAR H	COL	0-0019039	1059	1
KIDD WILLIAM T	COL	0-0048216	0867	1
KIDWELL FRANCES P	MAJ	L-0000222	0857	1
KIDWELL GAYLORD B	COL	0-0012029	0553	1
KIEFER HOMER W	M G	0-0012701	0753	1
KIEL ARTHUR G	COL	0-0042199	0663	1
KIELSMEIER SAMUEL G	COL	0-0009596	1046	2
KIELTY JOSEPH A	LTC	0-0015669	1046	1
KIELY CLARA M	LTC	N-0000101	0263	1
KIERNAN JOSEPH F	CW4	W-0903357	0363	1
KIERSCH THEODORE A	COL	0-0024386	0761	1
KIFNER DANIEL R	LTC	0-0037530	0962	1
KIGHT HARRY O	COL	0-0056904	1167	1
KIGHT JONATHAN M	LTC	0-0044919	1167	1
KILBOURNE JOSEPH C	CPT	0-0012114	1034	2
KILBURN CHARLES S	B G	0-0005295	1146	1
KILBURN JOHN W	LTC	0-0041700	0456	1
KILCOYNE JOHN T	COL	0-0019651	0762	1
KILDAY THOMAS T	COL	0-0019288	0759	1
KILGORE FLOYD V	COL	0-0008912	0150	2
KILIAN MYRTLE M	MAJ	N-0002372	0460	1
KILLELEA WILLIAM G	LTC	0-0051174	1162	1
KILLEN WADE O	COL	0-0011131	0949	1
KILLIAN JOSEPH O	COL	0-0019370	0764	1
KILLIAN NOE C	MAJ	0-0004892	1029	2
KILLIAN WILLIAM H	LTC	0-0007500	1022	2
KILLMAN HENRY P	LTC	0-0032538	1059	1
KILLOUGH JAMES S	LTC	0-0029697	0763	1
KILPATRICK WILLARD H	COL	0-0041895	0656	1
KILROY RAYMOND F	1LT	0-0012413	0522	2
KILROY VIRGINIA K	MAJ	N-0000040	1047	1
KIMBALL CURTIS Y	COL	0-0032852	0763	1
KIMBALL RALPH S	LTC	0-0003424	0138	1
KIMBALL RICHARD	COL	0-0042607	0665	1
KIMBALL ROBERT F	COL	0-0024586	0167	1
KIMBEL JOHN F	LTC	0-0026480	1165	1
KIMBERLY ALLEN	COL	0-0002206	0-45	2
KIMBRELL GORDON T	B G	0-0020851	0867	1
KIMBROUGH JR JAMES M	COL	0-0019816	0865	1
KIMM VIRGIL M	LTC	0-0016849	0252	1
KIMMEL JR MANNING M	COL	0-0003558	1044	2
KIMMELL JR JOHN R	COL	0-0019291	0554	1
KIMMET MARIE	MAJ	N-0002037	0559	1
KIMMICK JR LEONARD	LTC	0-0060558	0967	1
KIMMITT JOSEPH S	COL	0-0036343	0266	1

NAME	GRADE	SVC NO	DATE RET MO YR	RET CODE
KIMPTON MARGARET A	LTC	L-0000211	0359	2
KIMPTON THEODORE R	COL	0-0018226	0760	1
KINARD JR WILLIAM H	COL	0-0020180	0865	1
KINBERGER ALBERT G	COL	0-0008508	0846	2
KINCAID LEONARD C	COL	0-0031732	0864	1
KINCY JR WILLIAM R	COL	0-0078916	0567	1
KIND HENRY A	COL	0-0020986	0965	1
KINDERMAN HAROLD W	MAJ	0-0010749	1036	2
KINDERVATER ERNEST A	COL	0-0005727	0649	1
KINDRED WORTH L	COL	0-0029382	0758	1
KING ARCHIBALD	COL	0-0003323	0842	1
KING ARTHUR R	MAJ	0-0024915	0846	2
KING DALE M	COL	0-0039644	0660	1
KING DAVID C	CW4	W-0901805	0354	1
KING DICK A	COL	0-0030438	0863	1
KING EDGAR	B G	0-0002288	0146	1
KING EDGAR W	COL	0-0009705	0954	2
KING EDWARD W	COL	0-0030646	0267	1
KING ELNOR L	1LT	0-0056774	0451	1
KING FLORENCE H	MAJ	N-0002427	0265	1
KING FRANCIS J	LTC	0-0040265	0666	1
KING GEORGE A	COL	0-0005530	0549	2
KING GEORGE L	COL	0-0007865	0846	1
KING GLENNIS L	MAJ	0-0033661	0363	1
KING HARRISON	COL	0-0019078	0746	2
KING HELEN E	MAJ	N-0002409	0463	1
KING J CRAIG	MAJ	0-0013920	0420	2
KING JAMES B	LTC	0-0046196	0266	1
KING JAMES I	B G	0-0018534	0160	2
KING JOHN L	CPT	0-0025358	0246	2
KING JOSEPH C	COL	0-0002148	1142	2
KING JR CARY J	COL	0-0015574	0654	1
KING JR HARRY L	1LT	0-0027133	0448	2
KING JR JOHN H	COL	0-0020036	0755	1
KING JR JOHN L	LTC	0-0031491	0465	1
KING KENDALL E	CW4	W-0903359	0365	1
KING LAURENCE T	COL	0-0030713	0566	1
KING MARY L	LTC	N-0000321	0761	1
KING NORMAN E	LTC	0-00222[illegible]	0759	1
KING PAUL R	MAJ	0-0009482	0835	2
KING RALPH D	COL	0-0020115	0956	1
KING ROBERT A	LTC	0-0050797	0566	1
KING ROBERT W	COL	0-0051864	0365	1
KING ROGER O	LTC	0-0044600	1161	2
KING ROSEWELL H	COL	0-0028962	0158	1
KING RYAN W	COL	0-0079708	1263	1
KING THEODORE T	B G	0-0028889	1056	1
KING WARREN J	LTC	0-0042850	0464	2
KING WILLIAM I	COL	0-0036153	0566	1
KINGMAN ALLEN F	B G	0-0004749	0553	1
KINGMAN DAN C	LTC	0-0032045	1166	1
KINGMAN JR ALLEN F	LTC	0-0057556	0265	1
KINKE EMIL F	COL	0-0018034	0755	1
KINLEY MILES A	COL	0-0051718	0166	1
KINNAIRD RUBY L	MAJ	N-0000231	0963	1
KINNE JR HARRY L	COL	0-0029583	0761	1
KINNEY FREDERICK	CW4	W-0903360	0767	2
KINNEY OLIVER G	COL	0-0032067	0661	1
KINNISON LOIS F	MAJ	N-0000245	1264	1
KINNISON PAUL	COL	0-0032581	0666	1
KINSELLA HARRY F	COL	0-0031424	1266	1
KINSEY NANCY B	MAJ	N-0002025	0360	1
KINSLER DAVID E	COL	0-0041759	0664	1
KINSLOW ALBERT V	COL	0-0030808	0966	1
KINSON RICHARD L	LTC	0-0043955	1262	1
KINTNER WILLIAM R	COL	0-0023068	0861	1
KINTZ FRANCIS P	COL	0-0018937	1058	1
KIONKA JOHN	LTC	0-0051642	0960	2
KIRBY HARRY C	LTC	0-0017105	1044	2
KIRBY LEE W	LTC	0-0022048	0862	1
KIRBY PAULINE	COL	N-0000035	0757	1
KIRBY PIERRE P	LTC	0-0060624	1164	1
KIRBY WILLIAM F	COL	0-0028906	0557	1
KIRBY-SMITH EDMUND	COL	0-0021745	0167	1
KIRCHHOFF ARTHUR A G	COL	0-0016396	0656	1

NAME	GRADE	SVC NO	DATE RET MO YR	RET CODE
KIRCHOFF WAYNE F	COL	0-0043243	0866	1
KIRK JAMES	M G	0-0003372	0252	1
KIRK RAYMOND L	LTC	0-0087822	0467	1
KIRK ROBERT P	COL	0-0029710	0862	1
KIRK WARREN M	COL	0-0065674	1167	1
KIRKMAN BYRON J	CW4	W-0903363	0856	1
KIRKMAN LEWIS W	COL	0-0020066	0546	2
KIRKPATRICK C L	COL	0-0018642	0759	1
KIRKPATRICK HARRY F	COL	0-0039807	0463	1
KIRKPATRICK TRAVIS M	MAJ	0-0059924	0165	1
KIRKSEY FLAVIOUS W	CPT	0-0060363	0556	2
KIRPATRICK ELMER E	COL	0-0017660	1059	1
KIRSNER HARRY	COL	0-0011601	1146	1
KIRSTEN ELWYN N	COL	0-0020637	0560	1
KIRTLEY EDWIN L	COL	0-0024355	1164	1
KISER SHERMAN L	COL	0-0003498	0948	1
KISER WILLIAM M	LTC	0-0028329	0866	1
KISH WILLIAM E	LTC	0-0056818	0563	1
KITCHEN LLOYD	LTC	0-0065466	1166	1
KITCHINGS JR ROYCE D	COL	0-0041565	0159	1
KITSON ALFRED P	COL	0-0010043	0147	2
KITTRELL CLARK	COL	0-0005228	1049	1
KLASING WALDEMAR J	MAJ	0-0031478	1157	1
KLEFF PIERRE A	COL	0-0039799	0960	1
KLEIN BERTHA J	MAJ	N-0000481	0762	1
KLEIN EDWARD	CW4	W-0904144	0761	1
KLEIN JOHN A	M G	0-0007536	1056	2
KLEIN JR JOHN H	MAJ	0-0058176	0966	1
KLEINMANN MORTIMER V	LTC	0-0064975	1265	1
KLEIST ERWIN H	LTC	0-0026504	1066	2
KLEMM HELEN T	MAJ	R-0010073	0462	1
KLEMP HUBERT E	COL	0-0051076	0360	1
KLEMP IRENE J	LTC	N-0000556	0361	1
KLEPINGER WALTER J	COL	0-0014839	0854	1
KLIE HARRY K	LTC	0-0047792	0866	1
KLIM HENRY L	CPT	0-0060458	1163	1
KLIMA LAWRENCE J	LTC	0-0027188	0966	1
KLINCK EARL	COL	0-0028955	1057	1
KLINE EARL C	COL	0-0046466	0767	1
KLINE NICK	CW2	W-0901797	0748	1
KLINE ROBERT R	COL	0-0039780	0762	1
KLINETOP HOWARD A	COL	0-0039798	1262	1
KLINGAMAN MURIEL R	LTC	N-0000276	0767	1
KLINT EDMUND L	LTC	0-0042970	0263	1
KLOCK JR KARL T	COL	0-0020123	0965	2
KLOEPFER HANS E	COL	0-0006557	0146	2
KLUGE FRED	CW4	W-0903366	0658	1
KLUNDER JOSEPH D	LTC	0-0052947	0262	1
KNAPP ANNE F	MAJ	N-0002249	0661	1
KNAPP ERNEST C	COL	0-0038684	0660	1
KNAPP LAWRENCE M	COL	0-0041942	1161	1
KNAPP RAYMOND H	LTC	0-0042546	0261	1
KNAPP ROBERT H	LTC	0-0010234	0142	2
KNAUER JOHN G	COL	0-0006552	0653	1
KNEISL JERRY A	MAJ	0-0060499	0963	1
KNEYSE WALTER A	COL	0-0042227	0863	1
KNICKERBOCKER BARBAR	MAJ	J-0000033	0866	1
KNICKERBOCKER MAX E	LTC	0-0041151	0764	1
KNIER ALBERT A	LTC	0-0051137	0258	1
KNIER ALOYSIUS M	LTC	0-0068368	0965	1
KNIGHT ALFRED C	LTC	0-0029684	0152	1
KNIGHT ANDREW T	COL	0-0008052	0846	2
KNIGHT BUTLER L	MAJ	0-0007725	0934	2
KNIGHT DANIEL B	COL	0-0014735	0-45	2
KNIGHT ELWIN T	COL	0-0021380	1165	1
KNIGHT GLENNA E	MAJ	L-0000220	0257	1
KNIGHT GORDON C	CW4	W-0904145	0465	2
KNIGHT JOHN J	CW4	W-0903367	0155	1
KNIGHT JR CHARLES C	LTC	0-0009073	0142	1
KNIGHT LONNIE W	COL	0-0030885	1165	1
KNIGHT PAUL R	COL	0-0008317	0847	1
KNIGHT REMI C	1LT	0-0014403	0120	2
KNIPE WILLIS H	LTC	0-0050829	0866	1
KNIPS ALBERTA H	MAJ	N-0000971	1061	1
KNOBELOCH WILFRED	COL	0-0042464	1264	1

NAME	GRADE	SVC NO	DATE RET MO YR	RET CODE
KNOLL WILLIAM F	LTC	0-0043535	0163	1
KNOPF STACY	COL	0-0004919	1045	2
KNOTT JOSEPH W	LTC	0-0031350	1064	1
KNOTT WILLIAM C	COL	0-0018922	0856	1
KNOWLES WENDELL P	COL	0-0023953	0865	1
KNOWLTON HOMER C	LTC	0-0076803	0767	1
KNOWLTON JOSEPH L	COL	0-0023869	0167	1
KNOWLTON JR BRUCE R	CPT	0-0059861	0962	1
KNOWLTON STEWART H	COL	0-0030159	0464	1
KNOX ALICE T A	MAJ	R-0010062	0558	1
KNOX CAMERON	COL	0-0031815	0461	1
KNOX JASPER A	COL	0-0018283	0946	2
KNOX JOHN C	COL	0-0050897	0753	1
KNOX OHIC	LTC	0-0030572	1163	1
KNOX WILLIAM W	LTC	0-0041558	0257	1
KNUDSEN CHRISTIAN	COL	0-0012125	1046	2
KNUDSEN SR CHARLES E	LTC	0-0027829	0965	1
KNUTSON RALPH H	CW4	W-0906835	0563	1
KNUTSON SIDNEY A	LTC	0-0036199	1062	1
KOBRE HERMAN	COL	0-0002463	0543	2
KOCH ARTHUR L	LTC	0-0006389	0838	1
KOCH BRUCE C	LTC	0-0025947	0664	1
KOCH HARLAN G	LTC	0-0028725	0766	1
KOCH OSCAR W	B G	0-0010851	0954	2
KOCH RALPH A	COL	0-0015830	0854	1
KOCHEVAR JOHN H	COL	0-0016867	0757	1
KOCHLI JR FRED	LTC	0-0027611	0365	1
KOECKERT WILLIAM F	MAJ	0-0069715	0865	1
KOEHN CARL J	LTC	0-0052048	0264	1
KOENIG EGMONT F	B G	0-0004700	0448	1
KOERBEL FREDERICK	COL	0-0010007	1048	1
KOERNER JR RUDOLPH C	LTC	0-0052211	0163	2
KOERNER PAUL M	LTC	0-0040263	0666	2
KOESTER FRED W	COL	0-0009772	1047	1
KOHLER DONALD J	LTC	0-0027203	0766	1
KOHLOSS FABIUS H	COL	0-0010244	0846	2
KOHLS CARL W	COL	0-0018575	0761	1
KOHN JOSEPH R	COL	0-0005860	0753	1
KOHNSTAMM JOSEPH W	MAJ	0-0040645	1063	2
KOLB ROLAND L	COL	0-0025184	0167	1
KOLETTY JOHN W	COL	0-0040230	0763	1
KOLSTEE KENNETH K	LTC	0-0032886	0467	1
KOLTVET ANNA	MAJ	N-0000119	1060	1
KONKOL RALPH E	LTC	0-0052868	0862	2
KONOPASKA ROYDEN A	COL	0-0030787	0864	2
KONOPKA URBAN S	LTC	0-0041761	0462	2
KOOKEN JOHN J D	COL	0-0034743	0364	1
KOOKEN WILLIS E	COL	0-0043658	1066	1
KOON JR CARL C	CW2	W-0903373	0261	1
KOONS RAYMOND H	CW3	W-0903374	0660	1
KOPCSAK PETER J	COL	0-0019440	0964	2
KOPF JOHN B	MAJ	0-0040812	0863	1
KOPISCHKIE CARL E	LTC	0-0080433	0762	1
KORCHEK LOUIS	CW4	W-0903376	0467	2
KOREMAN EDWARD H	COL	0-0038953	1061	1
KORNFEIND HELEN A	LTC	N-0000105	0860	1
KOSCH LEWIS F	COL	0-0006511	0947	1
KOSCHMEDER JULIA F	MAJ	N-0002307	0467	1
KOSCIELNIAK ADAM A	LTC	0-0018159	0252	1
KOSHKO JR JOHN R	LTC	0-0043974	0767	1
KOSIOREK STEPHEN T	LTC	0-0023772	0262	1
KOSMACKI LEON F	LTC	0-0024194	0967	1
KOSTER ALFRED M	COL	0-0029796	1062	2
KOSTORA LEE H	LTC	0-0031598	0264	1
KOSZEWSKI STEPHEN S	COL	0-0015654	0854	1
KOTHE HERMAN H	COL	0-0029194	0261	1
KOTICK OTTMAR F	COL	0-0028924	0757	1
KOTOWSKI EVA T	MAJ	N-0002133	0560	1
KOTTE BERNARD J	COL	0-0029172	1059	1
KOTZEBUE LEON L	COL	0-0009700	0154	2
KOUNS CHARLES W	COL	0-0022129	0861	1
KOUP ELMER L	COL	0-0041999	0262	1
KOVACH FRANK Z	LTC	0-0080434	0765	1
KOVACIC EMMA C	MAJ	N-0001298	0566	1
KOVACS LESLIE R	COL	0-0051697	0266	2

UNITED STATES ARMY RETIRED LIST

NAME	GRADE	S/C NO	DATE RET MO YR	RET CODE
KOVACS LOUIS	WO1	W-0901461	1049	1
KOVAR PAUL J	COL	0-0058240	0867	1
KOWALSKI JR FRANK	COL	0-0018086	0858	2
KOZAK EDWIN J	COL	0-0043129	1266	1
KRACHT ARTHUR N	COL	0-0020923	0861	1
KRAFFT HENRY L	COL	0-0004043	1046	1
KRAFT ICELLE D	MAJ	N-0001056	0762	1
KRAFTSCHENK DOROTHY	LTC	N-0000287	0967	1
KRAMER ARTHUR	COL	0-0020140	0657	1
KRAMER JOHN J	LTC	0-0031221	0353	1
KRAMER JR THEODORE	LTC	0-0079881	0965	2
KRAMERS JOHN T	COL	0-0033890	0766	1
KRAMOLIS MARIE C	MAJ	N-0002358	0360	1
KRAMS CORTLANDT	COL	0-0010224	0553	1
KRANZ JUSTUS W	LTC	0-0028933	0955	1
KRAUS EDWARD	COL	0-0019789	0861	1
KRAUS HANNAH	1LT	R-0000652	0146	1
KRAUS WALTER E	COL	0-0017571	0859	1
KRAUSE ALBERT S	CW4	W-0904146	0964	1
KRAUSE WILLIAM O	LTC	0-0037448	0867	1
KRAUSKOPF FREDERICK	COL	0-0057053	0866	2
KRAUSS PAUL H	COL	0-0022932	0764	1
KREBS LOGAN A	CW3	W-0906839	0356	1
KREBS ROBERT C	CW4	W-0903380	0465	1
KREGEL HERMAN J	COL	0-0038845	1264	1
KREIDBERG MARVIN A	COL	0-0022733	0163	1
KREIDEL FRANCIS A	B G	0-0039553	0657	1
KREISER OSCAR G	COL	0-0020765	0759	1
KREITZER JAMES F	LTC	0-0023096	0763	1
KREN ROBERT E	LTC	0-0028277	0867	1
KRESGE MILES W	COL	0-0007014	0247	2
KRETLOW SIDNEY P	COL	0-0050908	0954	1
KRETLOW STANLEY A	COL	0-0039708	0859	1
KREUTER ROBERT H	COL	0-0012706	0750	1
KREUTZER RICHARD B	COL	0-0025037	0666	1
KRIECHBAUM FRED H	CW4	W-0903381	0164	1
KRIEGER MERVIN	LTC	0-0049000	0765	1
KRILLA MICHAEL N	CW4	W-0904147	0163	1
KROENING MARIAN E	MAJ	N-0001678	0665	1
KROHN HAROLD K	LTC	0-0042702	0861	2
KROLL MARILYN	MAJ	N-0000182	0662	1
KROMER JR PHILIP F	B G	0-0018030	0862	1
KRON JACK J	LTC	0-0045822	0262	1
KRON PHILIP H	COL	0-0010481	0842	2
KRONEMEYER SYLVIA M	MAJ	N-0000461	0761	1
KRONKE CHARLES J	LTC	0-0040371	0864	1
KROYER JOHN M	LTC	0-0060089	0867	1
KRUEGER AUGUST F	CW3	W-0903383	0861	1
KRUEGER JR WALTER	COL	0-0018351	0361	2
KRUEGER ORRIN C	COL	0-0018553	0261	1
KRUEGER PHILIP G	COL	0-0024677	0666	1
KRUEGER ROBERT H	COL	0-0015332	0455	2
KRUGER HERBERT W	COL	0-0015037	1047	1
KRUGER ROBERT E	LTC	0-0082035	1066	1
KRUKAR ANDREW	CW4	W-0903384	0565	2
KRUMPERMAN LUCILE	MAJ	N-0001338	0865	1
KRUPP OSCAR	COL	0-0003223	1145	2
KRZYZOSIAK STANLEY J	CW4	W-0903386	0855	2
KUBIN MILFORD T	COL	0-0018278	0360	1
KUEFLER KENNETH T	LTC	0-0059493	1067	1
KUEHLER WALTER W	COL	0-0030731	1065	2
KUEHLKE CHRISTIAN	LTC	0-0080435	0966	1
KUENNING HOWARD F	COL	0-0042739	0766	1
KUENTZ OSCAR O	COL	0-0003752	1146	1
KUHN FRANCIS H	COL	0-0012542	0747	2
KUHN FREDOLIN W	COL	0-0051734	0364	1
KUHN LUDWIG R	COL	0-0041752	1163	1
KUHN WILLIAM A	COL	0-0031419	1064	1
KUHNS DWIGHT M	COL	0-0018294	1055	2
KUHRE LELAND B	COL	0-0016056	0755	1
KUITERT JOHN H	COL	0-0041753	1163	1
KUJAWSKI JOSEPH S	COL	0-0021276	0864	1
KULP JAMES M	LTC	0-0080436	1061	1
KUMMER WILLIAM G	CW4	W-0903387	0962	1
KUMPE EDWARD F	COL	0-0018036	1054	1

NAME	GRADE	SVC NO	DATE RET MO YR	RET CODE
KUNA CHARLES S	COL	0-0020581	0964	1
KUNDEL TEWES	COL	0-0029037	1156	1
KUNESH FRED W	COL	0-0016768	0655	1
KUNITZ MARCELLUS	COL	0-0029642	1161	1
KUNZ ROBERT N	COL	0-0005293	0753	1
KUNZIG WILLIAM B	B G	0-0018825	0862	1
KURSTEDT HAROLD A	COL	0-0016735	1055	1
KURTH EDWARD H	COL	0-0021807	0761	1
KURTZ GUY G	B G	0-0007418	0753	1
KURTZ MYERS R	LTC	0-0078652	0867	1
KURTZ STANLEY L	CW3	W-0906844	1062	1
KURUTZ KATHERINE	MAJ	N-0001274	1165	1
KUSEWITT JR JOHN R	LTC	0-0027495	0166	1
KUSHNER GERSEN L	LTC	0-0019420	0862	1
KUSHNER LEONARD H	CPT	0-0060818	0753	1
KUSHNER WILLIAM H	WO1	W-0800303	1129	2
KUSKE ALBERT W	CPT	0-0021001	0-42	2
KUSTER JOHN G	COL	0-0042419	1064	1
KUTAC AGNES E	MAJ	N-0000086	0558	1
KUTCHINSKI HENRY P	LTC	0-0026734	0465	1
KUTSCHKO EMERICK	B G	0-0011434	0846	1
KUTZ CHARLES R	COL	0-0017763	0859	1
KUTZ HARRY R	B G	0-0002066	0646	2
KUYKENDALL VIRGIL L	CW2	W-0901798	0651	1
KUZIV MICHAEL	LTC	0-0023330	0965	1
KUZNIK JOSEPH V	LTC	0-0001407	1022	1
KVAM CONRAD T	COL	0-0020467	0167	1
KYDD MARJORIE W	MAJ	N-0000324	0265	1
LA BOUNTY JACK V	LTC	0-0034422	1165	1
LA CHAUSSEE CHARLES	LTC	0-0037164	0766	1
LA COMBE JAMES L	COL	0-0031284	0266	1
LA COUR JEAN P	COL	0-0039822	0363	1
LA CROIX HAROLD J	COL	0-0010273	0844	2
LA DUE PAUL E	COL	0-0019017	0957	1
LA FARGE WILLIAM F	COL	0-0042147	0363	1
LA FLARE BENJAMIN I	LTC	0-0052159	1262	1
LA FORCE CHARLES A	COL	0-0051349	1062	1
LA FORS CLAUD D	LTC	0-0021704	1162	1
LA FRANKIE REGINALD	MAJ	0-0041163	0761	1
LA HATTE WILLIAM F	COL	0-0024206	1266	1
LA MEE III WILLIAM S	COL	0-0032364	0567	1
LA MONT CHARLES E	LTC	0-0079885	1162	1
LA PLANTE THERESA S	LTC	N-0001917	0665	1
LA PRAD QUENTIN C	LTC	0-0027744	0765	1
LA ROCK RALPH I	LTC	0-0028159	0766	1
LA ROSE RAYMOND J	CPT	0-0023308	0744	2
LA RUE FRANK	COL	0-0010514	0947	2
LACHANCE JOSEPH R	LTC	0-0041500	0256	1
LACKAS JOHN C	COL	0-0029366	1059	1
LACKRO JR PAUL H	LTC	0-0030325	1262	1
LADD JOHN G	COL	0-0039509	1054	2
LADD MARGARET P	MAJ	M-0010115	0760	1
LAFAVER AMOS E	LTC	0-0042447	1162	1
LAGASSE FREDERICK	LTC	0-0031517	0463	1
LAGORIC ANTHONY P	COL	0-0008208	1148	1
LAHLUM ARTHUR H	COL	0-0023541	0763	1
LAHM LAWRENCE	COL	0-0024761	0764	1
LAMMER JOHN A	LTC	0-0079883	0266	1
LAHTI EDWARD H	COL	0-0021322	0662	1
LAIB JR ARTHUR J	COL	0-0043107	1167	1
LAIDLAW WALDO F	M G	0-0016414	0660	1
LAIN DALTON W	LTC	0-0040302	1166	1
LAIRD ROBERT A	LTC	0-0005565	1141	1
LAIRD WHEELER E	LTC	0-0058153	0167	1
LAITMAN MILTON A	LTC	0-0021805	0544	2
LAKE JACK F	LTC	0-0034291	1266	1
LAKE JOHN P	COL	0-0008366	0753	1
LALLY ESTELLA N	CPT	N-0000380	1051	1
LALLY LAWRENCE D	COL	0-0041674	0460	1
LAM GENE N	LTC	0-0062932	1166	1
LAMANSKY ETHEL A	LTC	N-0000041	1155	1
LAMAR JOSEPH R	COL	0-0043014	0366	1
LAMAR JR HENRY C	LTC	0-0058950	1065	1
LAMB EARNEST R	CW4	W-0906846	0564	1
LAMB ELIZABETH	MAJ	N-0000399	0361	1

NAME	GRADE	SVC NO	DATE RET MO YR	RET CODE
LAMB OAKLEY M	LTC	0-0032751	0661	2
LAMB SAMUEL S	COL	0-0016247	1146	2
LAMBERT BENJAMIN F	MAJ	0-0041131	1061	1
LAMBERT HARRY F	COL	0-0038919	0866	2
LAMBERT HERMAN J	COL	0-0010948	0253	1
LAMBERT JOSEPH I	COL	0-0009541	1046	2
LAMBERT KENT C	COL	0-0005591	0251	1
LAMBOURNE ROBERT C	LTC	0-0057851	0667	1
LAMING PERCY H	COL	0-0042000	0262	1
LAMOND JOHN B	LTC	0-0025309	0766	1
LAMONT JAMES M	COL	0-0017226	0157	2
LAMOREUX THOMAS L	MAJ	0-0004965	1136	2
LAMOTHE FRANK E	LTC	0-0065711	0965	1
LAMPERT JR LESTER L	LTC	0-0022100	0661	1
LAMUREY JUAN	CW4	W-0902070	1054	1
LANAHAN FRANCIS H	M G	0-0012735	0355	1
LANARD FRANCIS W	LTC	0-0025155	1064	1
LANCASTER ALEXANDER	COL	0-0041875	1061	1
LANCASTER HARRY R	COL	0-0030897	1058	1
LANCASTER JAMES L	CW4	W-0904148	0163	1
LANCASTER JOSEPH L	COL	0-0004779	1046	1
LANCEFIELD ROBERT L	COL	0-0018037	0959	1
LANCER THOMAS F	COL	0-0051317	0662	1
LAND CLIFTON E	CPT	0-0080254	1064	2
LAND JAMES C	COL	0-0030650	0665	1
LAND PETER W	WO1	W-0901049	0434	2
LAND RUFUS L	COL	0-0016392	0946	2
LANDAKER CHESTER L	COL	0-0018353	0761	2
LANDES SIDNEY W	LTC	0-0040397	0662	1
LANDIS LINCOLN	LTC	0-0027588	0965	1
LANDON DONALD C	COL	0-0030402	0565	1
LANDRESS SYLVA M	LTC	0-0084790	0266	1
LANDRUM JR EUGENE M	LTC	0-0055032	0864	1
LANDRUM JR JAMES E	M G	0-0020216	0866	1
LANDRY ERNEST S	LTC	0-0051932	0163	2
LANDRY JR WILSON A	MAJ	0-0063378	0766	1
LANDRY WILMER C	COL	0-0020208	0866	1
LANE ALBERT L	COL	0-0010178	0752	1
LANE ARTHUR W	B G	0-0002056	0845	1
LANE CECILE M	MAJ	L-0000074	0261	1
LANE DANNA L	COL	0-0051520	0864	1
LANE DOUGLAS H	COL	0-0040338	0866	1
LANE HERMAN O	COL	0-0010297	0854	1
LANE JAMES W	LTC	0-0053091	0466	1
LANE SAMUEL H	LTC	0-0017322	0830	2
LANE THOMAS A	M G	0-0017075	0762	2
LANE WILLIAM T	COL	0-0021714	1163	1
LANEY JR JAMES R	COL	0-0023942	0365	1
LANG ALBERT	1LT	0-0016582	0532	2
LANG CORNELIS O	B G	0-0019734	0766	1
LANG EDMUND H	COL	0-0043006	0467	1
LANG HAROLD G	COL	0-0051600	0961	1
LANG JAMES O	COL	0-0019728	0655	1
LANG NORBERT S	COL	0-0031062	0667	1
LANG RALPH W	COL	0-0033034	0764	1
LANG THELMA L	MAJ	N-0001979	1262	1
LANGBEIN LELAND H	LTC	0-0040473	0961	1
LANGDON HAZEL L	MAJ	N-0002138	1160	1
LANGDON WENDELL H	COL	0-0018101	0760	2
LANGE CHESTER E	COL	0-0030353	0165	1
LANGE WELLS B	LTC	0-0050767	0867	1
LANGENDORF WILLIAM H	LTC	0-0045551	0866	1
LANGEVIN JOSEPH L	COL	0-0012640	0554	1
LANGGUTH PAUL O	COL	0-0028923	0857	1
LANGLEY JOHN E	LTC	0-0008973	0-41	1
LANGLOIS SILAS R	COL	0-0029865	0563	2
LANGSTON CARL C	CW4	W-0903359	0259	1
LANHAM CHARLES T	M G	0-0015568	1054	1
LANKARD DELBERT W	CW4	W-0906849	1065	1
LANKENAU NORMAN H	COL	0-0018824	0552	1
LANNING HARLEY A	COL	0-0039720	0861	1
LANPHER ROLLIN A	LTC	0-0030636	0264	1
LANPHIER PAUL H	COL	0-0020949	1067	1
LANSFORD ERCIE O	COL	0-0030569	1163	1
LANSING ERNEST J	LTC	0-0063113	0766	1

NAME	GRADE	SVC NO	DATE RET MO YR	RET CODE
LANSING SAMUEL M	COL	0-0016271	0655	1
LAPIANA VINCENT F	COL	0-0051365	1262	1
LAPSLEY WILLIAM W	M G	0-0019727	1067	1
LARCHEVEQUE RUSSELL	CW4	W-0906850	0467	1
LARDIN HARRY E	COL	0-0019494	0660	1
LAREAU GEORGE D	CW4	W-0906851	0955	1
LAREW WALTER B	B G	0-0016643	1056	1
LARK MARTHA L	MAJ	N-0002418	0464	1
LARKIN ALWYN V	COL	0-0029809	0959	1
LARKIN GEORGE T	COL	0-0023293	0765	1
LARKIN THOMAS B	LTG	0-0003785	1052	1
LARNER THOMAS M	COL	0-0030223	0764	1
LARSEN GEORGE E	COL	0-0031550	0767	1
LARSON FLORIE M	MAJ	N-0002357	0858	1
LARSON GORDON P	LTC	0-0019124	0645	2
LARSON ROBERT C	COL	0-0041548	0958	1
LARSON ROBERT T	COL	0-0024506	0864	1
LARSON WERNER L	LTC	0-0029024	0956	1
LASH EUGENE L	COL	0-0042272	0866	1
LASH JR PERCY H	COL	0-0018458	0761	1
LASHER EDMUND C R	M G	0-0017624	0158	1
LASHLEY RALPH C	COL	0-0019982	0863	1
LASKOWSKY RUDOLPH	COL	0-0021243	0866	2
LASSETTER MARGARET N	MAJ	L-0000306	0761	1
LASSITER GEORGE L	LTC	0-0080957	1167	1
LASSITER JANIE L	LTC	N-0002041	0962	1
LASTAYO EDWARD H	B G	0-0012660	0853	1
LASTOVKA JOHN R	CW3	W-0901254	0247	1
LATHAM JR CHARLES C	LTC	0-0039950	0163	1
LATHEY CHARLES E	LTC	0-0081910	0261	1
LATHROP LESLIE T	COL	0-0006642	0450	1
LATHROPE FRANCES M	LTC	L-0000021	0558	1
LATIMER FARRIS N	LTC	0-0015935	0753	1
LATIMER RAYMOND L	COL	0-0034833	0867	1
LATOU ANDREW L	CW4	W-0906852	0467	1
LATTIN JAY D B	COL	0-0004637	0150	1
LATTIN JOHN H	COL	0-0029887	0263	1
LATZEN SAMUEL	CW4	W-0903401	0854	1
LAUBACH JAMES H	COL	0-0002278	0943	1
LAUBEN PHILIP S	COL	0-0039500	0854	1
LAUDANI ANGELO A	LTC	0-0024033	0762	1
LAUDERDALE JAMES M	LTC	0-0059552	0166	1
LAUDIERI MARIO F	LTC	0-0079887	0366	1
LAUER DAVID P	LTC	0-0030904	0155	2
LAUGERMAN JOHN B	COL	0-0030333	1264	1
LAUGHLIN GEORGE T	COL	0-0030723	0566	1
LAUGHLIN JOHN E	CW4	W-0906853	0657	1
LAUGHLIN THOMAS	LTC	0-0037414	0265	1
LAUGHLIN VIRGIL V	COL	0-0041059	1166	1
LAURIE PATRICK W	LTC	0-0040222	1162	1
LAURION LAWRENCE E	COL	0-0020150	0762	1
LAURSEN CHRIS N	CW4	W-0903402	0857	1
LAUTERBACH WALLACE M	COL	0-0023810	0665	1
LAUTZ EDWARD H	COL	0-0079711	0467	1
LAUX RAY J	M G	0-0042102	0967	2
LAVELL ROBERT G	LTC	0-0032080	1163	1
LAVELLEE LEO E	CW3	W-0903403	0967	1
LAVERICK BLENDA	MAJ	N-0000058	0951	1
LAVIN MARGUERITE	MAJ	N-0002071	0163	1
LAW ARTHUR G	LTC	0-0062977	0666	1
LAW CHARLES P	COL	0-0041684	0560	1
LAW WILLIAM	COL	0-0032169	0466	2
LAWES ROBERT C	LTC	0-0015571	0846	1
LAWLER WILLIAM H	LTC	0-0069722	0866	1
LAWLER WILLIAM J	1LT	0-0014358	0717	1
LAWLESS ROGER E J	COL	0-0080960	0767	1
LAWLEY JR EUGENE G	1LT	0-0063468	1054	2
LAWLOR JOHN D	B G	0-0019536	0864	1
LAWLOR ROBERT J	COL	0-0019036	0863	1
LAWLOR THOMAS J	COL	0-0020361	0864	1
LAWRANCE JACKSON S	COL	0-0032003	0965	1
LAWRENCE ABRAHAM M	COL	0-0008080	0644	2
LAWRENCE CARYL R	MAJ	N-0001242	1264	1
LAWRENCE CHARLES E	LTC	0-0052261	0367	1
LAWRENCE CHARLES S	COL	0-0014799	0949	1

NAME	GRADE	SVC NO	DATE RET MO YR	RET CODE
LAWRENCE FRANK J	COL	0-0011133	0947	1
LAWRENCE GEORGE H	MAJ	0-0017288	1147	1
LAWRENCE JACOB H	LTC	0-0006026	0142	1
LAWRENCE JAMES R	LTC	0-0058952	0266	2
LAWRENCE JR C W	COL	0-0041613	0859	1
LAWRENCE LESLIE F	COL	0-0006743	0848	1
LAWRENCE MARY S	LTC	N-0010103	0962	1
LAWRENCE PAUL H	COL	0-0041420	0455	1
LAWRENCE RAY G	LTC	0-0052606	0641	1
LAWRENCE RENN M	LTC	0-0057656	1067	1
LAWRENCE THOMAS E	LTC	0-0026835	0865	1
LAWRIE JOE S	M G	0-0020914	0667	1
LAWS WOODROW	LTC	0-0030677	0663	1
LAWSON DWIGHT	LTC	0-0018918	0643	2
LAWSON JOEL W	COL	0-0033298	0266	1
LAWSON JOSEPH F	CW3	W-0904149	0660	1
LAWSON PAUL F	LTC	0-0024525	0262	1
LAWSON RICHARD H	COL	0-0018526	0761	1
LAWSON RUTLEDGE	COL	0-0010493	0553	1
LAWSON THOMAS R	MAJ	0-0023907	0246	2
LAWSON WALTER R	COL	0-0020808	0867	1
LAWTHER J PAUL	COL	0-0041937	1061	1
LAWTON ELMORE G	COL	0-0038441	0966	1
LAWTON ELVA J	MAJ	N-0001978	1062	1
LAWTON KIRKE B	M G	0-0006805	0854	2
LAWTON ROSA T	LTC	L-0000254	0967	1
LAWTON WILLIAM S	LTG	0-0014924	0560	1
LAY KENNETH E	COL	0-0022224	0764	1
LAY SYLVAN P	LTC	0-0022638	0859	1
LAYER HARLAND W	COL	0-0019643	0855	1
LAYFIELD JR MOODY E	COL	0-0023939	0165	1
LAYMAN CHARLES A	LTC	0-0049778	0865	1
LAYMAN JR ERNEST W	LTC	0-0032455	1067	1
LAYMAN JR RALPH E	LTC	0-0049956	1064	1
LAYNE CLYDE L	COL	0-0020317	0866	1
LAYTON CHARLES B	COL	0-0030729	0666	2
LAYTON VICTOR J	COL	0-0059862	0867	1
LAZAR AARON M	COL	0-0018738	0862	2
LAZZARINI LOUIS T	COL	0-0043425	0862	1
LE BLANC WILLIAM P	CW3	W-0903406	0961	1
LE CLAIR JR NELSON	COL	0-0028797	0255	1
LE GETTE JAMES Y	COL	0-0011088	0646	1
LE GOLVAN PAUL C	COL	0-0024634	0466	1
LE MAY JR ROBERT W	LTC	0-0038236	0265	1
LE MAY ROLAND A	COL	0-0039987	0164	1
LE MONIER DONALD J	LTC	0-0080130	0767	1
LE MOON RALPH G	COL	0-0031264	0467	1
LE PENSKE JR F J	LTC	0-0039774	0660	2
LE STOURGEON PERCY E	COL	0-0014635	0753	1
LE VAN HUGH	LTC	0-0042514	1157	2
LE VIER EARL R	LTC	0-0059925	0365	1
LEACH ALICE L	MAJ	L-0000204	0953	1
LEAHY JOHN P	LTC	0-0033057	1161	1
LEAKEY FRANK N	COL	0-0016578	0656	1
LEAR FRANK L	COL	0-0039007	1163	1
LEARNARD JR HENRY G	COL	0-0029801	0660	2
LEARY JOHN E	B G	0-0018607	0361	1
LEARY THOMAS J	COL	0-0002572	0544	1
LEAVENGOOD LEO D	LTC	0-0044938	0262	1
LEAVER FRANK Y	COL	0-0018928	0563	2
LEAVEY EDMOND H	M G	0-0008559	0649	1
LEAVITT ALBERT H	LTC	0-0028218	0466	1
LEAVITT CHARLES A	COL	0-0051403	0563	1
LEBKICHER HARRY R	COL	0-0009995	1046	2
LECKIE WILLIAM F	COL	0-0040296	0966	1
LEDBETTER MCWESLEY	COL	0-0051096	0860	1
LEDERMAN MILTON D	COL	0-0023320	1066	1
LEDFORD EDWARD A	MAJ	0-0038496	0962	1
LEDFORD JR LEE H	LTC	0-0023775	0861	1
LEDGERWOOD HOWARD G	LTC	0-0079889	0861	1
LEE ARTHUR H	COL	0-0008216	0650	1
LEE DONALD C	LTC	0-0078940	0967	1
LEE EDWARD M	COL	0-0020661	0762	1
LEE EDWIN L	COL	0-0043030	0266	1
LEE ERNEST O	COL	0-0015517	0854	2

NAME	GRADE	SVC NO	DATE RET MO YR	RET CODE
LEE EUGENE M	COL	0-0031474	0664	1
LEE FAY W	COL	0-0014760	0247	2
LEE FLORENCE I	LTC	N-0000503	0149	1
LEE FRANK F	COL	0-0042775	0863	1
LEE FRANK M	COL	0-0014891	0850	1
LEE FREDERICK	COL	0-0039518	0955	1
LEE GAIL B	LTC	0-0033332	1060	1
LEE HARRIET S	COL	N-0010001	0360	1
LEE JOHN L	COL	0-0051088	0660	1
LEE JR JOHN K	COL	0-0030136	0364	1
LEE LEVIN L	LTC	0-0022172	0867	1
LEE LYNN C	COL	0-0023717	0765	1
LEE MARY F	MAJ	N-0002118	0360	1
LEE RICHARD	COL	0-0012057	0351	1
LEE ROBERT V	M G	0-0028882	0961	1
LEE STANTON W	CPT	0-0065719	1064	1
LEE TRUMAN	CW4	W-0904315	0766	1
LEE WAYNE H	LTC	0-0024469	1060	1
LEECH ROHAN F	COL	0-0021679	0865	1
LEECH ROBERT C	LTC	0-0040183	0364	1
LEEDHAM CHARLES L	COL	0-0017838	0855	1
LEEDY BYRON	COL	0-0014937	0348	2
LEEHEY DONALD J	COL	0-0012673	0546	1
LEFKA ALEC H	CW4	W-0903410	0465	1
LEEN EVELYN E	MAJ	N-0001945	0558	1
LEENEY LEWIS W	COL	0-0025206	1166	1
LEEPER BRYAN H	LTC	0-0026579	0864	1
LEER JAMES H	COL	0-0020270	0866	2
LEES FRANKLIN B	LTC	0-0007844	0-35	2
LEFFEL R ERNEST	COL	0-0021442	0846	2
LEFFERS JR RICHARD	COL	0-0031843	0766	1
LEGARE SR BEN W	COL	0-0039034	0866	1
LEGENDRE STEWART H	LTC	0-0042004	0260	1
LEGERE LAURENCE J	COL	0-0022937	0766	1
LEGGETT RUFUS L	LTC	0-0094609	0867	1
LEGLER MATTHEW L	LTC	0-0022114	0246	2
LEHMAN ASA M	COL	0-0004077	0149	1
LEHMAN GEORGE A	LTC	0-0030945	0563	1
LEHMAN ROBERT H	LTC	0-0079891	1266	1
LEHMANN GUS I	COL	0-0040001	0463	1
LEHNER CHARLES R	B G	0-0005740	0249	2
LEHRFELD IRVING	COL	0-0018586	0761	1
LEHTONEN REINO O	COL	0-0052532	0767	1
LEIBY KENNETH L	COL	0-0051286	0162	1
LEIDENHEIMER JOHN L	COL	0-0030795	0664	1
LEIDY MARIETTA M	CPT	N-0002269	0952	2
LEIDY ROYAL L	COL	0-0029886	1060	2
LEIGH JR BEVERLY M	COL	0-0039917	0864	1
LEIGHTON RALPH F	COL	0-0043688	0762	1
LEIN LORENCE G	CW2	W-0902675	0257	1
LEININGER DANIEL M	LTC	0-0027992	0867	1
LEINSTER ROY L	MAJ	0-0018589	0-44	2
LEIST GEORGE F	COL	0-0020657	0963	1
LEIST WILLIAM C	MAJ	0-0060220	0164	1
LELAND ALANSON F	COL	0-0042736	0963	1
LELAND HELENA M	MAJ	N-0000874	0965	1
LELAND LOUIS S	COL	0-0020990	1166	1
LEMA HENRY R	LTC	0-0039370	0965	1
LEMMON KELLY B	COL	0-0002552	0345	1
LENETEK JR CHARLES C	LTC	0-0063114	0963	1
LENEY HERBERT C	LTC	0-0035789	0761	2
LENHOFF RAYMOND J	CW3	W-0903415	1053	2
LENN CLAUDE R	MAJ	0-0037469	1161	2
LENNHOFF CHARLES O	LTC	0-0021882	0660	1
LENTINI ANTHONY R	LTC	0-0058479	0967	1
LENTZ BENJAMIN A	COL	0-0029401	0460	1
LENTZ HAROLD T	COL	0-0028766	0254	1
LENTZ II CARL	LTC	0-0021993	0966	1
LENTZ JOHN M	M G	0-0010343	0156	1
LENZ ADELINE H	MAJ	N-0000625	0160	1
LENZE GLADYS L	MAJ	N-0002224	1158	1
LENZNER EMIL	M G	0-0015810	0758	1
LEONARD ABEL I	COL	0-0015550	0654	1
LEONARD ANN M	CPT	N-0000683	0849	2
LEONARD EDGAR W	LTC	0-0037390	0561	1

NAME	GRADE	SVC NO	DATE RET MO YR	RET CODE
LEONARD JOHN W	LTG	0-0003840	0152	1
LEONARD JR CHARLES F	M G	0-0019829	0667	1
LEONARD JR ROBERT R	LTC	0-0060096	0966	1
LEONARD KATHARINE	MAJ	N-0010054	0558	1
LEONARD LAWRENCE C	COL	0-0014906	0652	1
LEONARD MARGARET W	MAJ	N-0000212	0157	1
LEONARD MARY T	MAJ	N-0002359	1058	1
LEONARD ROBERT T	LTC	0-0080965	1066	1
LEONARD WILLIAM	CW4	W-0906841	1058	1
LEONE GEORGE E	COL	0-0018287	0960	1
LEONE LOUIS R	COL	0-0015350	0854	1
LEOPARD WALTER D	CW3	W-0903417	0863	1
LEPPING ALOYSIUS J	COL	0-0016853	0757	1
LERETTE EARLE L	COL	0-0022133	1064	1
LERNER GERALD P	COL	0-0032199	0966	1
LERRO SANTINO J	COL	0-0020540	0661	1
LESLIE ROBERT C	COL	0-0018993	0959	1
LESLIE SAMUEL H	COL	0-0001511	1022	1
LESLIE WILLIAM T	LTC	0-0069524	0866	2
LESNESKI STANLEY V	LTC	0-0032053	1166	1
LESSER LOUIS L	LTC	0-0014771	0644	2
LESSLEY GEORGIA F	LTC	N-0001865	0959	1
LESTER GRAHAM W	COL	0-0004801	0854	1
LESTER ROBERT B	CW2	W-0901783	0247	1
LEVA FRANCIS L	LTC	0-0052627	1161	1
LEVARDSEN RICHARD W	LTC	0-0080307	0267	1
LEVASSEUR ARMAND R	LTC	0-0047280	0763	1
LEVENICK MAYNARD A	COL	0-0018514	0159	2
LEVENS ARTHUR J	COL	0-0031283	0766	1
LEVIE HOWARD S	COL	0-0038735	0263	1
LEVIN BEATRICE D	MAJ	L-0000018	0255	1
LEVIN EDWARD	LTC	0-0051510	0860	1
LEVIN MAURICE	COL	0-0039912	0764	1
LEVY JR RICHARD M	LTC	0-0023980	1165	1
LEVY JULIUS W	COL	0-0052466	0266	1
LEVY RICHARD M	COL	0-0004469	0450	1
LEWEY MERLE C	LTC	0-0080969	0167	1
LEWIS ARDEN I	COL	0-0043360	1163	1
LEWIS BERKELEY R	COL	0-0029065	0259	1
LEWIS BLANCHE Z	MAJ	N-0000714	0566	1
LEWIS BURTON O	B G	0-0002838	0747	1
LEWIS CHARLES	COL	0-0006821	0343	1
LEWIS CHARLES	1LT	0-0018257	0-37	2
LEWIS CHARLES W	COL	0-0004005	0344	2
LEWIS CLARENCE S	COL	0-0029039	0259	1
LEWIS DAVID C	B G	0-0029735	0762	1
LEWIS DONALD L	COL	0-0030119	0264	1
LEWIS EMMETT M	LTC	0-0032866	0166	1
LEWIS EMORY A	COL	0-0019584	1162	1
LEWIS EUGENE W	COL	0-0010847	1048	1
LEWIS EVAN H	COL	0-0040238	1167	1
LEWIS GABE W	COL	0-0042064	0761	1
LEWIS GARLAND B	COL	0-0079655	1065	1
LEWIS GEORGE G	LTC	0-0042240	1061	1
LEWIS GEORGE W	LTC	0-0038013	0862	1
LEWIS HAROLD J	LTC	0-0084321	1164	1
LEWIS HARRY J	COL	0-0019751	0762	1
LEWIS HUBERT D	COL	0-0018058	0758	1
LEWIS JAMES F	COL	0-0041915	1057	1
LEWIS JAMES L	COL	0-0021069	0167	1
LEWIS JESSE L	LTC	0-0024909	0459	2
LEWIS JETT W	CW4	W-0906864	0765	1
LEWIS JOHN T	LTG	0-0007000	0959	1
LEWIS JR JOHN H	COL	0-0012151	1048	1
LEWIS JR MARION A	LTC	0-0069737	0467	1
LEWIS LEHMAN J	LTC	0-0029537	0359	1
LEWIS PARRY W	COL	0-0008640	1146	1
LEWIS RALPH W	LTC	0-0020031	0843	2
LEWIS RAY H	COL	0-0005738	0951	1
LEWIS RICHARD L	COL	0-0042224	0863	1
LEWIS ROBERT B	LTC	0-0037802	0465	1
LEWIS ROBERT G	CW4	W-0902377	0366	1
LEWIS THOMAS E	B G	0-0015020	0653	1
LEWIS VERNON L	COL	0-0042628	1065	1
LEWIS WALDEN S	COL	0-0014811	1049	2

NAME	GRADE	SVC NO	DATE RET MO YR	RET CODE
LEWIS WARFIELD M	COL	0-0005242	0850	1
LEWIS WILLIAM H	COL	0-0020598	0758	1
LEWITZ EDWARD R	COL	0-0045325	0665	1
LEYDECKER CHARLES F	COL	0-0019227	0863	1
LEYKO CAROLYN A	MAJ	N-0001877	0558	1
LIAKOS ELIAS F	LTC	0-0032278	1156	2
LIBASCI ALFONSO M	COL	0-0019606	0461	1
LIBERSHAL FRANCIS M	COL	0-0023471	1046	2
LICHIRIE CORNELIUS	COL	0-0018371	0761	1
LICHTENWALTER LEON	COL	0-0012850	0954	1
LICKMAN EDWIN C	LTC	0-0011857	0840	1
LICORD FRANK A	LTC	0-0079895	0465	1
LIEBE HAROLD F	COL	0-0029334	0859	1
LIEBERBERG GEORGE	COL	0-0079896	0563	1
LIEBLICH JEROME F	COL	0-0033409	1163	1
LIEDING ROBERT K	LTC	0-0080438	0865	1
LIESKE BEATA M	MAJ	N-0000361	0560	1
LIESSMAN EMERSON O	CPT	0-0019949	0242	2
LIFFITCK WILLIAM T	LTC	0-0065249	0766	1
LIFSHUTZ OSCAR M	LTC	0-0052023	0865	1
LIGGETT DOYLE C	CW4	W-0902391	0457	1
LIGHT JOHN C	COL	0-0039611	0559	1
LIGHTCAP GEORGE E	COL	0-0015834	1046	2
LIGON THOMAS W	COL	0-0006656	0753	2
LIGON WALTER R	COL	0-0081912	0263	1
LIKENS JR ELLERY A	LTC	0-0079897	0565	1
LILE JOHN W	CPT	0-0007530	0233	2
LILES JAMES P	CW4	W-0903425	0762	1
LILES PAUL V S	LTC	0-0023876	0262	1
LILES ROY L	LTC	0-0058955	0766	1
LILL EUGENE M	LTC	0-0040011	0164	1
LILLARD ERMA L	MAJ	N-0002276	1263	1
LILLARD GERALD F	B G	0-0016770	0757	1
LILLY JR EDMUND J	COL	0-0007373	0753	1
LIMONCELLI DONALD D	COL	0-0042375	0664	1
LIMPUS JR CHARLES F	LTC	0-0027876	0167	1
LINCOLN JR RUSH B	M G	0-0018656	0265	1
LINCOLN RALPH A	COL	0-0016097	0755	1
LIND ELLIS R	CW2	W-0901590	0951	1
LIND HENRY O	COL	0-0020256	1060	1
LIND JR CARL J	COL	0-0029322	1059	1
LIND WILLIAM J	COL	0-0045230	0766	1
LINDBLOM VICTOR E	LTC	0-0091629	0567	1
LINDEN HENNING	B G	0-0007009	0952	1
LINDERMANN JOHN C	LTC	0-0023888	1047	2
LINDHOLM OSCAR W	CW3	W-0903427	0757	1
LINDMARK MARVIN L	LTC	0-0034393	0263	1
LINDNER KENNETH R	COL	0-0034650	0867	1
LINDORFF ROBERT L	MAJ	0-0077920	0863	1
LINDQUIST ALBERT A	COL	0-0041656	0360	1
LINDQUIST JOHN O	COL	0-0009614	0444	2
LINDQUIST ROY F	M G	0-0018125	0660	1
LINDSAY WALLACE W	COL	0-0038596	0856	1
LINDSEY JULIAN R	COL	0-0017772	0859	1
LINDSEY MALCOLM F	B G	0-0006914	0751	1
LINDSEY MORRIS L	LTC	0-0040935	1164	2
LINDSTROM HAROLD M	COL	0-0028932	1057	1
LINDT JOHN H	COL	0-0003379	0366	2
LINEBACK CARL W	LTC	0-0066037	0465	1
LINEBAUGH JOHN M	CPT	0-0140207	0467	2
LINEBERGER ERNEST C	LTC	0-0031297	0564	2
LINGAN WILLIAM J	LTC	0-0048851	0967	1
LINGENFELTER WILLIAM	LTC	0-0032829	0666	1
LINGER ALBERT F	1LT	0-0071219	0960	2
LINGNER FREDERICK	MAJ	0-0036387	0559	1
LININGER CLARENCE	COL	0-0001397	0642	1
LININGER JOHN H	LTC	0-0030059	1161	1
LINK LILLIAN G	CPT	N-0002644	0762	1
LINK WILLARD C	COL	0-0029028	1058	1
LINKSWILER GILBERT F	COL	0-0016098	0655	1
LINN EDNA J	MAJ	N-0000323	0764	1
LINN LAVON P	COL	0-0030757	0966	1
LINN PHILLIP J	LTC	0-0033391	0666	1
LINN SCOTT D	COL	0-0072260	1059	1
LINN WALTER A	COL	0-0041530	0658	1

NAME	GRADE	SVC NO	DATE RET MO YR	RET CODE
LINS HARRY W	COL	0-0009776	0749	1
LINSE FRANCIS D	LTC	0-0031858	C466	1
LINSERT HENRY	COL	0-000554C	C246	2
LINSMAN JOSEPH F	COL	C-0021476	0746	2
LINTHWAITE CEORGE F	COL	0-0029990	C963	1
LINTON JR WILLIAM C	LTC	0-0026140	1065	1
LIONAIS IRENE	MAJ	N-0001217	C264	1
LIPINSKI JAMES R	CW4	W-0903429	C760	1
LIROWSKI STELLA	MAJ	N-0001967	11AC	1
LIPPENCOTT GEORGE H	LTC	0-0080136	CR65	1
LIPPINCOTT AUBREY	COL	0-0000959	0541	2
LIPPINCOTT CLIFFCRO	LTC	0-0023429	C867	1
LIPSCOMB JOHN R	LTC	0-0C80977	1265	1
LIPSCOMB JR LAFAR	COL	0-0019054	C761	1
LIPTON SAMUEL M	COL	C-002439R	C762	1
LISK JR PERCY F	COL	0-005354C	C867	1
LISK ROBERT T	LTC	0-0039957	1055	1
LISTER RODERICK L	COL	0-0057753	0167	1
LISTON CAVIC E	COL	0-001782C	0356	1
LITTERAL EMMETT B	COL	C-00182R1	1055	1
LITTLE ANDY V	MAJ	C-0019700	C646	1
LITTLE OONALC C	COL	0-001838E	C761	1
LITTLE GERALD B	LTC	0-0040554	C766	1
LITTLE MURRAY A	COL	0-0039956	C864	1
LITTLE ROGER W	LTC	0-0065220	0666	1
LITTLE WILLIAM	COL	0-0018748	C656	1
LITTLEJOHN JAMES P	COL	0-0042837	C162	2
LITTLEJOHN ROBERT M	M G	0-0003373	1046	2
LITTLETON AUGUSTINE	LTC	0-0046066	0762	1
LITTON ANDREW L	LTC	0-0CR0979	0167	1
LITZ WAYNE P	COL	C-0030304	C261	1
LIVERMORE FRANCIS S	LTC	C-00322C3	C264	1
LIVESAY HARVEY R	COL	C-0008919	1050	1
LIVESAY WILLIAM G	M G	0-0004603	065C	1
LIVINGSTON JOHN J	COL	0-0039714	C361	1
LIVINGSTON LEON J	COL	0-0039512	C255	1
LIWSKI FRANCIS A	COL	0-0018777	0862	1
LIZARDI LUIS R	CW4	W-0907114	C760	1
LLOYO PETER J	COL	C-0007277	C753	1
LLCYO REES S	MAJ	C-0005993	C829	2
LLCYO ROBERT N	W01	W-0904252	0849	1
LO CICERO JOSEPHINE	MAJ	N-0001296	0863	1
LOBIT WILLIAM E	COL	C-0030699	C560	1
LOCHRIE ARTHUR J	LTC	C-0028142	C667	1
LOCK GREGORY J	COL	0-0051957	C566	1
LOCK JR EOWIN P	COL	0-0012064	1047	1
LOCKE JR THEODORE F	LTC	C-0059951	C966	1
LOCKE THOMAS W	LTC	0-0053105	C964	1
LOCKE WILLIAM A	LTC	0-0029967	C256	1
LOCKE WILLIAM J	LTC	C-0040512	0862	1
LOCKETT JAMES W	COL	C-0C17305	0758	1
LOCKETT JOHN	COL	C-0051292	C262	1
LOCKETT LANOON J	COL	0-0011107	C348	2
LOCKHART EUGENE E	COL	0-00201A1	C866	1
LOCKHART GECRGE A	COL	0-0007622	C448	1
LOCKHART MARIE L	MAJ	N-0CCC295	C861	1
LOCKSLEY NORMAN M C	COL	0-0025111	C863	1
LCCKWOOD DANIEL S	COL	0-0009106	C846	1
LCCKWOOD ESTHER M	MAJ	N-0001281	1164	1
LCCKWOCO JR B C	B G	0-0003090	0348	2
LOCKWOOD JR HENRY	CPT	0-0014372	C819	2
LOOGE EOWIN R	COL	0-0042252	0560	1
LOOLE ELWOOC G	MAJ	C-0059958	C266	1
LODMELL ELMER A	COL	0-0019315	C957	1
LODOEN GEORGE O N	M G	C-0016580	0461	1
LOEF JOSEPH W	COL	0-0006958	1147	2
LOEWUS JAMES O	COL	0-0023205	C867	2
LOFSTRANO ALBERT E	LTC	0-0042889	1051	1
LOFTIN HAROLDE T	COL	0-0039673	0460	1
LOFTUS JAMES V	LTC	C-0042451	1162	1
LOFTUS JR JOSEPH F	LTC	0-0084645	0267	1
LOGAN PAUL R	COL	0-0009078	C446	1
LOGAN WILLIAM J	LTC	0-0024470	C860	1
LOGSOON HARLAN V	LTC	0-0044347	C560	1
LOHMAN MARTHA E	MAJ	N-0001325	C465	1
LOHR MARY G	CPT	N-0CC0100	0657	1
LOHRMANN AGNES B	MAJ	N-0001329	0565	1
LOHRMANN IMELOA H	MAJ	N-0001254	0565	1
LOKUTA LORETTA L	MAJ	N-0000255	0164	1
LCLLI ANDREW R	M G	0-0029844	0966	1
LOMAN MAMIE V	MAJ	N-0001014	0365	1
LONCHAR HELEN T	LTC	N-0001012	0364	1
LONDAHL JOHN E	LTC	0-0C35829	0561	1
LONERO CHARLES	LTC	C-0043185	0460	1
LCNG ARTHUR R	COL	C-0C29287	C661	1
LONG FLCYD H	COL	C-0032889	1167	1
LONG GECRGE S	MAJ	0-0065082	1263	1
LONG HARLAN J	COL	0-0042994	0467	1
LONG HERNDON H	COL	0-0039759	0661	1
LCNG HOMER F	COL	0-0C3C176	0159	2
LONG JCHN H	CW4	W-0903443	0965	1
LONG JR HERBERT S	COL	C-0C31985	0765	1
LONG MARGARET A	LTC	L-0000127	0565	1
LONG MAURICE F	COL	0-0040422	0864	1
LCNG RICHARD L	COL	0-0C46931	1065	1
LONG RCBERT T	CPT	0-0C56536	0449	2
LCNG WILLIAM E	COL	C-0016221	0755	1
LCNG WILLIAM P	CW4	W-0903445	1165	1
LONGACRE TERRANCE M	COL	0-0030047	0759	1
LCNGAKER JR NCRRIS S	2LT	0-0017759	0232	2
LONGANECKER C R	COL	0-0C18707	1054	2
LONGBOTHAM RALPH M	LTC	0-0080985	0766	1
LCNGERICH HARRY	LTC	C-0053791	0563	1
LCNGFELLCW DCN	B G	C-0C16708	0357	1
LONGINC JAMES C	COL	0-0006702	1146	1
LONGINC MERCER P	LTC	0-0024024	0764	1
LCNGLEY JR CAM	COL	0-0C19112	0661	1
LONGLEY WILLIAM L	COL	0-0020274	1046	2
LONGWELL WILLIAM F	MAJ	C-0015125	1041	1
LONNINC STANLEY N	COL	C-0015281	0863	1
LONSINGER ROY W	LTC	0-0052192	0866	1
LOOME JAMES T	B G	0-0015584	1046	2
LOOMIS FRANCIS J	COL	0-0020551	0263	1
LCOMIS HAROLC F	B G	0-0003702	1146	2
LOOMIS JR JESTER M	COL	C-0C79899	0166	1
LOORER FLOY L	MAJ	N-0000744	0964	1
LOPER CALE F	CW4	W-0906865	1060	2
LCPEZ ANDRES	COL	0-0004843	1046	2
LOREZ FERNANCC	LTC	0-0080987	0767	1
LORCH ROBERT C	LTC	0-0058957	1166	2
LORCK HORACE C	LTC	0-0036359	0864	1
LCRD ERMA G	MAJ	R-0010069	C858	1
LCRO RCBERT H	COL	0-0006565	0747	1
LCRENCE MAX F	2LT	0-0060924	C551	2
LORENCE WALTER F	COL	0-0009317	1047	1
LORENZ JCHN T	LTC	0-0052408	0860	1
LORENZ JR ERNEST H	LTC	0-00235C5	1159	1
LORENZ RALPH A	COL	0-0030534	1264	2
LORENZ ROBERT M	LTC	0-0062036	1167	1
LOSCH ELMER H	CW3	W-0906866	0261	1
LOSCO FICRENZO D	LTC	0-0056579	0867	1
LOSEY MELVIN G	B G	0-0042235	0863	1
LOSTEN STEVEN W	LTC	0-0048412	0764	1
LCTHROP GUY C	COL	0-0018992	0561	1
LOTOZC JAMES A	LTC	0-0023109	0362	2
LCTT OCUGLAS A	1LT	0-0027227	0350	1
LOTT LYNWOCO O	COL	0-0041796	0557	1
LCUCKS CHARLES F	M G	0-0006949	0555	1
LOUCKS MARGARET L	MAJ	N-0002050	0760	1
LOUOEN RUSSELL R	COL	0-0010159	0252	1
LCUDENSLAGER ROBERT	LTC	0-0052155	C465	1
LOUGEE LAURENCE W	COL	0-0041933	1161	2
LOUGHLIN CHARLES C	COL	0-0007734	0642	2
LOUGHMAN JACK R	LTC	0-0026282	0963	1
LOUGHRAN JOSEPH S	CPT	0-0009435	0-21	2
LOUPRET GECRGE J	COL	0-0012676	0950	1
LCVE HENRY L	LTC	0-0014653	0952	1
LCVE RCBERT P	CW4	W-0906067	1165	1
LOVE RCBERT L	COL	0-0017774	0147	2
LOVE WALTER C	M G	0-0011506	0454	1
LOVELL HARRY F	COL	0-0042616	C559	1
LCVELL HERBERT R	LTC	0-0039253	0464	1
LOVELL JOSEPH M	LTC	0-0017648	0245	2
LOVELLY JR EDWARD A	MAJ	C-0008699	1022	2
LOVERING RICHARD S	MAJ	C-0023453	C547	2
LOVETT HILDA M	LTC	R-0010061	0558	1
LOVETT RALPH B	B G	0-0008092	C247	2
LOVETT ROBERT G	B G	0-0012062	0654	1
LOVIN HELEN B	MAJ	N-0002250	C761	1
LOVING ROGER C	LTC	0-0055885	C765	1
LOVSNE NEAL W	COL	C-0030540	1065	2
LOW HAROLO R	COL	C-0020234	C656	1
LOW JAMES L	COL	C-0030585	C166	1
LCW JOSEPH W	CW3	W-0903451	C459	1
LOWDEN CHARLES B	LTC	0-0060642	0767	1
LOWE ELWARD W	LTC	0-0054717	C562	1
LOWE PERCY S	COL	0-0CC9905	C949	2
LCWE ROBERT G	COL	C-0016800	C757	1
LOWE ROBERT L	COL	0-0042913	1165	1
LCWENSTERN SICNEY	LTC	C-0051285	C160	1
LOWERY JR AUSTIN	COL	0-0182282	C961	2
LOWERY WILLIAM B	LTC	0-0008083	C842	2
LOWREY CHARLES A	CW3	W-0903455	CR59	1
LOWREY JR AUSTIN	COL	0-0018282	CR61	1
LOWRIE ELVIN S	LTC	0-0079901	1066	1
LOWRY DEXTER	LTC	0-0017628	0150	1
LOWRY EARL C	COL	0-0020992	1058	1
LOWRY JR EVERETT E	COL	0-0025799	C666	1
LOWRY LEONARD	LTC	0-0080989	0967	1
LOWRY PORTER P	COL	C-0005567	C147	2
LOWRY RICHARD	COL	C-0039725	1052	1
LOWRY ROBERT H	COL	0-0004159	C747	1
LOYD FRANK R	COL	0-0016004	C854	2
LUBBE ALBERT J	LTC	0-0012523	1044	1
LUCAS BURTON L	COL	0-0CC7334	1050	1
LUCAS CHARLES E	CPT	C-0008908	C934	1
LUCAS ECWARD C	LTC	0-0023225	C660	1
LUCAS JR WILLIAM E	LTC	C-0004793	C142	1
LUCAS MASON H	B G	0-0016633	1056	1
LUCAS VIRGINIA G	MAJ	N-0001551	0965	1
LUCAS WILLIAM C	COL	0-0015309	C954	1
LUCE DEAN	COL	C-0012389	1050	1
LUCEY GEORGE A	COL	C-0024446	C466	1
LUCEY JOHN F	LTC	0-0042054	C249	2
LUCHWINKO JOSEPH	CW4	W-0903458	C266	1
LUCIER JR ALPHONSE F	LTC	0-0034832	0863	1
LUCK HARRY C	COL	0-0005119	C548	2
LUCKE EMIL A	COL	0-0042331	0364	1
LUCKE WILLIAM N	LTC	C-0024430	1159	1
LUCKETT JAMES S	COL	0-0018209	0760	1
LUCREE MORRIS J	COL	C-0033401	C966	1
LUDECKE FREO W	COL	0-0041898	0861	1
LUDEMAN RICHARC F	LTC	0-0022233	C759	1
LUDINGTON MARVIN W	COL	0-0029434	0860	2
LUCLAM COUGLAS G	COL	0-0C17207	C758	2
LUDWIKOSKY JOHN R	COL	0-0034228	C862	1
LUEBBERMAN HENRI A	COL	0-0016827	C549	2
LUKE ITTAI A	COL	0-0005541	C646	1
LUKE REGIS W	COL	0-0039859	0264	1
LUKEMAN JOHN M	COL	0-C061061	1167	1
LUKENS JAMES R	LTC	C-0063331	1265	1
LUKENS WALTER P	LTC	C-0050801	0467	1
LUKER CHARLES T	LTC	C-0038883	C161	1
LULL GEORGE F	M G	0-00C3516	C446	1
LULL JR GEORGE F	COL	0-0031114	0565	1
LUM NICK	CW4	W-0906868	C466	1
LUMIA SALVATORE	LTC	0-0080991	1165	1
LUMPKIN BENJAMIN E	LTC	C-0057425	C567	1
LUMPKIN JR CLAUOE C	LTC	0-0024941	C863	1
LUMPKIN JR WALTER L	COL	0-0037615	C764	1
LUMRY RAYMOND H	COL	0-0022199	C764	1
LUNA RAYMONC C	LTC	0-0C42403	0762	2
LUNCEFORD ROY L	LTC	0-0080992	0567	1
LUND GERTRUDE F	MAJ	L-0000217	C656	1
LUNDBERG FLOYD M	COL	0-0042136	0263	1
LUNDEBERG KARL R	COL	0-0017979	0454	1
LUNDQUIST CARL E	COL	C-0016885	0657	1
LUNDY IRVIN M	MAJ	0-0C410CC	0160	1
LUNDY JAMES T	MAJ	0-0067719	0567	1
LUNGER RICHARC T	COL	0-002538E	1262	1
LUNNEY DCNALD R	1LT	0-0027110	1147	2
LUNSFORD JR JAMES N	LTC	0-0033518	0867	1
LUNTZEL ADRIAN A	CW4	W-090346C	0167	1
LUONGO HENRY L	COL	C-0016683	1C56	1
LURA ECNA	LTC	M-0010034	0352	1
LUSCCMBE HARCLD B	COL	0-001829E	C356	1
LUSCOMBE JCHN B	COL	0-0012525	0946	2
LUSE ARTHUR H	COL	C-0007537	0848	2
LUSZKI WALTER A	LTC	0-0044073	1159	1
LUTES JR LERCY	COL	C-0020757	C866	1
LUTES LEROY	LTG	0-0005413	0152	1
LUTH WILLIAM C	CPT	0-0014409	0120	2
LUTHER HENRY	COL	0-0079713	0767	1
LUTHI IRVIN L	COL	0-0038830	0566	1
LUTTRELL JAMES A	LTC	0-0036363	0863	1
LUTZ CARL G	COL	0-004336E	0264	1
LUTZ RCBERT C	LTC	0-0027359	C865	1
LUTZ RCBERT C	COL	0-0028868	C854	1
LUTZ RCBERT R	COL	0-0030767	0766	1
LUX HERBERT C	COL	0-0042212	0863	1
LYBRANC ALBERT B	CW3	W-09C3461	1060	1
LYDAY CHARLES V	LTC	C-0065534	1266	1
LYDDON CCNALO W	LTC	0-0026413	1052	1
LYDICK JCHN M	COL	0-0041436	0956	1
LYDLE JR CRAWFORD H	LTC	0-0052349	0859	1
LYDCN JCSEPHINE	LTC	R-0010123	0565	2
LYKE CLARE N	LTC	0-0C24601	0262	1
LYLE JAMES R	COL	C-0C32348	0865	1
LYLE JAMES W	LTC	0-0035484	C761	1
LYLE JCHN R	LTC	0-0032700	0261	1
LYLE JR CLAYTCN B	COL	0-0040306	0767	1
LYLF PAUL B	LTC	0-0080993	0666	1
LYLE SHIRLEY M	MAJ	N-0000331	1059	1
LYMAN CHARLES B	B G	0-000359C	0346	1
LYMAN HARRY E	COL	C-0038903	0167	1
LYMAN IRVING R	COL	0-0024319	1C64	1
LYMAN JAMES H	1LT	0-0014444	C421	2
LYMAN REGINALO P	B G	0-0014872	0854	1
LYNCH CHARLES L	LTC	0-0057911	0766	1
LYNCH CHARLES P	COL	C-0C09247	0353	1
LYNCH FRANCIS H	1LT	0-0017748	1137	2
LYNCH FRANCIS T	MAJ	0-0056217	C863	1
LYNCM CECRGE E	M G	0-0017715	C257	1
LYNCH CECRGE R	B G	0-0016226	0556	1
LYNCH HARRY	LTC	0-0014766	1047	1
LYNCH HUBERT J	CW4	W-0903463	0261	1
LYNCH JAMES R	1LT	0-0026703	0546	2
LYNCH JCHN A	CPT	0-0070415	1C59	2
LYNCH JCHN F	CPT	0-0014371	0819	2
LYNCH JCHN M	COL	0-0020377	C866	1
LYNCH JOHN T	COL	0-0012841	1052	1
LYNCH JOHN T	CW3	W-0903464	C957	1
LYNCH JOHN W	LTC	0-0042984	C962	1
LYNCH JR BUFCRD A	1LT	0-0015881	0333	2
LYNCH JR GEORGE W	CW4	W-0903462	0959	1
LYNCH JR THOMAS D	MAJ	0-0080139	0361	1
LYNCH ROBERT J	MAJ	0-0060253	0665	1
LYNCH SUE	LTC	L-0000081	1164	1
LYNO RCY F	COL	0-0006146	0849	2
LYNDE JR NELSCN M	M G	0-001773C	0364	1
LYNES CCNALO L	LTC	0-006308C	0566	1
LYNN CLARK	COL	C-0001832	1138	1
LYNN DCSS O	COL	0-0021722	0363	2
LYNN JR CLARK	COL	0-0019456	0864	1
LYNN JR EDISCN A	COL	0-0023085	1262	1
LYNN LAURENCE E	COL	C-0042C59	0862	1
LYCN ARCHIBALD	B G	0-0018682	0862	1
LYON FREDERICK	CW3	W-0903465	0558	1
LYON HARCLD C	COL	0-0041832	0161	1
LYON HENRY Y	COL	0-0005868	0753	1

UNITED STATES ARMY RETIRED LIST

NAME	GRADE	SVC NO	DATE RET MO YR	RET CODE
LYONS CARL F	COL	0-0020824	C767	1
LYONS CATHERINE	LTC	L-0000073	1263	1
LYONS CHAUNCEY M	COL	0-0CC8105	0151	1
LYONS HARRY L	WO1	W-0901116	0425	1
LYONS JAMES P	COL	C-0006108	1146	1
LYONS JOHN H	LTC	0-0052079	1054	1
LYONS JOSEPH W	LTC	0-0059466	0567	1
LYONS JR GEORGE F	CW4	W-0906870	0767	1
LYTER CLINTON S	M G	0-0018291	0366	2
LYTLE JAMES R	LTC	0-0048021	0762	1
MAAS HARRY W	COL	0-0006573	C848	1
MABBOTT HAROLC C	COL	0-0006677	1047	1
MABBUTT CHARLES J	LTC	0-0007961	0934	2
MABEE RICHARD W	COL	0-0023241	1060	1
MABIE RUSSELL L	COL	0-0015626	0854	1
MABRY LELANC S	COL	C-0017034	0651	1
MABRY NED B	COL	0-0053148	0667	1
MABRY ROBERT A	CW4	W-0903467	C665	1
MAC ADAM LLOYD R	COL	0-0029513	1060	1
MAC ALLASTER W R	LTC	0-0051678	0157	1
MAC ARTHUR JOHN C	COL	0-0010115	C451	1
MAC ARTHUR JOHN E	MAJ	C-0040885	0162	1
MAC CONNELL III T	COL	C-0040286	0866	1
MAC DONALD ALECK F	COL	0-0022685	1065	1
MAC DONALD ALEXANE	LTC	0-0023341	C147	2
MAC DONALD AUGUSTINE	LTC	0-0036989	0661	1
MAC DONALD FRANCIS A	LTC	0-0041082	0664	1
MAC DONALD HENRY C	CW4	W-0902089	0662	1
MAC DONALD JOHN P	LTC	0-0039368	C965	1
MAC DONALD MALCOLM E	LTC	0-0028701	C766	1
MAC DONALD MARION C	1LT	R-0000266	1146	1
MAC DONALD STUART C	COL	C-0003854	1051	1
MAC DONALD VERNA E	MAJ	N-0002379	0261	1
MAC DONOUGH JOHN F	LTC	0-0052208	C965	1
MAC DOUGALL JAMES B	COL	C-0029335	C859	1
MAC EACHERN GEORGE A	COL	C-0039806	1065	1
MAC FARLAND JOHN J	COL	0-0018100	0260	2
MAC FARLANF WILLIAM	LTC	0-0036948	C864	2
MAC GREGOR CECIL M	COL	0-0042182	0763	1
MAC GREGOR LESTER E	COL	0-0007102	C546	1
MAC KELVIE JAY W	B G	C-0005476	C946	2
MAC KENZIE ALAN F S	COL	0-0C28806	0655	1
MAC KENZIE ALEXANC	COL	0-0012203	C446	2
MAC KENZIE FRANK P	COL	0-0010836	0248	1
MAC KINNON WILLIAM R	COL	0-0011408	0146	2
MAC KUSICK ARTHUR L	COL	0-0042695	0962	1
MAC LACHLAN DONALD J	MAJ	C-CCC2238	1022	1
MAC LAUGHLIN PAUL E	LTC	0-0017332	C252	1
MAC LEAN GERTRUDE A	LTC	N-0000506	1148	1
MAC LEAN ROBERT J	LTC	0-0044042	C862	1
MAC LECD JOHN W	COL	C-0041919	0961	1
MAC MILLAN KARL D	COL	0-0063822	0964	1
MAC MILLAN THOMAS R	MAJ	0-0037411	C861	1
MAC MORLAND EDWARD E	M G	C-0004653	0752	1
MAC NABB ALEXANDER	COL	0-0007436	0751	1
MAC NEILL FRANCIS W	LTC	0-0070416	0565	2
MAC QUIGG DAVID E	LTC	0-0061174	C167	1
MAC WILLIAMS JOHN	COL	C-0012555	0546	2
MAC WILLIE DONALD M	COL	0-0030152	0464	1
MACATEE EDWARD V	COL	C-0011366	0653	1
MACE DON L	LTC	C-0021737	C257	1
MACE RALPH R	M G	0-0017578	0664	1
MACHEREY EARL J	COL	C-0019158	0763	1
MACK JOHN D	COL	0-0080443	0765	1
MACK JR DANIEL D	COL	0-0030015	1263	1
MACK WILLIAM M	COL	0-0014866	0854	1
MACKEN JOHN J	LTC	0-0040304	1165	1
MACKENZIE GABRIEL T	COL	C-0004658	C951	1
MACKEY HAROLD V	LTC	0-0025046	C862	1
MACKIN JAMES H	COL	0-0029300	C166	2
MACKIN 3RD ROBERT N	MAJ	C-0023260	1152	2
MACKINTOSH HUGH	M G	C-0017716	0466	1
MACKINTOSH WILLIAM E	LTC	0-0051221	0250	1
MACLACHLAN WALTER L	COL	0-0050948	C657	1
MACOMBER JOHN A	LTC	0-0057965	1066	1
MACOMBER KENNETH D	COL	0-0042C05	0462	1
MACON JR FRANCIS A	COL	C-0005315	0753	1
MACON ROBERT C	M G	0-0C04733	0752	1
MADDALENA ARMAND S	CW4	W-0906872	1265	1
MADDEN IDA K	MAJ	L-0000252	0464	1
MADDEN JOSEPH C	COL	0-0C29656	0160	1
MADDEN TED J	LTC	0-0042537	0255	1
MADDING ALBERT S	LTC	0-0033680	0764	1
MADDOCKS RAY T	M G	0-0007291	0651	1
MADDOCKS THOMAS H	COL	0-0015000	0451	1
MADDOX EDWARD R	COL	0-0030036	1063	1
MADDOX GEORGE W	LTC	0-00C2090	0929	2
MADDOX HALLEY G	M G	0-0012852	0259	2
MADDOX J D	CW4	W-0903471	0464	1
MADIGAN JR JOHN J	COL	0-0039538	0956	1
MADIGAN MARIE J	MAJ	L-000CC69	0460	1
MAEROIAN FRANK R	COL	0-001725E	0758	1
MAERZ RICHARD H	LTC	0-0080444	0965	1
MAGE JACK D	COL	C-0028971	0258	1
MAGEE JAMES C	M G	C-0002565	0-43	1
MAGEE MERVYN M	M G	0-0018478	0667	1
MAGEE OSCAR J	LTC	0-0042158	0261	1
MAGNESS JR THOMAS H	COL	0-0051199	0261	1
MAGNUSSON JOHN R	COL	0-0031432	0165	1
MAGRUDER CARTER B	GEN	C-0015155	0661	1
MAGUIRE CEDRIC F	MAJ	C-0004932	0-35	2
MAGUIRE EDWARD F	LTC	0-0030332	1262	1
MAGUIRE EDWARD J	LTC	0-0042251	0961	1
MAGUIRE HAMILTON E	B G	0-0004433	0748	1
MAGUIRE ROBERT F	COL	0-0037528	1167	1
MAHAN DALE E	MAJ	C-0027642	0765	1
MAHER JR JOHN P	COL	0-0041490	1057	1
MAHER WILLIAM F	COL	C-0003747	0847	1
MAHONEY ELIZABETH	LTC	N-0000499	0252	1
MAHONEY JAMES H	COL	0-0051613	0565	1
MAHONEY JR WILLIAM C	COL	0-0023486	0861	1
MAHONEY MARGARET E	MAJ	M-0010017	0965	1
MAHONEY PAUL H	COL	C-0015022	0753	1
MAHONEY WILLIAM J	COL	C-0018616	0754	1
MAHR RAYMOND A	COL	0-0043157	0766	1
MAIDT RONALD A	COL	C-0042513	0762	1
MAIER ROBERT J	LTC	0-0063075	0367	1
MAILHEAU ROBERT T	LTC	0-0062172	0455	2
MAIN RALPH E	LTC	0-004120C	0665	1
MAINWARING JR JOHN W	LTC	0-0030865	0561	1
MAIORANC PASCUALE P	COL	0-0042316	0264	1
MAISER NEVA B	MAJ	L-0000228	0259	1
MAISH ALEXANDER	LTC	0-0026523	0767	1
MAITA WINIFRED Z	LTC	N-0002370	0463	1
MAJOR BERNARD P	COL	0-002075C	0467	1
MAJOR GEORGE C	MAJ	0-0046041	0762	1
MAKAROUNIS ALEXANDER	CPT	0-0058962	0556	2
MAKINNEY FRED W	COL	0-0012469	0146	2
MALANKOWSKI ANTHONY	LTC	0-0030500	C363	2
MALCOLM ROBERT	MAJ	0-0009442	0-34	2
MALDONADO JACK C	COL	0-0024447	0767	1
MALERBA AGNES C	MAJ	N-0001036	0366	1
MALEVICH STEVEN	COL	C-0030660	0663	1
MALEY AGNES A	COL	N-0000516	0658	2
MALIN HOWARD A	COL	0-0015821	0954	1
MALINA ANTHONY S	CW4	W-0903474	0863	1
MALING EDWIN C	COL	0-0014598	1047	1
MALISZEWSKI GEORGE H	COL	C-0020759	1067	2
MALL OSCAR A	COL	0-0031796	0767	1
MALLALIEU CHARLES F	LTC	0-0042333	0262	1
MALLETT PIERRE	B G	0-0008314	0550	1
MALLON FRANCIS B	M G	0-0003426	0946	2
MALLON JOHN B	LTC	0-0051123	1057	1
MALLONEE RICHARD C	COL	C-C008464	0854	1
MALLORY JOHN W	LTC	0-0056135	1066	1
MALLOY JOHN T	COL	0-0018576	0561	1
MALONE ARTHUR G	LTC	0-0023237	0761	1
MALONE DUANE W	LTC	0-0031479	0165	1
MALONE EVERETTE W	LTC	0-0049925	1061	1
MALONE FLORENCE C	MAJ	N-0002027	0558	1
MALONE JR ALBERT C	LTC	0-0063275	0967	1
MALONE JR EUBERT H	LTC	0-0038253	0965	1
MALONE MARIE L	LTC	L-0000198	1265	1
MALONE RHODA E	MAJ	N-0000364	C662	1
MALONE THOMAS R	COL	0-0029489	1160	1
MALONE WILLIAM F	LTC	0-0026044	0164	1
MALONEY ARTHUR A	COL	C-0021297	C846	2
MALONEY JAMES P	LTC	0-0039556	0150	1
MALONEY JR JAMES E	COL	C-001861C	0761	1
MALONY HARRY J	M G	0-0003385	C349	1
MALUMPHY CHARLES P	COL	0-0029131	C957	1
MALY LEWIS W	COL	C-0008755	0946	2
MAMER JAMES	1LT	0-0011559	1130	2
MANARY EUGENE D	LTC	0-0033216	0362	2
MANASCO RAYMOND O	LTC	0-0033608	0764	2
MANCUSO STEPHEN J	COL	C-0022006	C966	1
MANDEL ADRIAN D	LTC	0-0060889	C266	1
MANDELBAUM ALBERT J	COL	0-0018061	0660	2
MANDELL FRANK C	COL	0-0023234	C866	1
MANDERBACH HAROLD M	COL	0-0015984	C854	1
MANEES JAMES R	COL	0-0011664	0946	2
MANESS RALPH T	CW4	W-0906877	C560	1
MANGAN WALTER D	COL	0-0004511	C145	2
MANGINI MICHAEL	CW4	W-0903475	C862	1
MANGOLD HAROLD B	COL	0-0031522	C766	1
MANGONES ROBERT J	MAJ	C-0081004	C467	1
MANGUM ROBERT G	COL	C-0005983	1146	1
MANLEY NORBERT C	LTC	0-0007820	0545	1
MANLOVE ALMON W	COL	0-0019413	C864	1
MANLY LORRAINE L	COL	0-0051373	C758	1
MANN CHARLES C	MAJ	C-00C3990	C822	2
MANN HOWARD H	MAJ	0-0060259	C466	1
MANN JOHN P	CW3	W-0903478	0159	1
MANN JR HERBERT C	CW4	RW-0903476	0963	1
MANN ROBERT J	LTC	0-0027361	0766	1
MANNES JR CONRAD D	LTC	0-0032293	C459	1
MANNING EARL V	COL	0-0039941	C465	1
MANNING KENNETH T	MAJ	0-0060320	0760	1
MANNING RAMONA S	MAJ	N-0000446	C461	1
MANNING RICHARD I	LTC	0-0023439	0660	1
MANNING WALLACE A	LTC	0-0043386	1057	2
MANOV CHARLES F	COL	0-0051840	C467	2
MANRODT MANFRED P	CW4	W-0903479	0167	1
MANSAGER MERVIN E	COL	0-0041878	0661	1
MANSFIELD HERBERT V	COL	0-0080447	0861	1
MANSFIELD HERBERT W	COL	0-0018429	0761	1
MANSON PETER C	LTC	C-0023545	C660	1
MANTALAS JOHN G	CPT	0-0063064	1162	3
MANTELL LOUIS K	COL	C-0020035	C766	2
MANTER JR OTIS L	CW4	W-0906879	C566	1
MANTHEY ERWIN A	CPT	0-0006560	0134	2
MANTOR FRANCES C	LTC	N-0000813	C861	1
MANZANO NARCISO L	COL	0-001479C	0147	2
MAPES ROLAND H	COL	0-0030538	C256	1
MAPLES FREDERIC A	COL	0-0029017	1058	2
MARCH KENNETH F	COL	0-0016481	C856	1
MARCH MARY M	1LT	M-0000459	0544	1
MARCHEK CARLYLE S	COL	0-0029290	1158	1
MARCHUS JR DAVID F	LTC	C-0079636	C864	1
MARCONI SABATINE R	LTC	0-0036128	C866	1
MARCUS MORRIS H	COL	0-0014602	C954	1
MARCY ALFRED R	COL	0-0038597	C855	1
MARCY ROY W	COL	0-003138C	0763	2
MARDEN JR LYMAN P	COL	0-0040C86	0562	1
MARET RAYMOND	COL	C-0063666	1066	1
MARGESON HENRY B	COL	C-0016181	C655	1
MARGETIS NICHOLAS M	CPT	0-0060112	1151	1
MARGOLIN OLIVER	CW3	W-0903481	0361	1
MARGRAVE CHESTER E	COL	0-0016643	0846	2
MARIETTA SHELLEY U	M G	0-000329C	0145	2
MARINELLI JACK L	COL	0-0034331	0762	1
MARIS WARD H	M G	C-0006718	1152	1
MARKER HARRY J	COL	0-0051688	1265	1
MARKEY EDWARD W	COL	0-0035143	C365	1
MARKEY LAWRENCE B	B G	0-0038826	0867	1
MARKHAM HARRISON S	LTC	0-0020073	0156	1
MARKHAM MICHAEL C	LTC	0-0042986	0465	1
MARKLEY HARRISON M	COL	0-0038752	1163	1
MARKLEY MARTIN A	CPT	0-0063245	1158	2
MARKOWITZ ISIDOR	COL	0-0059511	1061	1
MARKS EDWIN H	B G	0-0002579	0747	2
MARKS WILLARD A	CPT	0-002672E	1047	2
MARKS YOUIR M F	LTC	0-0014155	0716	2
MARKWELL DICK R	LTC	0-0065758	0967	1
MARLAND JAMES R	MAJ	0-0039145	0255	2
MARNANE THOMAS J	COL	C-0018535	0761	1
MARPHIS JOSEPH C	LTC	0-0C51003	0956	1
MARQUETTE WILLIAM J	COL	C-0042231	0963	1
MARR JR HAROLD E	COL	0-0020729	0867	1
MARR LLOYD M	COL	0-0031420	0467	2
MARR RICHARD S	COL	0-0015447	1153	1
MARREN JOHN J	COL	0-0041706	0759	1
MARRERC JOHN	LTC	0-0054291	0964	1
MARRIOTT OWEN R	COL	0-0012587	0851	1
MARSDEN JR HENRY H	COL	0-0043643	1266	1
MARSH EDWARD T	LTC	0-0029325	0862	1
MARSH EDWIN S	LTC	0-0031307	0765	1
MARSH HOWARD M	CW2	W-0901865	1149	1
MARSH JAMES H	COL	0-0014610	0253	1
MARSH JR CURTIS N	COL	0-0079905	0766	1
MARSH JR RAYMOND	LTC	0-0067720	1167	1
MARSH LEON D	COL	0-0039739	0761	1
MARSH MARVIN W	COL	0-0008419	0854	1
MARSH RAYMOND	COL	0-0003798	0747	2
MARSH WILLIAM A	COL	0-0010608	1146	1
MARSHALL ALBERT B	COL	C-005235C	0962	1
MARSHALL CARLEY L	COL	0-0011765	0849	1
MARSHALL DAVID N	LTC	0-0052221	0864	1
MARSHALL EDWARD R	LTC	0-0022692	0764	1
MARSHALL ELEANOR M	LTC	M-0010040	0761	1
MARSHALL FURMAN W	LTC	0-0042925	C662	1
MARSHALL HARRY G	CW4	W-0903483	1061	1
MARSHALL HUBERT T	COL	0-0019689	0649	2
MARSHALL IRVINE H	COL	0-0039658	1160	1
MARSHALL JAMES C	B G	0-0009316	0347	2
MARSHALL MAX L	LTC	0-0026867	0764	1
MARSHALL MORRIS L	1LT	0-0093827	0263	2
MARSHALL RICHARD	LTC	0-0052416	0160	1
MARSHALL RICHARD J	M G	0-0004635	1146	1
MARSIC MARY A	MAJ	N-0001956	0558	1
MARSTON ANSON D	COL	0-0029427	0760	1
MARSTON MORRILL W	B G	0-0007126	0753	1
MARSTON OLIVER F	COL	0-0007174	0246	2
MARSZAL JOHN A	CW4	RW-0904442	0664	1
MARTAK CLYDE J	LTC	0-0054719	0763	1
MARTASIN WILLIAM N	COL	0-0044997	1166	1
MARTELINO AMADO	COL	0-0014881	0547	2
MARTENS HOWARD W	COL	0-0032324	0766	1
MARTIN ALFRED	COL	0-0023629	1165	1
MARTIN BRICE J	LTC	0-003362C	0159	2
MARTIN CHARLES H	COL	C-0011073	0749	1
MARTIN CLARENCE A	M G	0-0007007	0747	2
MARTIN CLARENCE E	CW4	W-0904155	1158	1
MARTIN CLYDE J	CW4	W-0903484	0158	1
MARTIN DANIEL J	COL	0-0015907	0946	1
MARTIN DARWIN O	COL	0-0015678	0854	1
MARTIN DAVID	LTC	0-0042947	0459	1
MARTIN EDWARD J	LTC	0-0041143	0661	1
MARTIN EDWARD R	COL	0-0016358	1052	1
MARTIN EMMOR G	COL	0-0016190	0847	2
MARTIN ETHEL M	MAJ	L-0000182	1264	1
MARTIN FLORENCE R	MAJ	L-0000036	0657	1
MARTIN GEORGE E	M G	0-0016802	0562	1
MARTIN HENRY F	CPT	0-0014443	0321	2
MARTIN JAMES E	MAJ	0-0081012	0364	1
MARTIN JAMES C	LTC	0-0C39035	0163	1
MARTIN JAMES J	LTC	0-0081013	0864	1
MARTIN JAMES M	LTC	0-0081015	0266	1
MARTIN JAMES S	MAJ	C-005766C	0766	1
MARTIN JOHN	COL	0-0068321	0855	2

NAME	GRADE	SVC NO	DATE RET MO YR	RET CODE
MARTIN JOHN A	COL	0-0024453	0661	1
MARTIN JOHN A	COL	0-0051419	0763	1
MARTIN JOHN B	LTC	0-0004563	0242	1
MARTIN JOHN T	LTC	0-0022694	1159	1
MARTIN L O KIRKWO	LTC	0-0037177	1163	1
MARTIN LAWRENCE A	COL	0-0043665	0565	2
MARTIN LEWIS T	COL	0-0030188	0762	1
MARTIN LINCOLN	COL	0-0006252	0835	2
MARTIN LORRAINE M	MAJ	N-0000351	0161	1
MARTIN LOUIS L	COL	0-0005277	0352	1
MARTIN LULUAH Y	MAJ	N-0000154	0261	1
MARTIN MARY L	MAJ	N-0000449	0364	1
MARTIN MERRITT P	LTC	0-0062215	0566	1
MARTIN MURRAY J	COL	0-0028775	0554	2
MARTIN NATHANIEL	COL	0-0019794	0857	1
MARTIN NORMAN E	COL	0-0051831	1166	1
MARTIN ORVILLE W	COL	0-0012253	1050	1
MARTIN PAUL H	COL	0-0018331	0155	1
MARTIN PAUL L	MAJ	0-0015055	0542	2
MARTIN ROBERT J	LTC	0-0062253	1166	1
MARTIN ROBERT T	LTC	0-0026641	0965	1
MARTIN RONALD L	COL	0-0019428	0660	1
MARTIN SARAH N	MAJ	N-0001532	0963	1
MARTIN SIDNEY T	COL	0-0021772	0865	1
MARTIN THOMAS L	B G	0-0004470	0451	1
MARTIN TRUBY C	LTC	0-0013944	0620	2
MARTIN WINFIELD L	COL	0-0020809	0665	1
MARTINEAU FREDERICK	COL	0-0042571	0864	1
MARTINEZ JOE I	LTC	0-0027446	0766	1
MARTINEZ JR SEVERIND	LTC	0-0024811	0263	1
MARTINI MARIAN E	MAJ	N-0000208	0463	1
MARTS FRED R	CW2	W-0903486	1050	1
MARTZ JR JOHN D	COL	0-0029769	0962	1
MARTZ WILLIAM V	COL	0-0019879	0862	1
MARVIN GEORGE W	COL	0-0014887	0753	1
MARVIN HORACE P	COL	0-0016957	0944	2
MARX RALPH L	COL	0-0022262	0258	1
MASLIN FRANCIS I	COL	0-0009040	0748	1
MASLOWSKI LADISLAUS	COL	0-0021789	0567	2
MASON ALFRED L	COL	0-0004405	1138	1
MASON BEN A	MAJ	0-0005182	0232	2
MASON CHARLES H	COL	0-0016045	1147	2
MASON DON A	COL	0-0031694	0266	1
MASON EDWARD R	COL	0-0031563	0666	2
MASON GRANT W	COL	0-0030738	0665	1
MASON JOHN P	LTC	0-0044587	1262	1
MASON JR MARSHALL A	LTC	0-0063462	1166	1
MASON KERMIT R	LTC	0-0046951	0664	1
MASON RICHARD R	COL	0-0020928	0861	1
MASON STANHOPE B	M G	0-0017295	0861	1
MASON TROXELL O	LTC	0-0023522	0761	1
MASON WILLIAM H	2LT	0-0082779	0559	2
MASSARO JOSEPH	LTC	0-0015798	0753	1
MASSELLO JR WILLIAM	COL	0-0018749	0760	1
MASSENGILL PAUL	CW4	W-0902368	0560	1
MASSEY CLYDE	B G	0-0015551	0954	1
MASSEY GEORGE W	CW4	W-0903488	1165	1
MASSEY JAMES L	COL	0-0018838	0262	1
MASSEY WILLIAM R	2LT	0-0057677	0550	2
MASSINGALE JOHN T	LTC	0-0051499	0562	1
MASSOGLIA MARTIN F	COL	0-0052831	1067	1
MASTELLONE ANIELLO F	COL	0-0043115	1165	1
MASTERS GEORGE C	COL	0-0028950	1057	1
MASTERS MEREDITH O	CPT	0-0016846	0937	2
MASTON VICTOR E	COL	0-0019075	0861	1
MASTROIANNI ELLEN	MAJ	N-0002252	0961	1
MASTRUCCI JOSEPH P	LTC	0-0031768	0166	1
MATCHETT HENRY J	B G	0-0005503	0250	1
MATCHETTE CLAUDE H	COL	0-0031490	0467	1
MATEJKA JERRY V	M G	0-0007496	1055	1
MATERI JOSEPH T	LTC	0-0024330	0764	1
MATHENY CHARLES W	COL	0-0024619	0762	1
MATHES EDWARD S	LTC	0-0030481	0763	1
MATHESON DAVID M	LTC	0-0021757	0667	1
MATHESON DONALD R	COL	0-0021213	0347	2

NAME	GRADE	SVC NO	DATE RET MO YR	RET CODE
MATHESON JOHN D	COL	0-0018962	0657	1
MATHESON MARIAN M	MAJ	N-0001875	0558	1
MATHESON MARJORIE	MAJ	N-0000928	0264	1
MATHEWS CLIFFORD J	COL	0-0003736	0850	1
MATHEWS DAVID J	CW4	W-0901885	0465	1
MATHEWS DON S	LTC	0-0030121	0162	1
MATHEWS ELMO S	COL	0-0017167	0658	1
MATHEWS FRANK H	COL	0-0039569	0452	1
MATHEWS JOEL L	MAJ	0-0019237	0448	2
MATHEWS LUDWIG L	CW4	RW-0903489	0262	1
MATHEWS WAYNE C	LTC	0-0070422	0667	1
MATHEWSON ELEANOR M	MAJ	R-0000026	0463	1
MATHEWSON JR DAVID A	COL	0-0038753	1163	1
MATHEWSON LEMUEL	LTG	0-0014980	0458	2
MATHEWSON NATHAN S	COL	0-0029771	0962	1
MATHIS WILLIAM H	LTC	0-0037653	0665	1
MATHOS HARRY G	COL	0-0045077	0465	1
MATHWIN ALBERT V	LTC	0-0037721	0967	1
MATLACK FRANK S	COL	0-0004171	0446	1
MATLACK TOM E	COL	0-0022238	0746	2
MATLAVAGE MATTHEW W	CW4	W-0903490	1064	1
MATLOCK HALLIE A	COL	0-0040377	0864	1
MATTE PAUL J	COL	0-0006722	0351	1
MATTER ROBERT A	COL	0-0022132	0867	1
MATTERNES LAWRENCE A	COL	0-0018295	0755	1
MATTESON JAMES S	LTC	0-0087847	0667	1
MATTESON MILO H	COL	0-0016127	0554	1
MATTESON WILLIAM J	COL	0-0017100	0242	2
MATTFELDT CYLBURN O	COL	0-0006128	0934	2
MATTHAIS EDITH F	MAJ	N-0001980	0263	1
MATTHEWS CLARA M	MAJ	L-0000058	0859	1
MATTHEWS FREDERICK	COL	0-0005625	1052	1
MATTHEWS HARVIE R	COL	0-0014680	0447	2
MATTHEWS JEWETT D	LTC	0-0006492	0241	1
MATTHEWS LESLIE M	WO1	W-0800155	0642	2
MATTHEWS STANLEY L	LTC	0-0060315	0163	1
MATTHEWS WILLIS S	M G	0-0016932	0163	1
MATTHIAS NORMAN A	COL	0-0016400	0656	1
MATTICE EARL	COL	0-00156C?	0854	1
MATTIE EDWARD C	LTC	0-0079671	0466	2
MATTINGLY HOWARD	LTC	0-0080144	0964	1
MATTINGLY THOMAS W	B G	0-0020068	0858	1
MATTISEN WILLIAM R	COL	0-0081018	0765	1
MATTOS ANTHONY R	LTC	0-0091325	0865	1
MATTSON OSCAR	CW2	W-0800212	0847	2
MATUSKA WALTER H	COL	0-0029155	1058	1
MATYAS ALBERT A	COL	0-0015928	0560	1
MAUBORGNE JOSEPH O	M G	0-0001783	0941	1
MAUPIN CLINTON S	COL	0-0056804	0660	1
MAURER FRED C	COL	0-0029324	0864	1
MAURICE KATHRYN	MAJ	J-0000038	0265	1
MAUSERT RYERSON N	COL	0-0079913	1262	1
MAUTZ MATTHEW C	COL	0-0022729	0765	1
MAUZ HENRY H	COL	0-0029799	0461	1
MAUZY HOYALL R	LTC	0-0039984	0562	1
MAKA RUDOLPH J	LTC	0-0081019	0364	2
MAKEIKER PAULINE G	MAJ	N-0000283	0860	1
MAXEY EDWARD C	LTC	0-0051955	0164	1
MAXEY PETER U	LTC	0-0051314	1052	1
MAXFIELD RALPH G	COL	0-0038683	0361	1
MAXIM CHESTER B	CW2	W-0901124	0145	2
MAXTON CORA J	LTC	N-0000509	1050	1
MAXWELL ARTHUR O	MAJ	0-0023173	0444	2
MAXWELL BENJAMIN R	LTC	0-0082048	0866	1
MAXWELL FOCIL C	CW2	W-0901522	1145	1
MAXWELL II JOHN B	COL	0-0021942	0166	1
MAXWELL JOHN W	COL	0-0039796	1162	1
MAXWELL LAVERN W	LTC	0-0059484	1165	1
MAXWELL MAMIE H	MAJ	N-0002380	0361	1
MAXWELL MARGARET A	MAJ	L-0000257	1164	1
MAXWELL ROY D	COL	0-0029265	0363	1
MAXWELL RUSSELL L	M G	0-0003350	0946	1
MAXWELL WILLIAM P	COL	0-0038636	0956	1
MAY ARTHUR G	LTC	0-0030335	0164	1
MAY CHARLES P	CPT	0-0060448	0760	1

NAME	GRADE	SVC NO	DATE RET MO YR	RET CODE
MAY DAVID D	MAJ	0-0024946	0161	2
MAY JOHN B	CW4	W-0901483	0356	1
MAY MARION H	LTC	0-0025576	0463	1
MAY METTICUS W	COL	0-0029394	0360	1
MAY RAY H	LTC	0-0038259	0963	1
MAY ROBERT W	COL	0-0039968	0665	1
MAY WALTER F	CW4	W-0903492	0757	1
MAYBEN JOHN W	MAJ	0-0008690	0831	2
MAYBERRY HUGH T	B G	0-0007065	1052	1
MAYER WILLIAM	COL	0-0006941	0152	1
MAYER WILLIAM E	LTC	0-0089897	0865	1
MAYERS THOMAS H	LTC	0-0030439	1163	2
MAYFIELD LUIE W	LTC	0-0042025	0660	1
MAYHUGH ELNA C	MAJ	R-0010132	0866	1
MAYNARD CHARLES D	COL	0-0023754	0865	1
MAYNARD STANLEY G	COL	0-0032515	0267	2
MAYNE ROBERT K	LTC	0-0067721	0767	1
MAYO ARTHUR A	CW4	W-0906886	0666	1
MAYO GEORGE	COL	0-0003913	0447	1
MAYO PAUL A	M G	0-0018621	1064	1
MAYO PERRY F	CW4	W-0903494	1262	1
MAYO RICHARD W	B G	0-0016430	0756	1
MAYO THOMAS T	1LT	0-0015483	0934	2
MAYS CHARLES W	COL	0-0008183	0452	1
MAYS WILLIAM L	COL	0-0008054	0847	1
MAYSON PRESTON R	COL	0-0039532	0256	2
MC ABEE FILMORE W	LTC	0-0076396	1061	1
MC ADAMS JOHN	MAJ	0-0024555	0349	2
MC AFEE BROADUS	COL	0-0029053	0159	1
MC AFEE CARLOS E	COL	0-0041629	1159	1
MC AFEE CHARLES C	WO1	W-0800049	1026	2
MC AFEE GEORGE O	MAJ	0-0026417	0846	2
MC AFEE GLEN R	LTC	0-0063410	0765	1
MC AFEE JAMES E	CW2	W-0903496	1159	1
MC AFEE JR CHARLES M	COL	0-002058C	0161	1
MC ALEAR JOHN H	COL	0-0018572	0955	1
MC ALEER WILLIAM A	COL	0-0042196	0763	1
MC ALISTER CHARLES K	COL	0-0011727	0853	1
MC ALISTER IRVINE L	MAJ	0-0014362	0319	2
MC ALLISTER CHARLES	LTC	0-0050056	0366	1
MC ALLISTER EDWIN J	COL	0-0012032	0649	1
MC ALLISTER MARTIN O	COL	0-0006808	0552	1
MC AMIS JR JAMES C	LTC	0-0060372	1165	1
MC ANDREWS BLANCHE M	MAJ	N-0000063	0759	1
MC ANENY GEORGE F	COL	0-0042075	1062	1
MC ANINCH WILLIAM T	LTC	0-0029601	0859	1
MC ANSH ANDREW T	B G	0-0038667	0560	1
MC ARDLE CHARLES E	LTC	0-0030695	1164	1
MC ARDLE JOHN F X	1LT	0-0026917	0346	2
MC ARTHUR DONALD E	LTC	0-0052892	1160	1
MC ARTOR WILLIAM S	LTC	0-0047849	0367	1
MC ATEER ROBERT H	COL	0-0029072	0359	1
MC AULEY JACK A	LTC	0-0036706	0364	1
MC AULIFFE ANTHONY C	GEN	0-0012263	0556	1
MC AULIFFE JOHN H	1LT	0-0056594	0349	2
MC BEE MARSHELL C	COL	0-0039015	0766	1
MC BRAYER CHARLES E	LTC	0-0003048	0926	2
MC BRIDE ARTHUR J	COL	0-0042870	1064	1
MC BRIDE CLYDE R	COL	0-0018424	0861	2
MC BRIDE FRANCIS G	COL	0-0033539	0966	1
MC BRIDE GLEN C	B G	0-0029004	0758	1
MC BRIDE JOHN	LTC	0-0006092	0244	2
MC BRIDE JR ROBERT B	B G	0-0004451	0752	1
MC BRIDE RICHARD M	LTC	0-0058071	1067	1
MC BRIDE ROBERT B	LTC	0-0037277	0664	1
MC BRIDE ROBERT J	COL	0-0015756	0754	1
MC BRIDE ROBERT J	COL	0-0030216	0764	1
MC BRIDE WILLIAM E	COL	0-0024587	0662	1
MC BURNEY HAROLD S	COL	0-0029248	0767	2
MC CABE EDWARD F	CW4	W-0903498	0465	1
MC CABE EDWARD R W	LTC	0-0040262	0666	1
MC CABE FRANK T	COL	0-0003315	C-33	2
MC CABE FREDERICK	B G	0-0004553	0947	1
MC CABE ROBERT C	COL	0-0021089	1046	2
MC CABE ROBERT E	COL	0-0020269	0866	1

NAME	GRADE	SVC NO	DATE RET MO YR	RET CODE
MC CADDEN WALTER L	LTC	0-0040239	0266	1
MC CAFFERY BENJAMIN	LTC	0-0023912	0766	1
MC CAHAN WALTER O	COL	0-0028936	1157	1
MC CAIG MILTON E	MAJ	0-0062240	0762	1
MC CAIN JOSEPH O	LTC	0-0003688	0142	1
MC CAIN RUBY E	MAJ	N-0000252	0762	1
MC CALL RAY N	MAJ	0-0037381	0861	1
MC CALLUM CHARLES F	LTC	0-0051952	1265	1
MC CALLUM JAMES A	B G	0-0009466	0153	1
MC CALLY MARY J	MAJ	N-0000770	0664	1
MC CALLY MILDRED A	MAJ	N-0000771	0664	1
MC CANN CLIFTON E	CW3	W-0903500	0655	1
MC CANN JR JAMES H	COL	0-0030468	0962	1
MC CANN WILLIE H	COL	0-0042603	1065	1
MC CARLEY THOMAS R	COL	0-0011953	0551	1
MC CARTHY CHARLES W	COL	0-0016667	1156	2
MC CARTHY DONALD E	CW3	W-0903501	0957	1
MC CARTHY EDGAR A	LTC	0-0032970	0566	1
MC CARTHY EILEEN L	LTC	N-0002143	0964	1
MC CARTHY GERALD P	COL	0-0041617	1159	1
MC CARTHY JOSEPH M	COL	0-0029043	0159	1
MC CARTHY LEO J	COL	0-0007146	0348	2
MC CARTHY THOMAS D	COL	0-0020954	0660	1
MC CARTHY THOMAS F	COL	0-0010068	0250	1
MC CARTHY WALTER W	COL	0-0040062	1064	1
MC CARTHY WILLIAM J	COL	0-0011516	1052	1
MC CARTY ROBERT S	LTC	0-0051970	1264	1
MC CARTY ROY C	COL	0-0020115	0866	1
MC CASKILL RALPH E	LTC	0-0020070	0843	2
MC CASLIN KERMIT J	LTC	0-0031096	0564	1
MC CATTY KENNETH	COL	0-0004691	0548	1
MC CAW ROBERT H	M G	0-0038722	0767	1
MC CHRYSTAL ARTHUR J	B G	0-0006913	0837	1
MC CLAIN DONALD H	COL	0-0042693	0861	1
MC CLAIN HARRY C	COL	0-0057697	0664	1
MC CLARY HUGH W	LTC	0-0023533	0860	1
MC CLEARY GORDON F	LTC	0-0037425	0862	1
MC CLEARY OLIVER S	LTC	0-0003095	0622	2
MC CLEARY ROBERT H	LTC	0-0041316	0164	1
MC CLEAVE ROBERT B	COL	0-0016702	1146	2
MC CLEAVE WILLIAM	COL	0-0002573	0934	2
MC CLELLAN ICLA R	LTC	N-0000278	0963	1
MC CLELLAND C B	COL	0-0017558	0859	1
MC CLELLAND CHALME	COL	0-0019011	1046	2
MC CLENAGHAN ROBERT	LTC	0-0014946	0649	1
MC CLENAHAN FRANK G	LTC	0-0082053	1066	1
MC CLINTIC BROWN S	COL	0-0004145	1146	2
MC CLISH ERNEST E	LTC	0-0030432	0562	1
MC CLOSKEY JOHN A	COL	0-0036372	0165	1
MC CLOSKEY OWEN T	COL	0-0030269	1064	2
MC CLUNG EARLE J	COL	0-0004026	0751	1
MC CLURE CLINTON I	COL	0-0004967	0850	1
MC CLURE GEORGE W	COL	0-0028794	0155	1
MC CLURE MARK	M G	0-0014935	0957	2
MC CLURE MARSHALL O	LTC	0-0056767	0765	1
MC CLURE MYRON	LTC	0-0032241	0961	1
MC CLURE ROBERT B	M G	0-0010356	0554	1
MC CLUSKEY VERNA A	LTC	L-0000215	0459	1
MC COACH 3RD DAVID	COL	0-0020177	0757	1
MC COLLAM ALBERT E	LTC	0-0021748	1262	1
MC COLLUM WILLIAM B	CPT	0-0006453	0833	2
MC COMMONS DAISY M	LTC	N-0000146	0858	1
MC CONAHAY ALVA M	COL	0-0051163	0563	1
MC CONAUGHY D S	B G	0-0009738	0753	1
MC CONEGHY JOHN K	LTC	0-0009582	0937	2
MC CONNELL C F	MAJ	N-0002219	0360	1
MC CONNELL CAMDEN W	COL	0-0018437	0761	1
MC CONNELL DAVID M	COL	0-0026385	0746	2
MC CONNELL EDWARD T	COL	0-0021996	1166	2
MC CONNELL FRANK C	B G	0-0014873	0957	1
MC CONNELL GLENN B	COL	0-0015556	0754	1
MC CONNELL GUY G	LTC	0-0049201	0865	1
MC CONNELL RICHARD S	COL	0-0041838	1057	1
MC CONNELL VEON M	LTC	0-0051333	0860	1
MC CONNELL VIOLA B	MAJ	N-0002231	0859	1

NAME	GRADE	SVC NO	DATE RET MO YR	RET CODE
MC CONNELL WILLIAM J	COL	0-0022052	C863	1
MC CCOL EDWARD J	LTC	0-0032024	C363	1
MC CORO FRANCIS S	MAJ	N-0002388	1061	1
MC CORO JAMES H	LTC	0-0032683	1266	1
MC CORMAC BILLY M	LTC	0-0027043	C563	1
MC CORMAC WESTON A	COL	0-0030716	C566	1
MC CORMACK BETTY T	LTC	L-0000149	1165	1
MC CORMICK ALOYSIUS	COL	0-0020363	C864	1
MC CORMICK ARTHUR B	COL	0-0009576	0145	2
MC CORMICK CHARLES J	COL	C-0051083	C460	1
MC CORMICK HAROLD D	COL	C-0042765	1166	2
MC CORMICK JOHN W	LTC	0-0006880	1042	2
MC CORMICK OTIS	COL	C-0015527	0754	1
MC CORMICK ROBIN E	LTC	0-0050905	C853	1
MC CORMICK THOMAS C	COL	0-0005850	0247	2
MC CORMICK VANE E	CW4	W-0906889	1164	1
MC CORMICK WALTER L	COL	C-0010775	1047	1
MC COWEN GEORGE A	LTC	C-0065480	C567	1
MC COY EDWIN D	COL	0-0010323	0753	1
MC COY EUGENE B	LTC	0-0063089	1264	1
MC COY FRANK L	COL	0-0008325	0549	2
MC COY GOLDIE M	MAJ	N-0002520	1067	1
MC COY JAMES M	LTC	0-0087558	0266	1
MC COY JOSEPH	LTC	0-C081028	C966	1
MC COY JR GEORGE W	COL	0-0019685	C756	1
MC CCY ROBERT G	LTC	0-0041003	0965	1
MC CRACKEN GERALD A	COL	0-0021695	C962	2
MC CRACY RICHARD E	LTC	0-0094319	1066	1
MC CRARY ARTHUR A	COL	C-0019037	0863	1
MC CRARY THOMAS A	COL	C-0019570	0165	1
MC CRARY THOMAS L	COL	C-0021258	C446	2
MC CRAVEY JAMES L	LTC	0-0060649	C464	1
MC CRAW ANNIE M	MAJ	N-0002116	C455	1
MC CREA WILLIAM S	COL	0-0020894	C664	1
MC CREARY JOHN M	LTC	C-0066180	1066	1
MC CREARY MELVIN L	COL	C-0007134	C752	1
MC CRILLIS PAUL L	COL	0-0045768	C765	1
MC CRIMMON KENNETH A	B G	C-0018336	C761	1
MC CRONE WILLARD P	COL	C-0020548	C664	1
MC CRORFY JR JAMES L	LTC	0-0022158	1064	1
MC CRORY DORSEY F	COL	0-0022683	C260	1
MC CRORY RAYMOND J	LTC	0-0037146	1165	1
MC CRUM RALPH C	LTC	C-0022643	C664	1
MC CULLER LOUIS P	LTC	0-0034636	0167	1
MC CULLOUGH GEORGE S	COL	0-0005749	C840	2
MC CULLCUGH HOMER C	LTC	0-0018314	0855	2
MC CURDFY NEWTON F	COL	0-0015085	0954	1
MC CURDY ROBERT M	CPT	0-0008376	0622	2
MC CURDY THOMAS E	CW4	W-0903504	C964	2
MC CUTCHEN ALAN J	COL	0-0017093	C756	1
MC CUTCHEN WILMOT R	COL	0-0021744	C366	1
MC CUTCHEON HOWARD S	LTC	0-0051703	1060	1
MC DANIEL EDWARD H	M G	0-0016497	1263	1
MC DANIEL LLOYD L	COL	C-0030513	1065	1
MC DANIEL MARION E	LTC	0-0033346	C762	1
MC DANIEL MYRA L	LTC	J-0000013	C667	1
MC DANIEL OTTO L	COL	0-0011846	0751	1
MC DANIEL SEATON F	COL	0-0043098	0767	1
MC DANIEL WILLIS C	LTC	0-0051900	1157	1
MC DIVITT JOSEPH B	COL	C-0053661	0766	1
MC DONALD AGNES C	MAJ	N-0002414	C963	1
MC DONALD CLIFFORD O	CW4	W-0903505	1054	1
MC DONALD DANIEL E	COL	0-0042884	C766	1
MC DONALD EUGENE C	COL	0-0023218	0867	1
MC DONALD HUGH	LTC	0-0028963	C156	1
MC DONALD JOHN W	COL	C-0004848	0750	1
MC DONALD JOHN H	COL	C-0029381	0260	1
MC DONALD LEE R	LTC	0-0052133	C366	1
MC DONALD LENIEL E	LTC	0-0030408	C960	1
MC DONALD LEO J	LTC	0-0017833	C248	1
MC DONALD MARY G	LTC	L-0000102	C567	2
MC DONALD MARY L	MAJ	N-0002290	0466	2
MC DONALD RAY L	1LT	0-0011560	1022	2
MC DONALD ROBERT C	COL	0-0019799	0863	1
MC DONALD THOMAS R	COL	0-0018892	1161	2
MC DONALD WILLIAM J	COL	C-003C169	0464	1
MC DONNELL HAROLD F	COL	0-0039549	0956	1
MC DONNELL PAUL J	COL	C-0004564	0647	2
MC DONNELL WILLIAM J	COL	0-0031698	0964	1
MC DONOUGH JAMES H	COL	0-0010110	0148	1
MC DONOUGH ROBERT J	LTC	0-0043591	0966	1
MC DONOUGH ROBERT K	COL	0-0016394	C656	1
MC DOWALL JOHN	COL	C-0008099	0947	2
MC DOWELL CHARLES T	LTC	0-0037309	0865	1
MC DOWELL EMERY J	CW4	W-0903506	0956	1
MC DOWELL JAMES R	COL	0-0011605	0947	1
MC DOWELL JAMES V	COL	0-0004756	0653	1
MC DOWELL JOELLA W	MAJ	N-0000355	0361	1
MC DOWELL MARION E	LTC	0-0057399	1164	1
MC DOWELL REX MC K	B G	C-0004011	1048	1
MC DOWELL RICHARD D	COL	C-0079919	0364	2
MC DOWELL ROBERT R	LTC	0-002598C	0763	1
MC DOWELL SAMUEL T	COL	0-0030321	0365	2
MC DUFF ROBERT J	COL	0-0028976	C658	2
MC EACHERN JOE A	LTC	C-0039907	1061	1
MC ELDOWNEY MORRIS C	LTC	0-0041715	0159	1
MC ELGIN HUGH J B	LTC	0-0001252	0221	1
MC ELHENNY WILLIAM S	COL	0-0039025	0265	2
MC ELHENY JOHN O	COL	0-0020170	0664	1
MC ELLIGOTT JOSEPH P	LTC	0-0031482	0365	1
MC ELROY ARVINE W	COL	C-003C093	0164	1
MC ELROY GEORGE R	COL	C-0010652	0546	2
MC ELROY JAMES E	LTC	0-0023917	1060	1
MC ELWEE FRANK O	COL	0-0025409	0867	1
MC ENTEE DUCAT	COL	0-0019932	0646	2
MC EVOY JOHN P	COL	0-0046774	0766	1
MC FADEEN GLENN M	COL	0-0031C04	0766	1
MC FADDEN MURDOCK A	COL	C-0008517	1044	2
MC FADDEN WILLIAM C	COL	0-0012726	0554	1
MC FALL JOHN H	COL	C-0011262	0748	2
MC FALL THOMAS A	COL	C-0029215	0961	2
MC FARLAND ANDREW J	B G	0-0005086	0547	2
MC FARLAND CHARLES N	COL	C-0012280	1151	1
MC FARLAND EARL	B G	0-0002128	0743	1
MC FARLAND JAMES O	LTC	0-0053149	1263	1
MC FARLAND JOHN A	COL	0-0016489	0756	1
MC FARLAND ROBERT R	CPT	0-0060479	1265	1
MC FEELY HENRY G	COL	0-0018810	0862	1
MC FEELY HORACE F	COL	0-0038812	0963	2
MC GAHEE HORACE S	CPT	0-0060690	0365	1
MC GARR LIONEL C	LTC	0-0017225	0762	2
MC GARRAUGH RILEY F	COL	C-0009706	0854	1
MC GARY THOMAS P	LTC	0-0051540	0962	1
MC GAW EDWARD J	M G	0-0012631	0261	1
MC GAW HUGH D	COL	0-0039537	0856	1
MC GEE ARTHUR P	COL	C-0007868	0846	1
MC GEE CHARLES E	COL	0-0029241	1162	1
MC GEE JOHN H	B G	0-0018600	0861	1
MC GEE JR GEORGE A	COL	0-0020806	C867	1
MC GEHEE JR ABNER J	COL	C-0015268	1038	2
MC GHAY DURWARD H	CW4	W-0903511	0557	1
MC GIFFERT STEPHEN Y	COL	C-0014865	C854	1
MC GILL JR DAN P	LTC	0-0029330	1054	1
MC GILL UPTON A	COL	0-0041659	0460	1
MC GILLIVRAY COLIN D	CW4	W-0903512	0957	1
MC GILTON HOWARD J	LTC	0-0082055	C867	1
MC GINLEY EUGENE	M G	0-0012318	1055	1
MC GINN FLOY W	COL	0-0042127	1262	1
MC GINNESS JOHN R	LTC	0-0016242	1045	1
MC GINNIS HARRY R	CW4	W-0903513	1265	1
MC GINNIS VELMER W	COL	0-0020059	1158	1
MC GLYNN EDWARD F	CW3	W-0906893	1060	1
MC GOLDRICK FRANCIS	M G	0-0019857	0766	1
MC GONAGLE LAURENCE	LTC	0-0062938	0766	1
MC GOOHAN JAMES J	LTC	C-0022753	1162	2
MC GOUCH GORDON H	LTC	0-0065041	0962	1
MC GOVERN JAMES C	MAJ	0-0004837	0934	2
MC GOVERN JOHN P	COL	C-0042391	0764	1
MC GOWAN GLENN J	COL	0-0042363	0761	1
MC GOWAN JAMES F	LTC	0-007992C	0664	1
MC GOWAN JOHN D	LTC	0-0025759	C864	1
MC GOWAN MURRAY E	COL	0-0015943	0854	1
MC GOWEN CLARENCE D	COL	0-00186C5	0356	1
MC GRADY HARPER L	COL	C-0030450	C657	1
MC GRAIL THOMAS M	COL	0-0039876	C758	1
MC GRANE EDWARD J	COL	0-0024027	C466	1
MC GRATH LUTA C	LTC	L-0000226	0261	1
MC GRATH M M	MAJ	N-0000298	C559	2
MC GRATH THOMAS W	COL	C-0043322	1167	1
MC GRATH VINCENT J	COL	0-0079921	0566	1
MC GRAW JAMES E	COL	0-0015672	C649	1
MC GRAW JAMES F	COL	0-0015446	1153	1
MC GRAW LEROY E	COL	0-0010088	0446	2
MC GRAW ROBERT E	COL	0-0039107	C866	1
MC GRAYNE DONALD	COL	0-0028762	0354	2
MC GREGOR DUNCAN G	COL	C-0008594	1050	1
MC GREGOR THOMAS	COL	C-0012305	C854	1
MC GREW GORDON W	CW4	W-0903516	0658	1
MC GUCKIAN AMBROSE T	COL	0-0042725	C764	2
MC GUIRE JOSEPH R	LTC	0-0024138	C866	1
MC GUIRE PAUL M	LTC	0-0035705	1262	1
MC GUIRE THOMAS C	COL	C-0033296	0762	1
MC GUIRE VERONA M	LTC	N-0002136	C960	1
MC HALE LARRY	COL	0-0005519	C546	1
MC HANEY GAILON M	COL	0-0021179	C764	1
MC HUGH HARRY D	COL	0-0015758	C954	1
MC HUGH JAMES F	COL	0-0039745	1161	1
MC HUGH JOHN J	LTC	0-0081031	1264	1
MC HUGH LOUIS J	CPT	0-0084324	1065	2
MC ILHINEY WILLIAM G	COL	0-0033005	1163	1
MC ILROY HORACE S	LTC	0-0030460	C563	1
MC ILWAIN SHIRLEY W	COL	0-0008252	0653	1
MC ILWRAITH CLARA B	MAJ	L-0000221	0257	1
MC INERNEY JAMES E B	COL	0-0015276	C554	1
MC INTIRE JOHN E	LTC	0-0082057	C967	1
MC INTOSH ALBERT E	LTC	C-0006771	C-41	1
MC INTOSH CHARLES A	COL	0-0045816	0766	1
MC INTYRE CLARENCE A	LTC	0-0016557	C545	2
MC INTYRE EDWARD J	LTC	0-0031152	C965	1
MC INTYRE JOHN C	LTC	0-0023976	0762	1
MC KAIG JR NELSON	COL	C-0028818	C953	1
MC KAY GRADY	CW4	W-0906894	C165	1
MC KAY HORTENSE E	LTC	N-0000110	C660	1
MC KAY JOHN I	COL	C-0011067	1144	2
MC KAY ROBERT R	COL	0-0041662	0360	1
MC KAY WINFIELD R	COL	0-0008450	0351	1
MC KEAN JOHN A	LTC	C-0042502	1061	1
MC KEAN STERLING J	COL	0-0079924	C766	1
MC KEE BASYE C	COL	0-0029041	C159	2
MC KEE GREGG L	COL	0-0023811	C462	1
MC KEE JOHN T	COL	0-0030383	0365	1
MC KEE JR EDWARD L	MAJ	C-0004983	0531	2
MC KEE MICHAEL R	CPT	C-0050276	1065	2
MC KEE RICHARD G	B G	0-0011217	C854	1
MC KEE RICHARD L	COL	0-0019453	0163	1
MC KELVEY LOWELL E	COL	0-0030967	0761	1
MC KENNA JOHN P	LTC	0-0042179	0361	1
MC KENNA ROBERT A	LTC	0-0051907	C865	1
MC KENNEY ALFRED E	COL	0-0011651	C754	2
MC KENZIE ALEX F	LTC	0-0039967	C663	1
MC KENZIE HENRY R	M G	0-0017623	C858	1
MC KENZIE JAMES	CW2	W-0901509	C547	1
MC KENZIE TIMOTHY H	COL	0-0039797	C760	1
MC KENZIE VERNON	COL	0-0094317	1167	1
MC KEON FRANCIS H	COL	C-0011421	0653	1
MC KEON VIRGINIA T	CPT	R-0000543	C946	1
MC KEOWN CLARENCE E	LTC	0-0031200	C766	1
MC KERRAL HOWARD A	LTC	0-0080452	C766	2
MC KIBBEN BYRON C	COL	C-0019633	C859	1
MC KIERNAN FREDERICK	LTC	0-0084395	C667	1
MC KIERNAN JOHN T	LTC	0-0081036	0866	1
MC KINLEY JR JAMES F	COL	C-0023893	C661	1
MC KINLEY KATHLEEN M	LTC	N-0000502	1148	1
MC KINNEY HARRY E	COL	0-0016888	C156	1
MC KINNEY HUGH L	LTC	0-0036986	0164	1
MC KINNEY RALPH O	COL	0-0019529	1156	1
MC KINNON JAMES L	COL	0-0015426	0649	1
MC KINNON ROBERT H	COL	0-0019590	0158	1
MC KITHAN QUINCY C	CW4	W-0905895	C460	1
MC KNIGHT ALVIE L	LTC	0-0022762	C960	1
MC KNIGHT CLYDE W	LTC	C-002976C	C760	1
MC KNIGHT JOE F	LTC	C-0017984	0350	1
MC LAIN EDWARD W	LTC	C-0020888	C165	1
MC LAMORE ROY T	COL	C-001C825	0645	2
MC LANACHAN JAMES D	LTC	0-0046037	0864	1
MC LANE ALTON O	COL	0-0038658	0755	1
MC LANE WILLIAM C	CW4	W-0903522	0164	1
MC LARREN EDMUND W	COL	C-0006662	0647	1
MC LAUCHLIN HENRY H	COL	0-0051752	0464	1
MC LAUGHLIN CHARLES	COL	0-0031639	1067	1
MC LAUGHLIN CHARLES	LTC	0-0037128	1163	1
MC LAUGHLIN CLENARD	COL	0-0000981	0642	1
MC LAUGHLIN EDWIN C	LTC	0-0044423	0661	1
MC LAUGHLIN HUGH S	LTC	0-0081914	0767	1
MC LAURIN COLIN H	CPT	0-0024493	0145	2
MC LEAN DAVID S	COL	0-0012472	1047	1
MC LEAN DONALD	COL	C-0015284	0753	1
MC LEAN EUGENE	CW2	W-0901256	0246	2
MC LEELAND JR W S	CW3	W-0903525	0160	1
MC LELLAN DOROTHY L	MAJ	L-0000255	1062	1
MC LEMORE EPHRAIM H	COL	C-0017184	1054	2
MC LENDON ERNEST L	COL	0-0005158	1047	2
MC LENNAN DONALD G	COL	0-0019475	0864	1
MC LEOD GREGG C	LTC	0-0030674	0462	2
MC LEOD JOHN J	LTC	0-0043036	0565	1
MC MACKIN CHARLES L	LTC	0-0031511	1048	2
MC MAHAN JOHN M	CW4	W-0903526	0762	1
MC MAHEA AGNES	MAJ	N-0001605	0765	1
MC MAHON BERNARD B	COL	0-0007040	0353	1
MC MAHON DENNIS J	COL	0-0019592	0862	1
MC MAHON JOHN A	LTC	0-0054182	0164	1
MC MAHON JR JOHN F	B G	0-0003541	0950	1
MC MAHON LEO T	B G	0-0010626	0248	1
MC MAHON MONA M	MAJ	N-0002139	0261	2
MC MAHON RALPH M	COL	0-0030526	1065	1
MC MAHON WILLIAM C	M G	0-0C0530C	0949	1
MC MAINS D M	COL	0-0080364	C764	1
MC MAKEN EDWARD	COL	0-0030318	1264	1
MC MANAWAY FRED	COL	0-0029335	C959	1
MC MANIS THAYNE F	COL	0-0021047	C867	1
MC MANUS HOWARD F	COL	0-0020346	C762	1
MC MANUS JR GEORGE H	COL	0-0018170	0655	1
MC MASTER RICHARD K	MAJ	0-0016439	0342	2
MC MATH JR CARROLL B	LTC	0-0042678	0164	1
MC MEEN EDWIN O	COL	0-0031109	C164	1
MC MILLAN DONALD L	COL	C-0023791	0765	1
MC MILLAN WILLIAM S	COL	0-0032703	0665	1
MC MILLIN JAMES M	COL	C-0012702	0753	1
MC MILLION WILLIE C	COL	0-0038668	0560	1
MC MINN JOHN H	LTC	0-0081039	0567	1
MC MORROW HUBERT A	COL	C-0006586	1047	2
MC MURDO HEW R	COL	0-0003305	1C47	2
MC MURRAY CLARENCE M	COL	0-0002753	0246	2
MC MURRAY RUSSELL F	LTC	0-0029389	0358	2
MC MURTREY GAIL B	LTC	0-0046748	0962	1
MC NAIR CHARLES F	COL	0-0018383	0761	1
MC NAIR JOEL N	COL	C-0C52075	C764	1
MC NALLY EDWARD J	B G	0-0017629	0859	1
MC NALLY JAMES R	LTC	0-0030192	0662	1
MC NALLY JAMES P	LTC	0-0042317	C659	2
MC NALLY JOSEPH D	COL	0-0035796	0862	2
MC NAMARA ANDREW T	LTG	0-0017324	0764	1
MC NAMARA DONALD G	LTC	0-0035085	0962	1
MC NAMARA WILSON C	LTC	0-0031738	1062	1
MC NAMEE JR ROLAND W	LTC	0-0027544	0765	1
MC NAMEE ROLAND W	COL	0-0012372	1151	1
MC NARY CHARLES H	COL	0-0038742	0663	1
MC NAUGHT WARREN H	B G	0-0007582	0751	1
MC NEAL JOHN L	LTC	0-0065174	0167	1
MC NEAL JOSEPH W	MAJ	0-0014159	0716	2

NAME	GRADE	SVC NO	DATE RET MO YR	RET CODE
MC NEELEY ARTHUR M	MAJ	0-0032792	0847	2
MC NEIL MURRELL B	LTC	0-0081915	1263	1
MC NEILL NORMAN	COL	0-0008631	0150	1
MC NELLIS RUSSELL	B G	0-0018935	1264	2
MC NICOL WALLACE K	CPT	0-0060820	0864	1
MC NINCH JOSEPH H	M G	0-0018645	0562	1
MC NINE RAYMOND W	CW3	W-0903528	1160	1
MC NITT ROBERT N	LTC	0-0065068	0860	1
MC NUTT CHARLES H	B G	0-0016751	0657	1
MC PEEK CLYDE O	1LT	0-0025026	1045	2
MC PHAIL THOMAS D	COL	0-0030613	0962	1
MC PHERON WESLEY F	COL	0-0030794	0964	1
MC PHERSON DON V	CW4	W-0903529	0662	1
MC PHERSON LEMOYNE	COL	0-0020309	0858	1
MC PHERSON ROBERT B	LTC	0-0065013	1164	1
MC PHERSON WILLIAM L	COL	0-0015464	0847	1
MC QUAIDE JOSEPH T	COL	0-0024247	0767	1
MC QUARRIE CLAUDE M	B G	0-0012830	0854	1
MC QUILLIN RAYMOND E	B G	0-0003274	0248	1
MC QUISTON MARIAN R	MAJ	N-0001567	0464	1
MC RELL DONALD W	COL	0-0029606	0961	1
MC REYNOLDS GEORGE B	COL	0-0012065	1148	1
MC SHANE JAMES E	LTC	0-0051884	0665	1
MC SHANE PATRICK I	COL	0-0020989	0856	1
MC SHEEHY ROBERT J	LTC	0-0030750	0664	1
MC SHERRY FRANK J	B G	0-0007118	1046	2
MC WATT ELIZABETH	MAJ	N-0002258	0662	1
MC WATTERS JOHN A	LTC	0-0034336	0462	1
MC WHORTER JOHN P	COL	0-0031692	0164	1
MC WILLIAMS EDWARD	COL	0-0031853	1066	1
MC WILLIAMS JOHN K	LTC	0-0032257	1061	2
MCCONKIE HOWARD S	COL	0-0017343	0459	2
MCNULTY WILLIAM A	COL	0-0018871	0862	1
MEACHAM HERBERT C	CW3	W-0903532	0163	1
MEAD ARMISTEAD	M G	0-0015767	0761	2
MEAD EVERETT V	LTC	0-0030317	1262	1
MEAD JOHN E	1LT	0-0019576	0342	1
MEAD WALTER P	LTC	0-0030972	0155	1
MEADE FRANK C	B G	0-0014777	1047	1
MEADE JOHN	COL	0-0016338	1055	1
MEADE JR EVERARD K	MAJ	0-0025808	0746	2
MEADE STEPHEN J	COL	0-0031834	1262	1
MEADE WARREN E	CW3	W-0903533	1155	1
MEADER GLENN S	COL	0-0028964	0158	1
MEADOR CLARK B	COL	0-0020395	0761	1
MEAGHER HARVEY E	LTC	0-0031305	1265	2
MEALS ROBERT W	COL	0-0019005	0656	1
MEANS DALE E	COL	0-0018756	0762	1
MEANS WILLIAM B	COL	0-0019920	0265	1
MEANS WILLIAM E	COL	0-0018901	0862	1
MEANY WILLIAM F	COL	0-0020287	1262	1
MEASE LEONA L	MAJ	N-0001981	0363	1
MECREDY JR HENRY F	LTC	0-0045091	0865	1
MEDARIS JOHN B	M G	0-0039554	0160	1
MEDDING WALTER L	COL	0-0008882	0753	1
MEDDING WALTER S	CPT	0-0058975	0664	1
MEDER LELAND G	COL	0-0017914	0260	1
MEDLAR WILLIAM P	CPT	0-0014272	0720	2
MEDLEN DALTON Y	LTC	0-0411634	1064	2
MEDLEY DONAL I	LTC	0-0033165	0662	1
MEDLIN DORIS E	LTC	N-0000510	0450	1
MEDOUSKY JOHN W	COL	0-0021756	1062	1
MEEHAN CHARLES G	COL	0-0015545	0754	2
MEEHAN PATRICK H	COL	0-0051889	0767	1
MEEHAN THOMAS G	CW4	W-0902372	0757	1
MEEK CHESTER H	COL	0-0029890	1059	1
MEEK JOHN A	COL	0-0051261	1061	1
MEEK JR JOHN W	LTC	0-0063095	0966	1
MEEK STERNER ST	COL	0-0007573	0147	2
MEEKER ROLAND J	COL	0-0052185	0566	1
MEEKS DAVIS D	CPT	N-0000059	0851	1
MEEKS JOHN A	COL	0-0018735	0756	1
MEEKS KERDIS E	CW4	W-0903534	1265	1
MEEKS WILBERT D	LTC	0-0045109	0267	1
MEETHER ARTHUR J L	MAJ	0-0084460	0964	1

NAME	GRADE	SVC NO	DATE RET MO YR	RET CODE
MEETZE ADAM W	B G	0-0030087	1263	1
MEGGS ERNEST L	COL	0-0035474	0267	1
MEGICA MARTIN G	COL	0-0021881	0660	1
MEHNER FRANK E	LTC	0-0027122	0765	1
MEHNERT ERICH C	LTC	0-0068385	0965	1
MEHRTENS DONALD J	LTC	0-0025877	0164	1
MEIDLING GEORGE A	COL	0-0042634	0666	2
MEIER WALTER M	COL	0-0030443	0664	1
MEINECKE HENRY W	COL	0-0042722	1265	2
MEINERT FRED H	COL	0-0029851	0163	1
MEINZEN LAWRENCE L	LTC	0-0007301	0444	2
MEISCH HENRY W	COL	0-0011461	0946	2
MEISELL HARRY E	LTC	0-0032812	0266	1
MEISNER HELEN B	MAJ	L-0000148	1167	1
MEISS JACK M	LTC	0-0062146	0764	1
MEISTER WILLIAM B	COL	0-0003288	0346	2
MELASKY HARRIS M	M G	0-0005319	0946	2
MELBERG REINOLD	COL	0-0003812	1149	1
MELCHER JOHN F	LTC	0-0080455	0166	1
MELHORN WILLIAM H	LTC	0-0051557	0359	1
MELIUS DONALD C	LTC	0-0044464	0158	1
MELLO RALPH T	CPT	0-0058976	0358	2
MELOY JR GUY S	GEN	0-0016892	0863	1
MELTESEN CLARENCE R	LTC	0-0040616	0864	1
MELTON G ELIZABET	MAJ	N-0001918	0464	1
MELTON JACK R	LTC	0-0033470	0662	1
MENARD NOEL A	COL	0-0020835	0763	1
MENCER EDWARD A	CW3	W-0906903	0958	1
MENDELL MARTIN M	COL	0-0042082	1055	1
MENDELSON JOSEPH A	LTC	0-0009505	0934	2
MENDENHALL CLARENCE	COL	0-0012218	0146	1
MENEGUS WILFRED F	COL	0-0042128	1262	1
MENGEL II RALPH H	LTC	0-0033504	0767	1
MENNIE MERLE L	COL	0-0039880	0264	1
MENOHER WILLIAM	COL	0-0018690	0955	1
MENOLD MARY V	MAJ	N-0001209	1063	1
MENTE JR ALVIN L	COL	0-0019974	0647	2
MENTZER DONALD O	CW4	W-0904253	0662	1
MENZIE JAMES T	COL	0-0006227	0949	1
MERCADER LEOPOLDO	COL	0-0002682	0-38	2
MERCADO LUIS F	COL	0-0020724	0867	1
MERCHANT EDWARD F	MAJ	0-0016687	0647	1
MERCHANT HUBERT W	COL	0-0063669	0866	1
MEREDITH LAWRENCE B	CW4	W-0903539	0862	1
MEREDITH OWEN R	COL	0-0002363	1045	2
MEREDITH PAUL E	LTC	0-0016829	0755	1
MERGENS GEORGE C	COL	0-0015300	0954	1
MERGLER VERNON T	LTC	0-0081044	0865	1
MERIGOLD FRANK A	LTC	0-0063050	0962	1
MERIKANGAS URHO R	COL	0-0019300	0860	1
MERITT JOHN F	LTC	0-0069743	0966	1
MERKLE ERNEST A	COL	0-0015597	0954	1
MERLE JR LEO V	LTC	0-0051778	0261	1
MERRIAM JOHN H	LTC	0-0033095	1163	1
MERRIAM LAUREN W	COL	0-0019002	0763	2
MERRIAM WHEELER G	B G	0-0030759	0766	1
MERRICK HERBERT F	CW3	W-0903541	0758	1
MERRIKEN JOHN E	LTC	0-0031253	0760	2
MERRILL ALBERTO E	COL	0-0008142	0935	2
MERRILL CHARLES C	COL	0-0010367	0346	1
MERRILL EARNEST D	COL	0-0039604	0157	1
MERRILL ELEANOR W	LTC	N-0000530	0748	2
MERRILL JOHN N	MAJ	0-0009229	1127	2
MERRILL MARIE E	MAJ	N-0000664	0864	1
MERRILL NELL W	COL	R-0010036	1054	1
MERRITT ANTHONY G	COL	0-0042255	1063	1
MERRITT CARLETON E	COL	0-0028867	0856	1
MERRITT WILMER B	COL	0-0012785	0753	1
MERRY LYNDON W	LTC	0-0051391	0261	1
MERRY WILLIAM T	COL	0-0000784	0-28	1
MESICK BENJAMIN S	COL	0-0015505	0854	1
MESICK JOHN	COL	0-0011207	0453	1
MESSAMERE LESLIE T	CW3	W-0903542	0859	1
MESSEC HARRY S	COL	0-0051682	0561	2
MESSER ELMER J	MAJ	0-0058977	1062	2

NAME	GRADE	SVC NO	DATE RET MO YR	RET CODE
MESSER HERBERT G	COL	0-0011724	1046	2
MESSER MELVIN	LTC	0-0069744	1167	2
MESSERSMITH BETTY E	MAJ	N-0002142	0761	1
MESSERSMITH JOSHUA R	COL	0-0019139	0561	1
MESSNER ARTHUR E	COL	0-0030181	1162	1
MESSNER E VALINE	LTC	N-0000013	0947	1
MESZAR MARJORIE	MAJ	N-0000675	0364	1
METCALF ELSIE J	CPT	L-0000342	0865	1
METCALF FREDERIC A	COL	0-0009724	1052	1
METCALF JAMES E	COL	0-0042288	1263	1
METCALF JR ROBERT L	COL	0-0053179	0765	1
METCALFE ALVIN C	LTC	0-0036809	0767	1
METCALFE CHARLES G	COL	0-0052749	0264	1
METCALFE GEORGE	LTC	0-0051637	0263	2
METCALFE SAMUEL L	COL	0-0009684	0854	1
METHENY LYAL C	B G	0-0039729	0858	1
METHVEN THERON G	COL	0-0004647	1146	2
METTE JR CLARENCE A	COL	0-0032776	1167	1
METTIE ELIZABETH	LTC	N-0000156	1164	1
METTLER CHARLES G	COL	0-0002123	0939	2
METTS JR WALTER A	COL	0-0009901	0550	1
METZ MICHAEL T	LTC	0-0042071	0860	1
METZ THOMAS M	COL	0-0020696	1166	1
METZGER EARL H	B G	0-0003253	0849	1
METZGER EDWARD H	COL	0-0011729	0753	1
METZGER ELIZABETH	MAJ	L-0000095	0763	1
MEWBORN NEECHAM P	LTC	0-0028645	0866	1
MEWSHAW HARRY C	COL	0-0011235	0754	1
MEYER CARL W	COL	0-0016071	0655	1
MEYER CHARLES R	B G	0-0020762	0867	1
MEYER HAROLD A	COL	0-0014960	0348	1
MEYER HENRY J D	B G	0-0012290	0952	2
MEYER JOHN S	CW4	W-0902379	0257	1
MEYER JR GEORGE F	COL	0-0031584	1167	1
MEYER JULES O	LTC	0-0060014	0365	1
MEYER RICHARD D	LTG	0-0018963	1067	1
MEYER RICHARD H	LTC	0-0025872	0763	1
MEYER ROBERT G H	COL	0-0017528	0759	1
MEYER ROBERT J	LTC	0-0069746	1265	1
MEYER THOMAS F	COL	0-0015105	0551	1
MEYER VINCENT	B G	0-0003143	1045	2
MEYER WALTER G	COL	0-0041653	0360	1
MEYER WALTER P	LTC	0-0063314	0767	1
MEYERDIRK ALVIN R	CW4	W-0906904	1164	1
MEYERS HARRY F	B G	0-0011877	0854	1
MEYERS HARRY T	COL	0-0041608	0959	1
MEYERS RUTH E	MAJ	L-0000005	0753	1
MIAL JOHN P	COL	0-0022157	1058	1
MICCIO JR EDWARD	LTC	0-0050013	0166	2
MICHAEL CLARENCE A	WO1	W-0901435	0841	1
MICHAEL JAMES R	COL	0-0025609	0866	1
MICHAEL JONATHAN H	COL	0-0039594	1058	1
MICHAELIS EMILY R	MAJ	N-0001613	0465	1
MICHAELIS LEON A	COL	0-0044486	0767	1
MICHAELS CHARLES B	CW2	W-0903545	1159	1
MICHAELS CHARLES E	COL	0-0038972	1165	1
MICHAELSON FRANKLYN	LTC	0-0048532	1262	1
MICHALAK EDWARD M	1LT	0-0027191	0449	2
MICHASIOW MYRON	CW4	W-0903548	0966	1
MICHENER WILLIAM	COL	0-0008270	0953	1
MICKEL GEORGE E	COL	0-0038793	0265	1
MICKEL LAURENCE	COL	0-0008259	0245	2
MICKELSON EARL L	COL	0-0028823	0955	1
MICKELWAIT CLAUDE B	M G	0-0010287	0756	2
MICKLE GERALD ST	B G	0-0012350	0946	2
MIDDLEBROOKS MARVIN	COL	0-0051440	0963	1
MIDDLEBROOKS RICHARD	COL	0-0038704	0162	2
MIDDLEKAUFF R M	CW4	W-0902014	0655	1
MIDDLETON EDWARD O	MAJ	0-0061107	0967	1
MIDDLETON EMERY O	COL	0-0030329	0163	2
MIDDLETON ETHEL W	MAJ	L-0000294	0659	1
MIDDLETON GEORGE R	COL	0-0005903	0547	2
MIDDLETON HARTER O	COL	0-0051767	0165	1
MIDDLETON SANDERS O	CPT	0-0060203	1162	1
MIDDLETON TROY H	LTG	0-0003476	0-37	1

NAME	GRADE	SVC NO	DATE RET MO YR	RET CODE
MIDDLETON WILLIAM R	LTC	0-0030338	0960	2
MIEHE WILLIAM J	COL	0-0006002	0951	2
MIESCHER JR WALTER H	LTC	0-0065017	0665	1
MIFFLIN THOMAS	COL	0-0018216	0760	1
MIGLIORA CHARLES A	CW2	W-0901721	0447	1
MIHOCH JOHN R	LTC	0-0069748	0964	1
MIKETINAC ANTHONY J	LTC	0-0045671	0667	1
MIKKELSEN HARRY E	COL	0-0020179	0757	1
MIKOWSKI FLORENCE J	MAJ	N-0001340	0365	1
MILAM JONAS C	CW3	W-0903550	1163	1
MILAN HAROLD L	COL	0-0008665	1147	1
MILANO JAMES V	COL	0-0046052	1266	1
MILBURN BRYAN L	M G	0-0007469	1156	1
MILBURN EUGENE	COL	0-0003978	0549	2
MILBURN WILLIAM R	LTC	0-0031599	0260	1
MILES BURTON F	COL	0-0042886	1160	1
MILES JR CHARLES H	COL	0-0019151	0158	2
MILEY JOHN D	LTC	0-0004501	0433	2
MILEY JOHN D	CPT	0-0028586	1154	2
MILEY WILLIAM M	M G	0-0011232	0755	1
MILLENER GEORGE A	COL	0-0015740	0954	1
MILLER ALEXANDER	COL	0-0016765	0757	1
MILLER ALICE M	MAJ	L-0000017	0854	1
MILLER ALVA E	COL	0-0022283	0760	1
MILLER ALVIN C	COL	0-0003302	1146	2
MILLER ARLES H	COL	0-0042287	0761	1
MILLER AUSTIN A	COL	0-0019228	0461	2
MILLER BOULTON B	COL	0-0033148	1064	1
MILLER CARL W	COL	0-0019740	0763	1
MILLER CAROLINE R	MAJ	N-0002374	0860	1
MILLER CHARLES F	LTC	0-0065222	0765	1
MILLER CLARENCE G	CW3	W-0904158	1159	1
MILLER DALE F	LTC	0-0084560	0466	2
MILLER DOT	MAJ	R-0010085	0760	1
MILLER EDGAR S	COL	0-0002401	0-37	1
MILLER EDNA R	LTC	L-0000038	0760	1
MILLER EDWARD G	COL	0-0041633	1059	1
MILLER EDWIN T	COL	0-0030006	1062	1
MILLER ELSIE K	MAJ	R-0010043	1263	1
MILLER EUGENE F	COL	0-0030156	0464	1
MILLER EUGENE L	COL	0-0011657	0450	1
MILLER EVERETT B	LTC	0-0040132	0365	1
MILLER FAUNTLEY M	LTC	0-0002283	0233	2
MILLER FRANCIS N	COL	0-0041791	0860	1
MILLER FREDERIC G	COL	0-0081052	0867	1
MILLER FREDERICK	LTC	0-0084561	0665	1
MILLER GAY E	LTC	0-0028842	0254	1
MILLER GEORGE A	B G	0-0007196	0248	2
MILLER GEORGE P	COL	0-0042475	1264	1
MILLER HAROLD H	1LT	0-0011738	0322	2
MILLER HAROLD R	COL	0-0053967	0767	1
MILLER HAROLD T	B G	0-0012633	0654	1
MILLER HARRY W	COL	0-0016005	0754	1
MILLER HELEN E	MAJ	N-0000149	0756	1
MILLER HENRY L	COL	0-0043302	0662	1
MILLER HOMER E	COL	0-0022227	0460	2
MILLER HUBERT S	COL	0-0014664	0854	2
MILLER JACK E	LTC	0-0023406	0864	1
MILLER JAMES A	COL	0-0040018	0760	2
MILLER JAMES B	COL	0-0030266	1064	1
MILLER JAMES B	COL	0-0084031	0667	2
MILLER JAMES P	CW4	W-0904160	0967	1
MILLER JESSIE L	MAJ	M-0010072	0360	1
MILLER JOHN E	LTC	0-0081053	1066	1
MILLER JOHN H	LTC	0-0038010	0964	1
MILLER JOHN K	COL	0-0028890	1056	1
MILLER JOHN P	CW4	W-0903553	0264	1
MILLER JOSIAH B	LTC	0-0032386	0765	1
MILLER JR BYRON L	LTC	0-0037630	1067	1
MILLER JR EDWARD C	COL	0-0038590	1054	1
MILLER JR EDWARD M	COL	0-0040167	0667	2
MILLER JR JAMES F	MAJ	0-0019353	1138	2
MILLER JR WILBUR O	LTC	0-0033126	0663	1
MILLER LEE C	COL	0-0019438	0864	1
MILLER LEHMAN W	B G	0-0003773	0844	2

NAME	GRADE	SVC NO	DATE RET MO YR	RET CODE
MILLER LELAND V	COL	0-0030235	0562	1
MILLER LEONARD C	COL	0-0024623	1065	2
MILLER LEROY	CW4	W-0904162	1060	1
MILLER LEWIS	MAJ	0-0089108	0966	1
MILLER LILLARD P	COL	0-0029511	1060	1
MILLER LOUISE	MAJ	N-0000544	0549	1
MILLER LUTHER O	M G	0-0011793	1149	1
MILLER LUTHER R	COL	0-0030737	0662	2
MILLER MABRY G	COL	0-0031486	0766	2
MILLER MARION C	COL	0-0051396	0463	1
MILLER MARY	MAJ	N-0000018	0448	1
MILLER MAURICE L	B G	0-0004490	1150	1
MILLER MAYNARD C	COL	0-0079928	0367	1
MILLER MELVIN O	MAJ	0-0040283	0658	1
MILLER MILLARD J	LTC	0-0047804	0762	1
MILLER NORBERT C	COL	0-0038905	0163	1
MILLER OPIE G	CW4	W-0903554	0862	1
MILLER PAUL A	COL	0-0030843	0165	1
MILLER PAUL R M	COL	0-0012500	0854	2
MILLER RAYMOND G	COL	0-0011586	0753	1
MILLER ROBERT B	COL	0-0019366	0864	1
MILLER ROBERT C	COL	0-0020625	0966	1
MILLER ROBERT C	COL	0-0037409	0762	1
MILLER ROBERT O	COL	0-0041448	0257	2
MILLER ROBERT L	COL	0-0009638	1146	1
MILLER ROBERT L	COL	0-0016575	0755	1
MILLER ROBERT S	COL	0-0007959	1047	2
MILLER ROGER G	COL	0-0017798	0859	1
MILLER RUSSELL J	LTC	0-0063388	0467	1
MILLER SAMUEL T	LTC	0-0031377	1055	1
MILLER THOMAS R	COL	0-0005109	0646	1
MILLER VERLE C	COL	0-0024396	0861	1
MILLER VERNE	CPT	0-0006058	1022	2
MILLER VERNON W	WO1	W-0901006	0836	1
MILLER VIRGIL R	COL	0-0015847	0854	1
MILLER WALTER W	LTC	0-0065541	0464	1
MILLER WHITSIDE	LTC	0-0017790	0757	1
MILLER WILLIAM A	COL	0-0012126	0350	1
MILLER WILLIAM L	CW3	W-0904163	0457	1
MILLER 2ND ALLEN C	COL	0-0020342	0758	1
MILLER 2ND C L	LTC	0-0022149	0960	1
MILLET STEPHEN J	COL	0-0038690	0760	1
MILLHOLLAND GEORGE H	COL	0-0007150	0446	1
MILLICAN RAYMOND W	COL	0-0023000	0762	1
MILLICE WILLARD F	COL	0-0015443	1046	1
MILLIGAN CAREY W	MAJ	0-0028125	0666	1
MILLIKEN CHARLES R	COL	0-0020340	0761	1
MILLIKEN WILLIAM S	LTC	0-0041017	0463	1
MILLIKIN JOHN	M G	0-0002856	0248	1
MILLS FRANCIS B	COL	0-0032544	1166	1
MILLS JENE F	COL	0-0023410	0267	1
MILLS JR ERIC R	COL	0-0047272	0766	1
MILLS MARION L	COL	0-0020038	0759	1
MILLS OLIVE E	LTC	L-0000085	0865	1
MILLS RUTH T	MAJ	N-0001580	0465	1
MILLS WILLIAM H	COL	0-0016376	0756	1
MILLS WILLIS E	MAJ	0-0014017	1020	1
MILLSON CYRIL A	COL	0-0042922	1266	1
MILLSTEIN CONAN H	LTC	0-0049920	0866	1
MILLWEE JOSEPH B	MAJ	0-0064388	0565	2
MILMORE CHARLES W	LTC	0-0026045	0767	2
MILNE WILLIAM O	COL	0-0020144	0656	1
MILNER FRED C	COL	0-0007230	0552	1
MILNER JAMES W	COL	0-0023124	0367	1
MILNER MORRIS E	COL	0-0041456	0357	1
MILNER WALKER W	COL	0-0018356	0758	1
MILNOR PHILIP L	MAJ	0-0002789	1022	1
MILTON THORNTON M	LTC	0-0028032	0867	1
MILVO JOHN D	CW3	RW-0907127	0664	1
MILWIT HERBERT	COL	0-0017514	0355	1
MINAHAN JR DANIEL J	COL	0-0021799	0664	1
MINAS FRANK A	COL	0-0019337	0147	2
MINCH HOWARD G	COL	0-0034945	1167	1
MINCKLER REX W	COL	0-0014599	0746	1
MINECCI JOSEPH R	LTC	0-0038823	0364	1

NAME	GRADE	SVC NO	DATE RET MO YR	RET CODE
MINER EARL M	COL	0-0011656	0753	1
MINER FLORENCE Z	MAJ	N-0000672	0264	1
MINER HAROLD E	LTC	0-0043019	0565	1
MINER HAROLD W	COL	0-0051102	0960	1
MINER HOWARD A	LTC	0-0039933	1162	1
MINER JOHN W	COL	0-0009847	0350	1
MINER RALPH E	LTC	0-0023285	0660	1
MINER RUSSELL M	COL	0-0015839	0762	1
MINER RUTH S	MAJ	L-0000087	0361	1
MINERVA FRANK D	COL	0-0051962	0766	1
MINICN EDWARD M	COL	0-0031601	0866	1
MINK ROBERT M	CW4	W-0906908	0660	1
MINNICH EDGAR R	COL	0-0051197	0161	1
MINOR FLOYD E	COL	0-0031668	0762	1
MINOR GEORGE H	COL	0-0020710	0246	2
MINTER JAMES W	LTC	0-0062015	0167	2
MINTON HENRY E	COL	0-0008262	1047	2
MINTON JOHN T	COL	0-0004790	0646	2
MINTON WARREN A	LTC	0-0045195	0859	1
MIRKIN MARJORIE	MAJ	N-0000216	0560	2
MIRRAS PETER W	COL	0-0052684	0367	1
MISOCH HOWELL E	COL	0-0079930	1166	2
MISEVIC GEORGE W	COL	0-0051782	0366	2
MISEVIC HELEN M L	MAJ	N-0001299	0361	1
MISSAL JR JOSEPH A	LTC	0-0021247	0866	1
MITCHELL BARRY H	COL	0-0079931	0765	1
MITCHELL CECIL W	CW3	W-0903558	0755	1
MITCHELL CHARLES H	COL	0-0041731	0662	1
MITCHELL CLAIR A	COL	0-0019899	0955	2
MITCHELL DONALD E	CPT	0-0088839	0763	2
MITCHELL DOUGLAS W	COL	0-0084399	0966	1
MITCHELL EARLE F	COL	0-0030272	0864	1
MITCHELL ELMO C	LTC	0-0018425	0945	2
MITCHELL EUGENE H	COL	0-0007463	0753	1
MITCHELL FRANKLIN	COL	0-0014665	0346	1
MITCHELL HARRIS T	LTC	0-0052670	0263	1
MITCHELL HARRY E	CPT	0-0014118	0909	2
MITCHELL HENRY F	MAJ	0-0068139	1167	1
MITCHELL HERBERT V	B G	0-0018073	0760	1
MITCHELL JAMES K	COL	0-0012647	1050	1
MITCHELL JOHN O	COL	0-0012713	0956	1
MITCHELL JR JOSEPH W	LTC	0-0036351	0762	1
MITCHELL LAWRENCE C	COL	0-0005304	0253	1
MITCHELL OTHELDA M	MAJ	L-0000229	0558	1
MITCHELL PAUL J	COL	0-0017314	0758	1
MITCHELL RICHARD F	LTC	0-0063338	0865	1
MITCHELL RICHARD T	COL	0-0015833	0654	2
MITCHELL ROBERT F	MAJ	0-0056291	0761	1
MITCHELL STEPHEN C	LTC	0-0080151	0767	1
MITCHELL STUART M	COL	0-0029305	0264	1
MITCHELL WILLIAM L	M G	0-0012832	1055	2
MITCHIM CHARLES F	COL	0-0020577	1061	1
MITER FRANK F	COL	0-0016477	0656	1
MITTENZWEI FRANCIS X	LTC	0-0081060	0267	1
MIX PERNIER A	MAJ	0-0008499	0934	2
MIXSON ELIZABETH	LTC	N-0000533	0758	1
MIZE PAUL H	COL	0-0032335	0767	1
MIZE WILLARD W	COL	0-0030204	0764	1
MIZELL WALTER S	LTC	0-0065438	1264	1
MOAK JAMES G	COL	0-0043454	1066	1
MOATS WILTON B	COL	0-0030336	0859	1
MOBERLEY KIRK B	COL	0-0051758	0666	1
MOBLEY JAMES C	CW4	W-0906910	0767	1
MOCKBEE JAMES B	COL	0-0011035	0448	1
MODRAK HENRY H	COL	0-0065415	0766	1
MOE ANNE C	LTC	L-0000034	0559	1
MOE GEORGE R	LTC	0-0026022	0264	1
MOEHLMANN F HERBERT	COL	0-0017986	1146	2
MOFFATT CARROLL K	COL	0-0029343	0959	1
MOFFETT CLEWIS C	COL	0-0039909	0764	1
MOFFETT JAMES R	LTC	0-0059441	0165	1
MOFFETT JR CHARLES W	CPT	0-0060807	1262	1
MOFFETT OREN F	LTC	0-0080460	0966	1
MOHLERE EDWARD D	COL	0-0020286	0466	1
MOHN EDWARD S	CW4	W-0903561	0660	1

NAME	GRADE	SVC NO	DATE RET MO YR	RET CODE
MOHRI RALPH W	COL	0-0017985	0758	1
MOLESKY WALTER F	COL	0-0023857	0967	1
MOLITOR ERIC S	B G	0-0012115	0854	2
MOLL RICHARD A	LTC	0-0049945	0959	2
MOLLOHAN CECIL S	COL	0-0019309	0757	1
MOLLOY FRANCIS P	2LT	0-0016440	0527	2
MOLYNEAUX HAROLD L	LTC	0-0056193	0465	2
MOMISTON ROBERT M	COL	0-0029242	0862	1
MOMM EDWIN C	CPT	0-0018864	0947	1
MONAHAN JOHN C	B G	0-0038706	0664	1
MONCRIEF JR JAMES S	COL	0-0031623	0865	1
MONETTE HELEN O	MAJ	N-0000900	0863	1
MONEYHUN JOSEPH A	LTC	0-0048065	0463	1
MONIHAN JAMES G	COL	0-0004593	0448	2
MONROE GRACE E	MAJ	N-0000563	1060	1
MONROE HAMMOND M	B G	0-0012132	0753	1
MONROE MELVIN C	LTC	0-0034552	0166	1
MONROE THOMAS H	COL	0-0003732	0446	1
MONSKE FREDA L	MAJ	N-0002135	0860	1
MONSON NELSON P	MAJ	0-0023996	1061	1
MONTAGUE ERNEST K	COL	0-0056890	1065	1
MONTAGUE MARY DO	1LT	R-0001226	0945	1
MONTAGUE THEODORE	1LT	0-0028332	0949	2
MONTESINOS MIGUEL	LTC	0-0010078	0142	1
MONTESINOS SERAFIN M	COL	0-0003197	0248	1
MONTGOMERY ALBERT E	COL	0-0057698	1262	1
MONTGOMERY AUSTIN J	B G	0-0051942	0867	1
MONTGOMERY BRIAN C	COL	0-0032529	0964	1
MONTGOMERY GUS H	COL	0-0029993	0863	1
MONTGOMERY JR JOHN H	COL	0-0020754	0867	1
MONTGOMERY LEE E	COL	0-0030958	0767	1
MONTGOMERY MURRAY M	COL	0-0007137	0653	1
MONTGOMERY ROBIN C	COL	0-0031525	0367	1
MONTGOMERY WALDO W	COL	0-0042890	0965	1
MONTI GILBERT A	LTC	0-0051641	0863	1
MONTILLA RAFAEL	COL	0-0051437	0863	1
MONTY PERCY A	LTC	0-0053945	0965	1
MOODY FLORENCE P	MAJ	L-0000116	1163	1
MOODY MARLIN S	COL	0-0028911	0557	1
MOOMAW OTHO A	LTC	0-0020905	0965	1
MOON HERBERT C	LTC	0-0084400	0663	1
MOON JACOB R	LTC	0-0015864	0448	1
MOON JAMES W	COL	0-0032540	0665	1
MOON JR WILLIAM P	LTC	0-0031589	0765	1
MOONEY HAROLD T	COL	0-0042918	1164	1
MOONEY JAMES S	LTC	0-0003402	0828	2
MOORE ALBERT F	LTC	0-0063364	1165	1
MOORE ANDERSON T	COL	0-0009327	0854	1
MOORE ARLICE J	COL	0-0031156	0664	1
MOORE ARTHUR L	COL	0-0012429	0451	1
MOORE ARTHUR P	COL	0-0010105	0151	1
MOORE AUDREY M	MAJ	N-0002452	0267	1
MOORE BICKELL	COL	0-0023248	0166	1
MOORE BUHL	COL	0-0007329	0947	1
MOORE CECIL R	M G	0-0006669	1046	2
MOORE CHARLES E	CPT	0-0004657	0622	2
MOORE CHARLES F	LTC	0-0051837	0265	1
MOORE CLARENCE A	COL	0-0050919	0756	1
MOORE DENIS G	COL	0-0030969	1265	1
MOORE DON G	COL	0-0003982	0646	2
MOORE ELMORE R	COL	0-0051460	0259	1
MOORE EUGENE M	CW4	W-0902193	0552	1
MOORE FRANK M	COL	0-0007891	1046	1
MOORE GEORGE A	COL	0-0005577	0945	2
MOORE GEORGE R	COL	0-0023804	1165	1
MOORE GLADYS	MAJ	N-0000239	0461	1
MOORE HARMON C	COL	0-0051971	0267	1
MOORE HERBERT K	COL	0-0010807	0851	1
MOORE HOWARD E	MAJ	0-0025816	0864	1
MOORE J MERRIAM	COL	0-0003487	0648	1
MOORE JAMES A	CW4	W-0904165	0164	1
MOORE JAMES E	GEN	0-0015650	0763	2
MOORE JEAN	MAJ	N-0002006	1067	1
MOORE JESSE N	LTC	0-0078993	0563	1
MOORE JOHN J	COL	0-0031355	0766	1

NAME	GRADE	SVC NO	DATE RET MO YR	RET CODE
MOORE JOHN M	COL	0-0012107	1146	1
MOORE JOHN M	MAJ	0-0016856	0444	2
MOORE JOHN V	LTC	0-0029093	0457	1
MOORE JOSEPH C	COL	0-0019791	0865	1
MOORE JOSEPH R	LTC	0-0050929	1154	1
MOORE JR CHARLES H	COL	0-0012201	0247	2
MOORE JR CLAYTON H	LTC	0-0035178	1263	1
MOORE JR FULESS B	LTC	0-0063300	0764	1
MOORE JR GEORGE B	COL	0-0016972	0945	2
MOORE KENNETH M	COL	0-0008558	0453	1
MOORE LESLIE S	COL	0-0051012	0259	1
MOORE LESTER B	CW4	W-0906914	1066	1
MOORE LISTER R	COL	0-0039947	1165	1
MOORE LOREN C	COL	0-0016527	1145	2
MOORE LOWELL G	LTC	0-0043539	0766	1
MOORE LOWREY R	COL	0-0029941	0462	1
MOORE NEO O	M G	0-0018212	0265	1
MOORE ORVILLE M	COL	0-0004804	0147	1
MOORE PIERCE M	CPT	0-0069227	0861	2
MOORE PRENTICE L	COL	0-0016023	0254	2
MOORE RICHARD H	COL	0-0030721	0563	1
MOORE ROBERT B	MAJ	0-0004821	0934	2
MOORE ROBERT B	COL	0-0051294	0462	2
MOORE ROBERT E	LTC	0-0032244	1062	1
MOORE ROBERT F	LTC	0-0018781	0757	1
MOORE ROBERT F	LTC	0-0036304	1167	1
MOORE ROBERT H	MAJ	0-0065147	0765	1
MOORE ROBERT J	CW4	W-0904166	1067	1
MOORE ROBERT S	M G	0-0011911	0854	1
MOORE ROY C	COL	0-0006633	0337	1
MOORE ROY E	COL	0-0018880	0862	1
MOORE SPURGEON A	LTC	0-0038370	0566	1
MOORE STERLIN C	LTC	0-0084061	0864	1
MOORE THOMAS E	COL	0-0014867	0452	1
MOORE THOMAS N	LTC	0-0037296	0464	1
MOORE VIVIAN M	MAJ	N-0000626	0860	1
MOORE WALTER E	LTC	0-0033145	0661	1
MOORE WAYNE S	COL	0-0012617	1050	1
MOORE WERNER W	COL	0-0011157	0753	2
MOORE WILLIAM H	COL	0-0018796	0862	1
MOORE WILLIAM C	COL	0-0004899	1048	1
MOORE WILLIAM P	COL	0-0051052	0555	1
MOORE WILLIAM S	COL	0-0030992	1165	1
MOORE WILLIAM T	COL	0-0017313	0758	1
MOOREFIELD JESSE P	COL	0-0022244	0867	2
MOORES ZACHERY W	COL	0-0015647	0954	2
MOORHEAD JAMES U	COL	0-0041957	1161	1
MOORING BRUCE O	COL	0-0051073	0258	1
MOORMAN FRANK W	M G	0-0019444	1065	1
MOORMAN HAROLD N	COL	0-0021095	0764	1
MOORMAN RICHARD R	COL	0-0019394	0864	2
MORAN JOHN J	LTC	0-0040004	1263	1
MORAN KATHLEEN A	2LT	R-0002170	1045	1
MORAN RICHARD B	B G	0-0005399	0450	1
MORAN THOMAS J	COL	0-0017266	0854	1
MORAN WILLIAM J	B G	0-0029195	0266	1
MORAWETZ FRANCIS E	COL	0-0028947	1057	1
MORDECAI ALFRED	COL	0-0009513	0-44	2
MOREAU ARTHUR	CW4	W-0903570	0966	1
MOREE MCATESCUE	COL	0-0041834	0361	1
MOREFIELD WILLIAM J	LTC	0-0081071	0463	1
MORELAND HOWARD B	MAJ	0-0029466	0850	1
MORELAND JOHN W	COL	0-0012616	0644	2
MORELOCK JR GEORGE L	LTC	0-0043960	0164	1
MOREMAN JR OTIS S	LTC	0-0051856	0963	1
MORENO ARTURE	COL	0-0002977	1140	1
MORGAN CHARLIE F	LTC	0-0051535	1262	2
MORGAN CLAYTON A	LTC	0-0085624	0961	1
MORGAN CLYDE H	COL	0-0008587	1046	1
MORGAN DALE L	COL	0-0045796	0265	1
MORGAN JAMES S	COL	0-0041696	0158	1
MORGAN JOHN B	COL	0-0019871	0865	1
MORGAN JOHN P	LTC	0-0081072	1066	1
MORGAN JOHN R	CW3	W-0904167	0558	1
MORGAN JOSEPH H	LTC	0-0051743	0464	1

UNITED STATES ARMY RETIRED LIST

NAME	GRADE	SVC NO	DATE RET MO YR	RET CODE
MORGAN JR CLAYTON A	LTC	0-0049124	C565	1
MORGAN MAURICE	COL	0-0005594	0546	2
MORGAN VERNON W	LTC	C-0045837	C966	1
MORGAN WILLIAM H	LTC	0-0024660	C763	1
MORIN MARTIN J	M G	0-0016911	0764	1
MORLEY AUBREY R	COL	0-0029758	C862	1
MORLEY HARRY C	LTC	0-0037341	C864	1
MORLEY JOHN D	COL	0-0019634	0247	2
MORLEY JR HARRISON A	LTC	0-0083611	C366	1
MORLOCK WALLACE J	COL	0-0019325	0457	1
MORREALE SAMUEL D	LTC	0-0041765	C862	1
MORRELL JOSEPH J	COL	0-0051996	1266	1
MORRIS CAVID A	COL	0-0014666	0354	1
MORRIS GEORGE W	COL	C-0009076	0749	1
MORRIS HOWARD A	B G	0-0020141	0266	2
MORRIS I SEWELL	M G	0-0018806	C563	1
MORRIS JAMES H	LTC	C-0081074	0866	1
MORRIS JOHN W	LTC	0-0080312	C963	1
MORRIS JR JOHN G	COL	0-0039657	C761	1
MORRIS MARIE C	MAJ	N-0002234	C560	1
MORRIS MARY C	MAJ	N-0002035	0360	1
MORRIS RAYMOND C	COL	C-0079939	1063	2
MORRIS ROBERT C	CW4	W-0904171	1265	1
MORRIS THURMAN W	COL	0-0020315	C759	1
MORRIS WILLIAM H	LTG	0-0003102	0352	1
MORRISETTE JAMES F	B G	0-0007839	0846	2
MORRISEY JR JOHN C	LTC	0-0080462	0765	1
MORRISON BURTON O	COL	0-0041658	C361	1
MORRISON CHARLES E	COL	C-0012109	C548	2
MORRISCN DOUGLAS E	COL	0-0007555	C145	2
MORRISON IDA B	MAJ	N-0001327	0465	1
MORRISON JAMES V	CW4	W-0903573	1158	1
MORRISON JOHN A	COL	0-0020945	1163	1
MORRISSEY STEPHEN B	LTC	0-002327C	C265	1
MORROW BERTRAN	COL	0-0005301	1047	1
MORROW JR SAMUEL L	COL	0-0018104	C760	1
MORROW SAMUEL H	COL	0-0015913	0948	2
MORROW THOMAS O	LTC	0-0081076	0666	1
MORSE FRANCIS H	COL	0-0012682	C854	1
MORSE GRANVILLE	COL	C-0015388	C846	2
MORSE MARY F	MAJ	N-0000860	C163	1
MORSE WILLIAM P	COL	0-0005106	C649	1
MORSE WOODROW W	LTC	0-0053048	C262	1
MORTIMER EDWARD C	CW4	W-0903575	0165	1
MORTON CLINTON O	COL	0-0051729	C366	1
MORTON JR WILLIAM J	COL	0-0015158	1033	2
MORTON PAUL A	LTC	C-0062127	C563	1
MOSCATELLI TITO G	COL	0-0017286	C758	1
MOSELEY CHARLES H	COL	0-0020402	C866	1
MOSELEY GEORGE V H	COL	0-0016893	0146	2
MOSELY SEABCRN H	LTC	0-0042399	C762	1
MOSEMAN MARTHA E	LTC	R-0010031	0565	1
MOSER ERNEST H	COL	0-0030960	1163	1
MOSES ALBERT R	LTC	0-0062235	C866	1
MOSES HARRIET N	LTC	L-0000056	C762	1
MOSES JAMES R	LTC	0-0041035	C267	1
MOSES JR JOHN G	LTC	0-0025528	1166	1
MOSES LLOYD R	M G	0-0C29362	1064	1
MOSES MERILLAT	COL	0-0018421	1059	2
MOSES RAYMOND G	B G	0-0004414	C549	1
MOSES RUSSELL L	LTC	0-0015843	C644	2
MOSLEY LAURA M	LTC	N-0001883	1159	1
MOSS ALFRED H	LTC	0-0080463	0862	1
MOSS JIMMIE O	LTC	L-0000179	C966	1
MOSS JOE D	COL	C-0012162	C854	1
MOSS MARGARET M	MAJ	N-0000054	C650	1
MOSS ROY P	COL	C-0028838	C156	1
MOSS VAUGHN R	MAJ	C-0034144	0962	1
MOSSMAN ALBERT P	COL	C-0019469	0162	1
MOTES PRESTON M	COL	C-0030372	0265	1
MOTOLA MARIO V	LTC	0-00634C6	0766	1
MOTT JOHN W	COL	C-0008400	C753	1
MOTT WILLIAM H	CW4	W-0903579	C858	1
MOTTER JOHN C	LTC	0-0032288	C667	1
MOTZ LESLIE L	LTC	0-0042596	0862	1

NAME	GRADE	SVC NO	DATE RET MO YR	RET CODE
MOUCHET WILLIAM O	COL	0-0043802	0566	1
MCUK RCBERT P	COL	0-0042368	0161	2
MOULTCN ROBERT J	COL	0-0016665	0852	1
MOULTRIE MARY L	MAJ	N-0001985	0664	1
MOUNSEY GLEN A	LTC	0-0C31607	0858	1
MOUNT CHARLES A	LTC	0-0041934	1059	1
MOUNTFCRD FRECERIC	COL	C-0002615	1146	1
MOURAT STEPHEN	LTC	0-0059515	0365	1
MOUSHEGIAN RICHARD	LTC	0-0022109	C160	2
MOWBRAY JAY B	LTC	0-0024450	1059	1
MOWERY WILLIAM A	LTC	0-0051492	0462	1
MOWREY FRED H	COL	0-0019687	0859	2
MOYER MAYNARD G	LTC	0-0023991	1057	2
MOYERS EUGENE E	COL	0-0041938	1061	2
MOYNAHAN JAMES M	COL	0-0042848	1066	1
MOYNAHAN JR CEORGE F	COL	0-0030210	1160	1
MOZLEY JOSEPH T	COL	0-0042611	0865	1
MRAZEK JAMES E	COL	0-0021268	0758	1
MUCCI HENRY A	COL	0-0020374	0447	2
MUCHA CANIEL	LTC	0-0044636	1061	1
MUDGETT CHARLES S	COL	0-0017815	0858	1
MUDGETT GILMAN C	M G	0-0014966	0361	1
MUDGETT JR CHARLES F	B G	0-0C30405	0565	1
MUDGETT LOUIS E	COL	0-0031069	0866	1
MUELLER EDWARD A	COL	0-0014829	1146	2
MUELLER JAMES M	LTC	0-0027121	0767	1
MUELLER WALDEMAR M	COL	0-0031553	1067	2
MUFFIE SAM F	COL	0-0051201	0559	1
MUIR JR JAMES B	COL	0-0006643	1048	1
MUIR JR JOHN E	LTC	0-0033754	0962	1
MUIR RCBERT P	LTC	0-0039105	0765	1
MUIR WILLARD A	COL	0-0044774	0864	1
MULCAHY JAMES P	COL	0-0024227	0866	1
MULCAHY JULIA J	MAJ	L-0000305	0561	1
MULCAHY MICHAEL J	COL	0-0007634	1047	2
MULHOLLAND RICHARD F	COL	0-0031124	0263	1
MULKEY JR STEVE W	LTC	0-0026724	C165	1
MULLANE WALTER R	LTC	0-0023987	C460	1
MULLANEY JCHN J	COL	0-0029150	1058	1
MULLARKEY JAMES P	LTC	0-0033030	0164	1
MULLEN CARROLL C	COL	0-0051456	1163	1
MULLEN LEMUEL T	CW4	W-0903584	0966	1
MULLEN WILLIAM J	COL	0-0019586	0864	1
MULLENIX JOHN C	COL	C-0004605	0946	2
MULLER JOHN K	LTC	0-0024570	1060	1
MULLER MATTHAUS E	CW3	W-0904173	0861	1
MULLER WALTER J	M G	0-0012224	1156	1
MULLER WILLIAM G	COL	0-0009161	0743	1
MULLETT DEWITT T	COL	C-0010352	0951	1
MULLIKEN DAVID F	LTC	0-0034948	0863	1
MULLIKIN ORVILLE W	LTC	0-0018893	1045	2
MULLIN WILLIAM H	LTC	0-0023015	0660	1
MULLINIX JCSEPH R	LTC	0-0032086	0962	1
MULLINS CLAYTCN E	COL	0-0019016	0646	2
MULLINS JR CHARLES L	M G	0-0005306	0153	1
MULLINS MABEL L	MAJ	N-0001942	0558	1
MULLINS WALTER F	COL	0-0006944	1145	2
MULRONEY FRANK A	MAJ	0-0035833	0863	1
MULVANITY RALPH T	COL	0-0029674	0262	1
MULVANY LLOYD T	CW4	W-0903587	0661	1
MULVIHILL FRANCIS X	MAJ	0-0C14947	1041	1
MUMMA HARLAN L	B G	0-0004508	0448	1
MUMMA JCHN R	LTC	0-0046819	0463	1
MUMMEY RCBERT M	LTC	0-0026610	1064	1
MUNDORF WILLIAM C	LTC	0-0067731	1167	1
MUNDY REUBEN W	COL	0-0025063	0766	1
MUNDY ROY L	LTC	0-0069997	0166	1
MUNERA JR ANTCNIO V	LTC	0-0049872	1165	1
MUNFORD JR CHARLES A	MAJ	C-0050838	0462	2
MUNRO PERRY A	COL	0-0032090	0764	2
MUNROE DCNALD A	COL	0-0084050	1067	2
MUNSON ETHEL C	LTC	L-0000091	0366	1
MUNSON FREDERICK	B G	0-0016505	C756	1
MUNSON JACK W	LTC	0-0039349	1167	1
MUNSON MERTON E	COL	C-0C29519	0261	1

NAME	GRADE	SVC NO	DATE RET MO YR	RET CODE
MUNSON ORVILLE O	LTC	0-0081080	C264	1
MUNSON THOMAS V	LTC	0-0042654	1062	1
MUNSTER IRENE V	LTC	L-0000110	0863	1
MURCH GORDON E	COL	0-0031651	0864	1
MURCHISON JAMES L	COL	0-0018920	1062	1
MURCHISON RCARY A	COL	0-0017808	0855	1
MURPHEY HENRY S	M G	C-0019338	1265	2
MURPHEY JAMES A	COL	0-0011818	1053	2
MURPHY ALLEN M	COL	0-0028764	C354	1
MURPHY ARTHUR A	LTC	0-0027951	C967	1
MURPHY ARTHUR M	LTC	0-0024156	0262	1
MURPHY ARTHUR P	COL	0-0052226	C665	1
MURPHY BINFORD W	CW4	W-0901891	0760	1
MURPHY CLARENCE J	COL	C-0039647	C460	1
MURPHY CORNELIUS	COL	C-0023146	C766	1
MURPHY DANIEL J	COL	0-0019776	1055	1
MURPHY DANIEL N	CPT	0-0014248	0520	2
MURPHY DENNIS P	COL	0-0010038	1147	2
MURPHY EARL J	COL	C-0016421	0656	1
MURPHY ECWARD A	LTC	C-0004695	C442	2
MURPHY EDWARD E	COL	0-0041634	1158	1
MURPHY EDWARD R	LTC	C-0052847	C166	1
MURPHY EILEEN K	LTC	N-0000098	0962	1
MURPHY ERNEST V	COL	C-0031663	1067	2
MURPHY FRANCIS J	LTC	0-0062156	0964	1
MURPHY GEORGE E	COL	0-C031047	0466	1
MURPHY JACK R	LTC	0-0051431	0761	1
MURPHY JAMES E	CPT	C-0066185	1164	1
MURPHY JAMES H	COL	0-0080465	C165	1
MURPHY JOHN R	M G	0-0012338	0758	2
MURPHY JOHN D	LTC	C-0027789	C867	1
MURPHY JOHN G	COL	C-0007111	0153	1
MURPHY JOHN T	LTC	0-0036776	0764	1
MURPHY JOSEPH A	COL	0-0044667	C966	1
MURPHY JOSEPH F	CW4	W-0906921	0763	1
MURPHY JR EDWARD J	COL	0-0042061	0962	1
MURPHY JR WILLIAM E	COL	C-0029437	C760	1
MURPHY KATHRYN V	MAJ	N-0001025	1163	2
MURPHY LENORE L	MAJ	N-0002131	C360	1
MURPHY LESLIE C	COL	C-0031021	C864	1
MURPHY LUTHER W	LTC	0-0043979	0865	1
MURPHY MARGARET M	MAJ	N-0002137	0960	1
MURPHY PAUL E	CW4	W-090359C	C656	1
MURPHY PAUL W	LTC	0-0037437	1065	1
MURPHY PRESTON J	COL	C-005093C	0257	1
MURPHY ROBERT V	LTC	0-0014975	0341	2
MURPHY VINCENT P	LTC	0-0042872	1158	2
MURPHY WALLACE S	LTC	0-0063174	C966	1
MURPHY WILLIAM O	LTC	0-0020944	1159	1
MURPHY WILLIAM F	LTC	0-0031441	C165	2
MURPHY WILLIAM M	WO1	W-0901714	1041	1
MURRAY ARTHUR R	CW4	W-0902076	C460	1
MURRAY BILLIE L	LTC	L-0000084	C765	2
MURRAY CHARLES M	MAJ	C-0060680	C666	1
MURRAY CHARLES R	COL	0-0018792	0561	1
MURRAY CLARENCE F	COL	C-C009066	1145	2
MURRAY DOROTHY H	MAJ	N-0001294	0563	1
MURRAY DOUGLAS C	COL	C-0024899	C667	1
MURRAY GEORGE J	COL	0-0020619	C360	1
MURRAY GORDON C	LTC	C-0031644	C759	1
MURRAY HARRY M	COL	0-0030610	0663	1
MURRAY JOHN F T	COL	0-0023768	C165	1
MURRAY JOHN W	COL	C-0029833	C862	2
MURRAY JR RUSSEL	LTC	0-0039655	C160	1
MURRAY ROBERT M	LTC	0-0052094	C164	1
MURRAY ROY A	COL	0-0042366	0564	1
MURRAY WALTER H	COL	0-0038693	C661	1
MURRAY WILLIAM R	CW4	W-0903592	0664	1
MURREL JOHN H	2LT	0-0018215	0924	2
MURZYN LUCIEN A	CW4	W-0903593	C956	1
MUSCHEL LOUIS H	LTC	C-0049922	C262	1
MUSHAM HARRY A	MAJ	0-0003268	1022	1
MUSHEN ROBERT L	COL	C-0043508	0963	1
MUSICK LAWRENCE A	LTC	0-0031811	0164	1
MUSICK RUSSELL G	CW4	W-0903594	0161	1

NAME	GRADE	SVC NO	DATE RET MO YR	RET CODE
MUTH EDWIN A	COL	0-0030670	0166	2
MUTH MARY B	MAJ	L-0000C89	1162	1
MUTH RCY W	COL	0-0018180	0560	1
MUTTONI CONALD S	LTC	0-0081083	0866	1
MUZYK ALEXANCER	COL	0-0024C1C	0964	1
MUZZY CLAUDE A	CW3	W-0902375	0856	1
MYER FRANCIS R	COL	0-0007109	0551	1
MYERS ALBERT F	LTC	0-0035239	0863	1
MYERS CHARLES M	COL	C-0010783	0749	1
MYERS COLLIN S	COL	0-0008356	0854	1
MYERS DONALD S	LTC	0-0057972	0964	1
MYERS GEORGE E	COL	0-0051765	0566	1
MYERS HERBERT A	COL	0-0006131	0449	1
MYERS JAMES R	LTC	0-0022209	0865	1
MYERS JR FREDERICK	LTC	0-0054959	0364	1
MYERS JR SHELLY P	COL	0-0030157	0161	1
MYERS PAUL E	LTC	0-0050062	0964	1
MYERS SAMUEL L	LTG	0-0017180	0463	1
MYERS WILLIAM R	MAJ	0-0025513	0864	1
MYNDERSE JACCB F	COL	0-0023523	0963	1
MYRICK CHARLES M	COL	0-0029675	0559	1
NACHOD ELIZABETH	LTC	J-0000050	1167	1
NADAL RAMONA	COL	C-001728C	0758	1
NAGLE FREDRICK W	COL	C-0C20904	0967	1
NAGLE JCHN J	LTC	0-0041726	0659	1
NAHAS JACK N	COL	0-0039990	0864	1
NAIMARK MAX	COL	0-0C19303	0862	2
NALER JCHN L	LTC	0-0063736	0366	1
NALLE WILLIAM	COL	0-000341C	0147	2
NANCE JOHN R	COL	C-0020663	1046	2
NAPIER HERMAN S	LTC	0-0027636	0965	1
NAPPER FRANK E	COL	0-0036416	1062	1
NASELLI GEORGE E	COL	0-0029133	1157	1
NASH ALLAN B C	LTC	0-0041438	0854	1
NASH BERTRAM I	LTC	0-0040361	1057	1
NASH GROVER E	LTC	0-0036182	1064	1
NASH JAMES H	LTC	0-0026153	0567	2
NASH LEONARD C	LTC	0-0081085	0366	1
NATHAN CHARLES C	CPT	0-0C06802	0722	2
NATIONS EMMETT L	COL	0-0041592	0559	1
NAUGLE PAUL T	LTC	0-0041075	0763	1
NAUMAN ARTHUR C	COL	C-0030467	0764	1
NAVAS MANUEL B	COL	0-0C0404C	0650	1
NAWROCKY LCUIS M	LTC	0-0030293	1062	1
NAYLOR ROBERT H	COL	0-0016739	0757	2
NAZARIC LUIS F	CW3	W-0906924	1162	1
NEAGLI CHARLES J	CW4	W-0903599	0355	1
NEAL CARROLL W	MAJ	C-001391C	0120	2
NEAL FCREST L	LTC	0-0038577	0766	1
NEAL PAUL L	B G	0-0011684	0854	1
NEAL RALPH M	COL	0-0015359	0554	1
NEALE CLAUDE L	LTC	0-0017826	0343	2
NEALON JOHN J	LTC	C-0008186	0244	2
NEARHOOD MADELINE L	MAJ	N-0000856	0861	1
NEBEL CHARLES A	COL	0-004204C	0762	1
NEE WILLIAM F	LTC	0-0050933	1154	1
NEEDELS EDWARD V R	COL	0-0030537	1165	1
NEEL JCHN S	COL	0-0051493	0464	1
NEELY JR JAMES E	LTC	0-0040093	0465	1
NEELY RCBERT B	B G	0-0019114	0363	1
NEELY WILLIAM G	COL	0-0042538	1C59	1
NEELY WILLIAM W	LTC	0-0024332	0863	1
NEESEMAN ARTHUR C	LTC	0-0057816	0366	1
NEFF ORRIN D	LTC	0-0062189	1166	2
NEGRON RAFAEL	LTC	0-0034115	0464	1
NEGROTTO SIDNEY H	COL	0-0006711	0151	1
NEIER THOMAS C	COL	C-0020698	0867	1
NEIL JAMES R	COL	0-005753C	0265	2
NEILL HAROLD A	LTC	0-0026271	0665	1
NEILL SAMUEL S	COL	0-0051447	0163	1
NEILSCN ALEXANDER	COL	0-0009321	1049	1
NEILSON HENRY	COL	C-0015588	0864	1
NEILSCN JR RCBERT W	2LT	0-0026256	0544	2
NEIMAN JR ROBERT E	LTC	0-0037683	0564	1
NEIMAN WATSCN E	COL	0-0031072	0763	1

NAME	GRADE	SVC NO	DATE RET MO YR	RET CODE
NEIRBY GLADYS O	MAJ	N-0002649	0265	1
NELLI HUMBERT O	COL	O-0038586	1155	1
NELSON ANDRE H	MAJ	O-0044271	0461	1
NELSON ANDREW C	LTC	O-0038676	0150	1
NELSON ARCHIE	CW2	RW-0903601	0662	1
NELSON ARTHUR H	COL	O-0023093	0964	1
NELSON BARTIL H	CW2	RW-0904431	0564	1
NELSON CARLTON	LTC	O-0047373	0762	1
NELSON CARLTON W	COL	O-0043381	0165	1
NELSON CHRIS C	CW3	W-0904178	0852	1
NELSON CHRISTIAN	COL	O-0016910	0757	1
NELSON CLARENCE F	COL	O-0043073	0667	1
NELSON CLARENCE J	COL	O-0050942	0555	1
NELSON CURTIS O	LTC	O-0084403	0866	1
NELSON DONALD H	COL	O-0012396	0949	1
NELSON EDNA M	MAJ	N-0000604	0363	1
NELSON FLORENCE R	MAJ	N-0002173	0464	1
NELSON GUSTIN M	COL	O-0014612	0348	1
NELSON HAROLD E	COL	O-0024487	1066	1
NELSON HAROLD F M	COL	O-0029351	0759	1
NELSON HARRY J	COL	O-0020053	1045	1
NELSON HENRY H	LTC	O-0031916	0746	1
NELSON HERBERT L	COL	O-0030232	0759	1
NELSON JOHN G	COL	O-0020886	0967	1
NELSON JOSEPH W	LTC	O-0034692	0661	1
NELSON JR OTTO L	M G	O-0015713	0346	1
NELSON JR RAYMOND N	MAJ	O-0059802	0764	1
NELSON JR WILLIAM H	COL	O-0031992	0567	1
NELSON KENNETH R	MAJ	O-0020508	0243	2
NELSON KENT J	CPT	O-0011969	0839	2
NELSON KNUTE R	COL	O-0061220	1165	1
NELSON LLOYD S	LTC	O-0052325	0762	1
NELSON OLA A	COL	O-0011878	0854	1
NELSON PAUL B	COL	O-0016698	1056	1
NELSON POPE M	CW2	W-0902151	1047	1
NELSON RALPH T	M G	O-0017308	0752	1
NELSON RAYMOND C	LTC	O-0052775	0965	1
NELSON ROBERT C	LTC	O-0027124	0966	1
NELSON ROBERT S	COL	O-0020111	0655	1
NELSON RUSSELL M	COL	O-0018674	0862	1
NELSON WILNER N J	COL	O-0079632	0867	1
NEMEC GODFREY B	LTC	O-0028967	0256	1
NEMO RALPH	COL	O-0008362	0657	1
NEPRUD LEIF	LTC	O-0016257	0753	1
NESBITT ALLAN P	LTC	O-0052782	0967	1
NESBITT GEORGE F	CW3	W-0903603	0659	2
NESLAND MARION L	CPT	N-0000347	0448	1
NESMITH VARDELL E	COL	O-0039669	0459	1
NETHERTON THOMAS H	MAJ	O-0065552	0361	1
NETHERY DONALD M	LTC	O-0054988	1163	1
NETT JOSEPH F	LTC	O-0025804	0864	1
NETTLES JR WILLIAM R	LTC	O-0050044	0666	1
NEUBAUER WILLIAM C	COL	O-0035572	0757	1
NEUBERT JR BERNARD F	LTC	O-0049637	0563	1
NEUMANN ANNA S	MAJ	N-0002306	0467	2
NEUMANN JAMES C	COL	O-0035956	1067	1
NEUMANN RICHARD T	COL	O-0039054	0561	1
NEVE JACK C	COL	O-0040893	0267	1
NEVELS ELIZABETH	MAJ	N-0010087	1262	1
NEVILLE FRED T	COL	O-0007806	0145	1
NEVIN JOHN I	LTC	O-0063804	0666	1
NEVIN STANLEY M	COL	O-0016552	0251	1
NEVINS ARTHUR S	B G	O-0007110	0846	1
NEW JAMES H	LTC	O-0043435	0266	1
NEWCOMB FIDELIS O	LTC	O-0022056	0959	1
NEWCOMB RALPH E	COL	O-0038727	1162	1
NEWCOMB RICHARD T	LTC	O-0042844	0864	1
NEWCOMER FRANCIS K	COL	O-0021898	0767	1
NEWELL CHARLES H	LTC	O-0028835	0154	1
NEWELL JOSEPH C	LTC	O-0084877	0467	1
NEWELL OLIN C	COL	O-0007507	0748	1
NEWELL ROBERT L	LTC	O-0035145	0965	1
NEWGARDEN GEORGE J	COL	O-0004500	0546	2
NEWHALL HENRY S	COL	O-0029717	0662	2
NEWMAN AUBREY S	M G	O-0016099	0360	1

NAME	GRADE	SVC NO	DATE RET MO YR	RET CODE
NEWMAN ERMAN M	COL	O-0030173	0564	1
NEWMAN GLENN	COL	O-0015902	0947	2
NEWMAN HAROLD H	COL	O-0038716	0862	1
NEWMAN JOHN T	COL	O-0024281	0366	1
NEWMAN JR FOREST P	LTC	O-0080313	0766	1
NEWMAN MARY F	MAJ	N-0000975	0263	1
NEWMAN OLIVER P	M G	O-0015016	0658	2
NEWMAN STANLEY	LTC	O-0062965	0866	2
NEWMAN WILLIAM J	COL	O-0051835	0865	1
NEWSOM JR MARION F	LTC	O-0043378	1163	1
NEWTON CARROLL T	COL	O-0020865	1163	1
NEWTON EDITH	MAJ	M-0010111	0766	1
NEWTON GEORGE D	LTC	O-0018286	0149	1
NEWTON JR CARLOS F	LTC	O-0061082	0263	1
NEWTON KENNETH F	LTC	O-0042875	0961	1
NEWTON LUCILE	MAJ	N-0000134	0561	1
NEWTON THOMAS J	COL	O-0042563	0565	1
NIBLACK EMMETT A	CPT	O-0011941	0138	2
NICCOLLS ROBERT S	LTC	O-0032317	0361	1
NICELY EDWARD L	LTC	O-0053251	0665	1
NICELY REBECCA M	2LT	M-0002162	1045	1
NICEWANDER DENNIS R	LTC	O-0071580	0867	1
NICHOL BYRON A	COL	O-0022286	0861	2
NICHOL ISAAC J	COL	O-0002692	0743	1
NICHOL WILLIAM W	COL	O-0018939	0662	2
NICHOLAS CHARLES P	COL	O-0016080	1067	1
NICHOLAS JACK V	COL	O-0051363	0761	1
NICHOLAS JEROME C	CW2	W-0902043	0144	2
NICHOLLS ANDREW B C	LTC	O-0031957	0866	1
NICHOLLS RUSSELL E	LTC	O-0019844	1143	2
NICHOLS CHRISTOPHE	CW4	W-0906930	0566	1
NICHOLS EARL R	COL	O-0030857	0565	1
NICHOLS GEORGE F	COL	O-0011875	0944	2
NICHOLS GEORGE W	LTC	O-0054033	0863	1
NICHOLS GLEN L	LTC	O-0058986	0962	1
NICHOLS HAROLD F	B G	O-0003076	0747	1
NICHOLS JAMES B	COL	O-0019693	0163	1
NICHOLS JOSEPH A	COL	O-0009699	0650	1
NICHOLS KENNETH O	M G	O-0017497	1053	1
NICHOLS MARK E	CW4	W-0906929	1165	1
NICHOLS MAURICE H	MAJ	O-0037532	0664	1
NICHOLS STEPHEN L	COL	O-0028844	0260	1
NICHOLS WALLACE J	COL	O-0030003	0161	1
NICK JAMES T	LTC	O-0082070	0866	1
NICKEL JOHN R	COL	O-0025553	0966	1
NICOL DAVID J	LTC	O-0038480	0167	1
NICOLARY CARL W	LTC	O-0031226	0164	1
NICOLSON WILLIAM H	LTC	O-0030804	0762	1
NIEDERFRUEM WILLIAM	COL	O-0007893	0248	1
NIEDZIELA EDWARD	CW4	W-0903612	0465	1
NIELSEN CARL H	LTC	O-0081091	0663	1
NIELSEN SVEND H	COL	O-0039753	0162	1
NIELSEN WILLARD L	COL	O-0021051	1166	1
NIEMI ARVO N	COL	O-0029753	0862	1
NIGHTINGALE GARDNER	LTC	O-0081093	0265	1
NIGRO GEORGE A	MAJ	O-0059270	0465	2
NILES ELLERY W	COL	O-0019763	0764	1
NILES EVELYN J	MAJ	N-0001656	0166	1
NILES GIBSON	COL	O-0023938	1065	2
NILES RICHARD H	MAJ	O-0035853	0663	1
NILES WALLACE E	COL	O-0014665	0949	2
NILON NILS J S	CW3	W-0903614	0664	2
NILSSON ERWIN G	COL	O-0031593	0764	1
NISHIMURA BERT N	COL	O-0081094	1166	1
NIST CECIL W	COL	O-0015274	0454	1
NIX ASBURY L	CW4	W-0903616	0762	1
NIXDORFF JAMES B	LTC	O-0040867	0862	1
NIXON JOSEPH J	CW4	W-0902144	0255	1
NIXON PAUL	COL	O-0017912	0846	2
NIXON ROBERT T	LTC	O-0026563	0864	1
NIXON THOMAS H	COL	O-0009326	0854	2
NIXON VICTOR M	LTC	O-0047617	0767	1
NOAKE DONALD W	COL	O-0020357	0864	1
NOBLE CHARLES L	COL	O-0012383	0649	1
NOBLE DORA A	LTC	N-0000025	0349	1

NAME	GRADE	SVC NO	DATE RET MO YR	RET CODE
NOBLE JR JOSEPH F	COL	O-0031973	0966	1
NOBLE WILLIAM E	MAJ	O-0063363	1159	1
NOBLES LAWRENCE E	COL	O-0029045	1058	1
NOCE DANIEL	LTG	O-0005226	1054	2
NOEL EDGAR A	LTC	O-0051570	1262	1
NOEL JR JOHN C	LTC	O-0031404	0462	1
NOID WILLIAM C	LTC	O-0038247	1066	1
NOLAN JAMES L	COL	O-0038689	0561	1
NOLAN WILLIAM	CW2	W-0904177	0463	2
NOLAND MARION B	LTC	O-0043603	0364	1
NOLD JAMES M	1LT	O-0062626	0753	2
NOLTE MARVIN C O	LTC	O-0036763	0267	1
NOONCASTER CLIFTON F	COL	O-0030061	1163	1
NORBY ALLEN R	MAJ	O-0065696	0962	1
NORBY THOMAS	LTC	O-0051548	0961	1
NOREEN ALBERT T	LTC	O-0060438	0464	2
NORELL JAMES A	B G	O-0039838	0763	1
NOREM ALBERT F	CW2	W-0902017	0349	1
NOREM LEROY K	LTC	O-0084749	0267	1
NORLING RALPH L	LTC	O-0032112	0266	1
NORMAN BROOKS O	COL	O-0035793	1065	1
NORMAN DANIEL P	COL	O-0015467	0954	1
NORMAN ERNEST C	COL	O-0012124	0854	1
NORMAN GEORGE B	CPT	O-0026784	0747	2
NORMAN JR FRANK P	COL	O-0020383	1047	2
NORMAN LEWIS S	COL	O-0010111	0749	1
NORMAN RANDOLPH G	COL	O-0039515	0655	1
NORMAND JOSEPH P E	CW4	W-0903625	0355	1
NORMINGTON JOSEPH M	LTC	O-0041157	0763	1
NORRIS BENJAMIN	COL	O-0004084	0945	2
NORRIS CLOVIS B	LTC	O-0051861	0162	1
NORRIS DON R	COL	O-0006500	0545	2
NORRIS JACK K	COL	O-0021865	0766	1
NORRIS LEON E	COL	O-0005633	0746	1
NORRIS NEO T	COL	O-0020222	0866	1
NORRIS WILLIAM H	LTC	O-0027295	0763	1
NORTH HARRIS J	COL	O-0052158	0766	1
NORTH THOMAS	B G	O-0011879	0553	1
NORTH WILLARD L	CW4	W-0903627	0861	1
NORTH WILLIAM O	COL	O-0017345	0948	2
NORTHAM WILLIAM F	COL	O-0019547	0864	1
NORTHCROSS WM H P	COL	O-0028793	0255	1
NORTHCUTT THADEUS P	LTC	O-0040677	0863	1
NORTHEN JR ERNEST E	LTC	O-0029297	1161	1
NORTHROP EDWARD C	COL	O-0040282	0762	1
NORTNER SYLVESTER	COL	O-0005595	0451	1
NORTON ANDERSON H	LTC	O-0008426	0934	2
NORTON AUGUSTUS	COL	O-0002668	0922	2
NORTON RICHARD A	COL	O-0041984	0462	1
NORTON ROBERT W	CPT	O-0005771	1122	2
NORVELL FRANK C	B G	O-0019471	0864	1
NORVELL JAMES E	COL	O-0020706	0967	1
NORWOOD JAMES L	LTC	O-0044048	1059	1
NORWOOD JR LEONARD L	LTC	O-0058990	1165	1
NORWOOD WAYNE O	LTC	O-0060693	0667	1
NOSECK KENNETH A	LTC	O-0045645	0866	1
NOSEK THADDEUS M	COL	O-0022934	0464	1
NOSSAMAN WARREN E	LTC	O-0025079	0466	1
NOTBOHM WILLIAM R	LTC	O-0060643	1064	1
NOTTINGHAM JONATHAN	LTC	O-0030482	0863	1
NOURSE ROBERT S	COL	O-0016484	0656	1
NOVICK JEHIEL	LTC	O-0061993	1265	1
NOWE CHARLES F	COL	O-0031460	0467	1
NOYES EDWARD P	COL	O-0002674	0745	2
NOYES MELVILLE F	COL	O-0039555	0657	1
NUGENT MARCUS Y	CW2	W-0903628	0253	1
NUMAINVILLE LEON J	COL	O-0021002	0862	1
NUNN DEWITT A	1LT	O-0027087	0748	2
NUNN JR CLIFFORD E	LTC	O-0060465	0767	1
NUSS RUDOLPH W	COL	O-0028981	0558	1
NUSSBAUM CHARLES W	COL	O-0051281	0262	1
NUTT JAMES C	COL	O-0030164	0464	1
NUTT JOHN W	CPT	O-0076474	0262	2
NUTTER WILLIAM H	M G	O-0016095	0462	1
NUTTMAN LOUIS M	B G	O-0000484	0138	1

NAME	GRADE	SVC NO	DATE RET MO YR	RET CODE
NYBERG ALMA M	MAJ	N-0001552	0564	1
NYE DAVID B	COL	O-0020695	0564	1
NYE ELWOOD L	COL	O-0009444	0146	2
NYE III CHARLES A	COL	O-0085058	0367	1
NYE WILBUR S	COL	O-0012797	0854	1
NYEZ WALBURGA G	MAJ	N-0001236	1064	1
NYFELER JR GEORGE L	MAJ	O-0096785	0567	2
NYGAARD JOHN R	LTC	O-0005331	0627	2
NYGARD WALTER E	LTC	O-0025665	0964	1
NYLEN ARTHUR H	COL	O-0006414	0250	1
NYPAVER MARY F	MAJ	N-0000576	0961	1
OAKES CURTISS W	LTC	O-0051471	1061	1
OAKES JOHN C	LTG	O-0017160	0163	2
OAKLEY SAMUEL H	LTC	O-0043841	0764	1
OARTEL JOHN S	COL	O-0057039	0261	1
OATES JR EUGENE C	COL	O-0044576	0864	1
OATMAN JR CLYDE O	COL	O-0020964	0962	1
OBERG CLARA R	MAJ	N-0002024	0360	1
OBERMEYER CHARLES R	LTC	O-0044755	0862	1
OBERST DONALD A	LTC	O-0031451	0759	1
OBOLER MAX	COL	O-0051287	0162	1
OBRADOVICH FRANCIS S	LTC	O-0063055	0767	1
OBRIEN DANIEL H	CW4	W-0903631	0660	1
OBRIEN EDMUND R	COL	O-0040032	0766	1
OBRIEN ELMER J	CW4	W-0906936	0466	1
OBRIEN JAMES V	LTC	O-0038230	0964	1
OBRIEN JOHN G	B G	O-0042171	0463	1
OBRIEN JR ROBERT E	COL	O-0020313	1163	1
OBRIEN THEO W	COL	O-0006665	0346	2
OBYRNE JOHN C	COL	O-0052910	0766	1
OCHOA LOIS W	LTC	L-0000063	1262	1
OCHS WILLIAM V	COL	O-0006592	0547	1
OCONNELL AUGUSTUS R	COL	O-0005527	0752	1
OCONNELL EDWARD M	COL	O-0019563	0258	1
OCONNELL FRANCIS J	LTC	O-0030667	0364	1
OCONNELL GEOFFREY M	COL	O-0009685	0447	2
OCONNELL JAMES O	LTG	O-0014965	0459	1
OCONNELL JOHN	LTC	O-0042422	1262	2
OCONNELL JOHN D	MAJ	O-0012546	0836	1
OCONNELL THOMAS C	MAJ	O-0023994	0660	1
OCONNOR DANIEL A	M G	O-0029454	0664	1
OCONNOR EDWARD F	LTC	O-0083585	0966	1
OCONNOR EDWIN	COL	O-0003170	0747	2
OCONNOR HERBERT J	COL	O-0051654	0965	1
OCONNOR JOHN F	CW3	W-0903635	1154	1
OCONNOR JOHN J	COL	O-0052160	0864	1
OCONNOR JR EDWIN	COL	O-0023539	1064	1
OCONNOR ROBERT J	COL	O-0041888	0661	1
OCONNOR THOMAS J	COL	O-0019125	0356	1
OCONNOR WALTER R	LTC	O-0051740	0364	1
OCONNOR WILLIAM W	B G	O-0016348	0656	1
ODAIR GEORGE W	CW4	W-0902376	0560	1
ODANIEL JOHN W	LTG	O-0007342	0256	1
ODAY RAY M	COL	O-0004918	0753	1
ODBERT LUCILE G	LTC	L-0000068	0363	1
ODEEN CARL H	COL	O-0008020	0846	2
ODELL DOROTHY J	MAJ	N-0000131	0461	2
ODELL JOSEPH C	B G	O-0012439	0854	1
ODENWELLER CHARLES J	LTC	O-0018135	0558	1
ODIAM CARL E	CW2	W-0902335	0948	1
ODLE SADIEBELLE	MAJ	N-0002394	0562	1
ODOM ALTON C	LTC	O-0081101	0567	1
ODOM CLEVE C	COL	O-0008679	0647	2
ODOM HERBERT R	LTC	O-0022086	0667	1
ODOM LOUIE W	LTC	O-0065231	1067	1
ODONNELL CHARLES M	COL	O-0029010	0357	1
ODONNELL JOHN W	COL	O-0019686	0447	2
ODONNELL ROBERT F	COL	O-0023228	0461	1
ODONNELL ROBERT J	COL	O-0051786	0666	2
ODOR RAYMOND W	COL	O-0012228	0647	2
ODWYER MAUREEN P	MAJ	N-0000425	0361	1
OELHAFEN WAYNE R	LTC	O-0037631	0664	1
OETTINGER VERNON S	LTC	O-0031262	1162	1
OFARRELL HUGH R	COL	O-0043888	0766	1
OFFLEY EDWARD M	COL	O-0001398	0-37	2

NAME	GRADE	SVC NO	DATE RET MO YR	RET CODE
OFFLEY ROBERT H	COL	0-0011205	0948	1
OFFUTT ANDREW C	MAJ	0-0025143	0449	2
OFFUTT HARRY D	B G	0-0003759	0351	1
OFFUTT RICHARD L	LTC	0-0040140	1167	1
OGDEN CHARLES L	LTC	0-0030689	0464	1
OGDEN CHARLES W	CPT	0-0006612	0928	2
OGDEN DAVID A D	LTG	0-0012051	1057	1
OGDEN LILY M	MAJ	N-0000173	0562	1
OGDEN MILTON L	B G	0-0018687	0762	1
OGG LESTER C	COL	0-0003911	0750	1
OGILVIE JR JOHN M	COL	0-0030773	0764	1
OGILVIE KENNETH W	CW2	W-0901761	0347	1
OGLE JOSEPH A	LTC	0-0024500	0661	1
OGLE MERLE W	COL	0-0022261	0164	1
OGLESBY GEORGE R	COL	0-0019877	0555	1
OGLETREE JAMES D	COL	0-0029492	0758	1
OGRADY GEORGE L	COL	0-0029282	0963	1
OGREN OSCAR J	B G	0-0020037	0866	1
OHANLON JOSEPH P	LTC	0-0027257	0965	1
OHARA JAMES	COL	0-0019593	0862	1
OHARA LEWIS B	LTC	0-0031887	0761	1
OHEA JOHN T	LTC	0-0035486	0163	1
OHERN ROBERT S	LTC	0-0079659	1162	1
OHLSSON LENNART Y	LTC	0-0030211	0762	1
OKEEFE ARTHUR J	CPT	0-0014241	0420	2
OKEEFE KEITH T	COL	0-0030669	0865	1
OLDAKER MARION J	CW4	W-0902682	0961	1
OLDFIELD HOMER R	M G	0-0002589	1046	1
OLEARY JOHN J	CW4	W-0904180	1265	1
OLHAUSEN JAMES N	COL	0-0040084	0267	1
OLIGHER HOWARD L	LTC	0-0080157	0866	1
OLIN CHARLES L	COL	0-0018190	0760	1
OLIVARES JOSE E	COL	0-0015377	0753	1
OLIVER EDWARD J	COL	0-0003238	1143	1
OLIVER GEORGE L	COL	0-0033118	1266	1
OLIVER JOHN E	COL	0-0039700	0159	2
OLIVER JR THAD S	LTC	0-0032553	0866	1
OLIVER LUNSFORD E	M G	0-0003536	0548	1
OLIVER RICHARD H	COL	0-0043586	1166	1
OLLEY CORNELIUS	CW4	W-0901829	0962	1
OLMSTEAD LOREN W	COL	0-0039721	0561	1
OLSEN HAROLD O	LTC	0-0031726	1265	1
OLSEN JR EDMUND S	COL	0-0031071	1163	1
OLSON CLARENCE O	LTC	0-0030734	1163	2
OLSON HARDIN L	COL	0-0019110	1159	2
OLSON HARRY C	COL	0-0031399	0167	1
OLSON HARRY H	LTC	0-0081108	0866	1
OLSON JOHN E	COL	0-0022125	0867	1
OLSSEN MARY J	MAJ	N-0001847	1067	1
OLSZOWY FRANCES F	MAJ	N-0001061	0264	1
OMALLEY JOHN F	LTC	0-0046050	0763	1
OMANS JOHN P	MAJ	0-0024771	0147	2
OMEARA ANDREW P	GEN	0-0018062	0667	2
OMEARA EDWIN F	CW2	W-0800369	0545	2
OMOHUNDRO WILEY H	COL	0-0008545	0854	1
ONDRICK JOHN G	B G	0-0018804	0862	1
ONEAL HARLLEE R	LTC	0-0042163	0459	2
ONEAL JR WILLIAM R	LTC	0-0019971	0863	1
ONEIL LARRY J	COL	0-0038761	0758	1
ONEIL PAUL F	COL	0-0022902	0267	1
ONEIL THOMAS A	COL	0-0019583	0864	1
ONEILL EDWARD J	LTG	0-0015952	0462	2
ONEILL GEORGE P	COL	0-0015773	0555	2
ONEILL HAROLD R	CW3	RW-0903640	1066	1
ONEILL JAMES H	B G	0-0016370	0152	1
ONEILL JOHN T	COL	0-0030166	0461	1
ONEILL RICHARD J	COL	0-0033536	0967	1
OOMS HENRICUS L	CW4	W-0902263	0753	1
OPELLO JUNE O	MAJ	N-0002113	0666	1
OPLE RICHARD E	COL	0-0011972	0846	2
OPPENHEIMER HUGH C	LTC	0-0027568	0765	1
OPPENHIMER JOHN S	LTC	0-0036490	0766	1
OPPY GLENN C	CPT	0-0006445	1028	1
OPSAHL HAROLD E	COL	0-0061057	1162	2
ORANGE ARTHUR J	LTC	0-0051986	0459	1

NAME	GRADE	SVC NO	DATE RET MO YR	RET CODE
ORCUTT JOHN W	COL	0-0008520	0249	1
ORD JOHN A	COL	0-0031532	0865	1
OREAR JOHN T H	COL	0-0002890	1045	2
OREILLY AUBREY J	LTC	0-0020537	1155	1
OREILLY GEORGE T	COL	0-0040120	0664	1
OREL BURNIS	CW3	W-0906939	0261	1
ORFALEA GEORGE A	MAJ	0-0060455	0962	1
ORMES MELVIN W	COL	0-0030549	1265	1
ORMISTON EDWARD J	COL	0-0029015	1057	1
ORMSTON MERCEDES M	MAJ	L-0000108	1264	1
ORDARK CULANEY L	COL	0-0029586	0863	1
ORDUARK GERALD A	COL	0-0012130	0228	2
OROURKE DONALD C	LTC	0-0036611	1166	1
OROURKE FRANKLYN S	MAJ	0-0084243	0865	2
OROURKE PETER J	LTC	0-0038923	1163	1
ORPHAN RICHARD C	LTC	0-0026039	0863	1
ORR RAYMOND	COL	0-0006691	1147	2
ORR URIAH N	LTC	0-0053877	0263	1
ORRINGER WILLIAM O	COL	0-0023343	0966	1
ORSINGER GUNTHER	LTC	0-0014264	0620	2
ORSINGER REMINGTON	COL	0-0006625	0651	1
ORSINI CLARA E	LTC	N-0002424	0867	1
ORTH GOTTLIEB L	COL	0-0020509	0859	1
ORTH JR EUGENE C	COL	0-0019863	0464	1
ORTH JR RAYMOND E	CPT	0-0028422	0652	1
ORTH RICHARD H	COL	0-0029308	0464	1
ORTON EUGENE M	COL	0-0051844	0367	1
ORTON RAYMOND L	LTC	0-0042306	0162	1
ORTON WILLIAM R	COL	0-0003724	0545	2
OSBORNE ERIC R	COL	0-0042299	1063	1
OSBORNE HAROLD C	COL	0-0028866	0556	1
OSBORNE HUGH P	COL	0-0030151	0464	1
OSBORNE NAOMI I	MAJ	N-0001225	1063	1
OSBORNE RALPH M	M G	0-0016399	1162	1
OSBORNE THEODORE M	B G	0-0015132	1047	1
OSBORNE VINCENT E	LTC	0-0033035	1062	1
OSBORNE WILLIAM L	COL	0-0032154	0166	1
OSETH INGOMAR M	COL	0-0007861	0646	2
OSHEROFF HYMAN R	COL	0-0021015	0755	1
OSMANSKI FRANK A	M G	0-0019745	0366	1
OSTENBERG FRANK T	COL	0-0016863	0757	1
OSTERHAUS LEO B	LTC	0-0084326	0964	1
OSTHUES HENRY E	LTC	0-0052512	0562	1
OSTNER CHARLES F	LTC	0-0024271	0661	1
OSTRANDER FORREST R	COL	0-0009165	0149	2
OSTROM CHARLES O	B G	0-0004641	0450	1
OSTROM HERBERT N	COL	0-0043614	0164	1
OSWALD DONALD C	LTC	0-0069762	1166	1
OSWALD EDWARD H	COL	0-0043330	1263	1
OSWALD MARIE A	MAJ	N-0002047	0160	1
OSWALD PAUL F	COL	0-0020160	1165	1
OSWALT JOHN W	COL	0-0046071	0763	1
OTT [illegible] R W	COL	0-0018338	1145	2
OTT EDWARD R	COL	[illegible]0050935	0257	1
OTT EDWARD S	B G	0-0007132	0247	2
OTT HAROLD G	COL	0-0016977	1057	1
OTTERBOURG CHARLES R	LTC	0-0080158	0763	2
OTTO CHARLES B	LTC	0-0088169	0667	1
OTTO SAMUEL E	COL	0-0019030	0863	1
OTTZENN HANS	COL	0-0006032	0946	2
OUTLAND ARLEY L	LTC	0-0044400	0661	1
OUTLAND GEORGE W	COL	0-0007035	0552	1
OUTSEN ROBERT	COL	0-0029595	0861	1
OUTWATER MURIEL	MAJ	L-0000307	0762	1
OVENSHINE ENGLEBERT	COL	0-0000627	0928	1
OVENSHINE RICHARD P	B G	0-0012303	0854	1
OVERALL III JESSE U	LTC	0-0046630	0966	1
OVERBY CARL F	COL	0-0030437	0665	1
OVERFELT CLIFFORD O	COL	0-0010227	0646	2
OVERSTREET SAMUEL	LTC	0-0041703	0357	2
OVERTON DANIEL	LTC	0-0027026	0566	1
OWEN GLENN B	COL	0-0032725	0864	1
OWEN JR HENRY M	LTC	0-0032083	0162	1
OWEN LOUELIA	MAJ	N-0002229	0559	1
OWEN THOMAS S	LTC	0-0028544	0766	1

NAME	GRADE	SVC NO	DATE RET MO YR	RET CODE
OWEN WILEY H	CW4	W-0903648	0561	2
OWEN WILLIAM V	COL	0-0041526	0658	1
OWENS ALEXANDER	B G	0-0006429	0246	2
OWENS CHARLES H	COL	0-0006957	0753	1
OWENS FREDERICK	COL	0-0043087	0661	1
OWENS GEORGE R	COL	0-0005856	0148	1
OWENS HARRY E	COL	0-0028786	1054	1
OWENS JOHN L	COL	0-0017035	1057	1
OXRIEDER RAYMOND B	COL	0-0016042	0755	1
OYSTER OALTES J	COL	0-0015456	0854	1
PACE BRICE	COL	0-0033035	0859	1
PACE GEORGE A	COL	0-0030552	0561	1
PACE GEORGE D	COL	0-0031531	0864	2
PACE GUY L	COL	0-0028826	1055	1
PACE HERBERT E	COL	0-0003016	0143	2
PACE LUCYLE M	MAJ	N-0001905	0162	1
PACE MARIE L	MAJ	N-0000066	1048	1
PACEY WILLIAM A	LTC	0-0031323	0966	1
PACHLER FRANCIS T	M G	0-0018488	0667	2
PACHOMSKI JOHN	LTC	0-0040252	0566	1
PACIOREK STANLEY J	MAJ	0-0033285	0863	1
PACIULLI ORLO C	LTC	0-0017427	0545	2
PACK CHARLES M	COL	0-0020378	0864	1
PACK DALLAS B	COL	0-0051517	0762	1
PACKARD FLORENCE M	MAJ	L-0000239	0461	1
PADDOCK JOHN W	COL	0-0020913	0867	1
PADDOCK JR RALPH L	LTC	0-0030740	1163	1
PADDOCK ROBERT E	CW3	W-0903649	0462	1
PADEN PAUL A	COL	0-0020981	0763	1
PADGETT JERRY E	LTC	0-0081117	0567	1
PADLEY HARRY E	LTC	0-0070464	0966	1
PAETZOLD ALMA M	MAJ	N-0000886	0763	1
PAGANO GERALD	CW4	W-0903651	0365	1
PAGANO PHILOMENA	LTC	N-0000354	1163	2
PAGE BENJAMIN N	COL	0-0032530	0966	1
PAGE DOUGLAS J	COL	0-0004495	0352	1
PAGE GORDON B	COL	0-0040046	0266	1
PAGE HENRY M	LTC	0-0042744	1263	1
PAGE JOHN W	COL	0-0040247	0760	1
PAGE JR CECIL W	LTC	0-0025723	0866	1
PAGE JR REGINALD	COL	0-0020149	0766	1
PAGE JR ROBERT W	COL	0-0022120	0267	1
PAGE JR ROGER M	LTC	0-0029430	0758	1
PAGE SIDNEY C	COL	0-0011718	0847	2
PAGE THOMAS N	COL	0-0018300	1058	1
PAHL GAYLORD G	LTC	0-0081119	0966	1
PAICH JACK J	CW4	W-0903652	0859	1
PAIGE RALPH E	COL	0-0031023	1055	2
PAINTER GEORGE E	LTC	0-0056813	1161	1
PAINTER MAURICE	LTC	0-0083613	1267	1
PAINTER VERE	COL	0-0008389	0146	1
PALIK THEODORE J	LTC	0-0043611	1064	1
PALIZZA MAURICE J	LTC	0-0033924	1061	1
PALM EUGENE W	MAJ	0-0035643	0763	1
PALMER CALLIE H	COL	0-0007235	1146	2
PALMER CHARLES D	GEN	0-0015519	0262	1
PALMER EDDY D	COL	0-0043224	0765	1
PALMER EDWIN S	COL	0-0030806	0864	1
PALMER EUGENE P	MAJ	0-0024245	0446	2
PALMER GEORGE W	COL	0-0015593	0754	1
PALMER GLENN H	COL	0-0015118	0854	1
PALMER HUGH A	1LT	0-0012086	0621	2
PALMER JAMES M	LTC	0-0004877	1022	2
PALMER JOHN M	COL	0-0042058	0862	1
PALMER JOHN R	LTC	0-0042758	0464	1
PALMER JR HARVEY K	LTC	0-0015311	0753	1
PALMER LESLIE F	LTC	0-0043531	0164	1
PALMER PAUL W	LTC	0-0060097	0966	1
PALMER RAYMOND O	COL	0-0015942	0854	1
PALMER ROBERT S	COL	0-0020611	0867	1
PALMER WILLISTON	GEN	0-0012246	1059	2
PALSROK JOHN	COL	0-0043722	1064	1
PAMPLIN DOUGLAS G	COL	0-0015192	0753	1
PANGBURN ELMER D	LTC	0-0010420	0142	1
PANISNICK GEORGE G	LTC	0-0089455	0367	1

NAME	GRADE	SVC NO	DATE RET MO YR	RET CODE
PANKER DOROTHY F	MAJ	N-0001997	1166	1
PAPA ANTHONY E	COL	0-0052294	0666	1
PAPE ROBIN B	B G	0-0015547	0654	1
PAPENFOTH WILLIAM H	COL	0-0011305	1047	2
PAPI EUGENE J	CW4	W-0901605	0556	2
PAPPAS CHRISTOPHE	COL	0-0051724	0366	1
PAPPAS JAMES P	COL	0-0021017	0564	1
PARASKA NICHOLAS	COL	0-0021765	0860	1
PARDUE THOMAS W	LTC	0-0028576	0966	1
PARHAM ALFRED H	LTC	0-0017304	0643	2
PARIS EDWARD J	LTC	0-0082073	0767	1
PARK EDNA K	LTC	N-0001945	0460	1
PARK HERMAN C	COL	0-0033163	0766	1
PARK JR RICHARD	COL	0-0019080	0863	2
PARK RICHARD	COL	0-0002211	1143	1
PARK ROY C S	WO1	W-0901012	1032	2
PARKER BEATRICE A	MAJ	L-0000247	0463	1
PARKER BENJAMIN M	CW4	W-0903655	0165	1
PARKER DANIEL	COL	0-0019038	0762	1
PARKER DORIS L	LTC	R-0010018	0766	1
PARKER EDNA M	LTC	N-0000271	0365	1
PARKER EDWARD M	COL	0-0018349	1146	2
PARKER EDWIN P	M G	0-0003457	0153	1
PARKER ELLIOTT G	LTC	0-0037540	0559	1
PARKER GILBERT E	COL	0-0007108	0749	1
PARKER HARRY F	COL	0-0084565	1264	1
PARKER HENRY B	COL	0-0004694	0146	2
PARKER JOHN C	COL	0-0031778	1164	1
PARKER JOHN F	LTC	0-0065015	1167	1
PARKER JOHN M	COL	0-0039018	0465	1
PARKER JOHN R	COL	0-0019735	0556	1
PARKER JOSEPH P	LTC	0-0040487	0660	1
PARKER JR GEORGE M	M G	0-0002783	0946	2
PARKER PAUL C	CW4	W-0906941	0661	1
PARKER R L	COL	0-0031057	1162	2
PARKER REUBEN O	LTC	0-0047214	0866	1
PARKER RICHARD B	CW4	W-0902390	0864	2
PARKER RICHARD C	LTC	0-0018230	0754	1
PARKER ROBERT J	CW4	W-0903657	0256	1
PARKER ROY H	M G	0-0012565	0552	1
PARKER WILL V	COL	0-0009170	1044	2
PARKIN CHARLES M	COL	0-0005206	0350	1
PARKIN JR CHARLES M	LTC	0-0024150	0761	1
PARKINS JAMES F	LTC	0-0036855	1157	2
PARKISON PETER A	CW4	W-0901681	0555	1
PARKMAN JR T G	1LT	0-0063860	0859	2
PARKS HENRY C	CW4	RW-0903658	0963	1
PARKS JEAN L	MAJ	N-0000377	0461	1
PARKS LEONARD F	LTC	0-0041207	1266	1
PARKS REBECCA S	LTC	L-0000008	1156	1
PARMELEE ARCHIBALD	COL	0-0009734	0153	1
PARMELEE CLYDE D	COL	0-0007831	1045	2
PARNELLE JR SAMUEL W	COL	0-0029501	0161	1
PARR CLIFFORD E	LTC	0-0051605	0463	1
PARR JR IVAN W	COL	0-0019255	0962	1
PARR MARVIN M	LTC	0-0053681	0963	1
PARR WAYLAND H	COL	0-0017565	0358	1
PARRISH ALICE A	LTC	L-0000016	0657	1
PARRISH CHARLES P	LTC	0-0053233	1163	1
PARRY ROBERT C	COL	0-0039508	0459	1
PARSEL JANE F	MAJ	L-0000067	0259	1
PARSELL SIDNEY I	COL	0-0028937	1157	1
PARSONS ARTHUR M	COL	0-0012344	0854	1
PARSONS HAROLD C	COL	0-0029816	1162	1
PARSONS JR GEORGE E	LTC	0-0036095	0662	1
PARSONS JR WALTER H	COL	0-0039782	0862	1
PARSONS NORMAN W	LTC	0-0030793	0762	1
PARSONS OTHAL T	LTC	0-0080162	0467	1
PARSONS RUFUS A	COL	0-0010077	0147	1
PARSONS WILLIAM J	COL	0-0040228	0265	1
PARTHUM JR ALFRED H	LTC	0-0035939	0767	1
PARTIN CALVIN L	COL	0-0017636	0759	1
PARTIN EVERETT W	COL	0-0019699	1059	1
PARTLOW FRANK A	COL	0-0031099	0163	1
PARTLOW LEO L	CPT	0-0009045	1034	1

NAME	GRADE	SVC NO	DATE RET MO YR	RET CODE
PARTRIDGE ALAN L	LTC	C-0026770	0763	1
PARTRIDGE CLARENCE E	COL	C-0002586	C846	1
PARTRIDGE DWIGHT	CPT	0-000630C	0722	2
PARTRIDGE FRANK H	M G	0-0007497	1053	1
PARTRIDGE RICHARD C	M G	0-0012630	0259	1
PARTRIDGE ROBERT B	COL	0-0020204	0465	1
PARTRIDGE STANLEY N	COL	C-0011622	0449	1
PASCAL ANDRE R	MAJ	C-0038573	C862	1
PASCHAL WALTER H	CPT	0-0017376	1138	2
PASCHALL WILLIAM C	COL	0-0015400	0654	1
PASCIAK LEONARD J	COL	0-0024765	C965	1
PASHLEY WALTER A	COL	0-0004796	0647	2
PASOLLI JR EMIL	COL	C-0028777	C754	1
PASSAILAIGUE EDWARD	COL	C-0010142	C951	1
PASSARELLA P FRANCIS	COL	C-0018485	C960	2
PASSINK CLARE	COL	0-0039734	0861	1
PASSMORE JACK W	COL	0-0060144	0967	1
PASTORE JAMES A	CW4	W-0903659	1154	1
PATE ROY H	LTC	0-0084407	C166	1
PATERICK GERALD A	LTC	C-0042853	C864	1
PATERSON KENNETH C	LTC	0-0051022	0357	1
PATERSON ROY D	1LT	0-0011198	C331	1
PATRICK BREAM C	COL	0-0018154	C146	1
PATRICK FRANCIS H	COL	C-0021235	C966	1
PATRICK LESTER R	LTC	C-0045212	1061	1
PATTERSON C A	CW3	W-0903660	0956	1
PATTERSON CECIL A	LTC	0-0084408	C963	1
PATTERSON CHARLES G	COL	0-0019073	0860	1
PATTERSON DALLAS W	LTC	C-0081124	C263	1
PATTERSON DONALD R	LTC	0-0018491	C651	1
PATTERSON EDWIN H	LTC	0-0054094	0966	1
PATTERSON FRANKLIN R	LTC	0-0038746	C661	1
PATTERSON FRED	MAJ	C-0035446	C863	1
PATTERSON JAMES C	COL	0-0008185	C452	1
PATTERSON JOHN C	COL	C-0057046	0765	1
PATTERSON LAWRENCE	LTC	0-0007571	0940	1
PATTERSON RALPH M	COL	C-0021013	C355	1
PATTERSON RICHARD A	1LT	0-0028445	C550	1
PATTERSON ROBERT F	LTC	0-0028302	C865	1
PATTERSON ROBERT W	CPT	0-0007438	C634	1
PATTERSON VICTOR	CPT	0-0014377	C919	2
PATTERSON WILLIAM G	COL	0-0004494	0934	2
PATTERSON WILLIAM H	COL	C-002211C	C567	2
PATTERSON WILLIAM P	COL	0-0019933	0763	1
PATTISON DONALD I	LTC	0-00291C8	C150	1
PATTISON HAL C	B G	0-0029683	0462	1
PATTON DEWEY C	CW4	W-0903662	0461	1
PATTON GORDON B	LTC	0-0024489	0767	1
PATTON HELEN H	LTC	N-0000514	0749	1
PATTON IRVIN L	CW4	W-0901687	0753	1
PATTON JOHN F	COL	C-0067949	1263	2
PATTON MAURICE V	COL	0-0008187	C552	1
PATTON TEDDY L	LTC	0-0082075	0767	1
PAUL ALBERT L	MAJ	0-0063461	1265	1
PAUL CATHERINE	CPT	N-000104C	0261	1
PAUL GERALDINE	MAJ	L-0000472	1065	1
PAUL RICHARD I	LTC	0-0036814	C866	1
PAULES EARL C	COL	C-0021447	C862	1
PAULES JOHN G	LTC	0-0050681	1066	1
PAULEY JR JOHN L	COL	0-0018194	0760	1
PAULL JOSEPH K	LTC	C-0081127	0966	1
PAULLIN HOLMES G	COL	0-0007166	0753	1
PAULSEN MARGARET J	CPT	N-0002974	C562	2
PAVEY KENNETH G	COL	0-0022207	C565	1
PAVIA FRANK N	LTC	0-0027791	0266	1
PAVILLARD RALPH A	CW4	W-0906944	0760	1
PAVLOVICH SYLVIA R	MAJ	N-0002028	0758	1
PAVY LAURENT D	MAJ	C-0026C88	0756	2
PAWLOWSKI IRENE M	MAJ	N-0001288	1264	1
PAXSON HARRY O	B G	0-0016764	0157	1
PAXTON JOHN W	COL	0-0024199	0760	1
PAXTON ORSEN E	LTC	0-0005050	C642	1
PAYNE CHARLES J	COL	0-0031554	0764	1
PAYNE IRVING P	LTC	0-0053878	0966	1
PAYNE JR CHARLES G	LTC	0-0060637	1066	1
PAYNE LAURANCE R	LTC	0-0051830	1064	2
PAYNE LESLIE W	LTC	0-0043797	1264	1
PAYNE OTHO C	LTC	0-0054764	0267	1
PAYNE RUTH	LTC	N-0000529	1054	1
PAYNE SAMUEL C	CPT	0-0009392	0433	1
PAYNTER EARL F	LTC	0-0007147	0-40	1
PEABODY PAUL E	B G	0-0004912	0350	1
PEACOCK EARL G	COL	0-0043873	0565	1
PEACOCK LEOLEEN I	LTC	N-000C831	1166	1
PEAIRS DOUGLAS D	LTC	0-0033479	0962	1
PEAK III HOWARD W	MAJ	0-0047981	0155	2
PEAKE ALBERT S	COL	0-0003024	0242	2
PEAKE AUGUSTA K	LTC	N-0000820	0166	1
PEALE EUGENE L	CPT	0-0060520	1263	1
PEALE JR JAMES N	COL	0-0020684	0867	1
PEARCE GERTRUDE C	LTC	N-0002387	1264	1
PEARCE MARTHA S	MAJ	N-0002183	0965	1
PEARCEY HAROLD W	LTC	0-0081128	1066	1
PEARS MARIA L	MAJ	N-000204C	0360	1
PEARSALL JR JAMES F	COL	0-0020774	0767	1
PEARSE MILDRED C	MAJ	N-0001951	0360	1
PEARSON FRANK J	COL	C-0007264	1151	1
PEARSON FREDERICK	COL	0-0012172	0753	1
PEARSON GENEVIEVE	MAJ	M-0001174	0463	1
PEARSON GEORGE C	COL	0-0039592	1058	1
PEARSON HAROLD J	COL	0-0042418	0864	1
PEARSON JR JAMES P	COL	0-0019157	0761	1
PEARSON MADISON	B G	0-0003607	0846	2
PEARSON MURBLE H	LTC	0-0023661	1059	1
PEARSON QUENNA A	LTC	C-0050923	0854	1
PEARSON RALPH A W	LTC	C-0004878	0637	2
PEARSON RALPH E	COL	0-0051077	0260	1
PEARSON RAYMOND W	COL	0-0003994	1046	1
PEARSON RICHARD W	COL	C-0016384	C355	1
PEARSON WILLYS H	LTC	C-0022660	0759	1
PECA PETER S	COL	0-0019392	0862	1
PECHACEK MELVIN L	MAJ	C-0081129	0762	1
PECK ALLEN L	COL	0-0020327	C866	1
PECK CLARENCE R	COL	0-0008312	0753	1
PECK LEUCELLE F	MAJ	N-0002045	0460	1
PECK MARVIN W	COL	0-0016472	0844	2
PECKHAM ELISHA O	COL	C-0031885	0965	1
PECKHAM HOWARD L	M G	0-0012058	1156	1
PECKINPAUGH EARL M	1LT	0-0010182	1029	2
PECORARO ANTHONY	LTC	0-0059873	0465	2
PEDDICORD EVERETT	COL	0-0017245	0158	1
PEDDICORD LLOYD F	COL	0-0043397	0366	2
PEDERSEN MAYNARD O	LTC	0-0019842	0660	1
PEDERSEN ROBERT W	LTC	0-003035C	0961	1
PEDLEY JR TIMOTHY A	COL	0-0007160	0649	1
PEEKE CHARLES M	COL	0-0019810	0265	1
PEEL ALFRED R	LTC	0-0029245	C859	1
PEEPLES EDWARD T	COL	C-0024537	0766	1
PEEPLES WILLIAM M	1LT	0-0014404	0120	2
PEER GEORGE F	COL	0-0019638	0758	1
PEERENBOOM MAURICE A	COL	0-0039684	0861	2
PEERY PAUL D	1LT	0-0017141	0835	2
PEGG LOREN O	COL	0-0016754	0757	1
PEGRAM EARL F	COL	0-0042487	0761	1
PEGRAM JOHN C	COL	C-0001693	0642	1
PEIFER FRANK A	CW3	W-0906946	0462	1
PEIRCE CHRISTOPHE	COL	0-0002788	0546	1
PEIRCE GEORGE F	COL	0-0016771	0757	1
PEISEL FRANCIS J	LTC	0-0059621	1065	1
PEISINGER ROMAN J	COL	0-0041920	1160	1
PEIKOTIC JAMES M	LTC	0-0047628	0765	1
PELL MARK G	LTC	0-0079948	0867	1
PELOSI JOHN J	COL	0-0021020	0461	2
PELTON SR EDWIN N	CW4	W-0902138	1153	1
PENAAT EDWARD F	B G	0-0029598	0963	1
PENCE DONALD C	MAJ	C-0025971	0746	2
PENCE GEORGE D	M G	0-0015625	0246	2
PENCE HARVEY J	COL	C-0043011	0466	1
PENCE JAMES H	COL	0-0016289	0548	1
PENCE WILLIAM P	B G	0-0016779	0757	1
PENDERGRAFT AMY R	LTC	N-0000028	0551	1
PENDLETON HARRY E	COL	0-0007395	1047	1
PENDLETON HENRY M	COL	0-0003829	0153	1
PENDLETON RANDOLPH T	B G	0-0003217	C849	2
PENDLETON RAYMOND L	MAJ	C-0024313	1045	2
PENDLETON RICHARD N	CW4	W-0903665	C662	1
PENDLETON ROSE A P	CPT	M-0001098	C947	1
PENDRAK THEODORE S	LTC	0-0070015	1166	2
PENFIELD WALTER A	LTC	0-0065707	0466	1
PENICK JACK G	LTC	0-0062218	C466	1
PENLY WILLIAM J	COL	C-0022300	1064	1
PENN JR WILLIAM S	COL	0-0019442	0762	1
PENNELL RALPH MC T	M G	0-0002150	C346	2
PENNEPACKER RUSSELL	COL	0-0052005	0662	1
PENNER RALPH S	LTC	C-0056223	C664	1
PENNIMAN CHARLES D	COL	0-0029616	C562	2
PENNINGTON ALVIE	CW3	W-0903666	0756	2
PENNINGTON EDWARD W	LTC	C-0029456	1058	1
PENNINGTON GEORGE H	CW4	W-0903667	C664	1
PENNINGTON JAMES C	COL	0-0042749	0466	1
PENNY ROBERT G	LTC	0-0059946	0967	1
PENNYPACKER LINDLEY	COL	0-0041851	0461	1
PENROD WILLIAM G	CPT	0-0060441	0962	1
PENROSE ARTHUR W	COL	C-0007913	0847	2
PENROSE CLIFFORD E	LTC	C-0080164	1265	1
PENSINGER BARBARA H	MAJ	N-0000422	C562	2
PEOPLES ROBERT H	LTC	0-0081132	C567	1
PEOT JOSEPH J	COL	0-0031536	0567	1
PEPLOE GEORGE B	M G	0-0016246	0956	1
PEPPER KELTON L	LTC	0-0001560	C621	2
PEPPLE LOYD K	COL	C-0020262	C150	1
PERCIVAL HAZEL	LTC	N-0000656	0866	1
PEREZ WILLIAM O	COL	0-0030324	0761	1
PERHAM WENDELL W	COL	C-0028999	1058	2
PERKINS DWAIN H	CW4	W-0903668	0462	1
PERKINS HAROLD T	COL	C-0051284	0162	1
PERKINS JAMES I	CPT	0-0063514	0566	1
PERKINS JR WILLIAM F	COL	0-0021691	C660	1
PERKINS LEONARD G	MAJ	0-0017982	0444	7
PERKINS SALLY M	MAJ	N-0000412	0163	1
PERLETT JOHN P	COL	0-0028956	0158	1
PERMAN JOHN F	COL	0-0016419	0756	1
PERREAULT MARSCIENE	LTC	N-0002396	C665	1
PERRILLIAT HOWARD A	2LT	0-0016813	1031	2
PERRIN RAY S	CPT	0-0005711	0933	2
PERRIN WILLIAM K	LTC	0-0030260	0459	2
PERRY ARTHUR G	LTC	0-0052985	0864	1
PERRY BEN W	LTC	0-0035447	0362	1
PERRY BENJAMIN F	LTC	C-0037328	C866	1
PERRY DONALD S	COL	0-0004770	1047	1
PERRY ELIZABETH	MAJ	N-0002524	0663	1
PERRY ERNEST L	COL	0-0053324	C764	1
PERRY FRED E	LTC	0-0038974	0367	1
PERRY JR GERALD L	LTC	0-0060184	0665	1
PERRY JR WILLIAM O	LTC	0-0027729	0765	1
PERRY MANLEY C	COL	C-0023024	0266	1
PERRY MILLER O	B G	0-0018427	0661	1
PERRY REDDING F	COL	C-0009900	1051	1
PERRY RUSSELL V	COL	C-0015383	1153	1
PERRY THEODORE O	COL	0-0031725	1163	1
PERRY WALTER L	COL	C-0008917	0449	1
PERRY WILLIS A	B G	C-0018131	C660	1
PERSELL ROBERT A	COL	0-0051608	C961	1
PERSHALL WILLIAM R	COL	0-0043825	1167	1
PERSIK VALENTINE	MAJ	C-0028854	C447	2
PERSON FRANK O	LTC	0-0051807	C964	1
PERSON JOHN L	B G	C-0017517	C759	2
PERSONS JR JOSEPH P	COL	C-0056776	C858	1
PERSONS WILTON B	M G	0-0007088	C649	2
PERTL MARTIN C	COL	0-0040349	C467	1
PERVIER GEORGE W	COL	C-0031736	0867	1
PERWEIN ALEXANDER	LTC	0-0012768	C548	1
PERWICH ALEXANDER	LTC	0-0028193	C967	1
PESEK JOHN M	COL	C-0015145	C954	1
PESUT ELIZABETH	MAJ	N-0000258	1058	1
PETER RICHARD H	COL	0-0025987	1263	2
PETERMAN JOHN D	COL	0-0029555	0763	1
PETERS EMANUEL P	LTC	0-0041006	1265	1
PETERS ERNEST C	COL	0-0018603	1160	2
PETERS GUSTON W	LTC	C-0035421	1058	1
PETERS JOANNA	LTC	N-0000005	0448	1
PETERS JOSEPH F	COL	0-0020075	0452	1
PETERS KENNETH A	LTC	0-004722C	0763	1
PETERS MARGUERITE	MAJ	N-0001575	0360	1
PETERS PETER	COL	0-0039561	0565	1
PETERS ROBERT E	B G	0-0031646	0865	1
PETERSEN BYRON K	COL	0-0042734	0466	1
PETERSEN GEORGE T	COL	0-0033771	0164	1
PETERSON ARTHUR C	COL	C-0018151	0161	2
PETERSON ARTHUR C	COL	C-0042555	0565	1
PETERSON CHARLES D	COL	0-0051633	0865	1
PETERSON DONALD R	COL	0-0020535	0956	1
PETERSON EMIL J	COL	0-0015523	0754	1
PETERSON EMMETT L	LTC	0-0031138	0565	1
PETERSON GERALD	COL	0-0028512	C556	1
PETERSON JAMES C	COL	C-0030311	0664	1
PETERSON JAMES H	LTC	0-0082356	0767	1
PETERSON JR PETER R	LTC	C-0047806	0667	1
PETERSON KENNETH H	LTC	0-0040035	C653	2
PETERSON KENNETH J	LTC	0-0031794	1262	1
PETERSON LEONARD T	COL	0-0018950	0946	1
PETERSON PAULINE F	CPT	N-000033C	1059	1
PETERSEN ROBERT D	COL	C-0029904	1061	1
PETERSEN SAMUEL R	LTC	0-0022904	0660	1
PETERSON TED W	LTC	0-005176C	0564	1
PETERSON VIRGINIA O	2LT	R-0000891	0345	1
PETERSON WALTER L	COL	C-0018292	0655	1
PETRELLI JOHN	LTC	C-0060413	0767	1
PETRI HOWARD R	CW4	W-090184C	0157	1
PETRINI BRUNO A	COL	C-0080317	1067	1
PETROLINO JOSEPH A	COL	0-0029712	0562	1
PETRONE ROCCO A	LTC	0-0027972	0766	1
PETROS HARRY C	LTC	0-0030184	0563	1
PETTERS FREDERICK	COL	C-0002923	0345	2
PETTEY FLORENCE L	MAJ	N-0001792	0665	1
PETTIN CHARLES F	LTC	0-008357C	1165	1
PETTIS CHARLES R	COL	0-0001885	1039	1
PETTIT FRANK A	COL	0-0016092	0755	2
PETTY JR EDGAR L	LTC	0-0062245	0667	1
PETTY TRAVIS L	COL	0-0019439	0656	1
PETZING EDWIN R	B G	C-0008463	0854	1
PEYTON ALBERT H	COL	0-0005021	0246	2
PEYTON HAMILTON M	COL	0-0018461	0761	1
PEYTON JOHN L	LTC	0-0029935	1157	1
PEYTON JOHN S	CW2	W-0903673	0850	1
PEYTON JR TOM L	LTC	0-0050117	0465	1
PEYTON JR WYTHE M	COL	0-004283C	0762	1
PEYTON ROBERT F	COL	C-0018263	0957	1
PFEFFER CHARLES A	COL	C-0004851	0850	1
PFEFFER HENRIETTA	LTC	N-0002413	0666	1
PFEFFER JR CHARLES A	LTC	0-0020613	0247	2
PFEFFER WILLIAM J	MAJ	0-0060593	0565	1
PFEIL ROBERT C	COL	C-0022921	0765	1
PHAIR TOM S	LTC	0-002352C	0761	1
PHARR MARION M	COL	C-0010251	0753	1
PHELAN CYRIL A	LTC	0-0003384	1022	2
PHELPS FRANKLIN E	MAJ	0-0079024	0666	1
PHELPS HARVEY W	LTC	0-0064935	0766	1
PHELPS JOSEPH V	B G	0-0012279	0549	1
PHELPS JR PHIL R	LTC	0-0026251	C864	1
PHELPS PRESTON V	COL	0-0040026	0566	1
PHELPS ROBERT H	CW4	W-0903675	0259	1
PHELPS VICTOR W	COL	0-0041455	C357	2
PHELPS WILLIAM G	LTC	0-0039369	C662	1
PHILBRICK ALTON H	CW4	W-0903676	0762	1
PHILBRICK KENNETH	LTC	C-0031642	0965	1
PHILIPS BURTON K	COL	0-0040048	0966	1
PHILIPS DAVID E	LTC	0-0081136	0767	1
PHILLIPS ADOLPH H	COL	0-0035888	0866	1
PHILLIPS ALBERT G	COL	0-0010156	0947	1

292-560 O - 68 - 4

NAME	GRADE	SVC NO	DATE RET MO YR	RET CODE
PHILLIPS BARRY F	COL	0-0051893	0760	1
PHILLIPS EDWIN R	CW2	W-0907147	0961	1
PHILLIPS HENRY G	LTC	0-0036383	0767	1
PHILLIPS HENRY L	COL	0-0051249	0961	1
PHILLIPS HUDSON B	COL	0-0018653	0257	1
PHILLIPS IVAN G	LTC	0-0032941	0867	1
PHILLIPS J COULSON	LTC	0-0049712	0867	1
PHILLIPS JAMES H	M G	0-0012331	0958	2
PHILLIPS JOHN D F	B G	0-0017584	0859	1
PHILLIPS JOHN R	CW3	W-0903677	0657	1
PHILLIPS JOSEPH F	LTC	0-0030170	0360	1
PHILLIPS JR ERNEST E	MAJ	0-0060942	0667	1
PHILLIPS JR EUGENE	MAJ	0-0065242	0764	1
PHILLIPS KATHLEEN W	LTC	N-0002458	0866	2
PHILLIPS MARY G	COL	N-0000512	0951	1
PHILLIPS MILTON B	LTC	0-0062210	0765	1
PHILLIPS MITCHELL W	COL	0-0022712	1167	1
PHILLIPS PAUL C	B G	0-0022939	0666	1
PHILLIPS ROBENA C	LTC	N-0002150	1264	2
PHILLIPS ROWELLA K	MAJ	N-0001212	1263	1
PHILLIPS STANLEY W	COL	0-0042407	0764	1
PHILLIPS WILMER S	COL	0-0004759	0753	1
PHILOON WALLACE C	M G	0-0002611	1045	2
PHILP WILLIAM R	COL	0-0007200	0852	1
PHIPPEN WILLIAM G	LTC	0-0059581	0865	1
PHYFE HERBERT L	COL	0-0029390	0360	1
PIBURN HURLBERT R	LTC	0-0042500	0163	1
PICCIOTTI ROMULUS A	LTC	0-0079951	1266	1
PICCIRILLI ALBERT A	LTC	0-0060342	0661	1
PICKARD JOHN G	CPT	0-0008289	1022	2
PICKARD OLIVER J	COL	0-0019723	0765	1
PICKARD RUTH A	LTC	N-0000350	0662	1
PICKELL CLYDE V	COL	0-0031376	0861	2
PICKELS WAYNE M	COL	0-0012586	0245	2
PICKENS ARTHUR	COL	0-0006466	0842	1
PICKENS ROBERT G	MAJ	0-0026808	0865	1
PICKERING CLIFFORD E	COL	0-0010741	0946	2
PICKERING ELLIS E	COL	0-0053113	0866	1
PICKERING JAMES A	B G	0-0004444	0946	2
PICKETT BENJAMIN L	COL	0-0042099	0962	1
PICKETT CHRISTIANC	COL	0-0005552	0653	1
PICKETT CLYDE	COL	0-0005098	0946	2
PICKETT EDMUND D	LTC	0-0027723	0966	1
PICKETT GENE G	MAJ	0-0075268	0365	1
PICKETT GEORGE F	COL	0-0042131	0562	1
PICKETT JEROME	LTC	0-0005494	1141	1
PICKETT JOSEPH R	LTC	0-0079952	0262	1
PICKETT LOWELL H	LTC	0-0031336	1064	1
PICKHARDT PAUL A	COL	0-0015772	0754	1
PICKHARDT WOODROW L	COL	0-0039497	0766	1
PICKNELL MILTON O	COL	0-0041952	1161	1
PIEL MELVIN	LTC	0-0084410	0965	1
PIERCE BRUCE	LTC	0-0040200	0865	1
PIERCE CHARLES S	LTC	0-0027888	0166	1
PIERCE HAROLD E	CW4	W-0903679	0657	1
PIERCE HARRY R	COL	0-0005302	0250	1
PIERCE HENRY J	LTC	0-0033989	0560	1
PIERCE HOSEA T	CW2	W-0901863	0646	2
PIERCE JAMES D	1LT	0-0011565	0521	2
PIERCE JAMES R	M G	0-0014979	0658	2
PIERCE JOHN A	CPT	0-0006974	1030	1
PIERCE JOHN T	B G	0-0004754	1147	2
PIERCE JR SAMUEL	COL	0-0038928	0858	1
PIERCE KENNETH	COL	0-0012385	1148	1
PIERCE THOMAS A	LTC	0-0079953	1166	1
PIERCE WILBUR R	COL	0-0015160	0554	1
PIERGALLINI ANNE R	MAJ	N-0001937	0965	1
PIERRE JOSEPH L	LTC	0-0084566	0766	1
PIERSON ALBERT	M G	0-0011838	0859	1
PIERSON FLORENCE P	CPT	R-0010038	0357	1
PIERSON LESLIE E	LTC	0-0087883	0265	1
PIERSON MILLARD	COL	0-0012803	0153	1
PIGG ALBERT M	COL	0-0010862	0752	1
PIGOTT JR WILLIAM T	COL	0-0003467	0934	2
PIKE ROBERT P	COL	0-0042023	0662	2

NAME	GRADE	SVC NO	DATE RET MO YR	RET CODE
PILANO OSCAR G	LTC	0-0052360	0762	1
PILEGARD ANNE K	MAJ	N-0000520	0349	1
PILET NUNEZ C	COL	0-0015531	0854	1
PILLIVANT RAY A	COL	0-0019761	0662	1
PILSBURY LAWRENCE B	MAJ	0-0009401	0934	2
PINCKNEY GLADYS H	MAJ	N-0000864	0365	1
PINE LYNN W	COL	0-0030392	0464	1
PINGER FRANK W	COL	0-0008698	1051	1
PINGER ROLAND W	COL	0-0002966	1144	2
PINZAN ANTHONY	WO1	W-0902217	1047	1
PIPIA FRANK P	LTC	0-0021720	0445	2
PIPPIN JR HARMON L	LTC	0-0040033	0664	1
PIRAINO VINCENT J	CW4	W-0903681	0967	1
PIRAM JOSEPH S	COL	0-0019411	0864	2
PIRKEY FRANK Z	COL	0-0014601	1146	2
PIRNER HILDEGARDE	MAJ	N-0002285	0959	2
PITCHER THOMAS A	COL	0-0039607	0159	1
PITNEY MAX L	COL	0-0022721	0266	1
PITTMAN BEUFORD A	COL	0-0041913	0961	2
PITTMAN FLORA V	MAJ	N-0000367	0165	1
PITTMAN JOSEPH M	COL	0-0019121	0861	1
PITTMAN LUSFORD C	COL	0-0039586	0958	1
PITTS FREDERICK	COL	0-0012743	0754	1
PITTS OGENE	COL	0-0044126	0866	1
PITTS THOMAS B	MAJ	0-0053951	0861	1
PITZ OTTO G	COL	0-0003430	0346	1
PITZER JOHN H	COL	0-0015293	0648	3
PITZER JOHN R	COL	0-0026378	0664	1
PIZZATI JR HENRY E	LTC	0-0031679	0664	1
PLACE OLNEY	LTC	0-0001539	0-22	1
PLAHTE FRED L	COL	0-0029536	0663	1
PLANK CLYDE H	COL	0-0010022	0446	2
PLANK EWART G	M G	0-0012649	0549	1
PLAPP HERBERT C	COL	0-0019059	0863	2
PLAPP PAUL V	LTC	0-0043362	1065	1
PLASSMEYER JOSEPH	LTC	0-0002633	0-35	1
PLATANIA GEORGE	CW4	W-0903682	1167	1
PLATT JR JOHN C	COL	0-0004815	0753	1
PLEASANT JAMES C	LTC	0-0036059	1160	1
PLEASANTS JOHN E	COL	0-0058701	0865	1
PLEMON EVONNE L	LTC	N-0001860	1065	1
PLEW RALPH V	COL	0-0018317	1060	1
PLICHTA FRANK	LTC	0-0040884	0863	1
PLOSMAY BERNARD J	LTC	0-0065309	0865	1
PLOWMAN FLOYD C	LTC	0-0031059	0564	1
PLUMB JOHN F	LTC	0-0059001	0167	1
PLUMMER ROOSEVELT	COL	0-0044412	0667	1
PLUNKETT OLLIE W	LTC	N-0002060	0364	1
PODBRECER HUBERT L	WO1	W-0906951	0253	1
POE JAMES E	LTC	0-0060700	0766	2
POFF ERNEST F	MAJ	0-0024020	0262	1
POGHYLA BENJAMIN H	M G	0-0030103	1066	1
POHL FRANCIS I	LTC	0-0019065	0636	2
POHL JR CLIFFORD H	LTC	0-0084660	0767	1
POHL MARION C	COL	0-0017176	0655	1
POINDEXTER WILLIAM C	COL	0-0008207	1048	2
POINIER ARTHUR E	COL	0-0021999	0265	1
POINIER NORMAN F	COL	0-0017581	0859	1
POLAK PHILIP B	LTC	0-0027193	0866	1
POLOFN DONALD F	LTC	0-0065308	0965	1
POLIFKA DONALD K	LTC	0-0060522	0366	1
POLK JOHN F	COL	0-0020859	0867	1
POLLACK JULIA R	MAJ	N-0001571	0463	1
POLLARD ARTHUR J	LTC	0-0042029	0958	2
POLLARD BERTHA E	LTC	N-0000566	0564	1
POLLARD GALE F	CW2	W-0906954	1062	1
POLLARD IRBY R	COL	0-0009497	0950	1
POLLARD JR JOHN S	LTC	0-0025291	1160	1
POLLARD MARTIN E	CW4	W-0903683	1062	2
POLLARD RICHARD J	COL	0-0042845	1066	2
POLLIN GEORGE A	COL	0-0004547	1046	2
POLLITT ALLEN W	MAJ	0-0008701	0339	1
POLLOCK BYRON F	COL	0-0020925	0960	2
POLLOCK ROLLA O	COL	0-0038832	0360	1
POLLOCK WILLIAM C	COL	0-0006433	0947	2

NAME	GRADE	SVC NO	DATE RET MO YR	RET CODE
POLUMBO FRED A	LTC	0-0042860	0964	1
POLZ ROBERT M	MAJ	0-0056431	0261	2
POMAR MIGUEL J	LTC	0-0042120	0261	1
PONDER SPEERS G	LTC	0-0041995	0460	2
PONDER WILLIAM A	CPT	0-0060589	0860	2
PONGONIS JOSEPH A	COL	0-0030301	1164	1
PONS PHILIP E	COL	0-0030621	0166	1
PONTICELLO ROSE L	MAJ	N-0002197	0765	1
POOLE JR CHARLES M	LTC	0-0089371	1167	1
POOLE JR THEODORE L	COL	0-0030606	1165	1
POOLEY NARDETH W	LTC	0-0081143	0666	1
POOP BENJAMIN W	COL	0-0041575	0459	2
POORMAN DONALD A	COL	0-0017631	0859	1
POPCKE JUNE H	MAJ	N-0001297	0566	1
POPE ARTHUR W	CPT	0-0014366	0619	2
POPE FRANCIS H	B G	0-0000543	0540	1
POPE GEORGE V W	B G	0-0007079	0754	1
POPE IDA A	MAJ	N-0001303	0666	1
POPE JOHN J	LTC	0-0031214	0663	1
POPE LILLIE S	CPT	N-0000810	0950	1
POPE PHILLIP H	COL	0-0019115	0863	1
POPE ROBERT F	COL	0-0040672	0965	1
POPE WILLIAM P	COL	0-0031981	0664	1
POPE WILLIAM R	COL	0-0001536	0-39	1
POPOVICH FRANCIS J	LTC	0-0040803	0760	1
POPOWSKI JR MICHAEL	COL	0-0031633	1163	1
POPPENBURG FRANCIS F	LTC	0-0025050	1060	1
PORTE WILLIAM L	LTC	0-0023322	0946	2
PORTER ERCIL C	COL	0-0006966	0753	1
PORTER FREDERICK	COL	0-0012492	0753	1
PORTER GWINN U	COL	0-0019210	0759	1
PORTER HOBERT H	CPT	0-0063311	0463	1
PORTER HORACE L	COL	0-0009883	1149	1
PORTER JOSEPH C	LTC	0-0029520	0359	1
PORTER OLIVER F	MAJ	0-0006531	0929	2
PORTER ROY V	COL	0-0031328	0763	1
PORTER WILLIAM N	M G	0-0002763	0346	1
PORTERFIELD BEN W	MAJ	0-0020685	0344	2
PORTERFIELD HERBER	COL	0-0004064	0842	2
POSEY ORLANDO J	COL	0-0006550	0149	2
POSEY REBER L	MAJ	N-0001067	1063	1
POSPISIL JAROMIR J	COL	0-0018183	0160	2
POSSE ERNEST W	COL	0-0029989	0263	1
POST CHARLES A	COL	0-0031524	0667	1
POSTLE JOHN A	CPT	0-0070018	0459	2
POSTLETHWAIT EDWARD	COL	0-0020718	0867	1
POSTON CARL M	COL	0-0030400	1063	1
POTEAT WILLIAM O	MAJ	0-0081145	1062	1
POTEET DANIEL P	COL	0-0015089	1046	1
POTHIER MATHEW V	COL	0-0019410	0655	1
POTOCHNIK ANNA M	MAJ	N-0002169	0966	1
POTTER ELEANOR M	MAJ	N-0002287	0565	1
POTTER GEORGE V	COL	0-0026434	1164	1
POTTER JR JOHN C	COL	0-0021439	0266	1
POTTER JR SEYMOUR A	B G	0-0029937	1062	1
POTTER JR WILSON	COL	0-0028798	0355	1
POTTER KENNETH B	COL	0-0030366	0662	2
POTTER WALDO C	B G	0-0002231	0346	1
POTTER WILLIAM E	M G	0-0017098	0760	1
POTTS ADAM E	COL	0-0003723	1048	2
POTTS FRANK G	LTC	0-0007819	0142	2
POTTS RUSSELL J	COL	0-0007241	0847	1
POULSEN WALDEMAR P	1LT	0-0096134	0364	2
POUST LUTHER R	COL	0-0003435	0946	2
POUTRE CLIFFORD A	COL	0-0029371	1059	1
POVENOU NICHOLAS A	COL	0-0079956	1066	1
POWELL CHARLES J	LTC	0-0085363	0466	1
POWELL CHARNER W	COL	0-0019284	0763	1
POWELL DAVID D	MAJ	0-0057662	0967	1
POWELL ELMER R	COL	0-0030414	0565	1
POWELL GROSVENOR	COL	0-0018382	0761	1
POWELL HERBERT B	GEN	0-0016684	0263	1
POWELL HERMAN L	CW4	W-0906958	0566	1
POWELL MALCOLM T	LTC	0-0051368	1160	1
POWELL MAURICE G	COL	0-0040259	1166	2

NAME	GRADE	SVC NO	DATE RET MO YR	RET CODE
POWER JOSEPH L	CPT	0-0062818	1152	1
POWER MARJORIE C	LTC	L-0000218	0959	1
POWER WILLIAM J	LTC	0-0019614	0259	1
POWERS EMORY S	CW3	W-0906959	0959	1
POWERS JAMES F	LTC	0-0039431	0564	1
POWERS JAMES W	COL	0-0083571	0766	1
POWERS JAY I	CW4	W-0903688	0963	1
POWERS JOHN L	COL	0-0020736	0865	1
POWERS LOWELL H	LTC	0-0042123	0161	1
POWERS PATRICK F	COL	0-0011659	0850	1
POWERS WILLIAM F	COL	0-0018672	0359	1
POWHIDA JOHN P	LTC	0-0051475	0162	1
POWLOSKI STANLEY	LTC	0-0011351	0346	1
POZERO JR JOE	CW4	W-0903689	0766	1
PRACHER JOHN R	LTC	0-0037622	0764	1
PRAHINSKI ALFRED	COL	0-0041620	1159	1
PRAHL ROBERT L	COL	0-0031555	0667	1
PRALL JOSEF A	COL	0-0051772	0666	1
PRATHER HUGH L	COL	0-0017810	0846	2
PRATHER LAWRENCE H	COL	0-0031722	0663	1
PRATHER RICHARD G	M G	0-0015698	0861	1
PRATT FLOYD G	COL	0-0019915	0661	1
PRATT FORD E	COL	0-0031433	0463	1
PRATT JAMES M	MAJ	0-0025135	1061	1
PRATT JR RAYMOND S	LTC	0-0018512	0859	1
PRATT OWEN M	CW4	W-0903690	0163	1
PRATT WARREN K	LTC	0-0051519	0762	1
PRAZAK GEORGE	COL	0-0018951	1062	1
PREBIL FRED C	COL	0-0079957	0764	1
PREBLE MERLE R	COL	0-0023524	0667	1
PREGALDIN CHARLES V	LTC	0-0034425	0863	1
PREISS HOLLIS J	COL	0-0081880	0967	1
PRENDERGAST JOHN O	COL	0-0040595	0665	1
PRENTICE JOSEPH C	COL	0-0031888	1266	1
PRENTISS AUGUSTIN M	B G	0-0003624	0846	1
PRENTISS LOUIS W	M G	0-0014672	0456	1
PRENTISS LOUISE M	LTC	N-0000515	0150	1
PRESSENTIN VERNON F	LTC	0-0035391	0866	2
PRESTON JR EDMUND R	LTC	0-0027525	0666	1
PRESTON JR WALTER J	COL	0-0042388	0859	1
PRESTON JR WILLIAM O	LTC	0-0032969	0764	1
PRESTON LEONARD L	MAJ	0-0057430	1166	2
PRESTON MARSHALL C	LTC	0-0038893	0964	1
PRESTON ROY W	CW3	W-0903691	0756	1
PRESTON WILLIAM M	COL	0-0022095	0867	1
PRETZER EMORY A	CW3	W-0906960	0263	1
PREUTZ EDWARD A	CW4	W-0901162	0452	1
PREWITT RICHARD R	LTC	0-0044603	0860	1
PRICE ALFRED J	LTC	0-0027397	0766	1
PRICE ALFRED L	COL	0-0014994	1047	1
PRICE CARTER C	COL	0-0051018	1054	1
PRICE DAVID B	LTC	0-0043842	0864	1
PRICE EARL M	CPT	0-0014170	0417	2
PRICE FOREST E	CW4	W-0903692	0463	1
PRICE GEORGE T	COL	0-0018647	0552	1
PRICE HERBERT H	COL	0-0009110	0945	2
PRICE HERBERT H	LTC	0-0081153	0166	1
PRICE IDA G	LTC	N-0002353	1060	1
PRICE JOHN W	COL	0-0083572	1066	1
PRICE JR HERBERT H	LTC	0-0027825	0766	1
PRICE MARVIN L	LTC	0-0027157	0766	1
PRICE MILTON H	LTC	0-0030518	0762	1
PRICE NEILL F	COL	0-0051841	0267	1
PRICE TERRILL E	COL	0-0004627	0752	1
PRICE WALLACE W	LTC	0-0065030	1064	1
PRICE WILLIAM D	CW4	W-0903694	0766	2
PRICE XENOPHON H	COL	0-0003666	0946	2
PRICKETT FAY B	M G	0-0004458	0453	1
PRIDDY LILLIAN F	MAJ	N-0001044	1062	1
PRIDE RONALD I	MAJ	0-0017002	0747	1
PRIDGEN CLAUDE L	COL	0-0038965	1263	1
PRIEST PERRY P	COL	0-0031562	0966	2
PRIMO ADRIAN H	CW4	W-0903696	0567	1
PRINCE ALTUS E	COL	0-0025714	0667	1
PRINCE CARL M	COL	0-0029288	0855	2

NAME	GRADE	SVC NO	DATE RET MO YR	RET CODE
PRINCE WILLIAM R	COL	0-0020219	0764	1
PRINOLE GEORGE L	COL	0-0008226	0747	1
PRINGLE HERNAN E	LTC	0-0030477	0263	2
PRIOR DAVID	LTC	0-0044304	0161	1
PRITCHARD JAMES R	COL	0-0019248	0863	1
PRITCHARD JOHN R	LTC	0-0052111	0765	1
PRITCHARD RUBY E	MAJ	N-0000690	0564	1
PRITCHARD WILLIAM C	COL	0-0029455	0960	1
PRITCHARD WILLIAM J	COL	0-0042258	1063	1
PRITCHETT JR HARRY H	COL	0-0025705	0267	1
PRIVETT FORBIE H	COL	0-0011975	0646	2
PRIVETT GEORGE P	COL	0-0015459	0954	1
PRIZER OLIVER H	COL	0-0010198	1052	1
PROBASCO NANCY A	CPT	N-0002208	1155	2
PROCTER GILBERT	COL	0-0010243	0846	2
PROCTOR MERT	COL	0-0003125	0646	1
PROCTOR WILLIAM M	LTC	0-0080171	0966	1
PROKOP JOHN J	LTC	0-0038797	0563	1
PROPST JULIAN C	LTC	0-0045943	0760	1
PROSSER CHARLES M	B G	0-0031945	0966	1
PROSSER WALTER E	M G	0-0002057	1045	2
PROSSER WILLIAM O	COL	0-0004052	0247	1
PROUTY AMOS L	CW4	W-0903698	0355	1
PROVENZANO THOMAS G	LTC	0-0028346	0766	1
PRUCHA MARY F	LTC	N-0000072	0454	1
PRUITT FRANCIS W	B G	0-0017812	0959	1
PRUNTY CARROLL A	COL	0-0017281	1053	2
PRUNTY THOMAS C	LTC	0-0032924	0761	1
PRYOR DELBERT A	COL	0-0018799	0660	1
PRYOR RALPH H	COL	0-0029996	0859	1
PRYSI HENRY F	LTC	0-0032904	1067	1
PUCKETT CHARLES D	MAJ	0-0026210	1061	1
PUE EDDIE B	LTC	0-0075272	0167	1
PUGH EUNITY F E	LTC	L-0000114	0463	1
PUGH JOHN R	M G	0-0018790	0466	1
PUGH RALPH H	COL	0-0024375	0966	1
PUGSLEY HELEN E	MAJ	N-0001969	0261	1
PUGSLEY MATTHEW C	COL	0-0017974	0147	2
PULASKI EDWIN J	COL	0-0041779	0765	1
PULLIAM JR GEORGE W	LTC	0-0062208	0867	1
PULSIFER ARTHUR	B G	0-0012211	0752	1
PULSIFER JR GEORGE	MAJ	0-0014006	0920	2
PULSIFER RALPH	B G	0-0015751	0945	2
PUMPELLY JAMES W	COL	0-0051384	0357	1
PUNSALAN LEON F	LTC	0-0042639	1163	1
PURCELL WILLIAM W	COL	0-0081881	0766	1
PURDIN WILLIAM H	LTC	0-0039504	0948	1
PURKHISER HARRY R	LTC	0-0088888	0765	1
PURKITT CLAUDE H	LTC	0-0035152	0356	2
PURKS NETA A	MAJ	N-0002356	0858	1
PURNELL EDWARD K	COL	0-0018539	0849	2
PURSALL ALFRED A	COL	0-0029491	1160	1
PURVIS ARTHUR C	COL	0-0008660	0949	2
PURVIS FRED M	CW4	W-0903703	0161	1
PUTNAM GEORGE D	LTC	0-0036328	0864	1
PUTNAM HELEN P	MAJ	N-0000171	0462	1
PUTNAM LINCOLN F	COL	0-0008712	0645	2
PUTNAM WEBSTER F	COL	0-0009831	1048	1
PUTNAM WILLIAM D	COL	0-0029605	1061	1
PUTNEY EDWARD W	COL	0-0002349	0141	2
PYLE CLYDE S	CW3	W-0903705	0964	2
PYNES OATS A	LTC	0-0036491	1166	1
PYUEN PYUENG S	COL	0-0041976	0162	1
QUACKENBUSH ROBERT E	COL	0-0018590	0761	1
QUAID THOMAS D	LTC	0-0022919	0761	1
QUANDT DOUGLAS P	M G	0-0020605	0866	1
QUANTZ RAOUL J	LTC	0-0028169	0866	1
QUARLES HUGH L	COL	0-0039614	0659	1
QUARTERMAN WILLIAM H	COL	0-0007476	0753	1
QUARTON REGINALD R	COL	0-0039663	1263	2
QUASHNOCK EMRO J	COL	0-0034321	0867	1
QUAVE JOSEPH	CW4	W-0907790	0964	1
QUENNEVILLE RENE C	COL	0-0039524	0356	1
QUETCHENBACK ALBERT	CW4	W-0903706	0565	1
QUICK GEORGE S	LTC	0-0044602	1167	1

NAME	GRADE	SVC NO	DATE RET MO YR	RET CODE
QUICK JOHN T	LTC	0-0053006	1066	1
QUICKEL HERBERT L	LTC	0-0004104	0142	1
QUIGG JOHN	CW4	W-0903707	0157	1
QUIGLEY EDWARDS M	COL	0-0014673	1046	2
QUIGLEY QUENTIN S	LTC	0-0029894	0153	1
QUIGLEY RAY E	LTC	0-0006037	0340	2
QUILL JAMES B	M G	0-0017673	0962	1
QUILLIAN EUGENE L	LTC	0-0084462	0967	1
QUIMBY JR JAMES O	COL	0-0035534	0764	1
QUIN BEATRICE M	LTC	N-0000494	1047	1
QUINLAN EDWARD W	LTC	0-0051617	0463	1
QUINLIN FRANK C	COL	0-0051860	1264	1
QUINN CCILE A	COL	0-0030571	0264	1
QUINN CORIS M	MAJ	N-0000381	0261	1
QUINN HELENA O	MAJ	R-0010066	0558	1
QUINN HORACE A	COL	0-0016820	1046	1
QUINN HOWARD W	COL	0-0018201	0650	1
QUINN JAMES F	COL	0-0031454	0267	1
QUINN JR EDWARD F	COL	0-0031031	0664	2
QUINN MICHAEL A	COL	0-0010882	0554	2
QUINN NATHAN M	LTC	0-0042574	1062	1
QUINN RAY R	LTC	0-0036604	0864	1
QUINN WILLIAM W	LTG	0-0019283	0366	1
QUINN 3RD DANIEL W	COL	0-0017697	0846	2
QUINNELL EARLE C	COL	0-0006256	0148	2
QUINNELLY JAMES L	LTC	0-0060177	0666	1
QUINTARO ALEXANDER	COL	0-0005581	0551	1
QUINTO MYRON A	COL	0-0018210	0760	1
QUINTON JR ALFRED R	M G	0-0003451	0852	1
QUIST FREDERICK	COL	0-0052178	0867	1
RAAB JR HENRY	CW4	W-0906965	0965	1
RAAEN JOHN C	COL	0-0012373	1047	1
RABER THOMAS J	COL	0-0030614	0961	1
RACE ANTHONY J	LTC	0-0052163	1158	2
RACKES ADAMS F	LTC	0-0042078	0249	2
RACKHAM KARL M	LTC	0-0083586	0767	1
RACKLEFF ANGUS N	LTC	0-0030488	0763	1
RADAM DAVID	COL	0-0051736	0257	1
RADCLIFF JOSEPH A	LTC	0-0081158	0262	2
RADCLIFFE MAURICE W	COL	0-0039787	0962	1
RADEBAUGH PHYLLIS R	1LT	R-0001248	0448	1
RADER DONALD C	CW4	W-0903711	0961	1
RADER ROBERT M	LTC	0-0031523	0157	1
RADER WILLIAM F	COL	0-0031543	0667	1
RADFORD LAWRENCE C	COL	0-0021462	0667	1
RADKE RYLE A	COL	0-0020522	0455	2
RADLEY BARBARA M	MAJ	N-0000445	1061	1
RADLINSKI JOHN C	LTC	0-0029156	0357	2
RADZWICH EDWARD R	LTC	0-0032691	0261	1
RAFF EDSON D	COL	0-0019261	1059	1
RAFF EDWARD G	LTC	0-0032588	1164	1
RAFFERTY JOHN F	LTC	0-0051150	0659	2
RAFFERTY KATHLEEN J	1LT	R-0000862	0346	1
RAFFERTY THOMAS A	COL	0-0031793	1166	1
RAFFERTY WILLIAM A	MAJ	0-0003600	1022	2
RAGER EDWARD F	COL	0-0022116	0762	1
RAGLAND WILLIAM W	COL	0-0018344	0761	1
RAGSDALE AGNES M	MAJ	N-0001239	1064	1
RAGUSE CARL W A	COL	0-0015598	0754	1
RAHMANN JOHN C	LTC	0-0066078	0767	1
RAIBL TONY J	COL	0-0051799	1061	2
RAILLAC JAMES M	LTC	0-0030593	1263	1
RAINES MARTIN L	COL	0-0035621	1064	1
RAINFORD WILLIAM R	COL	0-0029626	1061	1
RAINVILLE LEON H	MAJ	0-0032726	0361	1
RAJSKI LAURES B	MAJ	L-0000267	0766	1
RALEIGH ROBERT C	LTC	0-0023287	0261	1
RALEY LEROY W	LTC	0-0041733	0760	1
RALEY PERRY T	LTC	0-0031037	1266	1
RALL STATEN E	COL	0-0015410	0754	1
RALLS JR HOWARD L	LTC	0-0040186	0865	1
RALPH STEPHEN V	COL	0-0040080	0866	1
RAMEE FER	COL	0-0002758	0642	1
RAMEY RUFUS S	B G	0-0006614	0453	1
RAMSAY ALLAN B	COL	0-0018915	0557	1

NAME	GRADE	SVC NO	DATE RET MO YR	RET CODE
RAMSAY WILLIAM T	LTC	0-0056778	0657	1
RAMSEY ARTHUR C	COL	0-0015497	0554	1
RAMSEY DAVID L	LTC	0-0025072	0760	1
RAMSEY FOSTER G	LTC	0-0080319	0667	1
RAMSEY GEORGE L	COL	0-0007304	0945	2
RAMSEY HARRY E	COL	0-0029191	1160	2
RAMSEY JR ALBERT L	1LT	0-0027996	1150	1
RAMSEY JR DAVID M	COL	0-0053610	0764	1
RAMSEY LLOYD A	LTC	0-0033352	0961	1
RAMSEY THOMAS H	B G	0-0009728	0150	1
RAMSEY THURMAN F	LTC	0-0051571	0760	1
RANCK JOSEPH R	B G	0-0017647	0962	2
RANCOILTA JEAN C	MAJ	N-0000253	1266	1
RAND KENAN M	COL	0-0039795	0163	2
RAND OSCAR R	COL	0-0009953	0946	2
RANDALL CHARLES W	CW4	W-0904186	1057	1
RANDALL FRANK J	COL	0-0038842	0864	1
RANDALL HAL	COL	0-0050969	1157	1
RANDALL RAYMOND	COL	0-0009548	1049	2
RANDALL SAMUEL J	COL	0-0003980	1044	2
RANDLE EDWIN H	B G	0-0006745	0648	1
RANDLE ROBERT R	COL	0-0052570	1067	1
RANDOLPH THOMAS J	COL	0-0015050	0746	2
RANEY JOSEPH D	COL	0-0030285	0962	1
RANKIN ALEXANDER	COL	0-0032166	0365	1
RANKIN GEORGE H	COL	0-0032522	0267	1
RANKIN JAMES B	LTC	0-0018778	0246	2
RANKIN JOHN B	LTC	0-0040209	0963	1
RANKIN JR FRED W	LTC	0-0027073	0866	1
RANKIN SAMUEL P	CW4	W-0902142	0762	1
RANKIN SONJA M	MAJ	L-0000321	0764	1
RANNEY DANIEL A	COL	0-0039863	1059	1
RANSIER JOHN G	LTC	0-0063376	0767	1
RANSOM CHARLES H	LTC	0-0025841	0762	1
RANSOM JOHN P	LTC	0-0031140	0960	1
RANSOM PAUL L	M G	0-0004651	0548	1
RANSOM WALTER E	CW4	W-0903715	0965	1
RANSONE ALEXANDER	COL	0-0034142	1167	1
RAPALSKI ADAM J	COL	0-0041760	0966	2
RAPP ELIZABETH	MAJ	N-0002366	0360	1
RAPP PAUL C	LTC	0-0080479	0365	1
RAPSON WILLIAM F	LTC	0-0041166	1263	1
RASBACH JORIS R	COL	0-0015918	0854	1
RASCHE HERBERT H	COL	0-0051339	0862	1
RASCOE ROBERT F	CW4	W-0904276	0664	1
RASMUSON MARY L M	COL	L-0000080	0862	1
RASMUSSEN DONALD	CW4	W-0903716	0863	1
RASMUSSEN KAI E	COL	0-0017655	0955	1
RASOR SAM J	COL	0-0038769	0864	1
RASPER VINCENT W	LTC	0-0040615	1066	1
RASTETTER RICHARD J	COL	0-0023770	0664	1
RATAY JOHN P	B G	0-0006567	0846	1
RATCLIFFE LAMAR C	COL	0-0019034	0763	1
RATHBONE JR JOHN V	COL	0-0042424	0561	1
RATHJE THEODORE A	COL	0-0042311	0264	1
RATHLEV ARNOLD	COL	0-0059944	0666	1
RATLIFF FRANK G	COL	0-0022637	0767	1
RATTAN WILLIAM V	COL	0-0007178	1050	1
RAU CHARLES G	COL	0-0017721	0859	1
RAUENZAHN DANIEL A	LTC	0-0042528	0463	1
RAUKTIS HELEN D	MAJ	N-0000582	1061	1
RAULSTON JOHN W	COL	0-0020401	0862	1
RAWIE VERNON E R	COL	0-0022654	0962	1
RAWLEY ROGER A	LTC	0-0030648	0264	1
RAWLINGS JAMES G	COL	0-0033065	0163	1
RAWLINGS JOSEPH K	CPT	0-0064195	0358	2
RAWLINGS RICHARD J	LTC	0-0081164	0966	1
RAWLINGS WILLIAM K	COL	0-0042895	1062	1
RAWLINS GEORGE J	CPT	0-0011967	0235	1
RAWLINS WILLIAM A	LTC	0-0031258	0667	1
RAWLS CARLAS E	CW4	RW-0903717	0866	1
RAWLS ROBERT M	COL	0-0024675	0965	1
RAY CLAUDE E	COL	0-0051430	0863	1
RAY JEFF G	LTC	0-0031865	0566	1
RAY JIMMIE F	CW4	W-0903718	0855	1

NAME	GRADE	SVC NO	DATE RET MO YR	RET CODE
RAY JOHN E	COL	0-0008384	0854	1
RAYBURN ROBERT	LTC	0-0019295	0652	1
RAYCROFT HAROLD V	COL	0-0006815	0451	1
RAYENS CHARLES E	COL	0-0005456	0447	2
RAYHILL GILBERT L	CW4	W-0903720	0666	1
RAYLE ROY E	LTC	0-0025113	0163	1
RAYMOND ALLEN O	COL	0-0015366	0753	1
RAYMOND JULIAN F	COL	0-0012814	0954	1
RAYMOND MONTGOMERY	COL	0-0017227	0758	1
RAYMOND PHILIP H	1LT	0-0015015	1134	1
RAYMOND WILLIAM R	LTC	0-0084463	0866	1
RAYMOND 2ND C H	COL	0-0018403	0161	1
RAYNSFORD ROBERT W	COL	0-0014910	0854	1
REA EVERETT F	COL	0-0010523	1047	1
REA ROBERT P	COL	0-0019326	0854	1
READ BURTON Y	COL	0-0003433	0446	2
READ CLARENCE F	COL	0-0039602	0359	2
READ JOHN W	LTC	0-0018527	0153	1
READ JR GEORGE W	LTG	0-0012603	0860	2
READ MAHLON M	MAJ	0-0009817	0939	2
READ ROBERT A	COL	0-0038864	0566	1
REAFLEAG HARRY E	LTC	0-0036620	0960	2
REAGAN BRUCE W	LTC	0-0038975	0565	2
REAGAN THOMAS H	COL	0-0008485	1146	2
REAGAN WOODROW W	LTC	0-0043351	0962	1
REAGOR ELMER C	COL	0-0030639	0366	1
REAM ELLIS A	LTC	0-0036165	0964	1
REAM WILLIAM M	COL	0-0030905	0163	2
REAROCK RICHARD R	MAJ	0-0070484	1162	1
REAROCK WILLIAM J	COL	0-0015631	1049	1
REBER EDWARD C	COL	0-0017201	1055	1
REBER MILES	M G	0-0015123	1055	1
REBOVITCH MICHAEL J	CW4	W-0903721	0561	1
REDD JR THOMAS L	LTC	0-0035508	1264	1
REDD LEMUEL E	LTC	0-0043085	0765	2
REDDEN DONALD R	LTC	0-0033657	1166	1
REDDEN FREDERICK	COL	0-0018455	0859	1
REDDING JR FRANK J	COL	0-0043385	1158	1
REDDINGTON THOMAS C	LTC	0-0024401	0464	1
REDENIUS JOSEPHINE	LTC	L-0000189	0567	1
REDFIELD ROBERT S	COL	0-0030704	0566	1
REDLAND ARTHUR J	COL	0-0016947	0957	2
REDLINGER MATTHEW	MAJ	0-0024775	1148	2
REDMAN JR CHARLES L	COL	0-0032311	0566	1
REDMON WILLIAM F	CW2	W-0800037	0145	1
REDNER JR WALLACE J	LTC	0-0058767	1065	1
REDSHAW WARD F	MAJ	0-0079042	0863	1
REECE DONALD F	LTC	0-0083618	0667	1
REECE RUTH S	LTC	L-0000134	0565	1
REED ALBERT L	COL	0-0047380	0664	1
REED ARTHUR W	COL	0-0021878	0667	1
REED C WINGATE	COL	0-0011515	1049	1
REED CHARLES P	COL	0-0030193	0760	1
REED CHARLES H	COL	0-0014948	0249	1
REED CHARLES L	COL	0-0029475	0552	1
REED CHARLES R	LTC	0-0060017	0664	1
REED CHARLES S	COL	0-0009153	0846	1
REED FRANK F	COL	0-0008583	0753	1
REED HARRY F	COL	0-0011688	0753	1
REED HERBERT N	LTC	0-0051297	0360	1
REED HERMAN K	COL	0-0029081	0357	1
REED HOBART D	1LT	0-0011926	0133	2
REED JAMES W	COL	0-0035884	0967	1
REED JOHN F	COL	0-0051436	0963	1
REED JR PRENTISS A	LTC	0-0039841	0861	1
REED KATHERINE	MAJ	N-0000190	1162	1
REED KENNETH W	COL	0-0029203	0561	1
REED KENNETH D	LTC	0-0053107	0764	1
REED MELVIN W	COL	0-0029553	0561	1
REED PAUL A	COL	0-0065411	0367	1
REED RALPH M	LTC	0-0022760	0867	1
REED ROBERT J	LTC	0-0060900	1263	1
REED ROBERT W	COL	0-0041597	0959	2
REED RUSSELL R	COL	0-0052162	1066	1
REED WARREN F	LTC	0-0050231	0966	1

NAME	GRADE	SVC NO	DATE RET MO YR	RET CODE
REEDALL HARCLD M	COL	0-0010308	0246	2
REEDER JAMES R	LTC	0-0081167	C666	1
REEDER JR RUSSELL P	COL	0-0016494	0945	2
REEDER ROGER E	LTC	0-0080481	0966	1
REEDER WILLIAM D	M G	0-0008564	C153	1
REEDY LEONARD E	CW4	W-0903724	1165	1
REES ROGER S	LTC	0-0031652	0165	1
REES THOMAS H	COL	0-0003699	0651	1
REESE FREDERICK	COL	0-0039600	0159	1
REESE ROBERT M	LTC	0-0027975	C766	1
REESMAN WALTER L	COL	C-0003976	0248	2
REEVE ACATHA M	LTC	N-0000120	C856	1
REEVE ARNOLC M	LTC	0-0065453	C966	1
REEVE PARKER M	COL	0-0016390	0756	1
REEVES ANDREW R	COL	0-0006528	0353	1
REEVES ANN	MAJ	N-0000974	C263	1
REEVES CHARLES P	COL	0-0043996	C964	1
REEVES JOSEPH R	COL	0-0021820	C465	1
REEVES JR JAMES H	COL	0-0020665	C267	1
REGAD EUGENE D	COL	0-0015436	1153	1
REGAN JCHN F	LTC	0-0060859	0467	1
REGAN JOHN W	LTC	C-0022783	C761	1
REGAN JOSEPH B	LTC	0-0043105	C865	1
REGAN JULIA L	LTC	L-0000035	1059	2
REGAR PHILIP W	COL	0-0040053	1162	1
REGER HAMILTON	COL	0-0030700	1163	1
REGISTER CHARLES L	COL	0-0020594	1057	1
REGISTER WILLIAM F	COL	0-0043757	1165	1
REGNIER AUGUSTUS J	COL	C-0015720	0754	1
REGNIER FRANCIS W	COL	0-0022699	C265	2
REHM DONALD H	LTC	C-0027807	C766	1
REHM GEORGE A	B G	0-0012772	0955	1
REHM JR HAROLD W	LTC	0-0066080	0767	1
REHM WILLIAM F	COL	0-0007603	0553	1
REHMANN EDWARD J	COL	0-0005060	0344	1
REHMANN EDWARD L	COL	0-0030027	1063	1
REIBER MARTIN R	COL	0-0009165	1047	2
REICHEL MICHAEL J	B G	0-0040087	0666	1
REICHELDERFER HARRY	M G	0-0007547	1156	2
REICHLE PAUL A	COL	0-0010327	0749	1
REID ALEXANDER	COL	0-0015234	1054	1
REID CLARENCE E	COL	C-0031809	0867	1
REID ELIZABETH	MAJ	N-0002077	C961	1
REID GERALD J	COL	0-0015760	0648	1
REID MARION M	LTC	0-0079964	0665	1
REID ROBERT J	LTC	0-0084412	0765	1
REID WALLACE C	MAJ	0-0060361	0761	1
REIERSON JOHN E	COL	0-0012865	C952	1
REIFF STANLEY G	COL	C-0038688	C561	1
REIFSNYDER HAROLD R	COL	0-0039881	0364	1
REILLY FRANCIS W	LTC	0-0059009	0759	2
REILLY GEORGE M	COL	0-0017758	1046	2
REILLY ROBERT S	LTC	0-0023813	C164	1
REILLY STANLEY J	LTC	C-0019654	1147	2
REIMEL STEWART E	B G	0-0007449	0246	1
REINBURG WILLIAM H	COL	0-0008606	C447	2
REINEL ANTHONY A	LTC	0-0080321	0766	1
REINERS MARIE E	MAJ	N-0000534	1148	1
REING CORNELIUS	COL	0-0029637	1161	1
REINHARDT EMIL F	M G	0-0002887	0946	2
REINHARDT GEORGE C	COL	C-0015963	0854	1
REINHARDT WILLIAM R	LTC	0-0010843	C243	2
REINHART STANLEY E	M G	0-0004421	0946	2
REINIKKA ARNOLD J	LTC	0-0082084	0167	1
REIS MARGOT	MAJ	L-0000244	0862	1
REISER LLOYD M	COL	0-0039823	0363	1
REISNER RAYMOND W	COL	C-0051656	C964	1
REISS WILLIAM J	COL	0-0030853	C267	1
REITMEIER WOODROW A	LTC	0-0055144	0867	1
REITZ GEORGE W	COL	0-0030510	1065	1
REITZ JAMES T	COL	0-0033096	0664	1
REITZEL JR CLAUDE F	COL	0-0029404	0460	1
REMFREY CURT A	LTC	0-0040169	0461	1
REMICK CHARLES E	LTC	0-0034408	0766	1
REMUS JOSEPH A	COL	0-0019275	C863	1
RENFRO CHARLES G	COL	C-0024567	C966	1
RENFRO CURTIS D	COL	0-0016248	0755	1
RENFRO JOHN W	CW3	W-0903728	0962	1
RENOLA RAYMOND	COL	0-0022971	0760	1
RENSHAW CLARENCE	B G	0-0017708	1160	1
RENSHAW SOLON B	COL	0-0009468	1152	1
RENSHAW WILLARD S	COL	0-0029426	0760	1
RENTH EDWARD J	COL	0-0006355	C651	1
REPPA ROBERT B	LTC	0-0034978	0466	1
REPPARD ROY	COL	0-0029084	0459	1
REQUARTH JACK A	COL	0-0022189	0867	1
RESCH AGNES A	LTC	N-0000009	0748	1
RESING JOSEPH W F	1LT	0-0011740	0427	2
RESLER BARCLAY T	COL	0-0042068	0862	1
RESNICK SAUL M	CPT	0-0057190	0659	2
RESSEGIEU FRED E	COL	0-0020575	0358	1
RESSEGUIE GEORGE I	LTC	0-0053240	0761	1
RESSEGUIE ROY A	COL	0-0029306	C264	1
RESSIJAC LOUIS H	LTC	0-0023454	0661	1
RESTA FRANCIS E	LTC	M-0001000	0557	1
RESTA ROBERT	WO1	W-0901021	1038	1
RETTGERS FORREST I	COL	0-0036414	1066	1
REUBEL HARRY B	COL	0-0029050	0159	1
REUSCHLEIN JOHN W	CW4	W-0904256	0858	2
REUTENAUER MARGUERIT	LTC	N-0000206	0466	1
REUTER HERBERT C	COL	C-0012776	0854	1
REVIE CHARLES R	COL	0-0019369	0864	1
REYBOLD JOHN B	COL	0-0012842	0447	1
REYER GEORGE W	COL	0-0011343	0351	1
REYNOLDS ALEXANDER	1LT	0-0011811	1129	2
REYNOLDS BURKITT A	LTC	0-0030814	0964	1
REYNOLDS CARLOS F	COL	0-0029702	0354	2
REYNOLDS CHESTER A	LTC	0-0081171	0966	1
REYNOLDS EARL R	MAJ	0-0005111	0733	1
REYNOLDS EDWIN W	COL	0-0043969	0967	1
REYNOLDS EMBREE E	LTC	0-0051507	0554	1
REYNOLDS EUGENE F	LTC	0-0081173	0767	1
REYNOLDS HOUSTON C	MAJ	0-0059452	0265	1
REYNOLDS JACOB G	COL	0-0017612	0758	1
REYNOLDS JAMES H	LTC	0-0039919	0962	1
REYNOLDS JAMES H	COL	0-0042721	0963	1
REYNOLDS JOHN M	COL	0-0008347	0146	2
REYNOLDS JOSEPH E	LTC	0-0022151	0458	1
REYNOLDS JR ROYAL	B G	0-0019238	0863	1
REYNOLDS LAWRENCE S	COL	0-0042982	0966	2
REYNOLDS MAURICE W	COL	0-0011539	0248	1
REYNOLDS ROBERT W	COL	0-0042638	1165	1
REYNOLDS RONALD J	LTC	0-0084667	0366	1
REYNOLDS ROYAL	B G	0-0002814	1045	2
REYNOLDS RUSSEL B	M G	0-0008368	0849	1
REYNOLDSON CHARLES L	LTC	0-0027163	1065	1
REYNOLDSON JOHN R	1LT	0-0064678	0153	1
RHEA JOHN T	COL	C-0043117	0366	1
RHEA ROBERT L	COL	0-0030327	0862	1
RHEAUME JULIANNE M	MAJ	N-0001553	0965	1
RHINE ROBERT H	COL	0-0021317	0862	1
RHINEHART CLAUDE K	COL	0-0013935	0549	2
RHOADES JOHN F	COL	0-0019875	0865	1
RHOADS MARK	CPT	0-0012166	0337	2
RHODERS JR THOMAS A	CW4	W-0904303	0859	1
RHODES ELSIE G	LTC	N-0000493	0448	1
RHODES LESTER F	COL	0-0012265	0649	1
RHODY DEAN A	LTC	0-0030270	1062	1
RHYNE LLOYD T	CW3	W-0903730	1159	1
RHYNE MARION A	MAJ	L-0000210	1155	1
RIANI ALBERT	COL	0-0012093	1148	1
RIBBS EDWARD J	COL	0-0051713	0266	1
RICAMORE PHILIP W	COL	0-0010353	1046	2
RICCIARCELLI ANGELO	COL	0-0042208	0763	1
RICCIO JOSEPH A	LTC	0-0025737	1064	1
RICE ALBERT S	COL	C-0012501	0144	2
RICE CECIL R	COL	0-0042801	0866	1
RICE EDWARD S	COL	0-0025119	1067	1
RICE FRANKLYN O	CW3	W-0903731	0763	1
RICE HERBERT E	LTC	0-0023518	0761	1
RICE JAMES W	COL	0-0006986	0346	2
RICE JOHN K	M G	0-0007183	0153	1
RICE JOHN L	COL	0-0004889	0647	1
RICE JOHN S	COL	C-0024326	C563	1
RICE KENNETH E	COL	0-0079714	C766	1
RICE VERNON W	COL	0-0030189	C662	1
RICH JOSEPH	COL	0-0020562	C846	2
RICH THAIR C	COL	0-0019631	0563	1
RICHARD ELIZABETH	CPT	N-0000953	1053	2
RICHARD JOSEPH C	MAJ	0-0024236	0144	2
RICHARDS ALBERT P	COL	0-0023194	C164	1
RICHARDS DANIEL A	COL	0-0020689	C467	1
RICHARDS FRANK	COL	0-0009973	C847	2
RICHARDS FREDERICK	COL	0-0031565	C166	1
RICHARDS GEORGE J	M G	C-0003771	0153	1
RICHARDS HARRIS T	LTC	0-0038944	C847	2
RICHARDS JAMES T	COL	0-0021707	C959	1
RICHARDS JR GROVER C	LTC	0-0044139	C661	1
RICHARDS JR IRA B	COL	0-0022639	1065	1
RICHARDS RAYMOND	1LT	0-0023407	C942	1
RICHARDS WALTER L	COL	0-0005385	C547	1
RICHARDSON BERTHA D	MAJ	N-0001208	1063	1
RICHARDSON BEVERLY T	COL	0-0032864	0763	1
RICHARDSON CHESTER A	MAJ	C-0033259	1061	1
RICHARDSON EDWIN W	COL	0-0020830	0567	1
RICHARDSON FORD	COL	0-0003167	1041	1
RICHARDSON G S	MAJ	N-0002084	0261	1
RICHARDSON GEORGE M	LTC	0-0060843	1066	1
RICHARDSON HOUSTON H	CW3	W-0903732	0857	2
RICHARDSON HOWARD B	LTC	0-0036934	0465	1
RICHARDSON JAMES	LTC	0-0023993	0262	1
RICHARDSON JAMES A	M G	0-0029906	1166	1
RICHARDSON JAMES A	COL	0-0031395	1062	1
RICHARDSON JAMES O	LTC	0-0021761	C859	1
RICHARDSON JAMES L	GEN	0-0018232	C767	1
RICHARDSON JAMES R	MAJ	C-0025491	C860	1
RICHARDSON JOSEPH M	COL	0-0042269	1063	1
RICHARDSON JR JOHN B	COL	0-0019596	1062	1
RICHARDSON JR W H	LTC	0-0019082	0653	1
RICHARDSON JULES V	1LT	0-0019221	1041	1
RICHARDSON LEAVER	CPT	0-0014249	0520	2
RICHARDSON RICHARD L	COL	0-0044002	C866	1
RICHARDSON VELMA L	MAJ	R-0010014	1265	1
RICHARDSON WILLARD O	LTC	0-0045380	0164	1
RICHEK HERBERT G	LTC	0-0040139	0861	1
RICHERT JOEL H	LTC	0-0060145	0766	1
RICHEY GRANVILLE	LTC	0-0021721	1146	2
RICHEY JR RALPH C	LTC	0-0081177	0966	1
RICHHART EARL A	COL	0-0029210	C662	1
RICHMOND ALBERT M	COL	0-0019678	0655	1
RICHMOND BUDD W	LTC	0-0030658	C365	1
RICHMOND CLARENCE W	COL	0-0006824	C245	1
RICHMOND HAROLD R	LTC	0-0030265	1062	1
RICHMOND JACK B	LTC	0-0043515	C965	1
RICHMOND KIMBALL R	LTC	0-0047281	C461	1
RICHMOND VAN R	LTC	0-0057531	0263	1
RICHTERS ROBERT L	LTC	0-0065109	1265	1
RICHWINE FRANCIS K	LTC	0-0066084	C367	1
RICK MARSHALL	LTC	0-0088542	C262	1
RICKARD ROY V	M G	0-0008156	1051	1
RICKENBAUGH CARL L	COL	0-0020259	C763	1
RICKERSON HOMER O	CW4	W-0906967	0567	1
RICKETTS CURTIS T	COL	C-0051438	C863	1
RICKMAN EDGAR A	LTC	0-0024796	0955	2
RIDDLE HASTY W	LTC	0-0037456	0860	1
RIDDLE JOHN R	LTC	0-0032745	0267	1
RIDDLEMOSER FRANCIS	CPT	0-0059014	C862	1
RIDENOUR CLYDE B	CW4	W-0903734	0865	1
RIDEOUT JR MERLE C	COL	0-0060155	1266	1
RIDER ROBINSON B	COL	0-0051408	0563	1
RIDGE LAURA G	LTC	N-0000068	0156	1
RIDGE PAUL A	MAJ	C-0016590	1047	1
RIDGELL JR JOEL M	LTC	0-0030769	0764	1
RIDGELY DALE B	B G	0-0017797	0859	1
RIDGWAY MATTHEW B	GEN	0-0005264	0655	1
RIDINGS EUGENE W	M G	0-0015230	0258	1
RIDLEHUBER WALTER R	COL	0-0039902	0962	1
RIDLEY CLARENCE S	M G	0-0002024	0647	1
RIEDE REINHOLD C	COL	0-0045810	0363	1
RIEGER NATHANIEL	B G	0-0051027	0459	2
RIEKER MELVIN E	CW4	W-0903735	0167	1
RIEMENSCHNEIDER WALT	LTC	0-0019970	0563	2
RIENBOLT SAMUEL R	CW3	W-0903736	1058	1
RIEPE JOHN H	COL	0-0015515	0954	1
RIES ARTHUR W	COL	0-0044226	1166	1
RIGDON JONATHAN M	COL	0-0017981	0560	2
RIGDON MC DONALD	LTC	0-0028997	0656	1
RIGEL WILLIAM E	COL	0-0032894	0564	1
RIGELY GEORGE A	COL	0-0040204	1066	1
RIGG ROBERT O	COL	0-0076842	0866	1
RIGGINS LEWIS A	COL	0-0016111	0755	1
RIGGS DAN E	COL	0-0052285	0267	1
RIGGS THEODORE S	M G	0-0017076	1060	1
RILEY ELWYN A	COL	0-0040023	0666	1
RILEY FLETCHER S	1LT	0-0014387	1119	2
RILEY FRANCIS J	CW4	W-0904189	0165	1
RILEY GEORGE O	1LT	0-0014356	0717	2
RILEY HARRIE D W	COL	0-0008932	0547	1
RILEY HUGH W	COL	C-0018757	0946	2
RILEY JOHN F	LTC	0-0040465	0361	2
RILEY JOHN I	CW4	W-0903737	1163	1
RILEY JOHN R	COL	0-0038768	0762	1
RILEY JR FRANCIS J	LTC	0-0096714	0766	1
RILEY JR JACOB L	COL	0-0053161	1266	1
RILEY JR JASPER J	MAJ	0-0018244	0648	1
RILEY KEITH L	MAJ	0-0065346	0465	2
RILEY LOWELL M	COL	0-0008654	0652	1
RILEY WILLIAM E	LTC	0-0065553	0766	1
RILEY WINIFRED G	LTC	R-0010071	1264	1
RIME MABEL L	LTC	N-0001533	1166	1
RIMMER HARMON P	LTC	0-0023204	0760	1
RING JR WILLIAM P	COL	0-0029467	C960	1
RINGER MERRITT G	COL	0-0016532	1148	1
RINGGOLD CHARLES L	LTC	0-0030115	0161	1
RINGLER EARL L	COL	0-0016431	0656	1
RINGSAK ELTON W	LTC	0-0021409	0-45	2
RINGSDORF PASCHAL H	COL	0-0015287	0145	2
RINK RICHARD A	LTC	0-0064927	0667	1
RINKER CORNELIUS	COL	0-0030129	0364	2
RINQUE DONALD P	COL	0-0039874	0264	1
RIORDAN BERNARD N	COL	0-0056795	0655	1
RIOS EDWIN T	LTC	0-0063038	1064	1
RIOUX JOSEPH G	CPT	0-0028583	0754	2
RIPLEY MICHAEL E	CW2	W-0902369	1153	1
RIPPLE RICHARD W	COL	0-0020312	C866	1
RISDEN RICHARD A	B G	0-0019278	0963	1
RISHELL CLAIR L	LTC	0-0079049	0867	1
RISHOI STANLEY D	LTC	0-0051462	1061	1
RISING HARRY N	COL	0-0008652	1052	1
RITCHEL CHARLES S	COL	C-0003858	0646	2
RITCHEY ANDREW W	LTC	0-0031934	0766	1
RITCHEY STERLING J	COL	0-0022771	0260	1
RITCHIE ALVA L	COL	0-0039788	1162	1
RITCHIE CHARLES A	COL	0-0029586	0761	1
RITCHIE ERNEST L	COL	0-0029957	0262	1
RITCHIE ISAAC H	COL	0-0012321	0352	1
RITCHIE PAUL J	COL	0-0038808	0965	1
RITCHIE SCOTT B	COL	0-0005255	1146	1
RITTENMAR THEO R	CW4	W-0902062	0255	1
RITTER JAMES F	COL	0-0041578	0359	1
RITTER WILLIAM L	B G	0-0007437	1050	1
RITTGERS FOREST S	COL	0-0039557	1157	1
RITTS JAMES H	LTC	0-0038720	0660	1
RIVA HUMBERT L	COL	0-0026947	0661	1
RIVAS ERNEST G	COL	0-0037543	0266	1
RIVERS MAYNARD R	CW3	W-0903741	0160	2
RIVETTE DONALD F	MAJ	0-0034757	0863	1
RIXEY CHARLES O	COL	0-0039341	0866	1
RIXEY GEORGE F	B G	0-0009562	0348	1
RIZZO CORRINE C	MAJ	M-0010043	0666	1

UNITED STATES ARMY RETIRED LIST

NAME	GRADE	SVC NO	DATE RET MO YR	RET CODE
ROACH NEAL F	LTC	0-0060689	0167	1
ROADRUCK MAX J	COL	C-0042479	0761	1
RCAMER JAMES M	COL	0-0008406	1146	2
ROANE JR NATHAN A	LTC	0-0034156	0365	1
ROANE THOMAS W	COL	0-0011815	C753	1
ROBB HOLLAND L	COL	0-0004432	0753	1
ROBB JOHN E	COL	0-0042790	C666	1
ROBBE ALICE J	LTC	N-0000085	C960	1
ROBBINS ALVIN O	COL	0-0019769	0865	2
ROBBINS CHARLES	COL	0-0042512	0365	1
ROBBINS EARLE	LTC	0-0008729	0-41	2
ROBBINS HUGH W	LTC	0-0084415	C766	1
ROBBINS ISACORE	CW4	W-0903742	0756	1
ROBBINS JACK A	LTC	C-0043543	0766	1
ROBBINS JR P	COL	C-0017614	C859	1
ROBBINS LAWRENCE A	COL	0-0C51652	1165	1
ROBBINS ROBERT S	MAJ	C-0062192	0963	1
ROBBINS SIONEY	CW4	W-0903710	0967	2
ROBBINS WALTER F	LTC	0-0056929	C665	1
ROBBINS WILLIS G	COL	C-0051C81	0760	1
ROBBLEE PAUL A	COL	C-0042198	0766	1
ROBERSON GERALO L	COL	C-0019161	C657	1
ROBERSON WINFIELD S	MAJ	C-0010613	0736	1
ROBERTS BRUCE H	COL	C-0004001	1041	2
ROBERTS CECIL E	COL	0-0035232	1266	1
ROBERTS EOWIN H	B G	0-0006421	0350	1
ROBERTS ELEANOR W	MAJ	L-0000270	0167	1
ROBERTS FRANK N	M G	0-0012734	1157	2
ROBERTS FRANK W	COL	0-0039830	C962	1
ROBERTS HAYON P	COL	0-0014678	0145	2
ROBERTS HENRY G	LTC	0-0033733	0867	1
ROBERTS HEYWARD B	LTC	0-0015544	0847	1
ROBERTS JAMES F	COL	C-002192C	C561	1
ROBERTS JOHN E	LTC	0-0057833	0865	1
ROBERTS LITTLETON	COL	0-0028991	0959	2
ROBERTS NATHAN J	B G	0-0024345	1163	1
ROBERTS ROBERT V	LTC	0-0035584	0661	1
ROBERTS ROY F	COL	0-0029301	0762	1
ROBERTS THOMAS D	COL	C-0015529	0754	1
ROBERTS WILLIAM E	1LT	C-0014342	C410	2
ROBERTS WILLIAM E	COL	0-0030493	C865	1
ROBERTS WILLIAM H	COL	0-0010051	1146	2
ROBERTS WILLIAM L	B G	0-0003597	0950	1
ROBERTS WILLIAM W	LTC	0-0030264	C962	1
ROBERTSON CHARLES E	COL	C-0051756	0566	1
ROBERTSON DANIEL S	COL	0-0009484	1046	2
ROBERTSON DAVIO H	LTC	0-0080176	C665	1
ROBERTSCN EMANUEL M	LTC	0-0030149	0262	1
ROBERTSON HARRY J	LTC	0-0023683	C660	1
ROBERTSON KENNETH C	COL	C-0031845	C167	2
ROBERTSON ROBERT R	COL	C-0051357	1162	1
ROBERTSON STERLINC C	MAJ	C-0009608	0439	2
ROBERTSON SLE H	MAJ	N-0001244	C165	1
ROBERTSON WILLIAM W	COL	0-0014827	C348	1
ROBICHAUX DOUGLAS B	LTC	0-0080486	0765	1
ROBINETT PAUL MC O	B G	0-0010258	C846	2
ROBINETTE A INEZ	MAJ	N-0000453	C561	1
ROBINETTE ALBERT L	LTC	C-0021892	C261	1
ROBINETTE WILLIAM R	COL	0-0029539	C957	1
ROBINSON ALBERT H	COL	0-0018924	1057	1
ROBINSON BERNARD L	M G	0-0012652	1057	1
ROBINSON CARL	MAJ	0-0012288	0837	2
ROBINSON CHARLES A	COL	0-0008280	1047	1
ROBINSON DAYTON L	COL	C-0011084	0346	2
ROBINSON OELIA D	MAJ	L-0000278	C766	2
ROBINSON EOWARO A	LTC	0-0037735	1264	1
ROBINSON EDWARD N	CW4	W-0906970	1061	1
ROBINSON EUGENE	MAJ	C-0013984	0720	2
ROBINSON GEORGE B	LTC	0-0023428	0758	2
ROBINSON HOWARD F	LTC	D-0063077	C267	1
ROBINSON JAMES H	COL	0-0028988	C558	1
ROBINSON JOCA L	LTC	0-0051857	C365	1
ROBINSCN JOHN L	MAJ	C-0023929	0951	1
RCBINSON JOHN N	B G	0-0003870	C349	1
ROBINSCN JOHN S	LTC	0-0038948	1266	2
ROBINSCN JOSEPH S	B G	0-0011195	0850	1
ROBINSCN JOSEPH W	LTC	0-0086692	0965	1
ROBINSCN JR ARIN F	MAJ	0-0058793	0464	1
ROBINSCN JR ELISHA M	LTC	0-0028541	0767	1
ROBINSCN KARL	COL	C-0041857	0857	1
ROBINSCN LEONARO G	COL	0-0031448	0766	1
ROBINSCN PAUL I	M G	0-0017802	0858	1
ROBINSCN RALPH D	CW4	W-0903746	0966	1
ROBINSCN RAOUL L	CW4	W-0903747	1065	1
ROBINSCN ROBERT B	LTC	0-0026531	0964	1
ROBINSCN RUTH A	COL	J-0000045	0265	1
ROBINSCN SHAYER O L	COL	0-0028902	0457	1
ROBINSCN THOMAS	COL	0-0015395	0151	1
ROBINSCN VICTOR L	COL	0-0012019	1146	1
ROBINSCN WARREN A	COL	0-0015292	0854	1
ROBISON J SHELBURN	LTC	0-0006727	0530	2
ROBLES DARYL S	COL	0-0007590	1143	2
ROBSON ERNESTINE	MAJ	L-0000245	1162	1
ROCHFORD ALLAN B	COL	0-0042876	1266	1
RCCHFCRC CHARLES E	COL	0-0030707	0564	1
ROCK FAIRFIELD	LTC	0-0079053	0664	2
ROCKAFELLOW L HOYT	COL	0-0012369	0346	2
ROCKSTROH HENRY J	LTC	0-0056542	0864	1
ROCKWOOD CHARLES A	LTC	0-0027293	0263	1
RODDEN ROBERT M	LTC	0-0026588	0764	1
RODDY JOHN V	COL	0-0021356	0363	1
RODEHEFFER ALLEN W	LTC	0-0024602	0965	1
RODEMAN CHARLOTTE	LTC	N-0C00601	0763	1
RODGERS ELTON C	MAJ	0-0065100	1064	1
RODGERS HENRY H	COL	0-0029992	0863	1
RODGERS JOHN A	COL	0-0009799	0246	1
RODGERS JOHN W	COL	0-0042764	1163	1
RODGERS LOUIE N	LTC	0-0035941	0862	2
RODGERS ROBERT C	COL	0-0029540	0461	1
RODGERS THOMAS A	COL	0-004401C	0967	1
RODGERS THOMAS R	LTC	0-0043529	0766	1
RODGERS WILLIAM M	B G	0-0039812	0263	1
RODMAN FRAZER W	COL	0-0038741	0159	1
RODNEY DORSEY R	COL	0-0001817	0642	1
RODRIGUEZ MOCESTO F	COL	0-0004845	0348	1
ROE JR WILLIAM W	COL	C-0019675	0861	1
ROE THEODORE W	LTC	C-0052205	1066	1
ROEBUCK THOMAS W	CPT	0-0075776	0663	2
ROEHM JOHN F	COL	0-0007218	0753	1
ROELOFS THOMAS R	COL	0-0038764	0464	1
ROFFE A MORRELL	COL	0-0004654	1150	1
ROGERS ARTHUR M	B G	0-0006206	1046	2
ROGERS BENTON M	LTC	C-0059020	0764	1
ROGERS CARMON A	COL	0-0019952	0657	1
ROGERS CHARLES I	MAJ	0-0036778	0562	1
ROGERS CHARLES R	LTC	0-0024967	1062	1
ROGERS DIXON C	LTC	0-0026595	0765	1
ROGERS FRED P	COL	0-0C06100	0439	1
ROGERS GEORGE O	COL	0-0012409	0654	1
ROGERS GEORGE F	COL	0-0029544	0461	1
ROGERS GLENN F	COL	0-0018366	0761	1
ROGERS III HARRY L	LTC	0-0026578	0466	2
ROGERS JAMES L	COL	0-0022076	0865	1
ROGERS JAMES T	COL	0-0C58074	0764	2
ROGERS JOHN E	COL	0-0C41505	0558	1
ROGERS JR JESSE A	COL	0-0C08242	0450	1
ROGERS LLOYD R	CPT	0-0006799	1030	1
ROGERS PLEAS B	B G	0-0005170	0148	1
ROGERS POOLE	LTC	0-0079971	0967	1
ROGERS RALPH W	COL	0-0022943	0866	1
ROGERS RALPH W	COL	0-0012554	0248	1
ROGERS RICHARD	WO1	W-0901489	0139	2
ROGERS THEOA W	MAJ	N-0000444	0661	1
ROGERS THOMAS D	B G	0-0019351	0463	2
ROGERS WALTER C	MAJ	0-0005149	0833	2
RCGERS WARREN	LTC	0-0025913	0465	1
ROGERS WILLIAM C	COL	0-0031602	0967	1
RCHDE CTTO J	COL	0-0019725	0864	1
ROHR URBAN E	LTC	0-0038996	0164	1
ROJO FERNANDO S	LTC	0-0084833	0966	1
ROLAK BRUNO J	LTC	0-0046725	C862	1
RCLFE DOROTHY S	2LT	M-0000623	1144	1
ROLFE ONSLOW S	B G	0-0008637	C959	1
RCLLER HARRY G	COL	0-0018597	C757	1
ROLPH HERBERT F	LTC	0-0032091	0167	1
ROMAIN COLEMAN	COL	C-0028783	1054	1
RCMANS WARREN L	COL	C-003915C	C467	1
ROMEO NINA M	MAJ	N-0001633	1263	1
ROMINE BERNADETTE	MAJ	N-0001893	0660	1
RCMLEIN JOHN W	COL	0-0020197	C966	1
RONAN CHARLES F	LTC	0-0043750	0367	1
RODO JOHN W	COL	C-0052092	C266	1
ROOKER ROBERT L	MAJ	C-0026155	C662	1
ROOKS DAVID L	LTC	0-0063391	0366	1
ROOKS LOWELL W	M G	0-0005602	1045	2
ROONEY FRANCIS M	LTC	0-0023147	C960	1
ROONEY THOMAS O	COL	0-0042454	1064	1
ROONEY WILLIAM S	LTC	0-0060892	C965	1
ROOS PHYLLIS	MAJ	L-0C00509	0567	1
ROOSMA JOHN S	COL	0-0016486	C656	1
ROOT CHARLES W	CPT	0-0059950	0265	2
ROPER DANIEL W	CW4	W-0907116	0863	1
ROPER DAVID N	LTC	0-0031507	0759	1
ROPER HARRY M	M G	0-0015176	0855	1
ROPER ROBERT L	LTC	0-0042365	C162	2
ROQUE FRANCISCO	LTC	C-0063704	1165	1
RORABAUGH JAMES R	COL	0-0021445	1166	1
RORABAUGH JOHN R	CW3	W-0906971	1066	1
RORICK ALAN G	MAJ	0-0022959	1145	2
ROSADO SATURNINO	CW4	W-0902408	1054	1
ROSALER BENNIE	CW4	W-090375C	0567	1
ROSCH PAUL J	CPT	0-0074828	C259	2
ROSCOE DAVIC L	COL	C-0013985	C720	2
ROSE BUEL T	COL	0-0029592	C861	1
ROSE CHARLES E	LTC	0-0035066	0461	2
ROSE EDWARD C	COL	0-0003408	1050	1
ROSE MING	LTC	0-0042873	1064	1
ROSE RALPH E	LTC	0-0032C79	C667	1
RCSE ROBERT R	CW3	W-0903751	C865	2
ROSE WALTER A	COL	0-0008744	0350	1
ROSE WILLIAM C	M G	0-0003155	1046	1
ROSEBAUM DWIGHT A	COL	0-0012752	0854	1
ROSELL JR FRED E	LTC	0-0024682	0761	1
ROSEN MILTON L	COL	C-0019814	0255	1
ROSENBERG LYLE	COL	C-0015127	C846	2
ROSENGREN WALTER J	COL	0-0041392	C955	1
ROSENGREN WARREN J	MAJ	C-0062158	1055	2
ROSENTHAL SADYE M	LTC	N-0000497	0748	2
ROSKOSKY ELSIE	MAJ	M-0010033	0554	1
ROSS AARON P	LTC	0-0051754	C764	2
ROSS DAVID M N	LTC	C-0010355	C644	1
ROSS DOUGLAS M	LTC	0-0080178	C363	1
ROSS ESLIE N	CPT	0-0007016	0524	2
ROSS FRANK S	M G	0-0010213	0946	2
ROSS FRED L	COL	0-0030760	0766	1
ROSS GLENN A	COL	C-00052C8	1147	2
ROSS GLENN A	COL	0-0006229	1047	2
ROSS JAMES O	COL	C-0052442	C361	2
ROSS JR HEZEKIA J	LTC	0-0034112	C867	1
ROSS JR JOHN R	MAJ	0-0025688	C664	1
ROSS MARGARET C	MAJ	N-0002129	C260	1
ROSS MARY E	MAJ	N-C001947	0360	1
ROSS RAYMOND H	LTC	0-0036412	C559	1
ROSS RICHARD L	MAJ	C-0062901	C352	1
RCSS ROBERT C	COL	0-0016467	C354	2
ROSS ROSE F	MAJ	L-0000212	C959	2
ROSS SR FRANZ H	COL	0-0029871	0263	1
ROSS THOMAS P	COL	0-0040082	0267	1
ROSS WILLIAM A	LTC	C-0039003	1067	1
ROSS WILLIAM E	LTC	0-0050151	C666	1
ROSS WILLIAM E	LTC	0-0080324	0866	1
ROSS WINFRED A	COL	0-0021395	C757	1
ROSSELL JR JOHN E	LTC	0-0024011	0262	1
ROSSER FRANCIS C	MAJ	C-0061130	1162	1
ROSSO FRANK P	LTC	C-0039820	0164	2
ROSTENBERG LEO C	COL	0-0079119	0655	2
ROTH ALMON R	LTC	0-0027355	C167	1
ROTH ANDREW W	COL	C-0028980	0458	1
ROTH ARTHUR	COL	0-0016874	0757	1
ROTH HENRY D	COL	0-0029329	0864	1
ROTH IRVING E	COL	0-0018708	0859	1
ROTH LOUIS F	COL	0-0043387	0661	1
ROTH WENZEL O	LTC	0-0051392	0559	1
ROTHARMEL SAMUEL R	LTC	0-0051929	0864	1
RCTHBARD LEONARD	LTC	0-0054051	1263	1
ROTHERMICH ALBERT F	COL	0-0011164	0647	2
ROTHGEB CLARENCE C	COL	0-0015612	0654	1
ROTHROCK EVELYN A	MAJ	L-0000225	0258	2
ROTHSCHILD J H	B G	0-0018077	1162	1
ROTHWELL FRANKLIN G	COL	0-0019176	0763	1
ROTON WILLIAM F	COL	C-0023961	0967	1
ROUGE LEON J O	COL	0-0020882	0965	1
ROUILLARC CHESTER F	LTC	0-0038598	0953	1
ROUND ROSWELL E	COL	0-0014780	0751	1
ROUNTRE BILLY J	1LT	0-0059327	0753	2
ROUNTREE DENTON C	LTC	0-0033797	0466	1
ROURKE RITA V	LTC	N-0000677	0466	2
ROUSEK CHARLES	COL	C-0044030	1065	1
ROUSSEAU JR JOSEPH H	COL	0-0012762	0555	1
ROUSSEAU VINCENT P	MAJ	0-0014394	1119	2
ROUTH CLARENCE E	LTC	0-0039875	0262	1
ROUTH DAVID B	COL	0-0019437	0862	2
ROUTHEAU EDWARD A	COL	0-0012621	0753	1
ROUTLEDGE RODHAM C	LTC	0-0040143	1165	2
ROVEGNC EUGENE S	LTC	0-0088487	0667	1
ROW LATHE B	COL	0-0003601	0647	1
ROWAN CHARLES A	COL	0-0042615	0964	1
ROWAN EDMOND M	COL	0-0018841	0562	1
ROWAN HUGH W	B G	0-0009871	0753	1
RCWAN JOHN V	COL	C-0007787	0544	1
ROWAN ROBERT L	COL	0-0031727	0767	1
ROWE GERALD W	COL	0-0035810	0767	1
ROWE GUY I	B G	0-0002754	0846	2
ROWE HAROLD C	COL	0-0029413	0560	1
ROWE JOHN A	LTC	0-0008768	0-29	2
ROWLAND ARTHUR E	COL	C-0003245	0246	2
ROWLAND CHESTER A	COL	0-0015924	0754	1
ROWLAND GARLAND T	COL	0-0010245	1045	2
ROWLAND JR HENRY C	COL	0-0020940	1167	1
ROXBURY JR EDWARD J	LTC	0-0028075	0766	1
ROY ALFRED J	CW4	W-0902683	0361	1
ROY CHRISTINE	MAJ	N-0001196	0651	1
ROY HELEN M	MAJ	L-0000092	0361	1
RCY JAMES W	COL	0-0023762	0763	1
ROY PAUL A	COL	0-0018153	0760	1
ROY THOMAS H	CW4	W-0903756	0258	1
ROYALL HENRY E	COL	0-0018242	1047	2
ROYALS WALTER C	COL	0-0010991	1048	2
ROYCE CHARLES H	B G	0-0015769	1155	2
ROYCE PHILIP H	COL	C-0021814	0661	1
ROYSDON DORRANCE S	COL	0-0011135	0654	2
ROYSE FRANK	COL	0-0004828	1145	2
ROYSTER KATHRYN J	LTC	L-0000105	1067	1
ROZAMUS WALTER J	COL	C-0032892	1064	1
RCZYCKI ANNA	MAJ	N-0C00835	0758	2
RUBACK JOHN E	MAJ	0-0072643	0765	1
RUBENSTEIN SEYMOUR	COL	0-0024695	1065	1
RUBIN MORTON A	COL	0-0039962	0565	1
RUBIN SAMUEL	COL	0-0014819	1145	2
RUBY DONALD T	COL	0-0040151	0766	1
RUBY JACK W	LTC	0-0045871	1263	1
RUCKER CHOICE R	COL	0-0031610	0865	1
RUCKER HARRY E	COL	0-0041381	0255	2
RUDBERG ANGES J	MAJ	R-0010106	1166	1
RUDD AUGUSTIN G	COL	0-0014160	0716	2
RUDD DOROTHY T	MAJ	L-0000216	0556	1
RUDDLE NORMAN H	2LT	0-0063812	0453	2
RUDDY JOHN M	COL	0-0041426	0756	2
RUDE WALTER A	COL	0-0018732	0462	1
RUDELIUS ERNEST A	COL	0-0007045	0753	1

NAME	GRADE	SVC NO	DATE RET MO YR	RET CODE
RUOISILL JOHN W	LTC	0-0031128	C767	1
RUDOLPH JACK W	COL	0-0019135	C653	1
RUEDENAUER GEORGE A	CW4	W-0903758	0865	2
RUFFNER CLARK L	GEN	0-0015968	1162	1
RUFFNER DAVID L	M G	0-0006597	0653	1
RUGE HERBERT A	CW3	W-0903759	0665	1
RUGGABER JOHN C	COL	0-0028943	1057	1
RUGGLES JOHN F	M G	0-0018596	0866	1
RUHLEN GEORGE	COL	0-0002312	C-44	1
RULE DONALD D	LTC	0-0015611	C429	2
RULE MAX M	LTC	0-0041204	0865	1
RUMAGGI LOUIS J	M G	0-0014900	0659	1
RUMBOUGH WILLIAM S	M G	0-0005496	C546	1
RUMNEY JR MASON P	LTC	0-0028024	C766	1
RUMSEY IVAN C	COL	0-0019774	0963	1
RUND HENRY W	COL	0-0038606	0356	1
RUNDELL FRANCIS E	COL	0-0011228	C748	1
RUNDELL LILLA B	MAJ	N-0002392	C462	1
RUNDLE EDWARD P	CW3	W-0903760	C760	1
RUNFT HAROLD W	LTC	0-0063046	0666	1
RUPERT EVERETT O	CW4	W-0901871	1158	1
RUPLE CHARLES D	LTC	0-0085659	0266	1
RUPP PAUL B	COL	0-0009511	0447	1
RUPP ROBERT O	COL	C-0042103	1164	1
RUPPERT JOHN P	LTC	0-0062273	0864	1
RUSH PETER S	COL	C-0056793	C261	1
RUSH ROBERT I	LTC	0-0028660	C766	1
RUSS SAM W	COL	0-0041555	C159	1
RUSSEL EVELYN L	MAJ	N-0000661	0463	1
RUSSELL ALBERT	CW4	W-0902378	1054	1
RUSSELL CECIL R	LTC	0-0036600	0964	1
RUSSELL CLYDE M	LTC	0-0055518	0865	1
RUSSELL DAN C	COL	0-0020730	C967	1
RUSSELL EBER O	COL	0-0029591	0861	1
RUSSELL GEORGE B	COL	0-0051913	1264	1
RUSSELL GEORGE R	COL	C-0041827	0161	1
RUSSELL JAMES G	LTC	0-0032580	C359	1
RUSSELL JOHN A	LTC	0-0007793	C542	2
RUSSELL JOHN T	LTC	0-0025721	C764	1
RUSSELL JOSEPH P	COL	0-0018919	0659	2
RUSSELL JR GEORGE C	LTC	0-0059877	C965	1
RUSSELL JR ROGER L	MAJ	C-0024689	C863	1
RUSSELL JR WALTER B	LTC	0-0063994	1066	2
RUSSELL KATHERINE	MAJ	N-0002416	C164	1
RUSSELL LESTER F	LTC	0-0081195	C167	1
RUSSELL RANDOLPH	COL	0-0006890	0847	1
RUSSELL ROBERT C	LTC	0-0024557	C347	2
RUSSELL ROGER O	LTC	0-0022797	1062	2
RUSSELL WILLIAM I	COL	C-0042010	0262	1
RUSSEY JOHN W	COL	0-0007464	0753	1
RUSSI GILBERT C	COL	C-0033264	1266	1
RUSSO JEAN G	MAJ	N-0002159	0862	1
RUST CHARLES E	B G	0-0029965	C463	1
RUST JOHN H	COL	0-0020060	1158	1
RUST JR WILLIAM F	CPT	C-0025056	0244	2
RUSTEBERG EDWIN	COL	0-0019542	C864	1
RUSTEMEYER JOSEPH H	COL	0-0006056	0652	1
RUSTIGIAN BARJ A	COL	0-0031068	0566	1
RUTH HAROLD S	COL	0-0012481	C854	1
RUTHER WILLIAM J	CW3	W-0903761	0361	1
RUTHERFORD ALLAN	COL	C-0002071	0936	1
RUTHERFORD BENJAMIN	LTC	0-0080180	C866	1
RUTHERFORD DORSEY J	COL	0-0009037	C146	2
RUTHERMAN NILA P	MAJ	N-0000538	C451	1
RUTLEDGE BEN A	COL	0-0049950	0166	1
RUTLEDGE CECIL L	COL	0-0007298	0148	1
RUTLEDGE ELIZABETH	LTC	L-0000059	0962	1
RUTLEDGE HUGH M	LTC	0-0032201	C667	1
RUTLEDGE PAUL W	M G	0-0007289	C456	1
RUTTE LOUIS B	COL	0-0015928	C555	1
RUTTE ROLAND J	LTC	0-0019977	0661	1
RUTTEN PAUL G	COL	0-0007871	1047	2
RUTTER WARREN C	COL	0-0012628	0949	2
RUWET VINCENT L	COL	C-0024524	1066	1
RYAN CORNELIUS	M G	0-0007375	0757	1
RYAN EDWARD A	COL	0-0042795	1165	1
RYAN FRANCIS J	LTC	0-0056957	0964	1
RYAN GERALD J	CW3	W-0906973	0556	1
RYAN HELEN E	CW3	V-0904319	1163	1
RYAN JAMES W	CW3	W-0903763	0764	1
RYAN JOHN G	CW3	W-0904191	1066	1
RYAN JOSEPH S	LTC	0-0032300	0651	1
RYAN JR JOHN L	LTC	C-0016451	0863	1
RYAN JR JOHN L	LTC	0-0030234	C862	1
RYAN LEWIS S	COL	C-0001239	0639	1
RYAN PATRICK J	M G	0-0017363	1058	1
RYAN PHILLIP W	LTC	0-0033328	0560	1
RYAN THOMAS A	COL	0-0051795	1166	2
RYAN WILLIAM F	B G	C-0019142	0863	1
RYAN WILLIAM J	LTC	0-0009506	0542	1
RYCKAERT ELMER A	LTC	0-0079578	0662	1
RYCZEK STANISLAUS	COL	0-0019344	0644	2
RYDEN ETTA L	LTC	N-0002422	0867	1
RYDER FREDERICK	COL	0-0005548	0453	1
RYDER WILLIAM T	B G	0-0020298	0566	1
RYERSON IVAN L	CW4	W-0903766	0257	1
RYKER DON W	MAJ	0-0025349	C746	2
RYLANDER CARL M	COL	0-0017337	0654	2
RYNEARSON CHARLES R	COL	0-0019722	0863	1
RYNESKA JOSEPH F	COL	0-0032017	0566	1
SAAR OTTO T	COL	0-0042033	0662	1
SABAT JULIANNA	MAJ	N-0001874	C558	1
SABATELLI THOMAS A	LTC	0-0051525	0862	1
SABINE JOHN S	COL	0-0039860	1263	1
SABINI DOMINIC J	B G	0-0005719	1046	2
SABOLYK ROBERT	COL	0-0035475	0867	1
SACERDOTE SYDNEY E	COL	0-0038920	0667	1
SACHS EDWARD I	COL	0-0018185	0760	1
SACHS MARTHA S	LTC	L-0000317	0567	1
SACKVILLE WILLIAM	COL	0-0005276	1151	1
SADLER PERCY L	B G	0-0007408	1146	1
SAENZ RALPH	COL	0-0038762	0364	1
SAFER JOSEPH	LTC	0-0079980	0262	1
SAFFOLD EUGENE	COL	C-0043660	1266	1
SAFFORD HERMAN F	B G	0-0006692	0346	1
SAGER FLOYD C	COL	0-0009479	0548	2
SAHOLSKY BOLICK A	COL	0-0031331	0866	1
SAINE HAROLD J	LTC	0-0026291	0764	1
SAKOWSKI JOHN N	CPT	0-0061483	0954	2
SALADA REUBEN N	LTC	0-0032261	0667	1
SALGADO PETER P	COL	C-0005032	0753	1
SALING JAMES T	LTC	0-0037553	0767	1
SALISBURY HELEN M	MAJ	N-0000978	1052	2
SALISBURY HOWARD G	COL	0-0043510	0464	1
SALLEE ERNEST A	COL	0-0041523	0758	1
SALLEE JOHN T	COL	0-0005948	0246	2
SALLEY COLVIN W	COL	C-0029205	0661	1
SALLEY HENRY M	COL	0-0041430	0956	1
SALMON JOHN C	COL	0-0015937	0854	1
SALMON JR HENRY S	LTC	0-0079981	0965	1
SALTHOUSE WIRT C	LTC	0-0079982	0767	1
SALYER EVERETT G	LTC	0-0036107	0367	1
SALYER JOHN M	COL	0-0023570	0859	1
SALYERDS JAMES H	CW3	W-0903768	0562	1
SALZMAN CHARLES N	LTC	0-0079067	0867	1
SAMES HARRY B	COL	0-0042167	0463	1
SAMOUCE JAMES A	COL	0-0012666	0753	1
SAMOUCE WELLINGTON	COL	0-0015562	0954	1
SAMPLE CHARLES W	LTC	C-0023437	0859	1
SAMPSON GEORGE P	M G	0-0042926	0265	1
SAMPSON JR JOHN H	COL	0-0015974	0854	1
SAMS CRAWFORD F	B G	0-0018261	0755	1
SAMS GERALD A	COL	0-0041931	0464	1
SAMS JAMES O	COL	0-0018381	1060	1
SAMS JAMES F	COL	0-0022776	0462	1
SAMS JEAN P	COL	0-0043293	1064	1
SAMS THOMAS E	COL	0-0028989	0658	1
SAMSON CHARLES P	COL	0-0022204	1265	1
SAMUEL JR ALLEN T	LTC	0-0040045	0661	1
SAMUELS JR ANDREW	COL	0-0017552	0659	1
SANDBERG WILMA K	LTC	N-0000248	0463	1
SANDER ARNOLD R C	COL	0-0007628	0751	1
SANDERS BEN L	LTC	0-0063008	C867	1
SANDERS DONALD A	COL	C-0051489	0364	1
SANDERS EDGAR S	LTC	0-0052359	C461	1
SANDERS HENRY I	LTC	0-0042096	1060	1
SANDERS HORACE L	B G	0-0019445	C963	1
SANDERS JAMES R	WO1	W-0904192	0450	1
SANDERS JR ALLEN W	COL	C-0025305	C764	1
SANDERS JR WILLIAM O	LTC	0-0081201	0267	1
SANDERS LEO F	LTC	0-0089285	C665	1
SANDERS PAUL	MAJ	C-0059953	0965	1
SANDERS PAUL F	LTC	0-0053770	C866	1
SANDERS ROBERT W	LTC	0-0044296	1062	1
SANDERS SARAH L	MAJ	L-0000269	C165	1
SANDERS VERNON K	LTC	0-0025476	C562	1
SANDERS WALTER C	COL	C-0051246	C961	1
SANDERS WILBURN L	LTC	0-0084417	1167	1
SANDERS WILTON L	COL	C-0038794	1160	1
SANDERSON HELEN F	MAJ	N-0000220	C763	1
SANDERSON HENRY E	COL	0-0012352	0550	1
SANDERSON JOHN M	COL	C-0006710	0347	2
SANDIFER SAMUEL H	COL	0-0025158	C265	1
SANDIN RAMON A	COL	C-0039884	1263	2
SANDKAUT LOUIS G	MAJ	0-0057922	1265	1
SANDLIN TROY K	CW2	W-0902160	0945	2
SANDS JOSEPH N	LTC	0-0032957	C464	1
SANDS SIDNEY A	CPT	C-0006898	1022	2
SANDS THOMAS J	M G	0-0017521	0466	1
SANDUSKY RICHARD M	COL	C-0008291	C649	1
SANELLI ALFRED A	LTC	0-0060212	0765	1
SANFORD GEORGE A	COL	0-0003162	1146	1
SANFORD HENRY R	COL	0-0038827	C364	1
SANFORD JR ARTHUR L	COL	0-0031572	0566	1
SANFORD KENNETH H	1LT	C-0011930	0928	2
SANFORD TEDDY H	M G	0-0029893	C267	1
SANKEY WILLIAM E	COL	0-0010853	0750	1
SANTORA BERT	LTC	0-0031758	C564	1
SANTOS MELECIO M	LTC	0-0014683	0753	1
SAPIAGBOSCH T A	COL	0-0009805	0753	1
SAPP 3RD OSCAR L	MAJ	C-0058400	C458	2
SAR CECILIA M	LTC	N-0001876	0761	1
SARAZEN JOHN J	CPT	0-0057582	1162	1
SARGENT CHESTER E	COL	0-0010277	0150	1
SARGENT ELLWOOD W	COL	0-0039617	C559	1
SARGENT FRANK H	LTC	0-0048462	0462	2
SARGENT LOIS H	MAJ	J-0000063	C767	1
SARNECKI FLORIAN P	CW4	W-0904193	1163	2
SASSE FRANCIS M	COL	0-0029807	1262	2
SATHER JR PETER	COL	0-0015867	0450	1
SATTEM IVAN	MAJ	0-0022935	0544	2
SATTERTHWAITE R W	LTC	0-0051176	1053	2
SATTERWHITE SEYMOUR	COL	C-0031431	0167	1
SAUER ANNA M	CW3	V-0921330	0465	1
SAUER EDWARD F	COL	0-0050912	1053	1
SAUER JAMES H	CW2	W-0902189	0250	1
SAUL FRANCIS W	CPT	0-0026094	1146	2
SAUL LESLIE T	MAJ	C-0004442	0-33	2
SAULNIER DOROTHY N	LTC	N-0000249	0161	1
SAULNIER STANLEY G	COL	C-0005826	0751	1
SAUNDERS CLARENCE H	CW3	W-0903772	C857	1
SAUNDERS EDWIN O	COL	C-0001530	1141	1
SAUNDERS OSWALD H	COL	C-0002915	1048	1
SAUREL BENJAMIN W	COL	0-0042482	1264	1
SAUSER ARTHUR T	COL	0-0021379	C461	1
SAUTER IRENE M	LTC	N-0000388	0164	1
SAVACOOL EDWIN F	CW2	W-0901980	0654	1
SAVAGE LEONTINA M	MAJ	N-0002440	0466	1
SAVAGE MARY E	MAJ	L-0000052	0259	1
SAVAGE PAUL L	LTC	0-0058589	0867	1
SAVAN JULES	LTC	0-0080488	1064	1
SAWBRIDGE BEN M	M G	C-0005715	0746	1
SAWICKI STANLEY	COL	0-0018698	0762	1
SAWYER ALICE V	MAJ	L-0000132	1066	1
SAWYER BICKFORD E	M G	0-0008349	0855	1
SAWYER EDWARD W	M G	0-0019918	0864	1
SAWYER HAROLD G	CW4	W-0906979	0259	1
SAWYER JOHN A	COL	0-0017177	0555	2
SAX SAMUEL F	COL	0-0051267	0662	1
SAKE ROBERT K	COL	0-0043790	0965	1
SAXON MARTHA E	MAJ	L-0000272	1062	1
SAYLER HENRY B	M G	0-0007800	1149	1
SAYLOR PAUL	LTC	0-0084063	0966	1
SAYLORS JOHN H	COL	0-0031638	0967	1
SCALAN ENOCH J	LTC	0-0016240	0753	1
SCALES HOWARD N	LTC	0-0005055	1142	1
SCALES JOSEPH W	LTC	0-0079989	1165	1
SCANDRETT WILLIAM	COL	0-0023448	1165	2
SCANLON JOHN H	LTC	0-0033142	1061	1
SCANNON ANTHONY J	COL	0-0032393	1163	1
SCARBOROUGH LAWRENCE	COL	C-0051323	0862	1
SCARBOROUGH R F	COL	0-0041504	0358	1
SCARRITTA ANTHONY	LTC	0-0037519	0161	2
SCHABACKER C H	B G	0-0012714	1053	1
SCHABACKER GEORGE M	CPT	0-0064494	0457	2
SCHADE HOWARD G	LTC	0-0033311	0563	1
SCHAEFER CHESTER C	LTC	0-0042643	0463	1
SCHAEFER JOHN L	COL	0-0039999	0466	1
SCHAEFER PAUL R	LTC	0-0040562	0262	1
SCHAEFER WILLIAM H	COL	0-0015616	0454	1
SCHAFER WARREN	CW4	W-0903775	0461	1
SCHAFFER DONALD C	LTC	0-0038231	1163	1
SCHAFFER W HAROLD	COL	0-0015364	0853	1
SCHALL JOSEPH F	LTC	0-0065301	0866	1
SCHALLER REES F	MAJ	0-0037421	0658	1
SCHAMBER DEAN	COL	0-0020497	0259	1
SCHANER LOUIS T	LTC	0-0062200	0567	1
SCHANTZ OLIVER W	COL	0-0031795	1165	1
SCHANZE AUGUST E	COL	0-0015976	0854	1
SCHARDT BRUTCH B	LTC	0-0026757	0764	1
SCHARF HENRY W	LTC	0-0040683	0862	1
SCHARRF JR WILLIAM F	LTC	0-0028085	C264	1
SCHAS WILLIAM O	COL	0-0011819	0849	1
SCHATZ JOHN P	LTC	0-0026224	1163	1
SCHAUDT ELMER M	COL	0-0051664	1165	1
SCHAUDT HOWARD P	LTC	0-0031673	0764	1
SCHAUERS CHARLES J	LTC	0-0079991	0962	1
SCHAUPP MIRIAM C	LTC	N-0000144	0962	2
SCHFEL CHARLOTTE	MAJ	N-0002445	0866	1
SCHEELE ANDREW F	COL	0-0021475	C762	1
SCHEER JAMES H	LTC	0-0037749	1264	1
SCHEIBLA HARRY O	COL	0-0010107	0547	2
SCHEID ARTHUR M	COL	0-0042812	0766	1
SCHEIDENHELM ARLENE	LTC	L-0000049	0761	1
SCHELPER ANNA K	MAJ	N-0000414	0164	1
SCHENDEL JR HARRY A	COL	0-0023526	1263	1
SCHENKEN CARLTON G	COL	0-0039609	0259	1
SCHEPP DAVID G	COL	0-0042382	0764	2
SCHERER BERNARD J	COL	0-0052147	0864	1
SCHERER HAROLD E	LTC	0-0033032	0161	2
SCHERER HARRIS F	B G	0-0012275	0854	1
SCHERER JOHN W	LTC	0-0066093	1067	1
SCHERER KARL L	COL	0-0018784	0862	1
SCHERER MARY C	LTC	N-0000026	0848	1
SCHERMERHORN JOHN G	B G	0-0020610	0767	1
SCHEUMAN WILLIAM F	COL	0-0009135	0651	1
SCHEWE MARION W	B G	0-0029748	0661	1
SCHICK ROBERT	MAJ	0-0030970	0754	1
SCHIFFMAN MAURICE K	LTC	0-0031375	0561	1
SCHILD LAURA B	MAJ	N-0001652	0766	1
SCHILL GEORGE J	LTC	0-0051229	0859	1
SCHILLERSTROM MERL P	COL	0-0002638	0946	2
SCHIMMEL BERNARD H	COL	0-0079716	0667	1
SCHINDLING ROBERT C	CPT	0-0057645	0965	1
SCHINTZ THOMAS A	LTC	0-0039074	0866	1
SCHIRMER JACOB F	LTC	0-0063158	0865	1
SCHLAAK MELVIN V	COL	0-0029253	0361	1
SCHLOEMER BEULAH	CPT	N-0000588	1057	1
SCHLOSBERG RICHARD T	COL	0-0010311	0748	1
SCHLOTTER WILLIAM O	COL	0-0041495	0258	1

NAME	GRADE	SVC NO	DATE RET MO YR	RET CODE
SCHMELZ RUSSELL W	COL	O-0029353	1159	1
SCHMELZER JOHN F	COL	O-0019270	0761	1
SCHMELZLE CORNELIUS	COL	O-0031547	0767	1
SCHMICK PETER	B G	O-0018395	0161	1
SCHMID ELDON W	COL	O-0033627	0167	1
SCHMID HERBERT W	COL	O-0007907	0747	2
SCHMID WILLIAM K	LTC	O-0083620	0567	1
SCHMIDT ALVINE L	MAJ	N-0000039	0650	1
SCHMIDT GLEN L	COL	O-0028935	0955	2
SCHMIDT HOWARD H	LTC	O-0071960	0167	2
SCHMIDT HUGH F	LTC	O-0079992	0567	1
SCHMIDT JOSEPH J	COL	O-0007681	0642	2
SCHMIDT JR JOSEPH J	COL	O-0024672	0664	1
SCHMIDT ROBERT B	LTC	O-0062966	0666	2
SCHMIDT ROBERT J	LTC	O-0041088	0865	1
SCHMIDT RONALD W	LTC	O-0080450	1062	1
SCHMIDT VIRGINIA M	MAJ	L-0000034	0857	1
SCHMIDT WALTER A	LTC	O-0038346	0466	1
SCHMIDT WILLIAM C	CW4	W-0904194	1163	1
SCHMIDT WILLIAM F	LTC	O-0042423	0862	1
SCHMIDTKE REINHARDT	CPT	O-0019608	0242	2
SCHMITT HOWARD T	COL	O-0050987	0658	1
SCHNADER HELEN J	MAJ	N-0000834	1263	1
SCHNECKLOTH BARNEY G	LTC	O-0027756	0367	1
SCHNEIDER CARL P	LTC	O-0039688	0958	1
SCHNEIDER ELSIE E	LTC	N-0000014	0650	1
SCHNEIDER GEORGE A	CW3	W-0906981	0760	1
SCHNEIDER MILTON C	COL	O-0051639	0965	1
SCHNEIDER WALTER E	LTC	O-0038366	0764	1
SCHNEPF DONALD V	LTC	O-0050698	0167	1
SCHNITTKE RAYMOND E	COL	O-0023693	1165	1
SCHOCK ROBERT L	LTC	O-0022757	0759	2
SCHOEN JR WALTER A	LTC	O-0060737	1054	2
SCHOENBERGER SARA M	LTC	N-0000021	1047	1
SCHOENBUCHER ALBERT	COL	O-0058189	0467	1
SCHOENFELD WALTER E	COL	O-0031342	1066	1
SCHOENTHALER GEORGE	CW4	W-0903778	0754	1
SCHOLL JR WILLIAM F	COL	O-0032281	0266	1
SCHOLTZ JAMES H	CPT	O-0059349	0255	2
SCHOLZ ALLEN F	CPT	O-0064835	0159	2
SCHOMBURG AUGUST	LTG	O-0018422	0767	2
SCHONBERGER ADOLPH F	COL	O-0041461	0457	1
SCHONGALLA JR WILLIA	LTC	O-0080325	1167	1
SCHONHOLZ MORRIS	COL	O-0029761	0462	1
SCHONING RICHARD F	LTC	O-0037663	0863	1
SCHOONMAKER LUCAS E	COL	O-0006687	0547	2
SCHOONOVER HARRY F	MAJ	O-0007513	0935	2
SCHOONOVER JAMES E	LTC	O-0032304	0767	1
SCHOOS ROBERT B	MAJ	O-0037375	0764	1
SCHORR JR DAVID P	B G	O-0018861	1160	1
SCHOW ROBERT A	M G	O-0012180	1058	1
SCHRADER CURTIS B	COL	O-0019760	0862	1
SCHRADER JR JOHN F	COL	O-0021819	0166	1
SCHRADER OTTO H	COL	O-0002544	1041	1
SCHRADER PAUL J	LTC	O-0062897	0864	1
SCHRANK LAWRENCE L	MAJ	O-0062861	0664	1
SCHRATZ FRANK J	CW4	W-0904195	0757	1
SCHRECENGOST H E	LTC	O-0080182	0367	1
SCHREIBER ALOUIS A	CW3	W-0903780	0857	1
SCHREIBER THOMAS S	COL	O-0057918	1167	1
SCHREIBER WILLIAM I	COL	O-0034043	1165	1
SCHREPEL MAURICE F	MAJ	O-0073398	0765	1
SCHRIVER JR ANDREW J	COL	O-0011332	0846	1
SCHROEDER JOHN W	COL	O-0030637	0166	2
SCHROEDER PETER C	COL	O-0018651	0850	1
SCHROEDER HAL L	LTC	O-0025397	0252	1
SCHROEDER HENRY J	COL	O-0005231	0848	1
SCHROEDER JACK F	MAJ	O-0036460	1162	2
SCHROEDER NORMAN P	COL	O-0043002	0965	2
SCHROETER OSCAR A	COL	O-0051295	0462	1
SCHROY PAUL H	LTC	O-0061970	0567	1
SCHUCHMANN AMANDA	LTC	N-0002147	1064	1
SCHUCK EDWIN G	COL	O-0033606	0765	1
SCHUETZ RALPH J	COL	O-0050941	0357	1
SCHUH MARION E	MAJ	L-0000206	1054	1

NAME	GRADE	SVC NO	DATE RET MO YR	RET CODE
SCHUKNECHT LLOYD C	LTC	O-0081208	0564	1
SCHUKRAFT ROBERT E	COL	O-0018744	0862	1
SCHULL EDSON	COL	O-0019236	0263	1
SCHULL HERMAN W	B G	O-0000758	0538	1
SCHULL JR HERMAN W	COL	O-0016752	0757	1
SCHULTEN JR LEO E	COL	O-0040457	0866	1
SCHULTEN MARJORIE F	LTC	L-0000249	0866	1
SCHULTHEIS LEO J	COL	O-0029555	0561	1
SCHULTZ MARION H	COL	O-0038605	0254	1
SCHULTZ ROBERT D	MAJ	O-0079077	0567	2
SCHULZ HAROLD H	COL	O-0020074	0462	1
SCHULZ ROBERT L	B G	O-0042115	0163	1
SCHUMACHER GEORGE H	COL	O-0005394	0546	2
SCHUMAKER MARGARET E	2LT	R-0000304	0645	1
SCHUMANN HEINRICH G	COL	O-0039991	0166	2
SCHUMM FREDERICK	LTC	O-0032479	1167	1
SCHUTT CHARLES H	LTC	O-0020107	0855	1
SCHUTZ JOHN L	COL	O-0024225	0764	1
SCHUYLER C V R	GEN	O-0014905	1059	1
SCHUYLER ROY L	COL	O-0005875	1047	2
SCHWANEVELDT CLYDE J	LTC	O-0084052	0865	1
SCHWAB CARL I	LTC	O-0068048	0766	1
SCHWAB JOHN S	CPT	O-0008129	0930	2
SCHWANK BERNARD J	LTC	O-0081205	0160	1
SCHWARTZ FERDINAND	CPT	O-0059793	1062	1
SCHWARTZ JACK W	M G	O-0017823	1065	2
SCHWARTZ PHILLIP	COL	O-0014820	0753	1
SCHWARTZMAN JACK	COL	O-0040475	1167	1
SCHWARZ RICHARD A	CPT	O-0063957	0262	2
SCHWARZE HARRY M	COL	O-0010351	0652	1
SCHWARZWAELDER C A	COL	O-0006501	1146	2
SCHWATEL WILLIAM R	MAJ	O-0005819	0-34	2
SCHWEICKERT GRAHAM R	COL	O-0006787	1144	2
SCHWEIDEL KERMIT R	LTC	O-0019862	0863	1
SCHWEINLER DALE J	COL	O-0051930	1167	1
SCHWEITZER CHARLES H	COL	O-0021418	1066	1
SCHWIEN EDWIN E	B G	O-0004772	0-45	2
SCHWING EVELYN E	MAJ	N-0002410	0463	1
SCHWING RUTH M	MAJ	N-0000099	1057	1
SCHWINGHAMER W L	COL	O-0029184	0960	2
SCIPLE CARL M	COL	O-0018765	0762	1
SCITHERS GEORGE R	COL	O-0014885	0753	1
SCOFIELD FRANK C	COL	O-0004499	0247	1
SCOFIELD HERBERT L	M G	O-0029482	0163	1
SCOFIELD MARION E	CW4	W-0902182	0953	1
SCOFIELD NYE M	LTC	O-0023547	0661	1
SCORDAS PAUL M	COL	O-0038914	0465	1
SCOTHORN MARION W	COL	O-0051144	1060	1
SCOTT ADRIAN	MAJ	O-0060786	1162	1
SCOTT CHARLES C	CW4	W-0906982	0464	3
SCOTT CRAIG C	MAJ	O-0063079	1163	1
SCOTT DON M	COL	O-0007023	1050	1
SCOTT DONALD H	COL	O-0029018	0955	1
SCOTT EARL L	COL	O-0015805	0253	1
SCOTT ECCLES H	LTC	O-0030595	0261	1
SCOTT EDMOND L	1LT	O-0083988	0461	2
SCOTT EDWARD J	CW4	W-0903743	0765	1
SCOTT EMMETT G	COL	O-0043780	0865	1
SCOTT FRANCES M	MAJ	N-0001986	1064	1
SCOTT FRED W	COL	O-0044765	1166	1
SCOTT JAMES M	COL	O-0030422	1165	1
SCOTT JAMES M	LTC	O-0037201	0166	1
SCOTT JEAN D	COL	O-0015885	0754	2
SCOTT JESSE W	CW4	W-0904197	0459	1
SCOTT JOHN R	COL	O-0032213	0565	1
SCOTT JR EBRIN R	LTC	O-0060467	0467	1
SCOTT JR JAMES A	COL	O-0020652	0767	1
SCOTT JR MARVIN R	COL	O-0038898	1065	1
SCOTT JR RUSSELL F	LTC	O-0026325	0862	1
SCOTT JR SAMUEL B	LTC	O-0036312	0764	1
SCOTT JR THOMAS M	LTC	O-0052544	0660	1
SCOTT KENNETH L	COL	O-0022121	0664	1
SCOTT LEON C	LTC	O-0018166	0946	2
SCOTT MAYLON E	COL	O-0008407	0953	2
SCOTT ORLANDO A	COL	O-0042187	0563	1

NAME	GRADE	SVC NO	DATE RET MO YR	RET CODE
SCOTT OSBORNE E	LTC	O-0031188	1264	1
SCOTT PAUL T	COL	O-0030351	0165	1
SCOTT ROBERT S	COL	O-0043712	1066	1
SCOTT STANLEY L	M G	O-0004439	0354	1
SCOTT WALTER T	COL	O-0007340	0753	1
SCOTT WILLARD W	COL	O-0009827	1050	1
SCOTT WILLIAM J	LTC	O-0042718	0760	1
SCOTT WILLIAM R	COL	O-0001962	0642	1
SCOTT WINFIELD C	COL	O-0010624	0647	2
SCOTTGSMITH JR H H	LTC	O-0033817	0860	2
SCOVILL ELMER B	LTC	O-0035851	0966	1
SCOWDEN FRANK F	M G	O-0002863	1146	2
SCRITCHFIELD ARLYNN	CW3	W-0906984	0162	1
SCROGGS HOWARD R	COL	O-0037453	1164	1
SCROGGS JOHN R	COL	O-0021863	0766	1
SCULLEN ALLAN R	MAJ	O-0024984	0863	1
SEALE HARMON H	LTC	O-0032360	0661	1
SEALS JAMES F	COL	O-0041423	0756	1
SEAMAN JAMES B	COL	O-0020955	0657	1
SEAMAN JR OLEN J	LTC	O-0020825	0764	1
SEAMSTER DENNEY M	CW4	W-0903786	0761	1
SEARCY FRANK T	COL	O-0012819	0854	2
SEARING CARL B	CPT	O-0009637	0529	1
SEARLE VICTOR E	COL	O-0038697	0761	1
SEARLES JASPER L	COL	O-0039690	0960	1
SEARS CHARLES H	CPT	O-0007441	0926	2
SEARS HAYDEN A	COL	O-0012839	0854	1
SEARS RALPH R	COL	O-0016269	0551	1
SEARS ROBERT	COL	O-0002632	1144	1
SEARS WALLACE R	MAJ	O-0060447	0361	1
SEATON STUART M	COL	O-0034760	0762	1
SEAVER PHILIP R	LTC	O-0021916	0959	1
SEAWARD GORDON W	COL	O-0018809	0862	1
SEAY THOMAS R	COL	O-0030862	0565	1
SEBASTIAN EDWARD P	CW3	W-0903788	0264	1
SEBELIEN BERNICE K	MAJ	N-0000242	1063	1
SEBESTA ARTHUR J	LTC	O-0025644	0864	1
SECAN FRANK D	LTC	O-0060201	1265	1
SEDBERRY JR GEORGE R	COL	O-0025415	0764	1
SEDOR ELIZABETH	MAJ	N-0001972	1161	1
SEDER SOPHIA C	MAJ	N-0002079	0366	1
SEEBACH TIMOTHY M	2LT	O-0066390	0853	2
SEEGER WILLIAM H	CW4	W-0903790	0561	1
SEELEY BURTON A	COL	O-0004407	0248	1
SEELEY ROBERT B	LTC	O-0033436	0262	1
SEELEY SAM F	B G	O-0017344	0858	2
SEELY CHESLEY K	MAJ	O-0059025	1167	1
SEELY THEODORE A	COL	O-0016344	0355	1
SEEMAN LYLE E	M G	O-0017082	0965	2
SEESE HOMER P	1LT	O-0011549	0922	2
SEEWALD HUGHES	MAJ	O-0025381	0746	2
SEGARRA ANTULIO	COL	O-0016890	0757	1
SEIBEL PAUL	LTC	O-0036861	0962	1
SEIBERT DONALD W	LTC	O-0043613	0164	1
SEIBERT GERTRUDE C	MAJ	N-0000255	0164	1
SEIBERT LLOYD M	CW2	W-0901450	0644	2
SEID MARTIN J	CPT	O-0009450	0720	2
SEIDEMAN FRANK C	WO1	W-0800134	0740	1
SEIFERT ALBERT E	LTC	O-0024993	1163	1
SEIFERT RAYMOND A	COL	O-0052253	0865	2
SEIGLER JR THOMAS J	COL	O-0030789	1065	1
SEIPEL JR CLARENCE F	MAJ	O-0021847	0148	1
SEITZ J F R	M G	O-0017734	0466	2
SEITZMAN LEONARD F	COL	O-0040029	0867	1
SELBY ARTHUR L	COL	O-0038689	1159	1
SELBY GRANT A	LTC	O-0017906	0345	2
SELBY JOHN E	LTC	O-0005865	0341	1
SELDEN DUDLEY R	LTC	O-0051845	0260	1
SELEE RICHARDSON	COL	O-0014754	0748	1
SELEEN PAUL M	B G	O-0016139	0955	1
SELF AZILE	MAJ	N-0000228	0661	1
SELF GLADYS B	MAJ	N-0002246	0461	1
SELF JR SCOTT A	CPT	O-0084669	1061	1
SELF WILLARD	CW4	W-0903793	0364	1
SELIGMANN GUSTAV L	COL	O-0041400	0156	1

NAME	GRADE	SVC NO	DATE RET MO YR	RET CODE
SELL RUSSELL B	COL	O-0038918	0666	1
SELLARS JACQUELINE	MAJ	N-0000931	1263	1
SELLECK CLYDE A	COL	O-0002841	0447	2
SELLERS MELVIN B	LTC	O-0043981	0654	2
SELLERS RAYMOND W	LTC	O-0019217	0758	1
SELLERS THOMAS C	LTC	O-0065432	0667	2
SELLS CLARENCE K	LTC	O-0053600	1066	1
SELLS JOHN K	COL	O-0014770	0554	1
SELWYN ROBERT E	COL	O-0041704	0258	1
SEMBACH LEON	LTC	O-0026007	0764	1
SEMER JAMES	CW4	W-0902042	1154	1
SENAY CHARLES T	COL	O-0004699	0647	2
SENEFF GEORGE P	COL	O-0006954	1145	2
SENIOR WINFRED B	LTC	O-0056588	0567	1
SENN BURKHARDT	LTC	O-0052560	0266	1
SENN MERLE J	COL	O-0042322	0358	1
SEPTEONDS CHARLES E	LTC	O-0031837	0466	1
SERFASS BERNEDA A	MAJ	N-0000729	1163	1
SERFF PAUL C	COL	O-0015324	0954	1
SERGENT BYRD	COL	O-0052717	1162	1
SERREM EDWARD M	COL	O-0022090	0967	1
SESSIONS FRANK R	CPT	O-0014182	0717	2
SETCHFIELD CLARK W	CW4	W-0906986	0157	1
SETIAN ZADIG Y	LTC	O-0066095	0867	1
SETLIFFE TRUMAN H	COL	O-0024350	0763	1
SETTLE HENRY C	COL	O-0030665	0466	1
SEWALL ALEXANDER	COL	O-0016453	0656	1
SEWARD JOHN R	COL	O-0017698	0859	1
SEWELL GEORGE H	COL	O-0051595	0864	1
SEWELL TOXEY H	COL	O-0049609	1166	1
SEWELL WALTER E	COL	O-0039634	1059	1
SEXAUER LEO C	COL	O-0029251	0961	2
SEXTON LUTHER L	COL	O-0045778	1165	1
SEXTON MORRELL R	LTC	O-0034057	0366	1
SEXTON WILLIAM T	M G	O-0015777	0856	1
SEYBOLD JOHN S	M G	O-0012693	1155	1
SEYMORE DOROTHY L	LTC	N-0002268	1264	1
SEYMOUR FRED W	COL	O-0019671	1059	1
SEYMOUR PERCY W	1LT	O-0010242	0424	2
SEYMOUR WILLARD R	COL	O-0038772	0864	1
SHACTER JACOB	COL	O-0022724	0765	1
SHADE LESLIE N	LTC	O-0028698	0766	1
SHADEWALDT RUTH F	LTC	N-0000673	0367	1
SHADIE CLIVE P	MAJ	N-0000527	0750	1
SHADISH WILLIAM R	LTC	O-0071720	0766	1
SHADLE CHARLES S	B G	O-0010910	1047	2
SHADLE JR WILLIAM J	COL	O-0037262	0767	1
SHAFER HENRY L	COL	O-0078885	1056	1
SHAFER HOWARD T	LTC	O-0081882	0665	2
SHAFER WADE H	LTC	O-0027703	0767	1
SHAFFER FORREST C	COL	O-0008581	0246	1
SHAFFER FRANCIS W	COL	O-0057896	0867	1
SHAFFER FRANK J	COL	O-0022695	0964	2
SHAFFER LEWIS N	LTC	O-0031541	0465	1
SHAFFER WILLIAM Y	COL	O-0040635	0666	1
SHAKEL WILLIAM C	COL	O-0039612	0559	1
SHALER HARRISON	B G	O-0012080	0854	1
SHALLER HAROLD H	B G	O-0029657	1061	1
SHAMANSKY ANNA	MAJ	N-0000558	0459	1
SHAMBORA WILLIAM E	M G	O-0016540	0960	1
SHAMOTULSKI CHARLES	MAJ	O-0004898	0-32	2
SHANAHAN WILLIAM H	COL	O-0022950	0562	1
SHANER MILDRED M	MAJ	N-0001195	0763	1
SHANK GEORGE T	COL	O-0005148	1051	1
SHANKLE WADE L	COL	O-0028984	0558	1
SHANKS JOSEPH M	COL	O-0029061	0759	1
SHANLEY PAUL M	MAJ	O-0069791	1262	2
SHANLEY THOMAS J R	COL	O-0021828	0961	1
SHANNON JR ROBERT M	LTC	O-0024486	0861	1
SHANNON LELAND C	COL	O-0029346	1059	2
SHANNONHOUSE JOHN G	COL	O-0010984	0934	2
SHAPIRA NORMAN I	COL	O-0060239	0866	1
SHARP FREDERICK	COL	O-0008645	0237	1
SHARP JR FELIX C	MAJ	O-0039057	0948	2
SHARP JR WALTER C	LTC	O-0031408	0264	1

NAME	GRADE	SVC NO	DATE RET MO YR	RET CODE	NAME	GRADE	SVC NO	DATE RET MO YR	RET CODE	NAME	GRADE	SVC NO	DATE RET MO YR	RET CODE	NAME	GRADE	SVC NO	DATE RET MO YR	RET CODE
SHARP ROBERT	COL	0-0010121	C349	2	SHELOR WARREN S	COL	0-0050994	0858	1	SHOEMAKER JOSEPH A	LTC	0-0042993	0765	1	SILLS THOMAS H	COL	0-0028909	0557	1
SHARP TURNER R	COL	0-0005645	0748	1	SHELTON CLAUDE W	MAJ	0-0014421	0320	2	SHOEMAKER LEO W	LTC	0-0065028	0566	1	SILLS TOM W	COL	0-0029949	0663	1
SHARP WILLIAM B	COL	0-0010289	0447	2	SHELTON CYRUS O	B G	0-0010784	0854	1	SHOEMAKER PAUL S	COL	0-0029348	C858	2	SILMAN JAMES R	COL	C-0035048	0861	1
SHARP WILLIAM B	LTC	0-0038645	C260	2	SHELTON FRANK W	LTC	0-0033612	0161	1	SHOEMAKER RONALD Z	CPT	0-0072650	1265	2	SILVER MILTON R	CW2	W-0901804	0546	1
SHARPE HAROLD H	LTC	0-0043682	0962	1	SHELTON JOHNNIE F	CW4	W-0903806	1163	1	SHOEMAKER SAMUEL F	COL	0-0022661	0766	1	SILVER SAMUEL F	COL	0-0017770	0858	1
SHARPE THOMAS J	COL	C-0024181	C866	2	SHELTON JR JOSEPH R	LTC	0-0026781	0965	1	SHOEMAKER WILLIAM S	COL	C-0039694	1160	1	SILVERIA EDWIN D	CW4	W-0903822	0167	1
SHARPLESS FRANK E	COL	0-0005110	1047	2	SHELTON T J	LTC	0-0038570	0464	1	SHOMION ARTHUR M	LTC	0-0040094	C365	1	SILVERMAN LEO	LTC	0-0065435	1165	1
SHARPTON BENJAMIN T	MAJ	0-0011736	1138	2	SHELTON WILLIS E	COL	C-0051944	1264	1	SHOMO JOSEPH L	LTC	0-0061189	0165	1	SILVERS CHESTER O	COL	0-0039564	0358	1
SHARRER ROBERT A	LTC	0-0022229	0867	1	SHEMWELL VICTOR B	COL	0-0044395	0761	1	SHOOK LOUIS L	COL	0-0009470	1050	1	SILVERWOOD KERMIT J	COL	C-0042153	0363	1
SHATTUCK MILTON C	COL	0-0012835	0854	2	SHEPARD GEORGE	LTC	0-0087462	0767	1	SHORE MOYERS S	COL	0-0029589	0861	1	SILVEY ROBERT M	LTC	0-0033887	0161	1
SHAUG JAMES J	COL	0-0051645	0964	1	SHEPARD JR NORMAN C	LTC	0-0026654	0764	1	SHORT AUGUSTA L	LTC	N-0000024	1054	1	SIMCOX LAWRENCE S	COL	0-0030602	0461	2
SHAUGHNESSEY LEO W H	COL	C-CC19458	0962	1	SHEPARD WHITFIELD	M G	0-0011908	0156	1	SHORT DAVID S	LTC	0-0036603	1262	1	SIMENSON CLIFFORD G	COL	0-0019511	0864	1
SHAVALIER KENNETH	CW4	W-0903798	0367	1	SHEPARD WILLIAM M	COL	0-002511C	0962	1	SHORT EARL R	COL	0-0031685	C863	1	SIMERLY RUTH N	MAJ	L-0C00304	0861	1
SHAVER CLAUDE N	COL	0-0029333	C859	1	SHEPARDSON FRANK H	COL	0-0C19068	0959	2	SHORT JOHN J	COL	C-0024812	0767	1	SIMKINS TATTNALL D	LTC	0-000444C	0142	1
SHAVER JR ROBERT C	LTC	0-0078614	0667	1	SHEPHERD CHARLES	COL	0-0015904	0754	1	SHORTALL JR JOHN L	LTC	0-0025544	0663	1	SIMKUS CLYDE C	COL	0-0050998	0958	1
SHAVER JR WILEY F	LTC	0-0024459	0962	1	SHEPHERD DANIEL F	COL	C-004306C	0464	1	SHOWALTER WILBUR E	COL	0-0021794	0765	1	SIMMET BERNICE C	CPT	N-0000434	1047	1
SHAVER ROBERT T	LTC	0-0043928	1162	1	SHEPHERD ELIZABETH	MAJ	N-0000204	0263	1	SHPAKOWSKY ADAM P	CW4	W-0903814	C566	1	SIMMONS CHADWICK P	LTC	0-0042924	1164	2
SHAW CARL R	COL	0-0007652	0547	2	SHEPHERD GERALD D	COL	0-0031571	0762	2	SHRADER HAROLD D	COL	0-0039677	C660	1	SIMMONS ELDRIDGE C	LTC	0-0C56798	1159	1
SHAW DORIS L	MAJ	N-0002433	C865	1	SHEPHERD TYRON M	COL	0-0008021	0649	2	SHREVE ARTHUR L	COL	C-0011176	1052	1	SIMMONS GEORGE M	LTC	0-0020841	0459	1
SHAW FLOYD H	CW3	W-0903800	1058	1	SHEPLER LLOYD B	LTC	0-0037445	0762	2	SHROEDER MELVIN W	LTC	0-0094790	1067	1	SIMMONS HOWARD H	COL	0-0039C29	0866	1
SHAW FRANKLIN P	M G	0-0008168	1053	1	SHEPPARD HARVEY E	COL	C-0043086	0667	1	SHUBERT OSCAR A	CW2	W-0901213	0835	2	SIMMONS JOSEPH J	CW4	W-0903823	0256	1
SHAW HAROLD E	1LT	0-0018884	0242	1	SHEPPARD JEROME S	MAJ	0-0060468	0562	2	SHUEY HAROLD E	COL	0-002364C	0463	1	SIMMONS JR JAMES O	COL	0-004172C	0661	1
SHAW HARRY J	LTC	0-0027131	0666	1	SHEPPARD PAUL R E	COL	0-0004258	0646	1	SHUFELT JAMES V	COL	0-0007321	0551	1	SIMMONS JR TOM A	MAJ	0-0080326	1159	1
SHAW III WILLIAM C	LTC	0-0053248	C863	1	SHEPPECK MICHAEL L	COL	0-0021478	0865	1	SHUFORD LOUIS A	LTC	C-0045876	0262	1	SIMMONS JR VERNON N	COL	0-0039C63	0564	2
SHAW IRWIN T	LTC	0-0042679	1163	1	SHEPPER WILLIAM L	CW4	W-0904407	0365	1	SHUGG ROLAND R	B G	0-0004476	0552	1	SIMMS RAYMOND M	CW4	W-0903824	1061	1
SHAW JAMES L	CW4	W-0906987	1060	1	SHERBURNE EDWARD G	COL	0-0003845	0546	2	SHULER JR ALLEN C	COL	0-0031970	0563	1	SIMMS WILLIAM B	COL	C-0020968	0762	2
SHAW JOHN A	COL	0-0007720	0642	1	SHERBURNE JR T L	M G	0-0017293	1060	1	SHULER WILLIAM R	M G	0-0020118	C966	2	SIMON DONALD E	LTC	0-0024776	0464	1
SHAW JOHN C	MAJ	0-0014686	1142	2	SHEROEN JR JOHN P	COL	C-0019901	0965	1	SHULMAN FLORENCE	MAJ	L-0000319	0464	1	SIMON LESLIE E	M G	0-0015567	1155	2
SHAW JR FRANKLIN P	LTC	0-0025492	1064	1	SHERFY ROLLAND F	CPT	0-0010067	0127	2	SHUMARD GORDON H	LTC	0-0027497	C965	1	SIMON LINCOLN A	COL	0-0021961	0466	1
SHAW LAWRENCE E	COL	0-0016858	0356	1	SHERIDAN ANDREW J	CPT	0-0088928	1067	1	SHUMATE JOSEPH P	COL	0-0015537	C654	1	SIMONS ROBERT E	LTC	0-0025136	0162	1
SHAW LELAND B	COL	C-0028994	C658	1	SHERIDAN ARTHUR J	COL	0-0012074	1146	2	SHUMATE PAUL W	COL	C-0017547	C859	1	SIMPKINS MARTHA A	MAJ	N-0001265	0664	1
SHAW MILLARC	COL	0-0042313	0164	2	SHERIDAN JOHN W	COL	0-0043156	0666	1	SHUMWAY JR LESLIE E	MAJ	C-0038478	C862	2	SIMPSON ADA M	LTC	N-0000076	0754	1
SHAW RAUL A	COL	0-0042181	0563	1	SHERMAN HARRY B	B G	0-0011243	0153	1	SHUNK PETER W	COL	0-0015622	0754	1	SIMPSON CHARLES L	COL	0-0020325	0864	1
SHAW RONALD M	COL	0-0016103	0755	1	SHERMAN JOHN B	COL	0-0012160	1051	1	SHUPE JOSEPH B	LTC	0-0083588	0766	1	SIMPSON DONALD M	COL	0-0021986	0163	1
SHAW STANLEY H	COL	0-0080492	1066	1	SHERMAN JR JACQUES L	LTC	0-0059541	0964	1	SHURE WILLIAM C	COL	0-0022751	0367	2	SIMPSON EDWARD H	LTC	0-0030418	0463	1
SHAW THERON	CW2	W-0903802	0954	2	SHERMAN RAYMOND G	COL	0-0C07609	0351	1	SHURLING JOSEPH T	CW4	W-0903816	0159	1	SIMPSON GEORGE H	COL	0-0034704	1066	2
SHAW VERA F	LTC	N-0000155	1162	1	SHERMAN THOMAS J	CW4	W-0906988	0461	2	SHURN VERNON A	COL	C-0031436	C666	1	SIMPSON JOHN W	COL	0-0021480	0957	1
SHAW VIRGIL F	COL	0-0012340	0754	1	SHERMAN WILLIAM T	MAJ	0-0042667	0751	1	SHUTE BENJAMIN S	COL	0-0017097	0758	1	SIMPSON JR GEORGE L	LTC	0-0055818	0164	1
SHAW WALTER A	COL	0-0042343	C464	1	SHERRARD JOSEPH H	LTC	0-004C597	1065	1	SHUTT EDITH L	LTC	N-0000112	1163	1	SIMPSON MARIBETH T	LTC	L-0000106	1167	1
SHAY EDWARD B	WO1	W-0800135	C438	2	SHERRARD JR ROBERT G	COL	0-0019922	0962	1	SHUTT LOGAN O	COL	0-0012441	1049	1	SIMPSON RALPH T	COL	0-0029841	0859	1
SHEA DANIEL P	LTC	0-0081861	0665	1	SHERREIS DONALD C	LTC	0-0044781	0662	1	SHUTTLEWORTH W S	COL	C-0008898	1147	2	SIMPSON THOMAS B	B G	0-0020902	0167	1
SHEA EDWARD L	CW3	RW-0907158	0367	1	SHERRILL EVAN H	CPT	0-0007413	0722	2	SIBBALD GEORGE H	COL	0-0029958	C663	1	SIMPSON WALTER A	COL	0-0019778	0865	1
SHEA GEORGE D	M G	0-0005465	C153	1	SHERWOOD PHILIP H	MAJ	0-0004767	0846	2	SIBERT EDWIN L	M G	0-0011153	0154	1	SIMPSON WILLIAM H	GEN	0-0002645	1146	2
SHEA MICHAEL C	COL	C-0008415	C854	1	SHERWOOD ROBERT W	LTC	0-0063476	0164	1	SIBERT FRANKLIN C	M G	0-0003394	0646	2	SIMS HAROLD L	CW4	W-0906994	0955	1
SHEA PATRICK E	COL	0-0006545	C753	1	SHEVIAK FRANK G	LTC	0-0040878	0866	1	SIBERT FRANKLIN R	COL	0-0020329	0460	1	SIMS JULES V	COL	0-0011147	0750	1
SHEALEY PERCY R	LTC	0-0031164	1165	2	SHEWBRIDGE EDWIN C	COL	0-0038745	0663	1	SIBERT HERBERT F	COL	0-0030922	1066	1	SIMS LEONARD H	B G	0-0008383	0854	1
SHEALY NORRIS	LTC	0-0043088	0765	1	SHI JR JAMES C	LTC	0-0033230	1160	1	SIBLEY CLELAND C	B G	0-0015671	0954	1	SIMS RALPH	LTC	0-0035435	1264	2
SHEARER HUTTON A	MAJ	0-0020470	1144	2	SHICK DALE H	LTC	0-0033412	0661	1	SICHI WILLIAM T	COL	0-0019674	0655	1	SINCLAIR DUNCAN	COL	0-0019757	0163	2
SHEARER SPENCER E	MAJ	C-0002982	0233	2	SHIELDS JR HARRY H	LTC	0-0054994	0866	1	SICKS MARY E	MAJ	L-000033C	0766	1	SINCLAIR FORESTER H	LTC	0-0016834	0244	2
SHEAROUSE JAMES D	COL	0-0030337	0461	1	SHIELDS MAYNARD E	CPT	0-0077198	0864	2	SIDENSTRICKER HARRY	CW4	W-0907140	0967	1	SINCLAIR LACHLAN M	COL	0-0032369	0767	1
SHEDIVETZ CLAYTON L	MAJ	C-0037514	C564	1	SHIELDS PAUL A	COL	0-0041424	0756	1	SIDFRID LEROY D	MAJ	C-0039441	C866	1	SINCLAIR VICTOR E	LTC	0-0020795	1057	1
SHEEHAN DANIEL J	COL	0-0020929	1058	1	SHIERY FLOYD W	LTC	0-0051146	0259	1	SIDWAY RALPH W	CW4	W-0902323	1054	1	SINER JOSEPH L	LTC	0-0003C54	1022	2
SHEEHAN GERARD J	LTC	0-0043221	1062	2	SHIFLET ALBERT W	COL	C-0020507	0257	1	SIEBEN HERBERT U	MAJ	C-C033153	1061	1	SINGER LILLIAN	MAJ	L-0000340	0852	1
SHEEHAN HELEN R	LTC	J-0000046	0464	1	SHIMEK CECELIA H	MAJ	N-0002263	1062	1	SIEBENEICHEN PAUL C	LTC	0-0034729	0961	1	SINGER MERTON	COL	0-0021215	0165	1
SHEEHAN THOMAS F	COL	C-0011428	C148	1	SHIMOKER WILLIAM H	COL	0-0017745	0246	2	SIEBER JR HARRY F	LTC	0-0054161	1163	1	SINGER PAUL L	COL	0-0006797	0453	1
SHEEHY THOMAS W	LTC	0-0067614	1167	1	SHINKLE JOHN G	M G	0-0018979	0963	1	SIEBERT RITA M	MAJ	N-0002425	1164	1	SINGER RICHARD C	COL	0-0012756	0753	1
SHEEN CLARENCE E	COL	0-0040015	C266	2	SHIPE BURDWELL H	COL	0-0030065	1161	1	SIEGE ALFRED G	LTC	0-0059676	0466	1	SINGLES GORDON	COL	0-0018522	0761	1
SHEEN ERNEST T	COL	0-0029268	1055	1	SHIPLEY ALDEN R	LTC	0-0033699	0964	1	SIEGEL CHARLES L	COL	0-0042879	0662	2	SINGLEY JR GEORGE T	LTC	0-0055928	0365	1
SHEETS ARTHUR M	COL	C-0008028	0949	2	SHIPLEY BYRON M	COL	0-0039827	0463	1	SIEMERS HERMAN R	COL	0-0042162	0463	1	SINNREICH SIMON R	LTC	0-0021173	0956	1
SHEETS HENRY B	COL	0-0012460	0934	2	SHIPLEY WAYNE O	COL	0-0020491	0965	1	SIEMONS PHILLIP J	CW3	W-0903818	1167	1	SION EDWARD C	COL	0-0041744	0763	1
SHEETS JR CLARENCE E	COL	C-0021692	1163	1	SHIRMAN KENNETH	LTC	0-0060411	0963	1	SIEVERS HARRY L	COL	C-0029814	0962	1	SIPES KENNETH L	LTC	0-0041989	0162	2
SHEETZ JOSEF R	M G	C-0009720	0850	1	SHIPR BEVERLY A	COL	0-0008116	0748	1	SIEVERS HENRY R	COL	C-0030298	C762	1	SIPPLE BLANCHE I	LTC	N-0001204	0966	1
SHEFFER JR GEORGE E	MAJ	0-0028120	C567	1	SHIPSTEAD ALTON M	LTC	0-0026345	0965	1	SIEVERS RALPH H	COL	0-0017254	0858	1	SIREN VINCENT W	LTC	0-0021306	0866	1
SHEFFEY III JOHN P	COL	0-0024701	1065	1	SHIREY BURRELL P	LTC	C-0039969	0663	1	SIEVERS VERA A	LTC	L-0000020	1057	1	SISSON WINFIELD W	COL	C-0018096	1047	2
SHEFFIELD JR JAMES A	LTC	0-0088201	C765	1	SHIREY WILLIAM M	MAJ	C-0026635	C865	1	SIEVERS WILLIAM E	COL	0-0020299	1265	1	SITES EUGENE P	COL	0-0043526	1066	1
SHEFFIELD L O	COL	0-0021702	0959	1	SHIRK ROBERT V	MAJ	0-0056436	0163	1	SIGAFOOS ROLLAND B	COL	0-0022291	0266	1	SITES JR GEORGE E	MAJ	0-0079089	1162	1
SHEFFIELD ROBERT X	LTC	0-0028734	C467	1	SHIRLEY COURTNEY R	LTC	0-0059027	0366	1	SIGERFOOS EDWARD	COL	C-0020414	C866	1	SITLER HENRY C	LTC	0-0081227	0566	1
SHELBY RAYMOND T	LTC	0-0023504	C552	1	SHIRLEY JACKSON E	COL	0-0033577	0861	1	SIGHTLER JR S P	COL	0-0041824	116C	1	SITNEK WILLIAM G	LTC	0-0040142	0164	1
SHELDON GEORGE C	COL	C-0048236	C967	1	SHIRLEY LOUIS H	COL	0-0029372	1059	1	SIKES GLENN A	LTC	0-0020353	C66C	1	SIVIGNY JOSEPH A	LTC	0-0051385	C261	1
SHELL ROBERT H	COL	0-0031472	C766	1	SHIVE DONALD W	COL	0-0020628	0565	1	SILBAUGH VERNE R	LTC	0-0041489	0256	1	SIZEMORE BURLEY	MAJ	C-007909C	0762	1
SHELL VERNON MC	MAJ	C-0006696	0-35	2	SHIVER WILLIAM W	CW2	W-0906989	1059	1	SILBERMAN HENRY K	LTC	0-0066099	0965	1	SJOBERG JEANETTE E	MAJ	N-0002248	0561	1
SHELLENBERGER L C	COL	C-0020506	0655	1	SHOAFF ALMON L	LTC	0-0027866	0765	1	SILCOX MARSHALL W	LTC	0-0084671	0567	1	SKAGGS ROBERT N	COL	0-0039816	0158	1
SHELLEY ROYDEN R	CW4	RW-0903805	C664	1	SHOCKLEY PHILIP M	COL	0-0015485	1047	2	SILER ARNOLD M	MAJ	C-0011117	C539	1	SKARDON BEVERLY N	COL	0-0033939	0962	1
SHELLEY STONEY	COL	C-0042571	C964	1	SHOE ROBERT C	M G	0-0008119	0351	1	SILLIN WILLIAM E	LTC	C-0081221	1266	1	SKEATH ELBUR J	LTC	0-0079997	0864	1
SHELLUM ALFORD C	LTC	C-0033299	C262	1	SHOEMAKER JOHN J	COL	0-0030133	1163	1	SILLS CLARENCE F	COL	0-0024463	1163	1	SKEEHAN JR RAYMOND A	COL	0-0067959	0967	1

NAME	GRADE	SVC NO	DATE RET MO YR	RET CODE
SKEES HUGH S	COL	0-0079998	0565	1
SKEIBER STANLEY C	LTC	0-0080185	0865	1
SKELLS JAMES F	COL	0-0019830	0865	1
SKELLY FRANK H	COL	0-0029056	0159	1
SKELTON OSCAR G	COL	0-0003983	0946	2
SKELTON WINFRED C	B G	0-0012374	0854	2
SKENE CEDRIC M S	COL	0-0003209	0446	2
SKERRY HARRY A	COL	0-0005584	1147	2
SKERRY JR ARTHUR W	2LT	0-0071162	0-40	2
SKERRY LESLIE M	COL	0-0007313	0946	2
SKIBA SOPHIA C	MAJ	N-0000411	0662	1
SKIDMORE HERROL J	COL	0-0018664	0762	2
SKIDMORE WILBUR M	B G	0-0018440	0860	2
SKILLMAN CHARLES S	COL	0-0038989	0666	1
SKINNER ASA H	COL	0-0007996	0447	1
SKINNER EDWIN C	COL	0-0050985	0658	1
SKINNER ERNEST B	COL	0-0039710	0361	1
SKINNER HARRY E	COL	0-0021425	0863	1
SKINNER JAMES H	COL	0-0019144	0559	1
SKINNER JEAN E	MAJ	N-0000572	0761	1
SKINNER LAWRENCE L	COL	0-0015325	0954	1
SKINNER ROBERT A	B G	0-0019917	1162	1
SKINNER RUSSELL	COL	0-0007533	0349	1
SKINNER THOMAS R W	COL	0-0050971	0258	1
SKINROOD NORMAN A	COL	0-0019882	0865	1
SKIPPER JOHN O	LTC	0-0033083	0861	1
SKLADAL CONRAD	LTC	0-0003631	1139	1
SKOGSBERG PAUL L	LTC	0-0062134	0664	1
SKORINA ALEXANDER	MAJ	0-0052984	0555	2
SKVARCEK JR ANDREW	CW2	W-0903826	0849	1
SLACK ADA L	MAJ	N-0002222	0360	1
SLACK JULIUS F	B G	0-0012271	0951	1
SLAD HARRY A	LTC	0-0032088	0859	1
SLADE LAWRENCE	LTC	0-0008135	1141	2
SLADE TODD H	COL	0-0018789	0758	1
SLADEN JR FRED W	B G	0-0017677	0859	1
SLAGLE HALBERT J	LTC	0-0039865	0861	1
SLAPPEY EUGENE N	COL	0-0005163	1048	1
SLATE RALPH	COL	0-0005790	0746	1
SLAUGHTER DONALD F	COL	0-0022202	0965	1
SLAUGHTER JOHN E	LTC	0-0019921	0859	1
SLAUGHTER JR S C	COL	0-0029530	0361	1
SLAUGHTER PAGE H	COL	0-0030250	1064	1
SLAUGHTER WILLIS R	B G	0-0005296	0654	1
SLAWSON HARRY C	LTC	0-0055886	0865	1
SLAYDEN WILLIAM M	COL	0-0030754	0566	1
SLEDGE THEODORE J	COL	0-0005817	1044	2
SLIDER RICHARD H	LTC	0-0010309	0142	1
SLIGER JR IRA T	LTC	0-0059032	0667	1
SLISHER WELDON L	COL	0-0029787	0762	1
SLOAN EMERALD F	COL	0-0015084	1032	2
SLOAN GEORGE A	COL	0-0020821	0764	1
SLOAN JOHN F	M G	0-0003018	1046	1
SLOAN JR WILLIAM A	COL	0-0024235	0767	1
SLOANE JR CHARLES C	COL	0-0016456	0756	2
SLOANE NICHOLAS J	LTC	0-0043582	0866	1
SLOAT JAMES W	COL	0-0020556	1263	1
SLOAT JESSE I	COL	0-0004054	1166	2
SLOBE ELMER L	COL	0-0042867	1066	1
SLOCUM JR A N	COL	0-0039610	0259	1
SLOCUM LECOUNT H	B G	0-0009716	0754	1
SLOSSON JR CHARLES F	WO1	W-0900156	0841	2
SLOVER ROBERT H	COL	0-0043638	1264	1
SLUMPFF CARL F	LTC	0-0084573	1262	1
SLY GEORGE W	LTC	0-0081234	1153	1
SMALL ARTHUR C	COL	0-0052214	1263	1
SMALL BRAXTON E	COL	0-0042156	0363	1
SMALL JR BALLARD B	LTC	0-0081235	0766	1
SMALLE DANIEL E	COL	0-0041576	0259	1
SMALLEY HARRY E	COL	0-0004023	0248	1
SMALLEY HOWARD N	COL	0-0020853	0867	1
SMART DONALD V	COL	0-0031597	1263	1
SMEDILE JOSEPH A	COL	0-0020942	0764	2
SMELLOW SAMUEL	COL	0-0018439	0661	1
SMIGELOW HOWARD G	COL	0-0031791	0966	1

NAME	GRADE	SVC NO	DATE RET MO YR	RET CODE
SMILEY FRANK H	LTC	0-0037582	0862	1
SMILEY JAMES L	1LT	0-0023061	0148	1
SMILEY ROBERT E	LTC	0-0048683	1263	1
SMILEY STANLEY W	COL	0-0030160	0564	1
SMIT WALTER	COL	0-0020494	0965	1
SMITH ALBERT C	M G	0-0005265	0955	2
SMITH ALLEN T	LTC	0-0034320	0462	1
SMITH AUBURN H	COL	0-0031073	0764	1
SMITH BARTHOLOME	LTC	0-0060790	0960	2
SMITH BOYD L	COL	0-0008773	0851	1
SMITH BRADISH J	COL	0-0024049	0265	1
SMITH BYRON S	LTC	0-0043860	0767	1
SMITH C ELFORD	COL	0-0015074	0753	1
SMITH C RODNEY	M G	0-0016388	0857	1
SMITH CARL N	COL	0-0029105	0559	1
SMITH CAROLYN E	MAJ	R-0010009	1166	2
SMITH CECIL L	LTC	0-0023751	0759	1
SMITH CHARLES A	B G	0-0022113	0246	1
SMITH CHARLES C	LTC	0-0004497	1037	2
SMITH CHARLES M	LTC	0-0029199	0359	1
SMITH CHARLES R	COL	0-0011629	0549	1
SMITH CHARLES R	MAJ	0-0037608	0760	2
SMITH CHARLES W	CPT	0-0080186	1166	1
SMITH CLARKE S	COL	0-0000586	0624	1
SMITH CLAYTON J	MAJ	0-0060005	1265	1
SMITH CLIFFORD A	COL	0-0011424	0149	1
SMITH DANA E	COL	0-0038759	0362	2
SMITH DONALD H	COL	0-0016334	1055	1
SMITH DOUGLAS R	COL	0-0015699	0854	1
SMITH EDMUND C	CW4	W-0903830	0452	1
SMITH EDWIN A	COL	0-0007401	0947	1
SMITH EDWIN A	COL	0-0041459	0757	1
SMITH ELIZABETH	LTC	L-0000048	0861	1
SMITH ELLSWORTH	LTC	0-0048540	0367	2
SMITH EMIL J	LTC	0-0028860	0554	1
SMITH EMMETT W	COL	0-0029161	1057	1
SMITH EMMITT D	COL	0-0042788	0564	1
SMITH ERNEST F	COL	0-0029418	0759	2
SMITH ESTELLE	MAJ	N-0002193	0465	1
SMITH ESTIL V	COL	0-0003473	0646	1
SMITH EUGENE	LTC	0-0030559	0962	1
SMITH EUGENE A	LTC	0-0008747	0440	2
SMITH FLETCHER	MAJ	0-0044638	0262	1
SMITH FLOYD V	CW4	W-0904259	0863	1
SMITH FRANCIS M	LTC	0-0023634	0859	1
SMITH FRANK A	LTC	0-0027701	0966	1
SMITH FRANK P	LTC	0-0025888	0967	1
SMITH FRANK W	COL	0-0009088	0948	1
SMITH FRANKLIN G	B G	0-0019154	0963	1
SMITH FRED C	COL	0-0038703	1161	1
SMITH FRED C	COL	0-0044457	1165	1
SMITH FREDERICK	COL	0-0051997	0157	1
SMITH GEORGE	CW4	W-0904199	1059	1
SMITH GEORGE I	COL	0-0006517	1050	1
SMITH GEORGE S	B G	0-0015308	0754	2
SMITH GEORGE W	COL	0-0029013	0958	1
SMITH GLEN W	LTC	0-0038139	0866	1
SMITH GLENN K	COL	0-0020563	1066	1
SMITH GORDON K	COL	0-0029383	0260	1
SMITH GORDON L	LTC	0-0026029	0765	1
SMITH GROVER G	LTC	0-0080001	0866	1
SMITH H REX	CW4	W-0904305	0664	1
SMITH HAROLD A	LTC	0-0031615	0660	1
SMITH HAROLD H	LTC	0-0022677	0746	2
SMITH HARRY P	LTC	0-0006342	0941	2
SMITH HARRY W	LTC	0-0034041	0162	1
SMITH HARRY T	COL	0-0022001	0764	1
SMITH HARVEY H	COL	0-0010155	0252	1
SMITH HOMER A	CW4	W-0906997	0464	1
SMITH HORRELL H	LTC	0-0036562	0864	1
SMITH HULETT O	LTC	0-0081927	0167	1
SMITH II A MARK	COL	0-0029927	0563	1
SMITH II DAN L	COL	0-0040156	0567	1
SMITH JACK E	LTC	0-0060347	1167	1
SMITH JAMES B	LTC	0-0007508	0546	2

NAME	GRADE	SVC NO	DATE RET MO YR	RET CODE
SMITH JAMES B	LTC	0-0051491	0462	2
SMITH JAMES H	COL	0-0065410	0556	2
SMITH JAMES R	COL	0-0030772	0266	1
SMITH JAMES W	LTC	0-0032128	0564	1
SMITH JEROME F	LTC	0-0040406	1063	2
SMITH JEROME T	COL	0-0030874	0765	1
SMITH JOHN C	COL	0-0015656	0754	1
SMITH JOHN W	LTC	0-0010479	0729	2
SMITH JR ARTHUR J	COL	0-0021163	0648	2
SMITH JR C COBURN	B G	0-0018434	0761	1
SMITH JR DAVID C	LTC	0-0043394	1264	1
SMITH JR GEORGE F	LTC	0-0027247	0765	1
SMITH JR HERMAN R	LTC	0-0033922	0766	1
SMITH JR IRVING	1LT	0-0014465	0519	2
SMITH JR JOHN A	COL	0-0010228	0349	1
SMITH JR JOHN A	LTC	0-0063843	0966	1
SMITH JR MARTIN R	CPT	0-0059035	0663	1
SMITH JR RIDGWAY P	COL	0-0020243	0966	1
SMITH JR ROBERT G	COL	0-0029804	1060	1
SMITH JR ROBERT O	LTC	0-0031636	0765	1
SMITH JR SELWYN D	M G	0-0020194	0467	1
SMITH JR STILSON H	COL	0-0019480	0864	1
SMITH JR WILLIAM O	COL	0-0029850	0163	1
SMITH JR WILLIAM M	LTC	0-0080493	0867	2
SMITH JR WILLIAM R	COL	0-0018661	0259	1
SMITH JUDSON M	LTC	0-0016270	0753	1
SMITH JUNIUS R	COL	0-0017972	1053	1
SMITH KIMBALL C	COL	0-0029882	0459	2
SMITH KINGSLEY J	MAJ	0-0059034	0564	1
SMITH LELAND S	COL	0-0012799	0954	1
SMITH LEO A	COL	0-0030478	0865	1
SMITH LESLIE O	LTC	0-0033042	0863	1
SMITH LLOYD G	LTC	0-0038024	0562	1
SMITH LON H	COL	0-0018854	0762	2
SMITH LOWELL H	CPT	0-0060705	0862	1
SMITH LYNN D	B G	0-0029741	0764	1
SMITH MARK A H	COL	0-0041447	1056	1
SMITH MARK E	COL	0-0015796	0854	1
SMITH MARSHALL J	LTC	0-0080004	0966	1
SMITH MARY B	MAJ	N-0000413	0661	1
SMITH MARY I	LTC	N-0001005	1067	1
SMITH MERLE E	COL	0-0056785	0957	1
SMITH MERWIN H	COL	0-0042349	0464	1
SMITH MICHAEL G	COL	0-0012342	0547	2
SMITH MYRON D	LTC	0-0031860	0466	1
SMITH OSWALD C	LTC	0-0054531	0756	1
SMITH OSWALD H	CW4	W-0901998	1054	1
SMITH PAUL R	COL	0-0011960	0551	1
SMITH PHILIP J	COL	0-0021719	1059	1
SMITH PHILLIP B	COL	0-0030952	0862	1
SMITH PHILLIP R	COL	0-0035445	0764	1
SMITH PRESTON W	CPT	0-0009305	0-26	2
SMITH RALPH C	M G	0-0004723	1046	1
SMITH RALPH H	COL	0-0031614	1164	1
SMITH RICHARD A	LTC	0-0027490	0566	1
SMITH RICHARD D	COL	0-0029495	1160	1
SMITH ROBERT D	COL	0-0019690	1046	2
SMITH ROBERT L	LTC	0-0039350	0764	1
SMITH ROBERT L	LTC	0-0065129	0966	1
SMITH ROBERT M	COL	0-0015353	0847	1
SMITH ROBERT N	COL	0-0039709	0661	2
SMITH ROLLEN H	COL	0-0031367	0166	1
SMITH ROMAN A	CW4	W-0903835	0966	1
SMITH ROY E	LTC	0-0035777	0863	1
SMITH RUSSELL R	COL	0-0019953	0863	1
SMITH RUSSELL O	COL	0-0012698	0151	1
SMITH RUTH E	CPT	N-0001152	0657	2
SMITH RUTH P	MAJ	L-0000232	0359	1
SMITH SELWYN O	COL	0-0001209	0642	2
SMITH SR WILLIAM F	CPT	0-0074520	1062	2
SMITH STANLEY W	LTC	0-0043042	1062	1
SMITH STEPHEN E	COL	0-0020142	0466	1
SMITH TERENCE J	COL	0-0039585	0857	1
SMITH THOMAS E W	COL	0-0033064	0365	1
SMITH TRUMAN	COL	0-0004619	0142	2

NAME	GRADE	SVC NO	DATE RET MO YR	RET CODE
SMITH VALENTINE	COL	0-0015269	0854	2
SMITH VALLARD C	COL	0-0023543	0965	1
SMITH VERNON M	COL	0-0039993	0461	1
SMITH W DIXON	COL	0-0017085	0858	1
SMITH WALTER	MAJ	0-0013929	0620	2
SMITH WILLARD L	COL	0-0008048	0250	1
SMITH WILLIAM	LTC	0-0050717	0767	1
SMITH WILLIAM A	COL	0-0008674	0548	1
SMITH WILLIAM A	COL	0-0030079	1263	1
SMITH WILLIAM D	CW4	W-0904204	0760	1
SMITH WILLIAM E	CW4	W-0904205	1156	1
SMITH WILLIAM M	CW4	W-0904268	1056	1
SMITH WILLIAM R	LTC	0-0028562	0667	1
SMITH WILLIAM S	COL	0-0030968	0766	1
SMITH WILLIAM S	LTC	0-0038509	0963	1
SMITH WILLIAM T	COL	0-0024341	0762	1
SMITH WILLIS T	COL	0-0029518	0361	2
SMITH WOODROW M	COL	0-0022960	0762	1
SMITH WOODS B	LTC	0-0043438	0266	1
SMITHERS FLORENCE R	MAJ	N-0002158	0862	1
SMOAK JOHN R	COL	0-0031463	0267	1
SMOAK JR WILLIAM M	COL	0-0081857	0561	1
SMOAK MARION H	LTC	0-0043288	0861	1
SMOCK STANLEY C	COL	0-0009489	0150	1
SMOLENSKI FELIX S	LTC	0-0063037	1162	1
SMOLKA JOSEPH F	CW2	W-0901033	0342	1
SMOLLER JOHN F	M G	0-0019416	0864	1
SMOTHERS WILLIAM	LTC	0-0082098	0766	1
SMOYER RAYMOND E	CPT	0-0075295	0367	1
SMYKLO ALEXANDER	CW3	W-0903837	057	1
SMYLY JR JAMES W	COL	0-0016928	0757	1
SMYRL J T	LTC	0-0033732	0861	2
SMYSER CRAIG	COL	0-0019417	0754	1
SMYSER JR RUDOLPH E	COL	0-0017090	0758	1
SMYTHE GEORGE W	M G	0-0015816	0257	2
SNARE CONNIE	MAJ	N-0001904	1061	1
SNEDDEN HARRY O	CW3	RW-0903838	0458	1
SNEDEKER EUGENE C	LTC	0-0050011	0969	1
SNEE JAMES W	COL	0-0019516	0864	1
SNELLING WALTER H	LTC	0-0026752	0765	1
SNIDER VENNE E	LTC	0-0051341	1060	1
SNODGRASS EDGAR H	COL	0-0012478	0854	1
SNODGRASS JR JOHN W	LTC	0-0063477	0767	2
SNOOKS JR JAMES P	COL	0-0030011	0660	1
SNOW BEVERLY C	COL	0-0012056	1052	1
SNOW CHESTER R	LTC	0-0002483	1022	1
SNOW CLIFFORD M	COL	0-0029122	0859	1
SNOW FRANK G	CPT	0-0059875	0962	1
SNOW JAMES A	LTC	0-0060385	0864	1
SNOW ROBERT P	CW4	W-0902079	0762	1
SNOW ROBERT T	COL	0-0003417	0142	1
SNOWDEN HAZEL I	LTC	N-0001895	1163	1
SNOWDEN PAUL T	COL	0-0029811	1162	1
SNYDER AGNES R	LTC	M-0010003	0760	1
SNYDER BRADLEY J	CPT	0-0096646	0166	2
SNYDER CLIFFORD M	1LT	0-0018736	0437	2
SNYDER EMANUEL P	COL	0-0043286	0465	1
SNYDER FRANCES E	CPT	N-0002878	0762	2
SNYDER FRANK L	LTC	0-0043061	0964	1
SNYDER HARRY G	COL	0-0038854	1266	1
SNYDER HOLLICE H	LTC	0-0045998	0765	1
SNYDER HOWARD MCC	M G	0-0002412	1046	2
SNYDER JAMES L	M G	0-0019627	0465	1
SNYDER JAMES M	COL	0-0025036	0566	1
SNYDER JR HOWARD M	M G	0-0020213	0566	1
SNYDER MARVIN H	LTC	0-0030106	0162	1
SNYDER MYRTLE M	MAJ	N-0002446	0663	1
SNYDER OSCAR P	M G	0-0004008	1156	1
SNYDER RICHARD F	LTC	0-0039937	0660	1
SNYDER ROBERT I	COL	0-0052456	0962	1
SNYDER RUSSELL C	COL	0-0007456	0753	1
SOARES EDWARD J	COL	0-0030020	0360	1
SOCHON JOSEPH J	WO1	W-0902146	0446	1
SOCKOLOSKIE ALPHONSE	COL	0-0051945	0766	1
SOCKS HUGH J	COL	0-0039771	0762	2

NAME	GRADE	SVC NO	DATE RET MO YR	RET CODE
SODERBERG CHARLES A	1LT	0-0078512	0960	2
SODERHOLM NELS L	COL	0-0006199	0851	1
SODERHOLM WALTER F	COL	0-0007203	1146	2
SODERSTROM KENNETH M	1LT	0-0019684	0-36	2
SOGARD SIDNEY S	COL	0-0041518	0758	1
SOIK NILE W	1LT	C-0027140	0648	2
SOLLITTO BASIL J	LTC	0-0059796	0866	1
SOLLOHUB JULIAN V	COL	C-0020584	0567	1
SOLOMON EDWARD M	LTC	0-0032351	0766	1
SOLOMON MADDREY A	B G	0-0019194	0457	2
SOLOMON MORTON	COL	0-0051002	0858	1
SOLOMONSON LAWRENCE	2LT	0-0016318	0-29	2
SOLTZ ALICE E	MAJ	N-0000117	0958	1
SOMERS KENNETH	COL	0-0020413	0562	1
SOMERS RICHARD	CW4	W-0903842	0859	1
SOMERVILLE DUNCAN S	COL	C-0017109	0758	1
SOMMER HENRY J	COL	0-0029055	0159	1
SOMMERS LAWRENCE E	COL	0-0031405	0264	1
SOMMERS WILLIAM D	COL	0-0043270	0566	1
SOPER LEROY C	COL	0-0008554	1049	1
SOPRANO QUENTIN C	LTC	0-0037830	0165	1
SORBELLO ROSARIO	LTC	0-0025066	0163	1
SORENSEN LENNARD C	COL	0-0042710	1263	1
SORENSEN MARTIN D	LTC	0-0031784	0266	1
SORENSON MORRIS E	LTC	0-0031977	0858	1
SORINI CHARLOTTE	MAJ	N-0002270	0463	1
SORRELL ROY W	LTC	0-0030287	1262	1
SORRELLS JESSIE A	MAJ	N-0000600	1262	1
SORUM ARNE	COL	0-0011841	0948	1
SOTHERN RICHARD J	COL	0-0009290	1047	1
SOTO LILA D	MAJ	N-0001990	0466	1
SOULE JOHN E	COL	0-0050960	0957	1
SOULLIERE RALPH L	CW3	W-0903843	1062	1
SOUSA JOSEPH M	LTC	0-0084673	0265	1
SOUTHARD HARRY D	COL	0-0010837	0644	2
SOUTHARD WILLIAM W	COL	0-0004167	0147	2
SOUTHWORTH JOHN B	CW4	W-0901547	0157	1
SOWARDS MELVIN J	LTC	0-0039473	0265	1
SOWDER JOE W	CW4	W-0903844	0358	1
SOWERS KENNETH M	COL	0-0024357	0463	1
SOWERS LAWRENCE L	CW4	W-0903845	0463	1
SPACE FRED L	WO1	W-0800290	1037	1
SPAGNOLO JOSEPH A	LTC	0-0080495	0567	1
SPALDING ALBA C	COL	C-0014938	0350	1
SPALDING BASIL D	COL	0-0004541	1145	2
SPALDING DONALD P	COL	0-0006965	0648	1
SPALDING ISAAC	B G	0-0003383	0746	2
SPALDING SIDNEY P	M G	0-0003366	0849	1
SPANGLER RICHARD S	COL	0-0018457	0761	1
SPANN CHARLES W	LTC	0-0027135	0865	1
SPANN CHARLES W	MAJ	C-0034695	1061	1
SPANN CLAYTON D	1LT	0-0062113	0753	1
SPANN FRANKLIN L	COL	0-0023641	0764	1
SPANN GEORGE F	COL	0-0005115	1049	1
SPANN JAMES H	LTC	0-0045979	0863	1
SPANN JR CECIL E	COL	0-0020162	0460	1
SPANOGLE JOHN A	1LT	0-0014422	0320	2
SPARK JOHN R	LTC	0-0051812	1058	1
SPARKS JOHN W	COL	0-0030900	0566	1
SPARKS LEONARD C	COL	0-0002466	0845	1
SPARKS MURRAY E	LTC	0-0021374	0866	1
SPAULDING EDWARD C	COL	0-0020588	0867	1
SPAULDING THOMAS M	COL	0-0002030	0136	1
SPAULDING WILLIAM L	COL	0-0019704	1059	1
SPEAIRS ANSE H	COL	0-0084574	1265	1
SPEAKS ROBERT J	COL	0-0034196	0367	1
SPECIALE JOACHIM J	LTC	0-0045946	0461	1
SPECTOR SAM	LTC	0-0059037	0466	1
SPEED JR HORACE	COL	0-0012468	0951	1
SPEEDIE JOHN C	COL	0-0031730	0764	1
SPEER MILDRED	CPT	N-0002261	0459	1
SPEIDEL JR GEORGE S	B G	0-0018406	0761	1
SPEIDEL WILLIAM H	COL	0-0011074	1152	1
SPEIGELBERG FRANK J	LTC	0-0054373	0264	1
SPEIGHTS JR DURIS	LTC	C-0087924	0367	1

NAME	GRADE	SVC NO	DATE RET MO YR	RET CODE
SPEIR WILBERT A	COL	0-0041398	0855	1
SPEIRS RONALD C	LTC	0-0035820	0464	1
SPEISER ROBIN G	COL	C-0019104	0759	1
SPELLMAN CHARLES E	COL	0-0019655	0257	1
SPELLMAN JR SETH W	LTC	0-0070509	0867	2
SPELLMAN LAWRENCE E	LTC	0-0050267	0966	2
SPENCE RALPH W	MAJ	0-0052145	0366	1
SPENCE SR JUDSON C	LTC	0-0049771	0763	1
SPENCE WILLIAM	B G	0-0004447	0947	1
SPENCER ANDREW	LTC	C-0036076	0366	2
SPENCER HOUCK	COL	0-0034719	0664	1
SPENCER JOHN J	LTC	0-0044248	0163	1
SPENCER THOMAS C	COL	0-0002281	0644	2
SPENCER THOMAS K	1LT	0-0023327	0548	1
SPENDLOVE VENICE	MAJ	N-0001345	0367	1
SPERATI PAOLO H	COL	C-0009667	1149	1
SPERL FRANK	CW4	W-0902365	0660	1
SPERRY FREDERICK	COL	0-0051427	0863	1
SPETTEL FRANK J	LTC	0-0014613	0948	1
SPICER CYRIL B	COL	0-0006202	1046	2
SPICER WILLIAM H	COL	0-0029719	0661	1
SPIES CAGE H	COL	0-0029419	0660	1
SPIGELMEYER ROGER W	LTC	C-0052903	0262	1
SPIKA HOWARD J	LTC	0-0037593	0666	1
SPIKER ROBERT C	LTC	0-0035572	1064	1
SPILLANE JOHN H	LTC	0-0030932	0762	1
SPILLER EDWIN R	COL	0-0003445	0834	2
SPILLER OLIVER L	B G	C-0002978	0845	2
SPILLMAN LYNN	LTC	0-0050981	0456	1
SPILLMAN WILLIAM R	COL	0-0042345	0464	1
SPILLNER SIEGFRIED	COL	0-0035300	0766	1
SPINELLO MICHAEL S	LTC	0-0082101	0765	2
SPINKS LESLIE	COL	0-0029012	0858	1
SPINNEY RUSSELL G	COL	0-0030054	1263	1
SPITTLER AUGUST W	COL	0-0016954	1057	2
SPITZ HARRY	LTC	0-0057378	0756	1
SPITZMILLER BOB F	LTC	0-0060188	0761	1
SPIVA FORREST R	LTC	0-0084425	1166	1
SPIVEY EVA K	MAJ	N-0001897	1160	1
SPOHN EDWARD A	CW4	W-0903848	0365	1
SPOON THOMAS L	COL	0-0006385	0251	1
SPRAGINS ROBERT B	B G	0-0022080	0167	1
SPRAGUE HAROLD E	COL	0-0041940	1061	1
SPRAKE JAMES M	LTC	0-0029872	0161	1
SPRANKLE DANE D	COL	0-0042169	0961	1
SPRATT JAMES L	MAJ	C-0039233	0864	1
SPRING STONEY G	COL	C-0019770	0765	2
SPRINGER LOUIS F	COL	C-0079717	0567	1
SPRINGER ROBERT M	COL	0-0012422	0854	1
SPRINGER ROBERT R	COL	0-0030624	0666	1
SPRINGFIELD NORA G	LTC	L-0000062	0163	2
SPRINKLE LESTER A	COL	0-0004620	0151	1
SPROAT HARRY F	LTC	0-0057416	0266	1
SPROULL RALPH D	1LT	0-0010647	0828	2
SPURGIN WILLIAM F	COL	0-0018762	0960	1
SPURR JEROME L	LTC	0-0029398	0358	1
SPURRIER JAMES R	COL	0-0025273	0763	1
SQUIRES MONAS N	LTC	0-0038758	1061	1
SQUIRES WILLIAM A	COL	0-0003756	0445	2
ST HELENS BEATRICE	MAJ	L-0000040	1157	1
ST JAMES ROBERT G	COL	0-0009039	0146	2
ST JOHN CLEMENT F	M G	0-0018258	0461	1
ST JOHN FREDERICK	LTC	0-0031394	1264	1
ST JOHN RALPH P	COL	0-0039706	0161	1
ST JOHN RICHARD C	LTC	0-0043530	0862	2
ST LAWRENCE CLYDE P	CW4	W-0903850	0665	1
ST ONGE ROBERT J	LTC	0-0027844	0767	1
STAATS JR HARLAN H	CW3	W-0903851	0659	2
STACK ANDREW J	LTC	0-0031126	0365	1
STACK HELEN A	MAJ	N-0000104	0460	1
STACK JAMES	COL	0-0029005	0247	2
STACK MARY E	LTC	R-0010072	0165	1
STACK ROBERT I	B G	0-0007585	0753	1
STADFIELD HAROLD R	LTC	0-0039541	1054	1
STADIG NELS E	COL	0-0005112	1047	1

NAME	GRADE	SVC NO	DATE RET MO YR	RET CODE
STADLER JR JOHN H	B G	C-0015731	0150	1
STADTMAN CLAUD E	COL	0-0004549	0952	1
STAELENS MARTHA M	MAJ	N-0002360	1058	2
STAFFORD ALBERT T	LTC	0-0039866	1161	1
STAFFORD BEN	COL	0-0006840	1044	2
STAFFORD CHARLES E	COL	0-0010456	1046	1
STAFFORD HEZZIE W	CW3	W-0903852	1154	1
STAGG III SAMUEL T	CW4	W-0903853	1065	1
STAGLIANO FIORRE J	COL	0-0016389	0656	1
STAGNER CLYDE H	CPT	0-0065183	0564	2
STAGNER JOE P	CW4	W-0903854	0860	1
STAHL JOHN A	COL	C-0039934	1264	1
STAHLER CHARLES L	LTC	0-0032197	0966	1
STAHOVICH IRINA	MAJ	N-0000833	1166	1
STAIGER THEODORE S	LTC	0-0053879	0266	1
STAKES HARRY C	LTC	0-0030775	0764	1
STALCUP BYRON R	CW4	W-0903855	0264	1
STALEY JR HARRY L	CW4	W-0903856	0255	1
STALEY MORTIMER R	COL	0-0043620	1066	1
STALEY ROBERT B	LTC	0-0043331	0762	1
STALK THEODORE	LTC	0-0063208	0665	2
STALKER DANIEL E	LTC	0-0064959	0567	1
STAM CHARLES W	LTC	C-0081255	0966	1
STANCISKO STEPHEN F	COL	C-0011799	0954	1
STANDISH FREDERICK	LTC	0-0024581	0767	1
STANDLEE EARLE	M G	0-0016530	0457	1
STANDLEY JR C S	COL	0-0029840	1160	1
STANDLEY WILLIAM P	CW4	W-0903860	0163	1
STANFORD BLUNDEN	COL	0-0050578	0458	1
STANFORD FREDERICK	COL	0-0023812	0863	1
STANFORD WILLIAM A	COL	0-0043808	0666	1
STANGE CAROL	MAJ	M-0010058	0162	1
STANGEL LYMAN F	COL	0-0029449	0860	1
STANGLE JOSEPH H	COL	0-0021406	0962	1
STANKOVICH ALBERT A	LTC	0-0081256	0567	1
STANLEY ARTHUR W	COL	C-0008796	0742	2
STANLEY EDWARD	LTC	0-0061360	0967	1
STANLEY FORREST H	MAJ	C-0038545	0959	1
STANLEY HENRY C	CW4	W-0903863	1057	1
STANLEY JOHN B	COL	C-0019549	1060	1
STANLEY LESLIE W	COL	0-0038594	0655	1
STANLEY ORAMEL H	COL	C-0004080	0848	1
STANN EUGENE J	COL	0-0020573	0266	1
STANOWICZ JOSEPH J	LTC	C-0027869	0566	1
STANSILL JOHN T	LTC	0-0040738	0763	2
STANTON JULIUS D	COL	0-0019823	0757	1
STANTON RAYMUND G	COL	0-0016925	0757	1
STANTON WALTER C	COL	0-0016433	0656	1
STAPLES FRANKLIN F	MAJ	C-0065616	0563	1
STAPLES JAMES Y	LTC	0-0060444	0764	1
STAPLETON JAMES B	B G	0-0019656	0365	1
STAPLETON JOHN C	COL	0-0019878	0562	2
STAPLETON THOMAS J	LTC	0-0028285	0766	1
STAR REUBEN	LTC	0-0042920	0756	1
STARK AMELIA	MAJ	N-0000656	0263	1
STARK CHARLES R	COL	0-0028773	0354	1
STARK GILBERT J	COL	0-0042791	1162	1
STARK HARRY W	COL	0-0003437	0145	1
STARK HENRY J	COL	0-0051448	0863	1
STARK JOHN M	COL	0-0039622	0859	1
STARK JR ALEXANDER	B G	0-0005000	0246	2
STARK NORVELL R	LTC	C-0031335	0462	1
STARK THOMAS N	COL	0-0010368	0454	1
STARKEY ARTHUR W	COL	0-0025126	0762	1
STARKEY HENRY M M	LTC	0-0027422	0666	1
STARKS LESLIE F	LTC	0-0052029	0762	1
STARNES MERVYN B	COL	C-0029188	0960	1
STARR EDWARD M	COL	0-0012427	0854	1
STARR JAMES C	COL	0-0079640	0267	1
STARR LESTER L	CW4	W-0903867	0962	1
STARR ROBERT S	CW4	W-0903868	0666	1
STARR RUPERT E	B G	0-0011309	0550	1
STARR WILLIAM F	COL	C-0023843	1266	1
STARRATT THOMAS R	CPT	0-0017457	0340	2
STARRETT CARL H	MAJ	0-0009941	0939	2

NAME	GRADE	SVC NO	DATE RET MO YR	RET CODE
STATHAM HARLAN R	COL	0-0017672	1054	1
STAUB LESLIE J	COL	0-0029123	0859	1
STAUFFER CHARLES J	LTC	C-0032757	0666	1
STAVER DONALD F	LTC	0-0050422	0866	1
STAYER MORRISON C	M G	0-0002571	0746	2
STEADMAN FRANK M	COL	0-0017616	0459	1
STEARNS CUTHBERT P	B G	0-0002683	0246	2
STEARNS JOSEPH E	COL	0-0018791	0862	1
STEBBINS JR ALBERT K	COL	0-0015695	0854	1
STECK ERNEST E	LTC	0-0042490	0163	1
STECKEL GLENN A	LTC	0-0046036	0764	1
STEELE GORDON H	COL	0-0008175	1146	1
STEELE JOHN C	B G	0-0018668	0862	1
STEELE LOWELL R	COL	0-0025167	0765	1
STEELE MADA	MAJ	M-0010044	0464	1
STEELE PAUL	COL	0-0007509	0854	1
STEELE PRESTON	COL	0-0018729	0862	1
STEELE ROBERT L	LTC	0-0028429	0766	1
STEELE ROY H	COL	0-0041847	0361	1
STEELE RUSSELL D	LTC	0-0056800	0560	1
STEELE STANLEY F	COL	0-0020474	0759	1
STEEN ELSIE W	MAJ	M-0010109	0760	1
STEENBURGH RUTH M	MAJ	N-0002075	1060	1
STEERE JOHN A	COL	0-0006698	0947	1
STEERE THOMAS I	MAJ	0-0013988	0720	2
STEFANI LOUIS J	LTC	0-0040707	0166	1
STEFFEY WILLIAM G	LTC	0-0030404	0661	1
STEGALL JR OSCAR	LTC	0-0032014	1066	1
STEGMAIER ROBERT M	COL	0-0020725	0865	1
STEIGER WALLACE C	COL	0-0008196	0652	1
STEIN JOHN F	COL	0-0051538	1064	1
STEIN JR THOMAS F	LTC	0-0031411	0165	1
STEIN WILLIAM	COL	0-0063775	0465	1
STEINBACH ALOIS L	LTC	0-0048109	1166	1
STEINBACH RICHARD	M G	0-0018560	0761	2
STEINBRING MILTON E	LTC	0-0025946	0862	1
STEINER JAMES L	CW4	W-0903874	1165	1
STEINER RAYMOND B	COL	0-0051622	0165	1
STEINHARDT WALTER	CW2	W-0903875	1159	1
STEINIAGER DONALD H	LTC	0-0050599	1266	1
STEINKRAUSS ALBERT M	COL	0-0051843	0467	1
STEINMEYER GEORGE	COL	0-0016675	0451	1
STELMAN CHESTER R	LTC	0-0063352	1065	1
STELZENMULLER W B	COL	0-0021422	0660	1
STEMPIN HARRY J	LTC	0-0045786	0563	1
STEPCZYK FRANK	COL	0-0020051	1065	1
STEPHENS BLACKBURN	COL	0-0033060	0964	1
STEPHENS ERNEST T	CW4	W-0903877	0956	1
STEPHENS FREEMAN I	MAJ	0-0026372	0146	2
STEPHENS GEORGE R	B G	0-0027892	0261	2
STEPHENS HARVEY L	CW4	W-0902093	1162	2
STEPHENS HENRY J	CW4	W-0903878	0762	1
STEPHENS HERBERT W	MAJ	0-0069802	0765	1
STEPHENS JOHN F	COL	0-0025539	0863	1
STEPHENS JOSEPH W G	COL	0-0004622	0746	1
STEPHENS LEONARD E	1LT	0-0014967	0934	2
STEPHENS RICHARD W	M G	C-0015569	0658	1
STEPHENS ROY A	LTC	0-0038705	1059	1
STEPHENSON ANDREW D	COL	0-0019201	0863	1
STEPHENSON EDWARD	1LT	0-0021340	0442	2
STEPHENSON HARRY W	LTC	0-0002655	1122	1
STEPHENSON HORACE G	LTC	0-0055488	0965	1
STEPHENSON JAMES D	LTC	0-0017757	1046	1
STEPHENSON JR H W	LTC	0-0022722	1158	1
STEPPAN MARY M	LTC	N-0000113	1058	1
STERLING JOHN A	COL	0-0002693	0935	1
STERLING JR PHILIP C	LTC	0-0020848	0846	2
STERLING THOMAS M	LTC	0-0059655	0767	1
STERN BENJAMIN	COL	0-0015197	0854	1
STETEKLUH ROBERT F	LTC	0-0027575	0766	1
STEVENS ALFRED E	COL	0-0029916	1060	1
STEVENS ALFRED L	LTC	0-0051506	0562	1
STEVENS BURROWES G	COL	0-0012187	0753	1
STEVENS DOUGLAS	COL	0-0038816	1265	1
STEVENS ELI	COL	0-0018235	0948	2

NAME	GRADE	SVC NO	DATE RET MO YR	RET CODE
STEVENS GEORGE B	LTC	0-0044872	0764	1
STEVENS III PAT M	COL	0-0030557	1064	1
STEVENS JOHN D	B G	0-0019414	0764	1
STEVENS RAY F	CW4	W-0907008	0266	1
STEVENS RICHARD E	COL	C-0028954	C556	2
STEVENS VERNUM C	COL	0-0015526	0754	1
STEVENS WILBER A	COL	C-0030365	C262	1
STEVENSON DANIEL S	COL	0-0019696	0265	2
STEVENSON DON W	LTC	0-0034868	0763	1
STEVENSON FRANK E	COL	C-0038785	1264	1
STEVENSON HUGH W	COL	C-0017642	C859	1
STEVENSON JEROME M	LTC	0-0051897	1162	1
STEVENSON WALTER F	COL	0-0041705	C459	1
STEVENSON WILLIAM J	MAJ	0-0074856	0767	1
STEWART BLANCHE M	LTC	N-C002003	0866	1
STEWART CHARLES H	LTC	0-0032925	C261	1
STEWART DONALC E	MAJ	C-0069803	1164	1
STEWART DOROTHY I	MAJ	L-0000262	0962	1
STEWART GEORGE C	M G	0-0015349	1054	1
STEWART HARCLD R	COL	0-0009780	0547	2
STEWART HARRY T	LTC	0-0027331	0166	1
STEWART HOWELL F	MAJ	C-0056571	1265	1
STEWART JOHN A	COL	0-0005278	0244	2
STEWART JOSEPH C	COL	0-0029662	C162	1
STEWART JR JAMES J	LTC	0-0020901	C444	2
STEWART JR JODIE C	LTC	0-0023256	C661	1
STEWART JR MARION C	COL	0-0030246	0864	1
STEWART KEITH M	LTC	C-0027700	C867	1
STEWART LEROY J	B G	0-0014912	C451	1
STEWART MANLIUS R	LTC	C-0042503	C163	1
STEWART MATTHEW C	COL	0-0043541	C865	1
STEWART RALPH B	COL	0-0009527	C847	1
STEWART STANLEY L	LTC	C-0042274	0160	1
STEWART THOMAS R	COL	0-0039335	C866	1
STEWART WILLIAM B	COL	0-0008766	0952	1
STEWART WILLIAM R	COL	0-0004751	1044	2
STICKMAN WILLIAM R	COL	C-0006595	0249	2
STICKNEY LOUIS S	COL	0-0007515	1048	1
STIEBEL HENRY M	COL	0-0030198	C664	1
STIEFEL ARTHUR A	LTC	0-0038934	C856	2
STIER ROBERT J	COL	0-0080008	1167	1
STIESMEYER EDWARD F	COL	0-0060741	C667	1
STIEVENART LAVERNE	MAJ	N-0000260	0560	1
STIKA ROBERT W	COL	C-0015886	0446	2
STILL ALICE E	MAJ	N-0002052	C960	1
STILL DANIEL E	COL	0-0019510	0662	1
STILL EDGAR E	LTC	0-0081260	0765	1
STILL FAYF G	MAJ	N-0000539	0449	1
STILLINGER CECIL	LTC	0-0057926	C851	1
STILLINGER OTTO R	COL	0-0010320	0744	2
STILLMAN EDMUND H	LTC	0-0006645	0147	1
STILLMAN RICHARD J	COL	0-0025038	1265	1
STILLWAUGH ELVA M	MAJ	L-0000250	1063	1
STILSON GUY O	CW4	W-0903880	1167	1
STINESS PHILIP R	COL	0-0018398	C761	1
STINSON GERALD C	MAJ	0-0061997	0364	1
STIRLING WILLIAM E	CW4	W-0903881	1059	1
STITH MARION C	COL	0-0037385	1166	1
STIVLEN SYLVIA M	MAJ	N-0001432	0664	1
STOCK MARVIN H	LTC	C-0050633	C667	1
STOCKDALE GALE E	1LT	0-0028328	0149	2
STOCKOFR IRENE L	MAJ	N-0000547	045C	1
STOCKTON ERNEST L	COL	0-0039560	1057	1
STOCKTON JOHN B	COL	0-0026152	C867	1
STOCKTON JR M L	B G	0-0010619	0644	2
STOCKTON MARSH R	LTC	0-0051769	0762	1
STOCKWELL WARREN P	LTC	0-0040438	C660	1
STODGEL JAMES E	LTC	C-0067963	C866	1
STOOTER CHARLES E	COL	0-0000505	C435	1
STOOTER CHARLES S	COL	0-0016013	0954	1
STOOTER JOHN H	COL	0-0015018	0654	1
STOECKERT GEORGE I	LTC	0-0036757	0467	1
STOEVER ROBERT E	COL	0-0042114	1162	1
STOKELY CARLIN C	COL	0-0002639	C446	2
STOKES JR JOHN H	M G	C-0012181	1156	1
STOKES JR MARCUS B	B G	0-0015613	0854	2
STOKES ORVILLE N	COL	0-0020215	1058	1
STOKES ROBERT C	LTC	0-0057887	0361	1
STOLL IRWIN C	LTC	0-0029504	0148	2
STOLL JUSTIN W	B G	0-0030483	0765	1
STOLTZ RUTH M	LTC	N-0000586	0459	1
STOLZ STEPHEN H	LTC	0-0041707	0757	1
STONE ALEXANDER	COL	0-0018076	0657	1
STONE BERNICE A	MAJ	N-0002257	0662	1
STONE DON N	CW3	W-0903885	0260	1
STONE FRED O	MAJ	0-0009108	0-34	1
STONE GUY	MAJ	0-0060213	1153	2
STONE JR RAYMOND	COL	0-0015206	0854	1
STONE JR STEPHEN G	MAJ	C-004796C	0764	1
STONE KATRINE F	MAJ	N-0002386	0959	1
STONE LAURENCE A	COL	0-0040414	0465	1
STONE LLOYD E	MAJ	0-0037138	C561	1
STONE WILLIAM S	COL	0-0018277	0654	2
STONEBACK LEE S	COL	0-0044316	0764	1
STONEKING ROBERT E	CW4	W-0903888	1165	1
STOPP JOSEPH E	LTC	0-0031693	1265	1
STORAASLI GYNTHER	COL	0-0011751	0248	1
STORKE HARRY P	LTG	0-0016468	0961	2
STORMS HARRY F	COL	0-0005725	0951	1
STORRS BRUCE D	LTC	0-0061060	1065	1
STOTLAR WILLIAM G	LTC	0-0043662	0167	1
STOTT MABEL C	LTC	N-0000073	0558	1
STOUGH JR CHARLES S	LTC	0-0035187	C863	1
STOUGH PAUL A	CPT	0-0027429	1060	2
STOUT ARTHUR O	LTC	0-0031255	0161	1
STOUT CARRIE P	MAJ	N-0000889	1163	1
STOUT LOUIS W	CW4	W-0907012	0761	1
STOUT ROY A	COL	0-0008726	0949	2
STOVALL JR A S J	COL	0-0012434	0854	1
STOVER GLENN C	CW4	W-0907013	1062	1
STOVER WILLIAM J	COL	0-0031381	1266	1
STOW HAROLD E	LTC	0-0008446	0544	2
STOWBRIDGE ROBERT W	LTC	0-0036501	0362	2
STOWELL ALLEN L	COL	C-0010310	0452	1
STOWELL WILLIAM H	LTC	0-0026682	0862	1
STRADER RALPH B	COL	0-0017686	0859	2
STRADLEY SARAH C	CPT	N-0001233	0859	1
STRAIGHT CLIO F	B G	0-0024337	C661	1
STRAIN ETHEL L	CPT	N-0000811	0350	1
STRAIN JAMES F	COL	0-0008085	0850	1
STRAIN JAMES W	COL	C-0023719	0767	1
STRAND DONALD J	LTC	0-0057067	0865	1
STRANDBERG WILLIAM B	COL	0-0020579	0863	1
STRATTON CHARLES W	COL	0-0016661	1056	1
STRATTON CHESTER M	COL	C-0030431	0565	1
STRATTON FREDERICK	LTC	0-0039544	1154	1
STRATTON JAMES H	B G	0-0012656	0749	1
STRAUB RUTH M	MAJ	N-0000166	0157	1
STRAUSS RALPH V	COL	0-0017689	1054	1
STRAWBRIDGE JOHN T	LTC	0-0040287	0165	1
STRAWN CHRISTOPHE	COL	0-0007250	1047	1
STRAYHORN KATHLEEN M	MAJ	N-0000092	0656	1
STRECKER ROBERT H	COL	0-0026853	0767	1
STREET ANCIL L	CW3	W-0907014	C262	1
STREET FRANK L	COL	0-0030055	0962	1
STREET JACK B	LTC	0-0034272	0661	1
STREET JOHN C	LTC	0-0018686	1133	2
STREET ROBERT W	LTC	0-0059042	0166	1
STREETER HILBERT S	LTC	0-0020300	1057	1
STREETMAN JAMES R	LTC	0-0030086	0161	1
STREICHER FREDERICK	COL	0-0041485	1057	1
STREIT PAUL H	M G	0-0006254	0353	1
STREVIC JOHN R	LTC	0-0039656	1160	1
STRICKLAND ARTHUR T	COL	0-0044085	0266	2
STRICKLAND ERASMUS H	COL	0-0029355	0355	2
STRICKLAND HENRY F	COL	0-0016140	0755	1
STRICKLAND ICA R	MAJ	R-0010112	0365	1
STRICKLAND JR Z L	COL	0-0024176	1064	1
STRICKLAND ROBERT P	LTC	0-0030749	1058	1
STRICKLAND WILBURN L	COL	C-0029839	0163	2
STRICKLER EDWARD J	COL	0-0008677	0446	2
STRICKLER JOHN C	COL	C-0016445	0756	1
STRIDER NICHOLAS S	COL	C-0045585	C767	1
STRIEGEL JOHN O	COL	0-0029700	C761	1
STRINGFELLOW HORACE	MAJ	0-0014195	C119	2
STRIPLING COCK A	CW4	RW-0907015	1167	1
STROBEL PHYLLIS R	MAJ	M-0010069	C565	1
STROCK ALAN H	COL	C-0023099	1162	1
STRODE JOHN T B	COL	0-0019709	C163	2
STROEDE ROGER A	LTC	C-0049045	C667	1
STROEHER RUTH M	MAJ	N-0002104	0866	1
STROHBEHN EDWARD L	COL	0-0012312	C754	1
STROHM ROBERT H	CPT	0-0065152	0265	1
STROK MICHAEL J	COL	C-0052838	0667	1
STROKER JAMES F	COL	C-0018375	C947	2
STRONG CECIL H	COL	C-0022725	0366	2
STRONG EDWIN H	COL	0-0008538	C546	2
STRONG PASCHAL N	B G	0-0014904	0654	1
STRONG PAUL O	LTC	0-0007876	0342	2
STRONG ROBERT W	B G	0-0003832	C350	1
STROPES LLOYD R	LTC	0-0037629	0464	1
STROTHER KENNETH C	COL	0-0015738	C654	1
STROUBE ESTHEL O	COL	C-0041368	0954	1
STROUD JR JOSEPH C	LTC	0-0058693	C865	1
STROUD WILLIAM R	LTC	0-0028201	C966	1
STROUP DONALD F	CW4	W-0904316	0257	1
STRUBE RICHARD L	LTC	0-0082106	0567	1
STRUBLE H SPENCER	COL	C-0012953	1049	1
STRUBLE LAWRENCE A	CPT	0-0087396	C763	2
STRYKER WILLIAM R	COL	0-0019691	1060	1
STUART ALEXANDER	COL	0-0002307	1039	2
STUART ALEXANDER	COL	0-0019447	0762	1
STUART ARCHIBALD	M G	C-0019130	1058	1
STUART LARMETT L	B G	0-0003677	0751	1
STUART MARGARET	MAJ	R-0010064	C760	1
STUART WHITNEY O	LTC	0-0037788	1164	1
STUBBLEBINE JR A N	COL	0-0015768	0954	2
STUBBS JR HUGH P	LTC	0-0024530	0761	1
STUBBS MARSHALL	M G	0-0017706	1163	1
STUBBS WILLIAM H	COL	C-0022085	0946	2
STUCKERT JOHN M	LTC	0-0084427	1066	1
STUDLER RENE R	COL	0-0010398	0853	1
STULL KATHERINE	MAJ	L-0000002	0753	1
STULTING HARRY W	LTC	0-0022726	0160	1
STUMP GEORGE T	COL	0-0030023	1163	1
STUMP ROBERT C	LTC	C-0023518	C861	2
STUMPF ROBERT H	COL	0-0020707	C967	1
STURDIVANT LESLIE W	MAJ	0-0058620	0966	1
STURDY WILLIAM W	COL	0-0051043	0859	1
STURGEON JOHN H	COL	0-0004095	0848	1
STURGIS SARA L	LTC	L-0000029	1058	1
STURIES CARL H	COL	0-0017192	1053	2
STURMAN JR J FOXHALL	COL	C-0012720	C753	1
STUTZMAN OLIVER G	COL	0-0032771	0467	1
STUVERUD HOMER A	LTC	0-0043523	1164	1
STUWE KATHRYNE C	MAJ	N-0000298	1060	1
STYER WILHELM O	LTG	0-0004415	0447	1
STYLES SIDNEY S	CW3	W-0903894	0264	1
SUBE HERBERT P	LTC	0-0057723	0764	1
SUDDETH JAMES A	LTC	0-0055222	0865	1
SUGG DOUGLAS	COL	0-0011172	1150	1
SUGIYAMA SHIGEKI J	LTC	0-0092126	0966	1
SUGLIA ANTHONY S	LTC	0-0065108	1066	1
SULIT MARIANO S	CPT	0-0012869	0539	2
SULLIVAN ALEXANDER	COL	0-0003231	0147	1
SULLIVAN ARTHUR P	LTC	0-0030974	1162	2
SULLIVAN ELEANORE C	LTC	L-0000014	C257	1
SULLIVAN FRANCIS J	LTC	0-0039507	0753	1
SULLIVAN FRANCIS R	COL	C-0022923	C763	1
SULLIVAN GERALD J	1LT	0-0015511	0834	2
SULLIVAN JAMES J	MAJ	C-0059044	1063	1
SULLIVAN JOHN B	B G	0-0018363	C661	1
SULLIVAN JOHN M	COL	C-0030698	C766	2
SULLIVAN JOHN S	COL	C-0002271	1045	2
SULLIVAN JOSEPH P	M G	0-0005378	1053	2
SULLIVAN JOSEPH T	LTC	0-0059513	0763	2
SULLIVAN JR B H	COL	0-0022770	0161	1
SULLIVAN LEO J	MAJ	0-0037027	0658	2
SULLIVAN LEON F	CPT	0-0006749	0934	2
SULLIVAN MAURICE L	COL	C-0043165	1067	2
SULLIVAN MORTIMER F	COL	0-001066C	0854	2
SULLIVAN RICHARD C	LTC	0-0084808	0867	1
SULLIVAN WILLIAM E	B G	0-0029635	0162	2
SULLIVAN WILLIAM H	LTC	0-0050750	0666	1
SULLO ERWIN F	COL	0-0042491	0265	1
SULPIZIO VIRGINIA M	MAJ	N-0001802	C665	1
SUMMA GROVER A	COL	0-0011965	0153	1
SUMMERALL JR C P	COL	0-0015726	0754	1
SUMMERS EVELYN G	LTC	R-0010122	0667	1
SUMMERS IVERSON B	COL	0-000383C	0746	2
SUMMERS OWEN	B G	C-0008066	0647	2
SUMMERS WILLIAM M	COL	0-0021365	0566	2
SUMMERSETT JAMES A	LTC	0-0004882	1141	2
SUMMERSON DONALD J	LTC	0-0060747	1066	1
SUMNER EDWIN M	COL	0-0006894	0848	1
SUMNER GEORGE R	COL	0-0039689	1060	1
SUMNER HENRY A	COL	C-0002894	0544	2
SUMNICHT RUSSELL W	COL	C-0031208	0966	1
SUNDERLIN WILLIAM W	COL	0-0032678	1165	1
SUNDIN ALVAR R	COL	0-0021128	0366	1
SUNDLOF WILLIAM A	COL	0-0021236	0762	1
SUNDRE ROBERT L	LTC	0-0062950	1166	1
SUNDT DANIEL A	COL	0-0017604	0859	1
SUNDT HARALD S	COL	0-0018774	0862	1
SUNSHINE GEORGE R	LTC	0-0080497	0762	1
SUPPLE EDWARD L	COL	0-0009814	0350	1
SURPER CHARLES E	LTC	0-0032528	1057	1
SURRATT JOE F	COL	0-0019461	0661	1
SUTHERLAND ALEXANDER	COL	0-0018609	0661	1
SUTHERLAND CHARLES F	COL	0-0007107	0146	1
SUTHERLAND JOHN F	LTC	0-0030779	0764	1
SUTHERLAND KATHERINE	MAJ	L-0000296	0766	1
SUTTLES ERNEST A	COL	0-0016275	0255	1
SUTTON EARL	COL	0-0042961	0860	1
SUTTON GEORGE M	LTC	0-0035970	0363	1
SUTTON JR CLYDE T	LTC	0-0022128	0659	1
SUTTON STOWE T	COL	0-0011165	0748	1
SVARE CARROLL S	COL	0-0022313	0167	1
SVENSSON ERIC H F	B G	0-0017630	0859	1
SVILAR MATTHEW	LTC	0-0081210	1066	1
SWAIM ALLAN L	COL	0-0032871	0966	1
SWAIN OREN	COL	0-0020176	0866	1
SWALL ROSS F	LTC	0-0037511	0464	1
SWAN ELEANOR J	MAJ	N-0001901	0861	1
SWAN THOMAS H	COL	0-0031471	0367	1
SWANK MARCELL G	LTC	0-0082108	1166	2
SWANSON BYRON A	CW3	W-0907017	0964	2
SWANSON LEONARD N	COL	0-0018936	0760	1
SWANSON RAYMOND W	COL	0-0030925	1066	1
SWANSON RUTH M	MAJ	N-0002176	0767	1
SWANTON DONOVAN	COL	C-0005314	C951	1
SWARM WILLIAM R	COL	0-0043018	0666	1
SWARTZ ALVA W	LTC	0-0025077	C962	1
SWARTZ CHARLES H	B G	0-0012798	0457	1
SWARTZ DOROTHY L	MAJ	R-0010008	C364	1
SWARTZ ROBERT N	COL	C-0039903	0664	1
SWATTA FRANK A	COL	0-0022237	0867	1
SWEANY KENNETH S	B G	0-0015251	1155	1
SWEARINGEN JOHN C	LTC	0-0034711	0365	1
SWEARINGEN SAMUEL M	LTC	0-0021381	0866	1
SWEE RICHARD J	CW4	W-0907018	0467	1
SWEEK JACK G	COL	0-0030633	0366	1
SWEENEY ANNE E	LTC	L-0000119	0266	1
SWEENEY EUGENE J	COL	C-0021254	0860	1
SWEENEY FRANCIS P	LTC	0-0081271	0667	1
SWEENEY HARDIN C	COL	0-0004569	0654	1
SWEENEY JAMES L	LTC	0-0031457	0561	1
SWEENY ANNA C	CPT	N-000017[illegible]	0648	1
SWEET JOSEPH B	B G	0-0009694	0648	1
SWEET JR FRED W	LTC	0-0031266	0967	1

NAME	GRADE	SVC NO	DATE RET MO YR	RET CODE
SWEET JR WILLIAM J	LTC	0-0035814	C761	1
SWEET WILLIAM H	COL	0-0006579	1047	2
SWEETING JR HARRY H	COL	C-0019168	C863	1
SWENSON ALICE O	MAJ	N-0000196	0461	1
SWETT DANIEL H	LTC	0-0038984	0159	1
SWETT TREVOR W	COL	0-0007010	1032	2
SWICK CHARLES H	MAJ	C-0009019	0138	2
SWIDLER GEORGE J	CW4	W-0903901	C964	1
SWIFT EBEN F	COL	0-0023258	C965	1
SWIFT EDWARD V	LTC	0-0023636	C946	2
SWIFT IRA P	M G	0-0012205	C654	1
SWIFT MELVIN L	CW4	W-0902325	C156	1
SWINDLER CHARLES M	MAJ	C-0024641	1146	2
SWINDLER PERRY C	COL	0-0028827	0753	2
SWINEHART JR LEWIS S	LTC	0-0059880	C364	2
SWING JOSEPH M	LTG	0-0003801	0254	2
SWISHER ARTHUR C	COL	0-0051611	C565	2
SWITZER JOHN S	COL	0-0004747	0951	1
SWITZER WALTER E	LTC	C-0065442	0766	1
SWOFFORD JAMES L	LTC	0-0053451	C264	1
SWOGER FRANK R	COL	C-0029429	C759	1
SWOLLEY FRANK C	CW4	W-0903905	C662	2
SWOMLEY NEELY M	LTC	0-0059881	C866	1
SWOPE FRANCIS A	COL	C-0032774	C267	1
SWOPE HERMAN E	LTC	P-0080194	C566	1
SWOPE LESLIE J	LTC	C-0062216	C665	1
SYDENHAM HENRY R	B G	0-0018654	C661	1
SYDNOR JR WILLIAM C	LTC	C-0032618	C661	1
SYKES JR HORACE F	COL	0-0017494	0757	1
SYKES ORIN P	COL	0-0029003	0455	2
SYLVESTER ETHEL M	MAJ	N-0002157	0459	1
SYLVESTER LOREN H	MAJ	C-0062243	0763	1
SYLVESTER ROBERT W	COL	C-0051473	C164	1
SYMANOWSKI PETER P	CW4	W-0903906	C266	1
SYMBOL PAUL H	COL	0-0023452	C361	1
SYME LEANDER O	COL	C-0012334	C549	1
SYNNOTT DONALD A	LTC	0-0048542	C566	1
SYNOLDS DONALD L	CPT	C-005767C	0965	2
SYRON DARREL L	LTC	0-0025034	C764	1
SZABO JOSEPH	LTC	0-0024480	C861	2
TABER ALDEN P	B G	0-0018134	0657	1
TABER HAROLD	COL	0-0050940	C256	1
TABER JOHN H	COL	0-0020987	C467	1
TABER THOMAS R	COL	C-0009775	1046	1
TABER WILLIAM A	COL	C-0005628	C545	2
TABER WILLIAM R	LTC	C-0051927	1263	1
TABSCOTT ERNEST E	COL	0-0010126	0851	2
TACK WILLIS J	COL	0-0003691	0249	1
TAFT PHILIP H	LTC	0-0079116	C867	1
TAGGART OWEN H	LTC	0-0051696	0763	1
TAGGART SAMUEL J	COL	C-0041388	C755	1
TAINTOR CHARLES	MAJ	0-0003981	0224	2
TAIT ALBERT L	COL	C-0031568	1166	1
TAKAHASHI WILLIAM H	CW3	W-0904307	C564	1
TALBOT LAURENCE O	CPT	C-0011179	0137	2
TALBOT RAYMOND J	COL	0-00236C8	C963	1
TALBOTT SR CHARLIE Y	COL	C-0031664	1167	1
TALLEY BENJAMIN B	B G	0-0016668	C456	1
TALLEY JR JOSEPHUS B	COL	0-0023578	C946	2
TALSMA MARTIN L	LTC	CF-0103051	0967	1
TANCO KENNETH H	COL	0-0039695	1060	1
TANK CHARLES F	B G	0-0019350	1064	1
TANKERSLEY MILTON J	LTC	0-0080499	0965	1
TANKSLEY JEPTHA C	CPT	C-0026095	C147	2
TANNEHILL HELEN C	MAJ	N-0002172	C164	1
TANNER JOHN L	LTC	0-0033683	C564	2
TANOUS PETER S	COL	0-0024067	C766	1
TANSEY JR PATRICK H	COL	C-0023915	1066	1
TANSEY PATRICK H	M G	0-0009299	0553	1
TANSEY ROBERT F	LTC	0-0027456	0166	1
TAPPER GORDON U	LTC	C-0052314	C955	2
TARANTINO FRANK S	LTC	0-0080327	C167	1
TARANTOLA MICHAEL N	CW4	RW-0907020	0163	1
TARBET KENNETH D	MAJ	C-0091526	0967	2
TARBOY JAMES O	COL	C-0006776	0946	2
TARDY WALTER E	COL	0-0032532	0767	1
TARKINGTON HIRAM W	COL	0-0010618	0854	1
TARPLEY HERMAN V	LTC	0-0043121	0258	1
TARPLEY JR THOMAS M	COL	C-0017325	C457	2
TARR EUGENE S	COL	C-0042827	0864	1
TARR JR RAYMOND P	COL	0-0029358	1059	2
TARRANT JAMES E	COL	0-0028859	0458	1
TARRANT LEGARE K	B G	0-0017208	0958	2
TASKER ARTHUR N	COL	0-0002411	0838	2
TASKER HAROLD P	COL	0-0015557	0939	2
TATCH DAVID	COL	0-0031116	0666	1
TATE ALBERT	CPT	0-0014432	0620	2
TATE CLIFFORD H	COL	0-0004708	0947	1
TATE DOROTHY T	MAJ	N-0002272	0863	1
TATE FERDINAND	COL	0-0019355	0862	1
TATE FOSTER J	B G	0-0012287	0749	1
TATE JAMES E	LTC	0-0021709	0656	2
TATE JOHN C	CW3	W-0907911	0362	2
TATE NICHOLAS L	LTC	0-0038988	1058	1
TATE RALPH H	B G	0-0011949	0747	1
TATE ROY A	COL	0-007692C	0762	1
TATOM KEITH K	COL	0-0011742	0748	1
TATOM LOUIS J	COL	0-0014694	0753	1
TATUM JAMES E	CPT	0-0050846	1053	2
TAUBER BERNARD L	LTC	0-0036715	1164	1
TAUSCH EGON R	COL	0-0016452	0656	1
TAVEL HENRY	COL	0-0039652	0161	1
TAWES JOHN P	LTC	0-0031357	1064	1
TAYLOR A RHU	COL	0-0012646	0648	2
TAYLOR ANNA L	MAJ	N-0002163	1262	1
TAYLOR BARNEY C	CW4	W-0903912	0857	1
TAYLOR CHARLES M	COL	0-0004012	0748	1
TAYLOR CLARENCE L	COL	0-0019336	0962	1
TAYLOR CLAUDE E	COL	0-0045316	0865	1
TAYLOR CLOYD V	LTC	0-0047850	1263	1
TAYLOR DANIEL R	LTC	0-0018217	0551	1
TAYLOR DAVID A	COL	0-0012156	1048	1
TAYLOR EDGAR C	MAJ	0-0019024	1145	2
TAYLOR EDWARD G	MAJ	0-0014029	0121	1
TAYLOR EDWARD M	COL	0-0011388	0251	1
TAYLOR EDWARD W	COL	C-0032465	0959	1
TAYLOR ELWOOD	LTC	0-0084429	1066	1
TAYLOR GALEN M	COL	0-0012444	0947	1
TAYLOR GEORGE A	B G	0-0014992	1046	2
TAYLOR GEORGE F R	MAJ	0-0010744	0335	2
TAYLOR GLENN R	COL	0-0042387	0764	1
TAYLOR HARLAN H	COL	0-0058748	0359	1
TAYLOR HAROLD L	COL	0-0029694	0462	1
TAYLOR HAROLD W	COL	0-0039661	1063	1
TAYLOR HENRY F	COL	0-0038661	1059	1
TAYLOR HENRY P	1LT	0-0014381	0-19	2
TAYLOR HERBERT E	COL	0-0003147	0150	1
TAYLOR INEZ A	MAJ	N-0002160	1062	1
TAYLOR JAMES	B G	0-0007262	0848	1
TAYLOR JAMES C	COL	C-0030616	0266	1
TAYLOR JAMES S	COL	0-0019602	0451	1
TAYLOR JOHN C	COL	0-0016577	0956	2
TAYLOR JR FRANK F	COL	0-0015448	0546	1
TAYLOR JR JAMES	COL	C-0021184	C767	1
TAYLOR JR ROBERT R	LTC	0-0031619	0865	1
TAYLOR JR ROY M	LTC	0-0039419	0763	1
TAYLOR JR WILLIAM	COL	0-0018565	0761	1
TAYLOR KENNETH G	COL	0-0083573	0766	1
TAYLOR LLOYD W	COL	0-0031197	0862	1
TAYLOR MAXWELL O	GEN	0-0014898	0764	1
TAYLOR MILTON E	COL	C-0019867	C764	1
TAYLOR PAUL R	COL	0-0011747	1047	1
TAYLOR PERRY E	COL	0-0008128	0344	2
TAYLOR RALEIGH O	LTC	0-0076922	0466	1
TAYLOR RICHARD I	LTC	0-0036676	0767	1
TAYLOR ROBERT B	COL	0-0029903	0463	1
TAYLOR ROBERT L	COL	0-0014940	0854	1
TAYLOR ROYAL R	COL	C-0080195	0466	1
TAYLOR RUTH P	COL	N-0000302	1067	1
TAYLOR THOMAS F	COL	0-0003903	1149	2
TAYLOR THOMAS H	COL	0-0029931	C261	1
TAYLOR THOMAS H	CW2	W-0904363	1160	1
TAYLOR VICTOR B	LTC	0-0040130	C266	1
TAYLOR WALTER A	COL	C-0051566	1164	1
TAYLOR WENTWORTH	COL	0-0030280	1062	1
TAYLOR WILLIAM B	MAJ	C-0027077	C854	2
TAYLOR WILLIAM N	COL	C-0018168	C960	1
TAYNTON LEWIS C	COL	0-0034007	1265	2
TE SELLE JOHN	LTC	0-0050055	C964	1
TEABOLDT CHASE R	COL	0-0032082	1164	1
TEAGUE JACK	LTC	0-0026354	C866	1
TEAGUE MADGE M	LTC	N-0000201	0266	1
TEASLEY AGATHA B	MAJ	N-0002162	1162	1
TECCO ROBERT	CPT	0-0070525	C166	1
TECHEN EDMUND J	CW4	W-0902214	C356	1
TEDICK EUGENE	LTC	0-0059481	C264	1
TEENER DAVID R	MAJ	C-0060871	0567	1
TEESE JAMES L	MAJ	C-0063786	1066	1
TEETER EDGAR M	COL	C-0020688	C867	1
TEETERS BERNARD G	COL	0-0022081	C767	1
TEGNELL RUSSELL M	LTC	0-0042677	1163	1
TEIR WILLIAM	COL	0-0040701	0466	1
TEKSE LLOYD C	COL	0-0020062	1265	1
TELFORD CHARLES	LTC	C-0001789	1022	1
TELOUIST CLARK V	COL	0-0040443	0566	1
TEMME EUGENE J	CPT	C-0034553	C349	2
TEMPEL CARL W	M G	0-0018284	0962	2
TEMPLE HARRY D	COL	C-0051834	C966	1
TEMPLE JR CHARLES F	LTC	0-0047459	C863	1
TEMPLETON HAMILTON	COL	0-0003452	C142	1
TENCH CHARLES T	COL	C-0017502	0655	1
TENERY JOHN H	COL	0-0043172	C566	1
TENHAGEN CARL B	LTC	0-0043785	C767	1
TENNANT JOSEPH A	CW3	W-0907023	1053	1
TENNANT RICHARD S	COL	0-0051474	0264	1
TENNER ARMIN L	COL	0-0041428	C856	1
TENNESSON CHARLES E	COL	C-0024190	C760	1
TENNEY CLESEN H	B G	0-0003835	1146	2
TENNIES LESLIE G	COL	0-0041715	C261	1
TERRELL JR HENRY	M G	0-0003264	0446	1
TERRELL RALPH D	COL	0-0007017	C250	1
TERRY CARL C	COL	0-0004653	1044	2
TERRY DUDLEY K	LTC	0-0050076	1064	1
TERRY JR AUGUSTUS T	COL	C-0031781	C765	1
TESKE THEODORE I	CW2	W-0903915	0454	1
TESNEY CLYDE C	CW4	W-0903916	C256	1
TESSEN DOROTHY A	LTC	N-0001858	C364	1
TESSMER CARL F	COL	C-0024300	C863	1
TETER LESTER W	COL	C-0051312	C562	1
TEVIS JACK M	MAJ	C-0065717	1161	1
TEWELL MOLLIE A	MAJ	N-0000333	C862	2
TEXLEY ALFRED G	COL	0-0039539	0956	1
TEXTOR JEROME O	CPT	0-0023565	C542	2
THACKSTON JR A J	COL	0-0016607	C856	1
THALMANN WILLIAM G	COL	0-0024303	C862	1
THAMES JOHN W	COL	C-0030768	C866	2
THAMES JR WILLIAM M	B G	0-0029846	C762	1
THAMS ROBERT W	LTC	0-0065609	C867	1
THARP LLEWELLYN	COL	0-0008062	C550	1
THATCHER MARGARET K	MAJ	N-0000973	0263	1
THAYER ELMER B	COL	0-0017156	0758	1
THAYER HENRY C	COL	0-0019754	C459	1
THEBAUD DELPHIN E	COL	0-0004612	1049	1
THEBAUD JOSEPH V	COL	C-0009074	1048	2
THEE WALTER C	COL	C-0009701	0547	1
THEILMANN ETHEL M	MAJ	M-0010055	0155	1
THEIMER JOHN E	M G	0-0017566	0765	1
THEIRING ROBERT G	COL	0-0029982	C558	1
THEISEN GEORGE L	LTC	C-0023846	C262	1
THELEN EDWARD F	COL	0-0029649	1061	1
THERRELL JOHN W	COL	C-0040899	0567	1
THETFORD JAMES A	COL	0-0038913	C866	1
THEXTON MARGARET A	MAJ	N-0001034	C366	1
THIELE CLAUDE M	B G	0-00032C8	0948	2
THIELEN BERNARD	COL	0-0018782	0855	1
THIEME LEO V	LTC	0-0033561	0664	1
THIESSEN WYAN E	LTC	0-0051087	0655	2
THIGPEN HENRY S	LTC	0-0060264	0667	1
THOMA WILLIAM C	LTC	0-0063397	0766	1
THOMAS ARNOLD R	LTC	0-0023947	C661	1
THOMAS ARTHUR J	LTC	0-0035564	1059	1
THOMAS ARTHUR R	MAJ	C-0017211	0642	2
THOMAS ARTHUR R	WO1	W-09042C8	0250	2
THOMAS BENJAMIN A	COL	C-0010119	0148	1
THOMAS CHARLES M	LTC	0-0081282	0861	1
THOMAS DOUGLAS R	LTC	0-008050C	0366	1
THOMAS ELMER G	COL	0-0005995	C642	2
THOMAS FRANCIS J	CW4	W-0903919	0261	1
THOMAS GEORGE	MAJ	C-0037081	0859	1
THOMAS HARVEY G	CPT	0-0014407	0120	2
THOMAS HENRY L	CPT	OF-0101745	C267	2
THOMAS HOMER D	COL	0-0041621	0959	1
THOMAS HUGHIE C	LTC	0-0037462	0566	1
THOMAS IKE	CW4	W-0903920	0863	1
THOMAS JESSE F	COL	0-0021135	0858	2
THOMAS JESSE R	LTC	C-0036320	0966	1
THOMAS JOHN L	COL	0-0019958	0859	2
THOMAS JOHN W	CW4	W-0902046	1154	1
THOMAS JOSEPH W	LTC	0-0052015	0264	1
THOMAS JR ALFRED R	COL	0-0006297	1048	1
THOMAS JR EVERT S	B G	0-0030107	C164	1
THOMAS JR JESSE	LTC	0-002459C	0367	1
THOMAS JR WILLIAM G	CPT	0-0057144	C656	2
THOMAS JR WILLIAM N	COL	0-0007648	0653	1
THOMAS KRAMER	COL	0-0004705	0346	1
THOMAS LORRES C	LTC	0-002593C	0762	1
THOMAS LUCIUS G	COL	0-0019688	1163	1
THOMAS RALPH C	CPT	0-0007525	1034	1
THOMAS RICHARD G	COL	0-0023632	1C59	1
THOMAS ROBERT W	CW4	W-0904391	0267	1
THOMAS RODERICK M	LTC	0-0082110	1167	1
THOMAS THEODORE G	LTC	0-0030344	0967	1
THOMAS WESLEY F	MAJ	0-0060368	0862	1
THOMAS WILLIAM A	LTC	0-0015263	1047	2
THOMAS WILLIAM A	CW3	W-0903922	0961	1
THOMAS WILLIAM E	CW4	W-0904210	1055	1
THOMAS WILLIE N	COL	0-0029644	1061	1
THOMAS WILSON E	LTC	0-0082111	0867	1
THOMAS WINIFRED	MAJ	L-0000236	0260	1
THOMAS WRAY R	LTC	0-0060535	C766	1
THOMASESTAHLE C	COL	C-0003225	0346	1
THOMASON JOEL F	COL	0-0021867	1166	1
THOMILSON MATTHEW	COL	0-0001942	0840	2
THOMMEN LOUIS A	MAJ	0-0022922	1043	2
THOMPSON ALBERT N	COL	0-0024823	0367	1
THOMPSON CHESTER I	CW2	W-0902161	0146	2
THOMPSON CLARENCE A	COL	0-0033113	0765	2
THOMPSON DALE L B	COL	0-0039668	0865	1
THOMPSON DONALD F	COL	0-0020885	0866	1
THOMPSON EDWIN G	LTC	0-0081931	0766	1
THOMPSON ERNEST B	COL	0-0015242	0954	1
THOMPSON ESTEL A	LTC	0-0029653	0956	1
THOMPSON FRANK J	COL	0-0015609	0151	1
THOMPSON FREDERICK	COL	0-0015401	0653	1
THOMPSON FULTON G	COL	0-0050965	1057	1
THOMPSON GORDON K	CW4	W-0903923	0764	1
THOMPSON GUY D	COL	0-0005906	0854	1
THOMPSON HARRY F	B G	0-0007344	0646	1
THOMPSON HOWARD M	COL	0-0047399	1067	1
THOMPSON HUNDLEY	COL	0-0041663	0360	1
THOMPSON IDA M	MAJ	N-0000373	0261	1
THOMPSON II SAMUEL W	LTC	0-0056268	0267	1
THOMPSON JAMES F	MAJ	0-0084576	1065	1
THOMPSON JAMES V	B G	0-0016826	0757	2
THOMPSON JERRY V	LTC	0-0037451	1262	1
THOMPSON JOHN R	COL	C-0081289	0467	1
THOMPSON JOHN W	COL	C-0004975	C548	2
THOMPSON JR EDGAR H	COL	0-0020143	0966	1
THOMPSON LESLIE A	LTC	0-0023673	0367	1
THOMPSON LILLIAN G	LTC	N-0000015	1047	1

NAME	GRADE	SVC NO	DATE RET MO YR	RET CODE
THOMPSON LOUIS H	COL	0-0008411	0948	1
THOMPSON MAXWELL F	COL	0-0041998	0262	1
THOMPSON MERLE R	COL	0-0017534	0557	1
THOMPSON MILLARD	COL	0-0028951	0158	1
THOMPSON MILTON O	CW4	W-0902328	1056	1
THOMPSON MILTON S	COL	0-0029125	0758	1
THOMPSON NASH O	LTC	0-0031822	1052	2
THOMPSON PAUL W	B G	0-0017506	0746	1
THOMPSON PERCY W	COL	0-0016315	0855	1
THOMPSON RICHARD C	LTC	0-0084330	0564	1
THOMPSON RICHARD M	CW4	W-0904211	0963	1
THOMPSON ROBERT G	COL	0-0023568	0160	1
THOMPSON ROBERT M	LTC	0-0043794	0564	1
THOMPSON ROBERT P	COL	0-0019098	0662	2
THOMPSON SAMUEL W	COL	0-0041690	0658	1
THOMPSON WILLIAM J	B G	0-0017530	0859	1
THOMPSON WILLIAM L	COL	0-0011104	1151	1
THOMPSON WILLIAM V	COL	0-0019252	0157	1
THOMSON EARL F	COL	0-0014919	0854	1
THOMSON EDWARD P	COL	0-0029974	0963	1
THOMTE HUBERT O	COL	0-0022633	0966	1
THORKELSON WILLIAM L	COL	0-0022667	0460	1
THORLIN JOHN F	M G	0-0019067	0865	1
THORN HAMILTON	COL	0-0006877	0848	2
THORN JR WILLIAM R	CW4	W-0904212	0758	1
THORNBER HUBERT E	LTC	0-0041396	1053	1
THORNBURG ARTHUR W	CW3	W-0903925	1065	1
THORNE FREDERIC H	COL	0-0005922	0646	2
THORNHILL AVERY J	CW3	W-0907024	0259	1
THORNTON ALBERT L	COL	0-0031806	0761	1
THORNTON AUBREY O	LTC	0-0069816	0363	1
THORNTON JOSEPH A	COL	0-0031818	0365	1
THORNTON JOYCE A	LTC	N-0000267	0465	1
THORNTON MARGARET J	MAJ	R-0010077	0164	1
THORNTON MARGARET M	LTC	L-0000023	1058	1
THORNTON PAUL F	MAJ	0-0062815	0165	1
THORNTON VIRGIL H	LTC	0-0031503	0163	1
THORNTON WARREN G	LTC	0-0046663	0266	1
THOROUGHMAN ROY M	COL	0-0011509	0949	1
THORPE ELLIOTT R	B G	0-0011167	1149	1
THORPE FRED L	COL	0-0016935	0757	1
THORPE GEORGE M	COL	0-0040031	0766	1
THREADGILL FRANK W	COL	0-0021019	0766	2
THREADGILL WALTON C	COL	0-0025215	0664	1
THRELKELD LAWRENCE C	MAJ	0-0051501	0354	1
THRIFT RICHARD B	COL	0-0039849	0963	1
THROCKMORTON JOHN M	COL	0-0042711	1265	1
THROCKMORTON RUSSELL	COL	0-0005140	0246	2
THROM HAVEL I	LTC	N-0000549	0550	1
THUMMEL CLAUDE H	COL	0-0002591	1045	1
THURNESS ELIZABETH	LTC	N-0000436	0665	1
THURSTON BENJAMIN E	COL	0-0016409	0555	1
THURSTON CLAIR H	COL	0-0031453	0762	1
THUSS SR CHARLES J	COL	0-0067968	0166	1
THWEATT RICHMOND F	COL	0-0030766	0165	1
THYBONY WILLIAM W	COL	0-0039024	0564	1
TIBBETTS RALPH E	COL	0-0016156	1144	2
TIBBS RICHARD R	COL	0-0030688	0466	1
TIDLER CALVIN L	LTC	0-0061292	0665	1
TIEDE ROLAND V	COL	0-0031801	0964	1
TIEDT ELMER E	LTC	0-0019323	0846	2
TIFFANY RAYMOND H	COL	0-0020348	0866	1
TIFFANY WILLARD C	COL	0-0034230	0665	1
TIGHE JOHN R	COL	0-0009963	1146	2
TILGHMAN MAYO T	LTC	0-0051105	0359	2
TILLEY MATTIE F	LTC	N-0000008	0349	1
TILLMAN ERLAND A	COL	0-0020941	0765	1
TILLOTSON JOHN A	LTC	0-0081294	0766	1
TILLSON JR JOHN C F	COL	0-0002657	0243	2
TILSON GEORGE E	COL	0-0051838	0666	1
TILTON EUGENE H	CPT	0-0007894	0534	2
TILTON KENNETH E	COL	0-0029487	0860	1
TILTON ROLLIN L	B G	0-0002664	0248	1
TIMBERLAKE EDWARD W	B G	0-0008641	0750	1
TIMBERMAN THOMAS S	M G	0-0015328	0360	1

NAME	GRADE	SVC NO	DATE RET MO YR	RET CODE
TIMKE GEORGE H	COL	0-0020963	0866	1
TIMM EMANUEL A	LTC	0-0030615	0164	1
TIMMES CHARLES J	M G	0-0029777	0567	1
TIMMONS JOSEPH W	MAJ	0-0009543	1136	2
TIMOTHY PATRICK H	B G	0-0009297	1046	2
TIMOTHY ROBERT W	COL	0-0018141	0946	1
TINCHER MAXWELL A	COL	0-0020798	0859	1
TINDAL WINIFRED H	MAJ	L-0000237	0360	1
TINDALL RICHARD G	B G	0-0004800	0452	1
TINGAY LYNN H	B G	0-0005970	0453	2
TINKLE EVELYN F	MAJ	N-0000199	0263	1
TIPPETT EDWARD W	COL	0-0042570	0665	1
TIPTON DOROTHY G	LTC	M-0010020	0360	1
TIPTON HENRY C	LTC	0-0032777	0461	1
TIPTON NORMAN E	COL	0-0018408	0661	1
TIREY JAMES H	LTC	0-0033464	0466	1
TISCH DONALD C	MAJ	0-0090555	0765	2
TISDALE HENRY E	COL	0-0007568	0949	1
TISDALE WALTER M	COL	0-0018811	0162	1
TITLEY RICHARD J	LTC	0-0035582	0864	1
TITUS GEORGE F	COL	0-0038604	0356	1
TITUS REED M	LTC	0-0041879	0659	1
TITUS VIRGINIA I	MAJ	N-0000616	0657	2
TJOSTEM MARVIN L	COL	0-0030085	0164	1
TOBEY FRANK A	M G	0-0041698	1162	1
TOBEY MARY I	MAJ	N-0001039	1264	2
TOBIAS REBERT B	COL	0-0003985	1046	1
TOBIN EDWARD C	MAJ	0-0004607	0929	1
TOBIN NORA M	LTC	N-0001872	1160	1
TODD ALAN B	B G	0-0042088	1062	1
TODD ALBERT A	COL	0-0033878	0866	1
TODD GEORGE S	CW3	W-0903930	0864	1
TODD III WILLIAM N	LTC	0-0026846	1067	1
TODD JAMES C	COL	0-0041972	1061	1
TODD JR WILLIAM A	COL	0-0019598	0964	1
TODD JR WILLIAM N	COL	0-0009773	0653	1
TODD RALPH L	LTC	0-0033696	0162	1
TODD RALPH R	LTC	0-0040242	0466	1
TODD WALTER J	LTC	0-0040491	0264	1
TODD WILLIAM F	CW3	W-0904213	1066	1
TOFT DOUGLAS E	COL	0-0042183	0563	1
TOLAND HERBERT	CW4	W-0903931	1162	2
TOLBERT RAYMOND F	LTC	0-0031104	0855	1
TOLLIVER EDWARD M	COL	0-0033856	0964	1
TOLLY ROBERT J	COL	0-0031551	0367	2
TOLMAN JOHN D	COL	0-0051191	0161	1
TOLVE RALPH A	COL	0-0040027	0863	1
TOMEY WILLIAM R	COL	0-0012762	0846	2
TOMLIN JR JOHN W	LTC	0-0032249	1164	1
TOMLINSON CLARENCE M	COL	0-0014808	0248	1
TOMLINSON HUGH P	CPT	0-0061429	1064	2
TOMLINSON JR R H	COL	0-0038734	0960	1
TOMLINSON ROBERT R	COL	0-0031754	1066	1
TOMPKINS FRANCES P	COL	0-0011210	0747	1
TOMPKINS RAYMOND T	LTC	0-0014833	0346	2
TOMPKINS WILLIAM F	M G	0-0003780	0646	2
TONDA RICARDO D	1LT	0-0075841	1062	2
TONETTI OSCAR C	COL	0-0023864	0867	1
TONGUE ROBERT C	LTC	0-0027635	1165	1
TONNAR WILEY B	COL	0-0050955	0957	1
TOOHEY FRANCIS J	MAJ	0-0003603	0433	1
TOOLE CHARLES F	LTC	0-0083623	1167	1
TOOLE LENA A	MAJ	N-0001891	0360	1
TOOLE LESLIE F	COL	0-0007287	0753	1
TOOLEY JACK W	COL	0-0046860	0767	1
TOOMER HAROLD K	LTC	0-0040849	0662	1
TOON PHILIP P	LTC	0-0026795	0764	1
TOOTHILL EMMA A	MAJ	N-0001760	0765	1
TOPHAM DOUGLAS D	CW4	W-0903934	1055	1
TOPHAM WILLIAM O	CW2	W-0901266	1043	1
TORPING FREDERICK	COL	0-0005882	0349	2
TORRETT OSCAR C	LTC	0-0055654	0767	1
TORGERSON FERNANDO G	LTC	0-0037523	0862	1
TORMEY BERNARD A	COL	0-0015266	0854	2
TORNEY FRANCIS J	MAJ	0-0002900	1022	1

NAME	GRADE	SVC NO	DATE RET MO YR	RET CODE
TORNSTROM CLIFFORD H	COL	0-0043138	0967	1
TOROVSKY RICHARD F	LTC	0-0015478	0844	2
TORRENCE BRYCE J	LTC	0-0081298	0364	1
TORRENCE JR JAMES F	COL	0-0015151	0954	1
TORREY JR JOHN D	B G	0-0020217	0866	1
TOSNEY JOHN L	CW4	W-0903935	0259	1
TOTH ALFRED L	LTC	0-0025587	0764	1
TOUFANOFF ANATOLY I	CW4	W-0901310	0655	1
TOURTILLOTT RAYMOND	COL	0-0006932	0753	1
TOW WILLIAM M	COL	0-0010074	0350	1
TOWER JOHN V	COL	0-0015956	0854	1
TOWERS JACOB H	MAJ	0-0023883	1061	1
TOWNE CLAIR E	COL	0-0030385	0764	1
TOWNES JR JOHN F	LTC	0-0013991	0720	2
TOWNES MORTON E	B G	0-0018255	0960	2
TOWNLEY JOHN A	LTC	0-0041819	1158	1
TOWNSEND CLYDE E	COL	0-0031526	0962	1
TOWNSEND DURED E	COL	0-0031430	1066	1
TOWNSEND ELIZABETH	MAJ	M-0010077	0663	1
TOWNSEND FRANCIS W	CW2	RW-0907161	0962	1
TOWNSEND GEORGE L	COL	0-0010512	0148	1
TOWNSEND GLEN R	COL	0-0010001	0848	1
TOWNSEND HARRY F	LTC	0-0016832	0954	1
TOWNSEND HORACE E	COL	0-0030578	0765	1
TOWNSEND JAMES R	B G	0-0006357	0846	1
TOWNSEND ROBERT H	COL	0-0024890	0666	1
TOWNSEND SPENCER A	COL	0-0004479	0947	1
TOWNSEND WILBUR D	LTC	0-0042562	0563	1
TOWNSLEY CLARENCE P	B G	0-0011204	0753	1
TOWNSLEY FLOYD W	LTC	0-0033953	0162	1
TOYE ALFRED E	COL	0-0041723	0261	1
TRABER JR OSCAR W	LTC	0-0028030	0667	1
TRABUE WILLIAM	COL	0-0023625	1066	1
TRACEY BEATRICE E	MAJ	N-0001952	0259	1
TRACY ALOYSIUS J	LTC	0-0041724	0859	1
TRACY DONALD	MAJ	0-0044869	0462	2
TRACY MAXWELL W	COL	0-0015691	0147	2
TRAEGER GEORGE A	COL	0-0030746	0664	1
TRAIL HARRY E	COL	0-0030206	0461	2
TRAIN WILLIAM F	LTG	0-0018415	0667	1
TRAINOR ALFRED I	LTC	0-0033767	1058	2
TRAMEL HAROLD I	CW4	W-0903936	1166	1
TRAMMELL ADMIRAL P	COL	0-0041501	0358	2
TRAMMELL HOWARD A	LTC	0-0081300	1265	1
TRAMPE RAYMOND E	LTC	0-0042561	0661	1
TRAPNELL THOMAS J H	LTG	0-0016782	1262	1
TRAPOLINO GREGORIO	WO1	W-0901039	1040	2
TRAUB DAVID W	LTG	0-0017110	0862	1
TRAUB ROBERT	COL	0-0037450	0762	1
TRAVERS FRANCIS A	MAJ	0-0060709	1265	2
TRAVIS HARRISON G	1LT	0-0012833	0225	2
TRAVIS WILLIAM R	LTC	0-0020840	0865	1
TRAYWICK SR JESSIE T	COL	0-0015818	0954	1
TREADWAY JOSEPH E	LTC	0-0023617	0760	1
TREADWELL JOHN R	LTC	0-0027976	0367	1
TREADWELL LEWIS L	LTC	0-0053121	0252	1
TRECHTER OLIVER E G	COL	0-0005913	0854	1
TREDENICK JOHN C	COL	0-0023605	0962	1
TREDENNICK DONALD C	COL	0-0015335	0954	1
TRENEMAN ROBERT A	COL	0-0080506	0766	1
TRENHOLM DERRILL D	COL	0-0007501	0947	1
TRENHOLM JOHN H	COL	0-0037427	0666	1
TRENT JOSEPH F	COL	0-0017319	0858	1
TRETT EDWARD L	COL	0-0010402	0248	1
TREW FRANK C	COL	0-0015711	0854	1
TRIAL ERNEST T	COL	0-0030259	1164	1
TRIBE MERRILL L	B G	0-0042774	0764	1
TRICE HARLEY N	LTC	0-0018881	0949	2
TRICHEL GERVAIS W	COL	0-0012152	1146	1
TRIDEN JACK E	CW4	W-0903938	1058	2
TRIGG HARRY F	LTC	0-0060470	1066	1
TRIGG ROBERT F	LTC	0-0049819	0264	1
TRIMBLE FORD	COL	0-0028761	0954	1
TRIMMER JOHN C	LTC	0-0026633	0764	1
TRIMMER MILDRED L	LTC	N-0001911	0567	1

NAME	GRADE	SVC NO	DATE RET MO YR	RET CODE
TRINTER VERNON E	CPT	0-0025542	0446	2
TRIPLET WILLIAM S	COL	0-0015815	0854	1
TRIPP ROBERT C	B G	0-0018972	0863	1
TROESCHER EDWARD C	MAJ	0-0039055	0262	1
TROIANO CONSTANT A	COL	0-0022180	1164	1
TROLAND GIRARD B	COL	0-0008562	0854	1
TROLL JOHN F	COL	0-0043029	0767	1
TRONE JOHN H	COL	0-0039522	0850	1
TROSS RALPH G	LTC	0-0050257	0964	1
TROTH JAMES R	COL	0-0042270	1163	2
TROUP MALCOLM G	COL	0-0023862	0666	1
TROUT ROBERT J	COL	0-0020347	0966	1
TROUT ROBERT L	LTC	0-0043610	0858	1
TROXEL JR ORLANDO C	M G	0-0018487	0464	1
TROXLER PAUL C	COL	0-0041693	0760	1
TRUDEAU ARTHUR G	LTG	0-0015513	0762	1
TRUDEN JAMES R	COL	0-0042248	1061	1
TRUE GERALD F	COL	0-0038773	0864	1
TRUE RICHARD C	MAJ	0-0060864	0764	1
TRULSEN HERMAN H	CW4	W-0903940	1167	2
TRULY MERRICK H	COL	0-0018614	0761	1
TRUM BERNARD F	LTC	0-0020061	0658	1
TRUMAN LOUIS W	LTG	0-0018755	0867	2
TRUMBOWER WILLIAM C	CPT	0-0005866	0133	1
TRUXES ARTHUR H	COL	0-0004726	1047	1
TRYON MERLIN C	COL	0-0038810	1065	1
TUBBS HARRY S	COL	0-0019056	1057	1
TUBBS WILLIAM R	CW4	W-0903942	0866	2
TUCK WILLIAM R	COL	0-0024444	0665	1
TUCKER ANTHONY C	COL	0-0029130	0655	1
TUCKER ELON R	LTC	0-0052040	0462	1
TUCKER HENRY P	COL	0-0024232	0862	1
TUCKER JR ARNOLD R	1LT	0-0026124	0746	2
TUCKER LA MONTE A	COL	0-0042610	0865	1
TUCKER PRESCOTT S	MAJ	0-0004061	0-33	2
TUCKER RALPH A	CW4	W-0902191	0562	2
TUCKER REUBEN H	M G	0-0019894	0863	2
TUCKER ROBERT E	COL	0-0019538	0865	1
TUCKER ROY A	LTC	0-0084434	0866	1
TUDDER ELWIN B	LTC	0-0060541	0167	1
TUDOR OSCAR R	LTC	0-0010842	0536	1
TUFTS SUMNER P	COL	0-0028926	0855	1
TUGGLE JR WILLIAM P	COL	0-0042093	1162	2
TULLEY DAVID H	M G	0-0016075	0461	1
TULLEY EDGAR J	COL	0-0006036	0547	1
TULLY JAMES P	LTC	0-0031352	1064	1
TULLY TERENCE J	B G	0-0012823	0854	2
TUMIN HERBERT R	COL	0-0041367	0954	1
TUNBERG CLARENCE L	LTC	0-0065680	0865	1
TUPPER FRED A	LTC	0-0065032	1264	1
TUPPER MYRON W	COL	0-0005888	1139	2
TUPPER SEVIER R	COL	0-0004827	0453	1
TURGEON BEATRICE L	MAJ	N-0002734	0565	1
TURK STANLEY J	LTC	0-0080198	0367	1
TURLEY JR ROBERT E	COL	0-0004722	0349	1
TURMAN JOHN R	LTC	0-0042217	0761	1
TURNBULL FRANCIS W	LTC	0-0063112	0865	1
TURNBULL HAROLD T	COL	0-0012858	0748	1
TURNER ALEXANDER	LTC	0-0043136	0665	1
TURNER ALEXANDER	LTC	0-0051632	0461	1
TURNER ALFONSO	CW4	W-0907026	0558	1
TURNER CLAUDE E	LTC	0-0080230	0865	1
TURNER CLYDE M	COL	0-0043233	0864	1
TURNER DAVID R	CW4	W-0903945	0465	1
TURNER FRANK W	MAJ	0-0084679	0859	2
TURNER FRED H	COL	0-0001527	0240	1
TURNER HAROLD R	COL	0-0028752	1150	1
TURNER HARRISON F	COL	0-0019448	1146	2
TURNER HERBERT N	COL	0-0031921	1263	2
TURNER HOWARD W	COL	0-0005627	0851	1
TURNER IAN F	LTC	0-0032318	0767	1
TURNER JAMES H	COL	0-0017361	1058	2
TURNER JOHN E	B G	0-0031414	0166	1
TURNER JOHN R	COL	0-0039899	1062	1
TURNER JR PAUL L	LTC	0-0019558	0744	2

NAME	GRADE	SVC NO	DATE RET MO YR	RET CODE
TURNER MILDRED S	MAJ	N-0001856	0159	1
TURNER MORDAUNT V	COL	C-0007330	C653	1
TURNER ROBERT A	COL	C-0018987	C763	1
TURNER ROBERT G	COL	O-0016809	C757	1
TURPIN 3RD WILLIAM P	LTC	O-0018554	0344	2
TURTLE LEWIS	COL	O-0001803	C342	2
TURTON WILLIAM H	CW4	W-0902067	C256	1
TUSKEWICZ ERNEST	WO1	W-0907028	0251	1
TUTEUR CLIFFORD M	COL	O-0003243	1041	2
TUTTLE ALBERT L	LTC	O-0006330	0744	2
TUTTLE JAY F	LTC	O-0057703	0364	1
TUTTLE LAWRENCE O	LTC	O-0081303	C966	1
TWICHELL HEATH	COL	O-0012078	0854	1
TWINING ELMER E	COL	O-0030662	1163	1
TWITTY WILLIAM M	MAJ	O-0059808	C464	1
TWOMBLY III JOHN F	COL	O-0023519	C764	1
TWYMAN JOSEPH H	COL	O-0018116	0760	2
TYCHSEN ANDREW C	B G	C-0008256	0653	1
TYLER ANNE A	MAJ	N-0000263	0562	2
TYLER JAMES P	CW4	W-0903946	1265	1
TYLER JOHN S	COL	O-0043602	C966	1
TYLER JR ORVILLE Z	COL	O-0018511	C959	1
TYLER MAX C	M G	O-0001788	0944	1
TYLER WILLOUGHBY	COL	O-0031699	0966	1
TYNDALL 2ND JOHN G	LTC	O-0024014	0447	2
TYNES ACHILLES L	M G	C-0018916	1065	2
TYRALA ALFRED F	1LT	O-0026190	C845	2
TYSON ARTHUR W	COL	C-0019120	C863	1
TYSON ROBERT N	B G	O-0019594	0864	1
UCHEREK STEPHEN A	LTC	O-0031854	0961	1
UECKERT JON W	CW4	W-0903968	1065	1
UFTRING CELESTIA F	MAJ	N-0002042	1059	1
UHL FREDERICK	M G	C-0002874	C846	2
UHLMAN HAROLD R	1LT	O-0018577	C938	2
UHRBROCK HAROLD W	COL	O-0015990	C854	2
UHRHANE FRANCIS F	M G	O-0014071	0963	1
ULANS ROMAN I	COL	O-0052302	C966	1
ULLOM MADELINE M	LTC	N-0000123	0264	1
ULM OTIS M	COL	C-0023047	C959	2
ULMER JAMES C	LTC	O-0041792	C958	2
ULMER ROY C	COL	O-0041507	C356	1
ULMO HENRY W	COL	O-0010926	0942	1
ULRICH JOHN A	COL	O-0031527	0664	1
UMBACH EDNA D	LTC	N-0000007	C448	1
UMBERGER CLARENCE L	CW4	W-0907030	1054	1
UNDERCOFFER CHARLES	LTC	O-0081884	1067	1
UNDERDAHL CONRAD H	LTC	O-0033523	1167	1
UNDERDOWN C M	CPT	N-0000036	0248	1
UNDERHILL LEWIS K	COL	O-0003533	0646	1
UNDERWOOD CLARENCE R	COL	O-0031911	0666	1
UNDERWOOD EDGAR H	B G	C-0004768	C946	2
UNDERWOOD JEAN R	COL	O-0009230	1146	2
UNDERWOOD JOE S	COL	C-0008281	1045	2
UNDERWOOD JOHN M	LTC	O-0017621	0545	2
UNDERWOOD MILDRED R	CPT	N-0002226	0459	2
UNDERWOOD VERNON W	LTC	O-0036204	0762	1
UNDERWOOD WARREN A	COL	O-0016078	0755	1
UNORITZ FREDERICK	COL	C-0011827	1049	1
UNGER JESS P	COL	O-0023706	C765	1
UNVERFERTH JOHN E	COL	O-0023499	C767	1
UPHAM JR JOHN S	LTG	O-0017178	0764	1
UPHAM ROY W	LTC	O-0065551	C167	1
UPSHAW MARGARET M	MAJ	L-0000201	0753	1
UPTON RALPH R	COL	O-0024063	C565	1
URAM MICHAEL A	COL	O-0038648	C160	2
URBAN CHARLES R	LTC	O-0018490	0651	1
URBAN GEORGE	LTC	O-0080021	C962	1
URBAN JOHN G	COL	O-0021825	C759	1
URQUHART HENRY C	COL	O-0039754	0961	2
URRUTIA JR ENRIQUE	COL	C-0002976	0545	2
USCHOLD HERBERT J	CW4	W-0903951	C864	1
USERA VINCENT	COL	O-0039883	0463	2
USHER WILLIAM F	LTC	O-0055954	C865	1
USNICK EDWARD N	LTC	O-0042525	C762	1
UTKE RUSSELL O	COL	C-0028915	0657	1
UTTERBACK JAMES W	LTC	O-0040174	1062	2
UVAAS ISLA L	1LT	R-0000039	0846	1
VAIL BRUCE H	COL	O-0051533	0964	1
VAIL HOWARD K	MAJ	O-0016313	0644	2
VALENCOURT CHARLES W	LTC	O-0081933	0867	1
VALENTE ABEL A	LTC	O-0041687	0658	1
VALENTE FRANK A	COL	C-0028768	0354	1
VALENTINE CHARLES H	COL	O-0016325	0955	1
VALENTINE GEORGE C	LTC	O-0050385	0165	1
VALLASTER JR JOHN J	LTC	O-0027473	0765	2
VAN ALLEN WILLIAM G	COL	O-0020931	0265	1
VAN ATTA WARE H	COL	O-0020939	1167	1
VAN AUKEN HOWARD A	COL	O-0020096	0759	2
VAN AUKEN WILLIAM B	COL	O-0006972	1050	1
VAN BAAK LOUIS H A	MAJ	N-0000127	0859	1
VAN BENSCHOTEN ELMER	COL	O-0007929	0345	2
VAN BRUNT RINALDO	M G	O-0016225	0162	2
VAN BUSKIRK ROBERT J	COL	O-0005863	0547	2
VAN COURT LLOYD P	COL	O-0038966	0865	1
VAN DE VELDE LOUIS R	LTC	O-0031895	0661	1
VAN DE VOORT LEO D	LTC	O-0039071	0965	1
VAN DELDEN KARL H	MAJ	O-0067773	0165	1
VAN DERVEER ROBERT H	MAJ	C-0083101	0965	2
VAN DERVORT EDMUND H	COL	O-0020476	1264	1
VAN DEUSEN EDWIN R	COL	O-0002636	0446	1
VAN DEUSEN EDWIN S	COL	O-0007113	0547	2
VAN DEUSEN GEORGE L	M G	O-0002681	0846	1
VAN DINE WILLIAM H	COL	O-0030032	0364	2
VAN DUREN CORNELIUS	CW4	W-0907033	1165	1
VAN DUZEE FREDERIC P	COL	O-0012592	0650	1
VAN FLEET JAMES A	GEN	O-0003847	0353	1
VAN GIESON LEWIS M	COL	O-0009927	0344	1
VAN HOCK HENRY W	COL	O-0009173	0443	2
VAN HORN JAMES H	COL	O-0001996	0642	1
VAN HORNE EDWIN J	COL	O-0016468	0647	2
VAN HOLTEN JOHN G	M G	O-0016669	0761	2
VAN HOY JR JOHN W	COL	O-0023739	1064	1
VAN INGEN JAMES C	COL	O-0007228	1049	1
VAN KEUREN EDWIN	COL	O-00509[illegible]	0656	1
VAN LAETHEM GEORGE	LTC	O-0036342	1064	1
VAN NATTA THOMAS F	M G	O-0017086	0663	1
VAN NESS ROBERT G	LTC	O-0039646	0358	1
VAN OOSTEN ADRIANUS	COL	O-0040028	0962	1
VAN ORMER HENRY R	COL	O-0019787	0865	1
VAN ORME RONALD W	COL	O-0040725	0867	1
VAN ORNUM THURWOOD	CPT	O-0014434	0620	2
VAN ORSDEL ARTHUR D	COL	O-0041929	1061	1
VAN OSTRAND STUART D	CW4	W-0903958	0867	1
VAN SCHOICK ARTHUR W	LTC	O-0026017	C864	2
VAN SICKLER DONALD P	COL	C-0038585	0954	1
VAN STUDDIFORD G	COL	O-0010230	0553	1
VAN SYCKLE DAVID L	B G	O-0016425	0656	1
VAN TUYL HARRY E	COL	O-0009501	0954	1
VAN VLIET JR JOHN H	COL	O-0020828	0859	1
VAN VOLKENBURGH R H	B G	C-0003545	0250	1
VAN VOLKENBURGH ROBE	COL	O-0020758	0966	1
VAN WAGONER FRANK H	COL	O-0020095	0860	1
VAN WAGONER LOU G	B G	O-0041668	0360	1
VAN WAY GEORGE L	COL	O-0019693	0863	1
VAN WAY JR CHARLES W	COL	O-0015757	0754	1
VAN WIE GEORGE I	CW4	W-0903959	0757	1
VAN WYK HARRY	B G	O-0015555	0854	1
VANDEGEVELDE R W	COL	O-0020870	0357	1
VANCE DONOVAN M	COL	O-0029360	C348	2
VANCE JOHN R	COL	O-0012301	0854	1
VANCE LEE C	COL	O-0015382	1047	1
VANCE WILLIAM W	LTC	O-0051693	1050	1
VANDENBERG OLIVER W	COL	O-0016586	0956	1
VANDENBERG ROBERT E	COL	O-0038979	0367	1
VANDER HEIDE HERB	M G	O-0017754	0662	1
VANDER HYDEN WALT	COL	O-0005248	1046	1
VANDERBOGET CARLTO	COL	O-0004522	0147	2
VANDERGRIFT KENNARD	LTC	C-0042575	0463	1
VANDERHOFF DEAN T	COL	O-0022984	0660	1
VANDERPOOL JAY D	COL	O-0034570	0667	1
VANDERSLUIS HOWARD J	B G	C-0015213	C754	1
VANDERVEER HAROLD C	B G	O-0003262	0849	1
VANDERVOORT BENJAMIN	COL	C-0022715	C846	2
VANDERVORT RALPH E	COL	O-0025337	1165	1
VANDERWOOD LENA	MAJ	N-0000057	0951	1
VANN JOHN P	LTC	O-0038485	C863	1
VANN SR BENNIE T	CW4	W-0907034	0964	1
VARDAS CONSTANTIN	COL	O-0030236	C864	1
VARHALLA ROSE F	MAJ	N-0002403	1162	1
VARNER CURTIS L	COL	O-0028779	0854	1
VARS DONALD O	LTC	O-0019432	0657	1
VASSAR PHILIP M	CW3	W-0903962	0557	1
VASSETT FRANCIS J	COL	O-0084435	1167	1
VAUGHAN CURRY N	COL	C-0031407	C465	1
VAUGHAN ELTON O	COL	O-0047395	1065	1
VAUGHAN MARY E	MAJ	N-0001669	0967	1
VAUGHAN WILLIAM W	B G	O-0003649	1146	2
VAUGHAN WINSTON H	COL	C-0020927	0857	2
VAUGHN CLIFFORD H	LTC	C-0071618	0466	1
VAUGHN FRANCIS M	LTC	O-0031567	C665	1
VAUGHN GEORGE W	COL	C-0015747	C454	1
VAUGHN JACK E	LTC	O-0080511	0167	1
VAUGHN JR MCLLOY C	COL	O-0025393	0866	1
VAUGHT DONALD O	COL	C-0033308	C966	1
VEALE JOSEPH E	LTC	O-0021435	0866	1
VEDDER HENRY C	LTC	O-0020999	C865	1
VELASQUEZ BEN N	COL	O-0031779	0766	1
VELIE EARL R	LTC	O-0027410	1065	1
VELO MINNIE O	MAJ	N-0000535	1047	1
VENABLE BENJAMIN W	COL	O-0007130	0946	2
VENABLE RUSSELL V	COL	O-0001934	C642	2
VER MEY HAZEL	MAJ	L-0000256	1064	1
VERDE JOE	LTC	O-0040218	1265	1
VERFUERTH VINCENT P	COL	O-0079661	1066	1
VERMETTE RAYMOND F	COL	O-0009746	1146	2
VERNON EUGENE H	COL	O-0015417	0946	2
VERNON WILLIAM E	CPT	O-0007255	0-28	1
VERNOR KELSO O	LTC	O-0041988	0550	1
VERSACE HUMBERT J	COL	O-0019152	C863	1
VESS JACK M	LTC	O-0048639	0455	2
VEST HUGH A	COL	C-0039692	1060	1
VEST NETTIE L	MAJ	L-0000219	1156	1
VESTAL JOHN L	CPT	C-0069823	0966	1
VESTAL MARION R	MAJ	C-0013933	0620	2
VESTAL WILLIAM M	COL	O-0017596	0859	1
VEVIA PAUL J	COL	O-0007504	1043	2
VIA LERA V	MAJ	N-0000712	C361	1
VICHULES LEO D	CPT	O-0015599	0238	2
VICKERS FRANK	CW4	W-0907035	C966	1
VICKERS JAMES E	LTC	O-0024383	0246	2
VICKERS LOUIS T	COL	C-0017249	0758	1
VICKOREN ANGVALD	COL	O-0019680	C265	1
VICKREY LUSTER A	COL	O-0017592	0859	1
VICTORY HOMER J	COL	O-0031826	0264	1
VICTORY THOMAS F	COL	O-0041869	0761	2
VIDA FRANK J	COL	C-0012588	0748	2
VIEDT DORIS W	MAJ	N-0000731	0160	2
VIEMAN LEWIS D	COL	O-0022201	C560	1
VIGNES JOSEPH L	LTC	O-0080512	0267	1
VILLAMARIA AMELIA	MAJ	N-0002259	0862	1
VILLARET EUGENE	COL	O-0003695	0748	1
VILLARET JR GUSTAVE	COL	C-0007112	C552	1
VILLERE LEWIS G	COL	O-0042520	0164	1
VILLINES COLIN O	LTC	O-0063231	C865	2
VINCENT BERNARD E	CW4	W-0903965	1067	1
VINCENT CLIFTON F	CPT	O-0057440	0264	2
VINCENT EDWARD J	LTC	O-0038910	0365	1
VINCENT JOSEPH B	LTC	O-0042846	0756	2
VINCENT WILLIAM	CW4	W-0800347	0553	1
VINING OSMYN A	COL	O-0042398	0164	1
VINSON HAROLD A	COL	O-0021711	0457	1
VINSON JR FRANK M	LTC	O-0031990	C866	1
VINSON WILBUR H	COL	O-0010622	0753	1
VIOLANTE ANDRE L	COL	O-0010280	0846	2
VIRE HOWARD F	LTC	O-0056923	0667	1
VIRTUE CLARENCE M	COL	O-0016322	1151	1
VISSERING NORMAN H	M G	O-0041603	1162	1
VITA FRANK J	COL	C-0059664	1064	1
VITARIUS CHARLES A	LTC	O-0040544	0262	1
VITITOE VICTORIA O	MAJ	L-0000310	0562	1
VITTRUP RUSSELL L	LTG	O-0017681	0665	2
VIVAS JOSEPH R	COL	O-0022704	0559	1
VIVIAN GEORGE B	COL	O-0025272	0865	1
VIVIAN WILLIAM R	LTC	O-0031347	1064	1
VLAHOVICH FANNY E	LTC	N-0002573	0561	1
VOCKE LESTER	COL	C-0015047	0648	1
VOEGE ROY W	COL	O-0005509	1041	2
VOEGELI FRANCIS E	LTC	O-0024699	0863	1
VOEHL WILFORD E	COL	O-0019382	0864	1
VOGEL BERTHOLD	COL	O-0004871	0944	1
VOGEL EMMA E	COL	M-0010000	1151	1
VOGEL GUSTAVE H	B G	O-0012793	0854	1
VOGEL HERBERT D	B G	O-0015520	0854	1
VOGEL JOHN F	COL	O-0033585	0765	2
VOGEL LAWRENCE W	COL	O-0024661	C467	1
VOGNILD ALDEN E	LTC	O-0037080	0563	2
VOGT JOHN E	MAJ	O-0079131	C263	1
VOGT JR BRADY L	CPT	O-0060647	C664	1
VOGT ROBERT L	LTC	O-0060691	0664	1
VOINCHE MONA L	LTC	L-0000213	0359	1
VOLCKMANN RUSSELL W	B G	O-0019537	C757	2
VOLHEIM HERMAN M	LTC	O-0024593	C766	1
VOLKEL FORREST B	COL	O-0029361	0150	1
VOLKERS LOLITA M	CW3	V-0900984	0563	1
VOLLENDORFF ROBERT E	COL	O-0034398	C767	1
VOLLERTSEN ARTHUR H	COL	O-0038851	C265	1
VOLZ HEINZ H	CW4	W-0903968	C958	1
VON BERGE HERMAN H	LTC	O-0032237	C465	1
VON BURG ROBERT H	LTC	O-0035449	1264	1
VON GRENIP WALTER	CPT	O-0007614	0934	2
VON KAENEL HOWARD E	COL	O-0030527	1165	1
VON KANN CLIFTON F	M G	O-0021371	0365	1
VON KESSLER WILSON C	COL	O-0003656	0446	2
VON KOLNITZ HENRY	LTC	O-0030018	0961	1
VON SHOLLY FREDERICK	LTC	O-0080513	0166	1
VON TOAGELN WALTER W	MAJ	C-0038453	0960	1
VONNAHMEN FRANCIS H	LTC	O-0061952	0767	1
VOORHEES FREDERICK	B G	O-0029374	0160	2
VOORHES MARION I	COL	O-0007077	0948	2
VOORHIS NICHOLAS R	COL	O-0038691	0961	2
VORDERMARK JONATHAN	COL	O-0025917	C766	1
VOTAVA MARY T	LTC	N-0000448	0567	1
VOTE JR RALPH B	LTC	O-0051818	1064	1
VOYATZIS PAUL A	COL	O-0031499	0766	1
VOYER FRANCES A	MAJ	L-0000072	0960	1
VUKOMANOVISH SAVO	CW3	W-0907037	0962	1
WACHTER CHRISTIAN	COL	O-0017800	0155	1
WADDELL CHARLES C	LTC	O-0080023	0767	1
WADDELL EDWARD S	LTC	O-0063068	0666	1
WADDELL HUGH B	COL	O-0012319	0154	1
WADDELL JAMES C	COL	O-0013919	0320	2
WADDELL WILLIAM R	CW4	W-0907038	0766	1
WADDEN EDWARD P	COL	O-0008106	0151	1
WADDINGTON ROBERT B	LTC	O-0027527	0767	1
WADE DALLAS C	LTC	O-0030319	1262	1
WADE JAMES O	COL	O-0016518	0656	1
WADELTON WILLARD S	COL	O-0004714	1146	1
WADLE LOUIS J	LTC	O-0044059	0862	1
WADSWORTH JR LELAND	MAJ	O-0002272	0321	1
WAGENER MARY M	MAJ	N-0000153	0961	1
WAGGONER EDWARD F	COL	C-0042794	0763	1
WAGNER CARL N M	MAJ	O-0051225	0451	1
WAGNER HARRY D	CPT	O-0066592	0666	2
WAGNER HERMAN U	COL	O-0008567	0651	1
WAGNER JACOB F	LTC	O-0030475	0466	1
WAGNER JOHN C	LTC	O-0051348	0557	1
WAGNER JOHN H	COL	O-0042518	0662	1
WAGNER OTTO	COL	O-0003466	0347	1
WAGNER RICHARD C	1LT	O-0064340	1152	1
WAGSTAFF JR DAVID	COL	O-0019246	0955	1

NAME	GRADE	SVC NO	DATE RET MO YR	RET CODE
WAHL GEORGE D	B G	O-0005235	0649	1
WAHL JOHN	LTC	O-0027613	0765	1
WAID LEWIS C	LTC	O-0054314	0963	1
WAIKART WILLIAM H	LTC	O-0030504	0863	1
WAITE EILEEN M	MAJ	N-0002096	0665	1
WAITE FREDERICK	B G	O-0030358	1062	1
WAITE WILLIAM	LTC	O-0009271	0633	1
WAITS WARD B	COL	O-0040051	1163	1
WAITT ALDEN H	M G	O-0009606	0949	1
WAKEMAN JR PAUL M	CPT	O-0050500	0355	2
WAKEMAN PERCIVAL A	COL	O-0011068	0252	1
WALBRIDGE JOHN H	LTC	O-0054767	0864	1
WALBRIDGE VERN	COL	O-0015915	0854	2
WALD JOHN J	COL	O-0021804	0963	1
WALDEN II JOHN E	LTC	O-0057684	1167	1
WALDEN JACK T	COL	O-0037422	0662	1
WALDEN ROGER S	LTC	O-0041320	1066	1
WALDMAN MYRON	LTC	O-0081310	0467	1
WALDMANN CARL E	COL	O-0003447	0847	1
WALDNER STANLEY C	LTC	O-0039358	0662	1
WALDRON MIRIAM E	MAJ	N-0001202	0965	1
WALIGORA DANIEL J	COL	O-0020055	0855	2
WALINSKI LEEROY M	CW3	W-0903974	0866	1
WALITSCHEK KURT L	COL	O-0042241	0963	1
WALK GEORGE A	COL	O-0042796	0264	2
WALKER AQUILLYA M	MAJ	N-0002435	0166	1
WALKER ARCHIE S	COL	O-0052915	0665	2
WALKER BERRISFORD	COL	O-0036195	0967	1
WALKER BOYD F	COL	O-0024998	0165	1
WALKER CHARLES P	COL	O-0017903	0157	1
WALKER CHARLES S	CW4	W-0907039	0164	1
WALKER CLYDE W	CW4	W-0904348	0757	1
WALKER DANIEL F	LTC	O-0017727	0647	1
WALKER DELBERT F	CW4	W-0903976	0660	1
WALKER EDWARD E	MAJ	O-0005150	0132	1
WALKER ELMER H	COL	O-0019898	0159	1
WALKER FRED L	M G	O-0003029	0446	2
WALKER FREDERICK	LTC	O-0051655	1063	1
WALKER GEORGE L	COL	O-0041882	0959	1
WALKER HAROLD F	1LT	O-0015414	0335	2
WALKER ISAAC G	COL	O-0005154	0553	1
WALKER ISABELLE M	LTC	N-0000148	0964	1
WALKER JACK K	LTC	O-0032225	1265	1
WALKER JAMES F	COL	O-0002041	1030	2
WALKER JAMES H	B G	O-0012730	0846	2
WALKER JAMES T	COL	O-0029356	1059	1
WALKER JOEL T	COL	O-0022007	0964	1
WALKER JOHN E	COL	O-0021368	1066	1
WALKER JOHN R	CW4	W-0904215	0967	2
WALKER JR FRANK E	COL	O-0034691	0767	1
WALKER JR FRED L	COL	O-0020293	0866	1
WALKER JR JOHN H	COL	O-0042857	1166	1
WALKER JR LAWRENCE H	B G	O-0034243	0567	1
WALKER JR SAMUEL P	COL	O-0012179	0854	1
WALKER KEITH A	COL	O-0062910	0166	1
WALKER LELA A	MAJ	L-0000326	0355	1
WALKER LEONARD F	COL	O-0031344	0363	1
WALKER MARION W	COL	O-0023435	0867	1
WALKER NORVELL M	LTC	O-0034375	0367	1
WALKER PHILIP C	COL	O-0046287	0165	1
WALKER ROBERT H	LTC	O-0031740	0760	1
WALKER ROBERT T	COL	O-0031368	1066	2
WALKER ROY N	B G	O-0029112	0659	1
WALKER SIDNEY J	LTC	O-0063484	0867	1
WALKER STEPHEN M	LTC	O-0030561	1163	1
WALKER VIRGIL G	COL	O-0021700	0862	1
WALKER WELDON J	COL	O-0024307	0864	1
WALKER WILLIAM A	COL	O-0016410	0456	1
WALKER WILLIAM G	B G	O-0008073	0846	2
WALKER WILLIAM J	LTC	O-0036551	0566	1
WALKER WILLIAM L	LTC	O-0065022	0965	1
WALKOWSKI JOSEPH A	LTC	O-0051994	1159	1
WALL GEORGE R	COL	O-0040836	0867	1
WALL THOMAS F	LTC	O-0018207	0650	1
WALL THOMAS G	LTC	O-0033023	0466	1
WALLACE CHARLTON O	LTC	O-0042981	1163	1
WALLACE DAVID C	COL	O-0019715	0157	1
WALLACE EDWIN S	COL	O-0030859	0365	2
WALLACE ERNEST H	COL	O-0037552	0263	1
WALLACE EVERETT C	COL	O-0015525	0252	1
WALLACE FRANK R	CPT	O-0009063	0722	2
WALLACE II JOHN K	COL	O-0031131	0967	2
WALLACE JERRY G	LTC	O-0059812	1062	1
WALLACE JOHN B	LTC	O-0021680	1158	2
WALLACE JOSIAH A	COL	O-0006211	0545	2
WALLACE KENNETH W	COL	O-0032338	0964	1
WALLACE NEIL M	COL	O-0019101	0963	1
WALLAR HOMER R	COL	O-0051196	0361	2
WALLENDER ELMER F	B G	O-0005707	1049	1
WALLER ELBERT C	LTC	O-0082117	0961	1
WALLER JOHN L	WO1	W-0800680	0834	1
WALLER JR MORGAN L	LTC	O-0091716	0567	1
WALLER MARSHALL	LTC	O-0024758	0762	1
WALLER MARVIN E	LTC	O-0040294	1162	1
WALLINGTON EDWARD C	B G	O-0007838	0251	1
WALLIS JOHN W	MAJ	O-0014186	1017	2
WALLIS JR LUTHER D	LTC	O-0026592	0867	1
WALLNER MARGARET D	MAJ	N-0002145	0861	1
WALLS NELLIE F	MAJ	N-0002070	1162	1
WALMSLEY HAROLD	B G	O-0018769	0959	1
WALO ERNEST	CW4	W-0903975	0162	1
WALPOLE JAMES R	LTC	O-0038579	1164	1
WALRATH CHARLES F	LTC	O-0036207	0764	1
WALSH ALOYSIUS J	COL	O-0051792	0866	1
WALSH ARTHUR C	COL	O-0005402	0752	1
WALSH EDWARD J	COL	O-0014697	0753	1
WALSH HAROLD J	CW4	W-0907040	0366	1
WALSH HENRY	COL	O-0041408	0256	1
WALSH JOHN F	LTC	O-0033794	0863	1
WALSH JOHN X	LTC	O-0018090	0939	2
WALSH JR LOUIS A	M G	O-0019567	0766	2
WALSH MARGARET M	MAJ	N-0002420	0667	1
WALSH ORVILLE E	B G	O-0012094	0554	1
WALSH PATRICK J	COL	O-0029293	1263	1
WALT IVAN D	COL	O-0042286	1062	1
WALTER EDWARD C	LTC	O-0031578	0765	1
WALTER EDWARD H	COL	O-0014698	0449	1
WALTER EUGENE H	COL	O-0019836	0865	1
WALTERHOUSE HARRY F	LTC	O-0051882	0962	1
WALTERS ALLIE L	CPT	O-0055056	0761	1
WALTERS EDWARD E	LTC	O-0037710	0664	1
WALTERS ELSMERE J	COL	O-0011381	0748	1
WALTERS JAMES W	COL	O-0009791	0452	1
WALTERS PAUL R	COL	O-0019050	0863	1
WALTERS WARREN E	COL	O-0024200	0766	1
WALTON ARTHUR H	COL	O-0044746	0766	1
WALTON CHARLES H	LTC	O-0004010	0242	1
WALTON CHARLES W	COL	O-0006715	0847	1
WALTON JOSEPH R	COL	O-0039821	0463	1
WALTON LEON W	COL	O-0029062	0359	1
WALTON WILLIAM	LTC	O-0031459	0961	1
WALTZ WELCOME P	COL	O-0005429	1052	1
WALUSZ BERNARD P	CW3	W-0904437	0866	1
WALZ IVAN G	LTC	O-0028876	0954	1
WAMPLER BERT S	COL	O-0008013	0646	2
WANAMAKER WILLIAM W	B G	O-0012055	1149	1
WANDEL HUGH E	LTC	O-0045160	0859	1
WARD CHARLES R	COL	O-0019314	0863	1
WARD EDGAR R C	COL	O-0016585	0956	1
WARD FRANK	COL	O-0008041	0150	1
WARD FREDERICK	COL	O-0007566	0754	2
WARD FREDERICK	LTC	O-0039918	0962	1
WARD III NATHANIEL	COL	O-0019553	0864	1
WARD JR JUSTIN L	CW3	W-0903984	0956	2
WARD MARY A	MAJ	N-0000429	0561	1
WARD ORLANDO	M G	O-0003729	0153	1
WARD PATRICK B	LTC	O-0036739	0962	1
WARD PETER O	COL	O-0018574	0761	1
WARD ROBERT W	M G	O-0017637	0562	2
WARD WALTER R	CW4	W-0903985	0566	1
WARD WILLIAM R	COL	O-0043262	1062	1
WARDELL DENNIS J	LTC	O-0050237	0767	1
WARDELL PATRICK G	LTC	O-0025628	0965	1
WARDEN JOHN A	B G	O-0002473	0147	2
WARDLAW JOSEPH P	1LT	O-0014605	0428	2
WARDLOW RALPH C	LTC	O-0049516	0667	2
WARE JAMES V	COL	O-0004833	0951	1
WARE JOSEPH F	LTC	O-0001751	1022	2
WARE LAWRENCE R	LTC	O-0052317	0860	1
WARE WILLIAM A	LTC	O-0062114	0163	1
WARFIELD BENJAMIN M	COL	O-0020229	0864	1
WARFIELD CHARLES L	COL	O-0030590	1265	1
WARGUS EUGENE G	CW4	W-0903986	0364	1
WARING ROBERT C	LTC	O-0027721	0866	1
WARING ROBERT D	MAJ	O-0014648	1141	1
WARK JUDSON W	COL	O-0021428	0966	1
WARNER GORDON C	COL	O-0019466	0862	1
WARNER LEO V	B G	O-0009634	0854	1
WARNER MILO J	CPT	O-0014373	0819	2
WARNER OSCAR C	COL	O-0002550	1143	1
WARNER WALTER J	LTC	O-0034465	0867	1
WARNER WALTER W	COL	O-0005243	0153	1
WARNER WILLIAM A	LTC	O-0039771	0960	1
WARNKE JR JOHN J	MAJ	O-0058649	0464	2
WARNOCK ALN D	B G	O-0005162	0546	1
WARREN ARTHUR L	COL	O-0006993	0753	1
WARREN JOSEPH H	COL	O-0012451	0751	1
WARREN JR CARL K	COL	O-0023630	0463	1
WARREN JR SHIELDS	COL	O-0022103	0765	1
WARREN PRATT A	LTC	O-0023412	0761	1
WARREN ROBERT R	B G	O-0019380	0854	1
WARREN ROBERT E	COL	O-0076845	0866	1
WARREN ROSS B	COL	O-0007001	0752	1
WARREN STANLEY A	LTC	O-0045337	0864	1
WARREN VANCLEAVE	LTC	O-0024856	0263	1
WARREN WILLIAM E	LTC	O-0024852	0763	1
WARRICK FRED A	LTC	O-0081317	1167	1
WASHBURN ISRAEL R	COL	O-0029493	1058	1
WASHBURN MAURICE F	COL	O-0020475	1165	1
WASHINGTON DONALD	COL	O-0020894	0767	2
WASHINGTON WILLIAM C	COL	O-0003450	1144	2
WASKOWICZ ALOYSIUS T	COL	O-0019708	0757	1
WASSON VAL J	MAJ	O-0084836	0865	1
WASZAK EDWIN J	LTC	O-0035415	0767	1
WATERMAN BERNARD S	B G	O-0019746	0865	1
WATERMAN GLEN S	COL	O-0022239	0864	1
WATERMAN ROYCE A	CW4	W-0902366	0357	1
WATERS CHARLES H	COL	O-0020114	0866	1
WATERS DANIEL D	CPT	O-0025826	1144	2
WATERS EDWIN [illegible]	COL	O-0009974	0145	2
WATERS GRADEN C	COL	O-0041842	1058	2
WATERS II JOHN F	LTC	O-0037605	0165	1
WATERS JAMES H	LTC	O-0037327	0764	1
WATERS JOHN K	GEN	O-0018481	0966	2
WATERS JR FRED B	LTC	O-0025449	0265	1
WATERS JR JEROME J	B G	O-0005568	0551	1
WATERS THOMAS L	COL	O-0012417	0854	1
WATKINS ELLIOTT	COL	O-0012214	0454	1
WATKINS ERNEST S	LTC	O-0031028	0961	1
WATKINS HERBERT E	COL	O-0005867	1045	1
WATKINS JAMES G	COL	O-0007249	0448	1
WATKINS MABLE A	MAJ	N-0000540	0649	1
WATKINS ORLAN R	CW4	W-0901524	0355	1
WATKINS THEODORE R	CW4	W-0904216	0166	1
WATKINS WILLIAM A	COL	O-0051237	0861	1
WATLINGTON THOMAS M	M G	O-0016190	0661	1
WATMORE DONALD J	CW4	W-0903989	0762	1
WATROUS FREDERICK	LTC	O-0015073	0846	1
WATROUS JR LEE R	COL	O-0003247	0846	2
WATROUS LIVINGSTON	COL	O-0003176	1046	2
WATRY CLARA K	MAJ	N-0000700	0664	1
WATSON ARTHUR A	COL	O-0041918	0561	2
WATSON ARTHUR J	COL	O-0029730	0763	2
WATSON DONALD S	LTC	O-0028316	0766	1
WATSON DOUGLAS H	COL	O-0045908	0766	1
WATSON EDGERTON L	COL	O-0018208	0960	1
WATSON EDWIN A	LTC	O-0059469	0965	1
WATSON ERNEST C	COL	O-0029652	0861	1
WATSON GEORGE H	LTC	O-0025740	0263	1
WATSON HARRY L	COL	O-0012933	0445	2
WATSON II ALBERT	LTG	O-0018105	1166	1
WATSON JR ARTHUR E	1LT	O-0016517	1032	2
WATSON JR FRANCIS M	LTC	O-0039381	0866	1
WATSON LEROY H	M G	O-0007896	1153	1
WATSON NUMA A	M G	O-0014968	0956	1
WATSON RALPH H	LTC	O-0042458	1062	1
WATSON RICHARD R	COL	O-0034354	1166	1
WATSON ROBERT J	LTC	O-0018092	1044	2
WATSON RONALD	LTC	O-0052459	0963	1
WATSON RUSSELL B	COL	O-0023582	0859	1
WATSON RUTH V	MAJ	N-0000416	0261	1
WATSON WESLEY A	CW4	W-0907044	0765	1
WATSON WHITEFIELD	COL	O-0028802	0555	1
WATSON WILLIAM R	COL	O-0008354	0854	1
WATT JR DAVID A	COL	O-0017038	0758	1
WATTEN EINAR	COL	O-0044342	0466	1
WATTERS JOHN F	COL	O-0018994	0560	2
WATTERS WILLIAM E	COL	O-0015039	0753	1
WATTERSON TRAVIS K	LTC	O-0051008	1156	1
WATTS EUGENE A	COL	O-0081321	0766	1
WATTS FOSTER L	COL	O-0037569	0666	2
WATTS JAMES K	COL	O-0030752	0566	1
WATTS JR HARRY L	COL	O-0011714	0753	1
WATTS ROLAND S	COL	O-0050972	1057	1
WATTS WILLIAM F	LTC	O-0040291	0966	1
WAUGH JR WILLIAM H	COL	O-0015587	0864	1
WAY DAVID H	COL	O-0032341	1167	1
WAY EVERT C	LTC	O-0032888	0663	1
WAYMAN DUANE L	CPT	O-0060472	1162	1
WAYNE ROBERT P	LTC	O-0084681	1167	1
WEADOCK THOMAS A	COL	O-0039748	0159	1
WEAR GEORGE S	COL	O-0007337	0763	1
WEART DOUGLAS L	M G	O-0003774	0851	1
WEATHERBY FRANCIS F	COL	O-0005213	1048	1
WEAVER JAMES R	COL	O-0020278	0163	1
WEAVER JOHN C	COL	O-0041876	0561	1
WEAVER JOSEPH U	COL	O-0018941	1058	1
WEAVER JR WILLIAM K	LTC	O-0006192	1122	2
WEAVER LOGAN M	COL	O-0006368	0847	2
WEAVER MAYNARD R	COL	O-0032120	0264	1
WEAVER ROBERT M	MAJ	O-0067633	0665	2
WEAVER SR CARL A	COL	O-0030044	1061	1
WEAVER THERON D	B G	O-0007653	1052	1
WEAVER WILLIAM G	M G	O-0003413	0246	2
WEBB CHARLES C	LTC	O-0040620	0262	1
WEBB EDWARD E	CW4	W-0903497	0664	1
WEBB ELMER M	COL	O-0016908	0757	1
WEBB GEORGE E	COL	O-0041916	0462	2
WEBB JOSEPH F	COL	O-0051001	0866	1
WEBB JR CHARLES A	LTC	O-0040585	0956	1
WEBB JR HENDERSON	COL	O-0042527	0565	1
WEBB JR JOSEPH F	COL	O-0029271	0763	1
WEBB LESTER A	COL	O-0008451	0147	1
WEBB LYNN H	COL	O-0039946	1159	1
WEBB MAURICE E	COL	O-0030357	0863	1
WEBB MAXINE F	MAJ	N-0002267	1262	1
WEBB RALPH J	LTC	O-0065014	0766	1
WEBB RICHARD R	LTC	O-0004724	0133	2
WEBB ROBERT L	COL	O-0030207	0764	1
WEBB ROBERT M	MAJ	O-0035571	0863	1
WEBB WILLIAM H	LTC	O-0078263	1266	1
WEBBER CLARK	LTC	O-0030111	0162	1
WEBBER DONALD B	COL	O-0018392	0761	1
WEBBER IRA B	COL	O-0043375	0264	1
WEBBER REBECCA	MAJ	N-0002134	0760	2
WEBEL JAMES P	COL	O-0039463	0866	1
WEBER FREDERICK	COL	O-0018148	0760	1
WEBER JOHN H	B G	O-0018680	0762	1
WEBER JR RICHARD E	COL	O-0019421	0864	1
WEBER MILAN G	COL	O-0018444	0960	1

NAME	GRADE	SVC NO	DATE RET MO YR	RET CODE
WEBER ROBERT J	CPT	0-0065208	0856	2
WEBSTER AILEEN M	MAJ	L-0000293	0753	1
WEBSTER DANIEL	COL	0-0033071	0966	2
WEBSTER DONALD C	LTC	0-0081323	0567	1
WEBSTER HARRY W	LTC	0-0029294	1061	1
WEBSTER LOUIS C	COL	0-0010419	0-36	1
WEBSTER MONTGOMERY	COL	0-0021751	0667	1
WEBSTER SANFORD H	COL	0-0023222	0962	1
WEBSTER WILLIAM T	COL	0-0033858	0265	1
WECKERLING JOHN	B G	0-0011974	1054	1
WEDBUSH OTHON E	LTC	0-0055231	0966	1
WEDDELL WILLIAM A	COL	0-0016340	1055	1
WEDEMEYER ALBERT C	GEN	0-0012484	0751	1
WEED EARL D	COL	0-0009225	1046	2
WEED THOMAS J	COL	0-0010977	0852	1
WEEDON HERSCHEL R	LTC	0-0041741	0361	1
WEEGO GEORGE W	COL	0-0041484	0158	1
WEEKLEY DONALD W	CW4	W-0903994	1163	1
WEEKS BERTRAM A	COL	0-0026368	0264	1
WEEKS JOHN A	COL	0-0011211	0346	2
WEEKS RAYMOND W	LTC	0-0036173	0761	1
WEEKS ROBERT A	COL	0-0052011	1163	1
WEEMS MINER L	LTC	0-0040999	1163	1
WEGARD VICTOR L	CW3	W-0902382	1059	1
WEGGELAND JR HENRY N	LTC	0-0059882	0866	1
WEGNER CLARENCE A	CW2	W-0901739	0247	2
WEHLE PHILIP C	M G	0-0018067	0965	2
WEHRKAMP CLETUS J	CW4	W-0903995	0463	1
WEHRLE AWTRY P	COL	0-0051017	0459	2
WEHRLE MARGARET J	LTC	L-0000240	0264	1
WEIBEL RODNEY W	LTC	0-0079139	0867	1
WEIBLE WALTER L	LTG	0-0011308	0157	1
WEIDENKOPF STANLEY J	COL	0-0041771	0165	1
WEILAND PAUL H	COL	0-0008418	0950	1
WEINBERGER HOWARD W	LTC	0-0038234	0965	1
WEINERT MCDONALD C	COL	0-0014769	0954	2
WEINERTH STUART L	LTC	0-0042620	0963	1
WEINGARTEN WILLIAM H	CPT	0-0059605	0152	1
WEINLAND ARTHUR A	LTC	0-0030123	0162	1
WEINNING ALBERT J	COL	0-0021139	0660	1
WEINSTEIN ALICE E	LTC	N-0000976	0266	1
WEINSTEIN MARVIN S	LTC	0-0029149	0766	1
WEIR GEORGE M	LTC	0-0038623	0455	1
WEIR JR ROY T	COL	0-0038874	0862	1
WEIR REEA B	MAJ	N-0001881	0360	1
WEIR ROBERT W M	LTC	0-0042150	0161	1
WEISBERG BENJAMIN	COL	0-0040085	1162	2
WEISBROD JOSEPH J	CW4	W-0907046	0163	1
WEISEMANN HEINZ	COL	0-0021956	0167	1
WEISLER JULIAN E	COL	0-0042028	0562	1
WEISMAN LOUIS G	COL	0-0009464	0753	1
WEISS ALFRED V	LTC	0-0036287	0767	1
WEISSINGER WILLIAM T	COL	0-0004127	1146	2
WEISSINGER WILLIAM T	COL	0-0021154	0547	2
WEISSMAN EDWIN W	COL	0-0031559	0961	1
WEITZNER DANIEL N	CW3	W-0903997	1166	2
WELBORN JOHN C	COL	0-0018863	0859	1
WELCH GENE R	LTC	0-0024409	0261	1
WELCH GEORGE P	COL	0-0041422	0856	1
WELCH GLADYS M	MAJ	N-0002030	1058	1
WELCH GORDON P	COL	0-0004925	1146	1
WELCH JAMES C	COL	0-0012229	0251	1
WELCH JOHN M	COL	0-0009204	0852	1
WELCH JOHN P	COL	0-0008055	0146	2
WELCH JR JAMES C	LTC	0-0028367	0967	1
WELCH MARHL H	COL	0-0005972	0753	1
WELCH RAY O	COL	0-0012811	0954	1
WELD JR SETH L	B G	0-0019772	0865	1
WELDE GLENN A	COL	0-0040402	0166	1
WELGE CARL J	COL	0-0057041	0863	2
WELLBORN CHARLES G	LTC	0-0065273	0966	1
WELLBORN JR C J	CPT	0-0050665	0155	2
WELLENDORF LEONARD F	COL	0-0029538	0664	2
WELLENREITER F L	LTC	0-0028987	0456	1
WELLER WENDELL A	COL	0-0018290	0860	1

NAME	GRADE	SVC NO	DATE RET MO YR	RET CODE
WELLES GEORGE H	LTC	0-0024086	0965	1
WELLING ALVIN C	M G	0-0018983	0865	1
WELLS CLAYTON W	COL	0-0029962	0660	2
WELLS GEORGE R	LTC	0-0008070	0142	1
WELLS GORDON P	B G	0-0006689	0947	1
WELLS HARRY M	CW4	RW-0904000	1164	1
WELLS HOWARD B	COL	0-0083591	0965	1
WELLS JAMES B	COL	0-0019554	0862	1
WELLS JAMES F	COL	0-0030654	0466	2
WELLS JESSE B	COL	0-0015580	0654	1
WELLS JOHN A	MAJ	0-0036205	0762	1
WELLS JR ALBERT C	COL	0-0019838	0861	1
WELLS PAUL D	LTC	0-0020536	1055	1
WELLS RALPH H	LTC	0-0040014	0264	1
WELLS THOMAS J	COL	0-0017111	0758	1
WELLS WALTER J	COL	0-0021766	0962	1
WELLS WILLIAM L	COL	0-0033641	1265	1
WELSCH ALVIN P	LTC	0-0041786	0757	1
WELSCH JERALDINE	MAJ	N-0002331	0167	1
WELSH EARL G	COL	0-0009959	1046	1
WELSH JOHN B	COL	0-0030544	1165	1
WELSH STUART M	COL	0-0041498	0658	2
WELTNER JR NOYES	LTC	0-0080025	1067	2
WELTON KENNETH R	LTC	0-0042929	1264	1
WELTY JR REX G	CPT	0-0061280	0766	1
WENDEROTT MARCELLA	MAJ	N-0001548	0665	1
WENDLE HUGH M	LTC	0-0033764	1061	1
WENDORF HULEN O	COL	0-0021919	0859	1
WENDT WALTER W	COL	0-0032190	1266	1
WENTZ ROZENE	LTC	N-0000003	0348	1
WENZLAFF THEODORE C	COL	0-0016448	0655	1
WENZLICK GEORGE F	CW4	W-0904004	0859	1
WERGELAND DAVID A	CPT	0-0092144	1166	2
WERGELAND FLOYD L	M G	0-0019599	0864	1
WERLEY HARRIET H	LTC	N-0001241	0264	1
WERMUTH ANTHONY L	COL	0-0023252	1166	1
WERNER RICHARD J	B G	0-0029107	0159	1
WERNGREN MARTIN S	COL	0-0039006	0266	1
WERNITZNIG EDWARD R	COL	0-0020505	1065	2
WERTENBERGER IRENE	MAJ	N-0000468	1163	1
WERTZ JR GEORGE M	COL	0-0018357	1061	1
WESCOTT GEORGE R	COL	0-0007891	1133	2
WESKE JACK H	COL	0-0051054	0959	1
WESOLOWSKY CHARLES L	LTC	0-0028704	0966	1
WESSELS THEODORE F	B G	0-0006911	0552	1
WESSMILLER JOHN J	LTC	0-0054052	0862	2
WEST BLAND	COL	0-0031378	1264	1
WEST CHARLES P	COL	0-0029564	0763	1
WEST CHARLES W	B G	0-0012774	1162	1
WEST DARRELL W	CW3	W-0904005	0764	1
WEST ETHELBERT	CW4	W-0904006	0167	1
WEST EUGENE R	1LT	0-0014318	0805	2
WEST GEORGE C	LTC	0-0045153	0865	1
WEST GUSTAVUS W	COL	0-0016146	1049	1
WEST JOHN A	CW4	W-0904007	0660	2
WEST JR JOHN T	COL	0-0030825	0366	1
WEST JR ROBERT J	COL	0-0016925	0346	2
WEST MARTHA M	MAJ	N-0001230	0764	1
WEST ROLAND P	LTC	0-0034208	1162	1
WESTER SR RUSSELL N	CW4	W-0904009	0661	1
WESTERMEIER JOHN T	COL	0-0018493	0861	2
WESTERN GEORGE F	COL	0-0076930	0166	1
WESTERVELT F B	COL	0-0018630	0860	1
WESTFALL CHESTER C	LTC	0-0008204	1144	2
WESTFALL CLARENCE R	LTC	0-0026024	0764	2
WESTFALL ELEANOR J	MAJ	M-0010074	0558	1
WESTHAM JOHN P	LTC	0-0081327	0961	2
WESTON ALAN E	LTC	0-0026519	0764	1
WESTON JR ORVILLE M	1LT	0-0061830	0951	1
WESTPHALINGER HENRY	M G	0-0016130	1162	1
WESTPHELING CHARLES	COL	0-0018533	0761	1
WESTRUP CHARLES H	LTC	0-0051097	0758	1
WETHERBIE HAROLD B	COL	0-0041823	1160	1
WETHERBY LOREN A	COL	0-0007038	0351	1
WEYAND ALEXANDER	COL	0-0004510	0946	2

NAME	GRADE	SVC NO	DATE RET MO YR	RET CODE
WEYER DEROLT G	CW4	W-0904010	0365	1
WEYHER THEODORE A	B G	0-0016738	0657	1
WHALEN HORACE K	COL	0-0018727	0462	1
WHALEY BERT K	LTC	0-0042612	0763	1
WHALEY EUGENE B	LTC	0-0052150	1062	2
WHARTON WILLIAM L	COL	0-0008205	0643	2
WHATLEY JR VACHEL D	COL	0-0016886	0757	2
WHATLEY ROBERT J	LTC	0-0009844	0238	2
WHAYNE TOM F	COL	0-0019657	0655	1
WHEAT CLAYTON E	COL	0-0014810	0845	1
WHEAT LESLIE C	COL	0-0005769	0347	2
WHEATLEY ADELINE G	MAJ	L-0000076	1060	1
WHEATLEY EDWIN T	LTC	0-0008397	0739	2
WHEATLEY ROBERT E	LTC	0-0069828	0667	2
WHEATON HARRY J	COL	0-0016598	1056	1
WHEATON JAMES R	COL	0-0016458	0656	1
WHEATON PAUL R	LTC	0-0027800	0666	1
WHEELER CECIL G	COL	0-0039520	1053	1
WHEELER DRUID E	COL	0-0007443	1045	2
WHEELER ERNEST F	MAJ	0-0060418	0967	1
WHEELER ERNEST S	COL	0-0001373	0829	1
WHEELER EVELYN S	1LT	R-0000366	0846	1
WHEELER LESTER L	B G	0-0019951	0865	1
WHEELER MARGARET H	MAJ	N-0002068	0762	1
WHEELER RAYMOND A	LTG	0-0003064	0249	1
WHEELER ROBERT F	COL	0-0040872	0767	1
WHEELER WARREN N	LTC	0-0063176	1065	1
WHEELIN THOMAS J	LTC	0-0038856	1262	1
WHELCHEL JAMES L	COL	0-0012155	0754	2
WHELCHEL WILLIS W	COL	0-0016837	0757	2
WHELIHAN WILLIAM P	COL	0-0019102	0863	1
WHERLEY CLYDE H	LTC	0-0030675	0759	1
WHETSTONE RUSSELL E	COL	0-0053212	1064	1
WHICHER JOHN C	LTC	0-0039986	0962	1
WHIPPLE HOWARD R	COL	0-0039542	0662	1
WHIPPLE JOHN L	LTC	0-0043714	0164	1
WHIPPLE JR SHERBURNE	B G	0-0019130	0863	1
WHIPPLE WILLIAM	B G	0-0018024	0760	1
WHISNANT ISAAC E	LTC	0-0046983	0862	1
WHISNER EMOS B	B G	0-0007062	0753	1
WHISTLER JOHN M	COL	0-0015104	0845	2
WHITAKER DWIGHT R	LTC	0-0084441	1163	1
WHITAKER ERNEST J	COL	0-0023793	0765	1
WHITAKER JR W R	COL	0-0051272	0760	1
WHITCOMB BEATRICE	LTC	M-0010076	0562	1
WHITCOMB JOHN C	COL	0-0005321	1051	1
WHITCOMB RICHARD F	LTC	0-0041531	0656	1
WHITCOMB VIRGINIE G	MAJ	N-0002240	0860	1
WHITE ARTHUR A	M G	0-0003900	0949	1
WHITE ARTHUR E	COL	0-0019328	0656	1
WHITE ARTHUR N	MAJ	0-0004566	0622	2
WHITE BARNEY O	COL	0-0031606	0867	1
WHITE BOSWELL	CW4	W-0907053	0564	1
WHITE CECIL W	MAJ	0-0038208	0965	1
WHITE CHARLES H	M G	0-0002268	0746	2
WHITE CHARLES T	LTC	0-0052708	0163	1
WHITE CLAUDE W	LTC	0-0040448	1160	1
WHITE CLYDE E	LTC	0-0042700	0261	1
WHITE DAVID C	LTC	0-0060763	1167	1
WHITE DEAN	CPT	0-0084919	1165	1
WHITE DONALD G	COL	0-0012609	0448	1
WHITE EDMUND O	COL	0-0029077	0459	1
WHITE EDWARD C	COL	0-0039766	0462	1
WHITE EDWARD L	COL	0-0039885	0762	1
WHITE ELI F	COL	0-0041951	1061	1
WHITE EMETT R	COL	0-0031334	0966	2
WHITE FREDERICK	COL	0-0023326	0667	1
WHITE GEORGE W	B G	0-0019079	0561	1
WHITE GEORGE W	COL	0-0051200	0261	1
WHITE HILTON R	CW4	W-0904013	0763	1
WHITE HOWARD S	LTC	0-0032041	0267	2
WHITE ISAAC D	GEN	0-0015080	0461	2
WHITE IV WILLIAM B	MAJ	0-0026873	0965	1
WHITE JACK C	LTC	0-0040000	0962	1
WHITE JAMES C	COL	0-0011666	0653	1

NAME	GRADE	SVC NO	DATE RET MO YR	RET CODE
WHITE JOHN F	LTC	0-0025507	0867	1
WHITE JOHN N	COL	0-0009124	1048	2
WHITE JOHN W	COL	0-0021315	0859	1
WHITE JR CHARLES H	B G	0-0015407	0864	1
WHITE JR CHARLES T	LTC	0-0059059	0267	1
WHITE JR GEORGE E	COL	0-0020130	0557	1
WHITE JR REX H	COL	0-0045595	0864	1
WHITE JR ROBERT M	CPT	0-0028530	1059	2
WHITE LAWRENCE K	COL	0-0019241	0347	2
WHITE LEE A	MAJ	0-0041061	0361	1
WHITE LEON A	COL	0-0010770	0546	2
WHITE LESTER W	CW3	W-0907052	0864	1
WHITE RALPH W	COL	0-0039717	0561	1
WHITE ROBERT C	COL	0-0016851	0757	1
WHITE STEPHEN J	1LT	0-0059395	0851	2
WHITE VICTOR W	COL	0-0043475	0767	1
WHITE WILLIAM C	COL	0-0021457	0846	2
WHITE WILLIAM D	COL	0-0004024	0950	1
WHITE WILLIAM F	LTC	0-0037597	0264	1
WHITE WILLIAM N	COL	0-0011006	0854	1
WHITE WILLIAM R	B G	0-0003283	0946	2
WHITE WILSON E	LTC	0-0079663	0163	1
WHITEHEAD ARTHUR K	LTC	0-0043612	0863	1
WHITEHEAD JAMES R	LTC	0-0042095	1060	2
WHITEHEAD SAMUEL C	CW3	W-0904015	0161	1
WHITEHEAD THOMAS E	COL	0-0012780	0748	1
WHITEHORNE JOSEPH W	COL	0-0025277	0167	1
WHITEHOUSE BENJAMIN	COL	0-0028941	1057	1
WHITELAW JOHN L	B G	0-0012357	0755	1
WHITELEY EDWARD J	COL	0-0024627	0961	1
WHITELEY JOSEPH H	COL	0-0009378	0447	2
WHITESELL CARLIN H	COL	0-0020620	0863	1
WHITESIDE DAVID D	MAJ	0-0062149	0959	2
WHITFIELD MORGAN A	LTC	0-0036389	0163	1
WHITFIELD ROBERT L	COL	0-0029177	0660	2
WHITING EDWARD T	COL	0-0028855	0356	1
WHITING GEORGE W C	COL	0-0002484	1045	2
WHITLEY JACK R	LTC	0-0042705	0662	1
WHITLEY JESSE W	LTC	0-0050070	0365	1
WHITLEY JR FENNER H	COL	0-0031106	0766	1
WHITLOCK LESTER J	M G	0-0007138	0754	1
WHITLOCK ARCHIE B	LTC	0-0011916	0836	2
WHITMAN ELMER L	LTC	0-0029569	0659	1
WHITMORE HARRY E	LTC	0-0035993	0962	1
WHITNEY CARL L	COL	0-0031435	0267	1
WHITNEY CHARLES E	MAJ	0-0009878	0430	2
WHITNEY PHILIP M	COL	0-0012448	0446	2
WHITSETT WILLIAM L	COL	0-0051892	0164	1
WHITSON RAY W	COL	0-0030056	1263	1
WHITSON ROBERT K	COL	0-0004506	1144	2
WHITT RALPH L	COL	0-0080521	1167	1
WHITT SR DANIEL T	CW4	W-0904016	1161	1
WHITTAKER FRANK L	COL	0-0004766	1146	1
WHITTAKER HORACE L	B G	0-0004791	1146	1
WHITTAKER HOWARD R	B G	0-0029408	0760	2
WHITTEMORE FREDERICK	COL	0-0043255	0962	1
WHITTEMORE KENNETH S	COL	0-0007494	0349	1
WHITTEMORE PAUL B	CPT	0-0020648	0148	1
WHITTEN HAROLD L	COL	0-0042954	0661	1
WHITTEN RUDOLPH G	LTC	0-0003716	0928	2
WHITTET WILLARD A	COL	0-0028824	0252	1
WHITTING HENRY C	LTC	0-0044487	0862	1
WHITTLE CALVIN L	COL	0-0016913	0757	1
WHITTON JR JOSEPH F	COL	0-0051825	0167	1
WHITWORTH THOMAS C	LTC	0-0035231	0965	1
WHYBARK GEORGE W	LTC	0-0006283	0838	1
WICK ALBERT J	COL	0-0014822	1046	2
WICK THOMAS H	COL	0-0041685	0760	1
WICKENS PAUL A	COL	0-0041535	0756	1
WICKERT HOWARD T	LTC	0-0026312	0864	1
WICKEY HOWARD W	LTC	0-0030458	0663	1
WICKLINE WILLIAM A	COL	0-0001496	0833	1
WICKS ROGER M	B G	0-0012084	0550	1
WICKWARD ALICE C	LTC	N-0000033	0655	2
WIDENER TRAVIS F	CW4	W-0907054	1167	1

NAME	GRADE	SVC NO	DATE RET MO YR	RET CODE
WIDMANN HOMER	COL	0-0029032	1058	1
WIDMER ALPERT W	COL	0-0041911	0961	1
WIECHMANN JOSEPH H	COL	0-0019874	0762	1
WIEGAND CHARLES D	COL	0-0017731	0859	1
WIENECKE ROBERT H	M G	0-0041569	0264	2
WIENER WILLIAM M	CPT	0-0006686	0134	2
WIERSEMA KENNETH C	COL	0-0041624	0157	2
WIGGINS EDWARD G	LTC	0-0036457	0463	1
WIGHT JERMY B	MAJ	0-0074889	0964	1
WIGHTMAN RICHARD M	COL	0-0005267	0750	1
WIGHTMAN RICHARD C	CW4	W-0904019	1166	2
WIGTON EDWARD N	1LT	0-0014402	1019	2
WIKEN ARENT O	COL	0-0030426	0665	2
WIKOFF WILLIAM H	LTC	0-0032301	1063	1
WILBERT HARRY E	COL	0-0041535	1058	1
WILBUR WILLIAM H	B G	0-0003365	0347	2
WILBY LANGFITT B	COL	0-0019748	0263	1
WILCOX DICK	CW4	W-0904020	0255	1
WILCOX HERBERT B	COL	0-0012963	0345	2
WILCOX JR HOWARD E	LTC	0-0043347	0164	1
WILCOX JUDSON D	LTC	0-0030618	0761	2
WILCOX LESLIE R	COL	0-0032251	0764	1
WILCOX PERRY C	COL	0-0010685	0446	2
WILD HENRY H	COL	0-0051064	0360	2
WILDE ELIZABETH	MAJ	N-0002220	0360	1
WILDER CYRUS J	COL	0-0004744	0153	1
WILDER ERNEST B	LTC	0-0040271	1058	1
WILDER HAROLD W	LTC	0-0094969	0666	1
WILDER LYNDON S	COL	0-0056789	1060	1
WILDER WEBSTER	LTC	0-0051784	1060	1
WILDERMAN JORDAN J	COL	0-0023092	0867	1
WILDES THOMAS	LTC	0-0040778	0962	1
WILDEY ROBERT W	LTC	0-0052353	1167	1
WILDFOASTER FRIEDRIC	LTC	0-0030346	0762	1
WILDMAN THOMAS A	MAJ	0-0017793	1041	2
WILEMON WILLIAM K	COL	0-0029060	0556	2
WILES ISAIAH A	COL	0-0022709	1266	1
WILEY HENRY S	CW4	W-0904221	0757	1
WILEY IRVING B	LTC	0-0031132	0962	2
WILEY JR EARL T	COL	0-0040442	0665	1
WILEY JR NOBLE J	COL	0-0017228	0758	1
WILEY WILLIAM G	CW4	W-0901862	0653	1
WILHELM LELAND F	LTC	0-0048723	0967	1
WILHIDE GLENN C	COL	0-0028753	0653	1
WILHOIT EDWARD	LTC	0-0031166	0155	2
WILHOYT JR ELLIS E	B G	0-0020593	0367	1
WILKES GILBERT V	COL	0-0002581	1046	2
WILKES JOHN S	LTC	0-0030288	0959	2
WILKIN JOHN L	COL	0-0039847	0963	1
WILKINS ARTHUR L	LTC	0-0037438	1161	1
WILKINS FRANK F	COL	0-0039731	1061	1
WILKINS GEORGE R	COL	0-0019750	0863	1
WILKINS LOWELL V	CW4	W-0907056	1062	1
WILKINSON HARVEY W	COL	0-0017139	0347	2
WILKINSON WILLIAM C	CPT	0-0056407	1050	2
WILKINSON WILLIAM E	COL	0-0020525	1155	2
WILKOWSKI ANTHONY J	MAJ	0-0052748	0550	1
WILLARD LEROY E	MAJ	0-0063313	0863	1
WILLARD PAUL S	COL	0-0029541	0361	1
WILLARD SHERMAN F	COL	0-0011089	0647	1
WILLCOX EDWIN J	LTC	0-0025594	0766	1
WILLEMS JOHN M	M G	0-0016176	1061	1
WILLENZICK HAROLD	COL	0-0023342	0962	1
WILLERS KARL H	LTC	0-0021671	0661	1
WILLETS GEORGE D	LTC	0-0040281	0866	1
WILLETTE GEORGE C	COL	0-0017289	0858	1
WILLEY GEORGE L	LTC	0-0042408	0762	1
WILLEY JOHN P	B G	0-0015954	0854	1
WILLEY WILFORD L	LTC	0-0038961	0664	2
WILLIAMS URQUHART	COL	0-0019391	0864	1
WILLIAMS ALEX K	LTC	0-0041623	0758	1
WILLIAMS ALONZO K	MAJ	0-0041140	0864	1
WILLIAMS ANITA V	MAJ	M-0010053	0855	2
WILLIAMS BASIL P	COL	0-0051025	0559	1
WILLIAMS BENJAMIN P	LTC	0-0028519	0867	1

NAME	GRADE	SVC NO	DATE RET MO YR	RET CODE
WILLIAMS BYRON E	LTC	0-0030134	0163	2
WILLIAMS CARROLL J	COL	0-0030811	0361	1
WILLIAMS CHARLES L	COL	0-0018795	0362	2
WILLIAMS CHARLES S	COL	0-0009604	0151	1
WILLIAMS CLEON L	LTC	0-0011913	0844	2
WILLIAMS CLYDE W	CW4	W-0901886	0553	1
WILLIAMS CYRIL F	COL	0-0016882	0757	1
WILLIAMS DONALD B	COL	0-0038901	0766	1
WILLIAMS DONALD G	COL	0-0021071	0765	1
WILLIAMS EARL H	LTC	0-0020977	0346	2
WILLIAMS EDWARD T	LTG	0-0012818	0261	1
WILLIAMS EDWARD W	COL	0-0020205	0866	1
WILLIAMS ERNEST	COL	0-0007148	0553	1
WILLIAMS FREDDIE W	CPT	0-0095275	0267	2
WILLIAMS FREDERICK	LTC	0-0036227	1065	1
WILLIAMS GEORGE C	COL	0-0052146	0966	1
WILLIAMS GRANT A	COL	0-0016565	1048	1
WILLIAMS HAROLD C	LTC	0-0031372	1060	1
WILLIAMS HAROLD L	LTC	0-0056984	1064	1
WILLIAMS IRMA F	MAJ	N-0000830	0963	1
WILLIAMS J J B	COL	0-0005202	0846	1
WILLIAMS JAMES N	COL	0-0008800	0949	1
WILLIAMS JOHN A	COL	0-0042257	1063	1
WILLIAMS JOHN F	COL	0-0015548	1146	2
WILLIAMS JOHN J	LTC	0-0081935	0562	2
WILLIAMS JOHN M	COL	0-0020315	0765	1
WILLIAMS JOHN R	COL	0-0042996	0467	1
WILLIAMS JOHN W	COL	0-0034107	0766	1
WILLIAMS JR ALBERT S	COL	0-0025374	0965	1
WILLIAMS JR ALEX N	COL	0-0016810	1057	1
WILLIAMS JR ARTHUR H	COL	0-0043436	1167	1
WILLIAMS JR JAMES F	LTC	0-0023224	0960	1
WILLIAMS JR LEWIS C	COL	0-0040081	0266	1
WILLIAMS JR ROBERT C	COL	0-0022091	0765	1
WILLIAMS JR ROBERT L	COL	0-0018742	0756	2
WILLIAMS JR ROGER	COL	0-0005015	0246	1
WILLIAMS LAURIN L	LTG	0-0008425	0657	2
WILLIAMS LEE R	COL	0-0016821	0948	1
WILLIAMS LESLIE S	COL	0-0010637	1146	2
WILLIAMS LEWIS H	LTC	0-0080330	0265	1
WILLIAMS LOUIS F	COL	0-0018324	0959	1
WILLIAMS MARION G	COL	0-0044841	0864	1
WILLIAMS MARION R	CW4	W-0904029	1265	1
WILLIAMS MARVIN F	LTC	0-0035386	0161	1
WILLIAMS MAUDE O	LTC	N-0001871	0860	1
WILLIAMS MYRON L	COL	0-0030622	0862	1
WILLIAMS NORMAN L	LTC	0-0026173	1063	1
WILLIAMS NORMAN P	COL	0-0008523	0753	1
WILLIAMS RAYMOND M	COL	0-0020399	0164	1
WILLIAMS RICHARD G	LTC	0-0020751	0648	1
WILLIAMS RICHARD H	COL	0-0001238	0-38	1
WILLIAMS RICHARD W	LTC	0-0047344	0861	2
WILLIAMS ROBERT C	COL	0-0040352	0466	1
WILLIAMS ROBERT J	LTC	0-0049162	0561	1
WILLIAMS ROBERT P	B G	0-0003924	0851	1
WILLIAMS ROGER H	LTC	0-0040069	1050	1
WILLIAMS SAM S	LTC	0-0038902	1264	1
WILLIAMS SAMUEL T	LTG	0-0008472	0960	2
WILLIAMS SARAH E	LTC	N-0000508	0849	2
WILLIAMS SR GEORGE W	LTC	0-0052004	0667	1
WILLIAMS TIMOTHY C	COL	0-0030791	0766	1
WILLIAMS TREVETT	LTC	0-0052845	0463	1
WILLIAMS WALTER H	LTC	0-0038967	1266	1
WILLIAMS WILLIAM A	LTC	0-0032513	1167	1
WILLIAMS WILLIAM D	COL	0-0014708	0854	1
WILLIAMS WILLIAM R	LTC	0-0037675	0165	2
WILLIAMS WINNIE S	MAJ	N-0001961	0560	1
WILLIAMS ZACK M	COL	0-0050966	1157	1
WILLIAMS 2ND FRANK W	MAJ	0-0024911	0148	2
WILLIAMSON CARL F	COL	0-0030178	0564	1
WILLIAMSON ELLIS V	COL	0-0012345	0550	1
WILLIAMSON JOHN	COL	0-0019900	0863	1
WILLIAMSON LEO C	LTC	0-0059065	0861	1
WILLIAMSON LYNDALL E	CPT	0-0065234	1262	2
WILLIAMSON MELVIN S	COL	0-0005687	0546	2

NAME	GRADE	SVC NO	DATE RET MO YR	RET CODE
WILLIAMSON SAMUEL E	LTC	0-0039989	1063	1
WILLIAMSON WILLIAM F	COL	0-0050970	0158	1
WILLIARD WILLIS C	CW4	W-0902174	0962	1
WILLING ALEXANDER	B G	0-0038619	1162	2
WILLINGHAM CHESTER M	COL	0-0008442	0854	1
WILLINK ARTHUR	MAJ	0-0015933	0342	2
WILLIS ARTHUR N	COL	0-0014868	0552	1
WILLIS JACK E	LTC	0-0030313	0860	1
WILLIS JAMES S	B G	0-0015607	0954	1
WILLIS JAMES T	LTC	0-0020264	0657	2
WILLIS JEAN P	MAJ	0-0037283	0864	1
WILLIS JEFFERSON	COL	0-0011643	0847	2
WILLIS LUELLA R	LTC	N-0000340	1160	1
WILLIS NICHOLAS W	COL	0-0043099	0967	1
WILLIS ORAL G	LTC	0-0018628	0345	2
WILLIS RAYMOND E	COL	0-0006106	0347	2
WILLIS WILLIAM D	COL	0-0020496	0758	1
WILLIS WINSLOW N	COL	0-0051352	1167	1
WILLISON THOMAS L	W01	W-0901749	1042	2
WILLOUGHBY CHARLES A	M G	0-0004615	0851	1
WILLOUGHBY JESSE E	COL	0-0038787	0165	1
WILLOUGHBY WILLIAM H	COL	0-0030108	0764	1
WILLS LLOYD F	COL	0-0032060	0766	1
WILLSON ELMER J	LTC	0-0041445	0155	1
WILLSON RAY O	1LT	0-0014438	0820	2
WILLSON RICHARD T	COL	0-0015429	0555	1
WILMETH JAMES D	COL	0-0019519	0660	1
WILMOT FRED W	LTC	0-0059770	0667	1
WILSON ALBERT T	COL	0-0012574	1147	2
WILSON ARTHUR F	COL	0-0011873	0854	1
WILSON C FORREST	COL	0-0009559	0447	2
WILSON CHARLES F	CPT	0-0012363	0-33	1
WILSON CLAIRE A	MAJ	N-0002495	0364	2
WILSON CLIFFORD C	LTC	0-0059066	1266	1
WILSON DANIEL M	COL	0-0017144	0752	1
WILSON DONALD B	COL	0-0051198	0261	1
WILSON DONALD C	COL	0-0030248	0964	2
WILSON DURWARD S	M G	0-0002858	0146	2
WILSON EDWARD L	COL	0-0028969	0256	1
WILSON EDWIN C	LTC	0-0060650	0966	1
WILSON ELDON R	CW4	W-0904036	1165	1
WILSON ERNEST H	MAJ	0-0016160	0347	2
WILSON ERNEST L	MAJ	0-0008837	0724	2
WILSON FRANCIS H	COL	0-0006701	0753	1
WILSON FRANCIS J	COL	0-0014902	1046	2
WILSON FRANK B	LTC	0-0035162	0364	1
WILSON FRANKLIN L	LTC	0-0032350	0764	1
WILSON GARNETT H	COL	0-0010302	0753	1
WILSON GERALD R	LTC	0-0036338	0766	1
WILSON HAROLD D	MAJ	0-0027515	0664	1
WILSON HAROLD G	COL	0-0041384	0756	1
WILSON JAMES J	MAJ	0-0085703	0663	2
WILSON JAMES T	COL	0-0020103	0164	2
WILSON JOHN H	M G	0-0005930	0946	2
WILSON JOHN J	MAJ	0-0070566	0467	1
WILSON JOHN M	LTC	0-0025556	0464	1
WILSON JOHN W	COL	0-0033026	0766	1
WILSON JOSEPH	CW4	W-0800357	0751	1
WILSON JR AUSTON M	COL	0-0012178	0750	1
WILSON JR DAVID C	CPT	0-0058731	0452	1
WILSON JR FRANCIS H	LTC	0-0053452	1165	1
WILSON JR HARRY L	MAJ	0-0023064	1144	2
WILSON JR JAMES K	B G	0-0018218	0359	1
WILSON JR JOHN L	COL	0-0033268	0661	1
WILSON JR JOHN I	COL	0-0039597	0758	1
WILSON JR PENRHYN	LTC	0-0084690	0267	1
WILSON JR RAYMOND J	COL	0-0081345	0767	1
WILSON JR WALTER K	LTG	0-0017512	0765	1
WILSON KERMIT J	LTC	0-0060172	0667	1
WILSON LEONARD F	COL	0-0018943	1062	1
WILSON LLOYD G	LTC	0-0034685	0766	1
WILSON LOUIS A	LTC	0-0036129	0863	1
WILSON LUCILE A	CPT	N-0000394	0552	1
WILSON LYNNFORD S	COL	0-0051886	0866	1
WILSON MAYBIN H	COL	0-0010528	0851	1

NAME	GRADE	SVC NO	DATE RET MO YR	RET CODE
WILSON MILTON F	COL	0-0012020	0149	2
WILSON MINOR K	COL	0-0041626	1059	1
WILSON MURRAY C	COL	0-0010321	1046	1
WILSON NEIL E	COL	0-0029256	0761	2
WILSON NORTON B	COL	0-0018476	0761	1
WILSON OVID C	COL	0-0015887	0954	1
WILSON PAUL F	LTC	0-0038571	0764	1
WILSON PLANTER M	LTC	0-0050884	0567	1
WILSON RALPH W	COL	0-0002963	0744	1
WILSON RAY	CW4	W-0504038	0258	1
WILSON ROBERT B	LTC	0-0039685	0958	1
WILSON ROBERT B	MAJ	0-0084691	0764	1
WILSON ROBERT F	COL	0-0039687	0960	1
WILSON VENNARD	B G	0-0007207	0653	1
WILSON WELDON W	LTC	0-0032054	1166	1
WILSON WESTRAY F	COL	0-0041971	1061	2
WILSON WILBUR	COL	0-0042494	0165	1
WILSON WILLIAM E	LTC	0-0030542	1163	2
WILSON WILLIAM H	LTC	0-0032820	0662	2
WILSON WILLIAM I	COL	0-0008574	0948	1
WILSON WILLIAM L	B G	0-0016950	0956	1
WILSON WILLIAM R	LTC	0-0014192	0818	2
WILSON WOODROW W	COL	0-0021755	0864	1
WILTAMUTH RALPH	COL	0-0010407	1146	2
WILTRAKIS EDWARD J	LTC	0-0051575	0163	1
WIMBERLEY JERRY M	COL	0-0025049	0766	1
WIMBERLEY NORRIS A	COL	0-0008306	1147	1
WIMER BENJAMIN R	COL	0-0017516	0557	1
WIMMER JACOB F	CW4	W-0904042	0666	2
WINCKLER RUDOLPH G	COL	0-0051399	0463	1
WINDER WAYNE W	COL	0-0034420	1264	1
WINDHAM JAMES F	LTC	0-0030651	0364	1
WINERS FREDERIC P	CPT	0-0009972	1134	2
WINFIELD IRMA H	MAJ	N-0002282	0564	1
WINFIELD RICHARD M	LTC	0-0005858	1041	1
WINFREE WESLEY C	MAJ	0F-0105876	1067	2
WING ALBERT C	COL	0-0007602	0753	1
WING CHARLES K	COL	0-0002423	0847	1
WING JR FRANKLIN F	B G	0-0018107	0760	1
WINGET LEONARD W	COL	0-0041896	0961	1
WINGFIELD LINDSEY R	LTC	0-0016581	0748	1
WINGO CHARLES A	COL	0-0051451	0861	1
WINGO ROLAND H	COL	0-0031098	1160	2
WINIARCZYK ANDREW W	LTC	0-0047278	0463	1
WINK ALICE R	LTC	N-0000858	1167	2
WINKLER HARRIET F	MAJ	N-0002479	0767	1
WINN JAMES J	COL	0-0017724	0759	1
WINN JR DEAN F	LTC	0-0057959	0766	1
WINN JR JOHN S	B G	0-0012140	1148	1
WINN JR WALTER S	COL	0-0012355	1146	1
WINN NORMAN K	COL	0-0016567	0654	1
WINNIE FRANKLIN F	COL	0-0041992	0462	1
WINNINGSTAD OLAF P	COL	0-0007075	0653	1
WINSLOW EDWARD	CW4	W-0904043	0658	1
WINSLOW PAUL F	LTC	0-0041721	0259	1
WINSLOW RUBY Z	LTC	R-0010006	0164	1
WINSTEAD THOMAS E	COL	0-0011645	0549	1
WINSTED JOHN R	LTC	0-0051059	1057	1
WINSTON BARLOW	COL	0-0008438	0753	1
WINSTON CHARLES S	LTC	0-0021890	0859	1
WINSTON EDWARD D	MAJ	0-0018842	0546	2
WINSTON SANFORD H	LTC	0-0062154	0564	1
WINTERMUTE JR JOHN S	LTC	0-0022039	0146	2
WINTERSTEEN JOSEPH C	COL	0-0051168	0159	1
WINTHROP EDWARD L	LTC	0-0027560	0467	1
WINTON ARTHUR V	COL	0-0008189	0452	1
WIRAK LOUIS R	COL	0-0018342	0761	1
WIRT CHARLES A	LTC	0-0025725	1163	1
WIRTZ PETER	CPT	0-0014400	1019	2
WISE CLEMENT W	CW4	W-0907061	0665	1
WISE FRANK G	LTC	0-0039678	0658	1
WISE GEORGE S	COL	0-0038589	0754	1
WISE JAMES F	CPT	0-0024819	0-44	2
WISE JR JAMES R	LTC	0-0004951	0936	2
WISE RICHARD A	LTC	0-0038171	0264	1

NAME	GRADE	SVC NO	DATE RET MO YR	RET CODE
WISE 3RD SAMUEL P	MAJ	0-0057565	0554	2
WISELOGEL CHARLES C	COL	0-00166C6	0447	1
WISEMAN VERA H	CPT	0-0016989	1143	1
WISHART HENRY H	COL	0-0038935	C666	1
WISS JOHN W	LTC	0-0028154	C766	1
WITCZAK ANN M	LTC	N-0000610	0761	1
WITHERS EDWIN J	COL	0-0042921	1265	1
WITHERS WILLIAM P	COL	0-0012742	0854	1
WITMAN VINCENT B	CW4	W-0904045	C862	1
WITSELL EDWARD F	M G	0-0003455	0651	2
WITT GEORGE L	COL	0-0031382	0656	2
WITT JR EMITT C	LTC	0-0034027	0265	1
WITT ROSEMARY	MAJ	N-0001520	C865	1
WITT WILLIAM H	LTC	0-0039925	0460	2
WITTENBERG DAVID F	CW4	W-0907063	0859	1
WITTER KATHRYN G	LTC	N-0000082	0856	1
WITTMANN RICHARD C	COL	0-0025195	C962	1
WITTMAYER RAYMOND C	COL	0-0031631	0967	1
WOBBEKING BERNARD	COL	0-0042417	C864	1
WOERNER CHARLES A	CPT	0-0023592	C143	2
WOERNER LEO G	COL	0-0030341	C165	2
WOESTENBURG JOHN M	COL	0-0030004	C263	2
WOFFORD HOKE S	COL	0-0029480	1060	1
WOGAN JOHN B	M G	0-0003834	1046	2
WOHLFEIL CARL H	LTC	0-0021907	C766	2
WOICCAK EDWARD	CW3	W-0904047	0555	2
WOLCOTT WILLIAM J	LTC	0-0030496	0264	2
WOLD DONALD E	CW4	W-0904264	C466	1
WOLF JOHN F	COL	0-0058801	0265	1
WOLF KARL E	LTC	0-0026202	C663	1
WOLF SAMUEL S	COL	0-0038674	0960	1
WOLFE CLAUDIUS O	COL	0-0039536	0157	1
WOLFE HAROLD K	LTC	0-0031729	1265	1
WOLFE HENRY C	B G	0-0011349	0550	1
WOLFE III HIRAM M	LTC	0-0061090	0865	1
WOLFE LLOYD R	COL	0-0010117	0551	1
WOLFE RICHARD C	COL	0-0021743	C166	1
WOLFE WALTER J	COL	0-0014619	0754	1
WOLFE WALTER M	LTC	0-0057740	0865	1
WOLFE WILLIAM P	COL	0-0009457	1152	1
WOLFE YALE H	COL	0-0019415	C661	1
WOLFFE PETER O	MAJ	0-0091541	C266	1
WOLFINGER ANNA M	MAJ	N-0002326	0665	1
WOLFSON MORTON	LTC	0-0048975	0661	1
WOLLASTON PENNOCK H	COL	0-0019854	0264	1
WOLTHON JACK W	LTC	C-0060686	0864	1
WOLVERTON DAVID R	COL	0-0007775	1043	1
WOMACK CARL O	LTC	C-0019426	C862	1
WONES EDWARD M	COL	0-0016028	0954	1
WOOD BURL A	MAJ	0-0082128	C661	1
WOOD CAROLYN J	MAJ	N-0000584	0162	1
WOOD CHARLES H	COL	0-0019498	C160	1
WOOD DELMORE S	LTC	C-0004941	C934	2
WOOD ETHEL E	MAJ	N-0000887	C365	2
WOOD FRANCIS D	COL	0-0012327	C247	1
WOOD GEORGE W	LTC	0-0044203	C161	1
WOOD HARLAND G	LTC	0-0024154	0660	1
WOOD III ALLEN H	LTC	0-0028672	0766	1
WOOD JOSEPH S	CW2	W-0800348	C244	1
WOOD JR NORMAN E	LTC	0-0037596	C767	1
WOOD JR THOMAS C	COL	C-0015946	0854	1
WOOD JULIAN C	COL	0-0041651	C460	1
WOOD LINCOLN	COL	0-0029116	0859	2
WOOD OLIVER E	LTC	0-0021998	C867	1
WOOD OLIVER S	COL	C-0002491	0942	1
WOOD PHILIP S	COL	0-0004961	0648	1
WOOD ROBERT F	B G	0-0013847	C715	1
WOOD ROBERT J	GEN	0-0018064	0965	1
WOOD ROY L	LTC	0-0059071	0867	1
WOOD STARLING W	COL	C-0080527	1066	1
WOOD STUART	COL	C-0016857	0757	2
WOOD THOMAS E	COL	0-0019483	0959	1
WOOD WALTER S	COL	C-0007474	C550	1
WOOD WAYNE L	COL	0-0051250	C961	1
WOOD WILLIAM H	B G	0-0016135	C556	1

NAME	GRADE	SVC NO	DATE RET MO YR	RET CODE
WOODARD ANDREW J	LTC	0-0084445	0567	1
WOOOBERRY JOHN H	B G	0-0003701	0846	2
WOODBRIDGE WOODROW W	MAJ	0-0005469	0934	2
WOODBURN THOMAS B	COL	0-0007368	0951	1
WOODBURY HENRY J	COL	0-0014899	0852	1
WOODBURY JAMES A	COL	0-0042943	0267	2
WOODBURY KENNETH J	COL	0-0017601	0859	1
WOODES RAYMOND C	COL	0-0029067	0359	1
WOODLIFF CLIFFORD L	COL	0-0030796	0662	1
WOODMAN ERNEST A H	COL	0-0032822	0766	1
WOODMAN JOHN D	LTC	0-0040662	0263	1
WOODMAN NED H	COL	0-0029622	0861	1
WOODROW CHARLES E	COL	0-0032011	0364	1
WOODRUFF JAMES A	M G	0-0000748	0641	1
WOODRUFF JR C E	COL	0-0015283	0454	2
WOODRUFF JR CHEN E	COL	0-0036172	1063	2
WOODRUFF ROSCOE B	M G	0-0003819	0153	1
WOODRUFF VICTOR R	COL	0-0005684	1147	1
WOODS CAMERON F	COL	0-0042089	1162	1
WOODS CHARLES T	COL	0-0051069	1059	1
WOODS JAMES R	COL	0-0035812	0767	1
WOODS JOHN O	COL	0-0022755	1067	1
WOODS JR GEORGE E	COL	0-0041840	0161	1
WOODS JR LEE R	COL	0-0014851	0549	1
WOODS KENNETH J	LTC	0-0053413	0863	1
WOODS LAWRENCE	COL	0-0006349	0150	1
WOODS PAUL M	LTC	0-0025071	0361	1
WOODSON JR WILBERT Y	LTC	0-0049358	0665	2
WOODWARD DEAN R	LTC	0-0062237	0767	1
WOODWARD ERNEST A	CW4	W-0904056	0661	1
WOODWARD JR HORACE H	COL	0-0010188	0349	1
WOODWARD NICHOLAS O	COL	0-0009704	0854	1
WOODWARD SAMUEL M	MAJ	0-0059801	1262	1
WOODWARD WILLIAM R	B G	0-0004438	1050	1
WOODWARD WILLIAM R	B G	0-0018582	1059	1
WOODYARD DONALD H	LTC	0-0051564	1162	1
WOODYARD JR THOMAS W	COL	0-0019826	0865	1
WOOLEY JR GEORGE F	B G	0-001186C	0449	1
WOOLFLEY FRANCIS A	B G	0-0005699	0453	1
WOOLGAR WILLIAM A	COL	0-0017977	0454	1
WOOLLEY DONALD J	COL	0-0051478	1160	1
WOOLLEY HAROLD	COL	0-0006190	1145	2
WOOLSEY LAWRENCE S	1LT	0-0025403	0844	2
WOOTEN JOHN H	LTC	0-0053968	0367	1
WOOTEN JR CHARLES A	LTC	0-0044599	1064	1
WOOTEN SIDNEY C	M G	0-0018126	0865	1
WOOTTEN ANGUS E	LTC	0-0070572	0467	1
WORD JR ORVILLE C	COL	0-0050922	0754	1
WORKIZER BENJAMIN F	LTC	0-0020852	0944	2
WORKIZER DANIEL Y	COL	C-0018608	0352	1
WORKMAN JAMES H	COL	0-0015177	0954	1
WORKS JOHN M	COL	0-0012449	0845	2
WORKS ROBERT C	COL	0-0021221	0164	1
WORLEY CHARLES F	CW3	W-0907065	1062	1
WORLEY JANE E	MAJ	N-0000303	1060	1
WORLEY THOMAS G	LTC	C-0031494	0465	2
WORRALL JR JOSEPH A	LTC	0-0067975	0866	1
WORRALL LAWRENCE P	COL	0-0007738	0642	2
WORSHAM LUDSON D	B G	0-0004428	1148	2
WORTHINGTON JAMES M	B G	0-0019797	0865	1
WORTMAN VOLNEY W	COL	C-0010218	0453	1
WOZNIAK SR STANLEY V	CW4	W-0907066	0165	1
WREAN JOY T	COL	C-0016871	0757	2
WRIGHT ANDREW M	LTC	0-0018050	0546	1
WRIGHT BERTRAM S	LTC	0-0041137	0764	1
WRIGHT BRUCE E	CW4	W-0907067	0862	1
WRIGHT CHARLES E	LTC	0-0031564	0665	1
WRIGHT CLARENCE J	CPT	0-0008748	1021	2
WRIGHT DAVID B	LTC	0-0054276	0565	1
WRIGHT EDWARD M	COL	0-0024693	0764	1
WRIGHT EDWIN K	M G	0-0015475	C955	1
WRIGHT ERNEST C	MAJ	0-0014554	0717	1
WRIGHT ERNEST C	LTC	0-0053926	0863	1
WRIGHT JAY W	COL	0-0051516	1067	1
WRIGHT JOHN R	COL	C-0009537	1047	1

NAME	GRADE	SVC NO	DATE RET MO YR	RET CODE
WRIGHT JR CHARLES R	COL	C-0031388	C765	1
WRIGHT JR EDGAR	COL	0-0017736	0659	1
WRIGHT JR JOHN R	COL	C-0019817	C865	1
WRIGHT JR WILLIAM M	COL	0-0010433	0653	1
WRIGHT LESTER J	LTC	0-0037434	C362	2
WRIGHT LLOYD T	LTC	0-0092616	0767	1
WRIGHT LOWELL B	COL	0-0003918	0147	2
WRIGHT MARGARET M	MAJ	N-0002247	C561	2
WRIGHT ROBERT O	COL	0-0008396	0247	1
WRIGHT WILLARD L	LTC	0-0016114	C449	1
WRIGHT WILLIAM A	CW4	W-0904222	0962	1
WRIGHT WILLIAM H	LTG	0-0018129	1265	1
WRIGHT WILLIAM H	LTC	0-0059580	1065	1
WRIGHTSON SAMUEL H	COL	C-0039879	0264	1
WROCKLOFF JR G E	COL	0-0015781	C954	1
WUERDINGER GERTRUDE	MAJ	N-0000385	C361	1
WUEST CHARLES H	LTC	0-0039280	0961	1
WUEST MELVIN L	CPT	0-0073939	0365	2
WUEST WILLIAM J	COL	0-0029026	1058	1
WUNDERLICH F R	COL	C-0003999	0452	1
WURFEL SEYMOUR W	COL	0-0029835	C860	1
WURM URBAN J	COL	0-0030971	1065	1
WURTZLER HERBERT W	COL	0-0039596	0159	1
WYAND PRESTON W	COL	0-0044363	0766	1
WYATT OTHEL	COL	0-0080027	0166	1
WYATT THOMAS C	LTC	0-0066128	0767	1
WYATT WILLIAM L	LTC	0-0032310	0764	1
WYATT WILLIAM O	COL	0-0040020	C466	1
WYCHE IRA T	M G	0-0003112	C948	2
WYCOFF FRANCIS L	MAJ	0-0056391	0860	1
WYGANT ROBERT H	LTC	0-0031926	0262	1
WYMAN CHARLES L	LTC	0-0013997	0720	2
WYMAN JR THEODORE	COL	C-0007925	C-45	2
WYMAN PHILIP A	COL	0-0024854	C867	1
WYMAN WILLARD G	GEN	0-0012356	C758	1
WYMER HAROLD W	MAJ	C-0065587	1162	1
WYNNE ALBERT K	LTC	0-0081357	C567	1
WYNNE ANDREW J	COL	0-C007C74	0947	1
WYNNE CONSUELO R	2LT	N-0000571	0345	1
WYNNE GEORGE C	COL	0-0011874	0653	1
WYRUCHOWSKI EDWARD P	LTC	0-0065241	1067	1
WYSS ARNOLD V	COL	0-0029788	1062	1
YAGER ROBERT H	COL	0-0022761	C565	2
YAKSHE JOHN R	COL	0-0031820	0366	1
YALE V PAUL	MAJ	C-0022177	C147	2
YALE WESLEY W	COL	C-0014969	C854	1
YANCEY BENJAMIN A	MAJ	0-0004493	0-34	1
YANCEY MARTHA J	MAJ	N-0002149	1161	1
YANCEY THOMAS R	M G	0-0042256	0867	1
YANKA DONALD E	COL	0-0030252	0164	1
YANTIS MYRON O	LTC	0-0038014	0766	1
YARBROUGH JAMES E	COL	0-0017348	C755	2
YARBROUGH SAMUEL K J	COL	0-001946C	C764	1
YARRINGTON WILLIAM R	COL	0-0080028	0866	1
YASSEL LOUIS S	CW2	W-0901051	0642	1
YATES EAMES L	LTC	0-0050350	1163	1
YATES EDISON E	LTC	0-0039047	1167	1
YATES JULES D	LTC	0-0023127	C761	1
YATES VIRGIL T	COL	C-0052069	C866	1
YATSEVITCH GRATIAN M	COL	0-0031442	C267	1
YEAGER HAROLD R	LTC	0-0029567	C856	2
YEAGER MANFORD E	CW4	W-0907070	1262	1
YEAGER WALTER B	M G	0-0029464	0662	1
YEATON IVAN D	COL	C-0011648	0151	1
YEIK IRENE L	MAJ	N-0002383	0761	1
YEO STEWART	COL	0-0016664	0656	1
YERGER MARGUERITE	MAJ	N-0000555	1058	1
YERKS JR AUSTIN J	LTC	0-0027787	1165	1
YESSLER PAUL G	COL	0-0057C27	0966	1
YEUELL JR DONOVAN P	COL	0-C023C83	0660	2
YLIKORSA GEORGE A	CW4	W-0904061	0265	2
YLINEN LYDIA R	MAJ	R-0010007	C554	1
YODER LEVERETT G	COL	0-0012048	0854	1
YODER QUENTIN E	LTC	0-0048994	1163	1
YOOZIO STANLEY I	CW2	W-0901507	0543	2

NAME	GRADE	SVC NO	DATE RET MO YR	RET CODE
YORK JERALDINE	LTC	N-0001929	1167	1
YORK JEROME B	COL	0-0025327	0764	1
YORK JR E T	1LT	0-0027C18	1145	2
YORK ROBERT E	COL	0-0012083	0753	1
YORK WILLIAM E	CW3	W-0904062	1060	1
YORKE HAROLD W	CW3	W-0904063	0961	1
YOST CARL R	COL	0-0031542	0966	1
YOST HARVEY J	COL	0-0042277	0162	2
YOST JOSEPH B	COL	0-0020201	0866	1
YOST LOWELL A	COL	0-0039556	1057	1
YOUNG ADLAI C	COL	C-0004966	0851	1
YOUNG CHARLES G	COL	0-0020739	0967	1
YOUNG CHARLES T	COL	0-0017335	0657	1
YOUNG CLAUDE C	LTC	0-0031935	0163	1
YOUNG CLAUDE E	MAJ	0-0058792	0164	1
YOUNG CLYDE G	COL	C-002879C	0155	1
YOUNG DAVID R	LTC	0-0063091	0767	1
YOUNG DONALD A	COL	C-0006899	0847	1
YOUNG EDWARD H	COL	0-0012348	0854	2
YOUNG FOWARD R	COL	0-0028839	0256	1
YOUNG EDWARD R	1LT	0-0071899	0856	2
YOUNG ELLSWORTH	COL	0-0007483	0749	2
YOUNG ELMER W	B G	0-0016298	0859	1
YOUNG FREDERICK	COL	0-0001014	0934	1
YOUNG FREDERICK	COL	0-0018667	0653	1
YOUNG FREDERICK	LTC	0-0079157	0467	1
YOUNG GEORGE E	COL	0-0015659	0754	2
YOUNG HAMILTON R	COL	0-0056786	1159	1
YOUNG JAMES	1LT	0-0064774	0554	2
YOUNG JOHN B	CW2	W-0904223	0263	1
YOUNG JOHN J	COL	C-0051172	0859	1
YOUNG JR RALPH W	CW3	RW-0904068	0462	1
YOUNG JR RICHARD A	COL	0-0044524	0765	1
YOUNG MARION L	LTC	0-0006516	1041	2
YOUNG MASON J	B G	0-0003788	0753	1
YOUNG NELLIE M	LTC	L-0000325	1167	1
YOUNG NORMAN B	CW4	W-0904067	1262	1
YOUNG RANDALL M	CW4	W-0904069	0863	1
YOUNG RAYMOND E	LTC	0-0060484	0466	1
YOUNG ROBERT L	CW4	W-0904070	1065	1
YOUNG ROBERT M	LTC	C-0031891	0261	1
YOUNG ROSS	COL	C-0039001	0167	1
YOUNG SIDNEY H	MAJ	C-0005320	1036	1
YOUNG STANLEY A	COL	0-0051479	0364	1
YOUNG THOMAS H	COL	0-0011479	0753	1
YOUNG WILBUR P	COL	0-0084581	0367	1
YOUNG WILLIAM C	COL	0-0003537	0449	1
YOUNG WILLIAM H	LTC	C-0042753	0562	1
YOUNG WILLIAM V	MAJ	0-0060604	0165	1
YOUNGBLOOD NORMAN E	B G	0-0028996	1162	1
YOUNGBLOOD ROBERT C	LTC	0-0029423	0758	1
YOUNGER MARY M	LTC	N-0000288	0263	1
YOUNT PAUL F	M G	0-0018022	0158	1
YOUNTS JR JAMES O	COL	C-0029552	0461	1
YOW JOHN W	COL	0-0032361	1064	1
YUILL CHARLES W	COL	0-0005269	0447	2
YUILL HARRY F	LTC	0-0043571	0966	1
YULE RICHARD G	COL	0-0018948	0561	1
YUNCK RICHARD T	MAJ	0-0081355	0464	1
YUNKER SYLVESTER	CPT	0-007190C	0162	2
ZACHERLE ALARICH L	COL	P-0042817	0266	1
ZACHERLE JR GEORGE H	COL	0-0030868	0661	1
ZAHROBSKY RALPH E	COL	0-0023149	0766	1
ZAIS ANNE B	LTC	N-0000227	0858	1
ZAJICEK JOHN F	COL	0-0007866	0747	2
ZAK JOSEPH T	LTC	0-0011152	0838	2
ZALESNEY NELLIE J	MAJ	N-0001536	0264	1
ZALKAN GEORGE	COL	0-0021000	1166	2
ZANCA PETER	COL	0-0051167	0763	1
ZAREMBA EDWARD B	LTC	0-0024094	1060	2
ZARESKY ALEXANDER	LTC	0-0044353	0865	1
ZARTNER BERT	MAJ	C-0067889	0266	1
ZAUMEYER LAWRENCE M	COL	C-0032906	1065	1
ZAUTNER GEORGE H	LTC	0-0005337	0542	1
ZEBROWITZ MORRIS	COL	0-0080529	0767	2

NAME	GRADE	SVC NO	DATE RET MO YR	RET CODE
ZECCA MARIO J	COL	O-0032396	1064	1
ZEEFF DOROTHY M	MAJ	L-0000011	1053	1
ZEIDNER SAMUEL I	COL	O-0006104	0349	2
ZEIGLER ROBERT D	COL	O-0034726	0767	1
ZEITZ GORDON F	CPT	O-0060392	0764	1
ZELENIK JOHN S	COL	O-0043124	0666	1
ZELL QUENTIN L	COL	O-0081361	0966	1
ZELLEFROW ALBERT F	LTC	O-0040982	0967	1
ZELLER FRANK J	COL	O-0019043	0863	1
ZELLER GEORGE A	MAJ	O-0015975	1044	1
ZELLER HENRY M	COL	O-0016843	0757	2
ZELLER JAMES R	MAJ	O-0027567	0460	2
ZEOLI RICHARD F	COL	O-0032345	0861	1
ZEPF GEORGE E	WO1	W-0901053	0941	1
ZERBEE AUGUSTINE	COL	O-0004935	0344	2
ZIEGLER ARTHUR N	COL	O-0011886	0547	1
ZIEGLER CARL L	COL	O-0030707	0960	1
ZIEGLER ELDON F	LTC	O-0018873	1044	2
ZIELINSKI ALOYSIUS C	MAJ	O-0043162	0262	1
ZIERATH FREDERICK	M G	O-0019211	1167	1
ZIEROT JOHN G	M G	O-0020632	0767	1
ZIESENHEIM JOSEPH C	LTC	O-0066130	1264	1
ZIGMUND FRANK J	MAJ	O-0059075	0862	1
ZILER WILLIAM D	COL	O-0035412	0966	1
ZILLMER DAVID	LTC	O-0026722	1064	1
ZIMMER LAYTON A	COL	O-0016688	0856	1
ZIMMERMAN ARNOLD W	CPT	O-0010101	0824	2
ZIMMERMAN GEORGE J	COL	O-0016600	0854	1
ZIMMERMAN JOHN S	COL	O-0038945	0561	1
ZIMMERMAN ROBERT F	LTC	O-0024481	0361	1
ZIMMERMAN WAYNE C	M G	O-0012436	0156	1
ZINGALES JOSEPH A	LTC	O-0058750	0963	1
ZINNECKER GUS S	LTC	O-0042357	0562	1
ZINSER ROY F	COL	O-0030370	1064	1
ZIPF KARL A	COL	O-0039044	1166	1
ZISLIS LOUIS	LTC	O-0068066	0667	2
ZITZER FREDERICK	LTC	O-0021444	0360	1
ZITZMAN KENNETH F	B G	O-0018654	0859	1
ZIZON ANNE M	MAJ	N-0001271	0559	2
ZOLENAS JR ANTHONY J	COL	O-0031127	0961	1
ZOLLICOFFER MARION R	LTC	O-0065184	0767	1
ZORNIG HERMANN H	COL	O-0002969	0846	2
ZUCCARDY CHARLES A	LTC	O-0064991	1066	1
ZUCKERBROT IRVING	LTC	O-0036901	1064	1
ZUELZER WILHELM A	COL	O-0060730	0966	1
ZUERNER LURLINE V	MAJ	N-0001673	1067	2
ZUFELT DICK	LTC	O-0081363	0667	1
ZUNO EMIL A	LTC	O-0029169	1057	1
ZUNCEL EDWIN A	B G	O-0003792	0153	1
ZUNKER CLARA M	CPT	L-0000197	1262	1
ZWACK JOHN A	LTC	O-0031066	0757	1
ZWICKER RALPH W	M G	O-0016878	0560	2

SECTION 2

ARMY OF THE UNITED STATES RETIRED LIST

The Army of the United States Retired List is composed of officers other than Regular Army officers who are members and former members of the Reserve Components (Army Reserve and National Guard of the United States) and personnel who served in the Army of the United States without component, who are granted retired pay under any provision of law and retired warrant officers and enlisted personnel of the Regular Army who by reason of service in temporary commissioned grade are entitled to receive retired pay of the commissioned grade.

NAME	GRADE	SVC NO	DATE RET MO YR	RET CODE
E DITH	2LT	N-0751275	1044	1
U PALL	CPT	RW-0902792	1062	1
AABERG ROBERT R	CW2	W-2103829	0945	2
AAKKEN ALVIN T	MAJ	0-0265658	1055	3
AAMODT HUBERT N	LTC	0-1895467	0865	1
AAMODT JR JOHN F	CPT	0-0363887	0245	2
AANONSEN HERBERT E	CPT	0-2032968	0559	1
AARNI JOHN C	LTC	0-0363335	0565	3
AARNI WILLIAM H	CPT	0-0405314	0246	2
AARON GEORGE V	CW3	W-2146987	1059	1
AARON JOSEPH E	1LT	0-2061587	1147	2
AARON JR GERALD F	1LT	0-2208634	1051	1
AARON LAWRENCE T	CW3	W-2153379	1263	1
AARON MAX C	CPT	0-2289640	0462	1
AARON NORMA B	CPT	N-0725000	1146	2
AARON STANLEY	WO1	W-2149909	0959	1
AAS ERNEST I	CPT	0-1012486	1045	2
AASEN EDWIN K	LTC	0-0351130	0962	1
AASEN MINA A	CPT	N-0700460	1046	1
AASTROM HERMAN	LTC	0-0445820	0647	1
ABANTO RIZALITO	LTC	0-1301550	0363	1
ABAYA AMADEO	1LT	0-1896655	1149	1
ABBE JOHN A	LTC	0-1994376	0767	1
ABBETT JAMES W	MAJ	0-1132353	0261	1
ABBEY HARLAN I	COL	0-0221316	0962	3
ABBEY HOWARD O	CPT	0-0959067	0965	1
ABBEY JOSEPH A	MAJ	0-0333053	0146	2
ABBEY RUSSELL C	2LT	0-2035063	0345	2
ABBOTT ABBOTT O	LTC	0-1309153	0767	2
ABBOTT ALBERT W	LTC	0-0373312	1059	1
ABBOTT ALFRED A	LTC	0-1578086	0258	1
ABBOTT ARGYLE C	LTC	0-0241145	0358	2
ABBOTT CARROLL S	CW3	W-2147734	0263	1
ABBOTT CHARLES G	CPT	0-1703344	0945	2
ABBOTT CLYDE B	CPT	0-1700729	1145	2
ABBOTT ELMER W	MAJ	0-0107529	1055	3
ABBOTT FLOYD A	LTC	0-0298781	0667	3
ABBOTT GEORGE E	MAJ	0-1326688	0365	1
ABBOTT HAROLD S	LTC	0-0395025	0162	1
ABBOTT HARRY P	COL	0-0219676	0265	3
ABBOTT JAMES P	COL	0-0257156	1053	2
ABBOTT JOHN B	MAJ	0-0508010	0747	2
ABBOTT JOHN C	COL	0-0186525	0753	3
ABBOTT JOHN P	1LT	0-1321983	1045	2
ABBOTT JR MELVIN E	MAJ	0-1016610	0459	1
ABBOTT JULIA J	MAJ	N-0755199	1262	1
ABBOTT LARRY L	2LT	0-5504112	0358	2
ABBOTT LEE K	MAJ	0-1552219	0962	2
ABBOTT LOWELL W	MAJ	0-1300574	1053	2
ABBOTT PAUL J	MAJ	0-0269089	0665	3
ABBOTT ROBERT E	CPT	0-0235860	0154	3
ABBOTT ROBERT W	1LT	0-0470541	0643	2
ABBOTT TEMPLE W	LTC	0-0497365	0866	3
ABBOTT WALTER R	1LT	0-0406825	0345	2
ABBY ROBERT	CW2	W-2210821	0165	1
ABEE JOHN E	CPT	0-1919299	1062	1
ABEL AUGUST F	LTC	0-1182757	1262	1
ABEL DAREL M	CW3	W-2149497	0863	1
ABEL GOLDIE M	LTC	N-0724560	0761	1
ABEL HENRI E	MAJ	0-0501377	0240	2
ABEL JOHN F	CPT	0-0497118	0747	1
ABEL JR JAMES W	MAJ	0-1649423	0860	1
ABEL JR SIDNEY W	CW3	W-2150779	0963	1
ABEL ORAL J	MAJ	0-1294042	1160	1
ABEL RAYMOND L	COL	0-0100837	0556	3
ABEL ROY K	CPT	0-1648982	1059	1
ABEL STEWART W	COL	0-0290592	0562	1
ABEL THOMAS	CPT	0-0498318	0746	1
ABEL WALTER W	LTC	0-0281774	0462	1
ABEL WILLARD E	LTC	0-0320653	0966	3
ABELAIRAS ANDRES	MAJ	0-0487016	0640	1
ABELING LAWRENCE J	1LT	0-1322507	1145	2
ABELL FRANCIS V	MAJ	0-0503042	0557	1
ABELL HERBERT E	CPT	0-0416103	0142	2
ABELL MAURICE F	CW3	W-2143195	0567	1

NAME	GRADE	SVC NO	DATE RET MO YR	RET CODE
ABELL WILFORD	1LT	0-1639524	0663	1
ABELLAR CELESTINO	1LT	0-1896515	0563	1
ABELON SAMSON Z	COL	0-0187897	0954	1
ABENDROTH WILLIAM H	M G	0-0245795	1055	3
ABER JESS	2LT	0-1306525	0744	2
ABER WILLIAM A	CW2	W-2123059	0747	1
ABERBACH JULIAN J	2LT	0-1316880	0344	2
ABERCROMBIE LOIS	2LT	N-0744651	0145	1
ABERCROMBIE WILLARD	LTC	0-0483786	1063	1
ABERLE ALFRED L	MAJ	0-0505905	0154	1
ABERNATHY ROBERT B	MAJ	0-1640971	0966	3
ABERNETHY HENRY G	CPT	0-1101582	0646	1
ABERNETHY RAYMOND T	LTC	0-0329571	1166	3
ABERNETHY RICHARD	CPT	0-0438601	0453	1
ABERNETHY THOMAS J	COL	0-0100339	0955	3
ABERS BERNARD D	CPT	0-0375077	0146	2
ABERT ALBERT L	CW3	W-2206959	1265	1
ABEYTA MICHAEL G	CPT	0-0478682	1153	1
ABLAN MEL	CPT	0-1896662	1064	2
ABLANEDO ARMAND L	MAJ	0-1295482	0863	1
ABLE SCTHORON K	CPT	0-0460060	0446	1
ABLER JULIUS	CPT	0-1040861	0744	2
ABNER ROBERT	CPT	0-0335226	0951	3
ABNEY JOHN D	MAJ	0-0193055	0546	2
ABNEY JOHN J	MAJ	0-0991251	0863	1
ABNEY THOMAS B	CPT	0-0476627	0750	2
ABORJAILY ASSAD N	LTC	0-1081501	0467	1
ABPLANALP ARTHUR H	LTC	0-0431104	0962	3
ABRAHAM MICHAEL K	LTC	0-1010362	0361	1
ABRAHAM WILLIAM R	MAJ	0-2014642	0767	1
ABRAHAMS FRANK A	LTC	0-0496711	0557	1
ABRAHAMS JOHN T	CW2	W-2151845	0459	1
ABRAHAMS ROLLAND S	COL	0-0221860	0950	1
ABRAHAMSEN E J	2LT	N-0743392	1144	1
ABRAHAMSON GEORGE W	LTC	0-0393801	0966	1
ABRAHAMSON IRA A	COL	0-0140773	0346	2
ABRAHAMSON RAYMOND E	COL	0-0313155	1159	2
ABRAHAMSON WILLIAM R	MAJ	0-0160698	0151	3
ABRAMS BARNIE J	LTC	0-1579336	0655	2
ABRAMS EDWARD W	MAJ	0-0302238	0146	2
ABRAMS HARRY	LTC	0-0206487	0260	3
ABRAMS JOHN H	LTC	0-0270730	0155	1
ABRAMS LAWRENCE B	WO1	W-2121408	0744	2
ABRAMS LEONARD P	MAJ	0-0809074	0464	1
ABRAMS MAURICE	MAJ	0-1175754	0765	1
ABRAMS MAURICE J	LTC	0-0242900	1145	2
ABRAMS WILLIAM C	CPT	0-0912789	0345	2
ABRAMS WILLIAM W	LTC	0-0301658	0167	3
ABRAMSON ARTHUR S	CPT	0-0492867	1046	1
ABRAMSON EMANUEL	LTC	0-0529993	0565	3
ABRAMSON JUNIUS S	1LT	0-1547219	0346	1
ABREMSKI WILLIAM J	2LT	0-0552098	0246	2
ABRON JR JAMES A	MAJ	0-1292454	0661	2
ABSHIER ROBERT E	CPT	0-1173844	0848	1
ABSHIRE ROY W	CPT	0-0541497	0946	2
ABUYEN ERNESTO	2LT	0-1896390	0748	1
ABY CHARLES W	COL	0-0260606	0965	3
ACCARDI ROY R	1LT	0-1016633	0346	1
ACCARDI VINCENT	CPT	0-0496393	1045	2
ACE DREXEL M	MAJ	0-1309172	0361	1
ACEVEDO JR MANUEL	CPT	0-2263388	1162	1
ACEVEDO JR PLACIDO	CPT	0-0330882	0545	2
ACEVEDO RAMON	CW4	W-2101029	1254	1
ACEY RAYMOND E	LTC	0-0288814	1055	3
ACHARD FRANCIS H	LTC	0-0188269	0652	3
ACHAUER REED O	COL	0-0202126	0262	3
ACHENBACH JAY O	1LT	0-0244353	0664	3
ACHESON GEORGE J	LTC	0-1170616	1060	1
ACHESON ROBERT P	MAJ	0-0303279	0445	1
ACHEY KENNETH P	MAJ	0-1877154	1063	1
ACHOR JOHN R	COL	0-0407000	1164	3
ACHTERMANN ARIEL H	LTC	0-0360421	0259	1
ACKEMANN WILLIAM H	COL	0-0117655	1151	3
ACKENBACH HUGO G	CPT	0-2027492	0556	1
ACKER ALBERT L	MAJ	0-0187906	0551	3

NAME	GRADE	SVC NO	DATE RET MO YR	RET CODE
ACKER GRANT E	CW2	W-3100496	1163	1
ACKER RAYMOND	1LT	0-1032068	0746	2
ACKERLY ROBERT S	LTC	0-0225682	0446	2
ACKERMAN BARTLEY F	MAJ	0-0963386	1262	1
ACKERMAN DAVID M	COL	0-0271752	1264	1
ACKERMAN DON F	LTC	0-1581033	0763	1
ACKERMAN DONALD D	LTC	0-0370038	0766	3
ACKERMAN EDWARD A	LTC	0-0259147	0865	3
ACKERMAN EVERETT F	COL	0-0451623	0561	1
ACKERMAN EVERETT M	MAJ	0-1554485	0566	1
ACKERMAN GILBERT E	COL	0-0261635	0254	3
ACKERMAN GLENN A	CPT	0-0988044	0563	1
ACKERMAN HERMAN A	LTC	0-0210172	0648	3
ACKERMAN JR HENRY P	LTC	0-1324714	0763	1
ACKERMAN LOUIS	CPT	0-0367861	1047	1
ACKERMAN MELVIN J	LTC	0-2044373	0661	2
ACKERMAN MILTON N	CPT	0-1114899	1047	2
ACKERMAN RICHARD C	MAJ	0-0994282	0663	1
ACKERMAN SIDNEY	CPT	0-1547666	1046	2
ACKERMAN WARREN P	WO1	W-2101355	0944	2
ACKERMANN DAVID F	LTC	0-0188792	0646	1
ACKERS LOUIE F	1LT	0-1825871	0749	1
ACKERSON CLIFTON W	LTC	0-0128091	1056	3
ACKERT WILBUR A	LTC	0-1578567	0463	1
ACKLEY AVERON C	CW2	W-2152871	0458	1
ACKLEY JAMES B	CPT	0-0166329	0249	3
ACKLEY JOHN M	MAJ	0-2036038	1060	1
ACKLEY PHILIP J	1LT	0-0390861	0844	2
ACKLIN CHRISTOPHE	CPT	0-0384301	0945	1
ACLIN LOUIS	MAJ	0-1633043	0861	1
ACOMB ALLEN D	1LT	0-0392377	0944	2
ACOSTA ANTONIO J	CW3	W-2150923	0263	1
ACOSTA EMILIO V	CPT	0-0266852	0455	3
ACOSTA PEDRO F	1LT	0-0204286	0654	3
ACOSTA RAFAEL	COL	0-0230254	0566	3
ACOSTA-SANTINI FERNA	LTC	0-1951400	1166	1
ACREE CLARENCE P	MAJ	0-0478886	0754	1
ACREE FRANK M	MAJ	0-0480858	1045	2
ACRIVOS HAROLD N	MAJ	0-2007674	0561	2
ACTKINSON ARNOLD F	1LT	0-1303085	0346	1
ACTON CARL R	LTC	0-0123406	0756	3
ACTON CONRAD R	COL	0-0261181	1062	3
ACUFF CARL L	LTC	0-0272927	1266	3
ACUFF MILTON L	COL	0-0278319	1060	1
ACUFF RICHARD M	1LT	0-1327598	0447	2
ADAIR DANIEL L	MAJ	0-0482122	0651	1
ADAIR HORACE R	1LT	0-0250993	1161	3
ADAIR JAMES	CW4	W-2101310	0955	1
ADAIR JR JAMES T	LTC	0-0199739	0762	3
ADAIR JUNIUS M	MAJ	0-0365562	1159	1
ADAIR NORMAN	CPT	0-0489540	1043	2
ADAIR RUSSEL R	CW2	W-2147268	0957	1
ADAIR THOMAS E	MAJ	0-0452080	0457	1
ADAM CHARLES W	LTC	0-2014696	0867	1
ADAM DOUGLAS G	LTC	0-0243182	1165	3
ADAMAITIS WALTER J	MAJ	0-1650427	0961	1
ADAMCZYK LEO J	MAJ	0-2016126	1162	1
ADAMIETZ STEVE F	MAJ	0-0974455	1161	1
ADAMO FRANK S	COL	0-0181315	0746	2
ADAMS ADAM J	CPT	0-0499562	0347	1
ADAMS ALBERT H	LTC	0-0450215	0656	1
ADAMS ALFRED E	CPT	0-0384345	1045	2
ADAMS ALGERNON W	LTC	0-0264263	0151	3
ADAMS ALONZO R	MAJ	0-0120767	0648	3
ADAMS ALVIN S	COL	0-0266572	0760	1
ADAMS AMBROSE	LTC	0-1576866	0767	2
ADAMS ANDREW A	CPT	0-0476643	0456	1
ADAMS ANN A	1LT	N-0722861	0645	1
ADAMS ANTHONY B	LTC	0-0541058	0763	1
ADAMS ANTHONY O	COL	0-0126019	1048	1
ADAMS ARNEL R	COL	0-0222320	1061	3
ADAMS ARNOLD J	1LT	0-0543507	0448	2
ADAMS ARTHUR A	COL	0-0288809	0460	1
ADAMS ARTHUR A	MAJ	0-0505852	0157	1
ADAMS AUGUSTINE	1LT	0-0400780	0844	2

NAME	GRADE	SVC NO	DATE RET MO YR	RET CODE
ADAMS B F	LTC	0-0325642	0661	1
ADAMS BERNARD H	LTC	0-1017768	1162	1
ADAMS BERT	COL	0-0456186	0266	1
ADAMS CARL C	MAJ	0-1585656	0863	1
ADAMS CARL W	1LT	0-1598626	1056	1
ADAMS CARROLL E	COL	0-0398219	0446	1
ADAMS CHARLES C	LTC	0-0170238	0851	3
ADAMS CHARLES L	COL	0-0218943	0262	3
ADAMS CHESLEY M	LTC	0-0154207	0453	3
ADAMS CLARENCE G	LTC	0-1581089	0662	1
ADAMS CLAUDE A	2LT	0-0251118	0845	1
ADAMS CLYDE B	LTC	0-0369182	0846	1
ADAMS CRAWFORD M	LTC	0-0252508	0665	3
ADAMS CURTIS H	COL	0-0413145	0863	1
ADAMS DALLAS C	1LT	0-1055402	1046	2
ADAMS DANIEL B	COL	0-0301363	0566	1
ADAMS DAVID J	CPT	0-2020701	0155	2
ADAMS DAVID W	2LT	0-1513598	0337	1
ADAMS DONALD B	B G	0-0167551	0650	3
ADAMS DONALD C	LTC	0-0276107	0967	3
ADAMS DONALD K	MAJ	0-1633187	1058	1
ADAMS EARL F	MAJ	0-1996654	1159	1
ADAMS EARL P	COL	0-0301511	0766	3
ADAMS EDITH P	2LT	N-0743125	0946	1
ADAMS EDWARD	CW3	W-2147736	1262	1
ADAMS EDWARD H	MAJ	0-0128789	0-52	3
ADAMS EDWARD L	WO1	W-2140853	0550	1
ADAMS EDWIN B	CPT	0-0300192	0156	3
ADAMS ELDRED E	COL	0-0269666	0967	3
ADAMS ELIAS	MAJ	0-0240668	0965	3
ADAMS ELIZABETH	2LT	N-0764106	0845	1
ADAMS EPHRAIM	MAJ	0-0216968	0961	3
ADAMS EUGENE J	LTC	0-0304485	0148	2
ADAMS EUGENE V	1LT	0-2036039	0175	1
ADAMS FLORENCE A	1LT	L-0402790	0945	1
ADAMS FRANCIS C	MAJ	0-0963895	0266	1
ADAMS FRANK	MAJ	0-0105643	0848	1
ADAMS FRANK C	2LT	0-1051052	0344	2
ADAMS FRANKLIN P	LTC	0-1825921	0165	1
ADAMS GEORGE D	LTC	0-0451068	0457	1
ADAMS GEORGE J	LTC	0-0251380	0859	2
ADAMS GEORGE L	1LT	0-0519544	1145	2
ADAMS GEORGE M	MAJ	0-1116274	1160	1
ADAMS GEORGE R	CW3	W-2152777	0661	1
ADAMS GEORGE W	MAJ	0-0204377	0562	3
ADAMS GEORGE W	COL	0-0255288	0656	2
ADAMS HAROLD E	LTC	0-0173122	0960	3
ADAMS HAROLD P	MAJ	0-0559303	0765	1
ADAMS HARRY A	COL	0-0911403	0763	1
ADAMS HARRY L	MAJ	0-0109989	1022	1
ADAMS HARTMAN R	CW3	W-2141886	0659	1
ADAMS HOWARD G	LTC	0-0392673	0461	2
ADAMS HOYETT	CW2	W-2101267	0347	1
ADAMS HUGH M	WO1	W-2006771	0365	3
ADAMS ISAIAH K	2LT	0-1318505	0345	2
ADAMS JACK O	CW2	W-2151519	0561	1
ADAMS JACK R	LTC	0-0250542	0366	3
ADAMS JACK W	CPT	0-2033565	1056	1
ADAMS JAMES	LTC	0-0485260	0847	2
ADAMS JAMES C	CW3	W-2145048	0460	1
ADAMS JAMES H	1LT	0-0407158	0646	2
ADAMS JAMES M	LTC	0-1548611	0861	1
ADAMS JAMES O	CPT	0-0173205	0648	3
ADAMS JAMES S	CPT	0-1030205	0955	1
ADAMS JENNIE F	2LT	N-0786858	1050	1
ADAMS JESSE H	MAJ	0-1297644	1061	1
ADAMS JESSE R	LTC	0-0239355	0465	3
ADAMS JIMMIE E	CPT	0-2012543	0453	2
ADAMS JOHN C	MAJ	0-0227308	0146	1
ADAMS JOHN J	MAJ	0-0329787	1045	2
ADAMS JOHN J	CPT	0-0959269	0160	1
ADAMS JOHN K	LTC	0-1546265	0764	1
ADAMS JOHN L	MAJ	0-0810183	0164	1
ADAMS JOHN O	CPT	0-1331798	0947	1
ADAMS JOHN W	MAJ	0-1013995	0257	1

ARMY OF THE UNITED STATES RETIRED LIST

NAME	GRADE	SVC NO	DATE RET MO YR	RET CODE
ADAMS JOHN W	CW2	W-2207006	0763	1
ADAMS JOSEPH C	CW3	W-2108477	1254	1
ADAMS JOY C	CPT	0-0173574	0758	3
ADAMS JR DAVID L	1LT	0-2055790	1045	2
ADAMS JR ED	MAJ	0-1044159	0457	2
ADAMS JR EDWARD	MAJ	0-1284163	0257	1
ADAMS JR EDWARD F	LTC	0-0445457	0165	3
ADAMS JR EDWIN G	1LT	0-0334046	0646	2
ADAMS JR JAMES H	MAJ	0-0363787	1044	2
ADAMS JR JAMES W	1LT	0-1303956	1044	2
ADAMS JR JOHN P	LTC	0-0518857	0663	1
ADAMS JR LONNIE B	LTC	0-1318265	0264	1
ADAMS JR NORMAN I	LTC	0-0163307	0144	2
ADAMS JR ROY I	LTC	0-1058159	0961	1
ADAMS JR SAM J	LTC	0-1292814	0761	1
ADAMS JR THOMAS E	CW2	W-2146649	1064	1
ADAMS JR WALTER A	LTC	0-0465994	0647	2
ADAMS KIRK F	LTC	0-0363193	0859	1
ADAMS LEON L	CPT	0-0256671	1053	1
ADAMS LESLIE H	1LT	0-1017905	0845	1
ADAMS LESTER W	COL	0-0168771	0258	3
ADAMS LLOYD H	MAJ	0-1045995	0160	1
ADAMS LLOYD S	LTC	0-0152727	0553	3
ADAMS LOLA E	1LT	N-0777138	0448	1
ADAMS LUTHER	MAJ	0-0335706	0245	2
ADAMS MARION H	CW3	W-2147195	0962	1
ADAMS MARJORIE F	MAJ	L-1010064	0763	1
ADAMS MARY C	MAJ	N-0728238	0561	1
ADAMS MAX B	LTC	0-0240471	0363	3
ADAMS MELVIN F	LTC	0-0504256	0265	3
ADAMS MORRIS F	1LT	0-1310199	0946	2
ADAMS NORMAN H	COL	0-0280221	1055	1
ADAMS OLIVER	CW2	W-2210140	0461	1
ADAMS ORVILLE P	CW3	W-2113359	0354	1
ADAMS OTIS C	LTC	0-1294102	1060	1
ADAMS PAUL R	LTC	0-1017431	0652	1
ADAMS PEARL S	CPT	N-0756334	0546	1
ADAMS ROBERT	CPT	0-0150254	0360	3
ADAMS ROBERT C	LTC	0-1171862	0766	1
ADAMS ROBERT C	MAJ	0-2055200	0960	1
ADAMS ROBERT F	CPT	0-1310381	0945	2
ADAMS ROBERT H	MAJ	0-1897725	0264	1
ADAMS ROBERT L	MAJ	0-1919341	0966	1
ADAMS ROBERT P	1LT	0-0452350	1044	2
ADAMS ROBERT W	LTC	0-0276019	0667	3
ADAMS ROGER R	1LT	0-2007262	0446	2
ADAMS ROY C	CW3	W-2149323	0765	1
ADAMS ROY H	LTC	0-0355254	0966	3
ADAMS ROY J	MAJ	0-2050323	0361	1
ADAMS ROY W	CW3	W-2127887	0560	1
ADAMS ROYCE T	CPT	0-1289159	1151	1
ADAMS SAM H	LTC	0-0355721	1060	1
ADAMS SAMUEL	1LT	0-1178265	1045	2
ADAMS SAMUEL C	1LT	0-1315517	0745	2
ADAMS SAMUEL H	2LT	0-2202784	0453	1
ADAMS SAMUEL P	LTC	0-0156498	0959	3
ADAMS SHIRLEY S	2LT	N-0736494	0342	1
ADAMS SIDNEY M	LTC	0-0310372	0666	3
ADAMS STANLEY L	CPT	0-1055771	1165	3
ADAMS TYERUS F	CW4	W-2120711	1259	1
ADAMS VERNON J	MAJ	0-1825535	0763	1
ADAMS WALDEMAR P	COL	0-0123409	0751	3
ADAMS WALDO P	MAJ	0-2096982	1046	1
ADAMS WALLIS W	CW4	W-2118284	0855	1
ADAMS WARD A	MAJ	0-0242595	0152	3
ADAMS WARD W	MAJ	0-0248797	1166	3
ADAMS WELDON H	MAJ	0-0987521	0258	1
ADAMS WILBUR C	MAJ	0-0212903	0156	3
ADAMS WILEY J	COL	0-0123410	0555	3
ADAMS WILLIAM B	MAJ	0-0270491	1066	3
ADAMS WILLIAM B	MAJ	0-0370415	0550	2
ADAMS WILLIAM H	COL	0-0311363	0460	3
ADAMS WILLIAM H	COL	0-0365427	0765	1
ADAMS WILLIAM M	COL	0-0132952	0955	3
ADAMS WILLIAM O	MAJ	0-0324665	1160	1

NAME	GRADE	SVC NO	DATE RET MO YR	RET CODE
ADAMS WILLIAM W	LTC	0-0223166	0265	3
ADAMSEN JAMES H	LTC	0-0733251	1167	1
ADAMSKI FRANK J	1LT	0-1049714	0846	2
ADAMSKI LADIMIR S	MAJ	0-0490235	0850	1
ADAMSKY JOHN	MAJ	0-0335765	0161	1
ADAMSON BOYLE F	LTC	0-0399144	0161	1
ADAMSON GEORGE O	MAJ	0-0188929	0753	3
ADAMSON GEORGE E	MAJ	0-0206646	0458	3
ADAMSON HARRY R	CPT	0-1003436	1046	2
ADAMSON HOLTON R	LTC	0-0355030	0446	2
ADAMSON JASON	1LT	0-0108466	0540	1
ADAMSON MARVIN G	MAJ	0-0495556	1155	1
ADAMSON ORASTUS F	LTC	0-2042763	0866	1
ADAMSON OTIES A	MAJ	0-1292409	1060	1
ADATTO ALBERT	LTC	0-1641647	0862	1
ADCOCK CHARLES V	LTC	0-1542340	0361	1
ADCOCK ERNEST C	LTC	0-0444902	0653	1
ADCOCK LEE M	2LT	0-1320809	1144	2
ADCOCK MAURICE F	MAJ	0-1342063	0164	1
ADCOCK C T	CW3	W-2101357	0560	1
ADCOX GEORGE E	CPT	0-1044742	1161	2
ADCOX JOHN	CW4	W-2131440	1159	1
ADCOX WOODROW	CW2	W-2205380	0462	1
ADDERLEY JR JOSEPH F	LTC	0-0372312	0464	1
ADDINGTON JOHN M	CW4	W-2114810	0564	1
ADDIS RUSSELL E	LTC	0-0340174	0256	1
ADDISON DONALD E	MAJ	0-0988944	1164	1
ADDISON ELVIN R	2LT	0-1326953	1145	2
ADDISON JAMES F	LTC	0-0447553	0954	1
ADDISON JENNIE L	MAJ	N-0743120	0265	1
ADDISON JR WILLIAM P	MAJ	0-0330439	0546	2
ADDLEMAN THEODORE A	LTC	0-0277796	1053	3
ADDUCI FRANK R	CW3	W-2002549	0163	3
ADDY LESTER R	1LT	0-1299518	1045	2
ADDY ZIMRI N	1LT	0-0378920	0944	2
ADE GUY W	LTC	0-0118716	0951	3
ADE THEODORE	MAJ	0-1888620	0964	1
ADELSBERGER A R	CW2	W-2118870	1151	2
ADEN IRVING J	COL	0-0279041	0959	2
ADEN WILLIAM C	MAJ	0-0945694	0865	1
ADER SAMUEL	LTC	0-0222118	0257	3
ADERHOLT CLARA F	1LT	N-0759414	1145	1
ADESKO LEON R	CW3	W-2119352	0662	1
ADEST JACOB F	MAJ	0-0496146	0346	2
ADEY EDWIN A	LTC	0-0227132	0563	3
ADIE JOHN	CW2	W-2205844	0762	1
ADIMART FRANK J	LTC	0-1644434	0366	3
ADKINS CHARLIE H	CW3	W-2147555	0659	1
ADKINS CHARLIE S	MAJ	0-0488282	0254	1
ADKINS CLODECH	MAJ	0-1597975	0962	2
ADKINS CLYDE L	LTC	0-0327894	0164	1
ADKINS DAVID D	CPT	0-0520680	0849	1
ADKINS DONALD	CPT	0-0482385	1145	2
ADKINS EUGENE S	MAJ	0-1634594	0666	1
ADKINS HARRY T	LTC	0-0202880	1044	2
ADKINS HUGH F	CPT	0-0469634	0345	1
ADKINS JACK E	MAJ	0-1885587	0962	1
ADKINS JAMES B	2LT	0-1013570	0745	2
ADKINS JAMES R	MAJ	0-0269387	0363	1
ADKINS JAMES F	1LT	0-0449385	0146	2
ADKINS JOSEPH F	CPT	0-0341135	0666	3
ADKINS LUTHER H	CPT	0-2023427	0556	1
ADKINS PAUL	CPT	0-1035110	1045	2
ADKINS RAYMONT	CW2	W-2143005	0455	1
ADKINS ROBERT R	CW2	W-3200286	0966	1
ADKINS VIRGIL S	COL	0-0224734	0658	3
ADKINSON DALE W	CPT	0-0961588	0760	1
ADKINSON IVAN R	LTC	0-1284426	1163	1
ADKISON NORMAN R	COL	0-0245612	0356	3
ADKISON RICHARD F	1LT	0-1293412	0945	1
ADKISSON ALFRED J	MAJ	0-0332316	0345	2
ADKISSON GLEAN W	MAJ	0-1011809	1062	1
ADLER BENARD C	MAJ	0-0356490	0946	2
ADLER ERVIN A	CW3	W-2116183	0361	1
ADLER JUSTIN H	MAJ	0-0491505	0646	2

NAME	GRADE	SVC NO	DATE RET MO YR	RET CODE
ADLER LEO S	CPT	0-0483209	0146	2
ADLER WALTER	LTC	0-0215181	1156	3
ADLOW ELIJAH	COL	0-0259641	0855	3
ADMIRE ELMER E	LTC	0-1545471	0662	1
ADOLPHSON JOHN F	CPT	0-0258160	0867	3
ADRIAN GEORGE C	LTC	0-1323654	0863	1
ADRIAN JOSEPH H	MAJ	0-0970651	1165	1
ADRIAN ROBERT L	CW3	W-2152442	0467	1
AEBISCHER RAY R	LTC	0-1342075	0264	1
AENCHBACHER H L	CW2	W-2145929	1260	1
AERNE JR WALTER	LTC	0-1012955	0364	1
AERY JR LOUIS W	CPT	0-0786874	1164	1
AESCHLIMAN LEWIS C	MAJ	0-2263371	1162	1
AFF CHARLES E	LTC	0-1334944	0866	1
AGAN PIUS R	1LT	0-1896432	0559	1
AGARDY LOUIS	MAJ	0-1032649	0862	2
AGATE JOHN T	CPT	0-0473344	0245	2
AGEE GLADYS L	MAJ	L-0917538	0464	1
AGEE JOE H	LTC	0-0546547	0764	2
AGEE THOMAS H	CPT	0-0568165	0760	2
AGER ARTHUR F	LTC	0-0112432	1054	3
AGER JR CHARLES L	LTC	0-0231837	1060	3
AGIN PAUL L	MAJ	0-2033898	1065	1
AGNE HERBERT C	1LT	0-0517174	1146	1
AGNER JAMES F	1LT	0-1322299	0546	2
AGNEW CORNELIUS	MAJ	0-0241683	0766	3
AGNEW EDGAR T	1LT	0-0411787	0146	1
AGNEW JACK	LTC	0-1173140	0859	1
AGNEW THOMAS G	CPT	0-0382027	1144	2
AGNITSCH JOHN A	MAJ	0-1315996	0264	1
AGNOR GILMORE L	LTC	0-0174847	0359	3
AGOSTI VIRGIL P	2LT	0-1882108	1153	2
AGOSTINI GERMAN	COL	0-0191589	0862	3
AGRADA PACIFICO D	MAJ	0-1323652	0862	2
AGRCON TOMAS P	1LT	0-0890371	0750	1
AGRELIUS ROBERT J	LTC	0-1573918	0964	1
AGRICOLA THEODORE	CPT	0-0492902	0852	1
AGSTER WILLIAM C	COL	0-0234563	0356	3
AGUAS PRUDENCIO	CPT	0-1896897	0454	1
AGUD ALFRED	MAJ	0-1932276	0267	1
AGUERO CHARLES P	LTC	0-1186007	1264	1
AGUILAR CARLOS E	CW3	W-2151142	0762	1
AGUILAR PETER R	CW3	W-2147434	1262	1
AGUIRRE MARY E	CPT	N-2296361	1064	2
AGULE FRANK I	LTC	0-0232306	0149	1
AGUSTIN INOCENCIO	2LT	0-1896964	0762	1
AHANA KENNETH Y	MAJ	0-0955404	0862	2
AHEARN CLARENCE I	CPT	0-0128444	0753	3
AHEARN JOHN L	CPT	0-1011621	0746	2
AHERN CAROL A	1LT	N-0757721	0351	2
AHERN DANIEL K	COL	0-0249885	0357	3
AHERN DENNIS J	LTC	0-1636904	0265	2
AHERN JOHN E	MAJ	0-1877769	0765	1
AHERN JOHN F	COL	0-0382943	0261	1
AHERN JR ANDREW G	1LT	0-1311101	1046	2
AHERN ROBERT W	CPT	0-1293172	0446	1
AHERN WILLIAM A	CPT	0-1316818	0747	2
AHERN WILLIAM T	CPT	0-0382718	0944	2
AHIN GEORGE A	CPT	0-0330734	0643	3
AHLBERG ALVIN E	LTC	0-0195779	0340	3
AHLEMEYER EDWARD H	LTC	0-0345620	0262	1
AHLF ELMER G	LTC	0-0248187	0964	3
AHLSKOG IVER	MAJ	0-0189865	0958	3
AHLSTRAND FRANZ A	MAJ	0-0173642	0154	3
AHLSTROM NELS H	MAJ	0-1649427	0652	1
AHN HARRY H R	LTC	0-0955441	0867	1
AHN IANTHA M	MAJ	N-0772082	0564	3
AHNMARK OSCAR F	LTC	0-0217587	1061	3
AHRENBECK THEO	COL	0-0266163	0164	3
AHRENS DONALD W	WO1	W-2120710	0865	1
AHRENS JOHN H	COL	0-0190496	0648	3
AHRENS WALTER E	CW2	W-2209788	0560	1
AHRENS WILLIAM	CPT	0-0495404	0944	2
AICHELE JOHN H	LTC	0-2008415	0564	1
AIDALA THOMAS F	CPT	0-0351158	0547	2

NAME	GRADE	SVC NO	DATE RET MO YR	RET CODE
AIELLO JOSEPH T	CPT	0-1999766	0249	1
AIELLO RALPH P	MAJ	0-0397664	0256	1
AIELLO ROY G	1LT	0-1689087	1147	2
AIGNER ROBERT E	1LT	0-1323059	0846	2
AIKEN JOHN M	1LT	0-1013235	0847	2
AIKEN RICHARD S	MAJ	0-1167717	0860	1
AIKIN SYDNEY E	MAJ	0-2037029	1163	2
AIKIN WILLIAM T	MAJ	0-1311591	1060	1
AIL IRVING I	CPT	0-0292110	0245	2
AILSTOCK CORNELIUS	CPT	0-0482421	0246	2
AIMONE AUGUST L	MAJ	0-1042218	0267	3
AINLAY SR GEORGE W	COL	0-0322820	1155	3
AINSWORTH H MILLER	M G	0-0104004	1154	3
AINSWORTH JACK L	CW2	W-2148376	0766	1
AINSWORTH JAMES J	LTC	0-0450082	0158	1
AIR CLEMENTS W	LTC	0-0236110	1165	3
AIRHART BOYD L	MAJ	0-0350965	0461	1
AIRIS THOMAS F	COL	0-0276628	0666	3
AIROLDI ANTHONY J	LTC	0-0354097	0246	2
AIROV SAMUEL	1LT	0-1170618	0345	2
AIRSMAN JOHN W	LTC	0-0535501	0763	1
AISENSTADT F ALBERT	COL	0-0140113	1049	3
AISHECK DONALD F	1LT	0-0452333	1044	2
AISO DANIEL I	CW3	W-2145281	1164	1
AISON EMIL L	LTC	0-0106851	0545	2
AITKEN CARROLL H	MAJ	0-0314140	0646	1
AITKEN JOHN F	2LT	0-0395252	0642	2
AITKEN MARY E	CPT	N-0736600	0867	1
AJALAT MITRY P	CPT	0-0420419	1044	2
AJEMIAN CHARLES	MAJ	0-0259840	0660	1
AKAMATSU PETER K	LTC	0-0420502	1066	1
AKE LOREN F	LTC	0-0344712	1146	2
AKERS FRANK H	LTC	0-1317556	0960	1
AKERS FREDERICK	CPT	0-0468051	0747	1
AKERS GEORGE W	LTC	0-0435624	0353	1
AKERS JAMES C	CW3	W-2146437	0962	1
AKERS JR DEE F	CPT	0-0579442	0461	1
AKERS KENNETH P	LTC	0-0355815	0357	1
AKERS LEONARD A	LTC	0-0450570	0858	1
AKERS MARVIN L	CPT	0-0518969	1047	2
AKERSTROM OSCAR W	LTC	0-0395609	0560	1
AKEY ROBERT W	CPT	0-1767411	0850	1
AKIMOTO RALPH Y	CW3	W-2147897	0764	1
AKIMOTO THEODORE	1LT	0-1338039	1048	1
AKIN ALFRED K	COL	0-0321007	0461	1
AKIN AUBREY W	COL	0-0169695	0260	1
AKIN HENRY C R	COL	0-0142312	0649	3
AKIN KENNETH A	COL	0-0251991	0565	3
AKINS AUSTIN J	WO1	W-2119215	1046	1
AKINS CHARLES E	MAJ	0-1821573	1162	1
AKINS CLARENCE E	CW3	W-2143710	0464	1
AKINS COLUMBUS	CW3	W-2205132	0266	1
AKINS DONALD J	CPT	0-1836507	0860	1
AKINS J D	CW3	W-2124165	0661	1
AKINS MOSSIE C	LTC	0-1110985	0163	1
AKINS RACY L	LTC	0-0933325	0766	1
AKINS WALTER R	MAJ	0-0479186	1048	1
AKINS WILLIAM H	MAJ	0-1290524	1060	1
AKLEY CLARENCE V	1LT	0-0447461	0346	2
AKRIDGE CLYDE M	LTC	0-0452112	0159	1
AKROMAS ANTHONY	CW4	W-2101101	1154	1
AKSCMAITIS F J	LTC	0-1835252	0457	1
ALAIMO CARL V	LTC	0-1551997	0663	1
ALAIN THEODORE F	CW2	W-2151768	0861	1
ALAMEDA FRANK A	B G	0-0300306	1159	3
ALANIZ RAYMOND C	1LT	0-1312653	0267	1
ALARCON VERGILIO C	MAJ	0-0890535	0955	1
ALARIE JOHN P	MAJ	0-0401764	1047	2
ALATORRE FRANK F	MAJ	0-1338667	0563	1
ALAYON LEOPOLDO F	1LT	0-1896869	0958	1
ALBANO CAMILLO J	LTC	0-1546888	0667	3
ALBANO SALVATORE	CW2	W-2209085	0964	1
ALBAUGH JR KENNETH J	2LT	0-1327081	0844	2
ALBAUGH LYMAN P	1LT	0-1578095	0446	2
ALBEE EALE S	CPT	0-2004496	0460	1

NAME	GRADE	SVC NO	DATE RET MO YR	RET CODE
ALBEE JAMES H	2LT	0-0298919	C262	3
ALBEE JR STEPHEN	MAJ	0-0526858	0565	1
ALBEE MERTON A	COL	C-0110154	0648	3
ALBEE THOMAS L	COL	0-0202634	0461	3
ALBER PHILLIP R	COL	0-0187778	C456	3
ALBERG GUSTAVE W	1LT	0-0395576	0145	2
ALBERI EDVIN H	MAJ	C-1283531	C147	2
ALBERS ALBERT H	CPT	0-1914334	C243	1
ALBERS CLARENCE F	COL	0-0140774	0257	3
ALBERS HELEN J	1LT	N-0756605	0749	2
ALBERS RAYMOND H	LTC	0-0289538	0758	1
ALBERSHARDT HARRY F	MAJ	C-0206429	0555	3
ALBERSON HUGH T	MAJ	C-1641203	0767	1
ALBERSTADT NORMAN N	CPT	0-1718485	0850	2
ALBERT ALLEN D	LTC	0-0245503	0562	3
ALBERT BENJAMIN R	COL	0-0174726	C254	1
ALBERT OWEN S J	COL	0-0214815	C564	3
ALBERTELLI QUINTO J	CW3	W-2150669	1258	1
ALBERTI ALBERTO	MAJ	C-0763594	0246	1
ALBERTINE CAMELL	MAJ	0-0471716	0848	1
ALBERTINI ALBERT F	1LT	C-1999815	1146	1
ALBERTINI CONNELL	LTC	0-0290222	0757	3
ALBERTIS PAUL R	MAJ	C-0225703	0664	3
ALBERTO MELECIO P	1LT	0-2032266	0150	1
ALBERTS WILLIAM	COL	C-0181388	C655	3
ALBERTSON FRANK P	CPT	0-0358744	C545	2
ALBIG WILLIAM B	MAJ	C-1575663	C561	1
ALBIN LEON	COL	0-0398839	1059	1
ALBOSTA FRANK M	LTC	0-0384008	0765	3
ALBRECHT CARL W	LTC	0-0263065	C166	3
ALBRECHT CONRAD F	COL	0-0294342	C765	3
ALBRECHT DENVER D	MAJ	C-1308858	C866	1
ALBRECHT GERALD D	LTC	0-0400009	0145	2
ALBRECHT JOHN S	CPT	0-1288489	0444	2
ALBRECHT JR WILLIAM	MAJ	0-C140089	0257	3
ALBRECHT RALEIGH R	MAJ	0-1309488	0563	3
ALBRECHT WILLIAM H	LTC	C-1012176	0862	1
ALBREN EDWARD J	CPT	0-1171028	C547	2
ALBRICK EDGAR J	LTC	0-0450568	C364	1
ALBRIGHT BLANCHE C	MAJ	N-0728982	C766	1
ALBRIGHT DONALD E	1LT	0-1315258	C545	2
ALBRIGHT DONALD C	MAJ	C-2305750	0766	1
ALBRIGHT EVERETT W	2LT	0-2027062	C157	1
ALBRIGHT GEORGE O	WO1	W-2143828	C367	3
ALBRIGHT GEORGE R	MAJ	D-1585405	1058	1
ALBRIGHT LAWRENCE M	CW3	W-2105819	C860	1
ALBRIGHT MILES W	LTC	0-0476846	0857	3
ALBRIGHT OTUS W	LTC	0-0213693	0663	3
ALBRIGHT WILLIAM V	LTC	0-0285831	0764	3
ALBRITTON EMORY C	MAJ	C-0993286	0965	1
ALBRO LLOYD W	MAJ	0-0990354	0465	1
ALBRO RAYMOND L	MAJ	0-0988081	1266	1
ALBUCKER SAM	2LT	0-1314576	0545	2
ALCANTARA MICHAEL	1LT	0-1897013	0966	1
ALCINI ROY F	1LT	0-1179001	0945	2
ALCOCER RALPH R	CPT	0-2006441	0761	2
ALCOE EDGAR L	1LT	C-1316978	C845	2
ALCORN WILLIAM L	MAJ	0-0295312	C346	2
ALCOZE JOHNNIE W	CW3	W-2149746	1260	1
ALCEN SAM E	LTC	0-1104033	0755	1
ALCEN WILBUR L	CW2	W-2150046	1161	1
ALDERDYCE JOHN C	LTC	0-0128267	1044	2
ALDERFER ISADORE C	CPT	0-0382662	1145	2
ALDERMAN GORDON L	LTC	0-0479536	0962	1
ALDERMAN MARTHE R	MAJ	N-0724332	C561	1
ALDERMAN NORMAN E	CPT	0-1706025	0448	2
ALDERMAN OSCAR D	MAJ	0-0979351	1163	1
ALDERMAN WALTER A	CPT	C-0968899	C662	1
ALDERMAN WILLIAM R	MAJ	0-1304845	1060	1
ALDERTON JAMES R	COL	C-0384081	0661	2
ALDRICH FREDERIC C	LTC	0-0245579	0446	1
ALDRICH FREDERICK	MAJ	0-2210324	0167	1
ALDRICH HUGO C	LTC	0-0382585	1060	1
ALDRICH JR HARLEY J	MAJ	C-1181610	1165	2
ALDRICH LEON J	MAJ	C-1922663	0364	1

NAME	GRADE	SVC NO	DATE RET MO YR	RET CODE
ALDRICH LLOYD L	CPT	0-0318014	0852	1
ALDRICH RALPH L	LTC	0-1036890	1163	1
ALDRICH STANLEY B	LTC	0-1100525	0658	1
ALDRICH THEODORE A	CPT	0-0924936	0645	2
ALDRICH WARREN H	COL	0-0118753	1051	1
ALDRIDGE CLYDE S	MAJ	N-0735831	0563	2
ALDRIDGE EARL W	MAJ	0-1306216	1059	1
ALDRIDGE ELIZABETH	2LT	N-0700163	0837	1
ALDRIDGE IRA L	MAJ	0-0140446	0551	3
ALDRIDGE JAMES F	CW3	W-2205543	0766	1
ALDRIDGE JOHN S	1LT	0-1914107	0920	1
ALDRIDGE JOSEPH R	CW3	W-2144390	0557	1
ALDRIDGE RICHARD D	LTC	0-1285568	0756	2
ALDRIDGE RUSSELL C	2LT	0-0232741	1041	1
ALE CLARENCE K	CPT	C-0520234	C945	2
ALEFF KENNETH G	LTC	0-0330956	0263	1
ALENIK IRVING	2LT	0-1596563	0145	2
ALEO ANTONIO	MAJ	0-1116985	1060	1
ALESHIRE CLIFFORD W	MAJ	0-1548614	1058	2
ALEWINE MARION H	CPT	0-0488386	1046	2
ALEX MILLARD A	LTC	0-1545114	0162	1
ALEX STEPHAN H	CPT	0-0944226	0951	2
ALEXANDER A F J	2LT	0-1062802	0146	2
ALEXANDER ALBERT P	LTC	0-1551782	0757	1
ALEXANDER ALBERT W	LTC	0-0348720	0962	1
ALEXANDER ALEC	CPT	0-1038625	0947	2
ALEXANDER ALFRED L	MAJ	C-0445068	0849	1
ALEXANDER ANTHONY	CW3	W-2153127	0263	1
ALEXANDER ARTHUR A	COL	0-0237603	0854	3
ALEXANDER ARTHUR G	COL	0-0222143	1162	3
ALEXANDER ARTHUR P	MAJ	0-0120663	0853	3
ALEXANDER ARTHUR S	CPT	0-0367386	1042	1
ALEXANDER BENJAMIN K	CPT	0-1312859	0450	1
ALEXANDER BRYCE	LTC	0-0319638	0157	1
ALEXANDER CHARLES F	1LT	0-1290356	0444	2
ALEXANDER CHARLES F	MAJ	0-2016269	0761	1
ALEXANDER CHARLES H	COL	0-0453758	0565	1
ALEXANDER CHARLES H	MAJ	0-0497503	1152	1
ALEXANDER CLEON H	LTC	0-1636911	C164	1
ALEXANDER CLIFFORD	CW2	W-2144451	0562	1
ALEXANDER DONALD L	MAJ	0-0559996	0258	1
ALEXANDER DUANE F	LTC	0-1686424	0962	1
ALEXANDER EARLE L	MAJ	0-0268155	1058	3
ALEXANDER EDWARD	1LT	0-0185221	0630	1
ALEXANDER EDWARD A	1LT	0-1055517	0946	1
ALEXANDER EDWARD I	CPT	0-1922584	1162	1
ALEXANDER ERNEST	CPT	0-0483112	0848	1
ALEXANDER EUGENE	CW2	W-2209866	0166	1
ALEXANDER EVERETT G	LTC	0-1167718	0461	1
ALEXANDER FARRIS D	MAJ	C-2017793	1263	1
ALEXANDER FLOYD E	LTC	0-1325958	1062	1
ALEXANDER FLOYD R	LTC	0-0211863	0762	1
ALEXANDER FRED N	CW4	W-2129330	1264	2
ALEXANDER GARY F	MAJ	C-1185529	0657	1
ALEXANDER GEORGE W	1LT	0-1895293	0845	2
ALEXANDER GRANT H	LTC	0-0455609	0865	1
ALEXANDER HAROLD J	MAJ	0-0902068	1045	2
ALEXANDER HAROLD J	2LT	0-1323082	1044	2
ALEXANDER HARRY F	MAJ	C-0976925	0562	1
ALEXANDER HARRY W	COL	0-0463511	0762	3
ALEXANDER HARVEY A	CPT	0-2262723	1060	2
ALEXANDER HERMAN O	1LT	0-1317934	0845	1
ALEXANDER HILDA C	2LT	N-0764024	C745	1
ALEXANDER J W	CPT	0-0487560	0350	1
ALEXANDER JAMES C	CPT	0-1297556	0255	1
ALEXANDER JAMES E	CPT	0-0958208	0859	1
ALEXANDER JAMES F	CPT	0-2762523	1062	1
ALEXANDER JAMES N	MAJ	0-2206281	1265	1
ALEXANDER JEAN W	CPT	0-1798321	1154	1
ALEXANDER JOE S	1LT	0-1297955	0945	2
ALEXANDER JOSEPH R	LTC	0-1051967	0565	1
ALEXANDER JOSEPH M	COL	0-0238480	1162	3
ALEXANDER JOSEPH T	CPT	0-0929650	1052	2
ALEXANDER JR FRANK	CW3	W-2110828	0456	1
ALEXANDER LASSAR	CPT	0-0318232	0546	1

NAME	GRADE	SVC NO	DATE RET MO YR	RET CODE
ALEXANDER LAWRENCE J	COL	0-0269667	C667	3
ALEXANDER LEONARD C	CPT	0-0484918	1144	2
ALEXANDER LEROY T	CW4	W-2113364	1058	2
ALEXANDER LESLIE M	CPT	0-2041438	C364	1
ALEXANDER LESTER C	2LT	C-2026885	C360	1
ALEXANDER LEWIS F	MAJ	0-1337260	1164	1
ALEXANDER LYLE G	CW3	W-2150368	0555	1
ALEXANDER MARTIN P	MAJ	C-2040850	C364	1
ALEXANDER MARVIN T	1LT	0-1063026	0346	1
ALEXANDER MAURICE S	LTC	0-1100834	C461	1
ALEXANDER MELVILLE W	1LT	0-0308669	C744	2
ALEXANDER MORRIS C	MAJ	0-2015011	C661	1
ALEXANDER NEWTON W	COL	0-0100158	C857	3
ALEXANDER PAUL C	CPT	0-1290872	0145	2
ALEXANDER RALPH O	MAJ	C-0923701	0 0	2
ALEXANDER RAYMOND H	MAJ	C-0181129	0648	3
ALEXANDER RENA J	MAJ	N-0727701	1163	1
ALEXANDER RICHARD	LTC	0-0328538	1062	1
ALEXANDER RICHARD L	LTC	0-0274260	0348	2
ALEXANDER ROBERT A	LTC	0-1280102	C866	1
ALEXANDER ROBERT F	LTC	C-0271446	C166	3
ALEXANDER ROBERT C	LTC	C-0457209	1162	1
ALEXANDER ROBERT W	LTC	C-0287011	C260	1
ALEXANDER RUTH G	2LT	N-0775112	C145	1
ALEXANDER SAMUEL C	MAJ	C-1101055	1160	1
ALEXANDER SMITH K	LTC	0-1302101	C962	1
ALEXANDER SPENCER L	MAJ	0-0444321	C463	1
ALEXANDER THEODORE C	CW2	W-3250217	C767	1
ALEXANDER THOMAS B	LTC	0-0323451	1164	3
ALEXANDER THOMAS L	COL	C-0187486	C253	3
ALEXANDER THOMAS L	LTC	0-1166034	1162	1
ALEXANDER THOMAS L	MAJ	0-1822849	1264	1
ALEXANDER VINCENT A	2LT	0-1327486	C346	1
ALEXANDER WILLIAM M	CPT	0-1736243	1048	1
ALEXANDER WILLIAM P	CW4	W-2004246	0765	1
ALEXANDER WILLIE C	CW3	W-2148159	C464	1
ALEXANDER WRISTON C	CPT	0-1914108	C326	1
ALEXANDER YOUNG C	1LT	0-0212494	C857	3
ALEXICK EDWARD J	CPT	0-0484847	1049	1
ALFANO SYLVESTER	1LT	0-1310200	C645	2
ALFAR FRANCISCO	1LT	0-1896691	0450	1
ALFONSO CARL C	CPT	0-1296627	1045	1
ALFONSO JOSEPH C	CW4	W-2004209	C965	1
ALFORD CARL G	MAJ	0-2263505	C863	1
ALFORD CHARLES F	CPT	0-0920106	C745	2
ALFORD COLEMAN F	LTC	0-0916842	0366	3
ALFORD DEAN C	MAJ	0-1030743	C261	1
ALFORD HENRY M	COL	C-0238297	C365	3
ALFORD JR CLIFTON	MAJ	0-1885513	1066	1
ALFORD KENNETH W	MAJ	0-1060337	C465	1
ALFORD LEROY	CW3	W-2203271	0662	1
ALFORD PEARCE	CW3	W-2117955	1055	1
ALFORD RICHARD H	CPT	0-0921923	0146	1
ALFORD ROY A	COL	0-0407690	0556	1
ALFORD WILLIAM L	MAJ	C-0757146	C266	1
ALFORQUE PORFIRIO	CPT	0-0890546	C656	1
ALGAROTTI ROBERT A	MAJ	C-0450783	0764	1
ALGAZY EDWIN B	2LT	0-1044744	0645	2
ALCEO HAROLD L	COL	0-0117966	1149	3
ALGER CHARLES M	LTC	0-1302472	C866	1
ALGER DUANE L	CW3	W-2144082	1165	1
ALGER JOHN	MAJ	C-0230894	C560	1
ALGIE CECIL L	1LT	0-1591561	1159	1
ALGOOD REUBEN C	LTC	0-0340094	0162	1
ALGUIRE ADDISON D	COL	0-0142506	C157	3
ALICEA JUAN	MAJ	C-0980817	C961	1
ALICKI JOHN A	MAJ	C-1303076	C157	1
ALIFF CONRAD L C	CW2	W-2148426	C458	1
ALINE ROBERT F	MAJ	C-2046634	C857	2
ALISON JR JEFFERSON	LTC	0-0261155	0966	3
ALIX FRANCIS	MAJ	0-1170619	0656	1
ALKIM ALPHONSE F	CW4	W-2110495	C661	1
ALKIRE CHARLES R	LTC	C-1284980	1164	1
ALKIRE EDWARD M	COL	0-0263066	C467	3
ALKIRE FINFRED C	MAJ	C-1177263	1265	1

NAME	GRADE	SVC NO	DATE RET MO YR	RET CODE
ALL FRED H	COL	0-0169510	0450	3
ALLAIN CARL A	MAJ	C-0967640	0963	1
ALLAN ANDREW A	MAJ	C-0295919	0561	1
ALLAN HELEN V	1LT	N-0721601	0546	1
ALLAN WILLIAM	LTC	0-1001082	0163	1
ALLAN WILLIAM D	LTC	0-1284805	0656	1
ALLARD DWIGHT W	LTC	C-1579831	1166	1
ALLARD GERALD D	LTC	0-0231131	1264	3
ALLARD GORDON E	CPT	0-0482713	0454	1
ALLARD ROBERT D	LTC	0-1288346	1060	1
ALLARD WAYNE E	CPT	0-2009312	0853	1
ALLARDICE GEORGE M	CPT	0-1042471	0546	2
ALLBAUGH OKLA D	CW2	W-2001788	0665	1
ALLBEE CARL R	COL	0-0505325	0164	3
ALLBRIGHT JR JAMES J	LTC	0-1166879	1060	1
ALLBRIGHT PAUL H	CPT	0-0386980	0244	2
ALLBRIGHT WILLIAM J	MAJ	0-1114027	0658	1
ALLBRITTON BENJAMIN	LTC	0-0229614	0765	3
ALLCORN HUGH J	1LT	0-1294592	0745	2
ALLCORN JR LUTHER H	CPT	0-0294181	0345	1
ALLDREDGE BEUFORD H	LTC	0-0325776	0662	3
ALLEE RALPH E	MAJ	0-0402196	0154	2
ALLEGRA JAMES J	LTC	0-0506607	0263	1
ALLEGRA MICHAEL	MAJ	0-2212087	0262	1
ALLEMAN CHARLES H	MAJ	0-2025949	0265	1
ALLEMAN MABEL C	MAJ	N-0725779	0164	3
ALLEMEIER RALPH E	MAJ	0-1587047	0963	1
ALLEMEIER RALPH W	CW4	W-2102601	0859	1
ALLEN ALBERT A	MAJ	0-0245625	1163	3
ALLEN ALBERT L	CPT	0-0140091	0952	3
ALLEN ALBERT R	1LT	0-0539787	0146	2
ALLEN ALLEN L	LTC	0-1533242	1161	2
ALLEN ALVA J	CPT	0-0287332	1056	3
ALLEN ALVIN H	CW4	W-2145283	0856	1
ALLEN ANDRA W	MAJ	0-1323752	0164	1
ALLEN ARLISS C	LTC	0-0262981	0461	3
ALLEN ARTHUR E	COL	0-0228350	0460	3
ALLEN BEATRICE E	1LT	N-C722990	0346	2
ALLEN BERNARD F	LTC	0-1035224	0164	1
ALLEN BERNARD G	MAJ	0-0372704	0246	2
ALLEN BERTRAN L	MAJ	0-1585407	0662	1
ALLEN CHARLES D	CPT	0-0360098	1143	1
ALLEN CHARLES D	CPT	0-0890384	C853	1
ALLEN CHARLES E	LTC	0-0371420	1060	1
ALLEN CHARLES E	1LT	0-0450226	0146	2
ALLEN CHARLES E	LTC	0-1555936	0565	1
ALLEN CHARLES F	CW2	W-2152665	0560	1
ALLEN CHARLES H	MAJ	0-0959213	0567	1
ALLEN CHARLES L	LTC	0-1046709	0761	1
ALLEN CHARLES W	COL	0-0214814	1162	3
ALLEN CHARLES W	MAJ	C-1303598	1163	1
ALLEN CHESTER E	CPT	0-1342357	0261	1
ALLEN CHESTER R	LTC	0-1031617	0662	1
ALLEN CLAIR K	CPT	0-0144867	1153	3
ALLEN CLAUDE W	MAJ	0-0963458	0562	1
ALLEN CLEAROE	WO1	W-2146142	1151	2
ALLEN CLIFFORD	LTC	0-1311955	0962	1
ALLEN DANIEL A	CW2	W-2145378	0556	1
ALLEN DONALD E	LTC	0-0375459	0660	1
ALLEN DOUGLAS L	CW4	W-2153330	0259	1
ALLEN DWIGHT O	CW3	W-2203423	0465	1
ALLEN EDGAR W	LTC	0-1633034	1062	1
ALLEN EDWIN R	MAJ	C-0230255	0758	3
ALLEN ELBERT T	LTC	0-0213850	0464	3
ALLEN ELIZABETH	2LT	N-0729530	1045	1
ALLEN ELLEN R	CPT	N-0745532	0856	2
ALLEN EMERSON P	MAJ	0-0967011	0964	1
ALLEN ERNEST H	WO1	W-2109229	0750	1
ALLEN ERNEST W	LTC	0-0239658	0846	2
ALLEN ESTEL L	MAJ	D-1100413	0161	1
ALLEN ESTHER L	2LT	N-0722663	1143	1
ALLEN EUGENE C	LTC	0-0450444	0655	1
ALLEN EVELIN J	CPT	N-0773059	0446	1
ALLEN FORREST R	CW2	W-2150720	0859	1
ALLEN FRANK H	CPT	0-0224759	0847	1

ARMY OF THE UNITED STATES RETIRED LIST

NAME	GRADE	SVC NO	DATE RET MO YR	RET CODE
ALLEN FRANK L	LTC	O-0262652	0760	3
ALLEN FRED	CPT	O-0502569	1048	1
ALLEN FLRMAN	LTC	O-1012065	0965	1
ALLEN GEORGE F	LTC	O-1798544	1164	1
ALLEN GEORGE J	MAJ	O-2262729	0763	1
ALLEN GEORGE K	MAJ	O-0445838	0551	1
ALLEN GLEN V	MAJ	O-0310425	0867	3
ALLEN GLENN J	LTC	O-0260511	0856	2
ALLEN HARLAN K	LTC	O-0322395	0567	3
ALLEN HAROLD F	LTC	O-1645304	0163	1
ALLEN HAROLD I	CPT	O-2263030	0561	1
ALLEN HAROLD M	MAJ	O-0957519	0867	1
ALLEN HAROLD V	LTC	O-0419320	0259	1
ALLEN HAROLD W	COL	O-0312761	0251	1
ALLEN HARRY	LTC	O-1104701	0157	1
ALLEN HARRY A	LTC	O-0261034	1057	3
ALLEN HARRY D	LTC	O-0118454	0954	3
ALLEN HECTOR L	LTC	O-1103473	1262	1
ALLEN HERBERT W	CPT	O-0197574	0846	1
ALLEN HERMAN C	CPT	O-0399529	1043	2
ALLEN HERMAN R	MAJ	O-0278897	1050	1
ALLEN HILTON J	MAJ	O-2008365	1064	1
ALLEN HUBERT L	2LT	O-1996441	1045	2
ALLEN IDA M	MAJ	R-0000739	0763	1
ALLEN IVAN C	MAJ	O-1823684	0461	1
ALLEN IVAN J	LTC	O-0397769	0361	1
ALLEN IVOR H	CW3	W-2151869	0463	1
ALLEN JACK C	COL	O-0278601	0665	3
ALLEN JAMES E	MAJ	O-1894487	0955	1
ALLEN JAMES G	1LT	O-1321008	1045	2
ALLEN JAMES H	COL	O-0202149	0353	3
ALLEN JAMES J	1LT	O-0340127	1145	2
ALLEN JAMES N	CPT	O-0237839	0863	3
ALLEN JAMES P	LTC	O-0169350	0159	3
ALLEN JAMES W	LTC	O-2203746	0765	1
ALLEN JIMMIE C	LTC	O-1635555	0160	1
ALLEN JOHN C	MAJ	O-2038409	0264	1
ALLEN JOHN H	COL	O-0103843	1053	3
ALLEN JOHN J	LTC	O-1821952	0661	1
ALLEN JOHN R	LTC	O-0333631	0561	1
ALLEN JOHN W	1LT	O-0520872	0649	2
ALLEN JOSEPH	WO1	W-2147418	0555	1
ALLEN JOSEPH B	LTC	O-1314918	1062	1
ALLEN JOSEPH W	1LT	O-1640165	0645	2
ALLEN JR EDWARD I	MAJ	O-2102988	0167	1
ALLEN JR FRANK C	LTC	O-0232337	0565	3
ALLEN JR FRANK M	CW3	W-2151505	0267	1
ALLEN JR GEORGE W	MAJ	O-0962177	0462	1
ALLEN JR JAMES H	CPT	O-2264117	0660	2
ALLEN JR JOHN G	MAJ	O-0256698	0144	2
ALLEN JR JOHN H	1LT	O-1011006	1143	2
ALLEN JR JOHN H	MAJ	O-1294593	1060	1
ALLEN JR LAWRENCE J	1LT	O-0416072	1045	2
ALLEN JR LEONARD R	1LT	O-0537251	0646	2
ALLEN JR LOUIS A	LTC	O-0270790	0862	1
ALLEN JR OSCAR J	LTC	O-0269553	0146	2
ALLEN JR ROBERT H	LTC	O-1056622	0163	1
ALLEN KENNETH D	COL	O-0113382	0550	3
ALLEN KENNETH G	COL	O-0170059	0460	3
ALLEN KENNETH G	MAJ	O-1355518	1266	3
ALLEN LAWRENCE P	LTC	O-0397383	1161	1
ALLEN LAYTON E	LTC	O-0345317	1167	3
ALLEN LEE M	COL	O-0134415	0755	3
ALLEN LEONARD E	MAJ	O-1889848	0866	1
ALLEN LEWIS D	MAJ	O-2262951	1163	1
ALLEN LLOYD C	LTC	O-0278811	0867	3
ALLEN LLOYD D	1LT	O-2001947	1047	2
ALLEN LOUIS D	CW2	W-2152816	1257	1
ALLEN LOLA M	1LT	N-0773912	0646	1
ALLEN LYLE P	CW3	W-2147240	0566	1
ALLEN LYNN	1LT	O-0449351	0445	2
ALLEN MARGARET H	MAJ	N-0741690	1167	1
ALLEN MARY C	2LT	N-0741006	0645	1
ALLEN MARY S	2LT	N-0703076	0942	1
ALLEN MELVIN F	CW3	W-2146796	0263	1

NAME	GRADE	SVC NO	DATE RET MO YR	RET CODE
ALLEN MYRON A	CW4	W-2135224	1059	1
ALLEN NORMAN	1LT	O-1642595	1145	2
ALLEN NOEL H	MAJ	O-0955628	0962	1
ALLEN ODIE K	MAJ	O-2042981	0863	1
ALLEN OLA L	LTC	O-0278846	0255	2
ALLEN OLIVE I	CPT	M-0000499	0146	1
ALLEN ORLO R	MAJ	O-1304703	0959	1
ALLEN OTTO H	MAJ	O-0521310	0953	1
ALLEN OZNI F	LTC	O-0485707	1054	1
ALLEN PAUL A	LTC	O-0236820	0266	3
ALLEN PAUL J	CPT	O-1333160	0758	1
ALLEN PAUL L	CPT	O-1545202	0654	1
ALLEN PAUL W	LTC	O-0356951	0560	1
ALLEN PHILIP A	MAJ	O-0538792	0665	1
ALLEN RALPH E	LTC	O-0178355	0160	3
ALLEN RALPH C	COL	O-0128749	1152	3
ALLEN RAY C	COL	O-0267268	0467	2
ALLEN RAY L	LTC	O-0411441	0861	1
ALLEN RAYMOND	LTC	O-0346740	0660	1
ALLEN RAYMOND R	MAJ	O-1045702	0765	1
ALLEN RAYMOND S	CW2	W-2147436	0662	1
ALLEN RICHARD F	MAJ	O-0259670	1163	3
ALLEN RICHARD H	LTC	O-0420856	0960	1
ALLEN RICHARD L	1LT	O-0351210	0545	2
ALLEN ROBERT C	CPT	O-1299514	0750	1
ALLEN ROBERT D	CW2	W-2143020	0562	1
ALLEN ROBERT E	COL	O-0237666	0260	3
ALLEN ROBERT M	1LT	O-0476644	0157	1
ALLEN ROBERT N	CPT	O-0393565	0146	2
ALLEN ROBERT P	MAJ	O-2045165	1155	1
ALLEN ROBERT S	1LT	O-0445412	0644	2
ALLEN ROBERT S	COL	O-0481032	1046	1
ALLEN ROSCOE L	LTC	O-0274435	0859	3
ALLEN ROSS D	1LT	O-1580567	1144	2
ALLEN ROY C	MAJ	O-1642289	0357	1
ALLEN RUSSELL R	CPT	O-0493574	0259	1
ALLEN SAMUEL H	1LT	O-0340963	0244	2
ALLEN SIDNEY F	MAJ	O-1998298	0155	1
ALLEN SIMEON L	WO1	W-2120718	0445	2
ALLEN STANLEY C	LTC	O-1046335	0865	1
ALLEN STUART V	MAJ	O-1309254	0462	1
ALLEN THOMAS A	MAJ	O-0148926	0547	2
ALLEN THOMAS C N	MAJ	O-0224215	1058	3
ALLEN THOMAS L	COL	O-0152435	0358	3
ALLEN TOY J	LTC	O-0103498	0648	3
ALLEN ULYSSES W	CW2	W-2208188	0465	1
ALLEN VERNON E	CW3	W-2143759	0957	1
ALLEN VIRGIE	1LT	N-0734503	1045	1
ALLEN WADE W	MAJ	O-2011087	0260	1
ALLEN WALTER C	CW2	W-2147104	0461	1
ALLEN WALTER P	CPT	O-0987098	0562	2
ALLEN WARREN	COL	O-0120537	0756	3
ALLEN WARREN E	MAJ	O-1335373	0942	1
ALLEN WARREN G	LTC	O-1104035	1155	1
ALLEN WAYNE H	MAJ	O-1994556	0860	1
ALLEN WAYNE R	M G	O-0171232	0159	3
ALLEN WILBERT H	1LT	O-1165991	1262	2
ALLEN WILBURN D	MAJ	O-1109959	0955	1
ALLEN WILLARD J	CW4	W-2111716	0958	1
ALLEN WILLIAM E	LTC	O-0370188	0366	1
ALLEN WILLIAM F	CPT	O-1320005	0546	2
ALLEN WILLIAM H	COL	O-0223875	1066	3
ALLEN WILLIAM H	CW3	W-2206034	1067	1
ALLEN WILLIAM M	CPT	O-0212291	1062	3
ALLEN WILLIAM W	LTC	O-0489662	0256	1
ALLENSWORTH EVERETT	CPT	O-1007463	0666	1
ALLENTUCK SAMUEL	MAJ	O-0496597	1045	2
ALLERS WILLIAM E	MAJ	O-1821305	0347	2
ALLERTON PERRY	LTC	O-0215115	0657	3
ALLESEE MARVIN F	MAJ	O-0271604	0844	2
ALLEY HAROLD E	LTC	O-0232929	0362	3
ALLEY HERMAN L	LTC	O-1167719	0862	1
ALLEY JOHN M	MAJ	O-0968444	0261	1
ALLEY JR FRANK C	LTC	O-0142171	0744	1
ALLEY LEON A	COL	O-0226369	1052	3

NAME	GRADE	SVC NO	DATE RET MO YR	RET CODE
ALLEY LOFTON H	LTC	O-0410026	0161	1
ALLEY ROBERT G	LTC	O-1542580	1061	1
ALLEY THELMA L	CW3	V-2215659	0265	1
ALLEY WILLIAM P	MAJ	O-1290179	0865	1
ALLGEYER WILLIAM	2LT	O-1299515	0345	2
ALLGIRE JR ARCHIE C	MAJ	O-0381372	0960	1
ALLGOOD JOHN L	LTC	O-1292953	0657	1
ALLGOOD TOMMY L	MAJ	O-0490600	0856	1
ALLICON PHILLIP A	LTC	O-1284806	0261	1
ALLIE HENRY P	CPT	O-0982694	0162	1
ALLIN CHARLES W	1LT	O-1325847	0446	2
ALLINGHAM DAVID J	LTC	O-1283532	1165	1
ALLIS JOHN A	CPT	O-0239718	0864	3
ALLISON CHARLES F	LTC	O-1002565	1262	1
ALLISON DALE O	MAJ	O-0224775	0663	3
ALLISON DON O	LTC	O-0319349	1160	3
ALLISON DONALD G	CPT	O-0192920	1162	3
ALLISON EDGAR C	CPT	O-0511872	0151	1
ALLISON HOMER B	CW2	W-2206012	0962	1
ALLISON HOWELL P	CW2	W-2115759	0350	1
ALLISON JAMES R	1LT	O-1551561	1045	2
ALLISON JR ALEXANDER	MAJ	O-0360689	1044	2
ALLISON JR JAMES G	CW2	W-2141178	0561	1
ALLISON JR JAMES H	LTC	O-0273033	0766	3
ALLISON KENNETH F	2LT	O-1321730	0644	2
ALLISON KENNETH M	MAJ	O-2032946	0862	1
ALLISON NOAH C	B G	O-0278182	0259	3
ALLISON PAUL W	LTC	O-0496793	0462	1
ALLISON RODGERS W	LTC	O-0392961	0257	1
ALLISON SAMUEL C	LTC	O-0394115	0157	1
ALLISON WILLIAM H	CW2	W-2143703	0559	1
ALLMAN JAMES P	CPT	O-0360354	0563	3
ALLMAN JOSEPH R	CW3	W-2152922	1264	1
ALLMAN MORRIS	LTC	O-0885088	0254	2
ALLMAN SYDNEY J	LTC	O-0321937	0167	3
ALLNUTT JR ERNEST C	LTC	O-0451069	0646	2
ALLOTT THOMAS J	CPT	O-0430671	1047	2
ALLOU CHARLES A	LTC	O-1321276	0267	3
ALLOWAY FRANK L	LTC	O-0182512	0945	1
ALLPHIN CHARLES W	LTC	O-0245329	0152	3
ALLREAD JR DEWEY	LTC	O-1290359	0163	1
ALLRED ANTHON V	LTC	O-2210207	1067	1
ALLRED ELLA M	MAJ	N-0735555	0163	2
ALLRED JOE C	1LT	O-1109786	1045	1
ALLRED PAUL C	MAJ	O-2262884	0762	1
ALLRED ROBIN J	2LT	O-0548082	1145	2
ALLRED VINCENT C	COL	O-0330123	0866	3
ALLRED WILLIAM H	CW2	W-2210814	0363	1
ALLSOP MILDRED A	1LT	N-0759993	0246	1
ALLSTEAD EDITH M	2LT	N-0784705	1044	1
ALLUMS MARVIN M	MAJ	O-2204454	0566	1
ALLWINE JR ROBERT F	MAJ	O-1917769	0665	1
ALLYN CHESTER	CPT	O-0298408	0958	3
ALLYN WILLIAM R	COL	O-0103196	0556	3
ALLYNE ARTHUR B	LTC	O-0334401	0664	1
ALLYNE ROLLIN F	LTC	O-1574951	0665	3
ALMAS SAM	CW2	W-2151319	0560	1
ALMASSY LOUIS	CPT	O-1321472	1047	2
ALMASSY THOMAS G	CPT	O-1551559	0646	2
ALMEDA CHARLES	CW2	W-2142311	1260	1
ALMES GEORGE A	LTC	O-0135059	0346	2
ALMOND PHILIP C	MAJ	O-2015654	0664	1
ALMQUIST CARL T	LTC	O-0289963	0855	3
ALMQUIST JR ALLEN F	LTC	O-1176534	0367	1
ALMQUIST JR JOSEPH H	1LT	O-1323393	0146	2
ALMSTEAD GEORGE M	MAJ	O-0949216	1163	1
ALMY JR BENJAMIN F	CW3	W-2145786	1062	1
ALNUTT THOMAS L	LTC	O-0213389	1063	3
ALOISE SALVATORE	MAJ	O-1308457	0964	1
ALONZO ANTHONY L	MAJ	O-1037958	0363	1
ALONZO GERALD J	MAJ	O-0327153	0346	2
ALPAUGH STANLEY H	MAJ	O-1294247	0161	1
ALPER IRWIN I	COL	O-0230450	0362	3
ALPERT HERBERT R	1LT	O-1104705	0251	2
ALPERT IRVING E	LTC	O-0394060	1067	3

NAME	GRADE	SVC NO	DATE RET MO YR	RET CODE
ALPERT RAUL	1LT	O-1168997	0545	1
ALPS BAYARD G	MAJ	O-0180841	1152	3
ALS WILFRID R	MAJ	O-0199774	1157	3
ALSBERCE EDWARD W	LTC	O-0268020	0265	3
ALSBURY DENNIS P	CPT	O-2019543	1053	2
ALSBURY ROMAINE T	MAJ	O-1302934	0261	1
ALSHULER ROBERT E	1LT	O-0444751	0745	2
ALSPACH JERRY V	CPT	O-0939666	0158	1
ALSTERLUND JR C W	1LT	O-0435932	1045	2
ALSTON ARVILLE B	CPT	O-4006519	0167	1
ALSTON CHARLES N	MAJ	O-0176081	0549	3
ALSTON FRANK G	COL	O-0207735	1263	3
ALSTON WILLIAM K	COL	O-0176424	0756	3
ALSTROM JR JOHN T	MAJ	O-0381333	0252	2
ALSUP CECIL B	CW2	W-2105082	0946	2
ALSWORTH WILKINSON	LTC	O-0931661	0666	1
ALT GRACE F	LTC	N-0724122	0864	3
ALT WALTER F	COL	O-0237611	0456	3
ALTAFFER HARRY C	LTC	O-0233687	1060	3
ALTEE VINCENT J	LTC	O-0115182	0657	3
ALTENBURG CARL W	MAJ	O-1944856	0864	1
ALTENBURG SAMUEL L	MAJ	O-2020508	0264	1
ALTENDORF EDWARD L	MAJ	O-0230666	0562	3
ALTER DINSMORE	COL	O-0107645	0848	3
ALTERI ANTHONY M	MAJ	O-1332908	0559	1
ALTERMAN ROBERT H	CPT	O-1689962	1045	2
ALTERMATT RAYMOND C	LTC	O-0181413	0755	3
ALTHAUS JOHN W A	COL	O-0327234	1263	3
ALTHOFF ELEANOR R	2LT	N-0771702	0844	1
ALTHOUSE RAYMOND R	LTC	O-0251813	0566	3
ALTIERI JAMES J	CPT	O-2055876	0154	2
ALTMAN ELLIS F	COL	O-0115645	0449	3
ALTMAN FRANK A	MAJ	O-0234037	0357	3
ALTMAN GEORGE H	LTC	O-0465955	0562	1
ALTMAN JACOB	LTC	O-0321494	0446	1
ALTMAN LEON J	CPT	O-0511843	1146	2
ALTMAN MARTIN	2LT	O-1339596	0846	2
ALTMAN MARY R	1LT	N-0772103	0246	1
ALTMAN MILTON H	CPT	O-1573009	0245	2
ALTMAN RICHARD	COL	O-0277085	1264	3
ALTMAN WILLIAM T	MAJ	O-2097023	0866	1
ALTMANSBERGER R H	CW2	W-2114801	0746	1
ALTMEYER FRANK N	CW2	W-2152939	1061	1
ALTNOW GERALD H	LTC	O-0326176	0562	3
ALTON CHARLES	MAJ	O-0487988	0848	2
ALTOSE ALEXANDER	LTC	O-0360485	0546	2
ALTSHULER LOUIS N	COL	O-0482980	0864	1
ALTSTAETTER FREDERIC	LTC	O-0301548	0567	3
ALTUS NATHAN	WO1	W-2115287	0347	2
ALVAREZ FERNANDO L	MAJ	O-1301592	0763	1
ALVAREZ JOSE M	MAJ	O-1288669	1060	1
ALVAREZ JR JAMES J	2LT	O-0536618	0845	2
ALVAREZ LUIS A	MAJ	O-2055296	1154	1
ALVAREZ MIGUEL A	CPT	O-1303285	0561	1
ALVATER JAMES F	LTC	O-1181525	1163	1
ALVERSEN ROBERT M	LTC	O-0257664	1266	3
ALVERSEN WILLIAM G	CPT	O-1294596	0647	2
ALVES HENRY A	1LT	O-0357929	0844	2
ALVES VIRGINIA H	2LT	N-0720360	0943	1
ALVESTAD VERNON L	WO1	W-2112282	0463	1
ALVEY HASKEL D	2LT	O-0996787	1052	1
ALVIAR FREDERICK	MAJ	O-1326685	0264	1
ALVIN ALBERT	MAJ	O-1308901	0266	1
ALVIS AUBREY	CPT	O-0517564	0250	1
ALVIS ELMO H	COL	O-0340503	0862	1
ALVIS ROBERT L	MAJ	O-1950533	0664	1
ALWARD SHELBY C	MAJ	O-1645757	0761	1
ALWINE VIRGINIA E	1LT	N-0797234	0147	1
ALYEA COURTLAND	CW4	W-2003506	0764	3
ALZMANN HENRY F	MAJ	O-1017580	0661	1
AMADIO JOHN A	LTC	O-1559871	1166	1
AMAGUIN JOSE	2LT	O-1896627	0950	1
AMAKER JOHN B	LTC	O-1288670	1062	1
AMAN PAUL W	LTC	O-1053456	0661	1
AMANN ANDREW C	CPT	O-0235576	0352	3

NAME	GRADE	SVC NO	DATE RET MO YR	RET CODE
AMANN RALPH J	CPT	0-0452338	C646	2
AMANTI JEROME J	LTC	0-0265909	0262	1
AMARAL CLARENCE L	MAJ	C-1301761	C96C	1
AMARINE ROBERT F	CPT	0-2014665	C862	1
AMARO JAMES P	LTC	0-1315757	C366	1
AMASON MARY J	MAJ	N-0734593	0367	1
AMASON MATTIE M	CPT	N-0726002	C247	1
AMASON WARREN H	LTC	0-0310285	1160	2
AMATO JAMES P	LTC	0-0261329	1066	3
AMATO JOSEPH J	1LT	0-1041285	1047	2
AMATO LOUIS L	CPT	0-0361148	1145	1
AMATO PINO C	1LT	0-1036827	0545	1
AMATO SAM L	LTC	0-1176238	0766	1
AMATO VINCENT J	COL	0-0228313	C655	3
AMATO VINCENT L	1LT	0-1062958	0645	1
AMBERG JOHN A	COL	0-0234144	1064	3
AMBLER ALFRED C	CPT	0-0298176	0543	2
AMBLER JR CHARLES W	LTC	0-0248343	0866	3
AMBLER ROBERT T	CW2	W-2146560	1154	1
AMBOS ARNOLD H	1LT	0-1319593	1052	2
AMBRAZ SIMON P	LTC	0-0198368	1149	3
AMBRE RALPH A	LTC	0-1052235	C962	1
AMBROSE EDMOND G	LTC	0-0333982	0167	3
AMBROSE FELIX J	CW2	W-2143744	0563	1
AMBROSE JEFFERSON	LTC	C-0252053	0466	3
AMBROSE JOHN M C	1LT	0-1313185	1145	2
AMBROSE JR IKE H	MAJ	C-0425658	C959	1
AMBROSE JULIAN	1LT	0-0524713	C745	1
AMBROSE PAUL M	MAJ	0-1286756	0760	1
AMBROSIANO N R	CPT	0-C424010	1045	2
AMBROSOME JOSEPH P	1LT	0-0527733	1145	2
AMBUEHL JR LEO	CW3	W-2143475	C166	1
AMBURGEY GLENNIS A	LTC	0-2202812	0767	1
AMDUR HYMAN B	COL	C-0362690	0463	3
AMEEL ROSE F	MAJ	N-0772444	0464	1
AMEEN SAIAD W	MAJ	0-1587288	0663	1
AMELUNKE ALVIN E	1LT	0-1702999	1145	2
AMEN MARK	COL	C-0276253	C455	1
AMEND DAVID H	CPT	0-1326598	C547	1
AMENO EDWARD C	CW2	W-2109799	0545	2
AMENOF JAMES K	LTC	0-1040336	C962	1
AMENDOLA FREDERICK	MAJ	0-0445477	0743	2
AMENT MERTON J	LTC	0-0236268	1162	3
AMER ELI L	LTC	0-0335436	C857	2
AMERINE PAULINE F	2LT	N-0763265	C144	1
AMERMAN RICHARD H	MAJ	0-0948279	1067	3
AMERMAN WALTER G	CPT	0-1307632	0146	1
AMES EDWARD S	CPT	0-0185383	1143	2
AMES ERNEST D	LTC	0-0277652	C263	1
AMES FRANCIS H	CW4	W-2122181	C460	1
AMES HAROLD F	COL	0-0178472	0857	1
AMES HAROLD W	LTC	0-1181816	C163	1
AMES HARRY T	MAJ	C-0126997	C648	3
AMES HENRY P	MAJ	C-0260445	1050	3
AMES JEWEL F	WO1	W-2148685	1159	2
AMES JOHN H	CW3	W-2147907	0262	1
AMES JR JOHN L	COL	C-0148696	0755	3
AMES JR RALPH H	LTC	0-0415739	0657	1
AMES LOUIS F	MAJ	C-1325194	1061	1
AMES MAY K	CPT	N-0700115	1044	1
AMES ROY M	LTC	0-0168691	0957	3
AMES THOMAS T	WO1	W-2131966	0745	2
AMEY HARRY E	LTC	0-0243368	C466	3
AMICK JAMES F	CPT	0-0243731	C856	3
AMICK MELVIN M	LTC	0-1300907	0766	1
AMIDON DONALD A	LTC	0-2048543	0967	1
AMIDON ROGER E	LTC	0-0252212	0565	3
AMIRAL HIRAM H	LTC	0-0126153	0950	3
AMLIE PAUL J	1LT	0-0385994	0343	2
AMLING RAYMOND O	CPT	0-0510185	C246	2
AMMEL LOUIS J	LTC	0-0277161	0765	3
AMMON DAVID A	MAJ	0-1036828	0256	2
AMMON GEORGE L	LTC	0-0302023	0545	2
AMMONS EMMETT L	CW3	W-2107867	1160	3
AMMONS JAMES A	CW3	W-2147615	C862	1
AMMONS TELLER	LTC	0-0167464	1055	3
AMODEI FRANK V	CW3	W-2103838	0860	1
AMODIC GUDDIE P	CW3	W-2143254	0660	1
AMON THEODORE M	CPT	0-1321565	0655	1
AMOS EVERETT W	LTC	0-0357729	0660	1
AMOS FREDERICK	MAJ	0-0250131	0446	1
AMOS OSCAR G	COL	0-0115567	0158	3
AMOS RICHARD T	LTC	0-1283988	1162	1
AMOS ROBERT E	LTC	C-1292986	0961	1
AMOS ROBERT F	LTC	0-1286415	C657	1
AMOS SR ELBERT V	MAJ	0-1550308	0561	1
AMOS THOMAS G	MAJ	0-0198363	0948	3
AMOTT LAWRENCE G	LTC	0-0283695	1166	3
AMRHEIN LEO F	CPT	0-055361C	0346	2
AMSLER HILDRED S	LTC	0-0304707	0361	1
AMSLER OTTO L	COL	C-0118478	1053	3
AMSPACHER GEORGE L	MAJ	C-2000956	1265	1
AMSTER ADOLPH B	1LT	0-0540311	0845	2
AMSTER HENRY	1LT	0-0545945	1147	1
AMSTERDAM JULIUS	CPT	0-C547087	0965	2
AMUNDS GEORGE R	MAJ	0-0238819	0955	3
AMUNDSEN EARL	LTC	0-1015338	0361	1
AMUNDSEN EDWIN M	LTC	0-1822937	0767	1
AMUNRUD ARNOL A	LTC	0-0313157	1161	1
AMY ARMANDO	1LT	0-0954374	1154	2
AMY HENRY J	COL	0-0100856	0555	3
AMY MARY W	2LT	N-0764004	1044	1
AMY ROBERT N	CW3	W-2146212	1160	1
AMY RUPERT	LTC	0-0404337	0760	1
ANASCO HILARION	1LT	0-0890547	0150	1
ANCHEL DAVID	CPT	0-1689310	0746	2
ANCHETA CARLOS F	MAJ	0-1316979	0263	1
ANCHICKS CARL S	MAJ	C-0169172	0761	3
ANCHORS JR GARNER A	CPT	0-0206341	0245	2
ANDEL HENRY L	1LT	0-0537788	1045	2
ANDERMANN HENRY H	LTC	0-0381777	0166	1
ANDERS CHARLES H	MAJ	0-2010745	0163	1
ANDERS EMET R	LTC	0-0838023	0167	1
ANDERS FRANKLIN O	LTC	0-0337596	0347	2
ANDERS HARLEY D	2LT	0-1303442	0744	2
ANDERS STERLING H	LTC	0-0273939	0267	3
ANDERS VERION Z	CPT	0-0258049	0546	1
ANDERSEN ALFRED O	LTC	0-0481974	0466	1
ANDERSEN ANDREW L	MAJ	0-104827C	0260	1
ANDERSEN CYRIL C	MAJ	0-1010793	0148	1
ANDERSEN ELMER P	MAJ	0-1634784	C758	1
ANDERSEN HAROLD G	COL	C-0218499	0651	3
ANDERSEN HOMER N	LTC	0-0450719	0758	1
ANDERSEN IRVIN C	LTC	0-0443767	0663	1
ANDERSEN JOHN S	COL	0-0420158	0961	1
ANDERSEN LESLIE	1LT	0-1291384	1256	1
ANDERSEN LEW M	CW3	W-2141104	0662	1
ANDERSEN OSCAR W	LTC	0-1080338	1262	1
ANDERSEN RALPH M	LTC	0-0474498	1063	3
ANDERSEN RICHARD M	LTC	0-1798768	0867	1
ANDERSEN WILHELM A	COL	0-0164438	0754	3
ANDERSON ALAN F	CPT	0-1116072	C846	1
ANDERSON ALBERT M	CW3	W-2142795	1059	1
ANDERSON ALBERT S	MAJ	C-0959521	1164	1
ANDERSON ALBERTA M	2LT	N-0724624	1043	1
ANDERSON ALFRED D	1LT	0-0109261	0131	1
ANDERSON ALFRED L	CW4	W-2001725	1058	3
ANDERSON ALFRED W	CPT	0-0484175	C844	2
ANDERSON ALLEN O	LTC	0-0408991	0567	1
ANDERSON ALVAH W	MAJ	C-1281846	0561	1
ANDERSON ANDERS T	CPT	0-1306687	0546	2
ANDERSON ARNETT S	COL	0-0221831	0656	1
ANDERSON ARTHUR C	LTC	0-0231965	1058	3
ANDERSON ARTHUR O	CPT	0-0911405	C544	2
ANDERSON ARTHUR D	2LT	0-1573011	0843	1
ANDERSON ARTHUR E	CW3	W-2209048	0168	1
ANDERSEN ARTHUR G	LTC	0-0258399	0957	1
ANDERSON ARVAL L	COL	0-0223342	1062	3
ANDERSON BARNDT A	COL	0-0126999	1049	3
ANDERSON BARRELL E	COL	0-0265567	0958	3
ANDERSON BEAUFORD T	1LT	0-2103120	0952	2
ANDERSON BRYANT B	LTC	0-0286552	1067	3
ANDERSON BUEHREN O	CW2	W-2146302	C765	1
ANDERSON CARL A	LTC	0-0140108	C948	3
ANDERSON CARL A	LTC	C-0270919	0565	3
ANDERSON CARL F	LTC	0-0235974	0159	3
ANDERSON CARL F	COL	0-0261330	C565	3
ANDERSON CARL E	COL	0-0331057	C866	3
ANDERSON CARL E	CPT	0-0481718	0547	2
ANDERSON CARL F	COL	0-0287866	1062	3
ANDERSON CARL G	LTC	0-0327168	0459	1
ANDERSON CARL R	MAJ	0-1331461	C541	1
ANDERSON CARL S	1LT	0-1312112	C945	1
ANDERSON CARL T	CW2	W-2119589	1048	1
ANDERSON CHARLES	1LT	0-1914090	C229	1
ANDERSON CHARLES A	COL	0-0167095	C654	3
ANDERSON CHARLES A	LTC	0-0314914	1210	1
ANDERSON CHARLES C	MAJ	C-4006835	C667	1
ANDERSON CHARLES E	COL	0-0348456	C660	1
ANDERSON CHARLES L	MAJ	C-0362349	C743	2
ANDERSON CHARLES L	COL	0-0437179	0965	1
ANDERSON CHARLIE R	LTC	0-0498172	C256	1
ANDERSON CHESTER R	1LT	C-0545570	0846	2
ANDERSON CLARENCE C	LTC	0-0285441	0566	3
ANDERSON CLARENCE F	LTC	C-0445054	1162	3
ANDERSON CLARENCE M	CW3	W-2205469	C566	1
ANDERSON CLARENCE W	CPT	0-0209352	C557	3
ANDERSON CLAUDE C	LTC	0-1548974	0266	1
ANDERSON CLAYTON H	MAJ	0-1554849	C161	1
ANDERSON CLIFTON F	LTC	0-1575679	1266	1
ANDERSON CLINTON H	CW3	W-2144681	1165	1
ANDERSON CLYDE J	WO1	W-2115599	0645	2
ANDERSON COLEMAN P	MAJ	0-0206519	0461	3
ANDERSON CONRAD	CPT	0-0445067	C949	1
ANDERSON CURTIS E	LTC	0-0918336	0265	3
ANDERSON DAVID S	LTC	0-0425943	0856	2
ANDERSON DAVID V	CPT	0-1948140	C656	2
ANDERSON DON C	MAJ	C-0126955	0944	1
ANDERSON DONALD C	CPT	0-0438426	1046	2
ANDERSON DONALD P	CPT	0-0364254	0746	2
ANDERSON DONALD R	CW3	W-2150905	1062	1
ANDERSON DONALD W	MAJ	C-1685652	0461	2
ANDERSON DORIS L	CPT	W-0000444	0545	1
ANDERSON DORSEY B	MAJ	0-1826087	C459	1
ANDERSON EARL J	MAJ	C-2019268	1060	1
ANDERSON EARL L	MAJ	C-0289970	0747	2
ANDERSON EARL 1	CPT	0-1061608	0547	2
ANDERSON EDGAR N	MAJ	C-1175026	106C	1
ANDERSON EDNA L	1LT	N-0732892	0845	1
ANDERSON EDWARD	CPT	C-0992619	C162	1
ANDERSON EDWARD A	CPT	0-1119023	1052	2
ANDERSON EDWARD F	COL	0-0265113	0964	3
ANDERSON EDWARD H	1LT	0-0995123	1052	1
ANDERSON EDWARD M	LTC	0-1535856	0767	1
ANDERSON EDWARD P	CPT	0-0257473	1056	3
ANDERSON EDWIN C	CW2	W-2112234	C249	1
ANDERSON EDWIN S	MAJ	C-0967316	1061	1
ANDERSON ELBERT B	MAJ	C-0271607	0445	2
ANDERSON ELDON C	CPT	0-2289642	0562	1
ANDERSON ELLIOTT V	MAJ	0-0285383	0766	3
ANDERSON ELLSWORTH	CW3	W-2143856	1058	1
ANDERSON ELMER A	CW4	W-2146624	C861	1
ANDERSON EMIL S	CPT	0-1296631	0447	2
ANDERSON EMMETT C	LTC	0-0336987	1264	3
ANDERSON ERNEST	CW2	W-2102606	0445	2
ANDERSON EUGENE L	1LT	0-0780274	0545	2
ANDERSON EUGENE L	CW2	W-2118034	0960	1
ANDERSON FARRIS S	CW3	W-2205665	C167	1
ANDERSON FLOYD V	LTC	0-1293881	0861	1
ANDERSON FRANK A	LTC	0-0247219	0662	2
ANDERSON FRANK G	COL	0-0150305	1051	3
ANDERSON FRANKLIN K	CW2	W-2152899	1063	1
ANDERSON FRED R	CW3	W-2205617	0164	1
ANDERSON FRED T	MAJ	0-0206746	0656	3
ANDERSON FREDERICK	MAJ	C-0193274	0145	1
ANDERSON FREDERICK	LTC	0-0307234	0360	1
ANDERSON GARLAND D	1LT	0-1289191	0646	1
ANDERSON GEORGE	CPT	0-0464178	C444	2
ANDERSON GEORGE	MAJ	0-1540675	0862	1
ANDERSON GEORGE A	LTC	0-0563476	1264	1
ANDERSON GEORGE K P	CW3	W-2149199	0163	1
ANDERSON GEORGE R	LTC	0-0206577	0657	1
ANDERSON GEORGE R	CPT	0-0197744	0562	3
ANDERSON GEORGE R	LTC	0-0249357	0863	3
ANDERSON GEORGE R	MAJ	0-0285946	0550	1
ANDERSON GEORGE R	MAJ	0-0976584	0662	1
ANDERSON GEORGE S	MAJ	0-0517800	C457	1
ANDERSON GEORGE W	1LT	0-1015292	0346	2
ANDERSON GLASSELL B	2LT	0-0488701	1043	1
ANDERSON GLEN R	CPT	0-1825107	C462	1
ANDERSON GRANT S	LTC	0-0246621	1266	3
ANDERSON GUY R	1LT	0-0410158	0246	2
ANDERSON HAL A	1LT	0-1300909	1145	2
ANDERSON HAMPTON	B G	0-0243475	1150	3
ANDERSON HANS M	MAJ	C-0154077	1050	3
ANDERSON HARAMONT N	LTC	0-0120495	0648	3
ANDERSON HARLAN B	1LT	0-1764857	1046	1
ANDERSON HARLEY	CW3	W-2145603	1062	1
ANDERSON HAROLD	MAJ	0-0120498	0456	3
ANDERSON HAROLD J	COL	0-0120497	0752	1
ANDERSON HAROLD L	MAJ	C-1313944	0266	1
ANDERSON HAROLD W	COL	C-1289366	0561	1
ANDERSON HARRY W	COL	0-0187089	1050	3
ANDERSON HARVEY K	CW2	W-3430157	0467	1
ANDERSON HELEN G	2LT	N-0773845	0246	1
ANDERSON HENRY	CPT	0-0508161	1047	1
ANDERSEN HENRY C	LTC	0-0201175	C758	3
ANDERSON HENRY O	1LT	0-1182050	C546	2
ANDERSON HENRY G	LTC	0-0328256	0161	1
ANDERSON HENRY W	LTC	0-0321651	1056	3
ANDERSON HERBERT H	LTC	0-0260155	C266	3
ANDERSON HOLGER V	CPT	0-1062463	0346	2
ANDERSON HOLLY L	MAJ	0-0189259	0357	3
ANDERSON HOWARD J	CPT	0-0274856	0445	2
ANDERSON IRVING B	LTC	0-0383038	0267	1
ANDERSON ISAAC M	LTC	0-0519565	0663	3
ANDERSON IVAN A	WO1	W-2117537	0246	2
ANDERSON JACK J	1LT	0-1177266	0646	2
ANDERSON JAMES A	CPT	0-1114828	0963	1
ANDERSON JAMES C	CPT	0-101294C	0352	1
ANDERSON JAMES C	CPT	0-2018273	0261	1
ANDERSON JAMES E	MAJ	0-2262570	1067	1
ANDERSON JAMES H	MAJ	0-0237152	0664	3
ANDERSON JAMES L	1LT	0-1304654	0545	2
ANDERSON JAMES C	CPT	0-0518270	1147	2
ANDERSEN JEFFERSON	CPT	0-0498795	0446	2
ANDERSON JIMMY F	CW4	W-2141902	0862	1
ANDERSON JOE R	MAJ	0-0975959	0562	1
ANDERSON JOHN A	CPT	0-1056278	0447	2
ANDERSON JOHN A	MAJ	0-118539C	0457	1
ANDERSON JOHN A	LTC	0-1636922	C562	1
ANDERSON JOHN A	MAJ	0-2208003	0165	1
ANDERSON JOHN B	1LT	0-0328517	1044	2
ANDERSON JOHN B	CPT	0-0540731	0847	1
ANDERSON JOHN E	LTC	0-1636523	0664	1
ANDERSON JOHN E	WO1	W-2147562	1263	1
ANDERSON JOHN G	LTC	0-0290316	0567	3
ANDERSON JOHN I	LTC	0-1100002	0860	1
ANDERSON JOHN J	CPT	0-0450228	0249	1
ANDERSON JOHN K	LTC	0-0450219	0658	1
ANDERSON JOHN L	COL	0-0181053	0649	3
ANDERSON JOHN L	LTC	0-0507976	0766	2
ANDERSON JOHN W	LTC	0-1553544	0464	1
ANDERSON JOSEPH	1LT	0-0486075	0449	2
ANDERSON JOSEPH	CW4	W-2113906	1154	1
ANDERSON JOSEPH F	LTC	0-0245517	1057	3
ANDERSON JOSEPH H	MAJ	0-1325853	0261	1
ANDERSON JOSEPH W	MAJ	0-0166596	0750	2
ANDERSON JOSEPH W	1LT	0-1185710	1045	2
ANDERSON JR B F	LTC	0-0354454	1060	1

NAME	GRADE	SVC NO	DATE RET MO YR	RET CODE
ANDERSON JR EDWARD K	LTC	0-0193078	0246	2
ANDERSON JR FRANK C	CPT	0-1030321	0446	1
ANDERSON JR GUSTAVE	CW3	W-2147461	0964	1
ANDERSON JR HUGH C	MAJ	0-1594676	0165	1
ANDERSON JR JOHN C	MAJ	0-0257186	0666	3
ANDERSON JR JOHN R	1LT	0-1107078	0745	2
ANDERSON JUSTIN V G	CPT	0-0148912	0748	3
ANDERSON KARL G	MAJ	0-1179272	1062	1
ANDERSON KATHERINE	1LT	N-0764840	0650	1
ANDERSON KENNETH C	CPT	0-1285872	0559	1
ANDERSON KENNETH K	WO1	W-2106493	0552	1
ANDERSON KENNETH D	CPT	0-1030767	1047	2
ANDERSON KENNETH W	CW4	W-2111991	0966	3
ANDERSON KENT E	2LT	0-0887618	0146	2
ANDERSON KERMIT O	MAJ	0-2010787	0762	1
ANDERSON LAWRENCE B	LTC	0-0347336	0455	1
ANDERSON LAWRENCE R	CPT	0-1180791	0252	1
ANDERSON LEIF	COL	0-0254027	1265	3
ANDERSON LELAND R	CW2	W-2205111	0761	1
ANDERSON LELAND Z	1LT	0-0341601	0666	3
ANDERSON LEO	CW3	W-2153236	0762	1
ANDERSON LEO O	MAJ	0-2018631	0959	1
ANDERSON LEONARD J	WO1	W-2147967	1053	1
ANDERSON LEONARD T	CPT	0-0514043	0547	1
ANDERSON LEROY	CW3	W-2151856	0961	1
ANDERSON LEROY A	CPT	0-2096673	0763	1
ANDERSON LEROY H	M G	0-0239452	0366	3
ANDERSON LEROY R	MAJ	0-1170625	0161	1
ANDERSON LESLIE I	CPT	0-0963385	0261	1
ANDERSON LEWIS M	COL	0-0337938	1265	3
ANDERSON LILLY A	2LT	N-0700144	1038	1
ANDERSON LLOYD	2LT	0-1284446	0644	2
ANDERSON LLOYD F	LTC	0-0888339	0166	1
ANDERSON LLOYD H	CPT	0-0981892	0760	1
ANDERSON LLOYD L	CW3	W-2205768	0765	1
ANDERSON LOUIS A	MAJ	0-1000080	0655	1
ANDERSON LUTHER B	MAJ	0-1321277	0659	2
ANDERSON LYMAN C	LTC	0-1314140	0866	3
ANDERSON MARGOT M	1LT	N-0720602	0646	1
ANDERSON MARTIN V	CPT	0-0461221	0264	1
ANDERSON MARY J	CPT	L-0115641	0346	2
ANDERSON MAURICE	COL	0-0148703	0855	3
ANDERSON MAURICE F	LTC	0-0316875	0661	1
ANDERSON MAURICE T	LTC	0-0473359	1146	1
ANDERSON MELCHOIR G	LTC	0-0332403	1159	2
ANDERSON MELVIN B	1LT	0-1178685	0144	2
ANDERSON MELVIN F	LTC	0-0208915	0956	3
ANDERSON MERTON S	CPT	0-1307788	1145	2
ANDERSON MILFORD K	COL	0-0350073	0547	2
ANDERSON MILLARD T	CPT	0-0481727	0659	1
ANDERSON MILNER B	1LT	0-0392163	1043	2
ANDERSON NATHAN W	MAJ	0-0366587	0752	1
ANDERSON NELS A	COL	0-0121306	0852	3
ANDERSON NELSON J	LTC	0-0173435	1054	3
ANDERSON NEVIN B	COL	0-0274254	1154	3
ANDERSON NONNIE	MAJ	N-0786016	0765	1
ANDERSON NORMA J	1LT	N-0731014	0548	1
ANDERSON NORMAN E	LTC	0-1287643	0161	1
ANDERSON OLIVER C	1LT	0-1032187	0846	2
ANDERSON ORRIN E	LTC	0-0324513	1162	3
ANDERSON OSCAR H	LTC	0-0298892	1165	3
ANDERSON OSCAR S	CW2	W-2101377	0953	1
ANDERSON OTTIS C	2LT	0-1310667	0245	2
ANDERSON PAUL A	1LT	0-1587691	1263	1
ANDERSON PAUL E	MAJ	0-0387004	0960	1
ANDERSON PAUL F	CPT	0-1010543	0245	1
ANDERSON PAUL F	LTC	0-1573712	0865	1
ANDERSON PAUL V	LTC	0-0245368	0967	3
ANDERSON PAUL W	CPT	0-0251472	0353	3
ANDERSON PETER M	LTC	0-0339298	0462	1
ANDERSON PHILIP	CPT	0-1702755	0157	1
ANDERSON PHILIP S	MAJ	0-0248370	1066	3
ANDERSON POWELL A	LTC	0-1010876	0361	1
ANDERSON RALPH H	LTC	0-1114032	0262	1
ANDERSON RALPH O	LTC	0-1546338	0662	1
ANDERSON RALPH W	1LT	0-1822559	0246	2
ANDERSON RAY F	1LT	0-1303444	0945	2
ANDERSON RAYMOND A	CW4	W-2114651	1163	1
ANDERSON RAYMOND F	1LT	0-1032092	0246	2
ANDERSON RAYMOND F	CPT	0-0302065	0145	1
ANDERSON RAYMOND W	WO1	W-2146720	1053	1
ANDERSON RAYNA L	MAJ	L-0704403	0463	1
ANDERSON RAYNARD F	1LT	0-1284447	0145	2
ANDERSON RAYNOR E	COL	0-0193968	0761	3
ANDERSON REX N	COL	0-0246235	1066	3
ANDERSON RICHARD C	LTC	0-1338543	0565	2
ANDERSON RICHARD D	MAJ	0-0290670	0665	3
ANDERSON RICHARD C	CW4	W-2111651	1166	1
ANDERSON RICHARD F	COL	0-0177189	0546	2
ANDERSON RICHARD M	2LT	0-1056623	0244	2
ANDERSON ROBERT	1LT	0-0164144	0130	1
ANDERSON ROBERT	LTC	0-0339780	0450	1
ANDERSON ROBERT B	COL	0-0404740	0258	1
ANDERSON ROBERT C	LTC	0-0381332	0461	1
ANDERSON ROBERT D	MAJ	0-1876256	0667	1
ANDERSON ROBERT O	MAJ	0-2287135	1067	1
ANDERSON ROBERT E	LTC	0-1205691	0661	1
ANDERSON ROBERT F	1LT	0-1824388	1151	1
ANDERSON ROBERT J	1LT	0-1181818	1146	1
ANDERSON ROBERT J	CW4	RW-2143640	0965	1
ANDERSON ROBERT L	CPT	0-1293517	1045	2
ANDERSON ROBERT M	LTC	0-0452158	1157	2
ANDERSON ROBERT R	CPT	0-0132925	0345	2
ANDERSON ROBERT R	MAJ	0-1010952	0846	1
ANDERSON ROBERT R	MAJ	0-1918955	0264	1
ANDERSON ROBERT S	1LT	0-2021075	0352	1
ANDERSON ROBERT S	CW3	W-2148245	1062	1
ANDERSON ROBERT T	2LT	0-0269390	0466	3
ANDERSON ROBERT W	MAJ	0-0228628	0146	2
ANDERSON ROGER L	CW2	W-2210941	1064	1
ANDERSON ROY E	LTC	0-1634801	0162	1
ANDERSON ROY W	MAJ	0-1559289	0563	1
ANDERSON RUDOLPH D	CPT	0-1823079	1046	1
ANDERSON RUSSELL H	COL	0-0136982	0658	3
ANDERSON RUSSELL V	LTC	0-1287813	1058	1
ANDERSON RUTH	1LT	N-0720567	0846	1
ANDERSON RUTH C	LTC	N-0700381	0946	1
ANDERSON SAMUEL E	LTC	0-1185793	0363	1
ANDERSON SAMUEL P	LTC	0-0270492	1067	3
ANDERSON SIDNEY F	LTC	0-1288636	1061	1
ANDERSON SR JAMES E	CW3	W-2144092	0562	1
ANDERSON THEODORE H	LTC	0-0250937	0167	3
ANDERSON THEOPHILUS	MAJ	0-1181528	0265	1
ANDERSON THOMAS F	CPT	0-0975660	0762	1
ANDERSON THOMAS L	1LT	0-1333298	1048	1
ANDERSON THOMAS R	MAJ	0-1920237	0766	1
ANDERSON THOR S	COL	0-0385132	1160	1
ANDERSON THRAVES L	1LT	0-1106520	0746	2
ANDERSON VERNON J	LTC	0-0299354	0962	3
ANDERSON VERNON T	COL	0-0263860	1046	2
ANDERSON VICTOR E	LTC	0-0357896	0366	1
ANDERSON WADE H	2LT	0-0364079	0543	1
ANDERSON WALLACE G	MAJ	0-0259892	1045	2
ANDERSON WALLACE W	1LT	0-0536621	1045	2
ANDERSON WALLACE W	1LT	0-1173532	0946	2
ANDERSON WALTER A	MAJ	0-0192614	1047	1
ANDERSON WALTER A	LTC	0-0367614	0565	3
ANDERSON WALTER C	CPT	0-0421964	0644	2
ANDERSON WALTER L	B G	0-0232594	1053	3
ANDERSON WALTER R	CW2	W-2101017	0250	1
ANDERSON WALTER W	COL	0-0304113	1264	3
ANDERSON WENDELL B	LTC	0-0379666	0547	2
ANDERSON WESLEY H	CW3	W-2148427	0862	1
ANDERSON WILBERT D	CPT	0-1291212	1060	1
ANDERSON WILLARD	LTC	0-0339701	0767	1
ANDERSON WILLIAM A	MAJ	0-1288672	0860	1
ANDERSON WILLIAM A	MAJ	0-1798104	1060	1
ANDERSON WILLIAM A	WO1	W-2134503	0448	1
ANDERSON WILLIAM B	LTC	0-0150299	0546	2
ANDERSON WILLIAM B	MAJ	0-1573702	0954	1
ANDERSON WILLIAM C	CPT	0-1103037	0863	1
ANDERSON WILLIAM C	CPT	0-1173533	0545	2
ANDERSON WILLIAM C	COL	0-0321936	0666	3
ANDERSON WILLIAM D	LTC	0-1642202	1066	1
ANDERSON WILLIAM E	COL	0-0124534	1054	3
ANDERSON WILLIAM E	LTC	0-1109789	0862	1
ANDERSON WILLIAM F	LTC	0-0506628	0657	1
ANDERSON WILLIAM H	LTC	0-1283188	0963	1
ANDERSON WILLIAM H	2LT	0-1303445	0845	2
ANDERSON WILLIAM H	CPT	0-1689884	0446	2
ANDERSON WILLIAM J	MAJ	0-1289530	0662	1
ANDERSON WILLIAM L	LTC	0-1580027	0962	1
ANDERSON WILLIAM L	MAJ	0-1694233	0645	2
ANDERSON WILLIAM M	1LT	0-0315514	0846	2
ANDERSON ZANE L	MAJ	F-1010412	0758	2
ANDES ERNEST W	COL	0-0166248	0648	3
ANDES JAMES O	COL	0-0224859	1159	3
ANDES MARCELINO	1LT	0-1896882	0655	2
ANDIE JOHN R	MAJ	0-0223681	0564	3
ANDING GILBERT	CPT	0-1299567	0447	1
ANDO TOMOMI	MAJ	0-0957167	0867	1
ANDORA JUAN P	1LT	0-0890442	1048	1
ANDRAE WILLIAM F	LTC	0-1685005	0567	1
ANDRAIN MILTON D	LTC	0-0224932	1159	3
ANDRAKE JOHN	LTC	0-1947628	0766	1
ANDRAKE JOHN C	LTC	0-0150449	0454	3
ANDRASEK JOHN M	CW4	W-2155628	0662	1
ANDRASIK JR JOSEPH	LTC	0-0374307	0764	1
ANDRE DAVID L	LTC	0-0409954	0663	1
ANDRE EARL P	CW3	W-2203372	0763	1
ANDRE HARVEY M	MAJ	0-1687310	0546	2
ANDRE ROBERT J	MAJ	0-2011787	0163	1
ANDRE ROY D	LTC	0-0317561	0959	3
ANDRE WILLIAM M	CPT	0-0470919	0944	2
ANDREAS JOSEPH	LTC	0-1583987	0461	1
ANDREAS STEPHEN G	LTC	0-1301762	1262	1
ANDREASON NORMAN M	CPT	0-0278865	0857	3
ANDREASSEN EINAR C	COL	0-0266556	0152	3
ANDREE RICHARD J	CW2	W-2211821	0167	1
ANDREEN CARL O	LTC	0-0418786	1265	1
ANDREEN RUTH H	MAJ	N-0736826	1061	1
ANDREN KARL A	CPT	0-0338691	1045	2
ANDREOLI LOUIS	CW2	W-2142800	1052	2
ANDRES EDWARD J	MAJ	0-2288507	0767	1
ANDRESANO ROCCO J	CPT	0-1535120	0845	2
ANDRESEN ROSEMARY A	CPT	N-0771399	1047	1
ANDRESON WILLIAM H	2LT	0-1013988	1045	2
ANDRESS JESSE	MAJ	0-0501249	0157	2
ANDREUS FRANK C	CPT	0-0314477	0944	2
ANDREW FRED W	1LT	0-1340613	0449	2
ANDREW JR WILLIAM	WO1	W-2142747	0356	1
ANDREWS ALFRED C	LTC	0-0344645	0347	1
ANDREWS ARTHUR D	LTC	0-1171433	0367	1
ANDREWS AVANEAL E	2LT	N-0734122	1043	1
ANDREWS BENJAMIN C	CW2	W-2144983	0559	1
ANDREWS BILL L	LTC	0-0247307	0863	3
ANDREWS CARL W	CPT	0-1824555	1157	1
ANDREWS CHARLES	MAJ	0-1640188	0854	1
ANDREWS CHARLES E	CPT	0-0484764	1158	2
ANDREWS CHARLES H	COL	0-0185560	0859	1
ANDREWS CHARLES L	MAJ	0-0979156	0563	1
ANDREWS CLIFFORD T	LTC	0-0496860	0356	1
ANDREWS CLYDE L	CW3	W-2144899	0264	1
ANDREWS D LEE	CPT	0-0190307	0244	2
ANDREWS EARLE E	CPT	0-0124220	0749	3
ANDREWS ELMER	LTC	0-0241243	0764	3
ANDREWS EVERETT G	LTC	0-0530568	0763	1
ANDREWS FABIAN R	MAJ	0-1002571	0861	2
ANDREWS FLOOD S	LTC	0-0202451	0558	3
ANDREWS FRANCIS E	CW3	W-2148586	0962	1
ANDREWS FRANCIS J	COL	0-0162791	0265	3
ANDREWS FRED F	MAJ	0-0404032	1046	2
ANDREWS GEORGE C	MAJ	0-1306529	0161	1
ANDREWS GORDON G	LTC	0-1284262	0561	1
ANDREWS GRAHAM H	CPT	0-1341932	0959	1
ANDREWS HAL J	COL	0-0909716	0167	3
ANDREWS HARRY S	CW4	W-2002817	0658	3
ANDREWS HAYWARD	MAJ	0-0338114	0646	1
ANDREWS HUBERT L	CPT	0-0450220	1054	1
ANDREWS HUBERT T	MAJ	0-0234540	1052	3
ANDREWS HUNTER C	MAJ	0-2036419	0455	1
ANDREWS JACK B	LTC	0-1542905	0967	1
ANDREWS JACK E	LTC	0-1824394	0163	1
ANDREWS JACK R	LTC	0-1944861	0964	1
ANDREWS JAMES	COL	0-0163886	0256	3
ANDREWS JAMES C	LTC	0-0171131	0157	3
ANDREWS JAMES W	COL	0-0209387	0456	3
ANDREWS JOHN C	CPT	0-0554715	0747	2
ANDREWS JOHN J	MAJ	0-1308445	0761	1
ANDREWS JOHN N	P G	0-0150451	0356	3
ANDREWS JON E	MAJ	0-1556367	1061	1
ANDREWS JOSEPH V	2LT	0-1169413	0145	2
ANDREWS JR GEORGE A	CW2	W-2206320	1163	1
ANDREWS JR HERBERT G	2LT	0-1541660	0246	2
ANDREWS JR JAMES M	LTC	0-0974855	0962	1
ANDREWS JR LELAND E	MAJ	0-1881299	1067	2
ANDREWS JR MARTIN D	2LT	0-0479084	0245	2
ANDREWS LEWIS F	CW4	W-2142092	0166	1
ANDREWS LOMAX	MAJ	0-1321393	0661	1
ANDREWS LUTHER B	CPT	0-1173143	1058	1
ANDREWS MICHAEL F	CPT	0-0353802	0652	1
ANDREWS PATRICK H	MAJ	0-0347262	1163	1
ANDREWS RALPH C	LTC	0-1821528	0664	1
ANDREWS ROBERT E	MAJ	0-2025363	0965	1
ANDREWS ROBERT H	1LT	0-1165223	0144	2
ANDREWS ROBERT K	COL	0-0347874	1065	3
ANDREWS ROBERT C	CW2	W-2211964	0966	1
ANDREWS ROBERT R	LTC	0-1030637	0261	2
ANDREWS ROBERT S	CW4	W-2152291	1057	1
ANDREWS SAMUEL M	1LT	0-1051467	1147	2
ANDREWS SYDNEY P	CW2	W-2151395	0962	1
ANDREWS TALCOTT D	LTC	0-0545445	0167	1
ANDREWS TEOFCRO G	CPT	0-0284200	1064	3
ANDREWS WALTER F	LTC	0-0388990	0860	2
ANDREWS WARD B	1LT	0-1284263	0145	2
ANDREWS WILLIAM C	LTC	0-1041704	0457	1
ANDREWS WILLIAM M	CW2	W-2101241	1046	2
ANDREWS WILSON E	LTC	0-0372890	0867	1
ANDREWSEN WALTER D	LTC	0-1102603	0561	1
ANDRIOGE RICHARD S	1LT	0-1174211	0845	2
ANDRIST HARLAND F	LTC	0-1580577	0267	1
ANDROSKI WILLIAM A	CPT	0-1283893	0446	2
ANDROSKO FRANK J	MAJ	0-1300254	0159	1
ANDRULONIS VICTOR J	CW2	W-2110429	0855	1
ANDRUS CHARLES H	COL	0-0463490	0850	1
ANDRUS CLINTON F	CW2	W-2143857	0458	2
ANDRUS EDWARD D	LTC	0-0289731	0160	1
ANDRUSS WALTER E	LTC	0-0425227	0561	1
ANDRZEJEWSKI HENRY P	MAJ	0-0815081	0464	2
ANESI RICHARD A	1LT	0-1179004	0659	1
ANESTOS TASH P	LTC	0-0384014	0461	1
ANGEL FRED C	LTC	0-1171434	0867	1
ANGEL NICHOLAS C	MAJ	0-1100787	0746	2
ANGEL NORMAN B	CPT	0-1919100	1262	1
ANGELES GODOFREDO	COL	0-1897082	0267	1
ANGELI JR ERLANDO	CW3	W-2129732	0461	1
ANGELICH MARY E	MAJ	N-0773782	0864	1
ANGELIDES NICHOLAS	LTC	0-0383361	0360	1
ANGELILLIS PAUL	CPT	0-0264178	0458	3
ANGELL LESTER W	LTC	0-0972548	0866	3
ANGELL THEODORE F	LTC	0-0196149	0861	3
ANGELO ARTIE L	MAJ	0-0957249	1264	1
ANGELO EDWARD	CW2	W-2119910	0346	2
ANGELO MICHAEL D	CPT	0-2020510	1058	1
ANGELO WALTER L	MAJ	0-0232083	0646	2
ANGELOFF ELIA	MAJ	0-0970053	0565	1
ANGELOFF WILLIAM	CW2	W-2149374	0659	2
ANGER ROBERT T	LTC	0-1585444	1263	1
ANGERMAN CLYDE W	LTC	0-1541441	0866	1
ANGLAND THOMAS A	CPT	0-0494995	0945	2

NAME	GRADE	SVC NO	DATE RET MO YR	RET CODE
ANGLE DON L	MAJ	0-1003924	0358	1
ANGLE RAYMOND D	LTC	0-0386570	0265	3
ANGLEMAN LOUIS W	LTC	0-1587813	0862	2
ANGLEMYER JAMES L	LTC	0-1633272	0363	1
ANGLETON JAMES H	LTC	0-0117023	0246	2
ANGLEY ROLAND C	CW3	W-2151782	0162	1
ANGLIM EDWARD M	CPT	0-0397088	0746	2
ANGLIN SR THOMAS W	MAJ	0-1534421	0357	1
ANGLIN WILLIAM H	MAJ	0-0939698	0763	1
ANGONE ANTHONY C	MAJ	0-1937823	0366	1
ANGROS ANDREW G	CPT	0-0255837	0347	2
ANGSTADT RAYMOND W	CPT	0-1100422	0851	1
ANGSTREICH HERBERT S	CPT	0-0452260	0445	2
ANGUS ALEXANDER	LTC	0-0439478	0954	1
ANGUS HERSHEL F	LTC	0-0336109	0967	3
ANHALT EDWARD A	CPT	0-1104710	0446	1
ANJO OLIVER H	MAJ	0-2210027	0564	1
ANKELEIN WILLIAM J	MAJ	0-0286685	0344	2
ANKER HARRY	CPT	0-0493403	1144	2
ANKNEY GEORGE R	1LT	0-1111763	0147	1
ANKNEY ROBERT D	1LT	0-2085552	0452	1
ANKRUM HOMER R	LTC	0-1691731	0164	1
ANLOFF JR GARRY J	LTC	0-0269779	0360	1
ANNAS HOWARD G	COL	0-0333220	0358	1
ANNEN EDWIN H	CW2	W-3150606	0367	1
ANNESE JOSEPH J	CPT	0-1715112	0448	2
ANNINOS JOHN P	LTC	0-0506902	0263	1
ANNIS ORAL J	CW4	W-2122937	0167	2
ANNONI ALBERT F	WO1	W-2148873	0154	1
ANSBRO FRANCIS	CPT	0-0306792	1148	1
ANSCHICKS LOUISE M	CPT	N-0701940	0746	1
ANSEAUME CHARLES P	CPT	0-0953762	0559	1
ANSEL ROE C	LTC	0-0323350	0664	1
ANSELL LAWRENCE S	2LT	0-2201149	0952	2
ANSELMO PETER	MAJ	0-0493873	0648	1
ANSKE LEANDER H	LTC	0-0407609	1160	1
ANSLEY JOSIAH C	LTC	0-0280691	1266	3
ANSLEY OSCAR L	1LT	0-1035639	1045	2
ANSLEY WILLIAM T	LTC	0-1540658	0361	1
ANSLOAN GEORGE E	MAJ	0-1335875	0361	1
ANSLOW RALPH J	CPT	0-1822659	1148	2
ANSPACH HARRY S	2LT	0-2015013	0653	1
ANSPACH RAYMOND L	MAJ	0-0438272	0250	1
ANSPON ALWIN W	CPT	0-0299494	1044	2
ANSTED DAVID T	CPT	0-0310134	0458	1
ANSWINI RITA L	MAJ	N-0759864	0166	1
ANTANG ALFEO D	1LT	0-1896628	0561	1
ANTE SALVADOR P	CPT	0-1896768	0158	1
ANTELL GUNNARD J	CPT	0-0511948	0447	1
ANTELL HENRIK	COL	0-0166599	1055	3
ANTENUCCI MARIO M	LTC	0-0324609	0563	3
ANTES DONALD F	COL	0-0227497	1164	3
ANTHONY ALBERT J	LTC	0-0171997	1054	3
ANTHONY DELPHINE M	2LT	N-0760423	0745	1
ANTHONY EUGENE H	MAJ	0-0373425	0147	1
ANTHONY FLOYD L	LTC	0-0271861	1266	3
ANTHONY FRED M	CW2	W-2101387	0446	2
ANTHONY GEORGE L	CW4	W-2112238	1057	1
ANTHONY HAROLD H	1LT	0-1179746	0258	1
ANTHONY JAMES C	COL	0-0213910	0563	3
ANTHONY JAMES T	1LT	0-1287116	1043	2
ANTHONY JOSEPH G	1LT	0-1048272	0744	2
ANTHONY JR HENRY S	1LT	0-0436179	0445	2
ANTHONY JR THOMAS C	MAJ	0-0306647	0744	1
ANTHONY KELLY P	LTC	0-1546081	1062	2
ANTHONY MICHAEL I	1LT	0-1309199	0445	2
ANTHONY PERRY E	WO1	W-2143670	0853	1
ANTHONY RALPH W	MAJ	0-2020375	0361	1
ANTHONY ROBERT B	LTC	0-0359534	0367	3
ANTHONY TAYLOR C	LTC	0-0449178	0965	1
ANTHONY VICTOR A	LTC	0-1036720	0562	1
ANTHONY WILLIAM H	LTC	0-1171872	1066	1
ANTHONY WILLIAM W	MAJ	0-2263655	0265	1
ANTIGNAT RAYMOND F	MAJ	0-1591573	0163	1
ANTOINETTE JOHN L	CW2	W-2210883	0666	1

NAME	GRADE	SVC NO	DATE RET MO YR	RET CODE
ANTOL JR LOUIS	COL	0-0343170	0466	1
ANTOLINE SAMUEL	CPT	0-0181640	1060	3
ANTON GEORGE F	MAJ	0-0196927	0652	3
ANTON MICHAEL C	MAJ	0-0397522	0846	2
ANTON PHILIP A	CPT	0-0509975	0347	1
ANTONACCI MICHAEL H	LTC	0-0294879	0862	3
ANTONAKOS T	MAJ	0-0331530	0745	1
ANTONCHICK JOHN	LTC	0-0355354	0947	1
ANTONELLI ROBERT J	LTC	0-0396181	0448	2
ANTONITIS JOSEPH J	2LT	0-0453129	0544	2
ANTONSEN STANLEY P	MAJ	0-1542496	1266	1
ANTONUCCI JOSEPH A	1LT	0-1303618	1144	2
ANZALONE ANTHONY V	LTC	0-1575683	0859	1
ANZELMO SAM S	LTC	0-1596570	0263	1
ARABLASA SALVADOR C	LTC	0-0269780	0865	3
APEL ARNO M	MAJ	0-1876457	1066	1
APFEL CORNELIUS	LTC	0-0378906	0166	3
APGAR JOHN A	CW4	W-2142215	0459	1
APGAR JR HARRY E	LTC	0-1283894	0164	1
APGAR STERLING E	COL	0-0505443	0246	1
APLER JOHN H	WO1	W-2119635	0150	1
APOLLONY JOHN C	LTC	0-1638927	0862	1
APONE DOMINICK P	MAJ	0-1947888	1262	1
APONTE ALFREDO	CPT	0-0252437	1061	3
APONTE EMILIO E	MAJ	0-1913438	0763	1
APONTE FRANCISCO	2LT	0-1799683	0965	2
APOSTOLON GEORGE	CW2	W-2150039	0263	1
APOSTOLOS TIMOTHY	2LT	0-0922786	0145	2
APPEL HENRY	COL	0-0241378	0166	3
APPEL HENRY F	CW4	W-2117536	0361	1
APPELGATE JOSEPH M	COL	0-0389818	0563	3
APPELL LEONARD A	CPT	0-1283534	1045	2
APPELMAN GUSTAVE R	COL	0-0146326	0648	3
APPIARIUS JOHN C	LTC	0-0221847	0754	3
APPIARIUS WALTER P	LTC	0-0221596	0761	3
APPLE CHARLES D	MAJ	0-0207019	1048	3
APPLE HARRY	LTC	0-1286416	0961	1
APPLE HOWARD D	CPT	0-0416065	1144	2
APPLE OSBORNE F	LTC	0-0353105	0361	1
APPLEBAUM LEON B	LTC	0-0272962	0867	3
APPLEBY ALVA S	CPT	0-0474385	0645	2
APPLEBY JR J	1LT	0-1555502	0446	2
APPLEGARTH JR A R	CPT	0-0346876	0146	2
APPLEGATE DANIEL W	LTC	0-0304166	0267	3
APPLEGATE DELBERT P	LTC	0-1636934	0361	1
APPLEGATE EDNA H	2LT	N-0735280	0844	1
APPLEGATE JOHN	LTC	0-1280271	0160	1
APPLEGATE LAWRENCE W	CPT	0-0501365	0546	2
APPLEGATE LINDSAY M	LTC	0-0208842	0459	1
APPLEGATE ROBERT W	CW2	W-2143859	0261	1
APPLEGATE RODNEY W	MAJ	0-1013706	0161	1
APPLEMAN RUSSELL E	LTC	0-0486652	1055	1
APPLER HAROLD M	1LT	0-0514295	1045	1
APPLETON JR F P	LTC	0-0142229	0648	3
APPLETON WILLIAM C	LTC	0-0378472	1062	1
APPLETON WILLIAM F	LTC	0-0195937	0462	3
APPLEWHITE AUSTIN H	MAJ	0-0488484	0447	2
APPLEWHITE WARREN G	MAJ	0-0954577	0463	1
APPLING GRADY S	2LT	0-0152555	0456	3
APPLING HARRY C	MAJ	0-1289194	0464	2
APPLING ROBERT K	MAJ	0-1100858	0260	1
APPOLO DOROTHY M	1LT	N-0731422	0746	1
APRIL LEO M	1LT	0-1317864	1145	1
APRILL LIONEL J	1LT	0-1312356	0347	1
APT SAMUEL	LTC	0-0311153	1164	3
APTED CLARK H	COL	0-0182562	0754	3
APTER HARRY	CPT	0-0419536	0545	2
APTER LEONARD	MAJ	0-0682687	0363	1
AQUINO ANTONINO G	CPT	0-1640652	0661	3
AQUINO ENRIQUE J	CPT	0-1324126	0762	1
AQUINO JOSE S	1LT	0-1896405	1061	1
ACUINO RAYMUNDO	1LT	0-1896391	0659	1
ARAM SHIRLEY O	1LT	L-0502276	0645	2
ARANSON FLORENCE S	1LT	N-0755536	0847	1
ARANT FRANK S	LTC	0-0228723	0864	3

NAME	GRADE	SVC NO	DATE RET MO YR	RET CODE
ARANT PHILIP W	LTC	0-1041457	1264	1
ARANT WILLIAMS E	CPT	0-0244819	0766	3
ARAUJO JUAN	LTC	0-0155649	1055	3
ARAUJO URBAN J	CW3	W-2150693	1064	1
ARBENZ HERMAN L	CPT	0-0407634	0745	2
ARBOGAST EDWARD P	MAJ	0-1998433	0564	1
ARBOGAST JACK G	MAJ	0-0400148	0546	2
ARBOGAST LOUIS W	LTC	0-0464576	1059	3
ARBOGAST MEAD S	LTC	0-1643184	0163	1
ARBOGAST NORVILLE F	1LT	0-0524623	1045	2
ARBOUR LOUIS P	CW3	W-2103848	0160	1
ARBUCKLE ALEXANDER	COL	0-0213710	0162	3
ARBUCKLE ERNEST V	MAJ	0-0131522	0352	3
ARBUCKLE JR HOWARD B	COL	0-0248318	0566	3
ARBURUA JOSEPH M	LTC	0-0104230	0155	3
ARBURY HOWARD H	B G	0-0255103	0966	3
ARBUTHNOT WILLIAM B	MAJ	0-0238577	0366	3
ARCANA PETER S	LTC	0-1041077	0461	1
ARCAY LUIS	CPT	0-0203256	0949	1
ARCENEAUX CLESMAY J	CPT	0-0260604	1164	3
ARCENEAUX MILTON J	CW3	W-2145955	0962	1
ARCHAMBAULT JACK C	LTC	0-0395310	0457	1
ARCHAMBEAU GRANT F	1LT	0-1822763	0646	2
ARCHER CAYLEN	MAJ	0-1553022	1265	2
ARCHER HARRY O	CPT	0-0416188	0748	2
ARCHER HARRY E	MAJ	0-0957692	0866	1
ARCHER HOWARD L	COL	0-0174552	0854	3
ARCHER HOWARD L	1LT	0-0407567	0446	2
ARCHER JAMES B	CPT	0-1822092	0360	1
ARCHER JR BRUCE F	MAJ	0-1556238	0162	1
ARCHER JR RICHARD F	MAJ	0-1826036	0464	1
ARCHER KERMIT C	COL	0-0277679	1265	3
ARCHER RALPH J	MAJ	0-0585012	1062	1
ARCHER ROBERT B	CPT	0-0197253	1162	3
ARCHER ROBERT C	MAJ	0-0348919	0256	2
ARCHER ROY J	LTC	0-1587814	0962	1
ARCHER VERNON W	CPT	0-1114829	0765	1
ARCHIBALD GEORGE H	LTC	0-1634073	0864	1
ARCHIBALD ROBERT J	LTC	0-0384421	0557	1
ARCHIBALD THOMAS R	COL	0-0159940	0546	2
ARCHULETA JAMES M	CPT	0-2210030	0967	1
ARCINO FRANCISCO	CPT	0-1896629	0360	2
ARCISZ JOSEPH J	1LT	0-1048273	1144	2
ARCULEER JOHN H	LTC	0-1822926	1163	1
ARD MYRTLE E	1LT	N-0752967	0953	2
ARDISON ROBERT J	MAJ	0-0294309	0952	2
AREIAS RACHEL E	1LT	N-0783343	0746	1
ARELLANO ARSENIO Y	LTC	0-1301594	0766	3
ARENA ARTHUR A	LTC	0-1575686	0262	2
ARENA JOHN W	CW2	W-2145542	1265	1
ARENAS FELIPE G	2LT	0-1896354	1150	1
ARENDS G WILLIAM	CPT	0-1821306	1046	2
ARENGO RAFAEL A	CPT	0-1896760	0859	1
ARENSON ARTHUR N	LTC	0-0382172	1064	3
ARENZ ARNOLD H E	LTC	0-1330617	0665	1
ARENZ ARTHUR H	COL	0-0242530	0457	1
ARENZ MARK P	1LT	0-2031856	0448	2
ARETZ LAWRENCE I	CPT	0-0188419	1053	3
ARFORD CARROLL W	LTC	0-0284439	0565	3
ARGETSINGER DICK W	LTC	0-1105966	1262	1
ARGETSINGER JR L W	LTC	0-0207354	0650	3
ARGILLA JOSEPH	COL	0-0265836	0346	2
ARGO CLYDE R	MAJ	0-1173144	0161	1
ARGO ROBERT	LTC	0-0248853	0566	3
ARGUE ANSON J	LTC	0-0324409	0660	1
ARGUE JR ALEXANDER	MAJ	0-0474212	0657	2
ARGYRIS CHRIS A	CPT	0-1290181	0445	2
ARIAIL DAVID W	COL	0-0316647	0864	1
ARIAS ARMANDO	MAJ	0-1324386	0963	1
ARIENS MONROE J	MAJ	0-0331390	0962	1
ARIOLA DOMINIC S	CPT	0-0496054	0446	2
ARIS DEMETRIADE	1LT	0-0475153	1044	2
ARKET WILLIAM F	CW4	RW-2124466	1164	1
ARKIN MORRIS	1LT	0-1640674	0845	2
ARKUS ELLIS	COL	0-0279815	0561	1

NAME	GRADE	SVC NO	DATE RET MO YR	RET CODE
ARLAUD CARL F	LTC	0-0404436	0861	1
ARLEDGE ELZEY J	CW3	W-2103850	0160	1
ARLEDGE R F DEACON	COL	0-2051797	0767	3
ARLEIN MYRON S	MAJ	0-0369004	0845	2
ARMAGOST PETER H	LTC	0-1171436	0367	1
ARMAN ROBERT C	CPT	0-1297475	0854	2
ARMANO JOSEPH J	CPT	0-0495738	1051	1
ARMANDO MICHAEL	CW2	W-2148495	0359	1
ARMANN LOUIS L	CPT	0-0480088	0145	2
ARMBRECHT LOUIS A	MAJ	0-0223440	0954	3
ARMBRUSTER WILLIAM M	CPT	0-0265699	1155	3
ARMELLINO JOHN R	MAJ	0-0442775	1046	2
ARMENTROUT CARL O	LTC	0-1298012	1165	2
ARMENTROUT W W	CPT	0-1000195	0346	1
ARMER ALVIN L	CPT	0-0400574	0145	2
ARMIGER JESSE I	CW3	W-2148364	0664	1
ARMIJO FRANCIS C	CPT	0-0982002	1060	1
ARMIJO RICHARD A	CW2	W-2149898	0266	1
ARMINGTON ROBERT L	CPT	0-0447659	0146	2
ARMINTROUT FOREST C	CPT	0-1821530	0654	1
ARMISTEAD BEVERLY A	COL	0-0230440	0365	3
ARMISTEAD JR WIRT M	COL	0-0203469	0863	3
ARMITAGE ARTHUR N	MAJ	0-0224558	0648	3
ARMON AARON H	CPT	0-0136902	0648	3
ARMON THEODORE	CW2	W-2143524	0559	1
ARMOUR JOSEPH C	LTC	0-2002074	0762	1
ARMOUR PHIL B	LTC	0-1559290	1165	1
ARMOUR RICHARD W	COL	0-0244378	0866	3
ARMSTEAD JAMES H	WO1	W-2149659	0460	1
ARMSTRONG ALBERT E	LTC	0-0120418	0854	3
ARMSTRONG ANDREW C	CPT	0-1101314	0962	1
ARMSTRONG BENNIE	LTC	0-1314358	0263	1
ARMSTRONG CHARLES T	CW4	W-2142216	0559	2
ARMSTRONG CHARLES W	MAJ	0-0239453	0765	3
ARMSTRONG DOUGLAS A	CPT	0-1336025	0763	1
ARMSTRONG EARL F	LTC	0-0250740	0156	3
ARMSTRONG EDMOND G	MAJ	0-0378481	0561	2
ARMSTRONG EDWIN K	1LT	0-1057667	1046	1
ARMSTRONG EDWIN W	LTC	0-0249774	1154	3
ARMSTRONG ELMER S	COL	0-0108028	0754	3
ARMSTRONG EMMET E	LTC	0-0217630	0856	3
ARMSTRONG EUGENE A	LTC	0-1578118	1060	1
ARMSTRONG FORREST R	COL	0-0301255	1159	1
ARMSTRONG FRED W	CPT	0-1596251	0159	2
ARMSTRONG GEORGE A	MAJ	0-1948387	1263	1
ARMSTRONG GEORGE J	MAJ	0-0284579	0953	2
ARMSTRONG GEORGE W	2LT	0-1016714	0944	2
ARMSTRONG GERARD T	MAJ	0-1845077	1050	1
ARMSTRONG HAROLD E	CPT	0-0450221	1264	1
ARMSTRONG HENRY P	LTC	0-0268629	0852	3
ARMSTRONG HERBERT L	COL	0-0161803	1052	1
ARMSTRONG HERBERT T	LTC	0-1030887	0762	1
ARMSTRONG JACK H	CPT	0-1935549	0966	1
ARMSTRONG JAMES R	CPT	0-1168156	0948	2
ARMSTRONG JAMES B	1LT	0-1323511	0446	2
ARMSTRONG JAMES F	COL	0-0184635	0257	3
ARMSTRONG JAMES S	LTC	0-0267712	1067	3
ARMSTRONG JESSIE C	CPT	0-0200185	0558	1
ARMSTRONG JOHN E	MAJ	0-0229597	1262	3
ARMSTRONG JOHN H	MAJ	0-2039646	0661	1
ARMSTRONG JOHN R	MAJ	0-0242777	0465	3
ARMSTRONG JOSEPH E	LTC	0-1633318	0962	1
ARMSTRONG JOSEPH P	MAJ	0-1946428	0256	1
ARMSTRONG JR JAMES F	LTC	0-0343935	0567	1
ARMSTRONG JR LEROY	CPT	0-1111819	0362	2
ARMSTRONG JR R M	CPT	0-1061084	0555	2
ARMSTRONG KENNETH L	MAJ	0-0311362	0546	2
ARMSTRONG KENNETH W	MAJ	0-1541500	1266	1
ARMSTRONG LEE	CPT	0-1311277	0854	2
ARMSTRONG LEE ROY W	COL	0-0966576	0664	3
ARMSTRONG LESLIE R	LTC	0-0289600	0164	3
ARMSTRONG LUTHER L	CPT	0-0509406	0653	1
ARMSTRONG MICHAEL A	LTC	0-0266118	0262	3
ARMSTRONG MICHAEL E	MAJ	0-2017797	0662	1
ARMSTRONG NOAH	MAJ	0-1285873	1060	1

NAME	GRADE	SVC NO	DATE RET MO YR	RET CODE
ARMSTRONG NOEL	2LT	O-1170627	0843	2
ARMSTRONG NORMAN H	CPT	O-1050162	0846	2
ARMSTRONG RALPH A	LTC	O-0115063	0756	3
ARMSTRONG RALPH N	LTC	O-1280519	0261	1
ARMSTRONG RAYMOND F	CPT	O-0183276	0254	3
ARMSTRONG RAYMOND I	CPT	O-1287644	0345	2
ARMSTRONG RICHARD C	1LT	O-1924937	0353	1
ARMSTRONG ROBERT J	CW3	W-2203278	0365	1
ARMSTRONG ROBERT L	CW2	W-2211425	0966	1
ARMSTRONG ROBERT N	CW2	W-2149146	0959	1
ARMSTRONG ROBERT R	LTC	O-1314359	0763	1
ARMSTRONG ROLLIN S	LTC	O-0272101	0445	2
ARMSTRONG RUTH E	1LT	N-0768161	0146	1
ARMSTRONG THOMAS R	MAJ	O-2015907	1060	1
ARMSTRONG WILLIAM D	2LT	O-1176539	1145	2
ARMSTRONG WILLIAM H	MAJ	O-2026890	0157	1
ARMUS HARRY P	LTC	O-1573998	1067	3
ARNAU LOUIS J	CW2	W-2101063	0649	1
ARNBRECHT ELMER F	COL	O-0228816	0658	1
ARNDT GEORGE W	CW4	W-2104954	1056	1
ARNDT JR PAUL	MAJ	O-0300780	0847	1
ARNDT THEODORE A	B G	O-0257062	1163	3
ARNEBERG JOHN R	MAJ	O-0996961	0767	1
ARNER ERNEST S	1LT	O-1053457	0546	1
ARNER WELDON C	1LT	O-1307492	1045	2
ARNERT CARL M	WO1	W-2144091	0852	1
ARNESON CHARLES W	1LT	O-1326066	1145	2
ARNESON PAUL F	COL	O-0267916	1166	3
ARNEST HOWARD L	CPT	O-0455052	1148	2
ARNETT CLYDE E	LTC	O-0373613	0866	1
ARNETT HAROLD I	CPT	O-0154727	1053	3
ARNETT MARION L	MAJ	O-0966307	0663	1
ARNETT NOBLE L	MAJ	O-0397002	0346	1
ARNETT WILLIAM T	LTC	O-0248399	1065	3
ARNETTE RICHARD W	CW3	W-2141121	0453	1
ARNHOLD WILLIAM J	CW4	W-2151134	0365	2
ARNHOLS DANIEL	LTC	O-1290881	1061	1
ARNIM VICTOR T	MAJ	O-0216725	0663	3
ARNN EDWARD T	CPT	O-0466052	1046	1
ARNN ISAAC I	1LT	O-0925569	0445	2
ARNOLD BENJAMIN W	LTC	O-0246877	0948	3
ARNOLD CARL O	LTC	O-1036830	0261	1
ARNOLD CAROL E	CW3	W-2144900	0166	1
ARNOLD CHARLES E	LTC	O-1289674	1052	1
ARNOLD CHARLES F	LTC	O-0319265	1060	1
ARNOLD CHARLES J	LTC	O-1549422	0861	1
ARNOLD CHARLES W	CPT	O-0405650	0361	1
ARNOLD CHARLEY D	MAJ	O-1557245	0848	1
ARNOLD CLARENCE W	CW3	W-2152111	0365	1
ARNOLD CLEATIS A	CPT	O-2042971	0958	1
ARNOLD CLIFFORD F	LTC	O-0206145	0962	3
ARNOLD DAVID S	LTC	O-0442432	0562	1
ARNOLD DOUGLAS W	MAJ	O-0943008	0561	1
ARNOLD DOZIER P	LTC	O-1038216	0567	1
ARNOLD EDWARD P	COL	O-0293833	0265	1
ARNOLD EDWIN P	LTC	O-0383974	0360	2
ARNOLD EDWIN W	CW2	W-2152598	0359	1
ARNOLD ELMER C	CPT	O-0376703	0246	2
ARNOLD EMMETT L	MAJ	O-0185972	1149	3
ARNOLD ERNEST J	MAJ	O-1693972	0757	1
ARNOLD EVERETT A	LTC	O-0213870	1163	3
ARNOLD FERRIS L	LTC	O-0210025	1045	2
ARNOLD FLOYD S	COL	O-0162283	0958	3
ARNOLD FRANK J	LTC	O-0405383	0960	2
ARNOLD FRANK R	CPT	O-0107734	1042	2
ARNOLD FRAZER	COL	O-0105732	0648	3
ARNOLD GEORGE A	LTC	O-0239017	0365	3
ARNOLD GILBERT C	COL	O-0229505	0565	3
ARNOLD GLEN I	MAJ	O-2015685	0555	1
ARNOLD GRACE M	1LT	N-0741726	1045	1
ARNOLD HAROLD J	LTC	O-0439106	0848	1
ARNOLD HENRY C	CPT	O-2017170	0657	1
ARNOLD HORACE L	MAJ	O-0268438	0467	3
ARNOLD IGOR S	CPT	O-2026974	0554	2
ARNOLD JAMES M	COL	O-0241348	0566	3
ARNOLD JOE M	LTC	O-1165844	0267	2
ARNOLD JOHN T	1LT	O-1047858	0745	2
ARNOLD JOHN W	LTC	O-0118762	1059	3
ARNOLD JOSEPH M	MAJ	O-0243722	0462	3
ARNOLD JR GORDON L	1LT	O-1308448	1045	2
ARNOLD JR JAMES G	LTC	O-1118856	0766	1
ARNOLD JR JOHN C	CPT	O-0368629	1044	2
ARNOLD JR JULEAN	LTC	O-0343701	0246	2
ARNOLD JR WYATT A	LTC	O-2046364	1262	1
ARNOLD JULIA M	MAJ	N-0798892	0266	1
ARNOLD LAWRENCE E	LTC	O-0359726	0860	1
ARNOLD LOY L	CW2	W-2215480	1067	1
ARNOLD LYDIA	MAJ	N-0742385	1164	3
ARNOLD OPAL H	2LT	N-0765375	0346	1
ARNOLD OTIS M	1LT	O-1283358	0945	2
ARNOLD RALPH L	CPT	O-0520081	0245	2
ARNOLD RAY	1LT	O-1318852	0147	2
ARNOLD RICHARD E	COL	O-0287996	0665	3
ARNOLD RICHARD L	1LT	O-1308289	1065	1
ARNOLD RICHARD L	CW2	W-2152841	0563	1
ARNOLD ROBERT H	LTC	O-1640722	1058	1
ARNOLD ROBERT J	LTC	O-1040339	0461	1
ARNOLD ROBERT L	CPT	O-1031365	0648	1
ARNOLD ROBERT S	MAJ	O-0980826	0567	1
ARNOLD STEWART H	LTC	O-1558773	0765	1
ARNOLD TOM A	COL	O-0450027	1066	1
ARNOLD WALTER R	LTC	O-0370826	0267	3
ARNOLD WALTER T	1LT	O-1634042	0245	2
ARNOLD WILLARD C	LTC	O-0228629	0365	3
ARNOLD WILLIAM C	MAJ	O-0294429	0367	3
ARNOLD WILLIAM C	CW2	W-3430172	1066	1
ARNOLD WILLIAM H	MAJ	O-1636893	1057	1
ARNOLDY ELVIN D	MAJ	O-2036494	0457	1
ARNONE FRANCIS A	CW2	W-2146650	0959	1
ARNONE LOUIS F	LTC	O-0338507	1264	3
ARNTZ CLARENCE A	MAJ	O-0325745	0545	2
ARON FRED H	LTC	O-1101195	1060	1
ARONOFF SOLOMON	1LT	O-1014912	0646	2
ARONS HARRY	CPT	O-1692216	0346	2
ARONS NATHAN	LTC	O-0439920	0849	1
ARONSON EARLE	COL	O-0234742	1165	3
ARONSON SAMUEL S	2LT	O-0439109	0945	2
AROWESTY JOHN	1LT	O-1179007	0746	2
ARPKE CALVIN A	CPT	O-0226514	0945	2
ARPKE ROBERT S	CPT	O-1171037	1146	2
ARPS JR MERVIN H	LTC	O-0557986	0965	1
ARRADAJA MAR G	1LT	O-1896902	1063	2
ARRANTS CLAIR L	MAJ	O-1310204	0661	1
ARRAS MARGUERITE	1LT	N-0794345	1047	1
ARRIGO JOSEPH	LTC	O-1581492	0862	1
ARRIVAS SERAFIN B	1LT	O-1896973	1052	1
ARRONET HERBERT A	COL	O-0126892	0349	3
ARROWOOD RUFUS D	CW2	W-2149200	0858	1
ARROWSMITH GEORGE M	LTC	O-0232900	0648	3
ARROYAS JOHN D	CPT	O-1799563	0457	1
ARROYO ALFONSO S	CPT	O-0514895	0246	1
ARROYO AUGUSTO	MAJ	O-1315760	0257	1
ARSENAULT JAMES E	CW2	W-2206138	1163	1
ARTAMONOFF GEORGE L	COL	O-0240734	0562	3
ARTANDI TIBOR	1LT	O-0927477	1045	2
ARTASERSE GEORGE V	CPT	O-1692121	0445	2
ARTELL STEPHEN S	CPT	O-2055145	1054	1
ARTER JOHN B	COL	O-0507812	1162	3
ARTER THEODORE	COL	O-0204909	1054	3
ARTHER HUGH	CW3	W-2146461	1059	1
ARTHIN SAMUEL H	CW3	W-2148099	0664	1
ARTHUR CARLTON M	CPT	O-0231287	0959	3
ARTHUR DANIEL R	MAJ	O-1296571	0362	2
ARTHUR DONALD J	CPT	O-1331132	0152	1
ARTHUR EDWARD J	1LT	O-0335920	1054	3
ARTHUR FREDERICK	MAJ	O-0411012	0565	1
ARTHUR HAROLD J	MAJ	O-0300762	0364	3
ARTHUR HARRY M	B G	O-0148758	1059	3
ARTHUR HENRY G	MAJ	O-1640183	0256	1
ARTHUR JAMES F	LTC	O-0186409	1157	3
ITHUR JOHN O	LTC	O-1323655	0962	1
ARTHUR JR STEVE	1LT	O-1181629	0945	2
ARTHUR PERRY M	CW3	W-2145827	0164	1
ARTHUR RALPH W	COL	O-0451070	0460	1
ARTHUR ROBERT C	LTC	O-0304808	0547	2
ARTHURS JR JOHN F	COL	O-0244224	0765	3
ARTICOLA VICTOR J	CPT	O-1001507	1059	1
ARTIS SAUL S	CPT	O-0432344	0245	2
ARTLEY MILTON J	1LT	O-0456329	0744	2
ARTS JOSEPH B	LTC	O-0468061	1265	3
ARTZ NORMAN P	2LT	O-2055970	0753	1
ARVIDSON ROBERT A	MAJ	O-0497373	0557	1
ARVIN EDWARD B	MAJ	O-1323272	0463	1
ARWOOD JR FRANCIS M	LTC	O-0335120	0763	1
ASAI GEORGE N	MAJ	O-1335375	1264	1
ASAY FRANK F	2LT	O-2048833	0745	1
ASBELL DON C	LTC	O-1296972	1264	2
ASBELL ERNEST	MAJ	O-0265675	0447	2
ASBRIDGE ERNEST	MAJ	O-0450026	1151	1
ASBURY JR ROY W	MAJ	O-2005267	0764	1
ASBURY MARJORIE H	1LT	N-0755872	0845	1
ASBURY ROY W	MAJ	O-0464223	0647	1
ASCHE LEROY T	CPT	O-0132400	1048	3
ASCHWALD HOWARD A	MAJ	O-1334077	1161	1
ASCOLI LAWRENCE	COL	O-0400104	0160	1
ASEL NORMAN D	1LT	O-0472163	1146	1
ASH DWIGHT A	1LT	O-1113047	1044	2
ASH EDWARD T	CW3	W-2122130	1060	1
ASH FRANCIS G	B G	O-0154915	1153	3
ASH HENRY P	LTC	O-0124408	0256	3
ASH JAMES H	MAJ	O-0965959	1161	1
ASH JR MAURICE L	LTC	O-0253561	0265	3
ASHBACHER VERNON L	MAJ	O-1686273	0459	1
ASHBAUGH JAMES O	CW2	W-2152077	1055	1
ASHBRIDGE WHITNEY	COL	O-0229797	1264	3
ASHBY CARROLL A	CPT	O-1877126	0462	1
ASHBY CARROLL R	CPT	O-0369498	0446	1
ASHBY DANIEL M	CW2	W-2210908	0867	1
ASHBY FRANK G	LTC	O-0419031	0865	1
ASHBY JESSE W	2LT	O-0400322	0445	2
ASHBY MILTON L	CW3	W-2145003	1062	2
ASHBY RICHARD C	LTC	O-1319160	1064	1
ASHBY ROBERT K	LTC	O-1011259	0364	1
ASHCRAFT JR ROY L	1LT	O-1293518	0844	2
ASHCRAFT RAYMOND J	CW4	W-2120699	1154	1
ASHDOWN SAMUEL G	COL	O-0361016	0257	1
ASHE JOSEPH P	CW2	W-2102617	1043	2
ASHE RICHARD B	COL	O-0103173	0356	3
ASHE SILAS M P	1LT	O-0444258	1044	2
ASHELFORD RUTH A	MAJ	N-0774237	0165	1
ASHER CARL A	CPT	O-0483690	1046	1
ASHER JOHN T	MAJ	O-1288675	1060	1
ASHER JOHN W	1LT	O-0408270	0446	2
ASHER JR CHESTER A	COL	O-0174791	0095	1
ASHER JR JEFFERSON	1LT	O-1047429	0448	2
ASHER L D	LTC	O-0416861	0161	1
ASHERMAN DAVID G	MAJ	O-0454550	0548	2
ASHEY CLARENCE O	1LT	O-0493016	0561	1
ASHFORD EARNEST R	1LT	O-0358574	0347	1
ASHFORD ELLIOTT F	MAJ	O-0490168	0157	1
ASHLEY CARL E	MAJ	O-0961542	0863	2
ASHLEY CHARLES M	COL	O-0352019	0563	1
ASHLEY FLOY L	CPT	O-0254907	0145	2
ASHLEY FRANCIS S	LTC	O-0249737	0565	3
ASHLEY GEORGE E	1LT	O-1321137	1045	2
ASHLEY HALLAR B	1LT	O-1327799	0147	2
ASHLEY HARLEY R	CW3	W-2148307	0765	1
ASHLEY IRA J	MAJ	O-4010375	0866	1
ASHLEY JEROLD M	LTC	O-0150192	0648	3
ASHLEY JOE E	MAJ	O-0990107	0664	1
ASHLEY LEROY O	CW3	W-2147152	0964	1
ASHLEY MARK B	MAJ	O-0197611	0841	2
ASHLEY RAYMOND W	CW4	W-2135377	0760	1
ASHLEY ROBERT A	CPT	O-1948445	1055	1
ASHLEY SIDNEY J	1LT	O-0886904	0446	2
ASHLEY THOMAS D	MAJ	O-1823104	0762	1
ASHLEY WILLIAM E	MAJ	O-1686298	0963	1
ASHLOCK DONALD M	COL	O-0219043	0362	3
ASHMEAD ANITA H	MAJ	L-0300308	0263	1
ASHMORE CHARLES W	MAJ	O-0501755	0149	1
ASHMORE CLIFFORD G	CPT	O-0507890	0252	1
ASHMORE HUGIE	WO1	W-2141181	0552	2
ASHMORE PAUL R	CPT	O-1019312	0961	1
ASHMORE SHERMAN M	CPT	O-0396834	0947	2
ASHMORE SIDNEY A	MAJ	O-1173146	0755	1
ASHTON HAROLD D	MAJ	O-0124763	1044	2
ASHTON HERBERT H	MAJ	O-0275125	0557	3
ASHTON JEROME	MAJ	O-1102608	0859	1
ASHTON JOHN J	COL	O-0289203	0762	3
ASHTON MARY W	1LT	N-0734039	1047	1
ASHTON MERTON F	MAJ	O-0524555	1058	3
ASHURST EMORY B	CW2	W-2211029	0164	1
ASHWORTH JAMES	MAJ	O-0225301	0957	3
ASHWORTH JAMES L	MAJ	O-2262342	0865	1
ASHWORTH JR JOHN A	CPT	O-0397186	0147	2
ASHWORTH MAYNARD R	LTC	O-0146978	1044	2
ASKER EARL H	CPT	O-0456013	1046	2
ASKEW HUGH	COL	O-0171198	0456	3
ASKEW JOE B	CW2	W-2111537	1145	2
ASKEW JOHN F	1LT	O-1011443	0846	2
ASKEW PORTER L	CPT	O-0886367	0448	2
ASKEW SR RALPH C	CPT	O-1823923	1162	1
ASKINE IRVIN	MAJ	O-0232812	0647	2
ASKINS CHARLES M	1LT	O-1304954	0746	2
ASKINS JOHN K	1LT	O-1010684	1145	2
ASKINS LYNN C	MAJ	O-0811308	0767	1
ASLUND CHARLES P	2LT	O-1636538	0943	2
ASMAN HAROLD G	MAJ	O-0240888	0563	3
ASMAN HENRY P	MAJ	O-1685107	0146	2
ASMUS LEWIS O	LTC	O-0171725	0556	3
ASMUS LORAINE	1LT	O-1010747	0347	1
ASON STANLEY	COL	O-0528238	0963	3
ASP NCCI A	COL	O-0259856	1264	3
ASP STANLEY	MAJ	O-0109082	0649	3
ASPDEN WILLIAM U	LTC	O-1797414	1160	1
ASPINALL MURRAY C	LTC	O-0391827	0158	3
ASPIRAS JOHN O	CW2	W-2144056	0762	1
ASPNES GARNET S	LTC	O-0347187	0267	3
ASSEFF EMMETT G	2LT	O-1583760	1045	2
ASSELIN EDWARD C	MAJ	O-0262677	0346	2
ASSIRAN PHILIP J	CPT	O-1796018	1146	2
ASSMUS EDWARD A	LTC	O-1323897	0762	1
ASTBURY CHARLES	LTC	O-0277190	0161	3
ASTIN JOHN O	CW2	W-2146698	0454	2
ASTING NEIL J	LTC	O-0374852	0360	1
ASTLER DEWITT G	CPT	O-0499706	0645	2
ASTON LOUIE C	COL	O-0250276	1263	3
ASTOR HARRY W	LTC	O-1011412	0562	1
ASTRAB HARRY A	LTC	O-1172363	0662	1
ASTRUP MARK H	LTC	O-0430120	1261	3
ASUMA THOMAS V	CPT	O-2273272	0759	2
ATANASIC JOSEPH F	MAJ	O-0531738	0946	1
ATCHESON BELLFIELD	CPT	O-1684519	0245	2
ATCHINSON ARCHIE T	1LT	O-1574189	0552	1
ATCHISON ARTHUR L	LTC	O-0287096	0461	3
ATCHISON DICK E	CPT	O-1298783	0548	2
ATCHISON EDWARD R	LTC	O-0202437	0763	3
ATCHISON ELLIS C	LTC	O-1634942	1160	1
ATCHISON JAMES H	CPT	O-0487880	1046	1
ATEN FRANK N	CPT	O-1821553	0753	1
ATEN JOHN A	CPT	O-2017634	1059	1
ATEN JR JAY B	1LT	O-1596253	0146	2
ATEN LOUIS H	MAJ	O-0382739	0259	1
ATES ELLIS R	LTC	O-0400319	0663	1
ATHANASON NICHOLAS A	COL	O-0219847	0756	1
ATHAY JR ROLAND H	CPT	O-0451933	0246	2
ATHERTON DONALD H	LTC	O-0204726	0648	3
ATHERTON DONALD J	CW3	W-2142801	1160	1
ATHERTON JAMES P	CPT	O-0237840	0964	3
ATHERTON THOMAS H	COL	O-0179247	0648	3

NAME	GRADE	SVC NO	DATE RET MO YR	RET CODE
ATHEY JAMES R	CPT	0-2028660	0263	1
ATHY GREGG R	MAJ	C-1700286	0546	2
ATILES-CRESPO RAFAEL	CPT	0-192410S	C863	1
ATKESON THOMAS Z	CPT	0-0370343	C845	2
ATKINS ADMIRAL	CW3	W-2139804	0156	1
ATKINS CHARLES B	LTC	0-0295716	0565	3
ATKINS CLIFFORD F	LTC	0-0481131	0167	1
ATKINS CLINTON D	CW3	W-2145570	0359	1
ATKINS FRANK A	LTC	C-0248505	C167	3
ATKINS HARROLD C	CPT	0-0337016	C564	3
ATKINS JOE F	CPT	0-0497968	0746	1
ATKINS JOHN C	1LT	0-2036877	0264	1
ATKINS JOHN E	CPT	0-0971213	0961	1
ATKINS JOHN L	COL	C-0243555	C766	3
ATKINS KENNETH W	1LT	0-1317364	1145	2
ATKINS LOIS P	2LT	N-0743664	0944	1
ATKINS LOUIS H	CPT	0-0982680	1062	1
ATKINS MONTIVILLE	LTC	0-1304325	C762	1
ATKINS NORMAN D	LTC	0-0283356	C754	3
ATKINS PERRY C	CPT	0-1685705	C864	1
ATKINS ROBERT C	MAJ	0-0276316	C250	1
ATKINS THOMAS T	COL	0-0246315	C863	3
ATKINS WILLIAM O	CPT	0-2023954	0157	1
ATKINSON ALFRED O	COL	0-0353615	C463	1
ATKINSON ANN M	1LT	N-0744622	1046	1
ATKINSON BILLY	1LT	0-1284265	0845	2
ATKINSON CHARLES F	CPT	0-0150286	1158	3
ATKINSON CHARLES M	CPT	0-1110038	0953	1
ATKINSON CHARLES M	CW4	W-2114335	C659	1
ATKINSON DANIEL D	CPT	0-0176944	C555	3
ATKINSCN DONALD F	LTC	0-1032262	C666	1
ATKINSON ERNEST P	1LT	0-15919C5	C965	3
ATKINSON FREDDIE R	CPT	0-0327859	1044	1
ATKINSON GEORGE M	1LT	0-0179303	C355	3
ATKINSON GILBERT S	LTC	0-0395223	0766	3
ATKINSON HAROLD E	1LT	0-1011133	C945	1
ATKINSON HAROLD J	LTC	0-01319C2	1052	3
ATKINSON HARRY G	LTC	0-0183309	1150	3
ATKINSON HOWARD T	CPT	0-0504771	C447	1
ATKINSON JACK	MAJ	0-0981552	1263	1
ATKINSON JOHN A	MAJ	0-0254514	1163	3
ATKINSCN JOHN P	LTC	0-1107212	1166	1
ATKINSON JOHN H	1LT	0-0381594	0945	2
ATKINSCN JOSEPH F	MAJ	C-0978934	0262	1
ATKINSON JR WALTER G	MAJ	C-200530C	C860	1
ATKINSON LUTHER O	WO1	W-2118148	C856	1
ATKINSON LUTHER J	MAJ	C-1342033	C967	1
ATKINSON MARVIN F	CW3	W-2005656	0666	1
ATKINSCN ROBERT L	CPT	0-0449436	0248	1
ATKINSON ROBERT L	CW2	W-22056C0	0662	1
ATKINSON ROBERT M	COL	0-0256711	0967	3
ATKINSON THOMAS P	LTC	C-0191430	1044	2
ATKINSCN WALTER	COL	0-0249677	0165	3
ATKINSON WILLIAM J	COL	0-0235393	C859	3
ATKISON WILLIAM L	LTC	0-0252394	1146	2
ATLAS ANDOR H	CPT	0-0273383	0445	2
ATLAS CHARLES	2LT	0-1055775	C644	2
ATMAR LAURA B	CPT	N-0734678	1050	1
ATON THOMAS L	MAJ	0-2006400	1060	1
ATTARIAN EDWARD J	1LT	0-0464233	C145	1
ATTAWAY JAMES R	MAJ	0-1919429	1265	1
ATTAYA JR HENRY E	LTC	0-0354099	C463	1
ATTEBERRY DAVID G	LTC	C-0453131	0457	1
ATTEBERRY EMMETT M	MAJ	C-1294413	C960	1
ATTEBERRY HARRY M	1LT	0-1303830	1044	2
ATTEBERY JOHN J	LTC	0-0451823	0666	1
ATTEBURY EVERETT G	CPT	0-1821531	C146	2
ATTERBURY HENRY S	MAJ	0-1291758	C857	1
ATTICK WILLIAM E	MAJ	0-0970237	C263	1
ATTRIDGE FRANCIS L	MAJ	C-0486548	1047	2
ATTRIDGE PATRICK J	1LT	0-1925593	0354	2
ATTRIDGE ROBERT O	MAJ	0-1052659	1164	1
ATWATER MONTGOMERY	CPT	0-1300259	0945	2
ATWELL CHARLES F	LTC	0-0397206	0660	1
ATWELL HARRY B	CW3	W-2151697	1163	1
ATWELL RAYMOND B	LTC	0-0438850	0146	2
ATWOOD ARLICE G	MAJ	0-4043286	0567	1
ATWOOD JOSEPH	MAJ	0-0186511	1155	3
ATWOOD LAURENCE C	COL	0-0196253	0445	2
ATWOCD NORMAN C	COL	0-0214225	0163	3
ATWOOD ROBERT B	MAJ	0-0111740	0445	2
ATWOOD VERNON S	MAJ	0-0454334	0157	1
AUBREY GORDON K	MAJ	0-1318243	0257	1
AUBREY SAM B	1LT	0-0527770	1145	2
AUBURN HORACE T	LTC	0-0142453	1059	3
AUCHARC ROBERT R	2LT	0-1032501	0445	2
AUCHARE VIRGIL M	LTC	0-0221261	0645	2
AUD HERSCHEL B	2LT	0-0359294	0646	1
AUDA ANTHONY J	CPT	0-1302752	1047	1
AUDET NORMAN A	CW3	W-2145284	0361	1
AUDETTE RAUL J	1LT	0-0517092	1145	2
AUDETTE ROLAND D	CW3	W-2149007	0365	1
AUE CARLTON F	LTC	0-2036528	0465	2
AUERBACH CAESAR J	LTC	0-0504799	0563	3
AUERBACH EDWIN H	CPT	0-0233627	0146	2
AUERBACH JR EMIL E	MAJ	0-0264719	0565	3
AUERBACH MILTON G	CPT	0-0915306	0546	2
AUFDEMORTE JR M T	MAJ	0-1030542	C448	2
AUFFINGER JR G H	COL	0-0183639	0258	3
AUGENSTINE HELEN F	2LT	N-0733549	0644	1
AUGER CLARENCE A	CW2	W-2149317	1057	2
AUGER LEONARD S	LTC	0-1576893	0663	1
AUGUR ROBERT F	CPT	0-0301982	0546	2
AUGUST LOIS V	LTC	0-0354619	1147	2
AUGUSTAUSKAS ANTHONY	LTC	0-1284626	1163	1
AUGUSTINE CHARLES J	CW4	W-2113666	0958	1
AUGUSTINE JOHN	1LT	0-0887663	0857	1
AUGUSTINE LOUIS	CW2	W-2154660	1057	1
AUGUSTINE WALTER I	CPT	0-0535215	0945	2
AUGUSTINE WILLIAM H	2LT	0-13C8450	1044	2
AUGUSTINE WILLIAM J	CPT	0-0450787	0254	1
AUGUSTINOS PETER	MAJ	0-1047859	0657	1
AUGUSTYNCHICZ WALTER	CW3	W-2207243	1067	1
AUGUSTYNOWSKI E M	CPT	0-1293520	1048	1
AUK JULIA R	CW3	V-0313502	1164	1
AULD JR FRED G	CW2	W-215276	0161	1
AULOS HAROLD	CW2	W-215C889	1160	1
AULETTA ANTHONY J	LTC	0-0460153	0765	1
AULICK CARL H	B G	0-0260430	0665	3
AULMANN JR HERMAN E	1LT	0-0455949	0346	2
AULT DONALD V	MAJ	0-0967199	0563	1
AULT GLENN S	COL	0-0142216	0446	2
AULTMAN II DWIGHT E	COL	0-0181401	0262	3
AULTMAN ROBERT A	CW4	W-2117225	0960	1
AUMEND JEAN E	1LT	N-0728805	0251	1
AUMILLER FERD R	LTC	0-155263C	0264	1
AUMULLER EDWIN C	MAJ	0-1545045	1063	1
AUNGST FOSTER W	COL	C-0343491	0360	1
AURAND PAUL E	LTC	0-0341629	0463	1
AURE GARMON O	LTC	0-1184616	0766	1
AURELIC HONORIO V	CPT	0-0395564	0964	1
AURELIC SALVATORE	LTC	0-1685683	0467	1
AURELIUS LAWRENCE E	LTC	0-0217586	0656	3
AUREN WALTER I	CW4	W-2101393	0455	1
AURINGER FRANK J	CPT	0-1575697	1046	1
AURIT SAMUEL	LTC	0-0047925	0764	1
AUSAN FREDERICK	MAJ	0-1031885	0461	1
AUSAN JAMES V	LTC	0-1297649	0862	1
AUSANKA ALGERT F	2LT	0-0412287	0545	2
AUSBROCKS WILBUR O	CW3	W-2149190	1064	1
AUSHERMAN HAROLD P	LTC	0-012284E	0259	3
AUSLAND JOHN F	MAJ	C-0418525	0345	1
AUST ROBERT A	MAJ	0-1686628	0462	1
AUSTELL MICHAEL H	COL	0-0140215	0555	2
AUSTILL FREEMAN J	LTC	0-1944865	0960	1
AUSTILL WILLIAM E	COL	0-0337302	0961	3
AUSTIN ANDREW Y	MAJ	0-0290164	0760	1
AUSTIN ARCHIE C	LTC	0-2035280	0766	1
AUSTIN CARROLL F	CPT	0-0246307	0744	2
AUSTIN CHARLES D	LTC	0-0490065	0359	3
AUSTIN CALE J	LTC	0-04006C4	0146	2
AUSTIN EDWARD K	LTC	0-0292447	0367	3
AUSTIN FINIS H	LTC	0-0425149	0767	3
AUSTIN FRANK B	MAJ	0-1634997	0958	1
AUSTIN GEORGE W	1LT	0-1551345	C547	2
AUSTIN HAROLD D	LTC	0-0182373	0555	3
AUSTIN IRA W	2LT	0-08876C4	0246	2
AUSTIN IVAN D	LTC	0-0318263	C459	3
AUSTIN JESSIE L	1LT	N-0736689	0246	1
AUSTIN JOHN G	MAJ	0-0419921	0555	1
AUSTIN JR JOHN W	MAJ	C-0311954	0145	2
AUSTIN KATHLEEN M	1LT	N-0755557	0147	1
AUSTIN KAYLOR F	LTC	0-1573017	1160	1
AUSTIN LELAND A	COL	0-0222041	1C58	1
AUSTIN LESLIE H	MAJ	0-1644299	0761	1
AUSTIN LOUIS B	MAJ	C-1001509	C262	3
AUSTIN MARSHALL H	LTC	0-0170766	0960	1
AUSTIN NATHANIEL	1LT	0-1252638	1044	2
AUSTIN OTTO C	COL	0-0310071	0166	3
AUSTIN PATRICK J	CW4	W-2001874	1058	3
AUSTIN PERCY L	MAJ	0-0401765	1163	1
AUSTIN RALPH F	MAJ	0-0430154	1057	2
AUSTIN ROBERT D	LTC	0-0299978	1165	3
AUSTIN SAMUEL L	COL	C-0106261	1058	3
AUSTIN VERNE	COL	0-0184808	0254	3
AUSTIN WILLIAM B	LTC	0-1106559	0266	3
AUSTIN WILLIAM P	1LT	0-1106560	1145	2
AUSTIN WILLIAM R	1LT	0-1823654	0346	2
AUSTRAW JAMES L	COL	0-0248553	0866	3
AUTARC EUGENE J	1LT	0-0380749	0841	2
AUTEN MAURICE L	1LT	0-1313075	C345	2
AUTRAND SR VERNON L	MAJ	C-1301083	0961	1
AUTREY ERNEST R	COL	0-0443781	0453	1
AUTRY JOSEPH F	CW3	W-2145085	C960	1
AUTRY MAXIE M	MAJ	0-1580584	1155	1
AUTRY ROY	CPT	0-0499345	0646	2
AUTRY WILLIAM J	CW3	W-2152818	0166	1
AUVIL DANIEL M	LTC	0-2000007	0563	1
AUZAT EMILE T	CW4	W-212083C	C762	1
AVAKIAN RUPEN G	CPT	0-0462263	0946	1
AVANS JR JOSEPH	CPT	0-2016828	1155	2
AVANT ELIZABETH	2LT	N-0702513	1039	1
AVEDON HERBERT	LTC	C-164235C	1266	3
AVENDANO NUMA P	COL	0-0226352	C162	3
AVERA BERTIE L	LTC	0-0176399	1158	3
AVERA DOUGLAS J	CPT	0-1298337	C364	1
AVERILL BERYL R	LTC	0-0268669	1165	3
AVERILL EDWARD R	LTC	0-1334806	0766	1
AVERILL ERNEST P	CW4	W-2131494	1060	1
AVERILL JOHN M	CW3	W-2146615	C565	1
AVERILL ROBERT B	CPT	0-1043853	C147	1
AVERILL WILLIAM S	LTC	0-0148016	0-53	3
AVERITT JAMES R	LTC	0-0274340	0545	2
AVERKA CHARLES P	LTC	0-0385988	0546	2
AVERY ALPHONSO C	CPT	0-13C4849	0748	1
AVERY CHARLIE J	1LT	C-1546892	0346	2
AVERY CLIFFORD D	MAJ	C-0214634	1262	3
AVERY CLYDE K	CW2	W-2142802	0462	1
AVERY DORCAS C	MAJ	N-0701619	0947	1
AVERY EARLE S	LTC	0-0358149	1262	1
AVERY GEORGE W	MAJ	0-2000973	0165	1
AVERY HAROLD	CW4	W-2142803	1164	1
AVERY JAMES C	MAJ	C-0136970	C153	3
AVERY JAMES O	MAJ	0-1104474	0859	1
AVERY JOHN C	COL	0-0272548	C867	3
AVERY MARION D	COL	0-0168134	0358	3
AVERY NATHAN C	MAJ	C-0198816	0253	3
AVERY RAYMOND A	MAJ	C-0289532	0867	3
AVERY ROSCOE E	LTC	0-0492501	1145	1
AVERY ROY B	MAJ	0-1171877	1163	1
AVERY VESTAL O	COL	0-0391416	0660	1
AVERY VIVIEN H	1LT	N-0751035	C846	1
AVILES EMILIO F	CPT	0-0888084	1048	2
AVILLA FRANK A	1LT	0-1118156	0447	2
AVIN EDWARD	CW3	W-2144293	0964	1
AVISON JR GORDON W	MAJ	0-0938720	0264	2
AVON ROBERT	LTC	0-1331802	0267	1
AVRIETT BYRON A	LTC	0-2044596	0155	2
AVRIETT ROBERT J	MAJ	C-1329668	1161	1
AVVEDUTI LOUIS	2LT	0-2008651	0348	1
AWBREY DON C	CPT	0-154332C	0645	2
AWBREY LLOYD L	LTC	0-0308503	0765	3
AWE LESTER A	1LT	0-1301921	1046	2
AWTRY JOHN H	COL	0-0914101	0353	1
AXBERG NELS	WO1	W-2123062	0852	1
AXELSON JOHN M	CPT	0-0316040	0845	2
AXELSON OSCAR A	COL	0-0256857	1151	1
AXILROD ASHER A	MAJ	0-0331608	0665	3
AXTELL JR CLYDE R	CPT	0-1104718	0553	2
AXVALL CHESTER C	MAJ	C-0254724	1165	3
AYALIN HILARION S	2LT	0-1896968	0857	1
AYARS ALVIN E	CW2	W-3430440	1167	1
AYBAR JOSE A	COL	0-0240001	0764	2
AYCOCK BENNETT	COL	0-0299391	1057	2
AYCOCK CHARLES B	LTC	0-0277164	0245	2
AYCOCK EDNA M	LTC	N-0702984	0547	1
AYDELOTTE JR W W	1LT	0-1308584	0845	2
AYDLETT FRED H	MAJ	0-0451201	0253	1
AYER CORNELIA W	LTC	N-0736232	0461	1
AYER JASPER H	LTC	0-0362882	1061	1
AYER ROBERT G	1LT	0-0447206	0745	2
AYER WARONER O	COL	C-0195374	0648	3
AYERS CLAUDE G	CW4	W-2114635	C464	3
AYERS EDWARD G	MAJ	0-0366432	1045	2
AYERS HAROLD P	CW2	W-2121111	0651	1
AYERS HOWARD	COL	0-0195224	0859	3
AYERS JR CHARLES F	CW4	W-2205316	1166	1
AYERS KENNETH L	MAJ	0-1313042	1160	1
AYERS ROBERT S	LTC	0-1289855	0463	1
AYERS SEABORN A	COL	0-0214927	C856	3
AYERS SPILLMAN L	CPT	0-1290182	0747	1
AYERS WILLARD C	LTC	0-0261269	1061	1
AYLESWORTH HOWARD C	LTC	0-2272725	0862	1
AYLING RICHARD C	1LT	0-1170273	1145	2
AYLOR JOHN M	LTC	0-0409978	0157	1
AYLWARD FRANCIS T	MAJ	0-2000045	1060	1
AYMAT OCTAVIO	LTC	0-0386939	1060	1
AYNES ERMAN E	CPT	0-2000446	0957	1
AYNSLEY JAMES S	CW2	W-2109439	0647	1
AYOTTE PAUL J	CPT	0-1171039	1146	1
AYOUB EDWARD J	2LT	0-1291137	0745	2
AYOUB WILLIAM J	LTC	0-1294770	0267	1
AYRE JR DAVID	1LT	0-0300881	0646	2
AYRE RICHARD H	COL	0-0173533	0260	3
AYRES ALAN A	MAJ	0-1949694	0262	1
AYRES DENNIS A	LTC	0-1047013	0864	1
AYRES EDWARD R	COL	C-0189864	1053	3
AYRES JR CHARLES U	MAJ	C-0963056	0165	1
AYTES GLENN R	COL	0-0324655	1161	1
AZBELL SILAS C	1LT	0-0494076	0149	1
AZEVEDO JOHN V	LTC	0-0488902	0966	1
AZOFF SAMUEL	1LT	0-1725592	C246	1
AZZOPARDI JOHN	MAJ	C-0996608	0664	1
BAADE HENRY	MAJ	0-1643632	1061	1
BAAR FRANCES J	2LT	N-0702676	1035	1
BAAS EDWARD C	MAJ	0-1300911	1060	1
BABACY FRANK W	WO1	W-2109694	0248	1
BABALONIS ANTHONY J	CW2	W-2141923	0756	1
BABB CLYDE A	LTC	0-0283860	0267	3
BABB DOY H	CW4	W-2146213	1058	1
BABB EARL F	LTC	0-1307636	0964	1
BABB GEORGE A	CW3	W-2141184	0262	1
BABB HENRY R	MAJ	0-0203450	0361	3
BABB HOMER H	CPT	0-1944907	1045	1
BABB LEO D	MAJ	0-1C40866	0457	1
BABB MORRIS	1LT	0-05266C5	0648	1
BABBEY STEVE A	CW3	W-2144043	0956	1
BABBIT WORTH B	CPT	0-1322847	0246	2
BABBITT FREDERIC M	CPT	0-0214327	0663	3
BABBITT FREDERICK	WO1	W-2132762	0458	1

NAME	GRADE	SVC NO	DATE RET MO YR	RET CODE
BABBITT JAMES T	LTC	0-0287320	1161	1
BABBITT JOHN H	MAJ	0-4010794	1166	1
BABBITT PAUL L	COL	0-0359826	0461	1
BABBITT SR FRANK W	MAJ	0-1798902	0760	1
BABBITT THEODORE	COL	0-0136923	0257	3
BABBITZ ALBERT L	LTC	0-0310140	0665	3
BABBS CHARLES F	MAJ	0-0215219	0745	2
BABCOCK DANIEL W	COL	0-0269340	0664	3
BABCOCK EARL L	CPT	0-0475225	0949	1
BABCOCK JAMES O	LTC	0-0523504	0347	2
BABCOCK LEON E	LTC	0-1581410	0464	1
BABCOCK ROBERT A	CPT	0-1284989	0646	2
BABCOCK ROBERT E	MAJ	0-1881151	1167	1
BABCOCK ROBERT L	MAJ	0-1294414	1160	1
BABCOCK SAMUEL A	LTC	0-2046876	1166	2
BABCOCK WILBUR E	1LT	0-0175987	0753	3
BABEL PHILIP E	MAJ	0-0508672	0463	1
BABERS FRANK H	COL	0-0228835	0764	3
BABERS JOHN R	CW2	W-2215665	1167	1
BABES FRED J	LTC	0-1550537	0361	1
BABIARZ FRANK W	1LT	0-0934796	0162	2
BABIN JR ANDREW	LTC	0-1179279	0761	1
BABISH FRANK R	LTC	0-1062659	0866	1
BABJACK DENNIS B	CW2	W-3100539	0966	2
BABKIEWICH JOSEPH W	1LT	0-1299666	0746	2
BABLER MARY A	1LT	N-0743538	0347	1
BABLER OSCAR E	CPT	0-0520577	1045	2
BABSON JOHN C	COL	0-0197490	1162	3
BABYOCK NICHOLAS	1LT	0-1037799	0847	2
BACCAY CLARK	1LT	0-1896680	0758	1
BACCO ANTHONY J	2LT	0-1059354	1144	2
BACCUS EDWIN V	LTC	0-2055822	1161	1
BACH AUSTIN W	LTC	0-0545870	0964	1
BACH KENNETH J	LTC	0-0515798	0766	1
BACH ROLAND F	CPT	0-1996510	1066	2
BACH WILLIAM J	MAJ	0-1558998	0763	1
BACHAR PAUL W	2LT	0-1116199	1044	2
BACHAR PERRY H	LTC	0-0490116	1047	1
BACHAUD JEAN D	MAJ	0-2036849	0966	1
BACHE BENJAMIN A	LTC	0-0332400	0657	1
BACHELLER WESLEY M	MAJ	0-0267117	0966	3
BACHELLOR WILLIAM S	MAJ	0-0972805	0765	2
BACHENHEIMER RICHARD	1LT	0-0927940	1046	2
BACHISON ANDREW H	MAJ	0-1845139	0358	1
BACHMAN ARTHUR D	1LT	0-2048548	0146	2
BACHMAN EDWARD A	MAJ	0-0273663	0661	3
BACHMAN OSCAR G	LTC	0-0189743	0151	3
BACHMEIER IGNATIUS	CPT	0-1844980	0657	1
BACHMIRSKI STANLEY M	CW2	W-2206182	0862	1
BACHRACH JR CARL M	CPT	0-0456687	0246	2
BACHTELER WILLIAM F	CW2	W-2147727	0765	1
BACHTELL LEO M	1LT	0-1058165	0852	1
BACK ALBERT W	1LT	0-1643636	1146	1
BACK GEORGE A	CPT	0-1333299	0961	1
BACK HARLEY B	CW3	W-2153237	0565	1
BACK JOHN F	LTC	0-0451206	0865	1
BACK KENNETH	CPT	0-0452291	0551	2
BACK LEO W	CW3	W-2206338	1165	1
BACK SAMUEL H	COL	0-0327476	0263	3
BACKER JOHN H	LTC	0-1997750	1162	3
BACKER MAX B	CPT	0-0341190	0345	2
BACKES CHARLES C	LTC	0-0152565	0648	3
BACKES HARRY M	CPT	0-0493624	0957	1
BACKES JAMES M	COL	0-0304809	0153	2
BACKSTROM BERT H	LTC	0-0332146	0260	1
BACKUS HAROLD B	MAJ	0-1014458	0658	2
BACKUS WAYNE E	CPT	0-0237821	0346	2
BACOCH JR JOHN	1LT	0-1690943	1147	2
BACON ALLEN F	LTC	0-0299784	0146	2
BACON BERNARD J	CW2	W-2210707	0866	1
BACON CLARENCE B	LTC	0-1288676	0561	1
BACON EARL W	COL	0-0108783	0946	1
BACON EUGENE F	LTC	0-1283636	0161	1
BACON FORSYTH —	COL	0-0289096	0746	2
BACON FREEMAN C	LTC	0-0225796	0564	3

NAME	GRADE	SVC NO	DATE RET MO YR	RET CODE
BACON HENRY C	LTC	0-1556530	0163	1
BACON HENRY S	MAJ	0-0124098	0257	3
BACON HOWARD R	LTC	0-0168034	0549	3
BACON JAMES B	MAJ	0-1080698	0162	1
BACON JOHN A	COL	0-0272259	1266	1
BACON JOHN R	MAJ	0-0342149	0546	2
BACON JR ELBRIDGE	COL	0-0324170	0560	1
BACON ROBERT P	LTC	0-1287292	0466	1
BACON RONALD K	CPT	0-1010981	1147	2
BACON THOMAS F	1LT	0-0493777	1148	1
BACOS JOHN M	CPT	0-0544609	1047	2
BACZEK MARY A	2LT	N-0753366	0845	1
BADE ERNEST F	MAJ	0-0443901	0756	1
BADEEN LOUIS J	1LT	0-1775834	0945	2
BADELA ADAM	MAJ	0-1553214	0962	1
BADEN DAVID O	CPT	0-0553558	0946	2
BADENHOOP AUGUST G	LTC	0-0233569	0865	3
BADER FRANCIS A	LTC	0-0446946	0165	1
BADER GILBERT F	MAJ	0-0967552	0761	1
BADER PHILIP	CW3	W-2152154	1162	1
BADEY WILLIAM	COL	0-1043555	0966	1
BADGER CLAYTON I	CW3	W-2145355	0964	1
BADGER DARWIN H	CPT	0-1844953	0459	1
BADGER DONALD W	1LT	0-2211126	0853	1
BADGER EDWARD B	COL	0-0309824	0746	2
BADGER HARRY S	1LT	0-1650153	0947	1
BADGER MARION H	LTC	0-0260954	0362	3
BADGER WALTER E	LTC	0-0393628	0960	1
BADGER WALTER L	LTC	0-0275090	1164	3
BADGER WALTER M	LTC	0-0370989	1265	3
BADGETT CHARLES B	MAJ	0-2204072	0766	1
BADGETT LLOYD J	MAJ	0-0402708	0463	1
BADGETT WALTER H	COL	0-0260953	0167	3
BADGLEY FOREST R	LTC	0-1056029	0267	1
BADGLEY JOHN L	MAJ	0-1692938	1161	1
BADIN FRED P	MAJ	0-1553949	0860	1
BADO JOHN T	1LT	0-0991356	0453	2
BADOVINAC JOHN D	MAJ	0-1641136	0455	1
BADOVINUS CHARLOTTE	1LT	N-0775058	0446	1
BADT MORRIS B	COL	0-0150294	0648	3
BADURA DONALD R	1LT	0-1298000	1045	2
BAEBLER JR ARTHUR H	1LT	0-0541854	0847	1
BAEHR FRED W	LTC	0-0376274	0555	1
BAELLA RAFAEL A	LTC	0-0266882	0367	3
BAENZIGER ALBERT F	MAJ	0-1080341	0762	1
BAER FRANK A	MAJ	0-0920670	1044	2
BAER GEORGE W	CW2	W-2120143	0546	1
BAER HARRY	1LT	0-1038409	0346	1
BAER JOSEPH C	LTC	0-1041289	0363	1
BAER ROBERT D	LTC	0-0411167	0162	1
BAER ROBERT M	CPT	0-4031384	0567	1
BAER ROBERT O	MAJ	0-0500866	0850	1
BAER VICTOR	LTC	0-0324016	0245	2
BAER VINCENT T	CW2	W-2210005	0564	1
BAER WALTER	CW3	W-2149419	1064	1
BAER WALTER A	LTC	0-0244040	0460	1
BAERGEN JOHN	LTC	0-0518395	0363	1
BAES JEROME L	MAJ	0-2033628	0561	1
BAEZ RAMON E	CW2	W-2151642	1060	1
BAGAAN FREDDIE	2LT	0-1896484	0254	1
BAGACINA FELIX W	CPT	0-1896828	0159	1
BAGANZ HERBERT M	CPT	0-0120055	0658	3
BAGARIA JAMES C	2LT	0-1314582	0245	2
BAGBY HERBERT W	CW3	RW-2144254	0463	1
BAGBY JOHN	COL	0-0226051	1061	3
BAGBY LAWRENCE E	WO1	W-2115384	0945	2
BAGBY ROBERT T	LTC	0-1104476	1065	1
BAGBY WILLIAM R	MAJ	0-1643773	1060	1
BAGDONIS ALPHONSE J	MAJ	0-1173858	0761	1
BAGGERLY VAUGHN H	MAJ	0-1645133	1264	1
BAGGETT BOYD O	LTC	0-0265427	1060	3
BAGGETT JR ALLEN T	CW3	W-2000807	0166	3
BAGGETT KENNETH J	LTC	0-0338097	0666	1
BAGGETT LEO	CPT	0-1014208	0960	1
BAGGETT MARICK L	MAJ	0-0384798	0761	1

NAME	GRADE	SVC NO	DATE RET MO YR	RET CODE
BAGGETT STOKES E	CPT	0-1293351	0746	2
BAGGETT WARREN C	CPT	0-0268018	1059	1
BAGGETT WILBUR C	MAJ	0-0877348	1065	1
BAGGETT ZULA B	MAJ	N-0765610	0665	1
BAGLEY ALBERT G	COL	0-0104281	1051	3
BAGLEY CECIL C	COL	0-0187958	0748	3
BAGLEY DUANE W	MAJ	0-1291387	0161	1
BAGLEY EARL S	MAJ	0-0991051	0366	1
BAGLEY FERNALD S	LTC	0-0299294	1158	1
BAGLEY HARRY E	CPT	0-0493763	0745	2
BAGLEY HOWARD L	CPT	0-0463460	0152	1
BAGLEY JAMES H	LTC	0-0262025	1058	3
BAGLEY JAMES W	CW3	W-2142804	0661	1
BAGLEY JOHN P	MAJ	0-1280459	1047	2
BAGLEY JR JAMES P	1LT	0-1949048	0547	2
BAGLEY JR JOHN H	LTC	0-0348173	1060	1
BAGLEY LEO W	COL	0-0384166	0754	1
BAGLEY MASON R	LTC	0-0375461	0859	1
BAGLEY RICHARD D	CPT	0-0486485	0448	1
BAGLEY RUTH C	2LT	N-0752700	0445	1
BAGLEY THOMAS B	COL	0-0357805	0659	3
BAGLEY THOMAS D	CPT	0-1300119	0646	2
BAGLEY THOMAS J	MAJ	0-0486990	0756	1
BAGLEY TOM A	MAJ	0-0283213	0644	1
BAGLIEN SAMUEL	LTC	0-0237518	0145	2
BAGNALL ELMER R	LTC	0-0325390	0657	3
BAGNALL HARRY W	LTC	0-0142206	0644	1
BAGNELL DOUGLAS B	LTC	0-0267816	1059	3
BAGWELL JAMES H	MAJ	0-1031051	0262	1
BAGWELL JAMES P	CPT	0-1011081	0357	1
BAHME NATHAN	LTC	0-0316454	0261	1
BAHNER ALBERT R	MAJ	0-1998115	0163	1
BAHNSON FRANCIS H	CPT	0-1550740	0764	1
BAHORIC ALBERT J	LTC	0-1178692	0465	1
BAHR LELAND D	CW4	W-2108247	1262	2
BAHRKE CHESTER M	CW2	W-2147909	0461	1
BAIAS SAM	1LT	0-1305707	0644	2
BAICH STEVE	WO1	W-2135052	1154	2
BAICZER ABRAHAM I	LTC	0-0530323	1266	3
BAIER EDWARD A	COL	0-0247004	1163	3
BAIER FRANK E	MAJ	0-0443925	0847	1
BAIER VICTOR H	1LT	0-1012738	1045	1
BAILES JR ELBERT L	LTC	0-0359155	0366	3
BAILES LEONARD W	MAJ	0-0301201	1160	1
BAILES RUSSELL G	CPT	0-1308452	1146	2
BAILEY ALFRED H	COL	0-0170308	0847	1
BAILEY ARDITH BEL	1LT	N-0788603	1045	1
BAILEY ARTHUR F	CPT	0-0384117	0760	1
BAILEY BENJAMIN E	LTC	0-1340615	0866	1
BAILEY CHARLES C	CPT	0-0482985	0447	1
BAILEY CHARLES C	MAJ	0-0492828	0746	1
BAILEY CHARLES D	1LT	0-1103498	1145	2
BAILEY CHARLES T	MAJ	0-0957584	1061	1
BAILEY CLARK A	1LT	0-1944926	1044	2
BAILEY CLIFFORD H	MAJ	0-1692928	1162	1
BAILEY CLINTON B	WO1	W-2126177	0445	2
BAILEY DAVID W	MAJ	0-0507673	0854	1
BAILEY EDWARD B	CPT	0-1290875	0346	2
BAILEY EDWARD L	1LT	0-0375716	1043	2
BAILEY ELDON L	COL	0-0218668	0661	3
BAILEY ELLSWORTH	LTC	0-0452056	1164	1
BAILEY ELMA L	1LT	N-0729873	0346	1
BAILEY ERNEST O	CW3	W-2147337	0764	1
BAILEY ERNEST M	LTC	0-0377839	0454	2
BAILEY ERNEST M	LTC	0-0453983	0762	1
BAILEY EUGENE A	1LT	0-1305370	0645	2
BAILEY EVERARD A	CPT	0-0225491	0864	3
BAILEY EVERETT C	MAJ	0-1594692	1164	1
BAILEY FLORENCE A	2LT	N-0734575	1145	1
BAILEY FORD G	MAJ	0-2262327	1263	1
BAILEY GEORGE O	MAJ	0-1014051	0166	1
BAILEY GEORGE G	MAJ	0-0312904	0367	3
BAILEY GEORGE H	2LT	0-0888337	1044	2
BAILEY GEORGE W	CPT	0-0975231	0761	1
BAILEY GILBERT J	CW2	W-2108863	0552	1

NAME	GRADE	SVC NO	DATE RET MO YR	RET CODE
BAILEY GLENN A	1LT	0-2007221	0453	2
BAILEY GLENN G	LTC	0-1588416	0357	1
BAILEY GUY G	MAJ	0-0204815	0553	3
BAILEY HAROLD A	MAJ	0-0259459	0367	3
BAILEY HAROLD P	CW4	W-2001568	0862	3
BAILEY HARRY C	COL	0-0195866	0362	3
BAILEY HENRY C	MAJ	0-1823252	0562	1
BAILEY HERBERT	2LT	0-2262034	0752	1
BAILEY HEYWARD C	LTC	0-0201065	0763	3
BAILEY HORACE E	2LT	0-1062660	0345	2
BAILEY HUGH E	MAJ	0-0212500	0761	3
BAILEY JACK W	MAJ	0-1877070	0766	1
BAILEY JACKSON W	CPT	0-0432347	1145	2
BAILEY JAMES L	CW2	W-2208953	0663	1
BAILEY JAMES E	CPT	0-0461332	0345	2
BAILEY JAMES F	CW3	W-2148428	0960	1
BAILEY JAMES P	LTC	0-0228473	1160	3
BAILEY JAMES T	CPT	0-0204050	1048	1
BAILEY JAMES V	MAJ	0-0479440	1153	2
BAILEY JESSE L	LTC	0-0331039	0265	3
BAILEY JEWELL F	1LT	N-0763667	0546	1
BAILEY JOHN E	MAJ	0-0376495	1045	2
BAILEY JOHN F	CPT	0-1030114	0447	1
BAILEY JOHN W	LTC	0-0128510	0155	3
BAILEY JOHN W	1LT	0-4005401	0856	2
BAILEY JOSEPH W	MAJ	0-0297623	0944	2
BAILEY JR BENJAMIN P	LTC	0-0191355	0163	3
BAILEY JR CHARLES M	CW2	W-2147212	1162	1
BAILEY JR CLARENCE L	MAJ	0-1328870	0866	1
BAILEY JR FRANCIS M	CPT	0-0249782	1046	2
BAILEY JR FRED T	MAJ	0-0287483	0148	2
BAILEY JR HENRY V	LTC	0-1286587	0161	1
BAILEY JR ROBERT V	CPT	0-1313857	0647	1
BAILEY JR WILLIAM S	LTC	0-0136919	1058	3
BAILEY LEONARD E	LTC	0-1291378	0366	3
BAILEY LEONARD V	LTC	0-1308083	1162	1
BAILEY LESTER H	LTC	0-0200582	0460	3
BAILEY LEWIS G	CW4	W-2117906	0659	1
BAILEY LLOYD U	COL	0-0192922	0862	3
BAILEY MCDONALD	LTC	0-0479003	0157	1
BAILEY MORRIS H	WO1	W-2145710	0957	1
BAILEY MURIEL	CW3	V-0208653	0964	1
BAILEY NOEL R	CPT	0-0501285	0546	2
BAILEY ORVILLE R	CPT	0-0973840	0263	1
BAILEY OSCAR A	LTC	0-1291053	1165	1
BAILEY OTTO C	MAJ	0-4021546	0867	1
BAILEY PARK W	COL	0-0242216	0361	3
BAILEY PAUL H	1LT	0-1310043	1147	2
BAILEY PAUL S	CPT	0-0225052	0349	3
BAILEY PETER C	CW3	W-2147279	0263	1
BAILEY RALPH C	COL	0-0264984	0865	3
BAILEY ROBERT A	1LT	0-0547186	0346	2
BAILEY ROBERT C	LTC	0-0379958	0760	1
BAILEY ROBERT L	MAJ	0-2211010	0367	1
BAILEY ROBERT N	2LT	0-1105798	0945	2
BAILEY ROY W	COL	0-0102725	0152	3
BAILEY SAMUEL W	1LT	0-0419324	0146	2
BAILEY THERON P	CPT	0-0195894	0262	3
BAILEY THOMAS	CPT	0-2039441	0863	1
BAILEY VERNON E	MAJ	0-1948127	0561	1
BAILEY WILBERT L	LTC	0-0507707	1162	2
BAILEY WILLIAM A	LTC	0-1038803	0866	1
BAILEY WILLIAM F	MAJ	0-2208422	0666	1
BAILEY WILLIAM H	MAJ	0-0310052	0646	2
BAILEY WILLIAM J	LTC	0-1547873	0265	1
BAILEY WILLIAM N	COL	0-0264147	0763	3
BAILEY WILLIAM S	B G	0-0103209	1159	3
BAILEY WILSON L	LTC	0-1297301	1164	1
BAILIK JACOB B	LTC	0-0311719	0763	3
BAILIN MEYER M	LTC	0-4002690	0755	2
BAILLARGEON RAYMOND	CW2	W-2214515	0767	1
BAILLIE EDWARD P	MAJ	0-0242999	0863	3
BAILLIE MILTON C	MAJ	0-0277503	0550	1
BAILLOC YVONNE A	CPT	L-0408109	0348	2
BAILLY FLORENCE M	1LT	N-0700094	1145	1

NAME	GRADE	SVC NO	DATE RET MO YR	RET CODE
BAILLY RANDOLPH W	CPT	0-0548025	0447	1
BAILY LOUIS W	LTC	0-0248166	0164	3
BAIM CLARENCE K	WO1	W-2147346	0457	2
BAIN ARCHIE G	CW2	W-2150698	0258	2
BAIN CLARENCE W	LTC	0-1011103	0161	1
BAIN GEOFFREY C	COL	0-0313430	0262	1
BAIN GERALD E	LTC	0-1307354	0761	1
BAIN WESLEY T	MAJ	0-1302580	0557	1
BAINE CLYDE D	CPT	0-0259631	0566	3
BAINER FRANK A	CW2	W-2153238	0160	1
BAINES JESSE F	CW2	W-2146956	0461	1
BAINES THOMAS R	LTC	0-0397658	0261	1
BAINS ERSKINE	COL	0-0144535	0648	3
BAIR CLINTON E	CW3	W-2152426	0462	1
BAIR EUGENE B	MAJ	0-1288843	0159	1
BAIR GEORGE E	LTC	0-1575703	0361	1
BAIR LEIGHTON M	CW3	W-2112706	0858	1
BAIR LESTER W	CW4	W-2101450	0658	1
BAIRD ALBERT C	LTC	0-1551787	1061	1
BAIRD ALONZO E	LTC	0-0376930	1263	1
BAIRD ALTON T	LTC	0-1113088	0665	1
BAIRD BENJAMIN D	CPT	0-0517895	1054	1
BAIRD BERTRAM O	CPT	0-1922745	0867	1
BAIRD CHARLES T	2LT	0-1308414	0944	2
BAIRD EARL F	LTC	0-1012427	0256	1
BAIRD EUGENE F	LTC	0-0308988	1055	1
BAIRD FOSTER B	CW3	W-2141506	0761	1
BAIRD GILBERT B	LTC	0-0306815	0762	1
BAIRD HENRY	LTC	0-1795753	0463	1
BAIRD JAMES C	CPT	0-1582798	1145	2
BAIRD JAMES E	LTC	0-0148601	0755	3
BAIRD JOHN E	COL	0-0188461	0351	3
BAIRD JOHN R	LTC	0-0214545	0763	3
BAIRD JONATHAN L	LTC	0-1541287	0761	1
BAIRD JR CLETUS H	CW3	W-2149660	0763	1
BAIRD JR CUC T	LTC	0-0194257	0552	3
BAIRD JR HUGH	LTC	0-0325073	0267	3
BAIRD KENNETH W	LTC	0-0381407	0865	3
BAIRD PAUL E	LTC	0-0332112	0763	3
BAIRD RALPH W	LTC	0-0205652	1063	3
BAIRD RAYMOND O	CPT	0-0243067	0865	3
BAIRD RENNIE W	CPT	0-0249783	0166	3
BAIRD ROBERT C	2LT	0-1306960	1044	1
BAIRD RUTH B	CPT	N-0788601	1047	1
BAIRD WILLIAM D	LTC	0-0256856	0566	3
BAIRD WILLIAM F	CPT	0-1595360	0646	2
BAISDEN ARTHER M	MAJ	0-0352972	0861	1
BAISLEY THOMAS M	LTC	0-0439577	0366	1
BAIZ RAYMOND J	MAJ	0-1062661	0662	1
BAJ CASIMIR J	LTC	0-1795844	0565	1
BAJANDAS JOSE A	MAJ	0-1308291	1160	1
BAJORIN R J	MAJ	0-0517447	0454	1
BAJUK JOSEPH M	LTC	0-0919611	0664	1
BAKALIAN ARAM	LTC	0-1110914	0762	2
BAKASY ANDREW V	1LT	0-1286942	0956	1
BAKELESS JOHN F	COL	0-0126528	1054	3
BAKEN PALMER M	LTC	0-0336117	0254	3
BAKER ADOLPH	1LT	0-0373038	0146	1
BAKER ALBERT S	COL	0-0200830	0459	3
BAKER ALBERT U	MAJ	0-1557741	1160	1
BAKER ALFRED R	LTC	0-0335959	0663	3
BAKER ALONZO O	CPT	0-0307680	0648	1
BAKER ANDERSON L	CW2	W-2149485	0261	1
BAKER ANDREW O	LTC	0-0356281	0965	3
BAKER ANDREW Z	1LT	0-1037391	0646	1
BAKER ANSON R	CPT	0-1053904	0347	2
BAKER ARTHUR A	MAJ	0-0977424	1262	1
BAKER ARTHUR D	LTC	0-0506201	0854	1
BAKER ARTHUR R	LTC	0-0492217	0345	2
BAKER BERNARD	1LT	0-1306365	1045	2
BAKER BERTRAM	LTC	0-0204238	1054	1
BAKER CECIL B	MAJ	0-2040680	0357	1
BAKER CHARLES O	COL	0-0168615	0361	3
BAKER CHARLES H	CW2	W-2108408	0761	1
BAKER CHARLES J	MAJ	0-0171823	1052	3

NAME	GRADE	SVC NO	DATE RET MO YR	RET CODE
BAKER CHARLES L	LTC	0-1113553	0267	1
BAKER CHARLES M	CW2	W-2143861	1166	1
BAKER CLIFFORD V	CPT	0-1333407	0662	1
BAKER DALE R	CW3	W-2203524	1264	2
BAKER DARYL F	2LT	0-2262393		2
BAKER DONALD J	LTC	0-0436251	0357	1
BAKER DOUGLAS S	MAJ	0-1633008	1162	1
BAKER DUMOND H	CW3	W-2002789	0860	3
BAKER E E	1LT	0-1299836	1045	2
BAKER EDGAR A	LTC	0-1324803	0863	1
BAKER EDGAR F	CPT	0-1283644	0851	1
BAKER EDWARD D	LTC	0-1322616	1262	1
BAKER EDWARD F	LTC	0-1303448	0261	1
BAKER ELMER L	MAJ	0-0498137	0654	1
BAKER ERLINE	2LT	N-0735863	0645	1
BAKER ERNEST H	LTC	0-1183804	0263	1
BAKER ERNEST J	CPT	0-0226113	0956	3
BAKER EVELYN E	MAJ	N-0773098	1167	1
BAKER EZRA E	WO1	W-2118091	0255	1
BAKER FLAVEY F	LTC	0-1171879	1161	1
BAKER FLOROYCE W	MAJ	0-1573025	1145	2
BAKER FRANK E	1LT	0-0538590	0745	2
BAKER FRAYNE	B G	0-0134923	0851	3
BAKER FRED C	LTC	0-0315873	0266	3
BAKER FRED H	LTC	0-1177274	1063	1
BAKER FRED R	LTC	0-0298789	0759	1
BAKER FREDERICK	CW2	W-3200271	0366	1
BAKER GEORGE	LTC	0-1822851	0267	3
BAKER GEORGE A	LTC	0-0315515	0963	3
BAKER GEORGE A	MAJ	0-1040087	0158	1
BAKER GEORGE F	MAJ	0-0319461	0955	1
BAKER GEORGE H	MAJ	0-0265525	0845	1
BAKER GEORGE H	COL	0-0334654	0661	3
BAKER GEORGE V	COL	0-0189190	1054	2
BAKER GEORGE W	LTC	0-0468436	0366	3
BAKER GEORGE W	LTC	0-0900223	0563	3
BAKER GERTRUDE C	2LT	N-0794938	0946	1
BAKER GLEN	LTC	0-1043598	0961	1
BAKER HAROLD J	LTC	0-0281819	1065	3
BAKER HARRY A	1LT	0-0489170	1043	2
BAKER HARRY F	CPT	0-0490675	1049	1
BAKER HARRY S	MAJ	0-0470575	0660	1
BAKER HENRY R	CW3	W-2016492	1060	1
BAKER HOMER C	LTC	0-0502575	0464	3
BAKER HUGH C	LTC	0-1044446	0563	1
BAKER IRVIN H	LTC	0-1010422	0361	1
BAKER JACK C	COL	0-0286063	0865	3
BAKER JACK U	CW4	W-2146214	1160	1
BAKER JAMES A	COL	0-0361172	0766	3
BAKER JAMES E	CPT	0-1291561	0646	2
BAKER JAMES F	MAJ	0-0384506	0963	1
BAKER JAMES G	LTC	0-0209465	1159	1
BAKER JAMES H	LTC	0-0343241	0264	1
BAKER JAMES J	1LT	0-1301085	1045	2
BAKER JAMES L	COL	0-0302066	1055	1
BAKER JAMES L	CW3	W-2150548	0664	1
BAKER JAMES N	CW3	RW-2143048	1061	1
BAKER JAMES T	LTC	0-1015625	1162	1
BAKER JAMES W	1LT	0-0385746	1044	2
BAKER JAMES W	LTC	0-1049722	1065	3
BAKER JEAN L	MAJ	0-0981292	1063	1
BAKER JERRY	1LT	0-0491940	0847	1
BAKER JOHN B	COL	0-0194158	0657	3
BAKER JOHN F	CPT	0-2006552	0960	1
BAKER JOHN J	LTC	0-0369286	0862	1
BAKER JOHN M	LTC	0-0192392	0755	3
BAKER JOHN R	CW3	W-2152784	0465	1
BAKER JOHN W	1LT	0-1318853	1045	1
BAKER JOSEPH A	LTC	0-0401655	0860	1
BAKER JOSEPH D	LTC	0-0163885	0852	3
BAKER JOSEPH F	2LT	0-1329669	0748	2
BAKER JOSEPH H	CPT	0-0120302	1056	3
BAKER JOSEPH W	LTC	0-0386370	0460	1
BAKER JOSEPH W	CPT	0-1304660	1045	2
BAKER JR FURMAN J	1LT	0-0549410	0147	2

NAME	GRADE	SVC NO	DATE RET MO YR	RET CODE
BAKER JR HARRY L	LTC	0-0245785	0565	3
BAKER JR HARRY S	1LT	0-1286057	1044	2
BAKER JR JAMES F	CPT	0-4005457	1063	1
BAKER JR JOHN M	COL	0-0233229	0365	3
BAKER JR MAURICE H	2LT	0-1301923	0245	2
BAKER JR THEODORE R	1LT	0-2005948	0566	2
BAKER KENNETH D	1LT	0-1302754	0945	2
BAKER KENNETH R	LTC	0-0211337	1059	3
BAKER KIMBALL A	CPT	0-0509418	0145	2
BAKER LAWRENCE L	COL	0-0244958	0164	3
BAKER LEE H	CW3	W-2143601	0562	1
BAKER LEON H	LTC	0-0452213	0761	1
BAKER LYLE E	MAJ	0-1172739	0464	1
BAKER MARCUS	2LT	0-1583456	0944	2
BAKER MARCUS E	CW3	W-2146215	1060	1
BAKER MARION V	LTC	0-0405403	0865	1
BAKER MAURICE	CPT	0-0289658	0855	3
BAKER MCGAIL C	CW2	RW-2207005	0364	1
BAKER MELVIN O	LTC	0-1175931	0767	1
BAKER MENTER G	MAJ	0-0241914	0456	3
BAKER MILES R	2LT	0-1318855	0544	2
BAKER MORGAN W	CPT	0-0494836	1044	2
BAKER MOSES	1LT	0-0498939	0146	1
BAKER NED B	LTC	0-0551236	1266	1
BAKER NEIL C	LTC	0-1586416	1163	2
BAKER NELSON C	LTC	0-0453400	0561	1
BAKER NORMAN	CW3	W-2141185	0763	1
BAKER NORMAN J	COL	0-0250430	0167	3
BAKER ORLEN E	MAJ	0-0505097	0548	1
BAKER OTHA L	1LT	0-1169848	0750	1
BAKER PAUL D	LTC	0-1634360	0861	1
BAKER PAUL E	MAJ	0-1002861	0260	1
BAKER PAUL H	LTC	0-0171993	0852	1
BAKER PAUL J	1LT	0-1315997	0946	2
BAKER PERLEY O	LTC	0-0152213	0557	3
BAKER PHILIP I	COL	0-0284879	0554	3
BAKER PHILLIP E	1LT	0-1308907	0745	2
BAKER RALPH R	MAJ	0-0206536	0447	1
BAKER RALPH S	COL	0-0251400	1163	3
BAKER RALPH W	LTC	0-0156086	0953	3
BAKER RAYMOND A	MAJ	0-2018814	0163	1
BAKER RAYMOND E	CW3	W-2206121	1166	1
BAKER RAYMOND F	LTC	0-0406531	1054	1
BAKER RICHARD H	MAJ	0-0309032	0246	2
BAKER RILEY E	2LT	0-1336318	0446	2
BAKER ROBERT	CW3	W-2129192	0659	1
BAKER ROBERT B	MAJ	0-0215534	0257	1
BAKER ROBERT C	LTC	0-0354854	0647	2
BAKER ROBERT L	MAJ	0-1824469	0361	1
BAKER ROBERT W	LTC	0-0418930	1162	1
BAKER ROBERT W	LTC	0-1019683	1265	1
BAKER ROBERT W	LTC	0-1059738	1165	1
BAKER ROSCOE O	LTC	0-0146579	1053	3
BAKER ROSCOE G	MAJ	0-1332664	0764	1
BAKER ROY H	CPT	0-0156733	1054	3
BAKER RUFUS B	2LT	0-0386217	0442	2
BAKER RUSSELL G	B G	0-0291797	0165	3
BAKER RUSSELL L	LTC	0-0124056	0152	3
BAKER SEWARD J	CPT	0-1717517	0549	1
BAKER SILAS K	COL	0-0176754	0462	3
BAKER SR THOMAS A	COL	0-0277801	1160	3
BAKER STEWART J	LTC	0-0387163	0860	1
BAKER THELMA M	1LT	N-0735003	0346	1
BAKER THEODORE M	MAJ	0-0488939	1055	1
BAKER THOMAS H	CW3	W-2146501	0763	1
BAKER TRACY	LTC	0-0182592	0549	3
BAKER VAUGHN D	COL	0-0154781	0456	3
BAKER WARREN J	LTC	0-0259345	0467	3
BAKER WILLARD	MAJ	0-1583907	0361	1
BAKER WILLARD C	MAJ	0-1106566	0764	2
BAKER WILLIAM	LTC	0-0103272	0158	1
BAKER WILLIAM A	COL	0-0312444	0954	2
BAKER WILLIAM C	LTC	0-0338288	0761	1
BAKER WILLIAM D	MAJ	0-1635286	0348	2
BAKER WILLIAM H	LTC	0-1169008	0261	1

NAME	GRADE	SVC NO	DATE RET MO YR	RET CODE
BAKER WILLIAM C	COL	0-0370189	0461	1
BAKER WILLIAM W	2LT	0-0525343	1044	2
BAKER WINFRED H	CPT	0-1105576	0364	1
BAKER WINSTON A	CW2	W-2208854	0465	1
BAKER WOODROW W	CPT	0-1549349	0450	1
BAKER WRIGHT G	LTC	0-0144532	0551	3
BAKEY RUSSELL F	LTC	0-0391537	1163	1
BAKKE NORMAN W	LTC	0-0404269	1060	1
BAKKE WILLIS W	CW2	W-2208911	0466	1
BAKKEN WALTER	MAJ	0-0255760	0758	1
BAKKER JAMES R	CPT	0-1320224	0846	2
BAKKIE MILTON R	LTC	0-1637015	0459	3
BAKONIS JOSEPH A	1LT	0-1798827	0546	2
BALACANC SERGE	1LT	0-2027079	1148	1
BALANCA PAULY A	CPT	0-1896551	1059	1
BALASCLIDE MIGUEL A	LTC	0-0278006	0162	3
BALBARIN RUPERTO B	1LT	0-2030127	0864	1
BALBO MARY J	MAJ	N-0725768	0465	1
BALBONI HENRY F	CPT	0-1298169	1047	2
BALCAEN JR RAOUL G	LTC	0-1633462	1060	1
BALCAVAGE PAUL A	CPT	0-1920218	1163	1
BALCER JR FRANK A	MAJ	0-0191688	1049	3
BALCESZAK LIGE M	CPT	0-1289676	0148	1
BALCH ERNEST H	COL	0-0236974	1053	3
BALCH GLENN E	COL	0-0286138	0163	3
BALCHIUNAS BRUNO R	MAJ	0-1183659	0965	1
BALCIUS JOSEPH J	1LT	0-2006348	0847	1
BALCK LARS F O	LTC	0-0276383	0161	1
BALCOM E ROONEY	CPT	0-0547451	0566	1
BALCOMBE DEWEY W	MAJ	0-0978176	1263	1
BALDASSARI CARLO	LTC	0-0307418	0567	3
BALDES JOHN R	LTC	0-0301498	1053	1
BALDOCK CARROLL M	LTC	0-0260734	1064	3
BALDOCK RAWLEY M	LTC	0-0162645	0461	3
BALDRA FRED M	2LT	0-1549656	0743	2
BALDRIDGE JAMES D	LTC	0-0420440	0560	1
BALDRIDGE ROBERT L	LTC	0-0288503	1166	3
BALDWIN ARTHUR B	CPT	0-0364129	0560	3
BALDWIN BYRON C	LTC	0-1289536	0860	1
BALDWIN C B	LTC	0-1294771	0163	1
BALDWIN CLARENCE J	COL	0-0283694	1064	3
BALDWIN EARL E	LTC	0-1288678	0961	1
BALDWIN EDWARD T	LTC	0-0450701	0760	1
BALDWIN EDWIN A	MAJ	0-0196156	0956	3
BALDWIN ELBERT B	CPT	0-1999257	0156	1
BALDWIN ELLIOTT N	COL	0-0178861	0948	3
BALDWIN FRANCIS M	COL	0-0303012	1160	3
BALDWIN FRED W	LTC	0-0114033	0157	3
BALDWIN FREDERIC K	MAJ	0-1573721	0147	1
BALDWIN FREDERICK	LTC	0-0238997	0855	3
BALDWIN GEORGE M	MAJ	0-0304170	0145	2
BALDWIN GEORGE C	LTC	0-0450790	0261	1
BALDWIN IRVING R	LTC	0-1703248	0363	2
BALDWIN JAMES E	LTC	0-1636959	1060	1
BALDWIN JAMES L	CW2	W-2113426	0352	1
BALDWIN JOHN D C	LTC	0-0315833	1060	1
BALDWIN JOHN E	1LT	0-1016589	0545	2
BALDWIN JOHN H	CW3	W-2145289	0561	1
BALDWIN JOSEPH	CW2	W-2109523	1046	2
BALDWIN JR BUN	CPT	0-1173862	0846	1
BALDWIN JR WILLIAM B	CW3	W-2148085	0861	1
BALDWIN JR WILLIAM R	CPT	0-1553950	0447	1
BALDWIN LAURA E	MAJ	N-0727894	0465	1
BALDWIN MARIEN C L	LTC	0-0377344	0846	2
BALDWIN PAUL H	1LT	0-1541929	0345	2
BALDWIN RALPH R	1LT	0-1044447	1045	2
BALDWIN RICHARD D	LTC	0-0783491	0667	1
BALDWIN RICHARD S	1LT	0-1012267	1045	2
BALDWIN ROBERT B	1LT	0-0152994	0856	3
BALDWIN ROBERT C	MAJ	0-1062736	0663	1
BALDWIN RUSSELL I	LTC	0-0144569	0958	3
BALDWIN RUTH H	LTC	N-0742709	0862	1
BALDWIN THOMAS F	2LT	0-2000574	0446	2
BALDWIN VIRGIL H P	LTC	0-0266510	0261	3
BALDWIN WILLARD G	LTC	0-1184349	1066	1

NAME	GRADE	SVC NO	DATE RET MO YR	RET CODE
BALDY JOHN S	CW3	W-2145901	0761	1
BALE CLARENCE H	LTC	0-0310415	0557	1
BALE WILBER O	LTC	0-1580595	0961	1
BALENT LOUIS L	MAJ	0-0979802	1162	1
BALERVIEZ MICHAEL P	LTC	0-1555168	0466	1
BALES BARNETT L	LTC	0-1167306	1165	2
BALES CHARLES A	LTC	0-0262353	0866	3
BALES CHESTER L	2LT	0-0506068	0753	1
BALE EDWARD A	CPT	0-0489958	1046	1
BALFOUR CHARLES L	CPT	0-1552436	0647	2
BALFOUR JR CHARLES H	MAJ	0-0154632	0560	3
BALFOUR JR FRANK F	MAJ	0-0422360	0167	1
BALGROSKY STEVEN A	MAJ	0-1047868	0447	1
BALICKI HENRY S	MAJ	0-1306222	0961	1
BALIN ALBERT P	2LT	0-1797071	0944	2
BALINT RUTH L	2LT	N-0790906	0946	1
BALK VILAS D	MAJ	0-0674274	1263	1
BALKCOM MARSHALL W	LTC	0-1552632	0661	1
BALKEMA RAYMOND P	LTC	0-0336710	0760	3
BALKWELL LEROY G	1LT	0-1287985	1043	2
BALL ALLAN M	LTC	0-0266309	0454	3
BALL BENJAMIN W	CW2	W-2103860	0448	2
BALL BILLY E	CW3	W-2150380	0967	1
BALL CLAUDE	1LT	0-1821807	0460	1
BALL CLYDE S	CW2	W-2147937	1059	1
BALL DONALD R	CW3	W-2205873	0865	1
BALL EDGAR A	CW2	W-2151740	0659	1
BALL EUGENE N	MAJ	0-1946090	0363	1
BALL FRANKLIN P	MAJ	0-0489767	0646	2
BALL GEORGE A	1LT	0-0491689	0653	1
BALL GEORGE H	LTC	0-0397112	1159	1
BALL HARRY R	CPT	0-0247161	0453	3
BALL HOMER L	CW4	W-2117948	0756	1
BALL JAMES	1LT	0-2262147	0157	1
BALL JAMES A	LTC	0-1304486	0761	1
BALL JAMES D	LTC	0-0215015	0459	3
BALL JAMES S	1LT	0-0467837	0146	2
BALL JOHN F	CW3	W-2105529	0862	1
BALL JOHNNIE J	CW4	W-2118161	0959	1
BALL JR FRED S	MAJ	0-0366588	0458	2
BALL JR JAMES H	LTC	0-1101321	0463	1
BALL JR JOHN S	MAJ	0-1179772	0662	1
BALL LAURA M	LTC	N-0751278	1167	1
BALL LAWRENCE C	COL	0-0311247	0655	1
BALL LESLIE K	COL	0-0244506	0866	3
BALL MILLARD J	MAJ	0-0494079	0854	1
BALL OLIVER V	CPT	0-1290876	0546	2
BALL PRENTIS F	LTC	0-1533251	0661	1
BALL RICHARD D	MAJ	0-1308757	0865	1
BALL ROBERT D	MAJ	0-1182054	0761	1
BALL ROBERT P	LTC	0-0212035	1045	2
BALL ROBERT W	COL	0-0313066	0161	3
BALL SR MELVIN B	1LT	0-1103503	0662	1
BALL THEODORE B	CPT	0-1544183	0357	1
BALL THEODORE M	LTC	0-0226534	0557	1
BALL THOMAS L	LTC	0-1304326	1262	1
BALL URBAN H	1LT	0-0301309	0647	2
BALL WILLIAM L	COL	0-0290530	0962	3
BALL WILLIAM L	MAJ	0-0955142	0562	1
BALL WILLIAM N	MAJ	0-1116564	1059	1
BALL WOODROW W	MAJ	0-1017174	0161	1
BALLAGH JAMES C J	LTC	0-0184062	0858	3
BALLAM CYRIL J	CPT	0-0251643	1047	2
BALLANCE JAMES L	CW4	W-2148377	0562	1
BALLAND SAMUEL P	COL	0-0136831	0648	3
BALLANTINE JOHN J	CPT	0-0438926	0363	1
BALLANTINE LAURENCE	MAJ	0-0438851	0961	2
BALLARD CAROL B	CPT	0-0414551	0645	2
BALLARD CLAUDE H	LTC	0-0384648	0867	3
BALLARD CLAUDE T	LTC	0-0212519	0561	3
BALLARD FRANCIS J	CW4	W-2110187	0960	1
BALLARD FRED F	CW3	W-2149924	0263	1
BALLARD GEORGE W	LTC	0-0347590	0162	3
BALLARD HAZEL G	1LT	N-0762681	1048	1
BALLARD JR ROBERT M	LTC	0-0418263	1061	1
BALLARD LAWRENCE F	MAJ	0-0257666	1166	3
BALLARD LAWRENCE O	1LT	0-1120557	1265	2
BALLARD LEE F	CPT	0-1038257	0261	1
BALLARD LEVI	COL	0-0183165	1062	3
BALLARD LOCKETT F	1LT	0-1171881	1045	2
BALLARD MARY E	MAJ	N-0751226	0462	2
BALLARD MILTON E	LTC	0-1637614	0563	1
BALLARD RAYMOND H	CPT	0-0590642	0758	2
BALLARD RICHARD W	MAJ	0-0510626	0146	1
BALLARD RULON J	COL	0-0286877	0757	2
BALLARD ULYSSES G	CPT	0-1100434	0548	1
BALLARD WALTER	CPT	0-0486154	0647	1
BALLARD WILLIAM M	LTC	0-1184580	1262	1
BALLAS JOSEPH F	CW4	W-2145300	1166	1
BALLENGER JOHN F	MAJ	0-0111519	1048	3
BALLENGER RICHARD S	MAJ	0-0452208	0147	2
BALLENTINE K W	1LT	0-0381976	1044	2
BALLEW EVELYN M	CPT	L-0801316	0248	2
BALLEW JOE R	CPT	0-4031050	1065	1
BALLEW JOSEPH H	B G	0-0183226	0648	3
BALLEW THOMAS M	MAJ	0-1877756	0867	1
BALLF HAROLD P	COL	0-0236850	0662	3
BALLF HARRY A	COL	0-0236851	0662	3
BALLI ALFRED	CW2	W-3250189	1163	1
BALLIET CHARLES A	CW2	W-2142487	0255	1
BALLIET J PALMER	MAJ	0-2009724	0164	1
BALLIET KENNETH F	COL	0-0162424	1054	1
BALLIET THOMAS G	LTC	0-0393761	0760	1
BALLIK MICHAEL	CPT	0-0337566	0246	2
BALLINGER ERNE L	CPT	0-0261935	0850	2
BALLINGER LEWIS F	MAJ	0-1180109	1060	1
BALLINGER RODNEY P	MAJ	0-2012656	1062	1
BALLMEAT HAROLD F	LTC	0-0488624	0259	1
BALLMER EMERSON A	MAJ	0-0299804	1066	3
BALLON CHARLES	LTC	0-0518098	1045	1
BALLOU ALFRED F	LTC	0-0944664	1166	1
BALLOU CHARLES R	LTC	0-0354522	0546	2
BALLOU EDGAR W	1LT	0-1308454	0148	1
BALLOUGH WILMANS K	COL	0-0115223	0256	3
BALLYK PETER	CW4	W-2139609	0358	1
BALME CHARLES H	2LT	0-1547966	0146	2
BALMORES SILVINO R	1LT	0-1896905	1059	1
BALOGH STEPHEN F	LTC	0-0403873	0766	3
BALONA MARGARET B	CPT	N-0751252	0260	2
BALOUGH JOSEPH J	MAJ	0-0990740	1167	2
BALSAMO JOSEPH J	CPT	0-0499044	1045	2
BALSER JOSEPH F	MAJ	0-2200408	0565	1
BALSIS JOSEPH C	MAJ	0-0967831	0363	1
BALSLEY KENNETH R	LTC	0-1047017	0262	1
BALSLEY WILLIAM G	LTC	0-0295515	0767	3
BALSTERS ROBERT D	2LT	0-1178405	0444	2
BALTES GERARD W	WO1	W-2006595	0165	2
BALTES JAMES C	CW3	W-2147987	0460	1
BALTIER MICHAEL A	CPT	0-0969096	1161	1
BALTRUCKI EDMUND V	MAJ	0-0499176	0546	2
BALTZ EDWARD C	CW2	W-2205417	0861	1
BALTZ MARY C	MAJ	N-0779092	1063	1
BALTZ WILSON M	1LT	0-0482903	0944	2
BAMBERG EDMUND F	WO1	W-2131720	1046	2
BAMBERG GEORGE W	1LT	0-0226796	1063	3
BAMBERG ROBERT K	LTC	0-0421103	0663	1
BAMBERGER HENRY F	LTC	0-0235501	0554	3
BAMBERY JOHN T	CPT	0-1575705	0356	1
BAMBRICK EUGENE P	1LT	0-2006180	0746	1
BAME HARRY	CPT	0-0506823	0646	2
BAMFORD FREDERICK	1LT	0-2200076	0752	1
BAMFORD JR ARTHUR J	MAJ	0-0357932	0446	1
BAMFORD MALCOLM	MAJ	0-0982989	0867	1
BAMFORD WARREN H	LTC	0-0279793	1164	3
BANARES LINO R	1LT	0-2027040	1050	1
BANAS ANTHONY T	CPT	0-1176877	1161	2
BANASZAK SYLVESTER	CPT	0-0386536	0845	2
BANATAC BEN R	1LT	0-2027436	0450	1
BANCROFT HENRY K	COL	0-0217592	0563	3
BANCROFT JR LINCOLN	MAJ	0-1598309	0267	3
BANCROFT MARK W	MAJ	0-2052428	1165	3
BANCROFT RAYMOND F	MAJ	0-0295544	0663	3
BANDEL ALEXANDER	CPT	0-0975114	0260	1
BANDEL KENNETH W	LTC	0-0338545	0667	3
BANDIK MICHAEL G	1LT	0-1038600	0946	2
BANDURA ANTON J	CPT	0-0159789	0154	3
BANDY CLYDE R	MAJ	0-1641200	0365	1
BANDY JOE A	MAJ	0-2289766	1067	1
BANE ALFRED W	LTC	0-1045014	0563	1
BANE VERNON K	MAJ	0-1919144	0767	1
BANEN DAVID M	COL	0-0333667	0764	3
BANEY HAZEL S	2LT	N-0756050	0245	1
BANG ANTHON H	2LT	0-1305180	0445	2
BANG HANS	CW4	RW-2145234	0267	1
BANG JACOB	LTC	0-0249798	0464	3
BANGEMAN JOHN D	CPT	0-0366883	0545	2
BANGERT DONALD V	MAJ	0-1045015	1045	2
BANGHART ROBERT M	2LT	0-1303450	0844	2
BANGO HAROLD J	COL	0-0234751	0754	1
BANGS GERALD C	CW2	W-2211799	0964	1
BANGS HARRY E	LTC	0-0907882	0865	3
BANGSBOLL LEIF	LTC	0-1997738	0563	1
BANICK VINCENT W	LTC	0-0326777	0545	2
BANIGAN GEORGE E	LTC	0-1944389	0359	1
BANISTER ELLIS L	MAJ	0-2055281	0561	1
BANISTER JOHN R	COL	0-0159280	0848	3
BANISTER SAMUEL R	CPT	0-1922689	0462	1
BANISTER WELLMAN F	LTC	0-1541817	0361	1
BANK THEODORE P	COL	0-0142645	1057	3
BANKER JR WALTER F	LTC	0-1334081	0565	1
BANKERT CHARLES W	MAJ	0-0333153	0645	2
BANKES CLYDE W	LTC	0-1035191	0462	1
BANKHEAD MELVIN J	LTC	0-0269363	0845	2
BANKO JOHN P	MAJ	0-0332554	0961	1
BANKOWSKI JOHN R	CW3	W-2146779	1163	1
BANKS A B	LTC	0-0334589	0258	1
BANKS ALBERT C	CW3	W-2149192	0266	1
BANKS CHARLES F	CW2	W-2214367	0867	1
BANKS EARL R	CW4	W-2143098	0163	1
BANKS EDWIN B	COL	0-0422968	0967	1
BANKS ELMER F	MAJ	0-1550103	0757	1
BANKS ELWYN P	CW3	W-2152187	0164	2
BANKS EMIL	CW2	W-2205649	1163	1
BANKS FRED M	LTC	0-0209378	0453	3
BANKS GEORGE W	LTC	0-0381882	0360	1
BANKS GERALD F	LTC	0-0351207	0246	1
BANKS JAMES H	COL	0-0924622	0467	3
BANKS JAMES O	LTC	0-0286456	0564	3
BANKS JOHN F	MAJ	0-0259625	0166	3
BANKS JOHN H	CW2	W-2109490	0557	1
BANKS JOHN L	CPT	0-0504356	0857	1
BANKS KARL W	LTC	0-1544624	1060	1
BANKS OWEN G	WO1	W-2114369	0246	2
BANKS RAYMOND A	LTC	0-1285174	0563	1
BANKS ROBERT L	CPT	WN-2289417	0761	2
BANKS ROLAND W	MAJ	0-0283746	0946	2
BANKS ROY G	LTC	0-0223697	0461	3
BANKS SUMNER B	LTC	0-0274545	0565	3
BANKS WILLIAM E	MAJ	0-4031052	0867	1
BANKS WILLIAM F	2LT	0-1325733	0445	2
BANKS WILLIAM H	2LT	0-1013834	0245	2
BANKS WILLIAM M	CPT	0-0404215	0544	1
BANKS WILLIAM W	CPT	0-0435878	0647	2
BANKSTON BARNEY	MAJ	0-0450419	0654	1
BANKSTON BUFORD B	CW4	W-2119532	0355	1
BANKSTON H R	CPT	0-1184765	1157	1
BANNAN JAMES F	CW2	W-2203633	0660	1
BANNER FREDERICK	2LT	0-1166891	0445	2
BANNER JULIUS D	CW3	W-2148402	0561	1
BANNERMAN ROBERT H	CPT	0-1574381	1054	1
BANNICK JOHN H	COL	0-0326070	0363	1
BANNING FLOYD M	MAJ	0-2019698	0461	1
BANNING JOHN W	CPT	0-0511814	0548	1
BANNING ROBERT J	CPT	0-2036351	0457	1
BANNISTER JAMES	MAJ	0-1799469	0764	1
BANNISTER JR L G	2LT	0-1061051	0345	2
BANNON CORNELIUS	LTC	0-0492641	0954	2
BANNON EDWARD J	COL	0-1010019	0765	1
BANNON JAMES E	CPT	0-1313950	0947	2
BANOV ISADORE L	CPT	0-0259148	1065	3
BANOVITCH CARL A	2LT	0-1013613	0145	2
BANOWETZ LEONARD F	1LT	0-1168157	1045	2
BANOUER JACOB E	COL	0-0173984	0146	1
BANSBACK CHARLES L	CPT	0-0223861	0162	3
BANTA FRANK L	LTC	0-0510039	1054	1
BANTA NEIL W	1LT	0-0491547	1144	2
BANTHAM JR HARRY C	LTC	0-2200608	0966	1
BANTIN CARL	CW3	W-2150233	0565	1
BANTON HARTLEY L	1LT	0-0413646	1044	2
BANTON JAMES A	LTC	0-0239388	1064	3
BANZET FRANK B	LTC	0-1302542	0467	3
BAR EDWARD	LTC	0-1175031	1064	2
BARABE EMILE L	LTC	0-1014441	0962	1
BARABE JR CLIFFORD A	LTC	0-0327810	1044	1
BARAGER KENNETH M	COL	0-0112127	0753	1
BARALF GEORGE	WO1	W-2149100	1160	1
BARAN ADALBERT P	MAJ	0-0980562	0263	1
BARANOWSKI GEORGE J	LTC	0-0330189	0461	1
BARANOWSKI HENRY S	WO1	W-2151800	0158	1
BARANOWSKI RAYMOND C	LTC	0-1845382	0464	1
BARANSKI ROBERT J	CPT	0-4020503	1265	1
BARAT ERNEST	CW2	W-2147968	0556	1
BARAT LEON J	1LT	0-2025781	1149	1
BARATA VENTURA W	LTC	0-1169417	1060	1
BARATTA JOSEPH J	LTC	0-0366940	1059	1
BARATTINO EMANUEL J	LTC	0-1757418	0865	1
BARAY ROBERT R	CPT	0-0447973	0945	2
BARB PAUL F	MAJ	0-1685534	1163	1
BARBANO ALFRED J	CPT	0-0369562	0845	2
BARBATO ANGELO J	MAJ	0-0980306	0164	2
BARBATO NICHOLAS J	1LT	0-1302919	1144	2
BARBE HAROLD C	MAJ	0-1544391	0762	1
BARBEAU ARTHUR A	LTC	0-1284809	0665	1
BARBEE BILLIE M	LTC	0-1297478	0962	1
BARBEE ERNEST G	CW2	W-2146033	0659	1
BARBEE JAMES F	LTC	0-0283993	0766	3
BARBER ALVIN R	CW4	W-2144396	1263	1
BARBER BEN E	CPT	0-1114038	0252	1
BARBER CHARLES W	MAJ	0-1106571	1066	1
BARBER CLIFFORD A	CW2	W-3430284	1167	1
BARBER DARRELL C	CW4	W-2106099	0758	1
BARBER DEANE C	MAJ	0-0444073	1053	1
BARBER DELOSS H	COL	0-0121149	0446	1
BARBER EDGAR W	LTC	0-0446210	0246	2
BARBER GEORGE C	LTC	0-0498639	0860	1
BARBER GLENN F	CPT	0-1280145	0848	2
BARBER HAROLD L	MAJ	0-1927656	0765	1
BARBER HERBERT W	2LT	0-1545568	0844	2
BARBER JAMES E	COL	0-0373107	1262	1
BARBER JAMES M	CPT	0-0981016	0662	1
BARBER JOSEPH W	CPT	0-0482248	0246	2
BARBER JR HUGH T	1LT	0-0551551	0745	1
BARBER LEE H	WO1	W-2142947	0355	1
BARBER LEONARD O	LTC	0-1299178	0161	1
BARBER LOUIS E	LTC	0-0358820	0860	1
BARBER ROY M	CPT	0-2034070	0661	1
BARBER RUSSEL D	1LT	0-1172742	0645	2
BARBER RUTH J	MAJ	N-0779254	1263	1
BARBER WILLIAM A	2LT	0-0450420	0243	2
BARBER WILLIAM A	CPT	0-0477490	1046	1
BARBERA HAROLD J	LTC	0-2017491	0967	1
BARBERA HARRY J	MAJ	0-0395787	0350	1
BARBIE JOHN K	CPT	0-2051588	0757	2
BARBIER EVELYN	MAJ	N-0722370	0661	1
BARBOSA EUGENIO	MAJ	0-1315764	0761	1
BARBOSA GILBERTO	MAJ	0-0965370	1060	1
BARBOUR CHARLES H	MAJ	0-1011424	0857	1
BARBOUR DOUGLAS I	LTC	0-1636967	0162	1
BARBOUR EDMUND N	CPT	0-0530724	0346	2
BARBOUR GEORGE F	CPT	0-1688167	1045	2

NAME	GRADE	SVC NO	DATE RET MO YR	RET CODE
BARBOUR JOSEPH L	CPT	0-1899419	0660	1
BARBOUR JR LUTHER T	LTC	0-1290185	0161	1
BARBOUR LUTHER H	CPT	0-0208923	0353	3
BARBOUR MABEL M	MAJ	N-0741057	0560	2
BARBOUR NATHAN P	COL	0-0205474	0648	3
BARBOUR PAUL P	MAJ	0-1329552	0966	1
BARBOUR RICHARD H	CPT	0-1017460	0848	2
BARBOUR ROSCOE W	LTC	0-0255821	1062	3
BARBUTO ROCCO J	LTC	0-1016117	0366	1
BARCH RALPH P	LTC	0-1643137	1161	1
BARCHAN STANLEY S	COL	0-0183062	0356	3
BARCHARD FRANK V	COL	0-0273886	0165	3
BARCK WILLIAM F	COL	0-0132666	0648	3
BARCLAY CHARLES H	LTC	0-0251548	0461	2
BARCLAY DAVID W	MAJ	0-0255009	1044	1
BARCLAY ELTON W	MAJ	0-1995364	0756	1
BARCLAY HUGH	B G	0-0402854	0353	3
BARCLAY MORTON J	CW4	W-2147928	0667	1
BARCLAY ROBERT F	LTC	0-1308292	0664	1
BARCLAY WALTER P	LTC	0-0298545	0762	3
BARCLAY WALTER T	CPT	0-0385698	1145	2
BARCO NORMA L	LTC	N-0726022	1060	1
BARCUS WILLIAM D	MAJ	0-0236500	0557	3
BARD DONALD I	MAJ	0-0969251	0966	1
BARD ERNEST P	2LT	0-2266243	0453	2
BARD JAMES T	LTC	0-0506031	0367	3
BARD SOLT	CW2	W-2105042	1145	2
BARDEN ALBERT	COL	0-0148064	0449	3
BARDEN ARNOLD L	CW3	W-2144011	0761	2
BARDEN WILLIAM R	MAJ	0-0484814	1053	1
BARDES HERBERT C	1LT	0-0504853	0645	2
BARDES HOWARD G	LTC	0-0340730	0658	2
BARDES WILLIAM H	LTC	0-0286119	0663	3
BARDIN LEO H	LTC	0-0235382	0164	3
BARDIN OLLIE A	CPT	0-2046293	1050	1
BARDON BENNIE F	1LT	0-1822225	0544	2
BARDONNER WILMER J	LTC	0-0251927	0566	3
BARDWELL HARMON A	MAJ	0-0234807	0862	3
BARDWELL JOHN S	LTC	0-0454982	0961	2
BARDWELL MARJORIE S	2LT	N-0793865	0446	1
BARE ARNOLD W	WO1	W-2143829	0252	2
BARE HENRY M	LTC	0-0286201	0547	1
BARE JOHN W	CPT	0-0190669	0648	3
BARE LUCIEN K	2LT	0-1333919	0146	2
BAREFOOT EVERETTE A	CW3	W-2151806	0764	1
BAREFORD HAROLD S	MAJ	0-0132918	0454	3
BARENOSE ROBERT H	LTC	0-0452206	0465	1
BARERA ADLO	CW3	W-2150740	0865	1
BARFELL LLOYD M	CW2	W-2150043	0959	2
BARFIELD CEPHUS	CW3	W-2131999	0765	1
BARFIELD ELWOOD M	CW2	W-2144110	0559	1
BARFIELD JAMES J	COL	0-0128669	0946	1
BARFIELD LEONARD H	CPT	0-0980911	1158	1
BARFOOT DANIEL F	MAJ	0-0404154	0546	2
BARG RAYMOND J	LTC	0-1290186	0647	2
BARGAS JOSEPH E	COL	0-0207979	1162	3
BARGE JR ROBERT H	1LT	0-2020513	0352	1
BARGER ABRAHAM C	1LT	0-0438519	0645	2
BARGER ALPHONSO S	MAJ	0-0900276	0646	2
BARGER CHARLES M	MAJ	0-0998316	0265	1
BARGER JOSEPH M	LTC	0-0258096	0966	3
BARGERON RICHARD L	MAJ	0-0312613	0147	2
BARGERON WILLIAM R	CPT	0-1341319	0864	1
BARGLEBAUGH W M	2LT	0-1018813	0645	2
BARGMAN SAUL H	COL	0-0190119	0862	3
BARHAM CLIFFORD S	CPT	0-0974552	0161	2
BARHAM HUGH F	MAJ	0-0517247	0466	1
BARHAM JR THOMAS E	1LT	0-0322069	0745	2
BARHAM WILLIAM L	1LT	0-0550872	0346	2
BARIBAULT GEORGE J	CPT	0-0255078	0344	2
BARICUATRO ZACARIAS	CW3	W-2150539	0166	1
BARIL JOSEPH F	MAJ	0-0496906	0454	1
BARIL JOSEPH F R	LTC	0-1573030	0655	1
BARIL JOSEPH M R	MAJ	0-1011417	1058	1
BARINGER HENRY J	MAJ	0-1317469	0865	1

NAME	GRADE	SVC NO	DATE RET MO YR	RET CODE
BARINGER RAYMOND A	LTC	0-1167308	1062	1
BARISH LOUIS	LTC	0-0544536	0966	2
BARISKI ALEXANDER	CPT	0-1701445	0158	1
BARK FREDERICK	CPT	0-1081686	1055	1
BARK HURDMAN W	LTC	0-0259699	0759	3
BARKALOW JR F S	LTC	0-0329669	0546	2
BARKAS WILLIAM	CPT	0-0472614	0245	2
BARKEEN WALLACE I	LTC	0-0390987	1060	1
BARKELL JACK P	CPT	0-1339424	0254	2
BARKER ALBERT B	MAJ	0-1635887	0466	1
BARKER ALBERT R	LTC	0-1642008	0666	1
BARKER ALMAN J	MAJ	0-0943411	0264	1
BARKER ARTHUR W	LTC	0-2046881	1065	1
BARKER BERTRAM T	MAJ	0-1575808	0854	1
BARKER CARLETON J	COL	0-0251050	0159	3
BARKER CLARENCE D	COL	0-0224241	1147	2
BARKER CLARK A	COL	0-0281808	0457	1
BARKER DON A	LTC	0-0235173	0859	2
BARKER DOUGLAS P	MAJ	0-1924901	0965	1
BARKER ERNIE L	CW4	W-2115799	0964	1
BARKER GEORGE T	MAJ	0-0181411	1159	3
BARKER GERALD J	LTC	0-1642011	0964	1
BARKER HAROLD B	MAJ	0-1322302	0961	1
BARKER HAROLD E	COL	0-0336517	0963	3
BARKER HAROLD R	B G	0-0148571	0646	2
BARKER JAMES T	CW2	W-2141188	0861	1
BARKER JOSEPH W	LTC	0-0223627	0751	3
BARKER JR A C	CPT	0-0452790	0145	2
BARKER JR CHARLES F	1LT	0-1287646	0146	2
BARKER JR KENNETH A	CPT	0-0425643	1044	2
BARKER KARL M	MAJ	0-1634450	0357	1
BARKER LEAVITT R	MAJ	0-0128671	1052	3
BARKER LEE A	MAJ	0-0344633	0457	1
BARKER MARVIN T	CW2	RW-2142128	0364	1
BARKER MELVYN A	CPT	0-0291473	0748	2
BARKER NEAL M	LTC	0-0489623	0363	2
BARKER NORMAN C	2LT	0-1326450	1145	2
BARKER PRINCE P	LTC	0-0263945	0158	3
BARKER ROBERT C	LTC	0-0313639	1263	3
BARKER ROY F	LTC	0-0301328	0146	2
BARKER STANLEY G	LTC	0-0126236	0648	3
BARKER VALENTINE	MAJ	0-1283192	0361	1
BARKER WALTER B	LTC	0-1102757	0455	1
BARKER WAYNE G	LTC	0-1645198	1165	1
BARKER WILBURN N	CW3	W-2146183	0265	1
BARKER WILLIAM A	MAJ	0-0987646	0167	1
BARKER WILLIAM H	LTC	0-1284991	1060	1
BARKER WILLIAM L	LTC	0-0661693	1165	1
BARKER WILLIAM R	CW4	W-2124188	1154	1
BARKER WILLIAM S	2LT	0-1317870	1044	2
BARKER WITT H	LTC	0-1170275	0961	1
BARKLEY BRACKETT	CW3	W-2149748	0961	1
BARKLEY CLAUDE L	COL	0-0171738	0455	3
BARKLEY HILLARD R	MAJ	0-1324390	0960	1
BARKLEY JOHN	COL	0-0253806	1061	3
BARKLEY JOHN R	CPT	0-0523901	1048	1
BARKLEY JOHN W	CPT	0-1587100	0957	1
BARKLEY JOSEPH H	MAJ	0-1551160	1066	2
BARKLEY THOMAS J	MAJ	0-1687868	0546	2
BARKMAN HARRY F	CPT	0-0364809	0547	2
BARKMAN WILLIAM E	LTC	0-0189260	0158	3
BARKOVIC STEVE A	MAJ	0-1308753	0857	1
BARKSDALE DAN C	CW2	W-2152137	0557	1
BARKSDALE GARLAND R	MAJ	0-0498257	0346	1
BARKSDALE JELKS	CPT	0-0247239	1061	3
BARKSDALE SHULAR A	CW2	RW-2147404	1061	1
BARKUS SR ROBERT A	CW2	W-2212902	0867	1
BARLETTA MARY A	CPT	M-0000693	1047	1
BARLEY ARTHUR W	1LT	0-0310707	0445	2
BARLEY HAROLD S	CW4	W-2002277	0865	1
BARLEY JOHN J	CPT	0-1945752	0446	2
BARLOCK ROBERT J	LTC	0-0415111	0861	1
BARLOW EDWARD L	LTC	0-0189851	0349	3
BARLOW LEE A	CW2	W-2209280	0264	1
BARLOW PAUL J	CPT	0-0522742	0245	2

NAME	GRADE	SVC NO	DATE RET MO YR	RET CODE
BARLOW ROSCOE B	CW3	W-2145705	0361	1
BARLOW WILLIAM C	MAJ	0-0151473	0157	1
BARLOW WILLIAM H	CPT	0-1165813	0546	2
BARMORE CHARLES B	MAJ	0-0259126	1264	3
BARNA DANIEL	CW3	W-2143289	0660	1
BARNAK FRANK J	CW2	W-2154860	1263	1
BARNARD DONALD E	LTC	0-1017504	0265	1
BARNARD ERNEST J	CPT	0-0378861	0144	2
BARNARD EUGENE A	1LT	0-1552840	0545	2
BARNARD HARVIE	CPT	0-0223658	0246	2
BARNARD MAX C	LTC	0-1995211	0361	1
BARNARD MORTON J	LTC	0-0230305	0465	3
BARNARD PAUL C	MAJ	0-0163229	0354	3
BARNARD VIRGIL D	COL	0-0171875	1151	3
BARNARD WILLIAM H	LTC	0-0238243	0865	3
BARNARD WILLIAM R	1LT	0-1322670	1045	1
BARNEBURY HARVEY R	MAJ	0-0395198	0547	2
BARNES ADEN L	MAJ	0-1949050	1162	1
BARNES ADRIAN D	MAJ	0-0215074	0563	3
BARNES ALBERT F	LTC	0-0115788	0555	3
BARNES ALEXANDER	LTC	0-0242275	1159	3
BARNES ALLAN C	MAJ	0-1687184	0145	1
BARNES ARTHUR L	MAJ	0-1932359	0667	1
BARNES ASA	COL	0-0299595	0464	3
BARNES BENJAMIN F	MAJ	0-0506920	0645	2
BARNES BRUCE E	CPT	0-1945894	0157	1
BARNES BURRELL S	MAJ	0-0426655	0954	1
BARNES CARLTON J	MAJ	0-1326969	0457	1
BARNES CECIL J	LTC	0-0311384	0263	3
BARNES CHARLES E	CW4	W-2142435	0359	1
BARNES CLARK N	MAJ	0-1308455	0147	1
BARNES CYRIL A	LTC	0-0476213	0656	1
BARNES DEBBY E	CW2	W-2206630	0264	1
BARNES DELBERT P	MAJ	0-0331122	0245	2
BARNES DOUGLAS	LTC	0-1555660	0764	3
BARNES EDDIE W	2LT	0-1018588	0445	1
BARNES EDWARD M	MAJ	0-0273395	1065	1
BARNES EDWIN A	COL	0-0204360	0154	3
BARNES FERRIS F	LTC	0-0306303	0661	1
BARNES FLOYD H	MAJ	0-1168546	0964	1
BARNES FRANK J	1LT	0-1321279	1051	1
BARNES GEORGE G	LTC	0-0531820	0767	1
BARNES HAROLD F	LTC	0-0519261	0666	1
BARNES HAROLD J	1LT	0-1041960	0 5	2
BARNES HENRY C	CPT	0-0495962	1053	1
BARNES HERBERT W	CW2	W-2209861	1164	1
BARNES HUBERT D	COL	0-0267294	1062	3
BARNES ISOBEL C	MAJ	N-0737654	1162	1
BARNES JAMES A	LTC	0-0264766	0360	3
BARNES JAMES A	CPT	0-1701594	0547	2
BARNES JAMES A	CW3	W-2142179	0559	1
BARNES JAMES E	CW3	W-2144646	0364	1
BARNES JESSE E	CW3	W-2152923	1159	1
BARNES JESSE F	MAJ	0-1322848	1262	2
BARNES JR ALLEN F	CPT	0-1103505	0546	2
BARNES JR CHARLES N	LTC	0-0225232	0462	3
BARNES JR DAVID G	LTC	0-0450716	0958	1
BARNES JR HAL P	CPT	0-1312076	0847	1
BARNES JR JOHN T	MAJ	0-2096536	0565	1
BARNES JR WILLIAM J	MAJ	0-0370438	0344	2
BARNES LAWRENCE A	LTC	0-1012125	0866	1
BARNES LESTER H	LTC	0-0197228	0855	3
BARNES LYLE F	MAJ	0-0942947	0662	1
BARNES MARGARET L	2LT	N-0767377	0145	1
BARNES MATTHEW J	CPT	0-1171042	0954	2
BARNES MYRON C	LTC	0-0283592	0763	3
BARNES NELSON N	CPT	0-0395868	0345	2
BARNES NORMAN P	COL	0-0378019	0460	1
BARNES OTIS A	LTC	0-0190647	0644	2
BARNES PATRICK H	COL	0-0193656	0249	3
BARNES PAUL N	MAJ	0-0273118	0860	3
BARNES QUINTON E	MAJ	0-0491954	0661	1
BARNES RAYMOND C	MAJ	0-0177349	0345	2
BARNES REUBEN R	MAJ	0-2262472	0364	1
BARNES RICHARD A	2LT	0-1551791	0943	2

NAME	GRADE	SVC NO	DATE RET MO YR	RET CODE
BARNES RICHARD W	LTC	0-0270362	1262	3
BARNES ROBERT A	LTC	0-1534667	0565	1
BARNES ROBERT H	1LT	0-1113559	0944	1
BARNES ROBERT I	CPT	0-1578135	0546	2
BARNES ROBERT T	LTC	0-0362196	1163	1
BARNES ROBERT V	MAJ	0-0239449	0164	3
BARNES ROY H	LTC	0-1030116	0355	1
BARNES ROY M	MAJ	0-0257021	0765	3
BARNES RUSSELL M	MAJ	0-0385710	0146	2
BARNES SAMUEL E	MAJ	0-1893553	0767	2
BARNES SETH S	COL	0-0347803	0167	3
BARNES TERRY A	CPT	0-0496252	0546	1
BARNES TRAVIS P	1LT	0-0969278	0558	1
BARNES VERNON H	LTC	0-0244626	1060	3
BARNES VIRGIL K	MAJ	0-4010692	0867	1
BARNES WALTER L	LTC	0-0425612	0464	1
BARNES WALTER W	2LT	0-1318988	1145	2
BARNES WEBSTER R	2LT	0-2023627	0257	1
BARNES WILLARD D	MAJ	0-0466934	0854	1
BARNES WILLIAM B	2LT	0-0467400	0845	2
BARNES WILLIAM E	LTC	0-0256617	1051	1
BARNES WILLIAM E	MAJ	0-0486368	0947	1
BARNES WILLIAM H	COL	0-0340879	1262	1
BARNES WILLIAM L	CW3	W-2152078	1263	1
BARNES WILLIAM N	CPT	0-0315024	0643	2
BARNES WILLIAM S	COL	0-0371056	0364	1
BARNETSON ALFREDA B	2LT	N-0722076	0744	1
BARNETT ABE	1LT	0-1014099	0848	1
BARNETT BILLIE A	CW3	W-2124532	0656	1
BARNETT CHARLES M	CPT	0-1292457	0847	2
BARNETT CHARLEY R	CW3	W-2144090	1159	1
BARNETT CLARENCE C	LTC	0-0080554	0767	1
BARNETT DAN C	CPT	0-0528933	0248	2
BARNETT DOLPH	LTC	0-0182938	0522	3
BARNETT DOYLE F	MAJ	0-1685594	0864	1
BARNETT EARCELL R	CW3	W-2148365	0664	1
BARNETT EMMETT K	LTC	0-0450024	0361	1
BARNETT FRANK F	CW4	W-2114631	0659	1
BARNETT FRANKLIN	1LT	0-0321650	0745	2
BARNETT GENE H	MAJ	0-1306345	0361	1
BARNETT GORDON P	MAJ	0-0500204	0246	2
BARNETT HERBERT	LTC	0-1291289	0164	1
BARNETT HERBERT N	LTC	0-0152039	0648	3
BARNETT HERMAN H	1LT	0-1001510	0851	1
BARNETT IRVING H	CPT	0-1692197	0145	2
BARNETT JAMES C	COL	0-0185919	0156	3
BARNETT JAMES E	MAJ	0-1014736	0463	1
BARNETT JAMES G	LTC	0-0337013	0560	1
BARNETT JAMES S	CW2	W-2213117	0967	1
BARNETT JAMES W	MAJ	0-0452382	1159	1
BARNETT JESSIE F	CW3	W-2147389	0163	1
BARNETT JR JOSEPH S	COL	0-0159281	0952	3
BARNETT JR PAUL G	1LT	0-0555668	1046	2
BARNETT LOUIS L	CPT	0-1686901	1043	2
BARNETT MARION B	LTC	0-0195547	0663	3
BARNETT MAX K	LTC	0-1636883	0367	3
BARNETT MORTON L	1LT	0-0485506	0245	2
BARNETT OVAL C	CPT	0-0497810	0448	1
BARNETT PAUL W	1LT	0-1306196	0157	1
BARNETT RALPH T	CW2	W-2150038	0561	1
BARNETT RAYMOND R	MAJ	0-1878198	0965	1
BARNETT RICHARD B	1LT	0-1889790	0554	2
BARNETT RICHARD G	CW3	W-2142217	1062	1
BARNETT ROY L	CPT	0-1018744	1047	1
BARNETT RUSSELL F	LTC	0-1321280	0866	1
BARNETT WILLIAM E	CPT	0-0353093	1045	2
BARNETT WILLIAM K	LTC	0-0154976	0955	3
BARNETT WILLIAM R	CPT	0-0483404	0652	1
BARNEY ALFRED F	LTC	0-1293887	0164	1
BARNEY CHAUNCEY E	CPT	0-1314869	0846	2
BARNEY FRANK L	1LT	0-0126532	0252	3
BARNEY JAMES G	MAJ	0-0109939	0629	1
BARNEY JOHN A	LTC	0-0435004	0764	1
BARNEY JOSEPH	MAJ	0-0496970	0347	2
BARNEY WILLIAM V	MAJ	0-0200562	1055	3

NAME	GRADE	SVC NO	DATE RET MO YR	RET CODE
BARNHARDT GEORGE E	1LT	O-0190621	0655	3
BARNHART CHARLES F	LTC	O-1300746	0865	1
BARNHART DESTER A	CW4	W-2127574	0863	2
BARNHART JOSEPH F	MAJ	O-1541848	0446	2
BARNHART ROBERT A	CW2	W-2149894	0862	1
BARNHILL JAMES E	LTC	O-0370500	0361	1
BARNHILL PAUL P	LTC	O-1281140	1164	1
BARNHOUSE WILLIAM C	LTC	O-0926719	1264	1
BARNI ROY	2LT	O-1054471	1144	2
BARNO MICHAEL F	CW3	W-2144865	0659	1
BARNS BENJAMIN E	1LT	O-0280338	0943	1
BARNSBEE ALEXANDER	LTC	O-1636572	0763	1
BARNSLEY DAN R	COL	O-0233148	0756	3
BARNUM EDWARD F	LTC	O-0493576	0856	2
BARNUM FRANK L	LTC	O-0225443	0146	1
BARNWELL DANIEL J	LTC	O-1040090	0866	1
BARNWELL FRANK H	COL	O-0150052	1045	2
BARNWELL HOWARD R	MAJ	O-0545747	1046	2
BARNWELL JR JAMES R	LTC	O-0281996	0245	2
BARNY FREDERICK	2LT	O-0175298	0960	3
BARON CHARLES	COL	O-0383316	1067	3
BARON CHARLOTTE	2LT	N-0737754	0944	1
BARON HARRY	W01	W-2145310	0266	2
BARONCES DORCAS A	CPT	N-0783934	0863	1
BARONE AMICO J	MAJ	O-0224161	0359	3
BARONE FRANCIS A	LTC	O-0249679	0262	3
BARONE NICHOLAS L	LTC	O-0196645	0247	2
BAROTT KENNETH J	MAJ	O-0967119	0264	1
BAROWSKI EDWARD W	CW4	W-2103865	0659	1
BARR ALBERT R	CW4	W-2004927	0965	1
BARR ALEXANDER	COL	O-0135027	0961	3
BARR ANDREW	COL	O-0176447	0661	3
BARR ARTHUR W	LTC	O-1301241	0562	1
BARR BASIL C	LTC	O-0138839	1154	3
BARR BOWMAN F	LTC	O-1641850	0666	1
BARR CLIFFORD J	1LT	O-1822300	1045	1
BARR CLIFFORD N	CW2	W-2152413	1060	1
BARR CLINAL E	2LT	O-0401439	0543	1
BARR FRANCIS E	COL	O-0302606	0457	1
BARR FRANK E	COL	O-0165123	1051	3
BARR FREDERICK	MAJ	O-1169853	0661	1
BARR HARRY G	LTC	O-0251900	1164	3
BARR HENRY F	MAJ	O-0248069	1145	2
BARR HILDA M	1LT	N-0737208	0646	2
BARR HOWARD M	CW3	W-2148403	0960	1
BARR JAMES L	CW2	W-2151645	0164	1
BARR JOHN B	LTC	O-0475840	1057	1
BARR JOHN T	LTC	O-0483823	0458	3
BARR JOSEPH L	MAJ	O-0497801	1047	1
BARR JR CHARLES I	MAJ	O-0424536	0462	1
BARR MARSHALL D	COL	O-0218553	1059	1
BARR OLIVER F	LTC	O-1184894	0657	1
BARR RAYMOND C	CW3	W-2145042	0964	1
BARR RICHARD A	1LT	O-0537841	0945	2
BARR ROBERT C	CPT	O-0393760	0945	1
BARR ROBERT N	COL	O-0263452	1062	3
BARR WALTER J	MAJ	O-1169854	0665	1
BARR WARREN D	LTC	O-1795754	0862	1
BARR WILLARD D	COL	O-0292238	0465	3
BARR WILLIAM F	MAJ	O-0315822	0164	3
BARR WINSTON H	CPT	O-1586421	0852	2
BARRACLOUGH H H	CPT	O-0124225	0745	2
BARRACLOUGH JOHN F	W01	W-2128255	0745	2
BARRANCO ANTHONY J	CPT	O-0484068	0446	2
BARRANTE HENRY A	LTC	O-1294956	0962	1
BARRATT LEROY T	CPT	O-0346362	0663	3
BARRELL HARVEY W	COL	O-0373193	0764	1
BARREN RALPH E	LTC	O-1106574	0465	1
BARREN ROBERT J	MAJ	O-1031053	0166	1
BARRENTINE JAMES R	CPT	O-1167733	1165	1
BARRERA LAL R	CW3	W-2148587	0963	1
BARRERA MARK	1LT	O-1896809	0250	1
BARREST PETER A	2LT	O-1798637	0351	2
BARRET JOHN T	LTC	O-1554504	1163	3
BARRETT BERNARD	1LT	O-0567205	1044	2

NAME	GRADE	SVC NO	DATE RET MO YR	RET CODE
BARRETT CLARENCE L	CPT	O-0497688	1047	1
BARRETT CLINTON D	LTC	O-0175545	0760	3
BARRETT DANIEL W	CPT	O-0330874	0648	3
BARRETT DEXTER R	CPT	O-0382643	0647	1
BARRETT DONALD F	LTC	O-0349076	0267	3
BARRETT EARL H	CW3	W-2146651	1262	1
BARRETT FRED D	COL	O-0250431	1166	3
BARRETT FRED L	CPT	O-0223881	1164	3
BARRETT FREDERICK	LTC	O-1822660	0164	1
BARRETT GEORGE F	CPT	O-1177725	0349	2
BARRETT HELEN R	2LT	N-0795823	0146	1
BARRETT HIRAM E	1LT	O-0339097	0544	2
BARRETT HOWARD F	1LT	O-2048841	1045	2
BARRETT JAMES	1LT	O-1596538	0360	1
BARRETT JAMES A	MAJ	O-0794685	0464	1
BARRETT JAMES C	MAJ	O-1575715	0355	2
BARRETT JAMES F	LTC	O-1032191	0763	1
BARRETT JOHN A	CW3	W-2001855	0866	3
BARRETT JOSEPH W	LTC	O-1055212	0365	1
BARRETT JULIAN R	MAJ	O-0259720	1054	3
BARRETT KENNETH W	MAJ	O-2021470	1065	1
BARRETT ORION D	CW3	W-2205835	0866	1
BARRETT PATRICK J	LTC	O-0928398	0165	1
BARRETT PETER T	MAJ	O-2032082	0564	1
BARRETT RALPH W S	COL	O-0248233	0162	3
BARRETT ROGER M	1LT	O-0264185	1046	1
BARRETT ROLAND C	COL	O-0219212	0556	3
BARRETT THELMA A	MAJ	N-0744373	1162	1
BARRETT WILLIAM G	B G	O-0182445	0758	3
BARRETT WILLIAM T	COL	O-0195602	1060	3
BARRETTE CECIL E	COL	O-0922214	0265	3
BARRETTO ANITA T	2LT	N-0735389	0145	1
BARRIAGE ARCHIE R	1LT	O-0452303	1144	2
BARRICK CHARLES L	LTC	O-1113561	0366	1
BARRICK DALE L	LTC	O-0267013	0462	1
BARRICK MILFORD D	LTC	O-0334717	1059	1
BARRIE CHARLES F	LTC	O-1845016	0764	1
BARRIE FERDINAND	LTC	O-1576909	0361	1
BARRIER GEORGE L	LTC	O-0292319	0467	3
BARRIGA JULIO	1LT	O-1896799	0150	1
BARRINGTON PAUL S	MAJ	O-1030328	0964	1
BARRINGTON ROBERT B	CW2	W-2146303	0158	1
BARRINGTON VAN M	CW3	W-2142748	1060	1
BARRIOS-SANCHEZ FRAN	CW2	W-2205377	0661	1
BARRON CLARENCE B	COL	O-0220602	0564	3
BARRON EDWARD C	CPT	O-1647765	0361	1
BARRON ELBERT M	COL	O-0217479	0646	1
BARRON ERIC S	COL	O-0241526	0457	3
BARRON FLOYD T	LTC	O-1175976	1162	1
BARRON GAINES J	COL	O-0282554	0560	3
BARRON ROBERT E	COL	O-0242028	0162	3
BARRON ROUBLE C	MAJ	O-0283201	0948	1
BARRON STEPHEN F	COL	O-0111953	0648	3
BARRON WILLIAM F	LTC	O-0959259	0467	1
BARRONGNARCISE C	CPT	O-0306420	0345	2
BARRONIAN RICHARD	CPT	O-1168547	0446	2
BARRONTON JOHN C	CPT	O-1331254	0751	2
BARRONTON LESTER C	LTC	O-0487088	0746	1
BARROS RUSSELL D	COL	O-0298071	0460	1
BARROW CLAUDE A	2LT	O-1180415	1145	2
BARROW DOUGLAS A	CPT	O-1289858	0758	1
BARROW HERBERT A	COL	O-0222042	0861	3
BARROW JR EMMETT W	LTC	O-1052252	1164	1
BARROW VIRGINIA	2LT	N-0726487	0144	1
BARROW 2ND E R	LTC	O-0155024	1045	2
BARROWS BARNEY	MAJ	O-0290960	1047	3
BARROWS BRADFORD S	MAJ	O-1017764	0761	2
BARROWS GEORGE A	MAJ	O-1583674	0159	1
BARROWS HARRY	LTC	O-0225125	0149	3
BARROWS MAX W	LTC	O-0170103	0160	3
BARROWS PAUL	MAJ	O-1821533	0264	1
BARROWS RAYMOND R	LTC	O-0378496	0165	3
BARROWS RICHARD P	LTC	O-0265063	0965	3
BARROWS RICHARD S	CPT	O-2262155	1060	1
BARRY ALBERT C	LTC	O-0353700	0566	1

NAME	GRADE	SVC NO	DATE RET MO YR	RET CODE
BARRY AMBROSE C	CW2	W-2153174	0961	1
BARRY BERNARD V	LTC	O-1101325	0762	1
BARRY CALVIN E	B G	O-0271325	0158	3
BARRY CHARLES R	MAJ	O-0991317	0366	1
BARRY DANIEL T	CPT	O-1635921	0759	2
BARRY DONALD J	CPT	O-1302758	0164	1
BARRY EDGAR L	CPT	O-2262355	1060	1
BARRY EDWIN J	COL	O-0115260	0955	2
BARRY ELMO A	MAJ	O-0132849	1049	3
BARRY FRANK E	CPT	O-0493614	0254	1
BARRY HAROLD A	LTC	O-1046348	0967	1
BARRY HENRY F	LTC	O-0242603	0757	3
BARRY JEROME S	2LT	O-2265902	0953	2
BARRY JOHN F	CW3	W-2149058	0367	1
BARRY JOHN W	COL	O-0201480	0656	3
BARRY JR JOHN J	1LT	O-1317472	0547	2
BARRY LYMAN F	MAJ	O-0171207	0461	3
BARRY ROBERT E	LTC	O-1594017	0763	1
BARRY THOMAS A	LTC	O-0414954	0763	1
BARRY THOMAS F	LTC	O-0384324	0767	3
BARRY WILLIAM F	CPT	O-1053907	0447	1
BARSALOU ELIZABETH	MAJ	N-0761187	0963	1
BARSANTI GABRIEL W	CPT	O-0317002	1046	1
BARSI SAMUEL A	CW2	W-2146182	0559	1
BARSTIS ALBERT	LTC	O-0372051	0557	1
BARSTOW THOMAS I	COL	O-0262920	1057	3
BARSZCZ EDWARD J	LTC	O-1265354	0757	1
BARTA EDWARD J	COL	O-0238183	1059	3
BARTA EDWARD J	LTC	O-0397016	0763	1
BARTE GEORGE R	1LT	O-0262354	0651	1
BARTECCHI HENRY A	MAJ	O-2032091	0865	1
BARTELL DON J	LTC	O-0233037	0364	1
BARTELL JACK	MAJ	O-0359127	0646	2
BARTELLONI LOUIS	COL	O-0199859	0147	1
BARTELS HARRY H	CPT	O-0395745	0945	2
BARTELS JOHN C	COL	O-0274769	1165	3
BARTELT PAUL E	CW2	W-2208850	1164	1
BARTELT WILLIAM F	LTC	O-0183884	0647	2
BARTGIS JR JAMES E	COL	O-0330807	1165	3
BARTH EDWARD J	CPT	O-1019520	0158	1
BARTH GEORGE H	LTC	O-1945919	0763	1
BARTH JR ARTHUR W	1LT	O-1643837	0445	2
BARTH LEE O	COL	O-0286199	1160	1
BARTH TODD M	MAJ	O-1999366	1162	1
BARTHA NICHOLSA P	CPT	O-1689791	1044	2
BARTHEL ELMER W	1LT	O-2008412	1045	2
BARTHELME GENE A	MAJ	O-1192116	0556	1
BARTHELOW ADAM J	MAJ	O-0380515	0663	2
BARTHLOW CHARLES W	CPT	O-0420189	0645	2
BARTHOLME FRANCES M	MAJ	N-0800054	0765	1
BARTHOLOMAY EUGENE C	MAJ	O-2263064	0364	1
BARTHOLOMEW ALBERT S	LTC	O-1335728	0964	1
BARTHOLOMEW CARROLL	MAJ	O-2204034	0766	1
BARTHOLOMEW CECIL E	LTC	O-0349918	1059	2
BARTHOLOMEW CLAIR J	LTC	O-0254741	0763	3
BARTHOLOMEW EDWARD A	MAJ	O-0509895	0450	1
BARTHOLOMEW HERBERT	LTC	O-0246422	0763	3
BARTHOLOMEW LEE	CW3	W-2205057	1266	1
BARTHOLOMEW O T	1LT	O-1590982	0654	1
BARTHOLOMEW RALPH J	CW2	W-2147472	0963	1
BARTHOLOMEW ROBERT F	1LT	O-0967948	1052	1
BARTHOLOMEW WILLIAM	MAJ	O-1876327	0364	1
BARTHOLOW HOWARD R	CW4	W-2118094	0864	3
BARTICK PHILIP R	CW2	W-2146004	0360	1
BARTIZEK ALBERT	CPT	O-1059997	0544	1
BARTKUS EDWARD P	MAJ	O-0407759	0445	2
BARTLE FRANCIS C	COL	O-0370087	0764	1
BARTLES CLAUDE L	MAJ	O-0959441	1164	1
BARTLESON RICHARD J	CPT	O-1886736	0863	1
BARTLETT ASA	LTC	O-0298763	0758	3
BARTLETT BERNICE R	CPT	N-0761051	1147	1
BARTLETT CHARLES E	LTC	O-0245935	1066	3
BARTLETT CHARLES H	LTC	O-1036038	1163	1
BARTLETT CHARLES O	CW2	W-2144244	0360	1
BARTLETT CLIFFORD O	MAJ	O-4005876	1067	1

NAME	GRADE	SVC NO	DATE RET MO YR	RET CODE
BARTLETT DAVID E	1LT	O-1017375	1145	2
BARTLETT DOUGLAS P	MAJ	O-1322197	0559	2
BARTLETT FLOYD H	CW4	W-2113703	0960	3
BARTLETT FRANK	MAJ	O-2206415	1066	1
BARTLETT GENE R	CPT	O-1644956	0857	1
BARTLETT GEORGE H	LTC	O-1038025	1162	2
BARTLETT HENRY H	LTC	O-0300799	1061	3
BARTLETT HENRY L	COL	O-0264155	1147	2
BARTLETT ISABEL E	CW3	V-0400970	0265	1
BARTLETT JOHN E	COL	O-0402391	1061	1
BARTLETT JOHN L	COL	O-0159285	0252	3
BARTLETT JOSEPH B	2LT	O-0909864	0244	1
BARTLETT JR EBEN B	COL	O-0366695	0563	1
BARTLETT JR GEORGE G	COL	O-1045336	0562	1
BARTLETT JR LEE F	1LT	O-1002760	0845	2
BARTLETT LELAND D	LTC	O-0213258	0447	2
BARTLETT MERLIN O	CPT	O-1178408	0858	1
BARTLETT ROBERT L	LTC	O-1643867	0865	3
BARTLETT WALTER W	COL	O-0329845	0254	2
BARTLETT WILLIAM J	MAJ	O-1170641	0461	1
BARTLETT WILLIAM P	MAJ	O-0285258	1164	3
BARTLETT WOODROW J	LTC	O-1640275	0765	1
BARTLEY ANTHONY P	CW3	W-2142218	0559	1
BARTLEY CHARLES P	CPT	O-0390199	1145	2
BARTLEY CLAUD E	MAJ	O-2019979	1159	1
BARTLEY CORNELIUS	MAJ	O-1885675	1066	1
BARTLEY EDWARD W	COL	O-0178249	0162	3
BARTLEY JOSEPH F	1LT	O-1297640	1044	2
BARTLEY JOSEPH L	LTC	O-1582638	0463	1
BARTLEY JR JOHN A	CPT	O-0424342	0745	2
BARTLEY SAMUEL H	CPT	O-1951530	0262	1
BARTLEY THOMAS A	MAJ	O-0425537	1054	2
BARTLEY WALTER L	LTC	O-1994562	0163	1
BARTLEY WILLIAM E	CPT	O-0428221	0546	2
BARTLEY WILLIAM S	COL	O-0135235	1054	3
BARTMAN KENNETH E	CPT	O-0306655	1043	2
BARTNESS ADOLPH C	LTC	O-0272609	0155	1
BARTNIK HANS K	CW2	W-2142445	0455	2
BARTO EDWARD E	LTC	O-0401516	0662	1
BARTO JACK	CPT	O-0979373	1160	1
BARTO JASPER	LTC	O-1000010	0759	1
BARTOLEC SYLVESTE	1LT	O-0506208	0453	1
BARTOLINI ALFREDO	CW3	W-2207513	0267	1
BARTON BYRON	LTC	O-0479032	1156	1
BARTON CECIL L	CPT	O-0203329	1059	3
BARTON CHARLES W	LTC	O-0314051	1162	3
BARTON CORNELIUS	LTC	O-1543136	0661	1
BARTON GEOFFREY A	LTC	O-1047434	0762	1
BARTON GEORGE A	CW3	W-2150170	0463	1
BARTON GEORGE H	LTC	O-0313874	1064	3
BARTON HOWARD A	1LT	O-0312394	1045	2
BARTON JAMES E	CPT	O-0360157	0345	2
BARTON JEAN C	CPT	L-1010340	0964	1
BARTON JERRY W	MAJ	O-2055222	0361	1
BARTON JESS S	CPT	O-1289371	0645	1
BARTON JOHN V	LTC	O-0414960	0961	1
BARTON JR HARRY M	LTC	O-1035517	0365	1
BARTON JR ROBERT T	COL	O-0171824	1051	3
BARTON LAURENCE G	LTC	O-0123401	1055	3
BARTON LELAND H	LTC	O-0274532	0957	3
BARTON LOYD K	CW4	W-2103869	0860	2
BARTON RANDALL W	COL	O-0295686	0659	1
BARTON ROGER A	LTC	O-0369874	0164	3
BARTON THEODORE A	1LT	O-1844619	1145	2
BARTON WARREN D	1LT	O-0394030	0644	2
BARTON WILLIAM C	LTC	O-1946656	0667	1
BARTONI DONALD A	LTC	O-1284811	0264	1
BARTOSIK THOMAS J	MAJ	O-1120737	1063	1
BARTOSZWICZ H C	1LT	O-1304998	0645	2
BARTRAM JR WILLIAM J	CPT	O-1726775	1047	2
BARTSCH EDWARD J	W01	W-2108409	1048	1
BARTSCH FRANCIS P	CPT	O-0362122	0346	2
BARTZ AMOS D	CPT	O-1171451	0747	1
BARVIAN FRANCES A	1LT	N-0756557	0347	1
BARWICK CHARLES L	CW3	W-2151636	0261	1

ARMY OF THE UNITED STATES RETIRED LIST

NAME	GRADE	SVC NO	DATE RET MO YR	RET CODE
BARWICK LEON S	LTC	0-0472128	C954	1
BARWICK LIOF R	MAJ	C-1936694	C567	1
BASARA STELLA M	MAJ	N-0722240	0162	1
BASCO DAMASC K	1LT	0-0369415	C550	1
BASCO JOSEPH D	1LT	0-0890543	0159	1
BASFORC ALVIN T	LTC	0-0205867	1063	3
BASH JR JOHN	CW3	W-2153102	C862	1
BASHAM RAY	LTC	0-1633056	0166	3
BASHAM TRUMAN H	MAJ	0-0887666	C161	1
BASHAW WILLIAM N	LTC	0-0259490	1064	3
BASHISTA FRIEDA	1LT	N-0720323	1045	1
BASHORE KENNETH M	CW3	W-2148899	0765	1
BASILIERE DONALD E	CW2	W-2148703	0762	1
BASILICIO ATANACIO	2LT	0-0890496	115C	1
BASINSKI DANIEL H	CPT	0-0533824	0246	2
BASKETT EDGAR S	MAJ	0-C130010	1049	3
BASKETT JOHN L	LTC	0-0181769	0862	3
BASKETT JOHN W	1LT	0-0548297	0546	2
BASKETT MELVIN C	MAJ	C-1686599	1263	1
BASKIN LOUIS J	CPT	0-1690041	C844	1
BASKIN THOMAS C	MAJ	0-1946658	1265	2
BASKINS DONALD E	LTC	0-0454322	1062	1
BASLER BESSYE S	MAJ	N-C764087	1263	1
BASNER WILLARD J	MAJ	C-1018520	0863	1
BASNETT ESTEL W	CW4	W-2110555	1157	1
BASOM MERLE O	LTC	0-1296977	1060	1
BASON WILLIAM A	MAJ	0-0405398	C262	1
BASORA DEFILLO J	LTC	0-0251503	0763	3
BASORE BERNIECE M	MAJ	N-0735581	1166	3
BASS ANDREW J	LTC	0-0367227	0761	1
BASS BENNETT P	CW3	W-2151365	1060	1
BASS ELMER D	CW2	W-2141183	0756	1
BASS HENRY C	1LT	C-1635548	1045	2
BASS JAMES W	COL	C-C214852	0760	3
BASS LEROY P	LTC	0-1325544	C667	1
BASS MERVIN A	1LT	0-0557074	0447	2
BASS NOAH W	CPT	0-1107275	0954	1
BASS SILAS W	LTC	0-0288526	0565	1
BASS WILLIAM A	MAJ	0-157651C	C761	1
BASS WILLIAM E	CPT	0-1596577	C658	2
BASSAKIOFS GEORGE J	CW2	W-3430047	0166	1
BASSE HUGH	MAJ	C-1797420	0756	1
BASSEN EDWARD J	LTC	0-C439519	0346	2
BASSETT CHARLES F	LTC	0-0197726	0157	3
BASSETT DAVID M	MAJ	C-0263028	C546	1
BASSETT EUGENE W	LTC	0-0344114	C565	3
BASSETT FRANK F	CW2	W-2000107	0656	3
BASSETT HERBERT	MAJ	0-1173865	0257	1
BASSETT JOHN L O	2LT	0-C511081	0344	2
BASSETT JR JAMES E	CPT	0-0439943	1262	1
BASSETT JR RALPH F	MAJ	0-155914C	1163	1
BASSETT JR WILLIAM H	LTC	0-0111232	0157	3
BASSETT SANFORD S	CW4	W-2102634	0955	1
BASSETTI HENRY	LTC	0-1030006	1060	1
BASSFORD GEORGE E	1LT	0-0209236	0659	3
BASSHAM OLLIS	CPT	C-1795846	0849	1
BASSHAM WILLIAM L	MAJ	C-2039388	1163	1
BASSICH JR CYRIL	LTC	0-1183015	C267	1
BASSO JAMES	MAJ	0-1579365	C164	1
BAST JR ALBERT J	LTC	0-1897723	1067	1
BASTABLE CHARLES W	CPT	C-05034C1	0945	2
BASTENDORF WILLIAM L	1LT	C-0539892	0146	2
BASTEYNZ ACHILLE	MAJ	C-1913510	1047	1
BASTIAN KATHRYN V	MAJ	N-0742772	0767	2
BASTIAN THOMAS C	MAJ	C-0525609	0746	2
BASTIDA JOHN C	CPT	0-1108468	0246	2
BASTILLE ALBERT J	1LT	0-1324653	C746	1
BASTIN HARRY D	MAJ	C-1589046	0257	1
BASTINGS MARCEL S	CW3	W-21C9987	1060	1
BASTNAGEL GEORGE F	CPT	0-0375138	1049	1
BASTNAGEL RAYMOND	CPT	0-0887668	0756	1
BASYE CARL B	MAJ	0-0279658	0560	3
BASYE JOHN S	MAJ	C-1329673	0561	1
BATALIA DONALD C	CPT	0-1844529	0861	1
BATCHELDER JAMES H	LTC	0-0376155	C961	1

NAME	GRADE	SVC NO	DATE RET MO YR	RET CODE
BATCHELDER ROLAND C	COL	0-0199934	0655	1
BATCHELDER JOHN J	LTC	0-026414C	0555	3
BATCHELDER JR W P	LTC	C-02C1411	0461	3
BATCHELDER ROBERT E	CPT	0-0332596	0942	2
BATCHELDER VIRGIL R	MAJ	C-1546317	0746	2
BATDORF RICHARD O	LTC	0-0288931	0466	3
BATE ERNEST I	COL	C-0217711	0748	2
BATEMAN DICK S	WO1	W-2122941	1050	1
BATEMAN HAROLD C	LTC	0-0212544	0462	3
BATEMAN MARIE C	2LT	N-0724363	0945	1
BATEMAN WILLIAM C	LTC	0-0265874	0346	2
BATEMAN WILLIAM T	LTC	0-0503497	0157	1
BATES A E GRIFFI	LTC	0-0301926	0367	3
BATES ALFRED F	MAJ	0-154482C	0760	1
BATES ARTHUR B	LTC	0-0174555	0157	3
BATES CHARLES F	CW2	W-2150344	0861	2
BATES CHARLES R	1LT	0-0382048	0556	1
BATES CHARLIE M	MAJ	0-0485896	0250	1
BATES CLIFTON E	CPT	0-0240509	0341	2
BATES CREED F	LTC	0-0163616	0254	3
BATES DUANE H	2LT	0-1335C32	C746	2
BATES EDWARD R	MAJ	C-1797592	0161	1
BATES EUGENE	CPT	0-1574312	1050	2
BATES GEORGE H	1LT	0-1301414	0944	2
BATES HAROLD A	1LT	0-1544378	1146	2
BATES HAROLD L	MAJ	0-11C8470	0463	1
BATES JAMES L	MAJ	C-1015257	0658	1
BATES JAMES R	LTC	0-1637066	0964	1
BATES JESSE O	MAJ	C-1294774	1059	1
BATES JOHN F	1LT	0-229623C	0150	3
BATES JOHN L	COL	0-0331347	0658	1
BATES JOSEPH D	MAJ	0-125282C	0960	1
BATES JR CHARLES	CW2	W-335C352	0567	1
BATES JR JOSEPH D	LTC	0-0225409	0963	3
BATES JR ROBERT H	MAJ	0-203745C	0763	1
BATES KENNETH E	LTC	0-1533007	0457	1
BATES LYNN R	LTC	0-1635551	0761	1
BATES OSCAR L	LTC	0-0255586	1165	3
BATES PERRY A	CW2	W-2143653	1053	1
BATES RERVIS M	LTC	0-131319C	0967	1
BATES RALPH L	MAJ	0-0482381	1066	3
BATES RALPH R	CPT	0-0339783	1045	2
BATES RAYMOND B	MAJ	0-0223691	0357	3
BATES REXFORD B	CPT	0-1798547	0547	2
BATES ROBERT F	COL	0-0243892	0646	2
BATES ROBERT S	LTC	0-0332865	C660	2
BATES TEO R	LTC	0-1591584	0163	1
BATES THOMAS E	LTC	0-C18CC61	1050	3
BATES WILLIAM L	COL	0-0220855	0555	3
BATH PAUL L	CPT	0-158102C	0645	2
BATHEN JOHN P	1LT	0-4062599	0758	2
BATHORN JAMES J	CW2	W-2143183	1C53	2
BATOK STANISLAW	MAJ	C-2288C98	0667	1
BATOON CORNELIO	2LT	0-2032113	0150	1
BATOT MILTON J	CPT	0-0220776	0963	3
BATSFORD THEODORE H	MAJ	0-104475C	0261	1
BATSON CARROLL C	LTC	0-0208243	0252	3
BATSON CLYDE M	CPT	0-0489296	1045	2
BATSON FRANK E	COL	0-0240254	1063	3
BATSON HOWARD E	LTC	0-0264360	0566	3
BATSON WILLIAM K	1LT	0-1014519	0645	2
BATT LOUIS	CPT	0-1045664	0751	2
BATT ROBERT	MAJ	C-1312276	0665	1
BATTAFARANO W F	1LT	0-1583155	0245	2
BATTAGLIA ANGELO J	MAJ	C-019C281	1060	3
BATTELL FRANCES J	1LT	N-0786645	0353	2
BATTEN DOUGLASS H	CPT	0-0475929	1045	2
BATTEN JOHN L	1LT	0-1294068	0944	2
BATTENSLAG FRED G	LTC	0-0223073	0862	1
BATTERSBY MARK W	LTC	0-0372657	0146	2
BATTERSON JOHN E	LTC	0-0475841	0862	1
BATTERTON ROBERT V	COL	0-0309691	0661	3
BATTESTIN CHARLIE E	2LT	0-1010635	0745	2
BATTICE CARL C	COL	0-0296452	0765	3
BATTISSON JOSEPH T	1LT	0-1994533	0350	1

NAME	GRADE	SVC NO	DATE RET MO YR	RET CODE
BATTISTA WILLIAM L	MAJ	0-0414485	C960	2
BATTLE FOSTER L	CPT	0-1035193	C146	2
BATTLE HILTON L	MAJ	0-0347313	0361	1
BATTLE JR DORSEY	CW2	W-2206517	0563	1
BATTLE WILLIAM P	MAJ	C-0198656	0153	3
BATTLES FREDOL	LTC	0-0265859	1056	3
BATTON HOMER W	CW2	W-2142318	C755	1
BATTS VANCE C	MAJ	0-4043455	0367	1
BATTY ARTHUR R	LTC	0-0205017	1059	1
BATZ HERBERT	MAJ	0-1102144	C653	1
BAUCHLEY JR MICHAEL	CPT	0-1332459	C655	1
BAUCK LELAND	1LT	0-0285460	1144	2
BAUCUM RALPH L	LTC	0-1316723	C263	1
BAUDE WALTER A	COL	0-01704C1	C347	2
BAUDOIN JOSEPH C	LTC	0-0412028	0761	1
BAUDOUINE TEX G	LTC	0-0259635	C560	1
BAUER ALBERT H	LTC	0-C308627	1165	3
BAUER CHARLES B	CPT	C-0402874	C945	2
BAUER DEWITT C	COL	0-0266550	1058	3
BAUER FRANK J	MAJ	C-0386160	0457	1
BAUER HARRY C	CPT	0-1914014	1134	1
BAUER JR WILLIAM	CPT	0-0201279	1054	3
BAUER KENNETH N	1LT	C-1544858	C145	2
BAUER MARY N	MAJ	N-0796114	C466	1
BAUER MILTON E	CW3	W-2145230	C661	1
BAUER PAUL O	CW4	W-2103872	1057	1
BAUER RALPH C	COL	0-0182605	0956	3
BAUER ROSCOE W	COL	C-C198181	0860	3
BAUER WALTER R	CW2	W-2142386	0157	1
BAUER WILLIAM C	COL	0-0324816	C766	3
BAUER WILLIAM M	CPT	0-0136942	C749	1
BAUER WILLIAM R	LTC	0-0327483	C559	1
BAUERS WILLIAM	LTC	0-0544468	C465	2
BAUCH DANIEL P	COL	0-0175641	0855	1
BAUGH JOHN W	MAJ	C-0334030	0861	1
BAUGH JOSEPH R	MAJ	C-0345559	0563	1
BAUGH JR JAMES F R	MAJ	0-0262932	1167	3
BAUGH JR WILFORD A	MAJ	C-133934C	C465	1
BAUGH LESTER I	MAJ	C-5701482	0867	1
BAUGH ROBERT H	MAJ	C-0238263	0266	3
BAUGHER THOMAS J	LTC	0-1019046	0758	1
BAUGHMAN JIM T	LTC	0-0337677	0366	3
BAUGHMAN NED F	MAJ	C-1647869	0361	1
BAUGHMAN ROBERT W	CPT	0-0515602	0347	2
BAUGHN EARLE H	MAJ	C-1794896	0461	1
BAUCHN HERMAN C	COL	0-0225418	C457	3
BAUGHN JR MILTON H	LTC	0-0271229	0964	1
BAUM ALDEN H	LTC	0-0235163	0255	3
BAUM CLYDE C	LTC	0-0451072	0457	1
BAUM EDWIN K	COL	0-0170067	C360	3
BAUM HOWARD A	MAJ	C-0322133	C763	3
BAUM JOHN P	COL	0-0195343	0262	3
BAUM JOHN W	1LT	0-1299668	1045	2
BAUM LEE E	MAJ	C-0310688	1066	3
BAUM LYNN T	2LT	N-0764133	1045	1
BAUM ROBERT	LTC	0-0330835	1060	2
BAUM VICTOR	CPT	0-0438750	1145	2
BAUM WILLIAM W	2LT	0-2017637	0851	2
BAUMAN AVON	LTC	0-0354515	1159	1
BAUMAN CHARLES H	COL	0-0146400	0756	3
BAUMAN DARWIN T	LTC	C-0302084	C746	2
BAUMAN ERNEST N	B G	0-0262926	1056	3
BAUMAN JR ALBERT F	LTC	0-1169013	1061	1
BAUMAN OTTO F	WO1	W-2111366	0451	1
BAUMAN ROBERT O	MAJ	C-1331591	0762	1
BAUMAN WALTER J	CPT	0-2208509	1164	1
BAUMANN BERNARD J	MAJ	C-1959190	0460	1
BAUMANN CARL A	MAJ	C-0144481	1054	3
BAUMANN CHARLES H	CPT	0-1821231	C545	2
BAUMANN FRANZ	CPT	0-1702874	0146	2
BAUMANN HUBERT F	MAJ	C-1579367	C658	1
BAUMANN SR CHARLES J	LTC	0-0155100	0356	3
BAUMBACH ERNEST J	MAJ	C-1844898	0464	3
BAUMEISTER FRED S	CPT	0-1180806	0663	1
BAUMEISTER JR T A	1LT	0-0466469	1045	2

NAME	GRADE	SVC NO	DATE RET MO YR	RET CODE
BAUMGARDNER ARTHUR	LTC	0-204C681	0860	1
BAUMGARDNER HOMER T	MAJ	0-1330774	0563	1
BAUMGARDNER JOSEPH H	CPT	0-128746C	0563	1
BAUMGARDNER KENNETH	LTC	0-1316001	0866	1
BAUMGARDNER PEARLY L	CPT	0-0330824	0442	2
BAUMGART HANS	CW4	W-2108673	0359	1
BAUMGART SYLVESTER	LTC	0-0434574	1166	2
BAUMGARTEN GEORGE G	MAJ	0-0949191	0562	1
BAUMGARTEN JOHN H	LTC	0-0358063	1165	3
BAUMGARTNER DORST F	MAJ	0-0259491	0867	3
BAUMGARTNER GEORGE R	1LT	0-1057675	C146	1
BAUMGARTNER IRA P	CPT	0-0142902	0957	3
BAUMGARTNER RUPERT P	CPT	0-0248344	C145	2
BAUMGARTNER WALTER J	LTC	0-0277241	0861	3
BAUMOEHL ABRAHAM	CPT	0-0494712	0246	2
BAUSCHARD HAROLD C	MAJ	0-09C8977	0345	2
BAUSER MARGARET L	2LT	N-0797465	0947	1
BAUTISTA FRANK B	1LT	0-1896383	0952	1
BAUTISTA GUILLERMO	1LT	0-2030659	0464	1
BAVAGNOLI WILLIAM A	1LT	0-1926961	0554	2
BAVARIA ERNEST A	MAJ	0-0967C12	1163	1
BAVER JAMES M	1LT	0-0363567	1045	2
BAVOUSET JAMES S	1LT	0-1031465	0245	2
BAXLEY ALBERT N	CW2	W-2211401	0964	2
BAXTER ARTHUR	LTC	0-2289512	0767	1
BAXTER AUGUST C	LTC	C-1285881	0867	1
BAXTER CHARLES F	COL	0-0341602	0767	1
BAXTER COY L	MAJ	0-1014331	0158	1
BAXTER DONALD E	MAJ	0-1844542	1164	1
BAXTER EARL E	MAJ	0-0972587	0265	1
BAXTER EVERETT L	MAJ	C-1553C25	0466	1
BAXTER GEORGE B	LTC	0-0136576	1049	3
BAXTER GEORGE H	LTC	0-0393219	1060	1
BAXTER JACK	MAJ	0-1183467	1262	1
BAXTER JAMES A	MAJ	C-0731794	0363	1
BAXTER JOHN G	COL	0-0307495	1160	1
BAXTER JOSEPH	LTC	0-0360C11	086C	1
BAXTER JR CHARLES E	COL	C-C251097	1067	3
BAXTER LEVON C	MAJ	0-1184583	0461	1
BAXTER OWEN I	MAJ	C-1306223	1058	1
BAXTER RAY L	MAJ	0-0549792	0762	1
BAXTER RAYFIELD W	CPT	0-0319605	0245	2
BAXTER ROBERT E	CPT	0-1317473	0446	1
BAXTER ROSCOE	COL	0-0362837	1C63	1
BAXTER ROY J	1LT	0-2035915	0245	2
BAXTER STUART A	COL	0-0166064	C546	2
BAXTER THOMAS R	CPT	0-2023551	0346	1
BAXTER WILLIAM C	COL	0-0173675	0162	3
BAY EDWARD S	WO1	W-2146073	0254	1
BAYER ANTHONY P	COL	0-0359741	0966	1
BAYER EDWARD	CPT	0-1329787	C358	1
BAYER FREDERICK	LTC	0-0364858	0147	2
BAYER HENRY J	MAJ	0-0978989	1061	1
BAYER MICHAEL	CPT	0-0450222	0357	1
BAYER ROBERT L	CW3	W-2145711	0165	1
BAYERS ARTHUR J	CPT	0-0181374	C455	3
BAYLES DONALD O	2LT	0-1583526	0245	2
BAYLES WAYNE W	MAJ	C-129549C	0462	1
BAYLESS BILLY B	LTC	0-1168165	C863	1
BAYLESS REX S	LTC	0-0386809	0662	1
BAYLESS WILLIAM B	1LT	0-1030544	0946	2
BAYLEY ERNEST R	MAJ	0-0132156	0555	3
BAYLEY RUSSELL J	CPT	0-0467435	0647	1
BAYLIFF BERT P	1LT	0-0958274	0653	1
BAYLISS JAMES C	LTC	0-0407385	C863	1
BAYLISS ORVAL H	LTC	0-1641243	0862	1
BAYLISS WILLIAM R	COL	0-0343394	C765	2
BAYLOR JACK	MAJ	0-103664C	0946	2
BAYMON PORTER L	CPT	0-168831C	0862	1
BAYMOR MICHAEL	COL	0-037485C	0561	1
BAYNARD LUDLOW B	MAJ	0-0282252	0867	3
BAYNE JR JAMES W	CW4	W-2122309	0759	1
BAYNE ROBERT C	CW2	W-2208451	0667	1
BAYNE&JONES STANHOPE	B G	0-0170753	1049	3
BAYNHAM ROBERT	1LT	0-0280555	1144	2

NAME	GRADE	SVC NO	DATE RET MO YR	RET CODE
BAYSEK ALFRED J	MAJ	0-1825366	0461	1
BAYSINGER HOWARD F	MAJ	0-0303584	0747	2
BAYTEL JR LOUIS	1LT	0-1182507	0146	2
BAZARD WALTER S	MAJ	0-0142564	1153	3
BAZEMORE JAMES M	LTC	0-1689877	0648	2
BAZILUS JR JUSTIN W	2LT	0-1302104	0244	2
BAZYLOO JR STANLEY	MAJ	0-1329310	0461	1
BAZZANO JOHN J	CPT	0-0369225	1045	2
BEABER CHRIS	LTC	0-1552007	0166	1
BEACH ARVIC K	CW2	W-2207536	0564	1
BEACH BENJAMIN S	COL	0-0299915	0260	3
BEACH BURNETT B	LTC	0-1290364	1057	1
BEACH EARL E	LTC	0-1169015	1163	1
BEACH EUGENE H	CPT	0-0462550	1049	2
BEACH FRANCES C	CPT	N-0767281	0547	1
BEACH GEORGE A	LTC	0-0196429	0662	3
BEACH GEORGE I	WO1	W-2109623	0165	3
BEACH GILBERT A	MAJ	0-1116045	0262	2
BEACH GORDON L	COL	0-0250449	0858	1
BEACH IRVING F	LTC	0-0261169	0559	3
BEACH NORMAN A	LTC	0-0250360	0265	3
BEACH PERRY A	CPT	0-0178105	0955	3
BEACH RALPH P	CW2	W-2123043	0450	1
BEACH ROY E	1LT	0-0347349	0444	2
BEACH WILBER E	COL	0-0266051	1156	3
BEACH WILLIAM J	MAJ	0-1324821	0863	1
BEACH WILLIAM M	2LT	0-1321603	0344	2
BEACHBOARD THOMAS W	MAJ	0-0953639	0464	1
BEACHLEY FRANK A	1LT	0-0310829	0346	2
BEACHNAW DONALD C	CW3	W-2205964	0266	1
BEACOM JR JAMES E	MAJ	0-1284083	0546	2
BEAGLE HARRY	MAJ	0-1303451	0357	1
BEAGLE HARVEY L	WO1	W-2102639	0544	2
BEAHM ANDREW M	LTC	0-0428987	0763	3
BEAHM ARTHUR N	CW2	W-2114817	0150	1
BEAHM JR CARROLL R	MAJ	0-0495583	1062	1
BEAKLEY FELTON T	2LT	0-2055853	0745	2
BEAKLEY JULIAN	COL	0-0286390	0464	3
BEAL FREDERICK	CPT	0-0909828	0946	2
BEAL GEORGE C	CW3	W-2152030	0263	1
BEAL GORDON L	LTC	0-0383630	0361	1
BEAL PETER L	CPT	0-0440259	1045	2
BEALAND EDWIN P	CPT	0-1119783	0161	1
BEALE ALTON A	MAJ	0-0450697	0248	2
BEALE HARRY C	1LT	0-2021211	0752	1
BEALE JESSE M	LTC	0-1576915	1263	1
BEALE JOHN A	CPT	0-0384039	1045	2
BEALE LEO A	LTC	0-0468557	0448	1
BEALE LOUIS R	MAJ	0-0230109	1264	3
BEALE ROBERT C	MAJ	0-0975182	0363	1
BEALE RUDOLPH W	MAJ	0-4021214	0467	1
BEALE WARREN J	LTC	0-0400830	1061	1
BEALE WILLIAM A	MAJ	0-0496670	0154	2
BEALL BURTCH W	LTC	0-0142533	1148	3
BEALL CARL F	MAJ	0-0192309	0255	2
BEALL DAVID C	LTC	0-0240745	0665	3
BEALL EVERETT I	MAJ	0-1635992	0261	1
BEALL EWELL C	LTC	0-0468595	0964	3
BEALL IRVING A	MAJ	0-0263744	1060	3
BEALL JR JAMES F	MAJ	0-0262548	0366	3
BEALL ROBERT W	LTC	0-0114794	1155	3
BEALL THORNTON	LTC	0-0533679	1163	3
BEALS GEORGE W	COL	0-0322288	1045	1
BEALS RUSSELL M	LTC	0-0395013	0360	1
BEAM BURTON T	LTC	0-0451210	0160	1
BEAM GEORGE M	LTC	0-0371777	0457	1
BEAM JAMES C	MAJ	0-1290532	1046	1
BEAM JOHN A	1LT	0-0108242	1131	1
BEAM MARION J	CPT	0-0360496	0146	2
BEAM RICHARD L	MAJ	0-1688642	0665	1
BEAM SIM F	COL	0-0294791	1067	3
BEAMAN CHARLES D	CPT	0-1295982	0946	2
BEAMAN JOSEPH J	LTC	0-1558633	0763	1
BEAMAN MARVIN L	MAJ	0-1293182	0255	2
BEAMER CHARLES R	MAJ	0-0411759	1160	1

NAME	GRADE	SVC NO	DATE RET MO YR	RET CODE
BEAMER JR HENRY G	COL	0-0197734	0459	3
BEAMISH HAROLD L	COL	0-0172128	0160	3
BEAMS ALBERT I	LTC	0-1168548	0557	1
BEAN ABE K	1LT	0-1590987	1051	1
BEAN CHARLES L	COL	0-0270219	0162	3
BEAN CHARLES R	COL	0-0186832	0160	3
BEAN EARL C	MAJ	0-0226115	1044	1
BEAN EVERETT E	CPT	0-1045020	0258	1
BEAN GEORGE E	MAJ	0-1294964	0561	1
BEAN GOODING H	LTC	0-0408157	0763	1
BEAN JOHN J	CPT	0-1057349	0258	1
BEAN K CHARLES	COL	0-0155095	0648	3
BEAN LORENZO A	2LT	0-1589683	0444	2
BEAN RALPH W	LTC	0-0124576	0648	3
BEAN RICHARD A	COL	0-0210566	0259	3
BEAN ROBERT A	MAJ	0-1339247	0960	1
BEAN RORIE K	CPT	0-0264630	1167	3
BEAN SIMON K	MAJ	0-0262610	0463	3
BEAN THERON W	COL	0-0230042	1062	3
BEAN WALTER A	COL	0-0221804	0356	3
BEAN WILLARD F	COL	0-0249865	0367	3
BEAN WILLIAM F	MAJ	0-0978149	0465	1
BEAN WYONT R	COL	0-0277404	1265	3
BEANE BURL R	2LT	0-1324900	0645	2
BEANE NORMAN G	CPT	0-1090242	1047	2
BEANS ALVA R	CPT	0-0359193	0346	2
BEANS YANDELL S	COL	0-0219680	0858	3
BEANSTICK SAM	CPT	0-0370784	0445	2
BEAR CHARLES E	LTC	0-0245776	0954	1
BEAR HENRY H	LTC	0-0520676	0166	3
BEAR HERBERT K	COL	0-0103046	0648	3
BEAR JENNINGS B	CPT	0-0495248	0445	1
BEAR MANFORD C	CPT	0-0400702	0845	2
BEAR WILLIAM P	LTC	0-0116338	0648	3
BEARCE BOYDEN	MAJ	0-1593934	1058	1
BEARD ALVIN H	1LT	0-1535487	0451	1
BEARD BERNARD R	LTC	0-1576916	1264	1
BEARD CLETUS E	LTC	0-0450753	0656	1
BEARD FRED	MAJ	0-0142495	0753	3
BEARD FRED L	LTC	0-0327695	0446	2
BEARD HENRY J	MAJ	0-2018819	0165	1
BEARD HOWARD R	LTC	0-0397224	0664	3
BEARD IRA L	LTC	0-1173866	0662	1
BEARD JAMES F	1LT	0-1995368	0906	2
BEARD JESSE F	CPT	0-0967802	1160	1
BEARD JOHN M	LTC	0-0132115	0455	3
BEARD LAMBERT A	COL	0-0192878	0648	3
BEARD LAWSON R	MAJ	0-0450059	0960	1
BEARD NORMAN E	LTC	0-0407266	0954	1
BEARD ROBERT H	1LT	0-0293634	1046	2
BEARD ROBERT M	CPT	0-1549213	0164	1
BEARDEN ALVA G	LTC	0-1036838	1062	3
BEARDEN EUGENE I	CW2	W-3100514	0267	1
BEARDEN GARTH C	CW2	W-2147938	0955	1
BEARDEN J C	LTC	0-1016957	0463	1
BEARDEN JOHNNY L	MAJ	0-1286591	1057	1
BEARDEN NORMAN C	LTC	0-1104488	1265	1
BEARDEN RUFUS P	CW2	W-2205943	0663	1
BEARDEN WILLIAM R	MAJ	0-2030983	0964	1
BEARDMORE CHARLES C	1LT	0-0366933	0743	2
BEARDSLEE CHARLES G	LTC	0-0450575	1067	1
BEARDSLEE LEONARD L	COL	0-0210251	0746	2
BEARDSLEE VIRGIL K	1LT	0-1184770	1045	1
BEARDSLEY CHARLES H	COL	0-0230317	0864	3
BEARDSLEY HENRY S	COL	0-0261940	0655	3
BEARDSLEY MARVIN P	1LT	0-1300265	0158	1
BEARE JAMES C	CW2	W-2143562	0357	1
BEARLEY WILBER R	LTC	0-1695602	0966	1
BEARMAN EDWIN R	CW4	W-2143648	0167	1
BEARMAN EUGENE J	CPT	0-0447575	0146	2
BEAROK MAX	CPT	0-0251579	0167	3
BEAROR OLIVER W	LTC	0-1635556	1061	1
BEARR RICHARD J	LTC	0-1280462	0860	1
BEARSCOVE KARL D	MAJ	0-0411366	0847	1
BEARSCN BERNARD B	1LT	0-1895568	0945	1

NAME	GRADE	SVC NO	DATE RET MO YR	RET CODE
BEARUP ROSS M	LTC	0-1332566	1165	1
BEASLEY CHARLES M	MAJ	0-2018983	0762	1
BEASLEY CHARLIE R	MAJ	0-0965200	0563	1
BEASLEY FLOYD O	MAJ	0-0179209	0155	3
BEASLEY JAKE W	1LT	0-1180808	0245	1
BEASLEY JOE C	1LT	0-0238597	0663	3
BEASLEY JOHN G	MAJ	0-1318007	1158	1
BEASLEY JOHNEY W	CW2	W-2151110	0157	1
BEASLEY JOSEPH L	MAJ	0-0963798	0563	1
BEASLEY JR CLAUDE G	MAJ	0-2016456	1062	1
BEASLEY LEE H	1LT	0-1796564	1046	2
BEASLEY MARVIN J	MAJ	0-0984749	0865	1
BEASLEY ROBERT T	2LT	0-0334330	0543	1
BEASLEY SAM C	MAJ	0-1285357	0955	1
BEASLEY THEODORE L	LTC	0-1299842	0461	1
BEASLEY THOMAS G	CW3	W-2152000	1061	1
BEASLEY WILLIAM O	LTC	0-0916979	1162	1
BEASON JOHN T	LTC	0-0248975	0466	3
BEASTEY LEWIS	2LT	0-1323517	1144	1
BEASTON ALICE L	2LT	N-0784012	0945	1
BEATH JOHN R	CW4	W-2103663	0357	1
BEATON DONALD E	1LT	0-1822522	1146	2
BEATSON JOHN B	COL	0-0361850	1163	1
BEATTIE JAMES F	1LT	0-1011533	0846	2
BEATTIE JOHN C	LTC	0-0146785	0850	3
BEATTIE JR CHESTER M	MAJ	0-1534915	0656	1
BEATTIE LUCILLE M	2LT	N-0755150	0746	1
BEATTIE ROBERT W	CW4	W-2142523	0563	1
BEATTIE WALTER O	LTC	0-0239981	0963	3
BEATTY CHARLES G	CPT	0-1017794	1047	2
BEATTY DALE T	MAJ	0-1894620	0265	2
BEATTY FRANCIS J	COL	0-0171017	0853	3
BEATTY JR RICHARD F	CPT	0-0963992	0663	1
BEATTY ROBERT F	CW2	W-2208499	1066	1
BEATTY ROBERT L	LTC	0-0243421	0859	1
BEATTY VIVIAN B	CPT	N-0735808	0355	2
BEATY HERCHEL N	1LT	0-1184984	1057	1
BEATY JR ROBERT E	1LT	0-0520727	0246	2
BEATY LESTER C	CW4	W-2145035	0764	1
BEATY THOMAS C	MAJ	0-1013322	0848	1
BEAU HENRY P	CPT	0-1878683	1063	2
BEAUBIEN JOHN W	MAJ	0-2016449	0163	1
BEAUBIEN WILLIAM L	MAJ	0-1303620	0558	1
BEAUCHAMP GLENN A	LTC	0-1297141	0466	1
BEAUCHAMP HUBERT C	MAJ	0-1172748	0954	1
BEAUCHAMP JAMES D	CPT	0-0510826	0761	1
BEAUCHAMP JAMES W	CW2	W-2203377	1157	1
BEAUCHAMP JR E W	LTC	0-0396207	1060	1
BEAUCHAMP MARK L	CPT	0-0498552	0745	2
BEAUCHAMP ROBERT E	COL	0-0218843	0858	2
BEAUCHAMP ROBERT N	MAJ	0-1595548	1063	1
BEAUCHAMP S J	LTC	0-0168865	1060	3
BEAUCHAMP THOMAS O	CW4	W-2109358	1054	1
BEAUCHEMIN JOSEPH P	CW3	W-2143248	0861	1
BEAUDET CECELIA A	CPT	N-0752296	1047	1
BEAUDET JR GROSCH C	CPT	0-1107792	0547	1
BEAUDETTE GERALD J C	MAJ	0-2009235	1057	1
BEAUDIN THEODORE J	MAJ	0-1633612	1058	1
BEAUDOIN EUCLIDE P	CPT	0-1316004	0847	1
BEAUDOIN ROBERT L	MAJ	0-1282399	1060	1
BEAUDRY AIMIE H	LTC	0-1107284	0663	1
BEAUDRY EUGENE J	CW3	W-2207227	1165	2
BEAUDRY RICHARD C	LTC	0-0942851	0866	1
BEAUFORD FRANKIE F	CW2	W-2144741	0559	1
BEAULIEU ANTHONY A	CW4	W-2143220	0266	1
BEAULIEU DELTON C	COL	0-0155090	0359	3
BEAULIEU JAMES E	LTC	0-0274488	1060	1
BEAULIEU PHILIP F	MAJ	0-0407899	0561	1
BEAULIEU WILLIAM	1LT	0-1914012	0948	1
BEAUMONT WILLIAM D	MAJ	0-0290283	1060	1
BEAURABLANT JAMES H	LTC	0-1994565	0962	1
BEAUPERTHUY LOUIS F	CPT	0-4006382	1063	2
BEAUPRE AUGUSTUS J	COL	0-0124575	0954	3
BEAUREGARD JOSEPH A	LTC	0-1633621	0258	1
BEAUREGARD JOSEPH A	MAJ	0-2011766	0666	1

NAME	GRADE	SVC NO	DATE RET MO YR	RET CODE
BEAUREGARD PRESTON W	LTC	0-0238226	0358	3
BEAUREGARD RALPH F	CW2	W-2211463	0167	1
BEAUVAIS WILLIAM E	MAJ	0-0923681	1048	1
BEAVER ALFRED T	LTC	0-0385215	1061	1
BEAVER DAVID	1LT	0-1114045	0146	1
BEAVER HERMAN P	CPT	0-2036931	0752	1
BEAVER JOHN C	LTC	0-0379544	0560	1
BEAVER JOSEPH N	LTC	0-1280115	0958	1
BEAVER WILLIAM C	LTC	0-0424489	0746	1
BEAVERS DON L	LTC	0-0399461	0660	1
BEAVERS GEORGE F	CPT	0-0192068	0758	3
BEAVERS INMAN L	1LT	0-1293527	0446	2
BEAVERS VERNON E	MAJ	0-2011775	0163	1
BEAVERS VONIAL O	LTC	0-0386862	0360	1
BEAVERS WILLIAM R	COL	0-0281198	0261	2
BEBEE ELVIE I	CPT	N-0787228	1047	1
BEBENSEE SR FRED D	LTC	0-0363452	1054	1
BEBLER CLELL W	LTC	0-1047430	0167	1
BECHARAS JR GEORGE S	1LT	0-0517490	0446	2
BECHEL CHARLES R	LTC	0-1040092	0261	1
BECHEN VERNON T	MAJ	0-2036532	0163	1
BECHER JOHN C	LTC	0-2040722	0464	1
BECHET ALEXANDER	COL	0-0479811	0560	3
BECHT FREDERICK	CPT	0-1333167	0360	1
BECHT GRACE M	MAJ	N-0720528	0765	3
BECHTEL HAROLD A	CPT	0-0257005	0358	3
BECHTEL JACK O	MAJ	0-1923524	0565	1
BECHTEL JOHN M	LTC	0-1578151	0763	1
BECHTEL JR VICTOR J	MAJ	0-2018097	0762	1
BECHTELHEIMER ALICE	MAJ	N-0776338	0264	1
BECHTELL HOMER F	1LT	0-1925277	0554	2
BECHTLE EUGENE W	1LT	0-1324240	1145	2
BECHTOL JOHN L	1LT	0-1081197	0860	1
BECHTOLD EDWIN J	MAJ	0-2049467	0762	1
BECHTOLD HERBERT K	CW3	W-2152758	0563	1
BECK ALICE M	1LT	N-0784088	0148	1
BECK ARTHUR C	MAJ	0-0142857	1055	2
BECK BERT L	CW4	W-2101419	0358	1
BECK BJORN O	LTC	0-0244976	0966	3
BECK CLARENCE A	1LT	0-2055150	0753	1
BECK CLAYTON M	MAJ	0-1044450	1164	1
BECK DANIEL M	COL	0-0449560	0447	2
BECK DONALD W	1LT	0-0401613	0146	2
BECK EDWARD J	LTC	0-0337516	0562	1
BECK FLOYD A	LTC	0-1547877	0966	3
BECK FRANK E	CPT	0-0336684	0645	2
BECK GILBERT	MAJ	0-0369978	0246	2
BECK HAROLD J	MAJ	0-0326735	0146	2
BECK HARRY L	CPT	0-0109129	0640	1
BECK HENRY H	CPT	0-0225074	0747	1
BECK HERMAN L	LTC	0-2051043	1265	2
BECK JESSE A	COL	0-0255287	0351	1
BECK JOE T	LTC	0-1321988	0662	1
BECK JOHN F	LTC	0-0420117	0454	1
BECK JR HERMAN C	CPT	0-1580610	1047	2
BECK JR KONRAD C	COL	0-0205524	0959	1
BECK JR WILLIAM H	COL	0-0234311	1058	3
BECK L O	1LT	0-0511475	0743	2
BECK MALCOLM O	MAJ	0-1048279	0467	3
BECK MERRILL G	COL	0-0183406	1051	1
BECK MOXLEY L	LTC	0-0228176	0663	3
BECK ROBERT A	1LT	0-0464619	0745	2
BECK ROLAND L	MAJ	0-0981737	0565	1
BECK THEODORE S	MAJ	0-1053492	0165	3
BECK THOSS R	COL	0-0309434	0261	1
BECK WALTER D	MAJ	0-2017801	0762	1
BECK WESLEY W	CPT	0-0943764	1151	1
BECK WILLIAM A	LTC	0-0400832	0667	1
BECK WILSON	CW2	W-2145320	0960	1
BECKAGE PAUL	MAJ	0-1044452	1158	1
BECKEMEYER KARL D	MAJ	0-1003184	0457	1
BECKENHAUER R W	1LT	0-1174223	0945	2
BECKER ARNOLD A	LTC	0-0303406	0461	1
BECKER BENJAMIN	LTC	0-0273800	0261	3
BECKER BRUCE A	CPT	0-4067345	1058	[illegible]

NAME	GRADE	SVC NO	DATE RET MO YR	RET CODE
BECKER CARL H	LTC	0-2040775	0765	1
BECKER DAVID J	LTC	0-0294551	1058	1
BECKER ELMER W	COL	0-0202054	0362	3
BECKER EUGENE S	1LT	0-1322619	0845	2
BECKER GEORGE A	CW2	W-2102641	0851	1
BECKER HARLEY L	LTC	0-1550315	0559	1
BECKER HAROLD H	CW2	W-2209353	0162	1
BECKER HARRY F	COL	0-0198392	0246	2
BECKER HARRY G	COL	0-0322088	1165	3
BECKER HORACE G	LTC	0-0506202	0855	2
BECKER HOWARD J	MAJ	0-1324071	0266	1
BECKER JOHN H	MAJ	0-2026346	0165	1
BECKER JOHN R	1LT	0-1286944	1044	2
BECKER JOSEPH G	LTC	0-0253672	0748	2
BECKER JR JULIUS H	COL	0-0253219	1057	3
BECKER LEONARD S	LTC	0-0397149	0862	1
BECKER PHILIP A	MAJ	0-0363912	0759	2
BECKER ROBERT C	MAJ	0-1947636	1265	1
BECKER ROBERT J	MAJ	0-1798932	1263	1
BECKER ROLLIN F	COL	0-0319376	0446	2
BECKER SAMUEL	2LT	0-1296115	0644	2
BECKER SELDEN G	CPT	0-1342148	0261	1
BECKER WEST	LTC	0-0326338	0461	3
BECKER WILBERT H	MAJ	0-1558376	0157	1
BECKER WILLIAM	COL	0-0203141	0659	1
BECKERMAN WILLIAM	CPT	0-0477331	0450	1
BECKERT JOHN F	CPT	0-0320148	0445	2
BECKETT FRANCIS F	LTC	0-1113099	0365	1
BECKETT GERALD F	MAJ	0-0969805	1061	1
BECKETT HERBERT M	MAJ	0-1969701	0765	3
BECKETT IRVING R	MAJ	0-0175922	0745	1
BECKETT JOHN A	LTC	0-0462245	0966	3
BECKETT JOHN G	CW3	W-2203292	0962	1
BECKETT NEIL S	1LT	0-1302568	0946	2
BECKETT NICHOLAS S	COL	0-0253658	0660	3
BECKETT RICHARD L	CPT	0-1041710	1046	2
BECKETT WILLIAM H	CW4	W-2144351	1059	1
BECKHAM BENJAMIN M	LTC	0-0250580	0945	2
BECKHAM JAMES W	CPT	0-0963930	1060	1
BECKHAM LONA L	CPT	0-1166434	0448	1
BECKHAM MALCOLM F	COL	0-0337033	0157	1
BECKHAM ROBERT O	CPT	0-1174226	0763	1
BECKHAM THOMAS M	CPT	0-1047875	0866	1
BECKHAM WILLIE S	LTC	0-0245644	0662	1
BECKLEN ALICE A	LTC	N-0700172	1045	1
BECKLEY HARRY A	LTC	0-0302375	0659	3
BECKLEY LEO H	COL	0-0236865	0864	3
BECKLUND WALTER A	LTC	0-1636014	0363	1
BECKMAN ALBERT J	1LT	0-0121466	0451	3
BECKMAN CARL H	1LT	0-0549200	0146	3
BECKMAN CLETUS F	1LT	0-4028016	0358	2
BECKMAN DILL C	COL	0-0268974	0566	3
BECKMAN ELMER P	2LT	0-1030641	0744	2
BECKMAN FRED L	CPT	0-1825754	1046	2
BECKMAN FREDERIC P	COL	0-0325132	0960	1
BECKMAN JACK	CW2	W-2141903	0755	1
BECKMAN PAUL L	LTC	0-1823819	0962	1
BECKMANN GEORGE G	CPT	0-0179053	0157	3
BECKNELL ROBERT G	LTC	0-1051478	1062	1
BECKNER ROBERT R	CW2	W-2150892	0760	1
BECKNO JOHN	MAJ	0-0451074	0958	1
BECKORD DONALD C A	MAJ	0-0234925	1065	3
BECKSTEE G ELEANOR	MAJ	N-0755671	0463	1
BECKSTROM ALLAN D	CPT	0-0424191	0245	2
BECKWITH CARL A	MAJ	0-0394590	1263	1
BECKWITH CHARLES F	2LT	0-1547878	1143	2
BECKWITH HAROLD C	LTC	0-1578154	0764	2
BECKWITH MILLEDGE M	COL	0-0272050	0658	1
BECKWITH NANCY K	2LT	N-0762002	0545	1
BECKWITH RAYMOND W	CW3	W-2152173	0564	1
BECKWITH ROBERT L	MAJ	0-0391909	1045	2
BECKWITH SUTHERLAND	LTC	0-0116001	1050	3
BECKWITH THEODORE I	MAJ	0-0229595	1162	3
BECKWITH WARREN F	CW3	W-2144403	0460	1
BECQUE WILLIAM	2LT	0-1035589	0344	2

NAME	GRADE	SVC NO	DATE RET MO YR	RET CODE
BECTON THOMAS H	LTC	0-1287650	0767	1
BECTON WENDELL R	LTC	0-0917744	0565	3
BEDA STEPHEN W	LTC	0-0362704	0949	1
BEDARD LAWRENCE R	1LT	0-1322874	0246	2
BEDAYAN KEERKOR	MAJ	0-1545076	0657	1
BEDDINGFIELD WALTER	MAJ	0-0958178	0262	1
BEDELL ARCHER W	MAJ	0-0223690	0648	3
BEDELL FOREST L	MAJ	0-0227996	0164	3
BEDELL GEORGE W	LTC	0-1062328	0967	1
BEDELL HARRY P	LTC	0-0198163	0760	3
BEDELL JOHN A	CPT	0-1316122	0247	2
BEDELL JOHN F	COL	0-0136943	0354	1
BEDELL M JOSEPHIN	CPT	N-0720145	0846	2
BEDELL MATTHEW G	LTC	0-1104049	0156	1
BEDENBAUGH B H	MAJ	0-1798472	0656	1
BEDER MARVIN L	1LT	0-0512002	0845	2
BEDESSEM PHILIP M	COL	0-0325405	0451	3
BEDFORD ARCHIE G	2LT	0-0431547	1043	2
BEDFORD GEORGE J	LTC	0-0223156	1064	3
BEDFORD GORMAN L	LTC	0-1633657	0461	1
BEDFORD HIGH R	LTC	0-0451487	0954	1
BEDFORD JOSEPH S	LTC	0-0369270	0762	1
BEDFORD JR ALFRED C	CPT	0-1011333	0545	2
BEDFORD JR WILLIAM H	CPT	0-0463835	1146	1
BEDLE CRAIG P	LTC	0-0308401	0863	3
BEDNARZ HENRY	LTC	0-1555345	0763	1
BEDNARZ JOSEPH P P	MAJ	0-1336864	0563	1
BEDRICK DAVID N	1LT	0-1551352	0745	2
BEDSOLE NED	CW3	W-2143611	0660	1
BEDSOLE SR QUINCY L	CW4	W-2004297	1067	3
BEDWELL LYMAN C	LTC	0-1894550	0162	1
BEDZIS BENJAMIN	LTC	0-1308415	0261	1
BEE CARL E	COL	0-0286101	1152	1
BEEBE ALBERT H	LTC	0-0432507	0767	1
BEEBE EUGENE H	MAJ	0-1301766	0867	3
BEEBE FRANCES J	1LT	N-0797350	0146	2
BEEBE FRANCIS A	LTC	0-0220006	0650	3
BEEBE FRANK C	MAJ	0-0278904	0667	3
BEEBE RAYMOND L	CW3	W-2007442	0865	1
BEEBE REVERE H	LTC	0-0221290	0759	3
BEEBE THOMAS C	MAJ	0-0229536	1161	3
BEECH CHARLES W	MAJ	0-0249776	0554	3
BEECH CLIFFORD L	MAJ	0-1581024	0266	1
BEECH FRED P	MAJ	0-1104489	0660	1
BEECH GEORGE R	LTC	0-0220790	0762	3
BEECH JOHNSTONE	MAJ	0-0499933	1047	2
BEECH SIDNEY C	MAJ	0-1291939	0561	1
BEECH WILLIAM Y	CW3	W-2145558	0760	1
BEECHER VERNE L	CW4	W-2144483	1060	1
BEECHERL LOUIS A	MAJ	0-0152990	0654	3
BEECHINOR ROBERT M	COL	0-0384446	0764	1
BEECHLER JOHN G	1LT	0-1879006	0354	2
BEEDY STANTON L	CW3	W-2205966	0865	1
BEEKMAN FREDERIC	MAJ	0-0459873	0867	2
BEEKMAN WILLIAM N	LTC	0-0323541	0562	1
BEELER CARL G	CW3	W-2206431	0265	1
BEELER CHARLES F	MAJ	0-0142400	0558	3
BEELER HERBERT	LTC	0-0160494	1055	3
BEELMAN EMIL W	LTC	0-0180153	0561	3
BEEM FRANK C	CPT	0-0487858	0757	1
BEEM JACOB I	MAJ	0-0326183	1265	3
BEEM RICHARD C	LTC	0-0257556	0464	3
BEEMAN ALBERT F	CW4	W-2143302	1266	1
BEEMAN FRED	LTC	0-0230996	0758	3
BEEMAN JOHN A	COL	0-0250746	0567	3
BEEMAN LALLY	LTC	0-1823969	0962	1
BEEMAN ROBERT L	CPT	0-1292458	0247	2
BEEMER WILLIAM H	CPT	0-1320014	0662	1
BEENE JONATHAN J	MAJ	0-1342238	0764	1
BEER ANTON C	LTC	0-0370094	0965	1
BEER CARL A C	LTC	0-0200874	0648	3
BEER GEORGE R	MAJ	0-1283711	1065	1
BEER JR WILLIAM C	LTC	0-1047022	0366	3
BEER RALPH D	LTC	0-1001727	1166	2
BEERE HARRY W	CW4	W-2120026	0659	1

NAME	GRADE	SVC NO	DATE RET MO YR	RET CODE
BEERMAN HERMAN P	LTC	0-0286486	1056	3
BEERMAN MAX	LTC	0-0173370	0645	2
BEERS BARNET W	COL	0-0120516	0856	2
BEERS CARL K	MAJ	0-1996335	0261	1
BEERS DRYDEN N	MAJ	0-0247606	0566	3
BEERS INEZ F	MAJ	N-0725841	1067	1
BEERS JAMES F	LTC	0-1080509	0959	1
BEERS JOHN H	CPT	0-0379336	0945	2
BEERS RICHARD H	CPT	0-0537882	0847	1
BEERY EDWIN N	COL	0-0325016	0246	2
BEERY JR CLARENCE H	LTC	0-0387251	1062	1
BEERY SR WALLACE L	CPT	0-2014550	0766	1
BEESMER JOHN F	MAJ	0-1339549	0464	1
BEESON BILLY C	LTC	0-0536435	1264	1
BEESON EARL A	CPT	0-0498696	0254	1
BEESON JOHN R	1LT	0-0960363	1052	1
BEESON MARK T	MAJ	0-1013894	0662	1
BEESON WILLIAM W	1LT	0-1642877	1145	2
BEESTON WILLIAM H	1LT	0-1292293	0845	2
BEETHAM JR ROLAND M	CPT	0-1012266	0545	1
BEETLE MELVIN W	MAJ	0-1103059	0762	1
BEETS FREEMAN H	1LT	0-1062122	1045	1
BEEVES EARL J	CPT	0-1640209	0257	1
BEGALE JAMES W	MAJ	0-0291121	0346	2
BEGEMAN MYRON L	LTC	0-0158160	0953	3
BEGGEHLY ANDREW F	1LT	0-1317612	1145	2
BEGGS CHARLES G	LTC	0-0248900	0965	3
BEGGS GEORGE H	1LT	0-1293528	0645	1
BEGGS JOHN A	CPT	0-0793977	1054	2
BEGGS RICHARD J	CW2	W-2143171	0457	1
BEGIEN ROBERT S	COL	0-0308589	0564	3
BEGLEY MARCUS F	2LT	0-1591591	0544	1
BEGLEY RICHARD P	CW2	W-2142131	0656	1
BEGNAUD MELVIN	MAJ	0-2055479	1160	1
BEGOVICH JOHN C	2LT	0-2055253	1045	2
BEHAN SR WILLIAM F	MAJ	0-1688533	0163	2
BEHEE PAUL	CW3	W-2118194	0262	1
BEHERS JR BERNARD L	LTC	0-1633655	0261	1
BEHLE CALVIN A	COL	0-0487245	0467	3
BEHLING HARVEY W	MAJ	0-0888195	0364	1
BEHLKE WILLIAM D	CPT	0-0118421	0858	2
BEHNE FRANK J	CPT	0-1310674	0257	1
BEHNISCH ERWIN A	LTC	0-0154981	0444	2
BEHNKE DONALD A	MAJ	0-2032863	1062	1
BEHNKE DONALD W	CPT	0-0372749	0544	2
BEHNKE EWALD	MAJ	0-0510299	0153	1
BEHNKE RUSSELL O	CW2	W-2147722	0261	1
BEHNY HAROLD O	1LT	0-2020783	1151	1
BEHR ALEXANDER	CPT	0-1307182	0148	1
BEHR KENNETH P	CPT	0-0123302	0556	3
BEHRENBERG WILLIAM C	LTC	0-0354674	1060	1
BEHREND WILMER R	LTC	0-1053048	0263	1
BEHRENS CHARLES N	LTC	0-0240133	0949	3
BEHRENS CYRIL	1LT	0-1334873	1056	1
BEHRENS DAVID R	CW3	W-2103664	1054	1
BEHRENS HERMAN W	CW3	W-2200103	0666	3
BEHRENS WILLIAM C	LTC	0-0219859	0643	3
BEHRING CARL F	MAJ	0-0188218	0153	3
BEHRLE JR FRANK C	MAJ	0-0253725	0447	2
BEHRMAN ABRAHAM S	COL	0-0212187	1052	3
BEHRNS JOHN L	COL	0-0205704	0858	1
BEICHEK BORIS B	1LT	0-1633066	0347	2
BEICIUNAS PETER	CPT	0-0481756	0467	1
BEIDECK RUDOLPH R	MAJ	0-1583436	0261	1
BEIDLE JAMES C	CPT	0-1317873	1061	1
BEIDLER JOHN	LTC	0-0418690	1053	1
BEIER GAYLORD L	LTC	0-1286061	1063	1
BEIERSCHMITT ROBERT	LTC	0-1295151	0562	1
BEIGHLEY FRANK H	CPT	0-0984116	0462	1
BEIGHLEY HAZEL F	2LT	N-0734833	0345	1
BEILING WAYNE A	MAJ	0-0450403	0258	1
BEILSMITH LOWELL H	MAJ	0-1061057	1061	1
BEIN SOLOMON S	MAJ	0-0321965	0146	2
BEINECKE ALVIN A	LTC	0-1573035	0566	1
BEINECKE CHARLES R	MAJ	0-0955406	0363	1

NAME	GRADE	SVC NO	DATE RET MO YR	RET CODE
BEINSTEIN JOSEPH	CPT	0-0506266	0246	2
BEIRIGER WALTER F	MAJ	0-0312896	1162	3
BEIRNE JOHN F A	COL	0-0287462	0161	3
BEIRSTEIN SAMUEL S	MAJ	0-1689814	0444	2
BEISEL CLIFFORD L	CW4	W-2101428	0659	1
BEISEL JOHN E	2LT	0-1307345	1144	2
BEISEL LEON W	LTC	0-0201448	0461	3
BEISHEIM JOHN W	LTC	0-1115869	0265	3
BEISLER HAROLD A	LTC	0-0206614	0360	3
BEISTEL ARTHUR F	MAJ	0-0351258	0863	1
BEISTEL HENRY F	COL	0-0280287	0767	3
BEISTLE DONALD O	MAJ	0-0402659	0161	2
BEITIA-SALAME COSME	1LT	0-0155726	0255	3
BEITLER CLAUDE T	CW3	W-2151783	0863	1
BEJACH LOIS C	MAJ	0-0150578	0648	3
BEJASA GREGORIO O	1LT	0-1896278	0950	1
BEK RICHARD C	LTC	0-2036285	0667	1
BEKERIS LOUIS J	1LT	0-1646544	0745	2
BEKIER HENRY J	CPT	0-0532986	1048	2
BEKOWITZ SOLOMAN	CPT	0-1945551	1047	1
BELAIR EDWARD P	1LT	0-0393607	0145	1
BELAND OAKLEY B	COL	0-0325246	1165	3
BELANGER ALFRED V	MAJ	0-1044754	0261	1
BELANGER FRANCIS J	CW3	W-2143866	0762	1
BELANGER IRVING J	CPT	0-0106492	0758	3
BELANGER LEONARD S	1LT	0-0489294	0745	2
BELANGER LEWIS A	1LT	0-0395870	1045	2
BELASCO PHILIP	MAJ	0-2053829	0854	1
BELAWICH LEO B	1LT	0-1327922	0547	2
BELBA ISADORE M	LTC	0-1598367	0566	1
BELCH JAMES L	CPT	0-1333414	0557	1
BELCHER BASCOM A	LTC	0-0248131	1062	3
BELCHER CLIFFORD L	MAJ	0-0963739	0864	1
BELCHER EARL S	LTC	0-1575730	0253	2
BELCHER ORVAL	MAJ	0-2025362	0859	1
BELCHER TAYLOR	LTC	0-0140424	0648	3
BELCHER VERA M	2LT	N-0764131	0146	1
BELCOVSKY ADOLPH	MAJ	0-0480885	0647	1
BELDEN DARWIN J	2LT	0-1558115	0645	2
BELFT WILMER F	MAJ	0-0981102	0963	1
BELGARD CECIL C	LTC	0-0250337	0164	3
BELGRADE NATHAN B	MAJ	0-0320911	1058	1
BELICOSE RALPH J	CW4	W-2102643	0859	1
BELIE ROBERT A	CW2	W-2208528	1161	1
BELIKOVE SIDNEY C	CPT	0-1283007	0149	1
BELILES PEBLE	1LT	0-1686150	0349	1
BELISLE FRED	LTC	0-0215123	0363	3
BELITSKY FRANK C	LTC	0-1175038	0763	1
BELIVEAU EUGENE H	LTC	0-1289372	1055	1
BELK CLARENCE L	WO1	W-2120323	0855	1
BELK SAMUEL E	CPT	0-1323798	1146	2
BELKNAP CLIFFORD B	CPT	0-0486529	0445	1
BELKNAP FLORENCE M	LTC	L-0125022	0962	1
BELKNAP HOBART C	COL	0-0215798	0157	3
BELKNAPP JAMIESON R	LTC	0-0272510	0259	3
BELKOV SYLVIA	CPT	0-0385231	1144	2
BELKOVICZ JOHN A	1LT	0-1049725	1146	2
BELKY WILLIAM H	LTC	0-1799224	0761	1
BELL ALBERT J	1LT	0-1596265	0446	2
BELL ARTHUR H	LTC	0-0219479	0357	3
BELL ARTHUR R	CW2	W-2143017	0456	1
BELL ARTHUR S	COL	0-0155108	0546	2
BELL ARVIN	LTC	0-1173160	0665	1
BELL BANKS H	LTC	0-0271447	1067	3
BELL BENJAMIN	LTC	0-1047437	0761	1
BELL BERNARD O	2LT	0-1290766	0445	2
BELL BESSIE S	1LT	N-0700020	1033	1
BELL BILL	LTC	0-1643465	0963	1
BELL BYARD	MAJ	0-1640353	0562	1
BELL CARL	CPT	0-0300610	0754	3
BELL CHARLES L	COL	0-0266304	1061	3
BELL CHARLES L	MAJ	0-1011584	0547	2
BELL CHARLES R	1LT	0-1179293	1045	2
BELL CHESTER F	1LT	0-1284454	0745	2
BELL CLARENCE V	MAJ	0-0226310	0461	3

NAME	GRADE	SVC NO	DATE RET MO YR	RET CODE
BELL CLIFTON	LTC	O-0320035	0360	3
BELL CLYDE R	1LT	O-1573309	0248	2
BELL COOPER C	MAJ	O-1110367	1160	1
BELL DEWITT	1LT	O-2205719	1153	2
BELL DONALD A	LTC	O-1342235	0967	1
BELL DOROTHY M	MAJ	N-0772238	0767	2
BELL EDGAR V H	COL	O-0180702	0559	3
BELL EDGAR W	LTC	O-2049177	0963	1
BELL EDITH M	MAJ	L-1010009	0763	1
BELL EDWARD C	CPT	O-0301385	0648	3
BELL ERNEST T	CW3	W-2147245	0765	1
BELL EUGENE H	LTC	O-0245576	0863	3
BELL EUGENE M	MAJ	O-0437470	0848	1
BELL FOSTER F	CPT	O-2009573	0557	1
BELL FRANC W	CPT	O-1844863	0755	1
BELL FRANK F	B G	O-0173171	0948	3
BELL FRED O	CW3	W-2203424	0466	1
BELL GEORGE W J	MAJ	O-1342038	0262	1
BELL GEORGE R	1LT	O-2055191	0546	1
BELL GORDON F	MAJ	O-1284634	0346	2
BELL HARRY B	CW3	W-2145101	0361	1
BELL HENRY G	MAJ	O-0340345	1044	2
BELL HOWARD K	CW3	W-2151923	0263	1
BELL IRVING	1LT	O-1323709	1045	1
BELL JACK H	WO1	W-2148516	0656	1
BELL JAMES E	CW2	W-2149930	1263	1
BELL JAMES H	CPT	O-2010735	0958	2
BELL JAMES I	MAJ	O-0229294	0660	3
BELL JEAN N	LTC	O-0256986	1167	3
BELL JESS W	CW2	W-2132324	0262	2
BELL JOE W	CPT	O-1290706	1158	1
BELL JOHN E	CPT	O-1303291	1061	1
BELL JOHN R	MAJ	O-1633068	0747	1
BELL JOHN S	MAJ	O-0325173	0544	2
BELL JOHN T	LTC	O-0221255	1055	3
BELL JOHN T	LTC	O-0346145	0160	1
BELL JOSEPH	LTC	O-1300267	0561	1
BELL JOSEPH A	CW4	W-2143477	1162	1
BELL JR BRYAN	1LT	O-1313368	0945	2
BELL JR CLYDE C	1LT	O-0408158	0246	2
BELL JR ERNEST L	LTC	O-0206259	0460	3
BELL JR GLENN C	MAJ	O-1306751	0759	1
BELL JR GRALY I	CPT	O-0377782	0346	2
BELL JR HARVEY C	MAJ	O-0380598	1146	2
BELL JR HENRY N	CPT	O-0216738	0262	3
BELL JR WALLACE A	MAJ	O-1278145	1060	1
BELL JR WILLIAM T	COL	O-0419125	0466	1
BELL KENNETH D	CW3	W-2151134	0266	1
BELL LACOTE R	CW3	W-2143680	0560	1
BELL LEON R	CPT	O-1062366	0453	1
BELL LEON H	MAJ	O-1319208	0567	1
BELL LEONARD	LTC	O-1796407	0566	1
BELL LEROY A	1LT	O-1043365	0147	2
BELL [illegible] W	1LT	O-1256638	1043	2
BELL MARY E	2LT	N-0729444	0146	1
BELL MARY S	LTC	L-0702010	1053	2
BELL PAUL M	M G	O-0215450	0362	3
BELL PAUL A	COL	O-0253330	0647	1
BELL PERCY F	LTC	O-0918730	0763	3
BELL RALPH W	LTC	O-0402485	0146	2
BELL RAYMOND J	MAJ	O-0947848	0956	1
BELL RILEY [illegible]	MAJ	O-0970124	0765	2
BELL ROBERT	MAJ	O-0262138	0646	[illegible]
BELL ROBERT	CPT	O-1438863	0646	1
BELL ROBERT C	CW2	W-3440020	0367	1
BELL ROBERT J	MAJ	O-1100822	0846	1
BELL ROBERT W	CPT	O-1109137	0846	2
BELL ROY	MAJ	O-1885916	1266	1
BELL SIDNEY A	CPT	O-0401531	0549	2
BELL SPURGEON	LTC	O-0169927	0648	3
BELL VIRGIL W	CW3	W-2149784	0455	1
BELL WALTER H	LTC	[illegible]	1266	3
BELL WARREN J	MAJ	O-1552676	1055	1
BELL WILBURN K	CPT	O-0340128	0145	2
BELL WILLIAM [illegible]	CPT	O-1031483	1043	1
BELL WILLIAM H	COL	O-0205569	1061	3
BELL WILLIAM H	CW3	RW-2142537	0162	1
BELL WILLIAM K	1LT	O-0512817	1143	2
BELL WILLIAM P	COL	O-0247026	0665	3
BELL WILMER U	COL	O-0268865	1167	3
BELLAH JAMES H	LTC	O-1166006	0759	1
BELLAH JAMES W	COL	O-0219868	1059	3
BELLAMY JESSE P	COL	O-0177755	0958	3
BELLAMY JOHN A	LTC	O-0287615	0346	2
BELLAN JOHN M	MAJ	O-0254902	0552	3
BELLANTUONI JOSEPH	CPT	O-2055305	0156	1
BELLAS WILLIAM J	CW2	W-2152261	0264	1
BELLASSAI ANTHONY	MAJ	O-2287670	0667	1
BELLEFONTAINE JOHN P	CW2	W-2207231	1164	1
BELLEGANTE LOUIS	MAJ	O-0252613	1062	3
BELLEMAN WILLIAM I	CW3	W-2148954	0266	1
BELLEMARE ARTHUR J	CW3	W-2151921	0161	1
BELLER CHARLES H	WO1	W-2151409	0257	1
BELLER EARL J	LTC	O-0501538	0954	1
BELLES JOHN H	LTC	O-0415425	0958	1
BELLEVILLE TILO R F	COL	O-0179724	0458	3
BELLIEU LEO H	LTC	O-0513431	0863	2
BELLINGER FREDERICK	COL	O-0305358	0964	3
BELLINO VINCENT	MAJ	O-0957255	1163	1
BELLINY DANIEL S	2LT	O-1311966	0145	2
BELLIS CHARLES W	MAJ	O-0166790	0648	3
BELLIS LEON R	1LT	O-1585159	0145	2
BELLMAN MARTIN L	CW4	W-2108954	0655	1
BELLOCCHI ROBERT R	CPT	O-1294418	1145	2
BELLOIR ROBERT G	LTC	O-1286545	1058	1
BELLOMY OTIS E	1LT	O-1164453	0146	2
BELLOWS HAROLD S	MAJ	O-0981429	1263	1
BELLOWS LESLIE R	MAJ	O-1293186	0458	1
BELLOWS PAUL R	LTC	O-0900885	0745	2
BELLUCCI LAWRENCE Y	1LT	O-1290568	0745	2
BELLUCCI VINCENT	LTC	O-0916760	0363	1
BELLUSCI FRANK P	LTC	O-1638076	0766	1
BELMONT GAIL H	MAJ	O-2013183	0661	1
BELMONT MORRISON H	MAJ	O-1693481	0346	2
BELMONT PHILIP F	LTC	O-0532807	0861	1
BELMONT ROBERT	LTC	O-1055776	0866	1
BELNAP HOWARD Y	LTC	O-0285944	0346	2
BELOIT GUSTAVE H	CW4	W-2114475	0459	1
BELOTE JR GEORGE F	1LT	O-0356136	0444	1
BELOTE LEM Y	LTC	O-1101437	0960	1
BELOW WILLIAM W	MAJ	O-0197813	0953	3
BELSCHWENDER ROBERT	CW4	W-2152941	0764	1
BELSER IRVINE F	COL	O-0108475	0160	3
BELSER RICHARD R	LTC	O-0305605	0248	2
BELSHAW MARSHALL F	MAJ	O-0225445	0765	3
BELSHER HORACE I	COL	O-0245380	0565	3
BELSKY WILLIAM F	LTC	O-1580107	1062	1
BELSON NORVALL [illegible]	MAJ	O-1324241	0356	1
BELT CARL O	COL	O-0746542	0763	1
BELT CARLE H	COL	O-0122533	0648	3
BELT WILLIAM C	LTC	O-2055456	1162	1
BELTEN CHARLES C	MAJ	O-2006446	0466	1
BELTON GWILYM J	MAJ	O-1051849	0364	1
BELTRAN EVANS R	1LT	O-2027446	0552	1
BELTRAN LUDOVICO	1LT	O-2031840	1060	1
BELTZ JACK A	LTC	O-1016562	0366	1
BELVEL PAUL H	CPT	O-0538710	0455	2
BEMIS CLARA C	2LT	N-0700144	1043	1
BEMIS EDWARD C	MAJ	O-0225842	0661	3
BEMIS IFFLIN A	MAJ	O-0118793	0261	3
BEMIS RUSSELL R	LTC	O-1109138	0766	1
BEMONT RICHARD	LTC	O-1100015	1054	2
BENACK WILLIAM H	1LT	O-1318441	1045	1
BENASSI NORRIS R	CPT	N-0751008	0946	1
BENBOW EDGAR V	MAJ	O-0475192	0944	2
BENCH BERNARD H	LTC	O-0260702	0966	3
BENCH WILLIAM F	LTC	O-0201165	0745	1
BENCIVENNI RAOUL W	LTC	O-0371787	0561	1
BENDELE JR ALFRED	COL	O-0218586	0566	3
BENDER CLEBURNE S	LTC	O-0187228	0954	1
BENDER EARL	LTC	O-0194581	0453	3
BENDER ELMER P	CW3	W-2102646	0954	2
BENDER FOREST P	MAJ	O-0263486	1058	3
BENDER FRED	LTC	O-0120365	1054	3
BENDER FREDERICK	CPT	O-1942261	0665	2
BENDER GEORGE	CPT	O-1649696	0856	1
BENDER GLENNON F	1LT	O-1544347	1046	1
BENDER HARRY W	CPT	O-1013795	0854	1
BENDER HENRY A	MAJ	O-1765205	1047	2
BENDER JAMES W	COL	O-0297342	0861	1
BENDER JOHN P	LTC	O-0404663	0164	1
BENDER JR ALFRED J	LTC	O-0909346	0663	1
BENDER LLOYD C	LTC	O-1174772	0266	3
BENDER MATTHEW F	MAJ	O-1633859	0246	1
BENDER MICHAEL A	CPT	O-1689687	0645	2
BENDER NORMAN J	MAJ	O-0201840	0360	1
BENDER PAUL J	2LT	O-1182777	1144	2
BENDER ROBERT J	CW3	RW-2143460	0562	1
BENDER ROBERT O	CW4	W-2102648	1154	1
BENDER ROY W	LTC	O-0253114	1052	1
BENDER WILLIAM H	COL	O-0241394	0461	3
BENDER WILLIAM R	MAJ	O-1949496	0666	1
BENDERSON NATHAN	1LT	O-0921004	0645	2
BENDKOWSKI DOROTHY H	MAJ	N-0745550	0764	1
BENDKOWSKI JOSEF J	LTC	O-0376549	0960	1
BENDL ROBERT E	MAJ	O-1919424	1165	1
BENEDETTO ELMO J	1LT	O-2046888	0945	1
BENEDICT ALFONSO J	MAJ	O-0385697	0864	1
BENEDICT BRUCE W	CPT	O-0379934	0744	2
BENEDICT CHARLES A	MAJ	O-2096814	0765	1
BENEDICT DANIEL W	COL	O-1200103	0964	1
BENEDICT DONALD D	CPT	O-0364845	0845	1
BENEDICT EDWARD E	1LT	O-0505596	1044	2
BENEDICT HELEN G	CPT	N-0731137	1047	1
BENEDICT JR HOWARD W	2LT	O-1323900	0645	2
BENEDICT ROBERT E	LTC	O-1950577	0164	1
BENEDICT ROBERT M	MAJ	O-0452367	0661	1
BENEDOSSO VICTORIA T	2LT	N-0753083	0446	1
BENEFIEL JENNIE B	CPT	N-0729924	0652	1
BENEFIEL WILEY R	CW4	W-2111112	0659	1
BENEFIELD FREDERICK	CW3	W-2146495	0766	1
BENEGAR ARCHIE S	LTC	O-0394293	1060	1
BENET GEORGE	COL	O-0212066	0748	3
BENEVELLI ALEXANDER	CW3	W-2144819	0962	1
BENEVENTI JOHN K	CPT	O-0411147	1047	2
BENEZECH EDWARD P	LTC	O-0126188	0954	3
BENFORD FRANK S	CPT	O-1042232	1160	1
BENFORD GEORGE H	MAJ	O-1923625	0645	1
BENFORD MILTON A	LTC	O-0461469	1164	1
BENGE DAVID W	MAJ	O-1019289	0359	1
BENGE MARTHA F	CPT	N-0728433	0350	1
BENHAM LELAND F	CW4	W-2112016	0960	1
BENHAM SARAH M	MAJ	L-0202680	0463	1
BENHAM SOLOMON S	MAJ	O-1037037	0863	1
BENINI FLAVIO	CPT	O-1109139	0546	2
BENIOFF BEN	COL	O-0169145	0860	3
BENIT DUDLEY J	COL	O-0396342	0763	1
BENJAMIN FRANKLIN	MAJ	O-1114049	0860	1
BENJAMIN HAROLD	COL	O-0342449	0567	3
BENJAMIN HARRY	MAJ	O-2046639	1055	1
BENJAMIN IRVING	1LT	O-0495591	1145	2
BENJAMIN JASON	CW4	W-2114744	0157	1
BENJAMIN JR DAYTON	2LT	O-1112560	1143	2
BENJAMIN JULIEN	COL	O-0142844	1050	3
BENJAMIN KENNETH	COL	O-0348323	0150	1
BENJAMIN LESTER V	CPT	O-0126652	1053	3
BENJAMIN MILTON	CPT	O-0899084	0944	2
BENJAMIN WILLIAM F	CPT	O-0194531	1044	1
BENKE SR RALPH C	MAJ	O-1020065	1166	1
BENKENDORF DONNA V	CPT	O-0424355	1145	1
BENN BENJAMIN	CW2	W-2102651	0957	1
BENN FREDERICK	CPT	O-1578141	0952	1
BENNEFIELD LESTER	CW4	W-2152016	0760	1
BENNER CHRISTIANA	2LT	N-0735253	0445	1
BENNER FREDERICK	LTC	O-0212011	0563	3
BENNER HARRY L	CPT	O-0313111	1059	3
BENNER HULBERT H	CPT	O-1682487	0658	1
BENNER PEARL S	MAJ	O-1304666	0161	1
BENNER STANFORD P	LTC	O-0888584	1160	1
BENNERS JOHN S	CW3	W-2152103	0762	1
BENNETT ADOLPH J	CPT	O-1058438	0347	1
BENNETT ALBERT M	LTC	O-0305212	0347	1
BENNETT ALVIA E	WO1	W-2141711	0958	1
BENNETT ARCHIE	1LT	O-1698839	0845	2
BENNETT ARDEA L	LTC	O-0366931	1158	1
BENNETT ARTHUR A	MAJ	O-1642092	0158	2
BENNETT BENJAMIN H	LTC	O-1101333	1060	1
BENNETT BERT W	CPT	O-1016029	0756	1
BENNETT BYRON A	MAJ	O-0255345	0446	2
BENNETT CAROLINE E	1LT	N-0700600	0444	1
BENNETT CHARLES F	CPT	O-1300516	0147	1
BENNETT CHARLES W	MAJ	O-1168170	0763	1
BENNETT CHESTER N	LTC	O-0258713	0167	3
BENNETT CLARENCE H	CPT	O-0986286	1060	1
BENNETT CLAYTON C	1LT	O-1323997	0346	2
BENNETT CLYDE P	LTC	O-1795848	0862	1
BENNETT DAVID L	2LT	O-1303454	1144	1
BENNETT DENVER P	MAJ	O-1294256	0660	1
BENNETT DONALD H	LTC	O-0447843	0254	1
BENNETT EDWARD J	CW3	W-2145232	0862	1
BENNETT ERNEST R	1LT	O-1183240	0346	2
BENNETT EUGENE D	COL	O-0201988	1044	2
BENNETT EUGENE L	MAJ	O-0988893	0466	1
BENNETT EVERETT H	MAJ	O-1890385	1066	1
BENNETT FLOYD K	LTC	O-1175040	0962	2
BENNETT FOREMAN H	LTC	O-0238487	0466	3
BENNETT FRANK R	MAJ	O-1318953	0955	1
BENNETT FREDERICK	LTC	O-0336339	0960	1
BENNETT GEOFFREY W	COL	O-0318456	0806	3
BENNETT GEORGE A	COL	O-0264235	0165	3
BENNETT GEORGE F	LTC	O-0428456	1061	1
BENNETT GLENN L	LTC	O-0262106	0767	3
BENNETT GORDON C	MAJ	O-2071037	0765	1
BENNETT HAROLD T	CPT	O-0489936	0253	1
BENNETT HARRY J	LTC	O-0212730	0964	3
BENNETT HARRY W	CPT	O-0493174	0257	1
BENNETT HORACE M	LTC	O-0913115	0565	3
BENNETT HUBERT	CPT	O-0484072	1047	1
BENNETT IRA E	COL	O-0124335	0848	3
BENNETT IRA L	CPT	O-1080599	1057	1
BENNETT JACK	LTC	O-0947083	0967	1
BENNETT JAMES B	COL	O-0309960	0257	1
BENNETT JAMES C	1LT	O-1286947	1046	1
BENNETT JAMES G	LTC	O-0288013	0665	3
BENNETT JAMES H	LTC	O-0420655	0561	1
BENNETT JAMES R	MAJ	O-2262731	0863	1
BENNETT JEWEL E	CPT	O-0996458	0164	1
BENNETT JOE W	CPT	O-0978957	1060	1
BENNETT JOHN A	LTC	O-0229717	0355	3
BENNETT JOHN H	COL	O-0142738	0455	3
BENNETT JOHN R	LTC	O-0554021	0763	1
BENNETT JOSEPH F	MAJ	O-0116965	0648	3
BENNETT JOSEPH M	MAJ	O-1312485	0361	1
BENNETT JOSEPH R	LTC	O-0226664	0860	3
BENNETT JR FRANK W	LTC	O-0692267	0363	1
BENNETT JR JACOB C	LTC	O-1341391	0667	1
BENNETT JR JOE D	CPT	O-1324550	0559	2
BENNETT JR THOMAS W	MAJ	O-1058722	0165	1
BENNETT JUANITA L	MAJ	N-0759247	1162	1
BENNETT KENNETH C	CPT	O-2023490	1057	1
BENNETT KENNETH M	LTC	O-1295983	0961	1
BENNETT LENSEY R	MAJ	O-1925574	0967	1
BENNETT LOYD V	CPT	O-0458266	0154	1
BENNETT MARVIN C	LTC	O-1635571	0661	1
BENNETT MAX P	MAJ	O-1651915	0165	1
BENNETT OLIVER P	COL	O-0172709	1152	3
BENNETT OSCAR	2LT	O-0506653	1043	1
BENNETT PAULINE M	CPT	N-0728979	0847	1
BENNETT RAYMOND E	LTC	O-0360778	1061	1
BENNETT RICHARD F	COL	O-0286580	0362	3

NAME	GRADE	SVC NO	DATE RET MO YR	RET CODE	NAME	GRADE	SVC NO	DATE RET MO YR	RET CODE	NAME	GRADE	SVC NO	DATE RET MO YR	RET CODE	NAME	GRADE	SVC NO	DATE RET MO YR	RET CODE
BENNETT RICHARD S	MAJ	O-1058176	0761	1	BENSON WILLIAM F	LTC	O-0159268	1043	2	BERG ANNA M	MAJ	N-0762722	1264	1	BERGQUIST IVOR H	CW2	W-2205639	0863	1
BENNETT ROBERT A	MAJ	O-0433301	0962	1	BENT CARL O	CPT	O-1301597	0248	1	BERG ARNOLD	LTC	O-0296672	0267	3	BERGQUIST WALTER J	COL	O-0237215	0857	3
BENNETT ROBERT F	COL	O-0194532	0357	3	BENT EVERETT A	CW3	W-2145352	0861	1	BERG CHARLES R	CW3	W-2106439	1154	1	BERGSCHNEIDER F F	CPT	O-1165022	1160	1
BENNETT ROBERT N	MAJ	O-1637008	0260	1	BENT HARVEY G	CPT	O-0331451	1048	1	BERG DEL MONTE	MAJ	O-0354194	0160	1	BERGSCHNEIDER J G	1LT	O-1107292	0945	2
BENNETT ROBERT S	1LT	O-1102134	1045	2	BENTER JOSEPH V	1LT	O-1553565	0146	2	BERG DUANE P	MAJ	O-2265847	0365	1	BERGSTEN ROBERT E	MAJ	O-0452785	0456	1
BENNETT ROWLAND K	COL	O-0160814	1054	3	BENTIVEGLIO ISADORE	CW2	W-2150081	0959	1	BERG ESTHER	MAJ	N-0777413	0465	1	BERGSTROM M A	1LT	N-0752373	0248	2
BENNETT RUSSELL C	CPT	O-0258161	1066	3	BENTLEY ALBERT O	COL	O-0325768	0162	3	BERG HOWARD A	LTC	O-1057354	1062	1	BERGSTROM VINCENT A	LTC	O-0307636	0462	1
BENNETT SAMUEL L	MAJ	O-0975175	1262	1	BENTLEY DEWEY E	MAJ	O-1014855	0859	1	BERG HOWARD W	MAJ	O-0302470	1045	2	BERGUP FIN A	CPT	O-0464196	0250	1
BENNETT SANFORD A	CPT	O-0369958	0243	2	BENTLEY EDWARD L	CPT	O-0354620	0147	2	BERG JACK	MAJ	O-0327003	0346	2	BERICK JAMES	CPT	O-1044760	0446	1
BENNETT SPENCER W	MAJ	O-1644719	0658	1	BENTLEY FREDERICK	MAJ	O-1296160	0261	1	BERG JACK E	MAJ	O-1550745	0663	1	BERISFORD JOSEPH S	CPT	O-1914346	0332	2
BENNETT THOMAS E	LTC	O-0340227	0858	1	BENTLEY GEORGE	LTC	O-0480357	0662	3	BERG JANIS M	1LT	N-0795315	0347	1	BERK BRUCE W	MAJ	O-2019977	1164	1
BENNETT THOMAS H	1LT	O-1312269	0645	2	BENTLEY GEORGE F	LTC	O-0104036	0544	2	BERG LAWRENCE E	MAJ	O-0484865	0846	2	BERK HARRY B	2LT	O-0315697	1142	2
BENNETT TRUMAN L	MAJ	O-1061315	0955	1	BENTLEY HARLAND O	CPT	O-0379433	0745	2	BERG LAWRENCE P	MAJ	O-1315897	1162	1	BERK JACK E	MAJ	O-0345491	0246	2
BENNETT WILFRED C	1LT	O-1013342	1144	2	BENTLEY HOWARD H	COL	O-0184211	0858	3	BERG LLOYD G	MAJ	O-0971535	0865	1	BERK JOHN F	LTC	O-1302939	0766	1
BENNETT WILLIAM B	CPT	O-1637009	0355	1	BENTLEY JR ULLA M	CW2	W-2149685	0960	1	BERG MILTON E	LTC	O-0479450	0667	1	BERK RICHARD B	1LT	O-0546659	0646	2
BENNETT WILLIAM L	LTC	O-0318055	0146	2	BENTLEY JR WILLIAM E	LTC	O-0349811	0959	1	BERG NILS O	MAJ	O-2007477	0860	1	BERKE LOUIS J	MAJ	O-0263030	0764	3
BENNETT WILLIAM L	LTC	O-1286772	0860	1	BENTLEY LUCILLE R	2LT	N-0702360	0535	1	BERG PETER	WO1	W-2100033	1057	3	BERKE THOMAS J	CPT	O-0211590	1055	3
BENNETT WILLIAM T	LTC	O-0218442	0164	3	BENTLEY MARY E	2LT	N-0727076	1044	1	BERG ROBERT A	CPT	O-0955410	0361	1	BERKEBILE FRED D	MAJ	O-0506052	0847	2
BENNETTS EARL E	LTC	O-1634521	1161	1	BENTLEY MARY M	CPT	N-0737375	0757	2	BERG ROBERT J	MAJ	O-0467333	0648	1	BERKEBILE ROBERT R	MAJ	O-1186802	0664	1
BENNEY JOHN N	LTC	O-0193851	0263	3	BENTLEY ORVILLE G	MAJ	O-0444148	0546	2	BERG ROBERT O	MAJ	O-0289378	0656	3	BERKELEY CHARLES C	LTC	O-0280339	0367	1
BENNING WILLARD F	LTC	O-0278558	1048	1	BENTLEY ROBERT H	MAJ	O-2283921	0266	1	BERG ROLLAND H	CW3	W-2145120	0961	1	BERKENFIELD ROY K	LTC	O-0243428	0767	3
BENNINGER HERBERT P	CPT	O-0969308	0861	1	BENTLEY ROGER K	MAJ	O-2033780	0664	1	BERG THEODORE	MAJ	O-0461631	0346	2	BERKHEIMER WILLIAM J	CPT	O-0483258	0646	2
BENNINGTON CLAUDE F	MAJ	O-1797422	0663	1	BENTLEY WILLIAM C	LTC	O-1304490	0467	1	BERG WALTER T	LTC	O-0227255	0846	1	BERKOVE ALFRED R	COL	O-0287660	0864	3
BENNINGTON JOSEPH R	MAJ	O-0403965	0546	2	BENTON BENJAMIN J	LTC	O-1325625	0163	1	BERG WILLIAM A	MAJ	O-0406855	0147	2	BERKOVITZ EDWARD	1LT	O-1039456	1045	1
BENNIS JOSEPH F	CPT	O-1295153	0856	1	BENTON CHARLES R	LTC	O-0261625	0845	2	BERGAMINI HERBERT M	COL	O-0136526	0350	3	BERKOWICK BENJAMIN M	MAJ	O-2262616	1062	1
BENOIT GILBERT A	MAJ	O-0507936	0945	2	BENTON DARRELL W	2LT	O-1293702	0245	1	BERGAN CARL A	LTC	O-0262757	0265	3	BERKOWITZ GEORGE	1LT	O-1012476	1045	1
BENOIT JOSEPH J	COL	O-0176766	1061	3	BENTON EARL B	MAJ	O-0209022	1058	3	BERGE ADOLPH K	LTC	O-1574572	1162	1	BERKOWITZ MARVIN	CPT	O-1718222	0146	2
BENOIT RAYMOND L	MAJ	O-1544999	1061	2	BENTON EVERETT L	MAJ	O-0242427	0151	1	BERGEN CHANDLER W	LTC	O-1289537	0163	1	BERKQUIST ROBERT H	1LT	O-1290534	0244	2
BENS RICHARD A	LTC	O-0451212	0462	1	BENTON HARWOOD O	COL	O-0122168	1154	3	BERGEN HERBERT L	MAJ	O-1557595	1263	1	BERKSON SUZANNE O	2LT	N-0787296	1144	1
BENSCOTER DANIEL B	LTC	O-0168216	1059	3	BENTON HERBERT A	LTC	O-1111489	0562	1	BERGEN RAPHAEL J	LTC	O-1796409	0661	1	BERKY EUGENE R	LTC	O-1016987	1162	1
BENSER NORMA R	2LT	N-0768676	0846	1	BENTON HOWARD E	1LT	O-1546656	0959	1	BERGEN WILLIS	LTC	O-0235245	1046	2	BERL JESSE	MAJ	O-1689808	0946	2
BENSHOOF JULIAN L	MAJ	O-0183571	1164	3	BENTON ISHMAEL C	MAJ	O-1651932	1160	1	BERGENDAHL HAROLD A	CPT	O-0500308	0745	1	BERL JR WILLIAM	COL	O-0112559	0648	3
BENSKY ABRAHAM	1LT	O-0496807	0648	1	BENTON JAY A	LTC	O-1575732	0261	1	BERGER ALEXANDER	LTC	O-1051483	0566	2	BERLE CHARLES H	COL	O-0136542	0159	3
BENSLEY HARRY R	MAJ	O-0411584	0963	1	BENTON MARION L	CPT	O-0518491	0648	1	BERGER ARMISTEAD	MAJ	O-1542487	0658	1	BERLEME GEORGE H	2LT	O-1645507	0744	2
BENSON ALLEN G	COL	O-0261610	0856	3	BENTON RICHARDSON	COL	O-1304665	0462	1	BERGER ARTHUR J	LTC	O-0239183	0157	3	BERLEY BONNIE	1LT	O-1996336	0860	1
BENSON ARTHUR F	MAJ	O-0231017	0463	3	BENTON ROBERT A	LTC	O-0292432	0166	3	BERGER CHARLES J	1LT	O-0556180	0746	2	BERLIN CHARLES H	MAJ	O-2011940	1062	1
BENSON CARL	LTC	O-0168085	0660	3	BENTON ROBERT H	1LT	O-1109141	0944	2	BERGER DAVID Z	CPT	O-0486270	1145	2	BERLIN FREDERICK	MAJ	O-0398136	0246	2
BENSON CARL F	MAJ	O-1950842	1064	1	BENTON ROBERT R	CPT	O-0981832	0860	1	BERGER EMANUEL	LTC	O-0323261	0263	3	BERLIN MILTON D	LTC	O-0298541	1165	3
BENSON CARL S	CPT	O-0503944	1144	2	BENTON WILLIAM C	LTC	O-0244162	0664	3	BERGER ENGELBERT	LTC	O-0333912	0561	1	BERLINE JAMES H	1LT	O-1305712	0146	1
BENSON CHARLES M	LTC	O-0450755	0554	1	BENTSON WILLIAM A	MAJ	O-0958404	0963	1	BERGER FRANKLIN W	CW2	W-2131369	1051	1	BERLINER ORVAL S	MAJ	O-1578166	0761	1
BENSON CLARENCE M	CW3	W-2150772	1060	1	BENTY HERBERT A	1LT	O-1301769	0547	2	BERGER GEORGE J	MAJ	O-0965428	1162	1	BERLOVE DONALD L	1LT	O-1018983	0146	2
BENSON DAVIS A	MAJ	O-1687288	1046	1	BENTZ FRED F	MAJ	O-1544814	1060	1	BERGER JR GEORGE C	LTC	O-1283010	0763	1	BERLOVE IRA J	LTC	O-0478399	1145	2
BENSON EDWARD E	COL	O-0144821	0654	3	BENZ HAROLD J	1LT	O-0336617	0843	2	BERGER JR HERMAN W	1LT	O-0351094	0444	2	BERMAN HARRY	1LT	O-0530325	1045	2
BENSON FRANCIS M	LTC	O-0261183	0660	3	BENZ JR JOHN G	2LT	O-1330898	0346	2	BERGER MAROLF B	MAJ	O-0363678	1045	2	BERMAN JAMES C	1LT	O-1319166	1145	2
BENSON FRANK L	COL	O-0943765	0364	3	BENZ MORRIS	LTC	O-0295035	0246	2	BERGER MAURICE	MAJ	O-0201491	1045	2	BERMAN LOUIS	CPT	O-0479815	0547	2
BENSON FRANK R P	MAJ	O-1291061	0560	2	BENZA FRANK C	CPT	O-1690270	0246	2	BERGER MERTON M	CPT	O-1181540	0862	1	BERMAN MERITZ S	1LT	O-1184985	1045	2
BENSON GEORGE B	COL	O-0311058	1062	3	BENZICK ALLEN B	2LT	O-1060003	1044	2	BERGER ROBERT	MAJ	O-1641334	1064	1	BERMAN SAMUEL S	CPT	O-0486538	1045	2
BENSON GEORGE M	CW3	W-2124583	0263	1	BENZIGER ALICE C	1LT	L-0201545	0246	2	BERGER ROGER	LTC	O-0251736	0264	3	BERMAN SANFORD A	CPT	O-0308156	0645	2
BENSON GEORGE W	LTC	O-1547232	1066	1	BERANIA MELCHOR P	2LT	O-1897007	1048	1	BERGER THEODORE	CPT	O-1302583	0556	2	BERMAN SOL A	CPT	O-0419769	0344	2
BENSON GERHARD P	LTC	O-1795850	0966	1	BERARD ALBERT J	1LT	O-0128833	0648	3	BERGER VINCENT P	LTC	O-0280631	0667	3	BERMAN WILLIAM	COL	O-0128961	0354	2
BENSON HOWARD F	CPT	O-1580885	0247	2	BERARD JR WILBUR J	1LT	O-1013924	0545	2	BERGER WILLIAM J	CW2	W-2205986	0258	1	BERNARD ALBERT L	LTC	O-1796565	0862	1
BENSON JAMES C	LTC	O-1896216	0461	1	BERARD MARSHALL A	LTC	O-0435720	0155	1	BERGERON KENNETH T	CPT	O-1100442	0146	1	BERNARD BARBARA M	2LT	N-0725081	0745	1
BENSON JAMES P	MAJ	O-0497742	1053	1	BERARDCELLI JOSEPH H	CW3	W-2109157	0261	1	BERGERON PAUL E	CPT	O-1174776	0147	2	BERNARD EDWARD	LTC	O-0298935	0161	1
BENSON JEANETTE M	2LT	N-0732326	1044	1	BERARDI JAMES B	COL	O-0339826	0161	3	BERGHEIMER ALFRED	MAJ	O-1328002	0262	1	BERNARD JR HENRY O	CPT	O-1299181	0754	2
BENSON JESSE M	MAJ	O-0503276	0246	2	BERARDI RALPH J	MAJ	O-1302930	0960	1	BERGIN JOHN J	1LT	O-1298346	0353	2	BERNARD JUNIOR J	MAJ	O-1535726	1061	1
BENSON JOHN O	1LT	O-1043566	0444	2	BERASLEY MICHAEL	MAJ	O-1030118	1051	1	BERGIN LOUIS H	CW4	W-2141192	1064	1	BERNARD LOUIS	MAJ	O-1589696	0359	1
BENSON JOHN W	CW3	W-2152333	0561	1	BERBERIAN HERACH M	LTC	O-0441979	1067	1	BERGIN SAMUEL A	MAJ	O-1576925	0763	1	BERNARD LOUIS B	LTC	O-1797026	1263	1
BENSON JR WILLIAM V	MAJ	O-0559591	1163	1	BERBIGLIA JR NICKOLA	MAJ	O-0372825	1060	1	BERGIN WILLIAM A	CW3	W-2109273	0356	2	BERNARD PROSPER G	CPT	O-0246737	0644	2
BENSON LEO C	MAJ	O-1893746	0366	1	BERCAW WOODSON W	CPT	O-0107912	0556	3	BERGLUND CHARLES W	MAJ	O-0328458	0562	3	BERNARD WILLIAM J	MAJ	O-2018635	0863	1
BENSON LEROY I	CW2	W-2208773	0564	2	BERCH THOMAS H	LTC	O-0124963	1154	3	BERGLUND ELMER A	LTC	O-0261005	0367	3	BERNARDI EUGENE R	LTC	O-0258483	1059	3
BENSON LOUIS F	LTC	O-0301961	1057	3	BERCHENKO FRANK	MAJ	O-0348791	1045	2	BERGLUND FERN L	1LT	N-0733417	1045	1	BERNARDIC JOHN L	MAJ	O-1321990	0257	1
BENSON MURRAY	COL	O-0275067	1164	3	BERCKMAN ERNEST C	MAJ	O-0389821	0662	1	BERGLUND HARRY G	LTC	O-0234921	0846	2	BERNARDIN JOSEPH B	COL	O-0161156	0659	3
BENSON NOLDN J	MAJ	O-0960824	0262	1	BERCOT KATHRYN W	2LT	N-0759900	0445	1	BERGLUND LEONARD B	MAJ	O-1307498	0163	1	BERNARDO CARMELO J	LTC	O-0960826	1166	1
BENSON OLIN E	CW4	W-2132165	1163	2	BERDEEN THOMPSON N	MAJ	O-0264516	0667	3	BERGLUND ROBERT M	MAJ	O-2280059	0966	1	BERNARDONI BERNARD	LTC	O-0231677	0763	3
BENSON OLIVER G	COL	O-0309965	1065	3	BERDIN ELADIC N	1LT	O-0182561	0257	3	BERGMAN HAROLD D	CPT	O-1000084	1145	2	BERNATZ GRETCHEN R	1LT	N-0733098	0845	1
BENSON PAUL F	LTC	O-1294682	0764	1	BERDON LOUIS J	CPT	O-0311733	0145	2	BERGMAN JAMES A	MAJ	O-1180417	0163	1	BERNAUER NICHOLAS J	CPT	O-1165023	0346	2
BENSON RAYMOND I	COL	O-0203848	0854	3	BERENATO FRANK L	LTC	O-1638179	0461	1	BERGMAN KENNETH E	CW3	W-2148704	0961	1	BERNAYS HELEN M	1LT	N-0732828	0746	1
BENSON ROBERT G	LTC	O-0282929	1156	3	BERENDSEN HENRY F	MAJ	O-1315768	1160	1	BERGMAN ROBERT	1LT	O-1292114	1044	2	BERNAYS MURRAY C	COL	O-0506039	1145	2
BENSON ROBERT H	CW2	W-2114790	0147	1	BERENDSEN LLOYD H	CPT	O-0112445	1045	2	BERGMANN JEROME W	CPT	O-0496281	0845	2	BERNDSEN ALBERT J	MAJ	O-2096472	0266	1
BENSON SAMUEL L	LTC	O-0248192	0465	3	BERENDT ELMORE F	COL	O-0216733	1063	3	BERGMANN JOHN C	MAJ	O-0309708	0944	2	BERNE FREDERICK	1LT	O-1292115	1045	2
BENSON STERLING O	1LT	O-1926347	0554	2	BERESFORD CHARLES	MAJ	O-1941358	0766	1	BERGMANN PAUL K	1LT	O-1294071	0352	1	BERNE-ALLEN ALLAN	LTC	O-0226506	0962	3
BENSON THURSTON E	MAJ	O-0288279	1063	3	BERESFORD G F	MAJ	O-0424534	0547	1	BERGMANN ROBERT F	LTC	O-0288530	0560	1	BERNER ERIC P	MAJ	O-2028880	0356	1
BENSON VERNON W	CPT	O-0452239	1263	1	BERESWILL WILLIAM	MAJ	O-1335882	0662	1	BERGMANN RUSSELL A	LTC	O-1011757	0164	1	BERNER JACK L	1LT	O-1101335	0245	2
BENSON WALTER P	MAJ	O-2056270	0567	3	BERETTA JOHN W	COL	O-0185317	0359	3	BERGNER ELROY G	WO1	W-2139820	0352	1	BERNER LYLE C	MAJ	O-2319363	0867	1
BENSON WESLEY T	CPT	O-0284808	1144	2	BERG ALF M	MAJ	O-1920127	0765	1	BERGQUIST F W	LTC	O-0241742	0356	3	BERNHAGEN JAMES D	1LT	O-1301415	1045	2

NAME	GRADE	SVC NO	DATE RET MO YR	RET CODE
BERNHARD CARL W	MAJ	O-0248591	0367	3
BERNHARD JULIUS A	LTC	O-1321142	1162	1
BERNHARD ROBERT E	CPT	O-0352537	0146	2
BERNHARD STEVE J	MAJ	O-2016330	0564	1
BERNHARDT CHARLES J	CW3	W-2152573	0762	1
BERNHARDT DONALD R	CPT	O-1714834	0947	2
BERNHARDT FRANZ F	LTC	O-1174231	1064	1
BERNHARDT RALPH H	CW2	W-2214902	1066	1
BERNHARDT WILLIAM J	MAJ	O-2007930	0161	1
BERNHART ROBERT C	CW2	W-2214591	0866	1
BERNHEIM BERTHOL M	1LT	O-1580625	0546	2
BERNHEIM JACK W	LTC	O-1895987	1162	1
BERNICK FRANK M	CW2	W-2212922	0467	1
BERNIER DENNIS O	MAJ	O-0318209	0645	2
BERNIER JOSEPH L A	CPT	O-2024243	0353	1
BERNING JOSEPH F	LTC	O-1293531	0465	3
BERNING LAWRENCE H	MAJ	O-0300326	0854	1
BERNOTAS JOHN J	MAJ	O-2019414	0263	1
BERNS CHARLES	COL	O-0245693	0462	3
BERNSDORFF FLETCHER	LTC	O-0246943	0463	3
BERNSHAUSEN FRITZ	MAJ	O-1925560	0766	1
BERNSTEIN DAVID	MAJ	O-0332951	0146	2
BERNSTEIN DAVID	CPT	O-0918211	1055	2
BERNSTEIN DAVID	1LT	O-1796213	0146	2
BERNSTEIN ETHAN	1LT	O-1291766	0346	2
BERNSTEIN JOSEPH J	LTC	O-0258956	0267	3
BERNSTEIN LEO H T	LTC	O-0483931	0263	2
BERNSTEIN ROBERT	LTC	O-0444638	0667	1
BERNSTEIN WILLIAM H	CPT	O-1683874	0845	2
BERNSTROM HARRY O	CPT	O-0160801	0356	3
BERNT JR DANIEL M	MAJ	O-0916058	1045	1
BERNTHAL HERBERT I	1LT	O-0512011	1143	2
BERNUCCI KATHRYN T	CPT	N-0724626	1044	1
BEROJUNSKY ADOLPH L	1LT	O-1018018	0646	2
BERRENT SAMUEL G	LTC	O-0224959	1263	3
BERRET THOMAS J	CW2	W-2144511	1154	1
BERRETH CLARENCE J	LTC	O-0735511	0166	1
BERRIER CECIL G	MAJ	O-0968268	0863	1
BERRIER WILLIS H	MAJ	O-0277081	0260	3
BERRINGTON ZEMA W	MAJ	O-0167257	0347	1
BERRIOS JOSE R	COL	O-0108228	1053	1
BERRIOS-DIAZ TOMAS	1LT	O-0450848	0346	2
BERRY ARTHUR P	CW3	W-2142808	1159	1
BERRY CARL W	MAJ	O-0171425	0946	1
BERRY CAUSA E	LTC	O-1304329	1263	1
BERRY CECIL	CPT	O-0490953	0247	1
BERRY CHARLES M	CPT	O-1104747	0346	1
BERRY CHARLES P	MAJ	O-0970383	0664	1
BERRY CLIFFORD E	MAJ	O-1169024	0161	1
BERRY CONWARD R	COL	O-0365967	0761	1
BERRY DEE	COL	O-0212922	0853	3
BERRY DELTA B	MAJ	O-0971004	1163	1
BERRY DENZIL J	CPT	O-1051873	0847	1
BERRY DONALD F	MAJ	O-1688420	0862	1
BERRY EDWARD J	MAJ	O-1283011	0348	1
BERRY EDWARD W	COL	O-0244768	0762	3
BERRY ELIZABETH	2LT	N-0764667	1047	1
BERRY EUGENE J	COL	O-0187629	1148	3
BERRY EUGENE V	MAJ	O-2000508	0765	1
BERRY FERRIS M	COL	O-0345362	0564	1
BERRY FRANK B	B G	O-0166083	0552	3
BERRY FRANKLIN M	COL	O-0219393	0664	3
BERRY FREDERICK	MAJ	O-0353117	0946	1
BERRY GASSIWAY H	MAJ	O-1797423	0461	1
BERRY GEORGE G	COL	O-0276675	0363	3
BERRY HAROLD E	LTC	O-0332172	0160	1
BERRY IDA E	MAJ	N-0724523	0661	1
BERRY JACK T	LTC	O-1825618	1162	1
BERRY JAMES A	MAJ	O-1296801	0161	1
BERRY JAMES F	LTC	O-0918273	1264	3
BERRY JAMES L	MAJ	O-0254446	0166	3
BERRY JAMES M	LTC	O-0237112	0464	3
BERRY JAMES P	1LT	O-0416377	1045	2
BERRY JOHN C	MAJ	O-1876416	0665	1
BERRY JOHN F	CPT	O-1877767	0162	1
BERRY JOHN G	COL	O-0294490	0367	3
BERRY JOHN L	COL	O-0262675	0460	3
BERRY JOHN L	1LT	O-1175722	0947	1
BERRY JOHN T	LTC	O-0736952	1067	1
BERRY JOSEPH	LTC	O-1821667	1063	1
BERRY JOSEPH B	LTC	O-1327704	1167	1
BERRY JR CHARLES W	COL	O-0255057	1057	3
BERRY JR FRANCIS W	LTC	O-0155200	0157	3
BERRY JR GEORGE S	LTC	O-0166629	1057	3
BERRY JR JAMES B	COL	O-0361784	0960	1
BERRY JR ROBERT M	MAJ	O-1342362	0459	1
BERRY KENNETH O	CPT	O-1011504	1059	2
BERRY LELAND P	LTC	O-0239588	0863	3
BERRY LESLIE A	CW4	W-2127885	0957	1
BERRY LESTER	LTC	O-0469561	0247	1
BERRY LEWIS W	1LT	O-1311567	0845	2
BERRY MACK P	LTC	O-1119645	0966	1
BERRY OTHMAR P	MAJ	O-0914045	0146	2
BERRY PAUL	CW3	W-2127363	0157	1
BERRY PAUL N	MAJ	O-0447479	1046	2
BERRY RALPH U	MAJ	O-0353827	1145	2
BERRY REBECCA J	MAJ	N-0721440	1265	2
BERRY ROBERT F	LTC	O-1587123	0365	1
BERRY ROBERT H	2LT	O-1176253	0445	2
BERRY ROBERT L	1LT	O-2051962	1045	2
BERRY ROCKWOOD N	CPT	O-0413662	0245	1
BERRY WALLACE O	LTC	O-0369597	0167	3
BERRY WILLIAM A	MAJ	O-1922518	0967	1
BERRY WILLIAM H	MAJ	O-2021257	0666	1
BERRY WILLIAM J	2LT	O-0329903	0364	3
BERRY WILLIAM L	COL	O-0750332	0666	3
BERRYHILL RALPH O	MAJ	O-2055128	0760	1
BERRYMAN JR WALDO A	COL	O-0287847	0463	1
BERRYMAN MARY W	1LT	N-0779173	0446	1
BERSEY ARTHUR T	MAJ	O-0241525	0265	3
BERSHAD MILTON	MAJ	O-0241375	1265	3
BERSON ARTHUR I	MAJ	O-0246034	0260	2
BERSON JOSEPH	MAJ	O-0984292	0764	2
BERTAGNOLI ROBERT W	LTC	O-1637252	0861	1
BERTELS GLENN G	LTC	O-0325164	0660	3
BERTELSEN HENRY C	MAJ	O-0126951	0648	3
BERTELSMAN PATRICK F	CPT	O-0998178	1062	1
BERTHELSEN NELS M	MAJ	O-1554320	0460	1
BERTHELSEN WALTER L	LTC	O-0668044	0466	1
BERTINO FRED	LTC	O-0375390	1067	3
BERTOLET ALBERT G	CW4	W-2141974	0265	1
BERTRAM HENRY F	CW3	W-2143867	0662	1
BERTRAND CHARLES H	LTC	O-0347672	0367	3
BERTRAND JAY	COL	O-0260947	1066	3
BERTRAND JOHN W	MAJ	O-1557120	0961	1
BERTSCH LEO	LTC	O-0906103	0162	1
BERTSCH PIUS A	CPT	O-2049472	0746	2
BERTUGLI RUDOLPH	CW4	W-2141195	1046	1
BERTULIS SIMON J	1LT	O-1303647	0246	2
BERTZ HENRY	LTC	O-0164388	0546	1
BERUBE JOSEPH A P	MAJ	O-1587035	1164	1
BERWICK JOHN F	CW3	W-2141196	0862	1
BERZELIUS CARL F	LTC	O-0252214	1265	3
BERZINEC GEORGE G	1LT	O-0551230	0745	2
BERZOFF SYDNEY D	2LT	O-1944625	0244	2
BESANCENEY CHARLES E	LTC	O-0322055	0967	3
BESCHENBOSSEL A W	LTC	O-0236619	0454	3
BESECKER CLIFFORD A	MAJ	O-0519283	0853	1
BESENDORF GEORGE J	CPT	O-0215367	1153	3
BESHARA JOHN J	LTC	O-0235112	0758	3
BESHERS THOMAS H	MAJ	O-2007511	1162	1
BESLY CLAY A	COL	O-1168554	0261	1
BESNAH ALBERT N	LTC	O-0152959	0648	3
BESNIER WILLIAM C	MAJ	O-2006974	0857	1
BESS GORDON	MAJ	O-0324390	0646	2
BESS GORDON W	MAJ	O-1040497	0859	1
BESS JR JOHN F	LTC	O-1549888	0662	1
BESS WALDO R	LTC	O-0347414	0660	1
BESSELIEVRE ALLEN M	CPT	O-2043037	0646	2
BESSEN ROBERT E	CW3	W-2206294	1165	1
BESSENT EARL L	CPT	O-1923534	1162	1
BESSETTE ANITA E	MAJ	N-0799277	0765	1
BESSETTE LOUIS J	CPT	O-0239803	0753	3
BESSETTE ROLAND J	MAJ	O-0989010	1262	1
BESSEY ROY F	LTC	O-0111733	0949	3
BESSLER ALBERT O	LTC	O-1170651	0862	1
BESSUNGER THEODORE N	1LT	O-0920716	1045	2
BEST AUGUSTIE P	CPT	O-0492497	0547	2
BEST DALE D	LTC	O-1038741	0164	1
BEST GEORGE H	LTC	O-0244161	0864	3
BEST GEORGE P	CPT	O-2033667	0665	2
BEST HENRY L	LTC	O-0241910	0952	3
BEST HEPBURN I	1LT	O-1313545	0845	2
BEST HOWARD	MAJ	O-0207063	0648	3
BEST JANET C	2LT	N-0784323	0845	1
BEST JEWEL G	CPT	O-0497679	0459	1
BEST JOHN L	COL	O-0193618	0459	1
BEST LEALON L	CPT	O-2262202	0261	1
BEST LEE J	LTC	O-0202836	0955	3
BEST LEONIDAS W	MAJ	O-1176255	0861	1
BEST MELVIN R	LTC	O-1101736	0861	1
BEST NOLAN P	1LT	O-1548640	0444	2
BEST OSCAR V	LTC	O-0247733	0253	3
BEST RICHARD F	MAJ	O-2036352	0959	1
BEST RICHARD J	LTC	O-1102153	1161	1
BEST RICHARD R	MAJ	O-1114050	1060	1
BEST ROY L	2LT	O-1308586	1143	2
BEST RUSSELL C	2LT	O-1107803	0944	2
BEST TORREY L	CPT	O-1596464	0661	1
BEST WALTER E	LTC	O-0265275	0267	3
BEST WILLIAM	MAJ	O-0200750	0349	3
BEST WILLIAM T	2LT	O-1305882	0444	2
BESTE BENJAMIN F	CW2	W-2115813	1154	1
BESTENBOSTEL ANNE L	2LT	N-0720034	0544	1
BESTICK JAMES E	CW3	W-2114663	0461	1
BESTOR GEORGE C	MAJ	O-0194890	0862	3
BESWICK WILLIAM L	COL	O-0224225	0253	1
BETANCOURT ARTHUR	CPT	O-1341742	0958	1
BETHANCOURT WILTZ J	COL	O-0423624	1161	1
BETHARD ALVIN J	MAJ	O-0310686	0347	1
BETHARD MYRON G	CW3	W-2206336	1265	1
BETHEA CORA E	CPT	N-0762364	0849	2
BETHEA ROBERT J	CW2	W-2148465	0657	2
BETHEL CHARLES E	CW3	W-2206662	0666	1
BETHEL JR WILLIAM H	MAJ	O-0963140	0366	1
BETHEL LENSON	LTC	O-0205486	1057	3
BETHEL MILLIGAN	MAJ	O-0238488	1162	3
BETHERS CARL F	LTC	O-0290937	0446	1
BETHKE CLARENCE F	LTC	O-1633669	1161	1
BETHMAN JOHN J	LTC	O-0377987	0256	1
BETIT CLARENCE L	LTC	O-1010036	1165	1
BETKER CHRIS J	MAJ	O-0334580	0344	2
BETRUS THOMAS A	MAJ	O-1120624	0664	1
BETSON SR CASPER F	2LT	O-0425161	0245	2
BETT GEORGE F	MAJ	O-1646065	0762	1
BETTELHEIM BERNARD K	COL	O-0227763	0964	3
BETTENBURG PHILIP C	M G	O-0171936	1060	3
BETTENDORF HENRY J	MAJ	O-1287820	0559	1
BETTERLY JOHN A	COL	O-0251814	0266	3
BETTERLY WARREN A	MAJ	O-0144657	1047	2
BETTERS JR WILLIAM H	MAJ	O-1298487	0861	1
BETTGE HENRY M	LTC	O-0342918	0766	3
BETTI ALDER P	CPT	O-0959304	0261	1
BETTINGER JOHN	WO1	W-2102657	0345	2
BETTINGER JR JOHN C	1LT	O-0537952	0448	2
BETTINGER MAURICE E	COL	O-0249594	0657	1
BETTOLI FRANK S	2LT	O-1054910	0645	2
BETTONEY LAURICE A	1LT	N-0735052	0346	1
BETTS CHARLES F	1LT	O-0284839	1043	2
BETTS EDWIN J	MAJ	O-1295157	0157	1
BETTS HARRY H	MAJ	O-0225140	0265	3
BETTS JOHN W	CPT	O-1305001	0646	2
BETTS JOSEPH L	MAJ	O-0118714	0255	3
BETTS RICHARD H	LTC	O-1824910	0864	1
BETTS ROBERT A	LTC	O-0214263	0663	3
BETTS WILLIAM G	CW2	W-2110109	0945	2
BETZ GEORGE E	MAJ	O-0483976	0862	3
BETZ JOHN E	MAJ	O-0965519	0965	1
BETZER BOYCE F	COL	O-0298412	0564	3
BETZNER ROBERT C	LTC	O-0474420	1065	3
BEUCLER WILLIAM G	MAJ	O-0231018	0450	3
BEUTEL WILLIAM C	LTC	O-1169800	1266	1
BEUTTEL WILLIAM W	CPT	O-0514272	1048	2
BEVANS ROSCOE E	CW3	W-2143508	1067	1
BEVEL HAROLD W	MAJ	O-1918879	0463	1
BEVEL ROY F	MAJ	O-0322429	0648	1
BEVENS WRAY	LTC	O-0954560	0667	3
BEVER JAMES W	1LT	O-0501734	0147	2
BEVERAGE JR BOYD M	CW2	W-2150671	0760	1
BEVERAGE KEITH D	MAJ	O-1018515	0261	1
BEVERIDGE WILLIAM M	COL	O-0190607	0746	2
BEVERLEY JOHN H	MAJ	O-2031847	0766	1
BEVERLEY JR WILLIAM	CPT	O-0269422	0166	3
BEVERLY GRANT E	COL	O-0229530	0564	3
BEVERLY JR JOSEPH L	CW3	W-3150424	0867	1
BEVILACQUA FRANK	1LT	O-0485213	1043	2
BEVILL JOHN L	1LT	O-1112020	0346	2
BEVINGTON CLIFFORD R	LTC	O-0254455	0464	3
BEVINS JAMES R	MAJ	O-0948345	0863	1
BEVIS HARRY L	CPT	O-1180816	0456	2
BEVIS ROBERT E	1LT	O-0341615	1145	2
BEWIE EDWARD F	LTC	O-0364448	0258	2
BEWLEY JESSE W	CPT	O-0794481	0262	1
BEWLEY LOYAL V	COL	O-0231666	1058	3
BEWSHER ELEANOR W	CPT	N-0744040	0747	1
BEY BARNETT E	MAJ	O-0291838	0444	2
BEY FLORENCE L	CPT	R-0000271	0347	1
BEYATT EUGENE P	MAJ	O-0121642	0951	3
BEYDLER EARL S	MAJ	O-1824564	0761	2
BEYER CARL W	LTC	O-1795755	0262	1
BEYER ERWIN P	COL	O-0201544	0959	1
BEYER GEORGE W	1LT	O-1797075	0564	1
BEYER GEORGE W A	LTC	O-0346821	0758	1
BEYER JAMES S	LTC	O-1100446	0367	1
BEYER ROBERT W	LTC	O-0322957	0760	1
BEYER SR FRANCIS D	LTC	O-0278537	1053	3
BEYERLEIN RAYMOND H	1LT	O-2279415	1151	3
BEYERS CLIFFORD F	B G	O-0267530	0265	3
BEYERS JOHN A	LTC	O-1548642	0763	1
BEYERS JR WILLIAM F	CW2	W-3151989	0167	2
BEYERS ROBERT A	1LT	O-1825277	0947	2
BEYERSDORFER FRED A	LTC	O-0274441	1153	3
BEYL IRVIN A	LTC	O-1703024	1165	1
BEYMER CLYDE E	1LT	O-0889598	0247	2
BEYRER EDNA M	CPT	N-0700042	0740	1
BEZ JOHN A	LTC	O-1055781	1262	1
BEZIAT ROBERT L	LTC	O-0371342	0560	1
BEZLER ELEANOR J	1LT	N-0759342	1045	1
BEZUCHA ROBERT G	1LT	O-1165708	0144	2
BEZY EDWIN B	MAJ	O-1542842	0157	2
BIAFORA JOSEPH R	1LT	O-0446966	0345	2
BIAFORE SAM F	MAJ	O-1283712	0549	1
BIANCHI ANTHONY J	MAJ	O-1824412	0361	1
BIANCHI EMILIO R	LTC	O-1550109	1062	1
BIANCHI JOSEPH J	LTC	O-1041558	0264	1
BIANCO AUGUST J	LTC	O-0203013	0866	1
BIANCO FRANCIS R	CPT	O-1305529	1046	2
BIANCO FRANK C	COL	O-0185881	0556	3
BIAS DORSEY V	CPT	O-0495776	1262	2
BIAS WETZEL L	CPT	O-0980560	1060	1
BIASELLA HUMBERT F	COL	O-0316886	0760	1
BIBB EUGENE S	COL	O-0144077	0150	3
BIBB EVERETT I	LTC	O-0262498	0657	1
BIBB JR ARTHUR	1LT	O-0525521	0944	2
BIBBINS EDWARD A	CPT	O-0795549	0653	1
BIBICH NICK	MAJ	O-2096630	0464	1
BIBLE EDWARD M	MAJ	O-1335733	0765	1
BICE WALTER M	MAJ	O-1583946	0557	2
BICHKO ANDREW C	1LT	O-1695735	0159	1
BICKEL JOHN A	COL	O-0144486	0649	3

NAME	GRADE	SVC NO	DATE RET MO YR	RET CODE
BICKETT ROBERT J	1LT	O-1016978	0146	2
BICKFORD ROBERT J	COL	O-1797936	0766	2
BICKHAM CHARLES E	LTC	O-0177546	0661	3
BICKING JOHN W	LTC	O-1553223	0667	3
BICKLE LORENE A	2LT	N-0735392	0145	1
BICKLEY JR WILLIAM G	MAJ	O-0405161	0760	1
BICKMORE EUGENE G	MAJ	O-2007703	0765	1
BICKNELL GEORGE W	LTC	O-0275524	1265	3
BICKNELL RAY A	MAJ	O-1688484	0664	1
BICKNELL ROBERT L	1LT	O-0887449	0845	2
BICKSTON HAROLD A	CPT	O-0998773	0263	1
BIDART MARIE A	1LT	N-0736518	1045	1
BIDDIEX HAROLD L	2LT	O-1318911	0645	2
BIDDLE CLAYTON R	MAJ	O-1317749	0465	1
BIDDLE JAMES C	LTC	O-1575751	0662	1
BIDDLE JUANITA F	LTC	L-0900707	0964	1
BIDDLE KENNETH J	MAJ	O-1182065	1265	1
BIDDLE NICHOLAS	COL	O-0144488	0545	2
BIDDLE RUSSELL A	CW3	W-2147728	0964	1
BIDDLE SAM H	MAJ	O-1930984	0765	1
BIDDLE WALTER I	LTC	O-0448852	0762	3
BIDLACK CECIL S	CPT	O-0213296	0863	3
BIDLE PAUL J	LTC	O-0343055	0258	1
BIDUS LEO M	COL	O-0322215	1154	2
BIDWELL HAROLD F	LTC	O-0115640	0653	3
BIDWELL PAUL W	COL	O-0246597	0648	3
BIDWELL RAY B	CW3	W-2210815	0667	1
BIDWELL RAYMOND H	MAJ	O-1167742	0547	2
BIDWELL ROBERT L	LTC	O-0451077	0461	1
BIEBER BRUCE	MAJ	O-0230697	1049	1
BIEBER CHARLES V	COL	O-0324382	0365	3
BIEBER HAROLD J	LTC	O-1174502	0465	1
BIEBER HYMAN	2LT	O-1913525	0624	1
BIEBER JAMES B	CPT	O-2262208	0161	1
BIEBER MELVIN H	MAJ	O-2001069	0762	1
BIEBESHEIMER EDWARD	LTC	O-0203279	0959	3
BIEBLE LESLIE J	CPT	O-1549219	1160	2
BIEDA WALTER P	MAJ	O-1799090	0960	1
BIEDERMAN RICHARD E	MAJ	O-1011679	0347	2
BIEDLER ASHBY L	MAJ	O-0140878	0757	3
BIEDRZYCKI LEO J	1LT	O-1298174	0645	2
BIEG HENRY C	COL	O-0180925	0661	3
BIEGANSKI EDMUND	CPT	O-1591593	0459	1
BIEHL DAWSON D	CW2	W-2210043	0564	1
BIEHL JAMES A	LTC	O-0273906	1264	3
BIEHLER KARL F	LTC	O-0114089	1055	3
BIEHN FLORENCE O	LTC	O-0221157	0662	3
BIEL VINCENT E	CPT	O-1694344	1144	2
BIELAK RAYMOND L	LTC	O-0424189	0564	1
BIELAWSKI HILARY S	MAJ	O-2030843	0463	1
BIELEFELDT ROY A	CW3	W-2147080	0862	1
BIELFELDT CLAIRE J	1LT	N-0772573	0646	1
BIELSKI ROBERT F	1LT	O-2049473	0546	2
BIELSS AUGUST C	MAJ	O-0399156	0163	2
BIELUCKI CHESTER P	MAJ	O-1576933	1160	1
BIENEMAN ROBERT F	MAJ	O-0452029	0551	1
BIER ROBERT A	COL	O-0212248	0959	3
BIERBAUM LEWIS J	MAJ	O-1030952	1056	1
BIERBOWER JR C G	LTC	O-1548353	1060	1
BIERBOWER PARK P	CW3	W-2147437	1162	2
BIERER BION B	COL	O-0256670	1058	3
BIERKAN HOWARD E	MAJ	O-1573729	1145	1
BIERKORTTE GEORGE R	LTC	O-1113583	0867	1
BIERLEY DAVID H	1LT	O-1296639	0945	2
BIERLY ROBERT L	LTC	O-0958371	0866	1
BIERMAN GEORGE F	CPT	O-1557252	0646	2
BIERMAN GEORGE W	MAJ	O-1547235	0766	1
BIERMAN HARRY J	MAJ	O-0110229	0657	3
BIERMAN PHILIP W	COL	O-0265081	0267	3
BIERNAT JOHN J	1LT	O-1556841	0646	2
BIERNAT ROBERT L	2LT	O-2006413	0247	2
BIERNOFF JOSEPH	CPT	O-0331694	0144	2
BIERSTADT FRANCIS E	COL	O-0286429	0556	3
BIERSTEKER N O	LTC	O-0338847	0161	1
BIERY JAMES H	LTC	O-1080004	0361	1

NAME	GRADE	SVC NO	DATE RET MO YR	RET CODE
BIESE JOSEPH J	CPT	O-1014621	0549	2
BIESEMEYER HAROLD L	1LT	O-1322305	1145	2
BIESEMEYER HERBERT J	1LT	O-0332363	0844	2
BIEVER PHILIP M	LTC	O-0363120	0661	1
BIFANO SALVATORE	MAJ	O-1303097	0258	1
BIGART WILLIAM D	LTC	O-0926385	1065	3
BIGELOW ALBERT S	LTC	O-0181175	0649	3
BIGELOW ALLEN C	COL	O-0181860	0554	3
BIGELOW EDWARD R	LTC	O-0179422	0648	3
BIGELOW HARRY J	CPT	O-1012681	0846	1
BIGELOW LOUIS E	MAJ	O-1104754	0357	1
BIGELOW MAURICE H	COL	O-0919939	1163	3
BIGELOW ROBERT A	LTC	O-1305374	0167	1
BIGELOW ROBERT W	CW3	W-2207559	1067	1
BIGELOW WILLIAM F	COL	O-0124291	0360	3
BIGGAM JR RUSSELL F	1LT	O-1873328	0754	2
BIGGAR JR FRANK W	2LT	O-1287991	0543	2
BIGGAR WALTER T	LTC	O-0126423	0356	3
BIGGER CLARENCE V	COL	O-0277267	0959	3
BIGGER ERWIN A	LTC	O-0402126	0363	1
BIGGER WALTER K	MAJ	O-1080513	0854	1
BIGGERS WILLIAM G	1LT	O-1944402	0445	2
BIGGERSTAFF GEORGE W	LTC	O-0300279	0659	3
BIGGERSTAFF W H	COL	O-0381862	1054	1
BIGGINS PHILIP F	MAJ	O-0482013	0759	1
BIGGS ANSON W	1LT	O-0514580	0745	2
BIGGS GEORGE N	MAJ	O-0230806	0144	2
BIGGS GEORGE T	CPT	O-0430692	1044	1
BIGGS HAROLD W	LTC	O-1580633	0564	3
BIGGS HORACE F	MAJ	O-0467334	0847	2
BIGGS JACK H	CW2	W-2150270	0163	1
BIGGS JR JAMES E	2LT	O-0550653	1145	2
BIGGS JR JOSEPH P	MAJ	O-0396336	0960	1
BIGGS LAWRENCE W	MAJ	O-0452160	0658	1
BIGGS RAYMOND L	WO1	T-0193159	1065	2
BIGGS ROBERT C	MAJ	O-0121643	0845	2
BIGGS SR DAN T	LTC	O-1283013	1265	1
BIGHAM OCYLE B	CPT	O-0953986	1060	1
BIGHAM JR HUGHEY W	LTC	O-1300440	0366	2
BIGHAM ROCKWELL V	MAJ	O-1014170	0366	1
BIGLER EARL A	MAJ	O-0188320	0350	1
BIGLER LYNN E	CPT	O-0321536	1043	2
BIGLER THOMAS J	MAJ	O-2263096	0665	1
BIGLER THURMAN R	CW2	W-2149008	1160	1
BIGLIN WALLACE W	COL	O-0270002	0365	3
BIGLIN WELLMAN W	MAJ	O-1889823	0766	1
BIGNELL ARTHUR T	WO1	W-2103887	0857	1
BIGNELL SAMUEL E	COL	O-0298702	0457	1
BIHLMEYER EARL W	LTC	O-0361955	0862	1
BIHLMIRE JAMES M	1LT	O-1303098	1045	2
BIHN ROBERT M	1LT	O-0338233	0844	1
BIKLE JR CHARLES E	MAJ	O-0332696	0747	2
BILBO THOMAS J	LTC	O-1040179	0562	2
BILDERBACK FRANK	MAJ	O-1895921	0557	1
BILELLO JOSEPH W	COL	O-0291368	0163	1
BILES ALFRED F	LTC	O-0197009	0154	3
BILES DERWOOD C	LTC	O-1011034	0860	1
BILES GEORGE L	1LT	O-1687866	0543	2
BILES RANDALL H	MAJ	O-1113104	1162	1
BILES THOMAS H	LTC	O-0330889	0360	3
BILEWICZ ROGER L	LTC	O-0386927	0857	1
BILGER CECIL R	COL	O-0375833	0361	1
BILGER CHARLES E	CW2	W-2211146	0666	1
BILGER II ARTHUR S	LTC	O-0451555	0567	1
BILGER WALTER G	LTC	O-0334118	0762	1
BILINOVICH LOUIS P	1LT	O-1181541	0145	2
BILINS STEPHEN M	LTC	O-1549889	0763	1
BILIOKE ALBERT C	COL	O-0234994	0562	3
BILKS PATRICK S	CPT	O-0225230	1047	1
BILLADC REGINALD J	COL	O-0404257	1264	1
BILLBE MERRILL O	LTC	O-0477264	1057	1
BILLER LOREN H	CPT	O-0977253	0462	1
BILLETER FRANK J	COL	O-0210640	0451	3
BILLETT HARRY H	CPT	O-0242924	1163	3
BILLETT RUSSELL A	COL	O-0142122	0758	3

NAME	GRADE	SVC NO	DATE RET MO YR	RET CODE
BILLGER GERALD T	MAJ	O-0686967	0561	1
BILLIGMEIER ELMER E	CPT	O-1581032	0251	1
BILLIGMEIER RUBEN	CPT	O-1575752	0749	1
BILLINGER ELMER F	MAJ	O-2263151	0364	1
BILLINGER ROBERT H	CW2	W-2146217	0562	1
BILLINGS DONALD K	LTC	O-0146372	1045	2
BILLINGS HARRY G	COL	O-0226247	1062	3
BILLINGS HENRY J	CW3	W-2149284	1060	1
BILLINGS JOHN R	LTC	O-1303650	0165	1
BILLINGS JR THOMAS J	CPT	O-1286427	0746	2
BILLINGS RUFUS K	CW2	W-2101004	0253	2
BILLINGS WENDELL R	CW4	W-2105349	0866	1
BILLINGSLEY BOYCE	CPT	O-1701301	1045	2
BILLINGSLEY HARRISON	CPT	O-0109719	0540	2
BILLINGTON C A	1LT	O-2046294	1148	1
BILLINGTON KENNETH	CPT	O-0546023	0364	1
BILLINGTON SIMPSON T	MAJ	O-1291220	0457	1
BILLION CHARLES F	COL	O-0249616	0966	3
BILLIPP RUDOLPH A	LTC	O-0240486	0762	2
BILLMAN CALVIN J	1LT	O-1307793	1044	1
BILLMAN HARLAN F	CPT	O-1311474	0947	2
BILLMAN HERBERT C	CPT	O-1702976	0747	2
BILLMAN LEROY S	CPT	O-0280605	0145	2
BILLMIRE GARRETT O	LTC	O-0312255	0964	3
BILLS JR CLYDE A	COL	O-0913495	1062	1
BILLS KENNETH G	CPT	O-0404216	0144	2
BILLS REED G	1LT	O-1167743	0345	2
BILLS WELTON B	MAJ	O-1593457	0161	1
BILLUPS CRISTOPHER	LTC	O-0245951	0446	2
BILLUPS RUDOLPH R	COL	O-0475793	0265	3
BILLUPS WILLIAM D	MAJ	O-1686631	1162	1
BILLY MICHAEL	CPT	O-1585846	0554	2
BILLY SCHLICHT	2LT	O-2006051	0146	2
BILODEAU EDWARD G	MAJ	O-0927524	0666	3
BILOUS WILLIAM H	LTC	O-1945757	0859	1
BILTZ FREDERICK	COL	O-0273262	0852	3
BILYEU DICK	CW2	W-2145989	0861	1
BINCKLEY MILTON J	COL	O-0217619	0262	3
BINCO MICHAEL P	MAJ	O-0181461	1146	1
BINDA STANLEY J	CPT	O-0423703	0846	2
BINDER HERBERT	CPT	O-1716248	1054	2
BINDER JOHN A	MAJ	O-0408918	0760	1
BINDER LEON	LTC	O-1100019	0256	1
BINDER ROBERT O	1LT	O-0522583	0945	1
BINDER SAMUEL H	LTC	O-0359239	0160	1
BINDIG CHARLES H	MAJ	O-0205204	1157	3
BINDNER JOSEPH T	LTC	O-0922944	0684	3
BINDON LEONARD W	LTC	O-0307186	0346	2
BINFORD JOHN K	CPT	O-0979979	1160	1
BINGAMAN ROBERT L	MAJ	O-0959747	0564	1
BINGEN JOHN R	CPT	O-1826143	0252	1
BINGERT FRANK P	CW4	W-2129758	0858	1
BINGHAM DALE E	CPT	O-0305547	0945	2
BINGHAM DWIGHT W	LTC	O-0373616	1060	1
BINGHAM ERNEST S	MAJ	O-1951531	0561	1
BINGHAM GEORGE W	CPT	O-0144968	0349	3
BINGHAM GLENN F	CPT	O-0180644	0544	1
BINGHAM HOLLAND W	CW2	W-2143869	0563	1
BINGHAM JAMES F	CW2	W-2101023	0244	1
BINGHAM JR GEORGE G	LTC	O-0383689	1265	2
BINGHAM PAUL J	MAJ	O-2263337	0565	1
BINGHAM RALPH E	CPT	O-1918920	0661	1
BINGHAM SIDNEY H	COL	O-0477781	1145	2
BINGHAM STUART A	LTC	O-0217449	0863	3
BINKERD WILFRED W	1LT	O-1590287	0945	2
BINKLEY ALBERT L	1LT	O-1794761	0245	2
BINKLEY DAVID V	LTC	O-0266378	1059	3
BINKLEY HOWARD L	2LT	O-0549412	1045	2
BINKLEY JR JOHN E	1LT	O-0949128	0552	1
BINKLEY WILLIAM R	COL	O-0299967	0263	1
BINKO JR JOSEPH A	MAJ	O-1686634	0565	1
BINKOSKI JOSEPH J	1LT	O-2000954	1052	1
BINKS GEORGE A	MAJ	O-0199312	0943	2
BINNALL MARGARET H	2LT	N-0721169	1044	1
BINNEY HORACE	CPT	O-0252566	0448	2

NAME	GRADE	SVC NO	DATE RET MO YR	RET CODE
BINNICK JOHN E	1LT	O-1578171	1044	2
BINNS JAMES F	MAJ	O-0476550	0346	2
BINNS OTWAY P	COL	O-0325115	0662	1
BINSWANGER LEWIS W	WO1	W-2147063	0860	2
BINTNER MATTHEW S	MAJ	O-2262700	1162	1
BINZER HERMAN S	LTC	O-0247077	0264	3
BION BENJAMIN L	CPT	O-0217082	1061	3
BIONDI EUGENE	LTC	O-1017494	0862	1
BIONDO THOMAS	LTC	O-0228205	0261	3
BIPPUS HAROLD M	WO1	W-2127770	0355	1
BIRCH HAROLD H	LTC	O-0422186	1060	1
BIRCH HOWARD L	MAJ	O-1800128	0565	1
BIRCH MELVIN R	MAJ	O-2007670	0661	1
BIRCHER JOHN E	LTC	O-1326888	0366	1
BIRCHESS STEVE S	LTC	O-0493753	1054	1
BIRCHFIELD MILLARD F	CW2	W-2150536	0858	1
BIRCKHEAD EDWARD F	CPT	O-1051487	0254	2
BIRCUMSHAW JOHN H	1LT	O-1324719	1045	2
BIRD ALBERT R	LTC	O-0179860	1050	3
BIRD BYRON	COL	O-0178080	0848	3
BIRD CHARLES L	MAJ	O-0371278	0251	1
BIRD EDWARD F	LTC	O-1541723	0860	1
BIRD EDWARD W	COL	O-0400179	0746	2
BIRD ERNA D	1LT	N-0736727	0654	2
BIRD EUGENE K	LTC	O-2033122	1266	1
BIRD FRANK	CPT	O-1283196	0746	2
BIRD JAMES H	1LT	O-0518949	0553	1
BIRD JESUS J	1LT	O-1301090	0557	1
BIRD JOHN O	LTC	O-1578172	1060	1
BIRD JOHN R	COL	O-0298356	0765	3
BIRD WHITTIER S	COL	O-0172025	1158	3
BIRD WILLIAM A	COL	O-0280648	1164	3
BIRDSALL CHARLES H	LTC	O-1553224	1067	1
BIRDSELL JOHN J	LTC	O-1796746	0764	1
BIRDSONG CLAUD T	MAJ	O-1574586	0359	1
BIRDSONG ROY I	CW2	W-2144723	1061	1
BIRDSONG THOMAS B	COL	O-0184289	1054	3
BIRDSONG WITHERS G	COL	O-0299104	0561	1
BIRELY JOHN H	MAJ	O-0101925	0654	3
BIRGE ARTHUR B	CPT	O-1291395	1045	2
BIRGE JACKSON P	LTC	O-0486345	0846	2
BIRKBY VINCENT C	CW4	W-2144708	0259	1
BIRKEDAHL LEROY	MAJ	O-1688604	1163	2
BIRKENESS RALPH T	COL	O-0268584	0855	3
BIRKES CLEVE R	CW2	W-2147578	0359	1
BIRKHIMER DOW J	LTC	O-0417482	0861	1
BIRKHIMER ROBERT P	MAJ	O-1303455	1055	1
BIRKHOLZ CARL R	CPT	O-0254890	0556	3
BIRKINSHA HARRY E	MAJ	O-0994695	0864	1
BIRKNER ARCHIE G	LTC	O-0416862	0563	1
BIRKNER JACK W	1LT	O-1915796	0354	2
BIRKNER JOHN F	LTC	O-0495657	0465	1
BIRKS JOHN G	MAJ	O-0475277	0747	1
BIRMINGHAM CALVIN W	CPT	O-2212064	0361	2
BIRNBACH CHARLES	2LT	O-4006656	0654	2
BIRNBAUM GEORGE L	LTC	O-0256324	0662	3
BIRNBAUM NATHAN	COL	O-0901502	0867	3
BIRNEY DAVID T	LTC	O-0274855	0554	1
BIRNEY GEORGE H	LTC	O-0542236	0965	1
BIRNLEY FRANCIS W	MAJ	O-0385978	0661	1
BIROC DENNIS W	MAJ	O-1295817	0563	1
BIRON DONALD R	MAJ	O-0234732	0855	3
BIRON ERNEST M	MAJ	O-0319843	0555	3
BIRON PAUL E	LTC	O-1687950	0846	2
BIRRA ALFRED F	LTC	O-1104506	1161	1
BIRREN MURRELL F	MAJ	O-0206086	0544	2
BISAILLON ROLAND C	CW4	W-2105871	0565	1
BISBING LEWIS H	MAJ	O-1001090	1055	1
BISCHOFF ERIC E	COL	O-0420287	0562	1
BISCHOFF GEORGE H	CPT	O-0374535	0644	2
BISCHOFF MARIE S	1LT	N-0729127	0745	1
BISCOE JOHN S	LTC	O-0250582	1165	3
BISCOE STANLEY J	MAJ	O-0369902	0966	3
BISENIUS CHARLES F	COL	O-0216321	0560	3
BISER FRANK M	1LT	O-0488891	0648	1

NAME	GRADE	SVC NO	DATE RET MO YR	RET CODE
BISH SETH G	CW4	W-2142458	0564	1
BISHARD ELMORE H	CPT	0-1184354	0146	2
BISHER GEORGE M	CPT	0-0178974	0854	3
BISHER WILLIAM	LTC	0-0222483	0260	3
BISHOFF ROBERT G	MAJ	0-1917752	0965	1
BISHOP ALFRED W	CW4	W-2002838	0967	3
BISHOP ALVIN L	CW2	W-2153240	0160	1
BISHOP ANDREW R	1LT	0-1178711	0945	2
BISHOP BILLY G	MAJ	0-0959705	0862	1
BISHOP CECIL V	CW2	W-2142809	1060	1
BISHOP CHARLES W	CPT	0-0272549	1045	2
BISHOP CHARLIE L	CPT	0-2262852	0461	1
BISHOP CLARENCE	2LT	0-1999064	0157	1
BISHOP CLIFFORD	MAJ	0-1310676	0957	1
BISHOP DELBERT S	MAJ	0-2014822	0766	1
BISHOP ELDRIDGE L	1LT	0-1824271	1265	1
BISHOP ERRETT	LTC	0-0202641	0644	1
BISHOP ETHELBERT	2LT	0-1039156	0146	2
BISHOP GLEN O	LTC	0-0381175	0464	3
BISHOP HAROLD C	CPT	0-1294420	0546	1
BISHOP HARRY D	COL	0-0324967	0256	3
BISHOP HERBERT C	LTC	0-0290764	0460	1
BISHOP JACK W	LTC	0-1342236	1067	1
BISHOP JESSE F	COL	0-0222952	0255	3
BISHOP JOHN W	MAJ	0-1533735	0854	1
BISHOP JOSEPH I	LTC	0-0472317	0560	3
BISHOP JR ANDREW W	LTC	0-0254286	0764	3
BISHOP JR PAUL R	CPT	0-1578173	0744	2
BISHOP JR WILLIAM A	LTC	0-0327237	0346	1
BISHOP JR WILLIAM C	LTC	0-0028428	0967	1
BISHOP LUCILLE A	MAJ	N-0763961	1063	1
BISHOP LYNN R	MAJ	0-1923666	0167	1
BISHOP MARTHA B	2LT	N-0785210	0945	1
BISHOP MATTHEW F	LTC	0-1000709	0554	2
BISHOP OLIVE	1LT	N-0755250	1145	1
BISHOP PHILIP E	MAJ	0-1103063	0764	1
BISHOP PRESTON P	COL	0-0228836	0864	3
BISHOP RALPH C	COL	0-0136953	1051	3
BISHOP RAYMOND	MAJ	0-2026263	0859	1
BISHOP ROBERT A	1LT	0-1642180	0445	2
BISHOP ROBERT L	MAJ	0-0398121	0561	2
BISHOP SR JOHN J	MAJ	0-0973430	0263	1
BISHOP THOMAS J	COL	0-0292279	1159	1
BISHOP WALTER G	LTC	0-0264593	0957	3
BISHOP WALTER T	1LT	0-1010106	0445	1
BISHOP WENDELL C	2LT	0-1550544	1044	2
BISHOP WILLIAM A	COL	0-0289979	0565	3
BISHOP WILLIAM D	MAJ	0-1179724	0161	2
BISNOFF IRVIN	COL	0-0267909	0555	1
BISNOFF WILLIAM H	COL	0-0231241	0462	3
BISON THEODORE R	CPT	0-0193685	0560	3
BISS EDWARD C	CPT	0-0486397	1044	1
BISSELL EDWARD H	LTC	0-0312975	0359	1
BISSELL HARRY B	COL	0-0115544	0150	3
BISSELL INEZ M	MAJ	N-0737766	1164	3
BISSELL JR FLOYD H	CW2	W-2146825	0261	1
BISSELL NORMAN F	COL	0-0909426	0864	3
BISSET JR DAVID	LTC	0-0326333	0565	1
BISSON ROLAND P	LTC	0-0900061	0765	3
BISTANY VICTOR	MAJ	0-1287124	0361	1
BISTLINE CLARENCE H	COL	0-0285268	0467	3
BISTRITZ WILLIAM P	CW4	W-2105645	0866	1
BISZANT GEORGE P	MAJ	0-0508570	0853	3
BITLER EDWIN F	LTC	0-0206140	0463	3
BITLER RALPH M	COL	0-0255908	0358	1
BITNER HAROLD M	1LT	0-1821536	0444	2
BITTAKER LEROY F	CW4	W-2203296	0667	1
BITTENBENDER W R	MAJ	0-0359646	1146	2
BITTER REUBEN H	LTC	0-0224696	1055	3
BITTINGER JOHN V	1LT	0-0322964	1066	3
BITTINGER WILLIAM	1LT	0-0154897	0559	3
BITTLE DELBERT	CPT	0-0445604	0848	1
BITTLE GERALD F	COL	0-0178719	0547	2
BITTMAN EDWARD S	LTC	0-0121282	0253	3
BITTNER JR JOHN T	MAJ	0-1544725	0959	1
BITTNER NORMAN W	LTC	0-1100021	0457	1
BITTRICH LOUIS F	CPT	0-0382896	0949	1
BITTS CLARENCE A	MAJ	0-0260473	0466	3
BITZEL RENO	CPT	0-0323758	0745	2
BIVENS WOODROW R	CW2	RW-2143268	0661	1
BIVERT RAYMOND E	LTC	0-0227254	1062	3
BIVINGS JR YANCEY H	LTC	0-0453301	0961	1
BIVINS BRACK A	LTC	0-1011113	0265	1
BIVINS EDWARD A	CW4	W-2006336	0364	2
BIVINS JACK L	1LT	0-1283898	1147	1
BIVINS THOMAS E	CPT	0-0535260	0247	2
BIVINS THOMAS C	MAJ	0-2041667	0766	1
BIXBY FRANK H	CPT	0-0529696	0844	2
BIXBY FRANK J	MAJ	0-1548646	0959	1
BIXLER HENRY E	MAJ	0-1102518	0565	3
BIXLER RAY	MAJ	0-1327601	0164	1
BIXLER SALLY K	2LT	N-0725389	0344	1
BIXLER WILLIAM T	LTC	0-0417639	0863	1
BIZJAK WILLIAM J	LTC	0-1052675	0766	1
BIZZARO TONY	MAJ	0-1317676	0448	1
BIZZELL WILLIAM S	LTC	0-0162779	0961	3
BJERKE JEROY E	1LT	0-1587132	0944	2
BJERKE MARY K	2LT	N-0787398	0645	1
BJERKE MERLIN W	CW3	W-2147844	1063	1
BJERRE EDLMAR I	MAJ	0-0217596	0362	3
BJORGUM ROBERT T	1LT	0-1310556	1045	2
BJORKE ROLF C	1LT	0-0889883	0952	1
BJORKLUND ARNOLD L	1LT	0-1287993	0345	2
BJORKLUND EUGENE D	LTC	0-1568354	1162	1
BJORKLUND FLOYD H	MAJ	0-1040012	0258	1
BJORKLUND JESSE W	LTC	0-2050728	0863	1
BJORNBERG HARRY K	MAJ	0-1326374	0559	1
BJUGSTAD WILMER G	MAJ	0-1056041	1066	1
BLABER SR LEO R	1LT	0-1281818	1045	2
BLACH IVAN K	2LT	0-0523483	0145	2
BLACHER ALBERT E	2LT	0-1323999	1044	2
BLACK ALBERT W	1LT	0-1692596	0553	2
BLACK ALLEN R	MAJ	0-0444632	1148	1
BLACK ARTHUR W	LTC	0-0254310	0345	2
BLACK BRUCE H	LTC	0-1103064	0467	1
BLACK CARL R	LTC	0-0242829	1045	1
BLACK CHARLES H	MAJ	0-1877795	1063	1
BLACK CHARLES L	LTC	0-1124779	0864	1
BLACK CLARENCE R	CW2	W-2143201	0958	1
BLACK CLAYTON D	LTC	0-1100022	0860	1
BLACK DALE L	LTC	0-1114051	0864	1
BLACK DAVID H	2LT	0-1285696	0645	2
BLACK EDWARD L	LTC	0-0250088	1166	3
BLACK ELI	LTC	0-0417834	0856	1
BLACK ERNEST S	CPT	0-0508502	0655	1
BLACK GANES	LTC	0-1542533	0866	1
BLACK GLENN A	1LT	0-2000803	0846	1
BLACK HENRY B	1LT	0-1543613	0353	1
BLACK HENRY W	COL	0-0259095	0667	3
BLACK HOWARD R	CPT	0-1015871	0959	2
BLACK HUGH F	CPT	0-0116814	0643	2
BLACK IRENE D	CPT	N-0773625	1047	1
BLACK JAMES A	COL	0-0192581	1055	3
BLACK JAMES C	MAJ	0-1554136	0263	1
BLACK JOHN L	CW2	W-2147290	0861	2
BLACK JR ELBERT C	CPT	0-0383007	0846	2
BLACK JR JAMES R	MAJ	0-0259630	1264	3
BLACK JR ROBERT W	LTC	0-0233372	0164	3
BLACK JR THOMAS E	CPT	0-0387442	1145	2
BLACK JR WILLIAM J	LTC	0-0298145	1052	3
BLACK LEAHMAN C	LTC	0-1055552	0663	1
BLACK LONNIE W	CPT	0-1032323	0349	1
BLACK MERVIN T	CW3	W-2143871	1162	1
BLACK MINNIE M	LTC	N-0700723	0946	1
BLACK ORMOND C	LTC	0-0228178	0265	3
BLACK OTTIS E	MAJ	0-1895468	1157	1
BLACK PETER F	CPT	0-0405017	0845	2
BLACK PETER P	LTC	0-0450696	0954	1
BLACK RAYLSTON N	CW2	W-2147789	0562	1
BLACK RAYMOND	LTC	0-0481955	0553	1
BLACK RAYMOND H	LTC	0-2036354	0662	1
BLACK RUDY	MAJ	0-1330515	0862	1
BLACK SCOTT U	CPT	0-1179300	0756	1
BLACK SIDNEY M	CW2	W-2152446	0959	1
BLACK THOMAS B	CW3	W-2124095	1058	1
BLACK THOMAS R	COL	0-0499464	1061	3
BLACK WILLIAM A	MAJ	0-0327444	0447	2
BLACK WILLIAM E	LTC	0-0251647	0565	3
BLACK WILLIAM E	COL	0-0282633	1065	3
BLACK WILLIAM W	LTC	0-1167745	0865	1
BLACKBURN ASA O	MAJ	0-1885441	0767	1
BLACKBURN BOBBY L	MAJ	0-4011014	0867	1
BLACKBURN BUD	CPT	0-0490861	1047	2
BLACKBURN CHARLES W	LTC	0-0298800	0166	3
BLACKBURN CLARENCE R	CW2	W-2152819	0364	1
BLACKBURN CLARENCE V	CW2	W-2150968	0659	1
BLACKBURN CLARK K	WO1	W-2114496	1164	2
BLACKBURN ESTES M	COL	0-0331556		3
BLACKBURN EUNICE R	CPT	N-0773866	0247	1
BLACKBURN FRANK C	MAJ	0-0278015	0664	3
BLACKBURN GEORGE T	1LT	0-0549271	1047	2
BLACKBURN GLEN S	CPT	0-1031879	0861	1
BLACKBURN HARRY C	MAJ	0-1289683	0263	2
BLACKBURN HARRY F	LTC	0-1015640	0863	1
BLACKBURN JAMES H	CPT	0-1031466	0857	2
BLACKBURN JAMES K	CPT	0-1297305	1046	1
BLACKBURN JOHN S	CW3	W-2120780	0855	1
BLACKBURN LEROY F	CW2	W-2141198	0260	1
BLACKBURN REBECCA P	CPT	N-0724119	0646	1
BLACKBURN ROBERT C	MAJ	0-0409342	0646	2
BLACKBURN ROY V	MAJ	0-0291701	0962	1
BLACKBURN THOMAS P	1LT	0-1012072	0444	2
BLACKBURN TRACY R	1LT	0-1599104	1053	2
BLACKBURN WALTER R	1LT	0-0396718	0945	2
BLACKBURN WILLIAM L	1LT	0-0961370	0253	1
BLACKETT RAYMOND C	MAJ	0-0473044	0452	1
BLACKEY PHILIP R	LTC	0-1794763	0564	1
BLACKFORD ALBERT W	1LT	0-1284997	1145	2
BLACKFORD ERNEST J	MAJ	0-0403055	0260	2
BLACKFORD JOE F	MAJ	0-1049729	0160	1
BLACKFORD R F	MAJ	0-0243281	0750	3
BLACKLEDGE VICTOR R	LTC	0-0169742	0760	3
BLACKLEY LAWRENCE R	MAJ	0-2021096	0566	1
BLACKLIDGE GLENN R	MAJ	0-1640442	0160	2
BLACKMAN CARLE L	MAJ	0-1584164	0460	1
BLACKMAN HAROLD J	LTC	0-0181414	0457	3
BLACKMAN JAY V	COL	0-0179537	1051	1
BLACKMER BENJAMIN A	MAJ	0-1287652	0648	2
BLACKMER VIRGINIA H	CPT	L-0900770	0549	2
BLACKMORE EDWARD C	CW4	W-2130710	0157	1
BLACKMORE KENNETH P	CPT	0-2263713	1162	1
BLACKMORE NORMAN F	MAJ	0-2008338	0657	1
BLACKORRAY BRADIE P	1LT	0-0510470	1046	1
BLACKSHARE EVERRITT D	LTC	0-1051879	0467	3
BLACKSHEAR WILLIAM S	LTC	0-0150495	0253	3
BLACKSTOCK LEO G	COL	0-0349409	1059	3
BLACKWELDER LEROY J	LTC	0-1111497	0361	1
BLACKWELL CHARLES L	WO1	W-2108622	0847	2
BLACKWELL EUGENE R	LTC	0-1341141	0665	1
BLACKWELL FRANK Y	LTC	0-0163542	0357	3
BLACKWELL GEORGE C	MAJ	0-1327602	0161	1
BLACKWELL GEORGE W	CPT	0-1921094	0353	1
BLACKWELL HARRELSON	MAJ	0-0969737	0662	1
BLACKWELL JAMES E	MAJ	0-0315566	1064	1
BLACKWELL JAMES L	CPT	0-0560642	0762	1
BLACKWELL JOHN C	CPT	0-2262983	0463	1
BLACKWELL LOWELL L	LTC	0-0426055	1054	1
BLACKWELL MARVIN F	MAJ	0-2204068	1165	1
BLACKWELL NOAH M	CW4	W-2129619	0361	1
BLACKWELL PAUL	MAJ	0-1919895	0767	1
BLACKWELL RICHARD C	COL	0-0243688	0463	3
BLACKWELL SYLVESTER	COL	0-0245183	1062	3
BLACKWELL TED R	CPT	0-0503554	1059	1
BLACKWELL WALTER F	LTC	0-0261576	0667	3
BLACKWELL WILKIE D	CPT	0-2056261	0354	2
BLACKWELL WILLIAM H	MAJ	0-4007115	1165	1
BLACKWOOD BOB T	MAJ	0-1116204	0663	2
BLACKWOOD CHARLES J	LTC	0-0102686	0756	3
BLACKWOOD CHARLES M	COL	0-0224727	0864	3
BLACKWOOD DEWEY	MAJ	0-0351082	1043	2
BLACKWOOD HERMAN W	COL	0-0277179	1067	3
BLACKWOOD JAMES P	CPT	0-2007771	1148	2
BLACKWOOD WILLIAM F	1LT	0-0521814	0146	2
BLACKWOOD WILLIAM H	MAJ	0-1881730	0866	1
BLAETTLER PETER M	CPT	0-0415413	0545	2
BLAGDEN CRAWFORD	1LT	0-1308780	0945	1
BLAHA JR JOSEPH	COL	0-1100451	1067	3
BLAHNIK ROMAULD J	2LT	0-1307754	0945	2
BLAIN ROGER L	MAJ	0-1550546	0963	1
BLAIN THOMAS R	1LT	0-0338965	0642	2
BLAINE BELFORD C	CPT	0-0338497	0246	2
BLAINE FREDERICK	MAJ	0-2200212	0566	1
BLAINE WILLIAM J	CPT	0-1291769	0253	1
BLAIR ARLO	CW3	W-2142973	0462	1
BLAIR BOB E	MAJ	0-2011746	0462	1
BLAIR ELMER N	MAJ	0-1300921	1061	1
BLAIR EUGENE F	MAJ	0-1575755	0766	1
BLAIR FORREST L	1LT	0-0473768	1043	2
BLAIR GEORGE S	COL	0-0153590	1048	3
BLAIR HAROLD D	LTC	0-0278917	0460	3
BLAIR HENRY H	LTC	0-0498442	0163	3
BLAIR HENRY T	COL	0-0135056	0648	3
BLAIR HERBERT M	CPT	0-1687261	0845	2
BLAIR HOWARD W	LTC	0-0321156	0362	3
BLAIR JAMES L	LTC	0-1574200	1061	1
BLAIR JAMES L	CW3	W-2147285	0666	1
BLAIR JOHN G	LTC	0-0281372	0462	1
BLAIR JOSEPH R	1LT	0-1822524	1045	2
BLAIR JR CHARLES J	COL	0-0250583	1166	3
BLAIR JR FRED D	CPT	0-2262353	1060	1
BLAIR LESLIE W	CPT	0-1101336	0862	1
BLAIR LESTER W	MAJ	0-0158602	0649	3
BLAIR ORVILLE R	LTC	0-0276093	1163	3
BLAIR PAUL M	COL	0-0248401	0667	3
BLAIR PHILIP W	MAJ	0-0500345	1053	1
BLAIR RALPH P	2LT	0-1913528	1144	1
BLAIR RAY R	CPT	0-1895773	0147	2
BLAIR ROBERT C	COL	0-0205035	0661	3
BLAIR ROBERT W	LTC	0-1046726	0864	1
BLAIR RUSSELL T	MAJ	0-1311366	1057	1
BLAIR TROY	MAJ	0-1102358	0159	1
BLAIR VERNON N	CW3	W-2141904	0659	1
BLAIR VERNON W	COL	0-0335059	0159	3
BLAIR VICTOR J	CW3	W-2148646	0766	1
BLAIR WILLIAM F	MAJ	0-0299807	0261	3
BLAIR WILLIAM J	LTC	0-0321512	0159	1
BLAIS ARMAND	LTC	0-0312391	0954	2
BLAISDELL FRANK G	MAJ	0-0100792	0751	3
BLAISURE HAROLD	2LT	0-1308088	0645	2
BLAKE BERTRAM C	CW3	W-2208907	0567	1
BLAKE CLYDE W	LTC	0-0122414	0648	3
BLAKE CONNIE P	CPT	0-0224815	0254	2
BLAKE DAVID A	2LT	0-0423182	0545	2
BLAKE EDWARD K	CW2	W-2124237	0762	2
BLAKE ELWOOD C	CPT	0-0966400	0160	2
BLAKE ERNEST R	CPT	0-0213540	0453	1
BLAKE EVELYN M	2LT	N-0727229	1044	1
BLAKE FOREST R	1LT	0-1313336	0146	2
BLAKE FOSTER O	LTC	0-0451078	1155	1
BLAKE FRANK O	LTC	0-0234136	0656	3
BLAKE JAMES A	LTC	0-0223874	0859	1
BLAKE JAMES F	CPT	0-2289643	0860	1
BLAKE JOHN V	LTC	0-0293548	0864	3
BLAKE JOSEPH F	CW2	W-2143232	1262	1
BLAKE JOSEPH W	CW4	W-2142687	0563	1
BLAKE JR FRANK A	MAJ	0-1296982	0861	1
BLAKE JR RALPH J	LTC	0-1846247	1162	1
BLAKE JR WILLIAM G	LTC	0-0405968	0163	1
BLAKE JUNIOUS L	CW2	W-2141199	1062	1
BLAKE MILTON J	COL	0-0349707	1265	3

NAME	GRADE	SVC NO	DATE RET MO YR	RET CODE
BLAKE THOMAS W	MAJ	O-0946106	0864	1
BLAKE WALTER C	LTC	O-1633078	0960	1
BLAKE WALTER M	LTC	O-0364580	0361	1
BLAKELEY LUTHER D	MAJ	O-0292400	0656	2
BLAKELY CHARLES B	CPT	O-0507080	0357	1
BLAKELY FRANK E	LTC	O-2050730	0967	1
BLAKELY HOWARD M	MAJ	O-1284088	0860	1
BLAKELY HUGH J	LTC	O-1845386	0564	1
BLAKELY JR EUGENE J	COL	O-0172594	1057	3
BLAKELY PAUL G	MAJ	O-0414133	1145	2
BLAKELY RICHARD N	MAJ	O-2102920	0167	1
BLAKELY ROBERT W	MAJ	O-0466471	0765	1
BLAKENEY LEWIS B	LTC	O-0213467	1263	1
BLAKER JOHN W	MAJ	O-1295494	0361	1
BLAKESLEE ARNOLD B	CPT	O-1013976	0547	1
BLAKESLEE ERNEST L	CPT	O-0451217	0256	1
BLAKESLEE F O	CW2	W-2146187	0957	1
BLAKESLEE ROBERT B	MAJ	O-0334461	0146	2
BLAKEWAY WILLIAM R	CW4	W-2151759	0566	1
BLAKEY TOM	MAJ	O-1327804	1161	1
BLAKLEY JAMES C	CW3	W-2152002	0957	1
BLAKNEY HERMAN O	CW3	W-2141200	0958	1
BLALOCK JAMES H	MAJ	O-1300441	0954	1
BLALOCK JOSEPH G	CPT	O-0967797	0357	2
BLALOCK JR JOHN F	CPT	O-0359564	0545	1
BLAN OLLIE L	MAJ	O-0102513	0556	3
BLANAR ROBERT P	COL	O-0159269	0857	3
BLANC JOHN R	MAJ	O-1341621	0865	1
BLANCHARD ALBERT C	LTC	O-0394865	0267	3
BLANCHARD ARTHUR J	CW2	W-2206379	0763	1
BLANCHARD BASIL H	MAJ	O-1061064	0363	1
BLANCHARD DELIA F	2LT	N-0726644	0745	1
BLANCHARD ELWYN W	LTC	O-0341405	0546	2
BLANCHARD EMIL A	MAJ	O-0252395	0157	3
BLANCHARD ERNEST L	CPT	O-0271529	1066	3
BLANCHARD HAROLD J	CW2	W-2102662	0657	1
BLANCHARD JAMES L	2LT	O-1050184	0345	2
BLANCHARD JR JAMES C	1LT	O-1015609	0945	2
BLANCHARD JR JAMES F	CW3	W-2141905	0463	1
BLANCHARD LAWRENCE K	COL	O-0230947	1163	3
BLANCHARD LEO J	LTC	O-0181396	0746	2
BLANCHARD MELVIN H	LTC	O-2047925	0166	1
BLANCHARD WAYNE M	MAJ	O-0422265	0652	2
BLANCHARD WILLIE J	CW3	W-2150784	0764	1
BLANCHE LESTER M	CPT	O-0267840	0566	3
BLANCHETTE JOSEPH R	CPT	O-0976471	0461	2
BLANCHETTE LEON O	CW3	W-2152842	0463	1
BLANCHETTE NAPOLEON	1LT	O-0383253	0144	2
BLANCK WILLIAM R	CW3	RW-2145384	1164	1
BLANCO JOSE R	1LT	O-0156774	0147	2
BLANCO JUAN R	COL	O-0109959	0855	3
BLANC BLANCHARD	MAJ	O-0400752	0646	2
BLANE EUGENE H	COL	O-0286560	1266	3
BLAND GEORGE H	CPT	O-1169029	1046	2
BLAND GEORGE W	LTC	O-0271764	0265	3
BLAND IRVIN J	MAJ	O-0467782	0748	1
BLAND JR ROBERT T	MAJ	O-0449087	0846	2
BLAND LONNIE C	CW3	W-2141201	0466	1
BLANDFORD EARL F	1LT	O-1897740	0753	1
BLANDFORD ROBERT S	COL	O-0174483	0362	3
BLANDIN JR RAY W	MAJ	O-1312872	0860	1
BLANDING ALBERT H	M G	O-0222742	0648	3
BLANDING JOHN W	LTC	O-0187055	0648	3
BLANDING JR DONALD M	MAJ	O-0250089	0165	3
BLANEY FRED H	CPT	O-0372647	0346	2
BLANEY LAMSON	MAJ	O-0504163	0746	2
BLANFORD DAVID W	MAJ	O-4074360	1167	1
BLANFORD HOWARD L	LTC	O-2050731	1167	1
BLANK DAVID A	CPT	O-0482436	1147	1
BLANK HARRY C	CPT	O-0171406	0554	3
BLANK HOMER C	CPT	O-0961188	1262	1
BLANK JULIUS M	COL	O-0137112	0545	2
BLANK WILLIAM J	COL	O-0305210	0466	3
BLANKENBAKER GEORGE	CPT	O-0509587	0967	1
BLANKENBECKLER G K	LTC	O-0275062	0944	2
BLANKENBURG RUDOLPH	COL	O-0240819	0365	3
BLANKENHORN ROBERT D	COL	O-0372063	0154	1
BLANKENSHIP ARTHUR C	MAJ	O-1283014	0446	2
BLANKENSHIP BASIL R	MAJ	O-0576994	0665	2
BLANKENSHIP EDD	CW3	W-2145375	0857	1
BLANKENSHIP EDWARD W	CW4	W-2144125	1164	1
BLANKENSHIP FRED V	CW2	W-2207494	0963	1
BLANKENSHIP MICKEY O	1LT	O-1296802	0445	2
BLANKENSHIP ODIE V	LTC	O-0248863	0366	3
BLANKENSHIP ORA M	MAJ	O-0499726	0257	1
BLANKENSHIP OWEN	MAJ	O-1644300	0559	1
BLANKENSHIP PAUL E	MAJ	O-1168175	0656	1
BLANKENSHIP SHIRLEY	WO1	W-2128400	1051	1
BLANKENSHIP WADE A	1LT	O-1794901	0245	2
BLANKLEY CLIFTON T	MAJ	O-0237262	1063	3
BLANKLEY HAROLD W	MAJ	O-1643506	0258	1
BLANKS CLAYTON P	CW2	W-2147790	0961	1
BLANKS ISAAC R	CW3	W-2148198	0563	1
BLANKS RICHARD P	COL	O-1284637	0561	1
BLANN CLIFFORD L	1LT	O-1310969	1045	1
BLANTON ARTHUR	LTC	O-0490772	0557	1
BLANTON DORIS M	CPT	L-1010211	0966	1
BLANTON JR DENNIS M	MAJ	O-1298815	0563	1
BLANTON MARY E	2LT	N-0727900	1045	1
BLANTON ROBERT J	1LT	O-0507112	0446	2
BLASCO ALBERT	LTC	O-1627033	0865	1
BLASDEL CHARLES F	LTC	O-0450422	0655	1
BLASE ANDREW	COL	O-0382076	0663	2
BLASEN ROBERT E	LTC	O-0304134	0445	2
BLASER EUGENE S	CPT	O-2009627	0748	1
BLASER IDA A	1LT	N-0772725	0146	1
BLASER JOHN T	CW2	W-2150656	0860	1
BLASENCAME AMOS	CW2	W-2108714	0762	1
BLASIUS FRANK M	MAJ	O-0317964	0960	1
BLASKO RUDOLPH	MAJ	O-1285359	0657	1
BLASS JR LOUIS	MAJ	O-0178203	0347	2
BLATCH JOSEPH H	1LT	O-0413883	1045	2
BLATT DANIEL F	MAJ	O-2262295	1163	1
BLATT DONALD H	1LT	O-0546808	0247	1
BLATT SAMUEL E	LTC	O-0493231	0365	3
BLATTER ERWIN W	COL	O-0195716	0357	2
BLAU ELMER H	COL	O-0246421	0566	3
BLAUSTEIN MAURICE	MAJ	O-0230397	1043	1
BLAUSTEIN MORTON L	MAJ	O-0982162	0564	1
BLAUVELT ARTHUR F	LTC	O-0227176	1064	3
BLAUVELT JOSEPH W	WO1	W-2148837	1263	2
BLAUVELT ROBERT T	LTC	O-0920834	1266	3
BLAWUER CHANCE D	LTC	O-0299687	0765	3
BLAYLOCK FLOYD M	MAJ	O-1550547	0954	1
BLAYLOCK ROBERT G	COL	O-0509999	0862	1
BLAYNEY LINDSEY	LTC	O-0150487	0648	3
BLAZER FRANK	LTC	O-1284276	0459	1
BLAZETIC JOHN P	MAJ	O-0534913	0457	1
BLEAKLEY JR ELLIS F	2LT	O-0493037	0545	2
BLEASDALE JOHN W	MAJ	O-0195437	0657	3
BLECH JOSEPH	CPT	O-0182161	0945	1
BLECHA ARTHUR F	CW2	W-2150361	0661	1
BLEDSOE EVERETT J	MAJ	O-0496919	1152	1
BLEDSOE JAMES P	CW2	W-2210972	0166	1
BLEDSOE JR HENRY	CPT	O-1116687	0447	2
BLEDSOE RALEIGH C	CPT	O-1786382	0747	1
BLEDSOE ROBERT F	CW2	W-2142132	0657	1
BLEDSOE IRIS L	COL	O-0372641	0660	1
BLEIBERG JACOB	CPT	O-0465682	0645	2
BLEICE HERBERT M	WO1	W-2129245	0146	2
BLEICH JACK K	LTC	O-0256339	0967	3
BLEICHFELD SAMUEL	COL	O-0250258	0563	3
BLEIL LOUIS T	CPT	O-1103527	0462	1
BLEIL WALTER C	MAJ	O-0189334	0649	3
BLEKAITIS VEIC	COL	O-0401452	1060	1
BLENDER THOMAS K	LTC	O-0265937	0667	3
BLENKINSOP P M	LTC	O-0246065	0849	3
BLENKLE VICTOR A	LTC	O-0219328	0160	3
BLESER LOUIS W	MAJ	O-0269016	0644	2
BLESS GEORGE F	MAJ	O-0967058	0265	1
BLESSING JACK W	LTC	O-0318495	0552	1
BLESSING REX C	1LT	O-0291216	1145	1
BLESSINGER RAYMOND J	1LT	O-1299982	0945	2
BLETHEN ARNOLD P	LTC	O-1104763	0962	1
BLETTE JR JOHN	LTC	O-0294007	0260	1
BLEVANS JACK A	LTC	O-0287851	1265	3
BLEVINS JOHN M	CPT	O-0418729	0361	1
BLEVINS JOSEPH C	MAJ	O-0983702	0865	1
BLEVINS LESTER W	LTC	O-1331259	1265	2
BLEVINS PAUL W	1LT	O-2009571	0555	1
BLEVINS WILLIAM F	CW3	W-2152366	0765	2
BLEW MICHAEL J	COL	O-0118537	1151	3
BLEWITT JOHN J	CPT	O-0918076	0244	2
BLEZA FELICISIMO	2LT	O-1897014	0847	1
BLICKLE FREDERICK	LTC	O-2001704	1163	1
BLIED LEO J	COL	O-0181466	1053	3
BLIEM EMILE C	COL	O-0276572	0260	3
BLIGH ROGER J	LTC	O-1176886	0964	1
BLIND MILDRED M	CPT	N-0724274	0758	2
BLINKENBERG HAROLD G	LTC	O-0255230	0859	1
BLINKHORN GEORGE P	MAJ	O-0260491	0466	3
BLINSKEY JOHN	CPT	O-2046645	0757	1
BLISH MORRIS J	MAJ	O-0179418	0153	3
BLISS ARTHUR G	COL	O-0253918	1061	1
BLISS ARTHUR P	CPT	O-0110253	0848	3
BLISS BENJAMIN	COL	O-0268578	0959	1
BLISS EDWARD C	COL	O-0171900	0752	3
BLISS HOWARD C	MAJ	O-0334120	0862	1
BLISS JOHN N	CW3	W-2146613	1063	1
BLISS JR RAYMOND W	1LT	O-0385792	0446	2
BLISS PERCIVAL M	COL	O-0257995	0267	3
BLISS ROBERT J	MAJ	O-0381668	0246	2
BLISS WALTER S	MAJ	O-0455855	0346	2
BLISS WILLIAM C	COL	O-0130984	0453	3
BLISS WILLIAM H	LTC	O-0909542	0862	1
BLISS WILLIAM R	CW4	W-2145605	0667	1
BLISS ZENAS R	COL	O-0195832	0358	3
BLITCH HARVEY L	CPT	O-0256614	1165	3
BLITCHINGTON JOHN A	MAJ	O-0351856	1062	1
BLITZER MARTIN	MAJ	O-0979206	0862	1
BLIZZARD JOE W	LTC	O-1040877	0763	1
BLOCH EDMUND C	COL	O-0382301	1047	1
BLOCH JR WILLIAM	LTC	O-0171803	0452	3
BLOCH RALPH H	MAJ	O-1582804	0563	1
BLOCHER JR ARCH C	1LT	O-1308781	0246	2
BLOCHER SAMUEL J	COL	O-0200703	0154	2
BLOCK ABRAHAM M	1LT	O-1014339	0946	2
BLOCK AREND W	1LT	O-2036462	0446	2
BLOCK DONALD J	2LT	O-1178713	0145	1
BLOCK EDWARD	1LT	O-1012467	0346	2
BLOCK GEORGE F	CPT	O-0121332	0354	3
BLOCK HARRY	MAJ	O-0103973	0953	3
BLOCK JR JOHN H	CW2	W-2209296	0563	1
BLOCK MARTIN N	LTC	O-0301423	0462	1
BLOCK MARY B	CPT	N-0755145	0146	1
BLOCK PAUL L	2LT	O-1180820	1144	2
BLOCKER JR DANIEL J	LTC	O-1290189	0166	1
BLOCKER TOM B	COL	O-0177183	0353	3
BLODGETT ALOYSIUS L	CPT	O-0315703	0364	3
BLODGETT HAROLD E	LTC	O-0128915	1053	3
BLODGETT JAMES A	LTC	O-0366225	1060	1
BLODGETT JUAN J	CW2	W-2144733	0265	2
BLODGETT RILEY	1LT	O-1167321	1044	2
BLODGETT STANTON A	CPT	O-0316059	1044	1
BLODGETT WALTER R	LTC	O-1586445	0864	1
BLOECHL FRANK J	LTC	O-0337105	1166	3
BLOEMENDAAL GERRIT J	MAJ	O-0227111	0160	3
BLOGG AINSWORTH	COL	O-0174763	1059	3
BLOHM JACK	LTC	O-1174782	1160	1
BLOHM JOHN C	CPT	O-1052264	0864	1
BLOIR EDWARD	COL	O-0256723	1058	3
BLOIS ELLSWORTH	LTC	O-0915168	0964	1
BLOK JAMES	CPT	O-0345949	0260	3
BLOM ROBERT W	1LT	O-1016287	0546	1
BLOMBERG EARL H	1LT	O-1031998	0146	2
BLOMELEY LLOYD E	CW3	W-2152112	0364	1
BLOMME CHARLES R	COL	O-0278567	0460	1
BLOMQUIST ALLEN R	CPT	O-0298783	0944	2
BLOMQUIST CLAYTON A	1LT	O-1035067	0645	1
BLOMQUIST REINHOLD F	CPT	O-1642212	0657	1
BLOMQUIST RICHARD N	1LT	O-1325260	0545	2
BLOMQUIST VERNON R	CPT	O-1004420	0860	2
BLONDELL VERNON J	COL	O-0190200	0460	3
BLONDER ERWIN H	1LT	O-0524094	1045	2
BLOOD IVAN L	CPT	O-1797939	1061	1
BLOOD LEE H	1LT	O-1289684	0864	1
BLOOD MARGARET M	1LT	N-0741705	0645	1
BLOODWORTH JOSEPH A	CW2	RW-2145264	0862	1
BLOOM CHARLES W	1LT	O-1327924	0452	1
BLOOM D GEORGE	MAJ	O-0493928	1145	2
BLOOM EDWARD I	CPT	O-1695860	1144	2
BLOOM EDWIN J	1LT	O-0317557	0445	2
BLOOM EVERETT C	LTC	O-1115497	0163	1
BLOOM EVERETT D	LTC	O-0248800	1159	3
BLOOM FRANCIS J	LTC	O-1587136	0664	1
BLOOM FRANK	COL	O-0469826	0152	3
BLOOM HENRY C	2LT	O-1312102	0161	1
BLOOM HERBERT M	LTC	O-0389848	0462	1
BLOOM JAMES F	LTC	O-1117106	0866	1
BLOOM JEANETTE	1LT	N-0722964	0945	1
BLOOM JR GEORGE A	MAJ	O-2034091	0965	1
BLOOM LEWIS H	MAJ	O-1289034	0457	2
BLOOM PHILLIP	1LT	O-0451079	0246	2
BLOOM SAMUEL M	MAJ	O-0344720	1146	1
BLOOM SAUL S	LTC	O-0289874	0261	3
BLOOMENTHAL JOHN	1LT	O-0369055	0143	1
BLOOMFIELD CHESTER L	CPT	O-1317263	1045	1
BLOOMFIELD JOHN W	LTC	O-2009653	0965	1
BLOOMFIELD JR JOHN O	CW2	W-2143711	0260	1
BLOOMROSE RHODA V	2LT	N-0753526	1045	1
BLOPE RICHARD F	LTC	O-0217781	0157	1
BLOSE LEWIS A	LTC	O-1585179	0763	1
BLOSE PAUL M	MAJ	O-1167747	0557	1
BLOSJO ROLAND V	LTC	O-1574591	0264	1
BLOSS LORIMOR P	1LT	O-0975187	0156	1
BLOSSER GUY C	LTC	O-0294526	0560	1
BLOSSOM GEORGE L	COL	O-0173340	0454	3
BLOTZER JOHN W	COL	O-0412615	0867	1
BLOUGH ELMER	1LT	O-0495371	0746	1
BLOUGH GEORGE G	2LT	O-1644322	0844	2
BLOUGH ROBERT J	MAJ	O-1176898	1147	2
BLOUNT ALLEN T	COL	O-0290620	0162	3
BLOUNT BARBARA	MAJ	N-0755228	1262	1
BLOUNT BRADFORD G	2LT	O-0542966	1144	2
BLOUNT LEWIS O	LTC	O-0250842	0260	3
BLOUNT LORENZO	1LT	O-1287821	0845	2
BLOWE WILLIAM O	MAJ	O-0425739	0462	1
BLOWER BRUCE G	2LT	O-5001966	0360	2
BLOWERS RALPH F	MAJ	O-1109815	0265	3
BLOWERS TOM H	LTC	O-0300142	0364	1
BLOYS WILLIAM R	CW3	W-2143010	0360	1
BLOZE DANIEL M	2LT	O-1797237	0144	2
BLUE FORREST M	CPT	O-1168562	0960	1
BLUE JULIAN H	MAJ	O-0273917	0759	3
BLUEJACKET DONALD O	LTC	O-2026348	0864	1
BLUETHGEN ERNEST F	MAJ	O-0245044	1053	3
BLUETT JOHN H	WO1	W-2150302	1053	1
BLUHM FRITZ	CPT	O-0337222	0656	1
BLUHM HENRY C	LTC	O-1104511	0563	1
BLUHM HERBERT W	LTC	O-0210468	0559	3
BLUM ANDREW J	MAJ	O-1301093	0862	2
BLUM BEATRICE S	1LT	N-0723416	0346	1
BLUM CHARLES J	MAJ	O-0180961	1161	3
BLUM CHARLES J	COL	O-0324067	0265	3
BLUM FRANK J	MAJ	O-0311620	0860	1
BLUM HARVEY R	CW4	W-2108815	1055	1
BLUM HERMAN R	MAJ	O-2018822	1265	2
BLUM HOWARD M	LTC	O-1894898	0667	1
BLUM JOSEPH F	COL	O-0295663	1167	2
BLUM JR HARRY S	1LT	O-1305003	0745	2

NAME	GRADE	SVC NO	DATE RET MO YR	RET CODE
BLUM JULIUS F	CW2	W-2211729	1166	1
BLUM MAX	CPT	0-1944878	1146	2
BLUM MERLE C	MAJ	0-1048288	0863	1
BLUM MORRIS	CPT	0-0511324	1045	2
BLUM RUDOLPH A	LTC	0-0248450	0964	3
BLUM SIDNEY	LTC	0-1052265	0967	1
BLUM WALTER P	COL	0-0355809	0966	1
BLUMBERG SIDNEY H	CPT	0-0349046	0143	2
BLUME ARTHUR J	CPT	0-0232936	0364	3
BLUMENFELD IRVING	CPT	0-0400723	0346	2
BLUMENSAADT NORMAN S	LTC	0-0358062	1060	1
BLUMENSHINE HUGH W	1LT	0-1118848	1051	1
BLUMENSTEIN EDWARD J	MAJ	0-1100878	0462	1
BLUMENSTIEL MONROE A	MAJ	0-0215635	0256	3
BLUMENTHAL JACK	CW3	W-2151045	0964	1
BLUMER HOWARD D	1LT	0-0416379	1045	1
BLUMER MAX A	LTC	0-0543867	0247	2
BLUMHAGEN ROBERT F	MAJ	0-1297662	0461	1
BLUMSTEIN ALBERT	CPT	0-0335899	1163	3
BLUNK ACLAI S	CPT	0-0123281	1052	3
BLUNT ALAN R	CW2	W-2208645	0760	1
BLUNT ARTHUR E	1LT	0-1287126	0446	2
BLUNT WILLIAM J	CW2	W-2143427	1063	1
BLUNTZER WOODROW K	LTC	0-1556091	0664	1
BLUSH RUSSELL F	LTC	0-1595941	1066	2
BLUST CHARLES W	CPT	0-1169177	0857	1
BLUTEAU KENNETH R	LTC	0-1284998	0760	1
BLY ALBERT C	1LT	0-1031227	0844	2
BLY HARRY R	CW3	W-2150313	0562	1
BLY SYLVESTER	LTC	0-1040879	0763	1
BLYCKER LAWRENCE R	LTC	0-0507529	0555	1
BLYSKAL STANLEY	CPT	0-0490197	0455	2
BLYSTONE WILLIAM P	CW3	W-2206689	0766	1
BLYTH ROBERT P	CW2	W-2150336	1059	2
BLYTHE HARVEY C	CW3	W-2101456	1057	1
BOAG JOHN M	LTC	0-0230240	0752	1
BOAKS RAYMOND J	CPT	0-0504971	0549	2
BOAL GEORGE L	MAJ	0-0969448	1164	1
BOAL HOWARD W	1LT	0-0126340	0252	3
BOAN VURLYNE E	2LT	N-0720891	0744	1
BOARD JOHN S	CPT	0-0236725	0265	3
BOARDMAN EDWARD J	LTC	0-1285885	0760	1
BOARDMAN GEORGE F	LTC	0-0914417	0665	3
BOARDMAN JOSEPH A	MAJ	0-0977706	0563	1
BOARDMAN ROBERT P	LTC	0-0154836	0649	3
BOARDMAN THOMAS H	CPT	0-0265824	0158	3
BOATMAN RALPH A	LTC	0-0487187	1057	1
BOATNER YANCELL	1LT	0-1179303	0946	2
BOATRIGHT CHARLES C	LTC	0-0208528	0246	2
BOATRIGHT HENRY R	CW2	W-3200437	1167	1
BOATRIGHT LEAMON O	MAJ	0-1534679	0257	1
BOATRIGHT MELVIN C	CPT	0-1042765	0647	1
BOATWRIGHT GRIMES A	1LT	0-1303456	0446	2
BOATWRIGHT JOHN H	1LT	0-1178416	0346	1
BOATWRIGHT JR JOHN R	LTC	0-1292997	0561	2
BOATWRIGHT JUNIOUS T	LTC	0-1181826	0967	1
BOAZ RALPH A	LTC	0-0335232	0459	1
BOAZ THOMAS Z	LTC	0-0504355	1054	1
BOBB DONALD R	CW3	W-2143148	0858	1
BOBB LAWRENCE W	CW2	W-2113000	0450	1
BOBB ROBERT C	LTC	0-1011645	1060	1
BOBB WALLACE D	1LT	0-1824592	0746	2
BOBBITT HUBERT B	MAJ	0-1945996	0357	1
BOBBITT ROY R	CPT	0-0144023	0145	2
BOBBITT THOMAS A	CW2	W-2153223	0960	1
BOBER MARY E	2LT	N-0797536	0447	1
BOBERG DONALD E	CPT	0-1177291	0346	2
BOBERG RAYMOND W	LTC	0-0168599	0666	3
BOBERTZ CHARLES R	2LT	0-1327324	0745	2
BOBINGER WILLIAM F	LTC	0-0909508	1065	3
BOBKO ERNEST J	LTC	0-1293533	0961	1
BOBO CARL V	MAJ	0-0505427	0656	1
BOBO WILLIAM A	LTC	0-1014591	0462	1
BOBROW AARON H	CPT	0-1844499	1045	2
BOBROW LEON B	CPT	0-0470308	0146	1

NAME	GRADE	SVC NO	DATE RET MO YR	RET CODE
BOBST FRANCIS	CW2	W-2149326	0359	1
BOCCELLA HENRY J	MAJ	0-0574624	0165	1
BOCCELLI JOHN S	CW3	W-2149009	0666	1
BOCCHINO ELIOT J	LTC	0-0377876	0760	1
BOCCIERI JAMES N	MAJ	0-2006536	0263	1
BOCELATO JOSEPH A	LTC	0-1550968	0762	3
BOCH ALBERT R	1LT	0-1557568	0745	2
BOCHAT MILTON W	MAJ	0-0309654	1046	1
BOCK ABE	COL	0-0255188	0867	3
BOCK CHARLES H	COL	0-0310407	1050	1
BOCK GEORGE	CW2	W-2119591	1048	1
BOCK JOHN J	LTC	0-1846111	0665	3
BOCK JOSEPH J	MAJ	0-0390026	1262	1
BOCK JR HARRY E	LTC	0-0385172	1060	1
BOCKMAN ALFRED P	MAJ	0-1173163	0461	1
BOCKMON ROBERT W	COL	0-0288433	0660	1
BOCKOVEN JOHN S	CPT	0-0436712	0446	2
BOCKOVEN MILTON F	MAJ	0-1597365	0161	1
BOCKSEL RAYMOND A	CPT	0-0979378	1051	1
BOCKSTAHLER LOUIS A	LTC	0-1337131	0166	1
BOCKTING BERNARD H	CW3	W-2152695	0463	1
BOCKWITH JOHN C	2LT	0-1037397	0545	1
BOCOCK GORDON R	LTC	0-1014398	1166	3
BOCOOK JAMES S	CW2	W-2152760	0662	1
BODAK MICHAEL C	CPT	0-1286597	0147	2
BODAL EMIL K	LTC	0-0233064	1164	3
BODANSKY OSCAR	LTC	0-0494407	1046	1
BODDA ROBERT N	LTC	0-1637041	0863	1
BODDEN HARRIS L	LTC	0-0557357	0767	1
BODE JOSEPH H	MAJ	0-2034388	0861	2
BODELL DALE	MAJ	0-1301400	0358	1
BODELL WILLIAM J	LTC	0-0455324	0455	1
BODEN THOMAS H	LTC	0-0346797	0762	3
BODENHAMER GEORGIA S	MAJ	N-0776094	0966	1
BODENHAMER MILTON F	LTC	0-1013839	0863	1
BODENHAMER RICHARD C	LTC	0-0150381	0254	3
BODGE BASIL L	CPT	0-2038900	0655	1
BODIAN MARTIN	CPT	0-0351473	0446	2
BODINE CHARLES L	LTC	0-0206474	1159	1
BODINE HAROLD W	LTC	0-1290190	1066	2
BODINE JR GEORGE C	1LT	0-1102141	0745	2
BODINE LILLIAN A	1LT	N-0757610	0947	1
BODINE WILLIAM B	LTC	0-1636210	0562	1
BODKIN CHESTER C	CPT	0-1062665	0348	1
BODKIN JOHN P	MAJ	0-1080918	0267	1
BODLEY DONALD C	1LT	0-0418000	1043	2
BODNAR JOHN A	2LT	0-1308243	1144	2
BODNAR LESLIE M	CPT	0-0533623	1047	1
BODNAR STEPHEN	LTC	0-0450799	0959	1
BODNER MITCHELL	MAJ	0-0223353	0549	1
BODON GEORGE R	MAJ	0-0515845	1145	2
BODY LOWELL H	MAJ	0-0252773	1160	3
BODY RALPH C	LTC	0-0215264	0363	3
BODY RAYMOND F	MAJ	0-0209797	0851	3
BOE LESTER L	1LT	0-0217554	1263	3
BOE ORVIL M	CW4	W-2142789	0566	1
BOE ROLF T	2LT	0-1171057	0343	2
BOEBEL EARL F	COL	0-0288764	0165	3
BOECKH EVERARD H	LTC	0-0165786	0853	3
BOECKMAN RICHARD J	MAJ	0-1552234	0564	1
BOEDECKER HARRY W	1LT	0-0415028	1044	2
BOEFFER GUSTAV E	CPT	0-0197455	1062	3
BOEGLI WILBUR J	LTC	0-0373191	0457	1
BOEH DANIEL H	CPT	0-0484025	0146	2
BOEHLER CARL A	CPT	0-0520080	0346	2
BOEHM BENNIE H	LTC	0-1293360	0361	1
BOEHM EDWARD	1LT	0-1168565	0646	2
BOEHM HANS F	LTC	0-1309687	0962	1
BOEHM ROBERT C	CPT	0-0402182	1044	2
BOEHME DONALD W	MAJ	0-0408920	1047	2
BOEHME WERNER	MAJ	0-1596384	0157	1
BOEHNE BRUCE G	1LT	0-4022417	0562	2
BOEHNKE EMIL C	COL	0-0219902	0746	1
BOEHRINGER MILDRED	2LT	N-0768857	0745	1
BOEKEL WILLIAM A	COL	0-0114152	0854	3

NAME	GRADE	SVC NO	DATE RET MO YR	RET CODE
BOEKER WILLIAM E	CPT	0-1322978	1152	1
BOELTER AUGUST A	MAJ	0-1552844	0253	1
BOELTER RICHARD W	MAJ	0-5301580	0867	1
BOEMANNS HERMAN J	MAJ	0-1168566	1163	1
BOEPPLE GRAF A	LTC	0-1591601	0265	1
BOERBON ROBERT F	CW3	W-2126727	0760	1
BOERLAGE PETER J	MAJ	0-1799820	0167	1
BOERNER FRED H	CW3	W-2102667	1154	1
BOERSTLER FRANCIS W	CPT	0-0468435	0962	1
BOERTH WALTER H	CPT	0-0236656	0165	3
BOERTLEIN JULIUS P	1LT	0-1635596	1044	2
BOERUM JR ROBERT W	2LT	0-1053513	0344	2
BOES JOHN J	MAJ	0-0967309	0265	1
BOES JOSEPH H	1LT	0-1286066	0645	1
BOESCH JR JOHN C	LTC	0-0341206	0346	2
BOESE CLARENCE I	1LT	0-0375408	0142	2
BOESE HARVEY A	LTC	0-0330100	0657	1
BOESEL JACOB W	CPT	0-1284638	0146	2
BOESEL PAUL G	1LT	0-1054184	1145	2
BOESKE HOWARD E	1LT	0-2000002	0747	2
BOESLUND NORMAN N	1LT	0-1313069	0245	2
BOESSER ROBERT C	1LT	0-1185672	0752	1
BOESSNECK MAX	MAJ	0-0480862	0653	1
BOETTCHER ANDREW J	CPT	0-0968375	0857	1
BOETTCHER ARNOLD A	COL	0-0275224	0162	3
BOETTCHER ERVIN W	COL	0-0885038	0866	3
BOETTGER HANS F	MAJ	0-0469283	1057	2
BOEF ROBERT J	MAJ	0-1330377	1064	1
BOGAN DAVID E	LTC	0-1036860	1165	1
BOGAN ELAINE E	2LT	N-0733969	0845	1
BOGAN JOHN J	COL	0-0300424	1067	3
BOGAN JR JAMES J	CW3	W-2150767	0765	1
BOGAN TOLLIE	CW2	W-2146178	0557	1
BOGAR STEPHEN A	MAJ	0-0282044	0166	3
BOGARD THOMAS A	CPT	0-1001512	0946	2
BOGARDUS GEORGE M	CPT	0-1696558	0845	1
BOGART GEORGE D	CW2	W-2148199	0356	1
BOGART JAMES W	LTC	0-1051882	1167	1
BOGART JAMES W	MAJ	0-2006205	0762	1
BOGART WALTER J	LTC	0-1637045	1162	1
BOGASKI EDMUND	LTC	0-0518522	1054	1
BOGATIN ROBERT S	1LT	0-0550032	0746	2
BOGDAN WESLEY S	LTC	0-1307185	0662	1
BOGEN BEN	MAJ	0-0345295	0446	2
BOGEN JOHN F	CW3	W-2004618	0667	1
BOGER DANIEL J	COL	0-0294694	0958	3
BOGER JOHN D	COL	0-0146652	0349	3
BOGER JR GEORGE H	MAJ	0-1112030	1163	1
BOGER REINHARDT	LTC	0-1015082	0666	1
BOGERT DONALD C	CPT	0-1310214	0946	2
BOGES DAVID P	CPT	0-1930920	0565	1
BOGGESS CARTER T	LTC	0-0377877	0766	1
BOGGESS HARRY R	MAJ	0-1997368	0560	1
BOGGESS ROUGH A	MAJ	0-1325626	0164	1
BOGGIANO JR CHANCE F	LTC	0-0353192	0663	1
BOGGS CLARENCE E	COL	0-0116517	0648	3
BOGGS DONALD G	CPT	0-1895323	0348	1
BOGGS JAMES F	COL	0-0298951	0160	3
BOGGS KENNETH L	LTC	0-0277052	1057	1
BOGGS LEAMON	CW2	W-2214901	1066	1
BOGGS LYNN	CPT	0-1913561	0428	1
BOGGS ROY A	CW3	W-3150284	0767	1
BOGGS ROY L	CPT	0-1823391	0562	1
BOGGS 3RD GEORGE	1LT	0-0493716	0346	2
BOGH ROY E	COL	0-1043029	0866	1
BOGLE CLYDE E	CPT	0-1292118	0846	2
BOGLE EUGENE R	COL	0-0148419	0849	3
BOGLE JAMES A	MAJ	0-0994770	0267	1
BOGLE JAMES R	LTC	0-0560657	0159	1
BOGLE JOHN H	LTC	0-0460723	0557	1
BOGLE JOSEPH B	COL	0-0276647	0657	3
BOGLE RALPH H	LTC	0-0246276	0557	1
BOGLE ROBERT G	LTC	0-0260946	0967	3
BOGOSEWSKI ZYGMUND	CW3	W-2147081	1162	1
BOGOSEWSKI ZYGMUND	CW3	W-2147091	1162	1

NAME	GRADE	SVC NO	DATE RET MO YR	RET CODE
BOHAN JOHN J	CPT	0-1949615	1156	1
BOHAN PETER J	CW4	W-2142688	0164	1
BOHAN ROBERT J	MAJ	0-1169430	0566	1
BOHANNA GLENN A	LTC	0-0225685	1064	3
BOHANNAN CHARLES T	LTC	0-2034493	0761	1
BOHANNAN CLARK C	LTC	0-0450017	0960	1
BOHANNAN ROBERT C	COL	0-0176016	0257	3
BOHANNON EDWARD J	LTC	0-0375129	0462	1
BOHANNON JAMES P	CW3	W-2150282	0363	1
BOHANNON JOHNNIE L	MAJ	0-4006657	1066	1
BOHANNON RALPH M	LTC	0-0239213	1163	3
BOHANNON RALPH W	LTC	0-0450241	1054	1
BOHANNON THOMAS F	LTC	0-0430423	0262	1
BOHANON WOODROW W	1LT	0-0336433	0845	1
BOHDAN JOHN J	MAJ	0-2002230	0262	1
BOHIN JR HARRY	MAJ	0-2021186	0566	1
BOHIN TOM W	CPT	0-0489991	1061	1
BOHLENDER WILLIAM E	LTC	0-0181766	0956	3
BOHLER GEORGE M	MAJ	0-0146741	1146	2
BOHLER JAMES E	MAJ	0-1038540	0661	1
BOHLIN OSCAR C	LTC	0-0170806	0945	2
BOHLKEN JAMES D	LTC	0-1100880	0563	1
BOHM ALBERT	CPT	0-1115190	0945	2
BOHM GEORGE W	CPT	0-1636211	0846	2
BOHMER RUDOLPH J	LTC	0-0910608	1062	1
BOHN GUY F	MAJ	0-1703936	0559	1
BOHN JOSEPH F	MAJ	0-0969594	0664	1
BOHN MATHIAS	CPT	0-1185567	0756	1
BOHN WILLIAM	CPT	0-0504072	1052	1
BOHN WILLIAM F	LTC	0-1017593	1167	1
BOHNENBLUST CLARENCE	LTC	0-0238797	0566	3
BOHNER RAY B	CW4	W-2102669	0659	1
BOHNERT ALFRED E	LTC	0-0338269	0364	1
BOHNERT FRANCIS C	MAJ	0-2208703	0465	1
BOHNETT JR LEO F	1LT	0-1286950	1045	2
BOHR JOHN F	MAJ	0-1633680	1059	1
BOHREN DONALD E	2LT	0-4058909	0656	2
BOHREN JR ROBERT E	MAJ	0-1889673	1265	2
BOHRER MAX	CPT	0-0922117	0545	2
BOIAN GENTRY P	CPT	0-0290760	1066	3
BOIAN HAROLD L	LTC	0-2018990	1265	1
BOICE ROBERT C	LTC	0-0242288	1065	3
BOICH JOSEPH A	LTC	0-1101338	0861	1
BOICHOT DONALD F	COL	0-0320119	0457	1
BOID JOHN C	1LT	0-0371816	0245	2
BOIES HARRIETTE	2LT	N-0723597	0546	1
BOIES WILBER H	1LT	0-1323905	0545	2
BOIES WILTON R	MAJ	0-0993115	0465	1
BOILEAU 3RD WALLIS	1LT	0-0378637	0745	2
BOILES DAMON J	LTC	0-1046020	0960	1
BOISCLAIR HERMAN H	MAJ	0-0192311	1061	3
BOISVERT GEORGE A	MAJ	0-0966035	0764	1
BOISVERT JOSEPH A	MAJ	0-1018031	0762	1
BOITANO JOHN E	MAJ	0-1637046	0361	1
BOIVIN DOROTHY C	2LT	N-0722752	0745	1
BOJUS JOHN	LTC	0-0350832	0761	1
BOKAMPER JESSE W	CPT	0-0573837	1060	1
BOLAND CLEMENT R	1LT	0-1725011	0248	2
BOLAND EDWARD L	MAJ	0-0340720	0750	1
BOLAND JAMES C	MAJ	0-0382571	0855	1
BOLAND JAMES J	LTC	0-1559882	0466	1
BOLAND JOSEPH B	MAJ	0-0962775	1162	2
BOLAND JOSEPH J	CPT	0-1684256	0844	2
BOLAND JR CARL D	CPT	0-1646727	0847	1
BOLAND JR FRANCIS H	M G	0-0233853	0965	3
BOLAND PATRICIA R	1LT	N-0729980	0946	1
BOLAND WILLIAM L	COL	0-0288771	1054	1
BOLAND WILLIAM V	CPT	0-0358103	0246	2
BOLANTE AGAPITO	CW2	RW-2147405	0262	1
BOLATIN GEORGE	CPT	0-1939271	0955	2
BOLDIZAR JOSEPH A	CPT	0-1320091	0863	1
BOLDIZSAR JULIUS S	LTC	0-0888219	0465	1
BOLDT STEPHEN C	COL	0-0172378	0758	1
BOLDT WALDEMAR H	LTC	0-0490920	0446	2
BOLDUAN NILS W	MAJ	0-1690137	0246	2

NAME	GRADE	SVC NO	DATE RET MO YR	RET CODE
BOLDUC ANTONIO J	LTC	0-1044456	0956	1
BOLE JOHN C	COL	0-0225712	0463	3
BOLE JR DAVID C	1LT	0-1290047	1044	1
BOLEKY JR EDWARD J	MAJ	0-0384976	1046	2
BOLEN HARRY L	MG	0-0185986	0256	3
BOLENDER LYLE S	LTC	0-1319918	0564	1
BOLER GLEN	CPT	0-0958927	1160	1
BOLER JOHN P	1LT	0-1596273	1045	2
BOLES BOBBY P	CW2	W-2207953	0465	1
BOLES CARSIE L	WO1	W-2108424	0147	1
BOLES EDWARD N	CW2	W-2210141	0465	1
BOLES JANE L	1LT	N-0767782	0646	1
BOLES RICHARD	WO1	W-2127984	1052	1
BOLEWSKI JOSEPH M	MAJ	0-1824417	1060	1
BOLEY HAROLD C	COL	0-0271009	0867	3
BOLGER ALFRED F	MAJ	0-0235509	0954	1
BOLICK CLARENCE P	COL	0-0174447	0456	3
BOLICK SAM P	1LT	0-1104769	0245	2
BOLIN ARVID H	LTC	0-1011469	0761	1
BOLING VICTOR L	LTC	0-0376800	0160	1
BOLINGER CHARLES R	CPT	0-1000207	1053	1
BOLINGER JOHN J	CW2	W-2146145	0962	2
BOLIVER THOMAS E	LTC	0-0171010	0953	3
BOLKAN PETER	MAJ	0-0173689	1162	2
BOLL IOLA S	2LT	N-0744542	0845	1
BOLL JOHN H	CPT	0-0966035	0157	1
BOLLAG LAWRENCE M	LTC	0-0920700	0467	3
BOLLAND JAMES W	CPT	0-1044178	0947	2
BOLLENBACHER JAMES T	CPT	0-0265228	0562	3
BOLLES ELLSWORTH	LTC	0-1306231	0162	1
BOLLETTIERI P J	1LT	0-0551425	0147	2
BOLLINGER CHARLES M	MAJ	0-0504864	1154	1
BOLLINGER RAYMOND P	LTC	0-1328875	0767	1
BOLLMAN CLIFFORD R	CPT	0-0280262	0146	2
BOLLMAN HENRY F	MAJ	0-1170657	0964	2
BOLLUM EDWIN H	1LT	0-0265778	0655	3
BOLLWEG GEORGE C	MAJ	0-0477362	0154	1
BOLOGNA ANGELO R	CPT	0-1689402	0845	2
BOLON HARRY C	MAJ	0-0258130	0765	3
BOLSON JESSE A	MAJ	0-1011836	0661	1
BOLSTAD HAROLD J	CW3	W-2141514	0865	1
BOLT HARRY F	COL	0-0118749	0259	3
BOLT JACK W	MAJ	0-1170289	0258	1
BOLT LEWIS G	COL	0-0357727	0660	1
BOLT ROBERT A	LTC	0-1303624	0665	1
BOLTE CHARLES G	CW2	W-2142624	0161	1
BOLTE KATHRYN M	CPT	L-0702026	0747	1
BOLTER HARRY G	MAJ	0-1546910	0762	1
BOLTINGHOUSE TOMMY B	MAJ	0-1334087	0761	2
BOLTON ARTHUR K	CPT	0-0535356	1146	2
BOLTON CARLTON M	1LT	0-1840491	0647	2
BOLTON CHANNING M	COL	0-0213912	0563	3
BOLTON HAROLD M	CPT	0-1179789	0747	1
BOLTON HOWARD F	CW2	W-2210323	1062	1
BOLTON JAMES E	COL	0-0411772	1060	3
BOLTON JAMES J	CPT	0-0276232	0146	1
BOLTON JOHN C	COL	0-0335873	1160	1
BOLTON JOHN H	MAJ	0-0215191	1058	3
BOLTON LAWSON T	WO1	W-2143831	0855	1
BOLTON LEE B	LTC	0-0265539	0363	1
BOLTON LENWARD J	LTC	0-0321911	1053	1
BOLTON LEONARD T	LTC	0-1183243	1162	1
BOLTON RAYMOND E	MAJ	0-1575769	0457	1
BOLTON WILBUR M	COL	0-0227311	0558	3
BOLTZ THOMAS E	CW2	W-2208302	0363	1
BOLTZ THOMAS F	MAJ	0-1291399	0662	1
BOLVIN RALPH F	CPT	0-1634540	0557	1
BOLYARD CHARLES A	CPT	0-1309500	0547	2
BOMAR PORTER H	LTC	0-0213967	0563	3
BOMBARD GLENDON A	1LT	0-1327087	0746	1
BOMGARDNER MERRILL L	LTC	0-1010670	1060	1
BOMMARITO JOSEPH A	CPT	0-1944406	0845	2
BOMSTAD ROLAND G	CPT	0-0525945	1144	2
BONA ARTHUR P	LTC	0-1114850	0563	2
BONAGUIDI JOHN	LTC	0-1594049	1067	2

NAME	GRADE	SVC NO	DATE RET MO YR	RET CODE
BONANNO JOSEPH U	CPT	0-0404620	1044	2
BONAPARTE MARTIN	CW2	W-2147031	1162	1
BONAR HAROLD E	LTC	0-0148383	0252	3
BONAVENTURA CHARLES	MAJ	0-1314429	0761	1
BONCODIN EULALIO	2LT	0-1896380	0348	1
BOND ARTHUR L	MAJ	0-1589067	0960	1
BOND BENJAMIN B	MAJ	0-1583961	0165	1
BOND CHANNING A	CPT	0-1649253	0557	1
BOND CHARLES A	LTC	0-0239401	0662	3
BOND CICERO P	COL	0-0167690	0555	3
BOND CLIFFORD H	MAJ	0-1264639	1060	2
BOND DONALD H	MAJ	0-0271528	0845	2
BOND DONALD J	LTC	0-0303523	0662	1
BOND DOW G	MAJ	0-0405201	0747	2
BOND EDWARD C	CPT	0-0996094	0859	1
BOND EDWARD W P	COL	0-0190937	0648	3
BOND EUGENE A	COL	0-0114179	0550	3
BOND FLOYD D	LTC	0-0228120	0165	3
BOND GEORGE C	LTC	0-0370954	0864	1
BOND GLENN F	CW3	W-2147369	0663	1
BOND HENRY G	1LT	0-1016824	0845	1
BOND JAMES	CPT	0-0268597	1146	1
BOND JR GEORGE A	COL	0-0295771	1046	1
BOND JR RIGGELY B	BG	0-0237069	0765	3
BOND JUANITA R	MAJ	L-1010288	0264	1
BOND LEE F	LTC	0-0395570	0261	1
BOND MYRON D	CW4	W-2144167	0565	1
BOND STANLEY L	1LT	0-1693479	0145	2
BOND THOMAS H	COL	0-0281646	0561	1
BOND THOMAS W	CPT	0-1580660	0459	1
BOND WILMER K	LTC	0-0148454	1056	3
BONDE COILO A	CPT	0-2005647	0260	1
BONDI JOSEPH	CPT	0-0972511	1060	1
BONDI JOSEPH R	MAJ	0-0460648	0750	1
BONDS FEASTER W	2LT	0-1178075	0144	2
BONDS SAMUEL T	LTC	0-1035422	1163	1
BONDURANT JOHN F	MAJ	0-0415101	0346	2
BONDY DONALD H	2LT	0-1175645	0345	1
BONE JR WINSTEAD P	CPT	0-0501228	0144	2
BONE MAURICE C	MAJ	0-1175051	1160	1
BONE NORFLEET G	CPT	0-0184170	1032	2
BONEBRAKE JOSEPH R	LTC	0-0376026	0465	1
BONER GEORGE T	CW3	W-2135983	1062	1
BONESS OSCAR I	MAJ	0-1583981	1162	1
BONESTELL DEAN	LTC	0-0455097	1061	1
BONETTI ALBERT C	1LT	0-2046897	1145	2
BONEY EDWIN W	LTC	0-0104375	0954	3
BONEY JOHN C	CPT	0-0924609	0446	2
BONEY JR JOHN B	CPT	0-1647121	0247	2
BONFIGLIO JOSEPH	LTC	0-1285697	1062	1
BONFIGLIO JOSEPH H	1LT	0-0123475	1053	3
BONFORTE JOHN	LTC	0-0167237	1158	3
BONGARD CALVIN L	CW3	W-2150235	0165	1
BONHAM CLAUDE O	MAJ	0-0484086	0445	2
BONHAM JAMES H	CPT	0-1019035	0747	2
BONHAM JR BYRON M	LTC	0-1292825	0265	1
BONICH CATHERINE	2LT	N-0783651	1045	1
BONICORO LOUIS	CW3	W-2149424	0964	1
BONIFACE JOHN A	CPT	0-1031056	0248	2
BONIFAY SAMUEL A	CPT	0-0228727	1061	3
BONILLA THOMAS E	CPT	0-0217530	1047	1
BONILLA TOMAS E	MAJ	0-0371125	0760	1
BONIN ARTHUR L	WO1	W-2142815	1152	1
BONINE WILLIAM J	CPT	0-0229672	1056	3
BONINI JOHN R	CPT	0-1284278	0152	1
BONJEAN AMERICO F	CPT	0-0251018	0148	2
BONK JOHN A	MAJ	0-1641450	1146	1
BONKOWSKI JOHN S	MAJ	0-1594050	0556	2
BONNAVILLE JOHN E	CW2	W-2145073	0357	1
BONNEAU CHARLES R	CPT	0-0383563	0357	1
BONNELL FLOYD F	LTC	0-1167748	0162	1
BONNELL RALPH I	LTC	0-0218667	0256	3
BONNELL WILLIAM K	COL	0-0156592	0355	3
BONNELL WILLIAM L	CW3	W-2149327	1060	1
BONNER CHESTER C	MAJ	0-0271603	0648	3

NAME	GRADE	SVC NO	DATE RET MO YR	RET CODE
BONNER DAN F	MAJ	0-2018103	0864	1
BONNER EDWIN D	LTC	0-0461768	0954	1
BONNER EUGENE C	CW3	W-2152309	0162	1
BONNER FRANCIS C	CPT	0-0477214	1145	2
BONNER JAY W	CW3	W-2115855	0155	1
BONNER JOHN V	1LT	0-1583985	0745	2
BONNER JOHN W	COL	0-0318553	0862	3
BONNER MOFFATT G	LTC	0-0221629	0762	3
BONNER ROBERT A	MAJ	0-1325367	0667	1
BONNET CHRISTOPHE	MAJ	0-0392960	0261	1
BONNETT LEON	1LT	0-1583712	1045	2
BONNETTE JAMES L	MAJ	0-1578183	0757	1
BONNETTE ROLAND H	CPT	0-0261036	1066	3
BONNEY CHARLES J	MAJ	0-0364280	0360	1
BONNEY JR HARRY L	MAJ	0-1583991	0264	1
BONNING CHARLES W	MAJ	0-1283900	0261	1
BONNINGTON JAMES A	COL	0-0249277	1060	3
BONNIWELL CHARLES M	CPT	0-0426529	0746	2
BONS JILLES T	2LT	0-1176892	0145	2
BONSALL THOMAS F	COL	0-0308506	0560	3
BONTEMPS BENJAMIN W	MAJ	0-1633683	0660	1
BONUCCI LINO	LTC	0-0417429	0266	1
BONURA SR ROCCO F	LTC	0-0518199	0563	1
BONUS ROMAN A	MAJ	0-0934799	0763	1
BONZER WILLIAM A	LTC	0-1824974	1263	1
BOO CLINTON R	LTC	0-0233952	1057	3
BOOGE JOHN L	CPT	0-0302014	0262	1
BOOKER LYNN H	CW2	W-2143832	0660	1
BOOKER MILTON R	CPT	0-1945760	1059	3
BOOKHAMER JOSEPH A	LTC	0-0382539	0561	1
BOOKWALTER GEORGE R	COL	0-0142890	0852	3
BOOLE JR JAMES O	LTC	0-0888317	0857	1
BOOLOOKAS NICHOLAS H	1LT	0-1574595	0246	2
BOON CHARLES B	LTC	0-0478130	1263	3
BOONE CHARLES L	MAJ	0-2206400	0367	1
BOONE CLARENCE A	LTC	0-0259629	0463	3
BOONE DANA H	LTC	0-0200206	0757	3
BOONE DANIEL F	COL	0-0221957	0864	3
BOONE DANIEL H	CPT	0-2029867	0156	1
BOONE DANIEL L	CPT	0-1342237	1057	2
BOONE JEFFERSON	MAJ	0-1043872	0858	1
BOONE JR WILLIAM S	MAJ	0-0668885	1163	1
BOONE LEO E	CPT	0-1109822	0646	2
BOONE RALPH L	CW2	W-2204093	0562	1
BOONE RANKIN R	COL	0-0229398	0960	3
BOONE SAM H	LTC	0-0567376	0862	1
BOONE SAMUEL C	CPT	0-0168678	0258	3
BOONE WILLIAM E	COL	0-0199358	0755	2
BOONSTRA SAMUEL P	MAJ	0-0118732	0648	3
BOORAS THOMAS J	MAJ	0-2200327	0766	1
BOORON OWEN D	COL	0-0489965	0360	2
BOORSTEIN LOUIS S	1LT	0-1543787	0146	2
BOOSA JOHN R	MAJ	0-0264602	0646	2
BOOSE JR HOWARD H	COL	0-0376925	0261	1
BOOSE LLOYD	COL	0-0165769	0955	3
BOOT SAMUEL K	LTC	0-1585187	0467	1
BOOTH AUGUST M	COL	0-0269795	0264	1
BOOTH BENJAMIN J	LTC	0-1111502	0863	1
BOOTH BRUCE G	COL	0-0211148	0360	3
BOOTH CECIL V	CW4	W-2122649	0255	1
BOOTH EDWIN L	MAJ	0-1798552	0860	1
BOOTH EDWIN S	LTC	0-0250507	0747	1
BOOTH FREDERICK	MAJ	0-0378452	1045	1
BOOTH GEORGE L	CPT	0-0320750	0550	1
BOOTH GILBERT	MAJ	0-1540698	0860	1
BOOTH HAROLD R	COL	0-0114180	1054	1
BOOTH JOHN L	1LT	0-1323891	0346	2
BOOTH JR JOHN C	CPT	0-0241488	0564	3
BOOTH JR WAYNE E	1LT	0-1107306	0345	1
BOOTH MALCOLM C	CPT	0-0305408	0447	2
BOOTH MAYNARD B	LTC	0-0395521	1160	1
BOOTH ORBIN G	MAJ	0-0267018	0155	1
BOOTH PAUL M	COL	0-0327750	0560	1
BOOTH ROBERT	COL	0-0186477	0255	3
BOOTH ROBERT G	MAJ	0-1598747	1262	1

NAME	GRADE	SVC NO	DATE RET MO YR	RET CODE
BOOTH WALTER G	1LT	0-1300090	0945	2
BOOTH WILLIAM P	1LT	0-1315135	0745	2
BOOTHBY AUSTIN L	CW3	W-2148466	0166	1
BOOTHE HOWARD P	2LT	0-1578185	0944	2
BOOTHE LAWRENCE L	CW4	W-2144843	0864	1
BOOTHE RUBY F	2LT	N-0700238	0836	1
BOOTON LAWRENCE J	CW3	W-2004168	0559	3
BOOZE THOMAS W	CPT	0-1881409	0365	1
BOOZER JR GEORGE W	CPT	0-0403672	0646	2
BOOZER MATTHEW F	CPT	0-0315517	0345	2
BOOZER WILLIAM L	MAJ	0-0174084	0961	3
BORAH HARRY A	LTC	0-0237173	0362	3
BORAL HENRY	CPT	0-0495539	0849	2
BORAM GEORGE G	COL	0-0360972	0161	1
BORASCH EDWARD J	CW3	W-3150382	1167	1
BORCHERDT JACK A	CPT	0-1290886	1145	2
BORCHERS ROBERT B	CPT	0-0128310	0644	2
BORCHERT ERNEST F	CPT	0-0170807	0954	3
BORCHERT JOSEPH J	COL	0-0297890	0359	1
BORCHERT MAX A	MAJ	0-0256184	0248	1
BORCK CHARLES A	WO1	W-2114628	0366	3
BORCUK PETER J	LTC	0-1319171	0763	1
BORDE HARRY J	1LT	0-0464377	0144	2
BORDEN DANIEL L	COL	0-0186593	0648	3
BORDEN FRANK	MAJ	0-1574207	0460	1
BORDEN GARLAND A	LTC	0-1171910	0661	1
BORDEN HOKSEY J	LTC	0-0278268	0466	3
BORDEN NATHANIEL	COL	0-0241874	1059	1
BORDEN ROBERT B	LTC	0-1553029	0163	1
BORDEN WALTER J	LTC	0-1039180	0161	1
BORDER CHARLES R	LTC	0-0369388	0967	3
BORDER LENORA H	1LT	0-1031999	0552	1
BORDER WILLARD C	LTC	0-1302586	0162	1
BORDERS COLEMAN P	LTC	0-1113114	1061	1
BORDERS HUEY T	LTC	0-0298985	0166	3
BORDERS RAY W	LTC	0-1312165	0165	1
BORDERS WILLIAM A	COL	0-0222335	0964	3
BORDEWICH JOHN P	2LT	0-1015813	0245	2
BORDLEY ARTHUR W	MAJ	0-1039212	1061	1
BORDONARO ANTHONY C	CW2	W-2103897	0944	2
BORDONARO JAMES J	CW3	W-2203635	0463	1
BOREK JOHN W	1LT	0-1823824	0145	2
BOREL COLZEY	CW3	W-2113728	0555	1
BORELL ELDON W	LTC	0-0419609	1164	3
BORELL ROBERT W	LTC	0-1116827	1167	1
BOREN CLAUD W	MAJ	0-1300444	0856	1
BOREN DEAN A	MAJ	0-1182521	0160	1
BOREN EDGAR F	LTC	0-0371305	0560	1
BOREN JOHN C	LTC	0-0312354	0758	3
BOREN LESTER R	CPT	0-0489369	1050	1
BORENTZ DORA K	1LT	N-0728622	1045	1
BORER WILLIAM J	CPT	0-0529484	0346	2
BORESCH URBAN W	COL	0-0392227	0760	1
BORESON EVELYN A	CPT	N-0773100	0746	1
BORGATTI RAOUL F	1LT	0-1060016	0447	2
BORGELT PERSHING H	CPT	0-0467166	1046	2
BORGEN LLOYD C	LTC	0-1168179	0864	1
BORGENS CLARENCE	LTC	0-1329316	1062	1
BORGER WILMER F	MAJ	0-2035686	1060	1
BORGESON CARL A	COL	0-0207567	1263	3
BORGIA ANTHONY W	LTC	0-1637392	0862	1
BORICAN JR CHARLES H	MAJ	0-0247460	1162	1
BORIE HENRY P	MAJ	0-0322919	1160	3
BORING CLYDE C	LTC	0-1596276	0966	2
BORING HAROLD	CW3	W-2141202	0461	2
BORING JAMES W	LTC	0-1317753	0360	1
BORING JOHN S	LTC	0-0573987	0961	1
BORIS WALTER	CW3	W-2143412	0862	1
BORISS MARION E	LTC	0-0228662	0265	3
BORK LEROY V	2LT	0-1998097	0646	2
BORKIN EMILIA V	1LT	N-0755013	0745	1
BORKSTROM THEODORE W	1LT	0-1580548	0646	1
BORLANE JR WALLACE C	MAJ	0-0578953	0967	1
BORLAND WHITNEY M	LTC	0-1110939	1265	3
BORMAN WILLIAM R	MAJ	0-1885197	0864	1

NAME	GRADE	SVC NO	DATE RET MO YR	RET CODE
BORN RICHARD W	1LT	C-1288687	0146	2
BORNDAHL RICHARD I	LTC	0-0338260	C669	1
BORNE ANNE	CPT	L-0201406	1047	2
BORNEMAN ESTHER B	MAJ	N-0726918	0462	1
BORNEMAN JOHN K	COL	0-0266084	0450	1
BORNEMEIER WALTER C	MAJ	C-0174683	C561	3
BORNHOFFT JR HENRY J	CPT	C-0528393	C747	2
BORNHOLDT JOHN N	COL	0-0342327	C866	1
BORNKESSEL JULIUS G	LTC	0-0384018	C960	1
BORNMAN CASPER S	LTC	C-1051492	0962	1
BORNMAN JAMES A	LTC	0-0451824	1060	1
BORNSCHEUER WILLIAM	LTC	0-1054916	0165	1
BORNSTEIN LEON M	1LT	C-1846252	C445	2
BOROP LYLE E	1LT	0-1170290	C646	1
BOROS WILLIAM K	CPT	0-0539508	C546	2
BOROUGHS WILLIAM J	LTC	0-0362217	1156	3
BOROWITZ FRANK P	LTC	0-0980121	0266	1
BOROWSKI ANTHONY	LTC	0-0498155	0557	1
BOROWSKI JOHN D	LTC	0-0369156	0861	1
BORREGO ALBERTO M	1LT	C-0290651	1160	3
BORRELIZ ANTONIO	CW2	W-2210425	C766	1
BORRELL GERALD J	CW2	W-2143833	C559	1
BORRES MICHAEL G	MAJ	0-1341940	1263	1
BORROWMAN JOHN K	COL	0-0258115	0767	3
BORSHER IRVING P	CPT	0-0539075	C847	1
BORTIRI MAXIMUS	1LT	0-0538863	1144	2
BORTNER LESTER E	CW2	W-2146627	1154	1
BORUM VERNON L	LTC	0-0176353	0361	3
BORUSZAK NATHAN	COL	0-0189302	1262	3
BOSA JOSEPH R	LTC	C-0304030	C260	1
BOSAK JOHN R	LTC	0-1556389	0967	1
BOSCH EDMUND A	LTC	0-0288978	0861	3
BOSCH HENRY M	CW3	W-2148606	1063	1
BOSCHER HARRY W	MAJ	0-1043873	0561	1
BOSCHKE WILLIAM P	2LT	0-1048291	1044	2
BOSCO EDWARD J	LTC	0-1547883	C867	1
BOSEN HERBERT A	1LT	0-1936237	0755	2
BOSENBERG CHARLES F	CPT	C-0338352	C345	2
BOSFIELD HUGH H	CPT	0-0265908	0265	3
BOSHART MELVIN W	CW4	W-2119506	0762	1
BOSHOFF WILLIAM H	COL	C-0466828	0251	2
BOSINIO LOUIS L	CW3	W-2152188	0563	1
BOSKEY LOESER M	COL	0-0241686	0266	3
BOSKY WALTER F	LTC	0-0351823	0260	1
BOSKY ZIGMOND M	CPT	0-1573058	C645	1
BOSLEY BEATRICE M	LTC	N-0734346	0961	2
BOSLEY CHARLES H	LTC	0-0406932	0361	1
BOSLEY JAMES L	1LT	0-1285886	0558	3
BOSLEY JOHN O	CPT	0-0492137	0347	1
BOSMA CHARLES F	CPT	0-0523355	0546	2
BOSMA THEODORA C	LTC	L-0502131	0766	3
BOSOLD ROBERT F	CW3	W-2145131	C561	1
BOSS GERALD S	CW3	W-2148275	C163	1
BOSSARD SAMUEL L	LTC	0-0228065	0849	3
BOSSART DAVID H	MAJ	C-0559037	0658	1
BOSSE EDWARD V	LTC	0-0379205	0760	1
BOSSERT EUSEBIUS	1LT	0-2006046	C452	2
BOSSERT LESTER	CW4	W-2110124	C959	1
BOSSICK ANDY	WO1	W-2115661	0347	1
BOSSIDY REYNOLD J	COL	0-0379045	C662	2
BOSSINGHAM EARL N	LTC	0-0318260	0866	3
BOSSON DONAL C	1LT	0-0550430	C446	2
BOSSON HENRY	2LT	C-0187904	1161	1
BOSTEDO KATHRYN F	CPT	N-0744442	C353	2
BOSTER VERN	LTC	0-0383496	C557	1
BOSTIC JOHN H	COL	0-0355189	1161	1
BOSTICK BENJAMIN	LTC	0-0302283	1043	2
BOSTICK HARRY W	LTC	0-1046362	0258	1
BOSTICK JOSEPH F	LTC	C-0383933	C261	1
BOSTICK JR ARTHUR C	1LT	0-0398141	1043	2
BOSTICK MACON L	CPT	0-2012352	0861	1
BOSTICK ORBIE	LTC	0-0293977	1044	2
BOSTICK SAMUEL M	MAJ	0-1798775	0461	1
BOSTICK SIDNEY F	COL	C-0266448	1053	2
BOSTOCK GEORGE M	COL	C-0140131	1056	3
BOSTOCK THOMAS J	CPT	0-0479535	1046	1
BOSTOCK THOMAS J	2LT	0-1037403	0545	2
BOSTON DAVID	1LT	0-1544240	1144	2
BOSTON DONALD W	LTC	0-1636302	C861	2
BOSTON GEORGE A	MAJ	0-1822526	1161	1
BOSTON HOWARD R	MAJ	0-0955149	0864	1
BOSTON JOHN A	LTC	0-0192873	0749	3
BOSTWICK WILLIAM C	CPT	0-0553424	1047	1
BOSWELL ANDREW V	MAJ	0-0247446	0353	3
BOSWELL AUBREY	CPT	0-0333408	0346	2
BOSWELL CHARLES A	CPT	0-1292645	0446	2
BOSWELL CLARENCE H	LTC	0-0472263	0146	2
BOSWELL HENRY O	MAJ	0-1684980	1163	2
BOSWELL JAMES M	CW3	W-2149988	1062	1
BOSWELL JOHN H	LTC	0-1951003	0167	1
BOSWELL KENNETH B	MAJ	C-0367783	0761	1
BOSWELL LESTER R	2LT	0-1822097	C550	1
BOSWELL WILLIAM B	1LT	0-0511869	0145	2
BOSWELL WILLIAM P	MAJ	0-1302264	0661	1
BOSWELL WILSON S	MAJ	0-0450016	0854	1
BOSWORTH JULIAN E	CW4	W-2142222	1265	1
BOTDORF FREDERICK	CW2	W-2143872	0166	1
BOTDORF JR CHARLES E	LTC	0-1116355	1164	1
BOTELER LANHAM L	LTC	0-1114855	1165	1
BOTELHO BENJAMIN	CW4	W-2002060	1060	3
BOTERF CHESTER A	LTC	0-0482364	C563	1
BOTHE CHRISTOPHE	CPT	0-0318607	1045	2
BOTHWELL FLORA H	CPT	N-0731424	0747	2
BOTHWELL JAMES H	LTC	0-0208212	0861	3
BOTNICK ABRAHAM J	LTC	C-1172386	0466	1
BOTSFORD GERALD F	LTC	0-0206177	0556	3
BOTSFORD HARTLEY W	1LT	0-1323524	1145	2
BOTSFORD JR NORMAN L	LTC	0-0430473	0563	1
BOTT EDWARD	MAJ	C-1323525	C357	1
BOTTEMILLER HARLEY L	MAJ	C-2265310	0965	1
BOTTEMILLER HAROLD F	LTC	0-0345231	0446	2
BOTTING LEONARD P	COL	0-0172678	0657	3
BOTTOM NORMAN R	LTC	0-0255869	1062	1
BOTTOMLEY CORNELIUS	MAJ	0-0383327	0556	2
BOTTOMLEY HOWARD E	LTC	0-0347009	0860	1
BOTTOMS CHARLES B	COL	0-0206722	1263	3
BOTTOMS IRA G	CPT	0-0374578	1047	2
BOTTOMS WILMER R	LTC	0-0525504	0264	1
BOTTONI DOMINIC J	1LT	0-1047890	0944	1
BOTTORFF JAMES C	LTC	0-1031788	0862	2
BOTTORFF MARCUS G	LTC	0-1326377	C363	1
BOTTS PETE	CW3	W-2145386	0760	1
BOTTS ROBERT C	CPT	0-0466908	0645	2
BOUCHARD HOWARD S	LTC	0-0264033	1143	2
BOUCHARD PAUL E	CPT	0-1308782	0862	1
BOUCHARD PAUL H	LTC	0-2010445	C861	1
BOUCHARD RAYMOND E	LTC	0-1041972	0765	1
BOUCHER GEORGE H	LTC	0-0315561	0366	1
BOUCHER HARRY J	MAJ	0-1328965	1059	1
BOUCHER VERNON A	MAJ	0-0144433	0748	3
BOUCHEREAU DONALD P	1LT	0-1168180	1045	2
BOUCHEY WILFRID J	LTC	0-0402651	0565	3
BOUCK PERCY	COL	0-0111721	0854	1
BOUCEMAN FREDERICK	CPT	0-1031225	0847	2
BOUDINET HENRY H	LTC	0-0347314	0355	2
BOUDREAU BERNICE	MAJ	N-0721754	1162	1
BOUDREAU FLOYD T	CPT	0-0495767	0145	2
BOUDREAUX ARCHIE F	CW2	W-2101154	0246	2
BOUDREAUX JULES A	CPT	0-0404321	1045	2
BOUDREAUX LOUIS E	MAJ	0-1018243	0461	1
BOUEY DONALD E	1LT	0-1325196	1045	1
BOUFFARD CHARLES J	MAJ	0-0257109	1160	3
BOUFFARD HENRI J	LTC	0-1549433	0466	1
BOUFFARD ULRIC J	LTC	0-0188085	1156	3
BOUGARD JOSEPH G	WO1	W-2149804	1153	1
BOUGHNER DUNCAN S	MAJ	0-1041973	0361	1
BOUGHTON CHARLES A	MAJ	0-1593467	0464	1
BOUGHTON WELBY K	2LT	0-0398734	0344	2
BOUGHTON WILLIAM H	COL	0-0243886	0356	3
BOUK JUNIOR F	2LT	0-1319643	1043	2
BOUKNIGHT WILLIAM R	COL	0-0520010	C567	3
BOULAIS FREDERICK	MAJ	0-1332670	C161	1
BOULDEN JR HENRY W	MAJ	C-1951643	0166	1
BOULDEN MARION P	COL	0-0118806	1057	3
BOULDIN ALLEN H	LTC	0-1101342	1058	1
BOULDIN CHARLES E	CPT	0-1642944	0355	1
BOULDIN EDWARD J	CPT	0-1321146	1047	2
BOULDIN WILLIAM R	CPT	0-1287129	0246	1
BOULER WALTER T	LTC	0-1012066	0962	1
BOULEY ARTHUR G	CW4	W-2101106	0259	1
BOULLEMET MARSEILLE	MAJ	C-0228872	0155	3
BOULLION KENNETH L	LTC	0-1284089	0258	1
BOULTER ROBERT F	COL	0-0378621	C866	3
BOULTON ALBERT F	LTC	0-0271397	0967	3
BOULTON JOHN W	2LT	0-0436842	1045	2
BOULWARE CHARLIE L	CW2	W-2145700	0659	1
BOULWARE JOHN P	CPT	0-0497223	0148	1
BOUMENOT BEPPO	CPT	0-0442386	0147	1
BOUNDS JESSE C	1LT	0-0286424	C160	2
BOUNDS JOHN A	LTC	0-1589715	C167	1
BOUNDS SIDNEY V	MAJ	C-1296163	C961	1
BOUR LAWRENCE J	LTC	0-0408743	0861	1
BOURCEAU HERBERT F	LTC	0-0451630	0959	1
BOURDON WILLIAM P	LTC	C-0128111	1155	3
BOURGEOIS LAWRENCE J	MAJ	C-1590667	C160	1
BOURGEOIS MARCEL C	LTC	0-1647969	0264	1
BOURGOIN CARMEN M	MAJ	L-0221270	0164	1
BOURISSEAU DALE S	2LT	0-1311971	1144	2
BOURKE EDWARD	LTC	0-1166442	0457	1
BOURKE JOHN D	1LT	0-1323100	C346	2
BOURKE THOMAS C	COL	C-0130259	C653	3
BOURLAND PHILIP F M	LTC	0-0337832	1060	1
BOURLAND SAM P	CW3	W-2147226	0862	1
BOURNE ELDRED G	CW3	W-2153384	0966	1
BOURNE GORDON M	MAJ	0-0979079	1067	1
BOURNE ROBERT F	LTC	0-0347860	0746	2
BOURNE ROBERT L	CPT	0-1300751	0747	2
BOURNE WILLIAM O	MAJ	0-0179400	0750	3
BOURNS PAUL M	LTC	0-0387089	1163	3
BOURQUE JOSEPH A A	CW2	RW-2210907	1165	1
BOURQUIN RALPH H	MAJ	0-2026471	0261	1
BOUSCHOR CHARLES F	CPT	0-0490507	1145	2
BOUSE THERMAN	LTC	0-1581541	0565	1
BOUSH GILBERT W	COL	0-0228018	C361	3
BOUSQUET WILLIAM C	CW2	W-2143523	0953	1
BOUSQUIN SYLVIO L	LTC	0-0351412	0757	1
BOUST EDWARD B	LTC	0-0204391	0960	1
BOUTILIER FRANKLIN M	MAJ	0-1335225	0967	1
BOUTIN JOHN A	MAJ	C-0947298	0663	1
BOUTON JAY H	LTC	0-0268670	0646	1
BOUTON VERNON W	MAJ	C-2016248	C457	1
BOUTTE CLARENCE P	LTC	0-0282255	0467	3
BOUTWELL GENE A	1LT	0-1284641	0544	2
BOVE EMIL	MAJ	0-1691184	0745	2
BOVINO VICTOR J	LTC	0-1282317	1167	1
BOWAB ANTHONY J	MAJ	C-0103282	1058	3
BOWDEN AMBROSE H	CPT	0-0233072	1067	3
BOWDEN CLIFTON M	LTC	C-0271221	1067	3
BOWDEN HAYGOOD S	LTC	0-0329494	0465	3
BOWDEN HERMAN R	WO1	W-2150809	C861	1
BOWDEN HOWARD W	LTC	C-1312271	0261	1
BOWDEN JOHN W	COL	0-0352722	C861	1
BOWDEN JR JOHN W	MAJ	C-1115192	C857	1
BOWDEN JR THOMAS N	CW2	W-2147739	0756	1
BOWDEN MURRAY C	MAJ	0-0986768	C865	1
BOWDEN TROY C	CPT	0-2026574	0857	1
BOWDEN WALTER O	COL	C-0395769	0862	1
BOWDISH ARVINE C	CPT	0-0900310	1043	2
BOWDLE HARVEY C	LTC	0-0453406	0665	1
BOWE FRANKLIN G	WO1	W-2105384	0958	2
BOWEN CARL D	COL	0-0108770	1040	1
BOWEN CLARENCE W	LTC	0-0312443	0157	3
BOWEN E A	CPT	0-1288688	0546	2
BOWEN EMERY J	CPT	C-0221839	C349	3
BOWEN FLOYD L	CW4	W-2117006	0161	1
BOWEN GLENN R	COL	0-0351354	0764	1
BOWEN HAROLD F	LTC	0-0911782	1062	1
BOWEN HAROLD N	LTC	0-0277027	0464	3
BOWEN HARRY E	LTC	0-0481600	0455	2
BOWEN II RICHARD A	COL	0-0231931	0559	1
BOWEN ISAIAH F	LTC	0-0201332	0757	3
BOWEN JACK	MAJ	0-1293361	0661	1
BOWEN JOEL H	MAJ	0-0276535	0964	3
BOWEN JOHN J	LTC	0-1558539	0367	1
BOWEN JOHN P	MAJ	0-1549434	0366	1
BOWEN JR CLIFFORD D	LTC	0-1175054	1160	1
BOWEN JR HUBERT E	CPT	0-1169033	0546	2
BOWEN JR ROBERT E	1LT	0-0425625	1045	2
BOWEN KENNETH F	CPT	0-0255822	1058	3
BOWEN ORVAL W	LTC	0-0484218	0863	1
BOWEN PHILIP M	CW3	W-2144227	0461	1
BOWEN RAYMOND J	CPT	0-1691270	0545	2
BOWEN ROBERT W	CW2	W-2213129	0467	1
BOWEN WHEELER B	MAJ	0-0452290	0557	1
BOWEN WILLIAM C	COL	0-0191754	1162	3
BOWER BERNARD W	1LT	0-0539765	1045	2
BOWER CECIL L	LTC	0-0163573	1156	3
BOWER CHARLES W	MAJ	0-1050190	0164	1
BOWER EDWARD C	LTC	0-0233227	0762	3
BOWER FRED L	MAJ	0-0281416	0446	1
BOWER HAROLD C	2LT	0-1182780	0745	2
BOWER JACK W	CW2	W-2209862	0463	1
BOWER JOHN L	2LT	0-1181828	0944	2
BOWER LEWIS C	MAJ	0-1282357	0962	1
BOWER LOYS F	LTC	0-0243010	0157	3
BOWER RICHARD E	CPT	0-0483222	0946	2
BOWER WAYNE E	CW3	W-2150599	0365	1
BOWERMAN RALPH L	COL	0-0189553	0158	3
BOWERMAN THOMAS J	LTC	0-1796417	0261	1
BOWERMASTER FRED C	LTC	0-0414174	0667	3
BOWERMASTER JAMES W	1LT	0-1541580	1053	2
BOWERS ALBERT V	COL	0-0249564	0865	3
BOWERS BENJAMIN E	CW3	W-2150602	0659	1
BOWERS BYRON C	LTC	0-0274590	0156	3
BOWERS CARL E	MAJ	0-1037953	0761	1
BOWERS CHARLES E	MAJ	0-0972296	1064	1
BOWERS CLAUDE T	M G	0-0183291	0859	3
BOWERS EDWARD G	2LT	0-0108779	0545	1
BOWERS EDWARD W	LTC	0-0409997	0560	1
BOWERS EUGENE D	MAJ	0-1342151	1066	1
BOWERS FRANKLIN F	2LT	0-1301248	0745	2
BOWERS GAH T	CPT	0-0269119	0943	1
BOWERS HAROLD D	MAJ	0-0380790	0546	2
BOWERS III EATON J	MAJ	0-0407223	1160	1
BOWERS JACK G	CW2	W-2148026	0761	1
BOWERS JESSE W	COL	0-0231465	0648	3
BOWERS JOHN A	COL	0-0212638	1263	3
BOWERS JOHN A	2LT	0-1019285	0745	2
BOWERS JOHN E	1LT	0-1100884	0459	1
BOWERS JOSEPH J	MAJ	0-1549893	0357	1
BOWERS JOSEPH H	MAJ	0-1169433	0161	1
BOWERS JR J P	LTC	0-0269537	0463	1
BOWERS JR WILLIAM H	LTC	0-0197068	0758	3
BOWERS LAWRENCE J	MAJ	0-1030334	0456	1
BOWERS LEOLA C	CPT	N-0792560	0956	2
BOWERS LOWELL F	COL	0-0118805	0355	3
BOWERS RALPH K	MAJ	0-0203780	0145	2
BOWERS RICHARD G	1LT	0-0501757	0445	1
BOWERS RICHARD W	MAJ	C-1574737	0460	1
BOWERS ROBERT F	CW3	W-2147123	0162	1
BOWERS ROBERT J	CPT	0-0481954	0148	1
BOWERS RUSSELL S	MAJ	0-0213571	0549	3
BOWERS SR F A I	CPT	0-0195616	0660	3
BOWERS WARREN B	2LT	0-1299361	0544	2
BOWERS WILLIAM L	CPT	0-0495740	0647	1
BOWERS ZELOTIS P	1LT	0-1288506	0545	2
BOWERSOCK JOHN C	LTC	0-0446194	0262	1
BOWES ALMON A	COL	0-0146762	1155	3
BOWES JOHN G	COL	0-0330575	1163	3
BOWIE CLYDE F	MAJ	0-1683859	0246	2

NAME	GRADE	SVC NO	DATE RET MO YR	RET CODE
BOWIE DWAIN T	LTC	0-0329216	0861	1
BOWIE ELEAZAR R	COL	0-0121290	0349	3
BOWIE RALPH W	LTC	0-0254979	0867	3
BOWIE WILLIAM R	MAJ	0-1560404	0863	1
BOWIN LYNN L	COL	0-0327153	1165	1
BOWINGTON ELMER W	MAJ	0-1013646	0858	1
BOWKER IRVING A	1LT	0-1333923	1056	2
BOWLAND JR FRANK Y	LTC	0-0424188	0765	1
BOWLBY JAMES D	LTC	0-1548697	0665	2
BOWLBY JOHN G	CW3	W-2149690	0363	1
BOWLER DANIEL A	CPT	0-1114380	0147	2
BOWLER FRANCIS R	CPT	0-0124267	0259	3
BOWLER JOSEPH L	MAJ	0-0944658	0562	1
BOWLER ROBERT V	COL	0-0294619	0647	2
BOWLES ARTHUR L	WO1	W-2146870	0157	1
BOWLES CECIL C	1LT	0-0919735	0245	2
BOWLES GEORGE M	LTC	0-0322775	0459	1
BOWLES HERSHEL C	CPT	0-0499526	0847	1
BOWLES JOSEPH M	2LT	0-1541118	0344	2
BOWLES JR GEORGE R	1LT	0-0969057	0858	2
BOWLES JR HOWARD G	LTC	0-0425237	0463	1
BOWLES VICTOR D	2LT	0-2046902	0245	2
BOWLEY RAY A	CW3	W-2152367	0763	1
BOWLIN ALLAN K	LTC	0-0262925	0665	3
BOWLIN CLEO S	LTC	0-1581666	1062	1
BOWLIN DONALD W	CW2	W-2147563	1159	1
BOWLIN FOREST W	2LT	0-1014420	0645	2
BOWLIN FRANCIS R	COL	0-0291073	0559	1
BOWLIN WILLIAM D	MAJ	0-1109825	0663	1
BOWLING ROBERT H	1LT	0-1285366	0546	2
BOWLING SILAS B	CW3	W-2148276	0964	1
BOWLING TRULY T	MAJ	0-0503398	0755	1
BOWMAN BEATRICE	MAJ	L-0602965	0467	1
BOWMAN BRADLEY L	LTC	0-0315436	0958	2
BOWMAN CLAIR F	LTC	0-0245952	0760	3
BOWMAN CLARENCE	CW3	W-2205364	1065	1
BOWMAN CLARENCE W	WO1	W-2151834	0255	1
BOWMAN DORIS E	CPT	N-0742773	0448	1
BOWMAN EDWIN D	MAJ	0-1851544	0755	2
BOWMAN GEORGE H	LTC	0-0346618	0961	1
BOWMAN HAROLD M	MAJ	0-1937448	1266	1
BOWMAN HENRY L	MAJ	0-0121333	0556	3
BOWMAN HOWARD F	LTC	0-0218097	0952	3
BOWMAN HOWARD F	MAJ	0-0888601	0257	1
BOWMAN IRA G	CW4	W-2005868	0663	1
BOWMAN JACOB	CPT	0-0199391	0363	3
BOWMAN JAMES H	MAJ	0-1821541	0761	1
BOWMAN JAMES H	CW3	W-2205796	0167	1
BOWMAN JANET S	MAJ	N-0754548	0765	1
BOWMAN JOHN D	1LT	0-1015114	0146	2
BOWMAN JOSEPH J	LTC	0-0349209	0267	3
BOWMAN JR FRANK S	MAJ	0-1560337	0763	1
BOWMAN JR HARVEY R	LTC	0-1295988	0765	1
BOWMAN KENNETH D	2LT	0-1321283	0245	2
BOWMAN LAKIN A	1LT	0-0402016	0244	2
BOWMAN LAWRENCE R	2LT	0-1587145	0144	2
BOWMAN LELAND E	CPT	0-1288689	0246	1
BOWMAN MARTIN	CPT	0-1058201	0747	2
BOWMAN MAUDE	LTC	N-0700039	0846	1
BOWMAN MILTON S	COL	0-0162224	0946	1
BOWMAN OLIN F	CW3	W-2147277	1262	1
BOWMAN ORVILLE D	1LT	0-1913557	0723	1
BOWMAN RAYMOND X	LTC	0-1172769	0863	1
BOWMAN ROBERT L	1LT	0-0256152	0857	3
BOWMAN SAMUEL A	LTC	0-0382385	0161	1
BOWMAN SAMUEL H	MAJ	0-0146443	0555	3
BOWMAN TINSLEY	1LT	0-0255487	1160	3
BOWMAN VERNON D	LTC	0-0452481	0461	1
BOWMAN WESLEY W	COL	0-0221029	0160	3
BOWMAN WHEELER G	CPT	0-2036042	0861	1
BOWMAN WILLIAM	MAJ	0-0186504	0931	1
BOWMAN WILLIAM R	1LT	0-1305190	0161	2
BOWMAN WILLIAM M	MAJ	0-0522308	0460	2
BOWMAN WILLIAM T	1LT	0-1826145	1145	2
BOWMASTER CHARLES O	WO1	W-2112119	0444	2

NAME	GRADE	SVC NO	DATE RET MO YR	RET CODE
BOWRON JAMES E	COL	0-0103169	0253	3
BOWSER GEORGE M	LTC	0-0220014	1263	3
BOWSER JR HARRY F	CPT	0-1040350	0660	1
BOWSER ROBERT M	LTC	0-0288357	0866	3
BOWSHER PAUL L	LTC	0-0359681	0960	1
BOWSTEAD LEONARD A	2LT	0-0353223	0245	2
BOWYER DALE F	1LT	0-0543128	0146	2
BOWYER DELMAR M	CW3	W-2144569	1059	1
BOWYER JR CHARLES S	MAJ	0-0962457	0967	1
BOWYER MILFORD A	1LT	0-1313371	1045	2
BOWYER WESLEY C	CPT	0-1300123	0348	2
BOX HERMAN F	CPT	0-1303266	0760	1
BOX VERGIL M	LTC	0-1575776	0562	1
BOX WILLIAM G	CW3	W-2205411	1065	1
BOXER LEE M	LTC	0-0408494	0646	2
BOY GRACE A	CPT	N-0736653	0246	1
BOYACK ARCHIE R	COL	0-0268986	0161	1
BOYCE BINGHAM	COL	0-0225875	1060	1
BOYCE CARL R	LTC	0-1798435	0962	1
BOYCE DAVID C	MAJ	0-0977308	1262	1
BOYCE DAVID K	MAJ	0-1646784	1060	1
BOYCE HENRY H	COL	0-0107859	0648	3
BOYCE HUGH S	LTC	0-2034623	0466	1
BOYCE LARRY J	WO1	W-2110923	0945	2
BOYCE LLOYD L	LTC	0-0180015	0561	3
BOYCOTT CECIL M	COL	0-0171340	0956	3
BOYD ALLEN W	CW2	W-2151612	0762	1
BOYD ARTHUR L	LTC	0-1341500	0967	1
BOYD BERL	LTC	0-0184596	0356	3
BOYD BILLIE R	MAJ	0-1317068	0761	1
BOYD BUFORD E	COL	0-0256619	1165	3
BOYD CARTER	1LT	0-0392964	0544	2
BOYD CHARLES C	LTC	0-1318859	0566	3
BOYD CELLIA J	LTC	0-0284145	1060	1
BOYD DALE F	1LT	0-0447698	0246	2
BOYD DEMPSTER A	CW3	W-2150557	1164	1
BOYD DON C	CW2	W-2213859	1167	1
BOYD DUDLEY G	LTC	0-0929726	0665	1
BOYD DWIGHT I	LTC	0-0586553	0862	1
BOYD EMMETT T	CPT	0-0974980	0956	2
BOYD ENNIS F	MAJ	0-1552236	0557	1
BOYD FRANK K	LTC	0-0279249	0453	3
BOYD GEORGE W	CPT	0-0175650	0757	3
BOYD GRAYDON F	CPT	0-1182510	0358	1
BOYD HAROLD L	LTC	0-0239604	1062	3
BOYD HOWARD	1LT	0-0375311	1145	2
BOYD HOWARD R	1LT	0-1285180	0446	2
BOYD JAMES	COL	0-0236154	0165	3
BOYD JAMES C	1LT	0-1287654	0145	2
BOYD JAMES H	MAJ	0-2005421	0461	1
BOYD JAMES M	LTC	0-0227675	0563	3
BOYD JAMES R	COL	0-0279151	0952	3
BOY[illegible] C	COL	[illegible]338141	0662	1
BOYD JOHN L	MAJ	[illegible]	1061	1
BOYD JOHN S	CPT	0-1312400	1052	1
BOYD JOHN W	MAJ	0-0124266	[illegible]	[illegible]
BOYD JR CLYDE C	CW2	W-2145318	0461	1
BOYD JR DAVID J	CW2	RW-2144613	0163	1
BOYD JR EDGAR E	LTC	0-0509602	0567	1
BOYD JR ROBERT B	1LT	0-1926344	1054	2
BOYD JR THOMAS H	1LT	0-0328142	0344	2
BOYD LEON H	MAJ	0-0282810	0648	3
BOYD LESLIE C	LTC	0-1178417	1262	1
BOYD MARIE A	1LT	N-0724346	0345	2
BOYD MARIE K	MAJ	N-0722801	0162	1
BOYD MARY	1LT	N-0735358	0345	1
BOYD MARY G	1LT	N-0737568	0845	1
BOYD MAX W	MAJ	0-0971963	0763	1
BOYD OCEIS F	CW2	W-2143873	0461	2
BOYD PAUL S	COL	0-0553900	1067	3
BOYD PHILLIPS L	B G	0-0230117	0165	3
BOYD RALPH G	B G	0-0203104	1161	3
BOYD RALPH W	CW3	W-2205058	0364	1
BOYD RANDOLPH W	LTC	0-0269494	0560	1
BOYD RAYMOND K	2LT	0-1304627	0144	2

NAME	GRADE	SVC NO	DATE RET MO YR	RET CODE
BOYD ROBERT E	CW3	W-2152992	1061	1
BOYD ROBERT P	CPT	0-1692238	0146	2
BOYD RUDOLPH	CW2	W-2147994	0360	1
BOYD RUTH	MAJ	R-0000773	0160	1
BOYD RUTH G	1LT	N-0787097	0346	1
BOYD SPURGEON C	LTC	0-1548016	1263	1
BOYD THOMAS L	CPT	0-0291884	0844	2
BOYD THOMAS W	MAJ	0-1014810	0761	1
BOYD THURMAN L	LTC	0-1058152	1162	1
BOYD TILLMAN F	COL	0-0250041	0947	2
BOYD WARLAND F	CPT	0-1581683	0146	2
BOYD WESTON A	CW3	W-2149203	0961	1
BOYD WILLIAM C	LTC	0-0405788	0665	1
BOYD WILLIAM D	MAJ	0-0237357	0464	3
BOYDEN WILLIAM E	MAJ	0-0126252	0450	1
BOYDSTON JAMES E	LTC	0-0475237	0163	1
BOYEN WILLIAM A	COL	0-0373051	0166	1
BOYER BENJAMIN F	COL	0-0238364	1064	3
BOYER CHARLES M	COL	0-0148831	0648	3
BOYER CLARENCE A	CPT	0-0528019	0546	1
BOYER CLARENCE L	COL	0-0142755	0154	3
BOYER EDGAR J	2LT	0-0395080	0745	1
BOYER FRED A	LTC	0-0535712	0561	3
BOYER GEORGE C	LTC	0-0389822	0247	2
BOYER GEORGE H	LTC	0-0156961	0648	3
BOYER GERALD O	COL	0-0254128	0559	3
BOYER GROVER A	MAJ	0-0189412	0648	3
BOYER HOWARD E	COL	0-0218680	1062	3
BOYER JACK K	MAJ	0-0398138	0748	1
BOYER JAMES N	LTC	0-1543482	0661	1
BOYER JOHN A	MAJ	0-1548359	0157	1
BOYER LESLIE W	LTC	0-0324770	0567	3
BOYER LESTER L	MAJ	0-1547547	0258	1
BOYER MERIL A	LTC	0-0277229	0957	3
BOYER OTHA W	MAJ	0-0200795	0855	3
BOYER PAUL N	MAJ	0-1919179	1066	1
BOYER ROBERT M	1LT	0-0446912	0146	2
BOYER ROBERT R	1LT	0-1293194	0844	2
BOYER ROSWELL R	COL	0-0223124	1055	1
BOYER WILLIAM D	MAJ	0-1047463	0762	1
BOYER WILLIAM M	LTC	0-0120774	0858	3
BOYERS PAULINE J	MAJ	N-0767819	1263	1
BOYES BEDFORD W	COL	0-0174387	1052	3
BOYES JAMES G	1LT	0-0109824	1041	1
BOYKIN BREVARD	LTC	0-0245024	0561	3
BOYKIN CECIL A	LTC	0-1000086	1161	1
BOYKIN HERMAN N	1LT	0-1043876	1045	2
BOYKIN JR LEMUEL K	LTC	0-0317858	0554	3
BOYKIN JR STAPLEY N	COL	0-0260944	0248	2
BOYKIN SAMUEL	MAJ	0-0473521	0446	2
BOYLAN JAMES M	CPT	0-0503022	1046	1
BOYLAN JR PAUL C	LTC	0-1118551	0867	1
BOYLAN ROBERT F	1LT	0-1013144	1045	2
BOYLAN WILLIAM J	CW4	W-2002612	0267	1
BOYLE BERNARD	LTC	0-1552237	0466	3
BOYLE CHARLES F	MAJ	0-1101748	1047	2
BOYLE EDWARD W	LTC	0-0405860	0860	1
BOYLE FRANCIS P	CPT	0-0889762	0856	1
BOYLE IRVING C	CPT	0-0415801	0948	1
BOYLE JAMES H	CPT	0-0132811	0315	1
BOYLE JAMES J	MAJ	0-2263237	0962	1
BOYLE JOHN C	CW3	W-2141150	1163	1
BOYLE JOHN W	LTC	0-1299363	0165	2
BOYLE JOSEPH R	CPT	0-0472789	0247	1
BOYLE JR FRANK J	WO1	W-2127822	0645	2
BOYLE JR JAMES L	1LT	0-1056989	1045	2
BOYLE JR JOSEPH A	1LT	0-0498990	0944	2
BOYLE LEO M	M G	0-0266202	0859	3
BOYLE MICHAEL J	MAJ	0-0903249	1045	2
BOYLE MURAT	1LT	0-1010942	0345	1
BOYLE PATRICK J	LTC	0-0148815	0150	3
BOYLE PAUL E	CW3	W-2144004	1056	1
BOYLE PHILIP F	LTC	0-1945250	0361	1
BOYLE THOMAS F	MAJ	0-0902831	0944	2
BOYLE WILLIAM F	2LT	0-0527680	1144	2

NAME	GRADE	SVC NO	DATE RET MO YR	RET CODE
BOYLEN ERNEST L	MAJ	0-0231264	0445	2
BOYLES ALBERT E	CW3	W-2150199	0563	1
BOYLES EDWARD F	MAJ	0-1299673	0258	1
BOYLES FRANK R	CPT	0-1046731	0545	2
BOYLES FRED M	MAJ	0-0360921	0544	2
BOYLES JAMES L	CPT	0-2263458	1061	1
BOYLES RAYMOND F	MAJ	0-1302945	0556	1
BOYLES ROLLIN C	COL	0-0312046	0763	3
BOYNTON CHARLES I	COL	0-0173911	0850	3
BOYNTON EDGAR B	LTC	0-0154920	0459	3
BOYNTON HENRY R	COL	0-0154917	0459	3
BOYNTON JAMES W	LTC	0-0225537	1057	3
BOYNTON LEONIE C	MAJ	L-0903116	0466	3
BOYNTON MALCOLM B	COL	0-0124265	1154	3
BOYNTON MELVILLE S	CPT	0-0410689	1157	2
BOYNTON RALPH E	COL	0-0300716	0161	1
BOYS RALPH W	LTC	0-0383115	0267	1
BOYSON EDWARD W	MAJ	0-1935532	0465	1
BOYSON GLORIA D	1LT	N-0754980	0848	1
BOYSON WILLIAM A	COL	0-0247250	0954	3
BOYT SAMUEL W	MAJ	0-0411009	0559	1
BOZADA ALFONSO M	CPT	0-1329208	1047	2
BOZARDT MARION L	COL	0-0276824	0260	1
BOZARTH ESTEL A	COL	0-0375012	0657	1
BOZE JOSEPH M	MAJ	0-0200064	0562	3
BOZEMAN DAVID M	MAJ	0-1062801	0566	1
BOZICEVICH JOSEPH R	LTC	0-1330706	0466	1
BOZIGIAN HAIG	LTC	0-0416117	0346	2
BOZORTH III HARRY S	MAJ	0-2038888	1061	2
BOZORTH ROBERT E	LTC	0-1304007	0962	1
BOZZO AUGUST R	CPT	0-1296644	0746	2
BRAACK JOY W	LTC	0-0245701	0653	1
BRAASCH WALTER C	LTC	0-1557634	0865	3
BRAATEN INGVALD T	LTC	0-0186519	0754	3
BRAATHEN MELVIN A	2LT	0-2007433	0647	1
BRABANT ROBERT P	CW4	W-2142302	0865	1
BRABEC ROBERT	LTC	0-2034720	0761	1
BRABENEC JR JOHN J	MAJ	0-1167324	0257	1
BRABHAM WILLIAM R	MAJ	0-0579820	1060	1
BRABNER-SMITH JOHN W	COL	0-0368922	0763	3
BRABSON WILLIAM A	2LT	0-1300753	1043	2
BRACALELLO WILLIAM A	CW2	W-2142355	0659	1
BRACEWELL WILLIAM D	MAJ	0-1917822	1165	1
BRACEY KENNETH R	LTC	0-0477621	0261	2
BRACKEN CARL F	1LT	0-0322829	0344	2
BRACKENS PERCY	CW4	W-2105935	0156	2
BRACKETT CECIL F D	LTC	0-0298139	0565	3
BRACKETT EDWARD F	LTC	0-1302109	1062	1
BRACKETT FREDERICK	LTC	0-0286862	0760	1
BRACKETT GERALD C	MAJ	0-1576554	0154	1
BRACKETT MAX A	COL	0-0242184	0463	3
BRACKETT ROBERT M	LTC	0-1553229	0763	1
BRACY JOHN C	LTC	0-1298181	0962	1
BRADBERRY JR JOHN W	MAJ	0-1058447	0667	1
BRADBURY FRANK A	LTC	0-0384845	0261	1
BRADBURY GEORGE E	MAJ	0-2200126	0765	1
BRADBURY GEORGE L	MAJ	0-1305717	0358	2
BRADBURY HORACE C	COL	0-0335428	0664	1
BRADBURY JOHN F	LTC	0-1100027	1060	1
BRADBURY MAURICE J	COL	0-0224401	0263	3
BRADC PHILBIN M	MAJ	0-0585962	0955	1
BRADDOCK JOSEPH M	CPT	0-0252883	0455	3
BRADDOCK WILLIAM A	1LT	0-0497415	0455	1
BRADDOCK WILLIAM H	COL	0-0183735	0849	3
BRADDY JAMES A	MAJ	0-0983052	0765	1
BRADEN CLYDE E	CPT	0-0272363	0153	3
BRADEN CLYDE H C	MAJ	0-0275136	1060	1
BRADEN LAWRENCE A	MAJ	0-0301573	0245	1
BRADEN RALPH A	MAJ	0-0402070	0946	2
BRADEN ROBERT C	LTC	0-1035670	1263	1
BRADER LELLAND C	MAJ	0-1591005	0663	1
BRADER LORAN J	MAJ	0-1552021	0264	1
BRADEY ELMER J	MAJ	0-1053063	0860	2
BRADFIELD EARL F	LTC	0-0195662	0945	2
BRADFIELD HENRY F	CPT	0-0974700	0263	1

NAME	GRADE	SVC NO	DATE RET MO YR	RET CODE
BRACFIELD MAX E	MAJ	0-0364544	1052	1
BRADFORD BRAIN K	CPT	0-0467543	1147	1
BRADFORD BYRON B	LTC	0-0350320	0561	1
BRADFORD CARLTON C	1LT	0-1285888	1046	2
BRADFORD CHESTER	1LT	0-1316373	1145	2
BRADFORD DON C	CW4	W-2144783	0867	1
BRADFORD GARLAND B	LTC	0-1299674	0964	1
BRADFORD HARRY A	CPT	0-0105625	0648	3
BRADFORD JOSEPH E	CW4	W-2109234	C256	1
BRADFORD JR G I	LTC	0-0481575	0157	1
BRADFORD LLOYD L	LTC	0-0208543	0256	3
BRADFORD MARY P	1LT	N-0789542	1047	1
BRADFORD WILLIAM S	MAJ	0-1172771	0761	2
BRADFORD ZELDA E	MAJ	N-0763768	C165	3
BRADIN BENJAMIN M	LTC	0-1059721	0960	3
BRADISH JOHN A	LTC	0-0284157	0566	3
BRADLEY BERNARD W	COL	0-0248604	1164	3
BRADLEY CARMON J	MAJ	0-0493663	0256	1
BRADLEY CHARLES F	CW3	W-2144845	0562	1
BRADLEY CHARLES I	LTC	C-1796263	C656	1
BRADLEY CHARLES W	2LT	0-1913554	1143	1
BRADLEY CHARLIE A	CW4	W-2143835	C457	1
BRADLEY CLARENCE W	LTC	0-0477278	0157	1
BRADLEY CLAUDE L	LTC	0-0918956	0167	3
BRADLEY CLAY O	1LT	0-0164035	0646	2
BRADLEY EARL G	CW2	W-2215053	1166	1
BRADLEY EARL K	LTC	0-0530722	0456	3
BRADLEY EDWARD D	CPT	0-0146685	C648	3
BRADLEY GLENN P	2LT	0-0529810	0945	2
BRADLEY GORDON W	LTC	0-0443022	0856	1
BRADLEY HARRY E	COL	C-0154583	0954	3
BRADLEY HOMER C	CW3	W-2207495	0466	1
BRADLEY ISAAC M	LTC	0-0425178	0756	1
BRADLEY JAMES A	LTC	0-0204969	C762	3
BRADLEY JAMES F	MAJ	C-0384754	0547	2
BRADLEY JAMES M	LTC	0-1576957	1265	1
BRADLEY JAMES W	MAJ	0-0972976	0563	1
BRADLEY JOHN A	MAJ	C-1315775	1060	1
BRADLEY JOHN F	LTC	0-0259997	1262	2
BRADLEY JOHN J	LTC	0-0415705	C661	1
BRADLEY JOSEPH A	LTC	0-1296647	1160	1
BRADLEY JOSEPHINE	1LT	N-0732617	0446	1
BRADLEY JR JACK	CPT	C-0288697	0848	1
BRADLEY JR JOHN D	COL	0-0341714	0563	1
BRADLEY JR OSBORN W	1LT	C-1320417	C546	1
BRADLEY JR WILLIAM R	CW3	W-2145388	C662	1
BRADLEY MARION H	CPT	0-0351824	C446	2
BRADLEY MARSHALL F	LTC	0-0411973	0562	2
BRADLEY MARVIN C	COL	0-0174330	0855	3
BRADLEY NOAH O	1LT	0-0150406	0155	3
BRADLEY PAUL E	LTC	C-0921770	0363	2
BRADLEY PHIL F	CW4	W-2146155	0267	1
BRADLEY RICHARD	CW3	W-2205339	0265	1
BRADLEY RICHARD J	MAJ	C-1647396	0863	1
BRADLEY ROGER I	MAJ	C-1293534	0366	1
BRADLEY ROLAND H	COL	0-0184790	0657	3
BRADLEY ROY	COL	0-0332523	0752	3
BRADLEY RUFUS A	CPT	C-2263396	1266	1
BRADLEY SAM J	COL	0-1283539	C163	1
BRADLEY SR CECIL U	COL	0-0177215	1059	3
BRADLEY STANLEY A	LTC	C-0436447	0663	1
BRADLEY THOMAS H	COL	0-0205329	0755	3
BRADLEY VICTOR W	CPT	C-1010041	C959	1
BRADLEY VOLNEY E	COL	0-0205178	0155	3
BRADLEY WALTER C	W01	W-2109660	0145	2
BRADLEY WILBUR H	1LT	0-0920298	0245	2
BRADLEY WILLIAM C	MAJ	0-1167326	0164	2
BRADLEY WILLIAM E	LTC	0-1950954	1167	1
BRADLEY WILLIAM O	LTC	0-0904592	0742	1
BRADLEY WILLIAM W	CPT	C-1011062	C361	1
BRADLEY ZITA A	1LT	N-0788827	0450	1
BRADLOR DONALD G	MAJ	0-0969700	1064	1
BRADMAN JOHN	LTC	0-0383882	1162	1
BRADS ANDREW V	MAJ	C-1546294	1160	1
BRADSHAW ARNOLD F	CPT	0-1292287	0446	2
BRADSHAW ARNOLD W	1LT	0-1317221	1046	2
BRADSHAW ARTHUR L	LTC	0-0946730	0166	1
BRADSHAW CHARLES W	CW2	W-2105482	0862	3
BRADSHAW DELBERT L	MAJ	0-0965921	1262	1
BRADSHAW FREDERICK	COL	0-0321316	C964	3
BRADSHAW HENRY C	LTC	0-1116049	0265	1
BRADSHAW JAMES R	LTC	0-1053499	0965	1
BRADSHAW JESSE N	LTC	0-1001517	0257	1
BRADSHAW JOSEPH F	MAJ	0-2029693	1159	1
BRADSHAW JR AUBREY D	1LT	C-1319716	0246	2
BRADSHAW THOMAS F	CPT	0-1042246	0447	2
BRADSHAW WILLIAM W	LTC	0-0287137	0266	3
BRADSHAW WOODROW C	LTC	0-0455649	0261	1
BRADT EDWARD T	LTC	0-0244590	1045	2
BRADY BENJAMIN G	LTC	0-1015209	1263	1
BRADY BERNARD J	COL	0-0421721	0967	1
BRADY CALVIN O	CW2	W-3430108	0665	1
BRADY CARL M	LTC	0-1327499	0364	2
BRADY CECIL C	MAJ	0-0280680	0660	1
BRADY CHARLES F	LTC	0-0272633	0363	3
BRADY CHARLES P	CPT	0-1049422	0246	2
BRADY DAVID C	MAJ	C-0277248	0463	3
BRADY DONALD L	MAJ	C-1014203	C761	1
BRADY EDWARD C	MAJ	0-1573063	0747	2
BRADY ELMER J	LTC	0-1585202	0760	3
BRADY GEORGE D	CPT	0-1050192	0246	2
BRADY GEORGE S	COL	0-0110406	0648	3
BRADY GEORGE W	CW2	RW-2151035	1163	1
BRADY HARTSEL J	MAJ	0-0948701	0364	1
BRADY HERBERT P	CPT	C-1116205	0263	1
BRADY HUGH H	LTC	0-0487841	1062	1
BRADY HUGH W	LTC	0-1178077	1062	1
BRADY JACK E	MAJ	0-0953641	0661	1
BRADY JAMES E	LTC	0-1323801	0566	1
BRADY JAMES F	MAJ	0-1685654	0565	1
BRADY JAMES H	2LT	0-0157480	0941	1
BRADY JOHN F	MAJ	0-1031865	1146	2
BRADY JOHN F	1LT	0-1168573	1144	2
BRADY JOHN T	MAJ	C-0977129	1161	1
BRADY JOSEPH P	1LT	0-1309503	1145	2
BRADY JOSEPH T	MAJ	0-1542912	0557	1
BRADY JR BRUCE M	MAJ	0-1994287	0866	1
BRADY JR JOHN F	1LT	0-1304333	1045	2
BRADY JR JOHN J	2LT	0-1302768	1044	2
BRADY JR JOHN J	LTC	0-2017499	0967	1
BRADY JR LESTER D	LTC	0-0415071	1060	1
BRADY KYLE F	1LT	0-1297833	1045	2
BRADY PATRICK J	LTC	0-1647052	0364	1
BRADY RANDLE J	LTC	0-0266151	0563	3
BRADY SR THOMAS F	MAJ	0-1560008	1265	1
BRADY VESTER G	MAJ	0-0419683	1045	2
BRADY WALTER O	CW3	W-2152447	0164	1
BRADY WILLIAM A	CPT	0-0418818	1046	2
BRAENDLE WILLIAM F	LTC	0-2035212	1054	1
BRAGAN JAMES A	MAJ	0-0461478	0446	2
BRAGAN LAWRENCE	CW4	W-2124546	0659	1
BRAGDON GEORGE D	MAJ	0-0188236	0648	3
BRAGG CALVIN A	CW4	W-2112070	1154	1
BRAGG CHARLES D	CPT	0-2017644	0157	1
BRAGG GENE T	CPT	C-1937569	C466	1
BRAGG GORDON F	COL	0-0322706	C558	1
BRAGG HAROLD W	MAJ	0-0475765	0747	1
BRAGG JAMES G	CPT	0-0354579	C444	2
BRAGG JAMES H	1LT	0-0531998	0346	2
BRAGG JAMES H	LTC	0-1556848	0663	1
BRAGUNIER B BOWIE	LTC	0-0902067	0964	3
BRAHAM JAMES D	LTC	0-1317878	1162	1
BRAHMST GEORGE W	LTC	0-0248557	0861	3
BRAID WILLIAM D	1LT	0-0518709	1045	2
BRAIKER HAROLD R	CPT	0-1013211	0846	1
BRAIN MARION S	1LT	N-0727163	1045	1
BRAIN THOMAS	COL	0-0178635	0357	3
BRAINARD CARROLL D	CW2	W-2209166	0962	1
BRAINARD DWIGHT A	MAJ	0-0236826	0864	3
BRAINARD FRANCIS D	LTC	0-0242489	0962	3
BRAINARD STANLEY L	LTC	0-0303524	C261	1
BRAINARD WARREN M	CW4	W-2118278	1058	1
BRAINERD GARETH N	COL	C-0342330	0463	3
BRAISTED HARRY P	CW3	W-2003307	1060	3
BRAITHWAITE ROBERT J	CW2	W-2109511	0761	1
BRAITMAN MAX	1LT	C-0344379	1143	2
BRAKE FRED E	CPT	0-0258253	0855	2
BRAKE GEORGE E	MAJ	C-1550972	0760	3
BRAKE JOHN W	CPT	0-1635615	C746	1
BRAKE OTIS	CPT	0-2005552	1157	1
BRAKE RAYMOND C	LTC	0-1283369	0656	2
BRAKE WILLIAM P	MAJ	C-0946413	0962	1
BRAKKEN BOYD R	CPT	C-1575780	0554	1
BRALY BYRON D	CPT	0-1999142	0762	2
BRALY LONNIE B	MAJ	0-2007639	0960	1
BRAMAN ELMER C	LTC	0-0244812	0964	3
BRAMBLE JR ALBERT L	CPT	0-0174385	C460	3
BRAMBLE RUSSELL B	LTC	C-0252271	0264	1
BRAMBLETT MARY C	MAJ	N-C742004	1052	1
BRAMBLETT RARHF J	1LT	0-1318558	C945	2
BRAME FELIX J	MAJ	0-1636334	C553	1
BRAME WEBB	MAJ	0-0130291	C648	3
BRAME WILLIAM K	COL	0-0250654	1064	3
BRAMEIER CHARLES L	CW3	W-2203528	1046	1
BRAMI RUSSELL M	MAJ	C-2262844	C763	2
BRAMLETTE JOYCE D	CW2	W-2150639	0960	1
BRAMLEYHENRY D	MAJ	0-1310562	0963	1
BRAMLITT HUGH W	CW2	W-2149425	C860	1
BRAMMER DOUGLAS H	2LT	0-0507975	C844	2
BRAMMER FRED E	LTC	0-0230869	1150	3
BRAMMER HAROLD I	1LT	0-0539225	1146	2
BRAMSON EDWIN M	1LT	0-0558768	0348	2
BRAMSON JACK	LTC	C-1548652	0566	1
BRANAM FRED G	CW2	W-2150083	1058	1
BRANAMAN WILLIAM S	1LT	0-0528664	1146	2
BRANAN JOHN H	CPT	0-0406003	0146	1
BRANAUM EUGENE M	COL	0-0182563	0752	3
BRANCACCIO A A	CPT	0-2017191	0257	1
BRANCFIELD LEO N	LTC	0-0472418	0462	3
BRANCH DANIEL R	MAJ	C-0250850	1267	3
BRANCH EDWARD R	CW3	W-3150202	1166	1
BRANCH JAMES E	COL	0-0248662	0866	3
BRANCH JOSEPH H	CW2	W-2152262	0262	1
BRANCH JR HOUSTON	CW2	W-2211691	0367	1
BRANCH JULIAN O	MAJ	C-1552022	C967	3
BRANCH NORMAN R	LTC	0-0334999	C166	3
BRANCH OLIVE S	2LT	N-0759125	0544	1
BRANCH ROBERT K	CW3	W-2146891	0363	1
BRANCH WILLIAM M	CPT	C-0306550	0344	2
BRANCO SALVATORE	MAJ	C-4006023	0765	1
BRAND ALEX M	MAJ	C-1289596	0461	1
BRAND ELIAS R	LTC	0-0325213	C863	1
BRAND JOHN R	LTC	0-0361418	0667	1
BRAND JOHN W	MAJ	C-1104059	0759	1
BRAND JR HARRISON	COL	0-0103807	0851	3
BRAND LEONARD J	MAJ	C-1548018	0556	1
BRAND WILLIAM A	MAJ	0-4005766	0967	1
BRAND WILLIAM T	LTC	0-1580676	0364	1
BRANDARIZ CARLOS A	MAJ	C-1308297	1060	1
BRANDEIS ERVINE J	LTC	0-0210653	0756	3
BRANDEJSKY FRANK	1LT	0-0212823	1058	3
BRANDENBERGER F F	MAJ	0-1012528	0859	2
BRANDENBURG EDWIN W	CPT	C-0451501	C446	1
BRANDENBURG F H	CPT	0-0438076	0146	2
BRANDENBURG PARK H	LTC	0-0511565	1060	2
BRANDENBURG W G	CPT	0-1290889	1047	1
BRANDENBURG WALTER	CW3	W-2153341	1062	1
BRANDENBURG WILLIAM	LTC	0-0353095	1046	1
BRANDENHOFF HOWARD N	LTC	0-1166443	C358	1
BRANDES KONRAD G	CW4	W-2141087	C654	1
BRANDLEY PETER H	2LT	0-0925136	C445	2
BRANDLEY WILLIAM H	MAJ	0-0260985	1063	3
BRANDLY ROLAND L	COL	0-0353193	1161	1
BRANDMILL DINSMORE	LTC	C-0216952	0763	3
BRANDON CHARLES R	1LT	0-0445751	1045	2
BRANDON DAVID R	COL	0-0242144	1057	3
BRANDON ENZER L	LTC	0-0286328	0457	3
BRANDON LELAND P	MAJ	C-0192695	1C62	3
BRANDON LOREN E	CW3	W-2143378	0762	1
BRANDON SR JAMES W	LTC	0-0351084	0966	1
BRANDON WILLIAM P	CPT	0-0170830	1161	3
BRANDOW ROBERT C	LTC	0-1001956	0866	1
BRANDS WILLIAM H	LTC	0-1041510	0567	1
BRANDT ALFRED P	1LT	0-1825830	1145	2
BRANDT CHARLES J	COL	0-0287795	1060	1
BRANDT EDWIN	LTC	0-0290698	1164	2
BRANDT IRVING D	1LT	0-1183248	0945	1
BRANDT JOHN J	CW3	W-2203350	0967	1
BRANDT JR LEWIS F	2LT	0-1327706	0945	2
BRANDT JUSTIN	1LT	0-0464625	C146	2
BRANDT LLOYD H	CPT	0-0496969	1052	1
BRANDT MULFORD M	COL	C-0254578	1065	3
BRANDT ONEIL F	2LT	0-0382505	C653	1
BRANDT ROGER H	1LT	0-1106010	1043	2
BRANDVOLD FLORENCE C	MAJ	N-0776427	0364	1
BRANDYBURG FULTON C	WO1	W-2106554	0445	2
BRANEN FRED P	CPT	0-1114384	1053	1
BRANFORD WILLIAM J	LTC	0-1545077	0964	1
BRANHAM DONALD S	COL	0-0197978	0448	1
BRANICK WILLIAM G	MAJ	0-1103076	0857	1
BRANIGAN DANIEL A	MAJ	0-0169412	0647	2
BRANIGAN THOMAS L	MAJ	0-1016936	0662	1
BRANIN CHARLES F	MAJ	C-0142610	0654	3
BRANISEL JR JOHN	2LT	0-1111511	0346	2
BRANN WILLIAM T	CPT	0-0223900	1152	1
BRANNAM FINIS C	CW3	W-2146897	1058	1
BRANNAN JACK D	CPT	0-0980876	1060	1
BRANNAN JR ROBERT E	LTC	0-1171465	0766	1
BRANNAN LEE R	LTC	0-0287811	0160	3
BRANNEN JO A	MAJ	N-0726615	1066	1
BRANNEN MALCOLM D	LTC	0-0292262	0462	1
BRANNEN WILLIAM A	CPT	0-0510788	0653	1
BRANNER GEORGE L	MAJ	0-0180147	1154	3
BRANNIFF EARL C	LTC	C-0254917	0163	3
BRANNIGAN FRANK	LTC	0-0136585	1155	3
BRANNOCK WILLIAM R	CPT	C-0555958	1147	2
BRANNON ATHOS W	LTC	0-1299675	0861	1
BRANNON GEORGE M	CPT	0-0394409	0145	2
BRANNON HERBERT A	MAJ	0-1031387	0358	1
BRANNON JAMES G	MAJ	0-1877914	0765	1
BRANNON JR J BRUCE	CW3	W-2151808	0265	1
BRANNON PAUL F	2LT	0-1308417	0545	2
BRANNON WILLIAM C	LTC	0-0455613	0559	1
BRANNON WILLIAM H	LTC	0-1998453	0862	1
BRANON JOHN C	2LT	0-1307932	1044	2
BRANSCOMB RUSSELL	2LT	0-2263490	0461	1
BRANSCOMBE JAMES H	MAJ	C-0969816	1062	1
BRANSFORD HORTON W	MAJ	C-1048297	1166	1
BRANSFORD THOMAS L	LTC	0-0909276	0264	3
BRANSON ALBERT S	COL	0-0258729	1163	3
BRANSON CHARLES A	1LT	0-1314250	1147	1
BRANSON EUGENE H	CW2	W-2148429	0755	2
BRANSON LOUNSBURY	COL	C-0306842	0663	1
BRANSON MARION A	MAJ	0-0170567	0855	3
BRANSON ROBERT S	LTC	0-1641491	0363	1
BRANSON WILLIAM A	MAJ	0-1292288	1057	1
BRANSTAD WILLIAM	COL	0-0273480	0967	3
BRANSTETTER ROY	LTC	0-0108567	0347	1
BRANT ARTHUR A	CW2	W-2151761	0356	2
BRANT DONALD R	LTC	0-0336589	0760	1
BRANT FLORENCE M	2LT	N-0753041	0446	1
BRANT FREDERICK	LTC	0-0498842	0760	3
BRANT IRVIN L	CPT	0-0341077	1045	2
BRANT PAUL R	W01	W-2128538	0746	2
BRANT SANDI	CPT	L-1010012	1054	2
BRANT WILBUR J	1LT	0-0966752	0754	2
BRANTLEY JOE K	COL	0-0103346	1051	3
BRANTLEY JR ED	MAJ	0-2204028	0166	1
BRANTLEY RICHARD V	CPT	0-1877796	0663	1
BRANTLEY ROBERT H	LTC	0-0372306	0866	3

292-560 O - 68 - 7

NAME	GRADE	SVC NO	DATE RET MO YR	RET CODE
BRANTON CHARLES H	CW2	W-2143022	1055	2
BRANTON CHARLES K	LTC	0-0404600	1060	1
BRANTON DALTON E	CW3	W-2151157	0863	1
BRANUM ARTHUR M	CPT	0-0885894	0146	1
BRANUM MARVIN L	MAJ	0-0994085	0566	1
BRANUM ORRIS F	CW3	W-2146565	0764	1
BRANVAN CHARLES O	COL	0-0393605	0666	1
BRANYON WADE L	CPT	0-0973915	1160	1
BRARMANN EDWARD F	CPT	0-0351739	0745	2
BRAS PEDRO J	LTC	0-0155794	0556	3
BRASE WESLEY C	WO1	W-2131333	0263	1
BRASELTON ROSCOE	MAJ	0-0450404	0157	1
BRASH EDMOND J	1LT	0-1325861	1145	2
BRASHEAR FENTON W	MAJ	0-1559002	1262	1
BRASHEAR GOLDMAN T	LTC	0-0452022	0160	1
BRASHEAR ILO L	MAJ	0-0469339	0456	1
BRASHEAR JR JAMES L	LTC	0-1169870	0764	1
BRASHEARS GEORGE L	LTC	0-0376389	0162	1
BRASSELL RAY O	MAJ	0-1288850	0855	1
BRASSFIELD JOSEPH O	LTC	0-1330903	0467	1
BRASSIL JOHN	2LT	0-0164561	0039	1
BRASWELL CLOVIS L	CPT	0-1299366	0546	2
BRASWELL ERNEST	CW3	W-2143357	0462	2
BRASWELL JAMES L	1LT	0-2262711	1154	2
BRASWELL VERNON S	MAJ	0-1174237	0861	1
BRATCHELL HAROLD T	CPT	0-0491209	0662	1
BRATCHER ROBERT F	MAJ	0-1592631	0764	1
BRATLAND ADLER H	MAJ	0-1683434	0666	1
BRATTEBO NORMAN R	2LT	0-1315021	0843	2
BRATTIN WILLIAM C	MAJ	0-0228321	0663	3
BRATTLOF KENNETH W	2LT	0-1308262	0545	2
BRATTON ARGALUS B	LTC	0-0233935	1046	1
BRATTON JR NEIL A	1LT	0-1314431	0148	2
BRATTON PAUL E	MAJ	0-1796754	0657	1
BRAUCH JOSEPH F	CW3	W-2153120	0562	1
BRAUCHER JR JOHN L	1LT	0-1320275	0845	2
BRAUCHT JR GLEN R	1LT	0-1062470	0951	2
BRAUD WESTON M	LTC	0-1633091	0166	1
BRAUER ALBERT G	LTC	0-0363123	0463	1
BRAUER ALVIN P	CPT	0-0302358	0646	2
BRAUER EARLE W	CPT	0-0478029	0147	1
BRAUER EDWARD I	MAJ	0-0966169	0461	1
BRAUER EUGENE H	2LT	0-1324816	0345	2
BRAUER HARRY M	1LT	0-0466717	0846	2
BRAUER JOHN C	COL	0-0256443	1065	3
BRAUER ROBERT W	LTC	0-0463525	0158	1
BRAUN ALBERT F	MAJ	0-0966560	1062	1
BRAUN ALBERT W	LTC	0-0134329	1149	3
BRAUN ELMER H	LTC	0-0308667	1059	3
BRAUN ERIC J	LTC	0-0301303	1157	1
BRAUN ROBERT J	MAJ	0-1112582	1063	1
BRAUN ROLAND R	MAJ	0-0277079	0444	2
BRAUNECKER AUGUST J	MAJ	0-1695601	0958	1
BRAUNER FREDERICK	MAJ	0-1637073	0161	1
BRAUNS JOHN W	COL	0-0196689	0962	3
BRAUNSCHWEIGER OTTO	1LT	0-1315022	1146	1
BRAUNSTEIN ALBERT L	CPT	0-0482305	0145	2
BRAUNSTEIN ELIHU B	LTC	0-1166675	1167	1
BRAUNSTEIN LEONARD	CPT	0-0357673	1146	2
BRAUNWARTH WILLIAM W	LTC	0-0263124	0643	2
BRAUSA PAUL V	LTC	0-0307833	0562	1
BRAUSCH RAYMOND A	LTC	0-1948700	0565	1
BRAUTMAN ALVIN W	1LT	0-1012243	0646	2
BRAVERMAN LOUIS	MAJ	0-0484356	0349	1
BRAVOS GEORGE J	COL	0-0183018	0858	1
BRAWNER SELMA M	COL	N-0731302	1163	1
BRAXLEY SAMUEL E	MAJ	0-0427915	0263	1
BRAXTON DAVID	CW3	W-2150065	1063	1
BRAY ANN	MAJ	L-0514231	0863	1
BRAY CECIL H	MAJ	0-1324000	0960	1
BRAY DILLARD W	MAJ	0-0196681	0561	3
BRAY ELBERT W	1LT	0-0400895	0645	2
BRAY ELMER A	CPT	0-0360551	1060	1
BRAY FRANCIS G	LTC	0-0246662	0366	3
BRAY GEORGE	MAJ	0-1574604	1154	1

NAME	GRADE	SVC NO	DATE RET MO YR	RET CODE
BRAY HAROLD P	MAJ	0-0420953	0446	2
BRAY JOHN C	MAJ	0-0463952	0647	1
BRAY WILLIAM E	CW2	W-2147269	1057	1
BRAY WILLIAM H	COL	0-0220952	0355	3
BRAY WILLIAM M	CPT	0-1573066	1045	2
BRAY WILLIAM P	COL	0-0266987	0955	3
BRAYDEN ROBERT A	CW2	W-2150281	1161	1
BRAYE WILLIAM F	CW3	W-2148346	1262	1
BRAYFIELD RALPH S	CW2	W-2143875	1158	1
BRAYMAN JR HERBERT H	CW4	W-2119448	0159	1
BRAYTON JEAN H	CPT	0-0225828	1161	3
BRAYTON PAUL R	LTC	0-0270574	0967	3
BRAZDA FRANK F	MAJ	0-0524668	1047	2
BRAZEALE HERBERT R	MAJ	0-2262614	0663	2
BRAZEAL ALFRED L	MAJ	0-1340257	1065	2
BRAZELL FLOYD F	LTC	0-1109154	1160	1
BRAZEN FRANK J	MAJ	0-0423110	1047	2
BRAZIER MELVIN L	MAJ	0-0278315	0366	3
BRAZIER NESTER H	CPT	0-1100891	1052	2
BRAZIL THOMAS R	MAJ	0-1920353	1166	1
BRAZIL WILLIAM P	MAJ	0-0451505	0358	1
BREACH REGINALD A	LTC	0-0502043	0866	3
BREADON HUBERT R	LTC	0-0224806	1051	1
BREADY FREDERICK	CPT	0-2046343	0551	2
BREAKIRON HARRY T	MAJ	0-1063134	0163	1
BREARLEY JOSEPH W	LTC	0-0286569	0954	1
BREARLEY RALPH A	CPT	0-0521863	0146	1
BREARTY CHARLES R	LTC	0-0173852	0562	3
BREARTY FRANCIS W	CPT	0-0487029	0750	1
BREASHEARS WILLIAM F	MAJ	0-1334252	1263	1
BREATCHEL EDMUND O	1LT	0-1591008	0347	2
BREAUD JR C S	LTC	0-1580682	1160	1
BREAULT FRANK H	CW2	W-2144875	0463	1
BREAUX ALLEN C	MAJ	0-1641498	0860	1
BREAUX ROY C	CPT	0-1283016	0945	2
BREAUX WALTER J	CPT	0-0247295	0744	2
BREAZEALE JR T C	1LT	0-0460075	0346	2
BREBNER CHARLES E	COL	0-0284440	0958	1
BRECHBIEL FRANK W	CPT	0-0564896	0663	1
BRECHER CHARLES	LTC	0-1796036	0963	1
BRECHT JOHN W	1LT	0-1048298	0245	2
BRECHTEL DAVID W	MAJ	0-1280309	0857	1
BRECK ROGER S	LTC	0-0240814	0365	3
BRECKENRIDGE JR J G	1LT	0-1304607	1045	2
BRECKENRIDGE LEWIS R	CW3	W-2142224	0860	1
BRECKINRIDGE ETHELRE	MAJ	0-2005232	0662	1
BRECKONS WALTER H	LTC	0-1324978	1262	1
BREDAEL FRED B	1LT	0-0403999	0446	1
BREDBENNER AMBROSE M	MAJ	0-0278351	0761	3
BREDIN RYERSON A	LTC	0-0297346	1065	3
BREECE JAMES M	MAJ	0-0972319	0662	1
BREEDEN BERRY C	CPT	0-1324243	1264	2
BREEDEN CHARLES U	MAJ	0-0505288	0846	2
BREEDEN PERCY L	2LT	0-1824122	0844	2
BREEDEN SAM L	MAJ	0-0159157	1058	3
BREEDING CHARLES F	MAJ	0-1945264	1060	1
BREEDING CHARLES S	COL	0-0282559	0864	3
BREEDING DAVID N	LTC	0-0358862	0367	3
BREEDING HOWARD M	CW3	RW-2152369	1165	1
BREEDING WILLIAM C	CPT	0-0969873	0462	1
BREEDLOVE CONNER M	CPT	0-0197512	0655	3
BREEDLOVE GEORGE E	CW2	W-2214363	0767	1
BREEDLOVE JOHN C	LTC	0-0311829	0960	1
BREEDLOVE ROBERT E	CW3	W-2141934	0763	1
BREEDON DANIEL F	MAJ	0-1044185	0557	1
BREELAND GLENN E	CPT	0-2032907	0157	1
BREEN GERALD E	MAJ	0-0259001	0963	3
BREEN GLADYS M	1LT	N-0720820	1045	1
BREEN HARRY P	LTC	0-0274891	1164	3
BREEN JOHN D	CPT	0-2033188	0463	1
BREEN JOSEPH A	1LT	0-2292030	1149	3
BREEN JOSEPH M	LTC	0-0487867	0954	2
BREEN JR WILLIAM H	COL	0-0452384	0166	1
BREEN MARVIN	LTC	0-1169036	0567	3
BREEN MAURICE	1LT	0-1110396	1147	2

NAME	GRADE	SVC NO	DATE RET MO YR	RET CODE
BREEN ROBERT H	LTC	0-1172389	1165	1
BREEN THOMAS	CPT	0-0331295	0457	3
BREESE JOE W	CPT	0-2263717	0163	2
BREESE RALPH M	LTC	0-0485638	0657	1
BREESE THURLOW W	MAJ	0-1283540	0765	1
BREEZE JR THOMAS H	CPT	0-1042496	0248	1
BREEZLEY HENRY F	LTC	0-1548361	0558	1
BREEZLEY MARY B	1LT	N-0761031	0546	1
BREFCZYNSKI JOHN H	CW2	W-2208380	0962	1
BREGAN JOSEPH F	CW3	W-2208851	0167	1
BREGER SAMUEL	LTC	0-0331656	0965	3
BREGNARD ADRIAN L	LTC	0-0321695	0960	1
BREHAUT BURTON L	2LT	0-1313690	1044	2
BREHENY GEORGE R	CW3	W-2121104	1054	1
BREHM CLIFFORD A	CPT	0-1589078	1162	2
BREHM RUSSELL A	CW2	W-2214590	0866	1
BREIDENBACH AMELIA L	2LT	N-0728576	0844	1
BREIDENBACH GEORGE F	MAJ	0-0218594	0855	3
BREIDENBAUGH HENRY C	LTC	0-1844689	1065	3
BREIDSTER WALDEMAR F	MG	0-0221917	0760	3
BREILING OTTMAR A	LTC	0-0309646	0965	3
BREITENBACH R J	CPT	0-0103000	1147	2
BREITENBERG HARRY J	MAJ	0-1020526	0765	1
BREITENSTEIN JOHN J	CPT	0-1039605	0557	1
BREITFELLER JOSEPH C	CPT	0-1016973	0857	1
BREITHAUPT HOWARD M	LTC	0-1039544	0863	1
BREITLING GERALD E	LTC	0-0281896	0956	2
BREITMAN HARRY R	CPT	0-0233659	1043	2
BREITSMAN WILLIS J	WO1	W-2110551	0456	3
BREITWIESER CARL H	COL	0-0152440	0757	3
BREIZ FLORENTINO	2LT	0-0193249	1150	1
BREKKE MARTIN H	2LT	0-1327927	1145	2
BRELAND HENRY T	MAJ	0-2023916	0164	1
BRELAND JAMES E	LTC	0-0250965	1063	3
BRELL JAMES	CW2	W-2112147	0746	1
BREM JACOB	COL	0-0285742	1164	3
BREMEL GERHARD W	CW2	W-2144316	0560	1
BREMER AUGUST W	LTC	0-0456041	1061	1
BREMER FRED H	LTC	0-1895862	1266	3
BREMER HENRY M	LTC	0-0316442	0464	3
BREMER VIRGIL I	CW3	W-2149945	0263	1
BREMER WILLIAM R	LTC	0-1296986	1153	1
BREMERMAN F J	COL	0-0463647	0157	1
BREMERMAN FRANK E	CW2	W-2148311	0358	2
BREMSER EDWARD F	LTC	0-0245033	0760	3
BRENAMAN CHARLES	LTC	0-0280996	0746	2
BRENAN ALBERT	LTC	0-1542185	0457	1
BRENCE FRANK E	CPT	0-0296041	0544	2
BRENCHLEY GEORGE A	LTC	0-1589080	1062	1
BRENDEL ADOLPH P	CPT	0-0376558	0745	2
BRENDLE ROY C	MAJ	0-1289539	0457	1
BRENER LAZARD S	CPT	0-0542366	1045	2
BRENINGER ALFRED H	LTC	0-1283716	1057	1
BRENN GERALD C	1LT	0-1325548	1145	1
BRENN HARRY A	COL	0-0212413	0663	3
BRENNAN ALAN H	1LT	0-2014799	0165	2
BRENNAN DANIEL J	CW3	W-2131805	0365	1
BRENNAN EDWARD F	LTC	0-1169434	1167	1
BRENNAN EDWARD J	CPT	0-1295332	0347	2
BRENNAN FREDERICK	LTC	0-0359230	1055	3
BRENNAN JACK J	CW2	W-2150587	0361	1
BRENNAN JAMES D	LTC	0-1015053	0964	1
BRENNAN JOHN A	MAJ	0-1167334	0952	2
BRENNAN JOHN R	1LT	0-1590343	0146	2
BRENNAN JOHN T	LTC	0-1103077	0861	1
BRENNAN JOHN V	CPT	0-1297151	0647	2
BRENNAN JOSEPH	CPT	0-0497834	0849	1
BRENNAN JOSEPH G	CPT	0-1106012	0246	2
BRENNAN LEO W	CW4	W-2143208	0965	1
BRENNAN NORMAN G	LTC	0-0287815	0367	3
BRENNAN RAYMOND F	WO1	W-2123176	0447	2
BRENNAN ROBERT E	LTC	0-1107314	0861	1
BRENNAN WILLIAM	CPT	0-2008163	0756	1
BRENNAN WILLIAM C	MAJ	0-0491551	0557	2
BRENNECKE FRANCIS C	COL	0-0205865	0463	3

NAME	GRADE	SVC NO	DATE RET MO YR	RET CODE
BRENNEKE CHARLES H	COL	0-0263976	0346	2
BRENNEMAN FLOYD E	LTC	0-1556093	1060	1
BRENNEMAN ROBERT C	LTC	0-1113598	0265	1
BRENNEN HAROLD L	MAJ	0-0477494	0250	1
BRENNER GILBERT	MAJ	0-0348709	0165	1
BRENNER HUDSON O	MAJ	0-1014898	0859	1
BRENNER JOEL J	MAJ	0-0418242	0246	2
BRENNER JR HARRY F	CPT	0-1533740	0550	1
BRENNER LEON S	CPT	0-0493776	0245	2
BRENNER RICHARD J	LTC	0-0453141	0761	1
BRENNER THEODORE H	MAJ	0-2002233	1160	1
BRENNY MARTIN J	CPT	0-0452520	0145	2
BRENT JR EDWARD F	MAJ	0-0328956	0265	3
BRENT ROBERT A	CPT	0-0522757	0446	2
BRENTANO AUGUST	MAJ	0-0202261	0460	3
BRENTON ELMER	LTC	0-0162754	0757	3
BRENTS WALKER A	LTC	0-0282830	1056	3
BRERETON JOHN F	CPT	0-0306654	0451	1
BRERETON JOHN V	MAJ	0-0287721	1262	3
BRESCKA RUDOLPH S	MAJ	0-0233238	0461	3
BRESHEARS JAMES O	CW3	W-2153380	1163	1
BRESKE CHARLES C	CW4	W-2146576	1167	1
BRESLER ROBERT E	1LT	0-1042248	0346	2
BRESLIN EDWARD F	MAJ	0-0963529	0265	1
BRESLIN JAMES	LTC	0-0131851	0648	3
BRESLIN JR HUGH J	MAJ	0-1181546	0862	1
BRESNAHAN JOHN F	LTC	0-0102758	0346	2
BRESNICK SAMUEL	1LT	0-0359433	0245	1
BRESSAN ROBERT C	2LT	0-1115195	0645	2
BRESSETT FLORENCE L	CPT	N-0802018	1065	1
BRESSINCK EDWARD F	MAJ	0-0450243	0158	1
BRESSLER RICHARD E	MAJ	0-2263514	1066	1
BRESSLER SYDNEY	COL	0-0331745	0567	3
BRETANA ERNESTO	MAJ	0-0983917	0563	1
BRETH JAMES E	COL	0-0173712	0563	3
BRETON CLIFFORD F	CW4	W-2101474	0861	1
BRETON GUSTAVO A	CW2	W-2145132	0959	1
BRETON JOSEPH E	CPT	0-2002408	0858	1
BRETON PIERRE L	CPT	0-0505335	1144	2
BRETSCHNEIDER ARTHUR	CW3	W-2145390	0865	1
BRETT JOHN J	CW3	W-2152668	0563	1
BRETT JR GEORGE P	MAJ	0-0101696	0556	3
BRETT THOMAS J	LTC	0-0450224	0357	1
BRETTON WILLIAM J	2LT	0-0888907	1145	1
BRETZ BENJAMIN R	LTC	0-0294106	0767	3
BRETZ JR ANDREW	LTC	0-0416511	0961	1
BRETZ ROSS E	CPT	0-0971775	0958	1
BRETZER HERMAN	LTC	0-1000034	0657	1
BRETZKE LOUIS E	LTC	0-0267000	0851	3
BREUER ALFRED	CPT	0-0328857	0445	2
BREUER ARTHUR N	CPT	0-0507156	1045	2
BREUER WYLIE E	LTC	0-0328030	0347	2
BREVDA HARRY	MAJ	0-0330145	0245	2
BREVIG HJALMAR I	CPT	0-0494297	1263	1
BREVIK ROBERT T	1LT	0-0414661	1145	2
BREWER ALLEN L	COL	0-1035205	1064	1
BREWER ANGUS M	MAJ	0-2033322	0361	1
BREWER ARTHUR S	LTC	0-0507436	1263	3
BREWER BEACHER H	MAJ	0-1312272	0954	1
BREWER BOBBY J	MAJ	0-1581044	1060	1
BREWER CHARLES H	MAJ	0-0948970	0963	1
BREWER CHESTER O	COL	0-0308546	0261	1
BREWER DANIEL F	LTC	0-0347525	0460	1
BREWER DAVID L	LTC	0-0511211	0954	2
BREWER DEAN E	MAJ	0-1637077	0264	1
BREWER EDWARD G	WO1	W-2109994	0953	1
BREWER ELTO H	WO1	W-2117862	0762	2
BREWER FRANK J	CW4	W-2110657	0655	1
BREWER GARLAND S	CW3	W-2151918	0663	1
BREWER GEORGE F	MAJ	0-1798438	1061	1
BREWER HAROLD A	CPT	0-1702253	0264	1
BREWER HAROLD G	LTC	0-0146377	0257	3
BREWER HAROLD W	CW4	W-2109094	0758	1
BREWER HERCHELL E	CW4	W-2144165	1265	1
BREWER HOWELL	COL	0-0171412	0648	3

NAME	GRADE	SVC NO	DATE RET MO YR	RET CODE
BREWER JAMES D	MAJ	C-1550118	0761	1
BREWER JOHN F	LTC	0-0360077	1164	3
BREWER JOHN H	LTC	0-0390991	0962	1
BREWER JR GEORGE A	COL	0-0225014	0262	3
BREWER JR IRA V	MAJ	0-2016389	0663	1
BREWER JR JOSEPH C	1LT	0-1081463	1046	1
BREWER KAY W	CW2	W-2107225	0267	1
BREWER MARJORIE J	CPT	N-0728043	0246	1
BREWER ROBERT E	1LT	0-0504988	0653	1
BREWER ROBERT N	LTC	0-1552023	0466	1
BREWER ROY C	COL	0-0316654	0662	1
BREWER RUBEN N	CPT	0-0489144	0251	1
BREWER SR CLEO H	CPT	0-1292290	1160	1
BREWER THEODORE R	LTC	0-0349527	1164	3
BREWER VIRGIL O	WO1	W-2122940	0857	1
BREWER WESLEY B	2LT	0-1051047	0945	2
BREWER WILLIAM A	CW3	W-2146007	0966	1
BREWER WILLIAM C	LTC	0-0186774	0156	3
BREWER WILLIAM L	WO1	W-2145391	1056	1
BREWER WILLIAM M	COL	0-0251177	1262	3
BREWER WILLIAM S	CPT	0-1170294	0461	1
BREWINGTON ALLEN C	MAJ	0-0976215	0861	1
BREWRINK JAMES L	COL	0-0236372	0166	3
BREWSTER EDWARD S	LTC	0-0321194	1067	3
BREWSTER JOHN O	COL	0-0193894	0145	1
BREWSTER PHILIP H	LTC	0-0299492	0145	2
BREWSTER RICHARD T	LTC	0-0320117	0966	3
BREWTON MURRAY P	1LT	0-0434593	0947	2
BREWTON WILLIAM S	1LT	0-0415819	0845	2
BREX JR CHARLES J	1LT	0-1534684	0345	2
BREYLA FREDERICK	CW3	W-2129887	0561	1
BREZEE FREDERICK	MAJ	0-1653833	0656	1
BREZIN CAVIC	CPT	0-0371116	0346	2
BREZINA ECDIE B	CW3	W-2104648	0859	1
BREZNICKY JOSEPH J	CW3	W-2142135	0864	1
BRIA ALBERT J	CW3	W-2152513	0263	1
BRIARS NORMAN E	WO1	W-2122210	1047	2
BRICE ARTHUR T	COL	0-0167877	0952	3
BRICE JAMES P	COL	0-0504275	0465	3
BRICE MARSHALL M	COL	0-0205284	0858	3
BRICE WILLIAM A	COL	0-0173576	0162	3
BRICK EDWARD J	1LT	0-0541815	0445	2
BRICK JOHN J	MAJ	0-1691005	1045	2
BRICK JOHN P	CPT	0-0414176	0845	1
BRICKEN WILLIAM H	MAJ	0-0402608	0657	1
BRICKER ERNEST L	WO1	W-2121976	0252	1
BRICKER GARY R	LTC	0-0322712	1054	1
BRICKER HAROLD S	2LT	0-2012010	0743	2
BRICKER PETER C	MAJ	0-0230807	1064	3
BRICKER THOMAS G	LTC	0-0362935	1059	1
BRICKETTO EDWARD J	1LT	0-1951544	0151	1
BRICKEY CLARE R	CW2	W-2142402	0462	1
BRICKHOUSE GREGORY L	LTC	0-1103529	0363	1
BRICKMAN LLOYD F	CPT	0-2050736	1059	1
BRIDENSTINE FRANCIS	LTC	0-0447645	0962	2
BRIDGE CARL F	1LT	0-1319258	0546	2
BRIDGEFORTH WILLIAM	WO1	W-2129579	0446	2
BRIDGERS SAMSON K	CPT	0-0265776	1156	3
BRIDGES ARCHIE	CW3	W-2150625	0163	1
BRIDGES CLARA E	2LT	N-0764640	1145	1
BRIDGES IRA B	MAJ	0-0461561	1048	1
BRIDGES JAMES F	CPT	0-0267207	0263	1
BRIDGES JAMES P	MAJ	0-0377641	0844	2
BRIDGES JIMMIE H	MAJ	0-1010994	0948	1
BRIDGES JOHN T	CW2	W-2206882	0263	1
BRIDGES JOSEPH H	CPT	0-1579421	0157	1
BRIDGES JOSEPH L	MAJ	0-1056048	0862	1
BRIDGES MELVIN W	MAJ	0-0119092	0649	3
BRIDGES RICHARD B	LTC	0-1691931	0864	1
BRIDGES ROBERT M	CPT	0-0375851	0346	2
BRIDGES ROBERT L	CW3	W-2149872	0359	2
BRIDGES ROBINSON E	LTC	0-1598005	0765	1
BRIDGES ROLSTYN O	LTC	0-0144962	0151	3
BRIDGES STANLEY B	1LT	0-1844410	1045	2
BRIDGES WILLIAM C	MAJ	0-0976536	1161	1

NAME	GRADE	SVC NO	DATE RET MO YR	RET CODE
BRIDGHAM SAMUEL W	COL	0-1690163	0765	3
BRIDWELL CHARLES G	CPT	0-0437849	0647	1
BRIDWELL ERNEST A	LTC	0-1591610	0766	1
BRIDWELL WILLIAM E	MAJ	0-0210753	0648	3
BRIEGEL GEORGE F	WO1	W-2209292	0151	3
BRIEHL MARK R	CW2	W-2210568	0763	1
BRIEL FRED W	MAJ	0-0344479	1047	1
BRIENZA PAUL J	CPT	0-0394380	0345	2
BRIER GLEASON L	LTC	0-0195220	0962	3
BRIER HUBERT L	LTC	0-0253567	0667	3
BRIER JOHN C	COL	0-0284520	0546	2
BRIER MORRIS	1LT	0-2043121	1045	2
BRIERY CLIFFORD C	COL	0-0205909	0857	3
BRIGANTE LAWRENCE J	CPT	0-0498524	0346	1
BRIGEMAN RICHARD W	MAJ	0-1635623	0361	1
BRIGGMAN ROGERS C	1LT	0-2004049	0954	2
BRIGGS ALBERT F	LTC	0-0261500	0263	3
BRIGGS CHARLES W	LTC	0-0107885	0648	3
BRIGGS CLARK A	CPT	0-0167606	0853	3
BRIGGS ELMER H	MAJ	0-2028550	1164	1
BRIGGS GEORGE R	MAJ	0-0152831	0854	3
BRIGGS GLOW E	LTC	0-1315414	0757	1
BRIGGS JOHN C	MAJ	0-1030223	0660	1
BRIGGS JR MARVIN L	LTC	0-0370071	0363	1
BRIGGS LAWRENCE R	1LT	0-1020009	1052	1
BRIGGS LEROY E	MAJ	0-0219143	0649	3
BRIGGS MARK R	MAJ	0-0395215	0547	2
BRIGGS PAUL H	MAJ	0-0257654	0745	2
BRIGGS RALPH C	COL	0-0275763	0453	3
BRIGGS RAYMOND C	LTC	0-0240174	1165	3
BRIGGS THOMAS E	COL	0-0223942	0146	2
BRIGHAM EARNEST	CPT	0-1312510	0647	2
BRIGHAM EUGENE V	LTC	0-1181830	0258	1
BRIGHAM HERMAN C	LTC	0-0142494	1159	1
BRIGHAM LINCOLN F	MAJ	0-2208308	1067	1
BRIGHAM ROBERT A	MAJ	0-0315188	0544	2
BRIGHT CLYDE	CW2	W-2120062	1153	1
BRIGHT EVERETT W	LTC	0-0177763	0860	3
BRIGHT GRANT T	LTC	0-0191548	0247	1
BRIGHT HARRY R	LTC	0-0450244	0657	1
BRIGHT HENRY C	MAJ	0-0363607	0257	1
BRIGHT J T	CPT	0-1550549	0648	1
BRIGHT JAMES L	1LT	0-0495122	0548	1
BRIGHT JOHN E	CPT	0-1051049	0148	2
BRIGHT JR GEORGE H	CPT	0-0422146	0246	2
BRIGHT MARVIN L	CW2	W-2146318	0757	1
BRIGHT MERLE E	MAJ	0-1297152	1159	1
BRIGHT RICHARD	CW3	W-2147942	0861	1
BRIGHT WILLIAM F	LTC	0-0360902	0465	3
BRIGHTBILL ROGER D	1LT	0-0553761	0546	1
BRIGHTBILL ROLLIN M	LTC	0-0289987	1059	1
BRIGHTMAN JULIAN N	CPT	0-0511851	0947	1
BRIGHTWELL ROBERT L	COL	0-0179432	0948	1
BRIGHTWELL W G	CW3	W-2153016	0661	1
BRIGIDA GAETANO A	LTC	0-1039417	0167	1
BRIGNOLA JR RALPH D	MAJ	0-2265723	0165	1
BRILES ESTHER K	MAJ	L-0403164	0751	1
BRILEY ENOS C	COL	0-0286425	0760	1
BRILEY FRED L	CW3	W-2144659	0560	1
BRILEY KARL C	CW3	W-2148707	0665	1
BRILL CLINTON B	COL	0-0175436	0-53	3
BRILLANTE ORLANDO F	MAJ	0-1875130	0564	1
BRIM BYRON A	LTC	0-1291572	0261	1
BRIMBERRY JOHN H	COL	0-0109470	0146	2
BRIMMER FORREST F	MAJ	0-0350865	0246	2
BRIMMER WILLIAM C	MAJ	0-0432947	0161	1
BRINCKMANN EDWIN L	COL	0-0345882	0266	3
BRINDLEY SEARCY W	LTC	0-0469132	1054	1
BRINER CHARLES C	MAJ	0-0494417	0845	2
BRINGHURST EDMOND L	2LT	0-0262928	0754	3
BRINGLE CLARENCE F	CW2	W-2120829	1145	2
BRINING JOHN R	MAJ	0-1552024	1065	1
BRINK ARTHUR R	MAJ	0-1302590	1163	1
BRINK JAY F	MAJ	0-0148859	0852	3
BRINK LEE V	LTC	0-1327411	0266	1

NAME	GRADE	SVC NO	DATE RET MO YR	RET CODE
BRINKE ROBERT R	MAJ	0-1295823	0765	1
BRINKER CLARENCE T	MAJ	0-0239329	0761	3
BRINKER VIRGEL C	CW3	W-2151327	0764	1
BRINKERHOFF ARTHUR O	CW3	W-2142093	0756	1
BRINKERHOFF OLIVER J	MAJ	0-1554689	0557	1
BRINKERHOFF ROBERT	LTC	0-0236812	0263	1
BRINKERHOFF ROY A	CPT	0-0492378	0851	1
BRINKLEY ALBERT R	CPT	0-0544576	0747	2
BRINKLEY GEORGE A	CPT	0-0907122	0745	2
BRINKLEY GEORGE W	LTC	0-1823976	0766	1
BRINKLEY JIMMIE Y	CW2	W-2107540	0146	2
BRINKLEY WILLIS J	1LT	0-1080516	1155	1
BRINKMAN EMIL F	LTC	0-0227640	0656	1
BRINKMAN GERARD J	LTC	0-0323828	1265	3
BRINKMAN ROLLAND V	1LT	0-1322764	0247	2
BRINKMEYER JOHN E	LTC	0-0167015	1147	1
BRINKWART JR HUGO	LTC	0-1047458	0656	1
BRINKWORTH BEN	LTC	0-1951644	0467	1
BRINSFIELD JENNINGS	LTC	0-1175653	1266	1
BRINSMEAD HENRY	MAJ	0-1166235	0760	1
BRINSON ELMER J	WO1	W-2142419	0653	1
BRINSON JR CONNIE H	MAJ	0-0993438	0365	2
BRIODY THOMAS J	1LT	0-1284282	0745	1
BRION CLAY W	COL	0-0359834	0759	1
BRIONES DOMINADOR	1LT	0-0395565	1162	2
BRIOR JOHN E	CPT	0-0502980	1156	1
BRISBANE JULIUS S	MAJ	0-1637092	0562	1
BRISBEN WESLEY W	LTC	0-2045067	0563	1
BRISBINE DAWES E	COL	0-0195791	0346	2
BRISBINE JR TOM R	1LT	0-5514750	0466	2
BRISBOIS GERALD C	WO1	W-2119444	1145	2
BRISCO ELMER F	CW3	W-2144216	0663	1
BRISCOE ALBERT H	CPT	0-0142623	0156	3
BRISCOE EVELYN R	LTC	L-0800013	0163	1
BRISCOE GEORGE W	MAJ	0-1104466	0358	1
BRISCOE HENRY J	CPT	0-1573068	0159	1
BRISCOE PIERCE W	LTC	0-1325715	0766	1
BRISCOE WILLIAM A	COL	0-0191614	0355	3
BRISENTINE ROBERT A	CW2	W-3430054	1265	1
BRISK MICHAEL W	MAJ	0-2032589	0762	1
BRISKIN SAMUEL J	LTC	0-0398826	0743	1
BRISSETTE ALPHONSE L	MAJ	0-0948201	0166	1
BRISSON HERVEY R	MAJ	0-1552025	0563	1
BRISTER BENSON E	CPT	0-1318341	1062	1
BRISTER JAMES H	LTC	0-1168518	0962	1
BRISTER MARVIN C	MAJ	0-0453142	0546	2
BRISTO ELOIS F	LTC	0-1106015	0762	1
BRISTOL LELAND A	CW2	W-2101480	1148	2
BRISTOL ROBERT A	CPT	0-0363019	1044	2
BRISTOL WALTER L	LTC	0-0357883	0966	3
BRISTOW DON L	CPT	0-1560406	0855	2
BRISTOW JOHN A	LTC	0-1114391	1164	3
BRISTOW WALTER J	LTC	0-0169481	0952	3
BRISTOW WILLIAM A	LTC	0-1104287	1157	2
BRITAIN ERIC R	CPT	0-0162066	0557	3
BRITCHEY JEROME W	LTC	0-0349795	0946	2
BRITE BYRON H	LTC	0-1173173	0363	1
BRITE CHARLES R	1LT	0-1107827	0845	1
BRITO JOHN A	LTC	0-0480655	0157	1
BRITT CECIL A	CPT	0-1690809	1057	1
BRITT EDWARD J	CW3	W-2151315	1063	1
BRITT GERALD L	CW4	W-2121199	0454	1
BRITT III JAMES J	MAJ	0-1182523	0361	1
BRITT JOEL A	MAJ	0-1037414	0960	1
BRITT JR WILLIAM C	MAJ	0-0213837	0264	3
BRITT MAURICE L	CPT	0-0410156	1044	1
BRITT PAUL R	LTC	0-0132123	0157	3
BRITT REDDIN	MAJ	0-0480599	0346	2
BRITT ROBERT W	LTC	0-1182524	0166	1
BRITT THOMAS W	1LT	0-1182496	0557	2
BRITTAIN CECIL	CW2	W-2205105	0161	1
BRITTAIN CHARLES C	CPT	0-1541475	0756	2
BRITTAIN FREDERICK	LTC	0-1051050	0462	1
BRITTAIN HAROLD M	LTC	0-0221999	0847	2
BRITTAIN JOHN R	LTC	0-0280433	0860	3

NAME	GRADE	SVC NO	DATE RET MO YR	RET CODE
BRITTAIN WALTER	CW3	W-2152785	1167	1
BRITTAIN WILLIAM C	MAJ	0-0235731	1146	2
BRITTEN CHARLES H	LTC	0-0298594	1156	1
BRITTEN WILLIAM F	COL	0-0148163	0-53	3
BRITTENHAM EDWARD D	MAJ	0-2014540	0163	1
BRITTINGHAM ELMER A	MAJ	0-0300237	0867	3
BRITTINGHAM F A	CW3	W-2148336	1058	1
BRITTINGHAM GEORGE L	COL	0-0220637	0657	1
BRITTINGHAM HARRY A	2LT	0-0293053	0842	2
BRITTINGHAM LOUIS W	LTC	0-0197453	0761	3
BRITTO GEORGE R	LTC	0-1302655	1060	1
BRITTON ALTON C	LTC	0-0172703	0656	3
BRITTON CLARK V	MAJ	0-0301494	1162	3
BRITTON CLYDE V	LTC	0-1287298	1060	2
BRITTON DUDLEY J	LTC	0-0450560	0958	1
BRITTON EMMA L	LTC	N-0731265	1262	2
BRITTON ERNEST G	LTC	0-1174239	0961	1
BRITTON GLENN W	MAJ	0-0192261	0-49	3
BRITTON JACK A	MAJ	0-1922647	0765	1
BRITTON JAMES G	COL	0-0916437	0566	3
BRITTON JAMES W	MAJ	0-1683064	1044	2
BRITTON KIRBY L	MAJ	0-0962555	1262	1
BRITTON RAYMOND M	LTC	0-0364069	1045	2
BRITTON ROBERT S	CPT	0-1583978	1155	2
BRITTON WILLIAM F	LTC	0-1186991	0162	1
BRITTON WILLIAM P	LTC	0-1798242	0467	3
BRITTON WILLIAM S	CPT	0-0323915	0456	1
BRITTS CHESTER L	CW2	W-2103912	1045	2
BRIX JAMES A	CPT	0-0322645	1143	1
BRIZEE ROBERT F	LTC	0-0779773	1165	1
BRIZZOLARA CHARLES M	CPT	0-0407217	0246	2
BRIZZOLARA LOUIS A	CW3	W-2152501	1064	1
BROAD FAY E	MAJ	0-0118433	0444	2
BROAD GARDNER S	MAJ	0-0328601	0245	2
BROADAWAY JERRY L	CW3	W-2152031	0864	1
BROADBENT EVERETT F	LTC	0-0220346	0963	3
BROADDUS JACKSON A	CPT	0-0281434	0167	3
BROADDUS MALCOLM D	LTC	0-1300593	0762	1
BROADDUS MURRAY F	LTC	0-0333564	1144	2
BROADDUS RUSSELL G	COL	0-0314980	0866	1
BROADDUS THORBURN P	LTC	0-1310054	0665	1
BROADDUS WILLIAM L	2LT	0-4049351	0857	2
BROADHEAD WILLIAM C	LTC	0-0322962	0648	3
BROADHURST EDWARD E	MAJ	0-1575789	1061	1
BROADHURST LANSING E	LTC	0-1585083	0763	1
BROADHURST THOMAS I	MAJ	0-1878020	0667	1
BROADSTOCK LEONARD L	CW3	W-2146190	0961	1
BROADWELL ROLLAND E	LTC	0-1101346	0565	1
BROBERG JOHN A	CPT	0-0107870	0-53	3
BROBST CHARLES R	MAJ	0-0474993	1159	1
BROBST JR GEORGE W	LTC	0-1318756	0666	1
BROCK DARWIN A	COL	0-0453556	0667	1
BROCK DONALD L	LTC	0-0261880	0465	3
BROCK FRANK P	COL	0-0250777	0267	3
BROCK HOWELL E	LTC	0-1171921	1165	1
BROCK JOHN M	MAJ	0-1595144	1267	1
BROCK LEWIS D	LTC	0-1171063	1061	1
BROCK LLOYD S	CW3	W-2004804	0967	1
BROCK ROBERT L	CW3	W-2151089	0157	1
BROCK ROGERS E	CW2	W-2108314	0866	1
BROCK RONALD C	MG	0-0242225	0759	3
BROCK WALLACE W	CPT	0-1306371	0661	1
BROCK WALTER S	1LT	0-0255791	0444	2
BROCK WILLIAM C	CPT	0-0290664	0767	3
BROCK WILLIAM E	MAJ	0-0964091	0565	1
BROCKDORFF BEVERLY	LTC	0-1112048	0563	1
BROCKERT KENNETH E	CPT	0-2036293	0657	1
BROCKETT MILLAS B	LTC	0-0447963	0954	1
BROCKETT STANLEY W	CW2	W-2215074	0767	1
BROCKIE JR JOHN M	COL	0-0277251	0360	1
BROCKLEHURST R A	COL	0-0174521	0954	3
BROCKMAN CHARLES J	COL	0-0209360	0757	3
BROCKMAN EARL H	CPT	0-0116593	1052	3
BROCKMAN HARRY C	LTC	0-0216935	0163	3
BROCKMAN KARL W	LTC	0-0162397	0352	3

NAME	GRADE	SVC NO	DATE RET MO YR	RET CODE
BROCKMAN RAYMOND P	MAJ	0-0253182	0363	3
BROCKMAN ROBERT C	MAJ	0-1637086	0863	1
BROCKSIEPER CLARENCE	MAJ	0-1062471	0461	1
BROCKWAY ARTHUR J	LTC	0-1290196	0457	1
BROCKWAY GEORGE B	LTC	0-1114393	0764	1
BROCKWAY RONALD S	LTC	0-0490761	1162	1
BROCKWAY RUTH H	CPT	N-0784621	0847	1
BROCOPP HERMAN A	COL	0-0136185	0356	3
BRODBECK JAMES A	CPT	0-1304334	0647	1
BRODER ARNOLD	1LT	0-1044464	0346	2
BRODER SIMON	LTC	0-0312397	0164	3
BRODERICK CHARLES J	LTC	0-0438745	0662	1
BRODERICK CROCKETT B	LTC	0-0321609	1266	3
BRODERICK DAVID F	CW2	W-2114205	1145	1
BRODERICK FRED W	COL	0-0245228	0160	1
BRODERICK JOHN M	CPT	0-1306054	0548	2
BRODERICK THOMAS C	CPT	0-0389242	0245	2
BRODERICK WILLIAM J	1LT	0-1295333	0146	2
BRODEUR JOSEPH R	LTC	0-0267702	0450	3
BRODIE ARTHUR M	LTC	0-1333928	0167	1
BRODIE DONALD W	CPT	0-1684508	0245	1
BRODIE DUDLEY D	COL	0-0120524	0255	3
BRODIE JOHN T	LTC	0-0399938	0663	1
BRODKIN HENRY A	COL	0-0207258	0361	3
BRODKORB WALTER J	1LT	0-0160145	0455	3
BRODMAN HERBERT W	1LT	0-0471098	0749	1
BRODMAN KEEVE	MAJ	0-0244885	0444	1
BRODNAX MARION J	MAJ	0-0170258	1060	3
BRODRICK FRANK W	LTC	0-0150380	1045	2
BRODRICK GEORGE W	CW2	W-2142493	0856	1
BRODSKY ALEXANDER	1LT	0-0472333	0845	2
BRODY ALFRED W	CPT	0-0460731	1050	1
BRODY ARTHUR R	COL	0-0410462	1062	1
BRODY HERMAN	MAJ	0-0168550	1044	2
BRODY JAMES F	MAJ	0-0969881	0966	1
BRODY JOSEPH	CPT	0-1689403	0643	2
BRODY JOSEPH	1LT	0-1994389	0240	2
BRODY NATHANIEL	2LT	0-1314750	0645	2
BRODY WILLIAM	MAJ	0-0481997	0146	2
BRODZINSKY JACOB	MAJ	0-1109827	0567	1
BROE VARLEY F	MAJ	0-1310336	0862	1
BROEHM WALTER J	LTC	0-0183772	0847	2
BROFF MAURICE H	MAJ	0-0229100	1054	3
BROGAN JR WILLIAM A	MAJ	0-1062472	0461	1
BROGDON LELAND R	CPT	0-0495815	0750	1
BROILES JAMES O	CPT	0-1307501	0654	1
BROILLET EUGENE H	MAJ	0-1046465	0160	1
BROITMAN JACK	WO1	W-2105408	0946	2
BROKAW ALBERT R	MAJ	0-1996456	0661	1
BROKAW CHARLES E	COL	0-0170201	1158	3
BROKAW JOHN D	LTC	0-1015265	1062	1
BROKAW MAX V	LTC	0-0347639	0657	1
BROKAW STUART F	LTC	0-0220422	1051	3
BROKAW WILLIAM H	MAJ	0-0972067	0164	1
BROLINE ELINOR L	1LT	N-0776581	0347	1
BROM JACOB M	LTC	0-1035106	0364	1
BROMBLE EDWARD W	MAJ	0-0958098	1162	1
BROMLEY CHARLES D	COL	0-0193429	1059	3
BROMLEY JR W K	CPT	0-0528753	1046	2
BROMLEY ROBERT D	MAJ	0-0523043	0657	1
BROMS GUSTAVE A	LTC	0-0289478	0764	3
BROMSER PAUL F	MAJ	0-1823399	0261	1
BRONER RUSSELL A	LTC	0-0373366	0460	1
BRONISZ MATTHEW S	MAJ	0-0413907	1062	1
BRONNENBERG EDGAR M	LTC	0-1320096	0763	1
BRONNENBERG WILLIAM	MAJ	0-1543300	0761	1
BRONNER JR NELLIS B	CPT	0-0455346	1144	2
BRONNER LEONARD E	LTC	0-2001024	0564	1
BRONSON HARRY S	LTC	0-0167542	0645	2
BRONSON IRWIN P	CW3	W-2205400	0966	1
BRONSON RALPH P	COL	0-0438320	1046	1
BRONSON SIDNEY W	1LT	0-0267982	0650	1
BROOK OCOND	2LT	0-1112050	0545	2
BROOK R J	CW2	W-2152727	0861	1
BROOKE DONALD C	CW2	W-3430029	0666	1
BROOKE ELTON O	CPT	0-1306372	0146	2
BROOKE JR ARTHUR C	LTC	0-1081391	0962	1
BROOKE ROYAL G	COL	0-0307703	0867	3
BROOKE TYLER S	2LT	0-0467000	0745	2
BROOKENS NORMAN J	CW3	W-2206864	0167	1
BROOKER GORDON L	CPT	0-1112051	1047	1
BROOKES NORMA	2LT	N-0731297	0244	1
BROOKHART SMITH W	COL	0-0508524	1165	3
BROOKMAN STUART H	CW2	W-2214423	0866	1
BROOKMAN WILLIAM E	LTC	0-0411008	0760	1
BROOKNER JACK A	MAJ	0-1036875	0266	1
BROOKS ALBERT H	CPT	0-1291066	1044	2
BROOKS ALEXANDER	2LT	0-2006182	0146	2
BROOKS ALVIN L	CPT	0-2028882	0161	2
BROOKS BERNARD J	1LT	0-1285371	1045	1
BROOKS CARL R	CPT	0-1931867	0962	1
BROOKS CHARLES A	CPT	0-1301249	0352	1
BROOKS CHARLES H	CW4	W-2119343	0557	1
BROOKS CLOYCE H	LTC	0-1104791	1060	1
BROOKS CURTIS A	MAJ	0-0446018	0546	2
BROOKS DALE L	MAJ	0-1016536	0361	1
BROOKS DAVID F	LTC	0-1308092	0663	1
BROOKS DAVID M	CPT	0-1696080	1043	2
BROOKS EARL E	LTC	0-0219260	0648	3
BROOKS EARL T	CPT	0-0299296	0867	3
BROOKS EARLE C	LTC	0-1584080	0663	1
BROOKS EDGAR D	LTC	0-0454955	1162	1
BROOKS EDWARD H	1LT	0-0445627	0945	1
BROOKS ELTON G	1LT	0-2212003	0567	1
BROOKS EUGENE A	MAJ	0-1183251	0960	1
BROOKS EUGENE F	CPT	0-0504720	0446	2
BROOKS FRANK N	MAJ	0-2006538	0860	1
BROOKS GARMON W	CW3	W-2151382	0966	1
BROOKS GEORGE C	CW4	W-2102694	0357	1
BROOKS GILBERT	LTC	0-0320489	0666	3
BROOKS GILMON O	CW3	W-2147216	0366	1
BROOKS GLENN F	LTC	0-0369891	0556	1
BROOKS GRADY S	B G	0-0248317	0766	3
BROOKS HENRY L	LTC	0-1339605	1165	1
BROOKS HERBERT H	2LT	0-1823828	1044	2
BROOKS HERBERT J	CPT	0-0488834	0155	2
BROOKS HERBERT O	CW3	W-2142285	1058	1
BROOKS HERROLD E	COL	0-0179518	0163	3
BROOKS HOWARD R	1LT	0-0493083	0147	1
BROOKS JAMES B	MAJ	0-0406641	0447	2
BROOKS JAMES H	LTC	0-0932110	0665	3
BROOKS JOE F	CW3	W-2147740	0863	2
BROOKS JOHN E	COL	0-0309218	1158	3
BROOKS JOHN J	LTC	0-1944413	0463	1
BROOKS JOHN K	1LT	0-1061635	0945	2
BROOKS JOHN R	CPT	0-0407968	0246	2
BROOKS JOHN R	MAJ	0-2263013	0264	1
BROOKS JOHN S	MAJ	0-1293538	1160	1
BROOKS JOHN W	CPT	0-1010853	0144	2
BROOKS JOHNNY Y	LTC	0-1182782	1162	1
BROOKS JR ANDREW J	CPT	0-0372294	0565	1
BROOKS JR ARTHUR R	2LT	0-1051898	0445	2
BROOKS JR FRANK R	MAJ	0-1336476	0864	2
BROOKS JR GEORGE W	COL	0-0277250	0766	3
BROOKS LOREN R	COL	0-0158349	0449	3
BROOKS LYLE A	CPT	0-0195345	1062	3
BROOKS MATTHEW L	LTC	0-1317145	1162	1
BROOKS MAXWELL	2LT	0-1012662	0651	2
BROOKS MORTON P	COL	0-0294943	0864	1
BROOKS PAUL K	CW2	W-2118437	0648	1
BROOKS PAUL R	COL	0-0268087	0564	3
BROOKS PERRY R	MAJ	0-1950607	0264	1
BROOKS PHILIP M	CPT	0-0493415	0648	1
BROOKS RALPH C	LTC	0-0187204	0648	3
BROOKS RAYMOND A	LTC	0-0425809	1162	3
BROOKS ROBERT	WO1	W-2124108	1146	1
BROOKS ROBERT G	MAJ	0-1587753	1065	1
BROOKS ROBERT G	CW2	W-2122501	0753	1
BROOKS ROBERT G	WO1	W-2146757	0555	1
BROOKS ROBERT N	MAJ	0-1644470	1060	1
BROOKS RODNEY C	LTC	0-1165269	1165	1
BROOKS ROLAND	CPT	0-0160048	0153	3
BROOKS ROY T	COL	0-0308103	0759	1
BROOKS RUSSELL D	LTC	0-0275480	0467	3
BROOKS SAMMIE W	MAJ	0-2212008	0662	1
BROOKS STANLEY M	CW2	W-2147267	0464	1
BROOKS THOMAS G	CW4	W-2121961	0662	1
BROOKS VERNON R	MAJ	0-2024231	0856	1
BROOKS WALTER H	CPT	0-0263315	0363	3
BROOKS WILLARD A	MAJ	0-1646810	0557	1
BROOKS WILLARD R	2LT	0-1822232	1143	2
BROOKS WILLIAM F	CW2	W-2152858	0256	1
BROOKS WILLIAM J	WO1	W-2131124	1046	2
BROOKS WILLIAM V	1LT	0-1295825	1145	2
BROOKS WINFORD R	MAJ	0-1919353	0664	1
BROOKS WINSTON R	LTC	0-1598322	0462	1
BROOKS WINSTON S	LTC	0-0397079	0860	1
BROOKS WOODROW W	CPT	0-0496251	0253	1
BROOM CHARLES G	CPT	0-1926470	1164	1
BROOM DAVID	CPT	0-0528486	1050	1
BROOM EDWARD C	CW3	W-2149147	0364	1
BROOMALL FRED A	CPT	0-0171301	0542	1
BROOMALL SAMUEL C	MAJ	0-1558557	1162	1
BROOMFIELD ROBERT E	LTC	0-1043581	0760	1
BROPHY ALLEN D	LTC	0-0181956	1149	3
BROPHY EANES B	CPT	0-0507655	1052	1
BROPHY EDWARD A	MAJ	0-1994823	1062	3
BROPHY JAMES D	LTC	0-0328916	0860	1
BROPHY JOSEPH F	1LT	0-0226226	0850	3
BROPHY JR WILLIAM S	LTC	0-1548171	0267	1
BRORSEN JOHN J	MAJ	0-2211574	0967	1
BROSAMER JOHN J	CPT	0-1051500	1062	1
BROSE CARL E	LTC	0-0237147	0757	1
BROSHEAR JOHNNY W	MAJ	0-1822351	0561	1
BROSIN HENRY W	COL	0-0231426	0864	3
BROSIUS CHARLES C	MAJ	0-1688802	0466	1
BROSKE ABE	MAJ	0-0184671	1056	3
BROSKIE MARION L	2LT	N-0752474	0345	1
BROSNAN JOHN R	CPT	0-0192443	1041	2
BROSOKAS VICTOR P	LTC	0-0388976	0346	1
BROST BERNARD A	CPT	0-1560179	0865	1
BROSTEK ALEXANDER	LTC	0-0301001	0747	1
BROTEMARKLE W A	1LT	0-1050194	0452	1
BROTHERS HARRISON S	COL	0-0245815	0266	3
BROTHERS JOSEPH L	WO1	W-2114494	0344	2
BROTHERS MAURICE F	COL	0-0194942	0660	3
BROTHERS WILLIAM W	COL	0-0189122	0146	2
BROTHERTON DONALD R	MAJ	0-0973512	0164	1
BROTHERTON HENRY A	LTC	0-1553780	0563	2
BROTHERTON HOLMAN A	LTC	0-0519647	1263	1
BROTHERTON JAMES R	LTC	0-0347168	0258	1
BROTHERTON KENNETH F	MAJ	0-0479036	0350	1
BROTHERTON WILLIAM W	COL	0-0220791	0164	3
BROTMAN GERALD	LTC	0-1081201	0667	1
BROUGH HARRY R	LTC	0-0290902	0162	3
BROUGHAM JR JAMES P	MAJ	0-1310802	0257	1
BROUGHER GEORGE R	LTC	0-1180127	0965	3
BROUGHER JR COOPER	LTC	0-0362102	0266	3
BROUGHMAN WARNER A	CPT	0-0389459	0346	2
BROUS CHRIS J	CPT	0-0450653	1045	2
BROUSE KARL M	LTC	0-0140345	0153	3
BROUSSARD CHARLES C	LTC	0-0328259	0165	1
BROUSSARD DENIS	LTC	0-0481566	0857	1
BROUSSEAU LOUIS D	LTC	0-0262067	0866	3
BROWDER JESSE S	MAJ	0-0443858	1148	1
BROWDER JR EDWARD M	COL	0-0236155	0266	3
BROWER BESSIE L	MAJ	N-0779009	0765	1
BROWER JAMES F	MAJ	0-0112698	0954	1
BROWER JR DANIEL R	COL	0-0248691	0465	3
BROWERS HOWARD W	CW3	W-2141206	1059	1
BROWN A W	MAJ	0-1692933	0563	1
BROWN AARON C	COL	0-0410800	0667	1
BROWN ABE A	LTC	0-0148269	0954	3
BROWN ALAN	LTC	0-0314336	0266	3
BROWN ALBERT E	2LT	0-1552848	0345	2
BROWN ALBERT L	CPT	0-0205370	0859	3
BROWN ALBERT N	MAJ	0-0240143	0747	1
BROWN ALBERT S	MAJ	0-0969476	0465	1
BROWN ALFRED G	COL	0-0114468	0750	3
BROWN ALFRED W	1LT	0-1305375	1147	2
BROWN ALLAN H	MAJ	0-0138326	0845	2
BROWN ALMER G	CW3	W-2203634	0763	1
BROWN ALONZO L	MAJ	0-1048696	1162	1
BROWN ALSA R	LTC	0-0284950	0560	3
BROWN ALTON A	MAJ	0-2262990	0865	1
BROWN ANDREW J	MAJ	0-1290540	1163	1
BROWN ANN S	1LT	N-0759933	0246	1
BROWN ANTHONY J	CPT	0-0889011	0148	1
BROWN ARCHIE F	CPT	0-0470760	0645	2
BROWN ARDEN E	CPT	0-1913288	0967	1
BROWN ARNOLD L	MAJ	0-1296318	0658	1
BROWN ARRY L	LTC	0-0310288	1166	3
BROWN ARTHUR	CPT	0-0134887	0157	3
BROWN ARTHUR F	1LT	0-1285890	1145	1
BROWN ARTHUR W	2LT	0-1292828	0145	2
BROWN AUDREY R	CW4	W-2143165	0559	1
BROWN AUSY R	COL	0-0368781	0660	1
BROWN BEE H	MAJ	0-1322881	0859	1
BROWN BENJAMIN F	LTC	0-1313713	1066	1
BROWN BERNARD A	COL	0-0256766	0655	3
BROWN BERNARD N	LTC	0-1018994	1066	1
BROWN BERNARD W	CW3	W-2205584	0361	2
BROWN BOBBIE E	CPT	0-2053899	0350	1
BROWN BOYCE R	MAJ	0-1117371	0262	1
BROWN BRYAN B	MAJ	0-0211600	0346	1
BROWN BRYAN L	LTC	0-0276297	0567	3
BROWN BURRELL G	LTC	0-1697891	0158	1
BROWN BYRON F	LTC	0-0212967	0860	3
BROWN CALVIN B	CW2	W-2210175	0364	1
BROWN CAMERON	LTC	0-0369922	0246	2
BROWN CAMPBELL H	LTC	0-0401532	1049	1
BROWN CAREY H	COL	0-0276742	0648	3
BROWN CARL L	CPT	0-0978086	1060	1
BROWN CARL R	CPT	0-0329595	0446	2
BROWN CARLOS L	CPT	0-0155740	0757	3
BROWN CATHARINE	1LT	L-0601502	0245	1
BROWN CECIL E	COL	0-0338746	0561	1
BROWN CECIL J	LTC	0-1040886	0264	1
BROWN CHARLES A	LTC	0-1301250	1065	1
BROWN CHARLES A	CW2	W-3100523	0167	1
BROWN CHARLES B	MAJ	0-1046367	1264	1
BROWN CHARLES C	WO1	W-1440606	0656	3
BROWN CHARLES D	LTC	0-0345704	0958	3
BROWN CHARLES G	MAJ	0-1180763	0760	1
BROWN CHARLES H	MAJ	0-0375816	0246	2
BROWN CHARLES J	MAJ	0-0925023	0944	1
BROWN CHARLES L	CW4	W-2102696	0255	1
BROWN CHARLES M	LTC	0-0404367	0453	1
BROWN CHARLES M	LTC	0-1080689	1266	1
BROWN CHARLES M	LTC	0-1314590	0166	1
BROWN CHARLES S	CW4	W-2122989	1060	1
BROWN CHARLIE	CPT	0-0481710	0547	1
BROWN CHARLTON A	1LT	0-0400486	0442	2
BROWN CHESTER H	MAJ	0-2212001	0165	1
BROWN CHESTER T	LTC	0-0231573	1157	1
BROWN CLAIRE A	2LT	N-0742192	0745	1
BROWN CLAUDE P	LTC	0-0146350	1149	3
BROWN CLIFFORD A	CPT	0-1046026	1165	1
BROWN CLIFFORD A	MAJ	0-1894451	0961	1
BROWN CLIFFORD F	CW2	W-2114839	0455	2
BROWN CLIFFORD N	LTC	0-1533265	0753	1
BROWN CLIFTON D	CW3	W-2148786	0966	1
BROWN CLINTON H	MAJ	0-2208113	1165	1
BROWN COATS	CW3	W-2149426	1065	1
BROWN COLEMAN T	LTC	0-0181115	0152	3
BROWN COURTNEY P	COL	0-0243994	1264	3
BROWN CURTIS P	LTC	0-1320380	1063	1
BROWN DAVID F K	CW3	W-2147495	0762	1
BROWN DAVID C	LTC	0-0501649	0657	1
BROWN DAVID W	CW3	W-2145628	0166	1

NAME	GRADE	SVC NO	DATE RET MO YR	RET CODE
BROWN DECATER	LTC	O-0885510	0854	1
BROWN DEWAYNE G	1LT	O-1923978	0157	1
BROWN DONALD A	COL	O-0181651	0141	1
BROWN DONALD A	CPT	O-0376935	0146	2
BROWN DONALD P	1LT	O-1893809	1056	2
BROWN DONALD W	1LT	O-0405175	0743	2
BROWN DOUGLAS A	CW2	W-2214361	0966	1
BROWN EARL	LTC	O-1553781	0862	1
BROWN EARL J	1LT	O-1319821	0449	2
BROWN EARL S	LTC	O-1020178	0661	1
BROWN EARLE H	CPT	O-1297469	1146	2
BROWN EDGAR L	MAJ	O-0975470	0763	1
BROWN EDGAR T	CPT	O-1821672	0749	2
BROWN EDWARD	CW4	W-2132164	0656	1
BROWN EDWARD A	LTC	O-1046378	1165	3
BROWN EDWARD A	LTC	O-1949154	0365	1
BROWN EDWARD E	CW2	W-2209014	0961	1
BROWN EDWARD F	MAJ	O-1307798	0761	1
BROWN EDWARD M	COL	O-0164412	0153	3
BROWN EDWARD S	CPT	O-0405550	0146	1
BROWN EDWIN E	MAJ	O-1283017	0358	2
BROWN EDWIN H	MAJ	O-1894909	0167	1
BROWN EDWIN S	CW4	W-2113669	1262	1
BROWN ELVIE C	CW2	W-2109227	1044	2
BROWN EMIL	LTC	O-0115141	0255	3
BROWN EMMETT	CPT	O-0148927	0150	3
BROWN ERNEST A	CW3	W-2151885	1062	1
BROWN ERNEST J	COL	O-0503731	0760	3
BROWN ERNEST J	CW4	W-2101486	0158	1
BROWN ERNEST L	CPT	O-1581559	0256	1
BROWN EUGENE C	CPT	O-0307754	0346	1
BROWN EUGENE J	CPT	O-0914674	0344	2
BROWN EUGENE S	LTC	O-1106018	0465	1
BROWN FELIX B	MAJ	O-0468145	1145	2
BROWN FLETCHER H	CPT	O-1951039	1057	2
BROWN FLOYD D	1LT	O-1845325	1145	2
BROWN FLOYD L	LTC	O-0228728	0658	1
BROWN FLOYD S	CW4	W-2127548	0652	1
BROWN FLOYD W	COL	O-0286462	0648	1
BROWN FORREST D	COL	O-0319475	0960	1
BROWN FRANCES M	MAJ	N-0729820	0663	1
BROWN FRANCIS G	MAJ	O-0962620	0243	1
BROWN FRANK	CW2	W-2115687	0451	1
BROWN FRANK A	LTC	O-0217282	1263	3
BROWN FRANK J	CPT	O-0496935	0429	1
BROWN FRANK L	LTC	O-0450579	0457	1
BROWN FRANK M	COL	O-0188318	0257	3
BROWN FRED L	1LT	O-1173886	0147	2
BROWN FREDERIC R	CPT	O-0289845	0866	3
BROWN FREDERICK	MAJ	O-0971749	0763	1
BROWN FREDERICK	WO1	W-2115152	0747	2
BROWN FREDRICK J	CW3	W-2148074	0765	1
BROWN GALE C	CPT	R-0000083	0946	1
BROWN GALE L	1LT	O-1111516	0946	2
BROWN GARDNER W	MAJ	O-0276949	1145	2
BROWN GARNHART T	CPT	O-0693843	0252	1
BROWN GEORGE	COL	O-0328152	1061	1
BROWN GEORGE	CPT	O-0471637	0655	1
BROWN GEORGE A	LTC	O-0439640	1157	1
BROWN GEORGE B	LTC	O-0183238	1047	2
BROWN GEORGE B	CPT	O-0345492	0145	2
BROWN GEORGE C	LTC	O-0205800	0158	3
BROWN GEORGE C	MAJ	O-0305426	0445	2
BROWN GEORGE C	LTC	O-1031388	0557	1
BROWN GEORGE F	MAJ	O-0976367	0553	1
BROWN GEORGE H	MAJ	O-1874909	1065	1
BROWN GEORGE L	COL	O-0255870	0562	3
BROWN GEORGE S	COL	O-0144316	0754	3
BROWN GEORGE S	MAJ	O-0298158	1045	2
BROWN GEORGE W	1LT	O-1047453	1047	1
BROWN GERALD F	LTC	O-2050416	0364	1
BROWN GILBERT L	CPT	O-1015802	0446	2
BROWN GLENN J	1LT	O-0391530	0144	2
BROWN GLENN W	MAJ	O-1031156	0562	1
BROWN GRACE D	MAJ	L-0704036	0955	2

NAME	GRADE	SVC NO	DATE RET MO YR	RET CODE
BROWN HARLAN C	MAJ	O-0257092	0266	3
BROWN HARLEY L	LTC	O-1331370	0267	1
BROWN HARLEY W	MAJ	O-1312273	0761	1
BROWN HAROLD	LTC	O-0192645	0159	3
BROWN HAROLD A	1LT	O-2006608	0847	2
BROWN HAROLD G	LTC	O-0276640	1059	3
BROWN HAROLD H	MAJ	O-0447950	0667	1
BROWN HAROLD J	MAJ	O-0235967	0166	3
BROWN HAROLD O	LTC	O-0286530	0745	2
BROWN HARRISON E	LTC	O-0921365	0667	3
BROWN HARRY B	CPT	O-0225656	0554	3
BROWN HARRY E	COL	O-0235288	0865	3
BROWN HARRY E	CPT	O-0442587	0346	2
BROWN HARRY I	1LT	O-0403795	0959	1
BROWN HARRY R	MAJ	O-0280089	0962	3
BROWN HARRY W	MAJ	O-0296622	0945	1
BROWN HARVEY A	LTC	O-0105877	0259	3
BROWN HENRY A	CW3	W-2154642	0559	1
BROWN HENRY R	CPT	O-1169187	0745	2
BROWN HERBERT F	MAJ	O-0268642	0744	2
BROWN HERBERT F	WO1	W-2125039	0546	2
BROWN HERBERT J	CPT	O-1573748	1046	1
BROWN HOIT S	LTC	O-0482493	0255	2
BROWN HOMER J	MAJ	O-1547243	1262	1
BROWN HOMER P	CPT	O-0413742	0348	2
BROWN HORACE D	COL	O-0201728	1160	3
BROWN HOUSTON A	COL	O-0284648	0967	3
BROWN HOWARD E	COL	O-0403568	0667	1
BROWN HOWARD L	MAJ	O-0144307	1057	3
BROWN HOWARD S	CPT	O-0488752	0459	1
BROWN HOWARD T	CPT	O-0395428	1045	2
BROWN HOWARD W	LTC	O-0291849	0660	1
BROWN HUBERT L	MAJ	O-0471765	0645	1
BROWN HUBERT V	CW2	RW-2152820	0263	1
BROWN IRVEN S	LTC	O-1798113	0859	1
BROWN JACK F	CPT	O-1296588	0947	2
BROWN JACK M	1LT	O-0340734	0444	2
BROWN JACK W	MAJ	O-1298655	0557	1
BROWN JACOBS A	1LT	O-1032692	0945	1
BROWN JAMES A	LTC	O-0342779	0662	1
BROWN JAMES A	MAJ	O-1179313	0156	2
BROWN JAMES B	COL	O-0177023	0546	2
BROWN JAMES E	MAJ	O-0262444	0567	3
BROWN JAMES F	MAJ	O-4010991	0667	1
BROWN JAMES E	CW2	W-2149329	0362	2
BROWN JAMES G	CPT	O-0341761	1045	2
BROWN JAMES G	MAJ	O-1824420	1051	1
BROWN JAMES H	CPT	O-0219430	0754	3
BROWN JAMES H	CW2	W-2147930	0363	1
BROWN JAMES M	1LT	O-0373427	0845	2
BROWN JAMES M	MAJ	O-1913403	1264	1
BROWN JAMES R	LTC	O-0269761	0967	3
BROWN JAMES S	CPT	O-0449188	0766	2
BROWN JAMES T	COL	O-0226891	1264	3
BROWN JAMES W	MAJ	O-0516573	1163	1
BROWN JAMES W	LTC	O-1587164	0665	1
BROWN JASON L	CW2	O-1321698	1057	1
BROWN JESS W	WO1	W-2112845	0458	1
BROWN JESSE C	LTC	O-1328879	1265	1
BROWN JESSE F	COL	O-0101100	0648	3
BROWN JESSE H	LTC	O-0281200	0267	3
BROWN JESSIE E	MAJ	N-0752934	0864	1
BROWN JOHN A	LTC	O-0152648	0356	3
BROWN JOHN F	MAJ	O-0450691	0460	1
BROWN JOHN F	CPT	O-0485646	0146	2
BROWN JOHN H	LTC	O-0121708	0952	3
BROWN JOHN H	CPT	O-0450073	1145	2
BROWN JOHN H	CPT	O-0493406	0549	1
BROWN JOHN H	1LT	O-1291406	1144	1
BROWN JOHN H	CW3	W-2151874	0164	2
BROWN JOHN J	COL	O-0249438	0465	3
BROWN JOHN J	CPT	O-0314189	0743	2
BROWN JOHN L	CPT	O-0108608	0852	3
BROWN JOHN N	2LT	O-2313275	0261	3
BROWN JOHN R	MAJ	O-1011361	0461	1

NAME	GRADE	SVC NO	DATE RET MO YR	RET CODE
BROWN JOHN S	LTC	O-0268321	1166	3
BROWN JOHN T	CPT	O-1313968	1048	1
BROWN JOHN W	MAJ	O-0250058	1262	1
BROWN JOHN W	CPT	O-0383264	1044	1
BROWN JOSEPH B F	CPT	O-0305061	0844	2
BROWN JOSEPH W	LTC	O-1576615	0665	1
BROWN JOSEPH W	MAJ	O-1644822	0760	1
BROWN JR ALANSON O	MAJ	O-1825129	1063	1
BROWN JR ALBERT L	MAJ	O-1551959	0864	1
BROWN JR ARTHUR C	1LT	O-2262582	0859	2
BROWN JR ARTHUR G	MAJ	O-2032937	0862	1
BROWN JR CHARLES O	MAJ	O-1548660	0559	1
BROWN JR CHARLES F	MAJ	O-1109159	1061	1
BROWN JR CLYDE	CPT	O-0382126	0646	2
BROWN JR EUGENE L	MAJ	O-0116372	0648	3
BROWN JR FRANK M	CPT	O-0890107	0447	2
BROWN JR HAROLD A	CPT	O-0926414	0153	2
BROWN JR HAROLD E	LTC	O-0548971	1067	1
BROWN JR HARRY L	MAJ	O-1545500	0661	1
BROWN JR HARRY W	CPT	O-0317250	0644	2
BROWN JR JAMES	1LT	O-1114397	0645	2
BROWN JR JEFF G	CPT	O-1937081	0865	1
BROWN JR JOHN E	LTC	O-0335993	0263	3
BROWN JR NATHAN A	COL	O-1769917	0761	3
BROWN JR RALPH S	CW2	W-2146740	1060	1
BROWN JR ROBERT C	LTC	O-1640269	0863	1
BROWN JR ROBERT L	COL	O-0319865	0162	1
BROWN JR ROBERT L	LTC	O-1171066	0161	1
BROWN JR ROBERT L	MAJ	O-1999219	0861	1
BROWN JR ROBERT L	MAJ	O-2262388	0166	1
BROWN JR ROBISON	MAJ	O-0222333	0864	3
BROWN JR SAMUEL A	LTC	O-0241975	1054	3
BROWN JR SAMUEL A	2LT	O-1948095	0546	2
BROWN JR SELLERS B	LTC	O-2006315	0467	1
BROWN JR WALTER T	CPT	O-2036628	0859	1
BROWN JR WILEY W	CPT	O-1578213	0966	2
BROWN JR WILLARD H	2LT	O-4004740	1056	2
BROWN KARL J	CW2	W-2142037	1056	1
BROWN KELLY	CW3	W-2205754	0966	1
BROWN KENNETH A	LTC	O-1798976	0167	3
BROWN KENNETH C	COL	O-0118949	0755	3
BROWN KENNETH F	LTC	O-1177304	0263	1
BROWN KENNETH H	MAJ	O-0394266	0346	2
BROWN KENNETH R	LTC	O-0217823	0364	3
BROWN KENNETH W	CPT	O-1318277	0746	2
BROWN KENNETH W	CW3	W-2147476	0666	1
BROWN KERMIT K	CPT	O-0410809	0144	2
BROWN LAURENCE H	LTC	O-0176337	0659	3
BROWN LAURENCE R	LTC	O-0210563	1262	3
BROWN LAWRENCE F	MAJ	O-1845151	1051	1
BROWN LAWRENCE E	CW3	W-2203647	0864	1
BROWN LAWRENCE T	LTC	O-0113280	0854	3
BROWN LEO F	MAJ	O-1045400	0163	1
BROWN LEON G	COL	O-0261953	0661	3
BROWN LESTER A	LTC	O-1011084	0456	1
BROWN LESTER C	LTC	O-1894884	0960	1
BROWN LEWIS D	CPT	O-1945091	1047	2
BROWN LLOYD C	LTC	O-0360656	1064	1
BROWN LLOYD F	MAJ	O-0290042	0854	1
BROWN LLOYD M	MAJ	O-1640266		1
BROWN LONNIE V	CW2	W-2151043	0466	2
BROWN LOREN F	2LT	O-1058454	0445	2
BROWN LOUCKS R	COL	O-0179349	0848	3
BROWN LOUIS J	CW2	W-2107957	0762	1
BROWN LYMAN F	MAJ	O-0399993	0155	1
BROWN MAE L	MAJ	N-0797488	0665	1
BROWN MAJOR D	MAJ	O-2023354	1060	1
BROWN MALCOLM Z	LTC	O-0408923	1061	1
BROWN MARCELLUS	1LT	O-1319376	0645	2
BROWN MARGARET A	1LT	N-0741249	0546	1
BROWN MARIEM E	2LT	N-0787998	0844	1
BROWN MARION E	1LT	O-1106019	0745	2
BROWN MARY G	1LT	N-0761744	0247	1
BROWN MAX H	COL	O-0466962	0762	2
BROWN MCGREGOR E	CPT	O-0193166	0645	2

NAME	GRADE	SVC NO	DATE RET MO YR	RET CODE
BROWN MCKINLEY	CW2	W-2142136	0656	1
BROWN MELVIN C	CW2	W-2151806	0461	1
BROWN MERLE H	MAJ	O-1545895	0157	1
BROWN MERLE S	MAJ	O-2021282	0364	1
BROWN MERTON E	CW3	W-2149976	0961	1
BROWN MICHAEL J	LTC	O-1180826	0866	1
BROWN MILON I	1LT	O-1315903	0645	2
BROWN MILTON A	1LT	O-1180827	0845	2
BROWN MILTON L	CW2	W-2150298	0761	1
BROWN MINOT J	LTC	O-0184476	0648	3
BROWN MORRIS P	MAJ	O-0205227	1045	2
BROWN NEELY R	LTC	O-1185838	0264	1
BROWN NOEL C	COL	O-0351697	1161	1
BROWN NORMAN C	COL	O-0280302	0657	3
BROWN NORMAN F	LTC	O-1286956	1060	1
BROWN OSBORN H	CPT	O-0477489	1158	1
BROWN OSCAR R	LTC	O-1533019	0857	1
BROWN PAUL C	LTC	O-0450014	0255	1
BROWN PAUL F	LTC	O-0265795	0863	3
BROWN PAUL G	CW2	W-2205280	1056	2
BROWN PAUL R	2LT	O-0228324	0366	3
BROWN PHILIP G	COL	O-0344790	0361	1
BROWN PHILIP H	LTC	O-1001959	0862	1
BROWN QUINTON E	CW3	W-2147041	1266	1
BROWN RALPH	CPT	O-1289000	1045	2
BROWN RALPH C	LTC	O-0264974	0865	3
BROWN RALPH E	LTC	O-0268135	0355	3
BROWN RAY A	CPT	O-0507953	0446	1
BROWN RAYFORD F	CPT	O-1185383	0758	1
BROWN RAYMOND A.	COL	O-0177181	0648	3
BROWN RAYMOND D	MAJ	O-2017501	0858	1
BROWN RAYMOND J	COL	O-0265647	1266	3
BROWN RAYMOND W	MAJ	O-1013834	1263	1
BROWN REMBERT H	CW3	W-2150879	0663	1
BROWN RICHARD C	1LT	O-1285701	1045	1
BROWN RICHARD E	LTC	O-0329429	0163	1
BROWN RICHARD E	LTC	O-1320819	1165	1
BROWN RICHARD G	MAJ	O-1110959	0251	1
BROWN RICHARD G	CPT	O-1919234	0363	1
BROWN RICHARD L	1LT	O-1169875	1045	1
BROWN RICHARD P	MAJ	O-1321320	0363	1
BROWN RICHARD T	MAJ	O-0439632	0446	1
BROWN RICHARD W	LTC	O-1175391	0163	1
BROWN ROBERT A	1LT	O-0796075	1052	2
BROWN ROBERT B	CPT	O-0971826	0363	2
BROWN ROBERT C	COL	O-0234765	0558	3
BROWN ROBERT E	1LT	O-0148950	0363	3
BROWN ROBERT E	COL	O-0247461	0364	3
BROWN ROBERT E	LTC	O-1016677	0865	1
BROWN ROBERT E	CW2	W-2147319	1160	1
BROWN ROBERT F	LTC	O-1052274	0267	1
BROWN ROBERT H	LTC	O-1186565	0466	1
BROWN ROBERT J	2LT	O-1584107	1144	2
BROWN ROBERT L	MAJ	O-1342235	1166	2
BROWN ROBERT M	LTC	O-0413249	0861	1
BROWN ROBERT N	MAJ	O-1651580	0963	1
BROWN ROBERT O	MAJ	O-1882290	1067	1
BROWN ROBERT W	COL	O-0274312	0760	1
BROWN ROSEN T	1LT	O-1913512	0337	1
BROWN ROSS E	LTC	O-0144065	0457	3
BROWN ROSS G	LTC	O-1010604	0663	1
BROWN ROWLAND S	COL	O-0144834	0746	2
BROWN ROY	MAJ	O-0472324	0148	1
BROWN ROY C	MAJ	O-1120000	0664	1
BROWN ROY C	CPT	O-1285185	0946	2
BROWN ROY D	LTC	O-0183877	0948	3
BROWN ROY F	2LT	O-2016347	1047	1
BROWN ROY F	LTC	O-1305537	0962	1
BROWN ROY W	1LT	O-1754786	0847	2
BROWN ROYAL L	MAJ	O-0466340	1047	2
BROWN RUTH M	1LT	N-0776212	1145	1
BROWN SAMUEL	MAJ	O-1011353	1161	2
BROWN SAMUEL C	MAJ	O-0200059	1059	3
BROWN SAMUEL S	CPT	O-0916274	0845	2
BROWN SANFORD R	LTC	O-0185920	0355	3

NAME	GRADE	SVC NO	DATE RET MO YR	RET CODE
BROWN SARA M	MAJ	N-0765370	0465	1
BROWN SCRIBNER J	MAJ	C-1339041	1165	1
BROWN SHELDON	1LT	C-0385144	0845	2
BROWN SIDNEY S	1LT	0-1585218	0460	1
BROWN SILAS D	MAJ	C-1919050	0964	1
BROWN SIMON	2LT	0-1324502	C545	2
BROWN SPENCER A	LTC	0-0282870	0163	3
BROWN SR CARL H	MAJ	C-1080604	C561	1
BROWN STANLEY B	CPT	0-0395041	0560	1
BROWN STANLEY G	1LT	0-1289038	C445	2
BROWN STANLEY J	CPT	0-0499612	0156	1
BROWN STEPHEN L	LTC	0-1168583	0962	1
BROWN STEWART S	MAJ	C-0270431	C767	3
BROWN STUART D	COL	0-0207717	0755	3
BROWN THELMA A	CPT	N-0905027	C560	2
BROWN THEODORE D	CW3	W-2103914	C855	1
BROWN THEODORE R	CPT	0-0253103	0647	2
BROWN THOMAS	CPT	0-0485800	1047	1
BROWN THOMAS A	LTC	0-0239327	C657	1
BROWN THOMAS E	LTC	0-1054953	C166	1
BROWN THOMAS G	LTC	0-0918662	C346	2
BROWN THOMAS H	1LT	0-0378517	C245	2
BROWN THOMAS L	LTC	0-0232623	C360	3
BROWN THOMAS L	MAJ	C-2036045	C461	1
BROWN THOMAS M	LTC	0-0789896	0158	3
BROWN THOMAS M	LTC	C-1640270	1162	1
BROWN THOMAS M	MAJ	0-1640271	1160	1
BROWN THOMAS M	CW2	RW-2152429	C358	1
BROWN THOMAS R	LTC	0-0267634	0362	3
BROWN THURSTON D	MAJ	C-0192372	1162	3
BROWN VERNER O	COL	C-0351955	C267	3
BROWN VERNON M	LTC	0-0401752	0161	1
BROWN VERNON R	MAJ	0-0486077	C356	1
BROWN VERNON S	LTC	0-0256832	1064	3
BROWN VICTOR C	2LT	0-2035520	1044	2
BROWN VIVIAN C	MAJ	C-1051887	0157	1
BROWN WALKER T	MAJ	C-0372320	0867	3
BROWN WALTER C	COL	C-0250589	C567	3
BROWN WALTER E	MAJ	C-1541762	C557	1
BROWN WALTER J	MAJ	C-1636453	C956	1
BROWN WALTER L	LTC	0-0378511	0967	3
BROWN WARREN R	LTC	0-0299745	1051	1
BROWN WASHINGTON	LTC	0-0354220	0467	3
BROWN WENDELL W	LTC	C-0268533	C264	3
BROWN WILBUR A	CPT	0-1183029	C861	1
BROWN WILFRED S	CPT	0-0356045	C467	1
BROWN WILLARD H	MAJ	0-1170296	0761	1
BROWN WILLARD J	MAJ	0-0121139	C-52	3
BROWN WILLIAM A	COL	0-0124053	C355	3
BROWN WILLIAM A	LTC	0-1797428	1065	2
BROWN WILLIAM C	2LT	0-1799936	C754	2
BROWN WILLIAM F	MAJ	C-0164427	0346	1
BROWN WILLIAM F	MAJ	0-1281088	0354	2
BROWN WILLIAM F	LTC	0-1060023	0363	1
BROWN WILLIAM G	MAJ	0-1166918	C258	1
BROWN WILLIAM H	MAJ	C-0156249	1042	2
BROWN WILLIAM H	LTC	0-0199550	1160	3
BROWN WILLIAM H	CPT	0-1050180	0467	1
BROWN WILLIAM H	1LT	0-2005667	1045	2
BROWN WILLIAM H	MAJ	0-2206113	C363	2
BROWN WILLIAM H	CW3	W-2142120	0664	1
BROWN WILLIAM H	CW3	W-2209648	1067	1
BROWN WILLIAM J	COL	C-0253838	0265	3
BROWN WILLIAM J	MAJ	C-1637496	0163	1
BROWN WILLIAM L	WO1	W-2135097	C756	1
BROWN WILLIAM L	CW2	W-2206961	0661	1
BROWN WILLIAM M	LTC	0-1288000	0856	1
BROWN WILLIAM N	LTC	0-0290332	C465	1
BROWN WILLIAM S	LTC	0-1583990	C161	1
BROWN WILLIAM T	COL	0-0291245	C555	1
BROWN WINSTON W	CW2	W-2143700	0657	1
BROWN WOODROW W	MAJ	0-1180132	C664	1
BROWNBACK RUSSELL J	CPT	0-0146735	1053	3
BROWNCHWEIG SIDNEY R	MAJ	C-1634566	1154	2
BROWNE ARTHUR S	MAJ	0-0126232	0156	3

NAME	GRADE	SVC NO	DATE RET MO YR	RET CODE
BROWNE CARTER E	MAJ	0-1341504	0266	1
BROWNE GEORGE W	MAJ	0-0162506	0359	1
BROWNE HAROLD L	1LT	0-0498522	1045	2
BROWNE JOHN F	1LT	0-1703808	0645	2
BROWNE JOSEPH S	CPT	0-1917690	0162	1
BROWNE JR ROBERT E	MAJ	0-0150006	0956	3
BROWNE NORMAN E	LTC	0-1297670	0561	1
BROWNE RANDOLPH M	LTC	0-0301156	0661	1
BROWNE RICHARD E	1LT	0-1291943	0950	1
BROWNE RICHARD H	CPT	0-0184583	0154	3
BROWNE ROBERT W	LTC	0-1547552	1067	1
BROWNE THOMAS P	MAJ	0-0134379	0649	3
BROWNE THOMAS P	COL	0-0253097	0866	3
BROWNE THOMAS W	1LT	0-1035678	0644	2
BROWNE WILFRED P	MAJ	C-0188726	0252	3
BROWNE WILLIAM C	COL	0-0144123	0648	3
BROWNE WILLIAM F	1LT	0-1104530	0645	2
BROWNE WILLIAM F	1LT	0-1634567	C944	2
BROWNE WILLIAM G	LTC	0-0132029	0648	3
BROWNE WILLIAM H	COL	0-0253877	0247	1
BROWNELL ALBERT W	2LT	0-1325198	0745	2
BROWNELL EDWARD F	LTC	0-0217598	0460	3
BROWNELL GEORGE R	LTC	0-0215323	0160	3
BROWNELL HAROLD C	COL	0-0195219	0660	3
BROWNELL PAUL G	MAJ	0-0359107	0545	2
BROWNELL RALPH F	CW2	W-2214903	1167	1
BROWNELL VINCENT F	LTC	0-1103081	0865	1
BROWNELLER KENNETH E	LTC	0-1294476	1160	1
BROWNEWELL THELMA L	1LT	N-0728703	0447	1
BROWNFIELD BAYNE S	LTC	0-1058202	0167	1
BROWNFIELD JR A D	CPT	0-0462444	0247	2
BROWNFIELD STEPHON	2LT	N-0729968	1045	1
BROWNING ANTHONY	CPT	0-0209844	0146	2
BROWNING CECIL D	1LT	0-0352093	0644	2
BROWNING CLARENCE F	1LT	0-1305005	0756	2
BROWNING CLIFFORD F	LTC	0-0342456	0251	1
BROWNING CLIFTON M	CPT	0-0385158	0749	1
BROWNING FLOYD C	MAJ	0-1297671	0367	1
BROWNING FLOYD H	COL	0-0230483	0553	1
BROWNING FRANK W	COL	0-0150008	1057	3
BROWNING HERBERT H	MAJ	C-0972800	1057	1
BROWNING HOMER F	LTC	0-0279252	1046	3
BROWNING JAMES L	CPT	0-0468014	0943	2
BROWNING JOHN J	CPT	0-1305538	0847	2
BROWNING JOHN R	COL	0-0235533	1165	3
BROWNING JOHN W	MAJ	0-1635635	C561	1
BROWNING LOHA R	MAJ	N-0769666	1065	2
BROWNING LUTHER R	MAJ	0-0972508	1163	1
BROWNING MARTIN	LTC	0-1284819	0757	1
BROWNING ROLAND S	CPT	0-0473027	1045	2
BROWNING SAMUEL S	MAJ	0-1171469	0661	1
BROWNING WILLIAM L	COL	0-0233937	0965	3
BROWNLEE HENRY	1LT	0-1179314	1044	2
BROWNLEE JOHN H	1LT	0-0374136	0943	2
BROWNLEE JOHN H	MAJ	0-1104531	1055	1
BROWNLEE RICHARD H	1LT	0-1310566	0447	2
BROWNLEE WILLIAM J	LTC	0-1180133	0862	1
BROWNLOW JAMES C	LTC	0-1645042	0365	2
BROWNRIDGE GEORGE W	LTC	0-0305915	0865	3
BROWNSCOMBE TWILAR	CPT	N-0761278	0846	1
BROWNYER BURT W	MAJ	0-1637104	0466	1
BROXTON GEORGE F	CW2	W-2149662	0559	1
BROYLES EDWARD S	MAJ	0-0969433	0162	2
BROYLES GILMER P	MAJ	0-1170668	0660	1
BROYLES HENRY F	MAJ	0-0215559	0862	3
BROYLES JAMES N	1LT	0-1298656	0146	2
BROYLES LENA L	1LT	N-0733476	0745	1
BRU VIVIAN R	LTC	0-1548366	1066	1
BRUAW EUGENE H	1LT	0-1304496	0257	1
BRUBAKER ERNEST F	LTC	0-0197086	0363	3
BRUBAKER JOSEPH M	CPT	0-0508307	0952	1
BRUBAKER RALPH W	LTC	0-1575796	1061	1
BRUCCCLERI BART	MAJ	0-0969688	0966	1
BRUCE ALBERT W	LTC	0-0217878	0863	3
BRUCE ALFRED O	MAJ	0-2023550	0657	1

NAME	GRADE	SVC NO	DATE RET MO YR	RET CODE
BRUCE BYRON S	COL	0-0102643	C648	3
BRUCE CAROLINE H	LTC	N-0702482	0847	2
BRUCE CHARLES F	LTC	0-0889129	0562	1
BRUCE CLARENCE H	MAJ	0-0376550	0560	1
BRUCE DONALD A	MAJ	C-0346083	1266	3
BRUCE EVERETT C	MAJ	C-0218909	C263	3
BRUCE HAROLD O	LTC	0-1576973	0157	1
BRUCE HENRY A	COL	0-0254856	0661	3
BRUCE JOHN E	LTC	0-0252623	0965	3
BRUCE JOHN M	MAJ	0-0969477	C163	1
BRUCE JOSEPH F	MAJ	C-2036629	0762	1
BRUCE JR THOMAS M	1LT	0-1322517	C545	2
BRUCE JR WESLEY O	MAJ	0-2204152	1065	2
BRUCE MARGARET E	2LT	N-0784356	1044	1
BRUCE PETER P	CPT	0-0338753	C445	2
BRUCE RALPH	WO1	W-2127561	0949	1
BRUCE RICHARD J	MAJ	C-0223027	1046	1
BRUCE ROBERT A	CW2	W-3100262	C764	1
BRUCE ROBERT D	LTC	0-0284589	C864	3
BRUCE ROBERT H	CPT	0-1893894	1061	2
BRUCE ROBERT L	MAJ	C-0959281	0862	1
BRUCE ROBERT S	LTC	0-1293899	C364	1
BRUCE THOMAS E	MAJ	C-1031297	0657	1
BRUCE THOMAS K	MAJ	C-1999850	1061	1
BRUCE WILBUR C	MAJ	0-1020244	C265	1
BRUCE WILLIAM J	LTC	C-1053509	0165	1
BRUCE WILLIAM R	1LT	0-1919227	0367	2
BRUCK CARL R	MAJ	0-0447892	0254	2
BRUCKER HERBERT	MAJ	F-2045272	1160	1
BRUCKNER MAX D	LTC	0-1115199	0763	1
BRUDER MILDRED H	1LT	N-0703976	0246	1
BRUDERER PAUL J	MAJ	0-0482277	0147	2
BRUE LEIF J	LTC	0-0397172	0457	1
BRUE LEO K	MAJ	C-1310803	0259	1
BRUEDIGAM MARVIN J	LTC	0-0287034	0762	1
BRUEGGEMEIER CARL F	LTC	0-0487907	1067	3
BRUEHL GEORGE J	1LT	0-1317754	1046	2
BRUEHL WILLIAM O	MAJ	C-0253534	0566	3
BRUER JOE C	MAJ	C-1936361	0966	1
BRUETT WILLIAM F	LTC	0-0162985	0249	3
BRUFF THOMAS B	MAJ	0-2020388	0762	1
BRUFFEY JR LAWRENCE E	2LT	0-1185265	C545	2
BRUGGEMAN ELMER H	CPT	0-0471644	0663	1
BRUGGER ERNEST J	COL	C-0277103	1154	1
BRUGGERE WILLIAM H	MAJ	0-0130154	0944	2
BRUGH STANLEY G	LTC	0-1169876	C463	1
BRUHN ARTHUR K	CW2	W-2142949	C157	1
BRUHN HERMAN L	LTC	0-1100464	0958	2
BRUHY JAMES R	CPT	C-0966525	1161	1
BRULLE WILLIAM M	LTC	0-0299673	0560	1
BRUMBACK HENRY M	1LT	0-0390317	0742	2
BRUMBAUGH ALOYSISU M	MG	0-0225777	1161	3
BRUMBAUGH DAVID M	MAJ	0-1301938	1060	1
BRUMBAUGH ETHEL M	1LT	N-0761651	0746	1
BRUMBAUGH HARRY C	COL	0-0165468	C649	3
BRUMBAUGH JOHN C	LTC	0-0211544	0847	1
BRUMBERGER ALFRED	LTC	0-0136765	C648	3
BRUMBY PAUL R	MAJ	0-0543568	0546	2
BRUMER RUSSELL L	MAJ	0-2018831	0762	1
BRUMET CHESTER C	CPT	0-2020880	C859	1
BRUMFIELD ARTHUR W	1LT	C-0482422	0466	1
BRUMFIELD DAVID W	CW2	W-2145002	0359	1
BRUMFIELD MELBOURNE	1LT	0-1287299	C946	2
BRUMHALL JOHN H	MAJ	C-0167988	0149	3
BRUML LEONARD F	CPT	0-0339176	0441	2
BRUMLEY PAUL E	MAJ	0-1046027	0163	1
BRUMMITT GEORGE P	CW3	W-2203426	0666	1
BRUNACCI ALFRED W	CPT	0-0262216	0243	2
BRUNACCI GUY J	LTC	0-1114401	C367	1
BRUNDAGE ALBERT E	COL	0-0146674	0-52	3
BRUNDAGE ARTHUR F	CPT	0-0250322	0649	3
BRUNDAGE FRANK C	LTC	0-2048232	0457	1
BRUNDAGE LYLE D	LTC	0-0253026	0763	3
BRUNDICK LEROY	COL	C-0267174	1057	3
BRUNDICK WILLIAM T	COL	0-0245940	0450	3

NAME	GRADE	SVC NO	DATE RET MO YR	RET CODE
BRUNEAU PATRICIA	2LT	N-0784654	0445	1
BRUNELLE LOUIS W	1LT	0-1310056	0253	1
BRUNER CHARLES A	MAJ	C-0501255	1048	1
BRUNER DORSEY W	LTC	0-0357658	0167	3
BRUNER DOYLE B	MAJ	0-0574541	0563	1
BRUNER GEORGE O	COL	0-0375441	0761	1
BRUNER GEORGE E	MAJ	0-1821819	C361	1
BRUNER JULIAN M	LTC	0-0255346	0161	3
BRUNER ROBERT C	MAJ	0-1183668	C460	2
BRUNER SR HUGH H	LTC	0-0356814	1265	3
BRUNET LAWRENCE J	CPT	0-1001739	0357	1
BRUNET PAUL G	CPT	0-0423826	1145	2
BRUNETTE VIOLET L	1LT	N-0786937	1047	1
BRUNETTI VERA W	1LT	N-0760603	1145	1
BRUNEY RAYMOND R	LTC	0-1001961	1061	2
BRUNGER ERNEST G	COL	0-0275925	0960	3
BRUNHAVER GEORGE O	LTC	0-1845883	1064	1
BRUNI UBALD P	CW3	W-2151741	0863	1
BRUNICK MARVIN T	LTC	0-2035574	0161	1
BRUNJES JR MARTIN	CPT	0-1156022	0863	1
BRUNK EUGENE L	LTC	0-0943414	0666	1
BRUNKE HERMAN	LTC	0-0288280	1262	1
BRUNKHURST HENRY G	LTC	0-0267342	0752	3
BRUNKOW ALNDA F	1LT	0-2010695	0847	2
BRUNKOW PAUL H	MAJ	0-1103536	0665	1
BRUNNER FRANK F	LTC	0-0504465	C747	1
BRUNNER JOSEPH A	LTC	0-0292275	1061	1
BRUNNER MICHAEL C	COL	0-0217000	1059	3
BRUNNER ROBERT L	MAJ	0-0266290	0157	3
BRUNNER ROBERT L	1LT	0-0545538	0862	2
BRUNO ANTHONY J	LTC	0-0422217	1057	2
BRUNO HENRY A	MAJ	0-1302922	0762	1
BRUNO JAMES R	1LT	0-1324455	0446	2
BRUNO JOSEPH J	COL	0-0359146	0467	3
BRUNO PAUL W	LTC	0-1292293	0661	1
BRUNO RALPH	1LT	0-1052278	0245	2
BRUNO ROBERT G	LTC	0-0288113	0465	3
BRUNO RUDOLPH	MAJ	0-0373125	0157	1
BRUNOW MARCEL F J	COL	0-0163831	1153	1
BRUNS HENRY	CPT	0-1172779	0761	1
BRUNSON GAIL E	CW2	W-2101483	0947	1
BRUNSON HAROLD F	CW3	W-2152448	1163	1
BRUNSON JR GEORGE W	MAJ	0-0372691	1146	1
BRUNSON JR WADE W	CPT	0-0344115	0646	2
BRUNSON WILLIAM L	1LT	0-0460081	1144	2
BRUNSVOLD KENNEY T	COL	0-0211367	1054	1
BRUNSVOLD RICHARD I	CPT	0-1951580	0157	1
BRUNT ROBERT C	CW2	W-2205149	0561	1
BRUNTON JAMES	1LT	0-1179739	1145	2
BRUNTON LIONEL J	COL	0-0233982	1055	3
BRUSATI ANGELA J	CPT	N-0737001	0346	1
BRUSCHWEIN HAROLD F	CPT	0-0374513	1044	2
BRUSH ALFRED P	CW3	W-2141836	0262	1
BRUSH EDWARD N	LTC	0-0223253	0864	3
BRUSH GEORGE H	CPT	0-0322940	1061	1
BRUSH JR HERBERT S	1LT	0-0383766	0245	2
BRUSH OLIVER G	CPT	0-0196072	0554	3
BRUSH ROBERT J	CPT	0-1593478	0861	2
BRUSH WILLIAM F	CW3	W-2148840	0661	1
BRUSKI EUGENE A	MAJ	0-1185329	0764	1
BRUSSOW KARL W	CW3	W-2142817	0261	1
BRUSTAD MARVIN D	CPT	0-0254816	0846	2
BRUSTKERN VERN J	LTC	0-0332557	1059	3
BRUSTMAN WILLIAM F	LTC	0-1323532	0364	1
BRUTON CARROL T	COL	0-0440653	0747	2
BRUTON JOHN B	1LT	0-0418931	0551	1
BRUTON THOMAS W	COL	0-0213891	1062	3
BRUTON WALTER S	1LT	0-2055419	0454	2
BRYAN ARTHUR H	MAJ	0-0211377	0345	2
BRYAN CLARENCE P	MAJ	0-0275293	C350	1
BRYAN CORVAN S	LTC	0-0250207	0556	1
BRYAN DELBERT L	MAJ	0-0708642	0663	1
BRYAN EDWARD C	CPT	0-0486552	0646	2
BRYAN EUGENE R	CW3	W-2152799	0463	1
BRYAN FLOYD R	COL	0-0168137	1060	3

NAME	GRADE	SVC NO	DATE RET MO YR	RET CODE
BRYAN FRANK D	LTC	0-1584110	0767	1
BRYAN GORDON H	1LT	0-1310397	0646	2
BRYAN H ROSS	LTC	0-0309566	0961	1
BRYAN HARRISON R	LTC	0-0189588	0256	3
BRYAN JAMES W	CPT	0-2212036	0960	1
BRYAN JOHN C	MAJ	0-0499627	0157	1
BRYAN JOHN W	LTC	0-0308745	1163	3
BRYAN JOHN W	MAJ	0-1297155	0361	1
BRYAN JOSEPH O	LTC	0-0100866	0758	3
BRYAN JR DAVID C	1LT	0-0460082	0845	2
BRYAN JR EDWIN F	LTC	0-0235071	0758	3
BRYAN JR ROBERT L	CPT	0-1012311	1047	2
BRYAN JULIUS C	LTC	0-0279971	1151	1
BRYAN JUNIOR L	CW2	W-2152599	0161	1
BRYAN LESTER W	COL	0-0324378	0855	3
BRYAN LUCRETIA M	CPT	N-0704009	0761	1
BRYAN PINK E	CPT	0-0490415	1047	1
BRYAN ROBERT C	2LT	0-1103083	0745	2
BRYAN ROBERT E	MAJ	0-0386402	0653	1
BRYAN WILBUR F	COL	0-0279055	0665	3
BRYAN WILLIE E	LTC	0-0368240	0661	1
BRYANT ALFRED A	COL	0-0164989	1061	3
BRYANT ANDREW T	1LT	0-0990317	1047	1
BRYANT BARNARD M	CW3	W-2144157	0363	1
BRYANT CARROLL M	2LT	0-1018505	1044	2
BRYANT CHARLES G	CPT	0-1685255	0945	2
BRYANT CHARLES J	LTC	0-0282585	1067	3
BRYANT CLARENCE M	LTC	0-1322530	0241	1
BRYANT EARL R	LTC	0-0262508	0360	3
BRYANT EDGAR M	CW2	W-2142094	0355	1
BRYANT ELVIN J	MAJ	0-1543101	0463	1
BRYANT EVERETT C	1LT	0-1291774	0346	2
BRYANT GEORGE C	LTC	0-1293540	0461	1
BRYANT GEORGE W	MAJ	0-1951678	0962	1
BRYANT GORDON L	MAJ	0-0259360	0267	3
BRYANT GUY C	CW4	W-2115467	1262	1
BRYANT HARRY E	MAJ	0-0176932	1040	1
BRYANT HERBERT F	MAJ	0-0441951	0157	1
BRYANT HERBERT L	LTC	0-1324750	0263	1
BRYANT JAMES A	COL	0-0337654	1062	3
BRYANT JOAN N	1LT	N-0789820	0946	1
BRYANT JOHN L	MAJ	0-0966561	0862	1
BRYANT JOHN M	MAJ	0-0486247	1147	1
BRYANT JR NILES	COL	0-0144227	0653	3
BRYANT JR PINKEY A	CW3	W-2152062	0464	1
BRYANT KENNETH A	LTC	0-0367229	1046	1
BRYANT LEON S	MAJ	0-0152811	0349	3
BRYANT LESLIE L	COL	0-0348218	0954	2
BRYANT MALCOLM M	MAJ	0-0243191	0759	1
BRYANT MARION G	1LT	0-1581564	0445	2
BRYANT MARK F	LTC	0-0307291	0264	3
BRYANT MAURICE E	CPT	0-1702353	0344	2
BRYANT OLNEY H	1LT	0-0274813	1054	3
BRYANT PHINEAS R	1LT	0-0212556	0863	3
BRYANT RICHARD H	MAJ	0-0390491	0246	2
BRYANT ROGER O	CW3	W-2151854	0464	1
BRYANT RUSSELL A	MAJ	0-0258131	0666	3
BRYANT SAMUEL P	LTC	0-0347733	0860	1
BRYANT SIDNEY H	MAJ	0-1922523	0455	1
BRYANT SR WILLIAM J	CW3	W-2152032	0263	1
BRYANT THOMAS D	LTC	0-1109833	0457	2
BRYANT THOMAS F	1LT	0-1110974	0345	2
BRYANT THOMAS P	MAJ	0-1643066	0765	1
BRYANT VICTOR W	LTC	0-0277242	0167	3
BRYANT VIRGIL O	COL	0-1575800	0761	1
BRYANT WALTER T	MAJ	0-1305006	0354	2
BRYANT WELCH C	LTC	0-1031869	1161	1
BRYANT WILLARD A	MAJ	0-0501508	0953	1
BRYANT WILLIAM C	MAJ	0-0296050	0746	2
BRYANT WILLIAM C	CPT	0-0361786	0945	2
BRYANT WILLIAM C	CW3	W-2211084	0666	1
BRYANT WOODROW W	LTC	0-0316280	1053	2
BRYCE CHARLES H	MAJ	0-1917739	0864	1
BRYCE HAROLD F	CW4	W-2003367	1163	3
BRYCE HUGH W	MAJ	0-1896044	0851	1

NAME	GRADE	SVC NO	DATE RET MO YR	RET CODE
BRYCE JAMES	1LT	0-1298990	0545	2
BRYDAHL IRVING L	1LT	0-1649680	0346	2
BRYER BENJAMIN F	LTC	0-0356581	0646	2
BRYGIDYR JULIAN	CPT	0-1080179	0465	1
BRYHN CORNELL R	LTC	0-1287831	0261	1
BRYLA ADAM F	1LT	0-1317484	0747	1
BRYLA JOHN A	CPT	0-1544990	0358	1
BRYLA JOSEPH J	MAJ	0-1691384	0846	2
BRYLES MURPHY C	CW4	W-2132757	0761	1
BRYMER THOMAS H	CPT	0-1104798	1060	1
BRYNER LEON K	LTC	0-0368662	0766	3
BRYNIARSKI ALBERT J	CW2	W-2142818	1054	1
BRYSON JESSE D	CW4	W-2115889	0659	1
BRYSON JOHN V	CPT	0-0301974	0446	2
BRYSON JR WILLIAM J	LTC	0-0217409	0763	1
BRYSON LEO A	MAJ	0-0210274	0454	3
BRYSON RICHARD C	LTC	0-0399628	1060	2
BRYSON WILLIAM F	2LT	0-1018541	0545	2
BRZEZINSKI STANLEY R	1LT	0-0491640	0157	1
BSTANDIG PAUL J	LTC	0-2045487	1262	1
BUBA RAYMOND W	CW2	W-2142370	0357	1
BUBB RICHARD F	MAJ	0-1169442	0361	2
BUBLITZ KATHERINE	CPT	N-0751288	0646	1
BUBOLZ DANFORD J	1LT	0-1013249	0146	2
BUCALCY SIMON P	2LT	0-1896663	1055	1
BUCCIARELLI JOSEPH	CW3	W-2147150	0865	1
BUCCIARELLI TONY	1LT	0-0483687	0444	1
BUCEK CHESTER A	1LT	0-1013635	0645	1
BUCEK ROY F	1LT	0-0465333	1145	2
BUCH JOHN E	LTC	0-0150026	0751	3
BUCHAN HENRY W	MAJ	0-1167760	0861	1
BUCHAN WILLIAM R	1LT	0-1104066	1144	2
BUCHANAN ALFRED K	COL	0-0303753	0263	1
BUCHANAN BILLY C	MAJ	0-1685685	0165	1
BUCHANAN CHARLES W	CPT	0-0431094	0246	2
BUCHANAN DURANT T	CPT	0-1580695	0760	1
BUCHANAN ELIC L	CW2	W-2207535	1262	2
BUCHANAN ELMER R	MAJ	0-2035070	1065	1
BUCHANAN FELIX G	LTC	0-2043027	1266	1
BUCHANAN FRANCIS J	CPT	0-1295505	0647	2
BUCHANAN FRANKLIN R	MAJ	0-0505877	0351	1
BUCHANAN GENE W	MAJ	0-0453265	0361	1
BUCHANAN GEORGE W	LTC	0-0205422	0762	3
BUCHANAN GRAHAM C	COL	0-0216735	1262	3
BUCHANAN HALL	MAJ	0-0265781	0656	3
BUCHANAN HENRY O	LTC	0-0255537	0648	3
BUCHANAN HERBERT S	MAJ	0-1647240	0858	1
BUCHANAN HERBERT T	COL	0-0923158	0266	3
BUCHANAN HEYDON W	COL	0-0321472	0952	2
BUCHANAN JACK W	2LT	0-2045488	1044	2
BUCHANAN JAMES P	COL	0-0146715	0254	2
BUCHANAN JESSE F	LTC	0-0236373	0564	3
BUCHANAN JOHN C	LTC	0-1018728	0265	1
BUCHANAN JR FRANK R	COL	0-1584111	1264	1
BUCHANAN JR JAMES A	MAJ	0-0174404	1056	3
BUCHANAN JR W G	MAJ	0-0327505	0946	2
BUCHANAN LEIL	LTC	0-0243545	0566	3
BUCHANAN LESLIE	LTC	0-0326185	0647	2
BUCHANAN PAUL H	CPT	0-1324104	1047	1
BUCHANAN ROBERT C	LTC	0-2200532	1167	1
BUCHANAN ROBERT W	MAJ	0-0551565	0366	1
BUCHANAN ROY	MAJ	0-1591025	0557	1
BUCHANAN SAMMY W	2LT	0-1129746	0344	2
BUCHANAN SPENCER J	MAJ	0-0231626	0463	3
BUCHANAN VIVA G	MAJ	N-0775743	1163	1
BUCHBINDER MURRAY W	COL	0-0290868	0665	3
BUCHEN BAYARD K	2LT	0-1797947	0145	2
BUCHER LEE	MAJ	0-0945731	0567	3
BUCHER WALTER J	CPT	0-0240020	0545	2
BUCHHOLZ JAMES W	MAJ	0-1922595	0963	1
BUCHHOLZ MILTON F	MAJ	0-1556983	0459	2
BUCHHOLZ OSCAR T	LTC	0-1283904	0165	1
BUCHHOLZ RICHARD H	MAJ	0-1824570	0861	1
BUCHHOLZ RICHARD S	LTC	0-1644495	0859	1
BUCHHOLZ WILLIAM F	LTC	0-0734726	0465	3

NAME	GRADE	SVC NO	DATE RET MO YR	RET CODE
BUCHHOLZ WILLIAM F	1LT	0-1285892	0845	1
BUCHLER LLOYD G	COL	0-0247169	0167	3
BUCHMAN ROBERT A	MAJ	0-1019784	0765	1
BUCHNER RICHARD E	1LT	0-0246189	1043	2
BUCHNER RICHARD J	1LT	0-0337364	0645	2
BUCHSBAUM IRWIN	CPT	0-0330733	0444	2
BUCHSBAUM JOHN H	LTC	0-0583087	1063	2
BUCK BURTON H	CW2	W-2214592	0767	1
BUCK CAMELLUS W	MAJ	0-0988908	0865	1
BUCK CHARLES	1LT	0-1914093	0530	1
BUCK DONALD G	2LT	0-1052696	0944	2
BUCK EDWARD M	CW4	W-2149183	1264	1
BUCK FREDERIC C	LTC	0-1534224	0161	1
BUCK FREDERICK	MAJ	0-2009553	0156	1
BUCK GEORGE A	LTC	0-0461237	1263	1
BUCK HARPER R	LTC	0-0305890	1165	3
BUCK HENRY G	COL	0-0324089	0453	1
BUCK HOWARD F	LTC	0-0296492	0567	3
BUCK HOWARD H	CW2	W-2106482	0353	1
BUCK JAMES C	MAJ	0-1298815	1158	2
BUCK JAMES D	LTC	0-1175657	0662	1
BUCK JAMES H	LTC	0-1646274	0562	1
BUCK JOHN O	COL	0-0179291	0648	3
BUCK JOHN S	LTC	0-0253930	0857	3
BUCK JR EARLE H	MAJ	0-1326453	0765	1
BUCK JR GEORGE L	LTC	0-0368144	1147	2
BUCK JR HIRAM H	LTC	0-1533506	0864	1
BUCK KEITH O	MAJ	0-0461873	0662	1
BUCK MARSHALL G	COL	0-0309188	0357	3
BUCK MICHAEL M	CPT	0-1315905	0747	2
BUCK ORLAND D	LTC	0-0305000	1160	1
BUCK REER A	LTC	0-2055826	1160	1
BUCK SAMUEL L	LTC	0-0443859	0154	1
BUCK SHELBURNE	LTC	0-0405755	0465	3
BUCK THOMAS E	LTC	0-1692931	1263	1
BUCK WERNER	CPT	0-1316876	0847	1
BUCK WILLIAM E	1LT	0-0164367	0938	1
BUCK WILLIAM G	1LT	0-5505313	0662	2
BUCKALEW JAY R	CW3	W-2147885	0662	1
BUCKBEE CLIFFORD R	LTC	0-0324772	1262	1
BUCKHALT H J	CW2	W-3150174	0962	2
BUCKHAULTS JULIUS F	CW3	W-2108570	0960	1
BUCKHOLT BENNETT A	CW4	W-2144252	0366	1
BUCKHOLTS WALTER H	COL	0-0264271	1163	3
BUCKHOLTZ IRA E	LTC	0-0319193	0666	3
BUCKHOUT EGBERT C	MAJ	0-0793056	0967	1
BUCKINGHAM CHARLES H	LTC	0-0347243	0466	3
BUCKINGHAM CHARLES W	MAJ	0-0195301	0155	3
BUCKINGHAM EDWARD B	LTC	0-0484748	0363	1
BUCKIUS WILLIAM H	LTC	0-1330150	1266	1
BUCKLAND CHARLES C	COL	0-0487981	0554	1
BUCKLAND FLOYD H	LTC	0-0298179	0765	3
BUCKLAND FREDERICK	1LT	0-0532268	0247	2
BUCKLAND JAMES A	MAJ	0-2040861	0261	1
BUCKLER GEORGE F	CPT	0-1594011	0447	2
BUCKLES HARRY A	2LT	0-1012490	1144	2
BUCKLES LOUIS M	CPT	0-1019462	1056	1
BUCKLES PAUL H	LTC	0-0231504	0856	3
BUCKLES ROSCOE C	COL	0-0390668	0860	1
BUCKLEY ANTHONY	CW2	W-2150924	0662	1
BUCKLEY ARNOLD F	LTC	0-1300447	0262	1
BUCKLEY ARTHUR F	LTC	0-0377843	0963	1
BUCKLEY CHARLES A	MAJ	0-0502787	0954	1
BUCKLEY CHARLES C	COL	0-0319496	0267	3
BUCKLEY CHARLES H	MAJ	0-1169879	0960	1
BUCKLEY EARL E	CPT	0-0411421	0949	2
BUCKLEY EDWARD M	1LT	0-1062473	0462	2
BUCKLEY FRANCIS X	LTC	0-1101758	1062	2
BUCKLEY FREEMAN E	LTC	0-0250966	0563	3
BUCKLEY GERALD T	LTC	0-2012566	1167	1
BUCKLEY HELEN F	CPT	N-0722698	0446	1
BUCKLEY HOWARD	CW3	W-2150601	0163	1
BUCKLEY JACK C	CPT	0-2025480	0258	1
BUCKLEY JACK E	LTC	0-0170302	0658	3
BUCKLEY JOHN J	LTC	0-0324481	0164	3

NAME	GRADE	SVC NO	DATE RET MO YR	RET CODE
BUCKLEY JOHN L	LTC	0-1059383	0366	1
BUCKLEY JONATHAN F	LTC	0-1579441	0761	1
BUCKLEY LOUIS E	MAJ	0-0111422	0746	2
BUCKLEY PATRICK H	COL	0-0507317	0556	2
BUCKLEY ROBERT P	CPT	0-1011411	1045	2
BUCKLEY VERLIN J	CW3	W-2147939	0862	1
BUCKLEY WALTER L	LTC	0-0425616	0866	1
BUCKLEY WILLIAM F	MAJ	0-2037621	1062	1
BUCKLEY WILLIAM H	COL	0-1289204	0566	1
BUCKLIN JOHN W	MAJ	0-0475356	0159	2
BUCKMAN ALEX	MAJ	0-0450249	0758	1
BUCKMAN MORRIS E	1LT	0-0512848	1045	2
BUCKNELL JR ROMEO H	MAJ	0-1330151	0663	1
BUCKNER ARLEY V	CPT	0-0507869	0350	1
BUCKNER CHARLES G	CPT	0-0197938	0557	3
BUCKNER FREDERICK	1LT	0-1314435	0845	2
BUCKNER JESSE J	CW2	W-2213076	0767	1
BUCKNER JR LOUIS D	CW3	W-2145336	0665	1
BUCKNER JR WILLIAM A	LTC	0-2288860	0962	1
BUCKNER LESLIE M	MAJ	0-1693455	1045	2
BUCKNER LEWIS H	CW3	W-2114123	0461	1
BUCKNER LOUIS R	LTC	0-1285374	0165	1
BUCKNER ROBERT C	LTC	0-0255694	0363	3
BUCKNER WILLIS L	MAJ	0-1293198	0355	1
BUCKO JOHN P	CPT	0-1110965	0762	1
BUCKOVINSKY ANDREW T	CPT	0-0890200	0651	1
BUCKSPAN HAROLD	LTC	0-1306970	1163	1
BUCKTHAL ALBERT E	CPT	0-1796414	0346	2
BUCKWALD RUDOLPH A	CPT	0-0306151	0345	2
BUCKWALTER CHARLES K	LTC	0-0415355	1157	1
BUCKWALTER FRANKLIN	LTC	0-1642354	0366	3
BUCKWALTER JOHN B	CW2	W-2114995	0746	1
BUCY JR WILLIAM F	1LT	0-0519356	0747	2
BUCY LAWRENCE W	LTC	0-1642358	1155	1
BUCY ROBERT E	CW2	W-2148898	0359	1
BUCZEK JOHN	LTC	0-1017060	0962	1
BUCZKOWSKI FELIX J	LTC	0-1948869	0264	1
BUCZKOWSKI HARRY E	CPT	0-0510289	0749	1
BUDAHN EDSEL R	COL	0-1166922	0866	1
BUDATZ EARL	LTC	0-1293900	0761	1
BUDD ARTHUR C	MAJ	0-1311351	0367	1
BUDD CECIL G	2LT	0-1181556	0844	2
BUDD CHARLES C	COL	0-0148957	0450	1
BUDD CHARLES W	CW3	W-2154663	1262	1
BUDD RAYMOND F	2LT	0-1594738	0756	3
BUDDEMEYER HOMER J	1LT	0-1106618	0545	2
BUDDENHAGEN JR C G	MAJ	0-1637118	0460	1
BUDDIN CECIL E	CPT	0-1013653	1145	2
BUDERER JR GEORGE L	MAJ	0-0294729	1147	1
BUDGE BRUCE C	LTC	0-0312678	1146	2
BUDLONG THOMAS F	MAJ	0-1650395	0161	1
BUDNER SIMON	LTC	0-0290541	1046	2
BUDNY STANLEY J	CW2	W-2139466	0656	1
BUDNY WALLACE C	2LT	0-1310967	0445	2
BUDWAY EMIL	CW3	W-2152925	1162	1
BUDZ LOUIS R	CPT	0-2000125	0947	1
BUDZIK WALTER H	MAJ	0-0470442	0846	2
BUECHE CLEMENT A	1LT	0-1596597	1045	2
BUECHE FRANK	LTC	0-0259401	0867	3
BUECHLER ARTHUR J	LTC	0-1101349	0566	1
BUECHLER JR JOHN H	LTC	0-0455873	0866	1
BUECHNER FREDERICK	LTC	0-0232425	1045	1
BUEHL JR LOUIS H	LTC	0-0242745	0960	3
BUEHLER CARL W	MAJ	0-0204947	0156	3
BUEHRER KENNETH E	MAJ	0-1922978	0667	1
BUEHRER ROLLAND F	CPT	0-1285704	0246	2
BUELL CHARLOTTE	1LT	N-0726863	1145	1
BUELL FRANCES G	MAJ	L-0402015	0164	3
BUELL RAYMON C	COL	0-0490768	0547	2
BUELL VERNON C	MAJ	0-1289687	1060	1
BUENING BERNARD P	LTC	0-0506236	0-53	1
BUENTELLO JR ANTONIO	CW3	W-2144858	0666	1
BUERGE MYRON W	MAJ	0-1105291	0867	3
BUERGER OTTO H	MAJ	0-0199441	1058	3
BUERKE JAMES L	WO1	W-2112227	0553	1

NAME	GRADE	SVC NO	DATE RET MO YR	RET CODE
BUERKI WILLIAM C	MAJ	O-0508649	0764	1
BUERKLE JOHN G	COL	O-0242058	0852	3
BUETTELL ERNEST D	LTC	O-0152986	0651	3
BUETTNER HENRY F	COL	O-0221734	0347	2
BUEZO SALOMON	MAJ	O-0291236	0462	3
BUFANO JAMES T	LTC	O-2019982	0267	1
BUFFALANO FRANK A	LTC	O-1044770	1161	1
BUFFINGTON DALE W	MAJ	O-0992921	0867	1
BUFFINGTON FRANCIS S	CPT	O-0368684	1044	1
BUFFINGTON JOHN F	CPT	O-0130521	0644	1
BUFFINGTON JR C R	MAJ	O-1542590	0460	1
BUFFINGTON RALPH M	LTC	O-0252076	0367	3
BUFFINGTON THOMAS T	LTC	O-1168587	0166	3
BUFFKIN JR JOHN F	LTC	O-1286781	0960	1
BUFFO MICHAEL H	LTC	O-0919857	1262	1
BUFFONE JAMES V	CW4	W-2122033	0959	1
BUFFUM WILLIAM R	CW3	W-2152787	0963	1
BUFORD CECIL M	MAJ	O-0476385	0154	1
BUGAY LEE A	1LT	O-1059384	0945	1
BUGBEE JAMES T	COL	O-0251931	0566	3
BUGEL JOSEPH	LTC	O-1289866	1057	1
BUGEL JR JOHN	WO1	W-2123543	1060	1
BUHL BERNICE M	2LT	N-0773812	1045	1
BUHL LEON E	1LT	O-1320821	1144	2
BUHLER ALLEN C	2LT	O-2017346	1145	2
BUHRMAN MAC B	2LT	O-0200945	0246	2
BUIE HERMAN F	2LT	O-1540668	0945	2
BUIE NEIL D	COL	O-0253515	1163	3
BUIE NEILL D	LTC	O-0325027	0361	1
BUIRGE RAYMOND E	CPT	O-0326278	0945	2
BUISCH ARTHUR F	CW2	W-2210732	0663	1
BUJAC JAMES N	LTC	O-0150553	1057	3
BUJNOWSKI ANTHONY	1LT	O-0169076	0859	1
BUKACEK FRANK J	LTC	O-0905754	0363	3
BUKANTZ SAMUEL C	CPT	O-0425807	0146	1
BUKEY NORMAN J	COL	O-0244159	0763	3
BUKOVEC HELEN A	2LT	N-0737595	0645	1
BUKOVITZ STEVE L	LTC	O-0423722	1060	1
BUKOWSKI BARNARD V	1LT	O-1032577	1146	2
BUKOWSKI PHILIP S	2LT	O-0235079	0254	3
BUKSA EDWARD M	MAJ	O-1688465	0463	1
BULAT JOHN	CW4	W-2108885	0959	1
BULAWAN JUSTIN A	CPT	O-2027258	1049	1
BULGER JAMES E	MAJ	O-1822233	0465	3
BULILAN BIENVENIDO	1LT	O-2031860	0766	2
BULL CHARLES B	MAJ	O-0212493	0345	2
BULL DONALD E	MAJ	O-1339043	0764	1
BULL FREDERICK	LTC	O-0272553	0767	3
BULL FREDERICK	CW3	W-2151847	0662	1
BULL HORATIO W	1LT	O-0924437	1145	2
BULL HOWARD F	MAJ	O-0369348	0945	2
BULL NEWTON M	MAJ	O-0253840	0157	3
BULL ROGER L	1LT	O-0460084	0145	2
BULL THERON W	MAJ	O-1587051	0755	1
BULL WILLIAM R	CW4	W-2218218	1160	1
BULL WILLIE M	MAJ	O-0972000	1262	1
BULLA LOUIE L	CPT	O-2005945	1060	1
BULLARD CECIL G	LTC	O-1015321	0864	1
BULLARD CLARENCE P	MAJ	O-1174516	1055	1
BULLARD DAVID E	CPT	O-1642368	1059	1
BULLARD DOROTHY N	1LT	N-0727628	1145	1
BULLARD JR WILLIAM R	LTC	O-0455345	0960	1
BULLARD LEONARD M	CPT	O-1297311	0156	1
BULLARD LUCILE G	1LT	N-0789852	0645	1
BULLARD MERLIN A	LTC	O-1555180	0967	1
BULLARD NORMAN R	CPT	O-0334748	0355	2
BULLARD RAY E	MAJ	O-0330767	0246	2
BULLARD WALTER F	MAJ	O-2020252	1060	1
BULLEN SAMUEL R	MAJ	O-1688612	0663	1
BULLENS RICHARD S	CPT	O-1326203	0847	1
BULLINGTON WILLIAM T	CW3	W-2141208	0360	1
BULLION JAMES P	COL	O-0431349	1064	1
BULLIS HAROLD E	COL	O-0155616	0748	3
BULLIS PERRY D	MAJ	O-2008259	0960	1
BULLMAN BUFORD D	MAJ	O-2010351	0863	1

NAME	GRADE	SVC NO	DATE RET MO YR	RET CODE
BULLOCK BOYD W	LTC	O-0169405	1160	3
BULLOCK CHARLES L	LTC	O-0202723	1055	3
BULLOCK DEAN A	LTC	O-0465245	1162	1
BULLOCK EDWARD D	MAJ	O-1060724	1059	1
BULLOCK EDWARD S	LTC	O-0195384	0162	3
BULLOCK ELMORE C	MAJ	O-0357899	0146	2
BULLOCK GALE V	MAJ	O-1047468	1059	1
BULLOCK HAYWOOD W	MAJ	O-0488436	0358	1
BULLOCK JACK M	1LT	O-1915722	0554	2
BULLOCK JOHN E	LTC	O-0165388		2
BULLOCK JOHN R	CPT	O-1304167	0647	2
BULLOCK JOSEPH P	1LT	O-2055332	0346	2
BULLOCK LOREN J	LTC	O-0942991	1165	1
BULLOCK MARSHALL F	MAJ	O-0503264	1051	1
BULLOCK MARVIN C	CW3	W-2103923	0659	1
BULLOCK ORLINZA A	CW2	W-2153653	0560	1
BULLOCK ROBERT H	CPT	O-1291577	0753	1
BULLS JERALD D	CPT	O-1307191	0860	1
BULLUCK HEBER A	LTC	O-0502688	0656	1
BULMAN GUY	CW3	W-2145792	0263	1
BULMER JOHN C	LTC	O-0450567	0258	1
BUMGARDNER EDGAR	MAJ	O-0471057	0854	1
BUMGARNER FRANK E	LTC	O-0242656	0756	3
BUMGARNER GEORGE W	MAJ	O-1648862	0157	1
BUMGARNER JOHN R	MAJ	O-0381108	1046	1
BUMP SAMUEL C	LTC	O-0333535	0546	2
BUMP WILBUR T	MAJ	O-1324003	0459	1
BUMPAS CHARLES F	CW2	W-2145673	0960	1
BUMPUS ALTA M	1LT	N-0742383	0146	1
BUMSTEAD CHARLES M	LTC	O-1001523	0866	3
BUNCE HOMER T	MAJ	O-0244613	0866	3
BUNCH ALMER	CW4	W-2146438	0766	1
BUNCH CHARLES S	MAJ	O-0215305	0662	3
BUNCH CUEL F	MAJ	O-1999344	0563	1
BUNCH HERMAN L	LTC	O-0290400	0954	1
BUNCH JOHN R	MAJ	O-1186880	0765	1
BUNCH LEONARD	CW3	W-2143386	1263	1
BUNCH LVERNON	CPT	O-0268705	1054	3
BUNCH WILFORD W	CPT	O-0497640	1146	1
BUNCHMAN FLOYD M	1LT	O-0289040	1147	2
BUNDA JOSE	1LT	O-1896553	0762	1
BUNDARA WEJAY S	LTC	O-0361073	0361	1
BUNDICK EDWARD H	MAJ	O-0588997	0467	1
BUNDLIE HAROLD W	CW2	W-2108222	1045	2
BUNOD GEORGE R	CPT	O-1300272	0561	1
BUNDRANT JOHN W	1LT	O-0111366	0648	3
BUNDREN HERMAN R	WO1	W-2107917	0649	1
BUNDRICK HERMAN M	MAJ	O-1011158	1046	1
BUNDY ALMON S	1LT	O-1310216	0446	2
BUNDY GEORGE H	CPT	O-1321096	0146	2
BUNDY JAMES W	CW3	W-2143312	0959	1
BUNDY JOHN W	MAJ	O-0887350	1054	1
BUNDY ROY	LTC	O-2046548	1161	2
BUNGE WERNER E	MAJ	O-0100743	0159	3
BUNIS HENRY J	MAJ	O-1107834	0661	1
BUNKER EVANS C	LTC	O-0312871	0865	3
BUNKER NORMAN F	1LT	O-1016772	0146	2
BUNKER RUSSELL S	COL	O-0235720	0663	3
BUNKER THEODORE	MAJ	O-0188439	0157	3
BUNKER WILLIAM D	MAJ	O-2009682	0658	1
BUNKIN IRVING A	CPT	O-0512302	0145	2
BUNKLEY THOMAS H	CPT	O-1298816	0161	1
BUNN FLOON H	MAJ	O-0963179	0261	2
BUNN FRANK R	MAJ	O-1330264	0959	1
BUNN MARSHALL R	MAJ	O-1821820	0166	1
BUNN SARAH W	MAJ	N-0722210	1165	1
BUNN THOMAS G	MAJ	O-1301750	0557	1
BUNNELL ALBERT C	LTC	O-2036616	0562	1
BUNNELL JR GEORGE G	CW2	W-2211028	1263	1
BUNNELL LEE M	WO1	W-2101497	1047	1
BUNNER CHARLES M	CW3	W-2143551	0662	1
BUNTING LELAND K	1LT	O-1322885	0745	2
BUNTING LOUIS G	CPT	O-0468602	0745	1
BUNTING RICHARD P	CW3	W-2205167	1166	1
BUNTING STONEHAM E	CW3	W-2141518	0960	1

NAME	GRADE	SVC NO	DATE RET MO YR	RET CODE
BUNTING WILLIAM L	LTC	O-0196377	1060	3
BUNTING WILLISTON	MAJ	O-0381900	1045	1
BUNTON GEORGE R	LTC	O-0247955	1166	3
BUNTON HARRY H	LTC	O-1300757	0664	3
BUNTROCK ARNO W	1LT	O-1588463	0547	2
BUNTROCK WALTER F	LTC	O-0285874	0464	3
BUNTS KENNETH R	CW3	W-2208511	0367	1
BUNYAN ROBERT D	LTC	O-0229911	1164	3
BUNYON EDMUND F	COL	O-0244818	1262	3
BURACK PHILIP I	LTC	O-0267968	0660	3
BURANDT HAROLD F	MAJ	O-1102171	0461	1
BURANT ALEXANDER	MAJ	O-0471242	0746	2
BURBA JOSEPH W	COL	O-0245423	0160	3
BURBACH ERWIN E	LTC	O-0315121	1060	1
BURBANK DANIEL J	MAJ	O-1877759	0166	1
BURBANK NATT B	LTC	O-0217957	0164	3
BURBANK PETER	2LT	O-1823260	0845	2
BURBECK ROBERT T	CW4	W-2144380	1060	1
BURBINE THOMAS J	CW2	RW-2148233	1061	1
BURBRIDGE ALBERT D	CW2	W-2141712	0760	1
BURBY NORMAN V	CW2	W-2152337	0765	1
BURCELL ROBERT W	2LT	O-2024226	0945	2
BURCH ALVIN F	LTC	O-0513432	0263	1
BURCH ANDREW J	COL	O-0115128	0660	1
BURCH CHARLES A	1LT	O-0535062	0346	1
BURCH EDWARD H	LTC	O-0235352	0451	1
BURCH FELIX C	CW2	W-2109503	0154	1
BURCH GEORGE L	LTC	O-1114060	0966	3
BURCH JAY C	CPT	O-1335231	0465	1
BURCH JR JOHN A	1LT	O-1994729	0646	2
BURCH LEO L	MAJ	O-1102646	0754	1
BURCH LYMAN Y	LTC	O-0303979	1264	1
BURCH RAYMOND E	1LT	O-1298657	1045	2
BURCH RICHARD E	COL	O-0910869	0962	1
BURCHARD HENRY H	LTC	O-0323800	0960	3
BURCHARD SENECA R	MAJ	O-0469457	1158	2
BURCHARD THOMAS C	CPT	O-0212311	0444	2
BURCHELL ROBERT J	COL	O-0123447	0955	2
BURCHETT GEORGE R	CPT	O-0959471	1160	1
BURCHETT HARRY P	MAJ	O-2012787	0857	1
BURCHFIELD EVALYN G	MAJ	N-0722259	1263	3
BURCIN STEVE	CPT	O-1012843	0846	2
BURCK GEORGE D	CW3	W-2206737	0365	1
BURCKHARD FRANK A	CPT	O-1010292	1264	2
BURCKHARTT VIOLET M	LTC	L-0700111	1262	1
BURD EDWARD D	CPT	O-1324505	0946	2
BURD WILLIAM L	CPT	O-0987188	1060	1
BURDAN JACK H	CW4	W-2119485	1054	1
BURDEN JOHN A	COL	O-0344756	0947	2
BURDEN RUSSELL B	MAJ	O-0503713	0847	1
BURDEN WILLIAM H	LTC	O-0253128	0765	3
BURDESS ROBERT L	MAJ	O-1106027	0562	1
BURDETT JAMES B	CW3	W-2108927	0557	2
BURDETTE CLAUDE M	LTC	O-0261325	0667	3
BURDETTE HAROLD E	LTC	O-1046030	1061	1
BURDETTE JAMES A	CW3	W-2151138	1164	1
BURDETTE LEVI E	CW4	W-2143515	1066	1
BURDIC BURIC L	MAJ	O-0204984	0556	3
BURDICK ARTHUR A	1LT	O-1012180	1045	2
BURDICK FRANCIS D	MAJ	O-0368246	0947	2
BURDICK FREMONT R	LTC	O-0493565	1164	1
BURDICK HARVEY L	1LT	O-1755241	0146	1
BURDICK MARSHAL A	MAJ	O-1688419	0861	1
BURDICK RALPH M	CW4	W-0904405	0558	1
BURDICK RAYMOND R	MAJ	O-0237466	0464	3
BURDICK WALLACE I	2LT	O-1301102	0145	2
BURDIN EDWARD F	LTC	O-0917125	0365	3
BURDISH JOHN R	MAJ	O-1257487	0463	1
BURELBACH ARTHUR L	LTC	O-0264809	0162	1
BUREM HENRY S	CPT	O-0475419	1145	2
BUREN WOLCOTT E	LTC	O-0252274	0159	3
BURESH LUMIR F	CPT	O-0313232	0345	2
BURFETE JAMES A	1LT	O-1255168	0446	2
BURFORD DAVID R	LTC	O-0397832	0862	1
BURFORD JAMES L	MAJ	O-0977582	0962	1

NAME	GRADE	SVC NO	DATE RET MO YR	RET CODE
BURFORD JOHN C	LTC	O-0532491	1063	1
BURFORD OSCAR W	LTC	O-0279238	0561	1
BURG MORRIS H	MAJ	O-1596279	0657	1
BURGAMY RAYMOND E	MAJ	O-1306373	0660	1
BURGAN ATHAL E	MAJ	O-1303102	0159	1
BURGDOFER EVAN	CW2	W-2118285	1046	1
BURGE COLLIN M	CPT	O-0274611	0761	1
BURGE LOUIS C	MAJ	O-1291227	0261	1
BURGE NELSON J	COL	O-0380278	0662	1
BURGE PAUL	COL	O-0266315	0167	3
BURGE WILLIAM R	MAJ	O-1555799	0860	1
BURGER CLARENCE J	CPT	O-1297156	0367	3
BURGER HAROLD	LTC	O-0324041	0446	2
BURGER LAWRENCE J	LTC	O-1080651	0960	1
BURGER LYLE C	MAJ	O-1931525	0566	1
BURGER PAUL S	LTC	O-0451219	0457	1
BURGERT ROBERT R	MAJ	O-1049749	0361	1
BURGES MARVIN J	CW2	W-2149285	1159	1
BURGES PHILIP W	COL	O-0178095	0355	2
BURGESON JOHN C	MAJ	O-0300760	1058	2
BURGESS ALBERT H	2LT	O-1293501	0845	2
BURGESS CHARLES L	1LT	O-0918891	1043	2
BURGESS CLAYTON A	CPT	O-1337134	0756	2
BURGESS CLYDE C	CPT	O-1933927	0166	1
BURGESS EDWARD P	CW3	W-2148841	0467	1
BURGESS FRANK V	CPT	O-0501341	0351	1
BURGESS GEORGE O	1LT	O-1587864	0546	2
BURGESS HARRY C	CW2	W-2005377	0755	2
BURGESS JAMES	LTC	O-0490474	1057	2
BURGESS JAMES G	LTC	O-1055230	0765	1
BURGESS JOHN F	LTC	O-1556097	0263	1
BURGESS JOSEPH G	MAJ	O-1296478	1164	1
BURGESS JOSEPH J	LTC	O-0438734	0964	3
BURGESS JR JAMES R	MAJ	O-1169444	0962	1
BURGESS JR JOHN S	LTC	O-0238400	0264	3
BURGESS JR LUTHER G	MAJ	O-0979140	0665	1
BURGESS LAURENCE E	COL	O-0197235	0361	3
BURGESS NOAH	MAJ	O-0345200	1052	1
BURGESS RAYMOND N	LTC	O-0246285	0745	2
BURGESS RAYMOND R	2LT	O-1055234	0845	2
BURGESS RICHARD F	1LT	O-1104068	0244	2
BURGESS ROBERT A	MAJ	O-1922682	0967	1
BURGESS ROBERT T	MAJ	O-1633719	1162	1
BURGESS ROY E	MAJ	O-0338182	0447	2
BURGESS STANLEY K	LTC	O-0267321	0150	3
BURGESS VIRGIL W	MAJ	O-0366094	0167	3
BURGESS WILBUR H	COL	O-0350773	1060	1
BURGESS WILBUR T	LTC	O-0292873	0667	3
BURGESS WILLIAM F	CPT	O-1031506	1053	1
BURGESS WILLIAM K	LTC	O-1306973	0461	1
BURGESS WILLIAM M	CW2	W-2148496	0862	1
BURGESS WILLIAM O	CW4	W-2103925	0758	1
BURGESS WILLIS M	MAJ	O-2042813	0453	1
BURGETT ELDON J	LTC	O-1635648	0863	1
BURGETT GEORGE M	LTC	O-0322293	1160	1
BURGHARDT WALTER F	MAJ	O-1011166	0557	1
BURGHARDT WILLIAM C	LTC	O-0451912	0164	1
BURGIN JR ASBURY F	LTC	O-1635645	0662	1
BURGLAND FREDERICK	CPT	O-0262080	0743	2
BURGMEIER WILLIAM D	MAJ	O-1554870	1060	1
BURGNER ROBERT W	LTC	O-1167343	1265	1
BURGOON GARREL	LTC	O-0269473	0760	3
BURGOON PAUL L	MAJ	O-1550763	0561	2
BURGOS CANDIDO S	CPT	O-0191335	0648	3
BURGOS ELADIO A	MAJ	O-1301606	0660	1
BURGOS JOSE A	MAJ	O-1329085	0164	1
BURGOS&MACIAS RAFAEL	CPT	O-0155756	1054	3
BURGUSON EDWIN F	LTC	O-0261574	1066	3
BURHANS ROBERT O	COL	O-0345646	0161	1
BURHOE ROBERT D	1LT	O-1047907	0752	1
BURIAN CHARLES M	1LT	O-1181557	0446	2
BURINGRUC WENDELL F	MAJ	O-0563000	0664	1
BURK CLYDE J	LTC	O-0325037	0647	1
BURK E CHARLES	2LT	O-1545582	0844	2
BURK EUGENE C	MAJ	O-1290543	0662	2

NAME	GRADE	SVC NO	DATE RET MO YR	RET CODE
BURK FREAR	MAJ	0-0191773	0660	3
BURK JOSEPH E	CPT	0-0468020	0346	2
BURK LEROY R	LTC	0-0946178	1067	2
BURK PAUL J	CPT	0-0492049	1046	1
BURK THOMAS C	MAJ	0-1846396	0257	3
BURKART RICHARD G	2LT	0-1166449	0844	2
BURKE ALLEN T	LTC	0-0449586	0862	1
BURKE ANDREW J	COL	0-0244860	0764	3
BURKE ARCHIE	MAJ	0-0486001	0854	1
BURKE ARTHUR L	MAJ	0-2025123	0163	1
BURKE AUDREY A	1LT	N-0776819	0946	1
BURKE BARNEY F	MAJ	0-1292470	0266	1
BURKE CHARLES E	CPT	0-0475029	0553	1
BURKE CHARLES M	MAJ	0-1637580	0263	1
BURKE CLARE M	2LT	N-0789565	0545	1
BURKE DONALD	1LT	0-0552034	1145	2
BURKE DONALD F	MAJ	0-2263701	1265	1
BURKE DONALD J	LTC	0-0887943	0867	1
BURKE EDMUND J	CPT	0-2001759	0766	1
BURKE FRED	LTC	0-1291228	0760	1
BURKE GERARD J	MAJ	0-0386722	0762	1
BURKE HAROLD D	LTC	0-0481655	0163	1
BURKE HUGH F	COL	0-0252120	1264	3
BURKE IRENE M	1LT	N-0789011	1045	1
BURKE JACKSON D	LTC	0-0521007	0947	1
BURKE JACOB R	LTC	0-1283205	0160	1
BURKE JAMES A	CPT	0-1578221	1161	2
BURKE JAMES H	MAJ	0-0323403	1047	1
BURKE JAMES L	MAJ	0-1644542	0357	1
BURKE JAMES M	MAJ	0-1325187	0763	2
BURKE JOHN C	LTC	0-0264092	0764	3
BURKE JOHN D	COL	0-0244270	0657	1
BURKE JOHN E	LTC	0-0391811	0660	1
BURKE JOHN J	CW2	W-2144163	1161	2
BURKE JOSEPH F	LTC	0-0346853	0358	2
BURKE JOSEPH H	LTC	0-0290320	0754	1
BURKE JR ANDREW A	MAJ	0-1548665	0554	2
BURKE JR HARRY C	MAJ	0-2017955	0863	1
BURKE JR JAMES C	LTC	0-1315557	0967	1
BURKE MARTYN L	MAJ	0-1031540	0162	1
BURKE MAURICE J	CPT	0-2035623	1059	1
BURKE MAXWELL F	MAJ	0-0254503	0964	3
BURKE MERVYN F	COL	0-0212141	1059	3
BURKE MICHAEL	2LT	0-2008463	0157	1
BURKE PAUL F	CPT	0-0488471	0944	2
BURKE PERCY H	LTC	0-0906602	0764	1
BURKE PHILIP T	MAJ	0-0954337	0963	1
BURKE RALPH E	MAJ	0-2049491	0561	1
BURKE RALPH W	CPT	0-1175935	0547	2
BURKE RAYMOND J	LTC	0-0455954	0756	1
BURKE RICHARD	COL	0-0278691	0867	3
BURKE RICHARD M	LTC	0-2043079	1266	1
BURKE ROBERT J	CW4	W-2129302	0962	1
BURKE ROBERT P	2LT	0-1545502	0645	2
BURKE ROLLAND J	1LT	0-0464469	1045	1
BURKE STERLING C	COL	0-0206532	0961	3
BURKE THOMAS F	COL	0-0282364	1147	2
BURKE THOMAS F	MAJ	0-0969738	1161	1
BURKE THOMAS F	2LT	0-1533511	1043	2
BURKE THOMAS F	CW4	W-2119968	0459	1
BURKE THOMAS J	MAJ	0-0972048	0363	2
BURKE VINCENT H	LTC	0-1584152	1166	1
BURKE WAYNE H	1LT	0-0499506	0955	2
BURKE WILLIAM H	1LT	0-1824713	1045	2
BURKE WILLIAM V	CPT	0-0408043	0146	2
BURKE 3RD JAMES E	CW3	W-2114155	0756	1
BURKENPINE REESE A	CW3	W-2150807	0565	1
BURKERT CLIFFORD R	MAJ	0-1535662	1163	1
BURKERT HARRY J	LTC	0-0518629	0763	3
BURKES ROBERT A	MAJ	0-0300026	1059	2
BURKET JAMES M	MAJ	0-1321486	0161	1
BURKET PHILIP A	COL	0-0276679	1056	2
BURKET RAY S	MAJ	0-0305494	0846	1
BURKETT EVELYN G	2LT	N-0725055	1044	1
BURKETT HAROLD G	LTC	0-0348844	0161	1

NAME	GRADE	SVC NO	DATE RET MO YR	RET CODE
BURKETT JEROME E	MAJ	0-2001061	0263	1
BURKETT RAY W	MAJ	0-1318863	0860	1
BURKGREN MARVIN C	LTC	0-1000526	0961	1
BURKHALTER LEONARD L	CPT	0-0148433	0648	3
BURKHARDT HARRY A	LTC	0-1054198	0967	1
BURKHARDT HENRY S	MAJ	0-0220973	0853	3
BURKHARDT PHYLLIS T	MAJ	L-0200602	0555	2
BURKHART JAMES W	MAJ	0-0328829	0245	2
BURKHART JOHN T	CPT	0-1031791	1048	2
BURKHART JOSEPH H	LTC	0-0382440	1165	3
BURKHART MERLE P	COL	0-0146804	0153	3
BURKHART PEYTON H	1LT	0-1168589	0845	1
BURKHART THOMAS F	MAJ	0-0347240	0957	1
BURKHEAD MERVIN D	LTC	0-1557695	1164	1
BURKHOLDER JAMES A	LTC	0-0237296	1163	3
BURKHOLDER LLOYD A	LTC	0-1324097	1162	1
BURKHOLDER RICHARD D	MAJ	0-1342046	1060	1
BURKHOUSE FRANK X	MAJ	0-1999522	0757	1
BURKITT HENRY P	MAJ	0-0278684	0367	3
BURKITT JOEL L	LTC	0-0217191	1059	3
BURKLAND RICHARD L	MAJ	0-0315392	0744	2
BURKLE RALPH E	CW3	W-2119078	1151	1
BURKLEY JOSEPH A	LTC	0-2056689	0463	1
BURKS BARNEY	CPT	0-1580706	1046	2
BURKS FRANK J	COL	0-0211002	0756	3
BURKS GEORGE S	CPT	0-1290373	0146	1
BURKS JOHN B	WO1	W-2110259	1044	2
BURKS JULIAN	CPT	0-1100897	1046	2
BURKS ROY	LTC	0-0325375	1266	3
BURKS WILLIAM P	LTC	0-0247508	0957	1
BURL HARRY V	MAJ	0-0448334	1046	2
BURLA WILLIAM D	LTC	0-1317367	0363	3
BURLEIGH GEORGE N	COL	0-0325378	0865	3
BURLEIGH JOSEPH P	MAJ	0-1037421	0962	1
BURLESON JOE W	COL	0-0308774	0660	1
BURLESON PERCY L	CW3	W-2146130	0559	1
BURLEY DEXTER V	CW3	W-2145323	0265	2
BURLEY ROBERT D	MAJ	0-0356261	0645	1
BURLING FRANCIS P	CW2	W-2109918	0744	2
BURLINGAME ANSON H	1LT	0-1319719	0944	2
BURLINGAME CHARLES R	LTC	0-0245548	0653	3
BURLINGAME ELLMONT L	LTC	0-1322420	0764	1
BURLINGAME F W	CPT	0-0104357	0849	3
BURLINGAME GARNET J	MAJ	0-0246157	0244	2
BURLINGAME IVAN H	CW2	W-2146357	1154	1
BURMAN CHARLES H	LTC	0-1533978	0860	1
BURMAN JAMES A	MAJ	0-0988069	0864	1
BURMAN JOHN H	COL	0-0406380	0165	1
BURMAN MANNY	MAJ	0-0498417	0147	1
BURMEISTER HARRY K	LTC	0-0895677	0166	3
BURMESTER WILLIAM L	LTC	0-1636565	0760	1
BURNA GEORGE F	LTC	0-0349387	0262	2
BURNAP COURTNEY N	MAJ	0-0975966	0962	1
BURNAUGH CHARLES R	MAJ	0-0498177	0557	1
BURNELL HARRY T	LTC	0-1168195	0963	1
BURNELLE LOWELL E	LTC	0-0308157	0862	3
BURNER JR JACOB D	CPT	0-1701130	0146	2
BURNES JOSEPH A	CPT	0-0498089	1148	1
BURNES RALPH C	LTC	0-1598299	0866	1
BURNETT ALEXANDER	LTC	0-1645063	0263	1
BURNETT ALFRED S	MAJ	0-1286784	0161	1
BURNETT ALMER C	COL	0-0152155	1044	2
BURNETT BERRY H	COL	0-0140626	0648	3
BURNETT CHARLES A	LTC	0-0249127	0167	3
BURNETT CHARLES H	LTC	0-0138878	0548	2
BURNETT CLARENCE F	LTC	0-0304229	0557	1
BURNETT ELDON F	1LT	0-1011893	0157	1
BURNETT FRANCIS G	LTC	0-0250092	0667	3
BURNETT FRANCIS K	LTC	0-0132054	1151	3
BURNETT FRANK L	CW2	W-2151133	0562	1
BURNETT GLYNN N	CW3	W-2148106	0757	1
BURNETT HUGH B	COL	0-0326127	0867	3
BURNETT I D	MAJ	0-1685538	0662	1
BURNETT JAMES E	MAJ	0-2262859	1165	1
BURNETT JAMES E	CW3	W-2206801	1266	1

NAME	GRADE	SVC NO	DATE RET MO YR	RET CODE
BURNETT JOE	MAJ	0-1591622	0655	1
BURNETT JR ASTOR D	CPT	0-1701431	0146	2
BURNETT JR HAL A	LTC	0-1047470	0766	1
BURNETT LEWIS H	MAJ	0-0229675	0663	3
BURNETT MARK L	1LT	0-1017782	0945	1
BURNETT THOMAS C	COL	0-0287439	0458	3
BURNETT THOMAS K	LTC	0-1546783	0266	2
BURNETT THOMAS M	1LT	0-1914019	1043	1
BURNETTE ALBERT F	LTC	0-1174517	1055	1
BURNETTE FRANK D	CPT	0-1055231	1047	1
BURNETTE JAMES D	CPT	0-1844548	1052	2
BURNETTE MARSHALL J	LTC	0-0493619	0856	1
BURNETTE ROY L	CW4	W-2141211	0366	1
BURNETTE TALMADGE L	CPT	0-1283373	0745	1
BURNETTE WILLIAM R	CW4	W-2147053	0664	1
BURNEY WILLIAM E	COL	0-0198304	0953	3
BURNHAM ALAN B	COL	0-0259852	0958	3
BURNHAM ARCHER L	LTC	0-0130910	0648	3
BURNHAM ARTHUR L	LTC	0-0468670	0161	1
BURNHAM CHESTER W	CPT	0-0299212	0545	1
BURNHAM CLYDE R	1LT	0-0395821	0544	2
BURNHAM FRANK J	MAJ	0-1997970	0761	1
BURNHAM HAYNES G	2LT	0-2018287	0346	2
BURNHAM HERBERT W	MAJ	0-0230056	0663	3
BURNHAM JR PHILIP C	CPT	0-0372460	0746	1
BURNHAM JR ROY F	CW3	W-2206306	0966	1
BURNHAM LEE H	COL	0-0364800	0561	1
BURNHAM LEON	LTC	0-0523568	0265	3
BURNHAM PERCY C	LTC	0-0447785	0454	2
BURNIE WILLIAM T	CPT	0-0910579	0646	2
BURNIER AUGUST F	MAJ	0-1315478	1146	2
BURNLEY JAMES D	LTC	0-1104071	0766	1
BURNOTES WALTER A	CPT	0-0481507	0548	1
BURNS ALBERT S	LTC	0-0238643	0365	3
BURNS ARTHUR S	COL	0-0157689	1056	3
BURNS BRENDAN A	MG	0-0188865	0257	3
BURNS BURTON F	MAJ	0-0265947	0258	3
BURNS CHARLES P	LTC	0-0415426	0267	3
BURNS CLAUDE C	CPT	0-0107337	0648	3
BURNS COLEMAN C	CPT	0-0481005	0445	2
BURNS DARNCE B	COL	0-0332393	0954	3
BURNS DELBERT W	1LT	0-1030129	1144	2
BURNS EDGAR M	COL	0-0284342	0267	3
BURNS EDWARD	COL	0-0188634	1054	3
BURNS EDWARD J	MAJ	0-1294973	1060	1
BURNS ELIZABETH	CPT	N-0757093	0755	2
BURNS ELLSWORTH	COL	0-0450810	0167	1
BURNS ELLUS G	MAJ	0-1299987	0860	1
BURNS FELIX J	LTC	0-1643098	1066	1
BURNS FRANCIS H	LTC	0-0470764	0554	1
BURNS FRANK G	LTC	0-0219616	0559	3
BURNS FRANK H	LTC	0-1575809	0264	1
BURNS FRANK R	MAJ	0-0394258	0960	1
BURNS FRED M	COL	0-0442615	1154	1
BURNS GEORGE A	LTC	0-0398852	0457	1
BURNS GEORGE C	MAJ	0-0255131	0758	3
BURNS GERALD E	MAJ	0-1015459	0363	1
BURNS GERALD F	MAJ	0-0985684	0164	1
BURNS HARRY A	LTC	0-0166134	1060	3
BURNS HARRY K	1LT	0-1292122	0745	2
BURNS HUGH J	CPT	0-0481902	0546	2
BURNS JAMES C	LTC	0-0312555	0461	3
BURNS JAMES F	CPT	0-1011627	0946	2
BURNS JAMES J	MAJ	0-0242450	0565	3
BURNS JESSICA D	1LT	N-0726004	0347	2
BURNS JOHN A	LTC	0-1323534	0962	1
BURNS JOHN F	LTC	0-1012433	0565	1
BURNS JOHN J	1LT	0-0417214	1144	2
BURNS JOHN M	CPT	0-1166452	0647	1
BURNS JOHN R	LTC	0-1176273	0762	1
BURNS JOHN W	MAJ	0-2210124	0665	1
BURNS JOSEPH	CPT	0-0343493	0644	2
BURNS JOSEPH E	LTC	0-0306416	0762	1
BURNS JR FREDERICK	CPT	0-0269275	0944	2
BURNS JR MATTHEW A	1LT	0-1319720	1045	2

NAME	GRADE	SVC NO	DATE RET MO YR	RET CODE
BURNS JR ROBERT J	LTC	0-1645072	0764	1
BURNS JR THOMAS M	2LT	0-1295661	1044	2
BURNS JR WALTER W	1LT	0-0464630	0845	2
BURNS KELCIE H	CW2	W-2148908	1060	1
BURNS KENNETH B	LTC	0-0168293	1158	1
BURNS LAURENCE W	CPT	0-0338116	0544	2
BURNS LAWRENCE B	1LT	0-1286785	1145	2
BURNS LEE H	LTC	0-0447209	0862	1
BURNS LEATHO	CPT	0-1288930	0447	2
BURNS MARSDON S	LTC	0-0475717	0267	3
BURNS MARVIN P	CPT	0-0200047	0756	1
BURNS MARY A	1LT	N-0724023	0246	1
BURNS NELSON G	LTC	0-0916685	1047	2
BURNS NEWTON W	CPT	0-0889221	0956	1
BURNS ORAN F	COL	0-0354709	0966	1
BURNS PATRICK J	CW2	W-3150551	0567	1
BURNS PAUL J	LTC	0-1107836	0464	1
BURNS RALPH H	MAJ	0-1551582	1062	1
BURNS RAYMOND M	MAJ	0-1297488	1160	1
BURNS ROBERT E	MAJ	0-2017347	0863	1
BURNS ROBERT F	MAJ	0-0193728	1157	3
BURNS ROBERT H	1LT	0-1284647	1145	1
BURNS ROBERT J	CW4	W-2105110	0358	1
BURNS ROBERT M	2LT	0-1056996	1044	2
BURNS ROBERT W	LTC	0-1634579	0859	1
BURNS RUSSELL	LTC	0-0158528	0152	3
BURNS SAMMIE	LTC	0-1574010	0863	1
BURNS SAMUEL S	MAJ	0-1285541	1062	1
BURNS SOPHY M	CPT	N-0700017	0239	1
BURNS TERENCE F	CPT	0-0544199	1145	2
BURNS THOMAS	2LT	0-1913572	0838	1
BURNS THOMAS J	1LT	0-0540641	0546	2
BURNS VERNON P	MAJ	0-0366741	0547	1
BURNS WALTER J	1LT	0-0887401	1046	2
BURNS WILLIAM C	COL	0-0283642	0146	2
BURNS WILLIAM H	CW2	RW-2208375	0463	1
BURNS ZEO H	MAJ	0-0237890	1263	3
BURNSIDE HOWARD W M	2LT	0-0492608	0643	2
BURNSIDE VIRGIL J	CW2	W-2153021	0959	1
BURNSTEIN IRVING M	1LT	0-1994452	0646	2
BURPEE GERALD N	CPT	0-1109839	0961	1
BURPEE HARRY W	MAJ	0-1633723	0557	1
BURPITT JAMES W	LTC	0-0169093	0357	2
BURPO PAUL W	MAJ	0-2047582	0760	1
BURPO ROBERT C	MAJ	0-0965239	0862	1
BURR ALAN C	MAJ	0-1997375	1162	1
BURR ALBERT H	CPT	0-0533666	0746	2
BURR DAVID F	MAJ	0-0130470	0648	3
BURR DEPORTER	CW4	W-2126967	1155	1
BURR EDWIN M	CPT	0-0204545	0154	3
BURR GEORGE C	COL	0-0102253	1158	3
BURR HUGH	CPT	0-1167346	0946	2
BURR KENNETH D	LTC	0-1575811	1054	1
BURR ROLLIN D	CPT	0-0252381	0863	3
BURR ROSCOE C	LTC	0-0502836	0666	3
BURR SAMUEL F	LTC	0-0247375	1057	3
BURRAGE ROBERT H	COL	0-0126597	0352	3
BURRELL ETHELBERT	MAJ	0-0108150	1043	1
BURRELL FREDERICK	1LT	0-1541697	1145	2
BURRELL JACK R	CW2	W-2149805	0859	1
BURRELL MATTHEW J	LTC	0-0255100	1160	3
BURRIER LEON E	CPT	0-0189972	0554	3
BURRIL CHARLES F	MAJ	0-0154497	0456	3
BURRILL DON H	CW3	W-2152740	0863	1
BURRILL GERALD M	1LT	0-0538714	1145	2
BURRIS FELTON W	CPT	0-2012738	0257	1
BURRIS GARLAND F	2LT	0-1018246	0145	2
BURRIS HARRISON L	LTC	0-0118843	0848	3
BURRIS LEVI A	CW3	W-2148200	1066	1
BURRIS LUIS M	LTC	0-0453373	1063	1
BURRIS MYRA V	1LT	N-0734025	0246	1
BURRIS ORVAL F	WO1	W-2146358	0964	1
BURRIS THOMAS T	MAJ	0-1305888	0859	1
BURRISS CLIFTON A	COL	0-0193072	1062	3
BURRISS VIRGIL F	MAJ	0-0160358	0655	3

NAME	GRADE	SVC NO	DATE RET MO YR	RET CODE
BURRISS WALTER F	COL	O-0214470	0264	3
BURRITT HAROLD F	LTC	O-0213278	1060	1
BURRITT JOHN H	MAJ	O-0235236	0245	2
BURROUGHS ARTHUR T	LTC	O-1318410	0867	3
BURROUGHS DONALD L	MAJ	O-0990704	0266	1
BURROUGHS EARL T	1LT	O-0493175	0152	1
BURROUGHS JAMES A	LTC	O-0227872	0164	3
BURROUGHS JOHN D	2LT	O-0557655	1145	2
BURROUGHS JR EDGAR S	LTC	O-1287472	1066	1
BURROUGHS LISLE	COL	O-0124641	0559	3
BURROUGHS WILLIAM D	MAJ	O-1014211	0463	1
BURROWES HILLIER W	MAJ	O-0173795	0648	3
BURROWES ROBERT W	LTC	O-1297674	1266	1
BURROWS CARLOS W	MAJ	O-1290893	1057	2
BURROWS CHARLES A	LTC	O-0228531	1043	2
BURROWS DOUGLAS J	MAJ	O-1296480	0958	1
BURROWS HENRY	CPT	O-0253533	0966	3
BURROWS JOHN D	LTC	O-0221939	1160	3
BURROWS JOHN R	CPT	O-0508884	0446	2
BURROWS JOSEPH S	MAJ	O-0300935	0760	1
BURROWS JR STUART S	CW2	W-2212346	1166	2
BURROWS LEON S	CW3	W-2143469	0664	1
BURROWS STANLEY R	CPT	O-1585231	1046	2
BURROWS WALLER T	CPT	O-0257630	0860	3
BURRUS RUFUS R	COL	O-0253920	0560	3
BURSE DAVID A	CW3	W-2006984	0766	3
BURSELL WILLIAM R	MAJ	O-1998464	0961	1
BURSET MIGUEL A	COL	O-0382380	0761	1
BURSIEK RALPH C	LTC	O-0288660	1266	3
BURSLEY HARRY C	LTC	O-0268633	0859	3
BURSON CHARLES H	MAJ	O-2205896	1263	1
BURSON CURTIS E	MAJ	O-0354804	1045	1
BURSON JAMES C	MAJ	O-0233458	1148	1
BURSON MAURICE E	MAJ	O-0298305	0245	1
BURSTEIN MAX W	CPT	O-0479826	0847	2
BURSTEIN THEODORE	COL	O-0164734	0244	2
BURSTEN HAROLD R	CPT	O-1933719	0661	2
BURT CLARENCE D	CW4	W-2112553	0461	1
BURT DANIEL C	LTC	O-1037422	0562	1
BURT HERSEY F	CPT	O-0222130	1161	3
BURT JAMES B	CPT	O-1302427	1047	2
BURT JR ANDREW G	LTC	O-1633724	0363	1
BURT KENNETH L	MAJ	O-2035521	0760	1
BURT RALPH B	CPT	O-0310903	0546	2
BURT ROBERT D	CPT	O-2014641	1067	1
BURT ROWELL E	CPT	O-1175356	0446	2
BURT ROY A	COL	O-0184703	1052	3
BURT RUSSELL F	LTC	O-0252689	1059	1
BURTCH LYMAN D	LTC	O-1297489	0455	1
BURTIS KENNETH C	LTC	O-0184804	1162	3
BURTNER CALVIN R	LTC	O-0197819	0355	1
BURTNETT MERVIN	CPT	O-1107331	0561	1
BURTON ALVA A	1LT	O-0496979	0150	1
BURTON CECIL J	LTC	O-1685545	1065	1
BURTON CHARLES V	LTC	O-1318128	1162	1
BURTON CHESLEY F	CW2	W-2003643	1167	3
BURTON CLARK D	1LT	O-0416144	0245	1
BURTON CLYDE W	MAJ	O-1030226	0761	1
BURTON DAVID G	LTC	O-1060027	0962	1
BURTON EDWARD K	LTC	O-1947471	1066	1
BURTON EMERY W	CPT	O-0166713	0753	3
BURTON FRANK E	CW3	W-2002969	0366	3
BURTON HAROLD J	LTC	O-0912318	1062	1
BURTON HARRY	COL	O-0121426	0746	2
BURTON JOSEPH C	COL	O-0189286	0555	3
BURTON JOSEPH O	1LT	O-0115100	1052	3
BURTON JR LOUIS W	MAJ	O-2019283	0765	1
BURTON JR ROBERT A	COL	O-0425305	1263	3
BURTON KENNETH W	CW3	W-2206690	0166	1
BURTON LAWRENCE F	LTC	O-1032514	1264	1
BURTON LEON E	LTC	O-1180299	1061	1
BURTON LLOYD	LTC	O-0481038	0157	1
BURTON LLOYD E	LTC	O-0484333	1055	1
BURTON MARION J	CPT	O-0906592	0145	2
BURTON MELVIN F	1LT	O-1316142	0446	2
BURTON RAYMOND W	CPT	O-0507059	0745	2
BURTON RICHARD A	LTC	O-1173177	0361	1
BURTON ROBERT A	CPT	O-0266313	1053	3
BURTON ROBERT B	MAJ	O-0418443	0757	2
BURTON ROBERT H	MAJ	O-2265315	0764	1
BURTON ROYCE F	LTC	O-1635654	1163	1
BURTON THOMAS L	1LT	O-1300125	0852	1
BURTON WILFRED C	COL	O-1053928	0767	1
BURTON WILLIAM A	LTC	O-1647429	0367	1
BURTON WILLIAM H	1LT	O-0284571	0855	3
BURTON WILLIAM R	CPT	O-0498676	0745	2
BURUD WILLIAM N	LTC	O-1292123	0764	1
BURUM CARNETT M	MAJ	O-0516893	0260	1
BURWASSER JOSEPH	MAJ	O-0983944	1061	1
BURWELL JAMES W	LTC	O-1175061	0762	1
BURWINKLE WILLIAM M	CPT	O-1288176	0862	2
BURY JR COLIN J	1LT	O-0867480	0146	2
BURY LOYD A	COL	O-0297908	0866	3
BURY STANLEY	CW3	W-2142334	0161	1
BURZ ALEXANDER	LTC	O-1304677	1066	1
BUSBY ALBERT	MAJ	O-0976348	0765	1
BUSBY HUGH C	LTC	O-0417066	0861	1
BUSBY III OSCAR M	MAJ	O-1595403	1162	1
BUSBY JR YANCY L	MAJ	O-1579450	0261	1
BUSBY LONNIE L	CW3	W-2144701	0760	1
BUSBY PAUL H	CPT	O-0401458	0345	2
BUSBY SCOTT J	MAJ	O-1051063	1059	1
BUSCALL JR DAVID C	MAJ	O-0404331	0166	3
BUSCH CHARLES A	LTC	O-1307145	0863	1
BUSCH HENRY W	CPT	O-0443932	0648	1
BUSCH PHYLLIS M	CPT	N-0721688	1047	1
BUSCH RAY C	COL	O-0384458	0262	1
BUSCH WILLIAM F	MAJ	O-0329559	0567	3
BUSCHER CLEMENT F	MAJ	O-0376734	0445	2
BUSCHER KENNETH L	COL	O-0252643	0466	1
BUSCHKAMPER EDWARD	COL	O-0383326	0660	1
BUSCHMAN MELVIN C	1LT	O-0538103	0146	2
BUSER BERNARD R	CPT	O-1178430	0646	2
BUSER VERONICA H	MAJ	N-0732765	1062	1
BUSEY JR JOHN F	COL	O-0309417	0367	3
BUSH ANCUS M	CW3	W-2144346	1165	1
BUSH ARTHUR E	MAJ	O-0270213	0247	2
BUSH BREWSTER C	LTC	O-1533746	1066	1
BUSH CHARLES H	CW2	W-2110623	1044	2
BUSH CHARLES L	MAJ	O-0163086	0653	1
BUSH DONALD E	CW2	W-2213497	0267	1
BUSH DONALD P	LTC	O-0286543	0167	3
BUSH EDWARD L	1LT	O-0442278	0346	2
BUSH GERALD A	CPT	O-0400021	0945	2
BUSH HARLAND L	1LT	O-1325472	0556	1
BUSH HERMAN A	1LT	O-1320822	0445	2
BUSH JEPTHA H	MAJ	O-0257431	0947	1
BUSH JOE M	MAJ	O-0237029	0166	3
BUSH JOSEPH V	1LT	O-1013034	0846	2
BUSH JR CHARLES C	LTC	O-0168569	0660	3
BUSH JR HOUSTON L	2LT	O-1171933	0745	2
BUSH JR S M	1LT	O-0538973	0346	2
BUSH JULIUS L	MAJ	O-1589096	0763	2
BUSH KENNETH W	1LT	O-1325551	0 46	2
BUSH LAWRENCE G	1LT	O-0193547	0559	3
BUSH MARION E	MAJ	O-1556550	0562	1
BUSH MARSHALL F	B G	O-0298635	0867	3
BUSH MARVIN E	1LT	O-0320477	1044	2
BUSH MORGAN H	MAJ	O-1533975	0565	1
BUSH OTTIS R	CPT	O-0259992	0844	1
BUSH PAUL J	MAJ	O-1306974	0365	1
BUSH RALPH R	CPT	O-0373550	0245	2
BUSH RAYMOND B	COL	O-0231213	0959	3
BUSH RICHARD A	LTC	O-0357888	0167	3
BUSH RICHARD W	LTC	O-0911806	1067	3
BUSH RICHARD S	MAJ	O-0455155	0362	2
BUSH ROBERT N	CPT	O-1017368	0846	2
BUSH RUDOLPH M	COL	O-0240844	0162	1
BUSH SARGENT	CPT	O-0521005	0346	2
BUSH WEAVER L	LTC	O-0278697	0760	1
BUSHAW DELMON R H	CW3	W-2145396	1060	1
BUSHEK EMIL F	MAJ	O-1798440	0964	1
BUSHELL DORIS M	1LT	L-0909109	0644	2
BUSHERY LAWRENCE J	2LT	O-1291945	1144	2
BUSHEY DALE R	MAJ	O-1647266	0363	1
BUSHEY GEORGE O	CW4	W-2203632	0866	1
BUSHEY GORDON G	LTC	O-0215303	0158	1
BUSHEY HOWARD W	LTC	O-0372646	0263	1
BUSHEY JOHN M	LTC	O-0296294	0661	1
BUSHIE GORDON J	CW4	W-2004965	0865	1
BUSHMAN CHARLES S	COL	O-0121428	0656	3
BUSHNELL BYRON	COL	O-0116354	0355	3
BUSHNELL JOHN S	MAJ	O-1119390	0865	1
BUSHNELL JR THOMAS M	MAJ	O-0448333	0662	1
BUSHNELL LOUIS A K	LTC	O-0103695	0449	3
BUSHNELL WATROUS F	MAJ	O-0267873	0460	3
BUSHNELL WILFRED A	MAJ	O-0276415	0461	2
BUSHNER STANLEY	LTC	O-0504676	0661	1
BUSHOUSE ARTHUR A	MAJ	O-0888550	0757	1
BUSHOUSE WILLIAM J	CW4	W-2144271	0161	1
BUSHYHEAD JACK	CPT	O-1284822	0850	1
BUSI JOSEPH H	MAJ	O-0888299	0660	1
BUSKE HERMAN F	WO1	W-2106788	1146	1
BUSKETT BRUCE D	MAJ	O-2053918	0756	1
BUSKIRK HAROLD F	1LT	O-2002239	0448	2
BUSKIRK JAMES H	LTC	O-0224949	0246	2
BUSKNESS CARL O	CW2	W-2112741	0360	1
BUSKY ALBERT H	CPT	O-0213628	0862	3
BUSO WALTER	1LT	O-1299195	0645	2
BUSS JOE	1LT	O-1167762	1043	2
BUSS JOHN R	LTC	O-0238877	0764	3
BUSSE HERMAN A	CPT	O-2262818	0466	2
BUSSE MABEL K	CPT	L-0600080	0745	2
BUSSE OTTO C	LTC	O-0203744	1049	3
BUSSEN OLIVER J	LTC	O-1594744	1263	1
BUSSEY ARTHUR S	LTC	O-1333778	0967	1
BUSSEY CHARLES M	LTC	O-0804548	0366	1
BUSSEY DONALD S	COL	O-1299512	0567	2
BUSSEY FREDERICK	CPT	O-0322209	0546	2
BUSSEY GRANVILLE	COL	O-0347378	0864	1
BUSSEY HUGH D	CW3	W-2149332	0264	1
BUSSEY ROBERT H	LTC	O-0455558	0661	1
BUSSEY WILLARD D	MAJ	O-1575815	0661	1
BUSTARD WILLIAM W	CPT	O-1013997	0446	2
BUSTER THOMAS J	1LT	O-0509169	1147	1
BUSWELL CLARK J	MAJ	O-0257130	0867	3
BUSWELL DEWEY I	CPT	O-1541189	0864	1
BUSWELL EDWARD W	CW2	W-2113915	0557	1
BUSZTA JOSEPH J	2LT	O-1038927	0445	1
BUTCAVAGE ANTHONY J	MAJ	O-0972307	0665	1
BUTCH EDMUND R	LTC	O-0405085	0861	1
BUTCH LEO J	LTC	O-1102650	0763	1
BUTCH MICHAEL A	1LT	O-1036461	0945	2
BUTCHER DASH G	CW3	W-2145793	1164	1
BUTCHER DAVE E	LTC	O-0432858	0563	1
BUTCHER EDWARD T	MAJ	O-1312275	0562	1
BUTCHER ELMER H	MAJ	O-0356457	0162	2
BUTCHER HOWARD L	CW4	W-2144866	0866	1
BUTCHER JAMES P	MAJ	O-0201760	1046	2
BUTCHER MARY D	MAJ	N-0773887	0964	1
BUTCHER ORVILLE K	LTC	O-1324140	0363	1
BUTCHER WILLIAM E	LTC	O-1310976	1067	1
BUTCHER WILLIAM E	1LT	O-1318382	0945	2
BUTEAU FREEMAN H	CW4	W-2102715	0859	1
BUTHERUS HENRY	LTC	O-0310426	1157	1
BUTHORN WILLIAM F	1LT	O-0294223	0844	2
BUTIN PAUL	MAJ	O-1913505	1141	1
BUTKAS ALBERT A	MAJ	O-0397953	0946	2
BUTLER ALANSON H	MAJ	O-0424799	1160	1
BUTLER ALBERT M	COL	O-0335220	0962	1
BUTLER ARLIN S	CPT	N-0727799	0746	1
BUTLER BETTY I	MAJ	L-1010232	0863	1
BUTLER BURLIE C	CPT	O-0508318	0646	1
BUTLER BYRON N	LTC	O-0259459	0467	3
BUTLER CARL H	CPT	O-0171845	0653	3
BUTLER CARMON D	1LT	O-0200065	1055	3
BUTLER CHARLES A	COL	O-1641624	0155	1
BUTLER CHARLES E	LTC	O-0243226	1163	3
BUTLER CHARLES O	COL	O-0163672	0557	3
BUTLER CHARLES P	LTC	O-0370978	0260	1
BUTLER CHARLES W	CW2	W-2005142	0853	1
BUTLER CLETUS H	CPT	O-1317617	1062	1
BUTLER DAVID S	MAJ	O-0331348	0263	1
BUTLER DERUYTER A	LTC	O-0256999	0760	3
BUTLER DONALD R	CW2	W-2108494	1046	1
BUTLER EDWARD E	LTC	O-0300975	1052	1
BUTLER EDWARD F	MAJ	O-0490578	1145	2
BUTLER EDWARD R	1LT	O-1549235	0346	2
BUTLER ELLIS H	LTC	O-0511577	0266	3
BUTLER ELWYN H	MAJ	O-1800170	0665	1
BUTLER ETHAN F	LTC	O-0157979	0-53	3
BUTLER EUGENE R	LTC	O-0114127	0856	3
BUTLER EUGENE P	MAJ	O-1109170	0564	1
BUTLER EVERETT L	COL	O-0474142	0767	3
BUTLER FRANKLIN C	COL	O-0235354	0355	3
BUTLER FRED	1LT	O-0438273	1044	2
BUTLER GEORGE H	B G	O-0186922	0558	3
BUTLER GEORGE K	CPT	O-0322835	1045	2
BUTLER GRADY W	LTC	O-0354741	0856	1
BUTLER GRANT R	CW2	W-2152884	0162	1
BUTLER HAROLD A	LTC	O-0338469	1162	1
BUTLER HAROLD K	CW2	W-2118678	0454	1
BUTLER HAROLD R	1LT	O-0420026	0944	2
BUTLER HARRY	MAJ	O-0219920	0648	3
BUTLER HARRY G	LTC	O-0213621	0662	3
BUTLER HARVIE N	LTC	O-1305889	0264	1
BUTLER HENRY W	COL	O-0120530	0158	3
BUTLER HERBERT E	2LT	O-1328790	0546	1
BUTLER JACK C	1LT	O-0328260	0345	2
BUTLER JAMES F	COL	O-0255024	0757	1
BUTLER JAMES F	LTC	O-1549675	0661	1
BUTLER JAMES H	1LT	O-1324616	0647	2
BUTLER JAMES L	LTC	O-0306013	0560	1
BUTLER JAMES M	LTC	O-0405501	0847	2
BUTLER JAMES M	CW4	W-2143118	0263	1
BUTLER JAMES C	MAJ	O-0246824	1054	3
BUTLER JAMES W	CW2	W-2145039	0457	2
BUTLER JIMMIE L	MAJ	O-2051068	0261	1
BUTLER JOHN E	CW3	W-2141212	0762	1
BUTLER JOHN J	MAJ	O-1100468	1061	1
BUTLER JOHN J	CPT	O-1301608	0863	1
BUTLER JOHN L	MAJ	O-0974517	1262	1
BUTLER JOHN C	CW3	W-2143462	0262	1
BUTLER JOSEPH F	LTC	O-0451221	0657	1
BUTLER JOSEPH F	LTC	O-0475552	1047	2
BUTLER JR JAMES W	CW3	W-2146760	0265	1
BUTLER JR LUTHER B	1LT	O-2006894	0147	2
BUTLER KING S	LTC	O-0398131	0560	1
BUTLER LAUREL E	COL	O-0241817	0859	1
BUTLER LEONARD A	CW2	W-2145397	0456	1
BUTLER MELVIN	CPT	O-1923536	0264	1
BUTLER RAYMOND K	LTC	O-0214106	1059	3
BUTLER RAYMOND T	2LT	O-2055093	1144	2
BUTLER ROBERT C	LTC	O-0114876	1162	1
BUTLER ROBERT J	LTC	O-0435264	0662	1
BUTLER ROBERT W	COL	O-0373313	0761	1
BUTLER ROWLAND A	MAJ	O-0337410	1165	3
BUTLER ROY L	COL	O-0278870	1147	2
BUTLER SAM W	CPT	O-0480887	0346	1
BUTLER SUSANN K	MAJ	N-0757718	0966	1
BUTLER THOMAS F	CW4	W-2136645	0261	1
BUTLER VAUGHN V	CPT	O-0920547	1048	1
BUTLER WILLIAM E	1LT	O-0331226	0945	1
BUTLER WILLIAM F	CPT	O-0177288	0450	3
BUTLER WILLIS D	LTC	O-0142785	0145	2
BUTMAN BURTON B	MAJ	O-0365408	0546	2
BUTNER CORNELIUS	LTC	O-1107835	0663	1
BUTNER HUGH F	CPT	O-0306345	0345	2
BUTT CECIL G	CPT	O-0993432	0653	2
BUTT CLIFFORD W	COL	O-0175381	1264	3

NAME	GRADE	SVC NO	DATE RET MO YR	RET CODE
BUTT EUPHEMIA L	1LT	N-0752963	0546	1
BUTT HERBERT H	COL	O-0479678	0157	2
BUTT JR ARTHUR J	CPT	O-0383673	0544	1
BUTT JR RICHARD L	COL	O-0336856	1265	1
BUTT WILLIAM	WO1	W-2115956	0344	1
BUTTE CHARLES D	LTC	O-2029549	0367	1
BUTTERFIELD C L	1LT	O-0342316	0445	2
BUTTERFIELD LELAND W	LTC	O-0328921	1165	3
BUTTERFIELD MAX H	CPT	O-0265823	0246	2
BUTTERFIELD RUTH E	1LT	L-0115175	0745	2
BUTTERS BLAINE H	LTC	O-1580715	1061	2
BUTTERS FORREST H	CW4	W-2101512	0559	1
BUTTERS MANLY G	CPT	O-1697864	0745	2
BUTTERS WILLIAM F	LTC	O-0337407	1045	2
BUTTERSTEIN A F	2LT	O-0447700	1044	2
BUTTERWORTH JAMES E	COL	O-0103853	0855	3
BUTTERWORTH WALTON B	LTC	O-0186712	0459	3
BUTTGEN GEORGE A	MAJ	O-0967310	1061	1
BUTTLER JOHN F	CPT	O-1310569	1046	2
BUTTOLPH MILAN D	LTC	O-0296388	0846	2
BUTTON ALLEN M	LTC	O-0197892	0847	1
BUTTON FRANK P	MAJ	O-0200439	0857	3
BUTTON JAMES G	CPT	O-1637135	0558	1
BUTTON OSWALD W	MAJ	O-0959706	0661	1
BUTTON RONALD E	COL	O-0118810	1055	3
BUTTON WILLIAM B	LTC	O-0383861	0262	1
BUTTREY LINTON J	MAJ	O-0407113	0654	1
BUTTS CHARLES G	CPT	O-1004743	0647	2
BUTTS JACKSON K	CW3	W-2206208	0667	1
BUTTS JR DAVID T	MAJ	O-0361741	0562	2
BUTTS PAUL E	LTC	O-1318758	0267	1
BUTTS RALPH E	MAJ	O-1923501	1262	2
BUTTS SR SAMUEL T	CPT	O-1582927	0758	1
BUTTS WALTER	1LT	O-0492158	0744	1
BUTZKE EDWARD W	COL	O-0254686	0865	3
BUVENS RICHARD H	LTC	O-0162113	0145	1
BUWEN FREDERICK	CPT	O-0908383	0745	2
BUX ALBERT C	MAJ	O-0227815	0-50	3
BUXTON JOHN A	LTC	O-0161202	0157	3
BUXTON JOHN E	LTC	O-0168405	0752	3
BUYAK MITCHELL V	MAJ	O-0310512	1062	3
BUYS WILLIAM D	LTC	O-1110971	0464	1
BUYZE DANIEL	LTC	O-0360158	1061	1
BUZA ALFRED J	CW3	W-2145229	0862	1
BUZARD JOHN H	LTC	O-1105299	1067	1
BUZASH ALBERT S	LTC	O-0405814	0459	1
BUZZARD DONALD H	LTC	O-1010335	0561	1
BYALL WILLIAM F	MAJ	O-1917751	0565	1
BYARD RAYMOND J	MAJ	O-1920284	0426	1
BYARS CLARENCE E	CW2	W-2146938	0356	1
BYARS JOSEPH R	LTC	O-0338533	0762	3
BYARS RICHARD C	LTC	O-0261037	1066	3
BYARS ROBERT D	1LT	O-2018835	0851	1
BYARS WARNER S	CPT	O-1543734	1047	1
BYAS CARL H	MAJ	O-0452019	0957	1
BYASSEE MARSHALL C	MAJ	O-0967270	0464	1
BYBEE CLEADUS	CW3	W-2144641	0367	2
BYBEE JOE T	CW2	W-2149663	1262	1
BYBEE JOHN W	LTC	O-1294430	0262	1
BYCZYNSKI STANLEY J	CPT	O-0965857	1160	1
BYE SIGURD F	LTC	O-0743033	1160	3
BYE STANLEY F	MAJ	O-0244752	1044	2
BYE WILLIAM P	CPT	O-1822234	1045	2
BYER RUSSELL R	CPT	O-0138849	0657	3
BYERLEY WENDELL C	MAJ	O-2023958	0663	1
BYERLY FENTON H	CPT	O-1798441	0257	1
BYERLY JR GEORGE E	LTC	O-1287135	0161	1
BYERLY MATTHEW W	MAJ	O-0336132	0960	1
BYERS ALONZO C	LTC	O-0501440	0158	1
BYERS ANDREW	MAJ	O-0948502	1066	1
BYERS BENJAMIN H	LTC	O-0148868	0757	3
BYERS CARLOS L	MAJ	O-1036894	0461	1
BYERS DAVID F	LTC	O-1315264	0963	1
BYERS GEORGE	LTC	O-0170001	0753	3
BYERS HANS	CPT	O-2020523	0559	1
BYERS JASON H	LTC	O-0290942	0460	3
BYERS LAWRENCE W	COL	O-0169786	0657	1
BYERS MELVIN W	CW3	W-2150333	0164	1
BYERS RAYMOND A	COL	O-0243238	0558	3
BYERS ROBERT W	CW3	W-2209049	0966	1
BYERS ROLAND C	LTC	O-1171935	1262	1
BYKLE LAURA C	MAJ	N-0772431	1063	1
BYLAND WARREN T	MAJ	O-1301105	0764	1
BYLER RALPH J	COL	O-0318638	0246	2
BYLES HOWARD T	COL	O-0187175	0852	3
BYLES ROBERT E	LTC	O-0349174	0451	1
BYNUM HARTWELL T	COL	O-0267306	0858	3
BYNUM HENRY W	MAJ	O-0377680	1061	1
BYNUM JIMMIE D	MAJ	O-1688317	0164	1
BYNUM SR THOMAS W	LTC	O-0246261	0351	3
BYNUM WILLIAM L	LTC	O-0352705	0660	1
BYRAM CHARLES R	LTC	O-0439326	1053	3
BYRAM HERMAN F	MAJ	O-1302949	0464	1
BYRAM RUTH F	1LT	N-0785595	0947	1
BYRD AERAIN	LTC	O-1178727	0755	1
BYRD CLAYTON R	1LT	O-0955228	0952	2
BYRD COHEN R	COL	O-0410926	1061	1
BYRD DANIEL B	B G	O-0185002	1048	3
BYRD DAVID C	COL	O-0238264	0166	3
BYRD FELTON L	LTC	O-1049095	0858	1
BYRD GEORGE W	LTC	O-0270494	0766	3
BYRD HARDEN B	LTC	O-0348993	0657	1
BYRD HARVEY B	1LT	O-0340965	0845	2
BYRD HAZEL L	COL	O-0304497	0559	1
BYRD JAMES F	MAJ	O-2006101	0766	1
BYRD JESSE L	COL	O-0198514	0251	3
BYRD JR CECIL C	MAJ	O-0968681	0862	1
BYRD JR JIMMY R	CW3	W-2207102	0766	1
BYRD JR LARKIN A	MAJ	O-1328791	1262	1
BYRD JR LUCAS M	MAJ	O-0501767	0847	2
BYRD KURT	CPT	O-0956823	0257	2
BYRD LIONEL P	MAJ	O-0953925	1061	1
BYRD NELLIE B	MAJ	N-0727347	0846	1
BYRD PAUL F	LTC	O-0404271	0263	1
BYRD SAM	1LT	O-0488677	0650	1
BYRD SAM	MAJ	O-2046302	0954	1
BYRD SMITH T	2LT	O-1286435	0345	2
BYRD WILLIAM H	1LT	O-0491309	0146	2
BYRNE CLEMENT A	LTC	O-1573087	0157	1
BYRNE EDWARD G	CW2	W-2130673	0953	1
BYRNE EDWIN S	1LT	O-0414846	0450	1
BYRNE GERARD N	COL	O-0254282	0266	3
BYRNE JOHN F	LTC	O-1946450	0263	1
BYRNE JOHN J	CPT	O-1324004	0446	2
BYRNE JOHN P	MAJ	O-1579453	0465	1
BYRNE JOSEPH S	LTC	O-0497162	0862	1
BYRNE JR WILLIAM F	MAJ	O-0368227	0346	2
BYRNE MARK P	MAJ	O-0485184	0561	2
BYRNE MICHAEL	LTC	O-1291944	0363	1
BYRNE PAUL C	COL	O-0194842	0961	3
BYRNE RICHARD J	COL	O-0355777	0761	1
BYRNE ROBERT A	LTC	O-1533512	0962	1
BYRNE STEPHEN R	MAJ	O-1950563	1162	2
BYRNE THOMAS F	COL	O-0102103	0266	3
BYRNE THOMAS P	1LT	O-5023855	0867	2
BYRNE WILLIAM J	CPT	O-1573704	0456	1
BYRNES ALBERT F	CPT	O-1635660	0358	1
BYRNES ARTHUR A	CPT	O-1100470	0164	1
BYRNES GARRETT J	COL	O-0321225	0467	3
BYRNES GEORGE J	MAJ	O-0955545	0566	1
BYRNES JOHN P	1LT	O-1326354	0346	2
BYRNES JOSEPH R	MAJ	O-1043587	0560	1
BYRNES JR JAMES L	1LT	O-0349740	1147	2
BYRNES ROBERT J	CW3	W-2151198	0864	1
BYRNES THOMAS F	MAJ	O-1061325	0862	2
BYROM CASSIE N	2LT	N-0744546	0544	1
BYRON ALEXANDER	CPT	O-0124297	0150	3
BYRON CHARLES F	LTC	O-1293545	0561	1
BYRON CHRIS	1LT	O-0557991	0852	1
BYRON EDWARD S	COL	O-0210770	0-49	3
BYRON ELMER H	CW2	W-2148107	0662	1
BYRON FRANK J	LTC	O-1994395	1162	1
BYRON JOHN F	CPT	O-1289041	0954	1
BYRON WILLIAM E	1LT	O-1949223	0552	1
BYRUM JR GEORGE R	LTC	O-0213848	0747	2
BYRUM WILLIAM W	MAJ	O-1103543	1060	1
BYSTRAK PAUL	MAJ	O-0977286	1263	1
BYTHER PAUL F	LTC	O-0354042	0163	1
BYUS JR JOHN	LTC	O-0374754	1060	1
BYWATERS JAMES H	LTC	O-0262986	1067	3
BYWATERS RICHARD E	LTC	O-1826313	0763	1
BYZEK STEPHEN J	CPT	O-2055520	0959	1
BZOULA EDWARD B	CPT	O-1596602	0447	2
CABABAAN PABLO	1LT	O-1896567	0450	1
CABALLERO JOSE D	1LT	O-2030125	1050	1
CABANILLAS JUAN	MAJ	O-0934244	0765	1
CABANISS JR LEM	LTC	O-0966116	1266	1
CABANISS MARION I	CPT	O-1312748	1046	2
CABANISS WILLIAM L	COL	O-0293176	0546	2
CABBAGE VICTOR	2LT	O-1914017	1043	1
CABELL RANDOLPH M	COL	O-0189318	1155	3
CABIAO PROTACIO	1LT	O-2032075	1052	1
CABIL JUAN	1LT	O-0170615	0648	1
CABLE DONALD E	MAJ	O-0231464	1156	3
CABLE PAUL F	CW3	W-2146220	0162	2
CABLES GRACE M C	LTC	R-0001040	1165	3
CABOT RUSSELL C	LTC	O-0267432	1165	3
CABRER AGUSTIN	2LT	O-1081464	1045	2
CABRERA CHARLES T	LTC	O-0187263	0961	3
CABRERA DAGO	CW2	W-2149905	0667	1
CABRERA JUAN R	1LT	O-0527493	1045	2
CABRINHA ANTHONY M	LTC	O-0348171	0961	1
CABUNTALA STEVE	2LT	O-2031894	0652	1
CACCAMISE FRANCIS J	CW3	W-2142998	0959	1
CACCHIOTTI RALPH P	MAJ	O-1046032	1060	1
CACCIATO RICHARD C	LTC	O-0935273	0767	1
CACCIATORE DONALD E	CW2	W-2110608	0861	1
CACERES RALPH K	CPT	O-0450811	0547	2
CACHILLI FRED H	MAJ	O-1290545	0161	1
CADDELL CLYDE M	2LT	O-1311976	0445	2
CADDELL JR JAMES R	1LT	O-0535907	1045	2
CADDES ELMER E	LTC	O-0313537	0965	1
CADDINGTON WARD W	LTC	O-0231597	0945	2
CADDLE JOHN	LTC	O-0366365	0561	2
CADDY JR EDWARD W	MAJ	O-1554146	0961	1
CADE GEORGE F	MAJ	O-1550339	0364	1
CADE WILLIAM H	2LT	O-0553493	1045	2
CADIGAN ROBERT S	LTC	O-0426069	0664	1
CADIGAN WILLIAM J	MAJ	O-1110408	0962	1
CADMAN EUGENE E	LTC	O-0202985	0256	3
CADOGAN LARRY J	MAJ	O-1545644	0467	3
CADORET MARCEL A	1LT	O-0503255	0745	2
CADUNGUG DELFIN C	2LT	O-2032076	1048	1
CADWALADER HENRY	CPT	O-0340410	0744	2
CADWALLADER CHARLES	LTC	O-0144961	0951	3
CADWALLADER EDGAR C	CPT	O-1595407	0346	2
CADWELL CAROL V	COL	O-0150955	1054	1
CADWELL JOHN H	MAJ	O-0450253	0955	1
CADWELL VERN L	CPT	O-0173490	1145	2
CADY DUANE L	COL	O-0335065	0246	2
CADY FRED A	1LT	O-1301943	1157	1
CADY LAWRENCE R	LTC	O-1031542	0658	1
CADY LEE D	COL	O-0168429	1056	3
CADY MAX W	MAJ	O-0355693	0151	1
CAESAR GORDON M	CPT	O-1288177	0846	2
CAFARO SECONDO R	MAJ	O-0349741	0745	2
CAFFEY ROBERT C	MAJ	O-0347416	0847	1
CAFFO LOUIS L	CPT	O-0492302	0752	1
CAFFREY CHARLES F	MAJ	O-0534773	0448	2
CAFFREY CHARLES G	LTC	O-0375830	0364	3
CAFFREY DAVID P	LTC	O-1322203	0363	2
CAFFREY EDWIN J	MAJ	O-2056899	0766	1
CAFFREY GERALD C	1LT	O-2007423	0648	1
CAFFREY JAMES A	LTC	O-0246167	1160	3
CAFFREY JOSEPH G	CW2	W-2208321	0864	1
CAFFREY ROBERT J	LTC	O-1549441	0267	1
CAFONE JULIO J	CPT	O-1823835	1152	2
CAGANN ARNOLD R	MAJ	O-1174519	0962	1
CAGE ARNETT	CW3	W-2151378	0366	1
CAGGIULA VINCENT L	CPT	O-0351770	0346	2
CAGLE CHARLES D	MAJ	O-1016731	0747	1
CAGLE DARRELL J	CW4	W-2120969	0364	2
CAGLE JAMES M	CW4	W-2129268	0562	1
CAGLE PAUL M	MAJ	O-1919273	1264	1
CAGNONI GUIDO J	1LT	O-0345939	0544	2
CAGULADA LEONARDO	2LT	O-1896850	0151	1
CAHILL EDWARD H	MAJ	O-0100904	1044	2
CAHILL EDWIN D	CPT	O-1169450	0849	2
CAHILL HENRY F	LTC	O-1180142	0563	1
CAHILL JAMES T	CPT	O-0374958	0346	1
CAHILL JOHN B	CW4	W-2003740	0567	1
CAHILL JR THOMAS H	LTC	O-0188990	0755	3
CAHILL ROBERT P	MAJ	O-1799239	0263	1
CAHILL STANLEY E	2LT	O-1118555	1045	2
CAHILL THOMAS F	CPT	O-1287302	1047	2
CAHILL VINCENT F	CPT	O-1049429	0866	1
CAHOON AUGUST T	CPT	O-0361753	1145	2
CAHOY ANDY L	CPT	O-0283567	0246	2
CAIN ALVA N	LTC	O-0449577	0562	3
CAIN BEDFORD P	MAJ	O-1057000	0464	3
CAIN DANIEL E	CW2	W-2149883	0758	2
CAIN FREDERICK	COL	O-0244924	0562	3
CAIN GEORGE E	MAJ	O-0983241	0562	1
CAIN GLADYS C	MAJ	N-0751617	0867	1
CAIN HERVEY C	CPT	O-0496774	0646	2
CAIN JAMES S	LTC	O-2055885	1060	1
CAIN JOHN J	MAJ	O-0366731	0847	2
CAIN JOHN S	MAJ	O-0344674	0147	2
CAIN JR CLESSON C	MAJ	O-0968208	1062	2
CAIN JR FRANK D	1LT	O-0554497	0646	2
CAIN MEMORY H	COL	O-0232299	0147	1
CAIN RAY F	LTC	O-1321288	0862	1
CAIN ROLLIE W	1LT	O-1056655	0346	2
CAIN THOMAS E	LTC	O-0371462	0257	1
CAIN THOMAS R	1LT	O-0409095	0644	2
CAIN VINCENT C	MAJ	O-4009552	0766	1
CAIN WARREN E	LTC	O-0360608	0960	1
CAIN WILLIAM D	1LT	O-0543225	0846	2
CAIN WILLIAM F	MAJ	O-1041306	0462	2
CAINE IRVING	CPT	O-0471948	0445	2
CAINE JOSEPH P	CW3	W-2205275	0866	1
CAINE TRACY M	LTC	O-1062914	0767	1
CAINES THOMAS I	CPT	O-2039425	0557	1
CAIRNS MONIVAL A	LTC	O-0401962	0760	1
CAIRNS PAUL M	COL	O-0221610	0657	3
CAIRNS ROBERT T	MAJ	O-0125816	0746	2
CAIRY SCOTT A	LTC	O-0275662	0349	3
CAIVANO JAMES J	1LT	O-1292127	0146	2
CAKALIC ELINT M	LTC	O-0318271	1059	1
CAKE CHARLES	CPT	O-0508654	1046	2
CALABRESE DINO D	CPT	O-0419544	0145	2
CALABRESE EDWARD S	MAJ	O-0344965	0246	2
CALAHAN RICHARD A	CW3	W-2143282	1262	1
CALAMARI JOHN J	LTC	O-0305979	0767	3
CALAMARO ALFREDO A	CPT	O-1896758	0359	1
CALAPINI URBANO E	2LT	O-2030126	1050	1
CALARCO LOUIS D	COL	O-0410022	1065	1
CALAWAY GEORGE A	MAJ	O-0292401	1145	2
CALBOS FRANK	1LT	O-1821821	0946	2
CALCI HENRY V	1LT	O-1705374	1044	2
CALDER JOSEPH H	LTC	O-1313566	1163	1
CALDER NATHAN A	CPT	O-1308556	0746	2
CALDERON RAMON F	CPT	O-2020924	0260	1
CALDERONE JOSEPH J	CW3	W-2147950	0561	1
CALDERWOOD HOWARD N	LTC	O-0211463	0648	3
CALDERWOOD JOSEPH B	CW4	W-2110119	1057	1
CALDWELL ADRIAN A	LTC	O-1305159	0562	1
CALDWELL ALBERT B	1LT	O-1310977	0645	1
CALDWELL ALBERT L	MAJ	O-1017811	0161	1
CALDWELL ARNOLD E	CPT	O-1284651	0645	2

NAME	GRADE	SVC NO	DATE RET MO YR	RET CODE
CALDWELL ARTHUR N	LTC	0-0347708	0756	1
CALDWELL BEVERLY C	MAJ	0-0237098	1146	2
CALDWELL BYRON L	LTC	0-1585237	0766	3
CALDWELL CARL E	2LT	0-1049430	0845	2
CALDWELL CHARLES C	COL	0-0217778	0463	3
CALDWELL CHARLES I	MAJ	0-2034500	0262	1
CALDWELL CHARLIE	CPT	0-0166821	0652	3
CALDWELL CLOYD T	COL	0-0266527	0657	1
CALDWELL EARL	MAJ	0-1110972	1159	1
CALDWELL EDWARD G	LTC	0-2046303	1166	1
CALDWELL FREDERICK	CPT	0-0436952	0246	2
CALDWELL GEORGE D	COL	0-0125218	0551	3
CALDWELL GEORGE H	CPT	0-1174520	0550	1
CALDWELL HAMMOND D	LTC	0-0288780	0756	1
CALDWELL HAROLD C	CW3	W-2134050	0562	1
CALDWELL HAZLITT B	LTC	0-0165727	0455	3
CALDWELL HERMAN V	1LT	0-0965520	0962	1
CALDWELL HOWARD S	MAJ	0-0248374	1266	3
CALDWELL HUGH M	MAJ	0-1324313	0453	1
CALDWELL JAMES	MAJ	0-1913486	0565	1
CALDWELL JAMES F	CPT	0-0370928	0765	2
CALDWELL JAMES H	CW2	W-2150895	0562	1
CALDWELL JOHN A	LTC	0-1581790	1162	2
CALDWELL JOHN C	LTC	0-0480390	0855	2
CALDWELL JOHN E	CPT	0-0268860	0849	1
CALDWELL JOHN H	LTC	0-1109843	0763	1
CALDWELL JR ALLEN B	1LT	0-2043089	0446	2
CALDWELL JR JOHN E	MAJ	0-1341852	0865	2
CALDWELL JULIUS A	CPT	0-0339930	0146	2
CALDWELL LANGSTON H	LTC	0-0544283	0463	1
CALDWELL LEONARD A	CW3	W-2144002	1263	1
CALDWELL LESTER R	MAJ	0-1947183	0156	1
CALDWELL MELVIN H	CW3	W-2207607	0166	1
CALDWELL MILLARD F	LTC	0-0450208	0557	1
CALDWELL MILTON V	CPT	0-0474079	0745	2
CALDWELL RALPH D	MAJ	0-0264373	0943	2
CALDWELL RALPH W	LTC	0-0323920	1162	1
CALDWELL RALPH W	CW3	W-2153242	0863	1
CALDWELL ROBERT C	2LT	0-1112600	1044	2
CALDWELL ROBERT E L	CW3	W-2120775	1057	1
CALDWELL ROBERT M	1LT	0-1058465	1045	2
CALDWELL ROSS	CPT	0-0336597	1045	1
CALDWELL SHERRILL C	2LT	0-1547558	0445	2
CALDWELL THOMAS R	LTC	0-0229052	0864	3
CALDWELL TROY G	CPT	0-0493515	0746	1
CALDWELL VERNON	MAJ	0-1545823	0561	1
CALDWELL VIOLETTE M	2LT	N-0736768	0844	1
CALDWELL VIRGIL E	COL	0-0136361	0856	3
CALDWELL WILL H	LTC	0-0216731	0763	3
CALDWELL WILLIAM F	LTC	0-0245901	0245	2
CALDWELL WILLIAM H	CW3	W-2142040	0257	1
CALDWELL WILLIAM R	LTC	0-0493169	0855	1
CALDWELL WINSTON F	LTC	0-0366846	0264	1
CALE LUTHER T	LTC	0-0228729	0864	3
CALE RICHARD C	LTC	0-0336415	1064	3
CALER ROBERT S	COL	0-1580717	0661	1
CALEF RALPH E	1LT	0-1577245	0745	2
CALENDER ALLIE D	LTC	0-1557701	0566	1
CALERO AMILCAR R	MAJ	0-0962999	1063	1
CALESTINI JOSEPH C	CW4	W-2103932	0859	1
CALFEE LEE D	MAJ	0-1894956	0961	2
CALFEE RICHARD A	MAJ	0-2051425	1262	1
CALFEE WILLIAM A	LTC	0-1299711	1161	1
CALGOY PABLO C	1LT	0-0395420	1059	1
CALHOUN ALFORD E	COL	0-0323112	0664	1
CALHOUN ALISTAIR A	MAJ	0-2049495	0865	2
CALHOUN CHARLES E	LTC	0-1325553	0665	1
CALHOUN CHARLES L	MAJ	0-0236413	0758	3
CALHOUN EDWARD H	CPT	0-1302271	0949	1
CALHOUN GRIFF C	MAJ	0-0486507	0253	1
CALHOUN JACK	CPT	0-0409632	0146	2
CALHOUN JESSE E	MAJ	0-0434724	0347	2
CALHOUN JOHN N	LTC	0-1533271	0164	3
CALHOUN JR CHARLES H	LTC	0-0363284	0860	1
CALHOUN JR FORREST	1LT	0-1933668	0554	2

NAME	GRADE	SVC NO	DATE RET MO YR	RET CODE
CALHOUN PAUL R	LTC	0-2044318	0662	1
CALHOUN ROBERT S	1LT	0-1323256	0548	1
CALHOUN SAMUEL	MAJ	0-1311115	0560	1
CALHOUN SHELLACE T	LTC	0-1309212	0867	1
CALHOUN THOMAS	MAJ	0-0231888	0648	3
CALHOUN WESLEY P	CW2	W-2208449	0165	1
CALIFF JOHN W	LTC	0-0220384	0560	3
CALIGUIRI FRANCIS F	LTC	0-1184467	0263	1
CALISCH MERRIL H	MAJ	0-0706565	0765	1
CALKIN FREDERICK	LTC	0-0125817	0754	3
CALKIN GEORGE R	LTC	0-1051894	0563	1
CALKIN RALPH F	LTC	0-0341614	0260	1
CALKINS DELOS S	LTC	0-0284042	0661	1
CALKINS HARRY R	COL	0-0287444	0846	1
CALKINS JAMES E	LTC	0-0384430	0960	1
CALKINS JR JOHN D	LTC	0-1949063	0766	1
CALKINS JR JOHN U	M G	0-0114357	1149	3
CALKINS LUTHER S	LTC	0-1640750	0363	1
CALKINS MYRON L	1LT	0-0263484	1043	2
CALL CHAUNCY C	CPT	0-0271564	0647	2
CALL CORNELIUS	2LT	0-2011076	0747	2
CALL FREDERICK	MAJ	0-1556254	1163	1
CALL JR JOSEPH R	1LT	0-1296319	0745	2
CALL JR LUTHER P	COL	0-0125819	0258	3
CALL THOMAS C	LTC	0-0366567	1160	1
CALL 3RD LUTHER P	CPT	0-0975668	0858	2
CALLAGHAN ELLEN K	1LT	N-0787540	1146	1
CALLAGHAN EUGENE J	LTC	0-0450813	1060	2
CALLAGHAN GEORGE J	LTC	0-0453714	1153	1
CALLAGHAN HAROLD F	MAJ	0-1823401	1165	2
CALLAGHAN HENRY F	MAJ	0-2014472	0264	1
CALLAGHAN PATRICK E	LTC	0-1556551	1162	1
CALLAGHAN RICHARD P	MAJ	0-1315908	1063	1
CALLAGHAN ROBERT E	1LT	0-0544606	0646	2
CALLAHAN EDWARD J	1LT	0-1287833	0647	1
CALLAHAN JAMES F	COL	0-0260318	0767	3
CALLAHAN CHARLES F	2LT	0-1824631	0744	2
CALLAHAN FRANCIS R	LTC	0-1797245	0766	1
CALLAHAN FRANCIS P	LTC	0-1286958	0361	1
CALLAHAN FRANK J	1LT	0-1324456	104N	2
CALLAHAN GABRIEL P	CW4	W-2143107	0865	2
CALLAHAN GEORGE	1LT	0-0886318	0251	2
CALLAHAN HAROLD H	MAJ	0-0966310	0763	1
CALLAHAN HELENA M	MAJ	L-0115751	0363	1
CALLAHAN HORACE N	LTC	0-0336538	0346	2
CALLAHAN HUBERT A	MAJ	0-0984717	0766	1
CALLAHAN JAMES D	MAJ	0-0288511	0267	3
CALLAHAN JAMES E	LTC	0-0229603	0265	3
CALLAHAN JEAN G	MAJ	0-0298690	0266	2
CALLAHAN JOHN A	MAJ	0-1176911	0964	2
CALLAHAN JOHN D	CW3	PW-2142095	0263	1
CALLAHAN JOHN R	CW4	W-2109238	0652	1
CALLAHAN JR FRANK F	LTC	0-0340098	0446	2
CALLAHAN JR JOHN J	CW3	W-2144225	0564	1
CALLAHAN NOEL	LTC	0-0293135	1064	1
CALLAHAN RICHARD D	CW3	W-2150792	0966	1
CALLAHAN RICHARD L	MAJ	0-0974978	1163	1
CALLAHAN THOMAS J	LTC	0-0390706	1160	1
CALLAHAN WILLIAM C	CW2	W-2150114	0356	1
CALLAHAN WILLIAM J	MAJ	0-0302373	0348	1
CALLAHAN WILLIAM R	LTC	0-0407650	0261	1
CALLAN RAYMOND E	MAJ	0-1685651	0865	1
CALLANAN JOHN J	COL	0-0279797	0463	3
CALLANAN WILLIAM A	COL	0-0255935	1164	3
CALLANDER ADELBERT R	LTC	0-0273164	1058	3
CALLAWAY BRANTLEY B	LTC	0-0473228	0548	1
CALLAWAY GEORGE H	LTC	0-0979303	0763	1
CALLAWAY HOMER A	LTC	0-0200744	0355	3
CALLAWAY KERMIT H	LTC	0-0250157	1059	1
CALLAWAY OSWALD E	CPT	0-2262787	0963	1
CALLAWAY SAMUEL M	CPT	0-0959307	1060	1
CALLAWAY THOMAS W	CPT	0-1334254	0558	1
CALLEN JAMES W	CPT	0-0490017	0354	1
CALLENBERGER JAMES D	CW2	W-2148709	0160	1
CALLENDER WILLIAM R	COL	0-0222342	0965	3

NAME	GRADE	SVC NO	DATE RET MO YR	RET CODE
CALLERY JAMES B	LTC	0-2035624	0861	1
CALLIER STRATTON F	LTC	0-1283720	0960	2
CALLIER THOMAS P	1LT	0-0509854	1045	2
CALLIHAN AENID A	MAJ	N-0735716	0665	3
CALLIHAN CHAMPION M	2LT	0-1309909	1144	2
CALLIHAN CHARLES W	MAJ	0-1924766	0565	1
CALLIS OTIS W	LTC	0-1001312	0762	1
CALLIS RUSSELL S	LTC	0-1110410	0461	1
CALLISON EUGENE H	LTC	0-0171575	1161	3
CALLOW HERBERT T	CPT	0-0211433	0858	3
CALLOWAY LAWRENCE H	COL	0-0250967	1065	3
CALLOWAY RICHARD H	LTC	0-0383690	0461	1
CALLOWAY ROBERT F	CW3	RW-2149750	0263	1
CALLOWAY VICTOR L	MAJ	0-2265361	1266	1
CALM ELY	1LT	0-1896630	0249	1
CALNAN JAMES T	LTC	0-1796917	0765	1
CALOS SPERO W	MAJ	0-0963816	0761	1
CALPIN CATHERINE	2LT	N-0762380	0645	1
CALPIN MICHAEL J	LTC	0-1303661	0363	1
CALPO MAURICIO	1LT	0-1896417	0654	1
CALTON RALPH N	1LT	0-1579460	0945	2
CALUGAS JOSE	CPT	0-1896617	0457	1
CALVANESE IDEAL M	LTC	0-1585241	0862	1
CALVARY PAUL R	MAJ	0-1171076	0859	1
CALVERLEY CHARLES E	MAJ	0-0285480	0864	3
CALVERT BINNIE F	1LT	N-0700853	1138	1
CALVERT CECIL	CPT	0-0166409	1146	2
CALVERT FLORENCE	2LT	N-0700100	0938	1
CALVERT GEORGE H	LTC	0-0228229	0764	3
CALVERT LAWRENCE R	CPT	0-0324640	0157	1
CALVERT MICHAEL J	CPT	0-0130717	0954	3
CALVERT NORVAL K	CPT	0-1304016	0346	2
CALVERT PHILLIP E	CPT	0-1317880	0347	2
CALVERT RALPH D	1LT	0-1054508	0246	2
CALVERT ROBERT W	CPT	0-1110973	0556	2
CALVERT WILLIAM H	CW3	W-2142388	0161	1
CALVERT WILLIAM P	CW2	W-2152950	0859	1
CALVIN ASA E	MAJ	0-0298405	0862	3
CALVIN ELMER B	LTC	0-0195544	0961	3
CALWAY JAMES N	MAJ	0-1542497	1162	1
CALZA PETER	COL	0-0344311	0156	1
CAMACHO MIGUEL A	1LT	0-0410457	0743	2
CAMBELL CHARLES K	MAJ	0-1635666	1060	1
CAMBLIN JOHN W	1LT	0-2032971	0760	1
CAMBRE GERARD I	COL	0-0272504	0764	3
CAMERON ANDREW L	LTC	0-0249129	0666	3
CAMERON CHARLES E	1LT	0-1556696	0745	2
CAMERON CLARENCE P	MAJ	0-1688091	0146	1
CAMERON DORT A	1LT	0-0393545	1143	2
CAMERON EUSTACE R	CPT	0-1107337	0948	1
CAMERON FRANCES S	MAJ	L-0408158	0865	1
CAMERON FRANCIS	CW3	W-2128123	0661	2
CAMERON GERALD J	MAJ	0-1286305	0861	2
CAMERON HENRY M	LTC	0-0300431	0760	3
CAMERON JACK B	LTC	0-0477070	0256	1
CAMERON JOHN K	CPT	0-0405215	0745	2
CAMERON JR ARNOLD C	COL	0-0197196	0762	3
CAMERON JR DAVID A	MAJ	0-2034080	0966	2
CAMERON JR WILLIAM E	2LT	0-0926513	0146	2
CAMERON NEIL J	MAJ	0-1878052	0866	1
CAMERON NORMAN	CW3	W-2142951	0857	1
CAMERON RALPH H	COL	0-0265696	1152	3
CAMERON RALPH J	MAJ	0-0221750	0350	1
CAMERON RICHARD D	MAJ	0-1551368	0462	1
CAMERON ROBERT D	CW4	W-2110714	0664	3
CAMERON WILLIAM L	MAJ	0-1179320	0767	1
CAMERON WILLIAM P	MAJ	0-0292410	0648	3
CAMERON WILLIAM T	LTC	0-0244633	1056	3
CAMERUCI GLENN F	1LT	0-1284653	0745	2
CAMINER GERALD E	CW4	W-2136563	1164	1
CAMMACK OWEN F	MAJ	0-0901720	0246	2
CAMMACK RALPH I	MAJ	0-1289385	0563	1
CAMMACK WILLIAM R	2LT	0-0404183	0144	2
CAMP BERNARD L	CW2	W-2145074	0753	2
CAMP JAMES R	MAJ	0-2204431	1167	1

NAME	GRADE	SVC NO	DATE RET MO YR	RET CODE
CAMP JOSEPH J	MAJ	0-1014832	0460	1
CAMP JR FRANK	CW2	W-2207101	0461	1
CAMP JR GEORGE M	CPT	0-2005447	1057	2
CAMP LEWIS L	LTC	0-0904172	1065	3
CAMP MARSHALL F	MAJ	0-0246071	0866	3
CAMP MAURICE A	MAJ	0-1950270	0262	1
CAMP MERWIN J	LTC	0-0292567	0662	1
CAMP ORVILLE S	LTC	0-0423006	0860	1
CAMP RALPH M	1LT	0-1018066	0846	2
CAMP ROBERT L	CW3	W-2142225	0564	1
CAMP THOMAS E	CPT	0-0314027	0847	1
CAMPAGNA JOSEPH R	LTC	0-1172792	0767	2
CAMPAGNA SEBASTIAN	2LT	0-0361721	0444	2
CAMPAIN JOHN W	MAJ	0-0279154	1065	3
CAMPANILE MICHAEL	1LT	0-1056313	0845	2
CAMPBELL ALEXANDER	COL	0-0155568	0652	3
CAMPBELL ALFRED R	MAJ	0-1038931	0557	1
CAMPBELL ALLAN	LTC	0-0257514	0157	1
CAMPBELL ALLIE H	CW3	W-3150512	1067	1
CAMPBELL ANGUS L	COL	0-0201593	0356	2
CAMPBELL ARNOLD	MAJ	0-1581841	0367	3
CAMPBELL ARTHUR E	COL	0-0157114	1052	3
CAMPBELL BOBBIE D	CW3	W-2113410	0157	2
CAMPBELL BOWEN	LTC	0-0196594	0462	3
CAMPBELL BUFORD J	CW4	W-2116156	0664	1
CAMPBELL BURDETTE F	1LT	0-1299847	0945	2
CAMPBELL CALVIN C	COL	0-1100472	0761	1
CAMPBELL CARL	CW4	W-2123107	0666	1
CAMPBELL CHANDLER E	LTC	0-1015239	0666	1
CAMPBELL CHARLES E	1LT	0-0443987	1045	2
CAMPBELL CHARLES E	LTC	0-1640298	1166	1
CAMPBELL CHARLES H	COL	0-0183196	1053	1
CAMPBELL CHARLES K	MAJ	0-0177257	0157	3
CAMPBELL CHARLES M	1LT	0-0460085	0246	2
CAMPBELL CHARLES M	CW3	RW-2146504	0363	1
CAMPBELL CHARLES S	CPT	0-1702568	0944	2
CAMPBELL CHARLES S	CW3	W-2206784	0267	1
CAMPBELL CHARLES W	MAJ	0-0278643	0757	3
CAMPBELL CHARLES W	CPT	0-0399183	0644	2
CAMPBELL CLARENCE N	CPT	0-0507058	0245	2
CAMPBELL CLARK L	CPT	0-1165713	1158	1
CAMPBELL COLIN A	MAJ	0-0140178	0755	3
CAMPBELL COLIN C	LTC	0-0234463	0857	2
CAMPBELL DANIEL J	LTC	0-0190417	1148	3
CAMPBELL DAVID E	MAJ	0-2262969	0562	1
CAMPBELL DAVID F	LTC	0-1100902	0161	1
CAMPBELL DAVID H	2LT	0-1308470	0945	1
CAMPBELL DAY H	COL	0-0168140	0958	3
CAMPBELL DELVAN R	CW3	W-2151195	0166	1
CAMPBELL DONALD R	CW2	W-2207450	0463	1
CAMPBELL EARL M	LTC	0-0464795	0662	1
CAMPBELL EDITH B	2LT	N-0762024	0944	1
CAMPBELL EDITH M F	2LT	N-0755369	0944	1
CAMPBELL EDNA C	MAJ	N-0723451	1264	3
CAMPBELL EDWARD B	LTC	0-1100474	1160	1
CAMPBELL EDWARD C	LTC	0-1172793	0258	1
CAMPBELL EDWIN W	1LT	0-1556552	0646	2
CAMPBELL ELVIS S	LTC	0-0196036	0361	3
CAMPBELL ERNEST H	1LT	0-1100903	0645	2
CAMPBELL EUGENE D	WO1	W-2150115	0657	1
CAMPBELL FLOYD A	CW2	W-2206825	0862	1
CAMPBELL FORCYCE E	LTC	0-0195074	1054	1
CAMPBELL FRANCIS H	LTC	0-1176257	0765	1
CAMPBELL FRANCIS J	WO1	W-2110023	0948	1
CAMPBELL FRANK H	CPT	0-2150766	1057	1
CAMPBELL FRANK H	CPT	RO-2150766	1057	1
CAMPBELL FRANK J	LTC	0-0337015	1159	1
CAMPBELL FRED H	CPT	0-0105647	0155	3
CAMPBELL GEORGE A	1LT	0-0544230	1145	2
CAMPBELL GEORGE J	CW2	W-2117172	1046	2
CAMPBELL GEORGE L	CW2	W-2145715	0461	1
CAMPBELL GERALD D	LTC	0-0294819	0355	1
CAMPBELL GERTRUDE M	CPT	N-0729031	0948	1
CAMPBELL GLEN W	LTC	0-0207185	0656	3
CAMPBELL GORDON W	MAJ	0-1318760	0561	1

NAME	GRADE	SVC NO	DATE RET MO YR	RET CODE
CAMPBELL GORDON W	MAJ	0-1899451	1264	1
CAMPBELL GRAHAM G	LTC	0-0134191	0553	3
CAMPBELL GUY E	LTC	0-1284824	0260	1
CAMPBELL HAROLD R	CW4	W-2145122	0666	1
CAMPBELL HARRY M	LTC	0-0219918	0257	3
CAMPBELL HENRY C	COL	0-0115893	0446	2
CAMPBELL HERBERT C	CW2	W-2114991	1044	2
CAMPBELL HOLMES	MAJ	0-0244620	0259	2
CAMPBELL HOWARD N	1LT	0-1012983	0551	2
CAMPBELL HOWELL H	1LT	0-1320505	0346	2
CAMPBELL HUGH B	LTC	0-0367510	0264	1
CAMPBELL JACK H	CPT	0-1995062	1051	1
CAMPBELL JAMES	CPT	0-2097010	0162	1
CAMPBELL JAMES D	COL	0-0243258	1154	1
CAMPBELL JAMES E	MAJ	0-1798444	0967	1
CAMPBELL JAMES J	MAJ	0-0254398	0964	3
CAMPBELL JAMES J	LTC	0-0313493	0663	3
CAMPBELL JAMES M	MAJ	0-0513975	0437	1
CAMPBELL JAMES S	CPT	0-0944651	0860	1
CAMPBELL JAMES S	LTC	0-1588601	1262	1
CAMPBELL JAMES V	1LT	0-1298352	1045	2
CAMPBELL JAMES W	CW3	W-2207208	0867	1
CAMPBELL JOE C	1LT	0-0485658	0255	1
CAMPBELL JOHN	COL	0-0243514	0664	3
CAMPBELL JOHN E	1LT	0-1328114	1046	2
CAMPBELL JOHN F	CW2	W-2151809	0359	1
CAMPBELL JOHN G	2LT	0-0425866	0443	2
CAMPBELL JOHN H	LTC	0-0382000	0761	1
CAMPBELL JOHN M	1LT	0-0535905	1045	2
CAMPBELL JOHN N	1LT	0-0165681	0952	3
CAMPBELL JOHN P	COL	0-0115894	0648	3
CAMPBELL JOHN P	LTC	0-1169047	0561	1
CAMPBELL JOSEPH P	1LT	0-0400443	0244	2
CAMPBELL JR BRUCE B	1LT	0-0382744	0745	2
CAMPBELL JR BRUCE W	MAJ	0-0359177	0745	2
CAMPBELL JR FRANK S	MAJ	0-2029644	0465	1
CAMPBELL JR GEORGE W	CW2	W-2214904	1167	1
CAMPBELL JR JAMES	LTC	0-1115886	0264	1
CAMPBELL JR JAMES A	LTC	0-0249130	0766	3
CAMPBELL JR JOHN	MAJ	0-2203031	0767	1
CAMPBELL JR JOHN W	CW3	W-2146656	1065	1
CAMPBELL JR LELAND	MAJ	0-0778719	0656	2
CAMPBELL JR SAMUEL T	LTC	0-1316381	0666	1
CAMPBELL JULIA M	2LT	N-0736533	0444	1
CAMPBELL JUNIOR R	CW3	W-2147744	1264	2
CAMPBELL KENNETH A	LTC	0-0408829	0645	2
CAMPBELL KENNETH B	CW3	W-2149102	0265	1
CAMPBELL LAURIE P	MAJ	0-0423151	0149	2
CAMPBELL LAWRENCE J	LTC	0-0222427	0864	3
CAMPBELL LELAND E	CPT	0-0388511	0346	2
CAMPBELL LOUIS J	MAJ	0-0889617	0457	1
CAMPBELL MARION B	CW2	W-2143604	0656	1
CAMPBELL MARION L	LTC	0-0348975	1163	3
CAMPBELL MAVER J	MAJ	0-0271903	0366	3
CAMPBELL MAX F	CW3	W-2203658	0767	1
CAMPBELL MERLE E	MAJ	0-1051505	1262	1
CAMPBELL MONTGOMERY	LTC	0-0203344	1058	3
CAMPBELL MURDOCK A	B G	0-0186286	0952	3
CAMPBELL NELLIE D	2LT	N-0734614	1043	1
CAMPBELL OREN F	MAJ	0-0243872	0666	3
CAMPBELL PAUL L	LTC	0-0499813	0155	1
CAMPBELL PLEASANT P	CPT	0-1297158	0850	1
CAMPBELL RALPH L	LTC	0-0273521	0467	3
CAMPBELL RAY C	MAJ	0-0921003	0763	1
CAMPBELL RICHARD E	LTC	0-1044487	0863	1
CAMPBELL RICHARD H	LTC	0-0125205	0853	3
CAMPBELL RICHARD O	MAJ	0-0321197	0448	1
CAMPBELL ROBERT A	WO1	W-2101514	0845	2
CAMPBELL ROBERT H	MAJ	0-2017199	0164	1
CAMPBELL ROBERT J	LTC	0-1295990	0662	1
CAMPBELL ROBERT M	COL	0-0232139	0260	3
CAMPBELL ROBERT T	CW3	W-2142320	0261	1
CAMPBELL ROBERT W	CPT	0-0549388	0747	1
CAMPBELL ROBERT W	LTC	0-1312277	0161	1
CAMPBELL ROLLEN F	LTC	0-1594082	0767	1

NAME	GRADE	SVC NO	DATE RET MO YR	RET CODE
CAMPBELL RUSSELL A	MAJ	0-0401877	0860	1
CAMPBELL STEWART T	CW3	W-2145269	1065	1
CAMPBELL THEODORE	CW2	W-2101515	0350	1
CAMPBELL THEODORE	CW4	W-2144282	0161	1
CAMPBELL THEODORE M	MAJ	0-0510226	0546	2
CAMPBELL THERMAN L	CW2	W-2146691	0956	1
CAMPBELL THOMAS F	LTC	0-1042780	1161	1
CAMPBELL THOMAS G	MAJ	0-1553967	0565	1
CAMPBELL THOMAS H	MAJ	0-0385686	0760	1
CAMPBELL THOMAS J	MAJ	0-0469341	0452	1
CAMPBELL WALLACE J	CPT	0-0394267	0444	2
CAMPBELL WALTER F	LTC	0-0922274	0961	3
CAMPBELL WILLIAM B	LTC	0-0447657	0159	3
CAMPBELL WILLIAM C	LTC	0-0250121	0966	3
CAMPBELL WILLIAM F	COL	0-0160696	0354	2
CAMPBELL WILLIAM H	CPT	0-2288112	1262	1
CAMPBELL WILLIAM J	CPT	0-0915152	0445	2
CAMPBELL WILLIAM J	CPT	0-1306378	0550	1
CAMPBELL WILLIAM N	CW3	W-2148842	0662	1
CAMPBELL WINSTON E	CW3	W-2149250	0265	1
CAMPER DEWEY C	CW3	W-2141215	1165	1
CAMPER JR HARRY G	CPT	0-0517378	1046	2
CAMPER JR WILLIAM L	MAJ	0-1290547	1060	1
CAMPFIELD ALLAN B	COL	0-0142359	1154	3
CAMPFIELD ARTHUR M	CPT	0-0350050	0745	2
CAMPION ALBERT E	LTC	0-0276272	0967	3
CAMPISANO JOSEPH T	LTC	0-0302443	0666	3
CAMPISI ORLANDO A	MAJ	0-2262660	0566	1
CAMPLAN CHARLES W	CPT	0-0276097	0767	3
CAMPO DOMINIC	CPT	0-1857739	1158	1
CAMPORELLO SAMUEL	1LT	0-1062568	1045	2
CAMPRINI RODERICK P	LTC	0-1312375	0263	1
CAMUNEZ ARTHUR D	LTC	0-1313202	0762	1
CAMUTI LOUIS J	CPT	0-0140563	0853	3
CAMY LEON H	COL	0-0240337	0549	3
CANADA JAMES E	CPT	0-0172724	0648	3
CANADA JOHN R	MAJ	0-1108536	0363	2
CANADA JOHN R	CW3	W-2148784	1065	1
CANADA SAMUEL L	LTC	0-0947274	0866	3
CANADAY WILLIS L	MAJ	0-1876726	0666	1
CANALE ANTHONY J	1LT	0-5326853	1067	2
CANANT ERMER C	MAJ	0-2262856	1163	1
CANAS ENRIQUE J	CW3	W-2144702	0161	1
CANCELLARE ANTHONY D	LTC	0-0333094	0860	1
CANCIGLIA ALPHONSE	MAJ	0-0959097	0962	1
CANCIC LEONARDO D	1LT	0-2027039	1151	1
CANDELARIO JOSE M	2LT	0-1573756	0743	1
CANDLER JR ROBERT G	LTC	0-1014690	1167	1
CANDLER WILLIAM W	2LT	0-1304858	1044	2
CANDY JOE F	LTC	0-1166925	0161	2
CANE DONALD B	LTC	0-1633734	0657	1
CANELLOS PETER J	LTC	0-1048710	1061	1
CANET ROSE P	2LT	N-0763770	0145	1
CANFIELD BRUCE H	MAJ	0-0307588	1145	2
CANFIELD DONALD T	1LT	0-0120385	0955	3
CANFIELD GEORGE H	COL	0-0103796	0648	3
CANFIELD HENRY P	MAJ	0-0186478	0556	3
CANFIELD JOHN J	CPT	0-1695271	0746	2
CANFIELD MORRIS H	MAJ	0-1183297	1164	1
CANGELOSI IGNAZIO F	MAJ	0-1688412	0762	1
CANGER ANDREW J	2LT	0-1016997	0945	2
CANHA ALVIN A	CW3	W-2110718	1060	1
CANIFF THOMAS F	CW2	W-2116015	0648	1
CANILAC LUPO	1LT	0-1896903	0452	2
CANINOGJIMENEZ V M	LTC	0-1924308	0958	2
CANIPELLI EDWARD	CPT	0-0331242	0145	2
CANLETT FRANKLIN H	1LT	0-2103072	0162	2
CANN HOWARD L	LTC	0-0385640	1163	1
CANN JOSEPH R	CPT	0-1699962	0858	1
CANN JR ALFRED H	LTC	0-1180443	0166	1
CANNADY ELLEN B	2LT	N-0743893	1044	1
CANNAN EDWIN J	LTC	0-0450097	1059	2
CANNEFAX WARREN M	MAJ	0-1649722	0555	1
CANNEY BERNARD J	CPT	0-1284654	0647	1
CANNING CHARLES F	CW3	W-3000207	1266	1

NAME	GRADE	SVC NO	DATE RET MO YR	RET CODE
CANNING ROBERT A	MAJ	0-0232666	0463	3
CANNOM EARL D	1LT	0-0905829	0645	2
CANNON ANGUS B	1LT	0-0279402	0461	1
CANNON CECIL L	MAJ	0-1292300	0759	1
CANNON CHARLES E	LTC	0-1103090	0862	1
CANNON ESPEY F	MAJ	0-0345394	1045	2
CANNON FRANK W	MAJ	0-0243193	0851	3
CANNON GEORGE F P	MAJ	0-1799939	0463	1
CANNON GEORGE M	MAJ	0-0109166	1130	1
CANNON HARVEY P	MAJ	0-1051068	0657	1
CANNON JACK O	MAJ	0-1649723	1064	1
CANNON JAMES P	MAJ	0-0237956	0165	3
CANNON JOE E	LTC	0-0447757	1155	1
CANNON JOHN B	COL	0-0200174	0358	3
CANNON JOHN E	LTC	0-1309344	0962	1
CANNON JOHN P	CW3	W-2127106	0656	1
CANNON JOSEPH F	LTC	0-1289366	0366	1
CANNON JOSEPH H	CPT	0-0360804	1143	2
CANNON JOSEPH M	CPT	0-0108821	1027	1
CANNON JR MALLORY K	LTC	0-0215954	1262	3
CANNON JR OLIN B	CPT	0-0460090	0146	2
CANNON JR RAYMOND J	MAJ	0-0375991	0146	2
CANNON MALCOLM F	CW4	W-2141217	0465	1
CANON CLEO R	CW2	W-2147208	0662	1
CANONICA GEORGE	LTC	0-1554873	0765	1
CANOVA ENRIQUE C	COL	0-0235001	1056	3
CANRIGHT WARREN W	1LT	0-0430265	0547	1
CANTACO LUCIO	1LT	0-0890480	0548	1
CANTERBURY SHERMAN C	LTC	0-0345195	0266	1
CANTILLON THOMAS P	1LT	0-1293202	1046	2
CANTLEY CHARLES E	MAJ	0-0493813	0157	1
CANTLEY EUGENE H	MAJ	0-1578236	0859	1
CANTLEY HOMER H	MAJ	0-0971355	0662	1
CANTLEY JR CHARLES F	MAJ	0-0987825	0265	1
CANTLEY NORMAN J	LTC	0-0325076	0761	1
CANTLEY ROGER H	CPT	0-1999210	0646	2
CANTNER HARRY E	LTC	0-0191606	0648	3
CANTONI PETE J	1LT	0-2048241	0645	2
CANTOR JESSE E	LTC	0-0519174	1045	1
CANTOR MORTIMER J	LTC	0-0325167	1046	2
CANTOR PHILIP E	COL	0-0488955	0266	3
CANTORE THOMAS A	MAJ	0-2033077	0463	1
CANTPALL EVANS F	CPT	0-0118338	0648	3
CANTRELL ALLEN W	CPT	0-2032972	0764	1
CANTRELL BOYD T	MAJ	0-1582655	0965	1
CANTRELL DAVID M	CW3	W-2148687	1060	1
CANTRELL JACK G	CW2	W-2209577	0263	1
CANTRELL JAMES A	CW2	W-3200169	0764	1
CANTRELL JAMES C	MAJ	0-1341400	1165	1
CANTRELL LEONARD F	LTC	0-0676019	1166	1
CANTRELL LIGE L	CPT	0-0360654	0944	2
CANTRELL LYNDELL D	CW2	W-2146738	1059	1
CANTRELL OSCAR C	1LT	0-0887450	0556	1
CANTRELL RALPH E	LTC	0-0503011	0555	1
CANTRELL ROBERT B	MAJ	0-0399724	0862	1
CANTRELL THOMAS A	MAJ	0-0317971	0246	2
CANTRELL WILFRED O	CW3	W-2146706	0961	1
CANTRELL WILLIAM A	CPT	0-2026529	0154	1
CANTRELL WILLIAM P	CPT	0-1321744	0754	2
CANTRILL EVERETT R	MAJ	0-0975815	1155	1
CANTWELL CALVIN A	1LT	0-1175966	0645	2
CANTWELL JAMES W	MAJ	0-0303255	0244	2
CANTWELL JR JOHN J	2LT	0-1822956	0645	2
CANTWELL ORVILLE D	LTC	0-0243448	0963	3
CANTWELL ROBERT C	MAJ	0-2033626	0761	1
CANTY LEONARD C	1LT	0-0308982	0647	2
CANUTESON ELMORE C	CPT	0-0266492	1265	3
CANZANO JOSEPH	MAJ	0-0885732	0156	1
CAPARINO BRUNO	1LT	0-2030575	1049	1
CAPASSO ALEXANDER	MAJ	0-0352729	0260	1
CAPASSO SALVATORE	LTC	0-0403197	0860	1
CAPE GURNEE	1LT	0-1013252	0546	2
CAPE JOSEPH R	CW3	W-2150890	0263	1
CAPELLE WILMER B	CPT	0-1291230	0452	2
CAPEN EDGAR A	CPT	0-0163940	1044	2

NAME	GRADE	SVC NO	DATE RET MO YR	RET CODE
CAPERS HAROLD H	COL	0-0204559	0854	1
CAPERS ROBERT A	CPT	0-1301945	0347	2
CAPERTON LUCIEN M	MAJ	0-0304343	0745	2
CAPILOUTO ISAAC E	CPT	0-0353731	0545	2
CAPITELL ROBERT W	1LT	0-0396588	0344	2
CAPKA ADOLPH J	LTC	0-1703854	1263	1
CAPLAN CHARLES C	CPT	0-0537200	1045	2
CAPLAN LESLIE	MAJ	0-0413434	0746	2
CAPLE JR GEORGE H	LTC	0-0299266	0857	1
CAPLE JR JOHN A	CW3	W-2153349	0466	1
CAPLE RALPH G	LTC	0-1950643	0764	1
CAPLES ROBERT O	CPT	0-0481554	0345	1
CAPLES WILLIS H	LTC	0-0556902	0365	1
CAPLIN BERNARD	WO1	W-2121109	1144	2
CAPLINGER HAROLD S	COL	0-0264190	1060	3
CAPO MILFORD T	1LT	0-0417299	0945	2
CAPO RAFAEL	LTC	0-0279050	1065	3
CAPONE EDMUND P	COL	0-0225410	0564	3
CAPONEGRO ALFRED A	1LT	0-2041155	0552	1
CAPOZZI HENRY L	1LT	0-1102656	0146	2
CAPP GEORGE R	COL	0-0162771	0946	2
CAPPELEN JR JOHN J	MAJ	0-0598291	1262	1
CAPPELETTI LAWRENCE	MAJ	0-1998387	1060	1
CAPPELLETTI JOSEPH M	LTC	0-0450814	0759	1
CAPPER RANDOLPH B	MAJ	0-1587166	1060	1
CAPPS CARY F	LTC	0-1637150	0167	1
CAPPS JESSE L	CPT	0-0495247	0759	1
CAPPS JR WILLIAM T	2LT	0-1295826	0544	2
CAPPS RICHARD B	LTC	0-0386360	0346	2
CAPPS RODNEY O	LTC	0-0334655	0761	1
CAPPS TED	MAJ	0-1323285	0157	1
CAPPS WILLIAM P	MAJ	0-0328729	0754	2
CAPPUCCIO FRANK S	WO1	W-2126259	0745	2
CAPPY ANDREW L	LTC	0-1535146	0161	1
CAPRARO SALVATORE	1LT	0-0496218	0644	2
CAPRIELIAN LEON R	1LT	0-1166242	0745	2
CAPRIO MICHAEL J	1LT	0-1575829	1060	2
CAPROCK DOUGLAS M	2LT	0-5310853	0761	2
CAPSHAW JR ROY E	MAJ	0-1286789	0459	1
CAPSHAW LAWSON H	MAJ	0-2009292	0860	1
CAPSTICK DONALD R	LTC	0-1557129	1262	1
CAPTAIN GEORGE F	CW2	W-2209211	1264	1
CAPUANO ANDREW	CPT	0-1319598	0946	2
CAPUCILLE HENRY G	LTC	0-1998420	0712	1
CAPUTO MICHAEL L	1LT	0-1544535	0347	2
CAPUTO PETER A	MAJ	0-1895277	1054	2
CARAMAT RAFAEL	1LT	0-1896722	0951	1
CARANTO ERIBERTO	MAJ	0-1896462	0267	1
CARARIE ANTHONY	LTC	0-1166926	0861	1
CARAVAN ANTHONY	CW3	W-2144786	0563	1
CARAVATI CHARLES M	LTC	0-0481994	0646	1
CARAWAY JEWELL H	CW3	W-2150006	0264	1
CARAWAY LUTHER C	MAJ	0-4010214	0866	2
CARBALLO ABIGAIL	1LT	0-4028375	0857	2
CARBALLO DOMINADOR	1LT	0-1896611	1062	1
CARBAUCH KENNETH W	CPT	0-0291134	0945	2
CARBAUGH ROYCE A	CPT	0-0955451	0559	1
CARBERRY JAMES E	LTC	0-1017793	0965	1
CARBERRY WILLIAM F	CW2	W-2210665	0367	1
CARBIA MARIO	MAJ	0-0395353	0163	1
CARBIN JR JOHN P	LTC	0-1290897	0265	3
CARBIS WAYNE F	LTC	0-0159008	0756	3
CARBONE ALFONSO P	MAJ	0-1795861	1157	1
CARBONE FRANK A	MAJ	0-1637151	0161	1
CARBRY VINCENT N	CPT	0-0198903	0856	3
CARCHICI GEORGE M	CW3	W-2149404	0865	1
CARO JACK H	1LT	0-1821678	0745	2
CARO LLOYD S	CW4	W-2102727	0357	1
CARD THOMAS B	COL	0-0147154	0955	3
CARD WILLIAM R	CPT	0-1798779	0962	2
CARDAMON ALBERT J	LTC	0-0401482	0265	1
CARDE MANUEL D	CPT	0-0167885	0654	3
CARDELLA JAMES A	CW3	W-2147237	0463	1
CARDEN BLYTHE P L	COL	0-0195812	0960	3
CARDEN SR ALVA F	CPT	0-0232958	0357	1

NAME	GRADE	SVC NO	DATE RET MO YR	RET CODE
CARDER ALVA L	CPT	O-0246217	0648	3
CARDER FRANK R	MAJ	O-0444959	0149	1
CARDER JR WESLEY S	2LT	O-2010805	0945	2
CARDER NATHANIEL	COL	O-0266138	0458	3
CARDILLO LUCA F	LTC	O-0395352	0560	1
CARDINAL EUGENE C	CW3	W-2145381	0860	1
CARDLE GEORGE F	LTC	O-0486915	0165	3
CARDONA VICTOR	MAJ	O-0274202	1166	3
CARDONE MICHAEL A	CW3	W-2152801	0762	1
CARDOTT WAYNE N	MAJ	O-0265590	0267	3
CARDOZA HOWARD W	1LT	O-1177318	0551	1
CARDOZA HUGH L	COL	O-0357549	1165	1
CARDWELL ARJENTER R	MAJ	O-1012124	1055	1
CARDWELL CECIL L	MAJ	O-1281395	0555	1
CARDWELL CLIFTON C	MAJ	O-2036851	1060	1
CARDWELL FOSTER M	1LT	O-1796575	0944	2
CARDWELL JOHN E	CPT	O-0112896	0352	3
CARDWELL NICHOLAS	1LT	O-0491813	1046	1
CARDWELL OTIS R	CPT	O-1000921	0764	1
CARDWELL PERCY L	LTC	O-0179599	0354	3
CAREL MORRIS W	MAJ	O-0977372	0562	1
CAREL RALPH A	CPT	O-1588444	0657	1
CAREW JOHN H	1LT	O-1017345	0346	2
CAREW JOHN J	COL	O-0126433	0345	1
CAREW LAWRENCE F	COL	O-0234272	0246	2
CAREY ALFRED J	MAJ	O-0495992	0157	1
CAREY CHARLES W	MAJ	O-0472810	0544	2
CAREY CHARLOTTE	1LT	O-1103551	1045	1
CAREY EDWARD J	LTC	O-0232531	0163	3
CAREY FRANK J	COL	O-0165389	0452	3
CAREY GLENN W	COL	O-0171565	0542	2
CAREY HARRY H	LTC	O-0175988	0648	3
CAREY JAMES	CPT	O-1299682	0459	1
CAREY JAMES F	1LT	O-1011130	0945	2
CAREY JAMES F	LTC	O-0229821	0465	3
CAREY JAMES H	LTC	O-0443645	0365	1
CAREY JAMES T	MAJ	O-1796231	0657	1
CAREY JOHN A	2LT	O-1325373	0345	2
CAREY JOSEPH M	CW2	W-2206666	0262	1
CAREY JR JOHN J	1LT	O-1304859	1045	2
CAREY LAURENCE M	CPT	O-0902242	0745	2
CAREY LEO A	CPT	O-0489270	1146	1
CAREY MARC R	CPT	O-0167818	1155	3
CAREY NELSON B	LTC	O-1042511	0263	1
CAREY PERRY F	CPT	O-2026964	0757	1
CAREY THOMAS G	COL	O-0325545	1060	1
CAREY WILLIAM L	CPT	O-0361903	0244	2
CAREY WILLIAM M	CPT	O-1105307	0461	1
CAREY WILLIAM N	COL	O-0165788	0649	3
CAREY WILLIAM T	MAJ	O-2040783	0660	2
CARFAGNO JOSEPH J	MAJ	O-1589751	0958	1
CARFANO FRANCIS A	2LT	O-0439867	1042	2
CARFIELD WILLIAM E	MAJ	O-1917720	0264	1
CARGEN JOHN B	1LT	O-0528394	1145	2
CARGILE JR C B	CW3	W-2149841	0965	1
CARGILL DEXTER A	LTC	O-0272532	0758	3
CARGILL JR GEORGE S	MAJ	O-0227598	1164	3
CARGILL JR WILLIAM	CPT	O-1042781	1060	1
CARHARTT FORREST W	COL	O-0114232	0257	3
CARICH JOE	MAJ	O-0478521	1045	1
CARIDEO BIAGIO A	LTC	O-0273291	0667	3
CARIE JAMES J	MAJ	O-2265191	0167	1
CARIE JOSEPH	MAJ	O-0172045	0654	3
CARIGLIA MICHAEL W	LTC	O-0503750	1262	1
CARINI JIM	LTC	O-0489146	0456	2
CARIS JOHN A	CW3	W-2203646	0964	1
CARKEEK STANLEY N	LTC	O-0326167	0146	2
CARL DANIEL E	LTC	O-0484552	1051	1
CARL FLOYD C	COL	O-0103260	1145	2
CARL FRED W	CW2	W-2109510	0647	1
CARL GEORGE A	CW4	W-2001822	1161	3
CARL HARRY F	CPT	O-1170675	1047	2
CARL ROY G	MAJ	O-0247249	0160	3
CARL RUSSELL R	CPT	O-1573098	0446	2
CARLAW ROBERT H	1LT	O-1576995	0245	2
CARLENC ALBERT F	LTC	O-0498691	0655	1
CARLETON ALBION M	MAJ	O-1180146	0261	2
CARLETON CHARLES D	COL	O-0182940	0159	3
CARLETON GEORGE	LTC	O-0286910	0157	3
CARLETON GEORGE A	LTC	O-1108538	0862	1
CARLETON HARRY F	1LT	O-1061645	0146	2
CARLETON JR HOWARD	LTC	O-0166011	0447	2
CARLETON MILDRED I	1LT	N-0721617	0346	1
CARLIER JOHN W	MAJ	O-0311155	1165	3
CARLILE NORMAN A H	LTC	O-0315334	1264	1
CARLIN CLARA D	1LT	N-0731089	1145	2
CARLIN LOUIS	CPT	O-0533659	0447	2
CARLIN RAYMOND D	MAJ	O-0408151	0950	1
CARLISLE DOROTHY N	2LT	N-0775265	0145	2
CARLISLE FLOYD L	LTC	O-0221666	0156	3
CARLISLE FRANK B	LTC	O-1325075	0263	1
CARLISLE GLENN P	CPT	O-0315421	0758	2
CARLISLE HAROLD F	LTC	O-1107846	1161	2
CARLISLE JOHN S	LTC	O-0300626	0957	1
CARLISLE JOHN T	LTC	O-0169009	1060	3
CARLISLE JOSEPH Y	CW4	W-2113398	0366	3
CARLISLE RICHARD M	LTC	O-0365439	0265	3
CARLISLE ROBERT J	1LT	O-1319104	0945	2
CARLL FREDERICK	CW3	W-3150460	0967	1
CARLO ANGEL L	CPT	O-1301779	0860	1
CARLO JOSEPH F	1LT	O-0335042	0145	2
CARLO MICHAEL	MAJ	O-0286823	0847	1
CARLOCK HENRY A	LTC	O-0236114	1045	2
CARLOCK HORACE V	MAJ	O-0395543	0462	1
CARLOCK MARION F	MAJ	O-0268165	0565	3
CARLOCK NEIL S	LTC	O-0312663	0646	2
CARLOCK ROBERT H	CPT	O-1324507	0247	2
CARLOS WILLIAM	CW3	W-2145192	1062	1
CARLOVITCH FRANK	WO1	W-2148665	0655	1
CARLOW FRANK L	2LT	O-2010464	0167	3
CARLSEN CHARLES E	LTC	O-1307367	0466	1
CARLSEN EMANUEL	LTC	O-0468863	0163	1
CARLSEN WILLIS E	MAJ	O-1315458	0862	1
CARLSON ALBERT O	LTC	O-0243876	0262	3
CARLSON ALF B	MAJ	O-0503293	0450	1
CARLSON ARTHUR J	LTC	O-0192152	0457	1
CARLSON ARTHUR W	MAJ	O-1579465	0557	1
CARLSON BERNICE A	2LT	N-0742870	1044	1
CARLSON CARL A	LTC	O-0195144	0162	3
CARLSON CARL A	LTC	O-0303119	0855	3
CARLSON CARL A	MAJ	O-0966491	1262	1
CARLSON CARL C L	1LT	O-0413886	1144	2
CARLSON CHARLES P	LTC	O-0359045	0760	1
CARLSON CLARENCE W	LTC	O-0316874	0161	1
CARLSON CONRAD T	MAJ	O-2262992	0264	1
CARLSON CORINNE C	1LT	N-0744718	0845	1
CARLSON DALE W	MAJ	O-1308923	0865	1
CARLSON DOLPHINE H	CW4	W-2113910	0157	1
CARLSON EARL R	CW3	W-2150349	1065	1
CARLSON EDWIN O	LTC	O-0276143	1059	1
CARLSON ERNEST J	CPT	O-1285377	1045	2
CARLSON GEORGE C	LTC	O-0411511	0965	3
CARLSON GEORGE D	LTC	O-0456219	0461	1
CARLSON GLENN O	COL	O-0250791	0562	3
CARLSON GUSTAF M	MAJ	O-1105308	0967	3
CARLSON HENNING G	LTC	O-0242802	1153	3
CARLSON HERBERT A	MAJ	O-1333601	0461	1
CARLSON HERBERT E	CPT	O-1307193	0446	2
CARLSON JOHN A	LTC	O-1283210	0562	1
CARLSON JOHN F	MAJ	O-1799423	0961	1
CARLSON LAURANCE S	COL	O-0238101	0365	3
CARLSON LEONARD J	LTC	O-0144086	0-49	3
CARLSON LEONARD W	LTC	O-1646909	0367	2
CARLSON LESLIE R	CW2	W-2211370	0967	1
CARLSON LLOYD T	CW2	W-2141219	1060	2
CARLSON LLOYD V	MAJ	O-1110412	0666	2
CARLSON MAURICE L	1LT	O-0510533	0945	2
CARLSON MCKINLEY S	LTC	O-0212357	0761	3
CARLSON NORMAN V	COL	O-0283113	0364	3
CARLSON PAAVO D	COL	O-0306506	1266	1
CARLSON RALPH F	LTC	O-0201955	1162	3
CARLSON RAYMOND F	LTC	O-0126926	1150	3
CARLSON RICHARD	MAJ	O-1335744	0865	1
CARLSON ROBERT H	CPT	O-0451429	0346	2
CARLSON ROBERT H	CW3	W-2153113	0566	1
CARLSON ROBERT L	COL	O-0304819	0565	1
CARLSON ROBERT V	CW2	W-2144499	0960	1
CARLSON ROGER K	2LT	O-0975353	0853	1
CARLSON ROY E	LTC	O-1183480	0661	1
CARLSON SIDNEY A	CPT	O-0275616	1264	3
CARLSON SIGFRID F	COL	O-0351200	0162	1
CARLSON THEODORE C	CPT	O-0518992	0346	2
CARLSON TILFORD F	1LT	O-0245607	0961	3
CARLSON VERNON W	LTC	O-0544702	1167	1
CARLSON WINSTON L	MAJ	O-1823402	1263	1
CARLSTROM CHARLES H	MAJ	O-0288337	0767	3
CARLTON DUANE W	MAJ	O-0175295	0560	3
CARLTON GEORGE C	CPT	O-0509534	0357	1
CARLTON GEORGE S	CW2	W-2214655	1166	1
CARLTON JR CHARLES W	LTC	O-0186837	0762	3
CARLTON JR WILLIAM B	COL	O-0414915	0767	1
CARLTON MAURICE R	MAJ	O-0258148	0666	3
CARLTON RAY F	MAJ	O-1100906	1151	1
CARLTON RICHARD W	LTC	O-1030014	1264	1
CARLTON SR THAD M	CPT	O-0477473	0648	2
CARLTON TULLIE H	LTC	O-0182964	1155	3
CARLTON WILLIAM H	CW2	W-2205945	0960	1
CARLYLE CHARLES E	LTC	O-1533275	0860	1
CARMACK CRAIG S	LTC	O-0237332	0366	3
CARMACK JESSE	CPT	O-0443897	0944	1
CARMACK VERRA W	MAJ	O-0203761	0557	3
CARMAN CHARLES K	1LT	O-2028825	0750	1
CARMAN CHARLES M	1LT	O-0324062	1045	2
CARMAN DAVID B	2LT	O-1112072	0744	2
CARMAN DONALD L	MAJ	O-1010763	1047	2
CARMAN ROBERT M	CPT	O-1650461	0158	1
CARMEAN CHARLES C	MAJ	O-1633737	1161	1
CARMEL DAVID B	WO1	W-2128360	0545	2
CARMER CLARENCE W	1LT	O-0967311	1158	1
CARMER RALPH P	MAJ	O-0988112	0865	1
CARMICAL WILLIAM K	CW3	W-2149427	0367	1
CARMICHAEL EDWARD L	B G	O-0256012	1064	3
CARMICHAEL ELBERT E	LTC	O-0269211	1059	1
CARMICHAEL FRANCIS A	MAJ	O-0406625	0146	2
CARMICHAEL GEORGE W	CPT	O-0983441	0762	1
CARMICHAEL HOWARD E	MAJ	O-0183223	0648	3
CARMICHAEL HUBERT L	MAJ	O-2075529	0166	2
CARMICHAEL KENNETH C	MAJ	O-1923597	0465	1
CARMICHAEL THOMAS N	CPT	O-0440407	0246	1
CARMICHAEL TURNER F	CPT	O-2262664	1165	1
CARMICHAEL WILLIAM A	COL	O-0154303	0648	3
CARMICHAEL WILLIAM H	CPT	O-0389657	0844	2
CARMICHEAL WILLIAM A	LTC	O-1289544	0559	1
CARMODY DENNIS M	1LT	O-0419349	0544	2
CARMODY JOHN V	CPT	O-0488620	0650	1
CARNAGEY ERMAN P	MAJ	O-1686757	1165	1
CARNAGHAN RAYMOND S	CW4	W-2002355	0163	1
CARNAHAN ANDREW B	LTC	O-0415812	0561	1
CARNAHAN CLARENCE	CPT	O-0490447	0948	1
CARNAHAN HUGH L	COL	O-0122016	0251	3
CARNAHAN PAUL M	CPT	O-0218942	1056	3
CARNAHAN ROBERT S	CPT	O-0257131	0160	3
CARNAHAN WILLIAM G	1LT	O-0300631	0145	2
CARNAN JR CHARLES W	MAJ	O-0470163	1045	2
CARNE NORBERT O	CPT	O-1932329	0765	1
CARNER LESLIE	MAJ	O-0108572	1136	1
CARNER WILFORD R	LTC	O-0488923	1054	2
CARNES AVERY W	CPT	O-1032615	0156	1
CARNES CHARLES N	1LT	O-0497236	0246	2
CARNES CHARLES W	COL	O-0391298	0165	1
CARNES WILLIAM T	1LT	O-1297835	1045	2
CARNETT CHARLES D	MAJ	O-0263994	0753	3
CARNEY CHARLES A	COL	O-0241002	0158	1
CARNEY ELIZABETH	MAJ	N-0760080	0466	1
CARNEY HARRY R	COL	O-0270321	1263	3
CARNEY HENRY J	LTC	O-0245768	1059	3
CARNEY JAMES H	LTC	O-1552034	1162	1
CARNEY JOHN F	CW4	W-2110734	0758	1
CARNEY JOHN J	CPT	O-0924539	0745	2
CARNEY JOHN P	1LT	O-1316529	0845	1
CARNEY JR CHARLES P	MAJ	O-1298354	0346	2
CARNEY JR JOHN G	LTC	O-1590364	0862	1
CARNEY LAWRENCE B	LTC	O-0273610	0767	3
CARNEY LEONARD E	CW2	W-2145794	1160	1
CARNEY LEROY F	LTC	O-1114880	1067	1
CARNEY MARY L	2LT	N-0700830	0239	1
CARNEY SIDNEY	CPT	O-1169889	0446	2
CARNEY STANIS P	LTC	O-0510339	0557	2
CARNEY THOMAS M	1LT	O-1312103	0945	2
CARNEY WILLIAM	1LT	O-0178737	0241	1
CARNEY WILLIAM D	WO1	W-2105564	0146	2
CARNEY WILLIAM T	LTC	O-1038735	0364	2
CARNINE DONALD M	LTC	O-1822358	0661	1
CARNS ANDY M	LTC	O-1104076	0360	1
CARNS WILLIAM A	CPT	O-1913581	1023	1
CAROL HAROLD L	2LT	O-1013007	1043	2
CAROLIN JOHN V	LTC	O-1031470	1262	1
CARON JOSEPH G	CPT	O-0521273	1146	1
CARON JOSEPH R	CPT	O-1573760	0256	1
CAROTHERS ARTHUR W	LTC	O-1554874	0765	2
CAROTHERS PAUL L	WO1	W-2128325	1044	2
CAROTHERS VICTOR L	CPT	O-0267728	0656	3
CARP EDWARD M	MAJ	O-1341630	0363	1
CARP EDWIN H	2LT	O-1306240	0645	2
CARP FRED	COL	O-0218472	0748	3
CARP PETER F	MAJ	O-1104077	0264	1
CARPENTER ALVA C	COL	O-0290429	0262	3
CARPENTER CARL H	WO1	W-2127996	0346	2
CARPENTER CHARLES L	MAJ	O-1702256	1165	1
CARPENTER CHARLES M	LTC	O-0312540	0146	2
CARPENTER CHESTER F	LTC	O-2018481	0764	1
CARPENTER CLAIR F	1LT	O-1291413	0345	1
CARPENTER CLERON J	1LT	O-1297678	0 46	2
CARPENTER DELBERT O	LTC	O-1049433	0863	1
CARPENTER EDWIN J	COL	O-0300589	0859	1
CARPENTER EMMETT M	LTC	O-0430158	1264	3
CARPENTER FINLEY R	1LT	O-1310808	1046	2
CARPENTER FLAVE J	LTC	O-1691936	0266	1
CARPENTER FRANCIS W	MAJ	O-0255328	0867	3
CARPENTER FRANK G	2LT	O-0463904	0444	2
CARPENTER GEORGE K	LTC	O-0491892	1145	2
CARPENTER GEORGE L	1LT	O-1390172	1058	3
CARPENTER GILBERT R	LTC	O-1545815	1064	1
CARPENTER GROVER N	LTC	O-1595417	0367	1
CARPENTER HOWARD J	LTC	O-0483866	0458	2
CARPENTER HOWARD S	WO1	W-2114333	1043	2
CARPENTER HUGH	LTC	O-0924983	0364	3
CARPENTER JACK D	CPT	O-1296168	1159	1
CARPENTER JAMES H	LTC	O-0346782	0660	1
CARPENTER JAMES J	MAJ	O-1107340	0956	2
CARPENTER JAMES J	CW3	W-2143440	0257	1
CARPENTER JAMES L	MAJ	O-0488297	0950	1
CARPENTER JOAN G	1LT	N-0768969	1147	1
CARPENTER JOSEPH O	1LT	O-1019125	1062	2
CARPENTER JR ELLIOTT	CPT	O-1016118	0746	2
CARPENTER JR G Y	MAJ	O-0467679	0547	1
CARPENTER JR JOHN C	1LT	O-0446422	0646	2
CARPENTER KENNETH C	1LT	O-0492915	0153	1
CARPENTER KENNETH L	MAJ	O-0975887	1163	1
CARPENTER LAWRENCE E	CPT	O-0282178	0346	2
CARPENTER LESLIE B	LTC	O-0218170	0856	3
CARPENTER LYLE F	CW3	W-2147195	0266	1
CARPENTER MALCOLM Y	LTC	O-0266067	0756	3
CARPENTER MARY L	1LT	N-0734251	1047	1
CARPENTER MAURICE P	1LT	O-1304173	0346	2
CARPENTER MELVIN M	1LT	O-1307653	0546	2
CARPENTER ORVILLE E	MAJ	O-0441789	0448	2
CARPENTER PHILIP A	MAJ	O-1301429	0361	1
CARPENTER RALPH E	LTC	O-2018482	1163	1
CARPENTER RALPH G	MAJ	O-1308207	0859	1

NAME	GRADE	SVC NO	DATE RET MO YR	RET CODE
CARPENTER RAYMOND C	MAJ	0-1798114	0157	1
CARPENTER REED L	MAJ	0-1306701	0954	2
CARPENTER ROBERT C	CW3	W-2144404	0862	1
CARPENTER ROBERT R	LTC	0-1573761	0157	1
CARPENTER ROLAND F	1LT	0-1328119	0646	2
CARPENTER ROY R	LTC	0-1060387	0462	1
CARPENTER WALTER N	LTC	0-1286606	0966	1
CARPENTER WARNER H	CW2	W-2208740	0863	1
CARPENTER WILBUR R	MAJ	0-0219633	0947	1
CARPENTER WILLIAM J	MAJ	0-1640834	0767	1
CARPENTER WILLIAM J	MAJ	0-1949503	1262	1
CARPENTER WILLIAM R	LTC	0-0268641	0263	3
CARPENTER WILLIAM R	LTC	0-0387079	0461	1
CARPER HAROLD O	LTC	0-1894777	0361	1
CARPER ROBERT J	LTC	0-0107605	0153	3
CARPLES EDMOND N	MAJ	0-0109526	1155	3
CARPPI WALTER L	MAJ	0-0370313	0561	1
CARR ALFRED L	LTC	0-0115834	0756	3
CARR AMOS J	CPT	0-1913580	1028	1
CARR BERNARD	MAJ	0-0491216	0347	1
CARR CHARLES A	MAJ	0-0263485	0457	3
CARR CHESTER M	LTC	0-0451086	0854	1
CARR CLARENCE R	COL	0-0260108	1166	3
CARR CLAUDE J	1LT	0-1995557	0846	1
CARR CLINTON C	LTC	0-0401751	0763	1
CARR EDWARD J	CW4	W-2127932	1058	1
CARR FOSTER A	CPT	0-1849573	0356	2
CARR FRANCIS J	MAJ	0-1294618	0461	1
CARR FRANK C	LTC	0-0493874	0557	1
CARR GEORGE P	LTC	0-1106040	0463	1
CARR GEORGE W	MAJ	0-0126320	0547	2
CARR GUY F	MAJ	0-0373429	0346	2
CARR ISAAC N	LTC	0-0205660	0252	3
CARR JACK O	CPT	0-0460233	0945	2
CARR JAMES M	COL	0-0215827	0158	3
CARR JAMES W	CW3	W-2142137	0863	1
CARR JESSIE F	CW3	W-2121386	0856	1
CARR JOHN R	LTC	0-0349141	0960	2
CARR JOSEPH E	LTC	0-2049195	1162	1
CARR JR EDWARD A	CPT	0-1704914	1147	1
CARR JR RALPH W	LTC	0-1014256	0866	1
CARR JR SAM R	LTC	0-1169452	0162	1
CARR JR SHIRLEY N	CW3	W-2145400	0561	1
CARR LELAND F	LTC	0-0359589	0861	1
CARR LEMAR R	2LT	0-1998633	0945	2
CARR MILTON L	LTC	0-0452544	0561	2
CARR PHILLIP R	CPT	0-0972485	0562	1
CARR RAYMOND H	MAJ	0-2030526	0167	1
CARR RAYMOND O	MAJ	0-1081123	0156	1
CARR REX V	MAJ	0-0377256	0648	2
CARR RHEA	LTC	N-0741197	0165	3
CARR RICHARD R	MAJ	0-1885612	0865	1
CARR ROBERT W	MAJ	0-1307194	0863	1
CARR ROGER W	MAJ	0-2023326	1061	1
CARR SEYMOUR J	CPT	0-4014174	1054	2
CARR STEPHEN J	MAJ	0-0288972	1150	1
CARR THAD	CPT	0-0409382	0245	2
CARR THOMAS A	LTC	0-0150176	0857	3
CARR THOMAS J	CPT	0-1018842	1147	2
CARR WALTER L	LTC	0-1549680	0363	1
CARR WESLEY	1LT	0-1284290	0445	2
CARR WILLIAM F	1LT	0-0301953	0657	3
CARR WILLIAM P	LTC	0-1307195	0259	1
CARR WILLIAM R	LTC	0-0196824	1162	3
CARRABINO JOSEPH F	MAJ	0-0954058	1165	1
CARRAGHER TIMOTHY A	CW4	W-2118106	0155	1
CARRAWAY JR THOMAS L	1LT	0-0544173	0447	2
CARRELL STEPHEN E	CPT	0-0251091	1062	3
CARRELL VIRGEL R	CW2	W-2209274	0661	1
CARRERAS WILFRED C	MAJ	0-0502430	1046	1
CARRICK HAROLD T	CPT	0-0219935	0844	2
CARRICO ALFRED W	2LT	0-0503340	0644	2
CARRICO FRANK G	COL	0-0163875	0754	3
CARRICO III ANDREW	1LT	0-1010859	1045	2
CARRICO JOHN L	WO1	W-2126079	0545	2
CARRICO MELVILLE D	1LT	0-0108891	0633	1
CARRIER CLIFFORD C	1LT	0-1030646	1046	2
CARRIER ERNEST H	CPT	0-2043292	0556	1
CARRIER JOHN S	LTC	0-0333935	0750	2
CARRIER JOHN X	LTC	0-1176573	0667	1
CARRIER LUVERN J	CPT	0-0331981	0144	2
CARRIER NELL D	MAJ	N-0726111	0764	1
CARRIER ROLAND R	CPT	0-1332230	1059	2
CARRIER WILLIAM H	LTC	0-0183089	1055	3
CARRIERE EDGAR	1LT	0-2025952	0652	1
CARRIERE EDWARD E	COL	0-0248513	0565	3
CARRIG JR JOHN T	MAJ	0-1684974	1164	1
CARRIGAN MARY L S	2LT	N-0723119	1044	1
CARRIGER HERMAN D	1LT	0-1286791	0745	2
CARRIKER WALTER W	LTC	0-0337251	1146	2
CARRINGTON H K	CPT	0-0267161	0945	2
CARRINGTON HENRY P	CPT	0-0352502	1061	1
CARRINGTON LEON J	LTC	0-0298611	0560	2
CARRINGTON PAUL W	LTC	0-1180447	0565	3
CARRICK JOSEPH S	MAJ	0-1283375	1054	1
CARRIVEAU EDWARD T	CPT	0-1297317	0556	1
CARROLL ALFRED E	MAJ	0-1919043	1263	1
CARROLL BARNEY A	LTC	0-1633740	1065	1
CARROLL BERNICE	1LT	N-0730801	0446	1
CARROLL CHARLES	COL	0-0212391	0857	1
CARROLL CHARLES L	MAJ	0-1800064	1062	1
CARROLL CHARLES P	LTC	0-0282564	0263	2
CARROLL CHARLES T	MAJ	0-0381448	0246	2
CARROLL CLIFFORD C	MAJ	0-0150757	0753	3
CARROLL DELMAR B	LTC	0-0362830	0760	1
CARROLL DOYLE D	MAJ	0-0379100	0661	1
CARROLL EDWARD A	LTC	0-0921879	1166	3
CARROLL EDWARD R	LTC	0-0225094	0458	3
CARROLL EDWARD D	LTC	0-1172795	1165	1
CARROLL EDWARD J	MAJ	0-1004746	0557	1
CARROLL EDWARD J	1LT	0-1109184	0845	2
CARROLL ELMO D	LTC	0-2017351	1160	1
CARROLL ERVIN J	MAJ	0-0383996	0958	1
CARROLL FRANCIS R	COL	0-0264666	0962	1
CARROLL FRANK S	LTC	0-0286562	0360	3
CARROLL GEORGE E	MAJ	0-1684950	0862	1
CARROLL GEORGE P	LTC	0-0136928	1149	3
CARROLL HAROLD J	MAJ	0-1054203	1064	1
CARROLL HARRY M	COL	0-0191732	0351	3
CARROLL HARRY W	MAJ	0-1037429	0263	1
CARROLL HERBERT D	MAJ	0-1045653	0566	3
CARROLL HOMER D	CW3	W-2141837	0860	1
CARROLL JACK P	1LT	0-1307940	0147	2
CARROLL JAMES A	MAJ	0-0217344	1045	2
CARROLL JAMES J	LTC	0-0330470	0261	2
CARROLL JASPER G	1LT	0-2018840	1057	1
CARROLL JOHN	CW2	W-2145328	1160	1
CARROLL JOHN F	1LT	0-2034936	0452	1
CARROLL JOHN W	CPT	0-1165006	0546	2
CARROLL JOSEPH A	MAJ	0-0265746	0747	1
CARROLL JOSEPH J	MAJ	0-2025149	0563	1
CARROLL JR BERRY W	LTC	0-1046388	1064	1
CARROLL JR JABEZ F	1LT	0-1119161	0948	2
CARROLL JR JOHN E	LTC	0-0177281	0562	3
CARROLL JR ROBERT F	1LT	0-1308601	0745	2
CARROLL KENNETH L	1LT	0-1876452	0956	2
CARROLL KENT F	2LT	0-5701772	0259	2
CARROLL LAWRENCE W	CPT	0-0482470	0257	1
CARROLL LEONARD N	1LT	0-1110980	0246	2
CARROLL LEONARD S	COL	0-0292341	1155	1
CARROLL MACK M	CW3	W-2143395	0659	1
CARROLL MICHAEL L	CW3	W-2143712	0160	1
CARROLL OWEN J	LTC	0-1324141	1065	1
CARROLL PAUL E	1LT	0-1325571	0546	2
CARROLL PETER J	1LT	0-0557702	0546	1
CARROLL PHILLIP H	CPT	0-0412185	0945	2
CARROLL ROBERT E	LTC	0-0481182	0759	1
CARROLL ROBERT H	CPT	0-1325865	1158	1
CARROLL ROBERT J	MAJ	0-1540853	1162	1
CARROLL ROGER C	LTC	0-0264044	0759	1
CARROLL RULEY	CPT	0-1937997	0363	1
CARROLL SANFORD A	COL	0-0236833	1060	3
CARROLL SHELBY T	CW3	W-2149762	0761	1
CARROLL SR EVAN W	CPT	0-0163356	0559	3
CARROLL THOMAS F	LTC	0-0101020	0757	3
CARROLL VINCENT A	COL	0-0148806	0552	3
CARROLL WALKER K	COL	0-1100479	0163	2
CARROLL WESLEY W	CW2	W-2148108	0459	1
CARROLL WILLIAM F	CPT	0-0501756	0248	1
CARROLL WILLIAM G	1LT	0-1015369	0146	2
CARROLL WILLIAM R	M G	0-0246570	0456	3
CARROLL WILLIAM R	1LT	0-0924932	1145	2
CARROLL WINTON A J	MAJ	0-1014648	1059	1
CARROLLO JOHN J	LTC	0-0310209	1162	1
CARRON HECTOR M	MAJ	0-0174032	0150	3
CARROS COSTAS J	LTC	0-0487672	0853	1
CARROTHERS JOHN W	COL	0-0167282	0758	3
CARROUM OMER O	LTC	0-1284825	0761	1
CARROW WILFRED J	MAJ	0-1325374	1060	1
CARROZA ORLAND W	MAJ	0-1335511	0863	1
CARRUTH JAMES F	LTC	0-1104552	0158	1
CARRUTHERS GORDON F	1LT	0-2047591	0446	2
CARRUTHERS HECTOR K	MAJ	0-1058750	1059	2
CARRUTHERS JR J T	COL	0-0479653	0167	3
CARSCH HARRY	CW3	W-2149010	1065	1
CARSE STEWART L	LTC	0-0372147	1055	1
CARSKADEN LEWIS J	CPT	0-0157218	0954	3
CARSLEY ALBERT F	LTC	0-1300597	1264	1
CARSON ARCHIE K	CW3	W-2149039	0964	1
CARSON CARYL C	MAJ	0-0175135	1060	3
CARSON DAVID M	LTC	0-0407351	0562	1
CARSON DOUGLAS R	MAJ	0-1292833	0350	1
CARSON EARL J	2LT	0-0454299	1043	2
CARSON EDWARD C	CW3	W-2147137	0165	1
CARSON HARLIN C	CPT	0-0485400	0554	1
CARSON JAMES K	CW4	W-2110114	1155	1
CARSON JOHN L	MAJ	0-1824956	0861	2
CARSON JR BAYLIS R	MAJ	0-0374109	0862	1
CARSON KARL J	LTC	0-1170808	0764	1
CARSON PAT	MAJ	0-1111538	0963	1
CARSON REX W	WO1	W-2127037	0646	1
CARSON RICHARD L	MAJ	0-1331015	1064	1
CARSON ROBERT G	CW2	W-2143476	0865	1
CARSON ROBERT J	COL	0-0159178	1152	3
CARSON ROBERT L	MAJ	0-1173898	0461	1
CARSON THOMAS F	MAJ	0-0218860	0658	3
CARSON WILLIAM L	LTC	0-1293716	0358	1
CARSTARPHEN JACK	COL	0-1551816	0267	1
CARSTENS HENRY R	COL	0-0162758	1048	3
CARSWELL WILLIAM C	LTC	0-0348737	0863	1
CARTE CARL R	CW3	W-2118159	0959	1
CARTER ADGER M	COL	0-0259210	0860	1
CARTER ALBERT C	COL	0-0237910	1263	3
CARTER ALFRED H	CPT	0-0446423	0653	1
CARTER ARCEMUS	LTC	0-0109273	0337	1
CARTER ARTHUR	CPT	0-0519411	0546	2
CARTER ARTHUR R	CW3	W-2147351	1164	1
CARTER BOOKER W	LTC	0-1322204	0463	2
CARTER BRADLEY J	CPT	0-0275393	0355	3
CARTER BRYANT E	COL	0-0293814	0361	1
CARTER CARROLL S	LTC	0-0181198	1061	3
CARTER CHARLES	CPT	0-0191682	0452	3
CARTER CHARLES A	LTC	0-1102659	1162	1
CARTER CHARLES C	LTC	0-1589113	0761	1
CARTER CHARLES H	2LT	0-1180842	0645	2
CARTER CHARLES J	MAJ	0-1167765	1060	1
CARTER CHARLES M	CPT	0-1920308	0662	1
CARTER CHARLES R	LTC	0-1315558	0961	1
CARTER CHARLES R	MAJ	0-1649257	1164	1
CARTER CHARLES W	COL	0-0476804	0863	1
CARTER CHESTER	CPT	0-0248366	0365	3
CARTER CLAUDE E	COL	0-0319749	1061	3
CARTER DELL F	MAJ	0-1303810	0262	1
CARTER DONALD F	COL	0-0540128	0665	1
CARTER DOUGLAS E	CW3	W-2109046	0155	1
CARTER EARL	MAJ	0-0483615	0347	1
CARTER EDWARD F	MAJ	0-1175068	0957	1
CARTER ELIZABETH	1LT	N-0744864	0345	1
CARTER ELLERBE W	B G	0-0204334	0648	3
CARTER EVELYN M	2LT	N-0758343	0546	1
CARTER FRANK L	1LT	0-0189443	0836	1
CARTER GARRARD E	1LT	0-1591041	0745	2
CARTER GEORGE F	CPT	0-0492601	0145	2
CARTER GEORGE F	CW2	W-2127986	0547	2
CARTER GEORGE R	CW2	W-2147093	0861	1
CARTER GEORGE W	LTC	0-0227395	1163	3
CARTER GORDON L	COL	0-0123847	0453	3
CARTER HAROLD L	LTC	0-0267752	0551	1
CARTER HARRY P	LTC	0-0301632	0767	3
CARTER HORACE W	COL	0-0212222	0352	1
CARTER IVAN L	LTC	0-0297322	0454	3
CARTER J FLOYD	LTC	0-1004551	0962	1
CARTER JACKSON	CPT	0-0270772	0867	3
CARTER JAMES E	LTC	0-0932874	1066	3
CARTER JAMES H	MAJ	0-0272077	0345	2
CARTER JAMES R	LTC	0-1293204	1058	1
CARTER JAMES T	MAJ	0-1318513	1059	1
CARTER JERAL F	MAJ	0-0996674	0364	1
CARTER JESSE S	CPT	0-0186985	0627	1
CARTER JOE K	MAJ	0-0472361	0245	1
CARTER JOE T	CPT	0-1844595	0746	2
CARTER JOHN C	1LT	0-0277275	0857	3
CARTER JOHN C	LTC	0-0370812	0556	1
CARTER JOHN G	CPT	0-0359223	0447	2
CARTER JOHN H	COL	0-0276104	0346	2
CARTER JOHN H	COL	0-0410471	0460	1
CARTER JOHN J	CW4	W-2136751	0263	1
CARTER JOHN S	LTC	0-0217343	0756	3
CARTER JR GEORGE A	2LT	0-1175398	0745	2
CARTER JR HENRY E	1LT	0-0556525	0946	1
CARTER JR JACOB M	MAJ	0-0100448	1155	3
CARTER JR JAMES C	1LT	0-1316011	0845	2
CARTER JR JAMES N	LTC	0-2020709	0766	1
CARTER JR TONY L	COL	0-0279246	1057	3
CARTER JR WICKHAM P	MAJ	0-0354518	1046	2
CARTER JR WILLIAM H	MAJ	0-0391652	0645	2
CARTER JR WILLIAM P	LTC	0-1596289	0965	1
CARTER JR WILLIS	MAJ	0-1827359	0361	1
CARTER JULIAN H	MAJ	0-0374761	0563	3
CARTER KARL R	CW4	W-2131285	0659	1
CARTER KENNETH A	CW4	W-2107953	0659	1
CARTER KENNETH L	CW3	W-2144902	0960	1
CARTER LAWRENCE O	LTC	0-1580726	0863	1
CARTER LEROY H	1LT	0-1298659	1059	1
CARTER LLOYD W	MAJ	0-1922588	0963	1
CARTER LOUCIAN C	MAJ	0-0492700	0146	1
CARTER MABEL S	2LT	N-0769858	0446	1
CARTER MARGUERITE	1LT	N-0731728	0746	1
CARTER MARTIN S	MAJ	0-1306784	0860	1
CARTER MARY E	MAJ	N-0783500	1067	3
CARTER MELVILLE G	CPT	0-1305547	0147	2
CARTER MILTON P	MAJ	0-0300170	0663	3
CARTER NATHANIEL	MAJ	0-2262496	0363	1
CARTER NOAH J	2LT	0-2000503	0845	2
CARTER NUMA R	MAJ	0-0181991	1152	3
CARTER OWEN H	COL	0-0334313	0864	1
CARTER PAYSON D	MAJ	0-0924217	0846	1
CARTER RAYMOND F	CPT	0-0418684	0446	2
CARTER RICHARD E	MAJ	0-0301935	0564	3
CARTER RICHARD T	CW2	W-2142451	0758	1
CARTER ROBERT T	MAJ	0-1054204	0364	1
CARTER ROLLA N	MAJ	0-0175530	1160	3
CARTER ROLLAND O	CPT	0-1324143	0661	1
CARTER RONALD P	COL	0-0370782	0863	3
CARTER RUTH A	MAJ	N-0802138	0965	1
CARTER RUTH F	1LT	N-0790453	0746	1
CARTER SANFORD J	LTC	0-0430374	0861	1
CARTER SHERWOOD J	LTC	0-0960102	0667	1
CARTER SR AUBURN H	CPT	0-0167807	0858	3
CARTER SR CHARLES L	CPT	0-0255914	0757	3

NAME	GRADE	SVC NO	DATE RET MO YR	RET CODE
CARTER THOMAS B	LTC	0-0203915	0648	3
CARTER THOMAS M	COL	0-0115875	0648	3
CARTER THOMAS N	LTC	0-1303301	0163	1
CARTER VERNON L	CPT	0-1105319	1046	2
CARTER VICTOR S	LTC	0-0385758	0346	2
CARTER VILLA	LTC	0-0450557	0257	1
CARTER WILLIAM A	LTC	0-0289074	0762	1
CARTER WILLIAM C	MAJ	0-0244374	0757	1
CARTER WILLIAM L	MAJ	0-1031063	0662	1
CARTER WILLIAM R	LTC	0-0293459	0960	1
CARTER WOODROW W	LTC	0-1304338	0967	1
CARTER WYNN W	CPT	0-0327811	0144	2
CARTER ZINA R	MAJ	0-0306308	0962	1
CARTHEW IRVING G	MAJ	0-1308096	0762	1
CARTIER LOUIS F	1LT	0-1844596	0346	2
CARTLEDGE JAMES C	MAJ	0-1288854	1163	1
CARTMELL WILLIAM T	CPT	0-2262927	1067	1
CARTO DAVID S	2LT	0-1640840	0345	2
CARTON JOSEPH D	LTC	0-0245279	1264	3
CARTWRIGHT CHARLES B	MAJ	0-1314756	1060	1
CARTWRIGHT CHARLES R	LTC	0-0401396	0461	1
CARTWRIGHT CLARENCE	CPT	0-1414618	0446	1
CARTWRIGHT GENE H	CPT	0-1332928	0559	1
CARTWRIGHT GEORGE C	CPT	0-0495303	0747	1
CARTWRIGHT GEORGE T	MAJ	0-1291584	0360	1
CARTWRIGHT HERBERT L	LTC	0-2020786	0166	1
CARTWRIGHT JAMES J	CPT	0-0291077	0857	3
CARTWRIGHT JOHN E	MAJ	0-1684981	0154	1
CARTWRIGHT JR H A	CW3	W-2205044	0566	1
CARTWRIGHT KENNETH R	MAJ	0-2262835	0363	1
CARTWRIGHT MALCOLM F	MAJ	0-0970104	0765	1
CARTWRIGHT MYRTLE L	2LT	N-0733045	0445	1
CARTWRIGHT SAM F	1LT	0-1304020	0745	1
CARTWRIGHT WILLIAM D	COL	0-0203914	0947	2
CARTY CHARLES M	LTC	0-0399735	1160	1
CARTY GERALD J	1LT	0-1183032	1045	2
CARUGNO FRANK J	MAJ	0-0898949	0657	1
CARUS VICTOR	2LT	0-1550983	0845	2
CARUSO GEORGE A	MAJ	0-0235485	0258	3
CARUSO JOHN J	CPT	0-1690637	1045	2
CARUTHERS FRANK F	CPT	0-0471611	1058	1
CARVELL FATHEL C	CW3	W-2149286	0162	2
CARVER ARTHUR W	CW3	W-2144222	1262	1
CARVER CHARLES C	CW2	W-2114726	1164	3
CARVER CLARENCE D	MAJ	0-1591874	0765	3
CARVER DERL D	CW4	W-2125835	0659	1
CARVER JAMES L	CW3	W-2152200	0564	1
CARVER JR HENRY V	CW3	W-2142741	0762	1
CARVER KATHRYN E	1LT	N-0723048	1044	1
CARVER KENNETH F	CPT	0-0921920	0345	2
CARVER ROBERT I	MAJ	0-1919911	0467	1
CARVER WILLIAM H	LTC	0-1552245	0865	1
CARVILL JACK	1LT	0-0370344	1142	2
CARWILE ADDISON B	COL	0-0148807	1056	3
CARWILE JACK E	LTC	0-0109143	0646	1
CARY CARROLL F	LTC	0-1172404	1263	1
CARY HENRY B	COL	0-0410107	1057	1
CARY LOUIS A	MAJ	0-0211135	0354	3
CARY MAX E	LTC	0-1313495	0964	1
CARY WILLIAM F	1LT	0-0375835	1145	2
CASADA MARGARET V	MAJ	L-0605290	0767	1
CASADA MILTON T	2LT	0-1320427	0460	1
CASADY EDWIN L	CPT	0-1287809	1047	1
CASALE CHARLES E	COL	0-0257400	0358	3
CASAS GUILLERMO	CW2	W-2151636	0860	1
CASAUS JR CARLOS M	LTC	0-1053517	1062	1
CASAZZA CHARLES J	MAJ	0-1327812	0756	1
CASAZZAR EDWARD G	CPT	0-0462267	0546	2
CASCIO CARL W	LTC	0-1010598	0657	1
CASDORPH ROY A	CPT	0-2262437	1060	1
CASE ALBERT N	1LT	0-1286244	1045	2
CASE BEN F	CPT	0-0483983	0243	1
CASE BERNARD	COL	0-0194876	0959	3
CASE CHARLIE	1LT	0-0488673	0545	2
CASE DAVID L	LTC	0-1040191	0261	1

NAME	GRADE	SVC NO	DATE RET MO YR	RET CODE
CASE ELMER J	1LT	0-1546275	0448	2
CASE HAROLD T	CPT	0-0525944	0346	2
CASE HERSCHEL F	MAJ	0-0132012	1056	3
CASE HERSHEL C	LTC	0-0417237	1160	1
CASE JAMES R	LTC	0-0110145	1154	3
CASE KENNETH T	COL	0-0248874	0463	3
CASE LAWRENCE C	COL	0-0335454	0659	3
CASE LUTHER G	COL	0-0309384	0954	1
CASE MILTON L	MAJ	0-1824577	0262	1
CASE NORMAN S	COL	0-0166501	1048	3
CASE OLIVER L	MAJ	0-0430186	0157	1
CASE REX R	1LT	0-2009607	0753	1
CASE ROBERT J	2LT	0-5705909	1061	2
CASE ROY B	COL	0-0140042	0152	3
CASE ROY F	COL	0-0244693	1058	3
CASE WILLIAM L	LTC	0-2034839	0167	2
CASEBEER GAYLE M	MAJ	0-1015991	0361	1
CASEBEER JAMES R	MAJ	0-1593147	0657	1
CASELLAS ROZAS F N	1LT	0-1326891	0453	1
CASELLI ORLAND J	CPT	0-0346178	1044	2
CASERIC CHARLES C	LTC	0-1100480	0962	1
CASEY ALOYSIUS J	LTC	0-0233957	1162	3
CASEY EDWIN W	LTC	0-0554365	1064	1
CASEY GEORGE W	MAJ	0-1104715	0761	1
CASEY JAMES E	COL	0-0300239	0566	3
CASEY JAMES J	LTC	0-0396693	0463	1
CASEY JAMES W	MAJ	0-0325143	0762	1
CASEY JOHN F	LTC	0-1294468	0157	1
CASEY JOHN J	CPT	0-0512409	0645	2
CASEY JOHN J	CW4	W-2108664	0464	1
CASEY JOHN P	1LT	0-1016323	0346	2
CASEY JOHN P	CW3	W-2146446	0559	1
CASEY JOHN V	1LT	0-1182537	0246	2
CASEY JOHN W	COL	0-0289076	0160	1
CASEY JOSEPH A	LTC	0-0492901	1055	1
CASEY JR EDWARD J	LTC	0-1557823	0361	1
CASEY JR HERBERT D	MAJ	0-1017863	1163	1
CASEY LEE V	COL	0-0195810	0254	3
CASEY MARY A	1LT	N-0770001	0347	2
CASEY ROWELL A	LTC	0-0281301	1265	3
CASEY ROBERT F	CW3	W-2141525	1060	1
CASEY STEPHEN B	LTC	0-1325268	0367	1
CASEY TIMOTHY C	MAJ	0-2027375	0560	1
CASEY WALTER A	MAJ	0-0531978	0565	1
CASEY WILFRED	CW4	W-2135485	0556	1
CASEY WILLIAM C	LTC	0-1578249	0657	1
CASEY WILLIAM K	LTC	0-1312833	0361	1
CASEY WILLIAM L	COL	0-0125187	0953	3
CASH ARNOLD B	MAJ	0-0220598	0345	2
CASH GEORGE L	CPT	0-1058470	1060	1
CASH HAROLD E	LTC	0-1080836	0367	1
CASH PHILIP G	1LT	0-1058755	0546	2
CASH RALEIGH M	LTC	0-1703765	0358	1
CASH WALTER A	1LT	0-1321880	0146	2
CASH WARREN P	LTC	0-0227223	0565	3
CASH WILLIAM T	WO1	W-2124725	0650	2
CASH WILLIE F	CW3	W-2144867	0561	1
CASHIN DONALD F	1LT	0-0472307	0952	1
CASHION JOHN H	LTC	0-0462239	1064	1
CASHION MERRELL C	MAJ	0-1293908	0363	1
CASHMAN HARRY	MAJ	0-0978529	0167	1
CASHON IDA O	MAJ	N-0735434	1067	1
CASIANO-NAZARIO FERM	MAJ	0-4031039	0866	1
CASIMIR JOHN	1LT	0-1000094	1043	2
CASIMO ANTHONY J	CPT	0-1100147	0446	2
CASKEY EDWARD A	LTC	0-0904102	0251	1
CASKEY NEAL L	LTC	0-0407024	0460	1
CASKEY WILLIAM R	MAJ	0-0490731	0556	1
CASNER JR JOHN R	1LT	0-0534850	0846	2
CASNER LEETA L	1LT	0-1321488	0146	2
CASNER LEWIS E	MAJ	0-1183484	0359	2
CASON CLAUDE E	LTC	0-1311739	0261	1
CASON ELBERT H	CPT	0-0440873	0945	2
CASON GEORGE A	MAJ	0-1545242	0646	1
CASON JOSEPH H	MAJ	0-1304021	0161	1

NAME	GRADE	SVC NO	DATE RET MO YR	RET CODE
CASON WILLIS S	MAJ	0-0377355	0746	1
CASPER ANDREW F	COL	0-0171780	1060	3
CASPER CHARLES R	LTC	0-0888551	1060	1
CASPER JR RAYMOND E	1LT	0-0329837	1043	2
CASPER RAYMOND F	MAJ	0-0202697	0747	2
CASPERSON PETER C	COL	0-1296484	0967	1
CASS ROGER L	MAJ	0-1300598	0557	1
CASSADA JAMES C	MAJ	0-2000075	0464	1
CASSADY CHARLES A	LTC	0-0228803	0455	3
CASSADY MILBURNE C	MAJ	0-2263022	0463	1
CASSADY THOMAS C	LTC	0-0314369	0660	1
CASSARO ANGELO J	MAJ	0-1054936	0664	1
CASSAVANT THEODORE W	CPT	0-0144041	0356	3
CASSAVECCHIA WALTERE	CW3	W-2147456	0763	1
CASSCELLS SAMUEL R	CPT	0-0477283	0946	1
CASSEGRAND JR JOHN A	CW2	W-2211102	0765	1
CASSEL JONATHON F	MAJ	0-1533985	0957	1
CASSELBERRY WILLIAM	CPT	0-0990214	0763	1
CASSELL BENJAMIN F	COL	0-0407012	0267	3
CASSELL CHARLES G	COL	0-0302301	0358	1
CASSELL HARRIS	LTC	0-0556161	0963	1
CASSELL JR WILLIAM H	CW3	W-2141220	1060	1
CASSELL PAUL F	CPT	0-1310979	0846	1
CASSELL ROBERT S	LTC	0-0349803	0661	2
CASSELL THOMAS G	LTC	0-0471764	0153	1
CASSELLA PETER A	CPT	0-0327462	0146	2
CASSELMAN BERT W	LTC	0-0284727	1146	2
CASSELMAN LAWRENCE	CPT	0-1101772	1045	2
CASSETT GEORGE	LTC	0-0223851	0262	3
CASSETT WILLIAM C	MAJ	0-1549239	0158	1
CASSIDY ALBERT O	LTC	0-1101773	0761	1
CASSIDY ARTHUR E	LTC	0-0212112	0447	2
CASSIDY IRWIN F	CPT	0-0910133	0766	2
CASSIDY JAMES J	LTC	0-1297680	0664	1
CASSIDY JAMES J	CPT	0-2041003	0648	2
CASSIDY JOHN P	MAJ	0-0966157	0265	1
CASSIDY JOSEPH P	CPT	0-1012494	0346	1
CASSIDY JR LEONARD P	LTC	0-0676745	0163	1
CASSIDY LEWIS E	LTC	0-2294003	0765	1
CASSIDY LOUIS G	CPT	0-1945772	0347	2
CASSIDY MARGARET A	MAJ	N-0755704	0467	3
CASSIDY MARIE G	2LT	N-0722359	1043	1
CASSIDY MARK M	LTC	0-1945552	0860	1
CASSIDY MARY F	LTC	L-0202588	1066	3
CASSIDY RICHARD P	LTC	0-0965643	1067	1
CASSIDY WILEY L	MAJ	0-1298355	0563	1
CASSINELLI JR W J	CPT	0-1301948	1045	1
CASSITY GEORGE W	LTC	0-0248294	0563	3
CASSITY RICHARD P	1LT	0-2263384	0957	2
CASSODAY JOHN B	LTC	0-0296262	0564	3
CASSON HILLMAN C	CW2	W-2118158	0756	2
CASSON JOHN F	LTC	0-1304022	0962	1
CASTAGNETO FRANK C	COL	0-0338380	0864	2
CASTANARES SALVADOR	LTC	0-0473721	0446	2
CASTEEL BLAINE R	LTC	0-1592073	1262	1
CASTELL JOHN W	MAJ	0-0388252	0446	2
CASTELLA CHARLES C	LTC	0-0225163	1264	3
CASTER MAYNARD E	LTC	0-0384096	1062	1
CASTETTER CHARLES H	CW4	W-2142494	0657	1
CASTILLE SIMON	COL	0-0234762	1165	3
CASTILLO JOSE A	COL	0-0290344	0660	1
CASTILLO JOSE M	CPT	0-0507883	0544	2
CASTILLO RALPH	LTC	0-1575839	1060	1
CASTLE CLARENCE F	LTC	0-0252907	1166	3
CASTLE DON R	LTC	0-1321611	1063	1
CASTLE ELEANOR M	1LT	N-0720312	1044	1
CASTLE JOE F	LTC	0-1046037	1066	1
CASTLE JR KENDALL E	CPT	0-0235229	0561	3
CASTLE JR WILLIAM R	LTC	0-0179425	0457	3
CASTLE PHILLIP A	MAJ	0-0239518	1264	3
CASTLE ROBERT W	COL	0-0230213	0863	3
CASTLEBERRY GUY	MAJ	0-0182523	0743	2
CASTLEBERRY HARRALL	MAJ	0-1306243	1163	1
CASTLEBERRY L M	CPT	0-0550349	0547	1
CASTLEBERRY W M	1LT	0-0502578	1044	2

NAME	GRADE	SVC NO	DATE RET MO YR	RET CODE
CASTLEMAN WILLIAM L	1LT	0-1010165	1145	2
CASTLEN JOHN C	COL	0-0425217	0966	1
CASTLES RICHARD P	LTC	0-1581930	0662	2
CASTNER EARL L	LTC	0-0219632	1058	3
CASTNER JR LEWIS	MAJ	0-0579843	1262	2
CASTON BENJAMIN F	LTC	0-0453387	0859	1
CASTON SR CHARLES W	CPT	0-1593496	0746	2
CASTONGUAY ROLAND G	MAJ	0-0925161	0148	1
CASTOR TULLIUS R	CW4	W-2007999	0866	1
CASTORINA ALFRED R	MAJ	0-1108546	1060	1
CASTRIANNI SAM J	CW2	W-2150200	0261	1
CASTRILLO JACINTO	COL	0-0269840	0964	3
CASTRO ALFONSO A	LTC	0-1313496	0161	2
CASTRO EDWARD F	MAJ	0-0452512	0761	2
CASTRO TEODORO	1LT	0-1896677	0764	1
CASWELL ALAN R	LTC	0-2034812	0865	1
CASWELL ARTHUR D	LTC	0-0212866	0658	3
CASWELL GILBERT F	CPT	0-1796577	0548	2
CASWELL PAUL F	LTC	0-0329191	0767	3
CASWELL RALPH A	LTC	0-0381963	0462	1
CASWELL RAY	LTC	0-0405882	0560	1
CATALAN GUILLERMO	MAJ	0-1547976	1162	1
CATALANO ANTHONY C	CPT	0-0228586	0546	2
CATALANO BASIL R	CW3	W-3150319	0867	1
CATALANO EDWARD W	MAJ	0-0486594	0848	2
CATALANO SALVATORE	MAJ	0-1542427	0361	1
CATALDI ANTONIO A	MAJ	0-1878398	0867	1
CATALINE LEROY A	2LT	0-1824132	1044	2
CATANIA DANIEL	1LT	0-1797779	0348	1
CATANIA GUIDO R	MAJ	0-1046038	0562	1
CATANIA II JOSEPH J	MAJ	0-1599023	0962	1
CATE CHARLES V	LTC	0-0938010	1266	1
CATE CLIFTON J	LTC	0-0322384	1058	3
CATE HARRY R	CW2	W-2146205	0659	1
CATE HUGH C	MAJ	0-0169240	1158	3
CATE ROBERT C	CW3	W-2144178	0561	1
CATELLI CECILE M	MAJ	N-0793188	0865	3
CATENA JAMES J	CW3	W-2144048	0466	1
CATERSON RODMAN P	MAJ	0-1050587	1164	3
CATES CHARLES G	CPT	0-0255832	0656	3
CATES DAVID A	1LT	0-1182344	0245	2
CATES EDWIN H	COL	0-0239607	1265	3
CATES JOE M	LTC	0-0441927	1046	1
CATES JR JOHN H	LTC	0-0249463	0159	1
CATES JR ROBERT G	MAJ	0-0379911	1044	2
CATHELL WILLIAM T	MAJ	0-2030426	0366	1
CATHERMAN DONALD L	LTC	0-0367485	0563	1
CATHERMAN JR GUY W	LTC	0-1684959	0367	1
CATHEY CARL H	COL	0-0298035	0558	3
CATHEY CLYDE W	1LT	0-1544505	1045	2
CATHEY FRANCIS E	LTC	0-1043294	0267	1
CATHEY HARRIS H	LTC	0-1325269	1262	1
CATHEY JAMES W	LTC	0-0239433	0366	3
CATHEY JOSEPH G	COL	0-0289257	0564	1
CATHEY JR A M	2LT	0-1318761	1044	2
CATHEY WALTER K	COL	0-0299425	1060	1
CATHEY WILLIAM A	MAJ	0-0248319	1065	3
CATIZONE DOMINIC V	2LT	0-1313497	1044	2
CATLETT HAROLD G	LTC	0-1586479	0461	1
CATLETT JAMES G	COL	0-0115305	0256	3
CATLETT JAMES T	LTC	0-0144660	0158	3
CATLETT ROBERT L	CW2	W-2154103	0961	1
CATLIN HAMILTON P	CPT	0-0390092	1045	2
CATLIN VIRGIL G	LTC	0-0379591	0962	1
CATLIN WILLARD E	COL	0-0240408	0965	3
CATO ALLEN E	MAJ	0-0314062	0854	1
CATO REBECCA	MAJ	L-0903026	1163	3
CATON RUSSELL J	COL	0-0179275	0951	3
CATON WILLIAM R	CW2	W-2146179	1060	1
CATOR RICHARD O	CPT	0-1877901	1162	1
CATRAMBONE DOMINIC P	CW3	W-2148201	0167	1
CATRON ROBERT T	MAJ	0-0308528	0964	3
CATTANACH CHARLES G	MAJ	0-0994419	0566	1
CATTANACH GILBERT J	MAJ	0-1796758	0563	1
CATTANACH LACHLAN M	MAJ	0-0501189	0246	2

NAME	GRADE	SVC NO	DATE RET MO YR	RET CODE
CATTARUZZA ROBERT	MAJ	0-1699957	0662	1
CATTELL WILLIAM R	LTC	0-0372308	1067	3
CATTILINI EDWARD F	COL	0-0256811	0758	1
CATTS GEORGE W	CPT	0-0132019	1253	3
CAUBLE DALE W	1LT	0-1548374	1144	2
CAUCH JACK K	MAJ	0-2018290	0960	1
CAUCHON HERVE P	CPT	0-0187787	0149	3
CAUDILL RAYMOND	LTC	0-0885815	0954	1
CAUDILL WILLIAM S	WO1	W-2115447	0150	1
CAUDLE JR ROBERT C	CPT	0-1996704	0640	1
CAUDLE REUBEN D	CPT	0-0243400	0554	3
CAUDLE ROY C	CPT	0-0994737	1057	2
CAUGER JR ARTHUR V	MAJ	0-1637169	1060	1
CAUGHELL RALPH J	MAJ	0-2017811	0865	1
CAUGHLAN ARTHUR R	LTC	0-0252997	1155	2
CAUGHMAN ROBERT H	LTC	0-1633111	0162	1
CAULDER BARBARA F	1LT	N-0703975	0645	1
CAULEY ANTHONY	CPT	0-0972275	1061	1
CAULFIELD CHARLIE F	LTC	0-1550556	1057	1
CAULFIELD THOMAS F	2LT	0-0446425	0544	1
CAULK CARL D	CW3	W-2153340	1264	1
CAULKINS DANIEL P	COL	0-0136086	0757	3
CAULKINS JOHN P	CW3	W-2208472	1157	1
CAUM RICHARD H	CW3	W-2143676	1066	1
CAUMARTIN HUGH T	MAJ	0-0466261	0646	2
CAUSEY CHARLES D	LTC	0-1844624	0863	1
CAUSEY CHARLES M	2LT	0-1913575	0545	1
CAUSEY CHARLES M	CW2	W-2149428	0966	1
CAUSEY CHARLES O	2LT	0-0425288	1144	2
CAUSEY EDGAR	CPT	0-0885706	0550	1
CAUSEY JACK W	MAJ	0-1172406	1159	1
CAUSEY LILY F	CPT	N-0724818	0848	1
CAUTHEN JOHNNY M	CPT	0-0358955	1061	1
CAUTHEN JR IRBY R	1LT	0-1540564	0646	1
CAUTHEN WILBUR L	MAJ	0-1324824	0565	1
CAUTHEN WILLIAM C	COL	0-0239994	0960	3
CAUTHORN THOMAS E	MAJ	0-0415821	0347	2
CAVAGNARO MARGARET A	CPT	N-0759719	0846	1
CAVALCANTE JAMES J	CW3	W-2147249	0363	1
CAVALIER EUGENE H	CPT	0-0801244	1158	1
CAVALIER JOSEPH V	MAJ	0-0423109	1066	3
CAVALIERE VINCENT J	CPT	0-0443294	0946	2
CAVALIERI JULIA	CPT	N-0756989	1045	1
CAVALLO ANTHONY M	CPT	0-0359559	1045	1
CAVANAGH BERNARD P	MAJ	0-0235833	0145	2
CAVANAGH JOHN M	LTC	0-1016537	0962	1
CAVANAUGH DORA P	CPT	N-0702486	1044	1
CAVANAUGH EDWARD W	CW2	W-2144550	1164	1
CAVANAUGH JOHN P	2LT	0-1298995	1046	1
CAVANAUGH JOHN P	2LT	0-1322422	1144	2
CAVANAUGH JOSEPH P	2LT	0-1110982	0744	2
CAVANAUGH JR JOHN H	CW2	W-2207496	1164	1
CAVANAUGH PAUL W	CPT	0-0550270	1046	2
CAVANAUGH WILLIAM O	CW3	W-2144578	0662	2
CAVANESS WALTON R	2LT	0-1017951	0944	2
CAVANOR FRANK T	COL	0-0130232	0646	3
CAVAZOS SR IGNACIO	CW2	W-2209457	0961	1
CAVE FRANKLIN	LTC	0-1640887	0466	3
CAVE GLENN F	LTC	0-0411934	0960	1
CAVE JACK	MAJ	0-2039392	1160	1
CAVE JOHN E	CPT	0-1794779	0761	1
CAVE LESLIE C	COL	0-0265631	1262	3
CAVE RICHARD F	MAJ	0-1031302	0163	1
CAVE WILLIAM H	CPT	0-0268178	0246	2
CAVE WILLIAM R	MAJ	0-0985148	1067	1
CAVEN DONALD W	LTC	0-0144952	0648	3
CAVEN WALTER T	1LT	0-1319177	0145	2
CAVENAUGH DAVID F	CPT	0-0399377	1144	2
CAVENDER DONALD F	LTC	0-0525255	0465	3
CAVENDER MARVIN L	MAJ	0-2014792	1165	1
CAVENESS JAMES R	CW2	W-2147598	0662	1
CAVER EUGENE L	CPT	0-1573764	1057	1
CAVERLY JOHN P	LTC	0-1548026	1062	1
CAVERLY ROBERT P	CPT	0-1587878	0356	1
CAVIN DELMER L	CPT	0-1149653	0145	2

NAME	GRADE	SVC NO	DATE RET MO YR	RET CODE
CAVIN WALTER M	LTC	0-0320789	0255	3
CAVINESS DONALD G	CPT	0-0885737	0963	1
CAVINESS FRED R	LTC	0-0343488	1266	3
CAVINESS JAMES M	COL	0-0178278	1045	2
CAVINS JAMES N	COL	0-0313067	0160	1
CAWELTI JOHN R	MAJ	0-1598813	0964	1
CAWLEY AMOS	CPT	0-0497850	0350	1
CAWLEY ANN C	1LT	N-0786461	0552	1
CAWLEY EDWARD P	MAJ	0-1686917	0645	2
CAWLEY THOMAS A	LTC	0-1010006	0861	2
CAWTHON CHARLES P	COL	0-0407674	0764	1
CAWTHON KING W	CW2	W-2103946	0352	1
CAWTHORNE TEMPLAR S	COL	0-0199928	0461	3
CAWTHRON JR LEO	COL	0-1172407	0966	1
CAYCE WALTER R	COL	0-0150741	1156	3
CAYER JOSEPH C	LTC	0-1637171	0462	1
CAYLOR ED I	LTC	0-1040676	1060	1
CAYLOR HUGH L	CPT	0-0209926	1047	1
CAYTON BUELAH S	CW4	V-0600065	0666	1
CAYTON HENRY W	COL	0-0268885	0259	3
CAYWOOD GEORGE T	LTC	0-1289602	0757	1
CAZEAUX JR JOHN R	2LT	0-2008117	0246	2
CAZEL MAURICE H	MAJ	0-1001749	0163	1
CEAGLSKE BOYCE C	LTC	0-1552246	1262	1
CEASE ROBERT W	2LT	0-1323917	0345	2
CEBEL JOHN	MAJ	0-0374612	0255	1
CEBROWSKI CASIMIR C	1LT	0-1317489	0247	2
CECAN BENJAMIN R	2LT	0-0395794	0942	2
CECCHINI LOUIS A	COL	0-0450009	0567	1
CECIL CLARENCE C	MAJ	0-0218503	0253	3
CECIL ERNEST H	MAJ	0-0410745	1266	3
CECIL GEORGE H	MAJ	0-1641153	0960	1
CECIL JANET R	2LT	N-0703245	1040	1
CECIL JOHN L	LTC	0-1165052	0964	1
CECIL RICHARD F	MAJ	0-0315520	0946	1
CECIL ROY L	LTC	0-0182750	0648	3
CECIL SYLVESTER	LTC	0-0295221	0259	1
CECIL WAYNE A	LTC	0-1107854	1164	1
CECIL WILLIAM H	MAJ	0-0257671	0167	3
CECKA JAMES T	LTC	0-1293717	0165	1
CEDERVALL ANTON A	CPT	0-0934800	0656	2
CEGLAREK WALLACE J	CPT	0-1108548	0647	2
CEI PETER G	LTC	0-0337204	0647	1
CEJKA OLIVER J	LTC	0-0329593	0962	1
CELANI ALFRED J	MAJ	0-2263282	0167	1
CELANI FLORINO I	COL	0-0339067	0164	1
CELAYA LAURA F	MAJ	N-0737930	0865	1
CELEY J R	1LT	0-1337273	0661	1
CELIS DOMINGO	1LT	0-1896633	0149	2
CELKO JOSEPH F	CW3	W-2146001	0867	1
CELLA EDWARD L	MAJ	0-0338261	0362	2
CELLA FRANK F	CW2	W-2118141	0647	1
CELLIO LEWIS W	COL	0-0318327	0645	2
CELY TOM R	CPT	0-0356804	0245	2
CENIZA FLORENTINO	CPT	0-1896624	0559	1
CENSNER JOHN J	CW4	W-2124110	1059	2
CENTER FRANCIS C	1LT	0-1294976	0646	2
CENTRE DAVID	1LT	0-1314880	0146	1
CENTRONE PATRICK A	CPT	0-0352923	1045	2
CERALDI BERNARD A	CPT	0-0463729	0547	1
CERASOLI ANTHONY N	LTC	0-1795765	0261	1
CERECEDO JAVIER H	COL	0-0274777	0153	3
CERESI ANTHONY A	LTC	0-1283548	0561	1
CEREZO CARAFLE	MAJ	0-0184640	0257	3
CERNAGHAN ALBERT L	MAJ	0-0165967	1150	3
CERNY JEROME J	LTC	0-0116380	0648	3
CERNY JERRY	CW4	W-2106939	1055	1
CERNY JOSEPH	LTC	0-0261409	0766	3
CERRONE LUKE J	MAJ	0-0497467	0846	2
CERTAIN JACK	CPT	0-1285190	1068	2
CERVANTES ANTHONY V	1LT	0-0356887	1264	1
CERVERA SEVERO J	CW3	W-2147274	1063	1
CERVOLA JOHN	MAJ	0-1328465	0263	1
CERVONE ISADORE C	1LT	0-0177911	0654	3
CERVONI WALTER A	CPT	0-0976379	0552	1

NAME	GRADE	SVC NO	DATE RET MO YR	RET CODE
CERWINS JOSEPH M	COL	0-0309845	1164	3
CERWONKA FRANCIS W	MAJ	0-1950653	1164	1
CESAR CHARLES	MAJ	0-1633747	0258	1
CESKE WALLACE G	CPT	0-2034523	0866	1
CESSAR MATTHEW A	1LT	0-1185212	0346	2
CESTERO HERMAN J	LTC	0-0405148	0566	3
CETRULO PETER X	MAJ	0-2002054	1062	1
CEVAAL JOHN	MAJ	0-2024518	0660	1
CEWE LEROY G	MAJ	0-1017736	0762	1
CEY WILLIAM J	CW2	W-2203258	0562	1
CHABERT ALFRED A	LTC	0-0254531	0367	3
CHABOT ALBERT L	LTC	0-0237209	0358	1
CHABOT FELIX J	LTC	0-1533520	1063	1
CHABOT LOREN J	1LT	0-0425978	0345	2
CHACE MYRON D	COL	0-0464526	0257	3
CHACEY DANIEL K	COL	0-0506305	0166	3
CHACEY JOUETT A	LTC	0-0242015	0965	3
CHACON JOSE	CPT	0-0292323	0553	1
CHADDICK ELMER H	WO1	W-2131614	0146	2
CHADSEY MERLIN J	LTC	0-0274593	0960	3
CHADWELL RIXEY C	LTC	0-1580738	0861	1
CHADWICK JANET K	2LT	N-0736605	0943	1
CHADWICK JOHN S	LTC	0-0262758	1066	3
CHADWICK JR ARTHUR C	CPT	0-1300274	1046	1
CHADWICK JR FLOYD S	MAJ	0-2017812	1159	1
CHADWICK KERMIT V	LTC	0-0299178	0445	2
CHADWICK RUSSELL H	1LT	0-1101374	1045	2
CHADWICK SR FLOYD S	2LT	0-1913597	0244	1
CHADWICK STURGIS E	LTC	0-0246700	0366	3
CHADWICK WILLIE J	LTC	0-1303664	1054	1
CHADWICK WINFIELD S	MAJ	0-0401303	0561	1
CHAFFEE LEROY E	MAJ	0-1036903	0960	1
CHAFFEE THALIA A	CPT	N-0730596	0946	1
CHAFFEUR JOHN J	LTC	0-1999345	0763	1
CHAFFIN WENDEL T	LTC	0-0261618	0567	3
CHAFFIN WILLIAM A	MAJ	0-0574185	1055	1
CHAFIN WILLIAM V	LTC	0-0273102	1263	3
CHAGAMI RONALD T	CW3	W-2141065	0562	1
CHAILLE JAMES L	COL	0-0254303	0666	3
CHAILLE JOSEPH H	COL	0-0239434	0265	3
CHAIN JOHN S	LTC	0-0246433	0265	3
CHAIN JR BENJAMIN H	CW2	W-2149103	0861	2
CHAIRES WILLIAM R	MAJ	0-1646952	0160	1
CHAISSON GILBERT J	COL	0-0456022	0965	1
CHAIT MATTHEW W	LTC	0-0288109	0260	2
CHAIT ROBERT A	MAJ	0-0493946	0746	2
CHALFANT JAMES R	1LT	0-1317071	0845	2
CHALFIN SAMUEL L	CPT	0-1689009	1044	2
CHALIAN ALEXANDER	MAJ	0-0356519	0463	3
CHALKER SR JOHN O	CW3	W-2145797	0561	2
CHALKLEY JUDSON I	CPT	0-0418612	0845	2
CHALKLEY MARJORIE G	MAJ	N-0723599	0962	1
CHALKLEY SR BEN R	CPT	0-1307370	0266	1
CHALLAN JOHN A	MAJ	0-1175072	0757	1
CHALLENNER ANSEL P	LTC	0-0223610	1064	3
CHALLEY CLYDE	CPT	0-0236645	0963	3
CHALLIN ROBERT C	WO1	W-2108384	0464	2
CHALLMAN SAMUEL A	COL	0-0263450	0264	3
CHALMERS FRANKLIN S	COL	0-0118689	0252	3
CHALMERS GEORGE W	LTC	0-1019314	0862	1
CHAMBERLAIN ALMA	LTC	0-1173899	0762	1
CHAMBERLAIN CULVER B	1LT	0-0914019	0845	2
CHAMBERLAIN DON F	LTC	0-0138148	0648	3
CHAMBERLAIN EDWARD M	LTC	0-1635684	0962	1
CHAMBERLAIN ERVIN W	LTC	0-0175718	0443	2
CHAMBERLAIN F G	LTC	0-0150831	0648	3
CHAMBERLAIN FRANCIS	MAJ	0-1647211	0565	2
CHAMBERLAIN GEORGE L	2LT	0-1541210	0744	2
CHAMBERLAIN GEORGE M	MAJ	0-1688675	0467	1
CHAMBERLAIN GORDON W	LTC	0-1301950	1064	1
CHAMBERLAIN H G	1LT	0-1173900	0445	2
CHAMBERLAIN HARRY E	1LT	0-0437385	0957	1
CHAMBERLAIN HARRY E	CW2	W-2109954	0547	1
CHAMBERLAIN HOLCOMBE	MAJ	0-0908747	1145	2
CHAMBERLAIN HUGH D	CPT	0-0138067	0251	3

NAME	GRADE	SVC NO	DATE RET MO YR	RET CODE
CHAMBERLAIN JAMES R	LTC	0-2049502	0562	1
CHAMBERLAIN JOSEPH V	LTC	0-0302144	0945	2
CHAMBERLAIN LLOYD A	CW3	W-2206828	0965	1
CHAMBERLAIN LOUIS J	LTC	0-0887469	0563	1
CHAMBERLAIN MARIO C	LTC	0-0270419	1061	1
CHAMBERLAIN ROBERT L	CPT	0-0888611	0951	1
CHAMBERLAIN W H	COL	0-0238613	0951	3
CHAMBERLAIN WARD	1LT	0-1323106	0747	2
CHAMBERLAIN WILLIAM	CW2	W-2210405	1264	2
CHAMBERLIN FRANCIS A	1LT	0-0376597	0144	2
CHAMBERLIN HENRY R	MAJ	0-0467680	0263	1
CHAMBERLIN ROBERT M	CW3	W-2144101	1266	1
CHAMBERLIN ROBERT N	LTC	0-0286831	1060	3
CHAMBERLIN ROBERT W	B G	0-0279810	0660	3
CHAMBERLIN WILLIAM F	COL	0-0307335	0965	1
CHAMBERS ALAN R	CPT	0-0331422	0246	2
CHAMBERS ALBERT L	CPT	0-1303594	0546	2
CHAMBERS ANITA M	MAJ	N-0730062	0463	3
CHAMBERS ARTHUR D	MAJ	0-2017354	0863	1
CHAMBERS BAYARD S	LTC	0-0298133	0765	3
CHAMBERS BURGESS D	LTC	0-1010025	1060	1
CHAMBERS CHESTER H	COL	0-0169166	1046	2
CHAMBERS EDWIN P	COL	0-0316445	0259	3
CHAMBERS ELWOOD W	CW2	W-2152993	0360	1
CHAMBERS GORDON H	COL	0-0254701	0846	1
CHAMBERS HEWITT W	MAJ	0-0106120	0952	3
CHAMBERS JAMES O	1LT	0-1799828	0157	1
CHAMBERS JAMES S	LTC	0-1032072	1062	1
CHAMBERS JAMES T	1LT	0-0174354	1060	3
CHAMBERS JOHN A	COL	0-0251918	0459	3
CHAMBERS JOHN F	LTC	0-1313964	0467	1
CHAMBERS JOHN S	MAJ	0-0254082	0357	3
CHAMBERS JOHN T	COL	0-0276915	0158	3
CHAMBERS JOHN T	CPT	0-0397657	0761	2
CHAMBERS JR ANDREW	CPT	0-1165595	0346	2
CHAMBERS MARTIN M	MAJ	0-1115210	0561	1
CHAMBERS MARVIN A	CPT	0-1895261	1057	1
CHAMBERS MAX F	MAJ	0-2203408	1165	1
CHAMBERS PETER F	LTC	0-1030134	0262	3
CHAMBERS RALPH H	LTC	0-0500667	0457	2
CHAMBERS ROBERT L	MAJ	0-0146472	0254	3
CHAMBERS ROBERT P	LTC	0-0288811	0865	3
CHAMBERS ROBERT W	LTC	0-1542382	0962	1
CHAMBERS RUSSEL	CPT	0-0497881	0157	1
CHAMBERS STANLEY L	MAJ	0-0388554	0561	1
CHAMBERS THOMAS F	CPT	0-0501766	0851	1
CHAMBERS THOMAS L	CPT	0-0482005	0746	2
CHAMBERS TOFFY J	MAJ	0-1341256	0766	1
CHAMBERS WAYNE A	LTC	0-0506655	0447	2
CHAMBERS WILLARD F	LTC	0-1302429	0266	1
CHAMBERS WILLIAM L	CPT	0-0266544	0658	3
CHAMBERS WOODFIN C	LTC	0-0425472	0966	3
CHAMBERS WYLIE C	2LT	0-1308473	0445	2
CHAMBLISS JAMES R	LTC	0-0238599	0862	3
CHAMBREAU WILLIAM J	WO1	W-2133086	0945	2
CHAMNESS JOSEPH C	MAJ	0-1637174	0559	1
CHAMP CLIFFORD L	CW3	W-2108922	1155	1
CHAMPAGNE ANDRE	1LT	0-1043590	1155	1
CHAMPAGNE EDWARD E	MAJ	0-0972915	1160	1
CHAMPAGNE NORMAND H	CW2	W-2152271	1060	1
CHAMPAGNE ROLAND J	LTC	0-0421885	0366	1
CHAMPION ATWELL F	1LT	0-1314882	0545	2
CHAMPION GLENN R	LTC	0-0261331	0267	3
CHAMPION ROBERT L	MAJ	0-1938287	0966	1
CHAMPION WILLIAM H	MAJ	0-1119964	1063	1
CHAMPLIN DOUGLASS O	MAJ	0-0980964	1262	1
CHAMPLIN NATHANIEL	2LT	0-1112075	1044	2
CHAMPLIN NICHOLAS O	LTC	0-0310881	1166	3
CHAMPOUX FRANCIS L	LTC	0-1311981	0166	1
CHAN ROBERT J	LTC	0-1321994	0661	1
CHANCE HARRY C	CW2	W-2145287	0454	1
CHANCE S ETHEL	CPT	N-0724739	0646	1
CHANCE VERNON L	MAJ	0-1017844	0665	1
CHANCE WALTER R	LTC	0-0353500	1059	1
CHANCE WARD L	1LT	0-1684973	0752	1

292-560 O - 68 - 8

NAME	GRADE	SVC NO	DATE RET MO YR	RET CODE
CHANCE WAYNE A	LTC	O-1115523	0764	1
CHANCELLOR WILFORD O	LTC	O-1285382	0954	1
CHANCELLOR WILLIAM W	CPT	O-1114883	0261	1
CHANCEY NATHAN	MAJ	O-0275287	0666	3
CHANDLER ALBERT	LTC	O-1286962	0954	1
CHANDLER ARTHUR J	2LT	O-2204042	0656	2
CHANDLER CARL C	LTC	O-1551373	0662	1
CHANDLER CARL F	LTC	O-0412376	0167	1
CHANDLER CARLTON P	CPT	O-0364566	0346	2
CHANDLER CLINTON B	MAJ	O-0486905	0948	2
CHANDLER COVY B	CW2	W-2146131	1155	1
CHANDLER EARL F	2LT	O-0554417	0845	2
CHANDLER EARL P	LTC	O-0281674	1263	3
CHANDLER EDWARD R	CPT	O-1051515	1153	2
CHANDLER EDWIN M	CW3	W-2149104	0864	1
CHANDLER EKILLIS M	LTC	O-1057011	1262	1
CHANDLER ELI C	LTC	O-1112617	0862	1
CHANDLER EUGENE	2LT	O-1289693	0145	2
CHANDLER GEORGE A	LTC	O-0154047	0155	3
CHANDLER GEORGE A	MAJ	O-0219158	0955	3
CHANDLER GRAHAM L	MAJ	O-0372639	0862	3
CHANDLER HAROLD M	CW4	W-2114306	0257	1
CHANDLER HORTON L	COL	O-0130618	0558	3
CHANDLER JAMES C	LTC	O-0294432	0959	2
CHANDLER JOE F	MAJ	O-2009416	0661	1
CHANDLER JOHN A	MAJ	O-1044194	0358	1
CHANDLER JOHN H	MAJ	O-2028373	1167	1
CHANDLER JR ALBERT M	MAJ	O-1167358	1146	2
CHANDLER LEROY	CPT	O-0477947	1045	2
CHANDLER LOUIS J	LTC	O-0349551	0946	2
CHANDLER NOREEN C	1LT	N-0774412	0547	1
CHANDLER PATRICK M	CW3	W-2146322	0565	1
CHANDLER RALPH E	MAJ	O-1030230	0859	1
CHANDLER ROBERT L	MAJ	O-0292092	0846	1
CHANDLER SIDNEY P	LTC	O-0154676	0854	3
CHANDLER SR RAY J	MAJ	O-2263711	0266	1
CHANDLER STEPHEN J	MAJ	O-2011918	0959	1
CHANDLER VERNON M	LTC	O-0281089	0467	3
CHANDLER WALTER B	MAJ	O-0415578	0958	1
CHANDLER WALTER C	2LT	O-1171083	0743	2
CHANDLER WILLARD C	LTC	O-0168538	0144	2
CHANDLER WILLARD J	CPT	O-0356212	0646	2
CHANDLER WILLIAM H	CW2	W-2152885	1059	2
CHANDLER WOODROW W	CPT	O-2017009	0657	1
CHANEY EDWIN C	LTC	O-0450819	0456	1
CHANEY GEORGE L	CPT	O-1055559	0647	2
CHANEY HAROLD W	CPT	O-2029829	1058	1
CHANEY JAMES W	CPT	O-0890140	0148	2
CHANEY JOSEPH B	CW2	W-2203309	0761	1
CHANEY LUTHER M	LTC	O-1281724	0261	1
CHANG JAMES T M	MAJ	O-0249592	1159	1
CHANLEY HERMAN S	MAJ	O-1686318	0563	1
CHANNEY STEPHEN	LTC	O-0545784	0365	1
CHANNON HIRAM B	CPT	O-0130615	0854	3
CHANOSKI JOHN F	MAJ	O-1299373	0958	1
CHANOWSKI JOHN P	2LT	O-2002248	0546	2
CHANT HAROLD S	LTC	O-0223707	0157	3
CHANTRY ARTHUR S W	CPT	O-0508151	1047	1
CHAPA FRANK L	COL	O-0159185	0957	3
CHAPHE CARROLL G	LTC	O-0548565	1065	1
CHAPIN EARL L	1LT	O-1584425	0845	2
CHAPIN GERALD G	1LT	O-1168598	1045	2
CHAPIN JOHN L	1LT	O-1047063	0145	1
CHAPIN NORMAN G	MAJ	O-2010679	1265	1
CHAPIN STANLEY D	MAJ	O-0146422	0553	3
CHAPIN THEODORE	CPT	O-0368466	1244	2
CHAPIN WILLIAM B	CW3	W-2147986	0862	1
CHAPIN WILLIAM H	LTC	O-1553236	0563	1
CHAPIN WINONA M	1LT	N-0720140	0946	1
CHAPIN 3RD EDWARD Y	1LT	O-0528759	0146	2
CHAPLAIN JOHN R	CPT	O-0298968	0645	2
CHAPLESKY MARION P	CPT	O-2033528	0260	1
CHAPLIN EARNEST C	LTC	O-1533753	1066	1
CHAPLIN RALPH S	MAJ	O-2009389	1264	1
CHAPLIN ROBERT L	MAJ	O-0308397	0462	1

NAME	GRADE	SVC NO	DATE RET MO YR	RET CODE
CHAPLIN ROBERT M	CPT	O-1322423	0856	2
CHAPLIN SAXBY	COL	O-0185031	1060	3
CHAPLINSKI ANTHONY	CPT	O-1950129	1159	1
CHAPLINSKI CHARLES W	MAJ	O-1100046	0257	1
CHAPMAN ALBERT	COL	O-0217008	0264	3
CHAPMAN ALFRED E	CW3	W-2113386	0662	1
CHAPMAN ARTHUR J	MAJ	O-0254545	0266	3
CHAPMAN BRADY H	1LT	O-1821548	0750	1
CHAPMAN CAREY H	LTC	O-0176160	0557	1
CHAPMAN CARL E	MAJ	O-0118692	0845	2
CHAPMAN CECIL W	LTC	O-0301086	0347	2
CHAPMAN CHANEY	LTC	O-2024325	0962	1
CHAPMAN CHARLES F	CW2	W-2118126	0645	2
CHAPMAN CHARLES G	LTC	O-0298192	0165	3
CHAPMAN CLARENCE L	COL	O-0377425	0867	1
CHAPMAN CLYDE V	LTC	O-0386819	1257	1
CHAPMAN CORENE	CPT	N-0792315	0257	2
CHAPMAN DENMAN S	LTC	O-0324542	1065	1
CHAPMAN DONALD L	LTC	O-0318641	0856	2
CHAPMAN EARL H	COL	O-0105456	0756	3
CHAPMAN FORREST M	MAJ	O-1297497	0746	2
CHAPMAN FRANK H	COL	O-0136075	0349	3
CHAPMAN FREDERICK	LTC	O-2015057	1167	1
CHAPMAN GEORGE A	LTC	O-0285105	0263	1
CHAPMAN GERALD F	1LT	O-0550574	0246	2
CHAPMAN GERALD L	LTC	O-0124608	0454	3
CHAPMAN GORDON P	CPT	O-0287219	0345	1
CHAPMAN HAROLD L	CPT	O-1168199	1152	1
CHAPMAN HAROLD C W	LTC	O-0921129	0265	3
CHAPMAN HERBERT L	CPT	O-0483211	0247	1
CHAPMAN HESTER	MAJ	N-0736913	0467	1
CHAPMAN JAMES F	1LT	O-1036904	0345	1
CHAPMAN JAMES L	COL	O-0100573	1149	3
CHAPMAN JAMES R	LTC	O-0495817	0762	1
CHAPMAN JEFF H	CPT	O-0415670	0152	1
CHAPMAN JOHN C	CPT	O-0146420	1155	3
CHAPMAN JOHN C	MAJ	O-0348256	0546	2
CHAPMAN JOHN G	CW2	W-2112920	0746	2
CHAPMAN JR ARTHUR B	COL	O-0498009	1062	1
CHAPMAN JR CLARK R	2LT	O-1179811	0445	2
CHAPMAN JR HOWARD K	MAJ	O-0239336	1064	3
CHAPMAN LAWRENCE W	LTC	O-1175395	0862	2
CHAPMAN LEICESTER	LTC	O-0190127	0654	3
CHAPMAN LLOYD	LTC	O-1114417	0966	1
CHAPMAN LOIS B	2LT	N-0736402	0545	1
CHAPMAN MARION D	CW2	W-2149185	1160	1
CHAPMAN MARY	1LT	N-0755663	1147	1
CHAPMAN MIKE W	CW4	W-2142437	1065	1
CHAPMAN RAYMOND C	MAJ	O-1183827	0661	1
CHAPMAN RICHARD H	LTC	O-0452116	0856	1
CHAPMAN RICHARD I	MAJ	O-0478267	0154	1
CHAPMAN RICHARD W	LTC	O-0956349	1167	1
CHAPMAN ROBERT P	CW2	W-2207539	0166	1
CHAPMAN SR DONALD M	LTC	O-0290399	0455	1
CHAPMAN STANLEY	CPT	O-1175965	0450	1
CHAPMAN THOMAS L	MAJ	O-0558750	0163	1
CHAPMAN THOMAS S	LTC	O-0242151	1265	3
CHAPMAN WILLIAM C	CW4	W-2142821	0856	1
CHAPMAN WILLIAM H	LTC	O-1556985	1060	1
CHAPMAN WOODROW W	LTC	O-1556700	0266	1
CHAPNICK HENRY	LTC	O-1687103	1046	2
CHAPNICK RONALD	CPT	O-4046552	0962	2
CHAPPEL JR DONALD M	1LT	O-1296165	0347	2
CHAPPELEAR JOHN R	CW2	W-2148843	0960	1
CHAPPELL ALFRED H	LTC	O-1293371	1158	1
CHAPPELL CARL W	WO1	W-2106235	1045	2
CHAPPELL CLAUD W	MAJ	O-1685133	0745	2
CHAPPELL CLINTON C	CPT	O-0519315	0745	2
CHAPPELL DANIEL H	LTC	O-0211598	0161	3
CHAPPELL EDWIN J	MAJ	O-1685012	1164	1
CHAPPELL JAMES R	MAJ	O-1170311	0959	1
CHAPPELL JOHN L	CPT	O-2035241	0863	2
CHAPPELL JOHN M	LTC	O-0463586	0652	1
CHAPPELL WILLIAM B	MAJ	O-1293911	0461	1
CHAPPELLE VERGNE	COL	O-0142481	0648	3

NAME	GRADE	SVC NO	DATE RET MO YR	RET CODE
CHAPPLE WILLIAM F	CPT	O-0413425	0346	2
CHAPUT EDWARD L	MAJ	O-1638869	0859	1
CHAPUT JR LOUIS J	LTC	O-1542946	0561	1
CHAPUT OMER T	COL	O-0365453	0960	1
CHAQUETTE LAWRENCE T	LTC	O-0307862	0162	1
CHARBONNEAU LOUIS H	B G	O-0142965	0157	3
CHARDON CARLOS F	COL	O-0256034	1067	3
CHARETTE NORMAN A	CW3	W-2146223	0161	1
CHARETTE REGINALD W	LTC	O-1056316	0266	1
CHARITON RAYMOND C	MAJ	O-1540854	0761	1
CHARLES EARLE H	MAJ	O-0289640	0145	2
CHARLES HARRY M	LTC	O-1107341	1163	1
CHARLES MICHAEL P	CPT	O-1101375	0549	1
CHARLES RALPH	LTC	O-0176885	0562	3
CHARLES WILLIAM	COL	O-0355783	0367	2
CHARLESTON ELIZ M	2LT	N-0721139	0344	1
CHARLESWORTH JOHN R	CW4	W-2000317	0765	1
CHARLET REINHART F	1LT	O-0377023	0445	2
CHARLTON ARTHUR J	MAJ	O-0918715	0863	1
CHARLTON NELSON	MAJ	O-2036359	1262	1
CHARLTON ROBERT D	M G	O-0235009	0560	3
CHARLTON RUSSELL C	COL	O-0205558	1059	3
CHARNECO RAFAEL	LTC	O-0199348	0663	3
CHARON EDWARD J	LTC	O-1581952	1162	1
CHARON GEORGE	CW3	W-2147663	0966	1
CHARRIEZ GILBERTO O	CPT	O-0970810	1061	1
CHARTIER CURTIS R	CW2	W-2210143	1264	1
CHARTOCK WILLIAM	LTC	O-0274623	0360	1
CHARTRAND HELENE E	1LT	N-0721268	0246	1
CHARTRES GERARD	2LT	O-0464866	0244	2
CHARVAT ROSE C	1LT	N-0700419	0941	1
CHASE ALDEN	CW3	W-2206649	1266	1
CHASE ARCHIE R	MAJ	O-1052291	1262	1
CHASE ARTHUR R	LTC	O-1015721	0264	1
CHASE BENJAMIN O	MAJ	O-0917954	0258	2
CHASE BERNICE M	LTC	N-0720146	0461	1
CHASE CARL	CW4	W-2139465	0862	1
CHASE CARL E	MAJ	O-0252835	0262	3
CHASE CHARLES E	LTC	O-0241023	0364	3
CHASE CLIFFORD A	COL	O-0511085	0965	3
CHASE DAVID W	CPT	O-1048313	0463	1
CHASE DURWARD C	CPT	O-0312199	0153	2
CHASE EDMUND P	MAJ	O-0188766	0454	3
CHASE ELIZABETH	2LT	L-0116068	1044	2
CHASE EUGENE B	LTC	O-0301057	0361	3
CHASE EUGENE L	CW3	W-2142325	0662	1
CHASE FRED M	LTC	O-0244869	0966	3
CHASE FREDERICK	CPT	O-0419292	0946	2
CHASE GLENN	CW3	W-2142822	1062	1
CHASE HARLAN E	COL	O-0218422	0459	3
CHASE HOWARD H	MAJ	O-0272273	0659	1
CHASE HURLEY W	LTC	O-0334356	0958	1
CHASE HYMAN Y	COL	O-0212557	0960	1
CHASE IRENE F	2LT	N-0720256	0144	1
CHASE JACK M	CPT	O-1106642	0146	1
CHASE JACKSON B	MAJ	O-0193266	0950	3
CHASE JEAN L	LTC	O-1168200	0161	1
CHASE JR JAMES	CPT	O-1937237	1164	1
CHASE JR NATHANIEL	CPT	O-2016848	0461	1
CHASE LEONARD J	LTC	O-0412328	0161	1
CHASE LESTER J	LTC	O-0298059	0559	1
CHASE LOUIS S	MAJ	O-0499966	0346	2
CHASE LUCIUS P	COL	O-0178374	0262	3
CHASE MELVIN C	CW2	W-2118320	0953	1
CHASE PARAN E	CW3	W-2152202	0466	1
CHASE RICHARD G	1LT	O-1292834	1044	1
CHASE ROBERT L	LTC	O-0455040	0859	1
CHASE ROSS	COL	O-0167352	0558	3
CHASE S BRUCE	COL	O-0242449	0466	3
CHASE SAMUEL L	LTC	O-0412498	0466	3
CHASE STODDARD B	COL	O-0311455	0261	1
CHASE VOLNEY A	MAJ	O-0173954	0860	3
CHASE WILLIAM A	CPT	O-0379663	0346	2
CHASE WILLIAM D	LTC	O-0176231	0759	3
CHASE WILLIAM M	COL	O-0154340	0551	1

NAME	GRADE	SVC NO	DATE RET MO YR	RET CODE
CHASEN HAROLD	1LT	O-1080520	0745	2
CHASEN PHILIP	1LT	O-1307507	0545	2
CHASEN WILLIAM H	COL	O-0361118	0667	3
CHASNOFF JULIUS	COL	O-0247246	0962	3
CHASSE EDWARD D	2LT	O-1304862	0245	2
CHASSE MERIL J	CW3	W-2145798	0462	1
CHASSY GILBERT H	CPT	O-0381074	1145	2
CHAST ANN	2LT	N-0758083	0945	1
CHASTAIN CARL W	1LT	O-0527780	1045	2
CHASTAIN FRED A	LTC	O-0443895	0756	1
CHASTAIN JOHN F	CPT	O-0261615	0564	3
CHASTAIN JOHN T	CW2	W-2145153	0958	1
CHASTAIN KENNETH L	MAJ	O-1299850	0547	2
CHASTAIN MYRA E	MAJ	L-0403253	0263	1
CHASTAIN WALTER P	LTC	O-0258709	0565	3
CHASTAIN WILLIS L	MAJ	O-1535150	1054	1
CHASTEN STEPHEN M	MAJ	O-0488789	1151	1
CHASWOOD ERNEST E	WO1	W-2126514	0846	1
CHASZAR ELIZABETH	CPT	N-0729415	0946	1
CHATELAIN HARRY	WO1	W-2115686	0647	1
CHATELLE JOSEPH S	CW2	W-2151070	0963	1
CHATFIELD LEE W	LTC	O-0258286	0745	1
CHATHAM JOHN W	MAJ	O-1694382	0246	2
CHATHAM ROY L	LTC	O-0415851	0461	1
CHATIGNY ADRIAN G	MAJ	O-2101756	0966	1
CHATLAIN DEAN F	1LT	O-0453496	0244	2
CHATLAIN JOHN K	2LT	O-2006828	1045	1
CHATLEY ROBERT I	MAJ	O-0234360	0247	1
CHATLIN MORRIS	CPT	O-0922520	0945	2
CHATMAN JR RICHARD C	CW2	W-2207656	1061	1
CHATONNET BARTHELEM	CPT	O-2029625	0158	1
CHATTAWAY ERNEST H	MAJ	O-1550344	0561	1
CHATTERTON FLOYD E	CW2	W-2210137	0167	1
CHATTERTON FRANCIS C	MAJ	O-0245745	0757	3
CHAUDOIN ELIOT C	LTC	O-0197275	0261	3
CHAUDOIR WILLIAM	CPT	O-0492474	1054	1
CHAUNCEY PHILLIP T	1LT	O-4034421	0262	2
CHAUSSE LOUIS E	CPT	O-1052292	1164	1
CHAUVIN HUGH J	CW3	W-2205914	0966	1
CHAVARRIA CORENA R	CPT	N-0759619	0147	1
CHAVES CEFERINO	2LT	O-1897030	0249	1
CHAVET WALTER A	LTC	O-0451228	0960	1
CHAVEZ JOSEPH F	LTC	O-0450623	1160	1
CHAVEZ JR ANTHONY T	CPT	O-0384790	0945	2
CHAVEZ LEO	CPT	O-0978128	1062	1
CHAVIS JR DEANIE	LTC	O-0451312	0960	1
CHAVIS WILLIAM P	2LT	O-1645609	1044	2
CHAVKIN RALPH	MAJ	O-0455657	0546	2
CHAYES CHARLES M	CPT	O-0487601	0945	2
CHAYES EDWARD	COL	O-0115804	0554	3
CHEADLE EDWIN K	COL	O-0136814	0855	3
CHEADLE JOHN A	LTC	O-0205389	0863	3
CHEANEY FRANK H	MAJ	O-0237281	0662	3
CHEARY ELDON L	MAJ	O-1885152	1066	1
CHEATHAM ALBERT B	MAJ	O-1186262	0964	1
CHEATHAM CADER W	COL	O-0216167	1162	3
CHEATHAM GEORGE L	CW4	W-2119266	1160	1
CHEATHAM GUY C	MAJ	O-0225082	0245	2
CHEATHAM JAMES C	LTC	O-0190751	0163	3
CHEATHAM LEWIS W	LTC	O-1581562	0566	1
CHEATHAM ORME E	LTC	O-0264523	1167	3
CHEATHAM WILLIAM E	COL	O-0266584	1162	1
CHEATWOOD HERMAN A	CW4	W-2108458	0860	1
CHECKIE FABIAN L	LTC	O-1796578	0660	1
CHEDERQUIST ELMER C	LTC	O-1555523	1162	1
CHEDESTER FRANK M	LTC	O-0244870	0866	3
CHEDESTER MYRON O	LTC	O-0406773	0661	1
CHEDESTER RICHARD F	CPT	O-1323538	0446	2
CHEEK ISAAC E	LTC	O-1000724	1158	1
CHEEK JAMES E	LTC	O-0400102	0760	1
CHEEK JR LEE A	CPT	O-4006445	0667	1
CHEEK RICHARD C	CW2	W-2119675	1045	2
CHEEK RUBYE J	MAJ	N-0726878	0347	1
CHEEK VERNON E	CPT	O-0402511	0756	1
CHEEK WILLIAM W	LTC	O-1174528	1263	1

NAME	GRADE	SVC NO	DATE RET MO YR	RET CODE	NAME	GRADE	SVC NO	DATE RET MO YR	RET CODE	NAME	GRADE	SVC NO	DATE RET MO YR	RET CODE	NAME	GRADE	SVC NO	DATE RET MO YR	RET CODE
CHEELEY GRANVILLE	MAJ	0-0320627	1045	1	CHESTER ALBERT W	CPT	0-1633117	1146	1	CHILDS SR RALPH F	MAJ	0-1000332	0961	1	CHOLLAK JOSEPH P	CPT	0-0423442	0346	2
CHEESEMAN EVANS R	LTC	0-0113174	0848	3	CHESTER ARTHUR M	LTC	0-0196485	1054	1	CHILDS THOMAS M	COL	0-0134213	0-51	3	CHOMEAU HENRI	MAJ	0-0242706	0160	3
CHEESMAN BURT	1LT	0-0164802	0242	1	CHESTER CHARLES W	CW4	W-2115718	0365	2	CHILES HENRY L	CPT	0-2001130	0155	1	CHOMJACK JOHN	CW2	W-2117034	0447	2
CHEESMAN LEROY V	MAJ	0-2053935	0655	1	CHESTER III LEWIS S	1LT	0-0395383	0161	2	CHILES VERNON E	1LT	0-1304863	0845	2	CHOMKO PAUL	1LT	0-1291415	0844	2
CHEEZEM ROBERT L	CW4	W-2005682	1166	1	CHESTERMAN ALBERT F	1LT	0-0922317	0245	2	CHILMAN FRANCIS R	1LT	0-1012956	0744	2	CHOMOS STEVE V	LTC	0-1646359	0666	1
CHEEZUM THOMAS R	CW4	W-2108901	0758	1	CHESTERTON ALLAN B	CPT	0-0241266	0960	3	CHILSON CHARLES G	CW2	W-2147848	0860	1	CHONG KIN-FAN	LTC	0-0270480	0162	1
CHEKEL MARTIN A	CW3	W-2132184	0557	1	CHESTNUT JOHN S	CPT	0-0177738	0560	3	CHILSON FRANCIS A	COL	0-0318792	0860	1	CHONG PAUL	CW3	W-2151052	0563	1
CHELEDEN JOHN J	MAJ	0-0294345	0846	1	CHESTNUTWOOD JACK B	MAJ	0-1544001	0863	1	CHILSON GEORGE H	CPT	0-2671338	1060	1	CHONKO LILLIAN H	1LT	N-0725498	0246	2
CHELLEW EDWARD M	COL	0-0177691	0860	3	CHESTNUTWOOD ROBERT	1LT	0-0410378	0744	2	CHILSON VIRGAL R	COL	0-0311448	0262	1	CHOPP WILLIAM R	1LT	0-1767158	0245	2
CHELLIS RUEL B	COL	0-0162388	0556	3	CHETNIK ANTHONY J	1LT	0-1292477	1044	2	CHILTON CARL F	MAJ	0-1050594	0159	1	CHORSON EDWIN W	COL	0-0243625	0766	3
CHEMA THOMAS	LTC	0-2294014	0465	1	CHEVALIER ALAIN A	LTC	0-1037586	0864	1	CHILTON ELMORE F	LTC	0-0885544	0758	2	CHOQUETTE GRACE A	1LT	N-0756263	1145	1
CHEN JAMES E	MAJ	0-1895944	0765	1	CHEVALIER FRANK C	COL	0-0918459	0263	3	CHILTON FRANK	LTC	0-0375005	0155	1	CHORNYAK HELEN M	COL	N-0755305	0163	1
CHENERY CHARLES E	LTC	0-0903124	0654	2	CHEVALIER WILLIAM M	CPT	0-0505139	0447	2	CHILTON LLOYD	MAJ	0-2024103	0161	1	CHORNYAK JOHN	COL	0-0225878	0661	3
CHENERY HUBERT L	COL	0-0430349	1162	3	CHEVERIE JAMES P	MAJ	0-1926844	0167	1	CHILTON PAUL G	LTC	0-1042784	1162	1	CHOTAS MATTHEW E	COL	0-0317045	1060	1
CHENEY BENJAMIN F	COL	0-0112508	1155	3	CHEVES FOREST A	CPT	0-0889461	0457	1	CHIMINIELLO DOMINIC	COL	0-0308809	0166	1	CHOUINARD ARTHUR C	MAJ	0-1824578	0561	1
CHENEY CURTIS V	LTC	0-1080094	0466	1	CHEW LUN K	CPT	0-0320525	1045	2	CHIN WOODROW Y	MAJ	0-0974976	0663	1	CHOW WALKER	COL	0-1555026	0263	2
CHENEY ERVIN F	2LT	0-0333719	0444	2	CHEWNING JR ROBERT E	MAJ	0-0249785	0966	3	CHINDAHL ANITA G	CPT	N-0727992	0547	1	CHOWENHILL CHARLES F	LTC	0-0921981	0563	3
CHENEY JR ARTHUR M	MAJ	0-0330462	1066	3	CHEWNING REGINALD O	CW4	W-2127497	0157	1	CHINENE JON J	1LT	0-2046476	1047	2	CHOWNING RICHARD L	LTC	0-1295668	1061	2
CHENEY JR ISAAC P	CPT	0-0549897	0362	2	CHEWNING WILLIAM T	2LT	0-1324879	0445	2	CHING TAI TONG	CPT	0-0507662	0745	2	CHOWNING WILLIAM B	CPT	0-0949793	1159	1
CHENEY JR JOHN P	MAJ	0-1056664	0266	1	CHEYNE LESTER J	MAJ	0-0447853	0451	1	CHINKES STANLEY	MAJ	0-0958677	0663	1	CHRANE ROBERT N	CPT	0-0969796	1060	1
CHENEY LAURENCE B	LTC	0-0241151	1062	3	CHEYNE WILLIAM	LTC	0-2036360	0762	2	CHINLUND JOSEPH F	1LT	0-0466747	1146	1	CHREST JOHN F	LTC	0-0911808	0265	1
CHENEY LINWOOD G	1LT	0-1044195	0645	2	CHEYNEY RUSSELL G	1LT	0-1308474	0945	2	CHINN KEITH R	COL	0-0288424	0563	3	CHRIMES THEODORE D	MAJ	0-0202262	0846	2
CHENEY RUSSELL S	LTC	0-0296974	0362	3	CHEYNEY WALDRON J	COL	0-0105631	0345	2	CHINOWTH CHARLES C	CW2	W-2126894	0145	2	CHRISLEY JOHN R	CW3	W-2126176	0457	1
CHENEY WILLIAM D	CPT	0-0393396	0446	2	CHEYRICH LOUIS J	1LT	0-1281809	1047	1	CHINSKE RICHARD H	MAJ	0-2016588	1060	1	CHRISMAN CECIL M	WO1	W-2149691	0765	2
CHENOWETH C C	MAJ	0-1844948	0361	2	CHEZEM HAROLD R	LTC	0-1312835	1162	1	CHINWORTH JOHN L	CPT	0-0979767	0361	1	CHRISMAN ROBERT R	LTC	0-0211187	1063	3
CHENOWETH MARY N	MAJ	N-0742394	0766	1	CHEZMAR JULIUS	LTC	0-1542695	0561	1	CHIODO SANTO F	LTC	0-0451229	1262	1	CHRISTEN RUSSELL C	MAJ	0-1950654	1064	1
CHERAKIN BEN	LTC	0-0292550	0650	3	CHIANESE CAJETAN T	COL	0-0169198	0959	3	CHIOTAKIS VACILIOS A	LTC	0-1174249	0467	1	CHRISTENSEN ALAN W	LTC	0-0243571	1164	3
CHERBONNIER ANDRE V	LTC	0-0925568	0160	3	CHIARAMONTE JULIO	LTC	0-0348151	0161	1	CHIPLEY EHRLICH L	LTC	0-0305410	0562	1	CHRISTENSEN ALLEN D	CW3	W-2136684	1262	1
CHERNEY HYMAN	MAJ	0-2012651	0461	1	CHICATELLI JACOB J	CPT	0-1323238	0546	2	CHIPMAN ALBERT B	MAJ	0-0184857	1055	3	CHRISTENSEN ANDREW J	LTC	0-1635693	0463	1
CHERNOW HOWARD H	CPT	0-1786151	0348	2	CHICAZOLA MELVIN A	LTC	0-1104560	0464	2	CHIPMAN JR ALBERT B	1LT	0-0538397	0945	2	CHRISTENSEN ARLET C	CPT	0-0279720	0747	2
CHEROKE GEORGE	MAJ	0-0579858	0565	1	CHICHWAK LUCILLE C	1LT	N-0725556	0446	1	CHIPPEAUX HARRY L	MAJ	0-1119915	0461	1	CHRISTENSEN BURT P	CPT	0-0419153	0346	2
CHERRIE GEORGE M	MAJ	0-0188998	0157	3	CHICK LAMONT C	CPT	0-0236175	0258	2	CHIRICO ANTHONY R	MAJ	0-1946685	1164	1	CHRISTENSEN CAROL M	2LT	N-0775987	0345	1
CHERRINGTON ROBERT B	1LT	0-1055243	0745	2	CHICK LANGSTON F	CW2	W-2209354	1262	1	CHIRIGOTIS F F	LTC	0-1013071	0261	1	CHRISTENSEN CHRIST J	1LT	0-1886633	0658	2
CHERRINGTON VIRGIL A	LTC	0-0502365	0265	3	CHICKERING F L	CW4	W-2108242	1059	1	CHIRON ALBERT F	MAJ	0-0491244	0546	2	CHRISTENSEN EARL D	1LT	0-1305388	0345	2
CHERRON PETER	LTC	0-1647569	0962	1	CHICKERING M N	CPT	L-0105077	1054	2	CHIROS JIMMY	1LT	0-1183829	0946	2	CHRISTENSEN EARL E	1LT	0-2036535	0545	2
CHERRY ALFRED E	MAJ	0-0887698	0657	1	CHICO LUIS A	LTC	0-0229044	0265	3	CHISHOLM ELMER F	LTC	0-0234797	1263	3	CHRISTENSEN EDWARD	LTC	0-1294434	0761	1
CHERRY CHARLES C	LTC	0-1285547	0761	1	CHIDESTER CLARKE W	LTC	0-0341071	1059	1	CHISHOLM GORDON A	1LT	0-1288703	0545	2	CHRISTENSEN ELLIS G	COL	0-0280507	0656	3
CHERRY CHARLES M	2LT	0-1055244	0645	2	CHIDESTER GEORGE F	2LT	0-2016866	0746	1	CHISHOLM JOSEPH D	MAJ	0-0114287	0455	3	CHRISTENSEN FRANK P	COL	0-0216096	0953	1
CHERRY CHARLES S	LTC	0-0450425	1057	1	CHIEFFALO FRANK J	LTC	0-1578259	0967	1	CHISHOLM LAWRENCE W	1LT	0-1587734	0654	1	CHRISTENSEN FRED G	LTC	0-1587176	1167	1
CHERRY DITTMAR P	1LT	0-1043895	0344	2	CHIER REUBEN C	CPT	0-0338426	1045	2	CHISHOLM WILLIAM G	LTC	0-0392509	1264	1	CHRISTENSEN HALDOR F	LTC	0-0255480	0246	2
CHERRY EDMOND R	CW3	W-2142751	1060	1	CHIFSA ALOC C	LTC	0-0287230	0463	3	CHISHOLM WILLIAM H	CPT	0-0230808	0448	2	CHRISTENSEN HANS K	CPT	0-1766950	1047	2
CHERRY ELTON K	LTC	0-0921296	0557	2	CHILBERG GEORGE E	LTC	0-1544327	0667	2	CHISMAN THOMAS D	CW3	W-2141838	0958	1	CHRISTENSEN HOLGER	CPT	0-0494322	0351	1
CHERRY FRANK T	COL	0-0150756	0-49	3	CHILCOTE EARL H	CPT	0-1042783	0854	1	CHISMAR FRANK E	MAJ	0-0471641	0257	1	CHRISTENSEN HUGH W	1LT	0-1785321	0645	2
CHERRY JEFF F	MAJ	0-1884203	0867	1	CHILD BARBARA J	MAJ	L-1010078	0865	1	CHISMIRE FRANK E	MAJ	0-1291587	0561	1	CHRISTENSEN JENS	CPT	0-1913590	0836	1
CHERRY JERRY P	CPT	0-1185970	0258	1	CHILD HARRY M	LTC	0-1107857	0661	1	CHITTENDEN HERBERT M	LTC	0-0340826	0562	1	CHRISTENSEN JOHN B	LTC	0-0232887	1164	3
CHERRY JIM E	MAJ	0-1314732	1060	1	CHILD ROBERT W	COL	0-0173982	0158	3	CHITTENDEN MILES C	LTC	0-0112801	0955	3	CHRISTENSEN LESTER C	CPT	0-2262728	0361	1
CHERRY JOHN F	MAJ	0-1798448	0756	1	CHILDE JR JOHN W	1LT	0-1313570	0645	2	CHITTICK CLAIRE R	LTC	0-1306704	0856	1	CHRISTENSEN LESTER F	MAJ	0-1586762	0660	1
CHERRY JOSEPH A	LTC	0-1015046	0164	1	CHILDERS ARLIE M	MAJ	0-0969432	0867	1	CHITTICK GERVAISE S	COL	0-0903369	0662	1	CHRISTENSEN LINCOLN	CW3	W-2149808	0867	1
CHERUBINI AMERIGO J	MAJ	0-1533521	1055	1	CHILDERS CHESTER W	MAJ	0-1542402	0157	1	CHITTICK HARRY A	LTC	0-0293577	0263	3	CHRISTENSEN MELVIN	CW2	W-3100555	0567	1
CHESBRO IVAN A	COL	0-0119089	0651	3	CHILDERS DOROTHY T	MAJ	L-0900013	0565	1	CHITTICK JR HARRY S	LTC	0-0399870	0959	1	CHRISTENSEN NOAL A	LTC	0-1338922	0866	1
CHESCHEIR GEORGE M	COL	0-0189716	0849	3	CHILDERS EARL G	LTC	0-0388122	0760	1	CHITTICK MARTIN R	COL	0-0100258	0452	3	CHRISTENSEN PAUL E	CPT	0-0363126	0246	2
CHESHIRE GODFREY	COL	0-0181901	0153	3	CHILDERS FITZHUGH L	MAJ	0-0510348	0147	1	CHITTY CHARITA M	CPT	N-0763935	0747	1	CHRISTENSEN PETER A	LTC	0-0204635	0756	3
CHESHIRE JOSEPH B	LTC	0-0229153	0562	3	CHILDERS GEORGE T	LTC	0-0385461	0663	1	CHITWOOD ALBERT E	MAJ	0-1047918	0761	1	CHRISTENSEN R W	CPT	0-0488964	0246	2
CHESHIRE WILLIAM A	LTC	0-0323620	1266	3	CHILDERS JACK S	MAJ	0-1703058	0461	1	CHITWOOD GLENN W	MAJ	0-1822105	1157	1	CHRISTENSEN REX	MAJ	0-1634612	1160	1
CHESIRE JR JAMES C	MAJ	0-1177734	0461	1	CHILDERS JUNIOR A	MAJ	0-2005493	0361	1	CHITWOOD JULIUS R	MAJ	0-0447123	0346	2	CHRISTENSEN ROBERT	CW3	W-2147388	1062	1
CHESKI WILLIAM A	MAJ	0-0493177	0952	1	CHILDERS RAYMOND L	2LT	0-1049103	0844	2	CHITWOOD PAUL W	CW3	W-2117378	0560	1	CHRISTENSEN VIGGO	COL	0-0185784	0546	2
CHESKO JOSEPH W	1LT	0-1050593	1048	2	CHILDERS WARREN P	CPT	0-1637182	0952	1	CHIVINGTON FREDERICK	LTC	0-1111547	0163	1	CHRISTENSEN W BLAKE	CPT	0-0474980	0245	2
CHESLER MAURICE R	2LT	0-1587883	0144	2	CHILDRES JAMES P	LTC	0-0505393	0155	1	CHLADEK ARTHUR L	LTC	0-0246596	0366	3	CHRISTENSEN WIGGO	MAJ	0-1546157	0960	1
CHESLEY CATHERINE	1LT	N-0772147	0346	1	CHILDRESS CREED T	CW2	W-2150660	0559	1	CHLAPOWSKI THEODORE	MAJ	0-0981145	0245	1	CHRISTENSEN WILLIAM	1LT	0-5514636	0164	2
CHESLEY PHILIP R	MAJ	0-2020925	0663	1	CHILDRESS DENNIS R	2LT	0-1585272	0544	2	CHLEVIN JR B J	2LT	0-1050211	1144	2	CHRISTENSEN WOODROW	CPT	0-1294266	0657	1
CHESLEY WILLIAM C	1LT	0-1289045	0644	2	CHILDRESS HUGH J	MAJ	0-0277209	0653	3	CHLOUPEK CARL C	LTC	0-2289439	1166	1	CHRISTENSON ALBERT W	LTC	0-0209532	0345	2
CHESLOCK THEODORE J	MAJ	0-1937167	0466	1	CHILDRESS J T	2LT	0-1999222	0446	2	CHMIELEWSKI JANE T	1LT	N-0720455	1046	1	CHRISTENSON CONRAD W	CPT	0-0480356	0446	2
CHESMORE CARLTON R	LTC	0-0245898	1166	3	CHILDRESS LEWIS E	LTC	0-1554520	1166	1	CHMIELEWSKI SIGMUND	MAJ	0-1176280	1057	1	CHRISTENSON EARL D	LTC	0-0110007	1155	1
CHESNUTT JAMES G	COL	0-0906935	0667	3	CHILDRESS PAUL E	WO1	W-2150522	1154	1	CHO DAVID	MAJ	0-0977723	0763	1	CHRISTENSON HAROLD E	1LT	0-1295339	1146	2
CHESNUTT NORWOOD R	LTC	0-0168297	0746	2	CHILDS III DOMINIC J	MAJ	0-1031233	1160	1	CHO SAMUEL	CW3	W-2144179	0666	1	CHRISTENSON JEWELL C	LTC	0-0336544	867C	3
CHESROW EUGENE J	COL	0-0115806	0153	3	CHILDS J H	CPT	0-1305011	0947	2	CHOATE BENJAMIN D	COL	0-0257236	0648	3	CHRISTENSON JOHN C W	CW3	W-2150335	1162	1
CHESROW FRANK W	COL	0-0298680	0463	3	CHILDS JAMES N	1LT	0-1058473	0446	2	CHOATE HAROLD J	COL	0-0321782	0867	3	CHRISTENSON ROBERT L	LTC	0-1545067	0667	1
CHESS METKIN	CPT	0-0536967	0346	2	CHILDS JEANNE G	MAJ	L-0501178	0163	1	CHOATE JAMES F	1LT	0-0489756	0347	1	CHRISTIAN ALBERT O	2LT	0-0958647	0451	1
CHESSER FRED H	MAJ	0-1115212	0954	1	CHILDS JOHN P	2LT	0-1053086	0745	2	CHOATE JAMES F	MAJ	0-1919128	1263	1	CHRISTIAN BEATRICE M	1LT	N-0702500	1146	1
CHESSER JAMES L	1LT	0-0499480	0351	1	CHILDS JR EDWARD P	LTC	0-0189317	0556	3	CHOATE JOHN F	COL	0-0174426	1153	3	CHRISTIAN DEXTER I	CW3	W-2143884	1160	1
CHESSER JR JAMES A	1LT	0-1182082	1045	2	CHILDS LAWRENCE D	WO1	W-2150769	0155	1	CHOATE REGINALD C	CW4	W-2147513	1164	1	CHRISTIAN EARL H	LTC	0-0223567	0760	3
CHESSER LEWIS F	MAJ	0-1646350	0157	1	CHILDS LINCOLN B	CPT	0-0422647	0344	2	CHOFFREY MARIO J	LTC	0-1947553	0463	1	CHRISTIAN GEORGE W	CPT	0-0332959	0944	2
CHESSHIRE DOUGLAS	CPT	0-1542297	0661	1	CHILDS ORRICK A	LTC	0-1825592	0661	1	CHOINSKI WALTER F	COL	0-0246915	0558	1	CHRISTIAN GLEN H	LTC	0-0514108	0762	1
CHESSMAN JR CHARLES	CPT	0-1018652	0846	1	CHILDS RALPH S	COL	0-0246801	0959	3	CHOJECKI CHESTER J	LTC	0-1638874	0663	1	CHRISTIAN HENRY A	COL	0-0239704	0546	2
CHESSMAN JR WALTER F	1LT	0-0426750	0246	2	CHILDS ROBERT F	LTC	0-1296997	0463	1	CHOJNACKI ANDREW F	CW3	W-2144568	0662	1	CHRISTIAN HOWARD J	1LT	0-1635695	0146	2

NAME	GRADE	SVC NO	DATE RET MO YR	RET CODE
CHRISTIAN JACK	LTC	0-0219884	0856	3
CHRISTIAN JAMES T	1LT	0-1109197	0745	2
CHRISTIAN JOHN O	MAJ	0-1692548	0960	1
CHRISTIAN JOHN M	1LT	0-1080838	0246	2
CHRISTIAN JOSEPH L	1LT	0-1003895	0857	1
CHRISTIAN JR LOUIS C	MAJ	0-0451839	0647	2
CHRISTIAN MILTON B	LTC	0-1549908	0219	1
CHRISTIAN NICHOLAS J	2LT	0-1108552	0345	2
CHRISTIAN RUSSELL C	CW3	W-2143066	0357	1
CHRISTIAN WILLIAM G	CPT	0-1106644	0255	1
CHRISTIAN WILLIAM L	LTC	0-0207332	1243	3
CHRISTIANS CRYSTAL R	1LT	N-0742095	0945	1
CHRISTIANS JEROME J	LTC	0-0310427	0767	3
CHRISTIANSEN ALFRE	MAJ	0-1541781	0356	1
CHRISTIANSEN ARTHU	1LT	0-0298540	0845	2
CHRISTIANSEN ARTHUR	MAJ	0-1297839	0565	1
CHRISTIANSEN CARL P	CPT	0-0983191	1264	1
CHRISTIANSEN EMIL G	LTC	0-0389978	0363	1
CHRISTIANSEN ERNES	2LT	0-1015615	1044	2
CHRISTIANSEN GEORGE	LTC	0-1014923	1061	1
CHRISTIANSEN GEORGE	MAJ	0-1692647	0860	1
CHRISTIANSEN LAWRENC	MAJ	0-1334967	0862	1
CHRISTIANSEN VERNO	MAJ	0-1593238	0960	1
CHRISTIANSEN WALTER	MAJ	0-1324146	0364	2
CHRISTIANSON KENNETH	CPT	0-0447525	0946	2
CHRISTIE CLARENCE M	LTC	0-0269674	0467	3
CHRISTIE GOTTLIEB C	CW2	W-2149664	0260	1
CHRISTIE HAROLD R	LTC	0-0248770	0565	3
CHRISTIE JR GEORGE T	LTC	0-1309516	0764	3
CHRISTIE ROBERT M	LTC	0-0299031	0862	1
CHRISTIE ROBERT S	CPT	0-0220611	0660	3
CHRISTIE THOMAS M	MAJ	0-1014201	0167	2
CHRISTINA ANTHONY A	CPT	0-1288855	1157	1
CHRISTINE JAMES H	WO1	W-2118404	0849	1
CHRISTINE MILLER C	LTC	0-0446281	1160	2
CHRISTINE PAUL D	CW3	W-2152508	0762	1
CHRISTJOHN GLADYS R	2LT	N-0775665	1044	1
CHRISTL ERNEST M	MAJ	0-1041311	0146	2
CHRISTMAN ARTHUR V	CPT	0-1291952	0146	2
CHRISTMAN JOSEPH S	MAJ	0-0920461	1046	2
CHRISTMAN ROBERT J	1LT	0-2005340	0248	2
CHRISTMAS ELLIS H	CW3	W-2206847	0266	1
CHRISTMAS FRANK M	LTC	0-1283913	0961	1
CHRISTMAS JOE C	MAJ	0-0977849	0463	1
CHRISTNER EUGENE B	CW3	RW-2150156	0764	1
CHRISTOFFERSON HARLE	LTC	0-1036470	0662	1
CHRISTOPH CHARLES J	MAJ	0-1175075	0261	1
CHRISTOPHER ALVA J	LTC	0-1542821	1162	1
CHRISTOPHER ARTHUR C	LTC	0-0312811	1065	3
CHRISTOPHER DANIEL R	CW2	W-2141839	0756	1
CHRISTOPHER GLEN J	MAJ	0-1650469	0761	1
CHRISTOPHER JOHN	MAJ	0-1289121	0454	1
CHRISTOPHER JOHN O	LTC	0-1548177	0164	1
CHRISTOPHER LEON C	LTC	0-1334417	0864	1
CHRISTOPHER MILLARD	MAJ	0-2263448	0965	1
CHRISTOPHER SIDNEY L	CW2	W-2144162	0659	1
CHRISTOPHERSON CLIFF	LTC	0-0311038	0360	3
CHRISTOPHERSON GORDO	MAJ	0-0962892	0461	1
CHRISTOPHERSON OLAF	LTC	0-0330492	1064	1
CHRISTY GALE D	MAJ	0-1174530	0361	1
CHRISTY JOHN G	COL	0-0256819	0757	3
CHRISTY KENNETH R	LTC	0-0347606	0465	3
CHRISTY ROBERT J	MAJ	0-1100485	0566	2
CHRISTY THOMAS N	1LT	0-0440617	0446	2
CHRISWELL FRED O	LTC	0-0450582	0754	1
CHROMCIK BESSIE D	2LT	N-0792876	0751	1
CHROMI EDWARD	CW2	W-2152821	0757	1
CHRONIS LEONIDAS M	LTC	0-0313490	0961	3
CHRONQUIST GEORGE C	CPT	0-0484339	1143	2
CHRYSLER CLAYTON D	LTC	0-0236805	1057	3
CHRYST STANLEY T	MAJ	0-0488715	0753	1
CHRZAN WALTER S	1LT	0-1318651	0248	1
CHURAK WILLIAM J	MAJ	0-0450622	0455	1
CHUBB GEORGE F	CW3	W-2150040	0166	1
CHURBUCK FRANK M	CPT	0-0128927	0648	3
CHUM JR ANDREWS S	MAJ	0-1114887	0660	2
CHUMBLEY CHARLES M	LTC	0-1541235	0457	1
CHUN ARTHUR B	COL	0-0343577	0762	2
CHUN RICHARD S	MAJ	0-0953545	0862	1
CHUN-MING ARCHER	LTC	0-0308700	0548	2
CHUNG DAVID	MAJ	0-1340157	0765	1
CHUNG HENRY H	LTC	0-0322272	1065	3
CHUNG WAH N	1LT	0-0378070	0444	2
CHUNN FLOYD H	LTC	0-0315418	0858	3
CHUNN FRANCIS A	CPT	0-1032196	0258	1
CHUNN THOMAS H	2LT	0-0346754	0542	2
CHUPINSKY PETER	MAJ	0-1587178	0567	1
CHURAN DOROTHY	1LT	N-0785680	1046	1
CHURCH CLAUDE H	COL	0-0200642	0648	3
CHURCH ELVIN H	CPT	0-0146537	0257	3
CHURCH GERALD L	COL	0-0288207	0155	1
CHURCH HARRY J	2LT	0-1104084	0445	2
CHURCH HENRY H	LTC	0-0486468	0253	1
CHURCH JACOB F	MAJ	0-1173187	1058	1
CHURCH JAMES A	LTC	0-0888263	1160	1
CHURCH JOHN A	2LT	0-0468511	0745	2
CHURCH JOSEPH H	COL	0-0248168	0463	3
CHURCH JR ARCHIE W	LTC	0-1316383	0865	1
CHURCH JR CHARLES O	CW2	W-2143261	0666	1
CHURCH JR GEORGE B	LTC	0-0322545	0859	1
CHURCH JR GUY N	LTC	0-0398278	0263	1
CHURCH KENNETH W	CPT	0-0300082	1162	3
CHURCH MERTON E	LTC	0-0329610	0261	1
CHURCH ORVILLE T	LTC	0-0116144	0557	3
CHURCH RALPH C	CW4	W-2000324	1060	2
CHURCH RAYMOND B	MAJ	0-2055381	0656	1
CHURCH SAMUEL A	2LT	0-1550134	0643	2
CHURCH SANFORD F	LTC	0-0102910	0648	3
CHURCH WAYNE G	COL	0-0210727	0160	3
CHURCH WILLIAM K	MAJ	0-1281971	0262	1
CHURCHBOURNE HENRY	MAJ	0-1183038	0259	2
CHURCHILL DAVID R	LTC	0-1683453	1167	1
CHURCHILL HELEN K	CPT	N-0787471	0246	2
CHURCHILL MARJORIE P	MAJ	L-1000893	0664	1
CHURCHILL RALPH D	LTC	0-0340543	0764	1
CHURCHILL RICHARD T	CPT	0-0533422	1047	1
CHURCHILL RILEY V	CW2	W-2211382	1266	1
CHURCHILL WALTER R	MAJ	0-0142663	1049	3
CHURCHMAN DONALD A	LTC	0-1634615	1165	1
CHURCHMAN HENRY C	LTC	0-0122316	1055	3
CHURCHWELL SAMUEL B	MAJ	0-0253814	1054	3
CHYNOWETH JOHN H	CPT	0-1947185	0462	1
CHYNOWETH WILLIAM R	LTC	0-0183567	0648	3
CI MARCONE WILLIAM A	MAJ	0-1949507	0561	1
CIAGLO MICHAEL J	1LT	0-1172411	0346	2
CIAMPA RALPH P	CPT	0-0499649	1044	2
CIAMPA UBALDI J	CW2	W-2111600	0350	2
CIANI RAYMOND R	CW2	W-3000286	0966	1
CIANOS MICHAEL	LTC	0-1298662	0564	1
CIAPLO JR JOHN W	MAJ	0-2263028	1164	1
CIBOROWSKI MITCHELL	LTC	0-1039902	0862	1
CIBULA ALVIN M	COL	0-0256320	1067	3
CIBULSKI FRED C	MAJ	0-1042516	0954	1
CICCARELLI LAWRENCE	MAJ	0-0980818	0264	1
CICCIOLLO DOMINICK N	CW3	W-2145337	1061	1
CICCIU ANGELO	LTC	0-1177736	0166	1
CICCOLI MICHAEL J	LTC	0-1292659	0261	1
CICCONE ALEX P	LTC	0-1107861	1163	1
CICCOTELLI DOMINIC R	CW4	W-2147714	0766	1
CICERCHIA IOLANDA M	LTC	N-0721609	0767	1
CICHANSKI WILLIAM J	LTC	0-0411005	0766	1
CICHY JOSEPH J	CW4	W-2141977	1265	1
CICOLANI RENO R	CW4	W-2117879	1266	3
CICONE GAUDIC J	MAJ	0-1011832	1147	2
CIELINSKI EDWARD	LTC	0-1288856	0657	1
CIESIELSKI FRANCIS	LTC	0-0933326	0266	1
CIEZAK HENRY F	MAJ	0-1644667	1062	1
CIFORELLI BART L	LTC	0-1013443	1265	3
CIHOS CARL	CPT	0-1308208	0452	1
CILINO STEPHEN	LTC	0-1047922	0565	1
CILLEY GEORGE E	LTC	0-0336143	0460	1
CILLIS VINCENT A	LTC	0-1948104	0167	3
CIMINO JOSEPH N	CW3	W-2152203	1157	1
CIMINO JR VINCENT	MAJ	0-1696247	0563	1
CINI JULIAN A	MAJ	0-0976190	1165	1
CINQ-MARS PAUL R	LTC	0-0342446	0363	1
CINQUANTA FIORINO A	LTC	0-0782170	1167	1
CIOCHETTI HANNIBAL S	LTC	0-0164102	0552	1
CIOLA DOMINICK P	2LT	0-1185397	0545	2
CIPPES ISAAC B	MAJ	0-0237678	1043	2
CIPRIANO JOSEPH J	CW3	W-2147339	0265	1
CIPRIANO XAVIER V	LTC	0-0556666	0966	1
CIRELLI MARIO G	CPT	0-0534891	0446	2
CIRIACKS RUBEN H	LTC	0-1055248	1263	1
CIRILLO JOSEPH	MAJ	0-1595424	1060	1
CIROCCO CARMEL J	1LT	0-1553610	0645	1
CIROLIA PHILIP J	1LT	0-0553204	0146	1
CISCO JOSEPH A	MAJ	0-1313340	0955	1
CISEWSKI LAMBERT F	1LT	0-1291234	1144	2
CISZEK JULIUS G	CPT	0-1053521	0558	1
CISZEWSKI JOSEPH	CPT	0-0450709	1056	1
CITO ALBERT V	LTC	0-0326051	0360	1
CITRON ROBERT R	CPT	0-0337616	0645	2
CITRON WILLIAM M	MAJ	0-0478888	0344	2
CIUCHTA JOHN T	CW3	W-2151763	1062	1
CIULIK JOSEPH O	1LT	0-0931275	0346	2
CIVALIER JOSEPH J	CPT	0-1306064	0146	2
CIVELLO ANTHONY R	MAJ	0-1554521	0661	1
CIVICK RICHARD J	MAJ	0-0965346	0167	1
CIVIDANES MANUEL	MAJ	0-1315788	0461	1
CIVIK FRANK C	1LT	0-1798449	0848	1
CIVITELLA CAESAR J	MAJ	0-1918864	0964	1
CIZAN CLIFFORD L	MAJ	0-0976798	1063	1
CIZEK MELVIN A	LTC	0-1059740	0763	1
CLABAUGH RICHARD P	2LT	0-1053522	0344	2
CLABAUGH SAMUEL F	COL	0-0265446	0352	3
CLABEAUX HARRY W	CW2	W-2144903	1162	1
CLABO PETER	2LT	0-0422850	0442	2
CLAFF LESLIE A	COL	0-0530863	1064	3
CLAFFEY JAMES S	LTC	0-1822237	0766	1
CLAFLIN FREDERICK	LTC	0-0379751	0463	1
CLAGETT CARRELL M	MAJ	0-1173562	0258	1
CLAGETT DONALD R	1LT	0-1284473	0944	2
CLAGETT JOHN F	MAJ	0-0177622	0561	3
CLAGETT THOMAS B	LTC	0-1293011	1263	1
CLAGG JESSE F	MAJ	0-1541733	0157	1
CLAGGETT RICHARD F	1LT	0-1637727	0846	1
CLAGGETT THOMAS O	LTC	0-0308624	0864	3
CLAGHORN CLIFFORD H	LTC	0-0277269	1150	3
CLAGUE JOHN P	LTC	0-0244578	0861	3
CLAIN JR MARVIN R	MAJ	0-1554877	0661	1
CLAING GERARD J	LTC	0-1290554	0461	1
CLAIR CARL W	CPT	0-1590377	0346	1
CLAIR MARIE T	1LT	L-0120188	1050	2
CLAIRE GUY S	COL	0-0306823	0856	3
CLAITOR DAVID E	2LT	0-1037956	1044	2
CLAMPET JAMES R	LTC	0-0456542	0656	2
CLAMUCHA ANASTASIO	1LT	0-1896695	0151	1
CLANCY ANNA K	2LT	N-0700781	1036	1
CLANCY CLYDE O	COL	0-0310513	0963	1
CLANCY JOHN L	CW2	W-2150201	0761	1
CLANCY THADDEUS	CPT	0-0183569	0762	3
CLANCY THOMAS G	LTC	0-1948566	1266	1
CLANCY WILLIAM H	CPT	0-0172135	0155	3
CLANTON ALBERT O	CPT	0-1032145	0657	1
CLANTON DAVID L	LTC	0-1030135	0764	1
CLANTON THOMAS K	CW2	W-2105769	1147	2
CLAPHAM AUGUST J	CW3	W-2148577	1162	1
CLAPP ERNEST	1LT	0-0109074	0335	1
CLAPP EUGENE O	CW2	W-2144876	1055	1
CLAPP JR HARVEY R	CPT	0-0247527	0266	3
CLAPP LAURENCE W	CW2	W-2209167	0762	1
CLAPP LESTER L	MAJ	0-0217678	1057	3
CLAPP RALPH X	1LT	0-1313207	1055	1
CLAPP ROGER F	LTC	0-0260225	0867	3
CLAPP TILLMAN L	1LT	0-0977620	0859	1
CLAPP WILEY M	2LT	0-1913606	0336	1
CLAPP WINTHROP S	COL	0-0221525	1047	2
CLAPP 3RD RUSSELL A	2LT	0-0535591	0446	2
CLAPPER HUBBARD G	MAJ	0-1296488	1060	1
CLAPPER NEAL E	MAJ	0-0504279	0753	1
CLAPPER WILLARD C	LTC	0-1581599	0664	1
CLAPPISON CHARLES O	1LT	0-0492460	0946	2
CLARDY CARL C	CPT	0-0271233	0747	2
CLARE JOHN W	MAJ	0-1305730	0865	1
CLARE JOSEPH F	LTC	0-1638876	0665	3
CLARE LELAND T	1LT	0-0391124	0644	2
CLARE THOMAS H	1LT	0-1058474	1047	2
CLARENS HARRY F	LTC	0-1296998	0363	1
CLAREY JOHN C	LTC	0-2055099	0263	1
CLARICK MILDRED S	1LT	N-0751603	0146	2
CLARIDGE FREDERICK	LTC	0-0177316	0459	3
CLARK ALBERT C	MAJ	0-0272843	0367	3
CLARK ALBERT R	CPT	0-2200012	0555	2
CLARK ALFRED V	LTC	0-1053524	0865	1
CLARK ALLEN P	LTC	0-0416247	1062	1
CLARK ALLEN R	CPT	0-0375912	0746	2
CLARK ALVIN E	LTC	0-0374810	0766	1
CLARK ALVIN W	LTC	0-0196398	0862	3
CLARK ARCHIE E	COL	0-0498188	0761	2
CLARK ARTHUR F	CPT	0-2030433	1062	1
CLARK ARTHUR H	LTC	0-0291066	0445	2
CLARK AUBREY H	CPT	0-1298194	0447	2
CLARK AUREL R	LTC	0-0410123	0754	1
CLARK BENJAMIN F	COL	0-0308088	0566	3
CLARK BILLY C	MAJ	0-0396208	0257	2
CLARK BRADFORD A	CPT	0-0298052	0865	2
CLARK BROADUS	CW2	W-2151095	1057	1
CLARK CARROLL H	LTC	0-0232382	1057	3
CLARK CHARLES A	MAJ	0-0505228	0550	1
CLARK CHARLES C	LTC	0-0481948	0366	1
CLARK CHARLES C	MAJ	0-1287665	0160	1
CLARK CHARLES D	COL	0-0201707	0661	3
CLARK CHARLES E	COL	0-0144653	0252	3
CLARK CHARLES G	LTC	0-0338072	0555	3
CLARK CHARLES I	COL	0-0196442	0253	3
CLARK CHARLES K	CW2	W-2206930	1063	1
CLARK CHARLES L	MAJ	0-0288225	1067	3
CLARK CHARLES N	MAJ	0-1106055	0563	1
CLARK CHARLES T	MAJ	0-1031795	0161	1
CLARK CHESTER A	COL	0-0199426	1148	1
CLARK CHESTER F	MAJ	0-2263349	1264	1
CLARK CLAUDE C	LTC	0-0266443	0160	1
CLARK CLIFTON T	CW4	W-2107881	0659	1
CLARK CLYDE L	LTC	0-0250749	0167	3
CLARK CORBETT W	MAJ	0-0981212	1061	1
CLARK DANIEL J	MAJ	0-0551547	0963	1
CLARK DANIEL R	COL	0-0456541	0561	1
CLARK DEWITT H	MAJ	0-0183658	0749	3
CLARK DILBERT	MAJ	0-2263038	1164	1
CLARK DON B	LTC	0-2005665	0667	1
CLARK DONALD L	MAJ	0-0972824	1162	1
CLARK DONALD M	CW2	W-2150651	0662	1
CLARK DOYLE H	COL	0-0340638	0466	3
CLARK DUDLEY B	LTC	0-0471956	0157	1
CLARK DUNLAP C	COL	0-0115910	1156	3
CLARK EARL R	LTC	0-0113974	0648	3
CLARK EDITH M	MAJ	N-0730865	1067	1
CLARK EDMUND W	MAJ	0-0966143	1262	1
CLARK EDWARD	CPT	0-1318015	0547	2
CLARK EDWARD A	1LT	0-0527734	0646	2
CLARK EDWARD F	COL	0-0205961	0155	1
CLARK EDWARD J	CPT	0-1323539	1053	1
CLARK ELDRED S	CW3	W-2143886	1162	2
CLARK ELLWOOD	CW4	W-2133008	0263	1
CLARK ELMER F	LTC	0-1100913	0758	1
CLARK EMERSON	CW4	W-2122829	0754	1
CLARK ERNEST M	LTC	0-0225866	0864	3
CLARK ESTHER P	2LT	N-0702396	0733	1
CLARK EUGENE F	LTC	0-0362275	0945	1

NAME	GRADE	SVC NO	DATE RET MO YR	RET CODE
CLARK FLOYD H	LTC	O-1640933	0967	1
CLARK FRANK S	LTC	O-0309994	0559	3
CLARK FRANK W	CPT	O-0968850	0759	1
CLARK FRANKLIN D	CW3	W-2144237	0661	1
CLARK FRED G	COL	O-0234487	0754	3
CLARK FRED G	CW2	W-2143596	1056	1
CLARK FRED H	LTC	O-0193543	0555	3
CLARK FRED P	COL	O-0175054	0255	3
CLARK GEOFFREY	COL	O-0316999	0553	1
CLARK GEORGE A	CPT	O-0123276	0156	3
CLARK GEORGE D	CW2	W-2214888	1166	1
CLARK GEORGE E	LTC	O-0376765	0161	2
CLARK GEORGE E	MAJ	O-0415102	1060	1
CLARK GEORGE J	MAJ	O-0370232	0944	2
CLARK GEORGE M	MAJ	O-2019851	0463	1
CLARK GEORGE R	LTC	O-0320604	0861	1
CLARK GEORGE R	CPT	O-1303463	0958	1
CLARK GEORGE R	1LT	O-2055439	0860	1
CLARK GEORGE W	CPT	O-1018239	0862	1
CLARK GLEN	MAJ	O-2000968	0959	1
CLARK GLEN L	MAJ	O-0224661	0761	3
CLARK GLEN R	LTC	O-1115528	0962	1
CLARK GORDON C	CW2	RW-2143599	0561	1
CLARK HAROLD A	CW2	W-2150739	0157	1
CLARK HAROLD H	CPT	O-0381979	0354	2
CLARK HARRY A	CPT	O-0238080	0250	3
CLARK HARRY B	CPT	O-0495134	0347	2
CLARK HARRY E	MAJ	O-0174998	0353	2
CLARK HARRY K	COL	O-0140395	0951	3
CLARK HASKELL G	MAJ	O-1318016	0767	3
CLARK HENRY M	LTC	O-0192179	0753	3
CLARK HOWARD R	MAJ	O-1633125	0160	1
CLARK II RIDGWAY J	LTC	O-1055290	1062	1
CLARK IRVING T	LTC	O-0284917	0666	3
CLARK JACK A	LTC	O-0888302	0263	1
CLARK JACK A	MAJ	O-1290207	0261	1
CLARK JACK P	LTC	O-0260812	0446	2
CLARK JACK R	MAJ	O-1052721	0558	1
CLARK JAMES A	LTC	O-0288429	1067	3
CLARK JAMES A	MAJ	O-1295509	0459	1
CLARK JAMES C	1LT	O-1307944	1145	2
CLARK JAMES E	1LT	O-0506130	0445	2
CLARK JAMES F	MAJ	O-1925160	1166	1
CLARK JAMES L	CW2	W-2141778	0554	1
CLARK JAMES R	CPT	O-1171490	1055	1
CLARK JAMES R	LTC	O-1542974	0264	1
CLARK JAMES W	1LT	O-1326740	0248	2
CLARK JESSE R	MAJ	O-0251101	0660	3
CLARK JOE	1LT	O-1996652	0747	2
CLARK JOE W	CW3	W-2142096	0762	1
CLARK JOHN A	1LT	O-1002593	0546	2
CLARK JOHN B	LTC	O-0351998	[illegible]	1
CLARK JOHN H	MAJ	O-0249412	0542	3
CLARK JOHN H	MAJ	O-1599106	0763	1
CLARK JOHN N	COL	O-0197339	1161	3
CLARK JOHN P	MAJ	O-0907549	0146	2
CLARK JOHN R	MAJ	O-0142743	0650	3
CLARK JOHN R	LTC	O-0414858	1265	3
CLARK JOHN S	CPT	O-1323108	1046	2
CLARK JOHN S	LTC	O-1339613	0967	1
CLARK JOHN S	CPT	O-1998095	0955	1
CLARK JOHN T	MAJ	O-1633757	0453	1
CLARK JOSEPH	CW4	W-2111342	1054	2
CLARK JOSEPH F	LTC	O-1575862	0565	1
CLARK JR ARCHIE D	MAJ	O-0398001	0567	1
CLARK JR ARTHUR B	1LT	O-0441254	0745	2
CLARK JR ARTHUR W	MAJ	O-1104562	0764	1
CLARK JR CHARLES L	LTC	O-0300788	1164	1
CLARK JR CLEMENT W	LTC	O-0414900	0561	1
CLARK JR EDWARD P	COL	O-0126302	1158	3
CLARK JR EUGENE S	COL	O-0290853	0159	3
CLARK JR GEORGE A	MAJ	O-2051615	0563	1
CLARK JR HUGH O	CPT	O-1294909	1045	2
CLARK JR JAMES A	CPT	O-0427909	0346	2
CLARK JR MACK	MAJ	O-1105339	0965	1

NAME	GRADE	SVC NO	DATE RET MO YR	RET CODE
CLARK JR PORTER A	MAJ	O-1171948	0261	1
CLARK JR ROBERT F	CW4	W-2125936	0661	1
CLARK JR WALTER N	MAJ	O-0308568	0745	2
CLARK KENNETH	LTC	O-0444045	0751	1
CLARK KENNETH R	CPT	O-0222966	0444	2
CLARK LAWRENCE P	LTC	O-1167362	0261	1
CLARK LAWRENCE R	MAJ	O-1312664	0657	2
CLARK LAWRENCE C	CW2	W-2126226	0659	1
CLARK LAWRENCE F	COL	O-0246021	0754	3
CLARK LEROY K	MAJ	O-0475021	0347	1
CLARK LEX L	MAJ	O-0966364	0763	1
CLARK LINCOLN F	LTC	O-0387078	1060	1
CLARK LOIS L	CW4	V-0911145	0767	1
CLARK LOREN D	CPT	O-1324605	0947	1
CLARK LOUIS S	MAJ	O-2017813	0363	1
CLARK LOWELL L	LTC	O-0311740	0763	3
CLARK LUCIEN P	MAJ	O-2051623	0561	1
CLARK LYMAN J	COL	O-0401708	0760	3
CLARK MAJOR	LTC	O-1171088	0960	1
CLARK MANLEY W	LTC	O-1305896	0164	1
CLARK MARVIN C	COL	O-0193709	0162	3
CLARK MAURICE E	MAJ	O-0203476	0545	1
CLARK MAX A	LTC	O-2080330	0867	1
CLARK MERTON J	CPT	O-0296047	0345	2
CLARK MICHAEL I	LTC	O-2014461	0466	1
CLARK NATHANIEL	LTC	O-1107865	1064	1
CLARK NEIL W	MAJ	O-0402067	0746	2
CLARK NEWTON	1LT	O-0162704	0959	3
CLARK NORMAN E	MAJ	O-1922364	0962	1
CLARK OMER W	MAJ	O-0138770	0648	3
CLARK ORIE J	MAJ	O-1303245	0161	1
CLARK ORVAL C	MAJ	O-1998390	1154	1
CLARK OTHAR A	CW4	W-2004400	0866	1
CLARK PAUL	MAJ	O-0497855	0155	1
CLARK PAUL D	COL	O-0230925	1061	3
CLARK PAUL M	COL	O-0125363	0454	2
CLARK PHILO C	MAJ	O-0174161	0463	1
CLARK RALPH C	CPT	O-2025488	0859	1
CLARK RALPH W	LTC	O-0197466	0648	3
CLARK RAY O	LTC	O-1298026	1055	1
CLARK RAYMOND	MAJ	O-1108555	0560	1
CLARK RAYMOND J	LTC	O-0113570	0955	3
CLARK REX T	MAJ	O-2011201	1262	1
CLARK RICHARD A	MAJ	O-1553792	1062	1
CLARK RICHARD H	MAJ	O-0408832	0562	1
CLARK RICHARD H	MAJ	O-0981896	0967	1
CLARK RICHARD F	MAJ	O-0497450	0755	1
CLARK ROBERT C	CPT	O-1324007	0751	1
CLARK ROBERT F	CPT	O-2001211	0548	2
CLARK ROBERT E	1LT	O-2212015	0655	2
CLARK ROBERT H	1LT	O-1299345	0146	2
CLARK ROBERT K	CPT	O-0451740	0246	2
CLARK ROBERT K	CPT	O-1579487	0356	1
CLARK ROBERT L	LTC	O-1285389	0563	1
CLARK ROBERT L	CW2	W-2151736	0158	1
CLARK ROBERT P	CPT	O-1324511	0746	2
CLARK ROBERT W	CW3	W-2148716	0764	1
CLARK ROGER W	LTC	O-1301552	0264	1
CLARK ROSCOE E	LTC	O-1046097	0767	1
CLARK ROY B	LTC	O-0238851	1165	3
CLARK ROY D	CPT	O-1011800	1147	2
CLARK RUSSELL A	COL	O-0199667	0850	3
CLARK RUSSELL F	MAJ	O-0222893	1054	3
CLARK RUSSELL N	LTC	O-1797783	0667	1
CLARK STANLEY J	1LT	O-0924116	0744	2
CLARK STERLING H	LTC	O-0233075	0762	3
CLARK STROTHER J	MAJ	O-1845404	0450	2
CLARK THADDEUS J	MAJ	O-0485801	0157	1
CLARK THEODORE F	2LT	O-1545174	0744	2
CLARK THOMAS E	CW2	W-2210047	0660	1
CLARK THOMAS F	MAJ	O-1553420	0365	1
CLARK THOMAS W	CPT	O-0414799	0346	2
CLARK VICTOR L	LTC	O-0243333	0757	1
CLARK VIRGIL C	1LT	O-1311487	0945	2
CLARK VIRGIL W	LTC	O-0451460	1054	1

NAME	GRADE	SVC NO	DATE RET MO YR	RET CODE
CLARK WALTER K	MAJ	O-1877180	0765	2
CLARK WARREN F	MAJ	O-1923263	1163	1
CLARK WARREN W	CW4	W-2136687	0766	1
CLARK WILFORD L	CW2	W-2145164	0659	1
CLARK WILL M	COL	O-0258865	0964	3
CLARK WILLARD O	LTC	O-0296497	1157	1
CLARK WILLARD F	MAJ	O-0450415	0657	1
CLARK WILLIAM A	MAJ	O-0427680	1042	1
CLARK WILLIAM A	CPT	O-1313968	0444	2
CLARK WILLIAM B	CW2	W-3350234	0766	1
CLARK WILLIAM C	MAJ	O-1307802	0561	1
CLARK WILLIAM F	MAJ	O-0889039	0264	1
CLARK WILLIAM G	LTC	O-1533756	1061	1
CLARK WILLIAM G	LTC	O-1557261	0664	1
CLARK WILLIAM H	LTC	O-1821680	0962	1
CLARK WILLIAM M	CPT	O-1586493	0954	2
CLARK WILLIAM P	LTC	O-0288748	0252	1
CLARK WILLIAM R	LTC	O-0912914	0767	3
CLARK WILLIAM R	MAJ	O-0970514	0964	1
CLARK WILLIAM T	MAJ	O-1053541	1066	1
CLARK WILLIAM T	2LT	O-1323291	0245	2
CLARK WILLIAM W	LTC	O-0284225	0466	3
CLARK WILLIAM W	2LT	O-0403437	1047	2
CLARK WILLIE V	WO1	W-2110956	0566	3
CLARK WINDFIELD	CW2	W-2151075	0664	1
CLARKE ALAN K	LTC	O-0415186	1166	1
CLARKE ANDREW F	LTC	O-0260968	0862	3
CLARKE ARCHIE	CW3	W-2147020	0659	1
CLARKE BERNARD L	LTC	O-1798119	1060	1
CLARKE BRUCE F	COL	O-0150404	0950	3
CLARKE CHARLES J	CPT	O-0177816	0753	3
CLARKE CLAUDE R	MAJ	O-0109062	0637	1
CLARKE CREIGHTON	MAJ	O-1035222	0466	1
CLARKE CYRUS A	MAJ	O-0490858	0146	2
CLARKE EDWARD S	MAJ	O-2019433	0742	1
CLARKE ELIJAH S	LTC	O-1947658	1167	1
CLARKE FRANCIS J	1LT	O-1295175	1045	2
CLARKE GEORGE H	MAJ	O-1336879	0366	1
CLARKE GEORGE J	WO1	W-2114237	0755	1
CLARKE GEORGE L	COL	O-0170681	0758	3
CLARKE GEORGE W	1LT	O-1116762	0746	2
CLARKE GERARD T	1LT	O-0416145	0445	2
CLARKE JAMES E	LTC	O-0310482	0740	3
CLARKE JOHN J	LTC	O-0209933	0556	3
CLARKE JOSEPH G	CPT	O-0172625	0759	3
CLARKE JOSEPH V	1LT	O-0920565	0746	2
CLARKE JR ALFRED N	1LT	O-0454083	1045	1
CLARKE JR FRED M	COL	O-0242389	0166	3
CLARKE JR SAMUEL J	CW2	W-2150568	1263	1
CLARKE MAURICE L	MAJ	O-0190381	0761	3
CLARKE NEWELL W	LTC	O-0261788	1166	3
CLARKE RILEY H	MAJ	O-1342367	0162	1
CLARKE VAN A	LTC	O-0144084	1145	2
CLARKE WATTS R	MAJ	O-0278195	0958	3
CLARKE WILLIAM J	MAJ	O-1300607	0567	1
CLARKE WILLIAM L	LTC	O-1311065	0866	1
CLARKSON DALE F	CW2	W-2205644	0661	1
CLARKSON EDWARD D	MAJ	O-0155662	0144	2
CLARKSON JR EDWARD H	LTC	O-0264261	0953	3
CLARKSON MILAN E	CW3	W-2146916	0763	1
CLARKSON SAMUEL D	CPT	O-0239304	0665	3
CLARNO JOSEPH S	1LT	O-0482169	0244	2
CLARY JAMES O	CW3	W-2106337	1057	1
CLARY JOHN G	CW3	W-2143464	1160	1
CLARY JR HORACE F	LTC	O-0415052	1263	1
CLARY WILLIAM R	CPT	O-0359062	1060	3
CLASPILL BERTRAM A	MAJ	O-0275371	0647	1
CLASSEN EDWIN C	WO1	W-2124090	1044	2
CLAUDE WILLIAM T	1LT	O-0109411	1059	3
CLAUDIO JOSE F	CPT	O-1476311	0467	1
CLAUDIO LEONARDO C	1LT	O-0490549	0155	1
CLAUER LESTER J	LTC	O-1016466	1165	1
CLAUNCH GEORGE W	CW2	W-2145401	1158	1
CLAUNCH JR EMMETT S	1LT	O-1550378	0745	2
CLAUNCH THOMAS H	COL	O-0322868	1060	1

NAME	GRADE	SVC NO	DATE RET MO YR	RET CODE
CLAUS EVERETT C	COL	O-0312224	0660	3
CLAUSEL JR CALVIN L	1LT	O-0479223	0946	1
CLAUSEN ARTHUR C	MAJ	O-0165403	0659	3
CLAUSEN ERVIN H	COL	O-0100383	1149	3
CLAUSEN GEORGE F	MAJ	O-0331799	0746	2
CLAUSEN RALPH T	2LT	O-0517527	0545	2
CLAUSEN WILLIAM H	LTC	O-0516577	0967	1
CLAUSING GERALD A	LTC	O-1052712	0666	1
CLAUSON MARVIN A	CW2	W-2208817	0963	1
CLAUSS FRANCIS L	CW2	W-2002710	0263	3
CLAUSS FREDERICK	1LT	O-1638881	0646	2
CLAUSSEN GLEN O	LTC	O-1103102	0767	1
CLAUSSEN HARLEY M	LTC	O-2037225	1063	1
CLAUTICE JOSEPH W	LTC	O-0286591	0167	3
CLAVEL THOMAS S	1LT	O-1896510	0853	1
CLAVIN CHARLES P	COL	O-0211697	0959	3
CLAWSER JR SAMUEL M	LTC	O-0453669	1061	1
CLAWSON ARTHUR L	CPT	O-1541698	0755	1
CLAWSON CLARENCE A	MAJ	O-0980080	0362	2
CLAWSON EDWARD J	MAJ	O-0494539	0455	1
CLAWSON GORDON L	COL	O-0299004	0757	3
CLAWSON HENRY A	CPT	O-0109769	0241	2
CLAWSON IRWIN	LTC	O-0187234	0152	3
CLAWSON JR GREAR D	LTC	O-0483591	0764	1
CLAWSON JR THOMAS A	COL	O-0244565	0247	2
CLAWSON SAMUEL M	LTC	O-0489846	0555	1
CLAXTON GEORGE P	MAJ	O-2007479	0860	1
CLAXTON LAWRENCE L	CPT	O-1175078	0349	1
CLAY ALTON M	LTC	O-0295061	1266	3
CLAY BOYD V	CW2	W-2147397	1059	1
CLAY CECIL	CW2	W-2153243	0659	1
CLAY EDMOND G	2LT	O-1578270	0746	2
CLAY EUGENE H	MAJ	O-1108556	0657	1
CLAY GEORGE W	CW4	W-2102762	1154	1
CLAY GROVER C	MAJ	O-0130835	0253	3
CLAY HASKELL	CW3	W-2144943	0962	1
CLAY MORRISON F	MAJ	O-1053940	1060	1
CLAY PAUL V	MAJ	O-0166723	1150	3
CLAY ROGER A	CPT	O-1593500	0863	1
CLAY SHERMAN	MAJ	O-1703758	0357	1
CLAY UEL E	CW3	W-2150294	1263	1
CLAY WESLEY P	CPT	O-0285609	1045	2
CLAY WILLIAM W	MAJ	O-2206266	1266	1
CLAYBOURN GLEN L	LTC	O-0230668	0462	3
CLAYBOOK MAURICE	MAJ	O-0978236	1061	1
CLAYMAN SIGMUND J	MAJ	O-0384864	0747	2
CLAYPOOL BURRISS E	LTC	O-0222689	0964	3
CLAYPOOL CHARLES W	MAJ	O-4006027	0267	1
CLAYPOOL JOSEPH S	MAJ	O-0489151	0550	1
CLAYSON DEMAR	LTC	O-1167778	1262	1
CLAYSON LESTER V	MAJ	O-0503374	0161	1
CLAYTON BERT V	MAJ	O-0214862	0648	3
CLAYTON CURTIS F	CW3	W-2203879	0365	2
CLAYTON HAROLD C	CPT	O-0114704	0657	3
CLAYTON HARRY A	CPT	O-0322477	1165	3
CLAYTON J C	CPT	O-2011642	0657	1
CLAYTON JOEL W	COL	O-0116218	0157	3
CLAYTON JOHN D	LTC	O-0445067	0252	1
CLAYTON JR JOHN	1LT	O-1315521	1045	2
CLAYTON MICHAEL P	MAJ	O-2010429	1062	1
CLAYTON NEPHI W	CW2	W-2107859	0246	2
CLAYTON RAYMOND C	CW3	W-2207583	0267	1
CLAYTON ROBERT F	MAJ	O-2037664	0962	1
CLAYTON ROBERT G	MAJ	O-1180455	0459	1
CLAYTON SAMUEL	MAJ	O-0500674	0446	1
CLAYTON SAMUEL S	CPT	O-0420113	0862	1
CLAYTON WILLIAM N	LTC	O-0454649	0661	1
CLAYTOR ALTON R	CPT	O-0227260	0664	3
CLAYTOR FRANK W	CPT	O-0401308	0645	1
CLAYTOR JR JOHN B	MAJ	O-0404529	0746	2
CLEARY ALVA F	LTC	O-0400242	0954	1
CLEARY DAVID F	LTC	O-0403599	0760	1
CLEARY FRANCIS J	CPT	O-1302114	0846	2
CLEARY FRED K	LTC	O-1686754	1067	1
CLEARY HOWARD F	LTC	O-1641169	0962	1

NAME	GRADE	SVC NO	DATE RET MO YR	RET CODE
CLEARY JOHN D	CW3	W-2206498	1265	1
CLEARY JR DANIEL J	LTC	0-1320303	1163	1
CLEARY THOMAS D	LTC	0-1003696	0663	1
CLEARY THOMAS F	CPT	0-1108558	0164	1
CLEARY TIMOTHY	LTC	0-0264848	0657	1
CLEAVER GEORGE A	COL	0-0279613	1061	1
CLEAVER HAROLD J	CPT	0-1120533	0263	2
CLEAVER OSCAR P	COL	0-0912368	0265	3
CLEAVER THAYER	LTC	0-0225749	1163	3
CLEAVES MARK B	MAJ	0-0453423	0762	1
CLEAVES RICHARD H	MAJ	0-1303268	1063	1
CLECKLER FRANK S	COL	0-0190862	0454	3
CLECKLER WILLIAM F	LTC	0-0185412	1155	3
CLEGG JACK A	LTC	0-0927140	0667	1
CLEGG JAMES A	1LT	0-1573117	0644	1
CLEGG JOHN P	MAJ	0-0104731	0154	3
CLEGG KERMIT D	1LT	0-1318515	1045	1
CLEGG ROBERT J	1LT	0-0577148	1052	1
CLEGG SAM F	LTC	0-0420086	0860	1
CLEGG WILLIAM B	LTC	0-0255515	0954	3
CLEGHORN DAVID F	CW3	W-2143655	0163	1
CLEGHORN JOHN T	LTC	0-0464912	1053	1
CLELAND GAIL	COL	0-0126315	0755	3
CLELAND JOHN V	CW2	W-2118772	0647	1
CLELAND WILLIAM A	CW3	W-2141527	0659	1
CLEM JR JOHN T	MAJ	0-1332674	0264	1
CLEM ROBERT G	COL	0-0273566	0360	3
CLEM WILLIAM A	LTC	0-1995226	1167	1
CLEMANS CHARLES C	LTC	0-0304461	1063	3
CLEMENS JOHN E	CPT	0-0497129	0948	1
CLEMENS PAUL E	LTC	0-0248098	0954	2
CLEMENS PAUL J	CW4	W-2001776	0356	3
CLEMENS PAUL M	MAJ	0-1293552	0562	1
CLEMENS O VAN	CPT	0-0189610	0556	3
CLEMENS REUBEN B	1LT	0-1290899	0246	1
CLEMENS ROBERT E	2LT	0-1013658	1043	1
CLEMENS SIEGFRIED	LTC	0-1100918	1160	1
CLEMENT ALBERT V	MAJ	0-2263759	0964	1
CLEMENT ANDREW W	COL	0-0203133	0861	3
CLEMENT BAXTER L	CPT	0-0498677	1045	2
CLEMENT CURTIS D	LTC	0-0322981	1266	3
CLEMENT ELEANOR M	1LT	N-0753024	0648	1
CLEMENT FRANKLIN C	1LT	0-1302432	0758	2
CLEMENT JAMES H	CPT	0-0411053	0345	2
CLEMENT JAMES R	LTC	0-1316713	0267	1
CLEMENT JR RAYMOND I	LTC	0-0387381	0762	1
CLEMENT LAWRENCE P	2LT	0-1799614	0759	1
CLEMENT ROBERT W	CPT	0-0990765	0461	1
CLEMENT ROY C	CW2	W-2105642	0260	1
CLEMENT WALTER B	CPT	0-0324761	0245	2
CLEMENTE LEONARD J	LTC	0-0301633	0364	3
CLEMENTS ARNOLD	CW3	W-2145075	0956	1
CLEMENTS EDWARD S	CPT	0-1318448	0455	2
CLEMENTS JAMES R	CPT	0-0415715	0447	2
CLEMENTS JOHN P	MAJ	0-0990619	0964	1
CLEMENTS JR ALBERT B	MAJ	0-2016850	0364	1
CLEMENTS KENNETH	CPT	0-0359484	0648	1
CLEMENTS LEWIS M	CW4	W-2141228	0560	1
CLEMENTS MOSES R	MAJ	0-1049440	1264	1
CLEMENTS QUILLIAN D	MAJ	0-2263454	0766	1
CLEMENTS ROBERT E	CW2	W-2209787	1265	1
CLEMENTS WILLIAM C	MAJ	0-0973622	0563	1
CLEMINSON JR HALDANE	COL	0-0230302	1064	3
CLEMMENSEN PAUL V	MAJ	0-1591055	1162	1
CLEMMER JOHN S	CPT	0-2035075	1146	1
CLEMMER LEWIS M	CPT	0-1304688	0148	2
CLEMMONS LAWRENCE T	CPT	0-0972272	1060	1
CLEMONS CLETES V	CW3	W-2142694	0758	1
CLEMONS GEORGE F	CW2	W-2210438	1061	1
CLEMONS HARRISON L	COL	0-0155065	0846	2
CLEMONS JAMES	CW2	W-2151359	1159	1
CLEMONS RAYMOND J	MAJ	0-1698181	1159	1
CLEMONS WILLIAM L	LTC	0-1825595	0163	1
CLENDENIN RICHARD M	COL	0-0323305	0763	1
CLENDENNING MELVIN H	CW3	W-2153343	0465	1
CLENDINNING JR JOHN	MAJ	0-0136081	0449	3
CLEPPE JOHN E	CW2	W-2203710	1060	1
CLERICO JR LOUIS R	1LT	0-1298027	0245	2
CLESS GEORGE H	LTC	0-0243465	0146	2
CLESS JR RALPH S	1LT	0-1284103	1044	2
CLEVELAND ANSON H	MAJ	0-2035296	0363	1
CLEVELAND CHARLES N	MAJ	0-1111550	0954	1
CLEVELAND EDWARD K	LTC	0-0289108	0557	1
CLEVELAND GEORGE R	MAJ	0-1175668	0857	1
CLEVELAND HENRY F	CPT	0-0198252	0744	2
CLEVELAND JOSEPH S	CW4	W-2113271	0161	1
CLEVELAND JR RALPH L	1LT	0-1325376	1145	2
CLEVELAND MATHER	COL	0-0205765	0949	3
CLEVELAND REESE	CPT	0-0192038	0160	3
CLEVELAND STEWART E	MAJ	0-1105345	0861	1
CLEVELAND WILLIAM C	1LT	0-0390063	1044	2
CLEVELAND WILLIAM J	LTC	0-1170315	0966	1
CLEVENGER TRUMAN I	CPT	0-0445450	1143	1
CLEVERDON HERBERT S	LTC	0-0126456	0648	3
CLEVIDENCE GILBERT H	LTC	0-0264073	0557	3
CLEW MAURICE	CPT	0-0174577	0958	3
CLEW WILLIAM J	CPT	0-0902852	0343	1
CLEWELL WILLIAM L	LTC	0-0964468	0464	3
CLEWETT FRANK S	COL	0-0364585	0359	1
CLEWIS HOWARD R	COL	0-0355216	1066	3
CLEWORTH EARL W	LTC	0-0311339	0262	1
CLEWS WILLIAM R	CW2	W-2114270	0847	1
CLICK ALBERT F	MAJ	0-0401968	0753	1
CLICK ROBERT R	CPT	0-0453511	0845	2
CLICK ROBERT D	1LT	0-1325867	0450	2
CLIFF WILLIAM L	1LT	0-1824712	0346	2
CLIFFE EDWIN L	LTC	0-0349240	1266	3
CLIFFE HARRY L	CPT	0-1289695	0455	1
CLIFFE WILLIAM R	1LT	0-1309654	0146	2
CLIFFORD ALDEN F	LTC	0-0450621	1160	1
CLIFFORD BERNARD D	MAJ	0-0382218	0957	1
CLIFFORD CHARLES F	LTC	0-0345227	1061	1
CLIFFORD COOPER	CW3	W-2152088	0363	1
CLIFFORD DANIEL	CW4	W-2006120	0764	3
CLIFFORD DANIEL L	2LT	0-2026191	0657	1
CLIFFORD DENNIS J	CPT	0-1054943	0358	1
CLIFFORD PAUL J	LTC	0-1821973	0364	1
CLIFFORD SEWARD V	LTC	0-0102129	0559	3
CLIFFORD WESTELL J	LTC	0-1640946	1166	1
CLIFFORD WILLIAM V	CPT	0-0452152	1145	2
CLIFT CHARLES G	CPT	0-1312406	0546	2
CLIFT CRAYDON H	MAJ	0-1318017	1266	1
CLIFT HUBERT P	LTC	0-0963608	0963	1
CLIFT JAMES B	LTC	0-0331589	0662	1
CLIFT JOHN D	LTC	0-1115530	1060	1
CLIFT MAURICE G	COL	0-0334335	0960	1
CLIFT STANTON H	CW2	W-2144690	0361	1
CLIFTON CLIFFORD H	LTC	0-1796923	1263	1
CLIFTON DAVID A	2LT	0-2263750	0654	2
CLIFTON EDWARD E	MAJ	0-1584052	1161	1
CLIFTON EDWARD F	1LT	0-0419103	0344	2
CLIFTON FRANK R	1LT	0-0447925	0944	1
CLIFTON GEORGE M	CPT	0-0488371	0547	1
CLIFTON HARVEY B	COL	0-0219860	0457	1
CLIFTON JR JOHN H	1LT	0-1580760	0152	1
CLIFTON MCCORMICK	CW4	W-2107529	0462	1
CLIFTON RAYMOND K	2LT	0-1107866	0745	2
CLIFTON ROY F	LTC	0-0325374	0866	3
CLIFTON WARD R	CW2	W-2212627	0367	1
CLIFTON WILLIAM C	CPT	0-1332675	0157	1
CLIMIE ROBERT L	MAJ	0-2037782	0860	1
CLIMO HENRY J	COL	0-0436878	0665	3
CLINARD ALLIE L	CPT	0-1920001	1061	1
CLINE BURTON V	LTC	0-1015331	0862	1
CLINE DELBERT H	CW3	W-2144551	0562	1
CLINE FREDERICK	LTC	0-0927645	0567	3
CLINE GEORGE R	LTC	0-0228966	0763	3
CLINE HERBERT N	LTC	0-1999842	0564	1
CLINE J EDWARD	LTC	0-1173563	0463	1
CLINE JAMES O	COL	0-0451846	0960	1
CLINE JR HARRY G	MAJ	0-2046332	0657	1
CLINE LESTER L	MAJ	0-0325803	0546	2
CLINE LOUIS W	LTC	0-0173532	0158	3
CLINE MILTON O	2LT	0-2035297	0444	2
CLINE PAUL A	1LT	0-1049441	1144	2
CLINE RUSSELL F	CPT	0-0493213	1047	1
CLINE WILLIAM H	LTC	0-1534234	1061	1
CLINE WILLIAM J	COL	0-0178048	0656	1
CLINE WILLIAM P	LTC	0-0256002	1050	3
CLINESMITH JAMES M	LTC	0-1324512	1163	1
CLINGER EARL A	CPT	0-0412749	0961	2
CLINITE FLOYD E	LTC	0-0150444	0648	3
CLINK JACK J	MAJ	0-0391884	0945	1
CLINKINBEARD JOHN E	1LT	0-0383048	0945	2
CLINKSCALES RUBEN	1LT	0-0398766	0448	1
CLINTON CLEO S	MAJ	0-0331598	0362	3
CLINTON EDGAR T	CPT	0-0248694	1066	3
CLINTON GERTRUDE T	2LT	N-0720166	0744	1
CLINTON MICHAEL E	1LT	0-0925522	0845	2
CLINTON PAUL B	2LT	0-1309911	0245	2
CLINTON WESTCOTT	MAJ	0-1334829	0467	1
CLINTON WILLIAM H	MAJ	0-0249387	0466	3
CLINTON WILLIAM P	LTC	0-0300942	1163	1
CLIPPARD JAMES H	COL	0-0261326	0446	2
CLIPPINGER FRED B	CW4	W-2115110	0557	1
CLISBY KEITH M	COL	0-0315319	1065	3
CLISE JR FLOYD H	1LT	0-1299853	0246	2
CLISSOLD WALTER C	CPT	0-1166935	0944	2
CLISSON WILLIAM H	LTC	0-0404791	0860	1
CLODE HAROLD G	LTC	0-0365782	1060	1
CLODFELDER JAMES E	CW2	W-2146324	0463	1
CLOHOSEY BERNARD M	CPT	0-0493821	1049	1
CLONINGER FLOYD R	MAJ	0-1292133	0258	2
CLONINGER JOHN M	MAJ	0-0970844	0664	1
CLONTS JAMES E	CW4	W-2142319	0859	1
CLOORE HAROLD A	LTC	0-0284923	0460	1
CLOPINE RAYMOND L	CW4	W-2119238	0763	1
CLOPPER PAUL W	COL	0-0116282	0347	2
CLOPTON ROBERT H	LTC	0-2010924	1262	2
CLOPTON WILLIAM H	MAJ	0-1171090	0961	1
CLOR ALFRED L	CPT	0-1584529	0559	1
CLORE WALTER L	CPT	0-0509601	0546	2
CLOROFILLA ALFRED	1LT	0-0493160	0644	2
CLOSE ANN C	CPT	N-0725189	0746	1
CLOSE GERALD V	LTC	0-0162782	0755	3
CLOSE WILLIAM K	LTC	0-0318962	0263	3
CLOSSON ALVIN W	CW3	W-2146580	1262	1
CLOSSON JOHN L	MAJ	0-0887460	1154	1
CLOSTERMAN JOHN H	CW3	W-2152509	1063	1
CLOTFELTER ROY L	MAJ	0-1333314	0760	1
CLOTHAKIS CONSTANTIN	CPT	0-1080095	0463	1
CLOTHIER JR JOHN D	MAJ	0-0921980	0449	2
CLOTHIER LYLE R	MAJ	0-0272791	0457	3
CLOUD DONALD G	CW2	W-2210742	0865	1
CLOUD FREDERICK	MAJ	0-1287480	0459	1
CLOUD JR ARTHUR D	1LT	0-0456218	0245	2
CLOUD JR MASON C	CPT	0-1289545	0747	2
CLOUD MILTON H	LTC	0-0193242	0758	3
CLOUD RALPH M	CPT	0-1336880	0258	2
CLOUD SAMUEL F	CW2	W-2114193	0945	2
CLOUDT JR WALTER C	2LT	0-0382732	1041	2
CLOUDT WERNER H	MAJ	0-0980115	0461	1
CLOUGH ARTHUR M	LTC	0-0175753	0156	3
CLOUGH KENNETH M	MAJ	0-0229688	0762	3
CLOUGH LAWRENCE A	LTC	0-1175669	0461	1
CLOUSE CHARLES E	2LT	0-1297321	1143	2
CLOUSE HOWARD T	LTC	0-1575866	0563	1
CLOUSE WINFRED S	CW2	W-2145800	0658	1
CLOUSER SYLVIA M	CPT	N-0760847	0750	1
CLOUTIER ALBERT J	CPT	0-0486236	1047	1
CLOUTIER JOHN P	CW3	W-2145718	0760	1
CLOUTIER JR GEORGE A	MAJ	0-0179904	0454	3
CLOVER GLENN C	MAJ	0-1080352	1061	1
CLOW MELVIN L	LTC	0-0298519	0362	3
CLOWARD THOMAS M	LTC	0-0244546	0161	3
CLOWER ERNEST F	CW2	W-2207055	0760	1
CLOWER JAMES I	LTC	0-0174479	0160	3
CLOWES DUDLEY W	LTC	0-0444540	0767	1
CLOWNEY JR FRANK S	1LT	0-1182800	1044	2
CLOYD WILLIAM C	CW3	W-2206967	0366	1
CLUBA JR JOSEPH J	MAJ	0-2211824	1065	1
CLUCAS PHILIP D	1LT	0-1320430	0147	2
CLUCK HOMER E	1LT	0-1292134	0344	2
CLULEY FREDERICK	1LT	0-1337395	0850	1
CLURE DOUGLAS M	LTC	0-1323292	0962	1
CLUTCHKER JOSEPH M	LTC	0-0445266	0156	1
CLUTE GLEN C	LTC	0-1574646	0766	1
CLUTTER JR PAT C	CPT	0-0394556	0544	2
CLUTTER ROBERT D	CW3	W-2206734	0166	1
CLUTTER WADE C	MAJ	0-1584536	1265	1
CLYATT JOHN L	LTC	0-0354519	1159	1
CLYATT JR CLARENCE L	2LT	0-1055809	0545	2
CLYBURN ROYCE F	CW3	W-2205102	0864	1
CLYDE ALFRED M	CPT	0-0358752	0244	1
CLYDE THOMAS J	MAJ	0-0293117	0566	1
CLYDE WYLIE L	COL	0-0277709	1066	3
CLYMER CLARENCE O	WO1	W-2120962	1045	2
CLYMER MERYLE M	CPT	L-0900137	0845	2
CLYMER SAMUEL H	LTC	0-1585285	0563	1
CLYNE IRVING M	LTC	0-0336000	0646	2
CLYNES RICHARD J	LTC	0-0162680	0157	3
COAKLEY ANTHONY H	LTC	0-0397300	0763	1
COAKLEY BERTHA I	2LT	N-0722928	0145	1
COAKLEY FRANCIS H	LTC	0-0414297	0761	1
COAKLEY GEORGE E	LTC	0-0414298	0561	1
COAKLEY JOSEPH P	MAJ	0-1331268	1159	2
COALSON JAMES W	CW2	W-2141529	0261	1
COAN HERMAN S	CW2	W-2153022	0258	1
COANE RALPH W	B G	0-0209500	0346	2
COATE HAROLD O	LTC	0-0132425	0648	3
COATES AUSTIN M	CPT	0-0167094	0555	3
COATES EVERETT W	LTC	0-0236706	0648	3
COATES JOSEPH A	1LT	0-1303671	1045	2
COATES JR R N	1LT	0-0515370	1145	2
COATES LESLIE F	LTC	0-0338317	0161	1
COATES LESLIE R	CPT	0-1306200	0767	3
COATES MARVIN D	LTC	0-1282188	1066	1
COATES PALGRAVE H	CPT	0-1114420	0646	2
COATES ROBERT B	LTC	0-1582664	0966	1
COATS CHARLES F	CPT	0-1822238	0247	1
COATS JAMES M	CW2	W-2147723	0965	1
COATS MARVIN	CW3	W-2142825	0659	1
COATS MAURICE E	LTC	0-1109208	0467	1
COATS NORRIS W	CPT	0-0198862	0563	3
COATSWORTH JAMES T	COL	0-0335373	1063	3
COBAIN BURLE G	CW2	W-2149742	1160	1
COBB ARLON G	1LT	0-2005318	0562	1
COBB CECIL H	MAJ	0-1640951	0358	1
COBB DONALD W	CPT	0-1635704	1056	1
COBB EDWARD G	LTC	0-1555673	0561	1
COBB FARRAR M	LTC	0-0218001	0462	3
COBB GEORGE E	MAJ	0-0322982	0257	3
COBB HOWELL C	LTC	0-1311741	0665	1
COBB HOWELL E	LTC	0-0905724	0963	3
COBB IRVIN S	CPT	0-1291591	0246	2
COBB IVOREY	MAJ	0-1314994	0862	1
COBB JR ADOLPHUS O	1LT	0-1589127	1045	2
COBB JR ANDREW G	CW2	W-2210776	1064	1
COBB JR EUGENE S	CPT	0-0470377	0648	2
COBB JR LUTHER F	COL	0-0275271	0560	1
COBB JULIA M	1LT	N-0758628	0546	1
COBB KELLEY P	MAJ	0-1181205	0560	1
COBB MARION A	CW2	W-3200420	0267	1
COBB NELSON L	MAJ	0-1286965	1164	3
COBB NORMAN S	MAJ	0-1290033	0365	1
COBB ROBERT E	LTC	0-1010211	0866	1
COBB WILLIAM B	COL	0-0232640	1054	3
COBB WILLIAM H	COL	0-0919765	1064	3
COBB WILLIAM R	CW3	W-2146191	0461	1
COBB WILLIE R	LTC	0-0510824	0655	1

ARMY OF THE UNITED STATES RETIRED LIST

NAME	GRADE	SVC NO	DATE RET MO YR	RET CODE
COBBE CHARLES T	CPT	0-0318794	0962	1
COBBLE LYNNE M	CW2	W-2205618	0661	1
COBBS RICHARD H	MAJ	0-0214298	0963	3
COBEAN JR GEORGE C	CPT	0-0322422	0446	2
COBERG WALLACE H	MAJ	0-1051081	0561	1
COBIS JOSEPH F	MAJ	0-1878786	0167	1
COBLE EDWIN L	CPT	0-0366034	0644	2
COBLE MAX W	LTC	0-0265099	1266	3
COBLE OLIVER O	LTC	0-0150147	0858	3
COBLENTZ RALPH E	LTC	0-0271875	0566	3
COBLENTZ SIEGFRIED	COL	0-0209944	0154	3
COBLYN GEORGE H	MAJ	0-1303302	0461	1
COBO EDWARD A	CW2	W-2151919	0359	1
COBURN ANDERSON N	CPT	0-1291416	0459	1
COBURN BERNARD P	LTC	0-0392022	1060	1
COBURN CLARENCE O	LTC	0-0450827	1157	1
COBURN GEORGE J	CPT	0-0188843	0951	3
COBURN GEORGE J	1LT	0-1298028	1145	2
COBURN GLEN E	MAJ	0-1014419	1057	1
COBURN NICHOLAS W	COL	0-0232694	0465	3
COBURN PATRICK J	MAJ	0-2262345	0861	1
COBURN RALPH H	MAJ	0-0148577	0952	3
COBURN THEODORE J	CPT	0-0493343	0546	2
COBURN TRUMAN J	MAJ	0-2047952	0257	1
COCCA JOHN G	1LT	0-0334407	0442	2
COCCARI JAMES	LTC	0-1334259	0867	1
COCHARD EDMOND J	LTC	0-1114421	0467	1
COCHRAN AROYTH E	LTC	0-1167780	0263	1
COCHRAN CLARENCE	COL	0-0263221	1147	1
COCHRAN CLAUD H	CW3	W-2149751	0863	1
COCHRAN COLLINS C	CW3	W-2149287	0263	1
COCHRAN EDWIN C	CW2	W-3430170	0367	1
COCHRAN ELMO O	2LT	0-2008421	1147	2
COCHRAN GEORGE H	COL	0-0118497	1150	3
COCHRAN GEORGE H	LTC	0-0197223	0463	3
COCHRAN GEORGE M	CPT	0-0478121	0645	2
COCHRAN JACK W	MAJ	0-1013291	0663	1
COCHRAN JAY M	CW4	W-2141713	1065	1
COCHRAN JOEL L	LTC	0-0233582	0760	3
COCHRAN JOHN	CW3	W-2152189	0263	1
COCHRAN JOHN J	MAJ	0-2012467	1065	1
COCHRAN JR ALLEN J	CW3	W-2142512	0560	1
COCHRAN JR JOHN B	MAJ	0-1119865	0165	1
COCHRAN JR SAM L	MAJ	0-0887402	0862	1
COCHRAN LAWRENCE J	MAJ	0-0448147	0858	3
COCHRAN LESLIE	1LT	0-2042910	1145	2
COCHRAN LESTER D	MAJ	0-0497104	1047	2
COCHRAN LYLE A	CW3	W-2205664	0566	1
COCHRAN LYLE E	CPT	0-1297841	0457	1
COCHRAN LYNN E	LTC	0-1298828	0766	1
COCHRAN NEIL M	COL	0-0331055	0165	3
COCHRAN PRICE C	LTC	0-0279614	1059	2
COCHRAN RAYMOND J	MAJ	0-0430273	0163	1
COCHRAN RICHARD C	MAJ	0-1045377	1160	1
COCHRAN WALLACE J	LTC	0-0335292	0461	1
COCHRAN WILLIAM M	1LT	0-1035285	0850	1
COCHRANE BURTON C	LTC	0-0110163	0952	3
COCHRANE GEORGE M	1LT	0-1555957	1245	2
COCHRANE ROBERT B	LTC	0-0276372	1167	3
COCHRANE ROY	COL	0-0885009	1157	1
COCHRANE WILLIAM J	COL	0-1032198	0266	1
COCHRUN CLARENCE L	1LT	0-1001971	0445	2
COCHRUN EDGAR R	COL	0-0175905	0950	3
COCKE JR ERLE	MAJ	0-0441300	0247	2
COCKE PHILIP ST	COL	0-0885058	0464	1
COCKEFAIR GEORGE A	COL	0-0211751	0364	3
COCKERELL LONNIE L	CPT	0-1052715	0964	2
COCKERHAM DENVER H	CW2	W-2149139	0859	1
COCKEY MARY M	1LT	N-0742244	0845	1
COCKFIELD CHARLES O	LTC	0-0322724	1162	1
COCKRELL ELDRIDGE H	LTC	0-1103107	0261	1
COCKRELL HAROLD B	CPT	0-1289696	1057	1
COCKRELL HENRY B	MAJ	0-0271132	0648	3
COCKRELL THOMAS J	LTC	0-0169110	1060	3
COCKRELL WAYNE L	LTC	0-0202057	0463	3

NAME	GRADE	SVC NO	DATE RET MO YR	RET CODE
COCKRILL JAMES M	1LT	0-0104699	1057	3
COCKRUM HERBERT L	1LT	0-1559312	1046	2
COCO THEODORE A	CPT	0-1107868	0451	1
COCRERILL DONALD R	CW4	W-0904240	0659	1
CODD LEO A	COL	0-0205117	0455	3
CODDINGTON DAVID L	COL	0-0225717	0564	3
CODDINGTON ROY H	CPT	0-0460725	0461	1
CODE JR RALPH J	CPT	0-0365517	0945	2
CODER CLIFFORD F	CW2	W-3440000	1163	1
CODER HARRY F	COL	0-0411762	0865	1
CODIN KENNETH	1LT	0-0518928	0145	2
CODNER STANISLAUS	COL	0-0445066	0854	1
CODY BERNARD P	LTC	0-0223209	0347	2
CODY CHARLES L	MAJ	0-1170321	0463	1
CODY ERNEST H	CPT	0-0379963	0251	1
CODY FLOYD W	LTC	0-0478522	1154	1
CODY GEORGE L	COL	0-0292440	0864	3
CODY RICHARD R	2LT	0-1294622	0244	2
CODY RICHARD S	1LT	0-1305392	0945	2
COE CHARLES V	CW3	W-2142575	0158	1
COE HAROLD A	2LT	0-2000657	0246	2
COE HEARK D	CW3	W-2148312	0557	1
COE JR CHARLES A	LTC	0-1701473	1263	1
COE JR THOMAS H	LTC	0-0924246	0847	1
COE KENNETH C	LTC	0-0451230	0656	1
COE NOBLE W	COL	0-0184915	1051	3
COE ROBERT F	MAJ	0-1010320	0663	1
COE WARREN T	CPT	0-0378513	1045	2
COEN JOHN D	MAJ	0-1637203	0664	2
COEN KENDALL W	MAJ	0-1588475	0860	1
COEN WALTER L	WO1	W-2109925	0655	1
COERS DAVID H	CPT	0-0152936	0648	3
COERS JR DAVID H	LTC	0-1341748	1066	1
COFSTER EMIL H	COL	0-0215149	0163	3
COEY GROVER E	MAJ	0-1994405	1161	1
COFER CHARLES A	MAJ	0-1172415	1060	1
COFER CHARLES L	CPT	0-1581605	0945	2
COFER CHARLES R	MAJ	0-0983320	0364	1
COFER HERSTON H	CPT	0-2262793	0461	1
COFER HORACE J	LTC	0-1288860	1155	1
COFER LOUIS C	CPT	0-0479199	1144	2
COFER WAYNE H	MAJ	0-1178447	0962	1
COFFEE DAN F	CPT	0-0452552	0845	2
COFFEE RUSSELL F	CPT	0-1294088	0267	2
COFFEE VIRGIL O	MAJ	0-1544123	0156	1
COFFEEN KENNETH	CW3	W-2148100	0862	1
COFFEY CLARENCE W	1LT	0-0492156	1047	1
COFFEY EDWARD L	MAJ	0-1587533	1060	1
COFFEY ELMER J	MAJ	0-0455355	0657	1
COFFEY JOHN J	CW4	W-2004214	1063	3
COFFEY JOHN L	MAJ	0-0222900	0258	3
COFFEY JOHN W	LTC	0-1994580	1061	1
COFFEY RALPH R	MAJ	0-0265964	0246	2
COFFEY SPENCER F	CPT	0-0475238	0650	1
COFFEY THOMAS G	CPT	0-1823983	0161	1
COFFEY ULYSSES M	MAJ	0-1032658	1157	2
COFFEY WALTER A	CW2	W-2146197	1157	1
COFFIE JAMES	CW3	W-2140910	1162	1
COFFIE JAMES	CW3	W-2150910	0659	1
COFFIN EDWARD J	LTC	0-1299375	1060	1
COFFIN HAROLD W	COL	0-0181659	1051	3
COFFIN JAMES H	CPT	0-0450828	1265	1
COFFIN PAUL A	1LT	0-1821551	1043	2
COFFIN RAYMOND O	LTC	0-1112621	0763	1
COFFIN ROBERT T	1LT	0-1324984	0745	2
COFFMAN CHARLES A	CW4	W-2146893	1063	1
COFFMAN CLARENCE A	CW2	W-2211065	0965	1
COFFMAN CLARENCE F	CPT	0-1011608	0247	2
COFFMAN EARL R	MAJ	0-1031797	0263	1
COFFMAN HERSCHEL T	CPT	0-0885724	1046	1
COFFMAN JACOB F	1LT	0-1104569	0344	2
COFFMAN JENNINGS B	CPT	0-0370413	0859	1
COFFMAN JR CARL C	2LT	0-1300604	1144	2
COFFMAN TROY	MAJ	0-0102856	0245	2
COFFMAN WILLIS P	MAJ	0-0440780	0444	2

NAME	GRADE	SVC NO	DATE RET MO YR	RET CODE
COGAN JAMES R	1LT	0-1683932	0543	2
COGAN JOSEPH P	LTC	0-0195664	1058	3
COGAN LEO J	MAJ	0-0320733	0145	2
COGAN RICHARD H	2LT	0-1315909	0445	2
COGBILL JR JOHN V	CW2	W-2205746	0463	1
COGDALL THOMAS E	LTC	0-0334876	0547	2
COGDELL JAMES F	COL	0-0204845	1053	3
COGDILL RAY J	CW3	W-2146110	0959	1
COGER JOHN W	CW3	W-2141230	0461	1
COGGESHALL HOWARD L	CW2	W-2214899	1266	1
COGGHILL FRANCIS P	MAJ	0-0287489	0546	1
COGGIN EARLE R	MAJ	0-0343504	0760	1
COGGIN JOSEPH H	1LT	0-0183633	0632	1
COGGIN LA DEITRIC	MAJ	0-1580768	0466	1
COGGINS CYRIL M	MAJ	0-1037725	0658	2
COGGS THEODORE W	1LT	0-1302460	0745	2
COGHLAN CECIL L	LTC	0-1307657	0564	1
COGHLAN JOHN F	MAJ	0-1041314	1263	1
COGLEY JOHN P	LTC	0-0487780	1144	1
COGLEY JR FERNANDO	LTC	0-0450106	1263	2
COGLIATI DENNIS J	CPT	0-1824732	0261	1
COGSWELL DANIEL O	CW3	W-2148249	0964	1
COGSWELL MASON J	2LT	0-0374441	0641	2
COGSWELL RICHARD B	2LT	0-2006491	0845	2
COGSWELL WILLIAM C	LTC	0-0451231	0157	1
COHAN S HOWARD	LTC	0-0230865	0746	2
COHANE ARTHUR J	CPT	0-0527921	1045	1
COHEE GLENN O	CPT	0-1297162	0854	1
COHEN ABRAHAM B	LTC	0-0189956	0754	3
COHEN ABRAHAM J	MAJ	0-0979610	0466	1
COHEN ALBERT	CW3	W-2203298	0862	1
COHEN ALEXANDER	LTC	0-0535221	0657	1
COHEN ASHER Z	COL	0-0158252	0856	3
COHEN BEATRICE R	2LT	N-0720925	0745	1
COHEN BERNARD	CW2	W-2142482	0856	1
COHEN CLARENCE H	COL	0-0176291	0246	2
COHEN ELMER A	CPT	0-0384194	1145	2
COHEN GEORGE M	MAJ	0-0351310	0450	2
COHEN HAROLD	CPT	0-0399839	0245	2
COHEN HAROLD W	MAJ	0-0335001	1144	2
COHEN HARRY	MAJ	0-0189869	0157	1
COHEN HERBERT	1LT	0-0521199	0346	2
COHEN HERBERT J	LTC	0-0264445	0267	3
COHEN HOWARD T	1LT	0-1874932	0654	2
COHEN JACK B	LTC	0-0461886	0647	1
COHEN JASPER N	MAJ	0-1112089	1059	1
COHEN LEE	MAJ	0-0109163	0330	1
COHEN LEO	CPT	0-0230662	1162	3
COHEN LEO	LTC	0-0307525	1055	1
COHEN LEON	CPT	0-1286967	0346	2
COHEN LEONARD A	MAJ	0-1638889	0258	1
COHEN LOUIS M	CPT	0-1945556	0647	2
COHEN MANUEL W	CPT	0-1308791	0246	2
COHEN MAXWELL	MAJ	0-0220121	1041	2
COHEN MORRIS	MAJ	0-0476728	0264	1
COHEN MORRIS	1LT	0-1103109	0346	2
COHEN MORRIS C	CPT	0-1001115	0148	2
COHEN MOSES	MAJ	0-0477735	0845	2
COHEN MYER	MAJ	0-1289213	1156	1
COHEN NATHAN	CPT	0-0285412	0645	2
COHEN NATHAN N	MAJ	0-1691285	1146	2
COHEN NORMAN	CPT	0-0399980	0546	2
COHEN PHILIP	CPT	0-0498455	1057	1
COHEN RICHARD M	1LT	0-1579496	0745	2
COHEN SAMUEL	LTC	0-0509168	1054	1
COHEN SAMUEL	2LT	0-1643840	1045	2
COHEN SAMUEL A	COL	0-0101151	0763	3
COHEN SAMUEL H	LTC	0-0195962	0346	2
COHEN SHELDON G	CPT	0-0464563	0547	2
COHEN SIDNEY H	1LT	0-1311352	0445	2
COHEN STANLEY	MAJ	0-2055369	0158	2
COHEN WALLACE W	CPT	0-1015481	0448	1
COHEN WILLIAM	LTC	0-0282661	0966	3
COHEN WILLIAM R	COL	0-0232302	1059	3
COHEN YALE B	CPT	0-0452875	1145	2

NAME	GRADE	SVC NO	DATE RET MO YR	RET CODE
COHN BYRON S	CPT	0-0179381	0956	3
COHN EDWARD P	MAJ	0-1533029	0546	2
COHN GEORGE W	LTC	0-1313684	0363	1
COHN MELVIN J	CW3	W-2149175	1060	1
COHN RALPH	CPT	0-0126439	1052	3
COHN ROBERT C	LTC	0-1582667	1061	1
COHN SIDNEY	1LT	0-1320508	0645	2
COHOON GILBERT D	MAJ	0-1308209	1263	1
COHOON WILLIAM M	COL	0-0323355	0957	1
COIA GEORGE J	CPT	0-0484329	0551	1
COIL ARTHUR L	CPT	0-1310404	0246	1
COIL GEORGE J	1LT	0-1581608	0545	2
COIL WILFORD F	CW2	W-2115958	0846	1
COILE KATHLEEN R	1LT	N-0741004	1045	1
COIN CHARLES W	MAJ	0-1701674	0361	1
COINER DAVID T	LTC	0-0363725	0161	1
COING EDWARD F	LTC	0-1895591	0765	3
COIRO JOHN F	CW2	W-2145965	0655	1
COKELEY WILLIAM L	1LT	0-0534286	0147	2
COKER FRANK C	MAJ	0-0420101	0946	2
COKER JAMES R	MAJ	0-1179344	1160	1
COKER JOHN B	2LT	0-1324316	1045	2
COKER JOHN H	CPT	0-2262376	0461	1
COKER JR HAYDEN C	MAJ	0-1100923	0660	1
COKER MARION L	CW3	W-2207209	1166	1
COKER PAUL F	COL	0-1031394	0666	1
COLACINO JOHN F	MAJ	0-1825382	0361	2
COLANE VINCENT R	MAJ	0-1043595	0767	1
COLANGELO C C	MAJ	0-0507025	0247	2
COLAVITA HENRY J	LTC	0-0283015	1059	1
COLBERT CLIFFORD J	LTC	0-0368675	0867	3
COLBERT HERSCHEL M	COL	0-0130854	1051	3
COLBERT JACK A	LTC	0-1312407	0662	1
COLBERT JACK L	LTC	0-0347584	0847	2
COLBERT JAMES E	COL	0-0186720	0554	1
COLBERT JAMES R	CPT	0-1177339	0358	1
COLBERT LOUIS M	CPT	0-0506955	1055	1
COLBERT MAURICE R	LTC	0-0114742	0653	3
COLBERT RALEIGH F	CPT	0-1998479	1047	2
COLBERT ROBERT W	COL	0-0258801	0854	3
COLBERT SEYMOUR	CW3	W-2149062	1163	1
COLBORN JOHN W	LTC	0-0240662	0460	3
COLBURN EDWARD	2LT	0-1913615	0243	1
COLBURN WILLIAM R	CW2	W-2117543	0150	1
COLBY DEBORAH	MAJ	N-0757847	1265	3
COLBY J JESS	2LT	0-1012664	1045	2
COLBY JOHN H	MAJ	0-0297797	0364	3
COLBY MELVIN M	MAJ	0-1822534	0965	1
COLBY PAUL W	LTC	0-0121122	1054	3
COLBY SANFORD L	CW3	W-2147042	0656	1
COLBY THOMAS W	COL	0-0259156	0767	3
COLBY WALTER W	2LT	0-1107350	0545	2
COLBY WARD A	CPT	0-1914134	0746	2
COLCLASURE WYETT H	CPT	0-0367080	0445	1
COLDREN IRA P	COL	0-0215268	0462	3
COLDREN JOHN A	MAJ	0-0225488	0460	3
COLDREN LEON F	MAJ	0-1175080	0258	1
COLDSNOW LESLIE P	LTC	0-0254765	0965	3
COLE ALBERT C	LTC	0-1011524	0763	1
COLE ALBERT R	1LT	0-0310516	0867	3
COLE AMIS R	MAJ	0-1331277	0363	1
COLE ARTHUR L	MAJ	0-0496863	1146	1
COLE AUSTIN F	CPT	0-1176286	0163	1
COLE BERYL A	MAJ	N-0779068	1063	3
COLE CHARLES A	LTC	0-0182613	1048	2
COLE CHARLES C	LTC	0-0363378	0864	1
COLE CHARLES R	CPT	0-1640960	0358	1
COLE CHARLES R	MAJ	0-1825903	0163	1
COLE CHARLES T	1LT	0-5225758	0867	2
COLE CHESTER J	MAJ	0-1598962	0862	1
COLE CLIFTON	CW2	W-2153017	0761	1
COLE CULLEN E	CPT	0-2040687	1045	2
COLE DELBERT L	MAJ	0-1641176	0664	2
COLE DEWEY	CW4	W-2101535	1154	1
COLE DONALD F	COL	0-1686910	0566	3

NAME	GRADE	SVC NO	DATE RET MO YR	RET CODE
COLE EARL F	LTC	C-0243217	C462	3
COLE ELIZABETH	2LT	N-0722538	0445	1
COLE ELMER	MAJ	C-1307659	0262	1
COLE ERNEST J	CPT	0-0181783	0648	3
COLE FRANCIS J	CW3	W-2150503	0564	1
COLE FRANKF L	1LT	0-1317885	C446	2
COLE HAROLD C	CPT	0-0552218	C347	2
COLE HAROLD J	COL	0-0246891	1266	3
COLE HAROLD L	CW2	W-2430081	C666	1
COLE HARRY	MAJ	0-0446137	0447	1
COLE HAZEN W	1LT	0-0940753	0749	1
COLE HERBERT E	MAJ	C-0452507	1066	1
COLE HERBERT L	CW3	W-2139557	1055	1
COLE HORACE R	LTC	0-1114890	C365	1
COLE HOWARD P	LTC	0-1288708	0660	1
COLE HUGHIE B	CW3	W-2206576	0665	1
COLE JACK C	1LT	0-0349465	1043	2
COLE JAMES A	LTC	C-1586338	0462	1
COLE JAMES B	LTC	C-0180200	C757	3
COLE JAMES B	LTC	0-0408183	0161	1
COLE JEFFRIES G	MAJ	0-0263031	0764	3
COLE JENNINGS B	WO1	W-2106991	0447	2
COLE JESSE J	MAJ	C-1030748	1055	1
COLE JOE N	COL	C-C288990	0557	1
COLE JOHN C	1LT	0-5318330	0963	2
COLE JOHN J	LTC	0-1548695	C463	1
COLE JOHN M	LTC	0-0372004	1059	1
COLE JOHN W	MAJ	0-0450569	0946	2
COLE JOHN W	1LT	0-0965672	0652	1
COLE JOSEPH F	COL	C-0243345	C766	3
COLE JOSEPH G	CPT	0-0499773	0645	2
COLE JOSEPH G	CPT	0-1690169	1045	2
COLE JR DANIEL M	CW2	W-2147250	0962	1
COLE JR FELIX J	CW3	W-2207658	0866	1
COLE JR JOHN C	LTC	0-1040199	0566	1
COLE JR LEON L	COL	0-0288921	0566	3
COLE JR RUFUS L	MAJ	C-2263088	0363	1
COLE JR WILLIAM	MAJ	0-0396979	1147	2
COLE KENNETH J	LTC	C-0174288	0161	3
COLE LAWRENCE A	LTC	0-1645200	1167	1
COLE LAWRENCE R	COL	0-0233785	0659	3
COLE LOYAL J	MAJ	0-1633763	0258	1
COLE MAC	1LT	0-2046341	0945	2
COLE MARION C	1LT	C-1052301	0945	2
COLE MARION K	LTC	0-1285710	0764	1
COLE MARTIN G	CPT	0-0290842	0864	3
COLE MILTON J	COL	0-0414899	1264	3
COLE NATHANIEL	LTC	0-0262646	0446	1
COLE NEWELL C	1LT	0-0275257	0945	2
COLE OSCAR E	LTC	0-0469253	0645	2
COLE PAUL M	CW3	W-2145614	0463	1
COLE RALEIGH J	CPT	0-0456674	1148	1
COLE RALPH C	CPT	0-1303078	1047	2
COLE RALPH D	MAJ	0-1844633	0951	1
COLE RALPH E	COL	C-0226831	0265	3
COLE RAYMOND A	LTC	0-0415409	0660	1
COLE RICHARD G	LTC	0-0335540	C557	1
COLE RICHARD H	CPT	0-0365971	1045	2
COLE RICHARD J	1LT	0-1114423	0445	2
COLE RICHARD S	LTC	0-0291144	0858	3
COLE ROBERT E	MAJ	0-1294089	0763	1
COLE ROBERT J	MAJ	C-0355670	0853	2
COLE ROBERT K	CW4	W-2106920	0859	1
COLE ROBERT S	MAJ	0-1643871	1060	1
COLE ROSS R	LTC	0-0155676	0648	3
COLE ROY C	1LT	0-1016190	0545	2
COLE RUSSELL A	CPT	0-0365770	0644	2
COLE SCOTT	1LT	C-1295831	0545	2
COLE STANLEY W	CW4	W-2141531	1055	1
COLE THELMA M	2LT	N-0737060	0744	1
COLE THOMAS J	MAJ	0-1293210	1157	1
COLE TOM E	COL	0-0323339	C662	1
COLE VICTOR C	COL	C-0483161	0545	2
COLE WILLIAM A	CPT	0-0494795	0447	1
COLEBANK WILLIAM F	CW3	W-2115397	0656	1

NAME	GRADE	SVC NO	DATE RET MO YR	RET CODE
COLEBANK WILLIAM W	CPT	0-0554590	1160	1
COLEBURN JR JOSEPH L	MAJ	0-1647763	0263	1
COLEGROVE JACOB R	LTC	C-0257350	1045	2
COLEGROVE WESTLEY	LTC	0-0507826	0855	1
COLEHOUR MORRIS S	MAJ	0-0224254	0965	3
COLEMAN ALFRED I	MAJ	0-2014687	0266	1
COLEMAN BILLY J	MAJ	0-2206401	0165	1
COLEMAN CARL H	COL	0-0357728	0260	1
COLEMAN CARL C	LTC	0-0884903	0760	1
COLEMAN CHARLES S	CW3	W-2148828	0764	1
COLEMAN CHAUNCEY E	1LT	0-1282059	0653	1
COLEMAN CLARENCE M	MAJ	0-0463172	1146	2
COLEMAN CLARENCE N	COL	0-0420496	1162	2
COLEMAN CRANSTON R	MAJ	0-1574647	0761	1
COLEMAN DANIEL L	MAJ	C-0360205	1060	1
COLEMAN DELREY	COL	0-0196961	0262	3
COLEMAN EDMOND A	CPT	0-5318477	0866	2
COLEMAN EUGENE	2LT	0-2011581	0546	2
COLEMAN FLOYD E	CPT	0-1703800	0157	1
COLEMAN FLOYD M	CPT	C-0493879	0753	1
COLEMAN FRANCIS E	LTC	0-0207403	1063	3
COLEMAN FRANK P	LTC	0-1696423	0546	2
COLEMAN FREDERICK	LTC	0-1010433	0461	1
COLEMAN GEORGE J	LTC	0-1050603	1263	1
COLEMAN GERALD G	1LT	0-2034504	0855	1
COLEMAN HENRY	CW3	W-2203337	0764	1
COLEMAN HENRY C	LTC	0-0226432	0764	3
COLEMAN HENRY G	1LT	0-1684725	0145	1
COLEMAN HENRY H	LTC	C-0338445	0764	3
COLEMAN HENRY N	COL	0-0104016	0648	3
COLEMAN HERBERT L	LTC	0-1291236	0666	1
COLEMAN HOWARD S	CW2	W-2152080	0664	1
COLEMAN JAMES	1LT	0-0571755	0865	2
COLEMAN JAMES A	LTC	0-0122417	0648	3
COLEMAN JAMES B	CW2	W-2125278	0752	1
COLEMAN JAMES F	LTC	0-0901062	0545	2
COLEMAN JAMES F	MAJ	0-1311842	0446	2
COLEMAN JAMES P	MAJ	0-1336040	0963	1
COLEMAN JAMES T	1LT	0-1797785	0161	1
COLEMAN JAMES W	LTC	0-0177916	0854	2
COLEMAN JOE R S	MAJ	0-1304638	1060	1
COLEMAN JOHN E	COL	0-0256251	0667	3
COLEMAN JOHN G	2LT	0-1314445	0545	1
COLEMAN JOHN J	MAJ	0-1315793	1060	1
COLEMAN JOHN L	CPT	0-1289393	0763	1
COLEMAN JOHN R	LTC	0-0399878	1059	1
COLEMAN JOSEPH F	CPT	0-0150837	0345	2
COLEMAN JR DAVID J	LTC	0-0376394	0866	1
COLEMAN JR EDMUND A	MAJ	0-1116833	0663	2
COLEMAN JR LEWIS C	LTC	0-0338518	0956	1
COLEMAN JR THOMAS V	MAJ	0-1041737	0657	2
COLEMAN JUANITA V	CPT	N-0755308	0746	1
COLEMAN KENNETH G	MAJ	0-0290174	0362	3
COLEMAN KIRBY L	2LT	0-1319182	0545	2
COLEMAN LEONARD S	CW4	W-2109693	0562	1
COLEMAN LEWIS C	LTC	0-0164403	0144	1
COLEMAN MAOTE L	MAJ	N-0763971	1063	1
COLEMAN MICHAEL J	LTC	0-0267074	0654	3
COLEMAN ORAN S	LTC	0-0577172	0662	1
COLEMAN PHILIP E	LTC	0-0323809	0867	3
COLEMAN RAEPHEL V	1LT	0-1032419	0945	2
COLEMAN RAYMOND M	CW2	W-2147515	0663	1
COLEMAN ROBERT A	1LT	0-1573124	0364	1
COLEMAN ROBERT R	CPT	0-0310005	0545	2
COLEMAN ROBIN R	MAJ	0-0478621	1046	1
COLEMAN ROY E	LTC	0-1104572	0363	1
COLEMAN SAM J	CPT	0-0325795	0344	2
COLEMAN SAMUEL	LTC	0-0453092	0961	1
COLEMAN STAFFORD L	1LT	0-0257866	0267	3
COLEMAN STUART T	MAJ	0-0166404	0652	3
COLEMAN THEODORE F	COL	0-1003454	0566	3
COLEMAN THOMAS R	LTC	0-1291419	1162	1
COLEMAN V GLENN	1LT	N-0759009	0745	1
COLEMAN WARREN C	MAJ	0-1321157	0862	1
COLEMAN WILBUR R	MAJ	0-1299996	0161	1

NAME	GRADE	SVC NO	DATE RET MO YR	RET CODE
COLEMAN WOOD R	LTC	0-0238493	C560	3
COLEN JOSEPH E	CPT	0-0536646	1047	2
COLES FRANCIS A	LTC	0-0247664	0467	3
COLES FREDERICK	MAJ	C-1322312	0163	1
COLES JR RUSSELL A	CW3	W-2144768	C663	1
COLES JULIAN G	MAJ	0-2262386	1262	1
COLES PHILIP J	LTC	0-1799572	C958	1
COLETTA MARTIN M	MAJ	0-0403394	0945	2
COLETTO GEORGE G	MAJ	0-1114424	0162	1
COLEY ALBERT J	MAJ	C-1650894	1060	1
COLEY BERT R	CW2	W-2211638	0765	1
COLEY CLARENCE W	WO1	W-2149011	C853	1
COLEY LESLIE G	COL	0-0274316	0155	3
COLFORD LEONE M	2LT	N-0730361	1044	1
COLFORD ROBERT W	LTC	0-1306553	0462	1
COLGAN ROCHESTER	LTC	0-0964702	1066	3
COLGAN WILLIAM H	CPT	0-0136835	C950	3
COLGIN CLARENCE H	LTC	0-0409529	1062	1
COLGLAZIER JACK E	1LT	0-1313209	0845	2
COLGLAZIER ROBERT W	M G	0-0223635	0766	1
COLGLAZIER WALDO W	LTC	0-1994735	0161	1
COLHARC FRED T	MAJ	C-1056670	0360	2
COLIN IRVING	2LT	0-1643251	C245	2
COLIO EDISON P	LTC	0-0354520	C567	1
COLISON CHARLES W	COL	0-0444193	0765	3
COLLAER NICK D	CPT	0-0114017	0456	3
COLLAR CHARLES L	2LT	0-1179819	0245	2
COLLAR HENRY N	1LT	0-2046466	0845	2
COLLARD JOHN A	CPT	0-0971540	0361	1
COLLAZO FRANCISCO	MAJ	C-2263321	1265	2
COLLAZO JOSE A	CW3	W-2147627	C761	1
COLLAZO SANTIAGO	CW3	W-2147645	1060	1
COLLEARY JOHN C	CPT	0-0528497	0450	1
COLLESTER GAYNOR P	1LT	0-1289047	0145	2
COLLETT THEODORE J	1LT	C-0481621	0753	1
COLLETTE EDNA M	MAJ	N-0761302	1265	1
COLLETTE PATRICK W	CW3	W-2153075	C463	1
COLLETTI JR JOHN T	CPT	0-1923506	C262	1
COLLEY ARTHUR T	LTC	0-0271771	1065	3
COLLEY DWIGHT T	COL	0-0166222	0556	3
COLLEY JOHN	CW2	W-2110113	0553	1
COLLEY RALPH C	MAJ	C-0949732	0464	1
COLLEY TOLBY J	MAJ	C-0527019	C854	1
COLLEY WILLIAM B	LTC	0-1281112	1262	1
COLLIER ARCHER C	CPT	0-1798912	0754	1
COLLIER CALHOUN C	CPT	0-1295178	C248	2
COLLIER CHARLES F	COL	0-0230964	0762	3
COLLIER ERNEST J	1LT	C-1315142	1052	1
COLLIER ERNEST M	CPT	C-0195596	1143	2
COLLIER EVELYN O	MAJ	N-0736147	C361	1
COLLIER EVERETT R	CW3	W-2203274	0962	1
COLLIER GEORGE R	CPT	0-0514920	0547	2
COLLIER GERALD	MAJ	C-1118558	C663	1
COLLIER HAROLD L	LTC	0-0244285	0960	3
COLLIER HERMAN C	LTC	C-0271616	C359	1
COLLIER JAMES C	1LT	0-1010126	0655	2
COLLIER LEONARD L	LTC	0-1547252	1262	1
COLLIER PAUL R	MAJ	0-0201790	0763	3
COLLIER RAYMOND F	LTC	0-0262519	0160	1
COLLIER ROBERT	CPT	0-0493057	1047	2
COLLIER ROBERT B	COL	0-0307337	0166	1
COLLIER SAMUEL H	CPT	0-0275655	C648	3
COLLIER SOL R	CPT	0-1052304	1046	2
COLLIER THOMAS H	1LT	0-0497812	0148	1
COLLIER VINCENT R	MAJ	0-1946691	0663	1
COLLIER WILLIAM C	MAJ	C-0918701	0652	1
COLLIGAN JOHN W	LTC	0-1581610	0667	1
COLLIGAN LAWRENCE F	CPT	0-0964953	0661	1
COLLIGEN JAMES	2LT	0-1698001	0643	2
COLLIGNON RAMOLA R	2LT	N-0776100	0645	1
COLLIN II JONAS F	LTC	0-1299205	C761	1
COLLING JOHN G	MAJ	0-1284296	0546	2
COLLINGS ALFRED W	CPT	C-0342849	0345	2
COLLINGS JOHN B	COL	0-0351999	C662	1
COLLINGS WILLIAM J	CPT	0-1317494	0847	1

NAME	GRADE	SVC NO	DATE RET MO YR	RET CODE
COLLINGWOOD HAROLD O	COL	0-0276634	0858	3
COLLINS ADAM	LTC	0-1306987	0761	1
COLLINS ANDREW E	CW3	W-2143576	0659	1
COLLINS ANNE K	1LT	N-0789195	0746	1
COLLINS ANNE M	1LT	N-0721507	0745	1
COLLINS ARVIL R	CW2	W-2207140	1161	1
COLLINS ASA W	LTC	0-0284777	0360	3
COLLINS BERNHARD R	LTC	0-0314373	0359	1
COLLINS BILLINGS J	1LT	0-2035874	1145	2
COLLINS BURR W	MAJ	0-1107354	1166	2
COLLINS CARL E	MAJ	0-0498783	0354	1
COLLINS CHARLES D	COL	0-0461824	0965	1
COLLINS CHARLES N	MAJ	C-0480265	0954	1
COLLINS CHARLES R	1LT	0-1030344	1045	2
COLLINS CLARE O	LTC	0-1950321	1265	2
COLLINS CLARENCE L	CW3	W-2144754	1262	1
COLLINS DALE D	1LT	0-1315272	0146	2
COLLINS DAVID W	2LT	0-0537254	0845	2
COLLINS DOROTHIE E	CPT	N-0741344	1148	2
COLLINS EDNA M	LTC	N-0767217	0963	2
COLLINS EDWARD H	CPT	0-1640321	0355	2
COLLINS EDWARD V	CPT	0-0452035	1146	2
COLLINS ERNEST L	CPT	0-1290559	0964	3
COLLINS EUGENE L	MAJ	0-1920315	0266	1
COLLINS FLOYD	CPT	0-0229447	0947	1
COLLINS FLOYD M	1LT	0-2055048	1146	2
COLLINS FRANCIS E	1LT	0-1014161	0746	2
COLLINS FRANCIS X	CW4	W-2142826	0165	1
COLLINS FRANK B	MAJ	0-0298350	0247	1
COLLINS GEORGE A	LTC	0-1287145	1060	1
COLLINS GEORGE F	MAJ	0-1327333	0561	1
COLLINS GEORGE H	LTC	0-0108049	0745	2
COLLINS GEORGE H	2LT	0-1879119	0762	2
COLLINS GEORGE H	LTC	0-1994886	1067	1
COLLINS GEORGE W	LTC	0-0386042	1055	1
COLLINS HAROLD V	LTC	0-0416557	1060	1
COLLINS HELEN K	2LT	N-0720465	0445	1
COLLINS HENRY	CW2	W-2145402	0460	1
COLLINS HENRY H	COL	C-0365781	0567	3
COLLINS HOWARD	LTC	0-1633765	0460	1
COLLINS HOWARD B	CPT	0-0428298	1045	1
COLLINS HUGH C	MAJ	0-1058211	0762	1
COLLINS J B	CW4	W-2113397	1055	1
COLLINS JAMES D	1LT	0-1846405	0846	1
COLLINS JAMES G	LTC	0-0181325	1159	3
COLLINS JAMES M	MAJ	0-1106066	0661	1
COLLINS JAMES P	CW2	W-2141800	1057	1
COLLINS JASON J	LTC	0-0335638	0665	3
COLLINS JEFFERSON	LTC	0-0408192	0962	1
COLLINS JOHN B	MAJ	0-2025606	0960	1
COLLINS JOHN C	LTC	0-0902867	0263	3
COLLINS JOHN O	LTC	0-1548031	1063	1
COLLINS JOHN W	1LT	0-0409492	1044	1
COLLINS JOHN W	1LT	0-1822858	0346	2
COLLINS JOSEPH T	CW4	W-2116074	0456	1
COLLINS JOSEPH T	CW2	W-2142358	0X59	1
COLLINS JR ELIJAH A	LTC	0-1109211	0962	1
COLLINS JR EVERETT T	2LT	0-0465084	0944	2
COLLINS JR JOSEPH A	CW3	RW-2144895	0263	1
COLLINS JR SIDNEY H	COL	0-1945776	1263	3
COLLINS JR THOMAS A	CW2	W-2151017	0163	1
COLLINS KENNETH C	MAJ	0-1949811	0963	1
COLLINS LAFAYETTE	MAJ	0-0567133	0764	1
COLLINS LAFIECE D	LTC	C-0336764	0457	2
COLLINS LAWRENCE	COL	0-0114204	0958	3
COLLINS LEHMAN R	CPT	0-0294777	0762	1
COLLINS LEIGH G	CPT	0-0356676	1043	2
COLLINS LLOYD F	LTC	0-0287172	0759	3
COLLINS MELVIN P	MAJ	0-1877950	0864	1
COLLINS OTHO B	LTC	0-0402572	0762	2
COLLINS RALPH H	LTC	0-0463631	0454	1
COLLINS RAYMOND D	CPT	0-1289214	1145	2
COLLINS RAYMOND E	LTC	0-0918298	0266	3
COLLINS RAYMOND L	CPT	0-0949811	C860	1
COLLINS RICHARD H	LTC	0-2274612	0563	1

NAME	GRADE	SVC NO	DATE RET MO YR	RET CODE
COLLINS ROBERT E	COL	O-0253024	0566	3
COLLINS ROBERT S	LTC	O-1548184	1054	1
COLLINS ROBERT W	LTC	O-1167367	0763	1
COLLINS RUPERT	LTC	O-0290590	0462	1
COLLINS SHERWOOD E	LTC	O-0314445	0947	2
COLLINS THOMAS E	LTC	O-0500889	0555	2
COLLINS THOMAS H	1LT	O-0110926	1045	2
COLLINS THOMAS I	LTC	O-1558128	0165	1
COLLINS VIRGIL T	MAJ	O-2011992	1163	1
COLLINS WALTER H	CW3	W-2152802	0864	1
COLLINS WILLIAM	MAJ	O-2401007	0864	1
COLLINS WILLIAM E	MAJ	O-0311847	1167	3
COLLINS WILLIAM F	LTC	O-1638899	1066	1
COLLINS WILLIAM J	LTC	O-1117064	0767	1
COLLINS WILLIAM J	LTC	O-1314258	0867	3
COLLINS WILLIAM J	CPT	O-1317887	0946	2
COLLINS WILLIAM L	LTC	O-0246956	0266	3
COLLINS WILLIAM L	CPT	O-1204314	0954	2
COLLINS WILLIAM N	1LT	O-1548899	0846	1
COLLINS WILLIAM S	MAJ	O-0116183	0748	3
COLLINS WILLIAM S	MAJ	O-1175403	0555	1
COLLINSWORTH GORDON	CPT	O-0463259	0646	1
COLLISON BERNARD F	CPT	O-1917533	0462	1
COLLISTER LOREN O	CW3	W-2143133	0161	1
COLLITON ELLSWORTH	1LT	O-1041717	1145	2
COLLIVER JESSE Y	CPT	O-1577032	1058	1
COLLMAN ROLAND J	2LT	O-1303852	0445	2
COLLOM CHARLES R	CPT	O-1047484	0666	2
COLLOM HAROLD L	COL	O-0235613	0561	1
COLLORY JAMES S	MAJ	O-1291078	0366	1
COLLOTON FRANCIS T	CPT	O-0159731	0653	3
COLLUM THEODORE J	LTC	O-0384009	0966	1
COLLUMS JIM X	LTC	O-1641833	0862	1
COLLUP GEORGE W	CPT	O-1319135	1046	2
COLMAN CHARLES R	CW3	W-2215328	0767	1
COLMAN HOMER J	LTC	O-0358918	0567	1
COLMAN WILLIAM A	CPT	O-1552258	0146	2
COLMER MEYER J	CPT	O-0491490	0546	2
COLN CHESTER C	MAJ	O-0947270	1066	1
COLO FRANCIS W	MAJ	O-1054947	0960	1
COLOM JOSE I	COL	O-0174221	0749	3
COLOMBEL JR E F	1LT	O-1017942	1145	2
COLOMBO JAMES A	2LT	O-0975088	0744	2
COLOMBO JAMES A	CW2	W-2207064	0561	1
COLOMBO RAYMOND L	CW3	W-2145193	0764	1
COLON BELEN O	MAJ	N-0755538	0266	3
COLON VENANCIO	MAJ	O-0368631	0262	2
COLON-MALDONADO EFRN	MAJ	O-1063140	0765	1
COLONNA BENJAMIN A	LTC	O-0146517	1154	3
COLONNA DELIO	LTC	O-1156047	0167	1
COLOPRIT ANTHONY J	MAJ	O-2046087	1266	?
COLOSIMO JOSEPH	CW?	W-2104176	0966	1
COLOVOS NICHOLAS F	1LT	O-0642840	0845	1
COLOZZI CARL A	LTC	O-1181944	0767	2
COLSON ALEX G	CW?	W-2115691	0555	1
COLSON GARDNER	1LT	O-1325150	1046	?
COLSON GUY L	MAJ	O-0368103	0450	1
COLSON OLIVER W	LTC	O-1322310	1048	1
COLSTON CHARLES L	CW2	W-2152621	1060	1
COLT LEBARON C	LTC	O-0232847	0446	1
COLTON DONALD A	MAJ	O-1640324	1059	1
COLTRIN DONALD C	MAJ	O-0198469	0467	3
COLUMBIA FRANK L	LTC	O-0456530	1164	1
COLUMBO EUGENE	CW2	W-2206883	0261	1
COLUMBUS LEO M	1LT	O-0528059	0644	1
COLUMNA VICENTE U	MAJ	O-1886492	0861	1
COLUSSI LOUIS A	1LT	O-0377025	0544	3
COLVARD FREELAND A	LTC	O-0225167	0460	3
COLVERT THOMAS C	CW2	W-2148919	1055	1
COLVIN ARTHUR H	LTC	O-1285712	0460	1
COLVIN ERNEST E	LTC	O-0105946	0554	3
COLVIN FULA M	1LT	O-1735681	0145	2
COLVIN JAMES A	MAJ	O-1142051	0966	1
COLVIN JAMES F	LTC	O-1010919	0867	1
COLVIN KATHERINE	1LT	N-0744027	0845	1
COLVIN ROBERT A	WOJ	W-2116498	0743	2
COLVIN WILLIAM J	CPT	O-0535150	0746	1
COLWELL CLARK H	CW2	W-2149204	1262	2
COLWELL EVERETT L	LTC	O-0127388	1152	3
COLWELL HANFORD T	LTC	O-0495558	0364	1
COLWELL MARTIN A	CW2	W-2144840	0157	1
COLWELL RALPH W	LTC	O-0481351	0457	1
COLWELL ROBERT E	CW2	W-2134341	0648	2
COLYER CHARLES F	LTC	O-0402513	0258	1
COLYER DAVID J	COL	O-0130923	0854	3
COLYER WILLIAM N	LTC	O-0375207	0557	1
COMAN HOWARD J	MAJ	O-0968045	0763	1
COMBATALADE EDMOND A	LTC	O-0252672	0965	3
COMBEL GEORGE H	COL	O-0286887	0860	3
COMBEL OSBORNE P	LTC	O-1635713	0960	1
COMBES GEORGE F	WOJ	W-2146009	0653	1
COMBES J DERAISME	LTC	O-0138055	0251	3
COMBS ALONZO F	CPT	O-2036880	1159	1
COMBS CHARLIE A	CW3	W-2152602	0662	1
COMBS CLYDE W	MAJ	O-1560411	0860	1
COMBS CORNELIUS	LTC	O-0904922	0148	2
COMBS GEORGE F	LTC	O-1290379	0161	1
COMBS HAROLD D	2LT	O-1287262	0944	2
COMBS HENRY H	1LT	O-2000862	1147	1
COMBS HORACE E	LTC	O-2012216	0266	1
COMBS ISHMAEL T	WOJ	W-2151160	0157	1
COMBS JOHN A	MAJ	O-0445445	0953	2
COMBS JOHN D	1LT	O-1010395	0446	1
COMBS JR FRANKLIN	COL	O-0489198	0563	1
COMBS JR HERBERT L	LTC	O-1633766	1262	1
COMBS KERMIT S	LTC	O-0402506	1057	2
COMBS OLIVER R	LTC	O-0307587	0955	1
COMBS PALLAS E	CPT	O-1877034	1051	1
COMBS PAUL D	1LT	O-0324551	0549	2
COMBS RAYMOND W	COL	O-0114305	0753	3
COMBS SYDNEY E	MAJ	O-0387903	0346	2
COMBS THEODORE F	COL	O-0253003	0866	3
COMBS WATSON F	LTC	O-1626391	0263	1
COMBS ZENAS R	LTC	O-0224406	0761	3
COMEAU EDWARD J	2LT	O-1044483	0747	2
COMEAU EVANGELINE	CPT	N-0732280	0447	1
COMEAU LEAH A	MAJ	N-0752873	1066	3
COMER BARTHOLOMEW	MAJ	O-0461230	0346	1
COMER CHESTER J	LTC	O-0345872	0465	3
COMER EVERETT A	COL	O-0244925	0946	2
COMER HARRY I	MAJ	O-0468535	1047	1
COMER READIE	CPT	O-0437445	0144	1
COMER REUBEN H	1LT	O-0115477	0553	3
COMER THOMAS P	CPT	O-0492490	0446	2
COMER VIRGIL	CPT	O-0289338	1045	2
COMERFORD EDWARD P J	LTC	O-1103115	1162	1
COMERFORD MARTIN AJ	MAJ	O-0299022	1160	1
COMES FABIAN W	CPT	O-1403309	1052	1
COMESKY HARRY A	LTC	O-0295893	1066	1
COMEY EVERETT I	CW3	W-2146517	0561	2
COMEY LYMAN F	LTC	O-0325700	0260	3
COMFORT JOSEPH A	CPT	O-0461512	0545	2
COMINGS JAMES H	COL	O-0374201	0157	1
COMISKY BENEDICT J	MAJ	O-1846676	0464	1
COMMINS GEORGE J	CPT	O-2263213	0763	1
COMMINS SAUL	CPT	O-1691054	0146	1
COMMONS JR CHARLES W	CPT	O-0249436	0866	1
COMNES GREGORY A	LTC	O-1289049	1060	1
COMO MARTHA P	MAJ	N-0726007	0966	1
COMPARETTE HOMER J	MAJ	O-0382422	0448	1
COMPETENTE RAYMOND	2LT	O-1834438	0648	1
COMPTON DON E	1LT	O-1687813	1045	2
COMPTON EDWARD A	COL	O-0313294	0860	3
COMPTON EVELAND C	MAJ	O-0374395	0448	2
COMPTON GEORGE W	1LT	O-0414299	0145	2
COMPTON HARRY O	COL	O-0227449	1162	3
COMPTON JOHN P	LTC	O-0341218	0359	2
COMPTON MORGAN L	CPT	O-2000447	1066	1
COMPTON MUTT I	MAJ	O-1534456	1060	2
COMPTON ORBY	MAJ	O-1582339	1063	1
COMPTON ROBERT J	MAJ	O-0309031	0363	3
COMPTON SHERMAN W	CPT	O-0494560	1053	1
COMPTON WILLIAM F	2LT	O-1913608	0935	1
COMRIE RUSSELL W	LTC	O-0374514	0759	1
COMROE IRVING H	LTC	O-0309583	1063	3
COMSTOCK DONALD R	CW2	W-2148086	0860	1
COMSTOCK JR CARL P	CPT	O-0469597	0345	1
COMSTOCK OLIVER D	LTC	O-0275871	0460	3
COMSTOCK RAYMOND C	MAJ	O-0483258	1153	1
COMSTOCK ROBERT F	MAJ	O-1637813	0759	1
COMUNTZIS MARCOS C	CPT	O-0447058	1045	1
COMYACK GEORGE W	CW2	W-2209458	1263	1
CONA ANTHONY T	1LT	O-1017176	0646	2
CONAN JR NEAL J	1LT	O-0464565	1045	2
CONANT LEWIS T	MAJ	O-1951582	0360	1
CONANT LYNNE	1LT	O-0263788	0143	2
CONARD EUGENE S	MAJ	O-1101386	0759	1
CONARD HARRY W	CW3	W-2153185	0164	2
CONARD HORACE V	LTC	O-1533758	0362	3
CONARD WILLIAM F	LTC	O-1050606	0644	1
CONARTY EARL T	1LT	O-1303111	1045	2
CONARY GEORGE W	CPT	O-0128311	1055	3
CONATSER MAX C	LTC	O-1640325	0462	1
CONATSER TROY F	CW3	W-2143034	1058	1
CONAWAY CHARLES W	MAJ	O-0171080	0958	3
CONAWAY ROY W	MAJ	O-1695637	0464	1
CONAWAY RALPH C	CW2	W-2102276	0248	2
CONAWAY THOMAS W	MAJ	O-5205633	1067	2
CONBOY JOHN W P	LTC	O-1113149	0567	1
CONBOY RAY	CPT	O-0499431	0746	2
CONCAGH JOSEPH P	1LT	O-1650817	0647	1
CONCANNON JAMES W	1LT	O-0446020	0446	2
CONCAR MARY H	1LT	N-0747998	0846	1
CONCORDIA JOHN D	MAJ	O-1302777	0158	1
CONDAN WILLIAM H	1LT	O-0982101	1060	1
CONDELL WILLIAM J	COL	O-0165950	0456	3
CONDER FRANCIS E	COL	O-0179883	0860	1
CONDICT STEPHEN H	MAJ	O-1297605	0762	1
CONDIT HERBERT I	LTC	O-1534944	0767	1
CONDIT JOHN V	CPT	O-1263017	0560	1
CONDIT JR CHARLES P	MAJ	O-1186076	0866	1
CONDIT WILLIAM F	WOJ	W-2121440	1045	2
CONDON DEAN L	LTC	O-0314838	0861	1
CONDON EDWARD J	MAJ	O-0304027	0167	3
CONDON EDWARD V	COL	O-0209458	1153	3
CONDON JAMES L	1LT	O-2008796	0256	2
CONDON JOHN	1LT	O-1017190	0745	2
CONDON JOSEPH M	LTC	O-0907151	0265	3
CONDON JR HERBERT T	LTC	O-0351330	1062	1
CONDON KELLISON T	LTC	O-0016567	1063	3
CONDON RICHARD P	WOJ	W-2122001	1063	1
CONDON WILLIAM C	LTC	O-1044467	0164	1
CONDON WILLIAM F	1LT	O-1301356	0745	1
CONDON WILLIAM I	1LT	O-1645658	0545	2
CONDON WILLIAM W	LTC	O-0405180	1060	1
CONDREY DWIGHT L	1LT	O-2242083	0963	2
CONDRICK MAURICE P	1LT	O-0210926	0763	1
CONDRIN HARRY D	1LT	O-1315440	1145	2
CONDY HUGH H	LTC	O-1288710	0960	2
CONE ANTHONY C	CPT	O-0478184	1044	1
CONE JAMES P	WOJ	W-2125405	1143	2
CONE JR HUTCHINSON	LTC	O-0324133	1065	2
CONE RALPH N	LTC	O-1647281	0867	1
CONE ROY D	1LT	O-1114429	1263	1
CONE WILLIAM W	LTC	O-0198592	0761	1
CONEFREY FRANK A	MAJ	O-0243032	0857	1
CONEIN LUCIEN E	LTC	O-1322269	1061	1
CONELLEY WILLIAM P	MAJ	O-1341855	1166	1
CONELLY CHESTER L	CPT	O-0363201	0944	2
CONELLY RAYMOND J	COL	O-0288550	1060	1
CONERLY CECIL F	CPT	O-0323865	0344	2
CONERLY MAXWELL P	MAJ	O-2262432	0861	1
CONERLY ULDRIC E	MAJ	O-1080010	1056	1
CONEY DUDLEY E	COL	O-1015594	0165	1
CONEY JOHN D	COL	O-0297801	1161	1
CONEY JOHN S	CPT	O-0484330	0745	1
CONEY RICHARD H	MAJ	O-1994736	0862	1
CONEYBEER ROBERT T	LTC	O-1081206	0361	1
CONFEHR WILMER D	LTC	O-1895934	0767	2
CONFER ELMA I	MAJ	N-0724711	0464	1
CONFER WILLIAM R	MAJ	O-0887357	0756	1
CONGDON CHARLES C	CPT	O-1757031	0847	1
CONGDON JOHN	2LT	O-1400763	1144	2
CONGDON LEON A	MAJ	O-0142681	0554	3
CONGDON PAUL E	COL	O-0335455	0667	3
CONGER ALWYN D	CPT	O-0287446	0255	2
CONGLETON DEWEY S	MAJ	O-0246505	0244	2
CONINE HUBERT E	CPT	O-0277893	0946	2
CONISKI FRANK T	LTC	O-1309218	0862	1
CONKEL LLOYD J	LTC	O-0216502	1147	1
CONKELL JR FRANK	CW4	W-2110137	0265	1
CONKIN CHARLES A	CW2	W-2152503	0961	1
CONKLE JOHN C	LTC	O-1821825	0261	1
CONKLIN ALBERT R	COL	O-0287947	0560	1
CONKLIN CHARLES M	MAJ	O-1633138	0956	1
CONKLIN CLARENCE F	LTC	O-0284654	0964	3
CONKLIN DEANE L	1LT	O-0144018	0254	3
CONKLIN FRANK J	CW3	W-2145735	0465	1
CONKLIN GLENN G	CPT	O-2056241	0347	1
CONKLIN HARRY I	LTC	O-0309081	0962	3
CONKLIN JR EDWARD M	COL	O-0317520	0854	2
CONKLIN LEROY R	LTC	O-1302604	0866	1
CONKLIN MARY C	1LT	N-0754786	1048	2
CONKLIN ROSCOE R	MAJ	O-1686227	0159	1
CONKLING SAMUEL R	CPT	O-1637219	0452	1
CONLAN DAVID N	1LT	O-0315859	0445	2
CONLAN WILLIAM P	LTC	O-0255450	0466	3
CONLEY DON H	LTC	O-0321900	0747	2
CONLEY EARL C	1LT	O-1641097	0844	2
CONLEY EDWARD J	1LT	O-1031546	1150	1
CONLEY EDWARD P	MAJ	O-0507977	0654	1
CONLEY FRANK G G	MAJ	O-0316986	0267	3
CONLEY FRANK J	COL	O-0334739	1161	1
CONLEY GEORGE F	LTC	O-1107117	0661	1
CONLEY HARLAN L	1LT	O-1324085	1045	2
CONLEY IRVING L	MAJ	O-1834628	0241	1
CONLEY JAMES F	1LT	O-1559274	0846	1
CONLEY JOSEPH G	COL	O-0286588	0962	3
CONLEY LELAND H	LTC	O-0920141	0267	3
CONLEY MARGARET I	MAJ	N-0742444	0862	2
CONLEY PAUL P	1LT	O-1284246	0546	2
CONLEY PETER	CW3	W-2145882	0159	1
CONLEY RAYMOND F	MAJ	O-2265052	0767	1
CONLEY RUSSELL T	CPT	O-0267467	0757	1
CONLEY THOMAS W	CW2	W-2111680	0654	1
CONLEY WILLIAM R	CPT	O-5514006	0265	2
CONLEY WILLIAM S	CW3	W-2144859	0754	1
CONLIN ALVIN R	CPT	O-1312128	1060	1
CONLIN CHARLES A	COL	O-0317150	0866	1
CONLIN FRANK A	LTC	O-0177639	1157	1
CONLIN JOHN P	MAJ	O-0357804	0946	2
CONLIN JOHN T	MAJ	O-1104097	0748	2
CONLIN RICHARD G	LTC	O-1106576	0866	1
CONLIN THOMAS J	COL	O-0372171	0760	1
CONLON ARTHUR R	CPT	O-2044294	0460	1
CONLON THOMAS P	LTC	O-0401470	1060	1
CONLON WILLIAM F	LTC	O-0487093	0866	1
CONLOW JOHN J	1LT	O-1318867	1045	2
CONLYN JR WILLIAM J	CPT	O-0348103	1045	2
CONLYN PEARSTA C	COL	O-0254617	0165	3
CONN GARY R	CW2	W-2117990	1047	2
CONN KERMIT K	MAJ	O-1700130	0258	1
CONN LUCILLE Y	MAJ	N-0769936	0767	1
CONN MILTON H	1LT	O-1295863	0944	2
CONN ROBBINS L	COL	O-0100445	0756	3
CONN SOLOMON J	LTC	O-1108576	0658	1
CONN WILLIAM M	1LT	O-1552843	0257	1
CONNALLY CHARLES F	CW3	W-2145844	0650	1
CONNALLY DUDLEY B	MAJ	O-0274703	0563	3
CONNALLY LYNTON F	CPT	O-2208303	0358	2

NAME	GRADE	SVC NO	DATE RET MO YR	RET CODE
CONNARN JOHN P	CPT	O-0414143	0547	2
CONNELL CECIL H	COL	O-0336954	0363	3
CONNELL EDWIN M	COL	O-0378900	1060	1
CONNELL GEORGE B	CW2	W-2119340	1045	2
CONNELL HENRY L	LTC	O-0228845	0363	3
CONNELL JAMES B	1LT	O-0506670	0246	2
CONNELL JAMES K	LTC	O-0286567	0167	3
CONNELL NORMAN G	CPT	O-0414300	0864	2
CONNELL PAUL	CPT	O-0498228	1047	2
CONNELL WILBUR L	MAJ	O-0246559	0658	3
CONNELLAN GERALD V	MAJ	O-1645214	0460	1
CONNELLY ALLEN N	CPT	O-0266991	0947	2
CONNELLY FRANCIS J	MAJ	O-0348978	0346	2
CONNELLY GEORGE A	COL	O-0255259	0867	3
CONNELLY IRETON G	MAJ	O-0230660	1162	3
CONNELLY JAMES G	MAJ	O-1332932	0864	1
CONNELLY JOHN B	LTC	O-0369930	0660	1
CONNELLY JOHN K	COL	O-0337388	0961	1
CONNELLY ROBERT J	MAJ	O-2033203	0662	1
CONNELLY ROSE F	1LT	N-0751161	0745	1
CONNELLY THOMAS E	CPT	O-1303673	0746	1
CONNER CARROLL L	CW2	W-2151668	0659	1
CONNER CHARLES E	COL	O-0179246	0346	2
CONNER DAVID J	MAJ	O-0959309	1162	1
CONNER DONALD E	LTC	O-0455815	0160	1
CONNER EDGAR G	MAJ	O-1285159	0860	1
CONNER ELI T	LTC	O-0284918	1065	3
CONNER FRANK E	2LT	O-0317999	0659	3
CONNER HAROLD A	MAJ	O-2018846	0562	1
CONNER HARRY R	1LT	O-1315910	0747	2
CONNER HENRY F	LTC	O-0273523	0566	3
CONNER HOWARD W	2LT	O-1288711	0151	2
CONNER HOWARD W	CW2	RW-2209677	0966	1
CONNER IRA M	CPT	O-0297137	0547	2
CONNER IRIA O	1LT	O-2212016	0556	1
CONNER JAMES T	CW2	W-2148718	0656	1
CONNER JESSE H	1LT	O-0435913	1145	2
CONNER JOHN W	MAJ	O-0483566	0754	2
CONNER JOSEPH R	CW3	W-2143135	0358	1
CONNER JR BERTIS A	CPT	O-0708658	0147	2
CONNER JR OTTO R	LTC	O-0438212	0955	1
CONNER KENNETH H	MAJ	O-0325729	0566	3
CONNER LLOYD W	MAJ	O-1548702	0561	1
CONNER LOWELL L	CPT	O-0297800	0649	1
CONNER MEREDITH	1LT	O-1310813	0945	2
CONNER PHILIP H	LTC	O-0403499	1060	1
CONNER RANDAL E	CW2	W-2150810	1161	2
CONNER ROY F	1LT	O-0554024	0346	2
CONNER SIDNEY J	CPT	O-0286796	0346	2
CONNER WORTH C	LTC	O-1080183	0961	1
CONNERLEY MELVIN H	CW4	W-2131445	0761	1
CONNERS EDWARD D	CPT	O-1294787	1165	1
CONNERS JR DANIEL J	1LT	O-1012234	1046	2
CONNERS PAUL R	CW2	W-2206083	0963	1
CONNERS VINCENT P	MAJ	O-1691749	0763	1
CONNERTH SARA	2LT	N-0700826	0536	1
CONNERY RICHARD F	COL	O-0217671	0860	3
CONNICK JAMES R	LTC	O-0218108	1061	3
CONNICK ROBERT E	1LT	O-1287307	1145	2
CONNIFF JOHN J	CPT	O-1109862	1146	2
CONNINGTON CHARLES S	MAJ	O-0201848	0863	3
CONNOLLY BERNARD	1LT	O-0444707	1045	2
CONNOLLY BERNARD F	LTC	O-0419084	0961	1
CONNOLLY BERNARD T	CW3	W-2119581	0655	1
CONNOLLY CHARLES R	LTC	O-0254089	0762	3
CONNOLLY JAMES R	1LT	O-1310226	0446	2
CONNOLLY JOHN R	1LT	O-1799104	0246	2
CONNOLLY JOSEPH J	MAJ	O-1110426	0365	1
CONNOLLY JR JAMES J	MAJ	O-0908385	0862	2
CONNOLLY JR ROBERT D	LTC	O-1633139	0563	1
CONNOLLY JR W A	LTC	O-0329480	1160	1
CONNOLLY LEONARD W	LTC	O-0185389	0951	3
CONNOLLY REDMOND J	COL	O-0255066	0660	1
CONNOLLY ROBERT M	COL	O-0319372	1060	1
CONNOLLY THOMAS E	MAJ	O-1578294	0561	1
CONNOLLY THOMAS H	MAJ	O-1175980	0661	1
CONNOLLY THOMAS N	MAJ	O-2030145	1161	1
CONNOR BRIAN K	1LT	O-0916704	0944	2
CONNOR CLAUDE	CPT	O-0495341	0147	1
CONNOR DONALD G	LTC	O-1175083	0763	1
CONNOR EDWARD F	1LT	O-1325632	1045	2
CONNOR FRANCIS J	LTC	O-1822536	0563	1
CONNOR HERBERT C	MAJ	O-1169069	0960	1
CONNOR JAMES F	CW2	W-2213442	0867	1
CONNOR JAMES R	LTC	O-0394059	1164	1
CONNOR JAMES T	COL	O-0385243	0965	3
CONNOR JOHN J	MAJ	O-1535410	0657	2
CONNOR JOHN M	CPT	O-0259377	0367	3
CONNOR JOHN M	COL	O-0321714	0646	2
CONNOR JOHN W	MAJ	O-0338353	1145	2
CONNOR JOSEPH	MAJ	O-1298502	0563	1
CONNOR JR JOHN G	2LT	O-5007891	0761	2
CONNOR JR PRESTON B	CPT	O-0146880	0756	3
CONNOR MARGARET M	2LT	N-0757648	0345	1
CONNOR MYLES J	COL	O-0182391	0253	1
CONNOR ROBERT J	LTC	O-1170686	0664	1
CONNOR ROONEY V	1LT	O-0971167	1153	1
CONNOR SAMUEL W	COL	O-0220108	0549	3
CONNOR STANLEY R	LTC	O-0376766	0759	1
CONNOR THOMAS J	LTC	O-1061604	1163	1
CONNOR WILLIAM H	CW3	W-2149159	0563	1
CONNOR WILLIAM J	MAJ	O-1280187	0758	2
CONNOR WILLIAM J	MAJ	O-1341856	0561	1
CONNOR WILLIAM T	LTC	O-1796580	0763	1
CONNORS GERALD T	MAJ	O-0463341	0854	1
CONNORS HUGH M	COL	O-0229175	0859	3
CONNORS LAWRENCE P	LTC	O-1290903	0960	1
CONNORS MICHAEL J	MAJ	O-0488847	1045	2
CONNORS PANSY L	CW2	V-2211887	0866	1
CONOVER ARLIE B	MAJ	O-0235930	0648	3
CONOVER WOLFERT D	CPT	O-0163755	1055	1
CONRACE JOSEPH F C	MAJ	O-0189103	0256	3
CONRAD ALLISON A	COL	O-0327559	1058	1
CONRAD ARTHUR J	CW4	W-2117921	0659	1
CONRAD BERNARD R	1LT	O-0526646	0647	1
CONRAD CHESTER R	MAJ	O-1112628	0261	1
CONRAD DCOA	CPT	O-1691533	0347	2
CONRAD EDWARD	1LT	O-1291239	1055	1
CONRAD FRANK H	LTC	O-0184829	0862	3
CONRAD HARLAN C	MAJ	O-0308742	0148	1
CONRAD HAROLD C	LTC	O-0359386	0647	2
CONRAD HOWARD F	1LT	O-0408406	1045	2
CONRAD HUGH N	1LT	O-0888364	0264	3
CONRAD JAMES H	CW3	W-2206327	0166	1
CONRAD JAMES L	COL	O-0183985	1060	3
CONRAD JAMES P	1LT	O-1635717	0345	2
CONRAD JAMES R	CW3	W-2146686	1059	1
CONRAD JOSEPH F	2LT	O-1823586	1044	2
CONRAD LEON H	CW4	W-2102778	1157	1
CONRAD OLIVER H	MAJ	O-1047485	0667	1
CONRAD OMAR G	CPT	O-1542181	0346	2
CONRAD ROBERT L	CPT	O-0376955	0446	1
CONRAD STANLEY T	CW2	W-2150556	0260	1
CONRAD WARD E	LTC	O-0267905	0165	3
CONRAD WILBER D	MAJ	O-1822369	1155	2
CONROD ROBERT L	LTC	O-0126228	0257	3
CONROW JOSEPH M	LTC	O-0284655	0667	3
CONROY CHARLES W	MAJ	O-0974232	0165	1
CONROY GEORGE R	LTC	O-1287147	0364	1
CONROY HARRY A	COL	O-0255076	1148	3
CONROY JOSEPH F	COL	O-0331875	0760	1
CONROY LESLIE J	LTC	O-0472152	0954	1
CONROY RALPH J	LTC	O-0565081	0564	1
CONROY TERESA B	MAJ	N-0761041	0657	1
CONROY WALTER R	MAJ	O-1019778	1161	1
CONROY WILLIAM R	LTC	O-1017850	0862	1
CONSER FRANK M	MAJ	O-0436223	0946	2
CONSIDINE FLORENCE R	MAJ	O-1177345	1163	1
CONSIDINE LORETTA M	1LT	N-0771906	0646	2
CONSIDINE ROY J	CPT	O-1821826	0547	2
CONSOLETTI BENJAMIN	MAJ	O-0303533	1067	3
CONSTABLE EVERETT R	CW2	W-2142828	0862	2
CONSTABLE FRANCIS W	LTC	O-0200873	0756	3
CONSTANT JOE R	LTC	O-1640328	1066	1
CONSTANTINE JAMES	LTC	O-1011550	0656	1
CONSTANTINE JAMES T	CW3	W-2005258	1264	3
CONSTANTINE WALTER J	LTC	O-0419789	0563	1
CONTANT CHARLES F	LTC	O-0421249	0960	1
CONTAPAY FLORENTINO	1LT	O-1896618	0357	1
CONTE ANGELO J	LTC	O-0378678	1060	1
CONTE JOSEPH	CPT	O-1591065	0961	1
CONTE PETER A	MAJ	O-1550768	0157	1
CONTI AUGUSTO W	LTC	O-1549918	1263	1
CONTI DOMINIC L	CPT	O-1311983	0946	2
CONTI EDWARD J	LTC	O-1796581	0861	1
CONTOIS LEO A	CW2	W-2113705	1146	1
CONTOIS PAUL S	MAJ	O-1324911	1164	1
CONTOS DESPINA C	CPT	N-0784195	0247	1
CONTRAROS GEORGE J	CW3	W-2143260	0660	1
CONTRERAS JOSE T	1LT	O-1896635	0655	1
CONTROULIS THOMAS	CW3	W-2146170	0260	1
CONVERSE DUANE B	1LT	O-1290209	0245	2
CONVERSE GEORGE L	LTC	O-0291438	0759	1
CONVERSE JASON H	LTC	O-0253023	0865	3
CONVERY FREDRICK R	MAJ	O-0275487	1263	3
CONWAY BERNARD F	COL	O-0265759	0360	1
CONWAY CHARLES J	WO1	W-2141533	0457	1
CONWAY EDWARD H	LTC	O-0386858	1160	1
CONWAY FRAZIER M	MAJ	O-1185781	0461	1
CONWAY JAMES	CW3	W-2143887	0263	1
CONWAY JOHN A	LTC	O-0249919	0765	3
CONWAY JOHN F	1LT	O-1301439	0146	2
CONWAY JOHN F	CPT	O-1684299	1044	2
CONWAY JOHN R	2LT	O-1329806	0945	2
CONWAY JOHN V	CPT	O-0122460	1152	3
CONWAY JOSEPH M	LTC	O-0424522	0365	1
CONWAY MALACHI J	LTC	O-0433964	0363	1
CONWAY MARK F	COL	O-0270692	1165	3
CONWAY RAYMOND F	2LT	O-1822370	1043	2
CONWAY RICHARD H	MAJ	O-1339515	1164	1
CONWAY ROBERT H	MAJ	O-1640975	0764	1
CONWAY WILLIAM A	CPT	O-0453653	0844	2
CONWELL ROBERT W	CW3	W-2151609	0163	1
CONWELL STANTON A	MAJ	O-0205206	0962	1
CONYERS CHRISTOPHE	LTC	O-0170256	0759	3
CONYERS EDWARD	1LT	O-0109923	0632	1
CONYERS JR LUDGER B	MAJ	O-1061343	0564	1
CONZETT DONALD C	COL	O-0224796	0159	3
COOGAN BERNARD L	LTC	O-1555526	1062	1
COOK ADAM E	LTC	O-0502205	0256	1
COOK ALONZO E	MAJ	O-2262171	0862	1
COOK ARIE D	CW2	W-2151065	0857	1
COOK ARNOLD A	LTC	O-0487353	0266	3
COOK BILLIE G	CW4	W-2148314	0767	1
COOK BUFORD	CW4	W-2144212	0767	1
COOK BYRON J	LTC	O-0238745	0566	3
COOK CALLIE N	MAJ	O-1284105	1060	1
COOK CARL H	CPT	O-0390709	0445	2
COOK CARROLL K	CPT	O-0472402	0645	1
COOK CHARLES	CW4	W-2111209	0455	1
COOK CHARLES E	LTC	O-0182965	0962	3
COOK CHESTER L	CW2	RW-3150238	0466	1
COOK CLARENCE J	MAJ	O-0134985	0648	3
COOK CLIFFORD B	CPT	O-2055883	0758	1
COOK DARREL O	WO1	W-2112265	0348	1
COOK DAVID W	CPT	O-1287483	1147	1
COOK DEAN O	CW2	W-2211735	0167	1
COOK DENNIS S	MAJ	O-0399324	0645	2
COOK DON W	LTC	O-0308708	1060	1
COOK DONALD F	CPT	O-0972989	1062	1
COOK DONALD J	1LT	O-0534870	1045	1
COOK DONALD M	LTC	O-0128314	1153	3
COOK EDWIN W	CPT	O-1283215	0147	2
COOK EMORY J	LTC	O-0289844	1066	3
COOK ERNEST T	CPT	O-0495918	1147	2
COOK FRANK	CPT	O-0491449	0350	1
COOK FREDDIE	CW3	W-2143485	1162	1
COOK GEORGE A	CW4	W-2001611	0666	3
COOK GEORGE S	M G	O-0251434	0966	3
COOK GEORGE W	MAJ	O-0202683	0757	3
COOK GERALD C	COL	O-0450216	0764	1
COOK GILBERT W	CPT	O-1885925	0366	1
COOK HARRY A	LTC	O-0301333	0764	3
COOK HARVEY R	MAJ	O-0175299	0961	3
COOK HELEN A	1LT	N-0703899	0446	1
COOK HENRY G	LTC	O-1584696	0467	3
COOK HENRY R	MAJ	O-0397533	0361	1
COOK HERMAN W	COL	O-0173413	0361	3
COOK IVAN M	CW2	W-2152670	0561	1
COOK JACK C	LTC	O-1175084	0865	1
COOK JAMES A	MAJ	O-0282411	0367	3
COOK JAMES B	CW3	W-2205177	0565	1
COOK JAMES D	LTC	O-1303269	0962	1
COOK JAMES J	1LT	O-1016059	1147	2
COOK JAMES L	MAJ	O-1913366	0965	1
COOK JAMES T	COL	O-0227760	1064	3
COOK JAMES V	1LT	O-1062479	0747	2
COOK JAMES W	B G	O-0298148	0159	3
COOK JAMES W	MAJ	O-1844379	0558	1
COOK JOHN B	MAJ	O-1821684	1054	1
COOK JOHN C	COL	O-0329674	0559	1
COOK JOHN C	LTC	O-1637838	0960	1
COOK JOHN G	LTC	O-1010872	0156	1
COOK JOHN J	LTC	O-0284279	0757	1
COOK JOHN M	LTC	O-0403681	0346	2
COOK JOHN S	CPT	O-0522366	0151	1
COOK JOSEPH L	LTC	O-0198959	1150	3
COOK JOSEPH W	LTC	O-0480995	0355	1
COOK JOSEPH W	1LT	O-1308478	1146	2
COOK JR ALBERT R	LTC	O-0178788	1161	3
COOK JR CLARENCE C	CPT	O-0350421	0646	2
COOK JR CLIFFORD J	MAJ	O-0969387	0365	1
COOK JR GRIFFITH E	LTC	O-0448583	0557	1
COOK JR HARRY J	MAJ	O-2287137	0166	1
COOK JR HUGH D	2LT	O-1589133	0945	2
COOK JR JOHN A	1LT	O-2049208	0350	1
COOK JR THEODORE H	LTC	O-1544827	1064	1
COOK LAMAR H	1LT	O-1554882	0366	2
COOK LAURENCE	2LT	O-1031395	1045	2
COOK LAWRENCE E	CPT	O-0114028	0646	2
COOK LAWRENCE R	CW2	W-2153654	0560	1
COOK LELAND M	LTC	O-0450265	0357	1
COOK LEE H	MAJ	O-0504258	0158	1
COOK LEONARD J	1LT	O-0525002	0745	1
COOK LEWIS C	LTC	O-0262912	0166	3
COOK LEXIE W	CPT	O-1294269	0549	2
COOK LINDSLEY F	CPT	O-1010506	0246	2
COOK MADISON E	MAJ	O-0475736	0154	1
COOK MARIO V	CPT	O-0398164	0144	2
COOK MELVIN S	MAJ	O-1582104	0961	1
COOK MYRON O	COL	O-1166035	0461	1
COOK NATHANIEL	CW2	W-2145856	0257	1
COOK OLIN L	MAJ	O-0954743	1161	1
COOK OSSIAN L	LTC	O-0117769	0354	3
COOK OTIS S	CW3	W-2146132	0558	1
COOK OTTO G	LTC	O-0194064	1049	3
COOK OWEN E	2LT	O-1826259	0145	2
COOK PATRICK J	2LT	O-1304181	0746	2
COOK PAUL D	MAJ	O-1184027	0356	1
COOK PAUL F	MAJ	O-0517788	0556	1
COOK PAUL T	MAJ	O-0537146	0363	1
COOK PHILIP M	LTC	O-0330370	0459	1
COOK RALPH J	CW4	W-2144292	0367	1
COOK RAYMOND C	MAJ	O-0296699	0362	3
COOK RICHARD	M G	O-0107835	0658	3
COOK RICHARD L	LTC	O-0404590	1160	1
COOK RICHARD L	MAJ	O-1286971	0960	1
COOK ROBERT P	LTC	O-0439267	0967	1
COOK ROBERT R	LTC	O-1166036	0461	1
COOK ROBERT W	LTC	O-0476214	0155	1

NAME	GRADE	SVC NO	DATE RET MO YR	RET CODE
CCCK ROGER A	MAJ	C-0154345	1054	3
COOK ROLAND E	MAJ	0-07067C2	0961	1
COOK ROY H	LTC	0-1326255	1167	1
COOK RUSSELL O	COL	C-0367035	C964	1
COOK RUSSELL E	CPT	C-0394966	C747	2
COOK SHIRLEY S	LTC	0-0424484	0557	1
COOK STEWART G	LTC	C-0562763	C466	3
COOK THEODORE J	COL	0-0322984	0957	1
COOK THOMAS F	CPT	0-1300278	1060	1
COOK THOMAS J R	CW3	W-21467C3	C864	1
COOK TIM O	COL	0-0263796	1164	3
COOK WALTER G	CW4	W-2201047	1066	3
COOK WALTER R	MAJ	C-1917775	C563	1
COOK WAYNE R	LTC	0-0319129	0147	2
COOK WENDELL R	MAJ	C-C279016	0664	3
COOK WILLIAM B	LTC	0-0206632	1048	3
COOK WILLIAM B	MAJ	C-0245391	1264	3
COOK WILLIAM B	LTC	C-1552463	C767	1
COOK WILLIAM E	CPT	0-1304182	C847	2
COOK WILLIAM G	COL	0-0275468	0365	3
COOK WILLIAM G	2LT	0-1641877	0944	1
COOK WILLIAM H	MAJ	0-1102428	1059	1
COOK WILLIAM K	LTC	0-1302275	C662	1
COOK WILLIAM R	CPT	0-0887451	C349	2
COOKE BRONSON F	LTC	0-0278138	C858	1
COOKE BURDETTE E	CPT	0-2029657	1056	1
COOKE DON A	MAJ	0-0279518	0358	3
COOKE EDWIN T	COL	C-0198868	0251	3
COOKE ELLIS A	LTC	0-1578299	1061	2
COOKE ERNEST C	MAJ	C-0963352	C165	1
COOKE HCRACE G	LTC	0-1179822	C263	1
COOKE JAMES J	COL	C-0337465	C463	3
COOKE JOSEPH C	LTC	0-0473962	C954	1
COOKE JOSEPH E	CPT	0-2288504	0863	1
COOKE JOSEPH M	LTC	C-0251892	C156	3
COOKE JOSEPH R	COL	0-0100239	0753	3
COCKE LANE A	CPT	C-0966438	C161	1
COOKE LANE R	COL	C-0150563	1047	2
COOKE LEONARD C	COL	0-0316938	0560	1
COCKE OSCAR	MAJ	C-0277260	C863	3
COOKE PAUL R	MAJ	C-C975285	0761	1
COOKE RAFE	CW3	W-21155C7	0356	1
COCKE RAYMOND W	MAJ	C-0511018	1047	2
COOKE ROBERT A	CPT	0-0912581	0744	1
COOKE SAMUEL R	LTC	C-0223604	C560	3
COOKE THOMAS P	MAJ	C-0287274	0858	1
COOKE TOLBERT A	CPT	C-0244625	0250	1
COOKE WOODROW P	LTC	0-1647475	C365	1
COOKERLY VAN	COL	0-015056C	1047	2
COOKINGHAM THOMAS A	LTC	0-0434057	C962	1
COOKSEY DONALD W	MAJ	C-2033250	0765	1
COOKSLEY RICHARD F	CPT	0-1540843	C960	1
COOKSTON RAYMOND E	LTC	0-0909861	0467	3
COOL VALENTINE	MAJ	0-2262712	0663	1
COOLE HAROLD I	MAJ	C-2017360	C663	1
COOLEY ARTHUR E	LTC	0-0284411	C657	1
COOLEY CHARLES W	1LT	0-1755711	0946	1
COOLEY CANIEL S	CW3	W-215092C	0965	1
COOLEY FLOYC C	MAJ	C-0204394	C156	3
COOLEY FRED A	LTC	C-015092C	1049	3
CCOLEY HARRY A	CW3	W-2108960	1053	1
COOLEY HENRY	CW2	W-2148541	C161	1
COOLEY MARVIN G	MAJ	C-1001318	1155	1
COOLEY NORMAN E	MAJ	0-2023740	C862	1
COOLEY ORRIN F	1LT	0-1321020	1045	2
COOLEY PAUL S	CW2	W-2208454	0165	1
COOLEY RAY N	COL	0-0164815	0155	1
COOLEY RICHARD S	MAJ	0-0515539	1145	2
COOLEY THOMAS H	MAJ	C-0118568	0944	2
COOLEY THOMAS R	CPT	0-C272082	0754	2
COOLEY WARREN H	LTC	0-1043903	0464	1
COOLICAN MICHAEL J	LTC	0-0356807	1167	3
COOLICK JOHN	COL	0-0910539	C165	3
COOLIDGE FLOYD G	CPT	0-0163615	0150	3
COOLIDGE HAROLD J	MAJ	0-0925143	1045	2
COOLIDCE LYLE C	LTC	0-045C832	1157	1
COOMBE EWEN L	CPT	0-0416677	1145	1
CCOMBS FRANCIS P	MAJ	0-1020C90	C862	1
COOMBS FREDERICK	COL	0-0325927	0865	3
COOMBS JR ALBERT H	1LT	0-1041112	C349	1
COOMBS PERCY L	LTC	0-0337117	0867	3
CCOMBS WOODROW W	1LT	0-2007699	1046	2
CCOMER JOSEPH A	MAJ	0-1686673	0766	1
COOMES JR JAMES A	LTC	0-1046053	0563	1
COON HARRY W	LTC	0-0200027	0261	3
COON SIDNEY F	CPT	0-1283726	0646	2
COON WALTER P	1LT	0-0410453	1043	2
CCON WILLIAM F	CPT	0-2007226	1C62	3
CCON WILLIAM L	COL	0-0330421	1066	3
CCONE CERALD F	MAJ	0-0219713	1044	2
COONE MARGARET J	MAJ	L-0120113	0967	1
COONEN RAYMOND T	2LT	0-2007354	1045	2
CCONER ETHERICCE	MAJ	C-1647368	1163	1
CCONEY JOHN J	CW3	W-2203339	0164	1
CCONEY JCHN R	2LT	0-1057C20	0145	2
COONEY LEO A	MAJ	0-0297054	0753	3
COONEY WILLIAM H	LTC	C-0218573	0760	3
COONLEY DEAN E	COL	0-0192051	0966	2
COONRACT HARCLD L	MAJ	0-15547CC	0161	1
COONS BRADD B	LTC	0-2014328	0962	1
CCONS EARL R	LTC	0-1823266	0365	1
CCONS ELLEN F	2LT	N-0741567	0145	1
CCONS RCYAL E	CPT	0-1174541	0446	2
COOP ECNA	MAJ	N-0784493	1264	3
COOP NELCE I	LTC	0-C492338	1054	1
CCCPE RCBERT L	2LT	0-0959729	0751	1
CCOPER ACOLPH H	MAJ	C-1339565	0766	1
CCOPER ALBERT H	LTC	0-0324341	1266	3
CCOPER ANTHONY F	CW3	W-21479C4	1163	1
CCOPER BASIL P	LTC	0-0213916	0664	3
COOPER BEAUFORD O	LTC	0-01C3940	1056	3
CCOPER REMUS F	LTC	0-0922324	1167	3
CCOPER BRENT V	MAJ	C-188666E	1067	1
CCCPER CARL	WO1	W-2147652	0354	1
CCOPER CARL F	CPT	0-042C136	0144	2
CCOPER CARROLL C	LTC	0-0372416	1160	1
COOPER CECIL A	1LT	0-0960000	0361	2
COOPER CECIL P	CW2	W-2146902	0963	1
COOPER CHARLES A	CPT	0-1320433	0247	2
CCOPER CHARLIE G	CW3	W-2205382	1162	1
CECPER CLARENCE C	LTC	0-1112153	0662	1
CCOPER CURTIS	LTC	0-0403436	0156	1
COCPER DONALD R	2LT	0-1822565	C645	2
COOPER EDWARD	1LT	0-1303469	1045	2
CCOPER ECWARD H	CW3	W-2103567	0259	1
CCOPER ELTON R	MAJ	0-021C192	0164	3
COOPER EVERETT R	LTC	0-1014305	C757	1
CCOPER FRANCIS M	LTC	0-096243C	0667	3
COOPER CEORGE L	LTC	0-0243325	1065	3
COOPER GEORGE T	CPT	0-0256581	0764	3
CCOPER CERALD E	LTC	0-C359852	0166	3
CCOPER GERALD W	MAJ	C-098139C	0463	1
COOPER HAROLD L	MAJ	0-0486807	1049	1
CCOPER HARRY E	COL	0-0195473	0560	3
COOPER HENRY R	LTC	0-1041318	C861	1
CCOPER HERSTON M	MAJ	0-0241256	0245	2
COOPER HUGH R	MAJ	0-023233C	0765	3
CCOPER IRVIN F	LTC	0-01C681C	0457	3
CCOPER IVAN J	LTC	0-1037444	0361	1
CCOPER JAMES C	COL	0-0209195	1053	3
CCOPER JAMES H	LTC	0-0336819	1055	2
COOPER JAMES H	LTC	0-0673102	1066	1
CCOPER JAMES R	CW2	W-2144111	1160	1
COOPER JCHN P	LTC	0-0215942	1263	3
CCOPER JCHN B R	LTC	0-0232339	0765	3
CCOPER JOHN F	MAJ	0-0964411	0261	1
COOPER JCHN C	LTC	0-0199056	0757	1
COOPER JOHN V	1LT	0-1080271	0344	1
COOPER JCSEPH B	2LT	0-1598346	0147	1
CCOPER JOSEPH H	MAJ	0-0115691	C854	3
COOPER JR EMMETT	CPT	0-0293764	C246	2
COOPER JR JOHN W	LTC	0-0246626	0563	3
CCOPER JR RALPH W	B G	C-0266469	1165	3
COOPER JR WILLIAM H	CPT	0-0450112	C945	2
COOPER LEE	1LT	0-2008648	1154	1
COOPER LEON C	CW2	RW-2147877	0461	1
COOPER LEONARD S	CPT	0-1317495	0448	2
COOPER LESLIE M	LTC	C-0455661	C864	1
COOPER LOUIS A	LTC	0-0334434	0466	3
COOPER LOWELL M	MAJ	C-0966142	C665	1
COOPER LUTHER S	CPT	0-0494231	1048	1
COOPER MARK F	CW2	W-2105771	0547	2
COOPER MARTIN W	MAJ	0-1289549	0557	1
COOPER MELBOURNE	MAJ	0-0472512	1143	2
COOPER MICHAEL	CPT	0-179779C	0546	2
COOPER MURRAY T	CPT	0-1036240	C646	2
COOPER NATHANJ	1LT	0-0441995	1045	2
COOPER NEWSCM	COL	0-0254034	0267	3
COOPER NORMAN P	2LT	0-1305734	1044	2
COOPER NORMAN W	LTC	0-2037046	0263	1
COOPER OBIE W	MAJ	C-1703768	C360	1
COOPER OMER C	LTC	0-0282838	C164	3
COOPER OSWALD	CPT	C-0470938	C945	2
COOPER PAUL D	LTC	0-0296885	C658	2
COOPER RALPH C	MAJ	0-1893627	C667	1
COOPER RICHARC F	CPT	0-1012886	0450	1
COOPER RICHARC W	COL	0-0237470	1061	3
COOPER ROBERT C	CW2	W-2144354	C560	1
COOPER ROBERT R	LTC	0-0549712	1265	1
COOPER RUFUS A	LTC	0-0534582	1164	1
COOPER SCOTT	LTC	0-1281185	1262	1
COOPER STANLEY W	CW2	W-2146830	0261	1
COOPER THOMAS R	MAJ	C-0266049	C145	2
COOPER WALTER F	CPT	0-0477758	1048	1
COOPER WILLIAM	MAJ	0-0471116	1145	2
COOPER WILLIAM B	LTC	0-0419128	0562	1
COOPER WILLIAM J	1LT	0-1549686	0246	2
COOPER WILLIAM R	MAJ	C-1933851	1164	1
COOPER WILLIAM T	LTC	0-1294436	0965	1
COOPER WINFORD H	WO1	W-2108977	1160	1
COOPER WINSTON E	1LT	0-0510166	1151	1
COOPER WYLIE	LTC	0-0450266	1063	1
COOPER ZELIG	1LT	0-0557225	C846	2
COOPER 3RD JAMES S	MAJ	0-2036297	0960	1
COOPMAN WILLIAM C	CW4	W-2136639	1061	1
COOTS CLYDE	CW2	W-2147278	0460	1
COOVER ROBERT F	CW3	W-2203628	1163	1
COPADIS NICHOLAS C	1LT	C-2200923	0352	1
COPE ALFRED E	CW2	W-2142453	0561	1
COPE CYRIL H	2LT	0-C910023	0545	2
COPE HORIS F	CPT	0-0930060	0654	2
COPE JAMES F	CW4	W-2142696	0163	1
COPE LEE H	COL	C-0332852	0962	3
COPE OGLE R	LTC	0-1038946	0565	1
COPELAN EDGAR P	MAJ	0-2262721	C961	1
COPELAND ARTHUR J	COL	0-0289654	C265	3
COPELANC CAROL W	CPT	0-0323586	1045	1
COPELAND CHARLES A	MAJ	C-1957510	0661	1
COPELAND ELBRIDGE	MAJ	C-2019434	0465	1
COPELAND FRED M	MAJ	0-0227250	C760	3
COPELAND HAROLD R	CW3	W-2152033	1064	1
COPELAND HAROLD L	CW4	W-2106995	C665	1
COPELAND INA L	MAJ	N-0702078	0347	1
COPELAND JAMES C	MAJ	C-1031304	0762	1
COPELANC JOHN W	MAJ	C-0242955	C245	2
COPELAND JOHN W	COL	0-0247269	0167	3
COPELAND JR JOHN D	LTC	0-0264531	0560	1
COPELAND KENNETH L	MAJ	C-1108582	0165	1
COPELANC LEE R	CW3	W-2207488	0363	1
COPELANC LORD B	LTC	0-0292574	0163	1
COPELANC MARY F	CPT	N-0744657	C636	1
COPELAND MAURICE E	MAJ	0-1633774	1054	1
COPELAND RAYMOND F	LTC	0-0138765	1045	2
COPELAND RICHARD T	MAJ	C-0371610	0462	1
COPELAND ROYAL S	COL	0-0290405	C761	1
CCPELAND RUSSELL W	CW3	W-2102782	0256	1
COPELAND SHERMAN A	LTC	0-0323636	1162	1
CCPELLC FLORENCE H	MAJ	N-0722683	0264	1
COPEMAN ALBERT R	MAJ	0-1650C51	0865	1
COPENHAVER JR L L	MAJ	C-1294091	1146	2
COPENING JR FRANK L	LTC	0-0332671	0665	3
COPLAN BENJAMIN J	CPT	0-0255215	0158	3
COPLEN JCHN W	COL	0-0163145	0161	3
COPLEY ANDREW P	CPT	0-0346539	0546	2
COPP CHARLES A	LTC	0-0169342	0745	2
COPP CLARENCE W	CW3	W-2152104	0566	1
COPP JR ANDREW J	COL	C-0104498	0648	3
COPPAGE JOHN K	COL	0-0909559	1064	1
COPPAGE CRIS E	MAJ	0-1535411	0760	1
COPPARC VICTOR I	COL	0-0288624	0759	3
COPPERS NEIL T	1LT	0-0472745	0545	2
COPPINC DOMINICK	MAJ	0-1703C46	1265	1
COPPLE HARRY A	CW2	W-2149692	1157	1
COPPOCK EVERETT H	MAJ	0-1825659	0361	1
COPPOCK PAUL W	LTC	0-1018248	C267	1
COPPCLA LOUISE	2LT	N-0756731	0944	1
COPPS JAMES F	MAJ	0-0411474	0561	1
CORAY JEROME B	COL	0-0508438	1165	3
CORB MARCEL	2LT	0-0586806	0352	1
CCRBALEY LAURENCE H	MAJ	0-0187297	0554	3
CCRBE HUBERT A	LTC	0-0906987	0962	3
CORBETT EDWIN J	LTC	0-1591654	0967	3
CORBETT ELSIE H	CPT	N-0772377	0446	1
CORBETT FRANCIS J	1LT	0-2040729	0845	2
CORBETT JOHN F	LTC	0-1553613	1166	1
CCRBETT JR GEORGE C	LTC	0-0247637	0566	3
CORBETT JR JAMES J	LTC	0-1015035	1162	1
CORBETT KENNETH M	COL	0-0274041	0465	3
CORBETT MARGARET M	2LT	N-0735574	0345	1
CORBETT PAUL F	LTC	0-0405982	1264	3
CCRBETT PURCELL W	WO1	W-213997E	1145	2
CORBETT ROBERT J	CPT	0-1933830	0954	2
CORBETT WILLIAM A	CPT	0-052396C	0346	1
CORBETT WILLIAM J	MAJ	0-1170687	0565	1
CORBIN CAMCN E	CPT	0-0235341	0845	1
CORBIN FREDERICK	MAJ	0-2045176	0565	1
CORBIN JOHN R	1LT	0-1291726	0346	2
CORBIN JULES	WO1	W-2149245	1154	1
CORBIN PAUL E	MAJ	0-1289550	0560	1
CORBIN THOMAS J	COL	0-0262152	0562	3
CORBIN VIRGIL M	LTC	0-0236853	0664	3
CORBITT CLAUDE E	1LT	0-0548212	0646	2
CORBOFF JOHN J	CW3	W-22C536C	0963	2
CCRBOY JCSEPH V	1LT	0-15853C2	1045	2
CCRBY GEORGE E	MAJ	0-0138321	1055	3
CORBY HARRY C	LTC	0-0123259	0655	3
CORBY JR JCHN F	LTC	0-1169906	0463	1
CORBY RALPH F	LTC	0-0300623	1160	1
CORBY RCY A	LTC	0-0240032	0366	3
CORCORAN ECWARD M	MAJ	0-0592606	1264	1
CORCORAN GEORGE T	LTC	0-0297957	0760	1
CORCORAN JERCME J	MAJ	0-0942338	1165	1
CORCORAN JOHN R	LTC	0-0450833	1162	1
CORCORAN JOHN S	LTC	0-0353450	0865	3
CORCORAN JOSEPH A	LTC	0-0489402	1162	1
CCRCORAN JOSEPH J	CW3	W-21481C9	0565	1
CCRCORAN JR ECWARD J	1LT	0-1598029	1065	3
CORCORAN LAURENCE M	LTC	0-0370C45	0163	1
CCRCCRAN WILLIAM J	MAJ	0-1320305	0359	1
CORCOS LEON F	LTC	0-158977C	0764	1
CORO WILLIAM C	COL	0-0276083	0567	3
CORDEAN AUGUST F	LTC	0-1315796	0762	1
CORDELL CARRIE M	1LT	N-0770035	0547	1
CCRDELL HEWERL	CW3	W-214338C	0963	1
CORDELL JOE W	1LT	0-0462822	0546	2
CORDELL RAYMOND L	CPT	0-0979311	0562	1
CORDEN FREDERICK	LTC	0-1100499	0961	1
CORDER CLINTCN M	CPT	0-1580796	0654	1
CCRDER FRANK H	CPT	0-0334557	0245	1
CCRDER WILLIAM A	CW3	W-2003678	1161	3

ARMY OF THE UNITED STATES RETIRED LIST

NAME	GRADE	SVC NO	DATE RET MO YR	RET CODE
CORDER WILLIAM M	MAJ	C-0325756	C344	2
CORDERO ANTERO M	MAJ	0-1896811	C461	1
CORDES JIM C	1LT	0-0411245	C845	2
CORDES RAYMOND L	MAJ	C-0395249	0263	1
CORDES WALTER F	LTC	0-1577C45	0559	2
CORDICK CHARLES F	MAJ	C-2053917	0657	1
CORDIER VICTOR H	LTC	0-0361764	0963	1
CORDINGLY EDWIN H	LTC	C-0268078	C857	3
CORDNER CHARLES D	LTC	0-0253721	1055	3
CORDON CHARLES G	LTC	0-2035527	C366	1
CORDOVA ANTHONY C	MAJ	0-2096506	0765	1
CORDOVA JOHN B	MAJ	0-0969095	1162	1
CORDOVES WIFREDO	1LT	0-0386108	1045	2
CORDREY GEORGE F	LTC	0-0287647	C466	3
CORDREY MELVIN J	LTC	0-1587716	1162	1
CORE CARROLL B	MAJ	0-0257426	0956	3
CORE EARL F	1LT	0-0406179	0244	2
CORE EDWIN R	CPT	0-1689664	0645	2
COREY ALEXANDER	COL	0-0272917	1064	3
COREY GEORGE F	LTC	0-1100931	0360	2
COREY JR WILLIAM C	LTC	C-0542207	1063	1
COREY JULE F	LTC	0-0250482	C957	3
COREY KENNETH F	CW3	W-2142140	0359	1
CORFF MEYER	COL	0-0253288	1264	3
CORIDEN MARY H	CPT	N-0736489	C347	1
CORIGLIANO MATTHEW J	2LT	C-1031305	C245	2
CORKER NEWMAN	COL	0-0247797	C267	3
CORKHILL ROBERT K	1LT	0-1165717	C646	1
CORL ROBERT M	COL	0-0359673	0962	1
CORLESS JACK W	2LT	0-1313524	0945	2
CORLESS LEE M	COL	0-0269279	0965	3
CORLETT DONALD D	COL	C-0238482	1157	3
CORLEY BRUCE W	CW3	W-214184C	0659	1
CORLEY CHARLES G	MAJ	C-15865C8	C661	1
CORLEY JAMES F	CW2	W-3000091	0864	2
CORLEY KARL C	LTC	0-0294502	1166	3
CORLEY POMP	CPT	0-2262320	1162	1
CORLEY SAMUEL R	LTC	C-0248992	1162	3
CORLEY THOMAS J	MAJ	C-0362925	0961	1
CORLEY WILLIAM D	MAJ	0-1042525	C561	1
CORLIES MARIE H	2LT	N-0771119	0345	1
CORMACK JOSEPH M	LTC	0-0213137	0853	3
CORMAN MILLARD B	CPT	0-0510760	1048	1
CORMIER GUSTAV J	LTC	C-1109871	0266	1
CORMIER HENRY L	CPT	0-1312283	0746	1
CORMIER ULYSSE	LTC	C-0310488	C366	3
CORN EDWARD W	MAJ	0-0353841	0247	2
CORN FORREST A	MAJ	0-0475785	1044	2
CORN HORACE E	LTC	0-0226433	0564	3
CORN JAMES F	COL	C-0129126	1054	3
CORN RITA M	MAJ	N-0727112	C562	1
CORNABY LESLIE H	COL	0-0245604	1061	3
CORNAIRE RAYMOND F	LTC	0-1998389	0462	1
CORNEIL JR ROBERT F	LTC	0-0954949	1167	1
CORNEIL MARION G	MAJ	0-0931317	0263	1
CORNEL JOHN M	1LT	0-2030660	0555	1
CORNELISON HAROLD B	MAJ	C-0430406	0246	2
CORNELISON HARRY H	CW2	W-2148286	1059	1
CORNELISON JACK C	MAJ	C-1335126	0263	1
CORNELIUS GEORGE E	LTC	0-032431C	C565	3
CORNELIUS GEORGE W	MAJ	C-1053092	0264	1
CORNELIUS JONATHAN P	LTC	0-0361546	0246	2
CORNELIUS KENNETH C	CPT	0-0454347	1045	1
CORNELIUS LOWELL	MAJ	C-2025384	C462	1
CORNELIUS MARK E	CPT	0-2262671	0861	1
CORNELIUS REX	CW2	W-2142506	1062	1
CORNELIUS ROBERT J	CW2	W-3150189	1265	1
CORNELIUS WARREN C	1LT	0-1294789	0545	1
CORNELL DALE O	CPT	C-0948969	1061	1
CORNELL GLENN H	COL	0-0239232	0765	3
CORNELL HARRY L	LTC	C-1284829	0355	1
CORNELL HENRY W	COL	C-1100055	1264	3
CORNELL IRVING B	MAJ	0-2284555	1166	1
CORNELL JAMES H	CPT	0-0378620	0845	2
CORNELL KENNETH W	LTC	0-1012080	0565	1

NAME	GRADE	SVC NO	DATE RET MO YR	RET CODE
CORNELL MARK W	CW3	W-2207679	0666	1
CORNELL RAY F	1LT	0-1301112	0751	1
CORNELL RICHARD P	1LT	0-0299841	0946	2
CORNELL WALTER S	COL	0-0150002	0648	3
CORNELL WILLIAM W	MAJ	0-0280468	0264	3
CORNELL WILLIS E	LTC	0-1796234	0663	1
CORNER JR RICHARD	MAJ	0-0404583	0467	3
CORNETSKY ANTHONY F	LTC	0-1318964	0763	1
CORNETT ALAN C	LTC	0-0436902	0662	1
CORNETT BUSTER	LTC	0-0347335	0256	1
CORNETT CHARLES	LTC	0-1312667	0558	1
CORNETT EDNA MAY L	2LT	N-0700496	0439	2
CORNETT JESSE J	LTC	0-0107911	1144	2
CORNILLIE ISABELLE J	2LT	N-0801434	0946	1
CORNING BENJAMIN R	2LT	0-0502750	0944	2
CORNING GEORGE F	CPT	0-0477734	0446	2
CORNISH BRUCE B	1LT	0-1925314	C354	2
CORNISH CABELL C	COL	0-014464C	0658	3
CORNISH RUTH K	2LT	N-0720813	1044	1
CORNISH WILLIAM M	CW2	W-2145203	1153	2
CORNS JOSEPH B	LTC	0-0238496	0365	3
CORNWALL OSCAR L	MAJ	C-0116280	0150	3
CORNWALL PAUL W	CW3	W-2152451	0461	1
CORNWELL EUGENE W K	LTC	0-0857328	1266	1
CORNWELL FRANCIS E	LTC	0-0406121	0460	1
CORNWELL HAROLD J	MAJ	0-1581622	0960	1
CORNWELL JR JOHN B	CPT	0-0537383	0846	2
CORNWELL OZNI H	COL	0-0185475	0753	3
CORNWELL WILLIAM D	COL	0-0252075	0367	3
CORP JAMES H	CPT	0-0271336	1045	2
CORPENING ALBERT N	COL	0-0320631	1059	3
CORPORAN FREDERICK	LTC	0-0860100	0461	1
CORPUZ ROMUALDO D	2LT	0-0182935	0251	3
CORR JR JOSEPH J	LTC	0-1045382	C766	1
CORR WILLIAM P	COL	0-0213954	0360	3
CORRAN ROBERT L	LTC	0-0749811	0565	1
CORRE HAMERTO C	1LT	0-0890335	0258	1
CORREAL THOMAS R	LTC	0-1110429	1262	1
CORREALE WILLIAM H	LTC	0-0196483	1160	3
CORREIA EDMUND G	LTC	0-1573131	0758	1
CORRELL CHARLES L	MAJ	C-2005721	1060	1
CORRELL ERVIN T	CW3	W-2127848	1059	1
CORRELL FRANKLIN F	1LT	0-0325653	0945	2
CORRELL GERALD M	LTC	0-1037221	1161	1
CORRELL IRVIN H	MAJ	0-0534349	0965	1
CORRELL JIM E	WO1	W-2113846	0748	2
CORRELL JOSEPH T	CW3	W-2126178	1154	1
CORRELL MELVIN W	1LT	0-046848C	0745	2
CORRICK CONNELL D	MAJ	0-130028C	0365	3
CORRIGAN BURTON E	MAJ	0-1080841	0962	1
CORRIGAN EDWARD	2LT	0-0535594	0446	2
CORRIGAN ELAINE B	MAJ	N-0721251	0263	3
CORRIGAN HARVEY W	CPT	0-1584713	0747	2
CORRIGAN IRVING J	CW2	W-2150496	1060	1
CORRIGAN JAMES J	1LT	0-0191322	0758	3
CORRIGAN PAUL	MAJ	0-0329452	1045	2
CORRIGAN ROBERT F	LTC	0-0415951	1059	1
CORRIGAN ROBERT N	CPT	0-2045219	0246	2
CORRIGAN THOMAS J	MAJ	C-1638916	0562	1
CORRIN BROWNLEE S	MAJ	0-0464356	0847	1
CORRIN WILLIAM H	MAJ	0-111043C	0356	1
CORRINGTON LEWIS N	LTC	0-1016673	0165	1
CORRY JAMES W	CW2	W-2147625	0659	1
CORRY JOHN F	1LT	0-2002252	1054	1
CORSAUT EVELYN H	2LT	N-0773896	0945	1
CORSER GEORGE E	LTC	0-0484551	1054	1
CORSETTI MANUEL R	MAJ	0-1304352	0158	1
CORSO LEON	COL	0-0404852	0366	1
CORSO PHILIP J	LTC	0-104793C	0363	1
CORSON DAVID R	COL	0-0230459	0962	3
CORSON FRED J	LTC	0-0384548	0660	1
CORSON JR CLARENCE D	CW3	W-2206495	0167	1
CORSON ROY W	LTC	0-0233960	0744	2
CORSON WILLIAM	CPT	0-0306442	1045	2
CORTESE JOHN	MAJ	0-2018653	0662	1

NAME	GRADE	SVC NO	DATE RET MO YR	RET CODE
CORTHELL JR MARK A	CW4	W-2118521	1058	1
CORTRIGHT TOM	1LT	C-1290569	0545	2
CORTS GEORGE F	CPT	0-0456158	C146	2
CORUM JAMES F	MAJ	0-0944223	0565	1
CORWIN EMANUEL M	CPT	C-C285864	0543	2
CORWIN GERALD A	LTC	0-1036100	0966	1
CORWIN LEROY R	LTC	C-0148039	1055	3
CORWIN RICHARD W	LTC	C-0359553	0660	1
CORWIN THOMAS P	MAJ	C-1110431	C447	1
CORY ARTHUR M	COL	0-0287218	C767	3
CORY JR MARK E	COL	0-0314253	0563	2
CORY MAX E	MAJ	C-1766481	0946	2
CORY RUSSELL M	1LT	0-1313973	1145	2
CORYELL RALPH L	LTC	C-0221195	C961	3
CORZATT CHARLES W	MAJ	C-0985451	C665	1
CORZINE JAMES E	2LT	0-1949077	0246	2
CORZINE TROY B	1LT	0-12909C4	C744	2
COSBY CARL H	LTC	0-0383501	0657	1
COSBY EARL F	COL	E-0287325	0764	1
COSBY FRANK R	COL	0-0180405	0847	1
COSBY JR GEORGE H	B G	0-0167827	C661	3
COSBY RUFUS V	MAJ	C-0949877	0262	1
COSDEN GILBERT C	LTC	0-0343937	C261	3
COSENTINO FRANK F	MAJ	C-4051166	0967	1
COSENTINO GAETANO T	MAJ	C-095869C	0764	1
COSENTINO OSCAR	CW2	W-2209302	C966	1
COSEY VICTOR J	CW2	W-2205619	0860	2
COSGRAY HAROLD H	COL	0-0510424	C266	3
COSGROVE EDNA S	MAJ	N-0756580	0463	1
COSGROVE EMMET F	1LT	C-1640337	C249	2
COSGROVE FRANCIS K	CPT	0-1177348	C546	2
COSGROVE RICHARD A	LTC	0-0292499	1066	3
COSHEY JOHN R	CPT	0-0182446	0957	3
COSHOW GEORGE H	LTC	C-0214030	0563	3
COSHUN WILLIAM F	LTC	0-0398337	C161	1
COSKEY JACK W	CPT	0-1100933	1145	2
COSLETT CHARLES F	CW2	W-2150172	0457	1
COSLOW HAROLD H	LTC	0-0347850	0261	1
COSMAN EARL R	MAJ	C-2262840	C663	1
COSMEN FRANCIS G	COL	0-0256526	0246	2
COSNER ROBERT L	MAJ	C-2005320	0155	1
COSNER TROY L	CW3	W-2145412	0465	2
COSPER GORDON B	2LT	0-1167789	0745	2
COSPER JOHN H	COL	0-0161785	0954	2
COSS HARRY E	CPT	0-128801C	0246	1
COSSEY WOODROW V	CPT	0-0966122	1059	1
COSSICK WILLIAM	LTC	0-1306816	0863	1
COSSON CLARENCE	LTC	0-0323043	0566	3
COST CARL S	LTC	0-0178344	0552	3
COST EGBERT J	CPT	C-1017941	C462	1
COST JOHN W	LTC	0-0318165	1164	3
COSTA ALBERTA M	2LT	N-0761130	0546	2
COSTA ARTHUR J	CW2	W-2152034	C556	1
COSTA JUANITA	LTC	N-0743356	0862	1
COSTA JUNE E	1LT	N-0796856	0947	1
COSTA MICHAEL M	CW2	W-2145246	0461	1
COSTA SIERGE A	LTC	C-1949624	0266	1
COSTABILE VINCENT	CPT	0-0500351	C844	2
COSTALES VINCENT F	MAJ	C-1306707	0762	1
COSTANTINO JOSEPH S	MAJ	C-1638907	C960	1
COSTANZA HARRY J	CPT	0-0290909	0145	2
COSTANZA VINCENT F	1LT	0-1019341	0446	2
COSTAP SANTE P	LTC	0-1318138	1167	1
COSTELLO ALPHONSUS	MAJ	0-1555189	1061	1
COSTELLO CHARLES F	CPT	0-1552861	0847	1
COSTELLO EDWARD E	CW4	W-2141235	C365	1
COSTELLO EDWARD J	LTC	0-1165602	0265	1
COSTELLO JAMES B	COL	C-0917158	0257	2
COSTELLO JOHN H	WO1	W-2109509	0649	2
COSTELLO JOHN J	MAJ	C-0981229	0663	1
COSTELLO JOHN J	CW2	W-2213131	0567	1
COSTELLO PAUL J	CW4	W-2113850	1060	1
COSTELLO PHILIP J L	LTC	C-1846409	1066	3
COSTELLO SAMUEL J	LTC	C-1180156	0867	1
COSTELLO THOMAS J	1LT	C-1647798	C546	2

NAME	GRADE	SVC NO	DATE RET MO YR	RET CODE
COSTES JOSE P	1LT	0-1896465	C860	1
COSTIGAN DANIEL J	2LT	0-0442276	1C44	2
COSTIGAN HAROLD F	CPT	C-0366155	0247	2
COSTLEY ROBERT A	LTC	0-0510992	0963	3
COSTLOW WILLIAM H	LTC	0-0154132	0556	3
COSTOLC HAL P	LTC	0-0174832	0662	1
COSTON JAMES M	CPT	0-0278458	0445	2
COSTON MARY M	MAJ	L-0402413	0167	3
COSTON RALLS M	LTC	0-0195604	1162	3
COSTON TONY	CPT	0-1913620	0525	1
COTA ROBERT V	LTC	0-1035229	1060	1
COTE JOSEPH E	CW2	W-2209576	0361	1
COTE LEO J	MAJ	0-1575883	0661	1
COTE WILLIAM L	1LT	0-0972823	1058	1
COTET TROJAN I	2LT	0-1575512	0546	2
COTHAC WILLIAM Z	CPT	0-0414599	0246	2
COTHAM JR WILLIAM D	MAJ	0-1104103	0760	2
COTHES JOHN C	MAJ	0-0497171	1052	1
COTHRAN DONALD F	LTC	0-1288361	0761	1
COTHRAN ROBERT L	CW4	W-2150495	C864	1
COTNAM SIDNEY F	COL	C-0201315	0752	3
COTNER HERMAN F	LTC	0-0270558	0860	3
COTNER JR RAYMOND F	MAJ	0-2027020	1061	1
COTRONEC SALVATORE	1LT	0-1101392	0745	2
COTSENMOYER LLOYD G	MAJ	0-2015471	0666	1
COTSONIS DENUS A	MAJ	0-134175C	0961	1
COTTEN CHARLES G	MAJ	0-0159273	0551	3
COTTEN RAYMOND C	MAJ	0-0972015	0263	1
COTTER AMBROSE J	LTC	0-1846127	0966	3
COTTER CHARLES E	MAJ	0-2263311	1061	1
COTTER DANIEL S	COL	0-0242156	0465	3
COTTER HOWARD J	1LT	0-1796763	1044	2
COTTER JOHN	COL	0-0370658	1061	3
COTTER JOHN F	MAJ	C-0518947	0646	2
COTTER MICHAEL F	MAJ	0-1293556	0264	1
COTTER PAUL M	CPT	0-1298504	0146	2
COTTER WALTER H	MAJ	0-1821828	0361	1
COTTER WILLIAM H	1LT	0-1895037	0255	3
COTTER WILLIAM M	WO1	W-211528C	0748	1
COTTIER WEBSTER J	LTC	0-0262987	0665	3
COTTINGHAM BREMO T	LTC	0-0463572	0752	1
COTTINGHAM HARRY H	COL	0-033C595	0864	1
COTTINGHAM JAMES S	LTC	0-0313075	0964	3
COTTINGHAM WORTH M	2LT	0-0277262	1064	3
COTTLE NORMAN G	MAJ	0-049C237	1053	1
COTTON CHANDLER	MAJ	C-1294092	0662	1
COTTON GEORGE C	LTC	0-1557132	1262	1
COTTON JAMES	CW2	W-2141237	1054	1
COTTON JAMES M	MAJ	0-1635729	0161	1
COTTON JOHN V	MAJ	0-1044203	0764	1
COTTON LEWIS P	CPT	0-12952C2	1046	2
COTTON LOUIS H	LTC	0-0346404	1063	2
COTTON RAY E	COL	0-0165125	0851	3
COTTON WILLIAM O	LTC	0-0229623	0546	2
COTTON WILLIAM E	1LT	0-0375381	0245	2
COTTRELL ALVIN B	LTC	0-0176259	1056	3
COTTRELL CHARLES D	LTC	0-0493082	1154	1
COTTRELL HARRY P	1LT	0-0215085	0344	2
COTTRELL TURNER R	LTC	0-0222677	0660	3
COTTRELL WILLIAM W	CPT	0-163573C	0457	1
COTTRILL JR FRANK A	1LT	0-1310072	1045	2
COTTS CLIFFORD H	COL	0-0157044	0855	2
COTY PAUL M	CPT	0-1285388	0346	2
COUCH FRANK V B	COL	C-0322571	0660	1
COUCH FRANKLIN L	LTC	0-0124526	0352	3
COUCH GEORGE H F	1LT	0-1291261	0845	2
COUCH INEZ	MAJ	N-0764932	0567	1
COUCH JAMES C	2LT	0-0257457	0956	3
COUCH JAMES R	CPT	0-0988491	0761	1
COUCH MELVIN J	MAJ	0-2000028	1060	1
COUCH RAYMOND B	LTC	0-0915860	1064	1
COUCH STERLING S	MAJ	0-0999033	0867	1
COUCH WELDON M	LTC	0-0328643	0159	1
COUCHMAN HEBER	COL	0-0263480	0952	1
COUCHMAN JOHN P	MAJ	0-1183047	1064	1

NAME	GRADE	SVC NO	DATE RET MO YR	RET CODE
COUDRAY WYMAN E	COL	0-0207099	0247	1
COUGHER THOMAS F	CW4	W-2147674	0859	1
COUGHLAN VERNON H	LTC	0-0303437	1162	3
COUGHLIN DANIEL P	1LT	0-1797092	0545	2
COUGHLIN DANIEL J	MAJ	0-1319055	0361	1
COUGHLIN EDWARD J	COL	0-0483716	0566	3
COUGHLIN JOHN F	MAJ	0-2019558	1162	1
COUGHLIN LLOYD F	CW3	W-2152510	0265	1
COUGHLIN THOMAS P	MAJ	0-2006281	0165	1
COUGILL MILDRED N	MAJ	N-0772676	0963	1
COUGLE RAYMOND W	CPT	0-0450836	1061	1
COUK CLAUDE A	WO1	W-2123045	1044	2
COULAM DONALD M	CW4	W-2141536	0562	1
COULBOURN WILLIAM C	COL	0-0301299	0152	3
COULS WALTER F	WO1	W-2144905	0161	2
COULSON ARTHUR G	COL	0-0227036	0463	3
COULSON EUGENE H	2LT	0-1293724	0844	1
COULSON GEORGE H	LTC	0-0315452	0661	1
COULTER CHAN F	COL	0-0221082	1061	3
COULTER JACK W	LTC	0-1285016	0361	1
COULTER JOHN B	MAJ	0-0493015	0452	1
COULTER JOHN W	COL	0-0100282	0653	3
COULTER ROBERT	MAJ	0-1037740	0762	1
COULTER WILLIAM F	LTC	0-0364911	1054	1
COUNCIL CONWAY R	1LT	0-1039916	1150	1
COUNTERMAN HAROLD J	CW2	W-2151722	0665	1
COUNTRYMAN ROBERT N	MAJ	0-0348394	0648	3
COUNTS ERNEST L	2LT	0-2006150	0653	1
COUNTS MYRTLE I	2LT	N-0733700	0145	1
COUPE FREDERICK	CW4	W-2101560	0157	1
COUPENS JOSEPH P	MAJ	0-2262175	1061	1
COUPERUS THELMA	1LT	N-0776204	1046	1
COUPLAND RICHARD M	LTC	0-1686787	1067	1
COURAGE MAXWELL R	LTC	0-0430410	0966	1
COURAIN ROBERT C	LTC	0-1578309	0164	1
COURNOYER WILFRED W	CPT	0-0504915	1156	1
COURSEY MAURICE F	LTC	0-0450427	0557	1
COURT EVELYN W	1LT	L-0110001	0845	2
COURT JAMES W	CPT	0-1301113	0946	1
COURTEMANCHE HENRY P	MAJ	0-1103059	1053	2
COURTENAY BENTLEY	COL	0-0922370	1263	3
COURTENAY CHARLES H	WO1	W-2128823	0254	1
COURTENAY FRANK A	LTC	0-0192691	0644	2
COURTENAY JUSTIN A	COL	0-0168722	0360	3
COURTLAND ROGER	MAJ	0-0305838	0546	2
COURTNEY CHESTER C	CPT	0-0150935	1150	3
COURTNEY FRANCIS V	CPT	0-0338001	0146	2
COURTNEY HELEN P	2LT	N-0724604	0944	1
COURTNEY JOHN R	CPT	0-1996887	0340	2
COURTNEY LLOYD M	LTC	0-0515399	0763	1
COURTNEY LYNN C	LTC	0-0331729	0664	3
COURTNEY MARTIN	2LT	0-0112630	0450	3
COURTNEY NEWTON S	MAJ	0-0267795	0649	2
COURTNEY OSCEOLA S	CPT	0-1004054	0451	1
COURTNEY SAMUEL F	MAJ	0-0935061	0264	1
COURTNEY WILLIAM M	CPT	0-1102680	0956	1
COURTRIGHT ROBERT G	LTC	0-1014415	0763	1
COURTS EDWARD L	1LT	0-0347482	0144	1
COURVOISIER WILLIAM	CW2	W-2102789	0647	1
COUSINEAU IRVIN F	CPT	0-1553614	1157	2
COUSINS BERNARD F	CW3	W-2143218	0767	1
COUSINS HENRY W	MAJ	0-1016723	0364	2
COUSINS MORRIS W	LTC	0-0226614	0566	3
COUSINS RICHARD F	CPT	0-0928436	1162	1
COUSINS ROBERT O	CPT	0-2019854	0360	1
COUSINS WALLACE I	LTC	0-0162348	1060	3
COUSINS WAYNE A	LTC	0-1170329	0961	2
COUTO ANTONIO	CPT	0-0505958	0348	1
COUTURE FRANK S	1LT	0-1101394	0947	2
COUTURE JAMES F	MAJ	0-1321102	1262	1
COUTURE JOSEPH R	CPT	0-1313210	1158	1
COUTURIER EUGENE A	CW3	W-2147421	0966	1
COUVILLION YELDE	MAJ	0-0199410	1037	1
COUVILLON ANTHONY P	MAJ	0-2033582	0260	1
COVAK EDWARD L	MAJ	0-1798453	0656	1

NAME	GRADE	SVC NO	DATE RET MO YR	RET CODE
COVAULT CHARLES W	LTC	0-1596576	0765	1
COVE JOSEPH E	COL	0-0312417	0262	3
COVEL HAROLD O	2LT	0-1701676	0646	2
COVELL CRANSTON F	LTC	0-1041370	0261	1
COVELL ROBERT L	CPT	0-1302952	0546	1
COVELL SHELDON M	LTC	0-0273524	0866	3
COVELL STILLMAN D	LTC	0-0309405	0960	1
COVENEY JOHN A	MAJ	0-1302116	0662	1
COVENY JOHN P	MAJ	0-1637233	0961	1
COVERDALE RALPH T	MAJ	0-0110001	0255	3
COVERDELL VERA A	COL	0-0294862	1157	3
COVERT GEORGE W	COL	0-0532808	0364	3
COVERT GLENN O	LTC	0-1299854	0361	1
COVERT GRIFFIN J	MAJ	0-1824433	0562	1
COVINGTON ALBERT W	LTC	0-0506788	0366	3
COVINGTON AUBREY Y	COL	0-0339573	0466	3
COVINGTON D BRIAN	1LT	0-1294271	0346	2
COVINGTON DAVID L	CPT	0-0959310	0764	1
COVINGTON ELIAS W	CPT	0-0984961	0267	1
COVINGTON FEA H	MAJ	0-0385741	0346	2
COVINGTON HENRY L	LTC	0-1171592	0766	1
COVINGTON JAMES M	MAJ	0-0224100	1049	1
COVINGTON JR R W	LTC	0-0306422	1160	1
COVINGTON ROBERT E	LTC	0-0259456	0561	1
COVINGTON ROBERT L	CW3	W-2143651	0764	1
COVOTSOS CONSTANTIN	MAJ	0-2032069	0160	1
COWAN ADRIAN C	CPT	0-0498528	0545	1
COWAN AUORA W	CPT	0-1306246	1046	1
COWAN JAMES H	MAJ	0-0324194	0245	2
COWAN JOHN B	CPT	0-0252161	1160	3
COWAN JOHN D	COL	0-0244991	0461	3
COWAN JOSEPH H	CPT	0-0498122	1045	2
COWAN JR JOHN J	LTC	0-1325275	1167	3
COWAN KENNETH R	MAJ	0-1010857	1046	1
COWAN WALTER F	MAJ	0-1112632	1061	1
COWAN WILLIAM R	LTC	0-1574219	0862	1
COWAND JESSE R	MAJ	0-0272081	0247	2
COWARD ALGIER D	CW3	W-2141238	0159	1
COWARD AUBREY J	1LT	0-2005326	0761	1
COWARD JESSE M	CPT	0-0430294	0646	2
COWARD JR GEORGE S	CW3	W-2152452	0365	1
COWARD RICHARD W	COL	0-0177497	1146	2
COWART CLARENCE H	COL	0-0300438	0463	3
COWART JAMES N	CW3	W-2144333	1153	1
COWART JOHN W	MAJ	0-2262853	0764	1
COWART LEROY	LTC	0-0118448	0550	2
COWART C HIRAM	LTC	0-0295794	0961	3
COWART WALTER J	CPT	0-0259603	0266	3
COWDEN GERALD F	2LT	0-1879122	0453	2
COWDEN HARRY L	LTC	0-0229728	0161	3
COWDEN WILLIAM E	COL	0-0312707	1154	1
COWDREY CHARLES M	LTC	0-0308297	0960	1
COWELL ALVA R	1LT	0-0213700	1063	3
COWELL DAVID H	LTC	0-1051088	0567	1
COWELL WINFIELD S	CW4	W-2147745	0964	1
COWEN HENRY F	LTC	0-1061659	0662	1
COWEN HERMAN R	LTC	0-0211155	0264	3
COWGILL JOHN R	MAJ	0-1046057	0461	1
COWGILL NORMAN H	MAJ	0-1312768	0161	1
COWGILL PAUL K	LTC	0-1554702	0966	1
COWGILL RALPH R	COL	0-0142305	0648	3
COWGILL THURSTON	CPT	0-0516857	1147	1
COWGILL WILLIAM R	1LT	0-0526474	0346	2
COWHERD WILLIAM C	CPT	0-0179734	0153	3
COWHIG JOHN J	1LT	0-0496764	1157	1
COWIE ROBERT L	MAJ	0-1043303	0664	1
COWLES JR LONNIE M	1LT	0-2002064	0147	1
COWLES WALTER G	COL	0-0356539	0466	3
COWLEY EDWARD C	MAJ	0-0548840	0865	1
COWLEY JAMES F	LTC	0-1015212	0463	1
COWLEY JOHN H	CPT	0-1296000	1045	2
COWLEY LEONARD W	COL	0-0185078	0359	3
COWLEY WILLIAM F	LTC	0-0314376	0746	2
COWLING ALONZO N	CW3	W-2144024	0660	1
COWLING JR DEWEY	1LT	0-1178110	0745	2

NAME	GRADE	SVC NO	DATE RET MO YR	RET CODE
COWMAN FORREST M	LTC	0-0291854	0662	1
COWNE WILLIAM A	LTC	0-0314974	0862	1
COWSERT LEX H	LTC	0-0910665	0862	1
COX ALBERT P	COL	0-0112219	0648	3
COX ALBERT H	MAJ	0-0232549	0252	3
COX ALLEN H	MAJ	0-0150617	0555	3
COX ARTHUR A	CPT	0-0948659	0361	2
COX ARTHUR J	MAJ	0-0995627	1164	1
COX BENJAMIN J	MAJ	0-1595312	0461	1
COX BESSIE A	2LT	N-0735606	0345	1
COX BRISCOE C	LTC	0-1309348	0862	1
COX BURNS C	COL	0-0188960	0955	3
COX BURWELL H	WO1	W-2149743	1066	1
COX CARL A	CW2	W-2208814	0466	1
COX CHARLES B	LTC	0-0273363	0766	3
COX CHARLES M	1LT	0-0445088	1060	1
COX CLARENCE L	LTC	0-0251079	0346	2
COX DANIEL M	2LT	0-0462632	0544	2
COX DELBERT	LTC	0-1293385	0161	1
COX DEMMIE H	COL	0-0216765	0162	3
COX EARL W	1LT	0-0972684	0760	1
COX EARL R	LTC	0-1181847	1165	1
COX EDGAR C	CPT	0-0451236	1049	1
COX EDWARD A	MAJ	0-2026004	0762	1
COX EDWIN	COL	0-0221851	1062	3
COX EDWIN W	CPT	0-1691714	0457	2
COX ELDRIDGE H	COL	0-1577052	1165	1
COX ELMER C	LTC	0-0463357	0763	1
COX ERIC F	LTC	0-0180367	0254	3
COX EUGENE E	LTC	0-1171505	0561	1
COX FRANCES P	1LT	N-0720923	0146	1
COX FRANK A	LTC	0-1113155	0365	1
COX FRANKLIN	CPT	0-0400600	0844	2
COX FREDERIC R	CPT	0-0182811	0653	3
COX GEORGE	CPT	0-0375333	0146	2
COX GEORGE C	COL	0-0136953	1147	2
COX GEORGE F	1LT	0-0540335	1046	2
COX GEORGE E	1LT	0-1014358	1046	1
COX GERALD R	LTC	0-0339232	0246	2
COX HAROLD S	CW2	W-2205467	0563	1
COX HARRY F	MAJ	0-0323594	0159	1
COX HENRY E	COL	0-0140172	0357	3
COX HENRY F	MAJ	0-1336976	0865	1
COX HERBERT J	1LT	0-1547258	0146	2
COX HOBART C	CPT	0-1330162	0464	1
COX HOLLACE L	MAJ	0-0175848	0160	3
COX HUBERT L	CW4	W-2143840	1266	1
COX HUGH D	CW3	W-2111767	1154	1
COX HUGH J	BG	0-0244422	0853	3
COX IRVEN M	COL	0-0215126	0948	2
COX IRVIN L	CPT	0-2033631	1155	1
COX JAMES C	MAJ	0-2271532	0367	1
COX JAMES O	MAJ	0-2262824	0365	1
COX JAMES P	CPT	0-0250026	0663	3
COX JAMES S	CW3	W-2152310	0365	1
COX JOE R	MAJ	0-1177749	0463	1
COX JOHN A	CPT	0-0363734	0146	2
COX JOHN A	MAJ	0-0365124	0346	2
COX JOHN T	MAJ	0-2020791	0463	1
COX JOSEPH C	LTC	0-0293460	0351	1
COX JOSEPH D	CPT	0-0483312	1147	2
COX JOSEPH E	COL	0-0214665	0462	3
COX JOSEPH H	MAJ	0-0392697	0750	1
COX JOSEPH R	CW4	W-2144338	0967	1
COX JR EDGAR E	1LT	0-1295834	0846	2
COX JR GEDDES M	CPT	0-1020078	1167	1
COX JR HERBERT A	LTC	0-1824962	0864	1
COX JR HERMAN G	LTC	0-0260864	0645	2
COX JR HOMER J	CW3	W-2152372	0365	1
COX JR JAMES B	CPT	0-0337675	0146	2
COX JR JAMES W	MAJ	0-1913493	0366	1
COX JR JOHN P	LTC	0-1044789	0763	1
COX JR JOSEPH E	LTC	0-1550992	0367	3
COX JR OLIVER S	CPT	0-2010610	1065	1
COX JR WILLIAM F	1LT	0-1118866	0547	2

NAME	GRADE	SVC NO	DATE RET MO YR	RET CODE
COX LAWRENCE H	COL	0-0198411	0352	3
COX LENDAL D	CPT	0-0533008	1048	1
COX LEON C	MAJ	0-0198123	0648	3
COX LEONARD P	WO1	W-2150202	0754	1
COX LEONE M	2LT	N-0783020	1045	1
COX LLOYD J	MAJ	0-1283917	0447	1
COX LOGAN W	LTC	0-1295513	0462	1
COX LOUIE C	MAJ	0-0403556	0565	1
COX MARGARET I	1LT	N-0756909	1045	1
COX MARVIN W	CW2	W-2208107	0962	1
COX MARY L	2LT	N-0729027	0844	1
COX MELVIN R	LTC	0-0440736	0951	1
COX MICHAEL J	MAJ	0-0532817	0446	2
COX NORMAN F	WO1	W-2107891	0446	2
COX NORWOOD L	WO1	W-2146226	0159	2
COX OBERT T	1LT	0-0291179	0542	2
COX OMAR L	CPT	0-0492052	0149	1
COX OSBORNE S	LTC	0-0365868	0767	1
COX PHILIP J	1LT	0-0517900	0444	1
COX ROBERT L	COL	0-0156078	1156	3
COX ROBERT M	1LT	0-0496672	0946	1
COX ROBERT W	LTC	0-1594739	0865	1
COX ROWLAND E	MAJ	0-0970235	0267	1
COX ROY H	LTC	0-0167220	0945	2
COX ROY L	1LT	0-0969451	0551	1
COX ROY M	2LT	0-1080526	0245	2
COX ROY W	LTC	0-0195109	0252	3
COX RUBYE T	2LT	N-0764042	0847	1
COX SAMUEL V	LTC	0-1035642	0863	1
COX SARA S	1LT	N-0764307	0745	1
COX SHULER R	MAJ	0-0331223	0363	1
COX SR WILLIAM R	CW2	W-2149288	1059	1
COX THOMAS E	MAJ	0-1582173	0554	2
COX THOMAS M	2LT	0-2035078	0644	2
COX TOM C	CPT	0-0890133	1047	1
COX VERNON G	MAJ	0-0159161	0855	3
COX WARREN H	CPT	0-1541932	1044	2
COX WILBUR L	MAJ	0-1986196	0465	1
COX WILLARD W	CW3	W-2149817	0563	1
COX WILLIAM O	LTC	0-0227261	0265	3
COX WILLIAM F	CW2	W-2005326	0961	2
COX WILLIAM R	CPT	0-0236315	0253	3
COX WILLIAM R	MAJ	0-0581545	0457	1
COX WILLIAM S	MAJ	0-1637873	0258	1
COX 4TH THOMAS R	1LT	0-1646482	1145	2
COXE DWIGHT E	CW2	W-2142515	0160	1
COXE ROBERT E	LTC	0-0478175	0262	2
COXEY WYNATT F	2LT	0-1296426	0846	2
COXWELL JAMES M	CW3	W-2143738	0367	1
COYKENDALL FAYETTE L	MAJ	0-0247429	0863	1
COYLE CELLA M	CPT	N-0787858	0449	2
COYLE JOHN F	LTC	0-1285204	0366	1
COYLE JOHN J	MAJ	0-1061660	0357	1
COYLE JOHN W	CPT	0-1297688	0746	1
COYLE JR FRANCIS J	MAJ	0-2021166	0662	2
COYLE JR WILBUR F	LTC	0-0207405	1263	3
COYLE LOUELLA	1LT	N-0730730	0849	2
COYLE MICHAEL	CPT	0-1913817	0621	1
COYLE WILLIAM G	MAJ	0-0967408	1265	1
COYNE CHARLES A	CPT	0-1289551	0461	1
COYNE CLARENCE W	LTC	0-0386807	0966	1
COYNE EDWARD J	LTC	0-0288789	0646	2
COYNE FLOYD P	LTC	0-1282768	1065	1
COYNE JR JOHN W	CPT	0-0369215	1045	2
COYNE THOMAS J	CPT	0-1043907	1153	1
COYNE VINCENT P	BG	0-0236410	0562	3
COZART JESSE C	CW3	W-2206122	1165	1
COZART WILLIAM A	CPT	0-1303856	0146	2
COZENS BRADBURY R	CPT	0-1052725	0562	1
COZINE HENRY J	LTC	0-1637874	0856	1
COZINE WILLIAM K	CPT	0-0901935	0946	2
COZORT WILLIAM W	MAJ	0-1177352	0157	1
COZZATI BRUNO J	LTC	0-2025750	1064	1
CRABB JR LLOYD A	CPT	0-0540742	0846	2
CRABBE LELAND F	CW3	W-2144485	0164	1

NAME	GRADE	SVC NO	DATE RET MO YR	RET CODE
CRABBS FAYE L	2LT	0-2288327	0355	3
CRABILL CADMUS F	LTC	0-1649261	0667	1
CRABLE JACK B	MAJ	0-1556707	1162	1
CRABTREE CLARENCE	LTC	0-1305017	0166	1
CRABTREE DON R	MAJ	0-1917637	0663	1
CRABTREE DWIGHT E	MAJ	0-0293551	0757	3
CRABTREE EDWIN	1LT	0-0964036	1057	1
CRABTREE ERNEST B	CW3	W-2144944	0960	1
CRABTREE HOWARD W	CW3	W-2152206	0665	1
CRABTREE JOHN W	LTC	0-1101396	0666	1
CRABTREE MATTHEW I	COL	0-0266557	1058	3
CRABTREE PAUL F	CW3	W-2210317	0766	1
CRABTREE SAMUEL J	CPT	0-2024247	0459	2
CRABTREE VERNON D	CPT	0-0970533	0761	1
CRACKEL GEORGE E	LTC	0-1290720	0461	1
CRACRAFT MCLURE	COL	0-0319106	0163	1
CRADDOCK CLARENCE E	MAJ	0-0156076	0752	3
CRADDOCK FRANCIS R	MAJ	0-0287301	0947	2
CRADDOCK GEORGE J	2LT	0-1053095	0545	2
CRADDOCK IRA	CPT	0-0450005	0753	1
CRADDOCK ROBERT R	LTC	0-0291076	0562	1
CRADDUCK HALLEY H	1LT	0-1014349	0248	2
CRAFT CHARLES W	LTC	0-1300283	0966	1
CRAFT GEORGE W	LTC	0-0260492	0266	3
CRAFT LEE J	MAJ	0-0450116	1058	1
CRAFT MARTIN M	CPT	0-0473923	1047	1
CRAFT RONALD M	LTC	0-1824963	0965	1
CRAFTON DENNIS H	LTC	0-1331378	1067	1
CRAFTS CLAYTON E	LTC	0-0292094	0161	3
CRAGER JOSEPH L	COL	0-1167794	0161	1
CRAGG JOHN B	MAJ	0-1038568	0463	1
CRAGG WALTER	1LT	0-1301441	1145	2
CRAGG WILBUR W	MAJ	0-0180915	1149	3
CRAGHEAD MELVIN W	LTC	0-0415961	0863	1
CRAGIN ROBERT B	LTC	0-0193710	0346	2
CRAGO FELIX H	MAJ	0-0359430	0446	2
CRAGON HENRY D	COL	0-0308800	1263	3
CRAIG ALBERT	LTC	0-1643904	1061	1
CRAIG ALLAN C	CW3	W-2151688	0567	1
CRAIG ASHTON M	CW3	W-2152886	0960	1
CRAIG BENJAMIN K	1LT	0-1289216	0844	2
CRAIG BERTIE F	COL	0-0322720	0954	1
CRAIG CHARLES	CPT	0-0164460	0627	1
CRAIG CHASTEEN B	MAJ	0-1296328	0957	1
CRAIG DAVID K	LTC	0-0467337	0767	1
CRAIG DAVID M	COL	0-0249272	1058	1
CRAIG DONALD E	1LT	0-0534261	0746	2
CRAIG DONALD F	MAJ	0-1546940	1162	1
CRAIG DONALD J	MAJ	0-1013919	1265	1
CRAIG EDWARD W	LTC	0-0332192	0460	1
CRAIG ELMER C	1LT	0-0485258	0844	2
CRAIG HARRY M	COL	0-0250539	1261	1
CRAIG HERBERT B	LTC	0-0140187	0451	1
CRAIG HOMER G	MAJ	0-1047933	0164	1
CRAIG JAMES	MAJ	0-1036923	0562	1
CRAIG JAMES A	MAJ	0-0351086	0660	1
CRAIG JAMES R	MAJ	0-0452322	0660	1
CRAIG JR CHARLES R	CPT	0-1926603	1163	1
CRAIG JR HARRY N	LTC	0-1797959	0364	1
CRAIG JR JAMES A	LTC	0-1285555	0546	1
CRAIG JR JAMES L	COL	0-0316415	0563	1
CRAIG LAWRENCE W	MAJ	0-1311616	0457	1
CRAIG LEE E	CPT	0-0503712	0146	1
CRAIG LESLIE L	CPT	0-0924744	0744	2
CRAIG MALCOLM H	CW2	W-2205990	1163	1
CRAIG MAX W	MAJ	0-0487811	0854	1
CRAIG ORAN W	1LT	0-0387517	0345	2
CRAIG PAUL F	CPT	0-0493698	0445	2
CRAIG PHILIP C	LTC	0-1573830	0861	1
CRAIG REGINALD S	COL	0-0297500	0457	3
CRAIG RICHARD J	CW3	W-2148920	0263	1
CRAIG ROBERT	CW3	W-2146852	1262	1
CRAIG ROBERT E	CW3	W-2149105	0964	1
CRAIG ROBERT J	COL	0-0263226	1264	3
CRAIG ROBERT M	CPT	0-1323542	0452	1
CRAIG RONALD W	CW4	W-2105115	0359	1
CRAIG ROWLAND T	MAJ	0-0409330	0662	2
CRAIG SAMUEL E	LTC	0-0225529	1163	3
CRAIG SIDNEY C	CW3	W-2147646	0163	1
CRAIG SR CECIL P	CPT	0-1172425	1062	2
CRAIG THOMAS H	1LT	0-0504172	0147	1
CRAIG THOMAS K	MAJ	0-2262305	0763	1
CRAIG WILLIAM H	1LT	0-0420334	1046	2
CRAIG WILLIAM H	MAJ	0-1574663	1165	1
CRAIG WINIFRED S	MAJ	N-0768231	0866	1
CRAIGHILL EOLEY	COL	0-0335063	0754	3
CRAIGO RICHARD L	COL	0-0279816	0564	3
CRAIN ALFRED P	MAJ	0-0399750	0444	1
CRAIN BERNARD C	CPT	0-0355261	0446	2
CRAIN CHARLES N	MAJ	0-0493744	1054	1
CRAIN HALL S	COL	0-0202070	0955	3
CRAIN JR ROBERT F	CPT	0-4011025	0660	2
CRAIN L O	LTC	0-0229346	0847	2
CRAIN MARVIN E	CW3	W-2142753	0661	1
CRAIN RAY	CPT	0-1320509	1046	2
CRAIN TAFT F	CW2	W-2151156	1060	2
CRAIN VERNON J	CW2	W-2151801	0461	1
CRAIN WILLIAM H	1LT	0-0538887	1046	2
CRAIN WILLIAM H	CPT	0-0948728	0161	1
CRAINE NORBERT L	MAJ	0-0482643	0250	1
CRALL HERBERT D	COL	0-0235629	0147	1
CRALLE JEFFERSON	COL	0-0911508	0757	2
CRAM GEORGE D	LTC	0-0204400	0651	3
CRAMER CARL H	MAJ	0-0450428	0756	1
CRAMER CHARLES W	COL	0-0179712	0147	2
CRAMER EARL C	MAJ	0-0468867	0246	1
CRAMER FREDERICK	MAJ	0-0339308	0165	1
CRAMER HOWARD A	LTC	0-0207467	0152	3
CRAMER HOWARD K	CW4	W-2001943	0563	3
CRAMER JOHN R	LTC	0-1042045	0262	1
CRAMER JOHN W	COL	0-0242037	0256	3
CRAMER JR JOHN W	CW2	W-2152453	0161	1
CRAMER LEW W M	CPT	0-1844775	1057	2
CRAMER MERRITT	MAJ	0-0476937	0154	1
CRAMER NEIL F	LTC	0-0888241	0860	1
CRAMER WALTER R	COL	0-0134052	0552	1
CRAMER WILLIS A	1LT	0-1794786	0245	2
CRAMPTON ALEXANDER	MAJ	0-0421201	0345	2
CRAMSIE KENNETH J	COL	0-0238103	0760	1
CRANAGE JOSEPH L	MAJ	0-0383782	0663	1
CRANDALL AUSTIN R	MAJ	0-1337815	0467	1
CRANDALL CHARLES A	CW3	W-2136028	1060	1
CRANDALL DONALD L	LTC	0-1289699	0366	1
CRANDALL EUGENE F	LTC	0-1042003	0762	1
CRANDALL EVERETT F	MAJ	0-1324220	1263	1
CRANDALL FRANK B	MAJ	0-0198826	1043	2
CRANDALL GEORGE A	COL	0-0261467	0966	3
CRANDALL HUBERT E	CPT	0-0348191	0344	2
CRANDALL JESSE L	LTC	0-0275124	0956	3
CRANDALL KERN C	COL	0-0148897	1156	3
CRANDALL RICHARD	LTC	0-1061345	0464	1
CRANDALL ROBERT A	MAJ	0-0272794	0566	3
CRANDELL MALCOLM S	MAJ	0-2029189	1262	1
CRANDELL OLIN H	CPT	0-0274828	0962	3
CRANDELL WILLIAM R	CW2	W-2148202	0459	1
CRANE ALLEN R	COL	0-0150038	0453	3
CRANE CHARLES T	1LT	0-2209101	0952	2
CRANE COY A	MAJ	0-0994251	0365	1
CRANE DEWEY L	CW4	W-2144945	0567	1
CRANE DONALD R	LTC	0-1036487	0162	1
CRANE FRANK S	LTC	0-1795769	0261	1
CRANE FRED F	CPT	0-1000037	0946	1
CRANE GEORGE E	LTC	0-0320884	0446	2
CRANE HENRY M	CPT	0-0887403	0546	2
CRANE JAMES L	LTC	0-0324195	1052	1
CRANE JAMES L	LTC	0-0468978	0754	1
CRANE JOHN W	MAJ	0-0397226	0463	1
CRANE JOHN W	MAJ	0-1951078	0762	1
CRANE JR CLYDE C	1LT	0-1113650	0644	2
CRANE JR GEORGE H	1LT	0-1303676	0447	2
CRANE JR HERMAN T	MAJ	0-0704828	1060	1
CRANE LAWRENCE M	LTC	0-1294439	0266	1
CRANE NORMAN T	LTC	0-1692149	0146	1
CRANE RICHARD O	CW3	W-2149869	1064	1
CRANE TERRILL	LTC	0-0262570	0765	3
CRANE WILLIAM H	1LT	0-0535870	1145	2
CRANEY EDWARD R	LTC	0-1294626	0462	1
CRANFIELD REGINALD F	CPT	0-1320107	0346	2
CRANFILL HARVEY L	LTC	0-1051919	1062	1
CRANFORD JAMES R	LTC	0-0325470	0760	1
CRANFORD PAUL H	CPT	0-0546027	0663	2
CRANGLE EDWARD C	1LT	0-1999193	0247	2
CRANK CHARLES R	CW3	W-2122911	0859	1
CRANK MELVIN N	LTC	0-1309882	0760	1
CRANK RAWSER P	MAJ	0-0499857	0246	2
CRANKSHAW DAUNE W	LTC	0-0128967	0546	1
CRANKSHAW EDWARD D	MAJ	0-1535876	0164	1
CRANMER EUGENE W	CPT	0-0501090	0747	1
CRANMER RAYMOND H	MAJ	0-0497278	1150	1
CRANNA WILLIAM R	CW4	W-2126826	1263	1
CRAND JOHN A	1LT	0-1107369	0644	2
CRANSHAW WILLIAM	MAJ	0-0400745	1048	1
CRANSTON DONALD J	CPT	0-0207446	0253	3
CRANWELL JOHN P	LTC	0-0331482	0564	3
CRAPO EDWARD	COL	0-0164471	0146	1
CRAPO ISAAC A	COL	0-0187598	0650	3
CRAPSON CARMON L	MAJ	0-2032275	0664	1
CRARY ELISHA A	COL	0-0281006	0765	3
CRASS CLINTON W	CPT	0-0295669	0747	1
CRASSON SAMUEL L	CPT	0-0210607	0145	2
CRATHERN CHARLES F	LTC	0-0471073	0147	2
CRAVATAS JOSEPH H	LTC	0-0265910	0165	3
CRAVEN C L	CW4	W-2135338	1155	1
CRAVEN HAROLD E	COL	0-1304349	0865	1
CRAVEN JOHN C	LTC	0-0959871	1067	1
CRAVEN LAWRENCE A	CW4	W-2145123	0660	1
CRAVEN ROBERT W	COL	0-0190507	1053	1
CRAVEN WAYNE L	MAJ	0-0969704	1167	1
CRAVENS CHARLES	CPT	0-2011618	0663	1
CRAVENS IRA D	CPT	0-1183676	0846	1
CRAVENS JAMES J	MAJ	0-1177752	1062	1
CRAVENS MILDRED R	1LT	N-0702455	1042	1
CRAVER RICHARD L	LTC	0-0450429	0357	1
CRAVIS ROBERT M	1LT	0-1280813	1045	1
CRAWFORD ALBERT E	COL	0-0255502	0557	3
CRAWFORD ANDY W	COL	0-0275777	0364	3
CRAWFORD BENJAMIN B	MAJ	0-2000723	1160	1
CRAWFORD CHARLES O	LTC	0-1285205	0861	1
CRAWFORD CHARLES J	LTC	0-0297835	1061	2
CRAWFORD CHESTER H	LTC	0-1314449	0665	1
CRAWFORD CHESTER H	CW4	W-2115882	1057	1
CRAWFORD CLYDE L	WO1	W-2146228	0958	1
CRAWFORD DAVID J	MAJ	0-1306247	0161	1
CRAWFORD DAVID M	CW3	W-2152908	0162	1
CRAWFORD DONALD D	LTC	0-0175697	0652	3
CRAWFORD DONALD D	COL	0-0315234	0859	1
CRAWFORD EARL W	1LT	0-2040788	0645	2
CRAWFORD EDWARD W	COL	0-0366437	0961	1
CRAWFORD ELZIE L	CPT	0-1297845	0954	1
CRAWFORD FLOYD W	1LT	0-1638923	1145	2
CRAWFORD FRANK W	COL	0-0174604	0359	3
CRAWFORD FRED B	LTC	0-0157394	1154	3
CRAWFORD GARRETT O	MAJ	0-1342160	0365	1
CRAWFORD GEORGE D	CPT	0-0188965	0644	2
CRAWFORD GEORGE W	LTC	0-0260012	1166	3
CRAWFORD GEORGE W	CW2	W-2207727	1263	1
CRAWFORD GLEN M	1LT	0-1294094	1045	2
CRAWFORD GLENN O	COL	0-0214144	0456	3
CRAWFORD HARRY E	CPT	0-0184889	0344	2
CRAWFORD HERMAN H	CW3	W-2141907	0261	1
CRAWFORD IAN C	2LT	0-1556403	1243	2
CRAWFORD JAMES N	LTC	0-0174289	0454	3
CRAWFORD JAMES R	WO1	W-2103687	0745	1
CRAWFORD JAMES T	LTC	0-1944426	0667	1
CRAWFORD JESSIE E	MAJ	N-0702333	1060	1
CRAWFORD JOHN A	COL	0-0325261	1057	2
CRAWFORD JOHN D	CPT	0-1704917	0648	2
CRAWFORD JOHN E	CPT	0-0105623	0145	2
CRAWFORD JOHN N	CW2	W-2208815	1164	1
CRAWFORD JOHN T	COL	0-0237752	0962	3
CRAWFORD JOSEPH C	LTC	0-0191987	0462	3
CRAWFORD JOSEPH H	COL	0-0311190	0465	3
CRAWFORD JR GLEN C	1LT	0-1015125	1045	2
CRAWFORD JR JOHN C	LTC	0-1042532	0961	1
CRAWFORD KENNETH	MAJ	0-1824587	0163	1
CRAWFORD KENNETH F	CPT	0-1297500	1161	2
CRAWFORD LEO F	LTC	0-1288011	0859	1
CRAWFORD LETCHER	LTC	0-1313574	0463	1
CRAWFORD LINDSAY J	LTC	0-1643345	1066	3
CRAWFORD LLOYD C	COL	0-0285553	1161	2
CRAWFORD MARSHALL F	LTC	0-1036928	0267	1
CRAWFORD MAYNARD C	MAJ	0-0234826	0643	2
CRAWFORD OTTO M	MAJ	0-1011382	0757	1
CRAWFORD RALPH C	LTC	0-0294239	0446	2
CRAWFORD RANSOME H	CW4	W-2114336	0257	1
CRAWFORD RAY	WO1	W-2215389	0465	1
CRAWFORD RICHARD F	2LT	0-0415557	0145	2
CRAWFORD RICHARD G	LTC	0-0463004	0857	1
CRAWFORD ROBERT E	CPT	0-0488223	0247	1
CRAWFORD ROBERT M	CW3	W-2144612	0261	1
CRAWFORD ROBERT N	LTC	0-0325820	0747	2
CRAWFORD ROBERT P	LTC	0-1324585	0263	1
CRAWFORD SAMUEL T A	LTC	0-0332912	0860	2
CRAWFORD THOMAS B	MAJ	0-0225830	0365	3
CRAWFORD THOMAS K	MAJ	0-1928184	0267	1
CRAWFORD VERNE D	CPT	0-2033569	0462	1
CRAWFORD WALTER A	MAJ	0-0271351	1160	1
CRAWFORD WILLIAM H	COL	0-0273860	0156	3
CRAWFORD WILLIAM H	CPT	0-1001532	0146	2
CRAWFORD WILLIAM L	LTC	0-2042774	1054	1
CRAWFORD WILLIAM M	LTC	0-0323841	1056	3
CRAWFORD WM C	WO1	W-2106060	0444	2
CRAWLEY HAROLD G	LTC	0-1107881	0862	2
CRAWLEY HORACE L	MAJ	0-2102618	1167	1
CRAWLEY MANUEL E	1LT	0-1594114	0348	2
CRAWLEY NELSON M	1LT	0-1825156	1045	2
CRAWLEY SR LESLIE L	LTC	0-1283032	1161	1
CRAYNE BRUCE A	LTC	0-0246443	0360	1
CRAYS CHARLES G	CW3	W-2144425	1063	1
CREAGHE JOHN S	1LT	0-1325827	1145	2
CREAL WILLIAM R	MAJ	0-0341456	1145	2
CREAMER FORREST W	LTC	0-0252809	0960	2
CREAMER GEORGE M	CPT	0-0394956	0147	1
CREAMER JOHN S	CW2	W-2151773	0262	1
CREAN JULIAN J	1LT	0-0497819	1159	1
CREARY WILLIAM C	LTC	0-0228964	0663	1
CREASEY CHARLES W	CPT	0-0450704	1057	1
CREASEY JR GEORGE S	MAJ	0-0245242	0860	3
CREASON LYNN A	1LT	0-1165170	0444	2
CREATI JOSEPH A	LTC	0-1292839	0656	2
CRECELIUS OWEN L	COL	0-0221208	0955	3
CRECY WARREN G H	MAJ	0-2011754	0165	2
CREDE WILLIAM A	COL	0-0142394	0648	3
CREECH CLARENCE M	COL	0-0310238	0463	3
CREECH JOHN R	CPT	0-2019296	0161	1
CREECH WHITLEY	WO1	W-2120267	0553	1
CREED RITA M	1LT	N-0721453	0847	1
CREEDON FRANCIS O	LTC	0-0204937	0359	2
CREEGAN MARGARET M	CPT	N-0741022	0355	2
CREEGAN MATTHEW T	CPT	0-1948572	0759	1
CREEGAN THOMAS F	LTC	0-0450687	0765	1
CREEK HARRY J	CPT	0-1877857	0762	1
CREEKMUR ARNOLD J	CW2	W-2154664	1160	1
CREEL CLOYE L	MAJ	N-0726965	0364	1
CREEL JAMES C	LTC	0-0247960	0558	1
CREEL JR E D	CPT	0-1542341	0667	2
CREEL JR LAWRENCE E	1LT	0-0390506	0445	2
CREEL NORVEL E	MAJ	0-1056678	0258	1
CREELEY MATTHEW W	CW2	W-2205499	1165	1
CREELY ANDREW J	MAJ	0-0103503	0455	3

NAME	GRADE	SVC NO	DATE RET MO YR	RET CODE
CREESY CLYDE K	LTC	O-0111641	0954	3
CREGG JAMES L	LTC	O-0277857	0365	3
CREGO CLYDE A	LTC	O-1582227	1061	2
CREIGH CARL W	LTC	O-0920556	0163	1
CREIGHTON GEORGE W	LTC	O-2018654	0765	1
CREIGHTON LUTHER J	LTC	O-0325373	0367	3
CREIGHTON MILLAGE E	CW2	W-2102797	0147	1
CREIGHTON SR W S	CW2	W-2152926	0161	1
CREIGHTON WILBUR F	MAJ	O-0233706	1266	3
CREITH WILLIAM L	CW3	W-2148486	0464	1
CRELLIN STANLEY R	CW4	W-2002415	0264	1
CRENSHAW CALVIN L	CW4	W-2150901	0765	1
CRENSHAW CARLTON	MAJ	O-0237360	0465	3
CRENSHAW WILLIAM J	2LT	O-0538514	0545	2
CRERACK GEORGE	CW4	W-2131251	0559	1
CREPEAU CHARLES P	LTC	O-1291781	0861	2
CRESCENTA WILLIAM G	LTC	O-1544843	1065	3
CRESON ROBERT F	LTC	O-1341518	0767	1
CRESPO DEMETRIO	LTC	O-0230270	0156	3
CRESS CHARLES M	CW2	W-2146166	0760	1
CRESS HOWARD R	COL	O-0224271	0656	3
CRESS JAMES B	M G	O-0138001	0151	1
CRESS ROBERT E	CPT	O-0354685	0446	2
CRESSE HENRY A	MAJ	O-0263510	0954	3
CRESSEND JOHN B	2LT	O-1053548	0251	2
CRESSLER HARRY S	COL	O-0234783	1157	1
CRESSMAN HOWARD A	COL	O-0263125	1067	3
CRESSON KERMIT I	MAJ	O-2043299	1061	1
CRESSY ROBERT N	MAJ	O-1580809	0364	1
CRESTA GORI M	2LT	O-1054522	0944	2
CRETIN THEODORE D	MAJ	O-1688766	0265	1
CRETTON CLAYTON E	CW2	W-2215229	0766	1
CREVAR NICHOLAS	LTC	O-2042860	0367	1
CREVELING GUY L	CW2	RW-2209620	0166	1
CREVELT JAMES R	MAJ	O-0455673	0961	1
CREVENSTEN DANIEL C	LTC	O-1945336	0563	1
CREW WOODROW W	CW2	W-2152105	1157	1
CREWE JAMES A	COL	O-0367440	1060	1
CREWES SIDNEY L	CPT	O-0330275	0145	2
CREWS BOBBY F E	CPT	O-4006661	1066	1
CREWS CHARLES F	CPT	O-1919025	0254	2
CREWS DARIUS J	MAJ	O-0406905	1060	1
CREWS FRANK D	CPT	O-1325479	0547	2
CREWS HOWARD J	CW3	W-2203631	1063	1
CREWS JAMES R	CW3	W-2141239	0760	1
CREWS LYTLE F	CPT	O-0180563	0455	3
CREWS NORMAN C	MAJ	O-0259504	1066	3
CREWS PHILLIP W	1LT	O-5209024	1162	2
CREWS RALPH W	MAJ	O-0483740	0162	1
CREWS RUFUS	LTC	O-0370829	1066	3
CREWS WILLIAM H	LTC	O-1055567	0263	2
CRIBBINS JOSEPH P	LTC	O-1030967	0766	1
CRIBBS EDWARD S	LTC	O-1895791	0766	1
CRICE MILTON M	LTC	O-0271740	1162	3
CRICH JACK M	CW2	W-2153306	0660	1
CRICH WALTER H	COL	O-0325396	0852	1
CRICHFIELD MARCUS R	LTC	O-0289719	1057	3
CRICHTON DAVID F	MAJ	O-1324757	1060	1
CRICKMORE ISAAC C	MAJ	O-1302606	1165	1
CRIDER FRANK B	COL	O-0220902	0162	3
CRIDER HUBERT P	LTC	O-1579520	0763	1
CRIDER JR WILLIAM V	LTC	O-1050616	0566	1
CRIFASI PHILIP G	MAJ	O-1179694	1064	1
CRIGER RALPH D	LTC	O-0327538	0666	3
CRIGGER HARRY G	2LT	O-1186378	0950	2
CRIGHTON JOHN C	LTC	O-1945108	0164	3
CRIGLER THOMAS H	CPT	O-0234407	0262	3
CRILE HERMAN R	MAJ	O-0179668	0145	2
CRILEY FRANK W	CPT	O-1014038	0252	1
CRILL GEORGE H	CPT	O-0366396	1045	2
CRIM ERNEST M	CPT	O-0495925	1059	1
CRIM JOSEPH W	LTC	O-0290798	0148	1
CRIMMINS JAMES E	LTC	O-1698041	0961	1
CRIMMINS JOHN P	LTC	O-1112635	0961	1
CRIPE HERBERT W	LTC	O-0349602	0462	3

NAME	GRADE	SVC NO	DATE RET MO YR	RET CODE
CRIPPS GEORGE W	LTC	O-1041322	0656	1
CRIPPS JACKN	CW2	W-2142754	0957	1
CRIQUI HERBERT L	2LT	O-1533528	1043	2
CRISE WILLIAM F	LTC	O-1114081	0763	1
CRISFIELD JACK G	MAJ	O-1289553	1061	1
CRISLIP GENE	LTC	O-1339520	1165	1
CRISMAN GERALD W	1LT	O-1036488	1045	2
CRISMAN JR SEWELL W	LTC	O-0324910	0246	2
CRISMON LEO J	2LT	O-1316991	1143	2
CRISOSTOMO SERRY S	CW3	W-2150960	1066	1
CRISP CHARLES F	CW2	W-2144986	0657	1
CRISP JESSE M	1LT	O-1645726	0845	1
CRISP MELVIN L	1LT	O-0157546	1125	1
CRISP THOMAS F	1LT	O-1048730	0945	2
CRISPIN WILFRED T	LTC	O-2055371	1162	1
CRISSEY GILBERT W	LTC	O-0165060	0750	3
CRISSMAN ALONZO S	CPT	O-0365857	0645	2
CRISSMAN LEEROY A	1LT	O-2037204	0846	1
CRIST ALLARD D	1LT	O-1305524	0744	2
CRIST JERRY C	COL	O-0347135	0847	1
CRIST JOSEPH A	COL	O-0266431	1057	3
CRIST JR FRANCIS M	MAJ	O-0383997	0958	1
CRIST MILTON B	LTC	O-0468650	1263	3
CRISTE ANITA F	2LT	N-0726058	0244	1
CRISTOFENE FELIX E	CPT	O-0111244	0656	3
CRITCHLOW GEORGE C	MAJ	O-0291243	0657	1
CRITES CHARLES R	MAJ	O-2263335	0865	1
CRITTENDEN BRUCE S	2LT	O-1119164	1045	2
CRITTENDEN CHARLES E	1LT	O-1553794	0545	1
CROAD ROBERT G	LTC	O-1118867	1265	1
CROAK LEE M	MAJ	O-1641100	0258	1
CROAN MELVIN	COL	O-0127275	0648	3
CROAN MELVIN L	1LT	O-1995395	0647	2
CROAS PAUL R	WO1	W-2114612	1150	2
CROASDALE EMMETT F	CW3	W-2153278	1262	1
CROCHETIERE NORMAN R	1LT	O-1324009	0248	1
CROCKATT GEORGE W	COL	O-0144673	1051	3
CROCKER ALFRED	MAJ	O-0271236	0365	3
CROCKER ALVIN F	LTC	O-0250571	1058	1
CROCKER ATHEL W	LTC	O-1285714	0661	1
CROCKER FRANCES O	1LT	N-0742257	1145	2
CROCKER JOHN W	LTC	O-0454608	0257	1
CROCKER JR JOSEPH P	LTC	O-0279607	1161	1
CROCKER JR WALTER C	COL	O-0155064	1058	3
CROCKER LYMAN F	MAJ	O-1110434	0960	1
CROCKER RADFORD L	MAJ	O-1341858	0761	1
CROCKER REGINALD E	LTC	O-1117251	1167	1
CROCKER RICHARD P	1LT	O-0483914	0347	1
CROCKER THOMAS D	CW3	W-2151422	0867	1
CROCKER WILLIAM B	LTC	O-0449630	0862	1
CROCKER ZENAS 3D	1LT	O-1338925	0252	1
CROCKETT CHARLES B	COL	O-0444093	0767	1
CROCKETT CHARLES N	CPT	O-0202739	0456	3
CROCKETT DANIEL	MAJ	O-0205668	0555	3
CROCKETT DAVY B	CPT	O-1111003	0166	2
CROCKETT DORSEY C	1LT	O-0973024	0263	2
CROCKETT EDWARD D	CPT	O-0257721	0745	2
CROCKETT JOHN H	CPT	O-0363824	0646	2
CROCKETT JOHN W	COL	O-0300009	0767	3
CROCKETT JR JOHN R	CPT	O-1322834	1046	1
CROCKETT THOMAS P	1LT	O-1302277	0746	2
CROCKETT WILLIAM D	CW2	W-2124712	0265	2
CROCKETT WILLIAM L	CW3	W-2103982	0455	1
CROCKFORD F H	MAJ	O-1100507	0760	1
CROFOOT BRAINERD O	MAJ	O-1558845	0566	1
CROFOOT DEWEY V	MAJ	O-2033773	0265	1
CROFOOT GEORGE W	MAJ	O-0444284	0542	2
CROFOOT JACK F	LTC	O-0245100	0966	3
CROFT BLISS H	LTC	O-0948727	1067	1
CROFT CLAUDIA K	2LT	N-0761845	0645	1
CROFT GORDON Y	LTC	O-0162409	0943	2
CROFT HARRY P	COL	O-0191837	0857	3
CROFT NATHANIEL	1LT	O-0556382	0245	2
CROFT SAMPSON A	MAJ	O-0364935	0949	1
CROFT VIVIAN L	MAJ	O-0781528	0164	1

NAME	GRADE	SVC NO	DATE RET MO YR	RET CODE
CROFTON GEORGE R	LTC	O-0283079	0845	2
CROKE ALLAN R	CW2	W-2147462	0262	1
CROKEN HOWARD K	1LT	O-1644795	1053	1
CROKER BYRON P	2LT	O-1996886	0645	2
CROLL ALFRED W	LTC	O-0285571	0650	1
CROLL FORREST R	LTC	O-0179538	0549	3
CROLL RAYMOND H	COL	O-0228565	0664	3
CROMB VERNON F	CPT	O-1824284	0560	2
CROMELIN JULIAN T	MAJ	O-0219964	1063	3
CROMER FRANK X	CW2	W-2151002	0461	1
CROMER HOWARD E	LTC	O-1637900	0267	1
CRONER WALTER A	CPT	O-0260557	1143	2
CROMLISH VIRGIL	1LT	O-1317972	1047	1
CROMMETT RALPH L	LTC	O-2057572	0667	1
CROMWELL JAMES D	LTC	O-0309370	0965	3
CROMWELL RAYMOND F	1LT	O-1032699	0446	2
CROMWELL WILLIAM D	LTC	O-0337385	0459	1
CRON FREDERICK	LTC	O-0247279	0966	3
CRON GEORGE E	CW3	W-2148921	0764	1
CRONAN CHARLES J	LTC	O-0123564	0955	3
CRONAN FRANCIS W	LTC	O-0185365	0159	3
CRONAN FRANK X	1LT	O-2027437	0546	2
CRONAUER LEO A	MAJ	O-0571377	0964	1
CRONE CHARLES F	COL	O-0273576	1059	1
CRONE GEORGE K	CPT	O-1057715	1145	1
CRONE JOHN B	MAJ	O-0118948	0754	3
CRONHEIM KURT R	CPT	O-0510494	1045	2
CRONIA JAMES D	MAJ	O-2021049	0364	1
CRONIC HENRY T	LTC	O-2015513	0168	1
CRONIN ARTHUR F	1LT	O-1316970	0845	2
CRONIN DANIEL P	CPT	O-1303270	0246	2
CRONIN DENIS J	MAJ	O-0155150	0748	3
CRONIN JAMES J	COL	O-0922351	0765	3
CRONIN JOHN A	MAJ	O-2000905	0660	1
CRONIN JOHN F	LTC	O-0296621	0747	2
CRONIN JOHN F	MAJ	O-2239381	0963	1
CRONIN JOHN L	CPT	O-1295514	0446	2
CRONIN JR BERNARD M	LTC	O-1037452	0864	1
CRONIN JR JOSEPH M	1LT	O-0544235	0746	2
CRONIN KENNETH J	MAJ	O-2046588	1060	1
CRONIN LOUIS F	CPT	O-2026902	0855	1
CRONIN MARGARET M	LTC	N-0743396	0667	3
CRONIN MARY L	MAJ	N-0720201	0467	1
CRONIN MICHAEL E	CW2	W-2116280	0255	1
CRONIN PATRICK L	COL	O-0266888	1057	3
CRONIN ROBERT A	LTC	O-1109880	0764	1
CRONK JAMES R	CW4	W-2144604	0856	1
CRONK NORMAN H	LTC	O-0403321	1160	1
CRONK ROSE A	CPT	N-0722432	1047	1
CRONKHITE EDWARD J	LTC	O-1637243	0562	1
CROOK ARBA V	MAJ	O-0262030	0758	3
CROOK EVAN J	MAJ	O-0277393	0558	3
CROOK JOHN M	LTC	O-0426858	0766	1
CROOK KERMIT C	1LT	O-1036930	0546	2
CROOK ROWLAND O	1LT	O-0265542	1150	3
CROOK WELTON J	COL	O-0242716	1051	3
CROOK WILLIAM H	MAJ	O-1101796	1060	1
CROOKER HAROLD L	2LT	O-1297503	1044	2
CROOKS EDGAR D	COL	O-1100508	0655	1
CROOKS GEORGE C	COL	O-0279325	0265	3
CROOKS THOMAS O	MAJ	O-1298667	0361	1
CROOKS WILLIAM T	CW3	W-2141539	1061	1
CROOKSTON WILLIAM A	LTC	O-0106319	0352	3
CROON OSCAR G	1LT	O-0532102	1045	2
CROPP FORREST L	COL	O-0232673	1160	3
CROPP GARNET D	1LT	O-0505421	1058	1
CROPP HERBERT H	CPT	O-1574221	1044	2
CROPP RICHARD	LTC	O-0274437	1163	3
CROPPER PAUL E	CW3	W-2149840	0763	1
CROSBIE WILLIAM H	2LT	O-1318518	0944	2
CROSBY BRACEFORD D	CW2	W-2134765	1154	1
CROSBY ELMER L	CW4	W-2107919	1054	1
CROSBY GEORGE C	LTC	O-0923712	0966	3
CROSBY JOSEPH C	LTC	O-0489410	0855	1
CROSBY JOSEPH W	CW3	W-2148688	0664	1

NAME	GRADE	SVC NO	DATE RET MO YR	RET CODE
CROSBY JR ERNEST G	CPT	O-2262381	0461	1
CROSBY JR MANFORD E	COL	O-0324838	1166	1
CROSBY RALPH M	CPT	O-0490456	0445	2
CROSBY RAWLAND R	CW2	W-2151396	0262	2
CROSBY RAYMOND J	LTC	O-2048885	1166	2
CROSBY THOMAS F	2LT	O-1031708	0545	2
CROSBY WILL G	COL	O-0100291	0648	3
CROSKEY RALPH S	LTC	O-0150282	0652	3
CROSLEY CHARLES E	CW3	W-2152373	1064	1
CROSLIN CLYDE E	1LT	O-0932514	1046	1
CROSMAN CHARLES H	1LT	O-1535427	0845	2
CROSS ALFRED L	CW2	W-2108143	1046	2
CROSS ALLEN S	CPT	O-0330391	1045	2
CROSS CHARLES B	1LT	O-1287671	0547	1
CROSS CHARLES H	LTC	O-1551593	1262	1
CROSS CLINTON L	CW2	W-2146601	0958	1
CROSS CLYDE C	MAJ	O-1824144	1057	1
CROSS EDWIN S	MAJ	O-1296330	0847	2
CROSS FRANK M	CPT	O-2047961	0546	2
CROSS GEORGE C	MAJ	O-0489674	0747	2
CROSS GERALD B	2LT	O-1551380	1143	2
CROSS GERALD F	LTC	O-0359737	0462	3
CROSS HAYWOOD K	LTC	O-0427240	0562	1
CROSS HOMER V	MAJ	O-0278978	0149	1
CROSS JAY	1LT	O-0975496	1167	1
CROSS JR WILLIAM M	LTC	O-1300457	0765	1
CROSS LEO J	CPT	O-1175677	1053	1
CROSS LEONARD L	COL	O-0381227	0257	1
CROSS LLOYD A	COL	O-0147468	0250	3
CROSS MELVIN A	MAJ	O-2034507	0557	1
CROSS MILO J	2LT	O-2053833	0345	2
CROSS RALPH E	MAJ	O-0229866	1053	1
CROSS RALPH F	CPT	O-1735982	0446	2
CROSS RALPH H	LTC	O-1042534	0564	1
CROSS RICHARD A	MAJ	O-1285556	1058	1
CROSS ROBERT F	LTC	O-0423451	0662	3
CROSS ROSCOE	COL	O-0194705	0546	2
CROSS THEARON M	CW3	W-3150365	0667	1
CROSS WILLIAM H	MAJ	O-1324758	1062	1
CROSS WILLIAM R	CPT	O-0208421	0648	3
CROSSETT JESSE H	LTC	O-0177118	0853	3
CROSSETT WILLIAM A	2LT	O-1308927	0845	2
CROSSLAND ROBERT J	MAJ	O-1923626	0764	1
CROSSLEY CHARLES H	MAJ	O-1913484	0366	1
CROSSLEY SPENCER	MAJ	O-0916989	0847	1
CROSSLEY WALTER C	LTC	O-0240060	0466	3
CROSSLIN MACK S	MAJ	O-0970014	0463	1
CROSSMAN GILBERT C	LTC	O-0250912	0166	3
CROSSMAN LESTER E	CW4	W-2103984	0555	1
CROSSMAN MORTON	CPT	O-0263811	0845	2
CROSSMAN RAYMOND M	MAJ	O-0453115	0946	1
CROSSMAN ROBERT L	LTC	O-1558425	0764	2
CROSSON RAYMOND L	MAJ	O-0132071	0753	3
CROSTHWAITE LAURENCE	LTC	O-0260035	0863	3
CROTHERS FLOYD E	CW3	W-2143431	0561	1
CROTHERS JAMES A	B G	O-0189962	0753	3
CROTTY DANIEL	2LT	O-2008742	0950	1
CROTTY FRANCIS C	COL	O-0285078	1266	3
CROUCH ADAM L	LTC	O-1168616	1166	1
CROUCH CHARLES P	LTC	O-0493005	0366	2
CROUCH EDWARD P	COL	O-0211019	1263	3
CROUCH HENRY W	LTC	O-0168952	0360	3
CROUCH LLOYD G	COL	O-0150056	0949	3
CROUCH LOUIS C	COL	O-0278774	0464	1
CROUCH THEODORE	CPT	O-0450686	1148	1
CROUCH VERNON E	CW3	W-2111361	1155	1
CROUCH WILBUR S	LTC	O-0238339	0166	3
CROUSE FRANKLIN O	CPT	O-0493012	0157	1
CROUSE IRVING I	COL	O-0499220	0360	3
CROUSE JOHN C	LTC	O-0294092	0667	3
CROUSE JR JOHN C	MAJ	O-1996648	0465	1
CROUSE MARION W	COL	O-0391054	0257	1
CROUSE NEWT K	MAJ	O-0362918	0445	2
CROUSE WILEY H	1LT	O-1578318	0746	2
CROUSER CLAUDE S	LTC	O-0236707	0158	3

NAME	GRADE	SVC NO	DATE RET MO YR	RET CODE
CROVATTO LOUIS F	WO1	W-2110572	0744	2
CROVO EDMUND P	MAJ	O-2009380	0464	1
CROVO EDWARD P	MAJ	O-2011680	0463	1
CROW CLARENCE T	CW2	W-2209241	1061	1
CROW CLIFFORD C	1LT	O-0520787	0644	2
CROW DEE W	CW2	W-2208191	1162	1
CROW FRANK G	LTC	O-0233119	0865	3
CROW FRANK M	COL	O-0334339	0761	1
CROW HARRY S	LTC	O-0214553	0457	3
CROW HERCELL N	1LT	O-1323229	0446	2
CROW HOWARD R	WO1	W-2210336	1059	3
CROW JAMES W	LTC	O-0364130	0760	1
CROW JOHN H	MAJ	O-1300608	1060	1
CROW JR HORACE E	1LT	O-0394245	0145	2
CROW LAWRENCE M	MAJ	O-0365188	0846	2
CROW MILTON E	CPT	O-0407020	0645	2
CROW RALPH L	1LT	O-0190765	0845	1
CROW RAYMOND W	2LT	O-1030968	0543	2
CROW ROBERT H	CPT	O-0271067	0543	2
CROW SAM C	1LT	O-0446022	0146	2
CROW WALTER C	MAJ	O-1594409	0160	1
CROW WENDELL H	CPT	O-0366124	0944	2
CROW WILFRED M	CPT	O-0367618	0246	2
CROW WILLIAM J	COL	O-0221226	0262	3
CROWDER ARDEN B	LTC	O-0241890	1059	1
CROWDER JR JOHN F	MAJ	O-1644809	0757	1
CROWDER JR ROBERT P	CPT	O-0971083	0659	2
CROWDER KARL A	CPT	O-1322525	0466	2
CROWDER NILE O	1LT	O-1300768	0855	2
CROWDER RICHARD S	COL	O-0242861	0257	1
CROWDER WANDA M	MAJ	N-0760261	1163	1
CROWDER WILLIAM R	2LT	O-2016858	0446	2
CROWDUS ROBERT R	COL	O-0228124	0764	3
CROWE ALVIN L	LTC	O-0257796	0567	3
CROWE DAVID R	LTC	O-1169074	1061	1
CROWE FRANK H	CPT	O-0383525	1045	2
CROWE FRANK I	MAJ	O-0982067	0663	1
CROWE HUBERT L	CW3	W-2205539	0567	1
CROWE JOHN D	CW2	W-2210905	0665	1
CROWE JOHN W	MAJ	O-0185508	0337	1
CROWE JOSEPH E	WO1	W-2123195	1045	2
CROWELL DAN L	1LT	O-1821830	0163	2
CROWELL DONALD C	LTC	O-0347556	0467	3
CROWELL DOUGLAS D	CW2	W-2206800	1060	1
CROWELL GEORGE A	MAJ	O-2204414	1265	1
CROWELL HAMILTON T	COL	O-1643372	0765	1
CROWELL HAROLD L	1LT	O-1313574	1145	1
CROWELL HAROLD W	CPT	O-0287212	0462	1
CROWELL HARRIS C	LTC	O-1311489	0665	1
CROWELL JR HENRY P	LTC	O-0195387	0862	3
CROWELL RUPERT J	LTC	O-0140166	0456	3
CROWELL WILLIAM R	LTC	O-0414717	0563	1
CROWELL WILLIAM L	CW3	W-2145461	0860	1
CROWIE ROBERT C	2LT	O-1560344	0347	2
CROWL ALLEN L	CPT	O-0510899	1048	1
CROWL ELMER F	MAJ	O-2006687	1064	1
CROWLEY ALLEN P	MAJ	O-0354712	0646	2
CROWLEY ANNA J	MAJ	N-0700113	0246	1
CROWLEY FRANCIS	LTC	O-0242335	0358	1
CROWLEY JACK A	COL	O-0172799	0251	3
CROWLEY JARVIN G	LTC	O-1643922	0763	1
CROWLEY JOHN RICHA	WO1	W-2123177	1046	2
CROWLEY JOSEPH P	COL	O-0277297	0462	2
CROWLEY JR ARTHUR J	MAJ	O-1308109	0260	1
CROWLEY JR JAMES A	LTC	O-1647376	0865	1
CROWLEY JR WILLIAM J	MAJ	O-0994622	1266	1
CROWLEY LEO V	LTC	O-0544765	0564	1
CROWLEY MARY A	CPT	N-0722545	0947	1
CROWLEY MELVIN F	MAJ	O-0962309	0763	1
CROWLEY THOMAS N	LTC	O-0206496	1055	3
CROWLEY WILLIAM J	LTC	O-1036490	0366	3
CROWLEY WILLIAM S	MAJ	O-0992368	0663	1
CROWLIE JOHN R	1LT	O-0969934	0453	1
CROWLY JOSEPH H	LTC	O-0290406	1053	3
CROWN SAMUEL	LTC	O-0266168	0352	3

NAME	GRADE	SVC NO	DATE RET MO YR	RET CODE
CROWNOVER AUSTIN A	CPT	O-0342162	1046	2
CROWSON JAMES C	COL	O-0199898	0150	3
CROWSON JOHN F	1LT	O-1015475	1046	2
CROWTHER ADDISON C	LTC	O-0376813	1160	1
CROWTHER ALBERT R	B G	O-0306510	0958	3
CROWTHER FREDERICK	COL	O-0236854	0166	3
CROWTHER ROBERT W	LTC	O-0203436	0463	3
CROXTON AMOS B	CW2	W-2149375	0660	1
CROXTON JOHN M	MAJ	O-1019078	0258	1
CROZIER COURTENAY	COL	O-0100797	1154	3
CROZIER EDGAR F	MAJ	O-0571754	1262	1
CRUCE WILLIAM R	LTC	O-1823415	0363	1
CRUCHLEY ARNOLD D	LTC	O-1580816	1061	1
CRUEY RAY F	1LT	O-0469989	0545	2
CRUEY WENDLAND V	COL	O-0263071	0865	3
CRUGNALE CARL A	CW2	W-2210499	0264	1
CRUICKSHANK JAMES H	LTC	O-1283360	0865	1
CRUICKSHANK JOHN P	COL	O-0165026	0960	3
CRUICKSHANK KENNETH	MAJ	O-0280761	0764	3
CRUISE ROBERT R	LTC	O-1010915	0261	1
CRUIT GEORGE F	WO1	W-2126793	0445	2
CRULL JOHN S	LTC	O-0299502	0358	1
CRULL OSCAR C	CPT	O-0484332	0556	1
CRUM CARROLL M	LTC	O-0248195	0662	1
CRUM EDWARD M	1LT	O-1797259	0146	2
CRUM GEORGE E	CPT	O-0317170	0745	2
CRUM JAMES H	CW3	W-2209823	1167	1
CRUM JAMES W	COL	O-0114985	0948	3
CRUM MORRIS G	CW2	W-2124174	0964	1
CRUM WILLIAM P	COL	O-0237608	1060	3
CRUM WOODROW W	LTC	O-1043308	0567	1
CRUMB FRANCIS P	LTC	O-1100062	0757	1
CRUMBAKER CHARLES H	CW3	W-2122925	0657	1
CRUMBLISS JOSEPH P	MAJ	O-1289873	0861	1
CRUME HUGH L	1LT	O-1109219	0949	2
CRUME WOODROW W	2LT	O-0386869	0443	2
CRUMLEY GRADY M	CW4	W-2148250	0958	1
CRUMLEY HENRY C	LTC	O-0291575	1145	1
CRUMLEY JACK H	CPT	O-1062481	0747	2
CRUMLEY JAMES L	MAJ	O-0295164	1264	1
CRUMM CLIFTON J	LTC	O-0474411	0557	1
CRUMMETT CLOVIS V	MAJ	O-1646491	0163	1
CRUMP ORLANDUS	CW2	W-2152699	0762	1
CRUMP THOMAS E	LTC	O-0150584	0648	3
CRUMP WARREN R	LTC	O-0273928	0758	3
CRUMP WILLIAM W	LTC	O-0173986	0648	3
CRUMPACKER DANIEL L	LTC	O-0337170	0763	1
CRUMPTON SIDNEY R	COL	O-0293549	0162	1
CRUMRINE WILLIAM H	CPT	O-1304183	0747	1
CRUPE ROBERT I	CW4	W-2125201	0261	1
CRUPI ALBERT J	LTC	O-1316019	1067	1
CRUSE GORDON L	CPT	O-1822776	1045	2
CRUSE KENNETH	WO1	W-2143399	1053	2
CRUSE LENN R	MAJ	O-1643373	0967	3
CRUSH RAYMOND R	MAJ	O-0500281	0348	1
CRUSIE CLYDE E	MAJ	O-1794787	0161	1
CRUSON CLAUDE C	CPT	O-0103188	0648	3
CRUTCHER JOHN S	2LT	O-1012399	0745	2
CRUTCHER JR JOHN S	COL	O-0262972	0165	3
CRUTCHFIELD JACK M	CPT	L-0912156	0548	2
CRUTCHFIELD JAMES G	COL	O-0170385	0546	2
CRUTCHFIELD JAMES M	LTC	O-1010109	1166	1
CRUTCHFIELD JOSEPH M	LTC	O-0348535	1059	1
CRUTCHFIELD OWEN S	MAJ	O-1057395	0463	1
CRUTCHFIELD WILLIAM	LTC	O-1030352	0861	1
CRUZ ANTONIO W	1LT	O-1896532	0656	1
CRUZ EARIQUE E	1LT	O-0888097	0348	2
CRUZ JOSE L	MAJ	O-1284299	0661	1
CRUZ LORENZO H	LTC	O-0302853	0960	1
CRUZE ARTHUR O	MAJ	O-0975188	0163	1
CRYER CLIFFORD T	CPT	O-0212425	0453	3
CRYER WARRICK W	CW2	W-2102801	0944	2
CRYMES THOMAS P	COL	O-0235831	0254	3
CRYNOCK PETER D	1LT	O-1697075	0244	2
CSERGIE LOUIS	LTC	O-0924904	0964	1

NAME	GRADE	SVC NO	DATE RET MO YR	RET CODE
CUADRADO ANGEL R	MAJ	O-0995957	0653	2
CUANANG CELESTINO	1LT	O-1896475	0864	2
CUBBAGE LELAND F	LTC	O-1946704	0662	1
CUBBAGE RANSOM B	COL	O-0295597	0465	1
CUBBERLEY JAMES O	LTC	O-0518322	0667	1
CUCCIA EDWARD	MAJ	O-1947320	1064	1
CUCCINELLO DOMINIC S	CPT	O-1311618	0946	2
CUCITI ANTHONY C	MAJ	O-0976113	0966	1
CUDE WILLIAM C	LTC	O-0298008	0866	3
CUDINA JOHN M	1LT	O-1036932	0758	1
CUDMORE THOMAS J	MAJ	O-1107886	1162	1
CUE HOWARD F	LTC	O-0398947	0955	1
CUE LESLIE L	CPT	O-0946570	0555	2
CUEBAS RAFAEL	1LT	O-0164115	0547	1
CUERDA TOMAS	LTC	O-0198649	1162	3
CUERVO MABEL S	MAJ	N-0724136	0266	3
CUEVAS ALBERT J	LTC	O-0198313	0948	2
CUEVAS DOMINGO	CPT	O-0519622	1151	1
CUEVAS-BAEZ FRANK	LTC	O-1062995	0664	1
CUFF HAROLD J	CW3	W-2143671	0263	1
CUFFEE CLARENCE J	2LT	O-4002120	0954	2
CUFFNEY WILLIAM P	MAJ	O-2047286	0358	1
CUITE THOMAS J	LTC	O-1000341	1148	2
CULBERSON GEORGE E	CW3	W-2141240	0462	1
CULBERT JAMES N	CW3	W-2150027	1064	1
CULBERT OTTO L	MAJ	O-0281776	0265	3
CULBERT VINCENT J	MAJ	O-0973205	1064	2
CULBERT WILLIAM	COL	O-0348384	0763	3
CULBERTSON CARL C	2LT	O-1595447	0561	2
CULBERTSON CHARLES L	CPT	O-1314562	0449	1
CULBERTSON JOHN B	MAJ	O-1170694	0664	2
CULBERTSON ORRIE M	MAJ	O-2017517	0659	1
CULBERTSON PAUL M	LTC	O-0225626	0763	3
CULBERTSON ROBERT F	2LT	O-1324396	1044	2
CULBERTSON RONALD D	LTC	O-0287326	0446	2
CULBERTSON WEST	COL	O-0267015	0355	3
CULBERTSON WILLIAM L	LTC	O-1648239	0166	1
CULBRETH CECIL B	2LT	O-1581635	1159	1
CULBRETH DOUGLAS F	CPT	O-0385744	0660	1
CULBRETH PAUL	CW2	W-2214807	0866	1
CULHANE NICHOLAS J	CPT	O-1107375	0762	1
CULKIN KENNETH R	LTC	O-1300000	0861	1
CULL EOLINE C	CPT	L-0501176	0753	1
CULLAR JOHN W	CPT	O-1299006	0860	2
CULLATHER BERNARD D	MAJ	O-1032618	0557	1
CULLEN ERNEST O	2LT	O-2012237	1056	1
CULLEN FREDERICK	CW3	W-3150514	0467	1
CULLEN HARRY F	1LT	O-1293016	0245	2
CULLEN JOSEPH D	MAJ	O-1926250	0167	1
CULLEN JOSEPH F	LTC	O-1165721	0557	1
CULLEN JOSEPH W	CW3	W-2147911	0763	2
CULLEN JR JOHN B	MAJ	O-1641209	0960	1
CULLEN MARY A	2LT	N-0744656	0645	1
CULLEN MICHAEL R	MAJ	O-1184799	0562	1
CULLEN PAUL H	COL	O-0314377	0360	1
CULLEN RICHARD N	CW2	W-3150610	0665	1
CULLEN RICHARD S	CW3	W-2146947	0866	1
CULLEN ROBERT D	MAJ	O-1550353	0958	1
CULLEN THOMAS P	LTC	O-0277293	0264	3
CULLEN WILLIAM J	LTC	O-0100413	0648	3
CULLENS STEVE M	LTC	O-0411004	0147	2
CULLER HARRY G	CPT	O-0379715	0345	2
CULLEY FRANK L	COL	O-0250972	0264	3
CULLEY OTTO	CW4	W-2142472	0766	1
CULLEY TOM R	1LT	O-1018629	0146	2
CULLIFER JR LUTHER E	CPT	O-0970832	0764	2
CULLIGAN JOSEPH M	1LT	O-1308794	0745	2
CULLIMORE DOUGLAS	MAJ	O-0995383	0566	1
CULLINAN GEORGE L	CW3	W-2144449	0865	1
CULLINAN HENRY J	MAJ	O-0938978	0762	1
CULLINAN KENNETH J	1LT	O-1645254	0845	2
CULLINANE HENRY J	CPT	O-1585320	0261	1
CULLINGTON ALICE M	MAJ	N-0738023	1062	1
CULLISON CARL C	MAJ	O-0262738	0961	3
CULLITON ANNIE C	1LT	N-0722763	0145	1

NAME	GRADE	SVC NO	DATE RET MO YR	RET CODE
CULLOM EUGENE H	CW3	W-2152887	0959	1
CULLOTON EDWARD L	1LT	O-1320436	0446	2
CULLUM JR JAMES B	COL	O-0224446	1060	3
CULLY RALPH F	MAJ	O-0214645	0648	3
CULLYFORD JAMES S	LTC	O-0337155	1066	3
CULNAN EDGAR R	MAJ	O-0112151	0648	3
CULP ALLEN D	MAJ	O-1298507	0664	1
CULP ARNOLD C	MAJ	O-1936647	0666	1
CULP BENJAMIN R	CPT	O-0325655	0746	1
CULP EDWIN R	LTC	O-0238300	1263	3
CULP JR CLETUS C	MAJ	O-2204432	0963	1
CULP WILLARD E	LTC	O-1584733	0862	1
CULPEPPER CHARLES R	COL	O-0396635	1165	3
CULPEPPER DOUGLAS O	MAJ	O-1280820	1058	1
CULPEPPER PHIL L	CPT	O-1307516	0446	1
CULPEPPER WILLIAM F	CW3	W-2119770	0557	1
CULVER FRANK L	CPT	O-1014152	0563	1
CULVER JR FRANK P	COL	O-0154749	0949	3
CULVER ROBERT W	1LT	O-1166948	0844	2
CULVER THOMAS R	1LT	O-1542208	1153	2
CULVERHOUSE ROBERT C	MAJ	O-1923538	1063	1
CUMARELAS JOHN	MAJ	O-0494982	0746	1
CUMB RAYMOND F	MAJ	O-2017664	0960	1
CUMBERLAND DUANE K	LTC	O-0337561	1054	1
CUMBEY WILLIAM W	LTC	O-1030138	0557	1
CUMBOW ROBERT M	MAJ	O-0977506	0564	1
CUMBY BERT	LTC	O-1003213	0962	1
CUMISKEY FRANK	LTC	O-0492376	0849	1
CUMMING BRUCE H	MAJ	O-0957306	0666	1
CUMMING GORDON F	LTC	O-0413405	0863	1
CUMMING JAMES G	LTC	O-0122561	0648	3
CUMMING JOSEPH R	COL	O-0254292	1266	3
CUMMING RICHARD C	COL	O-0252451	1162	3
CUMMINGS BILL	CPT	O-2024158	0759	1
CUMMINGS CHARLES L	LTC	O-2049881	0564	1
CUMMINGS CHARLES M	COL	O-0279857	0560	3
CUMMINGS CHARLES W	MAJ	O-1824145	0266	1
CUMMINGS CLARENCE S	MAJ	O-0423447	0756	1
CUMMINGS DAVID L	CW2	W-2214712	0567	1
CUMMINGS EDWARD H	MAJ	O-1015719	0363	1
CUMMINGS ELBRIDGE H	LTC	O-0383366	0960	1
CUMMINGS FRED A	MAJ	O-2012366	0164	1
CUMMINGS FREDERICK	MAJ	O-1300609	0561	1
CUMMINGS GEORGE B	LTC	O-1635742	0657	1
CUMMINGS GEORGE E	CPT	O-0492900	1159	1
CUMMINGS JACK	CPT	O-0123500	0654	3
CUMMINGS JAMES B	CPT	O-1165835	0446	2
CUMMINGS JAMES H	WO1	W-2128250	1145	2
CUMMINGS JOE V	MAJ	O-1635744	0960	1
CUMMINGS JOHN C	CW2	W-2152454	0260	1
CUMMINGS JOHN E	MAJ	O-1014796	0562	1
CUMMINGS JOHN J	MAJ	O-0124516	0648	3
CUMMINGS JOHN L	LTC	O-0230573	0761	3
CUMMINGS JOHN P	CPT	O-0920339	1046	2
CUMMINGS JOSEPH H	LTC	O-0255055	1066	3
CUMMINGS LEIGHTON W	CPT	O-0180972	0360	3
CUMMINGS LEO C	CPT	O-2262132	1060	1
CUMMINGS LEONARD D	COL	O-0276867	0560	1
CUMMINGS MELVILLE F	2LT	O-0473654	0545	2
CUMMINGS MICHAEL P	CW3	W-2148011	1262	1
CUMMINGS RICHARD W	MAJ	O-0220354	1159	3
CUMMINGS STANLEY L	MAJ	O-1584097	0563	1
CUMMINGS TAFT	MAJ	O-0505391	0556	1
CUMMINGS THOMAS F	COL	O-1895707	0665	3
CUMMINGS VINCENT P	LTC	O-0360954	0666	3
CUMMINGS WALTER A	1LT	O-1294794	0446	2
CUMMINS EARL M	CPT	O-0522538	0646	2
CUMMINS GERALD J	MAJ	O-1010633	0564	3
CUMMINS HALDANE C	CPT	O-1703187	0146	2
CUMMINS JOHN F	CW3	W-2209456	0867	1
CUMMINS JR JAMES F	2LT	O-0466786	0445	2
CUMMINS KENNETH G	LTC	O-0282861	0667	3
CUMMISKEY JOHN T	MAJ	O-0321159	1166	3
CUNDELL ARTHUR B	MAJ	O-0150854	0648	3
CUNDIFF CARL H	COL	O-0447827	0863	3

ARMY OF THE UNITED STATES RETIRED LIST

NAME	GRADE	SVC NO	DATE RET MO YR	RET CODE
CUNDIFF CLARE R	MAJ	0-0286048	0548	1
CUNDIFF PAUL L	LTC	0-0321678	0660	1
CUNDIFF ROY	CPT	0-0364165	0346	1
CUNDIFF WILGUS B	CPT	0-1110439	1045	1
CUNEO RAYMOND F	2LT	0-1185357	0645	2
CUNJAK FRANKLIN J	CPT	0-1695251	0445	1
CUNNEEN LEONARD J	CPT	0-2023885	0761	1
CUNNINGHAM ALBERT	MAJ	0-1920066	1066	1
CUNNINGHAM ANDREW W	1LT	0-1056682	1048	2
CUNNINGHAM ARTHUR D	CPT	0-0299179	1160	1
CUNNINGHAM AUDREY W	MAJ	0-0940776	0960	1
CUNNINGHAM BERNARD W	CPT	0-0243216	0962	3
CUNNINGHAM CALHOUN D	LTC	0-0188590	1061	3
CUNNINGHAM CHARLES	COL	0-0281312	1064	3
CUNNINGHAM CHARLES C	LTC	0-2019994	0867	1
CUNNINGHAM CHARLES J	1LT	0-1287150	0446	2
CUNNINGHAM CHARLES J	LTC	0-1822538	0364	1
CUNNINGHAM CHARLES W	CPT	0-0171622	0545	2
CUNNINGHAM CLARK M	CPT	0-0335255	0245	2
CUNNINGHAM DANIEL L	MAJ	0-2042729	0965	1
CUNNINGHAM DAVID C	1LT	0-1549692	1262	1
CUNNINGHAM DENNIS R	LTC	0-1175679	0564	1
CUNNINGHAM DONALD S	CPT	0-5301510	0864	2
CUNNINGHAM EDMUND	COL	0-0152834	0560	3
CUNNINGHAM ELIJAH W	MAJ	0-1796242	0762	1
CUNNINGHAM EMORY B	CW2	W-2146825	0956	1
CUNNINGHAM EUGENE M	LTC	0-0244594	0154	3
CUNNINGHAM FINIS A	CPT	0-0493024	0450	1
CUNNINGHAM FRANCIS	1LT	0-1018159	1045	2
CUNNINGHAM FRED I	CW2	W-3200342	1166	1
CUNNINGHAM FREDRIC	2LT	0-1014971	0445	2
CUNNINGHAM GEORGE L	LTC	0-0226389	1064	3
CUNNINGHAM GEORGE M	MAJ	0-0259835	1267	3
CUNNINGHAM GEORGE W	1LT	0-1104596	1147	1
CUNNINGHAM GORDON L	LTC	0-1635747	1266	1
CUNNINGHAM HAROLD L	LTC	0-0453054	0261	1
CUNNINGHAM HARRY R	MAJ	0-1586519	0164	1
CUNNINGHAM HENRY K	MAJ	0-0167050	0756	3
CUNNINGHAM HENRY L	CPT	0-1018769	0454	2
CUNNINGHAM HERBERT B	MAJ	0-1303251	1058	2
CUNNINGHAM HUGH J	COL	0-0150281	0555	3
CUNNINGHAM HUSTON P	LTC	0-0366910	0263	3
CUNNINGHAM JACK	MAJ	0-1342164	0962	1
CUNNINGHAM JACK C	CPT	0-1311581	0747	1
CUNNINGHAM JACQUES A	LTC	0-2041090	1062	1
CUNNINGHAM JAMES A	COL	0-0111196	0950	3
CUNNINGHAM JAMES A	CW2	W-2145134	0858	1
CUNNINGHAM JAMES C	COL	0-0229410	0763	3
CUNNINGHAM JAMES E	CPT	0-1702366	0744	2
CUNNINGHAM JAMES M	LTC	0-0287625	0564	3
CUNNINGHAM JAMES M	CPT	0-0508189	0846	1
CUNNINGHAM JAMES P	LTC	0-1286252	0865	1
CUNNINGHAM JOHN F	1LT	0-1307517	0644	2
CUNNINGHAM JOHN J	CPT	0-0888269	1046	2
CUNNINGHAM JOHN J	CW3	RW-2147281	0662	1
CUNNINGHAM JOHN K	COL	0-0277284	1266	3
CUNNINGHAM JOHN L	LTC	0-0352620	0346	2
CUNNINGHAM JOHN L	LTC	0-1168619	0763	1
CUNNINGHAM JOHN D	MAJ	0-1172824	0762	1
CUNNINGHAM JOHN P	MAJ	0-1997962	0163	1
CUNNINGHAM JOHN R	MAJ	0-1100511	0961	1
CUNNINGHAM JOHN W	LTC	0-0496400	0655	1
CUNNINGHAM JOSEPH B	MAJ	0-0349125	0561	1
CUNNINGHAM JOSEPH H	MAJ	0-1640354	0160	1
CUNNINGHAM JR JOHN E	CPT	0-1304351	0146	1
CUNNINGHAM LAFAYETTE	LTC	0-0270588	1060	1
CUNNINGHAM LAWRENCE	MAJ	0-1018446	0263	1
CUNNINGHAM LEROY	LTC	0-0447298	1165	1
CUNNINGHAM MARY F	2LT	N-0703522	0944	1
CUNNINGHAM NOBLE E	LTC	0-1637249	1163	1
CUNNINGHAM OWEN	MAJ	0-0243511	0860	3
CUNNINGHAM PHILIP C	MAJ	0-0901266	0257	2
CUNNINGHAM RALPH F	LTC	0-1001119	0865	1
CUNNINGHAM RAYMOND J	COL	0-0117788	1056	3
CUNNINGHAM RICHARD T	CW3	W-2147538	0665	1

NAME	GRADE	SVC NO	DATE RET MO YR	RET CODE
CUNNINGHAM ROBERT D	MAJ	0-0182183	1056	3
CUNNINGHAM ROBERT E	LTC	0-0260119	0666	3
CUNNINGHAM ROBERT M	CPT	0-2300857	0765	1
CUNNINGHAM ROBERT R	1LT	0-2000175	0146	2
CUNNINGHAM ROBERT T	COL	0-0207400	0961	3
CUNNINGHAM ROY D	1LT	0-1015917	0151	1
CUNNINGHAM ROY W	MAJ	0-2202212	0166	1
CUNNINGHAM THOMAS J	COL	0-0234500	1065	3
CUNNINGHAM THOMAS P	MAJ	0-1649116	0161	1
CUNNINGHAM THOMAS S	1LT	0-1295344	0645	2
CUNNINGHAM VAN B	LTC	0-0157557	1049	1
CUNNINGHAM WALTER H	LTC	0-1317893	0962	1
CUNNINGHAM WILLIAM A	MAJ	0-1999200	1060	1
CUNNINGHAM WILLIAM H	1LT	0-2007102	0847	1
CUNNINGHAM WILLIAM L	CW3	W-2207680	0167	1
CUNYUS PAUL A	COL	0-0238501	0965	3
CUNZEMAN PAUL W	CW4	W-2141541	0964	1
CUOCO SALVATORE	MAJ	0-1339849	0164	1
CUPIT ELMER H	CW2	W-2150580	0661	1
CUPIT WILLIAM F	CW2	W-2145865	0566	1
CUPOLI CHARLES	CPT	0-1917733	0765	2
CUPP DONALD E	CPT	0-0510028	0345	2
CUPP HORACE P	COL	0-0312105	1063	3
CUPP WENDELL L	LTC	0-0450413	1054	1
CURR WILLIAM D	MAJ	0-2262743	0963	1
CURPLES REUBEN D	LTC	0-0450838	0757	1
CUPPS JR CECIL C	LTC	0-1061666	0463	1
CUPRYS FERDINAND	MAJ	0-1116216	0956	1
CURCIO LOUISE T	MAJ	N-0752115	1265	3
CURCIO MICHAEL S	CW4	W-2111364	1056	1
CURCIO ROCCO A	CW3	W-2152006	0765	1
CURO JOHN T	LTC	0-0338351	0361	1
CURO PAUL	CPT	0-0957604	0361	2
CURETON EDMUND H	MAJ	0-0232129	0563	3
CURETON HUGH B	CPT	0-0318180	0559	3
CURETON JR EVERARD E	1LT	0-1286799	1143	2
CURFMAN RALPH H	LTC	0-1288713	0261	1
CURIE ROBERT V	CPT	0-0455924	1043	2
CURIT LOUIS I	MAJ	0-0980264	1064	1
CURL FRED A	LTC	0-0234664	0765	3
CURL GILBERT W	LTC	0-0023418	1060	1
CURL JAMES P	MAJ	0-0472654	0351	1
CURL JR LOUIS J	MAJ	0-1292139	0946	1
CURL VINCENT L	LTC	0-0470047	0754	1
CURLEY ARTHUR L	CW3	W-2108023	0256	1
CURLEY BERNARD J	MAJ	0-1549245	0761	1
CURLEY DONALD W	LTC	0-1296662	1263	1
CURLEY LEO C	MAJ	0-0526409	0957	2
CURLEY WILFRED J	LTC	0-1797261	0658	1
CURLL RAYMOND A	MAJ	0-1794918	1060	2
CURNUTT SIDNEY K	MAJ	0-1540899	0661	1
CURRAN BOB L	MAJ	0-0973913	0164	1
CURRAN CHARLES L	LTC	0-0485007	0865	3
CURRAN DANIEL J	LTC	0-0322404	1149	3
CURRAN ELIZABETH	1LT	N-0731878	0646	1
CURRAN GEORGE A	1LT	0-0360172	0644	2
CURRAN GEORGE F	1LT	0-0422547	0645	1
CURRAN JAMES J	CPT	0-1307807	0255	2
CURRAN JOHN C	LTC	0-0485200	0859	1
CURRAN JOHN F	MAJ	0-0235129	0455	3
CURRAN JOHN J	2LT	0-0486735	0143	2
CURRAN JOHN K	CPT	0-1182806	1058	1
CURRAN JOHN M	1LT	0-1181856	1060	2
CURRAN JR JOHN J	MAJ	0-1324246	0967	3
CURRAN LOUIS F	1LT	0-1785754	0844	2
CURRAN MICHAEL F	1LT	0-2011078	0848	2
CURRAN MORRIS T	LTC	0-0271497	1066	3
CURRAN PATRICK H	1LT	0-1874404	0952	2
CURRAN PHILIP J	MAJ	0-1637252	0462	1
CURRAN WILLIAM P	LTC	0-0473756	1054	1
CURRAY JACK L	LTC	0-1056684	1262	1
CURRELL RALPH W	2LT	0-1179353	0545	2
CURREN FREDERICK	LTC	0-0211326	0850	3
CURRENCE DONALD R	1LT	0-1925385	0959	2
CURRENCE HOMER C	LTC	0-1116836	0264	1

NAME	GRADE	SVC NO	DATE RET MO YR	RET CODE
CURRENT ANDREW M	1LT	0-0367761	1043	2
CURRENT FRANCIS B	CPT	0-0406444	0348	1
CURREY CLARENCE A	CW3	W-2142071	0463	1
CURREY CLAUDE H	CPT	0-1947186	0363	1
CURREY JOHN R	COL	0-0176207	1059	3
CURREY NEIL P	1LT	0-1031066	1145	1
CURRIE JAMES W	LTC	0-0931964	0766	3
CURRIE RALPH H	1LT	0-0510031	0753	1
CURRIE WILLIAM B	COL	0-0242572	1062	3
CURRIE WILSIE A	LTC	0-0923848	0767	3
CURRIER DALLAS O	CPT	0-0888850	1048	1
CURRIER DONALD F	COL	0-0245107	1152	3
CURRIER FRANK T	MAJ	0-1287152	1264	1
CURRIER GREGORY F	MAJ	0-0481802	0356	1
CURRIER JOSEPH W	CPT	0-0464864	1045	2
CURRIER LELAND L	LTC	0-0215071	0664	3
CURRIER RUSSELL F	MAJ	0-1050619	1064	1
CURRIN JR FLEMING B	LTC	0-1588504	0961	1
CURRIN VIRGIL D	LTC	0-1055568	0565	3
CURRY DON C	LTC	0-0448851	1059	3
CURRY DONALD G	MAJ	0-1876335	0866	1
CURRY FLOYD L	CW4	W-2146770	0156	1
CURRY FRANK C	LTC	0-0379215	0447	2
CURRY GEORGE T	CPT	0-0385600	0746	2
CURRY HAROLD R	CW3	W-2119300	0659	1
CURRY HUGH J	LTC	0-0937878	0764	1
CURRY JAMES L	CW2	W-2003380	1146	1
CURRY JAMES R	MAJ	0-1533041	1263	1
CURRY JOHN H	2LT	0-1638935	0345	2
CURRY JOHN M	2LT	0-2036365	0645	2
CURRY JOHN W	1LT	0-0525004	1145	2
CURRY JR AL J	1LT	0-1106077	1145	2
CURRY JR HILLARY J	CW3	W-2146955	0962	1
CURRY JR JAMES D	1LT	0-1107376	1045	2
CURRY KENNETH E	LTC	0-1308312	0667	1
CURRY LASSIE	2LT	N-0767432	0439	2
CURRY MICHAEL F	LTC	0-0289209	1160	2
CURRY MORRIS J	CPT	0-1295345	1046	2
CURRY RAY H	CPT	0-1589145	0662	1
CURRY ROBERT E	CW2	W-2150246	0761	1
CURRY ULYSSES S	MAJ	0-1002191	0655	1
CURRY VIRGIL D	LTC	0-0237474	0466	3
CURRY WILLIAM M	CW3	W-2150847	1263	1
CURTES JOHN G	CPT	0-1548385	1055	1
CURTICE NORMAN B	MAJ	0-0108023	1155	3
CURTIN CHARLES J	MAJ	0-0344484	0154	2
CURTIN EDWARD N	2LT	0-1309668	1044	2
CURTIN ELDON R	1LT	0-1794916	1044	2
CURTIN ELMER P	LTC	0-0305653	0457	1
CURTIN JOSEPH S	LTC	0-1030870	1060	1
CURTIN JOSEPH T	MAJ	0-0158132	0749	3
CURTIN LAWRENCE R	CW3	W-2146150	0263	1
CURTIN MICHAEL F	LTC	0-2044397	1162	1
CURTIS ARTHUR W	COL	0-0903616	1166	3
CURTIS BENJAMIN C	LTC	0-1103122	0361	1
CURTIS BERNARD L	LTC	0-0464429	0954	1
CURTIS CLARENCE R	MAJ	0-1316621	0264	1
CURTIS CLARK C	MAJ	0-0202202	0462	3
CURTIS DONALD L	MAJ	0-1533763	0459	1
CURTIS DONALD S	MAJ	0-0277291	0363	3
CURTIS DONALD W	MAJ	0-2033885	0264	1
CURTIS EDWARD T	MAJ	0-0258752	1056	3
CURTIS ELGAR F	CPT	0-0168880	1046	1
CURTIS EUGENE L	MAJ	0-1686623	1063	1
CURTIS EUGENE M	2LT	0-1307202	0645	2
CURTIS EUGENE P	COL	0-0211910	1151	1
CURTIS FOREST J	LTC	0-0249105	1261	3
CURTIS FRED	CPT	0-0248407	1065	3
CURTIS HAL V	CPT	0-1924120	0162	1
CURTIS HAROLD E	CW3	W-2144152	0566	2
CURTIS HAROLD F	CPT	0-1644812	0157	1
CURTIS HENRY B	COL	0-0125355	1055	3
CURTIS HERBERT G	MAJ	0-0247794	0354	3
CURTIS JOHN L	MAJ	0-0336009	1158	3
CURTIS JOSEPH C	CW2	W-2148846	0361	1

NAME	GRADE	SVC NO	DATE RET MO YR	RET CODE
CURTIS JR CHARLES C	COL	0-0260172	0746	2
CURTIS JR CLARENCE F	COL	0-0298246	0564	3
CURTIS JR CLAUDE F	LTC	0-1324516	0163	1
CURTIS JR THEODORE E	COL	0-0254348	1159	1
CURTIS JR WILLIAM E	LTC	0-0240363	0166	3
CURTIS KARL W	COL	0-0183810	0855	3
CURTIS MELVIN L	MAJ	0-0561695	1162	2
CURTIS MERRILL J	LTC	0-0120217	1054	3
CURTIS MILTON H	1LT	0-1292313	0347	2
CURTIS OLEN R	COL	0-0255120	0766	3
CURTIS OWEN A	MAJ	0-0156045	0756	3
CURTIS REUBEN F	COL	0-0262460	0666	3
CURTIS ROBERT F	1LT	0-1011326	0545	2
CURTIS ROBERT MC	1LT	0-0395716	1144	2
CURTIS ROBERT W	MAJ	0-2262252	0364	1
CURTIS ROSS F	MAJ	0-1307377	0863	1
CURTIS RUSSEL J	CPT	0-0406373	1046	2
CURTIS RUSSELL W	LTC	0-0121081	0452	3
CURTIS SELVIE J	COL	0-0300642	0547	1
CURTIS VERL M	CW2	W-2111840	1058	1
CURTIS VERNON C	LTC	0-0322886	0560	3
CURTIS WALKER L	CPT	0-0441314	0945	2
CURTIS WILLIAM L	CPT	0-4005775	0566	1
CURTIS WILLIAM L	WO1	W-2151784	0164	1
CURTIS WILLIAM M	CW3	W-2205399	0167	1
CURTIS WILLMOTTE	LTC	0-0406807	1060	1
CURTISS CLAUDE O	COL	0-0183804	0455	3
CURTISS ROBERT A	LTC	0-0263242	0266	3
CURTISS ROBERT H	MAJ	0-1633788	0357	1
CURTIUS BENJAMIN L	CW3	W-2143428	0663	1
CURTNER MYRON L	COL	0-0214367	0749	3
CURTS CHARLES W	1LT	0-1179827	0847	1
CURTS HOLROYC A	MAJ	0-1100066	0647	2
CURZON MYRON W	MAJ	0-1894625	0546	2
CUSACK JR JOHN P	CPT	0-1315036	0646	2
CUSACK WILLIAM P	1LT	0-1298670	0244	2
CUSANELLI CARL F	LTC	0-1296495	1060	1
CUSHING ANTHONY	MAJ	0-1185866	0863	1
CUSHING CARL C	CW2	W-2110121	1052	1
CUSHING EMORY C	COL	0-0175235	0450	1
CUSHING EUGENE G	M G	0-0286447	0965	3
CUSHING JOSEPH	COL	0-0349677	0660	1
CUSHING LLOYD W	LTC	0-0419425	1062	1
CUSHMAN EDWIN P	COL	0-0275995	0867	3
CUSHMAN JOSEPH W	MAJ	0-1305735	0657	1
CUSHMAN ROBERT B	LTC	0-1641211	0566	1
CUSHMAN ROBERT P	1LT	0-0362863	0246	2
CUSHNER JOHN W	CPT	0-1305736	0346	2
CUSICK JOHN	MAJ	0-1044791	1157	1
CUSICK JOSEPH W	1LT	0-1039301	1056	1
CUSICK JR BART C	MAJ	0-1108596	0265	1
CUSTER PRICE C W	COL	0-0247445	0659	2
CUSTER CHALMERS R	MAJ	0-1643385	1060	1
CUSTER CHARLES A	COL	0-0277290	0961	1
CUSTER GEORGE W	LTC	0-0242157	0245	2
CUSTER HUBERT O	2LT	0-2005443	0246	1
CUSTER MARVIN B	COL	0-0455675	0862	1
CUSTIS EARL R	COL	0-0155311	0947	2
CUTCHINS JOHN A	COL	0-0154314	0648	3
CUTHBERT CLARENCE T	COL	0-0298077	0365	2
CUTHBERT DONALD A	COL	0-0276375	0167	3
CUTHBERT JR JAMES J	MAJ	0-0378761	0844	2
CUTHBERT RICHARD F	2LT	0-2036052	0445	2
CUTHBERTSON C C	CPT	0-1555192	0259	1
CUTHBERTSON WILLIAM	CW4	W-2148228	0667	2
CUTLER ALLEN G	2LT	0-1310580	0945	1
CUTLER CHESTER A	COL	0-0256629	0960	3
CUTLER DAVID	WO1	W-2122293	0149	1
CUTLER HARRY S	MAJ	0-0115335	0355	3
CUTLER IRVING	CPT	0-1299535	0159	1
CUTLER LEO J	1LT	0-0369554	1143	2
CUTLER MORTON T	MAJ	0-2047964	0964	1
CUTLER NORMAN P	1LT	0-1010998	1045	2
CUTLER QUENTIN R	CW2	W-2205667	0361	1
CUTLER RAYMOND H	LTC	0-1296822	0167	1

292-560 O - 68 - 9

NAME	GRADE	SVC NO	DATE RET MO YR	RET CODE
CUTLER SAMUEL	LTC	0-0208232	1163	3
CUTLER THORNTON L	COL	0-0124511	0555	3
CUTRER JAMES F	2LT	0-1303861	0445	2
CUTRER JR LEWIS W	2LT	0-4033959	0956	2
CUTSHALL LEONARD L	COL	0-0216453	1263	3
CUTSHALL LEONARD W	MAJ	0-0397698	0561	1
CUTTER JR HENRY T	LTC	0-1329329	0465	1
CUTTER LEON E	CPT	0-0165611	0653	3
CUTTER LLOYD A	LTC	0-0237183	0465	3
CUTTIN LUIGI W	CW2	W-2104990	0943	2
CUTTING ROBERT F	1LT	0-0961764	1152	2
CUTTS EVERETT T	CW2	RW-2146188	0263	1
CUTTS FRANCIS W	LTC	0-1057028	1167	1
CUTTS JR WARREN G	2LT	0-0539214	0245	2
CUVIELLO JOSEPH M	LTC	0-0309671	1166	3
CWALINSKI EDWARD J	CW3	W-2110769	0659	1
CYPRET CLELLA O	CPT	0-0479220	0659	1
CYR EUCLID J	1LT	0-1168622	1145	2
CYR HUBERT G	CW4	W-2101580	1154	1
CYR LUCIEN	1LT	0-1946941	0556	1
CYRIER BERNARD A	CPT	0-1313155	0447	1
CZACH MARY A	MAJ	N-0731473	0566	1
CZAJKOWSKI JOHN J	2LT	0-1015853	0845	2
CZAJKOWSKI WALTER S	LTC	0-0451521	0557	1
CZAPLA EDWIN H	LTC	0-0450742	0557	1
CZAPLA WALTER A	CPT	0-2017022	0266	2
CZAPRAN WALTER P	LTC	0-1058965	0764	1
CZARKOWSKI HARRY S	CW3	W-2150295	1262	1
CZARNIK RAYMOND T	LTC	0-1039302	0167	1
CZARNY KASMIR R	LTC	0-1039106	0163	1
CZECHOWICZ MARTIN C	LTC	0-0419936	0965	1
CZERNIEJEWSKI R C	CPT	0-0888853	0746	2
CZERNY WILLIAM	LTC	0-1052310	0763	1
CZERSKI EDWARD	LTC	0-1637255	0557	1
CZUHAJEWSKI FRANK J	MAJ	0-1315275	0566	1
CZWALINA PAUL F	CW3	W-2147022	0860	1
DA PRATO RAYMOND E	LTC	0-0438844	0764	1
DABB WAYNE C	1LT	0-0811324	1055	2
DABBS RALPH T	LTC	0-0065244	1167	1
DABERRY JOHN D	CW2	W-2150018	1160	2
DABLER HARRY L	MAJ	0-0270223	0752	3
DABNEY WALTER H	LTC	0-0267438	1162	1
DABOV ANTONY	MAJ	0-1043602	0861	1
DABRAVALSKAS JOHN P	MAJ	0-1557831	1066	1
DABROWSKI STANLEY J	1LT	0-1298360	0361	1
DACH RICHARD J	CPT	0-0485321	1145	2
DACHMAN BERNARD	2LT	0-1002403	0444	2
DACK MERLE F	CW3	W-2141242	0363	1
DACKLIN PAUL H	MAJ	0-1337402	0161	1
DADA THEODORE A	1LT	0-0467446	0645	2
DADDATO FRANK J	CW2	W-2151785	1162	1
DADDOW ELWOOD G	LTC	0-1332625	0161	1
DADICH MATTHEW	MAJ	0-2263150	1061	1
DADO JAMES	CPT	0-0211370	0644	2
DAFFRON CLYDE E	WO1	W-2119296	0150	1
DAFFRON MARGARET M	1LT	N-0736737	0253	2
DAFFRON PHILLIP L	CPT	0-0356110	0745	2
DAGENHART QUENTIN S	2LT	0-1296823	1144	2
DAGGETT BUFORD B	CPT	0-1284300	1053	1
DAGGETT FRED G	MAJ	0-1542494	0157	1
DAGGETT LYLE E	MAJ	0-1692578	0358	1
DAGGETT ROSS E	CW3	W-2126791	0854	2
DAGNALL JAMES D	LTC	0-1106061	0562	1
DAGNEY ISABELLA F	2LT	N-0703767	0844	1
DAGOSTINO ANGELO A	MAJ	0-2051432	0361	1
DAGOSTINO RALPH	WO1	W-2122188	1148	1
DAGUCON PEDRO	2LT	0-1896443	0465	1
DAGWORTHY JOHN H	CPT	0-0916499	0766	3
DAHL ARNOLD C	1LT	0-0285500	0945	2
DAHL ARTHUR G	COL	0-0231408	0761	3
DAHL ARVID P	LTC	0-0375760	0860	1
DAHL EARL B	LTC	0-0252297	0465	3
DAHL HERBERT A	1LT	0-1180158	0647	2
DAHL JACK V	2LT	0-1823845	0545	2
DAHL JOHN K	LTC	0-2034510	0265	1
DAHL JOHN S	MAJ	0-0887582	1266	1
DAHL JOSEPH V	1LT	0-1300288	1045	2
DAHL LAWRENCE K	1LT	0-1533764	1059	1
DAHL OWEN C	1LT	0-2055267	0748	2
DAHL RICHARD S	MAJ	0-1291427	1265	1
DAHL WILLIAM E	LTC	0-0238104	0263	3
DAHLBERG GEORGE P	1LT	0-0918700	0944	2
DAHLBERG LENEX V	CW2	W-2152763	0761	1
DAHLEN DUANE C	MAJ	0-0942992	0163	1
DAHLGREN ARNOLD W	LTC	0-1797263		1
DAHLGREN DALE A	MAJ	0-0354713	1050	2
DAHLIN LE ROY F	CPT	0-0325971	1045	2
DAHLIN TORALF A	CW3	W-2152544	0364	1
DAHLKE OTTO H	LTC	0-0410994	1063	1
DAHLMAN ORRIN J	MAJ	0-1030462	1157	1
DAHLQUIST LAWRENCE V	CW2	W-2151404	0758	1
DAHLSTROM CARROL A	CPT	0-0322998	0145	2
DAHMEN CHARLES A	LTC	0-0400014	1166	1
DAHMEN DANIEL J	1LT	0-1823416	0246	2
DAHN ROBERT C	MAJ	0-1877898	0767	1
DAHRLING BRUCE E	LTC	0-0364805	1263	1
DAIB WALTER C	LTC	0-0405380	0464	3
DAIGER JOHN G	LTC	0-0124726	0456	3
DAIGER WILLIAM H	LTC	0-0252359	0367	3
DAIGLE ALBERT J	MAJ	0-1556859	0854	1
DAIGLE ALBERT P	LTC	0-1001536	0658	1
DAIGLE DEBORAH	1LT	N-0720849	0346	1
DAIGLE HORACE F	CW2	W-2151211	0959	1
DAIGLE JOHN P	1LT	0-1339850	0752	1
DAIGLE JR ROYCEN E	LTC	0-1171567	0666	1
DAIGLE PAUL J	LTC	0-0316223	0161	1
DAIGLE RICHARD J	LTC	0-0472379	0151	1
DAILEY EDMOND R	CPT	0-0289695	0745	2
DAILEY ELLEN F	2LT	N-0722168	1043	1
DAILEY ERNEST W	1LT	0-1304036	1047	1
DAILEY JOSEPH M	1LT	0-0490393	0143	2
DAILEY MARION H	1LT	N-0776685	0945	1
DAILEY MARK C	MAJ	0-1589147	0857	2
DAILEY ROBERT C	LTC	0-1548387	0861	1
DAILEY WILLIAM G	MAJ	0-1947476	0161	1
DAILEY WILLIAM J	MAJ	0-0944673	0462	1
DAILY CLARENCE H	1LT	0-1302660	0745	2
DAILY GEORGE S	MAJ	0-2026573	0263	1
DAILY JR HENRY R	LTC	0-1547575	0166	1
DAILY RICHARD	COL	0-0201881	0856	3
DAILY ROBERT R	1LT	0-2025398	1060	1
DAILY SR ALLEN H	CW3	W-2010379	0958	3
DAILY VICTOR L	2LT	0-1310412	0943	2
DAINA MORDECAI M	LTC	0-0926988	1065	2
DAINES DELBERT A	CW3	W-2145409	1062	1
DAINES HAZEN B	LTC	0-0322294	0546	2
DAINTY CLEO L	CW3	W-2152945	1265	1
DAIS HENRY J	CPT	0-1174550	0448	2
DAIUTOLO CARMEN E	MAJ	0-1821689	0653	1
DAKAN FRANK P	COL	0-1101795	0366	1
DAKE III BENJAMIN F	MAJ	0-1120525	0665	1
DAKE JR JOHN P	MAJ	0-1686737	0765	1
DALATON MARK S	1LT	0-1896479	0466	1
DALBIAI MANLEY A	COL	0-1577067	1165	1
DALBOTTEN INGEBORG M	2LT	N-0701832	0933	1
DALBY CHRIS N	CW3	W-2138251	1160	1
DALBY HERBERT W	LTC	0-0320065	0362	1
DALBY RAYMOND E	CPT	0-2041006	0546	1
DALE ADRIAN S	CPT	0-0510520	0953	1
DALE BURIS C	LTC	0-0792003	1065	1
DALE CHARLES S	CPT	0-1283918	0546	2
DALE CLARENCE M	CPT	0-0213114	0357	3
DALE EDWARD J	MAJ	0-1285560	0361	1
DALE GEORGE H	LTC	0-0175953	0648	3
DALE IRVING H	COL	0-0251271	0861	3
DALE JAMES A	MAJ	0-1120612	0663	1
DALE JOE BOB	MAJ	0-2103020	0265	1
DALE JR REX R	2LT	0-1338318	0446	2
DALE LEROY	CW3	W-2143715	1060	1
DALE RAYMOND	MAJ	0-2055824	0257	1
DALE ROBERT J	MAJ	0-1548036	0161	1
DALEMBERTE CLINTON H	LTC	0-1533534	0365	1
DALEN ROSCOE E	MAJ	0-1641115	0363	1
DALES JR BERTRAM B	COL	0-0370504	0964	1
DALESSANDRO D T	1LT	0-1016317	1052	1
DALESSIO JOSEPH A	CPT	0-0487031	0644	2
DALESSIO WAGNER J	LTC	0-0262179	0567	3
DALEY ADALENE F	1LT	N-0730291	0646	1
DALEY CHARLES S	CPT	0-1304505	0446	2
DALEY FRANCIS G	MAJ	0-0546553	0166	1
DALEY GEORGE F	1LT	0-1846412	1045	2
DALEY JAMES P	CW2	W-2214619	1166	1
DALEY JEREMIAH	LTC	0-1283730	0557	1
DALEY PATRICK	CW2	W-2129709	0561	1
DALEY ROLAND R	CPT	0-0191320	0153	3
DALEY THOMAS F	LTC	0-0551043	0864	1
DALEY WALTER E	LTC	0-1308111	0557	1
DALEY WILLIAM	CPT	0-0333025	0648	3
DALGLIESH GEORGE E	LTC	0-0413928	0862	1
DALIPE JUAN	MAJ	0-0200848	0849	1
DALKE CLAYTON G	LTC	0-2035804	1160	1
DALKE RICHARD L	CW4	RW-2141243	1062	1
DALL CHARLES W	LTC	0-0101788	0648	3
DALL NORMAN F	1LT	0-0885441	0450	1
DALLAIRE ERNEST A	LTC	0-1553243	0462	1
DALLAS ALLEN K	LTC	0-2274769	0563	1
DALLAS BERTRAM J	MAJ	0-1294097	0164	1
DALLAS DOROTHY M	1LT	N-0722249	0346	1
DALLAS MAURICE H	CPT	0-0241861	1164	3
DALLAS RUSSELL L	MAJ	0-0227396	1144	2
DALLENBACH JOHN C	COL	0-0108553	0648	3
DALLENBACH KARL M	LTC	0-0159733	0648	3
DALMAO JOSEPH	1LT	0-1896861	0351	2
DALO PEDRO E	CW3	W-2147227	0465	2
DALRYMPLE DONALD I	LTC	0-1293213	0556	1
DALRYMPLE LAWRENCE A	CPT	0-0338186	0862	2
DALRYMPLE LESTER R	LTC	0-1179050	0662	1
DALRYMPLE ROBERT A	MAJ	0-1999879	0364	1
DALTON ALVIN J	CPT	0-0976488	0261	1
DALTON CHARLES E	CPT	0-2005616	0157	1
DALTON CHARLES W	CPT	0-0494099	0255	1
DALTON EDWARD J	MAJ	0-1913482	0962	1
DALTON ELBERT	CPT	0-0461454	0246	2
DALTON FRANCIS P	CW2	W-2113927	0644	2
DALTON HAROLD J	CW3	W-2145268	0363	1
DALTON HELEN L	1LT	N-0795519	0547	1
DALTON JACK	CW2	W-2122299	0749	1
DALTON JOHN B	MAJ	0-0244470	0154	3
DALTON JOHN S	1LT	0-0449495	1143	2
DALTON JOHN W	1LT	0-1179051	0546	2
DALTON JR JOHN T	2LT	0-1999819	0351	2
DALTON KENNETH W	COL	0-0297636	0460	1
DALTON LILLIAN F	1LT	N-0729083	0247	1
DALTON LUKE E	MAJ	0-0290202	1061	2
DALTON MARSHALL A	LTC	0-0425251	0561	1
DALTON ROBERT J	LTC	0-0295246	1263	3
DALTON THEODORE J	LTC	0-0338853	0757	1
DALTON THOMAS J	CW4	W-2106352	0862	1
DALTON WILLIAM A	CPT	0-2262498	0857	1
DALTON WILLIAM M	CPT	0-1056686	1256	2
DALTRY RAYMOND F	LTC	0-1318288	0763	1
DALWAY BENJAMIN C	MAJ	0-0379203	0245	2
DALY ANDREW	LTC	0-1825087	1154	1
DALY CHARLES B	LTC	0-0973470	0766	3
DALY DENIS A	LTC	0-0193433	0648	3
DALY FRANK A	1LT	0-0358726	0848	1
DALY FREDERICK	MAJ	0-1081061	0860	1
DALY HARRIET C	MAJ	N-0799473	0466	1
DALY HARRY A	LTC	0-0512351	0850	1
DALY JAMES E	COL	0-0109809	0347	1
DALY JAMES G	CPT	0-0269760	0765	3
DALY JAMES J	LTC	0-1638936	0762	1
DALY JAMES V	LTC	0-0463570	0657	1
DALY JAMES V	MAJ	0-1845697	0660	1
DALY JAMES W	CPT	0-0386538	0147	1
DALY JOHN A	LTC	0-1004098	1164	1
DALY JOHN F	MAJ	0-0234911	0646	2
DALY JOHN O	CW3	W-2206979	0665	1
DALY JOHN W	LTC	0-0304804	0161	1
DALY JR WILBUR T	LTC	0-0403225	1060	1
DALY LAWRENCE R	MAJ	0-1177356	0765	1
DALY LELAND J	LTC	0-1168625	0562	1
DALY MICHAEL J	CPT	0-1692630	0846	1
DALY OSWALD G	LTC	0-0125622	0754	3
DALY PAUL G	COL	0-0148189	1052	2
DALY PETER F	MAJ	0-0484550	0345	2
DALY THOMAS A	MAJ	0-0273747	0847	1
DALY WILLIAM H	CPT	0-0888289	0546	1
DALY WILLIAM J	2LT	0-1114446	0744	2
DALY WILLIAM J	LTC	0-1165173	0361	1
DALZELL JAMES E	CPT	0-1651782	0556	1
DALZELL JOHN A	MAJ	0-1332537	1162	1
DAM CYRUS K	COL	0-0248451	0865	3
DAMAN CHARLES R	COL	0-0292501	0267	3
DAMATO JOSEPH M	CW3	W-2148509	0163	1
DAME FRANK F	MAJ	0-0285110	0467	3
DAME MARY B	1LT	N-0775489	0548	1
DAME MERENCY R	LTC	0-1314451	1163	1
DAME RAYMOND F	MAJ	0-0455451	0147	2
DAMEN EDWARD M	LTC	0-0450839	0457	1
DAMER THOMAS T	1LT	0-1547580	0547	2
DAMERON JAMES H	CW2	W-2214606	0667	1
DAMERON THOMAS H	COL	0-0192414	0555	3
DAMERON WILLIAM G	LTC	0-0242158	0961	3
DAMEWOOD OSIE C	COL	0-0223241	0256	3
DAMEWOOD WALTER W	LTC	0-0260631	0766	3
DAMGEN EDWARD G	LTC	0-1550769	1061	1
DAMIANA JULES V	1LT	0-1322116	1145	2
DAMIANI COLUMBUS J	1LT	0-0436472	0955	1
DAMIANS PHILIP A	1LT	0-0410486	0845	2
DAMICO ANGELO F	LTC	0-1945110	0465	3
DAMICO ARTHUR	MAJ	0-0420182	0146	2
DAMICO FRANK J	2LT	0-1049123	1043	2
DAMICO JOSEPH P	MAJ	0-1327115	0464	1
DAMICO WILLIAM P	LTC	0-1054527	1165	1
DAMIENS JOSEPH N	MAJ	0-0257182	0145	2
DAMISH ADOLPH	MAJ	0-2017213	1159	1
DAMKOWITCH MICHAEL	LTC	0-1308483	0361	1
DAMMAN RAYMOND F	1LT	0-1644835	0445	1
DAMME WILLIAM H	LTC	0-0238894	0246	2
DAMMEN ARNOLD H	LTC	0-0296083	1067	2
DAMON CHARLES P	LTC	0-0372347	0763	1
DAMON RALPH P	LTC	0-0378428	0656	1
DAMOND JOSEPH L	LTC	0-0234603	0957	3
DAMORE ANTHONY M	1LT	0-1323296	0551	1
DAMORE JOSEPH E	CPT	0-0921487	0645	2
DAMORE ROY	LTC	0-1036499	0563	1
DAMOTH CHARLES F	MAJ	0-1285561	0664	1
DAMPIER CHARLES E	MAJ	0-1313010	0959	1
DAMREN JOHN E	CW3	W-2145765	0863	1
DAMRON SIDNEY F	CPT	0-0475063	0646	2
DAMRON WILBUR T	MAJ	0-0984508	0765	1
DAMROW ARTHUR E	LTC	0-0265655	0763	3
DANA RICHARD A	COL	0-0423622	0160	1
DANAHER RICHARD J	MAJ	0-1949517	1066	1
DANCAK EDWARD J	1LT	0-0507751	0844	2
DANCE CLAUDE A	COL	0-0171495	0961	3
DANCE EUGENE A	LTC	0-1290725	0666	1
DANCE LEE I	MAJ	0-0463471	1052	1
DANCE WILLIAM G	LTC	0-0402115	0266	1
DANCHERTSEN JOHN D	CPT	0-0291896	0752	1
DANCULOVICH GEORGE N	1LT	0-1286573	1045	2
DANDO EDWARD C	LTC	0-0420466	1160	1
DANDO JR ROBERT R	LTC	0-0399456	1060	1
DANDREIC JOSEPH	MAJ	0-1691515	1054	1
DANDRICCE WILLIAM M	MAJ	0-1332538	0765	1
DANDY IRVING E	CPT	0-0977223	0161	1
DANE CLARENCE R	MAJ	0-0260444	1062	2
DANE RALPH N	LTC	0-0419319	0961	1
DANE SIDNEY P	MAJ	0-1313343	0161	1

NAME	GRADE	SVC NO	DATE RET MO YR	RET CODE
DANEKER JOHN L	COL	O-0144465	0855	3
DANEKER JR CHARLES R	MAJ	O-0338957	0844	2
DANENHOUR GEORGE B	MAJ	O-2262398	0662	1
DANER VALENTINA	2LT	N-0725829	1143	1
DANFORD BEECHER	CPT	O-0166621	0648	3
DANFORD CHARLES A	CW3	W-2203487	0865	1
DANFORD ROBERT W	MAJ	O-1647520	0861	1
DANFORTH DWIGHT A	LTC	O-0902868	0665	3
DANFORTH JR E C B	B G	O-0234688	0854	2
DANFORTH LESTER F	LTC	O-0260134	1066	3
DANGELO ANTHONY F	COL	O-0241922	0560	3
DANGELO ANTHONY T	MAJ	O-1999092	0465	1
DANGELO JOHN P	CW2	W-2206029	0763	1
DANGELO VINCENT	MAJ	O-1186636	0765	1
DANGELONE ANTHONY JJ	CW3	W-2147283	1262	1
DANGLER RALPH B	LTC	O-1589783	0665	3
DANGREMOND LEROY M G	LTC	O-0169386	0346	2
DANHOUR GEORGE S	MAJ	O-0142792	0242	1
DANICO MARION L	2LT	N-0754946	0946	1
DANIEL ANDREWS F	WO1	W-2106967	0746	2
DANIEL CAMERON O	CW2	W-2144806	1056	1
DANIEL EARNEST J	MAJ	O-1894843	1161	1
DANIEL ELIJAH W	CW2	W-2121955	0346	2
DANIEL EMMETT W	1LT	O-2003153	0758	2
DANIEL FLOYD F	MAJ	O-0388728	0348	2
DANIEL HAROLD C	1LT	O-0555874	0546	2
DANIEL HENRY S	MAJ	O-0257355	0667	3
DANIEL HERBERT H	CW2	W-2149208	0861	1
DANIEL HERBERT L	MAJ	O-2263309	0765	1
DANIEL HUGH M	MAJ	O-0401406	0944	2
DANIEL JAMES G	LTC	O-0297435	0157	2
DANIEL JAMES M	MAJ	O-1844494	0658	1
DANIEL KENNETH J	LTC	O-0283570	1045	2
DANIEL LANDON G	LTC	O-0162874	0757	3
DANIEL LOUIE S	CPT	O-1693088	0246	2
DANIEL NIK J	1LT	O-2262335	0953	2
DANIEL ORVAL	MAJ	O-1996597	0860	1
DANIEL PENTECOST	CW2	W-2119450	0546	1
DANIEL RALPH	1LT	O-0504181	0263	1
DANIEL RALPH C	MAJ	O-1303679	0760	2
DANIEL RICHARD R	MAJ	O-1183679	0261	1
DANIEL ROBERT L	1LT	O-0336167	0158	3
DANIEL WELDON O	CW4	W-2123164	1264	1
DANIEL WILLIAM H	MAJ	O-1799709	1262	1
DANIELEK SR JAN	CW2	W-2142144	0457	1
DANIELEWICZ EDWARD J	CPT	O-1322133	0148	2
DANIELL JOHN T	LTC	O-0279746	0660	1
DANIELL SMITH C	MAJ	O-0201237	0849	3
DANIELLO ANTHONY A	MAJ	O-1994584	0657	2
DANIELS ANTHONY J	MAJ	O-0420501	0961	1
DANIELS ARTHUR C	MAJ	O-0486021	0445	1
DANIELS CHARLES F	MAJ	O-1300133	0854	2
DANIELS ERNEST W	LTC	O-1177828	0466	1
DANIELS EUGENE	MAJ	O-1549925	1054	1
DANIELS GILBERT	LTC	O-0482671	0457	1
DANIELS HARRISON W	1LT	O-1306069	0446	1
DANIELS HENRY	COL	O-0136778	0851	3
DANIELS HERMAN F	CPT	O-0389399	0446	2
DANIELS HOWARD	1LT	O-1173916	1045	2
DANIELS HOWARD A	MAJ	O-1547265	0959	1
DANIELS IRENE H	CPT	N-0795855	0555	2
DANIELS JAMES N	MAJ	O-1547267	0964	2
DANIELS JOHN T	MAJ	O-1304038	0159	1
DANIELS JOHN T	CW3	W-2150237	0164	1
DANIELS JR FRANK	CW3	W-2205745	1165	1
DANIELS JR HARRY R	MAJ	O-0387235	0646	2
DANIELS JR JOHN H	LTC	O-1293019	0463	1
DANIELS KENNETH W	MAJ	O-1924870	0866	1
DANIELS LEROY H	WO1	W-2143193	0663	1
DANIELS OREL M	CPT	O-2018307	0360	1
DANIELS PAUL R	COL	O-0321524	0661	2
DANIELS PAUL B	MAJ	O-1897732	0361	1
DANIELS PERCY E	MAJ	O-0247143	0262	3
DANIELS REUBEN W	LTC	O-0203842	1046	1
DANIELS REX D	LTC	O-0336245	0546	2

NAME	GRADE	SVC NO	DATE RET MO YR	RET CODE
DANIELS SR EUGENE B	LTC	O-0335512	0961	3
DANIELS SR HILLIARD	CW3	W-2145051	0263	1
DANIELS WALTER L	LTC	O-0255014	0457	3
DANIELS WILLIAM J	MAJ	O-1688479	1065	1
DANIELSON BERT L	MAJ	O-0967897	1060	1
DANIELSON ERNEST L	LTC	O-0162398	1044	2
DANIELSON LINNEA A	MAJ	N-0777537	1161	2
DANIELSON PAUL F	CPT	O-1306388	0048	2
DANIELSON RAYMOND W	MAJ	O-0248271	0265	3
DANIELSON RUEBEN J	CW4	W-2143505	0762	1
DANITZ ANSELM L	CPT	O-0258279	1044	2
DANKS GENE H	MAJ	O-0922067	1045	2
DANLEY JOSEPH C	COL	O-0247153	0457	1
DANLEY JR PRINCE H	MAJ	O-1551187	0556	1
DANN ARTHUR G	CPT	O-4005082	1165	1
DANN CLIFFORD H	LTC	O-1311125	1061	1
DANN JR ROSCOE E	MAJ	O-2202804	0466	1
DANNENMUELLER ELMER	CW4	W-2008170	0566	3
DANNER ELLIS	LTC	O-0259430	0467	3
DANNER EUGENE B	LTC	O-1055923	0563	1
DANNER LEROY M	LTC	O-1573834	0865	1
DANNER LYMAN F	WO1	W-2130179	0962	1
DANNER REX W	CW2	W-2119540	0665	1
DANNIS LOUIS W	1LT	O-0403322	0646	2
DANO BASIL W	LTC	O-1546942	0962	2
DANSBY BRADLEY L	LTC	O-0237361	1265	3
DANSER ROBERT C	LTC	O-0403217	1157	1
DANSON PAUL A	LTC	O-0217267	1160	1
DANTON RITA P	MAJ	L-1010212	0365	1
DANTONIC RINALDO N	CW2	W-2148847	0963	1
DANTZLER DANIEL B	CPT	O-0496156	0345	2
DANTZLER JR EDWARD A	LTC	O-0904258	1067	2
DANZENBAKER JOHN D	LTC	O-1296180	0964	1
DANZI RICHARD A	LTC	O-1822375	0746	2
DANZIGER DANIEL	LTC	O-0212857	0737	1
DARBE RAY E	CW3	W-2207630	0467	1
DARBY JEWELL F	MAJ	N-0735511	0663	1
DARBY JOHNIE T	LTC	O-1297690	0960	1
DARBY NORMAN D	LTC	O-1107892	0362	1
DARCANGELIS A F	CPT	O-1586470	0347	2
DARCHE LEO J	CW4	W-2102805	0859	1
DARCY ARTHUR F H	CPT	O-0265065	0455	3
DARCY HELEN K	1LT	N-0787034	1046	1
DARDEN ARNOLD W	CPT	O-1323544	0348	2
DARDEN DANIEL M	2LT	O-1318259	0245	2
DARDEN EDWIN H	CPT	O-0450841	1143	2
DARDEN JAMES W	LTC	O-0398206	0561	1
DARE AFTON	LTC	O-1179829	0664	1
DARE BEATRICE M	LTC	N-0701180	0446	1
DARE EDWARD	MAJ	O-0191347	0653	3
DARE EDWIN C	CW3	W-2145878	0564	1
DARGAN WALTER C	CPT	O-0248996	0946	2
DARGUSCH CARLTON S	B G	O-0246180	0947	2
DARISCH HENRY F	LTC	O-1111013	0567	3
DARK CARLETON W	LTC	O-0157089	0857	3
DARK FOY F	LTC	O-1341754	0767	1
DARKE FRANCIS J	COL	O-0291764	0547	2
DARKER EVELYN A	MAJ	N-0769177	0365	2
DARKEY GUY F	MAJ	O-0461812	0846	1
DARKEY KARL L	LTC	O-0343377	0659	3
DARKOW ALWIN J	LTC	O-0263385	0862	1
DARLEY WILLIAM H	MAJ	O-0395509	0860	1
DARLING BRICE H	CPT	O-1310688	1046	1
DARLING BRUCE R	2LT	O-1012832	1044	2
DARLING BYRON P	MAJ	O-1045459	1155	1
DARLING CLINTON S	MAJ	O-0117178	0865	1
DARLING FRANCIS W	COL	O-0265108	0966	3
DARLING GERALD S	LTC	O-0359644	0366	3
DARLING MAYO A	COL	O-0172647	0358	3
DARLING RICHARD W	1LT	O-1002897	0746	1
DARLING WILFRED O	COL	O-0257594	1067	3
DARLING WILLIAM V	CPT	O-0321473	0747	2
DARLINGTON BURLEY H	CPT	O-0498158	1048	1
DARLINGTON HARRY D	COL	O-0255142	0365	3
DARLINGTON JOHN E	LTC	O-1106672	1266	3

NAME	GRADE	SVC NO	DATE RET MO YR	RET CODE
DARMAND ROSCOE C	LTC	O-0209809	1052	3
DARMER EDWILL E	1LT	O-0483071	0345	1
DARMOPRAY MICHAEL	MAJ	O-0150171	0856	3
DARNALL JAMES W	LTC	O-0486003	0554	1
DARNELL GRACY P	CPT	O-0973557	0361	1
DARNELL ORVAL D	1LT	O-1923030	1053	2
DARNELL RALPH R	LTC	O-1166467	0556	1
DARNELL THOMAS F	MAJ	O-1633790	0954	1
DARNELL WILLIAM R	MAJ	O-0482469	1144	1
DARNER FLOYD W	MAJ	O-2262310	0563	1
DARNER OTIS L	MAJ	O-0348630	0759	3
DARR WILLIAM H	CPT	O-0486132	0852	1
DARRACOTT HALVOR T	COL	O-0391615	1062	1
DARRAGH JOHN C	CW3	W-2101587	0956	1
DARRAGH SCUDDER H	LTC	O-0525619	0965	3
DARRIGO JOSEPH	CPT	O-1325278	0451	1
DARRIN WILLIAM A	1LT	O-1317894	0446	2
DARROUGH GLENN E	LTC	O-1637258	1163	1
DARROUGH JOHN W	COL	O-0214672	0364	3
DARROUGH WILLIAM J	LTC	O-0233129	0955	3
DARROW ALBERT	MAJ	O-0499263	1051	1
DARROW ROBERT C	1LT	O-1180160	0945	2
DARROW RUSSELL E	MAJ	O-1534465	0357	1
DARST GEORGE I	MAJ	O-1164479	0664	1
DART JOHN	COL	O-0205781	0446	2
DARTENAY LEO P	LTC	O-1557438	1160	1
DARTEZ JOHN E	2LT	O-1795867	1159	2
DASDORF JOHN H	LTC	O-0494687	1261	3
DASHIELL SAMUEL C	MAJ	O-1111565	1265	1
DASHIELL WILLARD H	MAJ	O-0402586	0663	1
DASHNER RICHARD W	MAJ	O-0422625	1058	1
DASINGER ANTON F	1LT	O-0399448	0145	2
DASSE PIERRE L	CW4	W-2006856	0366	1
DASTOLI ANGELO N	CW3	W-2151690	0956	1
DATOC QUARDALOPE	1LT	O-2023827	1049	1
DATSON JOHN F	COL	O-0231953	0551	3
DATTLER JOHN C	LTC	O-2036367	0164	1
DAUBENFELD ALFRED F	LTC	O-0360144	0262	1
DAUBENSPECK LOUIS A	CW2	W-2208631	1060	1
DAUBENSPECK WAYNE M	COL	O-0336775	1264	3
DAUBER ELMER C	CW3	W-2144755	0162	1
DAUDELIN FREDERICK	CW4	W-2153144	1060	1
DAUDELIN JOE B	COL	O-0336127	1061	2
DAUDELIN NORMAN A	MAJ	O-0987407	0663	1
DAUE ARNOLD K	MAJ	O-2036368	0760	1
DAUGETTE CLARENCE W	COL	O-0326457	1063	3
DAUGHERTY CARY S	COL	O-0237033	0765	3
DAUGHERTY CHARLES B	LTC	O-0182240	0554	3
DAUGHERTY DURWOOD A	LTC	O-1289009	0557	1
DAUGHERTY FRED N	LTC	O-0279348	0657	3
DAUGHERTY HENRY S	LTC	O-0300320	0162	1
DAUGHERTY HERSCHEL	MAJ	O-0981499	1265	2
DAUGHERTY HUGH D	CPT	O-1573149	1045	2
DAUGHERTY JOSEPH P	CPT	O-0101002	0649	1
DAUGHERTY LEE F	LTC	O-0499535	0960	1
DAUGHERTY LYLE S	LTC	O-0340520	1159	1
DAUGHERTY SIMPSON B	COL	O-0254961	0551	3
DAUGHERTY TEMPLE J	MAJ	O-1080011	0261	1
DAUGHERTY THOMAS J	MAJ	O-1996670	1060	1
DAUGHTON KILMER E	CPT	O-0437949	0863	1
DAUGHTREY LYMAN C	MAJ	O-0197342	0263	3
DAUGHTRY EDWARD F	CW3	W-2143842	0659	1
DAUGUSTINE ANTHONY P	MAJ	O-1100941	0760	1
DAUGUSTINO PATRICK	CPT	O-2046562	0250	1
DAUME KENNETH R	1LT	O-0470588	0345	2
DAUN ARTHUR L	MAJ	O-1553245	0657	1
DAUNIS JOHN F	MAJ	O-0512477	0646	2
DAUPHIN LESTER R	MAJ	O-2042964	1058	1
DAUS ARCHIE H	MAJ	O-1692932	1058	1
DAUS MILTON J	MAJ	O-0258657	0945	2
DAUSEY FRANK W	LTC	O-1047493	0165	1
DAUWAY ALFONSO	CPT	O-0169316	0559	3
DAVANZO CHARLES S	CPT	O-0331541	1045	1
DAVEE CHARLES W	1LT	O-0971937	1152	1
DAVENPORT ARTHUR I	LTC	O-0234348	0765	3

NAME	GRADE	SVC NO	DATE RET MO YR	RET CODE
DAVENPORT ARTHUR R	MAJ	O-0961661	1163	1
DAVENPORT CHARLES F	2LT	O-1306248	0245	2
DAVENPORT CHESTER L	LTC	O-0348610	1262	2
DAVENPORT CLARA H	2LT	N-0764934	0446	1
DAVENPORT CLINTON M	MAJ	O-2103039	0964	1
DAVENPORT DARYL R	MAJ	O-0954673	0465	1
DAVENPORT DORSEY H	LTC	O-0290285	0264	3
DAVENPORT EDGAR E	MAJ	O-0961924	0965	1
DAVENPORT EDWARD I	LTC	O-0400911	0760	1
DAVENPORT ESTELLE E	MAJ	L-2291711	1067	1
DAVENPORT HAROLD D	MAJ	O-0310161	1059	1
DAVENPORT J C	LTC	O-1633152	0160	1
DAVENPORT JAMES M	COL	O-0358076	0865	2
DAVENPORT JOHN S	LTC	O-0487018	1062	1
DAVENPORT JOSEPH R	CPT	O-0164183	0836	1
DAVENPORT LEO R	CPT	O-1032425	0261	1
DAVENPORT MARSHALL R	1LT	O-1011172	1046	1
DAVENPORT MERLE F	1LT	O-1307670	0651	1
DAVENPORT NORMAN F	LTC	O-1173579	0662	1
DAVENPORT RALPH H	LTC	O-0567830	0864	1
DAVENPORT ROBERT E	MAJ	O-1686693	0465	1
DAVENPORT ROY C	LTC	O-0508710	0846	2
DAVENPORT ROY L	MAJ	O-2212058	0265	1
DAVES MAX F	MAJ	O-0565154	0256	1
DAVES ROBERT W	LTC	O-1798458	1161	1
DAVEY DONALD A	1LT	O-1295840	0645	2
DAVEY EDWARD J	CPT	O-1692946	0946	1
DAVEY KENNETH V	LTC	O-1100942	1057	1
DAVEY ROBERT G	LTC	O-0364816	0760	1
DAVEY THOMAS A	CW4	W-2146743	0564	1
DAVIA DAVID W	CW3	W-2142497	0859	1
DAVID ALEXANDER	MAJ	O-1334114	1263	1
DAVID CHARLES F	CPT	O-0493933	0753	1
DAVID EDWARD F	LTC	O-0297740	1045	1
DAVID FREDERICK	LTC	O-1826041	0363	1
DAVID HERMAN D	MAJ	O-0198724	1153	3
DAVID LAWRENCE P	MAJ	O-0994888	1065	1
DAVID LEON T	COL	O-0201780	0961	3
DAVID MARSHALL S	LTC	O-0265200	0166	3
DAVID ROBERT E	LTC	O-1012836	0766	1
DAVID ROSE	2LT	N-0790592	0746	1
DAVIDS THAD	1LT	O-0337625	1044	2
DAVIDSON ALTA F	1LT	N-0703757	0446	1
DAVIDSON ARCHIE B	LTC	O-1287312	0263	1
DAVIDSON BENJAMIN F	CW2	W-2144832	1060	1
DAVIDSON C G	1LT	O-1113657	1145	2
DAVIDSON CHARLES V	LTC	O-0376242	0156	1
DAVIDSON ELI L	CW2	W-2143894	0861	1
DAVIDSON ERNEST C	MAJ	O-1695712	1159	1
DAVIDSON EUGENE W	1LT	O-0420523	0545	2
DAVIDSON FRANK F	MAJ	O-1552655	0356	1
DAVIDSON FRED	LTC	O-2044531	0655	1
DAVIDSON HAROLD V	CPT	O-0917747	0145	2
DAVIDSON HARRY D	LTC	O-1107894	1060	1
DAVIDSON HEBERT	COL	O-0240079	0662	3
DAVIDSON HERBERT L	COL	O-0256521	0662	3
DAVIDSON HYATT L	LTC	O-0375913	1062	1
DAVIDSON IRVING E	CW2	W-2214501	0766	1
DAVIDSON JESSE H	COL	O-0255927	0556	3
DAVIDSON JEWEL L	1LT	O-1177357	0745	2
DAVIDSON JOHN L	LTC	O-1288714	1060	1
DAVIDSON JOHN R	1LT	O-0421394	0946	2
DAVIDSON JR JAMES F	COL	O-0312108	0759	1
DAVIDSON JR JAMES V	1LT	O-1546943	1045	2
DAVIDSON JR W S	LTC	O-0265450	0452	3
DAVIDSON JUSTUS S	MAJ	O-0173239	0855	3
DAVIDSON LESTER E	CW3	W-2148252	0761	1
DAVIDSON LILLIAN M	2LT	N-0777301	0446	1
DAVIDSON MARGARET M	2LT	N-0737438	0744	1
DAVIDSON MARION	1LT	O-2046396	1145	1
DAVIDSON MURRAY P	LTC	O-0275503	0766	3
DAVIDSON NORMAN H	MAJ	O-0144716	0354	3
DAVIDSON OLE K	MAJ	O-0278531	0554	3
DAVIDSON ROYCE L	MAJ	O-0973555	1064	1
DAVIDSON SAMUEL L	COL	O-0162543	1149	1

NAME	GRADE	SVC NO	DATE RET MO YR	RET CODE
DAVIDSON TEDDY R	CW2	W-2212572	1065	1
DAVIDSON WALLACE N	COL	0-0198015	0153	3
DAVIDSON WESLEY H	LTC	0-1304870	0961	1
DAVIDSON WILLIAM S	LTC	0-0484260	0665	1
DAVIDSON WILLIAM T	LTC	0-1592758	0767	3
DAVIE GEORGE A	MAJ	0-0464450	1054	1
DAVIE JAMES C	LTC	0-0309804	0462	3
DAVIE PAUL J	LTC	0-1310815	0862	1
DAVIE WARREN C	1LT	0-1637261	0845	2
DAVIES ADELAIDE A	MAJ	N-0756489	0563	1
DAVIES ALAN A	CPT	0-1177758	0847	2
DAVIES CLARENCE F	COL	0-0134089	0351	3
DAVIES CLYDE T	LTC	0-0197493	1160	1
DAVIES DAVID G	CPT	0-0227383	0564	3
DAVIES DAVID J	CPT	0-1030554	0361	1
DAVIES DAVID M	MAJ	0-1925899	0667	1
DAVIES EUGENE C	LTC	0-0308947	0660	1
DAVIES GEORGE N	LTC	0-0411033	0757	1
DAVIES HARRY H	LTC	0-0253625	0561	3
DAVIES HOMER G	MAJ	0-0138709	0648	3
DAVIES IVOR J	COL	0-0499026	1065	3
DAVIES JAMES E	MAJ	0-1036939	0461	2
DAVIES JOHN F	CW2	W-2117964	1049	1
DAVIES JOHN R	MAJ	0-0997098	1163	1
DAVIES JR CHARLES W	MAJ	0-1042540	0860	1
DAVIES PURCELL R	CPT	0-0244801	1159	3
DAVIES RAY J	LTC	0-0455587	1059	1
DAVIES RICHARD P	CW3	W-2143437	0561	1
DAVIES ROBERT P	1LT	0-1637262	0252	1
DAVIES ROBERT R	MAJ	0-1650818	1159	1
DAVIES RONALD E	MAJ	0-1895008	0662	1
DAVIES RUSSELL G	CPT	0-1169477	0846	2
DAVIES SAM L	LTC	0-0342728	0859	1
DAVIES SAMUEL D	LTC	0-0260446	0544	2
DAVIES STANLEY J	MAJ	0-1046762	0159	1
DAVIES THOMAS	LTC	0-2055891	0557	1
DAVIES WILLIAM	LTC	0-1302435	0366	1
DAVIES WILLIAM A	1LT	0-1558479	0246	2
DAVIES WILLIAM C	CW3	W-2112562	0660	1
DAVIES WILLIAM J	CPT	0-1299383	0147	2
DAVILA BENIGNO	MAJ	0-0227751	0365	3
DAVILA FERNANDO T	MAJ	0-1328677	0763	1
DAVILA LUIS A	CPT	0-2263291	0761	1
DAVILA RAFAEL	1LT	0-0167773	1052	3
DAVILA RUDOLPH B	1LT	0-1692556	0550	1
DAVIN HARRISON L	LTC	0-0489792	1164	3
DAVIS ADDISON C	1LT	0-0374063	0844	2
DAVIS ALBERT H	MAJ	0-0228847	1262	3
DAVIS ALBERT M	2LT	0-2034512	0545	2
DAVIS ALBERT R	CPT	0-0150423	0854	3
DAVIS ALEXANDER	LTC	0-0251780	0353	3
DAVIS ALLEN K	LTC	0-0207451	1056	1
DAVIS ALLIE F	CW4	W-2111195	0356	1
DAVIS ALVIN D	MAJ	0-1885368	1265	1
DAVIS ALVIN L	CPT	0-1053553	0460	2
DAVIS ANDREW A	MAJ	0-0181882	0255	3
DAVIS ANNA M	1LT	N-0768453	0348	1
DAVIS ARDIE M	MAJ	0-2025895	1059	1
DAVIS ARNOLD K	1LT	0-1647359	0246	2
DAVIS ARTHUR A	1LT	0-0179628	0360	3
DAVIS ARTHUR C	WO1	W-2129690	0645	2
DAVIS ARTHUR D	LTC	0-0489370	1055	1
DAVIS ARTHUR L	1LT	0-1103585	0547	2
DAVIS BAXTER C	LTC	0-0353502	1145	2
DAVIS BEN M	MAJ	0-0155014	0155	3
DAVIS BENJAMIN F	CPT	0-0167927	0558	3
DAVIS BENJAMIN H	CPT	0-0116175	1048	2
DAVIS BOWIE W	1LT	0-1304039	1045	2
DAVIS BRUCE A	MAJ	0-1686579	0662	1
DAVIS BURTON F	1LT	0-1314261	0845	2
DAVIS CALEB	MAJ	0-1703015	0258	1
DAVIS CARL F	CPT	0-0461673	0944	2
DAVIS CARL P	LTC	0-0248112	1050	2
DAVIS CARROL F	CW4	W-2122946	1054	1
DAVIS CARROLL R	MAJ	0-0157720	0145	2

NAME	GRADE	SVC NO	DATE RET MO YR	RET CODE
DAVIS CARY A	1LT	0-0208249	0253	3
DAVIS CATHERINE	MAJ	N-0737039	0464	3
DAVIS CHARLES C	CW2	W-2153664	1061	1
DAVIS CHARLES D	LTC	0-0215527	1061	3
DAVIS CHARLES D	MAJ	0-2262384	0463	1
DAVIS CHARLES E	LTC	0-0297250	0459	1
DAVIS CHARLES E	LTC	0-0382975	0660	1
DAVIS CHARLES F	1LT	0-1014454	0744	2
DAVIS CHARLES F	LTC	0-1309045	0562	2
DAVIS CHARLES E	CW2	W-2213454	1167	1
DAVIS CHARLES F	2LT	0-0978454	0352	1
DAVIS CHARLES H	CW3	W-2150582	0566	1
DAVIS CHARLES J	LTC	0-0248088	0846	1
DAVIS CHARLES L	MAJ	0-0225051	1057	3
DAVIS CHARLES M	COL	0-0184468	0439	1
DAVIS CHARLES W	CW4	W-2101591	1054	1
DAVIS CHARLIE	LTC	0-0464453	0258	1
DAVIS CHESTER P	LTC	0-1321376	1166	1
DAVIS CLARENCE C	COL	0-0245380	0766	3
DAVIS CLAUDE L	1LT	0-0490732	0447	1
DAVIS CLAUDE W	LTC	0-0299274	0164	3
DAVIS CLEO G	1LT	0-0446024	1045	2
DAVIS CLYDE	CW3	W-2144971	0563	2
DAVIS CLYDE E	MAJ	0-1642784	0557	1
DAVIS CLYDE M	MAJ	0-1285211	0263	2
DAVIS CURTIS C	MAJ	0-0497910	0157	1
DAVIS CURTIS C	WO1	W-2105928	1045	2
DAVIS DALE	MAJ	0-2036470	0564	1
DAVIS DAMON	1LT	0-2053903	1051	1
DAVIS DANIEL	CPT	0-0425709	1045	2
DAVIS DAVID E	WO1	W-2106684	0346	2
DAVIS DAVID C	LTC	0-0246795	0866	3
DAVIS DELMAR J	CW3	W-2153167	0764	1
DAVIS DELROY R	MAJ	0-0443250	0847	1
DAVIS DENVER E	1LT	0-0523304	0246	2
DAVIS DEVON A	LTC	0-0510646	0566	3
DAVIS DEWITT D	LTC	0-0220909	0764	3
DAVIS DONALD A	2LT	0-0299280	0544	1
DAVIS DONALD A	CPT	0-1287674	0345	2
DAVIS DONALD D	MAJ	0-0909913	0446	1
DAVIS DONALD S	MAJ	0-1919199	1166	1
DAVIS EARL	LTC	0-0399043	0557	1
DAVIS EARL L	MAJ	0-2262148	0761	2
DAVIS EDGAR C	MAJ	0-0496922	0747	1
DAVIS EDISON L	MAJ	0-1175412	0962	1
DAVIS EDISON O	COL	0-0244990	0360	3
DAVIS EDWARD F	CPT	0-2262782	1160	2
DAVIS EDWARD H	LTC	0-0182585	0954	3
DAVIS EDWARD J	CPT	0-0486761	0853	1
DAVIS EDWARD J	1LT	0-2302258	1257	1
DAVIS EDWIN A	LTC	0-0354192	0463	3
DAVIS EDWIN F	CPT	0-1292484	0459	1
DAVIS ELLSWORTH	COL	0-0359641	0165	1
DAVIS ELMER K	MAJ	0-0238774	0265	3
DAVIS EMMETT R	CPT	0-2044287	0900	1
DAVIS ERNEST G	LTC	0-0320023	0260	3
DAVIS ERVILLE A	CW2	W-2144908	0162	1
DAVIS EVERETT E	MAJ	0-1336490	0762	1
DAVIS FENIMORE E	COL	0-0335605	1165	3
DAVIS FLOYD E	LTC	0-1322979	0263	1
DAVIS FRANCIS E	COL	0-0257430	1067	3
DAVIS FRANCIS W	COL	0-0275021	0660	1
DAVIS FRANK A	CPT	0-1319725	0847	2
DAVIS FRANK F	MAJ	0-0374717	0146	2
DAVIS FRANK H	CPT	0-0487501	0945	2
DAVIS FRANK M	MAJ	0-0405152	0166	3
DAVIS FRANK R	CPT	0-0493626	0950	1
DAVIS FRANK W	CW3	W-2147647	0160	1
DAVIS FRANKLIN C	LTC	0-0245234	1059	1
DAVIS FRANKLIN C	LTC	0-0291926	0964	1
DAVIS FREDERICK	MAJ	0-1294273	0161	1
DAVIS FREDERICK	1LT	0-1800093	0151	1
DAVIS GEORGE	MAJ	0-0200818	0358	3
DAVIS GEORGE A	B G	0-0144767	0648	3
DAVIS GEORGE A	MAJ	0-1688605	1165	1

NAME	GRADE	SVC NO	DATE RET MO YR	RET CODE
DAVIS GEORGE C	LTC	0-0183485	0449	3
DAVIS GEORGE D	CPT	0-0267293	0147	1
DAVIS GEORGE H	COL	0-0307826	0167	3
DAVIS GEORGE M	COL	0-0193961	1060	1
DAVIS GEORGE M	CPT	0-1312751	0148	2
DAVIS GEORGE P	MAJ	0-0258645	0567	3
DAVIS GEORGE W	MAJ	0-0982905	0164	1
DAVIS GERALD E	LTC	0-1702833	1146	2
DAVIS GLEN E	LTC	0-0559719	1065	1
DAVIS GLEN M	MAJ	0-2051433	0261	1
DAVIS GRIFFIN L	LTC	0-0450843	0258	1
DAVIS GROVER C	LTC	0-0104968	0648	3
DAVIS HAROLD C	LTC	0-0164999	1159	3
DAVIS HAROLD F	LTC	0-0158668	1151	3
DAVIS HAROLD L	CPT	0-0497641	0749	1
DAVIS HAROLD L	LTC	0-1587915	0962	1
DAVIS HARRY C	LTC	0-0456336	1059	1
DAVIS HARRY E	LTC	0-0928438	1167	1
DAVIS HARRY G	MAJ	0-2096727	0963	1
DAVIS HARRY L	MAJ	0-0109617	1047	1
DAVIS HARRY L	LTC	0-0197898	0665	1
DAVIS HARRY O	LTC	0-1328239	0767	1
DAVIS HARRY V	LTC	0-1049791	0962	1
DAVIS HAYWOOD M	CPT	0-0498010	0845	2
DAVIS HENLEY H	MAJ	0-0271214	0566	3
DAVIS HENRY T	1LT	0-1315280	0945	2
DAVIS HOMER B	MAJ	0-0192690	0860	3
DAVIS HORACE B	CW3	W-2101553	0955	1
DAVIS HOWARD A	CPT	0-0105858	1054	3
DAVIS HOWARD F	CPT	0-0397821	0862	1
DAVIS HOWARD P	MAJ	0-0304103	0253	3
DAVIS HOWARD S	1LT	0-0496865	0858	1
DAVIS HUBERT L	CPT	0-2014561	0763	1
DAVIS HUBERT V	LTC	0-0173376	1058	3
DAVIS HUDSON T	CPT	0-0520932	0357	3
DAVIS HUGH D	MAJ	0-0420277	0747	2
DAVIS HUGH F	COL	0-0332404	0954	1
DAVIS HUGH O	COL	0-0245651	0959	3
DAVIS HUGO M	CPT	0-0275977	0948	1
DAVIS IRVING	MAJ	0-0317628	0447	2
DAVIS J C	MAJ	0-1823125	0861	1
DAVIS JACK 1	COL	0-0301288	1160	1
DAVIS JACK R	LTC	0-1108603	0962	1
DAVIS JACK R	1LT	0-2034705	0545	2
DAVIS JACK W	CW3	W-2145410	0657	1
DAVIS JAMES A	LTC	0-1633794	0660	1
DAVIS JAMES D	CW2	W-2145991	1060	1
DAVIS JAMES E	MAJ	0-0259108	0845	2
DAVIS JAMES E	MAJ	0-0371150	0966	1
DAVIS JAMES E	MAJ	0-0500393	0863	1
DAVIS JAMES E	CW3	W-2147886	0563	1
DAVIS JAMES H	CPT	0-0490972	0353	1
DAVIS JAMES H	LTC	0-0917368	1150	1
DAVIS JAMES H	MAJ	0-2019561	0466	1
DAVIS JAMES H	CPT	0-2032846	0457	1
DAVIS JAMES J	LTC	0-1555534	0667	1
DAVIS JAMES K	LTC	0-1015929	0559	1
DAVIS JAMES L	COL	0-0277299	0566	1
DAVIS JAMES L	MAJ	0-0477655	1146	1
DAVIS JAMES M	MAJ	0-0395720	0662	1
DAVIS JAMES T	CW2	W-2141246	1159	1
DAVIS JAMES W	COL	0-0265116	0959	1
DAVIS JAMES W	COL	0-0376299	0266	1
DAVIS JAMES W	MAJ	0-1693132	0963	1
DAVIS JAMES W	CW3	W-2147180	0966	1
DAVIS JAY B	MAJ	0-0972290	0661	1
DAVIS JAY M	LTC	0-0259211	1264	2
DAVIS JAY R	CW4	W-2146423	0967	1
DAVIS JENNIE G	MAJ	N-0723084	0263	1
DAVIS JESSE C	LTC	0-0226194	0862	3
DAVIS JOAN F	MAJ	N-0761324	1063	1
DAVIS JOE E	COL	0-0336049	1166	3
DAVIS JOE S	CW3	W-2145866	0262	1
DAVIS JOHN B	MAJ	0-1014065	0860	1
DAVIS JOHN C	LTC	0-0201365	1144	1

NAME	GRADE	SVC NO	DATE RET MO YR	RET CODE
DAVIS JOHN C	MAJ	0-1080777	0460	1
DAVIS JOHN F	CPT	0-0110132	0551	3
DAVIS JOHN F	LTC	0-1307520	1047	1
DAVIS JOHN L	MAJ	0-1585336	0264	1
DAVIS JOHN M	MAJ	0-0400213	0662	1
DAVIS JOHN M	CPT	0-0404415	0154	2
DAVIS JOHN P	MAJ	0-0316373	0446	2
DAVIS JOHN P	MAJ	0-1284672	0548	2
DAVIS JOHN P	CW3	W-2144036	0564	1
DAVIS JOHN R	LTC	0-0383617	1264	3
DAVIS JOHN R	1LT	0-0399025	0743	1
DAVIS JOHN R	LTC	0-1110450	1060	1
DAVIS JOHN S	LTC	0-0287913	0762	3
DAVIS JOHN S	2LT	0-0374065	1041	1
DAVIS JOHN T	LTC	0-0308748	0563	1
DAVIS JOHN V	MAJ	0-0684494	0865	1
DAVIS JOHN W	LTC	0-0256769	1041	2
DAVIS JOHN W	LTC	0-0454735	0463	1
DAVIS JOHN W	CPT	0-1308796	0246	2
DAVIS JOHNNIE F	CPT	0-1996700	0757	1
DAVIS JOSEPHINE	MAJ	N-0700665	1146	1
DAVIS JOSHUA W	COL	0-0208140	1056	3
DAVIS JR ALBERT B C	MAJ	0-1335630	0761	1
DAVIS JR AMOS R	1LT	0-0327573	0545	2
DAVIS JR CECIL A	LTC	0-2035080	0865	1
DAVIS JR CLYDE J	MAJ	0-1599027	0963	1
DAVIS JR EARL J	MAJ	0-1637897	0960	1
DAVIS JR ENOCH A	LTC	0-0226618	0760	3
DAVIS JR GESNA B	MAJ	0-0992922	0166	1
DAVIS JR GUILLETT G	LTC	0-0203089	0264	3
DAVIS JR HARRY L	MAJ	0-1036500	0862	1
DAVIS JR HOWELL A	MAJ	0-0498614	0557	1
DAVIS JR IRVIN C	LTC	0-1297169	0459	1
DAVIS JR JAMES E	LTC	0-0379890	1264	1
DAVIS JR JAMES L	LTC	0-0415808	0161	1
DAVIS JR MAURICE	CPT	0-1825402	1262	1
DAVIS JR MURRAY H	CPT	0-0262843	0664	3
DAVIS JR NOAH S	LTC	0-0242091	0346	2
DAVIS JR NORMAN H	COL	0-0236511	0266	3
DAVIS JR RICHARD H	MAJ	0-2005448	0860	1
DAVIS JR ROY	LTC	0-0422331	0961	1
DAVIS JR WILLIAM J	2LT	0-1328577	0945	2
DAVIS JR WILLIAM M	LTC	0-1181862	1062	1
DAVIS KARL R	MAJ	0-0112224	0255	3
DAVIS KENNETH F	MAJ	0-2289141	0960	1
DAVIS KENNETH G	WO1	W-2152115	1054	2
DAVIS KYLE F	COL	0-0423327	0962	1
DAVIS LAURENCE R	MAJ	0-1542456	0658	1
DAVIS LAWRENCE B	1LT	0-1044792	0345	2
DAVIS LAWRENCE C	LTC	0-0496683	0466	3
DAVIS LAWRENCE E	LTC	0-1102690	1065	1
DAVIS LAWRENCE J	1LT	0-0493807	0246	2
DAVIS LEE W	LTC	0-0165723	0655	3
DAVIS LEON M	CPT	0-1920228	0463	1
DAVIS LEON N	CPT	0-0321879	0546	2
DAVIS LEONARD E	CPT	0-1637591	1058	1
DAVIS LESLIE E	CPT	0-0226824	0764	3
DAVIS LESTER L	1LT	0-0206143	1054	4
DAVIS LESTER M	LTC	0-0164070	1049	1
DAVIS LESTER W	LTC	0-1324759	0967	1
DAVIS LLOYD F	MAJ	0-2035805	0657	1
DAVIS LONARD N	CW2	W-2214512	0767	1
DAVIS LORANZIA E	MAJ	0-1300136	0661	1
DAVIS LOUIS G	1LT	0-1309917	1145	2
DAVIS MACK A	CW3	W-2207728	0267	1
DAVIS MAJOR B	CW2	W-2144447	1160	1
DAVIS MAMIE E	CPT	N-0763592	0747	1
DAVIS MARION B	LTC	0-0382314	0466	3
DAVIS MARTIN L	LTC	0-0336888	0663	1
DAVIS MAYRON J	CW2	W-3151359	1067	1
DAVIS MELVILLE O	LTC	0-0277298	0960	3
DAVIS MELVIN C	MAJ	0-0410796	1046	2
DAVIS MICHAEL	CW3	W-2148922	0863	1
DAVIS MILDRED F	MAJ	N-0742477	0848	2
DAVIS MILES M	CPT	0-1574410	0146	2

NAME	GRADE	SVC NO	DATE RET MO YR	RET CODE
OAVIS MILFORO C	WO1	W-2206827	0956	2
OAVIS MILLARO Q	MAJ	0-1285391	C864	1
OAVIS MONTAGUE E	MAJ	C-1899398	1060	1
OAVIS NATHAN H	1LT	0-2025896	0955	1
OAVIS NEIL W	1LT	0-0366448	1144	2
OAVIS NELL M	MAJ	N-0730219	0465	3
CAVIS NELSON E	2LT	0-1304871	0145	2
OAVIS NORMAN S	CPT	0-0504304	C445	2
OAVIS OCTAVIUS C	LTC	0-0384319	0660	1
OAVIS OLE C	LTC	0-1036115	1163	1
OAVIS OLIVER E	CW2	W-2208753	0264	1
OAVIS ONNER O	COL	0-0132675	0153	3
DAVIS ORVILLE R	LTC	0-0197494	1060	3
DAVIS OSCAR L	MAJ	C-0510298	C955	1
OAVIS PAUL A	MAJ	0-104332C	C161	1
OAVIS PAUL E	CW2	W-2101305	1047	1
OAVIS PAUL M	LTC	0-0267081	0857	3
OAVIS PAUL M	MAJ	0-0527787	0663	1
OAVIS PAUL R	MAJ	C-0173599	0262	3
OAVIS PAUL V	LTC	0-0204482	0353	3
OAVIS PAUL V	CPT	C-0962556	0459	1
OAVIS PAUL W	LTC	0-0294583	1059	1
CAVIS PERK L	MAJ	0-0497213	0546	2
DAVIS PETER F	MAJ	0-1643974	1157	1
DAVIS RALEIGH H	MAJ	0-1551190	0865	1
OAVIS RALPH M	MAJ	C-0342379	1045	2
OAVIS RANDALL B	MAJ	0-1330794	0967	1
DAVIS RAY L	COL	0-0418102	1060	1
DAVIS RAY H	CPT	0-0210708	0645	2
OAVIS RAY M	WO1	W-2127967	C567	2
OAVIS RAYMOND A	CPT	0-1182811	0961	1
CAVIS REECE O	MAJ	C-0970532	0464	1
OAVIS REEO T	CW3	W-2146762	0663	1
OAVIS RICHARD B	MAJ	C-2016122	C563	1
OAVIS RICHARO E	LTC	0-1179830	C264	1
OAVIS RICHARO L	COL	0-0213229	0763	3
OAVIS RICHARO M	LTC	0-0451588	0261	1
OAVIS RICHARD W	1LT	0-0528766	0146	2
DAVIS ROBERT A	LTC	C-0887366	C564	1
OAVIS ROBERT F	LTC	0-0984475	0767	1
DAVIS ROBERT H	CPT	0-1799621	0258	1
DAVIS ROBERT L	LTC	0-0174834	0362	3
OAVIS ROBERT L	CW2	W-2148389	1059	1
DAVIS ROBERT M	MAJ	C-1305873	C861	1
OAVIS ROCKWELL A	LTC	0-0225959	0760	3
DAVIS ROGER C	CW2	W-2111172	C549	1
DAVIS ROSEMARY E	1LT	N-0773520	1046	1
OAVIS ROSS R	CW4	W-2145258	1067	1
OAVIS ROY A	LTC	0-0450206	0557	1
CAVIS SAMUEL L	LTC	0-0284292	0448	2
OAVIS SHERWOOD S	1LT	0-0468667	0844	2
OAVIS SIONEY S	COL	0-0226915	C760	1
DAVIS SR ECMOND H	CW2	W-2141245	C653	1
OAVIS SR MC LAIN	1LT	0-0988597	1058	1
OAVIS STANLEY E	1LT	0-1702997	1145	1
CAVIS STANLEY V	1LT	0-1015800	1045	2
DAVIS STEVE G	COL	0-1165842	0850	1
OAVIS SYLVIA	CPT	L-0204378	1046	2
OAVIS TANDY L	CPT	0-1293215	0161	1
DAVIS TEX	LTC	0-0441648	0954	1
DAVIS THEODORE E	CW3	W-2147263	1060	1
OAVIS THOMAS E	LTC	0-0672577	0867	1
OAVIS THOMAS F	MAJ	C-1004459	0650	1
OAVIS THOMAS H	LTC	C-0248487	C959	3
DAVIS THOMAS H	1LT	C-0291197	C167	3
OAVIS THOMAS J	LTC	0-1168628	0760	1
OAVIS TOMMYE H	MAJ	N-0727336	1263	3
CAVIS VANN B	CPT	0-0342055	0645	2
OAVIS VERNON E	LTC	0-1323670	0265	1
DAVIS VERNON T	1LT	0-1635760	0857	1
OAVIS VIRGIL R	1LT	C-0268862	C745	2
OAVIS VORIS B	1LT	0-1822376	1145	2
OAVIS W A	1LT	0-1283219	0845	2
OAVIS WALTER A	LTC	0-0555768	0767	1
DAVIS WALTER C	CPT	0-0574369	C152	1

NAME	GRADE	SVC NO	DATE RET MO YR	RET CODE
DAVIS WALTER G	MAJ	0-130639C	0359	1
OAVIS WAYNE E	MAJ	0-1920199	0465	1
OAVIS WENDELL T	CW2	W-2109855	1043	2
OAVIS WILBUR P	MAJ	0-0277303	0858	3
DAVIS WILLIAM A	LTC	0-1323546	C263	1
OAVIS WILLIAM E	MAJ	0-0245661	0953	3
DAVIS WILLIAM E	1LT	0-1174817	1044	2
OAVIS WILLIAM E	CPT	0-1946025	0447	1
OAVIS WILLIAM F	CW2	W-2152018	1156	1
DAVIS WILLIAM G	COL	0-0240362	0263	3
OAVIS WILLIAM G	LTC	0-0276137	1053	2
OAVIS WILLIAM G	CPT	0-0333985	0763	3
OAVIS WILLIAM G	MAJ	0-0885031	0956	1
DAVIS WILLIAM G	1LT	0-1797967	0944	2
DAVIS WILLIAM G	CW2	W-2213316	0867	1
DAVIS WILLIAM H	LTC	0-1302783	0766	1
OAVIS WILLIAM H	CW3	W-2206520	0166	1
OAVIS WILLIAM J	LTC	0-0117786	0245	2
DAVIS WILLIAM J	CPT	0-0548029	0547	2
OAVIS WILLIAM J	1LT	0-1101402	1045	2
OAVIS WILLIAM J	1LT	0-4006879	0856	2
DAVIS WILLIAM L	CW2	W-2145785	0756	1
OAVIS WILLIAM M	LTC	0-0504891	0161	1
OAVIS WILLIAM O	CPT	0-1590403	0161	2
OAVIS WILLIAM R	CPT	0-0465657	0646	2
OAVIS WILLIAM S	CW2	W-2209383	0266	1
DAVIS WILLIAM T	LTC	0-0387322	0767	3
OAVIS WILLIAM W	COL	0-0322164	0663	1
DAVIS WILLIE E	CW4	W-213299C	0960	1
OAVIS WILLSON	LTC	0-0253364	0267	3
OAVIS WILSON S	MAJ	0-1321571	1160	2
DAVIS WOODARO B	CW3	W-2145802	0462	1
DAVIS WORTH C	MAJ	0-0966414	0964	1
OAVISON ALLEN P	CPT	0-1281146	1062	1
OAVISON BURNS H	CPT	0-0119471	1158	3
OAVISON CHARLES H	1LT	0-0747764	0646	2
OAVISON CHRISTINE	MAJ	N-0702015	0366	3
DAVISON DAVID J	2LT	0-5206670	0160	2
OAVISON OONALD L	LTC	0-158534C	0662	1
OAVISON EDWARO H	MAJ	0-0251344	1165	3
OAVISON FLOYD A	LTC	0-0178600	1061	3
DAVISON KENNETH A	LTC	0-0355738	0959	1
OAVISON LEON R	MAJ	0-1280223	0354	1
OAVISON ROBERT H	CPT	0-1574411	0445	2
DAVISON TREADWELL	MAJ	0-0418444	0146	2
OAVISON WARREN R	MAJ	0-0388465	1045	2
DAVISON WILLIAM C	1LT	0-0397741	0245	2
OAVISSON ALEXANDER	COL	0-0298589	0757	1
OAVISSON CLAUDE R	CPT	0-0546636	0247	2
OAVISSON JOHN E	LTC	0-0225511	0460	1
DAVISSON RUSSELL W	MAJ	0-2006888	1165	1
OAVOLL WILLIAM C	MAJ	0-0373246	0760	1
OAVOUST NORBERT J	CPT	0-1100C72	0346	2
OAVY MARTIN E	LTC	0-0309924	0759	1
OAWE EDWARO J	MAJ	0-0374428	1046	2
DAWES CHARLES C	COL	0-0166510	0359	3
OAWES HENRY C	CPT	0-1577079	0149	1
OAWES RICHARO M	CPT	0-0285707	0665	3
OAWLEY CHARLES P	COL	0-0128305	0257	3
OAWS REX T	MAJ	0-0297846	0144	1
OAWSEY WILLIAM C	MAJ	0-0379248	1150	1
DAWSON ALVA C	COL	0-0223424	1164	1
OAWSON ARCH A	CPT	0-0304989	1045	2
OAWSON ARCHIE L	CPT	0-2008032	0656	1
OAWSON CHARLES C	CPT	0-1651733	0860	1
OAWSON CHARLES L	WO1	W-2115514	0247	1
OAWSON CHARLES O	COL	0-0262988	0167	3
OAWSON CHARLES P	WO1	W-2122422	0846	1
DAWSON CLAUO L	MAJ	0-0489547	0552	1
OAWSON OARREL W	CW2	W-2147600	0365	1
DAWSON DUOLEY T	COL	0-0203513	0648	3
OAWSON EDWARC	CPT	0-0509180	1046	1
OAWSON ELMER A	MAJ	0-0336540	1064	3
DAWSON FREDRICK	MAJ	0-0996491	1164	1
DAWSON GEORGE I	COL	0-0265919	0453	3

NAME	GRADE	SVC NO	DATE RET MO YR	RET CODE
OAWSON GEORGE P	MAJ	0-0946802	1067	1
OAWSON GEORGE W	CPT	0-0128710	C648	3
OAWSON HARWIN D	CPT	0-1633155	0361	1
OAWSON JACK W	MAJ	0-1587205	0957	1
DAWSON JAMES E	MAJ	C-1944913	0962	1
OAWSON JEROME W	CPT	0-2037224	0747	2
OAWSON JR EDWARD S	MAJ	C-0146740	0648	3
DAWSON JR LOUIS Y	COL	0-0222961	1045	2
DAWSON MERLE R	COL	C-0923654	C864	1
OAWSON MILLARO L	CW2	W-2209390	0664	1
DAWSON PAT W	LTC	0-0336300	0664	3
OAWSON REX H	MAJ	C-1823269	0661	1
DAWSON RICHARD	MAJ	C-0987531	1066	1
DAWSON ROBERT L	MAJ	C-0517112	0156	2
OAWSON ROBERTA R	1LT	L-0900831	1145	2
OAWSON RUSSELL H	LTC	0-1165843	0164	1
OAWSON THOMAS H	CPT	0-1796244	0849	1
OAWSON THURMAN E	MAJ	C-0382749	0146	2
DAWSON WILLIAM A	MAJ	C-0310463	1144	2
DAY ALANSON R	MAJ	C-1309046	C947	2
OAY ALFREO C	COL	0-0136537	C346	2
DAY CHARLES H	LTC	0-1062351	0667	1
DAY CHARLES W	CPT	0-0969390	0862	1
DAY CHARLIE E	2LT	0-1304874	0944	2
OAY CLAYTON E	CW3	W-2210974	C663	1
DAY OAINE L	LTC	0-0330642	1065	1
OAY DANIEL E	LTC	0-0422885	0261	2
CAY ECWARD H	MAJ	0-0489393	0954	1
DAY EKNNETH E	LTC	0-0382311	0460	1
OAY EVAN B	MAJ	C-1056073	0163	1
DAY GEORGE E	CW3	W-2207157	0367	1
OAY GEORGE H	LTC	C-0986892	0767	1
DAY HAL B	CPT	0-2000117	0761	1
OAY HARRY I	2LT	0-0281277	1064	3
DAY JOHN G	2LT	0-1081552	0265	3
DAY JOHN J	MAJ	C-0338453	C267	3
DAY JOHN S	LTC	C-1316940	1159	1
DAY JR ALFRED K	LTC	0-1104602	0962	1
DAY LAWRENCE H	CW4	W-2112038	0461	3
DAY LEONARO R	LTC	0-0394989	0756	1
DAY LEWIS A	LTC	0-0177313	0161	3
OAY MARION W	LTC	0-0290688	0446	2
CAY MYRON G	CW2	W-2206783	0960	1
DAY OSWALD N	CPT	0-0101682	1051	3
DAY OWENS L	CPT	0-0352356	0445	2
OAY ROBERT C	MAJ	C-2046943	C665	1
DAY ROBERT E	COL	0-0910386	0967	3
OAY ROGER O	COL	0-0212622	1160	3
DAY RUTH B	2LT	N-C751127	0545	1
DAY THOMAS L	CPT	0-0934091	0152	1
DAY THOMAS R	MAJ	0-1015286	0759	1
DAY THOMAS W	MAJ	C-1283922	0267	3
DAY WALTER L	LTC	0-0441089	0154	1
OAY WALTER W	CPT	0-2262618	0261	1
DAY WESSELS H	LTC	C-2033001	0266	1
OAY WILBUR	1LT	0-0451239	0245	2
DAY WILLIAM R	COL	C-018492C	0652	3
DAY WILLIAM W	MAJ	0-1573152	0457	1
DAY WILLIAM Z	CW4	W-2147746	0957	1
DAYE KHLAR J	MAJ	0-1319403	0161	1
CAYNES GERALO R	CPT	0-0265893	0145	2
OAYSH HARRISON J	1LT	0-1298362	0745	2
OAYTON EUGENE K	1LT	0-1318769	0545	2
DAYTON PERCY H	LTC	0-0509186	0761	1
OAYTON WILLIAM J	CW3	W-2142389	1160	1
OAYTON WILLIAM R	COL	C-0333295	1061	1
OAZE OAVIO J	2LT	0-1692600	0845	1
DAZEY WILLIAM B	2LT	0-2012325	C346	1
DE AGLE ELWELL T	LTC	0-1635763	C960	1
OE ANDREA ALFONSO R	CW4	W-2003921	1065	1
OE ANGELIS ALFREO	LTC	0-1292665	C959	1
OE ANGELIS FREOERICK	LTC	0-0199180	0263	3
OE ANGELIS MICHAEL L	LTC	0-1314263	0261	1
OE ANGELO JOHN A	MAJ	C-05027C4	1054	1
OE ANTONIO LOUIS	LTC	0-1823126	0262	1

NAME	GRADE	SVC NO	DATE RET MO YR	RET CODE
OE ARMAS LOUIS H	2LT	0-128802C	0245	2
DE ARMCNC ALBERT M	COL	0-0245748	0159	3
OE ARMCNC EBEN A	MAJ	0-0425879	0547	1
OE ARMCNO GRAVES L	LTC	0-0360622	0261	1
OE ARMCND JOE S	MAJ	0-1295518	0561	1
OE ASIS CESAREO	LTC	0-0204431	0356	3
OE AVEIRC CHARLES F	2LT	0-1324724	0645	2
DE BACKER RAYMOND H	CW2	W-2152764	0561	1
OE BAGGIS JOHN W	CPT	0-1549694	0947	2
OE BARPIERI THOMAS F	LTC	0-1542832	0661	1
DE BARC CARL O	M G	0-0288794	0864	3
OF BARRY JULIA	1LT	N-0741198	0246	1
OE BAT LUCILE A	CPT	L-0303858	1047	2
OE BELLEVUE CASSIUS	LTC	0-0482146	0566	3
OE BERNAROI L A	2LT	0-1C36502	0245	2
OE BEVCISE CHARLES P	LTC	0-1011022	0164	1
OE BIASE JOHN O	1LT	0-1180869	0746	2
OE BLCIS ERNEST F	LTC	0-0921309	0456	1
OE BLCIS RENE L	COL	0-0282807	0160	1
OE BOE FREEMAN C	LTC	0-0362705	0267	3
DF BOEF CLARENCE P	2LT	0-0888238	0444	2
OE BOER ARLEN M	MAJ	0-1282395	0562	1
DE BCER GUY W	CPT	0-1686998	0346	2
OE BOER RALPH E	1LT	0-1324518	C846	2
DE BOICE BENJAMIN S	MAJ	0-0119639	0249	3
DE BOIS WALTER	MAJ	0-0447965	0153	1
OE BOLT FRANCIS M	CPT	0-1703417	0465	1
OE BOLT PAUL L	LTC	0-1544052	0660	1
DE BONT LAWRENCE M	CW3	W-214451C	1163	1
OE BORO MARSHALL E	MAJ	0-0150602	0251	3
OE BORO PAUL S	CPT	0-0954172	1060	1
OE BOURKE JOHN M	MAJ	0-2263595	1164	1
OE BOY WILLIAM H	LTC	0-0366038	0966	1
DE BRABANDER PROSPER	MAJ	C-1341951	1262	1
DE BRUHL EDWARD C	CPT	0-1040517	C760	1
OF BRUHL PAUL K	MAJ	0-1285907	0945	2
DE BRULER DOUGLAS A	1LT	0-1894621	0744	2
OE BUSK FREO G	COL	0-0281598	0965	3
OF BUSK HARRY L	LTC	0-0492409	0457	1
OF BUYS WILLIAM E	LTC	0-0259865	0767	3
OE CAIR JR JESSE R	LTC	0-1186637	1266	1
OE CATRIC ALFCNZO	1LT	0-0291556	0546	2
OE CAMF CLARENCE A	LTC	0-0103508	0648	3
OE CARLO JESS	MAJ	0-0496327	0456	1
OE CARLO JOSEPH B	CW4	W-2144366	0766	2
DE CARLC MAURICE	CPT	0-0493885	1053	1
OE CARLC VINCENT J	WO1	W-2127206	0955	1
DE CESARIS ALFRED E	LTC	0-0280505	0867	3
DE CHAPLEROY ALBERT	LTC	0-0394271	0867	1
OE CHARLES RCGER Y	1LT	0-1175990	0745	1
OE CHOW CEORCEEN H	1LT	N-08C1234	0947	1
OE CLEENE CLARENCE B	MAJ	C-2208027	0762	1
OE CLUE CLYDE R	CW3	W-2147252	1165	1
DE CORY CLAUCE C	LTC	0-0391355	0560	1
OE COSTANZC NICHOLAS	LTC	0-1335756	0366	1
OE CRISTCFCRC W H E	CPT	0-0388921	1060	1
OE CRISTCFORC WALTER	LTC	0-0450844	0663	1
DE OIEGC MANUEL	CPT	0-0404792	0745	1
OE DOMENICO JOHN T	1LT	0-1010356	0945	2
OE FALCC MICHAEL	CW3	W-2150321	0165	1
OE FEEN MICHAEL A	MAJ	0-1290727	1157	1
DE FINA MICHAEL V	CPT	0-0347284	0966	3
OE FLCN LOUISE A	1LT	N-0737528	0646	1
OE FLORIA ANTHONY G	1LT	0-1637280	C345	1
OE FORC OON C	COL	0-0250178	0964	1
OE FORO LELANO F	CPT	0-0982593	0962	1
OE FORC LESTER J	CPT	0-0184555	0951	3
OE FOREST CARL B	MAJ	0-0174059	0648	3
OE FOREST EARLE W	LTC	0-0359532	0563	3
DE FOREST RALPH E	CPT	0-1755785	0248	1
OE FOY WALTER F	COL	0-0323956	0560	1
OE FRAIN RAY L	MAJ	0-1822245	0159	2
OE FRANCC MARY R	MAJ	N-0756912	1063	1
OE FRANCC RUTH O	1LT	N-0742214	0546	2
DE FREEST JAMES W	LTC	0-1316953	0561	2

NAME	GRADE	SVC NO	DATE RET MO YR	RET CODE
DE GARMO IVAN M	MAJ	0-1591087	0262	1
DE GARMO JAMES M	LTC	0-0406806	0463	1
DE GIACOMO FRANK	COL	0-0285035	0661	2
DE GRAFF FARRIS E	MAJ	0-1286452	1057	1
DE GRAM JOHN C	CW3	W-2145615	0761	1
DE GRANGE JUSTIN H	LTC	0-0475270	0251	1
DE GRAZIA EUGENE J	CPT	0-1684574	0545	2
DE GREGORIO ANTHONY	CW4	W-2143481	0564	2
DE GREGORIO JOSEPH J	MAJ	0-2212028	0763	1
DE GREW KENNETH E	COL	0-0216508	0363	3
DE GREY SIDNEY	1LT	0-0278642	1041	2
DE GROFF CHARLES E	COL	0-0323997	1166	3
DE GROODT FRANKLIN T	MAJ	0-1796587	1160	1
DE GROOT LAWRENCE R	LTC	0-0910402	0962	1
DE GROVE JOHN M	1LT	0-2016450	1046	1
DE GUINZBOURG VICTOR	LTC	0-1692515	0366	3
DE GUZMAN GERMAN C	1LT	0-2030661	0150	2
DE GUZMAN JOSE J	CPT	0-0278133	0860	3
DE HART LOWELL M	LTC	0-0204481	0959	3
DE HAVEN CLARENCE T	COL	0-0268867	0167	3
DE HAVEN JACOB G	LTC	0-0505432	0963	1
DE HAVEN ROLAND E	WO1	W-2106649	0854	1
DE HAVEN WILLIAM C	COL	0-0237034	0363	3
DE HAVEN WILLIAM E	CPT	0-0269859	0545	2
DE HOFF EMMETT	MAJ	0-1101405	0254	1
DE HORN RONALD E	LTC	0-0313160	0656	1
DE HORSEY REED D R	LTC	0-1641988	0765	1
DE JARNETT ELLIOTT H	LTC	0-0310667	0859	1
DE JARNETTE DAVID L	MAJ	0-0259127	0767	3
DE JARNETTE JAMES L	LTC	0-0239405	0764	3
DE JARNETTE WILLIAM	COL	0-0220036	0764	3
DE JESUS JOSE	1LT	0-1896486	0962	1
DE JONGE ALFRED R W	COL	0-0243318	0648	3
DE KASER RICHARD J	1LT	0-1178454	1146	2
DE KAY ORMONDE	LTC	0-0173314	1160	3
DE KENO RICHARD L	CW3	W-2145674	1063	1
DE KEYSER ERNEST	MAJ	0-1635770	0856	1
DE KLOTZ FRED W	COL	0-0216937	0561	3
DE KRUYFF RICHARD O	LTC	0-0213813	0361	3
DE LA JR MATER J A	LTC	0-0252741	1047	2
DE LA PENA MIGUE	LTC	0-1303119	0467	1
DE LA ROSA ROBER	WO1	W-2110839	0149	1
DE LACY CLIFFORD H	CPT	0-1310818	0448	2
DE LAMARTER RICHARD	LTC	0-1551598	1263	1
DE LAMATER WALTER A	B G	0-0142906	0648	3
DE LANCEY ZEB V	MAJ	0-0370749	0260	1
DE LANO MELVIN F	MAJ	0-2051436	1262	1
DE LANO PAUL K	1LT	0-1290729	0845	2
DE LANE JAMES K	MAJ	0-1638031	1265	1
DE LANEY CHARLES S	CPT	0-1176303	1046	2
DE LANEY THERON R	CW3	W-2145768	1162	1
DE LANEY VIRGIL L	MAJ	0-1185359	1160	1
DE LAP DAVID F	COL	0-0242740	1150	3
DE LAPPE GEORGE R	MAJ	0-2041093	0561	1
DE LARM FREDERICK	LTC	0-0362103	0664	3
DE LASHMET CARL A	LTC	0-1013850	1163	1
DE LAUNE WYBRA S	1LT	0-1293380	0745	2
DE LAURA VINCENT J	1LT	0-1315038	0945	2
DE LECLUSE EDMOND H	MAJ	0-1584912	0650	1
DE LEE MERINE	LTC	0-0175722	1059	3
DE LEO DAN A	1LT	0-1287315	1145	2
DE LEO FELIX R	CPT	0-0446612	0546	1
DE LEON EDWARD F	LTC	0-0452359	0957	1
DE LEON EUGENE P	MAJ	0-1301621	0560	1
DE LISO HENRY G	CPT	0-0469251	1044	2
DE LISSOVOY VLADIMIR	CPT	0-0426659	0345	1
DE LIT CLEMENT	CPT	0-1689490	0246	1
DE LOACH JAMES W	LTC	0-1286255	1060	1
DE LOACH SAM C	LTC	0-1944659	1057	1
DE LOACH SERRE D	LTC	0-0219892	1161	1
DE LOGE WILFRED T	CPT	0-1287156	1045	2
DE LONG CLEO W	MAJ	0-1107387	0561	1
DE LONG HOWARD M	LTC	0-1289557	0466	1
DE LONG ROBERT D	CPT	0-0556595	1147	2
DE LONG WALTER C	MAJ	0-0372095	1153	1

NAME	GRADE	SVC NO	DATE RET MO YR	RET CODE
DE LONG WALTER J	COL	0-0176195	0358	3
DE LOS RIOS LEO R	LTC	0-0904917	1266	3
DE LOZIER LEON S	1LT	0-1013875	0747	1
DE LUCA FRANK P	CPT	0-1690135	0445	2
DE LUCA JOHN V	LTC	0-1546745	1262	1
DE LUCA JOSEPH M	MAJ	0-1106087	0261	1
DE LUCA NICHOLAS J	2LT	0-2040733	0744	2
DE LUCCIA EMIL R	LTC	0-0241181	1064	3
DE MACKIEWICZ J H	LTC	0-0251741	0660	3
DE MAINE JR HENRY M	CPT	0-1057405	0651	1
DE MAIO ARMAND	MAJ	0-1322900	0260	1
DE MARCAY GEORGE A	LTC	0-1045351	0662	1
DE MARCO JOSEPH	LTC	0-1293022	0661	1
DE MARCO LOUIS R	MAJ	0-1299708	0662	1
DE MARCO MATTHEW	MAJ	0-0957568	1062	1
DE MARIO CHARLES A	CW2	W-2209815	0765	1
DE MARIO DAVID	1LT	0-1317278	0247	1
DE MARS ROBERT E	CPT	0-0566817	0363	1
DE MARTINO JAMES V	LTC	0-0275627	0551	2
DE MASSE THEODORE E	LTC	0-1577090	1161	1
DE MATTEO IGNATIUS M	CPT	0-0422087	0345	2
DE MELC ANGELO	CPT	0-0473043	0450	1
DE MENT RUSSELL D	MAJ	0-1337551	0864	1
DE MERCHANT CHESTER	CW2	W-2146962	0762	1
DE MERELL GEORGE S	LTC	0-0162171	0753	3
DE MERITT EDWIN W	CPT	0-1049797	0955	1
DE MERRITT ARTHUR L	MAJ	0-0533658	1054	1
DE MERSE ARTHUR F	LTC	0-0378057	1161	1
DE MEULENAERE JOHN C	CPT	0-0381024	0346	2
DE MEY MAURICE	MAJ	0-2263535	1264	1
DE MILHAU LOUIS J	LTC	0-0161523	0648	3
DE MILIA ALFRED F	CPT	0-0483936	0345	2
DE MILLE LYNN V	MAJ	0-1176932	0360	1
DE MILLER EDGAR A	MAJ	0-0228358	1262	1
DE MONC GERALD G	CW2	W-2105427	1160	1
DE MONE CHARLES J	LTC	0-0426052	0465	1
DE MONTFORT HAROLD	1LT	0-0312076	1163	3
DE MOOR LEONARD	LTC	0-0485775	1262	3
DE MOORE EUGENE W	LTC	0-0312250	0650	1
DE MOTT ARTHUR E	MAJ	0-0184881	0952	3
DE MOTT HARRY R	CPT	0-2032248	0563	1
DE MOTTE THEODORE M	LTC	0-1556713	0165	3
DE MUN OLIVER M	CW3	W-2145937	0157	1
DE MUTH EDGAR E	COL	0-0208086	1262	3
DE NEAU ROY E	CPT	0-0242120	0245	1
DE PALMA JR JOSEPH P	CPT	0-0966123	0960	1
DE PALO WILLIAM A	LTC	0-0344432	0661	1
DE PANE NATHANIEL	1LT	0-1897054	0659	2
DE PASCUALE FRANCIS	COL	0-0230759	0961	3
DE PASCUALE GEORGE L	LTC	0-0253854	0562	3
DE PASS MAURICE M	LTC	0-1040656	0666	1
DE PAUL ARTHUR	1LT	0-1051538	0445	2
DE PAUL ERNEST F	LTC	0-1045393	0766	1
DE PETRILLO VICTOR H	LTC	0-1081695	1165	1
DE PIERRE BRANTON A	MAJ	0-1337940	0963	1
DE PIETRO JAMES A	CW3	W-2147187	0464	1
DE PINTO DOMINIC A	CPT	0-1821459	0245	2
DE PRIEST ERNEST D	CPT	0-0530495	0849	1
DE PRINC JOSEPH G	LTC	0-1177364	1264	1
DE PRIZIO CARL J	LTC	0-0253070		2
DE PUMPO LESTER J	LTC	0-1544755	0964	1
DE QUOY ALFRED W	COL	0-0365341	0167	1
DE RAMUS INEZ	1LT	N-0734060	0947	1
DE RAMUS JUDSON O	COL	0-0184482	0656	3
DE RENNE ALFRED L	CPT	0-1283367	1046	2
DE RITA JOSEPH	COL	0-0307079	0260	1
DE ROCHE JOHN E	LTC	0-1010053	0366	1
DE ROCHE JOSEPH F	CPT	0-0498185	0357	1
DE ROO CLEMENT C	MAJ	0-0427682	0856	1
DE ROCOF RUDOLPH	CPT	0-0363627	0546	2
DE ROON JR LOUIS	CPT	0-0382541	0446	2
DE ROSA FRANK T	CW3	W-2205710	0865	1
DE ROSA HENRY T	MAJ	0-1553431	0462	1
DE ROSA JOHN J	LTC	0-0339033	0747	2
DE ROSA JR JOHN J	LTC	0-0447286	0662	1

NAME	GRADE	SVC NO	DATE RET MO YR	RET CODE
DE ROSA MICHAEL	LTC	0-1552265	1060	1
DE ROSA NICHOLAS J	CPT	0-0480940	0750	1
DE ROSIA JOHN J	MAJ	0-1327823	0862	2
DE ROSSET WILLIAM G	LTC	0-0124791	0648	3
DE SANDERS JR NEIL J	CPT	0-0375198	0845	2
DE SANDRE ARRIGO	LTC	0-0210984	1055	3
DE SANTIAGO ISAAC	2LT	0-0309086	0444	1
DE SCHWEINITZ LAWREN	MAJ	0-2033124	0660	1
DE SELMS WILBUR C	CPT	0-1000346	0550	1
DE SICO PHILIP A	COL	0-0256603	1165	3
DE SIMONE S V	1LT	0-0554922	1146	2
DE SOUCEY EDWARD H	LTC	0-1015396	0366	1
DE SPAIN BETTY L	1LT	N-0733194	0146	1
DE SPAIN LAWRENCE M	CW2	W-2150738	0562	1
DE STAEL NORBERT T	MAJ	0-1685633	0661	1
DE STASIO BARTHOLOME	LTC	0-1101810	1262	1
DE TEMPLE FRANKLIN H	CW3	W-2205597	1266	1
DE TONNANCOURT W	2LT	0-0164363	0648	3
DE TOSKEY PAUL R	MAJ	0-1324829	0662	1
DE VALL LOUIS D	MAJ	0-1297006	0862	1
DE VALL ROGER A	MAJ	0-0948350	1262	1
DE VAN JR WILLIAM T	1LT	0-1825845	0146	2
DE VANE HYBERT T	MAJ	0-1298199	0159	2
DE VAULT CHARLES C	COL	0-0337142	1059	1
DE VEAU LEON R	WO1	W-2120945	0861	2
DE VEAUX WALTER S	MAJ	0-0965983	0861	1
DE VERA DAMASO M	MAJ	0-1896355	0267	1
DE VERTER PAUL L	MAJ	0-0118986	0654	3
DE VILLE JOSEPH T	COL	0-0244492	1155	1
DE VILLE ODELL F	LTC	0-0328269	0267	3
DE VINCENT CHESTER J	LTC	0-1796049	1065	1
DE VIRGILIO LOUIS F	MAJ	0-1003504	0261	1
DE VITT EDWARD J	2LT	0-1179368	0445	2
DE VLAMING GEORGE W	MAJ	0-0375857	0461	1
DE VOE GEORGE M	LTC	0-0319949	0664	3
DE VOE JAY J	LTC	0-0169142	0660	3
DE VOR HAROLD V	MAJ	0-0252768	0565	3
DE VORE JANIE M	MAJ	N-0762732	1164	1
DE VORE JEROME L	LTC	0-1081471	0862	1
DE VOSS JAMES T	COL	0-0351360	0561	1
DE VRIES JOHN A	LTC	0-0269825	0765	3
DE WALD JOY H	MAJ	0-1049802	0761	1
DE WALL WALTER R	CW3	W-2146823	0961	1
DE WALT GORDON V	WO1	W-2146326	0153	2
DE WAR LLOYD K	MAJ	0-1013196	0561	1
DE WEERD JAMES A	CPT	0-0520591	0945	2
DE WEESE CALVIN S	MAJ	0-0502189	0744	2
DE WEESE JAMES A	CPT	0-0184586	0758	3
DE WEIN HAROLD J W	1LT	0-0371757	1262	2
DE WEY PAUL	LTC	0-1175415	0762	1
DE WITT DENNIS M	MAJ	0-0286171	0767	3
DE WITT GEORGE L	MAJ	0-2010822	1262	1
DE WITT JR EIRVIN M	MAJ	0-1885255	0867	1
DE WITT LEONARD A	WO1	W-2121139	0546	2
DE WITT ROSCOE H	LTC	0-0234920	0660	3
DE WITT VIRGIL B	CPT	0-0249837	0461	3
DE WOLF ANSON B	LTC	0-0174026	1061	3
DE WOLF HOWARD R	CPT	0-1913611	0339	1
DE WOLF LEWIS M	COL	0-0274912	1264	3
DE WOLFE THOMAS A	CPT	0-0383360	0241	2
DE WOODY GERALD M	CPT	0-0312327	0246	2
DE WOODY HUGH G	CPT	0-1303309	0248	2
DE YONG LOUIS W	LTC	0-0195711	0762	3
DE YOUNG KENNETH D	LTC	0-0310700	1159	1
DE YOUNG ROBERT M	MAJ	0-2016157	0164	1
DE&LA&CONCEPCIO A	CPT	0-1896409	0857	1
DE&LA&CRUZ JEREMIAS	2LT	0-1896584	0348	2
DE&ST&AUBIN VICTOR E	1LT	0-1297852	0646	2
DE-LOS-ANGELES F E	1LT	0-0172708	1147	1
DEABLER WALTER E	LTC	0-1281418	0463	1
DEACON JOSEPH F	MAJ	0-1111567	1060	1
DEACON MILTON L	LTC	0-1635762	0562	1
DEACY EDWARD O	LTC	0-0949394	1067	1
DEADY WILLIAM W	COL	0-0192464	0457	3
DEAKINS JR JOHN W	MAJ	0-1012787	0566	2

NAME	GRADE	SVC NO	DATE RET MO YR	RET CODE
DEAL CLAUDE V	LTC	0-0485627	0466	3
DEAL DANIEL W	1LT	0-1175094	0546	2
DEAL RAYMOND E	CW3	W-2146644	0360	1
DEAL ROBERT S	CW2	W-2145629	0461	1
DEAL SR WILLIAM E	CPT	0-0267441	1047	2
DEAL STANLEY V	1LT	0-0505545	0354	1
DEALE DANIEL G	MAJ	0-0500389	0546	2
DEAMUD WILDER S	MAJ	0-1289703	0860	1
DEAN ARCHIBALD	MAJ	0-1288015	0666	1
DEAN AVIS T	1LT	N-0733730	0546	1
DEAN CECIL R	MAJ	0-0205020	1061	3
DEAN CHARLES J	CW3	W-2141245	1159	1
DEAN CLARENCE	CW4	W-2127945	0659	1
DEAN EDWARD F	1LT	0-1166696	0147	2
DEAN ELMER W	LTC	0-1284834	1057	1
DEAN EVERETT	MAJ	0-0319743	0447	1
DEAN FRANKLIN A	CW2	W-2145304	1059	1
DEAN GEORGE L	CPT	0-0988028	0261	1
DEAN GEORGE M	COL	0-0195665	1261	3
DEAN GERTRUDE M	MAJ	N-0794749	0465	1
DEAN GRACE M	1LT	N-0701440	0643	1
DEAN GUY F	CPT	0-0451559	0357	1
DEAN HAROLD C	MAJ	0-1183498	0859	1
DEAN HAROLD S	COL	0-0276497	0847	2
DEAN HERBERT R	B G	0-0144648	0648	3
DEAN JAMES T	LTC	0-0487671	0157	1
DEAN JOEL L	LTC	0-0250095	0567	3
DEAN JOHN P	COL	0-0113820	0751	3
DEAN JOHN W	MAJ	0-0964518	0163	1
DEAN JOSEPH E	LTC	0-0494722	0459	1
DEAN JR BUFORD W	CPT	0-1637275	0346	2
DEAN JR JAMES M	1LT	0-0385071	1145	2
DEAN JR JOHN R	LTC	0-1950683	1266	3
DEAN JR WILLIAM W	LTC	0-1633795	0563	1
DEAN JR WILSON H	MAJ	0-0965126	0263	1
DEAN LEONARD M	1LT	0-0405517	0248	2
DEAN LEWIS W	WO1	W-2127944	1044	2
DEAN LLOYD A	CPT	0-0219521	0855	3
DEAN LUTHER J	LTC	0-1822678	0764	1
DEAN MATTHEW B	MAJ	0-2032129	0858	1
DEAN MERLIN F	MAJ	0-1300772	0854	2
DEAN NORMAN C	COL	0-0178888	1046	2
DEAN OLIN	CPT	0-1578344	0558	1
DEAN PATRICK C	LTC	0-1574412	0561	1
DEAN RALPH M	LTC	0-0189712	1058	3
DEAN ROBERT	MAJ	0-1165845	1162	1
DEAN ROBERT C	B G	0-0327502	0164	3
DEAN ROBERT C	MAJ	0-0249140	1265	3
DEAN ROBERT P	MAJ	0-1299537	0156	1
DEAN STANLEY E	MAJ	0-1171515	1166	1
DEAN THOMAS J	MAJ	0-0298099	0263	3
DEAN VERNICE F	CW4	W-2146448	1163	2
DEAN VIRGIL F	CPT	0-0920247	0745	2
DEAN WALLACE E	1LT	0-1306565	1045	2
DEAN WESLEY R	MAJ	0-1945112	0863	3
DEANE GEORGE J	CW3	W-2150583	0263	1
DEANE GLENN E	LTC	0-1321104	0962	1
DEANE HERBERT D	CPT	0-0277272	0442	2
DEANE JOHN J	COL	0-0185004	0154	1
DEANE LESTER C	CPT	0-0980989	0759	2
DEANE WILLIAM V	CW4	W-2141525	0459	1
DEANER ARCHER S	1LT	0-0461546	0645	2
DEANER JAMES F	CPT	0-0986665	0562	1
DEANS GLEN C	MAJ	0-1002198	1058	1
DEANS KENNETH V	LTC	0-0311210	1159	1
DEANS SYLVESTER	MAJ	0-1000343	0247	1
DEANS WILLIAM F	MAJ	0-0961017	0965	1
DEAR CHARLES B	MAJ	0-0332611	0967	3
DEARBORN DONALD H	CPT	0-1999043	0247	1
DEARDORFF RAYMOND A	LTC	0-1290385	0165	3
DEARIE WALTER E	CW2	W-2150110	0662	1
DEARMOND JR GEORGE W	1LT	0-0465866	0145	2
DEARTH JAMES A	MAJ	0-1296826	0547	1
DEARTH JAMES S	LTC	0-2034875	0864	1
DEARTH ROBERT D	LTC	0-1166469	0661	1

ARMY OF THE UNITED STATES RETIRED LIST

NAME	GRADE	SVC NO	DATE RET MO YR	RET CODE
DEASE JOSEPH M	2LT	0-1045061	1144	2
DEASON MARY C	1LT	L-0402470	0546	2
DEASON THOMAS B	CW3	W-2206536	1166	1
DEASY RICHARD M	MAJ	0-1999918	0363	1
DEATH RICHARD C	CW2	W-2146824	0561	1
DEATHERAGE CARL	CPT	0-0498268	0254	1
DEATHERAGE HUBERT D	MAJ	0-2005282	1163	1
DEATHERAGE LEON E	CW3	W-2146755	0161	1
DEATHERAGE WILLIAM R	MAJ	0-0254854	0554	3
DEATON ANDY N	LTC	0-0252992	0760	3
DEATON GEORGE V	LTC	0-1573154	0555	1
DEATON JAMES F	MAJ	0-1686640	0165	1
DEATON JAMES T	LTC	0-1637276	1060	1
DEATSCH ROBERT W	CW4	W-2108994	1265	1
DEAVOURS AUBRY H	CPT	0-1292487	0653	1
DEAVY JOHN	CPT	0-0191903	0221	1
DEBALD HARRY G	LTC	0-0920074	0665	3
DEBAR MAURICE	LTC	0-0325755	0463	3
DEBATES RALPH F	WO1	W-2116688	0744	2
DEBELAK WILLIAM F	MAJ	0-0343026	0746	2
DEBES DALE A	LTC	0-0364702	1154	1
DEBEUOISE PAUL	COL	0-0141239	0145	2
DEBIAS FRANK J	1LT	0-1292488	0645	2
DEBO WILLIAM	1LT	0-1822541	0345	2
DEBOER CLARENCE J	CPT	0-1686990	0346	2
DEBORD LEONARD D	1LT	0-1115547	0448	2
DEBRECHT JOSEPH C	1LT	0-1303117	0647	2
DEBROECK CARL F	CPT	0-1303118	0345	2
DEC JOHN J	MAJ	0-1683965	0563	1
DECESARE CARL R	CPT	0-0889359	1058	1
DECESARE FRANK J	CPT	0-0489945	0845	2
DECHANT EDWARD G	MAJ	0-1578348	0154	1
DECHON JOHN F	LTC	0-2014703	1167	1
DECHRISTOFORO ARTHUR	CPT	0-1689584	0145	1
DECK HENRY R	LTC	0-1534950	0764	1
DECK JR WALTER V	LTC	0-1298510	0663	1
DECK LEON C R	1LT	0-1597919	0351	2
DECK LUCIUS L	LTC	0-0227263	0957	3
DECKARD DEWEY	CPT	0-0225040	0349	1
DECKARD PERCY E	LTC	0-0146834	0648	3
DECKER ALFRED F	LTC	0-1040693	0963	1
DECKER ALPHONSE J	MAJ	0-1822117	0161	1
DECKER ALPINE N	CW3	W-2152636	0665	1
DECKER ARNOLD F	CW2	W-2212261	0864	2
DECKER ARTHUR	LTC	0-1300137	1265	1
DECKER CARL F	LTC	0-0318655	0661	1
DECKER CHARLES	CPT	0-0285792	0757	3
DECKER CHARLES A	COL	0-0273210	1067	3
DECKER CLIFFORD N	LTC	0-0380319	1160	1
DECKER DOYLE V	CPT	0-2027264	0551	2
DECKER ERVIN A	CW2	W-2212122	0866	1
DECKER FORREST E	LTC	0-1294799	0961	1
DECKER FORREST E	CW2	W-2207393	0861	1
DECKER FREDERICK	CPT	0-0164047	0545	1
DECKER FREDERICK	LTC	0-0497542	0457	1
DECKER FREDERICK	MAJ	0-1017898	0865	1
DECKER HARRY S	MAJ	0-0490637	0754	2
DECKER HOLLIS A	CPT	0-0518259	0452	1
DECKER JR CLIFFORD F	MAJ	0-0967740	0363	1
DECKER JR RALPH	1LT	0-1032272	0751	1
DECKER LEROY S	MAJ	0-1686614	0264	1
DECKER LESLIE F	CW4	W-2151301	0961	1
DECKER RICHARD F	LTC	0-1309156	0364	2
DECKER RUDOLPH F	CPT	0-0130316	0648	3
DECKER WILLIAM T	MAJ	0-1311621	0461	2
DECLERT ALBERT T	LTC	0-1555370	0163	1
DECLET CEFERINO	MAJ	0-2263294	0563	1
DECEAUX EUGENE J	MAJ	0-1643468	0462	1
DEDECKER JR ADRIAN F	CPT	0-1286450	0247	1
DEDERER HERMAN M	MAJ	0-0205193	0556	3
DEDI CHARLES A	COL	0-0358539	0960	1
DEDITZ FRANK L	CPT	0-0484553	0348	2
DEDMON JR JESSE O	CPT	0-0291474	1044	2
DEDMON ROBERT C	CPT	0-1030355	0348	1
DEDMON ROY L	LTC	0-1030140	0766	1

NAME	GRADE	SVC NO	DATE RET MO YR	RET CODE
DEDRICK WILLIAM T	1LT	0-0444542	0344	2
DEE ORVILLE F	LTC	0-1054532	0167	3
DEE SIDNEY F	CPT	0-0365178	0344	2
DEE WINFIELD S	LTC	0-0505592	1065	3
DEEBACH RALPH M	2LT	0-1118562	0457	1
DEEDS CLAUDE F	CW3	W-2151774	0565	1
DEEDS FRANK E	MAJ	0-1120313	0663	1
DEEDS JR FRANK H	2LT	0-2010806	0646	2
DEEDY EDWARD J	MAJ	0-0526206	0456	1
DEEG MILES F	1LT	0-1341952	0953	2
DEEGAN ROBERT J	CPT	0-1314394	0346	2
DEELEY JOSEPH M	COL	0-0267563	0264	3
DEELSTRA NICHOLAS J	LTC	0-1314453	1161	1
DEEMER CHARLES F	MAJ	0-0575298	0766	1
DEEMING GEORGE S	LTC	0-1108612	0166	1
DEEMS HAROLD F	LTC	0-0405210	0661	1
DEEMS IRWIN W	CW4	W-2114315	1160	1
DEEPE GEORGE S	LTC	0-1944657	0465	1
DEER THOMAS C	CW4	W-2104666	0859	1
DEER WILBER L	CW3	W-2147297	0465	1
DEERE WILLIAM R	WO1	W-2121204	0753	1
DEERING ROSS E	CW3	W-2148162	0263	1
DEERING WILLIAM A	LTC	0-1182812	0263	1
DEES RAYMOND J	LTC	0-0499856	0462	2
DEESE WALTER E	CPT	0-1101404	0747	1
DEETER EMMETT	COL	0-0298667	0564	3
DEETER MORTON L	MAJ	0-0399089	1151	1
DEETZ HENRY H	CPT	0-2019718	0958	1
DEFANDORF JAMES H	COL	0-0178688	0452	3
DEFFEYES THEODORE E	CPT	0-0488272	1049	1
DEFLON ERIC G	CPT	0-0472900	0145	2
DEFORD JOHN E	MAJ	0-0185320	0648	3
DEFOURNEAUX RENE J	MAJ	0-0887913	0265	1
DEFREES WILLIAM A	MAJ	0-0985648	0767	1
DEFUNIAK HERBERT R	MAJ	0-0450119	0164	1
DEGER LEON J	COL	0-0204827	1152	3
DEGLES GEORGE	MAJ	0-1876488	1065	1
DEGN SADIE AGNE	2LT	N-0730788	1044	1
DEGNAN JOHN M	MAJ	0-1010722	0567	1
DEGNER JR CARL F	LTC	0-0268863	0367	3
DEGOEY JOHN C	2LT	0-1996604	0945	2
DEGON VINCENT M	MAJ	0-0385040	0865	1
DEGONYCUN FREDERICK	CW2	W-2153157	1159	1
DEGOOD ALBERT F	CW3	W-2142953	0758	1
DEGRAW JOSEPH I	LTC	0-0451092	0356	1
DEGURSE JEAN R	2LT	N-0730713	0644	1
DEGUTIS EDWARD J	LTC	0-0396345	1060	1
DEHNER WALTER J	LTC	0-0175594	0462	3
DEIBERT FRANKLIN L	LTC	0-1040694	0264	1
DEIBLER HARRY M	LTC	0-0299759	1265	3
DEIGNAN FRANCIS W	1LT	0-0452723	1144	2
DEINES DAVID E	LTC	0-0240372	0759	1
DEIS HENRY M	CW4	W-2002837	1262	3
DEISS GWENDOLYN	CPT	N-0702850	0147	1
DEITCH EDWARD A	MAJ	0-1050228	1063	1
DEITCH LOUIS	2LT	0-1298674	1044	2
DEITERS FRIEDHELM	CW3	W-2148565	1164	1
DEITZ THAD R	CW2	W-2142422	0856	1
DEITZ WILLIAM C	1LT	0-1303472	1048	1
DEKALANDS ROBERT W	2LT	0-2019857	0950	1
DEKIS CONSTANTIN	1LT	0-1319467	0745	2
DEKKER CLARENCE E	LTC	0-1342325	0567	1
DEKKER JOHN L	LTC	0-1175993	0666	1
DEKTOR ABRAM A	LTC	0-0309256	0765	3
DEL BENE FRANCIS J	LTC	0-1293560	0462	1
DEL BENE JOSEPH A	LTC	0-1104120	0563	1
DEL BIAGGIO AMIL	CPT	0-0966894	0860	1
DEL CORRO IBARRA G	MAJ	0-1896381	0861	1
DEL CORSO ANDREW A	LTC	0-2043001	0767	1
DEL CUETO RENATO A	MAJ	0-1181224	0165	3
DEL ETOILE NORBERT	CW4	W-2120061	1159	1
DEL GIORGIO F M	1LT	0-1826130	1145	2
DEL GOERC VINCENT J	CW2	W-2143231	0859	1
DEL HOMME ELMER E	LTC	0-0230976	0464	3
DEL PORTE JACK R	MAJ	0-1342249	0767	1

NAME	GRADE	SVC NO	DATE RET MO YR	RET CODE
DEL PRETE EUGENE	LTC	0-1558134	0163	1
DEL REGNO LAWRENCE	MAJ	0-1111575	0764	1
DEL ROSARIO A	2LT	0-1896672	0757	1
DEL ROSARIO AMBROCCO	LTC	0-0496050	0354	1
DEL ROSARIO C	MAJ	0-1288365	0960	1
DEL TORO JOSE E	COL	0-0155797	1062	3
DEL TORO UBALDO	COL	0-0191507	0662	3
DEL VALLE ANTONIO	MAJ	0-1317224	1060	1
DEL-CHICCA SILVIO	CPT	0-0515967	0445	2
DELA CONCEPCION R	1LT	0-1896388	0952	1
DELA CRUZ JOSE	1LT	0-0890323	1149	1
DELA CRUZ VICTORIANO	2LT	0-1896871	0159	1
DELA PERRIERE JOHN J	MAJ	0-0236221	0365	3
DELACCRUZ LESCUM	CPT	0-2027361	0958	2
DELAFIELD JOSEPH L	CPT	0-0911611	0346	1
DELAHAY JR R T	2LT	0-1825844	0945	2
DELAHUNTY JOSEPH P	CW2	W-2117061	0256	1
DELAMATER GEORGE L	MAJ	0-1120537	1265	1
DELAMETER CHARLES M	LTC	0-0377027	0859	1
DELAND FRANCIS R	LTC	0-0214761	1262	3
DELANEY CARROLL S	1LT	0-1014784	1145	2
DELANEY CLAUDE R	MAJ	0-2037048	0263	1
DELANEY DANIEL T	LTC	0-0451663	0361	1
DELANEY FRANCES T	CPT	N-0756816	0347	1
DELANEY FRIEDA L	1LT	N-0779164	0845	1
DELANEY HARVEY R	CW4	W-2141947	0257	1
DELANEY JAMES A	LTC	0-0484998	0460	3
DELANEY JOSEPH H	MAJ	0-1951550	0364	1
DELANEY JR WILLIAM J	LTC	0-0417736	0461	1
DELANEY MARGARET A	1LT	N-0754429	0247	1
DELANEY NORMAN J	CW2	W-2144765	0657	1
DELANEY RALPH A	LTC	0-0397134	0262	1
DELANEY THOMAS F	MAJ	0-0983906	0364	1
DELANEY THOMAS J	CW4	W-2142303	0859	1
DELANEY WILLIAM E	CW2	W-2205737	0864	1
DELANEY WILLIAM H	2LT	0-0271315	1154	3
DELANEY WILLIAM L	CPT	0-0309237	1159	3
DELANO FRANK R	B G	0-0110597	1050	3
DELANO JOHN W	CPT	0-1875744	0957	2
DELANO NORMAN	CW3	W-2144877	0564	1
DELANY ARTHUR G	LTC	0-1281111	0762	2
DELANY GERALD M	CPT	0-1174819	0350	1
DELAUNAY ARTHUR J	MAJ	0-0444379	1044	2
DELEGRAM JR EMILE J	MAJ	0-1315804	1160	1
DELERUYELLE F J	2LT	0-2039597	0148	1
DELESHA LAVERN L	CPT	0-2289438	1162	1
DELFS HAMILTON D	1LT	0-1307951	1046	2
DELGADO ENRIQUE	2LT	0-0362563	1142	2
DELGREGO ARTHUR L	LTC	0-0272452	0646	2
DELHORNE ROOSEVELT	LTC	0-0452334	0463	1
DELIA JOSEPH L	CW2	W-2208647	0665	1
DELIA JR ANTHONY	LTC	0-0309867	0963	3
DELIA PIERRE J	MAJ	0-0326244	0467	3
DELICH PETER F	WO1	W-2130709	0645	2
DELISCU FRANCOIS	COL	0-0164542	1154	2
DELIZ JOHN F	MAJ	0-1688448	0163	1
DELK JOHN L	MAJ	0-0963778	0266	2
DELK JOHN W	LTC	0-0483998	0555	1
DELL LEWIS R	CW3	W-2130751	0457	1
DELL WALTER J	LTC	0-0223772	0655	3
DELLA ROCCA ANTH	COL	0-0242357	0262	3
DELLAGROCCA RENATO J	1LT	0-1310076	0546	2
DELLA-PENNA CARL F	1LT	0-1315917	0348	2
DELLAGO JOSEPH L	CW4	W-2143375	0967	1
DELLAPORT NORMAN	2LT	0-1329571	0945	2
DELLEPIANE HENRY C	LTC	0-0224076	0863	3
DELLERA JOSEPH L	MAJ	0-0101533	1057	3
DELLERT HOWARD C	COL	0-0397842	0958	1
DELLGREN CARL A	LTC	0-0282371	0861	1
DELLI-CARPINI DOMENI	LTC	0-0586606	0766	1
DELLIGATTI HENRY J	2LT	0-1998523	0846	2
DELLITT FRANK R	1LT	0-1061670	0346	2
DELMAGE SHERMAN H	MAJ	0-0969633	0465	1
DELMO ANTONIO	CPT	0-1587757	0755	1
DELMONICO JAMES R	CPT	0-1824438	1046	2

NAME	GRADE	SVC NO	DATE RET MO YR	RET CODE
DELO PERRY A	LTC	0-0465660	0745	2
DELOREY DONALD W	CPT	0-1308314	0447	2
DELOREY JOHN R	MAJ	0-2033572	1059	1
DELP JOHN P	MAJ	0-1302280	1062	1
DELPINO ROBERT A	LTC	0-0515924	0765	1
DELSON LEON	MAJ	0-0184003	1156	3
DEMA JOHN J	CW2	W-2111538	1058	1
DEMAREST JAMES V	COL	0-0137232	0449	3
DEMBERGER JAMES T	MAJ	0-0949056	1062	1
DEMBOSKY ANTHONY E	CPT	0-0479371	0752	1
DEMCHO NICK M	1LT	0-1313984	1145	2
DEMCHOK ANDREW J	LTC	0-1306708	0862	1
DEMENT RICHARD F	WO1	W-2112245	0650	1
DEMARANVILLE M I	CPT	0-1287316	0353	1
DEMERS ALBERT G	CW4	W-2115250	1054	1
DEMERS JACKSON J	CPT	0-1040695	1045	2
DEMERS LEON M	CPT	0-1165480	0561	1
DEMERS ROLAND P	MAJ	0-1179366	1165	1
DEMERS WILLIAM G	CPT	0-0385100	0146	1
DEMERY ROBERT L	CW3	W-2205477	0667	1
DEMETER MIKE	MAJ	0-2263412	1062	1
DEMETRAS LEO	2LT	0-1020046	0946	2
DEMICK FRANK W	LTC	0-1059762	0863	1
DEMICO JOSEPH H	CW4	W-2119750	0564	1
DEMING ALLEN C	LTC	0-1634665	1067	1
DEMING CLIFTON L	LTC	0-1554350	0363	1
DEMING CURTIS C	2LT	0-1016301	0446	2
DEMINGS CHARLES S	CW4	W-2115916	0463	1
DEMINT THOMAS W	COL	0-0290965	1156	2
DEMIR FRANCIS S	LTC	0-1283039	0961	1
DEMITRIADES CONSTANT	MAJ	0-1060410	1262	1
DEMKO WILLIAM	CW3	W-2149468	0163	1
DEMLING MARTIN A	CW4	W-2142559	0567	1
DEMLOW ROBERT E	1LT	0-1294101	1048	2
DEMMEL CLYDE K	LTC	0-0407756	1067	3
DEMMERS HENRY	1LT	0-0420188	0749	1
DEMO EDWARD L	CW2	W-2153246	0561	1
DEMO JOHN J	CPT	0-0338466	0245	2
DEMOS ALEXANDER	LTC	0-1176600	0261	1
DEMOUY MARSHALL F	CW3	W-2209527	0967	1
DEMPSEY EDWARD F	LTC	0-0240921	0464	3
DEMPSEY HARRY J	MAJ	0-1578352	0661	1
DEMPSEY JACOB P	2LT	0-0108325	0836	1
DEMPSEY JAMES C	COL	0-0255023	1051	1
DEMPSEY JOHN E	LTC	0-0373203	0752	1
DEMPSEY JOHN P	MAJ	0-1589157	0261	1
DEMPSEY JOHN T	WO1	W-2141841	0952	2
DEMPSEY JOSEPH E	MAJ	0-0464779	0344	2
DEMPSEY JR HENRY V	MAJ	0-1335906	0764	1
DEMPSEY JR JOHN T	1LT	0-1286094	1044	2
DEMPSEY LAWRENCE J	CPT	0-0461182	0850	1
DEMPSEY MARVIN F	MAJ	0-0931058	0859	1
DEMPSEY PERCY E	WO1	W-2113533	0350	2
DEMPSEY RALPH P	MAJ	0-2011723	0161	1
DEMPSEY S ELIZABET	1LT	N-0744437	1046	1
DEMPSEY SR ALFORD J	MAJ	0-1314603	0165	1
DEMPSEY WILLARD M	2LT	0-0863195	0545	2
DEMPSTER CLYDE R	COL	0-0199693	1153	3
DEMPSTER LESLIE J	CPT	0-0499532	0747	1
DEMSKI RAYMOND W	LTC	0-1104607	1165	1
DEMSKY THEODORE C	CPT	0-0537559	0550	1
DEMULLING JOSEPH J	CW2	W-3200130	0566	1
DEMUTH VICTOR J	CPT	0-1011983	1144	2
DEN BOER CORNE	1LT	N-0744566	0846	1
DEN-OUDEN CHRISTIAN	LTC	0-0350152	0554	2
DENARC RUSSELL G	MAJ	0-2049787	1263	1
DENAS JOSEPH M	LTC	0-1173585	0263	1
DENAULT HERBERT M	MAJ	0-0405158	0760	1
DENBEAU JOSEPH H	LTC	0-0371322	0260	1
DENBY OTIS E	MAJ	0-0547513	0564	1
DENEAU RUTH S	CPT	L-0304002	0146	2
DENEEN JR ARTHUR R	1LT	0-1292145	0645	2
DENFIP MYRTLE M	MAJ	N-0702296	1062	1
DENHAM CECIL W	CW3	W-2119756	0757	1
DENHAM CHARLIE A	CPT	0-1996596	0656	1

NAME	GRADE	SVC NO	DATE RET MO YR	RET CODE
DENHAM THOMAS J	MAJ	0-0282955	0144	2
DENHARD CHRISTOPHE	LTC	0-1051102	0567	1
DENICK WILLIAM A	LTC	0-1647841	0962	1
DENIO HOWARD I	LTC	0-0164454	0351	3
DENIS JEAN R	LTC	0-0270767	0246	2
DENISE FRANK L	LTC	0-0280041	0357	1
DENISON IRA J	2LT	0-1300292	0345	1
DENISON NELLIE M	MAJ	N-0700777	0346	1
DENISON WILLIAM R	MAJ	0-0211550	1058	3
DENISON WILLIAM R	CPT	0-0322311	0648	3
DENISTON DEAN T	CPT	0-1287844	1046	2
DENIT LEO A	COL	0-0189222	0355	3
DENKENBERGER JAMES V	MAJ	0-1306392	0960	1
DENLER WARREN A	MAJ	0-0443751	0962	1
DENLINGER EARLE B	LTC	0-0322254	0966	3
DENMAN JAN D	LTC	0-0291184	0267	3
DENMAN JOHN L	1LT	0-0378868	1144	2
DENMAN JR WILLIAM F	1LT	0-0481759	0343	1
DENMAN OLL C	WO1	W-2109272	0945	2
DENMAN RICHARD F	CW2	W-2151932	1057	1
DENMAN ROGER S	MAJ	0-0241368	0660	3
DENMAN WAYNE L	MAJ	0-0243265	0263	3
DENMARK HARRY A	2LT	0-1642794	0954	1
DENNARD BILLY C	2LT	0-1292843	1165	2
DENNELL ALFRED R	CPT	0-1313578	0347	2
DENNEN CHARLES A	MAJ	0-2204434	0666	1
DENNEN WILLIAM F	CW2	W-2145136	0758	1
DENNEN WILLIAM L	COL	0-0124661	0254	3
DENNER ROBERT E	1LT	0-0436428	0349	1
DENNETT FRANCIS J	CW4	W-2126820	1166	1
DENNEY CARL P	CPT	0-1178755	1053	1
DENNEY EDWIN R	MAJ	0-0965317	1163	1
DENNEY HUGH R	1LT	0-0507229	0457	1
DENNEY JOHN F	LTC	0-1410690	0862	1
DENNEY JUDD W	LTC	0-0552223	0967	1
DENNEY THOMAS V	LTC	0-1058491	0765	2
DENNEY WELLS H	LTC	0-0248070	0265	3
DENNIN JOHN H	LTC	0-0338600	0562	1
DENNING STANLEY P	CW3	RW-2206053	1065	1
DENNING WALTER S	COL	0-0262688	0963	3
DENNIS ANDREW D	MAJ	0-0502219	0547	2
DENNIS BENJAMIN F	CPT	0-1689804	0845	2
DENNIS BERTHA E	2LT	N-0759315	1044	1
DENNIS CAREY	LTC	0-0275594	0961	3
DENNIS CARL A	MAJ	0-1325189	0157	1
DENNIS CARL R	LTC	0-2288237	0867	1
DENNIS CAROL M	1LT	0-0274803	0744	2
DENNIS CHARLES E	LTC	0-1332152	0966	1
DENNIS EDWARD W	COL	0-0108892	1144	1
DENNIS EDWARD W	LTC	0-1055575	1262	1
DENNIS FREDERICK	COL	0-0182090	0854	1
DENNIS GUY G	CPT	0-0328501	1144	2
DENNIS JAMES A	LTC	0-1101806	0360	1
DENNIS JAMES A	CPT	0-1551385	0562	1
DENNIS JAMES A	1LT	0-2049219	0350	1
DENNIS JR JERRY T	1LT	0-0441526	0944	2
DENNIS LEONARD R	LTC	0-1691893	0967	1
DENNIS LORANCE L	COL	0-0383692	0861	2
DENNIS MARTHA R	MAJ	L-1010043	0167	1
DENNIS MILTON L	LTC	0-0900616	1046	2
DENNIS ORVILLE T	1LT	0-2008583	0951	1
DENNIS RAYMOND H	CW4	W-2142341	1264	1
DENNIS SIDNEY M	1LT	0-0491002	1053	1
DENNIS WALTER H	CPT	0-1697975	0346	2
DENNIS WALTER R	MAJ	0-0369610	0745	2
DENNIS WILLIAM F	LTC	0-0450845	0257	1
DENNISON JR JAY G	2LT	0-1293926	0345	1
DENNISON LAWRENCE E	MAJ	0-0490962	1058	1
DENNISON VEACHEL A	CPT	0-1011578	0449	1
DENNISTON GEORGE C	LTC	0-0243631	0766	3
DENNY CHARLES A	MAJ	0-1578354	0450	1
DENNY CHARLES H	LTC	0-1580855	0667	3
DENNY IRA F	CW2	W-2111083	0145	2
DENNY JASPER N	CPT	0-0231512	1148	3
DENNY JOHN L	MAJ	0-0172961	0258	3

NAME	GRADE	SVC NO	DATE RET MO YR	RET CODE
DENNY JOHN W	MAJ	0-0495312	0149	1
DENNY JR EDWARD R	LTC	0-0460101	0862	1
DENNY ROBERT M	LTC	0-1013921	0366	1
DENNY THOMAS	LTC	0-0253512	0359	3
DENNY WILLIAM M	MAJ	0-0404647	0847	2
DENSLOW WILLIAM R	CPT	0-0353198	0445	2
DENSMORE LEONARD D	COL	0-0181447	0956	3
DENSMORE RALPH A	COL	0-0169990	1055	3
DENT BRUCE	CW3	W-2142632	0361	1
DENT CARLOS E	WO1	W-2149668	0255	1
DENT DOROTHEA M	2LT	N-0741588	0845	1
DENT MARY R	1LT	N-0726520	0845	1
DENT PAUL L	MAJ	0-1685130	0845	2
DENT PERRY F	CW2	W-2148138	1159	1
DENT RAYMOND A	MAJ	0-1011138	0361	1
DENT TOWNSEND E	CPT	0-0264204	0346	1
DENTON CHARLES T	LTC	0-1114449	1061	1
DENTON CHARLES W	CPT	0-1579553	0145	2
DENTON DOROTHY A	2LT	N-0763354	0345	1
DENTON DWIGHT D	CPT	0-0361985	0645	2
DENTON GORDON R	CPT	0-0416525	0261	1
DENTON JR SAMUEL A	MAJ	0-1523598	0965	1
DENTON LEWIS F	MAJ	0-0356033	1061	2
DENTON MILLIS D	MAJ	0-1646553	1062	1
DENTON MONROE A	1LT	0-0320281	0743	2
DENTON ORRIN	LTC	0-0496584	0457	1
DENTON OWEN G	MAJ	0-0378701	0455	1
DENTON SAMUEL T	LTC	0-0499731	0654	1
DENTON SHELBY T	MAJ	0-0500530	0547	2
DENTON SR SAMUEL A	LTC	0-0184720	0750	1
DENTON WALTER F	CPT	0-0497988	0154	2
DENTON WILLIAM I	LTC	0-0216220	0563	3
DENTON WILLIAM M	1LT	0-1661363	0158	1
DENTREMONT EARL J	COL	0-0924650	0364	3
DENTREMONT JAMES F	LTC	0-1548725	1062	1
DENUNZIO VINCENT L	CPT	0-0175395	0545	2
DENVIR JAMES F	1LT	0-1311988	0547	2
DENZER RAYMOND	LTC	0-1036549	1166	1
DEO CLAUDE D	1LT	0-0888954	0146	2
DEORALE HARVEY J	LTC	0-0259442	0667	3
DEONIER WILLIAM C	LTC	0-0342319	1157	2
DEPEW HARLEY V	WO1	W-2128489	0145	2
DEPIERRO FRANK T	1LT	0-0436871	1044	2
DEPLER ROBERT E	MAJ	0-1117353	0765	1
DEPP DONALD S	CPT	0-0380368	0146	2
DEPPE ARLINGTON	MAJ	0-0109616	0844	1
DEPPE ROBERT F	MAJ	0-0386998	0665	1
DEPPEN GEORGE D	MAJ	0-1166041	1163	1
DEPPENSMITH LLOYD F	MAJ	0-1559446	0960	1
DEPRE RICHARD A	CW3	W-2141252	0156	1
DEPREZ ALEXANDER	MAJ	0-1327119	0764	1
DERT WILLIAM J	1LT	0-0492165	0556	1
DEPTULA FELIX A	1LT	0-0497112	0251	1
DEPTULA VINCENT	MAJ	0-1035148	0554	1
DEPUGLIA JOSEPH A	CPT	0-1797447	1058	1
DEQUAINE OWEN J	CW2	W-2214839	0966	1
DER MOTT WILLI	MAJ	0-0194556	0563	3
DERAS MARTIN W	1LT	0-1946472	0946	2
DERBER WARD H	1LT	0-1319141	1045	2
DERBES EARL M	LTC	0-0219818	0664	3
DERBIN CHARLES A	CW3	W-2152156	0363	1
DERBLICK MICHAEL	2LT	0-2030567	1047	1
DERBONNE JOHN K	LTC	0-1104124	1060	1
DERBY ALBERT C	CW4	W-2141253	1062	1
DERBY HENRY S	COL	0-0267562	0457	3
DERBY HENRY V	LTC	0-0261772	0862	3
DERBY HOWARD F	COL	0-0265780	0661	3
DERBY RAY L	LTC	0-0235915	0759	3
DERBY RICHARD G	MAJ	0-1845134	0564	1
DERBY STANLEY E	MAJ	0-0720808	0465	1
DERBY WILLIAM P	MAJ	0-0474437	0452	1
DERENZO AURELIO G	CPT	0-0928095	0646	1
DERGE RICHARD H	MAJ	0-1575555	0455	2
DERHAM EDGAR M	CPT	0-0220829	0446	2
DERIEUX WILLIAM T	1LT	0-2204548	0654	2

NAME	GRADE	SVC NO	DATE RET MO YR	RET CODE
DERINGER MAJORIE A	MAJ	N-0728753	0463	1
DERIS JR GEORGE F	1LT	0-1170705	0246	2
DERKSEN WILLIAM J	MAJ	0-0296850	0546	2
DERMIT LEE A	MAJ	0-0491283	0354	2
DERMONT JOHN G	1LT	0-4001705	1155	2
DEROSA JOHN F	1LT	0-1283041	0944	2
DEROSA MILTON A	2LT	0-1306710	0145	2
DEROSIER GEORGE H	1LT	0-1300138	0354	1
DEROY JUDITH M	1LT	N-0784138	0146	1
DERPA CHARLES R	MAJ	0-2047622	1057	2
DERRICK CEPHAS P	LTC	0-0222243	0657	3
DERRICK CHARLES D	MAJ	0-0451540	0559	1
DERRICK CHARLES W	COL	0-0255840	0967	3
DERRICK JOHN N	CW2	W-2152264	0464	2
DERRICO ARMAND J	MAJ	0-0335554	0646	2
DERRY EUGENE F	CW2	W-2143895	0755	1
DERRY JOHN A	COL	0-0262333	0667	3
DERRYBERRY I D	CPT	0-1018207	0346	2
DERSCHEID LYLE A	1LT	0-0522520	0446	2
DERTZO JOHN	LTC	0-0388325	1162	1
DERUS LEROY P	2LT	0-1013427	0344	2
DERUSSO LOUIS J	CPT	0-0167244	0257	3
DERVEY RAYMOND J	MAJ	0-0360473	0945	1
DERWIN JR JAMES J	WO1	W-2132769	0545	2
DERY ALEXANDER	CW4	W-2002182	0757	3
DES CHAMPS CLAUDIUS	COL	0-0243497	0766	3
DES JARDINS NORMAND	MAJ	0-1554533	0264	1
DES LAURIERS LAURENC	LTC	0-1548727	1062	1
DESANTIS LOUIS J	LTC	0-1306568	0962	1
DESAUTEL EDWARD	CPT	0-1179367	0361	1
DESCHENES HOMER	LTC	0-0497682	0554	2
DESCHNER FABIAN S	CPT	0-0261639	1264	3
DESERANO CHARLES F	MAJ	0-1106091	1054	1
DESFORGE WILLIAM V	1LT	0-0885765	1145	1
DESGUIN PAUL F	1LT	0-0450847	0349	1
DESHAIES GEORGE J	MAJ	0-1016684	0662	1
DESHANE ELMA A	2LT	N-0736053	1042	1
DESIST SAMUEL	MAJ	0-0980842	0664	1
DESJARDINE LOUIS P	MAJ	0-0255807	0944	2
DESJARDINS WILFRED A	CW3	W-2110079	0160	1
DESKIEWICZ T M	CW4	W-2144710	0960	1
DESKO MICHAEL D	LTC	0-1283388	0656	1
DESLANDES ELLERY C	CW2	W-2209454	0264	1
DESMOND GORDON R	MAJ	0-0942608	0155	2
DESMOND JOHN T	1LT	0-0435614	1043	2
DESMOND THOMAS J	COL	0-0265316	0465	3
DESMOND WALTER C	CW4	W-2119747	0862	1
DESNOYER ROY M	CPT	0-1597417	0253	1
DESONIE SR JAMES J	LTC	0-0354425	0566	3
DESONIER MARIE J	MAJ	N-0784464	0167	3
DESONIER ROLAND P	LTC	0-0257530	0562	1
DESPAIN CHARLES	2LT	0-1048330	0351	2
DESPRES LEONARD A	CPT	0-0527316	1045	2
DESROCHERS EDWARD J	CW3	W-2145786	0861	1
DESROCHERS JEAN B	LTC	0-0491712	0546	2
DESROCHES ALCIDE	COL	0-0484261	0956	1
DESROSIERS ROMEO J	CPT	0-1056689	0459	1
DESSEN SAMUEL	MAJ	0-1684272	0446	2
DESSUREAU DONALD A	LTC	0-1553432	0764	1
DESSUREAULT M J	CW2	W-2102834	0654	1
DESSUREAULT ROBERT L	2LT	0-1637293	1043	2
DESTEFANO JOSEPH	MAJ	0-1289876	0651	1
DESUTA FRANK J	LTC	0-0957569	0763	1
DESUYO AMBROSIO	1LT	0-2032077	0449	1
DETERRA JR JOSEPH B	1LT	0-0977387	1264	2
DETERS JACK	CW2	W-2209882	1160	1
DETERT CHARLES W	LTC	0-1333188	1264	1
DETIMER HENRY C	CW3	W-2152265	0264	1
DETLEFSEN BERNARD W	CPT	0-1119561	0561	1
DETLEFSEN MARVIN J	CPT	0-1112649	0257	1
DETRICK MERLE H	WO1	W-2111090	0950	1
DETRICK ROY M	2LT	0-1691716	1045	2
DETRIE ARTHUR	MAJ	0-0906372	0746	2
DETROIT LANCELOT L	CPT	0-0486541	0453	1
DETTMANN RALPH W	CPT	0-1697689	0446	2

NAME	GRADE	SVC NO	DATE RET MO YR	RET CODE
DETTMER HERMAN W	LTC	0-0256022	0967	3
DETTMER MARTIN W	LTC	0-1048331	0367	1
DETTMER STANLEY	LTC	0-0265252	0667	3
DETWEILER ERWIN E	CPT	0-0982057	1060	1
DETWILER HARRY L	LTC	0-0238644	0364	3
DETWILER ROBERT H	MAJ	0-0490852	0146	2
DETWILER SAMUEL S	MAJ	0-1001987	0765	3
DETWILLER ALBERT K	COL	0-0199153	0648	3
DETWILLER HARVEY C	MAJ	0-0508630	0450	1
DEU PREE CHARL	CPT	0-1057720	0446	2
DEUEL JOHN V	CPT	0-0100749	0959	3
DEUEL ROBERT L	1LT	0-1533535	0851	2
DEUELL ROBERT G	LTC	0-1300140	0263	1
DEUGAN LESTER A	CPT	0-1533769	0156	1
DEUGAW LLOYD	MAJ	0-0968074	0759	1
DEURREE JACK D	LTC	0-1308315	0762	1
DEUTCH MAX	LTC	0-0227882	0765	3
DEUTER CARL	COL	0-0283195	0955	2
DEUTSCH ALBERT C	MAJ	0-0156770	0154	3
DEUTSCH ALBERT C	COL	0-0193161	1061	3
DEUTSCH BERNARD B	CPT	0-0488340	0146	2
DEUTSCH HAROLD	MAJ	0-0254951	0351	1
DEUTSCH LAWRENCE M	2LT	0-1644906	0845	2
DEUTSCH MARTIN J	LTC	0-0274447	0367	3
DEUTSCH NICHOLAS J	LTC	0-1287317	0667	1
DEUTSCHLE JOSEPH S	LTC	0-0246503	0446	2
DEUTSCHMAN REYNOLD P	MAJ	0-0545636	1146	2
DEVALL ARCHIBALD	COL	0-0155657	1055	2
DEVALL SAMUEL S	COL	0-0185088	1156	3
DEVANY EUGENE P	1LT	0-1109892	0346	2
DEVENDORF CURTIS L	COL	0-0294692	1263	3
DEVENISH GEORGE P	MAJ	0-0188469	1157	3
DEVENPORT RUSSELL J	CW2	W-2150818	0463	2
DEVER RALPH E	LTC	0-0236456	0465	3
DEVERALL ROBERT L	CPT	0-0338210	0865	3
DEVEREUX RICHARD A	COL	0-0296831	0266	3
DEVERS JR ARVIN S	MAJ	0-1011049	0763	1
DEVERY GERALD P	1LT	0-1798653	1045	2
DEVICK ALVIN O	2LT	0-0378632	1142	2
DEVINE ANNA M	CW3	V-0800023	1265	1
DEVINE CRAIG W	CW4	W-2201186	0766	3
DEVINE DAVID	CW2	W-2215179	0567	1
DEVINE DONALD O	CPT	0-1585358	0547	2
DEVINE HAROLD A	MAJ	0-0202562	0158	3
DEVINE JAMES H	1LT	0-1823127	1046	2
DEVINE JOHN J	LTC	0-0279592	0964	3
DEVINE JOSEPH C	LTC	0-0288781	0165	3
DEVINE RICHARD C	2LT	0-1180165	0845	2
DEVINE ROBERT M	CW3	RW-2143213	0962	1
DEVINE RUTH T	1LT	N-0784389	0446	1
DEVINE THEODORE M	LTC	0-1184370	0767	1
DEVINE WILLIAM J	MAJ	0-0485673	0245	2
DEVINEY RUTH M	MAJ	N-0736444	0264	1
DEVIS DONALD A	LTC	0-1585359	0766	1
DEVLIN ALLAN W	MAJ	0-1821833	0662	1
DEVLIN CHARLES N	CPT	0-1015842	1145	2
DEVLIN GEORGE W	CW4	W-2001967	0358	3
DEVLIN JAMES W	LTC	0-1590406	1062	1
DEVLIN JOSEPH H	1LT	0-1311128	0546	1
DEVLIN JOSEPH J	CPT	0-1111576	0363	1
DEVLIN LAURANCE E	COL	0-0256080	0459	3
DEVLIN LAWRENCE F	LTC	0-0253466	0545	2
DEVLIN RAYMOND P	LTC	0-1050647	0762	1
DEVLIN THOMAS J	MAJ	0-0247438	1266	3
DEVOE CLIFTON B	CPT	0-2017822	0257	1
DEVOL DANA R	MAJ	0-1109136	0267	3
DEVOL HOWARD C	CW2	W-2207536	0464	1
DEVONALD 2ND DAVID H	1LT	0-0539125	0845	2
DEVORE DALE T	MAJ	0-0292073	1145	2
DEVRIES HENRY P	LTC	0-0912346	1044	1
DEW JOSEPH D	CPT	0-0314464	0145	2
DEW JR ROBERT J	2LT	0-0556940	0346	2
DEW PERRY T	CPT	0-1181864	1065	1
DEWALT HENRY J	CPT	0-0507816	0247	1
DEWAR DONALD B	MAJ	0-1112651	0964	1

NAME	GRADE	SVC NO	DATE RET MO YR	RET CODE
DEWART BENJAMIN B	LTC	0-0138568	1150	3
DEWEL CHARLES H	COL	0-0245026	1065	3
DEWEY ALBERT T	CPT	0-0116141	0650	3
DEWEY BLAIR H	LTC	0-2211248	0767	1
DEWEY CHARLES C	MAJ	0-0318320	1052	1
DEWEY CHARLES H	MAJ	0-0186968	0648	3
DEWEY CHARLES W	LTC	0-0236355	1051	3
DEWEY DONALD W	CPT	0-2018136	0558	1
DEWEY GEORGE	LTC	0-0251860	0345	2
DEWEY GEORGE A	LTC	0-1646584	1063	2
DEWEY GEORGE B	CPT	0-1012402	0353	1
DEWEY JR WILLIAM	MAJ	0-1633158	0646	2
DEWEY WILLIAM H	LTC	0-0364454	1064	1
DEWHIRST ROBERT B	CPT	0-4051052	0858	2
DEWHIRST VICTOR E	2LT	0-2006508	0546	2
DEWHURST DAVID H	CPT	0-0150605	1049	3
DEWHURST LAWRENCE	MAJ	0-1584133	0457	1
DEWITT FREDERICK	CPT	0-0261630	0448	2
DEWITT HENRY	2LT	0-2029433	1147	1
DEWS ELI M	MAJ	0-0347156	0756	1
DEWS JACK	MAJ	0-0206349	1052	3
DEWS SAMUEL C	COL	0-0336845	0165	3
DEWSNAP STANLEY	MAJ	0-0124872	1149	3
DEXTER ALLAN L	COL	0-0162523	0852	3
DEXTER FRANK	CPT	0-1913941	1029	1
DEXTER FREDERICK	CW3	W-2153317	0263	1
DEXTER HARRY A	LTC	0-2055317	1167	1
DEXTER JR HENRY V	MAJ	0-1328578	0561	1
DEXTER ROBERT V	LTC	0-0517523	0463	1
DEXTER RODNEY S	MAJ	0-0394208	1160	1
DEXTON HENRY A	MAJ	0-1038547	0657	1
DEY FLOYD M	MAJ	0-1924683	1266	1
DEYARMOND GEORGE E	LTC	0-0256205	1059	3
DEYESO FREDERICK	LTC	0-1798460	0666	1
DEYO HARRY N	COL	0-0215193	1052	3
DEYO RALPH F	CW2	W-2147748	0157	1
DEZULOVICH STEVE A	LTC	0-1554351	0761	1
DI BENEDETTE ANNE M	CPT	N-0724068	0650	1
DI BERTO ENIO D	MAJ	0-1290040	1160	1
DI BIANCO PASCHAL F	LTC	0-0359657	0766	1
DI BRIZZI THOMAS G	MAJ	0-0170689	1043	2
DI CAPRIO JOSEPH M	CPT	0-1922206	0659	2
DI CARLO GAETANO J	LTC	0-2001795	1165	1
DI CARLO PHILIP A	MAJ	0-0886902	0363	1
DI CRISTINA EDUARDO	LTC	0-0369175	0660	1
DI CRISTINA HUMBERT	LTC	0-0196742	1160	3
DI DOMENICO DONALD V	CW3	W-2145265	0663	1
DI FABION PAUL J	CW3	W-2150945	0765	1
DI GANGI MARION R	MAJ	0-0368574	0246	2
DI GIGLIA JOHN A	CPT	0-0489259	0544	1
DI GIOVANNI JOSEPH C	MAJ	0-2017671	1163	1
DI GIROLOMO FRANK E	MAJ	0-1014497	0465	1
DI GUISEPPI ERNEST	CW4	W-2153189	0466	1
DI LEO MICHAEL B	CPT	0-0524710	0645	2
DI LORENZO SAVERIO F	MAJ	0-0954060	1163	1
DI LORENZO VINCENT	MAJ	0-1289878	1157	2
DI MARCO JOHN J	CPT	0-1298040	0161	1
DI MARINO NICHOLAS J	LTC	0-1594798	0660	1
DI MASCIO CHARLES J	LTC	0-1104612	0862	1
DI MATTIA ARTHUR A	CW3	W-2146953	1163	1
DI MEO SAVERIO	COL	0-0288824		2
DI MONDA JR LEOPOLDO	CW2	W-2210139	0265	1
DI MUZIO ANGELO A	CW2	W-2147548	0460	2
DI PALMA ANELLO	1LT	0-1582681	0561	1
DI PASQUALE ROSATIO	CW3	W-2144238	1162	1
DI PIETRO JOSEPH A	LTC	0-0193566	0354	3
DI PIETRO LIETO P	MAJ	0-1116334	0763	1
DI RESTA GENE J	CW3	W-2147387	0962	1
DI SALLE RICHARD C	LTC	0-1541887	0962	1
DI SANTIS FRED J	WO1	W-2123175	0958	2
DI YORIO JOSEPH V	2LT	0-1018017	0244	2
DI ZEREGA PHILIP V	LTC	0-1111030	0167	3
DIAKOFF ALEXANDER	CW3	RW-2144310	1064	1
DIAL JR LEE J	LTC	0-1683451	0766	1
DIAL JR MATTHEW P	CPT	0-1281511	0446	2
DIAL PAUL E	1LT	0-1293219	1045	2
DIAMANT ALFRED	1LT	0-1016844	0645	2
DIAMOND ABRAHAM I	MAJ	0-0501179	1045	2
DIAMOND ABRAHAM J	MAJ	0-0500030	0447	2
DIAMOND ALBERT	CPT	0-1633159	0555	1
DIAMOND BENJAMIN C	1LT	0-0493674	0844	2
DIAMOND FRANK B	2LT	0-0547908	0945	2
DIAMOND FRANK J	LTC	0-1322626	0263	2
DIAMOND HERBERT D	MAJ	0-1636898	0360	1
DIAMOND JOSEF	COL	0-0356762	0467	3
DIAMOND LUCIUS L	MAJ	0-1289220	0160	1
DIAMOND SIDNEY	CPT	0-0358742	0667	3
DIAMOND SOLOMON	1LT	0-1062486	0347	2
DIAS APILIO	1LT	0-0489836	0749	1
DIAS DOUGLAS E	LTC	0-0225942	0954	3
DIASIC JOSEPH S	COL	0-0254848	0361	3
DIAZ CARLOS C	MAJ	0-2263358	1262	1
DIAZ FLORENCIO	1LT	0-1896909	0764	1
DIAZ-BETANCOURT ENRI	MAJ	0-1329103	0763	1
DIBBLE EDWARD C	1LT	0-1634676	1055	1
DIBBLE GEORGE B	LTC	0-0402145	0162	3
DIBBLE GEORGE F	CW4	W-2102836	0756	1
DIBBLE HAROLD A	MAJ	0-1946548	0657	1
DIBBLE LEROY	CPT	0-4004222	0166	2
DICE FRANCIS R	LTC	0-0274402	0864	3
DICK ALFRED R	LTC	0-0254371	0755	1
DICK ALLAN F	COL	0-0265906	0860	3
DICK ARTHUR C	LTC	0-0276022	0367	3
DICK ARTHUR J	LTC	0-1081646	0466	1
DICK DALLAS	MAJ	0-1289705	0855	1
DICK DAVID W	COL	0-0397358	1062	1
DICK EWART G	CPT	0-0488808	0944	2
DICK GEORGE A	CPT	0-1165846	1046	1
DICK JAMES	LTC	0-0382109	0163	1
DICK JOHN F	LTC	0-0514141	1067	3
DICK JR KENNETH R	MAJ	0-1685739	1165	1
DICK JR WALTER A	MAJ	0-0528534	0353	1
DICK RUSSELL G	LTC	0-0385675	0660	1
DICK VERNON S	LTC	0-1685944	1046	1
DICK WILLARD J	CW2	W-2209582	0564	1
DICKAS ROBERT B	LTC	0-0101113	1144	1
DICKENS GASTON L	MAJ	0-0348128	0245	2
DICKENS PITTS B	MAJ	0-1183271	0860	1
DICKENS ROBERT R	1LT	0-1309223	0645	1
DICKENS WILLIAM R	CPT	0-0187467	0256	3
DICKENSHEETS PAUL E	CPT	0-0193163	1055	3
DICKENSON HARRY	LTC	0-0491503	0954	1
DICKERMAN WILSON K	LTC	0-0739533	0759	1
DICKERSON BENJAMIN W	1LT	0-0389020	0845	2
DICKERSON BURL E	CW3	W-2146327	0863	1
DICKERSON GEORGE W	MAJ	0-0164080	1139	1
DICKERSON HENRY W	COL	0-0102963	0859	3
DICKERSON JAMES W	LTC	0-1284837	1064	1
DICKERSON JIM F	MAJ	0-0966492	0963	1
DICKERSON JOHN E	CW4	W-2102837	0858	1
DICKERSON MADELINE L	1LT	N-0773002	0546	1
DICKERSON PAUL S	LTC	0-1180872	0367	1
DICKERSON ROBERT C	LTC	0-1302614	0660	1
DICKERSON ROBERT V	1LT	0-0455654	0547	2
DICKERSON THOMAS W	MAJ	0-1314108	1263	1
DICKERSON WENDELL H	LTC	0-0405523	0560	1
DICKEY ALBERT R	LTC	0-0971111	0852	1
DICKEY BERGIN V	COL	0-0360244	0563	1
DICKEY DEAN R	LTC	0-0323965	0456	3
DICKEY ELIZABETH	1LT	N-0762991	0548	1
DICKEY GEORGE E	LTC	0-0266773	0247	2
DICKEY HAROLD	1LT	0-1307207	0146	2
DICKEY HARRY L	LTC	0-0282558	0965	3
DICKEY IVAN A	CPT	0-0467549	1148	1
DICKEY JACK D A	MAJ	0-1541827	1163	1
DICKEY JOSEPH B	MAJ	0-0506375	0452	2
DICKEY JR WALTER L	CPT	0-0994504	0361	1
DICKEY OTTO R	WO1	W-2126268	0452	1
DICKEY PHILIP A	COL	0-0188685	0852	3
DICKEY THOMAS F	MAJ	0-1185217	0563	1
DICKEY WAYNE S	CPT	0-0965885	1061	1
DICKHOFF CARL W	1LT	0-0407482	0145	2
DICKINSON ALBERT E	1LT	0-2210376	0353	1
DICKINSON ARNOLD W	2LT	0-1300616	0344	2
DICKINSON CHESTER J	LTC	0-0272853	0341	2
DICKINSON DAVID L	LTC	0-1052324	0262	1
DICKINSON DONALD C	LTC	0-0309678	0859	1
DICKINSON DONALD P	MAJ	0-0836741	1065	1
DICKINSON EDWARD B	1LT	0-1647892	0955	1
DICKINSON GEORGE E	CPT	0-1117394	1146	2
DICKINSON HAROLD G	CW3	W-2151299	0658	1
DICKINSON HARRY O	1LT	0-1293024	0945	2
DICKINSON JAMES H	LTC	0-0302127	0166	3
DICKINSON JESSE E	CPT	0-1553986	0155	1
DICKINSON KENNETH J	1LT	0-0334848	0744	2
DICKINSON MARSHALL C	MAJ	0-1180167	0956	1
DICKINSON NONNIE E	CW4	W-2143644	0166	1
DICKINSON ROBERT E	MAJ	0-1318520	0560	1
DICKINSON THEODORE M	LTC	0-0241310	1065	3
DICKINSON W C	LTC	0-0372800	1060	1
DICKINSON WILLIAM J	CW3	W-2147210	1065	1
DICKISON ANDREW J	CPT	0-1922646	0162	1
DICKISON LOREN W	MAJ	0-1920226	1163	1
DICKISON WILBERT	WO1	W-2122271	0248	1
DICKS EDWARD A	CW4	W-2121182	0464	1
DICKS MAXWELL E	MAJ	0-0993924	0466	1
DICKSON BENJAMIN A	COL	0-0184469	1045	2
DICKSON BYRON R	MAJ	0-1046768	0962	1
DICKSON CHARLES M	COL	0-0447766	1047	1
DICKSON DONALD R	CPT	0-1061136	1165	1
DICKSON EDWARD B	1LT	0-1647992	0955	1
DICKSON ELAINE R	MAJ	L-0202209	1266	3
DICKSON GEORGE A	CPT	0-1691942	0867	1
DICKSON GEORGE G	MAJ	0-0309002	1145	1
DICKSON GEORGE L	CPT	0-1824733	0662	2
DICKSON HARRY	2LT	0-1555810	0445	2
DICKSON JACK P	CPT	0-1574685	1059	1
DICKSON JAMES D	CPT	0-1884166	1262	1
DICKSON JAMES H	1LT	0-0150516	0652	3
DICKSON JAMES T	LTC	0-1178457	0565	1
DICKSON JOHN	CPT	0-0497046	0464	3
DICKSON JR IBER B	LTC	0-1316862	1162	1
DICKSON LOUIS A	CW3	W-2145925	0859	1
DICKSON MERWIN C	MAJ	0-0335121	1061	3
DICKSON PAUL	COL	0-0265507	0956	1
DICKSON RICHARD P	CPT	0-0152571	1057	3
DICKSON RICHARD S	LTC	0-1014014	0665	1
DICKSON ROBERT B	MAJ	0-0138562	0648	3
DICKSON ROBERT C	WO1	W-2132706	0945	2
DICKSON ROBERT H	LTC	0-0103032	0649	3
DICKSON WILLIAM A	LTC	0-1319607	0565	1
DICKSON WILLIAM K	COL	0-0138612	0555	3
DICKSON WILLIAM M	CPT	0-2262970	0257	1
DICKSON WILLIAM T	1LT	0-1316390	0246	2
DICUS GEORGE L	CPT	0-1116219	0450	1
DIDERRICK MARY K	2LT	N-0733567	0745	1
DIDUCH MICHAEL J	1LT	0-1318771	0646	2
DIEBELS JR WILLIAM J	1LT	0-5301598	0859	2
DIEBOLT JAMES L	CW2	W-2205834	1162	1
DIEDIKER VICTOR W	LTC	0-0392136	1160	2
DIEDRICH WILLIAM C	LTC	0-0254895	0567	3
DIEDRICHS MARTIN A	MAJ	0-0382401	0154	1
DIEFFENBACH GEORGE B	LTC	0-0286242	0947	2
DIEFFENBACH WILLARD F	MAJ	0-2019300	0363	1
DIEFFENDORF RANDALL A	2LT	0-0392821	0344	2
DIEFFENDORF RICHARD O	CPT	0-0510022	0845	2
DIEHL AUGUST P	MAJ	0-0177947	0445	2
DIEHL BRUCE E	MAJ	0-0432945	0266	1
DIEHL CHARLES E	LTC	0-0394925	0658	2
DIEHL CONDA H	LTC	0-0277525	0263	3
DIEHL EDWARD L	2LT	0-0554724	0645	2
DIEHL FRANK A	2LT	0-1645330	0745	2
DIEHL GEORGE W	CPT	0-1103596	0861	1
DIEHL HARRY A	MAJ	0-0423203	0557	1
DIEHL MAURICE	COL	0-0221093	0962	3
DIEHL PAUL J	MAJ	0-1103597	1151	1
DIEHL RAY F	COL	0-0209409	1155	3
DIEHL RAYMOND L	LTC	0-1011845	0164	1
DIEHL WALLACE J	1LT	0-1301447	1145	2
DIEHL WINIFRED F	MAJ	N-0725230	0464	3
DIEHOLD JAMES A	MAJ	0-2037123	1162	1
DIEM JACOB	MAJ	0-1796591	1155	1
DIEMER CARL A	MAJ	0-0221920	0653	3
DIEMER DONALD K	1LT	0-2035133	0147	1
DIENST CARL A	MAJ	0-0275061	0859	3
DIENST CHARLES F	LTC	0-0115869	0648	3
DIER CLIFFORD L	B G	0-0246655	0664	3
DIER STEPHEN C	COL	0-0381926	1057	3
DIERKES PAUL A	LTC	0-0450121	0161	1
DIESEL HALBERT M	MAJ	0-1557439	1060	1
DIETER EDWARD J	LTC	0-0298502	0660	3
DIETER GEORGE H	COL	0-0152241	0648	3
DIETER LOUISE C	MAJ	N-0736257	0563	2
DIETER OTTO A	LTC	0-0347065	1160	3
DIETERICH ALVAH M	1LT	0-1046411	0146	1
DIETERICH WARREN C	CW3	W-2120762	0760	1
DIETERMAN JOHN R	MAJ	0-1643495	0965	1
DIETLE JACK F	LTC	0-1171118	1160	1
DIETRICH BENNY S	1LT	0-1174559	0346	2
DIETRICH ELEANOR J	2LT	N-0723934	0845	1
DIETRICH LEO A	LTC	0-1647895	0361	1
DIETRICH ROBERT E	MAJ	0-2266365	1166	1
DIETSCH JR EMIL F	1LT	0-1582301	0245	2
DIETTRICH ROGER A	LTC	0-1995080	1162	1
DIETZ CARL I	CPT	0-0196683	1158	3
DIETZ CLARENCE C	CW2	W-2142756	0259	1
DIETZ FRED A	CPT	0-0107926	0848	3
DIETZ FREDERICK	MAJ	0-1280038	1055	1
DIETZ JR JOSEPH A	CW3	W-2143246	0962	1
DIETZ JR NICHOLAS	LTC	0-0338569	0161	3
DIETZ LOUIS H	LTC	0-1328130	1263	1
DIETZ NORBERT W	MAJ	0-0962251	0464	1
DIETZ PHIL G	MAJ	0-1012575	1047	2
DIETZ RAYMOND W	CW2	W-2141255	0460	1
DIETZE VICTOR E	MAJ	0-1703760	0450	1
DIFFEE GUY E	CW2	W-2151835	0857	1
DIFFENDERFER H C	1LT	0-1012190	0247	2
DIFFENDERFER HARRY S	LTC	0-0281288	0961	3
DIFFIN JOHN C	MAJ	0-0516339	0646	2
DIFFLEY THOMAS L	LTC	0-1184034	1063	1
DIGEORGE IGNATIUS J	1LT	0-1293025	0945	2
DIGGES JR ALEX P	MAJ	0-1101409	0561	1
DIGGINS VERNON T	MAJ	0-2262556	0465	1
DIGGS ARTHUR E	COL	0-0180120	0756	3
DIGGS JOHN C	LTC	0-0209509	0649	3
DIGGS JOHN W	COL	0-0359919	0456	3
DIGGS RAYMOND A	LTC	0-0304322	0561	1
DIGIACOMO WILLIAM H	CPT	0-0547104	1045	2
DIGIUNI LOUIS C	MAJ	0-1109896	0662	1
DIGMAN RITA A	1LT	N-0751147	0846	1
DIHM HENRY A	LTC	0-0116139	0153	3
DILBECK HENRY L	CW2	W-2146590	0657	1
DILBURN ERNEST L	WO1	W-2120701	0458	1
DILDINE WILLIAM F	LTC	0-0280266	0359	1
DILIONE ROBERT R	CPT	0-2034075	1061	1
DILKS KENNETH E	LTC	0-0410771	0960	1
DILL DONALD G	CW3	W-2109862	1055	1
DILL ERNEST W	CPT	0-1169486	1061	1
DILL FRANCIS W	LTC	0-1553067	0661	1
DILL JERRY L	CW3	W-2203208	0566	1
DILL JR CHARLES O	LTC	0-1586537	0461	1
DILL JR WALTER J	LTC	0-0256559	0966	3
DILL JR WILLIAM G	MAJ	0-1641239	0667	1
DILL LESTER C	MAJ	0-1541002	0854	1
DILL WILLIAM H	MAJ	0-2021245	0567	1
DILLAHEY WALTER R	LTC	0-0907864	1061	3
DILLAHUNT CHESTER A	LTC	0-1822246	0966	1
DILLARD HARDY C	COL	0-0440753	1162	3
DILLARD HENRY D	CPT	0-0395345	1043	2
DILLARD JAMES M	MAJ	0-1944663	0763	1

NAME	GRADE	SVC NO	DATE RET MO YR	RET CODE
DILLARD JAMES R	COL	O-0253528	1060	3
DILLARD WALTER S	CW3	W-2152138	0365	1
DILLAWAY JR GEORGE L	COL	O-0167528	0655	2
DILLE HENRY W	LTC	O-0390686	0760	1
DILLEHAY JAMES G	LTC	O-1573163	0363	1
DILLENBACK FRANK H	MAJ	O-0123371	0245	2
DILLENBECK WILLIAM H	LTC	O-0304974	0363	3
DILLER EVERELL W	COL	O-0276278	1066	3
DILLER JOHN C	COL	O-0150609	0555	3
DILLERY JOSEPH L	CPT	O-0273775	0545	2
DILLESHAW HOWARD D	CW3	W-2148253	0163	1
DILLEY CHESTER A	CPT	O-2053819	0554	1
DILLEY DONALD J	MAJ	O-1821692	0660	1
DILLINGHAM ALLAN M	2LT	O-1633163	0647	2
DILLINGHAM HAROLD S	BG	O-0315416	0565	3
DILLINGHAM PAUL W	COL	O-0200926	1058	1
DILLIPLANE CHARLES M	LTC	O-1946474	1265	1
DILLMAN DON W	MAJ	O-0980274	0762	1
DILLMAN JR CLIFTON J	CPT	O-1547587	0746	2
DILLMAN MELVIN A	COL	O-0410711	0866	3
DILLON ASAHEL S	COL	O-0184196	1153	3
DILLON CARSON L	CPT	O-0975294	0461	1
DILLON CLYDE J	MAJ	O-0682693	1055	2
DILLON GARLAND S	LTC	O-1309699	0964	1
DILLON GOMER S	LTC	O-0249889	0764	3
DILLON HENRY S	MAJ	O-1292147	0264	1
DILLON HOWARD E	CW2	W-2150805	0158	1
DILLON JACK J	LTC	O-1102533	1058	1
DILLON JAMES H	CPT	O-0305330	0145	2
DILLON JAMES R	LTC	O-0305432	0859	1
DILLON JOHN F	MAJ	O-1176305	0263	1
DILLON JOHN F	COL	O-1581093	1263	1
DILLON JOHN R	CPT	O-0161722	1153	3
DILLON JR ALVIN	MAJ	O-2014497	1165	1
DILLON JR EDWARD	LTC	O-0181850	0758	3
DILLON JR GEORGE F	CPT	O-1997520	0367	2
DILLON JR JOHN F	1LT	O-0383066	1045	2
DILLON JR JOHN R	MAJ	O-0248409	0766	3
DILLON LESTER R	LTC	O-0189920	0656	3
DILLON LLOYD H	LTC	O-0185654	1057	3
DILLON MARGARET F	CPT	N-0733151	0747	1
DILLON RALPH R	LTC	O-1551194	0767	1
DILLON STUART P	LTC	O-0197965	0360	3
DILLON WALTER	CPT	O-2011589	0853	1
DILLON WILLIAM G	1LT	O-0527232	0945	2
DILLOW TROY G	CPT	O-0571473	0153	1
DILLS ROWLAND H	MAJ	O-1544053	0762	1
DILMAN FRANK	CPT	O-0496788	0849	1
DILWITH LEWIS M	CPT	O-1301448	0147	2
DILWORTH FRANCIS H	LTC	O-0269763	0565	3
DIMARIA NICHOLAS	CPT	O-0484671	0445	2
DIMARIA VINCENT	2LT	O-1062160	1144	2
DIMENNA PAT	1LT	O-1298200	0944	2
DIMIT JR CHARLES H	CW2	W-3250354	0866	1
DIMLING JR JOHN N	1LT	O-1286803	0146	2
DIMMICK EDGAR L	MAJ	O-1689007	0752	2
DIMMICK HENRY S	LTC	O-0170197	1160	3
DINAN KATHLEEN M	2LT	N-0702674	1036	1
DINEEN ALOYSIOUS	MAJ	O-0253666	0648	3
DINEEN JOHN J	LTC	O-0300737	1056	3
DINEEN THOMAS P	MAJ	O-0938044	0363	1
DINELEY RICHARD L	CPT	O-0444678	0862	1
DINERMAN BENJAMIN	LTC	O-0227279	0260	3
DINGEE JOHN F	1LT	O-1320311	0645	2
DINGER JULIUS J	CPT	O-1574688	1046	2
DINGES GEORGE J	COL	O-0235780	1164	3
DINGES LINUS A	CPT	O-0445287	1147	2
DINGS PARLEY M	LTC	O-0311753	0767	3
DINGWALL KENNETH M	2LT	O-0150434	0455	3
DINKEL ALFRED J	LTC	O-1573165	0252	1
DINKELKAMP ARNOLD J	LTC	O-1035243	0663	1
DINKELSPIEL EDWARD A	MAJ	O-0264615	0645	2
DINNERVILLE R F	2LT	O-1038588	1144	2
DINNING WILLIAM L	COL	O-0259508	0867	3
DINNIS OSCAR E	CPT	O-0166820	0256	3

NAME	GRADE	SVC NO	DATE RET MO YR	RET CODE
DINSE MABEL	MAJ	N-0736728	1065	3
DINSMOOR CARLTON G	LTC	O-0246735	0966	3
DINSMORE ALBERT L	CPT	O-1649428	0356	2
DINSMORE ALDEN C	CPT	O-0368717	0244	2
DINSMORE GEORGE R	LTC	O-0272654	1264	3
DINSMORE JOSEPH S	LTC	O-0266072	0955	3
DINSMORE THOMAS D	LTC	O-0548260	0464	1
DINSMORE WAYNE A	LTC	O-1036123	0261	1
DINSTBIR JOHN F	CPT	O-1296667	1067	2
DINTEMAN WERNER	LTC	O-0361664	0459	2
DINWIDDIE CHARLES R	COL	O-0152576	0754	3
DINWIDDIE JACK O	LTC	O-0254460	1263	3
DINWIDDIE JOEL W	1LT	O-0492751	0347	2
DIOCSON CONRAD V	1LT	O-1896471	0559	1
DIOKNO MELCHOR V	MAJ	O-2026963	0257	1
DION DOROTHEA G	2LT	N-0741265	1144	1
DION POLYDORE F	CPT	O-0399085	0157	1
DIONNE ARTHUR D	CPT	O-2017029	0358	1
DIONNE GEORGE A	CW4	W-2115161	0354	2
DIONNE JOSEPH A	LTC	O-0481989	1155	1
DIONOLC THOMAS	LTC	O-1298007	0462	1
DIOTT THEODORE J	LTC	O-1306711	0658	2
DIPPO FRANK H	CPT	O-0204517	1151	3
DIPPO WILLIAM G	MAJ	O-1876719	0664	1
DIPPOLITO JOSEPH H	LTC	O-0364078	0865	1
DIRDEN DON S	1LT	O-1638961	1045	2
DIRKS EDWARD F	LTC	O-0218255	0264	3
DIRRIM PAUL E	CPT	O-0981971	0261	1
DISBROW HARRY C	2LT	O-1320512	0844	2
DISCH JOHN L	2LT	O-1326822	0546	2
DISCOE HENRY	CW4	W-2129877	1054	1
DISEKER ELLIS G	LTC	O-0249141	0363	3
DISHAROON JOHN C	LTC	O-0510722	0464	1
DISICK SOLOMON	MAJ	O-0331208	0845	2
DISKO MICHAEL	1LT	O-0388731	1045	2
DISLER ELLIOTT F	1LT	O-1319266	0945	2
DISMORE ALBERT R	MAJ	O-0233215	0847	1
DISMORE RAY A	MAJ	O-0475909	0947	1
DISMUKE GRACE M	CPT	N-0763528	0654	2
DISMUKE HENRY S	1LT	O-1010822	1151	2
DISNEY CYRIL C	LTC	O-1167395	0262	1
DISNEY ROBERT	COL	O-0237301	0465	3
DISNEY STANLEY E	MAJ	O-0513303	0147	2
DISPENZA SEBASTIAN	MAJ	O-0348382	0360	1
DISSER RALPH K	LTC	O-1286096	0465	1
DISSINGER ARTHUR W	LTC	O-1552659	0161	1
DISSPAIN ED	MAJ	O-1103136	0554	1
DISSTON HARRY	COL	O-0140374	1059	3
DISTELHORST FRED M	COL	O-0172875	0252	3
DITTBERNER VAN F	LTC	O-0401419	0566	2
DITTERT JESSE J	1LT	O-1303683	0945	2
DITTES PHILIP G	MAJ	O-0478557	0165	3
DITTMANN EARL E	CPT	O-0372566	0645	2
DITTMAR GUSTAVE C	COL	O-0191195	0955	3
DITTMAR MAX C	CW3	W-2151865	0363	1
DITTMAR RUSSELL E	COL	O-0224865	1059	1
DITTMAR RUSSELL W	CPT	O-0969736	1165	1
DITTMER CHARLES H	MAJ	O-0192353	0648	3
DITTMER JOHN S	COL	O-1030143	1163	1
DITTRICH FRANK	LTC	O-1058578	1065	1
DITTRICH KARL W	COL	O-0381571	0663	1
DITZEL JR WILLIAM E	LTC	O-1331161	0767	1
DIUGUID JOHN H	LTC	O-0231096	1163	3
DIVELBISS WILLIS	CW2	W-2203474	0762	2
DIVELEY REX L	COL	O-0201482	0156	3
DIVELY JOHN M	LTC	O-0472154	0557	1
DIVELY SHIRLEY F	MAJ	O-0956567	0963	1
DIVEN DANIEL C	MAJ	O-1917756	0665	1
DIVERS JESSE W	CW3	W-2143073	0664	1
DIVICH STEVE M	LTC	O-0317860	0146	2
DIVINE BERNICE M	1LT	N-0776516	1045	1
DIVINE JOHN E	1LT	O-1281836	0546	2
DIX HAROLD L	CPT	O-0969735	0161	1
DIXON ACES G	LTC	O-1342369	0767	1
DIXON ALTON W	CW2	W-2206286	1262	2

NAME	GRADE	SVC NO	DATE RET MO YR	RET CODE
DIXON BRYAN P	1LT	O-1342169	0752	1
DIXON CALVERT R	1LT	O-1573792	1045	2
DIXON CHARLES P	CW2	W-2212218	1066	1
DIXON COLIN A	MAJ	O-0279473	0157	3
DIXON DON S	1LT	O-1647537	1045	2
DIXON DON W	COL	O-0343066	0264	1
DIXON FLOYD N	LTC	O-1309700	0962	1
DIXON FLOYD V	MAJ	O-0242602	0262	3
DIXON FRANK J	LTC	O-1320443	1262	1
DIXON FRANK L	MAJ	O-0265493	1146	2
DIXON GEORGE M	CW2	W-2206095	0961	1
DIXON GILBERT W	MAJ	O-0243186	0245	2
DIXON HARLOW C	CPT	O-0287267	0845	2
DIXON HAROLD	CW2	W-2143227	1053	1
DIXON HOSEA J	MAJ	O-0200207	1044	2
DIXON JAMES A	LTC	O-0347640	0157	1
DIXON JESSE T	1LT	O-0487945	1047	1
DIXON JOHNNIE M	2LT	O-0409643	0643	2
DIXON JOSIE G	1LT	N-0726343	0146	1
DIXON JR WILLIAM P	LTC	O-1000349	0167	3
DIXON KENNETH J	MAJ	O-2016336	0366	3
DIXON LEE G	WO1	W-2115849	0646	1
DIXON LEONARD S	2LT	O-0514264	0345	2
DIXON LOIS E	1LT	N-0724827	0646	1
DIXON MARVIN H	COL	O-0205567	1163	3
DIXON MOSE E	CPT	O-1298676	0257	1
DIXON PAUL H	LTC	O-1175998	1065	1
DIXON PERRY M	LTC	O-0285833	1054	1
DIXON ROD P	2LT	O-1597394	0346	2
DIXON ROLAND B	CPT	O-1300943	0662	1
DIXON ROY F	MAJ	O-0304118	0446	2
DIXON SAMUEL C	MAJ	O-1994751	1055	2
DIXON SHERWOOD	COL	O-0119005	0656	3
DIXON THOMAS E	MAJ	O-0289989	1154	1
DIXON THOMAS S	MAJ	O-1919103	1266	1
DIXON TYLER F	LTC	O-0452600	0846	1
DIXON WALTER R	LTC	O-0315419	0860	3
DIXON WILLARD L	CW3	W-2147163	0664	1
DIXON WILLIAM R	LTC	O-0452270	0161	1
DIXON WILLIAM R	MAJ	O-1318654	1162	1
DIXON WORDEN E	LTC	O-1650065	1162	1
DIXON ZANDA B	CPT	N-0743812	1160	1
DIXSON JR I J	CPT	O-0970670	1060	1
DIXSON MONROE P	2LT	O-1292490	1044	2
DIXSON ROY H	CW3	W-2205950	0867	1
DJERNES ENTAR	MAJ	O-1301449	0464	1
DJIOVANIDIS JOHN C	2LT	O-1047093	0745	2
DLUGOSH LEONARD C	CW3	W-2150203	1263	1
DLUGOSZ STANLEY	1LT	O-2055102	1046	1
DMOHOWSKI ANTHONY	1LT	O-1182097	1145	2
DMUCHOWSKI ARTHUR M	1LT	O-1334555	0649	1
DOAK ALEXANDER	MAJ	O-1581663	0862	1
DOAK JOHN W	LTC	O-0285564	0562	1
DOAN MARTIN L	MAJ	O-2263484	1264	1
DOAN RAYMOND A	1LT	O-1794920	1045	1
DOAN ROBERT M	MAJ	O-1120051	1062	1
DOAN ROLAND E	LTC	O-0104452	0152	3
DOANE DWIGHT L	MAJ	O-5301599	0867	1
DOANE ELLIS B	CPT	O-2042828	1051	1
DOANE FRANCIS H	LTC	O-0226254	1046	2
DOANE JOHN E	LTC	O-1063119	0262	1
DOAR LEROY H	LTC	O-0193307	0455	2
DOBAK RAYNOLD S	LTC	O-0885621	1062	1
DOBBER STANLEY	1LT	O-1051933	0455	1
DOBBIE HARRY S	LTC	O-1584141	1061	1
DOBBIE JR JAMES N	LTC	O-1945786	1162	1
DOBBIN JOSEPH G	MAJ	O-1292149	0854	1
DOBBIN LOUISE	MAJ	N-0743726	1162	1
DOBBINS CLAUDE F	CPT	O-1554712	0446	1
DOBBINS ERNEST F	LTC	O-0292948	0859	1
DOBBINS FRANK P	COL	O-0481441	1160	3
DOBBINS JACK R	1LT	O-1823575	0845	2
DOBBINS JR WALTER E	COL	O-0221555	0556	1
DOBBINS THOMAS	COL	O-0102452	0648	3
DOBBINS WILLIAM F	MAJ	O-0980673	0366	1

NAME	GRADE	SVC NO	DATE RET MO YR	RET CODE
DOBBS BENJAMIN C	1LT	O-1324059	0945	2
DOBBS CHARLES H	COL	O-0239798	0759	3
DOBBS TOMMIE F	CPT	O-0535754	0157	1
DOBBS WILLIAM A	COL	O-0347197	0163	1
DOBBS WILLIAM H	MAJ	O-0506134	0255	1
DOBBS WILLIAM M	CPT	O-0284963	0946	1
DOBBYN HARRY W	LTC	O-0361015	0760	3
DOBER HARRY G	MAJ	O-1335759	0964	1
DOBIE CLYDE A	CW3	W-2203648	0665	1
DOBILES JOHN G	1LT	O-0497675	0550	1
DOBKIN ARTHUR	MAJ	O-0308186	0945	2
DOBLE JR HENRY P	MAJ	O-1342252	0667	1
DOBLE JR WILLIAM A	COL	O-0204145	0854	3
DOBLER GEORGE D	LTC	O-0413396	0763	1
DOBRESK SAMUEL	LTC	O-1599156	1167	1
DOBRICK HERBERT R	CPT	O-0481145	0853	1
DOBRINET CARL H	2LT	O-0529625	0744	2
DOBROLET GREGORY	MAJ	O-1535159	0463	1
DOBRY JAMES	MAJ	O-1103137	0646	2
DOBRZYNSKY CHARLOT	1LT	N-0720810	0646	1
DOBSON CATHERINE	CPT	N-0752964	0148	1
DOBSON CECIL R	MAJ	O-0237971	1263	3
DOBSON CHARLES W	LTC	O-0454046	0361	1
DOBSON LAWRENCE	LTC	O-1166047	0457	1
DOBSON ROBERT J B	1LT	O-1056337	1146	2
DOCHARTY MARGARET E	CPT	N-0793739	0847	1
DOCHERTY SADIE M	MAJ	N-0757623	0464	3
DOCHNEY JAMES J	CPT	O-1593542	0663	1
DOCK PAUL T	1LT	O-1533048	0245	1
DOCKA CLARENCE W	LTC	O-0276186	0466	3
DOCKAL LLOYD J	COL	O-0275420	1162	3
DOCKHAM RALPH A	CW3	W-2150689	0962	1
DOCKSTADER L A	CPT	O-0162100	1044	2
DOCKTER JACK G	MAJ	O-0494300	0357	1
DOCKUM OSCAR L	COL	O-0169108	1160	3
DODD A D	WO1	W-2127386	1047	2
DODD ABBY M	LTC	O-0268357	0646	2
DODD ALFRED H	MAJ	O-0493221	1054	1
DODD BENTLEY H	1LT	O-1011335	1044	2
DODD CARL H	MAJ	O-2262354	0765	1
DODD CHARLES E	CPT	O-1541488	0645	2
DODD EDWIN N	LTC	O-1573837	0253	1
DODD GEORGE K	CPT	O-0100651	1055	3
DODD GORDON R	CW4	W-2101623	0355	2
DODD HARRY J	MAJ	O-1295843	0361	1
DODD KENNETH H	LTC	O-1594803	1062	1
DODD LEWIS J	CPT	O-2017823	1160	1
DODD RAY M	1LT	O-1292318	1145	2
DODD STEPHEN F	LTC	O-0058372	1167	1
DODD WILBURN C	CPT	O-0164279	1138	2
DODD WILLIAM A	CPT	O-0512527	0745	2
DODD WILLIAM L	CPT	O-2025874	0757	1
DODDRIDGE THOMAS W	CPT	O-1844674	0547	2
DODDS ARTHUR C	LTC	O-0322130	0259	1
DODDS GERALD C	MAJ	O-0451095	0157	1
DODDS HORTON C	LTC	O-1584143	0764	1
DODDS JOHN F	MAJ	O-0516569	0667	1
DODDS JOHN H	LTC	O-0276428	1053	3
DODDS RUSSELL W	COL	O-0194035	0760	1
DODDS VERA L	1LT	N-0733085	0646	1
DODDS WILLIAM G	MAJ	O-1633164	0445	2
DODEL WALTER W	1LT	O-1172435	1045	1
DODGE ALBERT O	COL	O-0235131	0865	3
DODGE CLARENCE P	1LT	O-0259889	1045	2
DODGE CLAYTON E	MAJ	O-1886107	0267	1
DODGE DONALD J	CPT	O-1291087	1144	1
DODGE FRANK M	1LT	O-0509115	1146	1
DODGE GEORGE W	LTC	O-0393603	1059	1
DODGE ISRAEL R	MAJ	O-0221612	0954	3
DODGE JOSEPH A	COL	O-0465919	0365	1
DODGE JR HARRY W	LTC	O-1546235	1162	1
DODGE JR WARREN M	MAJ	O-0498420	0944	1
DODGE LAURENCE S	1LT	O-0105300	1055	1
DODGE LEONARD A	CW2	W-2105061	0845	2
DODGE LYNN O	MAJ	O-0267958	0246	2

NAME	GRADE	SVC NO	DATE RET MO YR	RET CODE
DODGE PHILIP R	COL	0-0265581	0160	3
DODGE ROBERT H	LTC	0-1331273	0267	2
DODGE ROBERT N	CW3	W-2204972	0763	1
DODGE WILBUR L	WO1	W-2125232	0157	1
DODGE WILLIAM H	LTC	0-0278854	0262	3
DODGE WILLIAM H	LTC	0-1183057	0967	1
DODGE WILLIAM P	MAJ	0-0148319	0648	3
DODGE WILLIS B	2LT	0-2020123	0951	1
DODGEN ALBERT J	LTC	0-0511360	0859	1
DODGEN FLORENCE D	LTC	0-2295345	0365	2
DODGEN JR THOMAS R	MAJ	0-1823274	0866	1
DODGION RAYMOND E	CW3	W-2143762	0460	1
DODSON FURLON G	MAJ	0-0193730	0858	3
DODSON JAMES A	CW2	W-2210520	1166	1
DODSON JOHN T	1LT	0-1585370	0844	2
DODSON LAVERE A	LTC	0-0507217	0663	3
DODSON LEONARD E	1LT	0-0449199	0546	2
DODSON ROGER S	CW2	W-2150307	0662	1
DODSON ROLAND S	MAJ	0-0278265	0759	3
DODSON WALTER S	1LT	0-1295135	0345	2
DODSON WILLARD F	COL	0-0174148	1059	3
DODSON WILLIAM C	CW2	W-2143763	0663	1
DODT WAYNE O	MAJ	0-1685648	0765	1
DOEBLIN ROBERT F	MAJ	0-1293026	1162	1
DOEDEN LESTER J	2LT	0-1015142	0645	2
DOEGE ARTHUR J	LTC	0-0349791	0660	3
DOELLINGER HERMAN C	COL	0-0286639	0450	3
DOERGES CLEON C	MAJ	0-2011776	0759	1
DOERING ANNE M	LTC	L-0800451	0467	1
DOERING CALVIN J	1LT	0-2030427	0765	2
DOERING CHARLES F	CW2	W-2150300	0661	1
DOERNBACH WILLIAM	CPT	0-2023686	0555	1
DOERR DAVID	CPT	0-1821835	1046	2
DOERR JEAN P	LTC	0-0416469	1163	1
DOERR NELSON E	MAJ	0-1181584	0465	3
DOERTY WALTER L	COL	0-0246922	0555	1
DOESBURG CHARLES F	LTC	0-2035877	0966	1
DOETTERL FRANK A	MAJ	0-0221442	0861	3
DOFF AARON	CPT	0-1310583	0946	1
DOFFLEMEYER NORMAN C	MAJ	0-2007971	0363	1
DOGGETT BENJAMIN F	1LT	0-0493820	1050	1
DOGGETT DENZIL	LTC	0-0107255	1054	3
DOGGETT WALTER L	1LT	0-1002412	0945	1
DOGGETTE JORDAN D	CPT	0-1303866	1046	2
DOHERTY DONALD R	MAJ	0-1119480	0162	1
DOHERTY EDWARD F	MAJ	0-1047054	0463	1
DOHERTY JACK	LTC	0-1166960	0462	1
DOHERTY MICHAEL	2LT	0-2010700	0753	1
DOHERTY OWEN F	LTC	0-1046769	1067	1
DOHERTY PATRICK L	LTC	0-1533301	0364	1
DOHERTY RAYMOND E	WO1	W-2120923	1057	1
DOHERTY VINCENT H	MAJ	0-1922552	0365	1
DOHERTY WILLIAM R	MAJ	0-0376743	0746	2
DOHM EDWARD C	COL	0-0175076	0648	3
DOHME JOHN F	2LT	0-1016578	1144	2
DOHN FRANCIS A	MAJ	0-1638966	0358	2
DOHR RAYMOND R	LTC	0-0267594	1161	3
DOHRMANN JACK F	LTC	0-0272515	0367	3
DOHY ALEXANDER	CW3	W-2152374	0563	1
DOIDGE HAROLD I	MAJ	0-2039384	0464	1
DOIG EDWIN A	LTC	0-0192014	0358	3
DOIL RALPH C	MAJ	0-2263074	0264	1
DOKE LOWELL V	1LT	0-1031307	0846	1
DOLAN BENJAMIN R	CPT	0-0171747	0457	3
DOLAN DANIEL F	CW4	W-2143024	1164	1
DOLAN EDWARD S	LTC	0-1647400	0766	3
DOLAN FRANCIS S	COL	0-0475385	0459	2
DOLAN GEORGE H	MAJ	0-1557271	0964	1
DOLAN GERALD	MAJ	0-0315394	0144	2
DOLAN JAMES H	1LT	0-0955079	0452	1
DOLAN JOHN	LTC	0-1994898	1163	1
DOLAN JOHN J	CPT	0-0341763	0445	2
DOLAN JOSEPH C	COL	0-0228092	0466	3
DOLAN JR CHESTER A	MAJ	0-0913657	1045	2
DOLAN JR JOHN E	MAJ	0-0223264	1045	2

NAME	GRADE	SVC NO	DATE RET MO YR	RET CODE
DOLAN KENNETH J	MAJ	0-0302646	0346	2
DOLAN LEONARD J	LTC	0-1170711	0967	1
DOLAN LESLIE C	LTC	0-1647542	0164	3
DOLAN MICHAEL J	LTC	0-1284839	0764	1
DOLAN PATRICK T	CPT	0-0369484	0546	2
DOLAN PETER F	COL	0-0202334	0261	3
DOLAN RONALD S	CW3	W-2145413	0760	1
DOLAN WILLIE L	WO1	W-2152994	0654	2
DOLBEARE RICHARD	LTC	0-0277412	1063	3
DOLBEE JR WALTER J	MAJ	0-0559084	0961	1
DOLBIER JOHN L	1LT	0-1112116	0757	1
DOLCE MATTHEW L	MAJ	0-1647545	0357	1
DOLE ROBERT J	CPT	0-1327518	0748	1
DOLEJSI FRANK C	MAJ	0-1302439	0258	1
DOLES ALVIN D	CW2	W-2117079	0653	1
DOLES EMMETT A	CPT	0-0482231	0345	2
DOLEZAL HENRY	MAJ	0-0232627	0265	3
DOLGOPOL RICHARD Z	1LT	0-1997060	0448	2
DOLIBER JR EARL L	CW3	W-2205454	0766	1
DOLITSKY MORRIS M	LTC	0-0450003	0366	3
DOLL CECIL T	COL	0-0915315	0965	3
DOLL CLIFFORD K	WO1	W-2127700	1061	2
DOLL GEORGE J	LTC	0-0206736	0955	3
DOLL JR CLARENCE E	MAJ	0-0309293	1059	1
DOLL WILLIAM E	MAJ	0-1922517	0565	1
DOLLAR CARMEL T	MAJ	0-1309148	0657	1
DOLLAR JAMES W	LTC	0-1322683	0962	1
DOLLAR LOUISE	CPT	N-0727762	1047	1
DOLLAR MAUREE E	MAJ	0-1796935	0959	1
DOLLINGER ROBERT F	2LT	0-1113172	0244	2
DOLLIVER HAROLD W	MAJ	0-1683443	0462	1
DOLLOFF HORACE A	CW4	W-2111834	0962	1
DOLMAGE GEORGE H	CPT	0-0499402	0145	2
DOLMAN HAROLD R	1LT	0-0428934	0345	2
DOLOZIK ANTHONY S	1LT	0-1823851	0347	2
DOLPH IVAR F	COL	0-0342225	0963	3
DOLSEY HERBERT S	LTC	0-1044209	1060	1
DOLSON IRMA A	MAJ	N-0736143	0765	1
DOLTON HENRY J	COL	0-0216803	0258	1
DOLVEN FRANK M	MAJ	0-0438573	1156	3
DOMAIGE GOMMAIRE L	CPT	0-0300162	0147	2
DOMAN ADOLPH C	MAJ	0-1292491	1061	1
DOMAN THURMAN S	COL	0-0298093	0360	1
DOMANSKI VINCENT P	CW2	W-2212025	0767	1
DOMBEK WALTER J	MAJ	0-2035246	0658	1
DOMBROSKI FRANK A	MAJ	0-1994589	0865	1
DOMBROSKI STANLEY T	2LT	0-1823275	0245	2
DOMBROWSKI EUGENE L	CW3	W-2152430	0462	1
DOMBROWSKI FRANCIS	1LT	0-0449625	1145	2
DOMBROWSKI HENRY F	MAJ	0-1102698	0357	1
DOMENIC RALPH E	CW3	W-2205712	0767	1
DOMER WILLIAM G	WO1	W-2108442	0347	1
DOMINE GENARO C	1LT	0-1896658	0667	1
DOMINGO DANIEL J	MAJ	0-1587530	0658	1
DOMINGOES JR FRANK A	MAJ	0-1597992	0761	1
DOMINGUEZ ALBERTO M	CPT	0-0402279	0945	2
DOMINGUEZ EDWARD SRA	1LT	0-1896759	0354	1
DOMINGUEZ ELISEO	CPT	0-1914341	1130	2
DOMINGUEZ JOSE R	MAJ	0-1326450	0561	1
DOMINGUEZ WILLIAM	CPT	0-2262638	0261	1
DOMINICK LEO H	LTC	0-0166411	0952	3
DOMINICK LOUIS	MAJ	0-1174827	0258	1
DOMINICK WILLIAM A	COL	0-0240088	0565	3
DOMINO THOMAS	CPT	0-0968070	0959	1
DOMME EDWARD J	2LT	0-1015182	0245	2
DOMMERT HOWARD F	MAJ	0-0966041	1061	1
DOMOKOS ALEX P	MAJ	0-2024125	0655	1
DOMOTOR JOSEPH J	CPT	0-1013470	0759	1
DOMS ALBERT R	LTC	0-0313206	0467	3
DON BATALLA RO	1LT	0-1896445	1062	1
DON LEAVY ALPH	LTC	0-1578379	0961	1
DONADIO SALVATORE	MAJ	0-1286982	0457	1
DONAGHY DONALD J	CW2	W-2111577	1045	2
DONAGHY GEORGE E	LTC	0-0335945	1266	3
DONAGHY WILLIAM R	LTC	0-0511618	0563	1

NAME	GRADE	SVC NO	DATE RET MO YR	RET CODE
DONAH DONALD A	CW2	W-2146231	0856	1
DONAHEY RAYMOND F	CPT	0-0213113	0145	2
DONAHO EDDIE L	CPT	0-0981836	0661	2
DONAHOE JR JOHN P	CPT	0-0423376	0746	2
DONAHUE DONALD L	CPT	0-1297693	0853	1
DONAHUE EDWARD L	CW4	W-2150504	1060	1
DONAHUE FRANK J	LTC	0-1060075	0465	3
DONAHUE HAROLD C	1LT	0-1317897	1045	2
DONAHUE HARRY F	LTC	0-0244961	0560	3
DONAHUE HARRY G	MAJ	0-1645796	0661	1
DONAHUE JOHN E	LTC	0-2046950	0967	2
DONAHUE JOHN P	1LT	0-1018038	0446	1
DONAHUE JOSEPH J	COL	0-0155398	1055	3
DONAHUE JOSEPH K	LTC	0-1043317	0761	1
DONAHUE JOSEPH P	LTC	0-1001321	0465	1
DONAHUE NINA E V	CPT	L-0115004	0455	2
DONAHUE ROBERT J	MAJ	0-2006446	0962	2
DONAHUE ROBERT V	LTC	0-1645344	0865	1
DONAHUE THEODORE P	LTC	0-1042795	1166	1
DONAHUE THOMAS F	CPT	0-2046617	1154	1
DONAHUE TIMOTHY M	CPT	0-0156073	0253	3
DONAHUE TIMOTHY S	MAJ	0-1633168	1057	1
DONALD H WEBSTER	LTC	0-0297315	0766	3
DONALD JEANETTE F	2LT	N-0801421	0947	1
DONALD JOHN	1LT	0-1184037	0446	2
DONALD WILLIAM S	LTC	0-1176601	0562	2
DONALDSON BEATRICE	1LT	N-0737724	0945	1
DONALDSON CALVIN L	LTC	0-0312366	0661	3
DONALDSON GEORGE	CPT	0-1635790	0747	1
DONALDSON GEORGE H	MAJ	0-1165281	0346	2
DONALDSON GEORGE M	LTC	0-0287511	0957	1
DONALDSON HAROLD A	COL	0-0479361	1064	3
DONALDSON HAROLD B	COL	0-0310552	0661	1
DONALDSON JAMES W	MAJ	0-0404601	1047	2
DONALDSON JOHN J	MAJ	0-0969391	0464	1
DONALDSON LEE F	LTC	0-1579571	0966	1
DONALDSON MAX A	MAJ	0-0359640	1265	3
DONALDSON RAE A	COL	0-0354109	0661	1
DONALDSON ROBERT B	LTC	0-1171123	0462	1
DONALDSON ROBERT F	MAJ	0-0208651	0231	2
DONALDSON SIDNEY S	MAJ	0-0372041	0962	1
DONALDSON VERNON H	LTC	0-0269280	0966	3
DONALDSON WAYNE R	MAJ	0-0224521	1054	3
DONALDSON WILLIAM C	COL	0-0265943	0657	3
DONALDSON WILLIAM E	MAJ	0-0187930	0947	1
DONALDSON WOODRUFF F	LTC	0-0498968	0955	2
DONAT ANTHONY D	LTC	0-0370852	0957	1
DONATH ROBERT T	MAJ	0-1933589	0167	1
DONATY ROBERT L	MAJ	0-1301450	0363	1
DONAVIN KIRKWOOD M	MAJ	0-0909171	0267	1
DONCHECK REMUS A	CPT	0-0407655	0646	2
DONEGAN JOHN J	MAJ	0-2037539	0563	1
DONEGAN THOMAS D	LTC	0-1321891	0265	1
DONELAN STEPHEN F	LTC	0-2016082	1167	1
DONELAN THOMAS E	LTC	0-0241290	0255	3
DONELSON DAVID K	COL	0-0275137	1158	1
DONELSON JR SAMUEL	1LT	0-0209265	0160	3
DONELSON ROYAL M	CW3	W-2207210	0466	1
DONERY MARY A	MAJ	N-0732413	1064	3
DONEY RICHARD J	MAJ	0-0392769	0845	2
DONG CHARLES	LTC	0-1054540	0361	2
DONHAUSER STEWART E	LTC	0-0305906	0661	1
DONIGAN BERCE R	LTC	0-0361412	1064	3
DONIGAN ROBERT L	COL	0-0263634	0463	3
DONIGAN WILLIAM R	LTC	0-0272708	0565	3
DONIVAN JR LEO R	CPT	0-0316659	0245	2
DONKLE MELVIN C	COL	0-0196099	0562	3
DONLAY WILLARD J	1LT	0-1640397	0545	1
DONLEVY JAMES H	CPT	0-1056339	0147	1
DONLEY DAVID E	LTC	0-0229409	0662	3
DONLEY DONALD	LTC	0-0214108	0258	3
DONLEY DONALD J	CPT	0-1304697	0357	1
DONLEY JOHN C	CPT	0-1283045	1045	2
DONLEY ROBERT M	WO1	W-2127901	0451	2
DONLEY WILLIAM J	MAJ	0-1116371	0858	1

NAME	GRADE	SVC NO	DATE RET MO YR	RET CODE
DONLIN DONALD J	1LT	0-0515669	0545	2
DONLON JOSEPH E	1LT	0-1318290	0146	2
DONLON MARGARET M	2LT	N-0793885	0946	1
DONLON VINCENT E	CPT	0-1950334	1162	1
DONNAL JR JOHN C	MAJ	0-0192888	0362	3
DONNELL HENRY J	COL	0-0300977	1160	3
DONNELL JOHN R	LTC	0-0339839	0346	2
DONNELLAN JOSEPH J	CPT	0-0200210	0455	3
DONNELLY ANDREW S	LTC	0-2040950	0657	1
DONNELLY ARTHUR E	MAJ	0-0901680	0562	1
DONNELLY CATHERINE	2LT	N-0729272	0546	1
DONNELLY CHARLES H	COL	0-0287435	0956	3
DONNELLY CLARENCE S	COL	0-0279213	0255	3
DONNELLY DESMOND B	1LT	0-1045399	0646	1
DONNELLY DONALD E	LTC	0-1589169	0667	1
DONNELLY EDWARD D	CPT	0-1081129	1146	1
DONNELLY EDWIN L	MAJ	0-1301793	0561	1
DONNELLY ELIZABETH	2LT	N-0787131	0944	1
DONNELLY EMMET F	LTC	0-1551833	0862	1
DONNELLY FRANK J	LTC	0-1063141	0461	1
DONNELLY GEORGE F	MAJ	0-1038591	0266	1
DONNELLY JAMES J	MAJ	0-1046426	0561	2
DONNELLY JOHN A	MAJ	0-0487225	0661	1
DONNELLY JOHN J	LTC	0-0204772	0153	3
DONNELLY JOSEPH E	LTC	0-1638103	1162	1
DONNELLY JR ANDREW J	MAJ	0-2032595	0561	1
DONNELLY JR W M	CPT	0-1176402	0648	2
DONNELLY PETER E	COL	0-0286835	0764	3
DONNELLY RICHARD E	CPT	0-1797450	0759	2
DONNELLY ROBERT E	MAJ	0-0931409	0363	1
DONNELLY ROBERT H	LTC	0-1844968	0566	3
DONNELLY THOMAS J	1LT	0-1319727	1045	2
DONNELLY WALTER P	LTC	0-1305165	1166	3
DONNELLY WILLIAM A	CPT	0-0466257	0246	1
DONNER WILBUR S	LTC	0-0119965	1059	3
DONNER WILLIAM C	MAJ	0-1933380	0867	1
DONNIGAN CLARKE E	LTC	0-0176600	0658	3
DONOFRIO NICHOLAS	MAJ	0-1647401	0762	1
DONOHO ELSMER E	CPT	0-1185270	0260	2
DONOHOE GUY F	CPT	0-0128803	0648	3
DONOHOE MARY E	1LT	N-0787445	0647	1
DONOHOE PATRICK	CPT	0-1176310	0454	2
DONOHOO DAVID D	COL	0-0136963	0648	3
DONOHUE EMMETT A	1LT	0-1037466	0360	1
DONOHUE JAMES J	CW2	W-2147824	0560	1
DONOHUE JR JOSEPH T	MAJ	0-1697929	0660	1
DONOHUE RITA G	1LT	N-0741737	1145	1
DONOHUE ROBERT E	1LT	0-0347031	0446	2
DONOHUE THOMAS A	LTC	0-0407414	0266	1
DONOHUE WALTER P	LTC	0-0493550	0161	1
DONOHUE WILLIAM M	LTC	0-1944664	0662	1
DONOVAN ALICE M	CPT	N-0756868	0946	1
DONOVAN BILLY R	MAJ	0-2262975	0567	1
DONOVAN EUGENE M	LTC	0-0248805	0458	1
DONOVAN FRANCIS	MAJ	0-0185393	0148	1
DONOVAN FRANCIS J	CPT	0-1557835	1060	2
DONOVAN GEORGE F	LTC	0-0223786	0258	3
DONOVAN GORDON J	MAJ	0-1325281	0261	1
DONOVAN HOWARD P	LTC	0-2044494	0655	1
DONOVAN JAMES H	CW4	W-2141891	1066	1
DONOVAN JAMES R	COL	0-0451096	0457	1
DONOVAN JEROME V	LTC	0-1644933	1164	1
DONOVAN JESSE F	MAJ	0-1550577	0661	1
DONOVAN JOHN J	COL	0-0204798	0154	1
DONOVAN JOSEPH M	LTC	0-0915437	0365	3
DONOVAN JOSEPH W	LTC	0-0420030	0963	1
DONOVAN JR WILLIAM J	CPT	0-1106097	0147	2
DONOVAN MIKE C	LTC	0-0287624	0660	1
DONOVAN MORTIMER W	LTC	0-0261949	0662	3
DONOVAN TIMOTHY J	1LT	0-1913299	0353	1
DONOVAN WILBUR L	1LT	0-1283389	0444	2
DONOVAN WILLIAM A	MAJ	0-1546788	0860	1
DONOWSKI STANLEY W	MAJ	0-1683458	0560	1
DONSKY JOSEPH J	MAJ	0-2049958	1163	1
DONZIGER IRVING S	1LT	0-0526281	0945	2

NAME	GRADE	SVC NO	DATE RET MO YR	RET CODE
DOOR FREDERICK	CPT	0-0472718	0245	2
DOODY WILLIAM F	LTC	0-1797796	0562	1
DOOHALUK ALFONZO J	MAJ	0-2041435	0866	1
DOOLEN ARTHUR H	MAJ	0-0226520	1051	1
DOOLEY ALBERT J	LTC	0-0243573	0265	3
DOOLEY BEN H	CW3	W-2146858	0565	1
DOOLEY DONALD W	LTC	0-1000548	0657	1
DOOLEY HARRY J	COL	0-0911813	0246	1
DOOLEY HERBERT J	LTC	0-0266675	0845	2
DOOLEY JAMES C	LTC	0-0322503	1057	1
DOOLEY JAMES L	1LT	0-1593545	0146	2
DOOLEY JOHN D	CW3	W-2151810	1263	1
DOOLEY JOHN J	CW3	W-2004434	0967	1
DOOLEY JOHN R	LTC	0-1311129	0763	1
DOOLEY JOSEPH M	CPT	0-1168223	0247	2
DOOLEY LEONARD	MAJ	0-2288009	0160	1
DOOLEY LESLIE W	CPT	0-0434863	1145	1
DOOLEY MERLE H	2LT	0-1824441	1044	2
DOOLEY THOMAS F	MAJ	0-2006577	0165	1
DOOLEY WALTER M	CW3	W-2122249	1060	1
DOOLEY WILLIAM L	COL	0-0209942	0846	2
DOOLIN ROBERT F	LTC	0-1648382	0364	1
DOOLITTLE CLARENCE	CPT	0-0246987	0350	1
DOOLITTLE DOUGLAS	2LT	0-1185540	1045	2
DOOLITTLE DWIGHT F	CPT	0-0259429	0867	3
DOOLITTLE ROBERT L	LTC	0-1822573	0361	1
DOOLITTLE SPIVEY A	2LT	0-1014427	1043	2
DOOLITTLE WILLIAM H	LTC	0-0247544	1166	3
DOONAN STEPHEN P	CPT	0-2262379	1265	1
DOONEIEF ALFRED S	LTC	0-0384651	0146	1
DOOP RALPH E	1LT	0-1171980	0645	2
DOOSE DONALD L	1LT	0-1053563	0446	2
DOPONA JOHN C	CW2	W-2147750	0764	1
DORAN ARTHUR F	LTC	0-0452506	0258	1
DORAN EDWIN	LTC	0-1104622	0662	1
DORAN FLOYD J	COL	0-0279350	1064	3
DORAN GEORGE W	LTC	0-0408889	0363	1
DORAN JAMES J	1LT	0-1112118	0466	1
DORAN JOHN GALBR	COL	0-0174450	1047	2
DORAN JOHN J	LTC	0-0268125	1266	3
DORAN JOHN P	LTC	0-0300756	0161	1
DORAN JOSEPH K	1LT	0-0368252	0945	2
DORAN JR HARRY G	1LT	0-1175689	0945	2
DORAN PATRICK R	LTC	0-0301872	0364	3
DORAN PHILLIP J	CW2	W-2214420	0866	1
DORAN ROBERT A	LTC	0-1994592	1263	1
DORAN ROBERT A	CW2	W-2211427	1167	1
DORAN WILLIAM P	CW2	W-2142633	0854	1
DORAN WILLIAM T	1LT	0-0010391	0337	2
DORATO LAWRENCE F	COL	0-0267453	0458	3
DORAZIO JOHN J	LTC	0-1011135	1163	1
DORBANDT JAMES C	COL	0-0346649	0565	3
DORBRITZ WILLIAM C	MAJ	0-0171007	0356	3
DORE ELIZABETH	2LT	N-0700688	0737	1
DORE FRANK L	CW4	W-2148203	0467	1
DORE ROBERT A	2LT	0-1324153	0544	2
DORECIAK JOHN J	LTC	0-1540937	0167	1
DORER GEORGE H	1LT	0-2262708	1167	1
DOREY LESTER F	MAJ	0-1685661	1063	1
DORF VICTOR	MAJ	0-0380865	1045	2
DORFMAN SAUL S	COL	0-0193611	0365	3
DORIA LOUIS C	CPT	0-1300095	0646	2
DORIE EDMOND L	LTC	0-1575922	1167	3
DORIGAN JAMES T	1LT	0-0402066	1144	2
DORIN CHARLES G	CPT	0-0331809	0864	3
DORIN JR WILLIAM H	LTC	0-0245583	0360	1
DORING GEORGE E	MAJ	0-1295185	0658	1
DORMAN DALE R	MAJ	0-0976212	0765	1
DORMAN GERALD D	COL	0-0404715	1263	3
DORMAN JOHN A	MAJ	0-1913272	0863	1
DORMAN LINSLEY B	LTC	0-1314457	0763	2
DORMAN WALTER E	1LT	0-2012360	0253	1
DORMER THOMAS L	MAJ	0-1325204	1060	1
DORMINEY JACK C	CW3	W-2147047	0366	1
DORMINEY WOODROW W	CW3	W-2143602	1058	1

NAME	GRADE	SVC NO	DATE RET MO YR	RET CODE
DORN EDWIN	MAJ	0-0278746	0265	3
DORN HAROLD C	1LT	0-1324248	0845	2
DORN JR FREDERICK	2LT	0-1168639	1044	2
DORN JR WALTER E	LTC	0-1341862	0967	1
DORN RICHARD M	CPT	0-0452015	0657	1
DORNBLATT BERNHARD M	LTC	0-0192280	1262	3
DORNEY JOHN W	2LT	0-2036369	0345	2
DORNEY MARION C	COL	0-0346131	0866	1
DORNSIFE EUGENE L	LTC	0-1642009	0866	1
DOROBIALA HENRY	CW4	W-2144745	1165	1
DORR EDGAR F	LTC	0-0301906	0764	3
DORR THOMAS W	CPT	0-1756180	0649	1
DORRE REYNOLD S	MAJ	0-0384640	0647	2
DORRIS HERBERT F	MAJ	0-0165685	1049	3
DORRIS LEWIS R	MAJ	0-1015716	0160	1
DORRITY THOMAS G	CPT	0-0438728	0546	2
DORROH GEORGE D	LTC	0-0335269	0345	2
DORROH GLENN U	COL	0-0298135	0461	3
DORROUGH JR THOMAS A	LTC	0-1080846	0463	1
DORSETT FRANCIS M	CPT	0-0405534	0261	2
DORSETT LESTER	CW3	W-2206275	1265	1
DORSETT NELLIE C	2LT	N-0704041	1144	2
DORSETT RICHARD H	MAJ	0-2044302	1158	2
DORSETT WILLIAM R	CW3	W-2141258	0661	1
DORSEY EDWARD V	1LT	0-1327721	0546	1
DORSEY FRANCIS L	2LT	0-1013107	1143	1
DORSEY FRED J	LTC	0-1578387	0462	1
DORSEY HORACE T	CPT	0-1550366	0954	1
DORSEY JAMES M	1LT	0-1316391	1145	2
DORSEY JOSEPH R	CPT	0-0452451	1045	2
DORSEY WILLIAM H	LTC	0-0177223	1160	3
DORSEY WILLIAM H	LTC	0-0263765	0766	3
DORSEY WOODROW F	2LT	0-0465511	1043	2
DORSHOW SAMUEL A	2LT	0-0887593	0845	2
DORST CLARENCE L	COL	0-0284868	1166	3
DORST HOWARD E	COL	0-0300270	1064	3
DORSTE GEORGE C	CPT	0-1056694	0657	1
DORT HELEN C	1LT	N-0720713	0746	1
DORTCH LEONARD J	MAJ	0-1919466	0164	1
DORTON HOWARD E	MAJ	0-0446138	0346	2
DORTON JAMES H	CW2	W-2149483	0562	1
DORTORT ISADORE	LTC	0-0237576	0464	3
DORULA WALTER S	2LT	0-1309178	0945	2
DORWART FREDERIC G	LTC	0-0144589	0853	3
DORY DELBERT A	CW2	W-3200165	0963	1
DORY REX G	MAJ	0-0196684	0162	3
DOSCHER ALBERT H	CW3	W-2143511	0665	1
DOSS ALTON	CPT	0-0485056	0355	1
DOSS ESTLE H	LTC	0-2011494	1066	1
DOSS HAROLD C	CW2	RW-2210901	0965	1
DOSS JAMES W	CW2	W-2141842	1055	1
DOSS JR WYATT C	MAJ	0-2033666	1163	1
DOSS ROBERT L	2LT	0-1183273	0145	1
DOSS SR WILLIAM R	LTC	0-1342254	1266	1
DOSS WINTHA T	CW2	W-2152417	0560	1
DOSSETT JOHN A	WO1	W-2149431	1154	2
DOSSETT ROBERT C	MAJ	0-0222240	1051	1
DOSSMAN PIERRE M	LTC	0-0887472	0963	1
DOSTALL DOUGLAS J	MAJ	0-1559167	0763	2
DOSTER HIRAM H	1LT	0-1058500	0853	1
DOSTER JIM B	CW3	W-2119510	1160	1
DOSTER JR PAUL C	MAJ	0-1060078	0162	1
DOSTIE JOSEPH F	LTC	0-0383522	0762	1
DOTEN HENRY L	LTC	0-0174384	0159	3
DOTEN ROBERT K	LTC	0-0241153	0166	3
DOTSON ARTHUR J	CPT	0-0384310	1265	2
DOTSON EARL J	LTC	0-1634684	1163	1
DOTSON GERALD W	CPT	0-1822974	0662	1
DOTSON JOHN C	LTC	0-0482007	0746	1
DOTSON JR RAYMOND S	MAJ	0-1575924	0960	1
DOTSON LEONARD	CPT	0-0424454	0943	2
DOTSON LLOYD J	CPT	0-0557683	0253	1
DOTSON ORVILLE R	WO1	W-2123214	0152	1
DOTTERER HAROLD A	MAJ	0-1917847	1063	1
DOTTIN DUNCAN A	2LT	0-1061101	0145	1

NAME	GRADE	SVC NO	DATE RET MO YR	RET CODE
DOTTS NEIL T	1LT	0-2030412	0754	2
DOTY CHESTER R	LTC	0-1642806	0464	1
DOTY EDOUARD R	COL	0-0312822	0561	3
DOTY HAROLD G	COL	0-0287734	0763	1
DOTY HENRY F	COL	0-0207926	0658	3
DOTY HERBERT K	CPT	0-1117014	0361	1
DOTY IRWIN T	LTC	0-0252822	1165	3
DOTY JOHN H	CW2	W-2107495	0647	2
DOTY JR JESSE B	1LT	0-0354046	1046	2
DOTY JR LUTHER L	CPT	0-1252844	1145	2
DOTY JR REGINALD J	CW3	W-2208649	0867	1
DOTY LYLE E	LTC	0-1104130	0863	1
DOTY NORMAN J	2LT	0-1947704	1046	1
DOTY REGINALD J	LTC	0-0906383	0460	3
DOTY RUSSELL E	LTC	0-0289455	0167	3
DOUBERLY ROSCOE	CW3	W-2142146	1057	1
DOUBLE JOSEPH E	CW4	W-2119903	0756	1
DOUBLET HAROLD J	LTC	0-1018814	1067	1
DOUBT MARY D	1LT	R-0000213	0346	2
DOUCET EDWIN J	1LT	0-1999477	0753	1
DOUCET LILLIAN N	1LT	N-0754555	0251	2
DOUCET ROBERT J	CPT	0-1296007	0860	1
DOUCET WILLS J	MAJ	0-0497054	0657	1
DOUCETT FRANCIS W	LTC	0-0320337	0860	1
DOUCETT JR RAYMOND G	LTC	0-0452615	0158	1
DOUCETTE JOSEPH J	MAJ	0-2037540	0861	1
DOUCETTE MYRON E	COL	0-0218254	1162	3
DOUD ALFRED H	B G	0-0266144	1164	3
DOUDS HAROLD L	LTC	0-0317572	1066	3
DOUDS PAULINE R	2LT	N-0759297	1144	1
DOUGALL JAMES L	CPT	0-0217025	0460	3
DOUGAN AULTON R	LTC	0-0331820	0945	2
DOUGAN CLARENCE R	CPT	0-1587759	0366	1
DOUGAN STEWART I	MAJ	0-1341863	0463	1
DOUGHERTY BUFORD T	CPT	0-1004756	0450	1
DOUGHERTY CHARLES F	COL	0-0102461	0649	3
DOUGHERTY CLYDE E	M G	0-0190855	0462	3
DOUGHERTY DANIEL V	CPT	0-0357834	1143	2
DOUGHERTY EDWARD A	LTC	0-1796436	0664	1
DOUGHERTY EDWARD D	LTC	0-1011444	0464	1
DOUGHERTY FRANK R	CPT	0-0279191	0745	2
DOUGHERTY HARRY S	CPT	0-1058782	0263	1
DOUGHERTY HUGH L	COL	0-0256749	0259	3
DOUGHERTY JAMES E	1LT	0-1311552	0645	2
DOUGHERTY JAMES J	1LT	0-1580873	0944	2
DOUGHERTY JOHN A	CW2	W-2147501	1064	1
DOUGHERTY JOHN P	LTC	0-1634688	0562	1
DOUGHERTY JR W B	1LT	0-0409644	0545	2
DOUGHERTY KENNETH D	MAJ	0-1598041	0962	1
DOUGHERTY MABRY A	CW3	W-2151058	0959	2
DOUGHERTY R W E	MAJ	0-1578389	0859	1
DOUGHERTY RICHARD S	LTC	0-1322430	0365	1
DOUGHERTY ROBERT L	COL	0-0312733	0663	3
DOUGHERTY ROBERT W	LTC	0-0344751	0364	3
DOUGHERTY SALLY C	1LT	N-0723025	0246	1
DOUGHERTY VIRGINIA	1LT	N-0779751	0352	1
DOUGHERTY WILLIAM C	MAJ	0-1115558	0559	1
DOUGHERTY WILLIAM H	LTC	0-1014262	0967	1
DOUGHERTY WILLIAM L	CPT	0-1591082	0359	1
DOUGHTIE HOWARD J	CPT	0-0246785	0744	2
DOUGHTIE JAMES D	MAJ	0-0888205	0954	1
DOUGHTON HOWARD F	MAJ	0-0367102	0647	2
DOUGHTY JR SEVERN B	2LT	0-1168641	0744	2
DOUGHTY JR WILLIAM D	LTC	0-0262439	0962	3
DOUGLAS ALLEN M	CPT	0-1642807	0548	2
DOUGLAS CHARLES L	LTC	0-0324315	0755	3
DOUGLAS DONALD B	CW2	W-2110849	0546	2
DOUGLAS EDMUND T	MAJ	0-0116236	1049	3
DOUGLAS ELMER A	CW3	W-2150308	0860	1
DOUGLAS FRANK E	CPT	0-1296500	0446	2
DOUGLAS FRANK W	CPT	0-0277094	0549	1
DOUGLAS GLENN R	LTC	0-0231424	0563	3
DOUGLAS GORDON W	CPT	0-0368467	0645	2
DOUGLAS HARRY V	CPT	0-0359142	1044	2
DOUGLAS HENRY C	MAJ	0-1547923	1263	1

NAME	GRADE	SVC NO	DATE RET MO YR	RET CODE
DOUGLAS IRVIN N	LTC	0-0349553	0466	3
DOUGLAS JAMES W	CW2	W-2210479	0265	1
DOUGLAS JESSE S	COL	0-0281504	1160	2
DOUGLAS JOHN M	CPT	0-1100954	1044	2
DOUGLAS JR JOHN R	MAJ	0-1119482	0861	1
DOUGLAS JR WILLIAM C	1LT	0-0445128	0244	1
DOUGLAS JULIAN L	LTC	0-0207604	0751	1
DOUGLAS LEE T	CW4	W-2000619	1062	1
DOUGLAS LEON D	CPT	0-1306394	0548	1
DOUGLAS LESTER E	CW3	W-2149385	0364	1
DOUGLAS MALCOLM	COL	0-0154234	0247	1
DOUGLAS MARVIN B	COL	0-0293138	0860	2
DOUGLAS RALPH	CW4	W-2114819	0657	1
DOUGLAS REYNOLDS E	LTC	0-0259143	0465	3
DOUGLAS ROBERT L	CW2	W-2203293	0861	1
DOUGLAS ROBERT M	1LT	0-1313580	0446	2
DOUGLAS WALLACE S	COL	0-0169714	0261	3
DOUGLAS WILLIAM A	CW2	W-2149854	0561	1
DOUGLASS DAVID R	COL	0-0281305	0452	3
DOUGLASS FRANK S	1LT	0-1845557	0146	2
DOUGLASS HAROLD E	LTC	0-0451856	0665	1
DOUGLASS HARRY S	LTC	0-0171461	0650	3
DOUGLASS HENRY S	MAJ	0-0235101	1044	2
DOUGLASS JOHN M	1LT	0-0511448	1143	2
DOUGLASS LOUIS R	LTC	0-0181875	0648	3
DOUGLASS ROBERT M	COL	0-0128015	1157	3
DOUGLASS TRUMAN L	1LT	0-0499846	0154	2
DOUGLASS WILLIAM R	LTC	0-1549698	0767	1
DOUGOVITC CARL J	LTC	0-0280007	0957	1
DOUM ALBERT C	MAJ	0-1796437	0258	1
DOUR WILLIAM W	LTC	0-1044800	0267	1
DOURESS PHILIP C	1LT	0-1173585	0945	2
DOURLET NESTOR J	LTC	0-0567934	0365	1
DOUTHIT HAROLD C	LTC	0-1012014	0467	1
DOUTHITT CHARLES L	LTC	0-1054543	0762	1
DOUTHITT JOHN	CPT	0-1599157	1262	1
DOUTHITT MERTON H	1LT	0-0417433	0444	2
DOUTHITT MERTON J	LTC	0-0117140	1153	3
DOUTNEY WILLIAM W	LTC	0-0240476	0561	3
DOUVIER GREGOR J	LTC	0-1300619	0867	1
DOUYOTAS WALTER F	MAJ	0-1638972	0358	1
DOVAL ARMANDO	LTC	0-0262227	1064	3
DOVALOSKY CHARLES R	LTC	0-0175568	1160	3
DOVE ALBERT C	LTC	0-0452546	1159	1
DOVE FREDERICK	MAJ	0-1052755	0760	1
DOVE JOHN C	LTC	0-0425215	1163	1
DOVER CARL L	CPT	0-2000996	0861	1
DOVER EARL L	MAJ	0-0959315	0562	1
DOVER JR GEORGE J	LTC	0-0349801	0961	1
DOVERS GEORGE W	MAJ	0-1553071	0356	1
DOVEY GORDON L	1LT	0-0418799	1045	2
DOVEY HOWARD	CPT	0-0448157	1047	1
DOVHOLUK PAUL	CPT	0-0887963	0448	2
DOW HOWARD B	LTC	0-1542628	0860	1
DOW JEREMIAH G	CPT	0-1080276	0847	2
DOW ORWIN F	MAJ	0-0154265	0857	3
DOW RAYMOND W	LTC	0-0489813	0445	2
DOW WENDALL W	MAJ	0-1948731	0164	1
DOW WILLIAM C	COL	0-1297511	0664	1
DOWD HELEN F	CPT	N-0732718	1046	1
DOWD HOMER F	LTC	0-0205212	1163	3
DOWD JAMES H	CPT	0-0411577	0446	2
DOWD JAMES J	2LT	0-2017523	1045	2
DOWD JOHN J	MAJ	0-1545420	1157	1
DOWD JOHN T	MAJ	0-0314420	0658	1
DOWD JR LAWRENCE V	LTC	0-0972672	0867	1
DOWD MORRIS D	CPT	0-1701760	1144	2
DOWD WILLIAM S	LTC	0-1543329	0662	2
DOWDELL HERMAN L	2LT	0-0984843	0352	1
DOWDEN ALVIN C	1LT	0-1185868	0550	1
DOWDEN JOHN F	CPT	0-0476449	0347	1
DOWDEN SR RUSSELL H	WO1	W-2150342	0160	2
DOWDLE HUGH J	MAJ	0-0282420	0146	2
DOWDY LEON	MAJ	0-2262367	0862	1
DOWELL GEORGE L	CW2	W-2209242	0661	1

NAME	GRADE	SVC NO	DATE RET MO YR	RET CODE
DOWELL LORENZO	CPT	O-0498626	1046	1
DOWELL WILBUR E	CW3	W-2104012	0853	1
DOWELL WILLIAM F	LTC	O-0534333	0663	1
DOWEN ROBERT H	CPT	O-0262335	0346	2
DOWGILLO ALEXANDER	MAJ	O-1080848	1157	1
DOWIS WELDON M	LTC	O-0241967	0360	1
DOWLER III FRANK H	COL	O-0371463	0860	1
DOWLING BERNARD J	1LT	O-0972258	0453	1
DOWLING CHARLES F	LTC	O-0289140	0254	1
DOWLING CHARLES R	LTC	O-1798132	0562	1
DOWLING DOLORES I	1LT	N-0728901	0846	1
DOWLING DONALD A	CW2	W-3430041	1164	1
DOWLING GEORGE E	LTC	O-1100083	0959	1
DOWLING GEORGE H	CPT	O-0580682	0454	2
DOWLING GORDON R	2LT	O-0207150	0363	3
DOWLING JOSEPH B	LTC	O-0360131	1060	1
DOWLING JOSEPH F	MAJ	O-0971837	1163	1
DOWLING JR MOYE C	2LT	O-0240877	1044	2
DOWLING REGINALD J	COL	O-0278421	1162	3
DOWLING SAMUEL F	LTC	O-2203041	0767	1
DOWNER HARRY M	LTC	O-0360942	0957	1
DOWNES CORNELIUS	1LT	O-1046074	0946	2
DOWNES DOROTHY E	2LT	N-0743673	0943	1
DOWNEY ARLIE L	LTC	O-0199557	1053	2
DOWNEY AUGUSTUS J	LTC	O-1579580	0764	1
DOWNEY BENJAMIN A	CPT	O-2042733	0257	1
DOWNEY DAVID H	MAJ	O-1688497	1165	1
DOWNEY DONALD L	MAJ	O-1337153	0161	2
DOWNEY EARL C	LTC	O-0411360	0963	1
DOWNEY EDWARD F	1LT	O-1019002	0252	2
DOWNEY GILBERT L	2LT	O-1925904	0253	2
DOWNEY JACK W	LTC	O-0450433	0358	1
DOWNEY JAMES B	CPT	O-1044213	0952	1
DOWNEY JAMES H	1LT	O-1284480	1145	2
DOWNEY JOHN A	MAJ	O-1644084	0361	1
DOWNEY JOSEPH F	CPT	O-1080782	1047	1
DOWNEY JR JAMES R	MAJ	O-0498385	0655	1
DOWNEY JR JOHN J	COL	O-0384228	0860	1
DOWNEY MICHAEL J	MAJ	O-2263867	0667	1
DOWNEY OLIVER E	MAJ	O-1111584	0967	1
DOWNEY REGINALD J	CPT	O-0225799	0263	3
DOWNEY ROBERT J	MAJ	O-1342060	1264	1
DOWNEY THOMAS W	MAJ	O-2035035	0662	1
DOWNEY TOM K	LTC	O-1549256	0163	1
DOWNEY WILLEM	CPT	O-1896574	0359	1
DOWNEY WILLIAM F	CW2	W-2151524	1157	1
DOWNING EARL L	COL	O-0179271	1154	1
DOWNING JAMES M	1LT	O-1573168	0345	2
DOWNING JOHN M	LTC	O-0258569	0965	3
DOWNING JOHN R	LTC	O-0294485	0767	3
DOWNING KENNETH C	COL	O-0222925	0760	3
DOWNING LELAND P	MAJ	O-1543593	1060	1
DOWNING ROLAND F	MAJ	O-1044802	0861	1
DOWNING SARAH P	CPT	N-0760727	0846	1
DOWNING THEODORE A	LTC	O-0268212	0364	3
DOWNING WILLIAM E	CPT	O-0245274	1047	1
DOWNING WILLIAM L	LTC	O-0266721	0764	1
DOWNS CLARENCE R	LTC	O-0418201	0266	3
DOWNS HAROLD T	MAJ	O-0252648	0561	3
DOWNS JAMES C	MAJ	O-1577109	0146	1
DOWNS JAMES C	MAJ	O-2263767	1164	1
DOWNS JOSEPH J	1LT	O-2049225	0146	2
DOWNS JOSEPH R	CW4	W-2144890	0764	1
DOWNS JR EDWARD J	CPT	O-1061038	0547	2
DOWNS JR FREDERICK	COL	O-0195508	0960	3
DOWNS THERESA M	CPT	N-0732170	1146	1
DOWNS WILLIAM W	2LT	O-2035807	0345	2
DOWS SAMUEL R	COL	O-0183084	0656	3
DOWTY JOHN A	CW3	W-2142834	1057	1
DOXSIE GERALD R	CPT	O-0383650	0662	1
DOYING WILLIAM W	CW3	W-2145867	1162	1
DOYLE ALBERT F	LTC	O-0321290	0265	3
DOYLE ALICE E	LTC	N-0720462	1263	1
DOYLE CURTIS W	CPT	O-2026214	0456	1
DOYLE DANIEL G	LTC	O-0251054	0562	1

NAME	GRADE	SVC NO	DATE RET MO YR	RET CODE
DOYLE EUGENE T	MAJ	O-0993007	1165	1
DOYLE FRANK	2LT	O-1030971	0345	2
DOYLE GEOFFREY W	LTC	O-1053111	0366	1
DOYLE GREGORY J	MAJ	O-0326083	0744	2
DOYLE HERSHEL L	WO1	W-2124722	1044	2
DOYLE HUGH	LTC	O-0109756	1047	2
DOYLE JACOBS H	MAJ	O-0233577	0944	2
DOYLE JAMES A	COL	O-0236421	0651	3
DOYLE JAMES J	COL	O-0244575	0955	3
DOYLE JAMES W	CPT	O-0125780	0945	2
DOYLE JAMES W	MAJ	O-0959316	0764	1
DOYLE JERRY F	1LT	O-2205230	0453	2
DOYLE JOHN C	COL	O-0138594	0258	3
DOYLE JOHN F	CW2	W-2207007	0364	1
DOYLE JOHN J	MAJ	O-1882033	0967	1
DOYLE JOHN M	LTC	O-0262366	0266	3
DOYLE JOSEPH A	LTC	O-1645353	1163	1
DOYLE JOSEPH H	COL	O-1042796	0763	1
DOYLE JOSEPH T	1LT	O-0448522	1045	2
DOYLE JR JOHN A	LTC	O-0421855	0163	1
DOYLE JUSTIN G	COL	O-0205111	0360	1
DOYLE KATHLEEN M	CPT	N-0723045	0746	1
DOYLE LAURENCE F	1LT	O-1019238	1045	2
DOYLE LEWIS W	LTC	O-1698096	1160	1
DOYLE LILLIAN	2LT	N-0700493	0834	1
DOYLE MARY C	MAJ	N-0752710	0464	1
DOYLE ROBERT	MAJ	O-0959031	0162	2
DOYLE WALTER J	LTC	O-0317970	0763	1
DOYLE WILLIAM C	MAJ	O-0960618	0763	1
DOYLE WILLIAM H	MAJ	O-0314153	0146	1
DOYLE WILLIAM H	WO1	W-2117923	1053	1
DOYLE WILLIAM J	1LT	O-1913650	1138	1
DOYLE WILLIAM M	COL	O-0370137	0267	1
DOYLE WILLIAM-DA	LTC	O-1573796	1161	1
DOYLE WILSON F	LTC	O-1300621	0462	1
DOYON ALBERT P	LTC	O-0399316	0864	1
DOZE CHARLES A	CPT	O-1281604	0667	1
DOZIER DAVID T	LTC	O-1177778	0666	1
DOZIER JR JAMES B	1LT	O-1059770	1046	1
DOZIER MARCELLUS	MAJ	O-1553801	1054	1
DOZIER MINNIE L	2LT	N-0742816	1144	1
DOZIER MORRIS	CW3	W-2143844	1162	1
DRABIC JOHN J	MAJ	O-1011275	0557	1
DRACHMAN FRANK F	1LT	O-1889126	0554	2
DRACK RUTH D	MAJ	N-0724310	0561	1
DRAEGER EMERY H	LTC	O-0504778	0754	1
DRAGANZA JOHN G	LTC	O-1103607	0465	1
DRAGNEFF NICHOLAS W	COL	O-0379990	0954	1
DRAGNETT WILLIAM V	LTC	O-0312173	0159	3
DRAGO GEORGE R	CPT	O-1300006	1045	1
DRAGO PAOLO	MAJ	O-1920163	0366	1
DRAGOIU ELY	MAJ	O-1185572	0863	2
DRAGOMANI LEO A	LTC	O-2033062	0166	1
DRAGON JOHN	CPT	O-1338573	0254	1
DRAGOO CHARLES M	LTC	O-0211862	0364	3
DRAGOO DON H	LTC	O-0380055	1262	1
DRAGOO RUSSELL N	MAJ	O-1640404	0359	1
DRAGOTIS BURT A	CPT	O-1547279	0854	2
DRAGSTEDT JR CARL A	MAJ	O-0935434	0564	1
DRAHEIM WILLIAM A	COL	O-0246210	1058	3
DRAIN FREDERICK	LTC	O-1797267	0662	1
DRAIN JAMES F A	MAJ	O-0387165	0852	2
DRAIN MILTON J	MAJ	O-0350142	0762	2
DRAINE OLIVER W	CPT	O-0390054	1046	2
DRAIZAR PAUL H	2LT	O-1179840	1044	2
DRAKE ALLEN H	CPT	O-1596310	0965	2
DRAKE ANTHONY F	CW3	W-2146742	0157	1
DRAKE ARTHUR D	MAJ	O-0295104	0666	3
DRAKE CHARLES A	COL	O-0165790	0554	3
DRAKE CLEATUS R	LTC	O-0239763	0565	3
DRAKE DAYTON O	LTC	O-0475805	0762	1
DRAKE DONALD W	LTC	O-1112661	0567	1
DRAKE EMERSON R	CPT	O-1824442	1046	2
DRAKE HARRIS P	MAJ	O-0415189	0246	1
DRAKE HARRY C	1LT	O-1291439	0645	2

NAME	GRADE	SVC NO	DATE RET MO YR	RET CODE
DRAKE HERMAN R	CW4	W-2124176	1059	1
DRAKE HORACE B	MAJ	O-0248998	0966	3
DRAKE HORACE L	CPT	O-0517279	1044	2
DRAKE JAMES F	CPT	O-0499816	0547	1
DRAKE JAMES R	CPT	O-0176983	0557	3
DRAKE JOHN T	CW4	W-2107996	1159	1
DRAKE JR DAVID H	1LT	O-1320613	1145	2
DRAKE JR JOSH M	1LT	O-1319268	0246	2
DRAKE LEO G	LTC	O-0277413	1261	3
DRAKE LINCOLN C	LTC	O-1104134	0761	1
DRAKE RAYMOND J	LTC	O-0352004	0462	1
DRAKE RICHARD N	MAJ	O-0472640	0353	1
DRAKE ROBERT J	CPT	O-0495540	0346	2
DRAKE RODGER E	MAJ	O-1893291	0467	1
DRAKE SIMEON F	CPT	O-0499531	0751	1
DRAKE THEODORE T	LTC	O-0334657	0448	1
DRAKE THOMAS A	CW2	W-2143899	0558	1
DRAKE WARREN A	LTC	O-0451272	1262	1
DRAKE WILLIAM J	1LT	O-2005674	0347	2
DRAKULICH ELI	MAJ	O-1551834	0861	1
DRALLE ROBERT B	MAJ	O-1825526	0661	1
DRANSFIELD GEORGE W	CW4	W-2120057	1064	1
DRAPER ANDREW J	LTC	O-1597001	0463	1
DRAPER CONSTANCE	1LT	N-0737922	1045	1
DRAPER DONALD E	MAJ	O-1285397	1054	1
DRAPER GEORGE L	MAJ	O-1638133	1058	1
DRAPER HOWARD A	LTC	O-1102705	0859	1
DRAPER JOHN I	CW3	W-2205436	1163	1
DRAPER JOHN W	MAJ	O-0498886	1045	2
DRAPER JR WILLIAM H	M G	O-0148333	0756	3
DRAPER PAUL J	LTC	O-1637325	1167	3
DRAPER ROBERT A	CPT	O-2262926	0664	1
DRAPER ROBERT C	CW2	W-2213503	0267	1
DRAPER WILLARD T	1LT	O-1321496	0945	2
DRAPES STANLEY E	MAJ	O-0403626	0960	1
DRASHEFF GEORGE	LTC	O-1037468	0565	1
DRASHPIL ALEX V	LTC	O-1796053	0464	1
DRATH FRANCIS S	COL	O-0222669	0462	1
DRATH WILFRED H	LTC	O-1055269	0266	1
DRAUGHON ROBERT W	COL	O-0256378	0160	3
DRAUTZ RUDOLPH A	CPT	O-1999373	0255	1
DRAVES NORMAN M	LTC	O-1165384	0455	1
DRAWBAUGH VICTOR R	CPT	O-0319722	1045	2
DRAWDY JR HOWELL F	CW2	W-2146011	0659	1
DRAY GENE E	MAJ	O-0981651	0266	1
DRAYER CALVIN S	LTC	O-0285205	0766	3
DRAYER JOSEPH H	CPT	O-0257341	0751	3
DRAYTON DOUGLAS C	LTC	O-0205109	0562	3
DRDA ROBERT J	MAJ	O-0437496	0365	1
DREBBER BERNARD S	MAJ	O-1337154	0663	1
DREDGE SR THOMAS E	COL	O-0252234	1062	3
DREGER RICHARD W	CPT	O-1553435	0546	2
DREGSETH IRVING A	1LT	O-1308118	1145	2
DREHER FRANCIS T	CW4	W-2117133	0659	1
DREIFUS CARL T	MAJ	O-0239164	0362	3
DREILING RICHARD J	CPT	O-0269525	0445	2
DREIS FRANK	CPT	O-0472746	0345	2
DREIS LEROY L	LTC	O-1183277	0561	1
DREISBACH HERBERT P	CPT	O-0235277	1164	3
DREISBACH ROBERT F	LTC	O-0485121	1156	1
DRENAN JOHN M	CPT	O-0490164	0342	1
DRENNAN GUY	LTC	O-1297331	0661	1
DRENNAN JR LEONARD	1LT	O-0446657	1145	2
DRENNEN CHARLES N	LTC	O-0233361	1163	3
DRENZEK ALFRED	LTC	O-1299016	0762	1
DRESBACH HOWARD T	LTC	O-0196808	0462	3
DRESBACH RICHARD E	COL	O-0295358	1162	1
DRESCHER WALTER	LTC	O-1949744	1163	1
DRESSEL MARTHA M	1LT	N-0725889	0246	1
DRESSER GREY	LTC	O-0394854	0760	1
DRESSER HOLLAND L	LTC	O-0275711	0263	1
DRESSER WILDER L	COL	O-0212470	1162	3
DRESSLER RAYMOND H	LTC	O-0251013	0246	1
DRESSOR WILFRED O	LTC	O-0279541	0161	3
DRESTE JOHN P	CW2	W-3100433	0167	1

NAME	GRADE	SVC NO	DATE RET MO YR	RET CODE
DREVER CRAWFORD H	MAJ	O-1822976	0361	1
DREVNO SANDER A	1LT	O-1176313	1045	2
DREW ARTHUR C	LTC	O-0451589	0255	1
DREW BERNARD J	COL	O-0361342	1057	1
DREW CHARLES A	CPT	O-1283738	0648	1
DREW DONALD W	MAJ	O-0228396	0464	3
DREW FRANCIS J	MAJ	O-1551605	0361	1
DREW FREDERICK	LTC	O-0249870	0266	3
DREW HARLEY R	MAJ	O-0974472	0165	1
DREW HAROLD F	COL	O-0291314	0457	3
DREW HAROLD C	CPT	O-0253751	0862	3
DREW JACK	LTC	O-0179566	0454	3
DREW JACK S	CW4	W-2147996	1164	2
DREW JAMES B	LTC	O-0279287	0463	3
DREW JOHN J	CPT	O-0508165	1147	1
DREW JOHN L	COL	O-0172074	0946	2
DREW JR SAMUEL M	MAJ	O-1038121	0361	1
DREW MICHAEL C	CW2	W-2147377	0562	1
DREW RAYMOND J	CW2	W-2148701	0359	1
DREWERY FRED C	LTC	O-1035748	0267	1
DREWES HENRY F	COL	O-0280783	0867	3
DREWS WILLIAM E	1LT	O-0335429	0445	2
DREXEL CONRAD G	COL	O-0257259	0154	1
DREXLER BERNARD	CPT	O-0333662	1145	2
DREXLER ERIC H	MAJ	O-0364588	0166	3
DREYER ALBERT	LTC	O-0256305	0165	3
DREYER CARL W	MAJ	O-2202647	1167	1
DREYER CHARLES H	COL	O-0253538	0361	3
DREYER EDWARD T	MAJ	O-1299217	0156	1
DREYER ROBERT D	CPT	O-1298042	0346	2
DREYER RODERICK G	CPT	O-1313082	0647	2
DREYER WAYNE J	MAJ	O-1047503	0364	1
DREYFOUS FELIX J	MAJ	O-0911173	0146	2
DREYFUS JR JOSEPH C	MAJ	O-0241451	0345	2
DREZMAL ALENE	LTC	L-0704017	1155	2
DRIER JR CHARLES H	LTC	O-0521349	0463	1
DRIES JOSEPH A	LTC	O-0885865	0358	1
DRIESBACH JOHN D	CW3	W-2207492	1166	1
DRIGGERS JULIAN K	CPT	O-0504857	1047	1
DRIGGERS LEE R	CW2	W-2000402	0465	3
DRIGGERS VAUGHAN W	LTC	O-0215494	1063	3
DRIGGS DALE M	CPT	O-0970266	0461	1
DRIGGS EDWIN O	LTC	O-0267820	1067	3
DRIGGS FRANCIS B	MAJ	O-1549257	0960	2
DRINKARD JOHN E	LTC	O-0365282	0260	1
DRINKWATER DOROTHY L	2LT	N-0742854	1044	1
DRISCHEL FRANK G	COL	O-0332657	1160	3
DRISCOLL CHARLES D	1LT	O-1050638	0944	2
DRISCOLL ELBERT A	CPT	O-0301552	0957	1
DRISCOLL J T M T	1LT	O-0916137	0945	2
DRISCOLL JOHN F	LTC	O-1105397	0265	3
DRISCOLL KEITH F	LTC	O-0254029	0146	1
DRISCOLL ROBERT F	CPT	O-0542757	0946	2
DRISCOLL ROBERT H	COL	O-0327598	0946	2
DRISCOLL ROBERT J	CW3	W-2144722	0663	1
DRISCOLL THERON W	MAJ	O-2038148	0463	1
DRISCOLL THOMAS D	LTC	O-0275111	0246	2
DRISCOLL WILLIAM J	CPT	O-2009792	0664	1
DRISKELL DELBERT W	CPT	O-1115501	0446	1
DRISKELL EZRA H	CW2	W-2209050	0963	1
DRISKELL HERMAN L	MAJ	O-0253360	1048	3
DRISKELL JOHN C	LTC	O-0270712	0767	3
DRISKELL JOSEPH L	COL	O-0284940	1158	1
DRISKI VINCENT P	1LT	O-1998325	0955	1
DRISLANE JAMES J	MAJ	O-1578397	0445	2
DRITTENBASS ALBERT R	2LT	O-0923006	1144	2
DRIVER ALTON C	CW3	W-2113365	0660	1
DRIVER DON	CPT	O-0477791	0148	1
DRIVER JOHN P	LTC	O-1316666	0864	1
DRIVER JR LOUIS F	LTC	O-0241745	0265	3
DRIVER PAUL R	CW2	W-2101635	0647	1
DRIVER ROBERT S	LTC	O-0112888	1053	2
DRNEK JOHN F	CW2	W-2151638	1156	1
DROBA PATRICIA L	2LT	N-0768758	1145	1
DROBEK OLGA M	MAJ	N-0742607	0767	1

NAME	GRADE	SVC NO	DATE RET MO YR	RET CODE
DROBEK PETER J	1LT	O-0890173	0560	1
DROBNIS DAVID D	LTC	O-0180956	0758	3
DRODDY PRUELLA H	MAJ	N-0700373	0345	1
DROEGE EDWARD H	COL	O-0248235	0260	3
DROEGEMUELLER W H	LTC	O-0395816	1045	1
DROGAN JOHN J	1LT	O-0468229	0247	1
DROGE WILLIAM B	LTC	O-0180804	1145	1
DROHAN THOMAS W	CPT	O-0370846	0247	2
DROHAN WILLIAM F	1LT	O-1314764	1145	2
DROKE HOWARD B	CW2	W-2151015	0657	1
DROLET RAYMOND A	MAJ	O-0423373	1056	1
DROMMOND MAY E	COL	O-0222356	0358	3
DROMS FRANK A	LTC	O-0190713	0251	3
DRON JOHN A	MAJ	O-0110606	0953	3
DRONBERGER CHARLES S	LTC	O-0375886	1159	1
DROSS HERBERT C	WO1	W-2128165	0357	1
DROSS MARION J	LTC	O-1320513	0467	3
DROSTE ELMER H	COL	O-0218641	0655	3
DROUIN FRANK H	CPT	O-0973507	0460	1
DROWN CLARENCE H	MAJ	O-0319409	0545	2
DROWNE JR HENRY R	B G	O-0136725	0757	3
DROWNS WILLIAM A	COL	O-0322115	0257	1
DROZO WALTER T	MAJ	O-2056921	0563	1
DROZESKI EDWARD F	CW3	W-2148527	0965	1
DRUBA ROYAL F	LTC	O-2042745	1159	1
DRUCKER ARTHUR	LTC	O-0866923	0865	1
DRUEN RALPH I	CW2	W-2206300	0563	1
DRUET ARTHUR L	1LT	O-2053913	0554	1
DRUM CLIFFORD H	LTC	O-1585383	1066	3
DRUM GEORGE	LTC	O-0298543	0657	1
DRUM THOMAS J	CPT	O-0359682	1143	2
DRUMM BYRON M	MAJ	O-1924567	0865	1
DRUMMOND ADDISON P	COL	O-0259120	0367	3
DRUMMOND ALFRED A	LTC	O-0146887	1056	3
DRUMMOND FREDERICK	LTC	O-0358214	1163	3
DRUMMOND JAMES	MAJ	O-2027754	1161	1
DRUMMOND JOSEPH R	CPT	O-0280471	0645	2
DRUMMOND MANCE E	LTC	O-1110465	0967	3
DRUMMOND PALMER R	MAJ	O-0239302	0845	2
DRUMMOND RAY D	CW4	W-2004226	1266	1
DRUMMY WILLIAM F	CPT	O-1794794	0445	2
DRUPIEWSKI JOSEPH	CW4	W-2003930	1060	3
DRURY BILL C	1LT	O-1304048	1045	2
DRURY CECIL H	LTC	O-0401832	0966	3
DRURY CHARLES H	MAJ	O-0243320	0160	3
DRURY EDWARD A	MAJ	O-1035749	0366	1
DRURY FORREST J	COL	O-0189680	0648	3
DRURY GEORGE A	LTC	O-0176008	0955	3
DRURY JOHN D	COL	O-0170024	0648	3
DRURY JR FREDERIC F	COL	O-0326705	0960	3
DRURY PERCIVAL P	LTC	O-0159314	0856	3
DRURY WILLIAM W	LTC	O-1060081	0766	1
DRUSS ABE R	LTC	O-1594133	0966	3
DRY ELMER D	MAJ	O-0119068	1145	2
DRY RALPH L	MAJ	O-0347758	1044	1
DRYDALE WILLIAM T	MAJ	O-1322138	0760	2
DRYDEN BEN	CW3	W-2147077	0361	1
DRYDEN DEAN W	MAJ	O-0514154	0158	2
DRYDEN JACK T	2LT	O-2000519	0656	1
DRYDEN JACK T	2LT	O-2000559	0656	1
DRYDEN JOHN F	CPT	O-1044503	0855	1
DRYDEN JOHN R	COL	O-0237475	1064	3
DRYDEN SHERMAN L	MAJ	O-0571515	0151	1
DRYER ADOLPH	1LT	O-1305219	0346	2
DRYER GENE F	2LT	O-1995411	0944	2
DRYER JR ARNOLD	MAJ	O-1015723	0164	1
DRYER JR JAMES C	LTC	O-0298231	0664	3
DRYER OLIN C	LTC	O-0132527	0652	3
DRYMON BRANDT C	MAJ	O-1016821	1060	1
DRYSDALE GEORGE H	MAJ	O-0278493	1056	3
DRYSDALE JR WALTER S	LTC	O-0327499	0356	2
DU BOIS BENJAMIN C	COL	O-0116480	0648	3
DU BOIS EARL D	COL	O-0215780	0858	3
DU BOIS FRANK A	LTC	O-1299863	0765	1
DU BOIS MARY E	1LT	N-0759554	0346	1

NAME	GRADE	SVC NO	DATE RET MO YR	RET CODE
DU BOIS ROBERT S	COL	O-0208072	0951	3
DU BOIS WILLIAM O	CW3	W-2146232	0661	1
DU BOSE CHARLES G	LTC	O-0315522	0161	1
DU BOSE FRANK H	LTC	O-0258521	0465	3
DU CHARME BENJAMIN J	2LT	O-0571519	1052	1
DU CONCE EDWIN J	CPT	O-1592786	0160	2
DU FLOCC EUGENE W	MAJ	O-0239782	0965	3
DU FRANE FRANCIS A	CW3	W-2142147	0960	1
DU MOULIN JULIA P	2LT	N-0720854	0547	1
DU PONT GEORGE J	MAJ	O-1178130	0765	1
DU PRE OSCAR L	COL	O-0231324	0565	3
DU PUIS ROBERT C	LTC	O-1310176	1061	1
DU PUIS ROBERT H	WO1	W-2106599	1044	2
DU PUY ELBERT N	COL	O-0254792	1164	3
DU RANT HARRY N	CPT	O-1915484	1263	1
DU RETTE CECIL A	MAJ	O-0189042	0355	3
DU TREMBLE LAURIEN R	CPT	O-1293732	0661	1
DU VAL JR HENRY W	1LT	O-1017161	1045	2
DU VALL EARL W	CW3	W-2207388	0661	1
DU VALL HERMAN C	LTC	O-0436250	0457	1
DU VALL THOMAS B	CW4	RW-2142836	0264	1
DU VARNEY EDWARD J	MAJ	O-1886462	1164	1
DUANE FRANCIS K	CPT	O-1322316	0147	2
DUANE STEPHEN A	COL	O-0136331	0257	3
DUARTE JR MANUEL J	CW2	W-2209567	1064	1
DUBBERLEY JOHN A	CPT	O-0379245	0348	2
DUBBS WILLIAM B	MAJ	O-1544051	0763	1
DUBE PAUL H	MAJ	O-0481854	0146	2
DUBES RUSSELL F	LTC	O-1647857	1067	1
DUBIN ABE	LTC	O-1845028	0566	3
DUBINSKI WILLIAM A	LTC	O-1284481	0854	1
DUBLIN SOLOMON	2LT	O-1177779	0944	2
DUBNICKA JOSEPH A	CPT	O-1185332	0746	2
DUBOIS EDWARD F	MAJ	O-2032287	1262	2
DUBOIS ETHELYN C	1LT	N-0727575	1045	1
DUBOIS JACK G	LTC	O-0231869	1263	3
DUBOSE ROBERT N	CPT	O-0339100	0944	2
DUBRISKE RAYMOND A	LTC	O-1577118	0961	1
DUBSON REUBEN F	LTC	O-0482467	0756	1
DUBUC JOSEPH A	LTC	O-1080099	0666	1
DUBUCLET WALTER M	MAJ	O-1799115	0462	1
DUCEY FREDERICK	MAJ	O-0169924	0355	3
DUCHAINE GEORGE F	LTC	O-1642018	0966	1
DUCHAINE JULIEN G F	CPT	O-0451273	0864	1
DUCHAJ JOHN H	LTC	O-1327127	0563	1
DUCHARME JOSEPH O C	LTC	O-0481416	0754	1
DUCHARME RAYMOND J	CW4	W-2102856	0157	1
DUCHEK CHARLES F	WO1	W-2106721	1044	2
DUCHEK JOSEPH D	LTC	O-0510067	0467	1
DUCHIEN WESLEY L	LTC	O-0485882	0753	1
DUCKER HAROLD P	MAJ	O-1335255	0164	1
DUCKETT OREN B	CPT	O-0923935	0745	2
DUCKETT PIERCE F	CPT	O-0450123	0258	1
DUCKMAN JOHN A	MAJ	O-1012013	0366	3
DUCKWITZ ALBERT H	CPT	O-1822119	0863	1
DUCKWORTH CARL L	LTC	O-0453337	1146	2
DUCKWORTH DOROTHY C	2LT	N-0794798	0846	1
DUCKWORTH ERNEST G	CW4	W-2143410	0959	1
DUCKWORTH GEORGE H	CPT	O-2262158	0960	1
DUCKWORTH GEORGE J	MAJ	O-0384832	1047	1
DUCKWORTH GLENN D	CPT	O-0504286	1055	1
DUCKWORTH JR JAMES C	CW3	W-2145416	1059	2
DUCKWORTH JR LEWIS F	1LT	O-0442859	1044	1
DUCKWORTH PHILLIP B	MAJ	O-1049812	0261	1
DUCKWORTH VIRGINIA	2LT	N-0784783	0945	1
DUCLON WARREN F	CPT	O-0551434	0547	1
DUCLOS CYRILLE A	CPT	O-1311495	0347	1
DUCOTE HAROLD A	1LT	O-1047100	0745	2
DUCOTE JR HARRY J	CW3	W-2146233	0762	1
DUDA ALBIN J	2LT	O-0337268	1044	2
DUDA GEORGE	MAJ	O-0450683	0356	1
DUDA MICHAEL	MAJ	O-1321109	1159	1
DUDAS STEPHEN	CPT	O-0975770	0857	1
DUDDING WILLIAM C	MAJ	O-2026069	0860	1
DUDDY JOSEPH J	WO1	W-2106109	1148	1

NAME	GRADE	SVC NO	DATE RET MO YR	RET CODE
DUDE LUDWIG	MAJ	O-1001992	0860	1
DUDEK ALEXANDER	2LT	O-5925000	0161	2
DUDEK ROMAN F	CW2	W-2203376	0963	1
DUDISH ANDREW C	1LT	O-0524684	1145	2
DUDLEY ARTHUR L	MAJ	O-0945810	0266	1
DUDLEY CHARLES W	LTC	O-1542997	0163	1
DUDLEY FRANK G	MAJ	O-0490639	0956	1
DUDLEY GORDON C	1LT	O-1111587	0846	2
DUDLEY HARRY E	COL	O-0235619	0754	3
DUDLEY HARRY C	CPT	O-0214675	0557	3
DUDLEY HARVARD E	LTC	O-1540562	0562	1
DUDLEY HENRY H	CPT	O-0130193	0251	3
DUDLEY JACK B	MAJ	O-0439365	0849	1
DUDLEY RICHARD S	2LT	O-2012079	0946	1
DUDLEY WILFRED	1LT	O-1640409	1043	2
DUDLEY WILLIAM R	CW2	W-2214489	0866	1
DUDMAN WILLIAM P	MAJ	O-0444519	0250	1
DUDONIS JOSEPH J	CPT	O-2055106	0156	1
DUDREY PHYLLIS G	1LT	N-0776050	1045	1
DUDYK PAUL P	CPT	O-1996899	0357	1
DUDZINSKI VINCENT P	CW3	W-2151631	0364	1
DUELL EVERETT A	LTC	O-0136727	1151	1
DUELL HOWARD S	1LT	O-0114802	0755	3
DUELL RONALD F	LTC	O-1172439	0766	1
DUENOW RICHARD F	LTC	O-1010042	0157	1
DUER ROBERT K	MAJ	O-1116713	1066	1
DUERNER LEWIS W	COL	O-0298331	1054	2
DUESER FRANK J	MAJ	O-1171520	0461	1
DUFF CARL L	COL	O-0905938	0863	1
DUFF LEONARD A	COL	O-0347855	1052	2
DUFF LOGAN	1LT	O-0109736	0130	1
DUFF OSCAR A	2LT	O-1299864	0844	1
DUFF PETER D	COL	O-0430540	0756	1
DUFF SYBIL K	MAJ	N-0743833	0865	1
DUFF THOMAS M	COL	O-0276832	0855	3
DUFF WILLIAM	1LT	O-1691602	0745	2
DUFFEY CATHERINE	CPT	N-0700591	0245	1
DUFFIE HAROLD R	B G	O-0126221	1054	3
DUFFIE JOHN M	MAJ	O-0243335	0960	3
DUFFIELD ELVOE W	LTC	O-0382986	0862	1
DUFFIELD JOHN M	LTC	O-0365405	0657	1
DUFFIELD KEITH P	MAJ	O-0575498	0961	1
DUFFIN DANIEL J	CPT	O-0903832	1044	2
DUFFIN EDSON C	MAJ	O-1548198	0161	1
DUFFY ADAM A	CPT	O-1535448	0146	2
DUFFY ALBERT W	CW3	W-2102857	0156	1
DUFFY FRANCIS K	LTC	O-0100252	0844	2
DUFFY FRANCIS X	CW4	W-2005157	1066	3
DUFFY HAROLD E	LTC	O-0452588	0960	1
DUFFY JAMES A	MAJ	O-2203010	0567	1
DUFFY JAMES J	LTC	O-1116373	1162	1
DUFFY JAMES M	1LT	O-1549700	0146	2
DUFFY JOHN H	1LT	O-1284303	0644	2
DUFFY JOHN J	CPT	O-0243043	0648	3
DUFFY JOHN J	CPT	O-0499377	1044	2
DUFFY JOHN P	MAJ	O-1799259	0561	2
DUFFY JOSEPH D	1LT	O-0387579	0245	2
DUFFY JR BERNARD J	MAJ	O-1587224	0161	1
DUFFY JR EDWARD F	CPT	O-0245964	0753	3
DUFFY JR ROBERT A	WO1	W-2144174	0367	2
DUFFY LAMBERT F	1LT	O-1549258	1145	2
DUFFY MARGARET G	MAJ	L-0610747	1163	1
DUFFY PAUL J	WO1	W-2125910	0146	2
DUFFY ROBERT N	MAJ	O-1286985	1059	1
DUFFY SR JAMES W	LTC	O-0177503	0156	3
DUFFY WILLIAM E	LTC	O-0410009	1060	1
DUFFY WILLIAM R	LTC	O-1299218	0764	1
DUFOE JR FABBIAN C	LTC	O-1181231	0666	1
DUFORT GERALD E	COL	O-0130169	0156	3
DUFORT LEO W	MAJ	O-0239667	0862	3
DUFRESNE ALFRED A	CW2	W-2143494	1154	1
DUFRESNE CARYL A	LTC	O-0379825	0566	1
DUFRESNE RAYMOND J	CW3	W-2144287	0267	1
DUGAN EDWARD C	1LT	O-0467178	0945	2
DUGAN EDWARD E	2LT	O-1178768	0245	1

NAME	GRADE	SVC NO	DATE RET MO YR	RET CODE
DUGAN FRANK C	LTC	O-0123495	0648	3
DUGAN JOHN J	LTC	O-0183402	0954	3
DUGAN JOIE A	1LT	N-0790040	1046	1
DUGAN RICHARD F	COL	O-0203374	0560	3
DUGAN THOMAS M	CPT	O-1726372	0549	1
DUGAN WALTER J	1LT	O-1289224	0246	1
DUGART ROBERT E	CW3	W-2152528	0467	1
DUGAS FRANK J	2LT	O-0922726	0344	2
DUGAS HENRY J	CW2	W-2123932	0360	1
DUGAS JR GUSTAVE H	MAJ	O-1796438	0761	1
DUGAS PAUL P	MAJ	O-1101417	1266	3
DUGGAN CHARLES W	CPT	O-1317767	0748	2
DUGGAN CLIFTON D	CW3	W-2143846	0461	2
DUGGAN CORNELIUS	CW4	W-2003205	1157	3
DUGGAN FRANCIS L	LTC	O-0319886	0756	2
DUGGAN JAMES F	CPT	O-1995242	0746	2
DUGGAN JAPSER T	MAJ	O-0184277	0250	3
DUGGAN JOHN S	1LT	O-1104626	0546	2
DUGGAN SAMUEL F	LTC	O-1101418	0762	1
DUGGAN WALTER L	CW3	W-2148960	0764	1
DUGGAY WILLIAM C	MAJ	O-0955798	0467	1
DUGGER JOHN	CPT	O-1633177	0248	1
DUGGER VIRGINIA N	2LT	N-0735896	0345	1
DUGHI PETER A	CPT	O-1308616	0147	2
DUGINGER LYNN C	CPT	O-1290017	1145	2
DUHANT ELIZABETH	2LT	N-0775127	0545	1
DUHART ROY S	LTC	O-0340290	0359	1
DUHE HENRY M	CPT	O-0417905	0446	2
DUHM WALTER T	MAJ	O-0430088	0546	2
DUHON WOODROW W	1LT	O-1825213	0745	2
DUISMAN JOE	CW4	W-2110200	0957	1
DUKAS ALEXANDER	LTC	O-1323295	0564	1
DUKE CHARLES L	LTC	O-0452521	0761	1
DUKE DURWARD A	MAJ	O-0986624	0163	2
DUKE FRANCIS	LTC	O-0906954	0466	3
DUKE FRANKLIN L	MAJ	O-2288515	0867	1
DUKE GRACY F	MAJ	O-1913405	0864	2
DUKE JOHN H	CPT	O-1647858	0246	2
DUKE JOHN P	COL	O-0150396	0457	3
DUKE JR THOMAS H	MAJ	O-1633178	0760	1
DUKE OSCAR	CPT	O-0503010	0952	1
DUKE PHILLIP W	MAJ	O-0159033	0648	3
DUKE RALPH L	LTC	O-1685031	0367	1
DUKE SPOTTSWOOD	COL	O-0154656	0554	3
DUKE WILLIAM R	CPT	O-1642817	0353	1
DUKEHART GRAHAM	MAJ	O-0302350	0465	3
DUKELOW BURTEN H	CW3	W-2148248	0165	1
DUKES EULA F	2LT	N-0761327	0245	1
DUKES JOHN D	LTC	O-0206953	1158	3
DUKES ROBERT J	LTC	O-0281979	0662	1
DUKES WILSON F	MAJ	O-1598417	1154	1
DULAN ELVA L J	2LT	N-0724860	0544	1
DULANEY EARL	MAJ	O-0312910	0942	2
DULANEY MARLAND D	MAJ	O-2021092	1064	1
DULANEY ROBERT A	CW3	W-3150264	0667	1
DULBERGER HOWARD	CPT	O-1013436	0946	1
DULEY FRANK R	MAJ	O-1036557	0461	1
DULIAN CLIFFORD V	CPT	O-1541845	1044	2
DULIN BYRON W	CW4	W-2002344	0867	3
DULIN CHARLEY	CPT	O-0981428	0161	1
DULIN GEORGE W	MAJ	O-0212745	0364	3
DULIN HOWARD C	MAJ	O-0494248	0849	1
DULIN JR RAMSEY W	1LT	O-1100558	0246	1
DULIN 3RD JOHN W	MAJ	O-0405191	0948	2
DULINA ANDREW S	MAJ	O-0980831	1167	2
DULING CLYDE S	CW3	W-2203297	0661	1
DULING EARL P	MAJ	O-1002616	0758	1
DULL DOROTHY A	2LT	N-0797854	1047	1
DULL FRANCIS A	MAJ	O-0556697	0265	1
DULL HAZEL E	1LT	N-0727295	0245	1
DULL JR CHARLES F	LTC	O-1581670	1065	1
DULL LLOYD W	LTC	O-1049815	1265	1
DULLEA MAURICE B	MAJ	O-1925393	0864	2
DULLNIG JR ADOLPH C	LTC	O-0380523	0147	2
DULMERY CURTIS V	CW3	RW-2145305	0361	1

NAME	GRADE	SVC NO	DATE RET MO YR	RET CODE
DULSKI STANLEY J	LTC	O-1844679	0561	1
DULUOF STEPHEN E	MAJ	O-1824294	0462	1
DUMAINE ALBERT L	2LT	O-0108353	0532	1
DUMAINE JOHN B	LTC	O-1294106	0860	1
DUMANOAN TIM C	1LT	O-1896729	0561	1
DUMANOIS HAROLD C	COL	O-0275204	0367	3
DUMANSKE MORRIS F	MAJ	O-1579590	1160	1
DUMAS ANDREW L	LTC	O-1011399	0961	1
DUMAS EDGAR J	CW3	W-2152116	0659	1
DUMBRIGUE ALEXANDER	MAJ	O-1924905	0966	1
DUMEY ARNOLD I	LTC	O-0921381	1266	3
DUMIC JOE	LTC	O-0451097	0155	1
DUMLAO MIGUEL P	MAJ	O-1896416	1058	1
DUMMER RUTH L	1LT	N-0731492	0845	1
DUMONT WOODROW M	MAJ	O-0364553	1045	1
DUMSER GERALD T	LTC	O-1549701	0263	1
DUNAVANT GEORGE A	COL	O-0401077	0463	1
DUNAWAY AUGUSTUS	LTC	O-0164110	0254	3
DUNAWAY MARION E	1LT	N-0742017	0445	1
DUNAWAY MARSHALL W	MAJ	O-1176941	1262	1
DUNBAR ARTHUR B	MAJ	O-0190499	0757	3
DUNBAR CLARENCE E	COL	O-0192761	0648	3
DUNBAR ERNEST J	WO1	W-2148594	0455	1
DUNBAR FREDERICK	CW3	W-2145884	0862	2
DUNBAR GERALD C	MAJ	O-0225997	1162	3
DUNBAR HANSON D	LTC	O-1587226	0265	3
DUNBAR HARVEY L	2LT	O-1017956	0545	2
DUNBAR JOHN C	COL	O-0218231	1163	3
DUNBAR JR QUINTIN R	CW3	W-2206537	0967	1
DUNBAR JR WALLACE B	CW3	W-2147330	0464	1
DUNBAR JR WILLIAM F	1LT	O-1061943	0546	1
DUNBAR PAUL A	CPT	O-0246781	0265	3
DUNBAR RICHARD B	COL	O-0192667	0746	2
DUNBAR ROBERT B	MAJ	O-1633181	0756	1
DUNBAR WILBUR R	CW4	W-2002118	0766	3
DUNCAN ANDREW	CPT	O-0109167	1026	1
DUNCAN ANDREW J	1LT	O-0273957	0845	1
DUNCAN AUBREY I	1LT	O-1548199	1157	1
DUNCAN AUBURN B	2LT	O-0556581	1044	2
DUNCAN CARL D	COL	O-1633182	0863	1
DUNCAN CHARLES A	MAJ	O-1297334	0960	1
DUNCAN CHARLES A	MAJ	O-2035217	0955	1
DUNCAN CLYDE W	CPT	O-1324991	0258	1
DUNCAN DANIEL E	COL	O-1288522	0367	1
DUNCAN DONALD E	MAJ	O-0554189	0863	1
DUNCAN DONALD W	CPT	O-1317080	0766	1
DUNCAN DORMAN L	LTC	O-0305380	0560	3
DUNCAN EARL L	MAJ	O-1170721	0561	1
DUNCAN EMORY L	MAJ	O-4006285	0367	1
DUNCAN EUGENE E	MAJ	O-0308531	0163	1
DUNCAN FRED	MAJ	O-1299865	0866	1
DUNCAN FRED J	LTC	O-0360148	0154	1
DUNCAN GEORGE A	LTC	O-1688244	0564	2
DUNCAN GEORGE H	MAJ	O-0271850	0962	1
DUNCAN HAROLD P	LTC	O-0209590	0960	3
DUNCAN HAROLD F	MAJ	O-1580887	0858	1
DUNCAN HARRY C	COL	O-0165433	0648	3
DUNCAN HARRY L	LTC	O-1290049	1055	1
DUNCAN HENRY T	COL	O-0231114	0863	3
DUNCAN HERBERT L	MAJ	O-0995144	0663	1
DUNCAN HORACE L	LTC	O-0405927	0960	2
DUNCAN JAMES	1LT	O-2027290	1152	1
DUNCAN JAMES B	COL	O-1287496	0263	2
DUNCAN JOE	MAJ	O-1174834	0154	1
DUNCAN JOHN A	1LT	O-2033309	0952	1
DUNCAN JOHN B	LTC	O-0317675	0759	1
DUNCAN JOHN V	MAJ	O-0974614	0667	1
DUNCAN JOSEPH D	CW3	W-2141843	1162	1
DUNCAN JR CHARLES M	LTC	O-0405858	0860	1
DUNCAN JR HIRAM A	MAJ	O-2036641	0661	1
DUNCAN JR WILLIAM C	CPT	O-1553074	0960	1
DUNCAN MADISON M	COL	O-0250659	0361	1
DUNCAN MARY E	1LT	N-0765509	0847	1
DUNCAN MARY V	MAJ	N-0741943	0762	1
DUNCAN ORAN W	COL	O-0238746	0562	3

NAME	GRADE	SVC NO	DATE RET MO YR	RET CODE
DUNCAN RALPH A	CPT	O-0508718	0245	2
DUNCAN RALPH F	CPT	O-0116487	0251	3
DUNCAN RALPH G	LTC	O-0325842	0860	1
DUNCAN RALPH M	CPT	O-2288111	0563	1
DUNCAN RAY H	1LT	O-0157438	1043	2
DUNCAN RAYMOND L	MAJ	O-0503354	0549	1
DUNCAN RICHARD F	MAJ	O-1923633	1066	1
DUNCAN ROBERT G	CW3	W-2143272	0962	1
DUNCAN ROBERT P	CW4	W-2133199	0559	1
DUNCAN ROBERT S	1LT	O-0249142	1266	3
DUNCAN ROBERT T	2LT	O-1559904	1146	2
DUNCAN ROY O	MAJ	O-1320514	0564	1
DUNCAN RUDOLPH L	COL	O-0219079	0755	3
DUNCAN RUSSELL T	MAJ	O-1917823	1165	2
DUNCAN SCOTT M	LTC	O-0126837	0653	3
DUNCAN SR JOHN C	MAJ	O-1950155	0463	2
DUNCAN THEODORE R	CW3	W-2145104	0159	1
DUNCAN WILBUR H	MAJ	O-0201880	1157	3
DUNCAN WILLIAM A	MAJ	O-1060082	0860	1
DUNCAN WILLIAM B	2LT	O-0713655	0246	2
DUNCAN WILLIE Y	LTC	O-0182186	0653	3
DUNCANSON DONALD D	LTC	O-0144737	0648	3
DUNCANSON JAY C	LTC	O-1037969	0967	1
DUNCANSON WILLIAM M	MAJ	O-0175486	1147	2
DUNCKEL RALPH L	COL	O-0215940	0549	2
DUNCKLEE HENRY W	2LT	O-0492814	0555	1
DUNCOMBE JR H S	COL	O-0144626	0356	3
DUNDA NICHOLAS	CPT	O-1180879	1163	1
DUNDAS HARRY B	MAJ	O-0470504	0945	2
DUNDAS JACK S	LTC	O-1634699	0865	1
DUNDAS JAMES E	MAJ	O-1341646	0663	1
DUNEGAN FRANCIS E	2LT	O-1321463	0945	2
DUNFEE JAMES F	CPT	O-0504609	0447	1
DUNFORD FREDERICK	MAJ	O-1113180	0661	1
DUNFORD JUNIUS E	LTC	O-0154246	0545	2
DUNG PURDESON D	MAJ	O-0961956	1164	1
DUNGAN DAVID V	CW4	W-2118287	0959	1
DUNGEE JOHN R	CPT	O-0460209	1046	2
DUNGEY LEONARD A	CW4	W-2114139	0661	1
DUNGEY LYNN F	MAJ	O-2039473	0163	1
DUNHAM CARL C	LTC	O-0411002	0663	1
DUNHAM CARL E	LTC	O-0342630	1058	3
DUNHAM DAN S	1LT	O-1825335	0850	1
DUNHAM EVERETT C	LTC	O-1051540	0963	1
DUNHAM FRED A	COL	O-0220388	1059	3
DUNHAM GEORGE F	CPT	O-0261790	0244	2
DUNHAM HOWARD R	LTC	O-0360301	0460	1
DUNHAM JAMES F	1LT	O-0265137	0146	2
DUNHAM JAMES F	MAJ	O-1288873	1155	1
DUNHAM JOSEPH F	CPT	O-0443474	0846	1
DUNHAM LEWIS L	LTC	O-1342255	0666	1
DUNHAM PAUL A	CW2	W-2144731	0660	1
DUNHAM RAYMOND L	CW3	W-2203711	0767	1
DUNHAM RICHARD R	CPT	O-0511094	0646	2
DUNHAM ROBERT L	LTC	O-0265613	0861	3
DUNHAM RUPERT F	LTC	O-0327213	0458	1
DUNHAM RUSSELL C	MAJ	O-0146877	1049	3
DUNHAM WALTER A	1LT	O-0535310	0949	1
DUNHAM WILLIAM C	LTC	O-1647861	0463	2
DUNHAM WILLIAM E	CW2	W-2145543	0461	1
DUNHAM WILLIAM H	COL	O-0253409	0161	3
DUNKEL LEONARD N	B G	O-0178133	0459	3
DUNKIN GLEN W	CPT	O-1284110	0658	1
DUNKIN LEON M	CW3	W-2147702	1262	1
DUNKIN SAMUEL J	LTC	O-0205190	0860	3
DUNKLE CYRUS G	MAJ	O-0222505	0561	3
DUNKLE SIMON P	COL	O-0194620	1062	3
DUNKLEE CARL D	LTC	O-0219134	1055	3
DUNKLEE THOMAS F	CW2	W-3200434	0767	1
DUNKLEY FRANK	B G	O-0240437	0557	3
DUNKLIN VOLNEY L	MAJ	O-0311282	0246	2
DUNLAP BRADY	MAJ	O-1051941	0959	1
DUNLAP EDWARD L	LTC	O-0168808	0658	3
DUNLAP FREDERICK	LTC	O-0383123	0147	2
DUNLAP GEORGE R	CW3	W-2141260	0760	1

NAME	GRADE	SVC NO	DATE RET MO YR	RET CODE
DUNLAP GORDON C	CW2	W-2146641	0557	1
DUNLAP HAROLD J	COL	O-0281572	0664	3
DUNLAP HERBERT P	COL	O-0217408	0563	3
DUNLAP JAMES O	COL	O-0101252	0256	3
DUNLAP JR CLAUDE E	COL	O-0410764	0161	1
DUNLAP JR JOSEPH H	LTC	O-1821983	0866	1
DUNLAP JR KINLOCH F	LTC	O-0252863	1266	3
DUNLAP MERRITT S	LTC	O-0274723	0966	3
DUNLAP RALPH E	CPT	O-2011344	0562	1
DUNLAP RICHARD O	MAJ	O-1174283	0753	1
DUNLAP ROBERT B	CPT	O-0361126	1065	1
DUNLAP ROBERT C	MAJ	O-0220242	0857	3
DUNLAP STEPHEN E	CPT	O-1726921	1046	1
DUNLAP WALLACE W	MAJ	O-0129175	0655	1
DUNLAP WALTER H	LTC	O-0353142	0963	1
DUNLAP WALTER T	CPT	O-1324830	0949	2
DUNLAP WILBUR	CW3	W-2124232	0561	1
DUNLAP WILLIAM A	1LT	O-0551020	0646	1
DUNLAP WILLIAM C	MAJ	O-2206188	0866	1
DUNLAP WILLIAM M	LTC	O-0152045	0955	3
DUNLAP ZAC R	1LT	O-0372348	1045	2
DUNLEAVY JAMES J	1LT	O-0501495	0747	2
DUNLEAVY ROY B	LTC	O-0399245	0261	1
DUNLEVEY DAVID R	LTC	O-0334130	0746	2
DUNMAN DOUGLAS W	CW3	W-2145747	0265	1
DUNMAR HAROLD	MAJ	O-2063998	0164	1
DUNMORE FRANCIS E	MAJ	O-4026450	1165	1
DUNN ALBERT A	COL	O-0157531	1052	1
DUNN ALBERT D	CW2	W-2145178	1060	1
DUNN ALBERT W	1LT	O-0885748	0859	1
DUNN ALFRED O	MAJ	O-1015939	0760	1
DUNN ANDREW M	COL	O-0348514	0859	1
DUNN ARLO M	CPT	O-0314921	0646	2
DUNN ARTHUR E	2LT	O-1797617	1044	2
DUNN ARTHUR M	CPT	O-1293030	0547	2
DUNN BYRON E	LTC	O-0233241	1264	3
DUNN CECIL G	COL	O-0275937	0364	3
DUNN CHARLES A	MAJ	O-1000357	1162	1
DUNN CHARLES C	MAJ	O-2262873	1062	1
DUNN CHARLES C	CW3	W-2147794	0366	1
DUNN CHARLES E	MAJ	O-0171782	0652	3
DUNN CLARENCE A	LTC	O-0281520	0451	1
DUNN O Y	LTC	O-0125252	0652	3
DUNN DARWIN A	MAJ	O-0324123	0746	2
DUNN DARWIN C	MAJ	O-1168640	1056	1
DUNN DAVID J	1LT	O-1306824	1045	2
DUNN DONALD J	2LT	O-1184195	0944	2
DUNN EDWARD	MAJ	O-1692536	0561	1
DUNN ELMORE	2LT	O-1913658	0444	1
DUNN ELVIS	1LT	O-2024283	1047	1
DUNN ESTHER M	CPT	N-0767645	0754	2
DUNN HAROLD W	LTC	O-0329376	0946	2
DUNN HOWARD J	MAJ	O-1313052	1155	1
DUNN HUGH P	LTC	O-0215037	0861	3
DUNN JAMES A	MAJ	O-1175691	1155	1
DUNN JAMES D	LTC	O-0509176	0661	1
DUNN JAMES H	MAJ	O-0509793	0155	1
DUNN JAMES W	LTC	O-1643511	1264	1
DUNN JEFF S	MAJ	O-0281094	1058	1
DUNN JOSEPH B	LTC	O-1168229	0258	1
DUNN JOSEPH L	1LT	O-0244736	0260	3
DUNN JR ANDERSON R	MAJ	O-0401878	0444	2
DUNN JR JAMES N	CPT	O-0495652	0350	2
DUNN JR PAUL C	LTC	O-1042551	1262	1
DUNN JR WALTER F	LTC	O-1101817	0363	1
DUNN JR WILLIAM E	LTC	O-1080620	0763	1
DUNN JULIA L	1LT	N-0730144	0746	1
DUNN LEO F	LTC	O-0245408	1062	3
DUNN MARY C	MAJ	N-0744195	0865	1
DUNN PAUL C	1LT	O-1032077	1152	1
DUNN PHILLIP L	LTC	O-1633183	0661	1
DUNN RAYMOND C	MAJ	O-2017975	0762	1
DUNN RICHARD O	LTC	O-0431952	0564	1
DUNN ROBERT H	MAJ	O-2026665	0963	1
DUNN ROBERT J	CW4	W-2111849	0655	1

NAME	GRADE	SVC NO	DATE RET MO YR	RET CODE
DUNN ROBERT L	1LT	O-1047507	1057	1
DUNN ROBERT R	2LT	O-1011536	0144	2
DUNN ROY F	LTC	O-0293001	0466	3
DUNN RUSSELL M	CW3	W-2152788	1166	1
DUNN SAMUEL C	LTC	O-0313468	1167	3
DUNN SAMUEL T	CPT	O-0347647	0964	1
DUNN SR WILLIAM M	LTC	O-1585077	0666	1
DUNN STANLEY	CPT	O-1011714	0846	2
DUNN THOMAS P	1LT	O-2055394	1044	2
DUNN THOMAS J	MAJ	O-0188404	0759	3
DUNN THOMAS J	1LT	O-1825459	0964	1
DUNN WARREN B	CPT	O-1176606	1059	1
DUNN WILLIAM	1LT	O-0506567	1047	1
DUNN WILLIAM A	LTC	O-1587939	0766	1
DUNN WILLIAM M	COL	O-0183724	0648	3
DUNN WILLIAM P	CW3	W-2144432	1165	1
DUNN WILSON H	COL	O-0302364	0163	3
DUNNAHOO JACK R	MAJ	O-1306076	1160	1
DUNNAM MILFORD A	CW2	W-2150007	1060	1
DUNNE EDWARD J	2LT	O-1697945	0744	2
DUNNE JOSEPH J	1LT	O-1292156	1045	2
DUNNE JR CHARLES J	LTC	O-0502156	1262	1
DUNNELL JR CHARLES A	LTC	O-0456035	0261	1
DUNNIGAN CATHERINE	MAJ	N-0788525	0963	1
DUNNING BARBARA T	1LT	N-0790370	0546	1
DUNNING ELLIS G	LTC	O-0296631	0667	3
DUNNING FLOYD S	COL	O-0277389	0560	1
DUNNING JACK R	CPT	O-1923539	0463	1
DUNNING JAMES E	COL	O-0352590	1266	1
DUNNING JAMES J	MAJ	O-0334073	1144	2
DUNNING THURLOW R	COL	O-0226516	0957	3
DUNNINGTON JR EARL V	CW3	W-2111770	0261	1
DUNNINGTON RAYMOND E	COL	O-0248170	1266	3
DUNPHEY PATRICIA E	2LT	N-0758564	0945	1
DUNPHY ALBERT C	COL	O-0171022	0457	3
DUNPHY CHARLES H	LTC	O-0317205	0246	2
DUNPHY CYRIL F	MAJ	O-0372806	0245	2
DUNPHY JOHN T	LTC	O-1337409	1162	1
DUNSHEE DONALD T	MAJ	O-0252218	1063	3
DUNSMOOR ELMER E	CW2	W-3430217	1066	1
DUNSMORE MURRAY K	LTC	O-0332774	0146	2
DUNSMORE RICHARD E	COL	O-1011998	0966	2
DUNSON DAVID A	CW3	W-2146364	0559	1
DUNSON NEIL B	MAJ	O-1169087	0164	1
DUNSTAN EDGAR M	COL	O-0257226	0462	3
DUNSTER ALBERT E	1LT	O-0178131	0233	1
DUNTON JR WALLACE A	COL	O-0209922	0454	3
DUNWIDDIE ROBERT B	LTC	O-0738120	0562	1
DUNWOODY JAY W	MAJ	O-1646648	1163	1
DUNWOODY LEONARD L	LTC	O-0319633	0357	2
DUPAS CAMILE J	MAJ	O-1285218	0260	1
DUPEE EDWARD L	MAJ	O-0964228	1264	1
DUPERE RAYMOND J	MAJ	O-0984942	0264	1
DUPES HENRY C	MAJ	O-0561880	0166	1
DUPIN PAUL E	MAJ	O-1556567	0466	1
DUPLANTIS JUSTIN A	2LT	O-1300144	1144	2
DUPLIS WILLIAM F	2LT	O-1311992	0544	2
DUPONT JR GEORGE H	1LT	O-1634704	0345	2
DUPONT LONIS J	CW3	W-2151194	0861	1
DUPRAS LEO A	LTC	O-1310586	0867	1
DUPRE LEO A	COL	O-0123601	0856	3
DUPREE DONALD J	LTC	O-0454204	1160	1
DUPREE LESTER E	1LT	O-0890389	0147	2
DUPREE LEWIS J	COL	O-0134439	0152	3
DUPREE SCOTT W	MAJ	O-0450584	0461	1
DURRES MARION R	LTC	O-0228077	0961	3
DUPREY FLOYD J	CW4	W-2143245	0859	1
DUPUIS ARTHUR N	MAJ	O-1119054	0860	1
DUPUIS CHARLES C	LTC	O-1585395	0461	1
DUPUIS PAUL H	LTC	O-1290570	0761	1
DUPUY HELEN C	CPT	M-0000679	0948	2
DUQUETTE HENRY B	MAJ	O-0271371	0445	2
DUQUETTE HERBERT E	MAJ	O-0188440	1057	3
DURALL BEN D	MAJ	O-1688454	1163	1
DURAN ALBERT E	LTC	O-0228522	0365	3

NAME	GRADE	SVC NO	DATE RET MO YR	RET CODE
DURAN JOHN	CPT	0-1927483	0360	2
DURAN JOHN A	MAJ	0-1919467	0165	1
DURAND CLIFFORD	MAJ	0-1944439	0861	1
DURAND PAUL J	CPT	0-1293699	0448	2
DURAND WILLIAM R	COL	0-0182973	0861	3
DURANT EDWARD J	LTC	0-2046473	0954	1
DURANT ROBERT J	LTC	0-0904741	0662	1
DURANTE VICTOR L	CW3	W-2152804	0567	1
DURBIN CLIFFORD J	LTC	0-0248298	1166	3
DURBIN GLENN R	MAJ	0-1647721	1165	1
DURBIN HARVEY	CW2	W-2144883	0260	1
DURBIN JOSEPH R	1LT	0-1292849	0146	2
DURBIN MARCELLUS	LTC	0-0397225	0265	3
DURBIN SR ROBERT F	COL	0-0119018	0457	3
DURDEN JR JOHN C	1LT	0-0445762	0245	2
DURDEN WILLIAM W	CW2	W-2121246	0848	1
DUREE JR CHARLES R	CPT	0-1822249	0445	2
DURELL HOWARD J	CPT	0-1798657	0861	1
DURETZ JACK	2LT	0-1322686	0245	2
DUREY THANE M	LTC	0-0146126	0858	3
DURFEE CHARLES W	1LT	0-1292850	0447	2
DURFEE DAVID W	MAJ	0-1796055	0759	1
DURFLINGER WILLARD L	MAJ	0-0252767	0462	3
DURFOR WALTER	MAJ	0-1165851	0161	1
DURGAN HERBERT L	1LT	0-0339644	0546	2
DURGIN SIDNEY L	CPT	0-0956815	0762	1
DURHAM ADAM W	MAJ	0-1288717	0159	1
DURHAM CHARLES T	MAJ	0-1309353	0657	1
DURHAM FELIPE	MAJ	0-1686271	0361	1
DURHAM GRACY C	LTC	0-0313390	0567	3
DURHAM JAMES F	MAJ	0-0164196	0739	1
DURHAM JOHN F	CW2	W-2210574	1163	1
DURHAM JOSEPH P	2LT	0-2206085	0951	1
DURHAM JR ISAIAH C	CPT	0-0452882	0544	2
DURHAM JR JAMES O	MAJ	0-0994746	0966	2
DURHAM LEWIS F	CW3	W-2146041	0166	1
DURHAM MAX J	LTC	0-0262529	0266	3
DURHAM WILLARD G	LTC	0-1307381	0757	1
DURHAM OSCAR L	CW2	W-2151042	1062	1
DURHAM WILLIAM C	LTC	0-0418202	0161	1
DURHAM WILLIAM M	2LT	0-1638172	0943	2
DURIE ROTH C	2LT	0-0475406	1060	1
DURIO GEORGIANNA	MAJ	L-1010555	0265	2
DURKEE DANIEL R	MAJ	0-0953626	0365	1
DURKEE HARRY O	CPT	0-0552163	0747	1
DURKEE MELVIN S	COL	0-0322845	0767	3
DURKEE RALPH H	COL	0-0159278	1048	3
DURKEE RICHARD W	CPT	0-1325809	0255	2
DURKIN HOWARD J	1LT	0-1644113	0645	2
DURKIN JR PATRICK J	WO1	W-2146424	0260	1
DURKIN PATRICK J	MAJ	0-1285911	0162	1
DURKIN ROBERT A	MAJ	0-0988668	0867	1
DURKIN ROBERT W	1LT	0-1335908	0847	2
DURKIN WILLIAM V	LTC	0-0451397	0757	1
DURNELL HOMER A	LTC	0-0423486	0164	1
DUROCHER RAYMOND E	CPT	0-1687335	1151	1
DURR GORDON V	LTC	0-0255757	0165	3
DURRETT HAROLD D	COL	0-0292450	0267	3
DURRETT JAMES B	1LT	0-1053569	1145	2
DURRETT WILLIAM B	MAJ	0-0939667	0262	1
DURSCHNITT SAMUEL	COL	0-0238074	1061	1
DURST GEORGE C	COL	0-0270788	0846	1
DURUZ WILLIS P	COL	0-0112605	0256	3
DURYEA WILBUR E	LTC	0-0235093	0166	3
DUSCHECK ROLAND P	1LT	0-1327612	0945	2
DUSELL WILLIAM H	1LT	0-0840918	0252	1
DUSHKO JR JOHN	2LT	0-1176319	0644	2
DUSINA ROBERT A	1LT	0-4042252	0264	2
DUSINBERRE PETER C J	1LT	0-0536725	0446	2
DUSK GEORGE M	LTC	0-0302985	0563	3
DUSOLD PAUL E	MAJ	0-1923663	1167	1
DUSSAULT HORACE J	LTC	0-2036240	0967	1
DUSSAULT LAWRENCE H	LTC	0-0420100	0355	1
DUSTIN HERMAN E	MAJ	0-0150595	0155	3
DUSTIN LAUREN L	MAJ	0-1300625	0557	1

NAME	GRADE	SVC NO	DATE RET MO YR	RET CODE
DUTASSY CHAPMAN	MAJ	0-1633822	0761	1
DUTCHER BURTT O	1LT	0-1642822	0546	2
DUTCHER HAROLD W	COL	0-0136406	0648	2
DUTCHER HENRY G	LTC	0-0926814	0563	1
DUTCHER JAMES T	MAJ	0-1014634	1264	1
DUTCHER SIDNEY H	CW3	W-2148720	0763	1
DUTCHESS DON D	CPT	0-2034087	0163	1
DUTKANYCH ANDREW	MAJ	0-0331389	0662	1
DUTKOWSKI CLARENCE H	2LT	0-1030755	0745	2
DUTO HENRY R	1LT	0-0289805	0549	2
DUTREAL CHARLES W	MAJ	0-1036558	0260	1
DUTT LORIS M	LTC	0-0264374	0364	3
DUTTENHOFER C S	COL	0-0182255	0954	3
DUTTENHOFER FRANCIS	MAJ	0-0411754	0346	1
DUTTON ARNOLD S	LTC	0-1310587	0266	1
DUTTON CALVIN P	MAJ	0-2033573	0365	1
DUTTON GEORGE L	LTC	0-0144621	0544	2
DUTTON JAMES B	CW2	W-2149888	0161	1
DUTTON RALPH A	COL	0-0229142	0858	1
DUTTON SHELLEY F	COL	0-0151490	0659	3
DUVA EDWARD A	MAJ	0-0347724	1165	3
DUVA NICHOLAS	LTC	0-1693855	0966	1
DUVAL CLAIBORNE	COL	0-0156771	1153	3
DUVAL CLAUDE	MAJ	0-0509746	0949	1
DUVAL ROBERT G	CPT	0-0986863	1060	1
DUVALL CHARLES T	MAJ	0-1644282	0160	1
DUVALL MEARLE D	2LT	0-0463518	0744	2
DUVALL RUFUS G	1LT	0-2010372	0951	1
DUVEL ALBERT W	LTC	0-0214635	0763	3
DUVOS LOUIS C	MAJ	0-1288874	0762	1
DUXBURY MAYNARD C	MAJ	0-0213082	1145	1
DUYSEN CARL C	MAJ	0-1577122	0454	1
DUZAN JAMES T	CW4	W-2117228	0967	1
DVOJACKY SYLVIA	1LT	N-0757058	0246	1
DVORAK ANTON E	CW3	W-2131794	1061	1
DVORSHAK ALVIN E	CW4	W-2102863	1056	1
DWIGHT FRANCIS M	MAJ	0-0138733	0956	3
DWIRE REGINALD B	LTC	0-0506469	0163	1
DWORAK ARTHUR F	MAJ	0-0246636	1265	3
DWORK KERMIT G	MAJ	0-1690709	0646	2
DWORKIN MAX M	CPT	0-0335240	1044	2
DWORKIN SAUL	CPT	0-0344944	1045	2
DWYER ELMER W	1LT	0-0220787	0865	3
DWYER FRANK H	LTC	0-1306571	0662	1
DWYER FREDERICK	CPT	0-0246774	0454	1
DWYER [illegible]ARD F	2LT	0-2043052	0445	2
DWYER GUSTAVE R	CPT	0-0917432	0847	2
DWYER HARRY S	MAJ	0-0146397	0745	2
DWYER JAMES J	MAJ	0-1320445	0159	1
DWYER JAMES F	1LT	0-1546034	0445	2
DWYER JEREMIAH H	LTC	0-[illegible]700	1266	1
DWYER [illegible] P	MAJ	[illegible]	0854	1
DWYER JOSEPH F	COL	[illegible]	0546	2
DWYER JOSEPH J	1LT	[illegible]	0346	2
DWYER JOSEPH P	CPT	0-0239650	0551	3
DWYER JR JAMES E	MAJ	0-1062581	0465	1
DWYER JR JAMES J	MAJ	0-2000843	1162	1
DWYER KENNETH J	MAJ	0-2014491	0464	1
DWYER LEO X	1LT	0-1589808	0146	1
DWYER RAYMOND F	MAJ	0-1116897	0261	1
DWYER VICTOR H	CW2	W-2209896	0865	1
DWYER WAYNE F	LTC	0-1169937	0161	1
DWYER WILLIAM J	LTC	0-1311086	0461	1
DWYER WILLIAM J	WO1	W-2128442	0146	2
DWYER WILLIAM R	LTC	0-0344931	0747	1
DYAKON MICHAEL	1LT	0-1822251	1145	2
DYAR LLOYD W	CPT	0-0967242	1061	1
DYAS JAMES H	CPT	0-0984326	0461	2
DYCUS JOHN E	CW2	W-2005555	0765	3
DYDEK FRANCIS J	MAJ	0-0974727	0567	1
DYE DALE W	LTC	0-1821695	0262	1
DYE DONALD H	COL	0-0215028	0164	3
DYE ELMER E	LTC	0-0253529	0462	3
DYE EMMETT C	MAJ	0-0152551	0857	3
DYE GEORGE F	CW3	W-2149335	1262	1

NAME	GRADE	SVC NO	DATE RET MO YR	RET CODE
DYE HAMPTON	LTC	0-0910441	0563	3
DYE HAROLD A	CPT	0-0385491	0344	2
DYE JR HOMER A	CPT	0-0190509	0553	3
DYE ROBERT K	MAJ	0-2098650	0764	1
DYE TANNER C	LTC	0-0184212	0856	3
DYE WILLIAM E	LTC	0-0378739	0764	1
DYER ALLAN D	MAJ	0-1047104	0662	1
DYER BERNARD J	MAJ	0-1297694	1061	1
DYER EDGAR N	MAJ	0-0320350	0453	1
DYER EDYTHE M	LTC	N-0736920	0964	1
DYER ELGIN F	MAJ	0-0110642	1150	3
DYER EMMETT B	CW4	W-2118307	0553	1
DYER FRANCES G	1LT	N-0768348	0946	1
DYER HAROLD D	LTC	0-2018494	0766	1
DYER JOHN W	MAJ	0-0499286	0662	1
DYER JOSEPH A	MAJ	0-0275509	0546	1
DYER JR JOHN F	MAJ	0-1541891	0758	1
DYER LARRY C	CW2	W-2150662	0566	2
DYER LOWELL	1LT	0-1312294	0845	2
DYER ROBERT A	MAJ	0-2262819	0665	1
DYER VERNON W	2LT	0-1540594	0347	2
DYER VOLNEY A	CPT	0-0328915	1166	3
DYER WILLIAM S	MAJ	0-2262821	0864	1
DYER WILLIS C	MAJ	0-0934560	0464	1
DYERS ORVILLE	COL	0-0418218	1045	2
DYESS CARLTON W	CW4	W-2101645	0659	1
DYGERT VINCENT D	LTC	0-1302789	0562	1
DYHRMANN FRED P	COL	0-0411000	1262	2
DYKE MARTIN T	LTC	0-0114056	0945	2
DYKE THEODORE	1LT	0-0435657	0145	2
DYKE WALTER J	MAJ	0-1647412	0563	1
DYKEMA RUTH D	2LT	N-0774483	0546	1
DYKEMAN CARL F	CPT	0-0372323	0549	1
DYKEMAN DANIEL W	1LT	0-1107924	0945	2
DYKEMAN RICHARD B	CPT	0-0449346	0647	1
DYKES CLAUDE R	LTC	0-1035454	1161	1
DYKES FRANKLIN B	1LT	0-0509990	0958	1
DYKES JAMES M	LTC	0-0340171	1265	3
DYKES JR WALTER W	MAJ	0-1913396	1066	1
DYKES LEONARD P	COL	0-0103934	0850	3
DYKHOUSE JAY	COL	0-0178814	0761	3
DYROFF EDMUND	MAJ	0-2012719	0855	1
DYROFF WILLIAM H	LTC	0-1284841	1048	2
DYSART GRADY L	WO1	W-2123178	0153	1
DYSART MAURICE S	LTC	0-0419978	0860	1
DYSART NELSON C	COL	0-0146178	0648	3
DYSART PALMER	CPT	0-0490661	0145	2
DYSON GEORGE T	MAJ	0-1703818	0557	1
DYSON JOHN D	LTC	0-0387099	0646	1
DYSON JOHN W	LTC	0-0220586	0563	3
DYSON RICHARD	COL	0-0229626	0161	3
DYSON WILLIAM A	CPT	0-2040772	0365	3
DYSTRA RAYMOND J	MAJ	0-2262534	1166	1
DZAMBA JOHN R	1LT	0-0391325	1044	1
DZIADUL ADAM C	LTC	0-2040795	0563	1
DZIADULA LOUIS	CPT	0-0488739	0251	1
DZIUK JOSEPH E	WO1	W-2118244	0648	1
DZURY OLGA	MAJ	N-0759300	0164	1
EABY JR WILLIAM O	CW3	W-2144580	0261	1
EACHUS CLIFFORD E	CW3	W-2149193	0863	1
EACHUS OLIVE H	MAJ	N-0756160	0463	1
EADDY BARBARA	1LT	N-0763588	1047	1
EADDY CARROLL M	1LT	0-0414318	0746	2
EADDY LIVINGSTON	CPT	0-0414319	0146	2
EADE CHARLES E	LTC	0-1950339	0964	1
EADES ERIC	LTC	0-0150377	0658	3
EADES OLIVER B	CW3	W-2147192	0961	1
EADS CHILON E	CW2	W-2150737	0655	1
EADS FORREST B	MAJ	0-1013886	1160	1
EADS JACK O	CW2	W-2210481	0761	1
EADS ROBERT L	MAJ	0-0980509	0965	1
EAGAN CHARLES C	MAJ	0-0146129	0356	3
EAGAN ROBERT W	MAJ	0-1885394	1067	2
EAGER ELWOOD B	MAJ	0-1171985	0660	1
EAGER SHERMAN W	LTC	0-0119021	0648	3

NAME	GRADE	SVC NO	DATE RET MO YR	RET CODE
EAGLE MYRON B	LTC	0-0252404	0965	3
EAGLE WILLIAM J	1LT	0-0244555	0753	3
EAKER ARTHUR T	LTC	0-0166935	0756	3
EAKER DOYLE W	CW3	W-2141262	1262	1
EAKER LAMONT J	LTC	0-0280298	1059	3
EAKINS RAY C	MAJ	0-0577429	1060	1
EALES KEITH	1LT	0-1047952	0345	2
EALY ELFRIEDA W	CPT	N-0772226	0347	1
EARDLEY CATHERINE	CPT	N-0772077	0448	1
EARDLEY JOHN K	CPT	0-0253472	1044	2
EARDLEY SAMUEL	2LT	0-1306826	1045	2
EARGLE ROY F	MAJ	0-0497368	0149	1
EARHART CHARLES E	LTC	0-0334600	0146	2
EARHART DANIEL E	LTC	0-1635822	0864	1
EARHART HUGH T	CW2	W-2152843	0666	1
EARL DALE E	CW4	W-2145721	0566	1
EARL DUNCAN O	WO1	W-2108068	0161	3
EARL EDWARD L	WO1	W-2105938	0148	1
EARL JR JAMES R	MAJ	0-1119695	0962	1
EARL JR N CLARKSON	LTC	0-0901946	0744	2
EARL JR TONY H	CW3	W-2151513	0766	1
EARL LLOYD R	LTC	0-0340568	0647	2
EARL ROBERT J	MAJ	0-4006899	0567	1
EARL VINCENT D	MAJ	0-1645354	1158	1
EARL WAYNE A	MAJ	0-1550581	1157	2
EARL WOODROW P	CPT	0-1303313	0446	2
EARLE FREDERICK	WO1	W-2110744	0147	1
EARLE GEORGE W	CPT	0-0971692	1160	1
EARLE JR MILTON H	LTC	0-0391589	1266	1
EARLE PIERCE	CPT	0-1306253	0945	2
EARLE RICHARD G	LTC	0-0306106	0462	1
EARLE WALLACE H	LTC	0-0355816	0661	1
EARLE WILLIAM A	CW3	W-2208963	0567	1
EARLEY HAROLD F	LTC	0-1167406	0261	2
EARLEY JANE S	2LT	N-0731307	1144	1
EARLEY JOHN J	LTC	0-0364653	0863	1
EARLIX LOUIS	LTC	0-0180765	0656	3
EARLL THEODORE R	LTC	0-0331584	0462	1
EARLY ALBERT C	MAJ	0-1016670	0862	1
EARLY CHARLES O	1LT	0-0907544	0345	2
EARLY EDWIN Y	CPT	0-1648413	0146	2
EARLY JOHN A	COL	0-1010100	0561	1
EARLY JOHN M	1LT	0-0173141	0744	2
EARLY JOHN W	COL	0-0201816	0753	3
EARLY JR STEPHEN T	1LT	0-1325382	1145	2
EARLY ROBERT	CW3	W-2122815	0261	1
EARNEST JAMES W	CW3	W-2101647	0354	1
EARNEY JR CHARLES E	CPT	0-1000744	0658	1
EARNHEART RICHARD L	COL	0-0236903	0765	3
EARP CARLYLE R	MAJ	0-0171085	0251	3
EARP JULIAN R	CPT	0-2262755	1061	1
EARP SR RALPH N	COL	0-0210384	0563	3
EASBY JOHN P	COL	0-0177754	0855	1
EASLER CARVIN R	LTC	0-0506114	0559	1
EASLER WILBUR O	MAJ	0-1918904	0565	1
EASLEY BERNICE	MAJ	N-0761213	1164	1
EASLEY CHARLES L	LTC	0-1019774	0166	1
EASLEY DAVE L	CW3	W-2207958	0666	1
EASLEY ELDON A	MAJ	0-1185489	0657	1
EASLEY JAMES L	1LT	0-1173225	1148	2
EASLEY JAMES P	LTC	0-0138135	1048	3
EASLEY JOHN R	LTC	0-1584168	0462	1
EASLEY JR DAVID C	LTC	0-0277584	0264	3
EASLEY MARION O	CW2	W-2149277	0660	1
EASLEY PURVIS F	CW3	W-2147718	1263	1
EASLEY RAY K	LTC	0-0104303	0458	3
EASLEY ROY W	B G	0-0172501	0251	3
EASLEY SMILEY T	CW3	W-2147038	0163	1
EASON ALTON W	CW2	W-2104675	0645	2
EASON CHESLEY A	CW3	W-2146113	1161	1
EASON EBEN O	WO1	W-2009250	1067	3
EASON GEORGE W	LTC	0-0363829	1060	2
EASON HENRY N	LTC	0-0223705	0543	1
EASON MILTON C	CPT	0-0289316	0966	3
EASON TALMADGE O	CPT	0-2039548	1157	1

NAME	GRADE	SVC NO	DATE RET MO YR	RET CODE
EASON WALTER T	CPT	O-0451970	0952	2
EASSON GRAEME S	LTC	O-0200425	0655	3
EASSON WILLIAM C	COL	O-0235257	0659	3
EAST ALTON M	CPT	O-0920221	0647	2
EAST EDGAR E	CPT	O-1287159	1143	2
EAST GARLAND M	1LT	O-0166850	0855	3
EAST HERMAN M	CPT	O-0394999	0962	1
EAST PAUL G	MAJ	O-1180478	0363	1
EAST ROBERT V	CW2	W-2116818	0546	2
EAST ROLAND L	LTC	O-0397231	1160	1
EASTER CARTER G	CPT	O-1300007	0555	1
EASTER CHARLES E	CW2	W-2143764	0559	1
EASTERDAY DAVID M	COL	O-0367790	0161	1
EASTERDAY KENNETH	MAJ	O-1684993	0765	1
EASTERDAY VANBUREN	CPT	O-0969823	0861	1
EASTERLING ALBERT C	MAJ	O-0963152	0667	3
EASTERLING CELCIS	1LT	O-1588108	0146	2
EASTERLING GEORGE R	MAJ	O-0274165	1165	3
EASTERLING MARCUS C	LTC	O-0271178	0347	2
EASTERLING OPAL B	2LT	N-0726204	0445	1
EASTERLING ROBERT C	COL	O-1000106	0762	1
EASTERLING WALTER D	LTC	O-1702201	0146	1
EASTHAM JR COWAN C	LTC	O-1330529	0267	1
EASTHAM RAMON G	CPT	O-1342067	1160	1
EASTHAM WILLIAM R	CW2	W-2144132	0552	1
EASTIN VERNON K	LTC	O-1010007	0461	1
EASTLAND FREDERIC R	LTC	O-0282899	0262	3
EASTLAND GEORGE A	CPT	O-0977628	0162	1
EASTLAND WALTON E	CW2	W-2105888	0648	1
EASTMAN ALBERT E	MAJ	O-1178773	0764	1
EASTMAN ARTHUR F	CPT	O-0192431	0263	3
EASTMAN CHARLES A	MAJ	O-1334988	1059	1
EASTMAN CYRUS D	LTC	O-0300775	0766	3
EASTMAN ERIC I	LTC	O-0402052	0361	1
EASTMAN GORDON E	CW3	W-2149289	0663	1
EASTMAN JAMES M	CW2	W-2116380	0958	1
EASTMAN JR WILLIAM A	1LT	O-1325588	0246	2
EASTMAN ORAN S	MAJ	O-1685701	0663	1
EASTMAN RAY	MAJ	O-0500000	0354	2
EASTMAN RUSSELL V	COL	O-0174251	0258	3
EASTMAN SEELEY H	LTC	O-1055273	0167	1
EASTMAN WALTER R	1LT	O-1293933	0246	2
EASTMAN WILLIAM E	MAJ	O-0494552	0347	2
EASTMEAD JOSEPH H	MAJ	O-2294697	0663	1
EASTON GEORGE D	MAJ	O-1876400	0867	1
EASTON JANE M	CPT	N-0722371	0646	1
EASTON JOHN W	COL	O-0225721	0664	3
EASTON JR OSCAR E	LTC	O-1587942	1061	1
EASTON MYRON N	1LT	O-1166474	1055	1
EASTON RALPH L	MAJ	O-1011148	0462	1
EASTON WALTER J	COL	O-0308641	0357	3
EASTRIDGE BENJAMIN R	CPT	O-1321759	0147	1
EASTWOLD JOHN D	MAJ	O-0154115	0347	2
EASTWOOD FRANCIS J	MAJ	O-1543935	0964	1
EASTWOOD HENRY C	1LT	O-1822546	0847	2
EATON ALLEN L	CW3	W-2152339	0563	1
EATON GEORGE E	COL	O-0323370	1153	1
EATON GEORGE S	1LT	O-1541353	0245	2
EATON HARRY E	COL	O-0365921	0864	1
EATON HUGH M	MAJ	O-1011030	0660	1
EATON JACK	LTC	O-1581678	0457	1
EATON JAMES A	MAJ	O-1642029	1058	2
EATON JAMES W	LTC	O-0464222	0154	1
EATON JR GEORGE W	CW2	W-2143157	0860	1
EATON JR HARVEY D	LTC	O-0188315	1152	3
EATON JR HOMER D	M G	O-0201691	0962	3
EATON LINDSEY F	LTC	O-0452200	0361	1
EATON MILDRED C	1LT	L-0909135	0645	2
EATON PETER J	LTC	O-1285027	1060	1
EATON RICHARD E	LTC	O-0394783	0461	1
EATON RICHARD J	LTC	O-0165737	0351	3
EATON RICHARD O	LTC	O-0309077	0967	3
EATON ROBERT L	CW3	W-2143409	0659	1
EATON WALTER J	MAJ	O-0223422	0353	3
EATON WILLIAM M	CW2	W-2105998	0345	2

NAME	GRADE	SVC NO	DATE RET MO YR	RET CODE
EAVENSON JOHN H	WO1	W-2109883	1045	2
EAVES LLOYD L	CW2	W-2152948	0360	1
EAVES ROBBY M	MAJ	O-1642030	1058	1
EAVEY HARRY R	CW3	W-2143504	0566	1
EAZARSKY THOMAS E	LTC	O-0980629	0563	1
EBAUGH DONALD D	CW2	W-2148315	1060	1
EBAUGH JR PAUL L	1LT	O-1061944	1145	2
EBBECKE GEORGE V	CPT	O-1303074	0259	1
EBBELER PAUL D	CPT	O-0349910	1065	3
EBBERT CHARLES A	MAJ	O-0304035	0452	1
EBBITT JOSEPH M	COL	O-1002207	0765	1
EBECK CHARLES F	MAJ	O-1052334	0661	2
EBEL ALFRED	COL	O-0361048	0567	3
EBEL HENRY N	MAJ	O-1081695	0463	1
EBELING JAMES C	MAJ	O-0495916	0657	1
EBER LESSER	1LT	O-2040936	1045	2
EBERHARD CLARENCE J	CW4	W-2123199	0356	1
EBERHARD JOHN L	MAJ	O-0979241	0662	1
EBERHARDT ELMER L B	MAJ	O-0111332	0753	3
EBERHARDT HARRY G	MAJ	O-1311748	0461	1
EBERHARDT JOHN J	MAJ	O-1284842	0949	2
EBERHARDT JR HIRAM C	MAJ	O-1301122	0961	1
EBERHARDT MARTIN W	CW3	W-2143198	0264	1
EBERHARDT ROBERT S	CW3	W-2154665	0562	1
EBERHART JOHN H	LTC	O-0194038	0756	3
EBERHART ROBERT D	1LT	O-1861886	0353	2
EBERHART VINCENT R	MAJ	O-1874711	1065	1
EBERLE HERMAN J	MAJ	O-0977258	1263	1
EBERLEIN CARL A	MAJ	O-1317153	1062	1
EBERLEIN CHARLES L	WO1	W-2127814	0645	2
EBERLEIN WILLIAM	MAJ	O-0100713	0256	3
EBERLY CHARLES W	LTC	O-1650511	0465	1
EBERLY GEORGE D	CPT	O-0323618	0445	2
EBERLY JACOB Y	MAJ	O-0201256	0153	1
EBERSOLE F LESLIE	COL	O-0275646	0446	2
EBERSOLE ROBERT P	CPT	O-0539531	0547	2
EBERSTEIN JULIUS S	COL	O-0398873	0965	3
EBERT CLAUDE S	CPT	O-0919179	0345	2
EBERT JOHN A	1LT	O-1580894	0950	1
EBERT LOUIS	MAJ	O-0313214	1044	2
EBERT RALPH L	CW2	RW-2203549	0264	1
EBERT ROBERT D	2LT	O-0442724	0743	2
EBERT ROBERT V	LTC	O-2046957	0263	1
EBERTS FRANCIS W	MAJ	O-1106111	0762	1
EBERTS JR RALPH T	1LT	O-1547283	0546	2
EBETINO MICHAEL T	LTC	O-2015426	0767	1
EBNER JR CHARLES F	CW3	W-2143136	0564	1
EBRIGHT ALBERT P	COL	O-0171377	1061	3
EBY CYRUS K	CPT	O-1920182	1164	1
EBY LOUIS R	MAJ	O-0293589	1051	3
ECCARD ALICE T	1LT	N-0755525	0845	1
ECCARD JOHN M	1LT	O-2047633	1145	2
ECCLES FRANK	COL	O-0361182	0556	1
ECCLESTON THOMAS A	LTC	O-1041337	0461	1
ECHANDI FRANCISCO	MAJ	O-1329105	1164	1
ECHOLS CHARLES L	2LT	O-1824833	0345	2
ECHOLS CLYDE F	2LT	O-1300626	0543	2
ECHOLS EUGENE S	LTC	O-0911505	1047	2
ECHOLS GEORGE P	CW2	W-2145637	0857	1
ECHOLS JOSEPH L	LTC	O-1296502	0563	1
ECHOLS RALPH W	LTC	O-0489833	0657	1
ECHTERHOFF HARRY R	LTC	O-1699803	0446	2
ECK ELDEN	CW4	W-2001850	0966	3
ECK JR HERMAN	CPT	O-2262495	0656	1
ECK PAUL J	CW2	W-2145022	0157	1
ECK STANLEY E	1LT	O-1591679	0246	2
ECKAM ANNA L	2LT	N-0700185	0637	1
ECKARD CHESTER R	CPT	O-1031634	0346	2
ECKARD GEORGE W	MAJ	O-1645542	1060	1
ECKAUS THEODORE M	LTC	O-1047280	1162	1
ECKBERG ORVILLE E	LTC	O-1683305	1164	1
ECKBURG JOHN T	1LT	O-1292492	0847	2
ECKDALL FRANK F	LTC	O-0300585	0667	3
ECKE ROBERT S	LTC	O-0438083	0546	2
ECKELS JACK C	CPT	O-0567602	0657	1

NAME	GRADE	SVC NO	DATE RET MO YR	RET CODE
ECKENFELS WILBUR C	CPT	O-1339150	0165	2
ECKER CHARLES T	WO1	W-2101281	0844	2
ECKER JR JOSEPH J	MAJ	O-0356854	0446	2
ECKER RAY E	LTC	O-0405162	0660	1
ECKERMAN DANIEL W	COL	O-0301414	0958	3
ECKERT ALBERT R	CW3	W-2145156	1062	1
ECKERT CHARLES J	1LT	O-1303125	0850	1
ECKERT JOHN C	LTC	O-0276371	0359	3
ECKERT JR HENRY G	1LT	O-0538086	1045	1
ECKERT RALPH G	LTC	O-1283227	0567	3
ECKERT ROBERT A	LTC	O-1115248	0264	1
ECKERT ROBERT W	1LT	O-1311381	0845	2
ECKERT THOMAS A	MAJ	O-1040213	0157	1
ECKFELDT ROGER W	M G	O-0177191	1051	3
ECKHART ARTHUR G	COL	O-0302678	1064	3
ECKHOFF EARL E	CPT	O-0490425	1053	1
ECKHOFF WILLIAM R	MAJ	O-1297176	0261	1
ECKHOUTE RENE V	CW2	W-2118027	0645	2
ECKLER JAMES A	WO1	W-2106779	0965	2
ECKLEY RALPH E	CW2	W-2207386	0761	1
ECKMAN IRVING I	CPT	O-1690580	0946	2
ECKMAN PAUL R	MAJ	O-2001672	0859	1
ECKMANN CLAUS	CW4	W-2145053	0157	1
ECKSTEIN DELBERT C	CW3	W-2142757	0861	1
ECKSTEIN HARRY	1LT	O-0289250	0962	3
ECKWALL ARVID O	MAJ	O-0497367	0956	1
ECOFF JAY M	CW3	W-2205602	0859	1
ECOFF JR ALFRED H	CPT	O-1184811	0747	2
ECOFF ROBERT W	LTC	O-1284113	0657	1
ECUYER ELMER O	MAJ	O-0916753	0646	1
EDBERG HOWARD L	LTC	O-1821696	0261	1
EDDEN JAMES A	LTC	O-0524476	0658	2
EDDINGER ADOLPH G	1LT	O-0150358	0755	3
EDDY ALLEN C	CPT	O-0956691	0159	1
EDDY DAVID W	LTC	O-0322994	0353	3
EDDY EMERSON W	CPT	O-0231933	0864	3
EDDY GEORGE P	CW2	W-3100259	0562	1
EDDY JOHN B	CPT	O-0453259	0144	2
EDDY JOHN L	COL	O-0121528	0255	3
EDDY LAURENCE W	COL	O-0162619	0560	3
EDDY LEVI C	COL	O-0198297	0647	2
EDDY MILTON A	LTC	O-1172442	0361	1
EDDY RICHARD T	LTC	O-0122404	0244	2
EDDY ROBERT A	MAJ	O-0262054	0356	3
EDDY ROBERT D	LTC	O-0164366	0154	3
EDDY ROGER W	MAJ	O-1291790	0946	1
EDDY SAMUEL G	COL	O-0283950	0858	1
EDDY THOMAS H	LTC	O-0243734	1053	3
EDDY WALDO O	MAJ	O-0384102	0559	1
EDE ALBERT B	COL	O-0208024	0353	3
EDEBURN PAUL W	CPT	O-0256055	0654	3
EDEL ARLYEEN E	CPT	N-0756142	1046	1
EDELE FRED L	MAJ	O-0154038	1049	3
EDELEN JOSEPH F	CPT	O-1289055	0745	1
EDELEN STEPHEN W	LTC	O-1012333	1264	1
EDELL NATHAN G	CPT	O-0447353	1045	2
EDELMAN BERNARD L	CPT	O-0230306	0164	3
EDELMAN MAURICE	LTC	O-0888465	0353	1
EDELSON EDMOND K	CPT	O-0367391	0144	1
EDELSON MARSHALL	CPT	O-4073403	0961	2
EDELSTEIN LEWIS	CW4	W-2103697	0659	1
EDELSTEIN MONROE M	CPT	O-1689645	0544	2
EDENFIELD ROBERT A	MAJ	O-1288877	0747	2
EDENFIELD ROY P	LTC	O-1030466	0666	1
EDENS ELVERT M	COL	O-1114911	0365	1
EDENS ORVILL E	1LT	O-0980557	0857	1
EDER FRED M	LTC	O-0226955	1164	3
EDER HELEN M C	CPT	N-0724510	0161	2
EDER HERBERT R	LTC	O-1175697	0163	1
EDER STEVE J	1LT	O-1042553	1044	2
EDERLE WILLIAM C	WO1	W-2148647	0363	1
EDFORS HUGO W	CPT	O-1058989	0752	1
EDGAR CLIFFORD M	MAJ	O-1826379	0557	1
EDGAR GERALD N	MAJ	O-1325205	0764	1
EDGAR HAROLD H	CPT	O-0114096	0256	3

NAME	GRADE	SVC NO	DATE RET MO YR	RET CODE
EDGAR HAROLD L	MAJ	O-0229861	0258	3
EDGAR JACKIE E	MAJ	O-1341764	0163	1
EDGAR JOHN L	LTC	O-0481323	0767	3
EDGAR JR FRANK M	LTC	O-2026501	0566	1
EDGAR LAWRENCE E	MAJ	O-1586553	0557	1
EDGAR LYLE W	MAJ	O-0490062	1055	1
EDGAR PERCY F	CPT	O-0142524	0648	3
EDGAR RALPH G	LTC	O-1295692	0264	1
EDGAR RICHARD N	CPT	O-1037365	1145	2
EDGAR ROBERT C	COL	O-0258257	0759	1
EDGAR THOMAS C	MAJ	O-1011152	0147	2
EDGAR WILLIAM A	COL	O-0386408	1054	1
EDGAR WILLIAM C	LTC	O-0185149	0157	3
EDGAR WILLIAM H	1LT	O-1303477	0447	2
EDGCOMB ROY H	CW4	W-2121253	0157	1
EDGE CORNELIUS	LTC	O-1060086	0967	1
EDGE JOHN B	1LT	O-1043614	0146	1
EDGE JOHN W	CPT	O-1046077	0746	2
EDGE JR WILLIAM N	2LT	O-0992531	0352	1
EDGERLY JOHN P	MAJ	O-1575940	0163	1
EDGERTON ERNEST B	LTC	O-0233983	1162	3
EDGERTON IRVINE A	LTC	O-0360920	0464	3
EDGERTON JR C F	LTC	O-0125248	1054	3
EDGERTON KARL A	COL	O-0174291	0359	2
EDGEWORTH HARVEY E	CPT	O-1312894	1145	2
EDGEWORTH JR R H	MAJ	O-2024151	0157	1
EDGING BOYD R	CW2	W-2207091	0864	2
EDGINGTON DONALD W	MAJ	O-1336048	0960	1
EDGINGTON OLGA M	LTC	N-0729029	1062	1
EDGMON DON T	LTC	O-1320717	0666	1
EDGMON WARD F	1LT	O-0399975	0344	2
EDINGTON ALFRED A	COL	O-0241992	1054	1
EDINGTON HELEN H	MAJ	N-0802155	1065	1
EDLAVITCH MARY W	MAJ	N-0742317	0767	3
EDLESTON ROBERT W	CW3	W-2145544	0863	1
EDLIN GUY	CPT	O-1101820	0448	2
EDLUND RICHARD E	CPT	O-0547710	0863	2
EDMARK RICHARD C	LTC	O-1010163	0762	1
EDMINSTER ROBERT M	CPT	O-1118571	0660	1
EDMISTEN EDWARD E	MAJ	O-2262444	1164	1
EDMISTON EDWARD J	MAJ	O-0885700	0457	1
EDMISTON FRED W	COL	O-0225258	1044	1
EDMISTON LEWIS L	LTC	O-1101821	0866	1
EDMISTON WALTER A	LTC	O-0331569	1264	3
EDMONDS ALONZO L	LTC	O-0287104	1165	3
EDMONDS CHARLES D	LTC	O-1080928	0265	3
EDMONDS EUGENE H	MAJ	O-1339523	0663	1
EDMONDS HOWARD L	LTC	O-1541750	1164	1
EDMONDS JAMES F	M G	O-0125247	0648	3
EDMONDS N F	CW2	W-2149860	0365	1
EDMONDS RAYMOND G	LTC	O-0565267	1164	1
EDMONDS ROBERT E	COL	O-0382042	0355	1
EDMONDS ROBERT E	MAJ	O-0995718	0966	1
EDMONDS WILLIAM S	2LT	O-1324249	1044	2
EDMONDSON C S R	COL	O-0216305	0258	3
EDMONDSON FRANK M	2LT	O-1321694	0744	2
EDMONDSON FRAZOR T	MAJ	O-0246884	0964	3
EDMONDSON JOHN R	1LT	O-1547285	0964	3
EDMONSON ROBERT G	MAJ	O-1824445	0561	1
EDMONSTON ALBERT E	LTC	O-1573177	0660	1
EDMONSTON ALEXANDER	COL	O-0199371	0563	3
EDMONSTON CHARLES M	MAJ	O-1106112	1157	1
EDMONSTON WEBSTER V	CW2	W-2151347	0460	2
EDMUNDS CHARLES R	CPT	O-0325976	0359	3
EDNEY CHARLES W	LTC	O-1575941	1061	1
EDRINGTON JOHN R	CW2	W-2152498	1062	1
EDRINGTON JOHN W	1LT	O-1294997	1045	2
EDRIS EDWIN N	LTC	O-0283083	1160	1
EDSALL CLARENCE A	1LT	O-1322535	1045	2
EDSALL JAMES P	MAJ	O-1323645	0461	1
EDSON CARROLL A	COL	O-0121087	1051	3
EDSON EDSON A	LTC	O-0241360	1265	3
EDSON JOHN C	MAJ	O-0191744	0263	3
EDSON MARIE L	MAJ	N-0730534	1061	1
EDSON RALPH A	LTC	O-0310987	0659	3

292-560 O - 68 - 10

NAME	GRADE	SVC NO	DATE RET MO YR	RET CODE
EDSON SAMUEL S	COL	0-0251903	0666	3
EDSTROM VIRGIL F	CW4	W-2117160	0860	1
EDWARDES LIONEL C	MAJ	0-0445054	0550	1
EDWARDS ALBERT B	CPT	0-0266984	0855	3
EDWARDS ALFRED C	LTC	0-0341618	0765	1
EDWARDS ALFRED H	2LT	0-2003970	0254	2
EDWARDS ALLEN	MAJ	0-1336896	1161	1
EDWARDS ALTON B	CPT	0-0482771	0146	2
EDWARDS AROL L	MAJ	0-2027287	0861	1
EDWARDS AULDON G	1LT	0-1305765	0146	2
EDWARDS BARNEY H	MAJ	0-0203568	0247	2
EDWARDS CHARLES F	CPT	0-1294109	0346	2
EDWARDS CHARLES H	COL	0-0182236	1057	3
EDWARDS CLARENCE	CW2	W-2151875	0761	1
EDWARDS CLARENCE W	MAJ	0-1306510	0261	1
EDWARDS CLARK	LTC	0-0467279	0862	1
EDWARDS CLIFFORD R	CW2	W-2206295	0365	1
EDWARDS CYRUS L	MAJ	0-0216718	0360	3
EDWARDS DAN M	1LT	0-0518824	0445	2
EDWARDS DAVE W	MAJ	0-1047106	0861	1
EDWARDS DENNIS W A	LTC	0-1180480	0854	1
EDWARDS EDWARD C	1LT	0-1289226	0944	1
EDWARDS EDWIN A	CW4	W-2114941	0360	1
EDWARDS ELMER W	LTC	0-1697883	1160	1
EDWARDS ELZIE F	1LT	0-1547597	0346	1
EDWARDS ERNEST A	MAJ	0-1032753	1161	1
EDWARDS ERNEST F	MAJ	0-0496864	0154	1
EDWARDS ERNEST P	COL	0-0261396	0754	1
EDWARDS FORREST W	COL	0-0290775	0953	3
EDWARDS FRANCIS R	MAJ	0-0246939	0847	2
EDWARDS FRANK J	CW3	W-2150723	0662	1
EDWARDS GEORGE A	CW4	W-2108157	0659	1
EDWARDS GEORGE F	MAJ	0-1589179	0859	1
EDWARDS GEORGE N	LTC	0-1588540	1264	1
EDWARDS GILBERT H	LTC	0-0229998	0264	3
EDWARDS GUY D	LTC	0-0222593	0948	3
EDWARDS HAROLD B	CW2	W-2147971	0160	1
EDWARDS HARRY A	LTC	0-0265277	0365	3
EDWARDS HELENE R	2LT	N-0755650	0845	1
EDWARDS HUGH F	CPT	0-0449155	0146	2
EDWARDS HUGH J	LTC	0-0405902	0660	1
EDWARDS J P	LTC	0-0452881	0364	1
EDWARDS JACK C	MAJ	0-2263196	0662	1
EDWARDS JACK G	CW3	W-2145105	0762	1
EDWARDS JAMES E	CPT	0-1822781	1060	1
EDWARDS JAMES H	1LT	0-1292853	0546	2
EDWARDS JAMES H	CPT	0-2000739	0457	1
EDWARDS JAMES W	CW3	RW-2152035	0265	1
EDWARDS JANE B	1LT	N-0755951	0945	1
EDWARDS JESSE W	1LT	0-1107401	0645	2
EDWARDS JOEL H	CW4	W-2113510	0760	1
EDWARDS JOHN G	COL	0-0155358	0953	1
EDWARDS JOHN H	MAJ	0-0403545	0646	2
EDWARDS JOHN W	MAJ	0-1286457	0859	1
EDWARDS JOHNSON P	COL	0-0235024	0661	3
EDWARDS JR F D	1LT	0-1172443	0246	1
EDWARDS JR GEORGE W	CPT	0-1289403	0248	2
EDWARDS JR JAMES H	LTC	0-1944673	1161	1
EDWARDS JR JAMES R	CW2	W-2203527	0963	1
EDWARDS JR JAMES S	MAJ	0-0371222	1045	2
EDWARDS JR KENNETH J	LTC	0-0519254	0666	1
EDWARDS JR T W	CPT	0-1106704	1045	2
EDWARDS KENNETH R	CPT	0-0504547	0547	1
EDWARDS L ROBERT J	COL	0-0199541	1150	3
EDWARDS LEGRONDE	LTC	0-1109265	0662	1
EDWARDS LELAND W	MAJ	0-2014580	1264	1
EDWARDS LEON E	CW3	W-2143214	0861	1
EDWARDS MANLEY W	CPT	0-0228344	1165	3
EDWARDS MARIAN R G	2LT	N-0756954	1044	1
EDWARDS NORMAN	MAJ	0-2263158	1162	1
EDWARDS NORMAN E	COL	0-0246054	0953	3
EDWARDS ODIS J	CW2	W-2147156	0357	1
EDWARDS PAUL L	LTC	0-0485120	0665	1
EDWARDS PERCY R	CW2	W-2143716	0861	1
EDWARDS POMEROY	1LT	0-0124899	0553	3
EDWARDS RALPH R	LTC	0-0241471	1057	3
EDWARDS REESE F	MAJ	0-1103615	1061	1
EDWARDS REXFORD C	CPT	0-0293300	0145	2
EDWARDS RICHARD R	CPT	0-0965600	0359	1
EDWARDS ROBERT A	MAJ	0-1342256	0862	1
EDWARDS ROBERT P	COL	0-0439491	0167	3
EDWARDS ROBERT W	COL	0-1308618	0867	1
EDWARDS ROY W	LTC	0-1114467	1262	1
EDWARDS SHERWOOD C	MAJ	0-0299998	0946	2
EDWARDS SMITH	LTC	0-1100564	0663	1
EDWARDS SOLOMON C	LTC	0-0257656	1062	1
EDWARDS SR ROBERT O	CW3	W-2203885	0767	1
EDWARDS SR WILBUR P	MAJ	0-1341765	0662	1
EDWARDS STANLEY	COL	0-0197962	0355	3
EDWARDS THOMAS L	LTC	0-0243038	1059	3
EDWARDS THOMAS M	CPT	0-0369292	0543	2
EDWARDS THOMAS W	CPT	0-0238340	1045	2
EDWARDS WALTER C	CW4	W-2114217	1160	1
EDWARDS WALTER R	CPT	0-1797800	0763	1
EDWARDS WALTON L	LTC	0-1178775	0363	1
EDWARDS WARREN C	1LT	0-1300627	0646	1
EDWARDS WILLIAM A	LTC	0-0271015	0563	3
EDWARDS WILLIAM A	LTC	0-0351514	0758	1
EDWARDS WILLIAM G	LTC	0-1845710	1158	3
EDWARDS WILLIAM H	MAJ	0-0242969	0963	3
EDWARDS WILLIAM J	LTC	0-0474704	0655	2
EDWARDS WILLIAM R	CW3	W-2143430	0956	1
EDWARDS WILLIAM W	LTC	0-1283568	0465	1
EDWARDS WOODROW W	WO1	W-2132077	0656	1
EELLS EARNEST E	LTC	0-0196250	1152	3
EFFINGER VICTOR W	MAJ	0-1536401	0962	1
EFFORD JOHN T	COL	0-0301202	1063	3
EFFRON DAVID V	CPT	0-0332871	0645	2
EFFRON MORTON	CPT	0-0424504	0246	2
EGAL HENRY J	LTC	0-1549932	0164	1
EGALKA MORRIS	CPT	0-1705270	0646	2
EGAN DONALD H	LTC	0-0388466	0761	1
EGAN EDWARD J	CPT	0-0531550	0645	2
EGAN ELIZABETH	1LT	N-0728357	1045	1
EGAN JAMES D	CPT	0-1824835	1146	2
EGAN JAMES J	LTC	0-0413625	0363	3
EGAN JAMES J	MAJ	0-1846421	0963	1
EGAN JR HORACE F	LTC	0-0310937	1052	1
EGAN THOMAS J	CPT	0-0359133	0947	1
EGBERT CLARENCE H	1LT	0-0435198	1045	2
EGBERT HAROLD S	LTC	0-1944674	0655	1
EGBERT HENRY C	MAJ	0-0409000	0547	2
EGBERT WALTER W	LTC	0-2042953	0564	1
EGDAHL LAWRENCE R	LTC	0-0298601	0963	3
EGELER IVAN P	LTC	0-1578417	0962	1
EGERER EGMONT A	MAJ	0-0302457	0545	2
EGERT CHESTER W	MAJ	0-0519333	1055	2
EGGAN FREDERICK	LTC	0-1950341	1166	1
EGGEN JOHN W	CW3	W-2204977	0266	1
EGGEN KARL M	COL	0-0263365	0466	3
EGGEN MILTON P	MAJ	0-0478754	0549	1
EGGER ALPHONSE J	LTC	0-1102714	0465	1
EGGERMAN WENDELL F	LTC	0-1535623	0865	1
EGGERS JULES H	CPT	0-1577127	1149	1
EGGERS RUTH H	CPT	N-0900079	0358	2
EGGERT HOWARD L	2LT	0-1323813	1144	2
EGGERT JAY R	1LT	0-1035752	1145	2
EGGIMAN FRED	CPT	0-0496790	0948	1
EGGIMANN EMIL L	COL	0-0451536	1066	1
EGGLER ALVIN F	CPT	0-1846278	0546	2
EGGLER HENRY J	MAJ	0-0297047	0966	3
EGGLESTON ANNA L	1LT	N-0761926	0846	1
EGGLESTON GEORGE L	LTC	0-0181376	0862	3
EGGLESTON HERBERT G	MAJ	0-0181429	0154	3
EGGLESTON HOMER L	CW4	W-2123030	1062	1
EGGLESTON ROBERT T	LTC	0-0318098	0363	3
EGGLETON LEO J	CPT	0-0147202	0842	2
EGGUM DONALD J	MAJ	0-0975062	0365	1
EGLESTON NATHANIEL	B G	0-0242017	0648	3
EGLOFF GEORGE J	CPT	0-0465012	0754	1
EGNER RAYMOND A	COL	0-0256064	0958	3
EHARDT HENRY	CPT	0-2036424	0851	1
EHINGER JOHN	COL	0-0169673	0750	3
EHLEN GEORGE H	2LT	0-0397179	0742	2
EHLENFELDT VERNON B	MAJ	0-0974091	0165	1
EHLER ERNEST W	LTC	0-0972975	0265	1
EHLERS ANTOINETTE	2LT	N-0724062	0145	2
EHLERS EDWARD C	MAJ	0-1799944	1061	1
EHLERS HARRY C	LTC	0-0452016	0361	1
EHLERS WALDO H	LTC	0-0248205	0962	3
EHLERT CHARLES O	COL	0-0309902	0566	3
EHLERT RAYMOND A	1LT	0-1304880	0446	2
EHLIN WILLIAM	2LT	0-1288878	0944	2
EHMKE ROBERT C	MAJ	0-1589809	0863	1
EHMSEN WALTER C	CW2	W-2151683	0861	1
EHNI JACOB	CPT	0-2010984	0755	1
EHREN ELMER B	1LT	0-0372987	0144	2
EHREN JOHN A	LTC	0-0193590	0959	3
EHRENBURG OTTO	LTC	0-0284154	1266	3
EHRESMANN STANLEY S	LTC	0-0450835	0756	1
EHRET DONALD M	WO1	W-2114617	0244	2
EHRET LESTER A	MAJ	0-0968140	0557	2
EHRGOTT WINSTON W	LTC	0-0241647	1061	3
EHRHARDT MARTIN W	CW3	W-2152995	0665	1
EHRHART EUGENE J	COL	0-0506966	0654	3
EHRLICH DAVID	LTC	0-0324925	0460	1
EHRLICH GERALD	2LT	0-1328582	0645	2
EHRLICH HERMAN	MAJ	0-1689638	1145	2
EHRMANN CHARLES H	LTC	0-1107928	1162	1
EHRSAM HARLEY A	2LT	0-0918407	1143	2
EHRSTEIN MARY A	1LT	N-0758136	0248	1
EIBER HAROLD B	MAJ	0-0492670	0246	2
EICHBAUM JOSEPH H	CPT	0-1647865	0847	2
EICHELBERGER JOHN C	CPT	0-1582679	0460	1
EICHELBERGER R R	MAJ	0-1584175	1060	1
EICHEN MARVIN A	1LT	0-1012343	0845	2
EICHENBERG HERMANN R	COL	0-0276982	0864	3
EICHENBERGER EARL R	LTC	0-0949748	0167	1
EICHENBERGER GENE R	2LT	0-0393746	0143	2
EICHERS ARMUND J	CW2	W-2214554	0867	1
EICHHOLTZ VERNER F	LTC	0-0300236	0147	2
EICHHORN ADRIAN A	MAJ	0-1020405	0463	1
EICHHORN DAVID M	LTC	0-0482124	0266	3
EICHHORN LEROY A	CW2	W-2152157	0161	1
EICHINGER JR JACK W	COL	0-0226940	1064	3
EICHLER ARTHUR L	LTC	0-0348515	1165	3
EICHLER THOMAS O	LTC	0-0352744	0461	1
EICHLING ROBERT E	MAJ	0-1825218	0161	1
EICHORN RUDOLPH M	LTC	0-1169500	0566	1
EICKENHORST WALTER F	CW2	W-2101053	1146	2
EICKHOFF DAVID L	LTC	0-1053122	1062	1
EICKHOFF FREDERICK	MAJ	0-1010498	1047	1
EIDMAN JR ARTHUR	2LT	0-1323675	1045	2
EIDY ADAM	MAJ	0-1058990	0360	1
EIFERT EUGENE C	2LT	0-1594816	0844	2
EIFERT SYLVESTER	LTC	0-0337799	0954	1
EIFFERT CECIL M	MAJ	0-0335310	1045	2
EIFLER CARL F	COL	0-0288691	0947	2
EIGABROADT EARL E	CPT	0-0970153	0161	1
EIGELBACH RICHARD E	LTC	0-0309437	0355	1
EIGNER EMMETT H	CW2	W-2145306	0660	1
EIGSTI ARTHUR E	1LT	0-1037971	0446	2
EIKENBERRY ROBERT W	CPT	0-1288879	0959	2
EIKLEBERRY MURRELL L	COL	0-0255802	1165	3
EILAND JR LIVY E	MAJ	0-0948387	1064	1
EILER DONALD L	MAJ	0-1057994	1059	1
EILERS BALDWIN C	LTC	0-0217601	0462	3
EILERT CHARLES T	LTC	0-1580900	1061	2
EILERT WILLIAM G	LTC	0-0337237	0846	2
EILERTSON JOHN E	LTC	0-0158986	0648	3
EIMERMAN LUCILLE B	CPT	N-0741361	1146	1
EIMERS JAY R	MAJ	0-1845562	1146	2
EINBECK AUGUST C	LTC	0-0357934	0661	1
EINFALT CARL R	LTC	0-0244157	0465	3
EININGER JR ROBERT S	LTC	0-0254619	0465	3
EINSTEIN ALFRED	2LT	0-1307213	0544	2
EINTRACHT IRA S	2LT	0-0131273	0361	1
EISEL JOSEPH R	MAJ	0-0290078	0663	3
EISELE EDWARD J	LTC	0-0277427	0247	2
EISELE PAUL L	LTC	0-0331241	0962	3
EISELT AUDREY A	1LT	N-0731587	0448	1
EISEN IRWIN R	MAJ	0-1545841	0765	1
EISEN JACOB	LTC	0-0290247	0261	3
EISEN JAY E	LTC	0-1799508	1165	1
EISEN NANCY J	MAJ	N-0757175	0866	1
EISENBERG BEN C	MAJ	0-0302558	0646	2
EISENBERG DAVID S	LTC	0-0309932	1167	3
EISENBERG ELI	CPT	0-1690553	0246	2
EISENBERG NATHAN P	CPT	0-0331741	1045	2
EISENBERG RANKIN H	CPT	0-1298842	1047	1
EISENBERG SOL	2LT	0-1691751	0545	2
EISENBERG STUART J	1LT	0-0441864	0645	2
EISENBERGER ROBERT R	CPT	0-2032974	0759	1
EISENHART MARION S	LTC	0-1298517	0361	1
EISENHAUER ADAM J	LTC	0-0393829	1159	1
EISENHAUER ACIES J	LTC	0-1642034	1062	1
EISENHAUER JOHN H	CPT	0-0480171	0148	2
EISENHAUER ROBERT F	LTC	0-1950159	0763	1
EISENHOWER FRANK L	CPT	0-1113677	0148	2
EISENHOWER ROY F	CW2	RW-2207262	0762	1
EISENHUT JOHN	1LT	0-1301123	0145	2
EISENMAN FRANCIS J	MAJ	0-0175077	0623	1
EISENSMITH ISADORE	MAJ	0-1587230	1262	1
EISENSTARK JULIUS	1LT	0-0541256	0945	2
EISENSTEIN EDWARD	CPT	0-1684332	0545	2
EISFELLER ROBERT C	CPT	0-0502671	0946	1
EISMEN SAMUEL N	CPT	0-1342327	1159	1
EISNITZ SHELDON R	LTC	0-2041008	0861	1
EISON FREDERIC J	LTC	0-0260342	0846	2
EISON ROY P	CPT	0-0299592	1045	2
EISS FRANK J	CPT	0-1166477	0745	2
EISSNER HARRY C	CPT	0-1035754	0750	1
EKBLAD EUGENE P	LTC	0-1001125	0960	1
EKDAHL SIGURD	LTC	0-0150658	0648	3
EKE REGINALD	1LT	0-1633012	0846	1
EKLUND CARL W	MAJ	0-0420300	0867	3
EKMAN GEORGE A	1LT	0-0176381	1043	1
EKRUT EDWIN H	1LT	0-1285221	0951	1
EKSTRAND LOYD J	MAJ	0-1109269	0763	1
EKSTROM ALTON C	MAJ	0-1173594	0959	1
ELA CLAYTON W	LTC	0-0237542	1057	1
ELAM EDWARD F	MAJ	0-1923584	0664	1
ELAM GEORGE T	LTC	0-0387715	0862	2
ELAM HARRY M	LTC	0-1325206	0966	1
ELAM JR CHARLES R	LTC	0-0270028	0461	1
ELAN MORRIS	1LT	0-1042556	0944	2
ELBEL JAMES A	MAJ	0-1595998	0262	1
ELBRADER WILLIAM C	LTC	0-0403591	0665	1
ELD VINCENT R	MAJ	0-1173936	1062	1
ELDER ARCHIBALD	LTC	0-0354205	1160	1
ELDER EARL F	MAJ	0-2263242	0765	1
ELDER FRANCIS B	COL	0-0353740	0566	3
ELDER FRANK R	LTC	0-0473230	0157	1
ELDER HAROLD R	LTC	0-0277428	0164	3
ELDER HUBERT B	COL	0-0213721	0761	3
ELDER JACK K	MAJ	0-1010843	0561	1
ELDER MILES M	MAJ	0-0221340	1151	3
ELDER NEIL M	LTC	0-0392498	0264	1
ELDER RALPH F	CW2	W-2152491	0761	1
ELDER ROBERT O	1LT	0-1535636	0347	2
ELDER RUFUS H	LTC	0-0278699	1161	3
ELDER SMITH L	LTC	0-0405834	0660	1
ELDER THOMAS C	LTC	0-0307482	0162	3
ELDER THOMAS H	CW3	W-2148690	0164	1
ELDER THOMAS J	COL	0-0295041	0166	1
ELDER 3RD GEORGE W	1LT	0-0546703	0550	1
ELDERDICE HUGH L	COL	0-0124901	1055	3
ELDERS JAMES F	1LT	0-0508034	0746	1
ELDRACHER JOSEPH J	MAJ	0-0977385	0962	1
ELDRED ARTHUR C	LTC	0-0294189	0167	3

NAME	GRADE	SVC NO	DATE RET MO YR	RET CODE
ELDRED PERCY D	LTC	O-0240556	0763	3
ELDRED ROBERT C	CPT	O-1174566	0246	2
ELDREDGE CHARLES J	1LT	O-1284115	0446	1
ELDREDGE JAMES C	CW2	W-2101656	1046	1
ELDRIDGE ALBERT C	MAJ	O-1861665	0763	1
ELDRIDGE ALLAN E	LTC	O-0308652	0660	3
ELDRIDGE BRUCE S	LTC	O-0353810	0562	1
ELDRIDGE EMORY M	CPT	O-1996552	0556	1
ELDRIDGE ERNEST R	MAJ	O-0175922	0246	2
ELDRIDGE GEORGE R	CPT	O-1303693	0155	2
ELDRIDGE HARRY E	LTC	O-0176311	0157	3
ELDRIDGE IRVING C	MAJ	O-0237734	0562	3
ELDRIDGE JAMES C	2LT	O-1913674	1130	1
ELDRIDGE LEO R	2LT	O-2262988	0852	2
ELDRIDGE WILLIE J	2LT	O-0426911	1143	2
ELERICK KERN	CPT	O-0290317	1044	2
ELEVELD SIDNEY Z	COL	O-0185895	0648	3
ELFERT BERNARD G	LTC	O-2204106	0966	1
ELGART JACOB M	LTC	O-1553990	1067	3
ELGIN CARL C	LTC	O-1314115	0263	1
ELGIN JAMES C	CPT	O-0381367	0645	2
ELGIN LOREN M	MAJ	O-0974973	0763	1
ELIAS CYRIL C	2LT	O-0901511	0246	2
ELIAS ELMER J	MAJ	O-0250382	1164	3
ELIAS GEORGE A	MAJ	O-1308316	0558	1
ELIAS MICHAEL A	LTC	O-1593970	0867	1
ELIAS MIGUEL G	MAJ	O-0492508	1043	2
ELIASON EVERETT J	LTC	O-0177696	0461	3
ELIASON RAYMOND D	COL	O-0222283	1051	3
ELIASSEN EVERETT C	CPT	O-1306255	0947	2
ELIASSON HILDA E	MAJ	N-0738047	0967	3
ELIOT JOHN A	MAJ	O-0272618	1044	2
ELK KENNETH M	MAJ	O-1642832	0366	1
ELKIN RAYMOND E	COL	O-0113551	0552	3
ELKINS DENNIE	CPT	O-0164001	0940	1
ELKINS ESTEL	LTC	O-1284484	0164	2
ELKINS JAMES W	1LT	O-1920286	0658	2
ELKINS THEODORE C	CW3	W-2142758	1162	1
ELKINS VERNON E	CPT	O-1691494	0954	1
ELLARD GEORGE E	MAJ	O-0235250	0958	3
ELLE KURT D	CW4	W-2136619	0263	1
ELLEDGE ELDON W	MAJ	O-0473382	0347	1
ELLEDGE EPHRAIM H	CW2	W-2148254	0555	1
ELLEDGE GEORGE R	MAJ	O-0501631	0359	2
ELLEDGE HORACE C	CW2	W-2149943	0361	1
ELLEDGE JOHN A	LTC	O-1042282	0566	1
ELLENBAST HENRY L	CW4	W-2111468	0266	2
ELLENBERGER DAVID T	CW2	W-2211088	0165	1
ELLENBURG CHARLES L	CW2	W-3151323	0267	1
ELLENBURG ROBERT E	MAJ	O-0519725	1151	1
ELLER CLEMON J	CW3	W-2145859	0460	1
ELLER DAVID A	CW2	W-2210431	0366	1
ELLER EDMUND R	1LT	O-1322774	0946	2
ELLER ELBERT H	LTC	O-0399352	0861	1
ELLER FLOYD E	COL	O-0166660	0953	3
ELLER HERMAN H	WO1	W-2123197	1049	1
ELLER JOHN H	LTC	O-1038602	0963	1
ELLERBE CONGRESS W	MAJ	O-1169093	0346	2
ELLERBE HENRY I	COL	O-0150789	0144	2
ELLERBE THOMAS H	LTC	O-0471425	0257	1
ELLERY ARTHUR D	1LT	O-0467264	0845	2
ELLETT ASA	CW2	W-3150646	0264	2
ELLETT HOMER C	MAJ	O-0478887	0662	1
ELLEY CHARLES R	CPT	O-2208460	0567	1
ELLIFRITT SYLVESTER	1LT	O-1287682	0346	1
ELLIGET EDWIN J	CPT	O-0397306	0744	2
ELLING CARL M	1LT	O-0354714	0146	2
ELLINGER JUNIOR J	2LT	O-1297513	0644	2
ELLINGER MAURICE R	MAJ	O-1100967	0765	1
ELLINGSWORTH C W	CW3	W-2141267	0557	1
ELLINGSWORTH WILLIAM	MAJ	O-1924131	0364	1
ELLINGTON CLAUDE	MAJ	O-0448002	1140	1
ELLINGTON GILMER	CW2	W-2210519	0165	1
ELLINGTON JOE W	LTC	O-0279133	0364	3
ELLINGTON JOHN C	WO1	W-2147579	1159	1

NAME	GRADE	SVC NO	DATE RET MO YR	RET CODE
ELLINGTON RAPLE C	CPT	O-0335881	0146	2
ELLIOT CARLISLE I	LTC	O-1550586	0766	1
ELLIOT CHARLES	CW4	W-2141552	1060	1
ELLIOT CHARLES W	COL	O-0493060	1160	1
ELLIOT CHESTER S	LTC	O-0176630	0648	3
ELLIOT PAUL R	MAJ	O-1338225	0663	1
ELLIOT PERCY J	LTC	O-0220406	0656	3
ELLIOTT BASS P	1LT	O-1335406	0352	1
ELLIOTT CARROLL W	COL	O-0224921	1163	3
ELLIOTT CECIL A	1LT	O-1285402	0444	2
ELLIOTT CLARENCE L	2LT	O-0452879	1143	2
ELLIOTT CLARENCE N	LTC	O-0885081	0551	1
ELLIOTT CLAUD	CPT	O-1318969	1166	3
ELLIOTT DALE N	CW4	W-2142545	1162	1
ELLIOTT DANIEL D	CW3	W-2147260	0863	1
ELLIOTT DAVID O	MAJ	O-0132027	0159	3
ELLIOTT DONALD F	COL	O-0334000	0865	3
ELLIOTT EDWARD B	MAJ	O-0358454	0858	1
ELLIOTT EDWARD C	MAJ	O-0351586	1044	2
ELLIOTT EDWARD J	CW2	W-2151125	0856	1
ELLIOTT EDWARD W	LTC	O-0205313	1053	3
ELLIOTT EDWIN	LTC	O-0451964	0364	1
ELLIOTT ELMER	LTC	O-1296188	1055	1
ELLIOTT ENNIS B	CPT	O-1640421	0954	1
ELLIOTT ERNEST O	LTC	O-0268459	1052	1
ELLIOTT EWING W	COL	O-0374987	1067	3
ELLIOTT GEORGE H	MAJ	O-1909372	0857	1
ELLIOTT GILBERT M	COL	O-0311817	0662	3
ELLIOTT GRANT R	LTC	O-0281601	0361	3
ELLIOTT HAROLD F	MAJ	O-1003721	0757	1
ELLIOTT HARRY R	1LT	O-0542333	1045	2
ELLIOTT HAYES	MAJ	O-2034607	0257	1
ELLIOTT HENRY	MAJ	O-1642036	0756	1
ELLIOTT HENRY F	2LT	O-1310695	0445	2
ELLIOTT HENRY W	CPT	O-1049473	0263	1
ELLIOTT HERBERT J	LTC	O-0368663	0466	3
ELLIOTT HOMER H	COL	O-0312911	0460	3
ELLIOTT HOWARD J	MAJ	O-0320197	1159	3
ELLIOTT IVAN A	LTC	O-0118734	1149	3
ELLIOTT JACK R	MAJ	O-1100968	1060	1
ELLIOTT JAMES A	LTC	O-0268762	0866	3
ELLIOTT JAMES C	2LT	O-1106709	0544	2
ELLIOTT JAMES R	CPT	O-2027430	0848	1
ELLIOTT JIMMY J	CPT	O-2265382	0764	1
ELLIOTT JOHN A	2LT	O-1106116	0744	2
ELLIOTT JOHN C	LTC	O-0319341	0560	1
ELLIOTT JOHN K	WO1	W-2129592	1050	1
ELLIOTT JOHN P	MAJ	O-1550781	0860	1
ELLIOTT JOHN W	CPT	O-0164885	1137	2
ELLIOTT JOSEPH	CPT	O-0501284	0649	1
ELLIOTT JOSEPH	WO1	W-2122615	0748	1
ELLIOTT JR GEORGE E	MAJ	O-2048606	0760	1
ELLIOTT JR HOWARD R	MAJ	O-2034513	0861	1
ELLIOTT JULIAN C	MAJ	O-1693077	0346	2
ELLIOTT KENNETH C	MAJ	O-0355505	1163	1
ELLIOTT MAX B	2LT	O-1541907	1045	2
ELLIOTT NATHANIEL	LTC	O-0179605	0558	1
ELLIOTT PAYTON F	1LT	O-1312295	0747	2
ELLIOTT RALPH A	COL	O-0438353	0566	3
ELLIOTT ROBERT E	CPT	O-1283744	0152	1
ELLIOTT ROBERT E	MAJ	O-2263445	0464	1
ELLIOTT ROBERT J	COL	O-1165284	0965	2
ELLIOTT RODNEY S	CPT	O-0416080	0446	2
ELLIOTT RUSSELL	CPT	O-0244995	0359	3
ELLIOTT RUTHEILEEN	1LT	N-0799388	1047	1
ELLIOTT SAM C	COL	O-0244798	1159	1
ELLIOTT SAMUEL F	1LT	O-1012689	1147	1
ELLIOTT SHELDEN D	R G	O-0519660	0766	3
ELLIOTT SIDNEY L	MAJ	O-1597211	0762	1
ELLIOTT SR CARL A	1LT	O-1305747	0944	2
ELLIOTT VIRGIL H	LTC	O-0327746	0561	1
ELLIOTT WALLACE W	COL	O-0331777	0865	3
ELLIOTT WALTER F	LTC	O-1293736	1163	1
ELLIOTT WILLIAM E	COL	O-0254106	1165	3
ELLIOTT WILLIAM E	LTC	O-0276877	1165	3

NAME	GRADE	SVC NO	DATE RET MO YR	RET CODE
ELLIOTT WILLIAM R	CPT	O-1580903	0759	2
ELLIS ALBERT	MAJ	O-0284303	1166	3
ELLIS ALFRED D	LTC	O-1049140	0859	1
ELLIS ALLEN J	CPT	O-1042017	0357	1
ELLIS ARTHUR A	CPT	O-0465248	0646	1
ELLIS BENJAMIN T	LTC	O-0351587	0365	2
ELLIS CARL E	CPT	O-1646708	0557	1
ELLIS CARLTON R	MAJ	O-0491243	0147	1
ELLIS CASSIUS M	LTC	O-0505543	1163	1
ELLIS CHARLES A	COL	O-0181368	0246	2
ELLIS CHARLES O	CW3	W-2142755	0659	1
ELLIS CHARLES R	CPT	O-2008542	1062	1
ELLIS CLARENCE R	CPT	O-1056704	0858	1
ELLIS CLYDE L	LTC	O-0910492	0262	3
ELLIS DAN B	1LT	O-1018888	0747	1
ELLIS DAVID E	CW2	W-2151174	0159	1
ELLIS DEE R	LTC	O-0123899	0357	3
ELLIS DONALD D	2LT	O-1012831	0144	1
ELLIS EARL M	LTC	O-0248434	0355	1
ELLIS EDWARD M	2LT	O-1642833	0444	2
ELLIS FORREST W	CW2	W-2209351	0163	1
ELLIS GERALD H	LTC	O-1297514	0461	1
ELLIS GLENN A	LTC	O-0420288	0463	1
ELLIS GRENVILLE	MAJ	O-0241640	0666	3
ELLIS HARRY N	CPT	O-0964315	0160	1
ELLIS HILLERY M	CW4	W-2146114	1164	1
ELLIS HUBERT H	LTC	O-1297338	0161	1
ELLIS HUGH R	MAJ	O-0257680	1044	2
ELLIS JAMES V	CPT	O-1290224	0849	1
ELLIS JR CHARLES L	CPT	O-0328403	0545	2
ELLIS JR JOHN R	LTC	O-0366485	0959	1
ELLIS KENNETH L	LTC	O-1109914	0363	1
ELLIS LAVERNE E	MAJ	O-1634720	0158	1
ELLIS LAWRENCE W	MAJ	O-0889070	1063	1
ELLIS LEONARD G	MAJ	O-0483163	1046	2
ELLIS LEWIS C	MAJ	O-0402864	0660	1
ELLIS MARCUS D	CW3	W-2152504	0864	1
ELLIS MARGUERITE	CPT	N-0751556	0545	2
ELLIS MILDRED C	2LT	N-0702444	0542	1
ELLIS MORRISS W	1LT	O-1010193	0944	2
ELLIS NATHAN W	LTC	O-0211683	1163	3
ELLIS NORMAN	CPT	O-0504714	1046	1
ELLIS NORMAN H	CW2	W-2151354	0762	1
ELLIS RAYMOND A	1LT	O-0489982	0554	1
ELLIS ROBERT C	MAJ	O-0206939	0553	3
ELLIS ROBERT E	MAJ	O-0142705	1152	3
ELLIS ROGER S	LTC	O-0208006	1263	3
ELLIS RONALD F	CPT	O-1047958	0358	1
ELLIS RUBY O	1LT	N-0761572	0846	1
ELLIS RUNNELL B	LTC	O-1633830	0357	1
ELLIS THEO H	1LT	O-0367235	0245	2
ELLIS THEODORE	LTC	O-1546966	0667	1
ELLIS THURMAN L	LTC	O-0402746	0660	1
ELLIS VIRGIL	CPT	O-1341865	0766	1
ELLIS WILLIAM A	MAJ	O-1649764	0762	1
ELLIS WILLIAM H	1LT	O-1055291	0761	2
ELLIS WILLIS T	COL	O-0239642	0360	1
ELLISON ALEXANDER	COL	O-0136821	0850	3
ELLISON CARROLL	CPT	O-0461823	1155	1
ELLISON CHARLES D	MAJ	O-1334557	0859	1
ELLISON DOROTHY M	MAJ	M-0000734	0666	1
ELLISON EDMOND C	CW2	W-2141935	0861	1
ELLISON FRANK S	LTC	O-0337277	0760	2
ELLISON HAROLD A	COL	O-0912303	0864	1
ELLISON HARRY E	CPT	O-1797269	0154	2
ELLISON IRVING J	CPT	O-1298843	0660	2
ELLISON JOHN G R	1LT	O-1304192	1045	2
ELLISON KENNETH E	LTC	O-0315498	0247	2
ELLISON LARRY R	1LT	O-5224263	0167	2
ELLISON MARLON L	LTC	O-0374654	0860	1
ELLISON NELSON M	LTC	O-0254574	0965	3
ELLISON NORMAN B	LTC	O-0256739	1054	3
ELLISON RALPH L	MAJ	O-1118714	0264	1
ELLISON RAYMOND D	LTC	O-1577134	1062	1
ELLISON ROY L	CPT	O-1576852	1154	1

NAME	GRADE	SVC NO	DATE RET MO YR	RET CODE
ELLISON STANLEY H	COL	O-0133973	0156	3
ELLISTON FRED A	LTC	O-0239641	1064	3
ELLMS EDGAR H	LTC	O-0245556	0354	3
ELLOIAN IRA P	CW4	W-2143244	0767	1
ELLOWITCH SHELDON H	1LT	O-0392325	1145	2
ELLSWORTH ALLEN E	2LT	O-1176950	0345	2
ELLSWORTH DE VON	LTC	O-0358727	1063	3
ELLSWORTH ELMAN K	LTC	O-0401510	0364	1
ELLSWORTH EUGENE	WO1	W-2126424	1046	1
ELLSWORTH JAMES R	CPT	O-1302795	0347	2
ELLSWORTH JOE K	MAJ	O-0267521	1165	3
ELLSWORTH LEONARD K	COL	O-0234974	0360	1
ELLSWORTH RAY O	CPT	O-1307528	0257	1
ELLSWORTH THEODORE D	COL	O-0502527	1065	3
ELLWANGER CLARA E	1LT	N-0701224	0135	1
ELLWOOD RICHARD M	CPT	O-1919154	0564	2
ELLZEY ROBERT C	LTC	O-1010540	0357	1
ELMAN MEYER J	LTC	O-0333931	0465	3
ELMBLAD VICTOR A	MAJ	O-0184627	1055	3
ELMEN PAUL H	MAJ	O-0528067	0646	2
ELMER ALBERT W	1LT	O-1306574	1145	2
ELMER CATHERINE	MAJ	N-0727918	0767	1
ELMES WILLIAM T	COL	O-0225978	0764	3
ELMGREN FLOYD E	MAJ	O-0335200	0949	1
ELMGREN LLOYD E	MAJ	O-2014987	0367	1
ELMORE ARTHUR J	MAJ	O-0450138	0657	1
ELMORE CLIFFORD L	CW2	W-2214784	0867	1
ELMORE HERBERT R	LTC	O-0532201	0457	1
ELMORE WILLIAM E	CW2	W-2148317	1060	1
ELMSTROM CLARENCE L	LTC	O-0474623	0766	3
ELOTT MILAN E	LTC	O-2036258	0664	1
ELROD FRED S	2LT	O-1004315	0444	1
ELROD JOHN O	MAJ	O-1998425	1160	1
ELROD ORVILLE F	CW2	W-2146133	0629	1
ELROD WELDON	MAJ	O-1825663	0766	1
ELSAM HAROLD G	COL	O-0435368	0467	3
ELSBERG WILLIAM	1LT	O-1014823	1045	2
ELSEA CARL A	LTC	O-0292729	1264	3
ELSEE WALTER R	1LT	O-1043615	0446	2
ELSEN VERNON H	1LT	O-1318528	1045	2
ELSER ROBERT W	CPT	O-1575952	0962	1
ELSHIRE JACK L	CW3	W-2116099	0561	1
ELSHOF HENRY	1LT	O-1289885	0745	2
ELSIFOR FLOYD D	COL	O-0369763	0661	1
ELSLER JR RICHARD J	LTC	O-0285180	0465	3
ELSOM RUSSELL L	LTC	O-0155292	0456	3
ELSON EDWARD L R	COL	O-0276662	0167	3
ELSON JULIUS	CPT	O-0544198	1045	2
ELSON MAURICE	1LT	O-1302619	1045	2
ELSTON HARRY S	MAJ	O-1103152	0546	2
ELSTON NORMAN E	MAJ	O-2084110	0563	1
ELSWEILER JOHN A	LTC	O-1041544	0461	1
ELTON CAREY F	CW2	W-2000401	0648	3
ELTON CHARLES E	LTC	O-1297359	0957	1
ELTON NORMAN W	COL	O-0122465	0757	2
ELTZROTH RICHARD T	CPT	O-1081600	0964	1
ELVIDGE BESSIE R	MAJ	N-0797162	0666	1
ELVIN ALMA G	2LT	N-0735455	0144	1
ELVIN NORRIS C	CPT	O-1690001	1145	2
ELWELL JR J STEWART	1LT	O-0323272	0145	2
ELWELL LEO D	LTC	O-0370335	0747	2
ELWIN JOHN	LTC	O-0191521	0761	3
ELWOOD LAVERN	CPT	O-0487878	0449	1
ELY CARLTON G	CPT	O-1304882	0446	1
ELY CHARLES R	LTC	O-0214193	1163	3
ELY CHARLES T	1LT	O-0386303	0245	2
ELY CHARLES W	MAJ	O-0971773	1163	1
ELY EIRVIN E	1LT	O-1003227	0945	2
ELY GEORGE C	1LT	O-1946722	1146	2
ELY GERALD F	LTC	O-0317743	0758	1
ELY HIRAM B	COL	O-0425123	0854	2
ELY HUDSON P	LTC	O-0476295	0155	2
ELY JOE T	LTC	O-1635840	0766	1
ELY JOSEPH C	CPT	O-1573182	0745	2
ELY JR JAMES H	COL	O-0306015	0665	3

NAME	GRADE	SVC NO	DATE RET MO YR	RET CODE
FLY JUNIOR R	LTC	0-0497509	0657	1
FLY KINGSTON G	1LT	C-1320828	C946	1
FLY NATHANIEL	COL	0-0219732	C563	3
FLY RAY	LTC	C-0262616	1165	3
FLY WILLIAM B	CPT	0-0313014	0146	2
FLYD MICHAEL	CW3	W-2151899	0563	1
ELZEA JOHN W	LTC	0-0268345	1266	3
EMANUEL EUGENE J	MAJ	C-1824447	C963	1
EMANUEL JAMES H	MAJ	C-0963466	C860	1
EMARD ALFRED J	LTC	0-0298738	0461	1
EMBACH HAROLD A	LTC	0-0104744	0648	3
EMBODY CALVIN F	CPT	0-C445145	C446	2
EMBREE ELISHA D	COL	C-0150803	1147	2
EMBREE FELIX V	MAJ	C-0155016	C356	3
EMBREE RAY O	COL	C-0274028	C859	1
EMBREE THOMAS R	CW3	W-2142701	C559	1
EMBREY CECIL L	CW3	W-2146234	1157	1
EMBREY LEMUEL J	CPT	0-0371438	C447	2
EMBRY SHERRILL F	1LT	0-0415314	C344	2
EMBURY MELVIN W	COL	C-0264750	0563	3
EMBURY ROY V	CW2	W-2154871	1058	2
EMDE JOHN M	COL	C-0172468	C153	3
EMDE RAYMOND J	CW4	W-2206760	C561	3
EMEIS RICHARD E	LTC	0-0300227	C765	3
EMELIA ALFREDO B	2LT	0-1896825	1050	1
EMENEKER CHARLIE	CW2	W-2148407	0757	1
EMENHISER LEE K	COL	C-0307238	C167	3
EMERICK CHARLES F	CW3	W-2144150	1059	1
EMERICK DAVE C	CPT	C-4063743	C667	1
EMERSON ALLEN M	LTC	0-0195259	1059	3
EMERSON ALLMON C	LTC	0-1171527	C262	1
EMERSON BURTON L	LTC	C-0313853	1161	3
EMERSON CALDWELL G	LTC	0-0267005	1262	2
EMERSON DONAHUE L	LTC	C-0165545	C647	1
EMERSON ELMER W	CW3	W-2152845	0464	1
EMERSON FITZHUGH L	MAJ	C-1585414	0363	2
EMERSON FRANK H	LTC	0-0358173	0664	1
EMERSON GEORGE F	MAJ	0-1686073	1046	2
EMERSON HAROLD S	CPT	0-0227161	1264	3
EMERSON JAMES H	MAJ	C-0684505	C766	1
EMERSON JAMES L	CPT	0-1010107	1062	2
EMERSON JAMES R	LTC	0-0401912	1160	1
EMERSON MACK	MAJ	0-0439152	0245	2
EMERSON PAUL J	CW2	W-2210666	0765	1
EMERSON TOM W	CPT	C-1101424	1160	1
EMERSON WILLIAM D	MAJ	C-1548401	0859	1
EMERSON WILLIAM H	COL	C-0189310	C453	3
EMERSON WINIFORD F	LTC	0-1178776	C663	1
EMERY ARLO A	COL	0-0180288	C350	3
EMERY CLYDE A	LTC	0-0333861	0564	3
EMERY CLYDE J	CW3	W-2153382	0565	1
EMERY DAVID G	MAJ	C-1020039	C761	1
EMERY DUNCAN M	LTC	0-1300300	C763	1
EMERY EARL E	LTC	0-1041756	0361	1
EMERY EDWIN L	1LT	0-1896006	1153	1
EMERY GEORGE W	1LT	0-1295188	0643	2
EMERY GEORGE W	WO1	W-2006204	0766	3
EMERY HARVEY F	1LT	C-0451277	0952	1
EMERY HERBERT T	MAJ	C-0266166	C459	3
EMERY JAMES I	LTC	0-1049821	1064	1
EMERY JOHN F	1LT	0-1176324	C656	1
EMERY JOSEPH S	LTC	C-0451591	0158	1
EMERY JR JOSEPH	LTC	0-1578424	0565	1
EMERY MARGARET F	1LT	N-C721040	0246	2
EMERY MARY S	CPT	N-0700769	C345	1
EMERY MYRON C	MAJ	0-1553258	C763	1
EMERY WALTER A	CPT	C-0482899	0448	1
EMHARDT FREDERICK	1LT	0-1290575	1046	2
EMIG CATHERINE	LTC	L-0215416	1062	1
EMIGH JR HARRY G	1LT	0-0958486	0452	1
EMM JOHN S	1LT	0-1326081	C152	2
EMMA GERARD J	1LT	C-1581686	C645	2
EMMANUEL KARL F	COL	0-0115685	C750	3
EMMANUEL MAX D	COL	0-0187947	0356	3
EMMANUELLI JUAN R	CPT	0-0255126	0244	2

NAME	GRADE	SVC NO	DATE RET MO YR	RET CODE
EMME JR ARTHUR H	LTC	0-1059778	1062	1
EMMECK LEROY S	1LT	0-1048757	0545	2
EMMERICH LAWRENCE H	CPT	0-1306396	1046	2
EMMERLING FRANK	CPT	0-0579921	0760	1
EMMERLING HERBERT J	2LT	0-1299867	0944	2
EMMERLING JOHN F	LTC	0-0269632	0246	2
EMMERSON ARTHUR	COL	0-0100813	0955	2
EMMERSON WILLIAM F	CPT	0-0949401	0361	1
EMMETT NED C	MAJ	0-1031635	1165	1
EMMONS CLARK W	LTC	0-1549705	0461	1
EMMONS CLAUDE D	CPT	0-0409732	0346	2
EMMONS DEIGHTON K	2LT	0-1525396	0853	1
EMMONS MARION C	1LT	N-0703061	0946	1
EMMONS RALPH L	CPT	0-1320829	0846	2
EMOND DANIEL L	MAJ	0-0238391	0655	3
EMORY MORRIS S	2LT	0-1327941	1045	1
EMPEY HOMER R	LTC	C-2048286	1164	1
EMPFIELD WARREN A	CW2	W-2152036	0561	1
EMRICH JACOB A	LTC	0-1581687	1262	1
EMRY JESS C	MAJ	0-0372509	1045	1
EMRY JR ALBERT	MAJ	0-0967197	1162	1
EMSHOFF LEE ROY H	CPT	0-1341866	1157	2
EMSLIE WILLIAM R	MAJ	C-1535707	C864	1
ENARSON RUTH E	1LT	N-0737649	1146	1
ENBODY CLARENCE	LTC	0-1177785	0462	1
ENCK FRANK F	LTC	0-0225585	0261	3
ENDE CARL F	COL	0-0168954	0459	3
ENDEBROCK JR JOHN C	MAJ	C-0254808	0165	3
ENDERLIN LEON W	MAJ	0-1547286	0161	1
ENDERS GORDON D	COL	C-0426588	C461	1
ENDERS MILDRED R	CPT	N-0724107	1146	1
ENDERUD WILLIAM L	LTC	0-0230044	0863	3
ENDICOTT JOSEPH A	LTC	0-1115567	0264	1
ENDICOTT RICHARD C	LTC	0-0209063	0547	2
ENDICOTT STEWART C	1LT	0-0401064	1044	2
ENDLER HAROLD A	LTC	0-0586633	0164	1
ENDLING REINHOLD A	MAJ	0-1845032	1053	1
ENDSLEY CLARENCE F	LTC	0-1548049	0357	1
ENDSLEY JAMES H	CPT	0-1794926	0247	1
ENEMARK ROY C	LTC	0-0451278	1067	2
ENFINGER ALLEN V	MAJ	0-1081131	0858	1
ENG ERNEST K H	LTC	0-1596318	1162	1
ENG SAMUEL Y	MAJ	0-0447790	0346	2
ENGARD MASON S	LTC	0-1030761	0162	1
ENGARDIO JOHN J	1LT	0-1177380	1045	2
ENGART HENRY S	CPT	0-0264906	0467	3
ENGBERG JOHN A	COL	C-0315360	1053	1
ENGDAHL HAROLD W	CPT	0-0570219	1061	1
ENGDAHL THEODORE N	CPT	0-1700706	0446	2
ENGEBRETSON M E	CPT	N-0703806	0546	1
ENGEL ANDREW H	LTC	0-1030144	0863	2
ENGEL BERNARD J	CW3	W-2104029	1159	1
ENGEL CARLTON B	CPT	0-0279545	1159	3
ENGEL CLINTON M	LTC	0-0443410	1054	1
ENGEL EDMUND J	CPT	0-0108121	0545	2
ENGEL HANS	LTC	0-1035149	0655	1
ENGEL KENNETH E	MAJ	0-0216720	1063	3
ENGEL RALPH E	LTC	0-0375428	0665	3
ENGEL RICHARD R	COL	0-0378184	0960	1
ENGEL WILBUR W	LTC	0-0318297	0967	3
ENGELBECK RANALD R	COL	0-0221966	0964	3
ENGELHARD SR WARD H	MAJ	0-1821988	C962	1
ENGELHARDT CHARLES W	MAJ	0-0965794	0563	1
ENGELHARDT RONALD	1LT	0-1049141	0945	2
ENGELHART GEORGE K	COL	0-0114578	0156	3
ENGELMAN EDWARD	LTC	0-0432915	1162	1
ENGELMANN WILLIAM G	LTC	0-1296190	0261	1
ENGELS JAMES F	CW2	W-2151821	1059	1
ENGELS VIRGINIA I	MAJ	L-1010016	1166	1
ENGELS WILLIAM N	LTC	0-0340293	0746	2
ENGER EARLE M	MAJ	0-0372594	0364	3
ENGER JAMES A	LTC	0-1543503	0462	1
ENGER WILLIAM T	COL	C-0192044	C657	3
ENGERT LLOYD S	LTC	0-1280112	0447	1
ENGESATH HENRY R	COL	0-0909181	1062	3

NAME	GRADE	SVC NO	DATE RET MO YR	RET CODE
ENGESSER GERALD W	CW4	W-2114558	C366	1
ENGLAND CHARLES F	COL	C-0337440	C364	2
ENGLAND JOE C	MAJ	C-0870740	0961	1
ENGLAND JOHN E	LTC	0-0214240	C463	3
ENGLAND JR JOHN M	MAJ	C-1282383	0965	1
ENGLAND RICHARD A	MAJ	C-1012612	C260	1
ENGLAND WARREN	MAJ	C-1575954	1059	1
ENGLE ADELINE R	2LT	N-0759365	C444	1
ENGLE BYRON E	CPT	0-0466118	C244	2
ENGLE CARL J	LTC	0-0319844	C747	2
ENGLE DONALD F	MAJ	0-1031477	0161	1
ENGLE ELDON B	LTC	0-0228789	1057	3
ENGLE FANNIE H	2LT	N-0759003	0945	1
ENGLE HARRY	CW2	W-2143154	0960	1
ENGLE HARRY O	CPT	0-0275926	0951	3
ENGLE HERMAN L	CW2	W-3200287	C866	1
ENGLE ROBERT J	MAJ	0-1688756	C465	1
ENGLE STOKES K	LTC	0-1641271	C960	1
ENGLEBERG JOHN J	CPT	0-0968813	0262	1
ENGLEBY JR LLOYD H	1LT	0-1928428	1154	2
ENGLEDOW JOE C	MAJ	0-1174287	C653	1
ENGLEHARDT ERNEST C	LTC	0-0399727	C557	1
ENGLEMAN SAMUEL	MAJ	0-1797270	0261	1
ENGLER GEORGE F	CPT	0-1283569	C446	2
ENGLERT WALTER F	LTC	C-0461770	1054	1
ENGLES FRANK	2LT	0-1945571	1145	2
ENGLEY THOMAS W	LTC	C-1635843	C663	1
ENGLISH ANTHONY G	1LT	0-1535166	0146	2
ENGLISH CLAUDE H	CW4	W-2145905	C859	1
ENGLISH DONALD L	LTC	0-1288720	0161	1
ENGLISH DORIS J	2LT	N-0790789	0445	1
ENGLISH EDWARD D	1LT	0-2035305	C152	1
ENGLISH EDWARD H	MAJ	C-1114115	C346	2
ENGLISH EDWARD L	MAJ	C-1685682	C363	1
ENGLISH ELIHU A	WO1	W-2112263	1043	1
ENGLISH EVERETT W	MAJ	0-1044504	1047	2
ENGLISH FITZHUGH A	MAJ	0-1293389	0963	1
ENGLISH FRANK C	LTC	0-0451495	1060	1
ENGLISH JAMES H	MAJ	0-0189384	0552	3
ENGLISH JOHN	WO1	W-2122716	C862	2
ENGLISH JR JESSE C	MAJ	C-2033141	C262	1
ENGLISH LEWIS K	1LT	0-1035112	0246	2
ENGLISH MILLARD C	LTC	0-1287684	0361	1
ENGLISH ROBERT C	1LT	0-1111047	0645	2
ENGLISH ROY C	WO1	W-2145266	0455	1
ENGLISH SAMUEL R	CPT	0-0132610	0648	3
ENGLISH THOMAS M	LTC	0-0378114	C567	3
ENGLISH TRACY L	LTC	0-0350778	0252	1
ENGLISH WILLIAM C	CPT	0-0389050	0761	1
ENGLISH WILLIAM O	MAJ	C-0259888	C266	3
ENGLUND ADELL B	CPT	0-0906384	0644	2
ENGLUND DEWITT W	1LT	C-0473347	C544	2
ENGQUIST MARVIN J	COL	0-0412586	0463	1
ENGRAM VANCE R	2LT	0-1695727	1045	2
ENGS ROBERT N	CPT	0-2203411	0864	1
ENGSTROM DALE M	LTC	0-1289886	0861	1
ENGSTROM PAUL V	COL	0-0222570	0757	3
ENGWELL LAVERN T	MAJ	0-2019303	0363	1
ENICH MITCHELL	MAJ	0-1822256	C561	1
ENLOE NEWMAN W	MAJ	C-0281283	C667	3
ENLOE THOMAS A	LTC	0-0482370	0761	1
ENLOW RALPH W	CW3	W-2145932	C160	1
ENNEN GORDON R	1LT	C-1317154	C146	2
ENNES CHARLES E	MAJ	0-2266367	1167	1
ENNIS CLARENCE H	COL	0-0394232	0960	1
ENNIS HILLIS H	LTC	0-0407586	0860	1
ENNIS JAMES P	1LT	0-0366706	1042	2
ENNIS RAYMOND G	MAJ	0-1293563	1262	1
ENNIS WILLIAM T	LTC	0-0212727	1057	1
ENOCH JOHN K	MAJ	C-0972901	0464	2
ENOCHS CARROLL A	CPT	0-0213993	0962	3
ENOCHS JOHN	CPT	0-0154123	0648	3
ENRIGHT CORNELIUS	COL	0-0242383	0764	3
ENRIGHT HAROLD F	MAJ	C-0236220	C547	2
ENRIGHT THOMAS F	1LT	0-1322406	C246	2

NAME	GRADE	SVC NO	DATE RET MO YR	RET CODE
ENRIQUEZ VICTOR M	CPT	0-0222555	0555	3
ENSEL LEE W	COL	0-0913178	0764	3
ENSIGN EDWIN W	MAJ	C-0288527	1043	2
ENSIGN PAUL R	COL	C-0218423	C146	1
ENSINGER LEAH M	LTC	N-0760987	0863	1
ENSLEN JR W M	MAJ	0-0245357	1057	3
ENSLEY SHERMAN W	MAJ	0-1336776	C565	1
ENSLOW RIDLEY M	LTC	0-0168566	1159	3
ENSMINGER HARRISON	MAJ	0-0326077	C660	1
ENSMINGER LEONARD A	1LT	0-1017062	0146	2
ENSMINGER PHILIP R	CW4	W-2108840	1164	1
ENSMINGER RAMAN V	MAJ	0-1051119	0763	1
ENSMINGER WILLIAM L	MAJ	0-2036501	0462	1
ENSWORTH GLENN E	CPT	0-1300781	0859	1
ENTERLINE HENRY M	LTC	0-0168607	0261	3
ENTREKIN WILLIAM W	MAJ	0-2017381	0961	1
ENTRINGER JOSEPH B	COL	0-0186963	0554	3
ENTWISTLE GEORGE H	CPT	0-0221547	1056	3
ENTZMINGER WILLIAM C	MAJ	0-0163079	0255	3
ENTZMINGER WILLIAM C	MAJ	C-1589812	0862	1
ENWALL HAYFORD C	COL	0-0332979	C865	3
ENYEART ROGER T	CW2	W-2207263	0662	1
ENZOR ELLEN A	MAJ	0-0420261	C846	1
EPAMINONDA JOHN G	LTC	0-0382573	0664	3
EPPERSON DEMPSTER F	COL	0-0366606	0165	1
EPPERSON GLENN I	COL	0-0260539	0457	1
EPPERSON JAMES E	CPT	0-0389707	0645	2
EPPERSON JESSE V	2LT	0-2000092	0146	2
EPPERSON JOHN I	2LT	0-1080362	0944	1
EPPERSON LESTER Y	1LT	0-1913672	C738	1
EPPERSON LLOYD A	MAJ	0-0975299	1064	1
EPPERSON MANUEL H	MAJ	0-0990769	0464	1
EPPINGER JR JOSUA	LTC	0-0290235	1162	3
EPPLER JAMES E	MAJ	0-1691530	C655	1
EPPLER JOSEPH M	MAJ	C-0160675	C449	3
EPPLER RUDOLF	MAJ	0-1179064	0457	1
EPPLEY GEARY F	COL	0-0112612	1055	3
EPPRIGHT CHARLES L	CW3	W-2206949	0966	1
EPPS ALFRED C	CW3	W-2148721	0563	1
EPPS CALVIN	CPT	0-0108257	1137	1
EPPS CHARLES K	LTC	0-0250097	1057	1
EPPS OLIVER C	CPT	0-1945123	0646	2
EPSARO AUSTIN F	LTC	0-0542653	0265	1
EPSOM GEORGE A	LTC	0-1796595	1264	1
EPSTEEN CASPER M	LTC	0-0446241	1045	2
EPSTEIN ABRAHAM	MAJ	0-2016865	0363	2
EPSTEIN ARNOLD	MAJ	0-0172177	0157	3
EPSTEIN BENJAMIN	1LT	0-1639005	0252	1
EPSTEIN LOUIS	CW4	W-2112233	0355	1
EPSTEIN PHILIP G	1LT	0-1109275	0246	2
EPSTEIN SIDNEY S	MAJ	0-0500416	0446	2
EPTING ELMER E	MAJ	0-0282423	0947	2
EPTING SYLVIAN W	1LT	0-0390515	1145	2
EPTING THOMAS H	1LT	0-0373432	1044	2
EPTON JOHN W	COL	0-0284766	0566	3
EPTON T L	1LT	0-0947921	1151	1
ERARD JR EDGAR B	CPT	0-0397118	0146	1
ERB CLARENCE L	CW3	W-2152209	0963	1
ERB GEORGE W	LTC	0-1295545	0462	1
ERB JOHN W	CPT	0-0191500	0651	2
ERBE OSCAR F	CW4	W-2122115	1C62	1
ERBES ALBERT C	LTC	0-2034672	0860	1
ERBST OTTO C	MAJ	0-1303127	0159	1
ERD GEORGIA H	MAJ	N-0774051	0165	1
ERDEL BEATRICE A	1LT	N-0772175	0448	2
ERDEL GEORGE T	1LT	0-1302956	0646	2
ERDESKY JOSEPH L	LTC	0-2008529	0965	1
ERDLEY ANNA F	1LT	N-0761089	0745	1
ERDMAN ALEXANDER	LTC	0-2032597	0167	1
ERDMAN ERVIN E	MAJ	0-0999035	C566	1
ERDMAN GEORGE B	CPT	0-1316395	1057	1
ERDMAN WILLIAM K	LTC	0-0918587	0747	2
ERDMANN ARTHUR C	MAJ	0-1010606	0247	1
ERDMANN JR EDWARD A	MAJ	0-1300301	0564	1
ERDMANN LOUIS E	LTC	0-0273482	0266	3

NAME	GRADE	SVC NO	DATE RET MO YR	RET CODE
EROMANN ROBERT E	LTC	0-2007507	1163	1
EROMANN ROY G	CPT	0-1014022	0146	2
EROOFY MAXWELL E	COL	0-0159943	1045	2
ERFURT HENRY F	MAJ	0-1051551	1057	1
ERGLE THEOROORE	LTC	0-0274272	1157	1
ERGOOD ALLEN M	CPT	0-0180249	1057	3
ERHAROT FRANCIS J	LTC	0-1284307	C563	1
ERHART FRANK H	COL	0-0182156	1151	3
ERHART HERMAN A	COL	0-0209409	0554	3
ERICKSEN ERLING	CW2	W-2152235	1060	1
ERICKSEN PAUL O	LTC	0-1018904	C263	2
ERICKSEN ROBERT E	CPT	0-1288207	C944	2
ERICKSON ALGOT E	LTC	0-0359655	1164	3
ERICKSON ALVIN	LTC	0-0349750	0665	3
ERICKSON CARL G	CPT	0-0178849	1155	3
ERICKSON CLARENCE P	LTC	0-0244975	1046	1
ERICKSON DWIGHT A	1LT	0-1050245	C445	2
ERICKSON EARL N	MAJ	C-1688425	C864	1
ERICKSON EDCAR C	M G	0-0171317	0559	1
ERICKSON EDGAR L	CPT	0-0181071	0262	3
ERICKSON EINAR A	LTC	0-0299121	0457	1
ERICKSON ERNST	LTC	0-0919692	0263	3
ERICKSON FLOYD C	LTC	0-1060764	C967	1
ERICKSON GENE C	LTC	C-1284308	0166	1
ERICKSON HARRY	COL	0-0164437	C749	2
ERICKSON HENRY T	MAJ	C-0271827	1067	3
ERICKSON JOHN F	CW4	W-2145420	0261	1
ERICKSON JOHN R	COL	0-0411753	0166	3
ERICKSON JOHN W	1LT	0-0920344	0545	2
ERICKSON JR EDWARD T	1LT	C-1302918	0346	2
ERICKSON JR WARREN D	LTC	0-1548756	C461	1
ERICKSON KARL F	LTC	0-0253213	C157	3
ERICKSON LEONARD A	1LT	0-1109276	C365	3
ERICKSON LOUIS	2LT	0-0195096	C418	1
ERICKSON OLIVER G	MAJ	0-0220106	0955	3
ERICKSON PETER A	LTC	C-1288372	C561	1
ERICKSON RALPH L	LTC	0-0348080	0460	3
ERICKSON REIDAR A	CW4	W-2143270	C967	2
ERICKSON RICHARD A	LTC	0-1184816	0962	1
ERICKSON RICHARD J	CW3	W-2149064	1162	1
ERICKSON ROBERT	LTC	0-0290381	C457	1
ERICKSON ROBERT C	1LT	0-1325207	C246	2
ERICKSON THORSTEN A	LTC	C-1166257	C159	1
ERICKSON VICTOR H	MAJ	0-1923513	0865	1
ERICKSON WILLIAM M	LTC	0-1315288	C962	1
ERICSON EVERETT F	CPT	0-1298520	0247	2
ERICSON JR JOSEPH H	MAJ	0-0527014	C557	2
ERICSON VINCENT H	CW3	W-2205962	0965	1
ERICSSON ADAM E	MAJ	C-0225365	C148	2
ERICSSON ARTHUR J	COL	0-0244419	1049	3
ERIE DEWITT W	LTC	0-0235655	C346	2
ERIKSEN ERIK	MAJ	0-1291968	C454	2
ERIKSEN NORMAN G	MAJ	0-2001735	0366	1
ERIKSON ALDEN F	LTC	0-0170195	1059	3
ERIKSON CARL A	WO1	W-2124703	1044	2
ERIKSON HERBERT R	CPT	0-0502825	1045	2
ERIKSSON NILES L	LTC	0-0331060	C761	1
ERISMAN ROBERT E	CPT	0-0355881	C545	2
ERKES MARION J	MAJ	C-0493273	1055	1
ERKKILA JACK	LTC	0-0294666	0667	3
ERKKILA MARTHA M	MAJ	N-0759158	0866	2
ERLE HAROLD	MAJ	0-0450414	0555	1
ERLE LUTHER M	MAJ	C-1644302	C861	1
ERMELBAUER CARL	CPT	0-1325186	0347	1
ERMENTROUT ROBERT A	LTC	0-0253610	0555	1
ERMERT CARL L	LTC	0-0423374	C658	1
ERMLER PETER J	CPT	C-0300890	0962	3
ERNESS LEE C	CPT	0-1594150	0262	1
ERNEST EDWARD F	MAJ	C-0486107	1152	1
ERNEST HENRY B	CPT	0-1575956	0350	1
ERNEST STANLEY S	MAJ	C-1341867	C864	1
ERNESTI ROGER	CPT	0-0345768	0146	2
ERNSER JOHN J	MAJ	0-1312856	0365	1
ERNST CLAUDE A	MAJ	C-1635847	1160	1
ERNST FRED G	2LT	0-1109277	C845	2

NAME	GRADE	SVC NO	DATE RET MO YR	RET CODE
ERNST GEORGE	MAJ	0-1551392	0263	1
ERNST JOSEPH L	COL	C-0190729	1050	3
ERNST MANFRIC P	LTC	0-1184379	C862	1
ERNST VICTOR L	LTC	0-0324090	0761	3
ERNSTEIN ARTHUR	LTC	0-0257642	0767	3
ERNSTING JR WILLIAM	CPT	0-0921455	0745	2
ERNYEI WILLIAM	CW3	W-2152949	0163	1
EROH JR HOBART V	CPT	C-1540912	0360	1
ERRICSON FREC M	MAJ	0-1823279	1262	2
ERRINGTON ROBERT N	LTC	0-0165167	0455	3
ERSAY EMIL F	LTC	0-0302587	1266	3
ERSIN HUBERT J	CPT	0-1175425	0551	1
ERSKINE ALEXANDER	MAJ	0-0195568	0662	3
ERSKINE FRANK G	MAJ	0-0319314	0566	3
ERSKINE HENRY F	CPT	0-1297698	0446	2
ERSKINE JOHN G	1LT	0-1010911	1045	2
ERSKINE ROBERT K	LTC	0-0194892	1061	3
ERTL CLARENCE E	CPT	0-1304512	0161	1
ERTWINE DOYLE C	WO1	W-2121992	C958	1
ERVIN DARBY E	LTC	0-1322321	1262	1
ERVIN FRED M	WO1	W-2129751	1145	2
ERVIN GLADYS C	CPT	N-0737330	C947	1
ERVIN JR ALVIN R	LTC	0-1558264	0766	1
ERVIN JR ROBERT T	COL	0-0209036	0462	3
ERWIN ANNE H	MAJ	N-0788979	1065	1
ERWIN BEVRL C	MAJ	C-0310595	0545	2
ERWIN EARL	LTC	0-0167923	1059	3
ERWIN ESTHER R	MAJ	N-0800214	0865	1
ERWIN HOWARD	MAJ	0-1648447	0759	1
ERWIN HUGH	CPT	C-0442375	0545	2
ERWIN JAMES E	LTC	0-0382282	0265	3
ERWIN JEFFERSON	CPT	0-2262313	1060	1
ERWIN JOHN T	MAJ	C-201687C	0162	2
ERWIN ROGER J	CPT	C-0450274	0244	2
ERWIN ROY C	MAJ	0-1288881	0258	1
ERWIN ROY M	2LT	0-0339358	1156	3
ERWIN WILLIAM R	COL	0-0453426	0661	1
ERYAVEC MARTIN F	CW4	W-2121275	0659	1
ESAACSON RICHARD L	CPT	0-1046779	0657	1
ESAIAS JOHN R	COL	C-0222010	0648	3
ESATOW THEODORE R	CPT	0-0395717	0549	1
ESCAMCS JOHNNY	1LT	0-0179409	0250	1
ESCH CHARLES A	MAJ	0-1288032	0754	1
ESCH ROLLAND D	CW2	W-214596C	0559	1
ESCH ROYAL L	CPT	0-0473101	0853	1
ESCHENBACHER A H	MAJ	C-1545394	0460	1
ESCOE LINDSY J	CPT	0-0477023	0445	2
ESCUDERO EDMUNDO	COL	0-0313914	0960	1
ESCUE JR CHARLES W	MAJ	0-1182822	1264	2
ESDERTS WILLIAM J	CW2	W-3430123	0966	1
ESENWEIN JR AUGUST	MAJ	C-1647965	0960	1
ESH LELAND D	LTC	0-029092C	0762	1
ESHELMAN CLARENCE F	CPT	0-1018053	0557	1
ESKELSEN RUEL M	LTC	0-0247148	1053	3
ESKOFF JOHN	MAJ	C-1173236	0358	2
ESKRIDGE CHARLES E	CW2	W-2143326	0159	1
ESLINGER WALLACE V	LTC	0-0353729	0754	1
ESMOND WILLIAM O	CPT	0-0414567	0645	1
ESPARAS MANUEL M	CPT	C-1896826	0859	2
ESPARZA ARTURO G	CW3	W-2147662	0862	1
ESPARZA MANUEL M	2LT	0-2055271	0645	2
ESPELIEN ERICK E	MAJ	0-0167101	0648	3
ESPEN JR JOHN M	LTC	0-1186535	0866	1
ESPENSCHADE PARK W	LTC	0-0239851	0166	3
ESPENSHADE PAUL S	LTC	0-0447770	1052	1
ESPERSEN RUBEN W	COL	0-0263448	0962	3
ESPEY HELEN E	MAJ	L-1010017	1264	1
ESPEY JAMES C	1LT	0-0112254	0344	2
ESPINOSA AURELIO M	LTC	0-0907331	0667	3
ESPINOSA MARIO A	CW3	W-2146759	0461	1
ESPOSITO EVA E	1LT	N-0735359	0146	1
ESPOSITO JOSEPH F	MAJ	0-1534475	1061	2
ESPY JR GOODMAN B	LTC	0-025913C	0167	3
ESSAM DUANE R	MAJ	0-0391097	0854	2
ESSECK RUDOLPH B	1LT	0-1298682	0551	2

NAME	GRADE	SVC NO	DATE RET MO YR	RET CODE
ESSER GILBERT F	LTC	0-0337558	C956	3
ESSEX JR GEORGE T	LTC	0-1061382	1263	1
ESSEX MARTIN J	1LT	0-1821989	C846	1
ESSEX WILLIAM	MAJ	C-1997523	C765	2
ESSRIG ROSE B	2LT	N-0758859	C346	1
ESTABROOK VIVIAN A	CW3	V-0104057	1263	1
ESTARIS MATEO	1LT	0-1896785	C250	1
ESTAVILLE LAWRENCE F	1LT	0-1017086	1045	2
ESTEL JR ADOLPH T	CPT	0-0407538	0247	1
ESTELL JAMES M	CW3	W-2129941	C766	2
ESTER JESSE M	1LT	0-1593560	1057	1
ESTERLY ARTHUR H	MAJ	0-0139610	0150	3
ESTES AUBREY C	CPT	0-0478150	1147	2
ESTES CHILTON J	CPT	0-0298067	1045	2
ESTES CLIFF M	CPT	0-0383609	0146	2
ESTES EUGENE J	CW3	W-2205446	0563	1
ESTES EZRA W	MAJ	C-0888525	0753	1
ESTES FRED K	COL	0-0199927	C258	3
ESTES HORACE O	CPT	0-1289404	0762	1
ESTES JR EDGAR S	LTC	0-0241794	C566	3
ESTES LOREN C	MAJ	C-1797106	0259	2
ESTES ROBERT M	MAJ	C-0367499	0156	1
ESTES WALTER	MAJ	C-0505288	C847	1
ESTES WARD M	LTC	0-0253007	C460	3
ESTES WELDON L	CPT	0-2273273	0758	2
ESTEVEZ MANUEL M	LTC	C-1326047	C563	1
ESTEY WILLIAM H	LTC	0-0439452	1264	1
ESTOCK JOHN A	LTC	0-1580907	0261	1
ESTOK FRANK W	MAJ	C-1186000	C465	1
ESTORGE LEONARD	CPT	0-0337053	C546	2
ESTRADA LEON R	CPT	C-0068098	0767	2
ESTRADA THOMAS E	LTC	0-2033605	C167	1
ESTRIDGE ROY W	CPT	0-0919889	1144	2
ESTRIDGE THOMAS W	CPT	0-0990880	0164	2
ESTUS ROBERT C	1LT	C-1797107	C246	1
ESTY LUCILLE M	1LT	N-0722664	1145	1
ESZES JOSEPH R	LTC	0-1558137	C865	1
ETHERIDGE FRANK W	CW3	W-2148616	0263	1
ETHERIDGE J T	MAJ	C-1642841	0358	1
ETHERIDGE WILLIAM C	CW2	W-2204983	0463	1
ETHERTON RAY E	CW2	W-2148561	0261	1
ETHINGTON IVAN C	1LT	0-1114917	C445	2
ETHINGTON WILLIAM M	MAJ	0-1923585	1164	1
ETHREDGE JACK R	MAJ	C-1877765	C765	1
ETHRIDGE JAMES C	1LT	0-0905111	1144	2
ETHRIDGE KENNETH M	CPT	0-1326541	C164	1
ETHRIDGE QUINN	MAJ	C-1996473	0465	1
ETINGOFF WILLIAM	CW2	W-2144534	1154	1
ETNIRE LEONARD H	CPT	0-1936961	C365	1
ETTENGER MORRIS S	CPT	0-1695938	C146	2
ETTER EDWARD F	LTC	0-0237735	C861	3
ETTER FORREST S	LTC	0-0245580	1145	2
ETTER HALL	LTC	0-0103435	0649	3
ETTER HAROLD K	CW2	W-2150806	0163	1
ETTER HELEN M	MAJ	N-0778675	0865	1
ETTER JOE W	LTC	0-0158792	C959	3
ETTER LEWIS E	LTC	0-0237798	0261	3
ETTINGER ARTHUR	CPT	0-0275152	0666	3
ETTINGER JEROME	1LT	0-1746822	0345	2
ETTINGER ROBERT C W	1LT	0-1320830	0348	2
ETZ EDWARD C	1LT	C-0520882	C545	2
ETZEL BERNARD A	1LT	0-0530045	C146	2
ETZWEILER ALBERT R	MAJ	C-0185024	1149	3
EUBANK CHARLES G	COL	0-0174262	C961	3
EUBANK DICK B	1LT	0-0286365	0645	2
EUBANK GEORGE R	MAJ	C-2007000	0267	1
EUBANK HENRY B	2LT	C-1317155	1045	2
EUBANK JAMES M	CW2	W-2149696	C161	1
EUBANK JARRELL M	MAJ	C-0506353	0567	2
EUBANK WILLIAM B	COL	0-0268815	C367	3
EUBANK WILLIAM H	CW2	W-2212209	0967	1
EUBANKS GEORGE W	LTC	0-0323079	C546	2
EUBANKS HERMAN T	COL	0-0255041	1265	3
EUBANKS JR BURNIE L	CW3	W-2144294	1060	1
EUBANKS MARTIN F	LTC	0-0451593	0358	1

NAME	GRADE	SVC NO	DATE RET MO YR	RET CODE
EUCHNER PERRY C	COL	C-0160785	0452	3
EUDY CHARLIE W	LTC	0-0493620	0155	1
EUKEL DONALD D	CW3	RW-2207986	0766	1
EULER HENRY J	LTC	0-0140008	1051	3
EULER ROLAND A	1LT	0-0494657	1045	2
EULLER RICHARD R	COL	0-0300982	0867	3
EUNICE DONALD A	CPT	0-1998653	1053	2
EURE JAMES C	LTC	0-1592803	0566	1
EURE OTHO A	MAJ	0-0520316	0746	2
EURE WILLIAM J	CW2	W-2146776	1060	1
EUSTACE CHARLES C	MAJ	C-0269170	0867	3
EUSTACE VIRGIL R	CPT	0-1000751	0946	7
EUSTROM HARVEY H	LTC	0-0177436	1047	2
EUTEMARK FRANK	MAJ	0-0947116	1165	2
EUTIZE WALTER J	MAJ	C-1111598	1162	1
EVANCHO ANDREW	CW2	W-2149319	0261	1
EVANDER DAN L	MAJ	0-0332194	0555	3
EVANGELISTA PETER J	CW2	W-2142634	0959	1
EVANICSKO MICHAEL	MAJ	C-1646735	0261	1
EVANOSKI JOSEPH	1LT	0-1018118	0246	1
EVANS ABEL W	1LT	0-1299391	0546	2
EVANS ARLEIGH U	LTC	0-0295696	1061	1
EVANS ARTHUR E	CPT	0-0249925	C645	2
EVANS ARTHUR P	LTC	0-0306350	0160	1
EVANS BENJAMIN F	COL	0-0174337	0648	3
EVANS BERT M	1LT	C-1119294	C550	1
EVANS BILLIE R	MAJ	N-0780335	C666	1
EVANS BLANCHE	MAJ	N-0759506	0163	1
EVANS CARLOS B	1LT	0-1305903	0645	2
EVANS CARVEL S	COL	0-0319357	0266	3
EVANS CATHERINE	MAJ	N-0771437	0847	1
EVANS CECIL F	LTC	0-0214875	0958	3
EVANS CHARLES R	1LT	0-1012116	0945	2
EVANS CLARENCE B	CPT	0-0490715	0160	2
EVANS DANIEL	MAJ	0-1040216	0161	1
EVANS DARYL C	1LT	0-1558265	0346	2
EVANS DAVID P	CW3	W-2147247	0563	1
EVANS DAVID C	CW3	W-2144842	0662	1
EVANS DAVID J	MAJ	C-0235075	0960	3
EVANS DAVID L	LTC	0-1703769	0361	1
EVANS DAVID W	COL	0-034726C	0266	1
EVANS DEAN P	1LT	0-0146131	1054	3
EVANS DON G	LTC	0-0223408	0150	3
EVANS DORIS Y	1LT	N-0723456	0546	1
EVANS DOYLE H	CW3	W-2205759	0365	1
EVANS EARL N	CW3	W-2151830	1063	1
EVANS EDGAR	1LT	0-1301972	0644	2
EVANS EDWARD A	B G	0-0122172	0955	3
EVANS EDWARD R	LTC	0-1102231	1163	1
EVANS ELDEN E	LTC	0-0402858	0161	1
EVANS ELDON E	CPT	C-035440R	1145	2
EVANS ELEANOR J	MAJ	N-0800007	0765	1
EVANS ERNEST A	LTC	0-0289454	0658	3
EVANS EVERETTE C	CPT	0-0972069	1061	1
EVANS FERDINAND	COL	0-040492C	0366	1
EVANS FRED C	LTC	C-0451275	0359	1
EVANS GEORGE F	LTC	0-1287686	1059	1
EVANS GEORGE G	COL	0-0150734	1050	3
EVANS GEORGE G	LTC	0-0451059	0958	2
EVANS GEORGE J	LTC	0-0146608	0653	3
EVANS GEORGE M	CPT	C-0265898	0445	2
EVANS GEORGE O	LTC	C-0226768	C360	3
EVANS GEORGE S	MAJ	C-1593562	0960	1
EVANS GEORGE T	MAJ	C-0387306	0346	2
EVANS GEORGE V	MAJ	0-1845272	0559	1
EVANS GERALD W	1LT	0-1534724	0746	2
EVANS GOLDEN F	LTC	0-1000938	1158	1
EVANS GORDON F	1LT	0-0285657	0343	2
EVANS HAROLE M	CW2	W-2141268	0257	1
EVANS HARLEY W	CW2	W-2211118	0864	1
EVANS HAROLD A	MAJ	0-2001821	1164	1
EVANS HAROLD J	CW3	W-2109635	0357	1
EVANS HARRY A	WO1	W-2108939	0251	2
EVANS HARRY D	CW3	W-2211438	0766	1
EVANS HENRY C	M G	0-0124891	0957	3

NAME	GRADE	SVC NO	DATE RET MO YR	RET CODE
EVANS HENRY M	LTC	0-C161038	0254	3
EVANS HILARY W	W01	W-2133221	0754	1
EVANS HORACE L	2LT	C-2048614	C245	2
EVANS HUGH F	COL	C-0308498	C161	3
EVANS J T	1LT	0-0548293	0446	1
EVANS JAMES	LTC	0-0404230	0859	1
EVANS JAMES C	CPT	0-1692612	0358	1
EVANS JAMES H	1LT	0-0414321	0943	2
EVANS JOHN B	COL	C-0259166	1046	2
EVANS JOHN F	LTC	0-0262751	0557	1
EVANS JOHN R	LTC	0-0255997	0166	3
EVANS JOHN T	LTC	0-0238424	0865	3
EVANS JOHN W	1LT	0-0326759	C547	2
EVANS JOHN W	CPT	0-2050223	0263	1
EVANS JON P	COL	C-0052010	0567	1
EVANS JR C J	LTC	0-0146167	C159	3
EVANS JR DAVID J	MAJ	C-1167826	1060	1
EVANS JR EDWARD V	CPT	0-1283745	1046	1
EVANS JR GILES L	COL	0-0020603	0660	1
EVANS JR HARRY B	CPT	0-C397364	1147	2
EVANS JR JOHN H	LTC	0-1172448	0762	1
EVANS JR LINTON H	LTC	C-1037479	C361	1
EVANS JR LONDON	CPT	0-4009441	1265	1
EVANS JR RICHARD W	COL	0-0285236	0846	2
EVANS JR WILLIAM A	1LT	0-1995086	1145	2
EVANS KENNETH B	LTC	0-1106718	0461	1
EVANS KENNETH K	LTC	C-0347953	1060	1
EVANS LEE	CPT	0-0305331	0744	2
EVANS LEONARD	MAJ	C-1644201	C461	1
EVANS LEONARD L	MAJ	0-0213836	0763	3
EVANS LESLIE L	B G	0-0246332	0659	3
EVANS LESTER J	LTC	0-0316975	0746	2
EVANS LESTER K	MAJ	C-1100974	0557	1
EVANS LLOYD A	CPT	0-0230625	1060	3
EVANS LLOYD E	1LT	0-1308938	1145	2
EVANS LOUIE G	CW3	W-2146127	0162	1
EVANS MARVIN J	B G	0-1100975	C167	3
EVANS MAX C	MAJ	C-1541159	C559	1
EVANS MELTON L	CW3	W-2150285	C161	1
EVANS MELVIN T	CW2	W-2206921	0264	1
EVANS MORGAN Z	MAJ	0-1634730	1060	1
EVANS NEAL T	COL	0-0232787	1164	3
EVANS NILE	COL	0-0460368	0353	1
EVANS OBIE F	CW4	W-2146561	0165	1
EVANS ORAL B	CPT	C-1322010	1058	1
EVANS ORVILLE T	CPT	0-1685138	1145	2
EVANS OSCAR	MAJ	C-1031636	C365	1
EVANS OWEN C	CPT	0-0981005	0852	1
EVANS PAUL	2LT	0-1300949	1043	2
EVANS PAUL B	LTC	0-0288307	0762	1
EVANS PAUL C	CPT	0-1010725	C954	1
EVANS PAUL J	LTC	0-1691786	0763	1
EVANS PAUL R	1LT	0-1000040	0354	2
EVANS PAUL R	MAJ	0-1552663	C555	1
EVANS PERCY W	COL	0-0115979	0848	3
EVANS PHILLIP I	MAJ	0-1298846	0661	1
EVANS RAYMOND W	1LT	0-1304362	1045	1
EVANS RICHARD H	CPT	0-0362568	0745	1
EVANS RICHARD J	MAJ	0-0574543	0560	1
EVANS RICHARD W	LTC	0-1177381	C966	1
EVANS ROBERT A	MAJ	0-1645827	C361	1
EVANS ROBERT C	LTC	0-1010953	1263	1
EVANS ROBLEY O	1LT	0-1895308	0745	2
EVANS RONALD M	CPT	0-1035114	0346	2
EVANS ROY O	W01	W-2127562	0948	1
EVANS RUTH	2LT	N-0724690	C644	1
EVANS STANLEY G	LTC	0-1946042	0264	1
EVANS STUART	LTC	0-0286015	0467	3
EVANS STUART A	CPT	0-1168655	1052	1
EVANS THOMAS A	CPT	0-0333628	0356	3
EVANS THOMAS H	COL	0-0261219	0566	3
EVANS THOMAS H	LTC	C-1168656	1167	1
EVANS THOMAS J	MAJ	0-2020002	0263	1
EVANS THOMAS M	MAJ	0-0107287	C656	3
EVANS TREVOR	MAJ	0-1306954	0161	1
EVANS VAUGHN M	LTC	0-1946243	0962	1
EVANS VAUHGN C	MAJ	0-1297699	0364	1
EVANS VIRGIL O	CPT	0-1287687	1060	1
EVANS WALKER W	LTC	0-0378141	C661	1
EVANS WALTER L	MAJ	C-1726621	1050	1
EVANS WAYNE L	LTC	0-0323179	C865	2
EVANS WILLIAM A	LTC	0-0368677	0361	1
EVANS WILLIAM D	MAJ	C-0181923	0862	3
EVANS WILLIAM F	CPT	0-0983063	0263	2
EVANS WILLIAM R	MAJ	0-1014440	0356	1
EVANS WILLIAM W	CPT	0-0504871	0546	2
EVANTS JOE F	CW2	W-2206289	1163	1
EVARTS FORREST S	CW3	W-2153183	1064	1
EVARTS SAMUEL W	1LT	0-0142643	0150	3
EVE ROBERT R	CW3	W-2149763	0761	1
EVEDON ROBERT A	1LT	0-1916844	1052	2
EVELAND THOMAS C	LTC	0-0338826	1160	1
EVELAND WILLIAM	LTC	0-0253060	1050	1
EVENBURGH RALPH L	LTC	0-0240268	0259	3
EVENS ALVEN	CW2	W-2109334	1053	2
EVENS WARREN M	2LT	0-1322011	0445	2
EVENSEN NORMAN	CW4	W-2144668	0660	1
EVENSON EDWIN F	LTC	0-0256525	0859	3
EVENSON FRED E	CPT	0-2262297	1160	1
EVEREST FOLSOM	COL	0-0180304	0446	2
EVERETT ADRIAN J	LTC	0-1635849	0765	1
EVERETT BILL B	MAJ	0-1293391	0263	1
EVERETT BURTON N	LTC	0-0334054	0854	1
EVERETT CECIL R	COL	0-0146604	0456	3
EVERETT DON W	LTC	0-1170728	0265	1
EVERETT EARL P	LTC	0-1301460	1164	1
EVERETT GOODMAN C	MAJ	0-1544315	C559	1
EVERETT HAROLD R	MAJ	0-0989116	0166	1
EVERETT JOHN A	MAJ	0-1555202	0457	2
EVERETT JOHN W	COL	0-0168798	0360	3
EVERETT LEROY	COL	0-0331168	0660	1
EVERETT LEWIS J	LTC	0-1109920	1162	1
EVERETT MYRON A	LTC	0-1102233	0954	1
EVERETT PERCY E	CW2	W-2102885	1148	1
EVERETT PERLEY L	COL	0-0289822	1160	1
EVERETT ROBERT L	CPT	0-0486248	0549	1
EVERETT VAUGHN R	LTC	0-0212256	0564	3
EVERETT WILLIAM J	CW3	W-2203344	0664	1
EVERETT WILLIAM R	MAJ	0-0402367	0646	2
EVERETT WILLIAM S	COL	0-0225063	0864	3
EVERHART EDGAR S	COL	0-0174822	0648	3
EVERHART WILLIAM G	1LT	0-0925440	1145	2
EVERITT DONALD R	CW3	W-2147752	0762	1
EVERLY RAYMOND H	MAJ	C-1100576	0862	1
EVERS FRANCIS O	LTC	0-1298645	0261	1
EVERS JOHN	MAJ	C-1575295	1054	1
EVERSOLE EDWIN A	MAJ	0-2262145	0662	1
EVERSOLE GARDNER S	CPT	0-0315735	1045	1
EVERSOLE JR FRANK R	LTC	0-1010839	0164	1
EVERSOLE JR JOSEPH	LTC	0-1574712	1163	1
EVERSOLE WILLIAM F	1LT	0-0326003	0944	2
EVERSON CLYDE W	MAJ	0-0994974	0464	1
EVERSON ROBERT F	LTC	0-1321111	1167	1
EVERT FLORENCE M	MAJ	N-0700703	0646	1
EVERT GERTRUDE S	MAJ	N-0700704	1045	1
EVETT ROBERT W	MAJ	0-1594597	1055	1
EVETTS JAMES K	LTC	0-0917350	1045	2
EVEY JOHN M	MAJ	0-0174235	0648	3
EVILSIZER LESTER J	2LT	0-0326663	0157	3
EVINGER FLOYD H	MAJ	0-0107317	0644	2
EVOY MARTIN	COL	0-0225638	1262	3
EVRARD SERVAIS L	LTC	0-0172032	0254	3
EWALD DONALD F	LTC	0-0222369	C646	1
EWALT LELAND G	LTC	0-0321163	1265	3
EWALT THEODORE A	LTC	0-1695687	0561	1
EWAN JOHN R	1LT	0-0400225	0642	2
EWART RYLAND K	LTC	0-0374029	0663	2
EWASKIE HARRY	1LT	0-0448112	0944	2
EWBANK GENE M	MAJ	0-0862737	0758	1
EWBANK JOHN M	LTC	0-0300809	0366	1
EWERS SCOTT H	LTC	0-0296943	1165	3
EWING CHARLES G	LTC	0-0387667	0566	1
EWING CHESNEY G	LTC	0-0245103	1056	3
EWING CLARKE L	COL	0-0253951	0156	3
EWING DONALD E	MAJ	C-1598556	0962	1
EWING DOROTHY A	MAJ	N-0769526	1166	1
EWING EARLE E	COL	C-0110470	1055	1
EWING EDWARD T	MAJ	C-1293740	0661	1
EWING HARRIET F	1LT	N-0760463	C146	1
EWING HARRY C	MAJ	0-1946044	1054	1
EWING HARRY G	CPT	0-1920107	1058	2
EWING HOWARD F	COL	0-0337144	C664	1
EWING JAMES C	2LT	C-0206534	0156	3
EWING JAMES W	COL	C-0259916	0847	1
EWING JOHN W	LTC	0-1948453	C966	2
EWING MARLIN B	CPT	0-0986940	C553	2
EWING MARTHA A	CPT	N-0702793	0147	1
EWING RALPH B	2LT	0-1946244	1144	2
EWING RAYMOND O	CPT	0-2055335	0546	2
EWING ROBERT E	CPT	C-0515513	C451	2
EWING ROY L	MAJ	C-0486135	C158	1
EWING THOMAS G	1LT	0-0497056	0646	2
EWING WILLIAM A	MAJ	C-1544229	0557	1
EWING WILLIAM H	MAJ	C-1588991	0466	1
EWING WILLIAM W	CW2	W-2146236	1160	1
EWING WYLIE B	1LT	0-C156079	1150	3
EWOLDT LEON H	CW4	W-2148152	C667	2
EWRY RALPH H	COL	0-0214465	0155	3
EWTON FRANCIS R	1LT	C-0376239	0344	2
EXLEY JOSEPH M	CPT	0-0324386	C954	3
EXLINE MAX R	MAJ	0-1686374	0556	1
EXNER JOSEPH H	CW2	W-2119594	1048	1
EXNER WILLARD B	CW2	W-2152455	C659	1
EXTON WALTER J	2LT	0-1300950	1144	2
EXUM CHARLES E	MAJ	0-0976490	0165	1
EXUM JAMES V	W01	W-2108976	0551	1
EY JR JOHN A	LTC	0-1701694	0164	1
EY LEO F	MAJ	C-0144122	0146	2
EYCLESHYMER HAROLD O	LTC	0-0299506	0565	3
EYER PHILIP F	MAJ	C-1635852	C457	1
EYESTONE RAYMOND T	COL	0-0438054	0658	1
EYHERABIDE STEPHEN P	1LT	0-1297862	0745	1
EYLE GEORGE W	LTC	0-1642844	0867	2
EYLER JR HARRY F	LTC	C-0293777	0866	3
EYMER CLARENCE M	COL	C-0196296	C346	2
EYRE HARLAN A	MAJ	0-1581120	1264	1
EYRICH ALBERT A	MAJ	0-1102720	0964	3
EYSTER JAMES A	MAJ	C-0148010	0156	3
EYSTER RICHARD W	2LT	0-1302287	C144	2
EZELL KINCHELOE	LTC	0-0300390	0762	2
EZZARD WILLIAM T	LTC	0-0315215	0167	1
EZZELL ALVIN O	CW3	W-2152524	C763	1
EZZELL JAMES M	CPT	0-1185616	0160	2
EZZELL LAURISTON	CPT	0-1693008	C346	2
FAASSE ADRIAN	MAJ	C-0468452	0946	2
FABE S SALEM	CPT	C-0398473	0744	2
FABEL DONALD C	COL	C-0144379	0857	3
FABER BENJAMIN L	1LT	0-0434868	1045	2
FABER EDWIN J	LTC	0-0232682	C762	3
FABER JR JOHN E	MAJ	C-0490968	1045	2
FABER WILLIAM M	MAJ	0-0975287	1061	1
FABERT MARVIN C	LTC	0-1031479	1263	1
FABIAN EMIL M	MAJ	C-0115980	1145	2
FABIAN EUGENE R	MAJ	C-1533310	1055	1
FABIAN ISAAC P	CW3	RW-2146973	0966	1
FABIAN JOSEPH A	MAJ	0-2212049	0463	1
FABIAN MARY J	MAJ	L-0200504	C865	3
FABLINGER WILLIAM O	CPT	0-1322213	0147	1
FABRIC FRED	1LT	0-0938169	C348	2
FABRICK JOHN	LTC	0-0529235	C866	1
FABRIZE ANGELO C	CW4	W-2117196	0355	1
FACE ALBERT R	1LT	0-0410598	1043	2
FACENDA ALBERT J	CW4	W-2120295	C262	3
FACER GRANT T	1LT	0-0550579	0446	2
FACEY JR FRED W	LTC	C-0902370	1266	3
FACKENTHALL ALLAN H	W01	W-2104037	1044	2
FACKRELL ALVIN P	CW3	W-2152176	1162	1
FACKLER JR JOHN M	1LT	0-0330146	0542	2
FACKO ROBERT E	LTC	0-0493371	0765	1
FACTEAU HENRY H	MAJ	C-0136053	0550	3
FADDEN VERNON J	LTC	0-0455855	0361	2
FADDIS CHARLES I	COL	0-0187211	0650	3
FADDIS CLIFFORD B	MAJ	0-0353166	0759	2
FADER CHARLES	CPT	0-0503359	0145	2
FADLEY KENNETH L	CPT	0-0505004	0548	1
FAES JESSE G	COL	C-0130201	0454	3
FAETH HENRY J	MAJ	0-1341528	0962	1
FAGAN LEMUEL T	COL	0-0357368	0863	3
FAGAN QUENTIN E	CW3	W-2152492	C165	1
FAGAN ROBERT F	2LT	0-1054559	0345	2
FAGAN WALTER F	LTC	0-1016387	0962	1
FAGERBERG EVERT C	1LT	0-1640433	0346	1
FAGGARD LIONEL E	MAJ	0-1552062	0860	1
FAGNANT PROSPER A	MAJ	0-0583754	0661	1
FAGONE FRANCIS A	COL	0-0265395	0159	3
FAGUET BENJAMIN B	CPT	0-0533150	0546	1
FAHEY BERNARD O	MAJ	0-2025641	0461	1
FAHEY GEORGE L	MAJ	C-0505527	0647	2
FAHEY JOHN J	COL	C-0385525	0360	1
FAHEY JOSEPH M	LTC	0-1894573	0365	3
FAHEY JR DANIEL C	COL	0-0247716	1266	3
FAHL MARTIN A	LTC	0-1318292	0563	1
FAHLEY ANTON N	CPT	0-1913670	0336	1
FAHNERT CURTIS F	MAJ	0-0160363	0354	3
FAHRINGER VICTOR T	COL	0-0158915	0646	2
FAHRICK LOUIS E	LTC	0-0189104	0951	3
FAIL JR JAMES F	MAJ	0-1798570	1160	1
FAILLACE GAETANO	MAJ	0-2030375	1264	1
FAILOR RALPH M	CPT	0-0382895	0246	2
FAIN BYRON R	1LT	C-0527373	1045	2
FAIN JR JAMES T	LTC	0-0250063	0467	3
FAIN STANSELL H	CPT	0-0407350	1146	2
FAIR CHARLES H	LTC	0-0395085	0854	1
FAIR CLIFTON D	CW2	W-3430478	0167	1
FAIR HAROLD	LTC	0-0442950	1150	1
FAIR HARRY	LTC	0-0954168	0667	1
FAIR JOSEPH K	MAJ	C-0108482	1036	1
FAIR ORSON F	1LT	0-1316634	0446	2
FAIR ROBERT J	LTC	0-1280818	0663	2
FAIR THEODORE	LTC	0-1017273	1266	1
FAIRBANKS CLIFTON A	COL	0-0287363	0667	3
FAIRBANKS LESTER L	LTC	0-1557839	0561	1
FAIRBANKS LYNN N	LTC	0-0321062	0365	3
FAIRBANKS RUSSELL	MAJ	0-1308802	0761	2
FAIRBANKS WESTON E	MAJ	0-2007585	0761	1
FAIRCHILD DUWAIN H	MAJ	0-1640435	0858	2
FAIRCHILD GEORGE W	COL	0-0138773	1151	3
FAIRCHILD JACKSON K	COL	0-0187028	0449	3
FAIRCHILD JOHN C	COL	0-0347067	0162	1
FAIRCHILD ORLC R	CW3	W-2147972	0763	1
FAIRCHILD TED	1LT	0-1589820	1266	2
FAIRCHILD WILLIAM H	COL	0-0454625	0761	1
FAIRES THOMAS F	MAJ	0-0252082	0646	2
FAIRFAX HARRY	CW2	W-2112073	0350	2
FAIRFIELD WILLIAM A	MAJ	C-0224999	1044	2
FAIRMAN CHARLES	COL	C-0118642	0757	3
FAIRWEATHER ELWYN B	MAJ	0-2049236	0163	1
FAIRWEATHER PATRICK	MAJ	0-0486676	0964	3
FAITH CHARLES M	LTC	0-1295854	1166	1
FAITZ EVERETT K	CPT	0-0298193	1163	3
FAJARDO AURELIO G	1LT	0-1896571	0149	1
FAKE GORDEN C	CPT	C-1284690	0545	2
FALANDERS EDWARD W	CPT	0-0152093	0250	3
FALASCA LAWRENCE J	LTC	0-1948588	1262	1
FALBE SR JOHN J	MAJ	0-1591706	0357	1
FALCK HAROLD E	LTC	0-1294284	0961	1
FALCON DAVIS P	LTC	0-0328273	0160	1
FALCON JR SIMON F	LTC	C-0275088	0954	1
FALCONER JAMES L	2LT	0-1178784	0445	2
FALCONER LEONARD J	CPT	0-1885817	1065	1

NAME	GRADE	SVC NO	DATE RET MO YR	RET CODE
FALEN AUGUST C	MAJ	O-1288725	0660	1
FALISE ALPHONSE	LTC	O-0138810	0254	3
FALK ALBION J	CPT	O-0488259	0847	1
FALK ARTHUR E	MAJ	O-1845881	0951	1
FALK BERNARD S	MAJ	O-1114920	1262	1
FALK DONALD A	LTC	O-0297058	0262	3
FALK MILTON	LTC	O-0307712	0966	1
FALKE THEODORE W	1LT	O-0490713	0543	2
FALKENAU ROBERT M	COL	O-0136601	0344	2
FALKENBERG GEORGE	1LT	O-0169400	1054	3
FALKENBURY ROBERT O	LTC	O-1300467	0964	1
FALKENRATH JOHN A	1LT	O-0452018	0646	2
FALKENSTINE ALLAN	LTC	O-0162950	0357	3
FALKENSTROM ARTHUR L	MAJ	O-1337286	1061	1
FALKNER MURRAY C	MAJ	O-0263713	0659	3
FALKNER SR JAMES E	MAJ	O-1341870	0764	1
FALKNER WILLIAM J	LTC	O-0391611	0561	1
FALKOVIC FRANK O	MAJ	O-1100578	0761	1
FALKOVICH MARK F	LTC	O-0384163	0557	1
FALLAI HOMER J	LTC	O-0235370	0662	3
FALLEUR JULIEN G	COL	O-0260463	0465	3
FALLIN EDMUND R	LTC	O-2010597	0566	1
FALLIN EDWARD O	MAJ	O-2035307	0263	1
FALLIS FRANK H	CW2	W-2147217	1164	1
FALLON JOHN W	LTC	O-1292856	0961	1
FALLON WILLIAM H	LTC	O-0199713	1053	3
FALLS LLOYD W	2LT	O-1319188	0645	2
FALLS RAYMOND O	COL	O-0319618	1060	3
FALLS ROLAND E	MAJ	O-0255752	0249	1
FALSEY EDWARD T	1LT	O-0529722	0646	2
FALSTICK CLEMENT J	CW2	W-2142761	0766	1
FALTINOW TOM J	MAJ	O-1038609	1162	1
FALVEY ARTHUR W	CPT	O-0130986	0252	3
FALZGRAF BENJIMAN A	LTC	O-0364166	0557	1
FALZONE CHARLES V	CW3	W-2147829	1062	1
FAMBROUGH JAMES M	COL	O-0216188	1062	3
FAMULARO NICHOLAS A	MAJ	O-0367477	0446	2
FANCHALSKY ELIZABETH	MAJ	N-0725765	0967	1
FANCHER HARVEY A	MAJ	O-0108656	0733	1
FANCHER HOWARD W	CW3	W-2143453	1060	2
FANDLE FRANK J	CPT	O-0108339	0250	1
FANEUF MARJORIE E	1LT	N-0721239	0546	1
FANGEROW WILLIAM E	LTC	O-0468655	0348	2
FANJOY ALLAN G	1LT	O-2204607	0853	1
FANJOY BERTHA J	MAJ	N-0756315	1065	1
FANKBONER WILSON M	CPT	O-1170358	0347	2
FANN BILLY M	CPT	O-2011098	0462	2
FANN WILLIAM E	CW4	W-2110606	0659	1
FANNIN ROBERT	MAJ	O-0980107	0163	1
FANNIN STELLA J	2LT	N-0735390	0645	1
FANNIN WILLIAM C	MAJ	O-0488415	0954	1
FANNING HOMER E	LTC	O-0269802	1263	3
FANNING JAMES C	LTC	O-0227584	1262	3
FANNING JOHN H	CPT	O-0110769	0213	1
FANNING MARY C	MAJ	R-0002281	0464	2
FANNING MERLE J	CW2	W-2214885	1166	1
FANNON WALTER C	1LT	O-1295002	0846	2
FANSLER EDWARD	MAJ	O-0499514	0157	1
FANSLER LYMAN C	MAJ	O-0979003	0167	1
FANT GLENN E	COL	O-0331752	0865	1
FANT HANDY R	COL	O-0208159	1263	3
FANT JOHN F	LTC	O-0172942	0158	3
FANT SHERMAN B	MAJ	O-1924775	0766	1
FANTAUZZI JOSE	CW4	W-2114068	0557	1
FANTOM ERNEST R	CPT	O-0174334	1054	3
FANUCCHI ANNA R	1LT	N-0728814	0246	1
FARACI FRANK J	MAJ	O-2029088	0563	1
FARAGHER JOHN H	1LT	O-1018426	0945	2
FARBER CHARLES F	LTC	O-1053127	0667	1
FARBER JACK E	CPT	O-1283228	0546	2
FARBES LOU J	COL	O-0224984	1054	3
FARDAHL NELS	LTC	O-0297580	0764	1
FARDEN BERNARD N	COL	O-0251148	0660	1
FARELL JOSEPH H	MAJ	O-1922585	0764	1
FARGO CHARLES C	COL	O-0245810	0559	1

NAME	GRADE	SVC NO	DATE RET MO YR	RET CODE
FARGO JAMES C	LTC	O-0188006	0648	3
FARGO MARY M	1LT	N-0725321	0546	2
FARGO WARREN C	COL	O-0237215	0450	3
FARGO WELLS	COL	O-0186674	1160	1
FARGUSSON RALPH M	MAJ	O-2212033	0962	1
FARHAT MAYNARD M	MAJ	O-0356679	1145	2
FARIA JUAN L	MAJ	O-0294534	0962	3
FARIEL WILLIAM D	CW2	W-2213540	0766	2
FARINA VINCENT F	MAJ	O-0453102	0945	2
FARINACCI MAURICE G	CPT	O-0343724	0745	2
FARINATO JOHN J	2LT	O-1999975	0246	2
FARINGTON IRWIN E	MAJ	O-0186643	1157	3
FARINHOLT WILLIAM W	LTC	O-0269460	1067	3
FARIS EDITH	2LT	N-0727042	0444	1
FARIS THOMAS M	COL	O-0193125	1159	3
FARKAS ARCHIE J	WO1	W-2115264	0854	1
FARLAND GEORGE A	CW3	W-2151811	0862	1
FARLEMAN MERWYN G	LTC	O-0253013	0566	3
FARLER FRED S	CPT	O-0509924	0947	2
FARLEY ARTHUR R	MAJ	O-0945578	0661	1
FARLEY FRANCIS A	LTC	O-1299018	0763	3
FARLEY FRANCIS J	MAJ	O-1285404	1061	1
FARLEY FRANK H	MAJ	O-0484817	0354	1
FARLEY FREDERICK	MAJ	O-1598557	0962	1
FARLEY GRACE E	LTC	N-0756631	0266	3
FARLEY JOHN C	1LT	O-0928063	0645	2
FARLEY JOHN L	COL	O-0174058	0452	3
FARLEY JOSEPH J	COL	O-0275583	0859	1
FARLEY JR ALBERT W	LTC	O-1080443	0562	1
FARLEY MATTHEW R	MAJ	O-0474060	0647	1
FARLEY PAUL J	COL	O-0134488	0456	3
FARLEY SAMUEL N	LTC	O-0901522	0265	3
FARLEY THOMAS J	CPT	O-1322012	0952	1
FARLEY THOMAS J	2LT	O-1590443	0244	2
FARLEY WIRT P	LTC	O-0319685	0853	1
FARMER ANTHONY X	WO1	W-2147480	0454	2
FARMER CHARLES D	MAJ	O-2266315	1167	1
FARMER CHARLIE H	CPT	O-0258486	0546	1
FARMER EDWARD S	MAJ	O-1284309	0457	1
FARMER FRAMPTON W	CPT	O-0324387	0553	3
FARMER GARY R	LTC	O-1105282	1060	1
FARMER GEORGE A	LTC	O-1336052	0964	1
FARMER GEORGE R	CPT	O-0157234	1145	2
FARMER HENRY C	MAJ	O-0972489	0965	1
FARMER HOLLY S	CPT	O-0523542	0553	2
FARMER HOWARD	CPT	O-0372281	1146	2
FARMER JACK J	MAJ	O-1105417	0157	1
FARMER JAMES E	LTC	O-1043622	0264	1
FARMER JAMES L	LTC	O-0385629	0557	1
FARMER JAMES R	CPT	O-1551202	1045	2
FARMER JAMES W	LTC	O-1030764	0463	1
FARMER JOHN H	CW2	W-2143070	0255	1
FARMER JOHN H	CW4	W-2143637	0756	1
FARMER JR FRED F	CW3	W-2205756	0767	1
FARMER JR JOHN G	LTC	O-0341902	0959	1
FARMER MAURICE A	2LT	O-1946726	1046	1
FARMER MURRAY W	CPT	O-0411862	0845	1
FARMER TRAVER H	MAJ	O-2262123	0661	1
FARMER VERE L	COL	O-0275076	0157	3
FARMER WALTER A	1LT	O-1995027	0646	2
FARMER WILLIAM A	LTC	O-0226445	0364	3
FARMER WILLIAM F	MAJ	O-0256593	1054	3
FARMER WILLIAM G	CPT	O-0438347	0849	1
FARMER YEWELL M	LTC	O-1011043	0760	1
FARNELL ERIC C	LTC	O-1596003	0662	1
FARNER KENNETH T	CPT	O-0306563	1144	2
FARNESS ORIN J	LTC	O-0322118	0247	2
FARNEY EMIL J	CPT	O-1110475	0657	1
FARNHAM JOHN A	LTC	O-1585168	0967	3
FARNHAM RAYMOND K	COL	O-0462074	0946	2
FARNHAM VERNON C	CW4	W-2205606	1266	1
FARNSLEY MURRY J	LTC	O-1111052	0867	1
FARNSWORTH CLAYTON B	CPT	O-1319190	0946	2
FARNSWORTH JOSEPH B	LTC	O-0358044	0662	1
FARNSWORTH L W	CPT	O-0312372	1047	1

NAME	GRADE	SVC NO	DATE RET MO YR	RET CODE
FARNSWORTH ORA L	COL	O-0444318	1053	1
FARNSWORTH RICHARD C	1LT	O-1080444	0645	2
FARNSWORTH W L	1LT	O-0494894	1044	2
FARNSWORTH WALLACE W	MAJ	O-1313084	0365	1
FARO HARRY	CW2	W-2118328	0347	1
FARQUHAR GEORGE A	COL	O-0242122	0665	3
FARQUHAR GUY L	1LT	O-0116037	0457	3
FARQUHAR JOSEPH H	MAJ	O-1319611	0957	1
FARQUHAR WILLIAM R	LTC	O-1176012	0562	1
FARQUHARSON CHARLES	WO1	W-2140391	1145	2
FARR HENRY L	LTC	O-0287065	0265	3
FARR JR WILLIAM	LTC	O-1102235	0358	2
FARR LEONARD W	1LT	O-1169948	0145	2
FARR RICHARD S	COL	O-0199150	0550	3
FARR STEPHEN A	LTC	O-1117601	0463	1
FARRA JOHN S	LTC	O-1040917	0954	1
FARRAGUT LOYALL D	LTC	O-0312130	0447	2
FARRALO HARRY E	MAJ	O-1322983	0658	1
FARRAR ANDREW J	MAJ	O-1011680	0160	1
FARRAR CHRISTY M	MAJ	O-0102198	0648	3
FARRAR CLAYTON P	1LT	O-1175704	0347	2
FARRAR EMMONS B	MAJ	O-0182201	0352	3
FARRAR FLOYD R	LTC	O-0202773	1057	3
FARRAR MARION L	LTC	O-1303696	0562	1
FARRAR RALPH W	COL	O-0226261	0863	3
FARRAR ROBERT G	MAJ	O-0990751	0867	1
FARREL THOMAS P	CPT	O-0255193	1046	1
FARRELL ALBERT M	CPT	O-1102236	1046	2
FARRELL ANDREW F	MAJ	O-0168655	0553	2
FARRELL EDWARD J	WO1	W-2111811	1262	3
FARRELL ERNEST R	LTC	O-0488156	0154	1
FARRELL ERWIN D	LTC	O-1317604	0865	1
FARRELL EUGENE J	LTC	O-0303935	0865	3
FARRELL FRANCIS D	CW2	W-2211772	0461	1
FARRELL FRANK J	1LT	O-0303391	1042	2
FARRELL HENRY F	1LT	O-1290734	0446	2
FARRELL HUGH R	LTC	O-0918923	1059	2
FARRELL JAMES W	MAJ	O-1175112	0165	1
FARRELL JEROME	LTC	O-0220537	0361	3
FARRELL JOHN R	CW3	W-2151634	0864	1
FARRELL JOSEPH F	MAJ	O-1013132	1061	1
FARRELL JOSEPH F	MAJ	O-1546970	1159	1
FARRELL JR LEE J	LTC	O-0379594	0365	1
FARRELL JR THOMAS J	LTC	O-0450858	0762	1
FARRELL LUTHER K	CPT	O-1304513	0664	1
FARRELL MARK A	CPT	O-0476978	0746	2
FARRELL NEIL K	MAJ	O-1923620	1165	2
FARRELL PHILIP V	CPT	O-0371489	0246	2
FARRELL RAYMOND G	MAJ	O-2018667	0463	2
FARRELL ROBERT G	LTC	O-0913473	0856	1
FARRELL ROBERT S	MAJ	O-1341650	0961	1
FARRELL ROLAND J	LTC	O-0426770	0565	1
FARRELL ROY W	MAJ	O-0502047	0147	2
FARRELL WALTER J	MAJ	O-0503836	1047	2
FARRELL WILLIAM F	CPT	O-2014535	0660	1
FARRELL WILLIAM J	MAJ	O-0179835	0658	3
FARREN ERNEST G	LTC	O-1010110	0565	1
FARRENS BEVERLY P	MAJ	O-2030222	1159	1
FARRER THOMAS J	CPT	O-0918791	0644	2
FARRIMOND JAMES W	COL	O-0244637	0866	3
FARRINGTON ALAN M	LTC	O-0499041	0157	1
FARRINGTON CARL S	1LT	O-0537819	0946	2
FARRINGTON CHARLIE L	CPT	O-1286808	0747	2
FARRINGTON FERRELL	MAJ	O-0262509	1060	3
FARRINGTON HOWARD F	1LT	O-1579630	0653	1
FARRINGTON JAMES T	MAJ	O-1298522	0863	1
FARRINGTON JAMES W	CPT	O-0323490	0457	1
FARRINGTON JOSEPH D	LTC	O-0468634	0646	2
FARRINGTON JR A A	MAJ	O-1057055	0161	1
FARRINGTON JR PAUL	CW3	W-2142072	0358	1
FARRIOR ALAN R	MAJ	O-0586637	0863	1
FARRIS BRUCE V D	LTC	O-1574716	1264	1
FARRIS CHARLES H	COL	O-0125214	1153	3
FARRIS DONALD M	COL	O-0220760	1158	3
FARRIS FRANK H	MAJ	O-1285224	0846	2

NAME	GRADE	SVC NO	DATE RET MO YR	RET CODE
FARRIS GARVIN R	COL	O-0287791	1047	2
FARRIS HOUSTON S	LTC	O-0309320	0456	2
FARRIS JOHN I	LTC	O-0389829	0463	1
FARRIS JOHN J	CPT	O-1736653	1050	1
FARRIS JOSEPH A	CPT	O-0429479	0646	2
FARRIS THAD L	LTC	O-1183512	1064	1
FARRISH FERDINAND	MAJ	O-1178137	0663	1
FARRISH THOMAS O	COL	O-0278806	0455	1
FARROW JOE R	MAJ	O-0959266	0563	1
FARROW JOE L	LTC	O-1175431	0862	1
FARROW JOE T	CW3	W-2141269	0165	1
FARRY LAWRENCE W	CPT	O-1323301	0747	2
FARSON WILBUR F	COL	O-0143685	0453	3
FARTHING ARTHUR C	COL	O-0274346	0867	3
FARTHING WILLIAM E	LTC	O-0023188	0660	1
FARVER WARREN L	CPT	O-0183247	1148	3
FARWELL RUDOLPH G	MAJ	O-1924077	0763	1
FARWIG WILLIS C	2LT	O-1038973	0445	2
FASANO DOMENIC T	CW2	W-3430542	0967	1
FASCE EGI V	LTC	O-0236271	1062	3
FASSETT JR HIRAM R	LTC	O-0245351	0350	3
FASSETT WILLIAM E	CPT	O-1300782	0454	2
FASSLER SALLY	2LT	N-0703265	0744	2
FASSNACHT PAUL L	MAJ	O-1643535	0463	1
FASTAIA MARTIN J	LTC	O-1302620	0363	1
FASTENBERG LOUIS J	1LT	O-1315152	0958	2
FATH LAURENCE M	LTC	O-1284486	1054	1
FATINA JOE J	1LT	O-1697906	0245	2
FATKIN GEORGE A	CW2	W-2108315	0460	3
FATORA JOHN A	MAJ	O-1120316	0163	1
FATULA JR JOHN	MAJ	O-1877110	0765	1
FAUBER EARL B	LTC	O-1100537	1161	1
FAUBER JOHN E	COL	O-0263178	0465	3
FAUBER ROBERT S	CPT	O-1923586	1262	1
FAUBERT VICTOR T	MAJ	O-0974055	0162	1
FAUBION ERNEST F	CW4	W-2105247	0461	1
FAUCETTE GEORGE R	COL	O-1000041	0761	1
FAUCHER RAYMOND E	MAJ	O-1913364	0465	1
FAUCON IVAN V	MAJ	O-0987510	0565	1
FAUGHT COLONEL H	LTC	O-0348573	1160	1
FAULCONER JAMES N	LTC	O-0255244	1045	2
FAULCONER SR E L	COL	O-0189349	1058	3
FAULOS JOHN W	COL	O-0163991	0753	3
FAULHABER GEORGE B	MAJ	O-1058996	1263	1
FAULK ARCHIE L	COL	O-0174495	0246	2
FAULK EVERETTE W	COL	O-0331414	1063	3
FAULK HARRY M	CW2	W-2215149	0967	1
FAULK WILEY C	LTC	O-0451101	1060	1
FAULKENBERRY M W	1LT	N-0763918	1045	1
FAULKINGHAM RICHARD	MAJ	O-1341767	0865	1
FAULKNER ACE F	LTC	O-0308507	0355	2
FAULKNER CLARENCE R	MAJ	O-0370959	0867	3
FAULKNER CLINTON E	MAJ	O-0319272	0258	1
FAULKNER DEWEY	CPT	O-0182733	0945	2
FAULKNER EDMUND B	2LT	O-1310589	0545	2
FAULKNER HOWARD G	COL	O-0202744	1055	1
FAULKNER JAMES D	LTC	O-0170799	0658	3
FAULKNER LIONEL E	LTC	O-0251898	0961	3
FAULKNER LOUIE L	CW4	W-2121218	0660	1
FAULKNER TRUEMAN E	MAJ	O-0217624	0157	3
FAULKS GLENN D	MAJ	O-0971337	0561	1
FAULS DOROTHY M	MAJ	L-0604503	1063	1
FAULVE MARCELO	1LT	O-0890487	0849	1
FAUNTLEROY LORENZO B	CW3	W-2129822	0863	1
FAUP JEAN H	LTC	O-1288726	0761	1
FAUROT BILLIE C	MAJ	O-2291443	1167	1
FAUROT EARL E	MAJ	O-1167829	1057	1
FAUS ROBERT R	COL	O-0199978	1157	3
FAUSEL EVERETT G	LTC	O-0213627	1061	3
FAUSEL WALTER F	CPT	O-0261865	0544	2
FAUSET MERL J	LTC	O-0254699	0351	1
FAUSEY FRANCIS S	1LT	O-2028907	0151	1
FAUSKE EINAR P	CW3	W-2147695	0964	1
FAUSSET DUANE S	MAJ	O-1185617	0160	1
FAUST ALMA V	2LT	N-0775595	0645	1

ARMY OF THE UNITED STATES RETIRED LIST

NAME	GRADE	SVC NO	DATE RET MO YR	RET CODE
FAUST CARLTON L	LTC	0-0196780	0162	3
FAUST ELEANOR S	CPT	N-0794630	0454	2
FAUST JOHN E	MAJ	0-0517246	0457	1
FAUX JAMES R	LTC	0-1554355	0162	1
FAVATA FRANCIS M	MAJ	0-0259013	0765	3
FAVERMAN BARNET	LTC	0-1052341	0467	1
FAVINGER CALVIN E	LTC	0-0321566	0862	3
FAVORITE RALPH S	MAJ	0-1111604	0859	1
FAVRE ILSE M	2LT	N-0737040	0445	1
FAVRE JOHN L	MAJ	0-0935366	1063	2
FAVREAU FRANK E	LTC	0-0377906	1057	1
FAVREAU WALDO S	LTC	0-0902781	0367	3
FAWCETT EDWARD G	1LT	0-1031076	1044	2
FAWCETT HARRY D	COL	0-0325163	1060	1
FAWCETT JR JOHN R	LTC	0-0415978	0664	1
FAWCETT PAUL W	LTC	0-0304909	0757	2
FAWCETT ROBERT A	CPT	0-1596321	0360	1
FAWCETT THEODORE L	2LT	0-1822122	1143	2
FAWCETT THOMAS E	MAJ	0-0114642	0553	3
FAXON HENRY H	MAJ	0-0399190	0745	1
FAXON JR ALFRED A	LTC	0-0361523	0667	3
FAY EUGENE F	MAJ	0-1540839	0664	1
FAY JOSEPH G	CW2	W-2144054	0358	1
FAY PATRICK B	COL	0-0333123	0559	3
FAY SR ELMER R	CPT	0-0488048	1044	2
FAY STANLEY A	LTC	0-0222227	1060	3
FAY THOMAS H	1LT	0-1312754	1057	1
FAY WILLIAM H	CW2	W-2152955	0563	1
FAYE EYVIND M	LTC	0-0236585	0166	3
FAYETTE NELSON C	CW3	W-2142762	0461	1
FAYLE LESLIE E	LTC	0-0256284	1262	3
FAYLE PERCY R	CPT	0-0379011	1045	2
FAYNE WILLIAM J	LTC	0-0470756	1147	1
FAYTLE URIEL F	CPT	0-1574717	0246	2
FAZAKERLEY F J	LTC	0-0268130	0759	3
FAZENBAKER EDGAR L	MAJ	0-1180179	1062	1
FAZENDIN ROGER A	1LT	0-0414574	0545	2
FAZIO HARRIET P	1LT	N-0728240	1145	1
FAZIO JOSEPH	CW2	W-2000607	0247	2
FEAGAN KENNETH M	MAJ	0-0288221	0964	3
FEAGANS WILLIAM C	LTC	0-1578446	1060	1
FEAGIN JOHN L	LTC	0-0237853	1165	3
FEAGIN OSCAR R	CPT	0-1310924	0845	1
FEAGLER DALTON G	CPT	0-0948792	0261	1
FEAGLES ROBERT W	CPT	0-0518826	0447	2
FEARING ALBERT H	LTC	0-0212471	0160	3
FEARING ARTHUR N	LTC	0-0371730	0466	1
FEARING OLIN K	MAJ	0-0245522	1155	3
FEARN ODELL E	MAJ	0-1650084	0660	1
FEASER ROBERT G	CW2	W-2118999	1047	1
FEAST HARRY C L	COL	0-0203302	0455	3
FEASTER BURNES L	MAJ	0-0116085	1058	3
FEASTER ORION O	LTC	0-0106052	0453	3
FEATHER JOHN W	2LT	0-0201373	1158	3
FEATHER JR ARTHUR C	CW2	W-2153190	0460	1
FEATHER RAYMOND O	MAJ	0-0215130	0463	3
FEATHERSTON ERNEST M	MAJ	0-0302220	0966	3
FEATHERSTON GEORGE O	MAJ	0-1541578	0457	1
FEATHERSTON THOMAS	1LT	0-0521151	1145	2
FEATHERSTONE FRED F	LTC	0-0418190	0462	1
FEATHERSTONE RALPH O	MAJ	0-0986825	1163	1
FEAY ROBERT W	LTC	0-0565325	0263	1
FEAZEL WILLIAM J	LTC	0-0448211	0159	1
FECHTER JR WILLIAM J	LTC	0-0450859	0657	1
FEDENETS ANDREW	MAJ	0-1175433	0755	1
FEDER EDWARD P	MAJ	0-0239477	1045	2
FEDERICK JOSEPH C	CPT	0-0500636	0445	2
FEDERICO JOSEPH L	CPT	0-1797803	0846	2
FEDERLIN FERDINAND	MAJ	0-0402445	0456	1
FEDERSPIEL FRANK J	CPT	0-0210162	0349	3
FEDERSPIEL JOHN A	CW4	W-2115549	0659	1
FEDOR GEORGE	LTC	0-1796256	0361	1
FEDORCHAK STEVE L	MAJ	0-1106723	1163	1
FEDOSI ALEC L	MAJ	0-1166977	0954	1
FEE ALBERT A	CPT	0-1300010	0963	1
FEE DARWIN O	LTC	0-1165287	0854	1
FEE ROBERT J	CPT	0-0134477	0648	3
FEELEY JR EDWARD J	MAJ	0-1796257	0261	1
FEELEY MICHAEL J	CPT	0-2287676	0765	2
FEEMSTER KENNETH L	1LT	0-2262896	1052	2
FEENAN JAMES J	CPT	0-0525497	0348	1
FEENER LESTER C	MAJ	0-0474006	0646	2
FEENEY ALFRED L	MAJ	0-0525634	0754	1
FEENEY BARTHOLOME	MAJ	0-1039338	0958	1
FEENEY CHARLES E	MAJ	0-1106724	1262	1
FEENEY CLINTON	LTC	0-0288652	1057	1
FEENEY ELTON C	LTC	0-0125212	0960	3
FEENEY IRENE C	MAJ	N-0752254	1163	1
FEENEY JOHN F A	MAJ	0-0219338	1054	3
FEENEY RICHARD T	LTC	0-1290401	0661	1
FEENEY ROBERT F	CW3	W-2152590	1263	1
FEESE ARTHUR J	WO1	W-2151999	0158	1
FEGAN JAMES J	MAJ	0-1109101	0861	1
FEGER JR GEORGE S H	MAJ	0-0392011	0562	1
FEGERT CARL R	LTC	0-0477619	1054	1
FEGLEY PAUL W	COL	0-0294731	0365	3
FEHLANDT PHILIP R	LTC	0-0497680	1060	3
FEHLMAN ROSS G	LTC	0-0235669	0160	3
FEHNER KENNETH C	MAJ	0-1316025	0266	1
FEHRENBACHER FRANK J	MAJ	0-0116088	1153	3
FEICHTINGER JOHN R	CPT	0-1106726	1145	2
FEIERABEND OTTO W	CPT	0-0290017	0867	3
FEIERLEIN OTTO F	LTC	0-1287850	0667	1
FEIGEL SR CLAYTON	CW2	W-2101285	1053	2
FEIGHERY EDWARD P	CW2	W-2147487	0663	1
FEIGIN EMANUEL V	MAJ	0-0335819	0646	2
FEIKE LAWRENCE V	LTC	0-0176930	0149	3
FEILD MAURICE A	LTC	0-1297018	1264	1
FEILD SAM C	1LT	0-1994758	0645	2
FEILEN JOHN T	1LT	0-1316030	0348	2
FEIMER THEODORE J	LTC	0-0358085	0156	1
FEIN EDWARD E	CW4	W-2120929	1065	2
FEIN MAURICE	CPT	0-0479735	0245	2
FEINBERG BERNARD S	CPT	0-1533779	0546	2
FEINBERG HARRY	CPT	0-0498305	0745	2
FEINBERG IRWIN	LTC	0-1182568	0865	1
FEINBERG RAYMOND	CPT	0-1647873	1262	1
FEINBERG SEYMOUR D	1LT	0-0483139	0245	2
FEINDEL HOWARD W	LTC	0-0305603	1060	1
FEINER EDWARD J	MAJ	0-0205060	1162	3
FEINSTEIN ISIDORE I	CPT	0-1304514	1166	2
FEITELL ARTHUR	MAJ	0-0345522	0346	2
FEITIG LOUIS R	CPT	0-1290053	0647	2
FEJDASZ JOSEPH F	CW2	W-2142584	0454	1
FEKETE ALFRED E	MAJ	0-0479651	0453	1
FEKETY STEPHEN	MAJ	0-0885713	0657	1
FELBER JR JULIUS J	MAJ	0-2021110	0363	1
FELBER STEPHEN	CW3	W-2141272	0159	1
FELBER THOMAS F	CW2	W-2127794	1046	1
FELCYN ROMAN C	2LT	0-1579633	1045	2
FELD ALBERT E	CPT	0-1578450	0446	2
FELD HARRY F	LTC	0-1556574	0367	1
FELDBUSH RICHARD L	MAJ	0-0967375	0464	1
FELDER DAVID J	MAJ	0-2263267	0463	1
FELDHACKER C J	MAJ	0-1288211	0457	1
FELDHAUS JAMES G	LTC	0-0249717	0266	3
FELDHUSEN FRANK H	1LT	0-1634736	0446	2
FELDMAN ARNOLD H	COL	0-0285525	0863	3
FELDMAN BENJAMIN W	MAJ	0-0275431	0967	3
FELDMAN DANIEL	2LT	0-1307809	0545	2
FELDMAN DANIEL J	MAJ	0-0442521	0846	2
FELDMAN HAROLD B	LTC	0-1590445	0664	1
FELDMAN HAROLD H	1LT	0-0336098	0844	2
FELDMAN HARRY H	CPT	0-0374265	0446	2
FELDMAN HERBERT	1LT	0-1013912	0448	2
FELDMAN IRWIN R	1LT	0-1885830	0454	2
FELDMAN JACK	1LT	0-2017040	0747	1
FELDMAN JEROME	MAJ	0-1043938	1165	1
FELDMAN MARY L	2LT	N-0741842	0844	2
FELDMAN MAX	MAJ	0-0360465	0346	2
FELDMAN SEYMOUR	MAJ	0-1821990	0562	1
FELDMAN THEODORE E	2LT	0-2009556	0246	1
FELDMANN GERALD C	MAJ	0-2033896	0764	1
FELDMILLER WILLIAM H	LTC	0-0281658	1158	3
FELDNER GEORGE D	LTC	0-0224109	0960	3
FELDSHUH ALFRED M	MAJ	0-0267670	0146	2
FELDSTEIN WILLIAM	CPT	0-1592809	1263	1
FELDT OTTO F	LTC	0-0220307	0747	2
FELESKI PAUL E	CW4	W-2146851	0960	1
FELICE JAMES C	LTC	0-1287500	1165	1
FELICIANO FERDINAND	LTC	0-0487850	1154	1
FELICIANO GEORGE	MAJ	0-4006266	0567	1
FELICIOTTI DOMINIC	LTC	0-1287163	0863	1
FELIX EDWARD A	WO1	W-2123422	0454	1
FELIX PAUL S	CPT	0-0446508	0944	2
FELIX ROBERT L	MAJ	0-0964107	0865	1
FELIX WARREN T	LTC	0-0285999	0161	1
FELIX WOODROW D	MAJ	0-0409488	1060	1
FELIZ EDWARD F	LTC	0-1637401	1262	1
FELKER JAMES V	CW2	W-2148848	1159	1
FELKER STANLEY V	CPT	0-1584205	0957	1
FELL GEORGE K	MAJ	0-0342056	0859	1
FELL RANALD H	LTC	0-0262793	0563	3
FELLENCER PAUL M	LTC	0-0288439	0961	3
FELLER ROSS P	CW2	W-2207486	0959	1
FELLERMAN HENRY S	MAJ	0-0971482	0862	1
FELLERS ALBERT G	MAJ	0-0980640	0763	1
FELLMAN LEON	CPT	0-0294270	0445	2
FELLMAN 2ND WILLIAM	LTC	0-0322317	0446	2
FELLON HAROLD C	CW3	W-2206638	1165	1
FELLOWS CARL H	MAJ	0-0144382	0554	1
FELLOWS CLIFFORD H	CPT	0-1645526	1050	1
FELLOWS FRANK C	MAJ	0-0307805	0448	1
FELMUS LAURENCE B	CPT	0-1690651	1145	2
FELS EUGENE E	LTC	0-1822259	1164	1
FELSTEAD CHARLES F	COL	0-0302380	0163	3
FELT STANTON W	1LT	0-1585686	0147	2
FELT WILLIAM A	LTC	0-1037483	0862	1
FELTENBERGER A L	1LT	0-0157549	0535	1
FELTER RANDALL H	LTC	0-0376468	0460	1
FELTMAN JAMES D	MAJ	0-2288295	0661	1
FELTMAN REUBEN	MAJ	0-0273187	0546	2
FELTNER JR BILL	LTC	0-1824003	0661	1
FELTON HAROLD V	CPT	0-1309237	0346	2
FELTON PHILIP K	LTC	0-0453442	0258	1
FELTS BUFORD B	WO1	W-2114661	1061	1
FELTS CARL R	CW2	W-2101675	0949	1
FELTS CLIFFORD F	CW2	W-2141273	0157	1
FELTS EUGENE A	CPT	0-2046397	0149	2
FELTS HEBER H	CPT	0-0391053	1045	2
FELTS JAMES K	MAJ	0-0248666	0664	3
FELTS JR JOHN R	CW3	W-2144134	0867	1
FELTY GEORGE M	2LT	0-1016566	0145	2
FELTY JAMES K	LTC	0-1308940	0263	2
FELTY WILLIAM F	LTC	0-1014575	0758	1
FELZ JAMES J	CPT	0-1797805	1046	2
FELZMAN JOHN H O C	CPT	0-1578454	0865	1
FENDER HARRY C	1LT	0-0404450	0845	1
FENDER RAY H	MAJ	0-0568110	0664	1
FENDRICH MANNING	CPT	0-0321652	1045	2
FENDRICK JOSEPH H	MAJ	0-0493950	1054	1
FENIGSON PHILIP M	WO1	W-2106633	0745	2
FENIMORE EARL R	CW3	W-2145175	0161	2
FENLEY JR JOHN H	CW2	W-2142678	1054	1
FENN ALVA L	COL	0-0190501	0762	3
FENN EDWARD P	LTC	0-0232874	0962	3
FENN FRED H	COL	0-0248521	1164	3
FENN HARLIN L	LTC	0-0275988	0760	2
FENN JACK B	1LT	0-0418200	0544	2
FENN MANNIE	1LT	0-1315572	0546	2
FENNELL ALEXANDER	MAJ	0-1924083	1264	1
FENNELL CHARLES H	CW3	W-2146831	1262	1
FENNELL JAMES	MAJ	0-0300605	1046	1
FENNELL JAMES	CW4	W-2115852	0257	1
FENNELL JAMES F	LTC	0-0480888	0859	1
FENNELL JAMES F	1LT	0-1294116	0246	2
FENNELL JAMES M	MAJ	0-0497882	0752	1
FENNELL JOSEPH W	2LT	0-1887608	0160	2
FENNELL WILLIAM F	COL	0-0313094	1057	1
FENNER JOHN E	LTC	0-1633850	0764	1
FENNER JR HENRY C	1LT	0-0326500	0745	2
FENNER REX N	CPT	0-1176956	1046	2
FENNESSEY FRANCIS P	CW3	W-2146692	0560	1
FENNO JOHN C	CPT	0-0334813	0946	2
FENNO WILLIAM A	CW4	W-2144445	0966	1
FENSCH CLARA M	CPT	N-0702048	0846	1
FENSKE HERBERT C	MAJ	0-1329576	1161	1
FENSTER LOUIS Z	1LT	0-1174849	0945	2
FENSTER ROBERT	1LT	0-1799122	0863	2
FENSTERMACHER EDWARD	1LT	0-0270708	0259	3
FENSTERMACHER H G	1LT	0-1297180	0145	2
FENSTERMACHER W A	LTC	0-0398418	0945	1
FENSTERMAKER J C	MAJ	0-2046568	0359	1
FENT ANSEL L	LTC	0-1285564	1159	1
FENTON HARRY M	LTC	0-0251739	0553	1
FENTON JAMES P	1LT	0-0245658	0355	3
FENTON JOEL V	CW2	W-2146237	1060	1
FENTON JOSEPH W	CPT	0-0494826	1046	2
FENTON JR MATTHEW C	LTC	0-0180389	0845	2
FENTON LEE M	CW3	W-2152293	1263	1
FENTRESS ROBERT B	LTC	0-0148905	0950	3
FENTRISS CHESTER R	CPT	0-1649272	0460	1
FENWICK GEORGE R	MAJ	0-0272093	0466	3
FENWICK HARRY D	CW3	W-2143485	0560	1
FENWICK OPAL T	MAJ	L-0701599	0463	1
FENWRICK GIL	CW2	W-2142474	1056	1
FERBER GERHARDT H	CPT	0-0482540	0243	2
FERBER SAMUEL J	MAJ	0-0489277	0246	2
FERDERBER WILLIAM	LTC	0-0302975	1061	3
FERDINAND HAROLD W	MAJ	0-1339528	1265	1
FEREBEE EDWARD S	LTC	0-0234435	0865	3
FERGUSON ALBERT E	LTC	0-0186037	0654	3
FERGUSON ALEXANDER	LTC	0-1596644	0667	3
FERGUSON ALFRED H	LTC	0-0226852	0666	3
FERGUSON ALONZO G	LTC	0-0187855	1055	3
FERGUSON ALVIN L	CPT	0-0970838	0762	1
FERGUSON ARTHUR W	LTC	0-0162285	0958	3
FERGUSON BEN F	CPT	0-0374460	0944	2
FERGUSON BILLY A	WO1	W-2126868	0345	2
FERGUSON BYRON F	MAJ	0-1178789	0667	1
FERGUSON CAROLYN E	MAJ	N-0725548	0767	1
FERGUSON CHARLES A	LTC	0-1297702	0161	1
FERGUSON CHARLES E	2LT	0-1825908	0445	2
FERGUSON CHARLIE W	CPT	0-1548407	0954	1
FERGUSON CLARENCE E	CPT	0-0488675	0650	1
FERGUSON CLIFFORD W	MAJ	0-0176663	0346	2
FERGUSON CLYDE W	WO1	W-2145127	0752	2
FERGUSON COMADORA M	CPT	0-0378801	1046	2
FERGUSON DONALD V	MAJ	0-0493062	0347	1
FERGUSON EARL A	MAJ	0-1541530	0862	2
FERGUSON EDWARD F	LTC	0-0181575	1161	3
FERGUSON EDWARD O	CW4	W-2005844	0767	1
FERGUSON EMANUEL R	CPT	0-0533822	0745	2
FERGUSON FRANK H	MAJ	0-0246731	0859	3
FERGUSON GEORGE X	MAJ	0-1294641	1060	1
FERGUSON GERALDINE	CPT	N-0702085	0646	1
FERGUSON GLEN E	CW3	RW-2151715	1065	1
FERGUSON HAROLD L	1LT	0-0955858	0352	2
FERGUSON HAYDEN R	2LT	0-1691759	0452	1
FERGUSON HAZEL M	1LT	L-0800636	0845	2
FERGUSON HENRY A	LTC	0-0170110	1160	3
FERGUSON J NEILE	LTC	0-1634743	0862	1
FERGUSON JACK L	CW2	W-2212523	0167	1
FERGUSON JAMES A	MAJ	0-1535893	1160	1
FERGUSON JAMES O	CW3	W-2207684	0467	1
FERGUSON JAMES R	MAJ	0-0517262	0549	1
FERGUSON JAMES R	1LT	0-1998434	0546	2
FERGUSON JOHN A	1LT	0-1557142	1146	2
FERGUSON JOHN C	LTC	0-0250855	1164	3
FERGUSON JOHN E	WO1	W-2148348	0653	1

NAME	GRADE	SVC NO	DATE RET MO YR	RET CODE
FERGUSON JOHN L	COL	0-0162558	0858	3
FERGUSON JR D H C	MAJ	0-0422417	0346	2
FERGUSON JR ERNEST L	1LT	0-1043336	0644	2
FERGUSON JR JAMES H	CPT	0-0422034	0945	2
FERGUSON JR JAMES W	CW2	W-2210230	0466	1
FERGUSON JR L J	CW2	W-2211794	0766	1
FERGUSON JR WADE D	LTC	0-1103158	0262	1
FERGUSON KARL E	MAJ	0-1999040	0866	1
FERGUSON KEITH W	MAJ	0-0888429	1263	1
FERGUSON LAURA B	1LT	N-0728583	0846	1
FERGUSON LORY E	CPT	0-0311119	0944	2
FERGUSON LOUIS F	LTC	0-0475962	0255	1
FERGUSON MELVIN S	CW3	W-2106558	0966	2
FERGUSON MOSES D	CW3	W-2149985	1164	1
FERGUSON NORMAN W	CW3	W-2153277	1164	1
FERGUSON PAUL E	MAJ	0-0245190	0154	3
FERGUSON ROBERT L	CW2	W-2114211	0553	1
FERGUSON ROBERT M	1LT	0-1882038	0159	2
FERGUSON ROBERT S	COL	0-0410119	1266	1
FERGUSON ROSCOE C	MAJ	0-0163278	0650	3
FERGUSON RUSSELL P	LTC	0-1295527	0867	2
FERGUSON SAMUEL H	CPT	0-0363233	0257	1
FERGUSON SIDNEY J	LTC	0-0176209	0556	1
FERGUSON SYRL K	CW2	W-2117354	0848	1
FERGUSON THOMAS L	LTC	0-0491745	0444	2
FERGUSON VERNON A	1LT	0-1295528	1044	2
FERGUSON W LOAR	LTC	0-0264880	0264	3
FERGUSON WADE H	LTC	0-0281204	0864	3
FERGUSON WILLIAM G	LTC	0-1540640	1167	1
FERGUSON WILLIAM H	MAJ	0-1185942	0161	1
FERGUSON WILLIAM R	MAJ	0-0247919	1166	3
FERGUSSON CECIL O	COL	0-0171625	0556	3
FERKINHOFF THEODORE	LTC	0-0213724	0963	3
FERLA SALVATORE	CPT	0-0488656	1146	1
FERNALD GORDON H	LTC	0-0104201	0648	3
FERNANDES ARTHUR M	MAJ	0-0888510	0853	1
FERNANDES JUDITH M	2LT	N-0901766	1054	2
FERNANDES ROBERT J	1LT	0-0425321	0646	1
FERNANDEZ CHARLES P	LTC	0-0328274	0861	2
FERNANDEZ EDWARD F	MAJ	0-2027344	0154	1
FERNANDEZ EUGENE	1LT	0-1896814	0557	1
FERNANDEZ F O	2LT	0-1896573	1147	2
FERNANDEZ FELIPE A	CPT	0-1896856	0767	1
FERNANDEZ JOHN S	CW4	W-2115860	1055	1
FERNANDEZ JR F L	MAJ	0-1320028	1155	1
FERNANDEZ JUAN R	1LT	0-0396833	0545	2
FERNANDEZ MARIO R	CPT	0-1797454	0761	1
FERNANDEZ MIGUEL A	LTC	0-1301628	0264	1
FERNANDEZ RAMON M	2LT	0-1896340	0550	1
FERNANDEZ VICTOR M	MAJ	0-0962218	0163	1
FERNER CHARLES P	LTC	0-1118369	0467	1
FERO JACOB	MAJ	0-0949566	0764	1
FERRANDINA JR A F	1LT	0-1698186	0546	2
FERRANDINO ROSARIO F	CW3	RW-2152493	1264	1
FERRANDO JOHN W	CW2	W-2208708	1265	1
FERRARA ANTHONY	2LT	0-1052765	0245	2
FERRARA DOMINICK	LTC	0-0451530	0457	1
FERRARESE CHARLES J	LTC	0-1599127	1067	1
FERRARI ALBERT N	LTC	0-1894928	1062	1
FERRARI FRANK L	MAJ	0-1049829	0167	1
FERRARI LEWIS J	2LT	0-0373198	0445	2
FERRARO GERALD J	MAJ	0-1319191	0864	1
FERREE ALBERT A	MAJ	0-0445060	1157	1
FERREIRA AUGUSTO	WO1	W-2135575	0646	2
FERREIRA JOSEPH	CW2	W-2153250	0462	1
FERRELL CHARLES O	CPT	0-0573822	0753	2
FERRELL GEORGE H	2LT	0-0407785	0444	2
FERRELL JAMES C	2LT	0-1310698	1044	2
FERRELL JOE R	1LT	0-1010556	0244	2
FERRELL JR CURTIS L	COL	0-1550163	1266	1
FERRELL JR SETH	CPT	0-1875124	0462	1
FERRELL JR THOMAS E	CPT	0-1699814	1143	2
FERRELL LEE A	MAJ	0-1592813	1160	1
FERRELL PALMORE A	COL	0-0390338	1262	1
FERRELL RICHARD S	MAJ	0-2036906	0661	1
FERRELL WILFORD L	LTC	0-0472326	0855	1
FERRER JR ALFRED	MAJ	0-0406108	0859	1
FERRERA MELVIN R	MAJ	0-2210166	0663	1
FERRERO MARTIN P	1LT	0-1822980	1146	2
FERRESE RALPH W	LTC	0-1291093	0261	1
FERRICK JAMES H	COL	0-0259743	0367	3
FERRICK JOHN V	MAJ	0-1003920	0657	2
FERRIE JOHN A	MAJ	0-1017392	0962	1
FERRIER WILLIAM W	LTC	0-0285904	0644	1
FERRILL OLIVER J	LTC	0-0444856	0852	1
FERRIS ASSAD G	MAJ	0-0482622	0943	2
FERRIS BERNHARDT	LTC	0-0249410	0466	3
FERRIS CHARLES B	B G	0-0213192	0464	3
FERRIS JAMES A	MAJ	0-0495459	0555	1
FERRIS JOHN W	LTC	0-2017526	0361	1
FERRIS ROBERT M	MAJ	0-1554357	0361	1
FERRIS ROY M	2LT	0-0442464	1044	2
FERRIS 3RD ROYAL A	CPT	0-1010367	0345	2
FERRO BENEDICT D	MAJ	0-1180890	0157	1
FERRO SALVATORE	CPT	0-0438839	1146	2
FERRON EARL	1LT	0-1639027	0645	2
FERRY JOHN J	CPT	0-0530934	1146	2
FERRY JOSEPH	CW2	W-2141555	1054	1
FERRY JR MILES	MAJ	0-1895080	0647	2
FERSHTMAN MAX B	CPT	0-1690498	0247	2
FERSTER NORMAN A	LTC	0-0474455	0366	3
FERTE JR JOHN G	CPT	0-0338292	1145	2
FERTIG CHARLES A	COL	0-0130208	0652	3
FERTIG JAMES C	1LT	0-1315675	0746	2
FERTITTA CENA V	CPT	0-0194474	0245	2
FERTITTA SAM R	1LT	0-0403980	0245	2
FESS FREDERICK	LTC	0-1302924	0661	1
FESSELMEYER ROBERT W	MAJ	0-0390021	0647	1
FESSENDEN BRADLEY M	LTC	0-0322255	0859	2
FESSLER GUENEVERE	1LT	N-0755275	0846	1
FESSLER HAROLD A	MAJ	0-1559911	1264	1
FEST THEODORE L	CW4	W-2122039	0858	1
FESTA CARMINE P	CPT	0-1314462	0247	1
FESTNER FRANCIS J	CPT	0-0194004	0654	3
FESTNER THOMAS E	1LT	0-1315047	0846	2
FETCHKO GEORGE	CW4	W-2117357	1155	1
FETGATTER HANEY C	CW2	W-2206785	1263	1
FETSCO PETER M	CPT	0-1294588	0347	1
FETTE WILLIAM F	CW3	W-2206460	1066	1
FETTER IVAN R	LTC	0-1634747	0162	1
FETTERHOFF HAROLD L	MAJ	0-1643542	0367	1
FETTERHOFF W M	MAJ	0-1579636	0547	2
FETTERMAN CLINTON F	LTC	0-1107944	0661	1
FETTERMAN JOSEPH	MAJ	0-0501662	0944	2
FETTERMAN ULYSSES G	LTC	0-0445459	0954	1
FETTERS DARWIN K	MAJ	0-1311384	1266	1
FETTERS OSCAR M	MAJ	0-0274783	0861	2
FETTY LILLIAN I	2LT	N-0729399	1044	1
FETZER EARL W	MAJ	0-1043001	0159	1
FETZER FRANCIS G	1LT	0-0507097	1045	2
FETZER JAMES J	CW2	W-2148166	0955	1
FETZER JR CHARLES K	1LT	0-1165854	1045	2
FEUERLICHT HENRY O	LTC	0-0181347	0856	3
FEUERMAN ZOLTON	MAJ	0-1948736	0564	1
FEULNER LOUIS H	MAJ	0-1315419	1063	1
FEUSTEL WILLIAM F	LTC	0-0146266	0352	1
FEW ARTHUR N	MAJ	0-0256020	1144	2
FEWSMITH JR JOSEPH	1LT	0-1178790	0146	2
FEWSTER JR JAMES F	COL	0-1575972	1262	1
FEXY GEORGE C	LTC	0-0241183	0364	3
FEY HOMER D	LTC	0-0250754	0165	3
FEYLER WARREN O	COL	0-0242996	0366	3
FIALA BARTH A	MAJ	0-0167617	0255	3
FIALA ROBERT	1LT	0-0885598	0346	2
FIANDACA JR PATSY M	COL	0-0368512	0766	1
FIANO JOSEPH	CW3	W-2151872	0962	1
FIBICH MICHAEL J	COL	0-0178052	0951	3
FICALORE VINCENT J	CW2	W-2141274	0259	1
FICHTER EMIL	MAJ	0-0184078	0849	3
FICHTER WILLIAM H	MAJ	0-1596645	0658	1
FICK ALBERT E	LTC	0-1544552	0763	1
FICK CHARLES B	1LT	0-1300012	0356	1
FICK JOHN H	MAJ	0-0298146	0567	3
FICKE CHARLES W	COL	0-0223759	1264	3
FICKESSEN JR W R	LTC	0-1280741	0261	1
FICKETT RICHARD N	LTC	0-0280569	0166	3
FICKLEN HOLMES	CPT	0-0322032	0645	2
FICKLIN MORTIMER T	1LT	0-0414322	0346	2
FICO GERALD J	LTC	0-1080101	0962	1
FIDDES EDWIN A	CPT	0-0301577	0246	2
FIDDES RITA H	1LT	N-0720853	0346	1
FIDLER WILLIS P	1LT	0-0927788	0247	2
FIDLOW HARRY	LTC	0-0377940	0960	1
FIEBIG HARRY A	2LT	0-0217072	0355	3
FIEDLER ROBERT W	CW2	W-2205963	0763	1
FIEJDASZ STANISLAW	CW2	W-2152652	0659	1
FIEL VICENTE	1LT	0-0890481	0550	1
FIELD ALMONT E	CW2	W-2143900	1060	1
FIELD ARTHUR W	COL	0-0269575	1061	3
FIELD CROSBY	COL	0-0138854	0349	3
FIELD DONALD E	CPT	0-1098792	0862	2
FIELD DWIGHT	MAJ	0-0518374	0561	3
FIELD EMMETT W	CW4	W-2110564	0659	1
FIELD ERNEST L	1LT	0-0396624	0445	1
FIELD EUGENE B	CW3	W-2203657	0864	1
FIELD FRANCIS C	1LT	0-0439489	0845	2
FIELD FRED H	COL	0-0235926	1262	3
FIELD GERTRUDE L	2LT	N-0700280	0734	1
FIELD GUY D	MAJ	0-0167991	0648	3
FIELD HENRY D	MAJ	0-0520814	1154	1
FIELD JOHN L	CPT	0-0912863	0944	1
FIELD JR JOHN W	2LT	0-1799437	0646	2
FIELD LACHLAN M	LTC	0-0372500	0661	1
FIELD LYMAN E	1LT	0-1544905	0245	2
FIELD MARSHALL N	1LT	0-1292162	0346	2
FIELD MARY E	1LT	N-0775219	0846	1
FIELD RICHARD O	MAJ	0-0290210	0665	3
FIELD RICHARD M	MAJ	0-0979585	1066	1
FIELD ROBERT G	MAJ	0-0480904	1052	1
FIELD ROBERT J	CW2	W-2145106	0763	1
FIELD THEODORE S	1LT	0-1173239	0845	2
FIELD THOMAS G	CPT	0-1105424	0547	1
FIELD VIRGIL F	COL	0-0470144	0455	1
FIELD WILLARD E	LTC	0-1057057	0264	1
FIELDER DANIEL W	COL	0-0345943	0259	1
FIELDER ROBERT A	LTC	0-0441621	0667	1
FIELDER WILLIAM R	1LT	0-1044511	0346	2
FIELDING JOSEPH F	1LT	0-0399351	0244	2
FIELDING JOSEPH H	1LT	0-1642051	0561	1
FIELDING JR JAMES M	COL	0-0322434	0467	3
FIELDING TEMPLE H	MAJ	0-0374072	0645	2
FIELDS ALLEN	CPT	0-0360785	1044	2
FIELDS CLARENCE O	CPT	0-0486508	0647	1
FIELDS ERNEST	MAJ	0-0496107	1047	1
FIELDS GEORGE G	MAJ	0-1317383	0955	1
FIELDS H MAXWELL	CPT	0-0502232	0445	1
FIELDS ISAAC R	CW2	W-2208546	0461	1
FIELDS JOE E	MAJ	0-2024266	0562	1
FIELDS JOEL B	LTC	0-0374238	0158	2
FIELDS JOHN R	CW3	W-2150077	0465	1
FIELDS JOSEPH A	LTC	0-1338329	0766	1
FIELDS LEON	COL	0-0302147	0563	3
FIELDS LEONARD B	MAJ	0-1046431	0361	1
FIELDS LLOYD C	CW2	W-2151111	1062	1
FIELDS MELVIN F	LTC	0-1169512	0960	1
FIELDS NORMAN E	CW2	W-2147530	1160	1
FIELDS ROSE M	MAJ	N-0722405	0661	1
FIELDS SANFORD W	CW2	W-3440033	1067	1
FIELDS SIDNEY	1LT	0-1589191	1045	2
FIELDS SINCLAIR	CW2	W-2208064	1162	2
FIELDS STANLEY E	MAJ	0-0414147	0366	1
FIELDS THOMAS B	CW3	W-2209275	0767	1
FIELDS WENDELL C	COL	0-0306693	0359	1
FIELDS ZANE W	MAJ	0-1693122	0164	1
FIEMAN PHILIP	CPT	0-0460759	1143	2
FIENHAGE WILFRED J	CW3	W-2122262	0856	1
FIERING ABRAHAM M	MAJ	0-1692015	1045	2
FIERO LUE E	COL	0-0126405	0852	3
FIERRAVANTI TERESA M	2LT	N-0754536	0946	1
FIERS JR WALTER H	CPT	0-0452955	0245	2
FIES ROBERT L	1LT	0-2203579	0952	1
FIESELER LOUIS O	MAJ	0-1328683	1160	1
FIESTER JOSEPH W	CPT	0-1686385	0657	1
FIFE FRANK H	LTC	0-1289567	1061	1
FIFE HENRY P	1LT	0-0164455	1044	1
FIFE JACK W	1LT	0-0410770	0446	1
FIFE PORTWOOD	LTC	0-0338207	0464	1
FIFE ROBERT G	1LT	0-0396264	0244	1
FIFIELD GERALD F	LTC	0-0407351	1166	1
FIFIELD GILBERT L	CW3	W-2148367	1262	1
FIGEL GEORGE E	LTC	0-2041144	0267	1
FIGGE GRACE H	MAJ	L-1010018	0364	1
FIGLER SEYMOUR J	1LT	0-1303485	1145	2
FIGUERAS JOSE	LTC	0-0161876	0553	3
FIGUEROA ARCADIO	MAJ	0-0156041	0353	3
FIGUEROA PASTOR	CW2	W-2113900	0246	2
FIGUEROA VICTOR A	LTC	0-0388405	0660	1
FIGUEROA-RIVERA RUBE	CPT	0-2034213	0962	2
FIGUEROA-SANTAN EMI	MAJ	0-2034212	0567	1
FIKE HAROLD E	LTC	0-0336714	0662	1
FIKE JAMES H	LTC	0-0210648	0255	3
FIKE WALTER B	WO1	W-2113745	0550	1
FIKENTSCHER ARTHUR	LTC	0-1052343	1062	1
FILAK JOHN J	1LT	0-2003531	0453	2
FILAN JOSEPH S	CPT	0-0452106	0343	1
FILBECK RAYMOND H	2LT	0-1015052	0152	1
FILBERT EARL J	CW3	W-2147215	0364	1
FILBERT JOHN A	LTC	0-1293034	0366	1
FILES ALONZO A	LTC	0-0150894	0252	3
FILES CHESTER A	B G	0-0297695	0351	3
FILES WILLIAM S	LTC	0-1644319	0562	1
FILIBERTI GEORGE J	LTC	0-0326504	0262	3
FILIPCZYK BOLESLAW C	CW3	W-2203342	1162	1
FILIPI EDWARD F	MAJ	0-0258280	0146	2
FILIPIAK JOHN J	LTC	0-0400082	0556	1
FILIPOVICH CARLO H	LTC	0-1110478	0764	1
FILIPPINI ALBERT R	WO1	W-3000324	1162	2
FILIPPONE JOSEPH	CW2	W-2107920	0152	2
FILIPSKI JOSEPH	CW2	W-2102895	0254	1
FILKINS WARREN D	CPT	0-0489054	0147	2
FILL LEON	CPT	0-0505126	0146	2
FILLE ARTHUR D	LTC	0-0348130	0546	2
FILLER WALTER S	LTC	0-0285168	1061	1
FILLER WILLIAM R	MAJ	0-1844979	1055	2
FILLEY CLARENCE E	CW3	W-2142042	1161	1
FILLIETTAZ CHARLES W	COL	0-0243642	0649	2
FILLINGHAM RALPH H	MAJ	0-0326202	1264	3
FILLMAN EDWARD R	MAJ	0-1046789	0859	1
FILLMAN GEORGE	LTC	0-1112685	0861	1
FILLMER HENRY A	LTC	0-0415371	0761	1
FILLMORE JAMES R	1LT	0-1284311	0744	2
FILLMORE ROBERT L	2LT	0-0554851	1145	1
FILOCCO MARIO A	CPT	0-0961570	0560	1
FILTEAU CLIFFORD E	CW2	W-2142956	0556	1
FILTER CHESTER	1LT	0-0346156	0843	2
FILUCCI JOHN	MAJ	0-4030804	0767	1
FILZER NATHAN	MAJ	0-1635872	1067	3
FINA JR PASCAL A	1LT	0-0577580	0960	1
FINAN JOHN J	LTC	0-1289059	0660	1
FINCH CHARLES S	COL	0-0395756	0462	1
FINCH DONALD F	CPT	0-2289548	1167	1
FINCH ELMER L	MAJ	0-0902904	0847	2
FINCH FRANK	CW3	W-2104047	0959	1
FINCH FRANK C	LTC	0-0169941	1059	3
FINCH JR ERNEST O	LTC	0-0232056	0660	3
FINCH KENNETH G	1LT	0-1185042	0446	2
FINCH ROGER A	1LT	0-1297704	0146	2
FINCH WILLIAM T	WO1	W-2128009	0546	2
FINCHER JR ROBERT C	CPT	0-1736682	1047	1
FINCHER WARREN C	CW2	W-2144911	0760	1

NAME	GRADE	SVC NO	DATE RET MO YR	RET CODE
FINCHER WILLIAM H	LTC	0-0241669	0564	3
FINCK ROBERT F	LTC	0-1797808	0361	1
FINCKE JR FRANK A	2LT	0-1176620	0144	2
FINCLE LOUIS P	LTC	C-0286622	0664	3
FINDEL SOLOMON	CPT	0-0526102	C846	2
FINDERUP ELMER P	1LT	0-1290404	C545	2
FINDLAY JAMES C	WO1	W-2143300	0153	2
FINDLAY JR R G	LTC	0-0348381	1046	2
FINDLAY ROBERT T	COL	0-0213002	1061	3
FINDLAY WALTER G	2LT	0-5710005	0965	2
FINDLEY JACKSON A	COL	0-0350006	1057	1
FINDLEY JAMES E	MAJ	0-1645244	0461	1
FINDLEY JR EVERETT E	CPT	C-1643710	0846	2
FINDLEY JR SEAB H	2LT	0-1299020	0943	2
FINDLEY MERYL G	CPT	0-0333826	0166	3
FINDLEY VIVIAN L	2LT	N-0760390	0345	1
FINE HENRY	WO1	W-2139924	0345	2
FINE HENRY R	COL	0-0287641	C662	3
FINE JAMES P	CW3	W-2209295	C866	1
FINE MERTON R	CW2	W-3150554	C865	1
FINE MORTIMER C	LTC	0-0273193	C467	3
FINE PAUL R	LTC	0-0497244	1162	1
FINE SIDNEY A	LTC	0-1168664	1265	1
FINE WILLIAM T	LTC	0-0393571	1266	1
FINEGAN CHARLES P	LTC	0-0480019	C853	1
FINEREN JR WILLIAM W	LTC	0-0914956	0963	3
FINGER HARVEY N	COL	0-1577159	0357	1
FINGERHUT WALTER C	LTC	0-1285406	C757	1
FINIELS RICHARD O	MAJ	C-1946051	0163	1
FINIGAN JOHN B	LTC	0-0386029	0560	1
FINK AUGUST O	LTC	0-0159456	1049	3
FINK EDWIN H	LTC	0-0252686	0158	3
FINK EMIL A	MAJ	0-0198404	0653	3
FINK FREDERICK	LTC	0-0241883	C246	2
FINK GEORGE	MAJ	C-0262154	0545	2
FINK HENRIETTA	1LT	N-0788823	1045	1
FINK HERBERT C	CW3	W-2147849	0464	1
FINK IRA S	MAJ	0-0414248	0547	1
FINK JOSEPH	CPT	C-0386307	1145	2
FINK LEROY M	LTC	0-0162196	0355	3
FINK RICHARD S	CW4	W-2004476	0865	1
FINK SOL P	COL	C-0136513	C358	3
FINK THEODORE H	LTC	0-0210570	1061	3
FINKEL JASON M	1LT	0-1182571	0146	2
FINKEL MAXWELL E	LTC	0-0276327	0567	3
FINKELMAN NATHAN	MAJ	0-1573200	0857	1
FINKELMAN SAMUEL	LTC	C-1542338	1262	1
FINKELSON JR JOHN M	MAJ	0-0307526	0645	2
FINKELSTEIN DAVID	CPT	0-1695765	C146	2
FINKELSTEIN LEON	CW4	W-2120194	0760	1
FINKLE FREDERICK	CPT	0-0275075	C653	1
FINKLE JAMES D	LTC	0-1053597	0962	1
FINKLE JOHN R	COL	0-0173687	0161	3
FINKS RAYMOND T	COL	C-0275582	1055	3
FINKS WILLIAM R	LTC	0-1533313	C757	1
FINLAY ANDREW N	2LT	0-0425736	C944	2
FINLAY WILLIAM O	LTC	0-1823716	C866	1
FINLAYSON DOUGLAS W	COL	0-0409886	1160	1
FINLAYSON FRANK E	1LT	0-1102242	C146	2
FINLAYSON ROBERT V	CPT	0-0889204	C559	1
FINLEY DEAN H	LTC	0-0303891	0960	1
FINLEY FRED L	CPT	0-0955807	0661	1
FINLEY GEORGE R	CPT	0-0360346	C462	2
FINLEY GEORGE V	MAJ	0-0225121	0454	3
FINLEY HARRISON C	CPT	0-0222871	1046	1
FINLEY JR OWEN J	2LT	C-0527152	C545	1
FINLEY MARK	LTC	0-0297439	C867	3
FINLEY MERLE F	LTC	0-1283052	0557	1
FINLEY SETH D	LTC	0-1320517	1262	1
FINLEY VICTOR G	LTC	0-1170735	C467	1
FINLEY WALTER C	MAJ	0-0305678	0944	2
FINLEY WILLARD L	LTC	0-0234070	1057	3
FINLEY WILLIS W	LTC	0-0152644	0555	3
FINN AIDAN A	1LT	0-1038616	1145	2
FINN BERNARD J	CW3	W-2204915	1067	3

NAME	GRADE	SVC NO	DATE RET MO YR	RET CODE
FINN CLEMENT E	LTC	C-0373256	1061	2
FINN DLANE L	MAJ	0-0988639	1164	1
FINN FRANK M	LTC	0-1308127	0866	1
FINN JAMES J	LTC	0-1102243	0561	1
FINN JOHN L	LTC	0-0995010	0567	2
FINN JR GEORGE J	1LT	0-1303486	0145	2
FINN JR PHILLIP S	LTC	C-0270791	0546	2
FINN MAURICE D	COL	C-0904181	0367	3
FINN SILAS M	LTC	0-0188094	0260	3
FINN THOMAS H	COL	0-0267560	1063	3
FINN WALTON C	LTC	0-0279762	0664	3
FINNEGAN ARTHUR M	LTC	0-0932656	0765	1
FINNEGAN DAVID F	MAJ	0-1951472	1060	1
FINNEGAN EDWARD B	LTC	0-2046608	0258	1
FINNEGAN JOHN J	MAJ	0-0968686	1162	1
FINNEGAN LEONARD J	LTC	0-1796444	1161	1
FINNEGAN MARGARET J	CW3	V-8200410	0364	1
FINNEGAN MILES J	LTC	0-0239178	1160	3
FINNEGAN RICHARD A	MAJ	C-1306516	0962	1
FINNEGAN RICHARD A	1LT	0-1311385	1045	2
FINNEGAN RUSSELL M	LTC	0-1113202	0761	1
FINNEGAN ZENUS E	LTC	0-0505148	1154	1
FINNELL GALEN F	CW2	W-2113676	0849	1
FINNELL JAMES K	1LT	0-1302960	1145	2
FINNELL JOHN W	LTC	0-1001554	0166	1
FINNELL JR WOOLSEY	COL	C-0250414	0766	3
FINNEMORE MERTON G	WO1	W-2152957	0853	1
FINNERTY CHARLES H	CPT	0-0922579	C844	2
FINNERTY JAMES H	MAJ	0-0307567	1059	3
FINNEY JAMES C	MAJ	0-0307260	1045	2
FINNEY NORMAN C	COL	0-0308426	0160	1
FINNEY PHILIP A	LTC	0-1638383	1065	1
FINNEY RAY C	LTC	0-0421810	1061	1
FINNEY THEODORE H	CW2	W-2144644	0863	1
FINNIGAN DONALD C	MAJ	0-0990814	0165	1
FINNIN RICHARD H	CPT	0-4074807	0862	2
FINNINC EDWARD C	MAJ	0-1297516	1054	1
FINSTER ROY R	MAJ	C-0367435	C467	3
FINT MELVIN J	CPT	0-1559016	0159	1
FINT RENEX G	LTC	0-1577163	0960	1
FINTON ALMON L	MAJ	0-1920268	0264	1
FIORE ANTOINETTE	2LT	N-0703435	C443	1
FIORE HENRY R	LTC	0-1180493	1062	1
FIORE MICHAEL N	LTC	0-1043337	1262	1
FIORELLA PASCUALE J	CPT	0-0266026	0557	3
FIORI GEORGE	MAJ	0-2262483	0862	1
FIPPS ELMER E	1LT	0-1109286	1045	2
FIREBAUGH ALBERT E	COL	0-0331411	0963	3
FIRESTONE MILTON H	MAJ	0-0480833	1145	1
FIRPO JOHN J	LTC	0-0380768	0146	2
FIRTH WILLIAM F	COL	C-0252170	1048	3
FISCHBACH CLIFTON M	COL	0-1696600	0962	1
FISCHER ALBERT C	MAJ	0-1117604	0860	1
FISCHER ANTHONY C	1LT	0-1322630	0648	2
FISCHER CARL B	CPT	0-0413762	0445	2
FISCHER CARL H	MAJ	C-0480264	0752	1
FISCHER CARL L	MAJ	C-1302622	0765	1
FISCHER DONALD R	CPT	0-1018658	1063	1
FISCHER EARL F	CPT	0-0356955	1048	2
FISCHER EUGENE A	MAJ	0-0283042	0961	3
FISCHER FRANK E	LTC	0-0233560	0865	3
FISCHER HERBERT M	CW4	W-2135096	1060	1
FISCHER JOHN H	CPT	0-1633209	0745	2
FISCHER JOHN J	MAJ	C-5405056	1067	1
FISCHER LAWRENCE R	1LT	0-1579645	0545	2
FISCHER LEONARD H	MAJ	0-1015495	0265	1
FISCHER LOUIS	CPT	0-0450860	0248	2
FISCHER LOUIS F	2LT	0-0370414	1060	2
FISCHER LYNN J	1LT	0-1328135	0846	2
FISCHER MARY H	CPT	N-0733063	1047	1
FISCHER MEYER	1LT	0-0353140	0746	1
FISCHER MORTON	LTC	0-0202570	0863	3
FISCHER MURIEL F	2LT	N-0730497	1042	1
FISCHER PERRY E	MAJ	0-0571503	0262	1
FISCHER VICTORIA M	MAJ	N-0731733	1064	1

NAME	GRADE	SVC NO	DATE RET MO YR	RET CODE
FISCHER WERNER	LTC	0-1100985	C765	3
FISCHER WILBUR H	LTC	0-0510023	1058	1
FISCHESSER CHARLES P	MAJ	C-1103630	0461	1
FISCHLE EDWARD J	MAJ	C-2036982	C161	1
FISCHLE EDWARD K	LTC	0-1297347	C662	1
FISCHLER JOSEPH	MAJ	0-1644256	0266	1
FISCUS ETHEL M	2LT	N-0735738	C445	1
FISCUS LLOYD	1LT	0-0195448	0556	3
FISCUS MILLARD W	MAJ	C-1595329	C565	3
FISET LEWIS H	MAJ	C-0452525	1046	1
FISH DAVID J	MAJ	C-0469359	0146	1
FISH DONALD O	CPT	0-1011538	0347	1
FISH ELBRIDGE G	LTC	0-0422591	0464	1
FISH FREDERICK	LTC	0-0266988	0146	2
FISH GORDON T	LTC	0-0165919	0546	2
FISH HAMILTON	COL	0-0168979	1048	3
FISH ISAAC W	CW2	W-2205611	0363	1
FISH JACK C	LTC	0-0341193	C666	3
FISH JAMES E	COL	0-0178358	1061	3
FISH LELLIE W	LTC	0-1303319	0454	1
FISH LESTER W	COL	C-0270461	0859	3
FISH RICHARD O	MAJ	C-0370981	C562	1
FISH VIRGIL O	COL	0-0272138	0567	3
FISH WILLIAM O	1LT	0-1081647	0246	2
FISH WILLIAM P	LTC	0-2048293	1167	1
FISHBACK AMOS M	MAJ	0-0332209	0860	1
FISHBACK DAVID B	CPT	C-0504865	C744	2
FISHBACK JOHN S	LTC	C-0175062	1045	1
FISHBACK JR LOUIS F	MAJ	0-0243480	C959	3
FISHBACK WILLIAM M	2LT	0-1320031	1045	2
FISHBURN RANDOLPH E	LTC	0-0407560	0661	1
FISHBURNE FRANCIS J	COL	0-0237977	C165	3
FISHEL DONALD R	CW4	W-2144154	0565	1
FISHER ABE A	CPT	0-1693779	0246	2
FISHER ALFRED S	CW3	W-2147587	C862	1
FISHER ALLAN G	MAJ	0-0188136	0552	3
FISHER ARTHUR F	COL	C-0246246	0747	2
FISHER BERNARD	CPT	0-0320727	C344	2
FISHER BILLY W	CW3	W-2144620	0965	1
FISHER BYRON G	MAJ	C-1321169	C361	2
FISHER BYRON J	LTC	0-0365454	C560	1
FISHER CARL J	CPT	0-0440495	1144	2
FISHER CHARLES	LTC	0-0403871	0761	1
FISHER CHARLES A	CPT	0-0318566	0245	2
FISHER CHARLES E	LTC	0-1551615	0962	2
FISHER CHARLES E	1LT	0-1646163	1160	1
FISHER CHARLES L	WO1	W-2113901	C147	1
FISHER CHARLES R	COL	0-0123484	0648	3
FISHER CHESTER E	MAJ	C-0990348	C862	1
FISHER CLYDE E	COL	0-0178829	0255	3
FISHER DALE R	1LT	0-0555909	0648	2
FISHER DONALD D	LTC	0-0477033	C457	1
FISHER DONALD R	MAJ	C-0956942	C163	1
FISHER EARL J	COL	0-0270652	C461	3
FISHER EDWARD	MAJ	0-0419039	0846	2
FISHER ELIZABETH	MAJ	N-0741303	C863	1
FISHER ERNEST L	CPT	0-1648017	0856	1
FISHER EUGENE L A	LTC	0-0481878	0754	2
FISHER EUGENE V	MAJ	0-0269510	C966	3
FISHER FRANCIS P	LTC	C-0251502	1147	2
FISHER FRANK E	MAJ	0-0271866	0967	3
FISHER FRANK R	1LT	0-1323304	C456	1
FISHER GEORGE	LTC	0-0411052	0761	1
FISHER GEORGE E	CPT	0-1183065	1045	2
FISHER GEORGE F	MAJ	C-1585212	C161	3
FISHER GEORGE W	COL	0-0248561	1065	3
FISHER GERALD F	MAJ	0-2026976	C562	1
FISHER GWYNDOLYN	CPT	N-0727199	1146	1
FISHER HAROLD B	LTC	0-0251943	0859	1
FISHER HAROLD E	COL	0-0212600	1262	3
FISHER HAROLD R	MAJ	C-0946887	1064	1
FISHER HENRY R	LTC	0-0286746	0665	3
FISHER HENRY T	MAJ	C-0133942	C955	3
FISHER HERMAN P	LTC	0-0249643	0966	3
FISHER HOWARD A	CPT	0-1597434	0657	1

NAME	GRADE	SVC NO	DATE RET MO YR	RET CODE
FISHER HYMAN	LTC	0-0256820	0263	3
FISHER HYMAN S	MAJ	0-1695686	0465	1
FISHER JACK D	LTC	0-0276617	0364	3
FISHER JACK E	MAJ	0-1922660	0366	1
FISHER JAMES C	MAJ	C-1590456	0663	1
FISHER JAMES R	COL	0-0294335	1067	3
FISHER JOHN	2LT	0-1914423	0749	1
FISHER JOHN H	LTC	0-1337289	C665	1
FISHER JOHN P	LTC	0-0290016	0167	3
FISHER JOHN W	MAJ	0-0186245	1048	3
FISHER JOSEPH S	1LT	0-1041066	0754	1
FISHER JR CHARLES H	1LT	0-1015174	0145	2
FISHER JR CHARLES L	MAJ	0-1169107	1067	3
FISHER JR DELPHIA F	LTC	0-0331595	0265	3
FISHER JR WILBERT D	COL	0-1104151	0866	1
FISHER JR WILLIAM H	CW3	W-2200558	0965	3
FISHER KATHERINE	2LT	N-0762650	0945	1
FISHER KENNETH M	CW4	W-2108488	0358	1
FISHER KENNETH W	MAJ	C-0887624	0957	1
FISHER LEO W	CPT	0-0451965	C146	2
FISHER LLOYD A	MAJ	0-0300651	1163	3
FISHER LLOYD W	LTC	0-1290522	0560	1
FISHER LYNWOOD W	COL	0-0243118	0560	1
FISHER MARY H	1LT	N-0759660	0745	1
FISHER MAX B	1LT	0-1310064	0846	2
FISHER MILTON R	LTC	0-0298174	0850	3
FISHER MORGAN C	WO1	W-2126320	0645	2
FISHER NELSON L	MAJ	0-0200768	0355	3
FISHER PAUL F	1LT	0-0497576	0447	1
FISHER PEARL C	LTC	N-0700798	0145	1
FISHER RAYMOND	MAJ	C-1047962	1165	1
FISHER RAYMOND A	CW4	W-2101686	0959	1
FISHER RAYMOND F	LTC	0-0337868	0763	1
FISHER RET H	CW2	W-2104938	1044	2
FISHER ROBERT A	LTC	0-0107554	1155	3
FISHER ROBERT H	LTC	0-1030025	0364	1
FISHER ROBERT S	1LT	0-1014674	0945	2
FISHER SAMUEL	CPT	0-0110091	0648	3
FISHER SEWALL	LTC	0-0308301	0861	1
FISHER THEODORE E	CPT	0-0245959	0843	1
FISHER THOMAS R	LTC	0-0180195	0855	3
FISHER VINCENT L	CPT	0-1281686	1146	2
FISHER VIRGIL S	CW2	W-2146705	1162	1
FISHER WALTER A	LTC	0-0303506	0662	1
FISHER WESLEY C	LTC	0-1320382	0667	1
FISHER WILLIAM C	COL	0-0158932	0753	1
FISHER WILLIAM C	LTC	0-0293513	0267	3
FISHER WILLIAM H	LTC	0-0228850	0962	3
FISHMAN MORRIS	CPT	0-0490724	0246	2
FISHPAW ELI I	LTC	0-1171140	1162	1
FISK DURWARD C	LTC	0-0408958	0461	1
FISK EARL A	MAJ	0-0988992	1062	1
FISK FRANK W	MAJ	0-0453505	0764	1
FISK GORDON A	1LT	0-0412208	0846	2
FISK HARRY H	LTC	0-0154122	0255	3
FISK HERBERT B	LTC	0-0445665	0964	3
FISKE DAVID L	MAJ	0-0161350	0758	3
FISKE JR EDWARD R	MAJ	0-0250909	0366	3
FISKE LEIGH G	CPT	0-1703178	0745	2
FISKE MAHLON F	LTC	0-0321475	1066	3
FISKE WILLIAM M	COL	C-0203517	1058	1
FISSEL GEORGE C	1LT	0-1326989	0746	1
FISSELL JOHN	LTC	0-0408089	0862	3
FISTER JR FRED M	COL	0-0257681	0466	3
FITCH CODY W	2LT	0-1593952	0460	2
FITCH CURRY F	CW3	W-2150952	0566	1
FITCH DAVID G	COL	0-0286551	0657	3
FITCH EDWARD W	CW2	W-2145180	0358	1
FITCH FRANKLIN G	2LT	C-1180182	1045	2
FITCH HANFORD M	2LT	0-1054361	1044	2
FITCH JAMES C	COL	0-0212131	0264	3
FITCH JAMES R	1LT	0-0501133	0944	1
FITCH JR ALBERT W	LTC	0-0664555	0262	1
FITCH JR FRANCIS B	LTC	0-0918150	1266	3
FITCH JR JAMES H	CW2	W-2210106	0464	2

NAME	GRADE	SVC NO	DATE RET MO YR	RET CODE
FITCH WILLIAM E	CW2	W-2214887	1167	1
FITCH WILLIAM L	LTC	0-1311752	1165	1
FITCHETT HELEN M	MAJ	N-0797421	0566	1
FITCHHORN RAY E	CW3	W-2205546	1065	1
FITE HARRISON F	MAJ	0-2262283	0162	1
FITE HUGH S	LTC	0-0310886	0663	1
FITE RANDOLPH V	COL	0-0381254	0757	1
FITE WILBER L	MAJ	0-0388558	1045	1
FITES EDWARD A	MAJ	0-2291672	0464	1
FITES ROBERT F	CPT	0-1544050	0346	2
FITKIN WILLIAM W	COL	0-0210549	0754	3
FITTING CHARLES L	CW2	W-2210024	1265	1
FITTS JAMES O	CW3	W-2151681	0663	1
FITTS PRYOR W	LTC	0-0265318	1064	3
FITTS RALPH L	LTC	0-0162368	1060	3
FITTS SAMUEL	CW3	W-2149752	0564	1
FITZ HARRIS RIC	MAJ	0-1289060	1060	1
FITZ SAMUEL B	CW2	W-2143328	0257	1
FITZGGIBBON GEORGE W	1LT	0-1310430	0246	2
FITZGGIBBON JAMES F	LTC	0-0103034	1056	3
FITZ-GIBBON GEORGE E	LTC	0-0121767	0648	3
FITZ-HUGH BERNICE R	2LT	N-0742432	0545	1
FITZGERALD CHARLES N	LTC	0-1799438	0767	1
FITZGERALD CHARLES R	COL	0-0206816	1048	3
FITZGERALD DERMOT T	2LT	0-2016875	1061	1
FITZGERALD DONALD E	MAJ	0-2262674	0566	1
FITZGERALD DONALD J	MAJ	0-2035085	0161	1
FITZGERALD EDWARD J	LTC	0-0258106	1064	3
FITZGERALD EDWARD J	CPT	0-0528916	0846	2
FITZGERALD EDWARD N	LTC	0-0386379	0760	1
FITZGERALD EUGENE J	MAJ	0-1315676	1160	1
FITZGERALD FRANCIS A	2LT	0-1111611	0145	2
FITZGERALD FRANCIS R	MAJ	0-1014210	1058	1
FITZGERALD FREDERICK	CW4	W-2142547	0863	1
FITZGERALD GERALD P	CW3	RW-2152623	0464	1
FITZGERALD GLENN L	MAJ	0-0226011	1161	3
FITZGERALD HOWARD A	MAJ	0-1114120	0758	1
FITZGERALD J MARION	LTC	0-0298330	1063	3
FITZGERALD J P	1LT	0-1173607	0744	2
FITZGERALD JAMES L	MAJ	0-0320809	0465	3
FITZGERALD JOHN F	MAJ	0-0228404	1052	3
FITZGERALD JOHN J	B G	0-0290834	0865	3
FITZGERALD JOSEPH C	COL	0-0263329	0965	3
FITZGERALD LESTER F	CPT	0-1548457	0857	1
FITZGERALD LOREN P	LTC	0-0888355	0261	1
FITZGERALD MARION J	MAJ	N-0736684	0459	2
FITZGERALD NORMAN F	MAJ	0-1548769	1060	1
FITZGERALD PAUL J	CPT	0-0503897	1147	1
FITZGERALD RALPH J	CW3	W-2146832	1061	1
FITZGERALD RICHARD H	1LT	0-1825462	0745	2
FITZGERALD RICHARD J	1LT	0-0411076	0344	2
FITZGERALD ROBERT M	MAJ	0-1947697	1058	2
FITZGERALD THOMAS C	CW3	W-2152605	0467	1
FITZGERALD THOMAS F	MAJ	0-0188808	0551	3
FITZGERALD WADE E	MAJ	0-0443941	0646	1
FITZGERALD WILLIAM E	MAJ	0-1553082	1056	1
FITZGERALD WILLIAM J	MAJ	0-1013874	0963	1
FITZGIBBONS THOMAS C	LTC	0-1552667	0962	2
FITZGIBBONS TIM L	MAJ	0-1327830	0661	1
FITZHUGH ANDREW F	MAJ	0-0330935	0347	2
FITZHUGH EDWARD B	MAJ	0-2033635	0661	2
FITZHUGH SAMUEL A	1LT	0-1058511	0646	2
FITZMAURICE F E	LTC	0-0309979	0359	1
FITZPATRICK CLYDE	CW2	W-2143901	0159	1
FITZPATRICK DAVID A	MAJ	0-1647884	1058	1
FITZPATRICK EDWARD J	MAJ	0-0155132	0355	3
FITZPATRICK EDWIN A	LTC	0-0193021	0146	1
FITZPATRICK F X	CPT	0-0477687	0546	2
FITZPATRICK FRANCIS	LTC	0-0254424	0766	3
FITZPATRICK FRANK R	LTC	0-0383610	1164	3
FITZPATRICK GORDON J	MAJ	0-1643547	0861	1
FITZPATRICK HAMILTON	LTC	0-0303566	0866	3
FITZPATRICK JAMES B	WO1	W-2116222	0244	2
FITZPATRICK JAMES D	2LT	0-2043211	0745	2
FITZPATRICK JAMES E	CPT	0-0983215	0760	2

NAME	GRADE	SVC NO	DATE RET MO YR	RET CODE
FITZPATRICK JAMES I	LTC	0-0383464	0860	1
FITZPATRICK JOHN D	CPT	0-1040380	0245	1
FITZPATRICK JOHN J	LTC	0-0212439	0562	3
FITZPATRICK JOHN J	LTC	0-0336864	0661	1
FITZPATRICK JOHN J	MAJ	0-1040525	1164	3
FITZPATRICK JOHN J	1LT	0-2041638	0554	2
FITZPATRICK LYLE J	COL	0-0300496	0559	1
FITZPATRICK PATRICK	MAJ	0-1946249	1262	1
FITZPATRICK ROBERT W	COL	0-0441611	1154	1
FITZPATRICK THOMAS A	COL	0-0184765	0147	2
FITZPATRICK THOMAS S	MAJ	0-1553631	0462	2
FITZPATRICK WILLIAM	LTC	0-0291255	0547	1
FITZSIMMONS JOHN P	MAJ	0-0447616	1145	2
FITZSIMMONS RICHARD	LTC	0-1060096	0263	2
FITZSIMMONS WALLACE	LTC	0-1541316	0661	1
FITZSIMONS ARCHIE L	LTC	0-0256049	1061	3
FITZWATER ROGER R	LTC	0-0451388	0954	1
FITZWILSON CRANE P	MAJ	0-1947870	0961	1
FIVEHOUSE NEAL R	CW2	W-2212118	0866	1
FIVES WILLIAM B	LTC	0-2055444	0967	1
FIX ALFRED E	LTC	0-0411607	1060	1
FIX HERMAN M	MAJ	0-0263901	0247	1
FIX JOSEPH E	COL	0-0173782	0857	3
FIX JR LESLIE N	MAJ	0-2096457	0565	1
FIXEL ROWLAND W	COL	0-0167941	0648	3
FLACH GEORGE L	MAJ	0-0245222	1152	3
FLACH JOSEPH R	LTC	0-0212427	0951	3
FLAGEL FRANK F	LTC	0-0198149	1048	1
FLAGG MARGARET C	2LT	N-0774630	0446	1
FLAGG MILDRED W	CPT	N-0743630	0647	1
FLAGG RAYMOND P	2LT	0-0392304	0243	2
FLAGG SEWELL L	CPT	0-0279070	0954	3
FLAGG STANLEY E	LTC	0-0162525	1044	2
FLAGG WILLARD G	LTC	0-0248667	0766	3
FLAHERTY EDWARD B	LTC	0-0371402	0646	2
FLAHERTY EILEEN V	LTC	N-0720526	0766	2
FLAHERTY JAMES J	1LT	0-1534968	1145	2
FLAHERTY JOHN J	LTC	0-1578468	0761	1
FLAHERTY JOHN L	LTC	0-2043002	0263	1
FLAHERTY JOSEPH P	LTC	0-0410422	1262	1
FLAHERTY JR R G	LTC	0-0450275	0955	1
FLAHERTY MATTHEW J	LTC	0-1050255	0563	1
FLAHERTY WALTER T	1LT	0-0525505	0645	1
FLAHIVE JOHN D	MAJ	0-0958441	0166	1
FLAHIVE JOHN R	2LT	0-0239200	1042	1
FLAHIVE ROBERT E	MAJ	0-1120276	0264	1
FLAIG FRANK J	CPT	0-1296350	0347	2
FLAIM RUDOLPH A	MAJ	0-1322538	0759	1
FLAITZ JAMES R	CW3	W-2146467	0461	2
FLAMER MORTIMER	MAJ	0-0523131	0746	2
FLAMICK LEO P	CPT	0-0253858	0658	3
FLAMM LEO M	1LT	0-0451542	1056	1
FLANAGAN CHARLES C	MAJ	0-0963512	0166	1
FLANAGAN CHARLES P	MAJ	0-2034516	0663	1
FLANAGAN DANIEL	LTC	0-1541843	1162	1
FLANAGAN FREDERICK	CW2	W-2151907	0361	1
FLANAGAN HARRY A	CPT	0-2032990	0959	2
FLANAGAN HARRY O	2LT	0-1551619	1044	2
FLANAGAN JAMES B	LTC	0-0528367	0863	2
FLANAGAN JIM W	CW2	W-2117855	0646	2
FLANAGAN JOHN D	CPT	0-1111058	0966	1
FLANAGAN JOSEPH E	CW3	W-2151371	1063	1
FLANAGAN JOSEPH R	CW4	W-2009156	0567	3
FLANAGAN JR JAMES L	MAJ	0-0565783	0366	1
FLANAGAN LAWRENCE M	MAJ	0-1332248	0664	1
FLANAGAN MILDRED H	2LT	N-0758000	0844	1
FLANAGAN PAUL R	LTC	0-0454283	1066	2
FLANAGIN MARVIN M	COL	0-0410691	0567	3
FLANAKIN HUBERT A	LTC	0-0921945	0365	3
FLANAKIN JEWELL B	2LT	N-0726372	0643	1
FLANARY JOHN	1LT	0-0495004	0945	2
FLANDERS CHARLES R	CW3	W-2152624	0463	1
FLANDERS EVERETT M	MAJ	0-1540715	0657	1
FLANDERS HERBERT P	MAJ	0-0294385	0845	2
FLANDERS RAY T	CW3	W-2147706	0563	1

NAME	GRADE	SVC NO	DATE RET MO YR	RET CODE
FLANDERS WILLIAM F	MAJ	0-1594079	0863	1
FLANDRO ARTHUR L	COL	0-0209052	0752	3
FLANIGAN ANGELA C	MAJ	N-0755078	0666	1
FLANIGAN JAMES P	CPT	0-1997076	0855	2
FLANIGAN PAUL T	2LT	0-0357804	0843	2
FLANIGAN RICHARD A	2LT	0-1998331	0545	2
FLANIGAN THOMAS J	1LT	0-0549631	0646	2
FLANIGAN WILLIAM M	B G	0-0265698	0354	3
FLANNIGAN CLAUD B	LTC	0-0491553	1155	1
FLANNIGAN ROBERT W	1LT	0-0449514	0745	2
FLANSBURG DALE M	CW2	W-2150676	0461	1
FLAPAN MAXWELL	LTC	0-0261236	0666	3
FLASCHNER IRA	CPT	0-0416664	0246	2
FLASH HOWARD S	CPT	0-1294811	0664	1
FLATLEY JOHN W	CPT	0-0423688	0346	2
FLATT ROBERT LIN	2LT	0-1319193	0551	2
FLATTLEY JR THOMAS M	LTC	0-0386318	1060	2
FLAUGHER THOMAS E	MAJ	0-1051956	0960	1
FLECHER JOHN	CW3	W-2109149	0756	1
FLECK BERNARD	WO1	W-2120000	0245	2
FLECK JAMES M	LTC	0-0548609	0365	3
FLECK LEROY S	LTC	0-0177175	0161	3
FLEEGE HERBERT W	1LT	0-0390005	0744	2
FLEEGLER SAUL M	CPT	0-0355896	0246	2
FLEEK DELBERT I	MAJ	0-1010562	0847	1
FLEEK NELSON	2LT	0-1031170	0845	2
FLEES FRANK J	1LT	0-1305406	1145	2
FLEET GLADYS M	CPT	N-0764350	1052	1
FLEET RUSSELL T	LTC	0-0441098	0661	3
FLEETWOOD RAYMOND	CPT	0-0454753	1153	1
FLEGAL CLAUDE P	CPT	0-0922076	0847	2
FLEGEL DAYLE F	MAJ	0-0410110	0361	1
FLEISCHAKER WILLIAM	LTC	0-1895662	1162	1
FLEISCHER IRVING S	LTC	0-0498764	1061	1
FLEISCHER JOSEPH	COL	0-0304042	0866	3
FLEISCHER JOSEPH K	MAJ	0-0962343	0763	1
FLEISCHER MILTON L	CPT	0-1114475	0661	1
FLEISCHMAN ANDREW	LTC	0-2019576	0366	1
FLEISCHMAN ARTHUR E	MAJ	0-0284834	0665	3
FLEISCHMAN FORREST G	COL	0-0344840	0661	1
FLEISHER ARLENE A	MAJ	N-0755074	1067	1
FLEITZ BENJAMIN F	MAJ	0-0148842	1054	3
FLEMENS NORRIS L	CPT	0-2007236	0957	1
FLEMIG ERNEST A	LTC	0-0340164	1159	1
FLEMING ANTHONY	COL	0-0274994	0562	1
FLEMING BALLARD	MAJ	0-2042140	0166	1
FLEMING CARL S	1LT	0-0495624	0550	1
FLEMING CHARLES A	MAJ	0-0469767	0747	1
FLEMING CHARLES C	MAJ	0-1313868	0166	1
FLEMING CHRISTOPHE	CW3	W-2143221	0959	1
FLEMING CLYDE	MAJ	0-2263200	0166	1
FLEMING DALE H	CPT	0-0973589	1161	1
FLEMING DANIEL O	CW3	W-2142942	0159	1
FLEMING DAVIDSON M	MAJ	0-0174824	0648	3
FLEMING EARL L	LTC	0-1280435	0360	1
FLEMING EDMOND C	MAJ	0-0309162	1053	3
FLEMING GEORGE A	MAJ	0-0953672	0862	1
FLEMING JAMES C	LTC	0-0238508	0662	3
FLEMING JAMES F	CPT	0-0338961	0146	2
FLEMING JAMES L	MAJ	0-1307215	0962	1
FLEMING JAMES T	LTC	0-0257682	0167	3
FLEMING JOHN	1LT	0-2002807	0954	2
FLEMING JOHN C	COL	0-0233512	0560	3
FLEMING JOHN E	CPT	0-1690960	0762	1
FLEMING JOHN H	1LT	0-1322399	1046	1
FLEMING JOSEPH	CPT	0-1104154	1145	2
FLEMING JOSEPH H	LTC	0-0903827	0958	3
FLEMING JOSEPH P	LTC	0-0128336	1053	3
FLEMING JR SAMUEL C	CW2	W-2147309	0764	1
FLEMING KARL J	2LT	0-1646166	0244	2
FLEMING KATHLEEN P	MAJ	N-0720273	0661	1
FLEMING MAURICE C	1LT	0-0387964	0342	2
FLEMING OMER J	CPT	0-1699980	0466	1
FLEMING RALPH O	CW2	RW-2209867	0464	1
FLEMING RAYMOND H	M G	0-0165022	0253	1

NAME	GRADE	SVC NO	DATE RET MO YR	RET CODE
FLEMING RAYMOND L	MAJ	0-1041343	1061	1
FLEMING REX	MAJ	0-0301218	0859	3
FLEMING RICHARD W	1LT	0-1584216	0446	2
FLEMING ROBERT J	CPT	0-1746695	0147	2
FLEMING ROBERT L	MAJ	0-1116774	0860	1
FLEMING SALVADOR	WO1	W-2123722	0757	1
FLEMING THOMAS T	MAJ	0-2035247	1160	1
FLEMING WALTER J	CPT	0-1301465	1048	2
FLEMING WILLIAM H	COL	0-0282479	0566	3
FLEMING WILLIAM M	CPT	0-0478547	1060	1
FLEMING WILLIAM M	LTC	0-2016499	0165	1
FLEMINGS MILTON B	LTC	0-1547934	0263	1
FLEMMING CHARLES W	CW4	W-2141276	0962	1
FLEMMING JOHN W	COL	0-0225136	0360	2
FLESCH LAWRENCE H	WO1	W-2108208	0946	1
FLESHER WILLIAM J	CPT	0-1103162	0561	1
FLETCHER ARCHIBALD	COL	0-0490514	0465	1
FLETCHER ARTHUR L	LTC	0-0101336	0648	3
FLETCHER CHARLES H	MAJ	0-0442003	1046	2
FLETCHER CHARLES J	LTC	0-1165558	0359	1
FLETCHER CHARLES M	CW3	W-2145332	0663	1
FLETCHER CHARLES R	LTC	0-1317510	0464	1
FLETCHER CHARLES V	COL	0-0298773	0259	3
FLETCHER CLAUDE C	COL	0-0126882	0954	3
FLETCHER DANIEL L	1LT	0-1309656	1045	1
FLETCHER DOZIER	LTC	0-1167837	0963	1
FLETCHER EDWARD A	1LT	0-1042563	0145	1
FLETCHER ELGIE C	LTC	0-1319938	0165	1
FLETCHER ELLSWORTH	1LT	0-0510341	0446	2
FLETCHER GERALD E	CW4	W-2141926	0764	2
FLETCHER HARRY W	CPT	0-0499898	0644	2
FLETCHER HARRY M	CW3	W-2153080	0365	1
FLETCHER HILBERT E	LTC	0-0478719	0265	3
FLETCHER JAMES H	MAJ	0-0411981	0761	1
FLETCHER JEANNE M	2LT	N-0722262	1044	1
FLETCHER JESS F	CPT	0-0488856	0645	2
FLETCHER JESSE H	LTC	0-1310085	0462	1
FLETCHER JOHN G	LTC	0-0226880	1264	3
FLETCHER JOHN V	CW2	W-2150339	1162	1
FLETCHER JOHN W	LTC	0-0126802	0748	3
FLETCHER JOSEPH F	CW3	W-2148349	0263	1
FLETCHER JR THOMAS H	CPT	0-0402965	1263	1
FLETCHER KENNETH L	1LT	0-0474936	1045	2
FLETCHER LA VERNE M	COL	0-0290434	0164	3
FLETCHER LEWIS A	LTC	0-0377794	0661	1
FLETCHER LOUIS W	LTC	0-0237870	0262	3
FLETCHER MARVIN H	LTC	0-1555208	0962	1
FLETCHER MILLARD M	LTC	0-1174572	0662	1
FLETCHER NANNIE B	CPT	N-0763845	0161	2
FLETCHER OSCAR E	CPT	0-1170368	0960	1
FLETCHER ROBERT D	CPT	0-0408082	0146	2
FLETCHER ROONEY	MAJ	0-2077785	0465	1
FLETCHER SAMUEL M	LTC	0-0270678	1055	1
FLETCHER WALTER C	CPT	0-1103631	0646	2
FLETCHER WALTER M	2LT	0-2001668	0546	2
FLETCHER WILLIAM F	LTC	0-0221292	0961	3
FLETT WILLIAM C	CPT	0-1061111	0347	1
FLEURY EDGAR	MAJ	0-2023875	1060	1
FLEURY JOHN R	2LT	0-0888461	1044	2
FLEWELLEN ROBERT H	1LT	0-1283402	1044	2
FLEWELLING MAX S	MAJ	0-0217188	0956	3
FLEWELLING MILTON F	MAJ	0-0525684	0547	2
FLEXSER EDWIN L	CW4	W-2126015	0867	1
FLICK FRANK C	LTC	0-0182655	1048	1
FLICK JOHN L	1LT	0-1298043	0146	1
FLICK LAWRENCE G	COL	0-0187137	0654	2
FLICK ROBERT L	WO1	W-2121771	0743	2
FLICKINGER ELMER E	LTC	0-1284172	1160	1
FLICKINGER LLOYD H	LTC	0-0235816	0364	3
FLICKINGER MALCOLM W	LTC	0-0370967	0965	1
FLIEGELMAN MAURICE T	MAJ	0-0381224	0346	2
FLIEGER JOHN H	MAJ	0-1635884	0756	1
FLINCHUM JAMES M	WO1	W-2147755	1162	1
FLINDERS DAVID C	CPT	0-1172859	0261	1
FLINN CHARLES D	LTC	0-1297705	0566	1

NAME	GRADE	SVC NO	DATE RET MO YR	RET CODE
FLINN GEORGE W	LTC	O-1031078	1265	1
FLINT CARL	MAJ	O-0861580	0764	1
FLINT CURTIS E	COL	O-1167421	0866	1
FLINT DONALD C	MAJ	O-0337127	0546	2
FLINT EARL P	2LT	O-0538272	0745	2
FLINT RAYMOND W	MAJ	O-0167698	0151	3
FLINT ROBERT J	CPT	O-1012030	0350	2
FLINT ROBERT N	LTC	O-0904810	0364	1
FLINTOSH JOSEPH	MAJ	O-0471639	0952	1
FLIPPO BETTYE P	MAJ	N-0724319	0949	2
FLOCCO THOMAS O	LTC	O-0398875	1266	3
FLOCKEN FRED H	LTC	O-0232539	0763	3
FLOCKS MAYER	CPT	O-0300968	0745	1
FLOM ANDREW M	MAJ	O-2015857	0262	1
FLOM CARL A	COL	O-0268006	0766	3
FLOM MERVIN O	LTC	O-0159369	0758	3
FLOOD ALBERT O	COL	O-0292542	0146	1
FLOOD ARNOLD O	LTC	O-2049885	1266	1
FLOOD ARTHUR P	COL	O-0915225	0362	3
FLOOD CLARENCE D	CPT	O-1045732	0550	1
FLOOD CLYDE F	CPT	O-0317832	0345	2
FLOOD EDWARD J	LTC	O-0919124	0266	3
FLOOD GERALD J	CW2	W-2146750	0662	1
FLOOD MARGARET E	2LT	N-0796965	0747	1
FLOOD MARY G	CPT	N-0752953	0147	1
FLOOD MATTHEW J	WO1	W-2148469	0356	1
FLOOD ORMOND K	CPT	O-0168089	0146	1
FLOOD RAYMOND J	CW2	W-2120985	0852	1
FLOOD ROGER A	COL	O-0107883	0553	2
FLOOD WILLIAM J	WO1	W-2115255	0345	2
FLOOK HARRY F	LTC	O-0126800	0646	2
FLOOK KENNETH G	LTC	O-0450862	0457	1
FLOOR ALBERT C	LTC	O-1558429	1063	1
FLORA HARRY D	CW4	W-2143951	1056	1
FLORENCE VICTOR G	CW4	W-2109861	0955	1
FLORES ARTHUR	CW2	W-2212742	0867	1
FLORES FLORO M	1LT	O-1896556	0350	1
FLORES JUSTINO	CPT	O-0980805	1161	1
FLORES PABLO J	CW3	W-2147659	0663	1
FLOREY JAMES R	2LT	O-0409734	0344	1
FLOREY THEODORE C	LTC	O-0402983	0660	1
FLORIDIS GREGORY C	COL	O-0321257	0566	3
FLORIMONT FRED S	LTC	O-0911657	0157	2
FLORO LAWRENCE A	LTC	O-0264327	0957	2
FLORY GAYLORD G	1LT	O-1172003	1045	1
FLORY HAROLD R	CW3	W-2148722	0966	1
FLORY JOHN W	LTC	O-1300784	0865	3
FLORY OLIVER E	LTC	O-0298885	1067	3
FLORY ROBERT C	LTC	O-0132105	0653	3
FLOURNOY III DAVID M	LTC	O-0254510	0666	3
FLOURNOY ROBERT E L	1LT	O-1019047	0845	2
FLOWER JR JAMES F	1LT	O-1017690	1147	2
FLOWERS BENJAMIN C	LTC	O-1172860	0163	1
FLOWERS DAVE	COL	O-0304718	1047	2
FLOWERS FARRAND	LTC	O-0261093	0167	3
FLOWERS FRED G	CPT	O-1172454	0246	2
FLOWERS JACK M	MAJ	O-0971470	0766	1
FLOWERS JOHN F	LTC	O-0256437	0461	3
FLOYD CHARLES J	LTC	O-1010584	0457	1
FLOYD CYRIL F	COL	O-0267443	0757	1
FLOYD EVERETT E	LTC	O-0224279	0160	1
FLOYD GEAVE	CW2	W-2212736	1265	1
FLOYD GEORGE W	MAJ	O-0414323	0847	2
FLOYD HAMILTON	LTC	O-0219930	0664	3
FLOYD HAROLD O	MAJ	O-1541836	0957	1
FLOYD HENRY C	COL	O-0234159	0146	2
FLOYD HENRY G	1LT	O-0974671	0363	2
FLOYD HILTON L	1LT	O-1685626	1052	1
FLOYD JOE R	COL	O-0324510	0546	2
FLOYD JOHN C	2LT	O-1112693	1143	2
FLOYD JR ALBERT J	LTC	O-0388983	0363	1
FLOYD MARCUS L	CW2	W-2208440	1162	1
FLOYD MONROE	1LT	O-2046300	0654	1
FLOYD RAY	LTC	O-1165729	0561	1
FLOYD RICHARD T	MAJ	O-0281756	0967	3
FLOYD SR PAUL H	MAJ	O-0201123	0559	3
FLOYD WALTER R	MAJ	O-0425420	0662	1
FLOYD WALTER R	LTC	O-1544083	0157	1
FLOYD WILLIAM E	MAJ	O-0300045	0465	2
FLOYD WILLIAM M	1LT	O-0503109	1044	2
FLOYD WILLIAM M	2LT	O-0537261	0245	2
FLOYD WILLIAM T	CW4	W-2124179	0761	1
FLUES ABRAM C	COL	O-0902712	0963	3
FLUHARTY JUNIOR J	CPT	O-1922566	0666	2
FLUKE MORRIS W	1LT	O-1547295	0547	2
FLUSCHE FREDRICK A	1LT	O-1176961	0545	2
FLY AUSTIN	COL	O-0279378	0456	2
FLYNN ARTHUR J	MAJ	O-1081473	0357	1
FLYNN CATHERINE	MAJ	N-0721060	0367	1
FLYNN CHELMER L	LTC	O-0341188	0564	1
FLYNN CENEEAR W	LTC	O-0450277	1057	1
FLYNN DONALD R	CPT	O-0287760	0545	2
FLYNN EDWARD J	1LT	O-0532089	0546	1
FLYNN FREEMAN J	LTC	O-0330795	0854	2
FLYNN GEORGE A	CW3	W-2205738	0867	1
FLYNN HAROLD D	LTC	O-0431362	0459	1
FLYNN HERBERT L	LTC	O-0265235	0162	3
FLYNN JAMES F	1LT	O-0887561	1154	1
FLYNN JAMES F	CPT	O-1044819	0450	1
FLYNN JAMES W	1LT	O-1295697	0447	2
FLYNN JOHN F	CW3	W-2141817	0462	1
FLYNN JOHN J	CPT	O-1030576	0746	2
FLYNN JOHN J	LTC	O-1580947	0763	1
FLYNN JOSEPH S	CPT	O-0110099	0648	3
FLYNN JOSEPH W	CPT	O-1166986	0257	1
FLYNN JR GRADY J	LTC	O-0397768	0662	1
FLYNN JR WILLIAM F	LTC	O-1115581	0561	1
FLYNN KATHERINE	MAJ	N-0757910	0364	1
FLYNN LESTER M	MAJ	O-0739175	0262	2
FLYNN MARIE D	2LT	L-0805638	1144	2
FLYNN MATTHEW A	LTC	O-0108989	0845	2
FLYNN PETER F	LTC	O-1341530	1066	1
FLYNN RAYFORD D	LTC	O-1056716	0867	1
FLYNN RICHARD T	COL	O-0261238	1057	3
FLYNN ROBERT M	LTC	O-1301978	0954	1
FLYNN THOMAS F	2LT	O-1549097	0346	2
FLYNN THOMAS J	MAJ	O-0358449	0465	3
FLYNN THOMAS L	LTC	O-0335453	0965	3
FLYNN THOMAS P	COL	O-0366126	1162	1
FLYNN VENCINE A	LTC	O-0324278	1265	3
FLYNN WALTER J	LTC	O-0394891	0460	1
FLYNN WALTER J	CPT	O-0414741	0445	2
FLYNN WALTER W	LTC	O-0298075	0767	3
FLYNN WILLIAM A	CPT	O-0941979	0459	1
FLYNN WILLIAM F	MAJ	O-2021230	1163	1
FLYNN WILLIAM L	CPT	O-1919134	0964	1
FLYNT JASON C	CW2	W-2145172	0356	1
FOARD ROBERT A	CPT	O-0184564	0252	3
FOBES ALFRED WEN	CPT	O-0359670	1051	1
FOBES RAMON O	LTC	O-0223989	1262	1
FOCHT WILLIS F	MAJ	O-1014367	1047	2
FODORA ALBERT A	CPT	O-0494353	1145	2
FODY EUGENE J	CPT	O-0948688	0666	1
FOE DONALD W	1LT	O-1172004	0246	2
FOE GLEN H	LTC	O-0206471	0956	3
FOEGLE ROBERT E	2LT	O-1913678	0442	1
FOEHRENBACH FRANK A	LTC	O-0302543	1065	3
FOEHSER ARTHUR W	LTC	O-1055851	1066	1
FOELEY ROGER R	MAJ	O-1107954	0462	1
FOELKER FRANK B	CPT	O-1287689	1159	1
FOERCH JR JOSEPH H	LTC	O-1637429	0361	1
FOERCH WILLIAM G	MAJ	O-0203625	0554	3
FOERSTER ERROL J	LTC	O-0235432	0159	3
FOERSTER HERVEY A	COL	O-0246052	1263	3
FOERSTER WILLIAM J	LTC	O-0278338	0660	3
FOERY FRANK R	LTC	O-1573203	0464	1
FOGARTY CLARENCE J	LTC	O-1011136	0461	1
FOGARTY DANIEL T	LTC	O-1822550	0464	1
FOGARTY HARRY B	MAJ	O-0148110	0651	3
FOGARTY JAMES S	CPT	O-0949572	1060	1
FOGARTY JOHN P	MAJ	O-1182824	0560	1
FOGARTY PHILIP F	1LT	O-0426843	0346	1
FOGARTY RICHARD F	LTC	O-1103165	1057	1
FOGARTY THOMAS C	LTC	O-1896186	0966	1
FOGARTY WILLIAM S	MAJ	O-2027815	1265	1
FOGEL ARTHUR A	CPT	O-1945130	1046	2
FOGEL HAROLD	2LT	O-1317553	1043	2
FOGEL ROY U	LTC	O-1165611	0258	1
FOGEL RUBEN H	LTC	O-1171143	1065	3
FOGEL SYDNEY M	CPT	O-0500316	1144	2
FOGG ALLSTON H	COL	O-0272640	0565	3
FOGG CHARLES E	COL	O-0289282	0847	2
FOGG CHARLES H	LTC	O-0507611	0566	1
FOGG SAMUEL H	2LT	O-1573204	0852	1
FOGG SUMNER S	LTC	O-0162073	0648	3
FOGLEMAN ELWOOD L	LTC	O-0461175	0462	1
FOGLEMAN HOMER T	2LT	O-2009924	0648	1
FOGLEMAN JOSEPH O	WO1	W-2126989	0947	2
FOGLER EDWARD N	COL	O-1010794	0961	1
FOGLI THOMAS W	2LT	O-2001064	0146	2
FOGO ALDEN E	CPT	O-1755879	0847	2
FOIZIE EARL W	LTC	O-0186514	1054	3
FOLAROS ARTHUR M	LTC	O-1594841	0563	1
FOLB HENRY	CPT	O-0495913	1045	2
FOLDEN PETER T	LTC	O-0262663	1064	3
FOLEY CECIL W	1LT	O-1013773	0359	1
FOLEY CHARLES E	COL	O-0360602	1165	3
FOLEY DAVID	CW3	W-2141556	0358	1
FOLEY FRANCES R	MAJ	N-0736414	0266	1
FOLEY FRANCIS J	MAJ	O-0437844	0646	2
FOLEY FRANCIS W	LTC	O-1049154	0264	1
FOLEY FRANCIS X	LTC	O-1058517	1165	3
FOLEY FREDERICK	MAJ	O-1300631	0862	1
FOLEY HENRY J	COL	O-0885518	0354	1
FOLEY JAMES M	COL	O-0265619	0264	3
FOLEY JOHN C	LTC	O-1585457	0762	1
FOLEY JOHN L	CPT	O-0124840	0435	1
FOLEY JOHN P	CPT	O-1286108	0747	1
FOLEY JOHN P	LTC	O-1287342	0361	1
FOLEY JOHN P	CW2	W-2214438	0867	1
FOLEY JOHN T	2LT	O-1333956	0246	2
FOLEY JR FREDERICK	MAJ	O-2263188	0666	1
FOLEY JR GEORGE F	MAJ	O-2103059	1064	1
FOLEY JR JAMES M	COL	O-0192723	0561	3
FOLEY LEONARD V	CPT	O-0400023	1144	1
FOLEY MAURICE J	LTC	O-0263615	1056	3
FOLEY OLLIE L	CW2	W-2125928	0853	1
FOLEY PATRICK H	1LT	O-1646167	0546	2
FOLEY ROBERT J	COL	O-0299855	0164	3
FOLEY WILLIAM H	2LT	O-2263526	0353	1
FOLEY WILLIAM V	CPT	O-1638404	0555	1
FOLGER JOSEPH J	LTC	O-1100541	0364	1
FOLK BRUCE W	CW4	W-2114128	0358	1
FOLK FREDERICK	CPT	O-2288302	0562	1
FOLK JOHN J	LTC	O-0480880	0964	2
FOLK THOMAS A	CPT	O-0227681	0944	2
FOLK WILLIAM H	CPT	O-1696435	1045	2
FOLKINS FLOYD L	COL	O-0426098	1164	1
FOLKMAN STANLEY M	LTC	O-0281494	0564	3
FOLKOFF CASPAR	LTC	O-0464331	0146	2
FOLLETT CHARLES O	1LT	O-0520250	1046	1
FOLLETT ELLSWORTH	CW2	W-2101292	0845	2
FOLLETT LESLIE C	LTC	O-0252697	1159	3
FOLLETTE ROGER L	LTC	O-1994909	0560	1
FOLLIS GEORGE M	2LT	O-0108675	0136	1
FOLLMAN CHARLES C	LTC	O-1038377	0767	1
FOLLMER WILLARD R	MAJ	O-0416081	0146	2
FOLRATH LAIRD O	MAJ	O-0299683	0563	3
FOLSOM EDWIN H	LTC	O-0200799	0263	3
FOLSOM HARRY L	1LT	O-0197316	0648	3
FOLSOM M B	CPT	O-1169514	0746	2
FOLTA ALFRED J	CW2	W-2107594	0145	2
FOLTS DAVID K	CPT	O-0254060	1147	2
FOLTZ FREDERICK	COL	O-0147177	1056	3
FOLTZ WENDELL A	1LT	O-1314463	0647	2
FOLTZER JR WILLIAM D	2LT	O-1286110	0445	2
FOLWELL PAUL A	CPT	O-1047963	0659	1
FONDA EDWARD S	LTC	O-0128058	1053	2
FONDREN JAMES C	CW3	W-2009830	1066	3
FONG CLIFTON	CPT	O-1921702	0652	1
FONG THEODORE C	COL	O-0197781	0760	3
FONGER BERNARD A	MAJ	O-0586208	1062	1
FONS AUGUST M	LTC	O-1059451	0465	1
FONT GILBERTO M	LTC	O-0198206	0163	3
FONT JR RAMON	MAJ	O-0194940	0361	3
FONT MANUEL	COL	O-0187488	0948	3
FONT WILLIAM A	COL	O-0191893	1062	3
FONTAINE LEWIS E	LTC	O-0484318	0367	3
FONTAINE RAYMOND V	LTC	O-1013389	0261	1
FONTAINE WILFRED H	CPT	O-1633857	0257	1
FONTANELLA RICHARD J	1LT	O-1328348	1147	2
FONTECCHIO THOMAS E	1LT	O-1290925	0445	2
FONTENOT NASEN J	CW3	W-2149044	1061	1
FONTENOT STEWART F	CW2	W-2112571	0748	1
FONTRON JR JOHN F	LTC	O-0507237	0164	3
FONZI NICHOLAS J	CW2	W-2149908	0860	1
FOOS JOHN L	CPT	O-2040693	0647	2
FOOSE FRANCIS I	1LT	O-1304531	0845	2
FOOTE BERNIE F	WO1	W-2008885	0254	3
FOOTE FRANCIS C	MAJ	O-0128304	0354	3
FOOTE GEORGE F	MAJ	O-0209819	0944	2
FOOTE GLEN L	LTC	O-0450438	0657	1
FOOTE JAMES E	MAJ	O-0298845	0364	3
FOOTE JR GEORGE C	LTC	O-1647642	1263	1
FOOTE RILEY F	1LT	O-1185577	0146	2
FOOTE WILLIAM A	LTC	O-0285561	0859	2
FOOTE WILLIAM G	MAJ	O-1923720	1167	1
FOOTE WILLIS B	MAJ	O-0262977	1047	2
FOPPE ANDREW J	CPT	O-1013425	0347	2
FORAKER CLARENCE M	LTC	O-0329097	0266	3
FORAN JAMES L	CW4	W-2148622	0662	1
FORBES CHARLES H	MAJ	O-2033194	0964	1
FORBES CLARENCE L	LTC	O-1684975	0967	1
FORBES GERALD W	LTC	O-1169517	1163	1
FORBES JACK R	LTC	O-1169518	1165	1
FORBES JACK W	CW3	W-2205838	0965	1
FORBES JAMES	2LT	O-1826266	0945	2
FORBES JOSEPH P	LTC	O-1589835	0366	3
FORBES JR WILLIAM H	MAJ	O-0474405	1047	1
FORBES LAUREN D	1LT	O-0972986	0657	1
FORBES LOUIS M	1LT	O-0198749	0253	3
FORBES LOWELL L	LTC	O-0101920	0154	3
FORBES MARRELL A	MAJ	O-0399717	0146	2
FORBES RICHARD W	CPT	O-0357274	0644	1
FORBES ROBERT W	COL	O-0154443	0557	3
FORBES THOMAS A	CPT	O-0168988	0344	2
FORBES THOMAS M	CW2	W-2005415	1265	1
FORBUSH CLIFTON H	COL	O-0176033	0857	3
FORBUSH EARL A	MAJ	O-1646168	1064	1
FORCE ROBERT C	1LT	O-0293203	0245	2
FORCHETTE DONALD G	MAJ	O-0995642	0265	1
FORCIER FRANCIS F	CW3	W-2150796	0659	1
FORCIER LOWELL A	CW3	W-2142795	0764	2
FORD ALEXANDER	CPT	O-0164456	0536	1
FORD ALICE M	1LT	N-0725486	0945	1
FORD ANDREW J	1LT	O-1796600	1145	1
FORD ALGOIL L	CPT	O-0468152	0444	2
FORD AZEL G	MAJ	O-0678217	0565	1
FORD BOBBIE B	LTC	O-0403524	1160	1
FORD CARL J	CPT	O-2263152	1062	1
FORD CARL L	CPT	O-1115258	0452	1
FORD CARLETON R	COL	O-0268927	0567	3
FORD CHARLES H	CPT	O-1002217	0458	1
FORD CLOVIS P	CPT	O-1289230	0246	2
FORD DALE M	MAJ	O-1035771	0262	1
FORD DANIEL W	CPT	O-1305563	0446	2
FORD DAVID A	WO1	W-2108355	0551	2
FORD DONALD A	CPT	O-1100542	0246	2
FORD DOUGLAS C	CPT	O-0515331	0347	1
FORD DUANE B	MAJ	O-1933438	0567	1

NAME	GRADE	SVC NO	DATE RET MO YR	RET CODE
FORD EDGAR	LTC	O-0332936	1159	1
FORD EDWARD L	CPT	O-1047122	0962	3
FORD EDWARD M	LTC	O-0400717	0664	1
FORD EDWARD P	CPT	O-0173912	1044	2
FORD EDWIN E	MAJ	O-1935440	0767	1
FORD ELBERT G	WO1	W-2106214	0160	1
FORD ERNEST H	MAJ	O-2016059	0163	1
FORD FRANK G	2LT	O-1303130	1144	2
FORD FREDERICK	CW2	W-2000812	1044	2
FORD GEORGE B	LTC	O-0486004	0256	1
FORD GEORGE J	LTC	O-0450863	0258	1
FORD GEORGE L	COL	O-0404999	0961	1
FORD GEORGE R	2LT	O-2001780	1059	2
FORD GEORGE W	LTC	O-0383261	0559	1
FORD HANSFORD D	LTC	O-0396847	1165	1
FORD HARRY S	CPT	O-0410089	1046	1
FORD HENRY H	CW3	W-2144180	0659	1
FORD HOWARD D	1LT	O-1058251	0646	2
FORD HOWARD G	WO1	W-2113538	1044	2
FORD HUBERT	MAJ	O-0975942	1167	1
FORD HUGH G	CW2	W-2143343	0462	1
FORD JAMES T	LTC	O-0475906	0947	1
FORD JAMES W	LTC	O-0189846	0351	3
FORD JOHN A	MAJ	O-1283232	0261	1
FORD JOHN D	CW3	W-2145033	0962	1
FORD JOHN H	1LT	O-2205264	0154	2
FORD JOHN J	CPT	O-0480310	0949	1
FORD JOHN N	MAJ	O-1338937	0865	1
FORD JOSEPH C	MAJ	O-0233885	0345	2
FORD JOSEPH C	1LT	O-0451449	0844	2
FORD JR EDWIN R	LTC	O-1318531	0961	1
FORD JR JOHN R	MAJ	O-1339979	0765	1
FORD JR JOSEPH A	MAJ	O-0356113	0363	1
FORD JR WILLIAM G	CW3	W-2147509	0463	1
FORD LEO W	CPT	O-0527793	0949	2
FORD LEONARD H	LTC	O-0102148	0648	3
FORD LESTER A	CW2	W-2145128	0659	1
FORD LUTHER E	MAJ	O-1177392	0960	1
FORD MABEL M	2LT	N-0700171	1138	1
FORD MARY	2LT	N-0700168	0840	1
FORD MARY J	MAJ	N-0731689	0163	1
FORD NORMAN A	2LT	O-0443986	0544	1
FORD PAUL F	COL	O-0289855	0360	1
FORD PERKINS	CPT	O-0415676	0850	1
FORD RALPH F	2LT	O-1291616	1044	2
FORD RAY W	CPT	O-0487080	0350	1
FORD RAYMOND E	COL	O-0259513	0867	3
FORD RAYMOND O	COL	O-0174149	0461	3
FORD RICHARD G	LTC	O-0371112	0265	1
FORD ROBERT F	CPT	O-1038378	0246	2
FORD ROBERT E	1LT	O-2000624	1147	2
FORD ROBERT L	MAJ	O-1030240	0854	1
FORD ROBERT M A	LTC	O-1056365	0363	1
FORD ROBERT P	CW4	W-2141557	0559	1
FORD ROBERT W	LTC	O-1287505	0861	1
FORD STANLEY B	CPT	O-0451710	0546	2
FORD STEPHEN K	LTC	O-0260213	1264	3
FORD WARREN A	LTC	O-0104266	1059	3
FORD WILLARD B	MAJ	O-2042566	0762	1
FORD WILLIAM E	CPT	O-1286991	1047	1
FORD WILLIAM H	MAJ	O-0258503	0158	3
FORD ZARVIS T	1LT	O-0414324	0844	2
FORDE ALBERT L	MAJ	O-0280405	0467	3
FORDHAM ADOLPH E	2LT	O-1051127	0245	2
FORDHAM HENRY B	CPT	O-2025951	1058	1
FORDYCE LESTER J	MAJ	O-0235301	0355	3
FORDYCE WENDELL L	CPT	O-2263734	0662	1
FORDYCE WILLIAM L	1LT	O-1013315	0761	2
FORE CHARLES H	LTC	O-0373423	0163	1
FORE CLYDE A	CPT	O-2014607	0756	2
FORE HOWARD T	MAJ	O-1289062	0158	1
FOREE ROBERT W	CW2	W-2108586	1045	2
FOREHAND RICHARD L	MAJ	O-1292228	0157	1
FOREMAN ALBERT S	LTC	O-0499060	0467	3
FOREMAN ARTHUR B	LTC	O-0115935	0549	3

NAME	GRADE	SVC NO	DATE RET MO YR	RET CODE
FOREMAN CLEMENS W	CPT	O-0102145	1055	3
FOREMAN GRAYSON A	CPT	O-0494120	0854	1
FOREMAN H H	1LT	O-2006060	0450	1
FOREMAN HARRY A	LTC	O-0209805	0164	3
FOREMAN JAMES N	LTC	O-0363342	0361	1
FOREMAN JOHN	COL	O-0200303	0459	3
FOREMAN LEONARD	CPT	O-0885712	0853	1
FOREMAN RICHARD G	CPT	O-4010570	0667	1
FOREMAN ROBERT O	MAJ	O-1685628	0864	1
FOREMAN ROBERT W	MAJ	O-0346196	1156	2
FOREMAN WALLACE G	LTC	O-0294775	0160	1
FOREMAN WILLIAM C	LTC	O-0359679	0766	1
FORESMAN HAROLD A	LTC	O-0361156	0163	3
FORESMAN HENRY J	CPT	O-0412794	0645	2
FOREST GEORGE F	CPT	O-1555041	0346	2
FORESTA ANGELO	CW2	W-2134771	0163	1
FORESTER ROBERT J	1LT	O-0502558	1045	2
FORGASON JACK P	COL	O-0348615	0460	3
FORGIONE PASCAL D	LTC	O-0360618	0567	3
FORINASH KYLE	MAJ	O-2262184	1062	1
FORKS LOUIS J	LTC	O-1050664	0662	1
FORLAND ARTHUR E	CW3	W-2150638	1264	1
FORMALEJO BERNARDINO	1LT	O-1896531	0650	1
FORMAN EDWARD	1LT	O-0432916	1046	2
FORMAN EVELYN K	MAJ	N-0731431	1262	1
FORMAN IRENE S	2LT	N-0727517	1044	1
FORMAN JAMES F	CPT	O-0419675	0745	2
FORMAN JOHN G	CPT	O-0447081	1046	2
FORMAN JOSEPH	CPT	O-1585837	0647	2
FORMAN MAURICE R	MAJ	O-0915116	1145	2
FORMAN ROBERT C	LTC	O-0339217	0162	1
FORMAN SEYMOUR	2LT	O-1054992	0745	2
FORMAN THEODORE M	MAJ	O-0212502	0861	3
FORMANACK ANGELA M	MAJ	N-0732811	1167	1
FORMHALS HARRY B	MAJ	O-0182284	1153	3
FORMSMA ROBERT J	2LT	O-1050665	0843	2
FORNASH JR LUKE	1LT	O-2041011	0945	2
FORNEA GENE F	CW2	W-2101695	0153	1
FORNELIUS CARL F	CPT	O-0495006	0448	1
FORNELL JOSEPH F	CPT	O-1552668	1045	2
FORNES HINTON E	LTC	O-1556414	0862	2
FORNEY DAVID H	CPT	O-1030555	0149	1
FORNEY HARRY R	COL	O-0150731	1055	3
FORNEY JOHN E	LTC	O-1112696	0661	1
FORNEY JOSEPH T	MAJ	O-1290226	0165	1
FORNEY LEON F	MAJ	O-1575316	0357	1
FORNEY RICHARD M	LTC	O-1598377	0464	1
FORNOF THEODORE W	CPT	O-1537501	0764	1
FORNOF WILBERT H	1LT	O-1172007	0146	2
FORONDA CRESCENCIO	2LT	O-1896605	0457	1
FORQUER WARREN K	CW3	W-2144299	1061	1
FORREST ARTHUR A	MAJ	O-1012547	0163	2
FORREST EDWARD F	1LT	O-2026569	0257	1
FORREST EUGENE R	LTC	O-0205835	0956	3
FORREST J O	1LT	O-1303695	0446	1
FORREST JAMES R	1LT	O-0454057	1047	1
FORREST JAMES R	2LT	O-0536232	0444	2
FORREST JOHN W	1LT	O-1691930	1146	2
FORREST JR ROBERT C	CW4	W-2111759	1161	1
FORREST KENNETH B	LTC	O-1639035	0762	1
FORREST MYRTLE I	MAJ	N-0777536	0465	1
FORREST NOLA G	LTC	N-0701473	0946	1
FORREST RAYMOND E	MAJ	O-0350768	0246	2
FORREST SAMUEL G	MAJ	O-0477284	0242	1
FORRESTAL WILLIAM T	CPT	O-1184383	0547	2
FORRESTER EDWIN C	CPT	O-1173947	0647	1
FORRESTER JERRY L	CW4	W-2145677	1066	1
FORRY THOMAS P	2LT	O-0900073	0542	2
FORRY WALTER E	COL	O-0299875	0363	3
FORSBERG CARL F	LTC	O-0360549	1164	1
FORSBURG OSCAR W	CPT	O-0164508	1053	3
FORSDICK WILFRED F	LTC	O-0108178	0245	2
FORSGREN FRED A	LTC	O-1010173	0263	1
FORSHA KENNETH D	MAJ	O-1015555	0861	1
FORSLUND CARL A	LTC	O-1822125	1266	1

NAME	GRADE	SVC NO	DATE RET MO YR	RET CODE
FORSMAN HUGH K	COL	O-0173844	1161	3
FORSSELL WILLIAM R	CPT	O-0276320	0257	3
FORST GEORGE H	COL	O-0170784	0948	1
FORSTNER DOROTHY I	CPT	N-0783376	1046	1
FORSYTH CHARLES L	CPT	O-0435721	0846	1
FORSYTH EARL N	LTC	O-0290148	0557	1
FORSYTHE BELMONT	LTC	O-2292056	0866	1
FORSYTHE EMMETT C	MAJ	O-0144166	0256	3
FORSYTHE ERWIN F	LTC	O-0451952	0860	2
FORSYTHE FRANK W	COL	O-0333358	1054	3
FORSYTHE JAMES V	CW3	W-2141801	0159	1
FORSYTHE ROBERT J	MAJ	O-0978135	0462	1
FORT ERNEST A	LTC	O-0204821	1063	3
FORT GLEN A	LTC	O-0921360	1062	1
FORT JR JAMES A	LTC	O-0169049	0760	3
FORT WAYNE W	LTC	O-0506940	0164	1
FORTE SALVATORE	CW2	W-2213113	1167	1
FORTENBERRY HARRY E	CPT	O-1041549	0561	1
FORTENBERRY JASPER H	CPT	O-0924952	0348	1
FORTES CLAUDIO	2LT	O-0890531	0248	1
FORTH FRANK E	1LT	O-0989963	1152	1
FORTH JR JOHN T	MAJ	O-1640459	0762	2
FORTIER ELMO A	LTC	O-1548774	0262	2
FORTIER ROMAINE M	MAJ	O-1646172	0856	1
FORTIER ROY M	LTC	O-0176508	1149	3
FORTIN CLARENCE C	MAJ	O-2019446	0263	1
FORTNER CARL	CPT	O-2044567	1053	1
FORTNER EDWARD F	MAJ	O-1172008	1158	1
FORTNER WILL M	1LT	O-1294118	0945	1
FORTNEY ARTHUR C	COL	O-0278668	0263	3
FORTNEY KENNETH R	MAJ	O-0252653	1066	3
FORTUNA PETER P	1LT	O-0528400	0545	2
FORTUNA VALENTINE	1LT	O-1331488	0348	2
FORTUNATO JOSEPH W	1LT	O-1119182	0946	2
FORTUNATO NICHOLAS A	COL	O-1305751	1165	1
FORTUNATO SAMUEL J	CPT	O-0345498	0845	2
FORTUNE DANIEL L	MAJ	O-0947159	0764	1
FORTUNE JOHN H	1LT	O-2036731	0355	1
FORTUNE MARVIN R	CPT	O-1047123	0747	2
FORTUNOFF SAUL	COL	O-1689037	0365	3
FORWARD DONALD D	LTC	O-0244566	0955	3
FORWARD FLETCHER C	LTC	O-0301591	1160	1
FORYS WALTER M	LTC	O-0442550	0459	1
FOSBURGH DAVID L	MAJ	O-0271365	0167	3
FOSDICK JACK R	1LT	O-1321501	0945	2
FOSEID OSCAR F	MAJ	O-0519793	0547	2
FOSHEE CLYDE H	MAJ	O-0273818	1045	2
FOSKO JR JOHN J	1LT	O-1535637	0246	2
FOSS ALVIN E	LTC	O-0124842	0851	3
FOSS DAVID F	CPT	O-0523168	0948	2
FOSS DONALD L	LTC	O-1534484	0163	1
FOSS HAROLD D	MAJ	O-0221926	0560	1
FOSS LAURISTON	COL	O-1100989	1163	1
FOSS REGINALD E	COL	O-0214958	0648	3
FOSS SHELDON H	MAJ	O-2033954	0465	1
FOSS SIMON A	LTC	O-0121652	1053	3
FOSSEL JULIUS D	2LT	O-1329697	1045	1
FOSSETT JR HARRY J	2LT	O-1109256	1044	2
FOSSUM JOHN W	1LT	O-1581716	1048	1
FOSTER ALBERT P	CW3	W-2144789	0761	1
FOSTER ALBERT W	CPT	O-1579658	0455	1
FOSTER ANNE C	MAJ	N-0756906	0663	1
FOSTER BEDFORD F	LTC	O-0275422	0965	3
FOSTER BILLY H	1LT	O-1294119	0347	2
FOSTER CECIL C	LTC	O-0887625	0463	1
FOSTER CHARLES C	MAJ	O-0314147	1046	1
FOSTER CHARLES D	LTC	O-0270918	1167	3
FOSTER CHARLES F	MAJ	O-2007016	1262	1
FOSTER CHARLES C	CPT	O-0550452	1046	1
FOSTER CHARLES M	MAJ	O-1104665	1266	1
FOSTER CLARENCE R	LTC	O-0297470	0866	3
FOSTER CLIFFORD D	CW3	W-2126244	0762	1
FOSTER DAVID A	CPT	O-0290444	1045	1
FOSTER DONALD L	MAJ	O-1172863	0861	1
FOSTER DOYLE F	LTC	O-1294120	1263	1

NAME	GRADE	SVC NO	DATE RET MO YR	RET CODE
FOSTER DWIGHT K	COL	O-0221420	0556	3
FOSTER EARL E	COL	O-0326181	0863	3
FOSTER EARL C	MAJ	O-1307291	0164	1
FOSTER EARL H	CPT	O-2262553	0864	1
FOSTER EDGAR M	1LT	O-0888230	0545	2
FOSTER EDWARD R	CPT	O-0283954	0246	2
FOSTER EDWARD T	COL	O-0276916	1064	3
FOSTER EDWIN T	MAJ	O-0490575	1262	1
FOSTER ELBERT F	LTC	O-0371577	0866	3
FOSTER ETHELBERT	MAJ	O-0112555	0950	3
FOSTER EUGENE C	MAJ	O-0172945	0247	1
FOSTER FRANKLYN H	CW3	W-2106297	1160	1
FOSTER FRED	CPT	O-0396923	0146	2
FOSTER GEORGE L	LTC	O-0289265	1165	1
FOSTER GEORGE L	LTC	O-0495334	0155	1
FOSTER GEORGE M	CPT	O-1042023	0346	2
FOSTER GEORGE R	MAJ	O-1545924	0660	1
FOSTER GILBERT J	LTC	O-0304651	0360	1
FOSTER GLENN A	MAJ	O-0339646	0547	2
FOSTER GUY W	MAJ	O-0496907	0154	1
FOSTER HARRY M	MAJ	O-0478380	0242	1
FOSTER HARRY W	MAJ	O-0212742	0563	3
FOSTER HART C	COL	O-0123331	0950	3
FOSTER HENRY	CW4	W-2106549	0358	1
FOSTER HERBERT M	MAJ	O-0222094	1048	3
FOSTER HUBERT E	CPT	O-0193488	0544	1
FOSTER JACK W	CPT	O-1080020	0261	1
FOSTER JAMES R	MAJ	O-0949262	0562	1
FOSTER JAMES R	MAJ	O-1016551	0961	1
FOSTER JAMES T	CW2	W-2142086	0463	2
FOSTER JOHN C	LTC	O-0268153	1059	1
FOSTER JOHN E	LTC	O-0423446	0961	3
FOSTER JOHN E	2LT	O-1513693	0134	1
FOSTER JOHN L	MAJ	O-1039349	0562	1
FOSTER JOHN R	MAJ	O-2001723	1262	1
FOSTER JOHN S	LTC	O-0910808	0667	3
FOSTER JOSEPH T	CPT	O-1797456	1047	2
FOSTER JR JAMES B	COL	O-0419161	0861	1
FOSTER JR LEMUEL L	1LT	O-1582693	0747	2
FOSTER JR LEWIS F	LTC	O-1102245	0267	1
FOSTER JR MAXWELL S	LTC	O-0337528	0560	1
FOSTER JR PAUL W	CW2	W-2115842	0155	1
FOSTER JULIAN S	MAJ	O-0976881	0865	1
FOSTER KATHERINE	1LT	N-0763856	1145	1
FOSTER KENNETH D	LTC	O-1112698	1064	1
FOSTER LAURENCE G	MAJ	O-0487992	0759	1
FOSTER LAWRENCE G	LTC	O-0261298	0566	1
FOSTER LEON M	LTC	O-0346515	0562	1
FOSTER LEROY E	1LT	O-1312532	1045	2
FOSTER LOREN N	CW3	W-3150367	0667	1
FOSTER MALCOLM L	CPT	O-0361929	0645	2
FOSTER MARSHALL P	CW3	W-2207961	1067	1
FOSTER MAX W	MAJ	O-1171146	0155	1
FOSTER MILO P	MAJ	O-1114480	1262	1
FOSTER MILTON M	1LT	O-0499245	0643	2
FOSTER MOSES A	LTC	O-0315595	0650	1
FOSTER NORMAN J	MAJ	O-2055984	0764	1
FOSTER NORMAAS	1LT	O-1017338	1046	2
FOSTER PAUL	CPT	O-0490054	0347	1
FOSTER PAUL	CW3	W-2142375	0557	1
FOSTER PAUL A	1LT	O-0507607	0550	1
FOSTER PAUL G	LTC	O-0358292	0450	1
FOSTER PAUL L	MAJ	O-0187696	0151	1
FOSTER RALPH D	LTC	O-0203768	1048	2
FOSTER ROBERT A	LTC	O-0500377	0657	1
FOSTER ROBERT A	1LT	O-1017394	0446	2
FOSTER ROBERT G	MAJ	O-1104159	0862	1
FOSTER ROBERT M	MAJ	O-0109040	0745	1
FOSTER ROGER H	CW4	W-2141277	0966	1
FOSTER ROGER W	WO1	W-2115484	0960	2
FOSTER SAMUEL F	LTC	O-1169561	1067	1
FOSTER SAMUEL W	LTC	O-2046491	0356	1
FOSTER SYBIL G	1LT	N-0726710	0745	1
FOSTER THEODORE P	LTC	O-1577179	1263	2
FOSTER THOMAS J	MAJ	O-1646175	0655	1

NAME	GRADE	SVC NO	DATE RET MO YR	RET CODE
FOSTER WALTER L	CW2	RW-2148279	0964	1
FOSTER WALTER W	1LT	0-0509592	0546	1
FOSTER WILLIAM B	LTC	0-0360650	0760	1
FOSTER WILLIAM G	LTC	0-0285749	0558	3
FOSTER WILLIAM H	CW4	W-2142573	0865	1
FOSTER WILLIAM S	MAJ	0-2015741	0263	1
FOSTER WILLIAM W	CW3	W-2152824	0364	1
FOSTER WINSLOW	COL	0-0222331	0360	3
FOTI SAMUEL J	LTC	0-1701699	0767	1
FOUCHS LAWRENCE E	COL	0-0181218	1059	1
FOULK ELDEN K	MAJ	0-2019578	0365	1
FOULK FRANK H	CPT	0-0488860	0747	2
FOULKE CARTER W	1LT	0-0536593	0146	2
FOULKE GEORGE A	LTC	0-0357997	1056	3
FOULKE PHILIP A	MAJ	0-1019316	0366	1
FOULKES HARVEY B	LTC	0-0130636	1155	1
FOULKS ERNEST E	COL	0-0228921	0963	3
FOULSTONE ROWLAND W	MAJ	0-1014011	0461	1
FOUNTAIN FLOYD G	CPT	0-1173948	0448	2
FOUNTAIN GEORGE L	LTC	0-0548503	1064	1
FOUNTAIN JESS W	1LT	0-1822871	0456	1
FOUNTAIN RAY C	M G	0-0121655	0954	3
FOUNTAIN RISDEN L	LTC	0-1010405	0561	1
FOUNTAINE ALFRED J	CW4	W-2102900	0559	1
FOUNTAINE ROBERT H	MAJ	0-2005592	1165	1
FOURACRE WILLIS A	MAJ	0-1295006	1047	2
FOUREMAN ROY R	LTC	0-0255112	0555	3
FOURNIER ALPHONSE J	MAJ	0-0456689	0357	1
FOURNIER CHARLES A	LTC	0-0748946	0567	1
FOURNIER JOSEPH A	LTC	0-1031927	0965	2
FOURNIER LEROY	CPT	0-0111063	0853	3
FOURNIER LOUIS O	MAJ	0-0291841	0163	1
FOURNIER ROLAND P	COL	0-0435623	0657	1
FOURNIER VINCENT C	MAJ	0-1645577	1064	1
FOURQUREAN LUDWELL N	LTC	0-0389222	1065	1
FOUSE DONALD W	MAJ	0-0341084	0146	2
FOUSHEE LEWIS F	LTC	0-0924493	0467	3
FOUSHEE SCHLESINGE	LTC	0-0304685	1064	3
FOUST BILLY	MAJ	0-1171530	0566	1
FOUST JOHN W	LTC	0-1821992	0663	1
FOUST PERRY E	MAJ	0-0405536	0961	1
FOUT JR JAMES R	LTC	0-1032081	0862	1
FOUTCH QUINTON W	LTC	0-0272729	1165	3
FOUTS ANDREW S	MAJ	0-0400767	1145	2
FOUTS HAROLD J	CPT	0-0910623	1043	2
FOWLER CECIL C	LTC	0-0450738	1055	1
FOWLER CECIL W	LTC	0-1298686	0361	1
FOWLER CHARLES E	CPT	0-1290228	0457	1
FOWLER CHARLES R	1LT	0-0527795	0546	2
FOWLER CHARLES R	CPT	0-1181888	0657	1
FOWLER CLARENCE A	CW2	W-2115724	1053	2
FOWLER CLARENCE W	1LT	0-1683312	0145	2
FOWLER CLYDE E	LTC	0-0921302	0363	1
FOWLER CARRELL	CPT	0-0255563	0345	2
FOWLER DELOS	MAJ	0-0175449	0456	3
FOWLER DONALD G	CW3	W-2151428	0666	1
FOWLER FORREST L	MAJ	0-1341088	0764	1
FOWLER GEORGE O	CPT	0-2263719	1262	1
FOWLER GILL	MAJ	0-0451556	1059	1
FOWLER GORDON C	LTC	0-0196186	0163	3
FOWLER GRACE H	MAJ	N-0700653	0346	1
FOWLER GRACE R	2LT	N-0731931	0644	1
FOWLER HARMON L	COL	0-0113287	0648	3
FOWLER HARRY R	COL	0-0167228	1155	3
FOWLER HENRY F	WO1	W-2149290	1054	1
FOWLER HENRY G	COL	0-0253899	0247	2
FOWLER HERBERT H	CW3	W-2146239	0862	1
FOWLER HERMAN W	CPT	0-1030472	0156	1
FOWLER HUPERT B	MAJ	0-0501045	1054	1
FOWLER JAMES C	LTC	0-1108667	0862	1
FOWLER JAMES E	CPT	0-1325884	0446	2
FOWLER JAMES H	2LT	0-0194344	0225	1
FOWLER JAY C	LTC	0-1641295	0867	3
FOWLER JESSE L	CW4	W-2108172	0960	1
FOWLER JOHN F	LTC	0-1031401	0561	1
FOWLER JOHN L	CPT	0-0486109	0448	1
FOWLER JOHN M	LTC	0-0306967	0460	1
FOWLER JOHN P	MAJ	0-1684944	0564	1
FOWLER JOHN R	CPT	0-0450199	0960	1
FOWLER JOSEPH D	CPT	0-0449793	0846	2
FOWLER JR BUTLER R	CPT	0-0409736	0145	2
FOWLER JR GEORGE W	CW3	W-2146833	1264	1
FOWLER JR JOSEPH H	WO1	W-2152210	0160	2
FOWLER LEO K	MAJ	0-0328119	1150	1
FOWLER LESTER D	LTC	0-2023286	0764	1
FOWLER MARION B	COL	0-0171554	0656	3
FOWLER MARION S	CPT	0-0301679	0146	2
FOWLER MAURICE R	LTC	0-0428308	0162	1
FOWLER PAUL I	MAJ	0-1114481	0565	2
FOWLER PAUL L	COL	0-0362004	0247	2
FOWLER ROBERT H	MAJ	0-0426209	0443	2
FOWLER ROBERT M	COL	0-0384792	0560	1
FOWLER ROBERT T	MAJ	0-2021219	0665	1
FOWLER ROLAND K	CPT	0-0484982	0549	1
FOWLER SID R	MAJ	0-2055148	1055	1
FOWLER STEPHEN	LTC	0-0389952	0366	1
FOWLER THOMAS A	CW2	W-2208306	1065	1
FOWLER WALTER R	LTC	0-0292943	0263	1
FOWLER WALTER H	MAJ	0-0573550	0361	1
FOWLER WILLIAM H	COL	0-0270339	1059	1
FOWLES LESLIE O	LTC	0-0330128	0145	2
FOWLIE ERVINE A	1LT	0-1796775	0557	1
FOWLKES JAMES H	CW2	W-2144535	0163	2
FOWLKES OTHO G	2LT	0-1913695	0947	1
FOWLKES REXFORD R	CW3	W-2151179	0664	1
FOWLKES RICHARD S	LTC	0-1041345	0166	3
FOWLKES ROBERT J	MAJ	0-0154769	0155	3
FOWSER MARK F	MAJ	0-1176015	0861	1
FOWSER WILLIAM C	MAJ	0-2200540	0764	1
FOX ALDEN E	2LT	0-0407882	0446	2
FOX ANNIE G	MAJ	N-0700454	1045	1
FOX ARTHUR C	LTC	0-0165106	0445	1
FOX ARTHUR W	MAJ	0-0235500	0856	3
FOX BUEL K	LTC	0-0503181	0954	1
FOX C LYN	M G	0-0154765	1156	3
FOX CARL J	LTC	0-0109572	0937	1
FOX CHARLES D	LTC	0-0412121	1162	1
FOX CHARLES F	1LT	0-0511989	0347	1
FOX CHARLES W	MAJ	0-0987376	1263	1
FOX CLIFFORD E	MAJ	0-0451843	0359	1
FOX DANIEL K	2LT	0-1055852	1044	2
FOX DEAN C	CW3	W-2148962	0465	1
FOX DONALD A	LTC	0-0549925	0767	1
FOX EARL L	1LT	0-1317772	0158	2
FOX EDWARD J	1LT	0-1116775	0447	2
FOX EDWARD V	CW2	W-2117016	0245	2
FOX ELMER M	LTC	0-1294645	0561	1
FOX ERNEST F	LTC	0-0229494	1162	3
FOX ERNEST L	MAJ	0-2263287	0662	1
FOX EUGENE C	MAJ	0-0128092	1155	3
FOX FRANCIS A	MAJ	0-1550592	0855	1
FOX FRANCIS E	MAJ	0-1945133	0566	1
FOX FRANCIS T	2LT	0-1321112	0444	2
FOX FRANCIS V	MAJ	0-2049555	0861	1
FOX FREDERICK	COL	0-0122607	0554	3
FOX FREDERICK	MAJ	0-0320052	0963	3
FOX GEORGE J	CW2	W-2210015	0161	1
FOX GERTRUDE T	1LT	N-0737155	1045	1
FOX HARRY L	COL	0-0041962	1060	1
FOX HARRY L	1LT	0-1689728	1043	1
FOX ISAAC B	1LT	0-2017428	0748	1
FOX JACK	LTC	0-0887439	0166	1
FOX JAMES B	1LT	0-1640462	0146	2
FOX JAMES C	2LT	0-1323820	0445	2
FOX JAMES H	LTC	0-0186646	0649	3
FOX JOHN F	2LT	0-1589619	0744	2
FOX JOHN G	MAJ	0-0200982	1055	3
FOX JOHN J	CW3	W-2145274	0765	1
FOX JOSEPH P	LTC	0-1330640	0966	1
FOX JR DON H	CW2	W-2214331	0667	1
FOX JR FREDERICK	COL	0-1283750	1266	1
FOX JR JERVIE P	MAJ	0-0962479	1263	1
FOX KENNETH E	1LT	0-1011433	0945	2
FOX LAWRENCE J	MAJ	0-0196908	1053	3
FOX LESTER I	MAJ	0-0368002	0946	1
FOX LEWIS B	2LT	0-1032012	0845	2
FOX LOUIS	MAJ	0-1697908	0745	2
FOX MAURICE P	CW2	W-2209104	0765	1
FOX MYEE F	2LT	N-0742408	0346	1
FOX NATHAN S	MAJ	0-0331679	0945	2
FOX NEWTON E	CW4	W-2145138	0960	1
FOX NOEL R	COL	0-0100379	0648	3
FOX RAYMOND C	CPT	0-1040922	0459	1
FOX RICHARD J	MAJ	0-0450864	0253	1
FOX RICHARD O	LTC	0-1312138	0266	1
FOX RICHARD W	CW3	W-2117208	0163	1
FOX ROBERT A	WO1	W-2120115	0960	2
FOX ROBERT L	COL	0-0902190	0567	3
FOX ROBERT M	LTC	0-0325920	0467	3
FOX ROYAL G	MAJ	0-0276541	1158	3
FOX SHELDON	CPT	0-0474786	0745	2
FOX SINCLAIRE	CW4	W-2101702	0859	1
FOX SR HENRY H	MAJ	0-0232127	0648	3
FOX THEODORE P	CPT	0-0969293	0860	1
FOX THOMAS O	LTC	0-1288884	0662	1
FOX THOMAS P	B G	0-0230823	0463	3
FOX VERNON A	CW3	W-2151786	0564	1
FOX WAYNE A	MAJ	0-0247652	0165	3
FOX WILLIAM H	MAJ	0-0340103	0762	1
FOX WILLIAM L	1LT	0-1303131	1044	2
FOX WILLIAM L	1LT	0-1821847	0246	2
FOX WILLIAM M	MAJ	0-0182450	0861	1
FOX WILLIAM M	CPT	0-0333799	0145	2
FOX WILLIAM M	LTC	0-1948135	0866	1
FOX WOODSON W	COL	0-1172865	0567	1
FOXWORTH LEWIS H	CPT	0-0494842	1047	1
FOY ALBERT J	LTC	0-0266938	0865	3
FOY GEORGE L	COL	0-0140017	0958	1
FOY NELSON E	MAJ	0-1309180	0864	1
FOY ROBERT E	LTC	0-1640463	0761	1
FOYE EDWARD D	MAJ	0-0147190	1045	2
FOYE KATHLEEN A	MAJ	L-0204280	0563	1
FOYLE JOHN O	MAJ	0-1081409	1164	3
FOYLE JR CHARLES M	LTC	0-1046439	0462	1
FOZ FREDRIC	MAJ	0-1896444	0661	1
FRADKIN IRVIN M	CPT	0-0495485	0446	2
FRADKIN JOSEPH	CPT	0-1541249	0346	2
FRADY CLARK K	1LT	0-1182363	1045	2
FRADY CLYDE H	CPT	0-0911415	1145	2
FRADY JAMES E	CW2	W-2205513	1264	1
FRADY PORTER R	MAJ	0-1590924	1266	1
FRAGGE STANLEY L	MAJ	0-1062813	1162	1
FRAIN JAMES F	1LT	0-1049839	0146	2
FRAINT SAUL	MAJ	0-1100991	0347	2
FRAIZER WAYNE O	LTC	0-1291254	0661	1
FRAKE CHESTER O	COL	0-0236328	1157	1
FRAKER HAROLD E	LTC	0-0451986	1165	1
FRAKES WILLIAM P	1LT	0-0422240	1044	2
FRALEY DANIEL W	CPT	0-0173979		1
FRALEY FLETCHER W	CPT	0-1703052	0759	1
FRALEY JR RAYMOND W	CPT	0-0954171	1058	1
FRALEY JR WILLIAM J	LTC	0-1106737	0267	1
FRALICK LAWRENCE R	MAJ	0-2028683	1065	1
FRAMBACH ARTHUR A	LTC	0-0185324	0853	3
FRAME JAMES W	LTC	0-0291465	0151	2
FRAME WILLIAM E	COL	0-0220711	0560	1
FRAMER DOROTHY M	MAJ	N-0733173	0962	1
FRAMPTON CHARLES R	1LT	0-0467715	1044	2
FRAMSON SELMA B	1LT	N-0762906	1047	1
FRANCAVILLA ANTHONY	MAJ	0-0991711	0364	1
FRANCAZI BRUNO A	LTC	0-2038800	1067	1
FRANCE DOUGLAS C	COL	0-0189015	1053	3
FRANCE JOHN J	MAJ	0-0265557	0364	3
FRANCE MILLARD R	CPT	0-1995596	0759	1
FRANCE ORVIL K	CW2	W-2145429	1157	1
FRANCE WILLIAM L	LTC	0-1318151	0366	1
FRANCES CHARLES A	LTC	0-0412659	0162	1
FRANCES WALLACE J	CW3	W-2142763	0659	1
FRANCHER HAROLD A	LTC	0-1291970	1160	1
FRANCHERE CHETWYND M	MAJ	0-0121786	0552	3
FRANCHINA CHARLES A	1LT	0-0449041	0246	2
FRANCHINA CHARLES T	LTC	0-1555687	0363	1
FRANCIS CLYDE D	CPT	0-1635903	0157	1
FRANCIS CRUSCE	CPT	0-1286467	0645	2
FRANCIS DONALD S	1LT	0-1558485	0646	1
FRANCIS FABIAN G	CPT	0-1534969	1050	1
FRANCIS FRANK	MAJ	0-0191915	1148	1
FRANCIS FRANK V	CPT	0-1799044	0357	1
FRANCIS GILBERT J	MAJ	0-0469503	0761	3
FRANCIS HARRY A	CW2	W-2149889	0861	1
FRANCIS HARRY B	LTC	0-0212720	1060	3
FRANCIS HERBERT M	LTC	0-0906647	0864	1
FRANCIS HORACE M	COL	0-0142728	0645	2
FRANCIS JOHN G	CPT	0-0497684	1146	1
FRANCIS JOHN J	1LT	0-0490860	0544	1
FRANCIS JOHN L	CW3	W-2119342	1164	1
FRANCIS JOSEPH	CW3	W-2141279	0860	1
FRANCIS JR ALFRED W	1LT	0-0265611	0364	3
FRANCIS LAWRENCE S	CW2	W-2145055	0658	1
FRANCIS LEO J	MAJ	0-1307532	0256	1
FRANCIS LEWIS E	MAJ	0-1176021	1263	1
FRANCIS MARGARET F	MAJ	N-0726244	1064	3
FRANCIS MARION E	LTC	0-1102728	0461	1
FRANCIS MELVIN C	LTC	0-1011793	1065	1
FRANCIS MORRIS F	LTC	0-1293233	0861	1
FRANCIS MORRIS J	CPT	0-0481725	0354	1
FRANCIS OLIVER J	LTC	0-1293575	0663	1
FRANCIS RAYMOND J	LTC	0-1110487	0967	1
FRANCIS SILVIO M	LTC	0-1050864	0962	1
FRANCIS THOMAS L	LTC	0-0252591	0365	3
FRANCIS URBAN L	LTC	0-1294121	0561	1
FRANCIS VINCENT O	COL	0-0346595	1262	3
FRANCIS WILLIAM H	LTC	0-0237854	0361	3
FRANCISCO FELIPE	1LT	0-1897022	1166	1
FRANCISCO FRANK F	MAJ	0-1116661	1262	1
FRANCISCO GEORGE L	1LT	0-1012134	0945	2
FRANCISCO WINSTON S	MAJ	0-0885893	0854	1
FRANCK HERBERT A	LTC	0-0334964	0662	1
FRANCK WALTER W	LTC	0-1595508	0363	1
FRANCKE ROY L	MAJ	0-0358994	0462	1
FRANCO BIAGIO	CPT	0-0343888	1045	2
FRANCO ERWIN J	CPT	0-1031240	0757	1
FRANCO JAMES W	LTC	0-1316501	0765	1
FRANCO LOUIS L	COL	0-0290228	0465	3
FRANCONA ANTHONY	CPT	0-0332005	1043	2
FRANCONE JOSEPH L	1LT	0-1103166	0349	2
FRANDEN NED W	CPT	0-1578481	0645	2
FRANDLER MONROE	CPT	0-0380400	0945	2
FRANDSEN DANA C	CPT	0-1283576	0646	2
FRANDSEN EARL F	CPT	0-1285407	1147	2
FRANEK ANTHONY A	2LT	0-1308320	0145	2
FRANGEDAKIS PANCALEO	LTC	0-1105440	0467	3
FRANGIE JAMES J	MAJ	0-1899371	0163	1
FRANGOS MICHAEL W	1LT	0-1875366	0355	2
FRANK ARNOLD F W	LTC	0-0543005	0965	1
FRANK BENJIMAN H	MAJ	0-0232043	0154	1
FRANK CHARLES P	CPT	0-1177800	0547	2
FRANK DAVID	LTC	0-0346321	0861	1
FRANK DAVID W	CPT	0-4030940	0666	1
FRANK EGON	WO1	W-2124121	0846	2
FRANK FREDERICK	WO1	W-2131346	0859	3
FRANK GEORGE F	MAJ	0-1636879	0660	1
FRANK GEORGE W	MAJ	0-0361614	1045	2
FRANK HAROLD W	LTC	0-0497672	0167	3
FRANK HOWARD	CPT	0-0384463	0146	2
FRANK ISRAEL R	COL	0-0297899	0865	3
FRANK JAMES L	LTC	0-1755183	0259	2
FRANK JOHN L	2LT	0-2047315	0245	2
FRANK JOHN M	LTC	0-1112155	1162	1
FRANK JOHN T	CW2	W-2207537	0661	1

NAME	GRADE	SVC NO	DATE RET MO YR	RET CODE
FRANK JOSEPH P	1LT	0-0517753	0550	1
FRANK JR HARRY C	LTC	0-1002920	0267	1
FRANK KENNETH L	CPT	0-0420524	1045	2
FRANK LOUIS W	LTC	0-0517574	0362	3
FRANK NATHAN	CPT	0-1692102	0346	2
FRANK PAUL J	1LT	0-1285408	1045	2
FRANK PAUL S	LTC	0-0177619	1160	3
FRANK PHILIP N	1LT	0-1061294	0845	2
FRANK SAMUEL S	LTC	0-0330180	1066	3
FRANK SIMON C	MAJ	0-0344264	0545	2
FRANK TONY C	COL	0-0479293	1153	1
FRANK WILLIAM B	LTC	0-0239353	0961	1
FRANK WILLIAM H	1LT	0-0239000	0355	3
FRANK WILLIAM M	MAJ	0-0243506	0666	3
FRANK WILLIAM R	1LT	0-2027779	0955	1
FRANK WILLIAM W	CW2	W-2209054	0560	1
FRANKE EDWARD F	LTC	0-1102247	0363	1
FRANKE HARRISON L	MAJ	0-1578483	0366	1
FRANKE THOMAS W	WO1	W-2153024	1055	2
FRANKE WILLIAM J	CPT	0-1693392	0346	2
FRANKE WILLIAM M	CW3	W-2143318	0662	1
FRANKEL HERBERT G	MAJ	0-0144232	0655	3
FRANKEL ISRAEL	CPT	0-0401415	0246	2
FRANKEL THEODORE	CPT	0-1305035	0248	1
FRANKEN PAUL L	CPT	0-0418302	1145	2
FRANKENBERGER J B	LTC	0-0195445	1053	3
FRANKENBURG FRANCIS	MAJ	0-1557147	0663	2
FRANKENBURGER M C	MAJ	0-1291797	0460	1
FRANKENFIELD JOHN J	CW3	W-2143075	0659	1
FRANKENFIELD KENNETH	MAJ	0-1053132	0961	1
FRANKHOUSER M L	2LT	N-0725330	0145	1
FRANKIE VALENTINE	CW3	W-2144915	0866	1
FRANKINA SAMUEL N	MAJ	0-2262357	0664	1
FRANKL ERNEST A W	LTC	0-0342972	0865	3
FRANKL JR STEPHEN	LTC	0-1311755	0866	1
FRANKLAND ROBERT E	M G	0-0277098	0364	3
FRANKLAND WALTER L	COL	0-0251710	0456	3
FRANKLIN ALFRED A	1LT	0-0385885	1042	2
FRANKLIN ARTHUR	2LT	0-1285918	1143	1
FRANKLIN ARTHUR L	CW4	W-2101706	1055	1
FRANKLIN BENJAMIN	CW4	W-2116042	0255	2
FRANKLIN BURTIS	2LT	0-1048360	0145	2
FRANKLIN CARL W	MAJ	0-2208402	1265	1
FRANKLIN CHESTER V	1LT	0-1692524	0647	1
FRANKLIN EDMOND L	CW4	W-2146014	0760	1
FRANKLIN EDWIN J	MAJ	0-1303701	0264	1
FRANKLIN ELGIE L	CPT	0-0237627	0261	3
FRANKLIN ELMER E	WO1	W-2119790	0154	1
FRANKLIN EMERSON	CPT	0-0967014	1060	1
FRANKLIN FREDRIC P	LTC	0-1319614	0962	1
FRANKLIN GEORGE H	LTC	0-1295860	0361	1
FRANKLIN GUSTAVE K	COL	0-0166708	0648	3
FRANKLIN HERBERT L	CPT	0-1173952	0754	2
FRANKLIN JAMES O	CPT	0-1641299	0860	1
FRANKLIN JAMES W	MAJ	0-1799725	1262	1
FRANKLIN JEFF L	CW2	W-2210167	0863	1
FRANKLIN JENNINGS R	CW2	W-2144175	0461	2
FRANKLIN JOHN D	MAJ	0-1298210	0361	1
FRANKLIN JOHN H	CW2	W-2150728	0462	1
FRANKLIN JOHN S	MAJ	0-0416481	1061	3
FRANKLIN JR CLAUD L	CW4	W-2147872	0264	2
FRANKLIN LAWSON O	MAJ	0-0435386	1062	1
FRANKLIN LESLIE	LTC	0-0261775	0859	3
FRANKLIN LESLIE R	CPT	0-1062175	0657	1
FRANKLIN MARY H	1LT	N-0763251	0145	1
FRANKLIN OLIN S	CW4	W-2119431	0858	1
FRANKLIN ORLAND A	2LT	0-1317773	0844	2
FRANKLIN RALPH H	LTC	0-0326461	0753	1
FRANKLIN RAYMOND	CPT	0-0514172	0346	1
FRANKLIN ROBERT B	CPT	0-0548744	0446	2
FRANKLIN ROBERT J	2LT	0-1581720	1044	2
FRANKLIN ROBERT S	1LT	0-1010567	0944	2
FRANKLIN THOMAS C	LTC	0-1950349	0866	1
FRANKLIN VERNAL H	MAJ	0-2288099	0667	1
FRANKLIN WILLIAM A	1LT	0-1165731	0246	2
FRANKLIN WILLIAM G	MAJ	0-1918913	1263	1
FRANKLYN EARL S	MAJ	0-0436862	0847	1
FRANKS BILLIE R	MAJ	L-0602017	1059	2
FRANKS CHARLES H	CW3	W-2150362	0163	1
FRANKS GARRET O	CW3	W-2206538	0866	1
FRANKS JR ROBERT H	MAJ	0-1314363	1062	1
FRANKS MILFORD R	MAJ	0-1877941	0567	1
FRANKS VICTOR L	MAJ	0-2208735	0966	1
FRANKVILLE DOMINICK	LTC	0-0395039	0562	1
FRANSEIN ELDON F	MAJ	0-0947371	0864	1
FRANSISCO FLOYD L	LTC	0-1574044	1060	1
FRANTZ CHARLES H	LTC	0-0320410	0744	1
FRANTZ DONALD E	1LT	0-1012151	0146	2
FRANTZ HARRISON S	1LT	0-1016588	1046	2
FRANTZ KARL L	LTC	0-1048778	0465	1
FRANTZ WILLIAM A	LTC	0-0174518	0651	3
FRANTZICH RICHARD H	MAJ	0-0404371	0661	2
FRANZ EDWIN F	LTC	0-0905703	0567	3
FRANZ LEO F	LTC	0-1577188	0657	1
FRANZ PAUL W	CW2	W-2101708	0149	1
FRANZ WALTER O	LTC	0-0445064	0349	1
FRANZEN IVAR P	1LT	0-1644967	0355	1
FRANZEN JAMES G	MAJ	0-1012170	0561	1
FRANZEN ROY C	LTC	0-0221934	0864	3
FRAPPIER JOSEPH F	CPT	0-0172188	0158	3
FRAPS JOSEPH A	LTC	0-0229732	0164	3
FRARY WILLARD E	CPT	0-1640465	0358	1
FRASER ANDREW S	CPT	0-0379864	0346	2
FRASER CARL A	LTC	0-0230548	0764	3
FRASER DEAN B	MAJ	0-0128057	0950	3
FRASER DONALD K	MAJ	0-2000567	0665	1
FRASER DONALD M	LTC	0-1106739	0762	1
FRASER DONALD R	MAJ	0-0231336	0665	3
FRASER DUNCAN F	MAJ	0-0429285	0557	1
FRASER FRANK E	M G	0-0222901	0958	3
FRASER HAROLD L	1LT	0-0390867	0646	2
FRASER HARRY C	LTC	0-0464521	0147	1
FRASER HUGH W	LTC	0-1013473	0366	1
FRASER JAMES G	LTC	0-0356933	0667	3
FRASER JAMES W	COL	0-0165792	1156	3
FRASER JOHN A	LTC	0-1283577	1163	3
FRASER JOHN W	1LT	0-1296356	0944	2
FRASER JOSEPH B	M G	0-0247121	0856	3
FRASER LLOYD O	LTC	0-0272950	0967	3
FRASER REGINALD S	CPT	0-0188493	0954	3
FRASER SHERMAN C	LTC	0-0487567	1146	2
FRASER THOMAS C	1LT	0-0437741	0645	2
FRASER WILLIAM M	MAJ	0-0553468	0865	1
FRASIER GWENDOLYN	LTC	0-1548779	0759	1
FRASIER RODERICK J	MAJ	0-2032881	0261	1
FRASL ETHEL J	2LT	N-0797347	1046	1
FRATICELLI EDDIE	MAJ	0-2033634	0261	1
FRATIS ELWOOD J	COL	0-0236538	0466	3
FRAVEL JESSE S	LTC	0-1553597	0663	1
FRAY LOREN M	1LT	0-0530482	1144	2
FRAYER WILSON A	1LT	0-2019307	1047	1
FRAZEE HARRY W	MAJ	0-0178837	0658	3
FRAZEE LOWELL B	CW4	W-2141559	0864	1
FRAZEE MARGARET L	LTC	N-0703602	1264	1
FRAZER DONALD O	CPT	0-0983548	0557	1
FRAZER PERCY W	MAJ	0-0259957	0966	3
FRAZIER BENJAMIN W	MAJ	0-0409965	0864	3
FRAZIER CECIL E	LTC	0-1697827	0561	1
FRAZIER DALE	CPT	0-0500893	0350	1
FRAZIER DANIEL H	CW3	W-2151424	0662	1
FRAZIER DERWOOD E	MAJ	0-0984411	0863	2
FRAZIER EARLY H	MAJ	0-0293403	0246	2
FRAZIER EDWIN	WO1	W-2154666	0956	1
FRAZIER FRANK A	MAJ	0-0370416	1155	2
FRAZIER GAEL M	LTC	0-1320938	1262	1
FRAZIER GEORGE F	CPT	0-0922430	1045	2
FRAZIER JAMES E	LTC	0-1293035	1167	1
FRAZIER JAMES E	CW3	W-2142586	1162	1
FRAZIER JAMES O	LTC	0-1115584	1262	1
FRAZIER JOHN	CW4	W-2115751	1154	1
FRAZIER JOHN M	LTC	0-0318085	0760	3
FRAZIER JULIUS O	LTC	0-0417602	0960	1
FRAZIER KENNETH H	CW4	W-2106897	1060	1
FRAZIER MURRAY	LTC	0-0383800	1160	1
FRAZIER NOAH L	CW3	W-2205720	0865	1
FRAZIER OSCAR H	LTC	0-0169180	0760	3
FRAZIER RAYMOND L	WO1	W-2146134	0853	1
FRAZIER ROBERT S	MAJ	0-4009146	1067	1
FRAZIER SHERVERT H	LTC	0-0322693	0646	2
FRAZIER THOMAS A	B G	0-0375140	0945	1
FRAZIER WILLIAM P	LTC	0-0302068	1147	1
FRAZIER WILLIE R	CW2	W-2149432	0762	1
FRAZIN BERNARD	LTC	0-0305638	0167	3
FRAZIOR DAVID M	COL	0-0272230	0964	3
FRAZY CESIRA A	CPT	M-0000779	0757	1
FREANEY WILLIAM J	LTC	0-0117870	1151	3
FREAR HARRY J	MAJ	0-1294814	1060	1
FREAS LILLIAN	MAJ	N-0723782	0960	2
FRECHETTE DONALD L	1LT	0-1331830	0347	2
FRECKLETON EARLE F	1LT	0-1289853	1045	1
FREDA ARMAND A	MAJ	0-0259376	0467	3
FREDA CESERE R	MAJ	0-2020935	0363	1
FREDEEN HARLAN L	CPT	0-0400048	0544	2
FREDEMAN FRANK H	LTC	0-0101681	0844	2
FREDEN GUNNAR O	LTC	0-0301512	0766	3
FREDENBURG DAVID L	LTC	0-0154792	0552	1
FREDERICK A F	LTC	0-0154053	0648	3
FREDERICK ALBERT R	COL	0-0259514	0867	3
FREDERICK ALVIN E	MAJ	0-2263331	0666	1
FREDERICK DONALD R	CPT	0-1019140	0346	2
FREDERICK ELMER E	LTC	0-0276839	0560	3
FREDERICK FRANCIS O	MAJ	0-0990152	0764	1
FREDERICK GEORGE F	LTC	0-0927620	0463	3
FREDERICK JAMES M	MAJ	0-0705677	0564	1
FREDERICK JOHN A	MAJ	0-1305161	0263	1
FREDERICK JOHN H	LTC	0-0183440	0652	3
FREDERICK LEO L	1LT	0-1574426	1047	2
FREDERICK ROBERT R	LTC	0-0214784	0462	3
FREDERICK ROSCOE	2LT	0-1185870	1045	2
FREDERICK THOMAS J	CPT	0-0290471	1163	3
FREDERICK WILLIAM C	COL	0-0290371	1056	3
FREDERICKS BORIS	LTC	0-1000118	1160	1
FREDERICKS JR PARKER	LTC	0-1106144	0867	1
FREDERICKS ROBERT F	CPT	0-0404069	0246	2
FREDERICKSEN PETER A	COL	0-0179024	0446	2
FREDETTE WARREN H	MAJ	0-1874901	0365	1
FREDIANI JACK F	MAJ	0-2102836	0764	1
FREDIN HUGH R	MAJ	0-2033690	0967	1
FREDIN JOHN E	COL	0-0225144	0961	1
FREDINE ALLAN R	COL	0-0513861	1163	1
FREDLUND THEODORE F	CW3	W-2007369	0265	1
FREDLUND VICTOR J	MAJ	0-1292681	0465	1
FREDREGILL JASPER I	LTC	0-0333701	0265	3
FREDRICK ANNA M	1LT	N-0771032	0845	1
FREDRICKS ERVIN Z	LTC	0-0292433	0662	3
FREDRICKS WILLIAM H	LTC	0-0325388	0365	3
FREDRICKSEN ARTHUR	MAJ	0-1825797	1163	1
FREDRICKSEN WILLIS L	MAJ	0-1547298	1060	1
FREDRICKSON CLYDE H	COL	0-0197979	0458	3
FREDRICKSON THEODORE	CW3	W-2110619	0659	1
FREE HELEN P	2LT	N-0733997	0945	1
FREEBLE THOMAS V	LTC	0-0142674	0758	3
FREEBORN ROBERT S	CPT	0-1325386	0846	1
FREEBURN HERBERT D	CW4	W-2127135	0259	1
FREED OLOF E	CPT	0-1018560	0854	1
FREEDMAN ALFRED	1LT	0-1321704	0947	1
FREEDMAN ARNOLD M	LTC	0-1310089	0862	1
FREEDMAN DAVID	CPT	0-0486414	0146	2
FREEDMAN DAVID T	MAJ	0-1640468	0547	2
FREEDMAN HARRY L	LTC	0-0253075	0160	3
FREEDMAN LEO	LTC	0-0191515	0562	3
FREEDMAN MILTON	1LT	0-1282102	1153	1
FREEDMAN ROBERT I	MAJ	0-1997081	1263	1
FREEDMAN SAMUEL A	CPT	0-1895050	0652	1
FREEDMAN STANLEY S	CPT	0-0335894	0146	2
FREEL WILFRED I	LTC	0-0213704	0663	3
FREELAND FREDERICK	LTC	0-1638475	1064	2
FREELAND NEWTON F	CW4	W-2129351	0756	1
FREELAND WALTER K	LTC	0-0397145	0461	1
FREELING RICHARD N	1LT	0-0439882	0845	2
FREELS FRANK H	LTC	0-1182828	0762	1
FREEMAN ALAN C	CPT	0-0524341	0154	2
FREEMAN ALBERT	CPT	0-0419746	1046	1
FREEMAN ALBERT S	LTC	0-1285033	0461	1
FREEMAN ALLYNE F	LTC	0-0138133	1154	2
FREEMAN ANNE C	1LT	N-0759217	0546	1
FREEMAN ARTHUR N	CPT	0-1290926	0347	2
FREEMAN CAROL J	LTC	0-0375209	0941	1
FREEMAN CHARLEY H	COL	0-0336781	0162	3
FREEMAN CLARENCE S	COL	0-0367100	1262	1
FREEMAN CLAUDE L	1LT	0-1310090	0148	2
FREEMAN CLIFFORD W	LTC	0-0406002	0560	1
FREEMAN CONRAD J	COL	0-0224719	1051	3
FREEMAN EARL K	CPT	0-0331567	0444	1
FREEMAN ED W	MAJ	0-1884184	0967	1
FREEMAN EDGAR I	CPT	0-0223057	1052	3
FREEMAN EDITH	2LT	N-0722244	0145	1
FREEMAN EDWARD H	CPT	0-0144408	0547	2
FREEMAN ERNEST	MAJ	0-0250153	0653	3
FREEMAN EUGENE C	1LT	0-0497857	0550	1
FREEMAN GEORGE W	1LT	0-0299593	0566	3
FREEMAN GERALD W	LTC	0-1001133	1160	1
FREEMAN GREGORY J	COL	0-0284397	0852	1
FREEMAN HAL W	CPT	0-0446116	0746	1
FREEMAN HAROLD F	1LT	0-1533554	0945	2
FREEMAN HARRY C	2LT	0-0992207	0452	2
FREEMAN HELEN L	1LT	N-0730639	0546	1
FREEMAN HERBERT C	CPT	0-0361615	0745	2
FREEMAN HOWARD L	LTC	0-0243570	1165	3
FREEMAN IRA	LTC	0-0158794	0249	3
FREEMAN JACK	1LT	0-1000115	0949	1
FREEMAN JACOB R	MAJ	0-0325873	1061	1
FREEMAN JAMES E	MAJ	0-0206714	0947	1
FREEMAN JAMES N	CW3	W-2146875	0762	1
FREEMAN JAMES W	2LT	0-1053602	0845	2
FREEMAN JOHN C	MAJ	0-1550982	1263	1
FREEMAN JONES M	COL	0-0101928	0655	3
FREEMAN JOSEPH L	WO1	W-2152312	1159	1
FREEMAN JOSEPH W	MAJ	0-0266023	0556	3
FREEMAN JR CURTIS W	LTC	0-1330056	0966	1
FREEMAN JR LOUIS C	COL	0-0236963	1265	3
FREEMAN JR MARTIN I	LTC	0-0386632	0263	1
FREEMAN JR RALPH C	MAJ	0-0587474	1162	1
FREEMAN LESLIE V	CPT	0-0167550	0853	3
FREEMAN LUTHER T	1LT	0-0889613	0957	1
FREEMAN LYNN A	LTC	0-2017389	0966	1
FREEMAN MARCUS	MAJ	0-0185241	0344	2
FREEMAN MERLE E	1LT	0-1061692	1146	2
FREEMAN NATHAN	LTC	0-0302011	0746	2
FREEMAN ORVILLE E	MAJ	0-0904061	0367	3
FREEMAN RALPH C	MAJ	0-0969472	0964	1
FREEMAN RAY M	COL	0-0322892	0661	3
FREEMAN RICHARD C	LTC	0-0297739	0567	3
FREEMAN RITA P	1LT	N-0751032	1045	1
FREEMAN ROBERT A	CW4	W-2113675	1157	1
FREEMAN ROBERT B	MAJ	0-1821593	0561	1
FREEMAN ROBERT L	CPT	0-0450198	0845	2
FREEMAN ROBERT S	MAJ	0-2097100	0164	1
FREEMAN ROGER A	CW4	W-2120288	0559	1
FREEMAN SUSAN E	CPT	N-0724383	0745	1
FREEMAN WALDO O	COL	0-0321037	0666	1
FREEMAN WALTER E	COL	0-0396780	0860	1
FREEMAN WILLIAM A	LTC	0-0175396	1060	3
FREEMAN WILLIAM C	2LT	0-0246313	0357	3
FREEMAN WILLIAM E	LTC	0-1171541	0561	1
FREEMAN WILLIAM H	MAJ	0-1305911	1165	3
FREER GEORGE C	COL	0-0256421	0560	3
FREER LOUIS E	LTC	0-0211285	0648	3
FREER WILLARD D	CPT	0-1640465	0157	1
FREESE CARLETON T	CW2	W-2110601	1154	1

NAME	GRADE	SVC NO	DATE RET MO YR	RET CODE
FREESE CHARLES A	CW3	W-2120073	0960	1
FREESLAND JOSEPH E	LTC	O-0340618	1062	1
FREEZE JR GEORGE G	CW2	W-2150205	0955	1
FREGEAU LAWRENCE P	CW3	W-2147155	1163	1
FREGOE HARRY B	CPT	O-0531204	0946	1
FREGOSI ALBERT	COL	O-0272905	0660	2
FREIBANC CARL A	LTC	O-0327777	0163	1
FREID JOSEPH A	1LT	O-0669030	0245	2
FREIDEN JOSEPH N	CPT	O-0474364	0945	2
FREIDKIN MARVIN J	CPT	O-0265643	1045	2
FREIHUPE JR ROBERT C	MAJ	O-0312604	0560	1
FREITAG MAC A	COL	O-0247486	0259	3
FREITAG ROY A	LTC	O-1011392	0961	1
FREITAS EDWARD W	CPT	O-2032318	0160	1
FREITCHEN LEROY C	CW3	W-2150994	0865	1
FRELIGH WILLIAM P	LTC	O-0563039	0663	1
FREMSTAD LISTON J	MAJ	O-0415778	0561	2
FRENCH ARCHIE	MAJ	O-0327385	0746	2
FRENCH ARLYN B	COL	O-0216587	0464	3
FRENCH CHARLES L	MAJ	O-1298046	0162	1
FRENCH CHARLES W	CPT	O-1302626	0558	1
FRENCH DANIEL C	1LT	O-0373068	0146	2
FRENCH DUDLEY L	LTC	O-1001786	0566	3
FRENCH EUGENIE G	MAJ	N-0752412	1263	1
FRENCH GEORGE R	1LT	O-0536726	1045	2
FRENCH GEORGE S	MAJ	O-2038135	1161	1
FRENCH GEORGE T	CW2	W-2203340	0262	1
FRENCH HOMER M	MAJ	O-0138654	1158	3
FRENCH IRVINE	2LT	O-0144229	1153	3
FRENCH ISAAC S	MAJ	O-2017984	0865	1
FRENCH JOHN A	MAJ	O-0249740	0765	3
FRENCH JOHN A	1LT	O-1011170	0461	1
FRENCH JOHN L	CW3	W-2104067	1051	2
FRENCH JOHN P	CPT	O-0904996	0344	2
FRENCH JR DEWITT H	CPT	O-1540721	1159	1
FRENCH JR GEORGE H	LTC	O-1100107	1163	1
FRENCH JR SHIRLEY S	1LT	O-1315420	1045	2
FRENCH KEITH A	LTC	O-0467186	0764	1
FRENCH LORNE	LTC	O-0443687	1047	2
FRENCH MARCUS R	MAJ	O-0980815	0563	1
FRENCH PAUL J	CW3	W-2147211	0962	1
FRENCH RALPH W	MAJ	O-0165184	0548	1
FRENCH RAY W	2LT	O-1304369	0644	2
FRENCH RICHARD E	LTC	O-0152131	0645	2
FRENCH RICHARD P	CW4	W-2105290	0860	1
FRENCH ROBERT M	CPT	O-0312004	1146	1
FRENCH ROLLIE L	MAJ	O-0272856	0759	1
FRENCH STEPHEN F	COL	O-0118628	0154	3
FRENCH VERNON L	MAJ	O-1110488	0961	1
FRENCH WALKER M	LTC	O-1108671	0167	3
FRENCH WILL C	CPT	O-0259936	0850	2
FRENCH WILLIAM C	LTC	O-1168675	1166	1
FRENCH WILLIAM T	CPT	O-1914353	1046	2
FRENCHER JOSEPH	MAJ	O-1016782	0457	1
FRENCK GARDEN	MAJ	O-1639047	0966	3
FRENKEL GEORGE L	MAJ	O-0552533	0664	1
FRENNA LEO C	COL	O-0167682	0555	3
FREPPEL PAUL L	LTC	O-1555965	0167	3
FRERICHS JOHN O	LTC	O-0350027	0167	3
FRESE GEORGE H	CPT	O-0226227	0955	2
FRESE WILLIAM O	LTC	O-0311674	0960	1
FRESHLEY LOWELL C	2LT	O-1177399	0345	2
FRESHOUR LARKIN W	LTC	O-1288729	0760	1
FRET JOSE A	2LT	O-0222463	0844	2
FRETER JOHN M	2LT	O-1327832	0146	2
FRETHEM ALLEN A	CPT	O-1766214	1049	1
FRETUEG KENNETH D	1LT	O-0577603	0860	2
FRETZ JOHN C	LTC	O-0219365	0160	3
FREUDENBERG WALTER	LTC	O-1299392	0563	1
FREUND JACK A	CPT	O-1311875	0347	2
FREUND PHIL W	LTC	O-0333371	0454	1
FREVELE ALBERT R	MAJ	O-0428605	0553	2
FREVERT WILLIAM	2LT	O-1039199	0544	2
FREW JR ARCHIE	CPT	O-0966108	1060	1
FREWIN NORMAN H	MAJ	O-1103641	1266	1

NAME	GRADE	SVC NO	DATE RET MO YR	RET CODE
FREY ARTHUR J	COL	O-0157661	1157	3
FREY ARTHUR W	LTC	O-0362045	0959	1
FREY EDWIN F	MAJ	O-0519133	1053	1
FREY FREDERICK	COL	O-0138981	0654	3
FREY HAROLD P	LTC	O-0258446	1165	3
FREY HARRY J	LTC	O-0140054	0954	3
FREY JR ARTHUR J	MAJ	O-1295008	0258	1
FREY JR HOWARD C	CW2	W-2208861	0559	1
FREY MARCY	COL	O-0311492	0165	3
FREY RAYMOND T	2LT	O-1100544	0843	2
FREY ROBERT F	LTC	O-0375479	0460	1
FREY WALTER J	CW2	W-2141282	0656	1
FREY WILLIAM C	MAJ	O-0409003	0646	1
FREY WILLIAM N	LTC	O-0523242	0365	1
FREYDER LEO F	COL	O-0271822	0166	3
FREYERMUTH JAMES R	COL	O-0262373	0267	3
FREYERMUTH JR OTT G	CPT	O-0443334	1045	1
FREYMUTH HARRY W	MAJ	O-1003106	0163	1
FREYTAG ROBERT F	MAJ	O-0542117	0962	1
FRIANT STUART T	COL	O-0186345	0447	2
FRIAR HERBERT H	LTC	O-1585470	0161	1
FRIBANCE AUSTIN E	MAJ	O-0273288	0867	3
FRIBERG ROBERT A	MAJ	O-0482043	0646	2
FRIBLEY EARL F	CPT	O-0118643	1064	3
FRICH JR GEORGE H	1LT	O-0265278	1044	1
FRICK CHARLES H	LTC	O-0144920	0648	3
FRICK CLARENCE F	MAJ	O-2263504	0665	1
FRICK DONALD S	CW2	W-3430049	0966	1
FRICK HARVEY L	CPT	O-0505715	0146	1
FRICK JOHN P	COL	O-0205855	0559	3
FRICK RALPH J	LTC	O-1170739	0261	1
FRICK RAYMOND R	MAJ	O-0257749	0546	2
FRICK RUPERT G	CPT	O-1825183	0957	1
FRICK WALTER H	LTC	O-0171447	0856	3
FRICKE HARRY C	1LT	O-0534889	0745	2
FRICKE JOHN W	1LT	O-1331279	0452	1
FRICKE LOWELL J	LTC	O-0468844	0964	1
FRICKER NORMAN K	MAJ	O-1293936	0662	2
FRIDAY EDWARD R	CPT	O-1290928	0346	2
FRIDAY JOE	MAJ	O-1920223	0264	1
FRIDAY JOHN D	COL	O-0171088	0760	1
FRIDAY RICHARD W	2LT	O-1996911	1145	2
FRIDELL MYRON D	MAJ	O-1686649	0964	1
FRIDIE DAVID H	1LT	O-2002879	0355	2
FRIDINGER WILLIAM T	1LT	O-0439821	0744	2
FRIDLEY JESSE R	COL	O-0150049	0648	3
FRIDRICH RICHARD L	MAJ	O-0179077	1056	3
FRIED GEORGE W	LTC	O-0235918	0855	3
FRIED HAROLD V	CPT	O-0247922	1165	3
FRIED JACOB V	MAJ	O-0574644	0762	1
FRIED JOSEPH A	CPT	O-1299394	0347	2
FRIED SAMUEL A	LTC	O-1004581	1264	3
FRIEDAH HAROLD F	CPT	O-1165859	0447	2
FRIEDBERG KARL M	LTC	O-1553446	0762	1
FRIEDENTHAL ADOLPH L	LTC	O-0112552	0557	3
FRIEDENTHAL RALPH F	LTC	O-0289531	0347	1
FRIEDENWALD AARON	LTC	O-0397823	0261	1
FRIEDERS CARL F	MAJ	O-0953671	0862	1
FRIEDFELD LOUIS	CPT	O-0500834	0444	1
FRIEDLAENDER ALEX S	MAJ	O-0351474	0843	2
FRIEDLAND GRACE R	1LT	N-0724521	0946	1
FRIEDLANDER JACKSON	MAJ	O-0430257	0446	2
FRIEDLANDER K R	MAJ	O-0257892	1055	3
FRIEDLI GOTTFRIED	1LT	O-1182830	1045	1
FRIEDMAN ALEXANDER	MAJ	O-0507642	0846	2
FRIEDMAN BERNARD E	1LT	O-1295530	1146	2
FRIEDMAN CHARLES	CPT	O-0533623	0546	1
FRIEDMAN CHARLES E	LTC	O-0423493	0361	1
FRIEDMAN EGON F	LTC	O-1017676	1264	1
FRIEDMAN FRANK	LTC	O-0503038	0857	1
FRIEDMAN HAROLD B	LTC	O-0254268	1164	3
FRIEDMAN HARRY	1LT	O-1013194	1145	2
FRIEDMAN HARRY	CPT	O-1690295	0346	2
FRIEDMAN HENRY T	1LT	O-0489226	0245	2
FRIEDMAN HERBERT S	MAJ	O-0344284	0146	2

NAME	GRADE	SVC NO	DATE RET MO YR	RET CODE
FRIEDMAN IRVING I	1LT	O-1014213	0346	2
FRIEDMAN MILTON J	MAJ	O-1584231	0446	2
FRIEDMAN PAUL S	CPT	O-0361551	0345	2
FRIEDMAN ROBERT L	CPT	O-0449639	1145	1
FRIEDMAN SAUL	2LT	O-1798253	0644	2
FRIEDMAN WILLIAM F	LTC	O-0166764	0951	3
FRIEDRICH DONALD F	MAJ	O-2263119	1065	1
FRIEDRICH HELEN E	MAJ	L-0203873	0667	1
FRIEDRICHS VICTOR	MAJ	O-0100200	0853	3
FRIEFELD NATHAN	MAJ	O-0508871	0446	2
FRIEL RAYMOND P	CW3	W-2205839	1166	1
FRIEMOTH AMEDEUS J	LTC	O-0263075	1064	3
FRIEND FREDERICK	MAJ	O-1288038	0854	1
FRIEND HILBERT E	1LT	O-1014260	0146	2
FRIEND JAMES W	COL	O-0314382	1162	1
FRIEND LESTER O	LTC	O-0198231	0758	3
FRIENDLY JR EDWIN S	CPT	O-0493717	0146	2
FRIERSON LUTHER	LTC	O-0473387	0954	1
FRIERSON PETE H	CPT	O-0462639	1144	2
FRIES DONALD E	MAJ	O-1926491	0864	1
FRIES HAROLD J	CPT	O-1112705	0246	2
FRIES JOSEPH B	CW2	W-2205843	1060	2
FRIES JR WALTER B	CPT	O-1312258	0547	2
FRIES ROBERT G	CW3	W-2001606	0266	3
FRIES WEYNAND J	COL	O-0371279	0966	2
FRIESE ROBERT E	MAJ	O-1590475	0856	1
FRIESEL DAVID	COL	O-0444437	0853	1
FRIESS HAROLD M	CPT	O-1285919	0346	1
FRIESZ LEONARD O	COL	O-0358172	0764	1
FRIGO LIONEL O	LTC	O-1293576	0561	2
FRILEY JR CHARLES E	MAJ	O-0337674	0845	2
FRILOT MATTHEW W	1LT	O-1302424	0145	2
FRINAK JOHN M	LTC	O-0405920	1060	1
FRINCHI LOUIS O	MAJ	O-1998347	1062	1
FRINDELL HAROLD M	COL	O-0363319	1163	1
FRIPP EDGAR W	MAJ	O-1535581	0958	1
FRISBEE CHARLES V	LTC	O-0298731	0760	1
FRISBIE WILLIAM E	1LT	O-1914354	0538	2
FRISBY CARL F	LTC	O-1633013	0350	1
FRISBY JACK O	MAJ	O-0289383	0444	2
FRISBY RALPH E	1LT	O-1325210	0449	2
FRISCH ARNOLD R	1LT	O-1314615	0447	2
FRISCH GEORGE A	LTC	O-0152615	0648	3
FRISCH ISAAC J	COL	O-0242778	0250	3
FRISCH JOSEPH	CPT	O-0509144	1145	2
FRISCHKNECHT REED L	2LT	O-1826078	0644	2
FRISHKEY FRANK	MAJ	O-0961085	0167	1
FRISHKEY NICK	CPT	O-0954840	0157	2
FRISTOE FRANK H	LTC	O-0911615	1265	3
FRISTOE KENNETH W	LTC	O-0516331	0563	1
FRITH CLIFFORD F	MAJ	O-0268713	0446	2
FRITH GILBERT R	COL	O-0343743	0763	3
FRITH ROBERT L	1LT	O-1004583	0146	2
FRITSCH CARL F	COL	O-0159891	0256	3
FRITSCH JAKE R	CPT	O-0519376	0447	2
FRITSCH JR HENRY F	2LT	O-0556910	0246	2
FRITSCH WILLIAM N	CPT	O-0235518	1050	3
FRITSCHE FREDERICK	CPT	O-0263519	0461	3
FRITSCHE JOHN R	CPT	O-0506042	0350	1
FRITSCHEL HERBERT E	COL	O-0175702	0655	3
FRITSCHLER JOHN C	COL	O-0253788	0159	3
FRITTS HARRY L	COL	O-0135031	0456	3
FRITTS MELVIN V	LTC	O-1286630	0757	1
FRITZ DANA R	2LT	O-1015107	0345	2
FRITZ FRANK J	MAJ	O-2055117	0457	1
FRITZ GEORGE	2LT	O-0451622	0154	2
FRITZ JOHN F	LTC	O-0192027	1152	3
FRITZ LAWRENCE J	2LT	O-1573853	0144	2
FRITZ SAMUEL F	LTC	O-0410379	0760	1
FRITZ WILLIAM O	COL	O-0220646	0363	3
FRITZ WILLIAM G	2LT	O-1301231	0445	2
FRITZ WILLIAM P	2LT	O-1049481	0644	2
FRITZE WALTER H	LTC	O-1322688	0163	1
FRITZEN CLAUS A	CPT	O-1313233	0848	2
FRIZ WILLARD C	LTC	O-0303986	1264	1

NAME	GRADE	SVC NO	DATE RET MO YR	RET CODE
FRIZELL LEWIS	LTC	O-0452107	1054	1
FRIZELL LEWIS E	CPT	O-2009225	0261	1
FRIZZELL EDWARD R	CPT	O-0101825	0648	3
FRIZZELL ROY E	1LT	O-2001134	0746	2
FRIZZELL TEDRCW B	CPT	O-0371070	0750	1
FRIZZELLE REGINALD E	COL	O-0332135	0460	1
FROBERGER GEORGE A J	CPT	O-0184141	0656	3
FROCK EARL M	CW4	W-2136738	1165	1
FROEDE ALEXANDER	LTC	O-0244496	0157	3
FROEHLICH THEODORE W	CW3	W-2141283	0760	1
FROELICH ARCHIE W	LTC	O-0107034	0254	3
FROEMEL EUGENE F	MAJ	O-1548787	0461	1
FROERER CARL	CPT	O-0506843	0344	1
FROGNER LESTER S	LTC	O-0326281	0763	3
FROHMAN HOWARD L	1LT	O-0449555	1144	2
FROHMAN IRVING G	COL	O-0186368	1262	3
FROHMAN LOUIS H	COL	O-0159856	0753	3
FROHNHOEFER FRANK	CW3	W-2147999	0264	1
FROMAN ANNA L	LTC	O-0248122	0365	3
FROMAN PAUL L	LTC	O-0920868	1057	3
FROME MANUEL M	1LT	O-1302803	0345	2
FROMENT HOWARD H	MAJ	O-1018555	0263	1
FROMER CHARLES L	MAJ	O-2268774	0963	1
FROMHART ROBERT E	LTC	O-2043280	0966	1
FROMM CHESTER E	CPT	O-0573464	0263	1
FROMM JOHN D	CW3	W-2105917	0852	1
FROMM JOHN O	LTC	O-1589845	1060	1
FROMMHAGEN F C	COL	O-0277989	1154	3
FROMUTH HERMAN C	LTC	O-0232357	0654	3
FRONAUER HENRY J	CPT	O-0939006	0464	1
FRONCILLO RENATO	MAJ	O-0347881	0146	2
FRONCZAK FLORIAN F	MAJ	O-0307937	0367	3
FRONK CLARENCE E	COL	O-0176571	0648	3
FRONK JOHN M	COL	O-0204016	0260	1
FRONK ROBERT A	LTC	O-0280801	0367	3
FRONTERA ENRIQUE	LTC	O-0402466	1165	1
FROOMAN MAURICE	WO1	W-2128177	1045	2
FROSH VOLLIE E	CPT	O-1166715	0546	2
FROST CAROL E	CPT	O-4030907	1066	1
FROST CHARLES G	MAJ	O-0126348	0648	3
FROST CAYTON H	COL	O-0527143	1163	3
FROST EARL G	LTC	O-0388910	1055	1
FROST EARLE R	CPT	O-0144004	0758	3
FROST FRANK A	LTC	O-0111373	0648	3
FROST JACK T	MAJ	O-1317082	0664	1
FROST JAMES F	LTC	O-1644971	1163	1
FROST JAY C	CPT	O-2289183	1164	1
FROST JOE M	1LT	O-1180185	0346	2
FROST JR JOHN F	LTC	O-0918628	0362	3
FROST KENNETH D	MAJ	O-0967026	0263	1
FROST KENNETH E	1LT	O-2004145	1055	2
FROST MERVIN J	CW3	W-2149211	1061	1
FROST MILLARD I	COL	O-0254541	1060	3
FROST NOEL C	CPT	O-1998100	0754	2
FROST OREN S	CPT	O-0383297	0745	2
FROST RAYMOND F	LTC	O-0289152	1263	1
FROST ROBERT J	LTC	O-0422232	0661	2
FROST ROBERT L	CW3	W-2203364	0365	1
FROST ROY L	1LT	O-1306262	0845	2
FROST WINSTON R	LTC	O-1555548	1162	1
FROUNFELKER FRANK A	MAJ	O-0379516	0265	3
FROYD ERWIN A	COL	O-0103318	0648	3
FROYD PAUL C	1LT	O-1302634	0546	2
FRUECHTENICHT G H	CPT	O-0205397	1161	3
FRUEHWALD RAYMOND M	CPT	O-1319942	0647	1
FRUIN CHARLES E	LTC	O-0297444	0565	3
FRUIN EMMETT G	LTC	O-0259426	0767	3
FRUIN MABEL E	2LT	N-0779278	0446	1
FRUMKES GEORGE	COL	O-0488350	0446	2
FRUSCELLA SALVATORE	MAJ	O-0324331	1263	1
FRUTCHEY RUSSELL H	LTC	O-0323676	0361	3
FRUZAN RALPH M	CPT	O-1056619	0161	1
FRY ARTHUR H	CW4	W-2109829	1154	1
FRY ARTHUR W	LTC	O-0326502	1060	1
FRY CHARLES V	LTC	O-0235121	0864	3

NAME	GRADE	SVC NO	DATE RET MO YR	RET CODE
FRY FRANKLYN D	LTC	O-0360928	1159	3
FRY HARVEY J	MAJ	O-0387369	1146	2
FRY JOHN A	LTC	O-0239037	0861	3
FRY JOHN W	COL	O-0321899	1047	2
FRY JR CHARLES A	LTC	O-1101833	0755	1
FRY KENNETH L	LTC	O-0354246	0462	1
FRY LEROY H	CPT	O-1882176	0264	1
FRY ROBERT W	MAJ	O-1923602	0566	1
FRY THOMAS C	LTC	O-0386200	0360	1
FRY WARREN N	LTC	O-1327616	0566	1
FRY WILLIAM H	LTC	O-1312535	0961	1
FRYAR JOHN H	CW2	W-2147912	1059	1
FRYDAY ALVORD C	2LT	O-1301288	0843	2
FRYDENLUND BERTHA A	1LT	N-0732654	0645	1
FRYE ALEX A	MAJ	O-1293752	0858	1
FRYE AUSTIN P	MAJ	O-0232884	0163	1
FRYE CHARLES L	2LT	O-1295534	0844	2
FRYE DELMAR O	MAJ	O-1290279	0861	1
FRYE HERBERT H	LTC	O-0342984	0961	1
FRYE JOHN H	COL	O-0202125	0262	3
FRYE JOSEPH W	LTC	O-0289264	0762	1
FRYE JR HARRY	CW3	W-2206595	1166	1
FRYE LUCIUS C	CW3	W-2153377	0865	1
FRYE MARCUS M	LTC	O-0230844	0359	1
FRYE ROBERT	COL	O-0243061	1161	3
FRYE ROBERT C	MAJ	O-0996492	0363	1
FRYE SHELDON B	LTC	O-1106745	0256	1
FRYER CHARLES W	CPT	O-2008341	0948	2
FRYER DOROTHY J	MAJ	N-0736585	0863	1
FRYER GORDON L	MAJ	O-1541124	0262	1
FRYER HERBERT F	CW4	W-2152958	1262	1
FRYER OSCAR G	MAJ	O-0188611	0156	3
FRYER SAMUEL R	CPT	O-1701759	0346	2
FRYKHOLM LLOYD D	2LT	O-0148063	0861	3
FRYKHOLM VERNON E	LTC	O-1284125	0663	1
FRYKLAND BASIL N	LTC	O-0251869	0459	3
FRYMIRE ALTON P	2LT	O-1165860	1045	2
FRYOU JR EUGENE J	CW2	W-2148378	1059	1
FRYSFEL JOHN	MAJ	O-1649273	0958	1
FUCCI CHARLES D	CW3	W-2143580	1162	1
FUCHS ARTHUR L	MAJ	O-0159276	0354	3
FUCHS EDMOND H	WO1	W-2117546	1049	1
FUCHS FREDERICK	MAJ	O-0341767	0744	2
FUCHS HENRY	CPT	O-0919588	1163	2
FUCHS JAMES R	1LT	O-0556916	0445	2
FUDGE ROBERT E	CW2	W-2209234	0763	1
FUDOLD JOHN H	LTC	O-1947707	1067	1
FUECKER FRED M	COL	O-0154055	0356	3
FUENTES JOSE	LTC	O-0265443	1050	1
FUERTES RAFAEL	1LT	O-0370820	0144	2
FUGATE DOUGLAS R	LTC	O-0246340	0966	3
FUGATE GLENN	CW4	W-2101209	0961	1
FUGATE ROBERT	LTC	O-0410735	1160	1
FUGE WILFRED W	COL	O-0353741	1265	3
FUGITCH JOHN	CW2	W-2144005	1055	1
FUGITT PRICE W	CPT	O-1290910	0247	1
FUGITT HOWARD D	LTC	O-1558978	1262	1
FUHR FAYE W	LTC	O-0166154	1157	1
FUHR MAX W	1LT	O-0518858	0445	2
FUHRMANN JOHN R	1LT	O-1296105	0645	2
FUKUCHI STANLEY T	CPT	O-0963000	0158	3
FUKUMOTO MASASHI	CW4	W-2133101	0767	1
FULBRIGHT WORTH	COL	O-0279211	0567	1
FULCHER MALCOLM W	MAJ	O-1896976	0762	1
FULENWIDER JR JOHN	CPT	O-0359565	0445	2
FULGHAM FRANK	CPT	O-0274861	1265	3
FULGHAM FRANK W	CPT	O-1307004	0746	1
FULK EDWIN	CPT	O-0275288	1248	1
FULK HUBERT A	LTC	O-0302483	1060	1
FULK WILLIAM W	MAJ	O-0421112	0859	1
FULKERSON JACK W	2LT	O-0531101	0145	2
FULKERSON THOMAS R	LTC	O-0361706	0566	3
FULKERSON WILLIAM	CW2	W-2117162	0767	1
FULKS HENRY	CPT	O-0120805	1050	3
FULLBRIGHT BESSIE V	LTC	N-0741127	0652	1
FULLBRIGHT MILDRED	2LT	N-0726652	1045	1
FULLBRIGHT PRESTON F	CW3	W-2151003	1157	1
FULLEN LILBURN S	LTC	O-0480157	0357	1
FULLENWIDER LEO	CW2	W-2147449	1060	1
FULLENWIDER RAY H	CPT	O-0243728	0249	3
FULLER ALBERT W	CPT	O-0279182	0544	2
FULLER ALONZEE H	WO1	W-2108670	1045	2
FULLER ANDREW J	LTC	O-0314855	0260	3
FULLER ARTHUR C	LTC	O-0241207	0561	1
FULLER ARTHUR H	COL	O-0242601	1155	3
FULLER BASIL R	MAJ	O-1420121	0167	1
FULLER BENJAMIN F	CPT	O-0498427	0547	1
FULLER BERNARD R	LTC	O-0272028	0957	3
FULLER CLARENCE H	MAJ	O-1332051	0365	1
FULLER CLIFFORD R	LTC	O-2007610	1161	2
FULLER DELBERT F	COL	O-0171586	0455	3
FULLER DONALD W	MAJ	O-0337120	0551	1
FULLER DORSEY P	LTC	O-1056720	0767	1
FULLER EDWARD F	CPT	O-0486720	1043	2
FULLER ELMER C	LTC	O-0144347	0845	2
FULLER ERNEST T	CW2	W-2112104	0749	1
FULLER FRANK H	LTC	O-0165636	0259	3
FULLER FRED	2LT	O-0108492	0341	1
FULLER GEORGE G	MAJ	O-0170755	1048	3
FULLER GEORGE S	LTC	O-0238424	0566	3
FULLER GRAYDON F	CPT	O-1101834	1062	1
FULLER HAROLD H	CW2	W-2150126	0959	2
FULLER HAROLD F	MAJ	O-1335140	1263	1
FULLER HARRY	CPT	O-0491579	0757	1
FULLER HENRY W	MAJ	O-1297183	1058	1
FULLER HERBERT W	LTC	O-1634779	0266	1
FULLER HOWARD F	B G	O-0130484	0946	2
FULLER HOWARD P	LTC	O-0198677	0648	3
FULLER IRWIN L	LTC	O-0291967	1162	1
FULLER J MURAS	CPT	O-0148885	1052	3
FULLER JACK P	1LT	O-0409654	1045	2
FULLER JAMES W	LTC	O-1104184	0261	1
FULLER JAMES N	LTC	O-0215349	1059	3
FULLER JOHN S	LTC	O-0405395	1160	1
FULLER JOHN F	LTC	O-1296357	0861	1
FULLER JOHN E	CW3	W-2165723	0663	1
FULLER JR ALFRED E	MAJ	O-0945689	1162	1
FULLER JR ELMER F	CPT	O-1112706	1046	2
FULLER JR JOHN	LTC	O-0240805	1262	3
FULLER JR JOSEPH W	LTC	O-0298104	0766	3
FULLER JR MYRON C	MAJ	O-1599162	0266	1
FULLER KATHERINE	CPT	L-0609658	0351	2
FULLER LEONARD H	COL	O-0333505	0860	1
FULLER LIVONIA W	LTC	O-0282962	0962	3
FULLER MCKINLEY L	CW2	W-2117916	1147	1
FULLER MELVYN H	LTC	O-1634780	0463	1
FULLER MORRIS G	MAJ	O-0187826	1056	3
FULLER ORVILLE M	LTC	O-1112707	0962	1
FULLER PAUL W	COL	O-1068860	1160	3
FULLER RAYMOND N	2LT	O-1010561	1146	2
FULLER RICHARD T	LTC	O-0526382	0864	1
FULLER ROBERT A	LTC	O-0317876	1162	1
FULLER ROBERT A	LTC	O-1104155	0662	1
FULLER ROBERT	LTC	O-0314046	0761	1
FULLER ROBERT W	CPT	O-2037971	0461	1
FULLER SPURGEON	1LT	O-1308804	0545	2
FULLER SR MELVIN	CPT	O-0986482	0161	1
FULLER THOMAS	B G	O-0248411	1066	3
FULLER VERNON F	MAJ	O-0262555	0664	3
FULLER WALTER	LTC	O-0256541	0163	3
FULLER WAYNE	CPT	O-1311295	0748	1
FULLER WAYNE R	MAJ	O-0888220	1065	2
FULLER WESLEY	LTC	O-1106147	1265	1
FULLER WILLIAM	CW3	W-2205391	0666	1
FULLER WILLIAM	CPT	O-0488812	0154	1
FULLER WILLIS	LTC	O-0258574	0266	3
FULLERTON ALBERT	MAJ	O-0364164	0147	1
FULLERTON CARLE	MAJ	O-1174859	0961	1
FULLERTON HUGH	COL	O-0285727	0540	3
FULLERTON PAUL A	MAJ	O-0361659	0455	1
FULLERTON RALPH O	MAJ	O-0305279	1067	2
FULLERTON 3RD ROBERT	COL	O-0354666	0946	1
FULLILOVE EMMA S	1LT	N-0793971	0951	1
FULLMER CYRIL C	CPT	O-0469531	1147	2
FULMER JAMES L	LTC	O-0337579	0960	3
FULMER WILLIAM A	LTC	O-0172088	0559	3
FULP SR ORVILLE H	LTC	O-1002922	0962	1
FULTON ALFRED	MAJ	O-0505342	1154	1
FULTON DONALD M	MAJ	O-1169968	0361	1
FULTON EDWIN H	CW3	W-2149292	0562	1
FULTON ETHAN A	CPT	O-2285438	1155	3
FULTON HAROLD J	CPT	O-0211982	1058	3
FULTON HARRIET V	1LT	N-0773275	0746	1
FULTON HENRY W	1LT	O-0347681	0442	2
FULTON JOHN D	CPT	O-1920277	0564	1
FULTON OLIVER A	MAJ	O-0266795	1160	1
FULTON ROBERT I	COL	O-0171351	1047	1
FULTON ROBERT L	CW3	W-2122491	0659	1
FULTON ROBERT M	LTC	O-0905063	0762	1
FULTON ROBERT W	WO1	W-2107842	0845	2
FULTON THOMPSON R	CPT	O-0507881	0254	1
FULTON WILLIAM P	LTC	O-0224886	0555	3
FULTZ ARTHUR O	MAJ	O-0949988	0662	1
FULTZ J LYSTON	LTC	O-0915086	1162	3
FUMAROLA NANCY J	1LT	N-0767736	0746	1
FUMICH VALENTINE	LTC	O-1633871	0965	1
FUNCHESS JESSE R	MAJ	O-0250976	1044	2
FUNGA FERDINAND	LTC	O-0274196	1051	1
FUNDERBURG GEORGE W	1LT	O-1293235	0747	2
FUNDERBURG L W	MAJ	O-0494508	0651	1
FUNDERBURK ROBERT W	MAJ	O-2036175	1061	1
FUNDERBURK WILBUR F	LTC	O-0232628	1063	3
FUNK BRIANT C	CW3	W-2206408	0967	1
FUNK CHARLES W	CW2	W-2143195	0955	1
FUNK DONALD A	LTC	O-1318931	0746	1
FUNK DONALD S	CPT	O-0215218	0162	3
FUNK DOROTHY M	2LT	N-0780057	1145	1
FUNK GARLAND E	1LT	O-0507746	1051	1
FUNK GENE D	CW3	W-2143187	0664	1
FUNK HAROLD I	LTC	O-1796453	0361	1
FUNK HARRY W	CW2	W-2113269	1146	1
FUNK IAN C	CPT	O-0469458	0646	2
FUNK IVERS L	MAJ	O-0383463	0460	1
FUNK JACK A	MAJ	O-0984520	0863	2
FUNK JAMES C	1LT	O-0538271	0946	2
FUNK JOHN	CPT	O-0349472	0544	2
FUNK JOHN S	CW2	W-2102917	0853	1
FUNK JOSEPH W	CPT	O-0413610	0648	1
FUNK MELVIN C	CW4	W-2141561	0861	1
FUNK NEIL E	COL	O-0205770	0648	3
FUNK THOMAS S	2LT	O-0904982	0443	2
FUNK WHARTON T	COL	O-0309253	1063	3
FUNKE ELMO G	LTC	O-0208171	1056	3
FUNKHOUSER CECIL R	CW2	W-2142587	1155	2
FUNSTON JOHN H	LTC	O-1584236	0862	1
FUQUA EALEY T	CW4	W-2101721	1154	1
FUQUA HARRY I	CW3	W-2150207	0962	1
FUQUA JACK R	MAJ	O-1543420	0257	1
FUQUA JOHN P	CW4	W-2101309	0758	1
FUQUA JR JOHN T	CW3	W-2206640	1165	1
FUQUA PAUL H	CPT	O-0150713	0649	3
FUQUARY HENRY W	CW3	W-2142638	1058	1
FURBEE BENJAMIN W	1LT	O-0192610	0636	1
FURBEE RAYMOND H	LTC	O-1325154	0563	1
FURBER CHARLES L	COL	O-0184779	0648	3
FURBER EDITH H	CPT	L-0400511	1045	1
FURBERSHAW WALTER I	COL	O-0182893	0648	3
FURBISH CHESTER A	COL	O-0266646	0157	2
FURCHES CLAYTON F	LTC	O-0213264	0164	3
FURCHES OOUTHIT I	LTC	O-1018989	0864	1
FURGIUELE PETER M	LTC	O-0364227	0762	1
FURHMEISTER ERNEST L	LTC	O-1544568	1062	1
FURIA ANNA L	CPT	N-0769325	1054	2
FURLO FRANK A	CPT	O-1316401	1265	1
FURLONG GERARD D	MAJ	O-1643565	0158	1
FURLONG HAROLD A	COL	O-0158405	0955	3
FURLONG JR C E	CPT	O-0971978	1060	1
FURLOUGH JR ARTHUR W	MAJ	O-0990533	0264	1
FURMAN ARTHUR E	CPT	O-0481888	0954	1
FURMAN EDITH I	1LT	N-0765416	1047	1
FURMAN NORMAN	1LT	O-1313085	0946	2
FURMAN SOL I	WO1	W-2129498	1145	2
FURMAN WALTER A	MAJ	O-1639054	0263	1
FURNER JR EDWARD M	CPT	O-1031081	1161	2
FURNISH EDWARD S	COL	O-0166273	1055	3
FURNISH WILLIE R	1LT	O-0199825	1035	1
FURNISS CLINTON C	MAJ	O-0388952	0461	1
FURR CARL J	COL	O-0278934	1063	3
FURR WILLIAM H	MAJ	O-1994603	0265	1
FURRY EMMERT F	LTC	O-0450868	0656	1
FURSE STEPHEN S	COL	O-0256086	0465	3
FURST ALAN S	LTC	O-1581138	1061	1
FURST ANTHONY R	1LT	O-0408723	1046	2
FURST HAROLD A	LTC	O-0270404	0246	2
FURST JACQUES	MAJ	O-1694503	0665	2
FURSTENAU THEODORE C	CPT	O-1543349	0356	1
FURTADO JOSEPH F	CPT	O-1303603	0655	1
FURUKAWA JAMES M	MAJ	O-0558193	0966	1
FUS BERNICE G	1LT	N-0730519	0646	1
FUSARO CLARENCE A	1LT	O-1042813	1045	2
FUSCO JEREMIAH A	LTC	O-1330174	0167	1
FUSELIER ALLEN J	1LT	O-1945801	0745	2
FUSELIER BURLEY P	MAJ	O-2024382	0464	1
FUSS JR CARL R	MAJ	O-0587405	0566	1
FUSS LEO J	CW2	W-2207138	0262	1
FUSSELL GEORGE W	MAJ	O-0970863	0264	1
FUSSELL HAROLD R	2LT	O-1063020	1044	2
FUSSELL JAMES R-	CPT	O-0489267	0457	1
FUSSELL JAMES R	LTC	O-1173250	0861	1
FUSSELMAN EARL C	CPT	O-1574047	1044	1
FUTCH HUBERT K	MAJ	O-2017682	0864	1
FYFFE BILLY L	MAJ	O-0994506	0364	1
FYFFE JOHN H	MAJ	O-1541401	0247	2
FYKE FRANK C	LTC	O-1698082	1060	1
FYOCK FLOYD C	CW4	W-2003628	0565	3
FYRNYS EDWARD L	MAJ	O-0319704	0965	1
GAA DONALD F	LTC	O-0289951	1263	3
GAALAAS ALBAN F	COL	O-0282836	0147	2
GABA HOWARD R	CPT	O-0560080	0146	2
GABARDI ALBERT I	1LT	O-1944683	0944	2
GABARREN GILES A	LTC	O-0391331	0860	1
GABHART EDWARD H	MAJ	O-0409875	0165	1
GABHART JAKE	MAJ	O-1290406	0867	2
GABBERT JOHN R	LTC	O-0335293	0460	1
GABEL BENJAMIN G	CW3	W-2205615	1265	1
GABEL FRANCIS S	COL	O-0284880	0658	1
GABEL GUS	LTC	O-1030660	0161	1
GABEL KURT	MAJ	O-1905383	0266	1
GABELMAN SR C G	MAJ	O-0161809	0668	3
GABERLEIN RAYMOND H	CW3	W-2168614	1164	1
GABERT LAWRENCE W	COL	O-0336839	0167	3
GABLE ELMER H	MAJ	O-0333311	1064	3
GABLE FRANK F	CPT	O-0397138	1060	1
GABLE HULETTE R	MAJ	O-0279174	0662	3
GABLE JACK M	1LT	O-1311877	0645	2
GABLE JOSEPH W	CPT	O-0171037	0456	3
GABLE LINWOOD M	COL	O-0164887	1051	1
GABLE ROMEE W	COL	O-0234277	1159	3
GABLER LOUIS	MAJ	O-0387420	1054	1
GABORSKY GODFREY V	LTC	O-0423370	0960	1
GABRIEL ALFRED R	MAJ	O-1896639	0263	1
GABRIEL CARMEN M	1LT	O-1119184	0747	2
GABRIEL CHARLES H	MAJ	O-0450156	0348	2
GABRIEL FRANK G	1LT	O-0440485	0745	2
GABRIEL JAMES C	COL	O-0220083	0455	1
GABRIEL JOHN DONAL	2LT	O-2018870	0351	2
GABRIEL NICHOLAS J	CPT	O-0413958	0346	2
GABRIEL WALTER A	CPT	O-0233766	0965	3
GABRINGER NORBERT J	2LT	O-1594940	0245	2
GABRYSCH CLAUDE J	1LT	O-1171015	0648	1

292-560 O - 68 - 11

NAME	GRADE	SVC NO	DATE RET MO YR	RET CODE
GACHAR AUGUST	CPT	0-0494134	0954	1
GACHES ROBERT A L	MAJ	0-2018500	0763	1
GACHET FRED	MAJ	0-0290914	0546	2
GACHETTE HEZEKIAH	CW2	W-2144305	1162	1
GACKOWSKI VERN A	CPT	0-1524720	0952	1
GADBERRY LUTHER C	MAJ	0-0144751	0555	3
GADD JR ROBERT F	LTC	0-0336227	1066	3
GADD RICHARD H	CPT	0-1641962	0457	1
GADD WILLIAM J	MAJ	0-2262312	0364	1
GADDIS GLEN D	1LT	0-0290809	0347	2
GADDY ERNEST C	CW3	W-2116127	0753	2
GADE MELVILLE R	LTC	0-0905526	1265	3
GADES JR FRED H	2LT	0-0530004	0845	2
GADEWOLTZ FRITZ A H	COL	0-0266797	0963	3
GADO ANTONIO L	COL	0-0181252	1051	1
GAEBLER EUGENE F	LTC	0-0174498	1152	3
GAECKLE WILLIAM H	COL	0-0041905	1060	1
GAEP WILLIAM C	CW4	W-2102918	0659	1
GAETZKE EUGENE V	CPT	0-1686784	1166	2
GAFEANEY ROBERT T	2LT	0-1309542	0545	2
GAFFEY EARL	MAJ	0-1296509	1054	1
GAFFNEY JOSEPH M	LTC	0-1640475	0763	1
GAFFNEY JR F G	CW2	W-2152341	0960	1
GAFFNEY JR JAMES J	LTC	0-0357736	1045	1
GAFFNEY LAWRENCE	1LT	0-1324015	1145	2
GAFFNEY RAYMOND A	MAJ	0-2263000	0164	1
GAFFNEY WALTER K	1LT	0-0507067	0249	1
GAFFNEY WILLIAM R	LTC	0-1002923	0662	1
GAFFORD CHARLES W	2LT	0-1031242	0451	2
GAFFORD VIRGIL S	COL	0-0211040	0552	3
GAGE EARL J	CPT	0-0488602	0246	2
GAGE EDGAR W	MAJ	0-0100507	1151	3
GAGE JOHN B	CPT	0-0452172	0746	2
GAGE JOSEPH M	LTC	0-1047976	1061	1
GAGE JR WILLIAM	CW3	W-2146367	0559	1
GAGE MORRIS V	MAJ	0-1996462	0958	1
GAGE ROBERT E	LTC	0-1306083	0363	1
GAGE WILLIAM L	COL	0-0261894	0466	3
GAGHAGEN HOWARD R	LTC	0-0150039	1057	1
GAGLIANO ANTHONY J	LTC	0-0381262	1060	1
GAGLIANO NICK G	LTC	0-1552882	0566	1
GAGNE ARMAND F J	MAJ	0-1701164	1167	1
GAGNE EMILE R	CW2	W-2105030	0250	1
GAGNER FREDERICK	MAJ	0-1553634	0367	1
GAGNON ARISTIDE	CW2	W-2120760	0352	1
GAGNON CLAYTON E	LTC	0-0401648	0661	1
GAGNON DAVID C	CPT	0-1016111	0647	2
GAGNON HOWARD A	MAJ	0-1293236	0461	1
GAGNON LORENZO A	LTC	0-0319415	1158	1
GAGNON MARIE J	2LT	N-0754446	0247	1
GAGNON NELSON C	MAJ	0-1081701	0762	1
GAGNON OMER A	MAJ	0-0973467	0662	1
GAGNON RAOUL A	CW2	W-2000105	0261	2
GAGNON VICTOR W	CPT	0-2200341	0757	2
GAHAGAN JR WALTER H	MAJ	0-0917360	0945	2
GAHAN WILLIAM J	LTC	0-0445873	0867	1
GAHNZ ELMER F	LTC	0-0276349	0363	3
GAHRING WILLIAM R	MAJ	0-0142998	0645	2
GAIBLE BENJAMIN J	2LT	0-1291976	0544	2
GAIDE JOHN F	MAJ	0-1540881	0564	1
GAIOSICK HAROLD G	LTC	0-0907625	1046	2
GAILLARD DAVID S	COL	0-0174224	0150	3
GAILLARD ELLEN L	MAJ	N-0763922	0365	1
GAILUS PAUL P	1LT	0-1541905	0145	2
GAILY JR WALTER	CW3	W-2148963	0262	1
GAIN MICHAEL L	MAJ	0-0975985	1162	1
GAINES BERNARD R	LTC	0-0348078	0450	1
GAINES CATHERINE	2LT	L-1000406	1045	2
GAINES CLARENCE L	1LT	0-1307961	0146	2
GAINES DONALD L	COL	0-0357552	0466	3
GAINES FRANK	LTC	0-0304841	0161	1
GAINES HARRY W	CPT	0-0178161	0854	3
GAINES HERMAN L	LTC	0-0169039	0261	3
GAINES KENNETH L	2LT	0-2212069	0252	1
GAINES LARRY	LTC	0-0266263	0155	2
GAINES RABUN M	MAJ	0-0450542	0457	1
GAINES ROBERT F	CPT	0-1307562	0646	2
GAINES SARAH E	MAJ	N-0726404	0566	1
GAINES SR CHARLES J	MAJ	0-0983554	0862	1
GAINES THOMAS R	LTC	0-0499304	0346	2
GAINES VIRGIL J	CPT	0-1176344	1145	1
GAINES WILLARD M	COL	0-0233697	1159	1
GAINES WILLIAM J	MAJ	0-0967862	0466	1
GAINES WILLIAM M	CW2	W-2107936	1151	1
GAINEY DAVID F	MAJ	0-1650875	1162	1
GAINEY FRANCIS J	CPT	0-0451489	0365	1
GAINEY NOEL R	CW2	W-2141285	0855	1
GAINEY REDMON R	1LT	0-1016119	0146	2
GAIRING JOHN A	LTC	0-0255074	0867	3
GAIRLOFF LESTER	MAJ	0-0958150	0366	1
GAIS ELMER S	COL	0-0442919	0746	2
GAITHER EDGAR	LTC	0-0419813	0563	1
GAITHER JR JAMES F	1LT	0-0497015	1045	2
GAITHER RALPH W	LTC	0-1286270	0764	1
GAITHER ROSCOE B	LTC	0-0292757	0954	3
GAITHER THOMAS P	LTC	0-0215975	0762	3
GAKEY JACK L	CW4	W-2150555	0562	1
GALAMBOS LOUIS	MAJ	0-1650101	1263	1
GALANG RICARDO C	LTC	0-0515082	0267	3
GALANIS HARRY W	LTC	0-1647899	0165	1
GALANTE DOMINICK A	LTC	0-1081213	0667	1
GALAWAY JR JOHN A	LTC	0-1587264	0862	1
GALBRAITH ALEXANDRIA	1LT	0-0453440	0644	1
GALBRAITH JOHN H	2LT	0-1044824	1043	2
GALBRAITH JOHN R	MAJ	0-0236625	0458	3
GALBRAITH JOSEPH M	LTC	0-0397191	0660	1
GALBRAITH LAWRENCE C	COL	0-0148671	0948	3
GALBRAITH LEO L	MAJ	0-0229769	0164	3
GALBRAITH WILLIAM J	LTC	0-0152179	0757	3
GALBREATH CHARLES S	MAJ	0-0372084	0745	2
GALBREATH JOHN C	LTC	0-0227398	0962	3
GALBREATH JR PAUL	MAJ	0-1290175	0163	2
GALBREATH LOYAL T	LTC	0-0248641	0566	3
GALBRONER HOMER C	COL	0-0144637	0857	3
GALE BERNARD G	CPT	0-1594175	0561	1
GALE CHARLES H	CW3	W-2148532	0659	1
GALE DAVID M	LTC	0-1533784	0361	1
GALE DEAN S	LTC	0-1049164	1061	1
GALE HOWARD C	LTC	0-1648063	1262	1
GALE JAMES M	COL	0-0456469	0767	1
GALE JOHN J	1LT	0-1592206	1045	2
GALE MILES W	CPT	0-1295777	1047	2
GALE STANLEY H	2LT	0-1060095	0245	2
GALE THOMAS L	MAJ	0-1002924	0858	1
GALE WALTER C	CPT	0-0309889	0245	2
GALE WALTER R	1LT	0-1327728	0450	1
GALE WILLIAM P	LTC	0-0416089	0650	1
GALEAZZI LEO J	2LT	0-1590475	0151	2
GALER ROBERT F	LTC	0-0392177	0165	1
GALES ARTHUR M	CW2	W-2147905	0761	1
GALES RICHARD C	COL	0-1011147	0367	1
GALFUND ALLEN W	LTC	0-2020280	1067	1
GALIANO MICHAEL C	R G	0-0269138	0666	3
GALIFFA WARREN V	MAJ	0-1120149	0164	1
GALIGHER THOMAS W	COL	0-0257523	0566	3
GALIPEAU DORIUS P	MAJ	0-0964360	0865	1
GALITELO PETER D	CW3	W-2144736	1166	1
GALL ANDREW L	LTC	0-1322632	0961	1
GALL EDWIN A	2LT	0-1313589	0245	2
GALL EWALD A	LTC	0-0163832	0953	3
GALL JOHN	LTC	0-1176633	0562	1
GALLACHER A J	CW2	W-2153191	0161	1
GALLAGHER ALICE H	MAJ	N-0700779	1146	1
GALLAGHER ANTHONY B	MAJ	0-1369116	0261	1
GALLAGHER ARTHUR R	COL	0-0319759	0767	3
GALLAGHER C E	CPT	0-0443350	0951	1
GALLAGHER C J H	1LT	0-0921330	0844	2
GALLAGHER DANIEL P	COL	0-1102136	0765	1
GALLAGHER DONALD J	MAJ	0-0963623	0466	1
GALLAGHER EDWARD	LTC	0-1796068	0766	3
GALLAGHER EDWARD F	LTC	0-0109712	0648	1
GALLAGHER EDWARD W	CW2	W-2146899	0463	1
GALLAGHER FRANCIS J	MAJ	0-0138093	0648	3
GALLAGHER FRANCIS J	1LT	0-2011676	0248	1
GALLAGHER FRANK	CPT	0-0488953	1044	2
GALLAGHER FRED R	CPT	0-1305566	0947	2
GALLAGHER HARRY L	LTC	0-0450736	0457	1
GALLAGHER HIRAM	MAJ	0-0312932	0546	2
GALLAGHER HOWARD J J	2LT	0-2037281	0546	2
GALLAGHER HUGH E	1LT	0-2049247	0846	2
GALLAGHER HUGH T	1LT	0-1580977	0744	2
GALLAGHER IRVING F	CPT	0-1588349	1046	2
GALLAGHER JAMES B	1LT	0-1011435	1045	2
GALLAGHER JAMES F	1LT	0-1697981	0763	1
GALLAGHER JAMES J	LTC	0-1061401	0146	1
GALLAGHER JAMES R	LTC	0-0522744	1055	1
GALLAGHER JAMES S	COL	0-0174034	0653	3
GALLAGHER JAMES T	LTC	0-1049483	0765	1
GALLAGHER JAMES T	CW2	W-2151787	0661	1
GALLAGHER JAMES W	CPT	0-2033625	0357	1
GALLAGHER JOHN J	2LT	0-0887354	0245	2
GALLAGHER JOHN J	CPT	0-1913686	1020	1
GALLAGHER JOSEPH G	LTC	0-1185790	0964	1
GALLAGHER JR T J	1LT	0-1057094	0247	2
GALLAGHER KENNETH N	LTC	0-2049800	0762	1
GALLAGHER LAVERGNE A	CW4	W-2141562	1058	1
GALLAGHER LAWRENCE J	CPT	0-2020413	0861	2
GALLAGHER M T	CPT	N-0760303	0846	1
GALLAGHER MARTIN L	MAJ	0-0446954	1045	1
GALLAGHER MICHAEL J	LTC	0-0454058	1165	1
GALLAGHER PATRICK J	LTC	0-0328002	0263	2
GALLAGHER PAUL	COL	0-0218280	0248	2
GALLAGHER PAUL L	MAJ	0-1303134	0463	1
GALLAGHER PHILIP N	LTC	0-0297775	0957	1
GALLAGHER THOMAS F	MAJ	0-4009811	0866	1
GALLAGHER THOMAS H	LTC	0-1291454	0566	1
GALLAGHER THOMAS J	1LT	0-1102565	0344	2
GALLAGHER WILLIAM	MAJ	0-0203210	1045	1
GALLAGHER WILLIAM F	LTC	0-0244098	0461	3
GALLAGHER WILLIAM F	1LT	0-2035420	1145	2
GALLAGHER WILLIAM G	CW2	W-2146507	0557	1
GALLAGHER WILLIAM J	LTC	0-1173956	0765	2
GALLAHER ELMER L	CW2	W-2150088	0363	1
GALLAMORE ROBERT F	1LT	0-2064200	0259	2
GALLAND MICHAEL R	1LT	0-0342991	1041	2
GALLANT EDWARD J	CPT	0-2033591	0857	1
GALLANT FRANCIS X	LTC	0-0409334	0860	1
GALLANT GEORGE W	MAJ	0-1109308	0265	1
GALLANT JOHN H	LTC	0-1635907	1058	1
GALLANT JOSEPH A	CW3	W-2144547	0162	1
GALLANT JOSEPH H	CPT	0-1299225	1263	1
GALLANT STEVEN H	LTC	0-1115590	0363	1
GALLARDO FRED F	2LT	0-1896763	0955	1
GALLARDO HORTENSE M	1LT	N-0735341	0247	1
GALLAUDET JOHN B	CPT	0-0910949	0845	2
GALLEGOS CAESAR A	CW3	W-2109270	0745	2
GALLEGOS CARLOS V	LTC	0-0257361	0663	3
GALLENA JOSEPH A	LTC	0-0441998	0965	1
GALLERO RAMON	2LT	0-1896699	1157	1
GALLERT EARL W	MAJ	0-1032707	0764	1
GALLET LARRY	CPT	0-1042028	0146	2
GALLETTE HENRY A	MAJ	0-0279451	0855	3
GALLIK JOSEPH J	LTC	0-0288569	0857	1
GALLINA JOSEPH O	LTC	0-1175441	0960	2
GALLINOTO MICHAEL R	LTC	0-1043635	0164	1
GALLION RALPH C	CW4	W-2148114	0564	1
GALLIONE FREDERIC W	LTC	0-0288485	0464	3
GALLIVAN III JOHN O	LTC	0-0865304	0264	1
GALLMAN ALVIN	MAJ	0-2030827	1059	1
GALLMAN HARRY E	LTC	0-1296314	0761	1
GALLMAN JOSEPH E	MAJ	0-0214937	0961	3
GALLO JR SALVATORE	MAJ	0-0571726	1060	1
GALLO WILLIAM H	CPT	0-1114492	1163	1
GALLOF JACK	MAJ	0-4021800	1165	1
GALLOGLY LAWRENCE V	MAJ	0-1319272	0964	1
GALLOTTE WILLARD A	LTC	0-0301592	0462	3
GALLOWAY ARTHUR L	LTC	0-1549273	0861	1
GALLOWAY DOW I	CW2	W-2101722	0347	1
GALLOWAY ENGLAND L	MAJ	0-2262696	0961	1
GALLOWAY ERNEST W	LTC	0-0264844	0663	3
GALLOWAY FRANK R	LTC	0-0404360	0646	2
GALLOWAY JAMES L	LTC	0-1550378	0457	1
GALLOWAY JOHN H	COL	0-0905301	1062	3
GALLOWAY JOSEPH S	1LT	0-1283407	0744	1
GALLOWAY JR HARVEY J	MAJ	0-0975085	1155	2
GALLOWAY PAUL W	CW2	RW-2152638	0961	1
GALLOWAY RAY L	1LT	0-2016356	0349	1
GALLOWAY ROBERT E	MAJ	0-0900703	0359	1
GALLOWAY SR WARREN P	LTC	0-1341961	0967	1
GALLOWAY VERNON H	CW3	W-2144379	0557	1
GALLOWAY WALTER G	MAJ	0-0311007	1044	2
GALLOWAY WILLIAM H	CPT	0-1643570	0946	1
GALLOWAY WILLIAM S	1LT	0-1116662	0746	2
GALLUCCIO ANTHONY C	MAJ	0-0242358	1045	2
GALLUP EARLE H	MAJ	0-1315421	0965	1
GALO JR GEORGE	2LT	0-1305037	0944	2
GALOT JOHN J	CPT	0-0498899	0949	1
GALPERIN LEON	LTC	0-1171153	1161	1
GALPIN ROBERT E	MAJ	0-2023894	0759	1
GALSTER BERNARD L	1LT	0-1323825	1046	1
GALT HENRY T	LTC	0-0222353	0964	3
GALUSAKA ANDREW J	MAJ	0-1548795	1157	1
GALUSKA EDWARD L	CW3	W-2150912	0265	1
GALVAN ALONZO M	CW4	W-2109056	1054	1
GALVAN ANTONIO J	MAJ	0-2030994	0764	1
GALVIN JACK P	MAJ	0-1010312	0548	1
GALVIN JOHN R	2LT	0-1331386	0346	2
GALVIN JR JOHN F	CPT	0-0462152	0745	2
GALVIN WILLIAM J	COL	0-0105776	0757	3
GALWAY RICHARD E	LTC	0-0347043	0265	1
GALYEN RICHARD L	CW3	W-2147873	1064	1
GALYON WALTER O	LTC	0-1595515	0766	1
GAMACHE PAUL L	LTC	0-1016069	0463	1
GAMACHE ROMEO J	COL	0-0426506	0964	1
GAMACK CHARLES A	CW2	W-3100529	0167	1
GAMARA NORBERT J	1LT	0-0923302	1044	2
GAMAS HORACE F	MAJ	0-2035421	1160	1
GAMBA JOSEPH	CPT	0-0491601	0844	2
GAMBEE JAMES J	COL	0-0261957	0164	3
GAMBERT CHARLES A	1LT	0-0930835	0547	1
GAMBERT LAWRENCE	CPT	0-0378840	1044	2
GAMBILL JOSEPH F	CPT	0-2041100	0547	1
GAMBILL MELBURN H	LTC	0-1328024	1262	1
GAMBINO RALPH R	CW2	W-2210738	0566	1
GAMBLE ALEXANDER	CPT	0-1310094	0348	1
GAMBLE CHARLES F	LTC	0-0917032	0467	3
GAMBLE DAVID S	LTC	0-0380397	1054	1
GAMBLE FRED R	1LT	0-1316286	1045	1
GAMBLE JR WILLIAM O	MAJ	0-0237366	1164	3
GAMBLE SAMUEL H	LTC	0-0238646	0465	3
GAMBLE SHELBY V	CPT	0-0109714	0844	2
GAMBLE WILLIAM A	MAJ	0-0177589	0654	3
GAMBLE WILLIAM F	MAJ	0-0792905	0864	1
GAMBOA EARNESTO A	CPT	0-1878770	1163	1
GAMBOA GEORGE T	1LT	0-1896653	0349	1
GAMBRELL JAMES H	LTC	0-0416093	0866	1
GAMBRELL RAY N	MAJ	0-0358121	0752	1
GAMBRELL ROBERT L	LTC	0-1292501	0964	1
GAMEL JAMES B	LTC	0-1296846	1166	1
GAMES WILLIAM J	LTC	0-2020014	0666	1
GAMM STANFORD T	1LT	0-1553635	0845	2
GAMMIE THOMAS G	LTC	0-0142259	1152	3
GAMMILL EVAN D	LTC	0-0450281	1057	1
GAMMILL LEE C	COL	0-0194428	0858	3
GAMMILL VINCENT M	1LT	0-1581727	0645	2
GAMMINO JOSEPH	WO1	W-2119896	0348	1
GAMMON EDWARD A	MAJ	0-1179861	0860	1
GAMMON FRANCIS D	CPT	0-0275632	0661	3
GAMMON FRANK M	CW2	W-2142746	0259	1
GAMMON ROBERT W	1LT	0-1998711	0945	2

NAME	GRADE	SVC NO	DATE RET MO YR	RET CODE
GAMWELL RICHARD L	MAJ	C-0383544	C745	2
GANDY CHARLES V	LTC	0-1548796	0461	1
GANDY JR THOMAS A	LTC	C-0401052	0764	1
GANE JOHN W	LTC	0-0488204	0363	1
GANEAU WILFRID F	LTC	0-1295864	C565	1
GANELLAS CONSTANTIN	CPT	0-0286913	0962	3
GANER GEORGE J	LTC	0-0354766	0463	1
GANEY JEROME	CW3	W-2207586	0766	1
GANG CARLOS D	LTC	0-1553813	0862	1
GANGE HAROLD H	LTC	0-0250550	0665	3
GANGNATH IRVIN T	CW3	W-2142703	C761	1
GANIO GINO	1LT	C-1012268	C746	2
GANN BRENT L	CPT	0-1283581	1147	2
GANN HENRY	MAJ	0-1689484	G146	2
GANN RUFUS J	MAJ	0-1325083	C561	1
GANN WILLIAM C	CW3	RW-2146325	C465	1
GANNARELLI JAMES	CW3	W-2205420	C464	1
GANNON EDWIN T	CW3	W-2150793	1262	1
GANNON EUGENE R	1LT	0-1172458	0746	2
GANNON JOHN E	LTC	0-0502095	C163	1
GANNON JOHN F	MAJ	C-0234673	0348	2
GANNON JOHN P	MAJ	C-0930712	1262	1
GANNON JOSEPH J	LTC	0-1637479	0962	1
GANNON JR THOMAS F	MAJ	0-2009698	106C	1
GANNON ROBERT L	LTC	0-1947993	1064	1
GANNON THOMAS P	LTC	0-1300017	C761	1
GANNON WENDELL C	LTC	0-0420887	1265	1
GANNON WILLIAM J	CPT	C-0408495	0446	2
GANO HERMAN C	CW2	W-2211120	1166	1
GANOUS BONNIE T	1LT	0-1301129	C246	2
GANOW GLEN C	LTC	0-1169971	1061	1
GANS EDWARD J	CPT	0-1036991	0656	1
GANSEL ROBERT W	MAJ	C-1599085	0963	1
GANT WILLIAM T	MAJ	C-0969392	C865	1
GANTENBEIN EARL D	CPT	C-0407268	C346	2
GANTER LEWIS E	MAJ	0-1633232	C466	1
GANTOS ALEX L	CW2	W-2209840	C561	1
GANTT BOB	CPT	0-0228668	C344	1
GANTT FRANK E	LTC	0-0352994	1266	1
GANTT GEORGE B	LTC	0-0335960	1263	3
GANTT HOUSTON H	MAJ	C-2011789	1060	1
GANTZ CHARLES F	CPT	C-1944450	C357	1
GANTZ MAURICE H	MAJ	0-0299813	C145	2
GANZ CARL D	LTC	0-0211981	0351	3
GAPINSKI WESLEY	1LT	0-0888571	0760	1
GARABEDIAN VAUGHAN	1LT	0-0401351	0945	2
GARAMELLA MICHAEL A	1LT	C-1040716	0945	1
GARBARINI URSULA B	2LT	L-0200199	C744	2
GARBARINO VICTOR J	COL	0-0171767	1059	1
GARBE JOE A	COL	0-1588573	C864	1
GARBER ALFRED E	LTC	0-0116941	0552	3
GARBER EDWARD E	CPT	0-1776271	0646	2
GARBER HOWARD A	LTC	0-0293404	1167	3
GARBER JACOB S	CPT	0-1689514	1045	2
GARBER JOSEPH	LTC	0-0296277	1066	3
GARBER LYNN L	MAJ	L-0401565	C563	1
GARBER MITCHEL W	1LT	0-1117861	C146	2
GARBER PAUL E	CPT	0-2263359	0762	1
GARBETT JOSEPH F	2LT	0-1914111	0138	1
GARBOW PHILIP	WO1	W-2148447	1053	1
GARCELON RAYMOND F	LTC	0-1633874	C261	1
GARCHIE RICHARD	CPT	0-1920310	1264	1
GARCIA AUGUSTO M	MAJ	C-0242797	C156	3
GARCIA BINO F	LTC	0-1587989	C665	1
GARCIA EDWARD V	COL	C-0173369	0947	2
GARCIA FELIX	MAJ	C-1031642	0860	1
GARCIA GREGORIO N	LTC	0-1574427	1054	1
GARCIA HECTOR D	MAJ	C-1541895	C259	1
GARCIA HERMAN	MAJ	C-1795031	1060	1
GARCIA JOSE	CPT	0-0250736	0145	2
GARCIA MIGUEL A	1LT	0-0450182	1145	2
GARCIA NICK D	MAJ	0-2006516	1262	1
GARCIA OBALDO	MAJ	C-1046808	0956	1
GARCIA RAFAEL A	CPT	0-0371330	116C	1
GARCIA ROBERTO R	MAJ	C-4031302	C867	1

NAME	GRADE	SVC NO	DATE RET MO YR	RET CODE
GARCIA SADY	MAJ	C-2263319	1061	1
GARCINA GEORGE M	1LT	0-0396551	1044	2
GARD JOHN I	MAJ	0-0451104	0657	1
GARD RAYMOND A	CW2	W-2147066	0459	1
GARD WILLIAM H	MAJ	0-1036992	0661	1
GARDELLA LEROY	MAJ	0-1699965	0663	1
GARDEN ALLAN C	LTC	0-0118650	1044	2
GARDEN HENRY R	MAJ	0-0175770	0360	3
GARDEN HENRY J	MAJ	0-1591735	0862	1
GARDENIER CHARLES K	LTC	0-0565405	C561	2
GARDENIER ROBERT C	LTC	0-1340548	0667	1
GARDINER ELMER W	LTC	0-1011556	0866	1
GARDINER ESTHER S	2LT	N-0745088	1043	1
GARDINER EVERETT E	LTC	0-0404662	0865	3
GARDINER GEORGE W	COL	0-0194699	1055	1
GARDINER HAROLD E	WO1	W-2112584	1147	1
GARDINER HAROLD W	COL	0-0210080	0463	3
GARDINER JAMES F W	LTC	0-0497653	0762	1
GARDINER JOHN F	LTC	0-0107035	C747	2
GARDINER WILLIAM P	WO1	W-2145181	0853	2
GARDNER AGNES R	LTC	N-0741199	0162	1
GARDNER ALLAN M	CPT	0-0290542	0465	2
GARDNER ANNETTE A	CPT	N-0762561	1154	2
GARDNER ARCHIE T	MAJ	0-0493272	0554	1
GARDNER CHARLES F	MAJ	C-1946C58	0550	1
GARDNER CHARLES H	B G	0-0273050	0967	3
GARDNER CLINTON G	1LT	0-0444549	1146	2
GARDNER DAVID O	1LT	0-1824299	1045	2
GARDNER DONALD L	MAJ	0-1297349	0560	1
GARDNER EARLE F	LTC	0-1184050	1062	1
GARDNER EDGAR W	WO1	W-2109221	0147	2
GARDNER EDWIN L	1LT	0-1319943	1045	2
GARDNER ELDON C	1LT	0-1319273	1C45	2
GARDNER EUGENE	MAJ	0-0990521	0365	1
GARDNER FRANK E	CPT	0-0970535	1161	1
GARDNER FRANKLIN T	LTC	0-0277457	0545	2
GARDNER FREDERICK	LTC	0-0386747	0463	1
GARDNER GEORGE F	1LT	0-1014813	1145	2
GARDNER GEORGE W	MAJ	C-1313392	0862	1
GARDNER HARRISON W	MAJ	0-0221677	0149	3
GARDNER HARRY B	LTC	0-1031807	0461	1
GARDNER HAZEL M	MAJ	N-0799010	0665	1
GARDNER HOWARD K	COL	0-0213846	0362	3
GARDNER HUGH H	LTC	0-1321300	0766	3
GARDNER JESS L	CPT	0-1019144	0947	1
GARDNER JESSE E	MAJ	0-1582832	0463	1
GARDNER JESSE J	LTC	0-0186174	0354	3
GARDNER JOHN J	CPT	0-1010575	0158	1
GARDNER JOHN L	LTC	0-1685725	0967	1
GARDNER JOHN N	1LT	0-0352056	0744	2
GARDNER JOSEPH M	2LT	0-1281157	0645	2
GARDNER JR DONALD R	CW4	W-2117283	C659	1
GARDNER JR FRANK H	1LT	0-0954783	1152	1
GARDNER JR JOHN P	LTC	0-1285738	0862	1
GARDNER KENNETH S	CW2	W-2151724	0762	1
GARDNER KENNETH W	LTC	0-0225595	0961	3
GARDNER LAMAR W	CPT	0-0265535	C146	2
GARDNER LEE H	CPT	0-0402910	C161	1
GARDNER LOUISE H	2LT	N-0767536	0744	1
GARDNER MADISON D	MAJ	0-2055279	1163	1
GARDNER MAN D	CPT	0-0202061	0863	3
GARDNER MICHAEL C	CPT	0-1894768	0161	2
GARDNER MILO S	LTC	0-0360427	0556	1
GARDNER MOFFAT A	MAJ	C-1340178	0263	1
GARDNER NORD A	LTC	0-0935348	0766	1
GARDNER ORVILLE K	LTC	0-0904141	0163	1
GARDNER PAUL H	CPT	0-0248890	0865	3
GARDNER ROBERT	MAJ	0-2262365	1163	1
GARDNER ROBERT A	LTC	0-0271404	0667	3
GARDNER ROBERT E	LTC	0-0217424	0551	3
GARDNER ROBERT P	LTC	0-0260518	1060	1
GARDNER ROBERT W	CPT	0-0512903	0346	1
GARDNER ROY E	MAJ	0-0221515	0955	3
GARDNER SIDNEY M	MAJ	0-0323625	0746	1
GARDNER WARREN F	CPT	0-0450343	1146	1

NAME	GRADE	SVC NO	DATE RET MO YR	RET CODE
GARDNER WESTON O	CPT	0-C470064	0845	2
GARDNER WILLIAM A	MAJ	0-0414327	1047	2
GARDNER WILLIAM B	MAJ	C-0444333	C447	1
GARDNER WILLIAM C	CPT	0-1051153	1055	1
GARDNER WILLIAM F	2LT	0-0504854	C845	2
GARDNER WILLIAM H	LTC	0-0546538	0863	1
GARDNER WILLIAM J	1LT	0-0890399	C849	1
GARDNER WILLIAM L	LTC	0-0250100	0146	2
GARDNER WILLIAM M	CPT	0-0185472	C747	2
GARDNER WILLIAM M	LTC	C-1055300	1162	1
GARDNER WILLIAM R	CW2	W-2107890	1053	1
GARDZINA EDWARD J	CW3	W-2145961	0664	1
GARE JOHN P	LTC	0-0332509	0765	3
GAREN JOSEPH F	MAJ	C-0252416	0467	3
GAREY ALVA E	COL	C-0154723	0648	3
GAREY GERARD S	CPT	0-0455407	0545	2
GAREY PHILIP	COL	0-0242064	1046	2
GARFIELD JAMES S	COL	0-0163794	0356	3
GARFIELD MELVIN G	1LT	0-1556722	0146	2
GARFIELD MORRIS	MAJ	0-0332401	C157	1
GARFIELD SEYMOUR F	CPT	0-1586590	C858	1
GARGAN MICHAEL T	CW2	W-2152046	C656	1
GARGANO HENRY N	1LT	0-1014072	1045	2
GARGARO ISADORE A	LTC	0-1574234	C163	1
GARGUILO ALFRED V	2LT	0-1301467	C245	2
GARGUREVICH LUKE T	CW2	W-2148292	0463	1
GARIBALDI LINN D	COL	0-0268031	0766	3
GARICK LAWRENCE T	CPT	0-0377373	C546	2
GARIEPY JR GEORGE H	LTC	0-0454612	C960	2
GARIGAN JR THOMAS P	CPT	0-1104674	0662	1
GARILLI HERBERT J	CPT	0-0317679	0745	2
GARINGER TRUMAN O	LTC	C-0257247	C751	3
GARLAND CYRUS G	MAJ	C-2020937	1162	1
GARLAND EDMUND S	COL	C-0263902	0155	3
GARLAND HOWARD Y	CW3	W-2149433	C465	1
GARLAND KENNETH D	CW2	W-3200139	0363	1
GARLAND MALVIN M	CPT	0-1100996	1046	2
GARLAND MAX L	MAJ	0-1165292	0557	1
GARLAND MYRTLE F	1LT	N-0726029	C846	1
GARLAND PAUL P	CW4	W-2114721	0764	3
GARLAND TEA	1LT	0-2006435	C456	1
GARLAND WILLIAM F	CW2	W-2147756	0158	1
GARLAND WILLIAM H	2LT	0-1081474	0645	2
GARLINER JACOB	CPT	0-0302903	1043	2
GARLINGER JOHN H	2LT	0-1169972	0144	2
GARLOCK EUGENE N	CW3	W-2146730	1060	1
GARLOCK FRED C	LTC	0-0253021	C665	3
GARLOCK JOHN R	LTC	0-1580984	0361	1
GARLOCK LEON M	MAJ	C-0973239	0463	1
GARLOCK SCHELLER L	MAJ	0-2000680	0561	1
GARMAN ROBERT L	CPT	0-0985575	1267	1
GARMENT EDWARD M	LTC	0-0369265	0166	3
GARMON HARRY H	LTC	C-0902124	C664	3
GARNAR THOMAS F	MAJ	0-0160581	1050	3
GARNEAU GASTON O	MAJ	0-1300787	C466	3
GARNER ARTHUR L	COL	0-0333679	1053	1
GARNER BLAINE W	1LT	0-1824450	1045	2
GARNER CARL	CW4	W-2101724	C259	1
GARNER GEORGE F	LTC	0-1036994	0762	1
GARNER GERVAIS J	COL	0-0405165	C848	2
GARNER HARRISON L	COL	0-0156793	0648	3
GARNER JACK G	LTC	0-1302451	C467	1
GARNER JAMES A	MAJ	C-0414328	1046	2
GARNER JAMES A	CW3	W-2207564	0166	1
GARNER JAMES O	LTC	0-0497951	0756	1
GARNER JAMES G	1LT	0-1291455	C346	2
GARNER JESSE A	MAJ	0-1297022	1060	1
GARNER JESSE P	CPT	0-0492339	1053	1
GARNER JOHN E	LTC	0-0916854	1162	1
GARNER JOHN J	COL	0-0242264	0954	3
GARNER JR ERNEST	MAJ	C-1120398	1263	1
GARNER JR GEORGE F	1LT	0-1637484	1048	2
GARNER JR INGRAM E	LTC	0-1592209	C365	1
GARNER JR PORTER S	1LT	0-0558276	C846	2
GARNER LAWTON F	COL	0-0240272	1161	1

NAME	GRADE	SVC NO	DATE RET MO YR	RET CODE
GARNER PASCAL G	MAJ	0-0490577	0154	1
GARNER PAUL N	LTC	0-1167429	0364	1
GARNER RICHARD F	MAJ	0-1935023	0966	1
GARNER SAMUEL B	LTC	0-0261309	0267	3
GARNER W H	LTC	0-0452038	0860	1
GARNER WILLIAM H	CPT	0-1286753	0645	2
GARNER WILLIAM M	CPT	0-1284316	0745	2
GARNETT EARL E	CW3	W-2205982	1164	2
GARNETT JAMES W	CW3	W-2149949	0364	1
GARNETT JR ROBERT J	1LT	0-1312536	0161	2
GARNHAM CHARLES W	CPT	0-1306263	1047	2
GARR MORRIS H	WO1	W-2149895	1051	1
GARRABRANT WILLIAM A	CPT	0-1013305	0963	1
GARRARD LEON A	1LT	0-4029307	0656	2
GARRETSON WILTON B	LTC	0-0293996	0662	1
GARRETT BECKHAM	CPT	0-0270740	0366	3
GARRETT BENJAMIN G	MAJ	0-0236755	0365	3
GARRETT BILL H	LTC	0-0959295	0967	1
GARRETT CHARLES A	1LT	0-2206749	0753	1
GARRETT CHARLES B	MAJ	0-0266606	0259	3
GARRETT CHARLES S	LTC	0-0111959	0246	2
GARRETT CHARLES W	CPT	0-2013983	0756	2
GARRETT DAVID R R	MAJ	0-0199515	0357	1
GARRETT EDGAR E	CPT	0-1320835	1047	2
GARRETT EMIL G	LTC	0-1103646	0366	1
GARRETT FELIX B	CW2	W-3150921	0766	1
GARRETT FRANKLIN H	MAJ	0-0267192	0556	3
GARRETT FREDERICK	CPT	0-1639064	0657	1
GARRETT GEORGE C	LTC	0-0428639	0662	1
GARRETT GEORGE E	LTC	0-044211C	0963	3
GARRETT GEORGE E C	LTC	0-0125752	1052	3
GARRETT GORDON H	LTC	0-0256021	1067	3
GARRETT HARRY W	MAJ	0-1878961	0267	1
GARRETT HERBERT K	MAJ	0-1103175	0953	1
GARRETT HOMER F	LTC	0-0383C47	0762	1
GARRETT HUGH W	MAJ	0-1286471	0159	1
GARRETT JAMES E	LTC	0-0226620	0646	2
GARRETT JESSE H	LTC	0-0205339	1154	3
GARRETT JOHN B	1LT	0-0498432	0645	2
GARRETT JR STEINER D	1LT	0-0522926	1045	2
GARRETT LEN J	LTC	0-1546988	1162	1
GARRETT MAHLON C	CPT	0-0231069	0463	3
GARRETT MARVIN D	MAJ	0-2067447	0660	1
GARRETT MORRIS G	LTC	0-1294648	1165	3
GARRETT ROBERT W	LTC	0-0251705	0966	3
GARRETT ROY C	CPT	0-0365225	0144	2
GARRETT SEXTUS D	MAJ	0-0477937	0744	2
GARRETT VERN T	CW3	W-2146241	1062	1
GARRETT WILLARD M	MAJ	0-1302452	0264	2
GARRICH ALAIN A	CW3	W-2152376	1163	1
GARRICK DAVID	MAJ	0-0319874	1044	1
GARRICK DAVID	CW4	W-2134418	0959	1
GARRICK KATHERINE	2LT	N-0732644	0343	1
GARRIGAN GEORGE A	LTC	0-0155C85	0654	3
GARRIGAN ROBERT F	LTC	0-0516798	0367	3
GARRIOTT COLBY I	CW2	W-2144602	0558	1
GARRISON ADELINE	2LT	N-0732458	1043	1
GARRISON DAVID W	1LT	0-1116951	0665	2
GARRISON DONAL D	CW2	W-2214622	0667	1
GARRISON DONALD L	1LT	0-1301468	1046	1
GARRISON DWIGHT	COL	C-0103221	0955	3
GARRISON EDWARD B	1LT	0-0969908	0153	1
GARRISON H R	CPT	0-1584242	0757	1
GARRISON HALSEY E	LTC	0-0286635	1054	3
GARRISON HARRY J	1LT	0-1290585	0745	2
GARRISON JAMES E	CW4	W-2003444	0266	1
GARRISON JOHN O	LTC	0-1284493	0161	1
GARRISON JOSEPH D	COL	0-0194996	0259	3
GARRISON JR DAVID M	CPT	0-1166068	0146	2
GARRISON JR JOHN J	LTC	0-0233118	0865	3
GARRISON NOLAND R	CPT	0-0915206	0348	2
GARRISON RAYMOND W	CPT	0-2263246	0962	1
GARRISON ROBERT H	COL	0-0247352	0267	3
GARRISON SAMUEL T	CPT	0-0491008	0845	2
GARRISON SR EDWIN E	CW3	W-2141563	0860	1

ARMY OF THE UNITED STATES RETIRED LIST

NAME	GRADE	SVC NO	DATE RET MO YR	RET CODE
GARRISON WALLACE P	LTC	0-1169525	C764	1
GARRISON WENDELL L	MAJ	0-0397778	C554	2
GARRISON WILLIAM F	CW2	W-2146583	0964	1
GARRISON X LEWELL	MAJ	0-0358686	C544	2
GARROD THEODORE A	MAJ	0-1102735	C157	1
GARROTTO JOSEPH P	LTC	0-1291257	1163	1
GARSETT JOHN M	CPT	0-158799C	0147	2
GARSON BARNETT	1LT	C-1586591	1045	2
GARSON JOHN	MAJ	0-1798468	0859	1
GARST RUTH R	MAJ	L-0400650	0163	1
GARSTAD EARL A	CW3	W-2141848	0258	1
GARTEN CHARLES E	MAJ	0-0488711	C155	1
GARTEN GERALD W	COL	C-0242079	0159	1
GARTH JR JAMES H	MAJ	C-2019582	1160	1
GARTLAND ARTHUR V	1LT	0-1112163	C246	2
GARTLAND JAMES B	CW3	W-2144748	0960	1
GARTLAND JAMES M	CPT	0-1646191	1146	2
GARTMAN EDWARD	COL	0-04864C5	1067	2
GARTNER FRED W	LTC	0-0242447	0663	3
GARTNER LEONARD G	LTC	C-0203615	C648	3
GARTON FLOYD E	LTC	0-0263795	1162	3
GARTON WILLIAM H	LTC	0-0336348	C463	2
GARTZKE GRAHAM O	CPT	0-0364902	0544	2
GARTZKE OPAL M	2LT	N-0733712	0345	1
GARVER ARTHUR S	LTC	0-0451105	1057	1
GARVER CARTER O	LTC	C-0245114	1246	1
GARVER CLYDE V	CPT	0-2012475	0658	1
GARVER HAROLD W	1LT	0-1286472	0448	1
GARVER JOHN T	LTC	0-1000566	0856	1
GARVER LESLIE A	MAJ	C-2262760	0163	1
GARVEY ARTHUR P	COL	0-0124950	C856	3
GARVEY DONN E	CPT	0-1285923	0745	2
GARVEY JOHN C	MAJ	C-1030662	C259	2
GARVEY JOHN W	MAJ	C-0512207	0657	1
GARVEY JR RAYMOND E	LTC	0-1111069	0962	1
GARVEY JR RAYMOND T	LTC	0-1543908	0961	1
GARVEY MARGARET A	MAJ	N-0761326	1163	2
GARVEY ROBERT J P	CPT	0-1114498	0746	2
GARVEY THOMAS A	1LT	0-1294454	C145	2
GARVEY VICTOR O	CW2	W-2150942	C659	1
GARVEY WILLIS A	CPT	0-0182097	1054	3
GARVILLE ARMAND J	1LT	0-1054580	1046	2
GARVIN ALBERT E	LTC	0-0222073	C449	3
GARVIN ARTHUR R	MAJ	C-0375918	C263	1
GARVIN JAMES E	MAJ	C-0990700	1264	1
GARVIN JAMES J	MAJ	C-0255129	C559	3
GARVIN JAMES M	1LT	0-1031243	C945	2
GARVIN JR WILLIAM C	1LT	0-0493876	0953	1
GARVIN PAUL C	1LT	0-1287691	0145	2
GARVIS HAROLD C	LTC	0-0264077	C462	3
GARWICK KENNETH S	CW4	W-2108296	0960	1
GARWOOD HAROLD W	LTC	0-0185939	0754	3
GARWOOD PAUL S	LTC	0-0247635	1166	3
GARY GORDON S	COL	0-0335737	C760	1
GARY HENRY G	CPT	0-1113698	0246	1
GARY JAMES R	1LT	0-1287692	0645	2
GARY JOSEPH E	LTC	C-0367749	1062	1
GARY KATHERINE	LTC	N-0759255	C863	3
GARY MICHAEL J	MAJ	C-1307535	0860	1
GARY THOMAS H	CPT	0-0378157	1045	2
GARZA ARTHUR	MAJ	C-1684948	C764	1
GARZA JOE L	CW3	W-2146330	1262	1
GARZA JR ISMAEL H	CPT	0-15473C3	1047	2
GARZARELLI RICHARD L	LTC	C-1295196	0566	1
GASATAYA FREDERICK	2LT	0-1896546	C362	1
GASCHEN MONROE L	LTC	0-1552068	1061	1
GASIOROWSKI THOMAS	LTC	0-0338134	1049	1
GASKE JOHN M	LTC	0-0405460	0862	1
GASKE MARION M	1LT	N-0758467	1046	1
GASKILL EARNEST R	CPT	0-1995256	0550	1
GASKILL HAROLD E	LTC	0-0268714	1266	3
GASKILL JAMES E	MAJ	0-0971821	0963	1
GASKILL JOHN H	1LT	0-0299747	0942	2
GASKILL PETER C	LTC	0-0508290	0164	3
GASKIN HUBERT W	CW3	W-2147795	1061	1

NAME	GRADE	SVC NO	DATE RET MO YR	RET CODE
GASKIN JR HUBERT S	CPT	0-2033256	0763	1
GASKINS DOUGLAS A	CW2	W-2112277	C750	1
GASKINS ORVILLE A	CW3	W-2146711	0162	1
GASKO JOSEPH J	CW4	W-2147425	1158	1
GASMAN ERLING	MAJ	C-0278776	1058	3
GASPER FRANK J	LTC	0-1934207	0666	2
GASS ROBERT H	MAJ	0-1103647	0259	1
GASS VIRGIL J	LTC	0-0406810	0164	1
GASSEL JACOB	2LT	0-1914189	1048	1
GASSER JAMES L	CPT	C-1113218	0547	2
GASSER JOHN R	LTC	0-0255195	1145	2
GASSERT LEE F	LTC	0-1010127	1264	1
GASSIE DONALD V	COL	0-0919273	0267	3
GAST GARRETT A	2LT	0-1317515	0344	2
GAST OTTO W	CPT	0-0404312	0746	2
GASTAUER WAHLERS H	CPT	0-1C32434	0148	1
GASTON HENRY J	LTC	0-0334464	0566	3
GASTON JAMES A	COL	0-0030138	1159	1
GASTON LAMAR D	LTC	0-0238025	0265	3
GASTON MARVIN C	MAJ	0-2208465	0467	1
GASTON RUTHERFORD	2LT	0-2C25869	0847	1
GATCH GORDON G	LTC	0-1312907	0664	1
GATCHELL CHARLES W	1LT	0-1585488	1045	2
GATELEY FRANK R	CW2	W-2131972	1065	1
GATELY JOHN E	MAJ	C-1685018	1066	1
GATELY THOMAS C	CPT	0-0334308	0745	2
GATEMAN MURRAY H	1LT	0-0499337	0543	2
GATES CHESTER M	LTC	0-0341554	0262	1
GATES CLARENCE G	MAJ	0-0567269	0565	1
GATES DELBERT C	LTC	0-1313394	0763	1
GATES DONALD O	LTC	0-0273910	0545	2
GATES EUGENE F	2LT	0-1301981	1043	2
GATES FRANCIS K	CPT	0-0320879	0246	1
GATES FRANKLIN F	MAJ	0-1304850	1062	1
GATES GEORGE D	CW2	W-2151355	C761	1
GATES GLEN F	MAJ	0-0169739	1058	3
GATES III RYERSON D	CPT	0-0464360	1162	1
GATES IRA E	CPT	0-1913688	0617	1
GATES JACK C	CPT	0-1290587	0546	2
GATES JAMES L	1LT	0-1308943	0451	2
GATES JOHN J	COL	C-0307450	0146	2
GATES JOSEPH	LTC	0-0378523	0960	1
GATES JR GEORGE O	LTC	0-1559562	1167	1
GATES JR WILBUR	CPT	0-2042001	0162	1
GATES JUNIOR D	MAJ	0-1923544	1264	1
GATES LLOYD R	COL	0-0249374	1263	3
GATES MARCIA L	1LT	N-0730145	0246	1
GATES REGINALD S	MAJ	0-0493639	1155	1
GATES ROBERT E	CW2	W-221066C	0463	1
GATES STANLEY M	LTC	0-0252735	0150	3
GATES THURMOND P	LTC	0-0280661	1151	1
GATES WALTER E	MAJ	0-048C568	0746	2
GATES WILLIAM G	CW2	W-3430476	1167	1
GATES WILLIAM O	CW2	W-2141975	0953	1
GATEWOOD WILLIAM M	CW4	W-2118288	1054	1
GATHRIGHT EMMETTE F	1LT	0-1328808	0946	2
GATLEY WILLIAM P	COL	C-0322450	1159	3
GATLIN CARL E	COL	0-02318C9	1061	3
GATLIN GRADY T	LTC	0-0488854	0557	1
GATLIN LEE B	MAJ	0-1549274	0161	1
GATLIN OLLIE H	LTC	0-1045435	0664	1
GATLIN ORRIN W	CPT	0-0515070	1147	1
GATLING JOHN	MAJ	C-0495789	0147	2
GATLING MERRCRNE P	LTC	0-0173131	1161	3
GATON ALBERT W	MAJ	0-0902446	1045	2
GATSKE CARL F	LTC	0-0393743	1060	1
GATT FREDERICK	CW2	W-2101727	0456	1
GATTAS FRED A	CPT	0-1756428	0948	2
GATTMAN LOUIS W	MAJ	0-0115403	0756	3
GATWOOD MILLARD F	CW3	W-2208166	0666	1
GATZ THOMAS	CW3	W-2206674	0765	1
GATZKE CARL W	LTC	0-04396CC	0862	1
GAU HENRY L	LTC	C-0319758	1159	3
GAUDET AUGUSTINE	MAJ	0-0451285	0658	1
GAUDET PERLEY I	CW3	W-2142155	0564	1

NAME	GRADE	SVC NO	DATE RET MO YR	RET CODE
GAUDIERI JOSEPH L	1LT	C-0267002	C845	2
GAUDREAU CHILSON P	MAJ	C-2020135	C959	1
GAUDREAU EUGENE L	LTC	0-0493321	0657	1
GAUDREAU ROBERT C	MAJ	0-0535731	0546	2
GAUDY WILLIAM T	COL	C-0447348	1264	1
GAUGER JR PAUL C	COL	C-0358244	C863	1
GAUGHAN ELMER M	CPT	0-0355752	C144	2
GAUGHAN MARY A	MAJ	N-0744438	C366	3
GAUGHAN WILLIAM G	LTC	0-0455060	0767	1
GAUKEL JR JOSEPH A	2LT	0-1581733	0544	2
GAULD GEORGE I	CPT	0-0400533	0943	2
GAULDING JR KARL J	2LT	C-1304517	C144	2
GAULE STEPHEN E	LTC	0-0268640	0654	3
GAULKE ALVIN T	MAJ	0-0313882	0265	3
GAULKE EDWARD E	MAJ	C-0949104	C163	1
GAULT BENJAMIN J	LTC	0-0936716	0660	1
GAULT CHARLES B	LTC	0-1533787	C761	1
GAULT J F	1LT	0-1998327	0557	1
GAULT JACK C	COL	C-0244796	1152	1
GAULT VACTOR J	1LT	0-1996625	1057	1
GAUMER ARDIS V	1LT	N-0760467	C646	1
GAUMER DAVID C	MAJ	C-2035469	1158	1
GAUMER EDMUND L	MAJ	C-0193495	0261	3
GAUMER OSCAR C	LTC	0-0235154	1149	3
GAUMNITZ FREDERICK	LTC	0-0148365	C154	3
GAUNT HARRY	LTC	C-1556422	1063	1
GAUNTT JAMES D	LTC	0-0465203	C567	1
GAUPER EMMETT G	MAJ	C-0477927	C947	1
GAUSE FREEMAN M	MAJ	C-1045098	1162	1
GAUSE THOMAS W	1LT	C-1295700	1143	2
GAUSE WILLIAM L	MAJ	C-1633879	1054	1
GAUSMAN WILLIAM C	CPT	0-0302888	C345	2
GAUSTAD JOHN W	MAJ	C-0450869	0146	2
GAUTHIER ARCHIE P	COL	0-0387677	1061	1
GAUTHIER BLUMES	1LT	0-1290588	0145	1
GAUTHIER FREDERICK	LTC	0-1167431	0561	1
GAUTHIER GEORGE A	MAJ	C-0319201	0465	3
GAUTHIER VERNESE M	CPT	N-0721653	C449	2
GAUTHREAUX ERVIN M	1LT	0-0888909	0345	2
GAUTIER THOMAS B	CPT	0-0904370	C844	2
GAUTSCHI WILLIAM I	CPT	0-0886212	1045	2
GAVA JR AUGUST	CW3	W-214800C	0763	1
GAVARINSKI FRANK J	1LT	0-1166069	1045	2
GAVIGAN JOHN J	CPT	C-1685178	1045	2
GAVIN CHARLES G	CPT	0-1291259	C346	2
GAVIN JOHN C	CPT	0-0375030	0145	1
GAVIN JOHN J	MAJ	C-0480749	0854	1
GAVIN JOHN R	2LT	0-1936221	C362	2
GAVIN MARY	LTC	N-0700063	0844	1
GAVIN RICHARD P	LTC	0-1322143	C266	1
GAVIN WILLIAM A	LTC	0-0171144	C858	1
GAVULA MICHAEL	LTC	0-2034944	0862	1
GAW ROBERT A	COL	0-0264956	0457	1
GAWENKA EVA	MAJ	N-0777541	1265	1
GAWKOWSKI PAUL	LTC	C-1181259	0163	1
GAWLAS FREDERICK	1LT	0-1303136	0345	1
GAWNE CHARLES B	CPT	0-1821420	C446	2
GAY ALDEN	MAJ	0-2009432	1061	1
GAY BRYAN W	MAJ	0-0969583	0263	1
GAY ELLERY C	LTC	0-0313177	0863	3
GAY ELMER D	COL	0-0290536	0167	3
GAY HERBERT	MAJ	C-0949044	0762	1
GAY JACK R	LTC	0-1297351	1061	1
GAY JAMES J	CPT	0-0528873	1046	2
GAY JAMES O	LTC	0-1338944	C267	1
GAY JAMES W	MAJ	C-1822263	C657	1
GAY JOE A	LTC	0-0320623	0864	3
GAY JR CHARLES HE	CPT	0-0525669	C847	2
GAY JR THOMAS H	1LT	0-1825665	C246	1
GAY MABELLE A	2LT	N-0751029	0444	1
GAY OTIS F	LTC	0-0461626	1146	2
GAY TOMMIE L	CPT	0-1300018	1047	2
GAY TRAVIS R	LTC	0-1949969	1067	1
GAY WILLIAM S	MAJ	C-02506C3	0245	2
GAYDON JR EMZY W	1LT	0-0415558	1046	2

NAME	GRADE	SVC NO	DATE RET MO YR	RET CODE
GAYDOSH LOUIS W	CPT	0-0294195	0267	3
GAYHART LLOYD W	CW2	W-2144055	0963	1
GAYLE JAMES C	LTC	C-0214727	0264	3
GAYLE WILLIAM T	COL	0-0229C87	0465	3
GAYLES JOHN L	MAJ	0-0426219	1060	1
GAYLOR ROSCOE O	COL	0-0232859	0964	3
GAYLORD CARL W	CPT	0-2C56090	0867	1
GAYLORD GEORGE F	LTC	0-1825528	C166	1
GAYNE ARTHUR G	LTC	0-1030366	0856	1
GAYNES SEYMOUR S	CW2	W-2111543	0644	2
GAYNIER WILLIAM M	2LT	0-0539899	0645	2
GAYNIN HENRY T	CPT	0-1690364	C845	2
GAYNOR DAVID R	1LT	0-1310959	0745	2
GAYNOR ELIZABETH	1LT	N-0721001	0346	1
GAYNOR GEORGE G	LTC	0-1017143	0562	1
GAYNOR HELEN A	LTC	L-0500009	0265	1
GAYNOR JR JOHN F	1LT	0-1016230	1145	2
GAYNOR PAUL F	LTC	0-0423108	1047	2
GAYNOR ROBERT M	LTC	0-0326696	1246	2
GAYNOR WAYNE J	MAJ	0-1895549	0664	1
GEAKE JR FRANCIS	CW2	W-2152827	0261	1
GEANEY JOHN J	1LT	0-1041767	0266	1
GEAR ALBREY C	CW2	W-2150667	0557	1
GEAR LELAND C	MAJ	0-1311386	1263	1
GEAR RICHARD H	COL	0-0488698	1064	1
GEAREN WALTER D	LTC	0-0170666	0257	3
GEARHART CARL P	MAJ	C-0484835	C647	2
GEARHART CHARLES H	COL	0-0274076	0361	3
GEARHART IRA D	CW4	W-2126123	0164	1
GEARHART JACK L	MAJ	0-0734334	0961	1
GEARHART RODMAN	1LT	0-1019249	0946	2
GEARING MILTON J	COL	0-0206863	0648	3
GEARING WILLIAM B	LTC	0-0457248	0263	1
GEARY JR JOSEPH W	CPT	0-0154949	0653	3
GEARY LEO A	CPT	0-1287513	0545	2
GEARY LEO P	LTC	0-0280476	0767	3
GEARY WILSON	CPT	0-0313539	0145	2
GEASE JR JOHN H	LTC	0-1574758	0764	1
GEBBEN ALBERT	CW4	W-2143906	0765	1
GEBERT CHARLES A	COL	0-0148115	1152	3
GEBHARDT CHARLES A	MAJ	C-0264187	0147	1
GEBHARDT EUGENE L	1LT	0-1294123	0145	2
GEBHARDT HARRISON W	LTC	0-0255538	1055	3
GEBHARDT KARL F	LTC	0-0275448	0462	3
GEBHART J D	LTC	0-1579681	1160	1
GEBHART JOHN F	LTC	0-0245487	0866	3
GEBHART MARK M	LTC	0-1000366	1054	1
GEBHART PEARL E	CW3	W-2148852	0264	1
GECIK MICHAEL G	LTC	0-1559915	0965	1
GECKLER JOHN H	CPT	0-0492148	0246	2
GEDDES GEORGE F	LTC	0-1944545	0165	1
GEDDES ROBERT W	MAJ	C-0326458	1266	3
GEDDES SR PAUL F	CW2	W-2148536	0659	1
GEDDES WILLIAM L	MAJ	0-0410755	1165	1
GEDDIE ROWLAND H	LTC	0-0921519	1065	3
GEDDINGS EUGENE N	MAJ	0-0254300	0666	3
GEDDINGS JOHN C	MAJ	0-1542711	1055	1
GEDEIST HOWARD S	LTC	0-0336553	1062	1
GEDRICH EDWARD	MAJ	0-1292867	0348	1
GEDULDIG CHARLES C	COL	0-1000122	0561	1
GEE CHARLES J	COL	0-0346676	0663	1
GEE CLAY H	CW2	W-2147543	0560	1
GEE EDWARD W	CPT	0-1306085	1153	2
GEE GRANT	LTC	0-0336412	0859	3
GEE JAMES A	CW2	W-2209923	0264	1
GEE JAMES G	COL	C-0164263	0547	2
GEER ELIHU	COL	0-0202045	0862	3
GEER FRANK	CW3	W-2102925	0459	1
GEER JR EDWARD W	COL	0-0402749	0860	1
GEER ROBERT C	LTC	0-2005967	0266	1
GEER WILLIAM C	MAJ	C-4014277	0267	1
GEERLINGS LEE T	MAJ	0-0421718	1263	1
GEERS PAUL F	CPT	0-1307343	0747	2
GEERTSEMA JOHN G	CPT	0-1011600	0151	2
GEESEMAN GORDON F	2LT	0-0541046	0145	2

NAME	GRADE	SVC NO	DATE RET MO YR	RET CODE
GEESLER FRED M	1LT	0-0278477	0546	2
GEESLIN WILLIAM F	COL	0-0250575	0655	3
GEEVER FRANCES R	2LT	N-0700476	0938	1
GEFFEN LOUIS	LTC	0-0359175	1264	3
GEFFERT ALVIN D	MAJ	0-0290939	0146	2
GEFOROS ELMER R	LTC	0-0399872	0960	1
GEGAN JOHN R	COL	0-0170192	0760	3
GEGECKAS DOROTHY T	2LT	N-0724629	0544	1
GEGESKY BENJAMIN W	MAJ	0-1637489	0264	1
GEHM EDWIN A	LTC	0-2055810	0155	1
GEHM ROBERT J	MAJ	0-2262308	1062	1
GEHMAN MIRIAM P	MAJ	N-0742864	0667	1
GEHR LAWRENCE A	CW2	W-2210454	0860	1
GEHR MIRES C	MAJ	0-0256660	0564	3
GEHRIG JR VICTOR J	1LT	0-1180508	1045	2
GEHRING HARRY G	CW2	W-2213305	0967	1
GEHRING JR HERMAN F	1LT	0-1032208	0545	2
GEHRMANN AUGUST J	MAJ	0-1541696	0757	3
GEIGENMULLER WARNER	LTC	0-0512180	1066	3
GEIGER CLARENCE E	COL	0-0230033	0465	3
GEIGER ELBERT C	MAJ	0-0313391	0945	2
GEIGER HARMON P	MAJ	0-0504365	0860	2
GEIGER HORACE W	MAJ	0-2051642	0866	1
GEIGER JOHN	1LT	0-0493508	0544	2
GEIGER ORVILLE T	LTC	0-1551408	0464	1
GEIGER WILLIAM D	MAJ	0-0132808	0648	3
GEIGLEIN JOHN C	COL	0-0406664	0163	1
GEIGLEY JOHN D	MAJ	0-1031403	0858	1
GEIKLER JOHN A	COL	0-0197167	0461	3
GEIMER EMIL J	LTC	0-1178807	0962	1
GEIS ROBERT J	MAJ	0-0506855	0653	3
GEIS ROBERT W	MAJ	0-0296513	1053	2
GEISE CHARLES R	1LT	0-0132981	0953	3
GEISE DANIEL F	1LT	0-1117013	1056	1
GEISEL JOHN G	MAJ	0-0326882	1159	1
GEISELMAN ROBERT C	COL	0-0176486	1161	3
GEISENDOHFER W C	CW2	W-2122913	0847	1
GEISER ELEANORE T	LTC	L-0200261	0765	1
GEISER FRANK F	MAJ	0-0177179	0550	3
GEISER JOHN E	COL	0-0247668	0160	1
GEISER ROBERT F	CW3	W-2206867	0567	1
GEISINGER EDWIN S	1LT	0-1080103	1045	2
GEISINGER LESLIE H	MAJ	0-0300473	0462	1
GEISLER ANDREW L	LTC	0-0452058	0358	1
GEISLER ARTHUR M	COL	0-0113187	0855	3
GEISLER RAYMOND J	MAJ	0-1299230	0661	1
GEISLER WILLIAM H	CPT	0-0489534	0645	1
GEISSINGER CARL R	LTC	0-1047131	0461	1
GEIST WILBUR F	MAJ	0-0395264	0258	1
GEIWITZ HERBERT J	LTC	0-0313194	0960	3
GELABERT JR LORENZO	2LT	0-0411582	1142	2
GELARDI ANTHONY	LTC	0-0377981	0862	1
GELBER JULIUS	CPT	0-0419694	0246	2
GELBER LOUIS J	MAJ	0-0466523	0545	2
GELDART WILLIAM A	CPT	0-0413959	0444	2
GELDER JOHN O	LTC	0-1107427	1065	1
GELDER JR EDWARD L	LTC	0-1111624	1265	1
GELETA LEO A	MAJ	0-2019730	0765	1
GELFAND DANIEL F	CPT	0-0439344	1147	2
GELFOND JOHN J	1LT	0-1319380	1145	2
GELINA HOWARD M	CPT	0-1633233	0560	1
GELINI ELMO E	1LT	0-1325885	1046	2
GELLER GEORGE R	LTC	0-0211417	0 46	2
GELLER MORRIS	CPT	0-1685891	0446	2
GELLER MORTON J	CPT	0-0440199	1045	2
GELLER PHILIP F	CPT	0-1293237	0146	2
GELLER PHILIP S	MAJ	0-0302036	0646	1
GELLER RALPH L	2LT	0-2034416	0444	2
GELLER ROBERT H	1LT	0-1647453	0646	2
GELMAN MURRAY C	MAJ	0-0363248	0645	2
GELONECK WILLIAM K	CPT	0-1580992	0254	1
GELSTHORPE FRANCIS D	LTC	0-1594231	0665	2
GELSTON WARREN W	MAJ	0-0296087	0165	1
GELTMACHER HARRY R	LTC	0-0279667	0662	1
GELTZ CHARLES C	MAJ	0-0166476	0256	3

NAME	GRADE	SVC NO	DATE RET MO YR	RET CODE
GELUSHIA WARREN G	2LT	0-1823285	0944	2
GELWICK ARTHUR R	LTC	0-0131761	1048	3
GELWICK ROBERT A	LTC	0-0465137	0762	1
GEMINIANI MARIO	LTC	0-0326460	0346	2
GEMMELL JAMES D	LTC	0-0352365	0161	1
GENARO JOSEPH F	LTC	0-2044283	0167	2
GENCO JASPER J	CW3	W-2152959	0464	1
GENDREAU ERNEST E J	1LT	0-1100114	1146	2
GENERALES C A	1LT	0-1705515	0647	2
GENERAUX CARNIE A	CPT	0-0925190	1044	2
GENEREAU EDMUND F	CPT	0-1994431	0646	1
GENERELY WALTER J	CW2	W-2152606	0266	1
GENG CHARLES E	COL	0-0336505	0958	3
GENGELBACH ROBERT O	LTC	0-0348736	0963	3
GENIN FRANCIS G	CPT	0-0493707	0645	2
GENNETT KENNETH A	CPT	0-0427927	0866	3
GENOVAR ROBERT L	CPT	0-0403608	0145	2
GENOVESE JOSEPH	LTC	0-0571765	0862	1
GENOVESE SEBASTIAN	1LT	0-0470274	0446	1
GENRE EMILE J	COL	0-1102740	0464	1
GENSCHAW JR WALTER W	LTC	0-1320836	1262	1
GENSON PAUL E	CW3	W-2101730	0456	1
GENT WARREN O	COL	0-0208591	0648	3
GENTER JOSEPH H	MAJ	0-0578665	1161	1
GENTES CHARLES E	MAJ	0-0308358	1262	1
GENTHON RENE M	COL	0-0134701	0154	3
GENTILE DOMINICK P	1LT	0-1289408	1045	1
GENTILE GEORGE	MAJ	0-1595521	0861	1
GENTILE JOSEPH P	2LT	0-1557286	0445	2
GENTILE ROY J	MAJ	0-1307220	0864	1
GENTINE PAUL W	CW3	W-2125853	0557	1
GENTLE HJALMAR T	LTC	0-0259471	1058	3
GENTLE JAMES C	COL	0-0296048	0864	3
GENTLE JAMES F	LTC	0-0451550	1060	1
GENTLE PAUL C	CPT	0-2037547	0854	1
GENTNER JOHN M	COL	0-0166960	0451	2
GENTON MAURICE F	MAJ	0-0556578	0663	1
GENTRY ALBERT R	MAJ	0-2204418	1163	1
GENTRY CHARLES F	COL	0-0328967	1060	3
GENTRY COY W	1LT	0-0256350	0642	1
GENTRY GERRY M	MAJ	0-1536175	1063	1
GENTRY HARRY L	MAJ	0-0467188	0346	2
GENTRY HERBERT C	1LT	0-0405390	1046	1
GENTRY JACK C	LTC	0-1284128	1263	1
GENTRY JOE C	MAJ	0-2211498	0766	1
GENTRY JOHN E	MAJ	0-1030245	0547	1
GENTRY JR CHARLES J	LTC	0-1342329	0464	1
GENTRY JULIUS A	CPT	0-0495783	0746	1
GENTRY LAWRENCE L	CW2	W-2101087	1147	1
GENTRY MARION M	MAJ	0-1282376	0860	1
GENTRY ORVILLE L	LTC	0-0885079	0555	1
GENTRY THOMAS F	MAJ	0-0152820	0756	3
GENTRY THOMAS F	COL	0-0251165	0167	3
GENTRY WILLIAM R	MAJ	0-0224642	0157	3
GENTRY WILLIAM R	LTC	0-0997241	1163	1
GENTRY WILLIAM R	CPT	0-2026506	0457	1
GENTZKOW MYLES J	1LT	0-0517662	0346	2
GENUA JOHN A	MAJ	0-1310553	1061	1
GENUNG JOEL M	LTC	0-0388379	0960	1
GEOFFRION RAYMOND J	LTC	0-1171157	0866	1
GEOGHEGAN JOSEPH F	LTC	0-2011395	0264	1
GEOHAGAN JAMES M	1LT	0-1648122	0346	2
GEORGE ALBERT	CPT	0-0982304	1061	1
GEORGE ALLAN	CPT	0-1017148	0667	2
GEORGE ALLEN M	CW3	W-2141287	0560	1
GEORGE ANNA L	CPT	N-0700051	0545	1
GEORGE ANTHONY R	MAJ	0-0341331	1046	1
GEORGE ARTHUR G	LTC	0-0131759	0149	3
GEORGE ATHOL W	LTC	0-0451106	0756	1
GEORGE CHARLES A	MAJ	0-1213735	0462	2
GEORGE CHARLES M	LTC	0-1316716	0661	2
GEORGE CHARLES W	MAJ	0-1010618	0261	1
GEORGE CHRISTIAN	LTC	0-1289409	0761	1
GEORGE CLAIR L	MAJ	0-1035260	1158	1
GEORGE CLARENCE J	COL	0-1576012	0264	2

NAME	GRADE	SVC NO	DATE RET MO YR	RET CODE
GEORGE DAVID E	LTC	0-0407452	0455	1
GEORGE DEWEY J	MAJ	0-1316287	0862	1
GEORGE DON R	MAJ	0-1557847	0261	1
GEORGE EDMUND T	CPT	0-0513858	0750	1
GEORGE EDWARD C	1LT	0-1315679	0946	2
GEORGE ELMER C	MAJ	0-2028877	0864	1
GEORGE ERNEST R	1LT	0-1013500	0745	1
GEORGE FRANK A	COL	0-0247128	1163	3
GEORGE GUSTAVE	LTC	0-0207174	1263	3
GEORGE HARRY C	MAJ	0-1824452	1060	1
GEORGE HERBERT E	LTC	0-0307673	1061	3
GEORGE JAMES H	CW2	W-2143660	0653	2
GEORGE JAMES V	CPT	0-0885612	0350	1
GEORGE JAMES W	LTC	0-2049560	0861	1
GEORGE JESSE M	LTC	0-0176982	1061	3
GEORGE JESSE R	CW4	W-2104085	0859	1
GEORGE JOHN J	MAJ	0-0947016	1165	1
GEORGE JOHN L	2LT	0-1302805	0145	2
GEORGE JOSEPH P	1LT	0-1295010	0246	2
GEORGE LLOYD F	1LT	0-0537182	0845	2
GEORGE RALPH A	LTC	0-1334451	0367	1
GEORGE RALPH K	CPT	0-2265131	1262	1
GEORGE RAMON T	LTC	0-2274645	1063	1
GEORGE ROBERT C	MAJ	0-1876299	0367	1
GEORGE ROBERT F	CW2	W-2208362	1064	1
GEORGE ROLLAND E	COL	0-0248283	1057	3
GEORGE SIDNEY L	LTC	0-2040694	0766	1
GEORGE SR MARTIN A	CPT	0-0297849	0544	2
GEORGE STUART N	LTC	0-0270945	0966	3
GEORGE TAFT L	1LT	0-1999052	0146	2
GEORGE TERRELL R	CPT	0-0486891	1145	2
GEORGE THOMAS A	COL	0-1285742	0467	1
GEORGE THOMAS J	CW2	W-2205353	1059	2
GEORGE WELTON L	WO1	W-2117029	0453	1
GEORGES JAMES	CW2	W-2147460	0363	1
GEORGES STANLEY	MAJ	0-1118895	0364	1
GEORGESKI ANTHONY J	LTC	0-0307517	0862	3
GEORGIA JR HAROLD P	2LT	0-1323120	1044	2
GEPHART MESEKE D	MAJ	0-0190563	0760	3
GEPHART STANTON L	LTC	0-1543724	1060	1
GERACI PHILIP C	LTC	0-1578511	1060	1
GERARD DARWIN P	LTC	0-1182838	0559	2
GERARD II JAMES W	COL	0-1577220	0161	1
GERARD JAMES N	2LT	0-0949899	0652	1
GERARD PAUL	LTC	0-0497797	0954	1
GERARD RAPHAEL C	COL	0-0246187	1263	3
GERARD STANLEY R	LTC	0-0402502	1060	1
GERARD WILLIAM F	LTC	0-1298853	0461	1
GERARD WILLIAM J	MAJ	0-1167854	0261	1
GERATY THOMAS H	MAJ	0-0359247	0346	2
GERBER ERNEST	LTC	0-0276965	0959	3
GERBER GALEN G	MAJ	0-1332253	0164	1
GERBER JACK H	MAJ	0-1182839	1265	1
GERBER JASPER F	MAJ	0-0278453	0959	1
GERDES NORMAN J	LTC	0-0416248	1060	2
GERDING PAUL R	COL	0-0161194	1155	3
GEREND ARTHUR J	CPT	0-1289898	1046	2
GERETY JOHN H	COL	0-0270173	0959	3
GERFEN CARL A	COL	0-0272730	1266	3
GERFEN HERBERT F	COL	0-0276723	1162	1
GERGELY JOHN P	CPT	0-2262699	0361	1
GERHARDSTEIN LEO F	MAJ	0-1599163	1062	1
GERICKE OTTO L	COL	0-0308439	0867	3
GERIG FERD L	LTC	0-0358610	0962	1
GERING GEORGE G	CPT	0-1689574	0346	2
GERIS JOSEPH D	MAJ	0-1922714	1066	1
GERKE FREDERICK	LTC	0-0349269	1046	2
GERKEN FRED E	LTC	0-0911334	0965	1
GERKEN FRED J	LTC	0-1310240	1262	2
GERKEN HENRY A	MAJ	0-0215944	0763	3
GERKEN RICHARD L	1LT	0-0416090	1144	2
GERKIN GEORGE F	LTC	0-0425857	0860	1
GERL JOHN G	MAJ	0-1322903	0960	1
GERLACH JOSEPH F	MAJ	0-1286994	1057	1
GERLACH RICHARD P	MAJ	0-1647455	0759	1

NAME	GRADE	SVC NO	DATE RET MO YR	RET CODE
GERLETT JOHN P	CW3	W-2147830	1164	1
GERLOCK JR FRANK G	CPT	0-0973312	0261	3
GERMAIN EDWARD L	1LT	0-2000051	1046	2
GERMAIN RAYMOND J	MAJ	0-0272186	0246	2
GERMAK MICHAEL J	1LT	0-1633234	0645	2
GERMAN AMBROSE H	CW2	W-2149034	0566	1
GERMAN DAVID P	MAJ	0-0509430	0346	2
GERMAN EDGAR P	LTC	0-0382678	0246	2
GERMAN FORREST A	1LT	0-2040875	0746	2
GERMAN FRANK C	COL	0-0183703	0855	3
GERMAN RALPH H	CW3	W-2152342	0258	1
GERMAN WALTER A	LTC	0-0277895	0966	3
GERMANE DOMINIC G	WO1	W-2129903	1059	1
GERMANN EDWARD H	LTC	0-2008135	0764	1
GERNAND CARL F	MAJ	0-2032581	0763	1
GERNER CHARLES S	LTC	0-1822557	0665	3
GERNER LOUIS J	LTC	0-1043639	1163	1
GERNHART JACK C	MAJ	0-1117135	0465	1
GERNON SR RICHARD W	CPT	0-0404630	0261	2
GERNON WILLIAM	MAJ	0-0490253	0646	2
GERO RALPH L	LTC	0-1287335	0864	1
GEROMANOS JR LEON A	CPT	0-0969543	0661	1
GEROMETTA EMANUEL	CPT	0-1183858	0154	1
GEROULD JUSTIN J	MAJ	0-2007446	0463	1
GEROW BENJAMIN R	CPT	0-2017686	0365	1
GEROW LUDWIG C	MAJ	0-0347683	0251	1
GERRARD ROBERT J	1LT	0-1597105	0949	2
GERRELLS TRAVIS A	LTC	0-0403571	1160	1
GERREN EMMET A	2LT	0-1914156	0746	1
GERRICK BERNARD H	WO1	W-2118858	0945	2
GERRIE PAUL F	1LT	0-1101842	0444	2
GERSHENSON LOUIS	CW2	W-2000215	0648	3
GERSHON GORDON M	LTC	0-0389438	0760	1
GERSHON SOL	LTC	0-0461258	0566	3
GERSON ALEX C	CPT	0-1693625	0446	2
GERSTEIN MICHAEL	1LT	0-1292868	0345	1
GERSTEN FELIX	MAJ	0-1549477	0960	1
GERSTEN JULIUS	LTC	0-0244465	1144	2
GERSTEN MAX	MAJ	0-1642090	1263	1
GERSTEN ROY	MAJ	0-0970658	0563	1
GERTH HENRY C	MAJ	0-1170747	0463	1
GERTH IRVIN W	LTC	0-0312633	0556	1
GERTIE STAN C	LTC	0-0253813	0663	3
GERTZ ROBERT E	LTC	0-0395201	0750	1
GERVAIS NARCISSE	MAJ	0-0245870	0759	2
GERVIG CHARLES W	1LT	0-0541108	0646	2
GERVIN JACK E	CPT	0-1293036	0446	1
GERVIN LEON W	CPT	0-2036374	0461	2
GERWIG JOHN H	MAJ	0-0416476	0547	2
GERY EUGENE A	2LT	0-1291977	0745	2
GERYE WALTER A	COL	0-0135319	0648	3
GESIN WALTER G	MAJ	0-0961705	0864	1
GESKER MITCHELL E	CPT	0-1895749	0151	1
GESREGEN ROBERT H	LTC	0-1591745	0562	1
GESS JERROLD P	COL	0-0338030	1154	3
GESS PAUL M	MAJ	0-1544777	0859	1
GESSER CARL	MAJ	0-0343808	0447	2
GEST JOHN F	LTC	0-0212776	0551	3
GESTER WALTER H	CW2	W-2109723	0947	2
GESTRING JOHN F	COL	0-0233786	1147	2
GETCHELL JR RALPH W	1LT	0-1047132	0145	2
GETCHELL MARY L	MAJ	N-0761351	1163	1
GETCHELL RALPH A	COL	0-0173482	1158	3
GETSINGER BOARDMAN G	MAJ	0-0148744	1156	3
GETSINGER JOHN G	1LT	0-0394435	1045	2
GETTER KERIN P	CW3	W-2110764	0956	1
GETTMAN HENRY	MAJ	0-1291622	0963	1
GETTNER FRANK E	LTC	0-2036732	0464	1
GETTSY WILLIAM J	MAJ	0-1937176	0867	1
GETTY CHARLES H	LTC	0-1000123	1060	1
GETTY CHESTER C	CPT	0-2262475	0759	1
GETTY GEORGE L	COL	0-0354956	0266	1
GETTY RICHART W	LTC	0-0122942	1149	3
GETZE ROLAND	CPT	0-0325585	1043	1
GETZINGER PHILIP L	COL	0-0352031	0764	1

NAME	GRADE	SVC NO	DATE RET MO YR	RET CODE
GETZOFF CYRUS G	1LT	0-1321623	1145	2
GEUSS EMIL W	MAJ	0-0475023	1052	1
GEVARTER HERMAN J	1LT	0-1318781	0146	2
GEVEDON OMER C	MAJ	0-1115556	1262	1
GEVERS CARL M	COL	0-0101940	1052	3
GEWINNER RAYMOND J	CPT	0-1303139	1045	2
GEYER CZERNEY D	CPT	0-0478745	0848	1
GEYER WALTER R	CPT	0-0313932	0246	2
GEZELMAN RALPH L	COL	0-0268199	0756	2
GHAN WILLIAM C	MAJ	0-0493076	0952	1
GHELARDI ANTHONY F	COL	0-0185708	1055	3
GHENT GEORGE W	MAJ	0-1647727	0662	1
GHENT IRA W	LTC	0-0368097	0362	1
GHENT WILLIAM F	LTC	0-1322144	0865	1
GHER RALPH G	LTC	0-0102175	0154	3
GHERARDI GUY J	1LT	0-1312393	0845	2
GHEZZI ANTHONY L	CPT	0-1823432	1046	2
GHINI GUIDO	MAJ	0-2037190	1264	1
GHIOTTO ANTHONY C	CW4	W-2145225	0166	1
GHIZ EDWARD M	COL	0-0342820	0463	1
GHOLSTON LAFAYETTE	1LT	0-0446740	0445	2
GHOLZ LORETTA E	1LT	N-0759757	0146	1
GIACOBBE WACIE	MAJ	0-1313395	1058	1
GIACOBBI SAMUEL N	CPT	0-2009992	0456	1
GIACOMAZZI RICHARD P	MAJ	0-1799729	0766	1
GIACOMO CASPER W	CPT	0-1324835	0847	1
GIAMMALVO FRANCESCO	MAJ	0-1281281	0459	1
GIAMMARCO DANTE A	LTC	0-1061403	1263	1
GIANDDMENICO FRANK A	COL	0-0144556	1155	3
GIANELLI JR A F	MAJ	0-1297353	1047	1
GIANFRANCESCO H B	CPT	0-0469478	1147	1
GIANNAKIS JOHN	CW3	W-2152960	0965	1
GIANNARIS JOHN	CPT	0-1322908	0146	2
GIANNI JOSEPH A	2LT	0-1112719	0946	1
GIARDINA ANTHONY L	MAJ	0-0250386	0865	3
GIARLA THOMAS C	MAJ	0-0365471	0650	1
GIARTH WILLIAM C	LTC	0-0247027	0646	2
GIATTINA ANGELINE	2LT	N-0754870	0147	1
GIBANICA SAMUEL	MAJ	0-0454384	1056	1
GIBB ADDISON R	COL	0-0222672	0258	3
GIBBARD CECIL D	1LT	0-1172023	0945	2
GIBBARD RODNEY H	1LT	0-0948758	0255	2
GIBBENS CHARLES A	MAJ	0-1295703	1160	1
GIBBINS KENNETH A	CW2	W-2145415	0856	1
GIBBLE HOWARD L	CW3	W-2144848	1060	1
GIBBON JR JOHN H	LTC	0-0399220	0246	2
GIBBONS CHARLES E	LTC	0-2053936	0256	1
GIBBONS CHARLES G	1LT	0-0316159	0845	2
GIBBONS CHARLES W	LTC	0-0450060	0455	1
GIBBONS DONALD L	CW3	W-2152037	0364	1
GIBBONS HARRIS A	1LT	0-0293278	0344	2
GIBBONS JAMES N	1LT	0-0441666	1145	2
GIBBONS JAMES R	CW3	W-2142381	0864	1
GIBBONS JOHN T	MAJ	0-0171133	0945	1
GIBBONS JR JOHN R	COL	0-0279376	0260	1
GIBBONS JR WILLIAM J	1LT	0-2203401	0658	2
GIBBONS LEO W	MAJ	0-0326482	0955	2
GIBBONS LEONARD L	CW2	W-2150637	0459	1
GIBBONS MAURICE C	LTC	0-1043958	0562	1
GIBBONS MURRAY F	COL	0-0144925	0251	3
GIBBONS ROBERT G	LTC	0-0346339	0961	3
GIBBONS ROBERT G	LTC	0-0346826	0758	1
GIBBONS WILLIAM E	COL	0-0310967	0666	1
GIBBS CHARLES W	COL	0-0408155	0861	1
GIBBS CLARENCE R	COL	0-0386843	0960	1
GIBBS DONALD R	CPT	0-0501308	1045	2
GIBBS DOUGLAS C	CPT	0-0312632	1146	1
GIBBS EDWIN M	COL	0-0257445	1156	3
GIBBS EVERETT P	MAJ	0-0969811	0261	1
GIBBS GRADY B	CW2	W-2147757	0761	1
GIBBS HOWARD W	MAJ	0-1588586	0861	1
GIBBS JACK	MAJ	0-0450637	0167	3
GIBBS JAMES R	LTC	0-0372602	1153	3
GIBBS JAMES L	CPT	0-1055859	0846	2
GIBBS JAMES M	MAJ	0-1108680	0761	1

NAME	GRADE	SVC NO	DATE RET MO YR	RET CODE
GIBBS JOE R	WO1	W-2129182	0152	1
GIBBS JOHN S	COL	0-0295839	1057	1
GIBBS JOHN W	CPT	0-0155121	0146	1
GIBBS JR JOHN L	MAJ	0-2040876	1164	1
GIBBS KENNETH C	LTC	0-1105451	0662	1
GIBBS PAUL J	CPT	0-0375368	1046	2
GIBBS RALPH	MAJ	0-0890308	1155	1
GIBBS ROYCE L	MAJ	0-1298528	1263	1
GIBBS SEYMOUR	LTC	0-1584255	1158	1
GIBBS THOMAS R	2LT	0-1058522	0844	2
GIBBS WILLIAM D	CPT	0-1894095	0167	1
GIBBS WILLIAM H	1LT	0-0299095	0962	3
GIBERSON DONALD K	1LT	0-1316894	0146	2
GIBLER JOHN W	MAJ	0-0301693	0747	2
GIBNEY JAMES J	1LT	0-0109693	1134	1
GIBNEY JR MATTHEW J	LTC	0-0318117	0864	1
GIBOULEAU M M	2LT	N-0787475	0345	1
GIBSON ALMA	1LT	N-0720168	0946	1
GIBSON BOAS E	CPT	0-0112917	0654	3
GIBSON CECIL C	LTC	0-0491980	0455	1
GIBSON CHARLES A	MAJ	0-1294293	0563	2
GIBSON CHARLES C	1LT	0-1014949	0546	2
GIBSON CHARLES H	CW3	W-3150582	1167	1
GIBSON CHARLES M	COL	0-0339617	0461	1
GIBSON CHARLES M	1LT	0-0571772	0965	3
GIBSON CLAIR R	MAJ	0-2020285	0164	1
GIBSON CLARENCE M	CPT	0-1700585	0345	2
GIBSON CLYDE W	LTC	0-0298577	0160	1
GIBSON DAVID C	MAJ	0-0178507	1154	3
GIBSON DONALD L	MAJ	0-1882044	0867	1
GIBSON EARL S	LTC	0-0192405	0363	3
GIBSON EARLE A	MAJ	0-0308600	0846	2
GIBSON EDMOND J	CPT	0-0341235	1145	2
GIBSON ELI W	CPT	0-2037913	1060	1
GIBSON ELMER H	LTC	0-0263693	0855	3
GIBSON EMILY	2LT	N-0700241	0538	1
GIBSON ERNEST V	MAJ	0-1307009	0961	1
GIBSON ERNEST W	COL	0-0175884	0461	3
GIBSON FLOYD D	LTC	0-0196695	0460	3
GIBSON FORD	MAJ	0-0510327	0348	1
GIBSON FOREST S	MAJ	0-0999616	0662	1
GIBSON FRANK A	CW3	W-2151166	0764	1
GIBSON FRANK H	CW4	W-2105877	0561	3
GIBSON GAYNOR A	LTC	0-1651744	0763	1
GIBSON GEORGE W	COL	0-0264324	0467	3
GIBSON GIFFORD G	MAJ	0-0454470	1166	1
GIBSON GLEN F	MAJ	0-2036648	0960	1
GIBSON GORDON J	MAJ	0-1107433	0761	1
GIBSON HAROLD C	MAJ	0-0241870	0350	1
GIBSON HAROLD L	MAJ	0-1693107	1062	1
GIBSON HERMAN N	CW3	W-2144724	1262	1
GIBSON II PAUL L	MAJ	0-1300635	0161	1
GIBSON JACK S	CW3	W-2207632	0766	2
GIBSON JACK W	CPT	0-0453039	1045	1
GIBSON JAMES A	MAJ	0-1639077	0361	1
GIBSON JAMES E	MAJ	0-0410204	0448	1
GIBSON JAMES T	CW2	W-2113300	0646	2
GIBSON JOHN C	CPT	0-1995440	0847	1
GIBSON JOHN C	CPT	0-0389633	1045	2
GIBSON JOHN R	MAJ	0-0453246	0346	2
GIBSON JOHN S	MAJ	0-2025917	0561	1
GIBSON JOSEPH F	COL	0-0333128	0157	3
GIBSON JR ARTHUR L	CW4	W-2118116	0559	1
GIBSON JR BOYD M	CW2	W-2152218	1262	1
GIBSON JR PERRY	CW2	W-2152577	0761	1
GIBSON JR REGINALD W	MAJ	0-1178811	1161	1
GIBSON JR RICHARD G	CPT	0-1058808	0847	2
GIBSON LEE P	LTC	0-0410091	0765	1
GIBSON LEO P	CW3	W-2141288	0459	1
GIBSON LLOYD L	CW4	W-2128809	0662	3
GIBSON LOYD D	LTC	0-0414199	0957	1
GIBSON MABRY H	MAJ	0-1294457	0659	1
GIBSON MARION E	MAJ	0-1335270	0464	1
GIBSON MARY A	MAJ	N-0724740	0861	1
GIBSON MOSES S	CPT	0-1798469	0657	1

NAME	GRADE	SVC NO	DATE RET MO YR	RET CODE
GIBSON OTHAR W	CW3	W-2142343	0364	1
GIBSON RAY S	CPT	0-1846437	0746	2
GIBSON RICHARD G	1LT	0-1311293	0945	1
GIBSON ROBERT A	MAJ	0-0154612	0454	3
GIBSON ROBERT M	LTC	0-1166070	0265	2
GIBSON ROLAND R	CPT	0-1885674	0664	1
GIBSON ROY C	MAJ	0-2033144	0165	1
GIBSON SAMUEL H	COL	0-0178546	1052	1
GIBSON SR DONNE E	MAJ	0-2056135	0954	1
GIBSON TERRY A	MAJ	0-1111072	0259	2
GIBSON TYLER W	CW3	W-2144340	0363	1
GIBSON VERL H	LTC	0-1325387	0661	1
GIBSON WARREN T	CPT	0-0492938	0746	1
GIBSON WILLIAM L	MAJ	0-2029648	0164	1
GIBSON WILLIE C	MAJ	0-2212097	0962	1
GICA THOMAS	1LT	0-1896946	0458	1
GIDDENS JESSIE D	MAJ	0-2263217	0962	1
GIDDINGS ALBERT A	LTC	0-1303706	0367	1
GIDDINGS CLYDE H	COL	0-0238296	1045	2
GIDUSKO ANDREW M	MAJ	0-0965384	0661	1
GIDWITZ VICTOR E	CPT	0-0425706	0246	1
GIEBNER FLORA M	2LT	N-0723413	1044	1
GIECK WILLIAM H	CPT	0-0398223	0161	2
GIEFER IRA	MAJ	0-0825148	0765	1
GIEGER MACK	LTC	0-1012677	1265	1
GIELLE FREDERICK	1LT	0-1321302	0345	2
GIELOW HOWARD J	CPT	0-1304713	0246	2
GIER EUGENE F	LTC	0-0119879	0650	3
GIER JACOB B	CPT	0-0336377	1145	2
GIERAS RICHARD	MAJ	0-0964206	1262	1
GIERE CARL N	CPT	0-0333749	0542	2
GIERE JOSEPH C	MAJ	0-0535516	0246	2
GIERISCH WILLIAM C	LTC	0-1165500	0361	1
GIERMAN GEORGE T	CW2	W-2142452	0953	1
GIES WILLIAM A	LTC	0-0288132	0158	1
GIESE DOUGLAS H	MAJ	0-0436868	0647	2
GIESE OSCAR A	MAJ	0-0494234	0154	1
GIESECKE LEONARD F	MAJ	0-0346658	0446	2
GIESECKE RAYMOND F	LTC	0-1845888	0866	1
GIESELMANN PAUL E	COL	0-0216233	0662	3
GIESEMANN JOSEPH	CPT	0-0446438	0653	1
GIESEN ARTHUR R	COL	0-0251688	1166	3
GIESER ALBERT F	MAJ	0-1894105	0166	1
GIESEY ALVIN F	MAJ	0-0275074	0658	3
GIESLER GARNETT J	LTC	0-0251552	0751	1
GIEZENTANNER ARCHIE	LTC	0-1052354	1065	3
GIEZENTANNER M N	MAJ	0-0269805	0161	1
GIFFE GEORGE M	LTC	0-0255269	0767	3
GIFFIN ARCH K	LTC	0-1001567	0766	3
GIFFIN JAMES L	MAJ	0-0131461	0856	3
GIFFORD ALLEN G	MAJ	0-0490087	1047	2
GIFFORD BILL	1LT	0-1031486	0556	1
GIFFORD BYRON G	LTC	0-0322680	0564	1
GIFFORD CHARLES C	CPT	0-2001695	0967	3
GIFFORD GEORGE H	LTC	0-0136625	0648	3
GIFFORD GEORGE T	COL	0-0296679	0167	3
GIFFORD JAMES A	MAJ	0-0986770	0366	2
GIFFORD JR STEPHEN J	MAJ	0-1107975	0761	1
GIFFORD LESLIE A	MAJ	0-0400878	0546	2
GIFFORD MILLARD H	LTC	0-1295538	1061	1
GIGANDET FRANCIS V	MAJ	0-0349880	0154	1
GIGANDET JOSEPH H	MAJ	0-1042575	0860	1
GIGGI ALPHONSE	LTC	0-1290742	1060	1
GIGLEVITCH VLADIMAR	1LT	0-0554916	1045	2
GIGLIA JR TONY R	CPT	0-0469103	0547	2
GIGLIO EDWARD	CW3	W-2147940	0464	1
GIGLIOTTI VINCENT W	1LT	0-1597780	0746	2
GIGLO WILLIAM F	CPT	0-0818654		2
GIGNILLIAT ARTHUR M	LTC	0-0249990	1264	3
GIGRAY JACK C	MAJ	0-0991640	1164	1
GIGUERE JR ALFRED J	LTC	0-1597013	0163	1
GIGUERE LOUIS N	1LT	0-1794934	0961	2
GIITTER LEO F	COL	0-0288861	0160	1
GIL DE LAMADRID JOSE	CPT	0-1924142	0363	1
GIL JOSE H	MAJ	0-1283060	0352	2

NAME	GRADE	SVC NO	DATE RET MO YR	RET CODE
GILBERT ALBERT	LTC	0-1037587	1064	1
GILBERT ALBERT A	CPT	0-1179864	0957	1
GILBERT ALBERT F	LTC	0-0347644	1161	3
GILBERT ALLEN L	CW3	W-2203265	0466	1
GILBERT ARTHUR S	2LT	0-1037000	0845	2
GILBERT BURTON R	COL	0-0277508	0760	1
GILBERT CHARLES E	LTC	0-0334814	0365	1
GILBERT DOUGLAS	CPT	0-1330811	0757	2
GILBERT EARL E	1LT	0-1545278	0546	2
GILBERT ELMER W	COL	0-0324752	0565	3
GILBERT FRANCIS M	MAJ	0-0221815	0158	3
GILBERT FRANK A	LTC	0-0170427	0460	3
GILBERT GAYLORD S	COL	0-0119408	0854	3
GILBERT GEORGE A	MAJ	0-0413019	0447	1
GILBERT GERALD E	LTC	0-0335871	0358	1
GILBERT GERALD F	COL	0-0173811	0853	3
GILBERT HARRY N	1LT	0-2026216	0952	1
GILBERT JOE W	MAJ	0-1924581	0466	1
GILBERT JOHN A	LTC	0-1290743	0962	1
GILBERT JOHN A	1LT	0-1305416	0445	2
GILBERT JOHN B	LTC	0-1180911	0861	1
GILBERT JOSEPH J	COL	0-0285737	0967	3
GILBERT JR THOMAS H	LTC	0-1014818	0966	2
GILBERT JR WALTER	1LT	0-1325722	1046	2
GILBERT JR WALTER L	2LT	0-0550770	0645	2
GILBERT KENNETH V	CPT	0-0194852	1047	1
GILBERT LEO	COL	0-0495258	0153	1
GILBERT LEROY C	COL	0-0254547	0563	3
GILBERT MATTHEW H	CPT	0-0352947	1046	2
GILBERT MELVIN P	MAJ	0-1165733	0656	1
GILBERT MILTON D	2LT	0-1106167	1044	2
GILBERT MORGAN W	MAJ	0-0240117	0265	3
GILBERT OWEN G	CPT	0-1312001	0847	2
GILBERT RAYMOND C	MAJ	0-0276211	0462	3
GILBERT RAYMOND R	CW4	W-2141567	0961	1
GILBERT RICHARD P	LTC	0-1543121	0861	1
GILBERT ROBERT F	MAJ	0-1641643	0363	1
GILBERT ROBERT M	CW3	W-2147609	0763	1
GILBERT SNOWDEN	1LT	0-0494334	0857	1
GILBERT STANLEY S	LTC	0-0328082	0866	3
GILBERT VAUGHN C	MAJ	0-1685645	0862	1
GILBERT VINCENT C	LTC	0-0320889	0546	2
GILBERT WALTER W	CW2	W-2143311	0557	1
GILBERT WARD T	LTC	0-1550799	0464	1
GILBERT WARREN F	MAJ	0-0274588	0158	3
GILBERT WILLIAM E	LTC	0-1594865	1162	1
GILBERT WILLIAM J	MAJ	0-1119702	1163	1
GILBERT WILLIS G	CW2	W-2119977	0946	1
GILBERTSON ARNOLD R	LTC	0-0266446	0566	3
GILBERTSON GERALD O	CPT	0-1183690	1164	1
GILBERTSON OSCAR F	COL	0-0236189	0164	3
GILBERTSON RALPH O	COL	0-0253639	0557	1
GILBOY JR JOHN P	CPT	0-0456664	0944	2
GILBRIDE LESLIE J	LTC	0-0204613	0556	3
GILCHRIST CHARLES A	LTC	0-1166271	0467	2
GILCHRIST FREDERIC	COL	0-0144769	0353	3
GILCHRIST HUGH A	LTC	0-0383127	0762	1
GILCHRIST JACK C	CPT	0-0390853	1044	2
GILCHRIST RICHARD W	LTC	0-0309056	0861	2
GILCHRIST ROBERT T	LTC	0-0278030	0964	3
GILDEA VADA M	2LT	N-0732722	0743	1
GILDEN BERNARD R	COL	0-0290176	0265	3
GILDEN JR CHARLES T	COL	0-0148121	1055	*3
GILDER CLYDE P	CW4	W-2102937	0455	1
GILDER JACKSON H	CPT	0-1645951	0864	1
GILDERSLEEVE HAROLD	LTC	0-1556285	1167	1
GILDERSLEEVE WILLIAM	COL	0-0301035	0663	3
GILE RICHARD E	LTC	0-0960389	1067	1
GILES GLADYS A	CPT	N-0702481	0346	1
GILES HOBERT L	2LT	0-0301700	0944	2
GILES JIMMIE	LTC	0-2017835	0866	1
GILES JR MALCOLM R	2LT	0-0475994	0644	2
GILES MALLIE T	1LT	0-0499061	0449	1
GILES MARGARET J	LTC	N-0783882	0863	1
GILES NORMAN R	WO1	W-2104093	1143	

NAME	GRADE	SVC NO	DATE RET MO YR	RET CODE
GILES WALTER V	COL	O-0287185	0658	3
GILES WILFRED	MAJ	O-1312002	0161	1
GILES WILLIAM T	1LT	O-1002430	0544	2
GILFILLAN A H	COL	O-0266512	0546	2
GILFILLAN WILLIAM F	LTC	O-1042576	0862	1
GILFORD IRVING	CW3	W-2119798	0662	1
GILFOY EDWIN G	1LT	O-1824608	0153	1
GILHOOLY WILLIAM P	MAJ	O-1048371	0161	1
GILKES WILLIAM J	CPT	O-4074812	0867	1
GILKESON VINCENT S	CPT	O-1112173	0662	1
GILL ANNETTE S	1LT	N-0722582	0549	2
GILL BERNICE E	MAJ	O-0270376	0766	3
GILL CHARLES A	LTC	O-1299727	0561	1
GILL CHARLES D	CW3	W-2140634	0461	1
GILL CHARLES H	CPT	O-0922155	0445	1
GILL EARL K	COL	O-0259574	0262	3
GILL EDWARD V	CPT	O-1587995	0262	1
GILL FREDERIC G	MAJ	O-1051145	0862	1
GILL JAMES	MAJ	O-0109676	0648	3
GILL JOHN D	WO1	W-2115696	0146	2
GILL JOHN J	1LT	O-1324404	0850	1
GILL JOHN W	LTC	O-0229397	1264	3
GILL JR JAMES L	MAJ	O-1935343	0467	1
GILL LAWRENCE H	CPT	O-1585499	0647	1
GILL MACLEAN J	CPT	O-0466639	0545	2
GILL MATTHEW J	CPT	O-1686864	0645	2
GILL NORMAN	CW3	W-2148001	1059	1
GILL OLIVER C	CPT	O-4009813	1061	2
GILL ROBERT F	CW2	W-2149109	0661	1
GILL VINCENT M	LTC	O-1598395	1163	1
GILL WALTER L	1LT	O-0507430	1045	2
GILL WILLIAM L	MAJ	O-0326459	0666	3
GILLAM CLAUDE E	CPT	O-0510215	0146	2
GILLAM FLOYD E	CW3	W-2146054	0264	1
GILLAM FRANK D	LTC	O-0921379	0163	3
GILLAM JR FRED	CPT	O-0352957	0446	2
GILLAM WILLIAM S	1LT	O-0386432	1045	2
GILLAN REAMER G	MAJ	O-0264400	0254	3
GILLAND EVERETT L	LTC	O-0326829	0163	1
GILLARD THOMAS W	COL	O-0101866	0953	3
GILLASPIE ROBERT A	LTC	O-1329110	1066	1
GILLASPIE TREVELYA	MAJ	O-0201341	0652	3
GILLELAND PALMER A	CW2	W-3200294	0265	1
GILLEN CHARLES R	LTC	O-1052355	0767	1
GILLEN EDWARD L	MAJ	O-1042297	0865	2
GILLEN JOHN R	1LT	O-1994916	1045	2
GILLEN JR MARION T	MAJ	O-0993447	0965	2
GILLEN WILLIAM C	MAJ	O-1582994	1163	1
GILLENS CHARLES H	LTC	O-1166071	1158	1
GILLENWATER ANDREW J	WO1	W-2110206	0358	1
GILLENWATER KENT L	LTC	O-0515310	0954	1
GILLENWATER WILLIAM	CW2	W-2152910	0361	1
GILLERAN THOMAS A	1LT	O-1552070	0646	2
GILLESPIE BRYCE	CPT	O-1043959	1160	1
GILLESPIE CHARLES R	MAJ	O-1996494	0859	1
GILLESPIE DANIEL	CW2	W-2210480	0262	1
GILLESPIE DAVID A	MAJ	O-0242423	0247	2
GILLESPIE DONALD L	1LT	O-1331493	0447	2
GILLESPIE EDWIN P	MAJ	O-1037499	0662	1
GILLESPIE EMERSON	MAJ	O-0495280	1145	2
GILLESPIE HARRY	MAJ	O-0386231	0546	2
GILLESPIE HARRY A	WO1	W-2123708	0845	2
GILLESPIE JAMES J	COL	O-0354218	0646	2
GILLESPIE JOHN C	LTC	O-0388361	0164	1
GILLESPIE JOSEPH F	MAJ	O-1937838	0765	1
GILLESPIE JR GLENN W	CW3	W-2151306	0767	1
GILLESPIE JR JACK O	CPT	O-1299033	0548	1
GILLESPIE JR JAMES O	CPT	O-0443305	0147	2
GILLESPIE JULIA B	MAJ	N-0726351	0661	1
GILLESPIE LAWRENCE C	WO1	W-2149791	0762	2
GILLESPIE MAX H	CW2	W-2148471	0558	1
GILLESPIE NORMAN E	LTC	O-0265138	0960	3
GILLESPIE RICHARD L	COL	O-0245821	0267	3
GILLESPIE ROBERT J	COL	O-0501229	0465	3
GILLESPIE ROBERT V	CW3	W-2149972	0766	1
GILLESPIE THOMAS M L	1LT	O-1643586	0946	2
GILLESPIE VICTOR P	COL	O-0245713	0765	3
GILLESPIE WILLIAM J	LTC	O-1302574	0562	1
GILLETTE EDWARD	COL	O-0183903	1055	3
GILLETTE GEORGE H	CPT	O-0254855	0244	2
GILLETTE GEORGE V	LTC	O-1171158	0667	1
GILLETTE GLENN	LTC	O-0321834	0867	3
GILLETTE JOSEPH A	CW4	W-2117949	1059	1
GILLETTE JOSEPH R	COL	O-0237916	0965	3
GILLETTE MYRON R	LTC	O-0122579	1054	3
GILLETTE PERCIVAL W	COL	O-0187882	1054	3
GILLEY WILLARD S	CPT	O-0520888	0647	1
GILLIAM CLUFFIE C	MAJ	O-0293141	0266	3
GILLIAM ROYCE B	CW2	W-2152379	0261	1
GILLICH PETER	MAJ	O-0439185	0147	1
GILLIE HENRY F	MAJ	O-0305896	0847	2
GILLIES LEROY D	1LT	O-1913685	0532	1
GILLIES ROBERT C	LTC	O-0338478	0262	3
GILLIGAN CARL M	1LT	O-1881428	0554	2
GILLIGAN DEVERN R	LTC	O-0298630	1263	1
GILLIGAN ELEANOR J	1LT	N-0788089	0546	1
GILLIGAN JOHN W	MAJ	O-0379204	0546	2
GILLIGAN THOMAS F	LTC	O-0204993	0360	3
GILLILAND ANNIE W	1LT	N-0765877	1147	1
GILLILAND DONALD C	MAJ	O-0969812	0264	1
GILLILAND JR JOHN O	MAJ	O-2032771	1265	1
GILLILAND ROBERT W	1LT	O-2263039	0454	2
GILLILAND WAYNE R	CW3	W-2141568	0660	1
GILLINGHAM C E	1LT	O-1638677	0246	2
GILLINGHAM CHARLES R	LTC	O-0312774	0657	1
GILLINGHAM GEORGE D	LTC	O-0100518	1054	3
GILLIS ANDREW J	CW2	W-2146874	0561	1
GILLIS CHARLES F	CW2	W-2104094	0545	2
GILLIS CHARLIE L	MAJ	O-1647942	0661	1
GILLIS GEORGE L	CW2	W-2118149	1046	1
GILLIS GLEN	MAJ	O-1183860	0259	1
GILLIS RICHARD E	LTC	O-0450441	0357	1
GILLMAN ELBERT D	CW2	W-3150909	0965	1
GILLMORE LLOYD J	CW4	W-2124355	0961	1
GILLOCK OLIVER P	MAJ	O-0314451	0346	2
GILLOTTE TONY	1LT	O-0497686	0947	1
GILLS JOSEPH A	CPT	O-0250661	0766	3
GILLULY GEORGE K	MAJ	O-1037500	0561	1
GILLY PAUL A	LTC	O-1166997	1060	1
GILLY WILFRED G	MAJ	O-1166598	0261	1
GILMAN EDWARD H	LTC	O-0171927	0648	3
GILMAN HAROLD D	MAJ	O-0192655	0656	3
GILMAN HARRIS H	1LT	O-1315053	1145	2
GILMAN HORTON P	CPT	O-1311879	0146	2
GILMAN JOHN S	CW2	W-2146867	0463	1
GILMAN JOSEPH	MAJ	O-0493790	0246	2
GILMAN JOSEPH R	LTC	O-0326693	0754	3
GILMAN MATTIE L	MAJ	N-0773121	0264	1
GILMAN RICHARD M	1LT	O-1014861	0945	2
GILMARTIN JR JAMES	CW3	W-2151788	0162	1
GILMER CARL E	LTC	O-1175719	1061	1
GILMER JAMES W	LTC	O-0271023	1058	3
GILMER LAWRENCE D	LTC	O-0255409	0866	3
GILMER MELVIN A	MAJ	O-1951570	1064	2
GILMOR DWINNELL	CPT	O-0326496	0944	2
GILMORE CARL F	LTC	O-0268015	1264	3
GILMORE CHARLES E	2LT	O-1322018	0545	2
GILMORE CLIFFORD E	CW3	W-2142796	1057	1
GILMORE FRANK	LTC	O-0312035	0665	3
GILMORE GAYLORD H	LTC	O-0407240	0661	1
GILMORE GERALD E	LTC	O-1317775	0563	1
GILMORE GLENN R	1LT	O-0888335	0145	2
GILMORE GORDON S	LTC	O-0247844	1156	3
GILMORE JOSEPH D	LTC	O-0314625	0160	1
GILMORE MARK A	1LT	O-1042817	0145	2
GILMORE RICHARD A	1LT	O-1179865	0146	2
GILMORE SHELDON C	MAJ	O-0300753	1065	3
GILMORE THOMAS H	2LT	O-1697998	1044	2
GILMORE THOMAS P	COL	O-0172612	0254	3
GILMORE WALTER E	CW3	W-2142840	0760	1
GILMORE WILLIAM E	MAJ	O-1324765	0462	1
GILMORE WINFRED T	2LT	O-1574239	0343	2
GILMOUR GEEN	CPT	O-0275414	0561	3
GILPATRICK GEORGE E	CW4	W-2008098	1057	3
GILPATRICK JAMES M	MAJ	O-0219840	0556	3
GILPIN VERNON T	LTC	O-1583002	1061	1
GILRAY GRANT N	2LT	O-1318423	1044	2
GILREATH DALE E	MAJ	O-1322440	0857	1
GILROY EDWARD F	LTC	O-0254585	0764	3
GILROY JOHN E	MAJ	O-1303815	0864	1
GILROY ROBERT J	LTC	O-1320626	1162	1
GILROY VINCENT J	MAJ	O-0377964	0351	1
GILSDORF ARTHUR F	LTC	O-0286761	0360	3
GILSDORF GEORGE S	LTC	O-1637508	0563	1
GILSDORFF HOWARD H	MAJ	O-0217863	0862	3
GILSON JOHN A	CW3	W-2151643	0864	1
GILSON THOMAS L	MAJ	O-1935444	0865	1
GILSTEIN CYRUS S	2LT	O-1044227	0251	2
GILSTRAP LEE F	LTC	O-0252500	0645	2
GIMESKY JOSEPH T	MAJ	O-2101869	0767	1
GIMPEL RICHARD W	LTC	O-1039357	0662	2
GINDELE CARL H	LTC	O-0384677	0662	1
GINDER NORINE D	MAJ	J-0101152	0366	1
GINGELL THOMAS B	LTC	O-1111626	0862	1
GINGERICH MARION C	LTC	O-0359053	0367	3
GINGERY LEWIS W	LTC	O-1030474	0861	1
GINGLES ERNEST F	CW4	W-2147225	0566	1
GINGRAS GEORGE J	MAJ	O-1291101	0861	1
GINGRICH KENNETH T	MAJ	O-1284129	0561	1
GINGRICH LEROY C	CPT	O-1823434	0861	1
GINN HARRY L	LTC	O-1300309	0560	1
GINN WILLIAM	COL	O-0316612	0367	2
GINN WILLIAM E	1LT	O-0285774	0351	3
GINNATY JOHN R	LTC	O-0263403	0265	3
GINNAVEN WILBUR D	MAJ	O-0183864	0552	3
GINSBERG ISADORE I	MAJ	O-0331193	0447	2
GINSBERG NATHAN N	MAJ	O-0250387	0664	3
GINSBERG STEWART I	COL	O-0320411	0566	3
GINSBURG ABRAHAM S	1LT	O-1638699	0745	2
GINSBURGH A S	LTC	O-0231297	0645	2
GINTER JOHN H	LTC	O-1584264	0961	1
GINTER MALAESKA M	LTC	O-0248173	0566	3
GINTHER FRANCIS C	LTC	O-1297522	1055	2
GINTHER FRED C	MAJ	O-0504357	0157	1
GIOGLIO FRED A	MAJ	O-0417821	0966	3
GIORDANO NICHOLAS	LTC	O-1103654	0963	1
GIORDANO OSCAR R	MAJ	O-0954627	0965	1
GIORLANDO CHARLES V	LTC	O-0301129	0460	1
GIOSCIA NICOLAI	MAJ	O-0493316	0547	2
GIOVETTI ALBERT	LTC	O-2007654	0564	1
GIOVINE LOUIS J	MAJ	O-1645993	0161	1
GIPPLE WILL C	CW2	W-2144656	1060	1
GIPSON CURTIS A	COL	O-0232334	0260	3
GIPSON JAMES M	COL	O-0905158	0365	3
GIPSON JAMES T	CW3	W-2143855	0260	1
GIPSON THOMAS E	CPT	O-0974370	0359	2
GIPSON WILLIAM H	CPT	O-0980892	0261	1
GIRANO CHARLES F	LTC	O-0284019	0967	3
GIRARD ARMAND E	CW3	W-2147573	1061	1
GIRARD BERNARD J	CPT	O-2032312	0959	2
GIRARD CHESTER H	MAJ	O-2050800	0266	3
GIRARD HAROLD H	LTC	O-0267701	0860	3
GIRARD JR MAURICE P	MAJ	O-2036907	0462	1
GIRARD WILLIAM	LTC	O-0286696	1062	3
GIRARDEAU MARVIN O	LTC	O-0174820	0658	3
GIRARDI GUY	CW2	W-3430214	0567	1
GIRAUD LYLE O	CW4	W-2143210	0567	1
GIRLINGHOUSE GUS N	COL	O-0180779	0558	3
GIRON PASCUAL M	CPT	O-0230057	0148	1
GIROUARD JR T J	LTC	O-2032603	0866	1
GIROUX ALBERT	CPT	O-1048372	0157	1
GIROUX LUCIUS A	MAJ	O-0424826	0447	1
GIROUX PAUL N	MAJ	O-1015314	0867	1
GIROUX ROBERT O	1LT	O-1102742	0944	1
GIRSTANTAS WALTER A	LTC	O-1000568	0961	1
GISH HENRY G	CPT	O-1593592	0355	1
GISH HERBERT O	COL	O-0334895	0658	3
GISCNOI FRANK A	MAJ	O-1587763	0561	1
GISSE FRED H	CPT	O-1015346	1047	2
GISSELL CLIFFORD J	CPT	O-1000949	0858	1
GIST LANDON E	LTC	O-0191128	0555	3
GITLIN HERMAN	CPT	O-1300475	0646	2
GITLIN SAUL	COL	O-0320654	1058	1
GITTELSON HERMAN	1LT	O-1015380	0445	2
GITTINGS BEN L	2LT	O-0328225	1142	2
GIULIANO ANNIELLIO	LTC	O-0425419	0462	1
GIUNTOLI WILLIAM M	2LT	O-1288374	0444	2
GIVAN GEORGE P	CW3	W-2141909	0659	1
GIVAN JR FRANK M	MAJ	O-1995604	0964	1
GIVEN ARTHUR G	LTC	O-0359347	0661	1
GIVEN GEORGE L	CW3	W-2147128	0363	1
GIVENS JOHN W	LTC	O-1174576	0264	1
GIVENS JR JAMES T	CW3	W-2143782	0666	1
GIVENS MALCOLM E	1LT	O-2201531	0753	2
GIVENS MARCEL	CW3	W-2147832	0564	1
GIVENS MITCHELL S	LTC	O-2047333	0267	2
GIVENS WILLIS R	COL	O-0239323	0556	1
GIVENTER EDWARD	LTC	O-1045089	0865	3
GIVHAN JOHN B	1LT	O-5314983	1064	2
GIVOTOFF HYMAN	MAJ	O-0359197	0467	3
GIZA JR JOSEPH J	MAJ	O-0987838	0564	1
GIZZI ERNEST R	LTC	O-0371600	0260	1
GIZZI TULLIO J	LTC	O-1584265	0967	1
GLAAB LAWRENCE H	LTC	O-1183862	0267	1
GLACEL JR EDWIN W	LTC	O-1590137	0163	1
GLACKIN JAMES A	LTC	O-0450154	0157	1
GLADDEN EMORY T	1LT	O-0315602	0346	2
GLADDEN MARTHA L	MAJ	N-0737319	1264	1
GLADDING PHILIP E	MAJ	O-0978977	0462	1
GLADIN CHANDLER B	LTC	O-0227588	0464	3
GLADING EUGENE J	LTC	O-1639078	0563	1
GLADNEY JR JAMES F	LTC	O-0419859	1047	1
GLADSON JAMES F	LTC	O-1298049	0657	1
GLADSTONE GEORGE L	LTC	O-0269156	0758	1
GLADWIN CHARLES C	MAJ	O-1047535	0565	1
GLADYS JOHN A	MAJ	O-1012242	0765	1
GLADYS STANLEY J	CPT	O-0890083	0756	2
GLADYSZ JOSEPH	CW4	W-2000112	1157	3
GLADZIK JR FERDINAND	LTC	O-0224213	1264	3
GLAESNER ROBERT O	CPT	O-1687121	0246	2
GLAISTER HENRY B	LTC	O-0293058	0761	1
GLAMORE JAMES H	CPT	O-1321303	0246	2
GLANCEY JAMES W	MAJ	O-1913273	0766	1
GLANCY LLOYD L	CPT	O-1637509	0747	1
GLANTZ ROBERT	LTC	O-1294294	0960	1
GLANZ WILLIAM H	COL	O-0247765	0961	1
GLASCO PERCY L	1LT	O-1040926	1144	2
GLASCOCK CHARLES L	LTC	O-1547309	0761	2
GLASCOCK FRANCIS R	CPT	O-0362216	0562	1
GLASER HERBERT R	LTC	O-0906735	1067	3
GLASER LELAND F	LTC	O-0311153	0446	2
GLASER LEO	CPT	O-1578519	0947	2
GLASGOW JOHN E	CW3	W-2152380	0565	1
GLASGOW RALPH H	CPT	O-0982782	0657	1
GLASGOW WILLIAM M	CPT	O-0155278	0648	3
GLASGOW WILLIAM R	CPT	O-0218622	0261	3
GLASGOW WILLIS H	CPT	O-0506821	1048	1
GLASHEEN GEORGE L	COL	O-0506844	1065	3
GLASIER EDWIN L	LTC	O-0114454	0450	3
GLASPEL CYRIL J	LTC	O-0136101	0353	3
GLASS CHARLES R	LTC	O-0425322	0161	1
GLASS CESSIE B	MAJ	O-0588789	1062	1
GLASS GARNET C	CPT	O-2005953	0647	2
GLASS JAMES F	MAJ	O-1011079	0862	1
GLASS JR NORMAN C	CPT	O-0409966	0145	2
GLASS MERTON L	MAJ	O-1037504	0155	2
GLASS THOMAS F	LTC	O-1014692	0560	1
GLASS THOMAS F	1LT	O-1301291	0845	2
GLASS VERNON E	CW2	W-2114727	0846	1
GLASSBURNER FRED R J	CPT	O-0361778	1045	1

NAME	GRADE	SVC NO	DATE RET MO YR	RET CODE
GLASSCOCK EARL C	COL	0-0348298	C660	1
GLASSCOCK MARGARET M	LTC	L-0800001	0767	3
GLASSEN CLIFFORD W	CPT	0-1284494	1145	2
GLASSER BENJAMIN F	MAJ	0-1688151	C147	1
GLASSER HYMIE	1LT	0-1321403	1047	2
GLASSER JOSEPH G	2LT	0-1997713	1145	1
GLASSER JULIUS M	LTC	0-0211257	0346	2
GLASSER ROBERT	MAJ	C-1294820	0967	3
GLASSFORD DAVID M	LTC	0-0342120	0767	3
GLASSMAN JAMES	LTC	0-1044527	C465	3
GLASSNER WILLIAM	LTC	0-0281505	C853	3
GLASTON MAX M	MAJ	0-1037004	0465	3
GLATHART CLIFFORD I	LTC	0-1573857	1057	2
GLATT RALPH A	COL	0-0241994	0854	3
GLAUBMAN WILLIAM A	1LT	0-0386566	0843	2
GLAUSER WILLIAM H	CPT	0-0498353	1048	1
GLAVE CHARLES W	MAJ	0-1686340	C566	1
GLAVES ALEXANDER	CPT	0-1639938	0957	1
GLAZE EDWARD L	1LT	0-1327139	C452	2
GLAZER FRED	1LT	0-1169126	0545	2
GLAZIER FRANK X	CW2	W-2141565	0253	2
GLAZIER HERBERT E	1LT	0-1825910	1145	2
GLAZIER SAMUEL	COL	0-0163240	1060	3
GLEADLE RUSSELL H	1LT	0-1794802	C944	2
GLEASNER JR LEO H	MAJ	0-0989219	0767	1
GLEASON DANIEL	LTC	0-1314558	0962	1
GLEASON GEORGE L	MAJ	C-0333959	0344	2
GLEASON GEORGE M	MAJ	C-2262271	C264	2
GLEASON JAMES A	COL	0-0249665	0365	3
GLEASON JAMES V	CPT	0-1301472	C850	1
GLEASON JOHN P	LTC	0-0476202	C147	1
GLEASON JOSEPH F	MAJ	0-0949337	C865	1
GLEASON JR GUS M	LTC	0-4001962	1155	2
GLEASON JR JOEL W	CW4	W-2102940	0659	1
GLEASON PERCY M	LTC	0-0174922	C648	3
GLEASON ROBERT E	CPT	0-0263979	1054	3
GLEASON ROBERT M	MAJ	0-2102972	1063	1
GLEASON THOMAS J	LTC	0-1171161	0267	1
GLEASON WALLACE A	COL	0-0263447	C764	3
GLEASON WALTER J	COL	C-0284957	1162	3
GLEASON WILLIAM C	LTC	0-2017836	C766	1
GLEESON ANDREW A	MAJ	0-0903557	C365	1
CLEESON EDITH M	1LT	N-0796282	1047	1
CLEFFE WILLIAM F	1LT	0-2009794	C761	1
GLEICHAUF WILLIAM P	CW4	W-2143229	0567	1
GLEICHER SOL H	1LT	0-1306265	C446	2
GLEIM EDNA A	CPT	J-0101150	0661	2
GLEISBERG WILLIAM P	MAJ	0-1553999	0656	1
GLEITSMAN ERNEST W	CW2	W-2209693	0866	2
GLEMSER ROBERT	CPT	0-0986155	C661	1
GLEN JOHN R	LTC	0-0248132	0966	3
GLENDENING DALE D	MAJ	0-1823725	C561	1
GLENDENING WILLIAM A	1LT	0-1320451	C757	1
GLENDY ROBERT E	LTC	0-0213896	1062	3
GLENN CARL B	1LT	0-1573232	0145	2
GLENN DELVIN C	MAJ	C-0955433	0463	1
GLENN EDWARD B	MAJ	C-0495981	0446	2
GLENN EDWARD R	MAJ	C-0148616	C857	3
GLENN EUGENE B	COL	C-0310948	C467	3
GLENN FRANCIS A	LTC	0-0274454	1045	2
GLENN HENRY L	COL	0-0162411	0861	3
GLENN JAMES L	LTC	0-1165502	0265	1
GLENN JAMES M	CPT	0-2006631	0157	1
GLENN JOSEPH S	CPT	0-0489850	1147	1
GLENN JR HARRY J	CPT	0-0366436	C847	2
GLENN JR JOSEPH W	CPT	0-0226675	C463	3
GLENN LORETTA E	CPT	N-0724880	C448	1
GLENN MARSHALL W	CPT	0-0314686	0646	2
GLENN MARTIN R	COL	0-0361541	0166	3
GLENN OTIS R	MAJ	C-0486581	0451	1
GLENN PAUL F	MAJ	C-1060105	C166	1
GLENN RAY	MAJ	0-1060101	0860	1
GLENN RICHARD C	MAJ	0-1644363	1060	1
GLENN ROBERT	LTC	0-0239521	C564	3
GLENN ROBERT L	MAJ	C-0419291	0346	2

NAME	GRADE	SVC NO	DATE RET MO YR	RET CODE
GLENA THOMAS C	MAJ	0-1557157	0364	1
GLENN WESLEY A	LTC	0-1634799	0761	2
GLENN WILLIAM T	MAJ	C-2035314	0663	1
GLENNAN JR JOHN F	LTC	0-0451474	0958	1
GLENNAN KENNETH A	MAJ	C-2078580	1066	1
GLENNEY JULIUS C	CPT	0-0316567	0545	2
GLENNON JOHN J	CPT	0-1321912	0646	2
GLEOGGLER FRED J	LTC	0-0202382	0453	3
GLERUM JR CORNELIUS	CPT	0-1169127	0647	1
GLERUM LAURENCE D	LTC	0-0252012	0567	3
GLESSNER FRANK J	LTC	0-2018155	0167	1
GLESSNER RUDOLF I	LTC	0-1305760	0465	1
GLEW GEORGE W	LTC	0-1556584	0761	1
GLEYE PAUL H	LTC	0-2008185	1067	1
GLICK ALBERT	2LT	0-1997085	1051	2
GLICK BERNARD W	CPT	0-0312038	0346	2
GLICK MARIE	2LT	N-0742685	0844	1
GLICKFELD WILLIAM	LTC	0-0453041	0746	2
GLICKMAN LEO G	MAJ	0-0235169	1259	3
GLIDDEN BURNETT E	MAJ	C-2007662	0361	1
GLIDDEN GORDON G	LTC	0-0274913	0765	3
GLIDDEN HAROLD L	CPT	0-1165865	C946	1
GLIDDEN HERBERT H	COL	0-0123635	C258	1
GLIDDEN HOWARD E	MAJ	0-1647591	0263	1
GLIDER JOSEPH	1LT	0-1297884	0246	2
GLIDEWELL JAMES B	MAJ	0-0887566	0361	1
GLINES VICTOR L	COL	0-0235276	1055	3
GLINSKI EDWARD J	LTC	0-0467625	0847	1
GLISAN ANDREW R	CW3	W-2152828	0361	1
GLISCH HARRY S	COL	0-0278637	0165	3
GLISH JOSEPH A	CW2	W-2120777	C547	1
GLISSON CHARLES J	CPT	0-1044829	0356	1
GLISSON JAMES P	LTC	0-1554367	0764	1
GLISSON MARION L	WO1	W-2101749	1053	1
GLOBUS ROBERT	CPT	0-0241654	0760	3
GLOCK ROBERT W	COL	0-0410816	0265	1
GLODELL LEROY M	COL	0-0292049	0760	1
GLOGOVCSAN RUDOLF	MAJ	0-1640489	0757	1
GLOMB LOUIS G	CW3	W-2150940	0667	1
GLOMINSKI JOHN A	MAJ	0-0128372	0648	3
GLOMSKI ARTHUR P	CW2	W-2143852	0261	1
GLOSSOP MARVIN	COL	0-1315297	0966	1
GLOTZBACH CLIFFORD W	LTC	0-0384335	1266	3
GLOVATZKY WADIN J	MAJ	0-1702356	0348	2
GLOVER ALFRED L	1LT	0-1320939	1145	1
GLOVER CHARLES C	CW3	W-2153128	0563	1
GLOVER HERBERT C	2LT	0-1176974	0544	2
GLOVER JOHN C	CW2	W-2147606	0762	1
GLOVER JOSEPH A	LTC	0-0255393	0260	2
GLOVER JR ROY A	LTC	0-1588482	0762	2
GLOVER KENNETH	MAJ	0-2045160	0165	1
GLOVER MERLE W	MAJ	0-0516938	0649	1
GLOVER PAUL G	LTC	0-0527148	1166	1
GLOVER RALPH C	COL	0-0333022	0865	3
GLOVER WELLINGTON	COL	C-0234431	0257	1
GLOVER WILLIAM P	LTC	0-0492526	0765	1
GLOVER WILLIAM S	MAJ	0-2263127	0962	1
GLOWACKI CLARENCE A	1LT	0-0388283	1145	2
GLOZER NORMAN L	MAJ	0-1080934	0962	1
GLUCH JR JOHN J	LTC	0-1045438	0463	1
GLUCHOWSKI FRANK W	LTC	C-1321175	1162	1
GLUCK ALVIN H	MAJ	C-1185490	0258	1
GLUCK EDWARD	COL	0-0239172	0357	3
GLUCK HAROLD	2LT	0-1306266	0244	2
GLUCK OSCAR W	LTC	0-0384150	0467	3
GLUCKHERTZ THOMAS F	CW3	W-2144210	0261	1
GLUMP FRANK	MAJ	C-1945588	0760	2
GLUNTZ EDWIN C	COL	C-0271024	0158	2
GLYNN FORREST B	LTC	0-0451107	0163	1
GLYNN HAZEL F	MAJ	L-0602912	0363	1
GLYNN JOHN L	COL	0-0371425	0258	3
GLYNN JOSEPH P	LTC	0-1944455	0463	1
GLYNN ROBERT F	MAJ	0-1293582	0361	1
GLYNN THOMAS J	CPT	0-0454087	0256	1
GLYNNE LAVINIA J	2LT	N-0722634	1C42	*1

NAME	GRADE	SVC NO	DATE RET MO YR	RET CODE
GMEINER LOREN L	COL	C-0246176	0454	2
GMYR BRONISLAW	CPT	0-1903885	C662	1
GNADT WILLIAM H	MAJ	C-1688414	C863	1
GNIADEK MARY M	MAJ	N-0751007	1164	1
GNIFFKE PAUL G	LTC	C-1306087	1265	1
GNUS MARIE	1LT	N-0761226	0446	1
GOAD SIDNEY E	MAJ	C-0252803	0866	3
GOATES FLOYD W	COL	0-0150783	C157	1
GOATES JOHN R	MAJ	C-1557851	0663	1
GOATLEY DURAND R	LTC	0-1010087	C757	1
GOBAR KENNETH W	LTC	C-1035079	0557	1
GOBLE ARTHUR L	CW2	W-2101751	0448	1
GOBLE CHESTER W	M G	0-0100210	0255	3
GOBLE NEIL T	CPT	0-0318803	1044	2
GOBLE ROBERT E	MAJ	C-1923603	1164	1
GOBLE ROBERT J	CPT	0-0338515	C446	2
GOBLE WILLIAM H	1LT	0-1019179	0446	2
GOBRECHT WALTER R	1LT	0-0522458	1043	2
GOCHENAUR FRED M	LTC	0-1641328	C565	1
GOCHENOUR FRANK D	CPT	0-1645998	C945	2
GOCHENOUR JOHN C	LTC	0-1949327	C565	1
GOCHENOUR JR OBED L	MAJ	C-1648160	0657	1
GOCHNAUER OSCAR B	MAJ	0-0272374	0961	3
GOCHNOUR FLOYD E	LTC	0-0318228	C560	2
GOCHNOUR ROSCOE J	MAJ	C-2042688	C155	1
GODBER JOHN T	MAJ	C-1589854	0962	1
GODBEY MERLE H	CPT	0-0373740	0346	2
GODBOUT JOHN P	MAJ	C-1554369	C356	1
GODBOUT MEDRIC M	WO1	W-2131964	C847	2
GODDARD BERNARD L	MAJ	C-0885085	1058	1
GODDARD CHARLES H	MAJ	C-0346892	C547	1
GODDARD GEORGE	CPT	C-1037006	C962	1
GODDARD HARRY E	LTC	0-0331602	C467	3
GODDARD JAMES E	COL	0-0251320	C966	3
GODDARD JAMES H	LTC	0-0293713	1047	2
GODDARD JOHN B	CPT	0-1323424	C846	2
GODDARD LAWRENCE L	LTC	0-1297524	1162	1
GODDARD LEWIS C	1LT	0-1895765	C646	1
GODDARD SR WILLIAM L	LTC	C-0453439	C261	1
GODDARD WILLIAM B	COL	0-0209216	C858	3
GOODEN ROSCOE H	MAJ	C-0363246	0557	1
GODFREY ALBERT J	LTC	0-0199503	0459	1
GODFREY ANSEL B	M G	0-0163566	1160	3
GODFREY CECIL H	COL	C-0216324	0863	3
GODFREY CLARENCE M	LTC	0-0503421	0364	3
GODFREY GEORGE H	LTC	0-0277909	C761	3
GODFREY JOHN F	CW3	W-2152505	C264	1
GODFREY THORNTON H	CPT	0-0988211	1160	1
GODFREY WILLIAM C	COL	0-0134892	0551	3
GODFREY XELIS W	LTC	0-0923973	C962	3
GODIN GEORGE V H	1LT	C-0466336	C746	2
GODING LLOYD A	CPT	0-0355265	C346	2
GODLEWSKI LEO A	CW3	W-2144045	0163	1
GODLEY JOSEPH	MAJ	C-0184608	C845	2
GODLEY ROBERT E	CPT	0-0488776	0945	2
GODLEY VES W	LTC	0-0256822	1044	2
GODSEY JR HOWARD E	CW2	W-2152627	1064	1
GODSMAN PAUL J	LTC	C-0408705	1064	1
GODSMAN SIDNEY P	COL	0-0238076	C950	3
GODSTREY HERBERT H	WO1	W-2145638	0654	1
GODWIN ALBERT S	CW3	W-2106194	1154	1
GODWIN DALE M	LTC	0-0298291	1062	3
GODWIN EARL J	CW3	W-2145772	0162	1
GODWIN GERALD S	CPT	C-1322329	C148	2
GODWIN GROVER	LTC	0-0132226	1057	3
GODWIN HARRY E	1LT	0-1826271	1144	2
GODWIN HOLLIS E	MAJ	C-1171555	0256	1
GODWIN JAMES A	LTC	0-0328524	0661	1
GODWIN JIMMIE J	COL	C-0187471	1056	3
GODWIN JOHN J	CW2	W-2147629	1057	1
GODWIN PAUL H	CPT	0-1640490	1056	1
GODWIN TULLIS M	1LT	0-0407840	0144	2
GODWIN WILLIAM D	CW3	W-2151610	1060	1
GOEBEL RALPH N	CPT	0-0175719	0557	3
GOECKER LOUIS E	LTC	0-0178918	1055	3

NAME	GRADE	SVC NO	DATE RET MO YR	RET CODE
GOEDDE VICTOR H	LTC	0-0166980	1057	3
GOEDEN LOUISE F	MAJ	L-0600306	0267	3
GOEDHART ROBERT G	2LT	C-0367165	0245	2
GOEDIKE JOHN G	COL	0-0152369	0648	3
GOEHRING RUFUS C	MAJ	C-0286654	1163	3
GOEN NEIL M	CPT	0-0506381	0555	3
GOERING GEORGE R	LTC	0-1011917	0766	1
GOERING WILLIAM H	LTC	0-0258981	0862	3
GOERISCH ROBERT W	MAJ	C-1031554	0256	1
GOERL MARTIN	COL	0-0231327	0855	3
GOESKE JOHN W	CW4	W-2142157	0961	1
GOESSENS LEONEL	MAJ	0-1338704	0666	1
GOETH CARL F	MAJ	0-0345155	1045	2
GOETHEL LOUIS N	LTC	0-0300215	0560	1
GOETTE JOSEPH A	MAJ	0-1281947	0166	1
GOETZ ALBERTA M	MAJ	N-0798983	0665	1
GOETZ CHARLES M	MAJ	0-1101845	0861	1
GOETZ FRED A	MAJ	C-1686320	0758	1
GOETZ JOHN A	CPT	C-0298822	0144	2
GOETZ JR WILLIAM L	MAJ	0-1330301	0163	1
GOETZ PAUL D	LTC	0-1173258	0466	2
GOETZ PHILLIP R	COL	0-0428265	0546	2
GOETZ ROBERT F	CPT	C-0474843	1047	1
GOETZKE GEORGE D	LTC	0-0916236	0362	1
GOEWEY JAMES H	LTC	0-0528599	1160	2
GOFF ABE M	COL	0-0173019	0160	3
GOFF ALLSTON S	MAJ	0-0282531	1045	2
GOFF CARLES A	LTC	0-1288043	0761	1
GOFF DIXWELL	LTC	0-0297554	1165	3
GOFF DONALD H	CPT	0-0417234	0347	2
GOFF FREDERICK	CPT	0-0257190	0344	2
GOFF JR LEE B	LTC	0-0247485	0656	3
GOFF LOUIS F	MAJ	0-1823288	0365	1
GOFF LYMAN E	2LT	0-1315054	1144	2
GOFF MARSHALL A	LTC	0-0154333	0545	2
GOFF PAUL	CPT	0-0450286	0761	1
GOFF ROBERT R	1LT	0-1315577	1145	2
GOFF SR EDDIE G	WO1	W-2153251	0958	2
GOFF VIRGIL R	MAJ	0-1876716	1263	1
GOFF WILLIAM J	MAJ	0-0941966	0161	1
GOFFAR ANNA K	MAJ	L-1010022	0766	1
GOFORTH DELBERT J	CW3	W-2141570	0859	1
GOFORTH HARRY J	1LT	0-1291804	0845	2
GOFOURTH THEODORE T	MAJ	0-1341774	0861	1
GOGATS JOHN C	CW4	W-2117386	0659	1
GOGGANS ELMER F	MAJ	0-0443980	0246	1
GOGGANS JR EMORY L	LTC	0-0452253	0562	1
GOGGANS JR OSCAR F	MAJ	C-1004590	0758	1
GOGGIN DANIEL F	CW4	W-2106010	0762	2
GOGGIN JOSEPH F	CPT	0-1283585	1045	1
GOGGIN ROY F	COL	0-0234412	0160	3
GOGGIN THOMAS W	LTC	0-0410732	1060	1
GOGLIA EDWARD G	1LT	0-0396637	0352	2
GOGLIO ALEXANDER	1LT	0-1061704	0447	2
GOGOLA BENJAMIN J	LTC	0-0415581	0461	1
GOGOLA MITCHELL A	CW4	W-2114168	0263	1
GOGUEN ARTHUR A J	LTC	0-0295097	0666	3
GOGUEN LEO A	MAJ	0-1014857	1060	1
GOHMERT EDWARD H	LTC	0-0201992	0860	3
GOHN ESTEL E	LTC	0-1635943	1060	1
GOHS FRANK J	CW4	W-2122216	0662	1
GOIN OTIS S	CW3	W-2143854	0163	1
GOING CHARLES F	COL	0-0265914	0152	3
GOINS RICHARD W	MAJ	0-1297525	0658	1
GOLAR LEWIS L	CPT	0-0199559	0648	1
GOLAR LOUIS L	CPT	0-0454730	0162	1
GOLBA SOPHIE K	MAJ	N-0722856	0964	2
GOLBEY FRANK A	LTC	0-0402961	0147	1
GOLBY LLOYD R	CPT	0-0887508	0648	1
GOLD ALEX F	CPT	0-0313688	0246	2
GOLD JR CLARENCE B	MAJ	0-1115600	0860	1
GOLD MORRIS A	MAJ	0-0336330	0346	2
GOLDA PETER A	WO1	W-2146744	0255	1
GOLDBACH FRANCIS H	2LT	0-1637522	0645	2
GOLOBECK JR BEN T	CPT	0-1168689	1044	2

NAME	GRADE	SVC NO	DATE RET MO YR	RET CODE
GOLDBERG BENJAMIN A	1LT	O-0364125	0444	2
GOLDBERG GEORGE	CW3	W-2150913	0964	1
GOLDBERG IRWIN	1LT	O-0278217	0944	2
GOLDBERG ISADORE	MAJ	O-0499871	0954	1
GOLDBERG LEON	LTC	O-0279928	0546	2
GOLDBERG LOUISE F	MAJ	N-0725262	0866	1
GOLDBERG NORMAN L	CPT	O-0510389	0545	2
GOLDBERG SAMUEL L	MAJ	O-0497896	0347	2
GOLDBERG STANLEY S	MAJ	O-0469313	0446	2
GOLDBERGER MAXWELL	COL	O-0140750	0250	3
GOLDBLATT LOUIS L	LTC	O-0167589	0648	3
GOLDBLATT MEYER G	CW2	W-2209926	0767	1
GOLDBURG NORMAN M	MAJ	O-0319814	0762	3
GOLDEN ABRAHAM	COL	O-0100485	0654	2
GOLDEN BEVERLY J	2LT	N-0777086	1045	1
GOLDEN ERNEST F	COL	O-0423107	0866	1
GOLDEN GEORGE J	1LT	O-1287338	1045	1
GOLDEN GERARD W	CPT	O-1556881	0746	2
GOLDEN GILBERT A	1LT	O-1045749	1046	2
GOLDEN HERMAN B	MAJ	O-2046580	0756	1
GOLDEN JOHN R	LTC	O-0519280	1067	3
GOLDEN JR HENRY J	2LT	O-1046102	0544	2
GOLDEN JULIUS	COL	O-0321435	0765	3
GOLDEN MARVIN L	MAJ	O-1895775	0460	3
GOLDEN PAUL F	MAJ	O-2096670	0865	1
GOLDEN PAUL M	CPT	O-2039459	0457	1
GOLDEN ROBERT F	CPT	O-0356620	0446	2
GOLDEN THEODORE S	MAJ	O-0497963	0546	2
GOLDEN WAYNE H	MAJ	O-1342175	1060	1
GOLDEN WILLIAM T	LTC	O-1179413	0867	1
GOLDENBERG AUBREY H	CPT	O-0984701	0457	1
GOLDENBOGEN ROBERT L	2LT	O-1577238	1043	1
GOLDENER DONALD	MAJ	O-4030733	0367	1
GOLDENSOHN ELI S	CPT	O-0388237	0644	1
GOLDER THOMAS E	CW4	W-2144991	0456	1
GOLDFARB HERMAN	CPT	O-1103181	0646	2
GOLDFARB JOSEPH S	1LT	O-0500124	0644	2
GOLDFARB MORRIS	MAJ	O-1995426	0963	2
GOLDFARB OSCAR	1LT	O-1534496	0146	2
GOLDIAN JOSEPH M	MAJ	O-1170750	1159	1
GOLDIN ABRAHAM W	1LT	O-1591753	1051	1
GOLDIN JOHN M	MAJ	O-0171722	0753	3
GOLDIN LEO N	MAJ	O-0502961	0346	2
GOLDING HAROLD B	CPT	O-0224132	1144	2
GOLDING HOWARD B	1LT	O-1310357	0845	1
GOLDMAN EPHRAIM J	CPT	O-0496604	0845	1
GOLDMAN ERNEST N	LTC	O-0104773	0556	3
GOLDMAN FRANKLIN J	MAJ	O-0253262	1164	3
GOLDMAN FREDERICK	COL	O-0105435	0150	3
GOLDMAN GEORGE	COL	O-0282995	0456	3
GOLDMAN HARRY	CPT	O-0886867	0856	1
GOLDMAN HERMAN L	LTC	O-1016127	0767	1
GOLDMAN IRVING	1LT	O-1995607	0746	2
GOLDMAN IRVING R	MAJ	O-0397115	0346	2
GOLDMAN LEONARD N	1LT	O-1322020	1045	2
GOLDMAN MARCUS S	COL	O-0231570	0554	3
GOLDMAN MARTIN I	LTC	O-1824301	0766	1
GOLDMAN MAX	MAJ	O-0344923	0345	1
GOLDMAN MAX R	CPT	O-0487810	0245	2
GOLDMAN MEYER N	CW2	W-2000301	0349	3
GOLDMAN NATHAN C	CPT	O-0921386	0244	2
GOLDMAN ROBERT	1LT	O-1324767	0345	2
GOLDMAN SIDNEY S	LTC	O-0227106	1162	3
GOLDMAN SYLVAN R	CW3	W-2151903	0864	1
GOLDNER ROBERT B	1LT	O-0493568	1045	2
GOLDSBERRY JOHN J	LTC	O-0313087	0962	3
GOLDSBERRY WILLIAM M	CPT	O-0193258	0747	1
GOLDSBY JOE C	LTC	O-0259515	0267	3
GOLDSCHMIDT HENRY C	LTC	O-0122845	1055	3
GOLDSMITH ARTHUR L	CPT	O-0411356	0944	2
GOLDSMITH CLARENCE A	1LT	O-0499489	1047	1
GOLDSMITH FRED J	LTC	O-1038644	0867	1
GOLDSMITH GORDON C	MAJ	O-1922609	0166	1
GOLDSMITH HENRY C	LTC	O-0138918	1156	3
GOLDSMITH IRWIN R	CPT	O-0311844	0743	2

NAME	GRADE	SVC NO	DATE RET MO YR	RET CODE
GOLDSMITH MYRON B	MAJ	O-0218536	0854	3
GOLDSMITH RICHARD L	MAJ	O-0410874	1049	1
GOLDSMITH ROBERT F	LTC	O-0395037	0760	2
GOLDSMITH SAM	LTC	O-0461642	0254	1
GOLDSMITH WILLIAM E	CPT	O-0223826	0957	3
GOLDSTEIN ARTHUR H	COL	O-0207404	0360	1
GOLDSTEIN DAVID	1LT	O-1534264	0845	1
GOLDSTEIN DAVID M	MAJ	O-0356433	0546	2
GOLDSTEIN GEORGE	LTC	O-0296847	0263	3
GOLDSTEIN HENRY	CPT	O-0230766	1167	3
GOLDSTEIN HOWARD J	CPT	O-1695821	0546	2
GOLDSTEIN JOSEPH	MAJ	O-0167519	0544	2
GOLDSTEIN MILTON	CW2	W-2104099	1046	1
GOLDSTEIN PHILIP	COL	O-0245051	1157	3
GOLDSTEIN QUENTEN E	MAJ	O-1338451	1265	1
GOLDSTEIN SAMPSON	LTC	O-0209636	1058	3
GOLDSTON WILLIAM M	COL	O-0202419	0254	3
GOLDT HENRY R	CPT	O-0357701	0146	1
GOLDTHWAITE DONALD E	1LT	O-1291102	0144	2
GOLDY CHARLES R	MAJ	O-1541871	0858	1
GOLEMAN OCIE A	LTC	O-0489055	0557	1
GOLEMON HARRY W	MAJ	O-0258522	0266	3
GOLER HAROLD K	LTC	O-0296901	0546	2
GOLEY WILLARD C	COL	O-0244760	0358	3
GOLIDAY FRANKLIN E	CW3	W-2143909	0461	1
GOLIGHTLY HAROLD E	CW3	W-2149874	0964	1
GOLISCH CLARENCE F	COL	O-0336047	0265	3
GOLKOPF WILLIAM A	1LT	O-1051147	1144	2
GOLKOWSKI ADELINE S	MAJ	N-0788420	0167	3
GOLL JOHN N	1LT	O-0448341	0945	2
GOLL MCKIE F	LTC	O-0301902	1059	3
GOLLA NICK	CPT	O-1896521	0559	1
GOLLER CHARLES G	CW4	W-2110290	0960	1
GOLLINGS FRANK J	COL	O-0364177	0967	3
GOLLNICK ALBERT H	MAJ	O-2009805	0359	1
GOLLOB HAROLD T	LTC	O-2035315	0767	1
GOLLUB MORRIS	MAJ	O-1590495	1060	2
GOLOJHICH FRANK J	1LT	O-1316490	1045	2
GOLSAN JOSEPH L	LTC	O-0378805	0146	2
GOLSAN WILLARD R	COL	O-0176812	0961	3
GOLTIAO HERMINIO	CPT	O-2027441	1158	1
GOLTMAN JOHN T	LTC	O-0268263	1262	3
GOLTZ SANFORD C	1LT	O-1549950	0246	2
GOLTZENE HOMER H	LTC	O-0183265	0356	3
GOLUBCK SAMUEL	CPT	O-0241381	0564	3
GOMAN CLIFFORD R	MAJ	O-0452141	1158	1
GOMBER JR HENRY A	MAJ	O-1291979	1060	1
GOMBERG CHARLES A	CPT	O-0921127	0463	1
GOMBERG JACK R	1LT	O-0527482	1045	2
GOMBOSH ARTHUR J	MAJ	O-2002279	0761	1
GOMEZ ABRAHAM	LTC	O-0444110	0563	1
GOMEZ BENJAMIN E	CPT	O-1039295	0547	2
GOMEZ HENRY W	LTC	O-1301913	0860	1
GOMEZ JOHN L	MAJ	O-1115601	0163	1
GOMEZ MARGARET M	1LT	N-0757972	0847	1
GOMEZ-CINTRON RAMON	CPT	O-0109083	0530	1
GOMIEN SCOTT	CPT	O-0216983	0254	3
GOMMESEN JACK	LTC	O-1181612	0364	1
GOMOLCHAK LEO A	MAJ	O-4009028	0366	1
GOMOLL OSCAR E	CPT	O-0494394	0346	2
GOMON HORACE	LTC	O-0238898	1262	3
GOMON LYLE G	LTC	O-0253317	0462	3
GOMORY GUSTAVE E	LTC	O-1291805	1166	2
GOMSAK PETER D	MAJ	O-0275913	0364	3
GONDA JR JOSEPH A	2LT	O-1594868	0244	2
GONDEK FRANK	WO1	W-2120680	0246	2
GONDERMAN LAMAR E	CW3	W-2145141	0562	1
GONDRAN ALBERT D	1LT	O-2207467	0553	1
GONEAU ERNEST R	CW3	W-2144869	0861	1
GONSALVES FRANK B	WO1	W-2131809	1151	1
GONYO WILLIAM C	CPT	O-0970210	0960	1
GONZALES EXECUIEL	1LT	O-0282960	0953	1
GONZALES LEO J	CW2	W-2150663	0861	1
GONZALES LISANDRO F	LTC	O-0359030	0658	1
GONZALES MOSES	CW2	W-2152459	0760	1

NAME	GRADE	SVC NO	DATE RET MO YR	RET CODE
GONZALES PABLO E	CPT	O-1896678	0559	1
GONZALES RALPH J	CW3	W-2208588	1167	1
GONZALES REGINALD R	CW3	W-2146834	1061	1
GONZALEZ ANCEL G	CPT	O-0502914	0944	2
GONZALEZ ERNESTO	LTC	O-0229046	0265	3
GONZALEZ ISHMAEL C	MAJ	O-2263333	0466	2
GONZALEZ JAIME	MAJ	O-0102156	0245	1
GONZALEZ JR ANDRES C	1LT	O-1541156	1043	2
GONZALEZ JR HIGINIO	CPT	O-0980712	0962	2
GONZALEZ JR JUAN C	MAJ	O-0408303	0148	1
GONZALEZ JUAN	1LT	O-0263643	1047	1
GONZALEZ MAXIMO	LTC	O-0203229	0660	1
GONZALEZ ORVIS L	MAJ	O-0132890	1052	3
GONZALEZ PRUDENCIO	CPT	O-0337555	0567	3
GONZALEZ REINALDO F	CPT	O-2033199	0762	2
GONZALEZ VICTOR	MAJ	O-1333625	0762	1
GONZALEZ-JULIA GILBE	MAJ	O-0334520	0661	1
GONZALEZ-MORALE FER	CW3	W-2147630	0962	1
GONZALEZ-RAMIRE LUI	COL	O-0310451	1063	3
GONZALVES GORDON P	CPT	O-0936633	1059	2
GOOCH CLIFFORD A	1LT	O-0405418	0445	1
GOOCH ELMER	1LT	O-1102263	0245	1
GOOCH GORDON R	MAJ	O-1897753	0164	1
GOOCH PAUL A	LTC	O-1321505	1066	1
GOOCH RAYMOND A	CW2	W-2110237	0947	2
GOOD BERNARD S	1LT	O-0360124	0945	2
GOOD CLIFTON H	MAJ	O-0286291	0246	2
GOOD CLYDE L	CPT	O-0512318	0466	3
GOOD DEAN K	LTC	O-0464845	0655	1
GOOD GEORGE W	CW3	W-2148449	0464	1
GOOD GILBERT G	2LT	O-1309715	0844	2
GOOD JOSEPH	MAJ	O-2011218	1160	1
GOOD MARVIN A	CPT	O-0397093	0644	2
GOOD PAUL E	MAJ	O-1283587	0959	1
GOOD RALPH E	CW3	W-2147657	1262	1
GOOD ROBERT N	CPT	O-0358405	0762	2
GOOD STANLEY J	LTC	O-0448462	0546	2
GOOD WALTER R	CPT	O-0535373	0646	1
GOODALE ROY F	CPT	O-0163090	0652	3
GOODALE THOMAS F	MAJ	O-0213489	0364	3
GOODALL JR FRANK A	LTC	O-1055305	0463	1
GOODALL ROBERT M	COL	O-0190297	1055	3
GOODBODY HENRY R	CPT	O-0509999	1044	1
GOODBOLD THOMAS G	LTC	O-1307010	0762	1
GOODBOUT ELENORE F	MAJ	N-0798980	0665	1
GOODBREAD WALTER L	MAJ	O-1296021	0258	1
GOODCHILD HOWARD H	CPT	O-1647910	1060	1
GOODE ALFRED L	MAJ	O-2103054	1064	2
GOODE ARCHIE E	CPT	O-0358258	1044	2
GOODE EDWARD A	2LT	O-0395276	0542	1
GOODE EDWIN F	1LT	O-1303329	0750	1
GOODE JAMES C	LTC	O-1179078	0262	1
GOODE JEWELL M	CW3	W-2148409	1263	1
GOODE LEMUEL	1LT	O-0447030	0945	2
GOODE SAMUEL W	MAJ	O-1686789	0165	1
GOODE THOMAS H	MAJ	O-1913404	0865	2
GOODE WALTER L	MAJ	O-0218356	0546	2
GOODE WAYNE T	2LT	O-1999798	1045	1
GOODE WILLIAM	LTC	O-0452564	1165	1
GOODE WILLIAM G	LTC	O-0885056	0864	3
GOODELL PAUL E	LTC	O-0326643	0260	3
GOODELL ROLLAND J	COL	O-0233794	0266	3
GOODELL STEWART A	CW2	W-2142548	1155	1
GOODEN JAMES H	LTC	O-1637529	0163	1
GOODENOUGH FRED H	MAJ	O-0405526	0660	1
GOODENOUGH NELSON B	CPT	O-0132200	0454	3
GOODENOW EDWIN R	COL	O-0336073	0756	1
GOODEVE JOHN G	LTC	O-0419750	0463	1
GOODFELLOW CAREY W	2LT	O-1557938	0944	2
GOODFELLOW JOHN J	COL	O-0568334	0767	1
GOODFELLOW MILLARD P	COL	O-0199214	0552	3
GOODFRIED MILTON S	LTC	O-0248040	0763	3
GOODFRIEND ARTHUR	LTC	O-0286300	0767	3
GOODHART ELLA M	2LT	N-0700515	0735	1
GOODHART JACOB A	CPT	O-1821158	0845	2

NAME	GRADE	SVC NO	DATE RET MO YR	RET CODE
GOODHART RAYMOND C	LTC	O-0110301	0346	2
GOODHEW JR JOHN W	LTC	O-0309976	1066	3
GOODIN WALTER B	2LT	O-1646202	0944	2
GOODIN WILLIAM L	MAJ	O-1786131	0548	2
GOODINE AMELIA I	1LT	N-0700035	0837	1
GOODING HUGH T	CPT	O-0306568	0844	2
GOODING ROBERT	CPT	O-1312841	1046	2
GOODLETT LLOYD	CPT	O-2036477	0754	1
GOODLETT WILLIAM D	CW4	W-2147009	0164	1
GOODLOE HENRY R	LTC	O-0165273	0648	3
GOODMAN ARTHUR J	1LT	O-1060782	0746	2
GOODMAN ARTHUR L	CPT	O-1167863	1147	2
GOODMAN AUSTIN	WO1	W-2125303	0253	1
GOODMAN BARNETT G	MAJ	O-0341370	0646	2
GOODMAN CALVIN B	MAJ	O-0314344	0447	1
GOODMAN CLARENCE F	MAJ	O-0465204	0165	1
GOODMAN DAVID R	MAJ	O-0592935	1165	1
GOODMAN EDWARD	CPT	O-0331565	1045	2
GOODMAN ETTA R	2LT	N-0736580	0745	1
GOODMAN GEORGE F	CW2	W-2143765	0359	1
GOODMAN GEORGE R	MAJ	O-2049254	0559	1
GOODMAN GERTRUDE F	2LT	N-0783584	0245	1
GOODMAN JACK	LTC	O-1585514	1262	1
GOODMAN JACK A	LTC	O-0240558	0464	3
GOODMAN JR ERNEST L	CW3	W-2151041	1063	1
GOODMAN MARGARET P	1LT	N-0731202	1245	2
GOODMAN MERVILLE L	LTC	O-0344650	0957	1
GOODMAN MILTON J	COL	O-0360143	0346	2
GOODMAN RICHARD W	CPT	O-1303140	1147	1
GOODMAN ROSCOE	MAJ	O-0181469	0449	1
GOODMAN SAMUEL	LTC	O-1634807	1262	1
GOODMAN SHELDON H	LTC	O-0222645	0257	3
GOODMAN SIDNEY	CPT	O-0490085	0445	2
GOODMAN STELLA H	CPT	N-0757540	0758	2
GOODMAN TRUMAN C	MAJ	O-1554370	0661	1
GOODMAN WILLIAM	1LT	O-1184056	0367	2
GOODMAN WILLIAM A	LTC	O-1316039	1065	1
GOODMAN WINIFRED E	MAJ	L-0204055	0966	3
GOODMANN CHARLES J	1LT	O-1016838	0945	1
GOODNIGHT CURTIS S	MAJ	O-1877305	0266	1
GOODNIGHT HULEN V	CW3	W-2150736	0559	2
GOODNOUGH CLEON W	LTC	O-0308977	0258	3
GOODNOUGH ROBERT C	MAJ	O-1165736	0459	1
GOODPASTER HOLMAN E	2LT	O-0286482	0866	3
GOODPASTURE CHARLES	MAJ	O-0466690	0762	1
GOODRICH ARTHUR F	MAJ	O-0275217	0360	3
GOODRICH DONALD F	CPT	O-0399862	0647	2
GOODRICH GAWIN L	CW3	W-2132763	0162	1
GOODRICH GEORGE A	CW3	W-2149753	0358	1
GOODRICH GEORGE M	COL	O-0242348	0851	3
GOODRICH GEORGE R	LTC	O-1101010	0261	1
GOODRICH HAROLD P	CPT	O-0573197	1162	1
GOODRICH HARVEY B	1LT	O-1588006	0646	1
GOODRICH JAMES L	CPT	O-0924950	0144	2
GOODRICH LEWIS E	COL	O-0140753	1045	2
GOODRICH LOUIS R	COL	O-0216110	0959	3
GOODRICH RAYMOND B	LTC	O-1579701	1166	1
GOODRICH SAMUEL J	CW3	W-2144987	0761	1
GOODRICK CARL H	LTC	O-0320726	0857	2
GOODRIDGE GEORGE L	COL	O-0124739	0156	3
GOODRUM RALPH C	MAJ	O-2096508	1265	1
GOODRUM WILLIAM H	MAJ	O-1303621	0964	1
GOODSON DORRIS M	CW2	W-2104907	0746	2
GOODSON JAMES R	2LT	O-0555755	1045	2
GOODSON OSCAR L	LTC	O-1292331	0164	1
GOODSON PAUL G	MAJ	O-1031555	0556	1
GOODSON ROBERT R	CPT	O-0242933	0354	3
GOODSPEED HOWARD A	LTC	O-0190914	0749	3
GOODSPEED JOHN W	1LT	O-0910685	1143	2
GOODWATER LEROY W	MAJ	O-0136567	0856	3
GOODWIN ARTHUR F	CW3	W-2152093	0565	1
GOODWIN CHARLES L	MAJ	O-0304061	0647	2
GOODWIN CHARLES W	COL	O-0204424	0759	1
GOODWIN CHESTER E	LTC	O-2042809	0261	1
GOODWIN DANIEL R	LTC	O-0140768	0553	3

NAME	GRADE	SVC NO	DATE RET MO YR	RET CODE
GOODWIN DURWARD T	LTC	0-0480144	0367	3
GOODWIN EDWARD L	LTC	0-0913180	0266	3
GOODWIN EDWIN A	LTC	0-0249871	1065	3
GOODWIN ELIZABETH	MAJ	N-0730458	0766	1
GOODWIN ELVIN C	LTC	0-1550388	0762	1
GOODWIN FRANCIS D	COL	0-0279129	0563	1
GOODWIN GEORGE H	COL	0-0290459	0367	3
GOODWIN GEORGE V	2LT	0-1825111	1145	2
GOODWIN HENRY C	CPT	0-1058525	0453	1
GOODWIN HOMER L	COL	0-0279814	0259	3
GOODWIN HUGH W	2LT	0-0547257	0546	2
GOODWIN JACK E	MAJ	0-2262219	0966	1
GOODWIN JAMES F	CPT	0-1107984	1046	2
GOODWIN JOHN W	CPT	0-2203019	0557	2
GOODWIN JR LEO	MAJ	0-0336964	0146	2
GOODWIN JR POWELL	CW2	W-2210856	0167	1
GOODWIN LEMUEL R	MAJ	0-0955843	0963	1
GOODWIN LOREN W	COL	0-0269050	0166	3
GOODWIN MAC N	CW2	W-2146331	0259	1
GOODWIN NORMAN E	MAJ	0-0402588	0661	1
GOODWIN NORMAN W	LTC	0-1174579	1061	1
GOODWIN OTIS D	CW3	W-2150068	0564	1
GOODWIN RANDOLPH	MAJ	0-2030993	0565	1
GOODWIN ROBERT M	1LT	0-0373079	0143	2
GOODWIN ROY L	COL	0-0255146	1067	3
GOODWIN WALTER I	MAJ	0-2210448	0764	1
GOODWIN WILLIAM I	COL	0-0124738	0256	3
GOODWIN WILLIAM M	COL	0-0263950	1059	3
GOODWIN WILLIAM M	CPT	0-0513247	0246	1
GOODWIN WILLIAM R	CPT	0-0253635	0444	2
GOODWIN WILLIAM V	MAJ	0-1693142	0965	1
GOODWIN WILLIAM W	1LT	0-1306837	0545	2
GOODWYN CHARLES A	LTC	0-0278187	0946	2
GOODYEAR AUGUSTUS S	COL	0-0165991	0547	2
GOODYEAR EMIL S	MAJ	0-0496416	0945	2
GOOGE PAUL H	COL	0-0115405	0956	3
GOOLMAN GEORGE V	LTC	0-1298217	0767	1
GOOLRICK JR W K	MAJ	0-0438144	1047	1
GOOLSBY CHARLES E	LTC	0-1588596	1162	1
GOOLSBY LACY R	CPT	0-1588008	0355	1
GOOLSBY LONNIE L	LTC	0-1012903	1061	1
GOOLSBY ROBERT R	MAJ	0-0917963	0863	2
GOOMBS FRANK R	CW2	W-2210006	0966	1
GOON THEODORE J	1LT	0-1312543	1145	2
GOORLEY JOHN T	LTC	0-0327231	0467	3
GOOTNICK ABRAHAM	CPT	0-0346966	0246	2
GOOZEE WILLIAM H	CPT	0-0985924	0361	1
GOPCEVIC RADE P	1LT	0-1296849	1054	1
GORANSON ROBERT A	LTC	0-1306838	0264	1
GORBEA RAFAEL	MAJ	0-1285231	0960	1
GORDEN DONALD L	MAJ	0-1592228	0255	1
GORDH SR GORDON	CW2	W-2144112	0659	1
GORDNER RALPH B	CW2	W-2147114	0661	1
GORDNIER TRUMAN W	LTC	0-1182370	0263	1
GORDON ALGERNON C	1LT	0-2003852	0853	2
GORDON ALVIN H	1LT	0-1303712	0960	1
GORDON BERTHA M	CPT	N-0759276	0846	1
GORDON CHARLES	MAJ	0-0501691	1047	1
GORDON CHARLES C	CPT	0-0987057	0259	2
GORDON CHARLES S	MAJ	0-1322441	0159	1
GORDON CHARLES W	COL	0-0222103	0158	3
GORDON CHESTER B	CW3	W-2150173	1061	1
GORDON CLARY D	CW3	W-2143792	0659	1
GORDON CLYDE W	CPT	0-0194099	0755	3
GORDON DONALD L	MAJ	0-1936107	0566	1
GORDON EDWARD S	MAJ	0-0286555	0646	2
GORDON FRANK L	CPT	0-1590497	0446	2
GORDON FREDERICK	LTC	0-0451110	0856	1
GORDON GILES D	LTC	0-1548420	0661	1
GORDON HAROLD L	LTC	0-0425898	1060	1
GORDON HARRY D	2LT	0-0389469	0343	1
GORDON HARRY H	CW2	W-2143910	0764	1
GORDON HENRY A	LTC	0-1056381	1264	1
GORDON HOWARD L	CW2	W-2101123	0251	1
GORDON JAMES	CPT	0-1689692	0246	2

NAME	GRADE	SVC NO	DATE RET MO YR	RET CODE
GORDON JAMES	CW2	W-2111204	1061	2
GORDON JAMES A	MAJ	0-2035053	0861	1
GORDON JAMES M	CPT	0-0485276	1044	2
GORDON JAMES W	LTC	0-1546575	0163	1
GORDON JESSE	CW2	W-2145076	0157	1
GORDON JR CHARLES B	CW2	W-2144446	0465	1
GORDON JR EARL C	LTC	0-1946738	0665	2
GORDON JR EDWARD W	MAJ	0-1645607	0161	1
GORDON JR JOSEPH R	LTC	0-1016892	1162	1
GORDON JR SAMUEL A	COL	0-0247395	0754	2
GORDON JR WILLIAM H	1LT	0-1646203	0546	2
GORDON KATHRYN W	MAJ	N-0724832	1061	1
GORDON KENNETH S	MAJ	0-0220754	0852	1
GORDON MARION B	CPT	0-0990654	0661	1
GORDON MARK H	LTC	0-1167443	0763	1
GORDON MAURICE	CPT	0-0925487	0745	2
GORDON MORTON	2LT	0-1080786	0445	2
GORDON MURDOC A	CW3	W-2142790	1160	1
GORDON NATHAN G	CPT	0-0369516	1045	1
GORDON OREN S	MAJ	0-2012748	0559	1
GORDON PAUL H	LTC	0-2010565	0562	1
GORDON PETER	MAJ	0-2039549	0363	1
GORDON PHILIP	LTC	0-1550806	0267	1
GORDON RICHARD	WO1	W-2106507	0447	1
GORDON RICHARD C	MAJ	0-1104687	1055	1
GORDON RICHARD M	MAJ	0-0962387	1060	1
GORDON ROBERT A	LTC	0-0503873	0257	1
GORDON ROBERT R	LTC	0-0175093	0162	3
GORDON ROY T	CPT	0-1103656	0262	2
GORDON ROYAL G	CW3	W-2144730	1263	1
GORDON SAMUEL J	MAJ	0-1588597	0660	1
GORDON SAMUEL M	LTC	0-0235698	0958	3
GORDON SIDNEY U	MAJ	0-1598971	0263	1
GORDON SR IVAN A	CW2	W-2105920	1048	2
GORDON STANLEY B	MAJ	0-1339352	0265	1
GORDON THEODORA A	CW4	W-2101016	1055	1
GORDON THOMAS C	WO1	W-2120681	0459	1
GORDON VIRGIL C	COL	0-0207502	0159	3
GORDON WALLACE H	CPT	0-0444151	1046	2
GORDON WALTER L	1LT	0-1174300	1044	2
GORDON WALTER S	LTC	0-0484495	1264	3
GORDON WILLIAM J	MAJ	0-0271510	0963	3
GORDON WILLIAM V	LTC	0-1549951	0462	1
GORDON WILSON	LTC	0-1327121	0163	1
GORDY RAYMOND E	CW3	W-2149338	0264	1
GORDY SAMUEL T	MAJ	0-0494692	0845	2
GORE AARON M	CPT	0-0495625	0250	1
GORE FRANK R	CW3	W-2108537	0163	1
GORE HILDRETH C	CPT	0-0494588	0447	1
GORE LAWRENCE L	CPT	0-0280874	0960	3
GORE MAHLON L	LTC	0-0225357	1056	3
GORE MELVIN T	1LT	0-1319089	0146	2
GORE RAYMOND S	CW3	W-2135056	0154	1
GORE ROY C	MAJ	0-0119897	0754	3
GORE WILLIAM A	LTC	0-0279670	0646	2
GORE WOODROW	MAJ	0-1822129	0261	2
GORECKI FRANK	CW3	W-2142100	0461	1
GOREHAM JAMES N	LTC	0-1174580	0763	1
GORELICK ALBERT P	MAJ	0-0979160	0562	1
GOREN SIDNEY M	CPT	0-0478551	0845	2
GOREY GEORGE F	COL	0-0118673	0654	3
GORGENSEN WILLIAM H	CW3	W-2141290	1262	1
GORGODIAN HENRY	COL	0-0264200	1046	2
GORHAM CHARLES S	MAJ	0-0113083	0452	3
GORHAM FORDYCE	MAJ	0-1283940	0446	2
GORHAM FRANCIS J	LTC	0-0522966	0464	1
GORHAM JOSEPH	CPT	0-1644371	0947	2
GORIN NORMAN	CW4	W-2144327	0967	1
GORING CHARLES	MAJ	0-1315422	0954	1
GORING HAROLD J	CW4	W-2141765	0764	1
GORING JACK F	MAJ	0-0490897	0644	1
GORK L HENRY	COL	0-0208577	0652	3
GORMAN ANGELINE L	1LT	N-0700070	1039	2
GORMAN CORNELIUS	COL	0-0292490	0167	3
GORMAN DAVID	MAJ	0-0409877	0946	2

NAME	GRADE	SVC NO	DATE RET MO YR	RET CODE
GORMAN DAVID B	LTC	0-0285716	0244	2
GORMAN DAVID H	MAJ	0-0158151	0648	3
GORMAN ELMER R	LTC	0-1036163	0367	1
GORMAN FRANCIS J	CPT	0-1289068	0946	1
GORMAN FRANK H	CPT	0-1063065	1147	2
GORMAN GERARD F	CPT	0-1533790	1046	2
GORMAN HENRY A	MAJ	0-0148222	0948	3
GORMAN HOWARD A	LTC	0-1573245	0364	1
GORMAN J FRANCIS	LTC	0-0417883	0962	1
GORMAN JAMES E	LTC	0-1339631	0966	1
GORMAN JOHN A	LTC	0-0175253	0858	3
GORMAN JOHN B	CPT	0-1318663	0446	1
GORMAN JOHN J	MAJ	0-1686775	0663	1
GORMAN JOHN J	CW3	W-2206868	1167	1
GORMAN JOHN M	1LT	0-0453465	0944	2
GORMAN JOSEPH P	LTC	0-0394914	1161	1
GORMAN LAURENCE G	LTC	0-0249282	0262	3
GORMAN LEONARD J	CPT	0-1541595	1044	2
GORMAN LESLIE F	CPT	0-0344204	0854	1
GORMAN PETER J	CW3	W-2149110	0466	1
GORMAN THOMAS	LTC	0-1012136	1165	1
GORMAN WILLIAM A	LTC	0-1114946	0563	1
GORMELY JOHN E	LTC	0-1174868	0164	1
GORMLEY HARRY	MAJ	0-0265324	1053	3
GORMLEY JR DANIEL J	MAJ	0-2205200	1067	1
GORMLEY WILLIAM J	2LT	0-1692626	0447	2
GORMLIE GEORGE F	LTC	0-0383812	0161	1
GORMSEN ALFRED N	COL	0-0253410	0864	3
GORMSEN NORMAN E	CPT	0-0390029	0645	2
GORNTO MILLSON B	MAJ	0-0333973	0258	1
GORRELL REX W	CW2	W-2106274	0750	2
GORRILL ATHOL B	LTC	0-0150619	1053	3
GORRILL GALEN A	LTC	0-0244585	0258	3
GORRY MICHAEL F	2LT	0-0970987	0452	1
GORSCH RUDOLPH V	COL	0-0172530	0545	2
GORSKI THADDEUS M	MAJ	0-0237786	0546	2
GORSKY JACK A	CW2	W-2151027	0766	2
GORSUCH CHARLES R	CPT	0-0522883	0746	2
GORSUCH ROBERT O	CW3	W-2146773	0666	1
GORTER RUSSELL T	CPT	0-2287870	0260	1
GORTON ALDEN C	LTC	0-0432417	0562	1
GORTON ANNA M A	1LT	L-0210159	0947	2
GORTON DONALD G	COL	0-0268295	1065	3
GORTON ELLIS H	LTC	0-0176765	0262	3
GORUM JAMES R	CW3	W-2144548	0463	1
GORWODA KARL E	MAJ	0-1643602	1060	1
GOSCH JR GEORGE	LTC	0-0297981	0866	3
GOSCH LENERT C	CPT	0-0294960	0344	2
GOSCIEWSKI ANTONI K	1LT	0-0233393	0847	1
GOSE EARLE M	CPT	0-0504175	1053	1
GOSHKO JOHN M	1LT	0-4035943	1162	2
GOSHORN EDWARD B	LTC	0-0510412	1154	3
GOSHORN FRANK R	1LT	0-1112729	0246	2
GOSLEE CHARLES F	LTC	0-1798665	0762	1
GOSLIN HAROLD W	CW4	W-2105060	0560	1
GOSMAN WILLIAM M	LTC	0-0309598	0463	1
GOSNELL JESSE L	CPT	0-2011269	0257	1
GOSNELL JOHN C	MAJ	0-0503352	0156	1
GOSORN LOUIS M	COL	0-0323238	0855	2
GOSS HAROLD L	B G	0-0201505	0750	3
GOSS JAMES H	CPT	0-1308764	0747	1
GOSS LEO E	CPT	0-1300022	0954	2
GOSS MARSHALL J	COL	0-0230147	0360	3
GOSS THEODORE C	MAJ	0-1175444	0355	2
GOSS VERNON V	1LT	0-0384067	1045	2
GOSSARD PETER D	2LT	0-0536502	1045	2
GOSSARD SYLVESTER	CW3	W-2143634	0164	1
GOSSARD THOMAS E	CPT	0-1322914	0848	1
GOSSE ANTHONY C	2LT	0-1545602	0845	2
GOSSEN CHARLES G	CW3	W-2147392	0565	1
GOSSEN ROBERT C	1LT	0-1546865	1146	2
GOSSERT GEORGE C	CPT	0-0946693	1062	1
GOSSETT GEORGE W	LTC	0-0921396	0158	2
GOSSETT JAMES C	MAJ	0-2025629	0761	1
GOSSIAUX JOSEPH A	1LT	0-0885643	0953	1

NAME	GRADE	SVC NO	DATE RET MO YR	RET CODE
GOSSMAN JR ALBERT J	2LT	0-2010680	0346	2
GOTAAS HAROLD B	COL	0-0242819	1066	3
GOTAY EMETERIC	COL	0-0156743	0352	3
GOTERA MARTIN	2LT	0-1896684	0248	2
GOTHAM FRED C	MAJ	0-1646204	0461	1
GOTHARD JOHN W	CPT	0-1597016	0547	1
GOTHIA JR MACK J	CW2	W-2211731	0666	1
GOTHOLD DAVID J	COL	0-0203239	1044	2
GOTT LEONARD K	MAJ	0-1044228	0859	1
GOTTER FRED B	LTC	0-1323560	1163	1
GOTTESMAN JOSEPH L	MAJ	0-0494216	0446	2
GOTTFREDSON DAVID	COL	0-0233589	0644	2
GOTTFRIED CHARLES J	MAJ	0-0307613	0146	2
GOTTLIEB MEYER P	LTC	0-0298685	0166	3
GOTTLOB JANET A	MAJ	N-0779249	1263	1
GOTTSACKER HAROLD A	1LT	0-1321115	0845	2
GOTTSCHALK ALBERT O	CPT	0-0296181	0447	2
GOTTSCHALK JERE L	CPT	0-1322331	0747	1
GOTTSCHALK WALTER R	LTC	0-0279023	0667	3
GOTTSCHALL ROBERT	LTC	0-1634813	1163	1
GOTZIAN HENRY L	LTC	0-1551215	0862	1
GOUCH CHESTER L	MAJ	0-1695748	0258	1
GOUCHER JR CHARLES A	MAJ	0-1015103	0161	1
GOUDEMOND ANTHONIE J	MAJ	0-1104176	1057	1
GOUDEY KEITH H	1LT	0-0476570	0545	2
GOUDREAU LEODORE	CW4	W-2113434	0959	1
GOUGEON EDWARD P	MAJ	0-2263058	0465	1
GOUGH EDWARD A	CPT	0-0199817	0648	3
GOUGH JAMES A	1LT	0-1031556	0144	2
GOUGH JR JAMES F	1LT	0-1592866	1046	2
GOUGH WILLIAM G	LTC	0-0103228	0656	3
GOUGHER ROSE L	MAJ	N-0725865	0867	1
GOUGUET LOUIS J E	LTC	0-0102884	0648	3
GOULARD LOWELL J	MAJ	0-1293941	1146	2
GOULARTE JOSEPH C	LTC	0-1040722	0665	1
GOULD ADRIAN G	COL	0-0209448	1052	3
GOULD CHARLES K	COL	0-0298119	0764	3
GOULD EDWARD A	COL	0-0222107	1046	1
GOULD EDWARD J	MAJ	0-2200113	1065	1
GOULD ERNEST E	CPT	0-0212871	0264	3
GOULD FRANK E	MAJ	0-0181426	0654	3
GOULD FRANK E	1LT	0-1283941	0546	2
GOULD FRED W	CW3	W-3200309	1266	1
GOULD HAROLD G	MAJ	0-0234749	1048	3
GOULD HAROLD S	COL	0-0297957	1060	1
GOULD JAMES A	LTC	0-0193260	0452	3
GOULD JEDEDIAH	CPT	0-0375194	0352	1
GOULD JERROLD	LTC	0-0348711	1262	1
GOULD JOHN A	MAJ	0-1062679	0765	1
GOULD JOHN D	1LT	0-1080107	1045	2
GOULD JOHN E	CPT	0-0351148	1044	1
GOULD JOHN J	CPT	0-0545759	1045	2
GOULD JOHN W	2LT	0-1016212	0844	2
GOULD JR WILLIAM J	1LT	0-1646206	0450	1
GOULD KINGDON J	2LT	0-2009589	0247	2
GOULD LEGRAND A	CPT	0-1303879	1045	1
GOULD RALPH C	CPT	0-1167446	0461	1
GOULD RALPH P	COL	0-0237144	0265	3
GOULD RICHARD G	CPT	0-0530597	0846	2
GOULD RUSSELL L	CPT	0-0343320	1044	1
GOULD VERNON G	LTC	0-0188814	0554	3
GOULD WILFRED E	LTC	0-0217801	1061	3
GOULDING VICTOR H	1LT	0-1101458	0845	2
GOULET BERTRAND L	MAJ	0-0184659	0650	3
GOULET ROBERT J	MAJ	0-1175721	0664	1
GOULSBY THEODORE	COL	0-0224019	0952	3
GOURD BERNARD M	CW2	W-2150883	0661	1
GOURGUES HAROLD W	COL	0-0282267	0457	1
GOURLEY JAMES L	CW2	W-2150898	0764	1
GOURLEY REX S	CPT	0-1049175	0845	2
GOUTIEREZ JAMES A	CW4	W-2152020	1167	1
GOVE GEORGE M	CPT	0-0253686	0653	3
GOVER ARTHUR F	LTC	0-1642117	1066	3
GOVER JESSE	MAJ	0-0111660	0648	3
GOVERNALE SAMUEL L	MAJ	0-0274710	0145	2

NAME	GRADE	SVC NO	DATE RET MO YR	RET CODE
GOW FRANCES R	2LT	N-0726512	1145	1
GOW RALPH F	COL	0-0236244	0463	3
GOWAN JAMES F	MAJ	0-0974673	1265	1
GOWANS ALBERT S	WO1	W-2119847	1047	2
GOWEN EDWARD J	1LT	0-1039649	0446	2
GOWEN FREDERICK	CW3	W-2115841	0457	1
GOWEN HARRY W	1LT	0-4032495	0757	2
GOWEN MAX F	1LT	0-1318535	0546	2
GOWER JOE R	MAJ	0-1032347	1265	1
GOWER WALTER R	MAJ	0-0243059	0864	3
GOWIN VIVIAN W	MAJ	N-0744929	0665	1
GOWKA WALTER W	2LT	0-1106172	0144	2
GOWLAND JOSEPH S	CPT	0-0918386	0246	1
GOYCOCHEA ALLAN G	CPT	0-5304112	0666	2
GOYETTE LINUS F G	COL	0-0379053	0667	3
GOZA RUFUS J	MAJ	0-0253654	0444	2
GRAB JOHN A	LTC	0-0154326	0755	3
GRABER EDWARD A	MAJ	0-0309231	0647	2
GRABER FRANK H	WO1	W-2130655	0147	1
GRABER LOUIS O	MAJ	0-1697764	0546	2
GRABERT EDWARD T	1LT	0-0931956	0346	1
GRABFIELD G PHILIP	COL	0-0163556	1045	2
GRABIAK GEORGE W	COL	0-0526972	0864	3
GRABICKI JOSEPH F	CW3	W-2142392	0758	1
GRABILL JOSEPH A	CPT	0-0498720	0546	1
GRABLE CARL F	CW3	W-2144203	0261	1
GRABOWSKI HENRY	LTC	0-1080860	0262	1
GRACE ANGUS D	CPT	0-1683863	0845	2
GRACE CORNELIUS	CPT	0-1299556	0246	1
GRACE GEORGE B	LTC	0-0415859	0863	1
GRACE GEORGE L	LTC	0-1553454	1262	1
GRACE GEORGE T	CW4	W-2128853	0557	1
GRACE HUBERT C	CW3	W-2112169	1154	1
GRACE JR CHARLES W	MAJ	0-1031557	1058	1
GRACE LUCILLE A	1LT	N-0703666	0245	1
GRACE WILLIAM G	MAJ	0-1180193	0465	1
GRACE WILLIAM S	1LT	0-1047986	0447	2
GRACIE EDWIN F	LTC	0-0452527	1060	1
GRACIE RAYMOND	CW3	W-2203267	0565	1
GRACY BRAINARD B	CPT	0-1166495	1046	2
GRACYK EDWIN O	2LT	0-1822130	0944	2
GRADALL GLEN P	CPT	0-0473963	0450	1
GRADO SR JOHN	MAJ	0-0497384	0949	1
GRADWELL GEORGE H	MAJ	0-1014577	0261	1
GRADY EDWARD F	LTC	0-0401447	1160	1
GRADY GLEN E	LTC	0-0477747	0966	1
GRADY JAMES W	CPT	0-0333150	0146	2
GRADY JOHN F	MAJ	0-0277451	1163	3
GRADY JOHN F	LTC	0-0292249	0654	1
GRADY JOHN W	COL	0-0378189	1160	1
GRADY PAUL J	COL	0-0326200	1060	3
GRADY ROBERT V	LTC	0-1296683	1061	1
GRADY WILLIAM H	MAJ	0-1685504	1263	1
GRADY WILLIAM J	CPT	0-1053147	0246	2
GRAEBENER JOHN R	COL	0-0346127	0961	1
GRAEBER DON E	2LT	0-2055903	0845	2
GRAEF JR FREDERICK	COL	0-0318024	0758	2
GRAEFF GEORGE R	LTC	0-1043968	1265	1
GRAEN LLOYD G	CW3	W-2149068	0263	1
GRAETZ MARION	LTC	0-0354842	0766	3
GRAF ERNEST W	MAJ	0-0206077	1046	1
GRAF FRANK J	COL	0-0225221	1166	2
GRAF GLENN F	LTC	0-0228567	0162	3
GRAF JEROME A	CPT	0-0236829	1063	3
GRAF LLOYD J	1LT	0-2010337	0346	2
GRAF ROBERT W	MAJ	0-1335273	1164	1
GRAFF EDWARD F	1LT	0-1304519	0646	2
GRAFF EDWARD S	MAJ	0-1691140	0146	2
GRAFF HUGH A	LTC	0-0240274	1264	3
GRAFF LESTER A	CW2	W-2212951	0867	1
GRAFF RUTH R	2LT	N-0721877	0645	1
GRAFFAGNINO PETER C	MAJ	0-0425300	1046	2
GRAFFAM CHARLES A	LTC	0-0316828	1047	2
GRAFFLIN ARTHUR C	CPT	0-0472352	0644	2
GRAFFUM ROBERT T	MAJ	0-1922507	0365	1

NAME	GRADE	SVC NO	DATE RET MO YR	RET CODE
GRAFTON CLEALON V	LTC	0-0213140	0450	1
GRAFTON ELDON C	LTC	0-0224966	1061	3
GRAFTON WILLIAM D	2LT	0-1038042	1044	2
GRAGARD JR EVERETT	CPT	0-1543105	0845	1
GRAHAM ANTHONY M	LTC	0-1288045	0463	1
GRAHAM ASA J	CW4	W-2001805	0855	3
GRAHAM BENJAMIN H	MAJ	0-1634815	0457	1
GRAHAM BERT W	1LT	0-1594609	0146	2
GRAHAM CHARLES H	LTC	0-0273936	1065	2
GRAHAM CLYDE H	MAJ	0-0290060	0962	3
GRAHAM CLYDE L	2LT	0-0278856	0851	3
GRAHAM CARL H	CW3	W-2142232	0259	1
GRAHAM DAVID	LTC	0-1172878	0664	1
GRAHAM DAVID F	LTC	0-1109960	0365	2
GRAHAM DORRIS C	LTC	0-0223685	0763	3
GRAHAM DOUGLAS R	1LT	0-0956091	1053	2
GRAHAM DRENNAN O	1LT	0-1796078	0758	1
GRAHAM EDWARD D	COL	0-0293590	0558	3
GRAHAM EDWARD E	CPT	0-0275437	0854	1
GRAHAM ELIZABETH	MAJ	L-0400521	0565	3
GRAHAM ELMER C	CPT	0-2037574	0963	2
GRAHAM EUGENE F	1LT	0-1550389	0844	2
GRAHAM EULOS F	1LT	0-0576864	0357	1
GRAHAM EZRA F	LTC	0-0277055	0449	1
GRAHAM FRANK D	LTC	0-1995095	0159	1
GRAHAM FRANK K	1LT	0-1032082	0945	2
GRAHAM FRED L	COL	0-0245497	1262	3
GRAHAM GEORGE A	1LT	0-0412922	0642	2
GRAHAM HAROLD G	CPT	0-0250606	0762	3
GRAHAM HAROLD M	LTC	0-0162764	0648	3
GRAHAM HAROLD W	CW3	W-2207566	0167	1
GRAHAM HARRY L	CPT	0-0474461	0347	2
GRAHAM HENRY S	MAJ	0-0222282	1053	3
GRAHAM HERSHAL M	MAJ	0-1336637	0561	1
GRAHAM HOWARD O	COL	0-0119591	0151	3
GRAHAM HURLIS V	MAJ	0-0966819	0961	1
GRAHAM JAMES M	MAJ	0-0122816	0250	3
GRAHAM JAMES M	LTC	0-1634817	1155	1
GRAHAM JAMES W	LTC	0-1597453	0763	1
GRAHAM JIMMIE	1LT	0-0594682	1054	2
GRAHAM JOHN F	LTC	0-0252713	1162	3
GRAHAM JOSEPH K	MAJ	0-0973838	0163	1
GRAHAM JOSEPH M	CW3	W-2141571	0762	1
GRAHAM JOSEPH N	MAJ	0-1314004	0258	1
GRAHAM JOY M	CPT	0-0216642	0164	3
GRAHAM JR BERT F	CPT	0-0568260	0361	1
GRAHAM JR GEORGE A	LTC	0-0353393	1162	1
GRAHAM JR JOSEPH	1LT	0-0416018	0246	2
GRAHAM JR WILLIAM T	1LT	0-0492704	0844	1
GRAHAM JULIAN D	LTC	0-0175022	0458	3
GRAHAM LAWRENCE M	COL	0-0102195	0648	3
GRAHAM LOIS C	CPT	N-0788681	0447	1
GRAHAM LYLE G	CW2	W-2111674	0547	2
GRAHAM MARGARET	MAJ	N-0737187	0662	1
GRAHAM MARY C	1LT	R-0000638	0346	1
GRAHAM NORVAL M	1LT	0-1311883	0845	2
GRAHAM RALPH F	COL	0-0345891	0860	1
GRAHAM RALPH W	MAJ	0-0194943	1162	3
GRAHAM RICHARD S	MAJ	0-1300436	0247	2
GRAHAM RICHARD W	LTC	0-0964394	0761	1
GRAHAM ROBERT B	LTC	0-2006062	0663	1
GRAHAM ROBERT C	LTC	0-0275336	0544	2
GRAHAM ROBERT C	LTC	0-0288417	1166	3
GRAHAM ROBERT H	MAJ	0-0155681	0548	2
GRAHAM RONALD M	CW2	W-2146765	0961	1
GRAHAM RUFUS F	LTC	0-0111636	0648	3
GRAHAM SIMON N	LTC	0-0293554	1163	2
GRAHAM THOMAS F	CPT	0-0541139	1147	2
GRAHAM THOMAS L	MAJ	0-0221158	1058	3
GRAHAM THOMAS P	MAJ	0-0183322	0647	2
GRAHAM WALTER C	LTC	0-0330260	0946	2
GRAHAM WESLEY J	1LT	0-2007651	1153	1
GRAHAM WILLIAM F	1LT	0-1177812	0246	2
GRAHAM WILLIAM L	CPT	0-0579208	1160	1
GRAHAM WILLIAM M	MAJ	0-0990451	1163	1

NAME	GRADE	SVC NO	DATE RET MO YR	RET CODE
GRAHEK FRANK E	CW2	W-2145885	1055	1
GRAHL CHARLES H	BG	0-0234562	0960	1
GRAHL MAURICE R	WO1	W-2102950	1044	2
GRAHLES ARMIN L	LTC	0-0178014	0650	1
GRAHLMAN JOSEPH S	MAJ	0-0262034	0267	3
GRAHN CLARENCE A	LTC	0-0248593	1263	3
GRAHN JR PETER M	LTC	0-0405714	0860	1
GRALAK VICTOR H	CPT	0-0358187	0145	2
GRALINSKI ALFRED	CPT	0-1289899	0355	1
GRAM RALPH L	LTC	0-0343477	0260	1
GRAM WILLIAM D	CW2	W-2144395	0461	1
GRAMATA GEORGE	1LT	0-0508322	0554	2
GRAMBORT EVERETT A	COL	0-0359736	0361	1
GRAMER WILLIAM L	COL	0-0260681	0166	3
GRAMLICH FRANCIS J	MAJ	0-2005406	0959	1
GRAMLICH WILLIAM	MAJ	0-0373297	0253	1
GRAMLING CHARLES A	LTC	0-0262205	0462	3
GRAMLING JR ROY M	LTC	0-0390536	0454	2
GRAMM HAROLD	MAJ	0-0959408	0465	1
GRAMMAR GLIDEWELL	MAJ	0-1644377	0159	1
GRAMMER GEORGE W	CPT	0-2018873	0857	1
GRAMMER WAYMON D	CPT	0-1822991	0158	1
GRAMMONT WILLARD C	CW2	W-2144240	0658	1
GRAMONT RAYMOND J	MAJ	0-0450874	1059	1
GRAMPIETRO ROBERT F	1LT	0-1289854	0352	1
GRAMS JOSEPH	1LT	0-2006955	0846	1
GRAMSTAD JIM	MAJ	0-1874622	0865	1
GRAMSTORFF THEODORE	COL	0-0258197	0962	3
GRAN CONRAD L	COL	0-0263402	0463	3
GRANADE JOE C	WO1	W-2121844	1045	2
GRANADE JR JAMES N	LTC	0-0354523	0859	1
GRANBACKA ALEXANDER	CPT	0-0233030	0347	1
GRANBERG MARTHA G	MAJ	N-0722112	1065	1
GRANBERRY HAROLD E	LTC	0-0301726	0260	3
GRANBERRY JAMES W	MAJ	0-1012536	1062	1
GRANDE GERARD F	LTC	0-1555819	1162	1
GRANDE JAMES L	CPT	0-2007263	0758	1
GRANDE NICHOLAS	CW2	W-2145436	0460	1
GRANDEA ANDRES G	1LT	0-2027388	0353	1
GRANDSTROM JOHN L	MAJ	0-1542209	0760	1
GRANDY LAURENS R	MAJ	0-1824302	0261	1
GRANECKI WALTER Z	LTC	0-1106173	0162	1
GRANFIELD EUGENE C	MAJ	0-1045757	0546	2
GRANGER AVERY L	MAJ	0-1116963	0163	1
GRANGER DAVID E	CW2	W-2109424	0148	1
GRANGER EARLE G	COL	0-0263843	0146	2
GRANGER EUGENE A	LTC	0-1175134	0762	1
GRANGER HOWARD C	CW3	W-2142841	1158	1
GRANGER ROBERT H	CW2	W-2208805	0965	1
GRANING MARTIN C	1LT	0-1547214	0446	2
GRANITO DANTE	CW3	W-2141291	0257	1
GRANNIS JOHN A	CPT	0-2102800	1262	1
GRANNIS JR JOHN D	COL	0-0198656	0761	3
GRANNIS ROBERT L	MAJ	0-1826411	1162	1
GRANO MARIO	CPT	0-2041102	0747	1
GRANQUIST KARL J	1LT	0-0312308	0645	2
GRANRATH CLARENCE W	MAJ	0-2212038	0865	1
GRANRUD WALTER H	LTC	0-0425279	0161	1
GRANSON NICHOLAS	LTC	0-1284010	1262	1
GRANT ALEXANDER	MAJ	0-2053830	0565	1
GRANT ANGUS G	MAJ	0-0491022	0145	2
GRANT ANTHONY H	MAJ	0-2033054	0662	1
GRANT ARTHUR B	COL	0-0239659	0163	3
GRANT ARTHUR E	CPT	0-1703823	0449	1
GRANT ARTHUR T	2LT	0-1642912	0944	2
GRANT ARVIN W	LTC	0-0325402	1065	3
GRANT BEN E	COL	0-0234887	0255	3
GRANT BEN R	CW3	W-2146541	1064	1
GRANT BENSON	LTC	0-1050684	1162	1
GRANT BYRON W	CPT	0-1001350	0246	1
GRANT CHARLES C	COL	0-0308106	0566	1
GRANT DAVID	MAJ	0-2033571	0561	1
GRANT DONALD I	MAJ	0-1050715	0960	1
GRANT EARLY T	2LT	0-0263858	0355	3
GRANT EDWARD C	LTC	0-0395183	0960	1

NAME	GRADE	SVC NO	DATE RET MO YR	RET CODE
GRANT ERNEST H	MAJ	0-0241267	1057	3
GRANT FRANCIS J	CW3	W-2146057	0162	1
GRANT FRANKLIN F	1LT	0-1336371	0950	1
GRANT FREDERICK	LTC	0-0372476	0460	2
GRANT GEORGE C	CPT	0-1012603	0657	1
GRANT GILBERT R	CPT	0-1052364	1045	2
GRANT GLEN D	MAJ	0-0446990	0660	1
GRANT GORDON H	CW3	W-2141292	0562	1
GRANT GORDON R	MAJ	0-0306789	1266	3
GRANT HAROLD C	1LT	0-0969165	0254	2
GRANT HAROLD D	CW3	W-2148147	0761	2
GRANT HARRY	CW2	W-2150186	0663	1
GRANT HENRY B	CPT	0-0462714	0146	2
GRANT HOWARD E	MAJ	0-1016322	0260	1
GRANT JAMES A	COL	0-0102832	0648	3
GRANT JAMES W	LTC	0-0382747	0859	1
GRANT JOHN F	1LT	0-1882452	0554	2
GRANT JOHN H	1LT	0-2049255	0746	2
GRANT JOHN N	CPT	0-0337629	0754	3
GRANT JOHN W	COL	0-0918906	1064	3
GRANT JR FRED S	LTC	0-0262477	0565	3
GRANT JR JAMES A G	CPT	0-0563150	0464	2
GRANT JR JOSEPH V	CW2	W-2144453	0561	1
GRANT JR RICHARD B	LTC	0-0290658	0545	2
GRANT LUTHER J	CPT	0-1894490	0147	2
GRANT MILTON N	LTC	0-1586618	0866	3
GRANT PAUL F	CW2	W-2147893	0457	1
GRANT PETER H	MAJ	0-0995581	0766	1
GRANT RAYMOND J	CPT	0-0358184	1043	2
GRANT ROBERT E	MAJ	0-1642121	0264	1
GRANT VIRGIL V	LTC	0-1585233	0263	1
GRANTHAM ALBA M	1LT	0-0462642	0344	2
GRANTHAM HENRY H	LTC	0-1311642	0466	1
GRANTHAM ROY E	LTC	0-0305719	0267	3
GRANTZ IRWIN A	LTC	0-0278614	0459	3
GRANVILLE GEORGE G	CW4	W-2145182	0566	1
GRANVILLE JOHN C	1LT	0-1173624	0146	2
GRAPATIN JOHN W	LTC	0-0485526	1067	3
GRAPEK HARVEY L	1LT	0-1051151	1045	2
GRAPES HOWARD F	CW3	W-2149837	0866	1
GRAPP HAROLD H	CW2	W-2142842	0356	1
GRASS EDWARDS J	COL	0-0238970	0757	3
GRASS MELVIN E	1LT	0-1795893	0445	2
GRASS PHILIP M	MAJ	0-2033957	0862	1
GRASS SAMUEL	CPT	0-0500752	1045	2
GRASSEY CHARLES	CPT	0-0146545	0249	3
GRASSL JOHN E	COL	0-0256228	0260	1
GRASSO LEONARD	2LT	T-0224371	1143	2
GRASSO MICHAEL L	CPT	0-0289715	0762	3
GRATER VINCENT M	1LT	0-0924037	0346	2
GRATHWOL JOHN D	WO1	W-2132829	0747	2
GRATRICK WILFORD D	COL	0-0322438	0764	1
GRAU BRYSON L	MAJ	0-1292332	0857	1
GRAU LESTER A	LTC	0-1049177	0665	1
GRAUEL JOHN E	CPT	0-1745984	0649	2
GRAVATT BASIL E	LTC	0-0268786	0764	3
GRAVATT JAMES H	CW3	W-2144746	0562	1
GRAVATT VERGIL C	MAJ	0-1797460	0360	3
GRAVEL JOSEPH M	WO1	W-2111447	0450	2
GRAVEL PAUL M	2LT	0-0440895	0145	2
GRAVELDINGER BERT	MAJ	0-0142823	0648	3
GRAVELIE ALBERT T	CPT	0-1995266	0947	1
GRAVELY JR LOUIS O	MG	0-0248412	1267	3
GRAVENSTEIN EDWIN L	MAJ	0-0983073	0765	1
GRAVER FREDERICK	LTC	0-0241100	0463	3
GRAVES CHARLES W	LTC	0-1823730	0167	1
GRAVES CLAUDE T	LTC	0-1165736	0358	1
GRAVES DONALD G	LTC	0-0219160	0563	3
GRAVES ELMER C	CPT	0-1015061	1060	1
GRAVES EVERETT C	CW2	W-2214753	1066	1
GRAVES HENRY R	CPT	0-1286995	0245	2
GRAVES JACK C	MAJ	0-1633899	0261	1
GRAVES JAMES W	CPT	0-0411579	1051	1
GRAVES JEFFERSON	COL	0-0112283	0648	3
GRAVES JR BEN S	CPT	0-1048790	0645	2

NAME	GRADE	SVC NO	DATE RET MO YR	RET CODE
GRAVES JR WYMAN A	W01	T-0010371	0965	2
GRAVES KENNETH K	1LT	0-0554315	1045	2
GRAVES LAMAR F	LTC	0-1845598	0656	2
GRAVES LEON	MAJ	0-0451111	0854	1
GRAVES LLOYD R	MAJ	0-1290622	1057	1
GRAVES MARVIN H	LTC	0-0293050	0265	3
GRAVES PAUL H	CW3	W-2146058	0661	1
GRAVES PERCY E	LTC	0-0309513	0257	3
GRAVES RALPH T	LTC	0-0111658	0648	3
GRAVES RAYFORD P	COL	0-0285410	0465	1
GRAVES RAYMOND C	LTC	0-1169986	0959	1
GRAVES RICHARD R	MAJ	0-2272272	0767	1
GRAVES ROBERT N	MAJ	0-0314319	1060	3
GRAVES WILLIAM L	CPT	0-0304694	0245	2
GRAVIN NORMAN R	LTC	0-0323038	0966	3
GRAVIS JOHN B	CPT	0-0491667	1043	2
GRAVLEY JACOB W	MAJ	0-1292169	1046	2
GRAVLIN ARTHUR M	LTC	0-1639094	0566	1
GRAW STONEY	MAJ	0-0942975	1060	1
GRAW WILLIAM K	LTC	0-0557363	0964	1
GRAY ANDREW S	CPT	0-0218624	0755	3
GRAY ARLINGTON	CPT	0-1172035	0946	1
GRAY ARTHUR L	2LT	0-1285743	0645	2
GRAY ARTHUR M	LTC	0-0466618	0365	2
GRAY ARTHUR R	CPT	0-1289573	0157	1
GRAY BASIL C	MAJ	0-0494232	0846	2
GRAY BERNADETTE	2LT	N-0700761	0139	1
GRAY BERNARD C	2LT	0-1310708	0345	2
GRAY CARROLL	COL	0-0105888	0754	3
GRAY CECIL L	CW3	W-2203522	0965	1
GRAY CHARLES H	CW4	W-2148338	0567	1
GRAY CHARLES T	CW3	W-2112002	1160	1
GRAY CHARLES W	MAJ	0-0447686	0346	1
GRAY CLARENCE O	CPT	0-0330517	0944	2
GRAY DANIEL A	CW2	W-2149726	0955	1
GRAY DAVID A	CPT	0-0441954	0346	2
GRAY DONALD D	LTC	0-0962159	0563	1
GRAY DONALD G	LTC	0-1031940	0463	1
GRAY EDGAR M	1LT	0-1824303	1045	2
GRAY ELDON A	CW2	W-2133565	0960	2
GRAY FRANK H	LTC	0-0287610	0661	2
GRAY FRED	CPT	0-1314468	1045	2
GRAY FREDERICK	W01	W-2126863	1045	2
GRAY GEORGE A	LTC	0-0228264	0658	3
GRAY GEORGE E	LTC	0-0335092	1165	3
GRAY GEORGE E	CPT	0-1017352	1062	1
GRAY GLEN O	CW3	W-2147220	0163	1
GRAY GORDON M	W01	W-2151320	1165	1
GRAY HAROLD T	COL	0-0146572	0454	3
GRAY HARRISON	CPT	0-0487073	1149	1
GRAY HERBERT C	COL	0-0205709	1061	3
GRAY HILLARD E	MAJ	0-1017393	1060	1
GRAY HOMER W	MAJ	0-0371130	0860	1
GRAY HOWARD F	1LT	0-1322916	1045	2
GRAY HOWARD R	CW3	W-2205451	0465	1
GRAY HOWARD W	LTC	0-1103657	0665	1
GRAY IRWIN H	MAJ	0-0484762	0548	2
GRAY JACK K	LTC	0-1168257	0459	1
GRAY JAMES	CPT	0-0292236	0347	1
GRAY JAMES A	LTC	0-0290921	1160	1
GRAY JAMES B	COL	0-0284088	0961	1
GRAY JAMES C	LTC	0-0165195	0648	3
GRAY JAMES W	CPT	0-0490220	1046	2
GRAY JEAN M	COL	0-0289625	1058	1
GRAY JERRY C	LTC	0-1103658	0962	1
GRAY JOHN C	2LT	0-1913699	0144	1
GRAY JOHN C R	CW3	W-2205862	0665	1
GRAY JOHN E	LTC	0-0300301	0360	1
GRAY JOHN H	LTC	0-0244130	0565	3
GRAY JOHN H	MAJ	0-1633900	1059	1
GRAY JOHN T	LTC	0-0196309	0446	2
GRAY JOHN T	1LT	0-0408177	0944	2
GRAY JOHN W	LTC	0-1101461	0165	1
GRAY JOSEPH A	MAJ	0-0172879	0849	3
GRAY JOSEPH R	MAJ	0-0395889	0647	2

NAME	GRADE	SVC NO	DATE RET MO YR	RET CODE
GRAY JR BENNETT G	LTC	0-0289552	0560	1
GRAY JR DOUGLAS T	MAJ	0-0408410	1146	2
GRAY JR ERNEST P	COL	0-0363031	0160	1
GRAY JR GEORGE A	2LT	0-0887712	0945	2
GRAY JR WILLIAM B	CPT	0-0378728	0450	1
GRAY KAY N	CW3	W-2147138	0166	1
GRAY KENNETH S	LTC	0-0298651	0666	3
GRAY KENNETH W	MAJ	0-1312004	0255	2
GRAY MALCOLM G	MAJ	0-0351589	0844	2
GRAY MARJORIE	1LT	N-0742566	0146	1
GRAY ORVILLE G	CW3	W-2210377	0167	1
GRAY OSCAR W	COL	0-0290558	0364	1
GRAY PAUL T	1LT	0-1323827	0645	2
GRAY RALPH J	MAJ	0-1587287	0161	1
GRAY RALPH W	LTC	0-0450619	0857	1
GRAY RAYMOND G	MAJ	0-2049256	0466	1
GRAY RAYMOND S	CW3	W-2146854	0964	1
GRAY REGIS L	2LT	0-1307153	0145	2
GRAY RICHARD E	CW3	RW-2207735	1166	1
GRAY RICHARD T	LTC	0-0909548	0267	3
GRAY ROBERT C	MAJ	0-2262806	0965	1
GRAY ROBERT E	MAJ	0-0142822	0952	3
GRAY ROBERT H	LTC	0-1043348	0965	1
GRAY ROBERT N	W01	W-2128344	0844	2
GRAY ROBERT R	CPT	0-1557456	0863	1
GRAY ROBERT W	LTC	0-1290746	0658	2
GRAY ROBINSON A	MAJ	0-2005336	0461	1
GRAY ROLLIE L	MAJ	0-0229922	1063	3
GRAY ROY F	MAJ	0-1317628	0558	1
GRAY RUSSELL A	LTC	0-0230905	0962	1
GRAY RUSSELL F	LTC	0-1293584	0862	1
GRAY VAUGHN T	CPT	0-0217697	0156	3
GRAY VELMA L	2LT	N-0789104	1044	1
GRAY VICTOR A	LTC	0-0403924	0660	1
GRAY VICTOR C	LTC	0-1106175	0261	1
GRAY WALDO G	LTC	0-1294827	0664	1
GRAY WALTER J	W01	W-2150305	1052	2
GRAY WAYNE W	LTC	0-0322666	0964	3
GRAY WHITFIELD	CPT	0-0136452	0648	3
GRAY WILLIAM A	MAJ	0-0359248	0245	2
GRAY WILLIAM A	CPT	0-0385084	0246	1
GRAY WILLIAM B	LTC	0-0762314	0463	1
GRAY WILLIAM G	CPT	0-1579716	0646	2
GRAYBEAL JESSE R	CPT	0-0903877	0746	2
GRAYBILL HERBERT A	1LT	0-1320627	0945	2
GRAYBILL JOHN W	CPT	0-1080544	1055	1
GRAYBILL JR HENRY M	CPT	0-1280178	0845	2
GRAYBILL WAYNE A	2LT	0-1326088	0645	2
GRAYDON CHARLES K	COL	0-0273657	0765	1
GRAYSON ARTHUR M	LTC	0-0222595	0556	3
GRAYSON II STEWART M	COL	0-0407673	0466	2
GRAYSON JOHN H	MAJ	0-0366271	0946	2
GRAYSON LINCOLN B	LTC	0-0326466	0767	3
GRAYSON LUTHER	2LT	0-2055169	0245	2
GRAYSON REX H	MAJ	0-0498451	0155	1
GRAYSON ROY C	LTC	0-0486834	1043	2
GRAZIANO MARIE E	1LT	N-0761955	1146	1
GRAZIER CHARLES S	LTC	0-1100564	1166	1
GRAZIER HOBART E	CPT	0-1286637	1047	1
GRBINICH FRANK	MAJ	0-0975059	0964	1
GREANEY RICHARD T	MAJ	0-1120112	0663	1
GREANY ANNE M	CPT	N-0501873	0662	2
GREASER EVERETT H	LTC	0-1640497	0164	1
GREASON SAMUEL	COL	0-0107929	0648	3
GREATHOUSE ALBERT T	COL	0-0265392	0463	3
GREATHOUSE CECIL E	CPT	0-1896022	0854	1
GREATHOUSE CHARLES I	LTC	0-0397914	0762	1
GREATHOUSE CICERO B	MAJ	0-0494233	0157	1
GREATHOUSE EVERETT F	1LT	0-2012267	0657	1
GREATHOUSE HERMAN	MAJ	0-0967195	0763	1
GREATHOUSE JACK M	CPT	0-0510697	1042	1
GREATHOUSE VERNON	CW3	W-2144009	1057	1
GREAVES DONALD L	MAJ	0-1303714	0259	1
GREAVES JR THOMAS G	CPT	0-0378648	0945	1
GREAVES VINCENT L	COL	0-0332513	0366	3

NAME	GRADE	SVC NO	DATE RET MO YR	RET CODE
GREAVY WALTER G	COL	0-0378307	0764	3
GREB MILLARD J	LTC	0-0224763	1154	2
GREBE FRANK F	COL	0-0383678	0461	1
GREBINGER CHARLES J	LTC	0-1012578	0661	1
GRECO FRANK	LTC	0-0406856	0560	1
GRECO SEBASTIAN	MAJ	0-0310136	0646	2
GRECSEK ERNEST R	CPT	0-0254098	0564	3
GREDINGER LAWRENCE M	COL	0-0205027	1162	3
GREEK ANGELO	CW2	W-2207403	0562	1
GREELEY JR JOHN B	LTC	0-0325748	1154	2
GREELEY LOYAL L	LTC	0-0155248	0753	3
GREELISH JOSEPH F	1LT	0-0170637	0641	1
GREEMAN GERALD B	MAJ	0-0360326	0747	1
GREEN ABRAHAM L	CPT	0-0497967	1044	2
GREEN ALBERT B	MAJ	0-1180194	1163	1
GREEN ALLEN E	LTC	0-0417603	0363	2
GREEN ALOYS J	CPT	0-1544114	1046	2
GREEN ALVIS G	MAJ	0-0367172	0146	2
GREEN ARCHIBALD	LTC	0-0279531	0653	3
GREEN ARTHUR L	CW2	W-2150930	1161	1
GREEN BENJAMIN	1LT	0-0441662	0645	2
GREEN BENTON H	CW2	W-2119507	1061	1
GREEN BERNARD W	MAJ	0-1114517	0760	1
GREEN BOYNTON M	MAJ	0-0229029	0851	3
GREEN CARL E	LTC	0-0428191	0363	1
GREEN CARL R	LTC	0-0248413	1165	3
GREEN CARL V	MAJ	0-0365385	0859	2
GREEN CARSON H	CW2	W-2208376	1060	1
GREEN CECIL C	CW2	W-2208607	0465	1
GREEN CHARLES A	LTC	0-0231538	0260	3
GREEN CHARLES C	MAJ	0-1111637	1262	1
GREEN CHARLES J	LTC	0-0298587	0262	3
GREEN CLARENCE J	LTC	0-0148230	0648	3
GREEN CLAUDE E	2LT	0-1881905	0753	2
GREEN CLELLAN H	CPT	0-1186412	0860	1
GREEN CURTIS E	CPT	0-2032901	0859	1
GREEN CYRIL C	COL	0-0368647	1163	1
GREEN DANIEL M	LTC	0-0291385	1045	2
GREEN DAVID	CW2	W-2148914	0361	1
GREEN DAVID G	CW2	W-2104106	0451	2
GREEN DONNA G	CPT	N-0733569	1046	1
GREEN DUANE M	CPT	0-0513939	1047	2
GREEN EDWARD C	LTC	0-1167866	1262	1
GREEN EDWARD J	MAJ	0-1331173	0263	1
GREEN EDWARD L	CW2	W-2152962	1262	1
GREEN EDWARD W	CW3	W-2102954	0757	1
GREEN EDWIN B	COL	0-0240222	0665	3
GREEN ELMER G	LTC	0-1289240	0867	1
GREEN EMANUEL	1LT	0-0518182	0345	2
GREEN ERNEST J	MAJ	0-1294654	0166	1
GREEN EUGENE	CPT	0-1257189	0267	1
GREEN FOREST T	LTC	0-0237630	1064	3
GREEN FRANK E	LTC	0-0320221	0561	1
GREEN FRED M	LTC	0-0234472	0447	2
GREEN GEORGE C	COL	0-0218076	0662	3
GREEN GEORGE D	LTC	0-0246346	0460	3
GREEN GLENN M	COL	0-0247866	0665	3
GREEN GRANT S	COL	0-0264558	0365	1
GREEN GUY B	CPT	0-0493168	1056	1
GREEN HAMPTON L	COL	0-0269907	1058	1
GREEN HAROLD	CW2	W-2126787	0545	2
GREEN HAROLD D	LTC	0-0298290	0762	3
GREEN HARRY F	CPT	0-1062501	0757	1
GREEN HARRY S	COL	0-0279571	0557	1
GREEN HARVEY O	CW4	W-2102955	0359	1
GREEN HENRY W	CPT	0-0331583	1145	2
GREEN HORACE F	MAJ	0-0483919	0462	1
GREEN HORACE F	CW4	W-2144185	0764	2
GREEN HOWARD M	CW3	W-2118108	1154	1
GREEN HUGH W	MAJ	0-0266529	0953	3
GREEN JACK P	MAJ	0-0236934	0445	2
GREEN JACOB M	1LT	0-0528825	1052	1
GREEN JAMES A	LTC	0-1643610	0962	1
GREEN JAMES C	CPT	0-0508329	0246	2
GREEN JAMES E	MAJ	0-2025780	0164	1

NAME	GRADE	SVC NO	DATE RET MO YR	RET CODE
GREEN JAMES H	MAJ	0-0979832	1061	1
GREEN JAMES L	2LT	0-0407930	1041	2
GREEN JAMES R	MAJ	0-1544694	0548	2
GREEN JAMES R	LTC	0-0342844	0961	1
GREEN JAMES W	CPT	0-1051576	0557	1
GREEN JOE H	LTC	0-0115516	0159	3
GREEN JOE S	LTC	0-0226821	1162	3
GREEN JOHN A	CPT	0-0217477	0757	3
GREEN JOHN A	CPT	0-2007705	0747	2
GREEN JOHN D	MAJ	0-0183216	1054	3
GREEN JOHN W	LTC	0-0209019	0449	3
GREEN JOSEPH R	MAJ	0-1291267	0163	1
GREEN JOSEPH S	LTC	0-0487285	0563	3
GREEN JR FRANK M	LTC	0-0386164	0661	1
GREEN JR MARTIN O	1LT	0-0924682	1143	2
GREEN JR NOAH A	MAJ	0-2019314	1160	1
GREEN JUDD N	LTC	0-0450259	0758	1
GREEN LAWRENCE E	CW3	RW-2208882	0467	1
GREEN LAYTON H	LTC	0-1288535	0765	1
GREEN LENARD J	MAJ	0-1826384	0358	1
GREEN LEONARD D	1LT	0-0958312	0954	2
GREEN LEROY	CPT	0-1550393	0156	1
GREEN LINWOOD O	LTC	0-0447359	0957	1
GREEN LLOYD C	LTC	0-0414731	1054	1
GREEN LOUIS S	MAJ	0-0243054	0363	3
GREEN LOYD W	LTC	0-0349120	0261	1
GREEN MANUEL	CPT	0-0517567	0146	2
GREEN MARIN W	LTC	0-2055146	1055	1
GREEN MELVIN C	MAJ	0-1117430	0962	1
GREEN MONROE H	LTC	0-1689220	0646	2
GREEN MONROE S	2LT	0-1055338	1044	2
GREEN MYRON J	LTC	0-0294388	0561	1
GREEN ORVIE L	COL	0-0346643	0367	3
GREEN PAUL P	W01	W-2148236	0157	1
GREEN RAYMOND B	MAJ	0-1688754	1064	1
GREEN RICHARD F	MAJ	0-0225726	0162	3
GREEN RICHARD I	MAJ	0-1106178	0662	1
GREEN ROBERT B	2LT	0-1633901	0443	2
GREEN ROBERT C	CPT	0-1912698	0546	1
GREEN ROBERT E	CW3	W-2144158	0861	1
GREEN ROBERT E	CW3	W-2209490	0867	1
GREEN ROBERT H	1LT	0-1290413	0546	2
GREEN ROBERT M	MAJ	0-1002637	0960	1
GREEN ROBERT T	CW3	W-2152314	0464	1
GREEN ROBERT W	1LT	0-1926079	1045	2
GREEN ROY	COL	0-0222729	1055	3
GREEN ROY A	M G	0-0226513	0557	3
GREEN ROY A	MAJ	0-0490171	0557	1
GREEN ROY F	MAJ	0-1300159	1160	1
GREEN SAMUEL	CPT	0-1304895	0146	2
GREEN SAMUEL G	COL	0-0183191	0250	3
GREEN SAMUEL T	MAJ	0-1107990	0761	1
GREEN SIGMUND	2LT	0-1589234	0844	2
GREEN THOMAS R	LTC	0-0401110	0861	1
GREEN THOMAS W	LTC	0-1058529	0265	1
GREEN VANZEL	MAJ	0-1646018	0756	1
GREEN VESTA D	1LT	N-0763931	0745	1
GREEN VIRGIL C	LTC	0-1305575	0765	1
GREEN WALLACE F	1LT	0-1055905	1045	1
GREEN WALTER E	CPT	0-1320628	0946	2
GREEN WARREN H	MAJ	0-1108693	0160	1
GREEN WARREN W	CPT	0-0492802	0944	1
GREEN WAVERLY S	CPT	0-1311885	0646	2
GREEN WILBUR V	MAJ	0-1923573	1063	1
GREEN WILLIAM E	COL	0-0224988	0164	3
GREEN WILLIAM J	LTC	0-1300023	1062	1
GREEN WILLIAM O	COL	0-0253569	1166	3
GREEN WILLIAM P	1LT	0-0447288	1046	2
GREEN WILLIAM S	LTC	0-0236182	0461	3
GREEN WILLIAM V	CPT	0-1041157	0959	1
GREENALL CHARLES H	COL	0-0500306	0352	1
GREENAWALT CLYDE W	LTC	0-0347434	0459	3
GREENAWALT EZMA F	MAJ	N-0724842	1066	1
GREENAWALT HOWARD A	LTC	0-1320523	0661	1
GREENAWAY ROBERT F	CW3	W-2152549	1060	1

NAME	GRADE	SVC NO	DATE RET MO YR	RET CODE	NAME	GRADE	SVC NO	DATE RET MO YR	RET CODE	NAME	GRADE	SVC NO	DATE RET MO YR	RET CODE	NAME	GRADE	SVC NO	DATE RET MO YR	RET CODE
GREENBAUM EDWARD S	B G	0-0132915	0254	3	GREENE THEODORE W	CPT	0-1533567	0247	2	GREER JIM	MAJ	0-0972264	0964	1	GREILICH EDMUND G	CPT	0-1180921	0559	1
GREENBERG ANNA K	1LT	N-0723800	0746	1	GREENE THOMAS G	LTC	0-0177347	0861	3	GREER JOHN C	LTC	0-0377193	0961	1	GREILING ROBERT E	1LT	0-0925411	1144	2
GREENBERG BENJAMIN	1LT	0-0534417	0146	2	GREENE VERNON F	LTC	0-0331258	1165	3	GREER JR CURTIS O	CPT	0-0995828	0761	1	GREIM WILLARD N	COL	0-0129885	0850	3
GREENBERG CHARLES	MAJ	0-0491079	1053	1	GREENE WALLACE J	LTC	0-0235411	0961	3	GREER MAURICE J	CW2	W-2208517	0462	1	GREINER JOHN B	LTC	0-0378698	1163	1
GREENBERG FRANK J	LTC	0-1587290	1162	1	GREENE WARREN F	MAJ	0-0179211	0863	1	GREER MELVIN A	MAJ	0-1692131	0446	2	GREINER NORBERT L	1LT	0-1593599	0945	1
GREENBERG HARRY A	LTC	0-2043102	1154	1	GREENE WELCH H	CPT	0-0343744	0945	2	GREER NEAL C	CPT	0-1179871	0960	1	GREINER WILLIAM E	MAJ	0-2284004	0762	1
GREENBERG HERBERT	CPT	0-1175723	0246	2	GREENE WILBUR M	CPT	0-4074599	0967	1	GREER ODAS A	CW3	W-2205137	1157	1	GREINER WILLIAM W	COL	0-0231095	0365	3
GREENBERG HERBERT A	CPT	0-0526123	1145	2	GREENE WILLIAM B	CPT	0-1290593	0546	2	GREER OLIVER W	COL	0-0200543	0758	3	GREINES ABRAHAM	COL	0-0308981	1059	1
GREENBERG MAX	MAJ	0-0312467	0366	3	GREENE WILLIAM D	CPT	0-1926740	0166	1	GREER RAYMOND L	CW2	W-2145439	0564	2	GREIR HAROLD F	COL	0-0260242	1057	3
GREENBERG MEYER	LTC	0-0321355	0565	3	GREENE WILLIAM D	CW3	W-2148965	1263	1	GREER RUSSELL A	COL	0-0198573	1162	3	GREISON HANS P	LTC	0-0192190	1151	3
GREENBERG MORRIS W	COL	0-0316987	0767	3	GREENE WILLIAM H	1LT	0-0538196	0945	2	GREER STANLEY W	LTC	0-0809127	1165	2	GREIST JOHN H	COL	0-0277466	0366	3
GREENBERG NORMAN S	LTC	0-1577251	0765	1	GREENE WILLIAM T	CPT	0-0448423	1146	1	GREER STEPHEN	MAJ	0-1550600	0361	1	GREMILLION GUY E	CW2	W-2121337	0560	1
GREENBERG ORRIN	CPT	0-0273197	0845	2	GREENE WILLIAM W	MAJ	0-0285209	1145	2	GREER WILLIAM E	LTC	0-1825530	0767	1	GREMILLION JACK P F	1LT	0-1309253	0645	2
GREENBLATT LOUIS T	CPT	0-1555693	0456	2	GREENE WILSON P	2LT	0-1318783	0945	2	GREER WILLIAM H	LTC	0-0323944	1060	1	GREMILLION JAMES D	MAJ	0-1594201	0965	1
GREENBROOK REGINAL	CPT	0-1320725	1047	2	GREENE WINTHROP S	LTC	0-0102010	0551	3	GREER WILLIAM O	MAJ	0-0436554	0364	1	GREMMELS ARNOLD C	LTC	0-1645615	0966	3
GREENBUSH WILLIAM E	CW2	W-2104107	0560	1	GREENEF GLENN L	COL	0-1011097	0564	1	GREESON DAVID P	2LT	0-1302639	0646	2	GREMORE WESLEY J	MAJ	0-1948747	1262	1
GREENE ALLYN W	LTC	0-1641342	1065	3	GREENFIELD ALFRED R	CPT	0-0423663	0546	2	GREESON ROBERT W	CPT	0-0509795	1153	1	GRENIG ROBERT E	LTC	0-0400701	0461	1
GREENE BENJAMIN R	MAJ	0-0213557	1057	3	GREENFIELD GEORGE A	MAJ	0-1030151	0558	1	GREESON WILLIAM R	CW2	W-2144573	0161	1	GRENNAN CHARLES A	COL	0-0259396	0865	3
GREENE CARROLL F	MAJ	0-1946269	0357	2	GREENFIELD HERMAN L	CW2	W-2108029	0444	2	GREEVER WILLIAM R	1LT	0-0371631	1044	2	GRENTZENBERG FLETCHE	LTC	0-1184503	0667	1
GREENE CHARLES E	CW2	W-2152381	0761	1	GREENFIELD LEONARD R	COL	0-0235677	0546	2	GREFE ARTHUR A	LTC	0-0494841	1155	1	GRENZEBACK JOE E	1LT	0-0524397	0645	2
GREENE CHARLES F	LTC	0-0352924	0953	1	GREENFIELD SAMUEL J	1LT	0-0225853	1164	3	GREGER ERWIN M	CW4	W-2105337	0666	1	GRESHAM GEORGE R	LTC	0-0288689	0661	3
GREENE CHARLES M	CW3	W-2206006	1066	1	GREENHAGEN MILTON F	LTC	0-1043645	1061	1	GREGERSON LELAND S	MAJ	0-1179082	0261	1	GRESHAM HENRY C	MAJ	0-1171168	0161	1
GREENE CLARENCE F	LTC	0-0361490	0263	3	GREENHALGH ROBERT A	LTC	0-1642124	1263	1	GREGG ALVA M	CPT	0-0237660	0365	3	GRESHAM LAMAR M	LTC	0-1557291	0765	1
GREENE CLIFTON S	CPT	0-1591764	1146	2	GREENHAW HERMAN H	MAJ	0-0305720	0845	2	GREGG CLIFFORD C	COL	0-0126732	0755	3	GRESHAM NORMAN C	COL	0-0251063	0267	3
GREENE DENMAN H	MAJ	0-1533793	0557	1	GREENHAW LEONARD F	1LT	0-0426672	0645	2	GREGG EARL T	CPT	0-1062194	0148	2	GRESHAM JR GLOVER C	1LT	0-1288732	0445	2
GREENE DOUGLASS	LTC	0-1582830	0865	1	GREENHILL NOBLE F	MAJ	0-0523733	0644	2	GREGG EVERITTE A	1LT	0-1949113	0762	1	GRESS KENNETH L	COL	0-0281342	0262	1
GREENE DUDLEY W	LTC	0-0430722	0961	2	GREENHILL SOLOMON	LTC	0-0292226	0665	3	GREGG FRANK P	MAJ	0-1703420	1067	1	GRESSANG WILLIAM H	1LT	0-1309363	0646	2
GREENE EARL F	LTC	0-0451602	0763	1	GREENHOUSE MAXWELL N	CPT	0-1918011	0953	2	GREGG HAROLD P	1LT	0-1321304	0246	2	GRESZLER PAUL R	MAJ	0-1540874	0264	1
GREENE EARL T	1LT	0-0488862	0745	1	GREENHUT FREDERICK	MAJ	0-0201736	1043	2	GREGG JAMES A	1LT	0-1309720	1146	2	GRETH EUGENE H	CW2	W-2214764	0967	1
GREENE EDDWARD C	WO1	W-2119717	0546	2	GREENIA LAWRENCE J	MAJ	0-2055142	0960	1	GREGG JESSE F	MAJ	0-0189954	0845	2	GRETTENBERG JACK O	MAJ	0-1291807	0261	1
GREENE EDWARD W	MAJ	0-1633902	1059	1	GREENING ELDRIDGE A	CW3	W-2141293	0162	1	GREGG JOSEPH W	CW4	W-2142843	0356	1	GREULICH FRANCIS A	MAJ	0-0382198	0766	3
GREENE EUGENE E	MAJ	0-0272070	0164	3	GREENING JAMES A	CW2	W-2146910	0661	1	GREGG JR JOSEPH J	LTC	0-0409980	0960	1	GREUNE FRANCIS W	2LT	0-1327620	1145	2
GREENE GERALD	COL	0-0302030	0865	3	GREENING THOMAS R	1LT	0-1176644	0745	1	GREGG LEROY B	CPT	0-0171877	0656	3	GREUNKE WILMA A	MAJ	N-0767279	0567	1
GREENE GLEN H	WO1	W-3430759	0467	2	GREENLAW WALTER R	MAJ	0-1047543	0561	1	GREGG SR WILLIAM A	LTC	0-0185698	1055	3	GREUP ERNST W	1LT	0-1301817	1047	1
GREENE GRANTLAND	CPT	0-0208647	1048	3	GREENLEE HAROLD E	COL	0-0274633	1061	3	GREGOR CLARA C	MAJ	N-0800032	0765	1	GREVE JOHN H	LTC	0-1548817	1165	1
GREENE GUTHRIE R	LTC	0-2035422	0264	1	GREENLEE RAE	MAJ	0-2283754	0764	2	GREGOR JOHN W	1LT	0-1062593	0446	2	GREVENBERG DUDLEY L	1LT	0-1590507	0660	1
GREENE HARLEY B	1LT	0-1643611	0745	2	GREENLEE RICHARD W	LTC	0-0488481	1154	1	GREGORIE JAMES B	COL	0-0172185	0953	3	GREWE HERBERT G	COL	0-0298574	0766	3
GREENE HERMAN L	WO1	W-2109377	0445	2	GREENLEE WILLIAM G	CW2	W-2149919	0965	1	GREGORY ALLEN L	CPT	0-2103784	1052	3	GREY ALLEN J	MAJ	0-0220538	0556	3
GREENE HOWARD G	MAJ	0-0549469	0865	1	GREENLEES DOROTHY E	1LT	N-0775967	1045	1	GREGORY ARTHUR L	MAJ	0-2020723	0860	1	GREY CALVIN	MAJ	0-1895125	0862	1
GREENE JAMES D	1LT	0-1307224	0944	2	GREENLEY CHARLES W	CW2	W-2210001	0564	2	GREGORY BEN M	LTC	0-0230321	0563	3	GREY EDGAR W	CPT	0-1014531	0255	2
GREENE JAMES T	1LT	0-0324313	0342	2	GREENOUGH FREDERICK	2LT	0-1175725	0144	2	GREGORY BERNICE B	LTC	0-0498289	0954	1	GREY FERNE P	MAJ	N-0742611	0465	1
GREENE JOHN D	MAJ	0-0163371	0347	2	GREENSTEIN GEORGE H	MAJ	0-0438755	0446	2	GREGORY BRYAN T	MAJ	0-0226056	0363	1	GREY HAROLD T	MAJ	0-0246174	0547	1
GREENE JOHN H	CPT	0-0409992	0345	2	GREENUF CHARLES N	LTC	0-0381878	0265	3	GREGORY BUNNIE E	CPT	0-1541557	0664	1	GREY JACK R	1LT	0-0543229	0946	2
GREENE JOSEPH F	LTC	0-0305999	0764	1	GREENWALD AARON T	LTC	0-0276948	1165	3	GREGORY CORBETT H	LTC	0-1635975	0266	1	GREY JOHN D	CPT	0-0496845	0647	1
GREENE JOSEPH L	CPT	0-0332636	0146	2	GREENWALD EDWARD J	LTC	0-2024456	0167	1	GREGORY DOUGLAS H	CPT	0-0380179	0644	2	GREY RICHARD R	LTC	0-2289554	0567	1
GREENE JR JOBE L	CW2	W-2143661	0657	1	GREENWALD IRVING	CPT	0-0430194	1045	2	GREGORY ELMER C	CPT	0-0672607	0354	2	GREY THOMAS A	MAJ	0-1299877	0963	1
GREENE JR VICTOR M	MAJ	0-1702270	1066	1	GREENWALD LOUIS	LTC	0-0306105	0165	3	GREGORY ENID	2LT	N-0743371	0345	1	GREYBILL JAMES R	MAJ	0-2014551	0262	1
GREENE JUSTIN L	MAJ	0-0511311	1045	2	GREENWALT EMMETT A	LTC	0-1314624	0867	3	GREGORY FRANCIS A	LTC	0-0455069	0364	1	GREYER CHARLES T	COL	0-0269157	0460	1
GREENE KENNETH A	CW2	W-2147000	0563	1	GREENWALT GILBERT C	COL	0-0102170	1148	2	GREGORY FRANK R	COL	0-0331030	0463	1	GRIB WALTER R	LTC	0-1037017	0767	1
GREENE KENNETH D	LTC	0-0243808	1163	3	GREENWAY EDWARD F	CPT	0-0531631	0547	2	GREGORY FRANK L	LTC	0-1533073	0461	1	GRIBBIN ROBERT E	LTC	0-0134293	1049	3
GREENE KENNETH J	MAJ	0-0986876	0463	1	GREENWAY JAMES C	COL	0-0253000	1164	3	GREGORY GABRIEL S	MAJ	0-0988310	0365	1	GRIBBLE ETHELBERT	CPT	0-1574782	1145	1
GREENE LAWRENCE W	LTC	0-0395765	1062	1	GREENWAY THOMAS O	CW2	W-2149293	0960	1	GREGORY GEORGE G	2LT	0-1014250	0245	2	GRIBBONS WILLIAM L	LTC	0-1315683	0663	1
GREENE LAWRENCE W	COL	0-0529912	1264	3	GREENWELL ROBERT J	MAJ	0-2014500	1167	1	GREGORY HUGH R	MAJ	0-0275459	0653	3	GRICE GERALD O	CPT	0-1307403	0846	2
GREENE LENWOOD	CW2	W-2142491	0157	1	GREENWELL WILLIAM J	LTC	0-1017145	0163	1	GREGORY IRVING F	CPT	0-0468903	1045	2	GRICE JOSEPH E	CPT	0-1105476	0464	1
GREENE LEON G	CW3	W-2149890	0363	1	GREENWOOD DEAN A	LTC	0-1300960	0266	1	GREGORY JAMES R	LTC	0-0379871	0767	1	GRICE STEPHEN H	LTC	0-0212601	0654	2
GREENE LESTER M	MAJ	0-0233399	0765	3	GREENWOOD GEORGE E	CPT	0-0489518	0653	1	GREGORY JAMES B	MAJ	0-2014718	1264	1	GRIDER LLOYD P	WO1	W-2123188	0749	1
GREENE LLEWELLYN	LTC	0-1101464	1266	3	GREENWOOD HENRY	CPT	0-1648191	0764	1	GREGORY JOHN M	LTC	0-0206153	0956	3	GRIDER ROSCOE R	CPT	0-0502701	0552	1
GREENE LLOYD B	MAJ	0-0403245	1053	3	GREENWOOD JAMES R	MAJ	0-0499059	0453	1	GREGORY JOSEPH F	MAJ	0-2204313	1166	1	GRIEB OLIVER W	CPT	0-0271020	0662	3
GREENE LUTHER W	COL	0-0168305	1060	3	GREENWOOD MOORE	LTC	0-0242600	1057	3	GREGORY JR CLAUDE W	2LT	0-1108696	0145	2	GRIECO JOHN A	CPT	0-1931863	1262	1
GREENE MARCELLUS	CPT	0-1050685	0257	1	GREENWOOD ROBERT L	CW3	W-2151046	1158	1	GREGORY LEO	MAJ	0-0318853	0446	2	GRIER CHARLES V	CPT	0-0488861	0649	2
GREENE MARION G	2LT	0-1310026	0245	2	GREENWOOD ROBERT R	CW2	W-2203470	0361	1	GREGORY LEROY J	CW3	W-2129454	0659	1	GRIER JOHN R	COL	0-0217681	0861	1
GREENE MAURICE L	LTC	0-0224333	1159	3	GREER RUDOLPH T	COL	0-0270965	0665	3	GREGORY ROBERT F	LTC	0-1017851	1062	1	GRIER WILLIAM H	CPT	0-1933802	1054	2
GREENE MAURICE W	CPT	0-0999003	1062	1	GREER ANDREW K	1LT	0-2206420	0162	2	GREGORY ROBERT L	COL	0-0195031	1062	3	GRIES ALBIN C	2LT	0-0165381	0855	3
GREENE MICHAEL I	CPT	0-1552681	1162	1	GREER BARRY D	COL	0-0238947	0151	3	GREGORY ROBERT O	LTC	0-0430354	0562	1	GRIESBAUER CHRISTIAN	1LT	0-2262144	0257	1
GREENE NATHANIEL	1LT	0-0517960	1144	2	GREER CHARLES W	CW3	W-2144116	0559	1	GREGORY RODGERS L	LTC	0-1112733	0462	1	GRIESE JAMES R	MAJ	0-2056088	1264	1
GREENE NELSON G	LTC	0-0918886	0157	2	GREER DRURY H	WO1	W-2122706	0445	2	GREGORY SIRAH K	CPT	0-1705717	0146	1	GRIESHABER HARRY F	CPT	0-0444969	1147	1
GREENE PAUL C	LTC	0-0198380	0454	3	GREER FREDERICK	LTC	0-1059793	0162	1	GREGORY STANLEY A	MAJ	0-1050282	0865	1	GRIESSER FRANK J	CPT	0-1039366	0347	2
GREENE PETER R	CW3	W-2145437	0861	1	GREER GEORGE	2LT	0-2055122	1044	1	GREGORY VIRGIL E	WO1	W-2149014	0351	1	GRIEST JOHN R	1LT	0-0367879	1145	2
GREENE PORTER C	LTC	0-0252903	0365	3	GREER GERALD L	1LT	0-0549481	0845	1	GREGORY WAYNE	CW2	W-2145142	0962	2	GRIFFEN JR FRANK A	1LT	0-0537778	0346	1
GREENE RALPH E	1LT	0-0469193	0745	2	GREER HAROLD E	LTC	0-2054014	0661	1	GREGORY WILLIAM T	LTC	0-1102269	1060	1	GRIFFES JAMES S	LTC	0-0521116	0265	3
GREENE RAY P	LTC	0-1826412	1062	1	GREER HERBERT K	COL	0-0411624	0463	1	GREGSON JR WILLIAM H	LTC	0-0369952	0546	2	GRIFFEY DURWARD P	MAJ	0-1289243	0561	1
GREENE RAYMOND A	CW3	W-2145752	0760	1	GREER JAMES A	MAJ	0-0283725	0260	3	GREIG BEN W	COL	0-0243210	0856	3	GRIFFEY JR MILTON	MAJ	0-2263166	0666	1
GREENE ROBERT A	MAJ	0-0276318	0544	2	GREER JAMES E	MAJ	0-2096478	0765	1	GREIG CLARENCE F	MAJ	0-0356344	1066	3	GRIFFIN ALICE E	1LT	N-0721671	0446	2
GREENE ROBERT C	COL	0-0299297	1061	1	GREER JAMES F	CPT	0-0522706	1051	1	GREIG ROBERT E	LTC	0-0286481	0363	3	GRIFFIN ANDREW D	CW2	W-2141294	0659	1
GREENE ROY W	1LT	0-2000560	0448	2	GREER JEAN M	1LT	N-0703272	0545	1	GREIG WALTER	LTC	0-0358456	1266	3	GRIFFIN ANGUS H	COL	0-0248902	1166	3

NAME	GRADE	SVC NO	DATE RET MO YR	RET CODE
GRIFFIN AUBREY C	MAJ	0-0417824	0646	1
GRIFFIN BARTON B	LTC	0-0454274	0461	1
GRIFFIN BENNIE H	MAJ	0-2025951	0363	1
GRIFFIN BERNARD M	2LT	0-1305242	0745	2
GRIFFIN BERTRAM F	LTC	0-0167615	1055	3
GRIFFIN BURL T	WO1	W-2102959	0855	1
GRIFFIN CARL H	LTC	0-0330961	0260	1
GRIFFIN CHARLES W	MAJ	0-0110401	1051	3
GRIFFIN DANIEL C	MAJ	0-1825911	0762	2
GRIFFIN EDWARD F	M G	0-0198652	1260	3
GRIFFIN ELMER E	LTC	0-0350905	0759	1
GRIFFIN EUGENE L	MAJ	0-0218952	0564	3
GRIFFIN FRANCIS E	MAJ	0-0337024	0460	1
GRIFFIN FRANCIS P	LTC	0-0267527	1044	1
GRIFFIN FRANK A	COL	0-0297143	0561	1
GRIFFIN GARLIN	CW3	W-2145441	0164	1
GRIFFIN GEORGE V	LTC	0-1639103	0661	1
GRIFFIN GERALD	COL	0-0169797	0459	3
GRIFFIN GUY E	LTC	0-0192430	0559	3
GRIFFIN HARRY D	LTC	0-0292600	0265	3
GRIFFIN HARRY S	1LT	0-2026532	1155	1
GRIFFIN HELEN R	CPT	N-0732278	0846	1
GRIFFIN HENRY J	LTC	0-0270358	0661	1
GRIFFIN HENRY W	LTC	0-2043051	0761	1
GRIFFIN HERSCHEL R	COL	0-0166893	0647	2
GRIFFIN HOWARD L	MAJ	0-1824305	0963	1
GRIFFIN IVY L	CPT	0-1293244	0448	2
GRIFFIN JAMES A	LTC	0-1554375	0962	1
GRIFFIN JAMES D	1LT	0-1052368	0858	1
GRIFFIN JAMES E	LTC	0-0231350	0556	3
GRIFFIN JAMES E	LTC	0-1288733	0347	2
GRIFFIN JAMES H	CW3	W-2149213	0860	1
GRIFFIN JAMES J	LTC	0-0298581	0660	2
GRIFFIN JAMES M	CW3	W-2152672	1062	1
GRIFFIN JAMES R	CPT	0-0971074	1060	2
GRIFFIN JERRY A	COL	0-0358644	0859	1
GRIFFIN JOE R	CW3	W-2205998	0166	1
GRIFFIN JOHN C	CPT	0-0352280	0246	2
GRIFFIN JOHN F	MAJ	0-1030152	0461	1
GRIFFIN JR CARRELL E	MAJ	0-0532730	0864	1
GRIFFIN JR FRED C	1LT	0-1060113	0846	2
GRIFFIN JR OLIN A	1LT	0-0438588	0845	1
GRIFFIN JR OSCAR R	MAJ	0-1104697	0259	1
GRIFFIN JR THOMAS F	LTC	0-0367731	0660	1
GRIFFIN JR WILLIAM H	MAJ	0-1281806	0161	1
GRIFFIN LAWRENCE W	CW3	W-2147335	0662	1
GRIFFIN LILLIAN R	2LT	L-0201502	0844	2
GRIFFIN MARGARET M	CPT	N-0727461	0947	1
GRIFFIN MARTIN J	MAJ	0-0387052	0864	3
GRIFFIN MARVIN E	CPT	0-1698202	0648	1
GRIFFIN MARY M	1LT	N-0758192	1147	1
GRIFFIN MEADE F	COL	0-0159279	0354	3
GRIFFIN MITCHELL	CW3	W-2213370	1067	1
GRIFFIN MOSE P	MAJ	0-0488467	0649	1
GRIFFIN NEWELL C	MAJ	0-0181522	0462	3
GRIFFIN NOEL H	MAJ	0-0443416	0459	1
GRIFFIN OLIVE D	MAJ	N-0722140	0361	1
GRIFFIN OSBOURNE A	LTC	0-1172882	0663	1
GRIFFIN PAUL V	WO1	W-2107670	0857	1
GRIFFIN REBA M	2LT	N-0737067	0945	1
GRIFFIN REYNOLDS M	LTC	0-0167900	0259	2
GRIFFIN ROBERT T	2LT	0-1948143	0346	2
GRIFFIN ROBERT V	MAJ	0-1102271	1060	1
GRIFFIN ROBERT W	CPT	0-1287866	1046	1
GRIFFIN ROYAL M	COL	0-0197718	1060	3
GRIFFIN SAMUEL A	1LT	0-2011747	0767	1
GRIFFIN SR GERALD E	LTC	0-1010283	1060	1
GRIFFIN THOMAS E	CPT	0-0942972	0758	1
GRIFFIN THOMAS F	LTC	0-1796611	1262	1
GRIFFIN THOMAS J	LTC	0-0827134	0363	1
GRIFFIN THOMAS M	WO1	W-2134441	0248	1
GRIFFIN WALTER C	MAJ	0-1918911	0566	1
GRIFFIN WAYNE H	1LT	0-1297025	0445	2
GRIFFIN WILBUR O	LTC	0-1037991	0960	1
GRIFFIN WILLIAM F	MAJ	0-0209002	1064	3

NAME	GRADE	SVC NO	DATE RET MO YR	RET CODE
GRIFFIN WILLIAM J	CW2	W-3430266	0867	1
GRIFFIN WILLIAM K	CPT	0-0342245	1145	2
GRIFFIN WILLIAM R	MAJ	0-0570261	1165	1
GRIFFIN WILLIAM W	COL	0-0234971	0654	3
GRIFFIN WILLIAM W	MAJ	0-1046462	0766	1
GRIFFIN WILLIE B	CW3	W-2141849	0760	1
GRIFFIN WILLIE C	CPT	0-1314133	0547	2
GRIFFIS HENRY H	LTC	0-0428163	0263	1
GRIFFIS HUGH C	1LT	0-1641344	1145	2
GRIFFIS WILLBERN O	CPT	0-1591164	0358	1
GRIFFITH ARCHIE L	LTC	0-1574784	1162	1
GRIFFITH ARTHUR E	1LT	0-1307538	0445	2
GRIFFITH BERTRAND A	LTC	0-0333555	1067	3
GRIFFITH BRANDON H	1LT	0-1111639	1045	2
GRIFFITH BRYAN	LTC	0-0497657	0457	1
GRIFFITH DEXTER K	COL	0-0324007	0860	1
GRIFFITH DONALD W	LTC	0-0323000	0965	3
GRIFFITH ERNEST F	MAJ	0-1633905	1060	1
GRIFFITH ESTES B	CPT	0-0363682	0446	2
GRIFFITH GORDON R	LTC	0-1017851	0264	1
GRIFFITH HAROLD H	COL	0-0280245	1056	3
GRIFFITH HENRY H	MAJ	0-1298534	1060	1
GRIFFITH HUGHEY L	CW3	W-2136698	0763	1
GRIFFITH JAMES	MAJ	0-0503094	1054	1
GRIFFITH JAMES A	MAJ	0-0298500	1165	3
GRIFFITH JAMES A	1LT	0-1633247	0544	2
GRIFFITH JAMES C	CPT	0-0246959	0162	3
GRIFFITH JAMES L	CPT	0-0443754	0864	1
GRIFFITH JAMES R	2LT	0-0424649	1044	2
GRIFFITH JOE F	MAJ	0-2204308	0366	1
GRIFFITH JOHN W	CW2	W-2142844	0254	1
GRIFFITH JOSEPH	LTC	0-0447950	0158	1
GRIFFITH JOSEPH L	1LT	0-0521854	0645	2
GRIFFITH JR BENNIE M	MAJ	0-1321032	0962	1
GRIFFITH JR FULLER O	LTC	0-0175227	1059	3
GRIFFITH JR HAROLD P	2LT	0-0546706	0345	2
GRIFFITH JR JAMES R	COL	0-0242878	1165	3
GRIFFITH JR LOUIS H	MAJ	0-1043646	0562	1
GRIFFITH KEAN	LTC	0-0114461	0154	3
GRIFFITH LESTER J	CW2	W-2208101	1062	2
GRIFFITH LEWIS S	CPT	0-0231116	0446	2
GRIFFITH LINDSAY J	COL	0-0242801	0754	3
GRIFFITH PHILLIP S	CW4	W-2119390	1263	1
GRIFFITH ROBERT D	CPT	0-1105445	0867	3
GRIFFITH ROBERT F	LTC	0-1058015	0565	3
GRIFFITH ROBERT J	CPT	0-2262322	0161	2
GRIFFITH ROBERT J S	1LT	0-1053149	0446	2
GRIFFITH WALTER D	COL	0-0166794	0956	3
GRIFFITH WILLIAM E	COL	0-0207262	1060	3
GRIFFITH WILLIAM H	MAJ	0-0231326	1056	3
GRIFFITH WILLIAM W	LTC	0-1558718	0862	1
GRIFFITHS ARTHUR L	MAJ	0-0347980	0661	1
GRIFFITHS BYRON R	CW3	W-2144104	0562	1
GRIFFITHS C B	1LT	0-1785317	0246	2
GRIFFITHS JR AARON C	LTC	0-1289902	1266	1
GRIFFITHS LIONEL L	CW3	W-2148463	1065	1
GRIFFITHS MORGAN D	LTC	0-1794937	0863	1
GRIFFITHS WILLIAM J	CPT	0-0497249	0546	1
GRIFFON CLARA ANN	1LT	L-0801200	1045	2
GRIGALAUSKAS JOSEPH	1LT	0-2006452	1046	2
GRIGG JERRY C	CW3	W-2146508	0565	1
GRIGG KENNETH C	LTC	0-1306581	0267	1
GRIGG MAX R	CW3	W-2143093	0165	1
GRIGGERS WILLIAM J	CW2	W-3100425	0367	1
GRIGGINS ANTHONY J	1LT	0-1294463	0946	2
GRIGGS BENJAMIN F	CPT	0-0502494	0546	1
GRIGGS EMMITTE H	1LT	0-1320318	0446	2
GRIGGS GRETCHEN	1LT	N-2295195	0862	2
GRIGGS HENRY H	CW2	W-2208917	0664	1
GRIGGS JR ERNEST L	COL	0-0234025	0965	3
GRIGGS JR THOMAS O	CW2	W-2212015	0466	1
GRIGSBY FRANCIS M	LTC	0-1579727	0661	1
GRIGSBY KENNETH R	LTC	0-0291298	0364	3
GRILL FREDERICK	CPT	0-0277805	0663	3
GRILL JACK	LTC	0-0452649	0161	1

NAME	GRADE	SVC NO	DATE RET MO YR	RET CODE
GRILL JAMES T	2LT	0-1016582	0444	2
GRILLO GEORGE F	1LT	0-0332660	1042	2
GRILZ JULIAN J	MAJ	0-0969286	1161	1
GRIM ORVILLE L	MAJ	0-1329352	0863	1
GRIMALDI MICHAEL	COL	0-0182849	0351	1
GRIMES ALTON W	CPT	0-1293403	0647	2
GRIMES CHARLES M	CW3	W-2004011	1265	1
GRIMES CLARENCE R	CPT	0-2262775	0261	1
GRIMES DAVID L	CW3	W-2208280	0967	1
GRIMES ERCELL A	CW4	W-2144182	0867	1
GRIMES GEORGE R	COL	0-0293108	1060	1
GRIMES HENRY J	CPT	0-1534272	0860	1
GRIMES JESSE R	MAJ	0-1642132	0157	1
GRIMES JOHN H	CPT	0-0226662	0845	2
GRIMES KENNETH A	COL	0-0265248	1263	1
GRIMES LADDIE J	LTC	0-1109335	0866	1
GRIMES PRIESTLY H	WO1	W-2106351	1047	1
GRIMES ROBERT H	WO1	W-2122030	0350	2
GRIMES VERNON S	CW3	W-2005981	0164	1
GRIMES WALTER B	COL	0-0264872	1067	3
GRIMKE GLEN D	MAJ	0-0218759	1154	3
GRIMM GLENN R	MAJ	0-2036055	1060	1
GRIMM JACK R	LTC	0-1104799	0761	1
GRIMM JR LAURENCE F	CPT	0-0406988	1145	2
GRIMM WILLIAM C	MAJ	0-1030980	0760	1
GRIMMER BRUCE H	MAJ	0-2210273	0365	1
GRIMMER DONALD R	COL	0-0414010	0867	3
GRIMMER WILLIAM N	LTC	0-1594877	0463	1
GRIMMETT HALL W	MAJ	0-0965920	0363	1
GRIMSLEY JAMES H	CPT	0-1309722	1147	1
GRINSLEY VERN O	CW3	W-2147181	0464	1
GRINAGER CLINTON F	MAJ	0-0959318	0366	1
GRINCH LAWRENCE R	MAJ	0-1559455	1263	1
GRINDELL JOHN E	MAJ	0-1799633	0164	2
GRINDELL JOHN R	LTC	0-0364570	0163	1
GRINDLAY RONALD B	WO1	W-2004212	0465	3
GRINDLEY JOSEPH F	MAJ	0-1796080	0661	1
GRINE EDWARD E	1LT	0-1100566	0745	1
GRINER EDNA W	MAJ	N-0771912	0563	1
GRINER MARTIN F	CPT	0-0418499	0957	1
GRINESTAFF WILLIAM E	MAJ	0-1315735	1262	1
GRINNELL JOHN H	MAJ	0-1172883	0461	1
GRINNELL JR ERNEST O	CPT	0-1174872	0246	2
GRINSLACE PHILLIP R	1LT	0-1552684	0145	2
GRINSTEAD RICHARD F	LTC	0-0114324	0345	2
GRINVALSKY STEPHEN A	1LT	0-0526561	0744	2
GRISBON ROSE M	MAJ	M-0002310	1166	3
GRISDALE EARLE G	CPT	0-1292689	1046	1
GRISDALE ERNEST E	2LT	0-1327621	0246	2
GRISE LEO J	2LT	0-2053932	0149	1
GRISET TEO A	CPT	0-1039657	0856	1
GRISHAM C R T	CW4	W-2146983	0656	1
GRISHAM FRED L	CW3	W-2142845	0559	1
GRISHAM HAROLD M	CW3	W-2141929	0261	1
GRISHAM QUITMAN O	LTC	0-0453650	0556	1
GRISHAM ROSCOE E	LTC	0-1118583	0664	1
GRISSINGER JOHN P	CPT	0-1323311	1046	2
GRISSOM GEORGE T	CW2	W-2147323	0957	1
GRISSOM HORACE B	2LT	0-1640502	0245	2
GRISSOM JOHN E	CW2	W-2119696	0845	2
GRISSOM LAWRENCE B	MAJ	0-0397774	0660	1
GRISSOM MERICA C.	LTC	0-0236147	1059	1
GRIST GEORGE E	1LT	0-2001796	0146	1
GRIST OLIVER E	LTC	0-0922590	1264	3
GRISTHUS ANTHONY	1LT	0-1302299	1152	1
GRISWOLD CARLTON P	CPT	0-0171502	0149	3
GRISWOLD FREDERICK	LTC	0-0393446	0664	1
GRISWOLD JAMES M	2LT	0-1317521	0744	2
GRISWOLD JAMES W	CW4	W-2142074	0461	1
GRISWOLD WESLEY C	1LT	0-1639107	0952	1
GRISWOLD WILLIAM H	LTC	0-0119283	0148	2
GRITMAN LINTON O	LTC	0-0499668	1061	3
GRITSAVAGE ALICE M	COL	N-0755518	1262	1
GRITTA PAUL B	MAJ	0-0455112	0653	1
GRITTON CLAUDE S	CW2	W-2148237	0358	1

NAME	GRADE	SVC NO	DATE RET MO YR	RET CODE
GRITTON HAROLD N	MAJ	0-0888585	0565	1
GRITZ WILLIAM	COL	0-0181762	1147	1
GRIVAS JAMES N	CPT	0-0164628	1155	3
GRIZZARD JACK H	LTC	0-1597228	0466	1
GRIZZARD JOSEPH E	LTC	0-1001135	0557	1
GRIZZARD PHIL S	LTC	0-1002538	0667	3
GRIZZLE CHARLES R	MAJ	0-0964825	0363	1
GROAH MILTON B	MAJ	0-2006191	0763	1
GROARK THOMAS P	1LT	0-1542441	0444	2
GROAT RICHARD D	CW3	W-2144135	0764	1
GROBMEIER B ARTHUR	LTC	0-0221358	1262	3
GRODBERG BURTON C	CPT	0-0541675	0146	2
GROESBECK BYRON	CPT	0-1318301	0247	2
GROETZINGER PHILIP W	LTC	0-1080285	1264	1
GROFF GEORGE M	1LT	0-1315579	0546	2
GROFF JESSE	CPT	0-1288536	0346	2
GROFF VICTOR L	COL	0-0239282	1162	3
GROGAN DORIS V	2LT	N-0785071	0146	1
GROGAN EDWARD M	CPT	0-0158982	1152	3
GROGAN JOHN	CW2	W-2210028	1163	1
GROGAN JOHN B	LTC	0-0401389	0161	1
GROGAN ROBERT J	MAJ	0-2014655	0564	1
GROGAN THOMAS W	LTC	0-1313028	0561	1
GROGG MILTON R	LTC	0-1167873	0861	1
GROH EDWIN G	LTC	0-1172884	1164	3
GROHL JOHN B	MAJ	0-0255777	0867	3
GROHNE WILLIAM G	1LT	0-1176646	0347	1
GROHS WILLIAM H	CPT	0-0242997	0149	3
GROKE LINTON R	COL	0-0274324	0956	3
GROLL DONALD J	MAJ	0-1015622	0657	1
GROLLMAN JAYE J	1LT	0-0345595	0741	2
GROMBACH JOHN V	COL	0-0252642	0852	1
GROMER TERRY J	LTC	0-1701143	0546	2
GROMKO JOSEPH W	CPT	0-1013262	0561	1
GRONAU AXEL R	1LT	0-0535798	1044	1
GRONBERG WILFRED E	LTC	0-0290663	0766	3
GRONEMYER RALPH F	CW2	W-2144894	0756	1
GRONKE OTTO H	MAJ	0-1947497	0465	1
GRONSETH INGVALD H	COL	0-0128546	0250	3
GRONVOLD THEODORE C	LTC	0-1107995	0165	1
GROOM JR HORACE E	1LT	0-0461019	1045	2
GROOM WINSTON F	MAJ	0-0499362	1066	3
GROOME CHERRY A	LTC	0-0291521	0563	1
GROOMS RUSSELL E	CW3	W-2149256	0762	1
GROOTMAN PAUL G	MAJ	0-0949287	0366	1
GROOVER FRED E	LTC	0-1823732	0266	1
GROPP FREDDIE L	MAJ	0-1554376	1061	1
GROPP WILLIAM H	COL	0-0293901	1264	3
GROSBERG SAMUEL	LTC	0-0358109	0246	2
GROSE DAVID L	MAJ	0-0289327	0360	3
GROSE EUDIE E	MAJ	0-1182124	0757	1
GROSECLOSE FORREST K	2LT	0-1642924	0345	2
GROSECLOSE FRANK F	COL	0-0255107	0659	3
GROSECLOSE JAMES H	MAJ	0-0408413	0466	1
GROSENBECK GRETCHEN	MAJ	N-0758169	1066	3
GROSGUTH JR JOSEPH	MAJ	0-0321063	0165	3
GROSHART OSCAR D	COL	0-0221207	1053	2
GROSHCK CRAIG G	1LT	0-1315300	0545	2
GROSOF WILLIAM S	CPT	0-0502082	0146	2
GROSS ARTHUR L	2LT	0-1300792	0744	2
GROSS BENJAMIN	CW2	W-2123050	0450	2
GROSS CHARLES L	MAJ	0-1114953	1158	1
GROSS CHARLES N	CPT	0-0360376	0346	2
GROSS CHRIS L	MAJ	0-0302688	0267	3
GROSS EARL R	LTC	0-1170397	0865	1
GROSS EDWARD C	2LT	0-0455339	0145	2
GROSS EDWARD L	MAJ	0-1014171	0361	1
GROSS EVERETT W	1LT	0-1102272	0744	1
GROSS FRANK F	1LT	0-0495586	0145	1
GROSS FRANK W	CW4	W-2131294	0659	1
GROSS HARRY W	MAJ	0-0150599	0356	3
GROSS HELEN R	MAJ	N-0798935	1265	1
GROSS HOWARD I	2LT	0-1799949	0446	1
GROSS IRVING	CW3	W-2152212	1264	1
GROSS JACQUES	LTC	0-0921291	1066	3

NAME	GRADE	SVC NO	DATE RET MO YR	RET CODE
GROSS JOHN G	CPT	0-0238187	C665	3
GROSS JOSEPH M	CPT	0-0341336	0144	1
GROSS KARL R	CPT	C-1299232	C546	2
GROSS LESTER E	COL	0-0340815	C562	1
GROSS MARGARET E	MAJ	N-0723156	C367	3
GROSS MARTIN L	LTC	0-1311143	0158	1
GROSS MURRAY M	2LT	0-1081748	0145	2
GROSS NICK	2LT	0-0108485	1029	1
GROSS NORMAN N	LTC	0-0391529	066C	1
GRCSS REYNOLDS C	LTC	0-0425309	1054	1
GROSS SAMUEL W	1LT	C-1327949	C646	2
GROSS THOMAS C	CW3	W-2149408	0662	1
GROSS WAYMON L	LTC	0-1316407	0765	2
GROSS WILMA M	LTC	N-0702058	C647	1
GROSSCUP BLANCHE R	LTC	N-0728886	1066	3
GROSSE WOODROW O	1LT	0-1316408	C546	2
GROSSER JAMES C	MAJ	0-1646213	0662	1
GROSSMAN AARON	1LT	0-0518319	0444	2
GROSSMAN ALEXANDER	LTC	0-0301112	0259	3
GROSSMAN HAROLD	LTC	0-1056019	1262	1
GROSSMAN JAMES M	MAJ	C-1854862	1223	1
GROSSMAN LESTER	MAJ	0-1330304	C567	1
GROSSMAN MARTIN M	1LT	0-1311765	C845	2
GROSSMAN MAX B	LTC	0-0292324	C447	2
GROSSMAN MORRIS J	WO1	W-2148293	1154	1
GROSSMAN PAUL W	LTC	C-1323312	1062	1
GROSSMAN ROYAL G	COL	0-0236123	1045	1
GROSSMAN SIDNEY W	MAJ	0-0321068	C845	2
GROSSMAN WILLIAM M	CPT	0-0538199	1046	2
CROSSTEPHAN ARTHUR R	COL	0-0220543	0564	3
GROSVENOR JACK L	CPT	0-1331282	1053	2
GROTE JR WILLIAM J	CPT	0-1715452	C648	2
GROTEFEND OLIVER C	COL	C-0321203	C964	3
GROTELUESCHEN E W	MAJ	C-0887376	C161	1
GROTENRATH JOSEPH A	COL	0-0253633	C154	2
GROTH ALFONS C	MAJ	C-1686538	0961	1
CROTH HOWARD G	LTC	0-1824857	C767	1
GROTHJAN CLETUS A	MAJ	C-0326483	C546	2
GROTHUSEN HAROLD D	LTC	C-0225751	C463	3
GROTTS JOHN J	MAJ	C-1649021	0657	1
GROTY JR CHARLES M	MAJ	C-0500270	1059	1
GROTZ CHARLES G	2LT	0-0109306	0227	1
GROTZ JR CLIFFORD C	MAJ	0-1922725	1066	1
GROUNDS MARIE	2LT	N-0761140	0345	1
GROUSE WALTER C	LTC	0-0499646	0648	3
GROUTT JAMES A	LTC	0-2034659	0962	1
GROVE CECIL V	CW4	W-2142846	0565	1
GROVE DON L	CW3	W-2147308	C861	1
GROVE ELLSWORTH	MAJ	C-0966417	C766	1
GROVE GEORGE W	LTC	0-0445535	0554	1
GROVE HARRY C	WO1	W-2106438	0453	2
GROVE HOMER T	CPT	0-0970380	1060	1
GROVE JOHN A	LTC	0-1685855	1045	2
GROVE LARENCE H	CPT	0-1303498	0246	2
GROVE PAUL C	MAJ	C-0272405	0246	2
GROVE PAUL C	MAJ	0-0310132	0246	2
GROVE PERCIVAL W	1LT	0-1995098	0946	1
GROVE ROBERT H	MAJ	C-0368584	C945	2
GROVE SAMUEL A C	MAJ	C-0406911	C366	3
GROVE STARKEY	LTC	0-0210425	C358	3
GROVE WENDELL P	CW2	W-2146860	0555	2
GROVER FRANK N	CPT	0-1324534	0147	2
GROVER FRED B	1LT	0-1320319	C146	1
GROVER FREDERICK	MAJ	C-1635983	C562	1
GROVER GEORGE B	CW4	W-2108326	C559	2
GRCVER MORRIS L	COL	0-0296698	0964	3
GROVER PHYLLIS P	1LT	N-0751484	0246	1
GROVER WARREN B	CPT	0-0485356	C145	2
GROVES ALFRED H	1LT	0-179873C	0950	1
GROVES CLAIRE F	LTC	0-0261776	C360	1
GROVES GERALD L	CW3	W-2208259	C366	1
GROVES JAMES F	MAJ	C-1181616	0759	1
GROVES LAURENCE W	CPT	0-1314280	C149	1
GROVES LYMAN M	CW4	W-2122593	1057	3
GROVES MELVIN J	LTC	0-0453895	C958	1

NAME	GRADE	SVC NO	DATE RET MO YR	RET CODE
GROVES PAUL A	MAJ	0-1548213	0452	1
GROVES ROBERT O	P G	0-0129915	0452	3
GROVES WILLIAM F	LTC	0-1576064	0462	1
GROVESTEEN LOYAL E	MAJ	0-204317C	0961	1
GROW NEVILLE L	LTC	0-0287535	C850	1
GROW PAUL C	LTC	0-0244082	1163	3
GROW STEWART L	MAJ	0-0368670	1045	2
GROWDON JAMES R	COL	0-0155229	0648	3
GRUBB HOMER J	CPT	0-0510087	1146	2
GRUBB JR WILLIAM F	MAJ	0-1298386	0364	1
GRUBB MILO W	CW3	W-2150655	0965	1
GRUBBS HORACE	MAJ	0-1112738	1160	1
GRUBBS IRVIN A	MAJ	0-1017872	0965	1
GRUBBS PAUL L	CW2	RW-2209318	0561	1
GRUBE NELSON E	MAJ	0-1118214	0667	3
GRUBE ROY O	LTC	0-0286417	0763	3
GRUBER CHARLES G	COL	0-0110218	C854	2
GRUBER CHARLES N	LTC	0-1000571	0356	2
GRUBER DAVID R	CPT	0-1166075	0246	1
GRUBER GEORGE W	MAJ	0-1342266	0262	1
GRUBER LOUIS G	CPT	0-0466976	0846	2
GRUBER RALPH A	LTC	0-0451112	0960	1
GRUBER RICHARD	1LT	0-1597802	0247	2
GRUBER ROBERT P	2LT	0-0957856	0550	1
GRUBER THOMAS H	LTC	0-1541909	1059	1
GRUBERT BILL	MAJ	0-2037166	1061	2
GRUBIN SAMUEL	LTC	0-0287063	0746	2
GRUBOWSKI JOSEPH N	CPT	0-1692011	0944	2
GRUDZIEN JOHN J	MAJ	C-2011254	0764	1
GRUELLE ORIE P	2LT	0-0439623	0860	1
GRUESS EMANUEL M	1LT	0-0502971	0643	2
GRUITS LAWRENCE T	MAJ	0-0484547	0154	1
GRULA JOE J	CW4	W-2111330	1054	1
GRUM MARY R	CPT	N-0783763	0146	1
GRUMAN DOROTHY J	1LT	L-0200182	1045	2
GRUMBEIN FRANKLIN K	CW3	W-2152343	0564	1
GRUMBLES TURMAN N	MAJ	0-1599041	1164	1
GRUMBLES WILLIAM H	CPT	0-1645012	0259	1
GRUMET MARVIN	2LT	0-1320726	0545	2
GRUMMISH CARROLL H	CW3	W-2126087	0962	1
GRUMMON STUART N	COL	C-0234610	0356	3
GRUNDBERG BERTEL H	COL	0-0305051	1058	1
GRUNDEN BERT C	CW2	W-2206238	1060	1
GRUNDER RICHARD R	CPT	0-1877221	0163	1
GRUNDMEIER LOWELL C	2LT	0-1333067	0946	2
GRUNDVIG HUGH R	COL	0-0282993	1160	1
GRUNDY MACK G	2LT	0-1015231	0857	1
GRUNDY THOMAS	CPT	0-0109574	0228	1
GRUNECK SIDNEY	COL	0-0174188	0258	1
GRUNER JR ERNEST F	CW2	W-2209161	0664	1
GRUNER JR LOUIS J	CPT	0-1534983	0853	2
GRUNEWALD ERNEST O	MAJ	0-0486772	0254	2
GRUNEWALD EUGENE F	LTC	0-0180509	0844	2
GRUNING ROLF R	MAJ	C-2263531	0365	1
GRUNKE ERIK B	MAJ	C-1324410	0557	1
GRUSINSKI FRED S	MAJ	0-2017051	0661	1
GRUSTAS EDWARD	1LT	0-2263144	1057	2
GRUTERS BERTRAM E	LTC	0-0329686	0446	2
GRUTZA JEROME S	CPT	0-1286116	0246	1
GRUVER JOHN J	LTC	0-0212127	1061	3
GRYMES HERBERT L	COL	C-0126905	0651	3
GRZEGORCWICZ VINCENT	LTC	0-1646750	1264	1
GRZESKOWIAK URBAN J	LTC	0-1639108	0561	1
GRZONKA EDWARD J	2LT	0-1328251	0845	2
GRZYBEK EDWARD F	MAJ	0-1045762	0247	2
GRZYBOWSKI CHARLES F	CPT	0-1300313	0561	1
GRZYMALA STELLA D	1LT	N-0774049	0348	1
GRZYWNEWICZ ZIGGI S	LTC	0-1643619	0867	1
GSCHWINDT GEORGE F	MAJ	0-0333204	0648	3
GUARDIOLA-PEREZ MIG	MAJ	0-1924151	0565	1
GUARIGLIA HUMBERT J	CW2	W-2117922	1044	2
GUARINO RUSSELL J	CW2	W-2143170	0956	1
GUARNIERI DAVID C	MAJ	0-0454213	0461	1
GUAS RAMON R	COL	C-0194051	0963	3
GUBIN EMIL K	COL	0-0922540	0566	3

NAME	GRADE	SVC NO	DATE RET MO YR	RET CODE
GUBIN IRVING P	LTC	0-0229252	C364	3
GUBITOSI CLEO A	1LT	0-1635984	C847	1
GUBITOSI VINCENT H	CPT	0-1039013	1046	2
GUBOW LAWRENCE	CPT	0-1308509	0748	2
GUDDAL IVAN C	CPT	0-1325389	C246	2
GUDENAS PAULINE M	MAJ	N-0795117	0565	1
GUDENKAUF BERNARD J	MAJ	C-0969814	C765	1
GUDGEON RUSSELL C	LTC	0-0910577	C964	3
GUDGER JESSE M	MAJ	C-0248320	C964	3
GUDIE GEORGE G	1LT	0-1797118	0654	1
GUDMUNDSON WAYNE A	COL	0-0237351	1158	3
GUDRIDGE FREDERICK	LTC	0-1994918	0267	1
GUDWIN ABRAHAM	CPT	0-0484408	C345	2
GUEDET JOSEPH J	MAJ	C-0383262	C964	1
GUELDNER JR WALTER J	CPT	0-1287518	1060	1
GUENARD JOHN R	LTC	0-0283852	C759	1
GUENTHER CLIFFORD E	LTC	0-0100752	0756	3
GUENTHER FRANK J	COL	0-0213585	C661	3
GUENTHER ROBERT H	LTC	0-1109968	1062	1
GUENTHER STANLEY H	LTC	0-0319266	0264	3
GUENTHNER FRED	CW4	W-2122178	C161	1
GUERIN COURTLAND	LTC	0-0312744	0467	1
GUERIN DONALD L	WO1	W-2125722	C246	2
GUERNSEY CHARLES	CPT	0-1327733	1167	1
GUERNSEY JAMES C	CW2	W-2153351	C560	2
GUERNSEY RICHARD C	CW3	W-2205196	C866	1
GUERNSEY RUSSELL L	1LT	0-0514596	C846	2
GUERRIERO HUMBERT	1LT	0-1182848	C963	3
GUERRISSI JOSEPH V	LTC	0-0860841	0267	1
GUERRO THOMAS M	LTC	0-0453428	C261	1
GUERTIN ALBERT R	MAJ	C-1104802	0666	1
GUESS JULIAN C	MAJ	C-1320837	C658	1
GUESS LUTHER H	MAJ	0-0399005	C762	1
GUESSAZ JR LOUIS A	COL	0-0259517	1160	1
GUEST FRANK	MAJ	C-0970128	C865	1
GUEST JOHN A	LTC	0-0289458	1059	3
GUEST JR WILLIAM C	2LT	0-1291981	0146	1
GUEST THOMAS W	CPT	0-1120682	0158	1
GUETSCHOW FRANK J	CPT	C-0262853	1145	2
GUEVARA ROBERTO	MAJ	C-0963511	0765	1
GUFFAIN TOMAS H	LTC	0-1287699	0165	1
GUFFEY CLARENCE L	MAJ	C-1320000	0758	1
GUFFEY HAROLD W	MAJ	C-0451293	1146	1
GUFFEY HUGH J	LTC	0-1012377	0261	1
GUFFIN WILLIAM B	1LT	0-1043094	1044	2
GUGELER RUSSELL A	LTC	0-1184834	C867	1
GUGGENHEIM MORRIS	LTC	0-0251314	1065	3
GUGGOLZ MURIEL F	MAJ	N-0742616	0364	3
GUGISBURG ALBERT W	LTC	0-0227925	C263	3
GUHL EDWARD R	MAJ	C-1178817	C265	1
GUICE JASON G	1LT	0-2319781	0451	3
GUIDA CRESCENZO	LTC	C-0387075	C662	1
GUIDA DOMINIC P	CPT	0-1309255	C347	2
GUIDO JOSEPH J	CPT	0-1923613	C462	1
GUIDOTTI FRANK P	LTC	0-0350147	C147	2
GUIER DAVID H	MAJ	0-1540852	0266	1
GUIJARRO ANTONIO	LTC	C-0287653	C657	3
GUILBAULT BRIEN L	CW2	W-2101774	C446	1
GUILD WALTER A	COL	0-0206210	C758	1
GUILE SAMUEL H	MAJ	C-1112740	0257	1
GUILFORD MADGE L	2LT	N-0773288	0447	1
GUILFORD WILLIAM B	MAJ	C-2021141	C565	1
GUILFOYLE FRANCIS L	CPT	0-1001796	C146	2
GUILFOYLE KENNETH H	CW3	W-2148902	1166	1
GUILLIAMS IRA	CW4	W-2143575	C466	1
GUILLORY KIRBY	LTC	0-0488432	1156	1
GUILLOT EARL L	LTC	0-0924812	C165	3
GUINAN EDWARD R	CPT	0-1012646	0161	1
GUINAN MATTHEW P	2LT	0-1012865	C345	2
GUINN FLETCHER	1LT	0-2036546	C754	1
GUINN JOSEPH P	LTC	0-1042586	C367	1
GUINN JR JOHN W	CPT	C-0698884	1057	2
GUINN JR WILLIAM H	LTC	0-2017052	1163	1
GUINN MARTHA S	1LT	N-0744284	C146	1
GUINNUP GORDON R	CPT	C-0296520	1145	2

NAME	GRADE	SVC NO	DATE RET MO YR	RET CODE
GUINOT LUIS	WO1	W-211562C	C359	1
GUINTO FAUSTINO G	1LT	0-1896387	1160	1
GUION JOHN P	CPT	0-2271658	0364	1
GUIOT FERNANDO M	MAJ	C-0508365	C264	1
GUISINGER CARLOS W	MAJ	0-1919231	0667	1
GUISINGER EARL C	COL	0-0240932	0846	2
GUIVER GOLDEN C	LTC	0-0309940	0146	2
GULA JR ANDREW	LTC	0-1000572	0463	1
GULBRANSON IRVIN V	MAJ	C-2030980	1166	1
GULCZYNSKI EDMUND C	MAJ	0-2039544	0563	1
GULDENZOPF ROBERT L	MAJ	C-1175726	1060	1
GULEKE JOSEPH	CW2	W-2206904	0663	1
GULIAN GEORGE	COL	0-0338700	1060	1
GULLANS OSCAR	COL	0-0231362	1262	3
GULLBORG HARRY E	1LT	0-1061710	0845	2
GULLEDGE GEORGE W	CW3	W-2152294	1159	1
GULLEKSEN CARL L	MAJ	0-2000615	0765	1
GULLETT PAUL C	2LT	0-0441772	0943	1
GULLETTE ROBERT F	LTC	0-020235C	0263	3
GULLICKSON CARMEN I	CPT	N-0775938	0546	2
GULLIFER WILLIAM H	MAJ	0-0126138	C853	3
GULLIKSEN ARTHUR G	COL	0-0304936	0858	1
GULLINGSRUD M J O	MAJ	0-0327720	0945	2
GULLION ROBERT C	2LT	0-0516589	0944	2
GULLIVER HERBERT J	CPT	0-1167012	0854	2
GULLIVER REGINALD E	MAJ	0-0259173	0166	3
GULLIXON RICHARD L	CPT	0-0452044	1045	2
GULMYER GEORGE J	MAJ	0-0228463	0463	3
GUMASKAS PETER J	LTC	0-0418283	1160	1
GUMBRELL ARTHUR J	2LT	0-1315301	0345	2
GUMBS ALFRED E	CPT	0-0156055	0648	3
GUMM CLARK L	CPT	0-1055021	0747	2
GUMMEL CHARLES P	LTC	0-0475964	1054	1
GUMMIG GEORGE J	2LT	0-4040907	0456	2
GUMP ALAN M	COL	0-0274087	0364	3
GUNBY RUSSELL A	MAJ	0-1019193	1060	1
GUNO LEON J	LTC	0-0378897	0554	1
GUNDECK WALTER S	MAJ	0-0198077	0557	3
GUNDERSEN GEORGE A	LTC	0-1546243	0366	3
GUNDERSON CARL F	CW2	W-2143743	0262	1
GUNDERSON COLEMAN G	LTC	0-0173062	1152	2
GUNDERSON ERNEST O	COL	0-0332033	0166	3
GUNDERSON FRANK N	COL	0-0283558	0464	3
GUNDERSON GEORGE M	MAJ	0-0171449	0554	3
GUNDERSON HARVEY J	LTC	0-0250254	C966	3
GUNDERSON RICHARD L	1LT	0-1324622	C245	2
GUNDERSON RUSSELL B	CPT	C-1016546	0947	2
GUNDLACH PHILIP J	LTC	0-0342498	1057	1
GUNDRUM JEROME C	1LT	0-1317906	0545	2
GUNDRY KENNETH E	MAJ	0-0322433	0847	2
GUNGL JOHN C	COL	0-0162684	0648	3
GUNHUS HARMS J	LTC	0-0930468	0465	1
GUNKEL WILLIAM F	LTC	0-0448356	0763	1
GUNN CYRUS L	LTC	0-0258631	0267	3
GUNN ELDON L	CPT	0-1996646	0547	1
GUNN GEORGE C	LTC	0-1309256	1166	1
GUNN JAN V	MAJ	0-0355328	0246	2
GUNN JOE C	MAJ	0-2018683	1162	1
GUNN JOHN H	LTC	0-0303585	0762	3
GUNN JR JOHN F	WO1	W-2120459	0862	2
GUNN NELLIE L	CPT	L-0200420	0346	1
GUNN RAYMOND F	COL	0-0192294	0561	1
GUNN ROBERT B	CPT	0-2035097	0662	1
GUNN ROBERT K	LTC	0-1824177	C765	1
GUNN SAMUEL A	MAJ	0-0370251	0446	2
GUNN THOMAS F	COL	0-0112193	0859	3
GUNNE MICHAEL J	MAJ	0-1291458	0960	1
GUNNELL EMMA R	MAJ	N-0783788	0863	1
GUNNERUD SWEN S	CPT	0-0224749	0561	3
GUNNING GORDON W	1LT	0-2025916	0247	1
GUNNING JOHN T	CPT	0-1321507	0746	1
GUNNING LAURENCE G	CW4	W-2152578	0765	1
GUNNOE WILBUR G	CPT	0-0473474	0546	2
GUNSEL ROBERT C	MAJ	0-2200513	0466	1
GUNSTON GEORGE T	COL	0-0194301	0259	3

NAME	GRADE	SVC NO	DATE RET MO YR	RET CODE
GUNTER ALBERT A	LTC	0-0485275	0954	1
GUNTER EDWARD R	1LT	0-0255333	0239	1
GUNTER ELMER E	CPT	0-0302160	0945	2
GUNTER LAWRENCE R	CPT	0-0493509	0148	1
GUNTER ROBERT E	MAJ	0-0292601	0444	2
GUNTER ROBERT L	CW3	W-2144885	1062	1
GUNTER SAM H	LTC	0-1635988	0162	1
GUNTHARP GEORGE D	LTC	0-0337281	0657	1
GUNTHARP PAUL M	LTC	0-1013289	0361	1
GUNTHER HERBERT J	COL	0-0267778	0158	1
GUNTHER RAYMOND C	COL	0-0369044	0365	3
GUNTHER WALTER	LTC	0-0132814	0556	3
GUNTHORP CECIL H	LTC	0-0360561	0863	3
GUNTZVILLER HARVEY L	1LT	0-2051159	1046	2
GURTON BENNETT L	CPT	0-0496366	0645	2
GURTON GROVER A	CW3	W-2204976	0663	1
GURTON SAMUEL A	LTC	0-1103190	0462	1
GURAN SIDNEY J	LTC	0-0332411	0646	2
GURAT PANTALEON	1LT	0-0890491	1050	1
GURBAL DOROTHY V	2LT	N-0795164	1046	1
GURIAN BERNARD	CPT	0-0486669	0245	2
GURLEY JAMES H	LTC	0-1649475	0861	1
GURLEY JOSEPH C	LTC	0-1633514	0860	1
GURNEE WILLIAM N	CW3	W-2146332	0962	1
GURNEY FAUNTLEROY	CW3	W-2144653	1264	1
GURNEY JR EDWARD J	LTC	0-1010115	1046	2
GURNEY MYRON F	CPT	0-0888209	1060	1
GURS GAY	MAJ	0-0400809	0163	1
GURSCH OTTO F	LTC	0-0358141	0663	3
GURTOV BERNARD M	1LT	0-1283759	0246	2
GURZNY JOSEPH L	MAJ	0-0271835	0257	3
GUSHIN PAUL P	LTC	0-1533330	0865	1
GUSIMAT GAVINO L	2LT	0-1896522	0358	1
GUSLER CYRIL L	LTC	0-0348279	0867	3
GUSMEROLI JOSEPH	1LT	0-1324411	0147	2
GUSSAK JOHN J	COL	0-0275458	0160	3
GUSSETT NORWICH B	LTC	0-0189403	0160	3
GUST GEORGE A	1LT	0-0448273	0344	2
GUSTAFSON ALICE C	1LT	N-0758203	0447	1
GUSTAFSON CARL G	CW3	W-2143194	0962	1
GUSTAFSON ERLAND W	1LT	0-1032711	0146	2
GUSTAFSON GERALD A	MAJ	0-0537593	0564	1
GUSTAFSON HARRY L	COL	0-0125927	0754	3
GUSTAFSON HERMAN C	LTC	0-0542428	0764	3
GUSTAFSON NILS R	LTC	0-0207338	0657	3
GUSTAFSON PAUL S	CW3	W-2152383	0763	1
GUSTAFSON VICTOR E	MAJ	0-0132119	0144	2
GUSTAFSON VICTOR V	CPT	0-0409147	1043	2
GUSTAFSON WALTER R	CW3	W-2005711	0167	1
GUSTAFSON WILLIAM C	WO1	W-2148255	0153	2
GUSTAVSON CARL B	LTC	0-1054763	1066	1
GUSTIN DALE O	CPT	0-1541852	0159	1
GUSTIN GEORGE W	LTC	0-1590511	0865	1
GUSTIN NICHOLAS L	CW4	W-2135684	0563	1
GUSTIN ROBERT V	LTC	0-0119793	0648	3
GUSTINA FRANCIS L	LTC	0-1101854	1160	1
GUSTOPF FRED	COL	0-0312010	0758	2
GUTH WILLIAM W	MAJ	0-1307685	1163	1
GUTHART WENDELL L	CPT	0-1179084	0946	2
GUTHRIE CHARLES M	MAJ	0-1289724	0246	1
GUTHRIE CLARENCE L	CPT	0-0533127	1145	2
GUTHRIE EDWARD H	MAJ	0-0229836	0845	2
GUTHRIE FRED G	1LT	0-1287701	0346	2
GUTHRIE GEORGE P	COL	0-0232937	0464	3
GUTHRIE GORDON J	MAJ	0-2011594	1162	1
GUTHRIE HUGH H	LTC	0-2289473	0365	1
GUTHRIE JAMES R	MAJ	0-0254304	0465	1
GUTHRIE JAMES C	LTC	0-2048941	1165	1
GUTHRIE JESSE L	MAJ	0-1996348	1160	1
GUTHRIE OTTO F	CW2	W-2150306	0162	1
GUTHRIE WARREN W	1LT	0-0252299	0446	2
GUTJAHR ARTHUR W	1LT	0-1030571	0645	2
GUTJAHR LYDIA	MAJ	N-0737847	0364	1
GUTMAKER HYMAN R	CPT	0-1696116	0246	2
GUTMANN ADDIS	COL	0-0219073	0261	3

NAME	GRADE	SVC NO	DATE RET MO YR	RET CODE
GUTOWSKY HERBERT S	CPT	0-0401051	0945	2
GUTSHALL RICHARD B	LTC	0-0399424	0860	1
GUTTERMAN GEORGE K	LTC	0-0382928	1060	1
GUTTMAN WILLIAM S	MAJ	0-1686596	1062	1
GUY ALFRED F	CPT	0-0268270	0346	1
GUY GEORGE F	COL	0-0213068	0664	3
GUY JAMES H	CPT	0-0524597	0246	2
GUY JAMES S	MAJ	0-1120060	0761	1
GUY LEONIDE J	MAJ	0-0185684	0842	1
GUY ROSS D	LTC	0-0138897	0648	3
GUY WILLIAM F	CW3	W-2148565	0567	1
GUYER NATHAN E	MAJ	0-0215195	1154	3
GUYER PAUL M	COL	0-0231780	1059	3
GUYETT HARVEY E	MAJ	0-0258582	0560	3
GUYTON JAY M	CPT	0-0524223	0447	2
GUYTON SAM M	MAJ	0-0471628	1046	2
GUZICKI RAYMOND A	LTC	0-0384541	1061	1
GUZMAN DONATO P	CPT	0-1896433	0358	1
GUZMAN HENRY M	CPT	0-1644388	0360	1
GUZMAN JR MANUEL	LTC	0-0293891	0246	2
GUZY STEPHEN W	LTC	0-0286667	0967	3
GUZZARDO SAM	LTC	0-1312760	0662	1
GWALTNEY PERRY M	LTC	0-0245433	1053	3
GWATHMEY CARELL	COL	0-0443908	0662	3
GWIAZDA EDWARD J	CW3	W-2147974	0761	1
GWILLIAM MARK R M	COL	0-0105575	1150	3
GWIN GARLAND L	CPT	0-1294299	0747	2
GWIN JAMES M	LTC	0-0282982	1166	3
GWINN FRANK W	LTC	0-0331898	1054	2
GWINN HUBERT E	1LT	0-1996364	1046	1
GWINN JOHN F	LTC	0-0420987	0563	2
GWINN JR FRED M	1LT	0-1644385	0745	2
GWINN MACK W	LTC	0-1181274	0167	1
GWINNER HAROLD H	LTC	0-0323360	1060	1
GWINNER JOHN K	MAJ	0-0960495	0264	1
GWOZDZ JOSEPH A	LTC	0-1283596	1264	1
GWYNN CHARLES B	COL	0-0223492	0262	3
GWYNN HAROLD V	LTC	0-1177816	0663	1
GWYNN THOMAS F	1LT	0-1996622	0552	1
GYAMI WILLIAM H	MAJ	0-1313696	0365	1
GYTE MILTON E	MAJ	0-0486579	0954	1
GYZEN KLESS	LTC	0-1340455	1166	1
HAAB HOWARD H	CPT	0-1293404	1047	1
HAACK ROBERT D	CPT	0-1319944	0347	1
HAAG CHARLES F	LTC	0-1588018	0163	1
HAAG ESTELLA W	2LT	N-0700392	0637	1
HAAG HAROLD H	LTC	0-0114972	0557	3
HAAG MERRALD H	CPT	0-0275058	1043	2
HAAG ROBERT H	LTC	0-0102930	0845	2
HAAG ROBERT V	CPT	0-0276203	0961	2
HAAKE HOWARD G	CPT	0-0381554	0545	2
HAAKER ELSIE C	MAJ	L-0220007	1167	3
HAALAND ADLER	LTC	0-0375261	0761	1
HAALAND OTTO E	LTC	0-0368654	0967	3
HAAN DANIEL A	CW3	W-2142681	0459	1
HAAR WALTER P	MAJ	0-1553831	0263	1
HAAS CHARLES W	1LT	0-1531297	1057	2
HAAS EDWARD F	1LT	0-2035846	0845	1
HAAS FRANK T	CW2	W-2142365	0858	1
HAAS GEORGE M	LTC	0-0307504	0564	3
HAAS JOSEPH	COL	0-0196248	1050	3
HAAS JR JOHN A	MAJ	0-2019875	0562	1
HAAS KENNETH W	COL	0-0311614	1146	1
HAAS LOUIS M	COL	0-0183372	1054	1
HAAS MABEL E	1LT	N-0752037	0845	1
HAAS DEAN C	LTC	0-1796460	0264	1
HAAS ROBERT F	WO1	W-2124707	0444	2
HAAS THEOPHIL W	LTC	0-0297191	0367	3
HAAS WILLIAM L	LTC	0-1642531	0267	3
HAASE ANTHONY C	LTC	0-0183464	0948	2
HAASE ELDON A	LTC	0-0384205	0760	1
HAASE ELTON L	CW4	W-2122272	0466	1
HAASE REX L	1LT	0-0298625	1145	2
HAASE WILLIAM F	MAJ	0-1107453	1059	1
HAASIS LOUIS C	LTC	0-1556433	0667	1

NAME	GRADE	SVC NO	DATE RET MO YR	RET CODE
HABAL DULCESIMO	1LT	0-1896474	1065	1
HABAS MILTON L	LTC	0-1283419	0561	2
HABEL HENRY W	CPT	0-0478470	1045	2
HABER JOSEPH	MAJ	0-1173262	0153	1
HABERCOM ALAN L	LTC	0-1043095	0765	1
HABERLE DAVID L	1LT	0-0389637	1145	2
HABERLE JACOB	CPT	0-0183349	0249	3
HABERLIN CHESTER E	COL	0-0162317	0559	3
HABERMAN EDWARD J	CPT	0-1299736	0746	2
HABERSTROH CHARLES F	LTC	0-0251617	0366	3
HABERSTZER D H	CW2	W-3100537	0267	1
HABURNE JAMES D	CPT	0-0890327	0348	2
HACHADORIAN CHARLES	CW2	W-2116212	0962	3
HACHET HARRY A	LTC	0-0301999	0764	3
HACK DON F	CPT	0-1894177	1065	1
HACK RAY B	1LT	0-0477730	0241	1
HACKARD CLIFFORD T	LTC	0-1296023	0262	1
HACKENBERGER R J	LTC	0-0299990	0264	3
HACKENYOS GEORGE E	CW2	W-2215362	0967	1
HACKER ALEX	LTC	0-1108709	1065	1
HACKER DONALD N	LTC	0-0398193	0966	1
HACKER HERMAN J	2LT	0-0437094	0945	2
HACKER HUBERT L	2LT	0-1294830	1144	2
HACKER HUGH A	LTC	0-1292171	0855	1
HACKER JR PHILIP C	LTC	0-0413331	0561	1
HACKER LAWRENCE W	LTC	0-0264053	0657	3
HACKER PHILIP C	MAJ	0-0239799	0753	3
HACKER RAYMOND G	LTC	0-1104186	0266	1
HACKETT JAMES W	CW3	W-2145175	0662	1
HACKETT KENNETH L	1LT	0-0535899	1145	1
HACKETT NEIL B	1LT	0-1894824	0846	2
HACKETT ROBERT A	2LT	0-1030476	0844	2
HACKETT THOMAS A	MAJ	0-0365174	0747	2
HACKETT WILLIAM O	MAJ	0-1327836	0263	1
HACKETT WILLIAM F	LTC	0-1591776	0163	1
HACKETT WILLIAM G	2LT	0-1016708	0645	2
HACKFORD LEIGH C	CPT	0-1691402	0845	2
HACKITT JACK	LTC	0-1312761	0663	1
HACKMAN HARRY C	MAJ	0-0126479	0850	3
HACKNEY CHARLES G	1LT	0-1331834	1046	1
HACKNEY JOE G	1LT	0-1175449	1044	2
HACKRADT OTTO A	CPT	0-0229756	0256	3
HACUMAN SIXTO	1LT	0-1896789	0948	1
HADAWAY JOHN W	MAJ	0-0887470	1058	1
HADAWAY WILLIAM C	CPT	0-1035276	0762	1
HADDAD EDWARD G	CPT	0-0299746	1050	1
HADDAD FREDERICK	COL	0-0339938	0560	1
HADDEN RALPH W	MAJ	0-0969649	1061	1
HADDEN ROBERT L	MAJ	0-1186413	0463	1
HADDICK JOHN K	LTC	0-0332478	0161	1
HADDIX PETER E	CPT	0-0164215	0929	2
HADDOCK JORGE G	CPT	0-1924075	0865	2
HADCOCK RAY O	MAJ	0-0144750	0152	3
HADDON WILLIAM S	CPT	0-0989466	0858	2
HADEN DONALD J	LTC	0-1120319	1065	1
HADEN ROBERT B	LTC	0-1181275	0865	1
HADEN WALTER R	LTC	0-1041781	0466	1
HADJY HARRY	1LT	0-1541702	1046	2
HADLEY BETTIE L A	MAJ	L-0804191	0966	1
HADLEY CHANNING L	LTC	0-0962516	0767	1
HADLEY CHARLES C	CW3	W-2149320	0659	1
HADLEY HERBERT	CPT	0-0110718	0544	2
HADLEY JAMES M	LTC	0-1291810	0166	1
HADLEY JOHN M	LTC	0-0906578	1062	3
HADLEY VIRLEN H	1LT	0-1698009	0146	2
HADLOCK ALBERT E	LTC	0-0907602	0463	3
HADLOW CHARLES F	LTC	0-1582356	1062	1
HAEBERLIN STANLEY M	1LT	0-1180927	0246	2
HAECKER ROSS R	LTC	0-1546028	0562	1
HAEFNER EUGENE A	1LT	0-1893976	0156	2
HAEFS GLENN H	WO1	RW-2148726	0858	1
HAEHL MARY J	2LT	N-0704144	0744	1
HAENDIGES WILLIAM A	MAJ	0-0329421	0756	1
HAENE WALTER H	MAJ	0-0415448	0346	2
HAENEL ROB B A	COL	0-0422190	1061	1

NAME	GRADE	SVC NO	DATE RET MO YR	RET CODE
HAENSEL FRANCIS S	MAJ	0-1799734	1162	1
HAERING MILSON C	CW4	W-2001677	1265	3
HAERING ROY W	2LT	0-1054258	0945	2
HAERLE CHARLES R	CW4	W-2101782	0560	1
HAERTEL GEORGE H	LTC	0-1697971	0667	1
HAERTEL VINCENT H	CW2	W-2143479	0456	1
HAFEMAN GEORGE E	LTC	0-1284326	0559	1
HAFER HAROLD	MAJ	0-1320693	0556	1
HAFFEN JOHN W	MAJ	0-0263838	0247	1
HAFFEY JR GEAN B	MAJ	0-1533331	0857	1
HAFFNER JR CHARLES C	M G	0-0142106	0658	3
HAFFORD JOHN L	1LT	0-0399365	0447	2
HAFLER MELBA	1LT	N-0734297	0146	1
HAFLEY GLEN C	CPT	0-1011288	1145	2
HAFLING ERNEST M	CPT	0-0488179	0145	2
HAFNER LENA A	2LT	N-0784184	0945	1
HAFNER RALPH A	LTC	0-0373451	1165	3
HAGA CECIL K	MAJ	0-1917850	0367	1
HAGA RALPH L	LTC	0-0520016	1164	3
HAGAN ALFRED E	LTC	0-0290216	1161	3
HAGAN CHARLES H	CPT	0-1581156	0845	2
HAGAN FRANK E	CPT	0-1312552	0451	1
HAGAN JAMES H	LTC	0-0207777	1047	2
HAGAN JOHN E	1LT	0-0532672	0646	2
HAGAN LLOYD O	MAJ	0-0322081	0746	2
HAGAN OSCAR P	MAJ	0-1328999	0466	1
HAGAN WILLIAM B	LTC	0-0281666	0357	3
HAGAN 3RD WILLIAM J	LTC	0-0386384	0446	2
HAGANS DONALD F	CPT	0-1596340	1060	1
HAGANS LYNDEN A	1LT	0-0361164	0542	2
HAGAR CLYDE V	1LT	0-1703011	1055	1
HAGARTY ELIZABETH	LTC	N-0736466	0961	1
HAGE SAM M	1LT	0-1545009	1145	1
HAGEDORN ENRIQUE	1LT	0-0890287	1152	1
HAGEDORN KENNETH F	CPT	0-0357375	1045	1
HAGEDORN RAYMOND E	MAJ	0-0265755	0244	2
HAGEDUS STEVEN R	CPT	0-1171570	0845	2
HAGEE GEORGE M	LTC	0-0132060	0749	3
HAGEL VINCENT	1LT	0-1300478	0845	2
HAGEMAN EARL L	MAJ	0-0177797	1049	3
HAGEMAN RICHARD F	CPT	0-0958856	0561	1
HAGEMANN MILTON H	LTC	0-1794938	0363	1
HAGEMEIER PAUL E	LTC	0-0409968	1060	2
HAGEMEYER JESSE F	MAJ	0-0311756	0154	1
HAGEN ARNOLD C	CPT	0-1288538	0246	2
HAGEN CHARLES M	1LT	0-0499736	0444	2
HAGEN CLIFFORD W	MAJ	0-0749232	0860	1
HAGEN DAVID R	LTC	0-0475366	0657	1
HAGEN DEAN C	LTC	0-1540544	0665	1
HAGEN DUANE L	CW3	W-2208010	1267	1
HAGEN EAGWARD H	MAJ	0-0286700	0544	2
HAGEN GUY R	LTC	0-1300961	0263	1
HAGEN JOHN F	CPT	0-0390793	0945	1
HAGEN LESLIE H	1LT	0-1304522	0350	1
HAGEN MILDRED A	1LT	N-0745241	0246	1
HAGEN ODIN M	CPT	0-0494381	1054	1
HAGEN WALLACE C	CPT	0-1309725	0847	1
HAGEN WAYNE S	COL	0-0257096	0467	3
HAGENBUCH FORREST H	LTC	0-0248152	0162	3
HAGENBUSH FRANK L	CW2	W-2144457	0665	1
HAGENDORFF HAROLD G	CPT	0-1341779	0457	1
HAGENMEYER ERNEST A	MAJ	0-0969598	1162	1
HAGENS DAVID K	LTC	0-1167876	0162	1
HAGER ANNA L	MAJ	N-0728187	1065	1
HAGER CARL J	LTC	0-0177667	0655	3
HAGER JAMES L	COL	0-0269019	1162	3
HAGER JOHN M	MAJ	0-0104655	0949	3
HAGER JR SAMUEL E	LTC	0-0277460	0459	3
HAGER REUBEN W	LTC	0-0341435	0346	2
HAGER VIRGIL G	CW4	W-2107941	0658	1
HAGER WALTER A	CW3	W-2147357	0568	1
HAGER WILLIAM M	MAJ	0-0242374	1056	3
HAGER WILSON C	CPT	0-0365854	1045	2
HAGERMAN DAVID O	MAJ	0-0528724	0565	1
HAGERMAN EDWIN B	LTC	0-1013689	0461	1

NAME	GRADE	SVC NO	DATE RET MO YR	RET CODE
HAGERTY CHARLES G	1LT	0-1012438	0445	2
HAGERTY DOROTHY G	CPT	N-0720754	0346	1
HAGERTY GEORGE L	LTC	0-1011552	0957	1
HAGERTY JAMES S	MAJ	0-0490900	0153	1
HAGERTY JOHN D	MAJ	0-0259339	1058	3
HAGERTY RICHARD C	CPT	0-1890410	1062	2
HAGERTY THOMAS L	MAJ	0-1298219	0248	1
HAGERTY WALTER H	LTC	0-1637585	1066	1
HAGEWOOD EUGENE C	CPT	0-1578562	0758	1
HAGEWOOD SHEPHERD C	CW3	W-2147894	0562	1
HAGG EARL R	WO1	W-2139539	0445	2
HAGGARD KENNETH L	MAJ	0-0283169	0945	2
HAGGARD LLOYD C	LTC	0-0234338	1264	1
HAGGARD MARION C	LTC	0-1291629	0265	1
HAGGARD MIKE L	CPT	0-0953642	1061	1
HAGGARD NEAL F	COL	0-0351806	0763	1
HAGGARD PAUL L	MAJ	0-0995684	0160	1
HAGGARD ROY S	LTC	0-0185163	0648	3
HAGGERTY CECIL J	LTC	0-0245557	1261	3
HAGGERTY CHARLES A	COL	0-0148369	0655	3
HAGGERTY CHARLES A	2LT	0-1825469	0845	2
HAGGERTY CLAUDE M	COL	0-0158648	0255	3
HAGGERTY RICHARD J	CW2	W-3151602	0367	1
HAGGERTY ROY H	LTC	0-0520071	1163	2
HAGGERTY WILLIAM D	LTC	0-1316548	1166	1
HAGLER CURTIS E	MAJ	0-0271524	0865	3
HAGLER WILLIAM	1LT	0-2056129	0645	2
HAGMAIER LOUIS C	CW3	W-2149698	1163	1
HAGMAN WILLIAM L	LTC	0-0247137	0858	3
HAGMANN EDWARD A	MAJ	0-0305950	0445	2
HAGNEY FRANK J	MAJ	0-1061711	0361	1
HAGON JOHN D	COL	0-0277461	1061	3
HAGOOD EUGENE A	CW2	W-2146960	1160	2
HAGOOD MONROE J	COL	0-0267972	0663	1
HAGSTROM JOHN H	LTC	0-2040740	0562	1
HAGSTROM JR OSCAR	1LT	0-1328485	0746	2
HAGSTROM WILLIAM F	MAJ	0-0464112	0947	2
HAGUE JR RICHARD H	MAJ	0-1166730	1061	1
HAGUE WILLIAM W	LTC	0-0158865	0955	3
HAGWOOD HENRY M	CW3	W-2141298	0459	1
HAGY EDWARD M	LTC	0-0467102	1165	1
HAHN AUGUST C	COL	0-0406912	0967	3
HAHN CHARLES J	LTC	0-1552687	0463	1
HAHN CLYDE R	1LT	0-0509189	1043	2
HAHN EUGENE G	CW3	W-2110932	0866	1
HAHN HAROLD W	2LT	0-0462272	0545	2
HAHN HARVEY L	MAJ	0-1690807	0767	1
HAHN HENRY W	CW2	W-2114999	0845	2
HAHN HUBERT C	LTC	0-0352926	0463	3
HAHN JOHN	MAJ	0-0487158	1049	1
HAHN JOHN H	COL	0-0259458	0359	1
HAHN JR FREDERICK	LTC	0-0425223	0862	1
HAHN NORBERT L	LTC	0-0281302	0666	3
HAHN PAUL R	CPT	0-0345804	0246	2
HAHN PAUL G	CPT	0-0155612	0354	3
HAHN RUDOLPH R	LTC	0-0321870	0561	1
HAHN WALTER S	COL	0-0243889	0766	3
HAHN WELDON J	CW4	W-2132550	0461	1
HAHN WILFERD K	CW2	W-2111071	0545	2
HAIG GEORGE	LTC	0-0204657	1061	3
HAIG JOSEPH A	COL	0-0167105	0758	3
HAIGH JAMES H	MAJ	0-0219556	1158	3
HAIGH RALPH H	LTC	0-1045445	1062	1
HAIGHT ARTHUR W	CPT	0-1548823	0762	1
HAIGHT ASHLEY R	LTC	0-0148367	0454	3
HAIGHT EARL R	MAJ	0-0291315	0747	2
HAIGHT LESLIE L	CPT	0-1311006	0747	2
HAIGHT WILLIAM C	2LT	0-1597121	1056	1
HAIGHT WILLIAM R	COL	0-0260588	0764	3
HAIGNEY VINCENT J	1LT	0-1635998	1043	2
HAIL CURTIS D	2LT	0-1691705	1145	2
HAIL DOUGLAS L	1LT	0-1309726	0346	2
HAILE HARRY W	1LT	0-1304207	1045	2
HAILE JR ELMER R	CPT	0-0281253	0446	2
HAILEY CARL C	2LT	0-1825952	0345	1
HAILEY JESSE S	MAJ	0-1688429	1263	1
HAILS GEORGE F	1LT	0-1294831	1144	2
HAILSTORK HOWARD H	2LT	0-1318892	0146	2
HAIMAN BERNARD A	MAJ	0-0919819	0847	2
HAIN HENRY F	LTC	0-0314717	0961	3
HAINER ALBION E	LTC	0-0245871	0245	2
HAINES ALFRED W	MAJ	0-0205966	0858	1
HAINES ARTHUR L	1LT	0-1014220	1046	2
HAINES BRUNETTO J	MAJ	0-0469571	0347	1
HAINES BURZELOUS	LTC	0-1797638	1266	1
HAINES CHARLES L	MAJ	0-2035607	0157	1
HAINES FRANCIS G	MAJ	0-1634840	0561	1
HAINES HILTON O	COL	0-0317834	1065	3
HAINES HOWARD F	B G	0-0173170	1161	3
HAINES JOHN H	COL	0-0261114	1167	3
HAINES JOHN W	MAJ	0-2262973	0665	1
HAINES JR WILLIAM A	LTC	0-1381789	1167	1
HAINES JUAN C	MAJ	0-2025324	0267	1
HAINES MELVIN E	CW3	W-2146820	0563	1
HAINES OBERT L	LTC	0-0472969	0257	1
HAINES PAUL E	COL	0-0202889	0755	1
HAINES PAUL L	LTC	0-0329848	1066	1
HAINES RICHARD E	CW2	W-2104120	0661	1
HAINES ROBERT W	LTC	0-1000956	1160	1
HAINES VICTOR H	2LT	0-1549486	0945	2
HAINES WILLIAM L	1LT	0-0890125	0350	1
HAINLINE FORREST A	LTC	0-0117396	0651	3
HAIR JR HARRISON B	1LT	0-0341242	0544	2
HAIR RAFORD	CW4	W-2112013	0958	1
HAIR ROBERT	CW3	W-2152607	1165	1
HAIR ROBERT W	CW3	W-2147334	0264	1
HAIR ROGER H	MAJ	0-1342267	1164	1
HAIRE JESSE L	COL	0-0398188	0960	1
HAIRSTON JOSEPH H	CPT	0-1171572	1060	1
HAIRSTON MCCOY F	CW3	W-2152213	0564	1
HAIRSTON ROBERT T	2LT	0-1039016	0146	2
HAIS HARRY I	1LT	0-0398140	1041	2
HAISER CARL J	LTC	0-1322795	0262	1
HAISLIP WILLIAM M	MAJ	0-0389112	0149	2
HAJDU FRANK R	CW2	W-2150269	1162	1
HAJEK JAMES W	MAJ	0-1314137	0861	1
HAKALA PENTTI J	CW3	W-2141295	1160	1
HAKE KEVIN	LTC	0-1050693	0264	1
HAKEN STONEY	LTC	0-1646048	0766	1
HAKES CHARLES C	MAJ	0-0909560	0944	2
HAKES JAMES D	CW2	W-2150874	1059	1
HALA OTTO	CPT	0-0339910	0462	1
HALAICC STEPHEN J	CW2	W-2150786	0258	1
HALAS LLOYD V	CW3	W-2203871	1066	1
HALASKA ANTON H	LTC	0-0312682	0657	1
HALBERG ROBERT L	2LT	0-1329118	0246	2
HALBERSTADT FRANK C	1LT	0-1555395	0745	2
HALBERSTADT HENRY J	LTC	0-0279972	0862	3
HALBERT HOWARD F	LTC	0-0395367	0261	1
HALBERT WILBAR	LTC	0-0202620	0663	3
HALBLEIB EDWARD K	LTC	0-0312144	0665	3
HALBROCK ALFRED F	MAJ	0-2288512	1264	1
HALCOMB WILLIAM F	1LT	0-1292024	1045	2
HALCOMB WILLIAM S	LTC	0-0144826	0353	3
HALDEMAN WELLINGTON	LTC	0-0126482	1043	2
HALE BARTLEY F	CPT	0-1318426	0556	1
HALE BERRY H	MAJ	0-2037053	0762	1
HALE BUNN O	COL	0-0382579	0761	1
HALE CLARENCE W	MAJ	0-1634841	0160	1
HALE DEKALB S	1LT	0-1016199	0646	2
HALE EDWARD T	LTC	0-1342179	1266	1
HALE FRANK S	CPT	0-0236157	0462	3
HALE GAITHER F	CPT	0-0142007	0853	3
HALE HARVEY M	CW3	W-2152384	0963	1
HALE HERMAN G	CPT	0-0132221	1054	3
HALE HOMER H	CPT	0-1542688	0653	1
HALE JAMES D	MAJ	0-0563980	0467	1
HALE JAMES F	MAJ	0-2026878	0161	1
HALE JOHN P	MAJ	0-2009688	0757	1
HALE JOSEPH W	MAJ	0-0426053	0146	1
HALE JR WILLIAM F	LTC	0-1180196	0457	1
HALE JULIUS	MAJ	0-0188803	0847	1
HALE KENNETH G	2LT	0-2011360	0251	2
HALE LELAND E	LTC	0-0355755	1060	1
HALE MURRILL E	MAJ	0-2012599	1161	1
HALE NORMAN H	MAJ	0-0253932	0766	3
HALE OLIVE M	2LT	N-0724072	1044	1
HALE PRESTON W	LTC	0-0918442	1162	3
HALE RICHARD S	LTC	0-1702876	0867	1
HALE RICHARD V	LTC	0-0550244	0664	1
HALE ROBERT E	LTC	0-1313399	0762	1
HALE ROBERT L	1LT	0-0456003	0147	2
HALE SAM T	LTC	0-0308347	1053	2
HALE SHERMAN A	CW3	W-2129496	1060	1
HALE VASCO O	1LT	0-1101470	0446	2
HALE WALTER T	MAJ	0-2018160	0662	1
HALE WARNER S	CPT	0-0406445	0346	2
HALE WARREN C	2LT	0-1317908	0245	2
HALE WILEY J	CPT	0-0365874	0363	3
HALE WILLIAM H	CPT	0-1167015	1045	2
HALE WILLIAM L	MAJ	0-1180523	1060	2
HALES GEORGE J	LTC	0-0251655	0167	3
HALES JOHN C	MAJ	0-0969196	0762	1
HALES JOHN D	CPT	0-1556143	0253	1
HALES MARVIN H	LTC	0-0264717	0561	3
HALETSKY ANTHONY D	CW3	W-2147224	0763	1
HALEY DONALD W	COL	0-0920439	0267	3
HALEY HENRY R	LTC	0-0382280	1166	3
HALEY JOHN	MAJ	0-0509221	1047	2
HALEY JOHN F	CPT	0-0461751	0745	2
HALEY JR WILLIAM R	LTC	0-1173632	1166	1
HALEY JULIUS F	1LT	0-0379688	1044	2
HALEY LAWRENCE C	CW2	W-2118092	0953	1
HALEY PAUL V	CPT	0-1308947	1047	1
HALEY ROBERT F	LTC	0-1011002	0163	1
HALEY ROBERT W	CPT	0-0969282	0161	1
HALEY VINCENT E	MAJ	0-0587209	0660	1
HALEY WILLIAM T	LTC	0-1321179	0465	1
HALFERTY ALMA	2LT	N-0700242	0832	1
HALFERTY ANGIE F	CPT	N-0775394	0947	1
HALFF MAYER H	COL	0-0272172	0166	3
HALFORD HARRY E	MAJ	0-2006850	0161	1
HALFORD WILLIAM D	MAJ	0-1573863	0357	1
HALISKY JOHN R	LTC	0-1554384	0264	1
HALKEWICZ JR MICHAEL	1LT	0-1051985	1146	2
HALL ALAN W	LTC	0-0240087	0247	1
HALL ALFONSO D	LTC	0-0379328	0153	1
HALL ALFRED H	COL	0-0290711	1154	1
HALL ALLEN C	MAJ	0-0477572	0745	1
HALL ALTON G	COL	0-0230252	0864	3
HALL ALVIN C	CPT	0-1292451	0847	2
HALL ANDREW A	COL	0-0296023	0460	1
HALL ANTHONY C	MAJ	0-1295203	0460	1
HALL ARTHUR A	MAJ	0-1063066	0258	1
HALL ARTHUR B	MAJ	0-0187624	0549	3
HALL BETTY J	MAJ	N-0792332	0864	2
HALL BILLY C	MAJ	0-0989363	0267	1
HALL BRUCE	MAJ	0-1923574	0766	1
HALL CARL E	MAJ	0-0327282	1045	2
HALL CARLISLE	CPT	0-0181105	1051	3
HALL CARLSON W	CPT	0-1303717	0358	1
HALL CECIL O	CPT	0-0218602	1157	3
HALL CHARLES D	CPT	0-0494445	0653	1
HALL CHARLES D	LTC	0-1323925	0761	1
HALL CHARLES E	LTC	0-0324407	1264	3
HALL CHARLES E	CW2	W-2214826	0567	1
HALL CHARLES K	MAJ	0-1116224	1057	1
HALL CHARLES L	CPT	0-0251782	1150	3
HALL CHARLES L	LTC	0-1575740	0563	1
HALL CHARLES W	COL	0-0329562	0565	3
HALL CLAIR L	MAJ	0-0291610	0160	1
HALL CLARENCE W	COL	0-0378335	0664	3
HALL CLOYD R	LTC	0-0323768	0347	1
HALL DALLAS A	2LT	0-1330421	1145	2
HALL DANIEL F	MAJ	0-0980547	1061	1
HALL DANIEL F	LTC	0-0476313	0867	1
HALL DANIEL W	CW3	W-2152461	0662	1
HALL DAVID B	CPT	0-1700741	0945	2
HALL DIXIE G	COL	0-0331832	0660	1
HALL DON	CW2	W-2149880	0562	1
HALL DON C	CPT	0-2202214	0658	2
HALL DONALD F	COL	0-0107297	0654	2
HALL DONALD S	CPT	0-2035098	1262	1
HALL EARL C	MAJ	0-0274537	0854	3
HALL EDGAR F	1LT	0-1314704	1145	2
HALL EDWARD P	LTC	0-0223588	0463	3
HALL EDWARD C	CW4	W-2106462	1057	1
HALL EDWIN P	LTC	0-0282523	1062	3
HALL ELLIS H	CPT	0-0377748	0744	2
HALL ERNEST B	COL	0-0323410	0966	1
HALL ERNEST J	COL	0-0206743	0648	3
HALL EVERETT C	1LT	0-1594882	0648	1
HALL FAYETTE G	COL	0-0270317	0561	1
HALL FLETCHER H	CW4	W-2108019	1058	1
HALL FLOYD A	LTC	0-1542856	1060	1
HALL FORREST D	MAJ	0-0980724	0363	1
HALL FRANCES W	MAJ	N-0735445	0163	1
HALL FRANK D	CPT	0-1011431	1045	2
HALL FRANK J	LTC	0-0327624	0848	3
HALL FRED A	MAJ	0-0165844	0754	3
HALL FRED C	LTC	0-1797124	1060	1
HALL FRED W	LTC	0-0131062	0355	3
HALL FREDERIC A	LTC	0-0138316	0359	3
HALL FREDERIC H	MAJ	0-1946275	0953	1
HALL FREDERICK	MAJ	0-0264240	0462	3
HALL GARNET E	LTC	0-0238359	0464	3
HALL GEORGE F	COL	0-0254703	0767	3
HALL GLENN O	COL	0-0287545	1065	1
HALL GORDON	COL	0-0128255	1055	3
HALL GORDON F	2LT	0-0441465	0344	2
HALL GORDON L	CW2	RW-3350135	0165	1
HALL GORDON S	CW2	W-2215283	1066	2
HALL HAROLD K	CPT	0-2262399	0261	1
HALL HAROLD L	MAJ	0-2262290	0863	2
HALL HARRY A	LTC	0-0115135	0744	2
HALL HARRY J	LTC	0-0355183	0863	3
HALL HARRY O	1LT	0-2030472	1053	2
HALL HARRY W	CW2	W-2209217	0564	1
HALL HARVEY A	MAJ	0-0103884	0155	3
HALL HENRY C	LTC	0-0235258	0153	3
HALL HENRY C	2LT	0-1998121	0149	1
HALL HENRY H	LTC	0-0124559	0648	3
HALL HENRY W	LTC	0-0247318	0564	3
HALL HERBERT H	MAJ	0-0148387	0551	3
HALL HIRAM C	COL	0-0292912	0858	1
HALL HIRAM R	CPT	0-1178169	0846	2
HALL HORACE L	LTC	0-0410866	1064	1
HALL HORACE W	CPT	0-0355610	0251	3
HALL HOWARD F	1LT	0-1325890	1045	2
HALL HUBERT P	CPT	0-0450879	0345	2
HALL HULON C	2LT	0-1308425	1144	2
HALL JACK T	LTC	0-1541328	0959	1
HALL JAMES C	LTC	0-0421951	1263	3
HALL JAMES D	LTC	0-1104809	0965	1
HALL JAMES L	LTC	0-0348888	0467	3
HALL JAMES M	MAJ	0-1018408	0457	1
HALL JAMES P	LTC	0-0265988	0544	2
HALL JAMES W	CPT	0-0900248	0845	2
HALL JAY L	LTC	0-0349614	0467	3
HALL JESSE E	MAJ	0-2018878	1266	1
HALL JESSE T	CW2	W-2149214	0762	1
HALL JOHN	COL	0-0207585	1163	3
HALL JOHN E	LTC	0-1301405	1065	3
HALL JOHN K	CPT	0-1997973	0656	1
HALL JOHN L	LTC	0-0488777	0254	1
HALL JOHN R W	LTC	0-0144352	1044	2
HALL JOHN W	CW2	W-2210375	0267	1
HALL JOSEPH	LTC	0-1824859	0666	1
HALL JOSEPH C	CPT	0-1286276	0446	1
HALL JR GEORGE A	COL	0-0909524	0966	3

292-560 O - 68 - 12

NAME	GRADE	SVC NO	DATE RET MO YR	RET CODE
HALL JR HILLARC	CW3	W-2149069	C762	1
HALL JR JAMES M	LTC	0-0291141	0466	3
HALL JR JAMES T	MAJ	C-1288539	0457	1
HALL JR REUBEN B	COL	0-1574249	C767	1
HALL JR ROBERT	CW3	W-2206283	0867	1
HALL JR ROBERT M	CW2	W-2147817	1061	2
HALL KARL S	LTC	0-0304845	C962	1
HALL LAURENCE W	LTC	0-0245788	0359	3
HALL LAWRENCE M	CW3	W-2152791	1163	1
HALL LAWRENCE P	CW2	W-2144532	0958	1
HALL LAWRENCE W	COL	0-0301381	C962	1
HALL LEON M	COL	C-0189382	0-49	3
HALL LEONA J	MAJ	N-0752466	C267	1
HALL LESTER H	COL	0-0242228	1155	3
HALL LUTHER B	CPT	0-027970C	0858	3
HALL MARTYN L	MAJ	0-0187318	1054	3
HALL MAC K	1LT	0-1293707	0246	2
HALL MERLE W	LTC	0-0362725	C964	1
HALL MERRITT W	CW2	W-2143391	C456	1
HALL MILLARC W	COL	0-0245542	0646	2
HALL MONROE	MAJ	0-1919105	C866	1
HALL MONROE S	MAJ	0-1168700	0267	1
HALL NOPHLEN R	2LT	0-0108378	0131	1
HALL NORMAN B	LTC	0-0249353	C659	3
HALL OLIVER H	CPT	0-0279144	C460	3
HALL OMER N	MAJ	0-1319199	C164	1
HALL PAUL L	LTC	0-0297084	1262	3
HALL PERCY G	COL	0-0246273	0953	3
HALL RALPH H	LTC	0-0922052	C-51	3
HALL RAYMONC C	MAJ	C-0510491	1060	1
HALL REGINALD S	LTC	0-0230070	1262	3
HALL RICHARC O	MAJ	C-1918977	C564	1
HALL ROBERT A	1LT	0-0497516	0953	1
HALL ROBERT E	MAJ	0-0978780	1264	1
HALL ROBERT M	MAJ	0-0367927	0645	1
HALL ROBERT P	CPT	0-0254281	0960	3
HALL ROBERT P	1LT	0-0366904	C245	2
HALL ROBERT W	LTC	0-0186337	C155	3
HALL ROSS C	CPT	0-0230502	C662	3
HALL ROSWELL B	WO1	W-2113830	0345	2
HALL RUPERT L	MAJ	0-2005494	0461	1
HALL RUTH I	MAJ	N-0742231	0463	1
HALL SAM W	MAJ	C-0380096	0645	2
HALL SAMMIE A	MAJ	0-1336503	C764	1
HALL SAMUEL B	CPT	0-0413920	0653	1
HALL SR JAMES N	LTC	0-1010420	0863	1
HALL SR PHIM	2LT	0-1289416	1045	2
HALL STANTON A	COL	0-0203487	0761	3
HALL STEPHEN E	LTC	0-0241660	0765	3
HALL STERLING J	MAJ	C-1182128	C164	1
HALL SYDNEY H	LTC	0-0230741	0857	3
HALL THOMAS B	CW4	W-2125297	0559	1
HALL THOMAS E	LTC	0-1175142	1162	1
HALL THOMAS L	COL	0-0911644	0647	2
HALL TOM	COL	0-0291795	C862	3
HALL VERNON	1LT	0-1049502	C259	1
HALL WALLACE B	LTC	0-0335743	1160	2
HALL WALTER E	MAJ	C-1332659	1155	2
HALL WALTER W	LTC	0-0474341	0657	1
HALL WARNER W	LTC	0-0223672	1164	3
HALL WARREN G	1LT	0-1647064	0150	1
HALL WENDELL L	LTC	C-2037978	0765	2
HALL WILBUR A	CPT	0-1307966	1046	1
HALL WILL E	CPT	0-0235148	C459	3
HALL WILLIAM E	CW3	W-2144072	0964	1
HALL WILLIAM L	LTC	0-0265913	0959	3
HALL WILLIAM M	1LT	0-1325751	1045	2
HALL WILLIAM P	LTC	C-1549959	0966	1
HALL WILLIAM R	LTC	C-1030667	1161	1
HALL WILLIAM R	WO1	W-2153085	1054	2
HALL WINDELL B	MAJ	0-2032920	1062	1
HALL WOODBURY K	LTC	0-0262662	0966	3
HALL WYATT E	MAJ	C-1340886	0765	1
HALLAHAN WILLIAM J	LTC	0-1012115	0563	1
HALLAHAN WILLIAM J	MAJ	C-1577276	1045	2

NAME	GRADE	SVC NO	DATE RET MO YR	RET CODE
HALLAM RICHARD E	CW3	W-214116C	0464	1
HALLAM ROBERT M	LTC	0-030024C	0567	3
HALLARMAN EDWIN	2LT	0-054C315	0945	2
HALLBECK CLARENCE F	CPT	0-0508059	0749	1
HALLBERG ROBERT E	CPT	0-0455637	0952	2
HALLOOW HARRY R	MAJ	0-1312006	0960	1
HALLE ARNE F	CPT	0-1645016	0247	2
HALLE EUGENE L	LTC	0-0374408	1163	1
HALLE HERMAN L	LTC	0-1292335	0261	2
HALLEN WALTER E	LTC	0-022527C	0555	3
HALLENBECK ALCNZO G	CPT	0-0168022	0453	3
HALLENBECK GEORGE G	MAJ	0-0195736	0246	2
HALLENBECK KENNETH L	COL	0-0223564	1060	3
HALLER JEROME B	LTC	0-0193152	1153	3
HALLER JR FRANKLIN P	COL	C-0177364	0944	2
HALLER ROBERT B	LTC	0-1054607	0465	1
HALLER WILLIAM M	LTC	0-1104813	1265	1
HALLER 3RD F P	1LT	0-0440896	0944	2
HALLETT CHARLES S	LTC	0-0315968	0462	1
HALLETT EDWARC A	COL	0-1100571	0463	1
HALLETT EMMALINE W	MAJ	N-0778345	0665	1
HALLETT JACK O	MAJ	C-1030668	1060	1
HALLEY HARRY L S	COL	0-0142333	0954	3
HALLEY THOMAS V	CW4	W-2127246	0859	1
HALLEY WILBUR G	2LT	0-0524437	C645	2
HALLFORD DANIEL C	CPT	0-0388737	0346	2
HALLIBURTON KENNETH	LTC	C-1582702	0467	1
HALLICAY EUGENE F	LTC	0-0494126	0555	1
HALLIDAY GRANT T	CW4	W-2121033	1057	1
HALLIDAY KENNETH G	LTC	0-1583045	1062	1
HALLIDAY MICHAEL	LTC	0-0371459	0657	1
HALLICAY RALPH H	LTC	0-1010045	1065	1
HALLICAY ROBERT J	COL	0-0331237	0467	3
HALLIN CYRIL A	LTC	0-1533079	0557	1
HALLINAN JCHN J	CPT	0-0131081	1050	3
HALLINAN JCHN J	MAJ	0-1633922	1057	1
HALLIWELL HARRY A	LTC	0-0568468	0465	1
HALLIWELL WARREN L	1LT	0-1061712	0854	1
HALLMAN PAUL F	LTC	0-0233922	0365	3
HALLMARK DALE E	MAJ	C-2263334	1264	1
HALLMARK SR KENITH V	MAJ	0-1011038	0557	1
HALLOR FREDERICK	COL	0-0246937	1047	2
HALLORAN ALFRED J	1LT	0-1019136	1045	2
HALLORAN HENRY E	COL	0-0220424	0262	3
HALLORAN PAULINE L	CW3	V-0820489	0365	1
HALLOWAY ECWARD A	CPT	0-0164021	0345	1
HALLOWELL NOEL E	LTC	C-0265005	1265	3
HALLOWELL RAYMOND M	MAJ	0-1114151	0954	1
HALLOWES WALTCN B	LTC	0-0910149	0263	1
HALLSTROM IRVING T	LTC	0-0214330	1061	3
HALLSTROM NILS F	MAJ	0-1030154	0956	1
HALLSWORTH HERBERT T	MAJ	0-2204101	0965	1
HALLUM FRANK F	LTC	0-0249431	1165	3
HALPERIN HERMAN J	CPT	0-0447733	0146	2
HALPERN HARRY L	CPT	0-0504929	1044	2
HALPERT WALTER	LTC	0-0320728	0967	3
HALPIN DAVID F	LTC	0-1560023	1263	1
HALPIN JAMES M	LTC	0-1060790	0167	1
HALPIN JR THOMAS F	1LT	0-2284007	0960	2
HALPIN MICHAEL R	LTC	0-0220838	0954	1
HALPIN ROBERT O	LTC	0-1305243	0562	1
HALPIN THOMAS A	LTC	0-0382262	0967	3
HALPRIN ROBERT S	1LT	0-1303718	0446	2
HALSALL JOHN S	MAJ	C-1337569	1263	1
HALSEY CLIFFORD W	CPT	0-1171175	1045	2
HALSEY JOHN E	1LT	0-1317294	0546	2
HALSEY JR EDWARD L	MAJ	0-1596344	0564	1
HALSEY RICHARD V	CW2	W-2144497	0261	1
HALSO ALTON K	CW3	W-2142159	1064	1
HALSTEAD ALICE S	CPT	N-0727775	0547	1
HALSTEAC EARL T	COL	0-0109786	0347	2
HALSTEAC FELIX G	COL	0-0161189	0754	3
HALSTEAD FRANK B	CW3	W-2205717	0467	1
HALSTEAD RAYMOND N	MAJ	0-1585553	0164	1
HALSTEAD T S	COL	0-0187623	0150	3

NAME	GRADE	SVC NO	DATE RET MO YR	RET CODE
HALSTEAD WOODROW W	CW2	W-2142705	0157	1
HALSTED HAROLD S	COL	0-0275266	0359	3
HALSTED JR WILLIAM B	LTC	0-1103672	0164	1
HALSTROM LLOYD C	MAJ	0-1895431	0762	1
HALTER SR WILLIAM F	MAJ	C-0971206	0663	1
HALTERMAN GEORGE A	MAJ	0-1101473	0764	1
HALVERSON CLARIBEL A	1LT	N-0771365	C345	1
HALVERSON KARL L	MAJ	0-05067C0	0954	1
HALVERSON KENNETH L	COL	0-0342280	1165	1
HALVERSON LESTER P	MAJ	C-0975684	1061	1
HALVERSON WALTER L	MAJ	C-0351021	0758	1
HALVERSON WILLIAM I	MAJ	0-1050287	1062	1
HALVIN MILTON S	CPT	0-1821862	C556	2
HALVORSEN CLIFFORD	MAJ	C-C258017	0450	2
HALVORSON EDWIN W	CPT	0-0532242	C845	2
HALVORSON GLADYS M	1LT	N-0741346	1045	1
HALVORSON HARRY A	LTC	0-0450258	1057	1
HALVORSON MELVIN A	1LT	0-0385204	C643	2
HALVORSON NORRIS R	MAJ	0-0346629	0364	3
HALVORSON THEODORE B	CPT	0-0234953	1056	3
HALVORSON VERNON C	MAJ	0-4074815	C567	1
HALWER MURRAY M	LTC	0-0452362	C267	3
HAM ARTHUR C	CPT	C-0522522	C747	2
HAM HARRY C	1LT	0-1323833	C546	2
HAM JR JOHN K	MAJ	0-5405016	0967	1
HAM JR WILLIAM P	COL	0-0311404	0562	3
HAM JULIUS W	CW4	W-2143588	0766	1
HAM LEWIS W	1LT	0-2207762	0353	1
HAM WALTER A	MAJ	C-0188555	C750	3
HAM WILLIAM E	LTC	C-0377991	1166	3
HAMAKER HAROLD E	CW2	W-2148728	0161	1
HAMAKER ROBERT F	COL	0-0330806	0257	1
HAMAN FRANK	CW2	W-2142640	0157	1
HAMASAKI RICHARD N	MAJ	0-1683429	0461	1
HAMBAUGH RAYMOND K	LTC	0-1100572	0364	1
HAMBLETON CECILE S	2LT	N-0745365	C845	1
HAMBLETON HARRY B	COL	0-0234731	C547	2
HAMBLEY HELEN E	2LT	N-0729134	1144	1
HAMBLIN MELVIN M	CPT	0-0370955	1144	2
HAMBLIN O B	1LT	0-1176043	0458	1
HAMBLIN WILLARD M	MAJ	C-0384143	0244	2
HAMBLIN WILLIE L	CPT	0-0968205	1057	1
HAMBURG JR HENRY	1LT	C-1337427	C151	1
HAMBURGER ALBERT C	MAJ	0-0448724	C847	2
HAMBURY ROLAND T	MAJ	0-0557767	C367	3
HAMBY FRANK M	LTC	0-0330465	0560	1
HAMBY LEWIS M	MAJ	C-0222508	1059	1
HAMBY MYRL W	MAJ	N-0779611	0566	2
HAMEL ALBERT L	CPT	0-0404066	0146	2
HAMEL EDWARC P	1LT	0-0177426	1147	2
HAMEL JR JCHN J	LTC	0-0173582	0662	3
HAMEL LEON A	CW2	W-2126003	C850	1
HAMEL RAUL R	CPT	0-0397076	0645	2
HAMEL RICHARD J	MAJ	C-1885735	C767	1
HAMEL RICHARD L	LTC	0-0723610	C563	1
HAMER GLENN R	LTC	0-1555827	C366	1
HAMER JOSEPH E	CPT	0-1043649	0164	1
HAMER LEONARD	MAJ	0-1103196	0562	1
HAMER ROBERT P	CPT	0-0282438	0467	3
HAMES JR LUTHER C	CPT	C-0101142	1045	2
HAMIL J O	CW2	W-2153027	1062	1
HAMIL JACK H	CPT	0-1303719	0762	1
HAMIL LEELON L	MAJ	0-1544923	0762	2
HAMILL CHARLES H	CPT	0-0158420	1046	1
HAMILL WARREN C	COL	0-0208683	1058	1
HAMILTON ALEXANDER	LTC	0-1170401	1164	1
HAMILTON ALLEN K	LTC	0-0218161	0344	2
HAMILTON ANTHONY R	LTC	0-1001355	C457	1
HAMILTON ARTHUR O	LTC	0-0262481	1266	3
HAMILTCN AUGUSTUS W	MAJ	0-1293945	C450	1
HAMILTON CHARLES C	CPT	0-1001143	0954	1
HAMILTON CHARLES E	CPT	0-1003246	0246	2
HAMILTON CHESTER O	1LT	0-0503450	1045	2
HAMILTON CHRISTOPHE	WO1	W-2147157	C564	2
HAMILTON CLARENCE W	LTC	0-0229110	1262	3

NAME	GRADE	SVC NO	DATE RET MO YR	RET CODE
HAMILTCN CLAUD C	MAJ	0-1637558	1056	1
HAMILTCN CONRAD F	COL	0-0119463	1058	1
HAMILTCN DANA R	COL	0-0233394	0557	3
HAMILTCN DELBERT S	CW2	W-2146244	0962	1
HAMILTCN DENNIS J	LTC	0-0385904	1164	3
HAMILTCN DEWEY C	1LT	0-0232733	1057	3
HAMILTCN EARL A	CPT	0-0508898	0246	2
HAMILTCN EARL O	CPT	0-0239664	0155	3
HAMILTCN EDISON K	CPT	0-1104187	1147	2
HAMILTCN EDWARD P	COL	0-0208420	0257	3
HAMILTCN ELINOR L	MAJ	N-075142C	0265	1
HAMILTCN ELIZABETH	MAJ	N-0751859	1063	1
HAMILTCN EMMETT A	1LT	0-1177427	0447	2
HAMILTCN ERNEST L	LTC	0-1290415	0761	1
HAMILTCN EUGENE A	MAJ	0-0406276	0546	2
HAMILTCN EZEKIEL A	LTC	0-0336374	0363	1
HAMILTCN FRED L	MAJ	0-0206376	0663	3
HAMILTCN G T	2LT	0-1686481	0446	1
HAMILTCN GEORGE A	CPT	0-1799049	0155	2
HAMILTCN GRACY R	LTC	C-1305244	0561	1
HAMILTCN HAROLD F	MAJ	0-0225576	1155	3
HAMILTCN HAROLD L	LTC	0-0276390	0758	1
HAMILTCN HAROLD R	LTC	0-0274853	0960	3
HAMILTCN HENRY A	CW3	W-2142848	0763	1
HAMILTCN HERALD H	CW4	W-2142234	0564	1
HAMILTCN HERBERT H	MAJ	C-0479502	0746	2
HAMILTCN HERSCHEL L	CW2	W-2115118	0550	2
HAMILTCN HOBART G	CPT	0-0440542	0746	1
HAMILTCN HOWARD G	1LT	0-1295542	1045	1
HAMILTCN HUBERT T	LTC	0-0290631	0745	2
HAMILTCN HUGH	MAJ	0-0965438	0465	1
HAMILTCN HUGH A	MAJ	0-0146676	0945	1
HAMILTCN IAN M	CPT	0-1297357	1145	2
HAMILTCN JACK E	1LT	0-0414339	0345	2
HAMILTCN JAMES C	COL	0-0230242	1361	3
HAMILTCN JAMES C	1LT	0-0527814	0346	2
HAMILTCN JAMES F	LTC	0-1169552	0663	1
HAMILTCN JAMES L	2LT	0-1544940	1044	1
HAMILTCN JAMES M	LTC	0-0167491	0648	3
HAMILTCN JAY M	LTC	0-0554299	0663	1
HAMILTCN JCHN	CW3	W-2146059	0861	1
HAMILTCN JOHN D	LTC	0-1296025	1062	1
HAMILTCN JOHN L	LTC	0-0165774	0844	2
HAMILTCN JCHN R	1LT	0-2055796	1046	2
HAMILTCN JCHN W	1LT	C-0382467	0645	2
HAMILTCN JR EDWARD S	MAJ	0-037248C	0147	2
HAMILTCN JR HENRY C	MAJ	C-097711C	0865	1
HAMILTCN JR W P	CPT	0-1041565	0645	1
HAMILTCN JR WALTER F	CPT	0-2305037	0766	1
HAMILTCN JR WASH H	CW2	W-2110205	0647	2
HAMILTCN KENNETH C	LTC	0-1586634	1160	2
HAMILTCN LAURENS A	LTC	0-0177680	0758	3
HAMILTCN LAWRENCE F	CPT	0-0278945	0544	2
HAMILTCN LENWOOD C	CW2	W-2211387	0766	1
HAMILTCN MARGARET C	2LT	N-0727327	C145	1
HAMILTCN MERWETHER	MAJ	0-C275887	0545	2
HAMILTCN MORRIS R	LTC	0-1590519	0967	1
HAMILTCN MORRIS R	LTC	0-0451297	0557	1
HAMILTCN OATHER L	WO1	W-2127652	0352	1
HAMILTCN PAUL J	MAJ	C-1286119	0657	1
HAMILTCN PHILIP M	CW3	W-2147254	0365	1
HAMILTCN RAY	1LT	0-0363583	0644	2
HAMILTCN RAY H	CW2	W-2144264	0457	1
HAMILTCN RAY W	MAJ	0-0147173	0355	3
HAMILTCN RICHARD	LTC	0-0253076	0262	3
HAMILTCN RICHARD O	CPT	0-1049870	1060	1
HAMILTCN ROBERT A	LTC	0-1014470	1157	1
HAMILTCN ROBERT F	COL	0-0106243	0648	3
HAMILTCN ROBERT M	COL	0-0127005	0152	3
HAMILTCN ROBERT M	MAJ	C-1000776	0655	1
HAMILTCN THEODORE L	CPT	0-0102571	0-52	3
HAMILTCN THOMAS J	MAJ	0-4009033	0767	1
HAMILTCN WARD L	COL	0-0243563	0364	3
HAMILTCN WESLEY B	B G	0-0172732	0658	3
HAMILTON WEST A	COL	0-0114687	0649	3

NAME	GRADE	SVC NO	DATE RET MO YR	RET CODE
HAMILTON WILLIAM E	MAJ	0-1300163	1160	1
HAMILTON WILLIAM H	1LT	0-1775152	1046	2
HAMILTON WILLIAM H	MAJ	C-2055147	1154	1
HAMILTON WILLIAM M	B G	0-0262501	0761	3
HAMILTON WILLIAM T	LTC	0-0359263	0259	1
HAMILTON WILLIAM W	LTC	0-0300414	C757	3
HAMILTON WILLIAM W	LTC	0-0341655	1066	1
HAMILTON WILLIAM W	CPT	0-0373744	0545	2
HAMILTON WILLIAM W	LTC	0-1305245	C866	3
HAMITER JOHN C	1LT	0-1541207	1045	1
HAMITER STANLEY M	1LT	0-0212954	0654	3
HAMLETT LAMAR	MAJ	0-1798668	1060	1
HAMLETT OTIS L	MAJ	0-2000607	0257	1
HAMLIN JAMES E	COL	0-0244284	0544	2
HAMLIN JOHN T	MAJ	C-0990305	C366	1
HAMLIN JR JAMES T	LTC	C-0479718	C147	2
HAMLIN MARGARET M	MAJ	N-0764351	0467	1
HAMLIN PERCY G	LTC	0-0201372	C354	3
HAMLIN ROBERT	CPT	0-1102748	1046	2
HAMLIN RUSSELL E	COL	0-0265974	0347	2
HAMM BRUCE S	MAJ	C-1588619	1160	1
HAMM CLIFTON M	COL	0-0181629	0857	3
HAMM RALPH E	CW3	W-2148792	1264	1
HAMM SR JACK W	CPT	0-1540903	0460	1
HAMM WILBUR V	2LT	0-1304070	C545	1
HAMM WILLIAM O	2LT	0-1114957	1144	2
HAMMACK EARL J	MAJ	0-1171573	0466	2
HAMMACK EMORY R	LTC	0-1115620	0463	1
HAMMACK JAMES W	MAJ	0-0168754	C260	3
HAMMACK LEWIS T	CPT	0-1013018	C357	1
HAMMACK ROBERT O	CPT	0-2033942	1061	1
HAMMACK ROBERT H	CPT	0-1015368	0960	1
HAMMACK WILLIAM J	MAJ	C-1581768	1053	2
HAMMAN FREO I	MAJ	C-0111010	0255	3
HAMMAN MARION A	CW3	W-2152295	C665	1
HAMMARLUND E R	CPT	C-0554317	C347	1
HAMME RICHARD J	CPT	0-1636000	C161	2
HAMMEL RICHARO L	MAJ	0-0949640	0667	1
HAMMELL MARJORIE	1LT	N-0723334	C552	1
HAMMELL ROBERT J	MAJ	0-2010838	1061	1
HAMMER AVERILL J	CPT	C-0278279	C161	3
HAMMER CHARLES R	LTC	0-0493487	C157	1
HAMMER EDWARO A	MAJ	C-0144929	0352	3
HAMMER HARRY C	MAJ	0-2006325	C158	1
HAMMER HELMUT E	2LT	0-0556397	0745	2
HAMMER HENRY	CW2	W-2115475	C846	2
HAMMER JOSEPH	CPT	0-0321299	C746	2
HAMMER MARTIN A	MAJ	0-0283047	C166	3
HAMMER PERRY C	MAJ	0-0148410	0753	3
HAMMER SIONEY	CPT	0-2026198	0758	1
HAMMER STEVENS F	1LT	0-0453494	C544	2
HAMMERICK JOHN M	MAJ	C-1576079	1060	1
HAMMERLUND JOHN M	LTC	0-0377482	C966	1
HAMMERNESS CARL E	LTC	0-0132714	C65C	3
HAMMERSLEY WARC	COL	0-0194379	C463	3
HAMMERSMITH AMOS F	1LT	0-1324700	C946	2
HAMMERSTONE JESSE	MAJ	0-0887422	0561	1
HAMMERSTROM R B	1LT	0-0550608	C847	2
HAMMETT CECIL E	MAJ	C-0258079	0566	3
HAMMETT JR FREO M	LTC	0-0249365	C566	3
HAMMETT THOMAS D	2LT	0-1300164	0661	2
HAMMETT WALTER M H	MAJ	0-1646222	0861	1
HAMMILL HENRY S	CPT	0-1316290	0947	2
HAMMOCK DELBERT J	MAJ	0-2262936	1164	1
HAMMOCK ROBERT E	2LT	0-1999885	0446	2
HAMMON JR GEORGE C	LTC	0-179627C	C262	1
HAMMCNO BENTON I	CPT	0-1285748	0357	2
HAMMONO BERTRAM L	LTC	0-0384224	1060	1
HAMMONO CELIA	2LT	N-0721942	1044	1
HAMMONO CHARLES F	LTC	0-1043355	0665	1
HAMMONC CHESTER L	MAJ	0-0969385	0263	1
HAMMOND DEWITTE	CW4	W-2116961	C755	2
HAMMOND ELORICH N	MAJ	0-1591169	C662	1
HAMMOND FORLINE	LTC	0-0517044	0954	1
HAMMONO FREO L	CPT	0-0376973	0143	2
HAMMONC FREDERICK	WO1	W-2107068	0945	2
HAMMONO GEORGE B	CW3	W-2210376	0766	2
HAMMONC GEORGE M	LTC	0-1054260	0861	1
HAMMONC GERALO E	1LT	0-1182591	0947	2
HAMMONC GILBERT C	WO1	W-2118218	C545	2
HAMMONC GOROCN B	COL	0-0119644	0857	3
HAMMONO HAROLC C	LTC	0-0406176	0461	1
HAMMONC HAROLD T	LTC	0-0298122	0667	3
HAMMCNO HOMER H	LTC	0-0033507	0158	2
HAMMONC JOHN A	1LT	0-1040236	0245	2
HAMMONC JOHN H	1LT	0-1286480	0645	2
HAMMONC JOHN M	WO1	W-2109988	0349	1
HAMMONO JOHN R	COL	0-0277048	1265	3
HAMMONC JR JOHN W	CPT	0-0246942	1166	3
HAMMONO JR WILLIAM C	COL	0-0270407	0460	1
HAMMONC LYLE R	MAJ	0-1284327	0255	1
HAMMONC MARTIN L	LTC	0-0483596	0761	1
HAMMONC MATTHEW	COL	C-0124562	0648	3
HAMMONC MATTHEW J	CW3	W-2004231	1166	3
HAMMONC MAURICE W	LTC	0-0297376	0665	3
HAMMONC CZIF G	CW2	W-2208888	0363	1
HAMMONC PAUL W	LTC	0-0262837	0861	2
HAMMONC RALEIGH L	2LT	0-1822796	0445	2
HAMMONC REGINALO W	MAJ	C-0506865	0246	2
HAMMONC RICHARD T	MAJ	0-0276661	0347	2
HAMMCNO ROBERT H	LTC	0-1117005	0866	1
HAMMONO RUTH P	2LT	N-0720831	0844	1
HAMMONO SR WCODROW W	1LT	0-0373114	1066	2
HAMMONC STEPHEN P	MAJ	0-2263020	0963	1
HAMMONC THOMAS B	LTC	0-0132713	0758	3
HAMMONC THOMAS T	1LT	0-1590520	1144	1
HAMMONO WILLIAM F	MAJ	C-0231906	0656	3
HAMMONC WILLIAM J	LTC	0-0419631	0964	2
HAMMONCS JCHN J	MAJ	0-2018510	0865	1
HAMMONCS KENNETH P	CPT	0-1574794	0466	1
HAMMONS TROY B	MAJ	0-118213C	0862	2
HAMNER GEORGE B	MAJ	C-044946C	0857	2
HAMNER LEWIS M	LTC	0-0404238	0556	2
HAMNER LCUIS	CPT	0-1181279	0758	1
HAMNER SHEPHERD L	CPT	0-0947743	0663	1
HAMNER WALTER C	MAJ	0-0583818	0161	1
HAMOR WACE H	1LT	0-1031091	0745	2
HAMRSHIRE FARL E	CPT	0-0510542	1144	2
HAMPSCN EDMUND R	MAJ	0-0197735	0754	3
HAMPSCN JR RUSSELL J	MAJ	0-1304640	0563	1
HAMPSON RONALO H	1LT	0-1946745	0146	2
HAMPTON CLARENCE R	MAJ	0-2021179	0965	1
HAMPTON CLIFFCRD A	CW3	W-2143912	1162	1
HAMPTON CURNEL S	COL	0-0297405	1060	1
HAMPTON EUGENE G	LTC	0-0179301	0944	2
HAMPTCN HAROLC O	LTC	0-0463640	1054	1
HAMPTCN JAMES H	MAJ	0-0216865	0847	2
HAMPTON JAMES H	1LT	0-4059058	1057	2
HAMPTON JAMES M	MAJ	0-1688825	0165	1
HAMPTON JAMES W	MAJ	0-0587101	0465	2
HAMPTON JASEPH A	CW2	W-2149437	0360	1
HAMPTON JR GEORGE S	MAJ	0-1554556	0754	2
HAMPTON JR CSCAR R	B G	0-0403301	0465	3
HAMPTON JR WALTER O	LTC	0-1046471	1058	1
HAMPTON LUTHER A	CW4	W-2146726	0167	1
HAMPTON RALPH W	LTC	0-0417501	1066	1
HAMRE JOSEPH	LTC	0-0128295	0450	3
HAMRICK GEORGE O	CPT	0-0493171	0846	1
HAMRICK NATHAN G	MAJ	0-2291950	1167	1
HAMRICK WALTERN C	MAJ	0-1048001	0661	1
HAMRICK WILLIAM H	COL	0-0219806	0657	3
HAMSHER KENNETH M	LTC	0-1184839	0360	1
HAMSON GEORGE V	LTC	0-1647067	0363	1
HANASEK FRANK J	LTC	0-0319810	0966	3
HANAVAN LOUIS W	1LT	0-1175145	0447	2
HANAW JUSTIN J	LTC	0-0202468	0363	3
HANAWAY BLANCHE F	CPT	N-0734700	1263	1
HANBERRY HOMER B	MAJ	0-0345005	0659	2
HANBURY REES G	CW4	W-2134346	1262	1
HANCANNCN WILLIAM H	LTC	0-0364187	0665	1
HANCHETT HACDEN L	1LT	0-0469177	1044	2
HANCHEY WILLIAM J	LTC	0-0228180	1162	1
HANCOCK ALBERTA W	1LT	N-0772651	1045	1
HANCOCK CLEC E	MAJ	0-1011054	0461	1
HANCOCK CLIFTON D	MAJ	C-1541033	C961	1
HANCOCK OARRELL B	1LT	0-1047153	1045	2
HANCOCK DOY L	LTC	0-0226057	C660	3
HANCOCK FREO J	LTC	0-0453437	C661	1
HANCOCK HAMPTON S	LTC	0-1640520	C866	1
HANCOCK HELMER W	LTC	0-0437076	0366	3
HANCOCK HENRY H	MAJ	0-1697040	0346	1
HANCOCK HOBART T	MAJ	0-0230981	C856	3
HANCOCK JOHN I	CPT	0-1002790	C556	1
HANCOCK JOHN W	LTC	C-0398383	C157	1
HANCOCK JOSEPH M	LTC	0-1053157	0463	1
HANCOCK LESTER A	COL	C-0253753	0254	3
HANCOCK LINDLE W	2LT	0-2030376	C964	2
HANCOCK LYNN O	COL	0-0336440	C966	3
HANCOCK MARVIN R	CW4	W-2108788	C761	1
HANCOCK MONTIE C	MAJ	C-0214453	1046	1
HANCOCK RALPH R	CW2	W-2147142	C661	1
HANCCCK ROBERT J	CW2	W-2127547	C946	1
HANCCCK ROMERO A	MAJ	0-0223047	1148	1
HANCOCK STANLEY M	CPT	0-1299881	C647	1
HANCOCK WILLIAM A	LTC	0-0259224	0361	1
HANCOCK WILLIAM I	2LT	0-1055312	C664	2
HANCOCK WINFIELD S	1LT	0-1031247	C945	2
HAND BENJAMIN F	COL	0-0357431	C346	2
HAND CHARLES R	1LT	0-0386088	1143	2
HAND CHARLIE T	CW2	W-2145906	1061	1
HAND CLIFFORD A	LTC	0-0333328	C760	3
HAND ELIZABETH	1LT	N-0742222	0346	1
HAND JOSEPH G	CPT	0-1166277	0548	2
HAND JR EDGAR L	MAJ	C-2042768	1061	1
HAND KENNETH W	CPT	0-1112195	C446	2
HAND MARK M	LTC	0-0490331	1045	2
HAND NOAH S	MAJ	0-0238287	C164	3
HAND OLIVER T	CW3	W-2205447	0165	1
HAND WILLIAM A	MAJ	C-1924510	1067	1
HAND WILLIAM O	MAJ	C-1686732	C864	1
HANDBERG ROGER B	MAJ	0-0383010	C859	1
HANDELMAN EUGENE V	CPT	0-1757070	0346	2
HANDELMAN SAMUEL R	MAJ	0-0240655	0364	3
HANDFIELD CHARLES K	MAJ	0-1636002	0860	1
HANDLER ALLEN A	CPT	0-0520021	1046	2
HANDLER IRVING	CPT	0-1825858	C447	2
HANDLER PHILIP E	CPT	0-0167972	0555	3
HANDLER WILLIAM	1LT	0-1306841	C846	2
HANDLEY ALVIE J	1LT	0-1647482	0852	1
HANDLEY ARTHUR	CW2	W-2153028	1059	1
HANDLEY CAMERON L	LTC	0-0321469	0163	3
HANDLEY JAMES J	MAJ	C-0152016	C846	2
HANDLEY JAMES P	MAJ	0-0344151	0246	2
HANDLEY KENNETH E	MAJ	0-1552292	C847	2
HANDLEY LEE R	MAJ	0-1824746	C966	1
HANDLEY PATRICK J	MAJ	0-C240056	0663	3
HANDLEY WALTER C	LTC	C-04504C6	0657	1
HANDLY RUSSELL E	MAJ	0-1287704	0361	1
HANDWERK ALLEN S	WO1	W-2134484	1058	1
HANDY OCNALD E	CW2	W-2205939	0263	1
HANDY ELSIE M	MAJ	N-0798118	0965	1
HANDY HARRY W	CPT	0-0143761	C648	3
HANCY JOSEPH L	LTC	0-1796463	0762	1
HANDY ROLAND L	WO1	W-2147271	0753	2
HANDZLIK LEON L	CW2	W-2000911	C445	2
HANER RUSSELL D	CPT	0-1592894	C466	3
HANER WILLIAM E	MAJ	0-1685715	C964	1
HANES ARCHIBALD	MAJ	0-4003617	0462	2
HANES ARTHUR E	2LT	C-1175729	1044	2
HANES CLARENCE W	LTC	0-021994C	0553	3
HANES GLEN C	MAJ	0-1045451	C256	1
HANES GUY L	1LT	N-0805848	0157	2
HANES RAYMOND G	MAJ	0-0496513	1055	1
HANES ROBERT C	COL	0-0216331	0763	3
HANESS MORRIS	CPT	0-1846444	1053	1
HANEWINCKEL WILLIAM	MAJ	0-1643633	0666	1
HANEY ANNE C	MAJ	N-0760684	0663	1
HANEY ARTHUR F	COL	0-0396846	0763	1
HANEY CHARLES T	CW4	W-2114977	0556	1
HANEY HARRY L	MAJ	C-2262834	0961	1
HANEY JILES W	LTC	0-0192403	0445	2
HANEY LELAND F	CPT	0-2309162	1066	2
HANEY CVEL M	LTC	0-0304244	1160	1
HANEY RCY R	MAJ	0-0114596	0858	3
HANEY THOMAS R	1LT	0-1325797	C446	2
HANGARTNER JOHN A	LTC	C-1016275	0363	2
HANGEN RUSSELL J	CPT	0-169534C	0343	2
HANGER JAMES F	LTC	0-0314632	0465	3
HANGER JR BRUCE B	LTC	0-0910254	C747	1
HANGER WALLACE C	CPT	0-1301296	0251	2
HANGER WALLACE S	2LT	0-0367756	0344	2
HANGERLD ERLING J	LTC	C-0258191	1057	3
HANIFIN JR RCBERT E	MAJ	C-1166079	0446	2
HANISCH CECIL L	CPT	0-1319493	0846	2
HANKENSCN JOHN A	LTC	0-0920326	1058	2
HANKINS COLEMAN	CW2	W-2144081	1059	1
HANKINS HENRY E	CW3	W-2142394	0760	2
HANKINS JOHN B	CPT	0-0372519	0147	2
HANKINS WILLIAM T	LTC	0-1946746	0463	1
HANKS ALGER	LTC	0-0109294	0549	1
HANKS CLIFTCN M	MAJ	C-1116497	1059	1
HANKS CALE L	CW2	W-2146664	0359	2
HANKS EVA B C	2LT	N-0787728	0945	1
HANKS JACK A	1LT	0-1313159	0947	1
HANKS JACK L	LTC	0-03180C8	0460	3
HANLEN GEORGE S	CW3	W-2146991	0561	1
HANLEY ARTHUR W	CW3	W-2208694	0667	1
HANLEY CHARLES W	LTC	0-1165865	0360	1
HANLEY CAVIO J	MAJ	0-1544465	0460	1
HANLEY CONALC B	CPT	0-0502613	1046	2
HANLEY ECWARC S	LTC	0-0304613	0467	3
HANLEY PAUL C	LTC	0-1578565	0860	1
HANLEY PHILIP W	CPT	0-1307817	1065	2
HANLEY WILLIAM E	LTC	0-1014635	1162	1
HANLEY WILLIAM J	MAJ	0-1043975	0661	1
HANLIN GEORGE B	LTC	0-1105491	0661	1
HANLIN JAMES E	MAJ	0-1951154	0263	1
HANLON CATHERINE	2LT	N-0721378	C345	1
HANLON ELIZABETH	CPT	N-0723533	1266	3
HANLCN FRANK E	COL	0-0382105	0767	3
HANLON JOHN J	LTC	0-0229298	0665	3
HANLCN JCHN P	2LT	0-1326396	1145	2
HANLON JCHN R	1LT	0-1035799	0845	1
HANLON JCSEPH W	MAJ	C-1293764	1060	1
HANLON PAUL A	LTC	0-1945369	0565	3
HANLON RAYMOND J	LTC	0-1593607	0867	1
HANLON ROBERT E	CW2	W-2213499	0167	1
HANLY EDWIN C	COL	0-0507918	0167	3
HANMER WILLIAM	CPT	C-117636C	0846	2
HANN CHARLES J	CW2	W-2110955	0246	2
HANN DALE E	MAJ	0-0810651	0866	1
HANN HARCLD C	LTC	0-130973C	0463	1
HANN JCHN R	COL	0-0183425	0957	3
HANN JR GEORGE C	LTC	0-035283C	0565	3
HANNA ARTHUR J	LTC	0-0136802	0152	3
HANNA AUSTIN P	LTC	C-0399455	0546	2
HANNA CARL	COL	0-0183285	0950	3
HANNA CHARLES C	1LT	0-2044296	0546	1
HANNA CHARLES T	CW3	W-2152296	1164	1
HANNA CLAIR E	CPT	0-1062200	0347	2
HANNA CLEVIS S	CPT	0-2001003	0357	1
HANNA CALIL	MAJ	C-1283762	0952	1
HANNA GEORGE W	CPT	0-1634849	1045	2
HANNA HUGH E	2LT	0-1895495	0244	2
HANNA JR LEE A	CW3	W-2206540	1067	1
HANNA JR ORA T	1LT	0-1060333	0346	2
HANNA MARTIN L	MAJ	0-1041566	0860	1
HANNA NELSON H	MAJ	C-1311250	0863	1
HANNA RALPH E	LTC	0-0217081	1063	3
HANNA ROBERT A	CPT	0-2263336	1262	1

NAME	GRADE	SVC NO	DATE RET MO YR	RET CODE
HANNA ROGER J	LTC	0-0473971	0446	2
HANNA VIRGINIA P	2LT	N-0732204	0645	1
HANNA WALTER J	M G	0-0171549	0164	3
HANNA WILLIAM A	MAJ	0-1285581	0657	1
HANNA WILLIAM C	LTC	0-0382766	1163	1
HANNABASS CARDWELL F	1LT	0-0408307	0644	2
HANNAH CARL W	MAJ	0-1796464	0555	1
HANNAH CLAUDE R	MAJ	0-0305556	0247	2
HANNAH HAROLD W	LTC	0-0295978	1045	2
HANNAH JOEL M	1LT	0-2202488	0453	2
HANNAH LAWRENCE W	LTC	0-0498193	1166	3
HANNAH PAUL D	LTC	0-0213969	0361	3
HANNAH RICHARD E	LTC	0-1257875	1264	3
HANNAH ROBERT W	MAJ	0-0207245	0151	3
HANNAN JOSEPH M	CPT	0-0518572	0216	2
HANNAN WILLIAM S	COL	0-0148971	0648	3
HANNAN WILLIAM T	MAJ	0-1685554	0562	1
HANNAWACKER FRANCIS	CPT	0-0335863	0963	3
HANNAY WILLIAM V	LTC	0-0257044	0556	3
HANNEGAN WILLIAM J	LTC	0-0494828	0555	1
HANNEKE IGNATIUS F	MAJ	0-1540904	1160	1
HANNEN HAROLD P	CW3	W-2145442	1063	1
HANNER KENNETH H	CPT	0-0329688	0547	2
HANNES EDWIN A	CW3	W-2143027	0264	1
HANNETT HENRY D	LTC	0-1042046	0861	1
HANNIGAN EDWARD V	1LT	0-1639126	0745	2
HANNIGAN FRANCIS	MAJ	0-0279438	1046	1
HANNIGAN WALTER J	MAJ	0-0995743	0364	1
HANNINGTON GEORGE A	CW3	W-2206943	1265	1
HANNON JOSEPH C	MAJ	0-0356740	0347	2
HANNON MILLARD W	MAJ	0-0272088	1165	3
HANNON PAUL E	CPT	0-0287286	1162	2
HANNON WILLIAM M	MAJ	0-1106791	1059	1
HANNULA JACK	MAJ	0-0474995	0747	1
HANNUM JOHN H	2LT	0-1640524	1044	1
HANNUSCH WILLIAM K	LTC	0-0519727	0765	3
HANNY AELLEN B	MAJ	0-0207401	0160	3
HANOLD CHRIS H	CW3	W-2104703	1154	1
HANON HARRY L	LTC	0-1316150	0366	1
HANOVER BILLY D	2LT	0-2000661	0646	2
HANOVER CHESTER F	LTC	0-0282138	0155	1
HANOVER FRANK J	CPT	0-1174881	0246	2
HANOVER JR CHARLES A	MAJ	0-0409333	0966	3
HANOVER LAURENCE R	LTC	0-0256076	0467	3
HANRAHAN CLEMENT J	CW4	W-2106497	0857	1
HANRAHAN MARGARET F	MAJ	N-0752670	0464	1
HANRETTY JOHN J	LTC	0-1585561	1265	1
HANSBEARRY ERNEST C	CPT	0-0319610	1145	2
HANSBROUGH ELIZABETH	MAJ	N-0700907	1044	1
HANSBROUGH JOHN H	LTC	0-0198230	0262	3
HANSCHEN JOHN A	1LT	0-1050701	0446	2
HANSCOM HOMER W	LTC	0-0232683	1264	3
HANSEL JACK H	MAJ	0-0426837	0557	1
HANSELL ADOPH	CPT	0-0278826	1148	1
HANSELL JR HOMER P	LTC	0-1298002	1060	1
HANSELL ROBERT J	CPT	0-0297213	1144	2
HANSELMAN WAYNE E	LTC	0-1169554	0461	1
HANSELMANN WALTER W	LTC	0-1037525	0561	1
HANSEN AGNES D	1LT	N-0756745	1045	1
HANSEN ALBERT W	2LT	0-0887685	0257	1
HANSEN ALFRED M	CPT	0-0481794	0347	2
HANSEN ALTON S	MAJ	0-1701105	0146	2
HANSEN ANITA M	1LT	N-0795429	0948	2
HANSEN ARNOLD A	MAJ	0-0299321	0464	3
HANSEN ARTHUR B	MAJ	0-0216058	0757	3
HANSEN BOYD S	MAJ	0-0406494	0657	1
HANSEN CARL V	MAJ	0-0119659	1147	2
HANSEN CHARLES G	CW3	W-2145443	0566	1
HANSEN CHARLES H	CW3	W-2142235	1159	1
HANSEN CLARENCE P	MAJ	0-1534750	0761	1
HANSEN CLARENCE W	MAJ	0-1822994	0257	1
HANSEN DONALD A	CPT	0-0962171	1064	1
HANSEN DONALD A	1LT	0-1177824	0945	2
HANSEN DOROTHY	2LT	N-0751781	0345	1
HANSEN EARL H	1LT	0-0321209	0646	2

NAME	GRADE	SVC NO	DATE RET MO YR	RET CODE
HANSEN EDWARD N	CPT	0-1644400	0358	1
HANSEN EDWIN	COL	0-0124563	1152	3
HANSEN ELLSWORTH	LTC	0-1289727	1160	1
HANSEN ERIC	CW3	W-2141733	0758	1
HANSEN EUGENE J	CPT	0-0345085	0150	1
HANSEN FRANKLIN C	MAJ	0-1544176	0662	1
HANSEN FRANKLIN S	LTC	0-1030372	0457	1
HANSEN FRED E	LTC	0-0155356	0253	3
HANSEN GEORGE R	LTC	0-0451295	0260	1
HANSEN GERHART H	MAJ	0-0134565	0550	1
HANSEN GLEN A	CW2	W-2145444	0659	1
HANSEN GODFRIED N	LTC	0-1329833	1265	1
HANSEN HAROLD M	1LT	0-1110532	0146	2
HANSEN HARRY	MAJ	0-0162261	0652	3
HANSEN HARRY P R	COL	0-0218906	0655	3
HANSEN JOHN C	CPT	0-0236201	0463	3
HANSEN JOHN C	CW3	W-2150286	1163	1
HANSEN JOHN E	LTC	0-0452621	1062	1
HANSEN JOHN H	LTC	0-0242142	0843	1
HANSEN KENNETH C	MAJ	0-0821160	0762	1
HANSEN LESTER E	MAJ	0-0450240	1046	2
HANSEN LOUIS A	COL	0-0410115	0465	1
HANSEN LOUIS A	MAJ	0-0987744	0963	1
HANSEN MABEL C	MAJ	N-0799337	0265	2
HANSEN MERLIN A	2LT	0-1598690	0845	2
HANSEN NEIL E	1LT	0-1633255	1145	2
HANSEN OTTO W	CW2	W-2114419	0949	1
HANSEN PAUL C	COL	0-0303357	0665	3
HANSEN PERCY M	COL	0-0143887	0150	3
HANSEN RALPH E	COL	0-0185147	0346	2
HANSEN RALPH W	MAJ	0-0245809	0447	2
HANSEN RALPH W	COL	0-0300198	1060	1
HANSEN RICHARD H	LTC	0-1582361	1164	1
HANSEN ROBERT H G	MAJ	0-1341538	0664	1
HANSEN ROBERT W	MAJ	0-0571294	0164	1
HANSEN RUSSELL H	CW4	W-2101799	0756	1
HANSEN SVEND C	MAJ	0-1645021	0756	1
HANSEN THEODORE B	COL	0-0238153	0964	3
HANSEN THEONE H	2LT	0-1108721	0944	2
HANSEN VERNON A	LTC	0-0239266	0166	3
HANSEN VICTOR L	LTC	0-0473008	1051	1
HANSEN VICTOR R	LTC	0-0217166	0466	3
HANSEN WELLS R	WO1	W-2115607	0561	2
HANSEN WILHELM G	CPT	0-1689461	0645	2
HANSEN WILLIAM H	LTC	0-0172752	0853	3
HANSER SAMUEL A	LTC	0-0355900	0146	2
HANSFORD GEORGE M	1LT	0-1288541	0545	2
HANSFORD JACK D	LTC	0-1307231	0262	1
HANSFORD JOHN W	MAJ	0-1291463	1060	1
HANSHAW EBBERT H	MAJ	0-0967345	1263	1
HANSHAW HORACE C	CW4	W-2112559	1159	1
HANSIS MARJORIE B	2LT	N-0742367	0844	1
HANSKETT JOSEPH F	CPT	0-1796785	1059	1
HANSMEIER ROBERT H	LTC	0-0308384	0457	2
HANSON ALTON D	CPT	0-1585562	0352	1
HANSON ARCHIE F	CPT	0-1292519	0157	1
HANSON ARTHUR C	CPT	0-0266580	0245	2
HANSON ARTHUR F	COL	0-0335203	0164	1
HANSON CARL R	MAJ	0-1304208	0266	1
HANSON CHARLES K	MAJ	0-2009795	0465	1
HANSON DANIEL	MAJ	0-1280716	0755	1
HANSON ERNEST C	1LT	0-1996591	0647	2
HANSON GEORGE W	COL	0-0263629	0158	1
HANSON JOHN A	LTC	0-0266148	0465	3
HANSON JOHN E	CPT	0-0423200	1144	2
HANSON JOHN E	1LT	0-1113727	0446	2
HANSON JOHN N	LTC	0-0194648	1059	3
HANSON JR HARRY A	MAJ	0-0976657	0862	1
HANSON KENNETH E	CPT	0-0954900	0358	2
HANSON LEO S	MAJ	0-2037130	1160	1
HANSON LINDLEY J	CPT	0-1544970	0762	2
HANSON LLOYD H	MAJ	0-1030572	0558	1
HANSON MERLE H	MAJ	0-1797463	1059	2
HANSON MERLE L	CPT	0-0961634	0860	1
HANSON OLIVER B	CPT	0-1113728	1146	1

NAME	GRADE	SVC NO	DATE RET MO YR	RET CODE
HANSON PHILIP F	CPT	0-1017890	1046	2
HANSON RICHARD F	CPT	0-0389067	0444	2
HANSON RICHARD H	LTC	0-1307686	1264	1
HANSON ROBERT E	CPT	0-0413442	0345	2
HANSON STEPHEN	LTC	0-0247575	1163	3
HANSON THOMAS C	CPT	0-0415620	0544	2
HANSON THOMAS S	LTC	0-2289382	0461	1
HANSON VIRGIL F	MAJ	0-1317007	0657	1
HANSON WARREN W	LTC	0-0548175	0663	1
HANSON WILLARD O	MAJ	0-0451300	0258	1
HANSON WILLIAM L	LTC	0-0117230	0152	3
HANSON ZELMA F	MAJ	L-0900134	0448	2
HANSS ARMAND W	MAJ	0-0328867	1045	2
HANSSEN HANS I	MAJ	0-0185313	0854	3
HANSSEN KEITH E	LTC	0-1542291	0667	1
HANST BENJAMIN F	LTC	0-0234722	0648	3
HANTELMANN HAROLD E	COL	0-0295837	1046	2
HANTKE RUSSELL C	LTC	0-0382985	1163	1
HANZEL CHARLES A	1LT	0-1797642	0567	1
HANZLIK JR CHARLES J	1LT	0-0541599	0845	2
HAPGOOD DAVID W	2LT	0-1996742	0346	2
HAPGOOD MILES M	MAJ	0-0162958	0156	3
HAPHEY ROBERT D	LTC	0-0316825	0960	1
HAPP WALTER J	CW3	W-2141983	0259	2
HAPPEL GEORGE W N	CPT	0-0224801	0747	2
HAPWORTH KENNETH C	COL	0-0369790	1060	1
HARABOSKY ROMAN H	WO1	W-2105792	0557	1
HARADA RAYMOND K	LTC	0-0979651	1166	1
HARADA SATORU	MAJ	0-1899432	0262	1
HARADEN ELMER F	LTC	0-0278260	1057	3
HARALSON CHESNEY C	1LT	0-1316749	1045	2
HARASIMOWICZ PAUL P	LTC	0-0297475	0146	2
HARBAUGH CHARLES W	LTC	0-1106796	1063	1
HARBAUGH HELEN H	MAJ	L-1020051	0866	1
HARBAUGH ORIL S	COL	0-0252277	0763	3
HARBECK GARNARD E	CPT	0-2005338	0158	1
HARBERGER CHARLES H	COL	0-0271379	0966	3
HARBERT EDGAR D	MAJ	0-2203301	0462	1
HARBERT EDWARD D	CPT	0-1845899	1155	2
HARBERT JAMES M	CW3	W-2148410	0966	1
HARBERT JASON T	LTC	0-0330582	0446	2
HARBIDGE KENNETH R	MAJ	0-0938977	0264	1
HARBIN THOMAS R	MAJ	0-0462232	0657	1
HARBIN WILLIAM R	MAJ	0-1551218	0860	1
HARBISON DOUGLAS H	MAJ	0-0274847	1157	3
HARBISON HUNTER G	LTC	0-1168705	0361	1
HARBISON JOHN C	1LT	0-1305050	0146	2
HARBISON JOSEPH S	COL	0-0205893	1054	3
HARBOR JOHN C	CW2	W-2149015	1060	1
HARBOUR WAYNE R	MAJ	0-2000919	0161	1
HARBRIDGE FREDERICK	LTC	0-0273060	1065	3
HARBULA MICHAEL G	MAJ	0-0106283	0455	3
HARBY HORACE D	COL	0-1015803	0566	1
HARD HELEN L	CPT	N-0779304	1147	1
HARD THORNTON F	LTC	0-1293407	0865	1
HARDAKER JOHN H W	LTC	0-1551021	0164	1
HARDART ROBERT J	CPT	0-1116156	0847	2
HARDCASTLE DALLAS C	LTC	0-1167883	0561	1
HARDCASTLE LOUIS V	LTC	0-1648282	0163	1
HARDEE FRANK S	LTC	0-0308470	0961	3
HARDEGREE HARMON B	CW3	W-2152996	0763	1
HARDEGREE WILLIAM P	COL	0-0276900	1061	3
HARDEMAN ALFRED A	WO1	W-2108346	0146	2
HARDEN BERNARD A	LTC	0-0308534	0367	3
HARDEN HOLLIS C	CPT	0-1323690	0346	2
HARDEN JAMES A	CPT	0-0361538	0846	2
HARDEN JR SAMUEL G	CPT	0-0248469	1066	3
HARDEN ROBERT E	1LT	0-1059137	0546	2
HARDEN THADDEUS E	CPT	0-0368355	1044	2
HARDENBERG WILBUR J	CW4	W-2104127	0656	1
HARDENBERGH W A	COL	0-0182732	0848	3
HARDENBURG WILLIAM L	LTC	0-0241044	1063	3
HARDER CARL F	LTC	0-0235122	0861	1
HARDER EDMUND A	LTC	0-0420092	1060	1
HARDESTY CHARLES M	LTC	0-1018359	0563	1

NAME	GRADE	SVC NO	DATE RET MO YR	RET CODE
HARDESTY CLAUDE A	MAJ	0-2015779	0261	1
HARDESTY JOHN R	LTC	0-1003249	0556	1
HARDESTY JR W H	COL	0-0305862	1060	1
HARDEY JR CHARLES A	MAJ	0-2014808	1065	1
HARDGRAVE LAWRENCE W	1LT	0-2012492	0862	1
HARDGROVE EVERETT A	LTC	0-0515776	1164	1
HARDGROVE GEORGE G	LTC	0-0405866	0663	1
HARDGROVE THOMAS J	COL	0-0492467	0265	3
HARDIE EMMETT F	MAJ	0-1039665	0964	1
HARDIE WADE E	LTC	0-0248300	1164	3
HARDIE WILBUR C	CW2	W-2149335	0157	1
HARDIMAN JOSEPH F	LTC	0-0450882	0457	1
HARDIMAN SYLVESTER	CW2	W-2119553	0347	1
HARDIN ARLTON W	LTC	0-1110533	1166	1
HARDIN BAKER B	CPT	0-0338529	1044	2
HARDIN CHARLES F	CPT	0-0332259	1044	2
HARDIN DAVID R	COL	0-0260922	0766	3
HARDIN DELL B	COL	0-0171321	1055	3
HARDIN FRED	CW2	W-2114591	0445	2
HARDIN HARRY T	LTC	0-1296365	0565	1
HARDIN HARVEY M	LTC	0-0469311	0662	1
HARDIN JAMES E	LTC	0-0443991	0854	1
HARDIN JAMES N	LTC	0-0530860	0765	3
HARDIN JAMES W	CPT	0-0485358	0145	2
HARDIN JOHN E	CW2	W-2105251	0546	1
HARDIN JR JOHN J	CPT	0-0465770	0846	2
HARDIN KENNETH E	LTC	0-1317786	0264	1
HARDIN LEO J	LTC	0-0198718	0962	3
HARDIN MERLE C	CW2	W-2150127	0661	1
HARDIN PARKER C	MAJ	0-0241295	0245	2
HARDIN THOMAS L	MAJ	0-0112116	0456	3
HARDIN VIRGIL L	CW2	W-2150130	0957	1
HARDIN WALTUS H	LTC	0-1845725	0662	1
HARDIN WILLIAM B	1LT	0-1317606	0365	2
HARDIN WILLIAM H	LTC	0-0319466	0157	1
HARDIN WILLIAM S	1LT	0-0538726	0945	2
HARDING ALARC C	1LT	0-1013424	0646	2
HARDING ARTHUR L	COL	0-0247067	0866	3
HARDING CHARLES O	MAJ	0-0274108	0656	3
HARDING EDGAR C	1LT	0-2045218	0147	2
HARDING ELIZABETH	LTC	N-0700050	0245	1
HARDING EMORY M	2LT	0-1039373	1044	2
HARDING FRANK P	LTC	0-0324334	0658	2
HARDING FREDERICK	CPT	0-1294657	1146	2
HARDING HAROLD F	M G	0-0263728	0464	3
HARDING HAROLD F	MAJ	0-1555829	0466	2
HARDING HARRISON W	CPT	0-0409864	0461	1
HARDING HARRY J	LTC	0-0392110	0849	2
HARDING HENRY A	COL	0-0224101	0655	3
HARDING JR EDWIN	LTC	0-0403971	0855	1
HARDING JR NEIL G	MAJ	0-1311890	1057	1
HARDING LEONARD B	1LT	0-1642943	1045	2
HARDING MABEL V	2LT	L-0902835	0345	2
HARDING ROBERT A	MAJ	0-1824179	0261	1
HARDING SR ROBERT R	LTC	0-1180936	0666	1
HARDING TOM D	LTC	0-0301320	1263	3
HARDING WARREN G	CPT	0-1876970	1164	2
HARDISON ROBERT S	MAJ	0-1172048	0361	1
HARDISON WALTER M	CPT	0-0489914	0653	1
HARDISTER CHARLES J	LTC	0-0404456	0364	1
HARDISTY DALE A	LTC	0-0351267	0363	1
HARDISTY HERSCHEL C	LTC	0-0362225	1145	2
HARDMAN SHERMAN W	MAJ	0-1326629	1163	1
HARDSOG HARRY N	COL	0-0261461	1263	3
HARDT DAN A	COL	0-0231170	0662	3
HARDT EDWARD J	CW4	W-2114867	0561	3
HARDT JOHN R	2LT	0-1301823	0844	2
HARDWICK EMMET V	COL	0-0262522	0551	3
HARDWICK JR EUGENE R	1LT	0-0524399	0146	2
HARDWICK ROY	MAJ	0-1011894	0856	1
HARDWICK RUSSELL V	CPT	0-0274907	0447	1
HARDWICK SYDNEY C	LTC	0-0261426	1066	3
HARDY ARTHUR W	LTC	0-0354209	1045	2
HARDY ASHBY W	LTC	0-1585566	0266	1
HARDY CHARLES H	LTC	0-1030573	0166	1

NAME	GRADE	SVC NO	DATE RET MO YR	RET CODE
HARDY CLYDE	CW2	W-2110753	0446	1
HARDY EDWARD J	LTC	O-0104779	0544	2
HARDY FRANK	COL	O-0201407	0262	3
HARDY GEORGE C	LTC	O-0440790	1266	3
HARDY GEORGE C	CW3	W-2141574	0159	1
HARDY GEORGE M	CPT	O-0545497	0946	2
HARDY GEORGE P	1LT	O-2262195	0557	1
HARDY HENRY W	COL	O-0163148	0961	3
HARDY HOLMES L	MAJ	O-1305766	0363	1
HARDY JACKSON L	LTC	O-0250977	0162	1
HARDY JOHN F	CW3	W-2142849	0662	1
HARDY JOHN G	COL	O-0212436	0561	3
HARDY JOHN H	LTC	O-1002023	0267	3
HARDY JOHN R	LTC	O-2007768	0167	1
HARDY JR BENJAMIN D	COL	O-0301886	0457	3
HARDY JR JOHN F	CPT	O-0361835	0845	2
HARDY JULIAN D	MAJ	O-1020533	0465	1
HARDY LEVI J	CPT	O-0518490	0447	1
HARDY OPAL	2LT	N-0726888	0445	1
HARDY OSCAR L	LTC	O-1823152	1061	2
HARDY RALPH L	CPT	O-1174882	0146	2
HARDY ROBERT M	COL	O-0237858	0166	3
HARDY RUPERT T	2LT	O-1544864	0845	2
HARDY RUSSELL L	1LT	O-1328033	0447	2
HARDY SILAS G	COL	O-1634851	0767	1
HARDY THOMAS J	CPT	O-0399699	0846	2
HARDY WILBERT C	LTC	O-0125712	0154	3
HARDY WILLARD J	MAJ	O-0887996	0861	1
HARDY WILLIAM F	CW3	W-2211479	0467	1
HARDZOG JAMES R	1LT	O-0539288	0946	2
HARE CHARLES A	LTC	O-0504368	0763	3
HARE HENRY H	LTC	O-0263891	1064	3
HARE JEAN M	MAJ	O-0948163	1167	1
HARE PERCY R	MAJ	O-2204408	0164	1
HARE WILLIAM W	CPT	O-1012986	1154	1
HAREN CHARLES G	MAJ	O-0243006	0960	3
HAREN FERDINAND	MAJ	O-0775342	0164	1
HARENZA JOSEPH M	MAJ	O-1590522	0360	1
HARFORD BERENICE K	1LT	N-0730710	1044	1
HARFORD DON L	COL	O-0207084	0355	3
HARGADON BERNARD A	LTC	O-1334284	0365	1
HARGENS AUGUSTM	1LT	O-1301140	0951	1
HARGER BERNARD A	CPT	O-0397936	1048	2
HARGETT CLAUDE F	LTC	O-1182377	0864	1
HARGETT YUELL S	MAJ	O-0415280	0546	1
HARGIS BERNIE S	LTC	O-0236409	0750	3
HARGIS JAMES	LTC	O-0450018	1154	1
HARGRAVE CLARENCE F	COL	O-0406844	0263	1
HARGRAVE CLIFFORD F	LTC	O-0927511	0764	1
HARGRAVE ELMO M	LTC	O-0388188	0647	2
HARGRAVE GARNETT D	MAJ	O-1299402	1057	1
HARGRAVES ALLEN P	2LT	O-1173270	0843	2
HARGRAVES RAYMOND	LTC	O-0116267	0155	3
HARGREAVES GEORGE M	COL	O-0280736	0666	3
HARGREAVES WILSON	LTC	O-0335346	1165	3
HARGROVE HARRY W	LTC	O-0373261	1265	3
HARGROVE JR GEORGE	MAJ	O-0387525	0346	1
HARGROVE RICHARD L	CPT	O-0974068	0861	1
HARGROVE ROY T	CW3	W-2145124	0757	1
HARGROVE WILLIAM H	MAJ	O-1996493	0855	1
HARIG OSCAR	MAJ	O-2263263	1061	2
HARING STUART F	LTC	O-0352718	1060	1
HARJES HERMAN H	CW3	W-2148529	0864	1
HARKCOM SAMUEL G	2LT	O-1323834	0644	2
HARKER ELROY F	CW3	W-2153319	0863	1
HARKINS CHARLES R	1LT	O-0530665	0146	2
HARKINS FREDERICK	MAJ	O-1686372	0361	1
HARKINS HAROLD E	LTC	O-0236324	1065	3
HARKINS KELLOGG W	COL	O-0213812	0558	3
HARKINS THOMAS P	LTC	O-0215554	0760	3
HARKNESS GEORGE W	MAJ	O-0234543	1065	3
HARKNESS LESLIE Y	CW3	W-2000624	1060	1
HARKNESS ROBERT R	COL	O-0245187	0162	3
HARLAN CLARENCE R	LTC	O-0299441	0467	3
HARLAN HAROLD R	LTC	O-0273201	0765	3
HARLAN JACK J	MAJ	O-1312915	0660	1
HARLAN JR ORVILLE A	CPT	O-1320366	0746	2
HARLAN STEWART M	LTC	O-1103679	0366	2
HARLAN WILLIAM H	LTC	O-0305386	0646	2
HARLAND ALDER G	MAJ	O-2039403	0964	1
HARLAND RUSSELL D	MAJ	O-1886336	1166	1
HARLANDER ALBERT C	COL	O-0277347	0858	3
HARLEM ALFRED F	LTC	O-0310951	1264	3
HARLEM ROBERT L	LTC	O-1171576	0763	1
HARLEMAN BERMAN C	MAJ	O-1647485	0657	1
HARLEY JAMES D	CW2	W-2149150	1058	1
HARLEY JAMES C	LTC	O-0337188	0758	1
HARLEY RICHARD J	MAJ	O-2033526	0761	1
HARLEY THOMAS	CPT	O-1287707	0246	2
HARLIN CLARENCE R	LTC	O-0392205	0760	1
HARLIN EDGAR F	1LT	O-0177129	0660	3
HARLIN HUGH F	CPT	O-0480854	0949	1
HARLINE EDWIN A	LTC	O-0349730	1162	1
HARLOW DOROTHY C	1LT	N-0755742	0946	1
HARLOW GERALD H	1LT	O-1313400	0745	2
HARLOW IRVIN L	COL	O-0371607	0660	1
HARLOW JAMES R	1LT	O-0244673	0154	3
HARM CHARLES J	WO1	W-2122644	0546	2
HARM HENRY W	1LT	O-1283765	0945	2
HARM WINFRED P	CPT	O-0126552	1153	3
HARMAN CAREY C	COL	O-0272776	0867	3
HARMAN CHARLES C	LTC	O-0250010	0667	3
HARMAN CLYDE E	CPT	O-1174883	0655	1
HARMAN LEO D	MAJ	O-0203194	0249	2
HARMAN ROBERT D	LTC	O-0265901	1043	2
HARMAN ROBERT J	MAJ	O-0974058	0463	1
HARMAN ROBERT L	MAJ	O-1317630	0165	1
HARMAN WILLIAM C	LTC	O-1294302	0965	1
HARMER JR EARLE J	COL	O-1541268	0466	1
HARMISON LIONEL L	MAJ	O-0266673	0257	3
HARMOLING KARL C	LTC	O-0231112	0563	3
HARMON ALTON E	LTC	O-0276074	1265	3
HARMON BENJAMIN C	CPT	O-0215101	0556	3
HARMON BILLY	MAJ	O-1884179	0167	1
HARMON CHARLIE P	CW2	W-2152030	1055	1
HARMON ELLIS D	LTC	O-0282239	1145	2
HARMON ERNEST S	1LT	O-1307408	0246	2
HARMON FREDERICK	1LT	O-1825121	1046	2
HARMON GEORGE G	CW3	W-2149402	1261	1
HARMON HARLEY R	CW2	W-2141303	0555	1
HARMON HAROLD M	LTC	O-0454692	0265	1
HARMON HERBERT H	LTC	O-0475177	0656	2
HARMON HOYT H	LTC	O-0110459	0151	3
HARMON JACK T	LTC	O-1289247	1160	1
HARMON JOHN C	MAJ	O-0205740	1055	3
HARMON JR DAVID M	MAJ	O-1116515	1160	1
HARMON LEO C	LTC	O-0405481	0363	1
HARMON LEO F	LTC	O-1177826	0962	1
HARMON LLOYD V	LTC	O-0245506	1051	3
HARMON NEALE K	MAJ	O-1341535	0365	1
HARMON ODIS L	COL	O-0240018	1063	3
HARMON PAUL C	WO1	W-2142850	0153	2
HARMON RICHARD A	CPT	O-1648251	0257	1
HARMON RICHARD W	LTC	O-1014946	0966	1
HARMON ROBERT	CW3	W-2208891	0467	1
HARMON ROBERT C	CW3	W-2106734	0359	1
HARMON RONALD C	CPT	O-0249645	0263	3
HARMON THOMAS D	MAJ	O-1321774	0562	1
HARMON WILMER P	CPT	O-0381762	0944	2
HARMS FRANK F	LTC	O-0293929	0562	1
HARMS GEORGE E	CPT	O-0435559	0546	2
HARMS GEORGE S	1LT	O-1321917	1147	2
HARMS GLENN L	LTC	O-0295782	0362	3
HARMS ROY C	LTC	O-1338229	0967	1
HARMS WILBUR C	LTC	O-1574798	0462	1
HARNED JOHN W	LTC	O-0168264	0461	3
HARNED LELAND D	1LT	O-1794940	0345	2
HARNED MARK L	COL	O-0232250	1151	3
HARNES ALVIN R	LTC	O-0170020	0454	3
HARNESS FOREST A	CPT	O-0119413	0655	3
HARNESS HAROLD O	CW3	W-2102981	0957	1
HARNESS LEROY R	LTC	O-0240278	0166	3
HARNESS MARSHALL C	CPT	O-1292877	0163	1
HARNETT ROBERT W	COL	O-0379206	1262	1
HARNETT SYDNEY G	COL	O-0174583	0554	3
HARNEY GLENN A	1LT	O-0435921	0546	2
HARNEY JAMES D	MAJ	O-1306717	0665	1
HARNEY JAMES M	MAJ	O-0452566	0746	2
HARNEY MARIE A	1LT	N-0751163	1045	2
HARNEY RALPH G	WO1	W-2149111	0157	1
HARNEY ROBERT G	MAJ	O-0957246	0962	1
HARNEY ROBERT G	LTC	O-1032090	1167	1
HARNISH ROBERT L	LTC	O-0371504	1265	3
HARNISH ROBERT O	MAJ	O-1050705	1064	1
HARNLY ROBERT C	COL	O-0325556	0660	1
HARONIAN FRANK J	CPT	O-0202585	1051	3
HAROVER ROBERT W	CPT	O-0974969	0161	1
HARP ALONZO M	CPT	O-0242911	0753	3
HARP PERCY F	MAJ	O-0202743	0446	2
HARP WILLIAM O	CW4	W-2149811	0862	1
HARPER ALLEN J	CPT	O-1290941	0747	2
HARPER BLANC F	MAJ	O-0252166	0553	3
HARPER CARL M	LTC	O-0499709	0155	1
HARPER CECIL K	MAJ	O-0472495	0555	1
HARPER CHARLES A	MAJ	O-1181288	1163	1
HARPER CHARLES I	MAJ	O-1996927	0662	1
HARPER CHARLES O	CPT	O-0331942	1244	2
HARPER CLIO A	COL	O-0232778	0765	3
HARPER DONALD A	1LT	O-0326373	0645	2
HARPER DOROTHY K	LTC	N-0722377	0561	1
HARPER EDWARD N	LTC	O-0278819	0656	3
HARPER EDWIN O	COL	O-0250159	0647	2
HARPER FRANK C	MAJ	O-1635857	0161	1
HARPER FREDERICK	LTC	O-0403328	0946	2
HARPER GEORGE G	CPT	O-1310837	0956	1
HARPER GERALD F	CW2	W-2210610	0866	2
HARPER GRANT F	CPT	O-0551753	1047	2
HARPER HAROLD	COL	O-0169566	0852	3
HARPER HAROLD I	MAJ	O-1113241	0358	1
HARPER HENRY C	LTC	O-0165089	1146	2
HARPER IVAN	1LT	O-0446834	0246	2
HARPER JAMES B	LTC	O-0254834	1156	3
HARPER JAMES K	LTC	O-0323759	1056	3
HARPER JAMES L	MAJ	O-1688452	0565	1
HARPER JAMES W	1LT	O-1114961	0246	2
HARPER JEAN C	MAJ	N-0804489	1162	2
HARPER JESSE R	CPT	O-0244576	1159	3
HARPER JOE T	1LT	O-1287708	0545	2
HARPER JOHN H	COL	O-0213733	1262	3
HARPER JOHN T	MAJ	O-2033096	0363	1
HARPER JR ARDIS C	MAJ	O-2014348	1262	1
HARPER JR WILLIAM F	COL	O-0238584	0457	1
HARPER LAMAR F	1LT	O-1636011	0546	2
HARPER LEWIS H	COL	O-0116195	0648	3
HARPER LOUIS M	CPT	O-1287344	0747	2
HARPER MILTON N	CPT	O-0735578	0866	1
HARPER OWEN F	MAJ	O-2020808	0164	1
HARPER PAUL F	COL	O-0274317	0860	3
HARPER RILEY A	MAJ	O-0335981	0546	2
HARPER RILEY A	MAJ	O-0355981	0559	2
HARPER ROBERT R	LTC	O-1633259	0162	1
HARPER ROBERT C	LTC	O-1015787	0861	2
HARPER ROBERT H	CPT	O-2263718	0163	2
HARPER ROBERT J	COL	O-0215051	0564	3
HARPER ROBERT J	CPT	O-0979355	0260	2
HARPER ROBERT S	MAJ	O-2014553	0663	1
HARPER ROY H	CW4	W-2116249	0161	1
HARPER VICTOR E	COL	O-0472457	1264	2
HARPER WALLACE T	MAJ	O-2007870	0161	1
HARPER WARD R	2LT	O-1301141	0744	2
HARPER WILLIAM L	LTC	O-0289147	0944	2
HARPER WILLIE F	LTC	O-1299742	0760	1
HARPIN CHARLES H	LTC	O-1589879	0367	2
HARR GERALD J	MAJ	O-0965429	0763	1
HARR JR HOWARD R	CPT	O-1288224	0346	2
HARR WILLIAM H	MAJ	O-1020499	1165	1
HARRAH CALVIN S	COL	O-0108134	0-53	3
HARREL THOMAS H	LTC	O-0304359	1045	2
HARRELL ARTHUR E	COL	O-0306807	0760	1
HARRELL BEVERLEY T	LTC	O-0225854	0364	3
HARRELL DAWSON L	CW3	W-2120963	0657	1
HARRELL EDWARD M	LTC	O-1285582	0862	1
HARRELL EUGENE J	CW4	W-2144918	0263	2
HARRELL FREDERICK	COL	O-0284779	0157	3
HARRELL GEORGE B	CW2	W-2146333	0560	1
HARRELL GEORGE C	LTC	O-0259058	0167	3
HARRELL GUS W	CPT	O-0455135	0645	2
HARRELL JR DALLAS W	CW3	W-2151056	1163	1
HARRELL LEIGHTON E	COL	O-0338414	1060	3
HARRELL LEROY J	CW2	W-2212023	0866	2
HARRELL ROBERT L	1LT	O-1999875	0646	2
HARRELL TRUMAN W	CW3	W-2142320	0157	1
HARRELL WALTER F	MAJ	O-0280045	1165	3
HARRELL WILLIAM R	CPT	O-1292447	0557	1
HARRELSON DARREL C	LTC	O-0281064	0865	1
HARRELSON LAWRENCE F	CW2	W-2152673	1060	1
HARRELSON WALTER N	CPT	O-0362888	0545	2
HARRIES BERNICE M	MAJ	N-0734449	0664	1
HARRIG MARION S	LTC	O-0442618	0464	3
HARRIGAN WILLIAM H	LTC	O-1319412	0763	1
HARRILL CHARLIE H	COL	O-0255876	1047	2
HARRILL ROBERT H	CPT	O-0258729	1043	2
HARRIMAN GRANT O	CPT	O-0317591	1144	2
HARRIMAN LOREN F	MAJ	O-1822397	1265	1
HARRIMAN ROGER L	LTC	O-0222082	0262	3
HARRIMAN WALLACE R	LTC	O-0278949	0864	3
HARRINGTON ALBERT T	COL	O-0217716	0454	3
HARRINGTON ARTHUR V	COL	O-0170114	0360	3
HARRINGTON DAVID B	LTC	O-0284720	1060	3
HARRINGTON EDWARD R	LTC	O-0919821	0365	3
HARRINGTON EUGENE S	CW2	W-2210190	1264	1
HARRINGTON FERDINAND	LTC	O-0251707	1266	3
HARRINGTON HARRY J	CW3	W-2142851	0359	1
HARRINGTON HUGH T	LTC	O-0906151	1167	3
HARRINGTON JACK	MAJ	O-1550399	1158	1
HARRINGTON JACK	MAJ	O-1557014	1161	1
HARRINGTON JACK P	CPT	O-1583064	0950	2
HARRINGTON JAMES A	MAJ	O-2031855	0363	1
HARRINGTON JAMES C	1LT	O-1321630	0746	2
HARRINGTON JAMES I	MAJ	O-1555980	0460	1
HARRINGTON JANET H	MAJ	N-0728117	0361	1
HARRINGTON JOHN J	LTC	O-1170408	1067	1
HARRINGTON JOHN J	LTC	O-1542675	1060	2
HARRINGTON JOHN V	CW3	W-2145445	1061	1
HARRINGTON LEO J	CPT	O-1556436	0454	1
HARRINGTON OMAR L	MAJ	O-1112199	0764	1
HARRINGTON PATRICK	1LT	O-1321918	0445	2
HARRINGTON PAUL F	MAJ	O-1586643	0861	2
HARRINGTON RALPH B	LTC	O-0188183	0358	3
HARRINGTON ROBERT C	CPT	O-0114613	0355	3
HARRINGTON ROBERTS	MAJ	O-0231037	0247	2
HARRINGTON SAMUEL H	MAJ	O-1578573	0757	1
HARRINGTON TIM J	1LT	O-1019074	0946	2
HARRINGTON V B	1LT	O-1045453	1044	2
HARRINGTON WILLIAM H	MAJ	O-1313601	0565	1
HARRINGTON WILLIAM J	CPT	O-0374234	0650	1
HARRINGTON WILLIAM J	LTC	O-1039375	0467	1
HARRIS ALBERT R	LTC	O-0263747	0961	3
HARRIS ALVIN V	LTC	O-1543476	0765	2
HARRIS ANTHONY R	LTC	O-0156156	0655	3
HARRIS ARCHIE M	LTC	O-0490966	0258	1
HARRIS ARTHUR O	LTC	O-0495957	0855	1
HARRIS AUGUST W	LTC	O-0189202	0746	2
HARRIS BARTON L	COL	O-0281638	0963	1
HARRIS BENJAMIN	COL	O-0137703	0852	3
HARRIS BENJAMIN F	CW3	W-2146451	1057	1
HARRIS BRACE W	2LT	O-0493104	0443	2
HARRIS BRUCE W	CW3	W-2206865	0666	1
HARRIS CARL M	LTC	O-1283251	1265	1
HARRIS CARMON C	LTC	O-0345016	1264	3

NAME	GRADE	SVC NO	DATE RET MO YR	RET CODE
HARRIS CARROLL T	COL	0-0187527	1051	3
HARRIS CATHERINE	MAJ	N-0735196	C962	1
HARRIS CECIL F	CW3	W-2148595	C564	1
HARRIS CECIL M	LTC	0-0119840	0750	3
HARRIS CECIL O	LTC	0-0419673	0562	1
HARRIS CECIL R	CW2	W-2150569	0361	1
HARRIS CHARLES A	LTC	C-1996744	0966	1
HARRIS CHARLES A	CPT	0-0451302	0647	2
HARRIS CHARLES C	CPT	0-1899396	0157	1
HARRIS CHARLES F	LTC	0-0279038	0958	3
HARRIS CHARLES E	LTC	0-0420465	C860	1
HARRIS CHAUNCY L	MAJ	C-0348773	0746	2
HARRIS CHESTER S	COL	C-0102898	0648	3
HARRIS CLEVELAND	LTC	0-1103680	C962	1
HARRIS CLIFFORD W	LTC	0-0372739	C360	1
HARRIS CLYDE A	MAJ	0-0301078	C766	3
HARRIS CURTIS A	2LT	0-1642154	C245	2
HARRIS DANIEL G	1LT	0-1341424	0649	2
HARRIS DAVID M	LTC	0-1591784	1162	1
HARRIS DON C	CPT	0-0921676	1045	2
HARRIS DUPONT G	LTC	0-0275754	1063	3
HARRIS EARL B	LTC	0-1018891	0867	1
HARRIS EARL R	MAJ	0-1822797	C262	1
HARRIS EDMUND R	CPT	0-1994925	C261	2
HARRIS EDWARD S	LTC	0-0290420	0263	2
HARRIS EDWIN M	1LT	0-1283068	C557	1
HARRIS ELMER J	MAJ	C-0417848	0347	2
HARRIS ELWOOD L	CPT	0-0361560	0346	2
HARRIS ELWOOD O	LTC	0-1176654	0763	1
HARRIS EUGENE	MAJ	0-2033146	0661	1
HARRIS EUGENE D	LTC	0-1637615	C264	1
HARRIS FORREST C	MAJ	C-2019736	0758	1
HARRIS FRANCIS J	CPT	0-0194461	C648	3
HARRIS FRANCIS W	MAJ	0-1542648	1165	1
HARRIS FRANK W	MAJ	C-0303000	0666	3
HARRIS FRED G	MAJ	0-1885275	C867	1
HARRIS FRED M	COL	0-0389405	0965	1
HARRIS FRED P	MAJ	C-0322550	C962	3
HARRIS FREDERICK	MAJ	0-0388785	C846	2
HARRIS GEORGE B	MAJ	0-0544855	C267	3
HARRIS GEORGE E	LTC	0-1308212	1266	1
HARRIS GEORGE H	CPT	0-1577289	1043	2
HARRIS GLEN W	LTC	0-1106800	1262	1
HARRIS GLYNN M	CPT	0-2204305	1063	2
HARRIS GOLON B	LTC	C-0182665	C351	3
HARRIS GUY J	LTC	0-1322221	C963	1
HARRIS HAROLD	CPT	0-2262251	C960	1
HARRIS HAROLD A	LTC	0-0168169	1055	3
HARRIS HAROLD B	MAJ	0-0356609	0745	1
HARRIS HAROLD E	MAJ	C-0983561	1262	1
HARRIS HARRY F	MAJ	0-0245160	1054	3
HARRIS HARRY L	WO1	W-2149194	0256	1
HARRIS HAWES C	LTC	0-0224890	0559	3
HARRIS HENRY C	LTC	0-0206404	C753	3
HARRIS HERBERT H	MAJ	C-0259573	C146	2
HARRIS HERBERT L	1LT	0-2030520	0458	2
HARRIS HERSHEL M	1LT	C-1167889	0744	2
HARRIS HIRAM S	1LT	0-0108744	C529	1
HARRIS HOWARD W	LTC	0-2033258	C965	1
HARRIS HOYETTE E	LTC	0-1285583	C555	1
HARRIS IRVING	CPT	0-0468823	1044	2
HARRIS IRVING C	1LT	C-0960747	0352	2
HARRIS IVAN H	LTC	0-0264500	0152	2
HARRIS J C	CW2	W-2151765	1163	1
HARRIS JACK M	1LT	0-1824311	C253	1
HARRIS JAMES C	LTC	0-0158082	0660	3
HARRIS JAMES C	CW3	W-2141850	0967	1
HARRIS JAMES E	LTC	0-0492972	0854	1
HARRIS JAMES E	CPT	0-1920224	0463	1
HARRIS JAMES F	1LT	C-1049873	1144	2
HARRIS JAMES O	CW2	W-2210406	0562	1
HARRIS JOHN D	1LT	0-0499845	1144	2
HARRIS JOHN E	LTC	0-0370107	0860	1
HARRIS JOHN E	MAJ	0-1174313	1060	1
HARRIS JOHN J	MAJ	C-0998380	C161	1
HARRIS JOHN L	MAJ	0-0243366	0864	3
HARRIS JOHN M	CPT	0-0317096	0446	2
HARRIS JOHN R	MAJ	0-0218312	0648	3
HARRIS JOHN R	COL	C-0154469	0451	3
HARRIS JOHN R	MAJ	0-2033200	0763	1
HARRIS JOSEPH A	MAJ	0-1298223	0960	1
HARRIS JOSEPH M	MAJ	0-0239716	0146	2
HARRIS JR EARL M	MAJ	0-1796616	0965	1
HARRIS JR EDWARD N	COL	0-0205238	0646	2
HARRIS JR FLETCHER W	2LT	0-0438987	0445	2
HARRIS JR HARDIE F	2LT	0-1039376	1044	2
HARRIS JR HENRY U	1LT	0-1339989	1047	2
HARRIS JR MARTIN H	LTC	0-0403176	0562	1
HARRIS JR ROBERT R	MAJ	0-2266396	0267	1
HARRIS KARL S	MAJ	0-1550183	1160	1
HARRIS KARL W	LTC	0-0262086	0964	3
HARRIS LEO E	1LT	0-1313240	0446	2
HARRIS LEONARD R	CW2	W-2144785	0862	1
HARRIS LESLIE H	MAJ	0-2037795	0863	1
HARRIS LESTER A	1LT	0-1048004	0447	2
HARRIS LLOYD F	COL	0-0204390	0346	2
HARRIS LOUIS C	LTC	0-0300046	0866	3
HARRIS LOWRY R	COL	0-0264290	0855	3
HARRIS LOYD E	COL	C-0215001	1060	3
HARRIS MAN E	LTC	0-0422348	0962	1
HARRIS MAURICE H	CPT	0-0281100	1043	2
HARRIS MCGREW	LTC	0-0250299	0859	1
HARRIS MEADE C	CPT	0-1108725	0647	2
HARRIS MERLE E	MAJ	C-1578574	0859	1
HARRIS MERRILL F	CPT	0-1110538	1046	2
HARRIS MILAM K	1LT	0-0399472	0145	2
HARRIS MILDRED G	2LT	N-0779012	0445	2
HARRIS NATHAN	MAJ	0-0129180	1045	2
HARRIS NEMI	CW2	W-2210158	1262	1
HARRIS NORMAN J	CPT	0-0321754	0144	2
HARRIS ONTY L	MAJ	0-0491943	1155	1
HARRIS PAUL	LTC	0-1114530	0762	1
HARRIS PAUL C	MAJ	0-2006625	C656	1
HARRIS PAUL C	CPT	0-1303500	0447	2
HARRIS PAUL D	LTC	0-1311646	0265	1
HARRIS PAUL R	1LT	0-1797820	0446	2
HARRIS PERRY F	CPT	0-1113243	1262	1
HARRIS PRICE F	MAJ	0-1599128	0563	1
HARRIS RAY A	1LT	0-1299743	0546	2
HARRIS RAY C	CPT	0-0416966	0546	2
HARRIS RAY M	COL	0-0900666	1067	3
HARRIS RAYMOND C	COL	0-0455641	0267	3
HARRIS RHETT C	COL	0-0445650	0667	1
HARRIS ROBERT A	1LT	0-1032715	1045	2
HARRIS ROBERT K	CPT	0-1046474	0847	2
HARRIS ROBERT L	COL	0-0255543	1057	3
HARRIS ROBERT L	CW2	W-2150636	1263	2
HARRIS ROBERT M	LTC	0-0235413	0865	1
HARRIS ROBERT W	LTC	0-1579755	0861	1
HARRIS RONALD M	COL	0-0223254	0451	3
HARRIS ROSS	1LT	0-1324332	0845	2
HARRIS ROY J	COL	0-0217844	1062	3
HARRIS RUSSELL B	2LT	0-1334568	0246	2
HARRIS SAMUEL M	LTC	0-1039022	1165	1
HARRIS SHIRLEY W	LTC	0-0473720	0863	1
HARRIS SIDNEY B	MAJ	0-0163044	0844	2
HARRIS STACY C	CW4	W-2106546	0358	1
HARRIS THEODORE D	CW4	W-2141576	0962	1
HARRIS THOMAS A	CPT	0-1341781	1060	1
HARRIS THOMAS G	CPT	0-1945559	0851	2
HARRIS THOMAS R	LTC	0-0902293	0663	1
HARRIS TOWNES M	LTC	0-0242497	0859	3
HARRIS TRUITT W	MAJ	0-1290942	0865	2
HARRIS VENDIA M	CPT	0-0307454	0944	2
HARRIS VERNER C	MAJ	0-1171578	0361	1
HARRIS VICTOR W	LTC	0-0348241	0560	1
HARRIS WARREN S	CPT	0-0994090	1159	2
HARRIS WEST J	CW3	W-2152067	0363	1
HARRIS WILLIAM C	CPT	0-1301138	1050	2
HARRIS WILLIAM C	MAJ	0-2262487	1061	1
HARRIS WILLIAM C	CPT	0-2262489	C161	1
HARRIS WILLIAM D	LTC	0-1300030	0959	1
HARRIS WILLIAM E	MAJ	0-1303501	0462	2
HARRIS WILLIAM F	MAJ	0-2262669	0266	1
HARRIS WILLIAM G	MAJ	C-2039652	1060	1
HARRIS WILLIAM H	MAJ	0-0405468	0865	1
HARRIS WILLIAM L	LTC	0-0502315	C856	1
HARRIS WILLIAM O	CW2	W-2150359	0662	1
HARRIS WILLIE P	MAJ	N-0700231	1044	1
HARRIS ZED C	LTC	0-0401427	0560	1
HARRISON ALFRED H	1LT	0-1310438	1044	2
HARRISON ANNA L	2LT	N-0777557	C746	1
HARRISON ARTHUR B	CW2	W-2145257	1058	1
HARRISON ARTHUR G	CPT	0-0513037	C649	1
HARRISON BENNIE J	LTC	0-1017561	0663	1
HARRISON BRUCE W	LTC	0-1013454	0758	1
HARRISON BUFORD M	MAJ	C-1002236	0861	1
HARRISON CECIL W	LTC	0-2000522	C965	1
HARRISON CHARLES R	CPT	0-0979224	1060	1
HARRISON CHARLES W	LTC	0-1167890	1262	1
HARRISON CLIFFORD W	CW3	W-2143339	0162	1
HARRISON CLINT H	COL	0-0163204	0255	3
HARRISON DAVID G	CPT	0-1253768	C146	2
HARRISON DAVID S	MAJ	C-1594218	1064	3
HARRISON EDMUND W	MAJ	C-0256879	C464	3
HARRISON EDWARD R	MAJ	0-1305922	1060	1
HARRISON EDWIN S	LTC	0-1019760	0567	1
HARRISON ERNEST L	MAJ	0-0932982	1065	2
HARRISON EUGENE L	LTC	0-1594219	0563	1
HARRISON FRANCIS L	CPT	0-0405950	0547	2
HARRISON FRANCIS M	LTC	0-0260554	C763	3
HARRISON FRANKLIN P	LTC	0-1587062	C463	1
HARRISON FRED L	COL	0-0224163	C355	2
HARRISON GEORGE R	LTC	0-1325390	C155	1
HARRISON GEORGE W	CPT	0-2034969	1145	2
HARRISON GRAYDON N	LTC	C-0279802	C260	1
HARRISON HAROLD J	1LT	0-1925631	0657	2
HARRISON HARRY	LTC	0-1295544	C666	1
HARRISON HARVEY G	CW4	W-2104129	0659	1
HARRISON HASKEL O	MAJ	C-0975499	0763	1
HARRISON HENRY H	COL	0-0195101	0648	3
HARRISON HOWARD W	CPT	0-1295016	C861	1
HARRISON IVAN H	LTC	0-1011440	C661	1
HARRISON JAMES C	MAJ	0-1183308	C961	1
HARRISON JESSE W	CW2	W-2146152	C856	1
HARRISON JOE T	LTC	0-1333970	C865	1
HARRISON JOHN E	COL	0-0497068	0163	1
HARRISON JR DESALES	1LT	0-1181900	1046	2
HARRISON JR FESTUS E	MAJ	C-1037826	0161	1
HARRISON JR JAMES O	2LT	0-1336062	C747	2
HARRISON JR JOHN E	CPT	0-0384036	0646	2
HARRISON JR LESLIE R	MAJ	0-0938013	0163	1
HARRISON JR LUDY C	MAJ	C-2210014	0263	1
HARRISON JR PETER J	2LT	0-1824460	0943	2
HARRISON JR W H	M G	0-0235649	0361	3
HARRISON JR WILLIAM	MAJ	C-0469752	0647	2
HARRISON LESLIE S	CPT	0-0528798	1145	2
HARRISON LESTER G	1LT	0-0108538	C539	1
HARRISON LOUIS H	CW3	W-2204981	0664	1
HARRISON LUCIEN E	LTC	0-0196650	1060	3
HARRISON LUCIUS A	MAJ	0-0199917	0756	3
HARRISON MERRIT F	COL	0-0232498	C260	1
HARRISON MICHAEL	1LT	C-1326630	C546	1
HARRISON OLIN C	LTC	0-1306584	0763	1
HARRISON OLSON A	MAJ	0-0495958	1050	1
HARRISON PAUL	MAJ	0-0482998	1046	1
HARRISON RICHARD B	CPT	0-1698866	0350	1
HARRISON RICHARD H	COL	C-0152584	0146	2
HARRISON RICHARD H	MAJ	0-0298035	C859	1
HARRISON RICHARD L	MAJ	0-0286936	1061	3
HARRISON ROBERT C	CW3	W-2153161	0763	1
HARRISON ROBERT O	LTC	0-0222663	C765	3
HARRISON ROBERT C	LTC	0-0182944	0749	1
HARRISON ROBERT M	LTC	C-0308305	C545	2
HARRISON ROLLIE M	LTC	0-0338969	1160	3
HARRISON ROYAL A	MAJ	C-0510573	1061	2
HARRISON SAMUEL G	COL	0-0184461	0851	3
HARRISON SAMUEL L	CW4	W-2122915	C456	1
HARRISON SEIDEL W	CW2	W-2151820	1059	2
HARRISON SHELBY A	MAJ	0-1552083	0759	1
HARRISON STANLEY L	COL	0-0272773	0367	3
HARRISON THOMAS D	LTC	0-0540392	0964	1
HARRISON VERGIL	CW2	W-2112224	C845	2
HARRISON WILBERT G	MAJ	C-1049874	C460	1
HARRISON WILLIAM F	MAJ	0-1560279	0363	1
HARRISON WILLIAM H	CW3	W-2149047	0365	1
HARRISON WILLIAM L	LTC	0-0313433	0854	1
HARRISS JR ANDREW H	COL	0-0204938	0458	3
HARRISS LYNN M F	LTC	0-0248644	0567	3
HARRITT GILBERT N	CPT	0-0225818	0762	3
HARROD CARROLL O	CPT	0-1178179	0951	2
HARROD DENNETTE A	CPT	0-0423194	1046	2
HARROD GEORGE W	CPT	0-1039023	0166	3
HARROD WILLIAM E	LTC	0-1331286	1167	1
HARROFF ROBERT E	COL	0-0271930	1067	3
HARROLD DONALD W	LTC	0-1013019	0364	2
HARROVER WILLIAM W	1LT	0-1291813	0446	2
HARROW NORMAN L	1LT	0-1049875	0845	2
HARROWER PAUL D	LTC	0-0124427	0153	3
HARRSCH SYLVANUS O	CW2	W-2150364	0563	1
HARRY EDWARD B	COL	0-0173200	0455	3
HARRY JAMES F	LTC	0-1328900	1265	1
HARRY JOSEPH H	LTC	0-0276118	0866	3
HARRY JR JOHN C	CPT	0-0503250	0845	2
HARRY ROBERT H	1LT	0-0527817	0446	2
HARRY WAYNE E	CW3	W-2150121	1265	1
HARSFIELD RAPHAEL E	1LT	0-2048077	0547	2
HARSHBARGER GLENN A	COL	0-0278982	0961	3
HARSHMAN CHARLES F	MAJ	0-0233812	0250	3
HARSHMAN CLARENCE C	COL	0-0180062	1153	3
HARSIN ALVA	MAJ	0-0501303	1053	1
HARSKI KAZIMIERZ	CW2	W-2211684	0567	1
HARSON JR MAYC	CW3	W-2146509	0264	1
HARSTER ARNOLD	1LT	0-1306093	1145	2
HART ALAN L	COL	0-0154184	0854	3
HART ALLAN S	1LT	0-1315823	0945	2
HART ANNA P	CPT	N-0700579	0945	1
HART BAYARD W	COL	0-0421879	0960	1
HART CHARLES W	LTC	0-0262990	0166	3
HART CLARENCE	COL	0-0410164	0767	1
HART CLARENCE R	LTC	0-1051588	0765	1
HART CLIFFORD C	CPT	0-1185405	0759	1
HART DANIEL F	CW3	W-2132546	1159	1
HART DEN O	MAJ	0-1165871	1050	1
HART DONALD F	CW2	W-2149439	0560	2
HART EARL E	CW4	W-2142462	1058	1
HART EARL P	CW3	W-2146775	0959	1
HART EDWARD F	LTC	0-0318601	0160	1
HART FRED L	LTC	0-1535190	0158	1
HART GEORGE H	MAJ	0-0146786	0748	3
HART HAL I	CPT	0-1319945	0946	2
HART HAROLD L	COL	0-0324325	0865	3
HART HARRY	1LT	0-0208048	0539	1
HART HUGH H	LTC	0-0241562	0265	3
HART IRVIN	CPT	0-1018423	0948	2
HART JAMES A	LTC	0-0252037	0765	3
HART JEROME G	1LT	0-1012526	0444	2
HART JOHN A	CPT	0-0267766	0445	2
HART JOHN P	CPT	0-0225299	0750	1
HART JOHN T	LTC	C-1291465	0766	1
HART JOSEPH F	COL	0-0322932	C657	1
HART JR ANDREW D	LTC	0-0443559	0245	2
HART JR CARROLL P	CPT	0-1307012	0246	2
HART JR CHARLES H	COL	0-0262474	0967	3
HART JR FRANK J	1LT	0-1287873	0645	2
HART JR H B	LTC	0-1319277	0165	1
HART KENNETH P	LTC	0-1645028	1162	1
HART LEONARD W	LTC	0-1108727	0865	1
HART LUTHER	MAJ	0-0472323	0953	1
HART NORMAN E	LTC	0-0180132	0450	2

NAME	GRADE	SVC NO	DATE RET MO YR	RET CODE
HART OLIVER J	CPT	0-0193361	0254	3
HART OLIVER J	COL	0-0230566	1161	3
HART PAUL H	COL	0-0276506	0361	3
HART PHIL C	MAJ	C-C332497	0465	3
HART RALPH L	1LT	C-1011723	C745	2
HART RICHARD L	LTC	0-1550815	0955	1
HART RICHARD M	CPT	0-0426660	C747	2
HART RICHARD W	2LT	0-1310102	0445	2
HART ROBERT E	CW3	W-2152546	0265	1
HART ROBERT H	LTC	C-1944960	1060	1
HART RUSSELL C	LTC	C-2036909	C465	1
HART SCOTT P	COL	0-0132717	1049	3
HART STANLEY E	LTC	0-1643647	1166	3
HART WALTER R	MAJ	0-0167311	0655	3
HART WILLARD L	LTC	0-0499727	0557	3
HART WILLIAM	COL	C-0231439	0864	3
HART WILLIAM S	MAJ	C-1104195	C961	1
HART WILLIAM S	CW2	W-2145007	C463	1
HART WILLIAM T	CPT	0-0293226	0146	2
HARTOEGEN RICHARD P	COL	0-0178112	C255	3
HARTE LAWRENCE A	MAJ	0-C191495	C762	3
HARTEL GUNTHER F	LTC	0-1105456	0261	1
HARTEN CLARENCE D	CPT	C-0263122	C345	2
HARTENSTINE ELIAS H	WO1	W-2113764	C547	1
HARTER DONALD H	MAJ	0-1288544	C158	1
HARTER JEAN A	CW3	V-0500835	C263	1
HARTER JOHN O	CPT	0-0442269	0447	2
HARTER PAUL O	COL	0-0194154	0758	3
HARTER RAYMOND A	LTC	C-0254778	C166	3
HARTFORD WILLIAM S	2LT	C-2009545	C448	1
HARTHCOCK CLYDE A	MAJ	0-1115919	0358	1
HARTLE HARVEY L	MAJ	C-1031490	C261	1
HARTLERODAD FRANK C	LTC	0-0223923	1047	2
HARTLEY ALBERT I	CPT	0-1879141	C863	2
HARTLEY CLYDE R	MAJ	N-0727268	C264	2
HARTLEY HARRY	MAJ	C-0187432	1047	1
HARTLEY JACK H	MAJ	0-1001145	C960	1
HARTLEY JAMES R	CW3	W-2148117	0562	1
HARTLEY RICHARD S	MAJ	C-0497062	1151	2
HARTLEY ROBERT D	COL	0-0274471	1065	3
HARTLEY RUSSELL W	2LT	0-1324727	C545	2
HARTLEY SAMUEL H	LTC	0-C903042	1062	3
HARTLEY WILLIAM A	CPT	0-2017541	C460	2
HARTLINE NOEL V	CPT	0-0498836	1153	2
HARTMAN AMMON N	COL	0-0317322	1060	1
HARTMAN CARL	MAJ	0-0970419	0762	1
HARTMAN EDWARD W	LTC	0-0319423	0159	1
HARTMAN FRED L	COL	0-0246993	0662	3
HARTMAN GEORGE J	CPT	0-0451116	0345	2
HARTMAN GEORGE L	MAJ	0-0371470	0545	2
HARTMAN GLENN W	LTC	C-04C2908	C161	1
HARTMAN HENRY H	WO1	W-2116465	0245	2
HARTMAN HIRAM W	MAJ	0-1341968	0961	1
HARTMAN IRA F	CPT	C-1697044	C745	2
HARTMAN JEAN F	CPT	0-1288225	C347	2
HARTMAN JOSEPH W P	MAJ	0-0987426	C764	1
HARTMAN JR ALBERT W	MAJ	0-0322328	0146	2
HARTMAN LEROY E	1LT	0-1297028	C844	2
HARTMAN MATTHEW J	CPT	0-1341969	0866	1
HARTMAN PAULINE A	1LT	N-0755843	0946	2
HARTMAN ROBERT W	LTC	C-0474092	0350	1
HARTMAN RUSSELL M	LTC	0-0478846	0859	2
HARTMAN SIDNEY J	MAJ	C-1542919	0557	1
HARTMAN STANLEY E	COL	0-0256165	0659	3
HARTMAN WILLIAM T	LTC	0-0307566	1067	1
HARTMANN CATHERINE	MAJ	N-0775664	C865	1
HARTMANN ELIZABETH	MAJ	N-0732882	C248	1
HARTMANN FRANKLYN J	LTC	0-0360342	C963	3
HARTMANN WILLIAM F	LTC	0-0309525	C267	3
HARTNER JR ALVIN H	LTC	0-1642162	1263	1
HARTNESS GEORGE Y	LTC	0-0279579	0860	3
HARTNESS ROBERT W	LTC	C-0324162	1060	3
HARTNESS WILLIAM H	LTC	0-0738553	0763	1
HARTNETT RICHARD J	CPT	0-0318809	C244	2
HARTNETT THOMAS T	CPT	0-1287874	C745	2
HARTOM ELBERT M	MAJ	C-0178232	0760	3
HARTON WILLIAM M	COL	C-0335116	0953	3
HARTS CLEMENT B	P G	0-0241711	0864	3
HARTSELL CHARLES F	MAJ	0-1548831	0558	1
HARTSELL JULIUS W	CW2	W-2208344	1063	1
HARTSHORN DUANE F	COL	C-0296731	0859	3
HARTSHORN JACK W	MAJ	0-0975880	0962	1
HARTSIC RALPH G	1LT	0-1016661	1145	2
HARTUNG ALBERT H	1LT	0-0277313	1045	2
HARTUNG JOHN S	WO1	W-2128670	0845	2
HARTUNG JOSEPH P	MAJ	0-1303502	0356	1
HARTUNG KENNETH B	LTC	0-0555376	0764	1
HARTWELL GEORGE N	MAJ	C-0424333	0948	2
HARTWELL OLIVER W	LTC	0-0323150	0267	3
HARTWELL VINTON J	MAJ	0-1045104	0461	1
HARTWICK FRED W	LTC	0-0270112	0863	3
HARTWICK ROBERT	CPT	0-1113732	0146	2
HARTWIG CARL J	LTC	0-0262245	0761	3
HARTWIG HARVEY H	LTC	0-0431351	0865	1
HARTY JAMES A	CPT	0-1284866	0755	1
HARTY JAMES F	LTC	0-0320390	0159	1
HARTY NORMAN C	1LT	0-1323692	0446	1
HARTY PATRICK H	MAJ	0-1047561	0161	1
HARTZ FRANCIS M	MAJ	0-0322699	1045	2
HARTZ WALTER F	MAJ	C-2017848	0262	1
HARTZEL NATHAN S	LTC	0-1795896	0562	1
HARTZELL CLYDE S	MAJ	0-0236260	0447	1
HARTZELL HAROLD P	COL	0-0292196	0759	1
HARTZELL HERBERT F	COL	C-1633935	0867	1
HARTZOG GEORGE A	LTC	0-0475273	0954	1
HARUTUN JAMES J	LTC	0-0270579	1066	3
HARVEL BENJAMIN H	CW4	W-2143277	0160	1
HARVELL CATHERINE	1LT	N-0721814	1146	1
HARVELL CLAUDIA M	CPT	N-0764234	1047	1
HARVEY ALBERT W	LTC	0-0397020	0557	2
HARVEY CARL S	CW2	W-2127172	0457	1
HARVEY CHARLES E	MAJ	C-0464523	0154	3
HARVEY CHARLES S	LTC	0-0955562	0767	1
HARVEY CLINTON C	LTC	0-1C28003	0564	1
HARVEY CURTIS B	CW2	W-3150903	0566	1
HARVEY EDWIN	CPT	0-1946981	0164	1
HARVEY FRANK E	LTC	0-1116961	0263	1
HARVEY FRANK F	CW2	W-2206367	0163	1
HARVEY FRANK N	CPT	C-0319499	0245	2
HARVEY GEORGE G	LTC	C-019670R	0358	3
HARVEY GEORGE M	MAJ	0-1052382	0747	2
HARVEY HOWARD A L	MAJ	0-0314538	0752	1
HARVEY JAMES H	MAJ	0-1010594	1062	1
HARVEY JAMES L	CPT	0-0155478	0450	3
HARVEY JAMES O	MAJ	0-0377294	0860	1
HARVEY JOHN E	CPT	0-095425C	0661	1
HARVEY JOHN F	COL	0-0214401	0254	3
HARVEY JOHN F	1LT	0-1633936	0644	2
HARVEY JOHN J	LTC	0-1043979	1162	1
HARVEY JR ALLEN P	1LT	0-1C12148	1045	2
HARVEY JR JOSEPH S	CPT	0-1317911	1046	2
HARVEY JR THOMAS J	COL	C-0238586	0565	3
HARVEY KENNETH L	CW4	W-2145059	0166	1
HARVEY LEAMAN C	MAJ	0-0963133	0662	1
HARVEY LILA P	CPT	N-0775974	1153	2
HARVEY MURLAN E	LTC	0-2029767	C467	1
HARVEY ORVILLE M	CW3	W-2141577	C659	1
HARVEY OWEN G	MAJ	C-1341542	0765	1
HARVEY QUINTON C	COL	0-0152983	0455	3
HARVEY RALPH A	LTC	0-0284889	1158	1
HARVEY RALPH E	CPT	0-0370690	0856	1
HARVEY RAYMOND	LTC	0-1286281	0562	1
HARVEY STEPHEN A	CPT	0-0477062	0554	1
HARVEY WALTER W	LTC	0-1297362	1162	2
HARVEY WARREN E	LTC	0-0453471	1157	1
HARVEY WILLIAM A	CPT	0-0214301	1062	3
HARVEY WILLIAM I	MAJ	0-1917979	0765	1
HARVEY WILLIAM V	CPT	0-1314629	1160	1
HARVILL HALBERT	LTC	0-0131580	1153	3
HARVIN CHARLES M	MAJ	0-0183825	1046	2
HARVIN JR LUCIUS H	2LT	0-0336319	1043	2
HARWARD JAMES R	MAJ	C-1951482	0364	1
HARWELL ALDEN C	1LT	0-1016154	1045	2
HARWELL JOHN O	LTC	0-1596351	0761	1
HARWELL JOHN T	2LT	0-1799446	C748	1
HARWELL WARNOCK O	LTC	0-0531981	0763	1
HARWOOD DEWEY S	LTC	0-0274709	0658	3
HARWOOD FREDRICK C	CPT	0-1650568	0647	2
HARWOOD GILBERT W	CW2	W-2110324	C653	1
HARWOOD HARRY L	1LT	0-0335442	0146	2
HARWOOD HORACE E	COL	C-0224578	C359	1
HARWOOD VICTOR K	LTC	0-1291112	0766	1
HASAL DIOGENES B	CPT	0-1896588	0557	1
HASBROOK WILLIAM	CPT	0-0383890	0746	2
HASBROUCK ELEANOR T	MAJ	N-0756145	0663	2
HASCALL FRANK L	CPT	0-0336265	C845	2
HASCALL JOHN L	COL	0-0131772	C648	3
HASCALL ROBERT E	COL	0-0289291	0861	1
HASE RAYMOND C	LTC	0-0239524	1265	3
HASELDEN JOSEPH H	1LT	0-1585587	0545	2
HASELTINE DUDLEY J	LTC	0-0374656	0964	1
HASEN JOHN S	CPT	0-0188086	C648	3
HASENRITTER ELBERT	COL	0-0250537	1166	3
HASFJORD HAROLD	LTC	0-0392279	C860	1
HASH AGNES R	1LT	L-0302632	1147	2
HASH CECIL J	CPT	0-2046609	0455	1
HASH CHARLES W	COL	C-03356C8	0265	1
HASH STANLEY G	LTC	0-1101478	C760	1
HASHAGEN ALBERT J	COL	C-0171477	C549	2
HASHAGEN EDWARD H	MAJ	0-0382555	C260	1
HASHAGEN RICHARD C	LTC	0-0317746	0360	1
HASHAM GEORGE J	MAJ	0-1080112	0260	1
HASHAM ROLUS K	MAJ	C-0203504	C755	3
HASHIMOTO MASAYUKI	CW4	W-2136381	C865	1
HASIE RAT W	MAJ	0-1645642	0361	1
HASIS HERBERT	LTC	0-1823294	C563	1
HASKELL CHARLES C	1LT	0-1059484	0746	2
HASKELL FRED L	CW3	W-2145678	0261	1
HASKELL GERALD G	CW4	W-2142044	C959	1
HASKELL HAROLD G	LTC	0-0470884	0240	2
HASKELL JOHN H F	COL	0-0222339	C246	2
HASKELL JOHN W	MAJ	C-1342331	0861	1
HASKELL LAURENT	LTC	0-0558049	0665	1
HASKELL LEROY	MAJ	C-0152704	0648	3
HASKELL WARREN R	LTC	0-0450473	0257	1
HASKETT REMEL	LTC	0-1303264	0761	1
HASKIN JOHN H	MAJ	C-0278414	0565	3
HASKIN JOHN J	MAJ	0-1054617	C859	1
HASKIN JOHN M	LTC	0-1010208	0164	1
HASKINS EDWARD T	MAJ	C-0410892	1146	2
HASKINS HAROLD A	MAJ	C-1341265	1065	1
HASKINS HOWARD E	MAJ	C-C412212	0162	1
HASKINS THOMAS C	LTC	0-1120114	C166	1
HASKINS WILLIAM R	CW3	W-2205168	1064	1
HASLAM JOHN H	WO1	W-2102986	0250	1
HASLAM JOHN W	CPT	0-1948118	1061	2
HASLAM LEGRAND	1LT	0-0377091	0451	2
HASLE HARTVICK K	MAJ	C-0461641	0246	2
HASLETT WILLIAM H	MAJ	C-1999025	C556	1
HASLIP JOHN L	LTC	0-1041568	C361	1
HASPEL JAMES E	2LT	0-2006409	1145	2
HASPETT HARRY A	CPT	0-1342269	0559	1
HASS ERNEST M	MAJ	0-0204405	1056	3
HASSE WILLIAM H	2LT	0-0542210	1045	2
HASSEL CLARENCE A	LTC	0-1062729	0767	1
HASSELBRINK DONALD H	CW3	W-2151756	C266	1
HASSELL ARTHUR S	COL	0-0208230	1063	3
HASSELL CHARLES H	MAJ	0-1286834	C465	1
HASSELL ELVIN	CW4	W-2132346	0763	1
HASSELL GEORGE E	MAJ	C-1876324	C765	1
HASSELL JOHN S	LTC	0-0319369	1160	1
HASSELL VERNON C	CPT	C-1305424	C959	1
HASSELO IRVING D	CPT	0-1298061	C647	2
HASSEMER ERWIN H	MAJ	0-0309375	C265	3
HASSEN ERWIN	CPT	0-0486757	0845	2
HASSETT WAMAN S	COL	0-0178083	0255	3
HASSIG JOHN L	LTC	0-0302409	0164	1
HASSLER MILBURN	LTC	0-0280065	0767	3
HASSMANN RUSSELL R	CPT	0-0949221	0163	1
HASTAIN JAMES E	COL	0-0243772	0960	3
HASTEN JOHN W	LTC	0-1039279	1163	1
HASTIE FRANCIS A	MAJ	0-1100584	0656	1
HASTIE FRANK B	LTC	0-0257500	0355	3
HASTIE ROBERT T	LTC	0-1703944	1061	1
HASTINGS CHARLES O	MAJ	0-0450884	1054	1
HASTINGS CHARLES W	1LT	0-0354647	0445	2
HASTINGS CLIFTON W	CW3	W-2203378	0766	1
HASTINGS DONALD H	MAJ	0-1301139	0167	1
HASTINGS DONALD W	CPT	0-1302096	0657	1
HASTINGS EMORY P	MAJ	0-0292364	1047	1
HASTINGS EUGENE F	MAJ	0-1117006	0263	1
HASTINGS JACK A	CPT	0-0439149	1048	2
HASTINGS JAMES L	MAJ	C-0360086	0549	1
HASTINGS RICHARD M	1LT	0-1055318	1145	2
HASTY FRANK C	LTC	0-0255191	0662	3
HASTY JR WINFRED L	LTC	0-0398480	0763	1
HASWELL JAMES H	1LT	0-1794941	1045	2
HATCH ALDEN C	COL	0-0306092	1060	1
HATCH AMOS C	LTC	0-C277056	0553	3
HATCH BERNARD F	COL	0-0218725	1057	3
HATCH DAVID R	MAJ	0-2025609	0461	1
HATCH DONALD R	1LT	0-5001161	1160	2
HATCH DONALD W	COL	0-1012006	0960	1
HATCH GRACE M	MAJ	N-0722109	0261	1
HATCH JR AZEL F	1LT	0-047638C	0344	2
HATCH JR FRANK M	LTC	0-0196356	0262	3
HATCH WILLARD C	LTC	0-0320393	1059	1
HATCH WILLARD C	LTC	0-2293991	0565	1
HATCH WILLIAM L	CPT	0-0317265	0146	2
HATCH WILLIAM M	LTC	0-0274355	0361	3
HATCHER CHARLES L	LTC	0-0157878	1045	2
HATCHER FREDERICK	LTC	0-0144743	0555	3
HATCHER GEORGE A	COL	0-0148454	0149	3
HATCHER HERBERT C	COL	0-0116222	0549	3
HATCHER HOWELL J	COL	0-0327179	0460	3
HATCHER JAMES E	COL	0-0186357	0558	3
HATCHER JAMES J	CPT	0-1651673	0958	2
HATCHER JOHN M	CW3	W-2146492	0960	1
HATCHER JR JOHN W	MAJ	0-045073C	0558	1
HATCHER JR WILLIAM F	MAJ	0-1101025	0161	1
HATCHER ROBERT J	LTC	0-0888599	1054	1
HATCHER THOMAS A	CPT	0-0180817	0163	3
HATCHER WILLIAM J	COL	0-0264151	0264	2
HATCHER WILLIAM L	CW2	W-214296C	0960	1
HATCHETT JAMES R	MAJ	0-132493C	C164	1
HATFIELD AMMON L	CPT	0-0438276	0455	1
HATFIELD ARTHUR R	LTC	0-1950177	0663	1
HATFIELD BENJAMIN F	COL	0-0272253	0866	3
HATFIELD CARSON A	MAJ	0-0156106	0650	3
HATFIELD CLYDE F	WO1	W-2146608	0866	3
HATFIELD ELMER L	2LT	0-1184222	0944	2
HATFIELD ELMER W	MAJ	0-2017689	C463	1
HATFIELD HILBERT H	CPT	0-2006375	0847	2
HATFIELD RAYMOND W	CW2	W-2144276	0661	1
HATFIELD ROBERT A	MAJ	0-2042703	0457	1
HATFIELD THEODORE C	CPT	0-0220562	0263	3
HATFIELD WEBSTER C	LTC	0-0162573	1C61	3
HATHAWAY CHARLES F	LTC	0-1280148	0361	1
HATHAWAY CLAYTON T	LTC	0-0398264	0257	1
HATHAWAY EUGENE F	LTC	0-0495175	0265	3
HATHAWAY GEORGE C	MAJ	0-1637633	0257	1
HATHAWAY JR THOMAS C	CPT	0-0966978	1266	1
HATHAWAY KENNETH E	LTC	0-1313403	0157	1
HATHAWAY ROY A	CPT	0-1001359	0759	1
HATHAWAY STILLMAN J	MAJ	0-0186576	1154	3
HATHAWAY VERNON L	CW2	W-2210624	0266	1
HATHAWAY WALTER H	COL	0-0251950	1265	3
HATHCOCK JESSE C	LTC	0-1298866	0867	1
HATHEWAY JR MAURICE	COL	0-0251464	0261	1
HATHORN RAUL A	COL	0-0348015	0162	3

NAME	GRADE	SVC NO	DATE RET MO YR	RET CODE
HATKE KENDALL J	LTC	O-0266875	0855	1
HATLEN CHARLES B	MAJ	O-0302281	0259	3
HATLEY CHARLES A	CW2	W-2145094	0659	1
HATLEY JAMES P	LTC	O-1173636	0857	1
HATLEY LLOYD E	MAJ	O-0425587	0247	2
HATSUKANO TOM S	MAJ	O-1699982	1061	1
HATT EARL	MAJ	O-0510517	0953	1
HATT KENDRICK A	MAJ	O-0119556	0358	3
HATT REGINALD L	COL	O-0208930	0161	3
HATTAN EMERSON W	MAJ	O-0711669	1262	1
HATTAWAY JOHN	CW2	W-2147874	0160	1
HATTEN CAS W	MAJ	O-2035189	0255	1
HATTEN GROVER C	LTC	O-0322029	0847	2
HATTEN JOHN H	MAJ	O-1176657	0861	1
HATTEN LEO A	LTC	O-1646235	0865	1
HATTEN WILLIAM W	CPT	O-0229441	0945	2
HATTENDORF ANTON P	MAJ	O-1684639	0346	2
HATTER MENZO E	CPT	O-1702977	0547	2
HATTERSLEY ELWOOD V	LTC	O-1048808	1165	1
HATTON BOYCE L	CPT	O-1598754	0557	1
HATTON ELMER	MAJ	O-0300034	0161	1
HATTON ELMO	MAJ	O-1001146	1055	1
HATTON THEODORE J	MAJ	O-0402250	1146	2
HATTORI EUGENE H	MAJ	O-2033622	0163	1
HATTOX JAMES H	2LT	O-1058539	1046	2
HATTY JR SAMUEL	CPT	O-0490295	1049	1
HAUBENNESTEL JOHN W	LTC	O-0207382	0659	3
HAUBERG HAROLD J	CPT	O-1342270	1058	1
HAUBNER WILLIAM P	MAJ	O-0974466	0266	1
HAUBRICK ROBERT T	WO1	W-2144387	0853	1
HAUBTMAN SYDNEY C	MAJ	O-0114422	1155	3
HAUCHMAN AARON	CW2	W-2148452	0654	2
HAUCK ARTHUR W	CPT	O-0237607	0554	3
HAUCK GEORGE F	COL	O-0213190	0363	3
HAUCK GEORGE K	CPT	O-0900513	0343	2
HAUCK RAYMOND L	LTC	O-0454099	1163	1
HAUCK WILLIAM F	1LT	O-1322334	1045	2
HAUER GEORGE T	1LT	O-0296063	0545	2
HAUER JOE M	LTC	O-1303882	1060	1
HAUER WALTER	CW3	W-2153156	0865	2
HAUFRECT FRED	CPT	O-0354788	0246	2
HAUG HAROLD J	2LT	O-1304384	0644	2
HAUG WARREN G	2LT	O-1314472	0245	2
HAUGE HARRY K	LTC	O-0435925	0651	1
HAUGE HOWARD L	LTC	O-0428733	0167	3
HAUGEN OBERT O	CW4	W-2135573	0964	1
HAUGENS EDWARD E	CPT	O-0543136	0846	2
HAUGH CALVIN J	1LT	O-1172897	1045	2
HAUGH JOSEPH G	MAJ	O-0509873	0747	2
HAUGHEY JOHN T	LTC	O-0227337	0961	3
HAUGHS HOMER	MAJ	O-0488710	0447	1
HAUGHT JR WILLIAM D	CW3	W-2150021	0265	1
HAUGHT LLOYD W	1LT	O-1821713	1044	2
HAUGNESS HAAKON A	1LT	O-1633940	0344	2
HAUGUM ELLA A	LTC	N-0732394	0464	3
HAUKENBERRY EVERETT	LTC	O-0225782	1163	3
HAUMAN ADAM J	CPT	O-1726214	0146	2
HAUMAN HAZEN L	MAJ	O-0491770	1045	2
HAUN BRUCE W	CW3	W-2148968	1064	1
HAUN LEROY W	WO1	W-2147521	0762	2
HAUN MADELINE M	MAJ	N-0795978	0865	1
HAUN PAUL	CPT	O-0473275	0246	2
HAUN ROLLAND C	LTC	O-0319866	0265	3
HAUPL JOHN	LTC	O-1575349	1162	1
HAUPT LOUIS L	LTC	O-0324377	0660	1
HAUPT MELVILLE I	1LT	O-1032447	0745	2
HAUPT WERNER R	LTC	O-1291466	0666	1
HAUPT WILLIAM G	LTC	O-0289312	0467	3
HAUPTMANN DAVID M	1LT	O-0523911	1045	2
HAUSAM HERBERT C	CPT	O-1646236	0765	1
HAUSAUER KARL F	MG	O-0142022	0257	3
HAUSE FRANK	CW2	W-2144119	0755	1
HAUSE HOWARD E	MAJ	O-0374633	0854	1
HAUSE WATSON L	1LT	O-1304526	0450	1
HAUSER FREDERICK	COL	O-0311304	0660	3

NAME	GRADE	SVC NO	DATE RET MO YR	RET CODE
HAUSER GEORGE J	LTC	O-1117441	0963	1
HAUSER GUS E	CPT	O-0401499	0246	2
HAUSER HENRY F	COL	O-0409744	0661	1
HAUSER ISADOR J	LTC	O-0300800	0246	2
HAUSER JOHN W	CPT	O-1693510	1145	2
HAUSER WALTER E	MAJ	O-1036186	0764	1
HAUSER WILLIAM F	MAJ	O-1186414	0762	1
HAUSER WILLIAM J	LTC	O-0288610	0263	3
HAUSLE PAUL M	CW2	W-2108498	0459	1
HAUSMAN JAMES H	LTC	O-0372397	0758	1
HAUSMANN ALBERTA	1LT	N-0723098	0845	1
HAUSWIRTH ERVING J	CPT	O-0254758	0463	3
HAVELY PAUL L	LTC	O-0350312	0767	3
HAVEN ALBERT D	LTC	O-0239267	0458	3
HAVEN FRANK S	MAJ	O-0257349	0446	2
HAVEN JAMES A	CPT	O-1933987	1265	2
HAVENICK NATHANIEL	COL	O-0348076	0560	2
HAVENS FLOYD	LTC	O-0446032	0862	1
HAVENS HENRY L	LTC	O-0397090	0766	1
HAVENS LEONARD M	MAJ	O-1651532	0465	1
HAVENS MILTON L	MAJ	O-0310812	0845	2
HAVENS ORIN D	CW3	W-2203363	1263	1
HAVENS RICHARD M	CW3	W-2148556	1063	1
HAVER JOHN H	CPT	O-1015260	0565	2
HAVER ROBERT W	1LT	O-1313744	0945	2
HAVERSTICK HARRY L	LTC	O-0185786	0447	2
HAVERSTICK HARRY R	MAJ	O-1030672	0454	2
HAVIG CHRISTIAN	LTC	O-0451781	0158	1
HAVIGHORST RUSSEL K	COL	O-0113127	0352	3
HAVILAND EUGENE	MAJ	O-1290243	0965	1
HAVILAND HAROLD L	COL	O-0288842	1061	3
HAVILAND SCOTT D	CPT	O-1307819	0561	1
HAVILAND WARREN F	1LT	O-1055320	1152	2
HAVILAND WILLIAM A	COL	O-0161169	0855	1
HAVILL REGINALD	MAJ	O-0134874	0552	3
HAVILLAND HARLAN L	1LT	O-0239137	1162	3
HAVLIK JOHN	MAJ	O-1038669	0964	1
HAVLIN WILLIAM G	1LT	O-1105500	0846	2
HAVRANEK JAMES C	1LT	O-0369486	1045	2
HAVRE ANDREW H	MAJ	O-0964894	0765	1
HAVRILLA JOSEPH M	MAJ	O-0956886	0262	2
HAW HARRY H	1LT	O-0134872	0154	3
HAW JR MARVIN T	MAJ	O-0330924	0145	2
HAW PHILLIP	WO1	W-2123434	1045	2
HAWEKOTTE JOHN W	1LT	O-1012318	1145	2
HAWES ALBERT L	1LT	O-0162375	0645	2
HAWES HOWARD R	LTC	O-0379193	0758	1
HAWES MILTON O	LTC	O-0239299	0554	2
HAWETHORNE ELLIOT G	1LT	O-1825123	0862	1
HAWFIELD ROBERT R	MAJ	O-0525321	1161	1
HAWK ALLEN D	CPT	O-0995689	0364	2
HAWK GEORGE W	MAJ	O-1291634	1160	1
HAWK JACK H	CPT	O-0367124	0960	2
HAWK JOHN F	1LT	O-2097187	1054	2
HAWK JR ASHER M	2LT	O-0441400	1143	2
HAWK JR ERNEST E	1LT	O-0452601	1044	2
HAWK JR JOE C	CPT	O-1169146	0646	2
HAWK LEWIS L	LTC	O-0327176	0262	3
HAWK OSMON R	LTC	O-0263123	0262	3
HAWK TOMMY C	MAJ	O-1890484	0766	1
HAWK WALTER D	CPT	O-0439320	0745	2
HAWKE HARRY L	1LT	O-0395312	0644	2
HAWKE LEONARD T	LTC	O-0415561	0163	1
HAWKER CHARLES W	MAJ	O-0476486	0757	1
HAWKES HOWARD G	MAJ	O-0185918	1054	3
HAWKES JR WINSLOW O	LTC	O-1697879	0164	1
HAWKES KENNETH	LTC	O-1552084	0460	1
HAWKES MAX V	CPT	O-2262583	0266	1
HAWKES THOMAS A	CPT	O-0181758	0845	2
HAWKING KENNETH T	COL	O-0469908	0764	1
HAWKINS CHARLES B	MAJ	O-1701526	0961	1
HAWKINS CHARLES F	CW2	W-2146885	1061	1
HAWKINS CLARENCE C	LTC	O-0340746	0561	1
HAWKINS DAMON	MAJ	O-1314286	0856	1
HAWKINS EDWARD S	MAJ	O-2016326	0265	1

NAME	GRADE	SVC NO	DATE RET MO YR	RET CODE
HAWKINS EDWIN D	CW3	W-2147270	0865	1
HAWKINS ELGIN G	CW3	W-2142424	0865	1
HAWKINS FORREST O	1LT	O-0425640	0945	2
HAWKINS FRED R	CPT	O-1884165	0964	1
HAWKINS GEORGE A	MAJ	O-0269513	1164	3
HAWKINS GEORGE B	CPT	O-2262114	1060	1
HAWKINS GEORGE F	COL	O-0233005	0765	3
HAWKINS GEORGE W	LTC	O-0353401	1059	1
HAWKINS GEORGIA M	MAJ	N-0734128	1266	3
HAWKINS HAROLD L	MAJ	O-1176658	0859	2
HAWKINS HARRY H	1LT	O-1184064	0749	1
HAWKINS HAZEL F	LTC	N-0730270	0962	1
HAWKINS HEFLIN N	MAJ	O-0407576	0264	3
HAWKINS HIRSCHLE F	LTC	O-1317733	0763	1
HAWKINS HUGH J	CPT	O-0395588	0544	2
HAWKINS JAMES F	LTC	O-1313602	0766	1
HAWKINS JAMES R	CPT	O-0454388	0453	2
HAWKINS JOHN C	2LT	O-1331359	0354	3
HAWKINS JOHN E	MAJ	O-1288546	0361	1
HAWKINS JOHN F	MAJ	O-1648611	0457	1
HAWKINS JOHN T	CPT	O-2262918	0367	2
HAWKINS JR LOUIS A	COL	O-0216201	0564	3
HAWKINS JR ROBERT R	MAJ	O-1050717	0562	1
HAWKINS JR WILLIAM A	LTC	O-1303883	0760	1
HAWKINS JR WILLIAM G	2LT	O-2026987	0246	2
HAWKINS JULIAN A	MAJ	O-1304074	1060	1
HAWKINS LESLIE L	CW2	W-2117529	0155	1
HAWKINS MALCOLM	LTC	O-0413711	0761	1
HAWKINS MARVIL P	LTC	O-0374121	0661	1
HAWKINS MARVIN L	MAJ	O-1107468	0461	1
HAWKINS MELVIN J	CPT	O-1922549	0764	1
HAWKINS MILDRED R	2LT	N-0768315	0347	1
HAWKINS MILTON	LTC	O-0469225	0146	2
HAWKINS OLIN L	MAJ	O-0971804	0264	1
HAWKINS ORINGTON H	LTC	O-1320383	0163	1
HAWKINS RALPH G	1LT	O-0435644	1045	2
HAWKINS REGINALD	MAJ	O-0360009	1060	1
HAWKINS ROBERT C	CW3	W-2206778	0266	1
HAWKINS ROBERT L	LTC	O-1298225	1161	1
HAWKINS RUFUS K	CW4	W-2118487	0361	1
HAWKINS THOMAS H	MAJ	O-1923547	1163	1
HAWKINS WESLEY F	LTC	O-0225056	1064	3
HAWKINS WIL	MAJ	O-1599042	1262	1
HAWKINS WILLIAM A	MAJ	O-1308426	0461	1
HAWKINS WILLIAM A	CW3	W-2151646	1165	1
HAWKINS WILLIAM B	COL	O-0310311	1263	1
HAWKINS WILLIAM K	CPT	O-0491515	0357	1
HAWKINS WILLIAM R	LTC	O-0451608	0256	1
HAWKINS WILLIAM S	CPT	O-0255274	0145	2
HAWKINS WILLIAM S	MAJ	O-0416747	0846	2
HAWKO RICHARD J	LTC	O-0402229	0764	3
HAWLEY CHARLES C	LTC	O-0452738	0766	1
HAWLEY CHARLES D	MAJ	O-0201589	1046	1
HAWLEY CHARLES L	LTC	O-1100515	0565	1
HAWLEY DORIS L	2LT	N-0760018	0545	1
HAWLEY GEORGE C	MAJ	O-0150315	0150	3
HAWLEY GEORGE F	MAJ	O-0375262	0461	1
HAWLEY HAROLD D	MAJ	O-2025332	0859	2
HAWLEY IVOR B	CW2	W-2145774	0365	1
HAWLEY MARGERY C	LTC	L-0909024	0862	1
HAWLEY PHILIP C	LTC	O-0167133	0955	3
HAWLEY RALPH S	COL	O-0153090	0150	3
HAWLEY RAY T	CW2	W-2145675	0561	1
HAWLEY RICHARD A	CPT	O-1289729	0546	2
HAWLEY ROBERT F	MAJ	O-0908694	1048	2
HAWLEY ROBERT L	LTC	O-0436880	0159	1
HAWLEY SHERMAN R	COL	O-0289933	1162	3
HAWLEY STANLEY S	LTC	O-0216463	0663	3
HAWLEY VERNON C	LTC	O-0189414	0955	3
HAWLEY WILLIAM G	CPT	O-4006451	0365	1
HAWN MATHEW	MAJ	O-1640538	0657	1
HAWORTH JAMES G	LTC	O-0148452	0648	3
HAWORTH JAMES G	MAJ	O-0987107	0962	1
HAWORTH LEONARD S	2LT	O-2055334	0353	2
HAWORTH MONTIE M	CPT	O-0500381	0654	1

NAME	GRADE	SVC NO	DATE RET MO YR	RET CODE
HAWORTH TEDDY L	LTC	O-0269543	1066	3
HAWRO VINCENT A	MAJ	O-0250266	0446	2
HAWRYLAK FRANK	MAJ	O-2018513	0863	1
HAWS LAWRENCE E	LTC	O-0271466	0565	3
HAWTHORNE EMIL F	LTC	O-1106805	0663	1
HAWTHORNE JAMES A	LTC	O-1576101	0564	1
HAWTHORNE JAMES E	1LT	O-1061722	0446	2
HAWTHORNE JOHN H	2LT	O-5405281	0460	2
HAWTHORNE RAMONA M	2LT	N-0797872	0646	1
HAWTHORNE ROY O	COL	O-0201442	0648	3
HAWTIN RAYMOND F	LTC	O-1321306	0662	1
HAWTOF E MANUEL	LTC	O-0276609	1059	3
HAY CARL F	MAJ	O-0463473	0456	1
HAY ELMER W	LTC	O-0263849	0650	3
HAY FLOYD B	CPT	O-0375213	0845	2
HAY KENNETH M	LTC	O-0525155	0764	3
HAY MALCOLM	MG	O-0284748	0667	3
HAY REGINALD W	LTC	O-0148426	0648	3
HAY ROBERT B	LTC	O-1080204	0461	1
HAYASHI HAJIME	MAJ	O-2030796	0863	1
HAYASHI RICHARD K	CPT	O-1326049	0263	1
HAYCOCK JR CHARLES A	CPT	O-0947573	1060	1
HAYCOCK ROBERT D	CPT	O-2036058	0646	2
HAYCOCK ROBERT W	CPT	O-1541731	0845	2
HAYDAHL JOHN T	CW4	W-2116007	0555	1
HAYDEN ALVIN C	CPT	O-0279209	1046	1
HAYDEN BERNARD	WO1	W-2104133	0853	1
HAYDEN CLIFFORD W	CPT	O-2011194	0658	1
HAYDEN CURTIS B	LTC	O-0452619	0161	1
HAYDEN DEBORAH F	1LT	N-0736757	0746	1
HAYDEN GEORGE F	MAJ	O-0524501	1146	2
HAYDEN HERMAN C	CW3	W-2152040	0466	1
HAYDEN JR RAYMOND W	LTC	O-0454270	0766	1
HAYDEN JR THOMAS C	MAJ	O-1584337	0960	1
HAYDEN VERNON L	CPT	O-1289080	0454	1
HAYDEN WILSON A	LTC	O-2017055	1163	1
HAYDON GERTRUDE M	MAJ	N-0773177	0364	2
HAYDON JULIUS H	MAJ	O-0888291	1062	1
HAYEK WILL J	COL	O-0163685	0756	3
HAYES ANDREW W	COL	O-0281103	0859	1
HAYES ARTHUR E	LTC	O-1001147	0964	1
HAYES BEDA M	1LT	N-0703915	1045	1
HAYES CATHERINE	CPT	N-0730102	0261	1
HAYES CLINTON C	CPT	O-1918917	0661	1
HAYES DONALD F	CPT	O-1291816	1045	2
HAYES DONALD R	LTC	O-1060474	1162	1
HAYES DOUGLAS A	1LT	O-1317913	0945	2
HAYES EDMOND M	CW2	W-2141985	1159	1
HAYES EDWARD J	1LT	O-1179884	1045	2
HAYES EDWARD K	LTC	O-0469769	0455	2
HAYES ERWIN M	LTC	O-1683489	1264	1
HAYES FLOYD M	COL	O-0208873	0655	2
HAYES GEORGE H	CW3	W-2205435	1164	1
HAYES GORDON B	CPT	O-0224220	1058	3
HAYES HARLEY L	WO1	W-2151039	1163	2
HAYES HAROLD E	LTC	O-1642952	0964	1
HAYES JAMES E	MAJ	O-0300547	0954	1
HAYES JAMES F	LTC	O-0518787	0663	1
HAYES JAMES H	MAJ	O-1283424	0957	1
HAYES JAMES J	MAJ	O-1650105	0261	1
HAYES JAMES M	CW4	W-2139549	0261	1
HAYES JAMES P	MAJ	O-0288628	0363	3
HAYES JAMES R	1LT	O-1284136	0845	2
HAYES JAMES T	CPT	O-0491633	1052	1
HAYES JEREMIAH F	LTC	O-1646238	0263	1
HAYES JESSE C	MAJ	O-0372702	0860	1
HAYES JOHN H	CPT	O-0311856	0345	2
HAYES JOHN J	1LT	O-1012477	114N	2
HAYES JOHN J	CPT	O-1797996	0547	2
HAYES JOHN R	LTC	O-0319397	1045	2
HAYES JOHN T	LTC	O-0446443	1264	1
HAYES JOHN T	MAJ	O-2203412	0965	1
HAYES JR ENOS W	MAJ	O-0348135	0566	1
HAYES JR GEORGE P	LTC	O-0337953	0962	3
HAYES JR THOMAS F	MAJ	O-0282375	1045	2

NAME	GRADE	SVC NO	DATE RET MO YR	RET CODE
HAYES JR WILLARD L	MAJ	O-0413689	1045	2
HAYES KENNETH M	CPT	O-1010128	1045	2
HAYES LEON C	CPT	O-1010188	0747	2
HAYES LUTHER Z	CPT	O-1878867	1066	1
HAYES REX S	1LT	O-2206811	0454	2
HAYES RICHARD G	2LT	O-1018701	0644	2
HAYES RICHARD L	COL	O-0109248	0546	2
HAYES RICHARD L	CPT	O-1293697	0554	2
HAYES ROBERT C	MAJ	O-0558085	1154	2
HAYES ROBERT L	COL	O-0155366	1155	3
HAYES ROBERT W	LTC	O-1035809	1163	1
HAYES RUDOLPH V	CW3	W-2207964	0666	1
HAYES SAMUEL E	CPT	O-0388295	0746	2
HAYES THOMAS E	COL	O-0311367	0664	3
HAYES THOMAS J	1LT	O-1286121	1043	2
HAYES THOMAS T H	1LT	O-5310888	0763	2
HAYES WALTER J	CW4	W-2111601	1067	1
HAYES WALTER L	CPT	O-0903755	0845	2
HAYES WARREN H	1LT	O-1307233	0845	2
HAYES WILLIAM G	MAJ	O-2263423	1266	1
HAYES WILTON B	CPT	O-1648614	0347	2
HAYGOOD EVERETT A	COL	O-0348351	0667	3
HAYHURST JERIMIAH V	MAJ	O-1918566	0663	1
HAYKEL NORMAN A	CW4	W-2143028	0664	1
HAYMAKER KENNETH G	COL	O-0398389	1055	1
HAYMAKER WEBB E	LTC	O-0291133	0762	3
HAYMAN ALAN P	LTC	O-0355661	0662	3
HAYMAN FIRMAN K	COL	O-0225647	0657	1
HAYMAN HARRY B	CPT	O-0237480	0464	3
HAYMAN JR ARLEY A	LTC	O-0331026	0561	1
HAYMON WILLARD	CW3	W-2149930	1162	1
HAYNE ORLANDO V	LTC	O-0524490	0965	1
HAYNE PAUL T	LTC	O-0215678	0364	3
HAYNE WILLARD W	COL	O-0325710	0566	3
HAYNER ROBERT L	CPT	O-1300031	0945	2
HAYNES ARTHUR L	CW4	W-2116101	0559	1
HAYNES ARTHUR S	2LT	O-1914401	0345	1
HAYNES BILLIE J	CW2	W-2211141	1265	1
HAYNES CHARLES J	CPT	O-1636021	0153	1
HAYNES CLIFFORD G	MAJ	O-0325052	0767	3
HAYNES CLIFFORD L	1LT	O-1301637	0348	2
HAYNES DAVID I	CW2	W-2149920	0661	1
HAYNES DEWITT	1LT	O-2034023	1063	2
HAYNES EARL F	LTC	O-1332814	1065	2
HAYNES EASIL E	CW3	W-2145158	0656	1
HAYNES EDWARD C	MAJ	O-1296370	0261	1
HAYNES EMERSON L	LTC	O-0452499	0153	1
HAYNES FRAZIER J	MAJ	O-1845049	0761	1
HAYNES FRED A	MAJ	O-1051591	1062	1
HAYNES GEORGE H	LTC	O-0275408	1043	2
HAYNES GORDON B	LTC	O-1996586	0265	1
HAYNES HORACE S	CW2	W-2127644	1151	1
HAYNES III WILLIAM P	LTC	O-1283951	0766	1
HAYNES JR BLANDY C	LTC	O-1282361	0567	1
HAYNES LEWIS M	MAJ	O-1548834	0565	1
HAYNES ORREN E	MAJ	O-0450885	1154	1
HAYNES PAUL E	LTC	O-1101483	0866	3
HAYNES PHILIP E	COL	O-0171548	1046	2
HAYNES RAY	COL	O-0172730	1059	1
HAYNES RUSSELL M	CPT	O-1317789	0267	3
HAYNES SCOTT C	CW3	W-2208864	0967	1
HAYNES STANLEY L	CPT	O-0120124	0654	3
HAYNES STUART G	2LT	O-2210396	1150	2
HAYNES THOMAS E	1LT	O-1551417	0445	2
HAYNES WALTER G	LTC	O-0369487	0246	2
HAYNES WHITWORTH	1LT	O-1313529	0146	2
HAYNES WILLIAM A	LTC	O-0454616	0263	1
HAYNES WILLIE E	CPT	O-0987607	0853	2
HAYNIE CLYDE M	CPT	O-0321372	0954	1
HAYNIE JACK D	CPT	O-0167724	0456	3
HAYNIE JEWELL G	LTC	O-0257248	0660	1
HAYNIE ROBERT C	COL	O-0921254	1046	2
HAYNOSCH FRED J	MAJ	O-1294836	1263	1
HAYNSWORTH THOMAS B	MAJ	O-0234162	0965	3
HAYS CLOYD A	COL	O-0308957	0846	2
HAYS FRED J	LTC	O-0451461	1156	1
HAYS GEORGE M	LTC	O-0352715	0546	2
HAYS HARRY F	LTC	O-0291471	0262	3
HAYS HUGH G	LTC	O-0323960	1161	3
HAYS JOHN W	CPT	O-0352281	1045	2
HAYS JR OTIS E	COL	O-0363584	1066	1
HAYS LEOPOLD M	LTC	O-0347342	0566	3
HAYS NORMAN M	CW3	W-2151416	0865	1
HAYS ORREN L	LTC	O-0272582	0263	3
HAYS RAY H	COL	O-0113566	0749	3
HAYS ROBERT L	CPT	O-2262612	0261	1
HAYS SAMUEL D	COL	O-0170950	0454	3
HAYS STANLEY	COL	O-0374722	0861	1
HAYS VERYL R	1LT	O-1036187	0845	2
HAYS WALTER L	MAJ	O-0413587	0461	1
HAYSON CECIL J	CW3	W-2143916	0262	1
HAYTON RALPH E	MAJ	O-1108008	0264	2
HAYUNGS HENRY A	LTC	O-0275367	0167	3
HAYWARD CHARLES P	COL	O-0129842	0760	3
HAYWARD DONALD R	2LT	O-0554347	0346	2
HAYWARD EVERETT F	LTC	O-0308138	0762	3
HAYWARD GEORGE E	CPT	O-0380449	1158	1
HAYWARD JOHN A	CPT	O-1922925	0867	2
HAYWARD JR EDWARD G	LTC	O-0191096	0649	3
HAYWARD LAURA F	2LT	N-0720023	0442	1
HAYWARD ORVILLE C	WO1	W-2123084	1049	2
HAYWARD PAUL H	COL	O-0107150	0445	2
HAYWARD VINCENT	CW2	W-2142961	0356	1
HAYWARD WILLIAM A	MAJ	O-0487157	0553	2
HAYWARD WINSTON R	COL	O-0281028	0260	1
HAYWOOD BLANCHE	1LT	N-0901630	0155	2
HAYWOOD HERALD E	LTC	O-0488289	0264	3
HAYWOOD TED M	COL	O-0278946	0561	3
HAYWOOD WILLIAM R	LTC	O-0321302	1265	3
HAYWOOD WILLIE	CPT	O-1328811	0753	1
HAZARD DOUGLAS O	CPT	O-0977613	0861	1
HAZARD FRANCIS J	LTC	O-0450412	1060	1
HAZARD FRED	LTC	O-1574057	1057	1
HAZEL ARTHUR T	LTC	O-1552694	0462	1
HAZEL HAROLD F	LTC	O-0262488	1160	1
HAZEL JOHN J	COL	O-0228093	0365	3
HAZEL R H	MAJ	O-0494263	0154	1
HAZELBAKER HARRY O	LTC	O-0230735	1062	3
HAZELBAKER PHILMON F	LTC	O-0505045	1057	2
HAZELET VINCENT H	MAJ	O-1324931	1061	1
HAZELIP WARNER S	LTC	O-0392116	0263	3
HAZELL WILLIAM C	1LT	O-0109813	0633	1
HAZELWOOD EDWARD L	1LT	O-1822877	0945	2
HAZELWOOD JAMES A	COL	O-0900684	1055	3
HAZELWOOD WENDELL H	LTC	O-0262719	1049	1
HAZEN JACK R	LTC	O-1293046	1063	1
HAZEN RAYMOND E	MAJ	O-1289081	0954	1
HAZEN RICHARD G	LTC	O-1058830	0663	1
HAZEN THOMAS F	LTC	O-0246525	0753	3
HAZENBUSH THOMAS G	COL	O-0188511	0252	3
HAZER KALEEM	LTC	O-1165398	0962	1
HAZLETT EDWARD A	COL	O-0220848	1055	1
HAZLETT WALTER R	MAJ	O-0991556	1265	2
HAZLETT WILLIAM L	MAJ	O-0354756	0162	3
HAZLEWOOD IVAN D	LTC	O-1533085	0954	1
HAZLEWOOD URSALA H	1LT	N-0725435	0646	1
HAZUCHA RUDOLPH F	MAJ	O-1553273	1061	1
HAZUDA ALEX W	LTC	O-0450886	0355	1
HAZZARD STEPHEN B	CPT	O-0446660	1044	2
HEACOCK CHESTER S	2LT	O-1172063	0444	2
HEACOCK FREDERICK	LTC	O-1327354	1065	2
HEACOCK HAROLD W	MAJ	O-0321851	0445	2
HEACOCK ROLAND T	CPT	O-0502079	0845	2
HEAD ALAN S	WO1	W-2111725	0845	2
HEAD ALLEN W	LTC	O-0405470	0363	1
HEAD ARNOLD T	LTC	O-0967637	1067	2
HEAD BERNARD B	CW4	W-2132863	0561	1
HEAD CLIFFORD M	LTC	O-1310440	0862	1
HEAD FREDERICK	LTC	O-1299744	1266	1
HEAD JOHN H	MAJ	O-2012524	1166	1
HEAD JR CHARLES S	COL	O-0254573	0466	3
HEAD JR HUGH G	LTC	O-0346630	0166	3
HEAD JR LAWRENCE W	LTC	O-1641376	0862	1
HEAD MORRIS W	CPT	O-1117142	0465	1
HEAD RAYMOND J	CPT	O-0381956	1145	2
HEAD WILLIAM	CPT	O-0204875	0128	1
HEADLAND VIOLET M	2LT	N-0700580	0535	1
HEADLEY CHALON S	LTC	O-1308951	1266	1
HEADLEY HOLLAND C	LTC	O-0122515	C-53	3
HEADLOUGH WARREN E	MAJ	O-1925712	1165	1
HEAGY CHARLES F	LTC	O-0289840	0264	1
HEALD GEORGE P	LTC	O-1301482	0466	1
HEALD HARRY C	MAJ	O-0222615	0644	2
HEALEY EDWARD F	CPT	O-0331666	0445	2
HEALEY EUGENE T	MAJ	O-1298703	0958	1
HEALEY GRANT	COL	O-2034424	0466	1
HEALEY JOSEPH T	CPT	O-0441572	1047	1
HEALEY JR ANDREW S	CPT	O-1304075	0347	2
HEALEY JR JOSEPH W	CPT	O-1110549	0564	1
HEALEY OWEN R	CPT	O-1049199	0746	2
HEALEY THEODORE	CPT	O-0885627	0250	1
HEALY ANNE P	1LT	N-0755986	0546	1
HEALY EDWARD A	MAJ	O-1796278	1060	1
HEALY EDWARD J	MAJ	O-0320184	0564	3
HEALY EDWARD W	MAJ	O-0336060	0347	2
HEALY FRANCIS D	LTC	O-0918722	0165	3
HEALY FRANCIS H	CPT	O-1032016	1162	1
HEALY JAMES K	LTC	O-0450019	1056	1
HEALY JOHN F	CPT	O-1036555	0546	2
HEALY JR EDWARD J	LTC	O-0311355	0562	1
HEALY JR JEREMIAH F	CPT	O-0453036	0846	2
HEALY MARTIN J	1LT	O-1307123	0945	2
HEALY MAURICE J	CPT	O-0356249	0246	2
HEALY MAURICE J	MAJ	O-1335003	0163	1
HEALY PAUL F	1LT	O-1324538	1145	2
HEALY RADCLIFFE	MAJ	O-0977900	1167	1
HEALY TIMOTHY J	COL	O-0204385	0261	3
HEALY TRACY K	COL	O-0159645	0751	3
HEANEY BERNARD F	CPT	O-1181626	0947	2
HEANEY ELBRIDGE	LTC	O-0318211	1263	3
HEANEY WILLIAM J	CW2	W-2148620	1055	1
HEAP GEORGE R	LTC	O-0155112	0648	3
HEAPE ARTIE M	LTC	O-0251330	1156	3
HEAPE GRAHAM	CW4	W-2113918	0763	2
HEAPHY JOHN J	MAJ	O-1578586	0361	1
HEARD ALBERT S	CW2	W-2146785	0557	1
HEARD CHARLES	MAJ	O-1303335	0961	1
HEARD CHARLES B	CPT	O-1535337	0746	2
HEARD EARL C	1LT	O-2212085	0966	2
HEARD GUNION M	LTC	O-0483218	0667	3
HEARD ISAAC J	WO1	W-2148658	1055	2
HEARD JAMES L	MAJ	O-0500092	0146	2
HEARD JOHN W	MAJ	O-1685655	0964	1
HEARD JR JOHN C	LTC	O-1169148	1160	1
HEARD JR WALTER S	MAJ	O-1046121	1263	1
HEARD SAMUEL P	1LT	O-1303336	0245	2
HEARFIELD HAROLD H	LTC	O-0112560	0450	3
HEARICK JAMES G	COL	O-1633949	0664	1
HEARLIN JR BERTRAM S	LTC	O-1100585	1060	1
HEARN ANNA E	MAJ	N-0760790	0764	1
HEARN CHARLES A	COL	O-0294025	1159	1
HEARN CHARLES L	MAJ	O-0406967	0146	2
HEARN CHAUNCEY M	COL	O-0257081	1264	3
HEARN FREDERICK	COL	O-0257185	0859	1
HEARN GEORGE R	2LT	O-1059805	1144	2
HEARN HENRY O	MAJ	O-0499915	0447	2
HEARN JR JAMES M	MAJ	O-1338091	0765	1
HEARN LYNN F	CPT	O-1314364	0446	1
HEARN OPA M	LTC	O-1014918	0160	1
HEARN THOMAS W	CPT	O-1320279	0964	2
HEARN VIRGINIA E	1LT	N-0762413	0650	1
HEARNE FRANK T	1LT	O-0422953	1144	2
HEARNE JR CHARLES E	CPT	O-1578587	0745	2
HEARNE JR JULIAN C	COL	O-0229386	0660	1
HEARTFIELD RICHARD C	COL	O-0180967	0662	3
HEARTSILL CHARLES E	MAJ	O-0260805	0158	2
HEASTY JOHN C	CPT	O-0984194	0862	1
HEATH CHARLES C	MAJ	O-1543128	1064	1
HEATH CLARENCE P	COL	O-0259726	0562	3
HEATH CLIFFORD S	CPT	O-0487913	0247	1
HEATH DENVER Y	CPT	O-0487946	0553	1
HEATH DONALD R	CPT	O-1020150	1059	1
HEATH FOY K	CW4	W-2112550	0659	1
HEATH FRANCIS C	LTC	O-1016373	0363	1
HEATH FREDERICK	MAJ	O-0482030	1059	1
HEATH FREDERICK	MAJ	O-1551220	0957	1
HEATH HARRIET	MAJ	N-0726510	0764	1
HEATH HENRY S	LTC	O-0314065	1047	2
HEATH JAMES W	LTC	O-1284137	1164	1
HEATH JOHN R	COL	O-0216294	0850	3
HEATH MORRIS L	LTC	O-1056114	0667	3
HEATH PAUL W	COL	O-0261717	1165	3
HEATH PHILLIP C	LTC	O-0463924	0962	1
HEATH RAYMOND A	LTC	O-0274354	0160	1
HEATH SR JAMES N	MAJ	O-0953932	0462	1
HEATH SR WILLIAM R	MAJ	O-1577303	1058	1
HEATH STANLEY H	MAJ	O-1288740	1158	1
HEATH THOMAS O	LTC	O-0229990	0344	2
HEATH WILLIAM S	2LT	O-1825675	0344	2
HEATHCOE EDWIN J	CPT	O-0985460	0162	1
HEATHCOTE CARLYLE J	MAJ	O-1186924	0366	1
HEATHER JR FRED H	MAJ	O-0498158	0348	2
HEATHERINGTON FRED R	CPT	O-1166282	0645	2
HEATHERLY EDWARD S	MAJ	O-1031648	0457	1
HEATHERLY JAMES A	MAJ	O-0501316	0747	1
HEATHMAN ROBERT C	LTC	O-1002442	0465	3
HEATLEY SELDEN E	CPT	O-1592265	0162	1
HEATLY CLYDE B	MAJ	O-1291636	0960	1
HEATLY HERBERT L	CW2	W-2141578	0161	2
HEATLY MAURICE O	MAJ	O-0379014	0246	2
HEATLY ROBERT L	CPT	O-1111660	0345	2
HEATON CHARLES C	LTC	O-0361792	0446	2
HEATON CHARLES F	MAJ	O-0885430	0653	1
HEATON CHARLES E	MAJ	O-1544716	0657	2
HEATON DOROTHY R	2LT	N-0745264	0345	1
HEATON EDWARD C	CPT	O-1648288	0956	1
HEATON GEORGE P	MAJ	O-0497522	1054	1
HEATON HUGH C	1LT	O-1055867	0664	1
HEATON JR JAMES H	CPT	O-0368764	0346	2
HEATON NELSON F	CPT	O-0261652	0956	3
HEATON RALPH S	CPT	O-1584342	0165	1
HEATON WILLIAM E	MAJ	O-0297494	0449	3
HEATON WILLIAM P	LTC	O-0456161	1060	1
HEAVEN PAUL J	LTC	O-1015670	1061	1
HEAVEY JOHN C	MAJ	O-0236483	0764	3
HEAVEY JR THOMAS J	LTC	O-0720499	0165	1
HEBARD GEORGE A	1LT	O-1286284	1044	2
HEBBE VERNE W	LTC	O-0403050	1060	1
HEBBLE JR JOHN C	CPT	O-0211099	0563	3
HEBBLETHWAITE L M	MAJ	O-0496866	1050	1
HEBEL AUGUST R	MAJ	O-0970432	0364	1
HEBERT ALFRED J	1LT	O-1637641	0446	1
HEBERT GLENN L	1LT	O-1113736	1045	2
HEBERT JULIEN A	CPT	O-0501378	0745	2
HEBERT ROBERT J	LTC	O-1315825	0564	1
HEBLICH FREDERICK	LTC	O-0263481	0845	2
HECHINGER RUSSELL W	LTC	O-1585600	1163	1
HECHT CHRIS M	LTC	O-0132233	0558	3
HECHT HARRY W	LTC	O-0205134	0247	2
HECHT JR LOUIS W	MAJ	O-1322448	0764	1
HECHT JR MORTON E	MAJ	O-1167896	0962	1
HECHT VERNON C	2LT	O-1322839	0845	2
HECHT WORTHY O	LTC	O-0917142	1166	3
HECK ALEXANDER	2LT	O-0389446	0647	2
HECK CHARLES A	MAJ	O-0980549	0564	1
HECK HAROLD J	COL	O-0236258	0966	3
HECK JR JESSE E	MAJ	O-2049572	0965	1
HECK LEWIS O	COL	O-0230478	0260	3
HECK ROBERT R	MAJ	O-2018515	0663	1
HECKER GEORGE L	LTC	O-0288071	0546	2

NAME	GRADE	SVC NO	DATE RET MO YR	RET CODE
HECKER GEORGE M	1LT	0-1297878	0645	2
HECKERMAN SEELEY E	LTC	0-0445558	0852	1
HECKMAN EDWARD A	CPT	0-1557606	0847	2
HECKMAN KENNETH A	CW3	W-2129916	0858	1
HECKMAN RAYMOND M	COL	0-0173540	0257	3
HECQ CHARLES A	LTC	0-1297363	0162	1
HEDBERG OSCAR G	MAJ	0-0332472	1054	3
HEDDAEUS GILBERT T	MAJ	0-0148547	0757	3
HEDDEN DOUGLAS J	2LT	0-1935248	1053	2
HEDDEN JULIUS C	LTC	0-0381256	0346	2
HEDDEN ORVE K	COL	0-0217767	0963	3
HEDDEN RANDALL	1LT	0-1589889	1044	2
HEDDLESTON ROY R	MAJ	0-1113737	0461	1
HEDERECK GEORGE H	LTC	0-0140907	0856	3
HEDGCOCK CHARLES C	MAJ	0-0134894	0648	3
HEDGE ALBERT A	COL	0-0174974	0550	3
HEDGE LAFAYETTE	LTC	0-0292843	0447	2
HEDGECOCK ARCHIE W	MAJ	0-1647491	0157	1
HEDGECOCK EDWARD F	LTC	0-1062682	0163	1
HEDGECOCK JOHNIE C	CPT	N-0726681	0347	1
HEDGECOCK LAVERNE L	CW2	RW-2149467	1164	1
HEDGER HAROLD E	COL	0-0224544	1058	3
HEDGES BEN W	LTC	0-1795898	0461	1
HEDGES FRANK H	MAJ	0-1821177	0446	2
HEDGES LAWRENCE P	LTC	0-1541724	1257	1
HEDGES WILLIAM R	MAJ	0-0981917	0263	1
HEDGLIN LESLIE H	CW2	W-2110107	0353	2
HEDGPETH LOUIS G	LTC	0-0520785	0465	1
HEDLESTON III WINN D	MAJ	0-1100586	0763	1
HEDLEY GEORGE A	MAJ	0-0370056	0654	1
HEDLEY JOSEPH J	MAJ	0-1338460	0264	1
HEDLUND CLIFFORD R	CW2	W-2153346	1263	1
HEDMAN FRITZ A	LTC	0-0921971	1066	3
HEDMAN HARRIS W	CW2	W-2148965	0456	1
HEDRICK CHARLES T	MAJ	0-1996650	1160	1
HEDRICK CLARENCE R	1LT	0-1017915	1045	2
HEDRICK JOHN R	MAJ	0-2029136	1060	1
HEDRICK JR CLYDE C	CW2	W-2211501	1264	1
HEDRICK JR GEORGE E	LTC	0-0325051	0962	1
HEDRICK WILLIAM P	CPT	0-1173280	1151	1
HEDSTROM FREDERICK	CW3	W-2144312	0959	1
HEEDUM LYLE F	MAJ	0-1179436	1163	1
HEEGEL GORDON C	CW3	W-2144184	0559	2
HEEKE ANGUS J	LTC	0-0272242	0262	1
HEELAN ROBERT W	MAJ	0-0162618	0858	3
HEER FRIDOLIN A	CPT	0-0198617	0662	3
HEER RUTH E	1LT	N-0767057	0347	1
HEERLEIN CHARLES E	CPT	0-0163695	0557	3
HEESCH HERMAN F	COL	0-0241932	0560	3
HEESCHEN ROBERT D	COL	0-0212056	1162	3
HEFFELFINGER H B	LTC	0-0405450	0261	2
HEFFELFINGER WARREN	MAJ	0-1014294	0965	2
HEFFERNAN HENRY J	LTC	0-0288092	1166	3
HEFFERNAN WILLIAM J	LTC	0-1173991	0563	1
HEFFNER JR J C	LTC	0-1577304	0866	1
HEFFNER RICHARD W	CPT	0-2032938	1056	1
HEFFNER WILLIAM W	CPT	0-1048401	0958	1
HEFLEY GENERAL P	LTC	0-1030373	0763	1
HEFLEY JESSE L	MAJ	0-0234246	0965	3
HEFLEY RAYMOND C	LTC	0-0370161	0860	1
HEFLEY ROGER E	2LT	0-0109220	0834	1
HEFLIN CARL W	COL	0-0125704	1052	1
HEFLIN EARL J	1LT	0-1289249	0761	2
HEFLIN FRANK O	MAJ	0-0159105	0456	3
HEFLIN HENRY O	CPT	0-2028697	1263	1
HEFLIN RANKIN W	LTC	0-0384868	1162	1
HEFT JR ROBERT G	MAJ	0-1309264	0960	1
HEG WINSLOW	CPT	0-1037045	0746	2
HEGARTY JR JAMES I	MAJ	0-1923587	1163	2
HEGARTY MARY M	MAJ	N-0759098	0866	1
HEGE FELIX D	LTC	0-0450617	0557	1
HEGELMAN THEODORE N	1LT	0-0401463	1045	2
HEGEMAN RICHARD C	LTC	0-1548221	0161	1
HEGEMANN OTTO H	LTC	0-0249429	0464	3
HEGGELUND EMIL M	CW4	W-2141307	0561	1

NAME	GRADE	SVC NO	DATE RET MO YR	RET CODE
HEGGIE WALTER B	CW4	W-2115545	0861	1
HEHOLT ALBERT C	1LT	0-1557607	0246	2
HEIB HARLEY F	LTC	0-0890424	0157	1
HEID JOHN B	1LT	0-0381817	1043	1
HEIDELBERG EDWARD W	CW3	W-2149215	0265	1
HEIDELBERG F H	MAJ	0-0497814	0546	2
HEIDEMANN WILLIAM B	1LT	0-1544138	0345	2
HEIDEN FLOYD A	WO1	W-2124378	0448	1
HEIDEN HARRY H	LTC	0-0327816	0648	3
HEIDENREICH JAMES F	CW3	W-2152964	0863	1
HEIDENREICH JOHN C	LTC	0-0116245	0949	3
HEIDER JULIUS F	CW2	W-2146855	1057	1
HEIDER LEWIS G	LTC	0-0110562	0648	3
HEIDGEN MARTIN F	CPT	0-0386492	1044	2
HEIDINGER EDWIN J	CW3	W-2141308	1058	1
HEIDINGER WILLIAM G	MAJ	0-1299745	1055	1
HEIDMANN HERBERT A	CPT	0-1535648	0464	1
HEIDT WOODROW W	CW2	W-2152768	0160	2
HEIDTMAN RALPH W	LTC	0-0248622	0254	1
HEIFETZ RALPH	LTC	0-0287981	1066	3
HEIKEN BYARD J	1LT	0-1591794	0645	2
HEIKENS GLADYS R	MAJ	N-0741809	0566	3
HEIKER ANTHONY E	1LT	0-2051468	0853	1
HEIKKINEN SULO H	MAJ	0-0976855	1165	1
HEIL RICHARD C	LTC	0-1312922	0867	1
HEILBRUN ROBERT M	LTC	0-0243329	0166	3
HEILIG JAMES L	MAJ	0-0226281	0864	3
HEILMAN EDWIN F	LTC	0-0174706	0145	2
HEILMAN EMMA H	MAJ	N-0727525	0964	1
HEILMAN GUS W	LTC	0-1289015	0449	2
HEILMAN JAMES M	MAJ	0-0268604	1144	2
HEILMAN MARION F	1LT	N-0728261	0645	1
HEILMAN RAYMOND J	LTC	0-0138161	1051	3
HEILPERN ALVIN	LTC	0-0283352	0559	1
HEIM LEWIS W	MAJ	0-0481114	0252	1
HEIMANN HERSCHEL G	CW3	W-2146042	0261	1
HEIMBAUGH HAYS M	LTC	0-0248723	1065	3
HEIMBRODT CARL E	COL	0-0200079	0651	3
HEIN ALVIN H	MAJ	0-2002293	0963	1
HEIN CORWIN E	LTC	0-0313499	1266	3
HEIN GORDON F	LTC	0-0401610	0345	2
HEIN MERRITT F	LTC	0-1320457	0266	1
HEINARD WHILDEN G	CPT	0-0544563	0347	2
HEINBACH CLAIR E	MAJ	0-0934205	1167	1
HEINDL LEOPOLD A	MAJ	0-1165507	0648	1
HEINE EDWIN J	CPT	0-1179438	1047	2
HEINE KARL G	COL	0-0246427	0766	3
HEINECCIUS BERYL R	1LT	N-0728726	0545	1
HEINEMAN ALBERT H	MAJ	0-2014997	0163	1
HEINEMAN PAUL E	MAJ	0-1312677	0261	1
HEINEMANN JOHN C	LTC	0-0322676	0662	2
HEINEMANN LAMBERT C	MAJ	0-1184065	0665	1
HEINEN JULIUS B	MAJ	0-0316460	1047	2
HEINETZ ALBERT	CW2	W-2146845	0157	1
HEINEY JOSEPH H	CPT	0-0198062	0357	3
HEINICHEN HENRY J	LTC	0-0337124	0660	1
HEINKE MARTHA M	1LT	N-0736834	0647	1
HEINKE ROBERT H	LTC	0-1583089	0365	1
HEINLEIN LAWRENCE L	B G	0-0233033	0960	3
HEINLY DALE H	2LT	0-0453452	1143	2
HEINMILLER CARL W	MAJ	0-0381754	1046	1
HEINRICH JOSEPH F	B G	0-0255083	0465	3
HEINRICH ROBERT L	CW3	W-2136714	1265	2
HEINRICHS LOUIS M	CPT	0-0234555	0451	3
HEINTZ LAMBERT W	CPT	0-0470423	0246	2
HEINTZELMAN ROBERT N	CPT	0-0343670	1044	2
HEINTZLEMAN ROBERT W	LTC	0-1300032	0962	1
HEINY FREDERICK	2LT	0-2050252	0446	2
HEINZ ALBERT R	CPT	0-1102286	0845	2
HEINZ CHARLES L	MAJ	0-1551866	0764	1
HEINZ ERNEST F	CPT	0-0391135	0252	2
HEINZ RICHARD J	COL	0-0268485	0364	2
HEINZE BERNARD T	LTC	0-0162581	0961	3
HEINZE MARION D	MAJ	0-2035582	0760	2
HEINZMANN FRANK M	MAJ	0-0245758	0957	3

NAME	GRADE	SVC NO	DATE RET MO YR	RET CODE
HEISE JOHN D	LTC	0-0209633	1160	3
HEISER ANN	MAJ	N-0772903	0760	2
HEISEY ELVIN N	LTC	0-1592269	1061	1
HEISEY JOHN W	CW2	W-3100528	0967	2
HEISHMAN CLAUDE R	MAJ	0-1012448	0355	1
HEISHMAN ROBERT L	1LT	0-2053975	0645	2
HEISIG JR GILBERT W	1LT	0-0552629	0946	2
HEISKELL EDWARD V	COL	0-0112714	0952	3
HEISLER JOSEPH C	CW3	W-2150711	0364	1
HEISLER KERMIT J	CW2	W-2143242	0756	1
HEISS EARL H	LTC	0-1321407	0967	1
HEISS SIMON W	LTC	0-0196005	0648	3
HEISS WILLIAM H	CPT	0-0131553	1049	3
HEIT GEORGE C	CPT	0-0146635	0751	3
HEIT PHILIP	CPT	0-0473104	1044	2
HEITHAUS JOHN	MAJ	0-2055214	1055	1
HEITMAN WALLACE H	MAJ	0-1171585	1165	1
HEITMEYER PAUL R	MAJ	0-0368742	0745	2
HEITMUELLER RUDOLF	MAJ	0-0450887	0958	1
HEITZ JOSEPH C	CW2	W-2106748	1047	1
HEITZMAN HARRY M	1LT	0-1285239	0545	2
HEIZER JAMES H	LTC	0-0323153	1048	1
HELBERG WALFRED J	MAJ	0-0965176	0966	1
HELBERT VICTOR C	CW3	W-2141309	0758	1
HELD ALBERT E	LTC	0-0499719	0646	2
HELD FREDERICK	MAJ	0-1558861	1062	1
HELD ISIDORE	1LT	0-1304212	0140	2
HELD JR GEORGE F	CPT	0-1170411	0747	2
HELD LEONARD J	1LT	0-1315164	1045	1
HELD SHELDON G	CW3	RW-2209545	0667	1
HELDE ERLING A	MAJ	0-0472863	1057	1
HELDENFELS GROVER C	COL	0-0268253	0756	3
HELDFOND ALFRED J	CPT	0-0486870	1045	1
HELDT WALTER H	MAJ	0-0269051	0566	3
HELES PATRICK F	MAJ	0-1319947	0357	1
HELFERTY JOHN K	LTC	0-0321065	0966	3
HELFF NORMAN E	1LT	0-0509341	0244	2
HELFRICK MURRAY D	LTC	0-0231338	0248	2
HELGREN DONALD H	CPT	0-0490357	0946	1
HELGREN ELVIRA H	LTC	N-0700099	0346	1
HELINSKI JOSEPH A	MAJ	0-1058833	1262	1
HELLAND ARNE A	CPT	0-1288380	0660	1
HELLAND CLARENCE W	LTC	0-1633956	1060	1
HELLAND ELMER D	MAJ	0-0494328	0547	1
HELLE ROBERT L	CW3	W-2145223	1157	1
HELLEBRANDT EDWIN T	LTC	0-0230303	0764	3
HELLENTHAL GEORGE M	CW2	W-2211921	1066	1
HELLER ARNOLD G	CPT	0-1310713	0246	2
HELLER BERNARD R	CPT	0-1284329	0145	2
HELLER EMIL E	LTC	0-1102761	0764	1
HELLER FRED F	CPT	0-0404353	0645	2
HELLER HARRY D	CW3	W-2129195	1065	3
HELLER HOMER K	COL	0-0222207	0864	3
HELLER JOHN S	1LT	0-1324539	0545	2
HELLER JOSEPH	CPT	0-0500412	0843	2
HELLER LAWRENCE R	CPT	0-1552699	1154	2
HELLER LOREN J	LTC	0-0318429	0265	1
HELLER RAYMOND G	LTC	0-1285753	0960	1
HELLER ROBERT C	CPT	0-0356962	0545	2
HELLER THEODORE M	CPT	0-0526181	0446	2
HELLIESEN HOWARD F	COL	0-0312905	0261	1
HELLINGER KENNETH F	LTC	0-0541090	0464	1
HELLMAN JOHN P	MAJ	0-0467505	0847	1
HELLMAN NATHANIEL	CPT	0-0554103	1046	2
HELLMAN ROGERS H	MAJ	0-2288096	0567	1
HELLMANN JACOB G	LTC	0-1038179	0263	1
HELLMIG RALPH E	LTC	0-1290751	0960	1
HELLWEGE JOHN K	LTC	0-1108011	1162	1
HELM DONALD L	2LT	0-1399887	0945	2
HELM HERBERT J	MAJ	0-1100588	1060	1
HELM JOHN R	CPT	0-5201545	0566	2
HELM LEONARD S	LTC	0-0334851	0265	3
HELM PRUETT B	CW2	W-3152839	0867	2
HELM THOMAS P	CW2	W-2146172	1160	1
HELM WILLIAM F	WO1	W-2116208	1044	2

NAME	GRADE	SVC NO	DATE RET MO YR	RET CODE
HELMAN NATHANIEL	CPT	0-1321512	0146	1
HELMBOLDT HENRY E	COL	0-0310312	0961	1
HELMERS RAYMOND A	1LT	0-1285240	1044	2
HELMICK CHARLES R	LTC	0-0461785	1165	3
HELMICK FLOYD F	LTC	0-0190534	1056	3
HELMICK ROBERT W	MAJ	0-1586654	1165	1
HELMICK RUDOLPH W	1LT	0-1176664	0246	2
HELMICKI EDWARD F	MAJ	0-1798790	1263	1
HELMKEN GILBERT M	CPT	0-0441401	0446	2
HELMLING RALPH W	CW3	W-2153226	1264	1
HELMOLD NORMAN C	MAJ	0-2014000	0562	1
HELMRATH NORMAN K	LTC	0-0307732	0248	1
HELMS AARON J	MAJ	0-2010799	1063	1
HELMS AUGUSTINE	LTC	0-1546481	0562	1
HELMS CHARLES L	LTC	0-0370308	0563	1
HELMS DONALD R	MAJ	0-2028698	0167	1
HELMS GEORGE W	WO1	W-2149216	1061	2
HELMS HAROLD H	CPT	0-0140279	0854	3
HELMS HUBERT O	LTC	0-0455788	0757	1
HELMS JACOB	LTC	0-0232642	0258	3
HELMS JAMES R	LTC	0-0204370	0659	3
HELMS LLOYD C	LTC	0-1063104	0267	1
HELMS MERCER D	MAJ	0-0258578	1043	2
HELMS RAYMOND W	CW2	W-2143517	0157	1
HELMS ROSCOE R	MAJ	0-2012189	1158	1
HELMS WALTER A	CW3	W-2152997	0264	1
HELMS WARREN E	CW3	W-2150508	1065	1
HELPBRINGER RALPH S	1LT	0-1581173	0644	2
HELPHINSTINE CARL B	COL	0-0327162	0758	3
HELPHREY LOUIS H	MAJ	0-0444082	0144	2
HELQUIST GEORGE B	LTC	0-0464855	0365	3
HELRINE WILLIAM J	MAJ	0-1295876	0961	1
HELSEL CLAUDE D	LTC	0-2048011	0962	1
HELSEL DONALD R	MAJ	0-0582296	1066	1
HELSEL FRANK H	1LT	0-0452617	0444	2
HELSEL MARIAN E	MAJ	N-0760762	0665	1
HELSER JOHN H	MAJ	0-0221729	0263	3
HELSLEY GORDON F	LTC	0-0244320	0850	3
HELSLEY OSCAR S	CPT	0-1846296	0262	2
HELTERBRAN ROBERT E	CW3	W-2145806	0361	1
HELTON HERMAN	CW3	W-2149701	1262	1
HELTON JR JAMES B	1LT	0-0439505	0845	2
HELTON ROY M	1LT	0-0865249		2
HELTON WILLIAM P	1LT	0-2011507	0747	2
HELWIG CARL	MAJ	0-1172489	0156	1
HELWIG CARL M	LTC	0-0213373	1161	3
HELWIG EDWARD W	LTC	0-1102287	0462	1
HELWIG FERDINAND	LTC	0-0204730	1058	3
HELWIG WALTER A	CPT	0-1037529	0361	1
HELY JOSEPH W	LTC	0-1329944	1264	1
HELZERMAN RALPH F	CPT	0-1687156	0146	2
HEMANN JAMES E	MAJ	0-0523776	0763	1
HEMBREE HUGH R	MAJ	0-0366162	0647	2
HEMBY NORMAN N	CW4	W-2121281	1057	1
HEMENWAY PAUL E	LTC	0-1994777	0862	1
HEMEYER KARL R M	LTC	0-0328120	0365	1
HEMINGER HAROLD R	MAJ	0-0160225	0457	3
HEMINGTON RALPH W	CPT	0-0313334	0246	2
HEMINGWAY WILLIAM W	CPT	0-1295877	0447	1
HEMKER JOSEPH F	COL	0-1000579	0867	1
HEMMER ANDREW P	CPT	0-0920085	1046	1
HEMMINGS ESTHER H	MAJ	N-0721196	0464	2
HEMMRICH FRED W	LTC	0-0453928	0358	1
HEMOVICH MICHAEL A	LTC	0-0388262	0567	1
HEMPERLY ROBERT W	MAJ	0-5210340	1061	2
HEMPHILL EDWARD S	COL	0-0116274	0852	3
HEMPHILL WILLIAM H	MAJ	0-2024172	0561	1
HEMPHILL WILLIAM T	MAJ	0-0405504	0349	1
HEMPLEY OSCAR L B	LTC	0-0301458	0555	1
HEMPSTEAD COURTNEY W	LTC	0-0335539	1061	3
HEMRY CHARLES S	COL	0-0226355	0565	3
HENAGAN JOHN C	M G	0-0163943	0157	3
HENAGE CADDIE L	MAJ	0-1306718	0561	1
HENRY ELIJAH B	LTC	0-0326375	0546	2
HENCHEY JR WILLIAM J	1LT	0-1017760	0746	2

NAME	GRADE	SVC NO	DATE RET MO YR	RET CODE
HENDEE CONN C	CPT	0-1334572	1263	1
HENDEE PAUL C	LTC	0-1895538	0361	1
HENDERSHOT EDGAR A	COL	0-0264329	0267	3
HENDERSHOT JOHN R	MAJ	0-1282334	0361	1
HENDERSHOT STERLING	CW2	W-2109886	0362	3
HENDERSHOTT H B	1LT	0-1043362	1045	2
HENDERSHOTT JACOB E	LTC	0-0376965	0756	1
HENDERSHOTT WALTER E	1LT	0-1165874	1146	2
HENDERSON ALBERT E	M G	0-0264146	0455	3
HENDERSON ALPHEUS L	COL	0-0212286	1156	3
HENDERSON ARLIE O	MAJ	0-0484511	0847	1
HENDERSON ARTHUR A	CW3	W-2005577	0966	1
HENDERSON ARTHUR E	MAJ	0-1553098	0157	1
HENDERSON ARTHUR H	COL	0-0191695	0962	3
HENDERSON CARL E	CW3	W-2152386	1264	1
HENDERSON CHARLES D	COL	0-0328148	1060	3
HENDERSON CHARLES R	CW2	W-3150661	0965	1
HENDERSON CHARLES W	LTC	0-0706174	0563	1
HENDERSON CHARLES W	MAJ	0-1299235	0462	1
HENDERSON CLAIR B	MAJ	0-1595552	0462	1
HENDERSON CLARENCE P	LTC	0-1844829	0762	1
HENDERSON CLYDE E	LTC	0-0307831	0265	3
HENDERSON CYRIL D	LTC	0-0507177	0864	3
HENDERSON DALE F	LTC	0-1013232	0463	1
HENDERSON DAVID L	2LT	0-1052811	0345	2
HENDERSON DICK K	MAJ	0-1825750	0360	2
HENDERSON DONALD A	COL	0-0236352	0859	1
HENDERSON DONALD R	LTC	0-2000844	1264	1
HENDERSON EDDIE C	CW4	W-2141310	0765	1
HENDERSON EDDYTH H	1LT	0-1104203	0745	2
HENDERSON EDGAR G	MAJ	0-0354798	0245	1
HENDERSON EDGAR L	LTC	0-0236319	0166	3
HENDERSON ELIZABETH	CPT	N-0720595	1150	1
HENDERSON ERNEST W	MAJ	0-0354903	1146	1
HENDERSON GENEVA F	MAJ	N-0727567	0863	3
HENDERSON GEORGE	COL	0-0125665	0648	3
HENDERSON GEORGE C	MAJ	0-1649484	0864	1
HENDERSON GEORGE H	LTC	0-0495430	1064	3
HENDERSON GEORGE H	CW4	W-2106046	0456	1
HENDERSON GEORGE M	LTC	0-2012707	0367	3
HENDERSON GEORGE R	MAJ	0-0310905	0344	1
HENDERSON GEORGE R	MAJ	0-0976135	0565	1
HENDERSON HAROLD	MAJ	0-0372986	0145	2
HENDERSON HUBERT C	CW2	W-2141176	1154	1
HENDERSON IRENE	MAJ	N-0736847	1264	1
HENDERSON J P	MAJ	0-2018882	0164	1
HENDERSON JACK	1LT	0-0499456	0847	1
HENDERSON JACKSON G	LTC	0-0239298	0266	3
HENDERSON JAMES E	LTC	0-1313241	0367	1
HENDERSON JAMES H	1LT	0-0945884	0853	1
HENDERSON JAMES R	2LT	0-0109274	0336	2
HENDERSON JESSIE T	1LT	N-0744263	0346	1
HENDERSON JOE R	MAJ	0-0336661	0241	3
HENDERSON JOHNNIE C	1LT	0-1288741	0945	2
HENDERSON JOSEPH J	LTC	0-1302816	0761	1
HENDERSON LESTER J	LTC	0-1113248	1262	1
HENDERSON LLOYD A	2LT	0-1297366	1043	2
HENDERSON LYLE H	MAJ	0-0248936	0763	3
HENDERSON MARVIN J	CW3	W-2114280	1154	1
HENDERSON MATTHEW G	LTC	0-0263853	0159	3
HENDERSON MAURICE F	COL	0-0242833	1154	3
HENDERSON MAXWELL	2LT	0-2323933	0648	3
HENDERSON OTIS W	LTC	0-1104836	0763	1
HENDERSON RALPH D	MAJ	0-0123080	0352	3
HENDERSON RALPH L	CPT	0-1168284	0454	1
HENDERSON RALPH W	MAJ	0-1639161	0765	3
HENDERSON RALPH W	CW2	W-2109328	1148	1
HENDERSON RAYMOND D	COL	0-0335228	0151	3
HENDERSON ROBERT C	MAJ	0-0450889	0459	1
HENDERSON ROBERT L	MAJ	0-1584346	1263	1
HENDERSON ROBERT M	CPT	0-0396589	0845	2
HENDERSON ROBERT P	CW3	W-2207476	0567	1
HENDERSON ROBERT W	LTC	0-0186543	0748	3
HENDERSON RUPERT C	LTC	0-0489727	0954	1
HENDERSON SIDNEY A	MAJ	0-1101864	0561	1
HENDERSON SIDNEY L	MAJ	0-0262709	0861	3
HENDERSON THOMAS E	CW3	W-2207444	0566	1
HENDERSON THOMAS J	MAJ	0-1294306	1147	2
HENDERSON THOMAS W	1LT	0-0506186	0844	2
HENDERSON VIRGIL L	LTC	0-0299365	0954	1
HENDERSON WALTER H	COL	0-0399792	0767	1
HENDERSON WILLIAM A	LTC	0-1103207	1066	1
HENDERSON WILLIAM B	LTC	0-0415969	0663	3
HENDERSON WILLIAM E	MAJ	0-1288050	0353	1
HENDERSON WILLIAM H	CW3	W-2152965	0965	1
HENDERSON WILLIAM R	MAJ	0-0354670	0246	2
HENDERSON WILLIAM R	CPT	0-1913727	0744	1
HENDLER FREDERIC E	COL	0-0494895	0458	2
HENDLEY ARCHIBALD	MAJ	0-1693114	1160	1
HENDON ROBERT R	COL	0-0109678	0354	3
HENDREN IRVIN K	COL	0-0279730	0566	3
HENDREN KENNETH H	MAJ	0-1794942	0760	1
HENDRESCHKE ROBERT H	CW3	W-3430004	0667	1
HENDRICK JR ROBERT M	LTC	0-1579774	0463	1
HENDRICK PAUL H	MAJ	0-1287350	0961	1
HENDRICK ROBERT E	MAJ	0-0280303	0567	3
HENDRICKS AZRO S	LTC	0-0247923	1266	3
HENDRICKS BILLY	MAJ	0-1338820	0363	1
HENDRICKS CHARLES S	COL	0-0176710	1150	3
HENDRICKS CHARLES Y	CPT	0-0402244	0445	1
HENDRICKS CLEO J	MAJ	0-0572519	0363	1
HENDRICKS EARL F	CPT	0-0286901	0245	2
HENDRICKS EDWARD	CPT	0-1306587	1052	1
HENDRICKS FRANK J	CW2	W-2142236	0160	1
HENDRICKS GEORGE H	MAJ	0-0291911	0760	2
HENDRICKS GLENN W	MAJ	0-0395978	0863	1
HENDRICKS HAROLD L	CW3	W-2101825	0761	1
HENDRICKS HARRY H	COL	0-0203253	0557	3
HENDRICKS JAMES H	MAJ	0-1301484	0757	1
HENDRICKS JEANIE K	MAJ	N-0757951	0265	3
HENDRICKS JOSEPH	MAJ	0-0483111	1053	1
HENDRICKS LAMBERT M	COL	0-0132219	0352	3
HENDRICKS PORTER	MAJ	0-0312987	1045	2
HENDRICKS RAPHAEL R	1LT	0-1012463	0445	2
HENDRICKS SHELBOUR	1LT	0-1293771	0245	2
HENDRICKS SIMON S	CPT	0-0246905	0855	3
HENDRICKS THOMAS A	LTC	0-0503203	1057	1
HENDRICKSON AGNES G	2LT	N-0784884	0345	1
HENDRICKSON ARTHUR	CPT	0-1319740	1048	2
HENDRICKSON BARNEY G	CPT	0-0353775	0844	2
HENDRICKSON BURTON L	LTC	0-1333572	0866	1
HENDRICKSON CHARLES	CW3	W-2206109	1066	1
HENDRICKSON DEAN M	MAJ	0-0392078	1146	2
HENDRICKSON F R	CPT	0-1010046	1147	2
HENDRICKSON FREDOLPH	MAJ	0-0463953	0546	2
HENDRICKSON GEORGE C	COL	0-0311127	0767	3
HENDRICKSON GEORGE G	MAJ	0-2007311	0164	1
HENDRICKSON GEORGE H	LTC	0-0917197	1264	3
HENDRICKSON HARLAN R	CW4	W-2102998	0659	1
HENDRICKSON HARRY R	CPT	0-1013560	0546	1
HENDRICKSON HUGH J	MAJ	0-1283771	0157	1
HENDRICKSON HUGO P	MAJ	0-1555059	0863	1
HENDRICKSON JACK M	CW3	W-2147550	1264	1
HENDRICKSON JAMES C	MAJ	0-0970124	0864	1
HENDRICKSON JOHN L	CPT	0-2035323	0348	1
HENDRICKSON L R	CPT	0-0488161	1155	1
HENDRICKSON LYDON E	WO1	W-2102999	0943	2
HENDRICKSON OLE O	LTC	0-0379820	0767	3
HENDRICKSON RALPH G	MAJ	0-0318224	0160	1
HENDRICKSON ROY G	MAJ	0-0024093	0157	1
HENDRICKSON W F	MAJ	0-1289423	0257	1
HENDRIE JONATHAN A	LTC	0-0502865	1266	3
HENDRIKS JOHN	MAJ	0-1874276	0566	1
HENDRIKSMA ELLERT	1LT	0-1317011	0646	1
HENDRIX ERNEST V	MAJ	0-0197138	0360	3
HENDRIX JACK S	CW2	W-2149255	0861	1
HENDRIX JAMES S	WO1	W-2107771	0646	2
HENDRIX JR SAMUEL B	LTC	0-1168285	0462	1
HENDRIX MIKE Y	COL	0-0417829	1167	1
HENDRIX PHILIP C	LTC	0-1824313	0862	1
HENDRIX RALPH L	MAJ	0-1533086	1148	2
HENDRIX RALPH W	CPT	0-1103208	1047	2
HENDRIX TRACY M	MAJ	0-0190845	0453	3
HENDRIX WILLIAM H	MAJ	0-0998502	0764	1
HENDRIXSON LOGAN R	MAJ	0-0279339	0547	1
HENDRY CHARLES	LTC	0-1796791	0864	1
HENDRY DONALD C	CW3	W-2205716	1165	1
HENDRY FRANK	LTC	0-1315932	0562	1
HENDRY GERALDINE	2LT	N-0773108	0345	1
HENDRY HENRY A	COL	0-0298626	0966	3
HENDRY JR JOHN E	LTC	0-0267511	0657	1
HENDRYX ANDREW R	1LT	0-0482403	1145	2
HENEBERY JR JOHN J	LTC	0-1054620	0866	1
HENEGAR ELMER	MAJ	0-1301640	0358	1
HENEGAR HELEN E	1LT	N-0732156	0846	1
HENEY EDWARD J	LTC	0-0346405	0861	3
HENFLING GEORGE W	MAJ	0-0385001	1047	2
HENGTGEN ARNOLD W	MAJ	0-1043104	1059	1
HENIKA ROBERT G	CPT	0-0317949	0545	2
HENIN ROBERT	CPT	0-1294838	0946	2
HENISE CHARLES E	LTC	0-0334222	0861	1
HENIUS HAROLD H H	COL	0-0359863	0864	3
HENKE KENNETH E	MAJ	0-1314141	0461	1
HENKEL BLAINE M	2LT	0-1314477	0144	2
HENKEL ROBERT S	1LT	0-0416482	0743	2
HENKLE CLAIRE V	LTC	0-0229299	0463	3
HENLE ELMO A	CW2	W-2144016	1060	2
HENLEY DELLIS L	CW3	RW-2144949	0761	1
HENLEY ESCOE B	CW3	W-2205136	0463	1
HENLEY GLADYS I	MAJ	N-0783452	0466	3
HENLEY JESS W	LTC	0-0452636	0859	1
HENLEY LOWELL D	LTC	0-0336721	0563	3
HENLEY MANFORD G	COL	0-0119204	0648	3
HENLEY MICHAEL E	WO1	W-3151258	0964	2
HENLEY ROBERT H	1LT	0-1298395	0945	2
HENLEY STEPHEN C	CPT	0-0474510	0945	1
HENLINE WENDELL Z	MAJ	0-0522533	0446	1
HENN EMMA C	1LT	N-0724084	1046	1
HENN ROBERT H	1LT	0-1039386	0745	2
HENNE CARL	LTC	0-0288687	0753	3
HENNEBERG ROBERT E	CW3	W-2144023	0258	1
HENNELL KENNITH I	MAJ	0-2046699	1161	1
HENNEMAN FREDERICK	COL	0-0273933	0746	2
HENNEMUTH JOHN R	CPT	0-1102763	0646	1
HENNESEY WILLIAM A	CPT	0-0905711	0946	2
HENNESSEE PATRICK H	WO1	W-2105650	0551	1
HENNESSEY DON P	WO1	W-2121051	0844	2
HENNESSEY JOSEPH J	CW2	W-2145447	0856	1
HENNESSEY JOSEPH W	CPT	0-0491281	0347	2
HENNESSEY THOMAS P	LTC	0-0530788	0167	1
HENNESSEY WILLIAM J	MAJ	0-2001092	0163	1
HENNESSEY WILLIAM L	1LT	0-0393234	0145	1
HENNESSY CARL D	MAJ	0-0311837	0460	1
HENNESSY CHARLES F	LTC	0-1293049	0663	1
HENNESSY EDWARD J	LTC	0-1295210	0461	1
HENNESSY FRANCIS W	CW2	W-2151616	0160	1
HENNESSY HAROLD R	COL	0-0275788	0963	3
HENNESSY HERBERT J	MAJ	0-0163301	0453	3
HENNESSY JOSEPH J	MAJ	0-0980981	0964	1
HENNESSY LEON G	MAJ	0-1650903	1065	1
HENNEY RICHARD B	CPT	0-1030674	0147	2
HENNICKE CAROLINE C	1LT	L-0900045	0645	2
HENNICKE RAYMOND G	LTC	0-1180535	0859	1
HENNIE OLIVER J	LTC	0-1552896	0367	1
HENNIGAN FRANCIS A	MAJ	0-0220898	0764	3
HENNIGAR WILLIAM C	CPT	0-0302615	0246	2
HENNING BERNARD A	CW2	W-2151389	1061	1
HENNING BERTHEL H	COL	0-0240602	0258	3
HENNING DORA M	LTC	N-0741655	0562	1
HENNING ERWIN P	LTC	0-1182597	0367	3
HENNING GEORGE F	LTC	0-1313607	1165	1
HENNING HARVEY P	2LT	0-1913724	1040	1
HENNING JOHN	1LT	0-1101865	0245	2
HENNING LUTHER T	CPT	0-1292881	0847	2
HENNING MARION M	2LT	N-0795719	0147	1
HENNINGER HALLIE B	MAJ	0-0503937	1054	1
HENNINGS ARNIT F	MAJ	0-0274445	0854	2
HENNINGS LAWRENCE R	COL	0-0299585	0160	3
HENNINGS WALTER D	COL	0-0278751	1160	3
HENNINGSEN MELVIN G	CPT	0-0535564	0346	2
HENNINGSGAARD B J	CPT	0-0515563	0846	2
HENNINGTON HAROLD M	MAJ	0-0750389	1060	2
HENNIS HARRY W	LTC	0-0179774	1053	3
HENNRIKUS ARTHUR W	1LT	0-1170004	1144	2
HENNRIKUS GEORGE F	LTC	0-0464194	0755	3
HENRECHON JOSEPH L	CPT	0-0275658	0951	3
HENRI ARTHUR V	LTC	0-2046337	0762	1
HENRICH CARL A	MAJ	0-0396542	0561	1
HENRICH MELVIN C	LTC	0-0317565	0864	3
HENRICHSEN ARTHUR L	CPT	0-0349338	1043	2
HENRICKS ALBERT M	LTC	0-1636029	0263	1
HENRICKSON JACOB	CPT	0-0128227	0648	3
HENRIETTA SR JOHN R	MAJ	0-1639164	0462	1
HENRIKSEN FRANCIS R	CPT	0-0321733	1048	1
HENRIKSEN VENITA B	2LT	N-0726925	0945	1
HENRY ANDREW J	CPT	0-4010845	1266	1
HENRY CHARLES E	COL	0-0353730	0557	1
HENRY CHARLES H	MAJ	0-0510889	0757	1
HENRY CHRISTOPHE	2LT	0-1994928	0644	2
HENRY CLARENCE R	CPT	0-0269516	1266	3
HENRY DALE E	MAJ	0-1536181	0765	1
HENRY DALE F	LTC	0-1544984	0962	1
HENRY DEAN T	MAJ	0-0400744	1145	2
HENRY EDWARD F	COL	0-0301584	0265	3
HENRY EDWARD R	MAJ	0-1685006	1264	1
HENRY ELLSWORTH	MAJ	0-0967033	1262	1
HENRY ELMER T	COL	0-0271679	0656	1
HENRY ERDEAN L	COL	0-0402798	1164	1
HENRY EUGENE D	MAJ	0-0302890	0245	2
HENRY EVART R	1LT	0-2023735	0847	2
HENRY FRANCIS J	LTC	0-1646142	0263	1
HENRY FRANK C	CPT	0-1885538	0365	1
HENRY FREDERICK	LTC	0-0515166	1065	3
HENRY G B	MAJ	0-1108733	0157	1
HENRY GEORGE	LTC	0-1040938	0363	1
HENRY GEORGE W	WO1	W-2150090	0556	1
HENRY HERBERT H	CW2	W-2105284	0449	1
HENRY HERMAN K	LTC	0-0216776	0263	3
HENRY JAMES A	CW3	W-2116055	0457	1
HENRY JAMES E	1LT	0-1112760	1044	2
HENRY JOHN	MAJ	0-0492424	0456	1
HENRY JOHN O	1LT	0-1289250	0744	2
HENRY JOHN W	CW3	W-2142237	0955	1
HENRY JR DEWITT C	MAJ	0-1175460	0762	2
HENRY JR JOSEPH P	LTC	0-1315063	1162	1
HENRY JR JUSTUS R	2LT	0-1303886	1044	2
HENRY LELAND D	CW3	W-2144878	0862	1
HENRY LOWELL G	LTC	0-0402453	0361	1
HENRY MARY R	MAJ	N-0726747	0356	2
HENRY MERRITT H	COL	0-0186401	0949	3
HENRY MERTON F	2LT	0-1576111	0245	2
HENRY MORDICA M	1LT	0-0274822	0756	3
HENRY NORMAN E	CPT	0-1104840	0962	3
HENRY PATRICK J	CW2	W-3430368	0866	1
HENRY PAUL D	CW2	W-2152387	0361	1
HENRY RALPH J	MAJ	0-0358757	0647	1
HENRY REX T	LTC	0-2042869	0463	1
HENRY ROBERT L	CW2	W-3430203	1166	1
HENRY ROBERT M	LTC	0-0399030	0757	2
HENRY RUSK G	LTC	0-2204074	0967	1
HENRY RUSSELL B	WO1	W-2111351	1053	1
HENRY SAMUEL C	LTC	0-1574822	0966	1
HENRY SR JOSEPH M	LTC	0-0183740	0862	3
HENRY THOMAS L	CPT	0-0450850	0853	2
HENRY TRUMAN K	CPT	0-1823871	0761	1
HENRY WALTER L	1LT	0-1288549	1045	2
HENRY WILLIAM B	MAJ	0-1588633	0355	1
HENRY WILLIAM G	MAJ	0-0721074	1060	2
HENRY WILLIAM J	MAJ	0-0181048	0946	1
HENRY WILLIAM J	1LT	0-0461526	1045	2

NAME	GRADE	SVC NO	DATE RET MO YR	RET CODE
HENRY WILLIAM J	CW4	W-2119838	0157	1
HENRY WILLIAM R	MAJ	O-0291809	0467	3
HENRY WILLIAM R	1LT	O-2043035	0246	2
HENSARLING THERON A	MAJ	O-0169188	0360	3
HENSCHEN HAROLD G	CW3	W-2145776	1262	1
HENSEL JOSEPH W	COL	O-0266185	0160	2
HENSEL WILLIAM A	CW3	W-2150914	0863	1
HENSEL WILLIAM R	CPT	O-1309182	0664	1
HENSEN ROBERT A	2LT	O-0968436	0151	1
HENSHAW FRED M	COL	O-0255509	0755	3
HENSHAW WILLIAM R	MAJ	O-1641384	0361	1
HENSKE WILLIAM C	LTC	O-0218686	0756	3
HENSLER DOROTHA E	1LT	N-0726910	0146	1
HENSLER HAROLD A	COL	O-0301076	0663	3
HENSLEY ARTHUR L	MAJ	O-0172797	0745	2
HENSLEY ARTHUR O	CW4	W-2108025	0660	1
HENSLEY BILLY G	MAJ	O-1879043	1264	1
HENSLEY HENRY	1LT	O-0496804	0846	1
HENSLEY JAMES E	CW2	W-2144682	0461	1
HENSLEY JOHN M	MAJ	O-1299746	0557	1
HENSLEY JR ROBERT J	CPT	O-1642178	0155	1
HENSLEY LESTER J	COL	O-0174226	0162	3
HENSLEY ROBERT B	COL	O-0303867	0560	1
HENSLEY ROBERT W	CPT	O-1685259	0846	2
HENSON BERNIE C	MAJ	O-2055957	0557	1
HENSON EDGAR L	CPT	O-0210717	0446	2
HENSON HAROLD E	LTC	O-0190960	1055	3
HENSON HOWARD W	LTC	O-0337911	0358	1
HENSON JAMES A	2LT	O-1298537	0945	2
HENSON JAMES L	MAJ	O-1581175	0656	2
HENSON JOHN W L	WO1	W-2143767	0152	2
HENSON OLEN D	LTC	O-0707691	0463	1
HENSON ROBERT G	WO1	W-2107217	0953	1
HENSON ROBERT J	MAJ	O-1919133	0964	1
HENSON ROBERT R	MAJ	O-0815698	0663	1
HENSON SR JAMES T	CW2	W-2121063	0955	1
HENSON WALTER A	CPT	O-1171186	0346	2
HENSTELL HENRY H	CPT	O-0360869	1044	2
HENTERLY JAMES K	2LT	O-1325702	0245	2
HENTGES KENNETH R	CW4	W-2142406	0464	1
HENTGES LESTER J	MAJ	O-2262643	1164	1
HENTGES ROBERT E	CW3	W-2144967	0862	1
HENTON JR RUFUS	CW3	W-2146019	0964	1
HENTSCHEL GEORGE W	CW2	W-2151669	0560	1
HEPBURN EARLE	COL	O-0164564	0652	3
HEPBURN JAMES W	LTC	O-1035012	0556	1
HEPBURN JOHN W	LTC	O-0973231	1067	1
HEPNER SERENE J	CW3	W-2152846	0562	1
HEPP DANIEL H	CPT	O-1030578	1046	1
HEPP WILLIAM	CPT	O-1693450	1145	2
HEPPARD GLENN R	2LT	O-0385297	0843	2
HEPPARD JOHN K	MAJ	O-1178502	1062	1
HEPPERLEN THOMAS A	CPT	O-0195700	0349	3
HEPPTING CHARLES F	CPT	O-0471514	0745	2
HERALD BANKS E	CW2	W-2107966	0753	1
HERALD VIRGIL H	LTC	O-0234251	0557	1
HERB CHARLES F	MAJ	O-1165876	0261	1
HERB FRANK H	LTC	O-0266622	1065	1
HERB ROBERT E	MAJ	O-0415418	1047	2
HERBERT CHARLES T	MAJ	O-0319406	1045	2
HERBERT EDWIN C	2LT	O-1183536	0645	2
HERBERT GERARD W	MAJ	O-1181630	0859	1
HERBERT GILBERT T	CPT	O-1284139	0758	1
HERBERT JR CHARLES E	CPT	O-2262183	1060	1
HERBERT JR FRANK L	CW2	W-2116287	1053	2
HERBERT MARDEN A	MAJ	O-0220298	1162	3
HERBERT PHILIP S	LTC	O-0102123	0655	3
HERBERT ROBERT L	LTC	O-1686665	0767	2
HERBERT WILLIAM S	CPT	O-0419244	1045	2
HERBERTS HERBERT L	COL	O-0142018	1155	3
HERBORN KENNETH D	MAJ	O-1015271	0261	1
HERBSLEB CARL F	LTC	O-0142026	0356	3
HERBST CARL S	COL	O-0216887	0463	3
HERBST JR EDWARD	LTC	O-1108013	0760	1
HERBST KENNETH J	LTC	O-1004781	0363	1

NAME	GRADE	SVC NO	DATE RET MO YR	RET CODE
HERBST PAUL W	LTC	O-0502764	0357	1
HERBST WALTER R	CPT	O-0513978	0148	2
HERBUY DAN	MAJ	O-2007203	0157	1
HERD FRANK E	CPT	O-1308818	0546	2
HERD WILFRED R	LTC	O-0245434	0565	3
HERDENER WILLIAM R	COL	O-0330688	1061	1
HERDMAN HAROLD	CPT	O-0483469	0747	1
HERDMAN ROBERT F	COL	O-0132640	0954	3
HEREDIA TRINIDAD M	MAJ	O-1281463	0757	1
HEREFORD JR LESLIE R	1LT	O-0519386	0 46	2
HERES SERAFIN O	1LT	O-1896621	1049	1
HERETH RAYMOND J	MAJ	O-1052387	0261	1
HERGENRATHER CHARL	1LT	O-1171187	0246	2
HERGENROEDER CHARL	2LT	O-0521211	0246	2
HERGERT FRED N	1LT	O-0491029	0258	1
HERGET GEORGE H	LTC	O-1642964	0663	1
HERIDER HARRY V	MAJ	O-0194318	0146	2
HERINA JOHN	LTC	O-1103689	1060	1
HERING JR ROBERT H	CPT	O-1552698	0553	1
HERICT JULIAN C	LTC	O-0376207	1263	1
HERIS GEORGE C	COL	O-0290976	0567	3
HERIT JOHN E	WO1	W-2148794	1064	1
HERITAGE WADE F	COL	O-1821202	0765	1
HERL MARGARET F	1LT	N-0729145	0746	1
HERLIHY FREDERICK	LTC	O-0473553	1066	3
HERLOCK ROBERT R	CPT	O-0964065	0159	2
HERLT ARTHUR J	1LT	O-0497873	0960	1
HERMAN ALPHONSE G	LTC	O-0195295	0259	3
HERMAN EARL F	CW3	W-2150174	0665	1
HERMAN ELMER B	1LT	O-1316414	0546	2
HERMAN MURRAY	LTC	O-0312338	0567	3
HERMAN RALPH	1LT	O-0444816	1145	2
HERMAN RAY E	MAJ	O-0255149	0361	3
HERMAN SANFORD	1LT	O-1286287	1045	1
HERMAN VINCENT J	LTC	O-1559022	0967	1
HERMAN WELDON P	1LT	O-1301301	0246	2
HERMAN WILLIAM J	LTC	O-1283427	0864	1
HERMANN CHARLES S	CPT	O-1015289	0846	2
HERMANSON HUGO E	CW3	W-2148537	0765	1
HERMANSON JACK	LTC	O-1545156	0462	1
HERMANSON JOHN H	MAJ	O-1636031	1060	1
HERMENING GLEN L	MAJ	O-1337707	0962	1
HERMES ROBERT B	1LT	O-1168286	114N	1
HERMEY WALTER E	MAJ	O-1104841	0762	1
HERMITAGE WILLIAM H	LTC	O-0216266	0648	3
HERNANDEZ ARMANDO	MAJ	O-2041427	0965	1
HERNANDEZ ELIGIO B A	1LT	O-1897060	0350	1
HERNANDEZ JOAQUIN	1LT	O-1310340	0945	2
HERNANDEZ JOSEPH C	2LT	O-1016436	0445	2
HERNANDEZ LAZARO M	MAJ	O-1597820	0660	1
HERNANDEZ LUIS F	MAJ	O-0993850	0266	1
HERNANDEZ MICHAEL R	MAJ	O-2005985	0263	1
HERNANDEZ RAFAEL	MAJ	O-0464520	0345	1
HERNANDEZ RAPHAEL S	COL	O-0177554	0961	3
HERNANDEZ RICHARD R	MAJ	O-1597476	0862	1
HERNANDEZ WALTER R	COL	O-1824183	1264	3
HERNANDEZ-MATOS JOSE	COL	O-0540709	0466	3
HERNANDO VALENTINE	WO1	W-2152792	1055	2
HERNDOBLER JOHN W	LTC	O-1646246	0464	3
HERNDON CLARENCE V	CPT	O-0435262	0746	2
HERNDON HUNTER V	COL	O-0179043	1060	3
HERNDON J PRUGH	COL	O-0182543	0757	3
HERNDON JACK V N	LTC	O-0293834	0860	1
HERNDON JAMES N	COL	O-1284512	0759	1
HERNDON JOHN S	CW2	W-2120104	0445	2
HERNDON MARY E	MAJ	N-0799105	0565	1
HERNDON QUINTUS T	2LT	O-2055136	0944	2
HERNDON WILBUR C	WO1	W-2149257	1060	1
HERNDON WILLIAM O	CW2	W-2214574	1166	1
HEROLD AMBROSE L	LTC	O-1102765	0464	1
HEROLD GERALD M	MAJ	O-1047567	0364	1
HEROLD MARY E	MAJ	N-0721615	1062	1
HERON CHARLES R	CPT	O-1914404	1135	1
HERON DAVID F	COL	O-0480234	0646	2
HERON JR WILLIAM E	LTC	O-0358260	0860	1

NAME	GRADE	SVC NO	DATE RET MO YR	RET CODE
HERPERS FERDINAND	CPT	O-0324220	104N	2
HERR JOSEPH E	MAJ	O-0949016	0462	1
HERR LAURISTON	LTC	O-0103870	1051	3
HERR NORMAN R	COL	O-0406323	0362	2
HERR PAUL S	MAJ	O-0323024	0445	2
HERREL GORDON K	CPT	O-1285938	0763	1
HERREN JOHN C	LTC	O-0264485	0661	1
HERREN JR JAMES M	LTC	O-0237859	0466	3
HERREN WESLEY M	LTC	O-0257709	0866	3
HERRERA FERNANDO A	MAJ	O-1641386	0464	1
HERRERA JOHN C	COL	O-0258813	0467	3
HERRERA RAYMOND M	LTC	O-0455254	1158	1
HERRERA WILLIAM	MAJ	O-1284330	0562	1
HERRICK BOBBY L	CW2	W-3200162	1065	1
HERRICK CHARLES C	COL	O-0172228	0251	3
HERRICK HAROLD A	LTC	O-0109320	0648	3
HERRICK JAMES A	MAJ	O-1004783	0457	1
HERRICK ROBERT D	MAJ	O-0157102	0657	3
HERRICK ROBERT F	CW3	W-2123215	0661	1
HERRICK WILLIAM H	MAJ	O-2262601	0165	1
HERRICKS ROBERT N	LTC	O-1010159	0160	1
HERRIN BURK Y	CPT	O-0356157	1146	2
HERRIN JR WILLIAM M	COL	O-0269307	0362	3
HERRIN NORMAN A	1LT	O-1324933	0854	1
HERRING CATHRYN C	1LT	N-0787015	0246	1
HERRING CHARLES R	LTC	O-0142337	1149	3
HERRING CLARENCE B	1LT	O-1112762	1047	2
HERRING GEORGE E	CPT	O-0363388	0646	2
HERRING HERBERT J	MAJ	O-1014238	0759	1
HERRING HERMAN R	CPT	O-0888598	1054	1
HERRING LESTER W	CPT	O-0291798	0564	3
HERRING THOMAS A	MAJ	O-1640547	0461	1
HERRING THOMAS F	LTC	O-0650530	1062	1
HERRING TULLIE S	MAJ	O-0885818	1044	1
HERRINGTON ARTHUR T	1LT	O-0502109	0744	1
HERRINGTON CECIL P	COL	O-0306826	0367	3
HERRINGTON ELMO	CW3	W-2206086	0766	1
HERRINGTON JOHN C	CW3	W-2145077	0365	1
HERRINGTON JOHN T	LTC	O-0422187	0957	1
HERRINGTON LINWOOD	CPT	O-0358123	1143	2
HERRIOTT RUSSELL K	LTC	O-1298704	0561	1
HERRIS WILLIAM W	MAJ	O-1337186	0465	1
HERRLICH WILLIAM E	MAJ	O-0179044	1061	3
HERRMAN RUSSELL T	CW2	W-2208901	0165	1
HERRMANN ALBERT	LTC	O-0246853	0264	3
HERRMANN ERNEST F	LTC	O-0281741	1066	3
HERRMANN FREDERICK	MAJ	O-0216646	0962	3
HERRMANN HARRY C	CPT	O-1184315	0347	2
HERRMANN HENRY J	MAJ	O-0247506	0550	3
HERRMANN HOWARD W	MAJ	O-0299348	1054	1
HERRMANN WESLEY P	LTC	O-0279929	0463	3
HERRMANN WILLIAM H	1LT	O-1032354	1145	2
HERRMANN WILLIAM J	CPT	O-0343530	0145	2
HERRON AUSTIN R	MAJ	O-0116911	0949	3
HERRON CLAIR E	CPT	O-0488160	0752	1
HERRON DURWARD P	MAJ	O-1826275	0557	1
HERRON EARL	COL	O-1821274	0764	3
HERRON FREDERICK	LTC	O-0171819	0648	3
HERRON JAMES R	LTC	O-0309073	0863	3
HERRON NAPOLEON	WO1	W-2108077	0861	1
HERRON RAYMOND K	LTC	O-0906820	0662	1
HERRON RICHARD A	COL	O-0259948	0365	3
HERRSTROM CHARLES E	COL	O-0195914	0263	3
HERSCHBACH SIGMUND R	MAJ	O-1018167	0961	1
HERSCHEL JR PAUL E	MAJ	O-0253358	0252	3
HERSCHLEDER FRED J	LTC	O-0451583	1060	1
HERSEY IRVING W	LTC	O-0919855	1262	3
HERSEY JAMES R	1LT	O-1331395	0846	2
HERSEY RALPH G	LTC	O-0173211	1147	1
HERSEY WALTER F	LTC	O-1183881	0464	1
HERSEY WINTHROP P	LTC	O-0247535	0466	3
HERSH ELMER B	MAJ	O-1584351	0362	1
HERSH HAROLD	MAJ	O-1534755	0666	1
HERSH HARRY	CW2	W-2142316	1054	1
HERSHBERGER HAROLD R	MAJ	O-0954538	0366	1

NAME	GRADE	SVC NO	DATE RET MO YR	RET CODE
HERSHBERGER RALPH E	CPT	O-1693789	1045	2
HERSHCUCK MICHAEL	1LT	O-1302900	104N	2
HERSHEY CHARLES E	CPT	O-0158873	1060	3
HERSHKOWITZ LEON	LTC	O-0225525	1263	3
HERSHON IRVING J	LTC	O-0293878	0966	3
HERSKER HERBERT S	2LT	O-0444116	0945	2
HERSMER GENE S	CW2	W-2146462	1060	1
HERSTEIN DAVID	CPT	O-1821444	1045	2
HERSUM HAROLD O	LTC	O-0183713	0856	3
HERSUM LEROY M	COL	O-0102375	0658	3
HERTEL OLIVER R	COL	O-0381328	1163	1
HERTGEN PAUL F	LTC	O-0915344	1165	3
HERTGES NICK F	LTC	O-0494051	0455	1
HERTHEL STEPHEN W	MAJ	O-1576116	0852	2
HERTSCHE JR JOEL C	COL	O-0236133	1065	3
HERTWECK EDWARD C	MAJ	O-0509442	0951	1
HERTZ ALBERT L	LTC	O-0918848	1047	2
HERTZ CLYDE E	COL	O-0165972	0757	3
HERTZ EVELINE R	MAJ	L-0201040	0163	1
HERTZ PAUL B	LTC	O-0464466	1067	3
HERTZ RAY E	1LT	O-1113252	0545	2
HERTZBERG LOUIS	CPT	O-0450022	1048	1
HERTZBERG ROBERT E	COL	O-0257139	0365	3
HERTZOG BERNARD E	CW2	W-2144223	0259	1
HERTZSCH JR C T	1LT	O-0350596	0145	2
HERTZSCH OTTO L	CW2	W-2000503	0253	3
HERVEY HARCOURT	B G	O-0108621	0846	2
HERVEY JR DAMON	CW2	W-2151790	0957	1
HERVOL EMIL C	1LT	O-2203642	1152	2
HERWICK JOHN T	CPT	O-1687100	1144	2
HERWITT HAROLD H	COL	O-0208922	0165	3
HERWITZ ROBERT I	2LT	O-1179094	0645	2
HERYFORD GLEN L	MAJ	O-1540914	0962	1
HERZBERGER ARTHUR C	MAJ	O-0381845	0446	2
HERZFELD JOHN G	LTC	O-0537021	1266	3
HERZKE WILLIAM J	LTC	O-1301824	0165	1
HERZOG LOUIS F	CPT	O-2046296	0949	1
HERZOG MANUEL	1LT	O-1321775	1045	2
HERZOG OTTO LA VE	1LT	O-1314478	0251	2
HERZOG PAUL E	CPT	O-0484294	0345	1
HERZOG VIRGINIA G	2LT	N-0785072	1045	1
HERZOG WILLIAM	LTC	O-0178534	0648	3
HERZOG WILLIAM	CPT	O-1298396	104N	2
HERZSTEIN BERNARD	1LT	O-1637660	0246	1
HESELTON CHARLES R	LTC	O-1017828	0561	1
HESFORD HUGH A	LTC	O-0491605	0954	1
HESKETH JAMES P	1LT	O-1335923	0453	2
HESKETT HARRISON A	CPT	O-0208051	0445	2
HESLEP EDWARD A	2LT	O-1043658	0243	2
HESLER ALGY E	COL	O-0119209	0649	3
HESLER GALEN J	LTC	O-0370604	1165	1
HESLIN WILLIAM G	MAJ	O-1038399	0262	2
HESS CHARLES J	CW2	W-2149113	0762	1
HESS CHARLES M	LTC	O-0919237	0467	3
HESS CHARLES W	2LT	O-1825124	0144	2
HESS CYRIL G	MAJ	O-0985949	0866	1
HESS EMIL F	MAJ	O-1554563	0464	1
HESS FRANK J	LTC	O-1044550	1167	1
HESS FREDERICK	LTC	O-1175157	0561	1
HESS GEORGE J	LTC	O-0888261	0263	1
HESS HAROLD E	MAJ	O-0223645	1154	3
HESS HAROLD S	MAJ	O-1293589	1160	1
HESS HOWARD J	1LT	O-1578598	0845	2
HESS IRWIN H	1LT	O-0978015	0353	2
HESS JAMES M	MAJ	O-0977243	1167	1
HESS JOHN J	CPT	O-0918696	0945	2
HESS KENNETH H	COL	O-0290342	0467	3
HESS LAURIE F	LTC	O-0272847	0961	3
HESS LAWRENCE E	LTC	O-0380039	0667	1
HESS MYRON T	CPT	O-0347703	0457	1
HESS ORVAN W	COL	O-0284820	0766	3
HESS SR JAY R	MAJ	O-0908160	1157	3
HESS WALTER F	LTC	O-0371618	0467	3
HESS WILLIAM F	CW2	W-2210668	1266	1
HESS WILLIAM J	MAJ	O-1846004	0255	1

NAME	GRADE	SVC NO	DATE RET MO YR	RET CODE
HESSE CLYDE F	LTC	0-0312542	1159	1
HESSE DAVID E	LTC	0-1542828	1165	1
HESSE GEORGE A	LTC	0-0306012	C863	3
HESSELBARTH PAUL K	1LT	0-1300326	1046	1
HESSELBERG ABRAHAM L	MAJ	0-0168051	0460	3
HESSER LOWELL W	LTC	C-1289424	C863	2
HESSER ROBERT N	CPT	0-0399404	1045	2
HESSEVICK GEORGE I	LTC	0-0502795	C658	1
HESSLER EDWARD A	CPT	0-0514151	0745	2
HESSON JAMES J	LTC	0-0348153	C767	3
HESTER BURDETTE L	LTC	0-1108737	0462	1
HESTER DAVID C	COL	0-0287113	C858	2
HESTER GEORGE C	CPT	C-0201948	C649	3
HESTER JOE A	MAJ	0-0964236	0164	1
HESTER JOSEPH L	CW3	W-2114487	C356	1
HESTER JR JOSEPH A	MAJ	0-0256132	1067	3
HESTER LEONARD C	LTC	0-1634881	0858	1
HESTER MARION W	CPT	C-0332088	C845	1
HESTER ROBERT J	MAJ	C-1589262	1055	1
HESTER WARREN E	CW3	W-2150158	C764	2
HESTON ROBERT B	CPT	0-0367799	0346	2
HETEJT PAUL S	1LT	0-0414854	C745	2
HETH MABEL S	MAJ	N-0732829	1263	3
HETHCOAT CHARLES L	MAJ	C-2015761	0262	1
HETHCOAT REUBEN	CW2	W-2141313	C753	1
HETHCOTE WILLIAM E	MAJ	0-1821584	C363	1
HETHERINGTON FERRALL	CW3	W-2141164	C561	1
HETHERINGTON JACK S	LTC	0-0449215	1066	1
HETHERINGTON RICHARD	MAJ	0-1846006	0359	1
HETHERINGTON VINCENT	LTC	0-0547580	1157	2
HETHERLY WILLIAM A	CW3	W-2147481	1065	1
HETLAND VICTOR A	LTC	0-0191485	0554	3
HETRICK DONALD R	MAJ	0-2018348	0865	1
HETRICK EDGAR C	MAJ	0-0499998	0753	1
HETTEL CHARLES L	MAJ	0-0990449	1165	1
HETTEL EARL F	LTC	0-0230373	0663	3
HETTLE DONALD R	CPT	0-0410799	1047	2
HETTLER WILLIAM F	LTC	C-0296157	C563	3
HETTRICH ALBERT L	COL	0-0356455	0657	1
HETZEL JR JOHN B	LTC	0-1104843	0966	1
HETZEL KATHARINE	MAJ	N-0786514	0665	1
HETZLER VAUGHN G	2LT	0-C107048	0353	3
HEUCK ROBERT A	CPT	0-1634882	C251	1
HEULER LOYAL J	1LT	0-1296373	C546	2
HEUSER CHARLES K	MAJ	0-2044573	0853	1
HEUVEL VIRGINIA C	1LT	N-0783644	C446	1
HEVERLIN JOSEPH W	CW2	W-2118114	1046	1
HEVERLY PAUL M	COL	0-0152154	0756	3
HEWES WILLIAM E	CPT	0-1059146	0557	1
HEWETT ARTHUR A	LTC	0-0268037	C167	3
HEWETT ERNEST W	LTC	0-0907915	C167	3
HEWETT GEORGE H	LTC	0-0182399	C160	3
HEWETT JAMES D	B G	0-0910307	1265	3
HEWETT JAMES F	CW2	W-2205266	0861	1
HEWITT CARTER F	LTC	0-0904564	1167	3
HEWITT CHARLES H	CW3	W-2152515	C664	1
HEWITT CHESTER J	LTC	0-0405876	0860	2
HEWITT FRANCIS M	LTC	0-0404316	0261	1
HEWITT JR ABEL N	MAJ	C-1042053	0262	1
HEWITT JR CHARLES F	LTC	0-1634883	1065	1
HEWITT JR CHARLES K	CPT	0-4026504	0860	2
HEWITT JR DANIEL A	LTC	0-1293773	0961	1
HEWITT LAWRENCE P	LTC	C-0289892	0665	3
HEWITT SR CHARLES K	MAJ	C-1636034	0156	1
HEWITT SR STEPHEN A	LTC	0-0233909	1160	1
HEWITT WALTER J O	LTC	0-0341418	0759	1
HEWITT WILLIAM C	LTC	0-1573275	0661	1
HEWLETT ARTHUR F	MAJ	C-0238324	0565	3
HEWSON HAROLD F	MAJ	C-0953846	0365	1
HEXT CHARLES M	LTC	0-0404369	C860	1
HEXTELL CLARE O	MAJ	0-1287880	0764	2
HEY RUSSELL	MAJ	C-0479453	0654	1
HEYDE ALBERT E	CW3	W-2150561	0762	1
HEYDT WILLIAM H	CPT	0-0989999	0661	1
HEYENGA LAWRENCE E	LTC	0-0367045	C859	1
HEYER GLENN A	LTC	0-0326771	0763	1
HEYING CLAIRMONT	MAJ	C-1822998	0966	1
HEYL HENRY L	CPT	0-0436847	0744	1
HEYL JR THOMAS D	LTC	0-0109444	0847	1
HEYL THEODORE C	1LT	0-0585017	0254	2
HEYLIGER FREDERICK	CPT	0-1010235	0147	2
HEYMAN LEO	COL	0-0266340	0-53	3
HEYMANNS PETER P	CPT	0-1106200	0355	2
HEYRMAN JOHN H	MAJ	0-1594899	0758	1
HIATT CHESTER L	LTC	0-1080031	0665	1
HIATT CLIFFORD R	LTC	0-0170701	1061	1
HIATT FRED	LTC	0-0534759	0163	1
HIATT JR ENAH C	LTC	0-0947424	1167	1
HIATT JR JOSEPH S	CPT	0-0464893	0145	2
HIATT LOUIS E	1LT	0-0146191	0357	3
HIATT MAURICE F	CPT	0-0973831	1162	2
HIATT NORMAN R	CPT	0-1293252	0447	1
HIATT PAUL F	MAJ	0-2018351	0563	1
HIBALA PAUL S	CPT	0-0503258	0152	1
HIBARD GEORGE	MAJ	0-0470607	0347	1
HIBARGER DON W	2LT	0-1547964	0345	2
HIBBARD CARL H	1LT	0-1115629	1045	2
HIBBARD CHARLES	COL	0-1101493	0263	1
HIBBARD CURT W	CPT	0-0178146	1045	2
HIBBARD KEZIAH	CPT	N-0701458	0145	1
HIBBARD LEE M	1LT	0-1287351	0544	2
HIBBARD WALTER C	COL	0-0270662	0560	1
HIBBARD WILLIAM J	MAJ	C-024563C	0258	3
HIBBERT CHESTER A	LTC	0-0166054	1160	3
HIBBETTS EDGAR M	1LT	0-1825272	0247	2
HIBBS CARL W	CW2	W-2148375	0161	1
HIBBS JERAL E	1LT	0-2023876	1047	1
HIBLER BERNARD C	COL	0-0261839	0566	3
HIBNER LOWELL J	LTC	0-2037058	0961	1
HICE GILBERT D	LTC	0-1844615	0967	2
HICHAK MICHAEL	LTC	0-1578601	0862	1
HICK FORD K	LTC	0-0291943	0146	2
HICKAMBOTTOM ELBIE J	MAJ	0-0988674	0567	1
HICKCOX PERCY M	COL	0-0256872	0854	3
HICKEL NED R	MAJ	C-1283257	0947	2
HICKERSON CHARLES W	1LT	0-2004014	0957	2
HICKERSON JR JOE R	CPT	0-1184070	0346	2
HICKERSON LEONARD A	CPT	0-1107476	0146	1
HICKEY CLARENCE A	COL	0-0450891	0655	1
HICKEY DENNIS A	1LT	0-0501148	1045	2
HICKEY EDWARD R	LTC	0-0351366	0667	2
HICKEY EDWARD J	MAJ	0-0103711	0648	3
HICKEY FREDERICK	LTC	0-0372700	0959	1
HICKEY GRANVILLE	MAJ	0-1894180	0367	1
HICKEY HARRY B	CPT	0-2262361	0161	1
HICKEY JAMES E	COL	0-0332047	0559	1
HICKEY JAMES H	MAJ	0-0344676	0346	2
HICKEY JOHN	CPT	0-1300485	0555	1
HICKEY JOHN F	COL	0-0373364	0867	3
HICKEY JR EDWARD J	CPT	0-1081475	0858	1
HICKEY JR EUGENE P	LTC	0-1535196	0262	1
HICKEY LEO K	2LT	0-1295019	1043	1
HICKEY MILDRED N	CPT	N-0786313	0857	2
HICKEY MORRIS J	MAJ	0-0364152	0346	2
HICKEY PATRICK V	CPT	C-1302971	0945	1
HICKEY PETER J	MAJ	0-0338512	1046	2
HICKEY RAYMOND P	CW4	W-2142160	0159	1
HICKEY RUBY P	MAJ	N-0765236	1066	1
HICKLIN HARRY M	CW2	W-2150808	0357	1
HICKLIN WENDELL C	MAJ	C-0920453	0567	3
HICKMAN ARTHUR J	LTC	0-0384495	0166	3
HICKMAN CARLOS S	CPT	0-0234664	0845	2
HICKMAN GEORGE F	MAJ	0-1340284	1165	1
HICKMAN GERALD H	1LT	0-1598756	0747	1
HICKMAN GLENN H	LTC	0-132624C	0367	1
HICKMAN HAROLD O	MAJ	C-1797133	1057	1
HICKMAN HOWARD D	COL	0-0104100	0558	3
HICKMAN JAMES R	LTC	0-1181299	1062	1
HICKMAN JEWETT C	CW2	W-2118255	0356	1
HICKMAN JOE C	MAJ	0-0272272	0359	1
HICKMAN JOHN W	LTC	0-0230327	0164	3
HICKMAN LYLE W	CW3	W-2152731	0463	1
HICKMAN PAUL W	CW3	W-2141584	1056	1
HICKMAN RAYMOND B	MAJ	C-2025403	0863	1
HICKMAN SPURGEON	CW3	W-2145664	1061	1
HICKMAN THOMAS F	LTC	C-0406011	1160	1
HICKMAN WILLIAM H	CW2	W-2142963	1053	2
HICKMAN WILLIAM R	1LT	0-1544022	0448	1
HICKOK ARNO J	CW2	W-2208233	0862	1
HICKOX CHARLES	1LT	0-1103212	1145	2
HICKOX SR DONALD L	LTC	C-1104209	C759	1
HICKS ARTHUR	1LT	0-2023800	1146	1
HICKS AUBREY	MAJ	0-1287007	C158	1
HICKS CARL F	LTC	0-1844381	0257	1
HICKS CHARLES E	LTC	0-0343549	0363	1
HICKS CHARLES W	CPT	0-1299863	0560	1
HICKS CLARENCE C	LTC	0-0346738	0764	1
HICKS CLARISSA	MAJ	M-0002734	1163	1
HICKS CLAUD M	1LT	0-1044242	1044	2
HICKS CLIFTON H	CW3	W-2209103	0367	1
HICKS DAVID N	MAJ	C-1331837	C664	1
HICKS EARL D	LTC	0-1646146	0765	1
HICKS ELMER B	COL	0-0209279	1059	3
HICKS FLOYD S	LTC	0-0492413	C855	1
HICKS FRANCIS O	1LT	0-1178188	C146	1
HICKS FREDERICK	MAJ	C-1823156	C859	1
HICKS HAROLD O	CW2	W-2148970	0261	1
HICKS HAROLD N	MAJ	0-0948651	0663	1
HICKS HAROLD W	CPT	0-0510745	0455	1
HICKS III THOMAS M B	LTC	0-0379455	0760	1
HICKS JAMES	1LT	0-0885624	C945	2
HICKS JAMES C	1LT	0-1319741	0652	1
HICKS JAMES F	1LT	0-1168719	0346	2
HICKS JAMES L	2LT	0-0466481	0144	2
HICKS JAMES M	CPT	0-1183702	0457	2
HICKS JOHN J	LTC	0-0381966	0655	1
HICKS JOHN R	2LT	0-1303727	1143	2
HICKS JR ACLE V	MAJ	0-1106816	0661	2
HICKS JR AMP F	1LT	0-0533904	1045	2
HICKS JR EARL A	LTC	0-1057100	0364	1
HICKS JR FRED C	LTC	0-0463925	C762	1
HICKS JR KENNETH C	LTC	0-1052390	C762	1
HICKS JR YALE	CPT	0-0412919	0745	2
HICKS LARUE C	1LT	0-1030880	C856	1
HICKS LOUIS E	LTC	0-1548435	C266	1
HICKS MATTIE D	MAJ	N-0765793	0466	1
HICKS MELVIN A	1LT	0-2010622	0153	2
HICKS MILFORD H	LTC	0-0290257	0456	3
HICKS ORA P	MAJ	N-0726589	C961	1
HICKS RAYMOND E	LTC	0-1296031	C258	1
HICKS ROBERT N	COL	0-0285411	C949	2
HICKS ROBERT O	CPT	0-1879143	C364	1
HICKS SAM E	LTC	0-0402700	0361	2
HICKS THOMAS J	CW3	W-2146247	0760	1
HICKS WESLEY	CPT	0-1823598	1044	2
HICKS WILLARD E	CW2	W-2212281	1265	1
HICKS WILLIAM L	LTC	0-0425289	C961	1
HICKS WILLIAM L	WO1	W-2151674	C956	1
HICKSON JOHN C	1LT	0-0421722	1044	2
HICKSON ROBERT W	CW3	W-2146972	0363	1
HICOCK RUSSELL	LTC	0-0244058	0965	3
HIDA MIRIAM I	1LT	N-0767126	1145	1
HIDALGO BENITO T	MAJ	0-0341151	1148	2
HIDALGO JACINTO	LTC	0-0255693	C764	3
HIDALGO JOHN P	CPT	0-128414C	C660	1
HIDALGO VINCENT M	COL	0-0245520	1262	3
HIDEN CHARLES S	LTC	0-0237201	C957	3
HIEFIELD ALFRED T	MAJ	C-1057466	0167	3
HIEGERT LEONARD P	MAJ	0-2038840	1058	1
HIEMSTRA CLIFFORD F	LTC	0-1339166	C466	1
HIEN CLARENCE R	LTC	0-0297303	0165	3
HIENTON TRUMAN E	COL	0-0253922	0558	3
HIEPLER JACOB F	MAJ	C-0946831	1062	1
HIERONYMUS CHARLES D	2LT	C-2044522	C445	1
HIERS ROBERT E	CPT	0-0981430	0960	1
HIETT CARRELL D	CPT	C-0884916	0147	2
HIETT EDWARD A	1LT	0-1336064	1051	2
HIGASHI YOSHIKAZU	LTC	0-2037059	0263	1
HIGBEE CLARENCE E	COL	0-0212694	0462	3
HIGBEE ELLSWORTH	2LT	0-1288742	0644	2
HIGBEE JR WALTER V	LTC	0-1041170	0767	1
HIGBY LEONARD G	CPT	0-0360478	0956	3
HIGDON EBB	CW3	W-2152344	0765	1
HIGDON EDGAR H	MAJ	0-2210454	0564	1
HIGDON GLENNIAL	CPT	0-1183462	0161	1
HIGDON KENNETH T	MAJ	0-1335005	0664	1
HIGDON RALPH T	CW3	W-2143205	0563	1
HIGGINBOTHAM EARL A	MAJ	C-0416232	0547	1
HIGGINBOTHAM GEORG	MAJ	0-0476253	1047	1
HIGGINBOTHAM ILIFF S	COL	0-025444C	0463	3
HIGGINBOTHAM IRA	1LT	0-1168720	1145	2
HIGGINBOTHAM MEADE	CPT	0-1924754	0961	1
HIGGINBOTHAM V M	1LT	N-0735453	0446	1
HIGGINBOTHAM WILLIAM	LTC	0-1300033	0361	1
HIGGINS ALBERT F	LTC	0-0487452	0265	3
HIGGINS CATHERINE	1LT	N-0720621	114N	1
HIGGINS CLIFTON L	LTC	0-1104848	1062	2
HIGGINS EDWARD F	LTC	0-0408897	0963	1
HIGGINS EDWARD J	LTC	0-0276583	0846	2
HIGGINS EDWIN L	MAJ	0-165359C	0646	2
HIGGINS EVERETT K	LTC	0-0162120	1046	2
HIGGINS FORREST W	CPT	0-2263641	1162	1
HIGGINS FRANCIS V	LTC	0-039912C	0867	3
HIGGINS HARVEY N	1LT	0-0497529	0453	1
HIGGINS HERBERT G	CW2	W-3150398	0767	1
HIGGINS HERMAN N	1LT	0-1285758	0745	2
HIGGINS HUBERT M	MAJ	C-0368164	0844	2
HIGGINS JAMES J	MAJ	0-0288902	0467	3
HIGGINS JAMES M	COL	0-0916271	0665	3
HIGGINS JOHN T	CW2	W-2150672	1057	1
HIGGINS JOSEPH A	2LT	0-1581177	0745	2
HIGGINS JOSEPH E	LTC	0-1645659	0960	1
HIGGINS JR JOHN F	LTC	0-1299336	0767	1
HIGGINS JR MICHAEL P	1LT	0-1302305	1145	2
HIGGINS LAWRENCE M	LTC	0-0422019	0661	1
HIGGINS LEMUEL W	MAJ	0-0207018	0656	3
HIGGINS LESLIE B	MAJ	0-1051177	0161	1
HIGGINS MARK R	CW4	W-2002246	0767	1
HIGGINS MILES W	2LT	0-2049277	1144	2
HIGGINS NORMAN F	MAJ	0-2262758	0864	1
HIGGINS OTTIS C	CPT	0-1690965	0248	1
HIGGINS OWEN W	CW2	W-2208892	0659	1
HIGGINS PAUL M	CW2	W-2210572	0465	1
HIGGINS RALPH P	CPT	0-0524938	1045	2
HIGGINS RAYMOND T	COL	0-0254206	1058	3
HIGGINS ROBERT E	MAJ	C-0571731	0364	1
HIGGINS ROY	MAJ	0-0985813	0358	1
HIGGINS STANLEY P	1LT	0-0395139	0145	2
HIGGINS TIMOTHY G	MAJ	0-0465096	0667	1
HIGGINS WALTER D	CPT	0-0488604	0545	2
HIGGINS WILLIAM B	COL	0-0219816	0356	3
HIGGINSON WILLIAM M	MAJ	0-2034534	0661	1
HIGGS ARDEN J	1LT	0-2033677	0554	2
HIGH CALVIN E	MAJ	0-1299885	0858	1
HIGH DLAY B	MAJ	0-2083351	0465	1
HIGH JR HOYLE O	WO1	W-2151090	0456	2
HIGH VINCENT C	LTC	0-0337303	0158	1
HIGHBERGER EDITH M K	1LT	N-0784550	0-48	2
HIGHBY PAUL R	LTC	0-0374617	0264	3
HIGHERS THOMAS P	WO1	W-2116691	0145	2
HIGHLEY GLEN H	WO1	W-2112893	1043	2
HIGHLEY HAROLD C	LTC	0-0199047	0258	2
HIGHSMITH LLOYD G	MAJ	0-1166740	0157	1
HIGHT ROBERT H	MAJ	C-2007604	0464	1
HIGHT WALTER	2LT	0-1637667	1048	1
HIGHTOWER GRACE L	CPT	N-0800092	0652	1
HIGHTOWER JR C L	CPT	0-0366305	1045	2
HIGHTOWER JR JOHN H	LTC	0-1168721	1167	1
HIGHTOWER NASH R	LTC	0-0450289	0161	1
HIGHTOWER RUPIN F	MAJ	0-1309062	0958	1

NAME	GRADE	SVC NO	DATE RET MO YR	RET CODE
HIGHTOWER WAYNE R	CPT	0-0432155	0756	2
HIGINBOTHAM WILLIAM	LTC	0-1320688	1162	1
HIGLEY ROBERT R	LTC	0-0374222	0263	1
HIGUCHI HIRO	COL	0-0527027	0267	3
HIKEL NOLAN G	COL	0-0292264	0857	1
HILARY HENRY R	LTC	0-0350501	1266	3
HILBURN NATHANIEL	LTC	0-0453721	0962	1
HILBURN WILLIAM S	1LT	0-1012378	1145	2
HILBUSH WILLIAM E	CW3	W-2143315	0864	1
HILDEBRAND GEORGE	CPT	0-0557524	1045	2
HILDEBRAND JR EUGENE	CPT	0-1684802	0344	2
HILDEBRAND MIKE	CPT	0-0492946	0350	1
HILDEBRAND PAUL R	COL	0-0317545	0766	3
HILDEBRAND RAYMOND	COL	0-0202793	0451	3
HILDEBRAND ROBERT W	LTC	0-0322605	0263	3
HILDEBRANDT FRANK B	LTC	0-2040802	0667	1
HILDEBRANDT H F	CW2	W-2142065	0755	1
HILDEBRANDT SIEGFRIE	CW3	RW-2151671	0364	1
HILDEBRANT LEO H	CPT	0-1765901	1045	2
HILDER PETER F	MAJ	0-0325723	0645	2
HILDERBRAND LEONARD	LTC	0-0258642	0660	3
HILDETON HILBERT C	LTC	0-0488767	1154	1
HILDRETH CLIFFORD W	CPT	0-0497055	0146	2
HILDRETH DONALD P	CW3	W-2207736	0967	1
HILDRETH EUGENE F	CW3	W-2146818	1162	1
HILDRETH GLENN W	LTC	0-0264502	1153	3
HILDRICH FRANCIS	CW2	W-3250445	1167	1
HILDYARD VICTOR H	CPT	0-0469295	0146	2
HILE WARREN J	CW2	W-2146774	0758	2
HILEY JULIAN	CPT	0-1044848	0961	2
HILFERTY WILLIAM R	CPT	0-0335374	0647	2
HILGERSON FRANK J	MAJ	0-2036548	1162	1
HILKE WILLIAM J	COL	0-0266017	0460	1
HILKERT WILLIAM P	MAJ	0-0194150	0545	2
HILL ALBERT E	MAJ	0-2200003	1165	1
HILL ALFRED O	LTC	0-1286288	0961	1
HILL ARCHIE O	2LT	0-1308336	0946	2
HILL ARTHUR A	CW2	W-2147489	0164	1
HILL ARTHUR B	CPT	0-2005657	1058	2
HILL ARTHUR E	LTC	0-0261862	0864	3
HILL BENJAMIN F	MAJ	0-0161360	0156	3
HILL BOYD B	COL	0-0204151	1044	2
HILL BOYD V	LTC	0-1103213	0961	1
HILL BURNIS E	1LT	0-1305925	1145	2
HILL BURTON S	COL	0-0198908	1049	3
HILL CATHERINE	1LT	N-0743503	0546	1
HILL CECIL R	COL	0-0243924	1158	1
HILL CHARLES E	CW2	RW-2147450	0463	1
HILL CHARLES F	1LT	0-0885793	0845	2
HILL CHARLEY R	1LT	0-0495993	1144	2
HILL CHAUNCEY V	CPT	0-0887433	0263	1
HILL CHESTER E	LTC	0-0408913	0361	1
HILL CLIFTON C	LTC	0-0196207	0660	3
HILL CYRUS N	LTC	0-0323911	0354	2
HILL DANA E	CPT	0-0152228	0455	3
HILL DARRELL F	LTC	0-0450054	0455	1
HILL DARRELL M	CPT	0-1311513	0847	2
HILL DARWIN M	LTC	0-1542718	0557	1
HILL DAVID O	MAJ	0-0446320	0663	1
HILL DAVID F	CPT	0-1287713	1159	1
HILL DOUGLAS O	CW2	W-2143325	1057	1
HILL EDGAR M	LTC	0-1172494	0663	1
HILL EDWARD B	LTC	0-1307013	0463	2
HILL EDWARD S	1LT	0-1644422	0553	1
HILL EDWARD W	2LT	0-1317793	0545	2
HILL ELLIOTT B	CPT	0-1045112	0859	1
HILL ELMER A	CW2	W-2149931	1162	1
HILL ELMER C	1LT	0-1291990	0146	1
HILL EUGENE L	MAJ	0-0263814	0949	3
HILL EUGENE R	CW4	W-2002774	1264	3
HILL EVAN	CPT	0-0417992	0848	2
HILL FORREST S	CPT	0-1178832	0661	1
HILL FRANCIS T	MAJ	0-1798260	0860	1
HILL FRED C	MAJ	0-0178612	0457	3
HILL FRED J	1LT	0-0405423	0145	2
HILL FREDERICK	COL	0-0298862	1066	3
HILL FREDRIC S	LTC	0-0417312	1262	1
HILL GEORGE	MAJ	0-0499638	0747	1
HILL GEORGE A	LTC	0-0390680	0146	2
HILL GEORGE H	MAJ	0-1030155	0258	2
HILL GEORGE M	COL	0-0224702	1054	3
HILL GEORGE W	CW4	W-2142382	0757	1
HILL GERALD W	MAJ	0-1185055	1060	1
HILL GRAHAM	CPT	0-0962951	1060	1
HILL GROVER L	CW2	W-2143484	0357	1
HILL HAROLD A	LTC	0-0195325	0562	3
HILL HAROLD R	MAJ	0-1043660	0962	1
HILL HARVEY W	CW2	W-2150691	0264	1
HILL HENRY F	1LT	0-1101868	0345	2
HILL HOMER F	CPT	0-2262112	0958	1
HILL HORACE H	LTC	0-1286124	0662	1
HILL HOWARD B	LTC	0-1184227	1167	1
HILL HOWARD C	COL	0-0179008	0355	3
HILL IRVING F	MAJ	0-1551869	0461	1
HILL JACK O	WO1	W-2125436	0945	2
HILL JAMES C	CW2	W-2205560	0363	1
HILL JAMES J	COL	0-0351368	0666	1
HILL JAMES O	CW3	W-2149956	1064	1
HILL JAMES R	MAJ	0-0547268	0962	2
HILL JAMES R P	MAJ	0-0298668	0546	1
HILL JAMES W	COL	0-0261395	0654	1
HILL JAMES W	LTC	0-0381654	0860	1
HILL JIM O	M G	0-0176433	0257	3
HILL JOE M	COL	0-0152186	0948	3
HILL JOHN A	CW3	W-2209878	0666	1
HILL JOHN B	COL	0-0191132	0857	3
HILL JOHN O	COL	0-0106115	0950	3
HILL JOHN E	CPT	0-0288457	0861	3
HILL JOHN F	1LT	0-1315167	0545	2
HILL JOHN J	LTC	0-1173285	0560	1
HILL JOHN L	COL	0-0359886	0162	1
HILL JOHN P	CPT	0-0473748	1044	2
HILL JOHN S	CPT	0-0376403	0244	2
HILL JOHN W	CPT	0-0173816	0852	3
HILL JR CHARLES L	2LT	0-1650882	1145	2
HILL JR ERNEST I	LTC	0-1167029	0460	1
HILL JR GEORGE	LTC	0-0284412	0967	3
HILL JR HARVEY G	CW3	W-2148856	0166	1
HILL JR HOYT B	2LT	0-0425231	1143	2
HILL JR JAMES R	MAJ	0-1685703	1265	1
HILL JR RAYMOND	MAJ	0-1305926	0758	1
HILL JR SAMUEL P	MAJ	0-1303504	0263	1
HILL JR VANCE V	LTC	0-0422518	1262	1
HILL JR WILLIAM A	CPT	0-0968435	0660	1
HILL KENNETH F	CPT	0-1290245	0947	2
HILL LEE O	LTC	0-1573278	0157	1
HILL LINFORD E	LTC	0-0451481	0457	1
HILL LLOYD M	1LT	0-1309930	0845	2
HILL LONNIE P	CPT	0-1897741	0462	1
HILL LOUIS A	LTC	0-0253101	1058	3
HILL MARION E	MAJ	0-1341786	0463	1
HILL NUGENT	CPT	0-0178149	0654	3
HILL OGDEN H	CPT	0-0377524	0446	2
HILL OLAN F	2LT	0-2012518	0746	2
HILL ORVILLE C	MAJ	0-0503576	0955	1
HILL RALPH O	CPT	0-0354465	0850	1
HILL RAYMOND H	MAJ	0-0299932	1044	2
HILL RICHARD V	CPT	0-1314618	0747	2
HILL ROBERT A	COL	0-0232567	1056	3
HILL ROBERT A	LTC	0-1100147	0662	1
HILL ROBERT L	COL	0-0319333	1059	3
HILL ROBERT L	MAJ	0-1118590	0664	1
HILL ROBERT N	COL	0-0243571	0763	3
HILL ROBERT W	1LT	0-1058024	1145	1
HILL ROY A	MAJ	0-0387054	0460	1
HILL ROYAL H	1LT	0-1998099	0346	2
HILL RUBY E	MAJ	N-0763533	1266	1
HILL SAMUEL O	LTC	0-0295473	1263	3
HILL SR HECTOR W	CW2	W-2139428	0962	1
HILL THOMAS G	MAJ	0-1640551	0163	1
HILL THOMAS P	LTC	0-0263038	0962	3
HILL URHO G	1LT	0-1325969	1046	2
HILL VANCE	CW2	W-2205689	0762	1
HILL VERNON	CPT	0-1012719	0148	1
HILL WALTER B	CPT	0-0416593	1145	1
HILL WALTER S	LTC	0-0186079	0554	3
HILL WARREN A	MAJ	0-0259303	0767	3
HILL WARREN W	MAJ	0-0335777	0845	1
HILL WAYNE	CPT	0-0182154	0731	1
HILL WETZEL	1LT	0-0451118	0949	1
HILL WILLIAM A	COL	0-0264435	1164	3
HILL WILLIAM F	CPT	0-0174341	1056	3
HILL WILLIAM G	CPT	0-1012291	0246	2
HILL WILLIAM H	MAJ	0-0247043	0966	3
HILL WILLIAM H	LTC	0-0319653	0454	1
HILL WILLIAM L	1LT	0-0490975	1047	1
HILL WILLIAM L	MAJ	0-0887896	1060	1
HILL WILLIAM M	LTC	0-0333298	0959	3
HILL WILLIAM R	1LT	0-0497379	0151	1
HILL WILLIAM T	LTC	0-0884917	0954	1
HILLARD THOMAS R	COL	0-0371060	0763	1
HILLARD WILLIAM J	LTC	0-1583109	0561	1
HILLARY MARK	LTC	0-0182696	1047	2
HILLEARY EARL W	CW2	W-2145860	0962	1
HILLEBERT LAWRENCE	CPT	0-1636043	0653	1
HILLEN JEANNE B	MAJ	N-0737980	0767	1
HILLER ELMER C	CW2	W-2153255	0958	1
HILLER JOHN A	MAJ	0-0125935	0656	3
HILLER JOHN W	2LT	0-1291992	0455	1
HILLER LA MOINE E	1LT	0-0360183	1143	2
HILLER ROBERT I	MAJ	0-0483337	1143	2
HILLER WILLIAM L	CPT	0-0299091	0945	2
HILLERY JR ARTHUR M	COL	0-0410116	1167	1
HILLEY LARRY T	CW3	W-2147758	0157	1
HILLEY PAUL E	1LT	0-2005707	1047	2
HILLHOUSE DOUGLAS P	LTC	0-1038401	0862	1
HILLIARD ALBERT L	COL	0-0336824	0267	3
HILLIARD CHARLES A	WO1	W-2103008	1046	2
HILLIARD CLARK	LTC	0-1314781	0762	1
HILLIARD CLAUDE R	CW2	W-2148623	0262	1
HILLIARD EMERSON E	MAJ	0-1010578	0261	1
HILLIARD EVELYN B	1LT	N-0741948	0346	1
HILLIARD JOHN H	CW3	W-2153256	1262	1
HILLIARD JOHN T	MAJ	0-1553470	0462	1
HILLIARD JR TEMPLE W	MAJ	0-0440741	0350	1
HILLIARD LEON W	COL	0-0212170	1052	3
HILLIARD MILDRED A	CPT	N-0733780	0847	1
HILLIARD OLEN	MAJ	0-0451579	0657	1
HILLIARD PAUL	2LT	0-1324839	1144	2
HILLIARD RUSSELL E	MAJ	0-0185819	0945	2
HILLIARD SHERMAN E	1LT	0-0491484	1046	1
HILLIARD SPENCER G	LTC	0-0212354	1061	3
HILLIARD WILLIAM F	CW2	W-2206941	0466	1
HILLIER ERNEST H	CPT	0-0279344	0267	3
HILLIKER HERBERT C	1LT	0-1303728	0346	2
HILLIS GEORGE W	LTC	0-0257108	1264	3
HILLIS JR LLOYD E	CW2	W-2210998	0367	1
HILLIS ROBERT O	COL	0-0922216	0664	2
HILLIS WILLIAM C	MAJ	0-0450288	0556	1
HILLMAN ARTHUR E	CW3	W-2135686	0860	1
HILLMAN ENOCCEN H	LTC	0-0177701	0660	3
HILLMAN HAROLD	CW3	W-2116659	1262	1
HILLMAN JIMMYE S	1LT	0-0446745	0545	2
HILLMAN JR JOHN A	CW4	W-2144520	0258	1
HILLMAN LEROY R	1LT	0-1549736	1056	2
HILLMAN LEWIS C	LTC	0-1292522	0966	1
HILLMAN WILLIAM O	COL	0-0258906	0466	3
HILLMANN FREDERICK	CPT	0-0238972	0545	2
HILLMON KENNETH K	WO1	W-2104144	0951	1
HILLMON WILLIAM R	MAJ	0-1637675	0656	1
HILLS LYMAN W	1LT	0-0129854	0354	3
HILLS RALPH W	1LT	0-1307015	0645	2
HILLSDALE CHARLES J	LTC	0-1013367	0866	2
HILLSMAN MARVIN C	COL	0-0269399	0957	2
HILLY ARTHUR J	CPT	0-1320320	1052	1
HILLYER JUSTIN O	LTC	0-0243510	0761	3
HILSHER JOHN M	COL	0-0241435	0463	3
HILT PAUL S	CPT	0-0503073	1049	1
HILTGEN WILLIAM F	CW4	W-2143392	0867	2
HILTNER JEROME M	1LT	0-1299564	1044	1
HILTON ARTHUR W	CW4	W-2142395	0456	1
HILTON EARL L	CPT	0-0240440	0646	2
HILTON ELMER R	MAJ	0-0450251	0154	1
HILTON EUGENE W	LTC	0-0200623	0659	2
HILTON HAROLD B	LTC	0-0235847	0847	1
HILTON HENRY R	CPT	0-1287176	1045	2
HILTON JAMES W	COL	0-0266360	0860	3
HILTON JOHN E	CPT	0-0451610	0245	2
HILTON JR GEORGE W	CW4	W-2114297	0359	1
HILTON RAY	COL	0-0328146	1266	1
HILTON WILLIAM W	LTC	0-0397792	0946	2
HILTY CHARLES F	LTC	0-0372447	0763	1
HILTY DONALD E	CPT	0-1693759	1044	2
HILTY ROBERT L	LTC	0-0367881	0861	1
HILTZ ROBERT C	1LT	0-1167470	0145	1
HIME LESLIE J	MAJ	0-0996796	0265	1
HIMEBAUGH WILLIAM K	MAJ	0-0235749	0364	3
HIMELSTEIN LOUIS	LTC	0-0251770	0848	2
HIMEON HAROLD T	LTC	0-0263980	0152	3
HIMES DELBERT R	MAJ	0-1642973	0361	1
HIMES JACK E	MAJ	0-2210180	0665	1
HIMES JOHN R	LTC	0-0516265	0663	1
HIMES JR CHESTER O	LTC	0-1541070	1066	1
HIMES ROBERT A	MAJ	0-1299886	0164	1
HIMMELE IRVIN H	COL	0-0217860	1163	3
HIMMELMAN GEORGE R	LTC	0-0259977	0555	3
HIMMELREICH HOWARD W	CW4	W-2134664	1163	1
HIMMELRIGHT JOHN R	LTC	0-1100148	1060	1
HINAMON HUBERT B	MAJ	0-0274539	0950	1
HINAU JOSEPH	1LT	0-0244389	1153	3
HINCH JR RICHARD L	LTC	0-0195005	0962	3
HINCHBERGER C C	MAJ	0-0247280	0346	2
HINCHBERGER PAUL A	CPT	0-0356587	0145	2
HINCHEY JAMES J	CW2	W-2205628	0262	1
HINCHLIFFE ARTHUR J	CPT	0-0303742	0545	2
HINCKLEY BENJAMIN H	1LT	0-1289864	0145	2
HINCKLEY CHARLES R	LTC	0-0274600	1055	3
HINCKLEY JAMES L	LTC	0-0363240	0666	3
HINCKLEY JOHN B	LTC	0-1636045	0966	3
HINCKLEY MARY J	1LT	N-0756834	0646	1
HINCKLEY ROBERT C	COL	0-0321742	1061	1
HINCKLEY ROBERT W	1LT	0-1303505	0346	2
HINCKLEY WILLIAM G	COL	0-0229918	0662	3
HINDEN EARL L	COL	0-0225783	0465	3
HINDEN ELIZABETH	1LT	N-0725827	0246	1
HINDIN HERMAN	MAJ	0-1035819	0659	2
HINDIN HERMAN	CPT	0-1702466	0945	1
HINDLEY CECIL J	CPT	0-1180541	0646	2
HINDLEY FREDERICK	LTC	0-0511533	1064	2
HINDMAN CURTIS D	MAJ	0-1284141	0761	1
HINDMAN HUBERT	MAJ	0-1577323	0457	1
HINDS BEN M	CW4	W-2148692	0957	1
HINDS GARLAND C	MAJ	0-1104850	0161	1
HINDS HOWARD K	1LT	0-1325089	1162	1
HINDS NORVIL T	LTC	0-0327014	0557	3
HINDS PAUL L	CW3	W-2149258	0267	1
HINDS WARREN E	MAJ	0-0425323	0459	1
HINDS WILLIAM T	CW2	W-2145886	0761	1
HINELINE EDWIN C	LTC	0-0377726	1162	1
HINEMAN RICHARD E	LTC	0-1765094	0167	1
HINENBURG LOUIS	CPT	0-1560174	0555	2
HINER GLENN L	LTC	0-1313406	0662	2
HINES CAROL C	COL	0-0336885	1059	1
HINES CHARLES G	CW3	W-2004341	1066	3
HINES EDWARD G	MAJ	0-1589269	0461	1
HINES EDWARD L	1LT	0-1949560	0661	1
HINES FLOYD W	COL	0-0260638	0866	3
HINES FRANK M	LTC	0-0373782	0764	1
HINES GAIL M	LTC	0-0516409	0964	3
HINES GEORGE P	CPT	0-0441384	1045	2

NAME	GRADE	SVC NO	DATE RET MO YR	RET CODE
HINES HORACE H	1LT	0-0450448	0645	1
HINES HUBERT C	1LT	0-0494072	0148	1
HINES III EMMETT L	LTC	0-1172907	1266	1
HINES JOSEPH F	LTC	0-0253987	1161	3
HINES LUCY R	CPT	N-0761085	0458	2
HINES MERRILL O	CPT	0-0475643	1144	2
HINES NICHOLAS J	MAJ	0-1172908	0761	1
HINES NORMAN F	COL	0-0183470	0262	1
HINES PERCY A	LTC	0-2034536	0660	1
HINES RALPH E	MAJ	0-1018863	0664	2
HINES RICHARD O	CW2	W-2142928	0554	1
HINES ROBERT E	COL	0-0180114	1148	3
HINES TED W	CPT	0-1997550	0861	1
HINES THOMAS G	MAJ	0-1637847	0859	1
HINES VANCE V	LTC	0-0442038	0664	1
HINES WALTER W	CW4	W-2144285	0267	1
HINESLEY DALE E	CPT	0-0488342	0546	2
HINESLEY JOSEPH O	MAJ	0-1556599	0262	2
HINEY MONROE N	MAJ	0-0370855	0949	1
HINGERTY JR OTIS J	CW3	W-2143188	0966	1
HINGLE JULES L	2LT	0-1822273	0344	2
HINISH JR JOHN E	2LT	0-1316553	0445	2
HINKEL JOHN V	COL	0-0270141	1266	3
HINKEL JOSEPH L	LTC	0-1030041	0557	1
HINKLE ELIZABETH	1LT	N-0776231	1045	1
HINKLE GEORGE R	CPT	0-0488431	0847	1
HINKLE HENRY L	COL	0-0312374	0365	3
HINKLE JOHNNIE J	CW3	W-2146990	0762	1
HINKLE KENNETH L	COL	0-0269220	0464	3
HINKLE OSCAR	LTC	0-0496934	0255	1
HINKLE WALTER J	MAJ	0-0375613	0346	2
HINKLE WILBUR E	MAJ	0-0450853	1055	1
HINKLE WILLIAM A	CPT	0-0495922	1151	1
HINKLEY FRANK R	COL	0-0272047	0159	1
HINKLEY HAROLD R	MAJ	0-1821585	0560	1
HINKLEY OLIN T	COL	0-0476454	0854	1
HINKO EDWARD N	1LT	0-0345518	0742	1
HINKSON DEHAVEN	LTC	0-0142156	1051	3
HINKSON EDWARD O	LTC	0-1286650	0463	1
HINKSON JR HAROLD H	2LT	0-0495576	1043	2
HINMAN ALANSON E	MAJ	0-0287271	0166	3
HINMAN CLIFTON F	CPT	0-0216384	1153	3
HINMAN GERALD H	CPT	0-0504291	0954	1
HINMAN HUBERT H	CW3	W-2205135	0265	1
HINMAN JR GEORGE W	COL	0-0220552	0653	3
HINMAN JR PAUL W	LTC	0-1037534	1061	1
HINNANT AUGUSTUS R	CPT	0-1533579	1053	2
HINNER RALPH F	LTC	0-0509496	1054	1
HINO KENNETH S	MAJ	0-0242002	0264	1
HINOJOSA JUAN H	LTC	0-0370944	0367	3
HINOTE RUSSELL C	COL	0-0217861	0355	1
HINRICHSEN JOHN C	MAJ	0-0961521	1163	1
HINRICHSEN ROBERT L	CW3	W-2144919	1056	1
HINSEY LOUIS E	LTC	0-0347295	0161	1
HINSHAW JACOB R	MAJ	0-0231977	0145	1
HINSON ARTHUR	LTC	0-0384851	1266	3
HINSON BENJAMIN F	MAJ	0-0108383	0938	1
HINSON CHARLES F	LTC	0-1288667	0462	1
HINSON CLYDE A	CW4	W-2143574	0661	1
HINSON ELVIS B	1LT	0-0366165	1043	1
HINSON ERNEST R	2LT	0-1999121	0845	2
HINSON JESSE J	COL	0-0245719	1060	3
HINSON LUTHER O	COL	0-0260353	0561	1
HINSON MARVIN G	MAJ	0-1179891	0265	1
HINSON MASON W	LTC	0-1045775	1266	1
HINSON ROBERT J	2LT	0-1325569	0545	2
HINSON SEDGIE V	MAJ	0-0395714	0746	2
HINTERMISTER F A	MAJ	0-0183040	0550	1
HINTON ANDREW H	LTC	0-0312681	1264	3
HINTON EARL D	MAJ	0-1546650	0258	2
HINTON EDGAR A	LTC	0-1647951	0863	1
HINTON HENRY W	MAJ	0-0249152	0866	3
HINTON HERMAN C	MAJ	0-0473274	1264	1
HINTON JONATHAN C	LTC	0-0147197	0648	3
HINTON JOSEPH F	LTC	0-0332299	0655	3
HINTON JR JOHN	LTC	0-1641393	0463	1
HINTON PUGH H	MAJ	0-0979935	0961	1
HINTON ROBERT L	CW4	W-2141585	0559	1
HINTON WALLACE R	MAJ	0-1688781	0265	1
HINTZ WARREN L	LTC	0-1052815	0165	1
HINTZ WILLIAM F	LTC	0-1316755	1262	1
HINTZ WILLIS A	MAJ	0-1336912	0763	1
HINUEBER ROBART C	1LT	0-1286487	0145	2
HINZ ROBERT H	CPT	0-0370932	0745	2
HINZ WALTER H	LTC	0-0244191	0862	3
HIOTT ROY	LTC	0-0271062	0261	1
HIPKINS OTHO F	MAJ	0-0912356	0847	1
HIPP DAVID W	CW3	W-2146894	0765	1
HIPP EDWARD B	CPT	0-1319742	0147	2
HIPP HAROLD W	LTC	0-1573867	0860	1
HIPP WILLIAM N	MAJ	0-1013181	0364	1
HIPPEY MARGARET	LTC	N-0722948	1066	3
HIPPLE JAMES B	COL	0-0265951	0263	3
HIPPLE JAMES W	LTC	0-0263182	0466	3
HIPPS EUFORD L	CPT	0-1317166	0854	2
HIPPS JUANITA R	LTC	N-0702902	0846	1
HIPSCHMAN IRVING S	1LT	0-1280759	0646	2
HIPSEN JOHN C	MAJ	0-1173644	0261	1
HIRABAYASHI TAKEO	MAJ	0-1899430	0162	1
HIRAI ERNEST	MAJ	0-0964947	0964	1
HIRANO ROY M	LTC	0-0425914	0467	1
HIRO THOMAS R	CPT	0-0925097	0448	2
HIRKO JR GEORGE J	LTC	0-1318432	0361	1
HIRONS KENNETH W	CPT	0-1041361	0748	2
HIRSCH CARL P	MAJ	0-0240896	1063	3
HIRSCH CONRAD G	LTC	0-0374551	1161	2
HIRSCH DONALD A	LTC	0-0309553	1264	3
HIRSCH GEORGE D	COL	0-0347286	0164	3
HIRSCH GUS J	LTC	0-1592927	1162	1
HIRSCH HARRY A	LTC	0-0207095	0446	2
HIRSCH LEO	MAJ	0-1314633	0162	1
HIRSCH OSCAR G	MAJ	0-1010709	0265	1
HIRSCH RICHARD C	MAJ	0-1111667	0161	1
HIRSCH SAMUEL	1LT	0-1017201	0346	2
HIRSCH SIDNEY	1LT	0-4000392	0355	2
HIRSCH STANLEY C	MAJ	0-1280809	1157	1
HIRSCH VICTOR H	MAJ	0-0150234	0247	1
HIRSCH WILLIAM L	MAJ	0-0981855	1264	1
HIRSCHBERG MICHAEL H	1LT	0-1934927	0354	2
HIRSCHLER RICHARD J	CW3	W-2152793	0464	1
HIRSCHMAN LOUIS J	LTC	0-0168340	0648	3
HIRSCHMAN RAYMOND S	MAJ	0-1170416	1266	1
HIRSCHOWITZ SIMON J	CW4	W-2109995	1155	1
HIRSCHY IRVIN A	COL	0-0210460	0854	1
HIRSCHY JAMES B	MAJ	0-1637681	1060	1
HIRSCHY LUTHER C	MAJ	0-1999130	0161	1
HIRSH BERNARD S	2LT	0-1588640	1044	2
HIRSH CLARENCE	MAJ	0-0228949	0365	3
HIRSH HARRY A	LTC	0-1316505	1062	1
HIRSHFIELD HOWARD A	1LT	0-1589906	0946	2
HIRT ARTHUR E	COL	0-0274787	0966	3
HIRT JAMES B	LTC	0-0288629	0965	3
HIRT RICHARD C	CPT	0-1287714	0246	2
HISAW BOBBIE L	CPT	0-2008407	0455	1
HISAW LUTHER G	CW2	W-2153105	0960	1
HISCOCK IRA V	COL	0-0170951	0552	3
HISE KENNETH W	MAJ	0-1913305	0967	1
HISER CLEM C	MAJ	0-0220859	0755	3
HISEY ROBERT G	CPT	0-1011073	0545	2
HISLE WILLIAM J	CW3	W-2144963	0764	2
HISS ALEXANDER	WO1	W-2135555	0246	2
HISSIGER HENRY L	LTC	0-0233736	0946	2
HISSONG JAMES S	CPT	0-0324165	0647	1
HITA JR VICENTE	LTC	0-0291062	0761	3
HITCH JR WILLIAM H	MAJ	0-0977556	0764	1
HITCH RICHARD J	MAJ	0-0248094	0966	3
HITCH ROBERT A	COL	0-0288190	0466	3
HITCHCOCK CLARENCE J	LTC	0-0275581	0763	3
HITCHCOCK DONALD G	MAJ	0-0885659	0261	1
HITCHCOCK EDWARD G	LTC	0-0259440	0466	3
HITCHCOCK GEORGE P	COL	0-0181803	0462	3
HITCHCOCK LAWRENCE S	COL	0-0132920	0958	3
HITCHCOCK LLOYD H	CW2	W-2152625	0161	1
HITCHCOCK LYMAN H	LTC	0-0229226	0563	3
HITCHCOCK ROBINSON	B G	0-0309266	0558	3
HITCHCOCK RUSSELL W	LTC	0-0269313	0359	1
HITCHCOCK WILLIAM L	CPT	0-0513503	0247	2
HITCHCOX GEORGE H	CPT	0-0253612	1046	1
HITCHINGS AUBREY C	MAJ	0-1298230	0461	1
HITCHNER CHARLES F	CW2	W-2101843	0646	1
HITCHNER RICHARD C	1LT	0-1014664	0745	2
HITE DOROTHY E	2LT	N-0783256	1043	1
HITE HENRY A	MAJ	0-1303729	0765	1
HITE JR JOSEPH N	MAJ	0-1648272	0559	1
HITSELBERGER JAMES F	LTC	0-0264444	1057	1
HITT ARNOLD D	COL	0-0129310	1055	3
HITT JAMES H	2LT	0-2009766	1045	2
HITTLE KENNETH T	LTC	0-0289522	0864	3
HITZEL JR JOSEPH M	LTC	0-0922544	0665	3
HITZEL RAYMOND C	2LT	0-0558521	0145	2
HITZGES EMMETT R	CW2	W-2214534	0966	1
HIVELY HARLAN P	CPT	0-0885631	0758	1
HIVELY JAMES P	CPT	0-1725517	1046	1
HIVELY SHERMAN E	LTC	0-0305723	0246	2
HIX CLAY W	MAJ	0-1173288	0462	2
HIX WILLIAM J	LTC	0-1179894	0463	1
HIXON JOHN L	CPT	0-1303341	0747	2
HIXON WALLACE C	CPT	0-0161895	0-53	3
HIXSON CHARLES H	CPT	0-1823872	0346	1
HIXSON CLAYTON H	LTC	0-0238973	0362	3
HIZAR DONALD A	CPT	0-0545809	0965	1
HJALMARSON DORI	LTC	0-0331841	0353	1
HJELMSTAD LOUIE O	MAJ	0-1181303	1062	1
HJELMSTROM ANDREW F	CPT	0-0283654	0962	1
HJELT GEORGE R	CW3	W-2150550	0464	1
HJELTNESS MELVIN J	MAJ	0-1291641	1046	1
HLAD RUDOLPH E	2LT	0-1031408	0943	1
HLADIK CHARLES A	CW2	W-2000217	0145	2
HLADKY FRANK P	LTC	0-0415733	1165	3
HLAVAC ALBERT	LTC	0-0136792	0648	3
HLUHANICH ALEXY M	2LT	0-1642187	0845	2
HOADLEY MAX L	1LT	0-1296210	1044	2
HOAG EDITH A	2LT	N-0745157	0545	1
HOAG GEORGE W	MAJ	0-1548840	0762	1
HOAG JAMES E	LTC	0-1582373	0363	2
HOAG JR JAMES H	CW2	RW-2208479	0465	1
HOAG MEREDITH W	2LT	0-1649161	1045	2
HOAG THOMAS R	COL	0-0334350	0561	1
HOAG VICTOR R	COL	0-0125411	0555	3
HOAG WILLIAM	1LT	0-0442106	104N	2
HOAGLAND CARROLL H	LTC	0-0414713	0760	1
HOAGLAND EARNEST R	MAJ	0-0479404	0154	1
HOAGLAND ELIZABETH	MAJ	L-1010068	1063	1
HOAGLAND KENNETH C	CPT	0-0526403	0246	2
HOAGLAND MELVIN J	1LT	0-1306097	0750	1
HOALT MARRIA M	MAJ	M-0002383	0963	1
HOAR JOHN	MAJ	0-0502782	0447	2
HOAR JOHN W	LTC	0-0398787	0166	1
HOAR JR JOHN B	COL	0-0276599	0761	1
HOAR RALPH D	CPT	0-0277537	0854	3
HOAR WALTER G	COL	0-0309682	0146	2
HOARD JAMES L	CPT	0-0299350	0267	3
HOBAN EUGENE F	CPT	0-0497965	1047	1
HOBAN THOMAS L	B G	0-0176644	1053	3
HOBAN VERN J	CPT	0-0517638	0548	1
HOBART JAMES H	1LT	0-1316048	1144	1
HOBBS CARL A	CPT	0-1291820	1145	1
HOBBS CREIGHTON	CW2	W-3430180	0267	1
HOBBS EARL R	1LT	0-1294473	1153	1
HOBBS EDWIN G	MAJ	0-0224992	0758	3
HOBBS EDWIN P	CW3	W-2152217	0565	1
HOBBS EUGENE S	MAJ	0-1056120	1262	1
HOBBS EVERETT G	CPT	0-0393019	0146	2
HOBBS FRANK C	MAJ	0-0432946	0146	2
HOBBS FRANK J	COL	0-0200955	0961	3
HOBBS HENRY R	CW3	W-2152190	0762	1
HOBBS HIBBERT	MAJ	0-1017836	0365	1
HOBBS J BRYAN	COL	0-0444332	1146	2
HOBBS JR JOHN O	COL	0-0245440	0167	3
HOBBS MARIAN	1LT	L-0701581	0746	2
HOBBS NORMAN H	CW4	W-2110460	0556	1
HOBBS RICHARD H	COL	0-0196169	1262	3
HOBBS ROBERT E	LTC	0-0466055	0346	2
HOBBS ROSSITER H	COL	0-0202355	1058	3
HOBBS STANLEY C	MAJ	0-2202817	0667	1
HOBBS VICTOR H	1LT	0-2055132	1148	1
HOBBS WILBUR G	MAJ	0-0887555	0662	1
HOBBS WILLIAM C	LTC	0-0286467	0959	1
HOBBS WILLIAM H	MAJ	0-0215107	0352	3
HOBBS WOODROW H	LTC	0-1030676	1264	1
HOBDY RICHARD O	MAJ	0-1640557	0162	1
HOBER ANTHONY R	LTC	0-1050720	0763	1
HOBER ISABELLE V	1LT	N-0751897	0546	1
HOBERG HENRY G	LTC	0-0142283	0154	3
HOBERG INGEMAR E	COL	0-0218055	1263	3
HOBERG INGOMAR A	LTC	0-0201645	1160	3
HOBERG WILBUR	CPT	0-1799141	0557	1
HOBGOOD RICHARD G	CPT	0-1776042	0450	1
HOBIN FRED J	CW3	W-2150019	0363	1
HOBLITZELL ALAN R	COL	0-0150311	0951	3
HOBSON ALLEN R	2LT	0-1797648	0245	2
HOBSON STANLEY L	CW3	RW-2152778	1167	1
HOBSON WALTER	LTC	0-0314006	0261	1
HOBSON WILLIAM S	CPT	0-1798734	1164	1
HOBSON WINFRED P	CPT	0-2011624	1060	1
HOCHBERG CLIFFORD M	MAJ	0-1112219	1164	1
HOCHBERG PAUL P	CPT	0-0504503	0246	2
HOCHSTADT JACK	MAJ	0-1637684	0162	2
HOCKE MERVIN P	MAJ	0-1176060	0561	1
HOCKEBORN CHESTER F	MAJ	0-1050303	0762	1
HOCKENBEAMER EMBREE	LTC	0-0224980	1163	3
HOCKENBERRY E D	COL	0-0269635	0947	2
HOCKENBERRY HAROLD L	LTC	0-1114167	1264	1
HOCKER AUGUSTUS S	COL	0-0266180	1158	1
HOCKETT KENNETH J	MAJ	0-0450898	0459	1
HOCKING ALBERT W	MAJ	0-0196378	0563	3
HOCKLANDER CECIL W	CPT	0-1297368	0247	2
HOCKMAN JOHN K	CPT	0-2055528	0756	1
HOCKMAN OLIVER W	MAJ	0-0982716	0662	1
HODAPP RAYMOND J	LTC	0-0248215	0446	2
HODEN BENJAMIN R	1LT	0-1113258	0745	2
HODES WILLIAM A	1LT	0-0917520	0744	2
HODGDON GEORGE E	1LT	0-1285941	0745	2
HODGE CHARLES J	B G	0-0332886	0967	3
HODGE CLAUDE W	CPT	0-0116812	0349	3
HODGE FREDERIC W	COL	0-0241338	1059	1
HODGE GEORGE C	LTC	0-0337849	0866	3
HODGE GERALD C	B G	0-0253172	0760	3
HODGE NORMAN L	CW3	W-2145093	0864	1
HODGE PAT E	MAJ	0-0308964	0245	2
HODGE ROY B	MAJ	0-2289396	0263	1
HODGE SAMUEL R	1LT	0-1913750	1146	1
HODGE WALTER	MAJ	0-2006425	1263	1
HODGES BURGESS G	COL	0-1290070	0561	1
HODGES CHARLES C	CPT	0-0495456	0261	3
HODGES CLARENCE W	LTC	0-0360647	0855	1
HODGES CLAUDE A	MAJ	0-0250609	1266	3
HODGES DALE F	MAJ	0-1052393	0958	1
HODGES DANIEL W	MAJ	0-0382313	1153	1
HODGES DEAN M	2LT	0-0520423	0145	2
HODGES DEAN W	LTC	0-0491083	1045	2
HODGES DUNCAN	COL	0-0449647	0956	3
HODGES GEORGE H	CPT	0-0499451	1154	1
HODGES GORDON S	CPT	0-1167032	0953	2
HODGES HAROLD W	CW3	W-2150148	0865	1
HODGES HARRY C	1LT	0-1598757	0752	1
HODGES HARRY M	CPT	0-1535476	0448	1
HODGES HARRY V	MAJ	0-1299045	0766	1
HODGES JAMES F	2LT	0-1881458	1052	3
HODGES JESSE W	MAJ	0-1289734	0357	1

NAME	GRADE	SVC NO	DATE RET MO YR	RET CODE
HODGES JOHN B	CPT	0-4005448	0866	1
HODGES JR ALLEN T	LTC	0-0493189	0465	1
HODGES LILLIE M F	CPT	N-0760526	0947	1
HODGES MARK L	MAJ	C-0406106	0247	2
HODGES RALPH O	LTC	0-0236762	0765	3
HODGES RAYMOND E	WO1	W-2149973	0753	1
HODGES WILLIAM H	LTC	0-0302116	0660	1
HODGIN JOHN L	LTC	0-0116813	0757	3
HODGKIN JR JOHN B	1LT	0-1591802	1045	2
HODGKINS HOWARD W	COL	0-0118559	0851	3
HODGKINS LAFOREST E	LTC	0-0538869	0565	3
HODGKINS LELAND M	CW4	W-2139849	0363	1
HODGKINS PIERCE N	MAJ	C-0126335	1151	3
HODGKINSON HENRY B	LTC	0-0273738	0557	1
HODGKINSON WILLIAM F	MAJ	0-0249930	0265	3
HODGKISS JOHN T	CPT	0-1633976	0250	1
HODGSON HAROLD B	CPT	0-0101277	1043	2
HODGSON JAMES F	COL	0-0146759	0254	3
HODGSON MELVIN E	LTC	0-0292197	1166	3
HODGSON RAY W	LTC	0-2036594	1262	1
HODGSON REGINALD M	COL	0-1574830	0765	1
HODNETT JOHN H	MAJ	C-2008394	1060	1
HODNETTE PAUL W	LTC	0-1307412	1262	1
HODSDON JR GEORGE M	CPT	C-0364572	0345	2
HODSHON PETER	2LT	0-1032531	0646	2
HODSON NEVILLE F	LTC	0-0313629	1045	2
HODSON RUSSEL L	CW3	W-2147852	0862	1
HODYKE STEPHEN S	MAJ	C-1796622	0561	1
HOECHSTETTER STANTON	LTC	C-0251872	0464	3
HOEFELMEYER HENRY L	CPT	0-0568642	1147	2
HOEFER CARL F	CPT	0-0277629	0854	3
HOEFER HAROLD W	CPT	0-0307617	0444	2
HOEFFLIGER FRANCIS L	CW3	W-2147044	0260	1
HOEFGEN NELSON G	1LT	0-1018932	1145	2
HOEHLE ARMAND F	COL	0-0225855	0163	3
HOEHN MARTIN C	LTC	0-0438949	0462	1
HOEHN ROBERT G	MAJ	C-1290602	0864	1
HOEHNEN EUGENE D	CPT	0-0428644	0347	2
HOEING HARLEY T	CW3	W-2143495	0963	1
HOELLER FRANCIS R	CPT	0-0311148	0552	1
HOELSCHER FRANK J	1LT	0-0553376	1047	2
HOELSCHER LEO J	CPT	0-0502686	0746	1
HOENER IRWIN R	LTC	0-0343096	0653	2
HOENINGER CARL L	CW3	W-2146567	0763	1
HOENSHELL FRANCIS E	MAJ	0-1946292	1065	3
HOERGER WINFIELD S	LTC	0-0208297	0359	3
HOERNER EMIL	MAJ	C-0481887	0754	1
HOERNSCHEMEYER JOSEP	LTC	0-0248248	0462	3
HOEY HARRISON	MAJ	0-2006232	0663	1
HOEY JR WILLIAM F	COL	0-0202517	0648	3
HOFACKER CARL F	CW2	W-2111197	1150	1
HOFF ARTHUR P	MAJ	0-1045776	0966	1
HOFF CLYDE W	MAJ	0-1331947	0560	1
HOFF CORNELL L	CPT	0-1702442	1145	2
HOFF EDWARD A	CPT	0-1106207	0544	2
HOFF HERBERT	LTC	0-0531226	1063	1
HOFF IVAN R	LTC	0-1948758	1067	3
HOFF ROBERT J	LTC	0-1822798	0962	1
HOFF WILLIAM J	2LT	0-1583120	0844	2
HOFFAY MEREDITH F	LTC	0-1555404	0964	1
HOFFENBACHER W F	COL	0-0237540	0259	3
HOFFENBERG JACOB	MAJ	0-0920724	1045	2
HOFFER GEORGE F	MAJ	C-0273778	0967	3
HOFFER MARIE F	1LT	N-0767062	1047	1
HOFFER WILSON L	CW4	W-2103012	0459	1
HOFFHINES JOHN W	CPT	0-1056121	0747	2
HOFFMAN ADAM H	2LT	C-2007300	0346	2
HOFFMAN ALBERT	WO1	W-2110111	0845	2
HOFFMAN ALBERT J	MAJ	0-0418025	0446	1
HOFFMAN ALBERT L	COL	0-0208043	0749	3
HOFFMAN ALBERT W	COL	0-0284924	1061	3
HOFFMAN ARTHUR A	MAJ	C-0154951	0952	3
HOFFMAN ARTHUR A	CPT	0-1102292	0762	1
HOFFMAN AUGUST A	CPT	C-1043984	0261	1
HOFFMAN BOYDELL	CPT	0-1540707	0758	2

NAME	GRADE	SVC NO	DATE RET MO YR	RET CODE
HOFFMAN CAMILLUS N	LTC	0-1175615	0464	1
HOFFMAN EDWIN H	LTC	0-0341617	0259	3
HOFFMAN EVERT E	MAJ	0-2212005	0663	1
HOFFMAN FLOYD H	1LT	0-1545606	1045	2
HOFFMAN FRANK D	CPT	0-0368811	0246	2
HOFFMAN FRANK G	MAJ	0-0188138	0546	2
HOFFMAN GEORGE N	MAJ	0-0916860	1063	3
HOFFMAN GEORGE W	LTC	0-1557730	0961	1
HOFFMAN GUSTAV	MAJ	0-0233702	0356	1
HOFFMAN HARRY W	LTC	0-1315446	0163	1
HOFFMAN HOMER D	MAJ	0-0266593	1057	3
HOFFMAN ISRAEL L	LTC	0-0335181	0666	3
HOFFMAN JACK N	LTC	0-0352911	0562	1
HOFFMAN JACK T	CW3	W-2148282	1167	1
HOFFMAN JACK W	CPT	0-2007294	0945	2
HOFFMAN JAMES F	MAJ	0-0220251	1058	3
HOFFMAN JAMES F	CPT	0-0373032	0945	2
HOFFMAN JAY B	CW2	W-2213701	1167	1
HOFFMAN JEAN M	CPT	N-0737769	0449	1
HOFFMAN JOHN C	COL	0-0220154	0157	3
HOFFMAN JOHN J	MAJ	0-0990615	0163	1
HOFFMAN JOHN J	MAJ	0-1000132	0353	1
HOFFMAN JOHN R	1LT	0-1010993	0646	2
HOFFMAN JOSEPH	LTC	0-0310722	0567	3
HOFFMAN JOSEPH A	CW2	W-2213087	0667	1
HOFFMAN JR HARRY O	1LT	0-0441261	1145	2
HOFFMAN LAWRENCE O	LTC	0-1289580	0457	1
HOFFMAN LEO L	COL	0-0246889	0167	3
HOFFMAN LLOYD H	MAJ	0-1101872	0861	1
HOFFMAN MARGARET R	1LT	L-0600027	0844	2
HOFFMAN MAX	1LT	0-1322027	0545	2
HOFFMAN MEREDITH F	CW3	W-2141782	0361	1
HOFFMAN MILTON S	LTC	0-0348155	0466	3
HOFFMAN MYRON P	MAJ	0-1112220	0559	1
HOFFMAN PHILIP	CPT	0-0510066	0145	2
HOFFMAN RALPH J	MAJ	0-1297036	0957	1
HOFFMAN RAYMOND H	LTC	0-0168535	0661	3
HOFFMAN ROBERT F	2LT	0-1316049	0844	2
HOFFMAN ROBERT G	CW2	W-2214632	0467	1
HOFFMAN ROBERT H	MAJ	0-1051600	0459	1
HOFFMAN ROBERT L	LTC	0-0450449	0359	1
HOFFMAN ROBERT R	CPT	0-0221959	0554	3
HOFFMAN RUDOLPH	MAJ	0-0562109	1262	1
HOFFMAN SIDNEY	MAJ	0-1081215	0759	1
HOFFMAN VIOLA E	CPT	N-0759554	0746	1
HOFFMAN WALTER F	WO1	W-2141084	0949	2
HOFFMAN WESLEY G	CPT	0-1534757	0754	2
HOFFMAN WILLIAM A	MAJ	0-2034971	0662	1
HOFFMAN WILLIAM F	LTC	0-1314634	0864	1
HOFFMANN ARTHUR F	CPT	0-0325667	1144	2
HOFFMANN BURTON E E	LTC	0-0492868	0454	2
HOFFMANN CHARLES W	COL	0-0174036	0848	2
HOFFMANN EDWARD D	CPT	0-1039396	1063	1
HOFFMANN GEORGE A	LTC	0-0254804	0766	3
HOFFMANN GREGORY J	MAJ	0-1112221	0361	1
HOFFMANN HERMAN F	MAJ	0-0301224	0555	1
HOFFMANN JACQUES G	1LT	0-0591736	0255	2
HOFFMANN JOSEPH S	LTC	0-0213729	0163	3
HOFFMANN JULIAN P	LTC	0-2047360	1167	1
HOFFMANN OTTO W	LTC	0-1116462	1062	1
HOFFMANN WILLIAM J	COL	0-0142237	0648	3
HOFFMEYER ARTHUR P	1LT	0-1295021	114N	2
HOFFMEYER WILLIAM T	LTC	0-0361365	0859	1
HOFFNAGEL IRVING	1LT	0-0904342	0345	2
HOFFNER BURTON P	CPT	0-5013078	0467	2
HOFFPAUIR JESSE S	LTC	0-0202713	0854	3
HOFFSTADT JOHN P	LTC	0-0264431	0742	2
HOFFSTATTER EDWARD W	LTC	0-0288518	0267	3
HOFMANN ADOLPH A	1LT	0-4000702	0962	2
HOFMANN GEORGE C	LTC	0-0328049	0265	3
HOFMANN JOSEPH E	LTC	0-0379857	0964	3
HOGAN ALBERT M	LTC	0-1052002	0565	1
HOGAN ARTHUR J	LTC	0-0281793	1266	3
HOGAN CHARLES D	CW2	W-2152095	1060	1
HOGAN CHARLES E	COL	0-0415266	1061	1

NAME	GRADE	SVC NO	DATE RET MO YR	RET CODE
HOGAN DANIEL J	LTC	0-1575364	1057	1
HOGAN DANIEL W	COL	0-0162772	0354	3
HOGAN EDGAR W	MAJ	C-1106823	0462	3
HOGAN EDWARD	CW3	W-2149114	0562	1
HOGAN EDWIN G	COL	0-0326768	0367	3
HOGAN ELTON R	LTC	0-0495606	1062	1
HOGAN GEORGE A	CPT	0-0176086	0355	3
HOGAN GEORGE J	CPT	0-0467336	0852	1
HOGAN GERALD E	MAJ	0-2206089	0867	1
HOGAN HENRY J	1LT	0-1559089	0546	2
HOGAN JAMES F	1LT	0-1315689	1045	1
HOGAN JAMES H	LTC	0-0124705	0849	3
HOGAN JAMES L	1LT	0-1013552	0948	1
HOGAN JOHN J	LTC	0-0255669	0867	3
HOGAN JR JOSEPH J	CW2	W-2148256	0461	1
HOGAN JR THOMAS F	MAJ	0-0320741	0145	2
HOGAN LULABEL S	1LT	N-0761184	104N	1
HOGAN MARY H	2LT	N-0728454	0644	1
HOGAN MICHAEL P	MAJ	0-1313522	0361	1
HOGAN RALPH W	CW3	W-2146043	1158	2
HOGAN ROBERT C	1LT	0-1825281	1045	2
HOGAN ROBERT D	MAJ	C-1579796	0464	1
HOGAN ROBERT L	MAJ	0-1341545	0561	1
HOGAN ROUE L	LTC	0-0314441	0261	2
HOGAN ROY E	LTC	0-0450287	0157	1
HOGAN SR GEORGE W	CW2	W-2151076	0163	1
HOGAN THOMAS J	CW3	W-3150436	0867	1
HOGAN WILLIAM R	2LT	0-1031641	1059	2
HOGAN WOODROW W	MAJ	C-1013800	1056	1
HOGBERG DAN A	1LT	0-1637689	0144	2
HOGE CHARLES S	LTC	0-1796280	0762	2
HOGE ELMER C	COL	0-0447872	0954	1
HOGE JR ROY D	LTC	0-0565667	1062	1
HOGEBOOM CORNELIUS	LTC	0-0249721	1065	3
HOGELAND LEONARD H	CPT	0-0508060	0653	1
HOGG ABNER C	CPT	0-1293253	1146	2
HOGG BRUCE M	MAJ	0-0497094	0745	2
HOGG EDWARD J	LTC	0-0349524	0967	3
HOGG HAROLD K	COL	0-0245634	1060	3
HOGG JAMES R	CPT	0-0406866	0761	1
HOGG JOHN H	CPT	0-1548074	1045	2
HOGG JOHN T	CPT	0-0411799	0246	1
HOGG JR ALEXANDER	CPT	0-0563328	0549	2
HOGG JR GEORGE B	MAJ	0-1945607	1265	3
HOGG JR HIRAM	CPT	0-0182043	0654	3
HOGG WILLIAM C	LTC	0-0320189	1061	3
HOGGAN MELVIN J	CPT	0-0278573	1044	2
HOGGAN WILFORD G	CW2	W-2146728	0661	1
HOGGE FRED M	MAJ	0-1925074	0367	1
HOGHAUG MAURICE A	COL	0-0310166	0964	3
HOGHAUG PHILIP A	CPT	0-0452490	0946	2
HOGLE ALBERT F	COL	0-0241918	0455	3
HOGLE JOHN R	CPT	0-1696808	0448	1
HOGQUIST KARL O	CPT	0-0505830	1047	1
HOGUE JOHN O	MAJ	C-0358378	1159	1
HOGUE JOHN V	CW3	W-2120842	0556	1
HOGUE PHILIP N	MAJ	0-0345770	0446	2
HOHAM JOHN C	1LT	0-1927690	0658	2
HOHL JOHN W	MAJ	0-1013925	0361	1
HOHL ROBERT A	CW2	W-2152913	0562	1
HOHM FRANK J	CW3	W-2145311	0664	1
HOHMAN JOHN L	LTC	0-1011011	1162	1
HOHMANN BENJAMIN W	CPT	0-1049207	0852	2
HOHNSTEIN CLAYTON J	1LT	0-0395979	0143	2
HOHU EDMUND K	CPT	0-0242669	1059	3
HOILMAN CLOYD R	MAJ	0-0264792	0167	3
HOIVIK TONY H	CPT	0-0530539	0845	2
HOJNACKI WILLIAM J	MAJ	0-1297370	0658	1
HOKE GEORGE A	CPT	0-0491863	1044	1
HOKE VERNON T	MAJ	C-1330072	0863	1
HOKEMSON EDWARD O	CW2	W-2150765	0758	1
HOKENSON HARRY S	2LT	0-2017695	0746	1
HOLADAY BEN G	1LT	0-1283604	0745	2
HOLADAY MELVIN E	CPT	0-1014104	1163	1
HOLAHAN DANIEL P	1LT	0-1173291	0644	2

NAME	GRADE	SVC NO	DATE RET MO YR	RET CODE
HOLAN MARIE E	2LT	N-0701183	0635	1
HOLANDA REORC P	WO1	W-2123051	0349	1
HOLANIK GEORGE V	MAJ	0-1284332	1158	1
HOLASO RAFAEL F	1LT	0-1896804	1062	1
HOLBERT JAMES R	2LT	0-0108981	0425	1
HOLBERT RAY L	MAJ	C-1016078	0761	1
HOLBERT ROY C	MAJ	0-0113693	0352	3
HOLBERTON TERRY H	COL	0-0112652	0160	1
HOLBRITTER MILTON A	CW4	W-2129612	1167	1
HOLBROCK ARTHUR A	LTC	0-0470511	0246	2
HOLBROCK BERTHAL A	MAJ	0-0442365	0855	1
HOLBROCK CHARLES F	LTC	0-1108024	1062	1
HOLBROCK EDWIN C	CPT	0-0126380	1049	3
HOLBROCK FRANK M	MAJ	0-2000719	1060	1
HOLBROCK GEORGE M	CPT	0-1176670	0546	2
HOLBROCK GORDON R	CW2	W-2148206	1262	1
HOLBROCK GUERNIE	MAJ	0-2006453	0863	1
HOLBROCK HAROLD B	LTC	0-0213104	0762	3
HOLBROCK HORACE N	1LT	0-0386393	114N	2
HOLBROCK JOHN L	LTC	0-0225591	1062	3
HOLBROCK JOHN S	LTC	0-1169574	0662	1
HOLBROCK PAUL E	LTC	0-0171681	0246	2
HOLBROCK SAMUEL S	CW3	W-2144808	0461	1
HOLBROCK WALTER C	1LT	0-0408658	0944	2
HOLBROCK WILLIAM	MAJ	C-1640562	0656	1
HOLBROCK WINIFRED V	1LT	N-0775312	0146	1
HOLCOMB FLOYD R	CPT	0-0298797	0644	2
HOLCOMB FREEBORN P	MAJ	0-0474574	0557	1
HOLCOMB GORDON V	COL	0-0224425	0964	3
HOLCOMB HARLEY J	LTC	0-0227244	0664	3
HOLCOMB HERBERT K	CPT	0-0888534	0849	1
HOLCOMB HOYT C	CPT	0-1289255	0945	2
HOLCOMB JOE A	1LT	0-0985986	0760	2
HOLCOMB JOSEPH W	LTC	0-1822699	0966	1
HOLCOMB LAMAR	MAJ	0-1335008	0160	1
HOLCOMB MONROE F	CW2	W-2145450	0459	1
HOLCOMB RUSSELL F	COL	0-0290907	1061	3
HOLCOMB THOMAS H	MAJ	0-0965866	0862	1
HOLCOMBE MILBURNE L	LTC	0-1575798	0565	1
HOLCOMBE ROLAND N	COL	0-0187588	0752	3
HOLCOMBE ROSS M	MAJ	0-0464157	0846	2
HOLCOMBE THEODORE G	COL	0-0172417	1058	3
HOLCOMBE THOMAS H	MAJ	0-1297037	0658	1
HOLCOMBE WILLIAM T	CW2	W-2152315	1263	1
HOLDE ERLING M	2LT	0-2053827	0245	2
HOLDEMAN BILLY F	CW3	W-2146717	0966	1
HOLDEN ALFRED W	CPT	0-0494105	0946	2
HOLDEN CHARLES A	COL	0-0173924	0648	3
HOLDEN FRANK H	COL	0-0112756	0447	2
HOLDEN HAROLD	CPT	0-2012838	0258	1
HOLDEN HAROLD K	COL	0-0193049	0954	3
HOLDEN JACKSON W	1LT	0-1031651	0847	2
HOLDEN JR FRANCIS W	LTC	0-1183318	1262	1
HOLDEN MILO E	LTC	0-1040037	0859	1
HOLDEN TIMOTHY N	CPT	0-0216365	0950	3
HOLDER ALLEN S	CPT	0-1040038	0753	1
HOLDER BALPHA W	CW3	W-2149978	0164	1
HOLDER DANIEL T	2LT	0-1309266	0844	2
HOLDER EVERTON A	MAJ	0-1598758	0164	1
HOLDER HALL C	COL	0-0292689	0159	3
HOLDER JOHN C	LTC	0-0238600	1052	1
HOLDERBY ROBERT A P	COL	C-0184413	0648	3
HOLDERER MADELINE	2LT	N-0700714	0436	1
HOLDERMAN WILLIAM F	LTC	0-1323928	0161	1
HOLDREN EDWARD A	MAJ	0-1534512	0359	1
HOLDRIDGE JOHN F	LTC	0-2023233	0267	1
HOLDSTOCK JAMES	COL	0-0257064	0663	3
HOLDSWORTH EDITH J	1LT	N-0735351	1144	1
HOLDSWORTH EDWARD H	COL	0-0332614	0459	1
HOLFORD LEWIS A	LTC	0-0474997	1048	1
HOLIEN GERALD M	CW3	W-2152237	0762	1
HOLIEN MAURICE J	LTC	0-1542282	1157	1
HOLINGER ERIC V	CPT	0-1649162	1162	2
HOLIWAY THOMAS C	CPT	0-0559410	0557	2
HOLK CHARLES	CPT	0-0498972	1145	1

NAME	GRADE	SVC NO	DATE RET MO YR	RET CODE
HOLLADAY CHARLES R	1LT	0-0558706	1045	2
HOLLADAY CHARLES T	1LT	0-1305429	0357	2
HOLLADAY WILLIAM A	LTC	0-0245968	1160	1
HOLLAHAN MARGARET E	CPT	N-0733501	0746	1
HOLLAHAN THOMAS W	1LT	0-1823300	0648	1
HOLLAND ALGIE B	MAJ	0-0264465	1067	3
HOLLAND ARTHUR C	CW2	W-2206797	1162	1
HOLLAND BENJAMIN F	MAJ	0-0496986	0853	1
HOLLAND BERNARD W	CPT	0-1899415	1160	1
HOLLAND CHARLES A	CW3	W-2149195	1262	1
HOLLAND CHARLES R	LTC	0-1592281	0763	1
HOLLAND CLYDE L	LTC	0-1173292	0658	1
HOLLAND DELBERT D	1LT	0-0353763	1158	3
HOLLAND EDMUND L	LTC	0-0246866	0966	3
HOLLAND EDWARD F	CPT	0-1540907	0562	1
HOLLAND ELWOOD W	COL	0-0310198	0667	3
HOLLAND FRANK	1LT	0-0290250	0844	2
HOLLAND FRANK W	WO1	W-2120296	0448	2
HOLLAND GEORGE C	MAJ	0-0411429	0545	2
HOLLAND HARRISON F	MAJ	0-1285552	0558	1
HOLLAND HENRY	CPT	0-1914145	1125	1
HOLLAND JACK G	LTC	0-0525406	0963	1
HOLLAND JAMES D	COL	0-0473478	0267	1
HOLLAND JAMES M	COL	0-0213728	0667	1
HOLLAND JESSE R	WO1	W-2131169	1149	1
HOLLAND JOHN D	LTC	0-0291232	0963	3
HOLLAND JOHN H	MAJ	0-1996575	0356	1
HOLLAND JOHN L	CW3	W-2142023	0662	1
HOLLAND JOSEPH A	LTC	0-0171940	0561	3
HOLLAND JOSEPH J	LTC	0-1166287	1161	1
HOLLAND JOSEPH P	CW3	W-3150327	0667	1
HOLLAND JR ARTHUR G	MAJ	0-1325496	0758	1
HOLLAND JR HARVEY H	1LT	0-0545150	0346	1
HOLLAND LOUNA W	CPT	0-0197161	0252	3
HOLLAND MARIE A D	1LT	N-0721752	0345	1
HOLLAND MARVIN L	MAJ	0-0488878	1154	1
HOLLAND MICHAEL J	CPT	0-0498325	0747	1
HOLLAND ROBERT P	LTC	0-0499132	0247	2
HOLLAND ROSCOE C	LTC	0-0496152	0257	1
HOLLAND SAM R	LTC	0-1283776	0857	1
HOLLAND URBAN D	CPT	0-0387473	0145	2
HOLLAND VON O	MAJ	0-2014572	0166	1
HOLLAND WILBUR F	LTC	0-0445702	1262	1
HOLLAND WILLIAM D	COL	0-0254165	1046	2
HOLLAND WILLIAM H	COL	0-0215521	0962	3
HOLLANDSWORTH ALBERT	LTC	0-0225438	0265	3
HOLLE HOBART M	1LT	0-1596910	0746	2
HOLLEB MELVYN G	CW2	W-2203861	0760	1
HOLLEMPEAK CHESTER D	LTC	0-1541227	1160	1
HOLLENBAUGH HOWARD G	CW2	W-2214633	0667	1
HOLLENBECK DALE V	MAJ	0-1591805	0862	1
HOLLENBECK MELVIN M	CPT	0-1951588	0856	2
HOLLENBECK THOMAS A	LTC	0-0925214	0254	2
HOLLERAN EDWARD J	1LT	0-0383822	0743	2
HOLLERBACH JOSEPH T	MAJ	0-1334290	0463	1
HOLLEY EMERSON	1LT	0-0344335	0542	1
HOLLEY FREDERICK	MAJ	0-0543788	0364	1
HOLLEY JOE W	CW3	W-2149378	0662	1
HOLLEY JOSEPH R	MAJ	0-0964520	0965	1
HOLLEY JR LEMUEL T	COL	0-0414180	1160	1
HOLLEY JR RICHMOND F	MAJ	0-0452526	1062	1
HOLLEY RICHARD T	MAJ	0-0946977	1265	1
HOLLEY SAM J	CW4	W-2144833	0367	1
HOLLICKF MERLE F	MAJ	0-0123131	0254	3
HOLLIDAY CARL H	CPT	0-0371512	0444	2
HOLLIDAY CLARENCE E	MAJ	0-1017944	0158	1
HOLLIDAY DENNIS H	LTC	0-0215800	0264	3
HOLLIDAY DONALD V	LTC	0-0216040	0264	3
HOLLIDAY FREDERICK	LTC	0-0420760	0256	1
HOLLIDAY JOHN C	CPT	0-0202519	0555	2
HOLLIDAY JOSEPH A	COL	0-0217476	0563	2
HOLLIDAY OSCAR W	CW2	W-2106705	0665	3
HOLLIDAY ROBERT D	LTC	0-1585629	0864	1
HOLLIDAY TERRELL C	LTC	0-1285241	0854	1
HOLLIDAY VERNA M	MAJ	N-0726017	1160	1
HOLLIDAY WILLIAM L	LTC	0-1646260	0561	1
HOLLIHAN JAMES R	CPT	0-1586670	0947	2
HOLLIHANC JAMES E	LTC	0-1056748	0861	1
HOLLIMAN CHARLES L	MAJ	0-0983968	0466	1
HOLLIMAN WILLIAM J	MAJ	0-0179999	0453	3
HOLLINGSHEAD JR L	CPT	0-1577228	1044	2
HOLLINGSHEAD LYMAN B	LTC	0-0931992	0667	1
HOLLINGSWORTH DAVID	LTC	0-2201444	0759	1
HOLLINGSWORTH GERALD	MAJ	N-0763766	1163	3
HOLLINGSWORTH HARRY	1LT	0-1060130	0646	2
HOLLINGSWORTH J L	1LT	0-2010495	0261	2
HOLLINGSWORTH J S	COL	0-0382335	0860	1
HOLLINGSWORTH J T	CW3	W-2146136	0656	1
HOLLINGSWORTH JAMES	LTC	0-1541178	0166	2
HOLLINGSWORTH JESSE	MAJ	0-1053641	0864	3
HOLLINGSWORTH L Z	WO1	W-2146248	1059	2
HOLLINGSWORTH MARION	LTC	0-0308367	0258	3
HOLLINGSWORTH NED W	MAJ	0-1327740	0859	1
HOLLINGSWORTH T G	MAJ	0-0355067	0445	1
HOLLINS SR EDWARD P	CW2	RW-2206420	0366	1
HOLLINSWORTH HANSEL	CW3	W-2143355	0966	1
HOLLIS BENJAMIN	LTC	0-0455867	0867	1
HOLLIS DERAL	CPT	0-0965052	0956	1
HOLLIS JAMES S	MAJ	0-1642193	0563	1
HOLLIS JR HAROLD E	CW2	W-2209874	0663	1
HOLLIS JR STEPHEN L	CPT	0-1688341	0358	1
HOLLIS KENNETH L	CPT	0-0115079	0855	3
HOLLIS LAWRENCE C	LTC	0-0178488	1060	3
HOLLIS LEVY V	CPT	0-2262168	0763	1
HOLLIS MARSHALL F	LTC	0-0407545	0863	1
HOLLIS PATRICK M	MAJ	0-0357324	0960	2
HOLLIS WILLIAM C	COL	0-0138446	1158	3
HOLLIS WILLIAM J	CW3	W-2150123	0865	1
HOLLISTER GEORGE F	LTC	0-0315104	1047	2
HOLLISTER HOWARD J	CPT	0-0239611	0445	2
HOLLISTER JOHN W	COL	0-0269570	1159	3
HOLLISTER KATHERINE	2LT	N-0743604	0445	1
HOLLIWAY HAROLD W	COL	0-0244579	0764	3
HOLLMAN THURMAN H	LTC	0-0413140	0266	1
HOLLOMAN HUBERT J	CW3	W-2103018	1057	1
HOLLOMAN JOSEPH P	CPT	0-0492985	0748	1
HOLLON LETTON H	LTC	0-0194517	0850	1
HOLLOWAY AUBREY T	LTC	0-0250979	0267	3
HOLLOWAY CARL L	MAJ	0-0310077	0646	2
HOLLOWAY CHARLES F	LTC	0-0346278	1061	1
HOLLOWAY GEORGE E	COL	0-0264946	0266	3
HOLLOWAY HAROLD K	COL	0-0286720	0361	1
HOLLOWAY HENRY G	MAJ	0-0995763	1065	1
HOLLOWAY HERBERT O	MAJ	0-1283606	0446	2
HOLLOWAY HERBERT K	LTC	0-0192688	1062	3
HOLLOWAY JESSE G	COL	0-0301946	0960	1
HOLLOWAY JR C E	CPT	0-1305774	0647	2
HOLLOWAY JR CLAUD L	2LT	0-1821588	0344	2
HOLLOWAY ROY L	LTC	0-1638901	0962	1
HOLLOWAY STEPHEN D	LTC	0-0503050	0766	3
HOLLOWAY WILLIAM	LTC	0-0281313	1162	3
HOLLOWELL CHARLES H	2LT	0-1176671	0444	2
HOLLOWELL EARL C	1LT	0-1824465	0745	2
HOLLOWELL ELMER A	CW3	W-2152316	0765	1
HOLLSTEIN CHARLES C	LTC	0-1280708	0360	1
HOLLSTEIN JOSEPH P	CPT	0-0497124	0147	1
HOLLSTEIN ROBERT W	CPT	0-0512307	0845	2
HOLLYFIELD MERWYN H	WO1	W-2128022	1046	2
HOLLYWOOD JAMES L	CPT	0-0535975	0445	2
HOLM AARON E	CPT	0-2263684	0862	1
HOLM ERNEST O	WO1	W-2115847	1051	1
HOLM JR EMIL G	CPT	0-0409668	1046	2
HOLM LIONEL C	MAJ	0-0225784	1264	3
HOLM PAUL C	MAJ	0-1296211	0661	1
HOLMAN CLYDE E	2LT	0-1318795	0844	2
HOLMAN EDWARD L	LTC	0-0225307	0854	3
HOLMAN EDWIN A	2LT	0-2043039	1044	2
HOLMAN HAROLD S	MAJ	0-0370891	0745	2
HOLMAN HORACE F	LTC	0-0224612	1264	3
HOLMAN JACK C	CW2	W-2141316	0655	1
HOLMAN LAWRENCE M	LTC	0-0352334	0157	1
HOLMAN ROSCOE E	2LT	0-1894588	0545	2
HOLMBERG ERNEST E	LTC	0-0272952	1066	3
HOLMBERG HAROLD R	MAJ	0-0251761	0445	1
HOLMBERG JEAN H	1LT	0-1287533	0146	2
HOLMBERG KENNETH N	LTC	0-1116551	0961	1
HOLMES ADOLPH	MAJ	0-1023158	0856	1
HOLMES ALPHEUS F	MAJ	0-2021259	0366	1
HOLMES ANDREW L	2LT	0-1796474	0645	2
HOLMES ARTHUR A	COL	0-0276591	0960	2
HOLMES ARTHUR D	MAJ	0-0385291	0947	1
HOLMES CHARLES K	COL	0-0162054	0452	3
HOLMES CHARLES M	2LT	0-1115924	1143	2
HOLMES CHARLES W	LTC	0-0400264	0163	1
HOLMES CLYDE R S	LTC	N-0727200	0466	3
HOLMES DAVID R	CW4	W-2119846	0559	1
HOLMES DELBERT H	MAJ	0-1292176	0958	1
HOLMES DELTON	CW2	W-2149948	0559	1
HOLMES EARL J	WO1	W-2123638	0257	1
HOLMES EDWARD R	MAJ	0-0333687	1145	2
HOLMES ELVIE H	LTC	0-1283608	1166	1
HOLMES FRANK O	1LT	0-0301186	0343	2
HOLMES FRANKLIN J	LTC	0-0402480	0757	1
HOLMES GASTON L	LTC	0-0172759	0648	3
HOLMES HAROLD H	1LT	0-1182860	0946	2
HOLMES HARRY G	MAJ	0-1105302	1060	1
HOLMES HELEN F	MAJ	L-0803000	0548	1
HOLMES JAMES D	LTC	0-0300415	1162	1
HOLMES JAMES E	MAJ	0-0134345	0449	3
HOLMES JAMES M	MAJ	0-1598093	0263	1
HOLMES JAMES R	MAJ	0-2010648	0859	1
HOLMES JAMES S	MAJ	0-2202912	0964	1
HOLMES JAY M	LTC	0-0168112	0850	3
HOLMES JOHN E	CPT	0-1949124	0955	1
HOLMES JOHN F	LTC	0-0474938	0661	1
HOLMES JOHN H	LTC	0-0361767	0355	1
HOLMES JOSEPH A	LTC	0-0154966	0555	3
HOLMES JOSEPH A	MAJ	0-0197071	0258	3
HOLMES JOSEPH P	CPT	0-1166509	0652	1
HOLMES JR ROBERT C	COL	0-1104855	1167	1
HOLMES JR RUSSEL A	1LT	0-0556883	0845	2
HOLMES K J	MAJ	0-1633980	1060	1
HOLMES LESLIE	1LT	0-0923563	0145	2
HOLMES LESTER R	LTC	0-0376074	0166	1
HOLMES LESTER L	LTC	0-0245978	0561	1
HOLMES MERLE V	LTC	0-0192795	0648	3
HOLMES NILS R	MAJ	0-2035222	0560	1
HOLMES OLIVER W	MAJ	0-1846448	0961	1
HOLMES PETER N	LTC	0-0514159	0563	1
HOLMES RAYMOND	WO1	W-2148730	0862	1
HOLMES REXFORD C	LTC	0-0357974	0860	3
HOLMES RICHARD R	MAJ	0-1051206	0962	1
HOLMES ROBERT B	1LT	0-4756681	0661	1
HOLMES RYLAND C	CW3	W-2146063	0262	1
HOLMES STERLING D	CW4	W-2120737	0563	2
HOLMES THOMAS J	LTC	0-0203971	0963	1
HOLMES THOMAS S	1LT	0-1049892	0246	2
HOLMES WENDELL S	COL	0-0359103	1167	3
HOLMES WILLIAM E	CPT	0-0541093	1145	2
HOLMES WILLIAM E	MAJ	0-1300487	1055	1
HOLMES WILLIAM F	CW3	W-2124248	0257	1
HOLMES WILLIAM H	LTC	0-0495632	0157	1
HOLMES WILLIAM O	MAJ	0-1555062	0161	1
HOLMES WILLIAM W	CPT	0-0184134	0353	3
HOLMGREN REINOLD A	2LT	0-0106638	1153	3
HOLMGREN SAMUEL T	COL	0-0205815	0745	2
HOLMGREN WARNER E	CPT	0-0445181	0445	2
HOLMQUIST GEORGE F	CPT	0-0110517	0850	3
HOLMQUIST HAROLD F	1LT	0-1291277	0746	2
HOLMSTROM HUGO R	CPT	0-1116552	1060	1
HOLMSTROM ROY C	1LT	0-2006968	1046	2
HOLMSTROM VICTOR R	CW3	W-2143390	0564	1
HOLMWOOD HARLAN W	MAJ	0-0193965	0363	3
HOLOCH ELROY O	LTC	0-1183885	0862	1
HOLOD JOSEPHINE	1LT	N-0794172	0547	1
HOLOM VICTOR	1LT	0-1304216	0845	2
HOLOMAN JR WILLIAM O	2LT	0-4063195	1157	2
HOLSAPFEL CLIFFORD A	CW2	W-2151054	0358	1
HOLSCHER GORDON H	MAJ	0-1999044	0164	1
HOLSINGER HARRIS W	LTC	0-0246345	0360	3
HOLST RALPH V	CW2	W-2152289	1157	1
HOLST WILLIAM W	LTC	0-0388569	0661	1
HOLSTE MERLIN L	CW3	W-2148021	0659	1
HOLSTEIN CHARLES F	2LT	0-1053642	0845	2
HOLSTEIN JANE F	MAJ	N-0741882	0862	2
HOLSTEIN RICHARD H	CPT	0-0292611	0445	2
HOLSTEN HERBERT N	COL	0-0334336	0460	1
HOLSTER HENRY P	LTC	0-1175467	0267	1
HOLSTLAW CHARLES H	LTC	0-0171195	0953	3
HOLSTON CLARENCE E	CW3	W-2148857	0161	1
HOLSTON SEYMOUR A	CPT	0-1185505	0648	1
HOLSTROM GEORGE	MAJ	0-1017584	0462	1
HOLSTROM JAMES R	CW3	W-2153344	1264	1
HOLSTUN BEVERLY R	CPT	0-0196138	1062	3
HOLT ARTHUR W	COL	0-0460185	0763	1
HOLT ELMER M	LTC	0-0224887	1054	3
HOLT ESTHER S	CPT	N-0767462	0546	1
HOLT FLOYD W	WO1	W-2127312	0749	1
HOLT FRANK R	MAJ	0-0977667	1062	1
HOLT FRANK F	LTC	0-1291642	0861	1
HOLT GEORGE T	COL	0-0235386	0965	3
HOLT HAROLD A	MAJ	0-0955431	0264	1
HOLT HERBERT	1LT	0-0535421	1044	2
HOLT HILAND J D	LTC	0-0306396	1167	3
HOLT HOWARD K	CPT	0-0979136	1061	1
HOLT JAMES M	LTC	0-1306098	0161	1
HOLT JOHN C	1LT	0-1913730	0132	1
HOLT JOHN P	MAJ	0-0359130	0865	3
HOLT JR TAYLOR	COL	0-0270614	0663	3
HOLT JR WILLIAM J	MAJ	0-1300036	1262	1
HOLT LAWRENCE E	CPT	0-1031096	0460	1
HOLT LORRAINE C	2LT	N-0774816	1046	1
HOLT MACK C	MAJ	0-1591208	0160	1
HOLT MARVIN W	CW3	W-2153111	0764	1
HOLT MONT	CW3	W-2141587	0860	1
HOLT RALPH J	1LT	0-1308645	0546	2
HOLT RANSOM A	CPT	0-1688262	1061	1
HOLT ROBERT A	CPT	0-1876277	0466	1
HOLT ROBERT T	COL	0-0312216	1262	3
HOLT SAMUEL E	MAJ	0-0220798	0858	3
HOLT SR RICHARD L	CW4	W-2005619	1265	1
HOLT THOMAS A	MAJ	0-2204407	0166	1
HOLT VICTOR R	CPT	0-1032156	1047	1
HOLT VINCENT J	CW2	W-2151662	0855	1
HOLT WAYLAND G	CPT	0-0454386	1045	2
HOLT WILLARD C	CPT	0-1548438	1160	2
HOLT WILTHELMA	1LT	N-0765382	0847	1
HOLTE ALFRED C	CPT	0-0441292	1045	2
HOLTE JR OLAV B	CW2	W-3410009	0867	1
HOLTEGAARD LEONARD F	CPT	0-1703028	0246	1
HOLTER HOWARD H	MAJ	0-2038857	0962	1
HOLTHAUS FRANCIS J	LTC	0-1108748	0663	1
HOLTMEIER MILTON J	1LT	0-1586672	0157	1
HOLTON CLARENCE A	MAJ	0-1182385	0562	1
HOLTON DARWIN S	LTC	0-0276183	1166	3
HOLTON FRANK N	CW3	W-2152579	1164	1
HOLTON GEORGE J	CW2	W-2153086	0462	1
HOLTON JAMES L	LTC	0-0170580	1059	3
HOLTON JR ARCHIE O	COL	0-0350609	0160	1
HOLTON JR CHARLES O	LTC	0-1104212	1067	1
HOLTON JR JAMES E	LTC	0-0299899	0166	3
HOLTON RAYMOND F	LTC	0-0498908	1155	1
HOLTON ROBERT G	LTC	0-1551226	1065	1
HOLTZ JOHN J	CPT	0-0167811	0752	3
HOLTZ PAUL R	COL	0-0280590	0155	3
HOLTZ ROBERT E	CPT	0-1113759	0862	1
HOLTZCLAW HARRY L	CPT	0-0281107	0665	3
HOLTZCLAW JR LOUIE H	1LT	0-0423208	1043	2
HOLTZMAN ABRAHAM	1LT	0-1061134	0645	2
HOLTZMAN RAYMOND S	COL	0-0212596	1057	1

NAME	GRADE	SVC NO	DATE RET MO YR	RET CODE
HOLUB JR CHARLES R	CW2	W-2154668	0564	1
HOLWAY ORLANDO G	CPT	0-0235886	0352	3
HOLY RUTH L	1LT	N-0772561	0848	2
HOLZ ARTHUR J	2LT	0-1319744	1044	2
HOLZ LOUIS F	MAJ	0-1321518	0457	2
HOLZ LOUIS T	MAJ	0-1897756	1063	1
HOLZAEPFEL DAVID W	1LT	0-2202321	1053	2
HOLZHAUER FRANKLIN L	MAJ	0-2010065	0962	1
HOLZMAN ROBERT A	COL	0-0422395	1062	1
HOLZMAN SIDNEY T	LTC	0-0205094	1146	2
HOLZMUELLER OSCAR W	CPT	0-0452656	1045	2
HOLZWORTH ELMER J	MAJ	0-0524319	C157	1
HOMAN CLARENCE A	LTC	0-0173539	0-51	3
HOMAN FREDERIC F	CPT	0-1683612	0744	2
HOMAN GEORGE F	LTC	0-1585637	1166	3
HOMAN HARRY	CPT	0-0395563	0345	2
HOMAN HARRY W	CPT	0-0275841	0859	3
HOMAN JR RALPH F	MAJ	0-1172499	1061	1
HOMAN LAWRENCE H	CPT	0-0371248	C246	2
HOMAN WAYNE E	COL	0-0173541	1051	1
HOMAN WILLIAM L	COL	0-0183865	C852	2
HOMANICH ANDREW	MAJ	C-0424195	C848	1
HOMER ARTHUR B	CPT	0-0200696	1042	2
HOMER DAVID	LTC	0-0284803	0765	3
HOMER LEROY W	CW3	W-2147311	1065	2
HOMER RUSSELL	CPT	0-1634899	0446	2
HOMERICK PAUL A	2LT	0-1325441	1144	2
HOMEWOOD CHARLES L	MAJ	C-1824619	0263	1
HOMFELD JOHN F	M G	0-0253221	0864	3
HOMME FRANKLIN F	LTC	0-1551427	0167	3
HOMME HERBERT T	LTC	0-1043667	C461	1
HOMMEL EDWARD H	1LT	0-0492174	1043	2
HOMMEYER PAUL G	COL	0-0255158	0762	3
HOMZA STEVE A	CW2	W-2147796	0561	1
HONACK FRANK R	MAJ	C-1946293	0662	1
HONAKER KEITH J	LTC	0-0407834	0563	1
HONAKER ROBERT L	2LT	0-2005565	C346	2
HONAKER SAMUEL A	COL	0-0125801	0749	3
HONAN JOSEPH C	2LT	0-1591809	1144	2
HONDOLERO FELIX S	CPT	0-1311893	0362	2
HONEA HENRY	2LT	0-2055841	1044	1
HONEA JR JAMES L	MAJ	C-0964195	C966	1
HONEA WILEY S	MAJ	0-1796624	0957	1
HONECK HOWARD D	MAJ	C-1030677	1164	1
HONECK ROBERT B	LTC	0-1556444	0466	1
HONEK MIKE S	MAJ	C-0512352	C755	1
HONEY ARTHUR G	LTC	C-0507462	0263	1
HONEY JOHN S	LTC	0-0322791	1059	1
HONEY WARREN	CPT	C-1285943	C545	1
HONEY WILLIAM V	LTC	0-0254484	C363	3
HONEYCUTT EUGENE J	MAJ	0-0228738	1164	3
HONEYCUTT LEE O	CW4	W-2134324	0957	1
HONEYCUTT TOWNSELL N	CPT	0-1586674	0746	2
HONEYCUTT WILLIS E	MAJ	C-1342378	1066	1
HONEYWELL ROY J	LTC	0-0132034	0648	3
HONEYWELL STANLEY S	MAJ	0-0976519	0263	[illegible]
HONIG RICHARD P	MAJ	0-2055100	0161	1
HONN TERRILL F	CW3	W-2141588	1061	1
HONODEL FRANCIS A	LTC	0-1695693	1064	1
HONOLD HENRY W	MAJ	C-0355212	0646	2
HONORE ALEXANDER	CPT	0-1796283	0764	2
HONORE MAGRETHE E	CPT	N-0784595	1047	1
HONOUR JOHN H	MAJ	0-1647506	1057	1
HONSA WILLIAM M	MAJ	0-0264969	C566	3
HONSBERGER JOHN H	LTC	0-1573288	0257	1
HONTS CHAYLON F	1LT	0-1119838	0352	2
HONTS EMORY R	COL	0-0200080	1045	1
HONTZ MARIE V	MAJ	N-0742292	1064	3
HOOBLER DANIEL B	LTC	0-1645056	0264	1
HOOD BOB C	MAJ	0-0995683	0865	1
HOOD CARL M	LTC	0-0360504	0646	2
HOOD CHARLES R	CPT	0-0499654	0946	1
HOOD DANIEL L	1LT	0-1913731	0520	1
HOOD DWIGHT L	COL	0-0251182	0462	3
HOOD ELMER C	1LT	0-1300037	0845	2

NAME	GRADE	SVC NO	DATE RET MO YR	RET CODE
HOOD ERNEST A	1LT	0-1117275	0460	1
HOOD FRANCES	MAJ	N-0764681	0563	1
HOOD FRANCIS C	COL	C-0274286	0853	1
HOOD FRANK	CW4	W-2145861	0567	1
HOOD FRANK C	COL	0-0146678	1048	3
HOOD FREDERICK	LTC	0-0212703	0845	2
HOOD GLEN D	CW3	W-2144186	0559	1
HOOD GUTHRIE H	CW4	W-2121059	0864	3
HOOD HOWARD H	LTC	0-1294132	C863	1
HOOD JAMES A	WO1	W-3200870	0967	1
HOOD JAMES V	CPT	0-0985687	0561	1
HOOD JOHN G	LTC	0-0278444	1159	3
HOOD JOHNNY	MAJ	0-2262802	1162	1
HOOD JR DAVID	LTC	0-1575367	0861	1
HOOD JULIAN R	CW3	W-2149184	0764	1
HOOD MARY E	2LT	N-0790846	0545	1
HOOD OLLIE A	LTC	0-0421839	1162	1
HOOD RANDOLPH P	MAJ	0-1547969	0756	1
HOOD THURMAN	MAJ	0-1647092	0955	1
HOOD WILLIAM B	CW2	W-2207479	0861	1
HOOD WILLIAM C	LTC	0-1030780	0465	1
HOOGLAND DIRK	CW3	W-2205507	0767	1
HOOK BRUCE F	CPT	0-4006395	0667	1
HOOK ENOS E	LTC	0-0920015	0446	1
HOOK GEORGE W V	1LT	0-1016836	1045	2
HOOK HAROLD J	LTC	0-1823876	1062	2
HOOK HAROLD C	LTC	0-030115C	0357	1
HOOK IRA T	MAJ	0-0115075	0648	3
HOOK LAWRENCE H	MAJ	0-0335738	0862	3
HOOK LILLIAN M	1LT	N-0760030	0946	1
HOOK LOUIS A	MAJ	0-0995685	1166	1
HOOK RALPH E	MAJ	0-0405381	0346	2
HOOK RALPH G	MAJ	0-1583126	0259	1
HOOK ROBERT W	CW3	W-2146335	1063	1
HOOK WALTER E	LTC	0-0406277	0346	2
HOOK WALTER S	CPT	0-1184521	1158	1
HOOKER ALLEN E	MAJ	0-1881767	1066	1
HOOKER DEWITT E	MAJ	0-C146012	1057	3
HOOKER JR JOHN C	LTC	0-1822007	C164	1
HOOKER LANGSFORD	CW2	W-2151633	0259	1
HOOKER WARREN L	CPT	0-1320919	0846	2
HOOKER WILLIAM A	2LT	0-1301489	0144	2
HOOKER WILLIAM F	MAJ	0-205541C	1158	1
HOOKIE LOWELL O	CPT	0-2032935	0457	1
HOOKS JOHN A	CW2	W-2145448	0761	1
HOOKS ROBERT G	LTC	0-0258683	0467	3
HOOKS ROBERT J	1LT	0-0694372	0346	2
HOOLE RALPH D	1LT	0-0405527	0453	2
HOOLIHAN WILLIAM J	CW2	W-2210C81	0167	1
HOOPER CHARLES H	LTC	0-0227580	C564	3
HOOPER FREDERICK	CPT	C-0307901	0345	2
HOOPER HENRY G	MAJ	0-0949722	1262	1
HOOPER JAMES F	LTC	0-0383877	0557	1
HOOPER JAMES R	COL	0-0438225	1154	1
HOOPER JR ALVIN F	MAJ	0-0973948	0567	1
HOOPER JR CHARLES R	CW3	W-2151C08	1162	1
HOOPER JR WILLIAM T	LTC	0-1317C14	1062	1
HOOPER LAWRENCE H	2LT	0-1576146	0445	2
HOOPER LORETTA A	1LT	N-0722484	0846	1
HOOPER MELVIN H	LTC	0-0254590	0562	1
HOOPER ROBERT W	MAJ	0-0498729	1044	2
HOOPER SIDNEY B	COL	C-0326834	1055	3
HOOPER SR JOHN C	MAJ	C-0970669	0363	1
HOOPER WALTER S	WO1	W-2110291	1C53	1
HOOPERT JOSEPH C	LTC	0-0371431	0260	1
HOOPMAN RICHARD B	LTC	0-1165514	0962	1
HOOPS RAYMOND	MAJ	0-1019301	0757	1
HOOPS THEODORE H	CW4	W-200C228	1159	3
HOOS HAROLD W	1LT	0-164C570	0646	2
HOOSE CLINTON M	MAJ	0-025322C	1057	2
HOOTS WILLIAM C	MAJ	0-0973458	0263	1
HOOVER CARL F	LTC	0-0273826	0246	2
HOOVER CLARENCE F	COL	0-0265957	0362	3
HOOVER DONALD D	COL	0-0264616	0264	3
HOOVER FRANCIS C	MAJ	0-2011121	1162	1

NAME	GRADE	SVC NO	DATE RET MO YR	RET CODE
HOOVER GILES N	CPT	0-0477221	0448	2
HOOVER HOBERT H	LTC	0-0364957	1264	1
HOOVER HOMER L	LTC	0-0169565	0648	3
HOOVER J O	1LT	0-2008405	C448	2
HOOVER JACOB C	MAJ	C-0250316	0862	3
HOOVER JOHN L	1LT	0-1331626	0546	2
HOOVER JOHN P	MAJ	C-0443857	C364	1
HOOVER JOSEPH H	CW3	W-2208503	0266	1
HOOVER JR FRANK B	LTC	0-0256354	C361	1
HOOVER JR SAMUEL R	LTC	C-1303816	0661	1
HOOVER JR WILLIAM M	COL	0-0330396	C751	1
HOOVER LLOYD H	COL	0-0252181	1064	3
HOOVER MARION J	2LT	0-2049585	C252	2
HOOVER MELVIN L	2LT	0-C887886	0845	2
HOOVER MERLE M	WO1	W-2123247	1145	2
HOOVER PHILLIP F	COL	C-0381163	1160	1
HOOVER ROBERT E	CW3	W-2152733	1164	1
HOOVER ROBERT V	2LT	0-2007114	C447	2
HOOVER ROSE E	MAJ	C-1541231	0760	1
HOOVER SAMUEL E	1LT	0-1686713	1051	1
HOOVER WILLIAM O	LTC	0-1636057	0958	1
HOOVLER JAMES A	1LT	0-1318306	0848	1
HOPCRAFT HARVEY J	CPT	0-0303330	1045	1
HOPE ALVIN C	COL	0-0163273	0855	3
HOPE CHARLES A	MAJ	0-0282591	0949	2
HOPE CHARLES W	MAJ	0-1289085	C760	1
HOPE GEORGE K	1LT	0-2055071	0745	1
HOPE JAMES C	CW3	W-2207056	1066	1
HOPE JR WILLIAM M	LTC	C-1178838	C562	1
HOPE MURL S	CW3	W-2145809	0561	1
HOPE ROBERT H	LTC	0-0226458	C964	3
HOPE ROBERT L	LTC	C-1112230	0964	1
HOPE ROBERT R	LTC	0-0914387	1159	3
HOPELAIN RICHARD	COL	0-0245960	1062	3
HOPEWELL ROLF K	CPT	C-1320532	1064	1
HOPFNER WALTER R C	MAJ	0-1874899	C865	1
HOPKE JACK A	LTC	0-0309841	0163	3
HOPKIN HENRY S	MAJ	0-1996482	0258	1
HOPKINS BILL H	LTC	0-1183703	C765	1
HOPKINS CECIL W	CPT	C-2010995	1160	1
HOPKINS CHARLES K	CW3	W-2144031	0461	1
HOPKINS CHARLES M	LTC	0-0453819	C157	1
HOPKINS CHARLES M	CPT	0-1312770	1149	1
HOPKINS CHRISTOPHE	LTC	0-0311002	0746	2
HOPKINS CLACK O	COL	0-0347340	1045	2
HOPKINS CLARENCE A	LTC	0-0213726	0263	3
HOPKINS CLARK	LTC	C-0166673	C955	3
HOPKINS DANIEL B	MAJ	0-1798262	C163	1
HOPKINS EDWARD E	MAJ	0-1314637	C461	1
HOPKINS EDWARD S	COL	0-0205045	1156	3
HOPKINS FLORIAN G	LTC	0-0357059	0264	3
HOPKINS GEORGE H	COL	0-0263835	0354	3
HOPKINS GEORGE J	1LT	0-1286291	1045	2
HOPKINS HARRY K	MAJ	0-1031812	1061	1
HOPKINS HENRY A	CW2	W-2206099	C66C	1
HOPKINS HENRY S	CPT	0-1289582	C449	1
HOPKINS HENRY U	LTC	0-0253268	C946	2
HOPKINS HOWARD H	1LT	0-1016113	0346	2
HOPKINS IRVING G	LTC	0-0141956	0257	3
HOPKINS JACK	LTC	0-0344306	0954	1
HOPKINS JOHN F	CW2	W-2211462	0967	1
HOPKINS JOHN S	COL	0-0245574	C566	3
HOPKINS JOHN T	1LT	0-1314484	0347	2
HOPKINS JOHN W	LTC	C-1173293	0557	1
HOPKINS JULIAN H	2LT	0-0530673	C645	2
HOPKINS LESLIE B	LTC	0-0446998	0150	1
HOPKINS LYMAN R	MAJ	C-1284876	0258	1
HOPKINS PAUL F	MAJ	0-2019744	0263	1
HOPKINS PAUL L	LTC	0-1304217	C862	1
HOPKINS RALPH L	MAJ	C-1080789	0660	1
HOPKINS RICHARD H	B G	0-0245902	0766	3
HOPKINS ROBERT F	CPT	C-1000382	0555	1
HOPKINS ROBERT W	MAJ	C-2208531	C666	1
HOPKINS ROSCOE B	MAJ	0-0308637	1067	3
HOPKINS ROY D	CW2	W-2209871	1063	1

NAME	GRADE	SVC NO	DATE RET MO YR	RET CODE
HOPKINS ROY H	MAJ	C-1648291	0157	1
HOPKINS THOMAS J	LTC	0-0174367	0561	3
HOPKINS WALTER F	CW4	W-2113954	0659	1
HOPKINS WALTER K	MAJ	0-0400916	1163	1
HOPKINS WAYNE O	MAJ	0-1176375	0561	1
HOPKINS WILLIAM C	MAJ	0-0222185	1145	2
HOPMANN URBAN C	CPT	0-0383804	0247	1
HOPP CHARLES T	CW3	W-2205355	C466	1
HOPP HARVEY W	COL	0-0190899	0158	3
HOPP RICHARD C	LTC	0-0206023	1160	3
HOPPE ARTHUR C	LTC	0-0428104	0364	1
HOPPE JR RICHARD E	1LT	0-0793772	1144	2
HOPPE LAWRENCE F	CW2	W-2144347	1156	2
HOPPE ROBERT C	LTC	0-0481343	0356	1
HOPPE WILLIAM G	MAJ	0-0454088	0346	2
HOPPE WOODROW C	MAJ	0-0407218	0864	1
HOPPER CLEO W	CW3	W-2149488	0363	1
HOPPER DAVID W	COL	0-0122526	1C59	3
HOPPER ELBERT B	MAJ	0-0461560	0549	1
HOPPER ELVIN C	MAJ	0-1548647	1160	1
HOPPER FRANCIS L	LTC	0-0378902	0660	1
HOPPER HERBERT W	CW3	W-2152266	1164	1
HOPPER JAMES A	MAJ	0-1584374	1060	1
HOPPER JOSEPH C	LTC	0-0509563	1055	1
HOPPER JR DANIEL A	LTC	0-0274273	0963	3
HOPPER JR FRED C	LTC	C-1010215	1264	1
HOPPER KATHERINE	2LT	N-0757669	0646	1
HOPPER M FRANCES	CPT	N-0759803	0546	1
HOPPER OBED A	LTC	0-1176068	0462	1
HOPPER RALPH T	MAJ	0-187716C	1266	1
HOPPER REX	LTC	0-1290753	1162	1
HOPPER STUART C	COL	0-0131928	0648	3
HOPPER WILLIAM F	1LT	0-1324169	C959	1
HOPPES JAMES K	1LT	0-0432791	0946	2
HOPPING JOHN S	MAJ	0-1689C44	0946	1
HOPPLE HOMER H	CPT	0-0513231	0650	1
HOPPOCK NOEL E	2LT	0-1174894	0445	2
HOPPS CARL W	MAJ	0-0191975	0749	3
HOPPUS HOWARD C	MAJ	0-1913472	0164	1
HOPSON EDISON	MAJ	0-1798353	0760	1
HOPSON TROY D	MAJ	0-1922674	C565	1
HOPSON WILLIAM H	LTC	0-0257075	0464	3
HOPTIAK TED J	CW2	W-214293C	0361	1
HOPWOOD DUANE J	CW3	W-2153347	0465	1
HORAK RUFUS V	2LT	0-1595578	0746	1
HORAMAN CHAUNCEY E	LTC	0-1648303	0461	1
HORAN ALICE M	1LT	N-075143C	0146	1
HORAN DONALD J	MAJ	0-2262621	0263	1
HORAN JAMES C	MAJ	0-1049894	0464	1
HORAN JOHN C	1LT	0-1041794	104N	2
HORAN JOHN F	MAJ	0-0347543	0261	1
HORAN JOHN P	LTC	0-0338284	0760	1
HORAN JR CHARLES A	LTC	0-1533815	0365	1
HORAN LYNOTT F	2LT	0-1591811	1043	2
HORAN MARY A	1LT	N-0721855	C646	1
HORAN THOMAS J	MAJ	0-0381646	0146	2
HORAN WILLIAM H	LTC	0-1291278	0660	1
HORBALY WILLIAM V	LTC	0-1941536	0256	2
HORD ASA A	LTC	0-0466C13	0367	1
HORD J T	CPT	0-0901205	1044	2
HORDAN RICHARD	LTC	0-0278896	0559	3
HORDECHUCK JOHN F	1LT	0-132744C	0152	2
HORDER HERBERT L	LTC	0-046868C	0854	1
HORDT CHARLES F	LTC	0-0921391	0766	3
HORESTA ELIZABETH	MAJ	N-0757587	0767	1
HORGAN FLORENCE F	1LT	N-0741481	0946	1
HORGAN WILLIAM O	CW2	W-2111889	0446	2
HORGEN CLARENCE A	LTC	0-0319875	0167	3
HORIMOTO WILLIAM S	MAJ	0-1923050	C765	1
HORKOTT JOHN	CPT	0-1081477	0 47	2
HORLANDER DERYL	LTC	0-0400092	0457	1
HORLOCK REGINALD J	MAJ	0-0185626	0656	3
HORMAN ARLAN W	MAJ	0-1101C45	0564	1
HORMAN DOROTHY	2LT	N-0729262	1043	2
HORMAN GLEN W	LTC	0-1169163	0265	1

NAME	GRADE	SVC NO	DATE RET MO YR	RET CODE
HORMEL HAROLD M	CPT	0-1040943	1146	2
HORN ALBERT N	LTC	0-0261944	0156	2
HORN ANDREW W	1LT	0-1179445	0160	2
HORN ANTHONY W	CPT	0-1042603	0247	2
HORN ARTHUR A	CW4	W-2136640	0459	1
HORN CHARLES W	COL	0-0374658	0263	1
HORN DONALD L	CPT	0-1307242	0857	2
HORN EDITH E	MAJ	N-0741844	1063	3
HORN ERLING	MAJ	0-0239069	0865	1
HORN GERALD R	LTC	0-0489061	0357	1
HORN JOHN M	MAJ	0-1553278	0767	3
HORN JOHN P	LTC	0-0228739	0365	3
HORN JOSEPH A	LTC	0-0221296	1163	3
HORN JULIUS J	MAJ	0-1634900	1060	1
HORN LESLIE O	LTC	0-0565685	0562	1
HORN LEWIS E	MAJ	0-0256244	0159	3
HORN MEZICK T	MAJ	0-1051188	0854	1
HORN ORLAND W	LTC	0-0361085	0864	1
HORN RICHARD W	LTC	0-0221789	0753	3
HORN ROY A	LTC	0-0228635	0264	3
HORN SIDNEY	MAJ	0-1169575	0560	1
HORN WALTER B	MAJ	0-0531270	0847	1
HORN WILLIAM G	CPT	0-2263668	0761	2
HORN WOODROW W	MAJ	0-0490480	0960	1
HORNADAY DONALD F	MAJ	0-0972268	0464	1
HORNADAY THOMAS P	COL	0-0267334	0550	1
HORNBEAK PAUL M	MAJ	0-0182502	0449	3
HORNBECK HUGH M	CPT	0-2033047	0762	2
HORNBERGER EVANS Z J	MAJ	0-0469007	1146	2
HORNBUCKLE CHARLES R	MAJ	0-0348067	0263	1
HORNBY WILLIAM E	COL	0-0372899	0665	1
HORNE GERARD F	1LT	0-1051607	0246	2
HORNE IVAN W	LTC	0-1104860	0361	1
HORNE JAMES W	WO1	W-2153257	0660	2
HORNE JR JOHN D	1LT	0-5300535	0459	2
HORNE JR THOMAS C	COL	0-0200882	0356	1
HORNE KENNETH	MAJ	0-0312371	0144	2
HORNE LEM D	CW2	W-3350246	0467	1
HORNE LLOYD F	CW3	W-2144187	0958	1
HORNE NORMAN P	LTC	0-1003257	0558	1
HORNE ROGER R	WO1	W-2107348	0846	2
HORNE STEPHEN F	CPT	0-0430249	0346	2
HORNE WILFORD W	CPT	0-0254517	1044	1
HORNE WILLIAM A	2LT	0-1175745	1143	2
HORNE WILSON R	MAJ	0-1690975	1066	1
HORNER BERNARD J	COL	0-0152843	0755	3
HORNER CHARLES E	1LT	0-1167906	1145	2
HORNER CLYDE L	MAJ	0-1030379	0158	1
HORNER DONALD C	WO1	W-2146667	0765	2
HORNER DONALD O	MAJ	0-1329482	0860	2
HORNER ELIJAH W	LTC	0-0265772	0553	3
HORNER FRANKLYN F	CPT	0-0143062	1055	3
HORNER FREEMAN V	MAJ	0-2014546	0962	1
HORNER HAROLD	LTC	0-0418652	0763	1
HORNER HAROLD A	CW2	W-2151066	0560	1
HORNER JACK C	MAJ	0-0356621	1046	2
HORNER JOHN E W	LTC	0-0374789	0264	1
HORNER MARION R	LTC	0-1586360	1163	1
HORNER NORMAN S	COL	0-0412352	0767	1
HORNER PENNINGTON	MAJ	0-1946990	0356	1
HORNER REUBEN	CPT	0-0164135	1139	1
HORNER REUBEN L	LTC	0-1313746	0163	1
HORNER ROBERT	2LT	0-1321087	0544	2
HORNER ROBERT W	LTC	0-0194587	1155	3
HORNESBY ERNEST F	LTC	0-4090113	0254	1
HORNEY DANIEL J	LTC	0-0321558	0965	3
HORNEY PHILIP S	CW4	W-2143051	0866	1
HORNICK HARRY	CPT	0-0274066	0345	2
HORNING CLYDE H	CW3	W-2143796	0667	1
HORNING GEORGE J	MAJ	0-0980395	0962	1
HORNING HAROLD F	COL	0-0320617	0163	3
HORNING JACKSON G	COL	0-0181021	0652	3
HORNING STEWART C	LTC	0-1551228	1264	3
HORNING THEODORE R	LTC	0-0283913	0364	3
HORNOR WILLIAM L	B G	0-0250277	0555	3

NAME	GRADE	SVC NO	DATE RET MO YR	RET CODE
HORNSBY IRVING R	CW3	W-2149070	0760	1
HORNSBY JOHN A	CW3	W-2151922	0266	1
HORNSBY ROBERT C	COL	0-0245252	1162	3
HORNSEY JR JOHN W	LTC	0-1119798	1166	2
HORNSTEIN ISIDORE	COL	0-0234525	0158	3
HORNUNG WILLIAM W	COL	0-0193775	1054	1
HORONY JAMES L	CW2	W-2214816	0766	1
HOROWITZ ABRAHAM H	MAJ	0-0215821	0555	3
HORR PHILIP F	COL	0-0218608	1059	1
HORR ROBERT J	COL	0-0171185	0757	3
HORRELL NORBERT C	1LT	0-1010355	1145	2
HORSEY FLORENCE J	MAJ	0-0451469	0157	1
HORSLEY JAMES L	CPT	0-1587328	0259	1
HORSLEY JOHN W	COL	0-0255162	1055	3
HORSMAN GEORGE L	LTC	0-0347605	0759	1
HORSMAN JR JESSE L	LTC	0-1328605	0865	1
HORST LRIAS S	MAJ	0-1799955	0243	1
HORST WALTER H	LTC	0-0305943	1162	3
HORSTMANN OTTO C	2LT	0-0916552	0344	2
HORT HENRY J	COL	0-0265593	1059	1
HORTA JUAN F	LTC	0-0253764	0266	3
HORTON ALFRED W	LTC	0-0171598	0748	3
HORTON ALTON E	MAJ	0-0190430	0760	3
HORTON ARNOLD G	CPT	0-1001154	0547	2
HORTON CHARLIE T	MAJ	0-1176377	0960	1
HORTON CLAUDE C	MAJ	0-2014563	1163	1
HORTON DENNIS W	CPT	0-0238247	0666	3
HORTON DONALD F	COL	0-0245393	0966	3
HORTON DONELSON B	2LT	0-1332495	0446	2
HORTON DWIGHT	COL	0-0103651	0648	3
HORTON EDGAR M	CW3	W-2141589	0259	1
HORTON EDWARD V	CPT	0-0362631	1044	2
HORTON FRANK R	COL	0-0269857	1060	3
HORTON FRED C	MAJ	0-2010489	0258	1
HORTON FREDERICK	LTC	0-0497102	0657	1
HORTON GERALD B	LTC	0-0333837	0463	3
HORTON GUY L	LTC	0-0120785	0648	3
HORTON HAL C	COL	0-0150307	0648	3
HORTON HARRY W	LTC	0-1111674	0664	1
HORTON JAMES D	CPT	0-0272141	0243	2
HORTON JOHN I	CPT	0-0414356	0345	2
HORTON JOHN T	MAJ	0-1697920	1057	1
HORTON LEE F	CPT	0-0198932	0944	2
HORTON MURRAY E	MAJ	0-1899453	0363	1
HORTON NORMAN B	LTC	0-0246789	1058	3
HORTON ORA L	CW2	W-2205889	1161	1
HORTON PAUL F	LTC	0-0242420	0964	3
HORTON ROBERT H	MAJ	0-0308555	0867	3
HORTON ROGER L	LTC	0-1307547	0463	1
HORTON RUTH K	2LT	N-0715870	0645	1
HORTON STERLING R	LTC	0-0915420	0563	2
HORTON TENTON N	2LT	0-1339997	0255	2
HORTON THOMAS R	LTC	0-0244926	0-52	3
HORTON WALTER	MAJ	0-1185207	0561	1
HORTON WILLIAM E	1LT	0-1016886	1045	1
HORTON WILLIAM F	CPT	0-2048658	0363	1
HORTON WILLIAM S	2LT	0-0929828	0351	2
HORTON ZACH A	CPT	0-0524338	0745	2
HORVATH ROSE V	LTC	N-0757107	0466	3
HORVATH WILLIAM S	2LT	0-1692557	0545	2
HORWATH FRANK S	1LT	0-0938045	0961	2
HORWITZ ALBERT	1LT	0-1181639	0946	2
HORWITZ ALEX	1LT	0-1302630	1145	2
HORWITZ DAVID	CW3	W-2145200	1061	1
HORWITZ MARTIN	1LT	0-1323320	0145	2
HOSCH JAMES E	MAJ	0-0565685	0151	1
HOSCH JOHN A	COL	0-0200305	0563	3
HOSE FRED H	CW2	W-2121157	0746	2
HOSE ORION F	LTC	0-0475240	0655	1
HOSEASCK NARRETT P	1LT	0-0172588	0643	2
HOSENFELD FLORENCE A	MAJ	N-0722271	0564	3
HOSEY CHARLIE M	MAJ	0-0495255	0854	1
HOSEY RICHARD L	CPT	0-1295883	0967	2
HOSHALL EDWARD M	COL	0-0255073	0867	3
HOSIER ROBERT O	2LT	0-1172512	0545	2

NAME	GRADE	SVC NO	DATE RET MO YR	RET CODE
HOSKIN ANDREW O	LTC	0-0258582	0166	3
HOSKINS ELEANOR	1LT	N-0742179	0846	1
HOSKINS FRANCIS	LTC	0-1310600	1263	1
HOSKINS JOHN H	MAJ	0-0496154	0554	2
HOSKINS MARSHALL O	LTC	0-1796960	0462	2
HOSKINS ORVILLE E	CW3	W-2145641	0364	1
HOSKINS STUART W	LTC	0-1575368	0467	2
HOSLER HAROLD M	COL	0-0370842	0161	1
HOSTAGE FABIAN	2LT	0-0326765	1062	3
HOSTER GEORGE M	LTC	0-0243389	1160	3
HOTALEN RUDOLPH B	LTC	0-0291364	0166	3
HOTCHKIN HARRY	MAJ	0-0200609	0554	3
HOTCHKISS DALE C	LTC	0-0885806	0359	1
HOTCHKISS HERVEY D	LTC	0-0351288	0267	3
HOTCHKISS JESSIE A	MAJ	L-0125890	1245	1
HOTCHKISS MERLE S	COL	0-0173168	0557	1
HOTCHKISS THOMAS A	LTC	0-0352530	0865	1
HOTELLING LEWIS A	1LT	0-0999546	1056	2
HOTOPP RAYMOND F	LTC	0-0454521	0258	1
HOTOVY GEORGE S	1LT	0-2047367	0746	2
HOTSENPILLER HARRY A	LTC	0-1545639	0763	1
HOTSKO GEORGE	LTC	0-2019037	0267	1
HOTT JAMES J	MAJ	0-0315307	0446	2
HOTT ROBERT J	CPT	0-0530101	1044	1
HOTT WILLIAM A	MAJ	0-0394789	0760	1
HOTTA YOSHIO	MAJ	0-0944659	1062	1
HOTTEN JACK	LTC	0-0484846	0657	1
HOTTENSTEIN CHARLES	MAJ	0-0288952	0756	3
HOTTINGER RAYMOND C	LTC	0-0278229	0265	3
HOTZ EUGENE R	LTC	0-1047159	0865	1
HOUBLER CLAUDE D	MAJ	0-1038011	0161	1
HOUCHIN EDWARD L	LTC	0-0501706	0563	1
HOUCK DAVID C	CPT	0-0522762	0746	1
HOUCK ELGG L	CW3	W-2205613	0965	1
HOUCK FREDERICK	LTC	0-0275930	0965	3
HOUCK RICHARD	CW2	W-2143203	0157	1
HOUFF CHARLES W	LTC	0-0474149	0163	1
HOUGEN JOHN H	COL	0-0260529	1154	2
HOUGH CECIL H	CPT	0-0504586	0949	1
HOUGH FLOYD W	LTC	0-0114626	0658	3
HOUGH GERALD L	LTC	0-1169576	0762	1
HOUGH HUGH P	LTC	0-1040244	0359	1
HOUGH KENNETH J	COL	0-0205551	0657	3
HOUGH ROBERT F	LTC	0-1588057	0563	1
HOUGH SUSANN Z	CPT	L-0502123	0450	1
HOUGHTALING HENRY M	MAJ	0-1799291	0264	1
HOUGHTALING JULES V	COL	0-0155552	0153	3
HOUGHTALING LESTER J	LTC	0-0431595	0566	2
HOUGHTON CHARLES W	CPT	0-0364479	1044	2
HOUGHTON GEORGE A	CPT	0-0999315	0561	1
HOUGHTON HOLDEN R	LTC	0-0235693	0762	3
HOUGHTON HORACE	MAJ	0-1797999	0757	1
HOUGHTON JR ALBERT R	LTC	0-0291930	0264	1
HOUGHTON RALPH H	MAJ	0-0263245	0367	3
HOUGHTON THURSTON T	COL	0-0187639	0556	3
HOUGHTON WENDELL Y	CPT	0-1951486	1162	1
HOUGHTON WILLIAM S	COL	0-0234946	0246	2
HOUGLAND ARNOLD L	LTC	0-1000244	0159	1
HOUGLAND GERALD T	LTC	0-0499031	1164	1
HOUGLUM EDGAR J	1LT	0-2006949	0947	2
HOUK EARL T	LTC	0-0333207	0359	2
HOUK ELIJAH P S	CPT	0-1747016	0548	2
HOUK JAMES N	MAJ	0-1946296	0958	1
HOUK THEODORE W	1LT	0-1702379	1042	2
HOULDIN JOSEPH F	COL	0-0261838	0367	3
HOULEHAN FORREST C	LTC	0-0201947	0253	3
HOULEY JOSEPH P	COL	0-0115273	0546	2
HOURIHAN MARGARET A	LTC	N-0722062	0261	1
HOUSAND CHARLES	MAJ	0-0916681	0447	1
HOUSE CHARLES O	LTC	0-0970095	0865	1
HOUSE DOYLE F	MAJ	0-2007002	0156	1
HOUSE ELMER S	CW4	W-2127036	1154	1
HOUSE FRANK W	COL	0-0104767	0-50	3
HOUSE GORDON H	LTC	0-1183091	1167	1
HOUSE HAROLD	2LT	0-1003550	0945	2

NAME	GRADE	SVC NO	DATE RET MO YR	RET CODE
HOUSE HOWARD H	LTC	0-0255303	1148	3
HOUSE JAMES H	LTC	0-1179106	0761	1
HOUSE JERRY C	LTC	0-0257502	0454	1
HOUSE JR LLOYD	LTC	0-1030254	0258	1
HOUSE KENNETH	COL	0-0330566	0860	1
HOUSE LEON F	CPT	0-0496106	0550	1
HOUSE ORVAL D	MAJ	0-0256245	0658	3
HOUSE RAY W	CPT	0-0536489	1047	2
HOUSE ROBERT J	CW2	W-2214822	0866	1
HOUSE RUFUS W	LTC	0-2042893	0656	1
HOUSE WILLIAM J	CPT	0-0265364	0147	1
HOUSECROFT MAURICE	LTC	0-0230988	0646	2
HOUSEHOLDER EDGAR S	CW3	W-2209101	0167	2
HOUSEHOLDER ERNEST O	COL	0-0113398	0648	3
HOUSEL JR JAMES R	1LT	0-0414801	0546	2
HOUSEMAN DONELSON M	1LT	0-1062541	1046	2
HOUSEMAN EDGAR W	CPT	0-1283609	0461	1
HOUSEMAN EUGENE B	COL	0-0126762	0648	3
HOUSER CARL F	CPT	0-1016011	0557	1
HOUSER CHARLES H	CW4	W-2110981	1055	1
HOUSER DONALD S	LTC	0-0349402	0761	1
HOUSER EDWARD C	LTC	0-0225002	0160	3
HOUSER EDWIN F	LTC	0-0330734	1063	1
HOUSER HARRY W	MAJ	0-1579809	0758	1
HOUSER JOHN A	CW3	W-2145555	0761	1
HOUSER JOHN F	LTC	0-1184670	0364	1
HOUSER JOHN F	CW3	W-2207098	1265	1
HOUSER RAYMOND L	1LT	0-2023884	1045	2
HOUSER RICHARD A	MAJ	0-1036573	0962	1
HOUSER STEWART L	COL	0-0329609	1153	2
HOUSER WILLIAM E	MAJ	0-1799292	0465	1
HOUSER WILLIAM F	CPT	0-1291469	0960	1
HOUSER WILLIAM F	CW4	W-2111887	1155	1
HOUSETON MARVIN	MAJ	0-1686530	1057	1
HOUSH ROSCOE P	MAJ	0-0271833	0650	1
HOUSHOLDER BAYLESS G	COL	0-0307202	1060	1
HOUSHOLDER EARL R	LTC	0-0142434	1053	3
HOUSHOLDER QUENTIN L	1LT	0-0401775	0445	2
HOUSMAN CLIFFORD A	LTC	0-1546433	0966	1
HOUSNER WILLIAM F	2LT	0-0445610	0145	2
HOUSTON ALBERT W	CPT	0-0917504	0346	2
HOUSTON CORNELIUS	1LT	0-0524918	0545	2
HOUSTON GEORGE H	CW3	W-2207054	0366	1
HOUSTON GEORGE H	MAJ	0-1633016	1056	1
HOUSTON GLENN N	MAJ	0-0345358	1156	2
HOUSTON HAROLD A	MAJ	0-0147195	0648	3
HOUSTON HARRY A	LTC	0-1648304	0546	1
HOUSTON JAMES A	MAJ	0-1019098	1262	1
HOUSTON JAMES L	MAJ	0-1914039	1021	1
HOUSTON JOSEPH A	LTC	0-0241571	1146	1
HOUSTON KEITH R R	LTC	0-0279850	1164	3
HOUSTON NEWELL E	CPT	0-0527553	0650	1
HOUSTON ROBERT W	LTC	0-0264741	0467	3
HOUSTON ROSCOE	CPT	0-0521297	0349	1
HOUSTON STEPHEN	LTC	0-1169577	0661	1
HOUY CHARLES F	CPT	0-1289584	0145	2
HOUY CORNELIUS	CPT	0-0525316	0154	2
HOUZE JESSE K	2LT	0-1536995	0647	2
HOUZVICKA OTTO A	MAJ	0-0274384	0960	3
HOVANEC JAMES F	LTC	0-1305872	0462	1
HOVANETZ CHARLES J	MAJ	0-1080205	0761	1
HOVANSKI AUGUSTINE	1LT	0-1873077	0154	2
HOVAS EDWARD F	LTC	0-0208299	0151	3
HOVDEN SR EARL C	CW4	W-0903275	0267	1
HOVE EVERETT G	2LT	0-0888221	0943	2
HOVE OLIVER P	CPT	0-0510739	1046	1
HOVER FRED H	COL	0-0264197	0649	3
HOVER CALEB W	LTC	0-0214117	0857	3
HOVER HARRY S	LTC	0-0229630	0664	3
HOVER THEODORE W	LTC	0-0333405	1154	1
HOVEY ALLEN J	CPT	0-1043365	0965	1
HOVIOUS JAMES W	MAJ	0-1322787	0265	1
HOVIS CARL A	LTC	0-0244568	0659	3
HOVIS EARL F	MAJ	0-1019157	1057	1
HOVIS HERBERT C	1LT	0-0291863	0944	2

NAME	GRADE	SVC NO	DATE RET MO YR	RET CODE
HOVLAND DENNIS A	LTC	0-1330185	1165	1
HOVLAND HAROLD L	1LT	0-1040407	0845	2
HOVLAND MELVIN L	1LT	0-0314412	0743	2
HOVORKA KEITH J	1LT	0-0453209	0644	2
HOVSEPIAN JOSEPH	2LT	0-1081652	0545	2
HOWARD ALVA B	LTC	0-1548442	0561	1
HOWARD AMPLUS O	CPT	0-0406052	1043	2
HOWARD ARNOLD J	LTC	0-0385190	0763	1
HOWARD ARTHUR G	CPT	0-0316923	1144	2
HOWARD BUCKLEY	CPT	0-0254832	0547	1
HOWARD CARROL J	MAJ	0-1018051	0657	1
HOWARD CHARLES A	MAJ	0-2263538	1065	1
HOWARD CHARLES B	LTC	0-0110895	0554	3
HOWARD CHARLES C	MAJ	0-1300489	0457	1
HOWARD CHARLES E	COL	0-0182482	0354	3
HOWARD CHARLES E	CPT	0-0491009	0754	1
HOWARD CHESTER R	LTC	0-0324630	0857	3
HOWARD CLAIR L	LTC	0-0302920	0561	2
HOWARD DAN	MAJ	0-0985361	1164	1
HOWARD DAVID R	CPT	0-0365577	0646	2
HOWARD DAVID L	1LT	0-1577334	0858	2
HOWARD DAVID S	MAJ	0-1650913	0962	1
HOWARD DONALD K	COL	0-0277847	0363	3
HOWARD EDGAR M	MAJ	0-2206278	0766	1
HOWARD EDWARD B	CW3	W-2146245	0166	1
HOWARD EDWARD W	CPT	0-1589650	0263	1
HOWARD ELMER H	MAJ	0-0974703	0644	1
HOWARD EZRA F	LTC	0-0212841	0759	3
HOWARD FRANCIS M	MAJ	0-1683435	1154	1
HOWARD FRANK E	MAJ	0-0486217	1047	1
HOWARD FRANK N	LTC	0-0445142	1062	3
HOWARD FRANKLIN V	LTC	0-0365446	0547	1
HOWARD FRED F	1LT	0-2096512	0557	2
HOWARD FREDERICK	CPT	0-0147413	0846	2
HOWARD GASTON S	COL	0-0178234	0758	3
HOWARD GORDON	LTC	0-1175468	0263	1
HOWARD GROVER C	MAJ	0-1642205	0265	1
HOWARD HARVEY F	CPT	0-0186389	0258	3
HOWARD HORACE G	2LT	0-1308822	0444	2
HOWARD IKE	CW2	W-2148012	0555	1
HOWARD IRA J	CW4	W-2105545	0260	1
HOWARD JAMES C	LTC	0-1551029	0762	1
HOWARD JAMES E	LTC	0-0284719	1265	3
HOWARD JAMES T	CW3	W-2152119	0864	1
HOWARD JEAN W	2LT	N-0744452	0546	1
HOWARD JENNINGS	1LT	0-1314486	0946	1
HOWARD JOHN	LTC	0-0271138	0966	3
HOWARD JOHN A	LTC	0-0467323	0267	1
HOWARD JOHN L	MAJ	0-1642954	1160	1
HOWARD JOHN T	CPT	0-0211684	0144	2
HOWARD JOHN W	LTC	0-0227343	0654	3
HOWARD JOSEPH A	MAJ	0-0285356	0349	2
HOWARD JOSEPH F	CW2	W-2152158	1163	1
HOWARD JOSEPH H	COL	0-0326698	0864	3
HOWARD JOSEPH J	MAJ	0-2049445	0457	1
HOWARD JR ANSE B	2LT	0-0538432	0646	2
HOWARD JR CHESTER A	1LT	0-1059156	0646	2
HOWARD JR ISERAL	CW2	W-2148926	0560	1
HOWARD JR JAMES O	LTC	0-0230451	0265	3
HOWARD KENNETH D	CW3	W-2206132	0866	1
HOWARD LAWRENCE J	LTC	0-1052822	0863	1
HOWARD LUCILLE E	MAJ	N-0761773	0964	1
HOWARD MARY C	1LT	L-0401064	0846	1
HOWARD MARY G	1LT	N-0720469	1144	1
HOWARD MELVIN W	CPT	0-1925929	0963	2
HOWARD RALPH L	CW3	W-2147685	0964	2
HOWARD RALPH M	LTC	0-1035490	0861	1
HOWARD RALPH S	LTC	0-1554753	0164	1
HOWARD RICHARD C	LTC	0-1546420	0165	1
HOWARD RICHARD F	COL	0-0192522	0862	3
HOWARD RICHARD H	CW3	RW-2141126	1161	1
HOWARD RICHMOND F	CPT	0-2028972	0655	1
HOWARD ROBERT	MAJ	0-1334708	0964	1
HOWARD ROBERT B	LTC	0-1338825	0866	1
HOWARD ROBERT B	MAJ	0-1591432	0667	3

NAME	GRADE	SVC NO	DATE RET MO YR	RET CODE
HOWARD ROBERT H	CPT	0-0370311	0146	2
HOWARD ROBERT L	CW4	W-2108637	0555	1
HOWARD ROBERT N	MAJ	0-1048025	0561	1
HOWARD ROBERT W	CW4	W-2143241	0562	1
HOWARD SAMUEL P	1LT	0-0497378	0552	1
HOWARD SANFORD S	CPT	0-0500266	0645	2
HOWARD SHELTON	WO1	W-2145811	0557	1
HOWARD SIMON	LTC	0-0300708	0960	1
HOWARD SR ROBERT L	CW2	W-2205976	0965	1
HOWARD STEPHEN R	CW3	W-2152743	0560	1
HOWARD STERLING B	COL	0-0221575	0157	1
HOWARD SUMNER E	MAJ	0-1581809	0859	2
HOWARD TAYLOR D	LTC	0-0400090	0760	2
HOWARD TELFORD C	MAJ	0-1824024	1263	1
HOWARD THOMAS L	LTC	0-0266780	1060	3
HOWARD VAUGHAN H	CPT	0-0463811	0447	2
HOWARD VIRGIL F	LTC	0-0306293	0462	3
HOWARD WALTER A	MAJ	0-0147048	0648	3
HOWARD WALTER C	MAJ	0-1047583	1163	1
HOWARD WALTER R	MAJ	0-1876251	1065	1
HOWARD WILLIAM	CPT	0-1944709	0858	1
HOWARD WILLIAM R	LTC	0-0252190	0764	3
HOWARTH GEORGE A	COL	0-0254264	0146	2
HOWARTH JACOB M	MAJ	0-0209989	0948	3
HOWARTH JAMES W	LTC	0-0485426	1164	3
HOWARTH ROBERT F	2LT	0-1294477	1143	2
HOWARTH WILLIAM F	LTC	0-0505317	0361	3
HOWATT LESTER C	LTC	0-1647956	0562	1
HOWDEN DAVID C	CW2	W-2212344	0466	1
HOWE ARLAND C	CW3	W-2151517	0663	1
HOWE CHARLES E	LTC	0-0410503	1145	2
HOWE CLARENCE S	COL	0-0221768	0958	2
HOWE CLIFFORD W	CW3	RW-2146752	0165	1
HOWE DONIVAN J	CW3	W-2125915	0756	1
HOWE EDWARD W	COL	0-0311510	0347	2
HOWE EDWIN S	CW3	W-2117885	0460	1
HOWE EUGENE C	LTC	0-0247319	0866	3
HOWE HAROLD W	COL	0-0150698	0648	3
HOWE JACK E	LTC	0-0391052	0261	1
HOWE JOHN H	MAJ	0-0569493	0762	1
HOWE JOSEPH G	COL	0-0273896	1061	3
HOWE NORMAN E	MAJ	0-0981607	1066	1
HOWE PAUL	LTC	0-0108019	1044	2
HOWE PAUL F	COL	0-0133473	0648	3
HOWE RALPH B	COL	0-0116682	0649	3
HOWE RUSSELL B	CPT	0-0297534	1044	2
HOWE WILLIAM M	CW3	W-2144886	0464	1
HOWE WISTAR C	MAJ	0-0217402	0844	2
HOWELL ALBERT	LTC	0-0436583	1067	2
HOWELL ALBERT D	MAJ	0-1081557	0767	1
HOWELL BEN O	CPT	0-0514304	0747	2
HOWELL BENJAMIN R	COL	0-0334097	1060	3
HOWELL CECILE M	2LT	N-0741109	0545	1
HOWELL CHARLES M	CW4	W-2203295	0766	1
HOWELL DALLAS C	2LT	0-1637710	0345	1
HOWELL DILLON J	LTC	0-0358538	0866	3
HOWELL EDGAR M	MAJ	0-0361620	0149	1
HOWELL ELI H	CPT	0-0452714	0645	1
HOWELL ERNEST W	COL	0-0269945	0159	1
HOWELL EUGENE J	COL	0-0169019	0161	3
HOWELL FRANKLIN H	MAJ	0-0235125	0260	3
HOWELL GEORGE E	1LT	0-0541130	0446	2
HOWELL GORMAN B	CPT	0-0237451	0853	3
HOWELL HELEN K	2LT	N-0790915	0545	1
HOWELL HOWARD L	MAJ	0-1645680	0564	1
HOWELL IRA L	MAJ	0-0374971	0446	2
HOWELL J ALLEN	CPT	0-0484904	0745	1
HOWELL JACK K	2LT	0-1692955	0451	1
HOWELL JAMES D	CW2	W-2211090	1266	1
HOWELL JAMES W	CPT	0-1941678	0161	2
HOWELL JEFF C	2LT	0-1913712	0737	1
HOWELL JOHN S	COL	0-0358830	1067	1
HOWELL JOSEPH C	2LT	0-2055057	1045	2
HOWELL JR EDWARD C	2LT	0-1591214	0644	2
HOWELL JR GEORGE H	LTC	0-1307696	0560	1

NAME	GRADE	SVC NO	DATE RET MO YR	RET CODE
HOWELL JR JOHN S	CW2	W-2205394	0263	1
HOWELL JR JOHNIE C	CW3	W-2149778	0563	1
HOWELL LEON	LTC	0-2031868	0855	2
HOWELL LESLIE D	LTC	0-0184616	0468	3
HOWELL LESSLIE S	COL	0-0150696	0357	3
HOWELL NED S	CPT	0-0172103	0953	3
HOWELL RALPH D	COL	0-0159900	0557	3
HOWELL ROBERT	CPT	0-1309884	1046	1
HOWELL ROBERT S	CPT	0-0312261	0546	2
HOWELL ROY R	MAJ	0-4030637	0666	2
HOWELL THOMAS P	CW3	W-2151911	0565	1
HOWELL VERNER L	CPT	0-0454248	0545	2
HOWELL WENDELL R	CW2	W-2202306	0367	3
HOWELL WILLIAM A	LTC	0-1294309	1163	1
HOWELL WILLIAM R	CPT	0-0323447	0345	2
HOWER EDWARD E	WO1	W-2147976	1053	1
HOWERTON MARION J	MAJ	0-0967032	0962	1
HOWERTON WILLIAM A	LTC	0-0249428	0262	3
HOWERY EMALETON R	LTC	0-0155045	0953	3
HOWES ALFRED L	COL	0-0347348	0566	3
HOWES JOHN E	CPT	0-1933976	0364	1
HOWEY CECIL A	CPT	0-1002945	0748	1
HOWEY ROBERT F	MAJ	0-2035326	0760	1
HOWEY STEPHEN H	1LT	0-0171178	0648	3
HOWEY THOMAS L	WO1	W-2114840	1147	2
HOWITZ CLIFTON I	LTC	0-1180962	1163	1
HOWLAND BERNARD F	LTC	0-0512552	0548	1
HOWLAND CHARLES F	COL	0-0909099	0958	2
HOWLAND CHARLES T	CW4	W-2120855	0859	3
HOWLAND FRANCIS C	LTC	0-0396887	1147	1
HOWLAND JOHN A	CPT	0-0285445	0965	3
HOWLAND MERLE B	CPT	0-1061137	1057	1
HOWLAND RALPH G	2LT	0-2001032	1045	2
HOWLAND ROBERT O	LTC	0-1545490	0363	1
HOWLAND STANLEY F	CPT	0-0223062	0461	3
HOWLE WAYNE H	CPT	0-1919290	0962	1
HOWLETT ALICE M	2LT	N-0726947	0445	1
HOWLETT ARTHUR F	LTC	0-0901058	0847	2
HOWLETT EMMETT T	2LT	0-1304528	1044	2
HOWLETT JR ERNEST	1LT	0-1015746	1144	2
HOWLETT WALTER M	LTC	0-0500772	0145	2
HOWLEY FRANK L	R G	0-0299977	0363	3
HOWLEY HELENA M	MAJ	N-0721442	1264	2
HOWLEY WALTER P	CW3	W-2203330	1265	1
HOWLEY WAYNE F	1LT	0-0949024	0254	2
HOWRY HAMILTON H	LTC	0-0204595	1053	3
HOWSE JOHN R	MAJ	0-1932445	1266	1
HOWSON CHARLES E	MAJ	0-0148769	0549	3
HOWSON LEO R	LTC	0-0361763	1050	1
HOWZE GEORGE W	LTC	0-0427924	1264	1
HOWZE JOHN W	LTC	0-0379337	0163	1
HOXIE ALBERT T	MAJ	0-1899417	0863	1
HOXIE HARRIE E	COL	0-0225642	1055	3
HOXIE THEORA G	1LT	N-0755993	0646	1
HOXSIE CLARENCE E	LTC	0-0272025	1066	3
HOXSIE NELSON C	LTC	0-0292407	0862	3
HOXSIE RUTH F	CPT	N-0722850	1047	1
HOY HENRY S	CPT	0-1290948	1048	1
HOY JAMES W	1LT	0-1045118	1045	2
HOYER HERBERT W	CPT	0-0949307	0360	1
HOYER JAMES R	2LT	0-2262541	1053	2
HOYER RAY E	CW3	W-2149115	0263	1
HOYLE IRBY H	LTC	0-0271026	0643	1
HOYLE IVAN T	MAJ	0-0976440	1064	1
HOYT CHARLES E	1LT	0-1584380	0445	2
HOYT CLIFFORD R	CW2	W-3430469	1266	1
HOYT EMMETT G	COL	0-0192458	0555	3
HOYT GENEVIEVE	2LT	N-0727110	0647	1
HOYT GEORGE H	CPT	0-1010555	1152	2
HOYT HAZEN L	COL	0-0188925	0648	3
HOYT HOWARD A	CW2	W-2211771	0866	1
HOYT JACK M	CW3	W-2150635	1265	1
HOYT JR RALPH W	CW2	W-2152238	0763	1
HOYT JR WILLIAM C	CW3	W-2208171	0661	1
HOYT KENNETH D	MAJ	0-1081520	0563	1

NAME	GRADE	SVC NO	DATE RET MO YR	RET CODE
HOYT OSCAR T	CPT	0-1557024	0557	2
HOYT RALPH F	CW2	W-2148604	0459	1
HOYT RICHARD L	CPT	0-0454526	0260	1
HOYT RICHARD M	LTC	0-0214091	0162	3
HOYT SR FRED L	LTC	0-0190142	0648	3
HOYT WARREN J	COL	0-0155402	1155	3
HOYT WILLIAM G	1LT	0-1302631	0646	2
HROY EUGENE E	CW3	W-2148412	0965	1
HRICINAK WILLIAM E	CW4	W-2145014	0859	1
HRITZ JOHN G	COL	0-0260220	0747	2
HRNCIR EDITH M	2LT	N-0734715	0746	1
HROMADKA NICOLAS J	CW4	W-2114338	0656	1
HROMADKA THEODORE V	MAJ	0-1825512	0655	1
HRYSENKO PHILIP M	LTC	0-1302632	0167	1
HUANG RAYMOND L	CPT	0-0546494	0647	2
HUARD EDWARD J	LTC	0-1061432	0163	1
HUBACH CLIFFORD E	MAJ	0-0243735	1161	3
HUBACH RALPH L	MAJ	0-0235381	0763	3
HUBAN GEORGE H	CPT	0-0370366	1051	2
HUBATA ROBERT	MAJ	0-0335218	1166	3
HUBBARD ALFRED W	CPT	0-0503228	1043	2
HUBBARD ARNOLD B	LTC	0-0323574	0364	3
HUBBARD ARTHUR W	CPT	0-0257325	0649	3
HUBBARD DOUGLAS G	LTC	0-0132162	0955	3
HUBBARD FRANK F	LTC	0-0205790	0346	2
HUBBARD FREDERICK	MAJ	0-1288840	0146	2
HUBBARD GEORGE R	1LT	0-0450263	0445	2
HUBBARD GILES B	LTC	0-0912672	0263	1
HUBBARD GLENN S	LTC	0-0326714	1063	3
HUBBARD HAROLD J	COL	0-0146581	1050	3
HUBBARD HENRY V S	MAJ	0-0117590	0649	3
HUBBARD JAMES R	CPT	0-1173297	0546	1
HUBBARD JOHN G	LTC	0-0169422	1158	3
HUBBARD JR JULIUS C	1LT	0-0461528	0146	2
HUBBARD JR KEITH B	LTC	0-0445097	0563	1
HUBBARD JR MACK J	CW2	W-2149217	0358	1
HUBBARD LEWIS E	LTC	0-0327758	0755	3
HUBBARD LOUIS D	LTC	0-0269400	0247	2
HUBBARD MAHLON G	LTC	0-0183411	0646	2
HUBBARD MCKINLEY	CW3	W-2145728	0860	1
HUBBARD PAUL W	COL	0-1547337	1067	1
HUBBARD SHELTON P	COL	0-0136858	0954	3
HUBBARD WILLIAM	COL	0-0228915	1047	2
HUBBARD WILLIAM D	LTC	0-0174562	0750	3
HUBBARD WILLIAM L	CW2	W-2149048	0460	1
HUBBARD WILLIAM M	MAJ	0-1323323	0357	1
HUBBARD WILLIAM R	COL	0-0212428	0954	3
HUBBELL EDWARD L	MAJ	0-0122389	0156	3
HUBBELL PORTER H	LTC	0-0343230	0467	3
HUBBELL RAYMOND M	MAJ	0-1303891	0457	1
HUBBELL WILBERT I	LTC	0-0309288	0958	3
HUBBERT CECIL F	COL	0-1845901	0666	3
HUBBS DONALD H	1LT	0-1283963	1044	2
HUBBS ROY S	COL	0-0273122	0156	3
HUBER ALBERT W	CW2	W-2208597	0267	1
HUBER ALFRED F	2LT	0-1294478	1043	2
HUBER CARL J	MAJ	0-0353383	1166	3
HUBER CHARLES B	LTC	0-0492278	0960	3
HUBER CHARLES R	MAJ	0-0196697	0848	2
HUBER ERNEST A	CPT	0-0298116	1064	3
HUBER FRANCIS D	MAJ	0-0466903	0844	2
HUBER JOSEPH P	1LT	0-1173999	1144	2
HUBER NATHAN	2LT	0-2306199	1061	1
HUBER WILLIAM J	LTC	0-0250907	0162	1
HUBER WILLIAM J	LTC	0-2208149	1158	1
HUBERT JR JAMES H	MAJ	0-0273089	0267	3
HUBERT MARION A	COL	0-0246028	0660	3
HUBERT ROLLAND E	LTC	0-0106322	0850	3
HUBIAK WILLIAM	MAJ	0-1177010	0258	1
HUBIN ELDOR F	CPT	0-0450189	0659	1
HUBKA CHARLES H	CW3	RW-2205940	0167	1
HUBKA MCCORCW W	CPT	0-1322030	0647	2
HUBLER NORMAN W	COL	0-0334136	0565	1
HUBNER KARL	2LT	0-1777574	0845	1
HUBNER ROBERT R	MAJ	0-0200023	0559	3

NAME	GRADE	SVC NO	DATE RET MO YR	RET CODE
HUBSCH ERWIN R	CW3	W-2142326	0361	1
HUC HARRY J	CW3	W-2148525	0264	1
HUCHISON ELDON A	COL	O-0189304	1150	3
HUCKABAY JOHN R	MAJ	O-0476157	0346	2
HUCKABAY JR BEN M	LTC	O-1168731	0960	1
HUCKABAY ZACHARY T	COL	O-1581812	1067	1
HUCKABEE JR JAMES G	1LT	O-1323432	1145	2
HUCKABY EDWARD V	MAJ	O-2000433	0562	2
HUCKABY THOMAS L	LTC	O-0248378	1265	3
HUCKINS JOSEPH	COL	O-0183637	1059	1
HUCKLEBERRY BOWEN C	LTC	O-0338158	0764	3
HUCKS JR HERBERT W	LTC	O-0293754	0647	2
HUDACEK JOSEPH M	MAJ	O-1796090	0262	1
HUDAK CHESTER A	CW3	W-2152023	1164	1
HUDAK CLARK J	1LT	O-0545152	0546	2
HUDAK DONALD M	MAJ	O-1546613	0267	1
HUDAK JR JOHN J	CPT	O-1584383	1144	2
HUDAK JR JOHN J	CW2	W-2148972	1155	1
HUDDART MAURICE	LTC	O-1313697	0161	1
HUDDELSON JR ALFRED	LTC	O-0135323	0653	3
HUDDERS EUGENE R	LTC	O-0927398	0765	1
HUDDLESON JAMES H	COL	O-0136700	0648	3
HUDDLESTON ALLAN E	CPT	O-1544555	1057	1
HUDDLESTON ARTHUR N	COL	O-0221102	0557	2
HUDDLESTON GRADY L	1LT	O-0513504	1145	2
HUDDLESTON JOSEPH R	CPT	O-0512589	0947	2
HUDDLESTON LESLIE F	LTC	O-1579817	1162	1
HUDDLESTON ORA L	LTC	O-0494942	0546	2
HUDDLESTON ROBERT A	LTC	O-0492159	1053	2
HUDDLESTON ROBERT C	CW3	W-2142643	0462	1
HUDDLESTON TERRELL O	LTC	O-1018753	0562	1
HUDDLESTON THOMAS	CPT	O-0919473	0344	2
HUDDY DONALD C	LTC	O-1946995	0563	1
HUDDY JR JAMES	CPT	O-0255720	0962	2
HUDELSON DANIEL H	M G	O-0247417	0562	3
HUDGINS JAMES W	LTC	O-0371018	0560	1
HUDGINS JETHRO T	LTC	O-0310669	1060	2
HUDGINS ROBERT J	LTC	O-0390289	0861	1
HUDGINS RUTH O	1LT	N-0764718	0547	1
HUDOCK JOSEPH A	MAJ	O-2015665	0263	1
HUDOCK STEVEN A	LTC	O-1585652	1162	1
HUDON JAMES R	MAJ	O-0310847	0560	1
HUDON RONALD F	CW3	W-2142965	1060	1
HUDSON ALFRED F A	MAJ	O-0443814	0847	2
HUDSON CARL R	1LT	O-0436604	0946	2
HUDSON CARY A	LTC	O-0141134	1050	3
HUDSON CHARLES F	1LT	O-2007192	0747	1
HUDSON CHARLES R	CPT	O-0446447	1146	2
HUDSON CHARLES W	LTC	O-0452274	1265	1
HUDSON CLYDE J	1LT	O-2016467	0748	1
HUDSON COLLIS P	COL	O-0205664	0559	3
HUDSON DOWELL B	MAJ	O-2018519	0665	1
HUDSON EDWARD B	CPT	O-1321928	0447	2
HUDSON EDWIN	CPT	O-0208347	0653	3
HUDSON ERNEST R	MAJ	O-1179453	0756	1
HUDSON EVERETT B	LTC	O-1165630	0656	1
HUDSON GEORGE E	LTC	O-0249023	0667	3
HUDSON GEORGE H	COL	O-0215379	0659	3
HUDSON GEORGE H	MAJ	O-1688206	1262	1
HUDSON GERALD W	LTC	O-1633951	1163	1
HUDSON HEARL E	LTC	O-1574847	0763	1
HUDSON HENRY E	LTC	O-0397586	0365	3
HUDSON HOWARD V	CPT	O-0953569	0960	1
HUDSON JACK F	MAJ	O-0409969	0555	1
HUDSON JOHN J	1LT	O-1019290	0745	1
HUDSON JOHN M	MAJ	O-0521093	0747	3
HUDSON JOHN N	LTC	O-0346575	1058	1
HUDSON JR CHARLES H	CW3	W-2146725	0860	1
HUDSON JR SUMNER	LTC	O-1574848	1265	1
HUDSON KING C	LTC	O-0106892	0354	3
HUDSON LLOYE D	1LT	O-1309150	0547	1
HUDSON LOIS	2LT	N-0726713	0146	1
HUDSON LYMAN I	WO1	W-2113867	1146	2
HUDSON NORMALL O	LTC	O-2000556	0766	1
HUDSON PAUL C	MAJ	O-1686722	0765	1
HUDSON PAUL L	LTC	O-1101050	0461	1
HUDSON PAUL R	CPT	O-0275476	0157	3
HUDSON RAYMOND B	CPT	O-1048027	1162	1
HUDSON RICHARD C	CW4	W-2142966	0663	1
HUDSON ROBERT C	1LT	O-2035945	0545	2
HUDSON ROBERT T	LTC	O-0450551	0960	1
HUDSON ROBERT T	MAJ	O-1018934	0161	1
HUDSON ROGER W	LTC	O-2035946	0960	1
HUDSON ROSS R	1LT	O-0332356	0264	3
HUDSON RUTH H	2LT	N-0722061	1143	1
HUDSON THEODORE W	LTC	O-1104871	0263	1
HUDSON TRUEMAN A	CPT	O-0345471	0447	2
HUDSON WALESTINE	CW3	W-2144749	0657	1
HUDSON WILBUR G	MAJ	O-2206398	0466	1
HUDSON WILLIAM A	CPT	O-1937185	1065	1
HUDSON WILLIAM F	1LT	O-0504127	0650	1
HUDSON WILLIAM R	WO1	W-2147035	0156	1
HUDSON WILLIAM T	LTC	O-0368365	0662	1
HUDSPETH BENJAMIN T	MAJ	O-0168093	0145	2
HUEBSCHWERLEN A S	MAJ	O-0493769	0146	1
HUEFFLEIN HOWARD B	MAJ	O-0315303	0965	3
HUELSENKAMP ROY C	WO1	W-2116005	0447	1
HUERTA SALVADOR J	MAJ	O-1821154	0346	2
HUESER JOHN L	CW3	W-2207665	0767	1
HUESTON NORMAN R	LTC	O-0270669	0861	1
HUET MARCEL A	LTC	O-1660575	0762	1
HUET MARGARET L	2LT	N-0725692	0245	1
HUETTER JR BERNARD R	LTC	O-1100601	0666	1
HUEY ELLA	MAJ	N-0700356	0246	1
HUEY ELLIS J	COL	O-0326699	0365	3
HUEY HAMILTON G	LTC	O-0293953	0858	3
HUEY JAMES R	MAJ	O-0959241	0664	1
HUEY JR JAMES T	1LT	O-0376772	1042	2
HUEY REX R	LTC	O-0525323	0951	1
HUEY ROBERT L	LTC	O-1293776	0862	1
HUEY VICTOR B	LTC	O-0400216	0457	1
HUEY WILLIAM C	MAJ	O-0406826	0156	1
HUFF ALVIN	CW2	W-3151321	0467	1
HUFF CECIL G	CW3	W-2150559	0459	1
HUFF CHESTER A	MAJ	O-2210167	1264	1
HUFF CLYDE	WO1	W-2123763	0747	1
HUFF DAVID H	MAJ	O-0307353	0545	1
HUFF EDGAR C	LTC	O-1331047	1067	1
HUFF EDWARD C	1LT	O-1000588	0346	2
HUFF EMMETTE C	LTC	O-0258682	1157	2
HUFF ERNEST H	LTC	O-0123934	0648	3
HUFF ERNEST R	COL	O-0241320	0350	1
HUFF GARD P	1LT	O-0535309	0146	2
HUFF GEORGE C	CW2	W-2120860	0253	2
HUFF GILMON A	COL	O-0408081	0957	1
HUFF GORDON R	LTC	O-0438791	0866	1
HUFF HORACE A	LTC	O-1649497	1067	1
HUFF HUGHLEN	CW4	W-2105909	0959	1
HUFF JAMES R	MAJ	O-1010281	1062	1
HUFF JOHN P	LTC	O-1113244	0365	1
HUFF JOHN R	MAJ	O-1312160	0259	1
HUFF JOHN W	CPT	O-1649498	0553	1
HUFF JR FRED L	MAJ	O-1019542	1163	1
HUFF JR LEE	LTC	O-0200491	0859	3
HUFF LEO F	LTC	O-0424444	1162	1
HUFF OWEN W	COL	O-0283557	1057	1
HUFF RALPH R	CW4	W-2115457	0661	1
HUFF REID R	LTC	O-0390555	0760	1
HUFF ROBERT F	MAJ	O-2266234	0665	1
HUFF RODERICK	LTC	O-1010967	0464	1
HUFFAKER HOWELL F	MAJ	O-0474027	1044	1
HUFFCUTT GORDON L	LTC	O-1633292	0965	1
HUFFER ELMER O	LTC	O-1017410	0866	1
HUFFER ROBERT W	CPT	O-0321249	1058	1
HUFFERD RALPH H	COL	O-0230956	0952	3
HUFFINE RODNEY C	MAJ	O-0390761	1161	1
HUFFINE ROY W	LTC	O-1584385	0367	3
HUFFMAN ARTIE C	CW3	W-2149703	1065	1
HUFFMAN CARROLL W	1LT	O-0419660	0542	2
HUFFMAN CLEO	CPT	O-0509578	0146	2
HUFFMAN DEAN D	LTC	O-0927177	1166	3
HUFFMAN FRANK L	MAJ	O-0504241	0456	1
HUFFMAN GEORGE H	LTC	O-0494380	1059	1
HUFFMAN HERBERT M	CW2	W-2145324	0459	1
HUFFMAN ISAIAH K	CPT	O-1919431	0462	1
HUFFMAN JAMES E	COL	O-0135322	0247	2
HUFFMAN JAMES V	CW3	W-2143598	0762	1
HUFFMAN ORVILLE L	CW3	W-2143000	0760	1
HUFFMAN ROBERT D	MAJ	O-0449769	0854	1
HUFFMAN RUSSELL L	MAJ	O-4074280	0867	1
HUFFMAN SAM H	MAJ	O-0237372	0566	3
HUFFORD BERLE K	LTC	O-0354872	0865	1
HUFFORD FLETCHER N	LTC	O-0121355	0154	3
HUFFORD FRANCIS G	COL	O-0164355	0758	3
HUFFSTUTLER THOMAS L	MAJ	O-0278000	1147	1
HUFFT RAYMOND F	LTC	O-0345018	1046	2
HUFSTADER ROBERT P	LTC	O-0243136	0659	3
HUGGETT EDWARD S	WO1	W-2148168	0457	1
HUGGINS CLEVELAND	LTC	O-1056752	0864	1
HUGGINS EDWARD J	LTC	O-1544222	1060	1
HUGGINS ELMER P	1LT	O-1574849	0447	1
HUGGINS JAMES H	MAJ	O-0489825	0152	1
HUGGINS JAMES R	CPT	O-0337817	0445	2
HUGGINS JR THOMAS V	CW4	W-2142518	0667	1
HUGGINS KENNETH L	MAJ	O-0346805	0663	3
HUGGINS MEREDITH W	LTC	O-0367960	0246	2
HUGGINS NEWMAN A	CW2	W-2152463	0663	1
HUGGINS NOAH L	CW4	W-2145887	1157	1
HUGGINS WILLIAM S	CPT	O-0394447	0245	1
HUGHES ALBERT G	1LT	O-1312418	0347	2
HUGHES ALBERT T	CW4	W-2109982	0959	1
HUGHES ARTHUR T	MAJ	O-0956066	0862	1
HUGHES AUGUST T	1LT	O-1949564	0546	2
HUGHES BODE	LTC	O-0214243	0662	1
HUGHES BYRON B	LTC	O-0392447	0361	1
HUGHES BYRON Z	LTC	O-0203706	0352	3
HUGHES CARL H	CPT	O-2015592	0960	1
HUGHES CARROLL V	LTC	O-1001369	0763	1
HUGHES CHARLES F	CPT	O-1534763	104N	2
HUGHES CHRISTOPHE	1LT	O-0553476	1147	2
HUGHES CLIFFORD H	CPT	O-0508033	1045	2
HUGHES DANIEL A	1LT	O-1825958	0146	2
HUGHES DANIEL F	LTC	O-1285055	1061	1
HUGHES DANIEL J	COL	O-0273327	0646	2
HUGHES DAVID W	LTC	O-1055334	0466	1
HUGHES DAVIS G	LTC	O-0385747	1047	2
HUGHES DONALD C	MAJ	O-1420239	0464	2
HUGHES DONALD M	LTC	O-0253153	0165	3
HUGHES EDWARD A	LTC	O-0277545	0756	3
HUGHES EDWARD J	1LT	O-1112770	1145	2
HUGHES EDWIN A	CW2	W-2145159	0859	1
HUGHES ERNEST V	COL	O-0146725	0855	3
HUGHES ETHELYN	MAJ	N-0737493	0264	1
HUGHES GORDON R	MAJ	O-1056753	0465	3
HUGHES GUSS C	CW3	W-2106918	0960	1
HUGHES HAROLD C	MAJ	O-1685558	0666	1
HUGHES HARRY J	LTC	O-0451120	0857	1
HUGHES HARRY W	COL	O-0261543	0766	3
HUGHES HAWTHORNE	CPT	O-0450198	0146	2
HUGHES HERBERT T	LTC	O-0247381	0256	3
HUGHES HOLLIS W	CPT	O-0378175	0466	2
HUGHES HONOR L	1LT	N-0723317	0946	1
HUGHES HORACE D	COL	O-0270638	0546	2
HUGHES HOWARD L	2LT	O-1058555	0345	2
HUGHES HOWELL R	CPT	O-1597520	1148	2
HUGHES HUGH A	MAJ	O-1168732	0662	1
HUGHES HUGH I	LTC	O-1107496	0767	3
HUGHES JAMES S	COL	O-0291135	0457	3
HUGHES JAMES T	MAJ	O-1651824	0461	1
HUGHES JESSE G	1LT	O-0317585	0642	2
HUGHES JOHN G	MAJ	O-0736766	0965	3
HUGHES JOHN G	MAJ	O-0370159	1065	2
HUGHES JOHN J	COL	O-0771022	0848	1
HUGHES JOHN W	LTC	O-0349509	0664	3
HUGHES JOSEPH E	MAJ	O-0919342	0644	2
HUGHES JOSEPH H	COL	O-0257084	0757	3
HUGHES JOSEPH W	CW3	W-2152805	1062	1
HUGHES JR ALLEN G	MAJ	O-2018520	0563	1
HUGHES JR ALVAH F	MAJ	O-2049590	0765	1
HUGHES JR ARTHUR J	2LT	O-1312377	0745	2
HUGHES JR EDWARD P	1LT	O-1321186	0448	2
HUGHES JR FRANK W	1LT	O-1114558	0945	2
HUGHES JR GEORGE B	LTC	O-1541518	0961	2
HUGHES JR JOHN A	COL	O-0275063	0555	3
HUGHES JR JOSEPH O	CW2	W-3430330	0567	1
HUGHES JR WILLIAM J	COL	O-0162756	0256	3
HUGHES KEVIN G	LTC	O-1645684	1163	1
HUGHES LAVERNE F	2LT	O-1175503	0445	2
HUGHES LOTUS P	LTC	O-1578632	0261	1
HUGHES MARCELLUS	LTC	O-0453529	0861	1
HUGHES MARK P	COL	O-1577345	1064	1
HUGHES MARY R	2LT	N-0734061	1142	1
HUGHES MELVERN C	MAJ	O-1013215	0866	1
HUGHES OWAIN J	COL	O-0167288	1055	3
HUGHES PAUL	MAJ	O-0480645	1154	2
HUGHES PAUL W	LTC	O-1173656	0763	1
HUGHES RAYMOND L	CW2	W-2105152	0946	2
HUGHES RICHARD M	1LT	O-1104874	0248	2
HUGHES RICHARD W	1LT	O-1283434	0346	2
HUGHES RICHARD W	1LT	O-1312162	0246	2
HUGHES ROBERT C	LTC	O-0144667	0461	1
HUGHES ROBERT G	MAJ	O-1327355	0562	1
HUGHES ROBERT S	LTC	O-1633992	1155	1
HUGHES ROBERT T	LTC	O-0251491	0766	3
HUGHES ROBERT W	COL	O-0232267	0156	3
HUGHES ROBERT W	1LT	O-1167037	0446	2
HUGHES ROY F	COL	O-0110519	0154	3
HUGHES ROY J	MAJ	O-1951623	0361	1
HUGHES SAM E	MAJ	O-0420242	0747	2
HUGHES SIDNEY	1LT	O-0510921	0553	1
HUGHES SIDNEY W	MAJ	O-0327246	0246	2
HUGHES SR BEN H	CW2	W-2000417	0157	3
HUGHES THOMAS H	2LT	O-1581185	0246	2
HUGHES THOMAS H	MAJ	O-1283777	0154	1
HUGHES THOMAS P	COL	O-0253536	0964	3
HUGHES WALTER B	LTC	O-0220572	0648	3
HUGHES WALTER J	MAJ	O-0216485	1057	3
HUGHES WARREN R	WO1	W-2126080	0245	2
HUGHES WILLIAM J	CW3	W-2152130	1162	2
HUGHES WILLIS B	1LT	O-1285056	0146	2
HUGHES WINIFRED A	MAJ	N-0723604	0163	1
HUGHETT GALEN A	MAJ	O-1285057	0360	2
HUGHEY ALBERT K	MAJ	O-0505497	0248	1
HUGHEY ALVIN H	CPT	O-0305443	0444	2
HUGHEY DANIEL W	CPT	O-1578634	0745	1
HUGHEY EUGENE V	LTC	O-0506241	0456	1
HUGHEY WILLIAM O	CPT	O-0571338	0860	1
HUGHLETT LANDON C	MAJ	O-1285546	1162	2
HUGHLETT RICHARD F	MAJ	O-0666397	0266	1
HUGHLING WALLACE C	LTC	O-0742423	1163	1
HUGHS MARVIN P	MAJ	O-0282592	0245	2
HUGHSON DAVID N	CPT	O-1823302	1264	1
HUGILL WILLIAM W	MAJ	O-0396848	0960	1
HUGINS HOLLIS N	LTC	O-0242642	1063	3
HUGO ALAN K	LTC	O-2034972	1067	1
HUGO HOWARD W	LTC	O-1574850	1060	1
HUGO MERRILL S	LTC	O-0251785	0858	3
HUGUELET ADALBERT F	MAJ	O-0506605	1146	2
HUGULEY THOMAS E	COL	O-0228181	0365	3
HUHN RICHARD C	1LT	O-1106836	1045	2
HUIE NELSON F	MAJ	O-0357972	0745	2
HUIET BEN T	COL	O-0188451	0355	3
HUINKER FLORIAN F	CW3	RW-2149828	1167	1
HUITT EVERT L	MAJ	O-2046393	1054	1
HUITT GEORGE J	LTC	O-1101881	0861	1
HUKING HARRY W	CPT	O-0137927	0656	3
HULBERT DAVID P	CPT	O-0465144	0446	2
HULBERT MILDRED Y	1LT	N-0727715	1045	1
HULBERT NORMAN P	CPT	O-2034794	1152	1
HULETT ALBERT G	COL	O-0180036	0550	3

ARMY OF THE UNITED STATES RETIRED LIST

NAME	GRADE	SVC NO	DATE RET MO YR	RET CODE
HULETT HENRY J	CPT	0-2262415	C161	1
HULIN DONALD F	MAJ	0-2035108	1062	1
HULIT CHARLES F	MAJ	C-1644955	1059	1
HULL ALBERT D	COL	0-0189752	C358	3
HULL CHARLES A	LTC	0-1000590	0657	1
HULL CHARLES L	LTC	0-0266121	C265	3
HULL HARMON H	MAJ	0-0195032	C663	3
HULL HARRY G	LTC	0-0259746	0367	3
HULL HARRY J	2LT	0-1301491	0744	2
HULL JAMES D	CW4	W-2005816	C867	1
HULL JOHN N	LTC	0-1592749	0357	1
HULL JOHN W	CPT	0-0252315	1266	3
HULL JOSEPH H	MAJ	C-1167478	C561	1
HULL JR HOWARD D	1LT	0-0535300	1046	2
HULL MARION L	CPT	0-1933705	C165	1
HULL MAURICE E	CW4	W-2110550	C863	3
HULL MILTON E	LTC	0-0242659	0559	3
HULL ROBERT A	MAJ	C-1591218	0163	1
HULL ROBERT J	2LT	C-1058030	C145	2
HULL T G	2LT	0-2000016	C946	2
HULL TRAVIS A	LTC	0-1039690	C764	1
HULL WALKER F	COL	0-0211923	0648	3
HULL WILLIAM E	MAJ	0-1118910	1163	1
HULL WILLIAM M	MAJ	C-1799297	C359	1
HULL WILLIS D	LTC	0-0276217	C264	3
HULLER VERNON W	COL	C-0909273	C862	1
HULLEY OLIVER S	COL	0-0195268	0862	3
HULLINGER CLARENCE W	COL	0-0272403	0766	3
HULMER ERIC C	MAJ	C-1169170	C350	1
HULSE CHARLES M	MAJ	0-0889573	0762	1
HULSE CHESTER T	MAJ	C-2055365	1055	1
HULSE KENNETH P	MAJ	0-0949784	1262	1
HULSE SR JOHN V	CW3	W-2141593	0163	1
HULSER JULIAN V	LTC	C-0919646	0763	3
HULSEY CHARLES E	LTC	0-1845602	1164	1
HULSEY JR JOHN M	COL	0-0321630	0967	3
HULSEY LLOYD W	CW3	W-2207666	0867	1
HULSLANDER DONALD J	MAJ	C-1476158	C564	1
HULSLANDER ROBERT F	MAJ	0-1288841	0847	2
HULTGREN HAROLD H	CPT	0-0170380	1051	3
HULTZ ROY E	LTC	0-0183355	C753	3
HULTZEN GILBERT N	MAJ	C-1104875	0762	1
HULVERSON FREDERIC	CPT	0-0484621	1047	1
HUMASON DAN W	MAJ	C-0283240	0545	2
HUMBERT LOCKE R	COL	0-0237633	1165	3
HUMBERT REUBEN L	LTC	0-0292368	C960	3
HUMBERTSON CHARLES E	1LT	0-1324264	C147	2
HUMBLE DRURY L	1LT	0-1307244	0947	2
HUMBLE JUNIOR R	1LT	0-0919126	0945	2
HUME FRANCES M	2LT	N-0735008	0545	1
HUME FRANCIS	MAJ	C-0964064	0762	1
HUME JAMES N	LTC	0-0197747	1062	3
HUME JAMES T	2LT	0-2012472	1045	2
HUME JOSEPH F	CW2	W-2104165	0748	1
HUME MANSON E	1LT	0-1642210	1046	2
HUME ROBERT	MAJ	C-0218083	0664	3
HUMENANSKY HELEN C	MAJ	N-0725861	C962	1
HUMENCZUK WILLIAM M	1LT	0-1106218	C745	2
HUMENICK DANIEL F	MAJ	0-1881287	1066	1
HUMISTON FLOYD E	MAJ	0-1926880	C867	1
HUMKE LEWIS H	CW3	W-2203384	0567	1
HUMM EDWARD L	CPT	0-1549298	C961	1
HUMMEL CHESTER R	CW3	W-2147570	1165	1
HUMMEL FREDERICK	COL	0-0117319	C648	3
HUMMEL GLEN O	1LT	0-1010378	C144	2
HUMMEL JOHN D	LTC	0-1638957	1161	1
HUMMEL MARSHALL L	LTC	0-1576855	C657	1
HUMMEL MARVIN J	LTC	0-0165936	0456	3
HUMMEL MATHIAS	LTC	C-0397092	C760	1
HUMMEL OSWALD R	COL	0-0318691	0660	1
HUMMEL VICTOR W	LTC	0-0451122	0656	1
HUMMEL WALTER A	LTC	0-1334150	0864	1
HUMMELL LUMAN A	MAJ	0-0126899	0353	3
HUMMER EARL E	1LT	0-1182864	0346	2
HUMMER JOHN F	MAJ	C-1922705	1266	1

NAME	GRADE	SVC NO	DATE RET MO YR	RET CODE
HUMMER ROBERT B F	1LT	0-2005786	0348	2
HUMMER ROBERT T	COL	0-1030781	1167	1
HUMMERT LLOYD C	LTC	0-1288555	1060	1
HUMMON DALE L	CPT	0-1633294	0760	3
HUMPHREY CHARLES O	MAJ	0-1330926	1163	1
HUMPHREY EDWARD L	MAJ	0-0414463	0546	2
HUMPHREY ELMER W	LTC	0-0323528	1162	3
HUMPHREY EUGENE I	LTC	0-1036204	0662	1
HUMPHREY FRANK L	LTC	0-0452376	0361	1
HUMPHREY FREDERIC G	CPT	0-0442403	0946	2
HUMPHREY GEORGE L	2LT	0-1052006	1144	2
HUMPHREY GLENN	CPT	0-1186978	0257	1
HUMPHREY GORDON K	LTC	0-1319951	0162	1
HUMPHREY HAROLD S	MAJ	0-0192037	0653	3
HUMPHREY HERMAN G	CPT	0-0503229	1046	1
HUMPHREY JAMES F	LTC	C-0239832	0164	3
HUMPHREY JOHN A	CW3	W-2147577	0867	1
HUMPHREY JOHNNIE W	1LT	0-0885774	1148	1
HUMPHREY JOSEPH F	MAJ	0-1545244	0349	1
HUMPHREY JOSEPH R	COL	0-0234079	0356	3
HUMPHREY JR CHAR J	LTC	0-0367274	C767	3
HUMPHREY NEAL C	MAJ	0-0510904	0949	1
HUMPHREY PAUL J	CW3	W-2143922	1164	1
HUMPHREY ROBERT A	LTC	0-0505286	0966	1
HUMPHREY ROBERT L	1LT	0-1042841	1145	2
HUMPHREY STEADMAN F	LTC	0-1175173	0165	1
HUMPHREY THOMAS	CW3	W-2142101	1157	1
HUMPHREYS BURTON W	LTC	0-0288907	0961	1
HUMPHREYS JOHN R	MAJ	0-0416085	1060	1
HUMPHREYS ROBERT F	LTC	0-0266581	0858	1
HUMPHREYS ROBERT L	LTC	0-0235384	0165	3
HUMPHREYS TREVOR R	1LT	0-1285058	0543	1
HUMPHREYS WILLIAM H	LTC	0-1553100	0662	2
HUMPHRIES CECIL L	CPT	0-0410530	0246	2
HUMPHRIES EDWARD G	CW4	W-2143052	1263	1
HUMPHRIES JAMES M	1LT	0-0432691	0847	2
HUMPHRIES JEAN B	CW2	W-2149071	1162	1
HUMPHRIES RUFUS R	CW3	W-2146066	1058	1
HUMPHRIES WILLIAM C	MAJ	C-0442545	0946	2
HUMPHRY ROBERT F	MAJ	0-1036575	0661	1
HUMRIGHOUSE EUGENE B	LTC	0-1180550	0765	2
HUNSTON JOHN L	LTC	0-1553101	1265	1
HUNCILMAN HARRY A	COL	0-0225325	C357	1
HUNDERTMARK HENRY	MAJ	0-2019745	1063	1
HUNDLEY DALLAS B	MAJ	0-0319522	0749	1
HUNDLEY EMMETT G	LTC	0-0260636	1166	3
HUNDLEY PRESTON J	COL	0-0359751	0164	1
HUNDLEY ROY W	CPT	0-1173657	0147	1
HUNDLEY SEYMOUR	CPT	0-0517597	0863	1
HUNEGS HARRY	LTC	0-0375767	0360	1
HUNEKEN FREDERICK	LTC	0-0919635	0464	3
HUNEYCUTT ANDREW J	LTC	0-0265837	0463	3
HUNEYCUTT WILLIAM H	MAJ	0-1165182	1148	2
HUNGATE JR WILLIAM C	COL	0-0466386	0562	2
HUNGER ROLF	CW3	W-2152051	0864	1
HUNGERFORD CHARLES F	CW2	W-2205351	0361	1
HUNGERFORD HARLEY	LTC	0-1695644	0363	1
HUNGERFORD JR VICTOR	MAJ	0-1300567	0460	2
HUNICHEN GEORGE A	CW3	W-2152041	1062	1
HUNKE HOWARD R	1LT	0-1292885	0745	2
HUNKE JR HARRY M	CPT	0-0965939	1061	1
HUNKIN ALFRED J	1LT	0-1048025	0246	2
HUNN CLIFTON E	CW4	W-2144827	0857	1
HUNNELL CHARLES H	LTC	0-0345867	0561	3
HUNNICUTT GEORGE S	MAJ	0-0565592	1262	1
HUNNICUTT J R	MAJ	0-0232973	0754	3
HUNNICUTT JACK C	COL	0-0182344	0862	3
HUNNICUTT LAURENCE F	MAJ	0-0508982	0947	1
HUNSAKER GRAHAM	1LT	0-0483408	0348	1
HUNSAKER HARRIE E	MAJ	0-0332510	0246	2
HUNSAKER JR WALTER S	LTC	0-1557945	1166	3
HUNSAKER LYNN M	MAJ	0-1299891	0261	1
HUNSICKER JOHN F	2LT	0-1062732	0145	2
HUNSINGER CARL J	LTC	0-0346556	1060	1
HUNSINGER PAUL O	CPT	0-0469912	1053	2

NAME	GRADE	SVC NO	DATE RET MO YR	RET CODE
HUNSTON THOMAS J	MAJ	C-0488986	0546	2
HUNSUCKER MARTIN R	MAJ	0-1648271	0365	1
HUNT ADAM L	CPT	0-0209344	C652	3
HUNT ARTIS	CPT	C-1289429	C261	1
HUNT DOUGLAS N	MAJ	C-2013838	0661	1
HUNT EDGAR C	WO1	W-2147933	C255	1
HUNT EDWIN T	MAJ	0-1190218	1162	2
HUNT EUGENE A	CPT	0-1109785	C467	1
HUNT FRANK M	CPT	0-1641422	0763	1
HUNT FREDERICK	LTC	0-0193211	0561	3
HUNT FREDERICK	1LT	0-1556448	0446	2
HUNT GEORGE C	LTC	0-0466119	C657	1
HUNT GEORGE W	COL	0-0287236	1061	3
HUNT HAROLD I	LTC	0-0285409	0356	3
HUNT HARRY A	MAJ	0-0478818	0955	1
HUNT HENRY	LTC	0-0241077	1265	3
HUNT HERBERT F	MAJ	C-1180551	0561	1
HUNT HERBERT P	MAJ	C-2008389	C263	1
HUNT HERBERT T	LTC	0-0114051	1144	2
HUNT HORACE S	CW4	W-2002864	0666	3
HUNT JACK R	LTC	0-1590554	1262	1
HUNT JAMES A	MAJ	0-1684955	C165	2
HUNT JOE W	MAJ	C-0966811	0365	1
HUNT JOHN H	LTC	0-0288621	0860	1
HUNT JOHN P	MAJ	C-0510460	0954	1
HUNT JOSEPH B	CW4	W-2115886	0659	1
HUNT JOSEPH F	LTC	0-0281521	1055	2
HUNT JR GRANT J	1LT	0-0514599	1145	2
HUNT JR RALPH S	LTC	0-0245502	0947	2
HUNT KATHLEEN H	1LT	N-C733709	0346	1
HUNT KENNETH A	LTC	0-0324415	C259	1
HUNT LESLIE R	LTC	0-1285763	C262	1
HUNT LINCOLN B	LTC	0-1557025	C167	1
HUNT MCCOWN E	LTC	0-0306091	1046	2
HUNT MELVIN B	MAJ	0-0312988	1145	2
HUNT MERWIN G	LTC	0-0450960	C257	1
HUNT NICHOLAS P	2LT	0-0109425	C447	1
HUNT PAUL D	MAJ	0-0298328	C367	3
HUNT PAUL R	LTC	0-0287938	C253	1
HUNT RALPH W	LTC	0-0422585	1163	1
HUNT ROBERT M	CPT	0-2096574	1161	1
HUNT RUTH B	1LT	L-0200257	1145	2
HUNT SINGLETON	CW2	W-2101870	C753	1
HUNT STANLEY B	COL	0-0324525	C865	3
HUNT THOMAS L	WO1	W-2106964	1157	1
HUNT WALTER E	LTC	0-0382141	0960	1
HUNT WARREN T	LTC	0-0888460	0765	1
HUNT WENDELL K	1LT	0-1301999	0145	2
HUNT WILLARD C	MAJ	C-1300491	C761	1
HUNT WILLIAM A	CW3	W-2151929	0864	1
HUNT WILLIAM H	MAJ	0-0143742	C658	3
HUNT WILLIAM H	LTC	0-0350477	0259	1
HUNT WILLIAM T	MAJ	0-1316232	1058	1
HUNT WILLIAM W	MAJ	C-1536482	0562	1
HUNT WILLIAM W	LTC	C-1576163	C319	1
HUNTER ALLEN M	LTC	0-1297895	C167	1
HUNTER ARNOLD A	1LT	0-2025140	C352	1
HUNTER BARTON H	LTC	0-1289430	C466	3
HUNTER BERNARD A	1LT	0-1553280	0445	2
HUNTER CETH T	CW3	W-2147761	0763	1
HUNTER CHARLES F	CW3	W-2144454	C459	1
HUNTER CHARLES S	LTC	0-0405172	C561	1
HUNTER CLYDE E	CW2	W-3430005	C866	1
HUNTER DAMIE R	LTC	0-0915052	1064	3
HUNTER DARALD E	CPT	0-1581619	0353	1
HUNTER EARL H	MAJ	0-1583148	1164	3
HUNTER EDGAR L	LTC	0-0215154	0462	3
HUNTER EDWARD H	MAJ	0-0407672	1060	1
HUNTER EDWARD J	CPT	0-0397143	1157	2
HUNTER ELMO J	1LT	0-1050318	0245	2
HUNTER ELVIE	2LT	N-0733539	0144	1
HUNTER EVERETT D	CW3	W-2142852	C961	1
HUNTER F DONIVAN	MAJ	C-1581820	1046	2
HUNTER FRANK A	COL	0-0143666	1148	3
HUNTER GEORGE C	LTC	0-1112774	C763	1

NAME	GRADE	SVC NO	DATE RET MO YR	RET CODE
HUNTER GEORGE W	MAJ	C-0366052	0447	2
HUNTER GEORGE W	MAJ	0-1318832	0963	1
HUNTER HAROLD H	LTC	0-1645685	0365	1
HUNTER HARRY M	CPT	0-0918568	0544	2
HUNTER HELEN B	MAJ	N-0786402	0665	1
HUNTER HENRY F	MAJ	0-0451258	1057	1
HUNTER HOWARD J	LTC	0-0194742	1062	3
HUNTER HOWARD V	LTC	0-0111978	0953	3
HUNTER IRENE M	2LT	N-0724952	0545	1
HUNTER JAMES E	LTC	0-1289261	0762	1
HUNTER JAMES W	MAJ	0-0301643	0263	3
HUNTER JOHN	CPT	0-1824321	1163	1
HUNTER JOHN C	MAJ	0-1177012	1161	1
HUNTER JOHN E	LTC	0-1578637	0360	1
HUNTER JOHN G	MAJ	0-1688343	0963	1
HUNTER JOHN H	CPT	0-0262573	1265	3
HUNTER JOHN M	CPT	0-0399959	1044	1
HUNTER JOHN W	CW3	W-2144791	1061	2
HUNTER JOSEPH L	COL	0-0296064	0758	1
HUNTER JR JOHN W	CPT	0-0364085	0246	2
HUNTER JR LILLARD C	MAJ	0-2008198	0663	1
HUNTER JR ROY V	LTC	0-2069781	0866	1
HUNTER KELVIN H	COL	0-0236203	0660	1
HUNTER KENNETH E	LTC	0-1633996	1163	1
HUNTER LEO F	MAJ	0-1591814	0862	1
HUNTER LESLIE C	LTC	0-0467517	0557	1
HUNTER NATHAN H	LTC	0-0118236	0955	3
HUNTER POLLY L	MAJ	N-0727520	1263	3
HUNTER RALPH L	LTC	0-0359088	0862	3
HUNTER RICHARD U	LTC	0-1576167	1162	1
HUNTER SYDNEY B	CW2	W-2209411	0663	1
HUNTER SYLVESTER	MAJ	C-1302468	0761	1
HUNTER THOMAS D	1LT	0-1325008	C146	2
HUNTER WALLACE L	MAJ	0-1688609	1262	1
HUNTER WALTER C	CPT	0-0456464	0446	2
HUNTER WILLARD N	MAJ	0-1342379	1060	1
HUNTER WILLIAM D	LTC	0-2042677	0655	1
HUNTER WILLIAM H	MAJ	0-1824026	1062	1
HUNTER WILLIAM R	LTC	0-1312934	C966	1
HUNTER WILMA A	1LT	N-0804147	0651	1
HUNTER WINFIELD K	LTC	0-0310724	0666	3
HUNTINGTON BEN	COL	0-0130828	1151	3
HUNTINGTON PARK W	COL	0-0180021	0755	3
HUNTINGTON RICHARD S	MAJ	0-0969868	0963	1
HUNTINGTON ROBERT A	LTC	0-0263253	1266	3
HUNTINGTON ROBERT W	MAJ	0-1114976	0757	1
HUNTINGTON ROY T	LTC	0-0373573	0963	1
HUNTLEY DUANE L	LTC	0-1316903	1066	1
HUNTLEY FRANK R	LTC	0-1577353	0760	1
HUNTLEY FRANK P	2LT	0-2034675	0744	2
HUNTLEY HARVEY J	1LT	0-1288747	C145	2
HUNTLEY OREN O	CW2	W-2143265	0563	1
HUNTLEY ROBERT M	CPT	0-0982263	0261	1
HUNTON 4TH EPPA	MAJ	0-0448389	0146	2
HUNTOON DAVID H	COL	0-0345772	1060	1
HUNTOON DONALD F	MAJ	0-0163592	0450	3
HUNTOON JOHN E	CW3	W-2103034	0957	1
HUNTSMAN GEORGE R	COL	0-0348057	0361	3
HUNTTER RAY E	CW2	W-2146836	0658	1
HUNZIKER LUTHER A	MAJ	0-1633998	0555	1
HUNZIKER ROBERT J	LTC	0-0371611	0258	1
HUPFER CLARENCE G	COL	0-0274322	0855	1
HUPFER JOHN H	CW2	W-2203476	1062	1
HUPP WILLIAM O	CPT	0-1704229	0758	1
HUPPE ARTHUR G	LTC	0-0222272	0454	3
HUPPERICH CHARLES M	1LT	0-1551874	1058	3
HURD ARCHIE G	CW4	W-2111695	0260	1
HURD ELINOR K	CW3	V-0712068	1164	2
HURD JARVIS C	1LT	0-0349943	0942	1
HURD JR ARNOLD H	MAJ	0-0535895	0763	1
HURD JR HERBERT N	CW2	W-2150541	1061	1
HURD WILLIAM	2LT	0-1042059	0345	2
HUREAU JR WILFRED J	CW3	W-2207291	0765	1
HUREWITZ MORTON M	CPT	0-0471806	0546	2
HUREWITZ SAMUEL	LTC	0-0488352	0466	1

NAME	GRADE	SVC NO	DATE RET MO YR	RET CODE
HURIANEK JEROME W	CPT	0-1845446	0566	1
HURLBERT CHARLES E	CPT	0-4006455	0464	1
HURLBERT DWIGHT E	LTC	0-0973230	0367	1
HURLBERT MARION R	CW4	W-2119543	0753	1
HURLBERT WILLIAM E	LTC	0-0219604	0456	3
HURLBUT HAROLD L	LTC	0-1286491	0555	1
HURLBUTT RALPH C	CPT	0-1646766	0846	2
HURLEN JR SEVERIN	CW4	W-2144156	1067	1
HURLEY ALICE K	LTC	N-0742358	0865	1
HURLEY EDWARD J	LTC	0-1634913	1262	1
HURLEY EDWIN P	COL	0-0901378	1263	3
HURLEY FLEMING K	MAJ	0-1584389	1162	1
HURLEY GLADYS E	1LT	N-0755161	0747	1
HURLEY HOWARD W	CW3	W-2141089	0364	1
HURLEY JOHN C	LTC	0-0299330	0257	1
HURLEY JOHN G	MAJ	0-2043263	1162	1
HURLEY JOHN S	1LT	0-1298710	0945	2
HURLEY JOHN S	CPT	0-2041434	0962	1
HURLEY JOSEPH W	2LT	0-1648311	0545	1
HURLEY JR JAMES E	LTC	0-1048832	0261	1
HURLEY MARSHALL R	MAJ	0-2014784	1262	1
HURLEY PAUL F	MAJ	0-0322309	0685	3
HURLEY PIERCE P	LTC	0-0336627	0163	3
HURLEY RANDALL V	LTC	0-0334447	0361	1
HURLEY ROBERT J	2LT	0-0946649	1051	1
HURLEY THOMAS F	CPT	0-1012679	0647	2
HURLEY THOMAS J	MAJ	0-2018005	0563	1
HURLEY WILLIAM L	CW3	W-2153369	1265	1
HURLEY WILLIAM T	LTC	0-2006084	0263	1
HURON BENJAMIN S	MAJ	0-0978571	0167	3
HURON HERBERT S	COL	0-0309683	0249	3
HURR HERMAN L	MAJ	0-2096795	1065	1
HURSEY FRANK H	CPT	0-0973477	0862	1
HURSEY WILBURN W	MAJ	0-1116603	1062	1
HURSH GUY C	MAJ	0-0510751	1047	1
HURST CHARLES E	MAJ	0-0498011	0346	2
HURST CHILTON N	CW2	W-3150872	0666	1
HURST COY F	LTC	0-1102310	1162	1
HURST ELMER F	LTC	0-1003947	0962	1
HURST FRANCIS M	CPT	0-0390560	0246	2
HURST HENRY L	MAJ	0-1283073	0555	1
HURST HOWARD R	LTC	0-1287883	0657	1
HURST ROBERT P	LTC	0-1059817	0466	1
HURST SAMUEL N	MAJ	0-2036605	0556	1
HURST SIDNEY J	CPT	0-0386176	0146	2
HURST THOMAS T	MAJ	0-0298484	0646	1
HURST WARREN L	MAJ	0-2014462	1167	1
HURST WILLIAM F	LTC	0-0185771	0655	3
HURST WILLIAM P	1LT	0-2055193	0845	1
HURT ANDREW	CPT	0-2262286	1160	1
HURT CECIL A	COL	0-0322051	0267	3
HURT CHARLES S	CPT	0-1319748	1047	1
HURT FREDERICK	LTC	0-1640581	0666	1
HURT HOLCOMBE H	COL	0-0326697	0461	3
HURT IRA H	COL	0-0204539	1150	3
HURT JAMES E	CW2	W-2141594	0955	1
HURT PETE E	CPT	0-0976882	1161	1
HURT ROBERT Z	LTC	0-0201931	0545	2
HURT SR JOSEPH G	CW2	W-2145920	0355	1
HURTEAU EVERETT F	MAJ	0-0356250	0446	2
HURTES MILTON	2LT	0-1306274	1044	2
HURTT CHARLES A	CW2	W-0906805	0157	1
HURTT JESSE H	CW3	W-2143421	0265	1
HURTT JOSEPH B	MAJ	0-2262458	0565	1
HURTT JOSEPH T	MAJ	0-0259550	0167	3
HURWITH ALBERT E	CPT	0-0478885	0445	2
HURWITT FRANK	LTC	0-0131090	0648	3
HURWITZ MORRIS H	LTC	0-0288428	0867	3
HUSBAND JR FRANK J	MAJ	0-0374249	0447	2
HUSBANDS SAMUEL	CPT	0-0973586	0562	1
HUSCH CHARLES J	CPT	0-1062210	0960	1
HUSCH LEWIS L	CW3	W-2111485	0456	1
HUSCHER EDWARD A	2LT	0-0558785	1145	2
HUSEBYE WILLIAM V	2LT	0-1291643	0144	2
HUSEMAN GEORGE F	CW3	W-2142592	0356	1
HUSEMANC ALTON	MAJ	0-0967757	0960	1
HUSING RUDOLPH C	1LT	0-0522418	0845	2
HUSKEA VICTOR G	CPT	0-0006099	0938	1
HUSKEY EUGENE C	1LT	0-0353483	0244	2
HUSKEY HOYLE M	MAJ	0-1588654	0157	1
HUSOS ALEXANDER	LTC	0-0448906	1060	1
HUSS LAWRENCE B	2LT	0-0299960	0843	2
HUSS WILLIAM J	CW2	W-2113620	0866	1
HUSSEY ALLIS F	MAJ	L-0706100	0763	1
HUSSEY ALPHONSE T	LTC	0-0110493	0848	3
HUSSEY BERNARD J	LTC	0-0450279	0651	1
HUSSEY JOE W	MAJ	0-0470132	0862	1
HUSSEY JOHN J	CPT	0-1322554	1047	1
HUSSEY JR JOHN C	2LT	0-2265996	0553	2
HUSSEY PIERCE L	LTC	0-0384432	0247	1
HUSSMAN CARL A	CPT	0-0159472	0355	3
HUSSMAN ROBERT R	2LT	0-1054275	0145	2
HUSSONG CYRUS C	MAJ	0-1884150	1166	1
HUSTACE JR CHARLES H	MAJ	0-1899375	0661	1
HUSTED ARTHUR L	1LT	0-0302022	1160	3
HUSTED DARWIN E	CW3	W-2144544	0262	1
HUSTED JR ARTHUR L	CPT	0-1589282	0163	1
HUSTED ROBERT C	CPT	0-1299412	0947	2
HUSTON CLYDE R	CPT	0-1595279	0446	2
HUSTON DWIGHT H	2LT	0-2006268	1145	1
HUSTON HARRY C	MAJ	0-1050731	0457	1
HUSTON JOHN L	LTC	0-0311401	0467	3
HUSTON PHILIP S	LTC	0-0372177	0556	1
HUSTRULID CLARENCE A	CPT	0-0525011	0546	2
HUSZCZA ANTHONY	CPT	0-1116086	0657	1
HUTCHENSON ESTELLA	MAJ	0-0491516	0851	1
HUTCHEON FRANK G	2LT	0-1645687	1144	2
HUTCHERSON ABNER C	COL	0-0351785	0155	1
HUTCHERSON GEORGE B	CPT	0-1120761	0457	1
HUTCHERSON KENNETH R	LTC	0-1319841	0962	1
HUTCHERSON PAUL M	LTC	0-0232706	0162	3
HUTCHERSON SAMUEL J	MAJ	0-0315241	0846	2
HUTCHESON CHARLES B	LTC	0-1555704	0263	1
HUTCHESON CHARLES E	MAJ	0-1002256	1158	1
HUTCHESON GUILFORD J	LTC	0-0296625	0766	3
HUTCHESON JACK R	LTC	0-0315618	0745	2
HUTCHESON PHILIP T	LTC	0-0946122	0667	1
HUTCHESON ROBERT W	CPT	0-1894760	0958	1
HUTCHESON WILLIAM M	CPT	0-0959320	0261	1
HUTCHINGS ARTHUR	CW2	W-2105004	0160	1
HUTCHINGS FRANK F	MAJ	0-0124967	0648	3
HUTCHINGS GEORGE F	LTC	0-1118224	0266	1
HUTCHINGS HAROLD E	COL	0-0259395	0567	3
HUTCHINGS JR CHARLES	COL	0-0439146	0-53	1
HUTCHINGS WILLIAM P	LTC	0-0487984	0855	1
HUTCHINS ANDREW F	LTC	0-1013030	0462	1
HUTCHINS BENTLEY S	LTC	0-0202197	0959	3
HUTCHINS CECIL C	LTC	0-0277028	0167	3
HUTCHINS CHARLES F	COL	0-0113299	0648	3
HUTCHINS ERNEST L	MAJ	0-0992429	1163	1
HUTCHINS JAMES P	CW2	W-2150577	1055	2
HUTCHINS JOE L	MAJ	0-1922544	0866	1
HUTCHINS JOHN P	1LT	0-0524382	1146	2
HUTCHINS JR DAVID W	CW2	W-3430023	0963	1
HUTCHINS JR JAMES G	1LT	0-1116852	0646	2
HUTCHINS LEONARD B	MAJ	0-1030382	0257	1
HUTCHINS LEROY W	LTC	0-1046498	0565	3
HUTCHINS PAUL A	CPT	0-1590556	0960	3
HUTCHINS ROBERT E	LTC	0-1019175	0457	1
HUTCHINS RUSSELL J	1LT	0-0386882	1048	2
HUTCHINS THOMAS M	2LT	0-1914114	0347	1
HUTCHINSON BRYAN W	CW3	W-2153383	0663	1
HUTCHINSON DORIS H	1LT	N-0756320	1145	2
HUTCHINSON GEORGE A	COL	0-0101910	1055	3
HUTCHINSON HENRY P	1LT	0-1166511	0545	2
HUTCHINSON JAMES H	LTC	0-0246148	1149	3
HUTCHINSON JOHN A	CPT	0-0278373	1263	3
HUTCHINSON LEWIS J	MAJ	0-0444775	1266	1
HUTCHINSON MANLY F	LTC	0-0236622	0355	3
HUTCHINSON MANNING E	LTC	0-1042847	0860	2
HUTCHINSON MILFORD B	LTC	0-1186107	1266	1
HUTCHINSON OLIVER H	LTC	0-0422392	1066	3
HUTCHINSON P C	COL	0-0192716	1060	3
HUTCHINSON PAUL V	CPT	0-0510065	0346	2
HUTCHINSON ROBERT	MAJ	0-2035330	0562	1
HUTCHINSON SAM C	LTC	0-0257973	0762	1
HUTCHINSON T G	LTC	0-1101883	1160	1
HUTCHINSON THOMAS H	LTC	0-1585658	0758	1
HUTCHINSON WILLIAM E	CW3	W-2205103	0864	1
HUTCHINSON WILLIAM H	COL	0-0254229	0659	3
HUTCHINSON WILLIAM L	MAJ	0-2042835	0559	1
HUTCHINSON WILLIAM T	CW3	W-2149072	0664	1
HUTCHINSON 3RD E S	1LT	0-0425672	0144	2
HUTCHISON ALEXANDER	CW3	W-2150771	0166	1
HUTCHISON AMOS M	CPT	0-0185020	0233	1
HUTCHISON BILLY J	MAJ	0-2012499	0366	1
HUTCHISON EMMA B	1LT	N-0722473	1044	1
HUTCHISON GUY T	MAJ	0-1822574	0662	1
HUTCHISON HERBERT A	CW3	W-2146924	0667	1
HUTCHISON JOSEPH C	M G	0-0209436	0954	3
HUTCHISON JR MACK J	LTC	0-1043115	0960	1
HUTCHISON JR R R	1LT	0-1011258	0745	1
HUTCHISON MELVIN L	MAJ	0-1177013	0159	2
HUTCHISON ROBERT L	MAJ	0-0307989	1144	2
HUTCHISON ROBERT S	CPT	0-0413712	1146	2
HUTCHISON ROBERT W	CPT	0-0286296	1061	3
HUTCHISON SHELTON M	MAJ	0-0316448	1062	3
HUTCHISON THOMAS O	CPT	0-0949426	0161	1
HUTEHKLES ALLEN G	LTC	0-0225754	0862	3
HUTESON JOHN R	1LT	0-1649168	0949	2
HUTH ELMORE P	1LT	0-0528172	1044	2
HUTH GILBERT H	1LT	0-1291123	0546	2
HUTH JOHN J	CW3	W-2146756	1160	1
HUTH MARGARET M	2LT	N-0725707	0745	1
HUTMAKER MATTHEW A	LTC	0-0297672	0547	2
HUTNER SYDNEY	MAJ	0-0492328	0545	2
HUTSCHLER HELEN O	2LT	N-0723979	1043	1
HUTSON ARTHUR E	COL	0-0247867	0167	3
HUTSON CLARENCE	LTC	0-1280431	0962	1
HUTSON CLYDE	1LT	0-0987643	1147	2
HUTSON JAMES W	LTC	0-1101508	0647	2
HUTSON ROY O	CPT	0-0252977	0356	3
HUTSON STANTON C	COL	0-2273266	1064	1
HUTT IRVIN C	CPT	0-1041580	0546	2
HUTT WILLIAM W	LTC	0-1014355	0667	1
HUTTAR JR RICHARD V	MAJ	0-1341883	0766	1
HUTTENHAUER EDWARD A	CW4	W-2002978	0866	3
HUTTER JAMES H	MAJ	0-1041799	1162	1
HUTTER ROBERT J	MAJ	0-1080291	1263	1
HUTTER STANLEY E	MAJ	0-0299343	1057	1
HUTTINGER WILLIAM O	1LT	0-0460566	0352	1
HUTTLIN FRANK L	1LT	0-0926834	0647	2
HUTTLINGER WILLIAM O	1LT	0-0943337	0653	1
HUTTO ALEXANDER	CW2	W-2123096	0452	2
HUTTO ARTHUR P	CW4	W-2142162	0860	1
HUTTO JR JAMES B	CW2	W-2146153	0158	1
HUTTO LIGE	1LT	0-1998404	0847	1
HUTTO TROY N	LTC	0-0252017	1255	3
HUTTON BRUCE M	LTC	0-1059818	0367	1
HUTTON DONALD J	COL	0-0276370	1064	3
HUTTON ELGIN T	CPT	0-1298402	0747	2
HUTTON FRANK V	MAJ	0-2006928	1060	1
HUTTON LORA E	1LT	N-0779071	0746	1
HUTTON LOUIS F	LTC	0-0195453	0653	3
HUTTON MAX P	MAJ	0-1019106	0163	1
HUTTON PHILIP W	LTC	0-0239370	1060	1
HUTTON ROBERT L	MAJ	0-0497660	0652	1
HUTTON ROBERT S	LTC	0-1170783	0966	2
HUTTON ROBERT W	MAJ	0-0355768	0446	2
HUTTY HENRY F	1LT	0-0138134	0751	3
HUXFORD WILLIAM F	MAJ	0-0436471	0146	1
HUXLEY WALTER F	MAJ	0-2033150	0563	1
HUXTABLE JAMES T	MAJ	0-0964242	0961	1
HUYLER FRANK K	1LT	0-0450630	0345	2
HYATT ALLEN T	LTC	0-0325271	1064	3
HYATT ARTHUR G	LTC	0-1541726	0161	1
HYATT FARRELL P	COL	0-0326655	1059	1
HYATT FRANKLIN G	1LT	0-1031548	0146	2
HYATT HAROLD B B	MAJ	0-1998411	0661	1
HYATT HOWARD C	MAJ	0-0979556	0864	1
HYATT PAUL L	MAJ	0-1913290	0766	1
HYATT VERLUS E	1LT	0-1295549	1044	2
HYDAKER VERNON F	COL	0-0221745	0459	3
HYDE ALBERT J	LTC	0-1551647	1162	2
HYDE ALLEN R	1LT	0-1102780	0443	2
HYDE ALVAN L	LTC	0-0194743	1162	3
HYDE BYRON G	LTC	0-0449553	0263	3
HYDE CLIFFORD C	1LT	0-1031326	1145	2
HYDE DAVID A	1LT	0-1645688	0148	1
HYDE DAVID T	1LT	0-1173301	1045	2
HYDE GARY	CPT	0-1178194	1056	1
HYDE GILBERT F	LTC	0-0336564	0163	3
HYDE HAROLD C	LTC	0-0241965	0452	3
HYDE HERBERT E	CW3	W-2146408	0463	1
HYDE JOHN B	MAJ	0-0230989	0856	3
HYDE MARTINA	MAJ	N-0767263	0765	3
HYDE ROBERT C	LTC	0-1167911	0760	1
HYDE ROBERT N	MAJ	0-1106222	1058	2
HYDE SYDNEY F	COL	0-0499610	1063	3
HYDE THEODORE L	MAJ	0-0241297	0744	2
HYDE THOMAS E	CW2	W-2210407	0865	1
HYDE VIRGIL E	CPT	0-0392001	0 45	2
HYDE WALTER H	LTC	0-0100531	1053	3
HYDE WILLARD N	CW4	W-2122508	0261	1
HYDE WILLIAM H	MAJ	0-0199396	0245	2
HYDEN CLYDE E	CPT	0-2016037	0358	1
HYDER BRYAN H	1LT	0-0255554	0967	3
HYDER WARREN L	CPT	0-0889746	0359	1
HYDRICK JOHN E	CPT	0-0249156	0465	3
HYDRICK ONAN A	COL	0-0102159	1048	3
HYDUK JAMES R	CPT	0-0907655	1147	2
HYDUSIK HARRY J	1LT	0-1636076	0945	2
HYER JOHN J	CW2	W-2145160	1055	1
HYER JULIEN C	COL	0-0199392	0454	3
HYER LAWRENCE F	1LT	0-4049704	1159	2
HYGYSCIAN PARASKA M	2LT	N-0704062	0244	1
HYKKONEN HERBERT W	1LT	0-1297727	1045	2
HYLAND CHARLES J	CPT	0-0425936	0445	2
HYLAND FREDERICK	COL	0-0921420	0567	3
HYLAND FREDERICK	LTC	0-1949998	0866	1
HYLAND GEORGE N	LTC	0-0144693	1054	3
HYLAND JOHN F	LTC	0-0302673	0948	1
HYLAND MARTIN J	LTC	0-0461549	1265	3
HYLER DONALD W	LTC	0-0971025	1164	1
HYLL FREDERICK	LTC	0-0451558	0452	1
HYLTON DOUGLAS M	LTC	0-1309370	0367	1
HYMAN BERNARD	MAJ	0-0278331	1146	2
HYMAN HARRY F	LTC	0-0208135	0944	2
HYMAN JOSEPH A	1LT	0-1583150	0245	2
HYMAN MORRIS	MAJ	0-0335504	0246	2
HYMAN MORRIS	1LT	0-1296361	0446	2
HYMES SYLVAN	CW3	W-2145107	0464	1
HYND ROBERT R	MAJ	0-0258391	0266	3
HYNDMAN JR THOMAS L	1LT	0-1877764	0755	2
HYNDS ANNE E	LTC	N-0701401	0746	1
HYNE HOWARD W	MAJ	0-0138045	0749	3
HYNES EDWARD P	WO1	W-2115151	0348	1
HYNES JAMES J	1LT	0-1014914	0147	2
HYNES JOHN J	LTC	0-0913035	0957	2
HYNES WALTER T	CW2	W-3200114	0366	1
HYNES WILLIAM P	LTC	0-0183642	0346	1
HYRODP GILBERT L	LTC	0-0337573	0849	2
HYROWSKI STANLEY	MAJ	0-2028504	0765	1
HYSICK ANDREW W	CPT	0-1012563	0140	2
HYSLOP GLEN	CW2	W-2205378	0157	1
HYSMITH PRICE E	1LT	0-1308647	1145	2
HYTER ELMER L	CW4	W-2117905	0664	1
HYZER LELAND	MAJ	0-0155628	0157	3
HYZINSKI WALTER V	LTC	0-1101054	0357	1
IACUVELLA RICHARD G	MAJ	0-1175174	0862	1

NAME	GRADE	SVC NO	DATE RET MO YR	RET CODE
IADANZA IGINO J	MAJ	C-1922650	C666	1
IAFRATI JOHN G	MAJ	O-2017701	0463	1
IANNELLA DANIEL R	MAJ	O-0367085	C646	1
IANNIELLO RALPH J	2LT	O-2055283	0745	1
IANNONE ROBERT C	CPT	O-1886357	C463	1
IBANEZ SARINIANO	MAJ	C-0369949	0257	1
IBBOTSON HARRY F	LTC	O-1293594	0263	1
IBSEN CHRISTIAN	CPT	O-1108759	C157	1
IBSEN MAXWELL	CPT	O-1038016	0446	2
ICENHOWER GEORGE A	MAJ	O-1633299	C760	1
ICENOGLE DALE F	CW2	W-2208297	0164	1
ICHIYASU BENJAMIN M	1LT	O-2030601	0751	1
ICKES CHARLES V	LTC	O-1310115	0465	1
ICKES SARAH M	1LT	N-0771720	0146	1
ICKS ROBERT J	COL	O-0236090	1060	3
IDE HARVEY W	CPT	O-0245582	C361	3
IDE HERVEY V	LTC	O-0309066	0662	1
IDEKER HENRY J	CPT	O-2019595	1162	1
IELMINI JOHN C	2LT	O-1824028	C944	2
IFFT DANIEL G	LTC	O-1308341	0962	1
IFFT MURRY M	MAJ	O-0290908	1165	3
IFLAND WILLIAM J	CW3	W-2146845	C663	2
IGLESIA FRED	CPT	O-0325033	0651	1
IGLOE MAX C	LTC	O-0274490	0961	3
IGNACIO MARCELINO	CW2	W-2151069	0361	1
IGNACIO RICARDO	CPT	C-0890550	0758	1
IGNELZI MICHAEL A	LTC	O-0425122	1264	3
IGOE JAMES P	MAJ	O-1342380	0664	2
IHARA ELEANOR C	MAJ	M-0002742	0967	3
IHLENFELD HANEY F	COL	O-0101889	C156	3
IHLENFELDT BRUCE C	LTC	O-0528244	0364	1
IHLING CHARLES E	CW3	W-2153181	1164	1
IIOA HARRY S	MAJ	C-2030797	C163	1
IJAMES FRED L	MAJ	O-1292886	0662	1
IKARD ANNIE L	MAJ	L-0402681	0264	1
IKE JOSEPH C	1LT	O-0887641	0146	1
IKEGUCHI JOSEPH	LTC	O-2024413	0966	1
IKELER EARL R	CPT	O-0174782	0546	2
IKERMAN CHARLES R	LTC	O-1103233	C765	1
ILARDI JOSEPH P	LTC	O-1035121	C962	1
ILGENFRITZ JOSEPH J	LTC	C-0250698	0467	3
ILLES JOSEPH W	CPT	O-4009160	0966	1
ILLINGSWORTH ONEICA	CPT	O-1172923	0558	1
ILLINGSWORTH R F	1LT	C-0501512	0946	1
ILLSCHE EDWARD A	1LT	O-0364520	1044	2
ILSLEY WILLIAM F	MAJ	O-4006342	0867	1
ILSON JACOB L	1LT	O-0229424	0643	2
ILYAS SHAKIR T	MAJ	O-0357613	0145	2
ILYUS EDMUND B	MAJ	O-0146258	0558	3
IMBER ROBERT J	1LT	O-1315425	C846	1
IMBLEAL LOUIS C	WO1	W-2107006	1049	1
IMBODEN WILEY P	MAJ	O-2008030	0565	1
IMBODY GERALD R	LTC	O-0250756	C664	3
IMBRIACO NICHOLAS	MAJ	O-0970867	1063	1
IMBURGIA FRANK J	COL	O-0303360	C267	3
IMER OSCAR A	MAJ	C-2289516	0962	1
IMERMAN CARLYLE P	CPT	O-0504832	0446	2
IMES JAMES K	MAJ	O-2011314	C666	1
IMHOF WILLIAM L	CPT	O-1113268	0761	1
IMMEL DONALD C	MAJ	O-1318437	0762	1
IMMELL RALPH M	M G	O-0155458	1054	3
IMMER WILLIAM L	COL	C-0225801	C864	3
IMMING MILDRED M	MAJ	L-0703099	0167	1
IMMLER JR CHARLES W	1LT	O-1341429	C949	1
IMMROTH FRANK H	MAJ	O-0857421	0767	1
IMORI HENRY T	MAJ	O-2033003	1161	1
IMSANDE LEMOINE E	LTC	O-0308634	1060	1
INABINET SHELTON F	1LT	O-1577360	0147	1
INANO TOM	CW2	W-2209503	C365	1
INBODY ROY M	LTC	O-0114435	0353	3
INCE MARION M	CW3	W-2153228	1057	1
IND ALLISON W	COL	O-0304920	1160	1
IND WALTER W	LTC	O-0309382	0758	3
INOACO ROBERT W	LTC	O-1301829	0265	1
INDERMILL ROY C	1LT	O-0370073	0845	2
INDERMILL WILLIAM G	LTC	O-2200203	1067	1
INDINGARC GEORGE T	1LT	O-0395646	1044	2
INDYK WALTER A	LTC	O-1647518	0958	1
INERFIELD ABRAHAM M	1LT	O-0531255	0245	2
INFANTI WALTER C	LTC	O-1C57116	0767	1
ING EDMUND T K	LTC	O-0214636	0362	3
ING KENNETH	CW2	W-2148288	0761	1
INGALLS FRANCIS G	CPT	O-0519823	1044	2
INGALLS KEITH I	LTC	O-0258392	0866	3
INGALLS PHINEAS H	2LT	O-0224802	1061	3
INGALLS ROBERT H	COL	O-0226934	0565	3
INGARGIOLA HENRY B	MAJ	O-2035583	0661	1
INGE GEORGE E	COL	O-0243053	0560	3
INGEBRITSEN MELVIN A	CW3	W-2143167	0659	1
INGERSOLL CHARLES F	LTC	O-0460271	0846	2
INGERSOLL HAROLD H	LTC	O-1054007	0766	1
INGHAM RAY L	MAJ	O-2007977	1065	1
INGLE CLEO G	COL	O-0192407	0762	3
INGLE DAWN V	CW2	W-2141320	0960	1
INGLE JOHN D	1LT	O-1775825	C645	2
INGLE WADE H.	LTC	O-0470487	0847	1
INGLEHART IRENE T	MAJ	N-0723336	C565	1
INGLIS LESTER B	LTC	O-0177290	0860	3
INGLIS PETE	1LT	O-0909836	0445	2
INGLIS WALTER	CW2	W-2114274	0653	1
INGLIS WEBSTER P	CPT	O-1329009	C163	1
INGLIS WILLIAM G	MAJ	O-0254441	0866	3
INGOJO JOSE P	MAJ	O-1595649	1061	1
INGOLD E DEE	COL	O-0345701	1065	1
INGOLD WINFRED L	LTC	O-0204648	0146	2
INGOLDSBY BERTRAM T	MAJ	O-0455571	0546	2
INGRAHAM ARTHUR K	LTC	O-0158671	0654	3
INGRAHAM ERIC F	LTC	O-1587340	0862	1
INGRAHAM HERBERT S	LTC	O-0123532	0460	1
INGRAHAM PAUL S	CPT	O-1323572	C946	1
INGRAHM MERTON	2LT	O-0109513	0329	1
INGRAM CHARLES L	WO1	W-2149116	0155	1
INGRAM CLAUDE R	COL	O-0286662	1059	1
INGRAM FRANK W	CPT	O-0239297	0964	3
INGRAM HAMILTON	CW2	W-2150003	0561	1
INGRAM JACK C	CW3	W-2149296	0561	1
INGRAM JAMES B	CPT	O-1951692	1159	1
INGRAM JAMES E	LTC	O-1179905	1163	1
INGRAM JR HENRY L	1LT	O-1334295	0453	2
INGRAM KENNETH	CW3	W-2206736	0866	1
INGRAM NEAL H	LTC	O-0250219	0965	3
INGRAM ROBERT C	COL	O-0315489	0962	3
INGRAM ROBERT W	CW4	W-2111353	1058	1
INGRAM RUBY K	2LT	N-0763415	0445	1
INGRAM TIMOTHY A	LTC	O-1595007	1265	1
INGRAM VERNON B	MAJ	O-0571815	0364	1
INGRAM WILLIAM I	LTC	O-1323434	0260	1
INGRAM WILLIAM W	CPT	O-0376315	1143	2
INGRASCI JOE	1LT	O-1306942	0945	2
INGRUM ROBERT P	COL	O-0311741	0367	3
INGUI THOMAS	CPT	O-1294842	1058	1
INLOW EDGAR B	2LT	O-1322996	0245	2
INLOW GEORGE E	MAJ	O-1643706	1060	1
INMAN DANIEL W	LTC	O-0446838	0263	1
INMAN ERNEST R	CW3	W-2152109	0563	1
INMAN HARRY H	WO1	W-2106907	0946	1
INMAN HOLLIS C	1LT	O-1549970	0245	2
INMAN JACK H	CW2	W-3420017	0967	1
INMAN JAMES E	COL	O-0217843	0862	3
INMAN MARJORIE C	2LT	N-0720868	1144	1
INMAN WILLIAM R	MAJ	O-0319923	0962	3
INNES CALDER	COL	O-0114045	0953	3
INNES RUCKER G	LTC	O-1288748	1266	1
INNES WILLIAM H	LTC	O-0102182	0648	3
INOMOTO SATORU T	MAJ	O-1999529	0564	1
INOUYE DANIEL K	CPT	O-1598638	0547	1
INOUYE KIYOSHI	CW4	W-2133700	1064	1
INOUYE MASATO	LTC	O-0983406	0867	1
INSCOE THOMAS W	CW3	W-2203365	1166	1
INSKEEP CURTIS B	WO1	W-2166087	0744	2
INSKEEP HAZEL M	1LT	N-0771605	C146	1
INSLEY ALAN W	1LT	O-1948765	C946	2
INTAS EDWARD D	MAJ	O-0249365	C665	3
INZER EUGENE G	1LT	O-2007106	0347	1
INZER RAY L	COL	C-1288560	0860	1
IOERGER GEORGE A	LTC	O-0451143	C755	1
IORIO FRANK P	CPT	O-0509550	C746	2
IORIO HERMAN	MAJ	O-1341975	0761	1
IORIO JOSEPH R	MAJ	O-1081348	C865	1
IOTT DONALD E	LTC	O-1294136	1166	1
IOVANELLA FRED	LTC	O-1844879	0763	1
IPPOLITO JOSEPH	CPT	O-1299571	C246	2
IPPOLITO LUCIANO	LTC	O-1576173	1156	1
IPSEN JAMES F	MAJ	O-4009161	0767	1
IPSON DONALD K	CPT	O-0368722	C146	2
IRBY R G	LTC	O-1301492	0664	1
IRBY WILLIAM I	CPT	O-0208185	0253	3
IRELAN WILLIAM E	LTC	O-0372411	C761	1
IRELAND EARL C	MAJ	C-1691951	C259	1
IRELAND EDWIN W	MAJ	O-1167913	0559	2
IRELAND EMMETT F	LTC	O-1316156	1264	1
IRELAND HARRY B	CPT	O-0410727	1044	2
IRELAND JOHN A	CPT	O-1922669	C564	1
IRELAND JOHN T	MAJ	C-2009289	C264	1
IRELAND LLOYD L	CPT	O-1165633	0355	1
IRELAND PAUL M	COL	O-0287277	C756	3
IRELAND THOMAS S	CPT	O-0278307	1043	2
IRELAND WILLIAM H	1LT	O-1546686	0146	2
IRESON ALFRED T	CPT	O-0548950	0347	2
IRGENS EDWIN R	LTC	C-0226759	C664	3
IRICK HAROLD L	CPT	O-1176073	0446	2
IRIE ROBERT K	1LT	O-1318438	1145	1
IRION VALENTINE	COL	O-0193283	1059	3
IRISH BLAINE S	MAJ	O-1015571	0364	1
IRISH EDWARD B	CPT	O-0179285	C648	3
IRISH EVERETT A	MAJ	C-0241119	0446	2
IRISH ROBERT J	COL	O-0180542	0450	1
IRISH WILLARD E	LTC	O-0368857	1066	1
IRIZARRY RAMIR-	CPT	O-0268111	0345	2
IRIZARRY RUDOLF F	MAJ	O-1326709	0165	1
IRLENBORN HENRY N	MAJ	O-0499575	1054	1
IRMEN CLAYTON R	CW3	W-2152847	1164	1
IRMISCH GEORGE W	CPT	O-0326838	0445	2
IRMSCHER ALDEN L	1LT	C-1116466	C346	2
IRONS GEORGE V	LTC	O-0195606	0962	3
IRONS MAURICE C	CW4	W-2109789	1061	3
IRONS WILLIAM	LTC	O-1581187	0861	1
IRSFELD HUBERT L	CPT	C-C338011	0447	2
IRTZ FREDEICK G	MAJ	C-0352819	0846	2
IRVIN DAVID F	CPT	O-1295721	C346	2
IRVIN FRANK P	CPT	O-1319418	C959	1
IRVIN GEORGE A	COL	O-0264007	C655	2
IRVIN JAMES M	1LT	O-1288901	1145	2
IRVIN JOHN W	CW2	W-2117963	0765	2
IRVIN RALPH D	MAJ	C-1935782	C167	1
IRVIN RAWLEIGH N	CW4	W-2149779	1164	1
IRVINE ATHILL H	CPT	O-0242946	0156	3
IRVINE GEORGE W	COL	O-0310440	1266	1
IRVINE JAMES A	LTC	O-0158672	0150	3
IRVINE JAMES P	COL	O-0290867	0660	1
IRVINE JAMES W C	LTC	O-0490774	1165	3
IRVINE JR PERCY S	LTC	O-0258960	C866	3
IRVINE JR RAYMOND G	1LT	O-5006799	0463	2
IRVINE JR WILLIAM L	1LT	O-0381985	C546	2
IRVINE RICHARD R	MAJ	O-2014653	1262	1
IRVINE ROBERT F	LTC	O-0240959	1263	3
IRVINE ROBERT M	CPT	O-0413669	0945	2
IRVINE STANLEY R	1LT	O-0342533	1043	1
IRVING BENJAMIN B	LTC	O-0140673	C652	3
IRVING CHARLES G	1LT	O-0992913	0253	2
IRVING EUGENE O	COL	O-0193054	1055	3
IRVING FRANK R	MAJ	O-0247858	0850	1
IRVING JAMES G	MAJ	C-0492541	1045	2
IRVING KENNETH J	LTC	O-1322748	1063	1
IRVING LOUIS C	LTC	O-0395485	C562	1
IRVING RICHARD H	CPT	O-0279782	0645	2
IRVING ROBERT L	COL	O-0224063	1160	3
IRVING WILLIAM	CPT	O-1284707	C146	2
IRWIN CARL H	COL	O-0307919	0457	1
IRWIN CHARLES W	1LT	O-0468843	0645	2
IRWIN DOUGLAS H	MAJ	O-2047693	0366	1
IRWIN EDWARD R	CPT	O-0506235	0356	1
IRWIN EMORY	CW3	W-2141110	1059	1
IRWIN FRANCIS L	COL	O-0233883	0865	3
IRWIN GEORGE A	LTC	O-0184886	0-53	3
IRWIN GERALD R	CW3	W-2206595	0766	1
IRWIN HAL F	COL	O-0197769	0749	2
IRWIN HAROLD S	CPT	O-0155457	0353	3
IRWIN JAMES H	1LT	O-1932461	0467	2
IRWIN JR KNOX H	1LT	O-1698024	1144	2
IRWIN LILBURN C	CPT	O-0971315	1161	1
IRWIN LUTHER W	COL	O-0281661	0662	3
IRWIN RICHARD C	MAJ	O-1002257	1156	1
IRWIN ROBERT B	LTC	O-1637734	0962	2
IRWIN RUEL C	MAJ	O-1543125	0954	1
IRWIN SAMUEL R	COL	C-0255291	0753	3
IRWIN THOMAS J	1LT	O-1102782	1C45	1
IRWIN THOMAS N	MAJ	O-0529949	0545	2
IRWIN WILLIAM C	MAJ	O-0347966	1266	3
ISAAC AARON A	CPT	O-1951533	0763	1
ISAAC THOMAS J	1LT	O-0467404	0546	2
ISAACS COLEMAN L	CPT	O-0474882	0244	2
ISAACS FREDERICK	2LT	O-1043000	0245	2
ISAACS LEONARD S	1LT	O-1581825	0145	2
ISAACS RAY C	COL	O-0284090	0462	1
ISAACS ROY R	LTC	O-1167914	0457	1
ISAACS SAM	1LT	O-1306721	1045	2
ISAACSON SAMUEL	2LT	O-1301830	0445	2
ISABELL JAMES C	CPT	O-1181494	0258	1
ISACCC ANDREW J	CPT	O-0921805	0146	2
ISACKSEN FRED R	COL	O-0482654	1063	3
ISBELL EARL B	2LT	O-1316422	0451	2
ISBELL FLETCHER F	LTC	O-0384689	0466	3
ISBELL JOSEPH B	MAJ	C-1583156	0457	1
ISBERG EDWIN S	MAJ	O-0166509	0-53	3
ISCH ALFRED E	LTC	O-1285764	0560	1
ISCH IRA L	MAJ	O-1933753	0467	1
ISEKE HAROLD J	MAJ	O-2043182	0860	1
ISEL JOHN W	1LT	O-1117883	0646	2
ISELEY WILLARD L	CW3	W-2152806	1262	1
ISELY JR CHARLES C	LTC	O-0268258	0565	3
ISEMINGER BERTRAND L	CW4	W-2128185	0659	1
ISEMINGER BOYD A	LTC	O-0192302	0660	3
ISENBARGER JOHN P	1LT	O-2019882	0452	1
ISENBERG BEATRICE T	1LT	N-0723808	C846	1
ISENBERG CARL L	COL	O-0236930	0163	1
ISENBERG FRANCIS R	MAJ	C-1106847	0264	1
ISENBERG GEORGE W	LTC	O-0445101	0166	1
ISENBERG WILBUR M	CW3	W-2153288	0867	1
ISENBERG WILLIAM G	LTC	O-0915606	1062	1
ISENHART JACK V	CW2	W-2211213	0165	1
ISERMAN FLOYD C	1LT	O-1551034	0146	2
ISERMANN CHRISTIAN	MAJ	O-0265965	0662	3
ISETT ROBERT L	LTC	O-1015281	0165	1
ISGRIGG JOHN G	LTC	O-0415076	0662	1
ISHAM HELEN J	1LT	N-0797859	0847	1
ISHAM ORVILLE A	LTC	O-0396860	0960	1
ISHEE VAUGHN E	LTC	O-0332028	0646	2
ISHLER ANSCEL I	LTC	O-1684505	0466	3
ISHMAEL JOHN R	CW3	W-2145301	1162	1
ISHMAEL WILLIAM K	MAJ	O-1701707	0246	2
ISHMAEL WILLIAM P	MAJ	O-1176075	0758	1
ISIKOFF MORRIS F	1LT	O-1316423	0346	2
ISLAN JR ALFRED F	1LT	O-1043371	104N	2
ISLER III SIMMONS H	LTC	O-1041582	0162	1
ISLER NATHANIEL	LTC	O-0244541	0663	3
ISLEY CARL J	LTC	O-0348085	1045	2
ISLEY LAMONT O	1LT	O-1289913	1045	2
ISOARD MAX C	LTC	O-0267266	0960	3
ISOLA CHARLES J	1LT	O-1303893	0246	1

NAME	GRADE	SVC NO	DATE RET MO YR	RET CODE
ISOM CLEBURNE R	CW3	W-2123148	0256	1
ISOM FRANCIS Z	2LT	O-0355116	0342	2
ISOM JR OLIN G	CPT	O-0363081	0845	2
ISON JR JASPER G	CW2	W-2208700	0864	1
ISON VENON H	MAJ	O-2014663	1262	1
ISRAEL HARRY P	LTC	O-1114175	0163	1
ISRAEL LEONARD	CPT	O-1306426	0946	1
ISRAEL MURRAY	CPT	O-0317984	1144	2
ISRAEL THEODORE J	MAJ	O-0183286	0-53	3
ISRAELSON CARL I	MAJ	O-0252572	0949	3
ISTA MYRON I	1LT	O-1318800	1045	2
ITERMAN GEORGE F	LTC	O-0205619	1049	3
ITO KANEMITSU	MAJ	O-1336220	0363	1
ITO PAUL H	CW3	W-2133589	0365	1
ITZEN HERBERT W	MAJ	O-1296216	1159	1
IVANHOE HERMAN	CPT	O-0520997	0147	2
IVANUSHKA MICHAEL	MAJ	O-1322155	0462	1
IVERS JERE J	LTC	O-0283583	0758	1
IVERS JERE J	MAJ	O-1925537	0263	1
IVERSEN ERNEST C	MAJ	O-1574265	0561	1
IVERSEN LYLE L	COL	O-0297912	0967	3
IVERSEN MERLE G	MAJ	O-0254495	0167	3
IVERSON JAMES R	2LT	O-1290424	0544	2
IVES ARTHUR D	COL	O-1306844	1067	1
IVES HOWARD S	COL	O-0204678	0860	3
IVES JOHN B	LTC	O-0496991	0756	1
IVES JOHN P	WO1	W-2148393	0752	1
IVES JR ROBERT P	CW2	W-2212541	1166	1
IVES LAVERN V	1LT	O-1996716	1049	1
IVES ROBERT M	B G	O-0140472	0459	3
IVES WILLIAM	CPT	O-1588657	0551	2
IVEY ALBERT J	LTC	O-0294028	1165	3
IVEY CURTIS	MAJ	O-1300493	0666	1
IVEY CURTIS J	LTC	O-0450034	1160	1
IVEY DANIEL W	MAJ	O-1002950	0756	1
IVEY EVAN W	CW2	W-2205134	0662	1
IVEY FRANCES [illegible]	MAJ	O-0450962	0858	1
IVEY JACK B	MAJ	O-0561349	0361	1
IVEY JOHN C	LTC	O-0369179	0955	1
IVEY JOHN D	MAJ	O-1113763	0949	2
IVEY OLIVER T	LTC	O-0246237	1167	3
IVEY PAUL B	1LT	O-1293439	0745	2
IVEY ROBERT U	MAJ	O-1280770	0266	1
IVINS RICHARD	1LT	O-1053190	0946	1
IVINS WILLIAM D	LTC	O-1643708	0365	1
IVORY MAURICE L	CPT	O-1999768	0860	1
IVY JAMES M	MAJ	O-2033261	0758	1
IVY ROBERT H	COL	O-0150639	0648	3
IVY SR ELDRIDGE L	MAJ	O-1931833	1066	1
IVY WILLIAM J	CW3	W-2141910	0559	1
IVY WILLIAM P	MAJ	O-0374129	0760	1
IWAI GERO	LTC	O-0282546	0657	1
IWAKIRI GEORGE K	CW4	W-2135973	0767	1
IWANAGA SAM S	MAJ	O-2030799	1263	1
IWASA WALTER M	1LT	O-2046476	0747	1
IZER JR STEWART C	LTC	O-1541656	1063	1
IZON JR GEORGE W	MAJ	O-1102783	1061	2
IZQUIERDO OSVALDO M	LTC	O-0349023	0260	1
IZZO WALLACE J	LTC	O-1634004	0661	1
JABBO JOHN J	CPT	O-0504839	0745	2
JACK ARCH M	MAJ	O-1299750	0564	3
JACK CARL P	LTC	O-0240287	1160	3
JACK CHARLES W	CPT	O-0464730	0146	2
JACK RALPH F	CW3	W-2144094	1057	1
JACK WHITFIELD	M G	O-0267915	0866	3
JACKETT ROBERT W	CW3	W-2147272	1162	1
JACKLEY LESTER J	MAJ	O-1016242	0262	1
JACKLIN BARBARA A	1LT	N-0741190	1045	1
JACKMAN GLEN R	LTC	O-0415813	0767	1
JACKMAN REESE W	COL	O-0441876	0854	1
JACKS CARL L	1LT	O-1319439	1046	2
JACKS GEORGE R	COL	O-0260352	0747	1
JACKS HERMAN P	LTC	O-1541425	0160	1
JACKS HILTON F	MAJ	O-0453483	0655	1
JACKSON ALBERT H	CW3	W-2141321	0564	1
JACKSON ALFRED C	CPT	O-0103491	0648	3
JACKSON ARCILOUS E	1LT	O-0411484	0946	2
JACKSON ARTHUR F	MAJ	O-2011598	0163	1
JACKSON AUBRA G	CW4	W-2150725	0558	1
JACKSON AUSTIN F	MAJ	O-1179461	0364	1
JACKSON BAYARD	CPT	O-1170433	0551	1
JACKSON BERNARD F	CPT	O-1288384	0747	2
JACKSON BESSIE M	2LT	N-0700246	0835	1
JACKSON BIRKHEAD	MAJ	O-1172924	0461	1
JACKSON BYRON B	1LT	O-0441753	1045	2
JACKSON CALVIN A	1LT	O-1302002	0446	2
JACKSON CALVIN G	COL	O-0282071	1053	2
JACKSON CECIL M	LTC	O-1290607	1161	1
JACKSON CHARLES A	MAJ	O-1541797	0362	2
JACKSON CHARLES F	LTC	O-1043672	0161	1
JACKSON CHARLES H	CPT	O-1574266	1061	1
JACKSON CHARLES K	CPT	O-0386346	1057	1
JACKSON CHARLES L	CW2	W-2147149	1166	1
JACKSON CHARLES S	1LT	O-1329992	1045	2
JACKSON CHESLEY C	MAJ	O-0414358	0647	2
JACKSON CHESTER T	MAJ	O-1999177	1157	1
JACKSON CHRISTENE	MAJ	N-0768550	0266	1
JACKSON CLAUDE L	MAJ	O-0251738	0346	2
JACKSON CLIFFORD C	1LT	O-0499777	0250	1
JACKSON CLIFFORD T	LTC	O-1634922	0261	1
JACKSON DALE	MAJ	O-1313350	0157	2
JACKSON DAVID G	LTC	O-0164014	1145	1
JACKSON DAVID H	CW2	W-2148859	1157	1
JACKSON DONALD F	MAJ	O-1323066	0865	1
JACKSON DONALD W	MAJ	O-1336068	0164	1
JACKSON DUANE P	LTC	O-1172850	1062	1
JACKSON DWIGHT W	CPT	O-0258583	0867	3
JACKSON EARL L	LTC	O-0348839	0557	3
JACKSON EDGAR A	CW4	W-2103047	0156	1
JACKSON EDWARD J	CW3	W-2109217	0450	1
JACKSON EDWARD R	CW2	W-2213145	0864	1
JACKSON EDWARD W	MAJ	O-1295751	0163	1
JACKSON EMERY D K	COL	O-0361657	1160	1
JACKSON EMERY L	LTC	O-0301529	0565	1
JACKSON EUGENE K	LTC	O-0909554	1265	3
JACKSON EVERETTE H	LTC	O-0103633	0648	3
JACKSON FLOYD L	LTC	O-0238738	0562	3
JACKSON FORREST A	CW3	W-2150768	0266	1
JACKSON FOSTER G	LTC	O-0216015	0945	2
JACKSON FRANK	2LT	O-2055816	1145	2
JACKSON FRED A	2LT	O-1013843	0844	2
JACKSON GAYLON C	LTC	O-1318801	0764	1
JACKSON GEORGE	MAJ	O-2053916	0157	1
JACKSON GEORGE A	MAJ	O-0258955	1266	3
JACKSON GEORGE D	MAJ	O-0969984	0762	1
JACKSON GEORGE S	CPT	O-1798871	1158	1
JACKSON GEORGE W	LTC	O-0272495	0967	3
JACKSON GERALD G	CW2	W-3410003	0866	1
JACKSON GERTRUDE O	MAJ	N-0755316	0161	2
JACKSON HAROLD	MAJ	O-1647522	1163	1
JACKSON HAROLD D	CPT	O-0280717	0545	2
JACKSON HARVEY C	LTC	O-1331052	0467	1
JACKSON HORACE R	LTC	O-1174604	0366	1
JACKSON HORACE W	COL	O-0261815	0361	3
JACKSON HOWARD	MAJ	O-1059507	0557	1
JACKSON HOWARD G	MAJ	O-1637740	0558	1
JACKSON HOWARD H	MAJ	O-0155534	0453	3
JACKSON HUGH C	1LT	O-0447756	0646	1
JACKSON IGAL C	LTC	O-1556736	1067	3
JACKSON JAMES	WO1	W-2150986	0957	1
JACKSON JAMES A	MAJ	O-0995669	0463	1
JACKSON JAMES C	COL	O-0146123	0856	3
JACKSON JAMES D	MAJ	O-0571325	0265	1
JACKSON JAMES L	MAJ	O-2263352	0563	1
JACKSON JAMES M	2LT	O-0556909	1045	2
JACKSON JAMES P	MAJ	O-1311896	0862	1
JACKSON JAMES T	1LT	O-1317308	0746	2
JACKSON JAMES T	CW3	W-2119651	0456	1
JACKSON JERRY	MAJ	O-1283779	0749	1
JACKSON JESSE A	LTC	O-0161782	0648	3
JACKSON JESSE R	LTC	O-0904506	1046	2
JACKSON JOE	1LT	O-1317242	0644	2
JACKSON JOE N	MAJ	O-1919436	0967	1
JACKSON JOHN F	LTC	O-0296148	0140	2
JACKSON JOHN F	1LT	O-0936121	0848	2
JACKSON JOHN M	CW4	W-2114227	1052	1
JACKSON JOHN W	LTC	O-1295591	0962	2
JACKSON JOHN W	CW3	W-2113841	1057	1
JACKSON JOSEPH	LTC	O-0461773	0-53	1
JACKSON JR ARTHUR A	LTC	O-1167915	1064	1
JACKSON JR CHARLES A	LTC	O-0260355	0767	3
JACKSON JR DUGALD C	COL	O-0125948	0855	3
JACKSON JR JAMES W	COL	O-0411245	1262	1
JACKSON JR LEWIS W	1LT	O-1002794	0545	2
JACKSON JR PAUL V	MAJ	O-1155585	0561	2
JACKSON JR SAMUEL T	MAJ	O-1304223	1162	2
JACKSON JR WILLIAM A	CPT	O-1294843	0755	1
JACKSON KENNETH	LTC	O-0321905	0662	1
JACKSON KENNETH L	LTC	O-1647964	0566	1
JACKSON KERMITT H	CPT	O-1299752	0957	2
JACKSON KIRBY E	LTC	O-0150462	0-53	3
JACKSON KYLE R	LTC	O-0888596	0560	1
JACKSON LELAND A	MAJ	O-0281065	0945	2
JACKSON LEO M	COL	O-0241757	1049	3
JACKSON LEWIS A	CPT	O-0289372	0662	3
JACKSON LLOYD S	MAJ	O-0671551	0764	1
JACKSON LONNIE H	CPT	O-0439999	0752	1
JACKSON LYNN S	MAJ	O-0249027	1059	2
JACKSON MARION C	MAJ	N-0720959	0965	3
JACKSON MAURICE W	1LT	O-1287886	0646	2
JACKSON MERVIN E	CW2	W-2110155	1046	1
JACKSON MILFORD G	LTC	O-1577366	0266	1
JACKSON NEIL	LTC	O-0393372	1160	1
JACKSON NEIL C	CPT	O-0385816	1045	2
JACKSON PAUL H	MAJ	O-1015385	0157	1
JACKSON PETER F	CW3	W-2150543	0743	1
JACKSON RALPH L	CW2	W-2147492	0563	1
JACKSON REUBEN A	CPT	O-0687993	0948	1
JACKSON REX H	CW3	W-2143923	0160	1
JACKSON RILEY V	COL	O-0368342	0167	1
JACKSON ROBERT C	CW3	W-2144476	0561	1
JACKSON ROBERT E	MAJ	O-0949185	0465	2
JACKSON ROBERT F	MAJ	O-1690937	1061	1
JACKSON ROBERT G	CPT	O-0690574	1063	1
JACKSON ROBERT H	MAJ	O-1646273	0562	1
JACKSON ROBERT I	1LT	O-0439602	0346	2
JACKSON ROBERT L	CPT	O-0485087	0450	1
JACKSON ROBERT T	CW3	W-2147977	0263	1
JACKSON ROBERT W	COL	O-0255320	0561	1
JACKSON S LESTER	CPT	O-1765098	0648	1
JACKSON SAM I	MAJ	O-0213491	1060	3
JACKSON SAMUEL D	CW4	W-2109338	0452	1
JACKSON SAMUEL S	WO1	W-2129967	0745	2
JACKSON STANFORD L	MAJ	O-0345544	0647	2
JACKSON TEDDY	CPT	O-0973442	1160	1
JACKSON THOMAS F	LTC	O-0517659	0866	3
JACKSON THOMAS H	1LT	O-1109380	1046	2
JACKSON THOMAS J	CW3	W-2205538	1065	1
JACKSON THOMAS K	MAJ	O-1293417	0857	1
JACKSON THOMAS R	COL	O-0121010	0556	3
JACKSON THOMAS S	CPT	O-0418595	1145	1
JACKSON VERNE O	LTC	O-0188125	0752	1
JACKSON VESTER A	LTC	O-0257686	0463	3
JACKSON WALLACE B	MAJ	O-1945173	0164	1
JACKSON WAYNE C	CPT	O-0396281	0645	2
JACKSON WILBUR P	CPT	O-0888906	0447	1
JACKSON WILBURN E	LTC	O-1062211	0766	1
JACKSON WILLIAM A	1LT	O-0989508	0153	1
JACKSON WILLIAM B	MAJ	O-1293967	0667	2
JACKSON WILLIAM B	1LT	O-2048028	1045	2
JACKSON WILLIAM C	COL	O-1633303	1163	1
JACKSON WILLIAM D	B G	O-0169669	0751	3
JACKSON WILLIAM E	LTC	O-0483483	0565	2
JACKSON WILLIAM F	CW3	RW-2208811	0766	1
JACKSON WILLIAM G	MAJ	O-0274365	0865	3
JACKSON WILLIAM H	COL	O-0115612	0351	3
JACKSON WILLIAM H	1LT	O-1316757	0146	2
JACKSON WILLIAM J	MAJ	O-0411432	1161	2
JACKSON WILLIAM L	CPT	O-1292530	0646	2
JACKSON WILLIAM M	COL	O-0202734	0556	3
JACKSON WILLIAM N	LTC	O-1324540	0767	1
JACKSON WILLIAM S	MAJ	O-0376831	1060	1
JACKSON WILLIE	CW2	W-2114588	0348	1
JACKSON WILLIS	1LT	O-1335009	0252	1
JACKY ALFRED W	MAJ	O-1935035	0167	1
JACO PAUL M	MAJ	O-0982552	0465	1
JACOB CARROLL D	2LT	O-1177851	0544	2
JACOB GLADYS L	CPT	N-0736423	0247	1
JACOB HAROLD O	MAJ	O-1985251	1165	1
JACOB PABLO	CW2	W-3440010	0866	1
JACOBBERGER BERNARD	MAJ	O-0224257	0164	3
JACOBELLI AMADEO J	LTC	O-0452858	0156	1
JACOBERGER PHILIP F	1LT	O-1945387	0957	1
JACOBI FRED W	COL	O-0349477	0865	1
JACOBI LEE	LTC	O-0117720	0953	3
JACOBS ARTHUR H	CW3	W-2148323	0162	1
JACOBS BURL	CW4	W-2148380	1266	1
JACOBS CHARLES E	LTC	O-1325395	0163	1
JACOBS CHARLES R	CPT	O-1300571	0346	2
JACOBS EDWARD J	CW4	W-2136700	0966	1
JACOBS FRANK H	LTC	O-0224803	1154	3
JACOBS GEORGE C	MAJ	O-0477360	0253	1
JACOBS HAROLD H	LTC	O-1594402	1266	3
JACOBS HELEN	MAJ	M-0002574	0366	1
JACOBS HERBERT	LTC	O-0502664	0964	3
JACOBS HERBERT S	MAJ	O-0312114	0145	2
JACOBS HUBERT L	COL	O-0114761	0160	3
JACOBS JAMES H	MAJ	O-1331053	0663	1
JACOBS JOHN R	COL	O-0237210	0458	3
JACOBS JOSEPH W	LTC	O-1541972	1161	1
JACOBS JR GERALD	LTC	O-0443753	1064	1
JACOBS JR LOUIS L	MAJ	O-1735010	0465	1
JACOBS JULIUS C	CPT	O-1304736	0566	2
JACOBS LESTER A	LTC	O-0182316	0845	2
JACOBS LEWIS	CPT	O-0484653	0945	2
JACOBS MARTIN H	CPT	O-0436240	0348	1
JACOBS MAURICE P	2LT	O-0108933	1040	1
JACOBS MELVIN W	CPT	O-0477934	0945	2
JACOBS MURRAY J	1LT	O-1639211	0646	2
JACOBS NELSON F	MAJ	O-2033974	1162	1
JACOBS NEWTON A	COL	O-0255001	0954	1
JACOBS PAUL E	COL	O-0251138	0767	3
JACOBS PAUL H	COL	O-0238503	0760	1
JACOBS RALPH F	CW3	W-2147257	0764	1
JACOBS REGINALD F	COL	O-0241186	0763	3
JACOBS RENE C	MAJ	O-0964850	0666	1
JACOBS ROBERT F	LTC	O-1895665	0966	1
JACOBS ROY M	MAJ	O-1322034	0865	2
JACOBS ROYAL A	COL	O-0298454	0360	1
JACOBS SAMUEL S	1LT	O-1310116	0945	2
JACOBS SHIRLEY C	MAJ	O-2033082	0461	1
JACOBS SIMSON	WO1	W-2124023	0745	2
JACOBS SR WILLIAM A	CPT	O-1919345	0562	1
JACOBS STANLEY J	CPT	O-1306276	1047	1
JACOBS STEPHEN T	LTC	O-0503353	0756	1
JACOBS UEDE L	CW4	W-2104720	0559	1
JACOBS VINCENT H	B G	O-0237721	0749	3
JACOBS WOODROW W	1LT	O-1300972	0945	2
JACOBSEN CARL E	LTC	O-0363522	0959	1
JACOBSEN CHARLES W	COL	O-0176712	0154	3
JACOBSEN EDWARD H	LTC	O-0137779	0648	3
JACOBSEN ERIC M	1LT	O-0465849	0546	1
JACOBSEN ERIC S	MAJ	O-1326305	0759	1
JACOBSEN FRANK E	LTC	O-0194856	0461	3
JACOBSEN GEORGE C	LTC	O-2035332	0667	1
JACOBSEN GORDON F	CPT	O-1053653	0755	1
JACOBSEN SOPHUS C	COL	O-0121535	0362	3
JACOBSEN WALTER C	1LT	O-1060820	1045	2
JACOBSON AL	CW3	W-2152298	0862	1
JACOBSON ALFRED H	LTC	O-0295767	1147	2

ARMY OF THE UNITED STATES RETIRED LIST

NAME	GRADE	SVC NO	DATE RET MO YR	RET CODE
JACOBSON ANDREW K	2LT	C-1297201	C644	2
JACOBSON CARL A	COL	0-0263399	C565	3
JACOBSON CLARENCE M	CW3	W-2144290	C661	1
JACOBSON GEORGE H	CW2	W-2118644	0162	2
JACOBSON GRANT H	CPT	0-0453870	0145	2
JACOBSON HJALMER A	LTC	0-0256997	C447	2
JACOBSON JAMES W	LTC	C-0242620	1065	3
JACOBSON JOHN P	MAJ	C-1105538	C357	1
JACOBSCN JOSEPH S	LTC	0-0323289	C559	1
JACOBSON JR JOHN	M G	0-0102326	0457	3
JACOBSON JULIUS	LTC	0-0255046	0745	2
JACOBSON LEONARD F	2LT	0-1059508	C145	2
JACOBSON RAYMOND L	LTC	0-1042344	0566	1
JACOBSCN ROLLAND F	CW3	W-2143117	1160	1
JACOBSON SAMUEL S	MAJ	0-0278140	1263	3
JACOBSON WILLIAM J	LTC	0-2047371	0865	1
JACOBUS FREDERIC A	2LT	0-0538798	C445	2
JACOBY BERNARD R	2LT	0-C531890	0246	2
JACOBY GLENN J	COL	0-0290884	1067	3
JACOBY HARRY J	LTC	0-0303340	1046	2
JACOMB WILLIAM M	1LT	0-1106849	0446	2
JACOT EARL C	CW2	W-2119479	C853	2
JACQUART DAVID R	CW2	W-2214545	0167	1
JACQUES BRYAN H	MAJ	C-0255881	0967	3
JACQUES ERNEST A	MAJ	C-0974445	1062	1
JACQUES FRED W	CW3	W-2147682	0464	1
JACQUES GABRIEL	CPT	0-0262922	0946	2
JACQUES GEORGE W	LTC	0-0206341	1059	3
JACQUES LEWIS H	MAJ	C-0438587	1146	2
JACQUES MYRON E	CW2	W-2143344	0958	1
JACQUOT HOWARD F	CPT	0-0326575	1146	2
JACQUOT ROBERT H	MAJ	C-0585790	0866	1
JAEGER ELEAINOR	CW3	W-2145340	C462	1
JAEGER EVELYN W	2LT	N-0772700	0744	1
JAEGER MARVIN F	LTC	0-1308148	C364	1
JAEGER RAYMOND B	MAJ	0-0416791	0945	2
JAEDER WALTER H F	COL	0-0186367	1062	3
JAEGY HUBERT J	LTC	0-0275540	1056	3
JAEKELS DALLAS C	COL	C-0370520	C964	1
JAFFA ROBERT R	LTC	0-0384833	C560	1
JAFFE AARON A	LTC	0-0184669	0450	3
JAFFE SEYMOUR A	1LT	0-1322831	0746	2
JAFFEE MORRIS	LTC	0-1030160	0656	1
JAGER ROLAND V	LTC	0-1048032	C964	1
JAGERS SAMUEL	CPT	C-0965009	0364	2
JAGGEARS JR MARVIN F	1LT	0-1294137	C646	2
JAGGERS HERMAN L	MAJ	C-1289434	0456	1
JAGGERS THEODORE	MAJ	C-2036382	0764	1
JAGGIE EDWARD A	LTC	0-0903332	0662	1
JAGO EARL F	LTC	C-C190048	0657	3
JAGODA STANLEY A	LTC	C-1177C17	1C57	2
JAGOE CHARLES W	LTC	0-1306427	C262	1
JAGOW EMIL B	MAJ	0-0916524	0948	2
JAHN WILLIAM M	LTC	0-0235159	0452	3
JAHNIGEN HERMAN H	2LT	0-1997800	1045	2
JAHNS LEWIS E	LTC	0-0121609	C648	3
JAHNSEN OSCAR J	B G	0-0943408	0959	3
JAHR LOWELL G	2LT	C-118056C	C344	2
JAILLET AQUILA	1LT	0-0497508	C647	1
JAILLET JR ENGLE L	1LT	0-1298068	C347	2
JAIME JR ALFRED C	MAJ	C-2055972	C954	1
JAIMES PHILIP M	MAJ	C-2206397	C867	1
JAKAITIS BRUNO L	COL	C-0320071	C865	1
JAKATIS ARTHUR O	2LT	0-1639009	C745	2
JAKCSY JOSEPH	CW3	W-2147148	C962	1
JAKES JR WILLIAM F	CPT	0-0405915	1045	2
JAKOB JOHN W	1LT	C-1292181	0246	2
JAKOPICH WILLIAM F	CPT	0-0504178	1043	2
JAKOVICH JR DANIEL	LTC	C-110151C	1262	1
JAKSHA BERNARD G	MAJ	C-1030991	0364	1
JAKUBIEC JOSEPH R	LTC	0-0486160	C667	1
JAKUBOWSKI JOHN J	MAJ	0-1634926	0457	1
JAKUBZAK CHARLOTTE	CPT	M-0000472	1047	1
JALBERT MAGLOIRE	1LT	0-0108443	1022	1
JAMERSON OSMOND T	COL	0-0245618	0866	3
JAMES ARCHIBALD	CPT	0-0258507	0444	2
JAMES BYRD L	MAJ	0-2000943	1059	1
JAMES EDGAR A	CPT	0-0360185	0656	2
JAMES EDWARD	MAJ	C-1685698	0263	2
JAMES EDWARD D	MAJ	0-2C18007	1062	1
JAMES ELIZABETH	CPT	N-0737430	0548	1
JAMES ELLIS L	WO1	W-2149179	0956	1
JAMES EMMETTE A	LTC	0-1576179	0662	1
JAMES ERNEST H	COL	0-0309493	0159	3
JAMES EVAN E	CPT	0-1030992	1047	2
JAMES FELTHAM S	MAJ	0-0249793	0846	2
JAMES FRANK	MAJ	0-2262449	0163	1
JAMES GEORGE L	LTC	0-0212808	0363	3
JAMES GEORGE M	1LT	0-0512104	1044	2
JAMES GEORGE R	MAJ	0-1796481	0761	1
JAMES GOMER	LTC	0-1110361	1262	1
JAMES HAROLD D	CPT	0-0381515	0346	2
JAMES HAROLD R	MAJ	0-1557617	0360	2
JAMES HARRY M	MAJ	0-1697868	0456	1
JAMES HOWARD E	MAJ	0-1042850	0864	1
JAMES HUBERT I	MAJ	0-1559576	1163	1
JAMES JAMES W	CW2	W-2206038	0659	1
JAMES JESSE R	CPT	0-1557858	0847	1
JAMES JOHN R C	CPT	0-0419173	1047	2
JAMES JOSEPH A	COL	0-0148520	0451	3
JAMES JOSEPH H	COL	0-1172085	0165	1
JAMES JR GEORGE R	MAJ	0-2704014	0767	1
JAMES JR HARRY	MAJ	0-1342381	0366	1
JAMES JR HARRY F	1LT	0-1322036	1045	1
JAMES JR HATCHER M	MAJ	0-1327957	1163	1
JAMES JR JOE	2LT	0-2027403	1151	2
JAMES JR WILLIAM F	LTC	0-0236095	0662	1
JAMES JR WILLIAM L	MAJ	0-0998774	1065	1
JAMES JR WILLIAM M	MAJ	0-2262765	0762	1
JAMES KENNETH L	LTC	0-1172926	0865	2
JAMES LAWRENCE C	MAJ	0-1166515	0761	1
JAMES LEE E	COL	0-0342172	0766	1
JAMES LEE E	MAJ	0-0390463	0446	2
JAMES LEONARD N	LTC	0-034934C	0760	1
JAMES LOUIE W	LTC	0-0269946	1067	3
JAMES LOUIS D	CW3	W-2144357	0766	1
JAMES MAURICE D	LTC	0-0244057	0366	3
JAMES MAXWELL	COL	0-0222145	0849	1
JAMES MELVIN F	MAJ	0-0254805	0166	3
JAMES MCWBRAY R	LTC	0-0359368	0646	2
JAMES NOYELLES L	MAJ	0-2023333	0762	1
JAMES PRESTON E	COL	0-0172462	0259	3
JAMES RICHARD E	MAJ	C-0309179	0754	3
JAMES RICHARD L	LTC	0-0450629	C161	1
JAMES ROBERT E	MAJ	0-1109381	1164	1
JAMES ROBERT S	MAJ	0-0497714	0855	1
JAMES SARA B	1LT	N-0768128	0946	1
JAMES THERESA V	MAJ	N-073253C	C667	1
JAMES THOMAS G	LTC	0-1178843	1167	1
JAMES THOMAS L	LTC	0-0172755	0245	2
JAMES ULRIC N	COL	0-0171127	0151	3
JAMES WALTER G	LTC	0-1636087	0766	1
JAMES WILARD	CW4	W-2144188	0764	1
JAMES WILLIAM O	COL	0-0349879	1166	3
JAMES WILLIAM H	CPT	0-095364C	0159	1
JAMES WILLIAM L	COL	0-0313426	0856	1
JAMES WILLIE R	CW3	W-2143283	0561	1
JAMESON EUGENE J	MAJ	0-1185711	0660	1
JAMESON KLIDE A	MAJ	0-2018357	0165	1
JAMESON LLOYD H	COL	0-0225664	1060	3
JAMESON MERRILL F	LTC	0-1177854	0167	1
JAMESON WALTER G	LTC	0-1557469	0263	1
JAMESON WILLIAM S	CPT	0-2040949	0764	1
JAMGOCHIAN VAUGHN M	COL	0-0224475	0158	3
JAMIESON GEORGE T	LTC	0-0542702	0367	3
JAMIESON ROBERT	LTC	0-0265555	0662	3
JAMISON CHARLES F	MAJ	0-1294672	0363	1
JAMISON FENTON W	CPT	0-0114499	1151	3
JAMISON HOMER C	CPT	0-0442275	1045	2
JAMISON MADISON L	CW3	W-2142766	1060	1
JAMISON THURSTON F	LTC	0-0324126	C462	1
JAMISON WILBUR G	MAJ	0-2006273	0465	1
JAMISON WILLIAM E	CPT	0-0391307	0745	2
JAMISON WILLIAM G	CPT	0-0359407	0645	2
JAMKOCHIAN KEHAN	LTC	0-2002457	0366	2
JAMMES JOSEPH M	MAJ	C-0973457	C862	1
JAMNICKI AUGUST	MAJ	0-2009532	0966	1
JAMPEL SYDNEY	CPT	0-1689081	0746	1
JAMROS JR JOSEPH J	1LT	0-1313248	1045	2
JANACEK FELIX V	MAJ	0-1167044	C757	1
JANAK MATILDA A	MAJ	N-0734402	0464	1
JANASIEWICZ JOHN F	WO1	W-2113766	1050	1
JANCO PETER P	WO1	W-2104721	0750	1
JANCURA CLARENCE J	MAJ	C-1639215	0957	1
JANDA WALTER M	1LT	0-2047372	0446	2
JANCRO DONALD H	MAJ	C-1688438	0663	1
JANEBA HUGO B	LTC	0-0961827	0465	3
JANERETTE VERSEAL A	CPT	0-0535827	0845	2
JANES BEN C	LTC	0-0268323	1065	3
JANES CHARLES F	LTC	0-0493881	0357	1
JANES CHARLES R	COL	0-0911793	0966	3
JANES EUGENE C	1LT	0-0236407	C648	3
JANES FRANK T	COL	0-0421282	C347	2
JANES RAYMOND L	1LT	0-1644445	0250	1
JANES WILLIAM D	CPT	0-1325899	C348	1
JANETIS JR MICHAEL	CW2	W-3430057	C566	1
JANEWAY AUGUSTINE	COL	0-0157793	0845	2
JANEWAY CHARLES H	MAJ	0-0148246	0257	3
JANICKI JOSEPH W	CPT	0-0138319	C852	3
JANIFER EDWARD F D	1LT	0-0245136	1151	3
JANIFER JAMES V	MAJ	C-1291995	0164	1
JANIGER NATHANIEL	CPT	0-0448354	1045	2
JANIN RICHARD A	LTC	0-1634929	C664	1
JANIS RAYMOND A	LTC	0-1574454	0461	1
JANISS HENRY W	CPT	0-2017549	0757	1
JANKOVICH JOSEPH S	LTC	0-1110584	1162	1
JANKOWIAK HENRY	LTC	C-1001814	1262	1
JANKOWSKI CHARLES J	CPT	0-1321373	C654	2
JANKUSKAS FRANK J	LTC	C-0358645	C966	1
JANNACE ATTILIO F	CPT	0-0527947	C645	2
JANNASCH JR JAMES R	2LT	0-2011900	0346	2
JANNELLE ARMAND F	MAJ	0-0217969	C455	3
JANNETTE LAWRENCE J	1LT	0-0383494	0146	2
JANNEY ELWOOD A	LTC	C-1291646	0760	1
JANNUSCH GLENWOOD L	CW3	W-2145454	1263	1
JANNUSCH HARRIS T	LTC	0-1640589	0562	1
JANNUZI WILLIAM R	MAJ	C-1548857	1046	2
JANOSIK GABRIEL E	MAJ	0-1284145	1146	2
JANOTA ERWIN J	LTC	0-1585668	1060	1
JANQUART MERVIN	1LT	C-0485710	0446	2
JANSEN CLARENCE T	MAJ	C-0410851	C746	1
JANSEN EDWARD T	CPT	0-1295723	0446	2
JANSEN ELMER	CPT	0-0172666	0858	3
JANSEN LAWRENCE C	LTC	0-1038194	0367	1
JANSEN MARIE T	MAJ	N-0756527	0963	1
JANSEN RAYMOND T	CPT	0-132901C	C355	2
JANSEN WILLARD S	MAJ	C-1917880	1066	1
JANSEY FELIX	LTC	0-0494598	0247	2
JANSKY ERNEST F	LTC	C-1795915	C657	1
JANSKY JR STEPHEN J	1LT	0-1309741	0845	2
JANSMA CLAYTON B	1LT	C-0410073	1044	2
JANSMA ROBERT K	MAJ	C-0966279	0863	1
JANSSEN HERMAN G	COL	0-0319236	1060	3
JANSSEN WILLIAM A	1LT	0-1001156	0444	2
JANUARY LEWIS E	MAJ	C-0356981	0446	2
JAPINGA MARTIN	LTC	0-0272823	0859	3
JAPPE FRANK K	CPT	0-2028926	0958	1
JAQUES CHARLES	LTC	C-1308149	1162	1
JAQUES ROBERT	MAJ	C-0199386	0648	3
JARAMILLO ELOY	CW3	W-2143603	1162	1
JARANILLA TIBURCIC	1LT	0-0890544	C750	1
JARDEE HERSCHEL H	CW3	W-2142855	C761	1
JARDINE BARBARA M	1LT	N-0721629	0745	1
JARDINE JR JOHN E	LTC	0-0112963	C859	3
JARED GEORGE B	LTC	0-0452682	0266	1
JARED MYRON S	LTC	0-0231039	1045	2
JARED RUSSELL W	LTC	0-1590564	1262	1
JARIS LOUIS C	MAJ	C-1183550	0260	2
JARK MARVIN A	LTC	0-1300173	0161	1
JARLETT JR OSCAR J	MAJ	0-1649832	1263	1
JARMAN CECIL C	COL	0-0102205	0156	3
JARMAN GORDON N	LTC	0-0243180	1264	3
JARMAN JR JOHN W S	LTC	0-159295C	0667	1
JARMON JOSEPH K	COL	C-0277047	1265	3
JARMON WILLIAM R	LTC	0-0260464	0766	3
JARNAGIN JAMES R	LTC	0-0105022	0655	3
JARDCH CHESTER J	LTC	0-1549506	0562	1
JAROMAY DELFIN	CPT	0-1896887	1266	1
JAROSKY WALTER	CW2	W-2213120	0767	1
JARRARD CLEMUEL L	2LT	0-1299513	1043	2
JARRARD FRANK C	MAJ	0-1185437	0461	1
JARRARD GEORGE V	LTC	0-2204062	0767	1
JARRATT HENRY M	LTC	0-1701427	1166	3
JARRELL HOWARD R	COL	0-0144639	0157	3
JARRELL RAYMOND E	MAJ	0-1951571	1165	1
JARRELL REMBERT L	1LT	0-0441964	1045	2
JARRETT EARL H	2LT	0-1296217	0944	2
JARRETT EDWIN S	LTC	0-1166296	0867	3
JARRETT ELMER J	MAJ	0-1331400	1059	1
JARRETT GEORGE B	COL	0-0241836	1161	3
JARRETT HARRIS H	CPT	0-1825914	1047	2
JARRETT IDELLA N	2LT	N-0702619	1036	1
JARRETT JR WILLIAM T	CW3	W-2206357	1167	1
JARRETT LOWEY F	2LT	0-1308241	0705	2
JARRETT PAUL J	COL	0-0346140	0661	1
JARRETT WALTER L	CW3	W-2148860	0966	1
JARRETT WILLIAM H	LTC	0-0416086	0861	2
JARRIEL ELLIS B	1LT	0-1306723	1045	1
JARVIS CHARLES W	MAJ	0-0403991	1044	2
JARVIS EDWARD J	2LT	0-1307160	0145	2
JARVIS GEORGE	COL	0-0229934	1064	3
JARVIS HAROLD O	LTC	0-1549972	0563	1
JARVIS JACK J	MAJ	0-0314115	0646	2
JARVIS JOHN E	LTC	0-0360982	0567	3
JARVIS JOHN S	CPT	0-1823604	0846	2
JARVIS NORMAN F	LTC	0-0374509	0863	1
JASEPH ROLAND H	LTC	0-0339926	0361	1
JASINSKI BERNARD M	LTC	0-1291282	1061	1
JASIO SR JOHN J	CW4	W-2117395	1060	1
JASPER CAROLINE E	1LT	N-0775513	1145	1
JASPER ROBERT B	CPT	0-0417763	0146	2
JASTROW PAUL W	1LT	0-0940747	0149	1
JASTRZEMBSKI JOHN R	MAJ	0-1042608	0158	1
JASUTA EDWARD B	LTC	0-1102315	0757	1
JAUBERT G WILFRED	LTC	0-0412052	0761	1
JAUCH ROLAND S	COL	0-0202231	0160	3
JAUCK WALTER M	1LT	0-1060144	0845	1
JAUDON ELBERT W	MAJ	0-0939665	1062	1
JAUVTIS ELIHU B	LTC	0-1995111	0466	3
JAVIER-BOSCIC BEN	CPT	0-0413007	0960	1
JAVINS REXFORD R	LTC	0-2055327	0963	1
JAVOIS ALEXANDER	LTC	0-0241879	0859	3
JAWOREK JOHN C	1LT	0-0415419	0666	3
JAWORSKI FRANK A	LTC	0-0370666	0760	1
JAWORSKI HENRY	CPT	0-0485652	0946	1
JAY ANDREW L	LTC	0-1583163	0563	1
JAY BYRON	WO1	W-2145729	1153	1
JAY JOSEPH E	LTC	0-0270233	0961	3
JAY JR THOMAS J	CW4	W-2143558	0767	1
JAYCOX CLAUDE E	CW2	W-2101883	0762	2
JAYJOCK LEO J	MAJ	0-1311154	1160	1
JEALDUS WILLIAM K	COL	0-0109136	0354	3
JEAN GUY B	CW3	W-2208401	0567	1
JEAN JR HOMER H	CPT	C-1701169	1265	1
JEAN WILLIAM W	LTC	0-1030680	0958	1
JEAN WILMER F	LTC	0-1286847	0847	1
JEANE HAROLD T	1LT	0-1554759	0950	1
JEANNETTE ROBERT F	CPT	0-1319885	1147	2
JEANSONNE FLOYD E	1LT	0-1106229	0452	1
JEBD ELMER H	1LT	0-1284708	0745	2

NAME	GRADE	SVC NO	DATE RET MO YR	RET CODE
JECKEL FREDERICK	MAJ	0-1283266	0264	1
JEDAMUS MARIE	2LT	N-0700725	0734	1
JEDEIKIN LAZARUS	2LT	0-1945618	0545	2
JEDLICKA ANTON G	LTC	0-0106797	1051	3
JEDLICKA FRANK C	MAJ	0-1321414	1057	1
JEEP CLEMENT S	CPT	0-0236454	0762	3
JEFFCOAT CLYDE E	CW3	W-2147880	0763	1
JEFFCOAT JR OTIS A	LTC	0-0261045	0766	3
JEFFE EPHRAIM F	BG	0-0138243	0256	3
JEFFERIES JOHN W	COL	0-0148427	1156	3
JEFFERS BERT M	MAJ	0-1111143	1162	1
JEFFERSON BILLY R	MAJ	0-1330821	1042	1
JEFFERSON EDWIN R	MAJ	0-0348758	0565	3
JEFFERSON JAMES R	CW2	W-2145645	1163	1
JEFFERSON JOSEPH F	CW2	W-2141325	1159	1
JEFFERSON PAUL L	1LT	0-1287887	0545	2
JEFFERSON WILLIAM M	LTC	0-0341625	0556	1
JEFFERY WILLIAM A	COL	0-0172360	0648	3
JEFFORDS ALEXANDER	MAJ	0-1296379	0260	2
JEFFREY ALLAN S	CPT	0-1313895	1145	2
JEFFREY ALVIS	MAJ	0-1998722	0264	1
JEFFREY BERNARD	LTC	0-0464213	0151	1
JEFFREY DORIS R	2LT	L-0602566	0345	2
JEFFREY JOHN G	1LT	0-5403215	0762	2
JEFFREY ROSS C	LTC	0-0340195	0360	3
JEFFREY WALTER R	COL	0-0117104	0752	3
JEFFREY-SMITH C W	CPT	0-0450965	1045	2
JEFFREYS DAVID E	CPT	0-2033541	0859	1
JEFFRIES ALBERT G	CPT	0-1167483	1147	1
JEFFRIES GURLEY T	MAJ	0-1922601	0866	1
JEFFRIES JAMES F	LTC	0-0172566	0959	3
JEFFRIES JOHN M	LTC	0-0236766	1064	3
JEFFRIES LYMAN B	CPT	0-1293961	1046	2
JEFFRIES LYNN	CPT	0-0281109	0344	2
JEFFRIES ONDE H	CPT	0-2262448	0963	1
JEFFRIES ROBERT F	1LT	0-1060146	0446	2
JEFFRY KENNETH W	CW4	W-2105241	0864	1
JEFFS DEAN R	LTC	0-0376473	0666	1
JEHLE EDWARD J	LTC	0-1554018	0566	1
JEKEL JR ALEX S	CW2	W-2215182	0667	1
JELINEK ENGELBERT	MAJ	0-0238430	0865	3
JELINEK JERRY R	LTC	0-1060497	1062	1
JELINEK JOSEPH J	CW2	W-2152388	0857	1
JELKS THOMAS O	MAJ	0-1997772	0666	1
JELLINGS HAZEL T	2LT	N-0789363	0645	1
JELLINGS RAYMOND P	MAJ	0-1311395	1060	1
JELLISON DONALD H	1LT	0-2034539	0561	2
JELLISON EDWARD C	LTC	0-0926830	1164	1
JELSMA MEREDITH H	LTC	0-0295854	0456	1
JELSCHINO SAMUEL J	CPT	0-0336666	0246	2
JELY OTTO	CW2	W-2147947	0555	1
JEMERIN EDWARD E	MAJ	0-0429233	1045	2
JEMISON JOHN H	MAJ	0-1045650	0561	1
JENCKS FREDERICK	LTC	0-0263540	0864	3
JENDRZEJCAK JOHN C	2LT	0-1688442	0450	1
JENEFSKY JOHN J	CW2	W-2143127	0554	1
JENISON DANIELL A	MAJ	0-1170435	1265	1
JENISTA JOHN E	LTC	0-0418915	0860	1
JENKE HERBERT P	MAJ	0-0981987	1061	1
JENKINS ALLISON W	CPT	0-0506931	1053	2
JENKINS ALTON A	COL	0-0311956	0964	3
JENKINS ALVIN R	MAJ	0-1304225	0963	1
JENKINS ARCHIE M	MAJ	0-0184490	0648	3
JENKINS ARTHUR L	CW2	W-2152219	1061	1
JENKINS CHARLES H	LTC	0-0495633	0767	1
JENKINS DANIEL P	LTC	0-0508955	1263	1
JENKINS DON A	LTC	0-0167537	0253	3
JENKINS EDWARD L	CW3	RW-2141596	0162	1
JENKINS ELLSWORTH	CW2	W-2152141	0261	1
JENKINS ELMER L	CPT	0-1177019	1158	2
JENKINS ELZIE H	1LT	0-1293595	0945	2
JENKINS EUGENE	CW2	W-2145939	1057	1
JENKINS EVERETT H	MAJ	0-0257141	0457	3
JENKINS FRANK P	LTC	0-0470964	0565	3
JENKINS FRANK W	CW2	W-2152317	0960	1

NAME	GRADE	SVC NO	DATE RET MO YR	RET CODE
JENKINS FRANKLIN M	CW3	W-2152229	1162	1
JENKINS GENEVA	1LT	N-0736283	0547	1
JENKINS GEORGE S	LTC	0-0481129	0155	1
JENKINS HADLEY E	COL	0-1548085	0661	1
JENKINS HAROLD A	LTC	0-0441117	0863	1
JENKINS HAZEL O	CPT	N-0783542	0646	1
JENKINS HERBERT G	CPT	0-0253110	0948	1
JENKINS HERBERT H	CPT	0-1318803	0546	2
JENKINS HORACE R	WO1	W-2149381	0557	2
JENKINS HUBERT A	2LT	0-2000482	0460	1
JENKINS HUGHES B	COL	0-0275384	0661	3
JENKINS JAMES M	CPT	0-0228744	0362	3
JENKINS JOHN P	MAJ	0-1101891	0164	1
JENKINS JOHNS K	CPT	0-1046145	0445	2
JENKINS JOSEPH D	CW3	W-2149770	1162	1
JENKINS JOSEPH H	CPT	0-0495049	0946	2
JENKINS JOSEPH W	LTC	0-1100165	0263	1
JENKINS JOSEPH W	LTC	0-1323136	0863	1
JENKINS JR CLAUDE	2LT	0-1292183	0544	2
JENKINS JR DELBERT R	CW2	W-2210186	0964	1
JENKINS JR GEORGE L	MAJ	0-1685731	0565	1
JENKINS JR HARRY S	LTC	0-1545218	0762	1
JENKINS JR ROBERT D	LTC	0-1103237	0662	1
JENKINS LEWIS R	1LT	0-0918844	0145	2
JENKINS LLOYD P	CW2	W-2120922	1049	1
JENKINS LYNN EARLE	MAJ	0-0361185	0762	1
JENKINS MARTIN H	MAJ	0-0438222	0154	1
JENKINS MELVIN	2LT	0-1053191	0644	2
JENKINS MITCHELL	LTC	0-0233967	0156	3
JENKINS NELSEN B	MAJ	0-0921266	1146	2
JENKINS NYE P	CPT	0-1302825	0947	1
JENKINS PLINY W	LTC	0-0410693	0761	1
JENKINS RICHARD V	MAJ	0-1645077	0756	1
JENKINS RICHARD W	LTC	0-1284340	0862	1
JENKINS SIDNEY C	LTC	0-0234720	0657	1
JENKINS STANLEY G	CPT	0-1557470	0248	2
JENKINS THOMAS	LTC	0-0146157	0544	2
JENKINS VERL P	LTC	0-0309006	0165	3
JENKINS VERNE W	CPT	0-0269852	0857	3
JENKINS WILBERT L	1LT	0-0385460	0545	2
JENKINS WILFORD M	MAJ	0-2034092	0166	1
JENKINS WILLIAM E	MAJ	0-1924117	0365	1
JENKINS WILLIAM F	MAJ	0-1555998	0557	1
JENKINS WILLIAM H	MAJ	0-1948323	1060	1
JENKINS WILLIAM J	LTC	0-1061984	0463	1
JENKINS WILLIAM N	COL	0-0210890	0955	3
JENKINS WILLIAM R	1LT	0-1058561	0846	2
JENKINS WILLIAM W	LTC	0-0263039	1262	3
JENKINS WOODROW R	1LT	0-1288060	0145	2
JENKINSON DONALD R	MAJ	0-2096481	0863	1
JENKS DONALD M	1LT	0-1945843	0146	2
JENKS JR WILLIAM S	1LT	0-0401651	0445	2
JENKS RICHARD L	LTC	0-1030257	1061	1
JENKS WILLIAM L	MAJ	0-0759939	1064	2
JENNE EDWARD S	LTC	0-0484291	0753	1
JENNER WILLIAM B	CW2	W-2000902	1262	3
JENNES SIDNEY W	1LT	0-0502131	1143	2
JENNESS KENNETH L	MAJ	0-0970625	0666	1
JENNEY ALEXANDER	MAJ	0-0420852	0766	3
JENNI CLARENCE M	COL	0-0277433	1156	3
JENNINGS ALBERT W	WO1	W-2106756	0646	1
JENNINGS ARTHUR J	COL	0-0224361	0963	3
JENNINGS CATLIN B	1LT	0-1167485	0448	2
JENNINGS CHARLES H	CPT	0-0515842	0846	2
JENNINGS CHARLES J	2LT	0-1641433	0246	2
JENNINGS CLAUDE C	2LT	0-1845055	0544	2
JENNINGS CLINTON S	CW3	W-2146895	0565	1
JENNINGS CURTIS E	CPT	0-1949806	0157	1
JENNINGS DOROTHY V	1LT	N-0901342	0155	2
JENNINGS EARL J	MAJ	0-1646285	0957	1
JENNINGS EDWARD O	CPT	0-1915452	1060	2
JENNINGS HAMLET G	1LT	0-0327924	0445	2
JENNINGS HARRY G	LTC	0-0438963	1163	1
JENNINGS HARRY T	CW3	W-2145455	1064	2
JENNINGS HOWARD M	LTC	0-1052406	1262	1

NAME	GRADE	SVC NO	DATE RET MO YR	RET CODE
JENNINGS HOWARD W	CPT	0-1305930	0452	1
JENNINGS JACK H	CPT	0-0336604	1145	1
JENNINGS JAMES H	CW4	W-2001521	0358	3
JENNINGS JAMES R	LTC	0-0268460	0657	1
JENNINGS JASON E	COL	0-0238451	0265	3
JENNINGS JOHN L	MAJ	0-0478387	0646	2
JENNINGS JR FLOYD C	1LT	0-1011282	0346	1
JENNINGS JR JOHN C	CPT	0-0324726	0146	2
JENNINGS JR JOHN F	LTC	0-1101512	0764	1
JENNINGS JR JOHN R	MAJ	0-1540860	0764	1
JENNINGS LESTER F	MAJ	0-0173950	0945	2
JENNINGS LOUIS A	MAJ	0-1107506	0761	1
JENNINGS LOUIS V	CPT	0-1926518	0464	1
JENNINGS MARY R	1LT	N-0792622	1150	2
JENNINGS MAURICE R	LTC	0-0234482	0962	3
JENNINGS OWEN R	CPT	0-0334842	1054	3
JENNINGS ROBERT S	CW3	W-2148796	0963	1
JENNINGS ROY A	CPT	0-1845448	1047	2
JENNINGS ROY L	2LT	0-1293418	1143	2
JENNINGS RUFUS F	CW3	W-2205918	1065	1
JENNINGS SAMUEL W	CPT	0-0977720	0760	2
JENNINGS T J	CW3	W-2205286	0666	1
JENNINGS THOMAS C	MAJ	0-1300650	0958	1
JENNINGS VERNE H	CPT	0-0148522	0757	3
JENNINGS WALTER F	MAJ	0-0463355	0446	2
JENNINGS WALTER G	COL	0-0174217	0157	3
JENNINGS WILLIAM I	MAJ	0-1321119	1058	1
JENNINGS ZACK O	CPT	0-0348053	1045	2
JENNY JR JOHN M	CPT	0-0412009	0745	2
JENNY LOUIS A	COL	0-0245627	0648	3
JENSEN ALFRED	CPT	0-0138844	1054	3
JENSEN ANON R	1LT	0-1295029	0246	2
JENSEN ARNOLD L	COL	0-0174743	0446	2
JENSEN AXEL	COL	0-0209635	0756	3
JENSEN CARL P N	LTC	0-0979807	0158	2
JENSEN CHESTER H	CW2	W-2147312	0261	1
JENSEN CHRISTIAN	LTC	0-0297348	0263	1
JENSEN ELERY N	MAJ	0-0327273	0365	3
JENSEN EVALYN D	2LT	N-0775107	1046	1
JENSEN GEORGE F	MAJ	0-1315468	0259	1
JENSEN HANS W	MAJ	0-0437001	0950	1
JENSEN HAROLD W	MAJ	0-0152304	0955	3
JENSEN HARRY P	LTC	0-1103027	0861	1
JENSEN JAMES H	CPT	0-0228438	0844	2
JENSEN JAMES W	LTC	0-1050325	0766	1
JENSEN JENS R	MAJ	0-0494757	0849	1
JENSEN JOHN T	LTC	0-0276191	0866	3
JENSEN JORGEN P	MAJ	0-0246073	1166	3
JENSEN LANDRY	1LT	0-0888958	0448	1
JENSEN LARS K	WO1	W-2141324	1053	1
JENSEN LEO R	COL	0-0905961	0562	1
JENSEN LEOTA M	CPT	N-0736752	0546	1
JENSEN LESLIE M	COL	0-0200134	0246	2
JENSEN LLOYD O	LTC	0-1330732	0766	1
JENSEN LYLE H	WO1	W-2141735	0654	2
JENSEN MARTIN E	LTC	0-0235549	0561	3
JENSEN NIELS P	MAJ	0-0503330	0346	2
JENSEN NORMAN C	LTC	0-0375770	0760	1
JENSEN NORMAN R	1LT	0-2010357	0147	2
JENSEN ROBERT J	CPT	0-1015098	1046	2
JENSEN ROBERT J	CPT	0-1306510	0146	2
JENSEN ROBERT L	LTC	0-1647970	0666	1
JENSEN ROSS E	LTC	0-0225598	0663	3
JENSEN UFFE T	CPT	0-0422669	0443	2
JENSEN VERNE M	LTC	0-1555574	0663	1
JENSEN WILLARD W	LTC	0-0454648	1158	1
JENSON GEORGE W	CW3	W-2152318	0263	1
JENTES CLARENCE L	CW3	W-2142035	1160	1
JENTZ GILBERT L	LTC	0-0261018	1266	3
JEPSON AUSTIN W	1LT	0-1010218	0346	2
JEPSON JR HERBERT A	CPT	0-0947429	0361	2
JERABECK JOSEPH R	LTC	0-0406012	0267	3
JERABEK MARGARET F	1LT	N-0751242	0146	1
JERAM JR FREDERICK	CPT	0-1327746	0947	1
JEREMIAS JOSEPH B	MAJ	0-1554566	0460	1

NAME	GRADE	SVC NO	DATE RET MO YR	RET CODE
JEREMIAS RICHARD A	CW3	W-2146510	1162	1
JERGE SUTTON	LTC	0-0498909	0550	1
JERKINS JR DANIEL M	CPT	0-0450725	1145	2
JERLES ROBERT F	MAJ	0-0252762	0246	2
JERMAIN LEONARD L	1LT	0-0388132	1044	2
JERNBERG JR CARL F	CPT	0-0360061	0545	2
JERNIGAN JACK	MAJ	0-1012369	1059	1
JERNIGAN JOHN H	MAJ	0-0889075	0954	1
JERNIGAN LAWRENCE C	CPT	0-1172929	0858	2
JERNIGAN OTIS H	LTC	0-0253442	0467	3
JERNIGIN RUSSELL C	LTC	0-0108044	0956	3
JEROME EDWARD	1LT	0-0462578	0345	2
JERRETT FRANCIS A	1LT	0-2035948	1046	2
JERRETT FRANKIE L	2LT	N-0703470	1046	2
JERRISON DOROTHY L	MAJ	L-1010359	1067	1
JERRY JR GEORGE	LTC	0-1798354	0766	1
JERSIN HAROLD E S	MAJ	0-0261199	0167	3
JERSIN PEARL D G	MAJ	N-0742262	0562	1
JERVEY CHARLES H	MAJ	0-0261557	0661	1
JERVEY JESSIE M	2LT	N-0763724	0145	1
JERVIS FREDERICK	1LT	0-0547320	0147	2
JESSE FRANCIS R	MAJ	0-1336652	0962	1
JESSE HAROLD L	CW3	W-2148002	1164	1
JESSE MARIE	2LT	N-0721984	0345	1
JESSEE GEORGE W	CPT	0-0405010	0645	2
JESSEE JR WILLIAM D	MAJ	0-1893739	0766	1
JESSEE ROBERT O	2LT	0-0105388	0355	3
JESSEN HOWARD W	CPT	0-2262522	1062	1
JESSUP DANIEL A	CPT	0-0375234	0144	2
JESSUP ERNEST O	COL	0-0354716	0148	1
JESSUP JR DALE C	MAJ	0-1214021	0761	1
JESSUP WALTER E	LTC	0-0105378	0548	3
JESTER JR JOHN C	MAJ	0-0257346	1167	3
JETER ANDREW H	CW3	W-2206284	1065	1
JETER LEWIS K	LTC	0-0348682	0360	1
JETER ROYAL C	CPT	0-0953637	0161	1
JETT BENNIE	CW2	W-2149844	0356	1
JETT CHARLES E	LTC	0-1252889	0966	1
JETT JACKSON R	1LT	0-0454308	0944	2
JETT JOHN D	MAJ	0-2033048	0662	1
JETT JR PRESTON R	CPT	0-0971298	0762	1
JETT OSCAR H R	LTC	0-1046837	1161	1
JETT SHELBY	2LT	0-0410978	0943	2
JETTON CLYDE T	MAJ	0-0454140	0547	1
JETTON MARION W	CPT	0-0309693	0461	3
JEWASINSKI STANLEY A	LTC	0-0190982	0456	3
JEWEL CHARLES A	LTC	0-0917076	0866	3
JEWELL DEAN K	LTC	0-0049924	0766	1
JEWELL EDWARD S	CPT	0-0248904	1163	3
JEWELL FRED J	LTC	0-0520673	0764	1
JEWELL HORACE J	CPT	0-2009972	0556	1
JEWELL JOSEPH L	CPT	0-2001014	0860	1
JEWELL JR FRANK	MAJ	0-1283968	0862	1
JEWELL LOIS R	LTC	N-0729397	0163	1
JEWELL WALTER H	MAJ	0-0554540	1262	1
JEWETT ALLEN C	MAJ	0-0985286	0467	2
JEWETT ARNO J	COL	0-0297516	0867	3
JEWETT DAVID G	1LT	0-0888281	0645	2
JEWETT HARVEY E	MAJ	0-1300335	0663	1
JEWETT KELSEY H	LTC	0-0177286	1059	3
JEWETT LOUIS F	LTC	0-0346604	0561	1
JEWETT MAURICE G	COL	0-0166442	0556	3
JILES JAMES W	MAJ	0-1579836	0756	2
JILES JULIAN C	MAJ	0-1307700	0859	1
JILES NEIL L	CPT	0-1286849	1045	2
JILES SR VIRGIL L	CW2	W-2205295	0261	1
JILL HERBERT G	MAJ	0-0369820	0154	2
JIMENEZ ERNEST J	CW2	W-2143052	1059	1
JIMENEZ JOSEPH W	CPT	0-1923149	0667	1
JIMENEZ RUFINO	1LT	0-1896815	0150	1
JIMERSON NORMAN C	1LT	0-0539296	0147	2
JIMERSON WILLIE J	CPT	0-1936972	0366	1
JIMMERSON ALLEN M	1LT	0-1647105	0445	2
JINDRA GEORGE V	MAJ	0-2039482	0361	1
JINES FRITE	LTC	0-1945174	1055	1

NAME	GRADE	SVC NO	DATE RET MO YR	RET CODE
JINKENS JR GEORGE W	LTC	O-0508560	0357	1
JINKS ALVIS H	CPT	O-1286653	1265	1
JINKS CLARENCE A	MAJ	O-1167920	0857	1
JIPSON JR FLOYD L	LTC	O-0380837	0565	1
JIRIKOWIC EDWARD L	MAJ	O-2023634	0862	2
JOBE WERNER H	CW2	W-2205381	0361	1
JOBERT ARTHUR H	MAJ	O-0277521	1058	3
JOBES JAMES E	COL	O-0269368	0263	3
JOBES JR CHARLES A	2LT	O-1316810	1044	2
JOBSON ROBERT C	LTC	O-1824753	0967	1
JOCA JOHN G	2LT	O-0462582	1045	2
JOCHEM ROBERT N	WO1	W-2121217	1044	2
JOE PHILLIP Y	MAJ	O-2266337	1164	1
JOERG THOMAS F	MAJ	O-1296530	1061	1
JOERIN WILLIAM A	MAJ	O-1687034	0547	2
JOERN ALBERT E	2LT	O-2025303	0761	1
JOERS WILLIAM H	CW3	W-2150211	1163	1
JOFFE SAMUEL M	CPT	O-1695882	0145	1
JOHANNES URBAN J	CPT	O-1296862	0258	1
JOHANNESSON BLANCHE	MAJ	N-0779280	0765	1
JOHANNESSON JOHN F	2LT	O-1309742	1044	2
JOHANSEN EINER W	CPT	O-0240881	0965	3
JOHANSEN WILLARD W	MAJ	O-0994500	1263	1
JOHANSON ELLIS C	LTC	O-0310942	0667	3
JOHANSON HANS C	CW4	W-2142056	1055	1
JOHENNING ALVY G	LTC	O-0280397	0660	1
JOHN CLINTON F	COL	O-0131631	0656	3
JOHN HENRY J	LTC	O-0219873	0750	3
JOHN THEODORE J	1LT	O-1308825	0546	2
JOHNOROW HAROLD F	CW2	W-3150650	0166	1
JOHNER PAUL	LTC	O-0357355	1063	3
JOHNS ALEXANDER	CPT	O-1693408	0143	2
JOHNS ARTHUR	MAJ	O-2012264	0461	1
JOHNS CECIL	LTC	O-1053192	1161	1
JOHNS DAVID E	CPT	O-1577375	0852	1
JOHNS DAVID M	MAJ	O-2020424	1062	1
JOHNS EDWARD J	CPT	O-1174010	0347	2
JOHNS FORREST R	2LT	O-1081015	0960	1
JOHNS GEORGE E	2LT	O-1598427	0247	1
JOHNS GEORGE J	MAJ	O-0169929	0559	3
JOHNS GEORGE W	LTC	O-0202979	0856	3
JOHNS GRANVILLE	MAJ	O-1296381	0461	1
JOHNS HYLAND R	LTC	O-0170857	0350	3
JOHNS JAMES B	CPT	O-1314495	0764	1
JOHNS JAMES T	2LT	O-2008406	1058	1
JOHNS JESSIE R	CPT	O-1103718	0253	1
JOHNS JOHN L	LTC	O-0505047	0263	1
JOHNS JOHN N	MAJ	O-1636095	1154	2
JOHNS SAMUEL L	MAJ	O-1576191	0655	1
JOHNS SAMUEL N	MAJ	O-0332512	0866	3
JOHNSEN JOHN L	2LT	O-1286133	1044	2
JOHNSEN MELVIN M	MAJ	O-1550199	1060	1
JOHNSEN NORMAN M	MAJ	O-0319364	0846	2
JOHNSEN RAYMOND K	CPT	O-1698177	0454	2
JOHNSON AARON J	1LT	O-0961468	0851	1
JOHNSON ABRAHAM L	WO1	W-2108067	0944	2
JOHNSON ADAM B	2LT	O-1310249	0245	2
JOHNSON ADOLPH F	LTC	O-0212433	0861	3
JOHNSON AINAR F	1LT	O-1314022	0246	2
JOHNSON ALBERT F	MAJ	O-0146886	0550	3
JOHNSON ALBERT S	LTC	O-0214532	1060	1
JOHNSON ALBERT S	LTC	O-0239733	1263	3
JOHNSON ALBERT S	M G	O-0269201	1058	3
JOHNSON ALBIN I	CW4	W-2105220	0766	1
JOHNSON ALEX	CW2	W-2118121	0361	1
JOHNSON ALFRED W	LTC	O-1031328	1060	2
JOHNSON ALGON B	COL	O-0118356	0855	3
JOHNSON ALLAN W	MAJ	O-0349774	0158	2
JOHNSON ALTEN R	1LT	O-0493386	1153	1
JOHNSON ALVIN B	MAJ	O-0258526	0966	3
JOHNSON ALVIN W	MAJ	O-1577378	0759	1
JOHNSON ANDREW	MAJ	O-0320635	0653	1
JOHNSON ANNIE B	2LT	N-0725920	1044	1
JOHNSON ARNIE A	2LT	N-0728605	0545	1
JOHNSON ARTHUR	CPT	O-1178202	0247	1

NAME	GRADE	SVC NO	DATE RET MO YR	RET CODE
JOHNSON ARTHUR C	MAJ	O-1285948	0361	1
JOHNSON ARTHUR D	LTC	O-1574868	0561	1
JOHNSON ARTHUR D	CW4	W-2115869	0156	2
JOHNSON ARTHUR L	MAJ	O-1314023	1059	1
JOHNSON ARTHUR O	CPT	O-0231878	0448	2
JOHNSON ARVID T	MAJ	O-0546640	1047	2
JOHNSON ARVIL E	CW4	W-2141911	0765	1
JOHNSON ASBURY H L	CW2	W-2148088	0958	2
JOHNSON ATWOOD N	MAJ	O-2039443	0363	1
JOHNSON AUGUSTUS R	CPT	O-1113279	1263	1
JOHNSON AYRES W	COL	O-0154169	1052	3
JOHNSON BERENDT E	COL	O-0106073	0255	3
JOHNSON BERNARD C	CPT	O-0516944	0654	1
JOHNSON BERNARD F	CPT	O-0351914	0450	2
JOHNSON BERT	CPT	O-0188802	0645	1
JOHNSON BERTEL R	1LT	O-0384821	0845	2
JOHNSON BETTY J	MAJ	L-1010130	0964	1
JOHNSON BOTHWELL R	COL	O-0327315	1265	3
JOHNSON BURKE	MAJ	O-0337630	0448	2
JOHNSON BYRON T	CPT	O-0152788	1048	3
JOHNSON CAIFSON	COL	O-0337085	0865	1
JOHNSON CAMPBELL C	COL	O-0114668	1055	2
JOHNSON CARL F	MAJ	O-1554019	1163	1
JOHNSON CARL H	LTC	O-2049594	1166	1
JOHNSON CARL L	CPT	O-1914032	0641	1
JOHNSON CARL R	CW2	W-2214544	0967	1
JOHNSON CARTER H	LTC	O-0486797	0655	1
JOHNSON CARTER S	LTC	O-0258818	1264	3
JOHNSON CHARLES C	1LT	O-1945175	0446	1
JOHNSON CHARLES E	CPT	O-0888035	1048	1
JOHNSON CHARLES F	CW3	W-2152889	1263	1
JOHNSON CHARLES F	LTC	O-0485255	1165	3
JOHNSON CHARLES F	WO1	W-2115168	0157	1
JOHNSON CHARLES G	2LT	O-1334156	0446	2
JOHNSON CHARLES H	LTC	O-0338848	0760	1
JOHNSON CHARLES L	CPT	O-0538615	1050	1
JOHNSON CHARLES O	CW3	W-2150212	0866	1
JOHNSON CHARLES R	1LT	O-1044565	1145	2
JOHNSON CHARLES R	1LT	O-1549744	0345	2
JOHNSON CHARLES R	MAJ	O-4030816	0167	1
JOHNSON CHARLES R	CW2	W-3430453	1266	1
JOHNSON CHARLES S	MAJ	O-0213493	0344	2
JOHNSON CHARLES V	COL	O-0188542	0648	3
JOHNSON CHARLES W	LTC	O-0543869	0364	1
JOHNSON CHARLES W	MAJ	O-1107508	0160	1
JOHNSON CHARLES W	1LT	O-1289435	0245	2
JOHNSON CHARLES W	CW2	W-2152551	0365	1
JOHNSON CLAIRE E	MAJ	O-2096522	1166	1
JOHNSON CLARENCE A	LTC	O-0225815	1164	3
JOHNSON CLARENCE B	LTC	O-0475903	0352	1
JOHNSON CLARENCE E	COL	O-0125764	0855	3
JOHNSON CLARENCE E	MAJ	O-0237942	0355	3
JOHNSON CLARENCE R	CPT	O-1168295	1057	1
JOHNSON CLARK E	LTC	O-1302005	0764	1
JOHNSON CLAUDE	CPT	O-0208711	0648	3
JOHNSON CLAUDE F	LTC	O-0169399	0958	3
JOHNSON CLIFFORD J	MAJ	O-0993291	0165	1
JOHNSON CLIFFORD J	CPT	O-1581838	1057	1
JOHNSON CLIFFORD L	CPT	O-0125755	0452	3
JOHNSON CLIFFORD M	CW2	W-2110602	1048	2
JOHNSON CLIFFORD R	CW2	RW-2144365	0664	1
JOHNSON CLIFTON E	LTC	O-0311333	0267	3
JOHNSON CLIFTON R	MAJ	O-1304226	0862	1
JOHNSON CLYDE D	MAJ	O-1685672	0664	1
JOHNSON CLYDE R	MAJ	O-1685588	0562	1
JOHNSON CURTISS S	1LT	O-1062895	1045	2
JOHNSON DALE N	LTC	O-1688453	0266	1
JOHNSON DARWIN L	LTC	O-0310111	0859	1
JOHNSON DAVID F	2LT	O-5505448	0860	2
JOHNSON DAVID R	1LT	O-1061743	0352	1
JOHNSON DECATUR	CPT	O-0293950	0648	1
JOHNSON DELOS L	1LT	O-0362398	0945	2
JOHNSON DENTON A	MAJ	O-2206161	0167	1
JOHNSON DONALD A	1LT	O-1599171	0950	1
JOHNSON DONALD B	COL	O-0329471	0364	3

NAME	GRADE	SVC NO	DATE RET MO YR	RET CODE
JOHNSON DONALD C	MAJ	O-1341435	0267	1
JOHNSON DONALD C	CW3	W-2207966	1265	1
JOHNSON DONALD E	MAJ	O-0977390	0365	1
JOHNSON DONALD F	CW3	W-2126086	0559	1
JOHNSON DONALD M	1LT	O-1031252	0845	2
JOHNSON EARL C	MAJ	O-1595598	1055	1
JOHNSON EARLE K	MAJ	O-0230340	1263	3
JOHNSON EARLING H	LTC	O-0451127	1059	1
JOHNSON EBEN C	1LT	O-1016147	0146	2
JOHNSON EDDIE L	CW3	W-2149117	0564	1
JOHNSON EDGAR A J	LTC	O-0165488	0260	3
JOHNSON EDGAR F	CPT	O-0465014	1046	1
JOHNSON EDGAR W	MAJ	O-2036662	0561	1
JOHNSON EDSEL I	CPT	O-0441958	0152	2
JOHNSON EDWARD	CPT	O-0196230	1046	1
JOHNSON EDWARD A	COL	O-0920578	0267	3
JOHNSON EDWARD H	CW2	W-2150966	0563	1
JOHNSON EDWARD J	LTC	O-0481602	1154	1
JOHNSON EDWARD L	CW2	RW-2209414	0461	1
JOHNSON EDWARD S	MAJ	O-0323815	0861	3
JOHNSON EDWIN H	MAJ	O-0174299	1060	3
JOHNSON EDWIN N	MAJ	O-1797469	0859	1
JOHNSON ELLSWORTH	2LT	O-1312938	0645	2
JOHNSON ELMER D	LTC	O-0174165	0658	3
JOHNSON ELMER G	LTC	O-1533356	1162	1
JOHNSON ELMER H	LTC	O-0283914	0166	3
JOHNSON ELMER R	MAJ	O-1109387	0665	1
JOHNSON ELVA K	COL	O-0192444	0858	1
JOHNSON ELWYN O	COL	O-0131878	1055	3
JOHNSON EMIL W	MAJ	O-0269677	0262	1
JOHNSON EMMETT N	1LT	O-1303897	0246	2
JOHNSON ERNEST A	MAJ	O-0487520	0354	1
JOHNSON ERNEST B	MAJ	O-0517777	0149	2
JOHNSON ERNEST C	CW4	W-2104176	0761	1
JOHNSON ERNEST S	LTC	O-0288273	0764	3
JOHNSON EUGENE C	CW4	W-2006440	0566	3
JOHNSON EUGENE E	LTC	O-1174604	0961	1
JOHNSON EVERETT H	MAJ	O-1335928	0565	1
JOHNSON FLORENCE L	1LT	N-0741479	0346	1
JOHNSON FLOYD M	1LT	O-1301313	0545	2
JOHNSON FLOYD W	MAJ	O-0183243	0853	3
JOHNSON FOBIAN E	MAJ	O-0237539	0655	3
JOHNSON FRANCIS M	CPT	O-1115303	0847	2
JOHNSON FRANCIS M	LTC	O-1577382	0463	1
JOHNSON FRANK A	MAJ	O-0902857	1044	2
JOHNSON FRANK C	CPT	O-0189536	1149	3
JOHNSON FRANK R	COL	O-0221977	0555	3
JOHNSON FRANK S	MAJ	O-0308235	0767	3
JOHNSON FRANK W	MAJ	O-1049228	0660	1
JOHNSON FRANKLIN C	COL	O-0261960	0158	1
JOHNSON FRANKLIN C	CPT	O-0449153	0247	2
JOHNSON FRANKLYN A	1LT	O-0444613	0845	2
JOHNSON FRED	LTC	O-0503770	0954	1
JOHNSON FREDERICK	COL	O-0232180	0860	1
JOHNSON FREDERICK	LTC	O-0353717	0162	1
JOHNSON GABRIEL	CW4	W-2142163	0466	1
JOHNSON GEORGE C	LTC	O-0268286	0254	2
JOHNSON GEORGE C	MAJ	O-1283782	1063	1
JOHNSON GEORGE E	MAJ	O-0468899	1262	1
JOHNSON GEORGE F	CW3	W-2208633	0367	1
JOHNSON GEORGE H	COL	O-0259644	1060	3
JOHNSON GEORGE L	CPT	O-0264655	0645	2
JOHNSON GEORGE M	LTC	O-0289353	1166	3
JOHNSON GEORGE R	1LT	O-0482029	0845	1
JOHNSON GEORGE T	LTC	O-0422634	0361	1
JOHNSON GEORGE W J	LTC	O-0916620	0858	2
JOHNSON GEORGE Y	MAJ	O-2025116	0862	1
JOHNSON GERALDINE	MAJ	N-0755060	0665	1
JOHNSON GERDEN F	COL	O-0303751	0747	1
JOHNSON GILBERT E	LTC	O-0284734	0265	3
JOHNSON GILMOR L	CPT	O-1317018	0457	1
JOHNSON GLEN H	MAJ	O-0976221	0162	1
JOHNSON GLENN A	CW2	W-2110018	0461	1
JOHNSON GORDON H	LTC	O-1181314	0663	1
JOHNSON GORDON R	MAJ	O-1319125	1063	1

NAME	GRADE	SVC NO	DATE RET MO YR	RET CODE
JOHNSON GORDON W	LTC	O-0356765	1160	1
JOHNSON GOVE	LTC	O-1011303	1062	1
JOHNSON GRACE L	MAJ	N-0778261	0665	1
JOHNSON GRANVILLE	MAJ	O-0336578	0862	1
JOHNSON GRANVILLE	CPT	O-1332707	0157	1
JOHNSON GREETA M E	CPT	L-0912231	0151	1
JOHNSON GROVER G	CW2	W-3400020	0267	1
JOHNSON GUSTAV F	COL	O-0309611	1166	3
JOHNSON GUSTAVE E	LTC	O-1314496	0964	1
JOHNSON GUY S	MAJ	O-1686622	0665	1
JOHNSON HAL C	LTC	O-0333651	0450	3
JOHNSON HARLEY E	COL	O-0107934	0648	3
JOHNSON HAROLD B	LTC	O-1285247	0661	1
JOHNSON HAROLD C	LTC	O-0324461	0446	2
JOHNSON HAROLD E	CPT	O-0249030	1051	1
JOHNSON HAROLD E	LTC	O-0324127	1060	1
JOHNSON HAROLD E	MAJ	O-2021635	0767	1
JOHNSON HAROLD F	CW4	W-2104178	0660	1
JOHNSON HAROLD J	LTC	O-0503623	0546	1
JOHNSON HAROLD L	1LT	O-1548865	1146	2
JOHNSON HAROLD R	2LT	O-1317534	0344	2
JOHNSON HAROLD S	LTC	O-1284882	0761	1
JOHNSON HAROLD T	CW3	W-2206110	1266	1
JOHNSON HARRIS E	COL	O-0320609	1067	3
JOHNSON HARRY A	COL	O-0247662	0965	3
JOHNSON HARRY B	LTC	O-0359908	1161	1
JOHNSON HARRY H	M G	O-0172820	0655	3
JOHNSON HARRY O	CW3	W-2120884	0154	1
JOHNSON HARVEY B	CPT	O-1175182	0646	2
JOHNSON HENRY N	CPT	O-0178691	0149	3
JOHNSON HENRY S	MAJ	O-0204471	0250	3
JOHNSON HENRY T	LTC	O-1042846	0561	1
JOHNSON HENRY W	MAJ	O-2056263	0967	3
JOHNSON HENSLEY S	LTC	O-0022305	1060	1
JOHNSON HERBERT B	CPT	O-1690112	0745	2
JOHNSON HERBERT W	MAJ	O-1585676	0765	3
JOHNSON HERMAN F	CW3	W-2007994	0566	3
JOHNSON HERMAN T	COL	O-0249157	0461	3
JOHNSON HILMER O F	COL	O-1581198	1066	1
JOHNSON HORACE L	COL	O-0181114	0959	3
JOHNSON HOWARD	MAJ	O-0969453	0562	1
JOHNSON HOWARD W	MAJ	O-1298070	0456	1
JOHNSON HUBERT V	COL	O-0330842	0565	1
JOHNSON IRA J	WO1	W-2146470	0253	1
JOHNSON IRA T	CPT	N-0763334	0652	1
JOHNSON IVAN S C	CPT	O-0197952	0145	2
JOHNSON JACK H	LTC	O-1183858	0167	1
JOHNSON JACK H	LTC	O-1332070	0463	1
JOHNSON JACK W	CPT	O-1183097	0257	1
JOHNSON JAMES A	CPT	O-1109388	0252	2
JOHNSON JAMES B	CPT	O-0487948	0250	1
JOHNSON JAMES B	MAJ	O-2019598	1162	1
JOHNSON JAMES D	1LT	O-1113773	1045	2
JOHNSON JAMES D	2LT	O-1302656	0446	1
JOHNSON JAMES D	CW4	W-2143925	1055	1
JOHNSON JAMES E	MAJ	O-0452066	0655	1
JOHNSON JAMES E	MAJ	O-0909986	0846	2
JOHNSON JAMES F	CPT	O-1317019	0457	1
JOHNSON JAMES H	LTC	O-0314237	0962	2
JOHNSON JAMES H	2LT	O-0446746	1044	2
JOHNSON JAMES O	MAJ	O-1636096	1058	1
JOHNSON JAMES P	CPT	O-2004965	0764	2
JOHNSON JAMES R	LTC	O-1117637	1263	1
JOHNSON JAMES V	CPT	O-1951624	0259	1
JOHNSON JAMES W	CPT	O-0266598	1263	3
JOHNSON JAY E	CPT	O-1017495	0147	2
JOHNSON JAY R	LTC	O-0390228	0766	1
JOHNSON JENNINGS B	CPT	O-0246335	1044	2
JOHNSON JENS C	LTC	O-1108766	1166	1
JOHNSON JERRELL G	LTC	O-1015224	0163	1
JOHNSON JESS K	MAJ	O-1293598	1060	1
JOHNSON JESSE J	LTC	O-1589930	1162	1
JOHNSON JESSE J	MAJ	O-2025368	0266	1
JOHNSON JESSE L	LTC	O-1595599	0967	1
JOHNSON JOE P	LTC	O-1594922	0859	1

NAME	GRADE	SVC NO	DATE RET MO YR	RET CODE
JOHNSON JOEL F	LTC	0-1303898	0762	1
JOHNSON JOHN	CPT	0-0495207	0847	1
JOHNSON JOHN C	MAJ	0-0173657	1148	3
JOHNSON JOHN C	CPT	0-1312170	1047	2
JOHNSON JOHN E	MAJ	0-0471291	0244	2
JOHNSON JOHN E	LTC	0-0490169	0357	2
JOHNSON JOHN H	CPT	0-2262898	0861	1
JOHNSON JOHN H	CW3	W-2149900	1262	1
JOHNSON JOHN J	COL	0-0205340	0752	3
JOHNSON JOHN R	COL	0-0290015	0765	1
JOHNSON JOHN R	CPT	0-1293965	0763	1
JOHNSON JOHN R	CW4	W-2104179	1054	1
JOHNSON JOHN S B	COL	0-0269112	0467	3
JOHNSON JOHN T	CPT	0-0352134	1145	2
JOHNSON JOHN W	2LT	0-1183553	0444	2
JOHNSON JOHNNIE	2LT	0-2055886	1044	2
JOHNSON JOHNNIE G	MAJ	0-1885428	1165	1
JOHNSON JONATHAN L	LTC	0-0115364	0160	3
JOHNSON JOSEPH	CPT	0-1575380	0155	1
JOHNSON JOSEPH C	LTC	0-0327797	0155	3
JOHNSON JOSEPH K	LTC	0-0182792	0157	3
JOHNSON JOSEPH M	COL	0-0287586	0159	1
JOHNSON JOSEPH M	LTC	0-0342994	0859	1
JOHNSON JOSEPH S	LTC	0-0687946	0964	1
JOHNSON JOSEPH T	LTC	0-0346960	1164	3
JOHNSON JR ALAN M	MAJ	0-0324490	0451	2
JOHNSON JR ALFRED L	CW2	W-2152193	0660	2
JOHNSON JR ANDREW J	MAJ	0-2262761	1064	1
JOHNSON JR ARTHUR W	CW3	W-2203497	1165	1
JOHNSON JR BASCOM	LTC	0-0333077	0266	3
JOHNSON JR CHARLIE W	LTC	0-0406703	0560	1
JOHNSON JR CLARKE E	1LT	0-0553497	0546	2
JOHNSON JR DAVID A	CW2	W-2147631	0562	1
JOHNSON JR DAVID T	MAJ	0-1013764	0163	1
JOHNSON JR EDWARD H	CPT	0-1111692	1163	1
JOHNSON JR FRANK E	MAJ	0-2020425	0563	1
JOHNSON JR FRANK W	CW3	W-2146982	1164	1
JOHNSON JR FRED H	1LT	0-1633312	0246	2
JOHNSON JR GRAYDON W	LTC	0-1578663	0662	1
JOHNSON JR HAROLD E	MAJ	0-2032958	0263	1
JOHNSON JR HAROLD H	MAJ	0-2289514	0962	1
JOHNSON JR HARRY	LTC	0-0172268	C-50	3
JOHNSON JR HENRY A	COL	0-0206579	0754	1
JOHNSON JR HERMAN J	CPT	0-0311177	1043	2
JOHNSON JR HOWARD A	CPT	0-0965264	1160	1
JOHNSON JR JAMES F	CW3	W-2141724	0360	1
JOHNSON JR JAMES T	COL	0-0195328	0561	1
JOHNSON JR JOHN J	1LT	0-1283616	1047	2
JOHNSON JR JOHN L	1LT	0-1061153	1045	1
JOHNSON JR JOSEPH A	LTC	0-0336504	0856	1
JOHNSON JR L R	LTC	0-0410072	0161	1
JOHNSON JR LAWRENCE	LTC	0-1176681	0667	1
JOHNSON JR ORESTES B	2LT	0-1059851	1044	1
JOHNSON JR OSCAR H	CW3	W-2151018	0463	1
JOHNSON JR PERCY S	CPT	0-0502461	0546	1
JOHNSON JR RAYMOND	MAJ	0-4006059	0567	1
JOHNSON JR ROGNAR P	CPT	0-4007069	0764	2
JOHNSON JR RUSSELL W	LTC	0-1905457	0566	1
JOHNSON JR SAMUEL N	1LT	0-0407361	0846	1
JOHNSON JR WALTER A	MAJ	0-1050776	0661	1
JOHNSON JR WALTER B	LTC	0-1640599	1265	1
JOHNSON JR WARREN W	1LT	0-1283078	0346	2
JOHNSON JR WILLIAM R	LTC	0-0241434	0364	3
JOHNSON JR WILLIAM S	CW4	W-2109662	1060	1
JOHNSON JUANITA G	MAJ	N-0798882	0665	1
JOHNSON JULIAN B	MAJ	0-1874876	0565	1
JOHNSON JULIE R	CPT	N-0776209	1046	1
JOHNSON KATHARINE	LTC	N-0720816	0162	1
JOHNSON KEITH E	CPT	0-0985688	0561	1
JOHNSON KELSEY R	LTC	0-0494846	0265	3
JOHNSON KENNETH A	LTC	0-0295950	0157	1
JOHNSON KENNETH A	1LT	0-1081521	0746	2
JOHNSON KENNETH S	MAJ	0-0234895	0765	3
JOHNSON KERMIT M	COL	0-0287486	0646	2
JOHNSON KIRBY W	CW2	W-2211847	1066	1

NAME	GRADE	SVC NO	DATE RET MO YR	RET CODE
JOHNSON KNUTH L	MAJ	0-0447988	0148	1
JOHNSON LACY L	1LT	0-2055797	0960	1
JOHNSON LANCELOT N	CW2	W-2151672	1060	1
JOHNSON LAVERNE F	WO1	W-2149073	0965	1
JOHNSON LAWRENCE C	MAJ	0-0409967	0844	2
JOHNSON LAWRENCE E	COL	0-0107071	0356	3
JOHNSON LAYMON A	CW2	W-2147129	0565	1
JOHNSON LEE F	CW2	W-3100508	1266	1
JOHNSON LEGRAND K	CPT	0-0415454	0346	1
JOHNSON LEIGH W	LTC	0-0298201	0255	2
JOHNSON LEMUEL R	LTC	0-1295030	0361	1
JOHNSON LEMUEL S	MAJ	0-1294062	0661	1
JOHNSON LEO L	MAJ	0-0976992	0961	1
JOHNSON LEON D	LTC	0-0427932	0266	1
JOHNSON LEONARD A	LTC	0-0927228	0765	1
JOHNSON LEONARD E	CW3	W-2144600	0160	2
JOHNSON LEROY G	1LT	0-0440615	0647	2
JOHNSON LESLIE H	1LT	0-0405334	1044	2
JOHNSON LEWIS M	LTC	0-0500757	0446	2
JOHNSON LEWIS N	2LT	0-1320046	0245	2
JOHNSON LEWIS S	LTC	0-1633214	0667	1
JOHNSON LLOYD F	WO1	W-2143029	1151	1
JOHNSON LORIN K	COL	0-0338745	0859	1
JOHNSON LOUIS F	MAJ	0-2262137	0364	1
JOHNSON LOYD R	MAJ	0-1030585	0759	1
JOHNSON LUTHER B	CPT	0-0370095	0462	2
JOHNSON LUTHER R	MAJ	0-2289190	0566	1
JOHNSON LUTHER O	CPT	0-0507789	1045	2
JOHNSON LYLE E	1LT	0-1039700	1047	1
JOHNSON LYMAN E	LTC	0-0228316	0761	3
JOHNSON MAJOR M	CW3	W-2151831	0562	2
JOHNSON MANNON A	MAJ	0-0410140	0656	2
JOHNSON MARCUS M	CW2	W-2113585	0247	2
JOHNSON MARGARET B	2LT	N-0743129	0944	1
JOHNSON MARION I	LTC	0-1181647	1262	1
JOHNSON MARION T	LTC	0-0229116	1158	1
JOHNSON MARK	CW2	W-2149215	0861	1
JOHNSON MARK H	COL	0-0319765	0257	1
JOHNSON MARTIN L	CW2	W-2150975	0159	1
JOHNSON MARTIN W	MAJ	0-1644459	0260	1
JOHNSON MARVIN E	1LT	0-0470846	1045	2
JOHNSON MAURICE E	LTC	0-0212566	0364	3
JOHNSON MAX E	MAJ	0-0232256	0246	2
JOHNSON MAX K	LTC	0-0389043	0361	1
JOHNSON MAXWELL	CPT	0-0508107	0647	1
JOHNSON MELVERN E	CPT	0-0373095	0244	2
JOHNSON MELVIN A	MAJ	0-1639058	0654	1
JOHNSON MELVIN A	CW2	W-2150919	0562	1
JOHNSON MELVIN I	1LT	0-1552527	0744	2
JOHNSON MELVIN W	LTC	0-0286688	0961	3
JOHNSON MELVIN W	LTC	0-0426848	0860	1
JOHNSON MERLIN S	MAJ	0-1553669	0762	1
JOHNSON MILDRED L	2LT	N-0700124	0531	1
JOHNSON MILO H	MAJ	0-0212826	1262	3
JOHNSON MIZE	CPT	0-0977099	1262	1
JOHNSON MOSES D	COL	0-0228747	0756	1
JOHNSON MOZELLE	CPT	L-0802041	0247	1
JOHNSON MURRY S	MAJ	0-1686387	0562	2
JOHNSON MYRON L	CPT	0-2055930	1046	1
JOHNSON NELLIS I	LTC	0-0385731	1167	1
JOHNSON NILS B	CPT	0-0168363	0853	3
JOHNSON NORMAN E	1LT	0-0466723	0546	2
JOHNSON NORRIS L	MAJ	0-0964196	0261	1
JOHNSON O B	2LT	0-1291373	0544	2
JOHNSON OLIVER	COL	0-0240388	0165	3
JOHNSON OSCAR HUGH	CW2	W-2146546	1058	1
JOHNSON PAUL	MAJ	0-1168302	0656	1
JOHNSON PAUL C	LTC	0-1105552	0965	1
JOHNSON PAUL H	2LT	0-0415027	0542	2
JOHNSON PAUL I	2LT	0-2023352	1046	2
JOHNSON PAUL L	CW3	W-2149321	1061	1
JOHNSON PAUL N	CPT	0-0347816	0753	1
JOHNSON PAUL W	CW3	W-2149443	0267	2
JOHNSON PEARL V	CPT	N-0732350	0849	2
JOHNSON PETER B	MAJ	0-2208566	0267	1

NAME	GRADE	SVC NO	DATE RET MO YR	RET CODE
JOHNSON PETER L	LTC	0-0178991	0648	3
JOHNSON PHILIP	LTC	0-0407957	0747	2
JOHNSON PHILIP M	COL	0-0123801	0955	2
JOHNSON PRESTON E	2LT	0-1003555	0144	2
JOHNSON QUENTIN L	CPT	0-1303512	0859	2
JOHNSON RALPH	LTC	0-0274407	0848	1
JOHNSON RALPH	MAJ	0-2025569	0760	1
JOHNSON RALPH C	LTC	0-1307250	0662	1
JOHNSON RALPH E	MAJ	0-0295864	1263	3
JOHNSON RALPH F	1LT	0-2011312	0853	1
JOHNSON RALPH J	MAJ	0-1559819	0159	1
JOHNSON RALPH V	1LT	0-1317536	0845	1
JOHNSON RANDOLPH L	2LT	0-0109515	1133	1
JOHNSON RAY E	LTC	0-1058998	0967	1
JOHNSON RAY M	LTC	0-1581200	1062	1
JOHNSON RAYBURN W	COL	0-0152034	0354	3
JOHNSON RAYMOND	MAJ	0-0450306	1047	1
JOHNSON RAYMOND	LTC	0-0551952	1062	1
JOHNSON RAYMOND C	LTC	0-0346705	0954	1
JOHNSON RAYMOND E	LTC	0-0358205	0567	3
JOHNSON RAYMOND H	2LT	0-1104889	0145	2
JOHNSON RAYMOND M	MAJ	0-1893538	0567	1
JOHNSON RAYMOND W	MAJ	0-1169588	1058	1
JOHNSON REUBEN H	CPT	0-2010330	0457	1
JOHNSON RICHARD A	2LT	0-2007358	1145	1
JOHNSON RICHARD C	LTC	0-0230095	C-53	1
JOHNSON RICHARD D	LTC	0-0355811	0261	1
JOHNSON RICHARD E	1LT	0-0970990	0552	1
JOHNSON RICHARD K	MAJ	0-0300813	1060	1
JOHNSON RICHARD L	LTC	0-0280576	1066	3
JOHNSON RICHARD L	1LT	0-1745202	0647	2
JOHNSON RILEY R	MAJ	0-0963700	0664	1
JOHNSON ROBERT B	LTC	0-0265638	0560	3
JOHNSON ROBERT B	1LT	0-1062230	1045	2
JOHNSON ROBERT D	MAJ	0-0576339	0765	1
JOHNSON ROBERT E	1LT	0-0548259	0346	2
JOHNSON ROBERT E	MAJ	0-1295886	1265	2
JOHNSON ROBERT E	MAJ	0-1305590	0358	1
JOHNSON ROBERT F	1LT	0-1312311	0845	2
JOHNSON ROBERT E	CW3	W-2153359	0264	1
JOHNSON ROBERT F L	MAJ	0-1554762	0357	2
JOHNSON ROBERT F	CW2	W-2149765	0857	1
JOHNSON ROBERT G	CPT	0-0422236	0146	2
JOHNSON ROBERT G	LTC	0-0444953	1054	1
JOHNSON ROBERT H	LTC	0-0377725	0759	1
JOHNSON ROBERT H	MAJ	0-0391137	0146	1
JOHNSON ROBERT H	CPT	0-0971208	0261	1
JOHNSON ROBERT J	LTC	0-0243110	0151	3
JOHNSON ROBERT L	COL	0-1001375	1161	1
JOHNSON ROBERT L	CPT	0-1917955	1061	1
JOHNSON ROBERT M	MAJ	0-0503137	0645	2
JOHNSON ROBERT M	CPT	0-1324338	0558	1
JOHNSON ROBERT W	COL	0-0252454	1163	3
JOHNSON ROONEY	1LT	0-0490374	0653	1
JOHNSON ROLAND	MAJ	0-1170022	0561	1
JOHNSON ROLAND	MAJ	0-2023286	0762	1
JOHNSON RONALD A	MAJ	0-1797828	0361	1
JOHNSON RONALD G	CPT	0-0104513	0849	3
JOHNSON ROWE	MAJ	0-0237897	1059	3
JOHNSON ROY B	CPT	0-0121711	1052	3
JOHNSON ROY E	CPT	0-0296683	0246	2
JOHNSON ROY M	CPT	0-0490416	1052	1
JOHNSON ROY W	MAJ	0-0182262	0952	3
JOHNSON ROY W	LTC	0-0467556	1160	3
JOHNSON RUFUS R	MAJ	0-1948937	1263	2
JOHNSON RUSSEL D	LTC	0-1585681	0960	1
JOHNSON RUTH E	1LT	N-0758543	0546	1
JOHNSON SAMUEL M	2LT	0-1316758	1044	2
JOHNSON SIDNEY E	CPT	0-1300496	1058	1
JOHNSON SIDNEY W	MAJ	0-0162501	1059	3
JOHNSON SR JOHN I	LTC	0-0359702	1067	3
JOHNSON STANFORD R	LTC	0-0342285	0161	1
JOHNSON STANLEY	LTC	0-0254708	0664	3
JOHNSON STANLEY B	1LT	0-1016398	0849	2
JOHNSON STEPHEN V	1LT	0-1322450	0851	2

NAME	GRADE	SVC NO	DATE RET MO YR	RET CODE
JOHNSON STEWART C	LTC	0-0274551	0867	3
JOHNSON STONE	CPT	0-1913744	0634	1
JOHNSON STUART L V	MAJ	0-0243338	1264	3
JOHNSON SVEN E	MAJ	0-2014156	0563	1
JOHNSON SWAN A	LTC	0-0913767	1262	3
JOHNSON SYLVESTER	CPT	0-1320329	1046	1
JOHNSON TED	COL	0-0309651	1067	3
JOHNSON THEODORE L	MAJ	0-0967030	0763	1
JOHNSON THOMAS E	LTC	0-1322342	1162	1
JOHNSON THOMAS L	LTC	0-1310119	0166	1
JOHNSON THOMAS S	LTC	0-2008051	0967	1
JOHNSON THOMAS T	CW3	W-2149247	0166	1
JOHNSON THOMAS W	LTC	0-0240181	0762	3
JOHNSON THOMAS W	LTC	0-0311059	0167	3
JOHNSON VANNER J	CW4	W-2001732	0762	3
JOHNSON VANO J	LTC	0-0280660	0665	3
JOHNSON VANSEL S	COL	0-0122541	0858	3
JOHNSON VERNON W	CW2	W-2119262	0647	2
JOHNSON VICTOR C	2LT	0-1574871	1044	2
JOHNSON VIRGINIA A	1LT	N-0727740	0946	1
JOHNSON WALLACE L	CPT	0-1556004	0346	1
JOHNSON WALTER A	MAJ	0-0114680	0352	3
JOHNSON WALTER A	MAJ	0-0511241	0646	2
JOHNSON WALTER C	CPT	0-0453531	0246	2
JOHNSON WALTER E	COL	0-0300290	0666	3
JOHNSON WALTER E	CW4	W-2144920	0966	1
JOHNSON WALTER G	CW2	W-2153321	0159	1
JOHNSON WALTER K	MAJ	0-0241187	0765	3
JOHNSON WALTER R	MAJ	0-1876320	0267	1
JOHNSON WALTER T	1LT	0-1170437	0345	2
JOHNSON WALTER T	CW2	W-2205356	0958	1
JOHNSON WARREN L	WO1	W-2115555	1156	1
JOHNSON WAYNE C	LTC	0-0245685	0760	3
JOHNSON WAYNE E	MAJ	0-1105554	0657	1
JOHNSON WAYNE H	LTC	0-0367254	0365	1
JOHNSON WAYNE L	COL	0-0333366	0348	2
JOHNSON WELBY K	CPT	0-0236204	1147	2
JOHNSON WELDON H	CPT	0-1165589	0551	1
JOHNSON WELDON S	CPT	0-1651538	0258	1
JOHNSON WENDALL S	MAJ	0-1639222	1062	1
JOHNSON WILDER A	MAJ	0-1895169	0858	1
JOHNSON WILLARD C	CPT	0-1303071	0646	1
JOHNSON WILLIAM	CPT	0-0505629	0246	2
JOHNSON WILLIAM A	LTC	0-0563433	1062	1
JOHNSON WILLIAM C	CPT	0-0249411	0947	2
JOHNSON WILLIAM E	LTC	0-0219948	0948	1
JOHNSON WILLIAM E	LTC	0-1037845	1162	1
JOHNSON WILLIAM G	COL	0-0319804	0657	1
JOHNSON WILLIAM G	MAJ	0-1167049	0658	1
JOHNSON WILLIAM G	MAJ	0-1284710	0759	1
JOHNSON WILLIAM J	CPT	0-0402701	1144	2
JOHNSON WILLIAM M	CPT	0-0266676	0265	3
JOHNSON WILLIAM M	LTC	0-0922698	0147	2
JOHNSON WILLIAM M	1LT	0-1182393	0453	1
JOHNSON WILLIAM P	CPT	0-1303606	1046	2
JOHNSON WILLIAM R	LTC	0-0395844	0760	1
JOHNSON WILLIAM R	WO1	W-2120024	0353	1
JOHNSON WILLIAM R	CW3	W-2144018	0157	1
JOHNSON WILLIAM R	CW2	W-2211903	0567	1
JOHNSON WILLIAM T	LTC	0-0110238	0648	3
JOHNSON WILLIAM T	MAJ	0-1166301	1054	1
JOHNSON WILLIAM T	MAJ	0-2007241	1060	1
JOHNSON WILLIAM T	CW3	W-2205166	1160	1
JOHNSON WILLIAM V	MAJ	0-1010063	0458	2
JOHNSON WILLIAM W	COL	0-0114425	0749	3
JOHNSON WILLIAM W	COL	0-0266698	0160	3
JOHNSON WILLIE H	CPT	0-4072235	0262	2
JOHNSON WILLIE L	WO1	W-2109940	0648	1
JOHNSON WINCE A J	CPT	0-0106055	1145	2
JOHNSON WINIFRED P	1LT	N-0744996	1045	1
JOHNSON WOODROW A	LTC	0-1114983	0667	1
JOHNSON WOODROW W	LTC	0-0451613	0858	1
JOHNSON YOUBERT T	LTC	0-0252237	0762	3
JOHNSON ZAC M	1LT	0-1896995	0949	1
JOHNSTON ADDY F	1LT	N-0734382	0147	1

NAME	GRADE	SVC NO	DATE RET MO YR	RET CODE
JOHNSTON ALAN C	MAJ	0-0170146	0661	3
JOHNSTON ALBERT M	LTC	0-0369374	0146	2
JOHNSTON AMBROSE F	COL	0-0335667	0761	3
JOHNSTON ARCHIE B	LTC	0-0431050	1160	1
JOHNSTON BYNUM G	MAJ	0-1685656	0564	1
JOHNSTON CARL R	MAJ	0-0208684	0651	3
JOHNSTON CECIL E	MAJ	0-2055135	0361	1
JOHNSTON CLOVIS H	CPT	N-0763575	0546	2
JOHNSTON CLYDE J	CPT	0-0423680	0546	2
JOHNSTON DEWEY S	MAJ	0-1598109	0763	1
JOHNSTON DONALD B	CW3	W-2143030	0559	1
JOHNSTON DONALD W	CW3	W-2205934	1265	1
JOHNSTON EDWARD G	COL	0-0265991	0655	3
JOHNSTON ELMER S	CW3	W-2143013	0161	1
JOHNSTON ELMO J	1LT	0-1032359	0346	1
JOHNSTON ETHEL L	CPT	N-0732165	0647	1
JOHNSTON EUGENE F	LTC	0-1293262	1163	1
JOHNSTON FLOYD R	LTC	0-1030681	0162	1
JOHNSTON FRANCIS I	MAJ	0-1051616	0261	1
JOHNSTON FRANK	LTC	0-0444449	0260	1
JOHNSTON FRANKLIN V	LTC	0-2205315	0758	1
JOHNSTON FREDERICK	LTC	0-0148195	0649	3
JOHNSTON FREDERICK	LTC	0-1639225	0666	1
JOHNSTON GEORGE A	COL	0-0218162	0850	3
JOHNSTON GEORGE F	LTC	0-0138892	0444	2
JOHNSTON GEORGE M	MAJ	0-1297544	0961	1
JOHNSTON GEORGE R	1LT	0-1104890	0444	2
JOHNSTON GORDON A	1LT	0-0405253	0745	2
JOHNSTON GORDON D	LTC	0-0254307	1263	3
JOHNSTON HANNAH A	2LT	N-0700192	0641	2
JOHNSTON HAROLD A	LTC	0-0496956	0266	1
JOHNSTON HAROLD H	MAJ	0-1015548	0860	1
JOHNSTON HAROLD W	LTC	0-0188607	1057	3
JOHNSTON HARRY A	COL	0-0172860	0955	3
JOHNSTON HARVEY G	LTC	0-0361999	0261	1
JOHNSTON HOMER W	LTC	0-1184241	0263	1
JOHNSTON HOWARD R	LTC	0-0308714	0566	3
JOHNSTON JACOB A	COL	0-0148641	0754	3
JOHNSTON JAMES H	MAJ	0-0269592	1057	3
JOHNSTON JAMES R	COL	0-0344996	0167	3
JOHNSTON JAMES R	LTC	0-1165518	0866	1
JOHNSTON JAMES V	COL	0-0208060	0950	3
JOHNSTON JAMES W	MAJ	0-1178520	1066	3
JOHNSTON JAMES W	WO1	W-2111118	1147	1
JOHNSTON JESSE E	COL	0-0354998	0566	1
JOHNSTON JOHN E	CPT	0-0487074	0446	1
JOHNSTON JOHN F	CPT	0-0235733	0151	3
JOHNSTON JOHN K	COL	0-0354227	1160	3
JOHNSTON JOHN L	COL	0-0235490	0858	3
JOHNSTON JOHN M	LTC	0-0264726	0166	3
JOHNSTON JOHN M	1LT	0-0548456	0346	2
JOHNSTON JOHN M	LTC	0-1575382	0763	1
JOHNSTON JOSEPH O	MAJ	0-1057794	0464	1
JOHNSTON JR ALBERT E	1LT	0-0495608	1044	2
JOHNSTON JR FRANK H	LTC	0-0472371	0167	1
JOHNSTON JR GEORGE H	CPT	0-2287823	1162	2
JOHNSTON JR GEORGE W	CPT	0-0408520	0246	2
JOHNSTON JR J C	CW3	W-2106054	1057	1
JOHNSTON JR JOHN C	CW2	W-2152267	0263	1
JOHNSTON JR JULIUS P	MAJ	0-0955456	0565	1
JOHNSTON JR RUFUS Z	LTC	0-1640601	0766	1
JOHNSTON LEE R	CW2	W-2146848	1059	2
JOHNSTON LEROY F	LTC	0-0254776	0265	3
JOHNSTON MARGARET M	CPT	N-0783796	0847	1
JOHNSTON MARION R	CW2	W-2145121	1059	1
JOHNSTON MELVIN T	MAJ	0-0322424	1045	2
JOHNSTON MILTON E	CPT	0-1689622	0152	1
JOHNSTON NATHAN J	LTC	0-0215490	0446	1
JOHNSTON OWEN A	MAJ	0-1284148	1057	1
JOHNSTON PAUL E	LTC	0-1114569	0664	1
JOHNSTON RALPH S	LTC	0-1105555	0762	1
JOHNSTON RICHARD B	2LT	0-1173665	1044	2
JOHNSTON RICHARD Y	CPT	0-0965630	0367	1
JOHNSTON ROBERT B	COL	0-0428223	0866	3
JOHNSTON ROBERT O	1LT	0-1323575	1145	2

NAME	GRADE	SVC NO	DATE RET MO YR	RET CODE
JOHNSTON ROBERT L	MAJ	0-0277084	0252	3
JOHNSTON ROY B	CW3	W-2205121	0965	1
JOHNSTON ROY C	LTC	0-0485409	0656	1
JOHNSTON ROY E	MAJ	0-0184735	0456	3
JOHNSTON ROY T	MAJ	0-1322156	0260	1
JOHNSTON RUSSELL S	COL	0-0195202	0652	3
JOHNSTON RUTH A	1LT	N-0735005	0445	1
JOHNSTON STANLEY J	CW3	W-2205199	1067	1
JOHNSTON TEDDY L	MAJ	0-0243709	0763	3
JOHNSTON THOMAS A	LTC	0-0288715	0562	3
JOHNSTON THOMAS B	MAJ	0-0258211	0749	2
JOHNSTON THOMAS N	LTC	0-0291259	1264	3
JOHNSTON TRUMAN J	1LT	0-1754993	0544	2
JOHNSTON WESLEY W	2LT	0-1951222	1046	2
JOHNSTON WILLARD A	COL	0-0172865	0360	3
JOHNSTON WILLARD T	CPT	0-0242790	0444	2
JOHNSTON WILLIAM A	LTC	0-0260538	0265	3
JOHNSTON WILLIAM A	CPT	0-1541251	1065	1
JOHNSTON WILLIAM C	1LT	0-0310215	1045	2
JOHNSTON WILLIAM D	COL	0-0266507	0857	1
JOHNSTON WILLIAM G	COL	0-0119145	0349	3
JOHNSTON WILLIAM H	LTC	0-0217080	0764	3
JOHNSTON WILLIAM J	LTC	0-0466724	0863	1
JOHNSTON WILLIAM J	MAJ	0-1327624	0361	1
JOHNSTON WILLIAM L	CPT	0-0462496	1145	2
JOHNSTON WILLIAM L	LTC	0-1289589	1159	1
JOHNSTON WILLIAM R	MAJ	0-1577389	0963	1
JOHNSTON WILLIAM R	MAJ	0-1882330	0966	1
JOHNSTON WILLIAM T	CPT	0-0974559	1060	1
JOHNSTON WOODROW K	1LT	0-1544508	0657	1
JOHNSTONE CHARLES W	CW3	W-2146693	1265	1
JOHNSTONE EDWARD L	LTC	0-0359540	0861	1
JOHNSTONE JOHN C	MAJ	0-1103241	0261	1
JOHNSTONE MYRON H	MAJ	0-1031889	0462	1
JOHNSTONE PARKER L	CPT	0-0311776	0645	2
JOHNSTONE RICHARD S	MAJ	0-2204172	0865	1
JOHNSTONE ROBERT H	MAJ	0-1049913	1062	1
JOHNSTONE RUTH B	CPT	N-0724636	0147	1
JOHNSTONE WILLIAM	COL	0-0450628	0963	1
JOHS ALBERT C	LTC	0-1003406	1262	1
JOINER GUS	1LT	0-1105556	0545	2
JOINER HARTWELL	LTC	0-0264424	1162	3
JOINER JOHN R	CPT	0-1584421	0754	2
JOINER KATHRYN L	2LT	N-0785246	0847	1
JOINER NANCY E	1LT	N-0702960	1045	1
JOINER ROWELL A	1LT	0-2025664	0847	2
JOINES ARMWELL J	1LT	0-1824193	1051	1
JOKI WILLIAM M	1LT	0-0384905	0244	2
JOLICOEUR LOUIS A	CPT	0-1114570	0162	2
JOLIE ROBERT P	MAJ	0-2028595	1265	1
JOLIN LEC E	MAJ	0-0327187	0764	3
JOLIN PHILIP W	1LT	0-1285432	0545	1
JOLLEY JAMES B	MAJ	0-1575384	0162	1
JOLLEY JR CHARLES A	MAJ	0-0415282	0246	2
JOLLEY ORAN R	MAJ	0-1044853	0258	1
JOLLIFFE KENNETH R	1LT	0-2262200	0460	1
JOLLIMORE ELIZABET	1LT	N-0758160	0945	1
JOLLY AB	MAJ	0-0242831	0859	3
JOLLY BENJAMIN R	CPT	0-0304067	0245	2
JOLLY BYRON F	LTC	0-0266670	0758	1
JOLLY JR THOMAS 3	COL	0-0243727	1151	3
JOLLY ROBERT V	CW3	W-2149409	0363	1
JOLLY ROY H	WO1	W-2146045	0858	1
JOMOK MARCELE G	1LT	0-1896670	0261	1
JONAS CHARLES R	COL	0-0224860	0165	3
JONAS CHARLES S	CPT	0-1688069	0845	2
JONAS HERMAN W	CPT	0-0293064	0945	2
JONAS JOHN F	LTC	0-0302035	0167	3
JONAS WILLIAM	MAJ	0-0177678	0846	2
JONELIS FRANK G	LTC	0-0362228	1158	1
JONES ADEN A	COL	0-0298786	0560	3
JONES ADRIAN H	LTC	0-1646294	1162	1
JONES ALBERT	LTC	0-0426300	0457	1
JONES ALBERT E	LTC	0-0452915	0361	2
JONES ALBERT W	MAJ	0-0942065	0963	1

NAME	GRADE	SVC NO	DATE RET MO YR	RET CODE
JONES ALEXANDER	MAJ	0-0281965	0858	1
JONES ALFRED	CPT	0-0455233	0467	1
JONES ALFRED B	CPT	0-0286764	1063	3
JONES ALFRED D	LTC	0-0250697	1065	3
JONES ALFRED P	CPT	0-1695360	0945	2
JONES ALFRED S	2LT	0-1004150	0245	2
JONES ALICE N	CPT	M-0000587	0147	1
JONES ANN	CPT	N-0721562	1059	2
JONES ARCHBOLD R	COL	0-0114497	1056	3
JONES ARCHIE A	2LT	0-1305156	0544	2
JONES ARNOLD C	MAJ	0-0360794	0466	1
JONES AUGUST E	MAJ	0-0975281	0861	1
JONES BARRY W	CW3	W-2152968	1162	1
JONES BENJAMIN C	COL	0-0148197	0656	3
JONES BERNICE F	LTC	0-0903263	1264	1
JONES BERRY E	LTC	0-0238471	1264	3
JONES BERTRAND H	MAJ	0-1046504	0261	1
JONES BEUFORD D	1LT	0-1297046	0146	2
JONES BILLY E	1LT	0-5317187	0565	2
JONES BOB R	1LT	0-1944980	0545	2
JONES BRUCE H	CW3	W-2142477	1064	1
JONES BUD L	MAJ	0-1340080	0764	1
JONES CALVIN	CW2	W-2211363	1166	1
JONES CARL S	LTC	0-0295127	0562	1
JONES CARL W	LTC	0-0348108	0355	1
JONES CAROL A	CPT	0-0494741	0946	1
JONES CARROLL E	1LT	0-1295559	0445	2
JONES CECIL R	MAJ	0-2043010	0962	1
JONES CHARLES B	CPT	0-0320560	0246	1
JONES CHARLES C	CPT	0-0170117	0161	3
JONES CHARLES C	LTC	0-0221582	0757	3
JONES CHARLES D	CW3	W-2146941	0664	1
JONES CHARLES F	1LT	0-1577391	1061	3
JONES CHARLES F	MAJ	0-1305592	1057	1
JONES CHARLES F	1LT	0-1329597	1045	2
JONES CHARLES H	COL	0-0224956	0165	3
JONES CHARLES H	COL	0-0307644	1047	2
JONES CHARLES L	LTC	0-0363543	0766	1
JONES CHARLES L	LTC	0-1053657	0661	1
JONES CHARLES R	LTC	0-0372926	1266	3
JONES CHARLES R	1LT	0-1999265	0547	1
JONES CHARLES S	LTC	0-0187192	0648	3
JONES CHARLES T	LTC	0-0267549	0645	2
JONES CHARLES T	MAJ	0-0527307	1054	1
JONES CHARLES W	LTC	0-0247925	0466	3
JONES CHARLIE P	LTC	0-0480757	0854	1
JONES CHILTON V	2LT	0-1914308	0932	1
JONES CLARENCE L	COL	0-0248036	0361	3
JONES CLARENCE M	LTC	0-0256801	1048	1
JONES CLARENCE O	LTC	0-0298243	0257	1
JONES CLAUDE A	MAJ	0-0887887	0656	1
JONES CLAUDE R	1LT	0-1016457	0746	2
JONES CLEO W	CW2	W-2150585	0357	1
JONES CLEVELAND	CW3	W-2143592	1059	1
JONES CLIFFORD B	CPT	0-0154480	0955	3
JONES CLYDE A	LTC	0-0323037	0547	2
JONES CLYDE W	MAJ	0-2007862	0662	1
JONES CONWAY B	LTC	0-1285597	0961	2
JONES DAN C	2LT	0-4063315	1058	2
JONES DANIEL H	CW2	W-2122377	0847	2
JONES DANIEL W	COL	0-0163455	1054	3
JONES DARWIN M	CW3	W-2150091	1066	1
JONES DAVID A	CPT	0-0381768	1057	1
JONES DAVID A	CPT	0-0447034	0447	2
JONES DEFOREST	MAJ	0-0456208	1160	1
JONES DEOLINDA C	MAJ	N-0736538	0966	1
JONES DEWITT	LTC	0-0259611	0364	3
JONES DILLARD F	LTC	0-0353009	0766	1
JONES DIXON H	LTC	0-1301753	0457	1
JONES DONALD B	LTC	0-1040742	0866	1
JONES DONALD C	1LT	0-1306280	0745	2
JONES DONALD F	1LT	0-1310252	1045	2
JONES DONALD R	CPT	0-0178223	1156	3
JONES DONALD S	1LT	0-1037846	1145	2
JONES DOVA L	MAJ	0-1115305	1262	1

NAME	GRADE	SVC NO	DATE RET MO YR	RET CODE
JONES DOYLE	1LT	0-1058279	0847	1
JONES DOYLE W	CW2	W-2131053	0862	1
JONES DUDLEY B	LTC	0-0154389	0354	3
JONES DUKE E	COL	0-0219568	0654	1
JONES EARL A	WO1	W-2116006	0745	2
JONES EARL W	COL	0-0185108	1052	3
JONES EBEN	1LT	0-1172938	0445	2
JONES EDGAR A	MAJ	0-2053871	1155	1
JONES EDGAR P	MAJ	0-0249158	1266	3
JONES EDMUND C	CPT	0-1644464	0560	1
JONES EDWARD	MAJ	0-0578207	0264	1
JONES EDWARD B	CPT	0-1598013	1162	1
JONES EDWARD C	MAJ	0-0236190	1064	3
JONES EDWARD C	1LT	0-1321313	0847	2
JONES EDWARD E	LTC	0-2018174	1167	1
JONES EDWARD L	LTC	0-0144901	0954	3
JONES EDWARD M	CW3	W-2147007	0667	1
JONES EDWARD P	1LT	0-1821876	0445	2
JONES EDWARD W	MAJ	0-1003266	1154	1
JONES EDWIN C	LTC	0-0902272	1054	2
JONES EDWIN G	CW2	W-3430062	1264	1
JONES EDWIN L	MAJ	0-0227047	0163	3
JONES EDWIN N	CW2	W-2143031	0957	1
JONES ELBERT T	LTC	0-0265464	0956	3
JONES ELLIE A	LTC	0-0238304	0262	3
JONES ELLIE C	MAJ	0-0187069	0852	3
JONES ELMER L	1LT	0-0404299	0142	1
JONES ELWOOD T	MAJ	0-0567183	0761	1
JONES EMERSON R	LTC	0-1293063	0766	1
JONES EMMETT B	CPT	0-0468631	0745	2
JONES ERNEST F	MAJ	0-1693794	1060	1
JONES ERNEST S	LTC	0-0179324	0648	3
JONES ERNEST T	MAJ	0-1168740	1160	1
JONES EUGENE L	COL	0-0232552	0864	3
JONES EVERETT L	MAJ	0-1548868	0860	1
JONES EVERTON	MAJ	0-0239558	1162	3
JONES FOREST A	MAJ	0-1944483	0260	1
JONES FORREST E	LTC	0-0190349	1152	3
JONES FRANK C	COL	0-0397755	0859	1
JONES FRANK E	CPT	0-0517632	0646	2
JONES FRANK M	MAJ	0-1333829	0262	1
JONES FRED L	LTC	0-0183358	1056	3
JONES FREDERICK	LTC	0-1035843	0761	1
JONES FREDERICK	MAJ	0-1291648	0157	1
JONES FREDERICK	LTC	0-1873455	1166	3
JONES FREEMAN	LTC	0-1798005	0861	1
JONES GEORGE A	MAJ	0-0978238	0964	1
JONES GEORGE A	MAJ	0-1876603	0765	1
JONES GEORGE D	LTC	0-0259783	0964	3
JONES GEORGE D	LTC	0-0320069	0460	3
JONES GEORGE W	CPT	0-0430264	0752	1
JONES GEORGE W	LTC	0-0580867	0963	3
JONES GEORGE W	2LT	0-1692513	0845	1
JONES GERALD A	CW3	W-2144546	0365	1
JONES GLEN W	1LT	0-0911354	1044	2
JONES GLEN W	LTC	0-2050842	1167	1
JONES GLENN L	CW4	W-2145731	1167	1
JONES GLENN W	LTC	0-0307691	0358	3
JONES GLENN W	CW3	W-2143926	0962	1
JONES GORDON L	1LT	0-0476017	0245	2
JONES GRANT R	LTC	0-0377156	0567	3
JONES GRANT S	CPT	0-1176682	0662	1
JONES GRIFFITH G	LTC	0-1951091	0166	1
JONES GUY D	MAJ	0-0418096	0760	1
JONES GUY H	CPT	0-0997911	0564	1
JONES HARLOW G	LTC	0-0258135	1064	3
JONES HAROLD	MAJ	0-0409296	0949	1
JONES HAROLD B	LTC	0-0319811	0159	1
JONES HAROLD J	CPT	0-1574456	0658	1
JONES HAROLD R	LTC	0-0354836	0161	1
JONES HARRY L	CW4	W-2104184	0255	1
JONES HARRY P	COL	0-0260778	1160	3
JONES HELEN J	MAJ	N-0744855	1062	1
JONES HENRIETTA	1LT	N-0783903	0446	1
JONES HENRY A	1LT	0-1320737	0645	2

NAME	GRADE	SVC NO	DATE RET MO YR	RET CODE
JONES HENRY H	LTC	0-1686589	0767	1
JONES HENRY W	CPT	0-0514007	0646	1
JONES HENRY W	CPT	0-1011642	0146	2
JONES HERBERT D	LTC	0-1794949	1065	1
JONES HERSCHEL C	MAJ	0-1923631	1067	1
JONES HILLERY D	CPT	0-0973178	0463	1
JONES HIRAM F	MAJ	0-0286268	0-53	1
JONES HOLMES A	COL	0-0249794	0363	1
JONES HOWARD B	LTC	0-0418206	0152	1
JONES HOWARD C	COL	0-0241041	0862	3
JONES HOWARD P	COL	0-0208883	0159	3
JONES HOWARD R	1LT	0-1164078	0845	2
JONES HOWARD R	2LT	0-1551651	0645	2
JONES HUGH D	MAJ	0-0964076	1062	1
JONES HUGH M	LTC	0-0154641	1153	3
JONES HUMPHREY B	CW2	W-2148653	0461	1
JONES II HENRY L	COL	0-0171546	1060	3
JONES II PHILIP I	LTC	0-1042851	0461	1
JONES JACK	MAJ	0-0975603	0964	1
JONES JACK A	CW3	W-2153352	1163	1
JONES JACK C	LTC	0-1554568	1262	1
JONES JACK I	LTC	0-1312010	0865	1
JONES JACK L	MAJ	0-1055878	0866	1
JONES JACK W	MAJ	0-1298240	0364	1
JONES JACKSON S	LTC	0-1577393	1064	1
JONES JAMES A	COL	0-0168857	0647	2
JONES JAMES A	CPT	0-0461070	0 45	2
JONES JAMES C	1LT	0-0519685	0146	2
JONES JAMES E	1LT	0-0219894	0-53	3
JONES JAMES F	1LT	0-0286392	0442	2
JONES JAMES H	MAJ	0-1172939	0561	1
JONES JAMES H	WO1	W-2115435	1053	1
JONES JAMES L	CPT	0-0504807	0245	2
JONES JAMES M	COL	0-0277141	0760	3
JONES JAMES M	MAJ	0-0960814	0863	1
JONES JAMES M	2LT	0-1913506	0747	1
JONES JAMES M	WO1	W-2146992	1157	1
JONES JAMES N	LTC	0-0422325	0262	1
JONES JAMES P	MAJ	0-0395437	0457	1
JONES JAMES R	MAJ	0-1325755	0863	1
JONES JAMES T	LTC	0-1116674	0264	1
JONES JAMES W	CW2	W-2206366	0861	1
JONES JAMES W	CW2	W-3411009	0965	1
JONES JANE C	2LT	N-0729899	0244	1
JONES JAY L	CPT	0-1030484	0147	1
JONES JAY M	CW3	W-2147440	0964	1
JONES JEFFERSON	1LT	0-1331841	0959	1
JONES JERALD R	1LT	0-1284149	0645	2
JONES JEROME B	LTC	0-0152773	0844	2
JONES JESSE J	COL	0-0888537	0854	1
JONES JESSIE M	CW4	W-2125074	1162	1
JONES JEWELL E	LTC	0-0299880	1165	3
JONES JOHN B	MAJ	0-0487427	0547	2
JONES JOHN B	WO1	W-2122811	0745	1
JONES JOHN C	LTC	0-0340817	1160	1
JONES JOHN C	CW2	W-2101901	0344	1
JONES JOHN E	MAJ	0-0972482	0265	1
JONES JOHN F	CW2	W-2205596	0561	1
JONES JOHN H	CPT	0-0363965	1044	2
JONES JOHN J	COL	0-0223454	1164	3
JONES JOHN L	CPT	0-0193156	0456	3
JONES JOHN P	MAJ	0-0148196	0648	3
JONES JOHN P	LTC	0-0275523	0662	3
JONES JOHN P	MAJ	0-0916953	1062	1
JONES JOHN P	1LT	0-1323576	0845	2
JONES JOHN R	LTC	0-0411430	0765	1
JONES JOHN R	WO1	W-2118306	0550	1
JONES JOHN W	COL	0-0197705	0263	3
JONES JOHN W	MAJ	0-1597146	0358	1
JONES JOSEPH A	LTC	0-0291045	1066	3
JONES JOSEPH A	LTC	0-1171209	0966	1
JONES JOSEPH J	MAJ	0-1044572	1263	1
JONES JOSEPH L	LTC	0-0225833	0365	3
JONES JOSEPH R	MAJ	0-0392726	0667	3
JONES JOSEPH R	MAJ	0-0491051	0146	2

NAME	GRADE	SVC NO	DATE RET MO YR	RET CODE
JONES JOSEPH W	MAJ	0-0973828	1165	1
JONES JR ALBERT S	CPT	0-2047657	0446	1
JONES JR BARNETT C	MAJ	0-1899421	0961	1
JONES JR BILL	MAJ	0-4031075	1266	1
JONES JR BILL T	MAJ	0-1577390	0960	1
JONES JR CHARLES A	CPT	0-1322451	0947	2
JONES JR CHARLES G	2LT	0-1032805	0351	2
JONES JR CHARLES H	COL	0-0216752	0160	1
JONES JR CHARLES H	CPT	0-0537859	0247	1
JONES JR CLARENCE F	LTC	0-0257719	0964	3
JONES JR CLEMENT R	LTC	0-0295192	1265	3
JONES JR DONALD B	LTC	0-0399857	0661	1
JONES JR EDGAR C	1LT	0-1173666	0646	1
JONES JR EDWARD T	CPT	0-0304253	0944	2
JONES JR EDWARD W	LTC	0-0524912	0763	1
JONES JR EDWIN T	MAJ	0-0404300	0662	1
JONES JR EMMETT L	LTC	0-0227080	0746	2
JONES JR EUGENE	MAJ	0-2014610	0967	1
JONES JR FRANK D	LTC	0-0253911	0767	3
JONES JR FRED K	LTC	0-0358816	0767	3
JONES JR HAROLD C	2LT	0-0390566	1242	2
JONES JR HOWARD S	MAJ	0-2035479	1160	1
JONES JR HUGH	LTC	0-0527809	1264	1
JONES JR JAMES C	MAJ	0-2262695	1065	1
JONES JR JAMES L	CPT	0-1824867	0861	1
JONES JR JAMES M	COL	0-0330151	1061	3
JONES JR JAMES S	COL	0-0192812	1059	3
JONES JR JOSEPH A	LTC	0-0249033	0664	3
JONES JR MARSHALL W	CPT	0-1300808	0446	2
JONES JR MARVIN L	MAJ	0-0966135	0664	1
JONES JR MILTON D	1LT	0-5323978	1066	2
JONES JR ROBERT H	CW2	W-2205630	0361	1
JONES JR SAMUEL A	MAJ	0-0995134	0465	1
JONES JR THOMAS	CW2	W-2207354	1263	1
JONES JR THOMAS W	MAJ	0-1922571	1163	1
JONES JR WILLIAM G	LTC	0-1634945	1264	1
JONES JULIET M	2LT	N-0726166	0644	1
JONES KATHERINE	2LT	N-0700179	1139	1
JONES KENNETH	1LT	0-0419530	0655	2
JONES LARREN L	CPT	0-1103244	0957	1
JONES LAWRENCE A	CW2	W-2214743	1067	1
JONES LAWRENCE H	MAJ	0-0982723	1062	1
JONES LELAND N	COL	0-0167383	1055	3
JONES LEO L	2LT	0-0504201	0743	2
JONES LEONARD M	LTC	0-1300336	0364	1
JONES LESLIE F	LTC	0-0446274	0966	3
JONES LEWIS H	COL	0-0204162	0360	3
JONES LINCOLN S	LTC	0-0212204	0264	3
JONES LINDBERGH	MAJ	0-4010795	0767	1
JONES LINZEY D	1LT	0-1321680	0745	2
JONES LLEWELLYN	LTC	0-0407531	0764	1
JONES LLOYD A	LTC	0-1314457	1165	1
JONES LLOYD C	MAJ	0-1339872	0464	1
JONES LOREN W	CPT	0-2103050	0962	2
JONES LOUIS K	CW4	W-2141329	0766	1
JONES LUTHER C	LTC	0-1540695	0965	1
JONES LYLE	CPT	0-1300807	0654	1
JONES LYLE V	LTC	0-0347709	0365	3
JONES LYLE W	LTC	0-0204722	0961	3
JONES LYNN R	1LT	0-0446747	1145	2
JONES LYTLE R	MAJ	0-0278419	0666	3
JONES MAJLE H	CW4	W-2146155	0767	1
JONES MALCOLM A	COL	0-0288056	0856	3
JONES MALCOLM S	COL	0-0182149	1155	3
JONES MANION F	CPT	0-0180266	0648	3
JONES MARCUS L	MAJ	0-1546401	0261	1
JONES MARGARET E	MAJ	L-0500995	0166	1
JONES MARGARET F	2LT	N-0761172	1044	1
JONES MARION A	LTC	0-1310120	0764	1
JONES MARION D	1LT	0-1318047	0146	2
JONES MARTHA R	MAJ	N-0761318	0865	3
JONES MARVIN	MAJ	0-0506388	0256	1
JONES MARVIN L	MAJ	0-1170023	0747	2
JONES MARVIN L	1LT	0-1175475	0346	2
JONES MARY F	2LT	N-0743809	0445	1

NAME	GRADE	SVC NO	DATE RET MO YR	RET CODE
JONES MELVIN H	COL	0-0199266	0855	1
JONES MELVIN R	LTC	0-1548233	1062	1
JONES MILFRED W	CW3	W-2149074	0763	1
JONES MILTON H	LTC	0-0297711	0162	1
JONES MINNIS M	1LT	0-1302473	1044	2
JONES MORRIS H	LTC	0-1637774	0964	1
JONES MORRIS W	MAJ	0-1115935	0964	1
JONES MORRIS W	1LT	0-1318181	0146	1
JONES MYRON S	CW3	W-2144472	1165	1
JONES NELSON R	MAJ	0-0418330	0663	1
JONES OLLIE F	LTC	0-0282488	0366	3
JONES ORION C	MAJ	0-0122177	0252	1
JONES ORVILLE H	MAJ	0-1051626	1058	1
JONES PAUL	MAJ	0-0359070	0854	1
JONES PAUL	CPT	0-0488774	0347	1
JONES PAUL	CW3	W-2150276	0659	1
JONES PAUL A	CW2	W-2115113	0351	1
JONES PAUL J	LTC	0-1111699	1062	1
JONES PAUL J	LTC	0-1296863	0562	1
JONES PAUL L	COL	0-0305788	0366	3
JONES PAUL L	LTC	0-0327182	0760	3
JONES PAUL S	MAJ	0-0111946	0648	3
JONES PAUL W	LTC	0-0194725	0746	2
JONES PAUL W	MAJ	0-1038021	0767	3
JONES PAULINE	MAJ	N-0729075	1062	1
JONES PRESTON F	LTC	0-1115306	0167	1
JONES RALPH C	MAJ	0-0258585	1162	1
JONES RALPH K	LTC	0-0361905	0459	1
JONES RALPH O	CW2	W-2214376	1266	1
JONES RALPH V	1LT	0-1333346	0549	2
JONES RAY	CW3	W-2148153	0660	1
JONES RAY B	COL	0-0247770	0556	2
JONES RAY E	MAJ	0-1301156	1059	1
JONES RAY J	2LT	0-1015050	0345	2
JONES RAY V	LTC	0-0136696	0454	3
JONES RAYMOND C	MAJ	0-0452125	1054	1
JONES RAYMOND E	CPT	0-0335313	0346	2
JONES RAYMOND E	1LT	0-1014532	0261	2
JONES REBEL J	CPT	0-0444954	1148	1
JONES RICHARD C	MAJ	0-1548872	0457	1
JONES RICHARD H	COL	0-0238409	1064	3
JONES RICHARD H	LTC	0-0503703	0157	1
JONES RICHARD H	MAJ	0-1296038	1146	1
JONES RICHARD L	LTC	0-0421426	0664	1
JONES RICHARD M	LTC	0-0273029	0257	3
JONES RICHARD R	MAJ	0-1552528	1164	3
JONES RICHARD S	1LT	0-1056774	0553	2
JONES RICHARD W	CPT	0-1684957	1060	1
JONES RILEY G	MAJ	0-0468285	0754	1
JONES ROBERT A	COL	0-0345653	0261	1
JONES ROBERT B	COL	0-0239269	0561	1
JONES ROBERT B	COL	0-0294455	0864	3
JONES ROBERT B	MAJ	0-1315004	0264	1
JONES ROBERT E	CW2	W-2148540	1163	1
JONES ROBERT F	MAJ	0-0472303	0858	1
JONES ROBERT G	MAJ	0-0260476	0164	3
JONES ROBERT J	MAJ	0-1032218	0157	2
JONES ROBERT J F	CW3	W-2145456	1060	1
JONES ROBERT K	LTC	0-1644466	1166	1
JONES ROBERT L	LTC	0-1325295	1162	1
JONES ROBERT M	1LT	0-1589626	0662	2
JONES ROBERT O	MAJ	0-0408580	1045	2
JONES ROBERT R	1LT	0-0440638	1143	2
JONES ROBERT R	MAJ	0-0973544	0861	1
JONES ROBERT R	LTC	0-2052210	0667	3
JONES ROBERT R	CW4	W-2113654	0155	1
JONES ROBERT S	LTC	0-0250614	0467	3
JONES ROBERT S	LTC	0-0273436	0963	3
JONES ROBERT T	CPT	0-1177475	0647	2
JONES ROBERT W	MAJ	0-0353930	0856	2
JONES ROBERT W	MAJ	0-0373794	0257	2
JONES RODNEY H	COL	0-0401840	0961	3
JONES ROSAMOND R	LTC	0-0407835	0657	1
JONES ROY	COL	0-0304857	0847	2
JONES ROY D	MAJ	0-1176087	0858	1

NAME	GRADE	SVC NO	DATE RET MO YR	RET CODE
JONES ROY L	COL	0-0336206	0858	3
JONES RUDOLPH M	LTC	0-0370312	0963	1
JONES RUFUS	CW2	W-2141330	0657	1
JONES RUTH E	MAJ	N-0771209	0867	1
JONES SALLIE T	MAJ	N-0722413	0765	3
JONES SAM H	MAJ	0-0207538	0757	3
JONES SCOTT S	LTC	0-0227812	0257	3
JONES SHERMAN A	CPT	0-1183101	0464	1
JONES SHERMAN F	CPT	0-0496266	0454	1
JONES SR AAREN L	WO1	W-2152675	0560	2
JONES SR CARROLL J	MAJ	0-1115934	0564	1
JONES SR ROBERT E	LTC	0-1574271	0267	1
JONES STANFORD F	MAJ	0-0237785	0763	3
JONES STANLEY E	1LT	0-0447220	0446	2
JONES STARR W	LTC	0-1285249	0266	3
JONES STENSON R	CPT	0-2103030	0662	1
JONES STUART M	MAJ	0-0262022	0664	3
JONES THOMAS B	MAJ	0-0201436	1155	3
JONES THOMAS B	CPT	0-1996351	0551	1
JONES THOMAS C	CPT	0-1286135	1045	2
JONES THOMAS G	CW4	W-2002787	0464	3
JONES THOMAS H	CW4	W-2141600	1060	1
JONES THOMAS K	MAJ	0-0273781	0945	2
JONES THOMAS N	COL	0-0249161	0764	3
JONES THOMAS R	MAJ	0-0358910	0546	2
JONES TORRENCE V	LTC	0-2006092	1163	1
JONES VERNA D	CW3	W-2145969	0166	1
JONES VERNON F	LTC	0-1103720	0861	1
JONES VERNON F	MAJ	0-1300337	0161	1
JONES VERNON C	MAJ	0-0572197	0562	1
JONES VERYL L	2LT	0-1032593	0445	2
JONES VIRGINIA D	1LT	N-0770051	0248	1
JONES WALTER	CW3	W-2141147	0863	1
JONES WALTER B	COL	0-0102768	0255	3
JONES WALTER E	2LT	0-1577396	0245	2
JONES WALTER H	CPT	0-1012298	0847	2
JONES WALTER P	LTC	0-0423283	0660	1
JONES WALTER S	LTC	0-0155500	0648	3
JONES WALTER T	LTC	0-0269856	0158	1
JONES WALTER W	LTC	0-0284685	0854	1
JONES WARD A	LTC	0-0246065	0862	3
JONES WAYNE T	MAJ	0-0572298	1061	1
JONES WENDELL H	1LT	0-1179114	0146	2
JONES WESLEY S	CW4	W-2113286	1055	1
JONES WILBERT L	MAJ	0-0383676	0460	1
JONES WILBUR A	MAJ	0-0997488	1266	1
JONES WILBUR M	1LT	0-1036582	1051	1
JONES WILFORD H	MAJ	0-1598428	1066	1
JONES WILLARD A	CPT	0-1951625	1057	1
JONES WILLARD L	LTC	0-0248472	0258	2
JONES WILLIAM	CW2	W-2108666	0853	1
JONES WILLIAM B	COL	0-0311529	1062	3
JONES WILLIAM B	CPT	0-0975035	0263	2
JONES WILLIAM B	MAJ	0-2017245	0764	1
JONES WILLIAM C	COL	0-0225001	0451	3
JONES WILLIAM C	CW3	W-2144572	0460	1
JONES WILLIAM H	MAJ	0-0966176	0563	1
JONES WILLIAM H	MAJ	0-1598400	0760	1
JONES WILLIAM J	LTC	0-0438619	0462	1
JONES WILLIAM J	1LT	0-1317607	0346	2
JONES WILLIAM J	CW3	W-2136680	1262	1
JONES WILLIAM L	CPT	0-0970211	0361	1
JONES WILLIAM L	LTC	0-1010154	0866	1
JONES WILLIAM M	MAJ	0-0177617	0861	3
JONES WILLIAM M	MAJ	0-1798158	1060	3
JONES WILLIAM R	1LT	0-1297735	0145	2
JONES WILLIAM S	2LT	0-1166097	1144	2
JONES WILLIAM T	MAJ	0-1176683	0864	2
JONES WILLIAM W	CPT	0-0117209	1155	3
JONES WILLIE A	CPT	0-1585685	0657	1
JONES WILLIE F	CW2	W-2145222	0358	1
JONES WILLIE L	MAJ	0-0946620	1263	1
JONES WINIFRED F	MAJ	L-1010723	0866	1
JONES WOODROW A	LTC	0-0395651	0358	1
JONES YOUNG G	WO1	W-2145921	0257	1

NAME	GRADE	SVC NO	DATE RET MO YR	RET CODE
JONES 3RD JOHN C	MAJ	C-0508477	1047	2
JONESCHILD WILLIAM R	LTC	0-0342562	1061	1
JONGEWAARD LAWRENCE	LTC	C-0403490	C661	3
JONSON LESLIE M	MAJ	0-0996580	0660	1
JOPLIN JOHNNIE R	CW3	W-2150010	0764	1
JOPLIN TROY M	LTC	0-1688514	0567	1
JOPLING DANIEL W	LTC	0-0417823	0561	2
JOPLING HARVEY M	LTC	0-0903835	1166	3
JORDAHL MARTIN	CPT	C-0307620	1144	2
JORDAN ALBERT B	CW4	W-2101906	0255	2
JORDAN ARLINGTON	CW2	W-2151878	0363	1
JORDAN ARTHUR L	CW3	W-2149259	C561	1
JORDAN ARTHUR W	LTC	0-0171634	1061	3
JORDAN ASHFORD T	COL	0-0397148	0760	1
JORDAN BENJAMIN R	CPT	0-0349926	0446	2
JORDAN BERTRAND	LTC	C-0321675	C766	3
JORDAN BUREN H	CW3	W-2142425	C965	1
JORDAN CECIL E	CW3	W-2141602	1059	1
JORDAN CHARLES A	LTC	0-0311677	C660	1
JORDAN CHARLES E	CW2	W-2151009	0859	1
JORDAN CONALD E	CPT	0-1289914	0847	2
JORDAN DONALD R	1LT	0-0379110	1145	2
JORDAN DOSIE	CPT	0-0486755	1145	2
JORDAN EARLAND R	LTC	0-0337166	0963	1
JORDAN EDMUND A	1LT	0-1313748	C845	2
JORDAN EDWARD B	MAJ	C-1302138	C355	1
JORDAN EDWARD M	LTC	0-0379266	0767	1
JORDAN ELAINE M	2LT	N-0735503	1044	1
JORDAN ELMO C	CPT	0-1010090	0446	2
JORDAN ERLAND R	CPT	C-1311784	C647	2
JORDAN EVERETT C	CPT	C-0260621	1147	2
JORDAN FRANCIS N	COL	0-0114288	1055	3
JORDAN FRANKLIN F	LTC	0-0271033	0464	3
JORDAN FRED W	MAJ	C-0444391	0357	3
JORDAN GEORGE F	LTC	0-1926151	C263	1
JORDAN GERARD A	CW3	W-2153125	1062	1
JORDAN GORDAN A	LTC	0-0336818	C860	1
JORDAN HARVIE R	CW2	W-2142932	1057	1
JORDAN HENRY M	LTC	0-0380141	0867	1
JORDAN HENRY S	CPT	C-2055162	0346	1
JORDAN HERBERT R	COL	C-0181117	1054	3
JORDAN HOWARD B	COL	0-0282053	C567	3
JORDAN JAMES A	CW3	W-2145558	1067	1
JORDAN JAMES E	1LT	0-0534348	0246	2
JORDAN JAMES L	CW3	W-2136536	0163	1
JORDAN JAMES M	1LT	0-2033529	0356	1
JORDAN JESSE A	MAJ	0-0249037	0866	3
JORDAN JOHN	LTC	C-1574879	0163	1
JORDAN JOHN A	CPT	0-0449052	C247	2
JORDAN JOHN R	COL	0-0235938	0460	3
JORDAN JOSEF C	MAJ	0-0327316	C860	3
JORDAN JR EARLE H	LTC	0-1293600	0561	1
JORDAN JR FRED A	CPT	0-0472956	0140	2
JORDAN JR H T	CPT	0-1591229	C347	2
JORDAN JR HARRY S	1LT	0-0480440	C347	2
JORDAN JR HENRY H	MAJ	0-0565784	0161	1
JORDAN JR STEVE	MAJ	0-0988049	1063	1
JORDAN LAURENCE O	MAJ	0-1030049	0665	1
JORDAN LAWRENCE H	LTC	0-0319628	0852	1
JORDAN LEON H	MAJ	0-0962415	C861	1
JORDAN LESTER F	COL	0-0264907	C167	3
JORDAN LEVI	COL	0-0334196	0263	1
JORDAN LOUIS L	LTC	0-0384153	1263	3
JORDAN OCTAVIO L	MAJ	C-0339600	1160	1
JORDAN PATRICK	LTC	0-0451458	1160	1
JORDAN PAUL H	M G	C-0241877	C964	3
JORDAN PAUL H	COL	0-0258585	0164	3
JORDAN ROBERT B	CW3	W-2141819	0957	1
JORDAN ROBERT H	MAJ	C-0377040	0561	1
JORDAN RUFUS P	CW2	W-2151339	0663	1
JORDAN RUSSELL C	LTC	0-0223951	0844	2
JORDAN THEODORE W	CPT	0-1166523	0645	2
JORDAN WALTER H	CPT	0-1120154	0564	1
JORDAN WILLIAM B	COL	0-0123854	C857	3
JORDAN WILLIAM M	CPT	0-1175759	0764	1

NAME	GRADE	SVC NO	DATE RET MO YR	RET CODE
JORDAN WILLIAM P	CPT	0-0344528	0545	2
JORDAN WILLIAM R	COL	0-0121575	0552	3
JORGENS JOSEPH	1LT	0-1765043	1044	2
JORGENSEN CHARLES J	LTC	0-0284501	1058	1
JORGENSEN CHRIST	CW2	W-2141332	1157	1
JORGENSEN CLEMENT A	CPT	0-0331443	0445	2
JORGENSEN GALE W	CW2	W-3200182	0165	1
JORGENSEN JR JAMES M	LTC	0-0465588	1066	1
JORGENSEN MABEL G	1LT	N-0732623	0146	1
JORGENSEN WILLIAM F	LTC	0-0183408	0758	3
JORGENSON DONALD K	1LT	0-1017406	0946	1
JORGENSON EARL A	1LT	0-1171615	0248	1
JORGENSON ROY E	CW4	W-2116004	1055	1
JORGENSON WALTER R	LTC	0-1285434	0658	1
JORNS HOMER F	1LT	0-1945848	0145	2
JORTE CHARLES H	CPT	0-0166855	0130	1
JORTH AARON M	CPT	0-0505535	0545	2
JOSEPH ALFRED A	LTC	0-0366133	0665	1
JOSEPH ALVIN A	CPT	0-1112785	0164	1
JOSEPH CHARLES N	MAJ	0-2049970	0361	1
JOSEPH EDWARD G	COL	0-0138440	0254	3
JOSEPH JOHN A	COL	0-0251523	1066	3
JOSEPH LESTER G	CPT	0-0378356	0145	1
JOSEPH MARGARET M	MAJ	N-0773598	0667	1
JOSEPH ROBERT D	MAJ	0-2263167	1162	1
JOSEPHS WILLIAM W	COL	0-0317977	0566	3
JOSEY ALLEN I	COL	0-0302692	0346	2
JOSIFEK LUCILLE H	2LT	N-0702292	0832	1
JOSLIN GEORGE R	CPT	0-0193928	1262	3
JOSSERAND NEWTON	CPT	0-1523548	0162	1
JOST GEORGE R	LTC	0-1287185	0965	1
JOST JR HERMAN H	LTC	0-0268282	0567	3
JOST LEWIS M	MAJ	0-1186647	0763	2
JOST LOYD G	LTC	0-0301542	0766	3
JOST WILLIAM R	LTC	0-0258353	1067	3
JOUBERT MARY L	MAJ	N-0729254	0965	3
JOUETT JOHN K	LTC	0-0439375	1064	1
JOUJON-ROCHE JEAN E	LTC	0-0254508	0666	3
JOURDAN PARMER L	MAJ	0-1683459	0762	1
JOURDEA FOREST J	CPT	0-0472012	1058	1
JOUROLMON NEIL	LTC	0-0261311	0667	3
JOUVRE PAUL A	CPT	0-1329755	0461	1
JOVES EUSEBIC P	1LT	0-1896836	1149	1
JOWELL LEWIS L	CW4	W-2114842	0559	1
JOWELL MAITLAND A	CW2	W-3150999	0467	1
JOY FREDERICK	CPT	0-0285954	0346	2
JOY HAROLD W	CPT	0-0123853	0751	3
JOY ROBERT A	LTC	0-0456299	0264	1
JOY ROBERT D	CPT	0-0408898	0945	2
JOYAL JEANNE G	CW4	V-0120144	1263	1
JOYCE EDWARD P	LTC	0-0917077	0263	3
JOYCE EDWARD P	MAJ	0-0963842	0266	1
JOYCE EUGENE V	LTC	0-0451320	0658	1
JOYCE HAROLD O	LTC	0-0324964	C762	3
JOYCE JOHN A	LTC	0-0388290	0650	1
JOYCE JOHN J	CW4	W-2105647	0557	1
JOYCE JOSEPH P J	CPT	0-0438811	0146	2
JOYCE MARY T	2LT	N-0731054	1044	1
JOYCE MERLE L	COL	0-0244898	0362	3
JOYCE MICHAEL	CW3	W-2148733	0662	1
JOYCE RAY T	LTC	0-0235279	0359	2
JOYCE RAYMOND N	CPT	0-1178852	0347	2
JOYCE ROBERT J	MAJ	0-1824871	0461	2
JOYCE THOMAS B F	LTC	0-0924036	0165	3
JOYCE THOMAS F	LTC	0-0903231	0655	2
JOYCE WALDO V	COL	0-0224704	0164	3
JOYCE WILLIAM A	CW2	W-2123431	1046	2
JOYCE WILLIAM G	CW3	W-2149985	1064	1
JOYCE WILLIAM J	LTC	0-0504672	0848	1
JOYCE WILLIAM L	CW3	W-2142791	0760	1
JOYE JAMES L	CW2	W-2208403	0863	1
JOYER BOYD J	LTC	0-0286728	0667	3
JOYNER HENRY C	MAJ	0-1554404	0658	1
JOYNER HOUSTON C	COL	C-0211284	C558	1
JOYNER JOHN P	MAJ	0-0199090	0949	1

NAME	GRADE	SVC NO	DATE RET MO YR	RET CODE
JOYNER JOHNY P	CPT	0-0505539	0157	1
JOYNER JONES S	LTC	0-0305099	0366	3
JOYNER LEGETTE L	WO1	W-2127713	1046	1
JOZWIAK CASS J	LTC	0-1307028	C367	2
JUBECK JOHN F	LTC	0-0286122	C560	1
JUCHNIK BOGUMIL F	LTC	0-1644468	0763	1
JUCKETT RUSSELL B	CPT	C-1015576	0146	1
JUDAH CARTER M	LTC	0-0229258	0964	3
JUDD JR ROLAND O	CPT	0-1174905	C263	1
JUDD JR WARREN C	CW3	W-2148257	0163	1
JUDD SR LEROY A	CPT	0-0988630	1061	1
JUDD VERNON C	2LT	0-0503827	1144	2
JUDD WENDELL O	WO1	W-2148973	0965	2
JUDD WILLABEL L	MAJ	L-0501294	C855	2
JUDGE THOMAS J	1LT	0-1583180	0451	2
JUDKINS DONALD S	MAJ	0-1061745	1265	1
JUDKINS PAUL A	LTC	0-0333933	1161	1
JUDKINS ROBERT D	CW2	W-2146464	1060	1
JUDKINS ROGER R	1LT	0-0448759	C545	2
JUDKINS ROY	CW3	W-2207014	C366	1
JUDKINS WELDON R	1LT	C-2287184	1161	2
JUDSON CARL J	LTC	0-0155505	0455	3
JUDSON FREDERICK	COL	0-0301120	C459	1
JUDSON LYMAN D	COL	0-0118250	0755	3
JUDSON SR HOWARD F	CW4	W-2118145	1054	2
JUDSON WILLIAM L	MAJ	C-0302171	0266	3
JUDY FERRIS M	COL	0-0144895	0957	3
JUDY JOHN H	LTC	0-1639105	C864	1
JUDY WILLIAM R	CPT	0-4022380	1265	1
JUELL ADOLPH B	COL	0-0230684	0762	3
JUENGER GREGORY M	MAJ	0-1552711	0760	1
JUGE JAMES J	WO1	W-2128054	0757	1
JUGO JOSE	2LT	0-1896606	1148	1
JUHL LEE K	LTC	0-0283491	C967	3
JUHL MILFORD L	LTC	0-0746360	C765	2
JUILFS ROBERT W	CPT	0-0980420	1060	1
JULA JOHN	CW2	W-2101910	1152	1
JULIAN ALLEN P	COL	0-0184492	0356	2
JULIAN DAVID P	2LT	0-0540377	0244	2
JULIAN ERLE H	COL	0-0138896	0155	3
JULIAN LAWRENCE C	CPT	0-1179115	1053	2
JULIAN ORMAND C	MAJ	0-0490238	0146	2
JULIANA HORACE F	CPT	0-0422151	C258	1
JULIANO AMORE V	LTC	0-1185368	0264	1
JULIEN RICHARD	CPT	0-0279528	0457	1
JUMP CLARENCE F	LTC	C-0243052	0863	3
JUMP GEORGE V	LTC	C-1170790	C860	1
JUN EDWARD J	LTC	0-0386215	C846	2
JUNE RALPH A	CW4	W-2108813	1154	1
JUNEAU CHARLES G	LTC	0-0382763	0760	1
JUNEAU LINUS M	LTC	0-1302979	1167	1
JUNEK LAVONNE K	MAJ	N-0775557	C664	2
JUNG ASHTON W	1LT	0-1296535	C545	2
JUNG GEORGE P	MAJ	0-0170795	C550	3
JUNG PHILIP E S	1LT	0-0348376	0446	2
JUNG WERNER F	MAJ	C-0213750	0460	3
JUNGE CARL L	COL	0-0166169	1059	3
JUNGE GORDON H	CPT	0-1646298	C650	1
JUNGE ROBERT O	CPT	0-0282342	C244	2
JUNGERS KENNETH G	MAJ	0-2263328	C765	1
JUNI ARTHUR H	CPT	0-0110411	0251	3
JUNIEWICZ ALEX J	CPT	0-0490565	C547	1
JUNKER CARL F	LTC	0-0922169	C765	3
JUNKERMANN CARL S	B G	0-0278976	C563	3
JUNKERMANN EDGAR P	LTC	0-0198465	C252	3
JUNKINS ROBERT A	MAJ	0-1037082	0359	1
JUNKINS WALTER F	MAJ	C-0979955	C463	1
JUPIN JOHN	1LT	0-1306850	0745	2
JURANTY EDWARD	MAJ	C-0568838	1154	1
JURBALA JOHN	LTC	0-1057480	1161	1
JURBERG EDWARD R	CW2	W-2152848	0655	1
JURDAK FLORIAN E	LTC	0-1050328	C862	1
JURGENS CHARLES J	CW2	W-2148473	1263	1
JURGENS HAROLD L	LTC	0-1557173	1066	1
JURGENSEN MERTON P	CW4	W-2109801	1065	3

NAME	GRADE	SVC NO	DATE RET MO YR	RET CODE
JURKOWSKI A C	MAJ	0-1290077	0248	2
JURUSZ ALFRED S	CPT	0-0546814	0146	2
JURY EARL W	CW3	W-2149911	0565	1
JUST BIENVENIDO	2LT	0-1896816	1047	2
JUSTESEN WAYNE O	CPT	0-1172943	1046	2
JUSTICE BIRCHETTE	CW2	W-2210198	1164	1
JUSTICE CARROLL J	CW2	W-2147221	0662	1
JUSTICE EUGENE P	CW3	W-2149871	0359	2
JUSTICE HAROLD G	MAJ	0-2262678	0462	1
JUSTICE HENRY G	2LT	0-1823010	0245	2
JUSTICE HOWARD	MAJ	0-0301948	0652	1
JUSTICE JAMES E	CPT	0-1341436	0860	1
JUSTICE MARVIN L	CPT	0-0260121	0865	3
JUSTICE PERRY T	CW4	W-2126329	0156	1
JUSTICE THELMA E	CPT	N-0745212	0445	1
JUSTICE VERNELL D	1LT	0-1913016	0153	1
JUSTICE WILLIAM C	LTC	0-1697950	0457	1
JUSTICE WILLIAM F	1LT	0-0303276	0844	2
JUSTIN JOSEPH A	MAJ	0-2026362	0865	1
JUSTINIANO RUBEN	CPT	0-1924108	1163	1
JUSTISS WILLIS	CW2	W-2149221	1057	1
JUSTUS HAL C	LTC	0-0243396	0345	2
JUSTUS JOHN H	CPT	0-0281066	1146	2
JUTH ROBERT J	2LT	0-0468533	1144	2
JUTRAS PHILIP L	CW2	W-2111607	0461	1
JUWIG GUENTHER P	MAJ	0-2006104	1159	1
JUZWIAK MICHAEL N	MAJ	0-1557311	1162	1
KAATZ ERVIN A	2LT	0-2010501	0248	2
KABACK EDNA M	1LT	N-0725314	C345	1
KABAKJIAN ARMON E	COL	0-0263148	0362	3
KABERLE OTTO H	LTC	0-0174712	0156	3
KABOT MEYER	1LT	0-5008941	1262	2
KACANDA JOHN A	1LT	0-1037562	1045	2
KACHMARIK MIKE	LTC	0-0500945	0357	1
KACKAUCKAS JOSEPH P	CW3	W-2145457	0167	1
KACZKA EDWARD F	CPT	0-1038706	0646	2
KACZOROWSKI FELIX F	CPT	0-1289915	0656	1
KACZYNSKI EDWARD J	LTC	0-1000007	0457	1
KADEL RICHARD C	LTC	0-0239912	1146	2
KADEL ROBERT B	LTC	0-1548453	0961	1
KADELA JOHN L	CPT	0-1167057	1045	2
KADES CHARLES L	COL	0-0254358	0466	3
KADIN MAURICE	CPT	0-0361283	0345	2
KADING LEE F	CPT	0-0491324	1147	2
KADOW ROBERT J	CPT	0-0919379	1044	2
KADOWAKI ROBERT N	1LT	0-2046477	1146	2
KADUCK WILLIAM W	LTC	0-1323436	0563	1
KADYSIEWSKI EDMUND	CW3	W-2145143	0661	1
KAEISER WILLIAM H	LTC	0-0345300	1266	3
KAELIN JR HARRY J	MAJ	0-1303255	0963	2
KAELLNER JOHN W	1LT	0-1549304	0545	2
KAEMPFE ILMER H W	LTC	0-1012573	0763	1
KAEPPEL ARTHUR E	LTC	0-0159960	0648	3
KAEPPLINGER R P	2LT	0-1552713	0944	2
KAETZER THOMAS H	LTC	0-1844871	1163	1
KAFTER THEODORE	LTC	0-1573705	0562	1
KAH CARL L	LTC	0-0103904	1159	1
KAHAN BORIS S	1LT	0-0526186	0644	2
KAHANAMOKU DAVID P	CPT	0-0248958	1054	3
KAHANIAK JOHN	MAJ	0-1103722	0258	1
KAHAPEA ALEXANDER	LTC	0-1300497	C465	1
KAHL GEORGE G	LTC	0-1640612	1163	1
KAHL KENNETH W	MAJ	0-2016685	0762	1
KAHL ROLAND E	MAJ	0-2006014	1264	1
KAHL-WINTER RANDOLF	MAJ	0-4006051	0167	1
KAHLER HARRY F	CW3	W-2203652	1061	1
KAHLER WALTER E	CPT	0-0536420	0848	1
KAHLSTROM CARL E	CPT	0-0336347	0546	2
KAHN EARL A	MAJ	0-2035583	1061	1
KAHN EDWARD	1LT	0-0469502	1043	2
KAHN FRANK D	LTC	0-0370112	0165	1
KAHN HARRY	LTC	0-1574460	0357	1
KAHN HARRY	MAJ	0-1586702	0161	1
KAHN HOWARD L	MAJ	C-0540989	0147	1
KAHN MARCIA L	1LT	N-0772616	0650	1

NAME	GRADE	SVC NO	DATE RET MO YR	RET CODE
KAHN MYER E	1LT	0-1308343	0752	1
KAHN RALPH H	MAJ	0-0963677	0764	1
KAHN RAYMOND A	MAJ	0-2051660	0862	1
KAHOE JR JOSEPH O	MAJ	0-1017761	0762	1
KAHRER LOUIS J	WO1	W-2111916	0746	1
KAI HERBERT U	CPT	0-0243466	0461	3
KAIGLER CHARLES G	LTC	0-1824474	0265	1
KAILEY JACK G	MAJ	0-0970639	1062	1
KAIN DONALD M	MAJ	0-1038023	0964	1
KAINER MARIAN B	MAJ	N-0730530	1061	1
KAISER CHARLES G	COL	0-0271943	0862	2
KAISER DAVID W	1LT	0-1583183	0846	2
KAISER ELIAS N	LTC	0-0426502	0746	2
KAISER EMANUEL	CW3	W-2150648	1263	1
KAISER FRANK	MAJ	0-1315005	1054	1
KAISER GEORGE E	MAJ	0-0238754	1064	3
KAISER JEROME	MAJ	0-0372911	0446	2
KAISER JOHN D	2LT	0-0502486	0445	1
KAISER JR WILLIAM J	MAJ	0-2019174	0564	1
KAISER ROBERT A	MAJ	0-0398960	0463	1
KAISER RUDOLPH	MAJ	0-1287016	0963	1
KAISER STANLEY C	CPT	0-0445806	1144	2
KAISER WALTER J	COL	0-0348478	0367	3
KAITIS CHESTER S	2LT	0-1016084	0645	2
KAITIS EILEEN M	MAJ	L-0504815	0363	1
KAITZ ROBERT	CPT	0-1578680	1045	2
KAITZ SIDNEY L	LTC	0-1534524	0261	1
KAJFAS JOHN	CPT	0-1013021	0550	2
KAKIMOTO TOMMY T	CPT	0-0969596	1161	1
KAKLIKIAN HARRY Z	MAJ	0-0990916	0265	1
KAKNAVICH WILLIAM A	CPT	0-1644471	1055	1
KALAHER CHARLES T	MAJ	0-2025424	0260	1
KALAMARIDES JOHN J	CPT	0-0378534	0545	2
KALB EVERETT L	CPT	0-0449710	0846	2
KALBERG TED	CPT	0-1305521	0352	1
KALBFELL ROBERT F	1LT	0-0384822	0544	2
KALBFLEISCH M C	CPT	N-0760633	0654	2
KALBUS CLARA W	CPT	N-0783238	0946	1
KALCOW MICHAEL	CW3	W-2145862	0663	1
KALDENBAUGH HENRY PR	1LT	0-1309373	0644	2
KALDIZAR LEWIS	MAJ	0-0438983	0848	1
KALE HERBERT W	LTC	0-0360514	0240	1
KALE SAMUEL S S	LTC	0-0326650	0860	2
KALEN SYLVESTER	CW4	W-2142483	0964	1
KALER OSCAR A	COL	0-0224735	0661	3
KALINOWSKA CZESLAW	CW2	W-2149957	0160	1
KALINOWSKI JOSEPH W	MAJ	0-2033204	0662	1
KALISCH BERTRAM	COL	0-0415761	0762	3
KALISH ARTHUR L	MAJ	0-1103724	1160	1
KALISH CHARLES	2LT	0-1636112	1044	2
KALISH DANIEL F	MAJ	0-1036218	0161	1
KALK RUSSELL F	CPT	0-1796292	0646	1
KALKUT LEON J	1LT	0-1310257	0146	2
KALLAM JOHN F	MAJ	0-0937945	0862	1
KALLBERG HARRY A	LTC	0-0373110	0256	2
KALLBRIER WILLIAM P	CW2	W-2208274	1061	1
KALLINA FREDERICK	CPT	0-0465830	0948	2
KALLMINZER MALCOLM A	1LT	0-1018208	0746	2
KALLMYER LEWIS K	LTC	0-0264791	0665	3
KALLOCH JR PARKER C	COL	0-0468004	1045	2
KALLUNKI WAYNE J	LTC	0-0522163	0155	1
KALMAN JOHN N	MAJ	0-1643029	0760	1
KALMAN MANUEL	LTC	0-0361819	0963	3
KALMAN ROSALIE C	1LT	N-0744281	1045	1
KALMBACH JACK R	CW3	RW-2210096	1166	1
KALMON MORRIS	LTC	0-0311334	0465	3
KALP JOHN R	CW3	W-2148861	0364	1
KALSOW ERNEST F	LTC	0-0220699	0646	2
KALTENBACH ERWIN J	LTC	0-0223653	0363	1
KALTSUKIS SPIROS G	CW3	W-2206596	1164	2
KALUSH PAUL J	CW3	W-2136757	0261	1
KALVAR EDWARD S	LTC	0-1113283	0662	1
KALVIN GEORGE B	MAJ	0-0298058	1058	1
KAMAR CHARLES M	CPT	0-1895420	0660	1
KAMBERG SAMUEL	COL	0-0474455	1162	3
KAMBOS GUS	CW3	W-2152066	0463	1
KAMIL CHARLES	1LT	0-1302139	0645	2
KAMIN ERVIN C	1LT	0-2024312	1151	2
KAMINESTER HERBERT M	MAJ	0-0498532	0446	2
KAMINSKE ROY	MAJ	0-0992313	0365	1
KAMINSKI MICHAEL B	MAJ	0-2055525	1057	1
KAMINSKY JOSEPH	COL	0-0471172	0554	1
KAMINSKY MORRIS	CPT	0-0371801	0245	2
KAMM ERNEST R	1LT	0-1881376	0857	2
KAMM WILBUR F	LTC	0-0205823	0651	3
KAMMAN COURTENAY	MAJ	0-0196845	0849	3
KAMMEL HARRY J	LTC	0-1055881	0266	1
KAMMERLING DONALD	LTC	0-0252760	0465	3
KAMP CHARLES F	LTC	0-0198061	0262	3
KAMP GORDON H	CW3	W-2141603	1057	1
KAMPS JOHN H	CPT	0-0451705	1145	1
KAMRIN BENJAMIN B	LTC	0-0290785	0245	2
KANA FRED J	CPT	0-0307457	0446	2
KANAK FRANK	LTC	0-0485000	0557	1
KANANEN EDWARD H	MAJ	0-0258046	0663	3
KANCIUS STANLEY C	2LT	0-0994833	1051	1
KANDEL ALFRED	CPT	0-0528048	1045	2
KANDELIN WALTER W	MAJ	0-1328727	0365	1
KANDIGAN CHARLES A	LTC	0-1061746	0463	1
KANDIS MARGARET A	1LT	N-0768757	0848	2
KANDLER JACOB P	LTC	0-1114580	1067	1
KANE AGNES E	CPT	N-0759142	0349	2
KANE ALLEN E	LTC	0-1545428	0962	1
KANE ANGELA M	2LT	N-0720178	1144	1
KANE ANTHONY S	CPT	0-1080458	0846	1
KANE ARNOLD	LTC	0-1042614	0261	1
KANE CARL L	LTC	0-0133412	1048	3
KANE DANIEL F	CPT	0-0451130	0552	1
KANE EDWIN A	COL	0-0100587	0852	3
KANE GENE L	CPT	0-1590172	1060	1
KANE GEORGE C	CPT	0-1666309	1047	1
KANE GEORGE R	LTC	0-1286473	0366	1
KANE HAROLD W	MAJ	0-1316298	0461	1
KANE HENRY S	MAJ	0-0163498	0648	3
KANE JOHN T	LTC	0-0328937	0859	1
KANE JOHN W	CW3	W-2152160	1059	1
KANE JOSEPH R	1LT	0-0491385	0745	2
KANE JOSEPHINE	MAJ	N-0783143	0566	3
KANE JR HERBERT W	WO1	W-2109740	1045	2
KANE JR JOHN K	CPT	0-1030164	0862	3
KANE LEO P	LTC	0-0451551	0457	1
KANE PAUL P	MAJ	0-1299830	1146	1
KANE RAYMOND E	COL	0-1165519	1167	1
KANE ROBERT J	CPT	0-1291546	0346	2
KANE THEODORE F	LTC	0-0346880	0360	1
KANE THOMAS C	MAJ	0-0164281	0545	1
KANE WALTER J	LTC	0-0276454	0265	3
KANEALLY FRANCES C	MAJ	N-0730420	0665	3
KANEALY JOHN F	CPT	0-0531263	0146	2
KANEGAI YOSHIO G	MAJ	0-2037067	0662	1
KANGAS TYKE R	LTC	0-1548879	0662	1
KANIA FRANK W	MAJ	0-1111156	0659	2
KANIA JOSEPH F	LTC	0-1167490	0166	2
KANNER SIDNEY	CPT	0-1314055	0163	1
KANOUSE CHESTER F	CPT	0-0924266	0747	2
KANOZA BERNARD	2LT	0-1030486	1043	2
KANSKY ELI	LTC	0-1038024	1067	3
KANSKY WALTER A	LTC	0-0234773	0557	2
KANSTRUP ARTHUR A	CPT	0-0327511	0866	3
KANTARIAN HAIG A	1LT	0-1560028	0348	2
KANTER MARVIN W	CPT	0-1172544	1048	2
KANTOLA HELEN E	2LT	N-0723999	0645	1
KANTOR GEORGE J	COL	0-0286418	0866	1
KANTOR JACK	CPT	0-1685762	0445	2
KANTORIK JOHN L	1LT	0-1641107	1155	1
KANTRIMAITIS JOHN	WO1	W-2148734	0154	1
KANZEKBACH MELVIN A	CW3	W-2214188	1167	1
KAPAUN WALLACE A	1LT	0-0411174	0745	2
KAPELOWITZ MAX	MAJ	0-0450969	1054	1
KAPICA FRANCIS A	LTC	0-0546784	0464	1
KAPINOS JOHN R	CW2	RW-2211052	1264	1
KAPLAN ABRAHAM H	CPT	0-0336283	1153	3
KAPLAN ALBERT	1LT	0-1002458	0646	2
KAPLAN ARTHUR	1LT	0-1289741	1045	2
KAPLAN ARTHUR T	LTC	0-0174929	1161	3
KAPLAN BEN B	1LT	0-0529308	0544	2
KAPLAN CHARLES	MAJ	0-0375136	0755	2
KAPLAN DAVID	CW2	W-2152177	0261	1
KAPLAN FRANK	WO1	W-2147898	0457	1
KAPLAN FRANK D	1LT	0-1302476	1146	1
KAPLAN GEORGE	LTC	0-0475357	0945	2
KAPLAN GEORGE G	LTC	0-0363744	0864	1
KAPLAN HAROLD L	MAJ	0-1015805	0955	1
KAPLAN HYMAN J	LTC	0-0309528	1045	2
KAPLAN ISADORE	MAJ	0-0371542	0445	1
KAPLAN ISADORE	MAJ	0-0485750	0249	2
KAPLAN JOSEPH	CPT	0-0333873	1145	2
KAPLAN JOSEPH A	LTC	0-0207597	0756	3
KAPLAN LEO	MAJ	0-1047603	0661	1
KAPLAN LOUIS	CPT	0-0507982	1145	1
KAPLAN MORRIS L	2LT	0-1578686	1044	2
KAPLAN MURRAY J	MAJ	0-0972904	0462	1
KAPLAN NATHAN	CW3	W-2146336	0264	2
KAPLAN RONALD R	COL	0-0374105	0964	3
KAPLAN SAMUEL D	MAJ	0-0413446	1046	2
KAPLAN SEYMOUR T	CPT	0-1534053	1145	2
KAPLAN SOL	2LT	0-2015782	1160	1
KAPLAN THEODORE H	1LT	0-0533958	1145	1
KAPLAN WILLIAM	2LT	0-1591841	0645	2
KAPLOW LEONARD S	1LT	0-1039315	0746	2
KAPNER WALTER H	LTC	0-0308403	0162	3
KAPOPOULOS GARY J	COL	0-0264450	1061	3
KAPP CHARLES L	1LT	0-1543253	0144	2
KAPP ERVIN J	CPT	0-0949095	1059	1
KAPP JOHN M	MAJ	0-1037087	0361	1
KAPP RICHARD C	2LT	0-2006391	0346	1
KAPP ROLLIN W	MAJ	0-1037088	0961	1
KAPP SERGIUS N	CPT	0-0451892	0952	1
KAPPANADZE ROMAN	CPT	0-0525285	1045	1
KAPPEL VERNON E	1LT	0-1314645	0345	2
KAPPELMAN LESTER B	CPT	0-1311094	1146	2
KAPPEN CHARLES V	MAJ	0-0305259	0653	1
KAPPIE ANTHONY	2LT	0-1592319	0145	2
KAPRAL JOSEPH J	LTC	0-0450195	1154	1
KAPS FRED A	LTC	0-1698187	0748	2
KAPSA RICHARD L	COL	0-0309097	0750	1
KAPUA JOSEPH K	1LT	0-0286934	0858	3
KAPUTA JOSEPH M	LTC	0-0378179	1059	1
KARABA MARTIN F	CW3	W-2142767	0165	2
KARAHALIS GREGORY G	CW4	W-2142858	0361	1
KARALIUS ALBERT L	CW3	W-2144804	1060	1
KARAM EMILE	MAJ	0-1059511	0467	1
KARAM ROBERT	MAJ	0-1534054	0861	1
KARAPATSKIE JOHN F	CW2	W-2151192	1057	1
KARAS STANLEY A	LTC	0-0885734	0557	1
KARAS WILLIAM J	LTC	0-0334805	0945	2
KARASEK JAMES J	1LT	0-1059512	0247	2
KARAU WILLIAM A	2LT	0-4068352	0458	2
KARBEL HOWARD W	LTC	0-0452720	1047	2
KARBER JON F	CPT	0-1039418	0366	1
KARBLEY HAROLD L	LTC	0-1577400	0860	1
KARCH HARRY A	MAJ	0-1824306	1060	1
KARCH HERBERT S	LTC	0-0203543	1058	3
KARCHER CHARLES F	CPT	0-1016891	0346	2
KARCHER FREDERICK	CPT	0-1282391	1059	1
KARDECG WALTER W	MAJ	0-2047601	0661	1
KAREIVA CHARLES T	MAJ	0-0578126	0164	1
KAREN JOSEPH W	2LT	0-1997421	0646	2
KARESH HARRY A	LTC	0-0246791	1063	3
KARESKY SIDNEY I	1LT	0-1294718	0550	1
KARGE THERON F	1LT	0-0372227	0445	1
KARGEL FREDDIE F	CPT	0-0495403	0358	1
KARGER ALFRED G	COL	0-0268810	0861	3
KARICHER NELSON R	LTC	0-1646787	0467	1
KARIG HOWARD L	COL	0-0505267	0863	3
KARIKA CHARLES	CW2	W-2151654	0761	1
KARIUS FRED	2LT	0-1913783	0844	1
KARKALAS ARTHUR A	LTC	0-0177415	0960	3
KARL BENJAMIN F	CW4	W-2151617	0963	1
KARL NORBERT F	2LT	0-1596680	0346	2
KARLAK JOHN W	CPT	0-1289094	1045	2
KARLEEN CONRAD E	LTC	0-0263420	0747	2
KARLEN HARVEY M	1LT	0-1010885	1044	2
KARLSON JOHN R	MAJ	0-0408700	0761	1
KARMATH JOHN I	CW4	W-2002357	1059	3
KARNES KENNETH F	MAJ	0-1543291	1063	1
KARNILOWICZ ANN C	2LT	N-0767925	0645	1
KARNS FREDERICK	MAJ	0-0165795	0750	3
KAROLCHUCK PHOEBE N	2LT	N-0701474	1131	1
KAROW JOSEPH J	COL	0-0263041	0864	3
KARP LEWIS S	1LT	0-0509831	0445	2
KARP ROSE	MAJ	N-0723997	0964	3
KARP STANLEY F	LTC	0-0250376	0666	3
KARP WILLIAM A	COL	0-0168226	0555	3
KARPE HENRY Z	LTC	0-1002039	0467	1
KARPEICHIK JOHN	2LT	0-1824755	0145	2
KARPEL SAUL	MAJ	0-0379839	0646	2
KARR ALBERT W	MAJ	0-0288782	0167	3
KARR CARL R	MAJ	0-0504199	0856	1
KARR FRANK W	CW2	W-2118531	0447	1
KARR RUSSELL B	MAJ	0-1633321	0561	1
KARSNITZ CHARLES R	LTC	0-1548878	0962	1
KARST JOSEPH R	CW4	W-2144608	0967	1
KARSTEN ERNST W	LTC	0-0349496	0863	1
KARWASKI LEOPOLD J	LTC	0-1109397	0960	1
KARWOSKI JOSEPH A	1LT	0-2042974	1055	1
KARYTA STANISLAW	MAJ	0-1548237	0753	1
KASARDA RALPH W	MAJ	0-1011125	1157	1
KASBEER MAX F	CW3	W-2152466	1262	1
KASCHAK HAROLD L	LTC	0-1167491	0862	1
KASCHEW ALEXANDER	MAJ	0-1894563	0860	1
KASCMER JOSEPH	2LT	0-1308517	1044	2
KASE CECIL B	LTC	0-0888242	1062	1
KASEFF BERNARD H	1LT	0-1302094	0845	2
KASEN JACOB	1LT	0-0537052	0245	2
KASHAFF HAZEL A	LTC	N-0728633	1266	3
KASHPUREFF NIKOLAI	CW2	W-2101282	0945	2
KASICH ANTHONY M	LTC	0-0228196	0146	2
KASIK OTTO	CPT	0-0499156	1046	2
KASKIN ALVIN	MAJ	0-0279584	0253	1
KASL GLEN M	MAJ	0-0258297	0267	3
KASMER JULIUS J	LTC	0-1579853	0661	1
KASOLD EDWARD F	LTC	0-1124018	0860	1
KASPAR ALBERT F L	CW3	W-2145081	0663	1
KASPAR JOE L	CPT	0-0531858	0847	2
KASPER EDWARD C	CPT	0-0460843	0845	2
KASPER HERBERT F	LTC	0-0886822	0557	1
KASPER RAYMOND I	LTC	0-0522102	0864	1
KASPER STANLEY F	LTC	0-0451453	0950	1
KASPER WALTER F	MAJ	0-2037871	0960	1
KASPRAK LEON	COL	0-0343478	1062	1
KASPROWSKI EDWARD	MAJ	0-2008634	0263	1
KASS ALBERT	MAJ	0-0424487	0547	1
KASS CHARLES	MAJ	0-2042781	0753	1
KASS DAVID R	CPT	0-0471436	1145	2
KASS HAROLD M	MAJ	0-0509145	0146	2
KASSAN DAVID	1LT	0-1796484	0444	2
KASSEL HARRY T	CPT	0-0288515	1146	2
KASSEL MAXWELL S	CPT	0-0509884	0446	2
KASSELS MAURICE F	CPT	0-0490239	0845	2
KASSEN WILLIAM [illegible]	COL	0-0184403	0562	3
KASSLER FRED W	1LT	0-1825297	1045	2
KASSNER ERNEST	MAJ	0-0962948	0663	1
KASTANOWSKI JOHN A	MAJ	0-2039379	0164	1
KASTEN EMIL W	MAJ	0-1306727	0364	2
KASTEN PETER H	CW3	W-2142353	0758	1
KASTENBAUM HARRY	CPT	0-0201287	0453	3
KASTLE JOHN	CW3	W-2206416	0665	1
KASTLER GEORGE J	CPT	0-1797144	0458	2
KASTLER PATRICK H	LTC	0-0202839	0857	3

292-560 O - 68 - 14

NAME	GRADE	SVC NO	DATE RET MO YR	RET CODE
KASTNER AUGUST A	LTC	0-0276649	C760	1
KASUN JOSEPH F	LTC	0-1296040	0264	1
KATALENICH THOMAS S	1LT	0-0371231	0145	2
KATALINAS JOSEPH A	LTC	0-0328994	C560	1
KATES DON B	COL	0-0267215	1067	3
KATES HOWARD A W	LTC	0-0266543	0154	3
KATH CHESTER	LTC	0-0276630	0647	1
KATIN JACQUES H	CW3	W-2136713	0664	2
KATO MATT J	LTC	0-1035086	0261	1
KATSCHKE WILLIAM	1LT	C-0976476	0657	1
KATSIAFICAS NICHOLAS	LTC	0-0448789	0165	1
KATSONES PALMER G	CPT	0-2263696	0265	1
KATTNER FRANCIS R	CPT	0-0503235	C947	2
KATZ ARTHUR	1LT	0-1302311	1045	2
KATZ CHARLES	CW3	W-2145201	0259	1
KATZ CHARLES I	COL	C-0297818	0767	3
KATZ GEORGE	LTC	0-1035039	C865	1
KATZ HAROLD	CW2	W-3430293	1265	1
KATZ HERMAN E	1LT	0-1114986	0146	2
KATZ IRVIN J	COL	0-0476775	0954	1
KATZ JULIAN H	1LT	0-0308356	1044	2
KATZ LESTER F	CW2	W-2209676	1166	1
KATZ LEWIS M	CPT	0-1716476	C645	2
KATZ MAX L	LTC	0-0509437	0156	1
KATZ MORRIS J	LTC	0-1577403	C364	1
KATZ RACHEL	2LT	N-0771383	0545	1
KATZ RAYMOND	1LT	0-1311018	C146	1
KATZ SEYMOUR M	MAJ	C-0404638	0645	2
KATZ SOL	MAJ	C-0332387	0246	2
KATZ STANLEY M	1LT	0-1002460	1045	2
KATZ STANLEY R	1LT	0-1305785	C246	2
KATZ WILLIAM J	1LT	0-1336511	1152	1
KATZBECK JOHN W	LTC	0-1101520	0161	1
KAUFER LAURENCE F	LTC	0-1037565	0463	1
KAUFFMAN CARL H	MAJ	0-0345122	0762	1
KAUFFMAN HARVEY E	COL	0-0111285	C851	3
KAUFFMAN HERBERT V	MAJ	0-2262282	0464	1
KAUFFMAN JAMES W	CPT	0-2014539	1162	1
KAUFFMAN JEROME A	CPT	0-1725521	0347	2
KAUFFMAN JOHN F	LTC	0-1341273	0665	1
KAUFFMAN JOHNNY G	MAJ	C-2085518	0163	1
KAUFFMAN STACY M	CW4	W-2129286	1058	1
KAUFFMAN WILLIAM A	2LT	0-2028708	C452	1
KAUFMAN ABRAHAM A	COL	0-0248738	0167	3
KAUFMAN ALKIE C	LTC	0-0336603	0460	1
KAUFMAN ALVIN J	CPT	0-1556157	0459	1
KAUFMAN CARL K	LTC	0-0322366	C367	3
KAUFMAN DON R	CPT	C-1685023	C855	2
KAUFMAN EDWARD	MAJ	0-0109108	0234	1
KAUFMAN ERNEST	MAJ	C-1318310	0151	1
KAUFMAN ERWIN R	1LT	0-1062215	C246	2
KAUFMAN HARRY	CPT	0-0498253	1263	1
KAUFMAN HERMAN P	LTC	0-0334706	0263	3
KAUFMAN JACK	CPT	0-1703582	0645	2
KAUFMAN JAMES K	MAJ	C-0381466	C443	2
KAUFMAN LOUIS A	LTC	C-0422101	0566	1
KAUFMAN LOUIS L	1LT	0-1112795	0858	1
KAUFMAN MARTHA M	MAJ	N-0790197	0364	1
KAUFMAN MORTON E	1LT	C-0944669	0848	1
KAUFMAN MORTON L	1LT	0-1287720	1045	2
KAUFMAN RALPH J	CPT	0-2262748	C857	1
KAUFMAN RUSSELL H	COL	0-0227321	C159	3
KAUFMAN SAUL O	1LT	0-0502866	0545	2
KAUFMAN WILLIAM	MAJ	0-2033938	0963	1
KAUFMANN BERTRAM	MAJ	C-0197727	0648	3
KAUFMANN MAURICE	CPT	C-0333954	0945	2
KAUFMANN ULRICH G	MAJ	C-0945757	0165	1
KAUFMANN WILLIAM R	MAJ	0-0958845	0463	1
KAUKA KAIPO F	LTC	0-0387314	1060	1
KAUL LLOYD K	CW3	W-3150331	1167	1
KAULAKIS EDWARD S	LTC	0-0452114	1155	1
KAUPPILA HANS N	CPT	0-0239150	0648	1
KAUSEK BERT G	MAJ	C-1595614	0461	1
KAUTH JOHN W	1LT	0-1824195	104N	1
KAUTZ GEORGE W	LTC	0-0419139	0763	3
KAUTZ HARRY G	LTC	0-0260294	0751	3
KAUTZ RICHARD W	MAJ	0-0977319	0962	1
KAUTZ WILLIAM W	LTC	0-0543605	0464	1
KAVADAS DANIEL S	LTC	0-1765358	1060	2
KAVANACH WILLIAM P	MAJ	0-0402444	0546	2
KAVANACH WILLIAM T	1LT	0-1296536	0945	2
KAVANAUGH FRANCIS E	COL	C-0265627	0566	3
KAVANAUGH MYLES T	CPT	0-1695207	0445	2
KAVANAUGH THOMAS E	LTC	0-1046511	0957	1
KAVANAUGH WINIFRED C	MAJ	N-0762521	0864	1
KAVENEY JOHN J	1LT	0-1590582	1045	2
KAVENEY WALTER J	CW2	W-2106319	0947	2
KAVITT HENRY HYMA	CPT	0-0370250	0246	1
KAVKA ANTHONY J	MAJ	0-1651101	0560	1
KAVLI EDWARD E	MAJ	0-1948487	0560	1
KAVNER IRVING	2LT	0-1046512	0146	2
KAVOVIT CHARLES	CPT	0-0475475	C446	2
KAWA CASMERE J	2LT	0-2000683	1145	2
KAWA WALTER	1LT	0-1295224	0445	2
KAWAGUCHI KATSUMI T	MAJ	0-1899378	0864	1
KAWALESKI FRANK	WO1	W-2108607	0255	1
KAWAMOTO NOBUO	MAJ	0-1925341	0166	1
KAWASAKI ISAAC A	MAJ	0-0420945	1046	2
KAWECKI EDWIN	CPT	0-1103252	0146	2
KAY CARNIG	LTC	0-0355140	1162	3
KAY FLOYD F	LTC	0-0216236	0763	3
KAY ISRAEL H	MAJ	0-1080870	0866	3
KAY JAMES G	MAJ	0-0971001	0564	1
KAY JR FRANK J	CW3	W-2148862	0766	1
KAY ROBERT R	CPT	0-1290613	0646	1
KAY ROBERT L	LTC	0-0543485	1063	1
KAY TED	MAJ	0-0451453	0854	1
KAY WILFRED S	COL	0-0186240	0848	3
KAYE BERNARD F	CPT	0-1533364	0545	2
KAYE JOHN P	COL	0-0165185	0751	3
KAYE PAUL W	CPT	0-0402335	0944	2
KAYES STEPHEN J	1LT	0-1108774	1048	1
KAYHS ERNEST W	CPT	0-1016249	0148	2
KAYLOR JOHN C	MAJ	0-2283917	0363	1
KAYLOR JOHN R	LTC	0-1845294	1162	1
KAYNER HOWARD L	LTC	0-0310856	0558	3
KAYRUKTIS ALFONSE F	2LT	0-1592964	1044	2
KAYS HAROLD V	LTC	0-1331192	0867	1
KAYSER FREDERICK	LTC	0-2041025	1167	1
KAZANJIAN BEARJ G	COL	0-0295616	0862	2
KAZARNOWICZ EDWARD J	LTC	0-1303735	0660	1
KAZERMAN JOSEPH	LTC	0-0349088	0860	1
KAZMAREK HELEN F	2LT	N-0728235	1143	1
KAZMIERCZAK STELLA	CPT	N-0727394	1162	2
KEACH WILLIAM P	MAJ	0-2044316	0958	1
KEADLE HOMER H	1LT	0-0383445	0745	2
KEAG HELEN G	CPT	N-0760031	1047	1
KEAGLE LEONADUS B	MAJ	0-1646304	1056	1
KEALA SAMUEL L	LTC	0-0242006	1059	1
KEALEY GEORGE I	MAJ	0-0273039	0455	1
KEALEY HORACE M	CW4	W-2111470	0658	1
KEAN JOHN R	1LT	0-1039715	1145	2
KEAN RUSSELL E	COL	0-0131673	1059	3
KEAN THOMAS V	LTC	0-0187542	0648	3
KEAN WILLIAM M	1LT	0-1688794	1051	1
KEANE CHARLES F	CW3	W-2150668	0366	1
KEANE JOHN M	LTC	0-1113290	1060	1
KEANE JOSEPH P	LTC	0-1948167	1162	1
KEANE THOMAS B	LTC	0-1184082	0967	3
KEANON SR FRANCIS P	MAJ	0-1114190	0461	1
KEARIN LAWRENCE E	LTC	0-1292001	0866	1
KEARINS JR BARTLEY E	MAJ	0-1320705	0261	1
KEARLEY ALICE G	2LT	N-0726870	1043	1
KEARNEY BERNARD W	B G	0-0161703	0649	3
KEARNEY BRYANT	COL	0-0274398	0664	3
KEARNEY CHARLES R	COL	0-0309819	0559	2
KEARNEY ERICK W	MAJ	0-0250862	0366	3
KEARNEY JOHN J	CW3	W-2151661	1263	1
KEARNEY JOHN O	1LT	0-1046514	0146	2
KEARNEY JOHN W	LTC	0-0478175	0553	1
KEARNEY JR JOHN A	CW3	W-2143274	0263	1
KEARNEY KENNETH J	LTC	0-1293786	0166	1
KEARNEY MARY F	MAJ	L-0125005	1066	3
KEARNEY RAYMOND C	LTC	0-1010619	0761	1
KEARNEY ROBERT M	1LT	0-1341792	0553	1
KEARNEY WILLIAM F	MAJ	C-2007719	1056	1
KEARNS CECIL	MAJ	0-0963473	1059	2
KEARNS CHARLES F	CPT	0-0462339	0746	2
KEARNS JOHN A	MAJ	C-1031183	C461	1
KEARNS JOHN F	LTC	0-1039425	1163	2
KEARNS JR CHARLES M	COL	0-0228706	C365	3
KEARNS RALPH E	LTC	0-2047379	C566	1
KEARNS ROBERT J	CW2	W-2150686	0857	1
KEARNS SR GILBERT P	LTC	C-0152991	0346	1
KEARNS SYLVESTER	CPT	0-0108624	1049	1
KEARNS WILLIAM S	LTC	0-1044575	C566	1
KEARNY CRESSON H	MAJ	0-0324605	1045	2
KEARTON JR JOHN G	1LT	0-0496742	0845	2
KEAS ARTHUR H	CW3	W-2146069	0964	1
KEASEY GEORGE	1LT	0-1174019	1045	2
KEAST WILLIAM J	1LT	0-1304395	0146	2
KEATHLEY CLAUDE C	CPT	0-0421497	1145	2
KEATING JAMES M	LTC	0-0289817	C960	3
KEATING JOHN A	LTC	0-1018691	0862	1
KEATING JR THOMAS	1LT	0-1823167	C246	2
KEATING LINDALE	CW4	W-2146126	0359	1
KEATING PAUL G	LTC	C-0359743	0256	1
KEATING RAYMOND G	LTC	C-1011237	0862	1
KEATING REGINALD B	LTC	0-0253411	C663	1
KEATON EARL R	MAJ	C-0410054	1160	1
KEATON MORGAN	COL	0-0113685	C-51	3
KEATS SIDNEY	MAJ	C-0391404	0845	2
KEAY LUTHER B	1LT	C-1015092	1145	2
KECKLER EVELYN L	CPT	0-0482134	C753	1
KECKLER RALPH J	LTC	0-0364690	C560	1
KEDZIOR CASIMIR J	CPT	0-1184083	C547	1
KEE GEORGE H	CW3	W-2209510	1166	2
KEE PAT M	MAJ	0-1061751	1162	1
KEE SAM R	MAJ	C-1646305	0361	1
KEE WILLIAM V	CPT	0-0507588	0245	2
KEEBLER JOSEPH F	LTC	0-1280920	C764	1
KEEFE ANSELM M	COL	0-0190892	0355	3
KEEFE CHARLES B	LTC	0-0166618	1154	3
KEEFE DONALD J	CPT	0-2032940	0357	1
KEEFE ETHEL A	CPT	L-0105072	0358	2
KEEFE JOHN D	LTC	C-0291407	1160	1
KEEFE JR JOHN E	LTC	0-0252558	1165	3
KEEFE ROND	LTC	0-0453114	0763	1
KEEFER HAROLD A	1LT	0-2024104	0747	2
KEEFER RUSSELL L	MAJ	0-1171216	1160	1
KEEGAN MICHAEL J	CPT	0-1307705	0847	2
KEEHN HARRY D	1LT	0-1320004	1045	2
KEEHNEN KENNETH K	LTC	0-1289270	C860	1
KEEL JAMES B	CPT	0-1327551	0760	2
KEEL PATRICK G	CPT	0-1288754	C947	2
KEELE JR JOHN C	LTC	0-1533106	0761	1
KEELER EDMUND L	LTC	0-0195033	0146	2
KEELER ELIZABETH	2LT	N-0720401	0144	1
KEELER ROBERT	CPT	0-2046400	C147	1
KEELER ROBERT C	1LT	0-0887431	0147	2
KEELER ROBERT O	CPT	0-1295893	1051	1
KEELER ROBERT J	LTC	0-0475976	0164	3
KEELER ROBERT L	LTC	0-2033270	C966	1
KEELER THADDEUS R	CW3	W-2146761	0764	1
KEELER WILLIAM	CPT	0-2016292	0257	1
KEELING FORREST E	COL	0-0119822	C657	3
KEELING REX G	LTC	0-0404550	0246	2
KEELING ROY E	COL	0-0149671	1054	3
KEELING WILLIAM R	2LT	0-0533452	C945	2
KEELY JAMES E	MAJ	0-0273340	0147	2
KEELY JR ROBERT W	2LT	0-1822885	C745	2
KEEN CLARENCE N	LTC	0-0365873	C255	1
KEEN DONALD E	MAJ	0-1885978	1166	2
KEEN FRANKLIN A	LTC	0-2040885	0766	1
KEEN MARLIN O	CW3	W-2205930	0465	1
KEENA CHARLIE F	LTC	0-C384059	0266	3
KEENA CLAIR S	LTC	0-1295895	0859	1
KEENAN FRANCIS	MAJ	0-0298302	0453	1
KEENAN JAMES B	CW3	W-2148227	1058	1
KEENAN JAMES P	1LT	0-1011194	0444	2
KEENAN JAMES P	CW3	W-2142970	0659	1
KEENAN JASPER F	CW3	W-2142164	0559	1
KEENAN JOHN T	CPT	0-0505455	1044	2
KEENAN JOHN V	MAJ	0-1010928	0550	1
KEENAN THOMAS G	LTC	0-1554918	1262	3
KEENE CECIL R	2LT	0-0548508	0847	2
KEENE ERNEST H	MAJ	0-0199953	0648	3
KEENE JOSEPH R	CW3	W-2149705	0962	1
KEENE LAWRENCE F	MAJ	0-1185369	0456	1
KEENE LYNDELL F	LTC	0-0426724	1062	1
KEENE PURLEY L	CPT	0-0188445	0151	3
KEENE RAYMOND E	MAJ	0-2200122	1266	1
KEENE RUDOLPH C	CW2	W-2149196	0161	1
KEENER CARL T	CW2	W-2149993	0958	1
KEENER GRACE E	CPT	N-0700415	0946	1
KEENEY FRANCIS R	LTC	0-1104902	1160	1
KEENEY HARRY C	COL	0-0455689	1059	1
KEENEY HERMAN F	CPT	0-0217794	0262	3
KEENON JOHN E	LTC	0-0228707	C859	1
KEENUM JOHN C	LTC	0-1637793	1062	1
KEENY LESLIE R	LTC	0-0256684	0857	3
KEEP ELINOR R	MAJ	N-0736940	1166	1
KEESE CHARLES J	CPT	0-0409561	1045	2
KEESE HENRY G	CW4	W-2136535	0559	1
KEESE OLIVER D	COL	0-0215051	0752	3
KEESEE RALPH V	LTC	0-1312312	0461	1
KEESHEN JR WILLIAM J	MAJ	0-2051194	0960	1
KEESLAR RALPH L	CPT	0-1286499	0246	2
KEESLING WILEY F	WO1	W-2107954	0650	1
KEESTER JOHN F	LTC	0-1169593	0760	1
KEESY EUGENE R	1LT	0-1168311	0746	1
KEETER CLINTON W	MAJ	0-2011528	0361	1
KEETER WALTER C	CPT	0-0502518	0948	2
KEETON HILLES G	CPT	0-1557622	0746	2
KEETON OZRO	CPT	0-0509850	0547	1
KEEVIL SIDNEY G	CW3	W-2200521	0966	3
KEGLEY GUY R	LTC	0-1573324	1060	1
KEGLOVITS WILLIAM F	CW3	W-2145915	0958	1
KEHM RONALD C	COL	0-0235899	0454	3
KEHOE BERNARD	MAJ	0-0108987	0344	1
KEHOE JAMES A	B G	0-0330837	1056	3
KEHOE ROBERT T	WO1	W-2121405	0344	2
KEHRER RICHARD F	CW2	W-2141607	0755	1
KEIDER JOHN C	LTC	0-0397548	1060	1
KEIDSER JOHN A	MAJ	0-0486124	0355	1
KEIFER GEORGE W	CW3	W-2143498	0562	1
KEIGHER CLINTON T	LTC	0-0243356	0955	3
KEIL LLOYD E	1LT	0-0391220	0445	1
KEIL MARCUS A	CPT	0-0430092	0645	2
KEIL WALTER F	CW2	W-2206288	0863	1
KEIL WILLIAM A	LTC	0-1949818	0467	1
KEILCH RALPH F	MAJ	0-2002088	0660	1
KEILEN DANIEL H	1LT	0-0969402	1061	1
KEILLOR GEORGE O	MAJ	0-1110593	0557	1
KEILMAN CHARLES H	MAJ	0-0497455	0657	1
KEIM HOWARD H	MAJ	C-0257176	0557	3
KEIM JOHN H	LTC	0-0454503	0760	1
KEINSLEY WALTER O	LTC	0-2047382	1162	1
KEIPE HENRY A	LTC	0-0221163	0862	3
KEIPER THEODORE W	LTC	0-0299353	1159	3
KEIR WILFRED G	2LT	0-0400381	0143	1
KEIRN IRA O	MAJ	0-0183053	0546	2
KEIRN JAMES C	LTC	0-0718662	0367	1
KEISER DONALD J	CPT	0-1166303	0946	2
KEISER ELLSWORTH	MAJ	0-0262392	0766	3
KEISER FRANK G	LTC	0-0964329	1067	1
KEISER GEORGE	CPT	0-1826781	0260	1
KEISER JOHN T	COL	0-0146692	0752	3
KEISER MARTIN F	MAJ	C-1166753	1157	1
KEISER ROBERT P	CPT	0-0511561	0845	2

NAME	GRADE	SVC NO	DATE RET MO YR	RET CODE
KEISERMAN JOSEPH	CPT	O-1695981	1045	2
KEISTER GUY A	LTC	O-0121623	1045	1
KEISTER STEVE E	CPT	O-1746087	0549	1
KEITH BERTHA B	MAJ	N-0761348	1263	1
KEITH CLARENCE M	1LT	O-1179118	0646	2
KEITH CLYDE D	COL	O-0131504	1057	3
KEITH DONALD M	COL	O-0333858	1054	3
KEITH EDWARD J	CPT	O-0328843	1044	2
KEITH FRANCIS C	LTC	O-0162319	0260	3
KEITH GLEN B	LTC	O-0374689	0760	1
KEITH JACK R	MAJ	O-1637796	0558	1
KEITH JAMES W	LTC	O-0204072	0557	1
KEITH JOHN O	LTC	O-0354022	0665	1
KEITH JOHN J	MAJ	O-0401514	0746	2
KEITH JR WILLIAM E	LTC	O-0335739	0860	1
KEITH LEWIS W	LTC	O-1105567	1062	1
KEITH PAUL R	CW4	W-2110637	0261	1
KEITH RICHARD W	1LT	O-0242384	0342	2
KEITH ROBERT G	1LT	O-1109404	0445	2
KEITH ROY L	2LT	O-1060838	1145	2
KEITH WARREN S	COL	O-0124708	0652	3
KEITH WILLIAM H	CW3	W-2141334	0858	1
KEITHAHN CHARLES H	MAJ	O-1845741	0847	2
KEITHLY OSCAR W	CPT	O-0359454	0846	2
KEITHLY PAUL E	MAJ	O-1822280	0261	1
KEIZUR WARREN S	MAJ	O-1885439	0866	1
KEKAHUNA JAMES I P	2LT	O-0276622	0455	3
KELCH PAUL	LTC	O-1895794	0863	1
KELCHAK PAUL J	LTC	O-1102326	0767	1
KELCHNER CLYDE H	MAJ	O-0501523	1046	1
KELCHNER WILLIAM R	1LT	O-1319214	0947	2
KELDER WILLIAM L	MAJ	O-1947206	0464	2
KELEMEN CHARLES	LTC	O-0375487	0562	1
KELEMEN PETE S	CPT	O-0355854	0346	2
KELKER JAMES J A	COL	O-0262378	0666	3
KELL CHARLES F	LTC	O-0367049	0567	1
KELL JAMES D	1LT	O-0890318	1162	1
KELL WILLIAM L	MAJ	O-1584447	0561	1
KELLAN DAYTON J	1LT	O-1039724	0346	2
KELLAR CLAYTON L	MAJ	O-1557314	0158	1
KELLAR KENDALL H	LTC	O-0228097	0954	1
KELLAS DONALD	2LT	O-0508865	0245	1
KELLEHER JAMES F	MAJ	O-0246252	0945	2
KELLEHER JAMES J	CPT	O-0486626	1147	1
KELLEHER JEROME M	CW3	W-2117184	1154	1
KELLEHER JOHN J	MAJ	O-1797474	0464	3
KELLEHER PAUL R	CW4	W-2001894	0566	3
KELLEHER THOMAS C	CPT	O-0492919	0546	2
KELLER ALVIN M	1LT	O-1320950	0947	2
KELLER ARTHUR F	LTC	O-0472967	0657	1
KELLER CARL J	CW4	W-2106232	0359	1
KELLER CHARLES	CW4	W-2144953	0365	1
KELLER CHARLES C	1LT	O-1114584	0445	1
KELLER DALLAS C	LTC	O-0287374	1055	3
KELLER DAVID M	MAJ	O-0946912	1167	1
KELLER DAVID W	1LT	O-1057125	0446	2
KELLER DOWNING D	COL	O-0229164	1164	3
KELLER DWIGHT L	CW3	RW-2148120	0262	1
KELLER EDWARD J	1LT	O-0517889	0944	2
KELLER ELLIS O	LTC	O-0230952	1057	3
KELLER ELVIN E	MAJ	O-1779150	0361	1
KELLER FRANK C	LTC	O-1578694	0364	1
KELLER FRANK G	CW3	W-2142860	0561	1
KELLER FRANK M	COL	O-0180763	0762	3
KELLER GEORGE W	MAJ	O-1010524	0155	1
KELLER GORDON H	MAJ	O-0115192	1150	3
KELLER HAROLD A	MAJ	O-1016837	0761	1
KELLER HAROLD E	LTC	O-0250123	0866	3
KELLER HAROLD W	COL	O-0223037	0455	3
KELLER HAROLD W	LTC	O-0409482	0261	1
KELLER HARRY D	COL	O-0233422	0460	3
KELLER HENRY W	COL	O-0256960	1262	3
KELLER HERMAN W	MAJ	O-0425493	0653	2
KELLER HERSCHEL W	COL	O-0296734	0155	3
KELLER II LUTHER	COL	O-1291129	0867	1

NAME	GRADE	SVC NO	DATE RET MO YR	RET CODE
KELLER JAMES S	COL	O-0230522	0257	1
KELLER JOHN	LTC	O-0473924	0357	1
KELLER JOHN F	LTC	O-0404775	0860	1
KELLER JOHN G	COL	O-0177707	0761	3
KELLER JOHN W	CPT	O-0304669	0345	2
KELLER JOSEPH F	CW2	W-2151862	1161	1
KELLER JR EUGENE	COL	O-0103324	0554	2
KELLER JR RAYMOND	CPT	O-0384070	0944	2
KELLER JR ROGER F	1LT	O-0547322	0946	1
KELLER KARL J	CW2	W-2148436	1156	1
KELLER KENNETH F	LTC	O-0359888	0954	1
KELLER LEONARD F	CPT	O-0286786	0445	1
KELLER MARVIN F	1LT	O-1055639	1044	2
KELLER MARVIN E	LTC	O-1639156	0663	1
KELLER NEIL	LTC	O-1305262	0962	1
KELLER NICHOLAS F	CW4	W-2148572	0659	1
KELLER OLIN T	1LT	O-1798356	0745	1
KELLER OSCAR S	MAJ	O-0147567	1151	3
KELLER OWEN V	LTC	O-0218509	0957	2
KELLER REX F	LTC	O-0113451	1155	3
KELLER WILFRED J	MAJ	O-0223122	0357	3
KELLER WILLIAM H	COL	O-0276579	1058	1
KELLER WILLIAM H	CW2	W-2151105	0361	1
KELLER WILLIAM J	CPT	O-0176729	0956	3
KELLETT HARRY R	CPT	O-0516226	1045	2
KELLETT NORMAN M	1LT	O-1180985	1045	2
KELLETT RALPH E	CPT	O-1922629	0662	1
KELLEY BARNEY L	MAJ	O-1179518	0761	1
KELLEY BYRON F	LTC	O-0460272	0866	3
KELLEY CARL C	CPT	O-4043198	0562	2
KELLEY CHARLES C	LTC	O-0171373	0560	3
KELLEY CHARLES E	COL	O-0278931	0157	3
KELLEY CHARLES F	MAJ	O-0262309	0967	1
KELLEY CHARLES W	CPT	O-0473476	0955	1
KELLEY EDGAR C	LTC	O-0202515	0656	3
KELLEY EDGAR D	COL	O-0318972	1263	3
KELLEY EDWARD W	LTC	O-1035847	0262	1
KELLEY ELLEN E	1LT	N-0793182	0849	1
KELLEY ELLERY E	LTC	O-0299877	0966	3
KELLEY EVERETT L	CPT	O-1175186	1160	1
KELLEY FRANCIS J	LTC	O-0178444	0760	3
KELLEY FRED	MAJ	O-0209435	0953	3
KELLEY FRED H	COL	O-0174046	0855	3
KELLEY FREDERICK	1LT	O-0490921	0953	1
KELLEY GEORGE P	CPT	O-0414258	0945	2
KELLEY GEORGE W	CPT	O-0492044	1155	1
KELLEY GEORGE W	LTC	O-1576226	0363	1
KELLEY GERARD W	B G	O-0235809	0263	3
KELLEY HAROLD L	MAJ	O-0270341	1266	3
KELLEY HAYWARD K	LTC	O-0143651	0857	3
KELLEY HENRY C	LTC	O-0270359	0467	3
KELLEY JAMES L	MAJ	O-0531428	0146	2
KELLEY JOHN R	CPT	O-0496168	0949	1
KELLEY JOSEPH C	LTC	O-0499800	0753	1
KELLEY JOSEPH J	MAJ	O-0502112	1152	1
KELLEY JR ERNEST L	CW3	W-2147233	0963	1
KELLEY JR HARMON	1LT	O-1317518	0845	2
KELLEY JR JOHN T	CPT	O-0367549	0545	2
KELLEY JR ROBERT L	CW3	W-2150111	0365	1
KELLEY KENDRICK K	LTC	O-0378974	1167	3
KELLEY LAWRENCE W	CW3	W-2146429	1162	1
KELLEY LEROY G	CW3	W-2142861	0961	1
KELLEY LOUIS R	CW3	W-2150315	1062	1
KELLEY MARY E	1LT	N-0752446	0646	1
KELLEY MORRIS S	LTC	O-1171219	0960	1
KELLEY NELLE A	MAJ	N-0767572	0365	1
KELLEY NICHOLAS L	LTC	O-0960581	0767	1
KELLEY PATRICK H	WO1	W-2151698	0458	2
KELLEY PAUL E	LTC	O-1102327	0157	1
KELLEY RALPH L	CPT	O-1052420	0261	1
KELLEY ROBERT J	MAJ	O-1951697	0366	1
KELLEY ROSALIND H	1LT	N-0756526	0646	1
KELLEY ROY A	CPT	O-0282963	0444	2
KELLEY SR KENT A	CPT	O-1924769	0963	1
KELLEY STANLEY R	COL	O-0255222	0360	1

NAME	GRADE	SVC NO	DATE RET MO YR	RET CODE
KELLEY STANLEY R	COL	O-0957175	0363	1
KELLEY THOMAS E	MAJ	O-1080940	0556	1
KELLEY THOMAS R	COL	O-0392669	0761	1
KELLEY TOM M	MAJ	O-1044860	1057	1
KELLEY TONY H	MAJ	O-1292188	1058	1
KELLEY VINCENT P	LTC	O-1290434	0861	1
KELLEY WARREN T	COL	O-0178222	1161	3
KELLEY WILLIAM B	MAJ	O-1337440	0264	1
KELLEY WILLIAM F	1LT	O-1304229	1145	2
KELLEY WILLIAM J	MAJ	O-0979215	1262	1
KELLEY WILLIAM J	MAJ	O-1048850	0461	1
KELLEY WILLIAM P	MAJ	O-1018692	0263	1
KELLEY WILLIAM P	LTC	O-0274443	0466	3
KELLEY WILLIS E	LTC	O-1824757	1062	1
KELLEY WINFORD R	MAJ	O-1311159	0361	1
KELLICK FRANK E	2LT	O-1110039	0444	2
KELLIHAN LOUIS L	CPT	O-1595704	0166	1
KELLIHER HENRY J	COL	O-0280247	0767	3
KELLNER HERMAN A	MAJ	O-0335315	0660	1
KELLNER JR JOHN	MAJ	O-0103880	0150	3
KELLNER LOUIS F	CPT	O-0397843	0263	1
KELLNOR ARTHUR	CPT	O-0343827	0544	2
KELLOGG ALBERT B	COL	O-0131505	0648	3
KELLOGG BESSIE T	2LT	N-0700226	0439	1
KELLOGG DOROTHY D	MAJ	J-0101288	1065	1
KELLOGG FREDERICK	COL	O-0284789	0766	3
KELLOGG GAYLE P	1LT	O-1318311	0352	2
KELLOGG HAMILTON H	COL	O-0257163	1059	3
KELLOGG HARRY W	1LT	O-1012902	0246	2
KELLOGG HENRY K	M G	O-0286132	1161	3
KELLOGG JESSE I	LTC	O-0166477	1056	3
KELLOGG JOHN G	LTC	O-0443619	0948	1
KELLOGG JOHN H	MAJ	O-0217764	0364	3
KELLOGG KENNETH O	1LT	O-0994290	0756	2
KELLOGG RAY E	2LT	O-1825862	0145	2
KELLOGG ROBERT P	LTC	O-0288791	1262	3
KELLOND JAMES K	MAJ	O-0361139	0746	2
KELLS RAYMOND G	LTC	O-0298046	1166	3
KELLSTROM CARL W	MAJ	O-0400219	0861	1
KELLUM FELIX	CPT	O-1596382	0852	1
KELLUM THOMAS B	COL	O-0206755	0956	3
KELLY AIDAN C	COL	O-0109178	0350	1
KELLY ALLAN B	1LT	O-1686427	1059	1
KELLY ALTON L	LTC	O-1037851	0761	1
KELLY ANTHONY O	LTC	O-1031099	1265	1
KELLY ARNOLD A	CW2	W-2205713	0161	1
KELLY ARTHUR F	1LT	O-1284523	104N	2
KELLY AUBREY R	LTC	O-0251410	0266	3
KELLY AUSTIN E	1LT	O-1311087	1146	2
KELLY BAYARD L	CPT	O-1292189	0955	1
KELLY BENNIE W	CW3	W-2152024	0164	1
KELLY BRUCE L	LTC	O-1105568	1263	2
KELLY CARROLL P	CW2	W-2144061	1059	1
KELLY CECIL R	CPT	O-2044301	1148	1
KELLY CHARLES C	CW4	W-2146070	0567	2
KELLY CHARLES G	COL	O-0268586	0467	3
KELLY CHESTER R	MAJ	O-2204086	0166	1
KELLY CLYDE W	1LT	O-0233517	0747	2
KELLY CYRIL A	LTC	O-0450971	1160	1
KELLY DANIEL D	CPT	O-0418624	1043	2
KELLY DAVID E	CW2	W-2151175	1158	1
KELLY DENNIS H	LTC	O-0486252	0545	1
KELLY DOROTHY N	1LT	N-0755804	0746	1
KELLY EARL B	LTC	O-1175188	1163	1
KELLY EDWARD	CPT	O-1690967	0557	2
KELLY EDWARD C	CW4	W-2114233	0858	1
KELLY EDWARD C C	CPT	O-0186384	0851	3
KELLY EDWARD F	MAJ	O-0488867	0757	2
KELLY EDWARD F	MAJ	O-1917611	1264	1
KELLY EDWARD G	CW3	W-2148355	0764	1
KELLY EDWARD J	LTC	O-1592973	1063	1
KELLY EDWARD L	CW4	W-2117138	0659	1
KELLY EDWARD L	CW3	W-2148864	0764	1
KELLY EDWARD S	CPT	O-1996765	1054	1
KELLY EDWARD T	1LT	O-1102328	0944	2

NAME	GRADE	SVC NO	DATE RET MO YR	RET CODE
KELLY ELMER R	CPT	O-1014442	0547	2
KELLY ERIC T	LTC	O-0130637	0953	3
KELLY ERNEST A	MAJ	O-0972063	0463	1
KELLY EUGENE C	MAJ	O-1645103	0364	1
KELLY EUGENE L	CPT	O-0246299	1058	3
KELLY FRANCIS J	1LT	O-1999952	0648	2
KELLY FRANCIS P	1LT	O-1309278	0445	2
KELLY FRANK A	CPT	O-0918705	0647	2
KELLY FRED A	LTC	O-0205671	0656	3
KELLY GEORGE W	CPT	O-0243424	0152	3
KELLY GEORGE W	1LT	O-1324420	1145	2
KELLY GEORGE W	MAJ	O-1543373	1058	1
KELLY GLENN M	LTC	O-1549308	0462	1
KELLY HARRY R	LTC	O-1104245	1055	1
KELLY HOWARD E	LTC	O-0223365	1158	3
KELLY HOWARD M	CPT	O-0487061	0549	1
KELLY HUGH J	MAJ	O-0248037	0565	3
KELLY IRA D S	COL	O-0173948	0560	3
KELLY IWYN V	CPT	O-1013553	0658	1
KELLY JACK S	LTC	O-1175479	1063	1
KELLY JAMES A	CW3	W-2147471	0865	1
KELLY JAMES M	MAJ	O-2035711	0960	1
KELLY JAMES P	CPT	O-0277626	1057	3
KELLY JAMES P	LTC	O-0300090	0546	2
KELLY JAMES T	CPT	O-0404383	0240	2
KELLY JAMES W	1LT	O-0383131	0146	2
KELLY JESSE T	MAJ	O-0220695	0847	1
KELLY JOHN A	COL	O-0480095	0762	3
KELLY JOHN B	WO1	W-2146173	0455	1
KELLY JOHN F	CPT	O-1304230	0947	1
KELLY JOHN F	LTC	O-1574891	0157	1
KELLY JOHN J	1LT	O-0509352	0245	2
KELLY JOHN J	MAJ	O-1646155	0861	1
KELLY JOHN M	LTC	O-0374988	0254	1
KELLY JOHN N	LTC	O-1308152	0267	3
KELLY JOHN P	COL	O-1292898	1066	1
KELLY JOHN T	CPT	O-0488200	0948	1
KELLY JOHN W	COL	O-0253421	1064	3
KELLY JOHN W	MAJ	O-0888320	0762	2
KELLY JOSEPH E	COL	O-0261366	0261	3
KELLY JOSEPH G	MAJ	O-1999818	0163	1
KELLY JOSEPH J	LTC	O-0324804	0156	2
KELLY JOSEPH J	1LT	O-1543479	0346	2
KELLY JOSEPH J	WO1	W-2124674	0745	2
KELLY JOSEPH P	MAJ	O-0267442	0463	3
KELLY JOSEPH Y	MAJ	O-0394820	0859	1
KELLY JP DAN	2LT	O-0351189	0945	2
KELLY JR EDWARD J	LTC	O-1335302	1167	1
KELLY JR JOHN J	CW4	W-2125246	0266	1
KELLY JR RICHARD B	CPT	O-1128934	0752	2
KELLY JR WALTER T	MAJ	O-1308815	0865	1
KELLY KATHRYN J	2LT	N-0733428	0845	1
KELLY KEITH C	1LT	O-1181925	1159	1
KELLY LAWRENCE R	LTC	O-1589305	0160	1
KELLY LEE C	LTC	O-1031655	0761	1
KELLY LEE W	LTC	O-1291832	0662	1
KELLY LESTER B	WO1	W-2153259	0560	1
KELLY LLOYD F	COL	O-0114560	0757	3
KELLY MARTIN J	CPT	O-0959268	0261	1
KELLY MARTIN J	1LT	O-1310605	0345	2
KELLY MAURICE F	MAJ	O-0919675	0355	2
KELLY MAURICE W	LTC	O-0461485	1166	3
KELLY MICHAEL J	COL	O-0125609	0648	3
KELLY MICHAEL W	LTC	O-0313665	0945	2
KELLY MILES F	1LT	O-0323901	0944	2
KELLY OLIVER H	COL	O-0445808	0662	1
KELLY PAUL J	CPT	O-1342384	1055	2
KELLY PAUL T	MAJ	O-1335428	0863	1
KELLY PHILIP A	CPT	O-0253100	1056	3
KELLY RALPH A	LTC	O-1558166	1062	1
KELLY RALPH C	MAJ	O-0167535	0957	3
KELLY RAYMOND F	MAJ	O-0441625	0260	1
KELLY RAYMOND J	COL	O-0140223	1154	3
KELLY RAYMOND J	LTC	O-0325610	0347	2
KELLY ROBERT A	LTC	O-1946086	1062	1

NAME	GRADE	SVC NO	DATE RET MO YR	RET CODE
KELLY ROBERT O	MAJ	0-1030788	0264	1
KELLY ROBERT F	MAJ	0-0976541	0764	1
KELLY ROBERT F	MAJ	0-1294319	1060	1
KELLY ROBERT G	CPT	0-0221751	0 43	2
KELLY ROBERT J	MAJ	0-0964081	0864	1
KELLY ROBERT M	CW3	W-2143930	0163	1
KELLY ROBERT S	MAJ	0-1598433	1264	1
KELLY RODERICK J	2LT	0-1798580	1157	2
KELLY RUSSELL M	LTC	0-1104246	0657	1
KELLY SAM	CW3	W-2145276	0363	1
KELLY SAMUEL E	LTC	0-1337716	0166	1
KELLY SYLVESTER	COL	0-0342923	0560	3
KELLY THOMAS A	1LT	0-0514713	1045	2
KELLY THOMAS A	LTC	0-2035813	1165	1
KELLY THOMAS J	MAJ	0-0251874	1059	3
KELLY THOMAS J	COL	0-0269351	1059	3
KELLY THOMAS J	1LT	0-1304231	0646	2
KELLY THOMAS J	LTC	0-1822582	0961	1
KELLY THOMAS R	MAJ	0-0496780	0657	3
KELLY VICTOR O	CPT	0-0532674	0147	1
KELLY WALTER H	MAJ	0-0188453	0748	3
KELLY WALTER L	LTC	0-0331042	0259	1
KELLY WALTER N	MAJ	0-0344504	1060	1
KELLY WALTER R	1LT	0-1019309	0747	1
KELLY WILLIAM A	LTC	0-0297037	1060	1
KELLY WILLIAM C	CW2	W-2110112	1047	2
KELLY WILLIAM D	LTC	0-0485654	0954	3
KELLY WILLIAM H	LTC	0-0222000	0157	1
KELLY WILLIAM M	COL	0-0189293	0656	3
KELLY WILLIAM P	LTC	0-0957402	0767	1
KELLY WOODROW W	CPT	0-2041030	0161	1
KELM CAROL V	MAJ	M-0002572	0266	1
KELM JACK R	LTC	0-1637799	0663	1
KELM PAUL H	LTC	0-0242752	1165	3
KELM ROBERT F	MAJ	0-1291650	0160	1
KELSAY JESSE D	COL	0-0885824	1160	1
KELSEY ALBERT J	MAJ	0-0231225	0960	3
KELSEY CLARENCE W	MAJ	0-0128603	1056	3
KELSEY JR OREN L	1LT	0-1288066	0245	2
KELSEY LOUIS E	MAJ	0-0337556	0966	3
KELSEY ROSS F	1LT	0-1293068	0345	2
KELSO BILLY P	2LT	0-1287362	0144	2
KELSO CHARITY T	2LT	N-0703007	0644	1
KELSO EARL H	COL	0-0279109	1159	1
KELSO ELMER G	LTC	0-0244296	0563	3
KELSO FRED O	COL	0-0170740	0352	3
KELSO HOMER C	MAJ	0-0473010	0852	1
KELSO MARIE L	2LT	N-0732074	0145	1
KELSO RUPERT E	MAJ	0-0300217	1064	3
KELSO VICTOR C	LTC	0-1798582	0563	1
KELSO WALTER F	COL	0-0447606	0862	1
KELSTON ROBERT H	CW2	W-2123327	0246	2
KELTNER JACOB G	CPT	0-0445742	1045	1
KELTNER JR EDGAR H	CPT	0-1302477	0246	2
KELTNER MARVIN B	CPT	0-1284154	0944	2
KELTON JOHN E	LTC	0-0388681	0660	1
KELTY HENRY J	CPT	0-0982488	0458	1
KELTY JAMES F	MAJ	0-1113780	0863	1
KELTZ CHARLES E	LTC	0-0321108	0560	1
KELTZ JR JOHN F	MAJ	0-0179329	1160	3
KEMBLE LEWIS G	LTC	0-1591849	0263	1
KEMELHOR MICHAEL C	MAJ	0-1690514	1045	2
KEMICK IRVIN A	CPT	0-0371436	1047	2
KEMMERER FRANK	LTC	0-0486914	0356	1
KEMNITZ JR WILLIAM H	LTC	0-1573880	0367	2
KEMNITZ LESTER E	CW2	W-2142971	0862	1
KEMP ARTHUR O	LTC	0-0368716	0867	3
KEMP ARTHUR H	COL	0-0258136	0967	3
KEMP CHARLES E	1LT	0-0452472	0145	2
KEMP FRED O	LTC	0-0994900	0665	1
KEMP GIBSON O	MAJ	0-1292349	0361	1
KEMP HARDY A	COL	0-0226089	0862	3
KEMP III HENRY O	MAJ	0-1951097	0661	1
KEMP IRA J	LTC	0-1950891	0766	2
KEMP JAMES M	CW3	RW-2145733	1163	1
KEMP JR PAUL H	LTC	0-1926153	1062	1
KEMP KARL	MAJ	0-1576228	0758	1
KEMP LAVERNE E	LTC	0-1314297	0163	1
KEMP LILBURN R	LTC	0-0252018	0964	3
KEMP MURRAY G	1LT	0-2001060	0147	2
KEMP NEAL R	LTC	0-1031733	1066	1
KEMP ROBERT M	LTC	0-1318808	0757	1
KEMP ROBERT W	1LT	0-1289788	0943	2
KEMP SILAS M	CPT	0-4009044	0563	1
KEMP VICTOR H	LTC	0-0406359	0663	1
KEMP WRIGHT C	LTC	0-0224493	0955	3
KEMP WYMAN W	LTC	0-0271355	0967	3
KEMPA WALTER	CW2	W-2144576	0664	1
KEMPER CECIL E	LTC	0-0188952	0758	3
KEMPER GEORGE E	LTC	0-1043381	0762	1
KEMPER RICHARD V	2LT	0-1647539	0745	2
KEMPER WAYNE D	MAJ	0-2030523	0967	1
KEMPER WILLIAM P	1LT	0-0907506	0444	2
KEMPF FRANCIS E	COL	0-0263780	1161	3
KEMPF FRANK J	LTC	0-0482055	0654	1
KEMPLE JOHN L	LTC	0-0906911	0566	3
KEMPSTER GEORGE A	MAJ	0-0370513	0746	2
KEMPTON JOHN	CW3	W-2149933	0862	2
KENDALL ANTOINETTE	2LT	N-0730443	0844	1
KENDALL ARTHUR W	LTC	0-0280434	0261	3
KENDALL BRUCE P	CPT	0-1041613	0245	2
KENDALL BURTON L	MAJ	0-2102528	1262	1
KENDALL CHARLES L	CPT	0-0450554	1053	1
KENDALL DONALD A	MAJ	0-1700179	0246	2
KENDALL DONALD L	MAJ	0-0392144	0363	1
KENDALL FREDERICK	COL	0-0174670	0853	2
KENDALL GEORGE P	1LT	0-0276932	1145	2
KENDALL GEORGE R	1LT	0-1301911	0546	2
KENDALL JACKSON W	LTC	0-0105380	0156	3
KENDALL MILTON	COL	0-0177923	0262	3
KENDALL OTHEL	MAJ	0-0235060	0954	3
KENDALL RALPH W	2LT	0-0127197	1056	3
KENDALL ROBERT M	LTC	0-0262740	1166	3
KENDALL ROBIA S	MAJ	0-2296604	1163	1
KENDALL WALLACE C	CPT	0-0412542	0945	2
KENDERCINE JOHN D	COL	0-0146176	0249	3
KENDLE ERNEST F	LTC	0-0426178	1161	1
KENDLE WALTER E	MAJ	0-0206877	0858	3
KENDRICK FRANK J	COL	0-0263876	0162	3
KENDRICK FREDERICK	CPT	0-1577413	0845	2
KENDRICK HAROLD C	CW3	W-2141988	0657	1
KENDRICK HAROLD P	CPT	0-1534527	0746	2
KENDRICK HARRISON F	MAJ	0-0287089	0558	3
KENDRICK JOSEPH F	MAJ	0-0103329	1154	3
KENDRICK JR GEORGE M	COL	0-0256424	1067	3
KENDRICK JR JAMES O	MAJ	0-2025152	0765	1
KENDRICK WILLIAM T	2LT	0-1306855	0444	2
KENDRIGAN MARTIN F	CPT	0-0490020	0948	1
KENEALY EDWARD R	LTC	0-0403404	0746	2
KENES KATHERINE	1LT	N-0723245	0746	1
KENESEY GEORGE F	CW3	W-2152419	0463	1
KENION JR ALONZO W	CPT	0-1310723	0646	2
KENISON AMELIA	MAJ	N-0703502	0666	1
KENLER MYRON L	CPT	0-1690644	0945	2
KENLEY MELVIN L	2LT	0-0538275	0545	2
KENLY GLENN H	MAJ	N-0762491	0864	1
KENNA ALPHA F	LTC	0-0170815	0648	3
KENNALEY JOHN J	COL	0-0384162	0361	2
KENNAMAN JACK R	CPT	0-0890141	0555	2
KENNARD ELEANOR F	MAJ	L-0200880	0263	2
KENNARD ERNEST W	CW2	W-2144355	0561	1
KENNARD FRANKLAND	LTC	0-0205808	1163	3
KENNAUGH MILTON C	CPT	0-1542691	0846	2
KENNEDY ALLEN B	CW4	W-2104518	0662	1
KENNEDY ALLEN K	CW2	W-2143310	0157	1
KENNEDY ALTA S	MAJ	N-0763721	0561	2
KENNEDY ARCHIBALD	MAJ	0-0908957	0747	2
KENNEDY ARCHIE J	LTC	0-1585709	1062	1
KENNEDY ARTHUR L	CW2	W-2144245	0255	1
KENNEDY CECIL J	M G	0-0243189	0360	3
KENNEDY CHARLES C	CPT	0-1320952	1047	2
KENNEDY CHARLES H	MAJ	0-0960221	0165	1
KENNEDY CHARLES H	MAJ	0-1177026	0657	1
KENNEDY CHARLES H	2LT	0-1549751	0145	2
KENNEDY CHARLES R	MAJ	0-2029464	0864	1
KENNEDY CLEMENT F	COL	0-0210104	0853	3
KENNEDY DALE E	LTC	0-0204750	1058	3
KENNEDY DAVID I	LTC	0-1002041	0367	1
KENNEDY DONALD D	CW2	W-2146688	0557	1
KENNEDY DONALD J	LTC	0-0386875	0147	1
KENNEDY EARL G	LTC	0-0495551	0952	1
KENNEDY EDMUND F	LTC	0-0287143	0562	3
KENNEDY EDWARD J	CW3	W-2205392	0264	1
KENNEDY EDWARD R	CPT	0-1325577	0346	2
KENNEDY ESTUS	MAJ	0-0108636	1047	1
KENNEDY EUGENE C	CW4	W-2003738	0865	1
KENNEDY FRANCIS I	COL	0-0140204	0553	3
KENNEDY FRANCIS J	CPT	0-0335267	0545	2
KENNEDY FRANCIS J	LTC	0-0907819	0455	1
KENNEDY FRANCIS J	CPT	0-2011324	0654	1
KENNEDY GARNETT L	CW2	W-2142996	1163	1
KENNEDY GEORGE E	MAJ	0-2262311	0664	1
KENNEDY GEORGE H	CPT	0-1341673	0458	2
KENNEDY GEORGE M	MAJ	0-1334586	0661	1
KENNEDY GEORGE W	CPT	0-1184681	1165	1
KENNEDY GLADYS	MAJ	M-0002577	0864	1
KENNEDY GORDON A	MAJ	0-1646793	0959	1
KENNEDY HAROLD M	LTC	0-0390571	0860	1
KENNEDY HARRY V	COL	0-0108871	1047	1
KENNEDY HELEN E	MAJ	N-0743168	0465	1
KENNEDY HELEN G	1LT	N-0752793	0747	1
KENNEDY HENRY	CPT	0-0422539	0446	2
KENNEDY HUGH H	COL	0-0255148	0864	3
KENNEDY III JOHN F	COL	0-0232684	0361	3
KENNEDY IRA W	WO1	W-2121268	0452	2
KENNEDY JAMES O	CW2	W-3430342	1067	1
KENNEDY JOHN A	MAJ	0-2020736	0767	1
KENNEDY JOHN C	LTC	0-0324080	1163	1
KENNEDY JOHN D	COL	0-0185280	0751	3
KENNEDY JOHN O	1LT	0-1551882	0346	2
KENNEDY JOHN E	MAJ	0-1168314	0960	1
KENNEDY JOHN J	1LT	0-1002959	0553	1
KENNEDY JOHN L	LTC	0-0308521	1057	1
KENNEDY JOHN N	MAJ	0-1320635	1062	1
KENNEDY JOHN T	LTC	0-1120198	0463	2
KENNEDY JOSEPH R	1LT	0-1316429	0346	2
KENNEDY JOSEPHINE	1LT	N-0700146	1141	1
KENNEDY JR DAVID C	LTC	0-0304256	0866	3
KENNEDY JR EDWIN R	COL	0-0345113	1262	3
KENNEDY JR JAMES F	CPT	0-2030193	0455	1
KENNEDY JR JOHN J	MAJ	0-0124601	0253	3
KENNEDY JR JOHN T	2LT	0-1319076	0146	2
KENNEDY JR REUBEN J	CW3	W-2104198	0357	1
KENNEDY JR WALTER J	CW2	W-2148552	0363	1
KENNEDY KENNETH E	WO1	W-2119592	0656	2
KENNEDY KLEIN W	LTC	0-0239415	1165	3
KENNEDY LAWRENCE F	MAJ	0-1298878	0662	1
KENNEDY LEO W	1LT	0-0522612	0746	2
KENNEDY LIONEL J	CW2	W-2000117	0146	2
KENNEDY LOWELL W	2LT	0-2000119	0447	2
KENNEDY LUTHER M	2LT	0-1824327	0744	2
KENNEDY LYLE J	LTC	0-0272854	0566	3
KENNEDY MARGARET M	LTC	N-0700629	0546	1
KENNEDY MAY D	2LT	N-0783463	1044	1
KENNEDY MILDRED D	MAJ	N-0724502	0661	1
KENNEDY OWEN R	CW4	W-2105919	0858	1
KENNEDY PAUL	2LT	0-2010638	0351	2
KENNEDY PAUL C	CW4	W-2149845	0467	1
KENNEDY PAUL J	1LT	0-2207531	0152	2
KENNEDY PAUL R	LTC	0-1280316	0367	3
KENNEDY PAUL T	1LT	0-1333484	0347	2
KENNEDY RALPH P	LTC	0-0984484	1165	1
KENNEDY RAYMOND J	MAJ	0-1114586	0762	2
KENNEDY ROBERT A	LTC	0-1292190	1061	1
KENNEDY ROBERT C	LTC	0-0211174	0154	3
KENNEDY ROBERT E	1LT	0-1573492	0260	2
KENNEDY ROBERT E	MAJ	0-1885533	0966	1
KENNEDY ROBERT H	2LT	0-0442406	0745	2
KENNEDY ROBERT H	LTC	0-0482132	0851	1
KENNEDY ROBERT M	COL	0-0231654	0565	3
KENNEDY ROBERT M	MAJ	0-0406448	0462	1
KENNEDY ROY L	CW4	W-2142304	1059	1
KENNEDY RUTH P	MAJ	N-0775335	0563	1
KENNEDY SHERROD O	CPT	0-1596922	1057	1
KENNEDY TAYLOR L	1LT	0-1168315	104N	2
KENNEDY TERRENCE S	LTC	0-0548538	1064	1
KENNEDY THOMAS J	CPT	0-0410845	0746	2
KENNEDY THOMAS J	LTC	0-1013257	0762	1
KENNEDY THOMAS J	MAJ	0-1302314	1060	1
KENNEDY THOMAS M	2LT	0-1001159	0344	1
KENNEDY WALTER J	MAJ	0-0126092	1055	3
KENNEDY WALTER U	COL	0-0120081	0648	3
KENNEDY WILLIAM	MAJ	0-1312660	0657	1
KENNEDY WILLIAM C	MAJ	0-0410342	0164	1
KENNEDY WILLIAM C	MAJ	0-2204189	1066	1
KENNEDY WILLIAM F	CPT	0-0213189	0446	2
KENNEDY WILLIAM M	COL	0-0249839	0362	3
KENNEDY WILLIE B	LTC	0-1543296	0157	1
KENNEDY WILLIS H	1LT	0-0209531	0858	3
KENNELLY EDWARD M	MAJ	0-0227122	0460	3
KENNERSON COLLIE C	MAJ	0-0498001	0946	2
KENNETH DONALD W	MAJ	0-0191336	0357	3
KENNEY ANDREW A	1LT	0-0269477	0949	1
KENNEY CHARLES W	MAJ	0-2018368	0557	1
KENNEY EARL E	CPT	0-1589545	0846	2
KENNEY GARDNER P	MAJ	0-0971341	1061	1
KENNEY HARVEY A	LTC	0-0386528	0367	3
KENNEY HESTER S	2LT	N-0751428	0944	1
KENNEY JACK P	LTC	0-1106250	0467	3
KENNEY JOHN F	CPT	0-0211445	0120	1
KENNEY JR AMASA R	LTC	0-0318376	0564	3
KENNEY JR WILLIAM N	LTC	0-1304356	0261	1
KENNEY MATTHEW R	MAJ	0-1825298	0455	1
KENNEY MILTON M	COL	0-0367304	0264	3
KENNEY OLNEY F	CW4	W-2117853	0967	3
KENNEY PATRICK J	LTC	0-1698005	0463	1
KENNEY PAUL J	LTC	0-0182667	0855	3
KENNEY ROBERT N	CPT	0-1296707	0346	1
KENNEY THOMAS J	MAJ	0-0489009	0155	2
KENNEY WILLIAM E	CPT	0-1101523	0145	2
KENNIGER CHARLES F	COL	0-0326828	0666	3
KENNING FRANK W	1LT	0-1053670	0245	1
KENNINGTON CLYDE B	LTC	0-0240061	0660	2
KENNISON SAMUEL M	LTC	0-2026815	1163	1
KENNON ROBERT F	COL	0-0185885	0962	3
KENNOY JOHN S	MAJ	0-0227537	0664	3
KENNY ELIZABETH	2LT	N-0700843	0641	2
KENNY JACK D	MAJ	0-0445507	0348	2
KENNY JOHN P	1LT	0-0377921	0344	2
KENNY MARY A	CPT	N-0700663	1044	1
KENNY RAYMOND J	1LT	0-1295384	0545	2
KENNY ROBERT W	B G	0-0205944	0362	3
KENNY ROY W	M G	0-0176730	0255	3
KENNY SIMON F	LTC	0-0524846	0867	1
KENOST ROBERT	CPT	0-1011812	0246	1
KENSOK EDMUND F	MAJ	0-1553486	1059	2
KENT ALBERT F	1LT	0-1798358	0945	2
KENT ALPHONSE J	1LT	0-1302829	0350	1
KENT ARTHUR	LTC	0-0287644	0966	3
KENT EARL W	COL	0-0190852	0260	3
KENT FRANCIS E	MAJ	0-0485656	1147	1
KENT FRED S	COL	0-0216103	0252	3
KENT GEORGE R	COL	0-0246364	1154	3
KENT GLEN W	MAJ	0-0418205	0646	2
KENT HAROLD W	COL	0-0118876	0460	3
KENT JAMES W	MAJ	0-1294848	1263	1
KENT JESSE M	CW3	W-2149821	0765	1
KENT JOHN R	CPT	0-1323935	1047	2
KENT JOSEPH J	COL	0-0470757	0353	1
KENT JOSEPH J	LTC	0-1579905	0363	1

NAME	GRADE	SVC NO	DATE RET MO YR	RET CODE
KENT JR FREDERICK	COL	O-0030172	1060	1
KENT JR JOHN H	MAJ	O-0415865	1046	2
KENT MALCOLM F	COL	O-0232939	0663	1
KENT MARK D	LTC	O-0460872	0657	1
KENT ROBERT C	MAJ	O-2263418	1061	1
KENT ROBERT F	1LT	O-1060153	1045	2
KENT ROBERT S	2LT	O-0540336	1045	2
KENT ROY L	2LT	O-1323145	0945	2
KENT ROYAL P	MAJ	O-1692508	0762	1
KENT THADDEUS F	CPT	O-1014268	0561	1
KENTY WILLIAM S	MAJ	O-1018202	1266	1
KENTZEL JOHN J	MAJ	O-1291651	0161	2
KENVIN CLARA R	1LT	N-0759912	0346	2
KENWORTHY HARRY S	MAJ	O-2009361	0360	1
KENWORTHY RAY W	MAJ	O-0247444	1158	3
KENWORTHY WILLIAM R	1LT	O-0491097	114	2
KENYON CHARLES W	COL	O-0289601	1058	1
KENYON ESTHER L	LTC	N-0751427	0865	3
KENYON FRANK C	LTC	O-0184092	1056	3
KENYON JAMES J	CPT	O-2009390	0657	1
KENYON LEE W	MAJ	O-1320134	0359	1
KENYON LEONARD G	1LT	O-1316831	0447	1
KENYON ORLAN E	MAJ	O-1922593	0665	1
KENYON PINCKNEY M	CPT	O-0266110	1054	1
KEOUGH JACK L	CPT	O-1924978	0864	1
KEOUGH JOHN	MAJ	O-0249644	0267	3
KEOUGH JOSEPH M	CW2	W-2211446	1265	1
KEOWN GORDON	CW3	W-2142103	0559	1
KEOWN LAURISTON	COL	O-0336274	0767	3
KEPHART CALVIN I	COL	O-0175037	0648	3
KEPHART SAMUEL W	CPT	O-0112211	0648	3
KEPLEY RODNEY S	LTC	O-1295227	0163	1
KEPPARD GORDON C	LTC	O-1577417	0261	1
KERBAUGH LESTER W	MAJ	O-0983741	0962	2
KERBER JOHN R	CPT	O-0301907	1045	2
KERBOW HERBERT L	CW2	W-2142711	0755	1
KERCE WOODROW	MAJ	O-1165247	1060	2
KERFOOT DONALD W	CW2	W-2209612	0267	2
KERG JAMES F	1LT	O-2265218	0254	2
KERKER HERBERT V	MAJ	O-1170449	1061	1
KERKSIS SYDNEY C	CW3	W-2136635	0957	1
KERL JULES J	CPT	O-0507127	1044	2
KERLEY THOMAS L	COL	O-1287363	0966	1
KERLEY WILLIAM G	CW3	W-2206993	0366	1
KERLIN HOMER F	CPT	O-1287364	1046	1
KERLIN ROBERT F	CPT	O-2262382	1062	1
KERLIN WILLIAM S	1LT	O-1321216	0746	1
KERMISCH ALBERT	LTC	O-1577419	0863	1
KERN ANNE C	1LT	N-0743446	0746	1
KERN DONALD R	MAJ	O-1297050	1158	1
KERN GEORGE F	COL	O-0320864	1067	3
KERN HARRY J	LTC	O-1167066	0145	1
KERN HERBERT	1LT	O-1171221	0153	2
KERN JOSEPH W	LTC	O-0214154	0257	3
KERN LEON W	LTC	O-0524469	1266	3
KERN RAY W	2LT	O-0489241	0445	2
KERN ROBERT I	CPT	O-1636135	0244	2
KERN THEOPHILUS	LTC	O-0230616	0165	3
KERN WALTER	MAJ	O-1047610	0757	1
KERN WILLIAM R	LTC	O-1000142	0262	1
KERNAN JR REDMOND F	B G	O-0173014	0147	2
KERNANDER WILLIAM H	CPT	O-1641464	1055	1
KERNELL LOUIS O	LTC	O-1554761	1166	1
KERNEN DELMAR L	CPT	O-0885445	0447	2
KERNEN WALTER R	2LT	O-0549851	1045	2
KERNER ROBERT H	MAJ	O-1553677	0259	1
KERNICK CHARLES F	CPT	O-0513670	0847	1
KERNODLE JOHN R	CPT	O-0539741	1046	2
KERNODLE MARION	2LT	O-0183347	0833	1
KERNODLE ROBERT E	COL	O-0129518	0248	2
KERNS BERTHA L	MAJ	N-0756890	0663	1
KERNS MALCOLM B	CW3	W-2152072	0564	1
KERNS MINNIE R	1LT	N-0743323	0546	2
KERNSTOCK ELWYN N	MAJ	O-1185075	1062	1
KERR ALLEN O	LTC	O-0297680	0958	1

NAME	GRADE	SVC NO	DATE RET MO YR	RET CODE
KERR CHARLES R	COL	O-0185899	1049	3
KERR CLAYTON O	MAJ	O-0259674	0563	3
KERR CLAYTON P	M G	O-0164979	0962	3
KERR DONNELL F	CW2	W-2113429	0945	2
KERR EDWARD F	1LT	O-0485418	0346	2
KERR EDWARD J	MAJ	O-1341551	0463	1
KERR FRANCIS R	B G	O-0232181	1050	3
KERR FRED M	CPT	O-1297381	0246	2
KERR GERALD J	1LT	O-1295897	1052	1
KERR GERALDINE	1LT	N-0767219	0745	1
KERR GLADYS	1LT	L-0602054	0445	1
KERR GLENN E	LTC	O-1597507	0364	1
KERR HARRY R	MAJ	O-0964237	0263	1
KERR HERBERT H	MAJ	O-1634965	0-53	1
KERR II CHARLES A	MAJ	O-1798740	0160	1
KERR JACK H	MAJ	O-2019179	0860	1
KERR JAMES F	CW2	W-2148553	0659	1
KERR JAMES F	COL	O-0175290	0760	3
KERR JOHN C	LTC	O-0272833	1160	3
KERR JR JAMES T	CPT	O-0996797	1061	1
KERR JR SAMUEL R	LTC	O-1172514	0462	1
KERR JR WILLIAM F	MAJ	O-1924759	0864	1
KERR KEITH I	MAJ	O-1341674	0862	1
KERR RAYMOND F	MAJ	O-0966618	0964	1
KERR RICHARD H	LTC	O-1310455	1066	1
KERR WENDELL H	LTC	O-0262090	0563	3
KERR WILLIAM C	CPT	O-0197751	0562	3
KERRIGAN JOHN T	CPT	O-1010847	0146	2
KERRIGAN WILLIAM C	MAJ	O-0305601	0967	3
KERRIN WILLIAM A	CW3	W-2126646	1162	1
KERRON SETH M	COL	O-0224044	0648	3
KERRY MARSHALL	LTC	O-0261725	1165	3
KERSBERGEN G P W	LTC	O-0374334	0461	1
KERSBERGEN JAY	LTC	O-0299123	0564	3
KERSBERGEN ROBERT M	MAJ	O-2288265	1166	1
KERSEY JOHN B	MAJ	O-1286299	0360	2
KERSH RUTH J	MAJ	N-0778243	0765	1
KERSHAW JAMES R	COL	O-0402712	1166	3
KERSHAW ROBERT C	CPT	O-1595130	0959	1
KERSHAW SELWYN	CPT	O-0298307	0561	3
KERSHINAR LOUIS R	MAJ	O-1062219	1161	1
KERSHNER GEORGE	MAJ	O-0481558	0346	1
KERSHNER JESS K	COL	O-0123199	0651	3
KERSHNER WARREN E	LTC	O-0167874	0649	3
KERSKI JOHN R	MAJ	O-1118921	0363	1
KERST FRANK	MAJ	O-0513295	0750	1
KERSTEIN CHESTER C	CW3	W-2122932	0160	1
KERSTEIN KARL W	CW3	W-2150778	0964	1
KERSTEN FREDERICK	COL	O-0370560	0964	1
KERSTNER WILLIAM F	WO1	W-2143086	1058	1
KERT MERTON	LTC	O-2035713	0265	1
KERTING WERNER H	MAJ	O-0925876	0560	1
KERTTULA WALTER T	LTC	O-0390744	0567	2
KERWIN EDWARD M	MAJ	O-0117776	0649	3
KERWIN EDWARD W	MAJ	O-1328374	0662	1
KERWIN JAMES J J	MAJ	O-0480985	1144	2
KERWIN WILLIAM	CPT	O-1014715	0346	2
KESECKER HARVEY R	1LT	O-0495379	0946	1
KESLER D CLAUDE	CPT	O-1309570	0648	2
KESLER JOHN W	CPT	O-0968394	0258	2
KESLER RAY	MAJ	O-4006827	0867	1
KESLER WINFRED A	MAJ	O-1301160	1060	1
KESLIK JOHN	MAJ	O-0889326	0163	1
KESLING CLIFFORD V	CW2	W-2145916	0657	1
KESNER SAM	MAJ	O-0465490	0646	2
KESSELRING HERBERT M	MAJ	O-1116089	0568	1
KESSELS ANN C	MAJ	N-0737698	1063	3
KESSIE MARSHALL H	1LT	O-0479119	0445	2
KESSINGER RICHARD S	MAJ	O-0438274	1046	1
KESSLER ALBERT F	CW2	W-2122827	0255	2
KESSLER ARTHUR G	LTC	O-1183332	0761	1
KESSLER EDWIN	LTC	O-0219819	1063	3
KESSLER FRANKLIN L	CPT	O-1889572	0945	2
KESSLER FRED J	MAJ	O-2007283	0765	1
KESSLER GEORGE D	COL	O-0427849	0463	1

NAME	GRADE	SVC NO	DATE RET MO YR	RET CODE
KESSLER HARRY	LTC	O-0490782	1166	3
KESSLER HERBERT F	MAJ	O-0292142	1166	3
KESSLER JAMES E	MAJ	O-0454362	1059	1
KESSLER JAMES H	CW3	W-2143493	0861	1
KESSLER JOHN	CPT	O-0385142	0546	2
KESSLER LAVIE F	CW2	W-2147432	0361	1
KESSLER MARY M	1LT	N-0790521	0147	1
KESSLER OLLA A	CPT	O-2043179	0-48	2
KESSLER RAYMOND L	LTC	O-0285990	0564	3
KESSLER SAM C	CPT	O-0493755	0547	1
KESSLING JOHN F	MAJ	O-0887336	0661	1
KESTER ALFRED J	CPT	O-1299250	0747	1
KESTER WILLIAM R	LTC	O-0223608	0152	3
KESTERSON JAMES C	MAJ	O-1317544	0359	1
KESTLE ROBERT C	MAJ	O-0262379	0146	2
KESTLINGER ROBERT S	CPT	O-1310359	1057	1
KETCH HERBERT L	LTC	O-0279638	1147	1
KETCHAM EARL F	COL	O-0159766	0755	3
KETCHAM FRANK G	COL	O-0224023	0558	1
KETCHAM GEORGE H	LTC	O-0192491	0860	3
KETCHAM HARRY T	COL	O-0218780	0546	2
KETCHER FREDERIC A	LTC	O-0339306	1046	2
KETCHERSID ROY R	CW3	RW-2209251	0866	1
KETCHERSIDE HILLARY	LTC	O-0200236	1045	2
KETCHUM ADDISON R	LTC	O-0358157	1166	3
KETCHUM DOUGLAS H	CPT	O-0405209	0859	1
KETKER EDWIN W	CW2	W-2147725	1262	1
KETNER ROBERT R	1LT	O-1587364	1045	2
KETRON HOBERT W	MAJ	O-0310033	0359	3
KETT CHARLES N	MAJ	O-0450307	0557	1
KETTELL HOLLISTER	MAJ	O-0497626	0155	1
KETTERER PAUL E	LTC	O-0240861	0965	3
KETTERING WILLARD S	CPT	O-0106646	1142	2
KETTERMAN CHARLES W	LTC	O-1576233	1045	2
KETTINGER JOHN P	LTC	O-1324422	0667	1
KETTLE STANLEY E	LTC	O-1015866	0965	1
KETTLE WILLIAM H	1LT	O-1591865	1149	1
KETTLER CHARLES J	LTC	O-0308656	0362	3
KETTNER EUGENE C	MAJ	O-0180809	1055	3
KETTRING LEON C W	LTC	O-0244877	0460	3
KETZ MAX T	COL	O-0237123	1061	3
KETZENBARGER CLIFFOR	LTC	O-0471743	0467	1
KETZLER KENNETH N	LTC	O-0275046	0252	1
KEULING RUSSELL J	MAJ	O-1596079	0560	1
KEVELIGHAN HOWARD J	1LT	O-1536188	0852	1
KEVELL WALTER M	LTC	O-0440763	0867	1
KEVER LUTHER O	MAJ	O-0971828	1062	1
KEVEREN KENNETH A	COL	O-0710514	0559	3
KEVIN RICHARD C	LTC	O-1294853	0266	1
KEY CARL F	CPT	O-0452687	0146	2
KEY CLAYTON N	CPT	O-0485733	1047	1
KEY GILBERT P	LTC	O-0258047	0466	3
KEY JAMES A	LTC	O-0194988	0562	3
KEY JOHNNIE J	WO1	W-2143595	0953	1
KEY JR WARREN E	MAJ	O-1290081	0461	1
KEY PERCY N	CPT	O-0572260	1157	2
KEY ROMULUS S	CPT	O-0480748	1045	1
KEY WALTER W	LTC	O-0265893	1063	3
KEYES BALDWIN L	COL	O-0140077	0556	3
KEYES CARLETON C	LTC	O-0290330	0460	1
KEYES EARL R	CPT	O-0270659	0264	3
KEYES FREDERICK	MAJ	O-0340676	0944	2
KEYES HARMON F	LTC	O-0230283	0-52	3
KEYES ROBERT C	1LT	O-1541125	1045	2
KEYES ROBERT M	1LT	O-1295730	1144	2
KEYES ROY R	1LT	O-1288907	1045	2
KEYES WILLIAM E	COL	O-0323361	0560	3
KEYFETZ BENJAMIN	CPT	O-0532329	0145	2
KEYMAS PETER G	MAJ	O-2020737	0765	1
KEYS CHARLES R	CPT	O-1294321	0764	1
KEYS DANA E	CW4	W-2122627	0656	1
KEYS EDWARD F	MAJ	O-0117105	0853	3
KEYS EDWARD M	MAJ	O-0346487	1157	2
KEYS JAMES H	MAJ	O-0947689	0465	1
KEYS JOHN J	LTC	O-0248647	0663	1

NAME	GRADE	SVC NO	DATE RET MO YR	RET CODE
KEYS JOHN J	1LT	O-1798584	1148	1
KEYS LEE F	MAJ	O-0525251	0961	2
KEYS THEODORE F	CW3	W-2146071	0661	1
KEYS THOMAS P	CPT	O-1286504	0746	2
KEYS WILLIAM C	CPT	O-2262866	0361	1
KEYS WILLIAM J	CW4	W-2114228	0756	1
KEYSER DAVID C	2LT	O-2005392	0845	2
KEYSER GAIL S	LTC	O-0359075	0561	1
KEYSER HAROLD W	MAJ	O-1015444	0762	1
KEYSER MERRIEL O	MAJ	O-0214615	0649	1
KEYSER RICHARD C	1LT	O-1291479	0545	2
KEYSON JOHN A	MAJ	O-0987177	1263	1
KEYSON WESLEY A	COL	O-0388063	0760	1
KHAIL EMIL	MAJ	O-0274293	0966	3
KHALIEL DAVID	MAJ	O-0264080	1050	1
KHALIL SAAD	LTC	O-1314149	0666	1
KHARITONOFF ALEXAND	LTC	O-0367468	1159	1
KIAUNIS PAUL N	CW2	W-2145183	0456	1
KIBBLE HARRY L	MAJ	O-0523289	0656	1
KIBBLE HOWARD P	CW3	W-2143532	0760	1
KIBBY SYDNEY V	LTC	O-0164687	0648	3
KIBELE ELBERT E	LTC	O-2040810	0862	1
KIBER DANIEL H	COL	O-0189393	0554	3
KIBLER HAROLD R	COL	O-0221711	0456	3
KIBLER JOHN W	LTC	O-0246410	0365	3
KIBLER NELSON E	LTC	O-0373200	0561	2
KIBLER THOMAS E	1LT	O-1016452	0449	2
KIBLINGER PAUL L	MAJ	O-1582405	1167	1
KICKLIGHTER JESSE W	LTC	O-1541074	1163	2
KICTAREK FLORIAN	CW2	W-2205559	0460	1
KIDD CHARLES H	COL	O-0396656	0866	1
KIDD COLIN R	MAJ	O-0260438	0557	3
KIDD ELVIN J	MAJ	O-2003836	0867	1
KIDD HOLLICE E	CPT	O-1920244	1261	1
KIDD JEFFERSON	COL	O-0195415	1161	3
KIDD WADE L	MAJ	O-1101904	0964	1
KIDD WESLEY S	LTC	O-0481121	0857	1
KIDD WILLIAM N	MAJ	O-1019278	0258	1
KIDDER GUY S	LTC	O-0174610	1060	3
KIDDER JAMES H	B G	O-0248043	0262	3
KIDDER SHELDON F	MAJ	O-1552531	0562	1
KIDDER WILLIAM	MAJ	O-1555233	0861	1
KIDNEY ANDREW N	CW3	W-2153260	0264	1
KIDDIE ERLAND O	MAJ	O-1544644	1059	1
KIDODO ROBERT W	LTC	O-1106251	1162	1
KIDNEY JOHN H	CPT	O-0164315	0638	2
KIDWELL HUBERT H	MAJ	O-0499494	0948	1
KIDWELL JOSEPH A	LTC	O-0291466	0145	2
KIDWELL WILLIAM M	LTC	O-0234098	0965	3
KIEF JOSEPH A	MAJ	O-1325996	1162	1
KIEF LEON A	LTC	O-1035040	0161	1
KIEFER EMIL C	2LT	O-1639250	0445	1
KIEFER OSCAR G	LTC	O-0231537	1057	3
KIEFFER CHARLES F	CPT	O-1171224	1160	1
KIEFFER GENE A	MAJ	O-2049671	0161	1
KIEFFER PAUL W	LTC	O-0253308	0961	3
KIEGLER DONALD F	CW3	W-2133202	1057	1
KIEHL MARVIN F	CW4	W-2145078	0167	1
KIEL HAROLD J	MAJ	O-2049815	1163	1
KIELBASA MITCHELL R	LTC	O-1011092	0361	1
KIELICH JR BRUNO A	MAJ	O-1691049	0346	1
KIELKOFF EDWARD C	COL	O-0101934	0249	2
KIELLMAN ALVIN J	MAJ	O-1342786	1262	1
KIELY RALPH J	MAJ	O-0320379	1145	2
KIENHOLZ MARFRED J	CPT	O-1311306	0149	2
KIENLY JR JOSEPH C	MAJ	O-0455698	0655	1
KIENZLE PAUL H	COL	O-0247297	0654	3
KIERAN JAMES J	1LT	O-1038028	0745	1
KIERAN JR JOHN F	1LT	O-0447442	0644	2
KIERNAN JR JOHN I	CPT	O-0890215	0249	1
KIERNAN JR JOHN M	LTC	O-1797307	0562	1
KIERNAN LOYD J	CPT	O-0151934	1055	3
KIERNAN WILLIAM T	1LT	O-0983270	0754	2
KIERULFF DUDLEY E H	1LT	O-1167496	1045	2
KIESELMANN HOWARD T	2LT	O-1825006	0544	2

NAME	GRADE	SVC NO	DATE RET MO YR	RET CODE
KIESSLING CHARLES J	CPT	0-0902871	C745	2
KIESZEK STANLEY J	CPT	0-1305595	0747	2
KIETZMAN CARL W	COL	0-0241545	C365	3
KIEVIT DONALD J	COL	0-0391835	0363	2
KIEWIK JOHN W	WO1	W-2151307	C960	2
KIFER JOSEPH H	LTC	0-0223945	1262	3
KIFFIN MONTE R	MAJ	0-0227065	0763	3
KIGER JACK A	CW3	W-2146320	0763	2
KIGER STANLEY M	COL	0-0292882	0160	1
KIGGEN JR THOMAS F	MAJ	C-0974480	0664	1
KIGGINS THOMAS R	LTC	0-1289095	0258	1
KIGHT ROBERT J	MAJ	0-0382997	C157	1
KIGIN LEO S	CPT	0-0204583	0254	3
KIHLGREN AXEL G	LTC	0-0507367	C263	1
KIJEK WALTER A	1LT	0-2200009	1053	2
KIJIMA MASARU	MAJ	0-1922681	1166	1
KIKER JR JOHN E	MAJ	C-0371793	0646	2
KIKER RUSSELL L	LTC	C-0109972	0948	2
KIL HENRY L	1LT	0-1305788	C346	1
KILANO THURLOW N	1LT	0-1323713	1045	2
KILBANKS LESTER H	1LT	0-1997258	0751	2
KILBOURN RUTH H	1LT	L-0900236	0346	2
KILBOURNE JAMES	LTC	0-0279256	0867	3
KILBOURNE LAWRENCE W	LTC	0-0279897	0167	3
KILBOURNE WILLIAM C	CW2	W-2213664	C867	1
KILBRIDE JOHN P	MAJ	0-1287017	0857	1
KILBURN LEW J	CPT	0-1302315	C245	2
KILCAULEY ELMER W	LTC	0-1639253	0467	1
KILCH CHARLES W	1LT	0-1311902	1046	2
KILCOYNE AUGUSTIN G	COL	0-0916066	1061	3
KILCREASE DALLAS F	CPT	0-0285899	C145	2
KILDAY JOHN	MAJ	0-0320319	C344	2
KILDUFF JR FRANCIS X	LTC	0-1167934	0561	1
KILE JOHN P	CPT	0-1312565	0551	1
KILE MORTON F	1LT	0-1302013	C347	2
KILE RAYMOND H	1LT	0-1311522	0246	2
KILE ROBERT F	MAJ	0-0456294	0647	2
KILE ROBERT W	MAJ	0-1116558	C557	1
KILESKI FRECERICK	LTC	0-0124809	C156	3
KILEY GERALD G	LTC	0-0265373	1262	3
KILEY RICHARD H	LTC	0-1643751	1065	2
KILEY THOMAS P	MAJ	C-0987952	1163	1
KILGALLEN RAYMONC F	MAJ	C-1170803	C261	1
KILGARIFF ANDREW J	MAJ	0-1166418	0162	1
KILGO STANLEY H	MAJ	C-0578176	1062	1
KILGORE AUSTIN J	LTC	0-0130032	1051	3
KILGORE BENJAMIN M	COL	0-0497420	C846	2
KILGORE JR WILEY M	CW3	W-2147121	0167	2
KILGORE LYNDON E	CPT	0-1315947	1046	2
KILGORE MAX G	LTC	0-1579876	C866	1
KILGORE WILLIAM D	MAJ	0-0947228	0661	1
KILGOUR HAROLD C	CW3	W-2142165	C863	1
KILGUS EDWARD J	1LT	0-1184247	1046	1
KILIAN JAMES F	MAJ	C-1342089	1262	1
KILKENNY BERNARD J	CW3	W-2145184	1060	1
KILKER JEROME V	CPT	0-1641467	C855	1
KILLABREW ROSS D	MAJ	0-1290766	0461	1
KILLEBREW JAMES A	CW4	W-2144121	0164	1
KILLEBREW ROBERT J	CW2	W-2151772	0157	1
KILLEEN FRANCIS M	MAJ	0-0964222	0162	1
KILLEEN JAMES R	1LT	0-1170029	1045	2
KILLEFFER JOHN J	MAJ	0-0329974	0246	2
KILLEN ROSS B	LTC	0-1555234	0665	1
KILLENE JR ELMER C	1LT	0-2055174	1045	2
KILLERLAIN WILLIAM C	2LT	0-1309750	0544	2
KILLETT ERNEST B	LTC	0-1017841	1263	1
KILLEY GLENN D	LTC	0-1996767	0266	2
KILLIMETT JR JOHN J	MAJ	C-1639254	1058	1
KILLIN ARTHUR H	COL	0-0271920	0767	3
KILLIN HUGH E	LTC	0-0193996	1044	2
KILLINGER WILMA R	1LT	R-0000417	0846	1
KILLINGSWORTH L J	CW3	W-2146253	1157	1
KILLION JAMES R	CW2	W-2146865	1059	1
KILLION WILLIAM J	MAJ	C-2262191	0965	1
KILLMASTER RICHARC G	1LT	0-0919054	C145	1
KILLMER CONALD F	COL	0-0314177	0764	1
KILLOUGH CLINTON W	MAJ	C-0384943	0862	1
KILLOUGH EDWARD M	LTC	0-0188492	0648	3
KILMAN HCWARC T	LTC	0-1180571	1162	1
KILMER DCNALD E	MAJ	0-4006978	0767	1
KILMER CEORGE M	MAJ	0-1182403	0163	1
KILPATRICK ALMER W	MAJ	0-1686341	0363	1
KILPATRICK BENJAMI	MAJ	0-2051488	1062	1
KILPATRICK CHARLES	CPT	0-1106874	1159	1
KILPATRICK CHARLES J	CPT	0-012865C	0354	3
KILPATRICK CHARLES W	MAJ	0-1291123	1056	1
KILPATRICK GECRGE E	COL	0-0103632	0754	3
KILPATRICK J M	WO1	W-212692C	0546	2
KILPATRICK JAMES E	2LT	0-1825137	C446	2
KILPATRICK JR R V	LTC	0-1325500	0161	1
KILPATRICK RICHARD T	LTC	0-1291288	0656	1
KILPATRICK RCBERT L	LTC	0-1119203	0665	1
KILPATRICK RCBERT W	CW4	W-2141137	0565	1
KILPATRICK WILLIAM B	MAJ	0-1325185	0860	1
KILROE JOHN C	LTC	0-0136758	0945	2
KILROE RCBERT H	COL	0-0193603	0861	3
KILTS CLINTON F	CW2	W-2206409	0364	1
KILTZ CHESTER V	1LT	0-0373931	0244	1
KIM ALBERT K H	CPT	0-1688408	0755	2
KIM ERNIE	CPT	0-1318675	0747	2
KIM PETER	MAJ	0-2024527	1164	1
KIM WALTER Y W	CW2	W-3400077	0167	2
KIM YCUN P	LTC	0-0544054	0661	1
KIM YOUAG O	MAJ	0-0956856	0166	1
KIMBALL BLANCHE	1LT	N-0702255	1046	1
KIMBALL CHASE	CPT	0-0217317	0262	3
KIMBALL EDGAR R	LTC	0-0902588	0266	3
KIMBALL ELBERT T	COL	0-0151255	0864	2
KIMBALL HUNTER H	MAJ	0-0129547	C347	2
KIMBALL JCHN W	LTC	0-0176334	0361	3
KIMBALL JR GEORGE H	LTC	0-0388444	1061	1
KIMBALL LESLIE G	CW3	W-2146988	0764	1
KIMBALL MILTCN S	LTC	0-0211727	0651	3
KIMBALL RALPH L	CPT	0-0227778	0646	2
KIMBALL RAYMCND H	CPT	0-1003565	0555	1
KIMBALL RICHARD V	LTC	0-1012288	0761	1
KIMBALL THCMAS F	1LT	0-1040255	1145	2
KIMBELL JACK G	1LT	0-0359000	0946	2
KIMBLE FRANCIS E	CPT	0-0371728	0661	1
KIMBLE HORTON E	CPT	0-0401617	0747	2
KIMBLE JOHN M	MAJ	0-0244204	0765	3
KIMBLE RALPH A	COL	0-0118168	0953	3
KIMBLE WILLIAM A	LTC	0-0158891	0-51	3
KIMBLE WILLIAM O	LTC	0-0250134	0746	2
KIMBRELL JAMES R	CPT	0-1337442	0358	2
KIMBROUGH JAMES D	CW2	W-2124224	0955	1
KIMBROUGH JOSEPH F	MAJ	0-2005278	0760	1
KIMBRCUGH CRMAN L	CPT	0-1299754	0450	1
KIME JAMES S	CPT	0-0318050	0246	2
KIME RCBERT C	1LT	0-0393656	1044	2
KIMEL RACHEL T	MAJ	N-0726269	0561	1
KIMLIN CONALD W	MAJ	0-1584461	0261	1
KIMMEL GEORGE C	LTC	0-0306802	1060	1
KIMMEL JCHN E	MAJ	0-0353821	0367	3
KIMMEL REED B	MAJ	0-0402023	0860	1
KIMMEL WILLIAM J	MAJ	0-027555C	0758	3
KIMMERLE FOREST E	LTC	0-0360746	0267	3
KIMMONS NEIL C	2LT	0-1054284	0645	2
KIMPEL ECWARD W	1LT	0-1317401	1046	2
KIMPTON EDWARD K	MAJ	0-0118167	0654	3
KIMSEY CHARLES L	COL	0-0373117	0866	1
KIMURA JIRCS	MAJ	0-0426755	0446	2
KINARD CHARLES M	LTC	0-0226778	0546	2
KINARD ETHEL S	LTC	0-1293423	0263	1
KINARD LYMAN V	CPT	0-1845510	0546	1
KINARD ULYSSES G	CW3	W-2144217	0361	1
KINARD WILLIAM C	CW4	W-2113636	0266	1
KINCADE GECRGE L	CW2	W-2147476	0860	1
KINCAID CLEMENT J	LTC	0-0241583	1060	3
KINCAID HENRY C	MAJ	0-1640628	0157	1
KINCAID JAMES L	B G	0-0522288	0648	3
KINCAID JOHN I	MAJ	0-0249506	1066	3
KINCAID ORESTUS J	1LT	C-0164033	0936	1
KINCER JR ALFRED L	LTC	0-1101905	0462	1
KINCHELOE JAMES M	CPT	0-0200812	C948	1
KINDELL JOHN W	LTC	0-0187601	1054	3
KINDER CHARLES H	LTC	0-0522097	C847	1
KINDER CHARLES W	CPT	0-2017554	C457	1
KINDER HAROLD	MAJ	C-0247546	0567	3
KINDER JACOB F	2LT	0-0939662	0848	2
KINDER SIDNEY R	WO1	W-2121007	C254	1
KINDER THURMAN A	COL	0-0268363	1046	2
KINDICK CHARLES M	MAJ	C-1055884	0164	1
KINDRED FRANK H	MAJ	C-0479907	0147	1
KINDRED WENDELL H	LTC	0-0510909	0347	2
KINEHAN VINCENT W	CW3	W-2147353	1064	1
KINER GEORGE A	CPT	0-2102902	1062	1
KINERK ROBERT L	CPT	0-1296866	0546	2
KING AARON L	MAJ	C-0114565	1052	3
KING ALBERT	CPT	0-1555236	1042	1
KING ALBERT B	LTC	0-0248154	1047	2
KING ALBERT K	COL	0-0415391	0461	1
KING ALBERT T	CPT	0-0235591	1265	3
KING ALFRED F	COL	0-0166704	C750	3
KING ALLYN P	CPT	0-0223333	0153	1
KING ALTON J	MAJ	C-2043185	0765	1
KING ANDRE R	COL	0-0117122	0252	3
KING ARDEN J	LTC	0-0493368	0455	1
KING ARTHUR G	COL	C-0273830	C966	1
KING ARTHUR R	1LT	0-1061441	1046	1
KING BAIRD A	LTC	0-1181326	C762	2
KING BEAUREGARD	CPT	0-0412501	0849	2
KING BENJAMIN F	MAJ	0-2008573	0263	1
KING BENJAMIN J	MAJ	C-0195095	0-51	3
KING BERNARD F	CPT	0-1767474	C348	1
KING BRON T	CW2	W-2208998	C865	1
KING BRUCE R	COL	0-0247245	C758	2
KING BYRON B	LTC	0-1314259	1062	1
KING BYRON F	LTC	0-0270436	0467	3
KING BYRON K	LTC	0-0300469	0359	1
KING CARLOS E	CW2	W-2213518	0566	1
KING CARSON H	CPT	0-1010366	0147	2
KING CECIL W	2LT	0-1298716	0744	1
KING CHARLES	LTC	0-1116386	0866	1
KING CHARLES A	1LT	0-1331519	C646	2
KING CHARLES F	MAJ	C-1554573	0361	1
KING CHARLES H	CW3	W-2149075	0165	1
KING CHARLES W	CW2	W-2103088	C750	1
KING CHARLEY L	1LT	0-1826209	0255	1
KING CHESTER L	1LT	0-1013965	C644	2
KING CLINTON A	LTC	0-0453065	C758	1
KING DAN W	CPT	0-0327451	1143	2
KING DANIEL P	COL	0-0196319	0761	3
KING DELBERT S	LTC	0-0237486	1263	3
KING DOWELL R	CPT	0-1919207	C363	1
KING EARL	CPT	C-1922677	C563	1
KING EARL C	MAJ	0-0502357	0555	1
KING EARL E	CPT	0-0220682	1057	3
KING EDMOND H	LTC	0-0369687	0860	1
KING ECWARD F	WO1	W-2111721	0958	1
KING EDWARD V	MAJ	0-0475815	C846	1
KING EDWIN D	COL	0-0254756	1164	3
KING EDWIN H	CPT	0-0111537	1054	3
KING EDWIN H	2LT	0-1548885	0843	2
KING ELIZABETH	1LT	N-0772488	0646	1
KING ELLIS R	COL	C-0107618	1045	2
KING ELMO C	CW3	W-2144849	1262	1
KING ELMO R	CPT	0-2033206	0361	1
KING ELZAH O	MAJ	C-0504180	0761	1
KING ERNEST G	CW3	0-2262845	0557	1
KING ERNEST L	MAJ	C-0360673	0667	3
KING ERNEST O	COL	C-0299340	1265	3
KING ESTUS R	CW2	W-2211444	C465	1
KING FRANK W	CW3	W-2148738	0561	1
KING FREDDIE L	CW4	W-2141338	1167	1
KING GECRGE P	LTC	0-0408242	1159	3
KING GECRGE P	1LT	0-1106253	0362	3
KING GECRGE J	1LT	0-1822584	0246	2
KING GECRGE W	LTC	0-1294486	0963	1
KING GERALD C	LTC	0-1845195	0365	1
KING GERALDINE	1LT	N-0770059	0247	1
KING GERARD W	MAJ	C-0179302	1053	3
KING GILBERT W	LTC	0-0268616	1061	1
KING GCRDON A	LTC	0-1587369	0962	1
KING HARCLD C	LTC	0-0371346	1060	1
KING HARRY L	MAJ	0-0245294	0967	3
KING HELEN	MAJ	N-0736083	0361	2
KING HENRY A	COL	C-0240214	0965	3
KING HERBERT G	COL	0-0288120	1160	3
KING HERBERT S	CPT	0-0476332	1047	2
KING HIRAM I	1LT	0-1285603	0448	2
KING HUBERT H	CW4	W-2142104	0666	1
KING HUGH J	CPT	0-2008509	0559	1
KING JAMES A	CPT	0-1010001	0847	1
KING JAMES D	1LT	0-1015255	0545	2
KING JAMES E	WO1	W-2109365	0146	2
KING JAMES F	LTC	0-1309071	0664	1
KING JAMES J	CW3	W-2144329	1163	1
KING JAMES T	MAJ	0-0378105	0845	2
KING JENKINS O	2LT	0-2035428	0645	2
KING JCHN C	CPT	0-0246617	0161	3
KING JCHN D	MAJ	0-101319C	0161	1
KING JCHN H	1LT	0-0488536	0745	2
KING JCHN H	LTC	0-1299755	0561	1
KING JCHN H	CW2	W-2150885	0663	1
KING JCHN J	CW4	W-2144269	1061	1
KING JCHN L	1LT	0-1011993	1145	2
KING JCHN L	CPT	0-1052425	0847	2
KING JCHN M	COL	0-0346800	1263	1
KING JCHN P	CPT	0-0255706	0967	3
KING JCHN P	COL	0-0474073	C859	1
KING JCHN R	LTC	0-1294145	0262	1
KING JCHN S	MAJ	C-0354919	1046	2
KING JOHN T	COL	0-0231533	0250	3
KING JCHN W	LTC	0-1284714	0965	1
KING JCSEPH D B	CPT	0-0474522	0447	1
KING JCSEPH M P	CW3	W-2142863	1160	1
KING JR CALEB J	COL	0-0238587	C666	3
KING JR CALTCN L	CPT	0-2023777	1057	1
KING JR E B	1LT	0-1306598	0645	2
KING JR ISAAC R	COL	0-1165888	0865	1
KING JR JAMES E	MAJ	0-1920267	1264	1
KING JR JAMES F	2LT	0-1031253	1044	2
KING JR JCHN C	1LT	0-0485932	1045	2
KING JR RAYMCND R	CW2	W-2147586	1064	1
KING JR RICHARD M	LTC	0-0382038	0262	1
KING JR STANHOPE H	LTC	0-0290313	0257	1
KING JR WILLIAM H	COL	0-0404532	0465	1
KING JR WILLIAM T	LTC	0-1035299	1266	1
KING KEITH O	1LT	0-1309072	0346	2
KING KENNETH E	1LT	0-1316062	0645	2
KING LAWRENCE A	MAJ	0-1644491	0961	1
KING LAWRENCE G	COL	0-0196305	0449	3
KING LECNARD	CW3	W-2150717	0765	2
KING LECNARD B	1LT	0-0488817	0844	2
KING LESLIE R	COL	0-0270986	0367	3
KING LESTER G	MAJ	0-0242975	0849	3
KING LEW	1LT	0-1945182	0945	2
KING LEWIS J	CW4	W-2117178	0261	2
KING LUDLCW	LTC	0-0278463	0945	2
KING LYLE T	LTC	0-0304942	0347	2
KING MARTIN L	1LT	0-1313501	0745	2
KING MARY D	CPT	N-075732C	0249	2
KING MAURICE E	LTC	0-0322622	0361	3
KING MERLE K	MAJ	0-1925524	C866	1
KING MCSES	COL	0-0146245	0648	3
KING MCSES G	MAJ	0-0461358	1146	1
KING NATHANIEL	MAJ	0-0320596	0361	1
KING NICHOLAS	CW3	W-2150882	1262	1
KING NCAN G	MAJ	0-1301650	1160	1

NAME	GRADE	SVC NO	DATE RET MO YR	RET CODE
KING NORMAN O	COL	0-0203021	0761	3
KING NORMAN J	LTC	0-1894740	1067	2
KING ORVAL A	CW2	W-2152268	0263	1
KING ORVILLE R	1LT	0-1104915	0745	2
KING OSCAR	COL	0-1289591	0157	1
KING OTIS W	2LT	0-2040952	0252	2
KING PAUL W	CW4	W-2101930	0560	1
KING PAULINE E	1LT	N-0729273	0946	1
KING PHILIP F	COL	0-0262737	0159	3
KING RALPH J	COL	0-0255695	1065	3
KING RANDOLPH C	MAJ	0-2042819	0760	1
KING RAYMOND W	MAJ	0-1540868	0164	1
KING RICHARD W	CPT	0-0299927	1163	3
KING ROBERT A	CW2	W-2144070	1265	1
KING ROBERT C	LTC	0-1997256	0966	1
KING ROBERT H	MAJ	0-1327853	0661	1
KING ROBERT J	CPT	0-1323937	0956	2
KING ROBERT V	CW3	W-2145278	0860	1
KING ROBERT W	1LT	0-1167936	0552	2
KING ROBERT W	MAJ	0-1299421	1147	2
KING ROBERT W	CW3	RW-2148003	0264	1
KING ROLLIN W	MAJ	0-0903260	0257	2
KING RUFUS G	CPT	0-0206721	1163	3
KING RUFUS F	CW2	W-2210523	0264	1
KING RUSSELL M	COL	0-0244102	0647	2
KING S EDWARD	COL	0-0256728	1060	3
KING SAMUEL L	LTC	0-0450038	0560	1
KING SAMUEL R	MAJ	0-0555570	1167	1
KING SEYMOUR O	MAJ	0-0970136	0163	1
KING SHERMONT L	CW3	W-2148004	0862	1
KING SLOAN	CW2	W-2146072	0757	1
KING STARR M	LTC	0-0124788	0355	3
KING STEPHEN H	MAJ	0-0353861	0346	2
KING THEODORE R	LTC	0-0281274	0257	1
KING THOMAS B	MAJ	0-1533105	1047	2
KING THOMAS C	1LT	0-1316559	0845	2
KING THOMAS F	MAJ	0-2046475	0454	2
KING THOMAS F	CW2	W-2115954	0654	1
KING THOMAS J	CPT	0-1291874	0146	2
KING THOMAS R	CW4	W-2002746	1165	1
KING TOMMY F	MAJ	0-0901027	1041	1
KING VERNE O	MAJ	0-2103004	0365	1
KING WALLACE N	MAJ	0-1056453	0264	1
KING WALTER P	MAJ	0-0148505	0648	3
KING WARREN L	2LT	0-5534248	1265	2
KING WILBUR R	LTC	0-0195329	0360	3
KING WILLIAM	MAJ	0-1796807	1060	1
KING WILLIAM A	MAJ	0-0471767	0353	1
KING WILLIAM C	CPT	0-0294939	0955	3
KING WILLIAM D	LTC	0-1944720	0562	1
KING WILLIAM E	COL	0-0268277	1060	3
KING WILLIAM E	MAJ	0-1037577	0164	1
KING WILLIAM F	MAJ	0-1306857	0957	1
KING WILLIAM G	LTC	0-1014973	0463	1
KING WILLIAM H	LTC	0-1323714	0163	2
KING WILLIAM H	CW2	W-2148579	0264	1
KING WILLIAM J	COL	0-0443105	1061	3
KING WILLIAM J	LTC	0-1284156	0666	1
KING WILLIAM M	LTC	0-0300825	1047	2
KING WILLIAM M	1LT	0-0447036	0146	2
KING WILLIAM P	LTC	0-1595624	1262	1
KING WILLIAM R	LTC	0-1794955	1263	1
KING WILLIAM S	CPT	0-0387692	1045	2
KING WILLIAM W	CW3	W-2144087	0660	1
KING WILLIE O	CW2	W-2150128	0262	1
KING WILLIS J	MAJ	0-1284200	0847	1
KING WOODROW H	1LT	0-0460570	0244	2
KINGDOM MARK W	LTC	0-1011134	0860	1
KINGERY DANIEL W	LTC	0-0172999	1158	3
KINGMAN JOHN P	LTC	0-0901703	0666	3
KINGMAN WARREN A	MAJ	0-0344722	0467	3
KINGREY LAWRENCE C	CW2	W-2210313	1063	1
KINGRY WILLIAM F	MAJ	0-1826240	1060	1
KINGSBURY FRANK F	CW2	W-2147819	0760	1
KINGSBURY HOWARD T	LTC	0-0229831	1064	3

NAME	GRADE	SVC NO	DATE RET MO YR	RET CODE
KINGSBURY JOHN B	MAJ	0-1634971	1050	1
KINGSBURY KENNETH R	MAJ	0-0509613	0348	2
KINGSBURY LEONARD L	LTC	0-0216898	0763	3
KINGSBURY RALPH N	CPT	0-0266560	1262	3
KINGSFORD CARLETON L	MAJ	0-0252634	0552	3
KINGSLAND FRANK C	LTC	0-0142709	0856	3
KINGSLAND LAWRENCE C	COL	0-0183836	0648	3
KINGSLEY EDWIN W	CPT	0-0273326	0943	2
KINGSLEY GEORGE R	LTC	0-0490302	0466	3
KINGSLEY JOHN G	LTC	0-1013199	0462	1
KINGSLEY NEIL S	LTC	0-0166219	0549	3
KINGSTEDT CHARLES H	LTC	0-1583212	0462	1
KINGSTON CLARENCE R	MAJ	0-0241311	1165	3
KINGSTON FRANK H	LTC	0-1081074	0662	1
KINGSTON THOMAS J	MAJ	0-2025126	0863	2
KINKEMA ALFRED C	LTC	0-0229222	0159	3
KINKENNON OMAR A	LTC	0-1055055	1162	1
KINKLE FRANKLIN S	LTC	0-1314787	0564	1
KINLEY JAMES D	LTC	0-0311780	1064	3
KINLEY NORMAN J	COL	0-0386938	0767	1
KINLOCH JAMES P	CW2	W-2146338	0762	1
KINMAN RUSSELL B	MAJ	0-0330466	0262	3
KINMONTH CHARLES R	MAJ	0-2033050	0561	1
KINNAMAN JR JOHN	CW2	W-2144468	0461	1
KINNE MILTON J	CPT	0-1043383	0465	2
KINNER EDGAR L	LTC	0-0376277	1262	1
KINNER ROBERT H	LTC	0-0266520	0563	3
KINNER STEPHEN G	MAJ	0-1325132	0664	1
KINNETT MAURICE F	CPT	0-1890141	0463	1
KINNEY CLARENCE P	MAJ	0-0252358	1054	3
KINNEY DANIEL J	CW4	W-2107117	0762	1
KINNEY EDWARD J	LTC	0-1641470	1062	2
KINNEY GEORGE F	CPT	0-1304358	1156	2
KINNEY HARRY A	LTC	0-1339450	0666	1
KINNEY JAMES L	CPT	0-0113953	1051	3
KINNEY JAMES W	2LT	0-1315952	0444	2
KINNEY JOHN E	COL	0-0312950	0158	1
KINNEY JOSEPH E	MAJ	0-2026469	1164	1
KINNEY KENNETH H	1LT	0-0113952	1056	3
KINNEY LAWRENCE E	MAJ	0-0453126	1060	1
KINNEY ROY W	CW2	W-2110459	0450	1
KINNEY WALTER W	COL	0-0366266	0859	1
KINNEY WILLIAM H	LTC	0-1103732	0664	1
KINNEY WILLIAM R	MAJ	0-0979906	0764	1
KINNS WILMOT J	LTC	0-1174615	0865	1
KINOSHITA ROBERT S	MAJ	0-0258299	0646	2
KINSAUL JR WILLIAM W	CPT	0-1589953	1047	2
KINSAUL WALLACE R	CPT	0-1016265	1060	1
KINSEL KENNETH C	MAJ	0-1031812	0261	2
KINSELLA JOHN J	LTC	0-1577428	1054	1
KINSEY CHARLES H	LTC	0-0410050	0966	1
KINSEY FREDERICK	2LT	0-1323329	1045	2
KINSEY GEORGE W	LTC	0-0905533	1065	3
KINSEY JOSEPH D	CPT	0-0524829	0545	2
KINSEY JR ROBERT S	1LT	0-1315968	0845	2
KINSEY PAUL S	1LT	0-2055832	0645	1
KINSEY ROY E	MAJ	0-0339572	1045	1
KINSEY SR GEORGE W	CW3	W-2144792	0762	1
KINSINGER JAMES R	MAJ	0-1552532	1060	1
KINSINGER JOSEPH	CPT	0-1303903	1159	1
KINSMAN JOHN W	MAJ	0-2019330	1161	1
KINSOLVING HERBERT L	LTC	0-0905567	0667	3
KINTER MARY A	LTC	N-0763032	0163	1
KINTLER FRANK C	LTC	0-0918942	1067	3
KINTNER FLOYD H	1LT	0-1293972	1145	2
KINTNER ROBERT E	LTC	0-0420703	0944	2
KINTZ JOHN S	LTC	0-0321514	0955	2
KINZER HUGH R	MAJ	0-0249165	0367	3
KINZER OSBORN A	LTC	0-0229928	0863	3
KINZER WALTER L	MAJ	0-0228749	0344	3
KINZIE CHARLES N	1LT	0-1307706	1044	2
KINZIE DONALD H	CW2	W-2130727	1060	1
KINZIE DONALD R	LTC	0-0242921	0863	1
KINZIE JOSEPH R	LTC	0-0455334	1062	1
KINZIE JULIAN M	1LT	0-1060842	0150	2

NAME	GRADE	SVC NO	DATE RET MO YR	RET CODE
KINZIE ROBERT D	MAJ	0-0964425	0867	1
KINZLER GEORGE G	LTC	0-0371375	0255	1
KIPLINGER JULES G	COL	0-0317870	0565	3
KIPP ARTHUR W	CPT	0-1101576	0161	1
KIPP WILLIAM A	LTC	0-0532482	0865	3
KIPPENBROCK MICHAEL	LTC	0-0509204	1063	3
KIPPS HAROLD R	CPT	0-0938178	0156	2
KIPPS HENRY E	LTC	0-1103734	0665	1
KIPPS LEWIS C	1LT	0-1114991	1044	2
KIPPS THOMAS C	1LT	0-1648336	1146	2
KIRBY ALEXANDER	COL	0-0212867	1055	1
KIRBY CHARLES R	MAJ	0-0223615	0762	3
KIRBY COURTNEY E	CPT	0-0387124	1045	1
KIRBY DARIOUS E	LTC	0-1173333	0165	1
KIRBY EDWARD M	COL	0-0245267	0766	3
KIRBY EDWARD P	1LT	0-1692512	0646	2
KIRBY EUGENE B	LTC	0-1581869	0762	1
KIRBY EUGENE W	LTC	0-1794818	0962	1
KIRBY FERNANDER	LTC	0-0455721	0858	1
KIRBY FRANK L	MAJ	0-0412764	0450	2
KIRBY GEORGE O	CPT	0-1332174	0563	1
KIRBY GORDON I	MAJ	0-0277136	0551	3
KIRBY HARLEY T	LTC	0-0370111	0657	1
KIRBY HILLIARD F	1LT	0-1014245	0146	2
KIRBY JAMES H	MAJ	0-1685666	0464	1
KIRBY JOHN L	1LT	0-0397817	0451	1
KIRBY JR GRANVILLE	MAJ	0-1049928	1265	1
KIRBY JR JEFFERSON	MAJ	0-1287365	0561	1
KIRBY KENNETH E	MAJ	0-0936175	0163	1
KIRBY MARION A	2LT	0-5875010	0161	2
KIRBY RANDALL G	CW2	W-2110516	0145	2
KIRBY RUSSELL	CPT	0-1284157	0152	1
KIRCHER JR EDWIN	1LT	0-2006067	1046	2
KIRCHHOFER MELVIN L	LTC	0-0297304	0463	3
KIRCHHOFF WILLIAM A	LTC	0-1108074	0161	1
KIRCHNER JOHN F	CW3	W-2149445	0665	1
KIRCHNER LOUIS P	CPT	0-0473025	0546	2
KIRCHNER MARVIN M	MAJ	0-1018543	1160	1
KIRCHNER PAUL C	MAJ	0-1174616	0262	1
KIRCHNER PHILLIP A	1LT	0-1030993	0246	2
KIRCHNER WILLIAM R	LTC	0-0287775	0856	1
KIRK DONOVAN	LTC	0-0475382	1151	1
KIRK EUGENE P	CPT	0-1319509	0547	2
KIRK FRANK J	COL	0-0327199	0561	2
KIRK FREDERIC D	LTC	0-0418479	0960	1
KIRK FREDERICK	MAJ	0-1004351	0163	1
KIRK GENE	LTC	0-1646319	1262	1
KIRK III ROBERT J	LTC	0-0535968	0763	1
KIRK ISIDOR L	1LT	0-1560215	0648	1
KIRK JESSE K	COL	0-0205990	1150	3
KIRK JOSEPH L	LTC	0-1634973	1166	1
KIRK JR CLEVELAND	MAJ	0-2010502	0161	1
KIRK JR LEWIS H	LTC	0-0396958	0560	2
KIRK KAY K	CPT	0-0498018	1044	2
KIRK NORRIS J	COL	0-0261745	0664	3
KIRK PATRICK J	MAJ	0-0464918	0849	2
KIRK PAUL G	COL	0-0201090	1044	3
KIRK RUFUS H	1LT	0-1645111	0146	2
KIRK THOMAS M	COL	0-0229724	0465	3
KIRK THURSTON S	2LT	0-2047390	0345	2
KIRK WILLIAM F	MAJ	0-0260453	0246	2
KIRK WYATT W	2LT	0-0924500	0844	2
KIRKEL SIDNEY	LTC	0-1550633	0865	1
KIRKENDALL CLARK F	LTC	0-0225984	0962	3
KIRKHAM BEUFORD C	MAJ	0-0490177	0247	1
KIRKHAM HENRY P	COL	0-0167010	0648	3
KIRKHAM JACK V	2LT	0-2009585	1158	1
KIRKHAM JOHN S	CW3	W-2143688	0557	1
KIRKHART ANDREW A	MAJ	0-1286505	0954	2
KIRKLAND CLIFFORD F	CW3	W-2148694	0761	1
KIRKLAND COLLIE	WO1	W-2145560	0855	1
KIRKLAND ELBERT H	MAJ	0-0475163	0360	1
KIRKLAND GEORGE A	2LT	0-1080298	0943	2
KIRKLAND GEORGE H	MAJ	0-1599109	0165	1
KIRKLAND HENRY D	CPT	0-0470467	0745	1

NAME	GRADE	SVC NO	DATE RET MO YR	RET CODE
KIRKLAND JAMES A	LTC	0-0232998	1045	2
KIRKLAND JAMES R	1LT	0-0450313	1051	1
KIRKLAND JAMES S	MAJ	0-0415653	0145	2
KIRKLAND JR LONNIE N	LTC	0-1289553	0267	1
KIRKLAND PARKS	CPT	0-1328706	0457	1
KIRKLEY DANIEL C	LTC	0-0235196	1265	3
KIRKLEY JIMMIE J	CW3	W-3150299	0467	1
KIRKMAN CLAUDE R	CPT	0-0493447	0650	1
KIRKMAN PAUL R	MAJ	0-0448581	0960	2
KIRKMAN VAUGHN E	MAJ	0-0570991	0764	1
KIRKPATRICK CHASE P	LTC	0-0252498	0144	1
KIRKPATRICK DAVID V	COL	0-0392561	0661	1
KIRKPATRICK EARL R	LTC	0-1317174	1164	1
KIRKPATRICK FRANK R	CPT	0-0418481	0646	2
KIRKPATRICK GRAHAM	LTC	0-0233899	0745	2
KIRKPATRICK H D	CPT	0-0270628	0354	2
KIRKPATRICK H E	CPT	0-0529844	0746	2
KIRKPATRICK HENRY	COL	0-1576238	0764	2
KIRKPATRICK JAMES F	LTC	0-0469038	1062	1
KIRKPATRICK JOSEPH O	LTC	0-1574277	0461	1
KIRKPATRICK JR R A	MAJ	0-1843759	1160	2
KIRKPATRICK JR T L	MAJ	0-0336737	1045	2
KIRKPATRICK MARK A	MAJ	0-1824761	0365	1
KIRKPATRICK MARTIN O	LTC	0-0262380	0866	3
KIRKPATRICK MAXWELL	MAJ	0-1691470	0759	1
KIRKPATRICK P E	LTC	0-0450184	0655	1
KIRKPATRICK WILLIAM	LTC	0-0419138	0861	1
KIRKS HENRY G	CPT	0-0439811	1148	1
KIRKSEY FRED	CPT	0-0966617	0259	1
KIRKSEY JR JAMES W	LTC	0-0290140	1067	3
KIRKSEY LOUIS A	CPT	0-0412858	0746	2
KIRKWOOD CLETUS F	MAJ	0-0976570	0166	1
KIRKWOOD GLADYS	CPT	L-0801499	0858	2
KIRKWOOD MAYWOOD	2LT	0-1513793	0942	1
KIRKWOOD ROBERT H	COL	0-0192304	0363	3
KIRLAND ERNEST J	CW4	W-2120835	0858	1
KIRLIN EUGENE O	MAJ	0-1012356	0161	1
KIRN JR HENRY	CPT	0-0291946	0847	2
KIRSCH DONALD H	1LT	0-0538616	0845	1
KIRSCH MYRON R	2LT	0-1535011	1144	2
KIRSCH RUSSELL O	LTC	0-0533635	0964	1
KIRSCHBAUM DAVID	MAJ	0-1285604	0961	1
KIRSCHBAUM WILLIAM F	LTC	0-1342190	1167	1
KIRSCHNER JOHN G	LTC	0-0410475	1160	1
KIRSCHNER KENNETH A	LTC	0-0451132	0764	1
KIRSH OLGA D	1LT	N-0761800	0746	1
KIRSHBAUM IRVING J	MAJ	0-0524582	0450	1
KIRSHE HENRY A	1LT	0-4034336	0658	2
KIRSTEIN MELVIN B	CPT	0-0485090	0446	2
KIRSTIEN MARTIN C	CW4	W-2002737	1163	1
KIRT NORMAN F	CPT	0-2035112	1145	2
KIRTHLINK TOWNSEND J	LTC	0-1298025	0262	1
KIRTLEY BUFORD S	LTC	0-0365407	0846	2
KIRTLEY JR GROVER C	LTC	0-1035504	0864	1
KIRTLEY ROBERT D	CW3	RW-2206024	0866	1
KIRTON GRAHAM G	LTC	0-0451324	0559	1
KIRVEN LAMAR L	MAJ	0-1951226	1162	1
KIRWAN JR FRANCIS M	LTC	0-1105575	0762	1
KIRWIN FRANCIS W	MAJ	0-1825477	0661	1
KISCH NICHOLAS M	MAJ	0-1550740	1163	1
KISE CHARLES D	COL	0-0343557	1265	1
KISELYK JOHN	MAJ	0-0384332	0259	1
KISER ADOLPHUS G	1LT	0-1303435	0444	2
KISER CARLTON H	1LT	0-1288398	0645	2
KISER FREDERICK	CPT	0-0347297	1057	1
KISER GEORGE F	1LT	0-0372178	1144	2
KISER HOWARD H	MAJ	0-1293793	0263	1
KISER ROBERT J	1LT	0-1012421	1051	1
KISER WILLIAM H	2LT	0-1316162	0545	2
KISER WILLIAM N	MAJ	0-0945111	0163	1
KISH FRANK S	CW4	W-2151803	0966	1
KISH GEORGE F	MAJ	0-2030475	0166	1
KISH HELEN L	2LT	N-0767-33	0944	1
KISH IVAN J	LTC	0-0290152	0664	3
KISH PETER J	MAJ	0-1299581	0957	1

NAME	GRADE	SVC NO	DATE RET MO YR	RET CODE
KISH STEPHEN A	LTC	0-1552309	0564	1
KISH WALTER C	CPT	0-0366134	1143	2
KISHIDA TATSUO	CW3	W-2144191	0764	1
KISHTER HARRY L	WO1	W-2128827	0348	1
KISINGER CHARLES E	CPT	0-1292194	1154	2
KISINGER JR HOWARD J	MAJ	0-1825544	0362	2
KISLIK ROBERT E	CPT	0-1583216	0246	2
KISLOW EDWARD E	CW2	W-0900991	1147	1
KISOR LORENZ	LTC	0-0130026	0158	3
KISPERT HENRY F	MAJ	0-2029753	0864	1
KISSAWETTER MARTHA K	MAJ	N-0742480	0662	1
KISSEL VICTOR T	CPT	0-0521722	0647	2
KISSELL DEWITT C	CPT	0-0345412	1045	2
KISSICK JAMES W	CW3	W-2136601	1165	1
KISSINGER LESTER G	MAJ	0-2010780	0961	1
KISSINGER MARVIN S	CPT	0-2011203	0757	1
KISSINGER PAUL L	MAJ	0-2262509	0366	1
KISTER CLAUDE V	LTC	0-0284570	1267	3
KISTLER NORMAN L	COL	0-0241336	0766	3
KITAGAWA KIYOSHI	MAJ	0-0336256	1163	1
KITCHELL ROBERT	MAJ	0-0202403	1058	3
KITCHEN BETHUEL M	COL	0-0310568	0657	1
KITCHEN CORTEZ A	LTC	0-0358416	0647	2
KITCHEN ELDON L	LTC	0-1533110	0761	1
KITCHEN GEORGE H	COL	0-0408699	1166	1
KITCHEN H DEAN	MAJ	0-0178498	0761	3
KITCHEN JAMES K	LTC	0-1594279	1060	1
KITCHEN JAMES W	LTC	0-1287194	1160	1
KITCHEN WILLIAM W	COL	0-0291804	1262	1
KITCHENS JOHN G	CPT	0-0352138	0946	2
KITCHENS MILTON G	CPT	0-2262106	1053	2
KITNER EDWIN F	MAJ	0-0983435	0561	1
KITSELMAN CHARLES H	COL	0-0125121	0855	3
KITSELMAN JR HENRY A	LTC	0-0376003	0859	1
KITSONAS NICHOLAS T	LTC	0-1047612	0866	1
KITT GUSTAV A	CW4	W-2106186	0962	1
KITT WILLIAM	MAJ	0-2000135	0662	1
KITTEL WILLIAM	LTC	0-0235907	0664	3
KITTELL ROY B	CPT	0-0980419	0761	1
KITTELSAA ERVIN	CPT	0-0504451	0750	1
KITTERMAN HOWARD I	CPT	0-1017267	0656	1
KITTERMAN JOHN W	CW2	W-2101935	0648	1
KITTINGER EDWARD R	CPT	0-0165827	1051	3
KITTINGER ROBERT L	LTC	0-0454221	0765	1
KITTLE KENNETH W	CPT	0-1315003	0646	2
KITTLE WALTER F	MAJ	0-0472540	0146	2
KITTLE WILLIAM R	MAJ	0-0917757	0346	2
KITTO LELAND H	CPT	0-1306286	0547	2
KITTRELL THOMAS S	COL	0-0183982	1159	3
KITTRELL WILBURN H	LTC	0-0192686	0262	3
KITTS ANDREW F	CW3	W-2150964	0365	1
KITTS HOWARD L	LTC	0-0919495	0364	3
KITZELMAN JAMES W	LTC	0-0498938	0954	1
KIVETT DAVID F	CPT	0-0353485	0146	2
KIVETT JR NOBLE W	CW3	W-2145161	0762	1
KIVO AARON L	CPT	0-1689375	0845	2
KIVEES JR ANDREW	MAJ	0-1648061	0961	1
KIYOTA WILLIE K	1LT	0-1999530	1045	2
KIZER RICHARD M	LTC	0-0422176	0163	1
KIZINSKI IGNATZ M	CPT	0-0499589	0145	2
KIZIS CLIFFORD E	LTC	0-1574905	0463	1
KJELLAND THOMAS K	CPT	0-1324340	0746	2
KJELLMAN HARRY A	MAJ	0-0149252	0754	3
KJELSTROM WILLIAM C	CPT	0-1286141	0247	1
KJER WINFRED E	1LT	0-1319574	0445	2
KJERNER MAX H	LTC	0-0495234	0663	3
KJONAAS ROBERT A	MAJ	0-0955474	0962	1
KLABANOFF BENJAMIN	MAJ	0-0381247	0548	1
KLACIK GEORGE	MAJ	0-1111713	0964	1
KLAES JR JAMES G	CPT	0-1341981	0860	1
KLAFFHN WILLARD J	LTC	0-1894961	0966	1
KLAHR ELLSWORTH	CPT	0-0417987	0744	2
KLAIBER JR JOHN J	CPT	0-0381710	0346	2
KLAINER MAX J	CPT	0-1686128	1145	2
KLAMER GEORGE F	MAJ	0-1289920	0958	1

NAME	GRADE	SVC NO	DATE RET MO YR	RET CODE
KLAMON CHARLES	CPT	0-1062921	0947	2
KLAMPERT MORRIS	CPT	0-1011848	0147	1
KLANCHER LADEIF F	CW2	W-2210889	1162	1
KLANIECKI EDWARD S	LTC	0-1177874	0862	1
KLAPMAN DAVID J	CPT	0-0400187	1045	2
KLAPPSA JOSEPH J	WO1	W-2107904	0945	2
KLARFIELD RICHARD	LTC	0-1846463	0767	3
KLARKOWSKI FRANK G	MAJ	0-2262420	1262	1
KLASE ROBERT F	LTC	0-0885028	1159	1
KLATT HAROLD O	MAJ	0-1292352	0348	2
KLAUBER LOUIS A	LTC	0-0229075	0665	3
KLAUDT MILTON	LTC	0-1581219	0363	1
KLAUS ADOLPH A	CPT	0-0224510	0956	3
KLAUSNER JOHN T	LTC	0-0235542	1165	3
KLAWITTER ARNOLD G	1LT	0-2055401	0145	2
KLEBER VICTOR A	COL	0-0167034	0452	3
KLECH WILLIAM S	MAJ	0-1040041	1052	1
KLECKNER EARL J	COL	0-0182983	0850	3
KLECKNER FRANK G	CW3	W-2145734	0464	1
KLECKNER LEONARD	LTC	0-1292900	0466	1
KLECZKA JOSEPH W	MAJ	0-1185947	1160	1
KLEE WILLIAM W	1LT	0-1183105	1144	2
KLEEB JR FREDERICK	CW4	W-2005737	1067	1
KLEEB WILLIAM H	CW4	W-2119449	1053	1
KLEEFIELD ELMER A	MAJ	0-0501088	0246	2
KLEEFISCH F R	1LT	0-1589955	0545	2
KLEESE JAMES G	LTC	0-0437663	1152	1
KLEIER JOSEPH	LTC	0-1646324	1167	1
KLEIKAMP HERMAN G	LTC	0-1017546	0562	1
KLEIMAN LEO	LTC	0-1012404	0564	1
KLEIMAN MAX	LTC	0-0161586	0157	3
KLEIN BERNARD H	2LT	0-1042336	1144	2
KLEIN CHARLES W	CPT	0-2020559	1058	1
KLEIN CLARENCE W	CW3	W-2150653	0962	1
KLEIN DAVID	CPT	0-0250389	0845	2
KLEIN DONALD C	1LT	0-1036233	0447	2
KLEIN EDITH M	1LT	N-0900062	0956	2
KLEIN ELIZABETH	MAJ	N-0702600	0359	1
KLEIN ELVIN W	LTC	0-1544800	0266	1
KLEIN ERNEST T	LTC	0-0276785	1062	3
KLEIN FRANK N	2LT	0-1913792	0542	1
KLEIN FRED	MAJ	0-1301162	0559	1
KLEIN GEORGE C	COL	0-0253744	0761	3
KLEIN HERMAN	CPT	0-0535218	0445	2
KLEIN HERMAN E	MAJ	0-0297875	1164	3
KLEIN JACK F	1LT	0-1316431	0146	2
KLEIN JAMES A	LTC	0-0467405	0962	1
KLEIN JENNINGS B	LTC	0-0261029	0449	2
KLEIN JEROME E	1LT	0-1594946	1145	2
KLEIN JOHN J	COL	0-0407195	1265	1
KLEIN JOSEPH	CPT	0-1291134	0446	1
KLEIN JOSEPH N	LTC	0-1535353	1162	1
KLEIN JULIUS	B G	0-0327822	1061	3
KLEIN LAURA M	MAJ	L-0405397	0966	3
KLEIN LOUIS H A	LTC	0-1534305	0262	1
KLEIN MILDRED J	1LT	N-0755043	0745	1
KLEIN MILTON A	LTC	0-0451609	0261	1
KLEIN MILTON E	LTC	0-4002318	0655	2
KLEIN MURRAY M	1LT	0-0522190	0745	2
KLEIN PATRICK L	LTC	0-1044862	0267	1
KLEIN PRESSLEY R	LTC	0-0149284	0853	3
KLEIN ROSE S	2LT	N-0762362	1144	1
KLEIN RUDOLPH	CPT	0-0524324	1145	2
KLEIN SAMUEL	2LT	0-1048047	1044	2
KLEIN THEODORE A	COL	0-0241061	0657	1
KLEIN TOBIAS	LTC	0-0919270	0446	2
KLEIN WILLIAM	MAJ	0-0492705	0957	1
KLEINAU CARL S	LTC	0-0171140	0359	3
KLEINBERG MAURICE S	COL	0-0498322	1167	1
KLEINECGER CHARLES J	LTC	0-0323116	0860	1
KLEINER ADELBERT F	LTC	0-1585725	1060	1
KLEINER MARY C	1LT	N-0759994	1045	1
KLEINFELD ABRAHAM H	1LT	0-0512968	0644	2
KLEINFIELD HERBERT L	1LT	0-0436968	1043	2
KLEINHANS RUSSELL W	CW2	W-2214540	0966	1

NAME	GRADE	SVC NO	DATE RET MO YR	RET CODE
KLEINKNIGHT L R	COL	0-0107218	1056	3
KLEINMAN ABRAHAM M	MAJ	0-1689246	1046	2
KLEINMAN FORREST K	LTC	0-0335972	1060	1
KLEINMAN WILLIAM W	COL	0-0200976	0564	3
KLEINMANN WILLIAM	1LT	0-1037103	1046	2
KLEINSASSER PAUL P	1LT	0-1547989	1145	2
KLEINSCHMIDT B W	CPT	0-0370992	0251	1
KLEISER ROY H	MAJ	0-0122225	0648	3
KLEKNER ARTHUR A	LTC	0-1325997	0366	1
KLEM STEPHEN	2LT	0-1302985	1043	2
KLEMANN JOHN H	CW3	W-2147358	0164	1
KLEMENS FRED W	CW3	W-2121223	0357	1
KLEMENS THADDEUS E	LTC	0-0406736	1059	1
KLEMES ISADORE S	CPT	0-0462136	0945	2
KLEMM DEWEY	CPT	0-0496809	0852	1
KLEMM GEORGE J	COL	0-0298403	0266	1
KLEMM WILLIAM H	1LT	0-0200846	1053	3
KLEMP RAYMOND A	CPT	0-0292078	1044	2
KLEMP WALTER A	2LT	0-1949368	0745	2
KLENIK RALPH L	MAJ	0-1048854	0761	1
KLENK FRED	CPT	0-0149784	0857	3
KLENK JOHN M	COL	0-0299982	0760	1
KLEPAC JOHN	1LT	0-0358078	0363	1
KLEPACZ MITCHELL V	LTC	0-1042622	1062	1
KLEPADLO WALTER E	MAJ	0-2097136	0265	1
KLEPEIS WALTER J	MAJ	0-1685011	0465	1
KLEPPEN NORMAN T	CW4	W-2141339	0765	1
KLEPEKOPER MAURICE R	LTC	0-1324868	1061	1
KLETT ELEANOR V	MAJ	M-0002034	1164	1
KLETT JOHN R	MAJ	0-0504517	1155	1
KLETT WILLIAM M	1LT	0-1308519	0446	2
KLIMA PAULINE M	1LT	N-0724236	1144	1
KLIMAS HELEN G	1LT	N-0729189	0646	1
KLIMAS WILLIAM J	WO1	W-2103099	0443	2
KLIMASZEWSKI WILFRED	CW2	W-3200265	0167	1
KLIMES GEORGE V	COL	0-0170713	0446	2
KLINCK JOHN H	LTC	0-0449973	0364	1
KLINDIENST EDWARD F	CPT	0-1040418	0952	1
KLINE ALFRED S	LTC	0-0428982	1063	3
KLINE CHARLES F	LTC	0-0263129	0767	3
KLINE CLAUDE N	1LT	0-0890240	0248	2
KLINE DORIS M	1LT	N-0751999	0546	1
KLINE FLOYD E	MAJ	0-1080212	0550	1
KLINE HARLAND R	LTC	0-0265350	0467	3
KLINE HARRY H	CW3	W-2147177	0862	1
KLINE HELEN	MAJ	N-0760036	0764	3
KLINE HELEN I B	1LT	N-0761888	0847	1
KLINE IRVING H	1LT	0-0248920	0446	2
KLINE JAMES H	1LT	0-0327541	0544	2
KLINE JR JAMES A	MAJ	0-0974511	1063	1
KLINE JR MARTIN L	MAJ	0-1041592	0261	1
KLINE LEE A	CPT	0-0197693	1262	3
KLINE MURRAY M	CW2	W-2101213	0346	2
KLINE NELSON F	CW2	W-2110117	0747	1
KLINE SIDNEY	CPT	0-0238431	0666	3
KLINE SR CONRAD W	MAJ	0-0162129	0648	3
KLINE STANLEY N	1LT	0-0428144	1043	2
KLINE WILLIAM P	LTC	0-1845676	0862	1
KLINEFELTER PAUL M	CPT	0-0547634	1147	1
KLING HERMAN A	CPT	0-0483382	0945	2
KLING JULIUS W	1LT	0-0549960	0347	2
KLINGBEIL HERMAN F	CPT	0-4006246	0664	1
KLINGENBECK ROBERT F	CW2	RW-2206111	0664	1
KLINGENSMITH M J	2LT	0-0158772	0756	3
KLINGER JR HARRY F	1LT	0-1292003	1045	2
KLINGER KENNETH P	LTC	0-0118192	1056	3
KLINGER WARREN V	1LT	0-1288071	0145	2
KLINGER WILLIAM H	LTC	0-0375170	0756	1
KLINGER WILLIAM L	LTC	0-1557031	1066	1
KLINKACEK FRANCIS	LTC	0-0482129	0962	1
KLINKBEIL CHARLES E	MAJ	0-2262253	0466	1
KLINKEL EDSON	CPT	0-0284915	0159	3
KLINKER DARRELL E	LTC	0-1296867	0163	1
KLINKO AGNES M	1LT	N-0722550	1046	1
KLIPA JR JOHN	CPT	0-1307709	0248	2

NAME	GRADE	SVC NO	DATE RET MO YR	RET CODE
KLIPSCH PAUL W	LTC	0-0225960	0464	3
KLIPSTINE CHARLES W	LTC	0-1319960	1262	1
KLISE CARLYLE	COL	0-0329798	1060	1
KLISS VICTOR L	MAJ	0-1174916	0164	1
KLITCH EDWIN M	MAJ	0-1297052	1064	1
KLOBY JOHN J	CPT	0-1692181	0845	2
KLOC CHESTER S	CPT	0-1050338	0258	2
KLOE DONALD R	CPT	0-0547099	0763	1
KLOEB WILLIAM C	LTC	0-1304952	1062	1
KLOECKLER CECILIA L	CPT	N-0735200	0549	2
KLOEPPERN EARL W	1LT	0-1171672	0546	2
KLOETZER ADELBERT D	MAJ	0-0226144	0863	3
KLOMAN CURT C	MAJ	0-2020165	0563	1
KLOO WALTER E	CPT	0-1332710	0265	3
KLOOSTERMAN JOHN	LTC	0-1014660	0567	1
KLOPFER HENRY T	CPT	0-1646327	0557	1
KLOPP CHARLES F	LTC	0-1584465	0364	1
KLOPP HARRY J	MAJ	0-0510770	1051	1
KLOPPEL KEITH M	2LT	0-1324223	0145	2
KLOPSTECK ARTHUR	COL	0-0198721	0253	1
KLORFINE MILTON	LTC	0-0235662	0764	3
KLOSKI HERMAN A	CPT	0-0346253	0745	2
KLOSS ELIZABETH	MAJ	N-0725935	1166	2
KLOSTER GEORGE D	CW2	W-2208896	0763	1
KLOSTER JR IVER J	LTC	0-0514489	0261	1
KLOSTER RUSH F	MAJ	0-1200657	0860	1
KLOSTERMAN WARREN W	LTC	0-0426106	0864	1
KLOTCH EDWARD P	LTC	0-1102806	1062	1
KLOTCH FREDERICK	2LT	0-1639261	1045	2
KLOTE EDWARD J	1LT	0-0375865	1145	2
KLOTHE CHARLES A	CW2	W-2118051	1145	2
KLOTZ MAURICE	COL	0-0324235	0766	3
KLOTZ WALTER	MAJ	0-0497030	1154	1
KLUBERTANZ ALBERT J	1LT	0-0221022	1147	1
KLUCHER GEORGE	CW3	W-2152468	0364	1
KLUCZINSKY VINCENT C	LTC	0-1703895	1056	1
KLUEGEL OSWALD E	MAJ	0-0344989	0645	2
KLUGLER JOSEPH	CPT	0-0526830	1046	2
KLUMBACH JOSEPH J	LTC	0-1282977	1165	3
KLUMP EMMETT J	CW3	W-2208283	1266	1
KLUMPP JOSEPH J	COL	0-0153094	1045	2
KLUMPP JOSEPH P	1LT	0-1314150	1145	2
KLUSKY RICHARD V	LTC	0-1314031	0565	1
KLUSMEIER FREDERICK	MAJ	0-0983838	0864	1
KLUSMEIER PAUL C	MAJ	0-0349147	0667	3
KLUTMAN WALTER J	2LT	0-1322832	1044	2
KLUTSCH JR JOSEPH	CPT	0-1289922	1046	2
KLUTTZ WALTER H	LTC	0-0304069	0966	3
KLUTTZ WILLIAM H	CW2	W-2151791	0563	1
KLYVERT EMMETH L	CW3	W-2205201	0867	1
KNAACK WILLIAM H	LTC	0-0337657	1259	1
KNABB JOSEPH H	CW2	W-2205026	0760	2
KNABE KATHRYN F	CPT	N-0728719	0247	1
KNABE RAY T	LTC	0-1579889	0765	3
KNABLE C ELKINS	COL	0-0149287	1049	3
KNACK WALLACE L	LTC	0-0260112	0764	3
KNACKSTEDT HENRY A	LTC	0-0406386	1060	1
KNADLER CHARLES N	LTC	0-0287351	0465	3
KNAFF MARTHA M	2LT	N-0730417	0844	1
KNAKE EDWIN C	LTC	0-0300992	0866	3
KNAPE DAVID R	LTC	0-0167036	0753	3
KNAPP ALLEN H	CPT	0-0333079	0642	2
KNAPP ARTHUR J	CW3	W-2144688	0959	1
KNAPP CHARLES J	CW3	W-2104735	1057	2
KNAPP CRAWFORD E	MAJ	0-0243769	0464	3
KNAPP EDWARD J	LTC	0-1000394	0267	3
KNAPP ETHEL M	2LT	N-0702206	0240	1
KNAPP FREDERICK	COL	0-0108285	0858	3
KNAPP GEORGE A	MAJ	0-0416164	0145	2
KNAPP GORDON A	MAJ	0-0130628	0452	3
KNAPP GORDON W	MAJ	0-1103262	0461	1
KNAPP HOWARD B	CW3	W-2150575	0962	2
KNAPP JR KENNETH J	LTC	0-1045137	1061	1
KNAPP KELVIN J	LTC	0-0392685	0746	2
KNAPP KINGSTON O	MAJ	0-0479471	0161	1

NAME	GRADE	SVC NO	DATE RET MO YR	RET CODE
KNAPP LLOYD B	LTC	O-1556302	1165	3
KNAPP RAYMOND S	LTC	O-0118193	0355	3
KNAPP ROBERT S	MAJ	O-0278239	0256	3
KNAPP VERNON R	CW2	W-2150776	0661	1
KNAPP WILLIAM A	LTC	O-0118270	1158	3
KNAPPEN JR CHARLES B	1LT	O-0514836	1045	2
KNAPPIK JACK E	MAJ	O-1589316	1158	1
KNAUB JR JACK	MAJ	O-0998540	0463	1
KNAUERHASE CARL O	LTC	O-0374693	1060	1
KNAUF CHARLES F	CPT	O-1699779	0945	2
KNAUF JR PAUL W	LTC	O-0170094	0760	3
KNAUF LAWRENCE W	COL	O-0302824	0663	1
KNAUF WILLIAM J	MAJ	O-0175157	0959	3
KNAUFF CHARLES H	MAJ	O-0961378	0862	1
KNAUFF FRANCIS T	1LT	O-0454129	0955	1
KNAUS FRED	1LT	O-0187154	0753	3
KNAUSS RUTH E	2LT	N-0724996	0345	1
KNAZOVICH ALEX	MAJ	O-1174918	1062	1
KNECHT LAWRENCE E	CW4	W-2118164	0659	1
KNECHTEL LLOYD W	LTC	O-0903360	0867	3
KNEE ROBERT G	LTC	O-0496460	0951	1
KNEECE ROLDRIDGE	LTC	O-0146409	0254	3
KNEECE THURMAN C	CPT	O-0970811	1060	1
KNEELAND BERNARD T	LTC	O-0432878	1262	1
KNEELAND THEODORE R	1LT	O-1305269	1048	2
KNEER BERNARD J	1LT	O-1169603	1045	2
KNEESE EDGAR A	LTC	O-1047191	1062	1
KNEFEL CLEMENT A	MAJ	O-0427953	0261	1
KNEIB CHARLES E	LTC	O-1641478	0465	1
KNEISEL WILLIAM G	1LT	O-0524130	0245	2
KNEISLER JAMES R	MAJ	O-1101906	1160	1
KNEISLER WALDEMAR	1LT	O-1302317	1045	1
KNEPHER JACK T	CW4	W-2127586	0859	2
KNEPKA EARL R	CW3	W-2145243	0267	1
KNEPLEY JAMES R	LTC	O-1103735	1164	1
KNERR LEWIS E	LTC	O-0101960	1149	3
KNETTLE LEROY J	LTC	O-0295426	0360	3
KNEUPPER WILFRED A	LTC	O-0348787	0946	2
KNEWITZ RALPH W	MAJ	O-0308065	0645	2
KNEZEVICH DONALD M	2LT	O-1574910	0744	1
KNEZOVICH FRANCIS M	MAJ	O-1108082	0157	1
KNICKERBOCKER E	MAJ	O-1548888	1054	1
KNICKERBOCKER G F	2LT	O-1558042	1044	2
KNICKERBOCKER WILLIA	LTC	O-1102333	1264	1
KNIE DONALD W	1LT	O-1042623	0446	1
KNIE WALTER M	CW3	W-2152914	0966	1
KNIERIEM JOHN P	LTC	O-0387397	0960	1
KNIERIM GEORGE W J	CPT	O-1314789	0653	1
KNIERIM HENRY E	MAJ	O-0140239	0254	3
KNIERIM JOHN H	1LT	O-1639230	0158	1
KNIESS SR GEORGE P	MAJ	O-0309717	0259	1
KNIESTEDT EWALD H	LTC	O-0282544	0862	3
KNIFFEN CECIL G	CW2	W-2141340	0655	1
KNIFONG EUGENE	CPT	O-0495409	1048	1
KNIFTON FRANCIS H	LTC	O-0226279	0663	1
KNIGHT ALBERT L	MAJ	O-2262937	0866	1
KNIGHT ALEXANDER	COL	O-0128718	0546	2
KNIGHT CHARLES R	LTC	O-2276376	0563	1
KNIGHT CHARLES F	CPT	O-1312018	1059	1
KNIGHT CHARLES W	LTC	O-0172624	1146	2
KNIGHT CHESTER R	MAJ	O-0976742	0663	1
KNIGHT CLARENCE G	MAJ	O-0945723	1066	1
KNIGHT EDWIN K	MAJ	O-1109424	1065	3
KNIGHT ERNEST E	COL	O-0451511	0766	2
KNIGHT ERNEST G	CW2	W-2149118	0761	1
KNIGHT FERRIS	MAJ	O-1320540	0859	1
KNIGHT GEORGE C	LTC	O-0243128	0861	3
KNIGHT GERALD E	1LT	O-1030487	1046	1
KNIGHT HANON	MAJ	O-1342082	0363	1
KNIGHT HENRY J	1LT	O-1049931	0347	2
KNIGHT HERBERT G	CPT	O-0109628	0438	1
KNIGHT HUGH E	MAJ	O-0215489	1058	3
KNIGHT HUGH F	COL	O-0348385	0860	1
KNIGHT JACK C	MAJ	O-0307184	0866	3
KNIGHT JEROME P	LTC	O-0287480	0357	1

NAME	GRADE	SVC NO	DATE RET MO YR	RET CODE
KNIGHT JOSEPH	WO1	W-2147188	0154	2
KNIGHT JR HOWARD W	CPT	O-0885740	0846	2
KNIGHT JR JOHN W	LTC	O-1116165	0661	1
KNIGHT JR WILEY	MAJ	O-0359843	0552	1
KNIGHT JULIUS A	LTC	O-1573336	1061	1
KNIGHT KENNETH L	1LT	O-0976569	0953	2
KNIGHT LAWRENCE O	LTC	O-2206259	1067	1
KNIGHT LEONARD M	1LT	O-0493518	1157	1
KNIGHT LEROY A	1LT	O-0141963	1153	3
KNIGHT LESTER R	MAJ	O-0528113	1154	1
KNIGHT LOUIS J	MAJ	O-0158054	0655	3
KNIGHT LOYD W	LTC	O-1825007	0667	1
KNIGHT MARION J	LTC	O-1284159	1161	1
KNIGHT MAX J	CPT	O-0519281	0844	2
KNIGHT PHILIP A	LTC	O-0453610	0662	1
KNIGHT RALPH T	COL	O-0177521	0648	3
KNIGHT RAYMOND	CW2	W-2208404	1263	1
KNIGHT RAYMOND F	MAJ	O-1322558	0363	1
KNIGHT REAMS R	CW4	W-2115520	0559	1
KNIGHT RICHARD E	MAJ	O-1309282	0659	2
KNIGHT ROBERT	MAJ	O-1999062	0460	1
KNIGHT ROBERT E	CW2	W-2143094	1155	1
KNIGHT ROBERT H	1LT	O-2004645	0554	2
KNIGHT ROBERT I	LTC	O-1080723	0258	1
KNIGHT RUSSELL F	MAJ	O-0589659	0466	3
KNIGHT SAMUEL R	COL	O-0243537	0963	1
KNIGHT THOMAS H	MAJ	O-0972033	0761	1
KNIGHT WILBURN W	CPT	O-0539442	0846	2
KNIGHT WILLIAM E	LTC	O-1543614	0163	1
KNIGHT WILLIAM F	LTC	O-1297741	0965	1
KNIGHT WILLIAM G	COL	O-0130141	0648	3
KNIGHT WILLMER F	CPT	O-0267276	0866	3
KNIGHTON HARRY A	LTC	O-1172122	0361	1
KNIGOFF MORRIS	CPT	O-0321325	1045	2
KNIPE GEORGE E	MAJ	O-1106260	0862	1
KNIPHFER DWIGHT O	CPT	O-2006741	0959	1
KNISELY EARL P	LTC	O-0381538	1045	2
KNISHKOWY EMANUEL S	CPT	O-0517242	0545	2
KNISLEY ELMER W	CPT	O-1293425	0763	1
KNISLEY EVERETT M	CW3	W-2152365	0964	2
KNISS GERTRUDE F	2LT	N-0774544	1047	1
KNITTEL RAYMOND W	CW3	W-2153279	0364	1
KNOBLAUCH ERNEST L	MAJ	O-0243822	1060	3
KNOBLAUCH KARL P	LTC	O-1596289	0661	1
KNOBLETT JR THOMAS F	CW3	W-2149119	0966	1
KNOBLOCH ELLIS C	MAJ	O-0417468	0944	2
KNOBLOCH HENRY P	1LT	O-1325810	0646	2
KNOBLOCK ROBERT J	1LT	O-1305937	1145	2
KNODE GEORGE H	LTC	O-0252173	0953	3
KNODE LEWIS H	MAJ	O-0102125	1153	3
KNODE THOMAS E	CPT	O-0349328	1143	2
KNOEBEL LAWRENCE W	CPT	O-1573338	0245	2
KNOELLER CHARLES R	MAJ	O-0504139	0258	1
KNOLL ALBERT H	LTC	O-0322929	1162	3
KNOLL KENNETH R	1LT	O-0554719	0646	2
KNOLLE IRENE M	MAJ	L-1010047	0764	1
KNOOP FREDERICK	CW3	W-2005373	0363	1
KNOPE FRANCIS N	MAJ	O-0221270	0863	3
KNOPF SAMUEL A	CPT	O-0524943	0745	2
KNOPP FRANCIS X	CPT	O-1015462	0847	2
KNOPP JAMES A	MAJ	O-1106261	1157	1
KNOPP JAMES H	CW3	W-2141612	0962	1
KNORR JAMES S	MAJ	O-0969878	1060	1
KNORR JR ERNEST A	LTC	O-0380205	0265	3
KNORZER NORVAL P	CPT	O-0510822	1055	1
KNOTT ARTHUR W	CPT	O-0218744	0-50	3
KNOTT ERNEST J	COL	O-0197098	1160	1
KNOTT JAMES F	MAJ	O-0180814	0657	3
KNOTT JR ARTHUR W	LTC	O-1166103	0161	1
KNOTT NORMAN I	1LT	O-0536373	0645	2
KNOTTS HALLECK S	CPT	O-4073684	0459	2
KNOTTS JR FRED	CPT	O-0405607	0945	2
KNOUF JAMES H	MAJ	O-0329799	0146	2
KNOUSE BILLY J	MAJ	O-2262125	0264	2
KNOUSE BOYD E	CPT	O-1062896	0255	1

NAME	GRADE	SVC NO	DATE RET MO YR	RET CODE
KNOWE BENJAMIN A	MAJ	O-0393277	0567	3
KNOWELS ROBERT J	1LT	O-1319753	0546	2
KNOWLDEN RONALD L	CPT	O-2012808	0156	1
KNOWLES CARL R	LTC	O-1797146	0267	1
KNOWLES CLARENCE H	MAJ	O-0148593	0349	3
KNOWLES CONRAD A	CPT	O-1588686	1266	3
KNOWLES DAVE G	2LT	O-0549597	1145	2
KNOWLES JAMES S	LTC	O-0131813	0549	3
KNOWLES JAMES W	1LT	O-1292901	0845	2
KNOWLES JOHN W	LTC	O-1577436	0461	1
KNOWLES JR ALFRED R	MAJ	O-1913368	0365	1
KNOWLES JR GEORGE E	MAJ	O-1935262	0866	1
KNOWLES LEWIS W	CPT	O-2300147	0160	3
KNOWLES ROBERT E	MAJ	O-1549753	1058	1
KNOWLES ROBERT G	CPT	O-1636158	1160	1
KNOWLES ROBERT P	MAJ	O-1557863	0764	1
KNOWLES ROBERT W	CW3	W-2203494	0666	1
KNOWLES WILLARD E	LTC	O-0388166	0146	2
KNOWLTON CHARLES F	COL	O-0294235	0159	1
KNOWLTON CHARLES P	CW2	W-2206282	0962	2
KNOWLTON DONALD F	CPT	O-1165026	0446	2
KNOWLTON HORACE A	MAJ	O-0465584	1045	2
KNOWLTON KENNETH F	COL	O-0101850	0557	3
KNOWLTON LEROY E	CPT	O-1596390	0963	1
KNOWLTON REX R	1LT	O-1590299	0752	1
KNOWLTON RICHARD P	LTC	O-1583221	0261	1
KNOX CARMEN R	MAJ	L-0303839	0764	3
KNOX CAROLINE C	1LT	N-0788473	0446	2
KNOX CHARLES V	MAJ	O-1032631	0663	1
KNOX CHESTER N	CW3	W-2147301	1263	1
KNOX EDDIE C	CPT	O-0490165	1048	1
KNOX ERMA J	MAJ	N-0777509	0365	1
KNOX GEORGE W	MAJ	O-0288732	0446	2
KNOX GLEN H	1LT	O-0958816	1051	2
KNOX HARRY	COL	O-0256118	1065	3
KNOX HENRY A	MAJ	O-0278208	0954	3
KNOX HENRY M	CPT	O-0423003	1060	1
KNOX JAMES W	1LT	O-1291836	1145	2
KNOX JOHN H	LTC	O-1293973	0463	1
KNOX JONATHAN F	MAJ	O-0982281	0163	1
KNOX JR FREDERICK	MAJ	O-0443360	0147	1
KNOX LAWRENCE A	1LT	O-0464659	0646	2
KNOX LEONARD L	1LT	O-2036062	0745	2
KNOX LLOYD A	LTC	O-0266634	0261	3
KNOX MARY C	1LT	N-0901900	0659	2
KNOX ROBERT W	CPT	O-0149595	1155	3
KNOX WALTER H	LTC	O-0351750	0553	2
KNOX WARREN P	CPT	O-0483729	0647	2
KNOX WILLIAM M	LTC	O-0463575	1148	1
KNOY NORRIS J	CPT	O-1746729	1152	1
KNOY VERLIE G	MAJ	O-2037993	0261	1
KNUCKLES C W	MAJ	O-1551658	0547	2
KNUDSEN FRED J	CPT	O-0315771	0845	2
KNUDSEN FREDRIK L	LTC	O-1286302	1262	1
KNUDSEN JENS M	CW3	W-2150606	0656	1
KNUDSEN JR MORGAN G	LTC	O-1556303	0767	1
KNUDSEN TORE H	CPT	O-2027345	1046	2
KNUDSON FOULKE D E	COL	O-0138335	1152	3
KNUDSON KENNETH E	COL	O-1576250	0261	1
KNUPP GILBERT B	CPT	O-1295730	0948	2
KNUTH EARL L	2LT	O-1016222	0253	2
KNUTSEN CLARA S	2LT	N-0700834	0738	1
KNUTSEN LLOYD R	COL	O-0285486	0967	3
KOART VIRGIL P	CPT	O-1340252	1057	1
KOBAR MAX J	CPT	O-1011805	0946	2
KOBECK BARNEY F	CPT	O-0406523	1060	2
KOBERNAT ARLEIGH L	LTC	O-0381560	0854	1
KOBLARCHICK PAUL W	CPT	O-1173334	0467	1
KOBLIS PETER S	CW2	W-2210506	1060	1
KOBS CHARLES J	LTC	O-0383486	0461	1
KOBS ELMER C	CPT	O-0285174	1066	3
KOBS RUDOLPH A	MAJ	O-0371559	0947	2
KOBUS ALEXANDIUM	LTC	O-0496714	1055	1
KOBUS WALTER S	CW4	W-2103103	0957	1
KOCER JAMES C	1LT	O-1054655	1045	2

NAME	GRADE	SVC NO	DATE RET MO YR	RET CODE
KOCH BERNARD	LTC	O-0334930	0665	3
KOCH CASPER F	MAJ	O-2019185	0264	1
KOCH CHESTER J	CW3	W-2142166	0767	1
KOCH CLINT M	MAJ	O-1299758	0959	1
KOCH EDWARD M	LTC	O-0268617	0462	1
KOCH EDWIN G	LTC	O-0247976	1065	3
KOCH EDWIN M	CPT	O-1014659	1047	1
KOCH ELLWOOD L	LTC	O-0377292	1154	1
KOCH ERNEST P	LTC	O-1551659	1265	3
KOCH GLENN F	1LT	O-1049933	0962	1
KOCH HAROLD C	LTC	O-0475511	0367	3
KOCH JAMES E	1LT	O-1170036	0146	2
KOCH LLOYD W	LTC	O-0320754	0161	1
KOCH LUTHER E	LTC	O-0272937	0663	3
KOCH STANLEY G	1LT	O-1285439	0745	2
KOCH THEODORE A	MAJ	O-0272381	0867	3
KOCH WALTER A	MAJ	O-1798679	0258	2
KOCH WALTER D	COL	O-0107918	0850	1
KOCH WILLIAM H	MAJ	O-0411675	1151	1
KOCH WILLIAM R	MAJ	O-2030448	0367	2
KOCHAN PETER S	CPT	O-0186472	1054	3
KOCHANSKI CHESTER	CPT	O-1556163	0964	2
KOCHANSKI JOSEPH	LTC	O-0311435	0366	3
KOCHER BERNARD R	MAJ	O-2014357	0764	1
KOCHERT JAMES F	MAJ	O-2203026	0363	1
KOCHNOWER WILLIAM	1LT	O-0523838	1045	2
KOCHY ERNEST A	MAJ	O-1874872	1065	1
KOCHY STEPHEN R	MAJ	O-1292004	0960	1
KOCIC DANIEL	MAJ	O-1924747	1264	1
KOCIEMBA VICTORIA E	MAJ	N-0786038	0565	1
KOCIURBASKA WANKA	1LT	N-0759416	0646	1
KOCZAK RICHARD	MAJ	O-1059836	0862	1
KOCZOK WILLIAM J	MAJ	O-1633338	0762	1
KODIS CHARLES	CW2	W-2146847	0161	1
KOEBBE NORVIL G	MAJ	O-1300576	0463	1
KOEBENSKY MICHAEL W	CPT	O-1308065	0654	2
KOEBER ERWIN C	LTC	O-0400703	1263	2
KOECHLIN ROBERT J	1LT	O-1288757	104N	2
KOEHLER ARNO P	LTC	O-1004352	0867	3
KOEHLER MILFORD A	LTC	O-0241716	0258	1
KOEHLER MILTON E	LTC	O-0241756	0260	3
KOEHLER WILLIAM M	LTC	O-1797147	0262	1
KOEHN GEORGE L	MAJ	O-0146365	0653	3
KOEHNE KENNETH K	CW2	W-2122177	0367	3
KOEHS SR ROBERT P	MAJ	O-1849965	0263	1
KOELLER REUBEN J	MAJ	O-1648341	0258	1
KOELLNER CARL G	COL	O-0319648	0160	1
KOELMEL WILLIAM A	MAJ	O-1798015	1060	1
KOEN JOSEPH T	MAJ	O-1043388	0860	1
KOENEMAN NATHANIEL	COL	O-0029106	0564	3
KOENEMAN THOMAS	LTC	O-1647557	0361	1
KOENIG AUGUST	LTC	O-0451326	0960	1
KOENIG FRANK J	LTC	O-0320229	0545	2
KOENIG FRED	LTC	O-0154370	1153	1
KOENIG JOSEPH A	CW3	W-2146597	0659	1
KOENIG JR FREDERICK	1LT	O-0549293	0346	2
KOENIG KARL J	1LT	O-0417407	0146	2
KOENIG RAYMOND R	MAJ	O-2262172	0163	1
KOENIG THOMAS J	MAJ	O-1640638	0859	1
KOENIG VICTOR L	1LT	O-0409478	0145	2
KOENIG WILBUR C	LTC	O-1000252	0957	2
KOENNE JAMES C	CW3	W-2205863	1167	1
KOEPKE ROBERT A	2LT	O-2006930	0357	1
KOEPP ARTHUR W	MAJ	O-0242865	0855	3
KOEPPE CLARENCE E	COL	O-0199942	0546	2
KOERBER HENRY A	CW2	W-2152678	0567	1
KOERNER CHARLES	MAJ	O-0480750	0455	1
KOERNER JULIAN A	CPT	O-0300446	1145	2
KOERNER PAUL C	LTC	O-0403532	0960	1
KOERNER ROBERT L	CPT	O-1292811	0546	2
KOERT CORNELIUS	CPT	O-0502746	1144	1
KOERTING VERNON R	CPT	O-0284165	0446	2
KOESTER HERMAN A	CPT	O-0887702	0858	1
KOESTER WILLIAM T	LTC	O-0300274	0262	1
KOETTNER FRANK X	CW4	W-2141117	0162	1

NAME	GRADE	SVC NO	DATE RET MO YR	RET CODE
KOFFLER BURTON A	LTC	0-0319882	1065	3
KOFFMAN CECIL W	MAJ	0-0146477	1053	3
KOFLER JOHN M	LTC	0-1822154	1162	1
KOFMAN JAMES W	CPT	0-0244891	0966	3
KOGEL MARCUS O	COL	0-0246239	1063	3
KOGER CARLINE F	MAJ	N-0760578	0167	1
KOGON SAMUEL E	1LT	0-0916337	0546	2
KOGUT FRANK	1LT	0-1012524	0146	2
KOHAN NATHAN H	CW3	W-2144038	0562	1
KOHANIK PAUL J	MAJ	0-1001166	0961	1
KOHL CLEMENT J	LTC	0-0385680	0661	1
KOHL GERALD C	MAJ	0-0250804	0463	3
KOHL JOHN M	CW2	W-2151895	0361	1
KOHL LEONARD L	LTC	0-1100184	0767	1
KOHL WILLIAM A	MAJ	0-1587378	1060	1
KOHLENBERG JR FRED	CPT	0-0444340	0246	2
KOHLER DANIEL E	CW2	W-2145079	0656	1
KOHLER FRANK L	2LT	0-1301327	0545	2
KOHLER GORDON E	CPT	0-1045797	0545	2
KOHLER JOHN J	MAJ	0-1106882	0564	1
KOHLER KENT F	MAJ	0-0235719	1164	3
KOHLER OTTO C	LTC	0-0285068	0263	3
KOHLER VINCENT O	MAJ	0-1645123	0361	1
KOHLHAGEN WERNER S	LTC	0-1049541	0361	1
KOHLOSS JR ROBERT A	COL	0-0396651	0844	2
KOHN ARNOLD	MAJ	0-1166758	0762	1
KOHN ARTHUR A	LTC	0-0495047	0867	3
KOHN FRANCIS M	MAJ	0-0235011	1165	3
KOHN JR ROY F	MAJ	0-0365706	0565	1
KOHUT MICHAEL J	1LT	0-0296167	0145	2
KOHUTEK WALTER W	MAJ	0-0987478	1265	1
KOHUTH ROBERT J	CW2	W-3152604	1067	2
KOIVISTO ALFRED K	MAJ	0-0450615	0446	2
KOJASSAR ARAM	COL	0-0464410	0650	1
KOKE OSCAR I	LTC	0-0111083	0358	3
KOKE RAYMOND O	MAJ	0-0352585	0246	2
KOKENZIE HENRY F	CPT	0-1002964	0646	1
KOKKO CARL W	CW2	W-2150612	0760	1
KOKOL MARY C	LTC	N-0760324	0563	2
KOLAR JOSEPH	MAJ	0-0177805	0347	1
KOLB ELMER R	LTC	0-0290445	0564	3
KOLB EUGENE J	LTC	0-0552569	0963	1
KOLB JAMES M	MAJ	0-0297861	1045	2
KOLB JOHN W	CPT	0-1324424	0458	2
KOLB JR FRED W	CW4	W-2103096	1057	1
KOLB ROBERT W	LTC	0-1287898	0461	1
KOLCUN EDWARD J	MAJ	0-2017077	0867	1
KOLDA CARL E	LTC	0-0303154	0664	3
KOLESAR JOE	LTC	0-0450183	1157	1
KOLHONEN BRUNO	LTC	0-1553860	1062	1
KOLKS RICHARD H	LTC	0-0444100	0367	3
KOLL CORNELIUS	LTC	0-1174030	1061	1
KOLLARS THOMAS M	MAJ	0-0959322	1066	1
KOLLIAS NICHOLAOS	CPT	0-0185399	1160	3
KOLM ALWIN S	LTC	0-0291756	0267	3
KOLMAN ALBERT J	LTC	0-0442960	0-53	1
KOLMAN LAWRENCE L	2LT	0-1823460	1144	2
KOLO JOHN F	LTC	0-0377149	1055	1
KOLODY JOHN F	1LT	0-0887496	0757	1
KOLODZIEJ PETER R	MAJ	0-0455195	0756	1
KOLOFER EDWARD A	LTC	0-0320190	1060	1
KOLOSKI JOSEPH L	LTC	0-1548893	0861	1
KOLPACK HERMAN W	LTC	0-0447840	0646	2
KOLSTAD HENRY C	1LT	0-0921696	1043	2
KOLTUN MICHAEL	LTC	0-1647559	0664	2
KOMANCSEK ALEXANDER	MAJ	0-0240242	0864	3
KOMAR JAMES R	1LT	0-1948011	0855	1
KOMAROSKI JOHN R	MAJ	0-0450977	0858	1
KOMMERS WILLIAM K	1LT	0-1583224	1143	2
KOMOROSKE ALEXANDER	LTC	0-1649303	1162	2
KOMOSA ADAM A	LTC	0-0378898	1057	1
KONAR ALBERT V	1LT	0-1293605	0945	2
KONAR GEORGE E	2LT	0-1299759	0844	2
KONOLER FRANK G	CPT	0-1283447	1154	1
KONECKI LEON W	COL	0-0374164	0161	1
KONEK EDWARD A	MAJ	0-1304913	0163	1
KONESKI CHESTER F	CPT	0-0510150	0446	2
KONIK EDWARD P	MAJ	0-0890185	0758	1
KONING JR IGNATIUS J	CW4	W-2136743	1066	1
KONKEL EDWARD G	1LT	0-1299906	1043	2
KONKRIGHT MILTON T	LTC	0-0220970	0958	3
KONO YEIJE	1LT	0-1019822	0950	1
KONOP MATT F C	COL	0-0261376	0366	3
KONOPASKE OTTO T	CW3	W-2004143	0865	1
KONOZA JOHN S	MAJ	0-1315696	0961	1
KONRAD ADOLF M	CPT	0-0201403	0762	3
KONRAD ELMER W	MAJ	0-2266260	0466	1
KONTRA GEORGE	LTC	0-1039064	0862	1
KONTZ JR ERNEST C	LTC	0-0253781	0167	3
KONZE ALICE S	MAJ	L-0910059	1163	1
KONZE WILLIAM K	LTC	0-1306217	1163	1
KOOISTRA JACK J	1LT	0-1634043	0246	2
KOOMJAN HELEN	1LT	N-0737376	0146	1
KOON WILLIAM B	CPT	0-0496794	0457	1
KOONCE VANCE T	LTC	0-0443667	0758	1
KOONS CRANDALL I	COL	0-0268527	0763	1
KOONS EVERETT A	LTC	0-0544743	1067	1
KOONS HERBERT N	MAJ	0-0481107	0547	2
KOONS VERNON C	MAJ	0-0166716	0749	3
KOONS WILLIAM B	LTC	0-1309575	1162	2
KOONTZ CLYDE F	LTC	0-0304302	0161	1
KOONTZ EMERY R	COL	0-0310369	0166	3
KOONTZ JR ELIAS A	CPT	0-1936571	1165	1
KOONTZ RUSSELL H	1LT	0-1823171	0245	2
KOONTZ WILLIAM F	LTC	0-1552724	0965	1
KOOP CHARLES F	MAJ	0-2263350	1265	1
KOOP JOHN L	LTC	0-1042338	1263	1
KOOP LOUIS O	MAJ	0-0138412	0648	3
KOOPERSTEIN SAMUEL I	LTC	0-0500798	0446	2
KOOPMAN ROBERT K	MAJ	0-0352769	0858	2
KOOPMANN FREDERICK	LTC	0-1313903	1162	2
KOOPS FRANK F	LTC	0-0244239	1044	2
KOOPS JR FREDERICK	LTC	0-0330021	0957	2
KOOS RICHARD B	LTC	0-0451638	0663	1
KOOSA FRED L	COL	0-0206959	0457	3
KOPANSKI STEPHEN	LTC	0-1293011	0164	1
KOPASZ JOHN C	1LT	0-1582409	0745	2
KOPCHAK JR JOHN	CPT	0-1017790	0347	1
KOPCHELL GILMORE R	MAJ	0-1541066	0647	2
KOPEC EMILY G	1LT	N-0731879	0646	1
KOPEC JOSEPH J	LTC	0-0497116	0756	1
KOPEIKIN ROBERT	2LT	0-1574913	0351	2
KOPELKE KEITH E	LTC	0-1822285	1060	1
KOPER EVA L J	CPT	N-0734376	0946	1
KOPESCHKA EDWARD C	MAJ	0-1930884	0967	1
KOPF FRANK A	COL	0-0202782	1045	2
KOPF JOHN H	LTC	0-1825626	1162	1
KOPICKI ANTHONY J	LTC	0-1640635	0862	1
KOPICKI CHESTER F	LTC	0-1824874	0462	1
KOPKE JOHN N	LTC	0-1012351	0363	1
KOPMAN PHILIP	1LT	0-1039830	0845	2
KOPNICKY ANDREW M	CW3	W-2145345	0162	1
KOPP ARTHUR R	MAJ	0-0982535	1065	1
KOPP FRED H	1LT	0-1045138	1145	2
KOPP WILLIAM L	COL	0-0242065	0554	2
KOPP WILLIAM R	LTC	0-0439392	0566	1
KOPPA KARL K	MAJ	0-1015664	0758	1
KOPPENHAVER FRED B	CPT	0-0503541	1045	2
KOPPENHOEFER ERVIN J	CW3	W-2141930	1058	1
KOPPERL JR BERTRAM B	1LT	0-1047195	0347	2
KOPPES LAWRENCE M	MAJ	0-1650617	0863	1
KOPPLER CARL E	1LT	0-2043023	0145	2
KOPS HERMAN	MAJ	0-1289924	0557	1
KOPSTEIN PHILIP E	MAJ	0-1798994	0967	3
KOR OLEG M	LTC	0-0466449	0862	1
KORACH SAMUEL	LTC	0-0493710	1165	1
KORANOCVITCH MIKE	1LT	0-0496167	0447	2
KORANEK JEROME	CW3	W-2205645	0464	1
KORB LELAND C	MAJ	0-0910512	0549	2
KORBAL FLOYD J	MAJ	0-0200392	0763	1
KORBHOLZ OSCAR	2LT	0-1300978	0744	2
KORDA ALEXANDER	CPT	0-1996512	1264	1
KORDECKI MELVIN A	LTC	0-0492124	0957	2
KORECKI STEVEN	MAJ	0-1051231	0157	1
KOREN MARY J	MAJ	L-0603229	1265	3
KORESODSKI FRANK	MAJ	0-0502859	0656	1
KORHAN HERMAN H	2LT	0-1288758	1044	2
KORIATH WILLIAM G	MAJ	0-1299265	1060	1
KORN DAVID	MAJ	0-0453500	1053	2
KORN MARTIN R	LTC	0-0144240	0648	3
KORN MATTHEW F	LTC	0-0239155	0865	3
KORN RICHARD R	2LT	0-1582849	0446	1
KORNEGAY SILAS	MAJ	0-2030197	1060	1
KORNFELD MURRAY I	1LT	0-1017429	0446	2
KORNHAUSER LESTER L	LTC	0-0220788	1051	2
KORNS WILLIAM L	2LT	0-0927147	1045	2
KOROL ALEXANDER	1LT	0-1303741	0546	2
KOROTSKY HENRY	MAJ	0-1897775	0661	1
KORP EDWARD M	MAJ	0-1337718	0463	1
KORPONIC ALEX J	MAJ	0-0337029	0853	1
KORRASIK SAMUEL	1LT	0-1634985	0446	2
KORRISON DAVID M	MAJ	0-1013027	0647	2
KORSCHGEN LEON M	LTC	0-0285599	0954	1
KORSE HARRY	CW2	W-2110277	0545	2
KORSGREN DAVID C	CPT	0-0199922	0153	3
KORSTANGE HERBERT J	CPT	0-2288263	0960	1
KORTEN HENRY J	MAJ	0-0923965	0845	2
KORTVESE STEPHEN J	LTC	0-0364457	0166	1
KORVER KENNETH J	LTC	0-1328709	0866	1
KORY JACK I	LTC	0-0581968	1162	1
KOSACK SUSAN E	1LT	N-0757204	1051	1
KOSAK ADAM A	CPT	0-2018121	0459	1
KOSAK JOSEPH C	MAJ	0-1285771	0962	1
KOSAKA FRED I	LTC	0-1544980	0165	1
KOSEBUTZKI VINCENT J	COL	0-1286144	0661	1
KOSEN JOSEPH	1LT	0-1289747	0246	2
KOSHIRE JOSEPH J	CW4	W-2120828	0166	1
KOSHOFFER JOSEPH T	LTC	0-1302988	1262	1
KOSICKI BERNARD A	COL	0-0211365	0660	3
KOSINSKI LEN V	2LT	0-1322189	1044	2
KOSKI WILLIAM A	LTC	0-0492648	1166	3
KOSKI WILLIAM N	LTC	0-1104257	0465	1
KOSMALSKI STEPHEN J	2LT	0-1311789	0244	2
KOSMATKA WITOLD C	2LT	0-1174921	0644	1
KOSON ANDRE D	MAJ	0-1950002	0264	1
KOSOREK VALERIE W	LTC	0-2055213	0565	1
KOSSA FRANK R	COL	0-0219748	1157	3
KOST HARRY	2LT	0-1546879	0644	2
KOST MICHAEL	CPT	0-1922658	0765	1
KOST WILLIAM L	LTC	0-0245515	1160	3
KOSTENBAUDER MARION	MAJ	N-0759394	0466	1
KOSTENICK STEVEN L	MAJ	0-1823888	0365	1
KOSTENSKI LESTER M	MAJ	0-1100627	0955	1
KOSTER CLIFFORD C	MAJ	0-0981878	0665	1
KOSTER DOROTHY B	2LT	L-0601416	1144	2
KOSTIN RUDOLPH A	LTC	0-0460661	1062	1
KOSTOCH FREDERICK	CPT	0-1540896	0862	1
KOSTOWICZ STEVEN	1LT	0-1303613	1145	2
KOSULAVAGE ADOLPH A	MAJ	0-1648422	0856	1
KOTARSKY JOSEPH M	LTC	0-1332973	0164	1
KOTCH DONALD J	MAJ	0-1579895	1159	1
KOTCH RICHARD E	LTC	0-1552921	0266	1
KOTELES JR ALEXANDER	1LT	0-1541055	0245	2
KOTH BEN	CW2	W-2146695	0761	1
KOTILAINEN REINO L	CW2	W-2143663	0657	2
KOTINEK JAMES J	MAJ	0-0982982	1062	1
KOTNIK VICTOR J	CW3	W-2106394	0461	1
KOTRE NICHOLAS D	1LT	0-1323006	1045	2
KOTTKE ELMER E	CPT	0-0174684	0944	1
KOTTLER JR CARL F	2LT	0-1536068	0745	2
KOTTMAN CLARENCE A	CPT	0-0471966	1046	1
KOTULAN ADOLPH	CPT	0-0277794	0847	1
KOUCKY GEORGE W	1LT	0-1948493	0448	2
KOUDELKA HAROLD A	MAJ	0-1639257	0156	1
KOUKES LEE N	MAJ	0-1597709	0866	1
KOUKOL JR AUGUST	COL	0-0320663	0562	1
KOUMJIAN PETER	MAJ	0-0456647	1061	2
KOUNTZE ELMER B	2LT	0-1284527	1043	2
KOVACH ALEXANDER	MAJ	0-0695354	0765	1
KOVACH JOHNNIE	MAJ	0-1651110	0662	1
KOVACH JOSEPH J	MAJ	0-0354543	0853	1
KOVACIC JOSEPH J	CW4	W-2151666	1265	1
KOVACS STEPHEN L	LTC	0-0268585	0762	3
KOVALCHIK JR GEORGE	CW3	W-2150526	0158	1
KOVE BERNARD S	COL	0-0296281	1065	3
KOWALCHICK MICHAEL	CPT	0-1000984	0546	2
KOWALESKI JOHN F	CPT	0-0212919	1044	2
KOWALKOWSKI STANLEY	MAJ	0-1030389	0258	1
KOWALSKI JEROME J	1LT	0-1314926	0845	2
KOWALSKI LEON A	CPT	0-4074612	1167	1
KOWALSKI STANLEY F	CW2	W-2148437	0954	1
KOWALYK WILLIAM	LTC	0-1107528	1064	1
KOWAR FRANK	CPT	0-1054291	0846	1
KOWELL JOSEPH A T	CPT	0-1297387	0746	2
KOYUTIS MARY E	MAJ	N-0752424	0364	2
KOZA ANDREW J	CPT	0-1035165	0557	1
KOZAL LAWRENCE J	CPT	0-0399086	0145	2
KOZBERG OSCAR	CPT	0-0337392	0245	1
KOZBIEL THEODORE E	LTC	0-1016646	0262	1
KOZEL ANTHONY R	LTC	0-1280794	0756	1
KOZIATEK THEODORE S	LTC	0-0187303	0854	1
KOZICH ALEXANDER	CW2	W-2146670	0963	1
KOZINN PHILIP J	CPT	0-0508890	0746	1
KOZIOL ELEANOR A	MAJ	N-0732254	0262	1
KOZLOW CASMER H	LTC	0-1648426	0563	1
KOZLOWSKI CHESTER P	WO1	W-2152052	0155	1
KOZLOWSKI ROBERT S	1LT	0-1300814	0945	2
KOZUB WALTER M	2LT	0-1641487	0344	2
KOZUSKO GEORGE J	MAJ	0-1587283	0464	1
KRABIEL WILLIAM F	LTC	0-0280880	0663	1
KRACALIK JOHN	CPT	0-2020035	0562	1
KRACKE LEE H	MAJ	0-0174913	0747	2
KRACKENBERGER EARL	MAJ	0-0497501	0748	1
KRAEMER GEORGE S	MAJ	0-0326080	1045	1
KRAEMER HORST C	CPT	0-0512493	0446	2
KRAEMER JR JOE	MAJ	0-0298142	0963	3
KRAEMER WENDELL J	MAJ	0-1175197	0866	1
KRAETTLI HAROLD J	MAJ	0-0366630	0248	2
KRAETZER KENNETH G	LTC	0-1170814	0261	1
KRAFFT ROBERT F	2LT	0-2032268	0946	1
KRAFT AL	CPT	0-1554415	1147	2
KRAFT ALLISON F	2LT	0-0544683	1045	2
KRAFT EMMITT E	CW3	W-2147324	0662	1
KRAFT HAROLD C	CPT	0-1165523	0157	2
KRAFT JOHN F	CW3	W-2142864	0161	1
KRAFT NED O	LTC	0-0237187	0166	3
KRAFT PAUL R	1LT	0-0325722	1043	2
KRAFTSCHIK ERNEST W	LTC	0-0333284	0360	1
KRAHN WILLIAM G	2LT	0-1317636	1144	2
KRAISEL MORRIS	LTC	0-0298678	0167	3
KRAJESKI WILLIAM S	LTC	0-0568977	1160	1
KRAJEWSKI STANLEY J	MAJ	0-1795924	1154	1
KRAKAUER MAX F	CPT	0-1542197	0367	1
KRAKAUSKAS WALTER A	LTC	0-1323938	0862	1
KRAKER JR JOHN	CW2	W-2148673	0964	1
KRAKOWER ARNOLD R	MAJ	0-1636168	0447	1
KRAL JOSEPH F	MAJ	0-1547359	0964	1
KRALL MICHAEL	MAJ	0-1823612	0762	1
KRALOVEC JOHN G	LTC	0-0173060	1060	3
KRAMER ALBERT A	MAJ	0-1293608	0661	1
KRAMER CHARLES T	LTC	0-0113112	0850	3
KRAMER CLARENCE A	2LT	0-2034546	0545	2
KRAMER CLAUDE J	LTC	0-0300364	0162	1
KRAMER DAVID F	MAJ	0-1540889	1266	1
KRAMER DONALD W	LTC	0-2036433	0361	1
KRAMER FRANK J	CPT	0-2262999	0461	1
KRAMER FRANK M	1LT	0-0277680	0943	2
KRAMER FREDERICK	CPT	0-0350042	1144	2
KRAMER GERTRUDE M	CPT	N-0784609	0747	1
KRAMER HERBERT J	1LT	0-1047196	0545	2

NAME	GRADE	SVC NO	DATE RET MO YR	RET CODE
KRAMER IRVIN H	CPT	0-1014110	0647	1
KRAMER JEROME D	CPT	0-0916139	0646	2
KRAMER JOHN	CPT	0-0508489	0646	1
KRAMER JOHN J	CW3	W-2141912	0959	1
KRAMER JOSEPH E	COL	0-0108291	0147	2
KRAMER JOSEPH E	MAJ	0-0808283	0767	1
KRAMER JR RICHARD A	MAJ	0-1644500	0662	1
KRAMER JR WILLIAM J	1LT	0-1012779	0246	2
KRAMER LEO J	LTC	0-2037069	0866	2
KRAMER MARCUS	CPT	0-0534326	0146	2
KRAMER PAUL R	1LT	0-1292905	0545	2
KRAMER RITA S	2LT	N-0721588	0944	1
KRAMER ROBERT O	LTC	0-0375122	0859	1
KRAMER ROBERT L	MAJ	0-0281280	0844	2
KRAMER SEYMORE	1LT	0-1592994	104N	2
KRAMER SR DEWIGHT F	MAJ	0-1924894	1066	1
KRAMER STEWART G	MAJ	0-2053836	1055	1
KRAMER WILBUR P	MAJ	0-0188708	0646	1
KRAMER WILLIAM R	1LT	0-1323146	1045	2
KRAMKOWSKI BENJAMIN	MAJ	0-1318187	0461	1
KRAMP MERLE W	CW2	W-2144610	0763	1
KRAMP RICHARD O	MAJ	0-0384632	0146	2
KRAN WILLIAM A	LTC	0-0290893	0954	1
KRANICHUCK JOHN M	MAJ	0-0492736	0547	2
KRANTZ HARRY	CPT	0-1689887	0245	2
KRANTZ MARVIN J	MAJ	0-0985938	1163	1
KRANTZ NORBERT J	2LT	0-1110054	1144	1
KRANTZ ROBERT L	CW2	RW-2210947	0664	1
KRANZ DWIGHT O	CW4	W-2005624	1265	1
KRANZ WALTER L	MAJ	0-1325820	1060	1
KRASHOC JOE T	LTC	0-1644502	1062	1
KRASNE LEO R	COL	0-0309808	0860	3
KRASNE PAUL W	1LT	0-0422211	0846	2
KRASNOFF HARRY M	COL	0-0489953	0863	3
KRASOWSKI REINHOLD C	CPT	0-0109446	0342	1
KRASSNER WILLIAM V	2LT	0-2048677	1044	2
KRASZEWSKI THAODELS	LTC	0-1050345	0864	1
KRATCH FRANCIS J	LTC	0-1113308	0664	1
KRATOCHVIL REGIS H	1LT	0-1319512	1045	2
KRATZ FRANCIS E	MAJ	0-1648980	0766	1
KRATZ GOLDEN P	COL	0-0203702	1052	1
KRATZ ORA A	2LT	0-1846018	0745	2
KRATZER DONALD A	CPT	0-1017859	1046	2
KRATZER NORWOOD W	CW3	W-2150848	0864	1
KRAU HAROLD N	LTC	0-0395809	0862	1
KRAUCHI CHARLES A	MAJ	0-0973503	0561	1
KRAUS ARTHUR I	LTC	0-0207562	0652	1
KRAUS CHARLES H	COL	0-0931705	0864	3
KRAUS FREDERICK	1LT	0-1705813	0645	2
KRAUS GEORGE H	CW2	W-2145458	0364	1
KRAUS JOHN L	CPT	0-0494479	0249	1
KRAUS JOSEPH A	1LT	0-1174922	1045	2
KRAUS LEO J	COL	0-0307551	1266	3
KRAUS RUSSELL E	2LT	0-2012480	0352	1
KRAUS WILLIAM	CW4	W-2136612	0666	1
KRAUS WILLIAM A	LTC	0-0199901	0544	2
KRAUS WILLIAM E	CPT	0-0367573	0145	2
KRAUSE ALBERT	LTC	0-1825010	0763	1
KRAUSE CHARLES F	MAJ	0-0153832	0648	3
KRAUSE CLARENCE R	CW3	W-2148324	0862	1
KRAUSE CLAUDE G	LTC	0-1292713	0263	1
KRAUSE DONALD A	MAJ	0-1845197	0361	1
KRAUSE EDWARD A	LTC	0-0243697	0845	2
KRAUSE EDWARD C	COL	0-0375296	0859	1
KRAUSE FRANCIS T	CPT	0-1542100	1144	2
KRAUSE GUSTAV J	LTC	0-0400034	0647	2
KRAUSE JAMES R	1LT	0-1644503	0646	2
KRAUSE MARTIN W	MAJ	0-0201581	0763	3
KRAUSE NELSON	LTC	0-1576257	1059	1
KRAUSE ROBERT R	MAJ	0-1014388	0161	1
KRAUSE VIRGIL E P	CW3	W-2205692	0766	1
KRAUSE WILLIAM J	MAJ	0-1824763	0361	1
KRAUSE WILLIAM O	CW2	W-3150682	0166	1
KRAUSHAR CARL	1LT	0-1588998	104N	2
KRAUSS ALBERT	2LT	0-0266491	1156	3
KRAUSS HERBERT M	CPT	0-1292714	0346	2
KRAUSS JOHN J	1LT	0-1047619	0445	2
KRAUSS WALTER F	CPT	0-2041377	0661	1
KRAUT ARTHUR M	LTC	0-0256685	0957	3
KRAVEC EMIL	MAJ	0-1637857	0859	1
KRAVITZ JAMES	LTC	0-0294122	0657	1
KRAVONTKA MICHAEL V	MAJ	0-1309659	0166	1
KRAWCHUK ARTHUR J	LTC	0-1647133	0863	1
KRAYENBUHL CRAIGIE	COL	0-0188798	0154	3
KRAYNICK MICHAEL	MAJ	0-1302017	1266	1
KREAMER JOHN H	1LT	0-0528195	0246	2
KREBER LEO M	M G	0-0171657	0658	3
KREBS CHARLES A	LTC	0-0398821	0161	1
KREBS EDWARD G	LTC	0-1030488	0657	1
KREBS FRED	1LT	0-2046566	0149	1
KREBS JR RAYMOND F	MAJ	0-0966958	1062	1
KREBS LEON A	CPT	0-0327515	0242	2
KREBS NITA	MAJ	N-0785656	0465	1
KREBS RUDOLPH J	COL	0-0302902	1162	3
KREBSBACH VERNON G	CPT	0-0984330	0461	1
KREGER CLARENCE J	MAJ	0-0887585	0161	1
KREH LEWIS V B	MAJ	0-0210663	0753	3
KREHER GERHARDT P	CPT	0-0328184	0746	2
KREIBICH ROBERT F	CW3	W-2142299	0860	1
KREIDER ABRAM H	CW3	W-2205511	0567	1
KREIDER GEORGE P	MAJ	0-0100517	0455	3
KREISA FRANCIS J	MAJ	0-0130631	0953	3
KREISER HENRY F	MAJ	0-1055360	0560	1
KREITNER HERMAN G	CPT	0-2034748	0145	2
KREITNER PAUL A	MAJ	0-1293795	1165	1
KREITZ WILLIAM P	LTC	0-1001384	1263	1
KREIZENBECK FRANK W	LTC	0-0172904	0352	3
KREIZENBECK JOHN W	MAJ	0-2050091	0961	1
KREJCI ERVIN C	CPT	0-1113310	1045	2
KRELL BESSIE S	CPT	N-0702418	1045	1
KREMBS DONALD W	LTC	0-1309941	1061	1
KREMENS VICTOR	1LT	0-1756590	0645	1
KREMER PAUL P	CW2	W-2146671	0463	1
KREML FRANKLIN M	B G	0-0909816	0267	3
KREMP FRED W	1LT	0-1287018	0447	2
KREMPECKI STANLEY W	1LT	0-1111720	114N	2
KREMPEL JANS A	LTC	0-0497536	0756	1
KRENCICKI THEODORE	CPT	0-2018373	0662	2
KRENITSKY THOMAS O	LTC	0-2040813	1065	1
KRENKEL HARRY N	COL	0-0125117	1055	3
KRENZ ROBERT W	LTC	0-0254429	1066	3
KREPAK MICHAEL	1LT	0-1644506	0945	1
KREPS ADAM	LTC	0-0414840	0766	1
KREPS JOSEPH L	CW4	W-2151979	0466	1
KRESKOSKY MIKE	1LT	0-1308227	0745	2
KRESS CYRIL G	COL	0-0255190	0564	3
KRESS JOHN J	1LT	0-1317313	0746	2
KRESS MARVIN	1LT	0-0512958	1145	1
KRESS WALTER J	COL	0-0141621	0653	3
KRESYMAN EDWARD J	CW2	W-2151905	0961	1
KRET FRANCIS J	CPT	0-0410046	0846	1
KRETSCHMER ALFRED A	MAJ	0-0335612	0963	3
KRETZ HAROLD	MAJ	0-0889892	0160	1
KRETZINGER WILLIAM	CW2	W-2103110	0650	1
KRETZMEIER CALVIN L	WO1	W-2146609	0457	1
KREUSLING EMIL W	MAJ	0-1048453	1162	1
KREUTER CHARLES L	CW4	W-2000903	0861	3
KREWITZ WILLIAM O	LTC	0-1108086	1165	3
KREWSCA CLAYTON B	LTC	0-1700598	0367	3
KREY NORBERT W	CW3	W-2146694	1263	1
KRICK CHARLES P	LTC	0-0307182	0355	3
KRICKL HOWARD F	1LT	0-1287368	0345	2
KRIDLER GEORGE G	2LT	0-1285772	1144	2
KRIECHBAUM JOSEPH R	COL	0-0200597	0855	3
KRIEG CAMERON E	1LT	0-1300342	1045	2
KRIEG JOHN L	LTC	0-0411090	0161	1
KRIEG JR FRED H	LTC	0-2047394	0466	1
KRIEG JR WILBERT A	MAJ	0-1553492	0966	1
KRIEGER BURTON E	CW3	W-2141342	1055	1
KRIEGER EDWIN H	1LT	0-1112270	1045	2
KRIEGER IRVING	CPT	0-1285441	0947	2
KRIEGER RICHARD H	CW2	W-2206720	1161	1
KRIENHAGEN LEE F	CW2	W-2148903	0860	1
KRIER HENRY L	LTC	0-0406847	1060	1
KRIESE CLINTON J	LTC	0-0346780	0560	1
KRIGBAUM WILLIAM L	COL	0-0187368	1046	2
KRIGER EONICE R	MAJ	0-2026160	0164	1
KRIGLINE EDMUND G	CPT	0-0235788	1148	1
KRIGSTEN WILLIAM M	COL	0-0270285	0446	2
KRIKAC STANLEY J	COL	0-0302377	0961	3
KRIM GEORGE A	COL	0-0446273	0854	1
KRIMBILL JACK B	LTC	0-0421206	0461	1
KRIMSLEY MALCOLM	1LT	0-1689588	0944	1
KRING HUGH E	COL	0-0275674	1264	3
KRINGS LOUIS W	MAJ	0-0254199	1064	3
KRISE LEO	CW4	W-2146254	0857	1
KRISH EDWARD P	LTC	0-0294736	1154	1
KRISHNA IKBAI	CPT	0-0483414	0245	2
KRISHNER THEODORE	MAJ	0-0303869	0951	2
KRISKE HERBERT A	MAJ	0-1647562	0657	1
KRIST CHESTER J	LTC	0-2292561	0766	1
KRIST LOUIS M	MAJ	0-1309073	1161	2
KRISTAL JACKSON J	MAJ	0-0371940	0146	2
KRISTIANSEN HARRY E	1LT	0-1317922	104N	2
KRISTIANSEN STANLEY	MAJ	0-0719963	1163	1
KRITKAUSKY ANTHONY R	1LT	0-0373095	0144	2
KRITZMAN CHARLES W	MAJ	0-2023633	0258	1
KRIVI ANDREW H	CPT	0-1306522	0364	1
KRIVONOS ABRAHAM F	MAJ	0-0536374	0945	1
KRIZ JACK J	1LT	0-0409187	1144	2
KRIZ JOSEPH R	COL	0-0323535	0963	3
KRIZ ROBERT F	COL	0-1553684	0665	1
KRIZAN EMIL J	WO1	W-2115700	0647	1
KROB DEAN M	MAJ	0-0968683	0863	1
KROCHMAL SR EMIL	CW3	W-2144170	0956	1
KROCHMALNY MICHAEL	MAJ	0-1823891	0261	1
KROCK RUPERT T	LTC	0-1281516	0765	3
KRODEL WILLIAM J	2LT	0-1035041	0343	2
KROEGER ARTHUR F	MAJ	0-0255246	0858	3
KROEGER CHARLES F	CW4	W-2107166	1057	1
KROEGER FRANK B	CPT	0-0320948	0545	2
KROEGER HOWARD E	MAJ	0-2103071	0764	1
KROEHL GEORGE F	LTC	0-0392387	0164	1
KROELL JOHN T	MAJ	0-0258380	0745	2
KROENCKE EDWARD J	COL	0-0220175	0560	3
KROENCKE FRED J	MAJ	0-0271716	0963	3
KROEPSCH KARL A	COL	0-0243588	1154	2
KROFCHICK JOHNNIE	MAJ	0-2000585	0459	1
KROFCHIK MICHAEL	MAJ	0-1637739	0756	1
KROFCHIK PAUL	LTC	0-0451327	0158	1
KROFT ANDREW P	CPT	0-1339281	1147	1
KROFT DAVID F	LTC	0-1056436	0967	1
KROGEL ROBERT W	LTC	0-1703897	0560	1
KROGH ELMER L	1LT	0-2210819	0854	2
KROGH RICHARD H	CPT	0-0221129	0863	3
KROHE THEODORE D	LTC	0-1533608	0765	1
KROHN NORRIS F	LTC	0-0327314	0566	3
KROKENBERGER JOHN	MAJ	0-0362023	1060	1
KROKUS THEODORE J	COL	0-0179937	0556	3
KROLAK GEORGE	MAJ	0-1115943	0163	1
KROLL MARGARET W	CPT	N-0728655	0556	2
KROMM FRED	1LT	0-0155239	0952	1
KROMREY ROBERT P	LTC	0-0216061	0364	3
KRON ARTHUR	MAJ	0-2025240	0462	1
KRONCKE ADELINE H	MAJ	N-0731978	0662	2
KRONE EARL M	MAJ	0-1115318	0257	1
KRONE MILTON F	CW3	W-2146074	1062	1
KRONENBERGER GEORGE	LTC	0-1312569	0663	1
KRONHEIM ALBERT S	MAJ	0-1288759	1145	2
KRONHEIM PAUL O	LTC	0-1636172	0857	1
KRONICK LLOYD	2LT	0-2036664	0645	2
KRONK ADAM B	CPT	0-1309074	0146	2
KRONTZ WENDELL K	1LT	0-4007013	0259	2
KROON PHILIP C	CPT	0-1170816	0465	1
KROPOSKY CHARLES P	LTC	0-0373205	0760	1
KROSCHEL JR FRED M	COL	0-0452418	0766	2
KROTTS PAUL G	LTC	0-0334555	0860	1
KROTZ DANIEL F	WO1	W-2119454	0545	2
KROULIK ALFRED R	LTC	0-0260868	0266	3
KROUNGOLD MILTON L	CPT	0-0436082	0146	2
KROUSEY WYMOND C	1LT	0-1541944	0457	1
KROVITSKY ELY Y	1LT	0-0451133	1045	2
KROWCHUN JOHN T	1LT	0-2000066	0248	2
KRSUL JOHN W	CW2	W-2145459	0159	1
KRUCKENBERG CARL W G	CW2	W-2150314	0860	1
KRUCKER HERBERT F	COL	0-0254436	0646	2
KRUCZEK BERNARD C	CW2	W-2205512	0160	1
KRUCZEK JOSEPH F	MAJ	0-1584481	1160	1
KRUCZEK WALLACE B	LTC	0-0387181	0657	1
KRUEGER ALBERT T	LTC	0-0232614	0364	3
KRUEGER CLARENCE J	COL	0-0242192	0364	3
KRUEGER ELMER J	CPT	0-0159413	0951	3
KRUEGER EUGENE F	LTC	0-1294148	0361	1
KRUEGER FRED	CPT	0-0488077	0857	1
KRUEGER FREDERICK	LTC	0-0182033	0659	3
KRUEGER GERARD	MAJ	0-0274456	0664	3
KRUEGER HERBERT A	2LT	0-1290617	0144	2
KRUEGER JESS	LTC	0-0240503	0648	3
KRUEGER LESLIE F	MAJ	0-2262257	0565	1
KRUEGER MARION H	MAJ	0-1120550	0965	1
KRUEGER NORBERT M	LTC	0-1284719	0665	1
KRUEGER PAUL M	CW2	W-3430151	0364	2
KRUEGER RALPH H	CW3	RW-2143173	1061	1
KRUEGER ROBERT F	CPT	0-1048055	1163	1
KRUEGER WILLIAM L	1LT	0-1297053	0745	1
KRUEGER WILLIS E	LTC	0-0252247	0263	3
KRUG JAMES M	LTC	0-0420992	0667	3
KRUG MARIE A	2LT	N-0795960	0845	1
KRUG RICHARD O	LTC	0-1305438	0767	1
KRUG ROBERT C	1LT	0-0556413	0152	1
KRUG ROBERT H	MAJ	0-1925344	1165	1
KRUGER ELMER L	LTC	0-0351068	1061	1
KRUGER JOHN H	MAJ	0-1589324	0547	2
KRUGER LESTER O	1LT	0-1549526	0146	2
KRUGER LOUIS E	LTC	0-0155872	1145	2
KRUGH ROBERT C	CPT	0-2288464	1264	1
KRUI FRANK	1LT	0-1108790	0247	2
KRUK JOHN S	LTC	0-1173339	1162	1
KRUKAR JOHN	MAJ	0-1548090	0455	1
KRULL GEORGE W	CW3	W-2143748	0263	1
KRULL HAROLD E	LTC	0-0346200	1059	1
KRULL SAMUEL	MAJ	0-0138606	0646	2
KRUMBHAAR CHARLES C	LTC	0-0311737	1262	1
KRUMDIECK NEWTON	MAJ	0-0427963	0146	2
KRUMENACKER GEORGE A	CPT	0-1308969	0647	2
KRUMHAR THOMAS B	1LT	0-0478242	1047	2
KRUML JOSEPH G	COL	0-0267803	0964	3
KRUMLAUF ERNEST J	2LT	0-1298720	0444	2
KRUMM CARL F	COL	0-0301842	0860	3
KRUMM ROBERT A	WO1	W-2120011	0746	2
KRUMM ROGER V	CPT	0-1035863	0446	2
KRUMMEY LLOYD E	MAJ	0-0453385	0357	1
KRUMPOCH QUIDO T	LTC	0-1182624	0766	1
KRUMSICK CALVIN P	CW2	W-2151619	0662	2
KRUPINSKI FRANCIS T	LTC	0-0353323	1061	1
KRUSE JACK H	LTC	0-1184685	1064	1
KRUSE JESSE E	CPT	0-1031735	0547	2
KRUSE JIM T	CPT	0-1693845	0557	1
KRUSE JR LOUIS F	LTC	0-0334404	0960	1
KRUSE LEE G	CPT	0-2016229	0656	1
KRUSEMARK LEO E	MAJ	0-0949471	0666	1
KRUSZYNSKY CHESTER	CW3	W-2142167	1156	1
KRUTAK FRANK J	CPT	0-1312570	0947	1
KRUTHERS JOHN V	CPT	0-1053678	1065	1
KRUTSCH DEXTER R	MAJ	0-1100629	0654	1
KRYLOFF EUGENE B	LTC	0-0298273	0560	2
KRYSTOK MATTHEW E	LTC	0-1583238	0261	1
KRYTER LAURENCE H	LTC	0-0407581	0765	1
KRYZAN FRANK X	1LT	0-1183340	0446	2
KRZYZANOWSKI W M	CPT	0-1691389	0445	2

NAME	GRADE	SVC NO	DATE RET MO YR	RET CODE
KUBA JOHN	W01	W-2131790	0650	1
KUBACH OSCAR C	COL	0-0267287	0956	3
KUBACKI PETER	LTC	0-0403620	0659	2
KUBE ROBERT B	LTC	0-0456435	0466	1
KUBELCK VERN F	2LT	0-0454519	0944	2
KUBELIUS ANTHONY J	LTC	0-1100186	0665	1
KUBIAK FRANK E	LTC	0-0496974	0657	1
KUBICEK ADOLPH R	CPT	0-0488691	1049	1
KUBICHEK FAYE M	1LT	N-0732619	0845	1
KUBISIAK NORBERT J	MAJ	0-1799526	0258	1
KUBISTAL LESTER M	CPT	0-1643054	0258	2
KUBISZEWSKI RAYMOND	LTC	0-1647564	0963	1
KUBIT THADDEUS A	MAJ	0-1558872	0464	1
KUBLICK WILLIAM G	1LT	0-1101533	0346	2
KUBOOSH EDWARD	CPT	0-1307033	0347	2
KUC WALTER J	CPT	0-0400415	0750	2
KUCERA WILLIE J	MAJ	0-0920269	1262	1
KUCHAR EMIL H	MAJ	0-1634994	0258	2
KUCHERA EARL A	LTC	0-1053679	0662	2
KUCHEVAR ANNE M	1LT	N-0730143	1146	1
KUCHINSKAS ERNEST V	MAJ	0-1598609	0760	1
KUCHINSKI WILLIAM H	CW3	W-2141344	0258	1
KUCHTA FRANK I	LTC	0-1589671	0567	1
KUCKUK ROLLAND A	LTC	0-0261016	0267	3
KUCZMARSKI LEO N	CPT	0-0327019	0746	2
KUDER BERNARD	LTC	0-0194297	0263	3
KUDER WILLIAM R	LTC	0-0333442	1060	1
KUDO FRANCIS M	2LT	0-2055905	0945	2
KUDRLE CHARLES A	LTC	0-1010123	1060	1
KUDZIA ALBERT G	MAJ	0-1306287	0753	1
KUEBER PAUL C	LTC	0-1171636	1164	1
KUEBLER WILLIAM D	COL	0-0268894	0764	3
KUEHL GREGORY J	MAJ	0-1329956	0364	2
KUEHL RUSSELL C	COL	0-0318545	0465	3
KUEHN CHARLES F	MAJ	0-2263794	0466	1
KUEHN MORTIMER H	MAJ	0-1578730	0262	2
KUEHN RILEY	COL	0-0227871	0960	3
KUEKER WILLIAM G	LTC	0-1542776	1161	1
KUEKES JOHN H	2LT	0-0539443	0345	2
KUENY JR GUSTAVE	CW3	W-2200110	0766	3
KUES OSCAR G	CPT	0-2007716	0648	2
KUESTER JR JOHN	2LT	0-1996667	1145	2
KUETHE RALPH W	LTC	0-1319289	1163	1
KUGEL CHARLES R	LTC	0-1053680	0167	3
KUGLER OLGA R	MAJ	N-0756911	1065	1
KUGLIN HERMAN E	CPT	0-0242932	1055	3
KUHAR ALBERT G	MAJ	0-1822286	0161	1
KUHAR STEVEN P	MAJ	0-1295037	0561	1
KUHFELD FRANK W	MAJ	0-0273531	0167	3
KUHL JR WALTER A	2LT	0-1012659	0444	2
KUHLING WALTER W	MAJ	0-1581885	0265	1
KUHLMAN MILTON F	1LT	0-0908739	0643	2
KUHLMAN ROSS E	MAJ	0-0200108	1054	3
KUHLMANN ROBERT L	CW2	W-2152654	0862	1
KUHN ARDELLA B	1LT	N-0730336	0246	1
KUHN CARL B	LTC	0-0274222	0965	3
KUHN CHARLES F	LTC	0-1293610	0657	1
KUHN CHRISTOPH	LTC	0-0537575	0466	3
KUHN CLIFFORD W	LTC	0-0311652	0866	3
KUHN DAVID R	CW3	W-2208889	1263	1
KUHN EDMUND O	COL	0-2053849	0967	3
KUHN ERNEST G	LTC	0-0221590	0559	3
KUHN GEORGE D	LTC	0-0366668	0763	1
KUHN HAROLD E	LTC	0-0246290	0557	3
KUHN HERMAN	MAJ	0-0499571	1057	1
KUHN HOWARD R	LTC	0-1120026	0867	1
KUHN IRVING	CPT	0-1169205	0346	2
KUHN JAMES R	CW3	W-2144458	1263	2
KUHN JOHN J	CW2	W-2153198	0758	1
KUHN JR FRANK J	MAJ	0-1109433	1161	1
KUHN JR RICHARD R	1LT	0-0531551	0346	2
KUHN KENNETH	COL	0-0325919	0265	3
KUHN LLOYD R	CW4	W-2109259	1165	3
KUHN NICHOLAS J	LTC	0-0392006	0161	1
KUHN RALPH R	1LT	0-0148004	0655	3

NAME	GRADE	SVC NO	DATE RET MO YR	RET CODE
KUHN WILLARD R	LTC	0-0166039	0650	1
KUHN WILLARD W	W01	W-2118537	0665	1
KUHN WILLIAM F	LTC	0-0296893	0159	1
KUHNE ROBERT E	LTC	0-0384128	0561	1
KUHNS CLINTON W	LTC	0-0325003	0761	2
KUHNS EDWIN J	MAJ	0-1298881	0664	3
KUHNS GLENN E	2LT	0-0335807	1045	2
KUHNS JAMES F	LTC	0-0623026	1046	2
KUHNS LLOYD L	LTC	0-0211536	0259	3
KUHNS LOGAN L	LTC	0-0212785	1063	3
KUHNS RUSSELL K	COL	0-0359599	0760	1
KUHNS WALTER A	MAJ	0-0483371	0355	2
KUHR LESTER F	LTC	0-1313257	1267	1
KUITE GEORGE B	MAJ	0-0239868	1062	3
KUJALA EARL W	CPT	0-1543839	0552	1
KUKA JOSEPH F	CW2	W-2211216	0764	1
KUKER EUGENE W	CW3	W-2141852	0959	1
KUKIELKA CASIMIR A	MAJ	0-1548901	1160	1
KUKLA EDWIN A	LTC	0-1640647	0563	1
KUKLA RALPH B	LTC	0-1335938	0367	1
KUKUCKA ANDREW J	LTC	0-1996440	0464	1
KULA HELEN S	2LT	N-0730957	1044	2
KULAS SOPHIA	1LT	N-0758704	0847	1
KULBES PHILIP A	MAJ	0-1109434	1262	1
KULESHA KASMIER J	1LT	0-0488059	0344	2
KULHAN EDWARD F	MAJ	0-0426131	0546	2
KULICK CHARLES G	CW3	W-2153170	1264	1
KULICK LEE R	CPT	0-0404201	0146	2
KULIK JOSEPH A	1LT	0-1312388	1045	2
KULINA PETER I	MAJ	0-1116092	0163	1
KULKOSKY FRANK	MAJ	0-1318050	0565	1
KULL BERTHA N	1LT	N-0742416	0146	1
KULL FRANCIS C	MAJ	0-1060161	0557	1
KULL FREDERICK	CPT	0-1308970	0246	2
KULL JR CHARLES W	LTC	0-0317813	1065	3
KULLBACK SOLOMON	COL	0-0300670	0567	3
KULLMAN JOHN T	1LT	0-1637869	1144	2
KULP SR DURWARD S	CW4	W-2152890	0165	1
KULZER FRANK W	W01	W-2106220	0644	2
KULZER NORBERT J	CPT	0-0307594	0246	2
KUMER MICHAEL R	2LT	0-1002801	0245	2
KUMM KARL G	LTC	0-0443096	0662	3
KUMPF MARGARET L	MAJ	N-0722514	0867	1
KUNCEK JCECK	1LT	0-0497752	0547	1
KUNCL JR JOSEPH	LTC	0-0255109	0146	2
KUNDERT REUMOND P	LTC	0-1300659	0962	1
KUNDRA PAUL R	1LT	0-0455317	0645	2
KUNDRAT ANN M	2LT	N-0741367	1144	1
KUNDRATH JOSEPH J	CW2	W-2007415	0361	3
KUNELLIS CHRIS E	CW2	W-2144491	0758	1
KUNEMAN LEO F	1LT	0-1080876	0654	1
KUNIHIRO SHIZUO	MAJ	0-0967756	0763	1
KUNKEL CLEMENTS E	1LT	0-1013373	1045	2
KUNKEL JR PAUL A	LTC	0-0400174	0446	2
KUNKEL RUDOLPH E	COL	0-0275635	0359	3
KUNKELMAN RAYMOND E	LTC	0-0222789	0355	3
KUNKLE GERALD F	LTC	0-0391043	0149	2
KUNKLE MARTIN L	CW4	W-2118360	0762	1
KUNKLE PAUL A	LTC	0-0284585	0562	1
KUNKLE WALTER F	2LT	0-2023857	0146	1
KUNS GEORGE G	COL	0-0271725	0264	1
KUNSEMILLER C F	CPT	0-0323199	0346	2
KUNSMAN GLENN H	1LT	0-2035952	0547	2
KUNTER THOMAS N	2LT	0-2089252	1050	2
KUNTZ JOSEPH T	CW3	W-2148741	0765	1
KUNTZ LOUIS F	MAJ	0-0133840	0648	3
KUNTZ PHILIP L	1LT	0-4036865	0356	2
KUNZ CLAUDE A	LTC	0-0322447	1060	3
KUNZ GEORGE P	MAJ	0-2032959	0360	2
KUNZ JOSEPH E	LTC	0-0436589	0264	1
KUNZ JR OTTO	1LT	0-1013575	1045	2
KUNZ K STUART	MAJ	0-2035118	1160	1
KUNZ RITA D	2LT	N-0702148	1031	1
KUNZE ARTHUR T	MAJ	0-0119143	0154	3
KUNZE JOHN H	CPT	0-1318051	1052	1

NAME	GRADE	SVC NO	DATE RET MO YR	RET CODE
KUNZE JOSEPH J	LTC	0-0182196	0157	3
KUNZI STANTON P	MAJ	0-1019315	0663	1
KUNZMAN HENRY W	1LT	0-1175199	0945	2
KUPERSTEIN ABNER D	CPT	0-0385612	1145	2
KUPFERIAN LAURANCE H	1LT	0-1645735	0847	2
KUPP HARLEN R	CW2	W-2211744	1166	1
KUPPER CHARLES J	LTC	0-0903658	1045	1
KUPSINEL HERBERT A	MAJ	0-0972512	0564	1
KURDY THOMAS J	LTC	0-0291337	0366	3
KURIATNYK STEVE	CW3	W-2152705	0862	1
KURIS DAVID B	MAJ	0-0375798	0246	1
KURITZKY WILLIAM	1LT	0-1311526	1044	2
KURKOWSKI JOSEPH P	CPT	0-1559359	1053	2
KURLAND LEON K	COL	0-0284283	0760	1
KURTENBACH EUGENE A	MAJ	0-1639281	1159	1
KURTH AGATHA R	1LT	N-0760584	0545	1
KURTH ARNO W	1LT	0-1103740	0545	2
KURTH ERVIN E	MAJ	0-0242202	0663	1
KURTH RICHARD A	CW2	W-2000106	0546	2
KURTH WILLARD C	CPT	0-1061162	0550	1
KURTII JOHN W	1LT	0-0316850	0543	2
KURTZ EDWARD F	1LT	0-0108986	1137	1
KURTZ FLOYD E	MAJ	0-0287093	1165	3
KURTZ IRVING M	CPT	0-0317943	0745	2
KURTZ JAMES M	CW2	W-2150028	0164	1
KURTZ JOHN R	1LT	0-1639283	1044	2
KURTZ JOHN W	1LT	0-2024272	0148	1
KURTZ MILLARD E	COL	0-0113385	0450	3
KURTZ WALTER H	MAJ	0-0530166	0146	1
KURTZ WILLIAM J	LTC	0-1823893	0961	1
KURTZWEIL SYLVESTER	CW3	W-2148866	0163	1
KURZ DONALD A	MAJ	0-1797313	0962	1
KURZ PHILIP W	LTC	0-0134034	0254	3
KURZAWSKI WILLIAM C	CW3	W-2143376	0462	1
KURZDORFER PERCE F	MAJ	0-1534065	1060	1
KURZEJEWSKI LOUIS S	MAJ	0-1650183	1057	1
KUSCHEL VICTOR H	COL	0-0288805	0365	3
KUSEL ROBERT L	CPT	0-1289750	0458	2
KUSENER WALTER C	MAJ	0-0578248	0560	1
KUSHMER FRED W	COL	0-0243339	0156	3
KUSHNER JOSEPH P	MAJ	0-0502512	0159	2
KUSHNER SAMUEL J	LTC	0-1103271	0461	1
KUSKA GEORGE W	CPT	0-0491359	0347	2
KUSKI JR PETER	CW3	W-2151673	1061	1
KUSMIERZ JOSEPH T	MAJ	0-1289097	0653	1
KUSNER FRANK	MAJ	0-0569001	0663	1
KUSSEROW OLIVER A	LTC	0-0414989	0961	1
KUSTER ALBERT J	1LT	0-1823310	1045	2
KUSTER KENNETH F	COL	0-0216853	1160	1
KUSTERMAN OSCAR B	LTC	0-0916306	0367	3
KUSZEWSKI BERNARD J	LTC	0-1290089	1063	1
KUTAUSKAS ANTHONY F	LTC	0-1296046	0361	1
KUTCHER NATHANIEL	COL	0-0451543	0967	3
KUTCHER THOMAS G	CW3	W-2144477	0461	1
KUTILEK FRANK A	CPT	0-1324937	1060	1
KUTLOV MILTON	LTC	0-1533376	1166	2
KUTSCHMENDE JOSEPH	CPT	0-0405124	0752	1
KUTTESCH FRED S	LTC	0-1178218	0663	1
KUTTLER ABNER K	CPT	0-0123239	0755	3
KUTTNER JAMES H	COL	0-0171252	0554	3
KUTTNER WILLIAM J	LTC	0-0279435	1266	3
KUTTNER WILLIAM J	2LT	0-0462278	0345	2
KUTY EUGENE	MAJ	0-0357651	0646	2
KUTYS JOSEPH J	CPT	0-1304539	1153	2
KUTZ RICHARD H	2LT	0-1002467	0244	1
KUTZ VERNON W	CPT	0-0885728	1047	2
KUTZENCO JACK	CPT	0-1292196	0140	2
KUTZER JEAN R	MAJ	0-1170043	1053	2
KUTZER MELVIN D	MAJ	0-0360755	0944	2
KUWABARA HENRY H	LTC	0-0937926	0163	1
KUWAYE SATORU	CW2	W-2215090	0167	1
KUYKENDALL JOE B	1LT	0-2019753	0951	1
KUZA ANTHONY J	CW4	W-2006420	0866	3
KUZMA JOHN J	CW4	W-2110305	1054	1
KUZNIK FLORENCE F	1LT	N-0759730	0646	1

NAME	GRADE	SVC NO	DATE RET MO YR	RET CODE
KVAAS MARTIN G	LTC	0-1329362	0267	1
KVESETH PER U	CPT	0-1703572	0347	1
KVIDT REUBEN O	MAJ	0-0966052	0561	1
KVITEK FRANCIS A	COL	0-0292062	0558	3
KVITEK RICHARD G	2LT	0-0535548	0945	2
KWAN HENRY A	MAJ	0-1896514	0761	1
KWIATKOWSKI EDWARD A	MAJ	0-1923051	0367	1
KWIECINSKI FRANK F	CPT	0-2032128	0556	1
KWINN FRANK C	CPT	0-0372835	0246	2
KWOCK JOHN F	LTC	0-1796681	0765	1
KYDLAND WALLACE A	LTC	0-1013231	0960	1
KYER CHARLES P	CW2	W-2148929	0959	1
KYLCE DONALD E C	LTC	0-1589315	1167	3
KYLE ANCEL F	CW2	W-2143605	0859	1
KYLE BRUDGE E	COL	0-0178766	1061	3
KYLE ERIE E	1LT	0-0491223	1046	1
KYLE FRANK K	1LT	0-0405094	1044	2
KYLE GEORGE R	MAJ	0-0154923	0447	2
KYLE JAY A	LTC	0-0917732	1266	3
KYLE LESTER F	LTC	0-0184835	0654	1
KYLE RICHARD E	COL	0-0233015	0765	3
KYLER MENTELL	MAJ	0-1300816	0961	1
KYLES CLAYTON R	CPT	0-0356327	0145	2
KYLES ROGER R	CW2	RW-2144828	0361	1
KYNES CHARLES A	CW3	W-2150633	1163	1
KYNETT LAURENCE E	LTC	0-0321700	0766	3
L HEUREUX HENRY F	LTC	0-0168110	1048	2
LA BARBERA VINCENT A	CW3	W-2149706	1064	1
LA BARRE RENE L	LTC	0-0276047	1266	3
LA BELLA JOHN J	MAJ	0-2019894	0962	1
LA BLANC DONALD E	1LT	0-2204192	1253	2
LA BOLLE RICHARD L	COL	0-0267089	0355	1
LA BONNE LEE	LTC	0-1058871	0367	1
LA BONTE SR JEVITE	CW4	W-2000124	0559	1
LA BOZETTA WILLIAM C	LTC	0-1323332	0563	1
LA BREE FRED W	LTC	0-0265738	0959	1
LA BRIE JR JOSEPH D	LTC	0-1549756	1065	3
LA BROAC RALPH G	LTC	0-0471419	0954	1
LA BUDA MARTHA E	MAJ	N-0759540	1067	1
LA BUTIS CONSTANTIN	LTC	0-0233192	0766	3
LA CAFF ROBERT F	LTC	0-2033281	0966	1
LA CAZE CECIL G	CPT	0-2262865	0461	1
LA CHANCE BERTRAND	1LT	0-1926888	0154	2
LA CHANCE PAUL A	CPT	0-0452419	0859	1
LA CONTE LEONARD	COL	0-0287695	0158	1
LA CORF IVAN A	MAJ	0-0491241	0246	2
LA COUR HARDIE J	LTC	0-0546687	0464	1
LA COUR HERBERT A	CPT	0-1920094	0162	1
LA COY ROBERT H	LTC	0-1105590	0163	1
LA CROIX DONALD R	LTC	0-1584489	0263	1
LA CROIX JAMES L	CPT	0-0511440	0746	2
LA DOUCEUR ALBERT J	CPT	0-0268815	0753	3
LA DU ROBERT W	1LT	0-0468515	0944	2
LA DUE CHARLES J	1LT	0-1177878	0147	1
LA DUE JACK W	MAJ	0-2097628	0367	1
LA FAVE KENNETH M	CW3	W-2150971	0163	1
LA FERNEY RUEL L	CW3	W-2152850	0959	1
LA FERRIERE REED J	MAJ	0-1895380	0461	1
LA FEVERS WARREN A	CPT	0-0329575	0746	2
LA FEVOR JAMES H	MAJ	0-0970511	0266	1
LA FLAMME VINCENT J	CPT	0-1646341	0163	1
LA FLEUR ALEXANDER	COL	0-0348118	0857	3
LA FOND ARTHUR F	MAJ	0-1822589	1264	1
LA FOND MARGARET R	2LT	N-0789837	1044	1
LA FOREST WILSON H	MAJ	0-2033630	0361	1
LA FRACE SUSAN W	COL	N-0743556	0962	1
LA FRANCE GILBERT	LTC	0-0500238	0157	2
LA FRANCIS CYRIL J	CW4	W-2000103	0255	2
LA FRENIERE IDA M	1LT	N-0757238	0547	1
LA GATTUTA JOSEPH W	LTC	0-1298411	0762	1
LA GRANGE RICHARD M	LTC	0-1894612	0566	1
LA GRONE WINFRED C	LTC	0-0370020	0865	3
LA HAIE JR ROBERT	LTC	0-0806701	0666	1
LA HAYE NORBERT E	1LT	0-1030996	0446	2
LA HAYE ROBERT G	LTC	0-1821881	0664	1

NAME	GRADE	SVC NO	DATE RET MO YR	RET CODE
LA JEUNESSE WILLIAM	LTC	0-1175776	0664	1
LA JOIE RUSSELL F	LTC	0-0332086	1064	1
LA LOGE DAVID	MAJ	0-1010982	0760	1
LA LONE RALPH E	CW3	W-2147382	0665	1
LA LUZ ENRIQUE	MAJ	0-0476225	1163	1
LA MANNA JOSEPH J	MAJ	0-0279940	0150	1
LA MAR ANDREW W	COL	0-0165154	1055	1
LA MARCA JOSEPH T	CW3	W-2105509	0961	1
LA MARCHE LOUIS J	1LT	0-1307426	0144	2
LA MARCHE PAUL J	MAJ	0-0147093	0649	3
LA MASTRA GERARD C	CW2	W-2214022	0866	1
LA MOE JR OMAR T	MAJ	0-1170817	0662	1
LA MONT KENNETH L	CW3	W-2147539	0566	1
LA MONTHE ARTHUR E	LTC	0-1177879	0461	1
LA MONTIA JOHN A	MAJ	0-2020565	1159	1
LA MOTHE RAYMOND I	LTC	0-1052854	0766	1
LA MOTTE FRANK W	COL	0-0211021	1063	3
LA MOTTE ROBERT S	LTC	0-0182559	0455	3
LA PISTO THOMAS R	MAJ	0-1178870	0862	1
LA PLANTE EDWARD J	CPT	0-1319514	1047	2
LA PLANTE JOHN B	CPT	0-0483756	1049	1
LA PLANTE RENE J	CW3	W-2113729	0657	1
LA POINT LEON	CW2	W-2002823	0566	3
LA POINT ROBERT E	LTC	0-1287226	0960	1
LA POINTE FRANK A	LTC	0-0452847	0958	1
LA POINTE HENRY J	CW2	RW-2209939	1064	1
LA POINTE PAUL A	LTC	0-1544566	0562	2
LA POINTE RAYMOND P	MAJ	0-1582731	1162	1
LA PORTE RAY B	LTC	0-0291910	0165	3
LA RAE EVA S	MAJ	N-0743156	0867	1
LA RAE LEWIS L	MAJ	0-1542075	0459	1
LA REAU HARVEY H	CW2	W-2152470	0361	1
LA REAU JOHN T	LTC	0-1574936	0758	1
LA ROCCA XAVIER W F	LTC	0-1594291	1164	1
LA ROCCO JACK A	1LT	0-1556013	0645	2
LA ROCCO JOSEPH L	1LT	0-1294324	0146	2
LA ROCQUE ERNEST A	CW3	W-2144656	1052	1
LA ROSA PETER A	CW3	W-2207990	0866	1
LA ROSA WILLARD F	COL	0-0179635	0964	3
LA RUE DENTON L	MAJ	0-0440054	0954	1
LA RUE HUGH B	MAJ	0-0119578	0648	3
LA RUE LEMUEL L	1LT	0-1175204	0845	1
LA RUE ROBERT G	LTC	0-0216396	0454	2
LA RUSSA PEARL F	2LT	N-0724065	0945	1
LA RUSSO ROCCO J	CW2	W-2111869	1047	2
LA SALLE ROBERT M	LTC	0-1684854	1045	2
LA SALLE WILBUR M	MAJ	0-0240295	1066	1
LA SCHELL MURRAY	COL	0-1945859	1163	1
LA SHELLE GEORGE W	1LT	0-0492407	0655	2
LA SHOMB LEON V	CW3	W-2207967	0266	1
LA SORSA FRANCIS I	MAJ	0-0303788	0346	2
LA TOUCHE ROBERT C	CW3	W-2152830	1062	1
LA TOURETTE W H	MAJ	0-1012905	0258	1
LA VAL VERNON R	MAJ	0-0365406	0866	3
LA VALLEE JOSEPH F	MAJ	0-1798744	0565	3
LA VALLEY LESLIE E	MAJ	0-0294121	0459	3
LA VELLE EDWARD H	CPT	0-1535790	0955	1
LA VERDE SANTO	MAJ	0-1047198	0561	1
LA VERE LARRY T	2LT	0-1998700	0559	1
LA VERTU BRUNO P	CPT	0-1341985	0862	1
LA VIGNE JR FRED	CW3	W-2141350	0361	1
LA VIOLETTE HOMER P	LTC	0-0327006	0163	3
LA VOICE BRUCE W	CW3	W-2205423	0964	1
LA VRENZ ROLAND H	2LT	0-1996562	1045	1
LAAS MOYLAN F	MAJ	0-0356127	1046	2
LABACZ HENRY A	MAJ	0-1994792	0658	1
LABADIE EMILE L	CPT	0-1784343	1146	1
LABARGE ALPHONSE	CW3	W-2146837	1164	1
LABART DORSEY M	MAJ	0-1332073	0263	2
LABBE FRANK F	CW2	W-2143290	0358	1
LABBE MARTIN	MAJ	0-0494710	0956	1
LABBE NORRIS M	COL	0-0197452	1149	1
LABELLE GEORGE A	2LT	0-1304915	1043	2
LABEN ROBERT C	CPT	0-0464660	0645	2
LABER ORVILLE J	MAJ	0-0484002	1166	1
LABONGE CARL A	LTC	0-0365023	1057	1
LABRAOER CHARLIE	MAJ	0-1896817	0561	1
LABRICLA CHARLES S	CPT	0-1690626	0245	2
LABRICLE JOHN	MAJ	0-2006492	0762	1
LACAGNINA PATSY M	MAJ	0-2011205	0467	1
LACAP TEOY N	CPT	0-1896499	0858	1
LACAPRIA ARTHUR	COL	0-0296764	0560	1
LACASSE ROBERT A	MAJ	0-0444075	1057	1
LACAVA FREDERICK	1LT	0-0512534	0645	2
LACE WILLIAM P	MAJ	0-0234152	0459	3
LACEDONIA JULIO R	LTC	0-0300495	1059	1
LACEFIELD EUGENIA M	1LT	N-0779002	0448	2
LACERTE OSWALD J	COL	0-0238781	0264	3
LACEY CLARENCE	COL	0-0446577	1054	1
LACEY DAVID T	1LT	0-1308348	0544	2
LACEY EARLYN W	MAJ	0-0421876	0662	1
LACEY EDWARD W	2LT	0-1031613	0944	2
LACEY JACK C	LTC	0-0724951	0961	1
LACEY JOHN F	COL	0-0216605	0962	3
LACEY JOHN H	CPT	0-0570845	0962	2
LACEY ROBERT D	1LT	0-0556755	0147	2
LACEY ROLLAND L	LTC	0-1030056	1054	1
LACEY ROSAMOND F	1LT	N-0721700	0945	1
LACHAT JULIETTE	2LT	N-0743428	1044	1
LACHENMAN ALFRED H	1LT	0-2018533	0459	1
LACHEY FRANCIS J	MAJ	0-1546461	0263	1
LACHICOTTE LOUIS H	MAJ	0-0151033	0858	3
LACHMAN MAX	LTC	0-0309723	0958	3
LACK ERNEST A	COL	0-0233907	1058	3
LACK NORMAN W	B G	0-0163445	1154	3
LACK ROBERT P	2LT	0-0922268	0644	1
LACKERMANN EARL E	2LT	0-1329131	1045	2
LACKEY CARVER M	LTC	0-0334837	0660	1
LACKEY LEE G	2LT	0-1913763	0140	1
LACKEY RAYMOND J	1LT	0-0349017	0142	2
LACKEY VADEN W	COL	0-0267322	0162	3
LACKEY WOODWARD H	1LT	0-0410391	1044	2
LACKNER CLARENCE	CPT	0-2262802	0460	2
LACKO JOHN R	WO1	W-2112578	1145	2
LACOCK WALTER R	COL	0-0213374	1057	3
LACOMBA MIGUEL A	LTC	0-1327246	0164	1
LACOUEMENT DELBERT S	CPT	0-0468966	0745	2
LACY AGNES	1LT	N-0735525	0446	1
LACY ALAN S	LTC	0-1173684	0961	1
LACY CLIVE W	COL	0-0204206	0253	3
LACY EUGENE L	MAJ	0-2262425	0861	1
LACY HAROLD G	COL	0-0236797	0953	3
LACY HENRY C	CPT	0-1284528	0246	2
LACY JACK B	1LT	0-1302018	0845	2
LACY JR CECIL C	CW3	W-2142665	0461	1
LACY LYNN C	CW2	W-2119248	0160	1
LACY VILAS F	LTC	0-0389068	0365	1
LACY WILLIAM C	CPT	0-1001612	0346	2
LACY WILLIAM D	CPT	0-0972062	1061	1
LADA CHARLES	CW2	W-2146375	1059	1
LADAS GEORGE	MAJ	0-2262300	0963	1
LADD ALMA D	LTC	N-0737564	1062	1
LADD ARCHIE	COL	0-0164481	0952	3
LADD ARNOLD R	2LT	0-1164765	1043	2
LADD EDGAR A	LTC	0-0256646	0167	3
LADD JR JOHN C	MAJ	0-2262915	0165	1
LADD LEON F	LTC	0-0405459	0463	1
LADD WILLIAM F	B G	0-0111693	0256	3
LADD WILLIAM R	CPT	0-0488206	1162	1
LADIEC ANDREW	CW2	W-2109468	0347	2
LADIGES RICHARD P	1LT	0-1319290	0546	2
LADNER HILLMON P	CW2	W-2144996	0957	1
LADNEY WILLIAM W	LTC	0-0451134	0157	1
LADSON WILLIAM F	COL	0-0364314	0965	1
LADUE DENNIS	MAJ	0-2000000	1061	1
LADWIG ARNOLD H	1LT	0-1042079	1044	2
LADY JAMES R	CPT	0-0402074	0545	2
LAEDLEIN WILLIAM A	CPT	0-0251817	0665	3
LAEVSKY MARCUS H	CPT	0-0216437	0256	3
LAFZZA ALBERT	CW3	W-2153146	0564	1
LAFACE DONALD A	LTC	0-0886118	0356	1
LAFAILLE JR PETER J	CPT	0-0497659	0754	1
LAFALGIO ANTHONY	2LT	0-1185727	1044	2
LAFAYETTE KENNETH	COL	0-0287383	035	2
LAFENE BENJAMIN W	CPT	0-0288196	0346	2
LAFEVER NANCY M	CPT	N-0727155	0554	2
LAFFAL LEON D	MAJ	0-0966695	0662	1
LAFFERTY CHARLES E	LTC	0-0153536	1052	3
LAFFERTY JEFF D	MAJ	0-0477472	0353	1
LAFFERTY LEROY E	LTC	0-1591889	0364	1
LAFFERTY THOMAS J	LTC	0-0885877	1162	1
LAFFERTY WARREN E	MAJ	0-1284720	0658	1
LAFFIN THOMAS M	CPT	0-0405852	0446	2
LAFFITTE CHARLES C	LTC	0-0348397	1061	1
LAFFLER JOSEPH A	CPT	0-0325065	0345	2
LAFIELD WILLIAM C	COL	0-0159255	0352	1
LAFLER CZERNA C	CPT	0-0221911	0345	1
LAFON LELAND F	CPT	0-1281838	0347	1
LAFORGE JR CHARLES V	2LT	0-1183562	1044	2
LAFOUNTAIN GEORGE J	LTC	0-1011967	0556	1
LAFRANCE RICHARD R	1LT	0-1017434	0545	2
LAGANA JAMES S	CW4	W-2143129	1163	1
LAGEN JOHN P	B G	0-0235968	0166	3
LAGEN ROBERT C	MAJ	0-1307424	1157	2
LAGER BUTLER H	1LT	0-1299760	1054	1
LAGER HERMAN J	CW3	W-2151082	0364	1
LAGER RALPH	CPT	0-1312022	1046	1
LAGERGREN MILTON A	CPT	0-0304622	0945	2
LAGERGREN OSCAR A	CW3	W-2144810	0761	1
LAGERQUIST EDWARD A	2LT	0-1589328	0644	2
LAGERQUIST HOWARD C	COL	0-0300126	0458	3
LAGERSTROM LEANDER A	CPT	0-0975929	1160	1
LAGISH GEORGE T	MAJ	0-0191514	0248	1
LAGOURCS JOHN F	LTC	0-0415660	1061	1
LAGOW WHITE F	CW4	W-2144407	0659	1
LAGRAND CHARLES A	MAJ	0-0162542	0-53	1
LAGREW EMORY D	COL	0-0298474	0346	2
LAGRONE GEORGE N	CPT	0-0249166	1065	3
LAHAR EDMOND F	CW2	W-2151814	0361	2
LAHAR RAYMOND T	MAJ	0-1293612	0648	1
LAHENS JR PIERRE P	CPT	0-0907282	0845	2
LAHEY GERALD R	COL	0-0348158	0567	1
LAHNER JR WILLIAM F	CPT	0-0537186	0646	1
LAHOURCADE SIDNEY F	MAJ	0-0329409	0944	2
LAIDLAW ELLIOT C	LTC	0-0268269	0646	2
LAIDLAW JR HARRY H	LTC	0-1547690	0567	3
LAIER OTTO J	MAJ	0-1648351	1060	1
LAIER SR LEO	2LT	0-0176850	0653	1
LAIGE RAYMOND J	LTC	0-0239495	0846	2
LAIN JAMES W	1LT	0-1323943	0145	1
LAINE ARTHUR J	MAJ	0-2103031	0766	1
LAINE FRANK R	CW2	W-2152641	1060	1
LAING FREDERICK	1LT	0-1293613	0545	2
LAING JOHN B	LTC	0-0287622	0464	3
LAIR HERLEY D	LTC	0-1185467	0767	1
LAIRD ARCHIBALD	COL	0-0261916	1067	3
LAIRD CLAIRE B	LTC	0-0201469	1055	3
LAIRD DONALD J	MAJ	0-0983439	0161	1
LAIRD EUGENE E	LTC	0-0272496	1167	3
LAIRD GEORGE A	MAJ	0-0490506	0-52	1
LAIRD JR WILLIAM J	1LT	0-1299584	1064	1
LAIRD WILLIAM D	CW2	W-2209097	1061	1
LAKE CLARK B	CPT	0-0264564	0764	3
LAKE DANIEL M	CPT	0-1115321	0256	1
LAKE DANIEL W	MAJ	0-0198501	0453	3
LAKE EARL W	MAJ	0-1040257	0761	1
LAKE JAMES A	B G	0-0234350	1065	3
LAKE JOHN I	MAJ	0-0960407	1263	1
LAKE JOHN R	2LT	0-1556744	0645	2
LAKE JOHN V	CW2	W-2143938	0962	1
LAKE LISLE R	LTC	0-0452416	0461	1
LAKE RICHARD H	LTC	0-0386487	0361	1
LAKE ROBERT A	LTC	0-1574075	0960	1
LAKE ROBERT E	CW3	W-2148454	0463	1
LAKE WILLARD	LTC	0-0189306	0648	3
LAKE WILLIAM F	COL	0-1001615	0365	1
LAKE WILLIAM S	CPT	0-1650196	0962	1
LAKEMAN WILLIAM O	LTC	0-0294867	0265	3
LAKEY CLETIS M	CW4	W-2101963	0757	1
LAKICH JOSEPH S	MAJ	0-1303355	0561	1
LAKITS GORDON F	1LT	0-1016148	0147	2
LALLANCE JOSEPH P	LTC	0-0422053	1060	1
LALLIS EVERETT	CW2	W-2152345	1058	1
LALLY JOHN M	LTC	0-1795927	0463	1
LALLY JR JAMES W	MAJ	0-0126008	0848	3
LALLY JR JOHN J	MAJ	0-0436900	1161	1
LALLY JR JOHN S	MAJ	0-0956082	0765	1
LALLY RICHARD M	LTC	0-1307425	0361	1
LALLY ROBERT F	1LT	0-0429217	0260	2
LALOS THOMAS K	2LT	0-1308834	0745	2
LAM DALE C	1LT	0-1336079	0750	2
LAMAN JOSEPH G	CPT	0-1285607	0848	1
LAMAR CARLOS P	CPT	0-0386672	1144	1
LAMAR FRANK L	CW4	W-2111854	0960	1
LAMAR JR BARNEY D	CPT	0-0959297	0861	1
LAMAR JR LAW	1LT	0-0523228	1045	2
LAMAR LUCIUS Q C	LTC	0-0912320	1266	3
LAMAR RALPH H	LTC	0-1574926	0867	1
LAMAR RAYMOND J	LTC	0-0446244	1147	1
LAMAR WILMER A	2LT	0-1309758	0144	2
LAMATSCH ROBERT J	LTC	0-0371960	0662	1
LAMB ALBERT W	WO1	W-2108962	1057	1
LAMB ALLAN I	COL	0-0359348	0267	1
LAMB ALVIN R	LTC	0-0119902	0459	3
LAMB ELAINE A	MAJ	L-1010030	0366	1
LAMB GAIL V	MAJ	0-2053868	1060	1
LAMB GEORGE I	CPT	0-2017714	1062	1
LAMB GILBERT R	COL	0-0255160	0564	3
LAMB HOWARD W	COL	0-0306471	0146	2
LAMB IVAN H	1LT	0-0984834	0451	2
LAMB JOHN A	LTC	0-1948342	0464	1
LAMB JOHN T	CW3	W-2143545	0864	1
LAMB JR EMMRICH O	LTC	0-0410547	0961	1
LAMB JR FREDERICK	COL	0-0332551	0161	3
LAMB JR JOHN W	CW3	W-2149369	0561	1
LAMB JR LEROY F	MAJ	0-1832412	1263	1
LAMB KENNETH O	COL	0-0181022	1154	3
LAMB MELVELL W	CW2	W-2152178	0656	1
LAMB MURRAY F	LTC	0-2023676	0167	1
LAMB NORMAN F	MAJ	0-1282981	0346	2
LAMB OTIS C	CW3	W-2125294	0257	1
LAMB PAUL A	COL	0-0177213	0455	2
LAMB PAUL J	LTC	0-0274119	0953	3
LAMB RAYMOND	WO1	W-2120501	0651	1
LAMB ROBERT F	MAJ	0-1555713	0961	1
LAMB THOMAS W	COL	0-0446302	0965	3
LAMBARD MASSEY S	COL	0-0396770	0867	1
LAMBDEN BILLIE G	1LT	0-2023659	0662	1
LAMBDIN ALLEN H	COL	0-0186043	0849	3
LAMBERSON CHARLES	CPT	0-1031333	0648	2
LAMBERSON RAYMOND E	CW3	W-2113907	1154	1
LAMBERSON RUSSELL	CW3	W-2149076	0763	1
LAMBERT ALBERT I	LTC	0-1104260	0563	1
LAMBERT CLAYER	CPT	0-1116856	1059	1
LAMBERT CRAIG W	LTC	0-1334174	0266	1
LAMBERT DANA C	MAJ	0-0119622	0356	3
LAMBERT EDWARD J	COL	0-0482714	0667	1
LAMBERT ELDON W	WO1	W-2142168	0454	1
LAMBERT ELLWOOD R	MAJ	0-1287196	1060	1
LAMBERT ERNEST F	CPT	0-0365307	1043	2
LAMBERT FRANCIS A	LTC	0-0324793	0460	1
LAMBERT HORACE W	LTC	0-1062855	1262	1
LAMBERT JAMES W	1LT	0-2056180	0869	1
LAMBERT JOSIAH	1LT	0-1825761	0746	2
LAMBERT LESLIE A	MAJ	0-0494907	1045	2
LAMBERT LUTHER R	COL	0-0245672	1056	3
LAMBERT MYLES R	MAJ	0-1283243	0961	1
LAMBERT ROBERT R	1LT	0-1308653	1145	2
LAMBERT SR FRANK P	LTC	0-0158386	0655	2
LAMBERT TRUMAN P	LTC	0-1306433	1165	1

NAME	GRADE	SVC NO	DATE RET MO YR	RET CODE
LAMBERT WARREN P	LTC	0-0332394	0460	1
LAMBERT WILLIAM A	2LT	0-4015323	0654	2
LAMBERT WILLIAM H	LTC	0-0381843	1059	1
LAMBERT WILLIAM H	CW4	W-2004521	1066	3
LAMBERTON FLOYD H	CW3	W-2146547	1264	1
LAMBERTON WILBUR H	LTC	0-0183263	0860	3
LAMBERTSON WAYNE C	LTC	0-0320815	0259	1
LAMBETH CHARLES J	LTC	0-0464995	0658	1
LAMBKINS FREDERICK	CW3	W-2141347	1058	1
LAMBRECHT CONRAD J	CW4	W-2143150	0159	1
LAMBRUSCATI PAUL	MAJ	0-0969784	0862	1
LAMEY JAMES L	MAJ	0-0386040	0346	2
LAMEY JOHN D	CPT	0-0257386	0346	2
LAMIRAND FRANKLIN W	CPT	0-0353862	0544	2
LAMKIN CHARLES E	LTC	0-1030685	0766	1
LAMKIN CLARENCE M	MAJ	0-0342104	0345	2
LAMM GEORGE D	MAJ	0-1287020	0361	1
LAMM GORDON W	LTC	0-1108794	0965	1
LAMM HERMAN R	COL	0-0257570	1166	3
LAMM IRVING	CW3	W-2115542	1157	1
LAMM VINCENT P	MAJ	0-0310490	0559	3
LAMM WILLIS O	LTC	0-1555242	1165	1
LAMMEL GEORGE A	2LT	0-1179929	0346	2
LAMMERS THEODORE G	CPT	0-0580898	0760	1
LAMOND JOHN P	MAJ	0-1913360	0865	1
LAMONDA MICHAEL J	1LT	0-2018896	0451	1
LAMONS CHARLES P	MAJ	0-1542707	0658	2
LAMONT CLAUDE W	CPT	0-0506430	1045	2
LAMONT GEORGE E	1LT	0-1287904	1145	1
LAMONT JACK O	MAJ	0-1765099	0147	2
LAMONT NEIL	LTC	0-0399730	1147	1
LAMONT WALTER S	LTC	0-0271326	0651	1
LAMOREAUX FRANCIS	CW2	W-2152679	0957	1
LAMORTE NICHOLAS D	COL	0-0245168	1061	3
LAMOTHE ANDREW H	MAJ	0-1547361	0657	1
LAMOURE PAUL A	LTC	0-0382404	0261	1
LAMOUREAUX ARMAND J	COL	0-0279032	1148	1
LAMOUREUX ARTHUR F	CPT	0-1114997	0446	2
LAMP JOHN	LTC	0-1556166	0964	1
LAMP JR FRED B	MAJ	0-2262423	C263	1
LAMPARTER CARL R	MAJ	0-1558950	C458	2
LAMPE ALFRD S	LTC	0-0362574	0262	1
LAMPE ELVAN W	CW4	W-2003232	0665	1
LAMPERT EMIL A	1LT	0-1304744	1147	1
LAMPERT HERBERT H	MAJ	C-1690592	1146	2
LAMPERT JOSEPH	LTC	0-0134848	0654	3
LAMPHEAR LAURENCE H	LTC	0-0444042	0953	2
LAMPHEAR RAY D	LTC	0-0297409	1167	3
LAMPKIN PHILIP	LTC	0-0372908	1265	3
LAMPKINS MYLES F	CW3	W-2135371	0858	1
LAMPL HOWARD J	CPT	0-2234079	0462	1
LAMPMAN GEORGE I R	LTC	C-0346532	0960	1
LAMPMAN ROY M	MAJ	C-0162533	0949	1
LAMPORT MORTON H	CPT	0-0507472	0346	2
LAMPORT WILLIAM A	CW2	RW-2143769	0461	1
LAMPOS NICHOLAS T	LTC	0-1633349	1059	1
LAMPRECHT ALAN F	LTC	0-1579915	0461	1
LAMPREY GEORGE W	1LT	0-1012158	0745	2
LAMPSON ALBERT W	2LT	0-1825354	C545	2
LAMPSON MERT M	COL	0-0523862	0963	1
LAMPTON WILLIAM R	MAJ	0-2020037	0361	1
LAMSON PERRY B	COL	0-0301841	0460	3
LAMUTT FREDERICK	LTC	0-0342481	0759	1
LANCASTER AUGUSTUS H	COL	0-0486636	0146	1
LANCASTER CLIFTON H	CW2	W-2151417	C664	2
LANCASTER EARLE W	COL	0-0198166	1143	2
LANCASTER FRED O	1LT	0-1287022	0944	2
LANCASTER GEORGE W	MAJ	0-0487060	0750	1
LANCASTER HARLAND F	MAJ	0-0464323	C146	2
LANCASTER JAMES J	CPT	C-0386469	C146	2
LANCASTER JOHN W	2LT	0-0887548	0653	2
LANCASTER LAMAR L	LTC	0-0310146	0464	3
LANCASTER LELON E	CPT	0-1821599	0157	1
LANCASTER OSCAR W	LTC	0-0217416	0463	3
LANCASTER RALPH A	COL	0-0174557	1155	3

NAME	GRADE	SVC NO	DATE RET MO YR	RET CODE
LANCASTER RUSSEL M	LTC	0-0288338	1266	3
LANCASTER VAL	CW2	W-2150816	0760	1
LANCASTER VIRGIL M	LTC	0-0262108	0565	3
LANCE ARVIL M	CPT	0-0504220	0247	1
LANCE LAWRENCE W	CPT	0-0405229	0345	2
LANCE WILLIAM J	CPT	0-0335884	1143	2
LANCER GEORGE	CPT	0-0505199	0846	1
LANCER JOHN J	LTC	0-0186190	1156	3
LANCON JR RAYMOND R	COL	0-0276144	0163	3
LANCTO JOSEPH W	1LT	0-C255992	1053	3
LAND CARROL P	MAJ	0-2033794	1265	1
LAND CECIL D	CPT	0-0382373	0649	1
LAND HARRY O	MAJ	0-0494142	1054	1
LAND HARVEY A	MAJ	0-169656C	0560	1
LAND JACK C	MAJ	0-0366799	1045	2
LAND LOGAN	1LT	0-0229499	1160	3
LAND PAUL E	1LT	0-129415C	0845	2
LAND WALTER C	LTC	0-0279323	1062	3
LAND WILLIAM E	LTC	0-0250981	0764	3
LAND WILLIAM H	MAJ	0-0266989	0348	1
LAND WILLIAM J	LTC	0-157335C	0261	1
LANDAU HAROLD S	CPT	0-1012435	0147	2
LANDAUER JOSEPH P	LTC	0-0279682	0360	1
LANDAUER NORMAN E	LTC	0-0247847	0167	3
LANDAW CLAUDE R	COL	0-0287389	0561	3
LANDBECK ALTON J	2LT	0-1581230	1044	2
LANDE ORIN	1LT	0-103C491	0146	2
LANDEN CORNELIUS	CPT	0-1693399	0945	2
LANDENBERGER J W	LTC	0-0497421	0960	3
LANDER ALICE M	2LT	N-0755212	0245	1
LANDER JR FRANK T	1LT	0-0378986	0844	2
LANDER QUINTIN S	COL	0-0261015	0859	1
LANDER STANTON N	MAJ	0-1636182	0866	1
LANDERS ALLAN R	LTC	0-0494158	0761	2
LANDERS HAROLD P	CPT	0-2262471	1060	1
LANDERS HARVEY J	1LT	0-1058292	0746	2
LANDERS JACK M	CPT	0-0520454	0645	2
LANDERS WARREN D	CW3	W-2141348	1057	1
LANDERS WILLIAM E	LTC	0-1104939	0862	1
LANDERS WILLIAM H	MAJ	0-1634050	0262	1
LANDES LEWIS	COL	0-0138767	0246	2
LANDFRIED ROBERT P	WO1	W-2145037	0653	1
LANDGRAFF JAMES A	CPT	0-1948776	1164	1
LANDINI AMELIA Z	1LT	N-0731712	0746	1
LANDIS ALBERT B	LTC	0-0330714	0561	1
LANDIS FRED S	LTC	0-0424343	0746	2
LANDIS NORMAN E	MAJ	0-1878676	0867	1
LANDIS RAYMOND B	LTC	0-1300051	1061	1
LANDIS ROBERT H	1LT	0-1293976	0745	2
LANDON FLOYD J	CW2	W-2109470	1046	1
LANDON LAWRENCE B	MAJ	0-2210028	0866	1
LANDRETH CHESTER G	1LT	0-1552729	1060	1
LANDRICAN HERBERT W	CPT	0-0497552	0347	2
LANDROCK ARTHUR H	1LT	0-1304605	0145	2
LANDRUM BERNARD L	1LT	0-1011058	1045	2
LANDRUM SR ARIE H	CW2	W-2101969	1155	1
LANDRUM WILLIAM K	LTC	0-0113382	0349	3
LANDRY ANTOINE	CW3	W-2149223	0463	1
LANDRY CATHERINE	MAJ	L-0303726	0564	1
LANDRY EMERY A	MAJ	0-1106272	1060	2
LANDRY ERNEST J	LTC	0-1059581	0567	1
LANDRY ERNEST J	MAJ	0-1692113	0345	2
LANDRY HOWARD P	LTC	0-0328285	0760	1
LANDRY JAMES A	CPT	0-1292199	1046	2
LANDRY JAMES P	CPT	0-099015C	0161	1
LANDRY JOHN J	1LT	0-0407564	0146	2
LANDRY JR WALTER J	LTC	0-0452053	0361	1
LANDRY MAURICE T	MAJ	0-0984682	1062	1
LANDRY MILTON J	LTC	0-0342179	0146	2
LANDRY PIERRE C	CPT	0-0122731	0654	3
LANDRY WALTER J	CW2	W-2150594	0959	1
LANDRY WILLIAM B	MAJ	C-1648352	0762	1
LANDSMAN HARRY	LTC	0-0309866	1058	3
LANDSMAN HARRY	LTC	0-1040964	0862	1
LANDSMAN SOL	LTC	0-1596093	0361	1

NAME	GRADE	SVC NO	DATE RET MO YR	RET CODE
LANDT HENRY L	LTC	0-1185233	0863	1
LANDVOIGT MILTON J	MAJ	0-0161986	0651	3
LANDY JAMES J	1LT	0-1173685	1045	1
LANE ALTON L	CPT	0-1040965	0351	1
LANE ARTHUR J	LTC	0-0510726	0255	1
LANE AUGUSTUS H	1LT	0-0455726	1144	2
LANE BILLIE I	MAJ	N-0786669	0467	1
LANE BOND E	LTC	0-0216945	1062	3
LANE CHARLES C	MAJ	0-0154798	0648	3
LANE CHARLES K	LTC	0-0469431	0546	2
LANE CHARLES L	LTC	0-0324279	0460	1
LANE CLARENCE L	LTC	0-0389433	0557	1
LANE CLARENCE M	CPT	0-0953844	1060	1
LANE DANIEL P	LTC	0-0104038	C648	3
LANE DARRELL T	LTC	0-0182484	C552	3
LANE DEWEY L	WO1	W-2133205	0357	1
LANE EDMUND T	MAJ	0-0274916	0146	1
LANE EDWARD	LTC	0-0229375	0956	3
LANE EDWARD W	LTC	0-0174191	0161	3
LANE ELTON A	CW2	W-2141349	1054	1
LANE FORREST L	CW2	W-2213032	1166	1
LANE GERARD F	1LT	0-2201809	0754	2
LANE GILBERT I	LTC	0-0451607	0462	1
LANE HAROLD A V	CW2	W-2152745	0564	1
LANE HARRY F	COL	C-0402285	0962	1
LANE HARRY W	LTC	0-0202185	0351	3
LANE HENRY A	MAJ	0-0887691	0459	1
LANE HIRAM T	MAJ	C-1636370	0953	1
LANE JAMES J	CW3	W-2106787	0461	1
LANE JOHN C	CPT	0-1698141	0964	2
LANE JOHN F	CW4	W-2118107	C755	1
LANE JOHN F	CPT	0-0289635	C464	3
LANE JOHN M	LTC	0-1172131	C766	1
LANE JOHN R	LTC	0-0358486	0160	1
LANE JOHN S	LTC	0-0905593	0453	1
LANE JR MERRITT	1LT	0-1182627	0345	2
LANE JR ROBERT J	CW2	W-3200496	0967	1
LANE JR WILLIAM T	LTC	C-0115530	0656	3
LANE JULIUS F	LTC	0-1325299	C163	1
LANE LAWRENCE G	MAJ	0-1297294	0564	1
LANE MARY P	2LT	N-0720113	0244	1
LANE RAYMOND J	COL	0-0255610	1157	3
LANE RICHARD J	CPT	C-1895189	1052	1
LANE RICHARD O	CW3	W-2146815	1157	1
LANE RICHARD S	MAJ	C-0330277	C146	2
LANE RICHARD S	CPT	0-1038213	0352	1
LANE ROBERT C	MAJ	0-1699958	0161	1
LANE ROBERT C	CW4	W-2111206	1055	1
LANE ROBERT W	MAJ	0-0172628	0656	3
LANE ROY L	LTC	0-0236598	1064	3
LANE RUSSELL G	1LT	0-1172132	C246	2
LANE STANLEY S	LTC	0-0314858	C855	1
LANE THERON I	COL	0-0254185	0654	2
LANE THOMAS J	CW3	W-2208351	0966	1
LANE VINCENT A	COL	0-0208424	0862	3
LANE WENDELL E	2LT	0-0220407	C360	3
LANELLI LESTER P	LTC	0-1040562	0266	1
LANEVE JOHN J	CPT	0-0525582	C845	2
LANEY JAMES D O	CW3	W-2206839	0866	1
LANFEAR ALMIRA A	LTC	N-0736827	0667	3
LANFORD LEROY C	MAJ	C-025866C	0960	3
LANG ABEL	LTC	0-1002267	0466	3
LANG ANTON A	MAJ	C-0199050	1045	2
LANG ARCHIE E	MAJ	0-0134039	0253	3
LANG ARTHUR P	1LT	0-0366167	C945	2
LANG CECIL H	COL	0-0147739	0351	3
LANG CHARLES M	CPT	0-0253502	0952	3
LANG CLEMENT M	MAJ	C-0162989	0546	2
LANG DAVID	MAJ	0-1325831	1059	1
LANG EMIL	CW2	W-2114181	1149	1
LANG FRANCIS C	LTC	0-0283037	1057	1
LANG GEORGE E	CPT	0-0230877	C846	1
LANG GEORGE H	MAJ	0-1948947	1163	1
LANG GEORGE K	CPT	0-0354640	0445	2
LANG GERALD M	LTC	0-132153C	C965	1

NAME	GRADE	SVC NO	DATE RET MO YR	RET CODE
LANG JAMES O	MAJ	0-1799454	0361	1
LANG JOHN M	CPT	0-0120547	0554	3
LANG JOSEPH	CPT	0-0492257	0645	2
LANG JR HENRY J	1LT	0-1335940	1053	2
LANG LAWRENCE P	COL	0-0177708	0262	3
LANG LAWRENCE R	1LT	0-1179495	0346	2
LANG LEROY F	WO1	W-2105664	0744	2
LANG ROBERT W	MAJ	0-2263763	0964	1
LANG ROBERT W	1LT	0-4031770	0157	2
LANG STANLEY B	MAJ	0-0194390	0362	3
LANG SYLVAN	COL	0-0185644	0751	3
LANG WALTER P	LTC	0-0323617	1057	1
LANG WILLIAM	CPT	0-1327015	1158	1
LANG WILLIAM E	LTC	0-0928361	0465	3
LANG WILLIAM J	CW2	W-2206655	0763	1
LANG WILMER J	MAJ	0-04C6940	1263	3
LANGAN JR DAVID D	COL	0-0331831	0565	1
LANGDON ROY B	MAJ	0-1573889	0151	1
LANGDON THOMAS J	1LT	0-1017266	0247	2
LANGE ALBERT	COL	0-0241676	0754	3
LANGE AUSTIN J	LTC	0-0327685	C566	3
LANGE CLARENCE C	MAJ	0-0109793	0855	3
LANGE EDWIN J	2LT	0-1913774	0640	1
LANGE ELMER A	CPT	0-1293074	1146	1
LANGE EUGENE W	LTC	0-1181937	1163	1
LANGE FRANK F E	LTC	0-1C19931	0166	1
LANGE FREDERICK	LTC	0-0133151	0949	3
LANGE GEORGE J	LTC	0-1030055	0265	1
LANGE JAMES A	CPT	0-1174345	0858	1
LANGE JOHN A	CW3	W-2146021	0967	1
LANGE LAWRENCE W	LTC	0-1294151	0758	1
LANGE LESLIE E	LTC	0-0888756	0363	1
LANGE WILLIAM A	CPT	0-1686874	1046	2
LANGEBARTEL RALPH W	1LT	0-1174C39	1045	2
LANGELUTTIG ALBERT C	LTC	0-0171236	1061	3
LANGENDERFER SYLVEST	CW4	W-2145618	0962	1
LANGER FRANK	MAJ	0-0435951	0254	1
LANGERAK DUDCK B	LTC	0-1178541	0758	1
LANGEVIN EVELYN	1LT	N-0785847	0649	2
LANGEVIN MARIE E L	1LT	N-0753058	1046	1
LANGFITT JOSEPH A	LTC	0-0107894	0350	3
LANGFORD CECIL T	CPT	0-0170043	0956	3
LANGFORD ELLIS C	MAJ	0-1185440	0961	1
LANGFORD JAMES A	CW2	W-2152025	0460	1
LANGFORD THEODORE H	MAJ	0-1292200	0157	1
LANGFORD WILLIAM B	LTC	0-0249508	0366	3
LANGGLE PAUL	CW2	W-2148742	0262	1
LANGGUTH ELMER E	LTC	0-1592363	0564	3
LANGHAM BURKE E	MAJ	0-1796811	1060	1
LANGHAM CECIL D	CPT	0-1062687	0747	2
LANGHAM JAMES W	LTC	0-0147761	0648	3
LANGHAM VERNON R	CW3	W-2150299	0466	1
LANGHER GORDON N	LTC	0-1574933	0766	3
LANGLAIS TEDDY	1LT	0-0100016	1037	2
LANGLEY CLAIRE	LTC	0-0307019	0360	1
LANGLEY FRANCIS H	COL	0-0225676	1159	3
LANGLEY HARRY J	LTC	0-1179128	0467	1
LANGLEY JR JAMES W	2LT	0-1553495	C845	2
LANGLEY LEOTA M	MAJ	N-0720740	1061	1
LANGLEY ROBERT P	LTC	0-0192713	1060	1
LANGLEY THORPE M	LTC	0-0153675	0352	3
LANGLEY WILLIAM A	CPT	0-1583249	1156	2
LANGLOIS ALFRED E	CPT	0-0982084	C653	2
LANGLOIS FLOYD A	MAJ	0-1637892	0862	1
LANGNER ROY W	LTC	0-1639331	0962	1
LANGO SAMUEL A	CPT	0-1824047	C764	1
LANGRUM GODFREY G	CW2	W-2145736	0357	1
LANGSTAFF CHARLES W	CW3	W-2000506	1253	3
LANGSTAFF JOHN M	1LT	0-1299588	0546	2
LANGSTON AUSTINN F	MAJ	0-1108796	0247	1
LANGSTON CHARLES R	1LT	0-1100634	1044	2
LANGSTON JAMES H	CW3	W-2148975	1164	1
LANGSTON JAMES L	MAJ	0-1844382	0855	1
LANGSTON JAMES T	MAJ	0-2289142	1165	1
LANGSTON JEAN C	LTC	0-1109438	0664	1

NAME	GRADE	SVC NO	DATE RET MO YR	RET CODE
LANGSTON JR CZAR C	2LT	0-2050540	0346	2
LANGSTON NORRIS D	MAJ	0-024339C	0544	2
LANGSTON PERRY O	CPT	0-0346693	0444	2
LANGSTON ROSS B	MAJ	C-1686669	0964	1
LANGSTON WILLIAM H	MAJ	C-15903CC	0465	1
LANGTON LUTHER L	CW3	W-2118104	0657	1
LANGUARO CHARLES J	WO1	W-2104191	0643	2
LANGUEMI FRANK C	MAJ	C-1013440	0546	2
LANGWASSER FRANK	LTC	0-1845063	0562	1
LANGWICK RALPH B	LTC	0-1633352	0261	1
LANGWORTHY WILLIAM J	LTC	0-0414070	0765	2
LANHAM HASKEL O	MAJ	C-0341031	C664	3
LANHAM RALPH E	LTC	0-0436467	1050	1
LANHAM STEPHEN A	MAJ	0-0257534	1065	3
LANHAM TRAVIS L	MAJ	0-0405145	0546	2
LANIER CLARK	CW2	W-2143720	1058	2
LANIER FELIX T	CPT	0-0334852	1048	3
LANIER HAROLD L	LTC	0-1339453	C966	1
LANIER JOHN E	CW2	W-2211639	C666	1
LANIER SR GENE O	CW3	W-2152106	0661	1
LANIER TEX B	2LT	0-1170047	1045	2
LANIER WILLIAM D	LTC	0-0102562	C249	3
LANIGAN JR JAMES M	LTC	0-0379352	1062	1
LANKER STANLEY	CPT	C-0495428	0546	1
LANKFORD B R	CW3	W-2143819	C959	1
LANKFORD CLINTON C	LTC	0-0921433	0463	2
LANKFORD HERMAN H	1LT	0-2262720	0463	1
LANKFORD JOHN L	1LT	0-0467725	0945	2
LANKFORD ROGER E	CW3	W-2146203	0662	1
LANKS VIOLA E	CPT	L-0305323	C756	2
LANMAN EDWARD O	MAJ	0-1172959	0262	1
LANN CLYDE E	CPT	0-0217471	0860	3
LANNAK LEONARD C	LTC	0-1946315	0761	1
LANNEN MARY K	MAJ	L-0604658	0965	1
LANNING EDWARD H	CPT	0-1004165	1050	1
LANNON CHARLES E	CW4	W-2108938	0364	1
LANPHERE CLARK P	CW2	W-2108763	1045	2
LANS WILLIAM J	LTC	0-0163299	0647	2
LANSFORD WILLIAM C	LTC	0-1583251	1065	1
LANSFORD WILLIS R	COL	0-0128645	0150	3
LANSFORD WILSON A	MAJ	C-0311287	0361	1
LANSING DANIEL H	LTC	0-0269348	0564	3
LANSING DUDLEY K	MAJ	C-0166361	0648	3
LANSING JR FRED	MAJ	C-0490196	0655	1
LANSING JR JESSE E	LTC	0-1003779	C566	1
LANSING LLOYD S	CPT	0-0288453	1045	2
LANSKI MAXWELL J	MAJ	0-0504497	0655	1
LANSTRUM GEORGE F	LTC	0-1298722	1066	1
LANTAU MARTIN	COL	C-0163040	0959	3
LANTHIER JOSEPH R	MAJ	C-1686793	C165	1
LANTIS JAMES R	MAJ	0-2020308	C364	1
LANTON JAMES R	CW3	W-2150319	0963	1
LANTZ ALFRED C	MAJ	0-1546341	1159	1
LANTZ CHARLES N	MAJ	C-1013755	C860	1
LANTZ DARRELL M	LTC	0-1552105	1160	1
LANTZ DAYLE R	LTC	C-1042347	1055	1
LANTZ ROBERT M	LTC	0-0289402	0460	1
LANTZ WARREN	MAJ	0-0534610	0946	1
LANZA ARTHUR J	1LT	0-1326286	0846	1
LANZA CHARLES V	CPT	C-2019334	0758	1
LANZILLI FERDINAND	1LT	C-1000607	0645	2
LAPERE EARL L	CW2	W-2212217	0167	1
LAPEYRI FERDINANC	COL	0-0264295	C660	3
LAPHAM DANA M	MAJ	C-0986076	0366	1
LAPHAM HOWARD H	WO1	W-2109340	0245	2
LAPHAM JR HARRY H	MAJ	C-1326855	0563	1
LAPHAM JR JOHN G	MAJ	C-1040966	0563	1
LAPHAM JR SAMUEL	COL	0-0188456	C952	3
LAPHAM ROBERT W	MAJ	C-1893930	1266	1
LAPIOUS REUBEN T	CPT	0-0344289	0745	2
LAPINE DOUGLAS P	MAJ	C-1949581	0155	1
LAPINE GLEN H	LTC	0-1997759	0663	1
LAPINER ARNOLD J	MAJ	C-1331847	1263	1
LAPINSKI ROMUALD J	MAJ	C-1845753	0657	1
LARKE ROBERT H	MAJ	0-1052040	0860	1

NAME	GRADE	SVC NO	DATE RET MO YR	RET CODE
LAPLANT PALMER L	LTC	0-1040753	0461	1
LAPLANTE BERNARD H	CPT	0-0410035	1044	2
LAPLANTE FRANCIS J	LTC	0-0237418	0263	3
LAPNIEWSKI CHESTER	MAJ	0-0473595	0645	2
LAPO CHESTER H	MAJ	0-2014564	0563	1
LAPOINTE ROGER J	LTC	0-0388474	0760	1
LAPOTA PAUL M	2LT	0-1108797	0244	1
LAPOTKA JOHN	LTC	0-0439605	0863	1
LAPPIN WILLIAM E	COL	0-0402827	0760	1
LAPPLEY WALTER F	CPT	0-0350043	0745	2
LAPRES JR THEODORE E	1LT	0-1307833	0845	2
LAPSLEY JOHN B	COL	0-0153139	0751	3
LAPUTKA MICHAEL	CW3	W-2117218	0353	1
LAQUIDARA SALVI J	MAJ	0-0409325	0661	1
LARA MANUEL P	1LT	0-2027042	0660	1
LARA PRIMITIVO	LTC	0-1574467	0556	1
LARABEE WAYNE O	LTC	0-1646347	0266	1
LARAIA HENRY X	COL	0-0302719	0858	1
LARAWAY BURRELL G	CPT	0-0182142	0248	2
LARCOM CHARLES C	CW2	W-2144311	0153	1
LARDINAIS LAURA J	2LT	N-0729139	1044	1
LAREW ISAAC L	LTC	0-1112273	1061	1
LAREW RUFUS W	1LT	0-1310266	0644	2
LARGAN JOSEPH A	MAJ	0-1015340	0657	2
LARGE BERNARD L	LTC	0-1313619	1263	1
LARGE CLOIS F	MAJ	0-0269546	0958	1
LARGE JAMES R	CPT	0-1286146	0147	1
LARIMER SIMON R	1LT	0-0175199	0455	3
LARIMORE DONALD E	MAJ	0-0367054	0946	2
LARIMORE PHILIP B	MAJ	0-0511609	0747	1
LARIOS ERNEST E	MAJ	0-0233985	1158	3
LARIOSA BENJAMIN	2LT	0-0890511	0947	2
LARIVEE BERNARD S	MAJ	0-0526055	0655	1
LARKE JR THOMAS H	CPT	0-0172910	0557	3
LARKIN CHARLES E	COL	0-0267856	0451	3
LARKIN EMMETT R	MAJ	0-0973616	0962	1
LARKIN GEORGE V	MAJ	0-0253960	0767	3
LARKIN HERSCHEL R	CPT	0-0463814	1045	1
LARKIN JOSEPH V	LTC	0-1589578	0562	1
LARKIN JR WILLIAM J	LTC	0-1686677	0767	1
LARKIN RALPH R	CW3	W-2145737	1166	1
LARKIN WALLACE S	MAJ	0-0297072	1166	3
LARKIN WILLIAM S	MAJ	0-1821732	0157	1
LARKINS JR JOHNB	WO1	W-2118090	0553	1
LARKINS SIMEON J	MAJ	0-1302147	0962	1
LARKINS WALTER W	MAJ	0-2262891	0766	1
LARKUM NEWTON W	COL	0-0229432	0757	3
LARMORE ROBERT C	CPT	0-0407539	0146	2
LARMOYEUX CYRUS	MAJ	0-0354120	0348	2
LARNER HUGH R	LTC	0-0363746	0866	1
LARNER RAY A	MAJ	0-0140698	0255	3
LARRABEE DWIGHT H	MAJ	0-1797481	0360	1
LARRABEE WILLIAM F	COL	0-0268498	1055	3
LARREMORE GENE F	MAJ	0-0455288	0456	1
LARRICK MYRON E	LTC	0-1533612	1165	1
LARRICK THOMAS	MAJ	0-0250125	0765	3
LARRIMER JOHN B	CW2	W-2146255	0756	1
LARRIMER WALTER D	CW4	W-2000306	0155	1
LARRINAGA CESAR	CPT	0-1326505	0266	1
LARRISON CHARLES B	CW4	W-2119556	1163	3
LARRIVEE ELPHEGE A	WO1	W-2145261	1053	1
LARROUX ROBERT W	LTC	0-0422332	0662	1
LARRY GEORGE	MAJ	0-1332612	0863	1
LARSEN AAGE	MAJ	0-0242259	0651	1
LARSEN ALBERT L	MAJ	0-0172636	0355	3
LARSEN ALF R	LTC	0-0483030	0241	1
LARSEN ANDERS	COL	0-0203145	0-53	3
LARSEN EMIL	MAJ	0-0393384	0146	2
LARSEN HANS C	COL	0-0197313	0553	3
LARSEN HAROLD W	CPT	0-1895782	0964	2
LARSEN IVY T	1LT	N-0736654	0145	1
LARSEN JOHN P	COL	0-0186867	0152	3
LARSEN JR FRED N	COL	0-0268007	0366	1
LARSEN LAWRENCE H	COL	0-0314138	0260	3
LARSEN LAWRENCE L	LTC	0-0352065	0360	1

NAME	GRADE	SVC NO	DATE RET MO YR	RET CODE
LARSEN MELVIN J	MAJ	0-1917845	0665	1
LARSEN WALTER T	MAJ	C-1185409	0958	1
LARSEN WILLIAM C	CW2	W-2144995	0357	1
LARSEN WILLIAM L	CW3	W-2144966	1165	1
LARSON ARTHUR A	COL	0-0215700	1054	1
LARSON ARTHUR H	LTC	C-0177795	0750	3
LARSON ARTHUR J	CPT	0-1014955	0746	1
LARSON CALVIN L	MAJ	0-1688449	0664	1
LARSON CHESTER G	LTC	0-1108798	0166	3
LARSON CONRAD L	CW4	W-2106810	0559	1
LARSON DAVID J	CPT	0-0524386	C546	2
LARSON DONALD G	CPT	0-0326207	0246	2
LARSON EDMOND H	LTC	0-0917187	1062	1
LARSON EDWARD L	1LT	0-1544059	0146	2
LARSON EDWIN C	CPT	0-0107886	0154	3
LARSON ELSA F	CPT	N-0736954	1046	1
LARSON FRANK L	LTC	0-1169610	0466	1
LARSON FRED D	1LT	0-1290441	1145	1
LARSON GEORGE R	LTC	0-1011157	0758	1
LARSON HARRY	LTC	0-0196584	0655	3
LARSON HARRY E	CPT	0-0401072	0445	2
LARSON JOANNA M	MAJ	N-0779303	C264	1
LARSON JOHN W	MAJ	0-0311440	1045	2
LARSON JR VERNET B	LTC	0-1318907	1167	1
LARSON KEITH O	MAJ	0-0515773	0947	2
LARSON KERMIT F	MAJ	0-1547362	C556	1
LARSON LEANDER T	CW2	W-2103124	C757	1
LARSON LELAND R	CPT	0-0426590	0246	2
LARSON LINNE C	MAJ	C-0169136	0259	3
LARSON LOUIS A	COL	0-0351269	0663	1
LARSON MARIAN L	1LT	N-0730612	1045	1
LARSON MEREDITH J	MAJ	0-1101539	0257	1
LARSON MERLE E	WO1	W-2108852	0255	1
LARSON MERRILL L	COL	0-0296664	0660	2
LARSON OLAF R	CPT	0-0182721	0954	3
LARSON OSCAR W	MAJ	0-0321647	1159	3
LARSON PETER	MAJ	0-0384739	0561	1
LARSON RAYMOND J	LTC	0-0253427	0757	3
LARSON RICHARD P	MAJ	0-1633356	1160	1
LARSON ROBERT A	LTC	0-1321374	0767	1
LARSON ROBERT A	1LT	0-1551893	0944	2
LARSON ROY E	MAJ	0-0481737	C146	2
LARSON SHERWOOD G	CPT	0-1103275	C746	2
LARSON STANLEY D	LTC	0-1592366	C861	1
LARSON SYDNEY S	1LT	0-1587398	0451	1
LARSON THOMAS A	LTC	0-2053934	0263	1
LARSON TURE L B	MAJ	C-0224606	0457	3
LARSON VERNON R	MAJ	0-1635004	0954	1
LARSON WALTER C	CW3	W-3150354	0767	1
LARSON WILLIAM B	LTC	0-1183112	1064	1
LARSSON BROR H	COL	0-0170691	0648	3
LARY JACK R	MAJ	0-1058295	0459	1
LARY JR VIRGIL P	1LT	0-1181338	C845	2
LASA RAFAEL A	1LT	C-0414590	0745	2
LASATER BUREN F	1LT	0-0957115	1053	2
LASATER DORSA L	LTC	0-0490373	C757	1
LASATER MERLE L	MAJ	0-2206201	0466	2
LASATER NORMAN E	WO1	W-2110882	0558	1
LASCOLA ANTHONY G	LTC	0-0395230	0461	1
LASEK EUGENE L	CW3	W-2203270	0862	1
LASELL MILO G	LTC	0-1297391	1165	1
LASH CLEO L	COL	0-0183069	0155	3
LASH JAMES W	COL	0-0649510	1166	1
LASH JOHN A	MAJ	0-0256853	1264	3
LASH RUSSELL J	2LT	0-1032536	0145	2
LASHE PETER	CW3	W-2105392	C861	1
LASHER WILLIS W	COL	C-0136968	C448	2
LASHKOFF GALENA	1LT	N-0756778	0646	1
LASHLEY WISTAR J	CW2	W-2145889	0960	1
LASHMAN RUTH E	2LT	N-0788848	0845	1
LASHUA WILLIAM C	CW3	W-2144700	0460	1
LASK WALTER M	MAJ	C-0305786	0950	1
LASKA LEONARD P	MAJ	0-1548906	0161	1
LASKO DONALD R	MAJ	0-1703450	1067	1
LASKOWSKI CLARENCE	MAJ	0-1997268	0767	1

NAME	GRADE	SVC NO	DATE RET MO YR	RET CODE
LASKOWSKI FRANK W	LTC	0-0349657	0661	1
LASKOWSKI HELEN C	1LT	N-0721209	0246	1
LASKY JOHN A	LTC	0-0485193	0953	1
LASKY JOHN F	1LT	0-2005658	0147	2
LASKY JOSEPH	CW4	W-2118196	1154	1
LASKY MORTIMER A	LTC	0-0244904	0364	3
LASLEY FRED	MAJ	0-0285388	0863	3
LASLEY HAROLD L	LTC	0-0953685	0567	1
LASLEY OLIVER P	CW4	W-2119373	0862	1
LASPINA GATIN T	MAJ	0-1032223	0160	1
LASSELLE HERBERT W	COL	0-0258394	1066	3
LASSELLE PERCY A	LTC	0-0173097	1060	3
LASSER CHARLES	CPT	0-0495129	0648	1
LASSETER PAUL L	CW2	W-3151611	0367	1
LASSETER WILLIAM W	CW2	W-2143053	0462	1
LASSETTER BURL G	LTC	0-0291598	0366	3
LASSITER BASIL	LTC	0-1173686	0962	1
LASSITER JAMES	CPT	0-1290769	0550	1
LASSITER RUBY S	LTC	L-0502525	1167	1
LASSOFF THEODORE	LTC	0-2001062	0661	1
LASSWELL J R	MAJ	0-0960063	1266	1
LASSWELL RICHARD E	CPT	0-1030794	0847	1
LASTER JOHN S	MAJ	0-1036247	0366	1
LASTON FREDERICK	MAJ	C-0476734	0946	2
LASWELL ROBERT A	LTC	0-1017972	1262	2
LATART LELANC J	1LT	0-1170458	0944	2
LATCHEW CLYDE G	LTC	0-0122825	1052	3
LATENDRESSE DONALD R	1LT	0-1106280	1045	2
LATENDRESSE WALDON G	MAJ	0-0962178	0961	1
LATERRIERE JOHN R	LTC	0-0393324	0261	1
LATEY KEITH P	CW3	W-2000712	0356	3
LATHAM ARTHUR A	LTC	0-1322641	0464	2
LATHAM BILL C	MAJ	0-1289595	0457	1
LATHAM BILL M	1LT	0-0389647	1045	2
LATHAM JR LEON D	COL	0-0315169	1065	3
LATHAM LYMAN A	MAJ	0-1635006	0266	1
LATHAM ROBERT F	CPT	0-1645750	0647	2
LATHAM RUDOLPH L	CW3	W-2152221	0161	1
LATHAM WALTER D	1LT	0-1797667	1049	1
LATHERS MARTIN L	CPT	0-0494009	0653	1
LATHOM HAROLD E	CW2	W-2103125	0955	1
LATHROP JR EARL S	CPT	0-0426088	0246	2
LATHROP LAURENCE L	LTC	0-0313407	0857	3
LATIMER CLAUDE A	COL	C-0211151	0149	3
LATIMER GEORGE W	COL	0-0174611	1060	3
LATIMER HUGH M	LTC	0-0258022	0857	1
LATIMER JR ROBERT G	CPT	0-0504909	0346	2
LATIMER WILLIAM G	CPT	0-0157423	1143	2
LATIMER WILLIAM H	LTC	0-1184870	0965	1
LATOFF THOMAS J	MAJ	0-1695789	1045	2
LATOUR ADRIAN R	LTC	0-0288340	0267	3
LATOUR LUCILE G	MAJ	N-0737818	0163	1
LATRONICO LOUIS	CPT	0-1574939	0655	1
LATSKO WILLIAM S	2LT	0-0538764	0845	2
LATSON CLAUDE H	LTC	0-0277830	1160	3
LATTA ALEXANDER	CPT	0-0276429	0865	3
LATTA SAMUEL C	MAJ	0-0153038	0745	2
LATTA WILLIAM M	MAJ	0-0334700	0265	3
LATTAL JR ANTON	LTC	0-0365929	0860	1
LATTARI DANIEL	1LT	0-1175484	0845	2
LATTERMAN ALBERT J	LTC	0-0134694	C754	3
LATTIMER GEORGE W	CW2	W-3430439	0867	1
LATUCHA ALBERT	CPT	0-1715974	0347	2
LATZ HELEN C	1LT	N-0761120	0746	1
LATZER PAUL J	COL	0-0201853	1061	3
LATZO JOSEPH	CPT	0-1554923	0556	1
LAU BENEDICT W	2LT	0-1019850	0943	2
LAU CHARLES E	MAJ	0-1284348	0345	2
LAU CHARLES F	2LT	0-1314227	0944	2
LAU FRANK D	CPT	0-0201081	1056	3
LAU JOSEPH F C	1LT	0-0405176	0843	1
LAU KENNETH K	LTC	0-0366921	0550	1
LAU ROBERT H	MAJ	0-0292884	0545	2
LAU WILSON R	1LT	0-1300344	C746	2
LAURENHEIMER WILLIAM	COL	0-0281642	0764	1

NAME	GRADE	SVC NO	DATE RET MO YR	RET CODE
LAUBER DANIEL A	CW2	W-2209397	0965	1
LAUCK MERRILL A	1LT	0-1181339	0745	2
LAUDENSLAYER OSCAR G	MAJ	0-1554030	1156	1
LAUDER EDWARD W	LTC	0-0243157	0563	3
LAUDER JOHN R	1LT	0-1174347	0744	2
LAUDERDALE GEORGE W	CW3	W-2146591	0364	1
LAUDERDALE SAMUEL M	MAJ	0-0913983	0546	2
LAUE ALBERT R	LTC	0-1648530	0767	1
LAUER ALBERT G	MAJ	0-0323143	1058	3
LAUER BYRON E	LTC	0-0258260	0567	3
LAUER CHARLES F	LTC	0-1101541	0166	1
LAUER JOSEPH G	LTC	0-1576278	0765	1
LAUER JR FRANK C	LTC	0-0406842	0445	2
LAUER MARGARET B	MAJ	N-0733980	0463	1
LAUER MARY H	2LT	N-0759807	0245	1
LAUFERSKI STANLEY P	LTC	0-0183841	1057	1
LAUGERMAN HAROLD W	1LT	0-1303166	0246	2
LAUGHLIN ALFRED J	MAJ	0-0335431	0546	1
LAUGHLIN CHARLES V	LTC	0-2051832	0667	3
LAUGHLIN JOHN C	1LT	0-2024324	0147	1
LAUGHLIN LORENZO C	MAJ	0-1949831	0663	2
LAUGHMAN HARRY E	CW2	W-2211403	1265	1
LAUGHNER JOHN H	COL	0-0316755	1264	3
LAUGHRUN WILLIAM A	MAJ	0-1702203	1044	1
LAUGHTER JOHN E	CPT	0-0428743	0647	1
LAUGHTER PAUL E	CPT	0-0372383	1043	2
LAUIGAN ESTANISLAO	2LT	0-0890499	0562	1
LAUKAITIS ADAM B	LTC	0-1045802	0461	1
LAULETTA CYPRIAN M	LTC	0-0484120	0467	1
LAUNDER JR JOHN E	CPT	0-0390139	1045	2
LAUR CLIFFORD N	MAJ	0-2263162	0262	1
LAUREA GERALD	MAJ	0-1305797	0655	1
LAURENCE LESLIE T	MAJ	0-2036248	0958	1
LAURIA PHILIP C	CW3	W-2146980	0964	1
LAURIE GEORGE C	LTC	0-0553095	1066	1
LAURIE ROBERT R	1LT	0-1301656	0146	2
LAURITANO EUGENE J	MAJ	0-1637899	1146	2
LAUSIER CLAUDE D	CW2	W-2153162	0565	1
LAUSMAN HAROLD J	1LT	0-2047038	0246	2
LAUTERBACH HERBERT G	COL	0-0199098	0948	3
LAUTH ALBERT W	CPT	0-2018535	1058	2
LAUTHERS CHARLES W	LTC	0-0179968	1153	3
LAUTNER ELMER F	MAJ	0-0919847	0447	2
LAUTZENHEISER C N	CPT	0-1945632	0547	2
LAUZZE ANTHONY R	CPT	0-1314032	1045	2
LAVALLE LAWRENCE L	COL	0-0324811	0364	3
LAVALLEE LEON J	COL	0-0206797	0953	3
LAVAN RAY E	LTC	0-0347905	0761	2
LAVELL JOHN B	MAJ	0-1331296	0762	1
LAVELLE JAMES J	MAJ	0-1325904	0863	1
LAVENDER CHARLES E	MAJ	0-0178646	1054	3
LAVENDER ROBERT P	MAJ	0-1298724	1264	1
LAVEROURE LOUIS A	MAJ	0-1578749	0460	1
LAVERY ARTHUR T	CW4	W-2103753	0757	1
LAVERY EUGENE H	1LT	0-1289928	0545	1
LAVERY EUGENE L	LTC	0-0884210	0465	1
LAVERY HAROLD S	CPT	0-1177045	1045	2
LAVETT JOHN S	1LT	0-1015561	0546	2
LAVEY PATRICK J	CW3	W-2146339	1163	1
LAVICK DONALD H	2LT	0-1642304	0745	2
LAVIGNE DAVID E	MAJ	0-1166538	0961	1
LAVIN JOHN A	COL	0-0165493	0156	3
LAVIN JULIA E	MAJ	N-0758300	0165	1
LAVIN MARGUERITE	LTC	N-0731436	1166	3
LAVIN MARSHALL R	2LT	0-2036822	0345	2
LAVINE BERNARD	CPT	0-1304407	1047	2
LAVIS FRANK J	1LT	0-1299911	0344	1
LAVOIE RICHARD J	MAJ	0-1704216	0957	1
LAVOIE WARREN R	MAJ	0-1113316	0261	1
LAVRAKAS CHARLES	LTC	0-0288968	0865	3
LAW ALLEN L	CW4	W-2132131	0857	1
LAW AUGUST	1LT	0-1288404	0551	1
LAW BUELL S	MAJ	0-0201479	0652	3
LAW CHARLTON E	MAJ	0-0239316	0166	3
LAW DAVID F	CPT	0-0499756	0450	1

NAME	GRADE	SVC NO	DATE RET MO YR	RET CODE
LAW DCA E	CPT	0-1798366	0566	3
LAW EARL J	MAJ	0-0965312	1061	1
LAW FRANCIS M	CW4	W-2143433	0164	1
LAW FRASER C	LTC	0-0219175	0263	3
LAW JAMES E	1LT	0-1548905	1150	1
LAW JOHN T	CPT	0-0505984	1048	1
LAW JR ELLIE C	LTC	0-0227690	0265	3
LAW JR ROBERT W	1LT	0-1294153	0447	2
LAW ROBERT S	MAJ	0-1550202	0764	1
LAW RUSSELL E	COL	0-0413124	0767	1
LAW RUSSELL E	MAJ	0-1289086	0857	1
LAW RUTH A	2LT	N-0762560	0746	1
LAW WYATT L	CPT	0-0939700	0457	1
LAWDER DOUGLASS J	CPT	0-0247732	1057	3
LAWER JAMES R	CW3	W-2151208	0264	1
LAWES CHARLES O	COL	0-0135743	0755	2
LAWLER AMY K C	CPT	N-0752430	0547	1
LAWLER EDWARD J	LTC	0-0380759	0557	1
LAWLER GEORGE R	LTC	0-0203301	0454	3
LAWLER GEORGE H	CPT	0-1186513	0957	2
LAWLER JACK R	MAJ	0-0981789	1165	1
LAWLER JOHN C	MAJ	0-1642305	0764	1
LAWLER JOHN M	LTC	0-0153801	1149	3
LAWLER RUSSELL P	MAJ	0-0236528	1265	3
LAWLER THOMAS H	MAJ	0-1017337	0265	1
LAWLER VERNON J	CW3	W-2111061	0960	1
LAWLESS CHARLES E	LTC	0-1035514	0367	1
LAWLESS JOHN J	CW3	W-2203284	0263	1
LAWLESS WILBUR D	2LT	0-1823314	0745	2
LAWLEY DOUGLAS N	COL	0-0149915	0955	3
LAWLEY JAMES M	WO1	W-2146055	0653	1
LAWLIS LAUREN L	CPT	0-2033066	1060	1
LAWLIS TILDEN T	LTC	0-1060527	0666	3
LAWLOR CLARENCE A	CW3	W-2145562	0861	1
LAWLOR FRANK E	MAJ	0-0292228	1056	3
LAWLOR HARRY J	CPT	0-1309577	0450	1
LAWLOR JAMES	COL	0-0245444	0863	3
LAWLOR JAMES P	CPT	0-0522220	1045	2
LAWLOR JOHN E	COL	0-0233976	1052	2
LAWLOR JOHN T	CPT	0-1574076	0855	1
LAWLOR WILLIAM J	LTC	0-1639341	0463	1
LAWRENCE ALBERT W	LTC	0-1574942	0557	1
LAWRENCE ALLAN R	COL	0-0305208	0862	2
LAWRENCE ALVIN P	CPT	0-1688542	1057	2
LAWRENCE ANTHONY A	1LT	0-0454929	1143	2
LAWRENCE ANTONIO J	LTC	0-0454077	0258	1
LAWRENCE ARTHUR J	CPT	0-0499440	1054	1
LAWRENCE BERTRAM I	COL	0-0200311	0648	3
LAWRENCE BESSIE	LTC	N-0742101	0164	3
LAWRENCE CHARLES R	1LT	0-1172141	0245	2
LAWRENCE CHENEY E	LTC	0-0297099	0648	3
LAWRENCE CLARENCE O	LTC	0-0438275	1047	1
LAWRENCE CLAUDE W	CW2	W-2152794	1262	1
LAWRENCE EDWIN T	MAJ	0-0312368	0762	3
LAWRENCE EUGENE A	MAJ	0-1796103	1059	1
LAWRENCE GEORGE E	LTC	0-1179499	1265	1
LAWRENCE GEORGE E	1LT	0-1576280	0344	1
LAWRENCE GEORGE H	MAJ	0-1283798	1064	1
LAWRENCE GERALD P	COL	0-0142275	0648	3
LAWRENCE GUY L	CW2	W-2149078	1064	1
LAWRENCE HANS W	COL	0-0246255	0546	2
LAWRENCE HARCLO	CPT	0-1845200	0747	1
LAWRENCE HARCLO M	COL	0-0404626	0766	3
LAWRENCE HELEN V	CPT	N-0763871	0547	1
LAWRENCE HENRY F	MAJ	0-1047630	0457	1
LAWRENCE HENRY J	COL	0-0311151	0360	3
LAWRENCE HENRY S	LTC	0-0202689	0159	3
LAWRENCE HOWARD J	CPT	0-0310404	0746	2
LAWRENCE JAMES P	LTC	0-1168772	0264	1
LAWRENCE JAMES S	1LT	0-1016774	0645	2
LAWRENCE JOHN D	MAJ	0-0242799	1154	3
LAWRENCE JR HARRY L	LTC	0-2056251	0265	1
LAWRENCE JR PHILIP L	2LT	0-0528793	0545	2
LAWRENCE JR ROBERT L	CPT	0-1178542	0947	1
LAWRENCE KENT E	COL	0-0183090	0563	3

NAME	GRADE	SVC NO	DATE RET MO YR	RET CODE
LAWRENCE LELAND F	CPT	0-0213737	1061	3
LAWRENCE LESLIE L	MAJ	0-0227617	0560	3
LAWRENCE LOUIS E	MAJ	0-1295038	0761	1
LAWRENCE MILTON M	LTC	0-1303167	0262	1
LAWRENCE MIZE L	1LT	0-0966779	0552	2
LAWRENCE O B	COL	0-0450040	0755	1
LAWRENCE PATRICK A	CPT	0-0490677	0747	1
LAWRENCE PAUL M	MAJ	0-0212492	0157	3
LAWRENCE PAUL M	CPT	0-1329493	0157	1
LAWRENCE RAY E	COL	0-0221084	0263	3
LAWRENCE ROBERT C	LTC	0-0372900	0964	1
LAWRENCE ROBERT F	MAJ	0-1951102	0267	1
LAWRENCE ROBERT J	CPT	0-0326389	0945	2
LAWRENCE ROY G	MAJ	0-1181670	0562	1
LAWRENCE STEWART S	LTC	0-0278087	1154	2
LAWRENCE WILLIAM A	CW3	W-2147477	1064	1
LAWRENCE WILLIAM F	COL	0-0450744	1058	1
LAWRENCE WILLIAM T	CPT	0-0308687	1046	1
LAWRENCE WILLIS R	1LT	0-1294154	0145	2
LAWRENCE WINSTON J	LTC	0-0419312	0665	1
LAWRENZ CHARLES A	LTC	0-1784162	1061	2
LAWRIE CLYDE H	CW2	W-2206364	1263	1
LAWRY ARTHUR T	LTC	0-0914875	1264	1
LAWRY LEE L	MAJ	0-0345080	0145	1
LAWS GEORGE M	MAJ	0-0145711	0648	3
LAWS HAROLD C	MAJ	0-1540911	0661	1
LAWS JAMES R	MAJ	0-1646353	1047	2
LAWS THOMAS F	CPT	0-1100191	1059	1
LAWS WALTER L	MAJ	0-0489834	0852	1
LAWSON ALBERT H	CW2	W-2150887	1162	1
LAWSON ALLAN L	LTC	0-1288075	1062	1
LAWSON ARTHUR O	LTC	0-0386934	0860	1
LAWSON CHARLES F	LTC	0-1947010	1262	1
LAWSON DAVID S	COL	0-0312079	1058	3
LAWSON EARL L	CPT	0-1702567	0246	2
LAWSON EDWARD J	CPT	0-0498463	0947	1
LAWSON ELMER L	MAJ	0-0525778	0349	1
LAWSON GEORGE M	1LT	0-1297390	0446	1
LAWSON GLASSELLE	MAJ	0-0450612	1155	1
LAWSON HAROLD L	1LT	0-1293616	0862	2
LAWSON HARRY A	LTC	0-1550641	0563	1
LAWSON J E	CPT	0-1018109	0863	1
LAWSON JOHN O	2LT	0-1636196	0144	2
LAWSON JOHN L	LTC	0-0476714	0565	1
LAWSON JOSEPH F	1LT	0-1576281	0547	2
LAWSON JOSEPH R	CPT	0-0271457	0445	2
LAWSON RUTH E	MAJ	M-0000479	0566	2
LAWSON WARREN G	CW3	W-2151333	0567	1
LAWSON WILLIAM	CPT	0-0444561	1144	2
LAWSON WILLIAM E	LTC	0-0171028	0260	3
LAWSON WILLIAM F	MAJ	0-1594969	0460	1
LAWSON WILLIS	CPT	0-0452117	1145	1
LAWTON ERNEST L	CW4	W-2144076	1066	1
LAWTON JAMES K	COL	0-0117701	0751	3
LAWTON JOHN D	LTC	0-1578751	0963	1
LAWTON MARION R	MAJ	0-0390578	1046	2
LAWTON MORGAN B	CPT	0-0907994	1045	2
LAWTON PHILIP C	LTC	0-0447764	1051	1
LAWTON ROBERT C	LTC	0-1311793	0563	1
LAWTON RODNEY E	LTC	0-1945192	1166	1
LAWTON VERA A	MAJ	N-0700948	1044	1
LAWYER CHARLES	CPT	0-0181151	0546	2
LAWYER HIRAM L	LTC	0-0906413	0766	3
LAX MARTIN J	1LT	0-0929249	0154	2
LAXTON AMON H	LTC	0-0262896	0467	3
LAY FOREST A	MAJ	0-1286511	0446	1
LAY JAMES S	MAJ	0-1685003	1064	1
LAY JOHN W	LTC	0-1313756	0865	1
LAY RUIL C	CW3	W-2144284	0456	1
LAY SR KERMIT R	CPT	0-0890211	0451	1
LAYBOURN EUGENE P	MAJ	0-0344648	0147	1
LAYCOCK CLAUDIA G	2LT	N-0761500	0645	1
LAYCOCK WALTER E	1LT	0-1896049	0845	2
LAYDEN CHARLES K	CPT	0-1557180	0864	1
LAYDEN JAMES F	MAJ	0-4006893	1066	2

NAME	GRADE	SVC NO	DATE RET MO YR	RET CODE
LAYDEN RICHARD J	MAJ	0-1336232	1161	1
LAYER BARBARA L	1LT	N-0721825	0946	1
LAYLE HERBERT F	COL	0-0322510	1059	3
LAYLE THEODORE W	LTC	0-0370711	1266	3
LAYMAN FRED F	MAJ	0-1308657	0557	2
LAYMAN JAMES W	LTC	0-0479798	0659	2
LAYMAN PHILLIP J	MAJ	0-1109444	1160	1
LAYMAN ROBERT P	CPT	0-1696549	0345	2
LAYMON HOWARD O	LTC	0-1798587	1264	1
LAYMON RICHARD S	2LT	0-1546624	1044	2
LAYNE LORENE	2LT	N-0702269	0132	1
LAYOS JOSEPH K	CPT	0-1821600	0344	2
LAYSON JUNIUS C	MAJ	0-1825867	0261	1
LAYTHE GATHEL C	MAJ	N-0727390	0862	1
LAYTON ALAN W	CPT	0-0416409	1045	1
LAYTON ARTHUR F	LTC	0-0265010	1265	3
LAYTON BENJAMIN T	LTC	0-1290351	0463	1
LAYTON CHARLES F	LTC	0-0475963	0653	1
LAYTON JR ROBERT R	COL	0-0404693	0946	2
LAYTON LEWIS L	CW3	W-2006467	0366	3
LAYTON MYRON M	COL	0-0270907	0859	2
LAYTON WILLIAM R	COL	0-0264732	0667	3
LAYUS AGUSTIN V	2LT	0-1896457	0762	1
LAYWELL RAYMOND L	MAJ	0-1796815	0360	1
LAZAR ISIDOR	MAJ	0-0490627	1155	1
LAZAR JR WILLIAM H	1LT	0-1179500	0546	1
LAZARUS FRANK L	B G	0-0242867	0861	3
LAZARUS JACOB	1LT	0-1593016	0946	1
LAZARUS LUCIUS T	CW2	W-2151197	0961	2
LAZARUS RICHARD S	1LT	0-1059525	0646	2
LAZICKI DANIEL F	MAJ	0-1542143	0762	1
LAZZARI AMERICO	LTC	0-0288573	0867	3
LE BLANC EDWARD H	COL	0-0297080	1166	3
LE BLANC LEO P	MAJ	0-0508040	0357	1
LE BOELF JOSEPH R	LTC	0-1293617	0863	1
LE BOEUF JR HERVEY J	LTC	0-1100638	1065	1
LE BRETON EDWIN L	MAJ	0-1104951	0763	1
LE CLAIR ADRIEN D	CW4	W-2104232	0157	1
LE CLAIR ARTHUR A	CPT	0-1080639	0157	1
LE CLAIR EDWARD C	LTC	0-1647573	0164	1
LE CLAIR ERNEST M	CW3	W-2002985	0963	1
LE CLAIR ISIDORE G	LTC	0-1822414	0965	1
LE CLEAR FRANCIS E	CPT	0-0393420	0561	1
LE CLERC LEON A	CPT	0-1044277	0955	1
LE CLERG VERNON C	COL	0-0267772	0463	3
LE COMPTE HOWARD C	CW3	W-2151203	0365	1
LE COMPTE THEODORE L	1LT	0-1321221	0246	1
LE COUNT ETHEL G	1LT	N-0772334	0446	1
LE COUNT LOUIS K	LTC	0-0234811	1065	3
LE CRAW ARTHUR E	LTC	0-0175791	1061	3
LE CRAW JOHN W	LTC	0-0116667	0945	2
LE CRONE NAOMI L	1LT	R-0000106	0247	1
LE CROY KERMIT P	MAJ	0-1296872	0866	3
LE DOUX EDWARD L	CPT	0-0480613	0848	2
LE DUC VINCENT J	CW3	W-2205178	1266	1
LE FEVRE JR GEORGE L	LTC	0-0223104	0955	3
LE FLEUR WAYNE O	LTC	0-1554926	0762	1
LE GATH EVERETT A	LTC	0-0289278	0167	3
LE GAULT MILTON L	LTC	0-1291138	0461	1
LE GORE LOY C	CW3	W-2148438	1065	1
LE GRAND EDWIN C	MAJ	0-0159534	0456	1
LE HARDY JULIUS C	1LT	0-2204117	1054	2
LE JEUNE JOSEPH H	CW3	W-2146341	1162	1
LE LACHEUR EMBERT A	LTC	0-0256180	1053	3
LE LIEVRE EFFIE	MAJ	N-0757474	1163	1
LE MAR DORIS	1LT	N-0736265	0746	1
LE MASTER FRED P	CW4	W-2121143	0864	1
LE MASTER IRA V	LTC	0-0261820	0466	3
LE MASTER ROBERT L	MAJ	0-4005819	0267	1
LE MASTER ROGER H	LTC	0-1043149	0760	1
LE MAY DAVID M	CW2	W-2148170	0959	1
LE MAY EDWARD F	MAJ	0-1547695	0561	2
LE MAY HAROLD W	CPT	0-1325501	1046	2
LE MCN TRUE E	MAJ	0-1951698	0564	1
LE NOIR JOSEPH T	CPT	0-1307984	0163	1

NAME	GRADE	SVC NO	DATE RET MO YR	RET CODE
LE PAGE MILTON E	LTC	0-0327756	C262	3
LE QUIRE JOHN B	CW3	W-2145740	1160	1
LE TANG LINUS L	LTC	0-0572401	0562	2
LE TRENT JOHN A	LTC	0-1304246	1067	1
LE VALLEY MILLER W	LTC	0-1048069	0562	1
LE VAN FRANKLIN P	CPT	0-0509727	1045	2
LE VAN RAYMOND E	LTC	0-1996661	C465	1
LE VASSEUR EDWARD F	CPT	0-1322048	C347	2
LE VASSEUR PROSPER J	CPT	0-0966290	0762	1
LE VEY ARTHUR E	LTC	0-0348696	0465	3
LE VIEN BERTRAM M	CPT	0-1030795	0662	1
LE VINE SAUL F	CPT	C-0355083	0845	1
LE VINES CHESTER W	CW4	W-2142242	C460	1
LE VITIN MORRIS L	LTC	0-0480611	0663	3
LEA EDWIN B	CW3	W-2146256	0962	1
LEA ELLIS	LTC	0-0288044	C859	1
LEA LUDWELL L	2LT	0-C415751	1042	1
LEA THOMAS R	LTC	C-036593C	0859	1
LEACH ALBERT A	CPT	0-C388065	0846	2
LEACH EDWARD M	CPT	0-1822289	C361	1
LEACH ELEANORE A	1LT	N-0733227	1145	1
LEACH HAROLD D	LTC	0-1995468	C962	2
LEACH HENRY C	COL	C-0358301	0862	1
LEACH HERMAN F	MAJ	C-1296871	C158	1
LEACH JOHN E	CPT	0-0444915	1045	2
LEACH JOSEPH A	CW3	W-2147055	C161	1
LEACH LOREN F	LTC	0-0949332	0866	1
LEACH RAYMOND E	LTC	0-0369957	0766	3
LEACH RICHARD F	MAJ	C-0338387	0946	2
LEACH TIMOTHY	MAJ	C-1047200	0361	1
LEACH WILLIAM P	LTC	0-0365423	0462	1
LEACHMAN THOMAS E	LTC	0-0358474	0461	1
LEACOCK CHARLES E	LTC	0-1913412	C867	1
LEACY BLANCHARD	1LT	0-2010583	0547	2
LEADBEATER HERBERT B	MAJ	0-0456112	1047	2
LEADER JR GLENN C	MAJ	C-0388761	0845	2
LEADER SAMUEL A	COL	0-0311834	C261	3
LEADY CLAUDE L	CW3	W-2152971	1265	1
LEAF JENNIE E	2LT	N-0724135	C244	1
LEAF JOHN M	MAJ	C-0955899	0765	2
LEAF LOUIS	COL	0-0268895	1166	3
LEAFSTONE JOHN H	1LT	0-1702998	C748	1
LEAGUE EDGAR A	CW3	W-2001718	1059	3
LEAGUE JAMES W	1LT	0-1598917	1047	2
LEAH LOUIS C	MAJ	C-1306109	0461	1
LEAHEY EDWARD W	LTC	C-0192077	1062	3
LEAHEY WALLACE J	LTC	0-1327017	0967	1
LEAHY ARTHUR F	CW3	W-2150714	0863	1
LEAHY ARTHUR L	1LT	C-1170822	1145	2
LEAHY BERNARD P	LTC	0-1585760	C762	1
LEAHY MARY E	MAJ	N-0736246	C166	1
LEAHY ROBERT G	MAJ	C-1308837	C165	1
LEAHY WALTER R	MAJ	0-1798868	1160	1
LEAIRD JR JOHN B	CW3	W-2147151	1062	1
LEAK EDWARD D	LTC	0-0953561	0567	1
LEAKE BAIN	CPT	C-1701359	C545	2
LEAKE HADLEY W	LTC	0-0445218	0247	2
LEAKE HARRY L	LTC	0-0116670	0753	3
LEAKE JOHN L	1LT	0-1321192	1147	2
LEAKEN RICHARD M	MAJ	0-1081659	0365	1
LEAKINS JOHN A	2LT	C-0106499	0720	1
LEAL GEORGE P	MAJ	C-1046169	1160	1
LEAMAN LEONARD S	1LT	C-1057498	C346	2
LEAMING ANDREW W	MAJ	C-0376979	0647	1
LEAMING ARTHUR C	1LT	0-1306605	C345	2
LEAMING EARL K	COL	0-0198402	0759	3
LEAMING JEREMIAH C	CPT	0-0177457	0662	3
LEAMING WILLIAM V	1LT	0-0537583	0545	2
LEAMON NICHOLAS J	MAJ	C-1102814	1C59	1
LEAMY FRANK P	COL	0-0900549	1265	3
LEAP ARTHUR G	LTC	0-1108802	0960	1
LEAP FRANCIS G	MAJ	C-1846311	0960	1
LEAPHEART SHELTON R	WO1	W-2145907	0657	1
LEAR IRA H	MAJ	C-0992283	0166	1
LEAR LESLIE A	CPT	0-1823016	C162	1

NAME	GRADE	SVC NO	DATE RET MO YR	RET CODE
LEARD ROBERT N	LTC	0-0338763	0860	1
LEARN GERALD H	MAJ	C-1546667	1262	1
LEARNED NORMA G	MAJ	J-0100135	1166	1
LEARNIHAN JR THOMAS	2LT	0-1305798	0757	2
LEARY ALEXANDER	MAJ	0-2008673	0365	1
LEARY DANIEL F	LTC	0-1302321	1262	1
LEARY EDGAR T	CPT	0-0506474	104N	2
LEARY EDWARD H	CPT	0-050437C	0343	2
LEARY EDWARD J	COL	0-0329499	0561	3
LEARY FRANCIS P	COL	0-0290627	1066	3
LEARY FRANK R	MAJ	0-0537476	0346	2
LEARY HOWARD R	LTC	0-0349255	1162	3
LEARY JR JOHN J	CPT	0-1016332	0147	1
LEARY JR WARREN F	LTC	0-1313422	0866	1
LEARY LEONARD W	1LT	C-1107546	0345	2
LEARY MARY E	MAJ	N-0751228	0865	1
LEARY WILBUR A	LTC	0-1000256	0457	1
LEARY WILLIAM E	LTC	0-0391609	0461	1
LEAS JOHN B	MAJ	0-1325302	0961	1
LEAS LARRY D	LTC	0-1290442	0861	1
LEASE STANLEY E	LTC	0-0355449	1055	1
LEASK ARTHUR A	MAJ	0-2021264	1165	1
LEASK GEORGE C	MAJ	0-0122826	1144	2
LEASURE CLYDE R	LTC	0-0186047	1148	3
LEASURE DAN S	LTC	0-1101088	0163	1
LEASURE ELMER F	MAJ	C-0106908	0754	3
LEASURE THOMAS J	MAJ	0-0287202	1161	3
LEASURE WILLIAM C	1LT	C-0403832	0244	2
LEATH HAROLD W	LTC	0-0323298	1161	3
LEATH JAMES G	CW3	W-2141879	0962	1
LEATHAM LOUIS S	LTC	0-0385131	1264	3
LEATHERMAN HAROLD E	2LT	0-1320469	1051	2
LEATHERMAN HARRY L	MAJ	C-0185907	0648	3
LEATHERMAN JAY C	LTC	0-1177499	0567	1
LEATHERS CECIL C	CPT	0-0502771	1047	1
LEATHERS CHARLES A	CPT	0-2036665	0448	2
LEATHERS ERNEST B	1LT	0-0288835	1264	3
LEATHERWOOD ABRAHAM	LTC	0-0228441	0465	3
LEAVELL FRED W	CPT	0-0288408	0356	3
LEAVELL LEWIS I	COL	0-0141686	0148	2
LEAVENS EDWIN T	CPT	0-1293274	0147	1
LEAVER ELMER R	CPT	0-2025264	0858	1
LEAVER THOMAS C	MAJ	0-022481C	0151	3
LEAVITT ARTHUR S	CPT	0-0297115	0446	2
LEAVITT ERNEST E	LTC	0-0244274	1160	3
LEAVITT GEORGE H	COL	C-0172183	0556	2
LEAVITT HARRY	CW4	W-2104231	0552	2
LEAVITT JAMES W	CW2	W-3200452	0267	1
LEAVITT JOHN M	CW2	W-2105967	0753	1
LEAVITT LEE R	2LT	0-2007032	1145	2
LEAVITT LEIGHTON T	CW2	W-214710C	0661	1
LEAVITT MERVYN W	COL	C-0430745	0261	1
LEAVITT MILO D	CPT	0-0477196	0345	2
LEAVITT MORRILL W	MAJ	0-0292251	0945	2
LEAVITT RAY M	MAJ	0-1648686	0865	1
LEAVITT STANLEY L	MAJ	0-1331298	1264	1
LEAVITT WENDELL D	2LT	0-0529115	0645	1
LEAX WILLIAM F	CPT	C-1295039	0546	2
LEAZAR MARVIN F	MAJ	0-1186044	0459	1
LEBAR JOSEPH	CW3	W-2110684	0357	1
LEBAY WILLIAM H	MAJ	0-0348306	0358	3
LEBB WALTER J	2LT	0-1300181	0994	2
LEBEL LUCIEN F	MAJ	0-2036666	0461	1
LEBER EUGENE I	LTC	0-0317478	1059	1
LEBLANC JR JOSEPH R	CPT	0-0982986	0161	1
LEBOEUF WILFRED F	CPT	0-0484848	1158	2
LEBRCN EDUVIGIS	1LT	0-0155976	0648	3
LEBRON LAMAR C	LTC	0-0168208	0959	3
LEBRUM ERNEST	CPT	0-0513412	0847	1
LECHLEITER EDWARD A	MAJ	0-0240348	0646	2
LECHMAN OTTO	MAJ	C-1648354	C854	1
LECHWAR MARTIN J	MAJ	0-0410868	0358	1
LECKAR LEO	MAJ	0-1648691	1263	1
LECKART HARVEY H	CPT	0-0487056	0246	2
LECKLITNER MYRON D	MAJ	0-1693315	0446	2

NAME	GRADE	SVC NO	DATE RET MO YR	RET CODE
LECKVARCIK NICHOLAS	WO1	W-2145738	0863	2
LECKY JOSEPH L	1LT	0-0281110	0946	2
LECLERC ADRIAN	CW4	W-2113731	0555	1
LECOCQ HENRY J	1LT	0-0237345	C255	3
LEDBETTER ARVOR M	CPT	0-0176536	1055	3
LEDBETTER CARL E	COL	0-0182694	C754	3
LEDBETTER CARL S	COL	0-0410688	1061	1
LEDBETTER CHARLES D	CPT	0-0385234	0943	1
LEDBETTER LAVERN E	LTC	0-1330327	C766	1
LEDBETTER ONIE C	CW2	W-2108961	0454	1
LEDBETTER PAUL L	CW2	W-2115848	0157	1
LEDBETTER VIRGIL K	MAJ	0-1824049	0258	1
LEDBETTER WILLIAM B	COL	0-0105674	0155	3
LEDBETTER WILLIAM M	MAJ	0-1950549	0860	1
LEDDON JR JAMES A	LTC	0-0426288	0263	1
LEDDY CHARLES P	MAJ	C-0372277	1066	3
LEDDY JOHN F	LTC	0-1542689	1063	1
LEDDY ORVILLE J	1LT	0-0351174	C745	2
LEDDY SAM W	LTC	0-1297058	1160	1
LEDERER WOLFGANG	CPT	0-1012737	C446	2
LEDESMAGDIAZ FRANK R	CPT	0-0482711	0746	2
LEDFORD JAMES J	2LT	0-1328496	1045	2
LEDFORD JR LARK	1LT	0-1306110	C546	1
LEDGERWOOD MARVIN C	1LT	0-0348617	C942	2
LEDIG ROY E	LTC	0-0409322	0961	1
LEDLIE JOHN P	CPT	0-1575409	C347	2
LEDOUX ALFRED C	LTC	0-0485430	1045	2
LEE AARON A	MAJ	C-1285776	0557	1
LEE ALAN S	1LT	C-1310464	0546	2
LEE ANNA V	2LT	N-0723064	C845	1
LEE ARVEL L	CW2	W-2142397	C861	1
LEE AUBRY E	CPT	0-1284579	1150	2
LEE AUGUSTUS S	CPT	0-0212283	C757	3
LEE BENOTE H	LTC	0-0333168	0350	3
LEE BUNNOE H	2LT	0-0108808	0833	1
LEE BYRON M	1LT	0-15819C2	1145	2
LEE CARL R	CPT	0-1307038	1047	2
LEE CARLETON H	CPT	0-0498771	0844	1
LEE CHANG W	LTC	0-0313400	1058	3
LEE CHARLES E	LTC	0-0477061	0246	2
LEE CHARLES W	LTC	0-0401958	0261	1
LEE CHESTER A	LTC	C-0172554	C859	1
LEE CLARENCE J	COL	0-0289619	0747	2
LEE CLARENCE J	MAJ	0-1309077	0762	1
LEE CLAUDE F	LTC	0-2034751	0864	1
LEE CLIFFORD M	CPT	0-1999851	1052	1
LEE CLIFTON H	1LT	C-0971261	0461	2
LEE CURTIS R	1LT	0-1032758	104N	1
LEE DARREL G	CPT	0-1294495	C446	2
LEE DONALD R	LTC	0-0922411	0263	1
LEE DONALD R	MAJ	0-1057500	0567	1
LEE DUDLEY	CW3	W-2148123	0659	1
LEE EDWARD V	CW2	W-2148143	0461	1
LEE EDWIN C M	MAJ	C-1101090	1046	2
LEE ELEANOR D	CPT	N-0703072	0747	1
LEE EMMETT C	LTC	0-0125145	C945	2
LEE ERIC	COL	0-0193691	0142	1
LEE ERNA F	MAJ	N-0783864	0165	3
LEE ERNEST W	MAJ	C-1306606	0256	1
LEE EUGENE	MAJ	C-0985115	0363	1
LEE FAIRMAN B	LTC	0-0237131	C656	3
LEE FELIX L	CW3	W-2153169	0766	1
LEE FRANK	CW3	W-2143939	0757	1
LEE FREDERICK	1LT	0-1578755	1052	1
LEE GEORGE YUN	CW3	W-2147383	C166	1
LEE GERALD V	LTC	C-0331038	1066	3
LEE GLENN A	LTC	C-1112816	0864	1
LEE GORDON S	COL	0-0204538	C363	3
LEE GROVER C	CPT	0-0499363	C853	1
LEE HAN K	LTC	0-1645756	0763	1
LEE HARLBERT R	MAJ	C-0424525	1060	1
LEE HAROLD D	LTC	C-1100193	0657	1
LEE HAROLD R	LTC	0-0274425	0355	3
LEE HARRELL F	LTC	C-0249781	C267	3
LEE HARRY S	COL	0-1642311	C567	1

NAME	GRADE	SVC NO	DATE RET MO YR	RET CODE
LEE HENRY P	1LT	0-1105606	0344	2
LEE HENRY H	CW2	W-2147117	0961	1
LEE HENRY L	MAJ	0-0247105	0660	1
LEE IRA L	CPT	0-1578756	0346	1
LEE IRWIN	LTC	0-0888575	0964	1
LEE JACK G	COL	0-0288223	0967	3
LEE JACK W	1LT	0-1315954	1045	2
LEE JAMES A	CW2	W-2144584	0761	1
LEE JAMES S	MAJ	0-0445137	0264	2
LEE JESSE V	CPT	0-1637908	0854	1
LEE JOHN	CW3	W-2149261	0862	1
LEE JOHN C	CPT	0-0544834	0950	2
LEE JOHN G	LTC	0-1102750	0457	1
LEE JOHN GRIDL	MAJ	0-0908106	1045	2
LEE JOHN L	COL	0-0164294	0946	2
LEE JOHN W	COL	0-0126000	1055	3
LEE JOHNSON C	LTC	0-0472618	0964	3
LEE JONAS R	LTC	0-0154682	1149	3
LEE JOSEPH R	CW4	W-2113908	0659	1
LEE JR BRUNER S	LTC	0-1167510	0963	1
LEE JR CLARENCE D	MAJ	0-1923588	1064	1
LEE JR DEN F	1LT	0-1306943	0846	2
LEE JR FRANK J	CPT	0-1324343	1047	2
LEE JR FRANK Y F	MAJ	0-0976053	0766	1
LEE JR HERMAN A	1LT	0-0462589	0544	2
LEE JR JESTWIN E	CPT	0-1646356	0946	2
LEE JR JOHN F	COL	0-0234448	0457	3
LEE JR MAJOR	CW3	W-2151726	0666	2
LEE JR ROBERT F	LTC	0-1309151	0261	1
LEE JULIAN R	CPT	0-1341887	0158	1
LEE JULIUS	LTC	0-0232C41	0248	1
LEE KIRWAN D	LTC	0-1325134	0465	1
LEE LAIN L	WO1	W-2108771	0744	2
LEE LAWRENCE J	MAJ	0-0967826	0465	1
LEE LEOPOLD L	MAJ	0-0501604	0547	2
LEE LESLIE E	2LT	0-0108261	1038	1
LEE LLOYD L	CPT	0-4026388	0965	1
LEE LOUIS W	1LT	0-1319077	0446	2
LEE MALVEN F	CW3	W-2147078	0265	1
LEE MARION M	CPT	0-0164459	1128	1
LEE MARY E	2LT	N-0726957	1144	1
LEE MARY V	1LT	N-0778332	0448	1
LEE MATTHEW J	CW2	W-2144028	1154	1
LEE MAXWELL F	1LT	0-1825479	1145	2
LEE MAYNARD E	CW4	W-2101263	1158	1
LEE NEWELL B	LTC	0-0156297	1055	3
LEE ORVILLE F	CPT	0-1307430	0661	1
LEE OSCAR B	1LT	0-C475875	0746	1
LEE PAUL	MAJ	0-0889890	0257	1
LEE PAUL D	MAJ	0-0228325	1046	1
LEE PHILIP A	LTC	0-0197031	1C59	3
LEE POWELL A	CPT	0-2037732	0360	2
LEE RANDAL E	LTC	0-0256242	1056	3
LEE RAYMOND A	LTC	0-0154428	1049	3
LEE RAYMOND C	CPT	0-0953544	0356	2
LEE RAYMOND J	1LT	0-1312023	0246	2
LEE RAYMOND N	COL	0-0269596	0360	3
LEE RICHARD P	LTC	0-1287024	C756	1
LEE RICHARD H	COL	0-0182052	0162	3
LEE RICHARD M	MAJ	0-1014198	0965	1
LEE ROBERT A	MAJ	0-2033685	0465	1
LEE ROBERT B	LTC	0-1579928	0761	1
LEE ROBERT F	CPT	0-027933C	0143	2
LEE ROBERT F	CPT	0-0424577	1045	1
LEE RCBERT F	MAJ	0-1310609	1063	1
LEE ROBERT F	LTC	0-1635012	1063	1
LEE ROBERT E	CPT	0-2263347	0366	1
LEE ROBERT F	CW3	W-2151337	0965	1
LEE ROBERT H	CW3	W-220505C	0765	1
LEE ROBERT H C	MAJ	0-0461762	0856	2
LEE ROBERT J	CPT	0-1534789	1048	2
LEE ROBERT N	MAJ	0-1316045	1162	1
LEE ROLAND P	LTC	0-0921161	0167	3
LEE ROY E	WO1	W-2147145	1154	1
LEE ROY W	MAJ	0-0305339	0446	2

292-560 O - 68 - 15

NAME	GRADE	SVC NO	DATE RET MO YR	RET CODE
LEE RUSSELL K	LTC	0-0503974	0965	2
LEE SMITH	LTC	0-0110741	0946	2
LEE THEODORE C	CPT	0-0311815	0145	2
LEE THOMAS E	MAJ	0-2033637	1061	1
LEE THOMAS F	LTC	0-1591885	0562	1
LEE THOMAS S	LTC	0-1824481	1066	3
LEE THURSTON L	MAJ	0-1166112	0359	1
LEE WILFRED C	2LT	0-1340784	0647	2
LEE WILLARD D	MAJ	0-1341800	1060	1
LEE WILLIAM	LTC	0-1651785	0966	1
LEE WILLIAM A	MAJ	0-1589986	0457	1
LEE WILLIAM B	COL	0-0258590	0764	1
LEE WILLIAM D	MAJ	0-1184092	1162	1
LEE WILLIAM D	CW3	W-2147729	0463	1
LEE WILLIAM E	CPT	0-1305799	0546	2
LEE WILLIAM E	CPT	0-2012060	1058	2
LEE WILLIAM EL	2LT	0-1307836	1144	1
LEE WILLIAM F	CPT	0-0203484	0863	3
LEE WILLIAM J	LTC	0-0383424	0461	1
LEE WILLIAM M	CPT	0-1109447	1046	2
LEE WILLIAM P	LTC	0-0153910	0448	2
LEE WILLIAM R	LTC	0-1291294	0763	1
LEE WILLIAM T	MAJ	0-0310099	0346	2
LEE WILSON A	CW2	W-2209845	0763	1
LEE WILTON A	LTC	0-0349581	0464	1
LEE 3RD ASBURY W	COL	0-0336510	0247	2
LEEB HENRY L	MAJ	0-0205028	0163	3
LEECH HARRY D	LTC	0-1558397	0765	1
LEECH HENRY F	MAJ	0-0473534	0360	3
LEEDLE ROBERT B	2LT	0-1324630	0644	2
LEEDOM JOE W	COL	0-0131231	0749	3
LEEDS DANIEL J	CPT	0-0320780	0645	2
LEEDS HARVEY S	LTC	0-1646364	0862	1
LEEDS JR CHARLES T	COL	0-0267703	0166	3
LEEGATE CARNEY B	CW2	W-2145564	0959	1
LEEK CALVIN R	LTC	0-0346816	0560	1
LEEK JAMES W	LTC	0-0319740	0567	3
LEEK NORMAN M	MAJ	0-1018141	1062	1
LEEL CHARLES W	LTC	0-0311695	0567	3
LEEN MARVIN J	CW4	W-2109843	0659	2
LEENERTS THEODORE H	CPT	0-0335498	0144	2
LEEP CHARLES M	CPT	0-1897720	1057	1
LEER EDWIN H	COL	0-0341910	1158	1
LEER RALPH H	LTC	0-0298927	1047	2
LEFROY ARTHUR	MAJ	0-0475405	0246	2
LEES GORDON S	LTC	0-1110068	0262	1
LEES HARRY C	CPT	0-1556016	0647	2
LEES HOWARD S	CPT	0-1290621	0146	2
LEES RICHARD S	1LT	0-1173689	0545	1
LEESE MERLE E	MAJ	0-0235223	1265	3
LEET WILLIAM L	COL	0-0183058	0962	3
LEETCH MARION L	CPT	0-1644946	0864	1
LEETY ROSS E	LTC	0-1287198	0166	1
LEFEBVRE HENRY C	1LT	0-0244451	1058	3
LEFF ABRAHAM	COL	0-0414231	0267	3
LEFF WILLIAM A	LTC	0-0374490	0445	1
LEFFEL VERNE M	LTC	0-1309078	0963	1
LEFFERTS JAMES C	MAJ	0-2203048	0763	1
LEFFERTS WILLIAM C	LTC	0-0252129	0466	3
LEFFINGWELL ROBERT B	MAJ	0-0494119	0145	2
LEFFINGWELL W M	LTC	0-0134805	0656	3
LEFKOVICH HAROLD H	2LT	0-1057504	0845	2
LEFKOVITS AARON M	LTC	0-0319905	0761	3
LEFKOWITZ MICHAEL P	CPT	0-0404777	1045	2
LEFLER DANIEL S	MAJ	0-0335514	0157	1
LEFLER JAMES H	LTC	0-0534807	1062	1
LEFLER JEWELL C	CPT	0-1320905	0846	1
LEFLER ROBERT C	MAJ	0-1165188	0446	2
LEFORS ARCHIE O	LTC	0-0247265	0563	3
LEFTON IRVIN M	CPT	0-1533120	0747	2
LEFTWICH JOE	LTC	0-0328045	0446	2
LEFTWICH JOHN V	MAJ	0-1010263	0456	1
LEGAN WANDLE	MAJ	0-1798018	1060	1
LEGARE JR EUGENE V	MAJ	0-0449978	0762	1
LEGAS FRANK	CPT	0-0981278	0960	1

NAME	GRADE	SVC NO	DATE RET MO YR	RET CODE
LEGAULT LEO A	CPT	0-0478681	0655	1
LEGER HERBERT J	COL	0-0503272	0664	1
LEGER LEROY A	LTC	0-0451262	0857	1
LEGER LOUIS P	CW3	W-2150842	0659	1
LEGG JACKIE C	MAJ	0-2262713	0463	1
LEGG LLOYD F	COL	0-0163785	0861	3
LEGG PHILLIP N	CW2	W-2142867	1056	1
LEGG ROBERT C	LTC	0-2033157	0367	1
LEGGE TOLLEY B	CW2	W-2147313	0364	2
LEGGETT JOHN W	COL	0-0166591	0948	3
LEGGETT JR JAMES L	CPT	0-0371518	1046	2
LEGGETT KENNETH E	MAJ	0-0989450	1167	1
LEGION ELBERT C	MAJ	0-1051249	0259	1
LEGNER HAROLD J	LTC	0-1637912	0764	1
LEGNER LUCIUS S	COL	0-0280594	0658	3
LEGRO ARCHIE W	MAJ	0-0171358	0351	3
LEGRO WILBUR H	CW3	W-2205509	0365	1
LEHAN ANDREW F	LTC	0-1056776	0965	1
LEHANE DECLAN R	MAJ	0-1039467	0661	1
LEHANE LAWRENCE L	MAJ	0-0325977	1045	2
LEHDE JOHN R	LTC	0-0327763	0459	2
LEHDE RAYMOND C	CPT	0-0227454	1262	3
LEHMAN ALFRED C	1LT	0-0242796	0860	3
LEHMAN EMORY V	LTC	0-0289562	0162	1
LEHMAN ERNEST F	LTC	0-1637513	0466	1
LEHMAN HENRY E	LTC	0-0323954	0346	2
LEHMAN LEON N	CW2	W-2209491	0361	1
LEHMAN LESTER	CPT	0-1689061	0246	2
LEHMAN ORIN A	CPT	0-0440430	0947	1
LEHMAN RAY	CW4	W-2106911	1054	1
LEHMAN ROBERT H	MAJ	0-1320955	0358	1
LEHMAN ROBERT H	LTC	0-2045212	0563	1
LEHMANN CORNELIUS	LTC	0-0157864	0555	3
LEHMANN RICHARD C	LTC	0-1044589	1163	1
LEHMANN ROBERT A	MAJ	0-2024300	0560	1
LEHMBERG FRITZ G	1LT	0-0490049	0145	2
LEHN DALLAS G	2LT	0-1296225	0445	2
LEHNE CHRISTIAN	LTC	0-0403234	0661	1
LEHNERT DIEDRICH	LTC	0-0205803	0858	3
LEHNERT FRANK H	LTC	0-0397308	0966	3
LEHNING JOHN W	WO1	W-2113091	0944	2
LEHNUS ELWOOD G	MAJ	0-0978662	0765	1
LEHR FREDERIC B	MAJ	0-0225632	0764	3
LEHR MILTON A	LTC	0-0182881	0956	3
LEHR WILLIAM	COL	0-0228253	0362	3
LEHRBASS MARY J	2LT	N-0784279	1045	1
LEHRER JOHN J	CW2	W-2147656	0456	1
LEIB CHARLES A	COL	0-0297328	1266	3
LEIBBRAND PHILO H	COL	0-0251525	1154	2
LEIBECKE ROBERT C	MAJ	0-1585763	0864	1
LEIBEL ROBERT M	2LT	0-2008404	0350	1
LEIBERT JULIUS A	LTC	0-0153418	0648	3
LEIBLY FRANK J	LTC	0-0290198	0463	3
LEIBOLD JOHN P	CPT	0-1726014	0647	2
LEIBROCK MARK S	MAJ	0-0311450	0662	1
LEIBSLE ROY W	COL	0-0119574	0352	3
LEICHTLING JULIUS J	CPT	0-0538312	0646	1
LEICHTMAN DAVID L	MAJ	0-0210039	0446	1
LEICK RUSSEL K	LTC	0-1338479	0867	1
LEIDAL FLOYD L	MAJ	0-0915703	0664	3
LEIDEL FREDERICK	LTC	0-0302670	0854	1
LEIDENHEIMER LARRY H	COL	0-0316064	1060	1
LEIDLEF FRANZ	1LT	0-0553800	0545	2
LEIGH ALFRED H	LTC	0-0241499	0464	3
LEIGH GEORGE H	1LT	0-2007898	1051	1
LEIGH KEITH B	MAJ	0-1845304	1059	1
LEIGH RALPH C	LTC	0-0450311	0960	1
LEIGH THOMAS E	LTC	0-0521923	0763	1
LEIGH THOMAS L	LTC	0-0130704	0855	3
LEIGHT WILLIAM J	COL	0-0317326	0261	1
LEIGHTENHEIMER W E	1LT	0-1184253	1047	2
LEIGHTON ALBERT C	CPT	0-0940777	0957	1
LEIGHTON GEORGE E	CW3	W-2007509	0866	3
LEIGHTON HENRY B	MAJ	0-0244328	1144	2
LEIGHTON HENRY P	MAJ	0-0515335	0549	1

NAME	GRADE	SVC NO	DATE RET MO YR	RET CODE
LEIGHTON JEFFRED W	COL	0-0246649	0254	1
LEIGHTON RICHARD A	MAJ	0-2096992	0665	1
LEIGHTTY RALPH S	MAJ	0-1535931	0564	1
LEIGHTY MAX	LTC	0-0420938	0357	1
LEIGHTY SR LESTER S	MAJ	0-1303519	1160	1
LEIHY CHARLES W	COL	0-0236216	0245	2
LEIKER SEVERIN F	1LT	0-0486675	0356	1
LEIKER VICTOR C	CPT	0-0372027	0146	2
LEIKIND ELIAS R	CPT	0-0335099	0944	2
LEIMKUEHLER PAUL F	2LT	0-1328159	0446	2
LEIN MARTIN F	CPT	0-0360789	1144	1
LEINBACH CHARLES L	WO1	W-2103134	0356	1
LEINEN CLETUS N	MAJ	0-0486080	0454	1
LEININGER OLIVER C	MAJ	0-0949480	0866	1
LEINSTER ESTEN B	LTC	0-0331830	0360	1
LEINWEBER ARTHUR R	COL	0-0302549	1265	3
LEINWEBER CHARLEY A	CPT	0-0490051	0251	1
LEINWEBER RAYMOND	WO1	W-2154869	1053	1
LEIPOLD CARL M	LTC	0-1574470	1152	1
LEISER GEORGE F	MAJ	0-1587464	0856	1
LEISER WILLIAM W	1LT	0-1018935	0547	2
LEISK JAMES H	MAJ	0-1315179	1266	3
LEISTER MICHAEL A	LTC	0-0404222	0761	1
LEISTER ORVILLE T	CW4	W-2122145	0563	1
LEITCH KENNETH H	COL	0-0338022	0167	1
LEITCH WILLIAM H	MAJ	0-0541958	0-48	1
LEITEM EDWARD E	CW3	W-2147707	0263	1
LEITER CLEMENT L	CW2	W-2150707	1060	1
LEITH ALEXANDER	LTC	0-0336121	0760	1
LEITH MILTON B	COL	0-0237723	0562	3
LEITNAKER JOHN M	LTC	0-2035011	1262	1
LEITNER CHARLES J	MAJ	0-1175489	0466	1
LEITNER GEORGE R	CPT	0-1296049	0658	1
LEITZ FRED	1LT	0-1945403	0653	1
LEITZEL HARRY M	LTC	0-1637915	1165	1
LEITZELL ROBERT A	LTC	0-1821883	0861	1
LEITZINGER W A E	COL	0-0190066	0958	3
LEJA EDWARD	1LT	0-0546334	0448	1
LEKNISKAS BENEDICT C	WO1	W-2115383	1043	2
LEKOM BEATRICE T	MAJ	N-0751468	0766	1
LELAND FRANK E	MAJ	0-0472663	0947	1
LELAND HERBERT A	CW2	W-2208608	0765	1
LELAND ROBERT O	1LT	0-0454372	0745	2
LELAND WALTER I	LTC	0-0327748	1060	3
LELAND WALTER J	1LT	0-0375924	0845	2
LELEKIS PETER J	LTC	0-1300182	0763	1
LELEVICH JOSEPH J	CPT	0-1112818	0349	1
LELONG ROBERT L	LTC	0-1341447	0966	1
LEMAITRE PAUL G	CPT	0-0508039	0945	2
LEMAN BROOKE W	LTC	0-0298598	1052	3
LEMAN LLOYD O	LTC	0-0193319	1157	3
LEMAN LOUIS	MAJ	0-1108809	0761	1
LEMANN ARTHUR A	MAJ	0-0373961	0246	2
LEMAY CHARLES M	CPT	0-1100197	0845	1
LEMBACH CARL L	CW2	W-2115977	0547	1
LEMBURG B HOMER	1LT	0-1292354	0746	1
LEMCHAK JOHN	CW2	W-2145302	0562	1
LEMCKE MARY F	2LT	N-0775723	0245	1
LEMENS WILLIAM V	LTC	0-0263453	1060	3
LEMERIS PAUL E	CW4	W-2125088	0262	1
LEMERISE DAVID B	MAJ	0-1285608	0461	1
LEMIEUX JOSEPH W	MAJ	0-0953559	0563	1
LEMING HOWELL E	LTC	0-0269703	0260	3
LEMIRE HENRY J	LTC	0-0371376	1160	1
LEMKE GORDON H	MAJ	0-1049950	1062	1
LEMKE WALTER R	COL	0-0321373	1159	3
LEMLEY FRED A	LTC	0-0279776	0463	1
LEMM RALPH H	MAJ	0-0241617	0-52	3
LEMM ROBERT J	MAJ	0-2009228	0764	1
LEMME RAYMOND W	MAJ	0-1649010	0164	1
LEMMON GLENN R	COL	0-0110742	0752	3
LEMMON JR JOHN M	LTC	0-0217400	1047	2
LEMMON MARY J K	MAJ	N-0778255	1265	1
LEMMOND JR WALTER H	LTC	0-0225644	0664	3
LEMMOND PARS H	LTC	0-0212125	0659	3

NAME	GRADE	SVC NO	DATE RET MO YR	RET CODE
LEMOINE CLAIRE	1LT	N-0745107	0646	1
LEMOINE HERBERT G	1LT	0-1861996	1053	2
LEMON BURTON J	COL	0-0107889	0648	3
LEMON CARL R	CPT	0-0284044	0244	2
LEMON CECIL W	MAJ	0-0436664	0446	1
LEMON CHARLES C	1LT	0-1285256	1145	2
LEMON FRED C	CW2	W-2115965	0545	2
LEMON GEORGE F	1LT	0-1100199	1043	2
LEMON JOSEPH F	LTC	0-0399815	0663	1
LEMONS CARL A	1LT	0-2262869	0267	1
LEMOS CARLOS R	CW3	W-2146971	1163	1
LEMP HARRY J	MAJ	0-0126189	0243	2
LEMP JOHN	COL	0-0273966	0367	3
LEMP WILLIAM A	LTC	0-0360815	1262	1
LENAHAN DANIEL W	COL	0-0223503	0464	3
LENAHAN GEORGE T	MAJ	0-1702812	1045	2
LENAHAN WALTER	1LT	0-0398696	0945	2
LENARD LEO L	1LT	0-0106291	0648	3
LENART CLARENCE P	COL	0-0185550	0953	3
LENCHNER GEORGE	1LT	0-1290093	0945	2
LENDVAY EUGENE F	MAJ	0-1057505	0560	1
LENETTI DOMINICK	WO1	W-2124122	0146	2
LENGYEL ALEXANDER	WO1	W-2125870	1046	1
LENGYEL JOSEPH W	MAJ	0-1015420	0160	1
LENHARDT BENJAMIN F	COL	0-0237999	1058	1
LENHARDT BERTRAM	LTC	0-1002269	1065	1
LENHART ALGERS N	CPT	0-0450981	0747	1
LENHART FRANK H	LTC	0-0372463	1263	3
LENHART HAROLD W	CPT	0-1302676	1057	1
LENHART HARRY A	LTC	0-0298296	0963	3
LENHART KENNETH G	LTC	0-0205015	0648	3
LENIC SIGMOND C	LTC	0-1551050	0564	1
LENIHAN JAMES W	1LT	0-1180242	0247	2
LENINGTON EARL F	1LT	0-1286147	0246	2
LENIUS JOHN E	CPT	0-0953683	0261	1
LENK DAVID A	COL	0-0223493	0656	3
LENN LLOYD L	CPT	0-1546321	1166	2
LENNA GEORGE	CPT	0-0501236	0550	1
LENNON FRANCIS A	COL	0-0238361	1164	3
LENNON JOHN W	LTC	0-0330661	0147	2
LENNON JOHN T	MAJ	0-1796648	1160	1
LENNON JOSEPH T	CPT	0-1307714	0246	1
LENNON MERWYN C	LTC	0-0250074	1265	3
LENNON ROBERT H	LTC	0-1284892	0463	1
LENNON WILLIAM T	MAJ	0-0506144	1146	2
LENNOX GEORGE	COL	0-0349674	0759	1
LENNOX RICHARD C	LTC	0-0195243	0363	3
LENNY MARY R	MAJ	N-0800141	0765	1
LENO JOHN J	LTC	0-1296545	0961	1
LENOIS ROY	CPT	0-1637916	0946	2
LENON JR JAMES E	LTC	0-1685714	1067	1
LENOX GEORGE H	COL	0-0232899	0961	3
LENT DAVID D	COL	0-0506507	0457	3
LENTINE JOSEPH	MAJ	0-0348315	0346	2
LENTINI VINCENT	COL	0-0321481	0763	3
LENTINI-ROTTEY PASCU	CW3	W-3150333	0667	1
LENTINO JOSEPH W	CPT	0-0354829	0750	1
LENTZ ELMER L	COL	0-0184531	0555	2
LENTZ JOHN C	LTC	0-0506569	0955	1
LENTZ JR RALPH F	LTC	0-1117288	0267	1
LENTZ LAWRENCE E	CW2	W-2143118	1157	2
LENTZ ROBERT F	LTC	0-0352652	0860	1
LENTZ THOMAS O	CPT	0-1330741	0657	1
LENTZ VALENTINE	LTC	0-0124024	0857	3
LENTZER FRANK M	2LT	0-1300564	0145	2
LENZ JOHN H	LTC	0-1015724	0462	1
LENZ JR GEORGE W	CW3	W-2123119	0661	1
LENZ LEONARD J	1LT	0-1305942	0546	2
LENZ OSCAR L	CW4	W-2002776	0862	3
LENZ ROBERT K	CPT	0-1691243	0845	2
LENZEN KENNETH R	MAJ	0-0481917	0849	1
LEO ARTHUR J	WO1	W-2122776	1058	1
LEO ROBERT T	MAJ	0-1686229	0364	1
LEO SAMUEL	CPT	0-0497113	1044	2
LEON LEO R	LTC	0-0369099	0764	3

NAME	GRADE	SVC NO	DATE RET MO YR	RET CODE
LEON THOMAS W C	LTC	0-1584513	0561	1
LEON VICTORIA A	2LT	N-0753738	1046	1
LEON WILFREDO	MAJ	0-0970127	0762	1
LEONARD ALFRED M	LTC	0-1284534	1162	1
LEONARD ARIEL J	LTC	0-1081755	0766	1
LEONARD ARTHUR L	WO1	W-2141353	1055	1
LEONARD BILL	CW2	W-2146900	0261	1
LEONARD BYRL C	WO1	W-2139607	0646	2
LEONARD CHARLES F	CW3	W-2145221	0161	2
LEONARD CLARENCE F	COL	0-0278285	0160	3
LEONARD DON E	MAJ	0-2011976	0256	1
LEONARD EMMETT T	CW3	W-2146160	0959	2
LEONARD GEORGE	CPT	0-0485194	0347	1
LEONARD GEORGE A	COL	0-0111174	0648	3
LEONARD GEORGE A	COL	0-0380820	0165	1
LEONARD HUBERT C	COL	0-0327753	0565	3
LEONARD JACK O	LTC	0-1544062	0866	1
LEONARD JAMES J	MAJ	0-1328713	1060	2
LEONARD JAMES M	LTC	0-0320429	0862	1
LEONARD JAMES M	CPT	0-2263561	1062	1
LEONARD JOHN H	CW3	W-2147213	0762	1
LEONARD JR JAMES W	LTC	0-1949833	0467	1
LEONARD KLEIN J	MAJ	0-1924537	0564	1
LEONARD LAURENCE E	CW3	W-2141913	0762	1
LEONARD LEO B	LTC	0-1691780	1155	1
LEONARD LLOYD	2LT	0-0496950	0944	2
LEONARD LOUISE K	MAJ	N-0765826	0567	1
LEONARD MATTHEW B	CPT	0-1285609	0845	2
LEONARD MAX S	CPT	0-1081350	0757	1
LEONARD QUIRINUS W	WO1	W-2002232	0467	3
LEONARD RALPH B	1LT	0-1294496	0844	2
LEONARD RALPH J	LTC	0-2042831	0158	1
LEONARD RAYMOND F	CW2	W-2213392	0867	1
LEONARD RAYMOND H	1LT	0-1285610	0845	2
LEONARD RICHARD A	1LT	0-0813532	0951	1
LEONARD RICHARD K	LTC	0-0273722	1060	1
LEONARD ROBERT J	MAJ	0-0969202	0564	1
LEONARD ROBERT L	MAJ	0-1535218	0862	1
LEONARD ROGER L	LTC	0-0362840	0463	1
LEONARD RUPERT A	CPT	0-0420120	0461	1
LEONARD SANFORD A	CW2	W-2209107	0661	1
LEONARD THOMAS B	MAJ	0-1646813	1264	1
LEONARD THOMAS J	CW2	W-2141783	0456	1
LEONARD WALLACE M	LTC	0-0275423	0657	3
LEONARD WILLIAM A	LTC	0-1557632	1166	1
LEONARDI MARK J J	LTC	0-0354838	0457	1
LEONARDO ALBERT	LTC	0-1315698	0261	1
LEONE JOHN A	CPT	0-1691228	0447	1
LEONE JOSEPH C	CPT	0-1284894	0162	1
LEONE SAM J	1LT	0-1301398	0645	2
LEONETTI CHARLES	MAJ	0-0248284	0155	3
LEONG HOP	MAJ	0-0964711	1263	1
LEONHARDT HANS A	LTC	0-0274169	0863	3
LEONHARDT HARRY H	LTC	0-0295742	0767	3
LEONHARDT JOHN W	COL	0-0158996	0155	3
LEONZANIDA QUIRINO	2LT	0-1896916	0654	1
LEOPOLD JESSE T	CW2	W-2109830	1047	1
LEPAGE FELIX	CPT	0-0208838	1043	2
LEPAK ALFRED J	CPT	0-0371211	0645	2
LEPAK LOUIS T	CPT	0-0348508	0145	2
LEPERA DOMINICK F	LTC	0-0888577	1154	1
LEPERA ERNEST O	MAJ	0-0453123	1054	1
LEPICIER LEONARD P	LTC	0-1290094	1161	1
LEPINE ADELAND	2LT	0-0153907	0443	1
LEPINE MARSHALL J	MAJ	0-1822023	0264	1
LEPISTO VICTOR E	CPT	0-0416129	0346	2
LEPKE RICHARD P	LTC	0-1113808	0565	1
LEPO PAUL P	MAJ	0-2020568	0563	1
LEPORS CHARLES	MAJ	0-1177050	0757	1
LEPOW HENRY N	CPT	0-1018895	0147	1
LEPP LOUIS P	COL	0-0268093	0763	3
LEPPER NORMAN	LTC	0-0502159	0364	3
LEPPER WILLIAM R	COL	0-0153021	0651	1
LEPPERT ROBERT O	CW2	W-2147424	0660	1
LEPPERT THEODORE J	2LT	0-1045811	0744	2

NAME	GRADE	SVC NO	DATE RET MO YR	RET CODE
LERCH PAUL F	1LT	0-1014034	0245	2
LERCH ROBERT W	COL	0-0399094	1060	3
LERDRUP JENS R	CPT	0-0450456	0552	1
LERNER DAVID G	CPT	0-0322054	1243	2
LERNER JAY S	LTC	0-0187690	0355	3
LERNER MARTIN H	LTC	0-0485169	1054	1
LERNER WILLIAM	1LT	0-1319148	0545	2
LEROE EDWARD R	CW4	W-2115859	1163	1
LEROY JOSEPH F	CPT	0-0451545	0758	1
LEROY LEO B	CPT	0-1101091	0246	1
LEROY WARREN S	COL	0-0347628	0259	2
LESAGE ARTHUR F	WO1	W-2125143	0746	2
LESAR WILLIAM J	LTC	0-1048873	0766	1
LESCARBEAU WILFRED J	CPT	0-1046864	0958	1
LESCH ALBERT S	MAJ	0-1581235	0657	1
LESCH JOSEPH A	CPT	0-1824769	0148	2
LESCHINSKY FRANK A	LTC	0-0261525	0165	3
LESEMANN EDWARD A	CPT	0-0256564	1039	1
LESEMANN JR F J	LTC	0-0406302	1047	2
LESENEY JOE M	LTC	0-0507327	1264	3
LESH EDNA M	2LT	N-0762295	0645	1
LESH WILLIAM T	MAJ	0-0252019	0966	3
LESHER JOHN H	COL	0-0341486	1066	3
LESHIN NORMAN	LTC	0-0511355	1045	2
LESHNE SAMUEL	CPT	0-1690430	0345	2
LESIKAR ADOLPH A	LTC	0-0269577	0166	3
LESIKAR GEORGE	LTC	0-0256650	0867	3
LESINSKI WALTER	MAJ	0-0452099	0660	1
LESKE HELMUTH F	MAJ	0-1293276	1162	3
LESKOVEC RAYMOND F	MAJ	0-1010439	0158	1
LESKOWITZ DAVID	LTC	0-0230269	1162	3
LESLEY CLETUS M	LTC	0-0305682	1060	1
LESLEY JAMES H	CW2	W-2149411	1060	1
LESLIE BENJAMIN L	CW4	W-2116106	1265	1
LESLIE BERTRAM L	MAJ	0-2014555	1262	1
LESLIE CHARLES A	CPT	0-0248221	0346	2
LESLIE CHARLES J	CPT	0-2103005	0962	1
LESLIE GAIL C	CPT	0-0452628	0945	2
LESLIE GRAHAM M	COL	0-0140614	0650	3
LESLIE HAROLD C	1LT	0-2035269	0845	1
LESLIE JR CLAUDE E	MAJ	0-1643794	0261	1
LESLIE JR JAMES R	COL	0-0246738	0566	3
LESLIE JR JESSE B	1LT	0-0521707	0646	2
LESLIE RICHARD C	MAJ	0-0938027	0762	1
LESLIE ROLAND R	LTC	0-0190956	0753	3
LESLIE ROMAN C	LTC	0-0248418	0766	3
LESLIE SHIRLEY	LTC	0-0253091	0158	3
LESLIE WESTRAY B	COL	L-0303512	0547	2
LESMERISES CONRAD R	WO1	W-2124172	0346	2
LESNESKI KATHERINE	2LT	N-0731181	0744	1
LESNICKI FRANK T	MAJ	0-1296788	1163	1
LESOWITZ EDWARD	LTC	0-1548475	0761	1
LESPERANCE L J	LTC	0-0349163	0557	1
LESPERANCE STANLEY G	LTC	0-0285070	1057	1
LESPIER MANFREDO E	MAJ	0-0970175	1065	1
LESSARD ROBERT J	MAJ	0-2018901	0363	1
LESSARD WILLIAM G	2LT	0-1310466	1043	2
LESSEL JAMES L	CW2	RW-2146315	0963	1
LESSER RINTELS	CW3	W-2144153	0357	1
LESSIG LESTER L	LTC	0-0150122	0653	3
LESSMAN DALE A	CPT	0-0569203	0561	1
LESSOR PETER J	MAJ	0-1579938	1052	1
LESTCHER STANLEY A	1LT	0-0509299	0345	2
LESTER BERTRAND M	CPT	0-0410907	0545	2
LESTER CALVIN D	WO1	W-2141061	0552	1
LESTER GUY D	LTC	0-0351468	0460	1
LESTER JAMES A	CW3	W-2153068	0664	1
LESTER JAMES V	LTC	0-1169617	0960	1
LESTER JR GRAHAM W	CPT	0-0520863	1047	2
LESTER JR JOHN C	MAJ	0-0970106	1165	1
LESTER JR VAN F	MAJ	0-1686389	0467	3
LESTER LEE O	1LT	0-1327635	0347	1
LESTER LEROY F	COL	0-0334415	0662	2
LESTER MELVIN D	1LT	0-1170461	0845	2
LESTER MICHAEL	CPT	0-1017076	0546	2

NAME	GRADE	SVC NO	DATE RET MO YR	RET CODE
LESTER SPURGEON	CW3	W-2144635	0863	1
LESTER SR ROBERT M	CW3	W-2151792	0564	2
LESTER VANCE B	CW3	W-2149396	0864	1
LESTER VESTAL R	CPT	0-1304245	0546	1
LESTER WILBURN L	LTC	0-1010144	1067	1
LESTER WILLIAM F	MAJ	0-0380628	0446	2
LESURE FLOYD A	MAJ	0-1543409	0661	1
LETALIEN ARTHUR	CPT	0-1300664	0546	2
LETCHER HARRISON G	2LT	0-1894797	0646	1
LETHCO EARL R	MAJ	0-1635020	0255	1
LETHERMON ROBERT H	MAJ	0-0109702	0945	2
LETHGO PERRY TURN	CPT	0-0450983	1051	2
LETKEMANN ADELLE F	2LT	N-0702801	1037	1
LETOURNEAU LESTER C	CW2	W-2203273	0357	1
LETOURNEAU ROGER N	LTC	0-1173351	0161	1
LETOURNEAU SYLVA J	MAJ	0-1017410	0961	1
LETSEN SR CARL W	CPT	0-1579939	0562	1
LETSON WILLIAM A	1LT	0-0313581	1144	2
LETT JOSEPH R	CPT	0-0424827	0345	2
LETT MAX A	MAJ	0-0230523	0144	2
LETT MAX E	MAJ	0-1299433	0860	1
LETTENMAIER NORBERT	MAJ	0-0980096	0364	1
LETTERMAN OSCAR	CPT	0-0113898	0251	3
LETTIRE WILLIAM J	MAJ	0-1637925	0960	1
LETTRICK LESLIE G	MAJ	N-0701259	0446	1
LEU HENRY G	LTC	0-1057147	0163	1
LEUCINGER JACOB	1LT	0-1844851	0349	2
LEUPP FRANCIS L	CPT	0-0350242	1047	2
LEUSMAN PATRICIA A	1LT	N-0776703	1145	1
LEUTHARD WALTER H	CW3	W-2152239	1163	1
LEUTHEN RUEL F	MAJ	0-0972294	0563	1
LEUTWYLER EDWARD T	CPT	0-0278500	1055	3
LEVADI SOLOMON S	MAJ	0-0275352	0258	3
LEVAKE CLIFFORD S	LTC	0-0252847	0166	3
LEVANTHAL HARRY	CW4	W-2126127	0653	1
LEVASSEUR GERARD L	CW3	W-2150214	0263	1
LEVECK HENRY H	COL	0-0215548	0164	3
LEVEILLE LOUIS A	LTC	0-0300817	1059	1
LEVEL JOSEPH P	WO1	W-2152496	1153	1
LEVELY JR HARRY P	MAJ	0-1010282	1160	1
LEVENDORF ABRAHAM	LTC	0-0153490	0156	3
LEVENDOSKY CHARLES L	CW4	W-2111897	0862	1
LEVENDUSKY HARRY G	LTC	0-0451333	0658	1
LEVENS FRANKLIN J	LTC	0-1947297	1265	1
LEVENSALER JAMES L	LTC	0-0262201	0967	3
LEVENSON DANIEL J	MAJ	0-1296051	0646	2
LEVENSON JOSEPH M	CPT	0-0366687	0745	2
LEVENSTEIN JOEL A	LTC	0-1636216	0961	1
LEVENTIS JR PETER P	MAJ	0-0422356	0347	2
LEVENTRITT DAVID	CPT	0-1310467	0546	2
LEVER SAMUEL R	CPT	0-1577474	0848	2
LEVER SHELBY N	LTC	0-0315900	0246	2
LEVERENZ EDWIN W	LTC	0-0434206	0462	1
LEVERET JR ROBERT L	1LT	0-1050353	0252	2
LEVERETTE JAMES W	COL	0-1101916	0861	2
LEVERETTE JR BLAND K	LTC	0-1103283	1166	1
LEVERING GEORGE H	CW2	W-2142241	1057	1
LEVERING WILLIAM C	2LT	0-1014869	0146	2
LEVERS RICHARD C	MAJ	0-1314503	0259	1
LEVESQUE ALBERT G	MAJ	0-1080043	0857	1
LEVESQUE ARTHUR J	MAJ	0-1899406	1162	1
LEVESQUE BARNEY J	1LT	0-1551666	0645	2
LEVETT JOSEPH E	LTC	0-1013908	0960	1
LEVEY MEYER L	LTC	0-0349666	0159	1
LEVEY SAMUEL	MAJ	0-0277993	0858	3
LEVI ELIEZER A	CPT	0-0888068	1045	2
LEVI EUGENE G	CPT	0-1299763	0846	1
LEVI ROBERT O	MAJ	0-1545666	0858	1
LEVIA HARRY F	LTC	0-1575418	0157	1
LEVIA LUCILLE A	MAJ	N-0722428	0763	1
LEVICKEY JAMES M	MAJ	0-2262160	0664	1
LEVIE JR JAMES K	LTC	0-0382883	0859	1
LEVIN AARON J	MAJ	0-0230829	0863	3
LEVIN CYRIL M	1LT	0-0368554	1041	2
LEVIN HARRY	MAJ	0-0912839	1047	2

NAME	GRADE	SVC NO	DATE RET MO YR	RET CODE
LEVIN HERBERT S	1LT	0-1288914	0245	2
LEVIN JEAN Z W	CPT	N-0760097	1046	1
LEVIN LEO M	MAJ	0-0318995	0646	2
LEVIN MOSES J	MAJ	0-0481314	0445	2
LEVIN ROBERT	1LT	0-1170058	0744	2
LEVIN SAMUEL	MAJ	0-0296100	1145	2
LEVIN WILLIAM	COL	0-0264259	1150	3
LEVINE ALEXANDER	LTC	0-1049554	0361	1
LEVINE DAVID	MAJ	0-0242364	0864	3
LEVINE DAVID B	LTC	0-0238976	0162	3
LEVINE DAVID L	CW3	W-2152999	0765	1
LEVINE EDWARD P	MAJ	0-0499873	0447	2
LEVINE EMANUEL	1LT	0-1061771	0646	2
LEVINE HARRY	LTC	0-1552735	0566	3
LEVINE IRVING	CPT	0-0487250	0845	2
LEVINE JOEL C	2LT	0-2006365	0846	2
LEVINE MAX A	CPT	0-0546777	0845	2
LEVINE MILTON A	1LT	0-1596100	0246	2
LEVINE RALPH	COL	0-0266189	1164	1
LEVINE RALPH M	MAJ	0-1045150	0464	1
LEVINE ROSE L	2LT	N-0762352	0646	1
LEVINE SAMUEL K	CPT	0-0506571	0745	2
LEVINE SOPHIE A	MAJ	N-0720749	0167	3
LEVINS EDWARD A	MAJ	0-0464234	1145	1
LEVINS EMANUEL	CW4	W-2101994	0557	1
LEVINS JAMES E	MAJ	0-0970585	0266	1
LEVINSOHN NATHAN	CPT	0-0307623	1044	2
LEVINSON CHARLES B	CPT	0-1533125	1047	1
LEVINSON JOSEPH	LTC	0-0984868	0867	1
LEVINSON JULIAN C	1LT	0-0402937	1045	2
LEVINSON MILTON A	MAJ	0-0322561	1146	2
LEVINSON NEWTON S	MAJ	0-0227335	0365	3
LEVINSEN PAUL	LTC	0-1535220	0761	1
LEVINSON ROBERT M	MAJ	0-0538118	0346	2
LEVINSON SOL	CPT	0-0472410	0745	2
LEVIS THOMAS C	CW3	W-2120423	0959	1
LEVISON RALPH D	COL	0-0242096	1064	3
LEVITIN JOSEPH	COL	0-0227559	1061	3
LEVITT ARTHUR	COL	0-0373480	0760	3
LEVITT EARL N	1LT	0-1822024	1043	2
LEVITT HARRY	MAJ	0-1308155	0361	1
LEVITT ROBERT	COL	0-0343518	0465	1
LEVITT THOMAS J	CW3	W-2109710	0959	1
LEVNO ANTHONY F	COL	0-0276836	0557	2
LEVOFF PHILIP	LTC	0-0466667	0754	1
LEVSTONE KENNETH J	MAJ	0-1112820	0758	1
LEVULIS ALBERT E	LTC	0-1341679	1167	1
LEVY ALFRED C	LTC	0-1311314	0663	1
LEVY BENJAMIN H	LTC	0-0242141	0466	3
LEVY BERNARD M	LTC	0-0193622	0561	3
LEVY DAVID	1LT	0-1692039	0545	2
LEVY EDWARD	CPT	0-0465600	0146	2
LEVY EDWARD R	LTC	0-1550645	0561	1
LEVY GEORGE V	2LT	0-1306436	0345	2
LEVY JACK H	MAJ	0-0460670	1146	2
LEVY JEROME S	LTC	0-0214894	1062	3
LEVY LILLIAN	2LT	N-0760863	0245	1
LEVY MILTON	1LT	0-0451559	0346	2
LEVY MILTON A	CPT	0-0253258	0564	3
LEVY MILTON G	MAJ	0-0357912	1043	2
LEVY RALPH	MAJ	0-0113721	1149	3
LEVY ROBERT E	1LT	0-1313103	1045	2
LEVY SAMUEL A	CPT	0-0466351	0646	1
LEVY SAMUEL B	MAJ	0-1689873	0346	2
LEVY SIDNEY W	CPT	0-0496983	0146	2
LEW HONOR W	2LT	N-0790059	0945	1
LEW SAM G	LTC	0-0361000	0964	1
LEWANDOWSKI C F	MAJ	0-1595590	0158	1
LEWANDOWSKI DANIEL R	MAJ	0-1301843	0960	1
LEWANDOWSKI EDMUND	CPT	0-1692237	0745	2
LEWANDOWSKI EDMUND W	LTC	0-1039751	0862	2
LEWANDOWSKI VICTOR J	LTC	0-0422225	0761	1
LEWELLEN JOE T	2LT	0-1322049	0645	2
LEWEN HERBERT E	CW2	W-2000223	0544	2
LEWICKA VICTORIA C	2LT	N-0731201	1145	1

NAME	GRADE	SVC NO	DATE RET MO YR	RET CODE
LEWIN CHARLES Y	CPT	0-0300738	0961	3
LEWIN JOHN F	CW3	W-2147045	0164	1
LEWIN ROSCOE B	COL	0-0277335	C465	3
LEWIN THEODORE F	COL	C-0355513	1064	1
LEWIS ACLAI R	LTC	0-0191525	0446	2
LEWIS ALBERT E	MAJ	0-1796651	0154	2
LEWIS ALEXANDER	MAJ	C-0926983	1164	1
LEWIS ARAMINTA E	MAJ	N-0752554	0966	3
LEWIS ARNOLD M	COL	0-0399798	1164	3
LEWIS ARTHUR N	COL	C-0225183	1264	3
LEWIS BARNEY V	MAJ	0-2033993	C963	1
LEWIS BERNARD M	LTC	0-0211814	C159	3
LEWIS BRUNER A	MAJ	0-1290770	0657	2
LEWIS BURTON W	LTC	0-0341169	0865	1
LEWIS CARLETON H	LTC	0-1110613	0866	3
LEWIS CAROL	2LT	0-182523C	0644	2
LEWIS CARROLL L	MAJ	C-1639307	C157	1
LEWIS CHARLES	CPT	0-1634068	C760	1
LEWIS CHARLES A	CW2	W-2153158	0160	1
LEWIS CHARLES E	LTC	0-1015768	0953	1
LEWIS CHARLES E	MAJ	C-1575421	0451	1
LEWIS CHARLES F	LTC	0-0254507	1265	3
LEWIS CHARLES F	1LT	0-0532198	0350	1
LEWIS CHARLES W	MAJ	C-2033937	C365	1
LEWIS CHESTER R	MAJ	C-0496376	1144	2
LEWIS CLARENCE D	CPT	0-1583282	0446	2
LEWIS CLAUDE E	CPT	0-0109177	1024	1
LEWIS CONDIE I	2LT	0-2000842	0960	1
LEWIS CRESLIE W	MAJ	C-2001745	1062	1
LEWIS DALE R	1LT	0-1319982	1045	2
LEWIS DARRELL E	2LT	0-1324550	0244	2
LEWIS DAVID	CW2	W-2101995	1146	2
LEWIS DELMAR J	LTC	0-0308645	0647	1
LEWIS DESSIE R	CPT	0-0486216	0947	2
LEWIS EARL R	CPT	0-1108106	0558	1
LEWIS EDWARD C	CPT	0-1306437	C447	1
LEWIS EDWARD J	COL	0-0170841	0752	1
LEWIS EDWARD L	LTC	0-0450984	1265	1
LEWIS EDWARD S	CW3	W-2207714	0667	1
LEWIS EDWIN M	LTC	0-0248028	0152	3
LEWIS ELDRIDGE O	CW2	W-2115496	0645	2
LEWIS ELIZABETH	1LT	N-0761058	C246	1
LEWIS ERIC L	LTC	0-1337592	1065	1
LEWIS EUGENE C	CPT	0-1182172	0647	2
LEWIS EUGENE F	1LT	0-0187038	0657	3
LEWIS FERRELL J	LTC	0-0394935	1160	3
LEWIS FLOYD V	CPT	C-0981777	0761	1
LEWIS FRED G	CW4	W-2101996	1158	1
LEWIS FREDERICK	LTC	0-0251628	C666	3
LEWIS GARLIN H	CW2	W-2211100	1166	1
LEWIS GORDON W	MAJ	0-2037387	0661	1
LEWIS GROVER C	COL	0-0259438	1266	3
LEWIS HAROLD C	1LT	0-1302150	0945	2
LEWIS HAROLD C	CW4	W-2144968	C367	1
LEWIS HAROLD E	LTC	0-1292206	1163	1
LEWIS HAROLD S	LTC	0-1325758	C863	1
LEWIS HARRY E	MAJ	C-1326254	1164	1
LEWIS HARRY I	LTC	0-0116788	C852	3
LEWIS HARRY L	MAJ	C-0937880	C762	1
LEWIS HARVEY D	COL	0-0196815	C662	3
LEWIS HARVEY H	LTC	0-0220615	1145	2
LEWIS HELEN A	1LT	N-0728423	C746	1
LEWIS HENRY H W	LTC	C-0215605	0364	3
LEWIS HENRY S	1LT	0-0112354	1157	3
LEWIS HENRY V	MAJ	C-0259105	C167	3
LEWIS HERALD F	LTC	0-0200732	C654	2
LEWIS HUGH S	CPT	0-1304085	0548	1
LEWIS ISAAC R	CPT	0-1174932	0853	1
LEWIS IVAN L	LTC	0-1001394	1162	1
LEWIS JACOB	1LT	0-0466562	1044	2
LEWIS JAMES C	MAJ	C-011926C	C648	3
LEWIS JAMES C	MAJ	0-0167661	1048	2
LEWIS JAMES H	CPT	0-1311657	0747	2
LEWIS JAMES M	LTC	0-0539813	0663	1
LEWIS JAMES N	COL	0-0326716	0263	1

NAME	GRADE	SVC NO	DATE RET MO YR	RET CODE
LEWIS JAMES C	LTC	0-0496202	0556	1
LEWIS JAMES R	LTC	0-1017230	0966	1
LEWIS JAMES W	LTC	0-1103752	1160	1
LEWIS JET D	MAJ	0-1647578	0259	1
LEWIS JOHN	WO1	W-2122717	1053	1
LEWIS JOHN D	MAJ	0-1015235	0962	2
LEWIS JOHN G	MAJ	0-0193343	0760	3
LEWIS JOHN P	CPT	0-0370243	1045	2
LEWIS JOHN P	1LT	0-1821884	0345	2
LEWIS JOHN W	CPT	0-1174627	0155	1
LEWIS JOSEPH H	B G	0-0182597	0843	2
LEWIS JOSEPH H	LTC	0-1112281	1162	1
LEWIS JOSEPH S	CW4	W-2115986	0357	1
LEWIS JOSEPH V	CW4	W-2145196	0765	2
LEWIS JR ALBERT B	MAJ	0-1648337	0162	1
LEWIS JR ALBERT M	CPT	0-035366C	0544	2
LEWIS JR EDGAR M	COL	0-0171322	0254	2
LEWIS JR HAROLD F	MAJ	0-1056147	0265	1
LEWIS JR HARRY J	COL	C-0254025	0361	3
LEWIS JR HARVEY C	LTC	0-1107551	0964	1
LEWIS JR HOWARD T	CPT	0-0475527	0747	2
LEWIS JR HOWELL C	LTC	0-0903536	1162	3
LEWIS JR JAMES M	MAJ	0-133323C	0359	1
LEWIS JR JOHN D	MAJ	0-1688526	0966	1
LEWIS JR JOHN F	LTC	0-1047263	0868	1
LEWIS JR JOHN W	LTC	0-0286918	0665	3
LEWIS JR LESTER H	MAJ	0-2204125	0167	1
LEWIS JR THOMAS O	1LT	0-1185284	0146	2
LEWIS JR THOMAS E	MAJ	0-1823020	0364	1
LEWIS JR WALTER K	CPT	0-0352147	1144	2
LEWIS JULIAN F	LTC	0-0312055	1162	3
LEWIS KARL R	1LT	0-1017053	0347	1
LEWIS KELLY H	COL	0-0172315	0654	1
LEWIS KENDRICK D	CW2	W-2141355	0961	2
LEWIS KENNETH R	MAJ	0-035080C	0544	2
LEWIS LAMONT	CW3	W-2146076	0367	1
LEWIS LAWRENCE E	LTC	0-0911912	1162	1
LEWIS LAWRENCE H	LTC	0-0150245	0156	3
LEWIS LEE R	LTC	0-1303357	0562	1
LEWIS LEROY A	LTC	0-0360560	0164	1
LEWIS LEWIS F	LTC	0-0364931	0547	2
LEWIS LINDSEY C	1LT	0-0376090	1145	2
LEWIS MARION S	CPT	0-0154514	C356	3
LEWIS MARTIN E	LTC	0-1110615	1062	1
LEWIS MARTIN G	LTC	0-1583283	0857	1
LEWIS MEREDITH T	COL	0-0238452	0665	3
LEWIS MERIWETHER	LTC	0-0252677	0456	3
LEWIS MICHAEL J	LTC	0-1647226	0364	1
LEWIS MILTON C	MAJ	0-1307716	0761	1
LEWIS MILTON P	LTC	0-0337224	1057	1
LEWIS MILTON T	MAJ	0-1877696	0764	1
LEWIS MIRIAM L	2LT	N-0788161	0445	1
LEWIS NELLIE C	1LT	N-0765512	0749	2
LEWIS OLIVER A	CPT	0-1017433	0261	1
LEWIS OLIVER C	LTC	0-1574283	0163	1
LEWIS OLIVER P	MAJ	C-0245920	0857	3
LEWIS OSBORNE F	COL	0-027662C	1164	3
LEWIS OSCAR M	LTC	0-0210053	0454	3
LEWIS PATRICIA A	1LT	N-0723993	0146	1
LEWIS PAUL B	LTC	0-1577476	1061	1
LEWIS PAUL W	LTC	C-0241282	1262	3
LEWIS PERLEY M	LTC	0-0329611	0646	1
LEWIS PHAON E	WO1	W-2122253	C153	2
LEWIS RALPH	LTC	0-1320638	0267	3
LEWIS RALPH A	COL	0-0333393	0456	3
LEWIS RAY N	COL	0-0231232	1160	3
LEWIS RAYMOND E	MAJ	0-1312176	1061	1
LEWIS RAYMOND J	COL	0-0271706	0260	1
LEWIS RAYMOND M	1LT	0-1311904	1045	2
LEWIS REBECCA	2LT	N-0799644	1046	1
LEWIS REECE H	COL	0-0288344	0166	3
LEWIS REUBEN C	COL	0-0183217	1150	3
LEWIS REX E	1LT	0-0461256	1045	2
LEWIS RICHARD A	LTC	0-1185718	1263	1
LEWIS RICHARD E	1LT	0-0467309	0145	2

NAME	GRADE	SVC NO	DATE RET MO YR	RET CODE
LEWIS RICHARD F	1LT	0-2211846	0653	1
LEWIS ROBERT A	COL	0-0210051	0-51	3
LEWIS ROBERT A	1LT	0-1170829	0246	2
LEWIS ROBERT A	MAJ	0-1920336	0966	1
LEWIS ROBERT B	COL	0-0176533	1153	3
LEWIS ROBERT B	CPT	C-0179074	1159	3
LEWIS ROBERT C	CW4	W-2105238	C559	1
LEWIS ROBERT F	1LT	0-0353144	C245	2
LEWIS ROBERT F	MAJ	C-1633366	0746	1
LEWIS ROBERT J	MAJ	0-1554422	0661	1
LEWIS ROBERT L	COL	0-0156226	0847	2
LEWIS ROBERT L	LTC	0-1286671	0761	1
LEWIS ROBERT M	CPT	0-0319982	C145	1
LEWIS ROBERT P	CPT	0-0238568	C955	3
LEWIS ROBERT R	CW3	W-2148931	0465	1
LEWIS ROGER E	MAJ	C-1030170	0254	1
LEWIS ROSWELL E	WO1	W-2209326	0359	1
LEWIS ROY	LTC	0-0276472	0356	3
LEWIS ROYAL C	LTC	0-1548918	0766	1
LEWIS ROYER K	COL	0-047231C	0653	1
LEWIS RUSSELL C	MAJ	0-0481916	1052	1
LEWIS RUSSELL M	MAJ	C-0991231	1266	1
LEWIS SAMUEL A	COL	0-0483415	C856	1
LEWIS SAMUEL F	1LT	C-1297745	C745	2
LEWIS SAMUEL L	LTC	0-0205107	1147	2
LEWIS SAUL	CPT	0-0435389	C245	2
LEWIS SPENCER R	MAJ	C-1115004	1060	1
LEWIS SR CHARLES R	LTC	0-1541964	C856	1
LEWIS STANLEY	MAJ	0-1011860	0761	1
LEWIS STANLEY D	LTC	0-0293749	0751	2
LEWIS STELLA C	2LT	N-0771890	1045	1
LEWIS STEPHEN A	MAJ	C-0220884	C750	1
LEWIS STUART	COL	0-0177190	C450	3
LEWIS THEODORE K	2LT	0-1296399	0143	2
LEWIS THOMAS A	LTC	0-0281111	1167	3
LEWIS THOMAS A	CPT	0-1309159	0946	1
LEWIS THOMAS J	MAJ	C-0493465	1152	1
LEWIS THOMAS P	LTC	0-1174045	0162	1
LEWIS THURL O	1LT	C-1306608	C246	2
LEWIS TOM	LTC	0-0221566	0354	3
LEWIS WALDON K	CPT	0-1168335	0445	1
LEWIS WARREN R	2LT	0-0526307	0146	2
LEWIS WAYNE H	CPT	0-C494029	0250	1
LEWIS WILBERT A	LTC	C-0237939	0946	2
LEWIS WILLIAM A	LTC	0-0224258	C762	1
LEWIS WILLIAM C	CW2	W-2149755	C963	1
LEWIS WILLIAM G	CW4	W-2001960	0866	3
LEWIS WILLIAM J	COL	0-0332277	0860	1
LEWIS WILLIAM M	LTC	0-1101920	0561	1
LEWIS WILLIAM P	1LT	0-1305801	0354	1
LEWIS WILLIE L	CW3	W-2149939	0164	1
LEWIS WODEA	1LT	N-0762765	C850	1
LEWISON MELVIN A	WO1	W-2132116	1145	2
LEWITZ ERWIN F	MAJ	0-0925453	0446	2
LEWMAN CHARLES O	MAJ	C-0341566	1056	3
LEWMAN R J	CPT	0-1317410	C446	2
LEWSEN RUDOLPH F	LTC	0-0916378	C464	3
LEWY EVERETT	COL	0-0234254	1065	3
LEX HENRY J	MAJ	C-1031416	0261	1
LEX IRWIN A	COL	0-0183427	0455	3
LEX ROLAND E	2LT	0-1288761	1044	2
LEY MAX O	1LT	C-1574080	0743	2
LEYBOURNE MALCOLM G	MAJ	0-0964581	0163	1
LEYDEN JR WILLIAM G	LTC	0-0462172	0765	1
LEYDEN THEODORE J	LTC	0-0337841	0864	3
LEYENDECKER C R	1LT	0-1185079	0856	1
LEYSER GEORGE E	LTC	0-1103286	0765	3
LEYSON JOE O	1LT	0-0890500	0362	1
LEYSON VICTORIO L	2LT	0-1896855	0554	1
LEZETTE GEORGE I	1LT	0-1302993	C945	2
LHAMON JAMES R	2LT	0-1644530	0345	2
LHEUREUX PHILIP L	LTC	0-1177887	C862	1
LHOMME JACQUES M	LTC	0-0267148	1061	1
LI VECCHI SALVATORE	LTC	0-1591267	1163	1
LIAKOS STEPHEN	CPT	C-1295041	C546	2

NAME	GRADE	SVC NO	DATE RET MO YR	RET CODE
LIBBERT CORNELIUS	COL	0-0120527	0154	2
LIBBY DONALD M	COL	0-0125236	0956	3
LIBBY FRED C	CW4	W-2141356	0660	1
LIBBY JAMES W	1LT	0-1550009	C247	1
LIBBY JR RALPH G	CPT	0-0425608	1143	2
LIBBY ROLAND O	LTC	0-0381575	C664	1
LIBBY THOMAS H	LTC	0-1329365	C265	1
LIBBY WILLIAM C	2LT	0-1102355	1043	2
LIBCKE JOHN W	M G	0-0233642	1061	3
LIBERATOR ERCOLE A	LTC	0-0922806	1265	3
LIBERATORI FRANCIS J	CPT	0-1100647	1146	2
LIBERTINI ROBERT M	MAJ	0-0254595	0-51	3
LIBERTY ALLEN P	MAJ	0-1112823	0360	1
LIBERTY JOHN F	MAJ	C-1018095	0662	1
LIBERTZ EDWARD F	CW2	W-2149075	1057	2
LIBOUREL HERBERT H	MAJ	0-0312442	0346	2
LIBY ROBERT A	LTC	0-0358285	1160	1
LICCIONE WILLIAM J	CPT	0-0380958	1144	2
LICHENE STEVE	COL	0-0384161	0954	1
LICHENSTEIN SIDNEY	CPT	0-1291842	0252	1
LICHTENBERGER JOHN W	LTC	C-1581239	C463	1
LICHTENBERGER L L	1LT	0-1318682	C546	2
LICHTENBERGER M M	1LT	N-0796316	C848	2
LICHTENBERGER WILLIA	LTC	0-0322895	C266	3
LICHTENEGGER SFIBO	MAJ	0-1048464	C858	1
LICHTENFELS ISAAC	LTC	0-0242265	C566	3
LICHTENSTEIN MEYER R	CPT	0-C498776	C446	2
LICHTMAN MELVIN I	1LT	0-1316169	1045	2
LICHTMAN WILLIAM T	1LT	0-1080123	1044	2
LICKEL WILLIAM C	CPT	0-1100648	1060	1
LICKLEY REX M	MAJ	0-0298037	1161	3
LICKLIDER BEECHER L	LTC	0-1171648	C963	1
LICKLITER WILLIAM F	CPT	0-0511400	C846	2
LIDFEN WALTER T	CW2	W-2147406	C962	1
LIDKE FRANK J	LTC	0-0262052	1144	2
LIEB FREDERICK	CW4	W-2132752	1162	1
LIEBENGUTH MARTIN F	CPT	0-0504538	1046	1
LIEBER GEORGE M	LTC	0-0140611	0358	3
LIEBER JR HARRY S	CPT	0-1320057	0547	1
LIEBER MARSHALL M	LTC	0-0271788	0546	2
LIEBER SIDNEY	1LT	0-1573366	1045	1
LIEBERMAN HARRY A	LTC	0-1315647	0862	1
LIEBERMAN HEIMAN G	MAJ	0-0488379	0246	2
LIEBERMAN HERMAN	MAJ	0-2010821	0566	1
LIEBERMAN JOHN I	MAJ	0-0495425	0350	1
LIEBERMAN LEO A	COL	0-0295447	0867	3
LIEBERMAN LEON R	COL	0-0371541	1167	3
LIEBERSTEIN J H	CPT	0-0495905	0246	2
LIEBERT HERBERT M	MAJ	0-1112824	0461	1
LIEBHARDT ROBERT G	LTC	0-0349662	1060	1
LIEBIG CHARLES J	CW4	W-2142868	1164	1
LIEBMAN HENRY	LTC	0-0195933	1162	3
LIEBNER BYRON E	1LT	0-1321381	0946	1
LIEBOWITZ HIRSCH R	MAJ	0-0497125	0246	2
LIEBRECHT CHARLES F	COL	0-0346155	0864	1
LIECHENSTEIN JOSEPH	LTC	0-0332127	1159	1
LIECHTY SHERMAN E	CPT	0-1055369	0446	1
LIEDER WILLIAM J	MAJ	0-1688607	0264	1
LIEDIGK WERNER M	MAJ	C-1917724	1265	1
LIEDMAN LYLE F	LTC	0-2049624	0766	1
LIEDTKE ALFRED W	LTC	0-0366426	0854	1
LIEN ALTON W	CW3	W-2151146	1062	1
LIEN FLOYD L	LTC	0-1323443	0267	1
LIEN VICTOR C	LTC	0-1287027	0263	1
LIESE RALPH F	1LT	0-0531865	0447	2
LIESINGER RUDOLPH O	1LT	0-0350288	1044	2
LIESKE HAROLD W	LTC	0-0273532	0766	3
LIESKE LOREN F	LTC	0-0998740	0466	1
LIETZ JAMES B	1LT	0-1325224	1045	2
LIEURANCE CHARLES H	CPT	0-0963188	0459	1
LIEURANCE LLOYD C	MAJ	0-0263822	1060	3
LIEVENS JACOB J	CW3	W-2144798	0761	1
LIFCHULTZ LEO B	CPT	0-0486903	0745	2
LIFE ARTHUR R	LTC	0-0170046	0859	3
LIFSCHUTZ MARY	2LT	N-0722245	1043	1

NAME	GRADE	SVC NO	DATE RET MO YR	RET CODE
LIFSEY JR JULIAN H	1LT	0-1637936	0145	2
LIGDA ANDREW V	LTC	0-2018687	0166	1
LIGEIKIS JOSEPH	1LT	0-1288250	0544	2
LIGGETT ALBERT L	LTC	0-0905418	0563	3
LIGGETT CLARENCE R	CW2	W-2146257	C858	1
LIGGETT ROBERT S	MAJ	0-0403327	C146	2
LIGHSTON JR RENOLD B	LTC	0-4002377	1066	3
LIGHT ALEXANDER	MAJ	0-0384241	0964	3
LIGHT GEORGE G	LTC	0-0245872	0966	3
LIGHT HARLEY E	MAJ	C-0339183	0862	1
LIGHT HARRY J	1LT	0-19461C1	C347	2
LIGHT JOHN M	CPT	C-2032941	C557	1
LIGHT JR CHARLES P	COL	0-0190273	0163	3
LIGHTBODY RAYMOND M	COL	0-0184473	1056	3
LIGHTBURN WILLIS C	1LT	0-1575425	C445	2
LIGHTBURNE WILLIAM J	LTC	0-0324024	1059	3
LIGHTCAP WILLIAM C	LTC	0-2017085	0965	1
LIGHTFOOT BENJAMIN H	1LT	0-0927964	1051	1
LIGHTFOOT ELLISON R	1LT	0-1284536	0744	2
LIGHTFOOT ROBERT H	CPT	0-4047966	0163	2
LIGHTFOOT WHITING R	MAJ	C-0947101	1163	1
LIGHTMAN PERCY	CPT	0-0200128	1056	3
LIGHTSEY G R	CW3	W-2108645	1057	1
LIGON JR EDWARD C	CPT	0-0318863	1144	2
LIGON RICHARD G	LTC	0-1634071	C864	1
LIGON ROY W	CW2	W-2101999	0749	1
LIGON SEBASTIAN	COL	C-0248474	1166	3
LIGON STANHOPE A	COL	C-0245230	1062	3
LIKAR FRANK	CPT	C-0504809	0453	1
LIKAS DONALD	LTC	0-1289759	C860	1
LIKAS JOSEPH F	LTC	0-0885844	1266	1
LIKES CREIGHTON	COL	0-0282171	C862	3
LIKES JOHN L	LTC	0-0417410	0748	1
LIKINS ROBERT A	MAJ	C-1167951	0347	1
LILES CLAUDE M	COL	C-0246135	C960	3
LILES JR LISTON D	MAJ	C-0918208	0746	2
LILES RAY L	CPT	0-0497851	1158	1
LILES WALLACE G	1LT	0-0436606	0546	2
LILEY WILLIAM L	MAJ	0-2203826	1167	1
LILIENTHAL WILBERT H	CPT	0-1295236	0845	2
LILJEGREEN LEROY R	CW4	W-2101198	C564	1
LILJEGREN HARRY E	MAJ	C-0233503	0147	1
LILL ARCHIE V	LTC	0-0197913	0748	3
LILLARD WALTER H	LTC	0-0101503	C648	3
LILLEY CLIFFORD A	LTC	0-1307432	0661	1
LILLEY FRANK S	COL	0-0320213	C865	1
LILLEY GEORGE F	MAJ	C-1598133	1058	1
LILLEY GEORGE P	CW2	W-2207133	0962	1
LILLEY HALDANE	CPT	0-1311658	1047	2
LILLEY ROY	LTC	0-0271550	0667	3
LILLGE KARL H	MAJ	C-1289760	C761	1
LILLI DOMINIC A	2LT	0-1546085	C944	2
LILLIBRIDGE HAROLD D	LTC	0-0244855	C857	3
LILLICRAP PAUL J	1LT	0-0231331	0943	2
LILLIE BERNARD J	MAJ	C-0349010	C164	2
LILLIE JOHN N	CW3	W-2146377	1060	1
LILLIE KENNETH H	LTC	0-0888444	1262	1
LILLIE LEROY D	COL	0-0236654	0761	3
LILLIS ROBERT E	CPT	0-0277294	1045	2
LILLY ALEXANDER	MAJ	C-0156444	0451	3
LILLY ALFRED	2LT	0-0109301	0530	1
LILLY BASIL G	LTC	C-0208710	0158	3
LILLY DONALD E	CW3	W-2205263	0563	1
LILLY FRANCIS W	2LT	0-1299592	0745	2
LILLY JR MAYFIELD	CW3	W-2143164	1266	1
LILLY ROBERT A	CPT	0-1309580	0947	1
LILLY SHELBY T	1LT	0-1169218	1045	2
LILLY THEODORE F	MAJ	C-0218599	C556	3
LILYGREN LLOYD E	COL	0-0244934	C848	3
LIM JR VINCENTE H	2LT	0-0549526	0745	2
LIMBACH WILTON G	MAJ	C-0276245	0943	2
LIMBECK JOHN A	LTC	C-1039078	1162	1
LIMBERG EARL W	COL	C-0355304	1060	1
LIMBOCKER THOMAS R	LTC	0-0113282	0558	3
LIMERICK JOE B	MAJ	0-0479800	C849	2
LIMERICK THOMAS J	MAJ	C-0981132	0363	1
LIMES JOSEPH K	LTC	0-0257895	1163	3
LIMOGES REGIS R	1LT	0-1290772	0547	1
LIMPERT DANIEL C	1LT	0-0890155	1046	2
LIMPIC JOHN	1LT	0-1290268	0945	2
LIMPUS LEROY D	MAJ	0-0416682	0761	1
LINAGEN EDWARD H	CW2	W-2141614	0257	1
LINARD CHAUNCEY C	LTC	0-0252815	C564	3
LINCAVAGE PAUL G	1LT	0-1798795	1058	1
LINCOLN ELMER D	CPT	0-0276157	0366	3
LINCOLN ELMER E	MAJ	0-1635033	0857	2
LINCOLN ELMER H	MAJ	0-1642324	C456	1
LINCOLN JOHN J	LTC	0-0372657	1166	3
LINCOLN LUCIUS F	LTC	0-0502514	C954	1
LINCOLN LYDIA R	MAJ	N-0737584	C663	1
LINCOLN MILAN A	2LT	0-1016535	0245	2
LINCOLN NELSON H	MAJ	0-0404361	0166	1
LINCOLN ROBERT A	LTC	0-0255372	0967	3
LINCOLN WILBERT J	LTC	0-0243750	0558	3
LIND ARTHUR H	LTC	0-1558661	1266	1
LIND CHARLES W	COL	0-0349961	0646	1
LIND EDMUND L	LTC	0-0320239	0260	3
LIND FREDERICK	LTC	0-0166672	1045	2
LIND HJALMAR A	MAJ	0-0452003	1157	1
LIND JAMES F	LTC	0-0279648	1160	3
LIND LAURIE P	COL	0-0215789	0860	3
LIND LESTER C	2LT	0-1167089	0145	2
LIND NORMAN	2LT	0-1649024	1045	2
LIND WILLIS T	LTC	0-0300086	0265	3
LINDAHL FRANK C	LTC	0-1584528	0662	1
LINDAHL FRANK O	COL	0-0261335	C166	3
LINDAHL JOHN C	MAJ	0-0129275	1053	3
LINDAMOOD ROBERT E	MAJ	0-1295737	0660	1
LINDAU FRED I	LTC	0-0225962	0762	3
LINDAUER BERNARD J	1LT	0-1293075	0645	2
LINDBERG ARTHUR M	CW3	W-2144567	0859	1
LINDBERG HARRY F	CPT	0-0182981	0553	3
LINDBERG JR ARTHUR J	CPT	0-0495777	0848	2
LINDBERG STANLEY J	LTC	0-1170463	1162	1
LINDBLOOM EDWIN O	CW4	W-2103755	0659	1
LINDBORG ARTHUR E	COL	0-0245055	0648	3
LINDE KNUD W	MAJ	0-0924713	0547	2
LINDEBERG RUTH R	2LT	N-0762567	0945	1
LINDEGREN GEORGE L	COL	0-0247697	0463	3
LINDELL KERMIT F	MAJ	C-0452857	0456	1
LINDEMAN ELMER H	MAJ	0-1184100	0663	1
LINDEMAN LEONARD K	CW4	W-2117128	0659	1
LINDEMAN MARK A	1LT	0-1637938	1046	2
LINDEMAN WILLIAM N	MAJ	0-0577845	0962	1
LINDEMANN THEODORE T	MAJ	C-0211092	0360	3
LINDEN EUGENE J	CPT	0-1297747	1147	1
LINDEN JOHN A	MAJ	0-1590609	0263	1
LINDEN JOHN R	LTC	0-0337126	0759	1
LINDEN JOHN W	CPT	0-0289216	1061	3
LINDEN SR JAMES E	LTC	0-1100202	0157	1
LINDENMAN SHEPARD	CPT	0-0486796	0445	2
LINDENMUTH LEROY A	CW3	W-2142244	1160	1
LINDENSTRUTH HENRY J	LTC	0-0344106	0263	1
LINDENSTRUTH R W	1LT	0-0384283	0545	2
LINDEQUIST DAVID C	CW3	W-2150094	1162	1
LINDER CLAUDE W	MAJ	0-0113283	0648	3
LINDER JAMES H	MAJ	C-0463051	0147	2
LINDER JESSE L	CW3	W-2146907	0463	1
LINDER ROY L	LTC	0-1575547	0863	1
LINDER VIRGIL R	MAJ	0-1302152	0263	1
LINDERER LAWRENCE W	COL	0-0336425	0865	2
LINDERMAN ALVIN A	CW3	W-2147318	0862	1
LINDERMAN GEORGE W	2LT	0-1291374	1044	2
LINDERMAN LONNIE E	CW4	W-2103145	0360	1
LINDEROSE WILLIAM C	MAJ	0-1020455	0763	1
LINDERSON HAROLD F	COL	0-0188264	0653	3
LINDGREN ALLAN G	MAJ	0-1165306	0662	1
LINDGREN ELMER A	MAJ	0-1318683	0457	1
LINDGREN FRANK W	CPT	0-0986449	1060	1
LINDGREN JOSEPH B	MAJ	0-1396307	C866	1
LINDGREN LLOYD A	CPT	0-1178226	1147	1
LINDHOLM GEORGE S	1LT	0-1308250	1045	2
LINDIMORE CHARLES F	MAJ	C-1286672	0663	1
LINDLE HERBERT A	LTC	0-0183620	1047	1
LINDLEY CHARLES L	1LT	0-1798592	1046	1
LINDLEY ELBERT O	CW2	W-2148124	0159	1
LINDLEY ERNEST E	CPT	C-1698890	0854	1
LINDLEY GEORGE F	1LT	0-0215194	0-49	3
LINDLEY ROBERT P	LTC	0-0479730	0457	1
LINDLEY THOMAS A	COL	C-0327212	C658	1
LINDLY HAROLD G	MAJ	0-1932205	1167	1
LINDMAN FRANCIS F	CPT	0-0382160	0347	2
LINDNER CLEMENT R	COL	0-0468974	1061	3
LINDNER JOHN A	LTC	0-0124058	C952	3
LINDNER KENNETH M	LTC	0-0547089	0666	3
LINDON JAMES T	2LT	0-0446041	1044	2
LINDQUIST GERALD E	MAJ	0-2036608	1057	1
LINDQUIST MABEL R	MAJ	N-0758219	1066	3
LINDQUIST MARSHALL C	MAJ	0-0487593	1054	1
LINDSAY ADAM S	MAJ	0-1037599	0744	1
LINDSAY GEORGE H	MAJ	0-0505240	1045	2
LINDSAY GEORGE M	LTC	0-1283095	0765	1
LINDSAY GEORGE T	1LT	0-1041826	1044	2
LINDSAY HAROLD E	CPT	0-0179948	C446	1
LINDSAY HAROLD J	CPT	0-0105671	0352	3
LINDSAY JAMES B	MAJ	C-0414366	1146	1
LINDSAY JESSE S	B G	0-0237198	0961	3
LINDSAY JOHN F	1LT	0-1299913	C546	2
LINDSAY ROBERT M	MAJ	0-2017086	0665	1
LINDSAY RUSSELL K	1LT	0-0505991	0147	1
LINDSAY WALTER A	MAJ	C-1897788	C765	1
LINDSAY WALTER I	CPT	0-1290269	0446	2
LINDSEY ADRIAN H	COL	0-0200836	0855	3
LINDSEY ALVA E	LTC	0-0279770	1055	3
LINDSEY ARLEN G	CW3	W-2203317	C467	1
LINDSEY CHARLES R	MAJ	C-1688435	C464	1
LINDSEY CLIFTON S	COL	0-0377868	0761	1
LINDSEY EDWARD L	LTC	0-0384546	0662	1
LINDSEY GILBERT F	1LT	0-1061173	0446	1
LINDSEY HOWARD S	CW2	W-2145917	0558	1
LINDSEY IRVIN B	MAJ	C-1546653	0257	1
LINDSEY JOHN R	CW2	W-2148208	C863	1
LINDSEY JOHN T	CPT	0-0450531	0557	1
LINDSEY JR MARTIN L	LTC	0-1795032	0766	1
LINDSEY JULIA S	1LT	N-0763464	1145	1
LINDSEY LOUIS G	CPT	C-0485989	1146	1
LINDSEY OREL B	LTC	0-0281844	0161	1
LINDSEY ROBERT E	LTC	0-0171946	0757	3
LINDSEY RUBLE	CPT	0-0499774	1052	1
LINDSEY SR GEORGE W	MAJ	0-2033601	1061	1
LINDSEY THEARON K	WO1	W-2124443	0353	1
LINDSEY TRAVIS	MAJ	C-1946550	0859	1
LINDSEY WILLIAM R	LTC	C-1553303	0465	1
LINDSKOG MAURICE B	CW2	W-2148352	1159	1
LINDSLEY CHARLES F	MAJ	0-1635036	1060	1
LINDSLEY LOUIS H	LTC	0-0317565	C858	3
LINDSTROM ALTON J	1LT	0-1105614	0345	2
LINDSTROM EDGAR V	MAJ	0-1172967	0364	1
LINDSTROM GUSTAV G	CPT	C-0370455	0346	1
LINDSTROM JR JOHN W	CW3	W-2141615	C462	1
LINDSTROM LEWIS I	MAJ	0-2210337	C866	1
LINDVALL BERT C	COL	0-0336039	C454	3
LINDY JOHN R	CPT	0-2033158	0855	1
LINE GERALD C	COL	0-0223414	0860	3
LINEAWEVER JOHN K	LTC	0-1052451	0362	1
LINEBARGER EDWARD C	CPT	C-0244450	C-53	3
LINEBARGER RAYMOND C	LTC	0-1845754	1265	1
LINEBAUGH GEORGE F	LTC	0-0450753	0560	1
LINEBERRY CHARLES T	LTC	0-1286859	0361	1
LINEHAN FRANCIS B	COL	0-0249642	0566	3
LINEHAN JR DANIEL J	LTC	0-0287700	0467	3
LINEHAN RAYMOND J	CW3	W-2146305	0662	1
LINEHAN ROBERT J	MAJ	C-0360913	C146	2
LINEK VICTOR	CW3	W-2103146	0755	1
LINES CLARENCE P	LTC	0-1044875	0666	1
LINES RAYMOND F	COL	0-2046320	0366	1
LINFORD TED R	LTC	0-1167952	0461	1
LING DAVID F	CPT	0-0965189	0261	2
LING THEODORE C	CPT	0-1018295	0547	1
LING WALTER J	CPT	0-1287028	0947	2
LINGELBACH DALE N	1LT	0-0526278	0647	2
LINGENFELTER JOHN F	CPT	0-0931958	0450	2
LINGG JAMES T	CW2	W-2150591	0164	1
LINGK GERHARD F	CW2	W-2105671	1053	1
LINGLE ARNOLD H	LTC	0-1173652	0465	1
LINGNER GEORGE A	CW4	W-2120273	C757	1
LINGO HENRY	CPT	0-1311659	0646	2
LINIK JOSEPH	1LT	0-1316564	0745	2
LINK ANDREW J	LTC	0-0264442	0667	3
LINK ELMER R	1LT	0-0973601	0460	2
LINK EUGENE F	CPT	0-0522209	0448	1
LINK GORDON S	LTC	0-0506221	0567	3
LINK HAROLD S	MAJ	0-1168337	0959	1
LINK HAZEL E	COL	0-0452420	0866	1
LINK HOWARD R	CPT	0-0382416	0446	2
LINK JESSE W	MAJ	0-1583291	0662	1
LINK JR JOHN B	CPT	0-0277030	1045	2
LINK RUSSELL L	1LT	0-1109454	0246	2
LINK SR MAX W	CPT	0-0498611	0852	1
LINK THEODORE W	WO1	W-2132128	0646	2
LINKA CLARA M	2LT	N-0702632	0548	1
LINKER AURAND E	LTC	0-0328454	1060	3
LINKER JOE B	LTC	0-0140078	0657	3
LINKER ROLAND C	COL	0-0451138	0860	1
LINKHART ROBERT C	CPT	0-0377491	0246	2
LINN ARTHUR C	COL	0-0268912	0852	3
LINN CHARLES A	COL	0-0334160	0465	3
LINN HOWARD M	LTC	0-0385050	0161	1
LINN IRVING	CPT	0-0471642	0648	1
LINN LESLIE A	MAJ	0-0286519	1060	3
LINN STANLEY T	MAJ	0-2203971	0365	1
LINN WALTER R	COL	0-0179186	0351	3
LINNELL JOHN M	LTC	0-0378305	0557	1
LINNERT CLEMENT W	CPT	0-0215414	0144	2
LINNEWEH WALTER L	CW4	W-2132193	0959	1
LINNVILLE RAYMOND A	CW3	W-2122842	0757	1
LINSCHEID HAROLD E	CPT	0-1700287	0145	2
LINSLEY BRUCE A	LTC	0-1320748	1063	1
LINSTAD HOWARD O	LTC	0-0410037	0161	1
LINT ROBERT S	2LT	0-1947014	1044	2
LINTER LEONARD M	CPT	0-0418991	0845	2
LINTH FRANK A	LTC	0-1636227	1162	2
LINTHICUM CECIL I	LTC	0-0253094	0658	3
LINTHICUM EUPERT W	CPT	0-0486065	0347	1
LINTHICUM EVERETTE	CPT	0-0495755	0756	1
LINTNER JULIUS H	COL	0-0213341	0963	3
LINTON GEORGE	LTC	0-0911941	0746	2
LINTON HOWARD L	LTC	0-0328950	0563	1
LINTON JAMES W	MAJ	0-1551448	0258	1
LINTON JOHN D	COL	0-0164151	0950	1
LINTON WALTER L	LTC	0-0302416	0261	1
LINTON WILLIAM E	CW3	W-2112041	0756	1
LINTZ HARRY F	CPT	0-1822026	1146	1
LINVILLE UNICE K	CPT	0-1179504	0650	1
LINVILLE VERA G	CW2	W-2214720	0267	1
LIOI ALBERT J	MAJ	0-1059858	0261	1
LIOTTA SALVATORE	CPT	0-1689824	0745	1
LIPARI JOSEPH	MAJ	0-2037627	0363	1
LIPE WILLIAM G	CW2	W-2106291	0960	1
LIPICH JOSEPH	MAJ	0-1597604	0160	1
LIPINSKI JOHN J	CPT	0-1766916	0755	2
LIPMAN ABRAHAM I	LTC	0-0291607	0954	1
LIPMAN BARNEY	CPT	0-0159662	0146	1
LIPMAN JACK M	1LT	0-1012155	0146	2
LIPP JOHN W	LTC	0-0290262	0557	1
LIPP LEONARD C	LTC	0-1287029	0559	2
LIPPAI STEPHEN A	CPT	0-4006738	0266	1
LIPPINCOTT HOWARD E	MAJ	0-1306113	1162	1
LIPPINCOTT LOUIS D	MAJ	0-0316057	C153	1
LIPPINCOTT ROBERT	MAJ	C-1796493	0461	1

NAME	GRADE	SVC NO	DATE RET MO YR	RET CODE
LIPPITT CHARLES W	COL	C-027283C	0554	3
LIPPITT LOUIS O	CPT	0-1696239	0346	2
LIPPITT SAMUEL R	COL	C-0189632	C756	3
LIPPMAN IRVIN W	MAJ	0-0439147	C649	1
LIPPMAN PAUL	CPT	C-1017813	1146	2
LIPPY HARRY G	MAJ	0-0239192	0563	3
LIPS FRANCIS W	WO1	W-2131946	0557	1
LIPSCH SIDNEY H	1LT	0-1595656	0745	2
LIPSCOMB CHARLES J	CPT	0-0901917	C345	2
LIPSCOMB CHARLES L	LTC	0-0296225	C467	3
LIPSCOMB DAVID H	1LT	0-0409319	0647	2
LIPSCOMB HAROLD J	COL	0-0284152	0363	3
LIPSCOMB JOHN W	COL	0-0178966	0-51	3
LIPSCOMB JR HUDSON P	LTC	0-0311406	0752	3
LIPSCOMB JR JOHN S	COL	0-0269405	1164	1
LIPSCOMB PATRICK C	LTC	0-0237288	1162	3
LIPSCOMB ROBERT L	MAJ	0-2263148	C566	1
LIPSCOMB THOMAS C	MAJ	C-0269437	C767	3
LIPSCOMB WILLIAM N	LTC	0-0122037	C249	3
LIPSCOMB WILLIAM W	CW3	W-2208933	0467	1
LIPSCOMBE ROBERT R	MAJ	C-2283835	C465	1
LIPSETT ZELNER M	COL	0-0179763	C855	3
LIPSEY ARCHIE L	MAJ	C-0499976	0353	1
LIPSEY RAYMOND E	LTC	0-0275761	0757	1
LIPSEY RICHARD C	LTC	0-0403413	0362	2
LIPSIUS ALBERT J	1LT	C-0889951	0759	1
LIPSIUS KURT R	MAJ	C-0193292	0857	3
LIPSKI PETER	MAJ	0-1797485	C257	1
LIPSKY ARTHUR A	LTC	0-0239945	C361	3
LIPSKY HARRY T	MAJ	0-0312195	C862	1
LIPSKY JOSEPH A	LTC	0-0324139	C767	1
LIPSON EDWARD	MAJ	0-0471730	0444	2
LIPSON ROY E	CW3	W-2151080	1163	1
LIPTON ALEXANDER	LTC	0-0253179	0262	3
LIPUT JOSEPH A	CPT	0-2006720	0657	1
LIPUT STANLEY	CPT	0-1321367	C958	1
LIQUE FRANCIS P	CW2	W-2109025	0547	2
LIQUORI VINCENT J	1LT	0-1302678	0945	2
LIS FLORIAN	CPT	0-1331524	0459	1
LIS JOHN J	1LT	0-1060172	C847	2
LIS PAUL M	1LT	0-2005931	1147	2
LISANTI DOMINIC C	CW3	W-2125244	1059	1
LISCINSKY ANDREW G	CPT	0-0411264	1145	2
LISCOMB JESSE R	LTC	0-1314707	0363	1
LISENBE JAMES C	CPT	0-1294160	1157	1
LISENBEE MILLARD K	1LT	C-C492935	C651	1
LISENBY ALBERT S	COL	0-0103566	0757	3
LISENBY RALPH W	MAJ	0-0976853	0762	1
LISH JAMES R	MAJ	C-1185236	1064	1
LISHNESS ARTHUR R	LTC	0-1106286	1158	2
LISK CLIFFORD L	CPT	0-1031959	0647	2
LISKA JOHN J	CW3	W-2152706	1066	1
LISMAN JR ANDREW J	CPT	0-1316651	C248	1
LISOVICZ LEONARD P	1LT	0-1316762	0345	2
LISS LEWIS L	1LT	0-1594307	0146	2
LISS VICTOR T	1LT	0-1309285	1045	2
LISSNER HENRY H	COL	0-0102510	0648	3
LISSNER JOHN J J	COL	0-1579949	0866	1
LISSY LEE W	CPT	0-1593031	C564	L
LIST EDWIN O	COL	0-0158541	1046	2
LISTON HOWARD F	LTC	0-0421220	0760	1
LISTON PAUL	MAJ	C-1051656	0665	1
LISZCZ STANLEY A	MAJ	C-0305499	1044	2
LISZT LAWRENCE S	1LT	C-1596405	C646	2
LITCH JR MILTON R	LTC	0-1103759	C561	1
LITCHFIELD VERNON A	LTC	C-0477118	1166	3
LITEHISER ROBERT R	COL	0-0141755	C453	3
LITHERLAND JOHN S	CPT	0-0298080	1263	1
LITHGOW MARION B	CPT	0-0244621	0362	3
LITKE WILLIAM E	COL	0-0244608	0261	3
LITMAN LEONARD R	LTC	0-0306950	1060	1
LITT EDWARD T	CPT	0-1696013	0545	2
LITTELL ELMER L	R G	0-0029823	1060	1
LITTELL HOWARD W	LTC	0-0359162	C160	1
LITTELL LEROY O	CPT	0-0370005	0750	1
LITTERAL KELLEY	CPT	0-1299260	1046	2
LITTERST FRANK C	1LT	0-0519592	1145	2
LITTLE ALFRED T	CPT	0-1795322	0961	3
LITTLE ANDREW T	1LT	0-0321393	0545	2
LITTLE CLAYTON N	MAJ	C-0456152	0346	2
LITTLE CLIFFORD F	MAJ	0-0286861	0966	3
LITTLE CLYDE L	CW3	W-2145111	1162	1
LITTLE DON D	1LT	0-0519238	0945	1
LITTLE EDWARD R	MAJ	0-0180290	0754	3
LITTLE EPHRAMS S	1LT	0-1796819	0562	1
LITTLE EUGENE T	LTC	0-1324427	0462	1
LITTLE FRED W	CW4	W-2102005	1C54	1
LITTLE FREDERICK	MAJ	0-1555424	0166	1
LITTLE GEORGE T	WO1	W-2113130	0946	2
LITTLE GEORGE W W	CPT	0-0502915	0545	2
LITTLE GUILBERT R	LTC	0-0232909	0960	3
LITTLE HAROLD C	LTC	0-0335046	0863	3
LITTLE JAMES L	CW3	W-2143102	0360	1
LITTLE JOE M	LTC	0-201659C	0565	1
LITTLE JR CARL C	CPT	0-1289446	0147	2
LITTLE JR JONATHAN F	CPT	0-0219858	1055	3
LITTLE KEITH A	LTC	0-1101553	0663	1
LITTLE LAMAR W	LTC	0-0248135	1045	2
LITTLE LAWRENCE F	CW3	W-2002388	1165	1
LITTLE LEWIS O	MAJ	0-2019479	0962	1
LITTLE LITTLETON	LTC	0-0296187	0546	2
LITTLE LONGINC	CPT	0-0349401	1045	2
LITTLE MARTIN B	LTC	0-0255C89	0962	3
LITTLE MILTON R	MAJ	C-0113705	1C53	3
LITTLE PERCY R	COL	0-0243667	0161	3
LITTLE RALPH V	MAJ	0-1300666	0761	1
LITTLE ROBERT E	CPT	0-0411350	1263	1
LITTLE ROBERT H	CW2	W-2148868	0761	1
LITTLE RUSSELL M	CPT	0-0247296	0557	3
LITTLE VERNA B	MAJ	N-0765652	0665	1
LITTLE WILLIAM J	MAJ	C-2016146	1058	1
LITTLE WILLIAM S	LTC	0-0254297	0266	3
LITTLEFIELD CHESTER	MAJ	0-2263230	0462	1
LITTLEFIELD ERNEST A	COL	0-0268573	0646	2
LITTLEFIELD HOWARD C	MAJ	0-2206093	0864	1
LITTLEFIELD JAMES C	COL	C-0174612	0562	3
LITTLEHALES WILLIAM	MAJ	0-0957394	C662	1
LITTLEJOHN ARON H	MAJ	C-2034976	0658	1
LITTLEJOHN CHARLES E	LTC	0-014784C	1155	3
LITTLEJOHN CLYDE	MAJ	0-1322243	0860	1
LITTLEPAGE NORRIS	2LT	0-1172148	0845	1
LITTLETON DARCY A	LTC	0-0337844	1059	3
LITTLETON HARRY M	CPT	0-0141758	0553	3
LITTLETON JR REX B	1LT	0-4043736	0361	2
LITTLETON MARVIN V	MAJ	0-1846025	0866	1
LITTMAN ABRAHAM	LTC	0-0247852	0567	3
LITTMAN HERMAN	LTC	0-0379058	1167	3
LITTMAN JEROME R	1LT	0-1053228	0346	2
LITTMAN MAXWELL	1LT	0-1048466	0444	2
LITTON BIRCHELL E	CW2	W-2211478	0766	1
LITTON STEPHEN M	CPT	0-0450179	0146	2
LITTRELL HOWARD F	MAJ	0-1116926	1063	1
LITTRELL LURA L	1LT	N-0733338	0245	1
LITTRELL WOODROW	WO1	W-2109854	0757	1
LITWIN DONALD J	CW2	W-2116119	0847	2
LITZELMAN JOHN H	MAJ	0-0141758	0857	3
LITZI JERRY	1LT	0-0561525	0653	1
LIUNI FRANK	COL	0-0138218	0558	3
LIUZZI ROCCO V	MAJ	0-0339067	104N	2
LIVAZER HERSH	LTC	0-0527131	0465	2
LIVE ISAAC C	MAJ	0-0335613	0766	3
LIVEAKOS GEORGE H	LTC	0-1186113	0766	1
LIVELY CHESTER A	LTC	0-0346055	0960	1
LIVELY JACK W	CW4	W-2142245	0556	1
LIVELY LABAN G	COL	0-0306318	0865	1
LIVELY RICHARD F	MAJ	0-200C448	0859	1
LIVELY RICHARD P	COL	0-0283172	0547	2
LIVELY ROBERT L	CW2	W-2141359	0858	1
LIVELY WILLIAM P	CPT	0-0182091	0357	3
LIVENGOOD NORMAN D	MAJ	0-0921554	0446	2
LIVENGOOD ROBERT R	1LT	C-1294329	C145	2
LIVENSPARGAR DAVENPO	LTC	0-0370841	0361	1
LIVERMORE EDWIN C	CW3	W-2141360	1057	1
LIVERNOIS EDWARD D	CPT	0-1014788	C464	1
LIVESAY TOLLAND D	CW4	W-2103149	C161	1
LIVESEY JR HERBERT B	LTC	0-0229502	C562	3
LIVINGSTON C E	CPT	0-0125232	1044	2
LIVINGSTON C E	LTC	0-0298814	C857	1
LIVINGSTON CHARLES H	LTC	0-0580929	0563	1
LIVINGSTON CHESTER	CW3	W-2148353	0760	1
LIVINGSTON DANIEL	MAJ	0-0265598	0664	1
LIVINGSTON DONALD B	LTC	0-0220255	C764	3
LIVINGSTON GUS	LTC	0-1999165	0962	2
LIVINGSTON JEROME M	MAJ	C-2046299	1154	1
LIVINGSTON JOE L	CW2	W-2152222	C961	1
LIVINGSTON JOSEPH D	CW2	W-2148744	1162	1
LIVINGSTON KNOX W	1LT	0-1042353	1047	2
LIVINGSTON LUNSFORD	LTC	0-0315305	0646	2
LIVINGSTON MORGAN L	LTC	C-0375153	0762	2
LIVINGSTON OLIVER E	CW3	W-2152727	0762	1
LIVINGSTON OLLIE B	1LT	0-0518145	1046	2
LIVINGSTON STANLEY R	MAJ	C-1639314	1062	1
LIVINGSTON STANTON K	COL	0-0224935	C458	3
LIVINGSTON THOMAS A	LTC	0-0328427	0662	1
LIVINGSTON WELLINGTO	LTC	0-1595319	0265	1
LIVINGSTON WILLIAM S	1LT	0-0524133	0846	2
LIVINGSTON WILLIS A	1LT	0-1014216	1145	2
LIVINGSTON WOODROW W	MAJ	0-1543881	C261	1
LIVINGSTONE CECIL G	LTC	0-0311179	1063	3
LIWSKI PETER P	COL	C-0312952	0758	1
LIZARDI JOSE C	CPT	0-0217529	1145	2
LIZON JAMES J	CW2	W-2148609	0163	1
LIZZI ARTHUR J	MAJ	0-042286C	C346	2
LJUNGDAHL WILLIAM A	1LT	0-0103190	0746	2
LLATO ANTONIO	1LT	0-1556465	C246	1
LLAVINA RAFAEL	CW2	W-2147664	0360	1
LLEWELLYN BERNARD J	CPT	0-1914384	1044	1
LLEWELLYN ENSLEY M	LTC	0-0246386	1165	3
LLEWELLYN JOHN G	COL	C-0232095	1050	3
LLEWELLYN KENDALL O	CPT	0-0379912	0246	1
LLEWELLYN RUSSELL W	MAJ	0-0199408	0155	1
LLOMPART JOSEPH A	LTC	0-0208691	1050	3
LLORENTE FLORENCIC	2LT	0-2030663	0548	1
LLOY HAROLD A	LTC	C-1558734	0463	1
LLOYD ADDINELL W	LTC	0-0286187	1062	3
LLOYD ARTHUR H	CW2	W-2150132	0564	1
LLOYD BENJAMIN J	1LT	0-1000993	0246	2
LLOYD CARLTON D	MAJ	0-1559720	1164	1
LLOYD CECIL C	CPT	0-1283099	0762	1
LLOYD CHESTER U	CW3	W-2142647	0561	2
LLOYD DAVID G	LTC	0-0292406	0367	3
LLOYD DOUGLAS P	MAJ	0-0245273	1162	3
LLOYD EARL K	MAJ	C-0996988	C464	1
LLOYD ERIC F	CW4	W-2114431	0857	1
LLOYD FRANK W	LTC	0-0327189	0659	2
LLOYD HENRY W	LTC	0-0330985	1166	1
LLOYD III WILLIAM C	MAJ	C-1919849	1165	1
LLOYD JAMES	CW3	W-2152161	0264	1
LLOYD JANE	MAJ	N-0745186	0867	1
LLOYD JOEL	CW3	W-2148833	0162	1
LLOYD JR JOHN W	MAJ	C-0252629	0167	3
LLOYD KATHERINE	1LT	N-0703320	0445	1
LLOYD LEON A	LTC	0-0158034	1057	3
LLOYD MARGARET C	CPT	L-1010317	C554	2
LLOYD MINTA	MAJ	N-0728554	0266	3
LLOYD ROBERT B	CPT	0-0336522	0749	2
LLOYD ROBERT J	MAJ	0-0244505	1262	3
LLOYD ROBERT W	1LT	0-0452465	1043	2
LLOYD THOMAS O	LTC	0-1285781	0461	1
LLOYD THOMAS R	WO1	W-2005350	1165	3
LLOYD WALTER R	MAJ	0-1338482	C363	1
LLUCH JOSE C	MAJ	C-017054C	0456	3
LO PRESTI JOSEPH M	CW3	W-2143055	1062	1
LO VECCHIO GUY F	LTC	0-0527343	0864	1
LOADER BYRON O	CW4	W-2141616	0767	1
LOADER CLIFFORD F	MAJ	0-052593C	0347	2
LOAR ROBERT R	2LT	0-1032636	1044	2
LOBBY MAURICE E	CW3	W-2150798	0962	1
LOBDELL ARTHUR T	COL	0-013C49C	1154	3
LOBEL JACOB	MAJ	0-1104959	0765	1
LOBEL MURRAY R	MAJ	0-0572584	0265	1
LOBERG LAURICE L	LTC	0-1305077	0562	1
LOBIANCO FRANK E	LTC	0-0346946	0351	1
LOBIT JAMES C	LTC	0-0496315	1162	1
LOBO ISMAEL Y	1LT	0-1896526	1157	1
LOBSINGER ALVIN P	LTC	0-105370C	0962	1
LOBUE NICHOLAS J	CPT	0-0359316	1044	2
LOCASCIO JOSEPH R	CW3	W-2206411	0166	1
LOCASCIO NICHOLAS R	MAJ	0-0284406	0246	2
LOCER HARVEY W	MAJ	C-1285448	0661	1
LOCH ELMER V	LTC	0-1303747	0159	1
LOCHEN EVERETTE L	LTC	0-0250441	0466	3
LOCHLIN CLIFFORD A	COL	0-0381008	0157	1
LOCK JAMES W	MAJ	0-2019480	0463	1
LOCK JR FRANK A	MAJ	0-2208581	0867	1
LOCKARD CLAIR R	MAJ	C-1319428	1060	1
LOCKARD CLARENCE H	CW2	W-2144642	1060	1
LOCKARD RICHARD J	MAJ	0-1846476	0160	2
LOCKARD WALTER S	CW2	W-3430275	0867	1
LOCKE BRUCE M	MAJ	0-1593035	0863	1
LOCKE CHARLES C	CPT	0-0107876	0752	3
LOCKE FREDERICK	1LT	0-0109173	0935	1
LOCKE HERBERT H	MAJ	0-2020741	0962	1
LOCKE JOHN P	LTC	0-0169467	0360	3
LOCKE JOHN R	COL	0-0301126	0466	3
LOCKE ROBERT	MAJ	0-1011713	0759	1
LOCKE ROBERT L	LTC	0-1577486	0667	1
LOCKE ROBERT M	CPT	0-1057806	1060	1
LOCKE ROLLIN K	MAJ	C-1591899	1160	1
LOCKE RUPERT A	LTC	0-0373342	0758	1
LOCKEN CARL M	MAJ	0-0280533	0566	3
LOCKER LUTHER M	LTC	0-0259133	0746	2
LOCKERMAN JULIAN F	LTC	0-1039443	0863	1
LOCKETT WENDELL W	LTC	0-0391249	1161	2
LOCKETT WILLIAM R	LTC	0-0360122	0766	3
LOCKHART CHARLES G	CPT	0-1103762	1064	1
LOCKHART HAROLD E	MAJ	0-1179506	0763	1
LOCKHART HOWARD C	LTC	0-0317298	0947	2
LOCKHART JACK N	MAJ	0-1177889	0461	1
LOCKHART JOSEPH	LTC	0-0170565	0945	2
LOCKHART JR ROBERT	MAJ	0-1168341	0762	1
LOCKHART RALPH M	COL	C-0241255	1262	3
LOCKLEAR ROBERT W	MAJ	0-1599C96	0759	1
LOCKLEAR WILLIAM C	MAJ	0-0509489	1053	1
LOCKLER FRANK T	CW2	W-2207543	0462	1
LOCKLIN HORACE M	LTC	0-0474127	0555	1
LOCKLIN ORVIL L	1LT	0-17963C8	0152	1
LOCKMAN EDGAR D	LTC	0-0307681	0458	3
LOCKMAN JR EDGAR P	CW2	W-2209928	1264	1
LOCKNANE BUSH W	MAJ	0-0232826	0460	3
LOCKSLEY HOWARD R	1LT	0-0341673	0246	1
LOCKWOOD ARTHUR W	CPT	0-1295395	0546	1
LOCKWOOD CHERRY L	1LT	J-0100151	0756	2
LOCKWOOD FREDERICK	LTC	0-1648361	0658	1
LOCKWOOD JOHN J	CW3	W-2112271	0256	1
LOCKWOOD JOHN S	CPT	0-0446772	1046	2
LOCKWOOD KENNETH V	CPT	0-1285257	0645	2
LOCKWOOD ROBERT J	MAJ	0-1113324	0165	1
LOCKWOOD RUSSELL A	LTC	0-0491382	0654	2
LOCKWOOD SAMUEL M	MAJ	0-1284723	1061	1
LOCKWOOD WILLIAM E	LTC	0-0117424	0754	3
LOCKWOOD WILLIAM W	LTC	0-0301415	0761	1
LOCKYER ROBERT H	LTC	0-1046182	0961	1
LOCKYER WILLIAM T	LTC	0-0341470	0647	1
LODATO JOHN F	LTC	0-0277761	0662	1
LODATO JR VICTOR	CPT	0-0495835	0145	2
LODEK CHARLES C	MAJ	0-0289155	0655	1
LODEN EARL	LTC	0-0271482	1056	3
LODER CHARLES	CPT	0-1642329	0654	2
LODER WILLIAM C	COL	0-0451336	0467	1

NAME	GRADE	SVC NO	DATE RET MO YR	RET CODE
LODGE SHENTON R	MAJ	0-1115677	0761	1
LODISE FRANCES R	1LT	N-0729064	0545	1
LODL JR JAMES	CW2	W-2110830	0556	1
LOEB ROBERT M	LTC	0-0296808	0964	3
LOEBEL GEORGE A	LTC	0-0510496	0762	1
LOEBS CARL H	LTC	0-0166328	1152	3
LOEFFLER ERWIN P	LTC	0-0555185	0565	1
LOEFFLER WILLIAM E	CPT	0-0515414	0249	1
LOEHNERTZ ELFRIEDA E	2LT	N-0774905	0845	1
LOEHR WILLIAM M	LTC	0-0332668	0753	1
LOER GEORGE W	MAJ	0-0349105	0764	3
LOES EDWIN B	MAJ	0-1297751	0264	1
LOES MURLAND F	COL	0-0350715	0557	1
LOES PAUL F	1LT	0-1325908	0446	2
LOESCH ROBERT J	LTC	0-0421204	0363	1
LOESER JOHN M	WO1	W-2131274	0747	2
LOEWE WILL R	COL	0-0277576	1161	3
LOEWEN FRANK W	CW2	W-2144385	1058	1
LOFFREDO ANTHONY P	MAJ	0-2047409	0261	1
LOFGREEN EARSTON A	CPT	0-0446845	0546	2
LOFGREN CARL R	LTC	0-1317552	1262	2
LOFGREN JAMES T	LTC	0-0383624	1060	1
LOFGREN PAUL F	1LT	0-1305611	0945	2
LOFLAND EDWARD O	CW3	W-2150801	1263	1
LOFLAND ROBERT R	1LT	0-1285612	0345	2
LOFLAND WILMER C	LTC	0-2029075	1263	1
LOFLEN LESTER A	MAJ	0-2016488	0660	1
LOFTESNESS CURTIS H	MAJ	0-1685659	0565	1
LOFTFIELD BERNER F	MAJ	0-0280640	0746	2
LOFTFIELD GORM	CPT	0-0199728	0551	3
LOFTHEIM HAAKON L	LTC	0-1032637	0861	1
LOFTIN JAMES C	MAJ	0-0251709	1046	2
LOFTIN ROBERT E	CPT	0-0386043	1043	2
LOFTON HARRY F	COL	0-0265634	1061	3
LOFTUS FRANCIS S	MAJ	0-0971198	0264	1
LOFTUS JOHN J	CW4	W-2148629	0656	1
LOFTUS MARGARET P	2LT	N-0797605	1147	1
LOGAN ALBERT N	2LT	0-1822159	0645	2
LOGAN BENNIE L	CW2	W-2124547	0650	1
LOGAN CHARLES F	MAJ	0-1935052	0966	1
LOGAN CHARLES O	LTC	0-0313173	0258	1
LOGAN CHARLES W	MAJ	0-1825232	1060	1
LOGAN CLYDE R	CW3	W-2152707	1263	2
LOGAN COOLIDGE A	MAJ	0-0963527	0861	1
LOGAN DULANEY C	CPT	0-0514410	0646	2
LOGAN EOSEL G	CPT	0-1533130	0851	2
LOGAN EMMETT M	LTC	0-0411080	0861	1
LOGAN ERNEST J	MAJ	0-0572469	1056	1
LOGAN GEORGE A	LTC	0-0403341	1066	3
LOGAN HENRY T	MAJ	0-0455588	0246	1
LOGAN HERBERT A	MAJ	0-2002482	0561	1
LOGAN JAMES W	COL	0-0288875	0860	1
LOGAN JOHN R	CW2	W-3150757	0367	1
LOGAN JOSEPH A	LTC	0-0111700	0453	3
LOGAN JOSEPH A	LTC	0-1845307	0765	3
LOGAN JOSEPH R	LTC	0-0397159	0261	1
LOGAN JR SHERMAN C	MAJ	0-0969783	0161	1
LOGAN JR WILLIAM B	1LT	0-1057151	0446	2
LOGAN JR WILLIAM G	CW3	W-2151648	1262	1
LOGAN RAYMOND M	2LT	0-0378088	1044	2
LOGAN ROBERT A	LTC	0-1699152	1144	2
LOGAN ROBERT G	COL	0-0411587	0161	1
LOGAN ROBERT L	COL	0-0101325	1154	3
LOGAN ROBERT M	LTC	0-0389737	1262	1
LOGAN RUSSELL S	MAJ	0-0358073	0945	2
LOGAN SR GORDON W	CPT	0-1937201	0864	1
LOGAN THEOPHILUS	MAJ	0-1311527	0762	1
LOGAN THOMAS H	CPT	0-0962710	1060	1
LOGAN WILBUR E	MAJ	0-0334329	1160	3
LOGAN WILLIAM B	1LT	0-1315703	0947	2
LOGAN WILLIAM N	2LT	0-1182635	1144	2
LOGAN WYATT Y	CPT	0-2212081	0860	1
LOGEL JOHN	WO1	W-2130729	0956	1
LOGIE MARC J	COL	0-0187529	0853	3
LOGSDON CALE M	LTC	0-0224131	1157	3
LOGUE CHARLES O	MAJ	0-2025630	1063	1
LOGUE CHARLES W	2LT	0-1016663	0545	2
LOHMAN KENNETH W	CPT	0-1289600	0257	1
LOHMILLER MATTHEW J	LTC	0-0133472	1056	3
LOHN OVID L	CPT	0-0497877	0547	1
LOHNES HALLET E	CPT	0-0187688	1053	2
LOHNES JAMES F	MAJ	0-1639319	0662	1
LOHR CURTIS H	COL	0-0275251	0157	3
LOHR JOHN M	LTC	0-0240182	0164	3
LOHR LAWRENCE J	CPT	0-0492151	0146	2
LOHSE MELVIN C	CW4	W-2124484	0964	1
LOIERO ALPHONSE J	CW2	W-2143196	1161	1
LOIZEAUX PAUL F	COL	0-0225670	0364	3
LOKEN HARRIS	1LT	0-1013648	0346	2
LOKEN LESLIE P	COL	0-0386341	1055	1
LOKEY BENJAMIN F	1LT	0-0424048	0346	2
LOKEY WILLIAM H	MAJ	0-0232243	0565	3
LOKKER HOMER C	MAJ	0-2035122	0261	1
LOLLAR LEON B	CPT	0-2016396	0561	1
LOLLAR RICHARD L	LTC	0-0208237	0654	3
LOLLAR VICTOR G	1LT	0-2204173	1053	2
LOLLIS GEORGE A	LTC	0-0518005	1264	1
LOMAN FREDERICK	CPT	0-0515091	0546	2
LOMAS ATHALEE A	MAJ	N-0703344	1165	1
LOMAS GEORGE A	CW3	W-2141618	0662	1
LOMASNEY JOHN W	LTC	0-0504349	1054	1
LOMBAES LEO	2LT	0-1174046	0445	2
LOMBARD ARTHUR G	COL	0-0910116	0966	1
LOMBARD EMMONS S	MAJ	0-0253614	0662	3
LOMBARD REGINALD T	COL	0-0196244	0856	3
LOMBARDI LUCIAN	LTC	0-0335036	0746	2
LOMBARDI PHILIP J	LTC	0-0547386	0967	1
LOMBARDO ETHEL M	1LT	N-0794572	1146	1
LOMBARDO LAWRENCE	CW2	W-3150404	0466	2
LOMBARDO ROBERT T	WO1	W-2150355	1153	2
LOMBARDO SAMUEL	LTC	0-1287551	0162	1
LOMET JR PIERRE	LTC	0-0211742	1061	3
LOMITOLA JOHN L	CPT	0-1298256	0863	1
LOMMLER PRYCE W	CPT	0-1321644	0547	2
LOMMORI JOSEPH P	MAJ	0-0358666	0646	2
LOMONACO JOSEPH	2LT	0-1308429	1143	2
LONABAUGH MARTHA M	MAJ	N-0725995	1167	1
LONBERGER FRANK R	1LT	0-0414072	0146	2
LONDON BENJAMIN C	LTC	0-1594628	0762	1
LONDON CLYDE F	MAJ	0-0570213	1061	1
LONDON DANIEL	CPT	0-0497950	0251	2
LONDON ELLIOTT F	CPT	0-0252899	0862	3
LONDON JOHN D	CW3	W-2152580	0664	1
LONERGAN FRANK F	LTC	0-1103764	0763	1
LONERGAN JOHN D	MAJ	0-0305621	0766	3
LONEY RALPH H	MAJ	0-0968675	0466	1
LONEY ROBERT S	LTC	0-0908137	0367	3
LONG AARON A	CW3	W-2150133	0456	1
LONG ADOLPHUS P	CW3	W-2144811	0862	1
LONG ALBERT W	MAJ	0-0448902	1055	1
LONG ARTHUR	MAJ	0-1994467	0863	1
LONG BROCKS R	2LT	0-2024322	0646	1
LONG BYFORD F	LTC	0-1287553	0665	1
LONG CALVIN	WO1	W-2115901	1044	2
LONG CARL F	MAJ	0-0355154	1166	1
LONG CHARLES F	1LT	0-1168782	0846	2
LONG CHARLES J	CPT	0-1010003	1051	1
LONG DON E	MAJ	0-1315849	1060	1
LONG DONALD F	LTC	0-0141656	0953	3
LONG EDWARD H	LTC	0-0283656	0467	3
LONG ELMER I	LTC	0-0331646	1067	3
LONG ERNEST W	LTC	0-0402446	0258	1
LONG EUGENE L	LTC	0-0327818	0366	3
LONG FAYE L	LTC	0-0373344	0161	1
LONG FLOYD M	2LT	0-1822890	0244	2
LONG FRANK C	CW3	W-2144711	0466	1
LONG FRANK E	MAJ	0-0118407	0648	3
LONG FRANK H	2LT	0-2005637	0356	2
LONG FRANK S	LTC	0-0111105	0648	3
LONG FRED P	LTC	0-0311126	0464	3
LONG GEORGE C	COL	0-0256349	0564	3
LONG GEORGE P	LTC	0-0336542	1154	2
LONG GLEN H	CW2	W-2109853	0857	1
LONG GLENDON R	COL	0-0359901	0563	1
LONG HAMILTON A	MAJ	0-0140380	0359	3
LONG HENRY A	CPT	0-0482079	0845	1
LONG HUBERT F	LTC	0-0299640	0359	1
LONG JAMES B	LTC	0-0235628	1044	2
LONG JAMES E	COL	0-0188220	0460	3
LONG JAMES F R	CPT	0-0171021	0648	3
LONG JAMES J	LTC	0-1541259	0364	1
LONG JAMES M	MAJ	0-2042880	0161	2
LONG JAMES R	MAJ	0-1108119	0663	1
LONG JAMES R	1LT	0-1287554	1145	2
LONG JOHN A	CPT	0-0302427	0546	1
LONG JOHN A	CPT	0-0376777	1045	2
LONG JOHN D	MAJ	0-1012647	1147	1
LONG JOHN L	CW2	W-2149226	0361	2
LONG JOHN W	COL	0-0190011	0355	3
LONG JOHN W	MAJ	0-0333779	1154	2
LONG JOSEPH S	MAJ	0-1637951	1046	1
LONG JR AVERY P	MAJ	0-0239105	0465	3
LONG JR EARL S	MAJ	0-1926294	0566	1
LONG JR LOUIS C	CW2	W-2109370	0156	2
LONG JR WILLIAM B	MAJ	0-1010220	0646	2
LONG LAWRENCE M	LTC	0-0372701	0656	1
LONG LAWRENCE W	COL	0-0239899	0462	3
LONG LEONARD H	1LT	0-1588129	1049	1
LONG MAURICE F	1LT	0-1304249	0245	2
LONG MAX H	CPT	0-0491131	1053	2
LONG NORMAN G	LTC	0-0290255	1164	3
LONG ODUS E	1LT	0-1293430	0752	2
LONG ORAN M	CPT	0-1030687	1048	1
LONG PAUL M	LTC	0-0278156	0758	3
LONG PAUL T	LTC	0-1825423	1166	1
LONG PAUL W	LTC	0-0308417	0466	1
LONG RAYMOND B	CPT	0-0219396	0457	3
LONG REGINALD	CPT	0-1924783	1262	2
LONG RICHARD J	1LT	0-1297060	0146	2
LONG RICHARD J	MAJ	0-2203067	0764	1
LONG ROBERT F	1LT	0-0449410	0344	2
LONG ROBERT F	CW2	W-2142170	0855	2
LONG ROBERT G	LTC	0-0254779	0954	1
LONG ROBERT N	CPT	0-0171920	0358	3
LONG ROBERT W	LTC	0-0201586	0663	1
LONG RUDOLPH A	CW3	W-2144750	0860	2
LONG RUSSELL A	CPT	0-0304903	0348	1
LONG SAM H	COL	0-0323054	0154	3
LONG SAMUEL M	2LT	0-1322640	0844	2
LONG THEODORE S	MAJ	0-1001398	0861	1
LONG THOMAS J	2LT	0-1304250	0345	2
LONG THOMAS J	1LT	0-1332836	0652	1
LONG THOMAS M	CPT	0-1598137	0165	1
LONG THOMAS TEL	COL	0-0242212	0951	1
LONG TOMMY L	LTC	0-0423851	0663	1
LONG VINCENT P	1LT	0-1319846	0546	2
LONG WARREN R	WO1	W-2120078	0654	1
LONG WAYNE E	MAJ	0-0238434	0864	3
LONG WENDELL B	LTC	0-0217854	0462	3
LONG WENDELL W	MAJ	0-1175784	0763	1
LONG WILLIAM	MAJ	0-0250163	0947	1
LONG WILLIAM C	CW3	W-2142246	1060	1
LONG WILLIAM F	MAJ	0-0151834	0455	3
LONG WILLIAM G	MAJ	0-2262903	0264	1
LONG WILLIAM H	CPT	0-0256924	0866	3
LONG WILLIAM J	MAJ	0-0218889	0254	3
LONG WILLIAM L	CW3	RW-2207647	0866	1
LONG WILLIAM M	CPT	0-0488819	0847	1
LONGACRE M ANNABEL	MAJ	N-0725120	0462	1
LONGENECKER ERNST A	MAJ	0-0156689	0456	3
LONGENECKER HARRY W	MAJ	0-0975473	0165	1
LONGEY LLOYD L	MAJ	0-0490115	0954	1
LONGFELLOW HENRY W	LTC	0-1100205	0963	1
LONGFELLOW LAWRENCE	LTC	0-1172152	0967	1
LONGFELLOW LYMAN E	CW3	W-2146606	0762	1
LONGFELLOW ROY C	LTC	0-0373272	1060	2
LONGLEY ANDREW J	COL	0-0231803	0365	3
LONGLEY FRANCIS F	MAJ	0-2262491	1265	1
LONGMIRE BYRON H	CW2	W-2112107	0450	1
LONGMIRE MARION A	CPT	0-0327821	0745	2
LONGNECKER THOMAS H	1LT	0-1959089	1046	2
LONGO AUGUSTINE	CW3	W-2141361	0461	1
LONGO DANIEL J	CW4	W-2115171	0959	1
LONGO JOHN M	LTC	0-2040892	0160	1
LONGOBARDI MARY S	2LT	N-0729149	0745	1
LONGORIA VICTOR M	CPT	0-0284684	0945	2
LONGPRE J H FERNAN	LTC	0-0483795	0346	2
LONGSDON MALCOLM J	MAJ	0-0481434	0546	2
LONGSDORF FORD H	COL	0-0298772	1060	3
LONGSDORF JAMES E	CPT	0-0954994	0467	1
LONGSHORE JOHN R	COL	0-0340185	0957	1
LONGSHORE PAUL J	LTC	0-0236701	0361	3
LONGSWORTH HAROLD J	LTC	0-0348582	0261	1
LONGTIN LUCGER P	CW2	W-2206335	0665	1
LONGWELL FREEMAN H	MAJ	0-0332962	0246	2
LONGWILL BENNY F	MAJ	0-2037073	0561	1
LONGWORTH EVERETT	CPT	0-0394858	0562	1
LONNQUIST T ESCARENA	MAJ	N-0741900	0864	3
LONON WILLIAM A	1LT	0-1168342	0747	1
LONSETH CLAYTON O	LTC	0-1550854	0563	1
LONSFORD CHARLES A	MAJ	0-0548805	1060	1
LONSINGER WALLACE F	2LT	0-1179508	0245	2
LONTOS CLARENCE J	MAJ	0-1932459	0667	1
LOOFBOURROW WADE H	LTC	0-0253511	0358	3
LOOMIS DONALD O	CPT	0-0890223	0147	2
LOOMIS JOSEPH M	CPT	0-2262289	0758	2
LOOMIS JR GUY A	COL	0-0261293	0667	3
LOOMIS LEE S	CW3	W-2150037	1060	1
LOOMIS MARVIN A	CPT	0-1297909	1147	1
LOOMIS PAUL A	COL	0-0350599	0366	2
LOOMIS PHILIP L	LTC	0-0351642	0759	1
LOOMIS WILLARD T	CPT	0-0343605	0744	1
LOOMIS WILLIAM R	LTC	0-0294773	0964	3
LOOMIS WILLIAM E	CW3	W-2109265	1060	1
LOONEY ENNIS M	CW3	W-2146758	0963	1
LOONEY HOUSTON G	LTC	0-1703759	1058	1
LOONEY JACK M	LTC	0-0541991	0767	1
LOONEY JAMES K	LTC	0-0198078	1056	3
LOONEY JR JAMES H	1LT	0-0461463	1144	1
LOONEY MICHAEL L	COL	0-0319850	0764	3
LOONEY MORRIS G	MAJ	0-2012772	0367	1
LOONEY QUENTEN S	MAJ	0-2262797	1062	1
LOOP ALFRED B	WO1	W-2114734	1049	2
LOOP ELVIN J	MAJ	0-0963858	0363	2
LOOP VINCENT C	LTC	0-0401826	0862	1
LOOPER RANSOME T	COL	0-0423260	0666	1
LOORAM JOHN J	CPT	0-1012175	1047	1
LOOS ALOC H	COL	0-0363503	1059	3
LOOS CARL O	LTC	0-1049250	1057	1
LOOS KARL O	CPT	0-0100047	0351	3
LOOSBROCK JOHN F	CPT	0-1286151	0345	2
LOOSER IRENE A	CPT	N-0730985	1047	1
LOPARDO ANTONIO A	CW3	W-2145216	0460	1
LOPER JAMES F	1LT	0-1319429	0749	2
LOPER JR WILLIAM H	LTC	0-0578362	0762	1
LOPES ALBERT V	CPT	0-2263307	0861	1
LOPEZ ALBERT C	LTC	0-1100653	0358	1
LOPEZ CARLOS	2LT	0-1017649	0945	2
LOPEZ DE VICTORI	1LT	0-1180589	0547	2
LOPEZ FRITCSC R	MAJ	0-1917614	1062	1
LOPEZ JR JULIAN	MAJ	0-1694994	0365	1
LOPEZ LAURENCE C	CW3	W-2153094	0163	1
LOPEZ LOUIS V	LTC	0-0186282	0154	3
LOPEZ LOUIS V	MAJ	0-0954056	1162	1
LOPICCOLO ERNEST K	LTC	0-1110627	0866	1
LOPSHIRE ARTHUR P	COL	0-0327147	0360	3
LOPUS LESTER R	COL	0-0197030	0454	3
LOPUSNIAK MACK S	1LT	0-0419864	1144	2
LOR ALFRED R	CPT	0-1306292	0857	1
LORAH BRUCE	CW3	W-2005876	0967	1

NAME	GRADE	SVC NO	DATE RET MO YR	RET CODE
LORANCE GEORGE A	CPT	0-0450987	1157	1
LORANCE JEROME	MAJ	0-1553502	1060	1
LORANGE HARRY	LTC	0-0278569	1264	3
LORANGER JOHN W	MAJ	0-1844817	0367	1
LORCH ROBERT B	LTC	0-0200850	0850	3
LORD AUSTIN R	MAJ	0-1319093	0565	1
LORD CHARLES E	MAJ	0-0263622	1058	3
LORD CHARLES G	LTC	0-0339355	0765	3
LORD E R	COL	0-0197753	0563	3
LORD FRANK H	WO1	W-2120361	0347	2
LORD GORDON C	MAJ	0-0251859	1057	3
LORD HANSEL L	CPT	0-1296723	0446	2
LORD HAROLD F	LTC	0-1000405	0261	1
LORD JR FREDERICK	CPT	0-0398404	0544	2
LORD JR WILLIAM A	COL	0-0231053	0364	3
LORD LAURENCE F	LTC	0-0473947	0162	3
LORD M D	MAJ	0-0935963	1163	1
LORD MEDERIC J	CW3	W-2148484	0163	1
LORD RALPH C	CPT	0-0494305	0548	1
LORD ROBERT E	CPT	0-1309766	0546	2
LORD RUSSELL R	COL	0-0253043	0566	3
LORD WILLFRED V	CPT	0-0415334	1044	2
LORD WILLIAM J	1LT	0-0555806	0247	1
LORDEN DANIEL F	1LT	0-0525324	0349	1
LORE GEORGE T W	MAJ	0-2262774	0762	1
LOREE JAMES T	COL	0-0299127	0648	3
LOREN WILLIAM H	LTC	0-1168785	0267	1
LORENTZ CARL R	WO1	W-2150169	1054	1
LORENTZEN JULIUS C	MAJ	0-0202991	0648	3
LORENZ FRANK	CW3	W-2207349	0966	1
LORENZ HERMAN A	MAJ	0-0166566	0545	2
LORENZ THEODORE E	LTC	0-0198949	1053	1
LORENZEN JOHN R	LTC	0-1558593	1167	1
LORENZO MICHAEL J	LTC	0-1634085	1164	1
LORENZO PEDRO	1LT	0-1896986	0859	1
LORENZO SEBASTIAN	MAJ	0-1301171	0762	2
LORETTE EDMOND O	CW4	W-2102014	0955	1
LORETTE FRANCIS B	CW4	W-2148258	0864	1
LORETTE SANFORD O	LTC	0-0449228	0263	1
LOREY JR PAUL R	2LT	0-0545475	1045	2
LORIA JR JOSEPH A	MAJ	0-1054680	0265	1
LORIE JAMES N	LTC	0-0475876	0454	1
LORIMER FRANK M	CPT	0-0476076	0446	2
LORIMER GEORGE H	LTC	0-0245573	0459	3
LORIMER III WILLIAM	COL	0-0297340	0560	1
LORING ALBERT W	CPT	0-1106913	0346	2
LORING ARTHUR P	LTC	0-0301101	1263	3
LORING GLADDON L	LTC	0-1548923	0267	1
LORSUNG LLOYD W	MAJ	0-1549535	0665	1
LORY EARL C	LTC	0-0249340	0766	3
LORY JOSEPH W	CW3	W-2203331	0465	1
LORZ NORBERT W	MAJ	0-0296057	0763	3
LOS BANOS BERN	MAJ	0-1331303	1162	1
LOSEF LOUIS C	MAJ	0-1556018	1060	1
LOSEE WILFRED J	MAJ	0-1699951	0962	1
LOSEL WILLIAM J	COL	0-0260070	0467	3
LOSER EARL G	LTC	0-0234997	0753	3
LOSER HENRY L	CPT	0-0822033	1166	2
LOSHBAUGH ALBERT O	MAJ	0-0405206	1146	2
LOSHNOWSKY HARRY W	1LT	0-1551051	1044	1
LOSPENNATO AMERICO W	2LT	0-1578786	0543	2
LOSS CHARLES R	LTC	0-0405233	0364	3
LOSSBOM KNUT E	CW4	W-2104249	1058	1
LOSSEF SAMUEL	1LT	0-0490264	0345	2
LOSSING FAY A	LTC	0-0234167	0965	3
LOSTUMBO DOMINICK J	LTC	0-1307923	0162	2
LOTH MORITZ A R	CPT	0-0183213	0254	3
LOTHNER ROY	LTC	0-1324428	1062	1
LOTHROP JACK W	2LT	0-0466486	0344	2
LOTHROP MELFORD M	MAJ	0-0234084	0645	2
LOTT COLON J	LTC	0-1289282	1057	1
LOTT DANIEL P	WO1	W-2119936	0244	2
LOTT DOYLE W	MAJ	0-1584535	1061	2
LOTT ELLIS T	CW3	W-2146430	0361	1
LOTT FREDERICK	CPT	0-0444203	0846	1

NAME	GRADE	SVC NO	DATE RET MO YR	RET CODE
LOTT HENRY E	LTC	0-0237461	0664	3
LOTT JOHN H	LTC	0-0294762	0257	3
LOTT JOSEPH W	CW2	W-2106758	0259	2
LOTT WILLIAM B	COL	0-0912404	0567	3
LOTTER CHARLES A	LTC	0-0267564	0157	1
LOTTI DOMINICO T	MAJ	0-0969460	0163	1
LOTTIE RAYMOND C	LTC	0-1117074	0862	1
LOTTIER RAYMOND L	MAJ	0-2033286	0465	1
LOTZ ARNOLD H	CPT	0-1293279	1262	1
LOTZ CHARLES J	1LT	0-1324429	0546	2
LOTZ HARRY B	1LT	0-0451038	0644	2
LOUCKS JOHN H	CW4	W-2133248	0158	1
LOUCKS JOSEPH A	CPT	0-1700739	0646	2
LOUD EMERY S	LTC	0-0229774	0563	3
LOUDEN MERRILL C	LTC	0-0372206	0860	1
LOUDEN RUSSELL	MAJ	0-0156895	0253	3
LOUDERMILK ALVIN E	CW2	W-2210185	1164	1
LOUDON EUGENE J	MAJ	0-1825145	0661	1
LOUDON JAMES D	MAJ	0-0380936	0746	1
LOUGEE BERNARD R	LTC	0-0557918	0167	1
LOUGH FRANK A	LTC	0-0255611	0360	1
LOUGH GEORGE E	LTC	0-0420864	1160	1
LOUGH JR CHARLES M	MAJ	0-0932077	0763	1
LOUGH LISLE S	CPT	0-1310612	0447	1
LOUGH SAMUEL R	LTC	0-0266082	0353	3
LOUGHEED CHARLES O	MAJ	0-1923522	1065	1
LOUGHRAN EUGENE P	1LT	0-5321972	1066	2
LOUGHRAN JOHN F	CW3	W-2107872	1061	1
LOUGHRAN JOHN J	COL	0-1040046	0466	1
LOUGHRY RICHARD F	MAJ	0-1325304	0161	1
LOUIS FRED W	COL	0-0434726	0462	1
LOUIS JOHN J	MAJ	0-4010509	0567	1
LOUN ELVA M	CW3	V-0322541	0765	1
LOUNSBERRY GEORGE H	MAJ	0-0285837	0862	3
LOUNSBERRY RALPH F	MAJ	0-1037135	0559	2
LOUPE SYLVAIN R	COL	0-0271551	0567	3
LOURDEAUX STANLEY J	CPT	0-0422851	1144	2
LOUSBERY ARTHUR E	LTC	0-0464227	0763	2
LOUSTEAU DANIEL T	LTC	0-1177568	0866	1
LOUT ELSA K	2LT	N-0723841	0645	1
LOVANYAK ERNEST J	LTC	0-1648550	1160	1
LOVAS WILLIAM S	MAJ	0-1687354	0546	2
LOVE AMANDA I	2LT	N-0743131	0846	2
LOVE ARTHUR	1LT	0-1896735	0350	1
LOVE CLAIR L	1LT	0-1646373	0846	2
LOVE DANA W	LTC	0-0212013	1156	3
LOVE DOYNE M	CW3	W-2150323	0963	1
LOVE ELBERT H	MAJ	0-0396630	0846	2
LOVE HARRY W	1LT	0-1081353	1045	1
LOVE HOWARD L	CW4	W-2136402	0865	2
LOVE JERRY I	LTC	0-1175216	0161	1
LOVE JOHN	1LT	0-2027443	0254	1
LOVE JOHN E	1LT	0-1108818	0246	2
LOVE JR WILLIAM A	CW3	W-2112841	1060	1
LOVE JR WILLIAM S	COL	0-0246751	0246	2
LOVE LAWRENCE E	MAJ	0-0446500	0954	1
LOVE LOWELL S	COL	0-0222612	0460	1
LOVE MELVIN V	CPT	0-0521351	1147	2
LOVE RAY	COL	0-0170287	1055	3
LOVE ROBERT B	LTC	0-0273386	1061	3
LOVE RUTH A	1LT	N-0728415	0646	1
LOVE WESLEY G	1LT	0-0188757	0535	1
LOVE WILBUR P	MAJ	0-1535022	0161	2
LOVE WILLIAM D	MAJ	0-1104964	0463	1
LOVEJOY CLARENCE E	COL	0-0219503	0654	3
LOVEJOY CLIFFORD O	COL	0-0308415	0362	3
LOVEJOY FRANK	MAJ	0-0450626	0660	1
LOVEJOY GEORGE F	LTC	0-0300383	0160	1
LOVEJOY LILLIAN L	1LT	N-0786070	0147	1
LOVEJOY RHEBA O	MAJ	N-0775389	0567	3
LOVEJOY THOMAS C	LTC	0-0257807	0567	3
LOVEJOY WALTER E	2LT	0-1308157	0445	2
LOVELACE HAROLD H	COL	0-0232931	0863	3
LOVELACY WILLIAM B	COL	0-0262588	0766	3
LOVELAND CARL H	MAJ	0-0931280	0566	1

NAME	GRADE	SVC NO	DATE RET MO YR	RET CODE
LOVELAND ERWIN H	CW3	W-2146884	1264	1
LOVELAND WILLIS H	CW2	W-2205433	1062	1
LOVELESS HOWARD A	CPT	0-1291661	1044	2
LOVELESS WALTER F	MAJ	0-1823546	0658	1
LOVELL DOW H	CPT	0-0268041	1046	2
LOVELL JAMES L	MAJ	0-1037605	0464	1
LOVELL JAMES W	MAJ	0-0334033	0246	2
LOVELL JOHN W	LTC	0-0384300	0346	2
LOVELL SAMUEL W	CPT	0-1018099	1160	3
LOVELL WILLIAM H	CW4	W-2110664	0860	1
LOVELY GUY R	CW2	W-2148125	1159	1
LOVELY JOHN F	2LT	0-0197116	1029	1
LOVELY JOSEPH O	CW3	W-2005973	1064	3
LOVEMAN ADOLPH B	MAJ	0-0476654	1045	2
LOVENTHAL MARTIN S J	2LT	0-1017714	0744	2
LOVERDE ALBERT A	CPT	0-0308066	0146	2
LOVERIDGE WILLIAM T	MAJ	0-1011822	0760	1
LOVERING FRANK R	LTC	0-0265296	0962	3
LOVERING HARRY O	LTC	0-0126632	0152	3
LOVESTEDT LOYD W	CPT	0-1170064	0446	2
LOVETERE ANGELO A	MAJ	0-0330401	0545	2
LOVETT CLARENCE J	MAJ	0-0181344	1056	3
LOVETT JOE T	COL	0-0210936	0245	2
LOVETT JR CLAUDE E	CPT	0-0521431	1047	2
LOVETTE JASON P	LTC	0-1313503	0961	1
LOVETTE JOE E	1LT	0-0497179	0946	1
LOVINGOOD ESTON A	LTC	0-0303942	0460	1
LOVITT ERNEST C	MAJ	0-2016163	1163	1
LOVKO JOHN F	COL	0-0327761	0263	3
LOVORN RICHARD T	CPT	0-1645772	0557	1
LOVRE STANTON C	MAJ	0-0343899	1045	2
LOVREIN LELAND C	MAJ	0-1894935	1060	1
LOVVORN JR WILLIAM B	LTC	0-1172969	0764	1
LOW CLARENCE O	MAJ	0-0365630	0456	1
LOW FREDERICK	MAJ	0-2208222	0367	1
LOW RICHARD C	COL	0-0316831	0960	1
LOW ROBERT J	COL	0-1166547	0164	1
LOWANDE WILLIAM B	1LT	0-1177062	104N	2
LOWDER JOHN W	CW3	W-2145683	0965	1
LOWDER PAUL J	LTC	0-1996774	0262	1
LOWDERMILK LEE D	COL	0-0279353	0950	1
LOWDERMILK ZEB B	CW3	W-2205542	0165	1
LOWE ACIE	1LT	0-0497647	0346	2
LOWE BENO P	CW2	W-2121116	0845	2
LOWE BESS G	1LT	N-0730285	0146	1
LOWE BILLY C	MAJ	0-2206422	0764	1
LOWE CARLTON M	MAJ	0-1329020	0865	1
LOWE CATHERINE	CPT	N-0736516	0951	1
LOWE CHARLES B	CW2	W-2004445	0164	1
LOWE CLARK	LTC	0-1180248	1060	1
LOWE DENZIL R	COL	0-0278598	0560	3
LOWE DONALD H	LTC	0-1285450	0759	1
LOWE EDGAR P	CW2	W-2144239	0656	1
LOWE EDWARD H	CPT	0-0450384	0356	1
LOWE EDWIN P	MAJ	0-0914214	0665	3
LOWE FARRELL O	LTC	0-0349000	0754	1
LOWE FRANK E	M G	0-0170395	0648	3
LOWE GERALD H	LTC	0-2048060	0244	1
LOWE GIDEON H	LTC	0-0265516	1153	3
LOWE HAROLD T	COL	0-0211491	0751	3
LOWE HENRY W	LTC	0-1994470	1264	1
LOWE HOWARD D	COL	0-0342310	1064	1
LOWE JAMES E	WO1	W-2128075	0447	1
LOWE JAMES L	LTC	0-0374696	0966	3
LOWE JERROL P	MAJ	0-0405931	0960	1
LOWE JOHN A	LTC	0-0160726	0848	3
LOWE JR CARL W	LTC	0-1030171	0357	1
LOWE JR CHARLES W	CW4	W-2142870	1064	1
LOWE JR JOHN L	CPT	0-1302025	0146	2
LOWE KATHRYN F	CPT	N-0751221	0363	1
LOWE MARY E	CPT	N-0763765	0649	2
LOWE MILLS T	2LT	0-2024287	1145	2
LOWE MILTON C	LTC	0-1012026	0655	1
LOWE MITCHELL	CW3	W-2152300	0662	2
LOWE OTTO B	2LT	0-1637958	1043	2

NAME	GRADE	SVC NO	DATE RET MO YR	RET CODE
LOWE RALPH W	MAJ	0-0359906	0160	1
LOWE RAYMOND P	MAJ	0-1950204	0564	1
LOWE ROBERT C	COL	0-0350544	0859	1
LOWE ROBERT W	LTC	0-1115681	0766	3
LOWE ROBERT W	MAJ	0-2283838	0859	1
LOWE SAM D	LTC	0-0237898	0863	3
LOWE THEODORE	COL	0-1105625	0266	3
LOWE THOMAS J	LTC	0-0241753	0460	2
LOWE WILLIAM A	MAJ	0-0969791	1263	2
LOWE WILLIAM A	LTC	0-1165858	0159	1
LOWELL EDDIE P	LTC	0-1182900	1262	1
LOWELL JAMES R	LTC	0-0343950	0646	2
LOWELL JOHN C	MAJ	0-1048878	0862	1
LOWELL JOHN H	LTC	0-0198524	1147	1
LOWELL PARKER	MAJ	0-0297544	0267	3
LOWELL ROBERT L	MAJ	0-1173360	0161	1
LOWENBERG MILTON A	COL	0-0196410	0350	3
LOWENSTINE JAMES R	2LT	0-0439208	0645	2
LOWER EDGAR R	COL	0-0194232	0354	3
LOWER ERNEST H	MAJ	0-0290030	0654	3
LOWER GRANT K	MAJ	0-1165252	0860	1
LOWER ROBERT W	LTC	0-1701568	1167	1
LOWERY AGNES R	MAJ	L-0305306	1165	1
LOWERY FRED T	MAJ	0-1518943	1265	1
LOWERY GEORGE W	CPT	0-0283059	1266	3
LOWERY H A	CPT	0-0969773	0261	2
LOWERY JOHN J	MAJ	0-2262790	0562	1
LOWERY LAWRENCE C	CW2	W-2148456	0559	1
LOWERY ONAS F	LTC	0-0109174	0146	2
LOWERY PAUL J	CPT	0-1038047	1047	1
LOWERY PERCY E	LTC	0-0182648	0846	1
LOWERY RALPH T	LTC	0-1292549	1262	1
LOWERY RAYMOND M	MAJ	0-0106033	0158	3
LOWERY SR JAMES C	LTC	0-0290756	1055	3
LOWES WILLIAM J	MAJ	0-1288252	1161	1
LOWI ALVIN R	MAJ	0-0103452	0246	1
LOWMAN ARDEN W	LTC	0-1299262	0562	1
LOWMAN CECIL B	1LT	0-0537424	1045	2
LOWMAN JENNINGS D	MAJ	0-0490259	0648	1
LOWN CHARLES R	1LT	0-1031192	0544	2
LOWN GROVER E	CW2	W-2118269	0946	2
LOWN JAMES M	MAJ	0-0408118	0157	1
LOWNES EDWARD O	COL	0-0195681	0762	3
LOWRANCE CARLOS U	MAJ	0-0187587	0557	1
LOWRANCE WILLIAM R	LTC	0-1635043	0461	1
LOWREY JAMES C	MAJ	0-1581918	0467	3
LOWREY JOHN C	CW2	W-2126737	0651	1
LOWREY JR ROBERT F	LTC	0-0300834		2
LOWREY NORTON R	LTC	0-0236818	1159	1
LOWREY ROBERT W	COL	0-0344894	1045	2
LOWREY WILLIS F	LTC	0-0397690	0561	1
LOWRY ALBERT H	CPT	0-0492936	0847	1
LOWRY BURRIS H	LTC	0-0271263	0166	3
LOWRY DOROTHY K	CPT	L-0800042	1162	1
LOWRY EARL D	MAJ	0-0146542	0653	3
LOWRY GEORGE B	MAJ	0-1112289	0959	1
LOWRY HARRY P	COL	0-0274217	0551	3
LOWRY J C	1LT	0-1920057	0753	1
LOWRY JAMES M	CW4	W-2142172	1162	1
LOWRY JEFFERSON	MAJ	0-1683578	1161	1
LOWRY JOHN A	2LT	0-0541577	0845	2
LOWRY JOHN C	COL	0-0107180	1057	1
LOWRY JOSEPH V	CW4	W-2118534	0155	1
LOWRY JR TAYLOR T	MAJ	0-1333090	0365	1
LOWRY JR THOMAS M	MAJ	0-0170548	1161	3
LOWRY KENNETH F	LTC	0-0490246	0346	2
LOWRY MAYMIE I	1LT	N-0771018	0646	1
LOWRY RICHARD E	LTC	0-1048470	0667	1
LOWRY SAMUEL N	COL	0-0262742	0456	2
LOWRY SR WILLIAM V	CPT	0-1181021	1060	2
LOWRY SUMTER L	M G	0-0170909	0853	3
LOWRY WILLIAM C	LTC	0-0270601	0862	3
LOWTHER BEN W	LTC	0-1646375	0767	1
LOY FRANKLIN L	LTC	0-0193820	0262	3
LOY JOHN H	CW3	W-2203318	1163	1

NAME	GRADE	SVC NO	DATE RET MO YR	RET CODE
LOY JOHN W	CPT	C-2011327	C257	1
LOY LELAND L	LTC	0-0471520	0365	1
LOY WILLIAM A	CPT	0-0360071	1145	2
LOYA MARY	2LT	N-0734863	0744	1
LOYD ALBERT S	CW2	W-2210818	0766	1
LOYD GARRITT W	CW2	W-2145288	0360	1
LOYD GILBERT M	MAJ	C-1297219	C762	1
LOYD KATHERINE	MAJ	N-0735329	C865	1
LOYD SAMUEL J	MAJ	C-0268047	C459	1
LOYD WILLIAM E	CW3	W-2205376	1166	1
LOYE HARLAN M	LTC	0-0397927	0760	1
LOZANO CONSUELO R	1LT	N-0728936	0945	1
LOZANO RAUL G	MAJ	0-0988043	0265	1
LOZEAU ROLLAND A	MAJ	C-1105629	0963	1
LOZIER LUE C	LTC	0-0130652	0246	2
LUBAN FRANCIS	MAJ	0-1899376	0561	1
LUBBEN JR JOHN F	LTC	0-0245673	0658	3
LUBCHANSKY HAROLD W	LTC	C-1101560	0462	1
LUBEN CONRAD J	MAJ	C-0942957	C466	1
LUBENS HERMAN	CPT	0-0444202	0545	2
LUBERT LOUIS	LTC	0-0346806	1161	3
LUBIN DAVID	1LT	0-1635044	0646	2
LUBIN FRANCES C	1LT	N-0759143	0845	1
LUBITZ BENJAMIN	COL	0-0261651	0160	3
LUBOTSKY IRVING J	MAJ	C-1307226	0964	1
LUBOVSKY BENJAMIN	LTC	0-0443671	C854	1
LUBRANO DOMINICK	CW2	W-2110436	0846	1
LUBY JOSEPH P	CPT	0-1014343	0854	1
LUCA SALVATORE	MAJ	0-0503985	C546	2
LUCANDER VICTOR	2LT	0-1310270	0557	1
LUCAS ALBERT	MAJ	C-0174022	0555	3
LUCAS CLARENCE P	2LT	0-1106914	C744	2
LUCAS CLARENCE R	MAJ	0-0451337	C660	1
LUCAS CLIFFORD R	MAJ	0-0475910	1053	1
LUCAS ERNEST	LTC	0-0335347	0760	1
LUCAS ERNEST L	COL	C-0203635	0752	3
LUCAS FRANCES R	1LT	N-0742031	0646	1
LUCAS FRANK C	MAJ	C-0257778	0966	3
LUCAS GEORGE	CW4	W-2111827	0659	1
LUCAS GEORGE	CW3	W-2206964	0267	1
LUCAS GEORGE A	1LT	0-1309675	0751	1
LUCAS GROVER E	MAJ	0-1877158	0165	1
LUCAS GUY P	1LT	0-0168748	0160	3
LUCAS HARLAN S	MAJ	C-0933933	C462	1
LUCAS HERBERT	CPT	0-1293621	1147	1
LUCAS HOWARD C	1LT	0-0365140	1142	2
LUCAS HOYT O	MAJ	0-0193813	1152	3
LUCAS JAMES A	CPT	0-0349110	0846	2
LUCAS JAMES F	MAJ	0-0491519	0453	1
LUCAS JOHN	LTC	C-0460117	1053	1
LUCAS JOHN A	MAJ	0-0526929	C155	1
LUCAS JOHN D	COL	0-0412396	C166	1
LUCAS JOHN J	MAJ	0-1695224	0246	2
LUCAS JOHN L	MAJ	C-1177063	0865	1
LUCAS JOHN P	MAJ	C-1548926	0761	1
LUCAS JOHN R	LTC	0-0355044	C660	1
LUCAS JOSEPH N	CPT	0-1011834	C847	2
LUCAS JR JAMES O	1LT	0-0537802	1045	2
LUCAS LOUIS F	COL	0-0407117	0546	2
LUCAS MARVIN H	LTC	0-0385794	0760	1
LUCAS MICHAEL	CW2	W-2109531	1152	2
LUCAS PAULINE R	MAJ	N-0724904	1061	1
LUCAS RAY O	CW2	W-2211279	C766	1
LUCAS RICHARD L	MAJ	0-1017939	0263	1
LUCAS ROBERT L	LTC	0-1185846	1062	2
LUCAS ROBERT L	WO1	W-2131792	1044	2
LUCAS ROSEMARY V	MAJ	N-0735591	1064	2
LUCAS RUSSELL S	CPT	C-0423535	1043	2
LUCAS STANLEY M	LTC	0-1050787	C263	1
LUCAS THOMAS C	2LT	0-2006069	C845	1
LUCAS WENDELL S	LTC	0-0444317	C853	2
LUCAS WILLARD J	CPT	0-1796113	1058	1
LUCAS WILMER F	COL	0-0242247	0757	3
LUCE CHARLES W	CPT	0-0580363	0645	1
LUCE EDWIN A	CW4	W-2110534	C957	1
LUCE FRANCIS N	MAJ	0-0251203	0155	3
LUCE GEORGE H	LTC	0-0383362	0660	1
LUCE GILBERT L	LTC	0-0278811	0763	3
LUCE WALTER A	CW3	W-2113626	0859	1
LUCERI VINCENT F	LTC	0-1168787	0563	1
LUCERO LEO L	MAJ	0-1104970	0960	1
LUCEY ALEXANDER	MAJ	0-0125975	0648	3
LUCHT HAROLD C	CPT	0-0912048	0244	2
LUCHT HERSHEL F	LTC	0-0445362	0463	1
LUCIAN JOHN A	CPT	0-0339802	0346	2
LUCIANO FRANK A	MAJ	0-0955589	0463	1
LUCIANO MICHAEL N	1LT	0-1295912	1044	2
LUCINSKI WILLIAM	LTC	0-0329439	1057	1
LUCIS EDWARD	CW3	W-2144360	0659	1
LUCK DONALD C	2LT	0-0515229	1043	2
LUCK EMORY H	CW2	W-2145890	0961	1
LUCK JULIAN W	LTC	0-0426047	0263	2
LUCK WILLIAM V	MAJ	0-0296540	0865	3
LUCKE CARL E	CPT	0-0117856	0650	3
LUCKES CLINTON E	MAJ	C-1686171	1060	1
LUCKETT GUSTUS	COL	0-0403573	0860	1
LUCKETT LUTHER J	LTC	0-0253347	0155	3
LUCKEY JR JULIUS J	CPT	0-0309404	1148	2
LUCKFIELD HERBERT M	LTC	0-1555721	0763	2
LUCKHURST CHARLES A	LTC	0-0176873	0648	3
LUCKIE CHARLES A	COL	0-0335074	1266	3
LUCKY SR VIRGLE E	CW3	W-2151144	0865	1
LUCKY VIRGIL M	MAJ	0-1924119	0663	1
LUCORE JAMES C	LTC	0-1635047	0862	1
LUCY CLAUD R	MAJ	0-0483623	0747	1
LUCZAK ARTHUR F	MAJ	0-2019341	0463	1
LUDDEN CHARLES F	LTC	0-0212360	0661	2
LUDDEN PAUL W	LTC	0-0510920	0363	1
LUDDEN WALTER E	MAJ	C-1103290	0165	1
LUDES GEORGE M	LTC	0-0318614	0566	3
LUDFORD AARON L	1LT	0-1298257	1145	2
LUDINGTON RALPH E	LTC	0-1016809	0465	1
LUDLOW GEORGE L	CW3	W-2142519	0667	1
LUDLOW PAUL L	CW3	W-2144193	0663	1
LUDOVICI PETER P	1LT	0-1546215	C446	1
LUDWIG DONALD W	LTC	0-0344045	1167	3
LUDWIG EDWARD P	CW4	W-2104254	0664	1
LUDWIG ERWIN P	COL	0-0313148	0767	3
LUDWIG GERALD E	LTC	0-0269519	0566	3
LUDWIG HENRY R	1LT	0-1182636	0946	2
LUDWIG JOHN J	CW2	W-2206848	0962	1
LUDWIG JR HOWARD G	CW3	W-2144691	0660	1
LUDWIG LEROY M	LTC	0-1040762	0861	1
LUDWIG LLEWELLYN	COL	0-0246406	0762	3
LUDWIG LLOYD A	LTC	0-0370126	0863	3
LUDWIG RODMAN W	LTC	0-1645774	0961	1
LUDWIG WILLIAM J	MAJ	0-0411349	0261	1
LUEBBE CLETUS L	CPT	0-1055371	0155	2
LUEBBERS RALPH H	LTC	0-0342611	0466	3
LUEBKERT BERNARD C	LTC	0-0285191	1058	1
LUEBKERT WILLIAM C	CPT	0-0299555	0944	1
LUEBSEN JOHN H	CPT	0-0317031	1044	2
LUEDDE FULLERTON	CPT	0-0345718	0743	2
LUEDEKE OTTO H	MAJ	C-1798021	0358	1
LUEDERS WILLIAM T	MAJ	0-1874397	0666	1
LUEDKE EDWARD A	LTC	0-0193394	0760	3
LUEDKE FREDERICK	CPT	0-0283752	0144	2
LUEDKE GEORGE E	1LT	0-1048474	1045	2
LUEDTKE LEO M	LTC	0-1041603	0367	1
LUELLMAN GEORGE V	CW2	W-2145923	1159	1
LUETH HAROLD C	BG	0-0285937	0864	3
LUFKIN BENJAMIN N	CPT	0-0280040	0254	3
LUFTMAN HARRY T	LTC	0-0487763	0946	2
LUFTY ANTHONY	1LT	0-1177510	114N	2
LUGO LUIS A	COL	0-0108281	1049	1
LUGO RAMON L	CPT	0-0198849	0562	3
LUGOWE BOLESLAUS	LTC	0-1331528	1162	1
LUGTU EMILIO L	MAJ	0-0373046	0157	1
LUHN JR EDGAR R	MAJ	0-1922651	1166	1
LUHORN VICTOR E	LTC	0-0444375	0755	2
LUHRING ELWIN E	MAJ	0-0217571	1161	3
LUIDOR CHARLES	CPT	0-0507962	1047	1
LUIKART GORDON A	1LT	C-2103226	1054	2
LUJAN JOE C	LTC	0-1291663	0860	1
LUJAN MANUEL S	MAJ	C-1329959	1061	1
LUKAS CHARLES J	MAJ	0-1171252	0261	1
LUKAS CHESTER T	MAJ	C-1181022	086C	1
LUKE CHARLES O	LTC	0-0299216	1167	3
LUKE FRANCIS F	MAJ	0-0311545	0757	3
LUKE GERALD M	MAJ	C-1644541	1060	3
LUKE JOHN L	2LT	0-0513508	1045	2
LUKE JULIAN S	WO1	W-2129317	1162	1
LUKE MARTIN	CPT	C-1292359	0445	2
LUKE WALDENE F	LTC	0-0232777	0765	3
LUKENS CHARLES E	CW2	W-2152973	0464	1
LUKENS REAVES C	COL	0-0167195	0148	2
LUKER WILBUR H	MAJ	C-1554424	0660	1
LUKEY PHILIP E	MAJ	C-1895434	1061	1
LUKITSCH JOSEPH F	LTC	0-1013420	C964	1
LUKOWSKI ANTHONY E	COL	0-0226856	1150	1
LUKOWSKI RAYMOND L	MAJ	0-1550432	0757	1
LULL EVERETT P	LTC	0-1312958	0962	1
LULL WILLIAM C	MAJ	C-2266144	0767	1
LUM CHARLES W	LTC	0-0348836	1266	1
LUM TOM K	LTC	0-0285431	C860	1
LUMAN HARRY J	MAJ	0-1329495	C465	1
LUMAN RALPH M	COL	0-0350086	0661	1
LUMBARDO JOSEPH E	CPT	0-0521133	0559	2
LUMLEY JAMES P	CPT	0-1639326	0962	1
LUMMEL JOSEPH J	LTC	C-0383193	C162	2
LUMMIS HELENE V	LTC	N-0722054	0566	3
LUMMUS J W	MAJ	0-1328913	0266	1
LUMPKIN OLIN H	COL	0-0279808	1150	1
LUMPKINS ROY G	MAJ	0-1325502	C860	1
LUMSDEN HOWARD R	CPT	0-2262742	0361	1
LUMSDEN JR VIRGIL M	1LT	C-1587423	C352	1
LUNA HAYES D	COL	C-0312746	0367	3
LUNA JOHN	CW2	W-2142976	0261	1
LUNA W C	CW2	W-2146578	0262	1
LUND ARNOLD	2LT	0-1170468	1144	2
LUND ARTHUR R	LTC	0-0504984	0556	1
LUND GLEN S	1LT	0-1285453	1045	2
LUND JR CARROLL R	CW4	W-2139469	1265	1
LUND JR OSCAR J	CW2	W-2147889	C861	1
LUND MELVIN C	CW3	W-2205500	0367	1
LUND MELVIN E	CW2	W-2209722	0363	1
LUND PAUL O	2LT	0-2043275	0346	2
LUNDAHL CHARLES A	MAJ	C-1317237	1166	3
LUNDAHL GEORGE E	1LT	0-1012822	1144	2
LUNDAHL SR JOHN H	CW2	W-2206975	C263	2
LUNDAY ARTHUR R	CW2	W-2149950	0161	2
LUNDBERG ANDREW M	COL	0-0373755	1162	1
LUNDBERG REUBEN C	MAJ	C-0254759	1263	3
LUNDBLAD JR FRANK W	LTC	0-1321793	0766	1
LUNDBLAD ROY A	CPT	C-1700762	C944	2
LUNDEBERG THURSTON R	LTC	0-0234848	C165	3
LUNDEEN WALTER S	CPT	0-0481576	1042	2
LUNDELL LESLIE J	LTC	0-0352208	C264	1
LUNDGREN JR FRED H	MAJ	0-0369513	0146	2
LUNDGREN ROY H	LTC	0-0403963	0960	1
LUNDGREN SIDNEY C	MAJ	C-2017876	C463	1
LUNDH JOHN	1LT	0-1017357	C246	2
LUNDHEIM ERLING J	CPT	0-0319208	C845	2
LUNDQUIST CARL K	MAJ	0-0452854	C152	2
LUNDQUIST CHARLES G	2LT	0-1688833	0351	1
LUNDQUIST DONALD N	MAJ	C-4074518	1166	1
LUNDQUIST HARRY T	LTC	0-0429568	1159	1
LUNDQUIST RAYNARD V	LTC	0-0227638	C862	3
LUNDSTROM JAMES E	CPT	0-1049961	0147	2
LUNDVALL MERLE E	1LT	0-1286861	1144	2
LUNDY CLAYTON J	MAJ	0-0118382	0556	3
LUNDY CONSTANCE	CPT	N-0752202	1047	1
LUNDY JR THOMAS F	COL	C-0252065	1263	3
LUNDY RICHARD P	MAJ	0-1551052	0747	2
LUNDY ROBERT A	LTC	0-0426277	C162	3
LUNDY ROBERT J	CPT	0-1598921	0157	1
LUNDY ROGER J	MAJ	0-1599088	0364	1
LUNDY SR WALTER A	MAJ	0-1316652	0462	3
LUNDY THOMAS G	1LT	0-1061777	0146	2
LUNDY WALTER O	COL	0-0258302	C165	1
LUNG ADOLPHUS V	CPT	0-1289107	1059	1
LUNGER CHARLES	LTC	0-1280065	0354	1
LUNN JESSIE C	CPT	0-1823025	C146	2
LUNN JR WALTER K	CPT	0-0553499	1047	2
LUNN MEREDITH A	1LT	0-1291846	0245	2
LUNN VERLE N	LTC	0-0257388	1046	2
LUNN WILBURN V	COL	0-0190586	0260	3
LUNNEY JR EDWARD J	MAJ	0-1302153	0661	1
LUNSFORD DOROTHY L	MAJ	L-0909416	1058	2
LUNSFORD JOHN A	LTC	0-0224386	C145	2
LUNSFORD PRESTON E	LTC	0-1120125	0467	1
LUNSFORD WILLIAM E	2LT	0-0108237	0238	1
LUNSKIS CHARLES P	LTC	0-2040702	0257	1
LUNT ARTHUR W	CPT	0-1586753	0763	1
LUNT CLINTON E	LTC	C-0320801	0960	3
LUNT HOMER K	MAJ	0-0279798	0166	3
LUNTZ BENJAMIN	MAJ	0-0111279	0251	3
LUPARELLO THOMAS G	COL	0-0347625	0665	3
LUPINACCI JOSEPH J	2LT	0-1315508	C145	2
LUPINACCI VINCENT P	COL	0-0225858	C265	3
LUPINOS JOSEPH	MAJ	0-0965876	C164	1
LUPO CARL W	COL	0-0114522	1153	3
LUPO JASPER	MAJ	0-1634089	C764	1
LUPO JOHN M	CW3	W-2207420	1167	1
LUPO RUTH A	MAJ	N-0727855	C867	1
LUPSA GEORGE J	CW2	W-2152030	C663	1
LUPTON GORDON L	MAJ	C-0166616	1158	3
LUPTON HELEN M	MAJ	N-0758784	C964	3
LUQUES DONALD L	LTC	0-0354377	C164	1
LUREY SAM	LTC	0-1111745	C663	1
LURIA SYDNEY	CPT	0-0386060	0140	2
LURIE PENNY	MAJ	0-0484275	0346	1
LURIE GUNTHER J	CW3	W-2149351	0964	1
LURIE JACK	CPT	C-1715087	0545	2
LURQUIN HENRY J	LTC	0-0219003	0253	3
LURVEY RALPH A	CW2	W-2144921	0859	1
LUSBY JAMES W H	LTC	0-0247451	0157	1
LUSCHER JR HENRY R	CPT	0-0399889	0645	2
LUSCHER WILLIAM G	CPT	0-1309770	1047	2
LUSCOMBE HERBERT A	CPT	0-0468875	C846	2
LUSCOMBE NICH A	LTC	0-0390771	1061	1
LUSE WALLACE K	LTC	0-0364124	1047	2
LUSH LEWIS C	MAJ	0-0231355	0260	3
LUSH RICHARD F	LTC	0-0278068	0157	3
LUSIGNAN GERARD A	CW3	W-2153175	0767	1
LUSK ALD E	MAJ	0-0187788	0753	3
LUSK DAVID F	MAJ	0-0431602	0646	2
LUSK DAVIS	LTC	0-0348800	0663	1
LUSK DONALD F	MAJ	0-0983538	0565	1
LUSK EARL W	CPT	0-0357420	0348	1
LUSK FRANK R	COL	0-0116856	0246	2
LUSK GEORGE V	LTC	C-1174051	0261	1
LUSK HAYWOOD W	CPT	0-1636245	0760	1
LUSK JAMES R	CPT	0-1341680	0254	2
LUSK ROBERT A	LTC	0-0223144	0964	3
LUSK ROBERT K	LTC	0-0360894	1165	1
LUSK RUTH L	1LT	N-0764171	0146	1
LUSK VERNON A	MAJ	C-1931401	0167	1
LUSKOSKI JR JOHN	CPT	0-2263576	0163	1
LUSSIER JOSEPH E	MAJ	0-1286316	1158	1
LUSSIER ROSARIO H	LTC	0-0394614	0457	1
LUSTRACER PHILIP F	CPT	0-0345586	0446	2
LUSTER HARRISON	1LT	0-0495302	1051	1
LUSTGARTEN EARL M	MAJ	C-1821315	C446	2
LUSTIG J MERWIN	LTC	0-0424026	1060	1
LUSTMAN JACK	CW2	W-2106037	1049	2
LUTCAVAGE ZIGMUND C	MAJ	0-1284538	0557	1
LUTEN CLARENCE R	LTC	0-1286517	0657	1
LUTER SR ASA B	MAJ	0-0313982	1059	1
LUTES JACK L	LTC	0-1182177	0567	1

NAME	GRADE	SVC NO	DATE RET MO YR	RET CODE
LUTES JR JOHN T	1LT	0-5204569	0361	2
LUTES ROBERT A	MAJ	0-4009570	0566	1
LUTFRING ANTHONY E	MAJ	C-0276566	C259	3
LUTGEN CONRAD J	MAJ	0-0229241	0363	3
LUTH BEN C	COL	C-0253719	1057	3
LUTH HERMAN W	MAJ	C-0506365	CR46	2
LUTH LOUIS H	COL	0-0100721	1051	3
LUTME M MARGARET	1LT	N-0773504	1145	1
LUTMER ARTHUR F	CPT	0-0487742	0259	1
LUTHER CHARLES C	MAJ	C-0296686	0867	3
LUTHER FRANCIS C	CPT	C-2262087	0361	1
LUTHER HAROLD S	1LT	0-1796977	1160	2
LUTHER LEE I	LTC	0-0583926	1164	1
LUTHER MARSHALL K	1LT	0-0493018	0154	1
LUTHER RALPH O	MAJ	C-0550277	0349	2
LUTHER STANLEY W	MAJ	C-0196736	0357	3
LUTHER STANLEY W	COL	0-0256891	1167	3
LUTICH LOUIS R	CPT	0-0890132	C846	1
LUTINSKI ALFRED M	LTC	0-1119087	0966	1
LUTMAN CHARLES W	MAJ	0-0437837	0861	1
LUTNER JR THOMAS R	1LT	0-0550355	0347	2
LUTON JAMES N	COL	0-0223344	0864	3
LUTTERBEIN RICHARD W	MAJ	C-0944139	0564	1
LUTTIG NORMAN W	LTC	0-1946556	0463	1
LUTTINGER WILLIAM W	MAJ	0-0969326	1061	1
LUTTON GLENN T	MAJ	0-1636246	0555	1
LUTTRELL EARNEST	LTC	0-0209823	0846	1
LUTTRELL LEWIS	CW4	W-2103162	1064	1
LUTTRELL THORNTON E	LTC	0-2047413	0962	1
LUTTRINGER WILLIAM B	LTC	0-0338000	0760	1
LUTWACK MAURICE	COL	0-0275727	0466	3
LUTYE WILLIAM B	CPT	0-1030798	C161	1
LUTZ ALVIN H	COL	0-0235866	0860	3
LUTZ CHRISTIAN	LTC	C-1105633	1262	1
LUTZ EARL E	LTC	0-0355383	C547	2
LUTZ GEORGE J	1LT	0-1032369	1044	2
LUTZ GEORGE L	MAJ	0-0531305	C956	2
LUTZ GEORGE W	CPT	0-1891104	1164	1
LUTZ HAROLD W	MAJ	C-1546400	0859	1
LUTZ HARRY J	LTC	0-0491313	0859	1
LUTZ HERMAN M	LTC	0-0242784	0567	3
LUTZ HOBART F	1LT	0-1825019	C945	2
LUTZ JOHN E	COL	C-0312083	0560	3
LUTZ JOHN W	CPT	0-0498058	0250	1
LUTZ JOSEPH	MAJ	0-0973444	1063	1
LUTZ JOSEPH C	LTC	0-0272105	C767	3
LUTZ KARL C	MAJ	C-1309286	0358	1
LUTZ PAUL F	LTC	0-0266242	0161	2
LUTZ RALPH H	CPT	0-0112789	0648	3
LUTZ RICHARD W	LTC	0-1311175	0764	1
LUTZ WALTER C	MAJ	0-1285076	0647	2
LUTZ WILLIAM O	LTC	0-0250927	0560	1
LUTZ 2ND JOHN E	MAJ	C-0398832	0446	2
LUTZE FRANK M	CPT	0-1794965	C949	1
LUX GEORGE L	2LT	0-1104275	1044	2
LUX JR TURNER S	2LT	0-0557728	0146	2
LUX SAMUEL P	1LT	0-2023680	0548	2
LUXBACHER JOHN W	MAJ	0-1011819	1263	1
LUXEM JOHN G	2LT	0-2024389	C646	1
LUXFORD RICHARD G	2LT	0-1798593	C445	2
LUXMORE BETTY M E	CW3	V-2205865	1265	1
LUXTON WILLIAM L	LTC	0-0171388	0747	1
LUZADER WILLIAM K	CW3	W-2148259	1067	1
LUZZIE EDWARD L	MAJ	0-0297014	0347	1
LYBARGER EARNEST W	CPT	0-2008220	0557	1
LYBECK CARL W	LTC	0-1646819	1062	1
LYBRAND WENCEL C	CW2	W-2151842	0562	1
LYBROOK ROBERT C	COL	0-0269407	0467	3
LYCETT WAYNE L	LTC	0-1000407	0457	1
LYDDON RICHARD E	CPT	0-2103101	0761	2
LYDECKER LEIGH K	COL	0-0133287	0648	3
LYDEN JOSEPH J	LTC	0-1592392	0648	1
LYDIARD CHARLES W	CPT	0-1165900	C745	1
LYDICK JESSE B	CW2	W-2131818	C246	2
LYDMAN ALVIN C	CPT	0-0374595	0445	2

NAME	GRADE	SVC NO	DATE RET MO YR	RET CODE
LYDON ANTHONY M	MAJ	0-1299438	0760	2
LYDON BERNARD J	CPT	0-0979306	0262	1
LYDON JAMES J	1LT	0-1299595	0365	2
LYDON JOHN E	MAJ	0-2037567	1062	1
LYELL JAMES P	CW2	W-2153C87	1061	1
LYELL ROSSLYN A	1LT	0-1113815	1C4N	2
LYERLY JOSEPH E	CPT	0-0909217	0263	1
LYGA THOMAS L	1LT	0-1996331	0347	2
LYKINS JOSEPH B	1LT	0-0450989	1154	2
LYLE ADRIAN B	CPT	0-1576316	1158	1
LYLE ARCY W	CW2	W-2215127	0667	1
LYLE CHARLES M	LTC	0-1581246	0762	1
LYLE CLARENCE L	LTC	0-0446262	0347	1
LYLE CLAUDE V	LTC	0-0287897	0862	1
LYLE DONALD F	CPT	0-0473182	0146	2
LYLE JAMES F	CW2	W-2148209	0461	1
LYLE JOHN T	1LT	0-0501238	0746	1
LYLE JR JAMES M	MAJ	0-0260997	1264	3
LYLE ORLANDO W	COL	0-0293004	0263	1
LYLE ROGER B	MAJ	0-0116731	1149	3
LYLES EDWARD H	MAJ	0-1186421	0264	1
LYLES FINIS J	CW3	W-2144669	0561	1
LYLES JOSEPH E	LTC	0-0163281	0246	2
LYMAN ANN S	1LT	N-0789213	1045	1
LYMAN EDWARD E	LTC	0-0212983	0362	3
LYMAN FRANK C	LTC	0-0370712	0159	2
LYMAN JOHN	LTC	0-0489048	0363	1
LYMAN JOHN F	CW2	W-2116325	0145	2
LYMAN LAUREN A	MAJ	0-1114629	0263	1
LYMAN LEW G	COL	0-0102915	1050	3
LYMAN RALPH G	MAJ	0-118601C	0464	1
LYMAN RICHARD F	LTC	0-0104159	0352	3
LYMAN WILLIAM S	LTC	0-1103768	0863	1
LYNAS JOHN W	CW3	W-2142648	0966	1
LYNCH ALBERT J	CPT	0-1167960	1046	2
LYNCH ARTHUR E	MAJ	0-1823026	0358	1
LYNCH ARTHUR W	COL	0-0262895	0967	3
LYNCH BERNARD P	LTC	0-1001179	0766	3
LYNCH CHARLES A	LTC	0-1054041	0465	1
LYNCH CHARLES E	LTC	0-0214643	0961	3
LYNCH CLARENCE R	LTC	0-0286197	0967	3
LYNCH DALLAS R	LTC	0-1101561	0761	1
LYNCH DAVID R	LTC	0-0205791	0757	3
LYNCH EARL	MAJ	0-0450386	0757	1
LYNCH EDMUND T	LTC	0-1105634	0765	3
LYNCH EDWARD J	LTC	0-0917002	0547	2
LYNCH EMZY H	LTC	0-0200759	1155	3
LYNCH FRANCIS A	2LT	0-0502547	0344	2
LYNCH FRANCIS J	1LT	0-1016793	1044	2
LYNCH FRANK J	MAJ	0-0480325	1046	2
LYNCH GEORGE C	1LT	0-1294685	0344	2
LYNCH GIRARD F J	2LT	0-1307044	0545	2
LYNCH GEFFREY J	LTC	0-0486986	1053	1
LYNCH GORDON C	LTC	0-0229024	0365	3
LYNCH GRAYSON L	CPT	0-0966311	1060	1
LYNCH HERBERT J	CPT	0-0900379	0347	1
LYNCH HILTON M	MAJ	0-0341748	0746	1
LYNCH JAMES A	COL	0-0361414	0266	3
LYNCH JAMES H	CPT	0-0133336	0552	3
LYNCH JAMES M	2LT	0-1016479	0245	2
LYNCH JAMES W	MAJ	0-0977447	0962	1
LYNCH JOHN C	CPT	0-0128445	0445	2
LYNCH JOHN C	CPT	0-0518894	0545	2
LYNCH JOHN E	LTC	0-0343676	0158	1
LYNCH JOHN J	MAJ	0-2209017	0466	1
LYNCH JOHN L	COL	0-0255672	1063	3
LYNCH JOHN M	CPT	0-1325226	0946	1
LYNCH JOHN M	CW4	W-2002030	1165	1
LYNCH JOHN W	MAJ	0-0348197	0846	2
LYNCH JOHN W	LTC	0-1555858	0967	3
LYNCH JOSEPH K	MAJ	0-0284389	1043	2
LYNCH JOSEPH P	1LT	0-1577498	0746	2
LYNCH JOSOPH E	LTC	0-0330823	0650	2
LYNCH JR EDGAR M	LTC	0-1334306	0867	1
LYNCH JR JOSEPH F	LTC	0-1576317	1061	1

NAME	GRADE	SVC NO	DATE RET MO YR	RET CODE
LYNCH JR THOMAS K	COL	0-0240576	0264	3
LYNCH KENNY E	LTC	0-0437852	0167	1
LYNCH LEO J	LTC	0-1546RC3	1265	1
LYNCH LEONARD P	LTC	0-1948352	1167	1
LYNCH LEONARD R	MAJ	0-0338319	0265	3
LYNCH MICHAEL J	LTC	0-0287813	0552	1
LYNCH MYRL C	LTC	0-1011402	0767	1
LYNCH PATRICK E	MAJ	C-1044597	C861	1
LYNCH PATRICK J	MAJ	C-0127903	0648	3
LYNCH PHILIP M	1LT	0-0375033	1045	1
LYNCH RAYMOND J	LTC	0-0330112	1046	2
LYNCH RICHARD P	MAJ	0-0263840	0351	1
LYNCH RUFF F	MAJ	0-1333988	0461	1
LYNCH SILAS W	MAJ	C-0494981	0854	1
LYNCH SR MAX A	CW3	W-2142124	0860	1
LYNCH THOMAS O	MAJ	C-0959361	C863	1
LYNCH WALTER J	LTC	0-0252495	0964	3
LYNCH WAYNE E	MAJ	0-1030799	0361	1
LYNCH WILFRED T	MAJ	0-0341567	0256	3
LYNCH WILLIAM O	COL	0-0264603	0963	3
LYNCH WILLIAM J	CPT	C-0337095	1145	1
LYNCH WILLIAM J	MAJ	C-2262143	0563	1
LYNCH WILLIAM P	MAJ	0-2262564	1266	1
LYNCH WILLIAM RY	MAJ	0-0128414	C247	2
LYNCH WILLIAM S	MAJ	0-0204069	1062	3
LYNCH WOODROW	MAJ	C-1004497	0854	1
LYNCH 3RD THOMAS	CPT	0-0415063	0646	2
LYNDE FRANK T	LTC	0-0208494	C156	3
LYNES GUY B	LTC	0-0229120	0663	3
LYNES WESLEY J	MAJ	0-0366346	C746	1
LYNG LESLIE V	COL	0-0180116	0846	2
LYNGE WILBUR J	MAJ	C-0354677	0854	1
LYNN CECIL S	MAJ	0-1117482	1059	1
LYNN CUSTER L	MAJ	C-0373459	C165	3
LYNN EDWIN A	2LT	0-1170469	0345	2
LYNN HAROLD R	LTC	0-1634092	0760	1
LYNN HUGH B	CPT	0-0411649	0346	2
LYNN JACK J	LTC	0-1578775	1067	1
LYNN JAMES	LTC	C-0451039	0358	1
LYNN JAMES E	MAJ	0-0496752	0157	1
LYNN JAMES J	MAJ	C-1576318	0962	1
LYNN JR DANIEL R	LTC	0-0456384	C759	1
LYNN JR ELLIS H	LTC	0-1297062	0161	1
LYNN JR JOSEPH R	LTC	0-1548928	0862	1
LYNN NOAH F	CPT	0-1305949	C246	2
LYNN ROBERT M	MAJ	C-0989759	1165	1
LYNN THOMAS U	WO1	W-2109242	0944	2
LYNN WILLIAM R	MAJ	0-0926828	C466	1
LYNN WILLIAM R	MAJ	0-0980169	0366	1
LYNNE ROBERT N	MAJ	0-0411168	0647	2
LYNSKEY JOSEPH P	COL	0-0230590	0463	3
LYNTON DALE W	MAJ	0-1875551	0966	1
LYNXWILER THOMAS L O	MAJ	0-0285628	C246	2
LYON ALBERT G	CW2	W-2214874	0766	1
LYON CHARLES A	MAJ	0-0479473	1155	1
LYON CLYDE	MAJ	0-C276069	0959	1
LYON DONALD S	LTC	0-2042739	0661	1
LYON ERNST F	CPT	0-0378704	1145	2
LYON GEORGE B	MAJ	0-0233134	1057	3
LYON GLOYD M	CPT	0-0387293	0246	2
LYON HARRY L	LTC	0-0253782	0163	3
LYON JAMES A	2LT	0-1080728	0744	2
LYON JENNINGS	1LT	0-1036609	0146	2
LYON JOHN F	CPT	C-0477716	0745	2
LYON JR ARTHUR J	2LT	0-1012837	0145	2
LYON MAX E	2LT	0-1011920	0545	2
LYON NEVEN R	MAJ	0-1951173	0663	1
LYON OLEN	LTC	0-1059538	0265	3
LYON ORVILLE Y	MAJ	0-1178233	0864	1
LYON PAUL E	LTC	0-1588134	1060	1
LYON RALPH M	MAJ	0-0221968	1262	3
LYON RICHARD J	LTC	0-0408985	1060	1
LYON ROBERT L	LTC	0-0295478	0759	3
LYON ROBERT R	CPT	0-1043411	1050	1
LYON ROSS M	LTC	0-0344849	0865	1

NAME	GRADE	SVC NO	DATE RET MO YR	RET CODE
LYON VELMA S	2LT	N-0721075	0145	1
LYON WIDNEY	MAJ	0-1014959	0658	2
LYON WINSLOW	COL	0-0140516	0549	3
LYONS BERNARD A	COL	0-0252679	0446	1
LYONS CATHERINE	MAJ	N-0741679	1166	1
LYONS CECIL R	CPT	0-038C741	0350	1
LYONS DANIEL T	CW3	W-2148470	1162	1
LYONS DEWEY B	LTC	0-0231370	1058	3
LYONS EDWARD A	MAJ	0-2017723	0764	1
LYONS EUGENE T	LTC	0-1317247	0866	1
LYONS HAROLD A	1LT	0-1179935	0361	2
LYONS HARRY A	LTC	0-0174767	1060	3
LYONS HARRY W	LTC	0-0319392	0964	3
LYONS JAMES P	CW3	W-2118103	1155	1
LYONS JAMES T	LTC	0-0219700	1146	1
LYONS JAMES V	CPT	0-0438618	1045	2
LYONS JOHN A	MAJ	C-1540906	0161	1
LYONS JOHN F B	COL	0-0225916	0864	3
LYONS JOSEPH L	CW3	W-2150605	1262	1
LYONS JR JAMES F	2LT	0-2034992	1050	2
LYONS JR JIM R	2LT	0-1305279	0744	2
LYONS JR OSCAR	CPT	0-0976233	0261	1
LYONS KATHLEEN J	MAJ	N-0730057	0261	1
LYONS LEONARD H	LTC	0-019448C	0962	3
LYONS MICHAEL J	LTC	0-04651C1	0246	2
LYONS MILTON H	LTC	0-0191453	0752	3
LYONS NELSON K	LTC	0-0158442	0257	3
LYONS OLIN F	CPT	0-2018192	0859	1
LYONS PAUL R	1LT	0-1109470	0245	1
LYONS RAYMOND J	LTC	0-0216095	1058	3
LYONS STANLEY	LTC	0-1291144	0461	1
LYONS THOMAS G	1LT	0-0145945	0755	3
LYONS THOMAS W	1LT	0-1016110	0445	2
LYONS ULRICH S	MAJ	0-0270955	1154	3
LYONS WILLIAM J	MAJ	0-1950557	0263	1
LYSAGHT CHARLES S	CPT	0-1166550	1145	2
LYSAKOWSKI EDWARD W	MAJ	0-0980258	0263	1
LYSINGER FREDERICK	MAJ	0-0970123	1163	1
LYSNE GERALDINE	1LT	N-0788798	0346	1
LYSNE PAYNEE C	LTC	0-0439108	0563	1
LYSTAC ANDY	LTC	0-0161963	0944	2
LYTAL WILLIAM L	MAJ	0-0973843	0364	1
LYTER RICHARD K	LTC	0-1171264	0562	2
LYTLE CARL S	LTC	0-0294363	0966	3
LYTLE CHARLES B	CPT	0-1299263	0547	2
LYTLE CLEVELAND	LTC	0-0326170	0152	2
LYTLE HUGH W	LTC	0-0267219	0362	3
LYTLE JAMES K	1LT	0-1012491	0845	2
LYTLE ROBERT P	LTC	0-0262279	0865	3
LYTLE THEODORE J	LTC	0-0497664	0155	1
LYTLE WILBUR C	CPT	0-045061C	0753	2
LYTLE WILLIAM W	MAJ	0-0324813	0945	2
LYTTON JACK W	MAJ	0-0386336	0747	2
LYUBLANOVITS ERNEST	LTC	0-1559591	1163	1
MA GEE WILLIAM M	MAJ	0-1312181	0862	1
MA HANNA WILLIAM R	CPT	0-0232192	0157	3
MAAHS RALPH F	CW3	W-2145081	0963	1
MAANUM JOHN C	1LT	0-1307720	1145	2
MAAS HYMAN T	CPT	0-1894659	0545	2
MAAS PAUL O	1LT	0-1292209	0147	2
MAASS VICTOR E	CW3	W-2146912	0960	1
MABBETTE EDWIN A	MAJ	0-0321235	0462	3
MABE RODERICK O	CW4	W-2104257	0557	1
MABEY JOSEPH G	CPT	0-0223020	0965	3
MABEY JR JOSEPH L	LTC	0-0341473	0546	2
MABILE ERNEST J	CW3	W-2145036	0461	1
MABRY AARON W	CW3	W-2141621	1157	1
MABRY BUFORD S	1LT	0-1306612	0346	2
MABRY JOHN F	CPT	0-0373438	0545	2
MABRY OLLIE B	MAJ	0-0269350	1050	3
MABUARY KENNEY C	1LT	0-2005449	1048	1
MAC ADAM DAVID A	LTC	0-0258673	0545	2
MAC ADAM FRANCIS A	LTC	0-0451452	0155	1
MAC ADAMS CHARLES W	MAJ	0-1314510	1163	1
MAC ADOFF JOHN	CPT	0-0982277	1061	1

NAME	GRADE	SVC NO	DATE RET MO YR	RET CODE
MAC ALISTER ALEXAN	LTC	0-0113033	0855	3
MAC ALUSO ALFRED C	1LT	0-0470465	1043	2
MAC AREVEY JAMES J	LTC	0-1288766	0966	1
MAC ARTHUR ALBERT O	MAJ	0-0360062	1045	2
MAC ARTHUR FLETCHE	CPT	0-0532553	0647	1
MAC ARTHUR JAMES	CW4	W-2101195	0255	2
MAC ARTHUR JOHN J	LTC	0-1825813	0263	1
MAC ARTHUR KENNETH R	LTC	0-0274762	0367	3
MAC AULAY THOMAS M	CPT	0-4011140	0566	2
MAC BETH NORBERT A	CW3	W-2146708	0264	1
MAC BRIDE MILTON F	2LT	0-1110079	0845	2
MAC CALLUM DANIEL R	COL	0-0120084	0158	3
MAC CARONE SEBASTIAN	CW3	W-2205276	0265	1
MAC CARTHY JR HOWARD	1LT	0-0915325	0744	2
MAC CARTNEY DONALD K	CW2	W-2206194	0360	1
MAC CHLERIE GEORGE W	MAJ	0-1798025	0754	1
MAC CLAIN ALBERT L	CPT	0-0151110	1154	3
MAC COMRIE HERBERT F	COL	0-0205739	1059	3
MAC CONNELL HERBERT	1LT	0-0525297	0358	3
MAC CORD HOWARD A	COL	0-1101098	1062	1
MAC COY PAUL W	LTC	0-0206929	0850	1
MAC CREADY DAVID B	LTC	0-0145684	0749	3
MAC DERMAID ALFRED R	LTC	0-1053235	0966	1
MAC DERMID JAMES H	CPT	0-1015442	0759	1
MAC DERMOTT W V	CPT	0-0288027	0944	2
MAC DERMUT EMANUEL G	MAJ	0-1844881	0758	3
MAC DEWITT EAMON O	1LT	0-0437818	0746	2
MAC DONALD ALAN F	MAJ	0-0785700	1064	1
MAC DONALD BERNARD H	MAJ	0-1920221	0767	1
MAC DONALD BRUCE W	MAJ	0-1329021	0365	1
MAC DONALD CATHERINE	MAJ	N-0720744	1162	3
MAC DONALD CHARLES	LTC	0-0165255	0349	3
MAC DONALD CHARLES F	1LT	0-2046521	0145	2
MAC DONALD CLARA B	MAJ	N-0759062	0165	2
MAC DONALD DANIEL A	COL	0-0422912	0262	1
MAC DONALD DANIEL P	LTC	0-1558304	0965	1
MAC DONALD DAVID J	CPT	0-1639488	0546	2
MAC DONALD DONALD F	COL	0-0120003	1158	3
MAC DONALD EDGAR C	LTC	0-0111185	0945	2
MAC DONALD ERIC D	LTC	0-0482392	0954	1
MAC DONALD FLORENCE	LTC	N-0700335	0746	1
MAC DONALD FLOYD P	LTC	0-0228379	1162	3
MAC DONALD GEORGE A	CPT	0-4007149	1064	1
MAC DONALD GEORGE F	MAJ	0-0428149	0662	1
MAC DONALD GORDON A	M G	0-0193923	0359	3
MAC DONALD GORDON J	2LT	0-4052510	0157	2
MAC DONALD HAROLD	COL	0-0302344	1053	1
MAC DONALD HENRY J	MAJ	0-0520978	0554	1
MAC DONALD IRA A	CPT	0-0411177	0845	2
MAC DONALD JAMES A	MAJ	0-1104340	0756	1
MAC DONALD JAMES L	CPT	0-1702873	0146	2
MAC DONALD JAMES W	MAJ	0-1541000	0754	1
MAC DONALD JEAN F	1LT	L-0700074	0745	2
MAC DONALD JOHN A	CPT	0-2208908	0756	2
MAC DONALD JOHN D	CW2	W-2207530	0761	1
MAC DONALD JOHN N	LTC	0-0418256	0861	1
MAC DONALD JOHN W	LTC	0-0202109	1060	1
MAC DONALD JR THOMAS	MAJ	0-0363804	1045	2
MAC DONALD KENNETH J	LTC	0-0358984	0262	1
MAC DONALD MAUDE C I	1LT	N-0752153	1047	1
MAC DONALD RALPH	COL	0-0216370	0357	3
MAC DONALD RALPH A	LTC	0-0175420	1059	3
MAC DONALD ROBERT B	1LT	0-1286317	0945	2
MAC DONALD THEODORE	LTC	0-1053706	1061	1
MAC DONALD TOMMYE S	2LT	N-0765295	0947	1
MAC DONALD VINCENT A	COL	0-0314351	0759	1
MAC DONALD WALLACE	COL	0-0183474	0554	3
MAC DONALD WILLIAM	MAJ	0-0294180	0344	1
MAC DONALD WILLIAM J	CW2	W-2142714	0760	1
MAC DONALD WINSTON A	CPT	0-1291490	0248	1
MAC DONELL ALAN M	LTC	0-0100867	0453	3
MAC DONELL JOHN R	CPT	0-0232807	0464	3
MAC DONNELL JAMES M	LTC	0-1559219	0767	1
MAC DONNELL RAYMOND	CPT	0-1555591	0146	2
MAC DONNELL REGINA	COL	0-0126174	0856	3

NAME	GRADE	SVC NO	DATE RET MO YR	RET CODE
MAC DOUGALD JOSEPH J	CW2	W-3350190	0565	1
MAC DOUGALL ANGUS W	LTC	0-0527602	0557	3
MAC DOWALL MARTHA E	CPT	N-0764082	1148	1
MAC DOWELL MATTHEW	CPT	0-0404975	0960	1
MAC DUFF DOUGLAS	COL	0-0261657	0265	3
MAC EACHERN ROBERT T	LTC	0-1796500	0361	1
MAC FADDIN JOHN W	MAJ	0-0172582	0165	3
MAC FADYEN ISABEL	CPT	N-0735720	0747	1
MAC FARLAN CHARLES W	LTC	0-0910031	1262	3
MAC FARLAN JOHN G	LTC	0-0263626	0162	3
MAC FARLAND GEORGE W	LTC	0-1327639	0263	1
MAC FARLANE EDWARD L	CPT	0-0153815	0453	3
MAC FARLANE JOHN R	MAJ	0-1688422	0361	1
MAC FARLANE RICHARD	LTC	0-0920655	0467	3
MAC FARLANE WINFIELD	LTC	0-0404596	0164	1
MAC FARLINE PAUL L	CW2	RW-2153031	1063	1
MAC FEDRIES GLADSTON	MAJ	0-0466959	0947	1
MAC GAFFICK CLYDE O	LTC	0-1574288	0954	1
MAC GEER DURWARD	1LT	0-0364696	0650	2
MAC GILL III ALLEN J	LTC	0-0371979	0463	1
MAC GILL ROBERT R	CPT	0-2040956	1146	2
MAC GILLIVRAY RAYNOR	MAJ	0-1946792	1165	1
MAC GRATH DONALD A	COL	0-0260431	0965	1
MAC GREGER DONALD L	COL	0-0174838	0162	3
MAC GREGOR ALAN A	LTC	0-0375064	0267	1
MAC GREGOR CHARLES W	CW2	W-2152852	1060	2
MAC GREGOR ROBERT T	CPT	0-1308980	0948	2
MAC GREGOR WALLACE D	LTC	0-0566117	0661	1
MAC GUIRE EUGENE B	CPT	0-1115947	0962	1
MAC HUGH ROBERT E	LTC	0-1324346	0867	1
MAC INNES MARION K	1LT	N-0720124	0646	1
MAC INNES ROY F	CW3	W-2205302	0965	1
MAC INNIS KENNETH O	1LT	0-1323589	0447	1
MAC INTIRE SAMUEL C	COL	0-0218549	0850	3
MAC INTOSH RICHARD N	LTC	0-0548221	0663	1
MAC INTYRE JOHN K	LTC	0-0330663	0860	1
MAC INTYRE NORMAN J	CW2	W-2146036	1158	1
MAC INTYRE ROBERT S	1LT	0-1286155	0544	2
MAC ISAAC CHARLES F	LTC	0-0430446	0561	1
MAC IVER ALEXANDER	1LT	0-1324034	0945	2
MAC IVER DONALD I	MAJ	0-1685667	0564	1
MAC KAY ALBERT A	MAJ	0-0267112	0164	3
MAC KAY DONALD K	LTC	0-0338741	0965	3
MAC KAY FRANCIS F	CW3	W-2147498	0259	1
MAC KAY JR JOSEPH J	COL	0-0229074	0464	3
MAC KAY STCLAIR C	MAJ	0-0903491	0245	1
MAC KAY WILLIAM C	LTC	0-0235786	0362	3
MAC KELLAR ROBERT S	LTC	0-0250948	0864	3
MAC KENDREE MOFFATT	CW3	W-2144717	0565	1
MAC KENZIE HOWARD A	LTC	0-0236565	0463	3
MAC KENZIE JOHN H	MAJ	0-0444630	0548	1
MAC KENZIE KEITH M	COL	0-0397911	1263	1
MAC KENZIE THOMAS T	LTC	0-0226278	0662	3
MAC KIEWICZ W S	CPT	0-0490466	0445	2
MAC KINNON WILLIAM G	COL	0-0235018	1165	3
MAC LACHLAN WILLIAM	1LT	0-1558050	1265	2
MAC LAFFERTY JAMES W	LTC	0-0234288	0965	3
MAC LAIRD KENNETH A	CW2	W-2104259	0147	1
MAC LAREN HORACE E	LTC	0-0305081	0965	1
MAC LAREN WILLIAM R	LTC	0-0100262	0157	1
MAC LAUGHLIN W C	LTC	0-0330995	0760	2
MAC LAUGHLIN WILLA	LTC	0-0125094	0556	3
MAC LEAN KENNETH J	1LT	0-1913350	1052	1
MAC LEAN WALLACE K	MAJ	0-1582737	0465	1
MAC LEAY FRANCIS R	2LT	0-1166318	0545	2
MAC LEAY RICHARD J	LTC	0-0920265	1262	3
MAC LELLAN ROBERT W	LTC	0-1287730	1161	1
MAC LENNAN NINA M	2LT	N-0754286	0646	1
MAC LEOD COLIN G	LTC	0-0275354	1052	3
MAC LEOD DAVID G	LTC	0-0548139	0967	3
MAC LEOD GREGOR A	LTC	0-0305452	1063	1
MAC LEOD HAROLD P	LTC	0-0224112	0163	3
MAC LEOD RALPH E	COL	0-0128748	0549	3
MAC LEOD ROBERT H	LTC	0-1822031	0462	1
MAC LEOD ROSS	CPT	0-0218054	0948	2

NAME	GRADE	SVC NO	DATE RET MO YR	RET CODE
MAC LEOD WALLACE W	LTC	0-1104977	0961	1
MAC LEOD WILFRID A	COL	0-0238681	1163	3
MAC MANNIS HENRY P	CPT	0-0181818	0760	3
MAC MASTER ARTHUR W	MAJ	0-1101935	0263	1
MAC MASTER DONALD B	MAJ	0-0278575	0344	2
MAC MASTER LYLE S	MAJ	0-0242855	0755	3
MAC MILLAN ANDREW R	LTC	0-0234459	1060	3
MAC MILLAN CATHERINE	MAJ	N-0759088	0665	1
MAC MILLAN EDWARD A	COL	0-0133426	0253	3
MAC MILLAN JOHN M	1LT	0-1001842	1045	2
MAC MILLAN MILDRED	1LT	N-0736078	0546	1
MAC MILLEN HESPER N	MAJ	0-0290923	0446	2
MAC MINN JR DAVID E	CW2	W-2148573	0959	1
MAC MURRAUGH ARTHUR	LTC	0-0250508	0664	3
MAC NAB DONALD H	LTC	0-0282944	0765	3
MAC NAB MARION L	1LT	N-0759022	0346	1
MAC NABB BARBARA A	2LT	N-0700200	0236	1
MAC NAMARA JAMES	CPT	0-0356943	0645	2
MAC NAMARA MAURICE E	MAJ	0-1010322	0261	1
MAC NAUGHTON HENRY O	MAJ	0-0322479	0849	3
MAC NEAL ROBERT C	CPT	0-0496060	1045	2
MAC NEIL EDMUND L	CW2	W-2126792	1060	1
MAC NEIL MARK K	MAJ	0-1043711	0960	1
MAC NEIL ROBERT E	CPT	0-4030586	1165	1
MAC NEILL JOHN P	COL	0-0172680	0255	2
MAC NEILL JR RALPH M	CW3	W-2146559	0365	1
MAC NEILL NEIL M	LTC	0-0103911	1149	3
MAC NICOL ALLAN E	COL	0-0117668	0855	3
MAC NICOL JAMES J	LTC	0-1592397	1164	1
MAC NIDER HANFORD	LTG	0-0108101	0951	3
MAC PHEE KATHERINE	MAJ	N-0783054	0363	1
MAC PHERSON ROBERT H	COL	0-1280231	0165	1
MAC PHERSON WILLIAM	1LT	0-0298406	0156	3
MAC PHETRIDGE EDWARD	1LT	0-1309288	0845	2
MAC QUEEN GEORGE F	COL	0-0365477	1165	1
MAC QUEENEY PATRIC	COL	0-0176532	0552	3
MAC QUIDDY HARROLD H	CPT	0-0451067	0545	2
MAC RAE COLIN D	COL	0-0205981	0658	3
MAC RAE GORDON C	COL	0-0289117	0658	3
MAC RAE JOHN D	MAJ	0-0192198	0959	3
MAC SLARROW JACK A	LTC	0-1823029	0264	1
MAC VANE GLENN E	CW2	W-2210232	1062	1
MAC VEAN JAMES M	LTC	0-0205185	0363	3
MAC VICAR NORMAN	MAJ	0-1287033	0954	1
MAC WILLIAMS JOHN D	CPT	0-1116239	0960	1
MACALI CHARLES M	MAJ	0-1639334	0358	1
MACARTNEY CLEMENT D	CPT	0-1185339	0164	1
MACATANGAY JUAN T	1LT	0-1896725	0854	1
MACATEE WALTER F	LTC	0-1104975	0463	1
MACAULAY EDWARD L	COL	0-0114166	0352	3
MACAULEY JR IRVING P	1LT	0-0517383	0247	2
MACCARONE LIORE	CPT	0-1799326	0858	1
MACCHIA JOHN J	1LT	0-1167523	0844	2
MACCOUL MELVIN	LTC	0-0520645	0554	1
MACDONALD PETER F	CPT	0-0461187	1046	2
MACDONALD ROBIN W	CPT	0-0461258	0849	2
MACE EUGENE E	CW3	W-2145567	0263	1
MACE GEORGE L	CPT	0-1895016	0457	1
MACE HERMAN A	LTC	0-0888952	1163	1
MACE JOHN W	MAJ	0-0976219	0562	1
MACE RECTOR T	COL	0-0234399	1053	3
MACE ROBERT H	CPT	0-1286518	0348	2
MACE WILLIAM E	LTC	0-1062238	0866	1
MACE WILLIAM M	CPT	0-2262319	1160	1
MACELLARO GOLDIE L	MAJ	N-0795837	0266	3
MACERA RAYMOND A	MAJ	0-1925202	0264	1
MACEWICZ JOHN G	MAJ	0-0452207	0959	1
MACEY ALLEN C	CW2	W-3150811	0363	1
MACEYAK MICHAEL A	CW3	W-2145646	1263	1
ACGREGOR ARTHUR S	CPT	0-0131802	1051	3
CHAMER WALDON K	2LT	0-2024273	0346	2
HAN HERBERT P	MAJ	0-0194654	0462	3
ANN JOSEPH A	MAJ	0-0280995	0760	1
TE JOSEPH V	MAJ	0-1105637	0761	1
A JOHN H	MAJ	0-1552737	0463	1

NAME	GRADE	SVC NO	DATE RET MO YR	RET CODE
MACHLE EDWARD P	LTC	0-0163362	0761	3
MACIEL FRANK H	2LT	0-1172154	0545	2
MACK ALONZO F	CPT	0-0460900	1265	2
MACK EDWARD B	MAJ	0-1166551	0663	1
MACK FRANCIS W	COL	0-0100623	0648	3
MACK FREDERICK	1LT	0-0514310	0246	2
MACK FREDERICK	CPT	0-0515323	0249	1
MACK GERALD C	LTC	0-0543633	0966	1
MACK HENRY D	MAJ	0-0112087	0648	3
MACK JAMES F	MAJ	0-1112831	0763	1
MACK JOHN D	CPT	0-0502035	0849	1
MACK JOSEPH J	COL	0-0297562	0362	3
MACK JR GEORGE L	MAJ	0-0984131	0266	1
MACK JR THOMAS F	MAJ	0-0450747	0557	1
MACK JR WALTER R	1LT	0-1301333	0645	2
MACK KENNETH R	MAJ	0-0285644	0944	2
MACK LAWRENCE G	CPT	0-0353270	0945	2
MACK LOUIS J	LTC	0-1289291	0164	1
MACK THOMAS E	LTC	0-0256825	0254	3
MACK VINCENT H	LTC	0-0990121	0764	1
MACK WARREN J	MAJ	0-2033159	1262	1
MACKAY HOWARD O	MAJ	0-1648016	0560	1
MACKAY JR BENTLEY B	MAJ	0-1290624	1060	1
MACKEL JOHN J	MAJ	0-0453839	1158	1
MACKENZIE DOUGLAS C	COL	0-0169135	0159	3
MACKENZIE GORDON S	LTC	0-1116930	0163	1
MACKENZIE IAN J	CPT	0-0750148	0445	2
MACKENZIE WILLIAM	MAJ	0-0126096	0356	3
MACKENZIE WILLIAM	CW3	W-2152680	0663	1
MACKERT JOHN H	LTC	0-0233158	0954	3
MACKEY BENJAMIN E	CPT	0-2263149	0761	1
MACKEY CATHLEEN M	2LT	N-0757624	0345	1
MACKEY CHARLES	CPT	0-1184884	0256	1
MACKEY EDWARD J	COL	0-0385900	1167	3
MACKEY FRANCIS L	CW4	W-2106433	0366	1
MACKEY JACK B	2LT	0-1300993	1044	2
MACKEY JAMES G	COL	0-0282291	0159	3
MACKEY JOHN J	MAJ	0-0328443	1262	3
MACKEY JR CLARENCE	CPT	0-0461555	1146	2
MACKEY MARY J	1LT	N-0729734	0947	1
MACKEY PATRICK D	CW3	W-2151822	0463	1
MACKEY PATRICK J	MAJ	0-0982151	0564	1
MACKEY PAUL N	1LT	0-0499939	0853	1
MACKEY SR CLARENCE H	COL	0-0298050	0264	1
MACKEY WALLACE R	WO1	W-2105784	0645	2
MACKEY WILLIAM R	LTC	0-0374521	0167	3
MACKIE ARTHUR	MAJ	0-1996545	0157	1
MACKIE FRED W	LTC	0-0248610	1166	3
MACKIE JAMES	WO1	W-2109627	1046	1
MACKIE WALTER H	LTC	0-1546675	0963	1
MACKIN HUGH F	LTC	0-0252985	0166	3
MACKIN JOHN R	MAJ	0-2037262	1062	1
MACKINNON GEORGE L	MAJ	0-1492443	0345	2
MACKINTOSH CHARLES O	LTC	0-0110143	0958	3
MACKINTOSH DONALD	CPT	0-0375265	0247	2
MACKINTOSH HOWARD O	MAJ	0-0504937	0654	1
MACKLEY EVERETT J	MAJ	0-2262846	0363	1
MACKLIN JACOB J	MAJ	0-0475853	0747	1
MACKLIN JOHN C	2LT	0-1914205	1037	1
MACKLIN THOMAS R	LTC	0-0506108	1057	1
MACKLIN WILLIAM	CPT	0-0524208	0849	1
MACKLIND PETRA	2LT	N-0731595	0746	1
MACKMULL GULDEN	MAJ	0-1696086	1045	2
MACKO JOSEPH J	MAJ	0-1048083	0860	1
MACKOFF ABE	1LT	0-0230656	0263	3
MACKOVEC JOHN P	COL	0-0274989	0764	3
MACKSCA CHESTER J	CPT	0-0540872	0947	2
MACLACHLAN CLIFTON L	MAJ	0-2000435	0656	1
MACNAK JOSEPH A	MAJ	0-1041607	0447	2
MACNAMARA HOMER P	COL	0-0278625	1249	3
MACNEILL ARTHUR I	MAJ	0-0419624	1044	2
MACOMBER DOROTHY M	2LT	N-0743649	0445	1
MACOMBER FREEMAN G	COL	0-0302040	0261	3
MACON DAVID	LTC	0-0225169	0363	1
MACON WILLIE B	MAJ	0-1592398	0261	1

NAME	GRADE	SVC NO	DATE RET MO YR	RET CODE
MACRI JAMES F	LTC	0-1058882	1163	1
MACSPADDEN ARNOLD	LTC	0-0900583	1044	2
MACWETHY RAYMOND E	2LT	0-1289602	1143	2
MACY GERALD A	CPT	0-1289451	0746	2
MACY HAROLD	COL	0-0165308	0155	3
MACY JOSIAH N	COL	0-0275505	0161	3
MACY MELVIN C	COL	0-0405816	0463	1
MACY SAMUEL C	CPT	0-0350354	0347	2
MADARA GUY F	LTC	0-0207410	0648	3
MADARY CHARLES R	LTC	0-0389947	1146	2
MADDEN ARTHUR R	LTC	0-0491658	0447	2
MADDEN CHARLIE A	MAJ	0-0371370	0447	1
MADDEN DAVID G	CW2	W-2146517	0566	1
MADDEN EDWARD A	COL	0-0179529	0147	2
MADDEN FRANCIS P	LTC	0-0903912	1063	1
MADDEN FRED	CPT	0-1168791	0346	2
MADDEN GRAHAM P	LTC	0-1015290	0463	1
MADDEN JAMES A	MAJ	0-0887329	1057	1
MADDEN JEROME P	1LT	0-1169224	0145	2
MADDEN JOHN B	COL	0-0145779	1052	3
MADDEN JOHN C	MAJ	0-1039501	0865	1
MADDEN JOHN J	LTC	0-0334417	0660	1
MADDEN JOHN W	CW2	W-2151503	1060	1
MADDEN JOSEPH P	LTC	0-0124051	0355	3
MADDEN LOUIS R	CW3	W-2148296	0559	1
MADDEN MARIETTA H	LTC	N-0759962	0767	3
MADDEN MARY J	MAJ	N-0759068	0263	1
MADDEN PAUL H	MAJ	0-2021232	0865	1
MADDEN SR THOMAS C	2LT	0-1825630	0145	2
MADDEN THOMAS E	MAJ	0-0505940	0147	2
MADDEN THOMAS H	LTC	0-0266326	0246	2
MADDEN THOMAS J	2LT	0-1316700	0544	2
MADDEN THOMAS J	CW4	W-2000611	0765	3
MADDEN WALTER L	1LT	0-1311025	0146	2
MADDEN WILLSON R	MAJ	0-0503279	0854	1
MADDOCK RUTH M	MAJ	N-0795477	0665	1
MADDOCK THEODORE P	LTC	0-1103774	0163	1
MADDOCKS EARLE F	LTC	0-0424809	0563	1
MADDOX ALFRED E	MAJ	0-4010856	0967	1
MADDOX ANDREW A	CW2	W-2148605	0462	1
MADDOX CHARLES W	CPT	0-0475016	0550	1
MADDOX EDWARD W	MAJ	0-0440773	0947	1
MADDOX ELVIS V	MAJ	0-1543735	1163	1
MADDOX JAMES R	1LT	0-0507236	0949	1
MADDOX JOHN B	LTC	0-0213395	1061	3
MADDOX JOHN C	LTC	0-0484286	0554	1
MADDOX JOHN W	MAJ	0-0211106	0849	3
MADDOX JOHN W	2LT	0-1311097	0645	2
MADDOX LINDSEY A	MAJ	0-0401932	0446	2
MADDOX LUTHER R	COL	0-0111176	0648	3
MADDOX WARNER V	COL	0-0271267	1166	3
MADDOX WILLIAM A	LTC	0-0239416	0864	3
MADDREY WILLIAM G	CW4	W-2141784	0761	1
MADDRY JOHN A	CPT	0-1941346	0466	1
MADDUX GERARD F	LTC	0-1576324	0454	1
MADDUX MILTON R	COL	0-0242020	0761	3
MADDY IRVIN S	LTC	0-0370138	0467	3
MADEAU JOSEPH I	CW3	W-2149355	0957	1
MADEIRA JR WARD A	1LT	0-1318199	0645	2
MADEN WILLIAM B	CW4	W-2102031	0354	1
MADER EDWARD R	LTC	0-0534747	0267	3
MADIAS DAVID	CW4	W-2102032	0664	1
MADIGAN DONALD L	COL	0-0335480	0646	2
MADIGAN JOHN J	COL	0-0117351	1252	3
MADIGAN JOHN J	CW2	W-2122902	0546	2
MADIGAN JR THOMAS J	LTC	0-1574988	0661	1
MADIGAN SID G	CPT	0-1044883	0552	1
MADISON ALFRED P	CPT	0-0263596	0647	1
MADISON CLAUDE O	MAJ	0-1582442	0858	2
MADISON CLEMENT C	CW3	W-2141968	1060	1
MADISON DALLAS E	MAJ	0-1119936	0166	2
MADISON DOROTHY E	MAJ	N-0734359	1161	1
MADISON EUGENE P	CPT	0-2263651	0263	1
MADISON FRANCES M	MAJ	N-0736802	1161	1
MADISON GILBERT C	LTC	0-0343941	1154	1

NAME	GRADE	SVC NO	DATE RET MO YR	RET CODE
MADISON GUY	CW3	W-2148745	0764	1
MADISON HERBERT L	WO1	W-2200006	0767	1
MADISON JAMES P	MAJ	0-1824645	0160	1
MADISON LEO H	MAJ	0-1286319	0155	1
MADISON MAURICE N	CPT	0-1112833	0960	1
MADISON MELVIN L	1LT	0-0491531	0654	1
MADISON ROBERT E	MAJ	0-2081516	1065	1
MADISON STANLEY	CPT	0-1104301	0660	1
MADISON TROY L	LTC	0-1172155	0263	1
MADISON WILLIAM H	CW3	W-2153119	1061	1
MADISON WILLIAM W	LTC	0-1173764	0261	1
MADOKORO SHIGESHI	LTC	0-1331965	0861	1
MADONIA PETER P	MAJ	0-1553505	0459	1
MADSEN EARL A	COL	0-0271688	0466	3
MADSEN EMIL	LTC	0-0288440	0767	3
MADSEN GEORGE P	1LT	0-1553305	0746	2
MADSEN HAROLD M	LTC	0-0219897	0164	3
MADSEN JAMES F	MAJ	0-1688759	1065	1
MADSEN LEO H	MAJ	0-2048062	0661	1
MADSEN SR OWEN M	LTC	0-2053986	1055	1
MADSEN NORRIS C	LTC	0-1644549	0361	1
MADZELAN JR VASIL	MAJ	0-1824053	0661	1
MAEKAWA GEORGE	CW2	W-2210899	0566	1
MAERZ FREDERICK	CPT	0-2262757	0361	1
MAES ANDREW J	LTC	0-0488459	1060	3
MAES ROBERT W	MAJ	0-0969255	0263	1
MAESER ARTHUR F	LTC	0-1542419	0367	2
MAFFEO PASQUALE E	1LT	0-1319759	1046	1
MAFFETT CHARLES R	LTC	0-0446325	1065	1
MAFFETT WALLACE G	2LT	0-1259439	0445	2
MAGAOLEU WALTER J	COL	0-0237277	0157	3
MAGALOTTI MARION F	CPT	0-0464470	0846	1
MAGARIAN ARAM	MAJ	0-1595669	0665	1
MAGARIAN HAROLD J	MAJ	0-1824208	0860	1
MAGARIAN OSCAR K	LTC	0-0504359	1165	3
MAGAURN ELTON L	LTC	0-1999877	0166	1
MAGAZIA GEORGE A	CW3	W-2143443	0365	1
MAGDITS EDWARD A	CPT	0-1058884	0747	2
MAGE SIGMUND	LTC	0-0486525	0446	1
MAGEE DUDLEY E	MAJ	0-0272085	0344	2
MAGEE FRANCIS J	COL	0-0172920	0858	3
MAGEE GEORGE R	CPT	0-0910277	0245	2
MAGEE HAROLD J	LTC	0-1585801	0661	1
MAGEE JEWEL L	CW4	W-2151507	0665	1
MAGEE JOHN A	LTC	0-0222776	0859	3
MAGEE LILLIAN F	1LT	N-0721558	0846	1
MAGEE LUTHER D	2LT	0-1172157	0145	2
MAGEE ROBERT D	MAJ	0-2048063	0161	1
MAGEE ROBERT E	LTC	0-1339551	0766	1
MAGEE ROBERT F	CPT	0-0487954	0246	2
MAGEE ROBERT W	MAJ	0-1799876	0163	1
MAGEE THEODORE F	COL	0-1292550	1162	1
MAGEE VERNON L R	LTC	0-1555426	0867	1
MAGEE VICTOR T	MAJ	0-1016041	0966	1
MAGEE WILLIAM G	CPT	0-0346091	0944	2
MAGEE WILLIAM L	MAJ	0-1646384	0161	2
MAGENOT FRED K	LTC	0-0323619	0153	1
MAGENS HANS J	LTC	0-0197728	0553	3
MAGERS FRANK J	COL	0-0503870	0847	1
MAGERS FREDERICK	LTC	0-0297411	0560	1
MAGERS JESSE E	MAJ	0-1290273	1060	1
MAGGIORE MICHAEL J	LTC	0-0345616	0364	3
MAGID ALLAN	LTC	0-0229372	1044	2
MAGILL GEORGE W	LTC	0-1292721	0167	1
MAGILL THOMAS C	MAJ	0-1047645	1162	1
MAGILL WALTER B	LTC	0-0359272	0666	1
MAGIN RALPH G	CPT	0-1945419	1045	2
MAGINNIS PATRICK C	LTC	0-0313745	0367	3
MAGLIO DENNIS C	1LT	0-0245805	0157	3
MAGLIO JR FRANK R	LTC	0-1012063	0767	3
MAGLIONE FRANK C	CPT	0-0970819	0758	2
MAGNAN JOSEPH P	CPT	0-0961626	1058	1
MAGNER GEORGE J	LTC	0-1296874	0765	1
MAGNES MAX	COL	0-0285213	1162	3
MAGNESS GUY A	COL	0-0251187	1059	3

NAME	GRADE	SVC NO	DATE RET MO YR	RET CODE
MAGNUS CLARENCE A	CPT	0-0268110	0847	2
MAGNUSEN LEWIS C	COL	0-0305535	1067	3
MAGNUSON GOSTA R	1LT	0-0525989	0944	2
MAGNUSON OSCAR W	MAJ	0-0236948	0264	3
MAGNUSON RICHARD	CW3	W-2144997	0858	1
MAGRI MICHAEL	LTC	0-1182905	0562	2
MAGRUDER ALFRED L	MAJ	0-2027534	0261	1
MAGRUDER HERBERT E	LTC	0-0450609	1058	1
MAGRUDER JERREL E	CPT	0-1290781	0153	1
MAGRUDER ROGER C	COL	0-0349145	0866	3
MAGRUDER VIRGIL E	MAJ	0-1043719	0761	1
MAGUE ALICE I	CW4	V-1001672	1264	1
MAGUFFEE BOBBY L	CW2	W-2211899	0167	1
MAGUIRE ANNA R	1LT	N-0725551	0947	1
MAGUIRE FRANK J	LTC	0-0252360	1266	3
MAGUIRE FRANK J	CPT	0-2263046	0861	1
MAGUIRE GEORGE T	MAJ	0-0526336	0949	2
MAGUIRE JAMES C	LTC	0-0363686	1059	1
MAGUIRE JAMES F	CPT	0-1299597	0266	2
MAGUIRE JOHN A	1LT	0-1295046	0454	1
MAGUIRE ROBERT R	MAJ	0-0976884	0664	1
MAGUIRE THOMAS	LTC	0-0284541	0858	2
MAGUIRE WILLIAM F	CPT	0-0297017	1044	2
MAGYAR CHARLES C	CPT	0-1307266	0463	1
MAGYAR STEPHEN J	WO1	W-2123610	1045	2
MAHADY FRANCIS L	LTC	0-0221527	0462	3
MAHADY STEPHEN C	CPT	0-0510401	0645	2
MAHALEY WALTER C	LTC	0-1100210	0760	1
MAHAN BERTHA M P	1LT	N-0783135	0845	1
MAHAN CHARLES E	MAJ	0-0451477	0856	1
MAHAN DAVID V	1LT	0-0438674	0346	2
MAHAN FRANCIS E	CW3	W-2143943	0862	2
MAHAN FRANCIS L	LTC	0-1287378	0666	1
MAHAN GUY S	LTC	0-0251321	0165	3
MAHAN JOHN P	MAJ	0-1947147	0960	1
MAHAN LORENZO B	MAJ	0-1114220	1064	1
MAHAN MILLARD	LTC	0-0453846	0959	1
MAHAN TALLMAN J	LTC	0-1108824	0462	1
MAHAN THOMAS L	CPT	0-1032726	0647	2
MAHANEY CHARLES E	LTC	0-0255940	1059	1
MAHAR EDNA L	LTC	N-0700175	0346	1
MAHAR EDWARD F	1LT	0-1302097	0346	2
MAHAR HAROLD W	CPT	0-1332616	1053	2
MAHAR THOMAS B	CW3	W-2141969	1161	2
MAHER EDMUND A	LTC	0-0173027	0860	3
MAHER EDWARD A	LTC	0-0255589	0763	3
MAHER EDWARD B	1LT	0-0499826	0754	1
MAHER EDWARD J	CPT	0-1285455	0745	2
MAHER JOHN F	MAJ	0-1693125	1263	1
MAHER JOHN L	1LT	0-1288767	0745	2
MAHER JOHN M	MAJ	0-0541637	1047	2
MAHER RAYMOND W	LTC	0-0451148	1159	1
MAHER ROBERT C	CW3	W-2133813	0360	1
MAHER THOMAS D	LTC	0-0147553	0854	3
MAHER WALTER G	LTC	0-0396862	0650	1
MAHER WILLIAM J	2LT	0-0507467	1144	2
MAHIKOA AINSLEY K	LTC	0-0315400	0561	1
MAHLE SR GERALD E	1LT	0-1799465	0559	1
MAHLER ARTHUR I	LTC	0-1547764	0765	1
MAHLER ERIC	MAJ	0-0466085	0648	1
MAHN FREDERICK	MAJ	0-1339075	0263	1
MAHOLTZ JOSEPH A	CW3	W-2132664	0956	1
MAHON GEORGE S	MAJ	0-0468133	0346	1
MAHON JAMES B	CPT	0-1015964	1146	1
MAHON JR BOYD B	1LT	0-1179940	1045	2
MAHON RUSSELL P	MAJ	0-1046545	0955	1
MAHONEY ARTHUR V	CW2	W-2148626	0357	1
MAHONEY BEULAH L	MAJ	N-0734167	0165	3
MAHONEY CATHERINE	LTC	N-0724674	0466	2
MAHONEY DANIEL J	LTC	0-0497990	1053	2
MAHONEY ELBERT W	CPT	0-0279042	1046	2
MAHONEY FRANCIS M	MAJ	0-1051270	0361	1
MAHONEY HAROLD J	LTC	0-0404372	0765	3
MAHONEY HARRY J	MAJ	0-0963254	0563	1
MAHONEY JAMES D	2LT	0-2012596	0746	2

NAME	GRADE	SVC NO	DATE RET MO YR	RET CODE
MAHONEY JAMES P	LTC	0-0297477	0666	3
MAHONEY JOHN J	1LT	0-0507705	0663	1
MAHONEY JOHN P	MAJ	0-0415906	0146	2
MAHONEY MICHAEL E	CPT	0-1304755	1146	1
MAHONEY MURIEL D	1LT	N-0752117	0546	1
MAHONEY ROBERT B	WO1	W-2113943	0145	2
MAHONEY ROSEMARY M	1LT	N-0703702	0645	1
MAHONEY WILLIAM J	LTC	0-0455389	0764	1
MAHONY EDWARD F	1LT	0-1325585	0646	2
MAHOOD FRANK C	COL	0-0250618	0567	3
MAHORIC FRANK	CW3	W-2207065	0465	1
MAHURIN KENNETH R	1LT	0-1651547	1048	2
MAIDEN JR BENJAMIN C	LTC	0-0348092	0662	1
MAIER FREDERICK	COL	0-0128549	0256	3
MAIER FREDERICK	LTC	0-0210833	0358	3
MAIER HEMO F	1LT	0-1324035	104N	2
MAIER JOHN G	CW2	W-2120127	1055	1
MAIER JOHN L	CPT	0-0419908	0946	2
MAIERS CLARENCE H	CPT	0-1590627	0864	2
MAILE BONIFACE	1LT	0-0911268	1144	2
MAILLARD CHARLES A	1LT	0-0420780	1145	2
MAILMAN EUGENE W	COL	0-0283824	0767	3
MAIN CHARLES L	COL	0-0149442	1057	3
MAIN DONALD C	1LT	0-1327640	0346	2
MAIN LESLIE J	1LT	0-1287556	0845	2
MAINAR BRUNO	1LT	0-1897031	0565	1
MAINAR JOSEPH D	2LT	0-1896468	0862	1
MAINES ALVIN R	CW2	W-2143645	0656	1
MAINORC HUGH I	COL	0-0109066	0955	3
MAINS CHARLES H	CPT	0-1312183	0147	2
MAINS JESSIE R	1LT	N-0736525	1146	1
MAINS JOHN R	MAJ	0-1310283	0264	1
MAINS PAUL G	LTC	0-0222584	0863	3
MAINS PAUL H	MAJ	0-1556756	0960	1
MAINS WILLIAM O	CPT	0-0406951	1044	2
MAINZ FRANCIS	LTC	0-0253762	1053	1
MAINZER FRANCIS S	LTC	0-0228135	1058	3
MAIORANA JOHN A	LTC	0-1826212	1264	1
MAIRE ROMAN W	MAJ	0-1168795	0258	1
MAISCH WILLIAM	LTC	0-0241426	0652	3
MAISEL FREDERICK	MAJ	0-0418335	1047	2
MAISENBACHER LEROY A	LTC	0-1824209	1266	1
MAISON HAROLD G	M G	0-0141515	0757	3
MAITEN SAMUEL J	1LT	0-1557323	0346	2
MAITLAND DAVID S	MAJ	0-0244148	0564	3
MAITLAND STEPHEN A	MAJ	0-2262328	0861	1
MAITLAND THOMAS F	LTC	0-0996384	0861	1
MAITLAND WILLIAM E	CPT	0-1081661	0247	1
MAIZE CLYDE H	COL	0-0225587	0565	3
MAIZE LLOYD H	CW2	W-2150996	0959	1
MAIZE WILLIAM	LTC	0-1289453	0461	1
MAJANE WILFRED C	1LT	0-1301508	1044	2
MAJERIC CHARLES	MAJ	0-0507540	0455	2
MAJEWSKI ALEXANDER	1LT	0-1010727	0744	2
MAJOR CLARENCE E	CPT	0-1292026	0146	1
MAJOR ELWOOD R	MAJ	0-0234910	0755	3
MAJOR FERDINAND	COL	0-0194481	1262	3
MAJOR RALPH B	LTC	0-0236300	0460	1
MAJOR RALPH H	LTC	0-0264238	1055	3
MAJOR TERRANCE A	MAJ	0-2006488	0957	1
MAJOR THOMAS H	LTC	0-1299442	0162	1
MAJOR THOMAS W	MAJ	0-1633386	0555	1
MAJOROS MICHAEL J	MAJ	0-2010386	1162	1
MAJORS ALLEN B	MAJ	0-1894436	0657	1
MAJORS GRADY D	LTC	0-1184888	0766	1
MAJORS N A	MAJ	0-1322753	0260	1
MAJORS WEBSTER B	LTC	0-0290523	0556	3
MAJURE ERNEST O	COL	0-0321066	0264	3
MAKAR WALTER V	LTC	0-1168796	0462	1
MAKAREVICH ANDREW J	1LT	0-1049968	0945	2
MAKER NAOMI N	2LT	N-0734011	1044	1
MAKHOLM ARTHUR E	LTC	0-1109479	0767	1
MAKI AUCIE	MAJ	0-1639524	1157	1
MAKI ELMER R	LTC	0-1048883	1062	1
MAKIN GRAHAM	MAJ	0-1595877	1262	1

NAME	GRADE	SVC NO	DATE RET MO YR	RET CODE
MAKOWSKI LEONARD D	MAJ	O-1016020	0262	1
MAKOWSKI RICHARD J	CW2	W-2214906	1166	1
MAKRIS JAMES C	CPT	O-0973820	0958	2
MAKUCH WALTER S	LTC	O-1174944	0367	1
MALABEO MAURICIO F	1LT	O-2032116	0851	1
MALACH MONTE	1LT	O-1917320	0754	2
MALACHOWSKI STANLEY	MAJ	O-0230348	0748	1
MALAMBRI WILLIAM F	CW3	W-2203356	0164	1
MALAN KENNETT H	MAJ	O-0311297	0844	2
MALANCA FRANCIS X	1LT	O-0501611	1043	2
MALANGA ANGELO P	CW4	W-2143304	0259	1
MALARKEY LEO L	1LT	O-0526058	0744	2
MALATESTA STEPHEN	MAJ	O-0104607	0648	3
MALAY WILLIAM J	MAJ	O-1584552	0862	1
MALCOLM BERNARD L	COL	O-0269145	0858	1
MALCOLM DON J	COL	O-0162499	0860	3
MALCOLM FRANK J	MAJ	O-0773412	0363	1
MALCOLM WALTER F	CPT	O-1945882	1262	1
MALDONADO JESUS M	CW4	W-2103168	0455	1
MALDONADO PEDRO J	MAJ	O-1924096	1063	1
MALDONADO PEDRO M	CPT	O-0298286	0446	2
MALEADY EUGENE L	LTC	O-0543785	0364	1
MALEK EDWARD R	LTC	O-2014468	0566	1
MALEK LEO E	1LT	O-1294501	1045	1
MALENFANT LAURENCE	MAJ	O-0234502	0345	2
MALENSKI ALBERT S	1LT	O-1306737	0767	2
MALET OLGA M	CPT	L-1005152	0847	2
MALEY EDMOND R	COL	O-0350943	0266	1
MALICK KENNETH R	1LT	O-1012085	1045	2
MALICK MARVIN P	WO1	W-2125242	0147	1
MALIKO JOSEPH	MAJ	O-1341987	0863	1
MALIKOWSKI STANLEY P	CW3	W-2206641	0166	1
MALIN EDGAR	1LT	O-0452664	0344	2
MALINAUSKI JOSEPH G	MAJ	O-1012932	1060	1
MALINIAK JOHN A	MAJ	O-1648370	0860	1
MALINICK GEORGE	CPT	O-1111751	0855	2
MALINOWSKI ROY E	CPT	O-0959292	0755	2
MALINSKI FLORIAN L	CPT	O-2015745	0760	1
MALISKEY DONALD C	LTC	O-0380676	1061	1
MALIZOLA JAMES	MAJ	O-1598924	0964	1
MALKEMUS GEORGE R	CW2	W-2109451	0647	1
MALKIN SIDNEY W	1LT	O-1308666	0245	2
MALKOWSKI EDWARD J	CW2	RW-2207062	0565	1
MALL JACOB O	COL	O-0287138	0962	3
MALL LEONARD W	MAJ	O-1845927	0763	1
MALL ROBERT R	MAJ	O-1302999	0965	1
MALLARO INMAN E	LTC	O-1305951	0463	1
MALLARI ELISEO V	CPT	O-0369767	0157	1
MALLAY JULES L	COL	O-0184780	0757	3
MALLEK JAMES R	CW2	W-2212303	0964	1
MALLEN ABRAHAM	LTC	O-0250286	0557	1
MALLENDER CHARLES W	LTC	O-1582445	0163	3
MALLETT CECILE A	MAJ	N-0753369	0965	1
MALLETT DIBRELL E	CW3	W-2136044	0662	1
MALLETT WINIFRED M	2LT	N-0703078	0643	1
MALLEY GEORGE F	1LT	O-1059869	0546	2
MALLEY LEO H	LTC	O-0401414	0966	2
MALLEY WALTER F	LTC	O-0305480	0358	1
MALLIA ANN T	MAJ	N-0729034	0962	1
MALLICOAT JAMES O	CPT	O-0188922	0648	3
MALLIN JOSEPH D	CPT	O-1299338	0246	2
MALLISON EARL O	COL	O-0178812	0458	3
MALLON ARTHUR	LTC	O-0220802	0664	3
MALLON EDWARD P	CPT	O-0887652	0747	2
MALLON ETHAN L	LTC	O-0290312	0467	3
MALLON FRANCIS P	CW2	W-2106104	0545	2
MALLON MAX K	CPT	O-0479353	0444	2
MALLONEE DAVID H	2LT	O-1913804	0642	1
MALLORY BURWELL S	CW4	W-2111461	0161	1
MALLORY EDWARD C	2LT	O-1313107	1045	2
MALLORY FREDERIC	CW2	W-2144524	1266	1
MALLORY GEORGE	CPT	O-0509663	0246	2
MALLORY HALSEY L	LTC	O-0239440	0666	3
MALLORY KIRK R	COL	O-0345786	0858	3
MALLORY MARGARET M	1LT	N-0722820	1146	1

NAME	GRADE	SVC NO	DATE RET MO YR	RET CODE
MALLORY ROBERT C	MAJ	O-0889271	1061	1
MALLORY WILLIAM T	LTC	O-0226812	1062	3
MALLOW ALFRED B	LTC	O-1323450	1167	1
MALLOW JR DONALD	CW3	W-2205181	1066	1
MALLOY AGNES A	1LT	N-0901143	0455	2
MALLOY EDWARD J	1LT	O-1576328	1053	1
MALLOY HOWARD F	1LT	O-0499795	1160	1
MALLOY JAMES T F	LTC	O-1577516	1060	1
MALLOY JOSEPH O	MAJ	O-0279271	1044	2
MALLOY JOSEPH J	COL	O-0306391	0657	3
MALLOY LUKE T	MAJ	O-1642345	0361	1
MALLOY ROBERT L	CPT	O-0446224	0744	2
MALLOY WESLEY J	LTC	O-1303362	0162	1
MALLOY WILLIAM F	LTC	O-0296150	0546	1
MALLOZZI PASQUALE J	CPT	O-0317306	0161	1
MALM PIERRE	LTC	O-1557488	0167	3
MALMBERG ARTHUR W	CPT	O-0193994	0662	3
MALMQUIST TORD V	LTC	O-1304416	0364	1
MALMSTROM CARL T	CPT	O-0485478	0761	2
MALMSTROM IVAR T	LTC	O-0261436	0367	3
MALMSTROM VINCENT F	LTC	O-0236107	0266	3
MALONE ALVIN P	LTC	O-0357477	0646	2
MALONE ANDREW	MAJ	O-0177090	0360	3
MALONE ARCHIE D	1LT	O-1319627	0445	2
MALONE BEN F	2LT	O-0274635	0543	1
MALONE BERT H	MAJ	O-1683850	0546	2
MALONE CHARLES B	LTC	O-0189910	0755	3
MALONE CLIFFORD A	MAJ	O-1556470	1162	1
MALONE DONALD J	LTC	O-1588140	0565	1
MALONE EDWARD W	COL	O-0275069	0860	3
MALONE FLOYD O	CW2	W-2209006	0565	1
MALONE FRANCIS H	1LT	O-0997645	0855	2
MALONE HENRY C	LTC	O-0421983	0765	3
MALONE ITHER C	CPT	O-1303913	0547	1
MALONE JAMES F	MAJ	O-0451344	0862	1
MALONE JAMES H	COL	O-0294214	0863	1
MALONE JOSEPH H	CW2	W-2143033	0160	1
MALONE JR ALBERT R	MAJ	O-1919386	1066	1
MALONE JR PAUL R	COL	O-0312074	1053	2
MALONE JR WILLIS	CW3	W-2203483	0766	1
MALONE MORRIS L	CPT	O-0169169	1059	3
MALONE ODIS L	MAJ	O-1999791	0461	1
MALONE ROBERT P	COL	O-0436929	0662	2
MALONE STEPHEN N	COL	O-0239339	1265	3
MALONE THOMAS C	LTC	O-0272212	1060	1
MALONE TOM W	CW3	W-2147762	0162	1
MALONE VICTOR A	CW3	W-2127496	1154	1
MALONE VICTOR E	CPT	O-0488380	0547	1
MALONE WILLIAM F	LTC	O-0471033	0851	1
MALONE WILLIAM J	CPT	O-0967827	0661	1
MALONEY ANDREW R	MAJ	O-0402255	0161	1
MALONEY EDWARD J	MAJ	O-0501140	0346	1
MALONEY EDWARD S	MAJ	O-0176330	0165	3
MALONEY ELDON T	MAJ	O-1634102	0860	1
MALONEY FRANK L	CW2	W-2147528	0760	2
MALONEY GORDON E	MAJ	O-0208707	0347	1
MALONEY HAROLD J	2LT	O-1584554	0344	2
MALONEY JAMES C	CW2	W-2209178	1062	1
MALONEY JAMES G	LTC	O-0299471	0465	3
MALONEY JAMES I	LTC	O-0307010	0460	1
MALONEY JAMES J	CPT	O-2025638	0655	1
MALONEY JOHN B	CPT	O-0315173	0949	1
MALONEY JOHN F	1LT	O-1295913	0246	2
MALONEY JOHN F	MAJ	O-2020449	1167	1
MALONEY JOHN F	CW3	W-2151886	1164	1
MALONEY JOHN P	MAJ	O-0587324	1061	2
MALONEY JOHN R	MAJ	O-0224048	0562	3
MALONEY JOHN T	COL	O-0490451	0267	1
MALONEY JOHN W	2LT	O-1056156	1044	2
MALONEY JR DENIS J	CPT	O-1018432	0747	2
MALONEY JR FRANCIS J	1LT	O-1686717	0551	1
MALONEY ORMAND	MAJ	O-0482877	0655	1
MALONEY ROBERT A	LTC	O-2006640	1163	1
MALONEY TED W	CPT	O-1326217	0347	2
MALOOF FREDERIC F	MAJ	O-0483154	0246	1

NAME	GRADE	SVC NO	DATE RET MO YR	RET CODE
MALOS LLOYD G	CPT	O-0425878	1047	1
MALOY EWELL W	MAJ	O-1030803	1057	1
MALPASS FRANCIS J	CW3	W-2206404	1264	2
MALSAM WENDELIN R	MAJ	O-0451345	0756	1
MALSBURY FRANK H	LTC	O-1288919	0867	1
MALSBURY JAMES S	LTC	O-0240304	0765	3
MALSBURY LIONEL A	LTC	O-0406410	0660	1
MALTAIS RENAUD J	COL	O-0496988	0859	1
MALTBA NEWT P	CW2	W-2114215	0647	1
MALTRY LEON M	MAJ	O-0537153	0466	3
MALTRY JR JOHN M	MAJ	O-1797847	0859	1
MALTZ FREDERICK	1LT	O-1284171	1045	2
MALVAL HENRY J	1LT	O-1048483	1044	2
MALZER ARNOLD	CPT	O-0555183	0946	2
MAMA MORA	CPT	O-0890532	0348	2
MAMUKARI JAMES	2LT	O-1305082	0444	2
MAMULA JEANNE O	1LT	N-0901151	0853	1
MANAHAN WILLIAM T	LTC	O-0230536	0347	2
MANARD HELEN L	2LT	N-0764533	0545	1
MANBECK FRANK E	COL	O-0282118	0166	3
MANCE JAMES E	LTC	O-1534800	1262	1
MANCIL COLEMAN M	CPT	O-0976983	0861	1
MANCIOCHI LOUIS J	CW2	W-2147890	0660	1
MANCK IRA	MAJ	O-1309582	0864	3
MANCUSO FRANK	MAJ	O-2055228	0660	1
MANCUSO MARCO S	CW3	W-2136620	0761	1
MANO IRWIN	CPT	O-0357890	0651	1
MANDEL GERALD S	CW3	W-2150721	0163	2
MANDEL J O	CW2	W-2144496	0760	1
MANDEL JEROME	LTC	O-0446288	0447	1
MANDEL NATHAN G	MAJ	O-0313612	0645	2
MANDELL HERMAN	LTC	O-0394553	0866	3
MANDELL HERMAN S	LTC	O-1105644	0266	1
MANDELL JR LOUIS E	LTC	O-0229504	0564	3
MANDELL LESTER	LTC	O-1043715	0664	1
MANDER DESMOND W	CPT	O-1183570	0347	2
MANDERS WILLIAM G	CPT	O-1010085	1046	1
MANDERSON WILLIAM T	MAJ	O-1913339	0763	1
MANDICH BENEDICT P	MAJ	O-0978801	0364	1
MANDL JOSEPH P	LTC	O-0313654	0660	3
MANDLE ALBERT	MAJ	O-1691459	0152	1
MANDOLADO CESARIO	2LT	O-1896660	0761	1
MANEE LEROY A	MAJ	O-0498284	0247	1
MANEGOLD JOHN E	LTC	O-0154005	1050	3
MANES CHARLES O	LTC	O-1579971	0961	1
MANES JOHN H	CW2	W-2101059	0248	2
MANEVAL ROBERT C	COL	O-0307005	0366	3
MANEY HOWARD S	MAJ	O-0964547	0565	1
MANEY JR WILLIAM F	LTC	O-1057155	0365	1
MANEY MARTIN F	1LT	O-1307438	0946	2
MANFRE JOHN G	LTC	O-1001843	0761	1
MANFREDI AUGUSTINE	CW2	W-2211861	0666	1
MANFREDO DOMINIC	CW3	RW-2146814	0264	1
MANGALINDAN PRIMITIV	2LT	O-1896377	0450	1
MANGAN BRUCE J	MAJ	O-1650218	0361	1
MANGAN EDWARD J	CPT	O-1012743	0645	2
MANGANARO PHILIP L	1LT	O-1045823	0745	2
MANGANELLO ARTHUR	CPT	O-0969655	0860	1
MANGELLY THOMAS	CPT	O-1640697	0660	1
MANGER LEO	LTC	O-0464915	0257	1
MANGES BINNIE L	1LT	N-0742694	1046	1
MANGHI GENE	CPT	O-1641540	0764	1
MANGIERI CHARLES E	2LT	O-1060544	1045	2
MANGIN CHARLES E	1LT	O-1826241	0745	2
MANGINE WILLIAM J	COL	O-0176734	0760	3
MANGINELLI VITUS W	COL	O-0448101	0665	3
MANGINI JOHN J	1LT	O-1030593	0944	2
MANGINI ROLAND A	COL	O-0239790	0852	3
MANGRUM ALTON J	LTC	O-1178883	1162	1
MANGUBAT DIOSCORO L	1LT	O-0890528	1046	1
MANGUM HOWEL C	WO1	W-2131583	0147	1
MANGUM JAMES E	COL	O-0157497	0753	3
MANGUM JR INGLIS P	CPT	O-1295574	1047	2
MANGUM JR ROBERT G	CPT	O-2262963	1266	1
MANGUM WILSON P	1LT	O-1307724	0345	2

NAME	GRADE	SVC NO	DATE RET MO YR	RET CODE
MANGUNO JOSEPH C	LTC	O-1292916	1061	1
MANGUSO ANTONINO H	LTC	O-0310672	0161	1
MANHART WALTER	CPT	O-0195808	0641	1
MANIFOLD GEORGE T	CW2	W-2152642	0660	1
MANIFOLD KENNETH M	LTC	O-1291849	0363	1
MANINGO FELIPE N	1LT	O-0890232	0447	2
MANION ESTHER L	2LT	N-0787969	0445	1
MANION JOSEPH P	1LT	O-0531210	0945	2
MANION THOMAS J	1LT	O-1325657	0348	2
MANION WAYNE H	MAJ	O-1291666	0662	1
MANIS JR CARL	LTC	O-0545432	0365	1
MANIX JOHN W	1LT	O-2035124	1045	2
MANKE ELDRED B	1LT	O-1111753	0845	2
MANKE FRED	CPT	O-0108183	1040	1
MANKE ROBERT L	CPT	O-1582447	0853	1
MANKER RAYMOND O	LTC	O-1035523	1062	1
MANKOWICH ABRAHAM	MAJ	O-0253591	0667	3
MANLEY CARL B	1LT	O-1635090	0661	3
MANLEY EUGENE H	COL	O-0378191	0765	1
MANLEY FRANCIS J	LTC	O-1040432	0366	1
MANLEY HENRY G	MAJ	O-0959381	0767	1
MANLEY JERRY R	2LT	O-1017543	0944	2
MANLEY JOSEPH W	CPT	O-0462723	0345	1
MANLEY JR JOSEPH P	1LT	O-0359520	0345	2
MANLEY ROBERT D	1LT	O-1298266	1145	1
MANLEY ROBERT F	MAJ	O-0969378	0267	1
MANLOVE JR CHARLES H	LTC	O-0176656	0648	3
MANLY CLARENCE H	CPT	O-0149577	1152	3
MANN ANTHONY A	CW2	W-2152553	0161	1
MANN BLAIR W	MAJ	O-1798489	1262	3
MANN CARL E	COL	O-0453178	1158	1
MANN CLAUS	CPT	O-1919485	1263	1
MANN CURTIS W	LTC	O-0302098	0758	1
MANN DOROTHY A	1LT	N-0742159	1145	1
MANN DORRANCE W	WO1	W-2109817	0157	3
MANN ELDON U	CW2	W-2002213	0867	3
MANN FRANK L	LTC	O-0305302	0660	1
MANN FREDERIC B	COL	O-0274106	0858	2
MANN GEORGE E	MAJ	O-0147813	0554	3
MANN GEORGE L	LTC	O-0143922	0656	3
MANN GRAMER L	1LT	O-1101565	0845	2
MANN HORACE	LTC	O-1578809	0361	1
MANN HOWARD C	MAJ	O-1311530	0864	1
MANN HUGO S	CW2	W-2151118	0264	1
MANN JACK	MAJ	O-2289274	1166	1
MANN JAMES G	LTC	O-0425285	0961	1
MANN JESS H	LTC	O-0486108	1058	1
MANN JOHN A	LTC	O-0492419	1048	1
MANN JR JOHN C	MAJ	O-0469925	1066	1
MANN JULIUS W	COL	O-0453180	1162	1
MANN LEROY S	COL	O-0245725	0860	3
MANN MAX W	CPT	O-0496344	0246	2
MANN NATHAN J	2LT	O-1643094	1052	2
MANN PAUL R	LTC	O-0350618	0357	1
MANN PAUL W	CW2	W-2142768	1154	1
MANN RALPH H	MAJ	O-0186625	1054	3
MANN ROBERT W	LTC	O-1045824	0964	1
MANN RUSSELL F	MAJ	O-0402257	1045	2
MANN THOMAS J	MAJ	O-1169628	1158	1
MANN THOMAS W	LTC	O-0578500	0358	1
MANN WALTER F	CW2	W-2109980	1049	2
MANN WAYNE G	LTC	O-0405505	1058	1
MANNE EDWARD	COL	O-0240648	0163	3
MANNEAR WILLIAM E	LTC	O-0146207	0648	3
MANNEN LESLIE E	MAJ	O-0267637	0346	2
MANNERSTEDT GORDON O	LTC	O-0446986	0546	2
MANNESCHMIDT GEORG	LTC	O-0257129	0453	1
MANNHEIMER ROBERT E	LTC	O-0322385	0765	1
MANNING BENJAMIN C	CW3	W-2150322	0959	1
MANNING BRECKAN J	CPT	O-0450534	0653	1
MANNING DANIEL F	COL	O-0219354	0559	3
MANNING DONALD V	WO1	W-2108967	0645	2
MANNING DREW A	1LT	O-1312577	0445	2
MANNING FORDYCE G	LTC	O-1010077	0259	1
MANNING FRANK R	LTC	O-1165904	0162	1

NAME	GRADE	SVC NO	DATE RET MO YR	RET CODE
MANNING FRED J	LTC	0-1588715	C162	1
MANNING FREDERICK	CPT	0-1577518	1058	1
MANNING GRACE H	MAJ	L-0220085	1163	1
MANNING GRANT W	LTC	0-0506017	1054	1
MANNING HAROLD L	CW3	W-2143616	0760	1
MANNING JACK R	CPT	0-1579973	0646	2
MANNING JAMES D	LTC	0-0398317	1062	1
MANNING JAMES F	1LT	0-1181026	0450	1
MANNING JAMES P	CW4	W-2113649	1154	1
MANNING JEFFREY H	2LT	0-1310929	1044	2
MANNING JERALD F	CW3	W-2203276	0767	1
MANNING JOHN C	MAJ	0-0941958	C463	1
MANNING JOHN F	LTC	0-0414970	0762	1
MANNING JOHN M	LTC	0-0259178	C860	1
MANNING JOHN W	COL	0-0219691	0459	3
MANNING JR ROBERT E	CPT	0-C461033	1047	1
MANNING MANFORD J	CPT	0-1041836	0446	2
MANNING RICHARD C	CPT	0-1298563	1047	2
MANNING VAUGHN E	CW4	W-2141363	C463	1
MANNING VIVIAN E	2LT	N-0702298	0235	1
MANNING WENDELL A	MAJ	0-2096467	1165	1
MANNING WILLIAM E	CW3	W-2141707	0657	1
MANNING WILLIAM J	CPT	C-1304418	1061	1
MANNING WILLIAM S	LTC	0-018948C	1158	3
MANNION JOSEPH W	MAJ	0-1545770	C965	1
MANNLE ROBERT A	LTC	0-1056457	0766	2
MANNON EUGENE L	MAJ	0-0250137	1145	2
MANNS EDDIE E	MAJ	0-0942802	0761	1
MANNY JAMES W	1LT	0-1933768	0355	2
MANO JOSEPH M	LTC	0-0419532	0261	1
MANOR ROBERT J	MAJ	C-0266915	C862	3
MANOS ANTHONY J	MAJ	C-2008537	C962	1
MANOWN JR VOYLE F	CPT	0-1062899	0346	2
MANRESA JR MIGUEL	CPT	0-0522941	1048	1
MANRIQUE BIENVENIDO	1LT	0-0890441	0858	1
MANROSS FREDERICK	COL	0-019155C	0161	3
MANRY JOHN C	MAJ	0-1305952	C757	1
MANS BILLIE	MAJ	N-0726549	C861	1
MANSEN THEODORE A	LTC	0-0513112	0166	3
MANSER HARRY M	COL	0-0178694	C758	3
MANSER JOHN A	LTC	0-0343381	C863	3
MANSER JULIEN G	CPT	0-0268529	0545	2
MANSFIELD EVE O	CPT	L-05001C1	C648	2
MANSFIELD FRANK S	MAJ	0-0121174	0658	3
MANSFIELD JOSEPH P	CW3	W-2008294	0266	3
MANSFIELD RICHARD D	MAJ	0-0342999	C645	2
MANSFIELD ROBERT C	COL	0-0254985	0153	1
MANSFIELD VIRGIL C	LTC	C-1588716	0862	1
MANSFIELD WILBUR L	LTC	0-0410360	0965	3
MANSFIELD WILLIAM A	LTC	0-0100183	0253	3
MANSHIP LAWRENCE L	LTC	0-0916148	0667	3
MANSKA JACK H	MAJ	0-0964031	1061	1
MANSKER JOSEPH S	LTC	0-0332721	C467	3
MANSON GORDON	1LT	0-C436993	0446	1
MANTELL FRANCIS J	LTC	0-0310158	0463	3
MANTER NELSON L	MAJ	C-0251300	1166	3
MANTER RALPH M	COL	0-0131514	0355	3
MANTEUFFEL ERWIN R	MAJ	C-C240005	1048	3
MANTHE CORNELIUS	LTC	0-1111214	1062	1
MANTHEI JOHN E	MAJ	0-1337727	0467	1
MANTIPLY SAMUEL T	1LT	0-0888450	0749	1
MANTO JOSEPH V	MAJ	0-2001784	C562	1
MANTONE PLINIO	MAJ	0-1014003	0966	1
MANTZ HARRY E	MAJ	0-0368520	1144	2
MANTZ JUANITA S	2LT	N-0736936	0445	1
MANUEL ANNIE J	1LT	N-0726756	0446	1
MANUEL FRANK J	MAJ	0-1286157	0547	2
MANUEL MILTON L	CPT	0-0414076	1045	2
MANUEL RALPH E	LTC	0-1294689	0860	2
MANUEL THOMAS B	COL	0-0249469	C146	2
MANUEL WEBSTER G	CW3	W-3150355	0667	1
MANULIK JOHN C	LTC	0-1542890	0861	1
MANWELL KARL R	MAJ	C-0889792	0555	1
MANWILLER JOHN A O	LTC	0-0356034	C463	1
MANZ HANS J	LTC	0-2200200	1066	1
MANZANO FLORENCIO	1LT	0-0268179	0447	2
MANZIONE JOSEPH A	MAJ	0-0279066	0154	3
MAPEL FRANK R	COL	0-0336161	0963	3
MAPES AMELIA C P	2LT	N-0753286	0546	1
MAPES LESTER R	MAJ	0-0123642	0750	3
MAPES LLOYD T	LTC	0-1331532	0164	1
MAPES MILTON C	COL	C-0193153	0648	3
MAPES WILLIAM M	CPT	0-0231062	0357	3
MAPLE ALPHEUS F	LTC	0-0346504	0662	3
MAPLE CHARLES W	CW3	W-2144308	0861	1
MAPLE HAROLD S	CW4	W-2113439	0461	1
MAPLE TELFORD G	1LT	0-0419358	0944	2
MAPLES FREDERICK	LTC	0-0341482	0647	2
MAPLESDEN GEORGE T	WO1	W-2131089	0546	2
MAR THOMAS A	CW3	W-2145025	1164	1
MAR THOMAS M	CPT	0-0421223	0246	2
MAR WILLIAM F	LTC	0-1949387	0662	1
MARA SAMUEL G	LTC	0-0234825	1154	3
MARABLE BEN F	LTC	0-0264510	0760	1
MARALDI CARL F	LTC	0-0246454	C755	3
MARANA ANDRO S	1LT	0-2031896	0649	1
MARANCHAK STEPHEN M	CW4	W-2151804	1060	1
MARANGONI BRUNO A	MAJ	0-0338956	0345	2
MARANVILLE KEATHLE	LTC	0-0450173	1158	1
MARATTA JOHN W	CPT	0-0410251	0146	2
MARAZZINI BERNARD J	LTC	0-0559253	0959	1
MARBERRY JOE D	MAJ	C-0451003	0657	2
MARBLE ALEXANDER	B G	0-0241298	0362	3
MARBLE CUSTER T	CW3	W-2141385	0659	1
MARBLE JOHN H	MAJ	0-1049970	1055	1
MARBLE ROBERT D	MAJ	0-191777C	0463	1
MARBLE ROLAND C	CPT	0-2006C93	0347	2
MARBRY GEORGE W	CPT	0-0494185	C346	2
MARBUT WILLIAM M	COL	0-0246304	0858	2
MARCAIS ARSENE F	CPT	0-0172452	0549	3
MARCANTONIO R C	1LT	0-2028391	0953	2
MARCEAU PAUL F	LTC	0-0504796	0164	3
MARCELL LEO J	MAJ	0-2055190	0756	1
MARCELYNAS ANTHONY F	LTC	0-0368747	0258	1
MARCENKUS ALBERT A	1LT	0-1322566	1045	2
MARCH HARRY S	LTC	0-022517C	0652	3
MARCH JOSEPH H	LTC	0-15961C6	0766	3
MARCH LEONARD W	LTC	0-0217688	1055	3
MARCH WILLIAM E	2LT	0-0451512	0544	1
MARCHAND CLAYTON P	LTC	0-0510804	0954	1
MARCHAND HANS L	CPT	0-1059542	0649	1
MARCHANT EDWARD J	WO1	W-2111690	0264	3
MARCHANT GORDON L	LTC	0-1550438	1161	1
MARCHANT JAMES O	LTC	0-0251659	0366	3
MARCHBANK ANDREW C	1LT	0-5022862	1067	2
MARCHBANKS JAMES L	MAJ	0-1287731	C954	1
MARCHBANKS VANCE H	CPT	0-0109537	1039	1
MARCHBANKS WILLIAM D	1LT	0-2212022	0656	1
MARCHE DON C	CPT	0-2033160	0662	1
MARCHESE FRANK J	CW3	W-2143584	1263	1
MARCHESELLI JR V F	MAJ	0-1042096	0459	1
MARCHETTI FRANK F	LTC	0-0187983	0847	2
MARCHI BRUNO G	LTC	0-0233093	1163	3
MARCHIONDO EDDIE	1LT	0-1826353	0346	2
MARCHITELLI HENRY A	LTC	0-1314037	1060	1
MARCHMAN MARY I	2LT	N-C773080	1045	1
MARCHMAN WILLIAM H	CW2	W-2215128	0567	1
MARCIN HILARY J	CPT	0-053522C	C545	2
MARCINAK CASPER F	WO1	W-2119927	1145	2
MARCINKO STEPHEN A	COL	0-0479005	1057	1
MARCINKOWSKI JULIAN	MAJ	0-0450607	0457	1
MARCINKOWSKI THADDEU	LTC	0-0383546	0263	1
MARCK WILLIAM J	MAJ	0-0312795	1044	2
MARCKS RAYMOND H	MAJ	0-0980124	0264	1
MARCO JOSEPH D	CPT	0-0305881	0845	2
MARCOTT HELEN M C	2LT	N-C758014	0146	1
MARCOTTE GERALD J	MAJ	0-1702281	0267	1
MARCOUS MARION H	1LT	N-0730350	0445	1
MARCOUX ELI A	LTC	0-0131516	1054	3
MARCROFT JOHN C	LTC	0-023816C	0764	3
MARCUCCI ALDO M	1LT	0-1593301	0746	1
MARCUM ALFRED L	LTC	0-0125162	0546	2
MARCUM HENRY F	2LT	0-1324634	C245	1
MARCUM HERSHEL	1LT	0-1643831	1045	2
MARCUM SAMUEL G	MAJ	0-0336903	0646	2
MARCUM WARREN E	1LT	0-1285967	C945	2
MARCUM WILLIAM H	LTC	0-1295916	1060	1
MARCUS IRWIN M	CPT	0-1756775	0946	2
MARCUS LAWRENCE F	CPT	0-0370714	0145	2
MARCUS LEO	1LT	0-1717555	0945	2
MARCUS LOUIS L	LTC	0-0297051	0260	3
MARCUS MAURICE	CPT	0-1312693	C847	1
MARCUS MORRIS D	CPT	0-0314202	0346	2
MARCUS PHILIP W	CPT	0-0333516	0844	2
MARCUS SAMUEL	CW3	W-2142251	0665	1
MARCUS SIDNEY R	MAJ	C-0284994	C157	2
MARCUS STANLEY	CPT	0-0511801	C146	2
MARCUS STANLEY S	1LT	C-1048887	C347	2
MARCUSSON WILLIAM B	LTC	0-0464075	0246	2
MARCY JR GUY E	CPT	0-0419008	0645	1
MARCYES PAUL F	MAJ	C-1043415	0661	1
MARDEN HAROLD C	COL	0-0242841	0860	3
MARDEN HARRY S	1LT	0-0279299	0538	1
MARDER SIDNEY S	CPT	0-0508861	0545	2
MARDIROS ARMEN N	COL	0-0279171	1066	3
MARDIS JOHN R	1LT	0-0408571	0345	2
MARDIS RALEIGH L	CW3	W-2141366	1161	1
MARDOS OTTO	MAJ	C-0969050	0163	1
MAREK CHARLES S	COL	0-0234053	C851	3
MAREK CHESTER J	2LT	0-1302683	C245	2
MAREK FRANK A	MAJ	C-1556175	0557	1
MAREK HATTIE L	MAJ	N-0701687	1163	3
MAREK NORBERT C	MAJ	0-1289934	0147	1
MAREK RICHARD G	CPT	0-0445638	C446	2
MAREKA EDWARD J	MAJ	0-0972667	1066	1
MAREN ADOLPH	CW2	W-2141367	1057	1
MARESCA JR ROBERT J	CW3	W-2152007	0765	1
MARESH EDWARD	MAJ	0-0165496	0447	1
MARFORI EDMUNDO J	LTC	0-130166C	C962	1
MARGESON JR EDWARD M	CW3	W-2152144	0964	1
MARGNER LOUIS J	MAJ	C-1038051	C461	1
MARGOLIASH JACOB S	CPT	0-0399026	0346	2
MARGOLIN BARACH	LTC	0-0321683	C161	1
MARGOLIN SAMUEL	MAJ	0-0250391	0165	3
MARGOLIS ARTHUR	MAJ	C-1001845	1155	2
MARGOLIS SAMUEL L	1LT	0-1543642	0245	2
MARGRAF RAYMOND	LTC	0-11C6925	0664	1
MARGULIES CHARLES	MAJ	0-1689285	C346	1
MARIAN JOHN B	COL	0-0192114	0551	3
MARIANI JOSEPH A	LTC	0-1548098	1062	1
MARICLE LECLAIRE R	MAJ	0-0314651	1045	2
MARICNEN PEDRO B	1LT	0-0280157	0157	1
MARIHUGH CLARENCE H	CW2	W-22059C8	0762	1
MARIN ALBERT G	COL	0-1285078	1157	1
MARINACCI ALBERTO A	MAJ	0-0370756	C846	1
MARINAN JOSEPH T	LTC	0-0170828	0349	3
MARINE MICHAEL	CW2	W-2148611	1061	1
MARINER FREEMAN B	MAJ	0-2010387	0864	1
MARING JR WILBUR F	COL	C-0160016	0757	1
MARINO ANTHONY L	CW3	W-2205704	0467	1
MARINO JOSEPH A	MAJ	C-0971308	C665	1
MARINO RAYMOND E	CW4	W-2118200	1065	1
MARINOS HARRY G	MAJ	0-0368262	0445	2
MARINZACK JOHN P	CPT	0-1691725	0457	1
MARION JOE E	MAJ	0-0441403	0445	2
MARION JOHN P	CPT	C-1322643	1047	2
MARION JR THOMAS F	CW4	W-2143770	0262	1
MARION MARIAN M	CPT	L-0400000	1144	2
MARION ROBERT D	LTC	0-1341279	1167	1
MARIS ANNE E	1LT	N-0726866	1046	1
MARIS JR THOMAS G	LTC	0-0363868	0347	2
MARIS LEE M	CPT	0-0491585	0346	2
MARK CECIL H	CPT	0-0324141	C944	2
MARK COLEMAN B	LTC	0-0189955	0648	3
MARK HILBERT	COL	0-0263440	0266	3
MARK JACK S	2LT	0-1703851	0645	2
MARKARIAN VARSING	2LT	N-0742969	0445	1
MARKEE JOSEPH E	LTC	0-1049972	1266	1
MARKEIM CHARLES H	2LT	0-1016461	C745	2
MARKEL BERNICE P	MAJ	N-0800273	C965	1
MARKEL NATHANIEL	CPT	0-1302835	0556	1
MARKEN DELOSS I	COL	0-0275539	1155	3
MARKER DANIEL I	LTC	0-0256149	0955	3
MARKER GEORGE L	LTC	0-1035311	C361	1
MARKER JOHN I	COL	0-C121088	C445	2
MARKER JR LOUIS W	1LT	0-1288420	1045	2
MARKER MARION R	CPT	0-2033162	0459	2
MARKETTE JR JOHN R	CPT	0-0487123	1043	2
MARKHAM CARL W	COL	0-0111181	1048	3
MARKHAM EDWARD D	LTC	0-0331570	0145	2
MARKHAM FAY F	CW2	W-2210181	0366	1
MARKHAM HARLEY R	MAJ	0-0261704	0165	3
MARKHAM JOHN M	LTC	0-0153914	C754	3
MARKHAM JOSEPH W	MAJ	0-128892C	C361	1
MARKHAM RAYMOND G	COL	0-0217485	0463	3
MARKHEIM HERBERT R	MAJ	0-0367677	1145	1
MARKIEWICZ JAMES	LTC	0-0729776	C264	1
MARKILLIE RICHARD C	LTC	0-1797323	0561	2
MARKIN JR CREL F	CW4	W-2119455	C462	1
MARKKULA RUSSELL F	1LT	0-0466733	0446	2
MARKLAND CURTIS W	COL	0-0308374	C960	1
MARKLAND JR OLIVER W	CW3	W-2206410	0966	1
MARKLAND WALTER H	MAJ	0-1185803	1159	1
MARKLE BYRON M	MAJ	0-0324348	1066	3
MARKLE EARL	1LT	0-1292211	0745	1
MARKLE EUGENE C	MAJ	0-1919420	0464	1
MARKLEY RAYMOND L	LTC	0-0231342	1150	3
MARKLEY ROBERT L	MAJ	0-1636267	C563	1
MARKOFF ABRAHAM	CPT	0-0504723	0346	2
MARKOLA HAROLD J	WO1	W-2118509	C144	2
MARKOVIC ERNEST J	LTC	0-0460186	0866	1
MARKOWICH EDWARD P	1LT	0-1180253	1147	2
MARKOWITZ MAX	MAJ	0-0438292	0246	2
MARKS ARTHUR	MAJ	0-0245674	0653	3
MARKS BERTRAM E	MAJ	0-0382675	0246	2
MARKS DUDLEY B	WO1	W-2149171	0156	1
MARKS FRANCIS W	COL	0-0180245	0863	3
MARKS FRANK H	LTC	0-0168555	0158	3
MARKS GEORGE E	CPT	0-0479214	0148	1
MARKS HARRY S	MAJ	0-0961725	0962	1
MARKS HERMAN	MAJ	0-1080126	1059	1
MARKS HILDA M	MAJ	N-0730887	0267	1
MARKS HOWARD E	WO1	W-2114877	0755	1
MARKS IRA G	1LT	0-1322698	C146	2
MARKS JAMES E	MAJ	0-0572511	1060	1
MARKS JULIAN I	COL	0-0138343	0648	3
MARKS KARL W	LTC	0-0218833	0752	3
MARKS LESLIE M	LTC	0-0347371	1067	3
MARKS MATTHEW O	1LT	0-0539718	1045	1
MARKS MAX	CPT	0-0496557	0646	2
MARKS PERRY C	MAJ	0-2028721	1066	1
MARKS SAMUEL F	MAJ	0-0287805	0360	3
MARKS THEODORE O	MAJ	0-1643633	1163	1
MARKS WILBUR C	MAJ	0-1824058	1162	1
MARKUNAS ELNOR M	1LT	N-0751279	0246	1
MARKUS MURELL F	MAJ	0-0223886	0245	2
MARKUSON REGINA W	MAJ	N-0757268	1163	1
MARLAN RAYMOND V	LTC	0-0210517	0852	3
MARLAND CLIFFORD R	MAJ	0-1645080	0756	1
MARLE WILLIAM D	LTC	0-1341452	0967	1
MARLER ALLEN C	MAJ	0-0976612	0865	1
MARLER JAMES O	LTC	0-0514627	0663	1
MARLEY GEORGE E	LTC	0-1821743	0763	1
MARLEY JOHN F	CPT	0-1106927	0947	2
MARLEY RALPH M	COL	0-0304142	0657	1
MARLEY WALLACE C	LTC	0-0814508	0467	1
MARLIER GASTON P	CW4	W-2142305	0256	1
MARLIN CLIFTON B	CPT	0-0514009	0847	2
MARLIN PERRY S	MAJ	0-0588297	0865	1
MARLIN WILLIAM E	MAJ	0-0982266	1264	1

NAME	GRADE	SVC NO	DATE RET MO YR	RET CODE
MARLOW SR GEORGE R	CW3	W-2146753	0559	1
MARLOWE ORVILLE E	MAJ	0-0267069	C760	3
MARMEN ROLANO A	MAJ	C-2018696	C363	1
MARNER PAUL B	COL	0-0188140	0962	3
MARNFELD ROBERT	MAJ	0-0451939	0457	1
MAROHN HAROLD	MAJ	0-1168802	0455	1
MAROHN RALPH L	CPT	C-1181947	0962	1
MAROLF JOHN F	MAJ	C-163627C	C959	1
MARONEY BERRY O	1LT	0-0508966	C959	1
MARONEY JOHN J	CPT	0-1295746	C857	1
MARONEY PAUL E	MAJ	C-2000831	0861	1
MAROON HABEEB Z	CPT	0-0500027	0246	2
MAROUKIAN MARTIN L	LTC	0-1575444	0266	1
MAROUARCT GEORGE W	LTC	C-0166718	1154	3
MAROUARCT OSWALD K	MAJ	0-037409C	0746	2
MAROUAROT VIOLA R	1LT	N-0732468	C246	1
MARQUES JR LEMUEL	MAJ	C-0251478	0164	3
MARQUESS ARTHUR C	1LT	0-1317182	0146	1
MARQUESS STANLEY F	CW3	RW-2147374	0763	1
MAROUEZ JOSE	MAJ	C-0466621	0147	1
MARQUEZ VICTOR	CPT	0-1340673	1160	1
MARQUIS JAMES F	LTC	0-0310615	0762	1
MARQUIS JR GEORGE W	MAJ	0-0264302	C454	3
MARQUIS VANCE B	COL	C-0295830	0559	1
MARQUIS WILLIAM C	1LT	0-1032466	1045	2
MARR CLIFFORO	LTC	C-0453816	0658	1
MARR IRVINE M	MAJ	C-0253937	0267	3
MARRA JOSEPH	MAJ	0-1336406	C264	1
MARRA PELLEGRINO	2LT	0-1104285	C445	2
MARRACCINI EUGENE M	2LT	0-1051669	0845	2
MARRAH GEORGE L	LTC	0-0339069	0846	2
MARRERO JUAN	CPT	0-0255465	C148	1
MARRIN JR JAMES G	LTC	0-0327555	1061	1
MARRIOTT FRANK	LTC	C-0264406	1165	3
MARRON JAMES M	1LT	0-1171661	0745	2
MARRON REGINA M	1LT	N-0758482	0646	1
MARROW WILLIAM M	CPT	C-0347931	1053	1
MARRS ALVERNA I	1LT	N-0784765	0846	1
MARRS BILLY J	CPT	C-0890468	1047	2
MARRS CARL O	MAJ	0-2016437	0258	1
MARRS GEORGE R	WO1	W-2111452	0647	2
MARRS HAROLC F	LTC	0-1047655	0463	1
MARS CHARLES	MAJ	0-0234355	1057	3
MARS ECWARO	CW2	W-2148869	0753	1
MARS EVERETT O	CPT	C-0395780	0961	1
MARSALA ANTHONY J	COL	0-1541293	C761	1
MARSOEN JR THOMAS A	LTC	0-0329458	C960	1
MARSOEN ROSS L	CPT	0-1697748	0145	2
MARSELLA CLARENCE B	MAJ	0-0230620	1057	3
MARSEY JOHN L	2LT	0-1649081	0445	2
MARSH ANOREW T	LTC	0-0261276	0560	1
MARSH AUBREY L	LTC	0-1288923	1266	1
MARSH CHARLES O	COL	0-0324478	C564	3
MARSH CHARLES E	1LT	0-0973561	0354	2
MARSH CHARLES W	1LT	0-1284900	0244	2
MARSH OANIEL J	MAJ	0-C384049	0267	3
MARSH OONALC L	COL	C-0233924	1054	1
MARSH EDGERLY B	MAJ	0-0374916	0147	2
MARSH EVELYN B	1LT	N-0760297	1145	1
MARSH EVIN H	CW2	W-2150189	0366	1
MARSH FRED	LTC	0-0443521	0851	1
MARSH GARVIS C	1LT	0-0527642	1145	2
MARSH GEORGE M	MAJ	C-2012803	0862	1
MARSH GLENN M	LTC	C-1297562	0757	1
MARSH HARVEY O	CW3	W-2206567	0266	1
MARSH JAMES V	LTC	0-1305953	C862	1
MARSH JOHN W	LTC	0-0252419	0453	3
MARSH JR ELLIS E	LTC	0-0269162	0760	1
MARSH JR EMER L	CW4	W-2118527	0361	1
MARSH KOSCIE H	1LT	C-1995128	0745	2
MARSH LOREN R	CW2	W-3430166	0467	1
MARSH LOUIS S	CW4	W-2124168	1160	1
MARSH MARION E	1LT	0-1031825	0960	1
MARSH RICHARO	LTC	0-1001010	0667	1
MARSH ROBERT E	LTC	0-0349903	0367	3

NAME	GRADE	SVC NO	DATE RET MO YR	RET CODE
MARSH RUTH M	1LT	N-0745237	0446	1
MARSH SAMUEL E	CPT	0-0493791	1059	2
MARSH VICTOR T	MAJ	0-2043221	0960	1
MARSH WILLIAM C	MAJ	C-1312780	1266	1
MARSH WILLIAM O	MAJ	0-1182644	0859	1
MARSHA EARL M	COL	0-0359891	0660	1
MARSHACK ROBERT C	LTC	0-1177897	0261	1
MARSHALL ARTHUR W	LTC	0-0363499	0859	1
MARSHALL BEAUFCRO C	CPT	0-1032226	0559	2
MARSHALL BENJAMIN E	CPT	0-1296150	1146	2
MARSHALL BENJAMIN F	COL	C-0103512	1C49	3
MARSHALL CARL A	MAJ	0-0253106	1263	3
MARSHALL CARL M	MAJ	0-0296665	0460	1
MARSHALL CHARLES C	MAJ	0-1015129	0466	3
MARSHALL CHARLES G	CW2	W-2119803	0960	1
MARSHALL CHARLES H	LTC	C-0389C33	0455	1
MARSHALL CHESTER R	CPT	C-0318189	0645	1
MARSHALL CLARENCE C	CPT	0-1013503	1154	1
MARSHALL CLARK	LTC	0-0506617	0453	1
MARSHALL CLEMON L	LTC	0-1177516	0760	1
MARSHALL OALLAS E	MAJ	0-0371493	0466	3
MARSHALL OAVIC E	LTC	0-0134221	0656	3
MARSHALL OAVIC L	2LT	0-0413205	0845	2
MARSHALL OCNALO	CW2	W-3430233	1266	1
MARSHALL OONALO R	2LT	0-1638001	0145	2
MARSHALL OCUGLAS G	MAJ	0-1040435	1165	1
MARSHALL EARL B	WO1	W-214252C	0757	1
MARSHALL EDWARO I	MAJ	0-0268109	0163	1
MARSHALL ECWARO V	WO1	W-2207165	0758	2
MARSHALL ECWARO W	MAJ	0-0217398	0464	3
MARSHALL EOWIN A	LTC	C-0348747	1161	3
MARSHALL ELIZABETH	1LT	R-0002157	0454	2
MARSHALL ELLWCOD J	CW4	W-2148462	0866	2
MARSHALL ELMER P	COL	C-0484151	0962	3
MARSHALL ERNEST O	LTC	0-1038053	0867	3
MARSHALL FRANK A	COL	0-0274032	0166	3
MARSHALL FRANK G	LTC	0-0239374	0666	3
MARSHALL FREDERICK	COL	0-0188790	0456	3
MARSHALL HARRY W	COL	0-0170342	0361	3
MARSHALL HERBERT O	MAJ	0-0275879	0261	3
MARSHALL HOWARO I	CPT	0-0204112	0648	3
MARSHALL JACK A	CPT	C-0451717	0546	2
MARSHALL JAMES E	2LT	0-1300347	0244	2
MARSHALL JAMES F	MAJ	0-1692988	0662	1
MARSHALL JESSE E	COL	0-0177361	0648	3
MARSHALL JCE S	CPT	0-0408666	0850	1
MARSHALL JOHN A	MAJ	0-0477555	0447	1
MARSHALL JOHN A	2LT	0-2026942	1048	1
MARSHALL JCHN H	MAJ	C-0358180	0544	2
MARSHALL JOHN H	CPT	0-0441138	0346	2
MARSHALL JCHN O	LTC	0-1002988	1266	3
MARSHALL JOHN S	LTC	0-0105727	1055	3
MARSHALL JOHN S	CPT	0-0474080	0645	1
MARSHALL JOHN W	LTC	0-0383634	0760	1
MARSHALL JCHN W	MAJ	0-1645791	0358	1
MARSHALL JOSEPH	LTC	0-0494689	0857	1
MARSHALL JR ALBERT L	MAJ	0-0335943	1045	2
MARSHALL JR ARTHUR A	1LT	0-1926899	0454	2
MARSHALL JR GEOFFREY	LTC	0-1535673	1164	1
MARSHALL JR JAMES C	CW3	W-2142872	0960	1
MARSHALL JULIA P	2LT	N-0761137	0445	1
MARSHALL LEHNHOLF S	COL	0-0228858	0562	3
MARSHALL LOUIS E	COL	0-0406404	1163	3
MARSHALL LYLE P	MAJ	0-1693129	0664	1
MARSHALL MITCHELL A	COL	0-0347637	0564	1
MARSHALL OSCAR E	WO1	W-211497C	0754	1
MARSHALL ROBERT A	CW3	W-2144630	0163	1
MARSHALL ROBERT I	CPT	0-1298267	0957	2
MARSHALL ROBERT P	CW4	W-2004577	0767	2
MARSHALL RUSSELL C	MAJ	0-0191502	1052	3
MARSHALL SAM L	B G	0-010292C	0860	3
MARSHALL SAMUEL	COL	0-0297504	0451	1
MARSHALL SAMUEL A	LTC	0-0116571	0360	3
MARSHALL SAMUEL G	MAJ	0-0954863	1162	1
MARSHALL SCHUYLER C	1LT	0-0999218	1154	2

NAME	GRADE	SVC NO	DATE RET MO YR	RET CODE
MARSHALL THEOOORE F	B G	0-0235213	C762	3
MARSHALL THOMAS L	CW3	W-2144242	C863	1
MARSHALL THOMAS T	MAJ	C-169571C	C163	1
MARSHALL VERN B	CPT	0-0165799	0648	3
MARSHALL VERNON T	LTC	0-1046549	1067	1
MARSHALL WILLIAM	1LT	0-1176719	0847	2
MARSHALL WILLIAM B	2LT	C-1914126	0342	1
MARSHALL WILLIAM J	LTC	0-0455286	C864	1
MARSHALL WILLIAM M	LTC	0-0124734	C950	1
MARSHALL WILLIAM R	CW3	W-2150652	0263	1
MARSHBURN CLARENCE E	1LT	0-1290101	0862	2
MARSHMAN GEORGE F	LTC	0-0216933	0862	3
MARSICO CLEMENT W	LTC	0-1303365	0165	1
MARSTON BURTON W	MAJ	C-0208653	C156	3
MARSTON CHARLES A	LTC	0-0311056	0464	3
MARSTON WALTER E	LTC	0-0321723	0366	3
MART ROY M	1LT	0-0390747	1044	2
MARTAUS JOSEPH A	LTC	0-1284357	C561	1
MARTEL CHARLES A	LTC	0-0919858	C865	3
MARTELL OAVIO	MAJ	0-130284C	C960	1
MARTELL OAYLF L	LTC	0-1050365	C666	1
MARTELL JAMES	CPT	0-0499574	0547	1
MARTELL LOUIS E	LTC	0-1000621	0754	1
MARTELL WILLIAM C	MAJ	0-104655C	0959	1
MARTELLO RUDOLF	CPT	C-0373762	1047	1
MARTELLO WALLACE	LTC	0-15481C0	1060	1
MARTENS EARL W	MAJ	C-0504763	0146	2
MARTENS IRVIN J	CPT	0-0556253	C746	2
MARTENS JOSEPH H	MAJ	0-0969026	0761	1
MARTENS LOUIS C	LTC	C-1824647	0764	1
MARTENS ROBERT P	1LT	0-2047421	1045	2
MARTH ALBERT F	LTC	0-0218616	0764	3
MARTHINSEN JOHN	2LT	0-0389164	1044	2
MARTHINSEN WILLIAM H	LTC	0-0360134	0960	1
MARTI ALFREO J	CPT	0-1697889	0346	1
MARTIG HOWARO J	2LT	0-1108140	0844	2
MARTIN ALBERT	CW3	W-2144443	1161	1
MARTIN ALBERT H	1LT	C-1317647	0345	1
MARTIN ALFREO J	COL	0-0267981	0359	3
MARTIN ALTON F	CW4	W-2205224	1064	3
MARTIN ALVIN W	MAJ	C-1031499	1158	1
MARTIN BENJAMIN G	CPT	0-0945897	0159	2
MARTIN BENJAMIN H	CW4	W-2152433	0867	1
MARTIN BILL M	1LT	0-1556177	1055	1
MARTIN BRUCE	COL	C-0481310	0661	1
MARTIN BUFORD L	CPT	0-0258593	0765	3
MARTIN BURL B	MAJ	C-1540767	1060	1
MARTIN BYRD C	CPT	0-0304543	0744	2
MARTIN CAMILO R	1LT	0-1896370	1148	1
MARTIN CARL H	CPT	0-0334001	0947	2
MARTIN CARL T	LTC	0-0103362	C648	3
MARTIN CHARLES D	MAJ	0-0986674	0967	1
MARTIN CHARLES E	COL	0-0278593	0265	3
MARTIN CHARLES E	WO1	W-2148598	1056	1
MARTIN CHARLES H	MAJ	C-0273056	0648	3
MARTIN CHARLES H	MAJ	0-2017093	1060	1
MARTIN CHARLES M	LTC	C-0134251	C648	3
MARTIN CHARLES W	MAJ	0-2032927	C765	1
MARTIN CHESTER C	1LT	0-0335359	0547	1
MARTIN CHESTER L	LTC	C-0404844	0760	1
MARTIN CHRISTINE	2LT	N-0743588	0844	1
MARTIN CLARENCE E	CW2	W-2210156	1066	1
MARTIN CLARENCE F	COL	0-0212364	C563	1
MARTIN CLARENCE V	MAJ	0-0230438	C558	3
MARTIN CLAUO M	1LT	C-2020572	0364	2
MARTIN CLIFFORO R	MAJ	0-1013432	0160	2
MARTIN CLYOE L	LTC	0-0382709	0456	2
MARTIN CANIEL	MAJ	C-1176419	0556	1
MARTIN CANIEL O	LTC	0-0450749	0752	1
MARTIN OOMINIC W	WO1	W-2152708	0656	1
MARTIN CONALO N	CPT	0-1170478	0862	2
MARTIN OONALO R	CPT	0-0342863	1065	1
MARTIN OOUGLAS B	LTC	C-1015087	C762	1
MARTIN OREW A	COL	C-0363590	1265	1
MARTIN CWIGHT E	CW2	W-2144533	1060	1

NAME	GRADE	SVC NO	DATE RET MO YR	RET CODE
MARTIN EARL J	MAJ	0-1799528	0361	1
MARTIN ECWARO A	CW2	W-2142934	0659	1
MARTIN ECWARC O	CPT	0-1030267	0161	1
MARTIN ECWARO L	1LT	0-1319298	0947	2
MARTIN ELBERT C	CPT	0-0121577	C947	2
MARTIN ELBERT W	COL	0-0103356	0858	3
MARTIN EMMETT J	CW4	W-2128032	1054	1
MARTIN EMMONS A	MAJ	0-0202306	0257	3
MARTIN EMORY H	1LT	0-1303752	1045	2
MARTIN ENOCH G	LTC	0-0373435	0167	1
MARTIN ENOLA M	1LT	N-0797709	0549	2
MARTIN ERNEST H	MAJ	0-1297561	1060	1
MARTIN EUGENE C	LTC	0-0293184	0562	2
MARTIN EVERETT E	LTC	0-0251348	0564	3
MARTIN FAY H	MAJ	0-0311951	0458	3
MARTIN FLOYO R	COL	0-0299916	0264	1
MARTIN FORO E	CPT	0-0391188	0346	2
MARTIN FRANK B	COL	0-0174652	0356	3
MARTIN FRANK B	LTC	0-0918775	1264	3
MARTIN FRANK R	1LT	0-0386931	0145	2
MARTIN FREC B	CPT	0-1703692	0745	2
MARTIN FREO M	CW4	W-2001598	0466	3
MARTIN FREO C	CW4	W-2005904	C964	3
MARTIN FREOERICK	1LT	0-1844797	0854	1
MARTIN FREDERICK	CW2	W-2152274	0661	1
MARTIN FREEMAN G	MAJ	0-0174101	0461	3
MARTIN GARNETT W	LTC	0-0256463	1161	3
MARTIN GENE J	CW2	W-2210696	0566	1
MARTIN GEORGE	LTC	0-0125154	0945	2
MARTIN GEORGE A	MAJ	0-1000815	0747	2
MARTIN CEORGE A	MAJ	0-1775720	1045	2
MARTIN GEORGE E	CPT	0-0490000	1043	1
MARTIN GEORGE G	LTC	0-1310360	0562	1
MARTIN CEORGE H	MAJ	C-0455277	0165	1
MARTIN GEORGE H	MAJ	0-0965091	0665	2
MARTIN GERALD J	CW3	W-2148676	0563	1
MARTIN GERTRUOE E	1LT	N-0721991	0646	1
MARTIN GLEN B	CW2	W-2209654	1265	1
MARTIN GLEN W	LTC	0-0234263	0947	2
MARTIN GORDON G	MAJ	0-2103028	1063	1
MARTIN GRANVILLE	1LT	C-0486971	0645	2
MARTIN GUY V	CPT	0-0328763	0754	2
MARTIN HAROLO J	LTC	0-0265037	0862	3
MARTIN HAROLC W	CPT	0-1876591	0967	1
MARTIN HARRY L	CPT	0-0519434	0949	1
MARTIN HARRY W	MAJ	C-1045165	0157	1
MARTIN HENRY F	CPT	C-0979575	C262	1
MARTIN HENRY J	MAJ	0-1080570	0162	1
MARTIN HERBERT D	CPT	0-0387633	1144	2
MARTIN HERSCHEL E	CW2	W-2147514	1060	1
MARTIN HERSHEL J	COL	0-0354423	0857	1
MARTIN HOWARO W	MAJ	0-0493637	0252	1
MARTIN HUBERT S	CW2	W-2147464	0157	1
MARTIN HUGH K	MAJ	C-0138490	0449	3
MARTIN IRL R	CPT	0-0980548	0359	2
MARTIN JAMES	MAJ	0-0202681	0858	3
MARTIN JAMES	CPT	0-2012526	0757	1
MARTIN JAMES A	CW3	W-2146306	0964	1
MARTIN JAMES C	MAJ	C-0943009	0765	1
MARTIN JAMES C	CW3	W-2141623	0559	1
MARTIN JAMES H	LTC	0-0550222	0265	1
MARTIN JAMES I	COL	0-0177161	0257	1
MARTIN JAMES M	CPT	0-0959460	0161	1
MARTIN JAMES M	CW2	W-2115851	0548	2
MARTIN JAMES T	CPT	0-1292366	1046	2
MARTIN JAMES W	LTC	0-1182645	0667	1
MARTIN JAMES W	MAJ	0-1923504	0665	1
MARTIN JESSE S	LTC	0-0302735	1065	3
MARTIN JCHN E	1LT	0-0512866	0547	1
MARTIN JOHN G	1LT	0-1318621	0745	2
MARTIN JCHN H	2LT	0-1289293	1044	2
MARTIN JOHN J	LTC	C-0223193	1046	1
MARTIN JOHN J	LTC	0-1181361	0361	1
MARTIN JCHN J	MAJ	C-1593701	0661	1
MARTIN JCHN R	MAJ	0-1328825	0163	1

NAME	GRADE	SVC NO	DATE RET MO YR	RET CODE
MARTIN JOHN S	COL	0-0181015	1060	3
MARTIN JOHN S	CPT	0-0510805	0649	1
MARTIN JOHN T	MAJ	C-2005675	0756	3
MARTIN JOHN W	MAJ	0-1182184	1060	1
MARTIN JOHN W	MAJ	C-2042866	0257	2
MARTIN JOSEPH V	1LT	0-0540507	0346	2
MARTIN JR CHARLES M	CW2	W-2114824	1044	2
MARTIN JR CHARLES S	CPT	0-0465782	0547	2
MARTIN JR CLARENCE V	LTC	0-0308237	C462	1
MARTIN JR ORED W	MAJ	C-1881937	C467	1
MARTIN JR ERNEST L	CPT	C-1303366	0848	1
MARTIN JR FRANK A	CW2	W-2113618	C746	2
MARTIN JR HENRY H	LTC	0-0354250	C563	3
MARTIN JR JOHN D	LTC	0-0277077	C863	3
MARTIN JR JOHN J	MAJ	0-0441461	0662	1
MARTIN JR WILFRED J	MAJ	0-1115341	0161	1
MARTIN JR WILLIAM C	LTC	0-1284541	0954	1
MARTIN JR WILLIAM T	LTC	0-0237226	0962	1
MARTIN JUSTIN E	MAJ	0-1045196	C765	1
MARTIN KEMP	MAJ	0-0245138	1063	3
MARTIN KENNETH H	CPT	0-0241355	1163	3
MARTIN KURT G	CW3	W-2136694	1061	1
MARTIN LANDRUM E	LTC	0-2060845	0563	1
MARTIN LAURIE C	LTC	0-0350155	0255	1
MARTIN LAWRENCE W	1LT	0-1061392	1045	2
MARTIN LEE M	LTC	0-0408641	0561	1
MARTIN LEON	CPT	0-1302495	0165	1
MARTIN LEONARD D	COL	0-0451140	0459	1
MARTIN LEROY E	MAJ	C-1922599	1163	1
MARTIN LEWE B	1LT	C-1119337	0846	2
MARTIN LEWIS E	LTC	0-0330785	1155	1
MARTIN LEWIS W	CW2	W-2143001	1160	1
MARTIN LINUS B	LTC	C-0304732	0560	1
MARTIN LIONEL F	CW4	W-2103757	1057	1
MARTIN LOCKETT B	CPT	0-0409513	0245	2
MARTIN LUTHER E	MAJ	C-1688532	0666	1
MARTIN LYLE B	1LT	0-1174637	1045	2
MARTIN MARGARET M	2LT	N-0796028	C446	1
MARTIN MARION R	LTC	0-0268962	C546	2
MARTIN MARION S	COL	0-0222449	0256	3
MARTIN MARVIN L	1LT	0-1306738	0545	1
MARTIN MAX A	1LT	0-1313266	0145	2
MARTIN MELROWE D	LTC	0-1185150	C163	1
MARTIN MELVIN L	LTC	0-0175026	C956	2
MARTIN MELVIN L	MAJ	0-1173367	C363	1
MARTIN MERLIN A	LTC	0-0321331	C959	3
MARTIN NORMAN	WO1	W-2144257	0459	2
MARTIN NORMAN H	2LT	0-1584565	C844	2
MARTIN OGLE J	LTC	0-0512544	0157	1
MARTIN ORLANDO A	LTC	0-0491920	116C	1
MARTIN OWEN C	LTC	0-0930670	C465	1
MARTIN PAUL	LTC	0-1590635	1067	1
MARTIN PAUL M	LTC	0-1015882	0461	1
MARTIN PAUL T	MAJ	C-0101971	1036	1
MARTIN PAUL W	1LT	C-1290784	0845	1
MARTIN RALPH A	2LT	0-1544687	1044	2
MARTIN RALPH L	LTC	0-1286321	C261	1
MARTIN RAYMOND C	CPT	0-1331200	1057	1
MARTIN RAYMOND D	CPT	0-1549777	C158	2
MARTIN RAYMOND H	CPT	0-0329460	0844	2
MARTIN RAYMOND L	LTC	0-1797682	1167	1
MARTIN REGINALD L	LTC	0-2030131	C266	1
MARTIN RESBERT R	CPT	0-1320356	1147	2
MARTIN RICHARD D	MAJ	0-1881792	C964	1
MARTIN RICHARD F	CPT	0-1014380	0945	2
MARTIN RICHARD R	LTC	0-0482069	0246	2
MARTIN RICHARD W	CW2	W-7146911	1165	1
MARTIN ROBERT E	LTC	C-1039455	C165	1
MARTIN ROBERT M	CW4	W-2104268	0659	1
MARTIN ROBERT O	LTC	0-0210273	0455	3
MARTIN ROBERT R	LTC	0-1322248	C566	1
MARTIN ROBERT S	LTC	0-0365635	0859	1
MARTIN ROBERT W	MAJ	C-1061434	1060	1
MARTIN ROGER C	LTC	0-0318536	0266	3
MARTIN ROLAND L	CW3	W-2205917	C567	1

NAME	GRADE	SVC NO	DATE RET MO YR	RET CODE
MARTIN ROY B	LTC	0-0423875	0847	2
MARTIN ROY L	CW3	W-2149775	0865	1
MARTIN ROY S	MAJ	0-0275442	1264	3
MARTIN SAM B	LTC	0-1306739	0566	3
MARTIN SIMPSON G	CW2	W-2149387	0756	1
MARTIN SOPHIA L	1LT	N-0732371	1045	1
MARTIN SPENCER O	MAJ	0-0956866	0563	1
MARTIN STEVE	CW4	W-2117893	0167	1
MARTIN STEVEN J	CPT	0-5323319	C867	2
MARTIN STEVENS J	COL	0-0348433	0866	3
MARTIN THEODORE R	LTC	0-1284540	0757	1
MARTIN THEODORE S	CPT	0-0252249	0865	3
MARTIN THOMAS	CPT	0-C184058	0644	2
MARTIN THOMAS A	CW2	W-2146551	1061	1
MARTIN THOMAS D	CPT	0-0231374	C859	3
MARTIN THOMAS J	LTC	0-0324347	C760	1
MARTIN THOMAS J	2LT	0-1881668	0853	2
MARTIN TOM B	COL	0-0125453	1049	3
MARTIN VAIDEN C	MAJ	0-0510611	0355	3
MARTIN VENVERT W	CPT	0-2033875	C562	2
MARTIN VERNON F	MAJ	0-1535228	C264	1
MARTIN VIRGIL G	LTC	0-0143852	0457	3
MARTIN WALLACE B	MAJ	0-1288C89	0859	1
MARTIN WALLACE R	LTC	0-1635097	0761	1
MARTIN WELLINGTON	CW4	W-2118523	1062	3
MARTIN WILLIAM B	2LT	0-1320397	0345	2
MARTIN WILLIAM C	CPT	0-0242781	0544	2
MARTIN WILLIAM C	MAJ	0-1174059	C961	1
MARTIN WILLIAM E	MAJ	0-0249052	1064	3
MARTIN WILLIAM F	MAJ	0-0374598	0146	2
MARTIN WILLIAM H	COL	0-0335128	0346	2
MARTIN WILLIAM H	MAJ	0-0585668	1057	1
MARTIN WILLIAM H	CW4	W-2142978	0963	2
MARTIN WILLIAM J	CPT	0-1110640	0846	2
MARTIN WILLIAM J	MAJ	0-1302841	0861	1
MARTIN WILLIAM L	CPT	0-0262095	0458	3
MARTIN WILLIAM M	CW2	W-2109012	1147	2
MARTIN WILLIAM R	LTC	0-C389035	0760	1
MARTIN WILLIAM R	MAJ	0-1634109	1162	1
MARTIN WILLIAM P	CW2	W-22C8940	1065	1
MARTIN WILLIAM S	2LT	0-0920694	1044	2
MARTIN WOODIE B	MAJ	0-0570665	0565	1
MARTIN WYATT	1LT	0-0476451	0547	1
MARTINA ALEFC J	1LT	0-1103300	0346	2
MARTINA GENO A	CW2	W-2143570	0358	2
MARTINA JR SAMUEL A	CPT	0-0392464	1145	2
MARTINDALE DICK	1LT	0-1105652	0845	2
MARTINDALE GEORGE H	MAJ	0-0199459	0859	3
MARTINDALE JOHN C	CPT	0-1055910	0163	2
MARTINDALE THOMAS	MAJ	0-0402739	0457	1
MARTINDALE WINFRED L	MAJ	0-0143889	0559	3
MARTINE JR RALPH L	CPT	0-2041221	0562	1
MARTINEAU JOHN A	LTC	0-1306298	1163	1
MARTINEE ROBERT F	MAJ	0-1541244	0847	1
MARTINEK RUDOLPH F	MAJ	0-1939094	0756	2
MARTINELLI JOHN	COL	0-0220297	0355	1
MARTINEZ DAMIAN	MAJ	0-2262645	0961	1
MARTINEZ DAVID S	MAJ	0-1048890	0966	1
MARTINEZ JAMES U	CPT	0-1305281	1062	1
MARTINEZ JOE	MAJ	0-1824337	C561	1
MARTINEZ JOSE M	LTC	0-0452009	1060	1
MARTINEZ JOSE R	CPT	0-1339897	0462	1
MARTINEZ MANUEL A	MAJ	0-1556020	0960	1
MARTINEZ MANUEL H	LTC	0-0386407	0560	1
MARTINEZ NICK M	1LT	0-1319523	0350	1
MARTINEZ RAFAEL G	CPT	0-0396768	0761	1
MARTINEZ RAMON P	MAJ	0-0406948	0960	1
MARTINEZ ROBERT J	MAJ	0-1703935	C361	1
MARTINEZ THOMAS H	LTC	0-1594631	0962	2
MARTINEZ-DAVILA ADRI	CW3	W-2151637	0366	1
MARTINEZ-DAVILA RAFA	LTC	0-1288414	0364	1
MARTINEZ-DE ANDINO F	CW2	W-2211962	0266	1
MARTINEZ-RIVERA VIRG	CPT	0-0219699	0165	3
MARTINI PAULINA M	1LT	N-0752396	0353	2
MARTINIAK LEONARD J	1LT	0-1100666	0745	2

NAME	GRADE	SVC NO	DATE RET MO YR	RET CODE
MARTINO CATHERINE	2LT	N-0751399	0645	1
MARTINO JOSEPH	CPT	0-0984556	0562	1
MARTINO PHILIP T	LTC	0-0451882	0261	1
MARTINO ROBERT A	COL	0-0272815	C859	3
MARTINOT PIERRE M	CPT	0-1313267	1045	2
MARTINSON BERNARD A	MAJ	C-1798874	0461	1
MARTINSON BRADY	CPT	0-2050884	0861	1
MARTINSON VERN H	CPT	0-1285260	0146	2
MARTINUS JOHN L	LTC	0-0302125	0860	1
MARTLEY WILLIAM P	LTC	0-1045531	C665	1
MARTON GEORGE L	MAJ	C-1080946	0859	1
MARTORANI WILLIAM	LTC	0-0386859	C560	1
MARTTILA REINO J	1LT	0-1018094	C847	2
MARTYNIAK STANLEY L	LTC	0-1584566	0762	1
MARTYNIAK WILLIAM	MAJ	0-1316306	0657	1
MARTZ ARTHUR A	CPT	C-1030690	1046	1
MARTZ FORREST L	COL	0-0218617	0658	1
MARTZ JOSEPH R	COL	0-0340569	0960	1
MARTZ KARL B	LTC	0-2046561	0257	1
MARULLO LOUIS J	MAJ	0-1998506	0161	1
MARUS GEORGE	LTC	0-0410643	1162	1
MARUSAK PETER	MAJ	C-1012994	0547	2
MARUTANI WILLIAM M	2LT	0-0936289	1047	1
MARVICH JR MARTIN O	CPT	0-1698173	0345	2
MARVILL HOWARD A	LTC	0-0286219	0450	1
MARVIN CHESTER J	CPT	0-1324175	C847	2
MARVIN EDWARD A	LTC	0-1048891	0564	1
MARVIN EDWIN J	MAJ	C-0974430	0264	1
MARVIN JR WILLIAM H	CPT	0-0422203	0447	2
MARVIN NEIL F	LTC	0-0286399	C163	3
MARVIN PAUL H	CW4	W-2136513	C966	2
MARWITZ JULIUS A	LTC	0-0916968	C266	3
MARX EMIL F	COL	0-C178916	1052	3
MARX GEORGE J	LTC	0-1297398	1061	1
MARX GERALD J	CW3	W-2148648	0267	1
MARX JOSEPH N	COL	0-017135C	0953	3
MARX MONROE F	2LT	0-1585829	0644	2
MARXEN EDWARD H	LTC	C-0164883	C550	3
MARXSON FRED R	LTC	0-0282754	0767	3
MARY JACOB	LTC	0-0157487	0948	2
MARY MILTON B	CPT	C-048714C	0844	2
MARYE MADISON E	MAJ	0-1925429	1165	1
MARYMEE JOHN O	CW4	W-2115934	0254	1
MARYNICK TEOFIL	MAJ	0-1825027	0355	1
MARZANO FRANK	LTC	0-0382341	C657	1
MARZANO GALLIO J	CW4	W-2002111	0762	3
MARZANO ROCCO G	MAJ	C-0406109	C546	2
MARZARI JR GUY J	LTC	C-0441965	0964	1
MASAR JOHN J	1LT	0-1317320	0546	1
MASARIK JR STEPHEN F	1LT	0-1823032	0644	2
MASARSKY HARRY	CW2	W-2149018	0761	1
MASBACH FLORES	LTC	N-0701400	1046	1
MASCARI PAUL F	1LT	0-1685013	0853	1
MASCETTE VINCENT J	2LT	0-1115764	0652	2
MASCHMANN JAMES W	LTC	0-1691914	C966	1
MASCHMEIER EMMETT C	LTC	0-0334976	C947	2
MASCHMEYER WILLIAM L	COL	0-0247928	1066	3
MASCIA FRANKLIN J	CPT	0-0374764	C746	2
MASCOLO ARNOLD D	MAJ	C-1638009	1060	1
MASEM MATTHEW C	MAJ	C-1316909	0761	1
MASEN JOHN M	MAJ	C-0502379	C250	1
MASENGILL HOWARD R	LTC	0-0251089	0260	1
MASHBIR SIDNEY F	COL	0-0191029	C951	3
MASHBURN FRANKLIN B	MAJ	0-1684982	C363	1
MASHBURN SNYDER F	LTC	0-1534553	0865	1
MASHEWSKE CHARLES F	1LT	C-130744C	C446	2
MASI ANTHONY	LTC	0-1549780	0164	1
MASI ROMEO J	MAJ	0-1635098	C766	1
MASICK RUTH V	2LT	N-0796344	0946	1
MASICLAT CIPRIANO	CPT	0-2027043	1149	1
MASIN FRANCIS A	CPT	0-0421796	0345	2
MASKEL JOSEPH A	LTC	C-1038753	0563	1
MASKELL JOHN W	LTC	0-1183358	C764	1
MASKIELL JR JAMES	CPT	0-0348196	0745	2
MASKOWITZ CHARLES W	CPT	0-1298466	C145	2

NAME	GRADE	SVC NO	DATE RET MO YR	RET CODE
MASLANSKY MANUEL M	LTC	0-0263476	1263	3
MASLIN MARY M	MAJ	N-0736867	0966	3
MASLOFF RAYMOND F	CW3	W-2143578	0762	1
MASLON VICTOR D	LTC	0-2049638	0766	1
MASLOSKI JOHN J	2LT	0-1644565	0144	2
MASLOWSKI STEPHEN A	MAJ	0-1292287	0661	1
MASLYK JULIAN A	LTC	0-1053714	1264	1
MASON ARTHUR R	CPT	0-1650548	0657	1
MASON BENTON A	LTC	0-2033648	0367	1
MASON BRUCE G	LTC	0-0428721	1066	1
MASON CARLE W	LTC	0-0229016	0964	3
MASON CHARLES E	COL	0-0319503	0565	3
MASON CHARLES J	CPT	0-0349993	1145	2
MASON CHARLES J	MAJ	0-1045828	1059	1
MASON CHARLES R	COL	0-1581267	0767	1
MASON CHARLES W	MAJ	0-0887988	0755	2
MASON DAVID P	MAJ	0-1292553	1060	1
MASON EDWARD W	LTC	0-0257531	0961	3
MASON EDWIN D	LTC	0-1044291	0467	1
MASON FRANCIS G	LTC	0-117406C	0665	3
MASON FRANCIS W	COL	0-0162871	0859	1
MASON FRED C	MAJ	0-2102930	0465	1
MASON GEORGE B	LTC	0-0282801	0460	1
MASON GEORGE E	LTC	0-0220495	0562	3
MASON GEORGE E	CW2	W-2142252	1C54	1
MASON GEORGE J	COL	0-0251322	0366	3
MASON GEORGE W	MAJ	0-0320951	0664	3
MASON HARRY E	1LT	0-1590021	0957	2
MASON HARRY F	MAJ	0-0412707	1144	2
MASON HAYDEN F	CW4	W-2141625	0559	1
MASON HORATIO C	COL	0-0252798	0965	3
MASON IRWIN	MAJ	0-0480637	0546	1
MASON JACOB W	CPT	0-0477981	0446	2
MASON JAMES B	B G	0-0219601	0458	3
MASON JAMES E	WO1	W-2147730	0654	2
MASON JAMES H	MAJ	0-4006765	0867	1
MASON JAMES J	CPT	0-0980034	0961	1
MASON JAMES L	1LT	0-1320544	C546	2
MASON JANET C	CW4	V-0311097	0466	1
MASON JOHN	CPT	0-2263626	0658	2
MASON JOHN C	CW4	W-2142046	0562	1
MASON JOHN E	LTC	0-1597185	0964	1
MASON JOHN H	LTC	0-1336409	1167	1
MASON JOHN M	WO1	W-2110491	0444	2
MASON JOY J	CW2	W-2113647	0961	2
MASON LEN J	CW3	W-2146680	0560	1
MASON LEONA M	CPT	N-0902533	1061	2
MASON LEROY W	LTC	0-1000053	0964	1
MASON MAURICE M	MAJ	0-0269289	0667	3
MASON MELVIN I	CPT	0-1287557	C946	2
MASON OMER E	MAJ	0-1585830	0163	1
MASON RALPH	MAJ	0-1285082	0752	1
MASON RAYMOND V	LTC	0-0905956	0264	3
MASON REGINALD P	CW2	W-2215381	0967	1
MASON RICHARD O	CW2	W-2152769	0565	1
MASON ROBERT D	MAJ	0-1020445	C562	1
MASON ROBERT F	CW4	W-2148104	0867	1
MASON ROBERT J	CPT	0-1060548	1046	2
MASON ROBERT P	MAJ	0-0215949	0264	3
MASON ROBERT S	MAJ	0-2049824	0557	1
MASON RUSSELL E	1LT	0-0343180	0141	2
MASON SAM	CPT	0-0331949	0146	1
MASON SAMUEL C	MAJ	0-0501772	1052	1
MASON THOMAS A	LTC	0-0214767	0960	1
MASON THOMAS J	CW3	W-2147856	0357	1
MASON THOMAS W	CW3	W-2112165	0454	1
MASON THOMAS Y	CPT	0-0455269	0446	2
MASON WALTER F	LTC	0-1010865	0366	1
MASON WATSY H	CW3	W-2143074	0258	1
MASON WILLIAM N	CPT	0-1541504	1145	2
MASON WILLIAM S	MAJ	0-0237100	0355	3
MASON WILLIAM W	1LT	0-0373340	0148	1
MASON WILLIAM W	1LT	0-1178.56	0646	2
MASON ZELNA V	MAJ	0-0505787	1046	2
MASONCUP SEWELL E	1LT	0-1313505	0945	2

NAME	GRADE	SVC NO	DATE RET MO YR	RET CODE
MASOTTI GEORGE M	CPT	0-0347527	0146	2
MASS LEON J	1LT	0-1553871	1045	2
MASSA JOSEPH M	1LT	0-0405912	1143	2
MASSA PAUL L	CPT	0-1167966	0246	2
MASSA RAPHAEL	CPT	0-0450459	0146	2
MASSARI SILVIO C	LTC	0-0206248	0562	3
MASSENGALE RAY	MAJ	0-0464913	0148	1
MASSEY ANDREW J	CW2	W-2206552	0264	1
MASSEY EARL D	LTC	0-0298905	0948	2
MASSEY HAROLD L	COL	0-0300147	0364	2
MASSEY JAMES W	MAJ	0-1106932	0860	2
MASSEY JR CALVIN L	CW3	W-2203643	1166	1
MASSEY OLIVER T	MAJ	0-0112329	1049	3
MASSEY SAM J	WO1	W-2144093	0358	1
MASSEY THOMAS J	MAJ	0-1294167	1052	1
MASSEY VIRGIL H	CPT	0-0484855	0848	1
MASSEY WALTER	MAJ	0-0329419	0260	3
MASSEY WILLIAM O	MAJ	0-1120769	0663	1
MASSEY WILLIAM M	LTC	0-1056163	1165	2
MASSIE HOMER B	MAJ	0-0500976	0347	2
MASSIE IRVIN L	CW2	W-2154867	1057	1
MASSIE JR WILLIAM K	MAJ	0-0357845	0846	1
MASSINGILL AARON W	MAJ	0-1937395	0566	1
MASSINGILL WILLIAM L	MAJ	0-1308529	0255	2
MASSO JOSE C	MAJ	0-2029534	0261	1
MASSON STANLEY F	CPT	0-0438759	1045	1
MASSOTH ALYSE C	1LT	N-0723676	1046	1
MASSOUD ALFRED P	MAJ	0-1295399	1160	1
MAST FRED R	COL	0-0154631	1056	3
MAST OSCAR P	LTC	0-0206112	0960	3
MAST RAYMOND E	CPT	0-0982684	0363	2
MASTELLAR BRUCE G	LTC	0-1044890	1162	1
MASTENBROOK FRED A	MAJ	0-0299870	1044	2
MASTER GUSTAVE W	LTC	0-0428032	1154	1
MASTERS CHARLES H	LTC	0-0359812	0559	1
MASTERS DONALD B	MAJ	0-1593703	1062	1
MASTERS DONALD F	CPT	0-1018740	0863	1
MASTERS DWIGHT S	LTC	0-0916388	0664	3
MASTERS GERALD R	CPT	0-1297914	0951	2
MASTERS JOHN	CPT	0-0100898	1038	1
MASTERS JR KENNETH	CW3	W-2206633	0566	1
MASTERS MILTON B	CW2	W-2149707	0361	1
MASTERS MYRL W	MAJ	0-1318205	0263	1
MASTERS REUBEN H	MAJ	0-1017936	0862	1
MASTERS ROBERT	MAJ	0-1311800	0562	2
MASTERS ROBERT E L	COL	0-0178254	1159	1
MASTERS STANLEY W	CPT	0-1014008	0248	2
MASTERSON ALVIN M	MAJ	0-0485892	1148	1
MASTERSON RUE B	LTC	0-1543260	1060	1
MASTERSON SAMUEL D	MAJ	0-0961624	0962	1
MASTERSON THOMAS P	CPT	0-0393784	1045	2
MASTERVICH JOHN	MAJ	0-0949829	1062	1
MASTICK MAX B	MAJ	0-0386548	0166	3
MASTIN SR CHARLES S	CPT	0-0984242	0464	1
MASTIN WILLIAM L	WO1	W-2108751	0345	2
MASTON AL	2LT	0-1641548	1044	2
MASTRO HENRY	COL	0-0349748	0460	1
MASTROIANNI ORIZZONT	COL	0-0428072	0966	1
MASTRONARDI FRANK J	CW3	W-2148610	0665	1
MASTROPOLO JOHN J	CPT	0-1690256	0446	2
MASUDA HIROSHI F	CW3	W-2136398	0265	1
MASUDA JOE Y	MAJ	0-0930027	0261	1
MASUR IRVING	CW2	W-2108683	0449	1
MASUYAMA HISAO L	MAJ	0-2030814	1263	1
MATCHAN JAMES A	CPT	0-0391584	0159	2
MATCHETTE GORDON T	CW4	W-2131815	0167	1
MATCHICK ANDREW	LTC	0-1169633	1163	1
MATCHIN TOM O	LTC	0-0513922	0865	2
MATECKO ANDY	LTC	0-1287379	0957	1
MATEER ROBERT F	LTC	0-0220430	0246	2
MATEJCZYK JOHN F	LTC	0-0363254	0566	3
MATEO LUCIANO E	1LT	0-1896746	0263	2
MATERA ALBERT A	LTC	0-1595676	1162	1
MATEREWICZ GEORGE L	LTC	0-2054015	0457	1
MATERNIAK ALVIN A	MAJ	0-1179950	0863	1
MATEYKA JR FRANK F	CPT	0-0578540	0961	2
MATHEKE CLARENCE C	MAJ	0-1933610	0466	1
MATHENEY WILLIAM L	MAJ	0-1037868	0560	1
MATHENY ALEXANDER	1LT	0-1303753	0646	2
MATHENY ARTHUR J	LTC	0-0383435	0760	1
MATHENY AUSTIN C	COL	0-0275241	0864	3
MATHENY ESTON G	LTC	0-0462652	0862	1
MATHENY REX	MAJ	0-0219757	0648	3
MATHENY WALTER P	CW3	W-2205703	0367	1
MATHER CLAYTON B	LTC	0-0324392	1145	2
MATHER HENRY S	COL	0-0267783	0857	3
MATHER JR JAMES R	1LT	0-4006274	1057	2
MATHER MARGARET P	1LT	N-0783760	1045	1
MATHER MILLARD L	MAJ	0-0496716	0161	3
MATHER THOMAS W	1LT	0-0538341	0945	2
MATHER WILLIAM J	COL	0-0121695	0451	1
MATHERS ROBERT L	MAJ	0-1036294	0960	1
MATHERS WILLIAM C	MAJ	0-1316178	0865	1
MATHES DONALD F	COL	0-0165280	1160	3
MATHES ROBERT C	LTC	0-0272239	0859	1
MATHESON MARVIN M	1LT	0-1167098	0159	1
MATHESON SR HUGH	MAJ	0-0366508	1045	1
MATHESON WENDELL H	MAJ	0-1062411	0261	2
MATHEW CHARLES R	WO1	W-2142594	0856	1
MATHEW THOMAS R	CPT	0-0357919	0545	2
MATHEWS ARTHUR E	MAJ	0-1030395	0854	2
MATHEWS CASEY P	CW3	W-2205483	1263	1
MATHEWS DAVIS L	CPT	0-1593704	1054	2
MATHEWS EARL B	MAJ	0-2007057	0562	1
MATHEWS EDWIN C	CPT	0-0532602	1046	2
MATHEWS EUGENE F	COL	0-0294835	0460	3
MATHEWS FRANK M	CW3	RW-2142296	0461	1
MATHEWS GLEN W	CW2	W-2148781	0855	1
MATHEWS HARVEY W	COL	0-0237769	1263	3
MATHEWS JOHN T	LTC	0-1535229	0862	1
MATHEWS JR WENDELL E	1LT	0-1872435	1053	2
MATHEWS LAFAYETTE	COL	0-0114368	0455	3
MATHEWS LEON L	M G	0-0255628	0267	3
MATHEWS LUCIUS D	COL	0-0274730	0453	3
MATHEWS LUKE G	LTC	0-0333401	0648	3
MATHEWS MILLARD F	MAJ	0-0488864	0153	1
MATHEWS MORRIS M	LTC	0-0547121	1064	3
MATHEWS OSCAR K	CW2	W-2210717	0461	2
MATHEWS PAUL L	1LT	0-1176123	0447	1
MATHEWS PERRY C	LTC	0-0167067	1053	3
MATHEWS RAYMOND A	LTC	0-1300348	0662	1
MATHEWS REX O	MAJ	0-0545526	0364	1
MATHEWS RICHARD T	LTC	0-0408198	1060	1
MATHEWS ROBERT J	MAJ	0-0111909	1150	3
MATHEWS ROBERT S	COL	0-0147733	0453	3
MATHEWS THOMAS O	COL	0-1533853	0463	1
MATHEWS THOMAS R	CW3	W-2141368	0760	1
MATHEWS TROUP H	2LT	0-1012589	1143	2
MATHEWS WILLIAM G	MAJ	0-0502090	0655	1
MATHEWSON DALLAS S	LTC	0-1035526	0167	2
MATHEWSON THEODORE P	LTC	0-0299905	0165	3
MATHEY CHARLES W	CPT	0-1110647	0646	2
MATHEY NORRIS A	MAJ	0-0276490	1165	3
MATHIAS JAMES F	2LT	0-0887522	0745	2
MATHIAS JOHN	1LT	0-1896538	0550	1
MATHIAS LEIGH H	LTC	0-0349659	0647	1
MATHIAS ROBERT D	MAJ	0-1685549	0464	1
MATHIESEN SR ROY A	CPT	0-0482579	0646	1
MATHIEU GEORGE F	LTC	0-0107777	0752	3
MATHIS ALTON P	LTC	0-0288157	1164	3
MATHIS BENJAMIN H	CW3	W-2149278	0864	1
MATHIS CHARLES B	CW3	W-2007231	0167	3
MATHIS JOHN H	MAJ	0-0329890	1145	2
MATHIS JR CHARLES C	LTC	0-0269524	1066	3
MATHIS JR JOHN E	LTC	0-1688406	1067	1
MATHIS MILLARD H	CW2	W-2144241	1163	1
MATHIS ROBERT B	LTC	0-0425906	0762	1
MATHIS ZACK C	LTC	0-0450076	0457	1
MATHISEN CHARLES A	LTC	0-1111222	0964	1
MATHLESS NORMAN	CPT	0-0451154	0345	2
MATHON GEORGE W	LTC	0-1543364	0661	1
MATHWIG WILLIAM H	MAJ	0-1293622	1146	2
MATIER FRANCIS A	MAJ	0-1329728	0862	1
MATIKIEWICZ CHARLE	1LT	0-1544480	0845	2
MATISH EDWARD J	MAJ	0-1101103	0963	1
MATIST ANTHONY F	MAJ	0-1938991	0454	2
MATISIN JOSEPH J	LTC	0-1297226	0857	1
MATISOFF MAURICE	COL	0-0312605	0657	1
MATLACK EDWARD A	CW2	W-2151742	0659	1
MATLOCK GEORGE J	2LT	0-1117670	0345	2
MATLOCK HOMER B	LTC	0-0403914	0562	1
MATLOCK LLOYD W	LTC	0-0321931	1055	1
MATLOCK RALPH S	1LT	0-0557135	1146	2
MATLOCK WESLEY J	WO1	W-2120094	0945	2
MATLOSZ ANNE K	1LT	N-0722823	0246	1
MATNEY CARL P	CPT	0-0407621	0147	2
MATNEY EUGENE D	CPT	0-0450461	0266	1
MATNEY JAMES B	MAJ	0-1168803	1060	1
MATNEY JAMES F	CW2	W-2205151	0461	1
MATNEY RICHARD L	MAJ	0-0974988	0164	1
MATNEY THOMAS H	MAJ	0-0974893	0863	1
MATOS FRANCISCO	CW2	W-2145001	0562	1
MATOS JORGE A	LTC	0-0927417	0666	1
MATOY JR GEORGE C	MAJ	0-1548101	0960	1
MATSCHE JOHN F	MAJ	0-1053715	0564	1
MATSCHKE ARNOLD W	LTC	0-0263214	0255	2
MATSCHULLAT W F	LTC	0-0250187	0646	2
MATSEN BRADFORD C	LTC	0-1168804	1058	1
MATSON CHARLES W	MAJ	0-1104997	0765	1
MATSON CLAUDE D	CW3	W-2150326	0765	1
MATSON GUSTAVE A	COL	0-0309147	0659	3
MATSON JOHN W	LTC	0-0374760	0746	2
MATSON JR ENOR K	LTC	0-0333598	0761	1
MATSON JR JOSEPH	COL	0-0233472	0865	3
MATSON RALPH A	LTC	0-0279045	0964	3
MATSON RANDALL F	1LT	0-1170071	0145	1
MATSON VICTOR T	LTC	0-0320317	0660	1
MATSUK AGNES A	2LT	N-0773138	1044	1
MATSUMOTO WALTER T	CPT	0-0315402	0946	1
MATSUNAGA ROY T	CW3	W-2152107	0665	1
MATT ROBERT H	1LT	0-1118425	0746	2
MATT WAYLAND P	CPT	0-0420949	0645	2
MATTAS JOHN A	CPT	0-2014534	0565	2
MATTAX JAMES O	CPT	0-0506751	0246	2
MATTE RUTH E	MAJ	N-0720510	0562	1
MATTEI JAMES J	LTC	0-0291792	0463	1
MATTEO GUS A	1LT	0-1534805	0745	2
MATTER ANTHONY J	CPT	0-0165878	0552	3
MATTERI ELY S	LTC	0-0877167	0766	1
MATTERN BURYL B	MAJ	0-1293808	0858	1
MATTES EDWIN L	MAJ	0-1685650	0264	1
MATTES LAWRENCE H	1LT	0-1054653	1045	2
MATTES MAX W	CPT	0-0423562	0146	2
MATTESON FLOYD A	CPT	0-0450504	0245	2
MATTESON FRED C	CW3	W-2205474	0466	1
MATTESON FREDERICK	MAJ	0-0214574	1162	3
MATTESON GRACE I	1LT	N-0731967	0546	1
MATTESON MARSHALL F	LTC	0-1312579	0966	1
MATTESON RICHARD L	LTC	0-0273446	1060	1
MATTHEW JOHN R	CPT	0-0297803	0146	2
MATTHEWS ALLEN L	MAJ	0-0304454	1047	2
MATTHEWS ANSEL H	LTC	0-0305472	0463	3
MATTHEWS AUBREY L	MAJ	0-0371617	0148	2
MATTHEWS AUBREY L	MAJ	0-1944742	0367	1
MATTHEWS BRUCE B	LTC	0-0524066	1265	3
MATTHEWS CHARLES M	LTC	0-1013456	0462	1
MATTHEWS CHARLES N	LTC	0-1168359	0258	1
MATTHEWS CHARLES W	LTC	0-0242203	1064	3
MATTHEWS CHARLES W	LTC	0-0374147	0860	1
MATTHEWS CLAUDE F	MAJ	0-2001790	0561	2
MATTHEWS CLAUDE I	CPT	0-0302721	0263	3
MATTHEWS DAISY R	CPT	N-0736023	1048	2
MATTHEWS DEE	CPT	0-0297848	1159	3
MATTHEWS EDITH A	MAJ	N-0722994	0165	1
MATTHEWS EDWARD H	1LT	0-1325603	0347	2
MATTHEWS ELMER L	LTC	0-0386358	0267	3
MATTHEWS ERIC F	LTC	0-1291852	0461	1
MATTHEWS FRANCIS B	LTC	0-0480726	0664	2
MATTHEWS GILBERT B	COL	0-0390365	0646	2
MATTHEWS HAZEN L	1LT	0-1010226	0446	2
MATTHEWS III HENRY S	MAJ	0-2049012	1266	1
MATTHEWS JOHN A	CPT	0-0499645	0551	1
MATTHEWS JOHN D	MAJ	0-1331306	1266	1
MATTHEWS JOHN H	1LT	0-0273031	1044	2
MATTHEWS JOHN P	MAJ	0-1182186	0763	1
MATTHEWS JOHN W	1LT	0-1795808	0258	3
MATTHEWS JOSEPH A	1LT	0-1102842	0847	2
MATTHEWS JOSEPH S	1LT	0-1002068	0154	1
MATTHEWS JR EDWARD D	CW2	W-2145741	0861	1
MATTHEWS JR GEORGE	LTC	0-0901516	0949	3
MATTHEWS JR HENRY S	COL	0-0234767	0956	3
MATTHEWS JR JAMES M	CPT	0-0419452	0544	2
MATTHEWS JR JOHN H	LTC	0-1048511	0463	1
MATTHEWS JR JOSEPH C	COL	0-0255569	0457	1
MATTHEWS JR PAUL J	CPT	0-1176124	0561	1
MATTHEWS JR ROBERT C	COL	0-0374230	0862	1
MATTHEWS KENNETH H	2LT	0-2034615	0344	2
MATTHEWS LLOYD P	LTC	0-0250188	0465	3
MATTHEWS MANASSES J	CW2	W-2210415	0864	1
MATTHEWS MAX A	LTC	0-0255846	0163	3
MATTHEWS MOORE	2LT	0-1038431	0544	2
MATTHEWS MYREL O	MAJ	0-0360319	0360	1
MATTHEWS OLLIE G	LTC	0-0171990	1048	3
MATTHEWS PALMER A	COL	0-0230182	0958	1
MATTHEWS PERCY B	MAJ	0-0348181	0947	2
MATTHEWS PHILIP A	CPT	0-2012858	1160	2
MATTHEWS ROBERT M	CW3	W-2148663	0965	1
MATTHEWS RUDOLPH S	COL	0-0336239	1063	3
MATTHEWS RUSSELL L	CPT	0-0543653	0351	1
MATTHEWS SAMUEL R	LTC	0-0221365	0863	3
MATTHEWS SEALE H	MAJ	0-1284542	0553	1
MATTHEWS THELMA L	MAJ	N-0742990	0665	1
MATTHEWS THOMAS	WO1	W-2130659	0446	2
MATTHEWS THOMAS J	CPT	0-0285721	0546	2
MATTHEWS THOMAS R	CPT	0-0925225	0246	2
MATTHEWS URA A	CPT	0-0263782	0845	2
MATTHEWS VIRGIL E	CPT	0-0990440	0662	1
MATTHEWS WALTER L S	CPT	0-0331911	0446	2
MATTHEWS WILLIAM F	MAJ	0-0973174	0264	1
MATTHIAS HOWARD C	LTC	0-0352633	0764	2
MATTHIAS RUSSELL H	LTC	0-0274276	0966	3
MATTHIAS WILLIAM T	MAJ	0-1949852	1160	1
MATTHIES HAROLD F	CPT	0-1292809	0447	2
MATTHYS HAROLD F	COL	0-0131848	0651	3
MATTICE CRAIG S	LTC	0-0309321	1160	3
MATTICE MICHAEL M	LTC	0-0167305	1055	3
MATTICK ROY W	CPT	0-1548490	0261	1
MATTINGLY FRED J	CPT	0-0189860	0452	3
MATTINGLY MARK E	WO1	W-2127498	0944	2
MATTINGLY ORVILLE B	CPT	0-0507056	0747	1
MATTIOLI JOSEPH	MAJ	0-0890174	0256	1
MATTIS MICHAEL C	COL	0-0277644	0164	3
MATTIS WILLIAM	LTC	0-0418730	1160	1
MATTISON ARTHUR C	COL	0-0174193	1059	3
MATTOCKS HAROLD P	MAJ	0-1171666	1158	1
MATTOCKS JESSE R	LTC	0-0314744	1167	3
MATTOX ERNEST E	LTC	0-1283807	0757	2
MATTOX HORACE	CPT	0-0490894	0750	1
MATTOX WILLIAM R	1LT	0-0910613	0743	2
MATTSON BERNARD H	LTC	0-0805950	0867	1
MATTSON BRUCE D	1LT	0-1824061	0446	2
MATTSON EDWARD J	LTC	0-0308137	0656	3
MATTSON EILLEEN J	2LT	N-0721469	0744	1
MATTSON HAROLD A	MAJ	0-1316179	1062	1
MATTSON HARRY W	MAJ	0-1996965	0163	1
MATTSON HERMAN G	LTC	0-0303269	1057	3
MATTSON PAUL J	CPT	0-0502302	0653	1
MATTSON ROBERT A	CW3	W-2148515	0864	1
MATTSON ROY A	MAJ	0-1291493	0661	1
MATTSON SELIM A	MAJ	0-0490619	1053	1

292-560 O - 68 - 16

ARMY OF THE UNITED STATES RETIRED LIST

NAME	GRADE	SVC NO	DATE RET MO YR	RET CODE
MATUCK GEORGE	CW4	W-2103185	1057	2
MATUKONIS ANTHONY M	MAJ	C-0885797	1056	1
MATULA THOMAS P	1LT	0-0511256	0745	2
MATULIS FRANK G	1LT	0-1895250	0357	1
MATULIS RAYMOND G	LTC	0-1592414	0363	1
MATUSZAK FRANK A	CPT	0-0492448	0254	2
MATUSZKO EDWARD J	CPT	0-1183360	0946	2
MATYSTIK EDMUND A	LTC	0-0499563	0762	2
MATZ ARTHUR	CPT	0-0157518	0840	1
MATZ FRANK P	LTC	0-1640706	0765	1
MATZ FRED W	1LT	0-0888231	1044	2
MATZ JOHN H	MAJ	C-0924540	0546	2
MATZ ROY W	LTC	0-1101943	0361	1
MATZEN HAROLD P	MAJ	0-0267046	0765	3
MATZKO MICHAEL A	LTC	0-0417830	0164	1
MAU LOWELL H	CW3	W-2147635	0161	1
MAUBORGNE BENJAMIN P	COL	0-0343930	0565	1
MAUCERI CHARLES	MAJ	C-1306790	1063	1
MAUCH ERNEST C	MAJ	0-0956053	0562	1
MAUER RONALD W	MAJ	0-1559945	0862	1
MAUER 3RD JOHN L	2LT	0-0444086	0344	2
MAUGANS JAMES W E	1LT	0-0398790	1144	2
MAUGEL JOHN P	1LT	0-0332765	0545	2
MAUGHAM CECIL L	CW3	W-2151137	1164	1
MAUK DESSIE A	COL	0-0441126	0860	1
MAUK JOHN D	CPT	0-0397237	1044	2
MAULDIN DENNIS E	CPT	0-0495505	1052	1
MAULDIN JR THOMAS R	MAJ	C-0554612	0364	1
MAULE JACK	2LT	0-1331643	0246	2
MAULE MAX O	LTC	0-1312695	0862	1
MAUM EUGENE	CW2	W-2147763	0560	1
MAUNEY JR SIDNEY F	LTC	0-0168315	0461	3
MAUPIN JAMES K	CPT	0-1013296	0346	2
MAURIN WARREN L	CPT	0-0557136	0347	1
MAUPIN WILLIAM A	1LT	0-1316492	0845	2
MAURELLO BERNARD J	1LT	0-1047760	1045	1
MAURER ARNOLD I	LTC	0-0333282	0465	3
MAURER BUD F	CPT	0-1305452	0947	2
MAURER FREDERICK	MAJ	0-0784744	0860	1
MAURER JOHN G	1LT	0-1054695	0447	2
MAURER JR CHARLES J	CW3	W-2148746	1066	1
MAURER LESLIE O	COL	0-0235417	0663	3
MAURER PAUL H	COL	C-0235474	0457	1
MAURER PHILIP E	CPT	0-0544139	1146	2
MAURER REGINALD A	B G	C-0180740	1159	3
MAURER RICHARD H	CW3	W-2146958	1263	1
MAURER ROBERT R	LTC	0-0388765	1060	1
MAURER ROY B	LTC	0-2053898	1154	1
MAURIER DAVID A	COL	0-0145748	0648	3
MAURITZ FRANK E	CPT	0-0312065	0143	2
MAURO CARL	CPT	0-1321795	0147	2
MAURO LUCIA G	1LT	N-0744538	0646	1
MAURY LEWIS A	COL	0-0172167	0352	3
MAURY MELVIN M	COL	0-1579999	0865	1
MAUS JOHN E	CPT	0-1166778	0647	2
MAUS ROGER G	COL	0-0102228	0155	3
MAUSERT CLAYTON L	COL	0-0183544	0957	1
MAUTE WILLIAM C	CPT	0-0125807	0156	3
MAUTNER RALPH A	2LT	0-1588724	0945	2
MAUZY BYRON F	CW2	W-2203636	1057	2
MAUZY CLAUDE R	COL	C-0350097	0846	2
MAVIS STEPHEN F	COL	0-0252797	0464	3
MAWBY ROBERT U	MAJ	0-1634115	0160	1
MAWHAR LAWRENCE F	CW2	W-2150142	0659	1
MAWHINNEY JAMES D	COL	0-0201060	1058	3
MAWN JOHN J	MAJ	C-2010475	0262	1
MAWN PETER R	MAJ	C-1596111	0760	3
MAX MOSES	MAJ	C-1578820	0361	1
MAX PAUL F	COL	0-0294805	0365	3
MAXAM HARRY A	CW3	W-2129706	0459	1
MAXEDON JAMES R	MAJ	C-1109491	0862	1
MAXEY BERNARD F	LTC	0-0238911	1162	3
MAXEY GEORGE F	MAJ	0-0228884	0357	3
MAXFIELD CHARLES E	LTC	0-0451347	0563	1
MAXFIELD CHARLES L	LTC	0-0165857	0358	3

NAME	GRADE	SVC NO	DATE RET MO YR	RET CODE
MAXFIELD DONALD V	CPT	0-0343002	1045	2
MAXFIELD GEORGE G	LTC	0-0242496	0461	1
MAXFIELD HAROLD A	COL	0-0187434	0953	3
MAXFIELD WILLIAM B	MAJ	0-1797328	0360	1
MAXIMINI BURT E	MAJ	0-1799591	0861	1
MAXON MILDRED E	2LT	N-0721146	0843	1
MAXSON KENNETH R	CPT	0-1181365	1063	1
MAXSON MELVIN L	LTC	0-0358736	0260	1
MAXSON PAUL A	LTC	0-1546421	1163	2
MAXSON RHEA F	MAJ	L-0201175	0763	3
MAXTED LAURENCE T	CW2	W-2141627	0159	1
MAXWELL ALEXANDER	MAJ	0-0211299	0549	1
MAXWELL ARTHUR A	CPT	0-0481585	0449	1
MAXWELL ARTHUR J	COL	0-0183032	0555	3
MAXWELL AUGUSTUS B	LTC	0-0401704	0364	1
MAXWELL CARL E	CW2	W-2144371	0157	1
MAXWELL CARLTON F	LTC	0-0473109	0962	1
MAXWELL CLARENCE M	CPT	0-0987401	0762	1
MAXWELL DAVID	1LT	0-1913818	0124	1
MAXWELL DAVID D	MAJ	0-1536420	0463	1
MAXWELL DONALD R	MAJ	0-0472858	0345	2
MAXWELL EDWARD H	MAJ	0-1037611	1262	1
MAXWELL EUGENE T	CW3	W-2205871	0962	1
MAXWELL FRANK W	1LT	0-1292028	0346	2
MAXWELL FREDERICK	COL	0-0198200	1153	1
MAXWELL GEORGE E	CW4	W-2143351	1060	1
MAXWELL GERALD C	COL	0-0358761	0160	1
MAXWELL HAROLD P	CW2	W-2143516	0260	2
MAXWELL HARVEY C	COL	0-0224771	0146	2
MAXWELL HUBERT J	CPT	0-0532861	1145	2
MAXWELL JAMES R	CW3	W-2152681	1064	1
MAXWELL JIM J	CW4	W-2110865	1058	1
MAXWELL JOHN C	COL	0-0925355	0567	3
MAXWELL JOHN E	LTC	0-1549541	0160	1
MAXWELL JOHN P	CW3	W-2102054	1154	1
MAXWELL JOHN W	COL	0-0922176	0663	3
MAXWELL JOSEPH L	LTC	0-0303395	0667	3
MAXWELL JOSEPH M	LTC	0-0259697	0166	3
MAXWELL JR CYRUS H	COL	0-0153700	0659	3
MAXWELL KENNETH L	MAJ	0-0813544	0661	1
MAXWELL LLOYD F	CW3	W-2151620	0361	1
MAXWELL LOREN C	COL	0-0235535	0146	2
MAXWELL NORRIS K	LTC	0-0450396	0561	1
MAXWELL OLIVER K	LTC	0-1638021	0161	1
MAXWELL PAUL R	CPT	0-0209245	0655	3
MAXWELL QUENTIN R	1LT	0-0702223	0245	2
MAXWELL RAYMOND	LTC	0-0460632	1046	1
MAXWELL ROBERT R	MAJ	0-4005319	1167	1
MAXWELL SAMUEL L	MAJ	0-1313506	0260	1
MAY ANTHONY A	LTC	0-0421984	1147	2
MAY BILLY R	MAJ	0-1919177	1163	1
MAY CLYDE V	LTC	0-0247225	1166	3
MAY CONDA E	1LT	0-0971548	0357	1
MAY DAVID E	CW3	W-2206332	1165	1
MAY DONAL R	1LT	0-1939784	0955	2
MAY DONALD R	1LT	0-1020311	0647	2
MAY EARL C	MAJ	0-0247929	0446	1
MAY EDISON L	MAJ	0-0981860	0865	1
MAY EMIL P	1LT	0-0377268	0245	2
MAY ERNEST V	LTC	0-0101324	0150	3
MAY FRANCIS P	MAJ	0-0907876	0750	1
MAY FREDERICK	LTC	0-0218030	0761	2
MAY GEORGE L	1LT	0-2055328	0147	1
MAY HAROLD F	MAJ	0-0358869	0661	1
MAY HERBERT C	COL	0-0156348	0149	2
MAY HERMAN J	LTC	0-1316517	0161	1
MAY HUGH R	MAJ	0-1540650	0563	1
MAY JAMES A	1LT	0-1030807	0957	1
MAY JAMES B	CW2	W-2143656	0661	1
MAY JAMES W	1LT	0-0583408	1062	2
MAY JOHN S	CPT	0-0456143	0644	2
MAY JOHN T	WO1	W-2109667	0145	2
MAY JOSEPH R	LTC	0-0348929	0856	1
MAY JR HARRY	COL	0-0253867	0767	3
MAY MABEL G	2LT	N-0700449	1038	1

NAME	GRADE	SVC NO	DATE RET MO YR	RET CODE
MAY MARJORIE O	MAJ	N-0760887	1166	1
MAY PERCY C	LTC	0-0247472	0466	3
MAY PETER G	LTC	0-0290973	1062	3
MAY ROBERT L	LTC	0-0451150	0257	1
MAY ROBERT T	MAJ	C-2263705	1166	1
MAY RUFUS H	CPT	0-1289605	0544	2
MAY SAMUEL	COL	0-0295650	1060	1
MAY STANLEY E	LTC	0-1577536	0761	1
MAY THEODORE S	LTC	0-1172982	0465	1
MAY WALTER R	MAJ	C-0984351	0563	1
MAY WALTER W	MAJ	0-1290968	1060	1
MAY WILLIAM M	CPT	0-1108143	0363	1
MAY WOODWARD J	MAJ	0-0165581	0157	3
MAYALL JAMES H	LTC	0-1285459	1067	3
MAYAUSKY BERNARD E	CPT	0-0963082	0361	1
MAYBEE ORRIN S	MAJ	0-1326247	0860	1
MAYBEE REGINALD W	1LT	0-2000463	1146	1
MAYBERRY ARCHER D	CW3	W-2151153	0764	1
MAYBERRY HENRY E	LTC	0-0365642	0460	1
MAYBERRY LESTER H	MAJ	C-1031259	0162	1
MAYBIN JOHN A	1LT	0-2033009	0551	1
MAYBIN JR ARTHUR H	1LT	0-0460041	0245	2
MAYBURY DANIEL C	COL	0-0246438	0664	1
MAYCUMBER GUY	MAJ	0-0231886	0445	2
MAYDEN WALTER S	COL	0-0248175	1062	3
MAYE HENRY R	CW4	W-2111862	0356	1
MAYE JOHN E	1LT	0-1055080	0346	2
MAYE VIRGIL F	CW3	W-2142769	0459	1
MAYE WARREN H	MAJ	C-1037612	1060	1
MAYEA ELIZABETH	1LT	N-0722167	0246	1
MAYER ALFRED F	1LT	0-1320249	0945	2
MAYER AUBREY E	CW3	W-2146751	0864	1
MAYER BENJAMIN J	LTC	0-1686384	0761	1
MAYER CARL P	COL	0-0216843	1154	3
MAYER DAVID E	B G	0-0178166	0961	3
MAYER FRANCIS L	LTC	0-0263357	0267	3
MAYER FRANK I	LTC	0-0214382	0652	3
MAYER GEORGE E	LTC	0-1165908	0162	1
MAYER GEORGE W	COL	0-0176069	1055	3
MAYER HAROLD F	1LT	0-1325587	0847	2
MAYER HARRY R	CW3	W-2144304	0363	1
MAYER HUGO E	LTC	0-0195422	1060	3
MAYER JAMES L	MAJ	0-1170073	0561	1
MAYER JOHN S	COL	0-0217175	1058	3
MAYER JOHN W	1LT	0-1301661	0644	1
MAYER JR ORLANDO B	COL	0-0207136	0857	3
MAYER MANETTE L	CPT	N-0733825	1046	1
MAYER MILVOY	MAJ	C-1800109	0161	1
MAYER ROBERT L	COL	0-0289678	0560	1
MAYER ROBERT R	1LT	0-1796666	0955	1
MAYER ROBERT W	LTC	0-1167967	1060	1
MAYER WERNER A	CW3	RW-2136690	1161	1
MAYER WILLIAM F	CW4	W-2141894	1163	1
MAYERHOFER ALFRED F	1LT	0-1062776	1046	2
MAYERS BENEDICT	MAJ	0-0256243	1166	3
MAYERS HENRY L	CPT	0-0486640	0846	2
MAYERS ISADORE	1LT	0-1294693	0845	2
MAYERS LEO V	CW4	W-2149807	1067	2
MAYES CULLUS M	LTC	0-0266435	0859	1
MAYES DON C	LTC	0-0266726	0667	3
MAYES FRANCIS B	MAJ	0-0193987	0861	3
MAYES HAROLD	MAJ	0-0238553	0865	3
MAYES JAMES L	LTC	0-0405934	0960	1
MAYES JESSE J	LTC	0-1059546	1264	1
MAYES LAWRENCE S	CPT	0-1054696	0564	2
MAYES LOUIS T	MAJ	C-1030808	0363	1
MAYES WALTER A	1LT	0-0403131	1144	2
MAYETTA FRANK P	COL	C-0320706	1161	1
MAYEUX LEVY C	2LT	0-0961737	0652	1
MAYFIELD ALFRED G	CW3	W-2127393	0958	1
MAYFIELD BEATRICE J	1LT	N-0727414	0846	1
MAYFIELD DON W	1LT	0-1322058	1045	2
MAYFIELD EDWARD T	1LT	0-1296555	0346	2
MAYFIELD FRANK G	LTC	0-0365828	0660	1
MAYFIELD GEORGE C	COL	0-0272147	0166	3

NAME	GRADE	SVC NO	DATE RET MO YR	RET CODE
MAYFIELD HARRY L	COL	0-0285829	0859	1
MAYFIELD HOWARD F	CW2	W-2149019	0159	1
MAYFIELD LAWRENCE A	CW4	W-2145466	0767	1
MAYFIELD ROBERT B	LTC	0-0418249	0964	3
MAYFIELD SAMUEL E	1LT	0-1012464	0751	2
MAYFIELD THOMAS M	M G	0-0168962	0161	3
MAYHALL EMMETT A	COL	0-0265121	0863	3
MAYHERCY ROBERT L	LTC	0-1167530	0361	1
MAYHEW JOHN P	MAJ	0-1312476	0658	1
MAYHEW JR WALTER P	MAJ	0-1298413	0361	2
MAYHEW WILLIAM M	MAJ	0-1257563	0261	1
MAYKOVICH ALBERT A	LTC	0-0451349	0657	1
MAYKOVICH JOHN J	MAJ	C-1050368	1153	1
MAYLARD JACK B	LTC	0-0888603	1160	1
MAYLE LESLIE	LTC	0-0493616	0949	1
MAYLUNAS JOHN A	CW3	W-2141725	0459	1
MAYNARD ALFRED A	LTC	0-0914285	1263	1
MAYNARD ALFRED C	CPT	0-0378988	0346	2
MAYNARD CECIL D	CPT	0-0527836	0147	2
MAYNARD CHARLES A	LTC	0-1550654	1060	1
MAYNARD HAROLD G	COL	0-0359276	0754	1
MAYNARD HIRAM H	COL	0-0185202	0746	2
MAYNARD HOY P	CW2	W-2112574	0846	1
MAYNARD PERRY C	COL	0-0195920	0662	3
MAYNE CARLTON A	MAJ	C-1588149	1065	2
MAYNE WARREN R	1LT	0-0485500	0145	2
MAYNHART JOHN	CPT	0-1576344	0749	1
MAYNOR CHARLES H	CW2	W-2149366	0660	1
MAYO ANDREW J	1LT	0-1062244	0146	2
MAYO ARTHUR	CPT	0-1913838	1133	1
MAYO CARL N	COL	0-0359546	1059	1
MAYO EDWIN A	CPT	0-1004373	1156	1
MAYO FRANK M	1LT	0-0461218	0845	2
MAYO GLENN M	LTC	0-1698194	0261	1
MAYO JOHN W	COL	0-0171773	1061	3
MAYO JOSH H	1LT	0-0408869	1145	2
MAYO LACIE L	2LT	0-1108144	1143	2
MAYO LEON G	MAJ	0-1998044	0360	1
MAYO PAUL E	CPT	0-1286159	0156	1
MAYO STEVEN R	LTC	0-1057163	1162	1
MAYO WILLIE A	LTC	0-1169233	0356	1
MAYOR JOSEPH J	WO1	W-2123101	0249	1
MAYORGA GEORGE W	LTC	0-0275948	0756	3
MAYOROS STEVE J	MAJ	0-0432586	0861	1
MAYOROS WILLIAM F	CPT	0-0550250	0764	1
MAYS DARYL F	1LT	0-1550861	0167	1
MAYS EARL R	CW2	W-2208218	0263	2
MAYS FRANK A	MAJ	0-1639364	0760	1
MAYS HELENA F	1LT	N-0720893	0147	1
MAYS JOHN P	MAJ	0-0468835	0862	1
MAYS JOSEPH R	MAJ	0-1172983	0762	1
MAYS JR JOHN W	MAJ	0-0974460	0964	1
MAYS NED G	LTC	0-1035527	0755	1
MAYS REAVUS C	COL	0-0347030	0557	1
MAYS RICHARD J	COL	0-0330072	0960	1
MAYS RICHARD J	LTC	0-0352895	0158	1
MAYS SAMUEL C	LTC	0-0335058	0265	3
MAYS SR ABRAHAM W	MAJ	0-0509482	1053	1
MAYSHARK JAMES P	CPT	0-0347088	1044	2
MAYSTER RONALD A	1LT	0-1037173	1045	2
MAZA HERBERT	CPT	0-0378859	0546	2
MAZAITIS EDGAR O	COL	0-0386310	0862	1
MAZE THOMAS A	MAJ	C-0442664	0552	1
MAZEAU JOHN Y	LTC	0-0256740	0960	3
MAZEKE WILSON	CW2	W-2147764	0261	1
MAZETIS WALTER P	LTC	0-1100221	1062	1
MAZIKE WALTER J	LTC	0-0493792	0656	1
MAZNEK NICHOLAS	1LT	0-1326104	1145	2
MAZOL JOSEPH J	LTC	0-0328446	0960	1
MAZUR EDWARD W	LTC	0-1283640	0258	1
MAZUR SEYMOUR	CPT	0-0119185	1153	3
MAZURKIEWICZ HENRY J	CW2	W-2115437	0155	1
MAZZA JOHN V	MAJ	0-1311802	0846	2
MAZZANTI VINCENT E	CPT	0-0471192	1045	2
MAZZARELLA ROBERT A	MAJ	0-0449454	1047	2

NAME	GRADE	SVC NO	DATE RET MO YR	RET CODE
MAZZARISI ERNEST S	1LT	0-1168807	1144	2
MAZZEI JOHN C	COL	0-0228045	1165	3
MAZZEI OTTO	CPT	0-1919874	0761	1
MAZZEO WILLIAM	LTC	0-1296232	0265	1
MAZZI EARL J	MAJ	0-1644570	0756	1
MAZZIE GASPERO P	LTC	0-0346388	0261	1
MAZZIE ROLAND R	CW2	W-2141629	0656	1
MAZZIOTTA ROBERT R	1LT	0-0537049	0345	2
MAZZOLA NICHOLAS C	LTC	0-1289936	0357	1
MAZZUCCO PETER P	CPT	0-2010704	1158	1
MC ABEE GARLAND J	MAJ	0-2263116	0763	1
MC ABEE JR ORMOND A	MAJ	0-1555862	0862	1
MC ADAM WILLIAM A	MAJ	0-0235310	1048	3
MC ADAMS DALE A	MAJ	0-0414371	0163	1
MC ADAMS JR CARL	COL	0-1576346	0867	1
MC ADAMS ROBERT L	CPT	0-0509554	1148	1
MC ADDO HOWARD F	1LT	0-1309170	1165	2
MC ADDO WILLIAM A	MAJ	0-0413995	1165	3
MC ADDO WINFRED E	2LT	0-1690744	0647	2
MC ADOW VIVIAN M	1LT	N-0732763	0746	1
MC AFEE DEVEAUX J	LTC	0-0299229	0961	3
MC AFEE FOREST S	MAJ	0-2020448	0264	1
MC AFEE JAMES P	CPT	0-1693368	0745	2
MC AFEE MILLS B	MAJ	0-1317034	0460	1
MC AHON JACK F	LTC	0-1315707	0767	1
MC ALEAR DORIS E	MAJ	L-1010358	1165	1
MC ALEVEY ALICE Z	CPT	N-0720222	0847	1
MC ALEXANDER HUGH R	CPT	0-0996747	0564	1
MC ALISTER CLINTON L	MAJ	0-0397124	0646	2
MC ALISTER GUY C	MAJ	0-1179953	0761	1
MC ALISTER JOHN R	LTC	0-0261405	1051	1
MC ALISTER JR JOHN M	LTC	0-0395879	1060	1
MC ALISTER REID W	MAJ	0-0337074	0946	1
MC ALISTER RENEAU S	LTC	0-0288832	0358	1
MC ALISTER ROBERT T	CW3	W-2146381	0662	1
MC ALLEN WILLIAM T	LTC	0-0498469	1162	1
MC ALLISTER CECIL M	LTC	0-0369824	1066	3
MC ALLISTER CHARLES	MAJ	0-1999027	0462	1
MC ALLISTER GEORGE	MAJ	0-1058893	0461	1
MC ALLISTER JAMES R	LTC	0-0242067	1044	2
MC ALLISTER MAX F	COL	0-0226061	0664	3
MC ALLISTER PHILMORE	LTC	0-0312760	1265	3
MC ALLISTER RICHARC	LTC	0-1592415	0365	1
MC ALLISTER ROBERT R	CPT	0-2034555	1145	2
MC ALLISTER THORNTON	LTC	0-0252438	0946	2
MC ALLISTER WILBUR B	LTC	0-0301037	1061	3
MC ALLISTER WILLIAM	CPT	0-1181033	1162	1
MC ALOON JOSEPH D	MAJ	0-1011325	1263	1
MC ALPIN ESTEL C	LTC	0-0510506	0854	1
MC ALPINE DONALD E	1LT	0-1322567	0945	2
MC ALPINE ELLAYNE F	COL	N-0744720	0767	2
MC ALPINE FRED F	MAJ	0-1297227	0358	1
MC ALPINE RODERICK K	MAJ	0-0213735	1263	3
MC ALPINE WAYNE D	LTC	0-0221469	0760	1
MC AMIS LEWIS A	MAJ	0-1543042	0961	1
MC ANALLY CHARLES W	LTC	0-0286076	1263	3
MC ANALLY HEARL R	CW2	W-2150727	0961	1
MC ANALLY WILLIAM F	COL	0-0197607	0947	2
MC ANDREW JOSEPH	CPT	0-2029454	0457	1
MC ANDREW NILUS F	LTC	0-0516184	0567	1
MC ANULTY DALE	LTC	0-1589002	0761	1
MC ANULTY HAWLEY D	WO1	W-2123416	0148	1
MC ANULTY JAMES S	LTC	0-0233125	0165	3
MC ANULTY WALLACE M	LTC	0-1794827	1061	1
MC ARDLE EDWARD J	CPT	0-1175507	0246	2
MC ARDLE JOSEPH J	CW4	W-2141990	0161	1
MC ARTHUR FRANCIS S	LTC	0-1308355	1167	1
MC ARTHUR STUART C	LTC	0-1115465	0767	1
MC ASKILL WILLIAM D	CPT	0-0559037	0945	1
MC ATAMNEY RICHARD W	2LT	0-1298740	0545	2
MC ATEE EUGENE M	2LT	0-2000738	0645	2
MC ATEE FRANK J	CPT	0-0509927	0745	2
MC ATEE LESLIE B	LTC	0-0195241	0960	3
MC AULEY WILLIAM C	CW3	W-2147102	0463	1
MC AULIFFE ALBERT	MAJ	0-1106338	0660	1

NAME	GRADE	SVC NO	DATE RET MO YR	RET CODE
MC AULIFFE FRANK B	LTC	0-0333169	0855	3
MC AUSLAN HAROLD L	LTC	0-0231832	1262	2
MC AVEY JR THOMAS J	MAJ	0-0180172	0958	3
MC AYEAL ROY C	MAJ	0-0924690	0547	2
MC BARRON JOSEPH P	LTC	0-0437743	1164	1
MC BEE JAMES W	CW3	RW-2143129	0761	1
MC BEE JOHN	MAJ	0-0941961	1262	1
MC BEE LEROY S	1LT	0-2012546	0447	2
MC BEE LLOYD W	CPT	0-0974431	0257	1
MC BEE WELDON H	LTC	0-0255299	0859	1
MC BRATNIE ELLEN J	MAJ	N-0726711	0863	1
MC BRAYER ELDON F	LTC	0-1549993	1159	2
MC BRAYER THOMAS F	LTC	0-0220101	1062	3
MC BREARTY CHARLES F	CPT	0-1552116	0163	1
MC BREEN WILLIAM T	MAJ	0-0954225	0166	1
MC BRIDE ANDREW C	1LT	0-1044293	0646	2
MC BRIDE ELZIE G	2LT	0-2009595	0146	2
MC BRIDE EMMA B	CPT	N-0755651	1046	1
MC BRIDE GEORGE	LTC	0-1043161	1060	1
MC BRIDE GEORGE A	MAJ	0-0244016	0865	3
MC BRIDE GEORGE W	WO1	W-2126717	1156	1
MC BRIDE JOHN S	1LT	0-1324038	0945	2
MC BRIDE JOHN T	CW3	W-2146693	0661	2
MC BRIDE JOSEPH L	MAJ	0-0450457	0855	1
MC BRIDE JOSEPHINE	MAJ	N-0760621	0566	1
MC BRIDE LAUREN E	LTC	0-0363427	0361	1
MC BRIDE LESTER H	LTC	0-0370288	1154	1
MC BRIDE MALCOLM R	CPT	0-1284732	0952	2
MC BRIDE PAUL T	CPT	0-0968388	0361	1
MC BRIDE RALPH F	CPT	0-0220371	0245	2
MC BRIDE ROBERT J	2LT	0-1012198	0144	2
MC BRIDE THOMAS W	CW3	W-2145685	0563	1
MC BRIDE WELDON C	LTC	0-1289286	0161	1
MC BRIDE WILLIAM F	MAJ	0-0480472	0557	1
MC BRIDE WILLIS T	CPT	0-1923615	0764	1
MC BRIEN RUTH E	MAJ	N-0720617	1163	1
MC BRIEN WALDO R	LTC	0-0366008	1165	3
MC BRIER CLYATT	CPT	0-0454452	0846	1
MC BRINN ROBERT J	LTC	0-0970304	1067	1
MC BROOM JAMES F	LTC	0-0384207	1160	1
MC BROOM JOHN C	MAJ	0-1997279	0164	1
MC BROOM ROBERT J	LTC	0-1592416	1263	2
MC BROOM WILLIAM H	MAJ	0-2046601	1155	1
MC BRYDE CHARLES M	2LT	0-1300508	1044	2
MC BURNEY HAROLD H	COL	0-0225884	0959	3
MC CABE ARTHUR T	MAJ	0-1290277	0157	1
MC CABE CHARLES J	CPT	0-1338834	0464	1
MC CABE DONNA S	MAJ	N-0723237	0265	1
MC CABE EDWARD J	1LT	0-0514511	0547	1
MC CABE FRANK J	LTC	0-1044609	0761	1
MC CABE GEORGE E	COL	0-0348434	1265	3
MC CABE GEORGE W	1LT	0-1314932	1047	2
MC CABE HENRY V	MAJ	0-1287208	1060	1
MC CABE JAMES F	MAJ	0-1650952	0263	1
MC CABE JAMES M	CW2	W-2107854	0847	2
MC CABE JR ARTHUR E	COL	0-0315142	1166	1
MC CABE JR LUKE V	CPT	0-1116795	1158	2
MC CABE JR WILLIAM S	CPT	0-1534558	0647	2
MC CABE LOUIS C	COL	0-0240760	0364	3
MC CABE MERRILL J	MAJ	0-0969511	0762	1
MC CABE THOMAS R	LTC	0-1057817	0163	1
MC CABE THOMAS W	MAJ	0-0538117	0646	1
MC CABE WILLIAM B	MAJ	0-2008752	0767	1
MC CABE WILLIAM F	1LT	0-0503584	0445	1
MC CAFFERTY ROBERT H	LTC	0-0925265	0964	3
MC CAFFERY HAROLD W	CW2	W-2144522	1060	1
MC CAFFERY PATRICK G	MAJ	0-1317322	1161	1
MC CAFFERY WALTER M	CW2	W-2141370	0360	1
MC CAFFREY HOWARD T	LTC	0-1302157	1062	1
MC CAFFREY JAMES A	LTC	0-1180604	0267	1
MC CAFFREY JAMES G	LTC	0-0238377	0961	3
MC CAFFREY JOSEPH E	COL	0-0190366	0856	3
MC CAFFREY JOSEPH F	1LT	0-1284360	0644	2
MC CAFFREY LEE E	CW3	W-2148126	1163	1
MC CAFFREY MICHAEL A	1LT	0-1294168	0246	2

NAME	GRADE	SVC NO	DATE RET MO YR	RET CODE
MC CAFFREY RICHARD	LTC	0-1695670	0762	1
MC CAFFREY THOMAS F	LTC	0-1697949	0962	1
MC CAGUE MICHAEL J	LTC	0-1037142	0867	1
MC CAHILL WILLIAM F	COL	0-0387227	0263	1
MC CAIG RAYMOND J	MAJ	0-1797851	0663	1
MC CAIN CLARENCE F	MAJ	0-0971753	1262	1
MC CAIN CLAWSON W	MAJ	0-1651345	0560	1
MC CAIN EARL F	MAJ	0-1015440	0257	1
MC CAIN EDWIN H	LTC	0-0923506	0567	3
MC CAIN HOWARD K	LTC	0-0330738	0967	3
MC CAIN WILLIAM D	B G	0-0288111	0467	3
MC CALE ALFRED F	COL	0-0265960	1058	3
MC CALEB ROBERT C	LTC	0-0452482	0361	1
MC CALL ANNA B	MAJ	N-0756824	1264	3
MC CALL BESSIE M	1LT	N-0728857	0546	1
MC CALL BILL C	CW4	W-2146161	0667	1
MC CALL FRANCIS L	1LT	0-1303918	1145	2
MC CALL GEORGE A	LTC	0-1548251	1160	1
MC CALL GERALD C	LTC	0-1044891	1066	1
MC CALL HOBBY H	CPT	0-0422737	1045	2
MC CALL IVER F	MAJ	0-1695649	0163	1
MC CALL JOSEPH H	LTC	0-0266909	0165	3
MC CALL JR CHARLES S	LTC	0-0381432	1046	2
MC CALL SR RUSSELL C	LTC	0-1295054	0463	1
MC CALL VIRGIL W	MAJ	0-0561566	0761	1
MC CALL WILFRED J	COL	0-0415680	0561	1
MC CALLA LOUIS S	CW3	W-2147069	0766	1
MC CALLEY WALTER S	CPT	0-0235462	1266	3
MC CALLION CHARLES L	CW2	W-2141371	0957	1
MC CALLISTER CURTI	MAJ	0-0159835	0955	3
MC CALLISTER RUSSELL	LTC	0-1183723	0463	1
MC CALLUM ARCHIBALD	MAJ	0-0253497	1065	3
MC CALLUM EDWARD J	CW2	W-2207136	0662	1
MC CALLUM GEORGE C	CPT	0-0419006	0645	2
MC CALLUM GEORGE L	LTC	0-1298259	0367	3
MC CALLUM GORDON A	CPT	0-0509906	0149	1
MC CALLUM HAROLD C	MAJ	0-0451339	1167	1
MC CALLUM HAYES S	MAJ	0-0177592	1045	2
MC CALLUM HERMAN D	LTC	0-1042361	0261	1
MC CALLUM LEROY	CW4	W-2103191	0955	1
MC CALLUM M ANNA	MAJ	N-0783034	0263	1
MC CALLUM ROBERT H	LTC	0-1552327	0161	1
MC CALLUM ROBERT S	LTC	0-0395450	0557	1
MC CAMEY JR JAMES F	1LT	0-1321796	1045	2
MC CAMMON JOSEPH R	COL	0-0279083	0859	1
MC CAMMON PAUL D	CW2	W-2149959	1062	1
MC CANCE CLYDE W	MAJ	0-0406455	0562	1
MC CANDLESS CHARLE	MAJ	0-0507053	0153	1
MC CANDLESS ELMER H	2LT	0-0753382	0750	2
MC CANDLESS GEORGE T	CPT	0-1597535	1065	3
MC CANDLESS JAMES B	CW3	W-2149081	0364	1
MC CANDLESS WILBERT	CW2	W-2147508	0963	1
MC CANDLISS CHARLE	CPT	0-1703319	1045	1
MC CANE GEORGE F	CW2	W-2152892	0161	1
MC CANLESS CHARLES L	LTC	0-0471556	1155	2
MC CANN DONN M	LTC	0-1044610	0261	1
MC CANN EDMUND T	CPT	0-0198190	0747	1
MC CANN EUGENE J	CPT	0-0890021	1147	1
MC CANN EUGENE J	2LT	0-2318371	0464	3
MC CANN HAROLD J	LTC	0-0124466	0350	3
MC CANN HOWARD	MAJ	0-2011240	0860	1
MC CANN JAMES R	1LT	0-1336524	0748	2
MC CANN JOHN F	1LT	0-0322244	0446	2
MC CANN JOHN R	COL	0-0156892	0455	3
MC CANN JOHN R	CPT	0-0386282	0245	2
MC CANN JOSEPH F	LTC	0-0456339	0766	1
MC CANN JR EDWARD T	2LT	0-1053245	1044	2
MC CANN LEONARD J	COL	0-0239167	0156	3
MC CANN PERCY J	CW2	W-2002790	0256	3
MC CANN RICHARD D	CPT	0-1305621	0546	2
MC CANN ROBERT J	1LT	0-0393660	0744	1
MC CANN THOMAS A	MAJ	0-1328164	0563	1
MC CANN WILLIS H	MAJ	0-0265456	0467	3
MC CANNA JR JOSEPH P	LTC	0-0427800	0763	1
MC CANNE JOE R	1LT	0-1182648	0946	2

NAME	GRADE	SVC NO	DATE RET MO YR	RET CODE
MC CANSE PHILIP	MAJ	0-1928321	1166	1
MC CANTS LESTER	LTC	0-0422066	0463	1
MC CARCELL FRANCIS J	CW3	W-2205860	0466	1
MC CARDIE CLARENCE F	CW2	W-2207522	0360	1
MC CARDLE JR JOHN	MAJ	0-2097006	1065	1
MC CARRICK MARJORIE	CPT	N-0732872	0647	1
MC CARRON EDMUND S	CPT	0-1301327	0546	2
MC CARRON ROBERT F	MAJ	0-0282116	1145	2
MC CART JOHN G	CW3	W-2151184	0965	1
MC CART KENNETH A	1LT	0-2042911	1054	1
MC CARTER LEE R	CPT	0-0476402	0147	1
MC CARTHEY RAYMOND M	LTC	0-1103787	0662	1
MC CARTHY ALLEN J	CPT	0-0172141	0951	3
MC CARTHY ALPHONSU	COL	0-0254260	0359	3
MC CARTHY ARNOLD B	MAJ	0-1183575	0261	1
MC CARTHY BARTHOLE	LTC	0-1287036	0657	1
MC CARTHY CORNELIUS	CPT	0-1048488	0859	1
MC CARTHY DAVID J	1LT	0-1174370	0745	2
MC CARTHY DONALD E	MAJ	0-1315708	0261	1
MC CARTHY EDMUND P	MAJ	0-1332840	1166	1
MC CARTHY EDWARD A	MAJ	0-0239029	0266	3
MC CARTHY EDWARD J	LTC	0-1338625	1066	1
MC CARTHY EDWARD R	CPT	0-1288588	0958	1
MC CARTHY FLORENCE J	CPT	0-1105338	1046	2
MC CARTHY FRANCIS J	MAJ	0-1050370	0461	1
MC CARTHY FRANK W	LTC	0-0112370	0852	3
MC CARTHY GEORGE V	CW3	W-2146485	0958	1
MC CARTHY HAROLD H	LTC	0-1108146	0462	1
MC CARTHY HENRY A	WO1	W-2118384	0846	2
MC CARTHY HERBERT J	1LT	0-1045171	0945	2
MC CARTHY JAMES A	CPT	0-0471024	0844	2
MC CARTHY JAMES F	MAJ	0-1947023	0662	1
MC CARTHY JAMES G	CW2	W-2208493	0360	1
MC CARTHY JAMES J	CPT	0-2018381	0456	1
MC CARTHY JAMES M	LTC	0-0359364	0760	1
MC CARTHY JOHN B	1LT	0-5704866	0365	2
MC CARTHY JOHN E	CPT	0-0885733	0155	1
MC CARTHY JOHN F	COL	0-0210475	0956	3
MC CARTHY JOHN J	MAJ	0-0182271	0862	3
MC CARTHY JOHN J	COL	0-0256199	0267	3
MC CARTHY JOHN J	LTC	0-0323278	0560	1
MC CARTHY JOHN J	MAJ	0-0443656	0954	1
MC CARTHY JOHN J	CPT	0-1181367	0846	2
MC CARTHY JOHN J	MAJ	0-1321384	1160	1
MC CARTHY JOHN R	CPT	0-2019624	0656	1
MC CARTHY JOHN W	1LT	0-0495324	0750	1
MC CARTHY JOSEPH H	MAJ	0-1587445	0346	2
MC CARTHY JOSEPH J	LTC	0-1576349	0862	1
MC CARTHY JOSEPHINE	1LT	N-0742068	1045	1
MC CARTHY LESTER	CW2	W-2150168	0860	1
MC CARTHY MARGARET	2LT	N-0700106	1038	1
MC CARTHY MARTIN J	MAJ	0-0463553	0246	2
MC CARTHY MICHAEL J	LTC	0-1112845	0467	1
MC CARTHY PATRICK D	LTC	0-0445055	1166	1
MC CARTHY PAUL E	2LT	0-1646400	0645	2
MC CARTHY PAUL V	COL	0-0220323	0859	3
MC CARTHY PHILIP J	MAJ	0-1574969	0747	1
MC CARTHY PHILIP O	LTC	0-0439628	0666	1
MC CARTHY QUENTIN R	CW2	W-2205505	0563	1
MC CARTHY RAYMOND R	1LT	0-1534088	1043	2
MC CARTHY ROBERT C	MAJ	0-2289515	1060	1
MC CARTHY STEPHEN R	LTC	0-0173623	0853	3
MC CARTHY THOMAS E	CPT	0-0169290	0755	3
MC CARTHY THOMAS J	CPT	0-1285462	0746	2
MC CARTHY THOMAS L	2LT	0-1293809	1044	2
MC CARTHY WILLIAM B	MAJ	0-0255458	0246	2
MC CARTHY WILLIAM F	LTC	0-0406954	0960	1
MC CARTHY WILLIAM J	CW4	W-2106936	0155	1
MC CARTHY WILLIS B	LTC	0-0454462	0161	1
MC CARTNEY CARL P	LTC	0-1945653	0266	1
MC CARTNEY CLINTON E	LTC	0-1585849	0962	1
MC CARTNEY HENRY A	LTC	0-0109901	1048	2
MC CARTNEY HERBERT M	CPT	0-0367464	0450	1
MC CARTNEY JAMES J	MAJ	0-1048489	1056	1
MC CARTNEY JAMES K	MAJ	0-1557045	0663	1

NAME	GRADE	SVC NO	DATE RET MO YR	RET CODE
MC CARTNEY JAMES R	LTC	0-1556182	1162	1
MC CARTNEY LOREN	LTC	0-2034796	1062	1
MC CARTNEY ROBERT J	LTC	0-1293079	1060	1
MC CARTNEY ROY C	MAJ	0-0484195	0145	2
MC CARTNEY WILLIAM A	LTC	0-0225500	1263	3
MC CARTY CECIL L	CPT	0-1307563	0347	2
MC CARTY CHESTER J	CW2	W-214741C	C761	1
MC CARTY JUSTIN J	LTC	0-1646401	0263	1
MC CARTY KENNETH T	LTC	0-1312189	1060	1
MC CARTY MARION C	LTC	0-0302793	0661	1
MC CARTY MATTHEW F	1LT	0-1649084	1146	2
MC CARTY OLIN C	MAJ	0-0398399	0946	2
MC CARTY RICHARD E	CPT	0-1080468	1049	2
MC CARTY THOMAS A	CPT	0-1946109	C265	2
MC CARTY THOMAS O	MAJ	0-1001180	0654	1
MC CARTY WILLIAM H	COL	0-0147115	1051	3
MC CARTY WILLIAM J	COL	0-0288864	0758	3
MC CARTY WILLIAM L	LTC	0-0322501	0446	2
MC CARVER EVERETT E	LTC	0-1177901	0763	1
MC CARY MASON B	MAJ	0-1557751	0759	1
MC CASKEY AMBROSE E	LTC	0-0280912	1146	2
MC CASKEY RAYMOND	CPT	0-2033067	1160	1
MC CASKILL MARVIN J	1LT	0-1886716	1054	2
MC CASKILL WILLIAM C	MAJ	0-0170658	0648	3
MC CASLAND STANFORD	LTC	C-0233154	0765	3
MC CASLIN GUY T	MAJ	0-1310859	0246	2
MC CASLIN JAMES F	COL	0-0336629	0553	3
MC CASLIN JOHN W	COL	0-0141603	0755	3
MC CASLIN JOSEPH L	MAJ	0-1185191	0257	1
MC CASTOR JOSEPH T	MAJ	0-0242686	0846	2
MC CAUGHEY PATRICK E	CPT	0-0258157	0267	3
MC CAUL THOMAS F	LTC	0-0405939	1164	3
MC CAULEY ALICE M	2LT	N-0700543	0838	1
MC CAULEY ANTHONY G	CW3	W-2148281	0664	1
MC CAULEY CHARLES	LTC	0-0216483	1161	3
MC CAULEY CHARLES	CPT	0-0545413	0847	1
MC CAULEY CHARLES O	CPT	0-0130947	1145	2
MC CAULEY DONNIE W	2LT	0-2000492	0558	2
MC CAULEY HARRY J	MAJ	0-0331432	C346	2
MC CAULEY JAMES O	LTC	0-0162712	1060	3
MC CAULEY JAMES R	LTC	0-0298083	0867	3
MC CAULEY JOHN B	1LT	0-1043419	1144	2
MC CAULEY JOHN J	LTC	0-1581250	0865	1
MC CAULEY ROBERT O	LTC	0-0450388	0161	1
MC CAULEY ROBERT M	MAJ	0-1323453	0461	1
MC CAULEY VINCENT P	1LT	0-1576350	C345	2
MC CAUSLAND CHARLES	LTC	0-0372606	0364	3
MC CAUSLAND PAUL W	1LT	0-0518719	0547	1
MC CAW THOMAS W	COL	0-0186192	0352	3
MC CAY ALFRED T	LTC	0-1308669	1262	1
MC CHESNEY ARTHUR	CPT	0-1765761	0847	2
MC CHESNEY CLAUDE M	LTC	0-1294170	C961	1
MC CHESNEY DON R	COL	0-0389538	0966	1
MC CHESNEY EDWARD R	CPT	0-0219267	0663	3
MC CHESNEY FRANK A	COL	0-0916942	0555	2
MC CHESNEY VERNETT	1LT	N-0732784	0645	1
MC CLAIN ARTHUR B	LTC	0-2039437	0167	2
MC CLAIN BRUCE M	CPT	0-1850139	1160	1
MC CLAIN CHARLES J	CPT	0-1795937	1045	2
MC CLAIN COLBERT C	COL	0-0147531	0649	3
MC CLAIN DELPHINA	2LT	N-0762531	0545	1
MC CLAIN EDGAR R	MAJ	C-0505829	1052	1
MC CLAIN ELIZABETH	MAJ	N-0727841	1262	1
MC CLAIN EUGENE F	LTC	0-1308531	0763	1
MC CLAIN GORDON M	CPT	0-0907885	0764	1
MC CLAIN JAMES R	MAJ	0-1946564	1060	1
MC CLAIN SYLVESTER	MAJ	0-1035933	0958	2
MC CLAIN THOMAS M	MAJ	0-1951496	0963	1
MC CLAIN VERNAL B	CPT	0-0518570	1047	1
MC CLAIN WILLIAM A	MAJ	C-2001746	0764	1
MC CLAIN WILDFORD A	CPT	0-0452441	1145	2
MC CLAMMA LOYAL	CPT	0-2018547	1054	2
MC CLANAHAN C J	MAJ	0-1643109	1060	1
MC CLANAMAN JAMES L	LTC	0-1051279	0162	1
MC CLANAHAN PAUL A	1LT	0-1585853	0945	2

NAME	GRADE	SVC NO	DATE RET MO YR	RET CODE
MC CLANAHAN ROBERT O	LTC	0-1580006	0662	1
MC CLANATHAN ROBER	LTC	0-0288998	0960	3
MC CLANNAHAN K E	CW4	W-2109841	0755	1
MC CLARNON JOHN T	MAJ	0-0961772	1060	1
MC CLARREN FREDERI	MAJ	0-1101946	1053	1
MC CLARREN RICHARD M	MAJ	0-1745905	0161	3
MC CLARY CLAUDE R	MAJ	0-1291667	0960	1
MC CLARY GEORGE R	LTC	0-0348192	0246	2
MC CLASKEY JAMES W	MAJ	0-1301849	0662	1
MC CLATCHEY DAVID H	MAJ	0-2033968	0163	1
MC CLAY ROBERT H	LTC	0-1308670	0166	1
MC CLEAR ROBERT O	COL	0-0251307	0866	3
MC CLELLAN DONALD	LTC	0-0383359	1060	1
MC CLELLAN ERNEST V	LTC	0-0257897	1054	1
MC CLELLAN FRANCIS R	CPT	0-0176397	0462	3
MC CLELLAN IRVIN R	COL	0-0320478	0565	3
MC CLELLAN JAMES T	CPT	0-0358541	0347	2
MC CLELLAN JOHN A	MAJ	0-1576251	0960	1
MC CLELLAN LLOYD G	LTC	0-1548943	0864	1
MC CLELLAN MAX O	CPT	0-1890037	1165	1
MC CLELLAN THOMAS F	CPT	0-1174945	1045	2
MC CLELLAN WEBSTER J	CPT	0-1641554	0667	3
MC CLELLAN WILLIAM A	MAJ	0-0957259	0364	1
MC CLELLAN WILLIAM O	LTC	0-0404968	0561	1
MC CLELLAND DAN R	LTC	0-0380017	0361	1
MC CLELLAND DONALD J	LTC	0-1042362	0164	1
MC CLELLAND FRANCES	MAJ	N-0728433	0364	2
MC CLELLAND FRANCIS	MAJ	0-0961194	C762	1
MC CLELLAND JAMES H	MAJ	0-0965431	0765	1
MC CLELLAND JAMES J	2LT	0-0551454	1045	1
MC CLELLAND PERRY G	2LT	0-1306872	0945	2
MC CLELLAND ROYCE S	COL	0-0140304	0948	3
MC CLELLAND SAMUEL	MAJ	0-1703832	1156	1
MC CLELLAND STANLEY	CPT	0-0317187	0845	2
MC CLELLAND WALTER B	MAJ	0-0263649	0861	3
MC CLELLAND WILLIAM	MAJ	0-0987787	1066	1
MC CLELLEN CECIL R	CW2	W-2206355	0860	2
MC CLEMENT VERE E	CPT	0-1293441	0446	2
MC CLENAHAN JOHN L	1LT	0-0413732	0544	1
MC CLENATHEN VERNE W	LTC	0-1542737	1164	1
MC CLENDON BERNARD	1LT	0-0366237	1045	2
MC CLENDON JESSE F	LTC	0-0128527	0648	3
MC CLENNY ERNEST B	MAJ	0-1333681	0761	1
MC CLESKEY CHARLES S	LTC	0-0176569	0357	3
MC CLESKEY DEE T	MAJ	0-0485191	0647	2
MC CLESKEY FELIX E	CW2	W-214681C	0461	1
MC CLEVEY ARTHUR M	LTC	0-0915364	0862	1
MC CLIMANS REUBEN L	MAJ	0-0450529	0357	1
MC CLINTIC GEORGE M	COL	0-0441924	0562	3
MC CLINTIC KENNETH	MAJ	0-0278554	1159	1
MC CLINTIC VIRGIL M	1LT	0-0463445	0845	2
MC CLINTOCK AUSTIN R	LTC	0-025937C	1264	3
MC CLINTOCK CHARLES	CW3	W-2145082	0962	1
MC CLINTOCK JOSEPH G	LTC	0-0408194	0860	2
MC CLINTOCK JR R O	CW4	W-2141630	0859	1
MC CLINTOCK RAYBURN	WO1	W-2124697	0445	2
MC CLINTOCK ROBERT A	CPT	0-1996498	1161	1
MC CLINTOCK VIRGIL H	LTC	0-0159211	0957	3
MC CLINTOCK WALTER L	CPT	0-0499858	0544	2
MC CLINTOCK WILLIA	LTC	0-0398311	0247	2
MC CLINTON JAMES W	MAJ	0-0497651	1162	1
MC CLISH JAMES O	LTC	0-1301236	0657	1
MC CLISTER CECIL M	CPT	0-130203C	0546	2
MC CLOONEY JAMES E	LTC	0-0541793	0763	1
MC CLOSKEY ANTHONY	LTC	0-1574972	0367	1
MC CLOSKEY BERNARD	1LT	0-1175794	0559	1
MC CLOSKEY CHARLES A	WO1	W-2142427	0256	1
MC CLOSKEY EDWARD B	MAJ	0-0992339	0166	1
MC CLOSKEY GERTRUD	1LT	N-0725263	1045	1
MC CLOSKEY JAMES	MAJ	0-1703762	0755	1
MC CLOSKEY JAMES W	LTC	0-1047669	0863	1
MC CLOSKEY JOHN	MAJ	0-0124468	0755	3
MC CLOSKEY JOHN	CW3	W-2146023	0464	1
MC CLOSKEY JOHN B	MAJ	0-0334424	0960	3
MC CLOSKEY JOHN E	MAJ	0-1327558	0662	1

NAME	GRADE	SVC NO	DATE RET MO YR	RET CODE
MC CLOSKEY JOHN T	MAJ	0-0435753	0450	1
MC CLOSKEY JOHN W	LTC	0-1534559	1061	1
MC CLOSKEY SHARON	COL	0-0145859	0846	2
MC CLOSKEY THOMAS	CPT	0-1325658	C947	1
MC CLOUD WALTER O	LTC	C-0244502	0164	3
MC CLOY JAMES S	2LT	0-0416412	0343	1
MC CLUNG ARTHUR J	CPT	0-0402859	C847	1
MC CLUNG BOYD E	LTC	0-1058895	0662	1
MC CLUNG FRED	CPT	0-0496718	0954	1
MC CLUNG J C	CPT	0-1690917	1266	1
MC CLUNG JAMES A	LTC	0-0265447	0261	1
MC CLUNG JOHN O	MAJ	0-0480973	0746	2
MC CLUNG MARGARET W	MAJ	M-0010075	0159	1
MC CLUNG WILLIAM A	LTC	0-1283642	0147	2
MC CLURE ALBERT J	MAJ	C-2208479	0867	1
MC CLURE ALMA G	MAJ	N-0786447	C665	1
MC CLURE BOYD E	CW2	W-3440062	0867	1
MC CLURE COVER G	WO1	W-2107527	0445	2
MC CLURE DEL B	LTC	0-0299282	C867	3
MC CLURE EDWARD J	CW2	W-2147479	1165	1
MC CLURE ERNEST W	LTC	0-0303320	1066	1
MC CLURE FRANK	1LT	0-C487979	0247	1
MC CLURE FREEMAN C	COL	C-0352901	1155	3
MC CLURE HAROLD L	2LT	0-1174063	0544	2
MC CLURE HORACE F	MAJ	C-1118084	C763	1
MC CLURE JAMES E	LTC	0-1120690	C266	1
MC CLURE JR JOHN B	LTC	0-0390585	C661	1
MC CLURE LINWOOD O	COL	0-0201182	0346	1
MC CLURE NATHAN F	LTC	0-0233406	0455	3
MC CLURE ROBERT W	LTC	0-1290787	CR63	2
MC CLURE ROSS	CPT	0-0959295	0560	1
MC CLURE WALTER C	1LT	0-2008218	1046	1
MC CLURE WALTER M	CW3	W-2144122	0559	1
MC CLURE WILLIAM K	COL	0-0178072	1054	3
MC CLURE WILLIAM M	LTC	0-1287559	0767	1
MC CLURG DONALD C	LTC	0-1949398	C966	2
MC CLUSKEY DONALD W	LTC	0-1894525	C263	1
MC CLUSKEY EAMONN	MAJ	0-0463524	1262	1
MC CLUSKEY RAYMOND V	CPT	0-1885837	C464	1
MC CLUSKY BETTY A	2LT	N-0725170	C145	1
MC CLYMONT JAMES R	MAJ	C-1059196	0361	1
MC COACH JAMES R	COL	C-0397800	0363	2
MC COID CHESTER B	COL	C-049138C	CR55	2
MC COIN JOHN F	MAJ	0-0334907	0662	2
MC COLERY CHARLES O	CW4	W-2151050	C665	1
MC COLGAN AUGUST T	LTC	0-1288262	0463	1
MC COLL BETTY A	1LT	N-0777538	1047	1
MC COLL CHARLES O	COL	0-0199576	0854	1
MC COLLISTER WILEY C	LTC	0-0454461	0761	1
MC COLLOM LAWRENCE S	LTC	0-1182649	C466	3
MC COLLOM WALTER W	LTC	0-0143734	1053	3
MC COLLOUGH SOLOMON	CW3	W-2146260	0765	1
MC COLLOUGH VINCEN	LTC	0-0342131	0546	2
MC COLLOUGH WALTER W	MAJ	C-1002276	0860	1
MC COLLUM BERT H	2LT	0-1053718	0744	2
MC COLLUM CHARLES T	CPT	0-2033317	C961	1
MC COLLUM CLARENCE E	LTC	0-1297400	0167	1
MC COLLUM EDWARD E	LTC	0-0404477	0464	1
MC COLLUM JEFFERSON	MAJ	0-1311668	0761	1
MC COLLUM JOSEPH E	CPT	0-1292029	0656	1
MC COLLUM JR FRED	COL	0-0284525	1066	3
MC COLLUM MARVIN E	LTC	0-1284362	1060	1
MC COLLUM REGINALD F	LTC	0-1118611	1067	1
MC COLLUM VESTAL P	LTC	0-1999189	0966	1
MC COLLUM VINCENT F	CPT	0-0481730	0246	2
MC COLLUM VIRGIL C	LTC	0-0253307	0947	2
MC COLLUM WENDELL O	MAJ	0-0289493	0247	2
MC COLLUM WILLIAM A	CPT	0-0116966	0153	3
MC COLLUM WILLIAM R	LTC	0-1552329	0167	3
MC COLLY HARRY A	COL	0-0200788	0255	1
MC COLPIN JOHN J	LTC	0-2009519	1167	1
MC COMAS BEN CURTIS	LTC	0-1823182	1165	1
MC COMAS EARL W	LTC	0-0189237	1154	3
MC COMB ALLAN W	CPT	0-0121951	1057	3
MC COMBS BILLY D	WO1	W-3410032	0967	1

NAME	GRADE	SVC NO	DATE RET MO YR	RET CODE
MC COMBS GEORGE R	MAJ	0-1798032	0660	1
MC COMBS NELSON C	CPT	0-0226696	0561	3
MC COMBS NORA	CPT	N-0725526	0448	1
MC COMMAS DONALD R	CW3	W-2150998	0463	1
MC COMMONS JOHN L	LTC	0-0217543	0549	3
MC CONAHAY JAMES A	LTC	0-0396886	0463	1
MC CONAHAY JAMES F	CPT	0-0237254	1056	3
MC CONAHAY WILLIAM C	LTC	0-0192663	1160	3
MC CONATHY EDWARD W	1LT	0-1576352	0146	2
MC CONAUGHEY DONALD	CW3	W-2147766	0966	2
MC CONCHIE JAMES K	COL	0-0538843	1165	1
MC CONIGLY RALPH O	COL	0-0310314	0767	3
MC CONN EARLE M	LTC	0-1593372	0862	1
MC CONNAUGHEY W E	LTC	0-0226315	1048	3
MC CONNAUGHHAY CLY	MAJ	0-1017346	0657	1
MC CONNEL JOHN P	MAJ	0-1102305	0967	1
MC CONNELL CLIFFOR	1LT	0-2056244	0546	2
MC CONNELL DELMER M	MAJ	0-2263581	0967	1
MC CONNELL ELBRIDGE	MAJ	0-4031024	0667	1
MC CONNELL FREDERICK	LTC	0-0371580	0167	1
MC CONNELL GEORGE E	LTC	0-0366014	1160	1
MC CONNELL HAROLD	MAJ	0-0145954	0554	3
MC CONNELL KENDRED C	LTC	0-0452014	0564	1
MC CONNELL LESTER O	LTC	0-1047670	1061	1
MC CONNELL LOUIS F	MAJ	0-0228751	0161	3
MC CONNELL OSCAR L	CW4	W-2109167	0553	2
MC CONNELL PAUL H	LTC	0-1037146	0666	1
MC CONNELL RICHARD M	LTC	0-1053719	0363	1
MC CONNELL ULYSSES S	COL	0-0333553	0561	1
MC CONNELL WILFORD O	MAJ	0-0264042	0354	3
MC CONNELL WILLIAM H	1LT	0-1107579	0448	2
MC CONNICO JAMES R	LTC	0-1338260	0166	1
MC CONNICO JARRETT C	MAJ	C-1017643	0465	1
MC CONVILLE ROBERT W	LTC	0-1633395	0559	1
MC CONVILLE THOMAS P	CW2	W-2150843	0559	1
MC CODEY VINCENT R	LTC	0-1581925	0260	1
MC COOK FRANK W	COL	0-0182516	1154	3
MC COOL DOROTHY N	MAJ	N-0724182	0162	1
MC COOL JAMES D	1LT	0-1549544	1045	2
MC COOL JOHN C	CPT	0-0885080	0555	1
MC COPPIN MARGARET	1LT	N-0737759	0646	1
MC CORC ANDREW	CPT	0-1168811	0759	1
MC CORC CAREY P	COL	0-0198783	0648	3
MC CORC EDGAR B	LTC	0-1534332	1264	1
MC CORC JOSEPH F	LTC	0-0224378	C945	2
MC CORC JR ELMER C	LTC	0-1181688	1066	1
MC CORD JR JAMES A	LTC	0-0381252	0860	1
MC CORC JR NED J	MAJ	0-0927643	0664	1
MC CORC RICHARD F	CW3	W-2147235	0464	1
MC CORD WALTER B	LTC	0-0346197	0660	1
MC CORKELL GORDON W	1LT	0-0525037	C647	2
MC CORKLE BEN W	CPT	0-0285413	0845	2
MC CORKLE ROBERT L	1LT	0-100082C	0752	1
MC CORKLE ROBERT W	MAJ	0-0967561	0463	1
MC CORKLE STANLEY A	MAJ	0-0300541	1062	1
MC CORLEW THOMAS J	MAJ	0-1298415	1060	1
MC CORMAC PAUL C	MAJ	0-034468C	0744	2
MC CORMACK CHARLES R	MAJ	0-0266743	1066	3
MC CORMACK DELOS W	LTC	0-0217570	0962	3
MC CORMACK ELDRIDGE	1LT	0-0491635	1148	1
MC CORMACK FREDERICK	CPT	0-1644575	0950	1
MC CORMACK GEORGE W	COL	0-0372247	0964	1
MC CORMACK HARRIS A	LTC	0-1047226	0164	1
MC CORMACK HARRY E	MAJ	0-1590051	0563	1
MC CORMACK JAMES M	LTC	0-0328933	1264	3
MC CORMACK JOHN C	COL	0-0416702	0365	1
MC CORMACK JOHN F	CPT	0-0397790	1045	2
MC CORMACK JOHN J	CPT	0-1591919	0754	2
MC CORMACK JOSEPH L	LTC	0-1168362	0162	1
MC CORMACK RICHARD	MAJ	0-0546557	0765	1
MC CORMACK ROBERT C	MAJ	0-0738993	0761	1
MC CORMACK ROBERT H	LTC	0-0265678	0549	2
MC CORMACK WILBUR	LTC	0-1301339	0364	1
MC CORMICK ALFRED A	MAJ	0-1304089	1060	3
MC CORMICK ALVIN G	CPT	0-1319150	1056	2

NAME	GRADE	SVC NO	DATE RET MO YR	RET CODE
MC CORMICK CHARLES	B G	0-0332054	0760	3
MC CORMICK CHARLES	MAJ	0-0479972	0646	2
MC CORMICK CHARLES E	CPT	0-0255874	0247	2
MC CORMICK CHRISTI	COL	0-0187429	1052	3
MC CORMICK CYRUS	MAJ	0-0483798	0943	2
MC CORMICK DONALD W	MAJ	0-0374530	1145	2
MC CORMICK EDWARD C	LTC	0-0176896	0846	2
MC CORMICK EVERETT L	MAJ	0-0572263	0766	1
MC CORMICK FRANCIS W	LTC	0-0358779	0262	1
MC CORMICK GEORGE	COL	0-0261650	0457	1
MC CORMICK HARRY	CPT	0-0225025	0759	3
MC CORMICK HARRY W	COL	0-0373126	0255	1
MC CORMICK HOWARD W	LTC	0-1554234	1062	1
MC CORMICK JAMES E	LTC	0-1693201	0246	2
MC CORMICK JOHN F	MAJ	0-1329374	1262	1
MC CORMICK LARRY W	CW2	W-2108473	0360	1
MC CORMICK LEIGHTON	LTC	0-0284663	1166	3
MC CORMICK LEONARD E	LTC	0-0302663	0755	2
MC CORMICK MORRISON	MAJ	0-0278342	0166	3
MC CORMICK RAYMOND C	CW2	W-2102067	0650	1
MC CORMICK RICHARD F	1LT	0-1322460	0546	1
MC CORMICK ROGER S	1LT	0-1041612	0644	2
MC CORMICK STANLEY	CPT	0-0925006	0345	2
MC CORMICK TERRENCE	LTC	0-1288589	0366	1
MC CORMICK THOMAS A	CW2	W-3411034	1266	1
MC CORMICK THOMAS W	LTC	0-1331850	0767	1
MC CORMICK WILFRED	LTC	0-0242464	0363	3
MC CORMICK WILLARD P	1LT	0-0538968	0945	2
MC CORMICK WILLIAM B	COL	0-0253191	0958	3
MC CORMICK WILLIAM H	MAJ	0-1583349	0263	1
MC CORMICK WILLIAM J	LTC	0-0495281	1055	1
MC CORMICK WILLIAM J	CPT	0-2292797	1266	2
MC CORMICK WILLIAM L	LTC	0-0231435	0565	3
MC CORMICK WILLIAM N	MAJ	0-4002102	0856	2
MC CORQUODALE ERNEST	CPT	0-1010651	0346	2
MC CORT MERCEDES A	MAJ	N-0759212	0464	1
MC COUCH NELSON	LTC	0-1105006	0152	1
MC COUN WILEY F	LTC	0-0328057	1060	1
MC COURT KEITH D	LTC	0-0465261	1162	1
MC COWAN EOSEL B	CW2	W-2119613	0657	1
MC COWEN RICHARD H	1LT	0-0431737	0646	2
MC COWN JOHN R	1LT	0-0318818	0944	2
MC COWN LLOYD L	CW2	W-2208082	1060	1
MC COWN LORIN S	CPT	0-0419817	0345	2
MC COWN MARJORIE P	LTC	L-0903592	0766	1
MC COWN ROBERT E	LTC	0-0213659	0556	3
MC COY ANDREW R	MAJ	0-1643494	1160	1
MC COY ARTHUR M	COL	0-0263250	1066	3
MC COY BURRILL F	1LT	0-1108840	0544	2
MC COY CARL M	LTC	0-1170850	0264	1
MC COY CAROLYN L	CPT	N-0773604	0648	1
MC COY CLYDE H	LTC	0-0302972	0263	3
MC COY DON L	1LT	0-1949399	1046	2
MC COY DONALD R	2LT	0-4045463	0857	2
MC COY DOUGLAS O	LTC	0-0344588	1047	2
MC COY ELMER R	CW3	W-2147767	0157	1
MC COY FRED W	CW4	W-2141372	0164	1
MC COY FREDERICK	LTC	0-0569201	0464	1
MC COY GEORGE W	CW2	W-2145004	1165	2
MC COY GERARD J	CW3	W-2147040	0864	1
MC COY HUBERT V	COL	0-0229600	1264	3
MC COY JAMES E	CW3	W-2152084	0361	1
MC COY JAMES H	MAJ	0-1310475	0762	1
MC COY JOHN F	MAJ	0-0909446	1046	1
MC COY JOHN J	1LT	0-1284545	0445	2
MC COY JOSEPH G	1LT	0-1030801	1045	2
MC COY JR EDWIN D	LTC	0-0533707	0463	1
MC COY JR JAMES M	MAJ	0-1002675	0566	3
MC COY JR JOSEPH H	1LT	0-0535875	0346	2
MC COY JR WILLIAM H	MAJ	0-1039778	0661	2
MC COY KEITH L	CPT	0-0370775	0345	2
MC COY MICHELLE R	1LT	N-0720072	0545	1
MC COY PASCHAL G	CPT	0-0887358	0247	2
MC COY PAUL	CPT	0-2007115	1147	2
MC COY ROBERT C	COL	0-0277712	0858	3
MC COY ROGER W	LTC	0-1003579	1062	1
MC COY STATES D	COL	0-0240963	0963	3
MC COY THOMAS A	1LT	0-0449229	0645	2
MC COY TIMOTHY J	COL	0-0153439	0451	3
MC COY WAYNE W	LTC	0-2048700	0166	1
MC COY WILLIAM M	LTC	0-0253340	1046	1
MC COY WILLIE F	MAJ	0-0969608	0167	1
MC CRACKEN BLAKE D	CPT	0-1551268	1047	2
MC CRACKEN CAROL A	CW3	W-2207466	0865	1
MC CRACKEN DAVID H	CW4	W-2133587	1065	1
MC CRACKEN HENRY F	LTC	0-0246633	1066	3
MC CRACKEN IVAN L	LTC	0-0432930	0756	1
MC CRACKEN JOHN T	MAJ	0-1119054	0964	1
MC CRACKEN REED J	LTC	0-0315097	0161	1
MC CRACKEN RICHARD S	CPT	0-1302496	1046	1
MC CRACKEN ROBERT F	2LT	0-1061475	0645	2
MC CRACKEN ROY G	LTC	0-1293998	0461	1
MC CRACKEN SARA	MAJ	N-0722896	0262	1
MC CRACKEN THOMAS F	LTC	0-0253847	0560	1
MC CRACKEN WALTER M	LTC	0-0365788	1160	1
MC CRACKIN EDWARD O	COL	0-0341543	0163	1
MC CRAE JAMES L	COL	0-0243621	0766	3
MC CRANEY DONALD	MAJ	0-0496265	1046	2
MC CRANEY THOMAS R	LTC	0-1557639	1065	1
MC CRARY GEORGE J	CPT	0-1035531	0260	1
MC CRARY HARVEY P	CW4	W-2134372	0957	1
MC CRARY JOHN M	CPT	0-1297758	0546	2
MC CRARY JR ROY P	LTC	0-2018384	0965	1
MC CRARY LAMAR	MAJ	0-0961197	0962	1
MC CRARY LEON F	LTC	0-0336970	0358	1
MC CRARY MARTHA F	LTC	N-0746985	1064	3
MC CRARY MARY S	CPT	N-0703969	0147	1
MC CRARY PAUL F	MAJ	0-0375868	0847	2
MC CRARY WALTER R	CW2	W-2144737	0656	1
MC CRARY WILLIAM R	MAJ	0-1577546	0258	1
MC CRAVY HOWARD W	MAJ	0-0147620	0855	3
MC CRAW HENRY G	COL	0-0277836	1060	3
MC CRAW ROY	LTC	0-0949973	0966	1
MC CRAY WILLIAM L	MAJ	0-1545717	0464	2
MC CREA DONALD M	LTC	0-0279597	1159	3
MC CREA JOHN A	1LT	0-1018598	1045	2
MC CREA JOHN H	CPT	0-0369066	0346	2
MC CREA ROBERT L	LTC	0-1822596	0665	1
MC CREA WILLIAM C	MAJ	0-0505124	0546	2
MC CREA WILLIAM W	COL	0-0249454	0566	3
MC CREADY CHARLES L	MAJ	0-0174049	0862	3
MC CREADY CLOYD E	MAJ	0-0122131	1052	3
MC CREADY DONALD D	1LT	0-0558097	0946	2
MC CREADY NORMAN J	CW3	W-2142247	0459	1
MC CREADY RICHARD J	1LT	0-1170486	0545	2
MC CREARY GERALD F	CPT	0-1111772	0248	2
MC CREARY JAMES M	MAJ	0-1876653	0367	1
MC CREARY LEROY	CW3	W-2006677	0863	3
MC CREARY ROBERT N	LTC	0-0203633	0853	3
MC CREARY WALTER W	LTC	0-1297070	0963	1
MC CREEDY JOHN J	MAJ	0-0469512	0346	2
MC CREERY JR SAMUEL	1LT	0-1634123	1144	2
MC CREIGHT IAN H	CPT	0-0218159	0758	3
MC CREIGHT REX	CPT	0-2010756	0260	1
MC CRELLEN RICHARD W	CPT	0-2012722	0858	1
MC CRICHT HOWARD L	CW2	W-2211778	0667	1
MC CRORIE JACK F	MAJ	0-1290279	0962	1
MC CRORY JOHN P	LTC	0-0291858	1266	3
MC CRORY ROBERT L	LTC	0-0374470	0859	1
MC CRORY ROY L	MAJ	0-1338835	0165	1
MC CRORY WALTER E	LTC	0-0377910	0266	1
MC CROSKEY NEWELL M	1LT	0-1081431	0246	2
MC CRUM JOHN O	1LT	0-0212805	0363	3
MC CRUM PHILIP H	COL	0-0246129	0959	3
MC CRYSTAL WILLIAM	LTC	0-0124181	0754	2
MC CUBBIN JODIE L	WO1	W-2108904	0760	1
MC CUBBINS ELIZABETH	MAJ	N-0755913	1063	3
MC CUDDEN EDWARD W	CW3	W-2149083	0462	1
MC CUE EARL H	CW3	W-2152974	0760	1
MC CUE ELMER S	MAJ	0-0507980	1149	1
MC CUE FRANK P	COL	0-0327183	0260	3
MC CUE HAROLD E	LTC	0-1039097	1153	1
MC CUE JOHN D	1LT	0-0447040	0746	2
MC CUE LEO M	CW3	W-2152275	0165	1
MC CUE LESLIE L	LTC	0-0535162	1064	3
MC CUEN JOHN W	MAJ	0-0170554	0855	3
MC CUGH LONNIE F	MAJ	0-1326414	0465	1
MC CUGH SIMON R	MAJ	0-2262136	0663	1
MC CUISTION ARTHUR W	WO1	W-2150588	0158	1
MC CUISTON TREMON W	LTC	0-0363609	0262	1
MC CULLA JAMES A	1LT	0-1645192	0245	2
MC CULLACH GEORGE H	COL	0-0280873	0167	3
MC CULLAGH THOMAS J	2LT	0-0409930	0244	1
MC CULLEN MATTHEW L	1LT	0-1314164	0146	2
MC CULLERS CECIL M	MAJ	0-0984550	0963	1
MC CULLERS EDGAR W	CPT	0-0166284	0254	3
MC CULLEY GEORGE H	LTC	0-0151051	1049	3
MC CULLEY JAMES A	MAJ	0-0387210	0746	1
MC CULLEY WAYNE L	LTC	0-0266907	1165	3
MC CULLION FRANCIS E	MAJ	0-1644260	1154	1
MC CULLOCH C P	WO1	W-2129308	0945	2
MC CULLOCH FRANK A	COL	0-0279008	0360	1
MC CULLOCH HORACE W	MAJ	0-1014142	0261	1
MC CULLOCH JAMES E	MAJ	0-0443016	0649	1
MC CULLOCH JAMES H	1LT	0-0455526	1144	2
MC CULLOCH MARGARET	1LT	N-0789917	0747	1
MC CULLOCH MAXWELL A	MAJ	0-0885723	0657	1
MC CULLOGH WILLIAM P	CW3	W-2004988	1262	2
MC CULLOH KENNETH E	1LT	0-0549653	1045	2
MC CULLOUGH CAMPBE	COL	0-0154168	0648	3
MC CULLOUGH FRANCIS	CW4	W-2001663	1061	3
MC CULLOUGH GEORGE F	LTC	0-0380018	0546	2
MC CULLOUGH HAROLD E	MAJ	0-1302031	0266	1
MC CULLOUGH HAROLD T	COL	0-0107182	1155	3
MC CULLOUGH HAROLD W	LTC	0-0237770	0764	1
MC CULLOUGH HELEN A	CPT	N-0742568	0351	2
MC CULLOUGH JACK D	MAJ	0-0450390	0853	1
MC CULLOUGH JAMES	MAJ	0-1298893	0760	1
MC CULLOUGH JAMES D	LTC	0-0227185	1064	3
MC CULLOUGH JESSE F	2LT	0-1055666	0145	2
MC CULLOUGH JOHN R	COL	0-0313702	0467	1
MC CULLOUGH JOSEPH F	MAJ	0-1320387	0565	1
MC CULLOUGH JR HIRAM	LTC	0-0225917	0265	3
MC CULLOUGH LORY L	MAJ	0-1289780	0958	1
MC CULLOUGH LOYD	CW4	W-2107071	1163	2
MC CULLOUGH MAURICE	LTC	0-0255774	0963	3
MC CULLOUGH ROBERT	LTC	0-0175073	0953	3
MC CULLOUGH THOMAS L	COL	0-0147345	0648	3
MC CULLOUGH WILLIA	MAJ	0-1636882	0855	1
MC CULLOUGH WILLIAM	2LT	0-1315595	0944	2
MC CUMBER JAMES B	COL	0-0183405	1060	3
MC CUNE GERALD F	2LT	0-1031007	0745	2
MC CUNE JAMES P	CW3	W-3150405	0767	1
MC CUNE MARVIN H	LTC	0-0301714	0359	3
MC CUNE WILLIAM W	CPT	0-0278276	1045	2
MC CURDY CHARLES F	MAJ	0-1101108	1164	1
MC CURDY DAVID S	LTC	0-0346463	0660	1
MC CURDY FORMAN D	LTC	0-0190598	1161	3
MC CURDY HARLEY F	CW3	W-2143034	1263	2
MC CURDY JOHN A	LTC	0-1038237	0764	1
MC CURDY JOHN E	CPT	0-1825151	0156	1
MC CURDY JOHN G	LTC	0-0328047	0560	1
MC CURDY LLOYD L	CPT	0-2018196	0358	1
MC CURDY RICHARD F	1LT	0-1323454	1045	2
MC CURDY ROBERT S	LTC	0-1168366	0666	1
MC CURDY WILLIAM C	LTC	0-0147713	0255	3
MC CURRY CLARENCE O	COL	0-0359032	0852	1
MC CURRY EDWARD R	LTC	0-1534561	0561	1
MC CUSKER ALOYSIUS E	CPT	0-0451145	0849	1
MC CUSKER GEORGE A	1LT	0-0275648	0158	3
MC CUSKER JOHN T	2LT	0-1325163	0844	2
MC CUSKER JOSEPH A	COL	0-0126170	0653	3
MC CUSKER JOSEPH X	1LT	0-1306443	0350	1
MC CUSKER SYLVESTER	1LT	0-2049017	0756	1
MC CUSKEY CHARLES F	LTC	0-0236487	1053	3
MC CUSKEY JOHN M	MAJ	0-0262280	0246	2
MC CUTCHAN HOWARD F	LTC	0-0344358	0647	2
MC CUTCHEN CHARLES C	CPT	0-0192285	1159	3
MC CUTCHEN DONALD P	LTC	0-0401632	0964	1
MC CUTCHEON GEORGE L	CPT	0-0155568	0452	3
MC CUTCHEON WILLIAM	LTC	0-1314372	0166	1
MC DADE WILLIAM P	CW2	W-2151426	0361	1
MC DANIEL ALVA F	1LT	N-0735986	0745	1
MC DANIEL CECIL A	LTC	0-1048899	1167	1
MC DANIEL CHARLES D	COL	0-0039696	1060	1
MC DANIEL DONOVAN	CPT	0-0405850	1150	1
MC DANIEL EARL	MAJ	0-2212074	0565	1
MC DANIEL EDWARD M	1LT	0-1648596	1045	2
MC DANIEL EDWARD P	CPT	0-0436256	0845	2
MC DANIEL EMERY	CPT	0-0316926	0943	2
MC DANIEL EUGENE	1LT	0-1554589	0450	1
MC DANIEL FAY A	CW3	W-2145472	0760	1
MC DANIEL GEORGE W	LTC	0-0251650	0663	1
MC DANIEL HAROLD C	LTC	0-0922439	0857	2
MC DANIEL HAROLD L	CPT	0-1182419	1164	2
MC DANIEL HARRY W	MAJ	0-1167533	0261	1
MC DANIEL J ZEB	LTC	0-0248095	0267	3
MC DANIEL JAMES C	CPT	0-1293442	0346	2
MC DANIEL JAMES H	LTC	0-1290788	0561	1
MC DANIEL JAMES W	CW4	W-2149197	0367	1
MC DANIEL JOHN F	CPT	0-1594324	1045	2
MC DANIEL LESTER G	CW2	W-2148747	0760	1
MC DANIEL MILTON R	CW3	W-2151500	0266	1
MC DANIEL MONTE	2LT	0-0485670	1161	1
MC DANIEL OLIVER H	LTC	0-0292637	1060	2
MC DANIEL PAUL H	CPT	0-0545107	0445	1
MC DANIEL PAUL L	CPT	0-0329160	0757	3
MC DANIEL PRESTON	CW2	W-3430038	1163	1
MC DANIEL RAYMOND F	CPT	0-0293473	0746	2
MC DANIEL ROBERT B	LTC	0-1182420	0960	1
MC DANIEL ROBERT C	CW4	W-2116976	0567	1
MC DANIEL ROBERT T	LTC	0-0265137	0560	1
MC DANIEL ROBERT W	MAJ	0-0255147	0262	3
MC DANIEL TALBOT A	1LT	0-1645804	0746	1
MC DANIEL VICTOR L	CPT	0-0975623	0665	2
MC DANIEL VIRGINIA	MAJ	N-0751103	0560	2
MC DANIEL WILMER K	COL	0-0224058	0760	1
MC DANIELS ARTHUR W	COL	0-0188426	0454	3
MC DANIELS ELMER L	CW2	W-2141993	0452	1
MC DANIELS FRANK L	MAJ	0-0179945	0155	3
MC DANIELS LYNN L	1LT	0-1822163	1045	2
MC DANIELS ORRIN D	LTC	0-0403714	0860	1
MC DAVITT JEROME A	LTC	0-0307358	0254	2
MC DAVITT JOHN F	2LT	0-1822814	1144	2
MC DEARMON GLADYS	CPT	N-0703278	0946	1
MC DEARMON LACY H	MAJ	0-0226841	0764	3
MC DERMOTT BERNICE M	1LT	N-0723881	0546	1
MC DERMOTT CLARENCE	1LT	0-1686506	1162	2
MC DERMOTT EDWARD E	LTC	0-1302032	0263	1
MC DERMOTT EDWARD T	1LT	0-1047228	1045	2
MC DERMOTT EMERSON M	COL	0-0356361	1058	1
MC DERMOTT FRANCIS O	WO1	W-2129264	1060	2
MC DERMOTT FRANCIS L	CPT	0-1015749	0966	2
MC DERMOTT JAMES P	CPT	0-1055383	0358	1
MC DERMOTT JAMES R	1LT	0-1060555	0746	1
MC DERMOTT JOHN F	LTC	0-1053249	0565	1
MC DERMOTT JOHN R	CPT	0-1924102	0763	1
MC DERMOTT MARY C	MAJ	N-0737504	0465	3
MC DERMOTT RAYMOND M	LTC	0-1101948	0863	2
MC DERMOTT RICHARD L	MAJ	0-1796117	0259	1
MC DERMOTT ROBERT F	LTC	0-2032856	0867	1
MC DERMOTT THOMAS C	COL	0-0200834	1155	3
MC DERMOTT VINCENT T	LTC	0-0439550	0146	2
MC DERMOTT WALTER J	CPT	0-1311413	0947	2
MC DEVITT DONALD I	LTC	0-1057523	0867	1
MC DEVITT FREDERICK	CPT	0-0518401	1145	2
MC DEVITT JAMES C	LTC	0-0408125	0965	1
MC DEVITT JOSEPH F	MAJ	0-1043421	0463	1
MC DEVITT RICHARD J	LTC	0-1894897	0861	1
MC DEVITT WILLIAM A	CW2	W-2206883	0167	1

NAME	GRADE	SVC NO	DATE RET MO YR	RET CODE
MC DEWELL DONALD S	1LT	0-0971748	0967	1
MC DIARMID JAMES C J	CPT	0-0524999	1143	1
MC DILL BRUCE M	MAJ	0-0175725	C851	3
MC DIVITT ARCHIE L	COL	0-0411347	0465	1
MC DONALD ADAM M	LTC	0-0498558	1162	1
MC DONALD ALMA F	2LT	N-0721223	1045	1
MC DONALD ARTHUR W	CPT	C-0244764	0462	3
MC DONALD CARL D	CW3	W-2149823	0664	1
MC DONALD CARSON C	CW4	W-2109052	C659	1
MC DONALD CLARENCE M	LTC	0-1011380	0464	1
MC DONALD CRAWFORD J	MAJ	0-2208555	0664	1
MC DONALD DAVID A	CPT	C-0519552	C146	2
MC DONALD DONALD L	CW3	W-2151849	0664	1
MC DONALD EARL B	MAJ	0-0355869	0563	1
MC DONALD EARL F	MAJ	0-0965426	0762	1
MC DONALD EARL L	MAJ	0-0356461	C653	1
MC DONALD EDWARD C J	MAJ	0-0381170	C646	2
MC DONALD ERNEST O	LTC	0-0409118	0761	1
MC DONALD EUGENE P	LTC	0-1057165	0262	1
MC DONALD FREEMAN W	CPT	0-1320855	C947	2
MC DONALD GEORGE	CW3	W-2103196	0260	1
MC DONALD GEORGE C	1LT	0-1947774	0247	2
MC DONALD HAROLD J	CPT	0-1298567	0461	2
MC DONALD HAROLD R	MAJ	0-1826423	0860	1
MC DONALD HARRY A	CPT	0-0117938	1053	3
MC DONALD HELEN C	MAJ	N-0759287	1061	2
MC DONALD HENRY T	MAJ	C-1110014	1264	1
MC DONALD HERBERT F	CW3	W-2147580	0564	1
MC DONALD HURLEY M	LTC	0-0450995	0562	1
MC DONALD JACK A	MAJ	C-1105664	0662	1
MC DONALD JACK W	LTC	0-0450996	0559	1
MC DONALD JAMES A	CPT	0-0499494	C347	1
MC DONALD JAMES A	LTC	0-1284001	0652	1
MC DONALD JAMES R	LTC	0-1329609	1262	1
MC DONALD JAMES D	2LT	0-1311033	0445	1
MC DONALD JAMES E	2LT	0-1038758	1044	2
MC DONALD JAMES J	CW2	W-2150354	0265	1
MC DONALD JOE M	1LT	0-0493519	0951	1
MC DONALD JOHN A	LTC	0-0164909	0855	3
MC DONALD JOHN A	LTC	0-0445823	0954	1
MC DONALD JOHN E	LTC	0-0236717	0365	3
MC DONALD JOHN E	CW3	W-2152145	0367	1
MC DONALD JOHN H	LTC	0-0162206	1060	3
MC DONALD JOHN R	LTC	0-1301002	0566	1
MC DONALD JOHN R	CW3	W-2141632	0659	1
MC DONALD JOHN T	CW3	W-2145357	1165	1
MC DONALD JOHN W	CW3	W-2112250	0757	1
MC DONALD JOSEPH F	LTC	0-1172987	1055	2
MC DONALD JR ARCH	MAJ	0-2001049	C263	1
MC DONALD JR CRAIG W	LTC	0-0376899	1262	1
MC DONALD JR HENRY S	COL	0-0946426	0558	1
MC DONALD KENNETH D	LTC	C-2014896	0966	1
MC DONALD MALCOLM W	CPT	0-1947262	1046	1
MC DONALD MARTIN H	CPT	0-1307126	0947	2
MC DONALD MAURICE H	MAJ	0-1062859	C762	1
MC DONALD MICHAEL	CW2	W-2144976	0157	1
MC DONALD NORTON L	LTC	C-0255929	0759	1
MC DONALD PAULINUS E	CPT	0-0236950	C166	3
MC DONALD QUINTON	CW4	W-2114216	C859	2
MC DONALD RALPH M	CPT	0-1684861	1145	1
MC DONALD RAYMOND J	CW4	W-2003849	0661	3
MC DONALD RICHARD F	LTC	0-0330379	1064	2
MC DONALD ROBERT A	LTC	0-1309781	C865	1
MC DONALD ROBERT F	COL	0-0371299	0261	1
MC DONALD ROBERT H	LTC	0-0163537	C349	3
MC DONALD ROBERT H	LTC	0-2051511	0166	1
MC DONALD ROBERT R	LTC	0-0294047	0660	1
MC DONALD ROGER W	CPT	C-2002072	0860	1
MC DONALD ROLLAND M	CW3	W-2146195	C560	1
MC DONALD RONALD B	LTC	C-0504455	1064	3
MC DONALD RONALD J	LTC	0-0172029	1046	1
MC DONALD ROSE M	1LT	N-0760246	1045	1
MC DONALD ROYCE C	MAJ	0-1300194	C161	1
MC DONALD THOMAS E	1LT	0-0380019	0144	2
MC DONALD THOMAS H	2LT	0-1913546	0447	1

NAME	GRADE	SVC NO	DATE RET MO YR	RET CODE
MC DONALD WALTER F	LTC	0-0352921	0258	1
MC DONALD WARD H	LTC	0-0407980	1166	1
MC DONALD WARREN R	MAJ	C-2001792	1061	1
MC DONALD WILLARD A	COL	0-0245131	0560	1
MC DONALD WILLIAM A	LTC	0-0158403	0150	3
MC DONALD WILLIAM A	LTC	0-1174951	1162	1
MC DONALD WILLIAM B	MAJ	0-0237919	0865	3
MC DONALD WILLIAM W	LTC	0-1323386	C567	2
MC DONALD WILLIS F	LTC	0-1011226	1163	1
MC DONELL GEORGE F	LTC	0-1296726	0860	1
MC DONELL JOHN P	MAJ	0-1058602	0261	1
MC DONIE CARL E	CPT	0-1294341	0346	2
MC DONNELL ALAN J	LTC	0-0489303	0766	3
MC DONNELL FRANCIS J	CW2	W-2146202	0966	1
MC DONNELL GEORGE O	2LT	0-2026996	0448	2
MC DONNELL JOHN P	LTC	0-1110111	1262	1
MC DONNELL JOHN P	CPT	0-1297759	0348	2
MC DONNELL JOSEPH W	2LT	0-0964878	1158	2
MC DONNELL JR H E	1LT	0-1289607	0246	2
MC DONNELL JR J F	CPT	0-1104294	1045	2
MC DONNELL ROBERT E	LTC	0-1018666	0962	1
MC DONNELL ROBERT F	CPT	0-1320065	0946	2
MC DONNELL THOMAS J	1LT	0-0346333	0842	2
MC DONNELL WILLIAM D	LTC	0-1299169	0754	1
MC DONOUGH CHARLES E	COL	0-0284143	1065	3
MC DONOUGH DANIEL J	LTC	0-1174066	0766	1
MC DONOUGH EDWARD M	1LT	0-1306618	1045	2
MC DONOUGH EDWARD W	MAJ	C-2017567	0965	1
MC DONOUGH FRANCIS T	1LT	0-1294885	0846	1
MC DONOUGH JOHN F	LTC	0-0102249	0256	3
MC DONOUGH JOHN H	CPT	0-1320151	0347	2
MC DONOUGH JOSEPH A	COL	0-0168267	0955	2
MC DONOUGH MARK D	LTC	0-0507398	0658	2
MC DONOUGH MILES V	LTC	0-0405071	0263	1
MC DONOUGH MENA	2LT	N-0727261	1144	1
MC DONOUGH RAYMOND E	LTC	0-1290102	0661	1
MC DONOUGH REDMOND A	LTC	0-1548496	1062	1
MC DONOUGH ROGERS M	LTC	0-0178544	0853	3
MC DONOUGH THOMAS J	CW3	W-2145973	0962	1
MC DONOUGH WILLIAM	1LT	0-1305956	0246	1
MC DONOUGH WILLIAM P	CW2	W-2149299	0760	1
MC DOUGAL HUBERT H	CPT	0-0468096	0246	2
MC DOUGAL LEO F	CPT	0-1587450	0860	2
MC DOUFALD CHARLIE	CW2	W-2152901	0161	1
MC DOUGALL BILLY E	1LT	0-1174953	0844	2
MC DOUGALL CHAUNCY L	CW3	W-2146078	0162	1
MC DOUGALL FRANCIS J	CPT	0-0471831	0945	2
MC DOUGALL HARRY G	COL	0-0287998	0359	1
MC DOUGALL LINDSAY M	CPT	0-0376236	0344	2
MC DOUGLE RAMEN E	CW4	W-2115564	0367	1
MC DOULETT RAYMOND P	CW2	W-2208646	1064	1
MC DOW ALLEN C	CW2	W-2150955	0358	1
MC DOWALL GRAVES H	MAJ	C-0308995	1161	2
MC DOWALL RAYMOND G	CW3	W-2151887	0461	1
MC DOWELL CARL A	CPT	0-0227238	1061	3
MC DOWELL CHARLES K	CW3	W-2141786	0863	1
MC DOWELL CLIFFORD	MAJ	0-0291046	0945	2
MC DOWELL DOUGLAS B	CPT	0-1687007	1045	2
MC DOWELL EDWARD H	CPT	0-1699979	0161	1
MC DOWELL ELISE	2LT	N-0738030	0745	1
MC DOWELL EUGENE A	LTC	0-0385323	0657	1
MC DOWELL EVALYN S	MAJ	N-0742447	0263	1
MC DOWELL HARVEY F	MAJ	0-0309571	0863	3
MC DOWELL JOHN D	1LT	0-1038064	0947	2
MC DOWELL JOUETT S	LTC	0-0281115	1067	3
MC DOWELL JR JAMES G	1LT	0-1845762	0647	2
MC DOWELL MALCOLM H	LTC	0-0454756	0261	1
MC DOWELL NEWTON D	LTC	0-1296065	0363	1
MC DOWELL PETER C	LTC	0-1315086	0762	1
MC DOWELL ROBERT L	CW3	W-2146414	1167	1
MC DOWELL VERN A	CPT	0-1020037	0965	2
MC DOWELL WALTER J	LTC	0-1035939	0767	1
MC DOWELL WILLIAM F	MAJ	0-1796978	0658	1
MC DOWELL WILLIAM J	1LT	0-1042647	0744	2
MC DUFF ALVIE L	COL	0-0357360	0960	1

NAME	GRADE	SVC NO	DATE RET MO YR	RET CODE
MC DUFF GRACY A	MAJ	0-1101573	0861	1
MC DUFF MELVIN A	COL	0-0389808	C265	1
MC DUFFEE DONALD V	LTC	0-0405689	0665	1
MC DUFFEE JAMES M	LTC	0-0214855	C562	3
MC DUFFEY JOHN C	CW3	W-2153657	0167	1
MC DUFFIE JR JAMES H	1LT	0-0407302	0645	2
MC DUFFIE JR LEON C	LTC	0-0904980	C566	3
MC EACHERAN DONALD	CPT	0-0154159	0854	3
MC EACHERN CHARLES	CPT	0-0525795	C252	2
MC EACHIN RAYMOND R	MAJ	0-1685541	0461	1
MC EADDY JAMES D	MAJ	C-0510366	1052	3
MC ELDOWNEY JOSEPH H	LTC	0-1638037	C663	1
MC ELDOWNEY ROBERT R	CPT	0-0241390	C648	3
MC ELFISH CHARLES J	MAJ	0-2037283	1065	1
MC ELHANEY EMERSON	CPT	0-0389032	C544	2
MC ELHANNON JAMES E	1LT	0-0445775	0745	2
MC ELHENY CLAIR C	COL	0-0260113	1263	3
MC ELHERNE FRANK P	CW4	W-2112334	0559	1
MC ELHOE ALBERT B	COL	0-0299566	0646	2
MC ELLIGOTT THOMAS J	CPT	0-0460436	1146	2
MC ELMURRAY GEORGE L	LTC	0-0357849	1059	1
MC ELREE JOHN W	CW3	W-2146406	0463	1
MC ELROY ALLEN A	LTC	0-1293443	0865	1
MC ELROY CECIL B J	LTC	0-1170856	1060	1
MC ELROY DANIEL R	CPT	C-1595691	C846	2
MC ELROY GEORGE E	LTC	0-0382834	0763	1
MC ELROY JAMES P	CPT	0-0423733	1048	2
MC ELROY JOHN H	LTC	0-0279254	0758	1
MC ELROY JUSTIN	LTC	0-0231562	0955	3
MC ELROY ORVAL J	CW2	W-2150574	1062	1
MC ELROY RAYMOND	CPT	0-0421460	1046	2
MC ELROY RUTH K	MAJ	N-0738032	C162	1
MC ELROY THEODORE J	CW4	W-2136574	0559	1
MC ELVANY GRAYSON E	MAJ	0-1999928	C656	1
MC ELWAINE EDWARD M	MAJ	0-1587451	0466	1
MC ELWEE DAWSON	CW4	W-2100019	0661	1
MC ELWEE PINCKNEY G	COL	0-0311642	0958	3
MC ELYEA ATWOOD M	2LT	0-2046692	0345	1
MC ELYEA BENNIE A	MAJ	0-0243947	C463	3
MC ENANY FRANCIS R	LTC	0-0400133	0860	1
MC ENDARFER MYRON E	MAJ	0-0256953	0264	3
MC ENEANY WILLIAM J	MAJ	0-0395349	0164	1
MC ENIRY CHARLES T	COL	C-0122041	C454	3
MC ENIRY DANIEL N	LTC	0-0122040	0648	3
MC ENROE ROBERT A	CW3	W-2143141	C262	1
MC ENTEE EDWARD J	LTC	0-0889069	C857	1
MC ENTEE JAMES J	LTC	0-1554235	1061	1
MC ENTYRE CLINTON F	LTC	0-0412865	0457	1
MC EOWEN ALMOND B	CPT	0-2002177	0357	1
MC EVER WILLIAM H	1LT	C-0359219	C542	2
MC EVILLA JAMES A	CW2	W-2213452	0767	1
MC EVOY DUDLEY J	LTC	0-0414602	C254	1
MC EVOY FRANK	MAJ	0-0456287	C646	2
MC EVOY FRED L	CW3	W-2005337	1066	1
MC EVOY HAROLD T	CW4	W-2006275	1065	3
MC EVOY JOHN A	COL	0-0336830	1065	3
MC EVOY RICHARD T	LTC	0-0349773	C860	1
MC EWAN DONALD H	LTC	0-1545623	C467	1
MC EWAN GERALD J	LTC	0-1535236	0964	1
MC EWAN JOHN J	LTC	0-0478042	1144	2
MC EWAN JOHN W	2LT	0-1113354	C844	2
MC EWEN CARL C	CPT	0-1298895	1060	1
MC EWEN LAURENCE B	LTC	C-0174538	C860	3
MC EWEN WILLIAM C	LTC	0-1639625	0563	1
MC FADDEN ALICE W	MAJ	R-0001330	C167	3
MC FADDEN DAVID J	COL	0-0224689	0457	1
MC FADDEN EMORY L	1LT	0-1549328	C466	3
MC FADDEN FRANK J	LTC	0-1284002	C864	1
MC FADDEN JOHN R	1LT	0-1315087	0146	2
MC FADDEN PHILLIP C	CW3	W-2152853	0164	1
MC FADDEN ROBERT E	MAJ	0-1174374	C446	2
MC FADDEN ROGER R	1LT	0-1109503	0947	2
MC FADDEN VINCENT B	LTC	0-0325707	C948	1
MC FADDEN VINCENT G	COL	0-0299871	0965	3
MC FADDEN WILLIAM G	CW3	W-2144408	C365	1

NAME	GRADE	SVC NO	DATE RET MO YR	RET CODE
MC FADDIN EDWARD F	CPT	0-0101996	1054	3
MC FADDIN NORMAN J	CPT	0-0383141	0260	2
MC FADIN OSCAR L	LTC	0-2027777	C962	1
MC FADYEN WILLIAM B	COL	C-0305737	1065	1
MC FALL STANLEY H	2LT	0-1798170	0146	2
MC FALL ELMER P	CPT	0-1180255	0559	1
MC FALL LOUISE A	MAJ	N-0800079	0765	1
MC FALL RUSSELL K	CW3	W-2114843	0154	1
MC FARLAND A J	MAJ	C-0970667	0859	1
MC FARLAND COWAN A	MAJ	C-0194249	1046	1
MC FARLAND ERWIN V	CW3	W-2153069	1164	1
MC FARLAND FRED C	COL	0-0133539	0758	3
MC FARLAND GEORGE H	LTC	0-1165651	0459	1
MC FARLAND HARRY L	MAJ	0-0973920	0863	1
MC FARLAND HENRY T	CW3	W-2120181	0962	1
MC FARLAND J B	CW2	W-2210216	1061	1
MC FARLAND JAMES E	MAJ	0-0463931	0165	1
MC FARLAND JAMES F	CPT	0-0243125	0854	3
MC FARLAND JOHN W	MAJ	0-2055144	0155	1
MC FARLAND JR JOHN R	MAJ	0-0452232	0346	2
MC FARLAND NELSON	1LT	0-1320757	C746	2
MC FARLAND OTTIS H	MAJ	0-0284262	0167	3
MC FARLAND PAUL T	LTC	0-0294516	1056	3
MC FARLAND ROBERT D	CPT	0-1298896	0346	2
MC FARLAND ROBERT M	COL	0-0290787	0561	3
MC FARLAND WILBUR G	MAJ	0-1582743	0562	1
MC FARLAND WILLIAM	1LT	C-0391923	C751	1
MC FARLANE PAUL S	LTC	0-1597193	1163	1
MC FARLANE SAMUEL J	1LT	0-1914062	1043	2
MC FARLIN GEORGE C	LTC	0-0265945	0958	3
MC FATE JR THOMAS J	1LT	0-1726015	0945	2
MC FAUL MARY E	MAJ	N-0756367	0463	1
MC FEE ALBERT A	CPT	0-0497458	0147	1
MC FEE WALTER E	LTC	0-0186770	0648	3
MC FEELY KENNETH D	MAJ	0-1317985	0563	2
MC FERREN ROBERT H	CPT	0-0552332	1163	2
MC FETRIDGE CAROL F	CPT	0-0582909	0162	1
MC GAFFIGAN JAMES A	CPT	0-0337537	0646	2
MC GAHA CHARLES L	MAJ	C-2027823	1061	1
MC GAHAN PAUL J	COL	C-0147271	1048	3
MC GAHEE NELSON M	CW3	W-2111947	1160	1
MC GALLIARD ALEXAN	LTC	0-0450957	1154	1
MC GALLIARD ANDREW H	CPT	0-0546043	0147	2
MC GANN WILLIAM G	MAJ	0-2007207	0561	1
MC GARR ROBERT L	WO1	W-2108903	0258	1
MC GARRETT ADDISON M	CW3	W-2144922	0462	1
MC GARRIGLE JOHN T	CW3	W-2139937	0860	1
MC GARRIGLE ROBERT J	CW2	W-2146925	1061	1
MC GARRY GERALD J	MAJ	0-1573408	0549	1
MC GARRY GERARD B	LTC	0-1584582	0666	1
MC GARRY JOSEPH J	LTC	0-1796979	0465	1
MC GARRY ROBERT L	1LT	0-1110653	0545	2
MC GARRY WILLIAM F	LTC	0-1045519	0762	1
MC GARRY WILLIAM L	LTC	0-1794971	0764	1
MC GARVEY EDMUND F	CW3	W-2152242	1063	1
MC GARVEY HERSCHEL G	MAJ	0-0889254	1264	1
MC GARVEY JOSEPH A	CW2	W-2146715	1263	1
MC GARVEY RICHARD C	COL	0-0454747	0464	1
MC GARVEY SAMUEL E	CW4	W-2141821	0861	1
MC GARVEY WILLIAM G	LTC	0-1104296	0563	1
MC GARY JOHN O	LTC	0-1594326	0366	1
MC GAUGHEY KENNETH E	MAJ	0-1688598	0865	1
MC GAUGHEY MUNSEY	CPT	0-0112074	0655	3
MC GAUHEY MILTON G	MAJ	C-0979702	0666	1
MC GAVOCK FRANCIS J	2LT	0-0979239	0352	1
MC GAW CHARLES F	2LT	0-1845067	1144	2
MC GEE CARL D	COL	0-0372381	0462	3
MC GEE CHARLES E	LTC	0-1535373	1162	1
MC GEE CHARLES F	2LT	0-1698164	0245	2
MC GEE CHARLES L	LTC	0-0254009	0862	3
MC GEE EDWARD F	2LT	0-1031899	0146	2
MC GEE ERNEST T	CW4	W-2142595	1265	1
MC GEE HOKE S	LTC	0-1546645	1262	1
MC GEE JR HENRY J	MAJ	0-1047673	1158	1
MC GEE JR JAMES E	LTC	0-1182191	1062	1

ARMY OF THE UNITED STATES RETIRED LIST

NAME	GRADE	SVC NO	DATE RET MO YR	RET CODE
MC GEE JR JOSEPH B	COL	0-0294448	1160	1
MC GEE JR WILLIAM N	1LT	0-0392655	0146	2
MC GEE LAWRENCE E	MAJ	0-1302846	0261	1
MC GEE MILOREO K	MAJ	N-0772393	0754	2
MC GEE MORGAN B	MAJ	0-1294655	0760	1
MC GEE MORRIS L	CPT	0-0984063	1060	1
MC GEE RALPH W	1LT	0-0518870	1045	2
MC GEE RAYMONO	WO1	W-2005939	1058	3
MC GEE REECE J	COL	0-0171858	1149	3
MC GEE ROBERT J	WO1	W-2129965	0846	2
MC GEE WILLIAM	1LT	0-0341168	C154	1
MC GEE WILLIAM B	LTC	0-0142948	1056	3
MC GEE ZETTIE A	1LT	N-0735187	C546	1
MC GEECHAN JAMES F	1LT	0-1315596	0146	2
MC GEHEE HARRY C	1LT	0-0546134	0846	2
MC GEHEE JR TURNER A	1LT	0-1010200	0146	2
MC GEHEE MARIA T	2LT	N-0702257	0635	1
MC GEHEE ROBERT J	1LT	0-0531122	1145	2
MC GERROW SAMUEL V	LTC	0-0327506	0661	2
MC GHEE OEWARO A	MAJ	0-1169641	1060	1
MC GHEE DONALD E	CW3	W-2145047	0164	1
MC GHEE EARL R	CPT	0-0109996	0755	3
MC GHEE JR AOOISON F	COL	0-0258592	C867	3
MC GHEE LEWIS M	MAJ	0-0270041	0447	1
MC GHEE ROBERT B	LTC	0-1824779	0466	1
MC GIBONEY CAVID P	1LT	0-1288773	0945	2
MC GILL ALFRED A	CPT	0-1895941	0567	3
MC GILL ALLAN C	LTC	0-1300350	C466	1
MC GILL ARTHUR A	LTC	C-0206031	0547	1
MC GILL OONALO K	COL	0-0436996	0462	1
MC GILL GRANT J	LTC	0-0276984	C855	3
MC GILL KENNETH H	LTC	0-1581253	1167	1
MC GILL LLOYO O	CPT	0-0885645	1147	2
MC GILL RICHARO H	CW4	W-2105469	0259	1
MC GILLICUOCY L D	LTC	C-1167538	1166	3
MC GILVERY LAWRENCE	CPT	C-0346408	C667	3
MC GILVRAY HAROLO R	CW3	W-2141633	1057	1
MC GILVRAY JOHN W	COL	0-0221838	C247	1
MC GIMPSEY WILLIAM T	CW4	W-2107942	C155	1
MC GIMSEY CECIL F	LTC	0-0252748	0649	1
MC GINITY JOSEPH T	CPT	0-1166132	0745	2
MC GINLEY ALICE C	MAJ	N-0720230	0461	1
MC GINLEY VINCENT J	MAJ	0-2014910	C167	1
MC GINN GEORGE F	COL	0-0145960	0853	1
MC GINN HAROLO J	MAJ	0-0125100	1051	3
MC GINN JOHN P	MAJ	C-0481291	0546	2
MC GINN JOSEPH G	LTC	0-1794829	0561	1
MC GINN JOSEPH L	MAJ	0-1167539	0364	1
MC GINN KATHLEEN	MAJ	N-0758486	C864	1
MC GINN MICHAEL J	MAJ	0-1635071	C648	1
MC GINNESS GEORGE L	LTC	C-0239807	0765	3
MC GINNESS JOHN A	MAJ	C-0520277	1146	2
MC GINNESS JOHN S	MAJ	0-1047229	1059	2
MC GINNIS EARL L	CW2	W-2124653	1045	2
MC GINNIS ECWARO J	CPT	0-0510084	1147	1
MC GINNIS EVERETT O	CW3	W-2146453	0760	1
MC GINNIS FRANCIS O	WO1	W-2139513	0745	2
MC GINNIS FREDERIC D	LTC	0-0261253	1262	1
MC GINNIS JOHN L	LTC	0-0422060	0547	1
MC GINNIS MARION L	CW3	W-2148211	0962	1
MC GINNIS PATRICK F	COL	C-1286326	0764	1
MC GINNIS PAUL W	1LT	0-1302847	C945	2
MC GINNIS ROBERT C	WO1	W-2139949	1145	2
MC GINNIS VINCENT F	MAJ	0-1165419	C461	1
MC GINNIS WILLIAM A	MAJ	0-1557328	0959	3
MC GINNIS WILLIAM H	CPT	C-0323291	1054	3
MC GINNIS WILLIAM H	MAJ	C-0491661	0546	1
MC GINTY GEORGE E	CPT	0-0524853	1146	2
MC GINTY HOWARO C	MAJ	0-0341155	C246	2
MC GINTY RICHARO R	LTC	0-1549330	C864	1
MC GINTY THOMAS F	MAJ	0-1822033	0164	1
MC GINTY WILLIAM R	MAJ	0-1584057	C146	2
MC GIRL JOHN J	MAJ	0-0138383	C853	3
MC GIRR JOHN P	1LT	0-1169243	C853	2
MC GIVEN PAUL L	LTC	0-0377100	1059	1

NAME	GRADE	SVC NO	DATE RET MO YR	RET CODE
MC GIVERN JR PETER M	MAJ	0-1299459	1162	1
MC GIVNEY ROBERT B	LTC	0-0354125	1065	1
MC GLAFERY JCHN W	CPT	0-0155808	1044	2
MC GLAUGHLIN W J	CW2	W-2119678	0348	2
MC GLAUN WILLIAM C	MAJ	0-0986436	0963	1
MC GLINN MARY E	CPT	L-0909021	1144	2
MC GLONE ANTHONY J	CW3	W-2200735	1266	3
MC GLONE CLARENCE	MAJ	C-0338246	0656	1
MC GLONE HAROLO W	LTC	0-1168812	0667	3
MC GLOTHLAN JCHN A	MAJ	0-0395007	0547	2
MC GLYNN EOWARO J	CPT	0-0359606	0545	2
MC GLYNN JAMES C	MAJ	0-0383192	0347	1
MC GLYNN JAMES D	LTC	0-0221107	1160	3
MC GLYNN THOMAS F	LTC	0-0393663	0262	1
MC GLYNN THOMAS J	CW3	W-2203312	0864	1
MC GOLCRICK JCHN P	MAJ	0-1549546	0950	1
MC GOLORICK LESTER C	LTC	0-1578835	0259	1
MC GONAGLE HCWARO F	MAJ	0-0966859	0661	1
MC GOUGAN ERNEST D	MAJ	0-0138551	1C54	3
MC GOUGH JOSEPH M	LTC	0-0336075	0464	3
MC GOUGH JCSEPH P	CPT	0-0399137	0346	2
MC GOUGH THOMAS L	CW3	W-2205160	1163	1
MC GOUGHRAN EOWARD H	LTC	0-1550657	1158	2
MC GOVERN ANN	MAJ	N-0720920	0364	3
MC GOVERN ARTHUR J	MAJ	C-0237233	0346	2
MC GOVERN CHARLES	LTC	0-0266276	0860	1
MC GOVERN FLCRENCE K	MAJ	N-0759078	1162	1
MC GOVERN FRANK A	LTC	0-0330586	0357	1
MC GCVERN JAMES F	MAJ	0-1041846	0354	2
MC GOVERN JOHN E	LTC	0-1167106	1061	1
MC GOVERN JR JAMES W	CW2	W-2145341	0461	1
MC GOVERN MILTON J	1LT	0-0884172	0644	2
MC GCVERN SYLVESTER	1LT	0-1895310	0944	2
MC GOVERN THCMAS F	CPT	0-1536422	0363	1
MC GOVERN THCMAS J	MAJ	C-0118041	0954	3
MC GOVERN WILLIAM R	2LT	0-1321805	1150	2
MC GOWAN ARTHUR O	CPT	0-1700279	0944	2
MC GCWAN CHARLES F	CPT	0-0266640	0245	1
MC GOWAN CHARLES S	LTC	0-1576359	C961	1
MC GOWAN CLARENCE M	CPT	0-2006684	0657	1
MC GOWAN EDWARD	1LT	0-1285096	0344	2
MC GOWAN EOWARO B	MAJ	0-0314899	0363	1
MC GOWAN FRANCIS	1LT	0-0885778	1153	1
MC GOWAN FRANCIS J	COL	0-0183258	1147	2
MC GOWAN FRANK B	MAJ	C-0959294	0563	1
MC GOWAN GRAEME	LTC	0-1115027	1264	3
MC GOWAN JAMES J	LTC	0-0477813	0355	1
MC GOWAN JCHN R	LTC	0-1324782	0563	1
MC GOWAN JR R I	CPT	0-0359281	0645	1
MC GOWAN MARCARET	LTC	N-0744396	0465	3
MC GOWAN MARTHA M	CPT	N-0732791	1046	1
MC GCWAN OREN H	CW3	W-2142878	0656	1
MC GOWAN PAUL W	MAJ	0-1103794	0858	2
MC GOWAN ROBERT F	1LT	0-1331646	1147	1
MC GOWAN SAMUEL F	LTC	0-0285511	0364	3
MC GOWAN SANFORO	CW3	W-2149472	0662	1
MC GOWAN THOMAS G	LTC	0-0288741	1064	3
MC GOWAN WILLIAM	LTC	0-1551C64	C764	1
MC GOWAN WILLIAM J	MAJ	0-1548951	0561	2
MC GOWAN WILLIAM J	WO1	W-2125104	1043	2
MC GOWAN WILLIAM P	LTC	0-025975C	1065	3
MC GRACE GFORGE E	CW3	W-2104760	L154	1
MC GRACY CATHERINE	MAJ	L-0115788	0367	1
MC GRACY J P	LTC	0-1106350	1064	1
MC GRACY MARICN M	LTC	0-1182911	0161	1
MC GRACY WILLIAM M	2LT	0-1016669	0944	2
MC GRAIN ROBERT A	CW4	W-2002068	0563	1
MC GRANE GFRALD J	1LT	0-1314811	0451	2
MC GRANE JCHN A	MAJ	0-1043423	0561	1
MC GRATH ALBERT J	MAJ	0-2019764	1160	1
MC GRATH ALBERT W	COL	0-0389029	0461	1
MC GRATH ANDREW T	LTC	0-1589369	0464	1
MC GRATH GFORGE F	MAJ	0-0956582	0463	1
MC GRATH GERALD A	MAJ	0-2016918	1162	1
MC GRATH HARCLO W	MAJ	0-1341893	0365	1

NAME	GRADE	SVC NO	DATE RET MO YR	RET CODE
MC GRATH HARRY J	LTC	0-0369432	0267	3
MC GRATH HOWARO L	LTC	0-0346958	C861	1
MC GRATH JAMES A	LTC	0-1177523	C161	1
MC GRATH JOHN C	COL	0-0210522	1064	3
MC GRATH JOHN R	CPT	0-4005832	0964	1
MC GRATH JOSEPH B	1LT	0-C536975	0946	1
MC GRATH JOSEPH S	CPT	0-0386415	C861	1
MC GRATH MAURICE A	MAJ	0-0386563	1145	2
MC GRATH RAY G	LTC	0-0218378	1059	3
MC GRATH ROY A	CW2	W-2110679	0653	1
MC GRATH THOMAS J	LTC	0-1559491	C863	1
MC GRATH VINCENT T	CPT	0-0118091	0858	3
MC GRATH WILLIAM H	LTC	0-0203053	0758	3
MC GRATH WILLIAM J	MAJ	0-1945427	1060	1
MC GRAW FRANK W	MAJ	C-1311183	0457	1
MC GRAW GEORGE	MAJ	C-1639381	0354	2
MC GREE NICHOLAS C	LTC	0-1043425	0761	1
MC GREEVY JOHN M	M G	0-0278060	C262	1
MC GREGOR ARDEN O	MAJ	0-2023893	0161	1
MC GREGOR CLIFFORO	WO1	W-2152122	1154	1
MC GREGOR ERNEST M	MAJ	C-2032290	0662	1
MC GREGOR JOEL I	1LT	C-1823754	0153	1
MC GREW DANIEL R	MAJ	0-0978982	C764	1
MC GREW JAMES W	LTC	0-1646408	0767	1
MC GREW JR EOWARO J	M G	0-0265015	1162	3
MC GREW THOMAS J	1LT	0-2033554	0559	1
MC GROGAN WILLIAM J	CPT	0-0307160	1145	2
MC GRUOER ANCERSON	CPT	0-2039430	C657	1
MC GRUOER CLEMENT W	1LT	0-1010573	C657	1
MC GRUOER ROLANO W	MAJ	0-1799762	1165	1
MC GUANE FRANK L	COL	0-0251622	0367	3
MC GUFFEY BILL E	CPT	0-1643113	C762	1
MC GUFFIN JOHN W	LTC	0-0285754	1163	3
MC GUIGAN CFORGF F	MAJ	C-2052223	1057	2
MC GUIGAN JOHN G	CW4	W-2004353	0964	3
MC GUIGAN LEONARO M	CPT	0-0489686	0246	2
MC GUINES ETHEL C	CPT	N-0721701	0746	1
MC GUINESS RICHARC M	CPT	0-1030065	0345	2
MC GUINESS WILLIAM J	1LT	0-1295407	C444	2
MC GUINNESS JAMES F	LTC	C-1173707	0560	1
MC GUINNESS JOHN P	COL	0-0183782	C753	3
MC GUIRE CHARLES F	CPT	0-1545492	C154	2
MC GUIRE CLEMENT J	CPT	0-1297566	C446	2
MC GUIRE CLYOE W	1LT	0-1181953	1145	2
MC GUIRE OAVIO T	CW2	W-2210617	1064	1
MC GUIRE ELMER L	LTC	0-1015793	C967	1
MC GUIRE ERNEST J	CW3	W-2151650	1262	1
MC GUIRE EVERETT A	MAJ	0-1284180	0758	1
MC GUIRE FRANCIS P	CPT	0-1551910	C859	1
MC GUIRE FRANK A	MAJ	0-0497708	1045	2
MC GUIRE CFCRGE F	MAJ	0-0217946	0162	3
MC GUIRE GERALD A	LTC	0-0232582	C359	3
MC GUIRF HERBERT	CPT	0-1914161	0427	1
MC GUIRE HERMAN M	MAJ	C-1042366	C148	1
MC GUIRE HUGH C	MAJ	0-1318370	C760	1
MC GUIRE JACK J	CPT	0-1323156	1152	1
MC GUIRE JAMES B	LTC	0-1000264	C757	1
MC GUIRE JOHN A	LTC	0-0234652	1164	3
MC GUIRE JOHN C	MAJ	C-0482445	0446	2
MC GUIRE JOHN M	MAJ	0-1922575	1064	1
MC GUIRE JOHN P	LTC	0-0294521	0358	3
MC GUIRF JOSEPH	LTC	0-1598130	0165	1
MC GUIRE JOSEPH F	COL	0-0439004	0453	1
MC GUIRE JR FRANK X	2LT	0-1596726	C245	2
MC GUIRF JR M J	1LT	0-1268592	C245	2
MC GUIRE JR WALTER T	1LT	0-1108157	C146	2
MC GUIRE LAWRENCE F	MAJ	0-1822597	C861	2
MC GUIRE MARTIN F	MAJ	0-1326004	1157	1
MC GUIRE ORLA E	COL	0-0519500	1163	3
MC GUIRE RALPH T	CW3	W-2146741	C866	1
MC GUIRE RAYMOND C	MAJ	0-0294291	0544	2
MC GUIRE RICHARD W	1LT	0-1290632	1145	1
MC GUIRE SEYMOUR J	CPT	0-0232965	1059	3
MC GUIRE THOMAS	2LT	0-2263722	C856	1
MC GUIRE THOMAS C	CPT	0-0283247	0966	3

NAME	GRADE	SVC NO	DATE RET MO YR	RET CODE
MC GUIRE WILLIAM T	CW4	W-2142521	1062	1
MC GUIRL DANIEL P	CPT	0-2000098	0861	2
MC GUYER GLENN C	MAJ	0-1821609	0558	1
MC HALE CONALO J	LTC	0-1796118	0367	3
MC HALE CONALD R	1LT	0-1643858	1058	2
MC HALF LAWRENCE	CW3	W-2141994	0762	1
MC HAN WALTER S	LTC	0-0302452	0347	1
MC HARG WILLIAM F	MAJ	0-1946569	0661	1
MC HENRY GUY T	MAJ	0-0290022	0163	3
MC HENRY HARVEY W	CPT	0-0245899	0550	3
MC HENRY HENRY T	LTC	0-0515424	0854	1
MC HENRY IRVIN	LTC	0-1012617	0357	1
MC HENRY JAMES L	LTC	0-1031461	0864	1
MC HENRY MELVIN C	LTC	0-0888344	1265	1
MC HENRY RCBERT M	LTC	0-0267315	0767	3
MC HENRY WILLIAM O	MAJ	0-1640725	1160	1
MC HONE JAMES R	1LT	0-1542511	0845	1
MC HUGH CATHERINE	2LT	N-0720723	1043	1
MC HUGH CHARLES X	LTC	0-1647602	0463	1
MC HUGH GECRGE M	CW2	W-2102075	1055	1
MC HUGH HAROLO J	LTC	0-0359365	0463	3
MC HUGH JOHN T	CPT	0-0509140	0655	1
MC HUGH JOSEPH C	COL	0-1578837	1164	3
MC HUGH KATHLEEN J	MAJ	N-0795454	1066	1
MC HUGH PATRICK H	CPT	0-0504833	0644	2
MC HUGH ROBERT F	LTC	0-0917025	0365	3
MC HUGH WILLIAM C	MAJ	0-0417259	0945	2
MC HUGH WILLIAM O	LTC	0-0497997	1048	1
MC HUGH WILLIAM P	CPT	0-0507696	0746	2
MC ILRAITH WILLIAM J	1LT	0-1287918	1146	2
MC ILREE JOHN L	WO1	W-2132217	0345	2
MC ILRCY FREC W	LTC	0-0474815	1153	1
MC ILRCY JAMES R	COL	0-0311807	0246	2
MC ILVAINE HCWARO F	WO1	W-2124496	1045	2
MC ILWAIN WALTER N	LTC	0-2015633	0767	1
MC ILWAIN WILLIAM T	LTC	0-0214306	0763	3
MC INANEY WILLIAM F	MAJ	0-2262888	0563	2
MC INOCE ELIZABETH	CPT	L-0906009	1045	2
MC INOCE JAMES E	LTC	0-0181162	0860	3
MC INOCF WILLIAM C	LTC	0-0154537	1054	3
MC INERNEY HENRY B	LTC	0-0376835	0667	1
MC INERNEY JOHN J	LTC	0-0397940	0346	2
MC INERNEY JOSEPH T	1LT	0-1101110	1145	2
MC INERNEY MARY M	1LT	N-0724365	1045	1
MC INERNEY MARY T	1LT	R-0002148	1045	2
MC INERNEY MICHAEL J	MAJ	0-2262855	1161	1
MC INNES JCHN P	CPT	0-1300831	1164	1
MC INNES JR CILBERT	1LT	0-1046562	0545	2
MC INNES MARGARET M	LTC	N-0751283	1167	1
MC INNES WILLIAM G	LTC	0-0526232	0366	3
MC INNIS GEORGE N	1LT	0-0866027	0146	2
MC INNIS MERRIN E	LTC	0-1548255	0563	1
MC INNIS JANE K	1LT	N-0784480	1148	1
MC INNIS JOHN W	CW3	W-2143657	1158	1
MC INNIS MERVILLE W	COL	C-0154545	0746	2
MC INNIS RICHARD J	LTC	0-0219004	1C59	3
MC INNIS RICHMOND R	2LT	0-020C821	1060	3
MC INNIS WILFREC C	MAJ	0-0358425	C145	2
MC INRCY OAVIO J	CW3	W-2153656	0665	2
MC INTIRE OONALO B	1LT	0-0454020	1044	2
MC INTIRE JOHN E	LTC	0-0258654	1165	3
MC INTIRF LEWIS W	COL	0-0183575	0861	1
MC INTIRE RILEY B	1LT	0-1323722	0646	2
MC INTIRE RCBERT B	LTC	0-0463815	0762	1
MC INTIRE RCLAND H	LTC	0-0450375	0258	1
MC INTIRE SCCTT L	LTC	0-0256248	0157	3
MC INTCSH CLAUDE	MAJ	C-0347617	0562	3
MC INTCSH EDWIN W	MAJ	0-0293747	1162	1
MC INTCSH ERNEST G	CW2	W-2121205	0564	1
MC INTOSH JESSE E	M G	0-0187985	0857	3
MC INTCSH JOSEPH R	LTC	0-0247550	0166	3
MC INTCSH KENNETH	LTC	0-0204150	0153	3
MC INTCSH REGINALD S	2LT	0-1312580	0145	2
MC INTCSH RICHARD I	COL	C-0235756	0266	3
MC INTCSH ROBERT M	1LT	0-0985331	0154	2

NAME	GRADE	SVC NO	DATE RET MO YR	RET CODE
MC INTOSH WILLIAM E	CPT	0-1298418	0446	2
MC INTOSH WILLIAM L	MAJ	0-1170489	1263	1
MC INTURFF HARLAND R	CW2	W-2146950	0161	1
MC INTURFF J H	CW4	W-2129364	0159	1
MC INTYRE ANDREW F	B G	0-0271317	0652	3
MC INTYRE ANTHONY	CPT	0-0360330	0960	1
MC INTYRE CARL M	LTC	0-0420127	0760	1
MC INTYRE CHARLES J	COL	0-0175207	0846	2
MC INTYRE EARL E	CPT	0-0153702	0955	3
MC INTYRE EDWARD J	1LT	0-1012056	0446	2
MC INTYRE EUGENE J	MAJ	0-0976064	0167	1
MC INTYRE GORDON P	LTC	0-0268394	1164	3
MC INTYRE JAMES B	LTC	0-0170901	0655	3
MC INTYRE JAMES O	1LT	0-1301514	0546	2
MC INTYRE JR ALEX	CPT	0-1304765	1045	2
MC INTYRE JR R J	LTC	0-0301530	1059	1
MC INTYRE JR WADE H	CPT	0-0396115	1046	2
MC INTYRE NATHANIEL	1LT	0-0300257	0665	3
MC INTYRE NILES J	MAJ	0-1011371	0859	1
MC INTYRE WILLIAM D	LTC	0-0424523	1060	1
MC INTYRE WILLIAM L	MAJ	0-1798870	1062	1
MC ISAAC MAURICE J	CW4	W-2122883	0562	2
MC IVER GEORGE O	CW2	W-2207473	0364	1
MC IVERS GRACE J	2LT	N-0790659	0545	1
MC IVERS PAUL T H	CPT	0-1283287	1045	2
MC KAGUE BERNARD F	MAJ	0-1578839	0762	1
MC KAIN JAMES H	LTC	0-1106944	0667	1
MC KAIN JR CHARLES L	1LT	0-1289781	0646	2
MC KALIP MARVIN S	MAJ	0-1294697	0963	1
MC KAMY THOMAS K	2LT	0-0485236	0644	2
MC KANNA NEAL B	CPT	0-1165309	0957	1
MC KAY ANDREW J	WO1	W-2146261	0352	2
MC KAY FRANCIS J	COL	0-1105668	0762	1
MC KAY GEORGE C	LTC	0-1016201	0263	1
MC KAY HAROLD W	LTC	0-0345797	0467	3
MC KAY HUNTER B	CPT	0-0206054	0158	3
MC KAY JAMES H	LTC	0-0455454	0758	1
MC KAY JAMES V	CPT	0-1913823	0828	1
MC KAY JOHN W	CPT	0-0246405	1055	3
MC KAY JR JAMES W	CPT	0-1292382	1046	1
MC KAY LOYD J	1LT	0-2304298	1060	2
MC KAY NEIL A	1LT	0-1533138	0743	2
MC KAY NEIL H	COL	0-0104944	0151	3
MC KAY NEIL R	B G	0-0173091	1055	3
MC KAY ROBERT O	CW4	W-2143286	0867	1
MC KAY TERRELL	LTC	0-0245158	0446	2
MC KAY WILLIAM	LTC	0-1297567	0962	1
MC KAY WILLIAM A	MAJ	0-1322462	0261	1
MC KEAGE THOMAS E	MAJ	0-1310280	0562	1
MC KEAN ALAN M	MAJ	0-1013759	0965	1
MC KEAN ALEXANDER	LTC	0-0260584	0864	3
MC KEAN ALVIN S	MAJ	0-1182193	1159	1
MC KEAN ELROY H	LTC	0-1288774	0955	1
MC KEAND JAMES M	LTC	0-0328052	1064	3
MC KEARNEY JR J B	1LT	0-1997810	1047	2
MC KECHNIE WILLIAM E	MAJ	0-0208599	0959	3
MC KEE ARTHUR R	1LT	0-0145578	0648	3
MC KEE CHARLES G	LTC	0-1109506	0265	1
MC KEE CLARENCE W	LTC	0-1550447	0261	1
MC KEE EDWIN	LTC	0-0910432	1046	2
MC KEE EUGENE C	CW3	W-2147768	0562	1
MC KEE FRANK	LTC	0-0189751	0362	3
MC KEE FRANK J	CPT	0-0493642	0246	2
MC KEE GEORGE R	CPT	0-0948641	0361	1
MC KEE GEORGE S	LTC	0-0195362	0462	3
MC KEE HERBERT A	MAJ	0-0181140	0245	2
MC KEE JAMES R	CPT	0-2036625	0359	2
MC KEE JOHN A	MAJ	0-0450999	0258	1
MC KEE JOHN C	LTC	0-0121704	0252	3
MC KEE JR JAMES E	2LT	0-1578840	0843	1
MC KEE JR JAMES W	MAJ	0-1821747	1160	1
MC KEE MORRIS R	CW3	W-2150328	0666	1
MC KEE RALPH H	M G	0-0234931	1165	3
MC KEE RAYMOND	COL	0-0313649	1060	1
MC KEE ROBERT A	CW2	W-2115530	0946	2
MC KEE ROBERT L	MAJ	0-1583358	1156	2
MC KEE THOMAS C	COL	0-0420767	0861	3
MC KEE WALDO C	MAJ	0-0348269	0444	2
MC KEE WILLIAM A	LTC	0-0152409	0649	3
MC KEEN CHESTER V	MAJ	0-1293623	0446	2
MC KEEN RAYMOND L	CPT	0-1315597	0346	2
MC KEEVER EDWARD L	MAJ	0-1876990	0265	1
MC KEEVER JAMES L	CPT	0-0554875	0948	2
MC KEEVER THOMAS E	LTC	0-1038761	0761	1
MC KEICH ROBERT W	CW4	W-2142505	1163	1
MC KEITH EARL J	CPT	0-0272484	0460	3
MC KEITHAN ERNEST H	CPT	0-0423039	0346	2
MC KEITHEN LONZIE	MAJ	0-0527993	1161	2
MC KEITHEN VANN E	CPT	0-0451716	1045	2
MC KELL WILLIAM M	LTC	0-1057531	1067	3
MC KELLEGET RICHARD	MAJ	0-0542994	0864	1
MC KELLOP BARNEY H	MAJ	0-1062984	0363	1
MC KELLY JOHN S	LTC	0-0350092	0760	1
MC KELVEY CLYDE C	CPT	0-0224035	0656	3
MC KELVEY PAUL G	MAJ	0-0145720	0246	2
MC KELVEY RUSSELL	CW3	W-2141376	0157	1
MC KELVEY WILLIAM T	CPT	0-0176845	0737	1
MC KELVIE CLYDE R	CPT	0-1166556	0866	1
MC KELVY GEORGE M	LTC	0-0401691	1160	1
MC KEMIE JAMES B	LTC	0-1312581	1264	3
MC KEMY JR WILLIAM L	CW3	W-2151140	1066	1
MC KENDREE JAMES L J	1LT	0-0536185	0946	2
MC KENDRICK JAMES	COL	0-0470913	1152	3
MC KENNA ALVIN	LTC	0-1548553	0665	1
MC KENNA CHARLES F	2LT	0-2000439	1145	2
MC KENNA DANIEL J	LTC	0-0330094	0645	2
MC KENNA ELEANOR C	2LT	N-0783090	1144	1
MC KENNA GERALD J	LTC	0-0924035	1066	3
MC KENNA HAROLD P	LTC	0-0348102	0346	2
MC KENNA JAMES E	LTC	0-0416959	1165	1
MC KENNA JAMES E	1LT	0-1648035	0146	2
MC KENNA JAMES F	2LT	0-1183927	0745	2
MC KENNA JAMES J	LTC	0-0402245	1262	1
MC KENNA JOHN F	CW2	W-2209657	0765	1
MC KENNA JOHN J	1LT	0-1010060	0346	2
MC KENNA JOHN V	LTC	0-1555861	1266	1
MC KENNA JR JOHN F	2LT	0-0528920	0544	2
MC KENNA JUNE M	1LT	N-0798858	0153	1
MC KENNA MICHAEL O	LTC	0-0524293	0963	1
MC KENNA ROBERT L	1LT	0-0494931	0245	2
MC KENNA WALTER D	LTC	0-0135589	1046	2
MC KENNAN BRADLEY	1LT	0-1032102	0246	2
MC KENNEY BEN	CW2	W-2148212	1154	1
MC KENNEY BERTRAM A	MAJ	0-1174069	0261	1
MC KENNEY CHARLES A	CPT	0-0298753	1064	3
MC KENNEY CHARLES L	MAJ	0-1294240	0557	1
MC KENNEY DOUGLAS C	1LT	0-1314168	0146	2
MC KENNEY HENRY J	MAJ	0-0143185	0151	3
MC KENNEY MARIE M	2LT	N-0700176	0837	1
MC KENZIE CHARLES R	CW4	W-2102076	0559	1
MC KENZIE DON M	MAJ	0-0968643	0667	1
MC KENZIE DONALD W	MAJ	0-2010433	1263	1
MC KENZIE DOUGLAS J	COL	0-0219187	0154	3
MC KENZIE GEORGE O	CPT	0-1582436	1145	1
MC KENZIE GERALD K	LTC	0-1040773	0666	1
MC KENZIE HUGH H	LTC	0-1057168	0865	1
MC KENZIE ISABEL C	MAJ	N-0751599	0866	1
MC KENZIE JAMES K	1LT	0-0888368	0345	2
MC KENZIE JOHN B	LTC	0-0215996	0249	3
MC KENZIE JOHN W	1LT	0-1293064	0944	2
MC KENZIE KENNETH D	COL	0-0356276	0248	2
MC KENZIE LEONARD C	LTC	0-0509403	0954	1
MC KENZIE LOUIS H	LTC	0-0528659	0865	1
MC KENZIE OLA E	COL	0-0207064	1051	3
MC KENZIE ROBERT L	MAJ	0-1821893	1047	2
MC KENZIE VIRGIL E	LTC	0-1796980	0864	1
MC KENZIE WALTER L	1LT	0-0453319	0744	2
MC KENZIE WILLIAM G	1LT	0-1284181	0744	1
MC KENZIE WILLIAM W	CPT	0-0491185	1144	2
MC KEON ANDREW J	LTC	0-0134865	0454	3
MC KEON CLIFFORD G	LTC	0-1319630	0665	1
MC KEON ELISHA J	LTC	0-0262459	0356	3
MC KEON HARRY	CW4	W-2152276	0264	1
MC KEON JOHN P	1LT	0-0222271	0557	3
MC KEON JR JOHN P	MAJ	0-0967059	0662	1
MC KEON KATHRYN R	2LT	N-0793717	0547	1
MC KEON RICHARD T	LTC	0-0212873	0562	3
MC KEON THEODORE	1LT	0-1643115	0958	1
MC KEOUGH DONALD J	MAJ	0-1047675	1060	1
MC KEOUGH JOSEPH F	MAJ	0-1543738	0762	1
MC KEOWN CAROLINE S	MAJ	L-0608150	1163	3
MC KEOWN DEWEY M	COL	0-0336380	0460	1
MC KEOWN FORREST C	LTC	0-0469557	0563	1
MC KEOWN LLOYD D	CPT	0-1181038	0946	2
MC KERLHAR ROY M	COL	0-0166594	0648	3
MC KERNAN DONALD	MAJ	0-1117491	1061	1
MC KERNAN EDWARD V	1LT	0-2036020	0745	2
MC KERNAN JOSEPH A	MAJ	0-1591301	0163	3
MC KEVITT JOHN G	1LT	0-1176428	0745	2
MC KEW JR JOSEPH E	CPT	0-1322568	0747	2
MC KEWEN WILLIAM R	CW4	W-2119616	0859	1
MC KIBBEN DONALD H	MAJ	0-2010633	1164	1
MC KIBBEN HERBERT O	LTC	0-1167541	0366	1
MC KIBBEN JR BEN B	LTC	0-1319304	0565	2
MC KIBBIN MARTIN H	1LT	0-0106440	0244	2
MC KIBBON JAMES J	CW2	W-2211443	0166	1
MC KIE FORREST W	COL	0-0452676	0361	1
MC KIE JR ARTHUR B	LTC	0-1318322	1062	1
MC KIE JR JAMES K	1LT	0-1288267	1045	2
MC KIE ROBERT B	LTC	0-0239030	1045	1
MC KIERNAN JOHN L	CW3	W-2146382	0966	1
MC KIERNON THOMAS B	CPT	0-1590649	1060	1
MC KILLOP DOUGLAS A	LTC	0-0884909	0660	1
MC KILLOP KENNETH	COL	0-0197645	0846	2
MC KIM HENRY D	LTC	0-1013584	0561	1
MC KIM JOHN V	LTC	0-2014255	0767	1
MC KIM WILLIAM J	LTC	0-1639646	0862	1
MC KIMM HARRY G	CW3	W-2145823	0665	1
MC KIMMEY LEROY L	CW2	W-2210654	0763	1
MC KIMMINS MARK	MAJ	0-0278347	1059	3
MC KINLAY DUNCAN E	MAJ	0-0104542	0648	3
MC KINLEY ALAN F	1LT	0-0378497	0144	2
MC KINLEY ARTHUR C	CPT	0-1684658	1145	2
MC KINLEY CARL E	CW3	W-2151332	0962	1
MC KINLEY HAROLD A	MAJ	0-0205686	0553	3
MC KINLEY HAROLD C	LTC	0-0476682	1052	1
MC KINLEY HUGH F	MAJ	0-0964162	0863	1
MC KINLEY JAMES R	COL	0-0248534	1163	3
MC KINLEY LAMAR M	COL	0-0104600	0648	3
MC KINLEY MERLE H	LTC	0-1054710	0766	1
MC KINLEY PAUL	LTC	0-0299489	0167	3
MC KINLEY RICHARD M	CW3	W-2208961	0967	1
MC KINLEY ROBERT P	COL	0-0902417	0364	3
MC KINLEY RUSSELL C	CW3	W-2145891	0562	1
MC KINLEY WILLIAM	CPT	0-1116102	0745	2
MC KINLEY WILLIAM J	LTC	0-1543220	0361	1
MC KINNEY ARTHUR J	MAJ	0-2204178	0664	1
MC KINNEY CHARLES B	MAJ	0-1288418	0459	2
MC KINNEY CHARLES H	MAJ	0-1303921	0861	1
MC KINNEY CLARENCE L	1LT	0-0946198	0862	2
MC KINNEY CLYDE T	MAJ	0-2056121	0157	1
MC KINNEY DONALD	CPT	0-2034797	1148	1
MC KINNEY DONALD E	CPT	0-2262323	0562	1
MC KINNEY GEORGE W	CPT	0-0509399	0944	2
MC KINNEY GLENN H	LTC	0-1546030	0357	1
MC KINNEY HAROLD P	LTC	0-0984375	1067	1
MC KINNEY ISAAC P	1LT	0-0186961	0336	1
MC KINNEY JAMES C	MAJ	0-1047234	1059	1
MC KINNEY JERALD F	MAJ	0-1019590	0464	2
MC KINNEY JOSEPH A	CPT	0-0212118	0648	3
MC KINNEY JOSEPH K	CW3	W-3200252	1067	1
MC KINNEY JOSEPH M	LTC	0-1167109	0461	1
MC KINNEY KENNETH G	CPT	0-0981839	0960	1
MC KINNEY MARVIN E	1LT	0-0970324	1053	2
MC KINNEY RALPH J	CPT	0-0514942	0247	2
MC KINNEY RALPH L	1LT	0-0389055	0245	2
MC KINNEY RALPH V	COL	0-0217183	0857	3
MC KINNEY REX	LTC	0-2044375	0855	1
MC KINNEY ROBERT L	COL	0-0453238	0965	1
MC KINNEY ROBERT L	2LT	0-1703043	0145	2
MC KINNEY ROLLO J	MAJ	0-0268891	0356	3
MC KINNEY STAN A	LTC	0-2035253	0761	1
MC KINNEY TROYCE R	MAJ	0-0977374	0264	2
MC KINNEY WALTER H	MAJ	0-1167973	1054	1
MC KINNEY WARREN L	MAJ	0-0288934	0765	3
MC KINNEY WESLEY B	CW2	W-2148297	0365	2
MC KINNEY WILLIAM	MAJ	0-1040050	0558	1
MC KINNEY WILLIAM B	COL	0-0257555	0760	3
MC KINNEY WILLIAM C	LTC	0-0465721	1266	1
MC KINNON ANGUS G	1LT	0-1309483	0345	1
MC KINNON DONALD A	COL	0-0179322	1055	3
MC KINNON EDWARD F	LTC	0-1043168	0957	2
MC KINNON JOHN L	MAJ	0-0460364	0232	1
MC KINNON RAY	MAJ	0-0183856	0346	2
MC KINNON WADE L	MAJ	0-1300195	1160	1
MC KINNON WILLIAM L	MAJ	0-0382552	0855	1
MC KINSEY HAROLD I	LTC	0-1323950	0366	3
MC KINSEY MILLARD F	LTC	0-0467734	0164	1
MC KINSEY ROY R	LTC	0-0266594	0565	3
MC KINSTRY EDWARD N	CPT	0-0280807	0664	3
MC KINSTRY ELWYN R	MAJ	0-1012520	0261	1
MC KINSTRY GEORGE C	LTC	0-0129283	0547	1
MC KINSTRY JEROME O	1LT	0-5217153	0864	2
MC KINSTRY JOHN O	CW3	W-2145197	0662	1
MC KINZIE LON	MAJ	0-1179533	1160	1
MC KISSICK DOUGLAS R	LTC	0-2047063	1162	1
MC KISSICK FRANK A	LTC	0-1552121	0563	1
MC KISSICK ROY	CW3	W-2143217	1160	1
MC KISSICK VERNON H	LTC	0-0259039	0365	3
MC KITTRICK KENNETH	MAJ	0-0338634	1144	2
MC KITTRICK PETER	MAJ	0-0510270	0554	3
MC KIVETT JAMES C A	1LT	0-0288489	0258	3
MC KNIGHT ALEXANDE	2LT	0-0102935	1155	3
MC KNIGHT CHARLES	COL	0-0100223	0951	3
MC KNIGHT EUEL E	MAJ	0-0159760	1044	2
MC KNIGHT FRANCIS H	CPT	0-0169438	0960	3
MC KNIGHT JAMES D	MAJ	0-1703806	0758	1
MC KNIGHT JOHN P	B G	0-0258303	0566	3
MC KNIGHT JOSEPH W	CPT	0-1176726	0360	1
MC KNIGHT RAY A	LTC	0-0202776	0863	3
MC KNIGHT ROBERT W	COL	0-0145761	0855	3
MC KNIGHT ROBERT W	MAJ	0-0233150	1263	3
MC KNIGHT STEWART D	LTC	0-0249172	0266	3
MC KNIGHT THOMAS J	MAJ	0-0264762	0445	2
MC KNIGHT WILLIAM H	LTC	0-0450042	0658	1
MC KNIGHT WILLIAM R	MAJ	0-0224662	0252	3
MC KOAN JOHN E	1LT	0-0928344	1051	1
MC KOAN JR JOHN W	COL	0-0255742	0445	2
MC KOAN THOMAS P	LTC	0-0292266	0366	3
MC KONE DON T	MAJ	0-0438363	1045	1
MC KONE SAMUEL A	MAJ	0-0107710	1143	2
MC KOWN CLARENCE D	LTC	0-0348813	0263	1
MC KOWN RUSSELL L	LTC	0-0305197	0155	3
MC KOY OTIS L	CW2	W-2105445	1045	2
MC KRILL EDWARD M	CPT	0-0335527	1144	2
MC KUIN JOHN W	CPT	0-2262456	1060	1
MC KULLA MARIE B	2LT	N-0734187	1043	1
MC LAIN GEORGE F	MAJ	0-0215545	0944	2
MC LAIN JOHN E	CPT	0-1171673	0946	2
MC LAIN LLOYD S	LTC	0-1291305	0361	1
MC LAIN LOWELL E	MAJ	0-1342158	0962	1
MC LAIN RALPH E	MAJ	0-0532091	0763	1
MC LAIN RONALD A	CPT	0-0468165	0753	1
MC LAIN RUSSELL K	CPT	0-0971801	1160	1
MC LAIN THERON N	LTC	0-0323936	0954	1
MC LAIN VOIL O	CW2	W-2150800	0156	1
MC LAINE WILLIAM H	MAJ	0-0238651	0762	3
MC LAIRD PAUL L	CPT	0-1695187	1265	1
MC LANE CAREY	1LT	0-1913824	1128	1
MC LANE DORIS M	MAJ	N-0741981	1067	1

NAME	GRADE	SVC NO	DATE RET MO YR	RET CODE
MC LANE NEIL G	1LT	0-0313545	0348	2
MC LANE WOODROW	CW2	W-2149185	1159	1
MC LAREN DONALD W	MAJ	0-0104509	0646	2
MC LAREN JR MILTON W	LTC	0-1032225	0664	1
MC LAUCHLIN ALBERT C	CW2	W-2211286	0765	1
MC LAUCHLIN THOMAS N	1LT	0-1332619	C448	2
MC LAUGHLIN AUBREY A	1LT	0-0547526	0246	2
MC LAUGHLIN BERYNE	COL	0-0346413	0960	1
MC LAUGHLIN CHARLE	LTC	0-0197856	0346	2
MC LAUGHLIN CHARLES	LTC	0-1013371	0866	1
MC LAUGHLIN CHARLES	MAJ	C-1651687	C867	1
MC LAUGHLIN CLAREN	MAJ	0-0141530	0648	3
MC LAUGHLIN CLAYTCN	CW3	W-2207740	0767	1
MC LAUGHLIN DEROY J	MAJ	C-0419337	0446	2
MC LAUGHLIN DONALD G	CPT	0-0418024	0744	2
MC LAUGHLIN EDWARC D	CPT	0-0218224	C763	3
MC LAUGHLIN ELIZAB	1LT	L-0602378	0947	2
MC LAUGHLIN ERNEST	1LT	C-0437724	0346	2
MC LAUGHLIN FRANCIS	MAJ	0-0252890	0167	3
MC LAUGHLIN FRANK	COL	0-0286130	0362	3
MC LAUGHLIN GEORGE J	CPT	0-0397294	0248	2
MC LAUGHLIN HAROLC A	LTC	0-0288742	C859	3
MC LAUGHLIN HARRY F	MAJ	C-0197603	1055	3
MC LAUGHLIN HARRY R	LTC	0-0297336	C546	2
MC LAUGHLIN HENRY F	CPT	0-0986866	C562	1
MC LAUGHLIN HOMER L	LTC	0-0238664	0164	3
MC LAUGHLIN JACK L	1LT	0-2040960	0246	2
MC LAUGHLIN JAMES J	CPT	0-2268763	1055	3
MC LAUGHLIN JOHN E	LTC	0-1014972	1263	1
MC LAUGHLIN JOHN E	LTC	0-1287919	1059	2
MC LAUGHLIN JOHN F	CW2	W-3150564	1266	1
MC LAUGHLIN JOHN W	1LT	0-1182912	1045	2
MC LAUGHLIN JOSEPH H	LTC	0-0498369	0147	2
MC LAUGHLIN JR M M	MAJ	0-1949405	0960	1
MC LAUGHLIN LEONARD	MAJ	C-1884167	1067	1
MC LAUGHLIN LESTER L	CW3	W-2146809	C164	2
MC LAUGHLIN MARY J	1LT	N-0742420	C945	1
MC LAUGHLIN MAX D	LTC	0-1011312	1262	1
MC LAUGHLIN MICHAEL	COL	0-0204673	1051	3
MC LAUGHLIN MICHAEL	CPT	0-0286903	0446	2
MC LAUGHLIN ORRIN L	MAJ	0-1308674	0355	2
MC LAUGHLIN ORVILLE	MAJ	0-0385597	0762	1
MC LAUGHLIN R B	CPT	C-0341317	1145	1
MC LAUGHLIN RALPH M	LTC	0-0279188	1164	3
MC LAUGHLIN THEODORE	LTC	0-0250370	0660	1
MC LAUGHLIN THOMAS A	LTC	0-1894714	C666	3
MC LAUGHLIN THOMAS J	MAJ	0-1177083	1066	1
MC LAUGHLIN W J	1LT	0-1290974	0945	2
MC LAUGHLIN WILLIA	LTC	0-0890331	0657	1
MC LAUGHLIN WILLIAM	COL	0-0237810	1162	3
MC LEAN ANDREW J	LTC	0-0141696	1050	3
MC LEAN ARTHUR O	LTC	0-0354616	0460	1
MC LEAN CECIL M	MAJ	L-0904566	0659	2
MC LEAN CLAUDE E	MAJ	C-0140805	0648	3
MC LEAN DANIEL R	CPT	0-0499158	0645	2
MC LEAN DONALC A	LTC	C-1798941	1266	3
MC LEAN DONALD M	CPT	0-05517C4	0647	2
MC LEAN FRANKLIN A	COL	0-0251353	1263	1
MC LEAN HAROLD A	COL	0-0281825	0660	2
MC LEAN JAMES C D	LTC	0-2048705	1164	1
MC LEAN JAMES F	LTC	C-1039108	0465	1
MC LEAN JOHN J	1LT	0-C517975	C944	2
MC LEAN JOSEPH I	MAJ	0-1039463	C665	1
MC LEAN JR DUNCAN N	CPT	0-0982792	1157	1
MC LEAN KEITH E	LTC	0-1017111	0762	1
MC LEAN LUCIEN M	CPT	0-0978674	0960	1
MC LEAN LYLE W	CPT	0-0288462	0457	3
MC LEAN PAUL F	MAJ	C-0966043	1166	1
MC LEAN ROBERT E	CPT	0-1573904	0547	1
MC LEAN ROBERT N	LTC	0-0130533	0153	3
MC LEAN SYDNEY S	CW2	W-2144074	0957	1
MC LEAN WILLIAM J	MAJ	0-1314169	0557	1
MC LEISH JR MURRAY M	1LT	0-0495623	0146	2
MC LELLAN ALLAN	LTC	0-0198479	1054	3
MC LELLAN CURTISS	CPT	0-2055157	1055	1
MC LELLAN EARL O	WO1	W-2107922	1046	1
MC LELLAN JAMES H	CPT	0-1317986	0747	2
MC LELLAN JESSE M	COL	0-0253445	0454	3
MC LELLAND JR W	CPT	0-0378819	0345	2
MC LEMORE CURTIS	CW4	W-2146976	0466	1
MC LENCON FRED S	MAJ	0-1114229	0265	1
MC LENCCK HENRY C	MAJ	0-1334880	0663	1
MC LENDCN HUBERT F	1LT	0-0462388	1046	2
MC LENDEN JAMES A	LTC	0-1001634	0666	3
MC LENDCN JAMES H	1LT	0-1102130	0545	2
MC LENNAN JAMES A	CPT	0-0177059	0759	3
MC LENNON PETER J	CPT	0-1841852	1044	2
MC LEOD ARCHIBALD	MAJ	C-1306620	0657	1
MC LECC ARCHIE H	LTC	0-0490906	1054	1
MC LEOC CHARLES H	LTC	0-030036C	0961	3
MC LEOC FRANCIS D	LTC	0-0420775	0461	1
MC LEOC HUGH S	M G	0-0143285	1156	3
MC LEOC JAMES G	CPT	0-034201C	0250	1
MC LEOD MURRAY	LTC	0-0360965	0560	1
MC LEOC PRENTISS R	CPT	C-0364753	0145	2
MC LECC RICHARD E	MAJ	0-0984087	0464	1
MC LEOD WAYNE L	CW2	W-2214926	0467	1
MC LEOD WILLIAM F	CPT	0-1583364	1058	2
MC LECD 3RD DAN	CPT	0-1821610	0945	2
MC LEOUD JACK	CPT	0-0498927	0650	1
MC LERCY JR JCHN O	1LT	C-0365254	0144	2
MC LESTER JAMES B	COL	0-0392945	0866	3
MC LIN ARTHUR N	CW2	W-2209721	0762	1
MC LINDEN HELEN F	1LT	N-0768818	0851	1
MC LINTCCK ADDISON W	MAJ	0-0492530	0647	2
MC LOUCHLIN ANTHONY	LTC	0-0409078	0766	3
MC LOUCHLIN JAMES M	MAJ	C-0274406	1162	3
MC LOUGHLIN JOHN A	MAJ	C-0439815	0348	1
MC LOUGHLIN JOHN H	CW3	W-2206018	1065	1
MC LOUGHLIN MICHAEL	LTC	0-0938028	0866	1
MC LOVICH ANDREW	1LT	0-1047235	0146	1
MC LURE JOHN J	COL	0-0154589	0648	3
MC LURE RICHARD A	1LT	0-1348962	0951	3
MC LURKIN CHARLES P	LTC	0-1554236	0763	1
MC MAHAN GEORGE T	COL	0-0249314	0361	3
MC MAHAN THEODORE W	COL	0-0342815	0157	1
MC MAHAN WILLIAM T	LTC	0-2046751	0667	1
MC MAHCN CHARLENE H	MAJ	L-0502117	1164	1
MC MAHCN EDMUND T	2LT	0-1051685	1044	1
MC MAHCN ECWARD A	COL	0-0233141	C648	3
MC MAHCN EDWARD J	CPT	0-0463271	0746	2
MC MAHCN HENRY J	MAJ	0-0264205	0154	3
MC MAHCN HUGH J	MAJ	0-1535799	0760	1
MC MAHCN JAMES J	1LT	0-1895192	0756	1
MC MAHON JAMES P	MAJ	0-0168882	1056	3
MC MAHCN JCHN E	LTC	0-1946332	1165	3
MC MAHCN JOHN F	LTC	0-108073C	0464	1
MC MAHCN JOHN F	CW2	W-2007564	0667	3
MC MAHCN JOHN T	MAJ	0-1823037	C361	2
MC MAHCN JOHN W	MAJ	0-0474886	0452	1
MC MAHON JOSEPH E	CW3	W-2119915	0655	1
MC MAHCN JOSEPH I	MAJ	0-1288268	1263	1
MC MAHCN JR EDWARD M	LTC	0-0473225	0656	1
MC MAHCN JR THOMAS G	LTC	0-0295308	0666	3
MC MAHCN LESLIE M	LTC	0-038165C	0763	1
MC MAHCN RAYMOND G	LTC	0-0264408	0862	3
MC MAHCN WALTER J	MAJ	0-1106947	0261	1
MC MAHCN WILLIAM J	MAJ	0-0548342	0564	1
MC MANAMNA ALAN A	MAJ	C-0428435	0263	1
MC MANIS HAROLD	CPT	0-0505360	1047	1
MC MANUELS ARTHUR J	CW3	W-2151164	1263	1
MC MANUS CHARLES F	COL	0-0172814	0259	3
MC MANUS CHARLES V	LTC	0-0357476	0446	1
MC MANUS FRANCIS G	2LT	0-1297467	0645	2
MC MANUS HENRY B	LTC	0-0249348	1264	3
MC MANUS JAMES J	MAJ	C-0173661	0753	3
MC MANUS JAMES L	MAJ	0-1318064	1160	1
MC MANUS JOSEPH W	COL	0-0202142	0954	1
MC MANUS JR ADRIAN C	1LT	0-0461061	0846	2
MC MANUS JR HUGH F	MAJ	0-0368213	0945	2
MC MANUS JR JOHN J	1LT	0-1110122	0546	2
MC MANUS JR PHILIP J	LTC	0-0437481	0764	1
MC MANUS MARGARET E	CPT	N-C759006	C947	1
MC MANUS ORVILLE D	LTC	0-1291307	1160	1
MC MANUS RAY J	LTC	0-0419073	1162	1
MC MANUS THOMAS L	LTC	0-0174274	0559	3
MC MANUS WOODROW F	CPT	0-1030904	1051	1
MC MARTIN FINLAY	1LT	0-1590934	0745	2
MC MASTER ARCHIE L	MAJ	C-0317527	0246	2
MC MASTER WILLIAM E	MAJ	0-1289762	0361	1
MC MASTERS JOHN R	LTC	C-0328054	1158	1
MC MATH MERCER B	LTC	0-0213246	1052	2
MC MAUGHAN GEORGE W	LTC	0-1100682	0662	1
MC MEANS HEATH L	MAJ	C-0187825	C849	3
MC MEANS THOMAS W	LTC	0-0344868	1067	3
MC MEEKIN ANDREW F	COL	C-0342249	0848	2
MC MELLEN ROBERT W	MAJ	0-1924556	C466	1
MC MENAMIN JOSEPH C	CPT	0-0337398	1045	2
MC MICAN STELLA M	2LT	N-0730402	C844	1
MC MICHAEL JOHN H	MAJ	0-0428107	C246	2
MC MICHAEL JOHN W	LTC	0-2007904	0363	1
MC MICHAEL MORRIS H	MAJ	C-C304015	C747	2
MC MILLAN ALBROSE C	LTC	0-0300699	0166	3
MC MILLAN CARLTON F	MAJ	0-1184549	0257	1
MC MILLAN CLARENCE T	CW3	W-214657C	0464	1
MC MILLAN DAVID G	LTC	0-0237378	C362	3
MC MILLAN DONALD J	MAJ	0-1115697	1162	1
MC MILLAN EUGENE A	CPT	0-1919250	1262	1
MC MILLAN EVERETT F	COL	C-0276146	0763	3
MC MILLAN GARLAND O	1LT	0-2016919	C852	1
MC MILLAN GEORGE	LTC	0-0319346	0859	3
MC MILLAN GORDON P	COL	0-0275824	C363	3
MC MILLAN HYDE	1LT	0-0461522	0146	2
MC MILLAN JAMES J	CPT	C-1558665	C263	1
MC MILLAN JAMES M	MAJ	0-146684C	0861	1
MC MILLAN JESSE M	MAJ	C-0305295	C767	3
MC MILLAN JOHN A	LTC	0-0270203	0365	3
MC MILLAN JOHN W	LTC	0-0302173	1063	1
MC MILLAN JR JACK W	MAJ	0-1171279	0661	1
MC MILLAN LENORE R	CPT	L-0304146	1150	1
MC MILLAN MARSHALL J	WO1	W-2122661	C846	2
MC MILLAN RICHARC J	LTC	0-1580023	0765	1
MC MILLAN ROBERT A	COL	0-0166804	C850	3
MC MILLAN ROGER J	1LT	C-1327753	1145	2
MC MILLAN ROLLAND H	MAJ	C-2033866	0463	1
MC MILLAN ROY A	LTC	0-0166890	0550	3
MC MILLEN ECWARD J	2LT	0-1331072	C864	2
MC MILLEN GERALD G	LTC	0-0266908	1059	3
MC MILLEN NORMAN W	LTC	C-0212451	0948	3
MC MILLIAN PORTER	MAJ	C-1307275	0257	1
MC MILLION OVID M	COL	C-0920572	0465	3
MC MINIMEE WALTER C	LTC	0-0917295	0765	3
MC MINN JACQUES S	MAJ	C-0153161	0-49	3
MC MINN JAMES	LTC	C-0405955	C951	2
MC MINN WALTER P	LTC	C-0497731	0954	1
MC MONAGLE CANIEL S	LTC	0-1824893	C567	1
MC MONICLE GLENN R	MAJ	C-1688831	0565	1
MC MONIGLE THOS J	1LT	0-1288269	0944	2
MC MORRIS ALFRED W	COL	C-0172466	1050	3
MC MORROW DAN A	1LT	0-1634128	C150	1
MC MORROW JOHN J	MAJ	0-0290781	1147	1
MC MORROW JOHN W	1LT	0-0973188	0353	2
MC MORROW LESLIE P	LTC	0-0323910	0762	1
MC MORROW RALPH J	1LT	0-1311320	C746	2
MC MULLAN JOHN J	1LT	0-1583365	0245	1
MC MULLEN CECIL J W	1LT	0-0270997	C667	3
MC MULLEN HERSCHEL H	LTC	0-0285902	C966	3
MC MULLEN JACK W	MAJ	0-1798688	C960	1
MC MULLEN JOHN A	CW3	W-2147068	1062	2
MC MULLEN JOSEPH E	COL	0-025014C	C766	3
MC MULLEN JR LEROY A	LTC	0-1287212	C163	1
MC MULLEN JR RAY W	LTC	C-1105018	C864	1
MC MULLEN PHILLIPS R	CPT	0-011726C	0257	3
MC MULLEN WILLIAM R	LTC	0-1845313	C158	2
MC MULLIN MICHAEL A	CPT	0-1340568	0358	2
MC MURCHY ERNEST L	2LT	0-0533894	0645	2
MC MURRAY CRAWFORD A	COL	0-0244413	0464	3
MC MURRAY FLEYD I	CPT	0-0117262	0151	3
MC MURRAY PAUL H	COL	0-0267663	0658	3
MC MURRAY ROBERT J	MAJ	0-2035485	0361	1
MC MURRAY TOM	COL	C-0183082	0854	3
MC MURRAY WILLIAM T	CPT	0-0451146	1055	1
MC MURREN IRVIN C	CPT	C-0499517	0449	1
MC MURRER JAMES E	CPT	0-0108836	0753	3
MC MURRY PEARL W	COL	0-0318427	0566	3
MC MURTRAY RCY S	LTC	0-0333367	0963	3
MC MURTRY LESLIE R	LTC	C-0168222	1054	3
MC NABB CHARLES J	MAJ	C-1919472	1265	1
MC NABB HUGH E	LTC	0-0179874	1045	1
MC NABB JAMES H	1LT	0-1313536	0260	1
MC NABB OSCAR J	MAJ	0-0235309	0563	3
MC NAGAY WILLIAM F	1LT	0-0493032	0145	1
MC NAIR ALBERT	CPT	C-4005704	0765	1
MC NAIR ELISHA B	LTC	0-0515551	0963	1
MC NAIR JAMES B	MAJ	0-0111191	0449	3
MC NAIR JAMES E P	COL	0-0244674	0846	2
MC NAIR JAMES R	1LT	0-0494993	0453	1
MC NAIR JOHN W	LTC	0-0153686	0853	3
MC NAIR JR WILLIAM H	1LT	C-1319631	1045	2
MC NALLAN JACK D	CW3	W-2152074	0966	1
MC NALLY GEORGE J	COL	C-0913024	1065	2
MC NALLY HENRY C	MAJ	0-0311243	0353	1
MC NALLY HUGH T	CPT	0-1169244	0546	2
MC NALLY JEANETTE M	1LT	N-0752563	1045	2
MC NALLY JOHN H	LTC	0-1536455	0766	1
MC NALLY JOHN W	LTC	C-027968C	0960	3
MC NALLY JOSEPH P	CPT	0-0478519	1045	2
MC NALLY JR CARL R	1LT	0-0528677	0146	2
MC NALLY JR IRA E	MAJ	0-1886042	0165	1
MC NALLY LEE D	1LT	0-0252724	0166	3
MC NALLY RICHARD S	LTC	0-155022C	0663	1
MC NALLY WILLIAM J	CW3	W-2147953	0962	1
MC NAMARA EDWARD O	LTC	0-1550448	0265	1
MC NAMARA JAMES E	MAJ	0-0990630	0463	1
MC NAMARA JAMES O	CPT	0-0497001	0553	1
MC NAMARA JOHN P	MAJ	0-0216093	1051	1
MC NAMARA JOSEPH P	COL	0-0917C84	0566	3
MC NAMARA MARVIN F	1LT	0-1823911	C244	2
MC NAMARA MICHAEL F	MAJ	C-0449565	0345	2
MC NAMARA ROBERT C	1LT	0-1012694	0745	2
MC NAMARA THOMAS	LTC	0-0153183	0648	3
MC NAMARA THOMAS	CPT	0-0496768	1048	1
MC NAMARA THOMAS F	LTC	0-1342199	1166	1
MC NAMARA WILLIAM F	CPT	0-0445922	0246	2
MC NAMARA WILLIAM J	CPT	0-1285263	0549	2
MC NAMEE EDMUND J	1LT	0-0717722	0745	2
MC NAMEE JOHN R	LTC	0-1534564	0765	1
MC NAMEE JR FRANK A	COL	0-014C490	1052	3
MC NARY ROBERT R	LTC	0-0232794	1163	3
MC NATT CRVILLE F	CPT	0-1103317	0346	2
MC NAUGHT PERCY C	CPT	0-0392518	1059	3
MC NAUCHTON JOHN N	CPT	0-1914127	0645	1
MC NAUGHTON LAWRENCE	LTC	0-0319779	0467	3
MC NAUGHTON RAY L D	CW3	W-2147574	1262	1
MC NAUGHTCN RODGER W	CPT	0-0379071	0245	2
MC NAUL WINFIELD H	COL	0-0410151	0461	2
MC NAY GEORGE H	LTC	0-0244947	0664	3
MC NEAL DAN H	LTC	0-0188541	0159	3
MC NEAL DAVID C	LTC	0-0509141	0547	2
MC NEAL FRED J	LTC	0-1552748	0962	1
MC NEAL THOMAS F	COL	0-0240050	1065	3
MC NEAL WILLIAM A	CW2	W-2206245	0459	1
MC NEARNY THOMAS L	MAJ	C-1015897	0165	2
MC NEE WILLIAM E	LTC	0-2042734	0466	1
MC NEELY JAMES H	LTC	0-0371890	1265	3
MC NEELY MARVIN	CW2	W-2153001	1060	1
MC NEER JAMES W	COL	0-0223703	1154	1
MC NEES HAROLD C	CPT	0-1683019	1144	2
MC NEES PHILIP M	CW4	W-2102083	0256	1
MC NEESE TURNER C	LTC	0-0510AC7	1060	1

ARMY OF THE UNITED STATES RETIRED LIST

NAME	GRADE	SVC NO	DATE RET MO YR	RET CODE
MC NEIGHT HARRY D	CW3	W-2203355	0165	1
MC NEIL BURTON E	LTC	0-1171674	0964	1
MC NEIL CHARLES J	MAJ	0-1580026	1061	1
MC NEIL DANIEL C	CW3	W-2202607	0567	1
MC NEIL DANIEL P	LTC	0-1581941	0456	1
MC NEIL DELBERT S	LTC	0-1304053	0864	1
MC NEIL FRANK J	MAJ	0-0331778	1044	2
MC NEIL HARRY E	CW2	W-2149300	0359	1
MC NEIL JACK G	LTC	0-1295754	1057	1
MC NEIL JOHN O	CPT	0-0507630	1047	1
MC NEIL MABEL B	1LT	N-0772008	0546	1
MC NEIL NEIL A	MAJ	0-1040443	0361	1
MC NEIL PERRY M	LTC	0-0301077	0267	3
MC NEIL RALPH G	MAJ	0-0194888	0152	3
MC NEIL ROBERT B	CPT	0-2024605	1053	2
MC NEIL ROY M	LTC	0-1287039	0961	1
MC NEIL STANLEY R	COL	0-0216015	0847	2
MC NEIL WILLIAM R	MAJ	0-0949545	0163	1
MC NEILL ALLISON	MAJ	0-1645813	0566	3
MC NEILL ALVIN J	WO1	W-2117108	1044	2
MC NEILL CHARLES L	COL	0-0366111	0264	1
MC NEILL JAMES C	MAJ	0-1304094	1060	1
MC NEILL JAMES M	CPT	0-0407746	0144	2
MC NEILL JOSEPH F	LTC	0-1314040	1162	1
MC NEILL JR FORD A	COL	0-0255587	0164	3
MC NEILL LOREN C	CPT	0-0358365	0944	2
MC NEILL THOMAS H	LTC	0-0316289	0252	1
MC NEISH PAUL M	LTC	0-0339474	0762	1
MC NELLY BERTRAM J	MAJ	0-1593080	0163	1
MC NELLY RICHARD L	B G	0-0256304	0662	3
MC NEMAR HAROLD B	LTC	0-0507074	1054	1
MC NERNEY DANIEL P	LTC	0-2036021	0962	1
MC NERNEY EDWARD W	1LT	0-1052076	1145	2
MC NERNEY GORDON	MAJ	0-1574985	1050	1
MC NERNEY THOMAS L	MAJ	0-0360201	0452	1
MC NERNY HERBERT C	COL	0-0134641	0946	2
MC NEVIN ALFRED C B	COL	0-0164797	0648	3
MC NEW JR HARRY C	CPT	0-0266897	1266	3
MC NEW LIESTER O	2LT	0-1326866	0146	2
MC NICHOL JR JOHN C	LTC	0-1313769	0562	1
MC NICHOL THEODORE	CW2	W-2149086	1058	2
MC NICHOLAS THOMAS G	LTC	0-0128457	0648	3
MC NICHOLL PATRICK J	LTC	0-0139095	0745	2
MC NICHOLL PATRICK J	MAJ	0-0980809	0964	1
MC NICHOLS ROBERT H	LTC	0-0419942	0161	1
MC NICKLE ARTHUR J	LTC	0-1040775	0461	1
MC NIFF MILES S	LTC	0-1106949	0563	1
MC NITT HENRY J R	LTC	0-0212260	1161	3
MC NULTY JAMES F	MAJ	0-1295579	0957	1
MC NULTY JAMES K	MAJ	0-1320760	0262	2
MC NULTY JOHN A	LTC	0-0449828	1266	1
MC NULTY JOHN N	LTC	0-2035353	0367	1
MC NULTY JOHN R	CW3	W-2146914	0266	1
MC NULTY JOSEPH O	2LT	0-2005424	0351	2
MC NULTY JR JOHN F	LTC	0-1316773	1164	1
MC NULTY SARSFIELD	LTC	0-1575462	0260	1
MC NULTY WARREN E	LTC	0-1320690	0763	1
MC NULTY WAYNE J	LTC	0-1686244	0366	1
MC NURLEN KEITH A	1LT	0-0513539	0945	2
MC NUTT DALTON W	2LT	0-1307276	0744	2
MC NUTT EUGENE C	2LT	0-2006429	0646	2
MC NUTT LAWRENCE E	MAJ	0-1305622	0159	1
MC NUTT LEONARD M	COL	0-0405852	0660	1
MC NUTT LEROY C	CPT	0-1288091	0556	1
MC NUTT LILLIE B	MAJ	N-0773269	0364	1
MC NUTT WILLIAM P	LTC	0-0272058	1166	3
MC PARTLAND HELEN J	MAJ	N-0720010	0146	1
MC PARTLAND MARION B	MAJ	N-0752236	0965	3
MC PEAK EDGAR M	LTC	0-0247744	0545	2
MC PECK EDWIN K	CPT	0-1649085	0648	1
MC PEEK FRANK O	CPT	0-2300984	1263	1
MC PEEK RICHARD W	LTC	0-1316701	0861	2
MC PHAIL ARTHUR M	LTC	0-0494536	0854	1
MC PHAIL BILLY B	MAJ	0-1174646	0860	1
MC PHAIL JAMES T	CW3	W-2146538	0165	1
MC PHAILL EARL	CPT	0-1703396	1145	2
MC PHAUL JOHN A	CPT	0-0275513	0166	3
MC PHEE EUGENE R	COL	0-0220462	0662	3
MC PHEE JOHN G	2LT	0-1015156	0244	2
MC PHEE MONICA K	1LT	N-0752909	0946	1
MC PHEETERS JAMES H	LTC	0-0471328	0762	1
MC PHERRAN PAUL L	LTC	0-0317706	0861	1
MC PHERSEN CHARLES M	CW4	W-2104293	0659	1
MC PHERSON CHARLES W	1LT	0-0450174	0344	2
MC PHERSON DONALD M	1LT	0-1298264	1045	2
MC PHERSON GEORGE R	LTC	0-0247698	0259	3
MC PHERSON HENRY A	CPT	0-0524983	1044	2
MC PHERSON HUE O	CW2	W-2123368	1058	1
MC PHERSON JACK K	CW3	W-2153322	0865	1
MC PHERSON JAMES R	MAJ	0-1332285	0963	1
MC PHERSON JESSE R	LTC	0-0278546	0954	3
MC PHERSON KENNETH M	COL	0-0345415	1066	3
MC PHERSON MARION V	MAJ	0-1313278	1162	1
MC PHERSON SADIE E	1LT	N-0743336	1145	1
MC PROUD CARL E	LTC	0-1822598	1061	1
MC QUADE EDWARD B	CW4	W-2147820	1155	1
MC QUADE JAMES F	1LT	0-2055251	0849	1
MC QUADE JOSEPH W	LTC	0-0286596	0462	3
MC QUAID KENNETH R	CPT	0-1576375	1145	2
MC QUAIG JAMES A	CW3	W-2205393	1063	1
MC QUAIL MARGARET B	2LT	N-0784833	0845	1
MC QUAIN GUY A	CPT	0-2034445	0258	1
MC QUARRIE HILTON B	CPT	0-0363605	0551	1
MC QUEEN FRANK T	MAJ	0-0162167	0355	3
MC QUEEN JOHN W	LTC	0-0268975	0967	3
MC QUEEN WILLIAM R	CPT	0-0304866	0247	2
MC QUEENEY WILLIAM A	LTC	0-0242608	0962	1
MC QUIDDY EUGENE R	CW3	W-2205070	0864	1
MC QUILKIN MARTIN F	MAJ	0-0100523	1055	3
MC QUILLAN FRANCIS C	1LT	0-1035946	0845	2
MC QUILLAN JOHN G	LTC	0-1542668	0966	3
MC QUILLAN JOHN J	CPT	0-2027809	0357	1
MC QUILLEN ALVIN K	MAJ	0-1541479	0754	1
MC QUILLEN PETER L	CPT	0-0108980	1038	1
MC QUISTON DANIEL H	COL	0-0147031	0546	2
MC QUISTON WILLIAM H	1LT	0-0259217	1045	2
MC QUOWN LEONARD A	COL	0-0147107	0853	3
MC RAE DAVID E	MAJ	0-0285790	1056	3
MC RAE JOHN S	1LT	0-1330840	1047	2
MC RAE MARGARET C	2LT	N-0723713	0145	1
MC RAINEY MALCOLM A	LTC	0-1284550	0861	1
MC REYNOLDS CHARLES	LTC	0-0203466	0563	3
MC REYNOLDS EDGAR	1LT	0-2024357	0466	2
MC REYNOLDS EDGAR L	MAJ	0-2263501	1262	1
MC REYNOLDS FRANK R	LTC	0-0114199	0648	3
MC RHOADS JAMES P	CPT	0-4006673	0167	1
MC ROBBIE EDITH	MAJ	L-0203219	0563	1
MC ROBERTS PAUL L	CW3	W-2209067	0966	1
MC ROBERTS WILLIAM N	LTC	0-0395083	0263	1
MC SHANE ADRIAN J	CW3	W-2146177	0662	2
MC SHANE FRANK R	CPT	0-1307730	0448	2
MC SHANE KENNETH J	MAJ	0-0487263	0660	1
MC SHERRY LEROY F	LTC	0-0455007	0566	1
MC SORLEY FRANK N	MAJ	0-1559492	1263	1
MC SPADDEN ROBERT S	MAJ	0-1641571	0465	1
MC SPADDEN WILLIAM B	2LT	0-0390291	0542	2
MC SPARREN GEORGE R	CW2	W-2212500	0867	1
MC SWAIN HAROLD V	1LT	0-1298898	1045	2
MC SWAIN OLA M	MAJ	N-0726041	0166	1
MC SWANE RAYMOND	CPT	0-0361191	1152	1
MC SWEEN F D	CW3	W-2143554	0859	1
MC SWEEN HARRY Y	LTC	0-0410271	0845	2
MC SWEEN JR JOHN M	MAJ	0-1635083	0258	1
MC SWEEN WHITT P	1LT	0-1011010	0146	2
MC SWEENEY JAMES J	LTC	0-2036022	0562	1
MC SWEENEY JAMES P	1LT	0-0530979	0646	1
MC SWEENEY JOHN	LTC	0-0164741	0753	3
MC SWEENY JOHN	CPT	0-0133227	0944	2
MC TAGGART ALASTAIR	MAJ	0-2021178	0167	1
MC TAGGART HARRY H	2LT	0-1913817	0237	1
MC TAMNEY JOSEPH J	MAJ	0-2200416	0666	1
MC TERNAN WILLIAM R	LTC	0-0204478	0157	1
MC TIER LINDY D	CW3	W-4150468	1167	1
MC TIGHE JOHN J	CPT	0-1551067	1146	2
MC VAY CLARENCE H	CW3	RW-2207614	0266	1
MC VAY LLOYD R	CW4	W-2141379	0764	1
MC VAY MELVIN J	CPT	0-0201673	0648	3
MC VEA JOHN B	MAJ	0-1018282	0263	1
MC VEIGH JAMES H	COL	0-0116330	1049	3
MC VEIGH SR GEORGE M	MAJ	0-1576378	0361	1
MC VEY ALBERT V	COL	0-0175141	0560	3
MC VEY DELBERT P	1LT	0-0177711	1261	3
MC VEY OTTO T	CPT	0-1634130	0647	1
MC VICAR JOSEPH K	LTC	0-0245551	0463	3
MC VICKER FOREST R	1LT	0-0519105	0146	1
MC VICKER GEORGE C	CW4	W-2115131	0857	2
MC VICKER PAUL M	CPT	0-0236492	1054	3
MC VOY JOHN A	LTC	0-0221457	1063	3
MC WADE JAMES	MAJ	0-1342288	0361	1
MC WATERS WILLIAM L	LTC	0-1301077	1062	1
MC WAYNE JR FRANK E	MAJ	0-0285725	1046	2
MC WEE NATHANIEL	MAJ	0-0378613	0555	1
MC WHIRTER BONNIE	MAJ	0-0241797	1144	2
MC WHIRTER EDWARD L	CPT	0-0413163	0946	2
MC WHIRTER OSCAR M	MAJ	0-0250012	0567	3
MC WHORTER FRANK R	CPT	0-1556023	0358	1
MC WHORTER JR JOHN C	1LT	0-0449506	0945	2
MC WHORTER ROBERT F	CW2	W-2120995	0348	1
MC WILLIAM JAMES T	LTC	0-1102858	1066	3
MC WILLIAMS ALVA L	MAJ	0-1878312	0767	1
MC WILLIAMS JOHN	CW2	W-2142250	0953	1
MC WILLIAMS JUDSON H	CPT	0-1593715	0647	2
MC WILLIAMS WILLIAM	COL	0-0321847	1159	3
MCCAWLEY HARRISON B	1LT	0-0548460	0946	2
MCDONALD LAWRENCE H	1LT	0-0488866	0654	1
MCGOVERN JAMES R	MAJ	0-1057527	0154	1
MCILWAIN JOSEPH E	COL	0-0208728	0456	3
MCKINLEY GEORGE R	CPT	0-1030591	0154	1
MCMENAMIN EDWARD C	1LT	0-0551924	0846	2
MCNULTY THOMAS J	LTC	0-0492138	1053	1
MEACHAM CARL J	COL	0-0106926	1055	2
MEACHAM GORDON F	CW3	RW-2209559	0467	1
MEACHAM MERLE A	LTC	0-0303610	0962	3
MEACHEN LORREN H	MAJ	0-0186499	0753	3
MEACHUM HUBERT J	1LT	0-1324351	0446	1
MEAD ALBERT H	MAJ	0-0206973	0147	2
MEAD ALFRED J	LTC	0-0192105	1157	3
MEAD AMOS R	LTC	0-0262543	0865	3
MEAD DOUGLAS O	MAJ	0-0219943	0154	3
MEAD EMORY A	LTC	0-0309406	0863	3
MEAD EUGENE W	MAJ	0-0230565	0644	2
MEAD JOHN G	LTC	0-1299774	0663	1
MEAD JR HARVEY L	LTC	0-0179115	1061	2
MEAD ROBERT F	CPT	0-0453855	0646	2
MEADE CHARLES H	CW4	W-2103764	0866	1
MEADE EUGENE L	MAJ	0-1945891	0564	1
MEADE JOHN E	LTC	0-0143054	1053	3
MEADE MARVIN W	1LT	0-1000822	0458	2
MEADE WILLIAM H	LTC	0-0503578	1045	2
MEADER EDWARD H	CPT	0-1017348	1060	2
MEADERS KIRK A	LTC	0-0397126	0447	2
MEADOR ARLINE R	2LT	N-0761589	0646	1
MEADOR BARCLAY F	COL	0-0140407	0958	3
MEADOR ELTON	WO1	W-2117247	0252	1
MEADOR JOHN D	CPT	0-0416030	0244	1
MEADOR JOHN G	MAJ	0-1577557	0455	1
MEADOR RILEY W	LTC	0-1309328	0358	1
MEADOR WILLIAM	WO1	W-2142997	0756	1
MEADORS JR JOHN H	CW2	W-2147834	1060	1
MEADORS RICHARD N	CW3	W-2144107	0756	1
MEADOW NATHAN	1LT	0-1284737	1143	2
MEADOWS ANDERSON C	LTC	0-0153790	1058	3
MEADOWS CHARLIE E	LTC	0-0386676	0357	1
MEADOWS CLARENCE C	MAJ	0-0266546	0244	2
MEADOWS CLYDE L	CW4	W-2109679	0857	1
MEADOWS ERNEST C	CW2	W-2152435	0461	1
MEADOWS FRED W	MAJ	0-1590655	1264	1
MEADOWS JAMES A	1LT	0-1287920	0245	2
MEADOWS JOHN R D	1LT	0-0251772	1055	3
MEADOWS JOHN W	CPT	0-1744795	0-48	1
MEADOWS MARSHALL D	MAJ	0-0330102	0846	2
MEADOWS OLIVER E	CPT	0-0465376	0447	2
MEADOWS WADE O	MAJ	0-1302501	0457	1
MEADOWS WILLIAM R	CW3	W-2141804	0360	1
MEADS OLIVER F	CPT	0-2008205	0557	1
MEAGHER JR THOMAS F	MAJ	0-1341561	0666	1
MEAGHER MARY C	MAJ	N-0771638	0864	1
MEAGHER STELLA M	MAJ	N-0737510	0166	3
MEALEY FRED T	CPT	0-0487155	1148	1
MEALEY JOHN A	MAJ	0-2000494	0264	1
MEALING JR JOHN R	LTC	0-0249055	0462	3
MEANEY JR WILLIAM J	LTC	0-0323319	0265	3
MEANEY MARTIN H	COL	0-0182202	0948	3
MEANEY ROD F	MAJ	0-1645816	0163	2
MEANLEY JR WILLIAM C	COL	0-0326057	0464	1
MEANS JOHN S	LTC	0-0110055	0453	3
MEANS LEWIS M	B G	0-0133499	0246	1
MEANS RALPH F	LTC	0-0293185	0765	1
MEANS RUSSELL R	MAJ	0-1176131	0765	1
MEANS WILLIAM J	CW4	W-2109848	0157	1
MEANY JOHN H	CPT	0-1685994	0845	2
MEARES WALTER A	LTC	0-0220071	0352	3
MEARS DOUGLAS C	2LT	0-1054714	0445	2
MEARS GLEN G	LTC	0-1047678	1061	1
MEARS JAMES E	LTC	0-1010034	0954	1
MEARS JOHN A	LTC	0-0255473	0967	3
MEARS JR KENNETH M	LTC	0-1823912	0264	1
MEARS RALPH E	MAJ	0-2006144	1163	1
MEASE RUSSELL S	CPT	0-1185291	0962	1
MEASLEY JR WILBUR T	MAJ	0-1326867	0163	1
MEAUT BERMOND J	LTC	0-1168816	0967	1
MEAUT WILLIAM M	2LT	0-0519697	0745	2
MEAUX ELTON J	CW2	W-2146454	0656	1
MEBUS GEORGE B	LTC	0-0197103	0563	3
MECARTEA LOUIS J	MAJ	0-1057823	0763	1
MECCA JR ANDREW L	LTC	0-0378326	0663	1
MECCA THEODORE F	MAJ	0-0969325	0463	1
MECHAM ROSS L	CPT	0-1174957	0251	1
MECHLER FLOYD A	CPT	0-1103799	0246	2
MECHLER WILLIAM J	MAJ	0-0286762	1059	3
MECHLING GEORGE S	LTC	0-0329587	0249	3
MECHTEL NORMAN F	MAJ	0-2262777	0162	1
MECORD PHILIP H	CPT	0-0980044	1060	1
MEDAGLIANI JOSEPH R	LTC	0-1691898	0561	1
MEDALIA LEON S	COL	0-0211525	0546	2
MEDARIS CHESTER T	LTC	0-0300677	1166	3
MEDBERY EDWARD W	LTC	0-0257754	0967	3
MEDCALF RICHARD A	CW2	W-2141995	0661	1
MEDCALF VAN C	LTC	0-0211448	0252	2
MEDD CHARLES B	MAJ	0-2326748	0466	3
MEDDAUGH RALPH T	CPT	0-0204134	0963	3
MEDEIROS WALTER L	CW3	W-2150902	0763	1
MEDER ALFRED C	CPT	0-1285083	1145	2
MEDESY WILLIAM A	CPT	0-0317969	0444	2
MEDFORD EDWARD E	CPT	0-1177087	0865	1
MEDFORD ERNEST C	MAJ	0-0986502	0864	1
MEDFORD WILLIAM T	COL	0-0128641	1055	2
MEDICK ROBERT L	CW2	W-2149934	0960	1
MEDICO SIMON P	CPT	0-2019060	0959	1
MEDINA ANGEL	2LT	0-1896441	0559	1
MEDINA ANTONIO	LTC	0-0267935	0760	1
MEDINA VICTOR	CW3	W-2144988	0861	1
MEDINGER ROBERT E	LTC	0-1110099	0967	1
MEDLEY ARTHUR W	MAJ	0-0487661	0463	1
MEDLEY CHARLES A	CPT	0-1922613	1161	1
MEDLEY MAX W	MAJ	0-1293252	0557	2
MEDLEY OSCAR W	CW3	W-2105019	0656	1
MEDLIN GEORGE C	CW2	W-2211601	0466	1
MEDLIN MAE	MAJ	N-0735821	0165	1
MEDLIN MOEF	LTC	0-0286741	0366	3

NAME	GRADE	SVC NO	DATE RET MO YR	RET CODE
MEDLIN NED O	CW3	W-2145899	1160	1
MEDLIN RAYMOND	LTC	0-1305288	0867	3
MEDLIN THOMAS F	CPT	0-2262972	1160	2
MEDLOCK AL S	MAJ	0-1877870	1266	1
MEDLOCK CLARENCE E	LTC	0-0211815	0164	3
MEDLOCK THOMAS L	MAJ	0-1923551	0866	1
MEDSKER ROY R	CW3	W-2153666	0264	1
MEDVED RAYMOND L	MAJ	0-0992736	0365	1
MEDZ GOHAR	1LT	N-0758379	0952	1
MEE JAMES H	CPT	0-0451744	0844	2
MEE JOSEPH W	CW3	W-2151005	0265	1
MEECE FRANK H	LTC	0-0271472	1164	3
MEECH ROBERT A	LTC	0-1104299	0862	1
MEEDS ROBERT E	COL	0-0252580	0959	3
MEEHAN DAVID R	MAJ	0-0499023	0147	2
MEEHAN JR FRANK J	CW3	W-2151667	0665	1
MEEHAN PAUL F	LTC	0-1319965	1062	1
MEEK EDWIN M	MAJ	0-0506264	0546	2
MEEK HIBBS S	MAJ	0-0510241	0557	1
MEEK JOSEPH C	CPT	0-0275849	1063	3
MEEK LEONARD L	CPT	0-0342059	0146	2
MEEK LESTER I	COL	0-0320351	0256	3
MEEK WILBUR J	LTC	0-0434226	0667	1
MEEK WILLIAM M	CPT	0-0521825	0347	2
MEEKER BRUNS	LTC	0-0395551	0860	1
MEEKER GEORGE E	COL	0-0201978	0161	3
MEEKER JR FRANK R	LTC	0-1646421	0563	1
MEEKER ROBERT M	CPT	0-1312032	0146	2
MEEKINS EDMUND L	LTC	0-0278490	0159	1
MEEKINS GEORGE E	MAJ	0-1172994	0561	1
MEEKINS JOSEPH A	CW2	W-2118459	0146	1
MEEKINS RAYMOND M	COL	0-0179465	0861	3
MEEKS CHARLIE C	MAJ	0-0358194	0347	1
MEEKS LAWRENCE F	COL	0-0299917	0360	1
MEEKS ROBERT B	LTC	0-0122861	0952	3
MEEKS SYDNEY M	CW4	W-2119453	0457	1
MEELER MARION F	CW2	W-2142306	1057	1
MEENAN IGNATIUS J	CPT	0-0182812	0751	3
MEERMAN WILLIAM A	MAJ	0-1296236	0862	1
MEES THOMAS L	1LT	0-1292215	0146	2
MEESE CHARLES M	LTC	0-0922558	0565	3
MEESKE JOHN M	CPT	0-1702352	0346	2
MEFFORD ANDY J	CW4	W-2110431	0361	1
MEFFORD ERNEST A	MAJ	0-0289306	0146	2
MEGAN LEE C	LTC	0-2040939	0566	3
MEGARGEE JR HENRY P	2LT	0-1555102	0445	2
MEGARITY JACK	CPT	0-0968217	0461	1
MEGERLE NEIL O	2LT	0-1913822	1039	1
MEGOWAN FRANK M	1LT	0-0519763	0846	2
MEGOWAN NORBERT F	LTC	0-0292836	0861	1
MEHAFFEY JACK E	MAJ	0-1588166	1160	1
MEHAFFEY JAMES L	MAJ	0-1293096	0366	3
MEHAFFEY JAY H	CPT	0-1321464	0247	2
MEHAFFEY JR ROBERT E	MAJ	0-0384153	0745	2
MEHAFFEY WILSON J	2LT	0-1320286	0944	2
MEHAFFIE HAROLD R	CPT	0-1044615	0154	1
MEHAFFIE KENNETH N	CPT	0-0204820	0362	1
MEHAFFIE TERRENCE C	2LT	0-1046196	0645	2
MEHAL ANDREW A	CPT	0-2262667	0861	2
MEHARG H T	2LT	0-1311913	1044	2
MEHCIZ RALPH C	CPT	0-4005326	0965	1
MEHEFKO JOHN J	CPT	0-1171468	0949	1
MEHEGAN JAMES D	MAJ	0-0533040	1047	2
MEHEULA DANIEL K	1LT	0-2012516	1048	2
MEHL FRED C	LTC	0-0100786	0657	3
MEHL LOUIS S	LTC	0-1031576	1264	1
MEHLE JAMES T	CPT	0-1948970	1051	1
MEHLICK CECELIA G	CPT	N-0773630	0764	1
MEHLIN ELIZABETH	MAJ	N-0731412	1162	1
MEHNER HANS H	CW3	W-2136650	0363	1
MEHOLIN JOSEPH W	CPT	0-0247284	1045	2
MEHRTEN DERYLE M	MAJ	0-1693115	1163	1
MEIER ALFRED A	CW3	W-2004721	0765	1
MEIER BERNHARDT	MAJ	0-0378498	0860	1
MEIER GEORGE A	CPT	0-1298092	0147	2

NAME	GRADE	SVC NO	DATE RET MO YR	RET CODE
MEIER JR CARL J	CPT	0-2007738	0457	1
MEIER MERVIN W	MAJ	0-1180615	0458	2
MEIER ROBERT A	LTC	0-0223045	0559	3
MEIER ROBERT J	CW4	W-2102089	0255	2
MEIER RUSSELL F	COL	0-0253923	1059	1
MEIERDIERCKS EDWARD	MAJ	0-1294872	0264	1
MEIGHAN SYLVESTER	LTC	0-0246329	0661	1
MEIGHEN CARL H	CW4	W-2132731	0361	1
MEIGHEN CHARLES P	MAJ	0-0151274	1155	3
MEIGHEN MILES P	CPT	0-0185195	0960	3
MEIGHEN PATRICK H	MAJ	0-1341352	1060	1
MEIGS CHARLES P	1LT	0-0108149	0839	1
MEIGS GEORGE A	LTC	0-0305387	0966	3
MEIHOFF AMIEL D	CPT	0-0521072	0248	2
MEIK FRANCIS J	LTC	0-0287668	1157	3
MEIKLEJOHN WILLIAM R	MAJ	0-1301854	0761	1
MEILSTRUP DREW R	MAJ	0-0347900	0346	2
MEINCKE WALDEMAR	MAJ	0-1799339	1262	1
MEINDERTSMA PETER	MAJ	0-2006946	0461	1
MEINDL JAMES A	LTC	0-0455521	1167	3
MEINERDING ROBERT R	MAJ	0-1320761	0562	1
MEINKE ARTHUR C	CPT	0-0888224	1045	2
MEINSCHEIN BERNARD J	1LT	0-1328381	0146	2
MEINSTEIN SIEGFRIED	1LT	0-0961622	0151	1
MEIS JOSEPH A	LTC	0-0478778	1048	1
MEISEL HAROLD L	LTC	0-1845071	0564	1
MEISENHEIMER JEROME	LTC	0-0244193	1061	3
MEISENHELDER LLOYD E	CPT	0-0904037	1044	2
MEISER EDWARD H	LTC	0-0461148	0862	1
MEISNER ROBERT F	1LT	0-1299925	1045	2
MEISS GUY C	LTC	0-1017397	0463	1
MEISSNER FRED	CPT	0-0182496	0431	1
MEISTER CARL J	MAJ	0-1283648	1046	2
MEISTER ELSIE M	MAJ	N-0742942	0965	1
MEISTER VICTOR M	MAJ	0-0242521	0257	3
MEIXELL SR GLENN E	MAJ	0-0994420	0365	1
MEIZLER FRANK	CPT	0-2006049	0160	1
MEJO WALTER L	MAJ	0-0250903	1166	3
MEKLAS JOHN F	2LT	0-0511831	0944	2
MELAD RAFAEL	2LT	0-1896491	0553	1
MELANCON JAMES L	CPT	0-0421159	1144	2
MELANSON JOSEPH W P	LTC	0-0395775	1160	1
MELANSON RICHARD C	MAJ	0-2289007	0763	1
MELBOURNE CLARENCE J	MAJ	0-1599049	0163	1
MELBOURNE RALPH V	CW3	W-2148502	0166	1
MELCHER GEORGE H	MAJ	0-0328155	0145	2
MELCHER PHILIP R	LTC	0-1041848	0862	1
MELCHERS DORA E	CPT	N-0762103	0854	2
MELCHERT HAROLD R	LTC	0-0499798	1263	3
MELCHIOR ARCHIBALD	COL	0-0134768	0454	3
MELDRUM CHARLES B	MAJ	0-0244323	0356	3
MELDRUM GORDON C	LTC	0-0333230	0863	3
MELEGARI WILLIAM	CW2	W-2200462	0562	2
MELENDEZ JUAN R	LTC	0-0404152	1164	1
MELGARD CHARLES G	2LT	0-0520258	0245	2
MELIM JOHN V	LTC	0-0363732	0563	3
MELINA SAMUEL R	LTC	0-1897081	0165	1
MELINE WILLIAM C	LTC	0-0378055	0665	3
MELISE SAMUEL	1LT	0-0380708	1144	2
MELISH JOHN R	LTC	0-0191763	0262	3
MELIUS ROBERT C	CW2	W-2204975	0160	1
MELKO JOHN T	MAJ	0-1284363	0457	1
MELKONIAN SAM	MAJ	0-1925535	0467	1
MELL CHARLES M	MAJ	0-1000824	0663	1
MELL CHARLES N	MAJ	0-0522705	1145	2
MELLA HUGO	COL	0-0485466	0846	2
MELLARD ROBERT R	CW2	W-2144704	1059	1
MELLARS JR THOMAS A	LTC	0-1058077	1166	1
MELLEN WILLIAM F	LTC	0-0295510	0166	3
MELLEN WILLIAM H	MAJ	0-0264942	0950	3
MELLER JOSEPH	MAJ	0-0274460	0165	3
MELLICK ALDEN B	LTC	0-1175237	1166	3
MELLIN CLIFFORD O	LTC	0-0280448	0247	2
MELLIN LEVI R	CPT	0-0121372	0355	3
MELLINGER OLIVER L	LTC	0-0497775	0767	3

NAME	GRADE	SVC NO	DATE RET MO YR	RET CODE
MELLION JACOB	COL	0-0276682	1057	3
MELLIS DONALD R	MAJ	0-0172966	1159	3
MELLISH FREDERICK	MAJ	0-0403265	1045	2
MELLMAN SANFORD S	CPT	0-0475019	0649	1
MELLOM JULIUS D	MAJ	0-1552334	1055	1
MELLON JAMES E	1LT	0-1934948	0854	2
MELLON JOHN	CPT	0-0496717	0750	1
MELLON JOSEPH R	LTC	0-1312491	0863	1
MELLOR MARY E K	CPT	N-0700141	0846	1
MELLOW JR THOMAS H	CPT	0-1305955	0548	2
MELNICK CARL J	COL	0-0443785	0954	1
MELNIKOFF VLADIMIR N	MAJ	0-0981211	1160	1
MELOAN JOHN H	COL	0-0145054	0856	3
MELOCHICK GEORGE	LTC	0-1312697	1057	1
MELODY MILNER D	CPT	0-0381555	0148	2
MELOGRANO VINCENT J	MAJ	0-1598635	0164	1
MELPIGNANO JOSEPH P	1LT	0-1298568	0353	1
MELRAGON HENRY A	CPT	0-0425931	1046	2
MELSON GRESHAM E	CPT	0-0971971	0567	2
MELTON ADRUS C	MAJ	0-0364692	0667	3
MELTON ALFRED E	MAJ	0-1947153	1060	1
MELTON CHARLES E	COL	0-0330103	0954	2
MELTON CLARENCE W	WO1	W-2145467	0862	1
MELTON DOYLE E	CW3	W-2208444	1166	1
MELTON EDWARD T	LTC	0-1641575	0265	1
MELTON EDWARD R	COL	0-0223239	1060	3
MELTON ELDRIDGE	COL	0-0223067	0254	3
MELTON ERNEST B	2LT	0-1032291	1044	2
MELTON EUGENE R	LTC	0-1280016	0854	1
MELTON FRANK	LTC	0-1542606	1058	2
MELTON GEORGE D	CW3	W-2142499	0859	1
MELTON JOSEPH	CPT	0-1689515	0146	2
MELTON JR ROBERT P	LTC	0-0549541	0564	1
MELTON LUTHER L	LTC	0-0403613	1263	1
MELTON NORMAN A	CPT	0-1171676	0156	1
MELTON OLIVER O	2LT	0-0514312	1045	2
MELTON ORVAL W	2LT	0-1897734	0452	1
MELTON ROBERT L	WO1	W-2118112	0758	1
MELTON ROMIE L	COL	0-0220624	0764	3
MELTON RUSCOE	CPT	0-1341895	0860	1
MELTON TALVIN R	CPT	0-1288932	0558	1
MELTON TILLMAN K	MAJ	0-0288839	0266	3
MELTON WILLIAM R	MAJ	0-0471031	0851	1
MELTZ ROBERT W	MAJ	0-1306302	0462	1
MELTZER JACK	MAJ	0-0336050	0246	2
MELTZER JAMES L	CPT	0-1304635	1147	2
MELVILLE ALBERT F	CW3	W-2144772	1055	1
MELVILLE JOHN W	MAJ	0-0299516	0246	2
MELVIN ALLISON O	LTC	0-1636318	0859	1
MELVIN DANIEL L	MAJ	0-1038066	0661	1
MELVIN GEORGE H	COL	0-0451006	0862	1
MELVIN HERSCHEL L	LTC	0-0288576	0954	1
MELVIN JOHN W	CW3	W-2205163	0766	1
MELVIN ROBERT F	LTC	0-1311807	1062	1
MELVIN THOMAS F	1LT	0-2034564	1044	2
MELVIN WALTER H	CPT	0-1686522	0554	1
MELVIN WILLIAM L	CPT	0-0948715	0361	1
MELZER CLIVE R	LTC	0-0474576	1153	2
MELZER PHILLIPS	LTC	0-1046567	0565	1
MELZER WILLIAM N	CPT	0-0466864	0245	2
MEMMINGER CHARLES B	MAJ	0-0140507	1152	3
MEMORY ROBERT A	CPT	0-0354093	0945	2
MENA ESTEBAN	LTC	0-0357958	0657	1
MENA JOSE A	MAJ	0-0376556	0157	1
MENAPACE LOUIS A	MAJ	0-1338733	1064	1
MENAPACE ROBERT R	COL	0-0169581	1053	3
MENARD JOHN R	MAJ	0-0404866	0248	1
MENARD LEO A	CW3	W-2151889	1065	1
MENARICK GEORGE E	MAJ	0-1639673	0267	1
MENCACCY ALBERT C	LTC	0-0283869	1060	3
MENCACCY FERNANDO C	M G	0-0278275	0762	3
MENCH EDWARD F	1LT	0-0912378	0745	2
MENCH LLOYD G	1LT	0-1101116	0446	2
MENCHER EDWARD W	CPT	0-0330539	0844	2
MENDE RALPH A	MAJ	0-0965177	0563	1

NAME	GRADE	SVC NO	DATE RET MO YR	RET CODE
MENDELSOHN ISADOR W	MAJ	0-0234424	0554	3
MENDELSOHN LESTER	WO1	W-2105532	0954	1
MENDELSON MARVIN	1LT	0-1306447	0745	2
MENDEN JULIAN	LTC	0-0250292	1165	3
MENDENHALL EDWIN L	CPT	0-1683501	0950	1
MENDENHALL HERBERT O	COL	0-0116377	0648	3
MENDENHALL JOHN B	COL	0-0331568	1164	3
MENDENHALL VIRGIL C	WO1	W-2123978	0844	2
MENDEZ EDRIS	LTC	0-0417742	0860	1
MENDEZ JOSE F	LTC	0-0453159	1060	1
MENDEZ JR PEDRO T	CPT	0-1313169	1060	1
MENDEZ-RIOS FRANCISC	CW2	W-2147655	0264	1
MENDLOW SAMUEL	1LT	0-1823035	0246	2
MENDOLA VINCENT S	1LT	0-1050812	0945	2
MENDOZA JOSE T	CPT	0-1313662	0863	1
MENDOZA JULIO F	MAJ	0-1037623	0260	1
MENDOZA NICK	2LT	0-1896671	1148	1
MENDOZA SOFIO P	LTC	0-0888136	0749	1
MENEGUS GRACE N	MAJ	L-0901371	0566	1
MENEGUZZI ENRICO	MAJ	0-1081085	0866	1
MENGEL GEORGE F	MAJ	0-0962937	0865	1
MENGES ALBERT C	LTC	0-0397125	1060	1
MENGES JOSEPH W	LTC	0-0255642	1163	3
MENGES WILBUR S	CPT	0-0361593	0145	2
MENGHINI ERMA P	1LT	N-0772100	0845	1
MENGHINI RENALDO R	MAJ	0-0318616	1045	2
MENIATIS ARTHUR	MAJ	0-0496373	0451	1
MENICON MENICOS N	LTC	0-0321699	0962	3
MENIFEE RUSSELL R	WO1	W-2126018	0154	1
MENKEMEYER HENRY	CPT	0-1165766	0245	1
MENKEN JOHN J	CW3	W-2136723	0163	1
MENKING ROBERT C	LTC	0-1634135	1067	1
MENMUIR JAMES B	LTC	0-0257169	1061	3
MENNEG PAUL F	CPT	0-1290637	0346	2
MENNELL LORNE F	CPT	0-1301183	0545	2
MENNING EUGENE W	LTC	0-1040270	1266	1
MENNINGER HENRY E	2LT	0-1794832	1145	2
MENSH JENNIE	CPT	N-0723635	0546	1
MENTEMEYER ALFRED D	1LT	0-1055917	1060	1
MENTKOWSKI JOSEPH T	MAJ	0-2262307	0364	1
MENTON CATHERINE	MAJ	N-0797771	0765	1
MENTZER BLISS A	1LT	0-1181957	0745	2
MENTZOS LEWIS G	MAJ	0-2007034	0859	1
MENUSTIK JR JOHN	CPT	0-0542521	0546	1
MENVILLE EUGENE F	LTC	0-0495402	0657	1
MENZIE MARY B	CPT	N-0739999	0947	1
MENZIES GORDON E	COL	0-0346100	0465	3
MENZIES GRACE	MAJ	L-0609389	0963	1
MERBACH EDWARD	MAJ	0-1059207	0459	1
MERBACK ARTHUR A	CPT	0-0535414	0549	2
MERCADO FELIX V	COL	0-0303993	0862	1
MERCADO RAUL	COL	0-0232438	0966	3
MERCAK ANDREW R	MAJ	0-2200128	0866	1
MERCER ARTHUR G	MAJ	0-0988494	0866	1
MERCER BEATRICE E	CW2	V-0135389	0165	1
MERCER CHARLTON W	2LT	0-1921896	0545	2
MERCER EDWIN W	LTC	0-0287369	1264	3
MERCER GARNET F	LTC	0-1313770	0966	1
MERCER GERALD L	1LT	0-1289768	0246	2
MERCER HORACE R	MAJ	0-1339380	0865	1
MERCER HOWELL P	COL	0-0906799	1262	1
MERCER JAMES A	COL	0-0283734	0647	2
MERCER JAMES A	COL	0-0470611	0455	1
MERCER JOE R	CW4	W-2143771	1060	1
MERCER JOHN W	LTC	0-0240935	1163	3
MERCER LEWIS P	CPT	0-1300677	0646	2
MERCER LOIS P	2LT	N-0741940	1043	1
MERCER NELSON	LTC	0-0151140	1251	3
MERCER RAY	COL	0-0117439	0648	3
MERCER RICHARD H	LTC	0-0240470	0763	3
MERCER ROBERT C	CPT	0-1295058	0146	2
MERCER ROY W	MAJ	0-0235051	0454	3
MERCER TIM	LTC	0-1103801	0867	1
MERCHANT AUSTIN W	COL	0-0262892	1066	3
MERCHANT CHARLES L	MAJ	0-1594333	0363	1

NAME	GRADE	SVC NO	DATE RET MO YR	RET CODE
MERCHANT HAROLD E	MAJ	0-1168818	0159	1
MERCHANT JR JESSE C	CW2	W-2104297	0347	2
MERCHANT MARCIUS F	MAJ	C-0247845	C648	3
MERCHANT MARTIN L V	LTC	0-1313113	C762	1
MERCHANT ROBERT P	LTC	0-0467814	0164	1
MERCHANT THCMAS D	CPT	0-0410858	0946	1
MERCHANT WILLARD R	COL	0-0296377	C265	2
MERCHANT WILLIAM A	CPT	0-0494850	0345	2
MERCHANT WILLIAM B	MAJ	C-0397121	0863	1
MERCIER FRANCIS B	MAJ	C-0454209	0261	1
MERCIER HAROLD A	LTC	0-0551807	1064	3
MERCIER HOWARD S	MAJ	C-1293445	C861	2
MERCIER JR ALBIN S	MAJ	C-2202018	C267	1
MERCIER ROMA R	1LT	N-0752833	1154	2
MERCIL SIMONE Y	MAJ	N-0755584	0965	1
MERCKER ALBERT D	COL	0-0237278	C460	3
MERCURIO ALBERT A	MAJ	0-1118615	0760	2
MERDELL MELVIN E	CPT	0-1101121	1055	2
MEREDITH ARVIN D	LTC	0-1042652	C762	1
MEREDITH CHARLES L	COL	0-0371790	1262	1
MEREDITH DOYLE C	LTC	0-1031666	0957	1
MEREDITH EARL E	LTC	C-1327366	C765	1
MEREDITH ERNEST L	CW4	W-2106048	0562	3
MEREDITH HERBERT J	MAJ	0-0962264	1165	1
MEREDITH JAMES C	MAJ	C-0228543	1156	3
MEREDITH JOSEPH W	1LT	0-0263430	0648	3
MEREDITH JR ROBERT M	MAJ	C-1685678	0364	2
MEREDITH KENNETH M	LTC	0-0318004	0455	1
MEREDITH PAUL F	LTC	0-0237978	0864	3
MEREDITH WILLIAM P	COL	0-0323047	C764	1
MEREHENT DALE D	MAJ	C-0195254	C462	3
MERENBACH WALTER	COL	0-0340814	0663	1
MERGARE VICTOR	MAJ	C-1796506	0759	1
MERGELE MARVIN E	CPT	C-0482577	0145	2
MERGENTHAL RAYMONC O	MAJ	C-2014467	C566	1
MERGET JOHN R	LTC	0-0313897	0661	3
MERICAL CLOYD A	MAJ	C-1648985	0857	1
MERICLE HAROLD F	LTC	0-0194266	0948	3
MERIDETH CLAUDE T	CW3	W-2145892	0464	1
MERIGLIANO JOSEPH J	CW2	W-2147407	C363	1
MERIN HERBERT L	CPT	0-1030908	104N	2
MERIWETHER DON R	1LT	0-0434705	1044	2
MERIWETHER JOHN B	MAJ	0-0162729	0356	3
MERIWETHER WILLIAM M	MAJ	0-1003989	C460	1
MERKEL ARTHUR V	LTC	0-0270120	1166	3
MERKEL ECWARD J	LTC	0-1577562	0266	1
MERKEL ELLEN H	MAJ	N-0800044	1165	2
MERKEL GORDON O	CPT	0-1325066	1047	2
MERKL FRANK M	LTC	0-0167914	1058	3
MERKLE CHARLES A	COL	0-027510C	0357	1
MERKLE NOLA J	2LT	N-0736420	0345	1
MERKLER FRANK C	CPT	C-1293293	0847	2
MERLE HENRI J	LTC	0-1328280	0563	1
MERLI PETER A	CW4	W-2148414	C967	1
MERLIN SAMUEL A	COL	0-0223870	1161	3
MERLINO LOUIS	CPT	0-1049579	0747	2
MERLO NICHOLAS A	1LT	0-2037860	1047	2
MEROLA ANTHONY A	LTC	0-1332397	C666	1
MERONEY RICHARD H	LTC	0-1042653	1060	1
MEROWIT CLEMENT E	CPT	0-0919438	1045	2
MERRELL HERMAN E	CPT	0-1946573	1060	2
MERRELL STANLEY S	COL	C-0287447	0566	3
MERRIAM BERNARD A	MAJ	0-0167860	0648	3
MERRIAM CHARLES	MAJ	0-0989882	0467	1
MERRIAM CHARLES S	LTC	C-0301344	C859	1
MERRIAM HOWARD K	LTC	0-1639398	C262	1
MERRIAM JR GEORGE C	LTC	0-0918333	1067	3
MERRIAM KENNETH G	COL	0-0171071	1061	3
MERRIAM LUCIUS B	LTC	0-0308608	0358	3
MERRIAM WALTER F	LTC	0-0243939	0943	2
MERRICK BERNARD V	COL	0-0184651	C853	1
MERRICK CHARLES M	MAJ	C-1553702	1067	3
MERRICK JANE A	1LT	N-0742353	C346	1
MERRICK JOSEPH W	LTC	0-1596731	0463	1
MERRICK RICHARD H	COL	0-0273724	0665	1

NAME	GRADE	SVC NO	DATE RET MO YR	RET CODE
MERRIFIELD CHARLES C	LTC	0-0252599	0-52	1
MERRIMEW JAMES L	1LT	0-1320155	1045	2
MERRILL ADELBERT H	MAJ	0-0254048	1057	3
MERRILL ALVIE L	COL	0-0207985	0346	2
MERRILL CHAUNCEY D	M G	0-0112486	0758	3
MERRILL EDWARC A	COL	0-0170186	0560	3
MERRILL EDWARC O	MAJ	0-1313771	0666	1
MERRILL ELWIN	MAJ	0-1116964	0463	1
MERRILL FRANKLIN R	LTC	0-1297516	0459	2
MERRILL HAMILTON	COL	0-0162202	0858	3
MERRILL HAROLD D	LTC	0-025425C	0960	3
MERRILL HARRY E	MAJ	0-1643123	0759	1
MERRILL HENRY B	COL	0-0216111	0754	3
MERRILL HOWARD C	LTC	0-1290282	0465	1
MERRILL JOHN P	COL	0-0181405	0559	1
MERRILL JR RCY A	MAJ	0-4018677	0466	1
MERRILL JR WILLIAM H	COL	0-0217017	0163	3
MERRILL KENNETH J	MAJ	0-1105026	0450	1
MERRILL LEW E	MAJ	0-0350093	1157	3
MERRILL LOUIS M	LTC	0-0296151	1160	3
MERRILL MARRINER W	CPT	0-0497199	0845	1
MERRILL MELVILLE L	LTC	0-0110553	0648	3
MERRILL MELVIN C	2LT	0-0772067	0146	2
MERRILL MICHAEL S	CPT	0-1166784	1C47	1
MERRILL RALPH H	CW3	W-2150096	1157	1
MERRILL ROBERT A	MAJ	0-0230255	0345	2
MERRILL ROBERT S	CW4	W-2146080	1067	1
MERRILL SAM D	MAJ	0-1313699	0661	1
MERRILL SR WILLIAM B	CW2	W-2208587	0662	1
MERRILL WENDELL W	LTC	0-0466450	1162	1
MERRIMAN TAYLOR	LTC	0-0909676	0766	3
MERRIMAN WILSCN C	MAJ	0-0506577	0846	2
MERRIOTT OTHELL O	LTC	0-1542951	0562	1
MERRIS GILBERT E	LTC	0-1167117	0266	1
MERRITT BUFORD A	COL	0-0233751	0963	3
MERRITT CELBERT L	CPT	0-1288595	0345	2
MERRITT EARL W	2LT	0-1322645	0645	2
MERRITT ELMER V	MAJ	0-1179967	0260	1
MERRITT EMMETT H	MAJ	0-0497489	0151	1
MERRITT GEORGE W	CPT	0-1016514	0546	2
MERRITT HARRY W	1LT	0-0131861	0554	3
MERRITT I T	CW3	W-2205781	0965	1
MERRITT JOHN M	LTC	0-1305382	0163	1
MERRITT JOSEPH W	CPT	0-0277282	1266	3
MERRITT JR NCRMAN F	CPT	0-1899386	1155	1
MERRITT MAURICE A	1LT	0-1016613	1145	2
MERRITT PAUL D	MAJ	0-1329860	C263	1
MERRITT ROLAND J	MAJ	C-0301705	C261	1
MERRITT SYLVESTER	LTC	C-0475085	0454	1
MERRITT WILLIAM R	MAJ	0-1533862	C759	1
MERROW ELMER J	LTC	0-0411626	1060	1
MERRYMAN JAMES H	CPT	0-0141521	0648	3
MERRYWELL HARRY H	CW2	W-2209515	0165	1
MERRYWELL LOREN W	CW2	W-2115286	0567	1
MERSCHOFF BAYLY E	LTC	0-0395855	1262	1
MERSENSKE J E	1LT	N-0742268	1044	1
MERSHCN FREDERICK	MAJ	0-0287073	1158	3
MERSHCN JR WILLIAM B	LTC	0-0141550	1149	3
MERTEN FRED W	CW4	W-2103214	0659	1
MERTENS HERMAN C	MAJ	C-0476861	0149	1
MERTZ LOWELL C	LTC	0-1585889	0164	1
MERTZ PAUL F	LTC	0-2037681	0866	1
MERULLC ROLAND A	MAJ	0-2007468	0864	1
MERVES LCUIS	MAJ	0-0461400	1145	2
MERVINE SAMUEL S	COL	0-0299831	1059	3
MERVINE WILLIAM H	CW3	W-2115366	0255	2
MERVIS WALTER J	LTC	0-1583372	0361	1
MERWIN DCNALC W	CW3	W-214941C	0463	1
MERWIN WILLIAM H	CPT	0-0525931	0146	2
MERWINE NETTIE K	1LT	N-0741002	1047	1
MERWORTH RCY C	MAJ	0-1950704	0760	1
MERZ RCBERT E	2LT	0-1081086	0545	2
MESA CELSO C	LTC	0-0888117	1063	1
MESARCH VICTOR M	LTC	0-129381C	0762	1
MESAROS ANTHONY C	CPT	0-0454505	0745	2

NAME	GRADE	SVC NO	DATE RET MO YR	RET CODE
MESCH FRED P	CW3	W-2147532	1067	1
MESCH JOSEPH A	2LT	C-1298094	C643	2
MESCHAN VINCENT R	1LT	0-1015631	1045	2
MESECK WALTER T	LTC	0-0223941	0954	3
MESEKE VICTCR H	COL	0-0248177	0564	1
MESEKE WILLIAM C	LTC	0-0236069	C163	3
MESHEY WILLIAM P	MAJ	C-2009736	0662	1
MESHKOFF PETER P	MAJ	0-0253659	0267	3
MESICK JACOB P	1LT	0-2035958	C245	2
MESKER THERMON D	1LT	0-1017253	1046	2
MESKIMEN JOSEPH E	MAJ	C-0204436	0755	3
MESSEC WENDEL C	LTC	0-0450046	0363	1
MESSENGER KENNETH W	1LT	0-1115700	0545	2
MESSER BERNARD A	CW3	W-2151020	1165	1
MESSER CHARLES F	MAJ	0-0369464	C161	1
MESSER DALLAS C	2LT	0-1032440	1044	2
MESSER CANIEL	MAJ	C-1047238	C657	2
MESSER DOROTHY B	MAJ	N-0752956	C864	1
MESSER DOROTHY S	LTC	L-0200747	1167	1
MESSER FRED W	2LT	C-2012427	C246	1
MESSER MARVIN A	CPT	0-1044304	C663	1
MESSER THOMAS A	CPT	0-2008269	C855	1
MESSER THOMAS V	MAJ	0-1645821	0963	1
MESSER ZORA	LTC	0-0450606	1157	1
MESSERLY JR NOEL	MAJ	0-1333851	0262	1
MESSERSMITH CHARLES	LTC	C-0240306	0862	3
MESSERSMITH LEO H	CW4	W-2108228	0157	1
MESSEY JACK	CPT	0-0233523	1159	3
MESSICK WALTER L	LTC	0-1298971	0461	1
MESSIER BERTRAND G	1LT	0-1013103	0961	1
MESSIER EDMUND G	CPT	0-0501773	0351	1
MESSINA JACK A	2LT	C-132123C	0345	2
MESSINA JOSEPH	LTC	C-1290453	C158	1
MESSINA JOSEPH C	CPT	0-0386835	C146	2
MESSINA PHILIP V	CPT	0-0504318	C645	2
MESSINER FRED	1LT	0-0537041	0145	2
MESSING FRECERICK	LTC	0-1103803	0960	1
MESSMER ROBERT L	LTC	0-15485C1	0960	1
MESSMORE RALPH E	CPT	0-2262798	C461	1
MESSNER GRANT J	CPT	0-1110662	C963	1
MESSNER LUCILE A	MAJ	N-0777784	0667	3
MESSNER MARK A	LTC	0-0189628	1055	3
MESSNER ROY G	LTC	0-0207692	0451	3
MESSURI JOHN R	LTC	0-1311514	C967	1
MESTAN ALBERT A	MAJ	C-1688488	0962	1
MESTAYER JOHN L	1LT	0-1256729	0546	2
METCALF ALLEN M	2LT	0-0532110	0544	2
METCALF ANNE C	1LT	N-0725926	0746	1
METCALF CHARLES E	1LT	0-1294514	0345	2
METCALF FREDERICK	LTC	0-1322859	C964	1
METCALF HAROLD B	LTC	0-0235663	C862	3
METCALF MAURICE	LTC	0-0508610	C965	1
METCALF ROBERT W	LTC	0-1551068	C361	1
METCALF STANLEY W	COL	C-0264611	0-53	3
METCALF THOMAS F	LTC	0-1285268	C263	1
METCALFE ARTHUR S	LTC	0-1177089	0967	1
METCALFE GEORGE S	LTC	0-0277611	0962	3
METCALFE HERBERT A	MAJ	C-0307677	C163	3
METCALFE REX	1LT	0-1305626	1045	2
METELSKI JOHN J	MAJ	C-0307500	C866	3
METENY ALBERT J	COL	0-0266150	1164	3
METEVELIS DON G	1LT	C-1301856	0147	2
METHENY ARLIE	CPT	0-0966654	0859	1
METHENY ELLSWORTH	LTC	0-0341159	0163	1
METHENY MARVIN D	1LT	0-1556763	C558	1
METHENY RALPH S	COL	0-0277220	0665	3
METHENY WILLIAM E	MAJ	0-1922524	C565	1
METHVEN ALBERT E	MAJ	C-1040776	0446	2
METOYER SR ALFRED L	CW2	W-2148976	1165	1
METTENHEIMER JOHN M	LTC	0-0253137	0559	3
METTLEN LEE R	MAJ	C-1174383	1265	1
METZ HERBERT H	MAJ	0-0203898	C860	3
METZ HERMAN A	CPT	C-1690382	1045	2
METZ JAMES L	MAJ	0-0333244	0562	1
METZ KARL H	COL	0-0138403	0252	3

NAME	GRADE	SVC NO	DATE RET MO YR	RET CODE
METZ PAUL E	CW2	W-2214763	1266	1
METZ THEODORE H	COL	0-0312669	0157	1
METZBOWER SAMUEL D	2LT	0-1338491	0546	2
METZE ALBERT	CPT	0-0108796	0929	1
METZEROTH ERIC C	COL	0-0225837	0862	3
METZEROTT KIRK A	COL	0-0113851	0754	3
METZGAR JOHN M	LTC	0-1176434	1061	1
METZGAR THOMAS I	LTC	0-0196870	1061	3
METZGER ALLEN C	MAJ	0-1341283	0461	1
METZGER ERNEST L	LTC	0-1165250	0363	2
METZGER FRITZ R	MAJ	0-0241405	0666	3
METZGER HARRISON A	LTC	0-2068713	0667	1
METZGER HENRY G	LTC	0-0325958	0760	1
METZGER JOHN M	CPT	0-1167981	0765	2
METZGER MICHAEL F	MAJ	0-1309949	0361	1
METZGER RALPH A	LTC	0-0340158	1060	1
METZGER RICHARD J	LTC	C-1597741	0763	1
METZGER RUDOLPH V	COL	0-0321564	0866	3
METZLER WILLIAM F	LTC	0-0276196	0764	3
MEULENERS RUPEN H	LTC	0-1299273	0761	1
MEUNIER HECTCR A	2LT	0-2023907	0553	1
MEUNIER MARCEL P	2LT	0-1080648	0445	2
MEUNIER PAUL A	LTC	0-1110104	1066	3
MEURER FREDERICK	CPT	0-0214096	0762	3
MEURLOTT BYRCN M	LTC	0-0264094	0149	1
MEWALDT LEONARD R	CPT	0-1595706	1046	2
MEWHIRTER SYDNEY A	COL	0-0103909	0854	3
MEYER ADOLPHA M	CPT	N-0732164	1049	1
MEYER ALEX	CW3	W-2142881	0257	1
MEYER ANDREW	CW3	W-2149485	0165	1
MEYER ARLEIGH G	MAJ	0-1323596	1060	2
MEYER CAPILLE A	CPT	0-0120902	0648	3
MEYER CARROLL C	LTC	0-1296884	0962	1
MEYER CHARLES Z	LTC	0-0203309	0755	3
MEYER CLEBURNE H	CPT	0-1C32229	1146	2
MEYER DAN C	1LT	0-1648605	1045	2
MEYER EARL L	CPT	0-0131341	0351	3
MEYER ECWARD J	LTC	0-1545463	1160	1
MEYER EDWIN H	LTC	0-0236265	0645	2
MEYER ELVIN L	MAJ	0-1300354	0665	2
MEYER FRANCIS P	CPT	0-0498132	1044	2
MEYER FRANK J	CW4	W-2144558	0767	1
MEYER FRED J	MAJ	0-0463956	0664	1
MEYER FREDERICK	LTC	0-0386508	0466	3
MEYER GECRGE E	COL	0-0190136	0651	3
MEYER HAROLD W	LTC	0-1017537	1262	1
MEYER HART E	2LT	0-1176731	0945	2
MEYER HENRY	1LT	0-1178563	114N	2
MEYER HENRY A	MAJ	C-0470583	0746	2
MEYER HENRY H	LTC	0-0254892	0167	3
MEYER HENRY I	CPT	0-1116799	0947	2
MEYER HENRY S	MAJ	0-0267902	0965	3
MEYER HERSHEL	CPT	0-1821390	0844	2
MEYER IVAN W	LTC	0-0196462	1045	2
MEYER JACK J	CPT	0-4011144	0661	2
MEYER JAKE K	CW4	W-2134476	0557	1
MEYER JOHN J	LTC	0-1549332	0164	1
MEYER JOSEPH F	CW3	W-2141932	0661	1
MEYER JR CHARLES C	2LT	0-1012637	0544	2
MEYER JR GEORGE C	LTC	0-1050387	0862	1
MEYER JR WILLIAM C	LTC	0-1019060	C967	1
MEYER KENNETH L	MAJ	0-0451155	0656	1
MEYER LEC J	COL	0-0166303	0955	3
MEYER LEONARC D	COL	0-0432911	0266	2
MEYER LEROY A	LTC	0-1327030	1065	1
MEYER LCUIS A	CPT	0-204971C	0156	1
MEYER LUTHER	LTC	0-0112777	0844	2
MEYER MANIE H	LTC	0-0238811	0961	3
MEYER MAURICE D	LTC	0-0270121	0258	1
MEYER CSCAR G	CPT	0-1286682	0346	2
MEYER CSCAR W	CPT	0-0251296	0463	3
MEYER PAUL R	LTC	0-0311C54	0145	2
MEYER RALPH E	CPT	0-1303371	0261	1
MEYER RALPH E	1LT	0-1305960	1044	2
MEYER RAYMCND F	MAJ	0-2048711	0664	1

NAME	GRADE	SVC NO	DATE RET MO YR	RET CODE
MEYER ROBERT J	MAJ	C-1165134	C664	1
MEYER RUSSELL A	MAJ	C-0350286	1163	1
MEYER STANTON H	MAJ	C-0230936	0762	3
MEYER STEPHEN J	CW2	W-2119777	1044	2
MEYER THEODORE D	LTC	O-1825966	C862	1
MEYER WALLACE A	LTC	O-2020324	C965	1
MEYER WILLIAM C	CPT	O-0162058	C560	3
MEYER WILLIAM C	MAJ	C-1999856	C361	1
MEYER WILLIAM L	CW3	W-2148801	C267	1
MEYER WILLIAM R	LTC	O-0113865	0855	3
MEYERS ANDREW J	CPT	O-0499788	C852	1
MEYERS BEN	1LT	O-1312858	0659	2
MEYERS CHESTER W	LTC	O-0387729	C364	3
MEYERS DAVID G	LTC	O-1175803	C864	1
MEYERS FRANK L	LTC	O-0389104	1060	1
MEYERS GARTH H	COL	O-0370859	1053	1
MEYERS GEORGE G	2LT	O-1292369	0445	2
MEYERS HAROLD A	MAJ	C-1999415	1262	1
MEYERS HENRY L	MAJ	O-1115960	1059	1
MEYERS J STUART	MAJ	C-0239634	C566	3
MEYERS JAMES L	WO1	W-2114367	0544	2
MEYERS JOHN P	CPT	O-0372849	0567	3
MEYERS JOSEPH H	COL	O-0522688	C864	3
MEYERS JR ALEXANDER	LTC	O-1593C89	0863	1
MEYERS LESTER A	MAJ	C-1948512	0157	1
MEYERS LUTHER D	MAJ	C-0194957	C344	2
MEYERS MARGUERITE	1LT	N-0775417	C146	1
MEYERS MARTIN D	COL	O-0244398	1064	3
MEYERS MAX E	MAJ	C-0451008	0253	1
MEYERS MELVIN C	LTC	O-2035130	0563	1
MEYERS ROBERT C	CPT	C-1919040	0262	1
MEYERS ROBERT D	CPT	O-0957703	1160	1
MEYERS RUSSELL P	1LT	O-1293294	C944	2
MEYERS STEWART F	COL	O-0241637	1165	3
MEYERS WALTER T	CPT	O-0505358	1148	1
MEYHAUS ROBERT H	LTC	O-0331176	0146	2
MEYUNG LEON J	COL	O-0145020	C648	3
MEYWES ROBERT A	1LT	C-1645826	0747	2
MEZROW RALPH R	CPT	O-1725381	C445	2
MEZUR FRANK A	LTC	O-1000023	0763	1
MHOON CECIL L	LTC	O-0471744	0755	2
MICACCHION RICHARD C	LTC	O-1543661	C666	1
MICCERI THEODORE	LTC	O-0406819	0656	1
MICCICHE CHARLES	CW2	W-2145975	C456	1
MICELI AUGUSTO P	COL	C-0347675	C862	3
MICELI JOHN N	CPT	O-0337119	1143	2
MICELI JOSEPH F	MAJ	O-1798693	1160	1
MICHAEL BARBARA S	2LT	N-0742277	0245	1
MICHAEL HORACE C	LTC	O-1176732	0267	3
MICHAEL HOWARD F	2LT	O-1012891	C944	2
MICHAEL JOHN M	LTC	O-0957640	1166	3
MICHAEL JOSEPH H	1LT	O-1845319	C545	2
MICHAEL SIDNEY J	LTC	O-0313370	0865	3
MICHAEL THOMAS D	MAJ	O-1311846	1162	1
MICHAEL WILLIAM F	CW2	W-2149447	0166	1
MICHAELS ABRAHAM J	MAJ	C-1690352	C447	1
MICHAELS ANTON S	CPT	O-2016205	C656	1
MICHAELS ARTHUR C	COL	O-0251964	1066	3
MICHAELS CHARLES F	CW3	W-2205444	0767	1
MICHAELS DAVID J	COL	C-0250223	C765	3
MICHAELS GEORGE M	MAJ	C-1826052	0356	2
MICHAELS HERMAN J	LTC	C-0887423	1167	1
MICHAELS JACOB A	CW2	W-2125055	1154	1
MICHAELS LOUIS A	CW3	W-2152854	C862	1
MICHAELS MICHAEL K	1LT	O-1292561	0644	2
MICHAELS MORRIS	1LT	O-0140180	C549	3
MICHAELS ROBERT M	CW3	W-2144850	0460	1
MICHAELS THOMAS W	2LT	O-2043302	C945	1
MICHAELSKI JOSEPH	LTC	C-1302853	C261	1
MICHAELY JACK	MAJ	O-1030505	1059	1
MICHAL WILLIAM R	MAJ	O-0976435	C562	1
MICHALAK RAYMOND F	COL	O-0278461	1165	3
MICHALOWSKI HELIODOR	CPT	O-0451471	0160	2
MICHALOWSKI ROMAN	LTC	O-0920687	C646	2
MICHALOWSKI V S	MAJ	C-0279572	C847	2

NAME	GRADE	SVC NO	DATE RET MO YR	RET CODE
MICHAU WERNER T	LTC	O-1017492	0263	1
MICHAUD OSCAR J	CW2	W-2152600	0460	1
MICHEK FRANK J	MAJ	C-0339131	0645	2
MICHEL GEORGE L	CW2	W-2139633	0858	1
MICHEL GUSTAVE	2LT	O-2007135	C346	2
MICHEL JR ALFRED	CPT	O-0966182	0760	1
MICHEL JULIUS F	CPT	O-0390243	0843	1
MICHELL ALLEN B	COL	C-0223102	0563	3
MICHELLON ROBERT L	MAJ	C-0990435	0365	1
MICHELS OLIVER A	MAJ	C-1308406	0561	1
MICHELSEN RICHARD C	1LT	O-0919344	C445	2
MICHENER ELIZABETH	MAJ	N-0700865	0646	1
MICHENER GEORGE G	MAJ	O-1316183	0364	1
MICHENER MILTON L	CPT	O-1595038	0147	2
MICHENER PERCY Z	COL	C-0285750	0264	3
MICHIE JR JOHN	LTC	O-1293813	C761	1
MICHIELS SYLVESTER	CW2	W-2211655	0367	1
MICHL JOSEPH P	LTC	O-0242463	1160	1
MICHNY FRANK J	MAJ	O-1597205	0859	1
MICHON STANLEY	CPT	O-2262715	0361	1
MICINOWSKI ANTHONY	MAJ	C-1181694	0264	1
MICIOTTO 3RD JOSEPH	1LT	C-1319307	0945	1
MICK WALLACE R	MAJ	O-1917548	0563	1
MICKA BENEDICT W	MAJ	O-1640737	1163	1
MICKELSEN EDGAR D	CPT	O-1011755	1047	1
MICKELSON WALFRED V	1LT	O-1103807	1145	2
MICKLE ROSS T	COL	O-0368548	0566	3
MICKLEBERRY STEPHEN	CPT	C-2262358	C261	1
MICUCCI ROSE A	MAJ	N-0724076	0361	1
MIDDLEBROOK CHARLES	LTC	O-0298096	0465	3
MIDDLEMAN ISADORE C	MAJ	O-0303371	1144	2
MIDDLEMAS JOHN A	MAJ	O-2262644	0162	1
MIDDLETON ALCINE M	CW4	W-2110626	0861	1
MIDDLETON CASTLEAR	LTC	O-2021294	C967	1
MIDDLETON CHARLES	LTC	O-0487560	0758	1
MIDDLETON CHARLES	CPT	O-1101579	1054	2
MIDDLETON CHARLES H	COL	O-0224905	1057	3
MIDDLETON CHARLES L	MAJ	O-1057174	0259	1
MIDDLETON FRANK V	MAJ	O-1580034	0361	3
MIDDLETON JAMES L	WO1	W-2135263	0146	1
MIDDLETON JOSEPH T	LTC	O-0383605	0647	1
MIDDLETON PAUL E	MAJ	O-0120963	0556	3
MIDDLETON PHILIP R	LTC	O-0229192	1163	3
MIDDLETON ROBERT D	MAJ	O-1922535	0763	1
MIDDLETON ROBERT S	1LT	O-1285269	0745	2
MIDDLETON WILLIAM D	COL	C-0176200	0648	3
MIDDLETON WILLIAM H	CPT	O-1316774	1146	2
MIDDLETON WILLIAM J	2LT	O-1112863	1044	2
MIDGETT DAVID P	LTC	O-0515580	0263	1
MIDGETT JOSEPH W	CPT	O-0243373	0347	1
MIDGLEY CHARLES E	1LT	O-0499787	0346	2
MIDGLEY ROBERT F	MAJ	O-1314525	1064	1
MIDKIFF HAROLD C	CW2	W-2005202	0667	1
MIDUSKI THEODORE A	MAJ	O-2036275	C161	1
MIDYETTE ELOISE H	1LT	N-0764353	0946	1
MIEHE PAUL H	LTC	O-0247966	0267	3
MIELE ADOLPH	LTC	O-0383643	0965	1
MIELE ANTHONY C	MAJ	O-2046297	0356	1
MIELKE JOHN W	LTC	O-1042887	0557	1
MIELLY PAUL F	LTC	O-0223578	0651	1
MIELNIK FRANK C	CW3	W-2203268	0763	1
MIESEGAES JULIUS T	COL	O-0221735	0754	3
MIETLOWSKI JOHN F	CW2	W-2150097	0959	1
MIETUS CONRAD A	CPT	O-1691011	0145	2
MIETZEL EWALD F	LTC	O-0256016	0160	2
MIFCOVIC FRANCIS S	LTC	O-0514338	0663	1
MIGDAIL CARL J	CPT	O-0432924	0750	1
MIGHT THOMAS E	MAJ	O-1294342	0463	1
MIGLIACCIO RICHARD P	CPT	O-1342095	1167	1
MIGUEL ANTONIO	1LT	O-0890501	1163	1
MIGUES GEORGE F	1LT	O-1293295	C845	2
MIHACHIK ALFRED D	LTC	O-0482573	1263	3
MIHAL GEORGE	CPT	O-1309790	0146	2
MIHALEK JOHN C	1LT	O-0470853	1145	2
MIHALIK MICHAEL	MAJ	O-1290639	0546	2

NAME	GRADE	SVC NO	DATE RET MO YR	RET CODE
MIHALKA JOHN G	CW3	W-2145342	0163	1
MIHARA LAWRENCE L	MAJ	O-0937978	C764	1
MIHUC GEORGE A	MAJ	C-1551C69	0461	1
MIJAL JR KAROL P	LTC	O-2200111	0767	1
MIKAL JOSEPH	CW3	W-2143385	0963	1
MIKELONIS FLORIAN F	CPT	O-1112321	C662	1
MIKESELL CARL L	LTC	O-0447755	C759	1
MIKESELL FREDERICK	1LT	O-1575003	1044	2
MIKESELL KEITH L	CPT	O-0402768	1046	2
MIKESELL RAY E	MAJ	O-0173821	0751	3
MIKESELL WILLIAM H	CPT	C-0506812	C246	2
MIKKELSEN JOHN E	LTC	O-0525017	0763	1
MIKLAUTSCH JOSEPH	MAJ	C-1054719	0166	1
MIKLES LOWELL	LTC	O-0779935	0767	1
MIKLES MARVIN E	MAJ	O-1824493	1160	1
MIKO RUDOLPH S	1LT	O-1060887	C452	1
MIKOS JOSEPH W	MAJ	C-0975975	0962	1
MIKU NICHOLAS	MAJ	C-2263562	C764	1
MIKULA HELEN M	1LT	N-0800196	0248	1
MIKULAK JOHN P	CPT	O-1580036	C860	1
MIKULAS JR JOHN	MAJ	O-1645829	1156	1
MIKULEKY BEN	MAJ	O-0281240	0963	1
MIKULENKA WILLIAM J	CW3	W-2142882	0261	2
MIKUS NICHOLAS M	LTC	C-1114656	C863	1
MILAM DENNIS W	CPT	C-0373735	C762	2
MILAM DEWITT T	MAJ	O-0331960	1041	1
MILAM GROVER C	MAJ	O-0221913	0947	1
MILAM HAROLD L	CPT	O-0493684	0145	2
MILAM JACK M	2LT	O-0439239	0645	2
MILAM ROBERT M	LTC	O-0336043	C160	1
MILAN EDWARD A	LTC	C-2035015	C555	1
MILAN FRED M	MAJ	O-1648045	0861	1
MILANI FRANK	COL	O-0179992	1051	1
MILANO ALFRED	MAJ	O-0757900	0261	1
MILANO LOUIS	CW2	W-2209645	1262	1
MILAVITZ LLOYD	1LT	C-1692582	0446	2
MILAZZO CHARLES J	LTC	O-1296730	1060	1
MILAZZO FRANK	MAJ	O-0982115	1161	1
MILBERGER JAMES B	CW3	W-2148977	0567	1
MILBERT ATHUR H	MAJ	O-0497749	1145	2
MILBURN GEORGE H	CPT	O-1946574	1162	1
MILBURN ROBERT W	COL	O-0117479	0648	3
MILBUT CHARLES W	MAJ	O-2064177	0660	1
MILCH ELMER	CPT	O-0403026	0145	1
MILDE GEORGE K	MAJ	O-1045185	C664	1
MILDNER RUSSELL F	MAJ	C-1311675	0664	1
MILDONIAN GEORGE A	COL	O-0328453	C954	1
MILEHAM RICHARD L	MAJ	C-2262631	1162	1
MILES ANDREW H	MAJ	C-1342886	0561	1
MILES AURELIUS B	MAJ	O-1322065	C647	1
MILES DEWITT M	MAJ	C-1003990	C855	2
MILES DONALD C	1LT	O-1016210	0945	2
MILES EARL W	CPT	O-1171679	0646	1
MILES EDGAR J	LTC	O-1583380	1161	1
MILES FRANK T	MAJ	O-0302737	0367	3
MILES GEORGE W	CW4	W-2111566	0761	1
MILES HARVEY W	CPT	O-0471965	C147	1
MILES HENRY P	CPT	O-1642389	C464	1
MILES JAMES C	MAJ	O-0307536	0654	1
MILES JOHN A	COL	O-0318226	0463	3
MILES JOHN H	MAJ	C-0195488	0762	3
MILES JOHN H	CW3	W-2141380	C661	1
MILES JOHN J	CPT	O-1303756	0455	1
MILES JOHN L	COL	O-0224888	C861	3
MILES JR LEONARD F	LTC	O-2014477	C666	2
MILES LAURENCE A	MAJ	O-1541467	0848	1
MILES LEE G	LTC	O-0326014	C660	1
MILES LOUIS A	CPT	O-1590050	C658	2
MILES MABEL M	1LT	N-0724878	C945	1
MILES MARION L	LTC	O-0216181	0263	3
MILES PAUL A	MAJ	O-1294241	0954	1
MILES RALPH F	COL	O-0247740	0959	1
MILES ROBERT C	CW3	W-2152166	1163	1
MILES STUART C	CPT	O-0463571	0748	1
MILES WARD R	CPT	O-0122892	0551	3

NAME	GRADE	SVC NO	DATE RET MO YR	RET CODE
MILES WILBUR O	WO1	W-2131636	1145	2
MILES WILLIAM R	MAJ	O-0371094	0352	1
MILES WOODROW W	CW3	W-2145688	0561	1
MILEWSKI JOHN A	CPT	O-0475679	0655	1
MILEWSKI JOSEPH S	CW2	W-2102095	0348	1
MILEY DAVID W	CPT	O-1825033	0346	2
MILEY DONALD H	CW2	W-2123070	1162	1
MILEY HARRY C	MAJ	O-0386293	0161	1
MILEY PERCY	COL	O-0245675	0966	3
MILEY WILLIAM F	CPT	O-0377401	0146	2
MILFORD HOMER C	COL	O-0370270	0447	2
MILFORD JESS F	LTC	O-0461568	0962	3
MILFORD PHILIP L	WO1	W-2133320	0945	2
MILHANS AMBROSE J	MAJ	O-2005380	1163	1
MILHEIM MADOLINE E	LTC	N-0700375	0447	1
MILHISLER JOSEPH J	LTC	O-1293814	0361	1
MILHOLLAND JR JAY G	CW2	W-2148328	0456	2
MILHOUS ATLAS W	LTC	O-1310620	1062	1
MILIANS MAX P	LTC	O-1597093	0667	3
MILJENOVICH NICHOLAS	MAJ	O-0382290	0862	1
MILJUS NATHANIEL	LTC	O-0359992	0860	1
MILKA CHESTER S	LTC	O-1304987	0764	1
MILKOVICH GEORGE	LTC	O-1591937	0965	1
MILKOVITCH JOHN J	MAJ	O-0495284	0657	1
MILKOWSKI STANLIS L	LTC	O-0359499	0360	1
MILL FREDRIC L	MAJ	C-1287739	0866	1
MILL GEORGE E	LTC	O-1322506	1263	1
MILLADC ISIDRO B	CPT	O-1896708	0459	1
MILLAM KENNETH F	CW4	W-2136719	0266	1
MILLAN LEWIS C	LTC	O-1049993	1266	1
MILLAR JAMES C	LTC	O-0384371	1266	3
MILLAR JR SAMUEL R	COL	C-0152508	0249	3
MILLAR JULIAN Z	COL	C-0177854	0861	3
MILLAR SR LUCIAN R	MAJ	O-0974680	1265	1
MILLARD ALLAN L	CW4	W-2112115	0256	1
MILLARD FRANK G	COL	O-0182140	0352	3
MILLARD JACK A	LTC	O-0301383	0667	3
MILLARD MOYER R	LTC	O-0918963	0766	3
MILLARD WILLIAM F	MAJ	C-1054720	0261	1
MILLARD WILLIAM J	MAJ	O-0146071	0648	3
MILLARE ULPIANO O	MAJ	O-0267768	0754	2
MILLAS JOHN G	1LT	O-0538150	1045	2
MILLBERRY HAROLD K E	LTC	O-0276885	0154	3
MILLEA EDWARD D	LTC	O-0166772	0656	3
MILLEN PHILIP H	1LT	O-0391251	0146	2
MILLENTHAL BENJAMI	COL	O-0131390	1052	3
MILLER A L	CW2	W-2150098	0556	1
MILLER ABBOTT R	CPT	O-2284130	1061	2
MILLER ABRAHAM L	CPT	O-2049028	0657	1
MILLER ABRAHAM W	LTC	O-0210728	0761	3
MILLER ADRIAN C	CW2	W-2209291	1159	2
MILLER ALBERT H	MAJ	O-0294761	0346	2
MILLER ALBERT K	CW3	W-2141381	0459	1
MILLER ALBERT L	LTC	O-0224298	0363	3
MILLER ALOFF G	CPT	O-1342100	0861	1
MILLER ALEXANDER	COL	O-0227622	0362	3
MILLER ALEXANDER	LTC	O-0264058	1154	3
MILLER ALFRED B	CPT	O-2042785	0251	2
MILLER ALLISON	COL	O-0227448	0155	3
MILLER ALTON L	CW4	W-2124677	1055	1
MILLER AMZIE E	LTC	O-0288745	0963	1
MILLER ANDREW A	MAJ	O-1046896	0359	1
MILLER ANDREW J	MAJ	O-0491152	0251	1
MILLER ANDREW J	LTC	O-1797685	0261	1
MILLER ANN K	2LT	N-0728740	C145	1
MILLER ANNA J	1LT	N-0703596	0746	1
MILLER ANNA L	MAJ	N-0722385	C562	1
MILLER ANNA T	MAJ	N-0755988	0152	1
MILLER ANSON S	LTC	O-0247898	1059	3
MILLER ARCHIBALD	LTC	O-1289771	0663	1
MILLER ARCHIBALD	CW3	W-2150797	0864	1
MILLER ARNOLD	LTC	O-1170088	0763	1
MILLER ARNOLD C	CW3	RW-2142980	0862	1
MILLER ART B	COL	O-0297487	0450	2
MILLER ARTHUR E	MAJ	O-2037471	0361	2

NAME	GRADE	SVC NO	DATE RET MO YR	RET CODE
MILLER ARTHUR E	CW2	W-2151515	C461	2
MILLER ARTHUR H	LTC	0-0203684	0647	1
MILLER ARTHUR J	CW3	W-214594C	0660	1
MILLER ARTHUR W	LTC	0-0259768	C867	3
MILLER AUGUST W	CW2	W-2151752	0862	1
MILLER BARNEY	MAJ	0-1583381	0860	1
MILLER BAYARD A	LTC	0-0308604	0954	1
MILLER BEN W	COL	0-0403582	1060	1
MILLER BENJAMIN H	CPT	0-2262348	1060	1
MILLER BERNARD	MAJ	0-0983380	0763	1
MILLER BERNARC I	WO1	W-2126310	C845	2
MILLER BERNARD N	CPT	0-1324783	C446	2
MILLER BERTHA A	MAJ	N-0730973	C465	3
MILLER BESSIE I	2LT	N-C700586	0337	1
MILLER BEVERLEY E	MAJ	0-1821897	1146	1
MILLER BILLY H	CW3	W-2205346	0367	1
MILLER BRUCE A	CW2	W-2152601	C561	1
MILLER BURNIE L	CW3	W-2147164	1163	1
MILLER CARL	2LT	0-0189342	C442	1
MILLER CARL F	MAJ	0-1332186	0462	1
MILLER CARL P	LTC	0-0255114	0663	3
MILLER CARL S	CPT	C-1300200	1045	2
MILLER CARMAN O	LTC	0-0230526	C364	3
MILLER CARSON E	MAJ	0-1174959	1061	1
MILLER CATHERINE	MAJ	L-0702037	1162	1
MILLER CECIL D	LTC	0-0320402	0161	1
MILLER CECIL G	LTC	0-1017842	0167	3
MILLER CHARLES A	LTC	0-0143533	0952	3
MILLER CHARLES E	LTC	0-0212775	1058	3
MILLER CHARLES E	MAJ	C-0451352	1046	2
MILLER CHARLES E	CPT	0-0958859	C361	1
MILLER CHARLES E	CW2	W-2103767	CT59	1
MILLER CHARLES G	LTC	0-0397175	1061	2
MILLER CHARLES H	CW2	W-2144892	0857	1
MILLER CHARLES J	COL	0-0268304	C967	3
MILLER CHARLES J	CW3	W-2145326	0959	1
MILLER CHARLES R	LTC	0-1036634	0867	1
MILLER CHARLES R	LTC	0-1312033	0263	1
MILLER CHARLES R	LTC	0-2042949	0964	1
MILLER CHARLES W	CW3	W-2142883	0862	1
MILLER CHARLEY W	LTC	0-0507313	C164	1
MILLER CHARLIE A	CPT	0-1290105	C666	1
MILLER CHRISTIAN	MAJ	C-0469211	1143	1
MILLER CHRISTOPHE	CW3	W-2144553	0458	1
MILLER CLARENCE G	2LT	0-1177530	1044	2
MILLER CLARENCE H	CW4	W-2120618	1057	2
MILLER CLARENCE T	LTC	C-1294174	C665	1
MILLER CLARENCE W	CPT	0-1552340	0958	1
MILLER CLARKE R	WO1	W-2110948	1058	1
MILLER CLAUDE R	CPT	0-1013940	1164	1
MILLER CLYDE C	COL	0-0137540	0850	3
MILLER CONRAD U	LTC	0-1048498	0763	1
MILLER CURTIS	COL	0-0141891	0660	1
MILLER DAN L	COL	C-0189278	1057	1
MILLER DANIEL H	COL	0-0309917	1159	3
MILLER DAVE	LTC	0-1290978	0861	1
MILLER DAVID	MAJ	0-0300695	0646	2
MILLER DAVID	1LT	0-0544916	0345	2
MILLER DAVIC C	CPT	0-0474470	0847	1
MILLER DAVIC C	CW3	W-2144670	0461	1
MILLER DAVIC E	CPT	0-0382079	C445	2
MILLER DAVID E	LTC	0-1335336	0767	1
MILLER DAVID G	CPT	0-0486968	0446	2
MILLER DAVID H	WO1	W-2145778	0855	1
MILLER DAVID M	MAJ	C-0408201	1045	2
MILLER DAVIC T	LTC	0-133898C	0766	1
MILLER DEARREL B	LTC	0-1299277	1061	1
MILLER DELBERT G	CW3	W-2152243	0964	1
MILLER DEWEY R	CPT	0-0488388	C546	1
MILLER DONALD C	2LT	0-1307989	1044	2
MILLER DONALD J	LTC	0-1016834	0762	1
MILLER DONALD L	LTC	C-1169654	0961	1
MILLER DONALD L	MAJ	0-2002497	1065	1
MILLER DONALD O	LTC	0-2017734	1166	2
MILLER DONALD T	LTC	0-0349953	0666	1

NAME	GRADE	SVC NO	DATE RET MO YR	RET CODE
MILLER DUDLEY O	LTC	0-0451502	0957	1
MILLER E C	CW2	W-2143772	1060	1
MILLER EARL B	COL	0-0117497	0445	2
MILLER EDGAR A	MAJ	0-0145978	0648	3
MILLER EDWARC C	LTC	0-1030910	0562	1
MILLER EDWARC J	LTC	0-0184485	C960	3
MILLER EDWARC L	MAJ	0-2014439	0165	1
MILLER EDWARD O	LTC	C-1594634	0861	1
MILLER EDWARD T	COL	0-0124344	0456	3
MILLER EDWARD T	MAJ	0-0171516	1050	3
MILLER EDWARD W	MAJ	0-0518877	0547	2
MILLER EDWARC Z	CW4	W-2150789	0360	2
MILLER EDWIN	COL	0-0256869	0964	3
MILLER EDWIN A	MAJ	0-0482224	0848	2
MILLER EDWIN E	MAJ	C-0330770	0965	3
MILLER EDWIN J	CW3	W-2136661	0762	1
MILLER ELDEN V	CPT	0-0471855	C348	2
MILLER ELLSWORTH	LTC	0-0282831	1254	1
MILLER ELMER L	COL	C-0247215	C860	3
MILLER ELMER L	CPT	0-1011171	1163	1
MILLER EMANUEL M	LTC	0-0920930	0964	3
MILLER EMILY U	LTC	L-0801003	0765	1
MILLER ERCIL D	LTC	0-1641584	0662	1
MILLER ERWIN E	MAJ	C-0254768	0546	2
MILLER ESTHER A	CPT	L-0304426	0950	1
MILLER EUGENE M	LTC	0-0397838	1262	1
MILLER EUGENE N	CW3	W-2126131	0659	1
MILLER FLOYD R	LTC	0-0190815	0555	3
MILLER FLOYD R	LTC	0-0452665	0161	1
MILLER FRANCES B	2LT	N-0730775	1043	1
MILLER FRANCIS G	MAJ	C-0229839	0562	3
MILLER FRANCIS L	CW3	W-2146407	0361	1
MILLER FRANCIS M	CW2	W-2212662	1266	1
MILLER FRANCIS X	WO1	W-2109647	0747	1
MILLER FRANK J	LTC	0-2046298	0955	2
MILLER FRANK W	COL	0-0254710	1165	3
MILLER FRED R	LTC	0-0165357	0359	3
MILLER FRED W	1LT	0-0921181	1045	2
MILLER FREDERICK	CPT	0-0131389	1149	3
MILLER FRECERICK	LTC	0-0257401	0262	3
MILLER FREDERICK	CPT	0-0501574	0245	2
MILLER FREDERICK	CW4	W-2002841	0957	3
MILLER FREDERICK	CW3	W-2142475	0863	1
MILLER GEORGE A	LTC	C-0492335	0867	3
MILLER GEORGE C	LTC	0-0251528	0566	3
MILLER GEORGE D	MAJ	0-0223902	0762	3
MILLER GEORGE F	CPT	0-0292582	0546	2
MILLER GEORGE F	1LT	0-0922872	0945	2
MILLER GEORGE F	CW3	W-2149344	0866	1
MILLER GEORGE F	CW3	W-2153323	1162	1
MILLER GEORGE H	LTC	C-0527353	0664	3
MILLER GEORGE J	CPT	0-1168825	0745	2
MILLER GEORGE K	CPT	0-0258734	1045	2
MILLER GEORGE L	COL	0-0122550	0648	3
MILLER GEORGE M	CPT	0-1032641	0247	2
MILLER GEORGE N	1LT	0-1010694	0344	2
MILLER GEORGE W	MAJ	C-0242075	0563	3
MILLER GEORGE W	2LT	0-1111789	0943	2
MILLER GERALD G	COL	0-0450398	0557	1
MILLER GERALD H	MAJ	0-1795810	0466	1
MILLER GLEN E	1LT	0-0208851	0645	2
MILLER GLEN I	LTC	C-0112278	1155	3
MILLER GRAY O	LTC	0-1180621	0762	1
MILLER GRETCHEN M	CPT	L-0104147	0847	2
MILLER GROVER C	MAJ	0-0164202	1144	2
MILLER GUSTAV A	MAJ	0-0254872	0964	3
MILLER GUY T	CPT	0-2282698	0666	3
MILLER HADLEY B	1LT	0-1044898	0745	1
MILLER HAROLD	WO1	W-2132183	1154	1
MILLER HAROLD A	MAJ	0-1554237	0261	1
MILLER HAROLC C	COL	0-0297193	1066	3
MILLER HAROLD D	LTC	0-0140933	0455	3
MILLER HAROLD O	1LT	0-1107593	1150	2
MILLER HAROLC E	MAJ	0-128912C	0266	1
MILLER HAROLC E	2LT	0-1598402	1046	1

NAME	GRADE	SVC NO	DATE RET MO YR	RET CODE
MILLER HAROLD F	LTC	0-0385067	C158	1
MILLER HAROLD G	2LT	C-0423184	0145	1
MILLER HAROLD H	CW2	W-2151832	0656	1
MILLER HAROLD N	MAJ	0-1693644	0146	2
MILLER HAROLD P	LTC	0-0316852	0361	1
MILLER HAROLD R	LTC	0-0217806	0162	3
MILLER HAROLD T	COL	0-0256008	C464	3
MILLER HARRY	CPT	0-4005707	0167	1
MILLER HARRY S	CW2	W-2113657	C848	2
MILLER HARVEY	CPT	0-1596938	C654	1
MILLER HENLEY E	COL	0-0401958	0347	2
MILLER HENRY	CPT	0-0404575	1045	2
MILLER HENRY C	LTC	0-0112414	0357	3
MILLER HENRY H	MAJ	0-0105284	1051	1
MILLER HENRY L	LTC	0-0308670	C562	3
MILLER HENRY S	MAJ	0-0137605	C852	3
MILLER HENRY W	COL	0-0128148	C648	3
MILLER HERBERT O	MAJ	0-0404474	0347	2
MILLER HERBERT E	MAJ	C-0509074	0748	2
MILLER HERBERT P	COL	C-0168239	1054	3
MILLER HERBERT R	MAJ	0-0304870	0467	3
MILLER HERMAN C	CPT	C-0274985	C249	3
MILLER HERMAN S	MAJ	0-1184739	0660	1
MILLER HIRAM A	COL	0-0125981	C156	3
MILLER HORATIO	COL	0-0101697	0952	3
MILLER HOWARD B	LTC	0-0407664	0461	1
MILLER HOWARD E	MAJ	C-1686661	0264	1
MILLER HOWARD F	1LT	0-1647184	C845	2
MILLER HOWARD F	MAJ	0-1951592	1064	1
MILLER HOWARD P	MAJ	0-1290106	1060	1
MILLER II DAVID A	CW2	W-2214886	0767	1
MILLER IRV I	1LT	0-1030067	1045	2
MILLER J ALLEE	CPT	0-0334874	1060	1
MILLER JACK	2LT	0-0494662	C445	1
MILLER JACK	1LT	0-1304098	C446	2
MILLER JACK	CPT	0-1306448	C955	1
MILLER JACK C	MAJ	0-1311417	0261	1
MILLER JACK R	1LT	0-1288422	1145	2
MILLER JACKSON H	CW2	W-2150554	1062	1
MILLER JACKSON P	LTC	0-1796833	C464	1
MILLER JACOB	CPT	0-0201260	0147	1
MILLER JAMES A	LTC	0-0131420	C648	3
MILLER JAMES A	CPT	0-1636337	C360	1
MILLER JAMES C	MAJ	0-0360833	1055	2
MILLER JAMES C	CW3	W-2142596	0460	1
MILLER JAMES D	LTC	0-0910016	0564	3
MILLER JAMES E	LTC	0-0569408	C461	1
MILLER JAMES F	COL	0-0190774	0162	3
MILLER JAMES H	MAJ	0-1168379	0364	1
MILLER JAMES K	COL	0-0404244	1060	1
MILLER JAMES M	COL	C-0456235	0861	1
MILLER JAMES P	COL	C-0904954	0365	3
MILLER JAMES R	LTC	0-1032374	C964	1
MILLER JAMES R	CW2	W-2152710	0562	1
MILLER JAMES S	CW3	RW-2147989	0861	1
MILLER JAMES T	MAJ	0-1308845	0461	1
MILLER JAMES W	LTC	0-0295518	0352	1
MILLER JAMES W	LTC	C-0453632	0661	1
MILLER JOE H	CPT	0-0514146	1145	2
MILLER JOE J	COL	C-0182171	C748	3
MILLER JOHN A	COL	0-0355517	C447	2
MILLER JOHN A	CW3	W-2150752	0358	1
MILLER JOHN B	MAJ	0-1824066	1163	1
MILLER JOHN D	MAJ	C-0282474	1167	3
MILLER JOHN O	2LT	0-1292217	C843	2
MILLER JOHN O	CW4	W-2001993	0365	1
MILLER JOHN E	LTC	0-0255225	C166	3
MILLER JOHN E	CPT	0-1109518	0467	2
MILLER JOHN E	LTC	0-1294515	1060	1
MILLER JOHN E	CPT	0-2200607	0664	2
MILLER JOHN G	CPT	0-0295829	1045	2
MILLER JOHN H	LTC	0-0238556	0365	3
MILLER JOHN H	1LT	0-0526270	0145	1
MILLER JOHN H	CPT	0-1297405	C147	1
MILLER JOHN M	MAJ	0-0450463	0658	1

NAME	GRADE	SVC NO	DATE RET MO YR	RET CODE
MILLER JOHN R	MAJ	0-1551072	0861	1
MILLER JOHN W	LTC	0-0215514	0245	2
MILLER JOHN W	LTC	0-0547130	0367	1
MILLER JOHN W	MAJ	0-0885652	0261	1
MILLER JOHNNIE C	CPT	0-1685616	0261	1
MILLER JOSEPH	CPT	0-0147425	0852	3
MILLER JOSEPH	COL	0-0368625	1264	1
MILLER JOSEPH	CPT	0-1100693	0446	2
MILLER JOSEPH B	LTC	0-0298989	0562	1
MILLER JOSEPH O	2LT	0-2049657	0545	2
MILLER JOSEPH H	LTC	0-1285472	0258	1
MILLER JOSEPH J	CPT	0-0447936	0744	2
MILLER JOSEPH J	CPT	0-4006595	1264	1
MILLER JOSEPH L	CW3	W-2150538	0167	1
MILLER JOSEPH R	MAJ	0-1828243	0261	1
MILLER JOSEPH W	2LT	0-0202524	1263	3
MILLER JR ARTHUR W	1LT	0-1302667	0146	2
MILLER JR CLARENCE M	LTC	0-1002C75	C363	2
MILLER JR EDWARD T	LTC	0-0241444	1165	3
MILLER JR ERNEST E	MAJ	0-2046459	1057	1
MILLER JR ERNEST R	LTC	0-1111788	0263	1
MILLER JR GEORGE E	CPT	0-1718614	0547	2
MILLER JR JAMES F	MAJ	C-0964941	0261	1
MILLER JR JAMES L	MAJ	C-0414114	1061	1
MILLER JR JOSEPH T	MAJ	0-1283087	0955	1
MILLER JR LEONARD L	LTC	0-1578867	0761	1
MILLER JR PAUL M	2LT	0-1055674	0545	2
MILLER JR WARREN S	COL	0-0208432	1056	3
MILLER JR WILLIAM J	CW2	W-2148283	0667	1
MILLER JR WILLIAM M	MAJ	C-1595710	1262	1
MILLER JULIUS A	CW4	W-2109161	1059	1
MILLER K C	CW3	W-2149301	0463	1
MILLER KELSIE E	COL	0-0201443	0858	3
MILLER KENNETH F	LTC	0-0237807	1263	3
MILLER KENNETH W	MAJ	0-1574294	0757	1
MILLER LA CLAIR P	LTC	0-1691855	0765	3
MILLER LARGENT M	MAJ	0-1649879	0965	1
MILLER LARRY C	1LT	0-1321800	0945	1
MILLER LAURANCE O	LTC	0-1110129	0361	3
MILLER LAWRENCE T	LTC	0-0471964	0855	1
MILLER LEO W	LTC	0-1635118	0462	1
MILLER LEON	CPT	C-1581278	0446	2
MILLER LEROY K	MAJ	0-0995515	C666	2
MILLER LEROY L	CW3	W-2205250	0863	1
MILLER LEWIS C	LTC	0-0451353	1163	1
MILLER LEWIS G	MAJ	0-1917586	0265	1
MILLER LLOYD E	LTC	0-0445885	0854	1
MILLER LLOYD E	WO1	W-2125447	0747	2
MILLER LOUELLA	MAJ	N-0784584	0364	1
MILLER LOUIS A	1LT	0-2008452	1046	1
MILLER MARCEL V	CPT	0-0302345	0845	2
MILLER MARCUS C	CW4	W-2003563	0464	1
MILLER MARCUS F	LTC	0-0235346	1063	3
MILLER MARGARET J	1LT	N-0767675	0845	1
MILLER MARIE B	MAJ	N-0737540	1162	1
MILLER MARION M	CW2	W-2149352	0659	1
MILLER MARK G	LTC	0-0483957	0163	3
MILLER MARLYN W	LTC	0-0317191	0746	2
MILLER MARTIN J	CW3	W-2142651	0265	1
MILLER MARTIN P	1LT	0-1328173	0147	2
MILLER MARVIN C	WO1	W-2146307	0153	2
MILLER MARY A	MAJ	N-0762377	0764	1
MILLER MARY M	2LT	N-0736129	0344	1
MILLER MARY S	1LT	N-0763335	1144	1
MILLER MARY W	MAJ	N-0737027	1063	1
MILLER MAURICE B	LTC	0-1639724	0761	1
MILLER MAXWELL	LTC	0-0492686	0161	1
MILLER MAXWELL E	1LT	0-1308677	0544	2
MILLER MAYNARD B	MAJ	0-0983407	0264	1
MILLER MELVILLE H	LTC	0-0147637	1146	2
MILLER MICHAEL W	MAJ	0-0462720	0945	2
MILLER MICHAEL S	LTC	0-0885766	0361	1
MILLER MILES C	CW3	W-2153331	0467	1
MILLER MILLARC C	MAJ	0-1031740	0158	1
MILLER MINNIE G	MAJ	N-0743134	0965	1

NAME	GRADE	SVC NO	DATE RET MO YR	RET CODE	NAME	GRADE	SVC NO	DATE RET MO YR	RET CODE	NAME	GRADE	SVC NO	DATE RET MO YR	RET CODE	NAME	GRADE	SVC NO	DATE RET MO YR	RET CODE
MILLER MOORE R	MAJ	O-0372072	0264	3	MILLER RUDOLPH A	CW4	W-2145468	0767	1	MILLETT EDWARD B	LTC	O-0450085	1056	1	MILLS PERCY H	1LT	O-1289297	0761	1
MILLER MORRIS	COL	O-0291069	0765	3	MILLER RUSSEL W	LTC	O-0453035	0555	1	MILLETT JR JOHN C	1LT	O-0452118	0-47	2	MILLS REVIS L	MAJ	O-0965267	1060	1
MILLER MORRIS A	LTC	O-0257444	0965	3	MILLER RUSSELL B	1LT	O-0310782	0746	2	MILLHAM MERLE P	CPT	O-1553875	0646	1	MILLS RICHARD F	1LT	O-1283109	1145	2
MILLER MORRIS E	2LT	O-0516324	0145	1	MILLER RUSSELL S	CW2	W-2208073	1060	2	MILLHISER II CHARLES	COL	O-0246017	0966	3	MILLS ROBERT E	LTC	O-1647186	1163	1
MILLER MYRA E	1LT	N-0796837	0255	2	MILLER SAMUEL A	MAJ	O-1185098	0759	1	MILLHOLLAND RANDOLPH	COL	O-0259648	1066	3	MILLS ROBERT L	LTC	O-1947781	0663	1
MILLER MYRTLE M	2LT	N-0724405	0145	1	MILLER SAMUEL D	1LT	O-0544988	1045	2	MILLICAN ARNIE L	LTC	O-0455326	0256	1	MILLS ROY	MAJ	O-1039802	1054	1
MILLER NATHAN	CPT	O-1692028	0546	2	MILLER SAMUEL E	2LT	O-0368931	0440	2	MILLICAN CHARLES R	COL	O-0168470	0659	3	MILLS ROY R	CPT	O-0491825	0148	1
MILLER NOEL	LTC	O-0284264	0167	3	MILLER SAMUEL H	LTC	O-1014451	0861	1	MILLICAN JR FRED J	LTC	O-1055096	0866	1	MILLS WALTER R	LTC	O-0178123	0153	3
MILLER NORMAN D	CPT	O-1114660	0348	2	MILLER SAMUEL L	MAJ	O-0289391	0245	2	MILLICAN JR LEWIS M	LTC	O-1324043	1061	2	MILLS WILLIAM H	COL	O-0243756	1163	3
MILLER NORMAN J	CW3	W-2152593	0662	1	MILLER SAMUEL R	CPT	O-1688143	0146	2	MILLICAN MAURICE E	CW3	W-2148750	0760	1	MILLS WILLIAM J	LTC	O-0215828	1044	1
MILLER NORMAN W	MAJ	O-0493931	0752	1	MILLER SANFORD L	1LT	O-1302162	0445	2	MILLICAN WOODROW M	WO1	W-2132841	0654	1	MILLSAPS ROBERT M	CW3	W-2149353	1163	1
MILLER OLEN E	LTC	O-0519652	0267	1	MILLER SAUL	CPT	O-0471863	0246	2	MILLIGAN ALEXANDER	LTC	O-0143867	0542	1	MILLSAPS WOODROW W	LTC	O-1303923	0457	1
MILLER ORAL O	LTC	O-1683315	0467	1	MILLER SEWELL A	CPT	O-2009709	0960	1	MILLIGAN ANDREW J	CPT	O-0272817	1049	1	MILLSTINE WALTER A	1LT	O-1102868	0745	2
MILLER ORAN J	CW3	W-2140687	0963	1	MILLER SEYMOUR M	1LT	O-0374245	0246	2	MILLIGAN CLARE B	LTC	O-0508805	0557	1	MILLWARD JAMES M	MAJ	O-0245164	1047	1
MILLER ORLA G	COL	O-0165260	1150	3	MILLER SIDNEY C	CPT	O-1286331	0746	2	MILLIGAN JAMES J	COL	O-0129695	0352	3	MILLWOOD WILLIAM H	MAJ	O-0975604	0863	1
MILLER ORVAL J	COL	O-0297219	0567	3	MILLER SR BERNARD A	CW4	RW-2143035	0164	1	MILLIGAN LIONEL C	LTC	O-0218038	0763	3	MILMORE JR JOHN F	1LT	O-1295926	0145	2
MILLER OTHMAR J	MAJ	O-0275064	0859	1	MILLER SR CHARLES A	MAJ	O-1576390	1161	1	MILLIGAN LOWELL A	COL	O-0289190	0763	3	MILNE DOUGLAS B	MAJ	O-0362269	0446	2
MILLER PAGE L	LTC	O-0339386	0562	1	MILLER STANLEY	1LT	O-1824897	1045	2	MILLIGAN RICHARD L	CW3	W-2145689	1266	1	MILNE WALTER L	MAJ	O-1012497	0764	1
MILLER PAUL	LTC	O-1311418	0457	1	MILLER STANLEY H	MAJ	O-1577570	1055	1	MILLIGAN ROBERT L	CPT	O-0329441	1043	2	MILNER ALFRED S	1LT	O-1326006	0845	2
MILLER PAUL C	LTC	O-1291308	1060	1	MILLER TAFT	MAJ	O-1648605	0160	1	MILLIKEN JOHN O	1LT	O-1327562	0446	2	MILNER DONALD S	CW3	W-2146704	0965	1
MILLER PAUL C	CW2	W-2152436	0758	1	MILLER THERMAN D	CW2	W-2146384	1158	1	MILLIKEN JR BASIL C	MAJ	O-0970992	0264	2	MILNER EVERETT W	CPT	O-0215048	0346	2
MILLER PAUL J	LTC	O-1585905	0763	1	MILLER THOMAS A	COL	O-0231720	0363	3	MILLIKEN LYMAN F	COL	O-0302278	0565	3	MILNER GIFF C	CPT	O-0331485	0850	1
MILLER PAUL J	CW4	W-2003318	0163	2	MILLER THOMAS A	CPT	O-1011289	0949	1	MILLIKEN RAYMOND W	1LT	O-1314175	0551	1	MILNER JAMES E	LTC	O-0397773	0160	1
MILLER PAUL R	LTC	O-0338840	1059	3	MILLER THOMAS B	LTC	O-0381770	0764	3	MILLIKEN ROBERT M	COL	O-1031198	0667	1	MILNER JOE W	1LT	O-0216134	0844	2
MILLER PAUL W	LTC	O-0342290	0663	1	MILLER THOMAS G	COL	O-0248057	0965	3	MILLIKEN TOM T	CPT	O-0531128	0248	2	MILNER JOSEPH A	LTC	O-0333203	0346	2
MILLER PHILIP A	MAJ	O-1549334	0655	1	MILLER THOMAS H	CW2	W-2105345	1048	1	MILLIKIN WILLIAM E	LTC	O-0157112	0950	3	MILNER PAUL	WO1	W-2121085	1045	2
MILLER PHILIP J	1LT	O-0450399	0246	2	MILLER VERN W	LTC	O-0273767	1265	3	MILLING JAMES W	CPT	O-1062825	1058	1	MILO CHARLES A	1LT	O-1693803	0346	2
MILLER PHILIP L	LTC	O-0384270	0161	1	MILLER VICTOR	1LT	O-1591318	1048	2	MILLINGTON CARL A	MAJ	O-0910322	1047	1	MILOGLAV OLGA H	2LT	N-0769216	1045	1
MILLER PHILLIP C	MAJ	O-1877762	0666	1	MILLER VICTOR N	MAJ	O-0169670	0356	3	MILLIREN JAMES L	MAJ	O-1186121	0764	1	MILOSOVIC ROBERT T	CPT	O-1115884	0258	1
MILLER PHILLIP H	LTC	O-1106314	1263	1	MILLER VINCENT B	COL	O-0311937	0963	3	MILLIS EDWARD L	COL	O-0203228	0754	3	MILROY LOIS M	MAJ	L-0909273	0867	1
MILLER RALPH D	MAJ	O-4005328	0765	1	MILLER VINCENT F	1LT	O-0528922	0746	2	MILLMAN HYMAN	CPT	O-0499187	0643	2	MILSTEAD CLAUDE W	1LT	O-1013564	0845	1
MILLER RALPH E	LTC	O-1548505	0162	1	MILLER VIRGIL J	CPT	O-0510577	1048	1	MILLNER ROSE	MAJ	N-0720760	0662	2	MILSTEAD FINLEY E	LTC	O-0370885	0962	2
MILLER RALPH K	2LT	O-2001046	0555	1	MILLER VIRGIL L	CW2	W-3430169	0566	1	MILLNER WILLIAM D	MAJ	O-0502762	0854	1	MILSTEAD JACK F	MAJ	O-1535379	0863	1
MILLER RALPH L	COL	O-1048112	0767	1	MILLER WALLACE C	LTC	O-1176134	0267	1	MILLON JOHN R	2LT	O-0379676	0541	2	MILSTEAD JR OSCAR V	CPT	O-1920133	0563	1
MILLER RAYMOND	CPT	O-0478194	0556	1	MILLER WALTER C	CW2	W-2114477	0345	2	MILLS ABRAHAM A	1LT	O-0507310	1144	2	MILSTEIN PHILIP	COL	O-0507374	0967	3
MILLER RAYMOND A	LTC	O-0343382	0855	1	MILLER WALTER J	MAJ	O-0503935	1054	1	MILLS ALBERT K	LTC	O-0307825	0364	3	MILSTER ARTHUR N	MAJ	O-0214915	0462	3
MILLER RAYMOND A	MAJ	O-0451010	1157	1	MILLER WALTER L	MAJ	O-0415970	1263	2	MILLS ANDREW J	MAJ	O-0103363	0245	2	MILTENBERGER EDWIN J	LTC	O-0914200	0464	3
MILLER RAYMOND C	1LT	O-0367479	0645	2	MILLER WALTER L	COL	O-0530956	1163	1	MILLS ARCHIBALD	COL	O-0195197	0457	3	MILTON JAMES A	MAJ	O-0166869	0456	3
MILLER RAYMOND D	CPT	O-0489753	0847	1	MILLER WALTER M	1LT	O-1113363	1144	2	MILLS ARTHUR E	LTC	O-0540017	0766	1	MILTON JOHN D	COL	O-0281807	0346	2
MILLER RAYMOND E	MAJ	O-1877080	1165	1	MILLER WALTER R	MAJ	O-1314309	0359	2	MILLS AVERY G	MAJ	O-1031010	1058	1	MILTON MAURICE D	MAJ	O-1312197	0758	1
MILLER RAYMOND M	CW3	W-2153063	0266	1	MILLER WAYLAND L	COL	O-0190144	0457	2	MILLS CHARLES F	MAJ	O-1057539	0562	1	MILTON PAUL H	COL	O-0302684	0657	1
MILLER RAYMOND W	CPT	O-0487982	0854	1	MILLER WAYNE	LTC	O-0263109	0662	3	MILLS CHARLES W	COL	O-0214538	1061	3	MILTON 2ND HUGH M	M G	O-0154541	0357	3
MILLER REUBEN S	CW3	W-2147906	0861	1	MILLER WAYNE J	MAJ	O-0808702	0566	1	MILLS CLARENCE L	LTC	O-1546070	0167	1	MILTONBERGER B B	M G	O-0197801	0947	1
MILLER REX K	COL	O-0240936	1045	2	MILLER WAYNE K	MAJ	O-2020325	0462	1	MILLS CLYDE R	LTC	O-0415788	1160	1	MILTZ CHARLES R	LTC	O-1174385	0763	1
MILLER RICHARD A	2LT	O-1306127	0744	2	MILLER WESLEY A	CPT	O-0312258	0345	2	MILLS DONALD C	LTC	O-0465011	1154	1	MILWARD STANLEY	MAJ	O-0265278	0867	3
MILLER RICHARD C	CPT	O-0540381	1046	2	MILLER WILBUR K	LTC	O-0298984	0645	2	MILLS DONALD D	MAJ	O-0443924	0446	1	MILYO RAYMOND L	LTC	O-1341685	1167	1
MILLER RICHARD S	MAJ	O-1923552	0465	1	MILLER WILBUR L	LTC	O-1118952	1063	1	MILLS DOYLE W	MAJ	O-1014830	0862	1	MIMNA CURTIS T	LTC	O-0452477	0557	1
MILLER ROBERT	LTC	O-1315089	0666	1	MILLER WILBURN M	MAJ	O-1044920	0958	1	MILLS DREXEL G	MAJ	O-1881215	0266	1	MIMONI LEONARD J	1LT	O-1017717	0945	2
MILLER ROBERT A	MAJ	O-1080128	0166	1	MILLER WILLARD W	MAJ	O-0494698	0759	2	MILLS EARL F	CW3	W-2118539	0262	1	MIMS FLOYD C	MAJ	O-0149915	0849	1
MILLER ROBERT A	LTC	O-1581968	0866	1	MILLER WILLIAM	1LT	O-1534815	0346	2	MILLS ELBERT B	CPT	O-1822600	0259	1	MIMS RICHARD B	LTC	O-0330997	1060	1
MILLER ROBERT B	CW3	W-2208195	1066	1	MILLER WILLIAM A	COL	O-0264108	1062	3	MILLS EMMA L	MAJ	N-0752851	1264	2	MIMS ROBERT H	MAJ	O-1046204	0665	3
MILLER ROBERT D	CPT	O-0247897	0564	3	MILLER WILLIAM A	CPT	O-0326303	0746	1	MILLS FRANK R	1LT	O-0108458	0124	1	MINARD ALDACE W	LTC	O-0244650	0866	3
MILLER ROBERT E	1LT	O-1108174	0945	2	MILLER WILLIAM D	1LT	O-1796834	0945	2	MILLS GUY G	COL	O-0163227	0648	3	MINARD CHARLES H	CPT	O-1011242	0359	1
MILLER ROBERT F	CPT	O-0536751	0847	1	MILLER WILLIAM F	WO1	T-0067512	0962	2	MILLS HAROLD N	LTC	O-0226731	1055	3	MINARIK GEORGE	LTC	O-0305177	0561	1
MILLER ROBERT F	LTC	O-1058328	0766	1	MILLER WILLIAM H	MAJ	O-0335423	0465	3	MILLS HENRY L	1LT	O-1016873	0246	2	MINCER CHARLES T	LTC	O-1283996	1064	1
MILLER ROBERT G	2LT	O-1591317	1044	2	MILLER WILLIAM H	CPT	O-1308359	1145	2	MILLS HENRY P	MAJ	O-0125022	1054	3	MINCEY TALMADGE W	CW2	W-2145825	0359	1
MILLER ROBERT H	COL	O-0362051	0661	1	MILLER WILLIAM J	LTC	O-0396269	0466	1	MILLS HERMAN W	MAJ	O-1951111	1058	1	MINCHEW JAMES C	LTC	O-1319308	0967	1
MILLER ROBERT J	LTC	O-0109354	0147	1	MILLER WILLIAM J	MAJ	O-0588548	1060	1	MILLS HOWARD M	CPT	O-0223464	0537	1	MINCKE JULIUS H	MAJ	O-0195713	0860	3
MILLER ROBERT M	LTC	O-0388301	1160	1	MILLER WILLIAM K	COL	O-0330280	0866	1	MILLS JAMES R	1LT	O-0318819	0146	2	MINEHAN EDWARD H	CW3	W-2144283	0866	1
MILLER ROBERT N	1LT	O-1288275	1145	2	MILLER WILLIAM L	CPT	O-1322646	1050	1	MILLS JOHN E	1LT	O-1018039	0348	2	MINEHAN ROBERT A	CPT	O-1333996	1060	1
MILLER ROBERT P	M G	O-0256068	1063	3	MILLER WILLIAM L	CW2	W-2148329	1262	1	MILLS JOHN E	LTC	O-1117687	0466	2	MINER CHESTER C	CPT	O-0183507	0-50	3
MILLER ROBERT P	1LT	O-1324641	0145	2	MILLER WILLIAM M	COL	O-0209920	0857	2	MILLS JOHN J	MAJ	O-1307053	0862	1	MINER GEORGE E	LTC	O-1168832	0161	1
MILLER ROBERT W	LTC	O-0555413	0865	2	MILLER WILLIAM R	MAJ	O-0997170	0961	1	MILLS JOSEPH A	MAJ	O-1552753	0764	1	MINER HARRY C	1LT	O-1053261	1144	2
MILLER RODMAN D	COL	O-0341921	0867	3	MILLER WILLIAM R	1LT	O-1047266	0745	2	MILLS JR RAYMOND C	CW3	W-2149122	0866	1	MINER HARRY E	LTC	O-0248501	1055	1
MILLER ROGER R	CW2	W-2142057	0553	1	MILLER WILLIAM R	LTC	O-1178257	1162	1	MILLS JR WILLIAM L	MAJ	O-1309591	0946	2	MINER JAMES G	CW3	W-2207995	0667	1
MILLER ROGER W	LTC	O-1041618	0267	2	MILLER WILLIAM T	CW4	W-2132890	1167	1	MILLS LAWRENCE F	1LT	O-1303177	0546	2	MINER JOE F	COL	O-0281796	0460	1
MILLER ROLLAND E	LTC	O-0228861	0163	3	MILLER WILLIAM V	CPT	O-0171228	0753	3	MILLS LEO W	COL	O-0202356	1059	3	MINER KENNETH L	CPT	O-0216314	0848	3
MILLER ROLLAND S	1LT	O-0176857	1044	2	MILLER WILLIE	CW3	W-2153002	0967	1	MILLS LEONARD J	MAJ	O-1651866	1265	2	MINER MARY C	MAJ	N-0703412	0666	1
MILLER RONALD D	LTC	O-0273175	1067	3	MILLER WILLIE F	LTC	O-0531127	0763	1	MILLS LOYD E	LTC	O-0382807	0560	1	MINER RILEY P	CW3	RW-2141636	1160	1
MILLER ROY A	CPT	O-1996567	0660	1	MILLER WILLIS T	MAJ	O-1174653	0557	1	MILLS MAMIE F	2LT	N-0702161	0837	1	MINER WILLIAM R	CPT	O-1299449	0846	2
MILLER ROY J	LTC	O-0108979	0439	1	MILLER WOODROW H	CPT	O-1043269	1146	2	MILLS MELBOURNE	LTC	O-0225492	0163	3	MINER WILLIS C	LTC	O-0214612	0652	1
MILLER ROY L	MAJ	O-1295580	1046	2	MILLER WYTHE R	1LT	O-1112868	0845	2	MILLS MILTON E	CW2	W-2139831	0763	1	MINERLEY ROBERT B	CW4	W-2120726	0766	3
MILLER ROY V	MAJ	O-0246716	1165	3	MILLERE EDMOND S	2LT	O-0117268	1052	3	MILLS ORBIN W	CW3	W-2148127	0460	1	MINERVA LOUIS L	CW2	W-2142105	0556	1
MILLER ROY W	2LT	O-1914181	0450	1	MILLERLILE WILLIAM A	CPT	O-1825242	1262	2	MILLS OTIS M	MAJ	O-1949610	0356	1	MINFORD 3RD LEVIS W	1LT	O-0403159	0245	2
MILLER RUBIN R	LTC	O-0295766	0566	3	MILLET GORDON Y	LTC	O-0265012	0367	3	MILLS PAUL T	CW2	W-2150016	1058	1	MINGHI LAWRENCE J	LTC	O-1112870	0761	1

NAME	GRADE	SVC NO	DATE RET MO YR	RET CODE
MINGLEDORFF MARVIN S	LTC	0-0260266	0864	3
MINGS JAMES W	CW3	W-2004832	0167	1
MINICHIELLO LEWIS A	COL	0-0228378	C463	1
MINICI JOE P	CPT	0-0904614	0545	2
MINICK FLETCHER E	CW3	W-2149672	1165	1
MINICK ROBERT O	CPT	0-0137236	0251	3
MINICUS JOHN E	CPT	0-0513196	1046	1
MINIE ALBERT G	CW2	W-2210521	0763	1
MINIER EARL E	LTC	0-0147687	1156	3
MINIETTA CHARLES	LTC	0-1179545	0763	1
MINIKES SOLETTE E	COL	0-0112356	C154	1
MINIUM DON	CPT	0-0210100	0247	1
MINKE KARL A	CPT	0-0319305	1148	2
MINKIN LUBA F	MAJ	N-0755130	0264	3
MINKIN SARAH R	MAJ	N-0796473	0465	3
MINKS FLOYD A	LTC	0-0287950	0866	3
MINNER MAURICE H	CW3	W-2147179	C662	1
MINNER MORRIS G	COL	0-0180552	C648	3
MINNEY HAROLD F	MAJ	0-1550662	C760	1
MINNICH SAMUEL T	LTC	0-1289942	C457	1
MINNICH THEODORE C	MAJ	0-1334194	0865	2
MINNICK JAMES H	1LT	0-1589004	114N	2
MINNICK KENNETH E	2LT	0-0411476	C245	2
MINNIS JESSE H	CPT	0-0507106	C647	1
MINNIS RAYMOND L	CPT	0-0507105	0448	1
MINNIX ELMER	CW3	W-2141383	0859	1
MINNS JOHN S	MAJ	0-0482313	C951	1
MINNS JR ALBERT E	COL	0-0388183	0661	1
MINOR BRUCE J	2LT	0-1056813	0944	2
MINOR EUGENE M	LTC	0-1575009	0259	1
MINOR JAMES A	CPT	0-0499580	0-53	1
MINOR JOE	COL	0-0211969	0146	2
MINOR MILLER G	1LT	0-2020832	C847	2
MINOR PAYSON S	CPT	0-0211689	0960	3
MINOR WALTER H	LTC	0-0233557	C165	3
MINOR WILLARD H	CPT	0-0491922	C953	1
MINOS ALEXIS P	LTC	0-0191672	1050	3
MINOTT ERNEST L	CPT	0-0282798	0024	1
MINSHAW WILLIAM C	LTC	0-0313437	C948	1
MINSON KENNETH M	MAJ	0-1595713	C961	1
MINSTER RICHARD F	1LT	0-0470930	0545	2
MINTER JR JOHN E	CPT	0-0367122	C345	2
MINTER LEE R	MAJ	0-1290981	C960	1
MINTER WILLIAM B	LTC	0-0215776	0663	3
MINTHORN BLAIR C	MAJ	0-0497371	C954	1
MINTO THOMAS M	MAJ	0-2014559	C164	1
MINTON RHEUBEN O	MAJ	0-1548260	1056	2
MINTON WILFRED M	LTC	0-1172553	1263	1
MINTZ ABRAHAM	1LT	0-1292040	C845	2
MINYARD ROBERT L	LTC	0-1309793	0167	1
MINYD ANDREW	MAJ	0-1643138	0261	1
MIRANDA ANTONIO	MAJ	0-0888977	C760	1
MIRANDA RAFAEL J	COL	0-0152050	1157	3
MIRE EVARICE C	LTC	0-0125019	C649	2
MIREE JAMES W C	LTC	0-0288908	1266	3
MIRSKY LOUIS H	1LT	0-0384706	0745	2
MISCHKE CHARLES G	CW2	W-2214839	0767	1
MISCHKER ERWIN J	MAJ	0-1181375	C163	2
MISCHLER PAUL B	MAJ	0-0988301	0166	1
MISCHO ISADORE W	CW2	W-2103768	C952	1
MISENER EARLE C	LTC	0-1314042	C764	1
MISENHEIMER HARVEY N	COL	0-0222236	0660	3
MISERENDINO ANTHONY	MAJ	0-1882362	C965	1
MISHLER IVAN N	1LT	0-1331539	C961	1
MISHOU JR THOMAS F	LTC	0-0113298	C653	3
MISIEWICZ CHESTER C	MAJ	0-1101580	0758	1
MISIEWICZ VICTOR J	MAJ	0-1535501	C161	1
MISKILL HOWARD P	CPT	0-1117919	C954	2
MISKIMON ROBERT M	CPT	0-0419830	0146	2
MISKOWICH DONALD T	MAJ	0-1053262	1164	1
MISKOWSKI MICHAEL	CW3	W-2150943	1061	1
MISLOCK RAYMOND A	LTC	0-0482480	0-52	1
MISS DAVID C	LTC	0-0404817	1060	1
MISSAL MORRIS E	LTC	0-0465627	C845	2
MISSALL JR MAYNARD M	LTC	0-0375302	1060	1

NAME	GRADE	SVC NO	DATE RET MO YR	RET CODE
MISSALL MAYNARD M	LTC	0-018298C	0453	3
MISSILDINE CHARLES E	MAJ	0-4010904	0967	1
MISSILDINE JACK A	2LT	0-2009353	0356	1
MISSIMER CARROLL	LTC	0-0188901	1053	3
MISTLER HERMAN C	LTC	0-1186267	1163	1
MISTRETTA JOSEPH F	MAJ	0-0912061	1067	3
MITCHAM CAMERON L	1LT	0-1284188	1145	2
MITCHAM EDWARD H	LTC	0-0195672	0446	2
MITCHELL ARCHIE B	1LT	0-1286871	1045	2
MITCHELL ARTHUR C	MAJ	0-1340010	0362	2
MITCHELL ARTHUR L	MAJ	0-0258942	1058	1
MITCHELL ARTHUR S	MAJ	0-0108043	0652	3
MITCHELL AUGUSTUS H	LTC	0-0303409	1061	1
MITCHELL BEN F	COL	0-0210697	0362	3
MITCHELL BERNARD A	MAJ	0-1703815	1053	1
MITCHELL BERTHA O	2LT	N-0728048	0343	1
MITCHELL BILL L	LTC	0-1639746	1161	1
MITCHELL BYRON C	MAJ	0-2024125	0466	1
MITCHELL CHARLES A	CW2	W-2152770	0762	1
MITCHELL CHARLES B	LTC	0-0203136	1043	2
MITCHELL CHARLES F	1LT	0-1043173	0145	2
MITCHELL CHESTER E	LTC	0-0276467	0445	2
MITCHELL CLIFFORD	MAJ	0-2010959	0457	1
MITCHELL CLYDE W	MAJ	0-2017102	0363	1
MITCHELL DONALD E	LTC	0-0900769	0364	3
MITCHELL DOUGLAS C	LTC	0-0231068	0263	3
MITCHELL EARL W	LTC	0-1542875	1163	1
MITCHELL EARLE W	LTC	0-0389354	C162	1
MITCHELL ED L	CW3	W-2147126	0164	1
MITCHELL EDWARD F	LTC	0-1283651	0961	1
MITCHELL EDWARD V	CW2	W-2142175	1053	1
MITCHELL EDWIN O	MAJ	0-0374020	0761	1
MITCHELL ELLIOTT C	CPT	0-1648395	0962	1
MITCHELL ELMER F	LTC	0-0256078	0460	1
MITCHELL EUGENE M	MAJ	0-1928160	C167	1
MITCHELL EVAN H	CPT	0-0326110	0644	2
MITCHELL FLOYD	CPT	0-1286532	0147	2
MITCHELL FRANKLIN A	LTC	0-0502254	1164	3
MITCHELL FRED	LTC	0-1319310	1165	1
MITCHELL FRED	CW3	W-2146934	0156	1
MITCHELL FRED G	LTC	0-0371572	1060	1
MITCHELL GABRIEL G	WO1	W-2118109	1044	2
MITCHELL GARLAND H	CPT	0-2006762	0757	1
MITCHELL GEORGE E	MAJ	0-2014794	0266	1
MITCHELL GEORGE F	COL	0-0277610	0260	3
MITCHELL GLADYCE V	CPT	N-0729023	0355	2
MITCHELL GOUVERNEUR	MAJ	0-1535944	1262	1
MITCHELL GUY	CW2	W-2148835	0457	1
MITCHELL HAROLD C	MAJ	0-0480761	0345	2
MITCHELL HAROLD E	CPT	0-0180305	0555	3
MITCHELL HARRY H	1LT	0-0432371	0445	2
MITCHELL HERBERT H	COL	0-0218635	1055	3
MITCHELL HOLLAND C	COL	0-0312767	1166	3
MITCHELL HUDEA A	LTC	0-1577580	0367	1
MITCHELL HUGH A	LTC	0-0334055	0846	2
MITCHELL IVERSON O	MAJ	0-1690911	1062	1
MITCHELL JAMES A	MAJ	0-0217237	C548	1
MITCHELL JAMES F	CPT	0-0369992	0944	2
MITCHELL JAMES F	1LT	0-1307282	0945	2
MITCHELL JAMES M	CPT	0-1319311	0767	2
MITCHELL JAMES W	CPT	0-2262526	0163	1
MITCHELL JESS	CW4	W-2104311	0259	1
MITCHELL JOHN A	COL	0-0101966	0655	3
MITCHELL JOHN B	CPT	0-0443958	0946	2
MITCHELL JOHN L	LTC	0-0351003	0761	1
MITCHELL JOHN P	1LT	0-2030503	0853	1
MITCHELL JOHN S	LTC	0-0481194	0657	1
MITCHELL JOSEPH A	CW4	W-2120015	0565	1
MITCHELL JOSEPH G	2LT	0-0408839	0844	2
MITCHELL JOSEPH H	LTC	0-0268888	0665	3
MITCHELL JOSEPH H	CW2	W-2152975	1062	1
MITCHELL JOSEPH L	MAJ	0-0275559	0961	3
MITCHELL JR CLAUDE O	CPT	0-1591943	1265	3
MITCHELL JR GEORGE J	LTC	0-0461738	1262	1
MITCHELL JR JAMES A	LTC	0-0174841	0760	3

NAME	GRADE	SVC NO	DATE RET MO YR	RET CODE
MITCHELL JR JAMES F	COL	0-0294760	1163	3
MITCHELL LAURENCE C	1LT	0-2033208	C264	2
MITCHELL LAWRANCE J	LTC	0-0416477	0466	3
MITCHELL LEONARD T	1LT	0-1305628	C146	2
MITCHELL LEROY S	MAJ	0-1581977	C561	2
MITCHELL LEWIS A	CW4	W-2122604	C466	1
MITCHELL LEWIS B	LTC	0-0511847	C564	2
MITCHELL LIONEL C	CPT	0-1923553	0363	1
MITCHELL LOUIS A	CPT	0-0124251	1049	3
MITCHELL MACK C	MAJ	0-0968371	1266	1
MITCHELL MALCOLM L	LTC	0-1181041	0862	1
MITCHELL MARVIN E	LTC	0-0342455	0657	1
MITCHELL MAURICE W	COL	0-0122871	0653	3
MITCHELL MERLE S	COL	0-0180305	0251	1
MITCHELL NORMAN L	MAJ	0-1825160	1060	1
MITCHELL OLIVER C	MAJ	0-0269117	0965	3
MITCHELL ORREN R	LTC	0-0465218	0967	1
MITCHELL PAUL E	CPT	0-1319433	1163	1
MITCHELL PAUL M	LTC	0-0169397	0758	3
MITCHELL PAUL O	COL	0-0238161	1054	1
MITCHELL PAUL W	MAJ	0-2047073	0665	1
MITCHELL PHILIP H	MAJ	0-0318562	C546	2
MITCHELL RALPH B	MAJ	0-0963857	0862	1
MITCHELL RALPH J	COL	0-0140483	1050	1
MITCHELL RICHARD L	COL	0-0308507	1065	3
MITCHELL ROBERT C	LTC	0-1047690	0761	1
MITCHELL ROBERT E	LTC	0-0237122	1265	3
MITCHELL ROBERT F	LTC	0-0365295	C859	1
MITCHELL ROBERT L	MAJ	0-0237438	C366	3
MITCHELL ROBERT L	CPT	0-0978766	C960	1
MITCHELL ROGER S	MAJ	0-0506263	C545	2
MITCHELL RUSSELL A	LTC	0-0301357	C967	3
MITCHELL SAMUEL C	1LT	0-1313035	C845	2
MITCHELL SAMUEL T	1LT	0-1031423	C246	1
MITCHELL SANDEFER	LTC	0-0959323	C965	1
MITCHELL SHELTON C	LTC	0-0962243	0766	1
MITCHELL SR LUTHER M	MAJ	0-1185917	C263	1
MITCHELL SR NEAL	MAJ	0-1998339	0657	1
MITCHELL STEVE F	LTC	0-0116404	0950	3
MITCHELL THOMAS A	LTC	0-1039120	C962	1
MITCHELL THOMAS O	COL	0-0316016	0158	3
MITCHELL THOMAS O	MAJ	0-1170095	C264	1
MITCHELL THOMAS R	MAJ	0-1875123	0764	1
MITCHELL VICTOR G	MAJ	0-2097585	1167	1
MITCHELL WALLACE A	LTC	0-0217850	0163	3
MITCHELL WALTER F	CW2	W-2145826	0457	2
MITCHELL WALTER L	MAJ	0-2032961	1064	1
MITCHELL WALTER M	CPT	0-0301386	0755	3
MITCHELL WILLIAM	CW2	W-2110106	1044	2
MITCHELL WILLIAM A	CPT	0-0370884	1144	2
MITCHELL WILLIAM A	LTC	0-2009327	1064	1
MITCHELL WILLIAM C	MAJ	0-1111247	0858	1
MITCHELL WILLIAM E	MAJ	0-1032033	C161	1
MITCHELL WILLIAM P	LTC	0-0451075	1146	1
MITCHELL WILLIAM S	LTC	0-0261157	C767	3
MITCHELL WILLIS F	LTC	0-1185590	C264	1
MITCHELL WINIFRED A	CPT	N-0784091	0657	2
MITCHEM WILLIAM E	2LT	0-1324465	C952	1
MITCHUM ARTHUR F	CPT	0-0371640	C247	2
MITMAN THOMAS R	MAJ	0-1287564	C661	1
MITNIK PAUL	CW3	W-2142177	0660	1
MITREGA JOHN P	MAJ	0-2047753	0859	1
MITRICK JOSEPH M	CPT	0-0423573	1045	2
MITRO JR GEORGE	MAJ	0-2000754	0763	1
MITROS ROBERT J	CW3	W-2148089	0563	1
MITTAG HERBERT C	MAJ	0-1115041	0367	3
MITTANCK ERHARD H	COL	0-0238457	C366	3
MITTELSTAEDT R E	B G	0-0102218	0648	3
MITTENTHAL HARRY H	MAJ	0-0890239	0154	1
MITTON WALTER G	MAJ	0-0269470	C866	3
MITTY WILLIAM F	LTC	0-1597872	0667	3
MITZEL PAUL C	CW2	W-2214521	C966	1
MITZEN LAWRENCE	LTC	0-0448383	C954	1
MITZEN STANLEY	COL	0-0885655	1154	1
MIX GALE L	MAJ	0-0212403	1262	3

NAME	GRADE	SVC NO	DATE RET MO YR	RET CODE
MIX STANLEY M	LTC	0-0399259	0161	1
MIX WILBUR M	CPT	0-0421918	0146	2
MIXON CHARLIE F	CW3	W-2146262	0764	1
MIXON CLAUDE R	LTC	0-0355028	0566	3
MIXON EARL R	CPT	0-0269583	0151	1
MIXON JACK C	CW2	W-2149053	0660	1
MIXON JOSEPH F	WO1	W-2145827	1155	2
MIXON QUINTON J	2LT	0-2212004	1052	1
MIXON WILLIAM M	1LT	0-2016277	1058	1
MIXON WINBOURN M	MAJ	0-1043437	0557	1
MIYAGISHIMA TERUO	MAJ	0-0996127	0865	1
MIYAKE HOWARD Y	CPT	0-2055907	1147	2
MIYAMOTO HARRY H	2LT	0-2055889	0645	2
MIYAMOTO THEODORE T	CW2	W-2214507	1167	1
MIZDAIL EUGENE R	MAJ	0-1172555	0561	1
MIZE ERVIN W	CW3	W-2141385	0761	1
MIZE WALLACE L	LTC	0-0313392	0954	1
MIZELL GEORGE C	LTC	0-2210004	0867	1
MIZELL JR JOE T	COL	0-0310853	0763	3
MIZELL WINTON R	LTC	0-0410532	0966	1
MIZER FLOYD R	CPT	0-1701090	0246	2
MIZER GEORGE L	LTC	0-1580045	0662	1
MIZER WARREN H	CW3	W-2205442	0764	1
MIZUHA JACK H	CPT	0-0331006	0944	1
MIZUTA RICHARD K	MAJ	0-0331007	1046	1
MIZZI DOMENICO	LTC	0-1895743	0567	3
MLAZGAR JOHN D	1LT	0-2035889	0545	1
MLINAR JOHN F	CW3	RW-2146460	0262	1
MLODZIANOWSKI FRANK	CW2	W-2207055	0766	1
MOA JOHN A	MAJ	0-1541368	0159	1
MOAK GIFFORD F	CW4	W-2112228	0965	1
MOAK HARRY G	1LT	0-1301009	0746	2
MOAK JR JOHN C	MAJ	0-1688359	0266	1
MOAK VERNON J	CW3	W-2117996	0653	1
MOALE JOHN F	MAJ	0-0462467	0662	1
MOATS GEORGE E	CW2	W-2151622	0463	1
MOATS WENDELL A	CPT	0-1311567	0147	2
MOBERG PHYLLIS H	MAJ	N-0754157	0665	1
MOBILIO JOSEPH A	LTC	0-0237701	0464	3
MOBLEY CLAIBORNE	LTC	0-0496933	1059	3
MOBLEY HUGH	LTC	0-0349286	1047	2
MOBLEY MARION R	LTC	0-0473710	0944	2
MOBLEY TILLMAN A	1LT	0-2007126	1054	1
MOCCIA LOUIS A	LTC	0-0923004	1265	2
MOCHAU MARSHALL F	COL	0-0317541	0449	1
MOCHEL LOREN G	MAJ	0-0311395	0662	2
MOCK ALVIN M	COL	0-0246924	0464	3
MOCK DONALD E	CW3	W-2205412	0966	1
MOCK EARL F	2LT	0-0120850	1159	1
MOCK FRED I	1LT	0-1320764	0845	2
MOCK GLEN O	CPT	0-2036069	0651	1
MOCK HARVEY B	1LT	0-1580046	0849	1
MOCK JOHN H	LTC	0-1318569	1161	1
MOCK JOSEPH B	CPT	0-0103650	0351	3
MOCK LEWIS V	CPT	0-1011239	0448	2
MOCK ORA R	CPT	0-1101123	0448	1
MOCK WALTER H	CPT	0-1307396	0664	1
MOCKBEE JACK	LTC	0-0498070	0854	1
MOCKUS JOHN	LTC	0-0302520	0946	2
MOCNIK JR JOHN	LTC	0-0399992	0457	2
MOCZYGEMBA NORBERT W	CW3	W-2153372	0267	1
MODDER LAWRENCE	CPT	0-0267945	0858	3
MODERN LOUISE	CPT	N-0737751	0646	1
MODICA MARTIN M	MAJ	0-2050304	0463	1
MODINE CARL F	LTC	0-1046569	0261	1
MODISETT SHIRLEY A	CPT	0-0412767	1045	2
MODISETT TOM F	MAJ	0-1339200	0265	1
MODLIN ELBRIDGE L	COL	0-0142756	1153	1
MODRAK JR JOHN J	1LT	0-1019141	0546	2
MODZIKOWSKI THADDEUS	CPT	0-0508421	1144	2
MOE CHARLES R	MAJ	0-0548345	1166	1
MOE FORREST L	1LT	0-0147261	0456	3
MOE GEORGE F	1LT	0-1181964	0846	2
MOE JAMES	LTC	0-1547722	0763	1
MOE JOHN J	MAJ	0-1540924	0564	1

NAME	GRADE	SVC NO	DATE RET MO YR	RET CODE
MOE LEWIS H	COL	O-0240883	0261	3
MOE LLOYD C	2LT	O-1110668	0245	2
MOE MAX E	LTC	O-0399172	0367	1
MOE THEODORE K	MAJ	O-0285284	1065	3
MOEBIUS MARY R	2LT	N-0777458	1046	1
MOEBIUS WILLIAM H	LTC	O-1648768	0267	3
MOECK HOWARD F	MAJ	O-1549555	0557	1
MOEGLE EDGAR L	COL	O-0221809	0756	3
MOEHLE EDWIN L	CPT	O-0404785	0645	2
MOEHLMAN ARTHUR H	COL	O-0357462	0367	3
MOELLER ALICE G	MAJ	L-0701347	0463	1
MOELLER GEORGE H	LTC	O-0414178	1065	1
MOELLER LOWELL J	LTC	O-0321229	0461	3
MOELLER SIGURD F	1LT	O-1167548	0745	2
MOELLER WALTER J	LTC	O-1290642	1060	1
MOELLERING CARL H	MAJ	O-0168818	0959	3
MOELLERS LAWRENCE T	LTC	O-0454680	0457	1
MOELLINGER JR MAX	LTC	O-0420562	0761	1
MOEN CHARLES B	1LT	O-1331540	1152	1
MOEN JAMES L	MAJ	O-1583395	0261	1
MOEN MARCUS M	LTC	O-0258902	0945	1
MOERLS JOHN H	MAJ	O-1173717	1060	1
MOESE OTTO H	MAJ	O-0304463	0664	3
MOESSNER KARL F	COL	O-0296125	0467	3
MOFFAT JR FRASER M	COL	O-0140651	0857	3
MOFFATT JOSEPH F	LTC	O-1108177	0462	1
MOFFET ROBERT E	B G	O-0220503	1058	3
MOFFETT ALBERT L	CPT	O-0475296	0947	1
MOFFETT COLEMAN J	LTC	O-1725606	0766	1
MOFFETT DONALD F	MAJ	O-2263097	0164	1
MOFFETT WILLIAM R	1LT	O-1302503	0544	2
MOFFIE ELEANOR F	MAJ	L-0300053	1062	1
MOFFIT FRANCIS C	LTC	O-1016954	1057	1
MOFFITT CARL F	MAJ	O-1302921	0657	1
MOFFITT EDWARD P	MAJ	O-1307732	0962	1
MOFFITT EDWARD V	CW3	W-2152893	0263	1
MOFFITT FREDERICK	MAJ	O-0287376	0646	2
MOFFITT GEORGE N	LTC	O-0268719	0457	3
MOFFITT JOSEPH H	CW3	W-2143222	1262	1
MOFFITT LAWRENCE C	COL	O-0308243	1065	3
MOFFITT LESTER W	CW3	W-2142564	0358	1
MOFFITT MARSHALL T	MAJ	O-2000500	0962	1
MOFFITT RUSSELL F	MAJ	O-0327734	1060	3
MOFFITT THOMAS O	CPT	O-0476234	0434	1
MOGAN JR FRANCIS M	MAJ	O-4006494	0867	1
MOGAN JR THOMAS E	MAJ	O-2006843	0262	1
MOGEL VICTOR L	CW3	W-2152497	0764	1
MOGILL CHARLES J	CW3	W-2009285	0267	3
MOGLIA JOHN J	CPT	O-2262260	0161	1
MOGUL ROBERT	MAJ	O-1535243	0264	1
MOHAN FRANK P	MAJ	O-0328086	1059	3
MOHAN JOHN J	2LT	O-1115042	0145	2
MOHAN RAYMOND P	1LT	O-1168382	0244	2
MOHAN STANLEY P	1LT	O-0372370	1266	3
MOHART HAROLD A	CW3	W-2104315	1054	1
MOHEN EUGENE J	LTC	O-0303602	1059	1
MOHER JEREMIAH W	LTC	O-1298900	0364	1
MOHLER ARTHUR E	MAJ	O-2011796	0465	1
MOHLER CHARLES E	MAJ	O-0122266	0648	3
MOHLER CHARLES R	MAJ	O-2051257	0963	1
MOHLER DON P	MAJ	O-0317963	1159	1
MOHLER DONALD P	1LT	O-1102871	0946	2
MOHLER FRANKLIN R	CW3	W-2109142	1060	1
MOHLER GALEN R	WO1	W-2126308	1058	1
MOHLER HARRY A	LTC	O-0278906	0863	3
MOHLER JOHN A	COL	O-0386389	0761	1
MOHLER JR SAMUEL C	MAJ	O-0355683	0660	1
MOHLER LEWIS H	CW3	W-2147442	0464	1
MOHLER RALPH H	LTC	O-1550005	1162	1
MOHLER SIDNEY C	CPT	O-0492057	1045	2
MOHLER WILLIAM A	CPT	O-1042115	1148	2
MOHN SAMUEL R	LTC	O-1080049	1061	1
MOHNEY JR EARL	2LT	O-1184264	0446	2
MOHNEY ROBERT R	CPT	O-1165657	0955	1
MOHOLY JOSEPH O	LTC	O-1047246	0764	1
MOHR DONALD W	1LT	O-0382142	0245	2
MOHR FREDERICK	COL	O-0262137	0366	3
MOHR GEORGE W	CPT	O-0515270	1047	2
MOHR GORDON C	LTC	O-1018564	0964	1
MOHR GUSTAV C	LTC	O-0255928	1161	3
MOHR HAROLD C	CW3	W-2147881	0263	1
MOHR HARRY C	LTC	O-1299605	0562	1
MOHR HENRY A	MAJ	O-1045533	0359	1
MOHR JAMES	CPT	O-1295758	0346	2
MOHR NORMAN F	MAJ	O-1184415	0164	1
MOHR RAY M	MAJ	O-0173731	0861	3
MOHR WALTER C	LTC	O-0274257	0347	2
MOHR WILLIAM H	COL	O-0250342	0866	3
MOHRHAUSER ROBERT W	MAJ	O-0265522	1157	3
MOHRMANN JOHN M	COL	O-0347389	0967	3
MOILAN DONALD H	LTC	O-2017737	0866	2
MOIR EDWIN G	CPT	O-0488640	0244	2
MOIR JACK R	LTC	O-0494984	0154	2
MOISAN PHILIP K	COL	O-0208175	0748	2
MOISELLE WILLIAM	LTC	O-0140650	0152	3
MOKLER JOHN F	CW3	W-2152933	0666	1
MOKRI FRANCIS J	CW3	W-2148555	0662	1
MOLD NEIL H	MAJ	O-2208440	0461	1
MOLDENHAUER OSCAR A	COL	O-0232749	1160	3
MOLE ALBERT L	LTC	O-1300065	0461	1
MOLENDA EDWIN A	CW2	W-2149935	0960	1
MOLENGRAFF CORNELIUS	COL	O-0309630	1262	3
MOLETTE ROBERT C	LTC	O-0251787	0465	3
MOLINARI PETER L	LTC	O-0291732	0967	3
MOLINARY VICTOR V	2LT	O-1012307	0244	1
MOLINE LEROY H	CPT	O-1112872	0862	1
MOLINI ANTONIO F	LTC	O-1324089	1066	1
MOLINO SALVATORE	WO1	W-2151850	0460	1
MOLITOR CHARLES J	CPT	O-2020184	0849	2
MOLL BONIFACE F	COL	O-0512294	0965	1
MOLL CARL E	LTC	O-0383681	0762	1
MOLLART ARTHUR G	LTC	O-0291569	1165	3
MOLLAUN JOSEPH W	MAJ	O-0267241	1047	1
MOLLEMA JOHN	MAJ	O-0450400	0954	1
MOLLENKOPF HUBER L	MAJ	O-0245904	0766	3
MOLLER JOHN H	MAJ	O-1800136	0163	1
MOLLICA ALFONSO A	CW2	W-2149912	0762	1
MOLLISH FRANK E	MAJ	O-0967895	0263	1
MOLLNER JOSEPH M	LTC	O-0550992	0367	3
MOLLOY EDWARD A	MAJ	O-1030175	0561	1
MOLLOY EDWARD T	MAJ	O-1686663	0363	1
MOLLOY JAMES A	1LT	O-0138497	0648	3
MOLLOY LOGAN H	1LT	O-0383034	0645	2
MOLLOY WILLIAM M	LTC	O-0171112	1158	3
MOLMEN ARMAN R	LTC	O-1290286	0364	1
MOLNAR LUDWIG S	CPT	O-0159676	1045	2
MOLNAR MIKE	CPT	O-0488708	0454	1
MOLNAR PAUL M	1LT	O-1106967	0545	2
MOLNAR STEPHEN C	LTC	O-0272352	0366	3
MOLNAR THEODORE T	COL	O-0267383	0359	3
MOLNER ALBERT Y	1LT	O-0321173	0564	3
MOLOHON ALBIN C	MAJ	O-0250147	0460	3
MOLOHON CHARLES W	MAJ	O-1821899	0861	1
MOLOHON MARTIN J	CW2	W-3430021	0765	1
MOLONEY ROBERT C	CPT	O-0453510	0346	2
MOLONY FRANK C	LTC	O-0125246	0648	3
MOLOVINSKY DAVID E	CW4	W-2146386	0566	1
MOLSEE DAVID C	CW2	W-2147265	0657	1
MOLTER ALBERT C	COL	O-0249936	0160	1
MOLTER HENRY J	LTC	O-1166423	1060	1
MOLTHAN ALBERT L	1LT	O-1341567	0259	1
MOLTRUP CHARLES H	CW3	W-2145044	0162	1
MOLTZ JR JOHN H	CPT	O-1584622	0746	1
MOLTZ LESTER M	LTC	O-1312318	1266	3
MOLUMBY JOHN R	MAJ	O-1555734	0259	1
MOMAN GEORGE H	MAJ	O-1292219	0361	1
MOMCILEVICH MICHAEL	LTC	O-1001196	0758	1
MOMEYER GERALD R	COL	O-0255257	0660	1
MOMEYER KENNETH W	COL	O-0179260	0356	3
MOMII TOM T	LTC	O-1330457	0965	1
MONA JOSEPH O	MAJ	O-0279612	1166	3
MONACO HUGO L	CW2	W-2210697	0865	1
MONACO RAYMOND T	1LT	O-1822431	0344	2
MONACO RAYMOND W	2LT	O-1297080	0344	2
MONAGAN III JOHN S	1LT	O-1575475	0344	2
MONAGHAN LORETTA F	1LT	N-0796175	0147	1
MONAGHAN ORLOFF	LTC	O-0452923	0465	3
MONAGHAN ROBERT W	MAJ	O-1824343	0464	1
MONAGHAN THOMAS J	LTC	O-1287565	0861	1
MONAHAN CHARLES E	CPT	O-0489602	0351	1
MONAHAN FRED V	1LT	O-1686568	0147	2
MONAHAN JOHN P	CPT	O-1170873	0348	2
MONAHAN JOSEPH W	CW2	W-2211149	0365	1
MONAHAN JR JAMES J	MAJ	O-1314043	0761	2
MONAHAN JR MARTIN C	CW2	W-2153126	1062	2
MONAHAN PATRICK	1LT	O-1324562	0550	1
MONAHAN PHILIP O	1LT	O-0408701	0744	2
MONAHAN STEPHEN O	LTC	O-0228152	0149	3
MONAHAN THOMAS F	MAJ	O-2021224	0466	2
MONASMITH MAURICE L	MAJ	O-0305965	0863	1
MONCK QUENTIN U	1LT	O-1167993	1145	2
MONCRIEF HAYWARD A	LTC	O-0302369	0565	3
MONCRIEF JOHN E	MAJ	O-2016632	0962	1
MONCRIEF LEWIS E	LTC	O-0394750	0162	1
MONCRIEF WALLACE B	CW4	W-2142178	1262	1
MONCUR JAMES W	1LT	O-1294914	0945	2
MONCURE WILLIAM A	LTC	O-2052234	1167	3
MONDA ANTHONY	CW2	W-2141386	1154	1
MONDELLI HUGO J	1LT	O-1297081	0546	1
MONDELLI LAVERNE N	CW3	V-0700123	0964	1
MONDUCK JOSEPH P	CPT	O-1294875	1047	1
MONELL FREDERICK	LTC	O-0320033	0459	3
MONETTE MAURICE H	COL	O-0477281	0662	1
MONEY ALLEN D	MAJ	O-0976424	0964	1
MONEYHAM DONALD R	CPT	O-1882081	0361	2
MONGE ALF	WO1	W-2103234	0252	2
MONGEAL PAUL V	MAJ	O-1043438	0765	1
MONGER LUTHER J	CPT	O-0481788	0247	1
MONGES CHARLES J	MAJ	O-0963987	0663	1
MONGRANDI RUDOLPH J	1LT	O-1014508	0450	1
MONICA LEILA J	1LT	N-0721548	0546	2
MONICAL WILLIAM B	LTC	O-0516632	0363	1
MONIHAN RICHARD J	1LT	O-1014753	1057	1
MONJAR HOWARD D	1LT	O-1301667	1146	2
MONJO NICOLAS Y	CW3	W-2152474	0265	1
MONK GALLOWAY	LTC	O-1553147	0460	1
MONK GEORGE F	LTC	O-0256717	0867	3
MONK JR JAMES R	MAJ	O-0217481	0564	3
MONK LEWIS J	MAJ	O-0923045	1164	3
MONK MARION M	LTC	O-1035317	0263	1
MONK ROBERT S	2LT	O-1302566	0943	2
MONKHOUSE GEORGE R	CPT	O-1024688	0663	1
MONKS JR CHARLES J	LTC	O-1797506	0262	1
MONLEON PETER D	MAJ	O-0523111	0453	1
MONLEZUN CLYDE J	LTC	O-1552341	0757	1
MONNERAT JR JOSEPH E	LTC	O-0419950	0161	1
MONNESS IRA H	LTC	O-1945647	1264	3
MONRO WILLIAM J	CW4	W-2144751	1057	1
MONRO 3RD WILLIAM L	1LT	O-0496731	0745	2
MONROE CHARLES H	MAJ	O-1688599	0566	1
MONROE CLYDE W	CPT	O-0283657	1044	2
MONROE ERNEST M	LTC	O-0267273	0147	1
MONROE HARLAN B	COL	O-0267055	0358	3
MONROE HARMON L	CPT	O-0463655	1045	2
MONROE HOWARD J	COL	O-0302846	0162	3
MONROE JAMES F	CW4	W-2115897	0359	1
MONROE JAMES LEWI	2LT	O-1990889	1051	2
MONROE JR JOHN	MAJ	O-1920315	0766	1
MONROE LEWIS A	1LT	O-2035962	0945	2
MONROE MARION H	1LT	O-1300684	0145	1
MONROE ROBERT H	LTC	O-1054068	1063	1
MONROE STEPHEN C	COL	O-0906558	0466	1
MONROE TONY F	CPT	O-0108514	0828	1
MONROE ULYSSES G	MAJ	O-1298098	0561	1
MONROE WILLIAM J	CPT	O-1174387	1146	2
MONROE WILLYS M	LTC	O-0202966	0850	3
MONSEES ALBERT J	CPT	O-1765987	0247	2
MONSEN MANLEY B	MAJ	O-0264014	0163	3
MONSERRATE LUIS A	CPT	O-1327368	0862	1
MONSON WENDELL L	LTC	O-2046428	0763	1
MONSOUR THOMAS B	LTC	O-1175808	0962	1
MONSSON C DOUGLAS	LTC	O-0242569	0164	3
MONT CHARLES R	CW4	W-2112034	0157	1
MONTAGUE DOROTHY S	2LT	N-0727236	0345	1
MONTAGUE EDGAR S	COL	O-0155971	0355	3
MONTAGUE EDWARD T	CPT	O-0415544	0445	2
MONTAGUE GLEN H	1LT	O-1639417	0648	2
MONTAGUE JAMES L	LTC	O-0175732	0755	3
MONTAGUE LUDWELL L	COL	O-0255454	0967	3
MONTANA FRANK R	CPT	O-0470610	0244	1
MONTANO ANTONIO	CW2	W-2126143	0648	1
MONTASSER AHMAD S	MAJ	O-1647192	0456	1
MONTAVON LORETTA V	1LT	N-0755304	0446	1
MONTBRIANO FRANCIS H	MAJ	O-1648051	0757	1
MONTE ANGELO J	LTC	O-1545833	0366	2
MONTE RUPERTO	1LT	O-1896597	1149	1
MONTEALEGRE FRANCISC	LTC	O-0235390	0564	3
MONTECALVO JOSEPH	CPT	O-0944661	0365	1
MONTEDONICO JAMES H	2LT	O-1587473	1044	2
MONTEE MATTHEW P	CPT	O-0742594	0859	1
MONTEFUSCO EDWARD	COL	O-0266239	0964	3
MONTEGUT JR JAMES J	MAJ	O-1582756	0263	1
MONTEITH CHARLES O	MAJ	O-0187060	0648	3
MONTEITH JAMES G	LTC	O-1305459	1266	1
MONTEITH JR COLIN S	COL	O-0193925	1262	3
MONTEITH ROBERT E	CPT	O-1291152	0759	1
MONTELEONE MAURICE O	LTC	O-0455268	1163	1
MONTEMARANO VINCEN	CPT	O-0331553	0246	2
MONTER GERALD	1LT	O-1018392	1045	2
MONTERO JOSE A	MAJ	O-0988302	0163	1
MONTES ABRAM	CPT	O-2007393	0566	1
MONTES ISIDRO	1LT	O-1896818	0259	1
MONTFORT GEORGE R	CW2	W-2212981	0467	1
MONTFORT WILLIAM H	CPT	O-0363238	0346	2
MONTGOMERY ALBERTIS	LTC	O-0172919	0450	3
MONTGOMERY ALF P	MAJ	O-1577585	0461	1
MONTGOMERY AVERY L	1LT	O-1050399	0345	2
MONTGOMERY CAL	WO1	W-2120031	0557	1
MONTGOMERY CARMEN	CPT	N-0779446	0847	1
MONTGOMERY CHARLES B	MAJ	O-0390838	0446	2
MONTGOMERY CHARLES R	MAJ	O-0989214	0666	1
MONTGOMERY CHARLES C	MAJ	O-0332710	1045	2
MONTGOMERY CHARLES W	LTC	O-1176736	0366	2
MONTGOMERY CLIFFORD	MAJ	O-0237640	1265	3
MONTGOMERY DEKALB F	1LT	O-0427801	1044	2
MONTGOMERY DOROTHEA	MAJ	L-0400814	0664	3
MONTGOMERY EARL R	LTC	O-1183310	1266	1
MONTGOMERY EARL W	1LT	O-1308846	0545	2
MONTGOMERY EARLE S	LTC	O-0141599	0553	3
MONTGOMERY EDWARD F	CPT	O-1325230	0248	1
MONTGOMERY EDWARD H	MAJ	O-2020185	0462	2
MONTGOMERY ELIJAH P	LTC	O-0259953	0467	3
MONTGOMERY FRANCIS C	LTC	O-0255015	0752	3
MONTGOMERY GEORGE W	1LT	O-0927578	1046	2
MONTGOMERY HARRY H	CW3	W-2144035	0661	1
MONTGOMERY HENRY K	CPT	O-0345147	0845	2
MONTGOMERY HERMAN F	MAJ	O-0956187	0761	1
MONTGOMERY HOMER T	LTC	O-1110137	0964	1
MONTGOMERY HUGH B	MAJ	O-0358114	0266	1
MONTGOMERY HUGH R	LTC	O-0188085	0649	3
MONTGOMERY JACK	LTC	O-1035545	1164	1
MONTGOMERY JAMES F	MAJ	O-0677104	0766	1
MONTGOMERY JEWEL O	1LT	O-0788380	0752	1
MONTGOMERY JOHN W	COL	O-0334082	0551	1
MONTGOMERY JONATHAN	CW2	W-2152163	1063	1
MONTGOMERY JOSEPH B	LTC	O-0286862	0646	2
MONTGOMERY JOSEPH R	LTC	O-1326163	0765	1
MONTGOMERY KENNETH A	CPT	O-0211858	1162	3
MONTGOMERY KENNETH L	CW4	W-2113294	0862	1
MONTGOMERY LLOYD P	CPT	O-1287741	0448	1

NAME	GRADE	SVC NO	DATE RET MO YR	RET CODE
MONTGOMERY MAYS E	1LT	0-0462876	C945	2
MONTGOMERY ORIN R	MAJ	0-0226151	C545	2
MONTGOMERY PAUL R	MAJ	0-2035433	1060	1
MONTGOMERY PHILIP V	MAJ	C-1330338	C766	1
MONTGOMERY QUINN F	CPT	0-0232391	0245	2
MONTGOMERY RAY	MAJ	C-1110138	C760	1
MONTGOMERY RAYMOND A	LTC	0-1296561	C361	1
MONTGOMERY ROBERT E	LTC	0-0452913	C357	1
MONTGOMERY ROBERT E	LTC	0-1533403	C462	1
MONTGOMERY ROBERT F	CPT	0-1577587	C656	1
MONTGOMERY ROBERT N	1LT	0-1329271	C147	2
MONTGOMERY THOMAS D	MAJ	0-0500137	C849	1
MONTGOMERY WILLIAM D	MAJ	0-0371780	C246	2
MONTGOMERY WILLIAM H	CPT	0-0890270	1147	2
MONTI DANIEL J	CPT	0-1317186	0155	1
MONTICH EMIL	MAJ	0-1172348	C963	1
MONTIETH LESTER E	CW4	W-2119362	0357	2
MONTJOY JR ROBERT H	LTC	0-1106322	C467	1
MONTO SAUL P	MAJ	C-0470885	C946	2
MONTOOTH CHARLES	CPT	0-0108977	1031	1
MONTOYA ALBERT	1LT	0-1683439	0262	1
MONTROSS HENRY E	MAJ	C-0230786	1047	2
MONTROY ROBERT E	CW3	W-2152554	0762	1
MONTS MILLES M	CW4	W-2103235	C659	1
MONTSTREAM WILLIAM L	MAJ	0-0261337	0666	3
MONYAK CHARLES	MAJ	0-2054023	0255	1
MONYEK MILTON S	1LT	0-0494252	0943	2
MOOD RENE L	CW3	W-2149793	0661	1
MOODY ALVAH E	LTC	0-0223787	0954	3
MOODY DAVID	CW3	W-2151902	0663	1
MOODY DONALD	MAJ	0-1949413	C961	1
MOODY DOUGLASS N	LTC	0-0293558	1163	3
MOODY EDWIN F	COL	0-0341984	1066	1
MOODY ELMER	CPT	0-1060895	0450	1
MOODY FRANK B	MAJ	C-0241027	0445	2
MOODY HARDY O	CW4	W-2143106	0366	1
MOODY JAMES E	1LT	0-0228676	1044	1
MOODY JAMES P	1LT	0-0887531	C667	1
MOODY JERALD J	LTC	0-1173390	0860	1
MOODY JOHN M	CW3	W-2145976	0861	1
MOODY LAFAYETTE	CPT	0-0206718	1142	2
MOODY NARVA L	1LT	C-1047248	C645	2
MOODY OTIS N	MAJ	0-1639776	C961	1
MOODY PHILIP H	CW3	W-2141915	1060	1
MOODY RAYMOND F	WO1	W-2145828	0654	1
MOODY REGINALD H	LTC	0-0174928	0648	3
MOODY WALTER L	CW4	W-2114978	0251	1
MOODY WILLIAM	MAJ	C-0949164	0962	1
MOOERS JR SAMUEL R	MAJ	C-1174656	1060	1
MOOK ANDREW W	LTC	0-0280549	0564	3
MOOK MILO M	1LT	0-0484849	1044	1
MOOK WALTER L	1LT	0-0924412	0648	2
MOOMAW JR BENJAMIN F	MAJ	0-0254827	C466	3
MOON EARNEST P	2LT	0-1299779	C644	2
MOON EDWIN E	MAJ	C-1824662	C465	1
MOON FREDERICK	CW4	W-2111019	C762	3
MOON JAMES R	CPT	0-0205225	1053	3
MOON JAMES W	1LT	0-0352161	C244	2
MOON JAY W	LTC	0-0322954	0166	1
MOON JOSEPH F	CW2	RW-2146685	1164	1
MOON LOYDE P	1LT	0-1592454	0652	2
MOON MAURICE J	COL	0-0145877	C256	3
MOON OSCAR O	LTC	0-0405702	1060	1
MOON SAMUEL	MAJ	C-1923059	1063	1
MOON WILLIAM A	MAJ	0-1303925	0761	1
MOON WILLIAM O	LTC	0-0474057	0457	1
MOONEY CHARLES E	LTC	C-1110139	C265	1
MOONEY DANIEL C	CPT	0-1822603	C566	1
MOONEY EARL R	CPT	0-0174454	1055	3
MOONEY EDWIN J	COL	0-0100062	C952	3
MOONEY GEORGE W	CW4	W-2113848	0257	1
MOONEY GLEN	CPT	0-1307057	C447	1
MOONEY HARRY F	COL	0-1043736	1067	1
MOONEY JAMES W	CW2	W-2111456	0753	1
MOONEY JOHN P	LTC	0-0432759	0765	1
MOONEY JR CHARLES P	MAJ	C-0270117	0965	3
MOONEY JR PAUL C	1LT	0-0281274	114N	2
MOONEY LAUREN M	MAJ	C-1634155	1160	1
MOONEY LEON C	MAJ	0-1103328	0666	1
MOONEY LESLIE L	MAJ	0-0227780	0463	3
MOONEY ROBERT	LTC	0-0372676	0762	1
MOONEY THOMAS L	MAJ	0-1167127	1055	2
MOONEY WILLIAM R	CW2	W-2142736	1061	1
MOONEYHAM BILL M	MAJ	0-2263072	0163	1
MOONEYHAM BOB R	CPT	0-2097061	0363	1
MOOR VINCENT C	MAJ	0-1318246	1165	1
MOORE ABNER B	MAJ	0-2019913	0662	1
MOORE ALBERT F	COL	0-0284740	0564	1
MOORE ALFRED O	MAJ	C-0983214	1262	1
MOORE ALFRED E	CW2	W-2211215	1164	1
MOORE ALLAN B	MAJ	0-1081155	0461	1
MOORE ALLEN L	MAJ	0-2018392	0463	1
MOORE ALLEN R	LTC	0-0177182	0655	3
MOORE ALTON M	LTC	0-0299182	1266	3
MOORE ALTON W	CPT	0-2032896	0257	1
MOORE ALVIN	LTC	0-0145878	0950	3
MOORE ALVIN H	LTC	0-0108682	0147	1
MOORE ALVIN L	CW3	W-2149415	0660	1
MOORE ALVIN R	COL	0-0300054	0454	2
MOORE ANDREW J	CW3	W-2144194	0662	1
MOORE ANGELA C	1LT	N-0775961	0446	1
MOORE ARCHIE	LTC	0-0278078	0263	3
MOORE ARTHUR H	1LT	0-1318624	0546	2
MOORE ARTHUR J	MAJ	0-0231722	0963	3
MOORE BARNETT J	1LT	0-1333998	0647	2
MOORE BENJAMIN F	CPT	0-1170097	1057	2
MOORE BERT E	LTC	C-0344415	0362	3
MOORE BESSIE L	MAJ	N-0780061	0767	1
MOORE BUNYAN B	MAJ	C-0228658	1137	1
MOORE BURTON L	LTC	0-0283933	0764	3
MOORE CALVIN L	CPT	0-0211775	1057	3
MOORE CARL C	CW3	W-2148261	1062	1
MOORE CARL R	CW2	W-2210326	0266	1
MOORE CARROTHERS	2LT	0-1584629	0646	1
MOORE CHARLES F	COL	0-0229895	0960	1
MOORE CHARLES H	COL	0-0199959	1162	3
MOORE CHARLES H	LTC	0-0242512	1055	3
MOORE CHARLES H	LTC	0-0425614	1166	1
MOORE CHARLES R	LTC	0-0297732	0763	3
MOORE CHASTAIN	LTC	0-0489922	1155	1
MOORE CLARENCE R	1LT	0-0922794	0745	2
MOORE CLARENCE W	MAJ	0-1315347	0765	1
MOORE CLAUDE I	CPT	0-0480330	1045	2
MOORE CLIFFORD C	MAJ	0-1951180	1162	1
MOORE CLINTON M	CW2	W-3151354	0667	1
MOORE CLYDE P	MAJ	0-0966109	0262	1
MOORE CORBITT R	LTC	0-1014227	0766	1
MOORE DAVID J	LTC	0-0451357	1058	1
MOORE DELMA G	CPT	N-0768289	0847	1
MOORE DEVERT	CW4	W-2115480	0866	1
MOORE DEWEY C	1LT	0-0291972	1065	2
MOORE DON W	MAJ	0-0505520	1144	2
MOORE DONALD E	COL	0-0194882	0861	3
MOORE DOWELL L	MAJ	0-1549793	0961	1
MOORE DOYLE L	2LT	0-0379555	0742	2
MOORE EDWARD N	LTC	0-0348074	0954	1
MOORE EDWARD W	1LT	0-1302035	0246	1
MOORE EDWIN C	CPT	0-0885837	0656	1
MOORE EDWIN C	LTC	0-1283652	0164	1
MOORE EDWIN J	CW4	W-2102108	0964	1
MOORE ELIASE L	MAJ	0-0484379	0954	1
MOORE ELLIS	LTC	0-0173774	0345	2
MOORE ELZIE K	COL	0-0223965	0564	3
MOORE ERNEST L	CPT	0-0311980	0365	3
MOORE ERNEST W	LTC	0-0143154	1154	3
MOORE ESCUM L	MAJ	0-0370260	0546	2
MOORE EUGENE M	CPT	0-1291929	1146	2
MOORE EVA E	MAJ	N-0727824	1264	1
MOORE FRANCIS C	LTC	0-1645840	1165	1
MOORE FRANCIS P	MAJ	0-0447560	0446	2
MOORE FRANCIS X	MAJ	0-0335257	0662	1
MOORE FRANK A	LTC	0-1636355	0259	1
MOORE FRANK C	CPT	0-4006066	0964	1
MOORE FRANK L	COL	C-0508743	1264	3
MOORE FRANK M	MAJ	C-0439833	1262	1
MOORE FRANK T	COL	0-0307015	C961	3
MOORE FRANKLIN D	LTC	0-0265603	0755	2
MOORE FRED A	1LT	0-1594343	C347	2
MOORE FRED W	MAJ	C-0179108	C959	3
MOORE FREDERICK	LTC	0-0309591	0660	1
MOORE GALE S	CPT	0-1301669	C364	2
MOORE GALLIE	2LT	0-0646247	0750	1
MOORE GARLAND J	MAJ	0-2262356	1164	1
MOORE GEORGE	COL	0-0248303	0367	3
MOORE GEORGE A	CPT	0-0383680	0367	3
MOORE GEORGE B	LTC	0-0360213	0260	1
MOORE GEORGE C	MAJ	C-2288319	1263	1
MOORE GEORGE F	LTC	0-1001857	1162	1
MOORE GEORGE M	MAJ	0-0354624	C255	2
MOORE GEORGE S	CPT	0-0495245	0948	1
MOORE GEORGE T	2LT	0-2011387	1046	1
MOORE GERALD K	LTC	C-0347906	0258	1
MOORE GERALD P	1LT	0-1299929	0846	2
MOORE GLENN A	MAJ	0-0257975	C267	3
MOORE GORDON E	1LT	0-0449063	0745	2
MOORE GRADY W	CW3	W-2149858	1262	1
MOORE GRANT W	1LT	0-0406808	0844	2
MOORE GUS R	CW3	W-2147486	0965	1
MOORE HARLAND B	CPT	0-0161473	C452	3
MOORE HARLIN A	LTC	0-0245504	0860	3
MOORE HAROLD E	MAJ	0-1688451	0364	1
MOORE HAROLD G	CPT	0-1035126	0661	1
MOORE HAROLD H	COL	0-0335728	C661	1
MOORE HAROLD Z	MAJ	C-1295582	0752	1
MOORE HARRY H	LTC	0-1170099	0562	1
MOORE HARRY L	MAJ	0-0263851	C864	3
MOORE HENRY D	CPT	C-0304029	C563	3
MOORE HENRY F	CPT	0-0187986	0349	1
MOORE HENRY W	MAJ	0-0252133	0665	3
MOORE HERBERT A	CPT	0-0407681	0562	1
MOORE HERBERT S	CPT	0-1306128	C447	2
MOORE HERMAN R	CPT	0-0174211	C353	3
MOORE HOLMES B	CPT	0-0379922	0562	1
MOORE HOMER L	MAJ	C-0978139	0664	1
MOORE HOOVER C	CW3	W-3150501	0466	1
MOORE HORACE	LTC	0-0925263	0265	3
MOORE HOWARD I	LTC	C-0191834	C762	3
MOORE HOWARD W	LTC	0-0276575	1161	3
MOORE HOWARD W	MAJ	0-1295062	C364	1
MOORE IDUS B	MAJ	0-0504280	0155	1
MOORE ILEAN	CPT	N-0729077	0946	1
MOORE JACK	1LT	0-0443968	0344	2
MOORE JACK B	CW2	W-3350347	C667	1
MOORE JACK M	LTC	0-1293629	C962	1
MOORE JACOB F J	LTC	0-1101124	1055	1
MOORE JAMES A	COL	0-0346936	0264	1
MOORE JAMES A	CW2	W-3420002	C266	1
MOORE JAMES C	LTC	0-0412607	0761	1
MOORE JAMES C	CPT	0-1046571	0762	1
MOORE JAMES D	CPT	C-0408329	C245	2
MOORE JAMES D	LTC	0-1596121	0363	1
MOORE JAMES E	LTC	0-0243068	0466	3
MOORE JAMES E	1LT	0-1589388	0346	2
MOORE JAMES E	1LT	0-1947039	0646	2
MOORE JAMES J	CW2	W-2152748	C363	1
MOORE JAMES L	MAJ	0-2019491	0363	1
MOORE JAMES M	COL	C-0237610	C845	2
MOORE JAMES O	MAJ	0-1548262	0754	2
MOORE JAMES O	CW3	W-2152098	0762	1
MOORE JAMES P	MAJ	0-0225521	0562	3
MOORE JAMES P	MAJ	0-1534099	0463	1
MOORE JAMES S	CPT	0-1686143	1050	1
MOORE JAMES W	LTC	0-0378081	1161	1
MOORE JAMES W	LTC	0-1638106	0564	2
MOORE JAMES W	CW3	W-2144673	0860	2
MOORE JARVIS B	2LT	0-1298424	0145	2
MOORE JAY K	MAJ	0-1050836	1263	1
MOORE JEROME W	MAJ	0-1557337	0256	1
MOORE JESSE W	CPT	0-2096817	0564	1
MOORE JOE L	CW3	W-2152796	0264	1
MOORE JOE P	MAJ	C-0290646	1059	3
MOORE JOE R	MAJ	C-1951701	0562	1
MOORE JOHN B	B G	0-0244989	0762	3
MOORE JOHN B	MAJ	0-1826425	0561	1
MOORE JOHN R	CW3	W-2142884	0161	1
MOORE JOHN D	COL	0-0209176	0846	2
MOORE JOHN F	LTC	0-0114183	0850	3
MOORE JOHN F	MAJ	0-1540917	0563	1
MOORE JOHN H	2LT	0-0466584	0743	2
MOORE JOHN H	2LT	0-2018910	0254	1
MOORE JOHN H	MAJ	0-2206124	1165	1
MOORE JOHN K	LTC	0-1287218	0465	3
MOORE JOHN K	MAJ	C-1287567	0461	1
MOORE JOHN M	MAJ	C-0258218	0467	3
MOORE JOHN T	CPT	0-0969436	0462	1
MOORE JOHN T	LTC	0-1308678	0667	2
MOORE JOSEPH A	COL	0-0285220	0864	3
MOORE JOSEPH D	LTC	0-1287219	0966	1
MOORE JOSEPH E	LTC	0-0431474	0162	1
MOORE JOSEPH E	MAJ	0-1945025	0565	3
MOORE JOSEPH M	CW3	W-2150980	1163	1
MOORE JOSEPH N	1LT	0-1299452	0246	2
MOORE JOSEPH C	COL	0-0319845	0-51	1
MOORE JR CHARLES E	LTC	0-0305638	0260	1
MOORE JR CLARENCE L	MAJ	0-1331973	1065	1
MOORE JR CLAUDE	CW3	W-2203324	0566	1
MOORE JR EDWARD C	COL	0-0231868	0660	1
MOORE JR IVEY J	CPT	0-2033986	1061	1
MOORE JR JAMES B	MAJ	0-1328918	1060	1
MOORE JR KENNETH M	CPT	0-2301019	0965	1
MOORE JR PAUL B	LTC	0-1288780	0261	1
MOORE JR RAY A	CPT	0-0460927	0448	2
MOORE JR REYNOLDS C	1LT	0-1115043	0846	2
MOORE JR ROBERT E	LTC	0-0254021	0246	2
MOORE JR ROBERT H	MAJ	0-1548970	1263	1
MOORE JR THOMAS V	CPT	0-0495702	0546	2
MOORE JR WILLIAM	LTC	0-0143116	1155	2
MOORE JR WILLIAM R	2LT	0-0549781	1145	1
MOORE JR WILLIAM T	1LT	0-0412219	0945	2
MOORE JR WILLIAM T	LTC	0-1573441	1159	1
MOORE JR WILLIE	MAJ	0-2028616	0165	1
MOORE JULIUS B	LTC	0-0549347	1066	1
MOORE KAY D	CPT	0-1031578	0147	2
MOORE LAWRENCE F	WO1	W-2132299	0854	1
MOORE LAWRENCE M	CW2	W-2147584	0857	1
MOORE LEC	MAJ	0-1698036	0655	1
MOORE LEC B	LTC	0-0354004	0346	2
MOORE LEONARD H	CPT	0-2002178	0659	2
MOORE LEWIS E	COL	0-0126834	0648	3
MOORE LOUIS E	MAJ	0-2055434	1054	1
MOORE LUCIUS L	COL	0-0197562	0456	3
MOORE LUKE R	MAJ	0-0938975	0662	1
MOORE LUKE W	LTC	0-0245079	0253	3
MOORE LUM H	CPT	0-1593732	1047	2
MOORE MARION N	CPT	N-0722790	0147	1
MOORE MARTHA D	2LT	N-0736236	1044	1
MOORE MARY M	2LT	N-0759907	1144	1
MOORE MATTHEW C	MAJ	0-0984999	0661	1
MOORE MATTHEW S	1LT	0-0454586	0545	2
MOORE MERLE E	MAJ	0-1822818	1061	1
MOORE MILLARD F	CW3	W-2153658	0665	1
MOORE MORRIS R	COL	0-0113954	0151	3
MOORE NELSON J	COL	C-0172651	0646	2
MOORE NEWELL V	1LT	0-1305460	0346	1
MOORE NORMAN M	MAJ	0-0914959	0945	2
MOORE OTIS E	CW2	W-2128044	0662	1
MOORE OLAF R	CPT	0-1312968	0546	2
MOORE ORVILLE A	CW4	W-2107902	1160	1
MOORE OSWALD C	CPT	0-0145817	0854	3
MOORE PAUL J	CPT	0-0347337	0964	3

NAME	GRADE	SVC NO	DATE RET MO YR	RET CODE
MOORE PERCY E	MAJ	0-0269216	1064	3
MOORE RALPH B	1LT	0-1014050	1046	2
MOORE RALPH E	MAJ	0-2005660	1262	1
MOORE RALPH H	2LT	0-1050390	0744	1
MOORE RALPH L	LTC	0-1002997	0564	1
MOORE RANDALL S	2LT	0-1330458	C146	2
MOORE RAY C	2LT	0-1646852	0345	2
MOORE RAYMOND L	LTC	0-0260958	1045	2
MOORE REX	2LT	0-1554941	1044	2
MOORE ROBERT A	LTC	0-0263684	1059	1
MOORE ROBERT B	LTC	0-0453276	0758	1
MOORE ROBERT B	1LT	0-1287742	C452	1
MOORE ROBERT C	CPT	0-1549560	C346	2
MOORE ROBERT E	2LT	0-1049999	0644	2
MOORE ROBERT E	CW4	W-2129443	C966	1
MOORE ROBERT H	MAJ	0-0209194	0260	3
MOORE ROBERT H	MAJ	0-1114663	C862	1
MOORE ROBERT J	2LT	0-1822432	1045	2
MOORE ROBERT L	LTC	0-0238604	C544	2
MOORE ROBERT L	LTC	0-0348825	C560	1
MOORE ROBERT M	1LT	0-1297573	1044	2
MOORE ROBERT M	CW3	W-2153373	1C66	1
MOORE ROBERT N	CW2	W-2150678	1161	1
MOORE ROBERT R	COL	0-0256307	C365	3
MOORE ROBERT R	LTC	0-1107603	0763	1
MOORE ROBERT S	CW3	W-2141387	0960	1
MOORE ROBERT W	2LT	0-1823916	1044	2
MOORE ROBERT W	LTC	0-2048086	0665	1
MOORE RODERICK G	1LT	0-0372356	0745	2
MOORE ROLAND	MAJ	0-1112875	C463	1
MOORE ROY A	CW4	W-2117926	1054	1
MOORE ROY E	MAJ	0-1015667	1266	1
MOORE ROY W	MAJ	C-2204104	1165	1
MOORE ROYCE L	CW2	W-2146879	0657	1
MOORE RUSSELL R	LTC	0-1010955	C661	1
MOORE SAM Y	MAJ	0-1300685	0161	1
MOORE SAMUEL A	LTC	0-0346046	1062	3
MOORE SAMUEL W	MAJ	0-0171469	0358	3
MOORE SARAH W	MAJ	N-0742056	0165	1
MOORE SCOTT	MAJ	C-1113847	0162	1
MOORE SHERIDAN B	MAJ	0-1051694	0462	1
MOORE SIDNEY S	2LT	0-0520753	0445	2
MOORE SR JOSEPH N	CPT	0-0249057	0762	2
MOORE SR LAWRENCE F	MAJ	0-0364879	1263	1
MOORE SR WALTER W	CPT	0-0116797	1159	3
MOORE STANLEY B	1LT	0-1317810	1045	2
MOORE STANLEY J	CPT	0-0973595	1060	1
MOORE THADDEUS S	CPT	0-1297408	C448	2
MOORE THEO L	MAJ	0-1999609	1060	1
MOORE THEOPHILUS	LTC	0-0319941	0461	1
MOORE THOMAS A	LTC	0-0299986	0361	3
MOORE THOMAS J	LTC	0-1314940	1163	1
MOORE TREVOR F	LTC	0-1042102	C462	2
MOORE TROY T	1LT	0-1645225	C855	1
MOORE TROY V	MAJ	0-0494952	C849	1
MOORE VERNON O	LTC	0-0393766	0264	1
MOORE VICTOR A	LTC	0-1010457	0767	1
MOORE VICTOR P	CPT	C-1822302	1058	1
MOORE VINCENT H	CPT	0-0924933	0745	2
MOORE VIRGIL S	MAJ	0-0317753	C553	2
MOORE VORDA B	1LT	0-2006320	1046	2
MOORE WALDO W	LTC	0-0129184	C455	3
MOORE WALLACE H	COL	0-0197922	C846	2
MOORE WALTER L	COL	C-0165067	0953	3
MOORE WALTER L	1LT	C-0454603	1045	2
MOORE WALTER S	LTC	0-0884101	0355	1
MOORE WALTER W	MAJ	0-0966639	0662	2
MOORE WARREN H	MAJ	0-2014661	0763	1
MOORE WAYMON L	MAJ	0-1311419	0956	1
MOORE WENDELL T	MAJ	0-0542610	1063	1
MOORE WESLEY G	CPT	0-1576408	0756	1
MOORE WILBUR H	LTC	0-0267722	C265	3
MOORE WILBUR M	MAJ	0-0316544	1144	2
MOORE WILLARD O	MAJ	C-0196277	0961	3
MOORE WILLIAM A	1LT	0-0443540	0745	2
MOORE WILLIAM A	LTC	0-1580056	1161	1
MOORE WILLIAM C	1LT	0-0547661	0546	2
MOORE WILLIAM C	WO1	W-2143692	0555	1
MOORE WILLIAM D	1LT	0-1339462	0448	2
MOORE WILLIAM F	MAJ	0-1823470	C661	1
MOORE WILLIAM H	MAJ	0-0193098	0163	3
MOORE WILLIAM H	1LT	0-0545985	0446	2
MOORE WILLIAM H	MAJ	0-0956659	0967	2
MOORE WILLIAM H	LTC	0-1584631	0261	1
MOORE WILLIAM H	CW2	W-2109372	0256	1
MOORE WILLIAM I	COL	0-0219688	0845	2
MOORE WILLIAM J	MAJ	C-0308919	0163	1
MOORE WILLIAM L	CPT	0-0372650	0750	1
MOORE WILLIAM R	LTC	0-1289775	0165	1
MOORE WILLIAM R	CW4	W-2143593	0162	1
MOORE WILSON P	CPT	0-1548504	0745	2
MOORE WOODFORD O	CPT	0-1293451	1047	2
MOORE WRIGHT C	MAJ	0-1554239	0361	1
MOORE WRIGHT T	COL	C-0129066	0853	3
MOOREHEAD CHARLES	LTC	0-0453111	0860	1
MOOREHEAD JOE N	1LT	0-1319528	0646	2
MOORER EDWARD A	MAJ	0-1286873	0760	1
MOORES JESSE T	LTC	0-1305291	0665	1
MOORHEAD JOHN T	COL	0-0278223	0559	3
MOORHEAD JOSEPH H	CPT	0-1878179	0355	2
MOORHEAD JR STEELE L	CPT	0-0473500	1044	2
MOORHEAD PAUL A	CPT	0-0336592	0744	2
MOORHEAD ROBERT D	CW3	W-2206939	0666	1
MOORHEAD ROBERT L	COL	0-0123658	0648	3
MOORHEAD WAYNE L	CW3	RW-2208764	0467	1
MOORHEAD WENDELL P	CW3	W-2143007	0456	1
MOORMAN ALAN W	LTC	0-0277806	0560	3
MOORMAN CHAPMAN S	MAJ	0-0245764	0653	3
MOORMAN CHARLES H	CW2	W-2149708	0261	1
MOORMAN CLINTON R	MAJ	0-2202336	0966	1
MOORMAN FRANK H	LTC	0-0184443	0756	3
MOORMAN JR JOHN H	CPT	0-0424466	0246	1
MOORMAN RALPH	CPT	0-1324887	0946	2
MOORS ARTHUR G	LTC	0-1550230	0264	1
MOORTEL JACK G	CW3	RW-2209724	0467	1
MOOSE ARCHIE E	LTC	0-2034826	0266	1
MOOSEN JOSEPH G	MAJ	0-2017572	0760	1
MORABITO JOHN	LTC	0-0252541	1166	3
MORACE JOHN J	CW3	W-2136672	0661	1
MORAGHAN ANNA G	2LT	N-0728974	0944	1
MORAINE JACK L	CPT	0-2036277	0954	2
MORALES BENITO	COL	0-0301225	0655	1
MORALES EDWARD B	1LT	0-1031347	0346	2
MORALES MARIANO	CW3	W-2145470	1061	1
MORALES RICHARD H	LTC	0-1548109	0257	1
MORAN ALLEN R	LTC	0-1049587	1166	1
MORAN BRIAN P	MAJ	0-1011119	0147	2
MORAN CARL H	CPT	0-1172558	0446	2
MORAN CLEMENT J	MAJ	C-0257616	0461	3
MORAN DAVID J	LTC	0-1014350	0462	1
MORAN EARL E	MAJ	0-0233816	1146	2
MORAN EDWARD B	1LT	0-2053954	0446	2
MORAN EDWARD F	MAJ	0-0215139	1063	3
MORAN EDWARD J	LTC	0-1574101	0858	1
MORAN ERNEST L	MAJ	0-0969051	1066	1
MORAN ETHEL S	LTC	L-0220003	0652	1
MORAN EVAN A	1LT	0-1320159	0745	2
MORAN FRANK R	LTC	0-0240058	0447	1
MORAN FRANK R	CPT	0-1019213	0361	1
MORAN GEORGE C	M G	0-0184043	0657	3
MORAN HALBERT S	LTC	0-0239081	0764	3
MORAN HAROLD A	CW2	W-2209334	C563	1
MORAN JAMES C	LTC	0-1300513	1161	1
MORAN JOHN F	LTC	0-0180301	0660	1
MORAN JOHN J	MAJ	0-0268932	0146	2
MORAN JOHN J	LTC	0-0487154	0557	1
MORAN JOHN S	COL	0-0166000	1051	3
MORAN JOSEPH R	CPT	0-1636608	0745	2
MORAN JR JACK T	MAJ	C-1580057	0557	1
MORAN JR JOSEPH F	CPT	0-1303634	0844	2
MORAN JR RAYMOND P	MAJ	C-1925655	C267	1
MORAN LUCILLE E	2LT	M-0002218	C446	1
MORAN OWEN W	MAJ	0-0278274	0754	3
MORAN RICHARD T	CW2	W-2211898	0867	1
MORAN ROBERT B	CW3	W-2150866	0865	1
MORAN ROBERT W	1LT	0-0420324	1144	2
MORAN THOMAS E	CPT	0-1288936	0447	2
MORAN THOMAS P	LTC	0-0361356	1061	1
MORAN TIMOTHY F	LTC	0-1695370	0445	2
MORAN VIRGINIA M	1LT	N-0762170	1046	1
MORAN WILLIAM	1LT	0-0959481	0452	1
MORAN WILLIAM D	CPT	0-0483965	C852	1
MORAN WILLIAM H	CPT	0-1703235	1044	2
MORAN WILLIAM J	CW3	W-2206597	0466	1
MORAN WILLIS T	LTC	0-0286584	0262	3
MORANCIE EDMOND J	MAJ	0-1309875	C656	1
MORANO RALPH	LTC	0-0446213	0667	3
MORAVEC RALPH A	2LT	0-2047080	0445	2
MORAVEK STEPHEN	COL	C-0236222	0963	3
MORAZ ALBERT P	CPT	0-1584635	C546	2
MORCE EARL M	CW3	W-2146919	0258	1
MORCOCK JR JOHN C	LTC	0-0244741	C363	3
MORDEN CARROLL V	MAJ	C-1052087	0258	1
MORDEN HOWARD C	CPT	0-0470248	0145	2
MORE CARLETON	LTC	0-0164435	C353	3
MORE GLENDALE	MAJ	C-1328623	C264	1
MORE JOSEPH F	LTC	0-0177765	C148	2
MORE WILLARD E	CW3	W-2148561	0464	1
MOREAU ALFRED	MAJ	0-1044904	C257	1
MOREAU CECIL J	LTC	0-2043173	0264	2
MOREAU DANIEL	CPT	0-1922630	1162	1
MOREAU GILBERT W	1LT	0-1283295	1045	1
MOREAU LAMAR J	CPT	C-0479350	C962	1
MOREAU LOUIS S	2LT	0-1299454	0345	2
MOREAU RAY A	MAJ	C-4009667	C166	1
MORECRAFT ELWOOD M	1LT	0-1015269	0845	2
MOREDA ARMAND E	MAJ	0-2008067	1060	1
MOREE JAMES A	LTC	0-1639424	0163	1
MOREHEAD GLENN E	LTC	0-0251350	1165	3
MOREHEAD JR LOUIS M	COL	0-0312506	1065	3
MOREHEAD LEMUEL Y	MAJ	0-0283873	1064	3
MOREHEAD WILLIAM F	LTC	0-1593734	0867	3
MOREHEAD WILLIAM H	CW3	W-2205362	0366	1
MOREHISER JR JOHN F	CPT	C-0428136	C344	2
MOREHOUSE COURTLAND	MAJ	0-0919319	1163	1
MOREHOUSE JOSEPH H	MAJ	C-0205361	1159	3
MOREHOUSE VIRGIL A	CW3	W-2150517	C663	1
MOREL VICTOR J	1LT	0-1638111	C947	2
MORELAND EARL E	CW4	W-2108718	C560	1
MORELAND EUGENE E	MAJ	C-0489729	0754	1
MORELAND HUGH E	CW3	W-2150647	C662	1
MORELAND J L	MAJ	0-1542097	0160	1
MORELAND JR JOHN W	1LT	0-0517677	1145	2
MORELAND KENNETH O	1LT	0-1319434	C450	1
MORELAND RANDALL R	COL	0-0359082	C547	2
MORELAND ROBERT G	LTC	0-1994662	C965	1
MORELAND SAMUEL J	CW3	W-2150815	0564	1
MORELAND WALTER T	LTC	0-1691929	C563	1
MORELL GUSTAVE A	CPT	0-0273554	1064	3
MORELLE GUY J	MAJ	C-0173047	1144	2
MORELLI TONY	2LT	0-1032467	C445	2
MOREN ALBERT A	LTC	0-0235126	0659	3
MOREN WILLIAM R	MAJ	C-1173393	1058	1
MORENCY ANTHONY J	CW2	W-2119961	C949	1
MORENCY JOHN E	MAJ	0-1280480	C860	2
MORENCY JR JOSEPH N	1LT	0-1314310	1045	2
MORENO VICENTE	1LT	0-0346144	0250	1
MORENO YOLANDA M	2LT	N-0798888	0646	1
MORERE RODERIC G	MAJ	C-0433254	0647	1
MOREST FREDERICK	MAJ	0-1699841	0146	2
MORET SIMON	1LT	0-0403267	C745	2
MOREY LEIGHTON G	COL	0-1300835	0567	1
MORFORD ALEXANDER	LTC	0-0280686	1062	3
MORFORD THEODORE	MAJ	C-0200007	0746	2
MORGAN ALOIS A	COL	0-1107C14	1167	1
MORGAN ANGELA J	1LT	N-0763826	0747	1
MORGAN ARTHUR C	1LT	0-1186268	0347	2
MORGAN BENJAMIN T	1LT	0-0197356	0161	3
MORGAN BILLY L	CW2	W-2150641	0657	1
MORGAN BOYCE M	CW4	W-2118370	0964	1
MORGAN CAMILLE G	CPT	0-1323160	1262	1
MORGAN CARL L	LTC	0-0452088	0255	1
MORGAN CARTHEL N	LTC	0-0342878	1058	1
MORGAN CHARLES A	MAJ	0-1289117	0358	1
MORGAN CHARLES E	CPT	C-1294703	0348	2
MORGAN CHARLES H	LTC	0-0334733	0257	1
MORGAN CLINTON D	MAJ	0-1294177	1157	1
MORGAN DAVID R	COL	0-0145644	0-53	3
MORGAN DON P	MAJ	C-0985328	0365	2
MORGAN DONALD H	LTC	0-2210327	1167	1
MORGAN DORSEY	CPT	0-0947729	0861	1
MORGAN EDNA L	2LT	N-0735926	0546	1
MORGAN EDWIN R	LTC	0-0300022	0166	3
MORGAN ELDON V	CW3	W-2142256	0659	1
MORGAN ELMER H	1LT	0-1286332	0946	2
MORGAN FLETCHER B	CPT	C-0333331	1053	2
MORGAN FRANCIS J	LTC	0-0470247	0651	1
MORGAN FRANK C	COL	0-0255235	0156	1
MORGAN FRANK C	CPT	0-1555109	0352	1
MORGAN FRED	CW3	W-2149466	0166	1
MORGAN FREDERICK	MAJ	0-0117425	0950	3
MORGAN GENE	1LT	0-1309299	0146	2
MORGAN GEORGE A	COL	0-0900096	0954	1
MORGAN GEORGE E	CW4	RW-2122105	C866	1
MORGAN GEORGE H	CPT	0-0887573	0646	2
MORGAN GEORGE H	2LT	0-1798945	0545	2
MORGAN GEORGE N	LTC	C-0342291	1160	1
MORGAN GEORGE W	CPT	0-2011656	0160	1
MORGAN GERALD C	COL	0-0451128	1160	1
MORGAN HAROLD A	COL	0-0215195	1054	3
MORGAN HARRIET P	CPT	N-0720973	1047	1
MORGAN HARRY T	LTC	0-0252987	0849	2
MORGAN HELEN M	2LT	N-0755236	0345	1
MORGAN HELEN S	1LT	N-0721573	0946	1
MORGAN HENRY G	1LT	0-1030579	0849	1
MORGAN HENRY T	LTC	0-1010172	0162	2
MORGAN HORACE R	MAJ	0-0994456	0165	1
MORGAN HOWELL E	CPT	0-0373465	0745	2
MORGAN II HENRY R	MAJ	0-2200220	0767	1
MORGAN IRVING B	LTC	0-0232976	0957	3
MORGAN JACK F	LTC	0-0358023	0461	1
MORGAN JAMES O	MAJ	0-1012523	0662	1
MORGAN JAMES F	2LT	0-1058092	0945	2
MORGAN JAMES C	LTC	0-0389654	0166	2
MORGAN JAMES R	MAJ	0-1820973	0166	1
MORGAN JESSE P	LTC	0-0258491	0746	2
MORGAN JESSIE M	MAJ	N-0755320	0163	1
MORGAN JOHN A	LTC	C-1550007	1263	1
MORGAN JOHN B	MAJ	0-0180812	0250	3
MORGAN JOHN B	MAJ	0-1587478	0858	1
MORGAN JOHN C	COL	0-0260818	0666	3
MORGAN JOHN D	COL	0-0133085	0648	3
MORGAN JOHN F	LTC	0-0296368	0165	3
MORGAN JOHN F	2LT	0-1297409	0944	2
MORGAN JOHN G	LTC	0-1643149	0665	2
MORGAN JOHN R	MAJ	C-1686721	0465	1
MORGAN JOHN T	COL	0-0105742	0152	3
MORGAN JOHN W	COL	0-1165918	0867	1
MORGAN JOHN W	MAJ	0-1924645	1263	1
MORGAN JOSEPH H	MAJ	0-0475017	0642	1
MORGAN JOSEPH L	CW2	W-2206646	1063	1
MORGAN JOSEPH W	COL	0-0285940	0166	3
MORGAN JR CLIFFORD O	1LT	0-3207949	0165	2
MORGAN JR JAMES A	WO1	W-2005635	1051	2
MORGAN JR JOHN D	COL	0-0238394	0-49	3
MORGAN JR JOHN R	1LT	0-0551743	1046	2
MORGAN JR JOSEPH H	CW3	W-2146498	0763	1
MORGAN JR LEONARD C	MAJ	C-2021129	0965	1
MORGAN JR LEROY	2LT	0-1311568	0645	2
MORGAN JR PAUL E	MAJ	0-0390602	0347	1

NAME	GRADE	SVC NO	DATE RET MO YR	RET CODE
MORGAN JR RALPH F	MAJ	0-0966086	0765	1
MORGAN JR WALTER R	MAJ	0-1295088	1046	2
MORGAN JR WILLIAM C	COL	0-0174464	0263	3
MORGAN KATHRYN M	LTC	N-0700058	0346	1
MORGAN KENNETH L	MAJ	0-0962162	0263	1
MORGAN LAURENCE C	1LT	0-1581984	0545	2
MORGAN LAURENCE S	1LT	0-1041201	0845	2
MORGAN LEANDER J	CW3	W-2118150	0557	1
MORGAN LEONARD F	CPT	0-2032892	1058	1
MORGAN LEROY E	MAJ	0-2000903	0760	1
MORGAN LONNIE	CW2	W-2205098	1060	1
MORGAN MARION N	LTC	0-1284744	0261	1
MORGAN MAURICE M	CPT	0-1796836	0246	2
MORGAN MILLARD	LTC	0-1285626	0165	1
MORGAN MYRON	LTC	0-1286333	0847	2
MORGAN NEIL B	LTC	0-0204073	0359	3
MORGAN NEWTON B	LTC	0-0149818	0852	3
MORGAN NOAH R	CW2	W-2145924	0562	2
MORGAN NORMAN	CPT	0-1919258	0462	1
MORGAN OLIN E	CW3	W-2147251	0965	1
MORGAN OLIN R	CW3	W-2147073	0161	1
MORGAN PATRICK H	LTC	0-0462401	1266	1
MORGAN PRENTICE G	LTC	0-0311202	0660	1
MORGAN PRESTON W	LTC	0-1308275	0767	1
MORGAN RALPH B	MAJ	0-0301335	0247	1
MORGAN RALPH L	LTC	0-0888375	0556	1
MORGAN RALPH S	LTC	0-0355386	0165	1
MORGAN RALPH W	LTC	0-0363477	0467	3
MORGAN RAYMOND A	CPT	0-2289500	0562	1
MORGAN RAYMOND E	LTC	0-1582468	0565	1
MORGAN RAYMOND O	1LT	0-0419149	0946	2
MORGAN RICHARD F	MAJ	0-1305963	0157	1
MORGAN RICHARD H	MAJ	0-1016964	1060	1
MORGAN RICHARD J	CPT	0-0910477	0747	1
MORGAN RICHARD L	COL	0-0297685	0660	1
MORGAN ROBERT G	MAJ	0-2043069	0657	1
MORGAN ROBERT H	2LT	0-1638117	0643	2
MORGAN ROBERT M	1LT	0-0425435	0643	2
MORGAN ROY L	CPT	0-0504084	1048	1
MORGAN ROY S	CPT	0-0307195	0244	2
MORGAN ROY W	CW2	W-2118329	0260	1
MORGAN RUFUS	CPT	0-0499502	1049	1
MORGAN SIDNEY	COL	0-0114527	0550	3
MORGAN STANLEY R	MAJ	0-0528115	0155	1
MORGAN STANTON A	MAJ	0-0465219	1062	1
MORGAN THEODORE J	CW2	W-2208610	0462	1
MORGAN THOMAS J	2LT	0-1292042	0945	2
MORGAN WARREN E	CW3	W-2147769	0964	1
MORGAN WENDELL H	MAJ	0-1541939	0466	3
MORGAN WILBER L	CW3	W-2151794	0264	1
MORGAN WILFRED A	COL	0-0170630	0153	3
MORGAN WILLIAM D	LTC	0-0344436	1159	1
MORGAN WILLIAM H	LTC	0-0103307	0549	3
MORGAN WILLIAM H	CW2	W-2211022	0666	1
MORGAN WILLIAM R	LTC	0-1340571	0767	1
MORGAN WILLIE E	CW3	W-2147527	0565	1
MORGAN WILMER G	LTC	0-0326226	0562	1
MORGAN WINSTON J	MAJ	0-1322802	0464	1
MORGAN WYNNE M	LTC	0-0237382	0664	3
MORGANSTERN ALFRED B	MAJ	0-0207643	0355	3
MORGANTI JOSEPH M	MAJ	0-1648615	0261	1
MORGENSTERN FLOYD V	1LT	0-1645846	0945	2
MORGENSTERN GEORGE E	MAJ	0-0297719	0145	2
MORGNER ARTHUR F	MAJ	0-1035548	0461	2
MORIAN HAROLD L	LTC	0-0282698	0156	2
MORIARITY WILLIAM J	CPT	0-1645847	1263	3
MORIARTY FRANCIS E	MAJ	0-1305252	0960	1
MORIARTY JAMES T	MAJ	0-0255241	0162	3
MORIARTY JOHN R	CPT	0-1174390	0246	2
MORIARTY LAUREN R	CPT	0-0367946	0145	2
MORIARTY RUSSELL S	MAJ	0-1328833	0263	1
MORIARTY VEALE F	LTC	0-0393729	0860	1
MORIARTY WILLIAM M	1LT	0-1934950	0654	2
MORICONI FRANK F	WO1	W-2151300	1066	1
MORIE GRACE D	1LT	N-0783122	0846	1

NAME	GRADE	SVC NO	DATE RET MO YR	RET CODE
MORIN ANDREW F	MAJ	0-0948833	1065	1
MORIN CHARLES E	CW2	W-2149709	1060	1
MORIN LEON	CW2	W-2108609	1055	1
MORIN MARGARET P	2LT	N-0720417	0444	1
MORIN MARGUERITE	MAJ	L-1010131	0164	1
MORIN ROGER J	LTC	0-1533868	0764	1
MORIN ROY E	CW3	W-2143228	1060	1
MORINE MYRON L	2LT	0-1301519	0843	2
MORING DAVIS C	CPT	0-1172559	0148	1
MORISON GARLAND M	MAJ	0-1587479	0457	1
MORISON JACK F	COL	0-0302028	0647	1
MORISSETTE BERTELL R	CW4	W-2143613	0767	1
MORITZ ROWLAND T	CPT	0-1845535	0162	1
MORITZ WILLIAM R	CPT	0-1032231	0847	2
MORIUCHI GUNJI	LTC	0-1330455	0464	1
MORK LEE D	COL	0-0259087	1264	3
MORLA RAFAEL	COL	0-0287456	1047	2
MORLAN ERNEST F	WO1	W-2148752	0158	2
MORLAN HAROLD E	WO1	W-2113197	0945	2
MORLEY ABNER S	COL	0-0188516	0949	3
MORLEY CHARLES P	CPT	0-2033287	1059	1
MORLEY JOHN H	MAJ	0-0284937	0946	1
MORLEY JOHN R	1LT	0-0527842	0946	2
MORLEY JOHN W	LTC	0-0441704	0662	1
MORNINGSTAR CLINTON	CW3	W-2205165	1064	1
MOROZ RAYMOND G	LTC	0-2048536	0960	1
MORPHEW SR WALTER L	LTC	0-1043739	0565	1
MORR DARRELL M	1LT	0-1100255	0843	2
MORRA DORIS M	1LT	N-0722424	0346	1
MORRELL IRA D	CPT	0-0505732	0854	1
MORRELL LEO A	1LT	0-1648616	0345	2
MORRELL PAUL A	LTC	0-1284555	0266	1
MORRELL RONALD F	CW2	W-2149453	1066	1
MORRIA JAMES I	CW2	W-2150124	0760	1
MORRILL HARVEY J	LTC	0-1645848	0165	1
MORRILL HORACE A	LTC	0-0204908	0750	3
MORRILL KEITH S	LTC	0-1102395	0962	1
MORRILL LESLIE S	COL	0-0118197	0754	3
MORRILL MARIAN A	1LT	N-0751954	0246	1
MORRIS AL K	LTC	0-1696548	0147	2
MORRIS ALBERT C	MAJ	0-0419969	0346	2
MORRIS ARCHIE	CPT	0-0173169	0254	1
MORRIS ARDEN S	LTC	0-0384642	0967	3
MORRIS ARTHUR C	CPT	0-1303525	0953	1
MORRIS ARVINE E	LTC	0-0220200	0250	3
MORRIS ASTOR A	LTC	0-1287744	0263	1
MORRIS BEE	2LT	N-0737485	0345	1
MORRIS CAROL	CPT	0-0488650	0656	1
MORRIS CECIL F	LTC	0-1169661	1060	1
MORRIS CLAUDE B	LTC	0-0365425	0946	2
MORRIS CLAUDE W	CW3	W-2141862	0358	1
MORRIS DANIEL R	LTC	0-0338337	0965	3
MORRIS DON L	MAJ	0-0969898	1160	1
MORRIS DONALD	CPT	0-0221897	0958	3
MORRIS DONALD K	COL	0-0365296	0363	1
MORRIS DONALD V	LTC	0-0384979	0846	2
MORRIS DOUGLAS	CW3	W-2142582	0758	1
MORRIS DOUGLAS B	MAJ	0-0983576	0764	1
MORRIS DREW W	LTC	0-1118955	1166	1
MORRIS EARL E	CW3	W-2151986	1064	1
MORRIS EDWARD H	CPT	0-0172499	0648	3
MORRIS EDWARD J	LTC	0-1184265	0566	1
MORRIS EDWARD J	1LT	0-1283465	0145	2
MORRIS EDWARD R	COL	0-0183525	0855	3
MORRIS ELISHA	CPT	0-2262460	0461	2
MORRIS ENA M	1LT	N-0772715	1045	1
MORRIS FLOYD C	CPT	0-0254769	0567	3
MORRIS FRANCIS S	LTC	0-1010155	1055	1
MORRIS FRANK E	MAJ	0-0286623	0944	2
MORRIS FRANK J	COL	0-0521454	0466	3
MORRIS FRED H	LTC	0-0337059	0555	3
MORRIS GEORGE A	B G	0-0266651	0867	3
MORRIS GEORGE E	1LT	0-0516870	0658	2
MORRIS GEORGE F	LTC	0-1169662	0561	1
MORRIS GEORGE P	CW4	W-2142683	0866	1

NAME	GRADE	SVC NO	DATE RET MO YR	RET CODE
MORRIS GEORGE R	LTC	0-0900408	0362	3
MORRIS GEORGE W	LTC	0-0397668	0461	1
MORRIS GLENN S	LTC	0-0209437	0755	3
MORRIS GRANT E	1LT	0-0293960	0641	2
MORRIS HARRY	LTC	0-0257903	0745	1
MORRIS HARRY D	COL	0-0247495	0167	3
MORRIS HARRY W	CPT	0-0175405	0658	3
MORRIS HENRY C	MAJ	0-1335818	0864	1
MORRIS HENRY L	LTC	0-0401673	0960	1
MORRIS HOBART A	1LT	0-2049662	0446	2
MORRIS HORACE M	LTC	0-0241257	0158	3
MORRIS HOWARD A	MAJ	0-0196871	0162	3
MORRIS HOWARD G	CPT	0-1110143	0646	2
MORRIS HUGH B	CPT	0-0373291	0445	1
MORRIS HUGH E	1LT	0-1312037	0747	1
MORRIS J D	CW3	W-2149087	1060	1
MORRIS JACK H	CPT	0-1300514	0459	1
MORRIS JAMES B	WO1	W-2109144	0962	1
MORRIS JAMES E	LTC	0-0453155	0461	1
MORRIS JAMES F	LTC	0-0928940	0166	1
MORRIS JAMES H	MAJ	0-1951556	0863	1
MORRIS JAMES K	LTC	0-0103358	0156	3
MORRIS JAMES L	CPT	0-0357608	0345	2
MORRIS JAMES S	COL	0-0309173	0460	2
MORRIS JAMES W	CPT	0-0423179	0163	1
MORRIS JIMMIE A	WO1	W-2150044	0954	1
MORRIS JOHN D	WO1	W-2151823	0357	1
MORRIS JOHN E	LTC	0-1101591	0961	1
MORRIS JOHN E	MAJ	0-2263095	0466	1
MORRIS JOHN H	CPT	0-0921478	0846	1
MORRIS JOHN R	MAJ	0-0502493	1146	2
MORRIS JOHN S	MAJ	0-0160895	0648	3
MORRIS JOHN S	CPT	0-1176740	0753	1
MORRIS JOHN T	MAJ	0-0253372	1262	3
MORRIS JOHN W	MAJ	0-2029521	0363	1
MORRIS JOHNIE L	CW2	W-2148678	0758	1
MORRIS JOSEPH A	1LT	0-2040895	0847	2
MORRIS JOSEPH E	COL	0-0278843	0446	2
MORRIS JOSEPH F	CW2	W-2148753	0561	1
MORRIS JOSEPH S	MAJ	0-1052489	0857	1
MORRIS JOSEPH W	CPT	0-0309474	0763	3
MORRIS JR ALBERT C	CPT	0-1553148	0246	1
MORRIS JR ALFRED M	COL	0-0244821	0465	3
MORRIS JR EDWARD P	CPT	0-1292043	1159	1
MORRIS JR EVERETTE W	CW2	W-2211615	1066	1
MORRIS JR FRANK S	CW3	W-2208445	0167	1
MORRIS JR FRED M	MAJ	0-0397851	0364	1
MORRIS JR JOHN A	CW3	W-2141822	0858	1
MORRIS JR LOVELL J	LTC	0-1589392	0664	1
MORRIS JR ROY C	1LT	0-2211233	0553	2
MORRIS JR WALTER J	2LT	0-1108182	0145	1
MORRIS JR WILLIAM B	MAJ	0-1822173	1160	1
MORRIS JR WILLIAM H	MAJ	0-1177915	0162	1
MORRIS JR WILLIAM W	LTC	0-1310749	0663	1
MORRIS LAVAL S	LTC	0-0173936	0160	3
MORRIS LEE	LTC	0-1294178	0754	1
MORRIS LEONARD S	LTC	0-0116820	0652	3
MORRIS LEW E	COL	0-0189360	0559	3
MORRIS LEWIS B	CW3	W-2148213	0762	1
MORRIS LEWIS E	MAJ	0-0472960	1048	2
MORRIS LLOYD M	COL	0-0149745	1055	3
MORRIS LOUIS W	1LT	0-0112270	0648	3
MORRIS MALCOLM E	MAJ	0-1634162	0364	2
MORRIS MANUEL R	CPT	0-1846324	0947	2
MORRIS MARK W	LTC	0-0287926	0666	3
MORRIS MARTIN M	1LT	0-1172433	1047	1
MORRIS MARVIN J	CW3	W-2142384	1164	1
MORRIS MELVIN EUG	2LT	0-1292567	0451	2
MORRIS MELVIN L	CW2	W-2150177	0864	1
MORRIS NORMAN	LTC	0-1114668	1061	1
MORRIS NORMAN W	LTC	0-1110675	0862	1
MORRIS ORVA E	CPT	0-1258574	0457	1
MORRIS OSCAR K	CW3	W-2116054	0660	1
MORRIS PAUL E	COL	0-0319558	1065	1
MORRIS PERRY L V	MAJ	0-1313116	1160	1

NAME	GRADE	SVC NO	DATE RET MO YR	RET CODE
MORRIS R V	WO1	W-2146348	0659	1
MORRIS RAWLINS M	MAJ	0-1168836	0258	1
MORRIS RAYMOND L	1LT	0-1894763	0958	1
MORRIS ROBERT	CW3	W-2145145	0862	1
MORRIS ROBERT F	CPT	0-0166546	0651	3
MORRIS ROBERT H	COL	0-0162361	0159	1
MORRIS ROBERT K	WO1	W-2126659	1061	2
MORRIS ROBERT L	LTC	0-1048505	0964	1
MORRIS ROBERT L	1LT	0-1591949	1264	2
MORRIS ROBERT M	MAJ	0-1115713	0757	1
MORRIS ROY L	CPT	0-1333105	0256	1
MORRIS SAMUEL R	COL	0-0246032	0462	1
MORRIS SIDNEY C	CW3	W-2144344	0664	1
MORRIS STEPHEN	LTC	0-1573450	1054	1
MORRIS STEPHEN E	COL	0-1633422	0560	1
MORRIS THEODORE F	CPT	0-0488816	0455	1
MORRIS THEODORE L	LTC	0-0507319	1065	3
MORRIS THEODORE N	1LT	0-0536117	0845	1
MORRIS THERON K	CW3	W-2142885	0158	1
MORRIS THOMAS B	COL	0-0100744	0648	3
MORRIS WALLACE E	CW4	W-2141390	0166	1
MORRIS WALLACE H	LTC	0-0321199	0157	1
MORRIS WALLACE M	MAJ	0-1945897	0966	3
MORRIS WALTER	MAJ	0-1308596	0760	1
MORRIS WALTER T	CW2	W-2102117	0949	1
MORRIS WILLIAM A	LTC	0-0384295	0767	3
MORRIS WILLIAM C	COL	0-0521542	1147	2
MORRIS WILLIAM C	CW2	W-2210689	1066	1
MORRIS WILLIAM D	CPT	0-0546873	0747	1
MORRIS WILLIAM H	LTC	0-0182784	1047	1
MORRIS WILLIAM H	MAJ	0-0389942	0445	1
MORRIS WILLIAM R	CW4	W-2141635	0867	1
MORRIS WILLIAM S	CPT	0-0415582	0953	2
MORRIS WILSON	MAJ	0-1323955	1160	1
MORRISON ALAN C	CW2	W-2108309	1059	1
MORRISON ALFRED E	CPT	0-1996653	0856	1
MORRISON ALVIN A	LTC	0-0273835	0664	3
MORRISON BENJAMIN A	CW2	W-2144647	1159	1
MORRISON CHARLES H	MAJ	0-0112344	0455	3
MORRISON CHARLES J	1LT	0-0537435	0847	2
MORRISON CHARLES W	1LT	0-1307565	0745	1
MORRISON CLARENCE E	LTC	0-2279330	1167	1
MORRISON CLAUDE B	2LT	0-1686527	0146	2
MORRISON CLIFFORD D	1LT	0-1177105	0562	1
MORRISON CLIFFORD R	COL	0-0300251	0367	3
MORRISON DANIEL W	CPT	0-0450460	0750	1
MORRISON DONALD A	1LT	0-1304770	0146	1
MORRISON DONALD J	MAJ	0-1951702	0266	1
MORRISON DONALD K	LTC	0-0103359	1152	3
MORRISON ELEANOR M	LTC	L-0600001	0163	2
MORRISON EVERT F	CW2	W-2146083	0365	1
MORRISON FRANCIS G	LTC	0-0910754	0765	3
MORRISON FRANK G	1LT	0-0116821	0652	3
MORRISON FRANK H	1LT	0-1321369	0246	2
MORRISON GARLAND V	CPT	0-0499496	0347	1
MORRISON GEORGE G	CPT	0-1684780	0246	2
MORRISON HARRY E	MAJ	0-0582160	0955	1
MORRISON HENRY C	CPT	0-1547410	0952	2
MORRISON HENRY G	WO1	W-2148415	0455	1
MORRISON HERMAN H	LTC	0-1031580	0160	1
MORRISON HOMER W	LTC	0-1318999	1066	1
MORRISON ISSAC F	LTC	0-0187218	0951	3
MORRISON IVAN L	2LT	0-1169261	1145	2
MORRISON J ATWOOD	COL	0-0302938	0160	1
MORRISON JEANNE E	1LT	N-0730551	1045	1
MORRISON JOHN A	LTC	0-1589393	1163	1
MORRISON JOHN L	LTC	0-0360859	0763	3
MORRISON JOHN W	MAJ	0-1318070	0561	1
MORRISON JOSEPH W	LTC	0-0351143	0159	1
MORRISON JOSEPH W	LTC	0-1328730	0563	1
MORRISON JR JAMES D	1LT	0-1285274	0845	2
MORRISON LORRAINE G	MAJ	0-0441782	0147	2
MORRISON LOUIS C	CW4	W-2121[illegible]68	0760	1
MORRISON LOUIS E	LTC	0-1290288	0461	1
MORRISON LUTHER S	2LT	0-1303375	0645	2

NAME	GRADE	SVC NO	DATE RET MO YR	RET CODE
MORRISON MARCUS E	MAJ	0-0369301	0446	2
MORRISON NORMAN B	MAJ	0-0291470	0344	2
MORRISON NORMAN T	MAJ	0-1044906	1164	1
MORRISON PAUL L	COL	0-0121799	1059	3
MORRISON PHILLIPS L	CPT	0-0490097	0343	2
MORRISON PRUDENZA S	MAJ	L-1010055	0163	1
MORRISON RAYMOND C	CPT	0-0498726	0550	1
MORRISON READ W	LTC	0-0495407	0154	2
MORRISON REGINALD G	1LT	0-0401679	0344	2
MORRISON RICHARD A	WO1	W-2139480	0646	2
MORRISON RICHARD R	COL	0-0334421	0648	3
MORRISON RICHARD R	LTC	0-0342190	0746	2
MORRISON ROBERT N	LTC	0-1294345	0563	1
MORRISON ROBERT T	CPT	0-0506149	0146	2
MORRISON SR FRED C	MAJ	0-0975181	0264	1
MORRISON THOMAS D	LTC	0-0277609	1266	3
MORRISON THOMAS E	LTC	0-0444359	0257	1
MORRISON VERNE B	MAJ	0-1645850	1166	3
MORRISON WHEELER J	LTC	0-1175252	0863	1
MORRISON WILLIAM C	LTC	0-0161285	0157	2
MORRISON WILLIAM E	MAJ	0-1044912	0666	1
MORRISON WILLIAM F	MAJ	0-1063071	1064	1
MORRISON WILLIAM C	MAJ	0-0258784	1066	3
MORRISON WILLIAM J	MAJ	0-1922590	1265	1
MORRISROE ROBERT	CW2	W-2150626	0157	1
MORRISS ABNER B	1LT	0-0915361	0744	2
MORRISSEY EDWARD L	LTC	0-0507614	0265	3
MORRISSEY FRANCIS C	MAJ	0-1322804	0263	1
MORRISSEY JAMES T	LTC	0-1104309	0562	1
MORRISSEY JOHN	MAJ	0-0286594	0166	3
MORRISSEY JOHN B	LTC	0-0323284	0247	2
MORRISSEY JOHN F	CPT	0-1031011	0459	1
MORRISSEY LAURENCE	LTC	0-1314542	0546	2
MORRISSEY PAUL A	CW3	W-2145779	0666	1
MORRISSEY RAYMOND E	1LT	0-1014408	0460	1
MORRISSEY THOMAS H	CW3	RW-2152164	0166	1
MORROW ALFRED	MAJ	0-1052090	0358	1
MORROW CHARLES H	MAJ	0-0473656	0858	1
MORROW CHARLES M	1LT	0-0513541	0346	2
MORROW DAVID C	LTC	0-1102880	0161	1
MORROW EUGENE F	1LT	0-0141882	0454	3
MORROW FRANK S	LTC	0-0910368	0264	3
MORROW HALF	MAJ	0-0286650	1044	2
MORROW HASKELL F	MAJ	0-0253451	1047	2
MORROW HENRY	1LT	0-0164213	0637	1
MORROW JACK C	1LT	0-2053900	1145	1
MORROW JAMES E	LTC	0-1048910	0866	1
MORROW JAMES F	LTC	0-1641601	0262	1
MORROW JAMES H	1LT	0-0536909	0845	2
MORROW JAMES R	2LT	0-0537436	0345	2
MORROW RAYMOND N	CPT	0-1309385	0754	2
MORROW ROBERT D	LTC	0-0168741	0444	2
MORROW ROBERT P	LTC	0-0315285	1059	1
MORROW ROBERT P	CPT	0-0358377	0246	1
MORROW ROBERT P	1LT	0-1056177	1051	1
MORROW SIDNEY S	2LT	0-1017572	0146	2
MORROW TALMADGE D	1LT	0-1825235	0767	1
MORROW THADDEUS L	LTC	0-0299854	0666	3
MORROW WALTER B	LTC	0-0334220	0958	1
MORROW WILEY W	MAJ	0-0981525	0667	1
MORROW WILLIAM H	2LT	0-1578882	0566	2
MORROW WILLIAM J	LTC	0-0349971	0246	2
MORROW WILLIAM T	2LT	0-2007671	0346	2
MORROW WINSTON V	LTC	0-0141834	0648	3
MORS GEORGE L	COL	0-0280853	0452	3
MORSE ANTHONY W	LTC	0-1280220	1060	1
MORSE ARNOLD A	CW4	W-2144224	1265	1
MORSE ARTHUR H	MAJ	0-0240845	1064	3
MORSE CALVIN	MAJ	0-0956057	0962	1
MORSE CLAYTON C	CPT	0-0214026	0264	3
MORSE DONALD S	CW4	W-2004760	0966	1
MORSE EDWARD J	MAJ	0-0976231	0762	1
MORSE FRANK E	MAJ	0-0128460	0350	3
MORSE GEORGE B	COL	0-0121796	0651	3
MORSE HENRY P	COL	0-0338673	1160	1
MORSE HOWARD C	CPT	0-1044311	0147	1
MORSE HOWARD W	1LT	0-1172561	1044	2
MORSE JACK W	MAJ	0-1059008	0762	1
MORSE JESSE S	MAJ	0-1588187	0260	1
MORSE JR ALBERT W	LTC	0-0158330	0760	3
MORSE JR HARRISON R	CPT	0-1018198	1046	1
MORSE LEWIS W	COL	0-0909172	0963	3
MORSE LOUIS L	COL	0-0174546	0866	2
MORSE MARIE A	2LT	N-0731605	0445	1
MORSE PERCY	LTC	0-0499561	1054	1
MORSE RAYMOND R	LTC	0-0213600	0955	3
MORSE RICHARD D	CW4	W-2122320	1060	1
MORSE RICHARD L	CW3	W-2144062	0461	1
MORSE ROY F	MAJ	0-0246391	0158	3
MORSE THELMA W	CW4	V-0120159	0967	1
MORSE WILFRED C	CPT	0-0973173	0961	1
MORSE WILLIAM R	LTC	0-0549409	1162	1
MORSON THERON D	1LT	0-0163337	0355	3
MORSS CLYDE L	CW3	W-2144452	0563	1
MORSS VIRGIL R	LTC	0-0242731	0864	3
MORT CHARLES L	MAJ	0-1051696	1066	3
MORT ROBERT T	LTC	0-2030848	0365	1
MORTENSEN DOUGLAS A	MAJ	0-2025138	0163	1
MORTENSEN EDWIN J	1LT	0-1057178	1045	2
MORTENSEN FREDERIC	COL	0-0186191	0253	3
MORTENSEN MARTIN A	2LT	0-1168387	0645	2
MORTENSEN RODNEY F	LTC	0-1171689	0466	1
MORTENSEN WILLIAM J	1LT	0-1057831	0146	2
MORTIMER WINFIELD S	LTC	0-0277665	0867	3
MORTON ALMON W	2LT	0-1308997	0944	2
MORTON CARL	MAJ	0-1289611	0147	1
MORTON EARL C	CPT	0-1298101	1045	2
MORTON EDWIN A	LTC	0-0522529	1163	3
MORTON EDWIN A	CW2	W-2214650	0767	1
MORTON HAROLD S	COL	0-0425611	0646	2
MORTON HENRY A	MAJ	0-0163708	1056	3
MORTON HOWARD W	WO1	W-2152302	1057	2
MORTON IRA H	CPT	0-0353275	1045	1
MORTON JAMES C	CPT	0-1060898	0462	2
MORTON JAMES F	MAJ	0-0228833	0748	1
MORTON JAMES G	CPT	0-0366352	0546	2
MORTON JAMES W	MAJ	0-1183934	0463	1
MORTON JAMES M	MAJ	0-1797859	0264	1
MORTON JOHN K	MAJ	0-0394613	0660	1
MORTON JOHN K	MAJ	0-0487108	0457	1
MORTON JR PAUL S	CPT	0-0432950	0646	2
MORTON JR RALPH W	1LT	0-1014172	1046	2
MORTON LELAND A	CW2	W-2118146	0553	1
MORTON LENA W	CPT	L-0514194	0458	2
MORTON MANUEL M	CPT	0-1042119	0456	1
MORTON MARY W	2LT	N-0759462	0544	1
MORTON MATTHEW W	MAJ	0-0933664	0757	1
MORTON NORMAN W	MAJ	0-0994505	0764	1
MORTON OLIVER F	LTC	0-0319222	0562	1
MORTON PAUL F	MAJ	0-1035481	0262	1
MORTON RALPH E	LTC	0-0490213	0456	1
MORTON RAY W	LTC	0-1947584	1062	1
MORTON ROBERT J	LTC	0-0171235	0460	3
MORTON ROY W	MAJ	0-0191466	1051	3
MORTON THOMAS C	MAJ	0-1323254	1159	2
MORTON WILLIAM C	CPT	0-1166788	1145	1
MORUD STANLEY J	MAJ	0-0756659	0667	1
MORYLE FELIX	CW3	W-2148262	1159	1
MOSBY BEATRICE C	2LT	N-0772208	0345	1
MOSBY CLARENCE L	MAJ	0-1297574	0261	1
MOSBY LEON	2LT	0-2027462	0547	1
MOSCICKE JR LEE F	LTC	0-0942577	1066	1
MOSEBACH JAMES A	LTC	0-0301716	0749	2
MOSELEY BRUCE W	MAJ	0-2020326	1065	1
MOSELEY CHAMP C	LTC	0-0219854	0664	3
MOSELEY CRAIG D	MAJ	0-2204041	1065	1
MOSELEY EDWARD F	MAJ	0-1636368	0160	1
MOSELEY FREDERICK	LTC	0-0380670	0462	1
MOSELEY GEORGE C	MAJ	0-1030598	0250	1
MOSELEY HOLSTON G	CW4	W-2147720	0464	1
MOSELEY JAMES L	MAJ	0-1340308	0765	2
MOSELEY JAMES R	CW2	W-2153003	1062	1
MOSELEY JR GEORGE C	CPT	0-1635140	0559	1
MOSELEY JR ROBERT F	LTC	0-0228185	0465	3
MOSELEY JR WILLIAM L	MAJ	0-1319818	0665	1
MOSELEY THOMAS F	CPT	0-1554446	0146	1
MOSER CHRIS J	CPT	0-0537895	0847	2
MOSER EUGENE R	MAJ	0-0315912	0162	1
MOSER HORACE G	MAJ	0-0966574	0161	2
MOSER JOHN G	LTC	0-1322360	0263	1
MOSER JR FLOYD D	MAJ	0-1557645	0961	1
MOSER JR JOSIAH L	LTC	0-1577599	0959	1
MOSER MORENO	CPT	0-0497370	0749	1
MOSER MORRIS K	1LT	0-1895874	0557	3
MOSER RICHARD H	1LT	0-0430492	0845	2
MOSER WALTER L	LTC	0-0275289	0854	3
MOSER ZACHUR	LTC	0-0505353	0257	1
MOSES ALAN W	MAJ	0-0116822	1054	3
MOSES BERNARD A	LTC	0-0299961	0462	1
MOSES EDWARD W	MAJ	0-0122955	0654	3
MOSES FRANK R	COL	0-0451360	0456	1
MOSES GEORGE W	CW3	W-2149124	1063	1
MOSES HAROLD T	COL	0-0314136	0462	1
MOSES HERMON L	MAJ	0-0335921	0844	2
MOSES JOHN R	1LT	0-1019183	1045	1
MOSES JR GEORGE W	LTC	0-0236861	0264	3
MOSES KELLIE H	LTC	0-0354127	0159	2
MOSES MAXMILLIAN	CPT	0-0505040	0744	1
MOSES PERCIVAL S	COL	0-0111551	0651	3
MOSES RUTH A	CPT	L-0800006	0347	1
MOSES WALTER F	LTC	0-0279564	0866	3
MOSES WILLIAM G	COL	0-0100078	0360	3
MOSES WILLIAM P	CW4	W-2004977	0267	3
MOSHBERGER MARTIN	COL	0-0249591	0359	1
MOSHER GRANT O	LTC	0-1310751	0367	1
MOSHER HAROLD S	LTC	0-1332514	0665	2
MOSHER HELEN M	CPT	N-0720317	1046	1
MOSHER JOHN F	COL	0-0240785	0663	1
MOSHER KENNETH A	MAJ	0-1042380	0962	1
MOSHER WILLIAM C	MAJ	0-0140737	0354	3
MOSHOLDER ROBERT M	CW3	W-2141863	0860	1
MOSIER ARTHUR I	CW4	W-2104774	0559	1
MOSIER JR ULYSSES G	CPT	0-0222251	0762	3
MOSIER 2ND LORAL	LTC	0-0429258	0655	2
MOSIG JOHN J	CPT	0-0545547	0747	2
MOSKOT EDWARD J	CPT	0-0499556	1053	2
MOSKOWITZ HENRY	CPT	0-0482103	0145	1
MOSKOWITZ IRVING L	LTC	0-0428582	0557	1
MOSLEY ARTHUR R	2LT	0-1994507	0546	2
MOSLEY DONALD C	CW3	W-2147082	0257	1
MOSLEY DOUGLAS	MAJ	0-2018201	0661	1
MOSLEY HUGH G	LTC	0-0296627	0259	3
MOSLEY JAMES W	CW2	W-2144578	0465	1
MOSLEY JOHN F	COL	0-0193883	1157	1
MOSLEY WASHINGTON	MAJ	0-0163793	0648	3
MOSLEY WILLIAM F	CPT	0-2005432	0757	2
MOSMAN HARRY W	1LT	0-0542205	0945	1
MOSMILLER WALTER E	COL	0-0255270	1162	3
MOSS CHESTER A	COL	0-0294265	0862	3
MOSS CLARENCE F	CPT	0-0104897	0648	4
MOSS CLAY B	MAJ	0-1182663	0658	1
MOSS CLIFFORD F	CPT	0-0258945	1165	3
MOSS DANIEL R	LTC	0-0502655	0760	3
MOSS DONALD E	CPT	0-1053743	0647	2
MOSS DURWOOD W	CPT	0-0166176	0153	3
MOSS EDWARD W	CPT	0-0978973	0461	1
MOSS FRANK H	LTC	0-0421004	1163	1
MOSS JACK E	LTC	0-1290794	0961	1
MOSS JACK C	MAJ	0-1167130	1060	1
MOSS JAMES M	MAJ	0-0416750	0348	1
MOSS JOHN R	LTC	0-0325614	0660	1
MOSS LEONARD	WO1	W-2121198	0148	1
MOSS MAYOR J	CPT	0-1684790	1045	2
MOSS NOVELLE H	LTC	0-0426912	0365	1
MOSS RAPHAEL S	2LT	0-0462342	0744	2
MOSS RAYMOND W	CW3	RW-2150330	0764	1
MOSS VERDIE S	LTC	0-1307059	0763	1
MOSS WALTER J	CW3	W-2142025	0959	2
MOSS WARREN R	LTC	0-1059566	0867	1
MOSS WILBERT	CPT	0-0109581	1121	1
MOSS WILLIAM K	CPT	0-0485883	0245	2
MOSSACK EDWARD L	CPT	0-0134183	1052	3
MOSSAWIR HARVEY H	MAJ	0-0321979	1265	3
MOSSER THOMAS M	2LT	0-1052894	0345	2
MOSTROM JR ALBERT C	LTC	0-1314821	0264	1
MOSTY ROBERT L	CPT	0-0316583	0347	2
MOSURE GAYLORD H	CW3	W-2148125	0461	2
MOTE ERSHAL L	CW3	W-2152131	0664	1
MOTE JOHN H	CPT	0-0261755	0446	2
MOTE JR CARL H	2LT	0-0359897	0944	2
MOTE WILLIAM A	MAJ	0-0192506	0957	3
MOTES PETE	WO1	W-2108656	0552	1
MOTHERSHEAD DORIS S	2LT	N-0788490	0644	1
MOTHERSHEAD EARL K	MAJ	0-0921008	0357	2
MOTHERSHEAD ROBERT A	LTC	0-0318360	0446	2
MOTHERWAY WILLIAM	CW4	W-2002570	0858	3
MOTICH MARK	CPT	0-0497201	1049	1
MOTKOWSKI BERNARD S	COL	0-0313164	1054	1
MOTKOWSKI CECELIA J	1LT	N-0796389	0647	2
MOTL ANNA	2LT	N-0700331	0839	2
MOTL JOSEPHINE	MAJ	N-0700344	0246	1
MOTLEY HENRY L	MAJ	0-0967128	0862	1
MOTLEY HULON E	CPT	0-0992063	0162	1
MOTLONG CHAUNCEY F	CPT	0-0147534	1154	3
MOTOGAWA LAWRENCE N	CW3	W-2136020	0364	1
MOTON RONALD C	LTC	0-1081569	0962	1
MOTSCHALL JAMES N	1LT	0-1047693	0144	2
MOTSCHALL ROBERT E	1LT	0-1796136	0244	2
MOTT CHARLES R	1LT	0-1305093	0345	2
MOTT FREDERICK	MAJ	0-0248439	0144	2
MOTT GEORGE E	COL	0-0254500	0767	3
MOTT GEORGE W	CPT	0-1635144	1045	2
MOTT HAROLD W	COL	0-0374190	1162	1
MOTT HUBERT A	LTC	0-1686653	0767	1
MOTT III MARSHALL L	LTC	0-1035549	0563	1
MOTT JAMES C	M G	0-0176119	1160	3
MOTT JAMES W	LTC	0-0196246	0253	3
MOTT SELDON R	COL	0-0243462	0158	3
MOTT VERN E	CPT	0-0255281	0162	3
MOTT WALTER C	MAJ	0-0140735	1057	3
MOTT WILLIARD C	LTC	0-1173394	0561	2
MOTTA ANTHONY F	LTC	0-1280875	0457	1
MOTTERN ALBERT J	LTC	0-0172756	0647	2
MOTTERN LAYTON R	COL	0-0210297	1154	3
MOTTILLA RICHARD A	1LT	0-1017986	0152	1
MOTTLEY ROBERT C	COL	0-0224717	0454	2
MOTTO ROCCO L	CPT	0-0435315	1046	2
MOTTORN JACOB R	COL	0-0248058	0862	3
MOTYLIASKI JOSEPH	CW2	W-2113007	1051	2
MOTZ JOHN R	LTC	0-0316248	0362	3
MOTZ WALTER R	MAJ	0-0492510	0266	3
MOTZNY JR LEON W	LTC	0-1106982	0864	1
MOUDY ALFRED L	LTC	0-0121147	0648	3
MOUDY RALPH W	LTC	0-0415555	0467	1
MOUKAD PAUL P	CW3	W-2153159	1152	1
MOULD GEORGE F	MAJ	0-1574104	0163	1
MOULTHROP HENRY S	MAJ	0-0177808	1051	3
MOULTIS CHARLES A	MAJ	0-1947926	0667	3
MOULTON ALVA H	1LT	0-1185792	0647	1
MOULTON EARL R	LTC	0-0236179	0862	1
MOULTON FREDRICK J	1LT	0-1294746	0945	2
MOULTON GEORGE D	CW3	W-2141640	0156	1
MOULTON JAMES A	LTC	0-0196235	0162	3
MOULTON ROBERT P	CW2	W-2150936	1157	1
MOUNCE KENNETH L	LTC	0-0284526	0866	3
MOUNGER OWYN W	LTC	0-0517598	0866	3
MOUNSEY CARY E	MAJ	0-0107234	0750	3
MOUNSEY WILLIAM R	MAJ	0-0450368	0864	1
MOUNT ERMON E	CPT	0-0287000	0655	3
MOUNT GEORGE F	1LT	0-1305631	0146	2

NAME	GRADE	SVC NO	DATE RET MO YR	RET CODE
MOUNT JR HARRY V	CPT	0-1107607	C146	2
MOUNT JR JOHN B	CPT	0-0254062	0567	3
MOUNT MARK L	LTC	0-0240309	C165	3
MOUNT ROBERT H	1LT	0-0266990	1045	2
MOUNT WILSON H	LTC	0-1796839	1262	3
MOUNTAIN DANIEL J	2LT	C-0495243	C648	1
MOUNTAIN EARLE	LTC	0-0400134	0762	1
MOUNTJOY PEARL B	MAJ	0-0361344	0455	1
MOUNTZ KENNETH B	MAJ	C-0387137	0460	1
MOURAS TED	CW2	W-3430173	1067	1
MOURHESS BERTRAND L	CPT	0-0188401	0144	2
MOVOLD CLINTON H	2LT	C-1173007	1043	2
MOW KUI P	CW3	W-2154669	0367	1
MOWAT EDITH F	LTC	N-0722629	0263	1
MOWAT JR WILLIAM J	LTC	0-0408677	1060	1
MOWATT GEORGE	CPT	0-0491565	C848	1
MOWBRAY EMMA H	CPT	N-0760627	1052	1
MOWBRAY ORVILLE H	LTC	C-0382566	0364	3
MOWBRAY RICHARD M	MAJ	0-0999552	C965	1
MOWEN JOHN H	CPT	0-0412548	104N	2
MOWER CHARLES J	1LT	C-0507592	0545	2
MOWER FRANK C	LTC	0-0235639	0965	3
MOWER NATHANIEL	COL	0-0319665	0767	3
MOWERS LEONARD F	MAJ	C-0256645	C256	2
MOWERY JAMES F	LTC	0-0448051	0662	1
MOWITZ JR ARNO P	COL	C-0296307	C560	1
MOWLOS WILLIAM L	LTC	0-0168443	C559	3
MOWRAR HAROLD M	MAJ	0-1886487	C864	1
MOWRY DON F	LTC	0-1182429	0762	1
MOWRY RICHMOND C	MAJ	0-1107608	0353	1
MOXHAM CYRIL B	MAJ	C-2263438	C665	1
MOXLEY CALVIN I	CPT	0-0495404	C657	1
MOXLEY GEORGE N	CW3	W-2151423	0363	1
MOXON JAMES A	MAJ	0-0324806	0446	2
MOY FRANK	MAJ	0-1580064	C557	1
MOYCO GUALBERTO	1LT	0-0890443	0158	1
MOYE JAMES E	CPT	0-0505111	1045	2
MOYE LEON B	COL	0-0300946	0252	1
MOYER BILL A	CW3	W-2205296	0267	1
MOYER CARL W	2LT	0-1295585	0445	2
MOYER CHARLES O	1LT	0-5201097	0959	2
MOYER CLIFFORD	CPT	0-0174671	0659	1
MOYER EDWARD F	MAJ	C-1296733	C760	1
MOYER ELSIE G	CPT	N-0700560	C644	1
MOYER HARRY	MAJ	0-1302333	0758	1
MOYER IRVIN P	MAJ	0-0151431	C361	2
MOYER JACK A	CPT	0-1289463	0657	1
MOYER JACOB E	MAJ	0-1588763	1058	1
MOYER JR EARL H	MAJ	C-1999155	C864	1
MOYER KENNETH G	CPT	0-0991974	0662	1
MOYER KERMIT W	LTC	0-0401461	C961	1
MOYER LAWRENCE R	LTC	0-1108186	0263	1
MOYER MARY E	2LT	N-0761284	0345	1
MOYER REX L	CW4	W-2122005	C559	1
MOYER REX M	LTC	0-0450678	0863	1
MOYER SHERMAN M	CW3	W-2120038	C159	1
MOYER WILBUR J	CW4	W-2001524	C667	3
MOYERS ALFRED J	WO1	W-2122965	C645	2
MOYERS JAMES P	1LT	0-1797336	C845	1
MOYES WILLIAM S	COL	C-0234721	1262	3
MOYLAN JAMES E	1LT	0-0492231	0246	2
MOYLE JOHN P	CW4	W-2144521	0266	1
MOYLE WALLACE A	COL	0-0171128	1157	3
MOYNIHAN PATRICK J	1LT	C-0494990	0348	1
MOYS NEAL O	MAJ	0-2043112	0761	1
MOYSE HERMANN	LTC	0-0108219	0951	3
MOZES EDWARD	MAJ	0-0326808	C146	2
MOZIAN GERARD H	MAJ	C-1578888	0454	2
MOZLEY HUGH A	COL	0-0403781	1060	1
MOZLEY JR JAMES H	MAJ	0-0103449	C645	2
MOZZER ALEXANDER	CPT	0-0465628	1045	2
MRAKAVA MICHAEL J	LTC	0-1633423	0962	1
MRAZ ALEX N	CW4	W-2102122	0656	1
MROCZKOWSKI CHARLES	MAJ	0-2262649	0263	1
MUCHA FRANK R	1LT	0-1634164	1044	2
MUCHEMORE FRANKLIN B	MAJ	0-1593115	0664	1
MUCHKA WALTER A	1LT	0-0420708	1144	2
MUCHMORE PETE M	2LT	C-1822175	C345	2
MUCHMORE WARREN G	1LT	0-1112334	0146	2
MUCK JAMES B	MAJ	0-4005021	1065	1
MUCKELROY ANTHONY	LTC	0-0357555	0762	3
MUCKEY MELVIN J	MAJ	0-0153736	0352	3
MUCKLE CRAIG W	LTC	C-0296339	1065	3
MUCKSTADT JOHN J	1LT	0-1015189	0546	2
MUDD WILLIAM C	CPT	0-1309386	0847	1
MUDGE JOHN W	COL	0-0293576	0861	3
MUDON GEORGE M	LTC	0-1037643	1264	3
MUDRY JOSEPH	CPT	0-0382256	0146	1
MUDSE JOSEPH W	1LT	0-0539701	0158	1
MUEDEN JR GEORGE F	CPT	0-0396187	0746	1
MUEHL FLORY M	1LT	0-1290110	0545	2
MUEHL JOSEPH W	CPT	0-1167995	1060	1
MUEHLBERGER C W	CW3	W-2142179	1157	1
MUELLER ADOLPH R	COL	0-0258180	0965	3
MUELLER CHARLES J	LTC	0-0360067	1057	2
MUELLER CHESTER	COL	0-0208506	0962	3
MUELLER CHESTER R	CPT	0-0554858	0447	2
MUELLER DON J	CPT	0-1999191	0657	1
MUELLER FRANK J	MAJ	0-0370238	0952	2
MUELLER FRANK J	MAJ	0-0988068	0663	1
MUELLER FREDERICK	LTC	0-1583413	0260	2
MUELLER GUSTAV C	MAJ	C-1178905	0256	2
MUELLER HARRIE S	COL	C-0102015	0651	3
MUELLER HOWARD G	CW3	W-2208640	1167	1
MUELLER JACKSON W	CW3	W-2149825	0464	1
MUELLER JOSEPH E	CPT	0-0406840	1046	1
MUELLER KEITH E	2LT	0-0528029	1045	2
MUELLER LEROY W	LTC	0-0429239	C261	1
MUELLER LESTER W	MAJ	C-2262275	1061	1
MUELLER MILTON O	CW3	W-2150528	1263	1
MUELLER MORRIS A	COL	0-1699868	0166	3
MUELLER OTTE J	MAJ	0-1633424	0262	1
MUELLER REINHOLD	CW3	W-2146811	0559	1
MUELLER ROY M	LTC	0-0314809	0467	2
MUELLER WALTER	1LT	0-1946646	1047	1
MUELLER WALTER E	LTC	C-0196332	0463	3
MUELLER WESLEY H	MAJ	0-0479827	0461	3
MUELLER WILLIAM G	CPT	0-0109311	0933	1
MUER JR JULIUS A	CW2	W-3430258	1066	1
MUES DONALD O	MAJ	C-1524799	0666	1
MUFFLEY ROBERT T	1LT	0-1634165	1045	2
MUGERDITCHIAN SHAR	1LT	0-1303009	0745	2
MUGFORD CHARLES	LTC	0-1046577	0162	2
MUHAR JR ANDREW V	LTC	0-1336105	0566	2
MUHL JAMES P	MAJ	0-1052491	0462	1
MUHLBAIER JAMES W	MAJ	0-2020997	0366	1
MUHLENBERG FREDERIC	COL	0-0167177	0648	3
MUHS ELEANOR J	CPT	N-0722208	0953	1
MUHSFELD E W	LTC	0-0442665	0446	2
MUILENBURG TEUNIS H	CPT	0-0309467	1145	2
MUIR CHARLES W	CPT	0-0523343	1045	2
MUIR HUGH B	1LT	0-0538623	1146	2
MUIR HUGH H	COL	0-0189251	0153	3
MUIR JR CHARLES H	LTC	0-0215977	0664	3
MUIR JR WILLIAM W	CPT	0-1292926	0846	2
MUIR KENNETH L	MAJ	0-0275200	1057	3
MUIR ROBERT L	LTC	0-0221388	0763	3
MUIR SYLVESTER	LTC	0-0298000	1165	3
MUIRHEAD GRACIEUSE	MAJ	N-0764249	0364	1
MUIRHEAD RAY J	MAJ	0-0989170	0765	1
MUIRHEAD RICHARD J	LTC	0-1994959	0863	1
MUIZERS JOHN F	CW3	W-2146486	1062	1
MUJICA FRANK E	1LT	0-0398023	0845	2
MUKENSNABLE L K	1LT	N-0731873	0546	1
MULADORE ROBERT W	LTC	0-1050003	0961	1
MULBERRY ALBERT F	LTC	C-1913217	0667	1
MULCAHEY JR JOHN T	LTC	0-1945651	1162	1
MULCAHY HUBERT F	MAJ	0-1552939	0658	1
MULCAHY JOHN J	MAJ	0-1328733	0565	1
MULCAHY ROBERT E	MAJ	0-2053862	0461	1
MULCAHY THOMAS A	LTC	0-1635148	C364	1
MULCAHY TIMOTHY J	MAJ	0-0163855	C846	2
MULDOON JAMES F	MAJ	0-0410562	1146	1
MULDOON MARY A	MAJ	N-0700528	0546	1
MULDROW HAL L	M G	0-0250319	0665	3
MULDROW JAMES J	LTC	0-0437951	0962	1
MULDROW JOSEPH F	COL	0-0118196	1049	3
MULFORD JAMES T	CPT	0-1059216	0246	1
MULFORD JAMES W	LTC	0-0426666	1266	1
MULFORD JOHN A	LTC	0-0293091	0961	2
MULFORD RALPH K	2LT	0-0554456	1145	2
MULFORD TODD M	LTC	0-0371671	1052	2
MULGANNON ROBERT E	CPT	0-1994483	0353	1
MULGREW EDWARD L	MAJ	C-0954202	1263	1
MULHALL LAWRENCE J	COL	0-0178412	0560	1
MULHERN FRANCIS L	LTC	0-1281212	0662	1
MULHERN JOHN J	LTC	0-0243996	0165	3
MULHOLLAN SHERMAN O	MAJ	0-1554942	1160	1
MULHOLLAND EDWARD J	LTC	0-1177112	0665	1
MULHOLLAND JAMES	1LT	0-0476512	C560	1
MULHOLLAND JOHN P	1LT	0-1329621	0746	2
MULHOLLAND JOSEPH E	1LT	0-1018971	0746	1
MULHOLLAND ROBERT T	LTC	0-0278543	1145	2
MULKERN JAMES A	CPT	0-1290795	C657	1
MULKERNE DONALD J G	1LT	0-0546819	C447	1
MULKEY OREN A	CPT	0-1340207	0263	1
MULKY FRANCIS P	LTC	0-0231209	0657	3
MULL CHARLES E	LTC	0-0486973	1065	3
MULL CLELLAND S	2LT	C-1031743	0344	2
MULL LEROY E	CW2	W-2144114	C259	1
MULL ROBERT S	CPT	0-2263748	C163	1
MULLAGHY EUGENE J	LTC	0-1533149	C861	1
MULLAHY WILLIAM J	LTC	0-1115044	0562	1
MULLALLY FRANCIS J	MAJ	0-1913280	1165	1
MULLALY DANIEL L	LTC	0-0448718	0449	1
MULLAN THOMAS L	MAJ	C-0499467	C461	2
MULLANE JAMES P	CPT	0-0450464	C845	2
MULLANE WILLIAM M	CW3	W-2002110	1155	3
MULLANEY BARTHOLOME	LTC	0-0503780	0157	1
MULLANEY CHARLES P	CW2	W-3200442	0267	1
MULLANEY JOHN T	LTC	0-0529100	1063	1
MULLANEY JOSEPH A	MAJ	C-1112877	1160	1
MULLANEY JOSEPH E	1LT	0-1913854	0543	1
MULLANEY THOMAS F	COL	0-0196495	1062	3
MULLANEY THOMAS J	LTC	0-0472652	0157	1
MULLANEY WILLIAM L	1LT	0-1052092	C845	2
MULLEN BEATRICE M	2LT	N-0744832	0144	1
MULLEN CLIFFORD J	LTC	C-0198423	1058	3
MULLEN DONALD A	CPT	0-1016810	0446	2
MULLEN FORREST H	2LT	0-1845629	C144	2
MULLEN FRANCIS A	CW3	W-2148493	C163	1
MULLEN FREDERICK	CPT	0-1299088	0547	1
MULLEN GEORGE E	CPT	0-1286536	C945	2
MULLEN GERALD B	1LT	0-1303930	0457	2
MULLEN JAMES F	LTC	C-1115966	C764	1
MULLEN JAMES R	COL	0-0153734	1051	3
MULLEN JOHN B	CPT	0-0505944	C745	1
MULLEN JOHN E	CPT	0-0454214	1145	2
MULLEN JOHN J	LTC	0-0499996	0657	2
MULLEN JOHN J	CW4	W-2143178	0667	1
MULLEN JOHN P	LTC	0-0236003	C-51	3
MULLEN JOSEPH T	WO1	W-2108959	0350	1
MULLEN JR JOHN J	1LT	0-1320340	1146	1
MULLEN JR WALTER J	LTC	0-1045191	1064	1
MULLEN KENNETH O	1LT	0-1583415	1045	2
MULLEN LEO F	LTC	C-0244664	1157	3
MULLEN MYRON C	LTC	0-0282813	1265	3
MULLEN OAKMAN E	CPT	0-0300071	0744	2
MULLEN RICHARD O	2LT	0-1641607	C845	2
MULLEN ROBERT V	2LT	0-1290796	0744	2
MULLEN THOMAS V	LTC	0-1325590	C564	1
MULLEN TIMOTHY F	COL	0-0251263	1263	3
MULLEN WILLIAM J	CW2	W-2150993	C260	1
MULLENAX VEE B H	1LT	0-1692567	C847	1
MULLENDER JOSEPH C	LTC	0-0267238	0662	3
MULLENIOUX WILLIAM H	MAJ	C-0974140	0562	1
MULLENIX JOSEPH R	CPT	0-0465962	0547	1
MULLENMEISTER HUGH F	MAJ	0-0280130	0346	2
MULLER ALBERT B	CPT	0-0216699	0364	3
MULLER ARNOLD	MAJ	0-0260547	1163	3
MULLER FLOYD M	1LT	0-1995306	0145	2
MULLER JAMES	MAJ	0-0973584	1062	1
MULLER JAMES F	LTC	0-0142058	0648	3
MULLER JR WILLIAM L	CPT	0-2051684	C459	1
MULLER LUIS	CPT	0-0371134	0960	1
MULLER MARCUS J	MAJ	0-0684386	0661	1
MULLER MARK T	COL	0-0375668	0267	1
MULLER MILTON E	COL	0-0305379	0358	1
MULLER PHILIP	CW2	W-2209441	0763	1
MULLER PHILIP H	1LT	0-0402517	0646	2
MULLER RICHARD F	CPT	0-1312203	0449	2
MULLER WALTER G	LTC	0-1040278	0859	1
MULLER WILLIAM F	MAJ	0-2018397	0663	2
MULLERY JAMES V	CPT	0-1183535	0662	1
MULLICAN JOHN A	COL	C-0294772	1264	3
MULLIGAN ARTHUR M	LTC	0-0267234	1063	3
MULLIGAN CLAIRE A	1LT	N-0745508	0646	1
MULLIGAN JOSEPHINE	MAJ	N-0758370	0864	1
MULLIGAN WELDON L	CW3	W-2151199	0561	1
MULLIN EDWARD P	MAJ	0-1052093	0865	1
MULLIN FRANCIS W	CW3	W-2152132	0265	2
MULLIN HOWARD L	MAJ	0-0258538	1065	3
MULLIN JOHN J	1LT	0-0443992	0945	2
MULLINAX EDWIN H	WO1	W-2143626	0157	1
MULLINC EUGENE G	COL	0-0234788	0247	2
MULLINES JOHN J	CPT	0-1030272	0847	1
MULLINIKS EDWARD C	LTC	0-0367692	1165	3
MULLINIX EARL L	COL	0-0236469	0461	3
MULLINIX RAY	MAJ	0-0264264	0158	3
MULLINS ALVA R	MAJ	0-0509986	0247	1
MULLINS CAROL H	LTC	0-1314312	0765	1
MULLINS HAROLD	LTC	0-1012522	0257	1
MULLINS HAROLD E	MAJ	0-2016158	0963	1
MULLINS JASPER C	WO1	W-2142567	1151	2
MULLINS JR JOHN W	CPT	0-1554057	0462	1
MULLINS LEONARD E	CW2	W-2119611	0852	1
MULLINS MARCUS G	MAJ	0-0407451	0861	2
MULLINS MERVIN E	MAJ	0-1101132	0361	1
MULLINS PAUL E	MAJ	C-1634168	0361	1
MULLINS RICHARD F	LTC	0-0276111	1144	2
MULLINS ROBIN F	MAJ	0-0385848	0761	1
MULLINS WALTER S	COL	0-0174806	0260	3
MULLINS WILLIAM B	MAJ	0-4030830	0866	1
MULLINS WILLIAM H	2LT	0-1595055	0645	2
MULLINS WILLIAM J	CW4	W-2109946	1164	3
MULLINS WILLICE R	CW4	W-2110528	0959	1
MULLOY PATRICK J	CPT	0-1101133	0546	1
MULQUIN WAYNE O	COL	0-0270344	1067	3
MULRAIN CHRISTOPHE	MAJ	0-0275511	0855	3
MULRINE GERALD J	LTC	0-1165195	1162	1
MULROONEY WALTER S	LTC	0-1316577	1166	1
MULVANEY BERNARD H	1LT	0-1305815	1044	2
MULVANEY JOHN J	CPT	0-1756343	0747	2
MULVANEY LOUIS C	LTC	0-1703794	0559	1
MULVENNA RICHARD F	MAJ	0-0439922	0551	1
MULVENON JOSEPH T	LTC	0-1110676	1065	1
MULVEY THOMAS P	LTC	0-0383437	0760	1
MULVIHILL JOHN R	CPT	0-1688491	0565	1
MUMBRALER CHARLES E	LTC	0-0359019	0867	3
MUMBY WILLIAM E	CPT	0-0155952	0648	3
MUMFORD HOWARD F	LTC	0-1059013	1263	1
MUMLER WILLIAM C	MAJ	0-0411537	0346	2
MUMM FRED E	LTC	0-1846041	1162	1
MUMM HARRY G	LTC	0-0252796	1265	3
MUMM KARL B	MAJ	C-0977445	1263	1
MUMMA CECIL J	LTC	0-0420944	0762	1
MUMME JR FRANK H	LTC	0-1312040	0562	2
MUMMEY PAUL F	CPT	0-2011034	0760	1
MUMPOWER WILLIAM B	COL	0-0326088	0160	1
MUNAKER ISRAEL N	MAJ	C-1995307	0564	2

NAME	GRADE	SVC NO	DATE RET MO YR	RET CODE
MUNBY WILLIAM A	MAJ	0-0980272	0866	1
MUNCH ARTHUR W	CPT	0-1285093	0746	2
MUNCH FRANCIS J	MAJ	0-1551472	0662	1
MUNCHMEYER LOUIS W	COL	0-0229402	0864	3
MUNCIE CLINTON J	LTC	0-0162231	0349	3
MUNCIE JAMES A	MAJ	0-2034691	1160	1
MUNCY LARKIN K	2LT	0-1913855	0832	1
MUNDALL BERNARD P	CPT	0-0551227	0246	2
MUNDAY AUDWERT L	MAJ	0-1301015	0363	1
MUNDELL GRACE I	LTC	N-0732294	0564	1
MUNDEM GUY O	MAJ	0-0161872	0259	2
MUNDEN CECIL L	COL	0-1055395	0567	3
MUNDEN ERNEST A	CPT	0-1697836	0955	1
MUNDEN KENNETH T	CPT	0-1284190	1055	1
MUNDORFF WILLIAM H	LTC	0-0463584	0854	1
MUNDT CARL R	1LT	0-1590068	1045	2
MUNDT DONALD A	MAJ	0-1331210	0164	1
MUNDT HENRY G	MAJ	0-1111802	1157	1
MUNDTH LYMAN K	2LT	0-1310292	0943	2
MUNDY CHARLES F	MAJ	0-1326652	0465	1
MUNDY HARRY K	2LT	0-0885879	0944	2
MUNDY HENRY L	LTC	0-1594371	0762	1
MUNDY JAMES R	LTC	0-1181383	0766	1
MUNDY JAMES T	CPT	0-0371039	0846	2
MUNDY JR JOHN T	LTC	0-0249058	1266	3
MUNFORD CHARLES W	LTC	0-0293904	1166	3
MUNFORD THOMAS T	1LT	0-1016390	0646	2
MUNGER HARRY A	MAJ	0-1332293	0867	2
MUNGER JR IRVIA C	LTC	0-0252704	0460	3
MUNGER PEARL M	2LT	N-0784255	1044	1
MUNGER RALPH L	LTC	0-0389817	1054	1
MUNGER RAY W	COL	0-0199850	1154	1
MUNGO ALFRED J	1LT	0-0328447	1043	2
MUNGOVAN JOHN F	COL	0-0277608	0565	3
MUNGUIA RAFAEL V	LTC	0-1047255	0263	1
MUNIAK JOHN J	CPT	0-0380791	0345	2
MUNIZ BRAULIO	CPT	0-0217528	0249	1
MUNK ROBERT E	CPT	0-1822435	0346	2
MUNKER FREDERICK	LTC	0-1105692	1160	1
MUNKRES GARLYN	LTC	0-0362057	0561	1
MUNN ARTHUR N	2LT	0-1949614	0646	2
MUNN CLEMMON F	LTC	0-0283342	1061	1
MUNN FREDERICK	MAJ	0-0966309	0459	1
MUNN GERALD H	LTC	0-0450168	1060	1
MUNN JAY A	CPT	0-0384753	0546	2
MUNN JOHN F	MAJ	0-1557760	0164	1
MUNN KELLY C	CPT	0-1951026	0259	1
MUNN LILLIAN M	2LT	N-0701823	1041	1
MUNN NEIL B	CW2	W-2207592	1162	1
MUNN RALPH B	LTC	0-0217198	0653	3
MUNN RICHARD R	LTC	0-0318489	0266	3
MUNN ROBERT W	CPT	0-0283594	0447	2
MUNN THELMA	LTC	N-0775056	0363	1
MUNNECKE CHARLES W	COL	0-0238096	0859	1
MUNNERLYN LAWRENCE A	CPT	0-1312204	0662	1
MUNOZ CARLOS F	COL	0-0273026	0155	1
MUNOZ CELESTINO	CPT	0-2032079	0263	2
MUNOZ FILBERT	2LT	0-1319152	0245	2
MUNOZ FRANK E	LTC	0-1319532	0563	1
MUNOZ JOHN C	MAJ	0-0198305	0253	1
MUNOZ MIGUEL A	COL	0-0102981	0247	2
MUNOZ WILLIAM P	LTC	0-0335729	0560	1
MUNRO ARTHUR W	CW4	W-2119632	0859	1
MUNRO DONALD M	MAJ	0-1335963	1159	1
MUNROE DUNCAN H	MAJ	0-0268241	0459	1
MUNROE ROBERT F	1LT	0-1019145	0446	2
MUNS JR GEORGE E	2LT	0-0538291	0845	2
MUNSEL HARLEY U	CW4	W-2122255	0259	1
MUNSELL BENJAMIN F	1LT	0-1297923	0248	2
MUNSHOWER ELMER F	COL	0-0210722	0648	3
MUNSKE CHARLES R	COL	0-0243021	0258	1
MUNSON ARTHUR E	MAJ	0-1172566	0361	1
MUNSON CHARLES H	CPT	0-0138338	1054	3
MUNSON DONALD C	CPT	0-1533870	0145	1
MUNSON EDWARD H	1LT	0-1010089	0445	2
MUNSON JOHN K	MAJ	0-0954485	0663	1
MUNSON JR CLARENCE S	MAJ	0-1317329	1164	1
MUNSON LEO A	CW3	W-2205601	0565	1
MUNSON LEONARD H	LTC	0-0411565	1061	3
MUNSON LEVI CHARL	CPT	0-0265827	0842	2
MUNSON NELSON C	MAJ	0-0511051	0447	1
MUNSON NICHOLAS S	LTC	0-0454670	0961	1
MUNSON WILBUR A	CW2	W-2114087	0858	1
MUNSON WILNER W	1LT	0-0885052	0644	2
MUNSTERMAN ALFRED H	CPT	0-1012893	1145	2
MUNYAN PAUL D C	CW3	RW-2142016	0761	1
MUNYER WILLIAM J	LTC	0-2042864	0466	1
MUNZ RUDOLPH P	LTC	0-0234685	0861	3
MUNZELL PETER C	LTC	0-1012058	0663	1
MURA ROMEO E	LTC	0-0234698	0964	3
MURANAKA REYNOLD T	MAJ	0-2030816	0162	1
MURANE EDWARD E	LTC	0-0245201	0962	3
MURATTI JOSE A	LTC	0-0368534	0660	1
MURAWSKI THEODORE M	MAJ	0-1057184	0162	1
MURAY ALBERT V	LTC	0-0323363	0852	1
MURBACH CLARENCE F	COL	0-0214007	0648	3
MURCH GREENWOOD	MAJ	0-1645233	0158	1
MURCH JAMES E	2LT	0-1287748	0845	1
MURCH ROBERT E	LTC	0-1321326	0363	1
MURCHISON ALBERT R	MAJ	0-0283063	1044	2
MURCHISON BRYAN	CW2	W-2112399	0651	1
MURCHISON JOHN T	COL	0-0238913	0366	3
MURCHISON JR CLYDE A	1LT	0-0552597	0646	2
MURCHISON LEWIS N	LTC	0-0201517	0563	3
MURCHISON ROBERT B	COL	0-0393804	0161	1
MURCHISON WALTER H	MAJ	0-1308363	0163	1
MURDOCH ALBERT R	LTC	0-0539265	0167	3
MURDOCK CHARLES E	MAJ	0-2212032	0962	1
MURDOCK EDWARD E	LTC	0-1309594	0264	1
MURDOCK FRED E	LTC	0-0239577	0162	3
MURDOCK JOHN T	CPT	0-2032931	0658	1
MURDOCK PATRICIA H	2LT	N-0785305	0546	1
MURDOCK ROBERT	1LT	0-1325138	0246	2
MURDZA JOHN L	2LT	0-1314944	0345	2
MURDZA JOSEPH L	CW4	W-2146264	0157	1
MURELLE CHARLES E	LTC	0-1041622	0964	1
MUREN GEORGE H	MAJ	0-0387244	0962	1
MURETTA JOE J	1LT	0-1178907	1145	2
MURFREE ERVIN E	CW3	W-2151135	0463	1
MURIEL RAFAEL A	CPT	0-0195801	0160	3
MURKBERG MAX A	LTC	0-1824071	1160	1
MURLEY FLORENCE	MAJ	M-0002830	0966	1
MURLIN JAMES S	MAJ	0-1048510	0948	1
MURNAN HERBERT B	COL	0-0300675	1059	1
MURNAN PAUL A	1LT	0-1286688	1044	1
MURNANE RAYMOND C	LTC	0-0508547	0954	1
MUROFF WILLIAM W	CW2	W-2145038	0559	1
MURPHEY ALBERT K	LTC	0-0146213	1054	3
MURPHEY ARLO L	MAJ	0-0318469	0746	2
MURPHEY HORACE F	MAJ	0-0251481	0864	3
MURPHEY MURIEL O	MAJ	0-1177539	0161	2
MURPHEY WALTER H	MAJ	0-1287220	0361	1
MURPHIE DONALD W	MAJ	0-1324354	1160	1
MURPHREE MARY L	MAJ	L-1010033	0864	1
MURPHREE WILLIAM M	LTC	0-0183450	0840	1
MURPHY ALBERT K	LTC	0-0284711	1061	3
MURPHY ALBERT W	CPT	0-1313358	0963	1
MURPHY ALFRED J	LTC	0-0290436	1164	3
MURPHY ALFRED L	1LT	0-1080310	0246	1
MURPHY ALFRED T	1LT	0-0481471	0345	2
MURPHY ALLEN H	LTC	0-0384174	0965	1
MURPHY CATHERINE	1LT	N-0793256	1047	1
MURPHY CHALMER S	1LT	0-0494238	0-48	2
MURPHY CHARLES A	LTC	0-0398889	0363	1
MURPHY CHARLES C	CPT	0-0410356	0246	2
MURPHY CHARLES E	LTC	0-0445920	1067	1
MURPHY CHARLES M	1LT	0-0501484	0146	2
MURPHY CHARLES V	CPT	0-0505548	0545	2
MURPHY CLAIR	LTC	0-0386553	0566	3
MURPHY CLEMENT R	LTC	0-0494482	0354	1
MURPHY CYRIL R	LTC	0-0304127	0760	1
MURPHY DANIEL J	LTC	0-0450677	1160	1
MURPHY DANIEL T	LTC	0-0390068	0660	1
MURPHY DAVID O	LTC	0-1559233	0963	1
MURPHY DONALD I	2LT	0-1291314	0943	2
MURPHY DORIS E	1LT	N-0759536	0846	1
MURPHY EARL J	CW2	W-2152711	0561	1
MURPHY EARLE W	LTC	0-1038775	0164	1
MURPHY EDGAR J	LTC	0-0226951	1061	3
MURPHY EDMUND C	LTC	0-0278607	0557	1
MURPHY EDWARD A	LTC	0-0242346	1044	2
MURPHY EDWARD B	LTC	0-0311052	1046	2
MURPHY EDWARD F	CPT	0-1581994	0746	2
MURPHY EDWARD J	CW3	W-2148755	0763	2
MURPHY EDWARD P	LTC	0-0448639	1054	1
MURPHY EMERY W	CW3	W-2205284	0766	1
MURPHY FRANCIS A	LTC	0-1691740	0561	1
MURPHY FRANCIS G	LTC	0-1017237	0763	1
MURPHY FRANCIS J	MAJ	0-2019069	0662	1
MURPHY FRANK E	1LT	0-0443755	0246	2
MURPHY FRANK W	COL	0-0370163	0853	1
MURPHY FRANK W	MAJ	0-1185104	0365	2
MURPHY FRED	CW3	W-2144734	0760	1
MURPHY FREDERICK	LTC	0-1585940	1064	1
MURPHY GLENN H	2LT	0-2043011	0445	2
MURPHY GORDON G	CW2	W-2149303	0860	1
MURPHY GUY H	COL	0-0285904	0960	1
MURPHY HAROLD J	LTC	0-0212535	0462	3
MURPHY HARRY G	1LT	0-0136675	0249	3
MURPHY HARRY M	MAJ	0-0403028	0346	2
MURPHY HENRY B	1LT	0-1323725	0845	2
MURPHY HENRY L	LTC	0-1112338	0265	1
MURPHY HERMAN A	1LT	0-0227220	1265	2
MURPHY HOLLIS E	MAJ	0-0962885	0665	1
MURPHY JAMES C	MAJ	0-1307568	0864	1
MURPHY JAMES D	LTC	0-2052237	0665	3
MURPHY JAMES E	LTC	0-0969323	1067	1
MURPHY JAMES W	LTC	0-0413514	1146	2
MURPHY JAMES R	MAJ	0-0969591	1264	1
MURPHY JEREMIAH P	2LT	0-1106328	0445	2
MURPHY JOE	CW3	W-2207691	0966	1
MURPHY JOHN C	LTC	0-0499468	1060	1
MURPHY JOHN C	MAJ	0-1186984	0361	1
MURPHY JOHN E	1LT	0-0441076	0345	2
MURPHY JOHN F	LTC	0-0407843	0163	1
MURPHY JOHN F	CPT	0-1299781	0646	2
MURPHY JOHN J	MAJ	0-1031427	0265	1
MURPHY JOHN J	MAJ	0-1280390	0246	2
MURPHY JOHN J	1LT	0-1585943	0853	1
MURPHY JOHN J	LTC	0-1689055	0754	2
MURPHY JOHN L	COL	0-0905222	1045	2
MURPHY JOHN L	LTC	0-1585944	0860	1
MURPHY JOHN L	CW2	W-2119572	1146	1
MURPHY JOHN R	COL	0-0336254	0167	3
MURPHY JOHN T	1LT	0-0382298	0941	2
MURPHY JOHN T	MAJ	0-1175256	0661	1
MURPHY JOSEPH B	MAJ	0-0426226	0546	2
MURPHY JOSEPH C	COL	0-0274358	0659	3
MURPHY JOSEPH P	MAJ	0-0256009	0942	1
MURPHY JOSEPH P	MAJ	0-0673866	1162	1
MURPHY JR CLARKE	1LT	0-0461963	114N	2
MURPHY JR DANIEL J	COL	0-0289447	0267	3
MURPHY JR JAMES A	MAJ	0-2262692	1065	2
MURPHY JR JAMES L	CPT	0-0352958	0944	2
MURPHY JR JOE H	CPT	0-1031581	0446	2
MURPHY JR JOHN L	MAJ	0-1060225	1065	1
MURPHY JR RAYMOND	1LT	0-4036531	0658	2
MURPHY LAWRENCE B	COL	0-0487617	0967	1
MURPHY LAWRENCE O	1LT	0-1823761	0546	2
MURPHY MARGARET L	2LT	N-0744129	0246	1
MURPHY MARVIN H	1LT	0-0468466	0348	2
MURPHY MARY L	MAJ	N-0742217	1064	3
MURPHY MATTHEW F	COL	0-0170752	1061	3
MURPHY MERRITT W	1LT	0-1309801	1046	2
MURPHY MICHAEL J	CPT	0-0328941	0642	2
MURPHY NIGEL C	CW3	W-2144851	1062	1
MURPHY OWEN F	COL	0-0261345	0657	3
MURPHY PATRICK C	1LT	0-1305173	0545	2
MURPHY PAUL J B	COL	0-0202186	0449	1
MURPHY PHILIP G	COL	0-0170848	0-49	3
MURPHY RALEIGH C	CPT	0-0321753	0645	2
MURPHY RAPHAEL A	LTC	0-0343276	1046	2
MURPHY RAYMOND H	LTC	0-1166338	1264	1
MURPHY RAYMOND L	CW4	W-2005163	0466	1
MURPHY RICHARD R	MAJ	0-1879071	0467	1
MURPHY ROBERT A	MAJ	0-1044319	0258	1
MURPHY ROBERT A	MAJ	0-2019205	1063	2
MURPHY ROBERT J	MAJ	0-0268324	0664	3
MURPHY ROBERT J	CPT	0-0380776	0645	1
MURPHY ROBERT M	LTC	0-1046590	0966	1
MURPHY ROLAND E	COL	0-0100686	1053	3
MURPHY ROY F	CPT	0-0281956	1145	2
MURPHY RUSSELL C	2LT	0-1106989	1044	2
MURPHY SAMUEL O	2LT	0-0374022	0142	1
MURPHY SAMUEL S	CW3	W-2143690	0564	1
MURPHY SR ROBERT J	COL	0-0255702	0961	1
MURPHY THEODORE E	LTC	0-0329902	0263	3
MURPHY THOMAS A	LTC	0-1292223	0461	1
MURPHY THOMAS E	CPT	0-1683515	0457	1
MURPHY THOMAS F	MAJ	0-0351779	0347	1
MURPHY THOMAS G	LTC	0-1341692	1066	1
MURPHY THOMAS J	LTC	0-0320267	0258	1
MURPHY THOMAS J	CPT	0-1595058	0553	1
MURPHY THOMAS O	CPT	0-0471558	0949	1
MURPHY THOMAS T	MAJ	0-1013377	1263	1
MURPHY TIMOTHY H	COL	0-0138469	0450	3
MURPHY TIMOTHY J	LTC	0-0450605	0860	1
MURPHY VALERIA K	MAJ	N-0745231	0865	1
MURPHY VIRGIL L	CPT	0-1684325	0546	2
MURPHY WAYMON T	LTC	0-1284920	0461	1
MURPHY WILLIAM C	LTC	0-1045534	0560	1
MURPHY WILLIAM E	COL	0-0400136	1062	1
MURPHY WILLIAM F	MAJ	0-1922898	0866	1
MURPHY WILLIAM F	LTC	0-0149778	0756	3
MURPHY WILLIAM F	LTC	0-1295067	1061	2
MURPHY WILLIAM H	LTC	0-0261697	0266	3
MURPHY WILLIAM J	CPT	0-1046209	0864	1
MURPHY WILLIAM R	CPT	0-1297768	0646	2
MURR CLYDE E	MAJ	0-1950911	1159	1
MURRAY ACY	MAJ	0-2042845	1059	1
MURRAY ALBERT S	1LT	0-0298144	0648	3
MURRAY ALFRED E	CPT	0-1645237	0961	1
MURRAY ARTHUR L	LTC	0-0395670	0547	2
MURRAY ARTHUR R	WO1	W-2110950	0461	3
MURRAY BETHEL R	1LT	0-1308681	0246	2
MURRAY BILLIE J	CPT	0-1922806	0164	1
MURRAY CARL W	CPT	0-0475674	0252	1
MURRAY CARL P	CW3	W-2105263	0662	1
MURRAY CHARLES A	LTC	0-0284140	1061	1
MURRAY CHARLES L	2LT	0-0216315	1042	1
MURRAY CHARLES W	MAJ	0-1048917	0661	1
MURRAY CHRISTOPHE	LTC	0-0479008	0546	2
MURRAY CLARENCE M	LTC	0-0227455	0664	3
MURRAY CLIFFORD E	COL	0-0322528	1059	3
MURRAY CLIVE E	COL	0-0291912	0955	3
MURRAY DAVID J	CPT	0-0461080	0648	1
MURRAY DAVID T	1LT	0-1012685	0945	2
MURRAY DENNIS F	CPT	0-0108249	0944	1
MURRAY EDWIN F	CW4	W-2117246	0862	1
MURRAY EMERY C	MAJ	0-1081157	0461	1
MURRAY FRANCIS O	CW2	RW-2206453	0361	1
MURRAY FREEMAN C	1LT	0-2035134	0645	1
MURRAY GEORGE E	MAJ	0-0415673	1057	1
MURRAY GERALD J	LTC	0-0450088	0762	1
MURRAY GERTRUDE J	MAJ	J-0100043	1266	1
MURRAY HAROLD W	LTC	0-1298576	0861	1
MURRAY HERMAN O	CPT	0-0283252	1067	3
MURRAY HERMAN T	1LT	0-0583991	0755	1
MURRAY HUBERT W	CPT	0-1797862	1060	1
MURRAY JACK S	1LT	0-0299112	0642	2

NAME	GRADE	SVC NO	DATE RET MO YR	RET CODE
MURRAY JAMES C	CW2	W-2147438	C360	1
MURRAY JAMES F	1LT	0-1560302	0955	1
MURRAY JAMES R	CPT	0-0451689	0246	2
MURRAY JOHN D	2LT	0-0113211	0655	3
MURRAY JOHN J	CPT	0-0479714	1143	2
MURRAY JOHN J	MAJ	C-0506115	1054	1
MURRAY JOHN L	LTC	0-1341569	0567	1
MURRAY JOSEPH D	LTC	0-0134004	C850	3
MURRAY JR LEONARD E	LTC	0-1291680	0960	1
MURRAY JR ROBERT M	2LT	0-1031260	1044	2
MURRAY KENNETH E	1LT	0-1306454	C546	2
MURRAY LEWIS G	LTC	0-0429458	0167	1
MURRAY LIONEL T	2LT	0-0555506	0247	2
MURRAY MELVILLE M	CPT	0-0451629	0757	1
MURRAY MICHAEL D	MAJ	0-0277606	1062	3
MURRAY NATHAN A	LTC	0-1584657	0361	1
MURRAY NORMAN C	LTC	0-1057548	C667	1
MURRAY OLIVER J	LTC	0-0478207	0255	1
MURRAY PHILIP F	LTC	0-0140942	0151	3
MURRAY RAYMOND A	LTC	0-1103827	C765	1
MURRAY RAYMOND A	CW3	W-2144989	0663	1
MURRAY RICHARD J	MAJ	0-1336679	1064	1
MURRAY RICHARD R	MAJ	0-0320250	0755	1
MURRAY ROBERT M	LTC	0-0453636	0860	1
MURRAY ROGER	CPT	0-0213015	0745	2
MURRAY ROSCOE L	COL	C-0171812	C347	2
MURRAY SAMUEL S	LTC	0-0208480	0351	3
MURRAY SARSFIELD	CW2	W-2149354	C561	1
MURRAY THADDEUS H	CW2	W-2151684	0161	1
MURRAY THEODORE C	MAJ	0-1591338	0263	1
MURRAY THOMAS C	COL	0-0405153	0461	2
MURRAY THOMAS E	CW3	W-2104328	C659	1
MURRAY THOMAS W	CW3	W-2153004	C567	1
MURRAY VIRGINIA M	1LT	N-0772922	C445	1
MURRAY WALTER G	LTC	0-0190795	0858	3
MURRAY WAVERLY C	MAJ	0-1634172	1047	1
MURRAY WILLIAM	MAJ	C-0460121	0746	1
MURRAY WILLIAM F	MAJ	0-0396585	C247	2
MURRAY WILLIAM J	COL	C-0251773	1159	1
MURRAY WILLIAM J	MAJ	0-0405709	1045	2
MURRAY WILLIAM J	2LT	0-1698108	1043	2
MURRAY WILLIAM J	2LT	0-2049042	0147	2
MURRAY WINTHROP P	LTC	0-1060567	C267	1
MURRELL BILLIE	CPT	0-0497005	0650	1
MURRELL PAUL M	LTC	0-0452288	0463	1
MURRELL POWELL G	LTC	0-0901893	0346	1
MURRELL WALTER L	CPT	0-0328076	0843	2
MURREY CHARLES T	COL	0-0264095	1059	3
MURRY MILTON J	CW2	W-2107950	1058	1
MURSELL GEORGE R	COL	0-0337942	1058	3
MURTAGH JAMES R	1LT	0-1045192	C745	2
MURTHA JOSEPH J	COL	0-0260553	0262	3
MUSARRA JOE S	CW3	W-2147248	1164	1
MUSCHANY GEORGE V	MAJ	0-1035928	0662	1
MUSE ALFRED L	CPT	0-1298275	1152	2
MUSE BRADFORD F	MAJ	0-1050394	0657	1
MUSE ERNEST O	MAJ	C-1647199	C954	1
MUSE JAMES A	MAJ	0-1686154	C461	1
MUSE JAMES G	WO1	W-2130496	1146	2
MUSE JR JAMES B	1LT	0-1300689	0846	2
MUSE JR RAYMOND W	CW2	W-2152146	0858	1
MUSE ROBERT S	CPT	0-1698180	0953	2
MUSE SAMUEL P	MAJ	0-2014460	C463	1
MUSEGADES WALTER E	LTC	0-0277166	1061	3
MUSGRAVE ARTHUR F	COL	0-0146276	1056	3
MUSGRAVE CLARENCE S	COL	0-0204902	1063	3
MUSGRAVE HARRY G	LTC	0-0113355	0648	3
MUSGROVE EARL E	MAJ	0-0970652	1062	1
MUSGROVE JAMES W	MAJ	C-0497037	0353	1
MUSGROVE ORA E	COL	0-0170309	C348	2
MUSHAKE WILLIAM I	COL	0-0184821	C461	3
MUSHET GERALD S	MAJ	0-0229271	0762	3
MUSICK EGBERT S	1LT	0-1573461	0861	1
MUSICK PAUL E	LTC	0-2000524	0666	1
MUSICK ROBERT M	MAJ	C-0262302	1047	1
MUSICO SEBASTIAN	2LT	0-1015864	0644	2
MUSIELEWICZ C A	1LT	0-1170107	1046	2
MUSIL FRANCIS J	CW2	W-2208150	0963	1
MUSINSKI SIGMUND M	CW4	W-2105651	1058	1
MUSKE HARRY E	CPT	0-1321370	0846	2
MUSKRAT JEFFIE M	LTC	0-0964066	0767	1
MUSOLF EARL R	CPT	0-0974709	1161	1
MUSSATTO KATHARINE	CPT	N-0783350	0547	1
MUSSELMAN JOHN M	MAJ	C-0396983	0246	2
MUSSELMAN LOUIS J	CW3	W-2142533	1C60	1
MUSSELWHITE EMORY L	LTC	0-1081158	0562	1
MUSSELWHITE JOHN O	CPT	0-1798948	0259	1
MUSSER CARROLL L	LTC	0-1575022	0161	2
MUSSER HARVEY H	LTC	0-0201964	1148	3
MUSSER MILTON S	COL	0-0379505	0259	2
MUSSER ROBERT S	2LT	0-1031744	0945	2
MUSSLER LOUIS H	COL	0-0333559	0947	1
MUSSOMELI MARINO	LTC	0-0455073	0663	1
MUSTAIN RHOADS	MAJ	0-0493652	1147	1
MUSTONE ALBERT A	LTC	0-2042790	0962	1
MUSZKIEWICZ STANLE	MAJ	0-1289947	0860	1
MUTERT LESTER F	MAJ	0-1560047	0264	1
MUTH DANIEL M	COL	0-0234295	1159	1
MUTHIG JAMES V	1LT	0-0547351	1046	2
MUTIK ADAM J	CW3	W-2141998	0659	1
MUTKALA WAINO J	1LT	0-1824350	0760	1
MUTTER ALVIE M	CPT	0-0149906	0950	3
MUTTER CLYDE S	CW4	W-2149125	0165	1
MUTTY JOHN E	COL	C-0221727	1056	3
MUXO EDUARDO	MAJ	0-1108882	1060	1
MUZZY EDWARD L	CPT	0-1290985	0947	2
MYATT FRED B	MAJ	0-0986859	0964	1
MYATT JR ALFRED R	LTC	0-0310227	0263	1
MYCOCK EDWIN S	CPT	0-1317656	0647	2
MYOLAND CLORIK B	LTC	0-0525101	C863	1
MYER ALFRED	WO1	W-2117234	0946	1
MYER AUSTIN H	LTC	0-0369838	1052	2
MYER CARL T	CPT	0-0242894	1150	3
MYER LLOYD M	CW4	W-2004194	0864	3
MYER THOMAS L	1LT	0-1170504	0545	2
MYERS ABEL	CW2	W-2147685	0757	1
MYERS ALBERT I	CW4	W-2134988	0959	1
MYERS ALVIN L	CPT	0-0334062	0145	2
MYERS ARTHUR E	LTC	0-1284921	0547	1
MYERS C B	LTC	0-1289612	0154	1
MYERS CARLTON B	MAJ	0-0104861	1155	3
MYERS CECIL L	1LT	0-0286849	0762	3
MYERS CHARLES A	MAJ	C-1645238	0655	1
MYERS CHARLES A	CW3	W-2206807	0367	1
MYERS CHARLES E	CPT	0-1315603	0148	2
MYERS CHARLES L	MAJ	0-1548979	1163	1
MYERS CHARLES R	CW3	W-2147182	1263	1
MYERS CHARLES W	LTC	0-0340562	0763	1
MYERS CHESTER C	MAJ	C-0426492	1157	1
MYERS CHESTER R	CPT	0-1104313	0465	1
MYERS CHRISTIAN	1LT	0-0152901	0942	2
MYERS CLIFFORD L	LTC	0-1011828	0264	1
MYERS DONALD C	LTC	0-0484371	0157	1
MYERS EDWIN M	WO1	W-2143515	0953	2
MYERS ELMER F	MAJ	0-0414618	1046	2
MYERS ELMER L	MAJ	0-1293092	0964	1
MYERS ERLAND F	LTC	0-1041854	0264	1
MYERS EUGENE B	CW3	W-2205913	1164	1
MYERS EVELYN L	MAJ	N-0727795	1262	1
MYERS FRANK R	MAJ	0-0219515	0749	3
MYERS FRED	CPT	0-0177715	0958	3
MYERS FRED J	1LT	0-1285277	0844	1
MYERS G TAYLOR	LTC	0-0472237	0945	2
MYERS GENE	COL	0-0354384	1265	1
MYERS GEORGE A	1LT	0-1298104	0145	2
MYERS GEORGE C	CW3	RW-2136645	0564	1
MYERS GEORGE N	COL	0-0301722	0760	1
MYERS GEORGE W	MAJ	0-0278117	1047	1
MYERS GERALD	CPT	0-0923023	0446	2
MYERS GLENN O	CW2	W-2147900	0763	1
MYERS HAROLD E	CW2	W-2147303	C263	1
MYERS HARRY	LTC	0-0103039	C848	2
MYERS HARRY A	MAJ	0-0189757	C250	3
MYERS HENRY B	LTC	0-1001649	1162	1
MYERS HENRY F	CW3	W-2104778	1152	2
MYERS HORACE W	MAJ	0-0276238	1266	3
MYERS IRVIN L	2LT	0-2047085	0944	2
MYERS IRVING	MAJ	C-0330833	C855	3
MYERS ISAAC C	LTC	0-0159308	0351	3
MYERS IVAN G	1LT	0-1312647	0746	2
MYERS JACK W	LTC	C-0487156	0555	1
MYERS JAMES K	MAJ	C-0450050	0151	1
MYERS JAMES L	MAJ	0-1685014	C765	1
MYERS JAMES M	LTC	0-0312591	0162	3
MYERS JAMES O	LTC	0-0912062	0567	3
MYERS JAMES R	LTC	0-1044908	0263	1
MYERS JAMES W	1LT	0-1312970	1045	2
MYERS JEFFERSON	COL	0-0238095	C666	3
MYERS JENNINGS	MAJ	C-1283467	C853	1
MYERS JESSE O	LTC	0-0491012	0547	2
MYERS JOE	CW4	W-2118499	0156	1
MYERS JOHN B	MAJ	C-0426031	0764	1
MYERS JOHN E	CW2	W-2210225	C865	1
MYERS JOHN T	MAJ	C-0947475	C765	1
MYERS JOHN W	2LT	0-0864753	1145	2
MYERS JOSEPH A	MAJ	0-0980968	0562	1
MYERS JR B F	MAJ	0-1185106	C560	1
MYERS JR COLLIN S	MAJ	0-1332090	C964	1
MYERS JR PELHAM L	MAJ	0-1595061	0163	1
MYERS JR ROBERT K	LTC	0-0350087	C161	1
MYERS JR THOMAS A	MAJ	0-0993963	C363	1
MYERS KEITH D	MAJ	0-1922874	C466	2
MYERS LEONARD O	LTC	0-0295305	C757	2
MYERS LEWIS E	LTC	0-0499740	0554	1
MYERS LLOYD V	MAJ	0-1016276	1060	1
MYERS LONNIE	2LT	0-1112885	0660	1
MYERS MARCUS A	MAJ	C-0585148	C962	1
MYERS MARVIN R	CW3	W-2146856	0962	2
MYERS MICHAEL J	LTC	0-1062777	C763	1
MYERS MILTON H	1LT	0-2005569	C850	1
MYERS ONNIE P	LTC	0-0337888	0965	3
MYERS ORVIS G	MAJ	0-0968382	0564	1
MYERS OSCAR L	LTC	0-0239540	0560	1
MYERS PAUL A	LTC	0-1296071	1165	1
MYERS PAUL A	2LT	0-2000100	1147	1
MYERS PHILIP	CPT	0-0216700	0962	3
MYERS PORTIA H	1LT	N-0729674	0645	1
MYERS RALPH N	LTC	0-0328158	0364	3
MYERS RALPH R	MAJ	0-1947156	C157	1
MYERS RAYMOND H	LTC	0-0471712	C549	1
MYERS RICHARD E	LTC	0-0323204	C945	2
MYERS RICHARD H	1LT	0-1313631	C247	2
MYERS ROBERT B	MAJ	0-1046210	C461	1
MYERS ROBERT D	2LT	0-0508680	1044	2
MYERS ROBERT E	COL	C-0349058	1060	1
MYERS ROBERT E	LTC	0-1032035	1062	1
MYERS ROBERT F	MAJ	0-1650667	C465	1
MYERS ROBERT H	COL	0-0276581	C845	2
MYERS ROBERT J	MAJ	0-1310752	0267	1
MYERS ROBERT J	CPT	0-1634173	C346	2
MYERS ROBERT N	MAJ	0-0183189	0-53	3
MYERS ROBERT O	1LT	C-0420532	C344	2
MYERS ROBERT O	CPT	0-0958653	0162	2
MYERS ROBERT O	MAJ	0-1645239	C160	1
MYERS ROY P	MAJ	0-1320699	0257	1
MYERS SAM M	COL	0-0260983	0864	3
MYERS SHERRY B	COL	C-0286810	1265	3
MYERS STANTON L	LTC	0-0266450	C860	1
MYERS TEX G	LTC	0-1325919	C263	1
MYERS THEODORE A	LTC	0-0246828	C846	2
MYERS THEODORE M	CPT	0-1018342	1163	1
MYERS THOMAS A	CW2	W-2208982	0166	1
MYERS THOMAS J	CW4	W-2143653	0766	2
MYERS THOMAS W	LTC	0-0915162	C663	1
MYERS TYNER W	LTC	0-0209435	C648	3
MYERS VIRGIL V	LTC	0-0518706	0965	3
MYERS WALTER E	MAJ	0-0191549	0346	2
MYERS WALTER P	LTC	0-0382551	0761	1
MYERS WILBUR J	COL	0-0403508	0166	1
MYERS WILLIAM F	LTC	0-0279876	0762	1
MYERS WILLIAM L	MAJ	0-0971399	1167	1
MYERS WILLIAM N	COL	0-0270043	0460	1
MYERS WILSON J	CPT	0-1169668	0448	1
MYETTE CHARLES L	CPT	0-0364186	1148	1
MYLAN CLYDE	CW3	W-2147133	0361	1
MYLAR JAMES L	LTC	0-0371465	C665	1
MYLAR WILBER K	COL	0-0156229	1050	3
MYLES RAYMOND J	MAJ	0-1545797	0461	1
MYLES WILLIAM S	1LT	0-5708088	0765	2
MYLKE ERNEST R	CPT	0-0489395	0450	1
MYLOD JAMES A	COL	0-0278694	1059	3
MYNCHENBERG GEORGE C	LTC	0-0248485	0543	2
MYNES JR CLARENCE M	MAJ	0-1919994	0466	1
MYNSBERGE MAURICE	LTC	0-2055420	0561	1
MYRA ELCENE L	CW3	W-2149810	1166	1
MYRANT ROBERT R	WO1	W-2144288	1160	1
MYRDEK JOHN F	MAJ	0-2053834	0456	1
MYRE HERMAN T	MAJ	0-1322581	C846	2
MYREN HATTIE L	MAJ	N-0742810	0766	1
MYRICE ALVIN G	MAJ	0-0469425	C747	2
MYRICK CHARLES E	LTC	0-0476384	1153	1
MYSAK FRANK C	CPT	0-1012615	0747	2
NAAR HENRY	COL	0-0106227	0650	3
NABB CLEAN R	MAJ	0-1284374	0259	1
NABRE PHILIP M	COL	0-0358059	1051	1
NABER EUGENE J	LTC	0-1178909	0962	1
NABORS JAMES F	COL	0-0397813	1160	1
NABORS JOHN H	CPT	0-0257359	1046	2
NABORS WILLIE R	CPT	0-1998338	0355	1
NACCI VINCENT	LTC	0-2029594	0966	1
NACE DAVID S	CPT	0-1103831	1146	1
NACE LLOYD E	CPT	0-0333191	0964	3
NACHAZEL CATHERINE	MAJ	N-0773977	0567	1
NACHIN JOSEPH J	LTC	0-1583428	1061	1
NACHTIGALL HENRY B	CPT	0-0368965	C246	1
NACK ARTHUR W	LTC	0-1302336	0260	1
NADDED MIKE	CPT	0-1319221	0148	2
NADEAU CHARLES E	MAJ	0-0343164	0446	2
NADEL HIRSCH	CPT	0-1118778	0148	2
NADELL MILTON J	LTC	C-0971310	0667	1
NADEN COYT M	LTC	C-0334316	1061	1
NADER CHARLES	CPT	0-1694362	0744	2
NADER ROBERT F	2LT	0-1590409	0345	2
NADER ROBERT L	CPT	0-1037197	0863	1
NADLER MAX	1LT	0-0298566	0546	2
NADOLA SANTO J	LTC	0-1115716	0463	1
NACOR GEORGE W	CPT	0-0385083	0346	2
NADWORNIK HANS A	CPT	0-0980235	1061	1
NAEGELI FLOYD C	COL	0-0217566	0163	3
NAEGELI HAROLD L	COL	0-0252251	0864	3
NAESS ERLING W	MAJ	0-0504912	0946	2
NAFE JOHN O	1LT	0-0430033	0647	2
NAFTULIN IRVING L	CPT	0-1693551	0146	2
NAGEL FRANCES	MAJ	L-1010036	0764	1
NAGEL HENRY	CPT	0-1039814	0862	2
NAGEL LEONARD E	1LT	0-1294889	1045	2
NAGEL RICHARD E	LTC	0-0451562	0859	1
NAGEL WALTER E	LTC	0-1108193	0461	1
NAGELMANN BERNARD R	LTC	0-0413632	0863	1
NAGLE BERNARD J	LTC	0-0301890	0762	1
NAGLE JR WILLIAM B	1LT	0-5316070	0467	2
NAGLE LOIS E	MAJ	N-0805665	1163	1
NAGLE VANCE E	MAJ	0-0515183	0453	1
NAGLEE COOPER M	MAJ	0-1693113	0263	1
NAGY ARNOLD A	CW3	W-2152192	0666	1
NAGY JAMES	1LT	0-1016802	1147	2
NAGY JOE H	1LT	0-2206436	0953	2
NAGY MICHAEL F	CPT	0-1927718	1067	2
NAHAN JOSEPH F	MAJ	0-0731406	0161	1
NAIRERT ARTHUR C	MAJ	C-0259008	1265	3

NAME	GRADE	SVC NO	DATE RET MO YR	RET CODE
NAIDORF CARROL P	COL	0-0471232	0664	3
NAILL WILLIAM Y	LTC	0-0237342	0463	3
NAIMO ALFRED J	LTC	0-0383246	1059	1
NAIRN HARRY J	CW2	W-2148589	0361	1
NAIRN JR WILLIAM W	COL	0-0207582	C-50	3
NAISBITT FRANK J	MAJ	0-0947436	0564	1
NAJOUCH MICHAEL J	MAJ	0-1548266	0756	1
NAJJAR SAMMY A	CW4	W-2102135	0659	1
NAKAMURA GEORGE T	MAJ	0-0985628	0864	1
NAKANISHI KOICHI	CW4	W-2136060	1066	1
NAKASHIAN SAMUEL J	1LT	0-0488979	1043	1
NAKATA CHARLES T	LTC	0-2027787	0564	1
NAKAYAMA JIMMIE T	MAJ	0-1998049	0963	1
NALBONE CHARLES J	MAJ	0-0347741	0263	1
NALER JR LAWSON H	MAJ	0-1036648	0661	1
NALL CARL B	1LT	0-0469550	0645	2
NALL JACK A	CW2	W-2142181	0157	1
NALL JAMES E	2LT	0-0787408		2
NALL JOHN R	CW4	W-2136015	0766	2
NALL VELMA E	CPT	N-0726649	1146	1
NALLE GEORGE S	LTC	0-0239055	0957	3
NALLEY EDWARD F	LTC	0-0414179	0749	1
NALLEY JAMES T	CW2	W-2146038	1161	1
NALLEY JOHN P	CPT	0-0505895	1047	1
NALLEY SR CHARLES F	CW3	W-2152807	0864	1
NALLI MARY J C	2LT	N-0756947	0945	1
NALLY JOHN F	CPT	0-0992821	1262	1
NALTY FRANK W	CPT	0-0885390	0150	1
NALUAI MOSES K	LTC	0-0375365	0365	3
NAMETH LYALL J	MAJ	0-1293053	0961	2
NANCARROW ROBERT C	CPT	0-1638154	0963	1
NANCE CLARENCE B	MAJ	0-1582000	1057	2
NANCE ELMER P	MAJ	0-1167137	0746	2
NANCE HERSCHEL G	LTC	0-1114681	0664	1
NANCE HUBERT M	LTC	0-1290292	0562	1
NANCE JACK A	MAJ	0-2206118	1153	1
NANCE JAMES W	LTC	0-0449163	0547	1
NANCE JOHN H	LTC	0-0482990	0453	2
NANCE RICHARD H	LTC	0-1323163	0263	1
NANCE ROGER J	MAJ	0-1647200	0859	1
NANCE TAYLOR H	CPT	0-0277666	1160	3
NANKERVIS BYRON J	MAJ	0-0184465	0754	3
NANTZ WILSON A	CPT	0-1011180	0161	1
NANZ ALBERT J	CPT	0-0286074	0245	2
NAOMI SR CHARLES A	COL	0-0255300	0862	3
NAPEROLA STANLEY J	CPT	0-1322070	0248	2
NAPIER CHARLES G	CPT	0-1014310	0747	2
NAPIER DAVID R	MAJ	0-0483790	0847	2
NAPIER FRANK C	MAJ	0-1165315	0448	1
NAPIER GREEN	MAJ	0-1322648	0859	1
NAPIER GUY J	MAJ	0-0221569	1149	1
NAPIER JAMES B	LTC	0-0282759	0766	3
NAPIER JOHN T	CPT	0-1030818	0258	1
NAPIER THURMAN W	LTC	0-1576433	0961	1
NAPIER WILLIAM T	CPT	0-0889081	0953	1
NAPLES ANGELO S	COL	0-0284826	0963	3
NAPLES RALPH V	LTC	0-0451359	0465	1
NAPOLIELLO CEASARE D	MAJ	0-2096511	0365	1
NAPOLITANO ANDREW J	MAJ	0-1894750	0757	1
NAPORA JOHN J	CW4	W-2115452	1065	1
NAPP RALPH R	2LT	0-0977170	1050	1
NAQUIN JOSEPH U	CPT	0-1593743	0165	1
NARA EDWIN A	LTC	0-1925245	1165	1
NARAMOR GILBERT E	LTC	0-0230938	0547	1
NARAMORE EARL	LTC	0-0199478	0545	2
NARAMORE STUART	LTC	0-0224590	0651	3
NARAMORE WILLIAM K	COL	0-0345529	0666	3
NARANJO LUCAS	MAJ	0-2030589	0650	1
NARDELLA CHARLES S	MAJ	0-1108195	0960	1
NARDELLA RALPH A	MAJ	0-1337073	1059	1
NARDI JR THOMAS	1LT	0-1014183	0446	2
NARDI PACIFICO A	2LT	0-1017126	1044	2
NARDIN GENE	CPT	0-0342908	0146	1
NARDIN JOHN G	COL	0-0296888	1265	1
NARDONE ANTHONY A	COL	0-0263156	0965	3

NAME	GRADE	SVC NO	DATE RET MO YR	RET CODE
NARDONE GEORGE J	LTC	0-1544518	0167	2
NARDUCCI JOSEPH J	1LT	0-0532683	0645	2
NARIGCA CHAIN M	MAJ	0-2046323	0262	1
NARINS SAMUEL R	CPT	0-1691009	0445	1
NARMORE JOSEPH W	MAJ	0-0450089	0846	2
NARUM ARTHUR J	LTC	0-0236217	0161	3
NARVIS CHARLES S	LTC	0-0194521	0450	3
NARWID RAYMOND J	1LT	0-1550667	1144	2
NARY THOMAS P	1LT	0-1293300	0646	2
NASAW JOSHUA J	2LT	0-1533410	0344	2
NASE JR DANIEL R	MAJ	0-1326511	1063	1
NASER VIRGIL S	LTC	0-0364832	0859	1
NASH ALFRED C	MAJ	0-0978055	1065	1
NASH BENJAMIN F	1LT	0-1059016	1145	2
NASH EDWIN B	1LT	0-1031345	0145	2
NASH ELMER N	MAJ	0-1120667	0662	2
NASH ELTON F	MAJ	0-0453164	0556	1
NASH GARVIN H	COL	0-0238309	0462	3
NASH GERALD S	COL	0-0278641	0661	1
NASH HERMAN P	CPT	0-0211369	0655	3
NASH JACK S	MAJ	0-0887320	0261	1
NASH JOHN C	CPT	0-0505019	1147	1
NASH JOHN E	2LT	0-0524353	0944	2
NASH JOHN W	MAJ	0-0295957	1045	2
NASH JOHN W	CPT	0-0996027	1060	1
NASH JOSEPH S	1LT	0-1063043	1044	2
NASH NEWMAN C	1LT	0-0360013	0645	1
NASH PERCY L	LTC	0-0284373	0154	1
NASH ROBERT E	LTC	0-0966772	1064	1
NASH ROBERT C	MAJ	0-1996577	0257	1
NASH SIMEON	COL	0-0143033	0648	3
NASH THOMAS H	LTC	0-0407838	0263	1
NASH THOMAS J	MAJ	0-1080311	0863	1
NASH TOM	CW3	W-2119897	0753	2
NASH WALLACE C	CPT	0-1341816	0960	1
NASH WALLIS G	1LT	0-1325410	0645	2
NASIS ALEJANDRO	CW2	W-2151392	1160	1
NASIS HELEN	1LT	N-0805651	1154	2
NASLUND JULIUS W	CPT	0-0370272	0444	2
NASON BENNETT E	LTC	0-0569542	1060	1
NASON GERALD J	1LT	0-1878823	0559	2
NASON JOHN	1LT	0-1320163	0947	1
NASON LEONARD H	COL	0-0171735	0955	3
NASON RICHARD A	LTC	0-1056479	0267	1
NASR FRED G	LTC	0-0397673	1047	1
NAST CHARLES C	M G	0-0298840	0165	3
NAST HERMAN F	1LT	0-1184555	0646	2
NAST WALTER H	LTC	0-0332820	0257	1
NASVIK ADOLPH C	LTC	0-0230686	0564	3
NATAL ERNEST C	MAJ	0-1047698	0859	1
NATAL STEVE W	MAJ	0-1042659	0159	1
NATALE ANTHONY J	1LT	0-1185842	0246	2
NATALINI CARLO A	LTC	0-1534581	1262	1
NATE CHARLES R	MAJ	0-0173980	1159	3
NATHAN AARON	LTC	0-1296245	0950	1
NATHAN ALBERT S	MAJ	0-0439657	1059	2
NATHAN DELORIS E	2LT	N-0786834	0746	1
NATHAN ELROY N	LTC	0-1949617	0962	1
NATHAN HERMAN	LTC	0-0261856	0667	3
NATHANSON NATHANIEL	LTC	0-0173288	0159	3
NATHANSON YALE S	LTC	0-0182155	0355	3
NATION FRANKLIN F	1LT	0-1920216	0865	2
NATIONS KENNETH L	CPT	0-2212052	0765	1
NATIONS OSCAR T	LTC	0-0312882	0257	2
NATKE STANLEY F	2LT	0-1945231	0445	2
NATTRESS JOHN A	CPT	0-0535379	1047	2
NATTRESS ROY K	CW2	RW-2143008	0163	1
NATZKE RICHARD H	LTC	0-0312272	0861	1
NAU GEORGE T	MAJ	0-1060901	0165	1
NAUCK DONALD A	LTC	0-0306114	0661	1
NAUDAIN GLENN G	COL	0-0213613	1054	3
NAUERT GEORGE V	1LT	0-2262828	0254	2
NAUGHER WILLIAM A	MAJ	0-1185241	0162	1
NAUGHTEN EDWARD T	LTC	0-0435642	1062	1
NAUGHTON FRANCIS L	LTC	0-1043447	0463	1

NAME	GRADE	SVC NO	DATE RET MO YR	RET CODE
NAUGHTON JOHN J	MAJ	0-0411021	0766	3
NAUGHTON THOMAS J	MAJ	0-2009297	0261	1
NAUGLE DONALD E	CW3	W-2150502	1064	1
NAUGLE JEFFERSON	MAJ	0-1100265	1162	1
NAUGLE WILLIAM R	CPT	0-1296407	0347	2
NAULT GERALD H	LTC	0-0451159	0157	1
NAULT ROLLAND F	CPT	0-2006431	0162	2
NAUM ALBERT A	LTC	0-0467837	0555	1
NAUMAN JR CHARLES F	CPT	0-0486184	1048	1
NAUMANN WILLIAM F	COL	0-0441445	0562	3
NAUSE FRANK X	MAJ	0-1578903	0957	1
NAVARRE CHRISTOPHE	CW3	W-2149710	0663	1
NAVARRE ELMER C	LTC	0-0404332	0760	1
NAVARRE GEORGE	LTC	0-1543874	1058	1
NAVARRE VINCENT J	CPT	0-0976679	1151	1
NAVARRETTE GABRIEL L	1LT	0-2055833	0845	2
NAVARRO PATRICK	CPT	0-0890320	0154	1
NAVARRO ROSENDO	1LT	0-2030387	1049	1
NAVAS STANLEY R	1LT	0-0412838	1045	1
NAVAS VICTOR M	MAJ	0-2262637	0961	1
NAVAZIO ATTILIO	CPT	0-0500566	1045	2
NAVE CLARENCE F	LTC	0-0360053	0157	1
NAVE JOHN A	LTC	0-1165768	0264	1
NAVIDOMSKIS JOHN N	MAJ	0-1016827	1161	1
NAVIN JOHN W	1LT	0-1182433	0746	2
NAVY SOPHIA I	MAJ	N-0763486	0664	1
NAWROCKI JR GEORGE J	MAJ	0-2033109	0764	1
NAY WARREN W	MAJ	0-1338633	0365	1
NAYFIELD CHESTER L	CPT	0-0494030	0446	2
NAYLON JOHN T	COL	0-0223921	0154	3
NAYLON JR GEORGE F	CPT	0-1165316	1044	2
NAYLOR ARTHUR S	COL	0-0268904	1160	1
NAYLOR CHARLES R	MAJ	0-1012963	0357	1
NAYLOR EUSTACE I	1LT	0-1548981	0959	3
NAYLOR JUSTUS R	LTC	0-0246338	1266	3
NAYLOR MYREL E	LTC	0-0289185	1061	1
NAYLOR ROBERT J	1LT	0-1590688	1045	2
NAYLOR WALTER C	1LT	0-0390780	1044	2
NAYLOR WILLIAM H	B G	0-0265997	0965	3
NAYLOR WILLIAM H	1LT	0-1030819	0250	1
NAYLOR WILLIAM R	MAJ	0-0470755	0247	2
NAZAK MICHAEL	2LT	0-1821902	0743	2
NAZARENO VICENTE V	CPT	0-1896537	1159	1
NAZARETE ALAS N	1LT	0-1896878	0751	1
NAZARIO MANUEL A	LTC	0-0245832	0753	3
NAZZARO JOHN J	LTC	0-2211317	1064	1
NEACE LAWRENCE T	CPT	0-0435053	0246	1
NEAGLE CHARLES W	LTC	0-1639866	0662	1
NEAL ALLEN B	WO1	W-2121331	0345	2
NEAL BILLIE J	MAJ	0-4074529	0867	1
NEAL CHARLEY G	CW2	W-2120789	0450	1
NEAL CLARK A	LTC	0-0448059	0962	1
NEAL CORNELIUS	1LT	0-0449239	0646	2
NEAL DAVID L	CW3	W-2147194	0964	1
NEAL EDWARD B	MAJ	0-0321628	0546	2
NEAL EDWARD J	MAJ	0-1926423	0767	2
NEAL HUGH A	LTC	0-0243951	0345	2
NEAL JACK O	1LT	0-1115362	0745	2
NEAL JAMES E	LTC	0-0340150	0446	2
NEAL JAMES P	MAJ	0-0260291	1147	1
NEAL JOSEPH D	1LT	0-0451430	0857	1
NEAL JR CHARLIE L	LTC	0-1303763	0861	1
NEAL JR HERESCHELL	LTC	0-0972707	0162	2
NEAL JR JOSEPH W	CPT	0-0398348	0144	2
NEAL JR THOMAS F	CW3	W-2143435	1163	1
NEAL JR WILLIAM A	LTC	0-0370120	0361	1
NEAL KENNETH R	1LT	0-1045858	1045	2
NEAL LENUAL C	CW3	W-2143426	0864	1
NEAL LETTY G	LTC	N-0702522	0960	1
NEAL LILY W	LTC	N-0772841	1263	1
NEAL MILLS F	COL	0-0172100	0857	3
NEAL OLIN F	MAJ	0-1555443	0561	1
NEAL REXFORD B	MAJ	0-0885741	1060	1
NEAL RICHARD K	CPT	0-0246976	0764	3
NEAL ROBERT W	LTC	0-0308715	1160	1

NAME	GRADE	SVC NO	DATE RET MO YR	RET CODE
NEAL ROBERT W	COL	0-1283468	0966	1
NEAL WILLIAM W	LTC	0-0374734	0267	1
NEALE ALTON D	COL	0-0505230	0266	3
NEALE JUSTICE R	COL	0-0338492	0366	1
NEALING WILLIAM H	COL	0-0444446	1054	1
NEALON JAMES F	LTC	0-1168004	0261	1
NEALON ROBERT T	CPT	0-1011306	1045	2
NEAMTZ JOHN C	MAJ	0-2265735	0266	1
NEARHOOF RALPH L	LTC	0-1555256	0566	1
NEARY JAMES E	MAJ	0-0451015	0455	1
NEARY JOHN S	LTC	0-1169670	0964	1
NEASE DARIUS H	MAJ	0-1036219	1047	1
NEAT LEYDEN K	CPT	0-0902414	0546	2
NEAVERTH ELMER J	COL	0-0305289	0966	3
NEAVLES JACKSEN C	CPT	0-0469740	0445	2
NEBEL DAVID A	CPT	0-1309301	0848	2
NEBEL HAROLD	LTC	0-0245780	0346	2
NEBINGER JOHN F	LTC	0-0333718	0563	1
NEBINGER RANKIN A	MAJ	0-0261757	1063	3
NEBLETT DOUGLAS C	CPT	0-0349917	0145	1
NEBLETT GEORGE L	LTC	0-0228219	1055	1
NECEL ROMUALD H	CW2	W-2144040	0761	1
NEDER ELLIS E	2LT	0-0920507	0145	2
NEDOPAC LOUIS F	MAJ	0-1533645	0457	1
NEDZELNITSKY OLEG V	2LT	0-1017155	0545	2
NEEB MILTON T	CPT	0-1302696	0548	2
NEED JR CHAR U	1LT	0-0335844	0943	2
NEEDHAM ARTHUR C	1LT	0-0397868	0244	2
NEEDHAM ARTIE C	LTC	0-0254317	0562	3
NEEDHAM DANIEL	M G	0-0179136	0551	3
NEEDHAM HARRY H	COL	0-0203824	0954	3
NEEDHAM JOHN A	LTC	0-0328926	0766	3
NEEDHAM JR SUMNER H	MAJ	0-0242858	0859	1
NEEDHAM LESLIE F	MAJ	0-0261970	0346	2
NEEDHAM RAYMOND H	2LT	0-1301018	0844	2
NEEDHAM WILLIAM A	1LT	0-1590685	0140	2
NEEDHAM WILLIAM A	MAJ	0-2200108	0566	1
NEEDLES FLOYD L	LTC	0-0499383	0962	1
NEEFE WARREN F	CW2	W-2205909	0763	1
NEEL JAMES F	MAJ	0-1283500	0960	1
NEEL TALLY M	LTC	0-0383562	1065	3
NEELEMAN LEONARD J	1LT	0-0465263	0145	2
NEELEY ANDERSON P	LTC	0-0238349	1064	3
NEELEY JOHN A	1LT	0-1030177	0845	1
NEELLY JOHN W	LTC	0-1287391	1166	3
NEELY ARNOL R	CPT	0-0366878	0246	2
NEELY CARL C	B G	0-0270845	0667	3
NEELY CECIL F	MAJ	0-0955771	0561	1
NEELY CHARLES V	CW4	W-2113912	0562	2
NEELY FRED P	CW2	W-2146719	0455	1
NEELY JAMES F	COL	0-0328441	0467	3
NEELY PAUL F	MAJ	0-1107615	0457	1
NEELY WORLEY R	CPT	0-0493217	1053	1
NEENER ELWOOD H	MAJ	0-0267034	0253	1
NEENER JR ELWOOD H	CPT	0-0990105	0961	1
NEER JAMES R	CPT	0-0182724	0648	3
NEES LEO C	CW4	W-2142182	0858	1
NEESON JAMES E	MAJ	0-2012108	1163	1
NEETZ HAROLD B	2LT	0-1305463	0644	2
NEFF ANDREW W	LTC	0-0198882	1153	3
NEFF CLYDE A	CPT	0-0120235	0853	3
NEFF ELSIE	LTC	N-0700021	0344	1
NEFF EMERY R	COL	0-0193482	0245	2
NEFF EUGENE R	MAJ	0-1633425	1065	1
NEFF GARLAND W	2LT	0-1331856	0446	2
NEFF JR CONRAD R	2LT	0-0528096	0944	2
NEFF JR PAT W	MAJ	0-0512005	0444	2
NEFF MARTIN H	CPT	0-1695874	1045	2
NEFF ROBERT C	CW2	W-2150545	0560	1
NEFF SAMUEL W	MAJ	0-0275199	0960	3
NEFF THEODORE H	2LT	0-1302173	1043	2
NEGLIA PHILIP P	CPT	0-1116737	1046	1
NEGRI MARY J	1LT	N-0786-84	1046	1
NEGRON CARLOS R	CW2	W-2151663	1060	1
NEGRON JESUS M	MAJ	0-0169963	0357	3

NAME	GRADE	SVC NO	DATE RET MO YR	RET CODE
NEHF ANDREW J	LTC	C-0254558	0366	3
NEHLS LAURA T	1LT	N-0759601	0845	1
NEHODA FLORENCE K	2LT	N-0794260	C346	1
NEHRLING ROBERT E	LTC	0-1115363	C165	1
NEICHTER JOSEPH C	CPT	0-0487575	1058	3
NEIDBALLA EDWARD G	CPT	0-1684598	0146	2
NEIDER DONALD F	MAJ	C-0379118	0260	1
NEIDER NORMAN L	LTC	0-1018130	1062	1
NEIDHAMER THOMAS V	LTC	0-1011268	1263	1
NEIDIG JR DESMOND E	MAJ	0-0370862	1048	2
NEIER RICHARD E	CPT	0-1011349	0347	2
NEIGHBARGER R M	CPT	0-1301673	0453	1
NEIGHBORS MELVIN H	MAJ	C-2019071	0862	1
NEIGHBORS WILLIAM R	LTC	0-1824668	C263	1
NEIGUM GOTLIEB G	1LT	0-0944682	C857	1
NEIL AUBREY R	MAJ	0-0500418	0653	1
NEIL TERRANCE	COL	0-0420187	C753	1
NEILL ANDRUS B	COL	0-0359884	0455	1
NEILL CHARLES R	CPT	0-0184878	C845	2
NEILL CHESTER H	CPT	0-1700692	C446	2
NEILL EUGENE P	CW3	W-2108838	C760	1
NEILL JEREMIAH F	MAJ	0-0223268	1060	3
NEILL JESSE L	1LT	0-1048119	C545	2
NEILL JOHN B	CW3	W-2203260	0666	1
NEILL JOHN L M	LTC	0-0295202	0665	3
NEILL LEX T	CPT	C-0472531	0146	2
NEILL OWEN C	CPT	0-0263088	0466	3
NEILL ROBERT G	MAJ	0-1289118	C159	1
NEILL ROBERT W	2LT	0-0529430	C945	1
NEILL THOMAS J	1LT	0-1294890	1044	2
NEILLY HAROLD J	CW3	W-2151695	1265	2
NEILON DANIEL F	MAJ	C-0296740	0843	2
NEILSON ROBERT C	CPT	0-1697874	C652	2
NEILSON ROBERT E	2LT	0-0464057	C245	2
NEIPLING LAWRENCE F	LTC	0-1341817	C563	1
NEIS BONNEVILLE	COL	0-0199299	0853	1
NEISS HELEN C	MAJ	N-0759283	1263	1
NEISWANGER HAROLD A	CW3	W-2143950	1262	1
NEISWENDER SR C P	LTC	0-0245250	1058	3
NEISWENDER WILLIAM G	MAJ	0-1284005	C361	2
NEIWIRTH LEO	1LT	0-1647621	0247	2
NEKICH JOSEPH	WO1	W-2112241	0348	1
NELCENGER EDWIN J	LTC	0-1585958	0361	3
NELL MARVEL G	LTC	0-0248306	0366	3
NELLEN ROBERT S	CPT	C-1016207	C864	1
NELLES JR PHILIP A	LTC	0-0288750	1056	3
NELLIGAN HARRY A	WO1	W-2004427	C458	3
NELLIS JOSEPH L	CW2	W-2109566	1058	1
NELLIS JR CHARLES N	LTC	0-0262021	0467	3
NELLOR EDWARD K	1LT	0-0450374	C544	2
NELLOR TUDOR M	1LT	C-1319567	1045	2
NELSEN HANS	2LT	0-1291681	1044	2
NELSEN KENNETH W	MAJ	C-1320767	C563	1
NELSON A JANE R	1LT	N-0724710	C846	1
NELSON AARON W	MAJ	0-0301167	1158	3
NELSON ADOLPH H	MAJ	0-0288743	C844	2
NELSON ALFRED H	CPT	0-0385118	C145	2
NELSON ANTON	CW4	W-2101086	1052	1
NELSON ARTHUR G	MAJ	C-2025119	0465	1
NELSON ARTHUR P	MAJ	0-1893738	C267	1
NELSON AUGUST W	CW3	W-2208677	C366	1
NELSON BERNICE A	MAJ	N-0771704	C448	1
NELSON CARL W	COL	C-0335637	0564	3
NELSON CARL W	LTC	C-1285278	C657	1
NELSON CHESTER H	CW4	W-2144871	C867	1
NELSON CHESTER L	MAJ	0-0210912	0648	3
NELSON CLARENCE A	LTC	0-0317003	1057	3
NELSON CLAUDE L	MAJ	C-0888275	1054	1
NELSON CLIFFORD R	WO1	W-2114445	C454	2
NELSON CLIFTON B	COL	0-0502250	1054	1
NELSON CLIFTON W	CPT	C-1282055	1054	1
NELSON CURTIS A	COL	0-0279146	0365	3
NELSON DAVID A	LTC	0-0240580	1152	1
NELSON DONALD M	LTC	0-1646448	C567	1
NELSON DONALD T	CPT	0-1165920	0346	2

NAME	GRADE	SVC NO	DATE RET MO YR	RET CODE
NELSON EARL J	LTC	0-0242326	0963	3
NELSON EARL W	CPT	0-0270345	1144	2
NELSON EDWARD G	CW3	W-2151534	0666	1
NELSON EDWARD H	MAJ	0-0256142	1063	3
NELSON EDWARD P	LTC	0-0257402	1265	3
NELSON EDWIN	MAJ	0-0286836	0653	3
NELSON EDWIN A	LTC	0-0487022	0357	1
NELSON EDWIN C	MAJ	0-0451160	0853	1
NELSON EDWIN J	LTC	0-1042660	0766	1
NELSON ELBERT L	COL	C-0245306	1158	3
NELSON ELMER L	LTC	0-1111805	1062	1
NELSON ELMER L	CW2	W-2147045	0663	1
NELSON ELVEN C	LTC	0-0529465	0967	3
NELSON EMIL H	1LT	0-1169268	1044	2
NELSON ERNEST L	1LT	0-1172754	0845	1
NELSON ETHEL M	1LT	N-0703015	C646	1
NELSON FRANCIS H	CPT	0-0252405	0965	3
NELSON FREDERICK	LTC	0-1010307	1262	1
NELSON FREDERICK	MAJ	0-1110153	0761	1
NELSON GEORGE E	COL	0-0256043	0159	3
NELSON GEORGE R	LTC	0-1646865	1162	1
NELSON GEORGE W	CW2	W-2113090	1151	1
NELSON GLENN E	LTC	C-1554449	0765	1
NELSON GORDON N	CW3	W-2141643	0959	1
NELSON GORDON W	1LT	0-1297771	1045	2
NELSON GRETCHEN A	2LT	N-0734403	0944	1
NELSON GRIFFIN G	1LT	0-1294891	0446	2
NELSON HAROLD A	COL	0-0353173	0166	1
NELSON HAROLD S	COL	0-0100559	0350	3
NELSON HARRY A	LTC	0-0232989	1060	3
NELSON HEDRICK C	MAJ	0-1030399	1060	3
NELSON HERBERT R	1LT	0-0921320	0544	2
NELSON HILDURE	1LT	N-0735659	0946	1
NELSON HOWARD C	LTC	0-0405241	1157	1
NELSON HOWARD W	MAJ	0-1305057	0363	1
NELSON III WILLIAM	LTC	0-0412771	0167	1
NELSON IRA	LTC	0-1010058	0257	1
NELSON IRA J	1LT	0-1300515	0454	1
NELSON IRENE M	1LT	N-0751765	0246	2
NELSON IRVING E	MAJ	0-0497136	1047	2
NELSON JACK J	MAJ	C-2033803	0865	1
NELSON JACK W	CW3	W-2150899	0862	1
NELSON JAMES A	CPT	0-2096900	0564	2
NELSON JAMES D	LTC	0-0404694	0546	1
NELSON JAMES H	CPT	0-0298722	0346	2
NELSON JAMES H	1LT	0-1285279	1045	2
NELSON JOHN A	COL	0-0173086	0753	3
NELSON JOHN A	CPT	0-0450051	1145	2
NELSON JOHN C	MAJ	0-0500691	0756	1
NELSON JOHN J	LTC	0-1577621	0755	1
NELSON JOHN L	CW2	W-2118406	0653	1
NELSON JOHN M	2LT	0-1633427	1044	2
NELSON JOHN R	CPT	0-0920250	0845	2
NELSON JOHN R	LTC	0-1546367	0363	1
NELSON JOHNNIE L	CW2	RW-2210416	1164	1
NELSON JOSEPH N	MAJ	0-0509879	0661	1
NELSON JR ALFRED W	1LT	0-1298745	0345	2
NELSON JR CHARLES G	CPT	0-1647623	0361	1
NELSON JR CLAYTON J	MAJ	0-0996656	0966	1
NELSON JR EDWARD O	LTC	0-1948025	0164	1
NELSON JR FRED C	2LT	0-1316579	1044	2
NELSON JR IVAR V	2LT	0-1110681	1044	2
NELSON JR JOHN L	MAJ	0-1338840	1060	1
NELSON JR WALTER S	LTC	0-1284924	0760	1
NELSON JR WILLIAM A	LTC	0-0454102	0859	1
NELSON JR WILLIAM S	COL	C-0174566	0358	3
NELSON KENNETH L	CPT	0-0261646	0166	3
NELSON KENNETH S	CPT	0-0456093	0745	2
NELSON KINLOCH	MAJ	0-0400345	0245	1
NELSON KLEMENS M	LTC	0-2034896	1060	1
NELSON LAWRENCE A	COL	0-0267617	0554	1
NELSON LAWRENCE J	LTC	0-0394215	C660	1
NELSON LAWRENCE M	MAJ	C-0290814	0146	2
NELSON LAWRENCE M	LTC	0-0377911	0662	1
NELSON LLOYD C	MAJ	0-1552943	0157	1

NAME	GRADE	SVC NO	DATE RET MO YR	RET CODE
NELSON LLOYD L	1LT	C-2042848	C348	1
NELSON LOWELL	LTC	0-0446978	0956	1
NELSON LYMAN A	LTC	0-0200076	0358	3
NELSON MANSFIELD	COL	0-0230627	C955	1
NELSON MARION M	LTC	0-1080890	0161	1
NELSON MARVIN L	CPT	C-0191598	C554	3
NELSON MARY E	MAJ	L-0906370	C166	1
NELSON MARY M	1LT	N-0763157	1045	1
NELSON MELVIN	CPT	0-2032889	1263	1
NELSON MELVIN E	CPT	0-1583435	C448	2
NELSON MELVIN W	CW2	W-2153043	0957	1
NELSON MERLIN N	LTC	C-0417550	0762	2
NELSON MURRAY R	CW3	W-2146455	1264	1
NELSON NEAL D	LTC	0-0226233	C464	3
NELSON NORMAN A	WO1	W-2104945	C946	2
NELSON ORVAL E	CW2	W-2151700	0561	1
NELSON ORVILLE L	CW2	W-2210214	1062	1
NELSON ORVIN E	1LT	0-1325509	C649	2
NELSON OSCAR H	CW4	W-2116143	C359	1
NELSON OTTO A	LTC	0-0364863	0859	1
NELSON OTTO F	MAJ	0-1574734	0365	1
NELSON QUENTIN V	CW3	W-2144342	C963	1
NELSON RALPH H	1LT	0-1054731	C346	2
NELSON RANDALL M	CPT	0-1036653	C347	2
NELSON RAYMOND A	COL	0-0286649	0655	1
NELSON RAYMOND F	2LT	0-1796139	C845	2
NELSON RAYMOND J	CPT	0-0387542	0144	2
NELSON RAYMOND N	2LT	0-1314398	C744	2
NELSON RICHARD O	MAJ	0-0977394	C264	1
NELSON RICHARD V	1LT	0-0160198	0854	3
NELSON RICHARD V	MAJ	0-0230873	C958	3
NELSON ROBERT A	CPT	0-1799068	C854	2
NELSON ROBERT C	LTC	0-1591341	0960	1
NELSON ROBERT D	MAJ	C-1318819	1063	1
NELSON ROBERT O	CW4	W-2105228	1060	1
NELSON ROY E	MAJ	0-0102250	0658	3
NELSON ROY E	COL	C-0294136	C866	3
NELSON ROY E	LTC	0-0750667	C761	1
NELSON ROY R	CPT	0-1324181	1047	2
NELSON ROY W	LTC	0-1063013	1062	1
NELSON RUSSELL C	LTC	0-0256045	1159	1
NELSON RUSSELL E	CW2	W-2151659	0361	1
NELSON SIGURD S	MAJ	C-0482712	1148	1
NELSON SR HENRY N	MAJ	C-0125857	C452	3
NELSON SR JAMES T	MAJ	C-0191468	0455	3
NELSON SR THOMAS C	MAJ	C-0974457	0764	1
NELSON STANLEY O	MAJ	0-1170111	1161	1
NELSON STEADMAN P	LTC	0-1944766	1265	1
NELSON SUE C	1LT	N-0763435	0346	1
NELSON SUMTER R	LTC	0-0420240	C660	1
NELSON TEDDY B	MAJ	0-1168391	C158	1
NELSON TERRY N	CPT	0-0913072	0445	2
NELSON THOMAS H	1LT	0-0250872	1044	2
NELSON THOMAS W	2LT	0-1052525	0245	2
NELSON THOMAS W	1LT	0-1845630	0446	2
NELSON THURSTON O	MAJ	C-0975931	C763	1
NELSON VINCENT H	MAJ	0-0978797	C364	1
NELSON WALDO	COL	0-0351054	0567	3
NELSON WALLACE E	MAJ	C-2262188	1263	1
NELSON WARREN H	CW4	W-2004440	1167	1
NELSON WILLIAM A	MAJ	0-1080651	0863	1
NELSON WILLIAM A	CW2	W-2102144	C846	1
NELSON WILLIAM F	MAJ	0-1181970	1062	1
NELSON WILLOUGHBY	MAJ	0-0965143	C966	2
NELSON WOODFORD O	LTC	0-0255755	0560	1
NELSON WOODROW L	LTC	0-0412285	1060	1
NEMEC FRANK A	CPT	0-0517258	0445	2
NEMETH ALBERT J	1LT	0-0885791	1145	2
NEMETH ERNEST A	CPT	C-2263137	C761	1
NEMETH JR STEPHEN	MAJ	0-0488480	0457	1
NEMETH JR THEODORE W	CPT	0-1055680	C147	1
NEMETH LELIA L	MAJ	N-0797837	C765	1
NEMIC ALBERT L	LTC	0-0350061	0566	3
NEMISH CHARLES	LTC	0-1323021	1162	1
NENN WILLIAM H	CW2	W-2006562	1057	2

NAME	GRADE	SVC NO	DATE RET MO YR	RET CODE
NENNINGER HAROLD F	LTC	0-1823336	0562	1
NENNO ARTHUR C	MAJ	C-1548982	0161	1
NENOW NIKOLAI	CW2	W-2210841	1265	1
NERI FRANK O	MAJ	0-0494495	C350	1
NERI HENRY J	LTC	0-0359280	0367	3
NERRIE JR ROBERT A	MAJ	0-0252884	0460	1
NESBETT JR GEORGE H	COL	0-0313384	0961	1
NESBIT ARTHUR P	COL	C-0244574	0357	1
NESBIT VIRGIL C	CW3	W-2148874	C563	1
NESBITT CARL E	COL	0-0192853	0146	2
NESBITT DAVID A	CW3	W-2148574	0862	2
NESBITT GARVEN S	LTC	0-0925250	0666	3
NESBITT GEORGE B	WO1	W-2126752	0145	2
NESBITT JR THOMAS M	COL	0-0223246	1064	3
NESBITT LEROY J	LTC	0-0322010	1062	1
NESBITT RUSSELL G	MAJ	C-0201136	0958	3
NESBITT WILLIAM E	CPT	0-0249595	0762	3
NESBITT WILLIAM J	1LT	0-1309805	0146	2
NESEWICH MARTIN	CW3	W-2148357	1262	1
NESLEN CLARENCE C	COL	0-0368733	0267	3
NESMITH II JAMES	COL	0-0163241	1C61	3
NESS DONALD L	LTC	0-0419311	0263	1
NESS JULIUS B	CPT	0-1285479	0945	1
NESS MARTIN K	MAJ	0-1173728	0656	1
NESS PAUL F	CW2	W-2152976	1057	1
NESS RICHARD C	LTC	0-1322071	1066	1
NESS VERNELLE J	CPT	0-1698201	0646	1
NESSELHOF WILLIAM	CPT	0-0133905	0254	3
NESSLEY EDWARD J	LTC	0-1703892	0163	1
NESSMITH REX C	WO1	W-2117962	0759	1
NESSON JOHN H	LTC	0-0220385	1058	3
NESTER GILBERT C	LTC	0-1634176	0960	1
NESTER NORMAN W	LTC	0-0282761	0865	3
NESTOR MARION E	LTC	L-0203227	0667	1
NESTOR MONA E S	1LT	N-0742988	1046	1
NETHERLAND RAYMOND A	CPT	0-1320769	1146	2
NETHERTON CHARLES J	MAJ	0-1109555	0865	1
NETHERTON GROVER T	CPT	0-0446464	0645	2
NETHERY SAMUEL C	LTC	0-0234867	1159	1
NETHERY WILLIAM M	LTC	0-0322004	0566	3
NETSKY MARGARET P	1LT	N-0743611	0747	1
NETTERS JIMMIE C	1LT	0-0360051	1043	2
NETTLES ALBERT A	CPT	0-0330906	1045	2
NETTLES EARL W	LTC	0-0428341	0162	1
NETTLES FRANK K	WO1	W-2147343	0853	2
NETTLES HOWARD C	MAJ	0-1639451	1160	1
NETTLES ROBERT L	MAJ	0-0249903	1057	3
NETZER ERWIN	MAJ	0-1889862	0766	1
NETZLOFF HAROLD H	MAJ	0-1287045	1060	1
NEU EUGENE G	WO1	W-2119381	1044	2
NEU WARREN E	COL	0-0369942	0862	1
NEUBAUER ADOLPH	CW3	W-2118064	1060	1
NEUBAUER KENNETH H	MAJ	0-1062031	0762	1
NEUBAUM FREDERICK	CW3	W-2206377	0966	1
NEUDEK ELSIE V	2LT	N-0728999	0145	1
NEUDORFF KARL A	CW2	W-2150347	1066	1
NEUENDORF RAY C	LTC	0-0484316	0655	1
NEUFELD CHARLES M	LTC	0-0581221	1063	1
NEUFELD LEWIS	2LT	0-1597877	104N	2
NEUGEBAUER WILLIAM F	COL	0-1994666	0562	1
NEUHAUSER HARRY M	LTC	0-0235424	0760	1
NEUMANN ARTHUR	LTC	0-1281037	0766	1
NEUMANN ARTHUR T	CPT	0-1290987	0249	1
NEUMANN CARL E	CW3	W-2148357	1062	1
NEUMANN EARNEST O	MAJ	0-1936344	C967	1
NEUMANN EDWARD E	COL	0-0279600	0254	1
NEUMANN OSCAR O	LTC	0-0374430	0860	1
NEUMANN PAUL M	LTC	0-0376918	1060	1
NEUMANN RAYMOND J	LTC	0-1944535	1060	1
NEUMANN SIDNEY S	CPT	0-1308849	0947	1
NEUMANN WALTER E	CPT	0-0425940	0954	1
NEUMARK GEORGE	COL	C-0254403	0765	3
NEUMYER ROBERT J	LTC	0-1582831	0863	1
NEUNEWS ROY T	CPT	0-1303010	0146	2
NEUROCK JOHN	MAJ	0-1336682	1161	1

NAME	GRADE	SVC NO	DATE RET MO YR	RET CODE
NEUWIRTH ABRAHAM	MAJ	C-1554947	0756	1
NEUWIRTH ABRAHAM A	LTC	0-0274171	0544	2
NEVELING WALDO	1LT	0-2032300	0646	1
NEVELLS FREDERICK	LTC	0-0241272	0762	3
NEVELS ALICE P	CPT	L-0401524	0445	2
NEVILL GALE E	COL	0-028606C	C167	3
NEVILLE ANDREW P	COL	0-0510313	0660	3
NEVILLE CATHERINE	MAJ	N-0751945	0666	1
NEVILLE HOWARD T	2LT	0-1947265	0345	2
NEVILLE JAMES M	LTC	0-4021577	1059	2
NEVILLE JOHN F	1LT	0-1030179	1044	2
NEVILLE JOHN W	1LT	0-0958911	C554	2
NEVILLE JOSEPH M	COL	0-0114956	0754	3
NEVILLE JR JOSEPH H	1LT	0-0269525	0445	2
NEVILLE JR WILLIAM H	2LT	0-1292047	0545	2
NEVILLE LEWIS J	MAJ	0-2263114	0465	1
NEVILLE WALTER L	LTC	C-0289686	1060	3
NEVILLE WILLIAM O	CPT	0-0130045	0453	3
NEVILLE WILLIAM G	LTC	0-0452778	0547	2
NEVIN JR JOSEPH P	MAJ	0-1583438	0357	1
NEVINS GLEN	1LT	0-1316915	1045	2
NEVINS WILLIAM B	MAJ	0-1923599	C665	2
NEVITT JAMES R	COL	C-0321833	0959	3
NEVITT OLNEY L	MAJ	0-1577625	0761	1
NEVITT PEYTON G	COL	0-0178264	1154	3
NEVITT THOMAS R	MAJ	0-0173732	1060	3
NEVIUS CARL W	MAJ	0-0309576	1153	3
NEVLING CLAYTON T	MAJ	0-0969463	1263	1
NEVUE FRANCIS E	MAJ	C-1634179	0657	1
NEW CHARLES A	COL	0-0226473	1063	3
NEW CHARLES J	LTC	0-1032545	1266	1
NEW JAMES D	CW2	W-2213521	0566	1
NEW JOHN R	CPT	0-0460044	0647	2
NEW MARVIN H	1LT	0-1179553	0945	2
NEW WILLIAM J	COL	0-0237900	0665	3
NEWBEGIN FRANCIS N	MAJ	0-1299284	0564	1
NEWBERG MILDRED	MAJ	L-0100089	C965	1
NEWBERN HOWARD E	LTC	0-0355976	1067	3
NEWBERRY DONALD C	MAJ	C-2203250	1166	1
NEWBERRY GUY F	2LT	0-1549799	1043	2
NEWBERRY JARREL M	CPT	0-2262392	1160	1
NEWBERRY LOUIS M	LTC	C-0954162	0367	1
NEWBERRY MARK	WO1	W-2146977	0659	1
NEWBERRY ROY W	CW3	W-2152335	C763	2
NEWBERRY Y T	CW4	W-2109971	1062	1
NEWBILL MARION L	CW3	W-2144852	0661	1
NEWBILL ROBERT N	LTC	0-0454816	1161	1
NEWBOLD JOHN W	1LT	0-0441319	C544	2
NEWBURGER JR SIDNEY	LTC	0-0243248	C365	3
NEWBURGER STANLEY W	WO1	W-2107176	1045	2
NEWBURN ALVA C	LTC	0-0490479	0159	3
NEWBURY FRED L	CPT	0-0485186	0647	1
NEWBY RALPH C	LTC	0-1170113	C563	1
NEWCOMB ARTHUR M	CW4	W-2131484	0760	1
NEWCOMB GEORGE L	CW4	W-2111703	C559	1
NEWCOMP JR CARMEN A	MAJ	0-0303003	0245	2
NEWCOMB LESTER D	1LT	0-0925226	C445	2
NEWCOMBE HAZEL J	2LT	N-0720556	C545	1
NEWCOMER DONALD R	CW3	W-2205108	1067	1
NEWCOMER ROBERT	CW4	W-2124709	1060	1
NEWELL ALBERT C	LTC	0-0151682	0755	3
NEWELL BEN A	1LT	0-0413864	0343	2
NEWELL CLYDE R	MAJ	0-0135827	C648	3
NEWELL FRANCIS M	LTC	0-0274205	1061	3
NEWELL HAROLD L	CPT	0-032316C	C351	1
NEWELL HARVEY P	2LT	0-1104319	0855	1
NEWELL JACK D	2LT	0-1114686	1044	1
NEWELL JAMES J	CW3	W-2149797	0462	1
NEWELL JOHN L	MAJ	0-0273837	1043	2
NEWELL JR JOSEPH J	CW3	W-215261C	1163	1
NEWELL JR ROBERT L	CW2	W-3151848	C966	2
NEWELL LELAND R	LTC	0-1844959	C862	3
NEWELL LOU P	1LT	N-0726011	C646	1
NEWELL MELVIN S	CW2	W-2111718	0945	2
NEWELL RICHARD E	MAJ	0-2042909	0258	1

NAME	GRADE	SVC NO	DATE RET MO YR	RET CODE
NEWELL SHEPARD B	MAJ	C-0977562	0763	1
NEWELL WESLEY S	1LT	0-1550880	1158	1
NEWELL 3RD JOHN	1LT	0-0538805	0246	2
NEWGARD JOSEPH M	MAJ	0-0119972	0648	3
NEWHALL HARRY R	LTC	0-1170114	0864	1
NEWHARD CHARLES H	1LT	0-1298107	1045	2
NEWHARDT CLIFFORD J	2LT	0-0966507	0550	2
NEWHART ARTHUR H	MAJ	0-2024105	0860	1
NEWHOUSE ELBERT A	LTC	0-0278536	1066	3
NEWHOUSE FRED L	MAJ	0-2211504	0667	1
NEWHOUSE JESSE P	MAJ	0-2262882	0567	1
NEWHOUSE WILLIAM C	CPT	0-1325920	0856	1
NEWINGTON ELMER J	MAJ	0-1298578	1262	1
NEWITT BERENICE E	2LT	N-0700986	0737	1
NEWKIRK ARTHUR C	COL	0-0119C81	1150	3
NEWKIRK HAROLD J	1LT	0-1038779	0146	2
NEWKIRK JAMES R	LTC	0-0364415	1266	1
NEWKIRK KENNETH L	CPT	0-0384606	0346	1
NEWKIRK LEWIS R	MAJ	0-1646868	0162	1
NEWKIRK MARION J	LTC	0-0516992	1167	1
NEWKIRK WILLIAM G	LTC	0-1333372	0166	1
NEWLAND FLETCHER E	MAJ	0-2279879	0366	1
NEWLAND HAROLD	COL	0-0123883	C953	3
NEWLAND JR LEROY T	MAJ	0-0889794	0263	1
NEWLANDER JULIAN A	COL	0-0269989	0860	1
NEWLIN DALE A	COL	0-0221176	0150	1
NEWLIN FLOYD W	1LT	0-1542501	1045	2
NEWLIN LEWIS K	LTC	0-1558186	0467	1
NEWMAN BERNARD J	1LT	0-1172574	0246	1
NEWMAN BERYL R	CPT	0-0346726	1045	2
NEWMAN CARL F	1LT	0-1113374	104N	2
NEWMAN CHARLES C	CPT	0-0508492	0946	1
NEWMAN CHARLES E	COL	0-0193139	0553	3
NEWMAN CHARLES F	CW3	W-2148875	1266	1
NEWMAN CHARLES W	LTC	0-0244778	0964	3
NEWMAN DELMAR J	CPT	0-0361166	1045	2
NEWMAN DONALD R	LTC	0-0518842	0767	1
NEWMAN DWIGHT R	CW2	W-2150153	1160	1
NEWMAN EARL L B	CPT	C-0501427	0145	2
NEWMAN EARL W	CPT	0-0167669	1150	3
NEWMAN ELMER C	LTC	0-0365773	0760	1
NEWMAN ELMER K	MAJ	0-0185120	0156	3
NEWMAN FLOYD W	MAJ	0-C179097	0944	2
NEWMAN FRED O	MAJ	0-1874692	1061	1
NEWMAN GEORGE J	CW3	W-2142090	0859	1
NEWMAN HAROLD T	LTC	0-0220847	1061	3
NEWMAN HENRY	2LT	0-0395267	0345	2
NEWMAN HENRY E	MAJ	0-1185506	0255	2
NEWMAN HOWARD E	LTC	0-1312586	1166	1
NEWMAN IRVING J	COL	0-0248735	0367	3
NEWMAN JACK W	1LT	0-1314823	1045	1
NEWMAN JAMES S	MAJ	C-1918878	0863	1
NEWMAN JESSE V	1LT	0-0479016	0447	1
NEWMAN JOE L	1LT	0-0373003	0544	2
NEWMAN JOE W	2LT	0-2101162	1045	2
NEWMAN JOHN F	CPT	0-0361508	0945	2
NEWMAN JOSEPH	WO1	W-2115377	0845	2
NEWMAN JR EZRA H	LTC	0-1165254	C263	1
NEWMAN JR MOSES C	CW2	W-2210642	0466	1
NEWMAN KENNETH F	CW2	W-2209024	1062	1
NEWMAN KENNETH F	LTC	0-0387412	0258	1
NEWMAN LESLIE	CPT	0-0167755	0745	2
NEWMAN MARCEL J	CPT	0-1341233	1058	1
NEWMAN MARTIN C	LTC	0-0302716	0167	3
NEWMAN MAURICE A	LTC	0-1541951	0661	1
NEWMAN MILTON B	1LT	C-1594358	0446	2
NEWMAN NEFUS L	1LT	0-0487726	0844	1
NEWMAN OLIVER L	LTC	C-1297928	0962	1
NEWMAN PATT C	MAJ	0-0488206	0451	1
NEWMAN PAUL C	CPT	0-0511397	1045	2
NEWMAN PETER J	CPT	0-1925217	0764	1
NEWMAN PHILIP H	CPT	0-0485514	1045	2
NEWMAN RALPH C	WO1	W-2117840	1046	2
NEWMAN SAMUEL W	CW2	W-2152475	1161	1
NEWMAN SR MARCEL L	LTC	0-0499730	0654	2

NAME	GRADE	SVC NO	DATE RET MO YR	RET CODE
NEWMAN STEWART L	MAJ	C-1684988	C564	1
NEWMAN TAYLOR F	CW2	W-2115933	C949	2
NEWMAN THOMAS C	MAJ	0-1100702	0359	1
NEWMAN WALTER C	LTC	0-0327155	1265	3
NEWMANN NORMAN F	LTC	0-1322651	1262	1
NEWMARK PHILIP M	MAJ	C-1001203	0347	2
NEWMARK TED	LTC	0-1001864	0567	3
NEWNAM ALONZO R	LTC	0-1316580	C466	1
NEWNAM JOHN H	CPT	0-0480979	0447	1
NEWNAN HERMAN R	LTC	0-0205930	0150	3
NEWPORT EARL M	2LT	0-0391988	0741	1
NEWSHAM ARTHUR J	CPT	0-1315092	0747	1
NEWSOM HAROLD R	MAJ	C-0504917	0457	1
NEWSOM HERMAN L	1LT	0-0171602	C355	3
NEWSOME CHARLES H	MAJ	0-1547414	0462	2
NEWTON ABRAM M	COL	0-0224539	C648	3
NEWTON ALBERT	CW3	W-2205260	C464	1
NEWTON ARTHUR P	MAJ	0-0322177	1165	1
NEWTON CECIL J	LTC	0-0915388	1067	3
NEWTON GORDON E	CPT	0-1120668	C760	1
NEWTON HAROLD O	MAJ	0-0137271	0355	3
NEWTON HARVEY P	1LT	0-0555150	C446	2
NEWTON HENRY C	B G	0-0104029	0756	3
NEWTON HERBERT R	MAJ	C-0267374	C261	3
NEWTON IOUS W	CW3	W-2145894	0866	1
NEWTON JAMES E	COL	C-0290054	1064	3
NEWTON JAMES S	LTC	0-0322597	0365	3
NEWTON JOHN G	1LT	0-2002693	0753	1
NEWTON JOHN H	LTC	0-0255882	0967	3
NEWTON JOSEPH B	MAJ	C-1302042	0462	1
NEWTON JOSEPH C	CW4	W-2114199	0655	3
NEWTON JOSEPH L	CPT	0-1289471	0146	1
NEWTON LAWRENCE R	LTC	0-0328437	C763	3
NEWTON LULU J	LTC	N-0700371	1046	1
NEWTON PAUL V	LTC	0-1105061	0862	1
NEWTON PERCY W	LTC	0-0198442	0348	1
NEWTON PETER J	LTC	0-0359139	0647	2
NEWTON RUFFUS H	MAJ	C-0976054	0962	1
NEWTON WILLIAM A	MAJ	C-1894193	C167	1
NEWTON WILLIAM H	COL	0-0277999	0159	3
NEWTON WILLIAM T	CW3	W-2149229	1265	1
NEXSEN SAMUEL M	1LT	0-0460045	0845	2
NEY VIRGIL	COL	0-0227473	1057	1
NG-MUN-TAYNE HELEN B	CW3	V-0906970	C164	1
NIBALI VINCENT C	MAJ	C-1598986	C462	1
NIBBELINK HARRY L	MAJ	C-1548985	0164	1
NIBBELINK WAYNE R	1LT	0-0467220	0445	2
NIBERT WILLIAM E	LTC	0-0408942	0765	1
NIBLACK CHARLES K	COL	0-C174889	1054	3
NIBLACK JR CARLTON O	LTC	0-0296230	1161	1
NICCOLLS FRANCIS A	LTC	C-1796142	C361	1
NICCUM JOHN F	CPT	0-0959998	1061	1
NICCUM LEWIS L	CW2	W-2105726	C845	2
NICE HERBERT O	COL	0-0171524	C864	3
NICELY ROY E	CW3	W-2203261	0266	1
NICEWANDER WILLIAM A	MAJ	C-2202225	C866	1
NICHOL DEANE M	CPT	0-1324566	C746	2
NICHOL EFFIE B	MAJ	N-0788572	C963	1
NICHOL ERNEST R	COL	0-0262044	0165	3
NICHOL RAYMOND R	CPT	0-1039823	C862	1
NICHOLAS GEORGE D	LTC	0-1289472	0763	1
NICHOLAS GEORGE W	CW2	W-2141396	0667	2
NICHOLAS JESSE T	COL	C-0261951	1157	3
NICHOLAS JOSEPH	MAJ	C-1580088	C960	1
NICHOLAS JR JOHN F	LTC	0-0392659	0761	1
NICHOLAS JR ROBERT W	CPT	0-0525069	1057	1
NICHOLAS LANDON G	CPT	0-1290647	0748	1
NICHOLLS HAROLD C	COL	C-0317492	0265	3
NICHOLLS JOHN F	CPT	C-0141007	C459	3
NICHOLLS JR EARLE R	MAJ	0-1639871	C165	1
NICHOLLS MALCOLM A	CW3	W-2146119	0264	1
NICHOLS ARTHUR T	LTC	C-0291581	0167	3
NICHOLS BENNIE B	LTC	0-2017888	0967	1
NICHOLS BRYANT L	LTC	0-1303765	C464	1
NICHOLS BYRON D	MAJ	C-1928037	0167	1

NAME	GRADE	SVC NO	DATE RET MO YR	RET CODE
NICHOLS CARNIE F	WO1	W-2115173	0750	1
NICHOLS CHESTER A	COL	0-0255671	0160	1
NICHOLS CHESTER W	LTC	0-0229776	0165	3
NICHOLS DEAN M	1LT	0-1018444	0246	2
NICHOLS EDWIN O	LTC	0-0309796	1063	1
NICHOLS ERNEST A	CPT	0-15741C8	0664	1
NICHOLS FLOY L	CPT	0-0239663	1065	3
NICHOLS FRANCIS L	CPT	0-0222946	0860	3
NICHOLS FRANK	CPT	0-0497456	0447	1
NICHOLS FRANKLIN L	MAJ	C-1081828	1166	1
NICHOLS FREDERIC H	COL	0-0155985	0355	3
NICHOLS FREDERICK	LTC	0-0507780	0363	1
NICHOLS GAYLE H	LTC	0-0321348	0459	3
NICHOLS HENRY C	MAJ	0-0186169	0155	3
NICHOLS HERBERT A	2LT	0-1688282	1054	1
NICHOLS HERSHEL R	MAJ	0-0576895	0666	1
NICHOLS JAMES A	COL	0-0224989	1058	1
NICHOLS JAMES A	CW3	W-2147255	0361	1
NICHOLS JASPER W	MAJ	0-0151391	1150	3
NICHOLS JOHN A	CPT	0-0353254	0444	2
NICHOLS JOHN H	COL	0-0336909	0465	3
NICHOLS JOHN H	MAJ	C-1554791	0447	2
NICHOLS JOHN L	LTC	0-0496317	0463	1
NICHOLS JOHN M	CW3	W-2208438	0866	1
NICHOLS JOHN W	MAJ	0-1798288	0556	2
NICHOLS JR ELIJAH E	2LT	0-1822440	0252	2
NICHOLS JR FRED Z	CPT	0-1040988	0447	2
NICHOLS JR JAMES R	MAJ	C-0270044	0667	3
NICHOLS LAWRENCE G	LTC	0-0450642	0561	2
NICHOLS LEON H	CW4	W-2142026	1164	1
NICHOLS LEONARD T	MAJ	0-0284865	0566	3
NICHOLS MARON J	CPT	0-0987710	1057	1
NICHOLS MAURICE L	1LT	0-0401659	0544	2
NICHOLS ORVIN N	COL	C-0358C54	0354	3
NICHOLS RALPH M	MAJ	C-2026804	0563	2
NICHOLS RICHARD D	1LT	0-164863C	0653	1
NICHOLS RICHARD T	COL	0-0206550	1155	1
NICHOLS ROBERT E	CPT	0-2263516	0764	1
NICHOLS ROBERT F	CW3	W-2203361	0565	1
NICHOLS ROBERT J	COL	0-0210064	1057	3
NICHOLS SR EARL T	CW2	W-2145331	0758	1
NICHOLS THEODORE J	1LT	0-1636876	0849	2
NICHOLS WALTER R	COL	C-0301532	1057	2
NICHOLS WALTER S	MAJ	0-1824073	0264	1
NICHOLS WALTER V	LTC	0-0481946	0566	1
NICHOLS WALTER W	MAJ	0-1172575	1265	1
NICHOLS WILLIAM C	LTC	0-1593750	0862	1
NICHOLS WILLIAM F	CPT	0-0379281	0447	1
NICHOLS WILLIAM G	LTC	0-1168393	1163	1
NICHOLS WILLIAM H	CPT	0-1882370	0267	1
NICHOLS WILLIAM V	COL	0-0908968	0862	1
NICHOLS WILLIS F	MAJ	0-0259789	0267	3
NICHOLS WOODROW E	LTC	0-0396953	0961	1
NICHOLSON ALFRED O	COL	0-0238561	0566	3
NICHOLSON ALVIN F	1LT	0-1285098	0944	1
NICHOLSON DAVID S	MAJ	0-164687C	0561	1
NICHOLSON ERNEST R	CPT	0-0394004	0862	1
NICHOLSON EUGENE C	LTC	0-0397766	1060	1
NICHOLSON FLORENCE C	LTC	L-0700205	0363	1
NICHOLSON FRANCIS L	CW3	W-2103261	0356	1
NICHOLSON FRANK A	MAJ	C-1040989	0961	1
NICHOLSON FRANKLIN W	MAJ	0-1286692	0850	1
NICHOLSON FRED E	COL	0-0185424	1158	3
NICHOLSON FREEMAN M	WO1	W-2122636	0951	1
NICHOLSON HARRY L	LTC	C-2055275	C866	1
NICHOLSON HENRY H	MAJ	C-0266814	C257	3
NICHOLSON JAMES G	1LT	0-1320770	0747	1
NICHOLSON JAMES L	LTC	0-0287171	0165	3
NICHOLSON JR S J	1LT	0-0437793	0846	2
NICHOLSON JR W R	CPT	0-1100269	C248	1
NICHOLSON KENNETH B	LTC	0-1043003	1061	1
NICHOLSON MALCOLM F	CW4	W-2122943	0859	1
NICHOLSON MILTON E	COL	C-0301539	0566	3
NICHOLSON NELSON C	1LT	0-1293457	0746	2
NICHOLSON RENAUD	CPT	0-0454309	1145	2

NAME	GRADE	SVC NO	DATE RET MO YR	RET CODE
NICHOLSON ROBERT H	COL	0-0182727	1149	3
NICHOLSON ROBERT V	CPT	0-0130040	0950	3
NICHOLSON THOMAS I	CPT	0-0481408	0244	2
NICHOLSON WILLIAM S	1LT	0-1300840	0546	1
NICKEL ALBERT W	COL	C-0408559	0561	1
NICKEL LOUIS F	COL	C-0200669	C646	2
NICKEL PAUL H	LTC	0-0499433	1154	1
NICKELL DENNIS C	MAJ	C-0523015	C448	1
NICKELL JOE	M G	0-0246192	0658	3
NICKELL WALLACE H	B G	0-0234267	1161	3
NICKELS DONALD R	LTC	0-1315353	C164	2
NICKELS ORVIN F	1LT	C-1179556	1045	2
NICKERSON GEORGE D	CW3	W-2150059	C764	1
NICKERSON GEORGE L	CW2	W-2151914	C561	1
NICKERSON MAXWELL E	COL	C-0249382	0665	3
NICKERSON OSGOOD A	COL	0-0168518	1052	1
NICKERSON WENDELL R	2LT	0-1825969	1044	2
NICKETAKIS GEORGE	1LT	0-1045862	C844	2
NICKEY SR RALPH	MAJ	C-1308850	C161	1
NICKLAS WILLIAM G	COL	0-0223346	0362	3
NICKLE FERN L	LTC	0-0254155	C864	3
NICKLES HERBERT L	MAJ	C-0248361	0762	3
NICKLIN BRYAN G	CW2	W-2211500	C563	1
NICKOLAISEN DARREL I	1LT	C-4006934	C157	2
NICKOLAUS HENRY F	LTC	0-0178532	0146	2
NICKOLI THOMAS R	1LT	0-2289829	C962	2
NICKROSE JOHN J	CW2	W-2104342	C648	1
NICKS BRYAN	MAJ	0-0246994	1056	3
NICKS CLIFFORD W	1LT	0-1298909	0248	2
NICKS FRANK I	MAJ	C-0318241	0346	2
NICKUS VINCENT	CW4	W-2142183	C659	1
NICOL WILLIAM D	CPT	0-1304935	C962	3
NICOLAI NORMAN A	COL	0-0199943	C751	3
NICOLAIT EUGENE B	2LT	0-1593132	C944	2
NICOLETIF ANGELO D	MAJ	C-2012340	C860	1
NICOLL JR HARRY A	LTC	0-1641625	C466	1
NICOLOSI AMEDEO A	MAJ	C-0291733	C258	1
NICOLSON DANIEL M	LTC	0-1063087	C367	1
NICOLSON JR W P	COL	0-0193326	0553	3
NIDA ORR L	MAJ	C-1595737	C363	1
NIDAY MARY D	2LT	N-0783723	0744	1
NIDEVER ELZA E	CW4	W-2002C85	C964	3
NIDOSITKO MICHAEL	MAJ	C-1824904	C661	1
NIERLING LOUIS H	LTC	0-0255605	C366	3
NIEBRUEGGE LYLE H	CPT	0-1933526	0265	1
NIEBUR CLARENCE H	LTC	0-0298333	C265	3
NIEC STANISLAW	LTC	0-C395006	0356	1
NIEDER SAMUEL	CPT	0-0393265	C844	2
NIEDERHAUSER ALBERT	1LT	C-0453684	1044	2
NIEDERMAYER WALTER T	LTC	0-1326209	C465	1
NIEDERNHOFER SADIE M	CPT	N-0728157	1046	1
NIEDORACH CHARLES A	1LT	0-1288782	1048	2
NIEDRICH WILLIAM V	LTC	0-1576443	0961	1
NIEHANS ALFRED A	CPT	0-0555610	0946	2
NIEHAUS GOLDIE A	2LT	N-0765083	1146	1
NIEHAUS SMITH S	CW3	W-2148804	C565	1
NIEHOFF ERNEST H	WO1	W-2153033	C165	2
NIELSEN ANDRES F	LTC	0-0233925	C254	3
NIELSEN ANDREW J	2LT	0-0131029	0249	3
NIELSEN BERNICE C	MAJ	N-0774998	1265	1
NIELSEN CARL E	MAJ	C-1334612	0564	1
NIELSEN CHARLES W	LTC	C-0254852	C854	1
NIELSEN EARL W	MAJ	0-1913220	0665	1
NIELSEN EDWARD V	CPT	0-1640775	1147	2
NIELSEN EMMA J	2LT	N-0732308	C443	1
NIELSEN GLENN Z	LTC	0-0383591	0759	3
NIELSEN HENRY M	MAJ	C-1321543	0163	1
NIELSEN HOLGER D	CPT	0-0212989	1163	3
NIELSEN HOWARD R	CW3	W-2144530	C263	1
NIELSEN JAMES J	LTC	0-1018858	C666	1
NIELSEN KAJ T G	CPT	0-0497369	0553	1
NIELSEN MAURICE D	MAJ	C-1590697	C561	1
NIELSEN NIEL W	1LT	0-1038078	0745	2
NIELSEN NORMAN I	CPT	0-1541006	0246	2
NIELSEN RALPH W	WO1	W-2123111	C246	2
NIELSEN RAY	LTC	0-1111271	0858	1
NIELSEN RAYMOND H	MAJ	0-0452119	0658	1
NIELSEN RICHARD W	1LT	0-1295761	0446	2
NIELSON CARREL R	1LT	0-2016525	0746	1
NIELSON DAVID J	COL	0-0135938	0855	3
NIELSON JAMES G	MAJ	0-1288283	0546	2
NIEMAN CHARLES H	CW3	W-2146084	0765	1
NIEMAN HERBERT A	LTC	0-0225026	1152	3
NIEMAN WALTER E	MAJ	C-0340822	1045	2
NIEMAND HENRY O	1LT	0-0141428	0251	3
NIEMCZURA BENNIE S	CW3	W-2152629	0263	1
NIEMCZYK PAUL M	CPT	0-2033069	0257	1
NIEMEN ANN N	1LT	N-0784316	0447	2
NIEMEYER CLARENCE A	1LT	0-0356362	1154	1
NIEMEYER NELSON F	MAJ	0-2263154	C762	2
NIEMI ELVIN F	MAJ	C-1046591	1157	2
NIEMI WILLIAM J	COL	0-0228905	0464	3
NIEMIRC BERNARD J	CPT	0-0309039	0745	2
NIEMZ ARTHUR W	LTC	0-0102747	1049	3
NIEMZ RICHARD F	COL	0-0274424	1163	3
NIER MARTIN L	MAJ	C-0973508	0963	1
NIERGARTH JOHN E	MAJ	0-1180646	0263	1
NIERMANN FRED W	LTC	0-0404666	0761	2
NIESSE JOHN L	LTC	0-0119109	0155	3
NIETSCH CLARENCE H	CPT	0-0488482	0549	1
NIEVES JOSE M	MAJ	C-0387465	1160	1
NIEVES RAUL	MAJ	C-2262193	0766	1
NIFFENEGGER CRA E	LTC	0-0324817	0166	3
NIFFENEGGER RALPH E	LTC	0-0033084	1060	1
NIFORD CHESTER R	1LT	0-0405829	1046	1
NIFORTH WARREN M	MAJ	0-1822819	0560	1
NIGALAN PEDRO	2LT	0-1896601	0151	1
NIGHTINGALE ROBERT L	CW3	W-2152682	0962	1
NIGHTINGALE WILLIAM	CW3	W-2203471	1164	1
NIGRO DOMINIC	CPT	0-0512492	1145	2
NIGRO THEODORE M	CPT	0-1548112	0246	2
NIHART GEORGE W	CPT	0-0983366	0962	1
NIKKEL DONALD A	1LT	0-1302176	1045	2
NIKKEL GEORGE W	LTC	C-0262219	0560	1
NIKSTAITIS WALTER C	2LT	0-1288942	0244	2
NILAND JACK N	LTC	C-1634185	0161	1
NILAND JR THOMAS J	1LT	0-1309955	0845	2
NILAYAN CARRIC V	MAJ	0-1896253	0662	1
NILES CHARLES E	COL	0-0217522	0958	3
NILES LELAND G	MAJ	C-0123054	1057	3
NILES LYLE E	CPT	C-1290294	0247	2
NILES ROBERT G	CPT	0-0451020	0960	1
NILL JACK G	CW3	W-2136633	0865	1
NILLES AL C	CPT	0-1173729	1161	2
NILO ALPHONSC	LTC	0-1103839	0263	1
NILSEN NILS	LTC	0-1534825	1061	1
NILSSON CHARLES J	LTC	0-0355419	0763	1
NIMITZ ERNEST H	MAJ	0-0175282	1060	3
NIMMER RAYMOND F	2LT	0-1797339	1144	2
NIMMERFROH RAYMOND J	MAJ	0-1341900	0261	1
NIMS HENRY M	MAJ	0-1120484	0864	1
NIN LUIS L	COL	0-0238367	0965	3
NIOLET JAMES W	MAJ	0-2288311	0463	1
NIPPER JAMES L	MAJ	C-1798603	0657	1
NIPPS THOMAS H	MAJ	0-1292450	0555	1
NISBET LEIGH M	COL	0-0162233	0157	3
NISBET ROY O	CPT	0-0386954	0261	1
NISBETT JAMES M	LTC	0-0222476	1156	3
NISBETT STUART L	MAJ	C-0373034	0665	3
NISEVICH STANLEY J	CW2	W-2147654	0858	1
NISEWANER RAYMOND E	LTC	C-0256357	1059	1
NISHIKAWA JAY K	CW2	W-2215160	0167	1
NISHIMURA THOMAS H	CW3	W-2133592	0662	1
NIST FRANK J	CPT	0-1295258	0556	1
NISKA CIVA R	MAJ	0-1105062	1060	1
NISLEY JOHN F	CW2	RW-2214852	0866	1
NISLEY RICHARD E	1LT	0-1316916	0445	2
NISSBLATT EDWARD	CW3	W-2146808	0957	1
NISSEN WALLACE F	LTC	0-0484133	0646	2
NISSENBAUM JAMES	CPT	0-0502503	0946	2
NITCH JAMES E	LTC	0-1040054	C666	1
NITKOSKI KAROL A	MAJ	C-0986228	0664	1
NITSCHE RICHARD E	CPT	0-1081294	0754	2
NITTISKIE JOSEPH N	CW3	W-2142654	1055	1
NITZ WILLIAM C	LTC	0-1542795	C464	1
NIVER LISLE H	LTC	0-0320157	C460	1
NIX DILLARD L	CPT	0-1735738	0656	2
NIX HENRY B	CW3	W-2143037	0161	1
NIX HENRY E	CW2	W-3150713	0467	1
NIX JAMES C	MAJ	C-2017577	0462	1
NIX JR JAMES H	LTC	0-1055927	C764	1
NIX ROBERT R	MAJ	C-1558891	0763	1
NIX WILLIAM M	1LT	0-1111811	C146	2
NIX WILLIAM T	CPT	0-0979237	0761	1
NIXDORF JAMES R	LTC	0-1335452	C966	1
NIXDORFF ROYCE G	LTC	C-0278100	0267	3
NIXON ALBERT M	WO1	W-2112358	C854	1
NIXON BRYAN W	MAJ	C-0220827	0756	3
NIXON DRURY M	LTC	0-0163512	C861	3
NIXON EWING M	MAJ	C-0381094	0446	2
NIXON GWINN H	LTC	0-0301543	C266	3
NIXON HUBERT A	MAJ	C-1924830	C467	1
NIXON JACK H	WO1	W-2143336	0457	1
NIXON JR VINCENT F	CW2	RW-2152165	1062	1
NIXON RAY A	COL	0-0290461	0462	1
NIZENSKI STANLEY F	CPT	0-1013899	1047	1
NOACK HAROLD R	LTC	0-C297033	C565	3
NOACK WILLIAM R	LTC	C-0244077	0463	3
NOAH EDWARD C	CW3	W-2148805	0165	1
NOAH EMERAL O	MAJ	C-1280961	C856	1
NOAH GHOLSTON N	1LT	0-1302043	1045	2
NOAH LEOPOLD S	2LT	0-1845631	0145	2
NOAKES RAY W	MAJ	0-1688283	1163	1
NOARC JOHN W	MAJ	C-1290114	0757	1
NOBILE JEANETTE M	1LT	N-0755980	0845	1
NOBLE CARTER	1LT	0-0440608	C845	2
NOBLE CHARLES L	CW2	W-2209468	1264	1
NOBLE CURTIS A	COL	C-0178886	0547	2
NOBLE DAVID H	CPT	0-2019072	0161	1
NOBLE EDNA L	CPT	N-0795541	1160	2
NOBLE HAZEL P	MAJ	L-0503105	1162	1
NOBLE HENRY J	LTC	C-0286680	1266	3
NOBLE HOWARD T	MAJ	C-0225240	C450	3
NOBLE JAMES W	CPT	0-1921743	0252	1
NOBLE JR HENRY P	LTC	0-0260725	C267	3
NOBLE KENNETH L	COL	0-0360235	C364	3
NOBLE MARVIN B	CPT	0-0420085	0246	2
NOBLE MYRTLE E	2LT	N-0729562	1144	1
NOBLE NATHAN M	COL	0-0326658	C566	3
NOBLE ROYCE J	COL	0-0220702	C857	3
NOBLE RUFUS B	WO1	W-2146266	1051	2
NOBLE RUSL R	CPT	0-0464298	C145	2
NOBLE SPENCER C	MAJ	C-0242925	C354	3
NOBLE THEODORE R	MAJ	C-0977561	0963	1
NOBLE WILLIAM H	LTC	0-1176146	C767	1
NOBLES BOB T	LTC	0-0959325	C567	1
NOBLES CLARENCE G	CW2	W-2206418	1263	1
NOBLES GERRY	CW4	W-2108957	C756	1
NOBLES JAMES L	MAJ	C-0327751	C667	3
NOBLES JR LAWRENCE F	MAJ	C-2020192	C763	1
NOBOA JR JUAN	COL	0-0191260	0462	3
NOBUNAGA TADASHI	CW3	W-2144422	C266	1
NOCELLA ROCCO J	1LT	0-0522871	0445	2
NOCH CLIFFORD J	1LT	0-1544967	C646	2
NODDER WILLIAM R	LTC	0-0254683	C767	3
NODDINGS FREDERICK	MAJ	C-2262179	1161	1
NODEN ROGER H	CPT	0-0521994	C347	2
NOE JR ROBERT S	MAJ	C-1945441	0460	2
NOE LAWRENCE J	MAJ	0-2050107	1060	1
NOECKER LEWIS R	MAJ	C-0373027	C467	3
NOEL ALBERT E	CPT	0-0268428	0544	2
NOEL CHESLEY J	LTC	0-1102889	0465	2
NOEL EARL E	LTC	C-0331119	C161	1
NOEL ELIZABETH	2LT	N-0730743	C845	1
NOEL FRED V	LTC	0-0418493	1060	1
NOEL JAMES O B	LTC	C-0170995	1055	3
NOEL JOSEPH W R	CPT	0-1926670	1163	1
NOEL JR CLAUDE B	WO1	W-2119293	1145	2
NOEL LOUIS A	MAJ	0-1589408	1054	1
NOEL MAE H	1LT	N-0786721	0749	1
NOEL MARSHALL E	MAJ	C-2033665	0264	1
NOEL WRAY H	LTC	C-0319848	1148	2
NOELL CHARLES E	LTC	0-0962507	1160	1
NOESGES THOMAS M	1LT	0-2056715	1147	2
NOETH JOHN A	CW4	W-2136712	0966	1
NOFTE MONTELL S	CPT	0-0528492	0745	2
NOFTZ GEORGE P	1LT	0-1559109	0251	2
NOFZIGER JAMES C	1LT	0-0525039	0847	2
NOGAR EDMOND J	LTC	0-0495818	0460	1
NOGAY EDWARD	1LT	0-1018368	0247	1
NOGGLE MYRL K	LTC	0-1287572	0765	1
NOGUERA IGNACIO	2LT	0-1949422	1045	2
NOGUERA JOSE R	MAJ	C-1947785	1163	1
NOKES JAMES C	CW3	W-2141645	1059	1
NOKES JR ARTHUR J	CW2	W-2210483	0962	1
NOKES LEWIS H	MAJ	C-0505901	1046	1
NOLAN CHARLES H	COL	0-0172210	1056	3
NOLAN CONWAY G	CPT	0-1015766	0155	2
NOLAN DANIEL B	CPT	0-1322861	0747	2
NOLAN DONALD J	CPT	C-0486687	1145	2
NOLAN EDWARD T	CW3	W-2148950	0662	1
NOLAN FRANCIS A	MAJ	0-0339447	0947	2
NOLAN FRANCIS J	CPT	0-1318921	1047	1
NOLAN JOHN E	LTC	0-0335793	0563	1
NOLAN JOHN R	LTC	0-1590081	1065	1
NOLAN JR JOHN F	MAJ	0-1598753	0861	1
NOLAN JR MAURICE J	MAJ	C-1184914	0266	1
NOLAN JR THOMAS F	1LT	0-1825434	0545	2
NOLAN LAWRENCE F	MAJ	C-0955590	1060	1
NOLAN PAUL H	LTC	0-1593137	0561	1
NOLAN RICHARD J	LTC	0-1166797	0463	1
NOLAN THOMAS J	LTC	0-0364508	0465	1
NOLAN WALTER H	MAJ	0-0127776	0-50	3
NOLAN WILLIAM A	LTC	0-0910225	0762	3
NOLAN WILLIAM F	CW2	W-2148018	0961	1
NOLAN WILLIAM H	1LT	0-1306311	0746	2
NOLAN WILLIAM J	2LT	0-0373221	0442	2
NOLAN WILLIAM J	MAJ	C-1168845	1059	1
NOLAND ALLEN K	MAJ	C-1685702	1064	1
NOLAND AUGUSTUS T	LTC	0-0419301	1160	1
NOLAND CLIFTON M	LTC	0-1171300	0266	2
NOLAND HORACE V	LTC	0-0246951	0866	3
NOLAND LOREN D	CW4	W-2143951	0367	1
NOLAND VERNON	MAJ	0-0889176	0560	1
NOLEN BOB H	CPT	0-0483787	0745	2
NOLEN CALVIN E	LTC	0-0911016	0866	3
NOLEN CHARLES A	MAJ	0-1173730	0958	1
NOLEN CHARLES W	LTC	0-0394001	1162	1
NOLEN GEORGE M	COL	0-0482477	1054	1
NOLEN NEIL D	LTC	0-0281918	0660	1
NOLEN TITUS R	CW2	W-2145474	0761	1
NOLF JR JAMES H	CPT	0-1303933	1146	1
NOLFO LOUIS A	COL	0-0279538	0563	3
NOLIN ALBERT R	MAJ	0-0139722	1057	3
NOLKER WILLIAM F	MAJ	0-1650677	0567	1
NOLL ELOISE A	2LT	N-0769557	1046	1
NOLL JR JOHN V	MAJ	0-0081095	0566	1
NOLL WILLARD J	CPT	0-1312437	0547	1
NOLLEN FREDERICK	MAJ	0-0502277	1154	1
NOLLENBERGER ROBERT	LTC	0-1299093	0965	1
NOLLER WALTER H	LTC	0-0203465	0659	3
NOLLETTE FRANCIS C	MAJ	0-2262457	0663	1
NOLLKAMPER RALPH W	1LT	0-0338917	1045	2
NOLT ROY E	MAJ	C-0966601	0862	1
NOLTE HANS F	CW4	W-2144793	1166	1
NOLTE JOHN F	LTC	0-0145130	0648	3
NOLTE JR HENRY A	LTC	0-1288602	0167	1
NOLTE LAWRENCE W	COL	0-0239064	1065	3
NOLTEN EVERT	MAJ	0-1284560	0353	1
NOLTENSMEYER M H	CPT	0-0418770	0846	1

NAME	GRADE	SVC NO	DATE RET MO YR	RET CODE
NOLTING JOHN P	LTC	0-0261255	0366	3
NOLTING PAULA J	MAJ	N-0742958	0646	1
NONEMAKER AUBREY G	1LT	0-0412635	C344	2
NONES BENITO D	CPT	0-0282303	C949	1
NONES JR ROBERT H	COL	C-0145131	C648	3
NONTE JR GEORGE C	MAJ	0-1688654	0764	1
NOON JR THEODORE W	CPT	0-1285480	C146	2
NOON SAMUEL H	1LT	0-1319535	C446	2
NOONAN CHARLES J	CPT	0-1292048	C848	2
NOONAN CHARLES J	MAJ	C-1946822	C865	1
NOONAN EDWARD J	MAJ	0-2032067	C963	1
NOONAN FRANCIS J	CPT	0-0353778	0446	2
NOONAN GEORGE S	1LT	0-1285280	0851	2
NOONAN THOMAS F	CPT	C-1309388	C147	2
NOONAN THOMAS J	LTC	C-0251586	1061	3
NOONS EDWARD J	COL	0-0260289	0452	3
NORAT ANGEL R	CPT	0-1924125	0263	1
NORAT DOMINGO	1LT	0-0452010	0956	1
NORBERG ERNEST L	LTC	0-0104225	C-49	3
NORBERG JOHN H	LTC	0-0461338	C263	3
NORBERG SHERWOOD M	1LT	C-1324436	C246	2
NORBUT ALEX J	MAJ	0-0394756	C644	2
NORCROSS ELLSWORTH	CW2	W-2146388	C559	1
NORCROSS FERNANDO T	COL	0-0173258	C352	3
NORCROSS ORION	LTC	0-0189875	C655	3
NORCROSS WILLIAM H	MAJ	C-1282073	1162	1
NORD EDGAR R	1LT	0-1300365	C146	2
NORDEAN MAURICE E	1LT	C-2055456	1146	2
NORDELL CHARLES A	MAJ	C-0413756	C447	1
NORDELL ELMER	MAJ	0-1301867	C960	1
NORDGREN EDWIN J	CW2	W-2115781	0552	1
NORDGREN KARL E	COL	0-0264143	C465	3
NORDIN JAMES T	CW3	W-2148046	0865	1
NORDIN WILLIAM J	MAJ	0-0498240	0754	1
NORDLING JOHN H	MAJ	0-1013786	1265	1
NORDLINGER LEROY F	CW3	W-2144498	0862	1
NORDLINGER STEPHEN L	COL	0-0201113	0358	3
NORDLUND HOWARD D	CW3	W-2147916	0861	1
NORDLUND KEITH L	LTC	0-1288783	0662	1
NORDMANN BERNARD J	LTC	0-0367194	C964	1
NORDMANN FRED M	1LT	0-0353672	C142	2
NORDMANN OLAF	CPT	0-1825435	C154	1
NORDQUIST HARRY O V	CPT	0-0170435	1152	3
NORDSTROM ARTHUR H	COL	0-0228068	C357	3
NORDSTROM CARL T	COL	0-0167942	0450	3
NORDSTROM MAURICE O	LTC	C-0901110	C148	1
NORDWELL ALFRED W	LTC	0-0104324	C648	3
NORDYKE DALTON L	LTC	0-0450377	C557	1
NORDYKE HERBERT F	CW2	W-2214588	C866	1
NOREEN EUGENE L	LTC	0-0453147	0361	1
NORELIUS EMIL F	COL	0-0217964	0648	3
NOREN WILLIAM L	MAJ	0-2028731	0965	1
NORFLEET WILLIAM J	COL	C-0262071	C845	2
NORGARD CARL E	CW3	W-2143952	1159	1
NORLEY EARL M	CPT	0-0359354	C463	3
NORLIN JAMES E	COL	0-0237414	1150	3
NORLING MALCOLM R	MAJ	0-1042127	1060	1
NORLING OSCAR S	CPT	C-0278035	C354	3
NORMAN ABRAHAM	COL	C-0268570	0861	3
NORMAN AUSTIN H	LTC	0-1587499	C461	1
NORMAN BERKIE E	MAJ	0-1885193	C867	1
NORMAN CHARLES J	COL	0-0217653	0154	1
NORMAN EARLE T	COL	0-0249315	C462	3
NORMAN FRED W	2LT	0-1004387	0545	2
NORMAN GENE L	2LT	0-1327973	C439	2
NORMAN HENRY A	MAJ	C-1182211	C862	1
NORMAN HENRY R	LTC	0-0507594	C946	2
NORMAN HUGH W	MAJ	C-0970802	0267	1
NORMAN JACK J	MAJ	C-1016804	0463	1
NORMAN JAMES C	CW4	W-2113308	0559	1
NORMAN JAMES O	LTC	C-1585975	C166	2
NORMAN JAMES R	1LT	0-1184558	C758	1
NORMAN JANET H	2LT	N-0703000	054C	1
NORMAN JOHN	MAJ	C-1651491	0261	1
NORMAN JOHN A	LTC	0-0288753	0666	3
NORMAN JR GEORGE S	LTC	0-1312042	0862	1
NORMAN LEWIS E	LTC	0-1298108	0662	1
NORMAN MEADE B	LTC	0-0234471	1062	1
NORMAN OLIVER V	MAJ	C-1178274	0960	1
NORMAN RAYMOND	CPT	0-0967107	0262	2
NORMAN RICHARD L	CW2	W-2212429	0567	1
NORMAN ROBERT A	COL	0-0404481	0661	1
NORMAN ROBERT T	COL	0-0246528	1266	3
NORMAN THOMAS G	MAJ	0-0502019	0959	1
NORMAN WILLIAM L	CPT	0-0199023	0563	3
NORMAN WILLIAM S	LTC	0-0511716	1059	1
NORMAN WILLIAM T	LTC	C-0285495	0862	3
NORMAND JR FELIX A	CW2	W-2207529	0960	1
NORMANDIN LOUIS A	CW3	W-2209176	1266	1
NORMINGTON LEONARD R	CW3	W-2152977	0465	1
NORQUIST SAMUEL G	CPT	0-0441267	0947	2
NORQUIST STANLEY E	CW4	W-2112555	0759	2
NORRED LLOYD H	MAJ	C-1100704	0353	1
NORRELL LUCIAN H	1LT	0-1296891	0645	2
NORRGARD WARREN J	CW2	W-2149979	0463	1
NORRICK GORDON D	1LT	0-1533158	1264	1
NORRIS ALBERT M	CPT	0-1303012	0447	2
NORRIS ARTHUR H	CPT	0-0174541	0648	3
NORRIS BERGERON J	CW3	W-2152712	0762	1
NORRIS CHARLES A	LTC	0-0498484	0265	3
NORRIS GEORGE W	CPT	0-0973571	1161	1
NORRIS HARRY R	LTC	0-0391842	0965	1
NORRIS HUGH H	LTC	0-0259805	0567	3
NORRIS IDA M	1LT	N-0730306	0345	1
NORRIS JOHN C	LTC	0-048304C	0962	1
NORRIS JOHN G	MAJ	C-0978859	1061	1
NORRIS JOHN L	CPT	0-0513369	0946	1
NORRIS JR JOHN M	LTC	0-1825876	0767	1
NORRIS JR RAYMOND C	CW2	W-2210112	0365	1
NORRIS KATHRYN N	2LT	N-0760871	0744	1
NORRIS LOUIS	2LT	0-1913868	0634	1
NORRIS LYNN W	LTC	0-1545772	0161	2
NORRIS MILTON R	CPT	0-0516067	0846	2
NORRIS OSCAR J	CPT	0-0263231	0745	2
NORRIS OTIS L	COL	0-0358917	0264	3
NORRIS PAUL T	COL	0-0292587	0260	1
NORRIS RICHARD M	MAJ	C-0264917	0645	1
NORRIS RIDLEY L	CW3	W-2147075	0560	1
NORRIS SAMUEL D	MAJ	0-1999801	1060	1
NORRIS WALTER C	MAJ	C-1038448	0663	1
NORRIS WALTZ W	CPT	0-0103697	114N	2
NORRIS WILLARD	COL	0-0367155	0165	1
NORRIS WILLIAM L	LTC	0-1172200	0261	1
NORRISH VERNON M	LTC	0-022576C	0664	3
NORSWORTHY BERNARD A	LTC	C-0187230	1054	3
NORTH EDGAR	LTC	0-1324284	1167	1
NORTH EVERETT K	MAJ	C-1576446	0860	1
NORTH JIMMIE	1LT	0-1323164	1045	2
NORTH JOHN F	CW3	W-2151857	1060	1
NORTH JOHN P	COL	C-0230783	0261	3
NORTH JOHN W	1LT	0-1290463	0945	2
NORTH JR CARL E	MAJ	C-0975621	0963	1
NORTH ROBERT E	CPT	0-1642430	0364	1
NORTH THOMAS M	2LT	0-1305972	0445	2
NORTHAM EDWARD A	MAJ	0-0149429	0857	3
NORTHAM FLOYD A	CW3	W-2153659	0464	1
NORTHAM HOWARD L	CPT	0-0242440	1264	3
NORTHCUTT JACK E	LTC	0-1015944	0962	1
NORTHEY WILBERT	WO1	W-2114768		2
NORTHFIELD IVAN H	COL	0-0127979	0551	3
NORTHRIDGE BEN J	COL	0-0275C42	1263	3
NORTHROP ALLEN C	LTC	0-1107CC0	1165	1
NORTHROP HENRY H	MAJ	C-0813561	1262	1
NORTHROP LEROY M	LTC	0-0454555	0758	1
NORTHROP MARY E	LTC	N-0701782	0346	1
NORTHROP THOMAS E	LTC	0-0322658	0467	3
NORTHRUP HARRY E	LTC	0-0275026	0159	2
NORTHRUP HOBART E	COL	0-0185047	0454	1
NORTHRUP JOSEPH	MAJ	0-2283946	1160	1
NORTHRUP ROBERT C	MAJ	C-1920360	C166	1
NORTHUP HARRISON	CPT	0-0127154	C153	3
NORTON ALLYN S	1LT	0-0285801	1044	2
NORTON ARTHUR D	MAJ	C-0161198	1052	3
NORTON CLARK L	MAJ	0-1797654	1160	1
NORTON CLIFFORD J	MAJ	0-1031430	C261	1
NORTON CURTIS C	MAJ	C-1017001	1057	1
NORTON EDWIN W	LTC	C-0497465	C764	3
NORTON EUGENE E	MAJ	C-2204169	0265	1
NORTON FRED L	CPT	0-0333142	0246	2
NORTON GRADY H	MAJ	0-1016338	1262	1
NORTON JEAN G	LTC	0-0336169	C247	2
NORTON JERRY J	MAJ	0-1951664	C166	1
NORTON JOHN D	1LT	C-0541186	0844	2
NORTON JOHN D	CW2	W-2147431	C661	1
NORTON JOHN E	MAJ	0-0476615	C844	1
NORTON JOHN H	LTC	0-1041210	C361	1
NORTON JOHN W	LTC	0-1950025	C767	1
NORTON JOHN W R	COL	0-0287167	0758	3
NORTON JR ELLIOTT M	LTC	C-0374886	0361	1
NORTON JR MAXFIELD W	CPT	C-0394857	C246	2
NORTON LEROY P	CW4	W-2115448	1057	1
NORTON LESTER C	1LT	0-1325923	C346	2
NORTON MATTHEW V	CPT	C-0463342	C645	2
NORTON MICHAEL E	LTC	0-0370657	C161	3
NORTON ROBERT H	1LT	0-1913871	0446	1
NORTON ROBERT S	LTC	C-0217435	C648	3
NORTON WILLIAM	2LT	0-1646457	C744	2
NORTON WILLIAM D	LTC	0-0337828	C266	3
NORTON WILLIE B	CW3	W-2151145	C863	1
NORUK HAROLD A	1LT	0-1319324	1052	1
NORUM ELMER C	MAJ	C-1338121	0363	1
NORUM MILTON G	LTC	C-0357867	0457	1
NORVE LESTER H	1LT	C-1998651	1151	1
NORVELL ROY E	COL	0-0265029	0962	3
NORVIEL JOHN W	LTC	0-0194962	0759	1
NORVILLE ATKINS W	LTC	0-0480574	1054	1
NORWOOD ANTHONY F	CPT	C-1573482	C746	1
NORWOOD AUBURN	MAJ	C-0992928	0265	1
NORWOOD EARL	CW2	W-2142110	0254	1
NORWOOD JAMES W	LTC	C-1300071	C361	1
NORWOOD JR ARTHUR H	LTC	0-0299763	066C	1
NORWOOD LUTHER M	CW2	W-2150024	0961	1
NORWOOD RAY A	CW3	W-2149675	C861	1
NOSSAL LEWIS R	MAJ	C-0975624	1163	1
NOSSAMAN CALVIN W	MAJ	C-1879074	1167	1
NOSSOV MORRIS A	CPT	0-0380351	C545	2
NOSUN ALBERT H	B G	0-0264243	1163	3
NOTARO MARIANNE F	1LT	L-0500328	1046	2
NOTGRASS CHARLES D	LTC	0-0435237	C944	2
NOTGRASS JR JAMES C	LTC	0-1290649	C761	1
NOTHDURFT ROBERT H	LTC	C-163640L	0765	1
NOTT CARTER	1LT	0-1052502	1045	2
NOTTINGHAM COLBY M	CW3	W-2148876	0466	1
NOTTROOT RUDOLPH F	LTC	C-1560557	C866	1
NOTTROTT CARL G	LTC	0-0349034	1263	3
NOURSE KEITH C	LTC	0-128330C	C564	1
NOVACK DAVID	CPT	0-1298647	0447	2
NOVACK FELIX	COL	0-0252669	C851	1
NOVACK FRANCIS L	MAJ	C-1289122	C858	1
NOVACK JOHN A	LTC	0-1004389	C767	1
NOVACK LOUIS	CPT	0-0490355	C645	2
NOVAK ANDREW J	CPT	0-2262622	0361	1
NOVAK FRANK	LTC	C-0403221	C258	1
NOVAK FRANK W	LTC	0-0329558	C454	1
NOVAK GEORGE A	LTC	0-0209030	C556	3
NOVAK LEONARD J	LTC	0-1018372	C663	1
NOVAK MARION H	1LT	0-1016283	1045	2
NOVAK ROBERT A	1LT	0-1335040	C252	1
NOVAK THEODORE W	MAJ	C-0308196	0546	2
NOVAK WALTER S	CPT	C-0465725	C246	2
NOVAKY FRANK S	MAJ	C-2011181	0261	1
NOVARO JOSEPH A	LTC	0-0230743	0165	3
NOVASCONE MARJORIE F	1LT	N-0731433	C646	1
NOVELLINO JOSEPH J	MAJ	0-0339890	C140	2
NOVEY ERNEST F	COL	0-0240017	L051	3
NOVGRCO IRVING	LTC	0-1643177	0565	1
NOVICK JOHNNY T	LTC	0-1043185	0166	1
NOVINSKI CLEMENT J	2LT	0-202747C	0557	2
NOVIS CARMIN C	LTC	0-0310236	1147	2
NOVITT NORTON T	2LT	0-1574303	0745	2
NOVO AMERICO L	2LT	0-1949877	0745	2
NOVOSAC JERRY J	MAJ	0-0964576	1065	1
NOVOSAC ROMAN R	CPT	0-1300366	0747	2
NOVOSEL NICHOLAS	COL	0-0393387	0760	1
NOVOTNEY JOSEPH W	MAJ	C-1011200	0457	1
NOVOTNY ARCHIE A	CPT	0-0451518	0258	1
NOVOTNY FRANK C	LTC	C-0258898	0266	3
NOVOTNY REGINA A	MAJ	N-0762623	1064	1
NOWACK EUGENE E	1LT	0-4038357	0159	2
NOWAK SYLVESTER	LTC	0-2033129	0866	1
NOWASKI JOE L	1LT	0-C564533	0951	1
NOWELL ALVIN H	1LT	0-0236223	0137	1
NOWELL CLAUDE R	MAJ	0-0232276	1054	3
NOWELL III JOHN M	MAJ	0-1995314	0461	2
NOWELL JAMES W	MAJ	0-1018718	0557	1
NOWELL JR TOM E	LTC	0-0347948	0462	1
NOWELL WILLIAM D	CW3	W-2109741	0157	1
NOWERS GEORGE C	LTC	C-1035952	0361	1
NOWICK JOE	LTC	0-0359995	C560	1
NOWICKI ALBERT L	LTC	0-0314330	0367	3
NOWICKI JAMES J	LTC	0-1303014	0462	2
NOWICKI JOSEPH M	MAJ	0-1300516	0756	2
NOWICKI JR JOHN S	CW3	RW-2209596	0167	1
NOWICKI WILLIAM J	CW2	W-2146932	0355	1
NOWILL WILLIAM K	CPT	C-0475118	0647	1
NOWINSKI STANLEY M	LTC	0-1288426	0761	1
NOWLAND LEE J	LTC	0-0472339	0461	1
NOWLIN EDGAR E	CW3	W-2151987	0962	1
NOWLIN GEORGE A	1LT	0-0371646	0845	2
NOWLIN IRVIN J	COL	C-0294302	0563	3
NOWLIN KATHERINE	MAJ	L-0800676	0358	2
NOWLIN OTIS C	CPT	0-2005357	1159	1
NOWLIN STANLEY E	MAJ	0-2005317	0957	1
NOWOSLAWSKY WALTER F	CW2	W-2126921	1144	2
NOXON JAMES A	LTC	0-0165962	0850	3
NOXON WILLARD M	1LT	C-0887542	0546	2
NOYES ALBERT L	CPT	0-1589412	0656	1
NOYES FRANK E	COL	0-0186536	0156	3
NOYES JR HARRISON C	1LT	0-0548466	1046	2
NOYES JR SHERMAN F	LTC	0-1285986	1060	1
NOYES ROBERT H	LTC	0-0910227	0165	3
NOYES STEPHEN D	LTC	0-1039492	1263	1
NOYES WILFRED	CW2	W-2117125	0559	1
NUGE HARRY R	CPT	0-0212210	1157	3
NUCKELS CLIFFORD R	CW2	W-2152181	1162	1
NUCKOLLS DRUSILLA N	CPT	N-0792603	0758	2
NUCKOLLS LEONARD A	LTC	0-1110691	0262	1
NUCKOLS GEORGE W	MAJ	C-1176754	0859	1
NUCKOLS MILTON F	MAJ	C-0260775	C347	2
NUERENBERG KARL A	CPT	0-0530981	0346	2
NUGENT AMBROSE H	LTC	0-0387162	0460	1
NUGENT CATHERINE	1LT	N-0724006	1044	1
NUGENT GEORGE L	LTC	0-1650259	1262	1
NUGENT III ROBERT P	LTC	0-028265C	0167	1
NUGENT JOHN	MAJ	0-1040992	0856	1
NUGENT JOHN J	LTC	0-0908501	1066	3
NUGENT JOHN P	CW2	W-2142111	1159	1
NUGENT MICHAEL	LTC	0-1292572	0263	1
NUGENT OLAN	MAJ	0-0979307	0965	1
NUGENT REGEENA	1LT	N-0783325	0146	1
NUGENT WILLIAM F	1LT	0-1297238	0146	2
NULL CARROLL H	2LT	0-0960105	0751	1
NULTA MAURICE C	LTC	0-15743C4	0455	2
NULTON HENRY G	M G	0-0205635	0161	3
NUNES RICHARD E	COL	0-0360390	0762	1
NUNEZ JR ROBERT F	MAJ	0-0288914	1053	3
NUNGESSER WILLIAM C	MAJ	C-0263089	0265	3
NUNLEY CHESLEY C	LTC	0-1327650	0965	1
NUNLEY ROY M	MAJ	0-0997867	0267	1
NUNN CARROLL L	LTC	0-1289787	0658	1

NAME	GRADE	SVC NO	DATE RET MO YR	RET CODE
NUNN CHARLES F	LTC	0-1169675	1059	1
NUNN CLIFFORD T	2LT	0-1055689	1044	2
NUNN ERNEST W	MAJ	C-1030275	C857	1
NUNN JOHN T	MAJ	0-2017269	0561	1
NUNN JR WILLIAM A	COL	0-0231161	C359	1
NUNN LESLIE L	COL	C-0213016	1058	3
NUNN WALTER A	CW3	W-2203279	C659	1
NUNN WILLIAM J	CPT	0-1170121	1045	2
NUNNALLY JR W B	CPT	0-1105713	C446	2
NUNNALLY OTIS	CW3	W-2146039	0861	1
NUNNELLEY JR JAMES R	CPT	0-0305351	C459	1
NUNVAR FRANCIS E	LTC	C-0184367	C860	3
NUQUI DANIEL	2LT	0-1896971	C950	1
NUQUI RENE B	1LT	0-1896590	1061	2
NURNEY BERNARD T	CW2	W-2152978	C359	1
NURSS RICHARD E	CPT	0-0888533	0160	1
NUSBAUM CHARLES S	LTC	C-0337056	0261	2
NUSBAUM JACK B	1LT	0-1315095	1045	2
NUSE GEORGE H	MAJ	C-1333252	C663	2
NUSSBAUM WILLIAM V	MAJ	0-1582015	C662	1
NUSSDORFER ALFRED F	MAJ	0-0262874	C864	3
NUSSDORFER JOHN H	COL	0-0182251	0646	2
NUSSE DANIEL T	CPT	0-1822180	C960	1
NUSSER WILLIAM A	COL	C-0369320	C962	1
NUTLEY VICTOR L	LTC	0-0155848	0952	3
NUTT CECIL E	MAJ	C-1648938	C457	1
NUTT JOHN F	COL	0-045291C	C763	1
NUTTER LLOYD B	CPT	0-0255667	C544	2
NUTTER ROBERT L	MAJ	C-1014834	0760	2
NUTTING DANIEL C	COL	0-0216473	0563	3
NUTTING JR HARRY O	COL	0-0252609	1165	3
NUTTING LOWELL O	LTC	0-2045143	C564	1
NUWER JOHN E	LTC	0-0350002	0561	1
NUZIE SAMUEL B	MAJ	C-0500136	0546	2
NUZUM JOHN B	LTC	0-1114245	C764	1
NUZUM PAUL B	CW2	W-2114959	0848	1
NUZZO JOHN	2LT	0-1038252	0454	1
NUZZO JOSEPHINE	2LT	N-0753186	0546	1
NUZZOLO CHARLES A	CPT	0-0508897	C752	1
NYBURG WILLARD M	LTC	0-0221794	1061	1
NYE DOUGLAS B	CW3	W-2143038	C862	1
NYE MAURICE R	COL	C-0221014	0456	3
NYE STEPHEN G	LTC	0-0165599	0258	3
NYE WILLIAM F	COL	C-0163877	C648	3
NYEMASTER MARC	CW2	W-2150687	1063	1
NYENHUIS EDWARD J	LTC	0-0394053	C960	1
NYERS JAMES J	1LT	0-1307291	0348	1
NYGARD WILBUR A	MAJ	0-0991829	1262	1
NYGREN BURDETTE J	LTC	C-1184275	C767	1
NYHAN STANLEY L	LTC	0-2274644	0463	1
NYITRAY JOSEPH A	1LT	0-1289305	C544	2
NYLAND LAWRENCE E	CPT	0-1312208	C463	1
NYLANDER EVA	CPT	N-0756610	C647	1
NYMAN ROBERT A	2LT	0-C392892	C647	1
NYMAN WILLIAM M	MAJ	C-0964562	C862	1
NYQUIST ELBERT A	LTC	0-0384133	1150	1
NYSTROM ERNEST G	LTC	0-0213096	0551	3
NYSTROM JOSEPH B	2LT	0-1305298	1061	2
NYSTROM MARIAN A	2LT	N-0732245	0145	1
OAKES MILTON C	LTC	0-0283068	C764	3
OAKES THEODORE C	2LT	0-1288605	1044	2
OAKES WALTER H	LTC	C-0314048	0349	1
OAKES WILLIAM F	LTC	0-1052105	0662	1
OAKEY GEORGE J	LTC	0-1185244	0762	1
OAKLEY ALBERT R	MAJ	C-1797866	0663	1
OAKLEY CARL L	MAJ	0-1294179	0858	1
OAKLEY DONALD L	1LT	0-1175817	C549	2
OAKLEY JACK O	CPT	0-1799977	0456	1
OAKLEY RALPH W	COL	C-0183119	1055	3
OAKLEY WARD S	MAJ	C-1055408	1062	1
OAKNER MERVYN G	2LT	0-1948202	0945	1
OAKS ELDRED W	LTC	0-1844608	0462	1
OAKS THOMAS R F	MAJ	0-1055409	0366	2
OAKSFORD JR HOMER H	LTC	0-1289124	0461	1
OAS CLAYTON S	MAJ	C-1311345	1158	1

NAME	GRADE	SVC NO	DATE RET MO YR	RET CODE
OATES AGNES	1LT	N-0764536	1047	1
OATES CALVIN W	MAJ	0-0955543	0765	1
OATES CHARLES R	LTC	0-1047277	0263	1
OATES JR EDWARD F	CPT	0-1182671	0965	2
OATES OTIE F	MAJ	0-0208991	1054	3
OATES WALTER M	MAJ	0-0230982	0450	1
OATES WILLIAM A	MAJ	0-0346606	0450	1
OATES WILLIAM H	LTC	0-1548991	0661	1
OATIS ALICE S	1LT	N-078872C	0646	1
OATLEY CHARLES W	MAJ	0-0325489	0264	1
OATMAN ALFRED S	MAJ	0-1105068	1160	3
OATMAN CHESTER G	2LT	T-0003234	1047	2
OBAN NEMISIO	1LT	0-2030388	1047	2
OBANNON JAMES B	1LT	0-1293459	0346	2
OBANNON LLOYD W	CPT	0-0402325	0453	1
OBANNON ROBERT E	LTC	0-1282354	0466	1
OBARR HUGH A	CW3	W-2144207	0660	1
OBATA BENJAMIN T	LTC	0-2030779	1263	1
OBAUGH FREDERICK	CPT	0-1036658	0353	1
OBBINK JACK O	CPT	0-0405344	0646	2
OBEN JOHN H	LTC	0-0307705	0665	3
OBENAUF HOMER A	MAJ	0-0234985	0251	3
OBENOUR MERLE W	COL	0-0287515	0955	3
OBENOUR WILLIAM H	COL	0-0243089	0658	3
OBER THEODORE M	LTC	0-0908473	0263	3
OBER WILLIAM L	CW2	W-2117547	0251	2
OBERFELL GEORGE J	1LT	0-1299618	0745	2
OBERG ALICE I	CPT	N-0731530	0646	1
OBERG JOHN A	1LT	0-1301868	0845	2
OBERLANDER MAURICE I	1LT	0-1588779	0450	1
OBERLE EDWARD F	1LT	0-0408506	0861	2
OBERLE HENRY J	2LT	0-1557963	0345	2
OBERLIN BENJAMIN G	MAJ	0-0139739	1054	3
OBERLIN WILLIAM W	MAJ	0-0442039	0946	2
OBERMEIER CHARLES F	CW3	W-2148905	0363	1
OBERNDORFER ABBOTT	COL	0-0139706	0154	3
OBERSCHLAKE ALBERT F	CW3	W-2205388	1065	1
OBERSEIDER JOHN R C	CW3	W-2142597	0559	1
OBERST ARTHUR L	LTC	0-0215184	1151	3
OBERST MARY J	CPT	N-0702985	0947	1
OBERSTER HOWARD J	1LT	0-1287048	1059	1
OBERWEGNER MARION T	LTC	0-0300337	0562	1
OBETZ ROBIN C	MAJ	0-0500586	1044	2
OBITZ FREDERICK	LTC	0-1001422	1163	1
OBLACK ELMER F	CW2	W-2212609	0266	1
OBLEY WILLIAM M	MAJ	C-1287573	0164	1
OBLINGER FRANK D	CW2	W-2199547	0248	1
OBRANOVICH JOHN	MAJ	0-1591960	0957	1
OBRANOVICH PETE	WO1	W-214777C	0854	1
OBRASKY GEORGE H	COL	0-0202658	1046	2
OBREMSKI EGAN A	MAJ	0-0974715	1063	1
OBRIAN JR GEORGE R	CPT	0-1285100	1146	1
OBRIEN ALVIN E	CW3	W-2146185	0857	1
OBRIEN AMBROSE R	LTC	0-0382965	0559	2
OBRIEN CARLTON P	CPT	0-0538292	0447	2
OBRIEN CHARLES E	LTC	0-1108896	0962	1
OBRIEN DALE F	LTC	0-1108897	0263	1
OBRIEN DANIEL A	COL	0-0369366	0766	3
OBRIEN DAVID B	1LT	0-0481653	0845	2
OBRIEN EDWARD B	CPT	0-0491528	0855	1
OBRIEN EDWARD J	LTC	0-0812124	1262	1
OBRIEN EDWARD J	1LT	0-1575496	1043	2
OBRIEN EDWARD J	CPT	0-2043025	1046	2
OBRIEN EDWARD T	LTC	0-0236365	0567	3
OBRIEN EVERETT M	LTC	0-1285806	1162	1
OBRIEN FRANCIS R	1LT	0-0387615	1145	2
OBRIEN FRED E	MAJ	0-0969859	1060	1
OBRIEN FREDERICK	MAJ	0-0967332	0865	1
OBRIEN GERALD J	2LT	0-0479268	0445	2
OBRIEN HARRY J	COL	0-1040587	0366	1
OBRIEN HELEN J	CPT	N-0724558	0147	1
OBRIEN HENRY W	CW2	W-2146086	0956	1
OBRIEN ISABEL M	MAJ	N-0776728	1166	1
OBRIEN IVAN T	LTC	0-0358206	0263	1
OBRIEN JAMES E	LTC	0-1798505	0765	1

NAME	GRADE	SVC NO	DATE RET MO YR	RET CODE
OBRIEN JAMES J	LTC	0-1032380	0465	1
OBRIEN JOHN A	CW4	W-2116079	1158	1
OBRIEN JOHN D	MAJ	0-0139740	0257	3
OBRIEN JOHN J	CPT	0-0515793	1045	2
OBRIEN JOHN J	CPT	0-1105717	C455	2
OBRIEN JOHN J	CPT	0-1305100	C146	2
OBRIEN JOHN L	MAJ	C-1634187	C664	1
OBRIEN JOHN W	LTC	0-0209814	0661	3
OBRIEN JOSEPH C	CW4	W-2148241	0867	2
OBRIEN JOSEPH E	LTC	0-0995082	0463	1
OBRIEN JOSEPH F	LTC	0-0202717	C857	3
OBRIEN JOSEPH F	LTC	0-1578932	0662	1
OBRIEN JOSEPH L	CPT	0-0261393	C545	2
OBRIEN JOSEPH L	LTC	0-0293009	0758	1
OBRIEN JR GEORGE L	COL	0-0269746	1064	1
OBRIEN JR JOHN M	MAJ	C-0250413	0365	3
OBRIEN JR JOHN P	LTC	0-1641116	1167	1
OBRIEN LAURENCE A	LTC	0-040476C	0660	1
OBRIEN LEONARD C	LTC	0-1000057	C461	1
OBRIEN LYNN H	CPT	0-0297749	0248	1
OBRIEN MADELINE J	CPT	N-0722315	C848	1
OBRIEN MARRIN J	MAJ	0-1015807	0165	3
OBRIEN MARY ANN E	MAJ	N-0794306	0365	1
OBRIEN MARY E	MAJ	N-0723981	1162	1
OBRIEN MAXWELL A	B G	0-0295693	1150	3
OBRIEN MAYO M	CPT	0-0496487	1060	1
OBRIEN MICHAEL	1LT	0-1913900	1019	1
OBRIEN MICHAEL J	LTC	0-C482097	0654	2
OBRIEN MICHAEL L	LTC	0-0276680	0957	3
OBRIEN PATRICK C	MAJ	C-1111816	C861	1
OBRIEN PATRICK J	CPT	0-0227501	C463	3
OBRIEN PATRICK J	CPT	0-1041409	C744	2
OBRIEN RAYMOND F	1LT	0-2021285	0954	2
OBRIEN RAYMOND J	LTC	0-0411023	0363	1
OBRIEN RICHARD A	MAJ	C-0247995	C842	2
OBRIEN RICHARD C	MAJ	0-1922577	C164	1
OBRIEN RICHARD C	CPT	0-0970525	C363	1
OBRIEN ROBERT A	LTC	0-0569624	0762	2
OBRIEN ROBERT F	LTC	0-0330160	1060	1
OBRIEN ROBERT E	CPT	0-1306133	1147	2
OBRIEN ROBERT E	CPT	0-1316778	C347	2
OBRIEN ROBERT G	CPT	C-1697973	1046	2
OBRIEN ROBERT L	1LT	0-1316918	1045	2
OBRIEN ROGER J	CPT	0-1291157	1045	2
OBRIEN THOMAS	LTC	0-0919555	0467	3
OBRIEN THOMAS A	MAJ	C-1314374	C762	1
OBRIEN THOMAS J	CPT	0-1324473	0847	2
OBRIEN THOMAS L	MAJ	C-2021093	0766	1
OBRIEN TYRRELL W	CW3	W-2136038	C862	1
OBRIEN WALTER H	MAJ	C-0450539	0560	1
OBRIEN WILLIAM F	COL	0-0299919	0446	1
OBRIEN WILLIAM H	COL	0-0307803	1062	1
OBRIEN WILLIAM J	LTC	0-0301287	C867	3
OBRIEN WILLIAM J	LTC	0-0345945	0962	1
OBRIEN WILLIAM J	CPT	C-0439442	1046	2
OBRIEN WILLIAM J	LTC	0-1287223	C466	1
OBRIEN WILLIAM L	CPT	0-0404205	C445	2
OBRIEN WILLIAM M	COL	0-0303372	0146	2
OBRIEN WILLIAM M	CPT	0-0511815	C347	1
OBRIENE PATRICK E	CW2	W-2142259	1057	1
OBRIST ROBERT A	MAJ	C-0522367	C266	1
OBROCK JOHN C	CPT	C-0515676	0854	1
OBRYAN JR HARRY L	COL	0-0454879	0266	1
OBRYAN LARRY E	CPT	0-1304105	C947	1
OBRYAN RAPHAEL L	1LT	0-C493787	1049	1
OBRYAN RONALD I	LTC	0-1304936	0766	1
OBRYANT ALBERT H	1LT	0-18257C3	0146	1
OBRYANT CHARLES W	M G	0-0328896	1059	3
OBUCHOWSKI ALPHONSE	LTC	0-2047766	0662	1
OBURG JR HAROLD G	CPT	0-0348695	1164	1
OBYE CHARLES H	LTC	0-0119768	0854	3
OBYRNE THOMAS W	CW3	W-2145114	0659	1
OCALLAGHAN EDMUND J	LTC	C-1574305	C963	2
OCALLAGHAN ROBERT J	LTC	0-1101145	1060	1
OCAMPO ALFREDO	CPT	C-0984312	1062	1

NAME	GRADE	SVC NO	DATE RET MO YR	RET CODE
OCAMPO-EUSTAQUI	2LT	0-1896591	0555	1
OCARROLL MARY A	MAJ	N-0756727	0663	1
OCASEK MILES F	CPT	0-0499328	0445	2
OCHOJSKI B CHARLES	1LT	0-0416170	0945	2
OCHRAN EDWARD P	CPT	0-05008C9	1048	1
OCHS ADOLPH S	MAJ	0-0151353	0643	2
OCHS ISIDOR	MAJ	C-0311705	0144	2
OCHS JR ERVIN G	MAJ	0-1292049	1060	1
OCKER III HENRY	CW3	W-2151795	1165	1
OCKINGA HAROLD H	MAJ	0-0972815	0466	1
OCKULY EUGENE A	MAJ	0-0515877	0545	1
OCONNELL ANNETTE M	CPT	N-0805493	0555	2
OCONNELL BARTHOLOME	LTC	0-1176148	0464	1
OCONNELL DANIEL F	CPT	0-1533416	0844	2
OCONNELL EARL J	1LT	0-1548992	1044	2
OCONNELL EARLE R	1LT	0-0133146	0357	3
OCONNELL EDMUND W	CPT	0-1299619	0446	2
OCONNELL FRANK B	COL	0-0190132	0252	3
OCONNELL FRANK V	2LT	0-1051310	1043	2
OCONNELL GEORGE E	COL	0-0911785	0864	3
OCONNELL GERALD F	CW3	W-2147280	0862	1
OCONNELL JOHN	LTC	0-1171704	0-53	1
OCONNELL JOHN A	LTC	0-1003003	1065	1
OCONNELL JOSEPH A	LTC	0-1323469	0567	1
OCONNELL LAWRENCE O	CPT	0-1166148	0845	2
OCONNELL MARY C	MAJ	L-0115997	1065	3
OCONNELL PAUL R	LTC	0-1176455	C161	1
OCONNELL PHILLIP D	COL	0-0269526	1167	3
OCONNELL PHYLLIS A	2LT	N-0721193	1043	1
OCONNELL RICHARD C	COL	0-018243C	0152	3
OCONNELL ROY I	CW2	W-2147417	0259	1
OCONNELL THOMAS B	MAJ	0-2023688	0161	1
OCONNELL THOMAS M	1LT	0-1176456	1150	2
OCONNELL THOMAS P	MAJ	0-1000273	0366	1
OCONNELL THOMAS R	CPT	0-0538754	0247	2
OCONNELL WILLIAM	CPT	0-0468566	1047	1
OCONNELL WILLIAM H	LTC	0-0475922	0256	1
OCONNELL WILLIAM J	CPT	0-0344454	0346	2
OCONNELL WILLIAM J	CPT	0-1584690	0347	2
OCONNOR ALBERT R	CPT	0-0887710	1046	2
OCONNOR ANSON	MAJ	0-1998524	1054	1
OCONNOR BERNARD C	MAJ	0-0373574	0747	2
OCONNOR DANIEL J	MAJ	0-1639467	0656	1
OCONNOR DAVID J	CPT	0-0509431	0148	1
OCONNOR EMMET L	LTC	0-0270707	1161	1
OCONNOR EVERETT W	CW3	W-2150593	0566	1
OCONNOR FRANCIS B	MAJ	0-0301814	0547	1
OCONNOR FRANCIS E	1LT	0-1322945	0246	2
OCONNOR FRANCIS J	CPT	0-0386309	0961	1
OCONNOR FRANCIS J	2LT	0-042446C	0944	2
OCONNOR FRANK A	CW3	W-2144552	0663	1
OCONNOR FRANK W	LTC	0-0287487	0645	2
OCONNOR FREDERICK	LTC	0-1323388	1262	1
OCONNOR GEORGE L	MAJ	0-2038016	0865	1
OCONNOR GEORGE M	COL	0-0178379	0362	3
OCONNOR GERALD A	CPT	0-1686497	0954	2
OCONNOR GERALD J	LTC	0-1947355	0164	1
OCONNOR GERALD T	MAJ	0-0482556	0747	2
OCONNOR HOWARD	COL	0-0339823	1157	3
OCONNOR JAMES	CPT	0-1913897	0924	1
OCONNOR JAMES J	1LT	0-1011821	0945	2
OCONNOR JAMES W	MAJ	0-1049290	1060	1
OCONNOR JOHN A	MAJ	0-1578933	0564	1
OCONNOR JOHN D	1LT	0-1305820	0853	1
OCONNOR JOHN J	CPT	0-0298327	0245	2
OCONNOR JOHN J	LTC	0-1015830	0263	2
OCONNOR JOHN M	COL	0-0311187	0861	2
OCONNOR JOSEPH F	CPT	0-0191257	0361	3
OCONNOR JOSEPH L	MAJ	0-1302866	0861	1
OCONNOR JOSEPH M	1LT	0-0922783	1043	1
OCONNOR JR GEORGE M	LTC	0-1060912	0467	1
OCONNOR JR JOSEPH R	CPT	0-0445039	0463	1
OCONNOR KEVNEY	MAJ	0-047744C	0-50	3
OCONNOR MARIE I	MAJ	N-0759115	1162	1
OCONNOR MORGAN P	COL	0-0381892	0562	1

NAME	GRADE	SVC NO	DATE RET MO YR	RET CODE
OCONNOR NORMAN J	WO1	W-2116221	0544	2
OCONNOR PATRICK J	CPT	0-1638181	0455	1
OCONNOR PAUL E	LTC	0-1001206	0862	1
OCONNOR PHILIP J	LTC	0-0518206	0467	3
OCONNOR RICHARD P	1LT	0-0370015	0346	2
OCONNOR ROBERT G	LTC	0-1043450	1262	2
OCONNOR THOMAS	CPT	0-1012539	1265	1
OCONNOR THOMAS J	LTC	0-0888542	0663	1
OCONNOR THOMAS J	1LT	0-1321943	1045	2
OCONNOR THOMAS W	LTC	0-1596943	0163	1
OCONNOR WILLIAM D	CW2	W-2212253	0267	1
OCONNOR WILLIAM H	LTC	0-0192183	1053	3
OCONNOR WILLIAM J	CPT	0-0193821	0453	3
OCONNOR WILLIAM R	MAJ	0-1291158	0261	1
ODA WILLIAM S	LTC	0-1695654	0967	1
ODAHL WILLIAM R	CPT	0-1542010	0754	1
ODANIEL PAUL A	CW2	W-2211678	0766	1
ODAWE NICHOLAS	CPT	0-0370486	0946	1
ODAY MARY M	CPT	N-0725512	1046	1
ODAY THOMAS H	CPT	0-1044327	1153	1
ODDI VICTOR L	LTC	0-0335210	0864	1
ODEA EDWARD B	LTC	0-0258419	0565	3
ODEA JAMES J	CPT	0-1303625	0646	2
ODEA MILTON L	CW4	W-2104167	0659	1
ODEA PADRAIG M	LTC	0-1030181	0963	1
ODEGAARD ERLING A	2LT	0-1172203	1044	2
ODEGARD HENRY D	LTC	0-1177559	0965	1
ODELL ALBERT M	COL	0-0210109	0249	1
ODELL BILLIE E	CW2	W-2214674	0667	1
ODELL BRUCE	MAJ	0-0431606	0757	1
ODELL CLAUDE W	MAJ	0-0246896	0455	3
ODELL COURTNEY J	COL	0-0235919	1061	3
ODELL DONALD E	CW3	W-2143724	0159	1
ODELL DOUGLAS V	CPT	0-1309306	0446	1
ODELL EDWARD P	1LT	0-1172579	0146	1
ODELL ERNEST F	MAJ	0-1341693	0463	1
ODELL GORDON E	CW3	W-2206588	1165	1
ODELL HAROLD H	LTC	0-1105070	1266	3
ODELL HAROLD S	MAJ	0-1683967	0954	1
ODELL JACK C	CPT	0-2009612	0864	1
ODELL JAMES L	1LT	0-0545988	0147	2
ODELL JAMES W	CW3	W-2139701	1062	2
ODELL JOSEPH F	CW2	W-2210083	1264	1
ODELL JR LORRENCE	LTC	0-2018739	0466	1
ODELL JR VIRGIL L	MAJ	0-1338843	0867	1
ODELL MARION C	CPT	0-0973480	0561	1
ODELL RALPH E	LTC	0-1822043	0567	2
ODELL ROBERT E	COL	0-0209219	0253	3
ODELL WILLIAM R	MAJ	0-1108210	0267	1
ODEM NORMAN H	LTC	0-1314537	0867	3
ODEN PHILIP W	CPT	0-0322494	0143	2
ODEN WILLIAM D	MAJ	0-0423216	0560	1
ODENBRETT JOSEPH J	MAJ	0-1303381	0159	1
ODENWALDER CHARLES M	LTC	0-0412129	0960	1
ODENWELLER RICHARD F	LTC	0-0180701	0553	1
ODER JOHN T	MAJ	0-0490167	0356	1
ODESS SAMUEL L	1LT	0-1292574	0545	2
ODETTE MARJORIE F	2LT	N-0772477	0834	1
ODIL EMMETT C	1LT	0-1172906	0646	2
ODIOSO RAYMOND C	1LT	0-0549112	0346	2
ODLAND THEODORE E	COL	0-0220399	0652	3
ODLEY RALPH L	MAJ	0-0319649	0146	2
ODLIN WALTER C	CW2	W-2141788	0758	1
ODOM ALFRED D	CPT	0-0147515	0748	3
ODOM ANN W C	MAJ	N-0737807	0366	3
ODOM BERRYMAN H	CPT	0-1316194	0359	1
ODOM BOBBIE M	WO1	W-2110389	1044	2
ODOM CLIFFORD K	CPT	0-1594365	0849	2
ODOM EDWARD E	MAJ	0-0105734	0552	3
ODOM HAYNES	LTC	0-0164048	0335	1
ODOM HUPERT L	MAJ	0-0927267	0957	1
ODOM IRA D	CW3	W-2206591	0966	1
ODOM JAMES J	MAJ	0-0237874	0765	3
ODOM JOHN W	CPT	0-0988987	0461	2
ODOM JR OWEN W	LTC	0-1116979	1062	1

NAME	GRADE	SVC NO	DATE RET MO YR	RET CODE
ODOM ROBERT H	MAJ	0-1541303	0761	1
ODOM WILLIAM F	CW3	W-2142717	0661	1
ODONNAL MELVIN C	LTC	0-0396879	0960	1
ODONNELL ANTHONY W	1LT	0-1876252	1055	2
ODONNELL BERNARD J	LTC	0-1060234	0363	1
ODONNELL CORNELIUS	CPT	0-1320910	0257	1
ODONNELL DANIEL P	LTC	0-0127245	0648	3
ODONNELL FRANCIS J	1LT	0-1102410	0145	2
ODONNELL JAMES D	LTC	0-0344985	0463	1
ODONNELL JAMES P	LTC	0-1796338	1161	2
ODONNELL JAMES T	CPT	0-1080892	0748	2
ODONNELL JOHN B	MAJ	0-1585975	0466	3
ODONNELL JOSEPH G	CW3	W-2141864	1060	1
ODONNELL JOSEPH J	CPT	0-0905323	1145	2
ODONNELL JOSEPH M	MAJ	0-0969254	1063	1
ODONNELL LEO P	MAJ	0-0229201	1056	3
ODONNELL MALCOLM F	COL	0-0350013	0346	2
ODONNELL MORGAN J	CW3	W-2141398	0262	1
ODONNELL PAUL T	LTC	0-0549030	0566	1
ODONNELL ROBERT W	LTC	0-0181399	0646	2
ODONNELL THOMAS H	COL	0-0210680	0554	3
ODONNELL THOMAS W	CW2	W-2144605	0259	1
ODONNELL VINCENT R	CPT	0-1283823	0846	2
ODONNELL WALDROP L	COL	0-0177056	0560	3
ODONOGHUE FRANCIS E	1LT	0-0499511	1043	2
ODONOGHUE NICHOLAS R	CPT	0-0441093	0743	1
ODONOHUE EDWARD	LTC	0-0498564	0153	1
ODONOVICH PAUL	LTC	0-1698133	1263	1
ODOR HUGH E	LTC	0-0906164	0866	3
ODUM OTIS R	CW2	W-2149172	0461	1
ODWYER BERNARD L	MAJ	0-1833418	0960	1
OECHSLE ELMER H	COL	0-0195715	0762	3
OECHSLE HERMAN P	1LT	0-1315606	1044	2
OED PAUL	COL	0-0463583	0950	1
OEDER LAMBERT R	MAJ	0-0255243	0151	3
OEHLER JAMES C	COL	0-0162708	0155	3
OEHMKE BENJAMIN H	COL	0-0328930	1264	1
OEHNE FORD A	2LT	0-1031354	1045	2
OELKERS ALBERT L	LTC	0-1110694	1164	3
OELRICH WILFRED C	LTC	0-0465108	0567	1
OELSCHLAGER JAMES A	2LT	0-1165770	1044	2
OELTJEN GUS J	CPT	0-0487024	0350	1
OENNING SR LESTER C	LTC	0-1325387	0966	1
OERTEL WILLY H	CW4	W-2115682	0658	1
OERTER HERBERT L	MAJ	0-2046395	0956	1
OERTER KARL C	CW4	W-2122139	1160	1
OESCH WILLIAM H	LTC	0-0133147	0459	3
OESER RICHARD W	MAJ	0-1642443	1264	1
OESTREICH FORREST C	LTC	0-0381007	0157	1
OESTREICH ROY H	LTC	0-1298278	0860	1
OETINGER JR GEORGE	COL	0-0218245	0859	1
OETJEN GEORGE F	MAJ	0-0199757	0745	2
OETKEN BYRON W	CW3	W-2144065	0766	1
OETTINGER JR LEON	1LT	0-0539719	0146	2
OFARRELL FRANCES M	1LT	N-0735830	0946	1
OFFEN JR ROGER L	CPT	0-0361632	0945	2
OFFER PAUL J	CPT	0-1639469	1060	1
OFFER RICHARD F	1LT	0-2037085	0247	2
OFFERMAN JACOB	CW2	W-2148696	0859	1
OFFICER BREARON A	LTC	0-2020754	0766	1
OFFICER VERNON W	LTC	0-0275722	1160	3
OFFIE SAMUEL J	LTC	0-1944772	0660	2
OFFNER DAVID I	CW2	W-3430216	0863	2
OFFNER JOSEPH A	MAJ	0-1588782	0361	1
OFFNER WILBUR H	LTC	0-1180651	1059	1
OFFRIL PAUL C	1LT	0-1896966	0551	1
OFFRINGA ROBERT J	1LT	0-1330107	0747	1
OFFUTT JR EDWARD W	MAJ	0-1685656	0366	1
OFFUTT REGINALD J	CPT	0-0149696	0150	3
OFFUTT ROBERT K	MAJ	0-0119176	0952	3
OFLAHERTY JOHN C	MAJ	0-0179829	1145	2
OFLYNN GEOFFREY J	COL	0-0101392	0648	3
OGAN BOYINGTON	MAJ	0-1590708	1063	1
OGARA HERRICK J	LTC	0-0501250	0755	2
OGARA JOHN E	2LT	0-1552762	0544	2

NAME	GRADE	SVC NO	DATE RET MO YR	RET CODE
OGAWA HARUJI	MAJ	0-0958733	0563	1
OGAWA KATSUMI	2LT	N-0784086	0545	1
OGBURN LORANZY O	1LT	0-1289951	0347	2
OGDAHL HARMON T	CPT	0-1316319	0646	2
OGDEN CARL J	CW3	W-2147901	0666	1
OGDEN CARLOS C	CPT	0-1299287	0448	2
OGDEN CLAIR F	LTC	0-1551922	0657	1
OGDEN CLAUDE H	LTC	0-0115709	0251	3
OGDEN FREDERICK	CPT	0-0305640	0246	2
OGDEN HAROLD F	COL	0-0204623	0557	3
OGDEN JAMES D	1LT	0-1746362	0645	2
OGDEN JAMES P	1LT	0-0392338	1143	2
OGDEN VAN L	LTC	0-0261296	0565	3
OGDEN WALTER H	MAJ	0-0162938	1151	3
OGESEN EVER J	CPT	0-0239562	0745	2
OGG JACK L	CPT	0-0528680	0846	2
OGG RICHARD L	1LT	0-0762486	1067	2
OGG STODDARD L	CPT	0-1013983	0247	1
OGILBEE HARRY L	CW2	W-2147637	0259	1
OGILVIE JOHN D	MAJ	0-0454123	0755	1
OGINSKY THEODORE J	1LT	0-1292929	1044	2
OGLE ELMER E	COL	0-0182425	0559	3
OGLE WALTER A	MAJ	0-1556195	0358	1
OGLE WILLIAM E	CW4	W-2135378	1055	1
OGLES OTIS R	LTC	0-0373396	0760	1
OGLESBY JR DAVID F	CPT	0-1692643	0663	1
OGLESBY JR ERNEST J	CPT	0-0449004	0750	1
OGLESBY OSCAR O	CPT	0-1339386	0858	1
OGLESBY PAUL C	CPT	0-1774793	1054	2
OGLESBY WALTER R	CW4	W-2119769	1263	1
OGLETHORPE RAYMOND J	MAJ	0-1636421	0560	1
OGLETREE CLYDE	MAJ	N-0727702	0365	1
OGRADY FRANCIS O	CW2	W-2148263	0261	1
OGRADY GERALD B	COL	0-0164475	1056	3
OGRADY JOHN J	MAJ	0-0499844	1045	2
OGRADY MICHAEL P	CPT	0-0925069	0446	2
OGREEN RUDOLPH C	LTC	0-0259051	0155	3
OGREN CECIL C	CPT	0-0229811	0261	3
OGWYNN PAUL D	LTC	0-1044636	0562	1
OHACO MICHEL J	CPT	0-0446852	0847	2
OHAGAN FRANCIS G	CPT	0-1796515	0163	1
OHAIR JOHN E	COL	0-0237115	0556	1
OHALLORAN MARY A	MAJ	N-0744796	1162	1
OHANLON FRANCIS R	1LT	0-0904505	0845	2
OHANLON JAMES F	LTC	0-0217676	1047	1
OHANLON JOSEPH O	LTC	0-0282328	0558	1
OHARA CHARLES R	LTC	0-0415679	0161	1
OHARA CHRISTOPHE	COL	0-0403390	0966	1
OHARA FRANCIS D	CW3	W-2150754	0163	1
OHARA JAMES T	COL	0-1107002	0567	1
OHARA JOHN C	CW2	W-2119313	0447	2
OHARA JOHN J	MAJ	0-1296411	0755	2
OHARA RICHARD C	LTC	0-1290550	0561	1
OHARA SR THOMAS J	CW2	W-2148341	0457	1
OHARA THOMAS P	MAJ	0-0968682	0163	1
OHARAN PAUL F	LTC	0-0541059	0466	1
OHARE FRANK J	COL	0-0349695	0466	3
OHARE JACK	LTC	0-1646467	1163	1
OHARE JAMES P	LTC	0-1825972	0463	2
OHARE JAMES P	CW3	W-2144295	0562	1
OHARE JOHN F	MAJ	0-1288785	0564	1
OHARE KENNETH W	LTC	0-0300188	0546	2
OHARE WILLIAM E	1LT	0-2017271	1166	1
OHARRA JAMES J	MAJ	0-1325926	0760	1
OHARROW JOHN W	CPT	0-0492356	0447	1
OHART THEODORE C	MAJ	0-0260115	0767	3
OHEARN JAMES P	WO1	W-2137302	0345	2
OHEARN RAYMOND L	LTC	0-1946352	0566	1
OHEARN WILLIAM J	COL	0-0192519	0362	3
OHEREN PAT	MAJ	0-1596560	0959	2
OHL THOMAS H	LTC	0-0375784	1064	1
OHLAND FREDRICK C	CPT	0-1107004	0347	2
OHLHEISER HAROLD R	LTC	0-0242139	0163	3
OHLINGER NORBERT P	CW2	W-2148090	0157	1
OHLMAN GERALD G	MAJ	0-1297932	0761	1

NAME	GRADE	SVC NO	DATE RET MO YR	RET CODE
OHLRICH VIRGIL C	MAJ	0-1062775	0363	1
OHLSEN HENRY L	WO1	W-2151778	0361	2
OHLSEN WALTER C	LTC	0-0252317	0163	3
OHLSON LEROY J	1LT	0-1184560	0147	2
OHLSON RUTH H	2LT	N-0736540	0244	1
OHMAN CARL S	CPT	0-0495057	0746	2
OHMAN RINOLD L	LTC	0-0280260	0652	3
OHMER ROBERT F	COL	0-0160347	0450	3
OHMERT WINFIELD L	COL	0-0151245	0648	3
OHRBECK JOSEPH E	CPT	0-0129749	1059	3
OHRVALL ADOLPH F	LTC	0-0288554	1060	1
OJA CARL A	LTC	0-1305821	0266	1
OJE LYLE F	MAJ	0-1591349	1162	1
OJI SUKEO	MAJ	0-1339091	0863	1
OJIBWAY PHILIP J	CPT	0-0424655	0845	1
OKADA ICHIRO	1LT	0-0410147	0246	2
OKANE MORTIMER J	COL	0-0247071	0959	1
OKANE ROY	1LT	0-1914070	0748	1
OKEEFE DANIEL M	MAJ	0-1324183	0862	1
OKEEFE FRANCIS A	LTC	0-1165139	0159	1
OKEEFE FRED T	MAJ	0-0465381	0365	1
OKEEFE JOHN A	COL	0-0277514	0551	1
OKEEFE JOHN F	LTC	0-0369837	0862	1
OKEEFE JOHN P	CPT	0-1532162	0645	2
OKEEFE JOHN P	MAJ	0-1645886	0958	2
OKEEFE JOHN W	CPT	0-1035953	0246	2
OKEEFE MAURICE P	CPT	0-1301869	0960	1
OKEEFE PAUL T	LTC	0-0248261	0759	3
OKEEFE ROBERT P	LTC	0-1547788	0965	1
OKEEFE SR HERBERT A	CPT	0-1326109	0347	2
OKEEFFE ELBERT B	LTC	0-0416856	1060	1
OKEEFFE ELLEN L	MAJ	N-0745391	0664	1
OKEEFFE JR JAMES	1LT	0-0449005	0645	2
OKELLEY GOLMER P	MAJ	N-0727632	0962	1
OKELLEY HOKE S	CPT	0-0135849	0747	2
OKELLEY HORACE M	CPT	0-0510880	0647	1
OKELLY ARTHUR P	1LT	0-1013531	0645	2
OKELLY JR FIELDING K	CPT	0-1578935	0145	2
OKEN MORRIS H	CPT	0-0512411	1044	2
OKERT FRED H	CPT	0-0495166	0849	1
OKEY ELMER E	MAJ	0-0115713	0556	3
OKEY KEITH M	CW2	W-2151173	0966	1
OKIE FREDERICK	COL	0-0259965	0767	3
OKIN HARRY	MAJ	0-0119766	0950	3
OKOLOWICH THOMAS J	MAJ	0-0413337	0647	2
OKONOGI HUGO S	COL	0-0527069	1065	3
OKONSKI LEONARD J	MAJ	0-2097082	0867	1
OKULICK AMBROSE	CW2	W-2115176	0457	1
OKUMURA MAKOTO	MAJ	0-2030780	1061	1
OKUSA MUNEO M	MAJ	0-0935440	0765	1
OLAH THOMAS F	MAJ	0-1580119	0164	1
OLANDER EDWIN J	1LT	0-2055861	0445	2
OLANDER FRANK H	LTC	0-0349133	0860	1
OLANDER RALPH C	CPT	0-0272585	0545	2
OLAUGHLIN PHILIP J	LTC	0-0309043	0259	1
OLAZABA JR AURELIO R	CW3	W-2146345	0364	1
OLBON CLAY	B G	0-0246675	0663	3
OLD ALVY O	MAJ	0-2046374	0447	2
OLD GEORGE H	CPT	0-0397913	0546	2
OLDENDORFF ERNEST	MAJ	0-1593763	1156	1
OLDHAM OWEN L	MAJ	0-1119106	0365	1
OLDHAM RODNEY L	LTC	0-1100707	0964	1
OLDOM FRED	CPT	0-0508487	0347	1
OLDS CORWIN H	COL	0-0265810	0455	3
OLDS OMAR G	COL	0-0191489	0859	3
OLDZIEWSKI LEO M	MAJ	0-1575041	0557	1
OLEAIR JOHN J	CPT	0-0302403	0166	3
OLEARCZYK STANLEY R	MAJ	0-0939629	0764	1
OLEARY ARTHUR E	LTC	0-0441778	0748	1
OLEARY CORNELIUS	LTC	0-0123614	0361	3
OLEARY DANIEL R	CPT	0-1014452	1060	1
OLEARY FRANCIS A	CPT	0-0577204	0956	1
OLEARY GLENA B	CPT	N-0763636	1046	1
OLEARY LAWRENCE A	COL	0-0261808	1067	3
OLEARY LEO W	LTC	0-0500349	1262	1

NAME	GRADE	SVC NO	DATE RET MO YR	RET CODE
OLECH RAY A	CPT	0-0535521	C146	1
OLECK CAVIO	1LT	0-1547093	1045	2
OLEFIROWICZ C P	CPT	0-1845223		2
OLEJAR PAUL O	LTC	0-0911598	1066	3
OLENAFRGER JR CARL F	1LT	0-0405346	0246	2
OLENTINE JULIE E	CPT	0-0528280	1045	2
OLES FLOYO	LTC	0-0189508	0556	3
OLES PAUL F	CW2	W-2141647	C556	1
OLESHEYTZ MIKE	MAJ	0-2039501	C666	1
OLESON EVERETT E	MAJ	0-1014673	0565	1
OLESON LLOYC F	CPT	0-0366962	C545	2
OLESZAK MAX W	MAJ	C-0887342	0261	1
OLEZ GLENN	2LT	0-1896607	0666	1
OLFKY ANTHONY E	MAJ	C-1534108	C546	2
OLIG FRANCIS A	LTC	0-1826217	C164	2
CLIHOVIK JOHN	LTC	0-0799622	0562	1
OLIJAR MICHAEL	LTC	0-1177926	1163	1
OLIN FRANK R	COL	0-0203254	0646	2
OLIN JOHN H	LTC	0-0324955	C358	1
OLIN MORSE E	LTC	0-0322710	0457	1
OLINO JOHN H	CPT	0-0110583	0355	3
OLINO JR JOHN H	CW2	W-2206629	1063	1
OLINE JOSEPH R	LTC	0-0390795	C366	3
OLINGER JR ALLEN M	1LT	0-1702791	0645	2
CLINGER WILLIAM A	CPT	0-0469788	0945	2
OLIPHANT CHARLES F	CPT	C-1054742	1047	2
OLIPHANT FLOYO W	COL	0-0235017	C260	3
OLISZEWSKI CASIMIR	COL	0-0300907	1056	1
OLIVARI-ANILL WILLIA	LTC	0-1325772	1162	1
OLIVE CEORGE S	MAJ	C-1280304	C446	2
OLIVE HAROLC P	WO1	W-21501CC	0855	1
OLIVE JR LEONARO J	CW3	W-2203369	0963	1
OLIVE JR ROBERT H	MAJ	0-1331979	C960	1
OLIVE JR WILLIAM M	MAJ	C-1590710	0262	1
CLIVER ALFRED	LTC	0-0149406	C654	3
OLIVER ALFREO L	COL	0-0269527	C860	1
OLIVER CALVIN C	CW2	W-2102162	C866	2
OLIVER CHARLES W	MAJ	C-0255582	0351	3
CLIVER CLARENCE R	MAJ	C-1920264	1163	1
OLIVER EVERETT J	CPT	0-0967061	1060	1
OLIVER FRANCIS J	MAJ	C-1291868	C860	1
OLIVER GEORGE L	LTC	0-0286338	0246	2
OLIVER HENRY C	CPT	0-1283122	0546	2
OLIVER JACK L	LTC	0-2070542	0867	1
OLIVER JAMES G	COL	0-0506051	0266	3
OLIVER JESSE	CW4	W-2145869	0765	1
OLIVER JOHN G	MAJ	0-0971200	0365	1
OLIVER JOHN W	COL	0-0205398	C659	3
OLIVER JR DONALD B	LTC	0-1116967	0467	1
OLIVER LEO P	MAJ	C-1548115	0559	1
OLIVER LEONARC E	MAJ	C-1578937	1054	1
OLIVER LOUIS U	MAJ	0-1899405	C263	1
OLIVER NORMAN	MAJ	C-0442262	0146	1
OLIVER RALPH	CW2	W-2151314	1160	2
OLIVER THOMAS H	LTC	0-1573489	0961	1
OLIVER THURMAN W	LTC	0-1305973	0266	1
CLIVER WALTER E	MAJ	0-1922573	1263	1
CLIVER WILLARC E	CPT	0-0989036	0161	1
OLIVER WILLIAM H	MAJ	C-0342230	C346	2
OLIVER WILLIAM P	MAJ	0-0220733	1158	3
OLIVER WILLIAM R	COL	0-1310139	0466	1
OLIVER WILLIAM W	LTC	0-0910454	0864	3
OLIVERAS RAFAEL	1LT	0-0425552	C446	2
OLLER J C	CW2	W-2152392	C563	1
OLLER JOSE A	COL	0-0523909	C667	1
OLLER JCSEPH W	1LT	0-1319327	0646	2
OLLIFFE ARTHUR J	CW2	W-2150358	1161	1
OLLS VICTOR	LTC	0-1290295	0663	1
OLMSTEAC ALFREO S	MAJ	C-2263443	0367	1
CLMSTEAO KENNETH A	LTC	0-1549804	C961	1
CLMSTEAD THOMAS	1LT	0-1340797	1152	2
OLMSTED ALFREO M	MAJ	0-0373968	1160	1
OLMSTEO GENE S	COL	0-0244935	C447	2
OLMSTEO GEORGE H	M G	0-0199581	0461	3
OLMSTEO RANCOLPH F	COL	0-0290457	C659	3
OLMSTED ROBERT O	CPT	0-1010718	0346	2
OLMSTEC WALTER C	1LT	0-0396890	0245	2
OLNEY FRANCIS X	LTC	0-0341358	1159	1
OLOANS JCHN M	CW3	W-2136361	0163	1
OLOUGHLIN ROSEMARY	MAJ	L-0311291	1163	1
OLSCHEWSKE JCHN A	COL	0-0421916	1061	1
OLSEN AARON B	MAJ	0-0401643	0649	1
OLSEN ALBERT L	LTC	0-0248307	1164	3
OLSEN ALBERT M	LTC	0-0301651	0461	1
OLSEN ALFREO W	CPT	0-0496976	0249	1
OLSEN ARNOLO	LTC	0-0201821	0455	3
OLSEN ARNOLO C	MAJ	0-2018043	0264	1
OLSEN ARTHUR T	WO1	W-2152244	0557	1
OLSEN BOB G	LTC	0-0451364	0758	1
OLSEN BUOD	CW3	W-2148299	1061	1
OLSEN BURGA P	LTC	0-1105722	1062	1
OLSEN CARL T	CPT	0-0223237	0756	3
OLSEN CLARENCE M	LTC	0-0233467	1050	1
OLSEN DONALD H	MAJ	0-2090150	0966	1
OLSEN EARL	CW2	W-2109539	0949	2
OLSEN EARL M	MAJ	0-0973224	1160	1
OLSEN ECHARD H	LTC	0-0422757	0856	1
OLSEN GCRDON N	COL	0-0244795	1055	3
OLSEN HANFORC T	LTC	0-0901865	0666	3
OLSEN IVAN C E	CW2	W-2214539	0667	1
OLSEN JAMES E	LTC	0-0283676	0864	3
OLSEN JCHN R O	MAJ	0-1115369	0958	1
OLSEN JR BEN	CPT	0-0365730	0246	2
OLSEN JR SAMUEL G	MAJ	0-1798388	0764	1
OLSEN KAUO	CPT	0-0278975	0447	1
OLSEN LERCY J	1LT	0-1595080	0146	2
OLSEN CDIN T	MAJ	0-1330953	0163	1
OLSEN ROBERT N	LTC	0-1594370	0566	1
OLSEN ROLF	MAJ	0-0992458	0764	1
OLSEN ROY J	MAJ	0-1308367	0164	1
OLSEN SAM N	CPT	0-0888359	1145	2
OLSEN VICTOR L	COL	0-0297916	1162	3
OLSEN WILLIAM S	CPT	0-1306882	0447	1
OLSH JCHN Z	CPT	0-0324144	1048	1
OLSON ALBERT J	MAJ	0-1894700	1053	2
OLSON ALBERT N	MAJ	C-2007117	1265	1
CLSON ALBIN J	CW3	W-2150093	0363	1
OLSON ALLAN M	CPT	0-1765343	1045	2
OLSON ANOREW G	CW4	W-2107818	0562	1
OLSON CARL A	1LT	0-0487084	0744	1
OLSON CARL G	CW4	W-2109834	0959	1
OLSON CARROLL A	CPT	0-1020C28	0252	2
CLSON CHARLES H	LTC	0-1167147	0166	1
OLSON CHARLES W	CPT	0-1293821	0258	1
OLSON CLARENCE H	COL	0-0201092	0560	3
OLSON CLINTON W	MAJ	0-2021181	0565	1
OLSON CONALO O	CW2	W-2148216	0962	1
OLSON EARL J	MAJ	C-1684271	0346	2
OLSON EDWARD	1LT	0-1322166	1046	2
OLSON EOWARO	LTC	0-1585985	1262	1
OLSON EOWARO T	CPT	0-1341034	0265	1
OLSON EDWIN C	CPT	0-0232591	0355	3
OLSON EINO O	CPT	0-0329632	0146	1
OLSON ELLEN M	LTC	N-0728322	1161	1
OLSON ELMER J	1LT	0-0549966	0946	2
OLSON ELMER M	MAJ	0-2026946	0467	1
OLSON ELVIN A	MAJ	0-2097007	0864	1
OLSON FRANCIS J	MAJ	0-0487611	0863	3
OLSON FRANKLIN R	LTC	0-1039493	0964	1
OLSON FRANZ L	LTC	0-1036664	0162	1
OLSON FREDERICK	WO1	W-2128101	0456	1
OLSON GECRGE H	LTC	0-1311042	0662	1
OLSON GECRGE W	LTC	0-0475020	0762	1
OLSON GUSTAF P	B G	0-0275721	1062	3
OLSON HAROLD H	LTC	0-1557764	0564	1
OLSON HARRY E	CW2	W-2113563	0947	1
OLSON IHLINE G	2LT	N-0732606	0843	1
OLSON JAMES C	MAJ	0-0376428	0846	2
OLSON JCHN F	MAJ	0-0246155	0463	3
OLSON JCHN E	MAJ	0-1103845	0859	1
CLSCN JOHN R	1LT	0-0372399	1143	2
OLSON JR ELMER A	CPT	0-0520545	C146	2
CLSON LEONARO A	LTC	0-1797174	1162	1
OLSON LEROY B	CPT	0-1555115	C661	2
OLSON LESTER E	CPT	C-0503271	0746	2
OLSON LUDWIG E	WO1	W-2103274	1056	1
CLSON MARVIN A	CW3	W-2207223	1165	1
OLSON MARVIN V	LTC	0-1182674	0563	1
OLSON MELVIN W	LTC	0-1284927	0665	2
CLSON OLIVE	2LT	N-C783041	0944	1
CLSON OLIVER S	COL	C-0180111	C457	1
CLSON OSCAR	2LT	0-1324184	C544	2
CLSON OSCAR A	LTC	0-0182367	C357	3
CLSON PALMER F	CPT	0-1291161	0662	1
CLSON RICHARD	CPT	0-0504962	0745	1
OLSON RICHARO A	CW2	W-2213047	0667	1
CLSON RICHARO W	CPT	C-0948898	C161	1
OLSON ROBERT B	LTC	0-1697845	C363	1
OLSON ROBERT M	1LT	0-1322806	C148	2
OLSON ROBERT R	CW3	W-2113658	0658	2
OLSON RUSSELL L	MAJ	C-1114693	0959	1
CLSON SIGURO	LTC	0-2046324	C466	1
OLSON THEODORE A	LTC	0-0369628	0246	2
OLSON THEODORE P	MAJ	C-0950438	0466	1
OLSON THOMAS O	2LT	0-1913886	1038	1
CLSON VERNON G	2LT	0-0888239	0744	2
CLSON WALTER L	1LT	0-0452943	0848	2
OLSON WALTER P	LTC	0-0350467	C964	1
OLSON WALTER W	MAJ	C-0270928	0667	3
CLSON WALTON S	MAJ	C-1698184	C861	1
CLSON WILLIAM A	LTC	0-1106378	C664	1
CLSON WILLIAM P	LTC	0-0486694	C156	2
OLSON WILLIS E	1LT	0-1312706	C845	2
OLSOWSKY EDWARD C	WO1	W-2108372	C445	2
CLSSON JOHN E	LTC	0-0264993	1060	3
OLSSON SR ROY H	MAJ	C-1891227	0167	1
OLSTAO MYRTLE A	LTC	N-0721096	1165	3
OLSZEWSKI JOHN P	MAJ	0-1946125	1154	1
OLSZEWSKI WALTER J	2LT	0-1288427	0745	2
OLTARZEWSKI WALTER J	CPT	0-039787C	0867	1
OLTJENBRUNS ELIZABET	MAJ	L-0801279	1065	1
OLTJENBRUNS WALTER W	MAJ	C-1032106	0460	1
OLTMAN ALBERT O	1LT	0-13C1198	0548	2
OLTMANN OSCAR F	MAJ	0-1019277	C361	1
CLTS CHARLES A	LTC	0-0453655	1061	1
CLVER THOMAS M	LTC	0-1281357	0864	2
OLVERSON JR JOHN B	MAJ	C-0900528	0146	2
OLVIS CHARLES J	COL	0-0290522	1059	3
OLWIN JOHN H	LTC	C-0259418	C667	3
OLYNICK MILTON	CW3	W-2152269	1264	1
OMALLEY EOWARO A	LTC	0-0291024	0260	1
OMALLEY EDWARD F	1LT	0-1000636	0750	2
OMALLEY EDWARD P	LTC	0-0308495	1065	3
OMALLEY FRANCIS E	1LT	0-1916517	0452	1
OMALLEY FRANK W	CPT	C-0444661	0245	1
CMALLEY GEORGE E	MAJ	0-1016721	C467	1
OMALLEY JAMES E	LTC	0-1636428	C761	1
OMALLEY JAMES F	CW3	W-2149711	0461	1
CMALLEY JOHN E	CPT	0-0143883	0751	3
OMALLEY VIRGINIA L	1LT	0-0539933	0750	2
OMALLEY WILLIAM D	1LT	0-0349937	0957	1
OMAN ERNEST H	MAJ	C-0319767	C266	3
OMAN RALPH W	MAJ	C-0166871	0657	3
OMARA JAMES J	CPT	0-0408508	1045	2
CMARA THOMAS J	1LT	0-1317736	1145	1
CMEARA ARTHUR A	LTC	0-0905136	0662	1
ONEARA CHARLES E	CW2	W-2142385	1055	1
CMEARA HOWARO F	LTC	0-1556031	1262	1
CMEARA JAMES J	CPT	0-1822607	1162	1
OMEARA MILORED M	1LT	N-0724094	0146	1
CMEARA WILLIAM F	MAJ	0-0204802	0759	3
OMELANUK MICHAEL	CW3	W-22C3862	0965	1
OMELIA JOSEPH J	CW3	W-2152734	C564	1
CMELIA MALCOLM B	CPT	0-1323728	1264	1
OMER DANIEL O	COL	0-0195630	C960	3
OMER JAMES M	MAJ	C-1296074	0546	1
OMHOLT ELMER V	1LT	0-1294351	0145	1
OMHOLT GARTH D	MAJ	C-4010593	1167	1
OMOHUNCRO ROBERT L	LTC	0-1041413	0962	1
OMCRI RICHARC T	MAJ	0-2030794	0866	1
OMSTEAC FREO A	CW4	W-2118032	1053	1
ONASCH WILLIS E	CW2	W-22C9400	0763	1
ONOFCK MICHAEL	LTC	0-1336548	0466	1
ONDECKER ANDREW M	MAJ	C-0406796	0947	2
ONDO JCSEPH	LTC	0-1542849	1161	2
ONEAL ARVIL C	LTC	0-1288106	0755	1
ONEAL AUBREY M	MAJ	0-2011718	1056	1
ONEAL BUFORO L	LTC	0-0295494	0867	3
ONEAL CECIL S	MAJ	C-2263113	0865	1
ONEAL CECIL T	CPT	0-0192590	0151	3
ONEAL CCCK L	CW3	W-2143365	0861	1
ONEAL ECMUNO J	CPT	0-0532434	0946	2
ONEAL FRANK W	LTC	0-1056496	0365	1
ONEAL HAROLO F	LTC	0-0238871	0760	3
ONEAL JACK O	MAJ	C-0988881	1065	2
ONEAL JAMES G	CW3	RW-2149741	1163	1
ONEAL JAMES M	LTC	0-0383537	1044	2
ONEAL JR GEORGE A	LTC	0-0439797	1262	1
ONEAL JR WILLIAM L	MAJ	0-1938025	0367	1
ONEAL LECN H	CW3	W-2149798	0667	2
ONEAL LOWELL W	MAJ	0-1108215	0760	1
ONEAL MCNCURE C	LTC	0-0248329	0567	3
ONEAL THCMAS F	CW2	W-2115863	0754	1
ONEAL WALTER D	MAJ	0-2032311	0960	1
ONEAL WILLIAM H	CW2	W-2211221	1165	1
ONEAL WILLIAM T	MAJ	0-2042870	1157	1
ONEAL WILTON K	COL	C-0348056	1063	1
ONEALE MINERVA	LTC	N-0700135	C846	1
ONEIL ALBERT O	CW4	W-2145162	0767	1
ONEIL ARTHUR	CPT	0-0977921	0160	2
ONEIL GILBERT M	LTC	0-0292375	0859	1
ONEIL JAMES E	LTC	0-0181248	0953	3
ONEIL JCHN P	LTC	0-1112899	1062	1
ONEIL JOSEPH F	MAJ	C-1947790	1165	1
ONEIL MABELLE M	LTC	N-0751261	0266	3
ONEIL CRLANO J	CPT	0-2097059	0762	1
ONEIL RAYMONC F	LTC	0-1338504	0466	1
ONEIL RCBERT	COL	0-0346053	0667	3
ONEIL THOMAS F	CPT	0-0101817	0648	3
ONEIL THCMAS F	CW4	W-2135576	0766	1
ONEILL CHARLES T	COL	0-0191567	0748	3
ONEILL CLIFFCRD L	1LT	0-1176757	1046	1
ONEILL OCNALD F	CW2	W-2147602	0766	1
ONEILL EDWARD M	CPT	0-1646472	0348	1
ONEILL ELEANCR E	CPT	N-0700666	0446	1
ONEILL ELIZABETH	1LT	N-0763568	0746	1
ONEILL FREDERICK	COL	0-0281043	0866	3
ONEILL GERALC M	LTC	0-1305467	0561	1
ONEILL HARCLC L	MAJ	0-1109569	0861	1
ONEILL JAMES O	CW4	W-2006890	1067	1
ONEILL JAMES E	CW3	W-2144678	1060	1
ONEILL JAMES J	CPT	0-0381006	0647	2
ONEILL JAMES W	MAJ	0-1297578	1157	2
ONEILL JEREMIAH F	LTC	0-0131039	0353	3
ONEILL JCSEPH A	LTC	0-0361262	0756	1
ONEILL JCSEPH L	MAJ	0-0887355	0564	1
ONEILL JR JAMES L	MAJ	0-1298114	0864	1
ONEILL KATHRYN M	MAJ	N-0758770	1264	1
ONEILL LEANDER W	LTC	0-1328392	0765	1
ONEILL PAUL S	MAJ	0-2033945	0664	2
ONEILL PETER M	LTC	0-0189753	0558	1
ONEILL RICHARD F	CW3	W-2144053	0564	1
ONEILL RCBERT B	MAJ	0-0454222	0261	1
ONEILL THOMAS J	MAJ	C-1650682	1062	1
ONEILL THOMAS P	MAJ	C-1294002	1060	1
ONEILL TIMOTHY J	2LT	0-1644637	0146	2
ONEILL WALTER L	CPT	0-1004392	0962	1
ONEILL WILLIAM H	MAJ	0-0369043	0267	3
ONEILL WILLIAM J	CPT	0-0479558	1144	2
ONEILL WILLIAM R	CPT	0-2017579	1057	2

NAME	GRADE	SVC NO	DATE RET MO YR	RET CODE
ONELLICN WILLARC M	1LT	0-0480139	024P	1
ONEY WALTER	MAJ	0-2C07204	1157	1
ONGERT WALTER J	CPT	C-1280235	C760	2
ONGIES JEROME H	LTC	0-1698789	0767	1
CNION 3RD WILLIAM F	1LT	0-1284379	C346	2
ONKES WILLIAM R	CPT	0-0450468	C847	1
ONKST DOROTHY O	1LT	N-0767746	0147	1
ONSRUD MYRTLE S	CPT	N-0736615	C946	1
ONSTOT CLEMENT C	CW3	W-2123023	C361	1
ONSTOTT EDWIN C	LTC	0-1845326	1062	1
OOLEY WAYMAN R	CPT	0-0197139	C262	3
OOSTERLING WALTER H	LTC	0-0266032	C653	2
OPAL EDWARC A	CPT	0-1998388	C750	2
OPALEK ELLA	MAJ	N-0793429	0365	1
OPENSHAW FRANK	CPT	0-0407912	0245	2
OPENSHAW FRED	MAJ	C-01C4330	1058	3
OPENSHAW GLEN A	CW2	W-2205156	1163	1
OPENSHAW JAMES	LTC	0-1634188	0665	1
OPENSHAW THOMAS E	1LT	0-2043266	1046	2
OPHAUG ORVILLE H	LTC	0-1300519	0463	1
OPIE EVARTS W	B G	0-0172561	C953	3
OPIE SICNEY P	LTC	0-0353607	0559	1
OPILLA PAUL C	CW2	W-2209665	0464	1
OPITZ WILLIAM A	CW2	W-2123826	1256	2
OPLIGER PAUL G	MAJ	C-1948365	C460	1
OPPENBERG IRVING L	1LT	0-1822901	C547	2
OPPENHEIM ARMAND	1LT	0-1288428	1045	2
OPPENHEIM NORMAN W	COL	0-0291873	C847	2
OPPENHEIMER LOUIS H	CPT	0-1010039	C960	1
OPPER CHARLES G	LTC	0-0331749	C161	1
OPPIDO ALBERT A	1LT	0-0915145	1047	2
OPPLEMAN HERMAN F	CPT	0-0428292	C144	2
OPUDA JOHN	LTC	0-0485030	C363	1
OQUINN JAMES D	MAJ	C-0260380	1266	3
OQUINN THOMAS J	CW2	W-2125153	C161	1
OQUINN TRUEMAN E	COL	0-0917160	0665	3
OQUINN WILLIAM A	LTC	0-1322167	C766	1
ORAM GEORGE F	WO1	W-2125199	C647	2
ORAMAS FELIX	CW4	W-2113844	0760	1
ORATE BRAULIO O	CW3	W-2135150	1063	1
ORAVEC ANDREW H	CPT	0-1686564	0946	1
ORAVEZ JAMES J	MAJ	0-0372731	0954	1
ORAZEN JOHN	MAJ	C-0471096	1154	1
ORBECK MARTIN J	LTC	0-0165416	0450	3
ORBESEN CLIFFORD E	LTC	0-0312925	0562	1
ORBISON FRANK H	MAJ	0-0486043	0547	2
ORCHARD WINIFRED M	MAJ	N-0783925	C963	1
ORCUTT HAROLD H	COL	C-0393762	0557	1
ORCUTT ROBERT D	LTC	0-0364494	1065	3
ORDAHL STAFFORD N	COL	C-0273570	0165	2
ORDOYNE LUCIEN P	MAJ	0-1302868	0761	1
ORDWAY FRED D	LTC	0-0130099	1049	3
ORDWAY ROBERT F	2LT	C-1698079	0145	2
OREAR JOHN F	MAJ	0-1540636	0757	1
OREARDON DANIEL C	MAJ	C-0207825	C455	3
OREBAUGH LOUIS E	CW3	W-2208329	0366	2
OREFICE WILLIAM R	CPT	0-1288287	C647	2
OREGAN SAMUEL G	LTC	0-0350838	0662	1
OREGAN TERENCE P	MAJ	C-1303533	0361	1
OREILLEY JAMES H	COL	C-0151663	1054	3
OREILLEY WILLIAM C	WO1	W-2108304	1064	3
OREILLY BERNARD E	MAJ	C-1015379	C861	1
OREILLY DANIEL E	CPT	0-0438940	0246	2
OREILLY HUGH R	MAJ	0-1339208	1060	1
OREILLY JOHN V	MAJ	0-0406958	0961	1
OREILLY JOSEPH G	1LT	C-1323346	114N	2
OREILLY ROBERT M	MAJ	C-1826293	0666	2
OREM CHARLES W	CPT	0-0318723	1044	2
OREM WILLIAM W	MAJ	C-0208231	C257	3
ORENO JACK F	LTC	0-1585988	0766	1
ORENDORF CARROLL A	1LT	0-117646C	0945	2
ORENDORFF LLOYD E	CPT	0-0117859	0554	3
ORENDORFF ROBERT O	MAJ	C-2012665	C663	1
ORENSTEIN LEO L	MAJ	0-0346845	C446	2
ORESCHAK ANDREW	1LT	0-2007045	C647	1
ORESS CHARLES F	CW3	W-2148582	0964	1
ORF ROBERT C	MAJ	0-0390145	0847	2
ORFANCS CONSTANTIN	LTC	0-0908532	0166	3
ORFF DALE V	MAJ	0-1285484	0163	1
ORGEL SAMUEL Z	LTC	0-0104405	0255	3
ORI GEORGE	LTC	0-1309008	0261	1
ORI STEPHEN J	MAJ	0-1173026	1060	1
ORILEY LESTER E	LTC	0-1011852	0163	1
ORILEY ROBERT M	LTC	0-2010615	0866	1
ORIN LAWRENCE E	LTC	0-1108216	0962	1
ORINGDERFF LOYD G	CPT	0-200C493	0956	1
ORIORDAN CHARLES P	LTC	0-1583463	0662	1
ORITT LOUIS	1LT	0-159249C	0645	2
ORIVIS HARRIET S	MAJ	L-0909571	0463	1
ORLANDI MANUEL	CW2	W-2005005	0767	3
ORLANDC THOMAS	COL	0-131063C	0567	1
ORLOFSKY CHARLES F	CPT	0-1555452	1060	1
ORLUK ALPHONSE J	1LT	0-1325234	1045	2
ORMOND CLYDE B	MAJ	0-0975476	0765	1
ORMSBY DONALD F	CW2	W-2107923	0257	1
ORMSBY EDWARD T	CPT	0-0904121	0847	2
ORMSBY JUSTIN R	LTC	0-1050846	0961	1
ORMSBY THOMAS C	CW2	W-2152612	0262	1
ORMSBY WADE E	1LT	0-0428539	1045	2
ORNDOFF JOSEF M	CPT	0-2263675	0263	1
ORNDORF WENDELL R	LTC	0-0913385	1165	3
ORNDORFF CLARENCE A	COL	C-0174803	0646	2
ORNELAS MANUEL	CPT	0-1287575	1047	1
ORNSTEIN DAVID	LTC	0-0485678	1265	1
ORNSTEIN HAROLD A	LTC	0-0300174	0262	3
OROSCO ERNEST D	MAJ	0-1325349	0859	1
CROURKE ALEXANDER	LTC	C-0208723	0447	1
CROURKE DAVIC J	LTC	0-1698130	0364	2
OROURKE JAMES J	LTC	0-0309594	1065	3
OROURKE JOSEPH V	MAJ	0-0361452	0246	2
OROZCO EMIL M	1LT	0-1315002	0347	2
ORR CLAUDE H	MAJ	0-0456677	0557	1
ORR DONALD J	CPT	0-0135863	0156	3
ORR DOROTHY L	MAJ	N-0754526	0665	1
ORR ELI H	COL	0-0286382	0658	3
ORR FRANK M	LTC	0-0193848	0661	3
ORR FREDERICK	LTC	0-0885525	0861	1
ORR FREDERICK	CW3	W-2205946	0764	1
ORR HILOUR O	2LT	N-0742904	0545	1
ORR JAMES F	CW3	W-2146587	0361	1
ORR JR JOHN K	MAJ	0-0394151	0547	2
ORR JR SAMUEL S	CW3	W-2203277	1266	2
ORR LEWIS P	MAJ	0-1000438	0155	1
ORR MORRIS M	MAJ	0-0123577	0550	3
ORR RONALD H	CPT	0-0501205	1045	2
ORR SAMUEL V	CPT	0-0456166	0646	2
ORR WILLIAM F	LTC	0-0328931	0360	1
ORR WILLIAM T	CPT	0-0329105	0446	2
ORRELL ELISE	2LT	N-0727885	0745	1
ORRICK CHARLES H	MAJ	0-0264C06	0561	3
ORRICK LUTHER E	M G	0-0357391	0667	3
ORRIS HAROLD J	MAJ	C-0317842	0745	2
ORRISON HOWARD C	MAJ	0-1031503	0661	1
ORSAY ELMER P	1LT	0-1112351	1145	2
ORSBORN ERNEST V	LTC	0-0319827	0264	3
ORSBORN JR GEORGE E	1LT	0-0443610	0345	2
ORSER LYON C	MAJ	0-1582333	0862	2
ORSINI PAUL	LTC	0-1002701	0658	1
ORSON ELLIOTT A	CPT	0-0468163	0745	2
ORSON OLIVER W	MAJ	0-0301522	0147	2
ORSTAD EDWARD L	COL	0-0298776	0857	1
ORSZULAK MICHAEL J	MAJ	0-1323266	0261	1
ORT JOHN P	MAJ	C-0225795	C165	3
ORTEGA MANUEL M	CW2	W-2209157	0964	1
ORTEGC CRESENCIO	WO1	W-2129629	1146	2
ORTH HAYES J	MAJ	0-1031671	0960	1
ORTH JOHN M	CPT	0-0153923	0751	3
ORTHEY GEORGE F	LTC	0-0185187	0653	3
ORTHNER WALTER H	MAJ	0-0480583	0657	1
ORTIZ ALEJANDRO	CPT	0-0108224	0848	2
ORTIZ CLEMENTE M	1LT	0-1896679	0365	2
ORTIZ JOSE A	CPT	C-0401879	0461	1
CRTIZ JOSE R	2LT	C-1318820	C445	2
ORTIZ SILVESTRE	LTC	0-0382119	C960	1
ORTIZ-CUENCAS JOSE	CW2	W-2210743	C865	1
ORTLER LESLIE A	LTC	0-1683441	1065	1
ORTLIP HENRY T	COL	0-0332093	0760	1
ORTMANN ARNOLD E	MAJ	C-0278221	0365	3
ORTNER RICHARD F	CPT	0-157392C	0946	2
ORTON JACK L	LTC	C-1648658	C762	1
ORTON LEONARD C	CPT	0-1557201	0453	2
ORTON RAY	MAJ	C-1285988	C957	1
ORTZMAN PHILIP	LTC	0-1100712	1061	1
ORVINO JOSEPH R	CPT	0-2049675	0346	2
ORY MURPHY A	COL	C-0348261	0860	1
ORYAN JAMES E L	MAJ	0-0137825	C648	3
ORZECHOWSKI EDWARC A	MAJ	C-2012774	0962	1
ORZECHOWSKI HENRY E	LTC	C-0487708	0657	1
ORZEPOWSKI WALTER S	CPT	0-1303383	C647	2
OSAGE ANTHONY J	CPT	0-1179169	0750	2
OSBORN ARTHUR W	LTC	C-0323211	0962	3
OSBORN BILL E	MAJ	0-1030279	C447	2
CSBORN DAVIC A	LTC	0-0969643	1167	1
OSBORN FRED P	LTC	0-0177896	1155	3
OSBORN JAMES E	MAJ	0-1303626	0761	1
OSBORN JR GEORGE C	MAJ	0-0340691	0646	2
OSBORN NORTON J	LTC	0-0264000	C666	3
OSBORN PRESTON H	MAJ	C-1300846	1061	1
OSBORNE ALBERT B	MAJ	0-0369355	0867	3
OSBORNE ALBERT C	CPT	0-0512255	C755	1
OSBORNE ALBERT J	MAJ	0-1105077	0556	1
OSBORNE ALICE L	1LT	N-0793327	1046	1
OSBORNE ARTHUR H	CPT	C-0259711	0363	3
OSBORNE CECIL M	CW3	W-2144556	0565	1
CSBORNE CHARLES C	CPT	0-1280954	C460	2
OSBORNE CLARENCE F	MAJ	0-0311420	1144	2
CSBORNE EARL E	MAJ	0-0488880	1148	1
OSBORNE ERNEST T	CPT	0-0491923	0349	1
OSBORNE FRANCIS H	CPT	N-0726177	C147	1
OSBORNE GEORGE M	CPT	0-1106381	1045	2
CSBORNE HAROLD L	LTC	0-0555421	0765	1
CSBORNE HUGH D	CPT	0-1017889	0466	2
OSBORNE JOSEPH E	MAJ	C-0994496	1066	1
OSBORNE JR CHESTER M	MAJ	C-1285485	1060	1
OSBORNE JR RUPERT S	CW3	W-2203305	0861	1
CSBORNE JULIUS F	MAJ	C-1588213	0262	1
OSBORNE LOUIS	MAJ	C-1845336	C461	1
OSBORNE LOUIS G	COL	0-0102317	C158	3
OSBORNE OTIS S	LTC	0-1299784	C261	2
OSBORNE RICHARD	CPT	0-0371448	C346	2
OSBORNE ROBERT E	LTC	0-0229270	1263	3
OSBORNE SYDNEY G	LTC	0-0474818	0647	2
OSBORNE THOMAS B E	CW2	W-2147070	1154	1
OSBORNE VINCENT C	CW2	W-2148217	0757	1
OSBORNE WALTON L H	COL	0-0147059	0648	3
OSBORNE WILLIAM	CW4	W-2131047	C566	1
OSBOURN GEORGE R	CPT	0-2032942	C859	1
OSBOURN WARREN E	CPT	0-2263271	0961	1
OSBURN BENJAMIN F	LTC	0-1584703	1054	1
OSBURN EMMITT W	CW4	RW-2133714	C564	1
OSBURN GABRIEL W	1LT	0-0532149	1047	2
CSBURN JAMES C	MAJ	0-1178923	C161	1
OSBURN LEROY	LTC	0-1295262	0954	1
OSBURN RICHARD P	MAJ	C-1799979	0658	1
OSCHWALD EMIL C	CW2	W-2111341	0650	2
OSCHWALD LAWRENCE W	MAJ	0-0340813	0966	3
OSEKOWSKI THOMAS J	LTC	0-1101149	1160	1
OSEN BERT O	MAJ	0-1686197	0166	1
OSENKOWSKI KAROL P	WO1	W-2122710	0345	2
CSGOOD BASIL R	MAJ	0-1046559	1061	1
OSGOOD DEXTER T	LTC	0-0273283	0367	3
OSGOOD DONALD W	LTC	0-1292744	0262	1
CSGOOD FRANK G	CPT	0-0220153	1050	3
CSGOOD FRANKLIN B	COL	0-0305623	1164	3
OSHAUGHNESSY JOHN	1LT	0-1799069	0851	2
OSHAUGHNESSY JOHN F	MAJ	0-1824356	C459	2
OSHAUGHNESSY PATRI	1LT	0-1017747	0846	1
OSHEA EDWARD A	LTC	0-0258474	0466	3
OSHEA HOWARD F	1LT	0-1177562	0446	2
OSHEA JAMES	CW3	W-2142362	0561	1
OSHEA JOHN F	LTC	0-0308591	0159	3
OSHEA ERIE M	MAJ	0-0498140	1052	1
OSHEE PATRICK C	COL	0-0216153	1063	3
OSHEROFF WILLIAM	MAJ	0-0426611	0645	2
OSHIRO WILLIAM C	1LT	0-1998050	0147	2
OSICKEY BENJAMIN L	LTC	0-1647216	0267	1
OSIER ROLLAN	1LT	0-1183151	0747	1
OSLER RALPH	MAJ	0-0991484	1265	2
OSMAN JAMES A	CPT	0-1285989	1151	1
OSMAN LEO D	CPT	0-0196449	0944	2
OSMAN LEROY J	MAJ	0-1794843	1060	2
OSMANSKY MORTIMER	MAJ	C-0285380	0460	3
CSMUN ELMER E	MAJ	C-0242138	0263	3
OSMUN JOHN B	LTC	0-0247235	0758	3
OSMUN JR JAMES W	1LT	0-2037581	1047	1
CSMUN JR WALTER	CW3	W-2148758	1062	1
OSMUN WILLIS R	CPT	0-0133189	0648	3
OSMUSSEN JOHN S	1LT	0-1177563	0246	2
OSOSKY BERNARD H	CW2	W-2143273	1056	2
OSTEEN BERNARD V	CW3	W-2144332	0961	1
OSTEEN JACK A	CPT	0-0959358	1064	1
OSTENDORF WALTER A	COL	0-0213614	0550	3
OSTERBY BARBARA M	2LT	N-0778196	0147	1
OSTERCAHL ETHEL V	CPT	N-0793684	0956	2
OSTERHOLM ORRIN C	2LT	0-1307292	0144	2
OSTERHOUDT PHILIP J	LTC	0-0192147	0156	3
OSTERKAMP FRANCIS R	MAJ	0-0474962	0647	1
OSTERMAN ARTHUR H	MAJ	0-0969555	0765	2
OSTERMAN JAMES K	COL	0-0378433	0461	1
OSTERMAN MARTIN G	MAJ	0-1884092	1066	1
OSTERMANN RAYMOND J	MAJ	C-0562883	1266	1
OSTERMEIER RUSSELL L	LTC	0-0242396	0757	1
OSTERNDORF LOGAN C	1LT	0-0372981	0147	1
OSTERSTOCK GEORGE A	LTC	0-1291872	0960	1
OSTERWALD HERBERT R	MAJ	0-0258138	0766	3
OSTEYEE WILLIAM W	CW3	W-2105776	0456	2
OSTLUNC VICTOR S	1LT	0-1180654	0545	2
OSTRANC CHARLES J	MAJ	C-4021162	0167	1
OSTRANDER GILBERT G	MAJ	0-0423867	1162	1
OSTRANDER WILLIAM G	CW2	W-2148144	C659	1
OSTREM VICTOR L	LTC	0-0463472	0954	1
OSTRO HARRY	1LT	0-0563969	0845	2
OSTROFF DAVID S	CPT	0-1313786	104N	1
OSTROM ERNEST S	LTC	0-1315356	1062	1
OSTROM PAUL G	LTC	0-1646475	0367	3
OSTROM PAUL L	2LT	0-1825877	0845	2
OSTROM RALPH K	CPT	0-0343776	0854	2
OSTROW JAMES D	LTC	0-0330621	0446	1
OSTROW LOUIS B	CPT	0-0209897	0661	3
OSULLIVAN DELLA E	2LT	N-0752736	0246	1
OSULLIVAN EDMOND J	LTC	0-1011329	0860	1
OSULLIVAN FRANK D	1LT	0-1310869	104N	2
OSULLIVAN GEORGE W	COL	0-0284871	0646	2
OSULLIVAN JACK M	CPT	0-0338920	0445	1
OSULLIVAN JAMES V	1LT	0-0562623	0157	1
OSULLIVAN JOHN F	CPT	0-1014318	0448	2
OSWALC CLETUS J	LTC	0-0263866	1057	3
OSWALD RALPH J W	COL	0-0294657	0863	1
OSWALT JAMES O	2LT	0-1181398	0944	2
OTENBERGER JOHN L	MAJ	0-2263383	1065	1
OTERT JOHN	CW4	W-2110317	0859	1
OTERO TULIO	CW3	W-2147638	1160	1
OTEY IVO F	COL	C-0246568	1264	3
OTIS FREDERIC S	MAJ	0-1305101	0665	3
OTIS HAROLD	CPT	0-0477958	0247	1
OTIS WILLIAM L	MAJ	0-1042665	0859	1
OTOOLE CHARLES V	CPT	0-0938143	0956	1
OTOOLE JOHN H	MAJ	0-0312499	0946	1
OTOOLE JOSEPH F	CPT	0-1593156	0457	1
OTOOLE WILLIAM F	CW4	W-2142307	0758	2

292-560 O - 68 - 18

NAME	GRADE	SVC NO	DATE RET MO YR	RET CODE
OTOOLE WILLIAM J	2LT	0-1054744	0645	2
OTOOLE WILLIAM L	CPT	0-1172933	C949	2
OTOUSA JANE C	2LT	N-0762090	0245	1
OTSEA MARSHALL S	MAJ	C-1339305	0365	1
CTSTOT RICHARD G	LTC	0-0295563	0666	3
OTT ARTHUR A	LTC	0-1168402	1060	1
OTT CLIFFORD S	LTC	0-0297025	0263	1
OTT DOYLE C	MAJ	C-0508917	0646	1
OTT EDWARD V	1LT	0-1311199	0945	2
OTT GLENN J	1LT	0-0382090	1044	2
OTT JOHN F	LTC	0-0318035	0762	1
OTT JOSEPH T	CPT	0-0333097	0450	1
OTT JR CHARLES H	COL	0-0218491	0159	2
OTT JR JOHN J	CPT	0-0464204	C744	2
OTT RALPH J W	CPT	0-1322365	C847	2
OTT RICHARD B	MAJ	0-0151726	0357	3
CTT ROBERT S	CW2	W-2141400	1057	1
OTT ROBERT T	CW2	W-2146890	0661	1
OTT ROBERT W	LTC	C-1036665	0664	2
OTTAVI ROMOLO F	LTC	0-1302871	0767	1
OTTAVIANO ANTONIO F	CW2	W-2145476	0660	1
OTTAWAY LESTER B	WO1	W-2116023	1055	1
OTTE FREDERICK	WO1	W-2114665	0756	1
OTTE RALPH E	LTC	0-0242019	0456	3
OTTEN JACK A	MAJ	0-0364545	0667	3
OTTEN JOHN H	MAJ	0-1307065	0459	1
OTTEN WILLIAM C	B G	0-0470649	0761	3
OTTERPOHL HENRY J	2LT	0-1914152	1046	1
OTTINGER GEORGE W	CW3	W-2142598	0161	1
OTTINGER LOWELL T	LTC	0-0454089	0561	1
OTTMANN EDWARD C	MAJ	0-0455988	0757	1
OTTO CARL E	LTC	C-0235939	1155	3
OTTO EMIL H	1LT	0-1032383	C845	2
OTTO GEORGE N	MAJ	C-0337802	0567	3
OTTO JOHN	LTC	0-1030182	0661	1
OTTO RAYMOND H	MAJ	0-0229777	0365	3
OTTO ROBERT G	CW2	W-2146889	0764	1
OTTOFY LADIS H	1LT	0-0131120	0657	3
OTTS SHERMAN R	CW2	W-2142121	0662	1
OTTMILLER ROBERT F	CW2	W-2210893	0762	1
OUELLETTE CHARLES E	CW4	W-2106323	1066	1
OUILETTE JAMES J	CPT	0-0410376	1144	2
OUSLEY IVON L	CW2	W-2145900	1057	1
OUSTAD CARL B	LTC	0-0194898	0259	3
OUTEN DEWEY L	MAJ	0-0220938	1051	1
OUTLAND ORLAND T	MAJ	C-0948897	C462	1
OUTLAW ARTHUR T	LTC	0-1584705	0963	1
OUTLAW VENIRA E	MAJ	N-0763230	0966	2
OUTMAN HARL F	MAJ	0-1103849	0863	1
OUTSEN ROBERT K	1LT	0-1549001	0145	2
OUTTEN ALMA J	1LT	N-0743610	1145	1
OUTTEN EDGAR C	LTC	0-0153650	0-51	3
OUTTERSON CHARLES W	CPT	0-0256112	1160	3
OVELMEN HERMAN O	COL	0-0289573	0965	3
OVENS MELVON J	MAJ	0-C284053	1166	3
OVER JR FRANK	LTC	0-0103033	0256	3
OVERACKER ALVIN G	CW2	W-3430442	C966	1
OVERBAY CLARENCE M	CW3	W-2142014	C764	1
OVERBAY ROY V	2LT	0-1322587	0745	2
OVERBECK ALVIN H	MAJ	0-0552007	0664	1
OVERBY CARL L	CW2	W-2121439	1053	2
OVERBY EDWARD J	MAJ	0-0525219	1045	2
OVERCASH DENNIS B	MAJ	0-0162580	0158	3
OVERFIELD ELIJAH H	LTC	0-0487651	0452	1
OVERGAARD TERANCE E	LTC	0-0264314	0866	3
OVERHOLSER DEWEY L	MAJ	0-0242622	1058	3
OVERHOLTZER HARRY A	LTC	0-0332234	0461	1
OVERLEE DONALD	CPT	0-1553329	0755	1
OVERLEY RAYMOND J	CW2	W-2143518	1156	1
OVERLOCK JR WALTER E	MAJ	C-1590088	0761	1
OVERMAN GERARD B	MAJ	0-1897800	1162	1
OVERMYER CALVIN J	COL	0-0218884	0257	3
OVERMYER CHARLES E	MAJ	0-0400482	0462	1
OVERSTREET CHARLES O	MAJ	0-1000836	0860	1
OVERSTREET CLAUDE L	MAJ	C-2002513	0762	1

NAME	GRADE	SVC NO	DATE RET MO YR	RET CODE
OVERTON AMOS	CW2	W-2205568	0961	1
OVERTON GLEN D	1LT	0-1304781	0646	2
OVERTON IRVING J	CPT	0-0527125	0345	2
OVERTON LEMUEL H	1LT	0-0281225	C345	2
OVERTON MACK W	1LT	0-0483157	0447	1
OVERTON ROBERT H	LTC	0-0271857	0361	3
OVERTURF ARCHIE M	1LT	0-0506237	0351	1
OVERTURF ARNOLD A	LTC	0-2048737	0564	1
OVERTURF VERNON F	MAJ	0-0979458	0762	1
OVIATT WELLS	MAJ	0-0168986	0647	2
OWEN ALBERT E	1LT	0-1325351	0147	2
OWEN ALBERT S	COL	0-0247659	1265	3
OWEN CHARLES J	LTC	0-0313585	1058	1
OWEN CHARLES R	LTC	0-0371227	1064	3
OWEN CLARENCE I	COL	0-0210363	1156	3
OWEN EDWARD E	MAJ	C-2006071	1160	1
OWEN GARLAND M	MAJ	0-0287408	0264	3
OWEN GEORGE R	LTC	0-0343412	0759	1
OWEN HARRY M	MAJ	0-015364C	0456	3
OWEN HOWARD P	CW2	W-2150773	1061	1
OWEN JACK D	MAJ	0-0358568	0449	1
OWEN JACK S	COL	C-0363845	0761	1
OWEN JAMES B	LTC	0-1824907	C867	1
OWEN JAMES D	1LT	0-0885727	1045	2
OWEN JAMES G	CPT	0-0968077	0461	1
OWEN JAMES R	1LT	0-0108535	0134	1
OWEN JOSEPH A	MAJ	0-0252138	1166	3
OWEN JOSEPH H	MAJ	0-1996623	0162	1
OWEN RICHARD W	LTC	0-0205494	0145	2
OWEN RICHARD W	COL	0-0211765	0960	1
OWEN ROBERT D	CPT	0-1048522	0647	1
OWEN ROBERT W	COL	0-0358421	0461	1
OWEN ROY W	LTC	0-1174095	0461	1
OWEN RUTH W	MAJ	N-0741645	0164	3
OWEN SAMMIE H	MAJ	0-1048131	1060	1
OWEN SEWARD E	COL	0-0201536	1058	3
OWEN WALTER D	CPT	0-0413993	1062	2
OWEN WESLEY C	LTC	0-0220752	0461	1
OWEN WILLIAM W	MAJ	0-2014057	0567	1
OWEN WILLIE J	CPT	0-0409572	0146	2
OWENS ANDRE H	MAJ	0-1001025	0664	1
OWENS BENJAMIN T	MAJ	0-0328932	1164	3
OWENS BENNETT G	COL	0-0224270	0361	3
OWENS BILLIE G	CW2	W-3430427	0966	1
OWENS CHARLES F	LTC	0-1171303	0962	1
OWENS CLARENCE P	CW4	W-2000628	0261	3
OWENS CLEO H	LTC	0-1052113	0166	1
OWENS EARL H	CPT	0-0969228	1061	2
OWENS EDWARD A	CPT	0-1726066	0146	2
OWENS EDWARD H	CW2	W-2142888	0764	1
OWENS EDWARD J	MAJ	0-0137488	0648	3
OWENS EUGENE R	1LT	0-1111820	1046	2
OWENS FRED	CW4	W-2146677	0757	1
OWENS FREDERICK	1LT	0-4030832	0459	2
OWENS GLADYS E	MAJ	N-0759878	0263	1
OWENS HAROLD C	MAJ	0-1636435	0960	1
OWENS HENRY M	LTC	0-1580130	0658	1
OWENS HERBERT T	MAJ	0-1057556	0865	1
OWENS HERMAN	2LT	0-195163C	0750	1
OWENS JAMES C	LTC	0-1180655	0663	1
OWENS JAMES E	MAJ	C-1578945	0261	1
OWENS JAMES M	1LT	0-1015162	0367	1
OWENS JESSE L	CW4	W-2153265	0166	1
OWENS JOHN B	MAJ	0-1108908	0466	1
OWENS JOSEPH E	LTC	0-1108909	0962	1
OWENS JOSEPH H	LTC	0-0230093	1165	3
OWENS JR CHARLES W	MAJ	0-2212C19	0464	1
OWENS JR JAMES W	CPT	0-0309861	0442	2
OWENS JR JOHN D	CPT	0-1326015	0647	2
OWENS JR JUDSON F	LTC	0-0555567	1265	1
OWENS JR WILLIAM H	CPT	0-1303384	C147	2
OWENS KENNETH G	1LT	0-1590714	0245	2
OWENS LAWRENCE H	MAJ	0-1323024	0963	1
OWENS LAWTON K	MAJ	0-0462605	0862	1
OWENS MARVIN A	CW2	W-3150536	0365	1

NAME	GRADE	SVC NO	DATE RET MO YR	RET CODE
OWENS MARY H	1LT	N-0723333	C146	1
OWENS MATTHEW J	CPT	0-0157787	1059	3
OWENS MAURICE J	LTC	0-0336916	0762	3
OWENS MAURICE T	LTC	0-0259389	1166	3
OWENS MERVIL C	MAJ	C-2262288	0863	1
OWENS ROBERT E	MAJ	0-2047098	0759	1
OWENS ROBERT H	LTC	0-0336821	1054	3
OWENS ROBERT V	LTC	0-0524053	C763	1
OWENS ROBERT W	1LT	0-1823924	C546	2
OWENS ROSS	COL	0-0263873	0966	3
OWENS THEODORE R	LTC	0-0558201	1064	1
OWENS THOMAS M	LTC	C-0420739	C566	1
OWENS TRACY C	LTC	0-0490887	C545	2
OWENS WILLIAM C	1LT	0-2026911	1046	1
OWENS WILLIAM F	CPT	0-0918660	0445	2
OWENS WILLIAM H	LTC	0-0444895	0747	1
OWENS WILLIAM I	CPT	0-0472007	1047	2
OWENS WILLIAM L	CW2	W-2152831	0557	1
OWINGS DORSEY	COL	0-0286618	0256	3
OWINGS ORVILLE M	LTC	0-1289478	0157	1
OWINGS WALTON A	2LT	0-0507896	0144	2
OWNBY KEITH M	MAJ	C-1304108	1163	1
OWNEY HOLMAN F	MAJ	0-1016070	0561	1
OWSLEY EDWARD A	COL	0-0414501	0466	1
OWSLEY GUY A	COL	0-0254641	0364	3
OWSLEY LINTON L	MAJ	0-0981680	C764	1
OXENDINE MELYAR R	MAJ	0-2014445	0662	1
OXFORD WILLIAM D	CPT	0-0238589	0761	3
OXLEY DELBERT F	2LT	0-1999304	0448	1
OXLEY JOSEPH C	LTC	C-0204148	0756	3
OXLEY LAWRENCE A	1LT	0-0127499	0648	3
OXLEY LEWIS P	MAJ	0-4074732	0967	1
OXTON CHARLES A	2LT	0-1946128	1144	2
OXWANG MARGARET	1LT	N-0736483	0247	1
OYLER DONALD D	CW3	W-2147364	0165	1
OYLER FRANK H	CPT	0-1556774	0561	1
OYLER URAL E	MAJ	C-1013294	0860	1
OZDOWSKI FRANK C	CPT	0-0384987	0244	2
OZENBERGER PETER F	MAJ	C-1285284	1056	1
OZIER SR RAYFIELD	CW2	W-2141401	C856	2
OZMUN CHARLES G	CPT	0-0279175	C844	2
OZSVATH DANIEL R	CPT	0-C500057	1046	2
PAAR EDWARD G	LTC	0-C258649	0159	1
PAAR ROBERT J	MAJ	C-1688496	0765	1
PABLO AGAPITO B	1LT	0-1896490	C366	1
PABONRAMIREZ M	WO1	W-2113970	0446	2
PABST EDWIN D	1LT	0-0516715	1047	2
PACE BONNIE L	CW3	W-2150035	0962	1
PACE CHARLES M	CPT	0-1535611	0366	1
PACE FRED C	1LT	0-1103358	1045	2
PACE GEORGE A	MAJ	C-1107018	C267	3
PACE GEORGE D	2LT	0-1039499	1044	2
PACE JR SMITH H	LTC	0-1578946	0461	1
PACE LORAN A	LTC	0-0545451	0364	1
PACE OTIS	MAJ	C-1634194	0854	1
PACE RENTIS E	LTC	0-1548273	0757	1
PACEK LOUIS E	CW2	W-2143393	1157	2
PACELLA RALPH M	1LT	0-1169854	0146	2
PACETTI AMEDEO E	CPT	0-0517459	0545	2
PACHECO EDWARD F	LTC	0-1100714	1160	1
PACHECO EDWARD J	CW2	W-2146737	0561	1
PACHECO ESTHER M	CPT	N-0900805	C263	2
PACHL LADDIE J	CPT	0-0255656	0862	3
PACIFICO ALEXANDER	MAJ	0-0969838	1064	2
PACK JR HENRY B	MAJ	0-0315065	C646	2
PACK LAMONT A	LTC	0-0232389	0757	3
PACK MYRTLE I	1LT	N-0730647	0946	1
PACK PHILIP C	COL	0-0170735	0556	3
PACKARD BRUCE G	MAJ	C-0285931	1064	3
PACKARD EDWARD N	COL	0-0202025	0648	3
PACKARD JOHN K	MAJ	0-0172335	104N	1
PACKARD LYLE D	MAJ	0-0390934	0861	1
PACKARD RUSSEL L	LTC	0-1039277	0962	1
PACKER ALMA S	COL	0-0199890	0-52	3
PACKER DAVID A	LTC	0-2051271	1166	1

NAME	GRADE	SVC NO	DATE RET MO YR	RET CODE
PACKER JACOB L	MAJ	0-0400694	0163	1
PACKER NORMAN N	1LT	0-1040597	0445	2
PACKER ROY F	CPT	0-1060575	0447	2
PACOCHA EDMUND S	CPT	0-1684346	0545	2
PACULA STEVEN J	1LT	0-0402302	1044	2
PACULIS GEORGE B	MAJ	0-1062622	0164	1
PADALINO MARTIN L	LTC	0-0070463	1167	1
PADAN FRANK L	2LT	0-1116536	0946	2
PADAONC CONSTANTIN	1LT	0-203192C	0149	1
PADDENBURG JOHN A	LTC	0-0451370	0660	1
PADDOCK CLINTON T	LTC	0-0232005	0465	3
PADDOCK FREDERICK	MAJ	0-0417328	0946	1
PADDOCK HOWARD P	LTC	0-0178103	0648	3
PADDOCK LEROY	CW4	W-2103782	0957	1
PADDOCK RALF C	COL	0-0182590	0446	2
PADDOCK ROBERT H	COL	C-0234415	1065	3
PADDOCK STILES R	LTC	0-0300501	1065	1
PADEN DONALD G	CW4	W-2176333	1160	1
PADEN JOHN K	LTC	0-0210629	1053	2
PADGET JR HENRY F	1LT	0-0540402	0446	2
PADGETT BENNIE	MAJ	0-1303017	0459	1
PADGETT EDMOND J	LTC	0-0345017	0660	1
PADGETT EUGENE C	COL	0-0314533	0559	1
PADGETT JOEL J	LTC	0-0209103	1147	2
PADGETT JOHN L	MAJ	0-1876933	1166	1
PADGETT LORENZO O	MAJ	0-0497004	0756	1
PADGETT MEADE H	CW2	W-2207366	0762	1
PADGETT PAUL J	MAJ	0-2033068	1262	1
PADGETT PHILIP G	CPT	0-0482455	0447	2
PADGETT ROBERT G	LTC	0-0177274	1161	3
PADGITT JAMES T	MAJ	0-0244920	1144	2
PADIAL ISABEL R	MAJ	N-0800252	0865	1
PADILLA JAIME L	CPT	0-0450379	1060	1
PADLAR PEGGY A	2LT	L-0210160	0645	2
PADLEY EVERETT J	LTC	0-0297913	0864	3
PAOLON JOSEPH F	COL	0-0205557	0760	3
PADMORE WILLIAM G	CW3	W-2149876	0663	1
PADRICK WALTER R	LTC	0-0254414	0162	1
PAORTA NORMAN L	2LT	0-1590093	0344	2
PADUA MARIANO	2LT	0-1896608	0750	1
PADVORAC VICTOR A	1LT	0-1308853	1044	2
PAEPER HENRY	MAJ	0-0256353	0662	3
PAEPKE HAROLD M	MAJ	0-1181069	0963	1
PAFENBERG ROY E	MAJ	0-2027357	0562	1
PAFFORD JR ROBERT B	MAJ	0-0960103	0264	1
PAFFORD PARNELL M	COL	0-0272214	0563	1
PAGAC BENEDICT P	LTC	0-1339559	1066	1
PAGAN FRANCISCO	LTC	0-0298806	0467	3
PAGAN LUIS R	CW2	W-2154862	1060	1
PAGANI JR FEDERICO	CPT	0-2262642	0261	1
PAGANO RICHARD L	CPT	0-1017855	0346	1
PAGE CANNON R	MAJ	C-0241933	0962	3
PAGE CHARLES A	LTC	0-0361734	C859	1
PAGE CHARLES E	LTC	0-0422077	0760	1
PAGE DAVID E	CPT	0-0497616	0854	1
PAGE DAVID P	COL	0-0204809	0262	3
PAGE EDSEL F	CPT	0-2014548	0366	1
PAGE EDWIN R	MAJ	0-0199862	0648	3
PAGE GEORGE H	LTC	0-1635187	1266	1
PAGE HERMAN F	LTC	0-0151845	1054	3
PAGE JAMES A	MAJ	0-0272102	1166	3
PAGE JAMES F	CPT	0-1290991	0348	2
PAGE JESSE B	MAJ	0-0247281	0167	3
PAGE JOHN B	1LT	0-0498039	0846	1
PAGE JOHN E	CPT	0-0515866	0247	1
PAGE JOSEPH E	LTC	0-2030621	0267	1
PAGE JR HENRY L	MAJ	0-0990415	1064	2
PAGE JR JOHN G	MAJ	0-1012226	0361	1
PAGE JR JOHN W	MAJ	0-0385136	0646	2
PAGE JR ROBERT L	2LT	0-1289789	0645	2
PAGE KENNETH J	1LT	0-1645859	0145	2
PAGE LESLIE K	MAJ	0-0972813	0962	1
PAGE NOBLE W	1LT	0-0404282	0745	2
PAGE OTTO C	CPT	0-0448618	0547	1
PAGE PAUL E	MAJ	0-1340924	1163	1

NAME	GRADE	SVC NO	DATE RET MO YR	RET CODE
PAGE ROBERT C	MAJ	0-0324117	1145	2
PAGE VICTOR S	MAJ	0-0475727	0953	1
PAGE WILLIAM E	CPT	0-1881954	0963	1
PAGE WILLIAM M	MAJ	C-2208586	0766	1
PAGE WILLIS M	MAJ	C-1104328	C961	1
PAGEL HERBERT E	MAJ	C-1045546	1065	1
PAGELS EDWARD A	CPT	0-2262921	0361	1
PAGLIERANI LOUIS J	LTC	0-1101981	0161	1
PAGNOTTA FRANK R	LTC	0-2000817	0965	1
PAGTER AMOS T	LTC	0-0127827	C251	3
PAHL JOSEPH W	1LT	0-0539209	0446	2
PAHLE JOSEPH R	1LT	0-0524626	1046	1
PAIGE BYRON L	COL	0-0018704	1060	1
PAIGE CLAUDE	CPT	0-1323607	C455	2
PAIGE JOSEPH	1LT	0-1596460	114N	2
PAIGE ROLANC W	MAJ	0-1895512	0466	3
PAINE ALBERT W	COL	C-0151120	0648	3
PAINE ANDREW	LTC	0-0815226	C767	1
PAINE CHARLES B	LTC	0-0359132	1046	2
PAINE EDWARD V	1LT	0-1547098	C266	1
PAINE EUGENE M	CPT	0-0401873	0645	2
PAINE FRANK L	CPT	0-0256979	1064	3
PAINE HENRY E	MAJ	C-118140C	0760	1
PAINE JOHN R	LTC	0-0284794	1266	3
PAINE JR CHARLES C	2LT	0-2010796	0746	2
PAINE MELVIN R	WO1	W-2151635	1053	1
PAINE ROBERT L	CW3	W-214635C	0363	1
PAINTER BENJAMIN F	CPT	0-0149083	0653	3
PAINTER DAVID R	WO1	W-2142773	0756	1
PAINTER FREDERICK	MAJ	C-1585996	C447	2
PAINTER HARRY J	LTC	0-0941993	C366	1
PAINTER JAMES P	1LT	0-0447044	1145	2
PAINTER KENNETH O	1LT	0-1924797	0753	1
PAINTER LOWELL	1LT	0-1107021	1051	1
PAINTER MARY L	1LT	N-0755031	0646	2
PAIRSH JOHN R	CPT	0-1546019	1051	1
PAISLEY HAROLD	CW2	W-2141403	1054	1
PAISLEY OLDHAM	COL	0-0120285	0553	3
PAISTE ALBERT J	MAJ	0-1985650	1166	1
PAJELA FELIPE R	2LT	0-1896837	0858	1
PAJU OLAF E	CPT	0-2033097	C959	1
PAJUNAS ALBERT	LTC	C-0384447	1060	1
PAKELE JR PETER N	LTC	0-0224738	C954	3
PALACIO FRANK J	MAJ	0-0398123	C248	2
PALACKY FRANK A	LTC	0-1536209	0263	1
PALAGI SETH	LTC	0-0372551	0658	1
PALASKY FRANK	CW2	W-2149936	0261	1
PALAU OTTO G	2LT	C-2009644	0646	2
PALDA ROBERT R	LTC	0-0953903	C764	1
PALEDES NICHOLAS P	LTC	C-1294892	0961	1
PALERMO JOSEPH D	MAJ	C-1297414	C757	1
PALETZ EUGENE	LTC	0-0248086	1058	1
PALEY AARON	CPT	0-0428323	C745	1
PALEY JAMES E	LTC	0-0322368	C662	1
PALFREY THOMAS R	COL	C-0178635	1055	3
PALIN AGNES J	MAJ	N-0757411	0164	3
PALKA STANLEY J	CW2	W-2152280	0860	1
PALKOVIC MICHAEL J	CPT	0-0478880	1059	1
PALL THOMAS O	1LT	0-1796995	1060	1
PALLA RINALDO F	LTC	C-164864C	0166	1
PALLASCH PAUL V	CPT	0-0117746	0647	2
PALLMAN GEORGE H	LTC	0-0282985	C760	1
PALLO GEORGE S	1LT	0-0515634	0446	2
PALM WILLIAM J	1LT	0-1035332	1045	2
PALMA ANTHONY V	MAJ	0-0346304	C764	3
PALMACCIO CHARLES P	LTC	0-1052913	1167	1
PALMATARY ERNEST F	CPT	0-034619C	0245	1
PALMER ALBERT J	CPT	C-0524533	C845	2
PALMER ALFRED H	COL	0-0284096	1067	3
PALMER ALGER A	MAJ	C-0168549	0551	3
PALMER ALONZO S	MAJ	C-0970812	1161	1
PALMER ARTHUR C	LTC	0-0273736	1264	3
PALMER BEATRICE B	MAJ	L-1010010	C165	1
PALMER CARL J	MAJ	0-1311047	0862	1
PALMER CARL L	LTC	0-1030701	C865	1

NAME	GRADE	SVC NO	DATE RET MO YR	RET CODE
PALMER CHARLES B	LTC	0-0451024	0258	2
PALMER CHARLES E	LTC	0-1111286	0464	1
PALMER CHARLES K	CW3	W-2205899	0266	1
PALMER CHARLES L	CPT	0-0202124	0362	3
PALMER CLARENCE E	LTC	0-0285815	0665	3
PALMER CLARK F	CPT	0-132396C	1048	1
PALMER CLETUS T	1LT	0-1280375	0945	2
PALMER CUSTIN C	MAJ	C-1184518	0761	1
PALMER DOMINIC M	MAJ	0-0469827	1045	1
PALMER DONALD B	LTC	0-0166974	0648	3
PALMER ERNEST D	MAJ	0-0226475	0763	3
PALMER FRANCIS J	LTC	0-0388839	1060	1
PALMER FRANK	LTC	0-0492154	0157	1
PALMER FRANK C	CPT	0-1577668	1048	2
PALMER FREDERICK	LTC	0-1290992	0959	1
PALMER GAIL A	CW2	W-2104788	1044	2
PALMER HARRY O	CW2	W-2205164	0758	1
PALMER HELEN L	LTC	N-0723014	0562	1
PALMER HENRY U	LTC	0-1057557	0166	1
PALMER JACK	CPT	0-130037C	1053	1
PALMER JACK M	CPT	0-2012844	0457	1
PALMER JAMES R	MAJ	0-0257215	1159	3
PALMER JESSE I	CPT	0-0255262	0766	3
PALMER JEWEL H	CW3	W-2151324	0564	1
PALMER JOHN L	1LT	C-1822721	1145	2
PALMER JOHN W	2LT	0-1332150	0746	2
PALMER JOSEPH H	1LT	C-0201939	0753	3
PALMER JOSEPH P	1LT	0-1320170	1045	1
PALMER JOSEPH W	COL	0-0110603	0754	3
PALMER JR EARL J	LTC	0-0407863	0663	1
PALMER JR EDWARD J	1LT	0-0983007	0458	1
PALMER JR THERA O	MAJ	C-0268801	1046	2
PALMER KARL V	COL	C-012359C	0755	3
PALMER LELAND H	LTC	0-1533882	0461	2
PALMER MAC A	LTC	0-0401497	0453	2
PALMER MARVIN E	1LT	0-1185115	0645	2
PALMER MC KEE A	MAJ	0-0300097	0167	3
PALMER NOBLE E	LTC	0-1551286	0462	1
PALMER NOYES S	MAJ	0-1318077	0457	1
PALMER OSBORN	LTC	0-0100314	0648	3
PALMER OTIS B	COL	0-0390721	1266	1
PALMER R V	LTC	0-0540396	1063	1
PALMER RALPH J	CW3	W-2145218	1160	1
PALMER RANDOLPH M	MAJ	0-1030400	0459	1
PALMER RAY H	MAJ	C-021228C	0453	3
PALMER RAYMOND C	MAJ	0-0127307	C844	2
PALMER RICHARD H	LTC	0-091164C	0665	3
PALMER ROBERT E	1LT	0-1019973	0647	2
PALMER ROBERT R	CPT	0-0182567	1043	2
PALMER STANLEY A	LTC	0-0367957	0667	3
PALMER THURSTON J	MAJ	0-0317135	0367	3
PALMER TRUMAN G	LTC	0-0299873	0960	1
PALMER WALTER E	COL	0-0115125	0648	3
PALMER WILLIAM E	LTC	0-117220P	1066	1
PALMER WILLIAM G	1LT	0-1825249	0346	2
PALMER WILLIAM H	MAJ	0-0392010	1262	1
PALMERLEE JOHN O	1LT	0-0481336	0445	2
PALMERTON RUSSELL J	MAJ	0-1313441	0858	2
PALMIERI FRANK F	WO1	W-2124067	0443	2
PALMORE AARON D	LTC	0-0412866	0560	1
PALMQUIST HOWARD D	MAJ	0-0963863	0761	1
PALMQUIST MILFORD H	MAJ	0-0508058	0159	1
PALMQUIST ROY M	CPT	0-1313787	0159	2
PALUMBO ANTHONY A	LTC	0-037296C	1164	1
PALUMBO GERALD A	MAJ	0-0397068	0146	2
PALUMBO JOSEPH G	CPT	0-0240964	1161	3
PALUMBO LEONARD J	MAJ	0-0423164	1262	1
PALUMBO RICHARD J	LTC	0-1580137	1066	1
PALYOK JR JOHN	MAJ	0-1171306	0262	1
PALZKILL ANNA M	LTC	N-0730227	C561	1
PAMER JR JOHN A	1LT	0-1326229	1145	2
PAMPLIN LLOYD	CPT	0-1575052	0358	1
PANAGOPOULOS PETER P	CW3	W-2144978	0962	1
PANAGOT GEORGE J	2LT	0-1302872	1044	1
PANAK VINCENT	CPT	0-1101608	0747	2

NAME	GRADE	SVC NO	DATE RET MO YR	RET CODE
PANAPOLIS PETER J	CPT	0-0274859	0160	3
PANCOAST KATHERINE	CPT	N-0729053	C646	2
PANCOOK ARTHUR J	COL	C-0299366	C567	3
PANEK JOHN M	1LT	0-163420C	C947	2
PANETTIERE BARTHOLOM	LTC	C-1592496	C967	3
PANGBORN RICHARD K	CW3	W-2208127	C566	1
PANGLE HAROLD J	COL	0-0418496	0761	1
PANIAN DONALD J	MAJ	0-1876994	1264	1
PANICH HAROLD L	1LT	0-1171307	0346	2
PANISH CHARLES K	COL	C-0908231	C567	3
PANKER JOSEPH F	LTC	0-1535049	1266	1
PANKEY ELDRIDGE T	MAJ	C-1301202	0761	1
PANKEY HENRY G	WO1	W-2127650	0550	1
PANKEY JAMES E	CW2	W-2143341	0162	1
PANKOSKY JOHN J	LTC	0-1283475	C657	1
PANKRATZ ROBERT R	CW2	W-2210842	C765	2
PANNEBAKER CHARLES P	CW2	W-2142568	C761	1
PANNECK THEODORE W	LTC	0-0407704	1060	1
PANNELL EARL R	1LT	0-1318572	1045	2
PANNELL GEORGE E	LTC	0-1050855	0162	1
PANORA ANTHONY	MAJ	C-0125985	C858	3
PANOS MICHAEL	CPT	0-0941998	0657	1
PANOTES RICARDO	1LT	0-1896757	C862	1
PANTALEO FRANK A	1LT	0-1003425	C652	1
PANTAZI SPIROS G	1LT	0-0550183	1045	2
PANTERA ALBIN M	CPT	0-1717800	1046	2
PANTON WILLIAM A	LTC	0-0203771	0553	3
PANTSARI ERIC W	MAJ	C-1306137	C563	1
PANUZIO FRANK L	LTC	0-0273647	0867	3
PANZARINO ANGELO	MAJ	C-1298585	C461	1
PAOLI LOUIS S	1LT	0-1317106	0645	2
PAOLINI MARIO	MAJ	0-1039587	C860	1
PAOLUCCI VINCENT P	LTC	0-C540812	0667	2
PAONESSA ROBERT A	MAJ	0-0968640	0764	1
PAPA ANTHONY T	MAJ	0-0420351	C863	1
PAPAE NORMAN	LTC	0-0229696	C262	3
PAPAS ALEXANDER	CPT	0-0510202	114N	2
PAPAZOGLOU GEORGE	CPT	0-1301355	C646	2
PAPE GLENN W	LTC	0-0332584	0561	1
PAPE LEWIS C	2LT	0-1522902	C344	2
PAPE MIRIAM A	CPT	N-0773313	C348	1
PAPEN BERNARD P	COL	0-0236606	C758	1
PAPERNO SAMUEL	CW3	W-2142000	0159	1
PAPIERNIK ADOLPH J	WO1	W-2105891	1146	1
PAPKEE EDWARD E	CPT	0-1535511	0647	2
PAPKEE GUSTAVE A	1LT	0-0127458	C753	3
PAPP EDWARD A	MAJ	0-1636443	C960	1
PAPP EDWIN A	1LT	C-1331326	C946	1
PAPPALARDO CARMELO	CW4	W-2121633	C862	1
PAPPALARDO JOHN	1LT	0-5019627	0566	2
PAPPAS ANGELO	1LT	0-1547738	C146	2
PAPPAS ANTHONY	CPT	0-1718586	1049	1
PAPPAS ANTHONY J	1LT	C-0438715	C844	2
PAPPAS CONSTANTIN	LTC	0-1041624	0163	1
PAPPAS ERIC W	2LT	0-1996342	C246	2
PAPPAS GEORGE W	1LT	0-2008001	0652	1
PAPPAS JR NICK G	CPT	0-2265239	C765	1
PAPPAS NICHOLAS G	LTC	0-1324571	0763	1
PAPPERITZ ALVIN N	1LT	C-0490114	1050	1
PAPROCI LEONARD C	CPT	0-0544888	C246	2
PAQUETTE HENRY L	LTC	0-1640800	0765	1
PAQUETTE MAURICE G	MAJ	C-2011270	1060	1
PARADIS OMAR M	CW4	W-2001602	1265	3
PARADIS ROGER	2LT	0-1299785	C544	2
PARADISE HAROLD W	2LT	C-0420454	0344	2
PARADY JR RANSOM D	WO1	W-2108634	C844	2
PARAGON LOUIS	LTC	0-0531223	1264	1
PARAISO RUDY V	LTC	0-2210134	1067	1
PARANGAN ANDRES M	2LT	0-189701C	0652	1
PARANO JOSEPH	2LT	0-1176154	0545	2
PARAS BENJAMIN P	2LT	C-189660Z	0662	2
PARAYOS STEVE	CW3	W-2142067	0862	1
PARCHMAN SR DAVID S	1LT	0-0493992	C650	1
PARDI RICHARD A	1LT	0-4085201	0260	2
PARDILLA CRISPIN C	2LT	0-2031888	1047	2

NAME	GRADE	SVC NO	DATE RET MO YR	RET CODE
PARDO JAMES	CPT	0-0516706	1153	1
PARDUE ROBERT J	MAJ	0-2289822	0967	1
PARDUE VICTOR E	MAJ	0-1794845	0560	1
PARDUE WOODROW W	1LT	0-0518953	1045	2
PAROUN ERNEST W	1LT	0-1017999	0346	2
PARELLA WILLIAM P	2LT	0-1589424	0444	1
PARENT FRANK R	CPT	0-1299954	1060	1
PARENT JOSEPH L C	1LT	0-2046511	0755	1
PARENT JR JOSEPH A	CPT	0-2017745	0762	1
PARENT LEO J	LTC	0-2208507	0667	1
PARENT ROBERT L	MAJ	0-2035435	1060	1
PARES CÉSAR	MAJ	0-0270615	0247	1
PARFITT CARL L	LTC	0-1280775	0160	1
PARHAM BILLY S	CPT	0-0527868	0846	2
PARHAM CHARLOTTE	2LT	N-0701925	0647	1
PARHAM CLAUDE	CPT	0-049638C	0647	1
PARHAM FOSTER B	MAJ	C-0491822	1049	1
PARHAM HARRY C	1LT	0-0462660	1045	2
PARHAM JOHN A	1LT	0-0541386	0946	1
PARHAM JR ROBERT W	LTC	0-0227404	0964	3
PARHAM LLOYD	CPT	0-1301204	0347	1
PARHAM MALVIN J	1LT	0-0833984	1147	2
PARHAM ROBERT H	CW2	W-2147234	0763	1
PARIENT WILLIAM R	LTC	0-0345865	0 47	2
PARILLA JOSEPH	COL	C-017225C	0250	3
PARIS FRANKLYN G	COL	0-0327280	1060	1
PARIS JEWEL W	1LT	0-1294182	0967	1
PARIS JOSEPH	1LT	0-101354C	0945	1
PARIS JOSEPH W	1LT	0-1926184	0454	2
PARIS WILLIAM W	LTC	0-1166804	0266	1
PARISE PETER	1LT	0-2007266	1064	1
PARISEAU WILLIAM E	LTC	0-128948C	0757	1
PARISH JAMES W	CW3	W-2121017	0456	1
PARISH JOHN E	MAJ	0-0310222	0645	2
PARISH JOHN P	LTC	0-1284383	0661	1
PARISH WYATT M	1LT	0-2265154	0354	2
PARISOT LEE J	1LT	0-1686801	0752	1
PARK ALTON E	LTC	0-1332521	1266	1
PARK ARTHUR	MAJ	0-0190133	0259	3
PARK BRYCE W	LTC	0-1583473	1161	1
PARK EDWARD L	LTC	0-1795962	1163	1
PARK FRANCIS C	CW4	W-2110422	0258	1
PARK GEORGE A	MAJ	0-4043698	0767	1
PARK GLENN M	LTC	0-0131319	0854	2
PARK HALL C	COL	0-0261095	0667	3
PARK IV ANDREW	LTC	0-0261338	0462	1
PARK JAMES H	CPT	0-1283659	0945	2
PARK JAMES K	LTC	0-1016736	0464	1
PARK JR RALPH R	LTC	0-2033214	0966	1
PARK LUTHER A	CPT	0-0149089	0950	3
PARK MARY B	1LT	N-0729841	0546	1
PARK PRINTES V	CPT	0-0447116	0745	2
PARKE FRANCIS W	LTC	0-0182019	0357	3
PARKE JAMES W	LTC	0-0423829	1063	3
PARKE JR ORLANDO M	CPT	0-1285107	0946	2
PARKE LOUIS L	LTC	0-0223528	0262	3
PARKER ADAM C	CPT	0-1051324	C651	1
PARKER ADEAN	CPT	N-0735495	0649	2
PARKER ALFRED C	LTC	0-0410125	0565	1
PARKER ALVIN H	COL	0-0341985	0861	1
PARKER ARNOLD G	MAJ	0-2017444	0367	1
PARKER AUSTIN J	MAJ	0-0795621	0866	1
PARKER AUSTIN L	MAJ	C-1825169	0566	1
PARKER BRAXTON C	CPT	0-1303773	1055	1
PARKER BURTON E	LTC	0-0219292	104N	2
PARKER CHALMERS M	LTC	0-0141012	0256	3
PARKER CHARLES D	CPT	0-0257755	0467	3
PARKER CHARLIE H	LTC	0-0507677	0154	1
PARKER CLARABEL	CPT	N-0735755	1048	2
PARKER CLARENCE F	COL	0-0102390	1054	3
PARKER CLARENCE	CPT	0-0127303	0253	3
PARKER CRAYTON A	LTC	0-1182-75	0867	1
PARKER DAVID P	LTC	0-1290-93	1164	1
PARKER DELBERT	MAJ	C-0454771	0448	2
PARKER DONALD E	CW2	W-3440005	0967	1

NAME	GRADE	SVC NO	DATE RET MO YR	RET CODE
PARKER DONALD R	LTC	0-0400271	1060	1
PARKER DONOVAN W	1LT	0-1331764	0347	2
PARKER DUYANE A	LTC	0-0975606	1167	1
PARKER EDGAR A	COL	0-0397877	0860	1
PARKER EDWARD A	CPT	0-1894938	0354	3
PARKER ELMER K	MAJ	0-1300521	0658	1
PARKER EMULON B	1LT	0-0500762	1043	2
PARKER EUAN J	CPT	0-1174098	0661	1
PARKER FORREST R	CW2	W-2145930	0555	1
PARKER FRANKLIN D	CW3	W-2143773	0764	1
PARKER FRED H	MAJ	0-0413165	1161	1
PARKER FREDERIC T	COL	0-0195994	1157	3
PARKER GARDNER E	CW2	W-2148218	0657	1
PARKER GEORGE C	WO1	W-2114266	0545	2
PARKER GEORGE E	MAJ	0-2263067	1064	1
PARKER GEORGE F	COL	0-0249063	0460	1
PARKER GEORGE J	LTC	0-0305148	1047	2
PARKER GEORGE M	MAJ	0-1639479	1060	1
PARKER HAROLD O	LTC	0-1640802	1165	1
PARKER HARRISON D	MAJ	0-0163028	1048	3
PARKER HARRY	CPT	0-0231121	0949	3
PARKER HARRY S	LTC	0-0229368	1058	3
PARKER HARVEY C	CW3	W-2142125	0662	1
PARKER HOWARD M	MAJ	0-1101610	1053	2
PARKER JACK C	WO1	W-2146839	0755	1
PARKER JAMES A	LTC	0-1310870	0163	1
PARKER JAMES R	LTC	0-0386484	0761	1
PARKER JIMMY W	MAJ	0-1998501	0460	1
PARKER JOEL R	LTC	0-1010182	1047	2
PARKER JOHN A	2LT	0-0538806	0844	2
PARKER JOHN A	CW2	W-3250453	0167	1
PARKER JOHN B	LTC	0-0271347	0666	3
PARKER JOHN L	MAJ	0-0241050	0266	3
PARKER JOHN L	MAJ	0-1577663	0761	1
PARKER JOHN R	LTC	0-0451635	0756	1
PARKER JOHNNIE G	CW3	W-2206378	1065	1
PARKER JOSEPH B	LTC	0-1048134	0764	1
PARKER JR EDGAR L	LTC	0-1168858	0661	1
PARKER JR FRANCIS W	COL	0-0175056	0648	3
PARKER JR HOMER V	2LT	0-1037666	0745	2
PARKER JR JOHN B	CW2	W-2211054	1167	1
PARKER JR LEREN L	CPT	0-1595751	0748	2
PARKER JR NELSON H	MAJ	0-0276294	0967	3
PARKER KERMIT R	MAJ	0-1640803	1057	1
PARKER LAURANCE T	MAJ	0-2037087	0866	1
PARKER LEE T F	LTC	0-1946125	1165	3
PARKER LEON	LTC	0-0531649	0746	2
PARKER LEONARD F	MAJ	0-1115731	0559	1
PARKER LESLIE E	LTC	0-0249750	0855	3
PARKER LESLIE T	LTC	0-1641652	0164	1
PARKER LOUIS E	CW2	W-2210640	1065	1
PARKER LOWELL W	MAJ	0-1924052	0963	1
PARKER LUTHER C	CPT	0-1046225	0346	2
PARKER LYLE A	MAJ	0-1643950	0563	1
PARKER MARGARETTE	LTC	L-0701119	1167	1
PARKER MARY B	LTC	L-0510098	0664	1
PARKER MEYER H	CPT	0-0493868	0345	2
PARKER OLIVER F	COL	0-0312552	0157	1
PARKER OSCAR E	MAJ	0-0957668	0264	1
PARKER PARKER	COL	0-0220849	1047	2
PARKER PAUL E	MAJ	0-0517937	1045	2
PARKER PAUL R	LTC	0-1331327	0165	1
PARKER PERCY E	LTC	0-0309887	0465	3
PARKER PERCY O	COL	0-0312257	1164	3
PARKER PETER A	MAJ	0-1640804	0760	1
PARKER PHILANDER	CW4	W-2123138	0462	2
PARKER RALPH M	CPT	0-0198644	0954	3
PARKER RAY C	CW2	W-2144079	0959	1
PARKER RAY J	1LT	0-0361382	0445	2
PARKER RICHARD L	CPT	0-1168859	0446	2
PARKER RICHARD M	LTC	0-0350297	0265	1
PARKER RICHARD W	MAJ	0-1639480	0363	1
PARKER RONALD	CW3	W-2117156	0755	1
PARKER SAMUEL I	LTC	0-0180686	1051	3
PARKER SHERROW G	COL	0-0169207	1158	3
PARKER STANTON C	LTC	0-0276236	0157	1
PARKER STEPHEN E	LTC	0-1171710	0261	1
PARKER STEVIE B	MAJ	0-0277592	1046	2
PARKER THOMAS R	LTC	0-0275501	0961	3
PARKER THOMAS S	COL	0-0288816	0665	3
PARKER VIRGIL A	1LT	0-0174948	0362	3
PARKER WALTER J	CPT	0-1292053	0348	2
PARKER WALTER J	CPT	0-2021039	0166	1
PARKER WALTER L	LTC	0-0245980	0155	1
PARKER WALTER L	WO1	W-2117239	1055	1
PARKER WILBUR E	LTC	0-0194460	1156	3
PARKER WILLARD V	MAJ	0-1690791	0960	1
PARKER WILLIAM	CPT	0-4030533	0765	1
PARKER WILLIAM C	CPT	0-1550675	0661	1
PARKER WILLIAM C	MAJ	0-1686288	1155	1
PARKER WILLIAM D	CPT	0-0417995	0645	2
PARKER WILLIAM F	COL	0-0169349	1060	1
PARKER WILLIAM F	MAJ	0-1885324	1067	1
PARKER WILLIAM M	MAJ	0-0133510	0156	3
PARKER WILLIAM R	CW2	W-2000809	0745	2
PARKER 3RD HERVEY E	1LT	0-0466737	0344	2
PARKERSON HAROLD C	LTC	0-1546868	0662	1
PARKERSON SR W W	WO1	W-2110893	0346	2
PARKES COLIN G	MAJ	0-1100720	0346	2
PARKEY JACK L	CW3	W-2143824	0764	1
PARKHURST CHARLES	1LT	0-1294405	1044	2
PARKHURST DAVID S	MAJ	0-1877812	1266	1
PARKHURST ORVILLE J	MAJ	0-0269653	1057	3
PARKIN CLAIR A	1LT	0-2027426	0646	2
PARKIN HENRY E	CW4	W-2002482	1060	3
PARKINS FREDERICK	MAJ	0-2014470	0865	1
PARKINS GUY W	MAJ	0-0210679	0852	3
PARKINSON DEE R	CPT	0-0478493	0346	1
PARKINSON ODA M	1LT	0-1017236	0446	2
PARKINSON GILBERT N	MAJ	0-2055042	0961	1
PARKINSON JOHN F	LTC	0-0135732	1057	3
PARKINSON THOMAS V	MAJ	0-1177120	1163	1
PARKISON RALPH R	CW3	W-2152393	0563	1
PARKO HENRY J	MAJ	0-2000766	0661	1
PARKS ALVIN J	CW3	W-2144888	1160	1
PARKS BERYL F	LTC	0-1284384	0561	1
PARKS CECIL W	MAJ	0-1285487	0856	1
PARKS CECIL W	CPT	0-1822046	0161	2
PARKS CLARENCE C	LTC	0-0445063	1047	2
PARKS CLARENCE F	LTC	0-0273925	1064	3
PARKS DOROTHY R	MAJ	L-1010203	0766	1
PARKS EARL H	LTC	0-0106254	0857	3
PARKS EDWARD C	MAJ	0-1101982	0160	1
PARKS GEORGE M	LTC	0-1895832	0562	1
PARKS GORDON W	LTC	0-2010834	0963	1
PARKS GROVER T	CPT	0-2033291	0554	2
PARKS HARRY E	1LT	0-2055163	0146	2
PARKS HOMER H	CW2	W-2145666	0657	1
PARKS JAMES E	MAJ	0-2017893	0862	1
PARKS JAMES C	COL	0-0153005	0754	3
PARKS JAMES F	MAJ	0-1592498	0859	1
PARKS JAMES L	1LT	0-0492184	0350	1
PARKS JASPER D	1LT	0-1312576	1044	2
PARKS JOHN H	LTC	0-0217807	1262	3
PARKS JOSEPH W	1LT	0-0536437	0145	2
PARKS JR WILLIAM T	LTC	0-1634202	0761	1
PARKS LAWRENCE	COL	0-0270346	0766	3
PARKS LORENZO L	COL	0-0247996	0466	3
PARKS RALPH G	WO1	W-2116220	0344	2
PARKS RALPH R	COL	0-0221112	0362	3
PARKS ROWLAND M	LTC	0-0511578	0360	1
PARKS SAMUEL F	MAJ	0-2020459	0161	1
PARKS VELLA E	MAJ	M-0002250	0667	3
PARKS WARREN E	CW2	W-2207506	0663	1
PARKS WILLIAM E	MAJ	0-0386251	0661	1
PARKS WILLIAM F	1LT	0-1950918	0650	1
PARLAS JOSEPH L	1LT	0-0483032	0944	2
PARLEE ARTHUR F	LTC	0-0182141	0457	3
PARLIAMENT ALLEN D	MAJ	0-1341186	1265	1
PARLIN GEORGE S	LTC	0-0508804	0246	2
PARLINI CATHERINE	1LT	N-0758750	0847	1
PARMELE LESLIE P	LTC	0-0270085	0467	3
PARMELEE ERNEST B	LTC	0-0295117	0658	3
PARMELEE GLENN C	COL	0-1544021	0661	3
PARMELEE JAMES T	LTC	0-0377895	0646	1
PARMELEE THERON S	LTC	0-0207654	0656	3
PARMENTER ALFRED C	CPT	0-0393242	0646	2
PARMENTER CAROLINE S	1LT	N-0764153	0846	1
PARMENTER EDWARD E	MAJ	0-0387247	0960	1
PARMENTIER HAROLD J	1LT	0-2035664	0945	2
PARMER GLENN G	COL	0-0399914	1262	1
PARMETER BERNARD W	2LT	0-1294525	0645	2
PARMETT ALAN	2LT	0-1638221	0944	2
PARNASS EMANUEL R	LTC	0-0171701	0653	3
PARNELL CHARLES E	CW3	W-2152735	1063	1
PARNELL CHARLIE L	CPT	0-0238058	0745	2
PARNELL GEORGE A	LTC	0-1103852	0162	1
PARNELL HUBERT N	LTC	0-0168648	1060	3
PARNELL RICHARD	LTC	0-0160310	1056	3
PARNELL SAMUEL A	CW3	W-2142048	0863	1
PARNELL WILLIAM C	LTC	0-0199729	1045	1
PARNELLE MILTON H	LTC	0-1171711	0960	1
PARNESS HENRY	LTC	0-1165771	0562	1
PARNIN JOHN R	COL	0-0201334	0957	3
PAROLARI BERT W	LTC	0-1020491	0866	1
PARR CHARLES H	MAJ	0-1327038	1061	1
PARR FRANKLIN A	CW3	W-2149400	0263	1
PARR GEORGE W	LTC	0-1001658	0463	1
PARR J C	MAJ	0-0472647	0955	1
PARR JOHN E	MAJ	0-0496952	1047	1
PARR PERRY L	LTC	0-0175561	0756	3
PARR VIRON P	COL	0-0231727	0763	3
PARRA FRANCISCO	COL	0-0253714	0646	2
PARRACK CECIL T	MAJ	0-1181072	0358	1
PARRACK DONALD L	MAJ	0-1703002	1060	1
PARRAMORE BENJAMIN B	LTC	0-1306463	0763	1
PARREN JOSEPH S	LTC	0-1186774	0567	2
PARRES LAWRENCE J	CW3	W-2150101	0564	1
PARRETT HENRY E	1LT	0-1913898	0238	1
PARRETT JOSEPH W	MAJ	0-1558603	0863	1
PARRILLO ANTHONY C	CPT	0-0502829	0146	2
PARRINO PAUL S	LTC	0-0198992	0561	3
PARRIS RALPH O	LTC	0-1310144	0263	1
PARRIS TOM B	LTC	0-1307776	1063	1
PARRIS WARREN M	1LT	0-0539297	0645	2
PARRISH COLIN D	MAJ	0-1336951	0464	1
PARRISH DUDLEY T	COL	0-0926221	1162	1
PARRISH EDWIN T	LTC	0-1111823	0263	1
PARRISH JAMES M	CPT	0-1592499	1056	1
PARRISH JOSEPH W	LTC	0-0468044	0347	1
PARRISH LESLIE H	MAJ	0-1643951	0757	2
PARRISH MINTON O	MAJ	0-0322478	0352	1
PARRISH ROBERT B	MAJ	0-0488548	0355	2
PARRISH SIDNEY F	1LT	0-0536545	0759	1
PARRISH SPENCER O	MAJ	0-1638223	0860	1
PARRISH SR JAMES W	LTC	0-1284011	0658	1
PARRO WILLIAM J	2LT	0-1119356	0246	2
PARRON JR WALTER C	2LT	0-1296417	0244	2
PARROT DAVID L	CPT	0-0396141	0545	2
PARROTT ARTHUR E	COL	0-0249522	0265	3
PARROTT BEN C	LTC	0-0344461	0563	1
PARROTT ERNEST M	LTC	0-0490352	0164	3
PARROTT JOHN B	COL	0-0282024	0660	1
PARROTT JOHN H	MAJ	0-0331763	0846	2
PARROTT JOHN R	CW4	W-2146389	0962	1
PARROTT WILLIAM R	LTC	0-0887434	0666	1
PARRY HOWELL J	LTC	0-1635194	0960	1
PARRY JR EDWARD A	MAJ	0-0388854	0861	1
PARRY PRISCILLA	MAJ	N-0759338	1262	1
PARRY ROBERT S	1LT	0-1317238	0446	2
PARRY STEPHEN H	MAJ	0-1342345	1163	1
PARSEK CLARENCE R	MAJ	0-1796997	0361	1
PARSHALL CECIL S	MAJ	0-1284201	0352	1
PARSHALL CHARLES J	LTC	0-0279125	0962	3
PARSHALL FRED N	MAJ	0-1643204	0860	1
PARSHALL HARVEY G	MAJ	0-1308857	1160	1
PARSON JOHN	1LT	0-0450381	0345	2
PARSON KENNETH B	MAJ	0-0502673	0347	2
PARSONS CARY C	CPT	0-0289375	1163	3
PARSONS CHARLES A	1LT	0-1184706	0745	2
PARSONS CHARLES L	CW4	W-2143446	1066	1
PARSONS CHESTER N	LTC	0-0307368	1067	3
PARSONS CLAIRE K	CW4	W-2109815	1061	3
PARSONS DAVID B	LTC	0-1554604	0967	1
PARSONS DOROTHY	LTC	N-0720025	0161	1
PARSONS GEORGE C	LTC	0-1578953	1061	1
PARSONS HAROLD K	COL	0-0197578	0750	3
PARSONS J D	MAJ	0-1291749	0359	1
PARSONS JACK G	COL	0-0343358	0466	1
PARSONS JAMES M	LTC	0-1105083	1161	1
PARSONS JOHN F	MAJ	0-1107028	1264	1
PARSONS JOHN G	1LT	0-0360870	1043	2
PARSONS KELLY	1LT	0-0462163	0444	2
PARSONS LAWRENCE B	CPT	0-0248104	1043	2
PARSONS LYMAN	MAJ	0-0227576	0665	3
PARSONS MARIAN C	1LT	N-0789171	0546	2
PARSONS PRESTON	1LT	0-0109458	0637	1
PARSONS PRESTON P	MAJ	0-1825250	1057	1
PARSONS RALPH A	COL	0-0168874	1055	3
PARSONS RICHARD W	CW3	W-2205787	0566	1
PARSONS ROBERT B	MAJ	0-1174095	0665	1
PARSONS ROBERT L	CPT	0-1846047	1045	2
PARSONS RODNEY T	MAJ	0-0386970	0547	1
PARSONS THEODORE W	LTC	0-0369810	1057	1
PARSONS VERIL D	MAJ	0-1949185	0759	1
PARSONS WILLIAM B	COL	0-0221205	0264	3
PARSONS WILLIAM G	CW3	RW-2148013	1163	1
PARTANEN GEORGE O	CPT	0-1287053	1046	2
PARTCH ELDON B	MAJ	0-1951504	0465	1
PARTEN JOHN C	MAJ	0-0986835	1264	2
PARTHUM CHARLES F	2LT	0-1004657	0944	2
PARTIN IRA	LTC	0-0157539	0345	2
PARTIN WALTER F	COL	0-0407006	1163	1
PARTLOW GEORGE L	LTC	0-0350357	0459	1
PARTLOW RAY W	CW4	W-2006400	0866	2
PARTON BENJAMIN F	CPT	0-1299625	1051	1
PARTON JR GEORGE P	LTC	0-0491867	0366	1
PARTRIDGE GEORGE F	CPT	0-0412221	0245	2
PARTRIDGE JOHN S	MAJ	0-0266334	0262	1
PARTRIDGE LEON S	CPT	0-0231728	0165	3
PARTRIDGE STANLEY H	COL	0-0378455	0160	2
PARTRIDGE WILLIAM J	MAJ	0-2033298	0662	1
PARTRIDGE WILLIAM T	MAJ	0-2203051	0566	1
PARULIS DANIEL A	2LT	0-2040575	0944	2
PARUN BERNARD	MAJ	0-0276135	0664	3
PARVEY MARCUS A	1LT	0-0384704	0646	2
PARVIS CHARLES F	CW3	W-2145363	0165	1
PARZNIK JOHN T	CW4	W-2106554	0259	1
PASAHOW SAMUEL	CW3	W-2142655	1164	1
PASCAL LOUIS R	1LT	0-1177131	1047	2
PASCALE FRANK L	1LT	0-1321810	0345	2
PASCALE VITO P	CPT	0-1287935	0648	1
PASCH HARRY A	LTC	0-0553607	0765	1
PASCH LOUIS A	CPT	0-0411671	0545	2
PASCH THOMAS C	CW2	W-2212935	0767	1
PASCHAL MERLE B	LTC	0-0182371	0157	1
PASCHAL WALTER R	MAJ	0-1105084	0761	1
PASCHALL CHARLES R	CW3	W-2152902	0263	2
PASCHALL HUNTER H	LTC	0-1590586	1262	1
PASCOE BENJAMIN D	1LT	0-0888197	1045	2
PASCOE JOHN T	MAJ	0-2102980	1165	1
PASCUAL NICOLAS	CPT	0-1297773	0246	1
PASCUCCI LUCIEN M	MAJ	0-0357139	0246	2
PASH BORIS T	COL	0-0275706	1157	2
PASH LEONARD O	CPT	0-0459515	0446	1
PASKELL ARCHIBALD	CW2	W-2129724	0566	3
PASKLER JUNIUS	2LT	0-1541533	0552	1
PASKO JOSEPH W	MAJ	0-1335573	0764	1
PASKOPOULOS GEORGE F	COL	0-0243685	1062	3
PASKUS JOHN G	1LT	0-2008369	0450	1

NAME	GRADE	SVC NO	DATE RET MO YR	RET CODE
PASMORE JOHN L	MAJ	0-0323943	0345	2
PASOLA JOSEPH	2LT	0-2008515	0446	1
PASQUALINO FELIX	LTC	0-0524440	0946	2
PASQUARIELLO VINCENT	CPT	0-1874821	1167	1
PASQUINO JR JOSEPH	CW4	W-2143418	0866	1
PASS BERNARD J	CPT	0-1821497	0145	2
PASS PASQUAL E	CW2	W-2110327	0762	1
PASSER JEROME	1LT	0-0514150	0345	2
PASSEY WILLIAM H	MAJ	0-0979985	1062	1
PASSON WALTER	CPT	0-1917762	0263	1
PASSONS ROBERT J	MAJ	0-1691774	0563	1
PASTELL JOHN S	LTC	0-2018046	0266	1
PASTER EMANUEL	1LT	0-1592197	0853	2
PASTERNAK CHESTER J	MAJ	0-1283661	0746	1
PASTERNAK JOSEPH A	MAJ	0-1292227	0366	1
PASTON DAVID G	COL	0-0189428	0647	2
PASTOR AMELIA	CPT	N-0757027	0247	1
PASTOR JOHN E	1LT	0-1320911	0346	2
PASTOR LOUIS J	CPT	0-1310871	0747	1
PASTORET AL L	LTC	0-0135312	0352	3
PASTUSZYNSKI EDWARD	MAJ	0-1999315	0156	1
PASVOLSKY VALENTINE	MAJ	0-0184269	0759	1
PATACSIL LAUREANA F	2LT	N-0783899	0246	1
PATAKI GEORGE D	COL	0-1643952	0566	1
PATANE JOSEPH S	MAJ	0-1280943	0657	1
PATANIA JOSEPH M	CW3	W-2141805	0661	1
PATCH JR EDGAR M	MAJ	0-2262229	1167	1
PATCH RUSSELL B	CPT	0-0290865	0244	2
PATCH VERNON T	MAJ	0-0183969	0362	3
PATCHETT HOWARD F	CW2	W-2205851	1162	2
PATCHIN WILLIAM F	CPT	0-0108982	1035	1
PATE ARTHUR A	CPT	0-0497788	0553	1
PATE CHARLES G	MAJ	0-1342208	0963	1
PATE DAVID C	CW4	W-2149263	1166	1
PATE DURWOOD L	CW3	W-2142523	0263	1
PATE EUGENE H	CW3	W-2141405	0662	1
PATE GERALD B	CW3	W-2108257	1057	1
PATE JEWELL M	1LT	0-1636449	1054	1
PATE JOE N	WO1	W-2151509	0255	1
PATE JOHN L	MAJ	0-1324703	0561	1
PATE JR JAMES F	1LT	0-4024060	0159	2
PATE JR JOSEPH B	LTC	0-1010298	1061	1
PATE LEO R	1LT	0-1322946	1045	2
PATE OTHO S	1LT	0-0528063	0744	2
PATE RALPH R	LTC	0-0413633	0657	1
PATE TOM D	1LT	0-0505831	0855	1
PATE VERNE E	COL	0-0361205	0567	1
PATEE JAMES C	MAJ	0-0993226	0864	1
PATER EDWIN F	MAJ	0-2032979	0961	2
PATERSON CHARLES	LTC	0-1286175	1060	1
PATERSON GLEN S	MAJ	0-0257757	0865	3
PATERSON JAMES R	MAJ	0-1798608	0262	2
PATEY ELWOOD K	MAJ	0-1303020	0560	1
PATHE TIMOTHY J	CPT	0-0925842	0347	2
PATIN TADDY	CPT	0-1574498	0958	1
PATNESKY EDWARD	CPT	0-1535392	0746	2
PATREM JOHN R	MAJ	0-1337084	0963	1
PATRENOS FRANCIS P	CPT	0-0961232	0463	1
PATRICIO RAYMOND	MAJ	0-1110172	0962	1
PATRICK CARL	CPT	0-0486611	0548	1
PATRICK CLAUDE B	LTC	0-1535512	0165	1
PATRICK FLAY P	CPT	0-1644651	0256	1
PATRICK FOREST	CPT	0-1037217	0959	1
PATRICK FRANK J	MAJ	0-1549807	0363	1
PATRICK GEORGE A	MAJ	0-1105085	0157	1
PATRICK GEORGE M	2LT	0-2011808	0146	2
PATRICK GEORGE P	1LT	0-0444863	0744	2
PATRICK HARTFORD L	2LT	0-0467225	0744	2
PATRICK JAMES P	LTC	0-0113918	0253	3
PATRICK JASPER R	CW2	W-2147534	0860	1
PATRICK JOHN D	CW4	W-2103295	1058	1
PATRICK JOHN F D	COL	0-0290515	0560	1
PATRICK JOHN K	CW3	W-2148578	0965	1
PATRICK JOHN N	MAJ	0-0291721	1044	2
PATRICK KENNETH J	LTC	0-1325165	0663	1

NAME	GRADE	SVC NO	DATE RET MO YR	RET CODE
PATRICK MARION L	CPT	0-0104811	0821	1
PATRICK MILTON L	2LT	0-1182934	1044	2
PATRICK NOBLE M	LTC	0-1172588	1265	1
PATRICK OSCAR F	MAJ	0-2081349	1066	1
PATRICK THOMAS E	CPT	0-1047716	0160	1
PATRINELIS JOHN E	COL	0-0178905	0753	3
PATRITCH JOHN J	LTC	0-0389827	0561	1
PATRYLC RUDOLPH M	CPT	0-1113386	1262	1
PATSCHKE MILDRED L	1LT	N-0794919	1047	1
PATSY GLORIO J	LTC	0-1534357	0857	1
PATT EMANUEL	CPT	0-0553820	0346	2
PATTEE KARL H	COL	0-0208962	0457	3
PATTEN ALBERT J	CW3	W-2144985	0962	1
PATTEN ALLEN P	1LT	0-1296418	1045	2
PATTEN FRANKLIN W	LTC	0-0168150	0760	3
PATTEN LAWTON M	CPT	0-0239083	0565	3
PATTEN RAYMOND L	LTC	0-0481389	1157	3
PATTEN WILLIAM W	MAJ	0-1586005	0359	1
PATTERSON ADNA R	MAJ	0-2049679	1262	1
PATTERSON ALAN F	CW3	W-2146862	0765	1
PATTERSON ALLEN A	LTC	0-0170070	1057	3
PATTERSON ARTHUR J	MAJ	0-1917574	1064	1
PATTERSON ARTHUR S	LTC	0-0285834	0757	2
PATTERSON BEN	CW2	W-2144353	0659	1
PATTERSON BRUCE E	2LT	0-0336267	0666	3
PATTERSON BUEL R	LTC	0-0248158	0664	3
PATTERSON BUNYAN L	MAJ	0-1285488	1154	1
PATTERSON BURTON R	LTC	0-0478161	0858	2
PATTERSON CALVIN W	1LT	0-2042871	0851	1
PATTERSON CARROLL G	LTC	0-1053766	0865	3
PATTERSON CECIL	MAJ	0-2262285	0761	1
PATTERSON CHARLES C	COL	0-0204232	0547	2
PATTERSON CHARLES H	CPT	0-0488822	0153	1
PATTERSON CHARLES L	MAJ	0-2262615	0764	1
PATTERSON CHARLIE L	LTC	0-0278103	0366	3
PATTERSON CUTHBERT	MAJ	0-0482977	0547	1
PATTERSON DANIEL S	MAJ	0-0499043	0257	1
PATTERSON DONALD W	CW3	W-2150073	0566	1
PATTERSON DOROTHY D	CPT	N-0763685	0747	1
PATTERSON DREXEL P	MAJ	0-0189698	0647	2
PATTERSON EDWARD L	WO1	W-2115183	0844	2
PATTERSON EDWIN M	MAJ	0-0351574	1047	2
PATTERSON EMERY F	LTC	0-1000839	0358	2
PATTERSON EUGENE K	CPT	0-0145029	1055	3
PATTERSON EUGENE R	COL	0-0999481	0963	2
PATTERSON FARREL S	CPT	0-1287397	1047	1
PATTERSON FRANK B	LTC	0-0135012	1056	3
PATTERSON FRANK S	WO1	W-2112285	0859	1
PATTERSON GEORGE P	CW4	W-2136699	0666	1
PATTERSON GORDON E	CPT	0-0361769	0345	2
PATTERSON HAROLD J	CW2	W-2153266	0261	1
PATTERSON HAROLD R	LTC	0-1342108	0167	1
PATTERSON HARRY F	CPT	0-0489907	0352	1
PATTERSON HOWARD A	CPT	0-1108920	0359	1
PATTERSON HOWARD L	1LT	0-2055089	0849	2
PATTERSON HOWARD S	COL	0-0125844	0648	3
PATTERSON ISAAC N	CPT	0-0473175	0943	1
PATTERSON JAMES D	2LT	0-2006025	0945	2
PATTERSON JAMES N	COL	0-0255586	0656	3
PATTERSON JAMES P	MAJ	0-1298751	0561	1
PATTERSON JOHN C	COL	0-0366882	0864	1
PATTERSON JOHN C	LTC	0-0392197	0262	1
PATTERSON JOHN H	CPT	0-0256803	0952	1
PATTERSON JOHN J	1LT	0-1698071	0245	2
PATTERSON JOHN K	COL	0-0193473	1160	3
PATTERSON JR CARL O	LTC	0-1165928	0161	1
PATTERSON JR FRED L	MAJ	0-0335105	0745	2
PATTERSON JR LUTHER	COL	0-0269810	1067	3
PATTERSON LAWRENCE P	MAJ	0-0112674	0645	2
PATTERSON LEON C	MAJ	0-0129514	0648	3
PATTERSON LLOYD E	CPT	0-0452690	1043	2
PATTERSON LOWELL H	LTC	0-1002706	1166	1
PATTERSON LYNN T	CW2	W-2102187	0958	1
PATTERSON MATTIE L	2LT	N-0701964	0243	1
PATTERSON MC LEOD	LTC	0-0381437	0347	1

NAME	GRADE	SVC NO	DATE RET MO YR	RET CODE
PATTERSON OSCAR A	CPT	0-0995076	1161	1
PATTERSON PAUL H	2LT	0-0581068	0945	2
PATTERSON PAUL J	MAJ	0-0278723	1060	3
PATTERSON RALPH B	MAJ	0-1307571	0657	1
PATTERSON RALPH E	COL	0-0201550	0751	3
PATTERSON RAY C	2LT	0-1597237	0945	2
PATTERSON RAYMOND	CW2	W-2205603	0760	1
PATTERSON ROBERT A	1LT	0-0416417	0444	2
PATTERSON ROBERT A	MAJ	0-0421001	0161	1
PATTERSON ROBERT B	LTC	0-0261383	1265	3
PATTERSON ROBERT B	1LT	0-1290651	0946	2
PATTERSON ROBERT C	COL	0-0262952	0964	3
PATTERSON ROBERT C	LTC	0-0350408	0562	1
PATTERSON ROBERT E	MAJ	0-1922512	0965	1
PATTERSON ROBERT G	COL	0-0218143	1047	2
PATTERSON ROBERT H	CPT	0-1323168	1047	2
PATTERSON ROBERT M	LTC	0-0153811	0355	3
PATTERSON ROBERT M	MAJ	0-2055079	0857	1
PATTERSON ROY J	MAJ	0-1304109	0266	1
PATTERSON ROY M	1LT	0-1301531	1045	2
PATTERSON STANLEY J	LTC	0-1294183	0261	1
PATTERSON THADDEUS M	LTC	0-1593167	1067	1
PATTERSON THOMAS C	LTC	0-0180439	0746	2
PATTERSON THOMAS D	LTC	0-0287492	0661	1
PATTERSON THOMAS J	1LT	0-1309600	1045	2
PATTERSON THOMAS L	CW3	W-2142410	0361	1
PATTERSON WARREN J	MAJ	0-2097589	0667	1
PATTERSON WILLIAM D	LTC	0-0260126	0264	1
PATTERSON WILLIAM G	LTC	0-1295591	0763	1
PATTERSON WILLIAM M	CW2	W-2214748	1066	1
PATTERSON WILLIAM T	LTC	0-1320556	1262	1
PATTERSON WILLIS C	LTC	0-1019840	1066	1
PATTERSON WINFRED E	MAJ	0-0931190	0260	1
PATTI ARCHIMEDES	LTC	0-0372453	0757	1
PATTI JOSEPH A	MAJ	0-2023922	0559	1
PATTIE CHARLES M	LTC	0-0349650	0657	1
PATTIE MARY T	CPT	N-0742073	1046	1
PATTILLO LEWIS C	B G	0-0244386	1063	3
PATTIS GEORGE J	LTC	0-1332857	0667	1
PATTISON CLARENCE L	MAJ	0-2202211	0665	1
PATTISON GEORGE P	2LT	0-0919386	0545	2
PATTISON HARLAND C	LTC	0-0268746	1063	3
PATTISON PAUL F	LTC	0-0753921	0163	1
PATTISON PHILIP R	COL	0-0188917	0558	3
PATTISON RAYLINN	CPT	0-1170131	0953	2
PATTISON VIRGINIA R	1LT	N-0776312	0147	2
PATTON BYRON R	COL	0-0103082	1056	3
PATTON CHARLES G	CPT	0-1591974	0954	1
PATTON CHARLES M	CPT	0-1001872	1145	2
PATTON CLIFFORD M	CW2	W-2147639	0357	1
PATTON CLOYD E	CPT	0-1576479	0546	2
PATTON COREY E	COL	0-0244766	0561	3
PATTON DOUGLAS J	CPT	0-0336341	0648	3
PATTON EDWARD C	COL	0-0239564	0961	3
PATTON EDWARD K	2LT	0-1321660	0344	2
PATTON ELMO L	B G	0-0229128	0463	3
PATTON FREDERICK	2LT	0-2019777	0846	2
PATTON JACK F	LTC	0-1549576	0765	1
PATTON JAMES B	COL	0-0179705	0755	3
PATTON JAY O	LTC	0-0266996	1067	3
PATTON JOHN A	COL	0-0201965	0753	3
PATTON JOHN B	MAJ	0-1825705	0363	1
PATTON JOHN D	MAJ	0-0450644	1054	1
PATTON JOHN W	COL	0-0149119	0855	3
PATTON JR JAMES H	MAJ	0-1295932	0163	1
PATTON JR JOHN W	COL	0-0256699	0758	2
PATTON JR STEWART H	CPT	0-0465251	0559	1
PATTON KARL S	LTC	0-1184919	0564	1
PATTON KENDALL K	2LT	0-1080655	0844	2
PATTON RAYMON E	1LT	0-1298915	0246	1
PATTON ROBERT L	CPT	0-0153810	0527	1
PATTON SAMUEL A	CPT	0-0994231	1061	1
PATTON THOMAS E	MAJ	0-0350044	0745	2
PATTON THOMAS R	MAJ	0-0474643	0559	1
PATTON WENDELL B	LTC	0-0220999	1057	2

NAME	GRADE	SVC NO	DATE RET MO YR	RET CODE
PATTON WILLIAM E	CPT	0-1685873	0844	1
PATTON WILLIAM M	1LT	0-1824358	0845	1
PATTON WILLIAM T	CPT	0-2033553	0566	1
PATTUGALAN SANTIAGO	1LT	0-2030550	0950	1
PATTY DAVID O	MAJ	0-0234258	0844	2
PATURZC MICHAEL R	1LT	0-1925830	0254	2
PATY JR BYRD F	1LT	0-0538807	0446	2
PATY WILLIAM W	CPT	0-0481656	0846	2
PATZE RICHARD A	LTC	0-1102418	0860	1
PATZIG W J	CW2	W-3150656	0466	1
PAUGH DELMER I	LTC	0-1293466	1062	1
PAUL ARTHUR T	LTC	0-1172214	1067	1
PAUL CALVIN	WO1	W-2145575	0560	2
PAUL CARROLL O	LTC	0-0164084	0647	2
PAUL CHESTER V	MAJ	0-0947156	0765	2
PAUL DONALD K	MAJ	0-0959244	1266	1
PAUL GROVER S	MAJ	0-1798392	0361	1
PAUL HARLOW L	LTC	0-1183155	1065	1
PAUL JACK O	MAJ	0-0305265	0846	1
PAUL JAMES H	CW3	W-2152476	1263	1
PAUL JAMES P	MAJ	0-1031115	0658	1
PAUL JAMES R	CPT	0-2010876	0256	1
PAUL JR JESSIE W	CW3	W-2208415	0765	2
PAUL JR JOSEPH B	WO1	W-2149057	0254	2
PAUL JR WILLIS L	LTC	0-1115057	1066	1
PAUL LACY W	CW2	W-2103297	0854	1
PAUL LELAND H	LTC	0-2032980	0765	1
PAUL LEMUEL R	CW3	W-2119817	0159	1
PAUL LESLIE J	COL	0-0176650	0950	3
PAUL NICHOLAS T	CW4	W-2111542	1065	1
PAUL RACHEL L	1LT	N-0745375	1146	1
PAUL ROBERT C	MAJ	0-1703407	0946	2
PAUL RODGER R	LTC	0-0229941	1061	3
PAUL ROLAND N	LTC	0-0408088	0263	1
PAUL SR LEO J	1LT	0-1012090	0159	1
PAUL THEODORE S	COL	0-0176640	0250	3
PAUL THOMAS R	MAJ	0-0596291	0164	1
PAUL WARREN C	LTC	0-0116272	1056	3
PAUL WERNER W	MAJ	0-1800159	0264	1
PAUL WILLIAM E	LTC	0-0233607	0648	3
PAUL WILLIAM G	CPT	0-0378414	0246	2
PAULDING JOHN	CPT	0-0255665	0364	3
PAULETTE DAVID W	COL	0-0302871	1152	3
PAULETTE WILLIE N	MAJ	0-1593168	0763	1
PAULEY ARTHUR R	LTC	0-0506889	0163	1
PAULEY DENVER	CPT	0-1182677	1162	1
PAULEY WARREN B	LTC	0-1286545	0261	1
PAULHAMUS KENNETH H	LTC	0-0450544	0656	1
PAULI AUGUST	2LT	0-2006218	0646	2
PAULIN ALBERT A	WO1	W-2115516	1046	1
PAULIN ANDREW C	LTC	0-1546000	0862	1
PAULIN HOWARD P	MAJ	0-0236640	0166	3
PAULINC DANIC	CW2	W-2152245	0263	1
PAULK BILLIE B	2LT	0-1048968	0345	2
PAULL FREDERICK	CW3	W-2143774	1060	1
PAULL JULIUS J	MAJ	0-1292935	0662	1
PAULL ROBERT R	2LT	0-1049969	0744	2
PAULL ROSS	COL	0-0267130	0746	1
PAULLIN PERRY E	1LT	0-1575505	0366	3
PAULLUS JR GEORGE E	MAJ	0-0340947	1043	2
PAULS HENRY J	MAJ	0-0493017	1151	1
PAULSEN ARTHUR F	LTC	0-1105090	1163	1
PAULSEN CARL G	COL	0-0371477	0756	1
PAULSEN CLARENCE I	MAJ	0-0900430	0245	2
PAULSEN EDWARD D	2LT	0-0520756	0445	2
PAULSEN OSCAR	CPT	0-1540543	0349	1
PAULSON EUGENE C	MAJ	0-1646489	0461	1
PAULSON JACK C	CPT	0-0321892	0744	2
PAULSON KENNETH D	CW2	W-3250480	1167	1
PAULSON MARGARET M	CPT	N-0745325	1147	1
PAULSON ROBERT L	CPT	0-0401516	0146	2
PAULSON ROY P	CW3	W-2142774	1162	1
PAULSON WILLIAM C	CPT	0-0342870	0945	1
PAUS JOSEPH H	LTC	0-2033545	0965	1
PAUSTIAN MARGRET K	1LT	N-0799510	0747	1

NAME	GRADE	SVC NO	DATE RET MO YR	RET CODE
PAUTENIS EDWARD R	MAJ	0-1051327	C265	1
PAUTSCH LAWRENCE O	COL	0-0907472	0162	2
PAVELKA MILTON F	CPT	C-1016049	C949	2
PAVELKA STANLEY G	CPT	0-1548278	1166	2
PAVEY ROBERT E	MAJ	0-1881809	0967	1
PAVIA ALBERT J	CPT	0-2262730	0361	1
PAVLAK ALEXANDER	MAJ	0-2045102	0455	1
PAVLICK JOHN J	MAJ	C-1895539	0261	1
PAVLICK MARY A	MAJ	N-0728374	0962	1
PAVLIK ALEX G	1LT	0-1291163	C144	2
PAVLIK JOSEPH R	1LT	0-1181724	0246	2
PAVLCCK EDWARD S	LTC	0-C496086	1154	1
PAVLOVICH PAUL L	1LT	0-1324948	C246	1
PAVY ECMOND E	CPT	0-0260575	0145	1
PAWL WALTER F	CW4	W-2146909	0861	1
PAWLAN NORMAN C	2LT	0-1823053	C245	2
PAWLENOK ALEX	LTC	0-1284931	C959	2
PAWLING GEORGE F	LTC	C-0343006	0163	1
PAXMAN RALPH S	MAJ	C-1185415	C361	1
PAXTON ALEXANDER	M G	0-0129178	1059	3
PAXTON CALVIN N	CPT	C-1554RC1	0465	1
PAXTON FLOYC M	MAJ	0-0350572	C447	2
PAXTON JACK L	LTC	0-1000442	0461	1
PAXTON JEROME M	MAJ	0-1634207	1047	2
PAXTON JOSEPH M	CPT	0-1013665	0547	2
PAXTON JR GEORGE W	CW3	W-2150724	0164	1
PAYETTE ANDRE H	LTC	0-0504985	C163	1
PAYNE ADAM G	LTC	C-0303071	0154	1
PAYNE ARCHIE L	LTC	0-1041626	1062	1
PAYNE BROWN H	WO1	W-2119405	1143	2
PAYNE CARLOS	CW4	W-2127911	1165	1
PAYNE CARTER H	CW2	W-2206681	0463	1
PAYNE CHARLES B	LTC	0-1535950	0965	1
PAYNE CHARLES E	MAJ	C-1688286	C663	1
PAYNE CHARLES M	CPT	0-0382449	C843	2
PAYNE CLAUD M	MAJ	0-1304562	0160	1
PAYNE CYRIL J	1LT	0-1014300	C845	2
PAYNE ELMER P	LTC	0-0189396	0646	1
PAYNE ELWOOD M	LTC	0-0365998	0566	3
PAYNE GEORGE A	LTC	0-0924022	1264	3
PAYNE GEORGE A	MAJ	C-2014269	C76C	1
PAYNE GEORGE R	CPT	0-0123726	1055	3
PAYNE GEORGE S	CW2	W-2102192	C349	1
PAYNE HAROLD J	MAJ	C-1697944	C557	1
PAYNE HARRY N	LTC	0-0310691	C658	1
PAYNE HENRY C	CPT	C-1312215	C550	1
PAYNE HERBERT M	LTC	0-0252819	0863	3
PAYNE HOUSTON	MAJ	0-1013971	0862	1
PAYNE JOHN E	2LT	0-2008478	0157	1
PAYNE JOHN J	LTC	0-0479784	1067	3
PAYNE JR GLENN A	LTC	0-1594384	0966	1
PAYNE JR JAMES E	MAJ	C-2262117	1263	2
PAYNE JR JOHN R	LTC	0-0151860	C259	3
PAYNE JR WILLIAM F	LTC	0-0325122	0562	1
PAYNE KENNETH B	2LT	0-1298916	C644	2
PAYNE LUTHER	LTC	0-1101156	0758	1
PAYNE OTHA E	LTC	0-1295078	0964	1
PAYNE RALPH S	LTC	0-0209690	0955	3
PAYNE RICHARD H	MAJ	C-1016753	0954	1
PAYNE RICHARD M	LTC	0-1328838	1067	1
PAYNE ROBERT E	LTC	0-0337998	C565	3
PAYNE ROBERT E	CW2	W-2210813	0865	1
PAYNE THOMAS L	LTC	0-0382032	1165	3
PAYNE VERA E	1LT	N-0756287	0546	1
PAYNE WALTER K	COL	0-0198278	0656	1
PAYNE WILLIAM H	MAJ	C-0179088	0948	3
PAYNE WILLIAM H	CPT	0-2042972	0755	1
PAYNE WILLIAM N	LTC	0-1324704	C165	1
PAYNTER FLOYD L	LTC	0-0212966	0358	3
PAYONK ANDREW L	MAJ	0-1311923	0761	1
PAYSON MICHAEL J	1LT	C-1822451	0747	1
PAYTE JR SAMUEL G	1LT	0-1314322	C945	2
PAYTON JR ROY A	MAJ	C-1946594	C754	2
PAYTON LELAND E	LTC	0-0123722	0554	3
PAYTON RALPH H	LTC	0-1104331	0961	1
PAYTON ROBERT C	CPT	0-0116273	1157	3
PAYTON VERCLD H	CW4	W-2146562	0666	2
PAZICH STEPHEN	2LT	0-1308043	0844	2
PAZZELLI LOUIS P	2LT	0-0430461	0445	2
PEABODY BURTON H	MAJ	C-0901518	1043	2
PEABODY CARY S	CPT	0-0411501		2
PEABODY HUGH D	LTC	0-1638233	1164	1
PEABODY JOHN W	MAJ	0-1951032	0261	1
PEABODY SELIM D	COL	0-0156281	0355	1
PEACE JAMES M	WO1	W-2108263	0245	2
PEACH ERIC A	COL	0-0328475	1163	3
PEACH JR ROBERT E	LTC	0-1636455	1061	1
PEACH THOMAS F	CPT	0-2019360	1159	1
PEACH WILLIAM C	CPT	0-0477470	0546	1
PEACOCK CORTEZ A	MAJ	0-1846503	1060	1
PEACOCK FREDERICK	MAJ	0-1035964	0760	1
PEACOCK GORDON H	CPT	0-1894013	0763	1
PEACOCK JAMES H	LTC	0-0299276	0863	3
PEACOCK JAMES J	1LT	0-1046921	0447	1
PEACOCK JOSEPH A	LTC	0-1320476	0461	1
PEACOCK RICHARD B	MAJ	0-1059031	1064	1
PEACOCK WILLIAM R	LTC	0-0118032	0249	3
PEAK ELSIE M	2LT	N-0727897	C944	1
PEAK RAYMOND M	LTC	0-020335C	0859	1
PEAK REUBEN T	MAJ	0-0131330	0451	3
PEAKE CHARLES U	CPT	0-0184958	0856	3
PEAKE MARTHA C	MAJ	N-0759341	0967	1
PEAKE RALPH A	LTC	0-0359685	0959	1
PEARCE ALTON A	MAJ	C-2021128	0264	1
PEARCE CHARLES M	LTC	0-0139909	0648	3
PEARCE EDWIN L	LTC	0-1555746	0965	3
PEARCE FRANKLIN E	LTC	0-1116112	0665	3
PEARCE JACK R	LTC	0-0888557	0657	1
PEARCE JAMES M	LTC	0-0221936	0563	3
PEARCE JOHN F	LTC	0-0215484	0862	3
PEARCE JOHNSCN L	WO1	W-2134293	C660	1
PEARCE JR ARTHUR B	LTC	0-0372534	0667	3
PEARCE JR FRANCIS M	2LT	0-0494471	1143	2
PEARCE JR WILLIAM H	1LT	0-199643C	0847	2
PEARCE KENNETH E	LTC	0-0280669	0266	3
PEARCE LOVICK B	COL	0-0137716	0554	3
PEARCE MARGARET H	CPT	N-0752898	0952	2
PEARCE NIEL A	CPT	C-1301206	0646	2
PEARCE RUFUS B	LTC	0-0185113	1148	3
PEARCE VERA B	1LT	N-0700759	0246	1
PEARCE WESLEY C	1LT	0-0382833	1145	2
PEARCE WILLIAM J	CW2	W-2151322	0765	1
PEARCE WILLIAM N	COL	0-0235875	0462	3
PEARCY EVANS C	CW4	W-2108806	0656	1
PEARLMAN HUBERT S	CPT	0-0999551	0854	2
PEARMAN EARL C	CPT	0-0507865	0546	2
PEARMAN JR JAMES N	LTC	0-0390615	0860	1
PEARS DONALD R	CPT	0-0180816	1059	3
PEARSALL ARTHUR J	LTC	0-C414772	0763	1
PEARSALL MARTIN L	CPT	0-1294185	0546	2
PEARSCN ALEXANDER	LTC	0-1105092	0163	1
PEARSCN AUBREY O	1LT	0-1590099	0246	2
PEARSON BENJAMIN F	COL	0-0383145	0147	1
PEARSON CARL L	CW4	W-2128069	1054	1
PEARSON CHARLES B	COL	0-0352071	0165	1
PEARSON CHARLES L	MAJ	0-2206424	1166	1
PEARSON CHARLES T	LTC	0-0505014	0157	1
PEARSCN CLARENCE E	MAJ	0-0973172	0365	2
PEARSON CLEMENS P	LTC	0-1285290	1155	1
PEARSON ELINOR	MAJ	R-0000531	0766	1
PEARSON EMMET F	COL	0-0272145	0466	3
PEARSON GEORGE C	LTC	0-0113146	0648	3
PEARSCN HERBERT C	1LT	C-1012535	0145	2
PEARSCN HOWARD E	LTC	0-0320143	0544	2
PEARSON HUBERT R	CPT	0-0436960	0846	1
PEARSCN JOHN R	LTC	0-0325400	0647	1
PEARSCN JOSEPH E	LTC	0-0271503	0547	2
PEARSON JR CARL A	MAJ	0-1925831	C566	1
PEARSCN JR THOMAS V	MAJ	0-1340576	0364	1
PEARSON JULIUS R	MAJ	0-1683871	0546	2
PEARSON KARL M	LTC	0-0230034	C465	3
PEARSON LENDON P	MAJ	0-0578833	1164	1
PEARSON LEROY	COL	0-0127299	C648	3
PEARSON LEROY F	MAJ	C-1638237	0261	1
PEARSON LOYCE E	1LT	0-2026850	C148	1
PEARSON MORRIS	1LT	0-1309010	1045	2
PEARSON OLEN	CW2	W-2145896	1054	2
PEARSON OVIC F	LTC	0-0253096	0240	2
PEARSON RAYMOND C	1LT	0-1644654	C860	1
PEARSON RICHARD H	CPT	0-1643957	C658	1
PEARSON ROBERT L	CW4	W-2145830	1061	1
PEARSON RUSSELL C	1LT	0-1312793	1045	2
PEARSON THOMAS D	LTC	0-0359288	0965	1
PEARSON THOMAS J	LTC	C-0133562	C950	3
PEARSON THOMAS R	MAJ	0-1951631	0263	1
PEARSON VED K	1LT	0-1795963	C844	2
PEARSON WHITMAN	LTC	0-0357818	C866	3
PEASE AUSTIN H	CW3	W-2147710	1061	1
PEASE EDWIN J	COL	0-1172218	1164	1
PEASE JAMES N	COL	0-0214497	C648	3
PEASE LAURENCE T	LTC	C-0366564	0463	3
PEASE LOYAL M	LTC	0-1548123	1060	1
PEASE ROOSEVELT	CPT	0-0224332	C747	1
PEASE WILLIAM H	LTC	0-1020389	C966	1
PEASE WILLIAM K	CPT	0-1172219	0555	1
PEASLEY ELMUS O	LTC	0-0257314	0663	1
PEASNER ALMA W	1LT	0-0516707	C848	1
PEATROSS 3RD SETH C	CPT	0-0520898	1045	2
PEATTIE JOHN J	LTC	0-0450469	0858	1
PEAVEY FRANK H	COL	0-0266490	1163	3
PEAVY JERRY L	LTC	0-1289617	0664	1
PEAVY JR HENRY J	MAJ	0-0213955	1145	2
PEAY ROBERT E	MAJ	C-1581316	0261	1
PEBLER CAROLINE M	MAJ	N-0795431	0167	1
PECAUT RAYMOND H	MAJ	0-0499017	C655	1
PECAWICZ JOHN W	MAJ	0-1591361	C862	1
PECHIN FREDERIC H	MAJ	0-1287754	0361	1
PECHIN JAMES R	CPT	0-0974795	0666	1
PECHON ERNEST F	CPT	C-1580147	C253	1
PECHULIS FRANK V	LTC	0-1041216	1163	1
PECK ALBERT B	2LT	0-1173417	C444	2
PECK CALVIN R	MAJ	0-1919937	0963	1
PECK EARL W	CW3	W-214165C	0559	1
PECK ELAM A	MAJ	C-0260907	0365	3
PECK ERNEST	LTC	0-0321478	1058	1
PECK HARLAND K	MAJ	0-0810210	C263	2
PECK HARRY M	COL	0-0163234	0948	3
PECK JAMES C	MAJ	C-1924598	C867	1
PECK JAMES E	COL	C-0338204	0467	1
PECK JESSE M	CPT	C-0109336	0527	1
PECK JOHN C	1LT	0-1302703	104N	2
PECK JR ALLEN S	LTC	0-0331955	1060	1
PECK JR GEORGE A	LTC	0-1035336	0661	1
PECK KENNETH	LTC	C-0289854	C757	3
PECK LOUIS P	CPT	0-0418983	1047	1
PECK PHILIP B	CPT	0-0254285	1065	3
PECK RALPH W	CW2	W-2209573	1060	1
PECK ROBERT G	CPT	0-1292937	0247	2
PECK ROLAND B	LTC	0-0229525	C545	2
PECK SAMUEL W	MAJ	0-1305978	0561	1
PECK SR JOHN S	CPT	0-1175532	0562	1
PECK WYATT N	MAJ	0-0102084	0856	3
PECKENS MARK R	CW2	W-2109610	0456	1
PECKHAM CHARLES L	LTC	0-1287938	0367	2
PECKHAM GEORGE M	MAJ	0-0331670	1046	2
PECKHAM VIVIAN B	COL	0-0201150	0763	3
PECKINPAUGH R L	CPT	0-1575506	0446	2
PECKLERS HERBERT R	2LT	0-1545728	1044	2
PECOR ROBERT E	MAJ	C-1885431	C966	1
PECOR VIRGEL E	CPT	0-0483031	0154	1
PEDDICORD JAMES O	CW3	W-2141806	C158	1
PEDDIE EDGAR C	CW3	W-2145041	0963	1
PEDDIE JAMES	LTC	0-0494136	0657	1
PEDDRICK ELMER M	COL	0-0180194	0752	3
PEDDY ROY L	CW3	W-2141406	0659	1
PEDEN ROSIE L	2LT	N-0703797	1042	1
PEDERSEN ANKER C	LTC	0-1584724	0957	1
PEDERSEN CHRISTIAN	COL	0-0104176	0648	3
PEDERSEN CONRAD H	COL	0-0201855	C860	3
PEDERSEN CORA M	MAJ	M-0002630	1164	1
PEDERSEN FRANK S	MAJ	0-0276148	0963	3
PEDERSEN HAROLD	MAJ	0-0984537	0862	1
PEDERSEN JOHN H	2LT	0-15925C3	0446	2
PEDERSEN NORMAN C	CW3	W-2152394	0866	1
PEDERSEN WARREN E	MAJ	0-1308432	0861	1
PEDERSEN WILLIAM W	MAJ	C-4006745	1067	1
PEDERSCN DALE V	MAJ	0-2048104	0763	1
PEDERSCN ERNEST O	LTC	0-0275712	0567	3
PEDERSCN HANS F	CPT	0-0235838	0752	3
PEDERSON HAROLD W	WO1	W-2108611	1044	2
PEDIGO PAUL C	CPT	0-0406089	0344	1
PEDIGO ROGER L	MAJ	0-0366535	0961	1
PEDNEAULT GEORGE J	LTC	0-0301887	0152	1
PEDONE GASPAR J	2LT	0-0965078	1151	1
PEDONE JOSEPH J	LTC	0-1595093	0864	1
PEDREIRA LUIS A	LTC	0-0262057	0448	2
PEDRONI PETER J	1LT	0-1111827	0745	2
PEDROTTI PETER W	LTC	0-036167C	0358	1
PEEBLES BARCLAY	LTC	0-1319438	0566	3
PEEBLES FRANCIS E	CPT	0-1304110	1146	1
PEEBLES SNYDER L	B G	0-0238690	0862	3
PEEBLES THOMAS A	MAJ	0-0204341	1052	2
PEEBLES WARD K	MAJ	0-2033675	1065	1
PEED JAMES E	CW3	W-2149264	1265	1
PEEK CLIFFORD L	LTC	0-0917164	0765	3
PEEK DUNCAN G	LTC	0-0309644	0364	3
PEEK GEORGE J	CW3	W-2152856	0764	1
PEEK JAMES E	MAJ	0-2014783	0165	1
PEEK NCHEA O A	COL	0-0245525	0161	3
PEEK ROBERT P	LTC	0-0453710	C656	1
PEEKE RAYMOND G	COL	C-0203608	1055	3
PEELER ALLEN L	LTC	0-0305473	0661	2
PEELING ORRAL J	MAJ	0-0247369	0749	3
PEEPLES HAZAEL L	MAJ	0-1342294	0867	1
PEEPLES HEARL A	MAJ	0-0235763	0565	3
PEEPLES JR WILLIAM H	MAJ	C-0204633	1062	3
PEER CHARLES W	LTC	0-2210018	1167	1
PEERSCN JAMES H	1LT	0-1048136	0548	1
PEET MARLIN O	MAJ	0-0268122	0759	3
PEET WILLIAM H	CPT	0-0312969	0545	2
PEET WILLIAM W	MAJ	0-0118031	0648	3
PEETOON PETER W	LTC	0-0341563	0252	1
PEGELOW EDWIN F	LTC	0-1059032	0767	1
PEGG HAROLD J	LTC	0-0236279	0457	3
PEGG ROBERT W	COL	0-0404164	1060	1
PEGRAM ALBERT A	MAJ	0-0373611	0964	1
PEGRAM HOWARD M	LTC	0-04954CC	0955	1
PEGRAM JAMES C	MAJ	0-110242C	0359	1
PEHRKCN ARTHUR J	LTC	0-0299951	0966	1
PEIFER ELSIE S	MAJ	N-0723632	0965	1
PEIFER GEORGE T	CPT	0-0147918	0559	3
PEIFFER DONALD R	CW2	W-2214506	0866	1
PEIFFER JAMES L	LTC	0-0450757	0857	2
PEIFFER RAY C	CW3	W-2111715	1054	1
PEIFFER ROBERT O	LTC	0-1580152	1056	1
PEIKERT ALBERT B	CPT	0-0277743	0850	1
PEIL RODMAN H	1LT	0-2033247	0450	1
PEINE PATRICK E	MAJ	0-1550479	0960	1
PEIRCE BYRON H	LTC	0-0272005	1166	3
PEIRCE EUGENE W	LTC	0-0237139	0664	3
PEIRCE HEMAN W	CW2	W-2104794	0853	1
PEIRCE LEONARD K	LTC	0-1589437	1164	1
PEIRCE MERVIN W	CW3	W-2146025	0960	1
PEIRCE SHELDON J	CPT	0-0254752	0267	3
PEISER HARRY	LTC	0-0499215	0150	1
PEISER MILDRED B	MAJ	N-0795848	0465	1
PEISER WILLIAM S	CPT	0-0421924	0547	1
PEITROWSKI EDWARD E	CPT	0-1545364	0351	1
PEITZER BERNARD	LTC	0-0499368	0965	3
PEIXOTTO EDGAR R	CPT	0-0234832	0844	2

ARMY OF THE UNITED STATES RETIRED LIST

NAME	GRADE	SVC NO	DATE RET MO YR	RET CODE
PELAK WILLIAM T	1LT	0-1030077	C144	2
PELAVA MIKE	CW3	W-2145344	0659	1
PELEBECKY GEORGE W	1LT	0-0436280	0744	1
PELET MARISKA J	MAJ	N-0726646	1162	1
PELFREY WILLIAM C	2LT	0-2010884	0449	1
PELHAM JR THOMAS W	LTC	0-0174461	0147	2
PELHAM WALTER C	MAJ	0-0888437	C860	1
PELINSKI P ELEANOR	1LT	N-0730677	C646	1
PELISH MAX	2LT	0-1297417	0943	2
PELISSIER LOUIS R	CW2	W-2145253	0660	1
PELL CLEMENS A	LTC	C-0271718	0663	1
PELL EARL R	CW3	W-2205948	C965	1
PELL FRANCIS H	MAJ	0-1688368	1262	1
PELL HARRY S	LTC	0-1044921	1066	1
PELL JR HOWLAND H	COL	0-0139975	C957	3
PELL WENCE P	1LT	0-0289181	1042	2
PELLACANI ROMOLO	LTC	0-1639504	0666	1
PELLE JOHN J	CPT	0-0953870	0461	1
PELLEGRENE ADA O	MAJ	N-0727807	C165	1
PELLEGRINI MARIO	CW3	W-2152147	C663	1
PELLEGRINO HAROLD L	MAJ	0-0416867	0646	2
PELLEGRINO PETE A	CPT	0-0234785	0563	3
PELLEGRINO PETER J	1LT	0-0404139	0346	2
PELLENS GERARD G	MAJ	0-2263057	0865	1
PELLER IVAN W	MAJ	C-0486782	0563	1
PELLER JOSEPH R	COL	0-0145929	C456	3
PELLETIER CHARLES E	WO1	W-2104795	0346	2
PELLETIER IRVING	CW4	W-2000113	C165	3
PELLETIER JAMES J	LTC	0-1294186	0761	1
PELLETTIERI JAMES E	COL	C-0282308	0356	3
PELLING PETER	1LT	0-1178285	C646	2
PELLISH ALEX	LTC	0-0390212	C258	1
PELLISH MAXWELL C	LTC	0-0193465	1159	3
PELLOUX ROBERT L	LTC	0-0378525	0261	2
PELLOWSKI JOSEPH A	CW3	W-2104879	0860	1
PELLS HARRISON W	LTC	0-0385101	0161	1
PELOSI LEON	CW3	W-2145290	1063	1
PELOT NELL S	LTC	0-1546188	0867	1
PELOUZE CANNING C	LTC	0-0362142	1059	1
PELOW CHARLES A	1LT	0-1326295	0246	2
PELT AUGUSTUS H	MAJ	0-0980438	1266	1
PELT JOSEPH S	MAJ	0-1104333	C846	1
PELTIER REGINALD A	LTC	0-2026564	0366	1
PELTON CHARLES E	CW3	W-2148807	0564	1
PELTON WILLIAM C	LTC	0-0371514	0161	1
PELUSO SAMUEL A	CW2	W-2150242	0265	1
PELZER GROSS A	LTC	0-0250371	0367	3
PELZMAN IVY A	LTC	0-0197221	0146	2
PEMBERTON BILLIE J	CPT	0-1999323	0847	2
PEMBERTON CHARLES S	MAJ	C-1320173	C563	1
PEMBERTON FRANK S	LTC	0-1586012	1162	2
PEMBERTON HOWARD L	2LT	0-2000137	1145	2
PEMBERTON JR JAMES E	COL	0-0112677	1058	3
PEMBERTON WILFRED G	LTC	0-0398965	C862	1
PENA JOSEPH A	LTC	0-1301207	0263	1
PENA WILLIAM W	CPT	0-0465382	C647	1
PENAS FRANK C	LTC	0-2033166	0366	1
PENCE ALFRED H	LTC	0-0250044	0565	3
PENCE ARTHUR P	CW3	W-2141652	1058	1
PENCE DAN	1LT	0-0221858	1044	2
PENCE HARRY S	LTC	0-0289287	0661	3
PENCE JR YARD W	MAJ	C-4005253	1067	1
PENCHAN BENJAMIN	CPT	0-1587528	C461	1
PENDARVIS ADRIAN E	1LT	0-0450505	0345	2
PENDER HAROLD E	CPT	0-0309648	0255	2
PENDER HENRY L	1LT	0-2054039	0747	1
PENDER HERBERT W	CW3	W-2151910	1163	1
PENDER MURRAY T	CPT	0-0390616	0146	2
PENDER RICHARD H	LTC	0-0485672	0159	1
PENDERGAST HERBERT C	LTC	C-0198441	0455	3
PENDERGRAFT GEORGE W	CPT	C-0445626	0447	1
PENDERGRAFT HENRY C	CPT	0-2331637	1166	3
PENDERVILLE EDGAR R	CPT	0-0467C10	C448	2
PENDLETON ARTHUR G	LTC	C-0451462	0960	1
PENDLETON FRANK S	2LT	C-0494666	0345	2
PENDLETCN HUNTER A	CPT	0-0184576	1057	3
PENDLETCN ROBERT W	LTC	0-0450342	1054	1
PENDLETCN THOMAS H	MAJ	0-1341698	0166	1
PENDLETCN WILLIAM E	1LT	0-1115058	0946	2
PENDLETCN WILLIAM E	CW2	RW-2211288	0764	1
PENDLETON WILLIAM W	1LT	0-1295079	0646	1
PENDLETON WILLIE G	CPT	0-1101989	0447	2
PENER WILLIAM H	LTC	0-1324092	1262	1
PENFIELD JOEL F	MAJ	C-0207910	1146	2
PENFIELD JOHN B	LTC	0-1002709	0866	1
PENFIELD RICHARD	COL	0-0133618	1051	3
PENFIELD RONALD W	LTC	0-0256505	0563	3
PENGELLY HAROLD	COL	0-0360761	0154	1
PENGILLY JOSEPH H	COL	0-0103755	0648	3
PENHALLOW DAVID P	LTC	C-0227802	0446	2
PENHALLOW RICHARD	LTC	0-0242757	0266	3
PENICK JR EDGAR C	MAJ	0-1643214	C963	3
PENINGTCN RALPH A	LTC	0-1185300	1061	1
PENKUNAS ISABELL C	MAJ	N-0725488	0767	1
PENMAN JAMES T	CPT	0-1822613	0447	2
PENN CLARK J	LTC	0-1650690	0765	1
PENN JULIUS H	MAJ	0-0168717	0959	3
PENN MARION B	LTC	0-0226773	0962	3
PENN WILLIAM A	MAJ	0-0502883	0850	1
PENNDORF WILLIAM B	CPT	0-0498215	0946	1
PENNEFATHER RICHARD	2LT	0-1104334	0445	2
PENNELL GLENN E	CW2	W-2152134	0361	1
PENNELL HENRY B	2LT	0-0231308	1062	3
PENNELL LOCKWOOD M	LTC	0-0274890	0466	3
PENNELL VIRGINIA H	1LT	N-0731130	1C46	1
PENNER ELWOOD G	MAJ	0-1951186	1059	1
PENNER EMANUEL J	CW3	W-2147115	0763	1
PENNETT JOHN A	LTC	0-1013171	0962	1
PENNEWELL NOAH A	LTC	0-0280456	0261	1
PENNEY HAROLD C	MAJ	0-0575870	1159	1
PENNEY JR DAVID E	COL	0-0320260	0866	3
PENNEY JR EDWARD O	1LT	0-1556930	0746	2
PENNEY MAYNARD M	MAJ	0-0109433	0946	2
PENNEY MYERS F	MAJ	C-1941324	0966	1
PENNEY THOMAS F	LTC	0-0451374	0658	1
PENNIMAN EDWARD G	CPT	0-1315205	1047	1
PENNING EDWIN W	CPT	0-1166152	0260	1
PENNINGA WILLIAM J	LTC	0-0361460	0161	1
PENNINGTON ALTON R	1LT	0-1931279	0357	2
PENNINGTON CLARK W	LTC	0-0254551	0954	1
PENNINGTON CLYDE H	CW3	W-2146456	0859	1
PENNINGTON CLYDE L	LTC	0-0305618	0549	1
PENNINGTCN DAVID	LTC	0-1168863	1065	1
PENNINGTCN FRED P	1LT	0-0564004	0956	1
PENNINGTON JAMES H	LTC	0-1550240	0666	1
PENNINGTON JOHN A	MAJ	0-0301529	0160	3
PENNINGTCN JOHN M	CPT	0-1289131	0647	1
PENNINGTCN LORETTA N	1LT	N-0756245	0546	1
PENNINGTCN LUTHER T	1LT	0-1736095	0645	2
PENNINGTCN RALPH W	CW3	W-2145694	0166	1
PENNINGTCN REGUS M	MAJ	0-0497642	0156	1
PENNINGTON WILLIAM R	MAJ	0-1821763	1056	2
PENNINC WALTER A	LTC	C-0371010	1059	1
PENNOCK JOHN S	MAJ	0-0453107	0356	1
PENNOCK JOSEPH L	CW3	W-2152421	0663	1
PENNOYER GEORGE O	MAJ	0-1686221	1265	1
PENNY ALLEN L	MAJ	0-0984895	0763	1
PENNY FOREST L	1LT	0-0887680	1145	2
PENNY HAROLD G	COL	0-0191995	0157	1
PENNY LEON J	LTC	0-1C45209	1165	1
PENNY NEWTON W	CPT	0-0308539	0545	2
PENNY WILFRED F	CW2	W-2206644	0661	1
PENNYWITT LESLIE H	2LT	0-2050825	0250	3
PENOFF ALEXANDER	CPT	0-2015805	0359	1
PENOYER MARK H	LTC	0-0406260	0464	1
PENROD CHARLES W	CW3	W-2149676	0162	1
PENROD CLAUDE W	LTC	0-0497492	0355	1
PENROD HAROLD L	LTC	0-1582042	0567	1
PENROD HOMER F	CW2	W-2144097	0960	2
PENROD PAUL E	CW3	W-2148975	0962	1
PENROSE CHARLES	LTC	0-1291508	C954	1
PENRY WILLARD W	LTC	0-0194750	1060	3
PENSKE WILLIAM W	LTC	C-0145468	C351	3
PENSTONE GILES H	MAJ	C-0256908	0867	3
PENSYL JOSEPH O	CW3	W-2143506	C867	1
PENSYL WILLIAM H	LTC	0-0546887	C265	1
PENTECOST FATE J	CPT	C-1290118	1163	1
PENTER KENNETH L	1LT	0-1290997	1145	1
PENTON GUY	CPT	0-0493957	0550	1
PENTON JAMES R	CPT	C-1822614	1047	2
PENTZ CARL M	WO1	W-2111763	0851	2
PENTZ WILLIAM R	MAJ	C-0216876	C755	3
PENUEL JR BENJAMIN H	MAJ	C-2014692	C465	1
PENWELL GUY D	LTC	0-0191368	0162	3
PENZENIK JR JOHN J	MAJ	C-C395026	0257	1
PEOPLES AVERY G	MAJ	0-0981134	0961	1
PEOPLES CLAUDE F	CPT	C-0308326	C346	2
PEOPLES HOWARD C	LTC	0-1104335	C860	1
PEOPLES PAUL E	1LT	0-1109584	1045	2
PEPAS JOHN J	MAJ	C-1000841	0462	2
PEPIN BERNARD J	MAJ	0-1551486	0161	1
PEPLAU WALTER C	MAJ	0-1169282	C857	1
PEPPARD HAROLD J	MAJ	C-2009351	1162	1
PEPPEL BLAIR W	MAJ	C-1300524	C561	1
PEPPER DICKINSON	COL	0-0296317	C667	3
PEPPER GRADY S	LTC	C-0911830	1062	3
PEPPER JACK A	1LT	0-C484997	1046	1
PEPPER JOE C	MAJ	C-2026891	0260	1
PEPPER ROBERT H	1LT	0-1288610	C750	2
PEPPERDENE JOHN H	MAJ	C-1825170	1262	1
PEPPERS DONALD F	COL	0-0211217	0453	3
PEPPERS TRACY O	LTC	0-0224152	1044	2
PEPPIN HULL C	LTC	0-0298604	0261	3
PEPPLE RAYMOND F	MAJ	0-0270163	0151	1
PERAK JOHN S	2LT	C-5325476	0366	2
PERANTONI DAVID T	1LT	0-5706838	0565	2
PERCEFULL PAYNE H	CPT	0-2024211	1058	1
PERCIFIELD JAMES O	LTC	0-1105095	C261	1
PERCIVAL GEORGE W	COL	0-0114533	0254	3
PERCIVAL HAROLD C	COL	0-0117958	0454	3
PERCIVAL RICHARD G	CW3	W-2145653	0663	1
PERCIVAL WILLIAM J	MAJ	0-4074736	0367	1
PERCOCO FRANK A	WO1	W-2120822	C745	2
PERCY RANDOLPH H	LTC	0-0103685	1056	1
PERCY ROBERT J	LTC	0-1549010	0967	1
PERDELWITZ LEE F	MAJ	0-1341288	C766	2
PERDUE EDWARD F	LTC	0-0181385	0455	3
PERDUE JR GEORGE T	MAJ	C-1643215	C159	1
PERDUE JR LOVIC P	LTC	0-0260786	1264	1
PERDUE LOREE V	1LT	N-0770790	C547	1
PERDUE WILLIAM L	1LT	C-0525884	C646	2
PERE HENRY J	CPT	C-0219598	1156	3
PEREDO FRED U	CPT	0-C890288	0150	1
PEREGO FORCYCE L	LTC	0-01C7805	0648	1
PEREIRA FRED E	COL	C-0206204	C746	2
PEREL MILTON	CPT	0-0360512	1044	2
PERELL SYDNEY C	COL	0-0242681	0346	2
PERELLA DORWIN H	LTC	0-0315977	C760	1
PERETTI SERAFINO	CPT	0-1846048	115C	1
PERETTIE DANIEL J	COL	C-01C9568	0148	2
PEREZ CHARLES F	LTC	C-1296420	1061	2
PEREZ ERNESTO	CPT	0-0156277	0655	3
PEREZ EUGENE R	LTC	0-0372172	C845	2
PEREZ JOSE M	CPT	0-2027328	0557	1
PEREZ JR OVIDIO	CW3	W-2144996	0361	1
PEREZ MANUEL S	CPT	0-0156276	0653	3
PEREZ REVESTER	CRT	N-0804211	0357	2
PEREZ ROBERT	COL	C-0278105	1065	3
PEREZ TEMISTOCLE	1LT	0-1896919	0162	1
PEREZ-GARCIA RAFAEL	LTC	0-0322056	0461	1
PEREZ-VEGA HECTOR	MAJ	0-0988480	1162	1
PERFATER GEORGE M	COL	0-026764C	0454	1
PERFETT FLORENCE A	1LT	N-0722467	C346	1
PERHAM BERTRAM S	CPT	0-1692350	1045	2
PERHAM CLIFFORD A	LTC	0-0240025	C859	1
PERHAM MARSHALL	LTC	0-0488865	0964	1
PERICONE VINCENT J	CW2	W-2146964	0854	1
PERIGNY CHARLES H	LTC	0-0491897	0365	1
PERIM CHARLES	CW3	W-215121C	0865	1
PERILLI CHARLES	LTC	0-1323731	0163	1
PERILLOUX FELIX F	WO1	W-2109111	0545	2
PERINA JR FRANK A	1LT	0-2055298	0146	2
PERING CHARLES L	CW2	RW-2211208	0165	1
PERKIN FRANK S	MAJ	0-0470591	1045	1
PERKINS ALBERT H	LTC	0-0375871	0664	1
PERKINS AUGUST T	LTC	0-0494289	1166	3
PERKINS CALVIN E	LTC	0-0496542	0664	3
PERKINS CHARLES F	CW3	W-2149407	0565	1
PERKINS CHARLES L	MAJ	C-0395829	0547	2
PERKINS CHYDE A	CPT	0-0333807	0166	3
PERKINS CLARENCE A	1LT	0-0268990	1054	3
PERKINS CLAUD E	MAJ	0-1287756	0358	2
PERKINS CLIFFORD A	MAJ	0-0477479	0944	1
PERKINS DAVID M	LTC	0-0448179	0560	3
PERKINS DUNCAN C	LTC	0-1306139	0165	2
PERKINS EARL	CW3	W-215137C	0665	1
PERKINS EARLE F	MAJ	0-1650281	0956	1
PERKINS EDWARD	CW2	W-2108686	0650	2
PERKINS EDWARD M	LTC	0-0281287	0363	3
PERKINS ELDON R	MAJ	0-1933577	0665	1
PERKINS ELGIN A	MAJ	0-1582044	C762	1
PERKINS ERWIN F	COL	C-0255141	1054	3
PERKINS FRANK A	MAJ	0-2056114	0762	1
PERKINS FRED FRED	CPT	0-0494052	0852	1
PERKINS GEORGE H	CW4	W-2131831	0762	1
PERKINS GRADY R	1LT	0-1043752	0545	2
PERKINS HANSON T	MAJ	C-0200661	0959	3
PERKINS HARRISON H	COL	0-0439841	0-53	1
PERKINS HUGH V	MAJ	0-0204381	0151	3
PERKINS JAMES R	1LT	0-2208142	1152	1
PERKINS JAMES W	COL	0-0279636	0861	3
PERKINS JOHN	COL	C-0103397	0648	3
PERKINS JOHN H	MAJ	C-1797345	0561	1
PERKINS JOHN T	CW2	W-2210641	0263	1
PERKINS JOHN W	CW3	W-2142349	0659	1
PERKINS JOHN W	CW2	W-2147496	1058	1
PERKINS JR HENRY N	CW3	W-2149231	0466	1
PERKINS JR PERCY H	COL	0-0239342	1065	3
PERKINS JR ROSCOE	COL	0-0149123	0651	3
PERKINS LEON W	LTC	0-0181935	0150	3
PERKINS LLOYD A	LTC	0-045047C	0955	1
PERKINS MELVILLE F	COL	0-0170762	0554	3
PERKINS NORRIS H	MAJ	0-0325782	0246	2
PERKINS ORVILLE O	1LT	0-1690945	1047	2
PERKINS OSCAR L	LTC	0-0180551	0862	3
PERKINS RAY	COL	0-0142725	0855	3
PERKINS RAYMOND K	COL	0-0908549	C466	3
PERKINS ROBERT	LTC	0-1703784	1060	1
PERKINS ROBERT A	CW2	W-2152659	0960	2
PERKINS RODNEY	CW2	W-2119677	1060	1
PERKINS RUSSELL V	MAJ	0-1650541	0259	1
PERKINS SAMUEL W	LTC	C-1297244	0361	1
PERKINS WHEELER R	COL	C-0250625	0466	3
PERKINS WILLIAM A	LTC	0-0236053	0449	3
PERKOWSKI JOHN	MAJ	0-1688424	0561	1
PERKOWSKI STEPHEN P	CW3	W-2144881	0960	1
PERKOWSKY WILLIAM	MAJ	0-1311814	1058	2
PERL WILLIAM R	LTC	0-0555149	1066	3
PERLEY ALLAN H	CW2	W-2146026	0259	1
PERLEY SYDNEY H	LTC	0-0124279	0345	2
PERLMAN JEROME	CW3	W-2145831	0163	1
PERLMAN SAM S	LTC	0-1549011	1064	1
PERLOFF WILLIAM H	CPT	0-0465633	0945	1
PERLOW DAVID	LTC	0-0221212	0-53	1
PERLSWEIG BERNARD I	CPT	0-1311537	1046	1
PERMAN MAXWELL L	MAJ	0-0434710	0446	2
PERMENTER GAIL W	2LT	0-2048108	0544	2
PERNA ALFONSO A	MAJ	0-0334901	0846	2
PERNETTI ANTHONY H	CPT	0-0310977	1045	2
PERNICK HARRY C	COL	0-0510666	1167	1

NAME	GRADE	SVC NO	DATE RET MO YR	RET CODE
PERNISH PAUL J	LTC	0-0348225	0965	3
PERO JAMES P	MAJ	0-1014838	0862	1
PERONE NICHOLAS A	MAJ	0-1796147	0458	2
PEROTTI JAMES O	LTC	0-0379600	0663	1
PERREAULT ALBERT F	MAJ	0-1874288	0664	1
PERRETTA CANIO D	CPT	0-1549013	0447	1
PERREY JOSEPH I	COL	0-0240311	0964	3
PERREY RAPHAEL F	LTC	0-0319875	1160	1
PERRIN AUBREY H	LTC	0-0224675	0662	3
PERRIN FRANK Y	1LT	0-1108225	0562	1
PERRIN HORACE C	2LT	0-1050860	0743	2
PERRIN HUBERT E	CW3	W-2142984	0960	1
PERRIN VIRGIL C	MAJ	0-1312326	0559	1
PERRINE ALFRED T	CPT	0-0469123	0946	1
PERRINE EARL R	CW3	W-2208545	0866	1
PERRINE FLOYD V	LTC	0-0384766	0666	1
PERRINE JR NAT S	LTC	0-0406897	0461	1
PERRINGTON ALBERT W	MAJ	0-1292747	0558	1
PERRON HENRY F	LTC	0-1576491	0157	1
PERRON ROBERT C	MAJ	0-1595756	0157	1
PERRONE DOMINIC A	MAJ	0-1795034	1058	1
PERRONE VICTOR E	MAJ	0-4021477	0855	2
PERRONE VINCENT R	MAJ	0-2200222	0563	1
PERROTTA DONATO F	CPT	0-1047290	0353	1
PERROW EARNEST A	LTC	0-0162232	0146	2
PERRY ALBERT N	MAJ	0-2023306	0467	1
PERRY ALEXANDER	COL	0-0378492	0365	3
PERRY ANNA A	CPT	N-0731147	0547	1
PERRY ANTHONY G	CW2	W-2123318	0963	3
PERRY ARVEL H	MAJ	0-1322404	0158	1
PERRY BREWSTER	COL	0-0450163	1162	1
PERRY CARL B	CPT	0-1302705	1054	1
PERRY CHARLES E	LTC	0-0127159	1156	3
PERRY CHARLES H	LTC	0-1645908	1266	3
PERRY CLARENCE L	LTC	0-1287232	0661	1
PERRY CLAUDE S	COL	0-0227626	0659	3
PERRY CLYDE L	MAJ	0-1183592	0860	1
PERRY COLLINS R	LTC	0-0270368	0345	1
PERRY DOUGLAS B	CW4	W-2121777	0963	1
PERRY EDWIN R	COL	0-1107033	0463	1
PERRY ELTON L	CW4	W-2142599	0464	1
PERRY EVERETT W	1LT	0-1309816	0845	1
PERRY EZRA B	CPT	0-0466237	0546	2
PERRY FANNY S	2LT	N-0767374	0145	1
PERRY FRANCIS F	1LT	0-0443131	0345	2
PERRY FRANK O	MAJ	0-1578962	1062	1
PERRY GEORGE J	CW2	W-2000115	0354	3
PERRY GERALD F	CPT	0-0191974	0158	3
PERRY GLENN G	MAJ	0-0441331	0346	2
PERRY HAROLD E	CW3	W-2150220	0166	1
PERRY HAROLD W	CW2	W-2212234	0367	1
PERRY HASKELL O	CW4	W-2104367	0659	1
PERRY HERBERT J	CPT	0-1169684	0863	1
PERRY HERMAN A	2LT	0-1914169	0348	1
PERRY HERMAN M	MAJ	0-0252685	0550	1
PERRY HIRAM S	LTC	0-0205596	0648	3
PERRY HOWARD E	2LT	0-2019502	0354	2
PERRY HOWARD W	MAJ	0-2034899	0462	1
PERRY JAMES A	LTC	0-0311057	0866	3
PERRY JAMES F	LTC	0-1315610	1162	1
PERRY JAMES G	1LT	0-0920481	1045	2
PERRY JAMES M	CPT	0-2293414	0666	1
PERRY JAMES Z	1LT	0-0430651	0845	1
PERRY JASON A	LTC	0-0250255	0654	2
PERRY JOHN B	MAJ	0-0995628	1064	1
PERRY JOHN C	MAJ	0-0331360	0851	1
PERRY JOHN W	COL	0-0257066	0854	1
PERRY JOSEPH H	1LT	0-2263425	0461	1
PERRY JOSEPH R	2LT	0-2034454	1044	2
PERRY JOSEPH W	LTC	0-1310489	0562	1
PERRY JR JAMES I	CPT	0-2212099	0960	1
PERRY JR JOHN P	LTC	0-0397171	0561	1
PERRY LAYTON M	MAJ	0-1166351	0546	1
PERRY LEBERT F	CPT	0-0410098	0647	1
PERRY LEE C	CPT	0-1013640	1047	1

NAME	GRADE	SVC NO	DATE RET MO YR	RET CODE
PERRY LEE G	CW3	W-2129091	0461	2
PERRY LEE ROY	1LT	0-1583491	0447	2
PERRY LEON J	2LT	0-1288437	0744	2
PERRY LESTER E	MAJ	0-1309310	0661	1
PERRY LONNIE W	MAJ	0-2016018	0860	1
PERRY LYNN	LTC	0-0166512	0648	3
PERRY MARLIN F	1LT	0-1081093	1045	2
PERRY MARSHALL E	MAJ	0-0563206	0863	1
PERRY MARVIN J	CW4	W-2132192	0659	1
PERRY MERLIN H	LTC	0-1181728	0762	1
PERRY NORBERT V	CPT	0-0333426	0140	1
PERRY REGINA B	2LT	N-0788806	0744	1
PERRY RICHARD T	MAJ	0-0244660	0562	3
PERRY ROBERT E	LTC	0-1287581	0661	2
PERRY ROBERT K	1LT	0-0404805	0245	2
PERRY RONALD H	MAJ	0-2029435	0763	1
PERRY RYLAND B	CPT	0-0309478	0345	2
PERRY SANFORD C	MAJ	0-0305352	1067	3
PERRY THEODORE A	MAJ	0-0545770	0464	1
PERRY THERON H	LTC	0-2017275	0367	1
PERRY THOMAS C	MAJ	0-0203961	0647	1
PERRY THOMAS E	CW4	W-2107208	0656	1
PERRY THOMAS L	2LT	0-1050032	0145	2
PERRY THURSTON R	MAJ	0-1560378	0263	1
PERRY VERNON R	CW2	W-2145345	0255	2
PERRY VIRGIL L	CW3	W-2152713	0564	1
PERRY WADE B	MAJ	0-0320261	0546	2
PERRY WALTER S	CPT	0-1301208	0747	2
PERRY WARREN B	LTC	0-0505206	0264	3
PERRY WELDON W	CPT	0-2020199	0561	1
PERRY WILLIAM	LTC	0-0180556	0444	1
PERRY WILLIAM	MAJ	0-0501603	1046	2
PERRY WILLIAM A	MAJ	0-1589435	0861	1
PERRY WILLIAM H	CW3	W-2142657	0860	1
PERRY WILLIAM K	COL	0-0443840	0565	3
PERRY WILLIAM O	COL	0-0181268	1055	3
PERRY WILLIAM W	CW2	W-2214845	0667	1
PERRY WINFRED O	MAJ	0-0166270	0353	3
PERRYMAN JULIAN G	WO1	W-2115997	0156	1
PERRYMAN KENNETH C	2LT	0-2018406	0547	1
PERRYMAN LEON T	LTC	0-0267257	0960	3
PERRYMAN MARK F	1LT	0-0888881	0350	1
PERRYMAN TAYLOR O	LTC	0-0267020	0157	1
PERRYMAN VIRGIL D	LTC	0-1597238	0666	1
PERSICHINI ARCHIE O	CPT	0-2053591	0756	1
PERSION MATTHEW M	MAJ	0-0209693	0558	3
PERSON DON E	LTC	0-0491798	0959	1
PERSON EPHRAIM E	MAJ	0-0265996	0859	3
PERSON ERNEST A	LTC	0-0934864	1266	1
PERSON JR RUFUS M	CPT	0-0250873	1166	3
PERSON LAWRENCE E	MAJ	0-1312379	1163	1
PERSON VERNON E	LTC	0-1105097	0863	1
PERSON WILLIAM E	MAJ	0-0123555	1052	3
PERSONETT CHESTER A	CW2	W-2118131	0447	1
PERSONETTE CHESTER A	LTC	0-2069107	0866	1
PERSONS DONALD B	LTC	0-1639900	0760	1
PERSONS ELAINE O	2LT	N-0737043	0444	1
PERSONS JOHN C	M G	0-0203751	0648	3
PERSONS JOSEPH H	CPT	0-1102901	0762	1
PERSONS LAWRENCE L	LTC	0-0402050	0464	1
PERUGINI MORRIS F	MAJ	0-0965933	0864	1
PERUSO LOUIS R	1LT	0-1012489	0945	2
PESANO JAMES	CW2	W-2123410	1044	2
PESAVENTO ROBERT F	LTC	0-1314053	0862	1
PESCATORE VINCENT V	LTC	0-1576492	1162	1
PESCI RICHARD G	CPT	0-1557060	1147	2
PESHAK GEORGE J	1LT	0-1183390	0546	1
PESHMALYAN BARUYR	MAJ	0-0242817	0448	2
PESKIN AARON R	MAJ	0-0236129	1043	2
PESSA JOSEPH J	COL	0-1101991	0867	1
PESSIN JOSEPH	LTC	0-0473463	0546	2
PESSUTTI JOSEPH P	1LT	0-1046608	0546	2
PESTER EARL H	1LT	0-1825314	0346	2
PETER ALBERT G	COL	0-0202671	0450	3
PETER ALEXANDER	LTC	0-0243896	0646	2

NAME	GRADE	SVC NO	DATE RET MO YR	RET CODE
PETER DONALD R	2LT	0-1316084	0745	2
PETER JOHN A	1LT	0-0513647	0445	2
PETER MAURICE G	LTC	0-0239090	0758	3
PETERKA CHARLES	MAJ	0-0230652	0260	3
PETERKIN JR GEORGE W	MAJ	0-1945453	0954	1
PETERKIN WILBUR J	COL	0-0270347	0364	3
PETERS ALEXANDER	MAJ	0-0165079	0-49	3
PETERS BENARD	LTC	0-0183104	0157	1
PETERS BURNHAM L	1LT	0-0888267	0145	1
PETERS CARL F	CW3	W-2206652	0766	1
PETERS CECIL A	CW2	W-2150360	0160	1
PETERS CLARENCE C	MAJ	0-1105362	0660	2
PETERS CLAUDE P	CPT	0-0114001	1154	3
PETERS CLIFFORD	1LT	0-1913201	0553	1
PETERS DONALD W	MAJ	0-2034980	1060	1
PETERS DWAIN P	1LT	0-1316200	0645	1
PETERS EARL V	1LT	0-1012277	0744	2
PETERS EDWARD A	CW3	RW-2144398	0365	1
PETERS EDWARD R	CW2	W-2205281	0761	1
PETERS EVA G	1LT	N-0721125	0446	1
PETERS GERALD D	1LT	0-1636464	0544	2
PETERS GORDON K	MAJ	0-1582495	0363	1
PETERS HARRY C	MAJ	0-1019601	0461	1
PETERS HARRY E	LTC	0-0399371	0164	1
PETERS HENRY T	MAJ	0-1081669	1060	1
PETERS IONE H	2LT	N-0733334	1044	1
PETERS JAMES G	COL	0-0212784	0362	3
PETERS JOHN A	COL	0-0376228	0261	1
PETERS JOHN D	COL	0-0348995	0767	3
PETERS JOHN L	MAJ	0-1328289	1061	1
PETERS JOSEPH A	CW2	W-2144516	0557	1
PETERS JOSEPH F	LTC	0-0450471	0657	1
PETERS JR WALTER H	CW3	W-2150312	1064	1
PETERS JR WALTER J	LTC	0-1011551	0961	1
PETERS JR WILLIAM H	COL	0-0161886	0356	3
PETERS KENNETH C	CPT	0-1822447	0966	2
PETERS KENNETH F	CPT	0-2012376	0457	1
PETERS LAWRENCE E	1LT	0-1312710	0745	2
PETERS LEO J	MAJ	0-2262396	0862	1
PETERS MARIN A	LTC	0-1294168	0859	1
PETERS NYREN L	CW3	W-2147134	0760	1
PETERS PAUL E	CW3	W-2148628	0762	1
PETERS PETER H	LTC	0-0377948	0667	3
PETERS RAYMOND	MAJ	0-2035553	0661	2
PETERS RAYMOND S	2LT	0-1691588	1045	1
PETERS ROBERT H	COL	0-0228620	0663	3
PETERS RUPERT E	MAJ	0-0889772	1262	1
PETERS VERNON E	MAJ	0-0969025	1160	1
PETERS WALTER	MAJ	0-1011238	0858	1
PETERS WALTER C	LTC	0-0169074	0660	3
PETERS WAYNE A	CW4	W-2115898	0359	1
PETERS WILLIAM C	LTC	0-1547108	1262	1
PETERS WILLIAM E	CPT	0-2036738	0759	1
PETERS WILLIAM H	CPT	0-0166125	0648	3
PETERS WILLIAM I	CPT	0-0471949	0846	1
PETERS WILLIAM R	MAJ	0-0379286	0560	1
PETERSEN ALLEN L	CW3	RW-2146807	0562	1
PETERSEN CHRISTIAN	LTC	0-0463470	0748	1
PETERSEN CLARENCE W	1LT	0-1946833	0246	2
PETERSEN DONALD F	MAJ	0-0453561	0161	1
PETERSEN EMIL	MAJ	0-0966964	0964	1
PETERSEN ERNEST	MAJ	0-1575510	0557	1
PETERSEN FRED M	1LT	0-1306641	1062	1
PETERSEN GLEN N	1LT	0-1311925	0646	2
PETERSEN HANS G	COL	0-0153212	0652	3
PETERSEN HAROLD W	CPT	0-0495739	1045	2
PETERSEN HENRY E	MAJ	0-0242380	0158	3
PETERSEN HENRY E	CW3	W-2003877	1064	3
PETERSEN HENRY R	LTC	0-0425006	0662	1
PETERSEN JIMMIE P	1LT	0-1699973	0965	2
PETERSEN JOHNS W	CW2	W-2148301	0757	1
PETERSEN JOSEPH C	CPT	0-1102902	0646	2
PETERSEN KERMIT	MAJ	0-0752017	0661	1
PETERSEN LAVERNE H	LTC	0-1305104	1067	1
PETERSEN MELVIN E	CW3	W-2142308	0558	1

NAME	GRADE	SVC NO	DATE RET MO YR	RET CODE
PETERSEN NORMAN F	MAJ	0-1332529	0263	1
PETERSEN PATRICK J	CPT	0-0509882	1045	2
PETERSEN RAYMOND L	CW2	W-2143806	0664	1
PETERSEN SIDNEY O	MAJ	0-0214543	0963	3
PETERSEN SIDNEY M	LTC	0-1115738	0263	1
PETERSEN WILLIAM B	CPT	0-1583498	0557	1
PETERSEN WILLIAM H	CPT	0-2033567	0859	1
PETERSEN WILLIAM W	LTC	0-1292750	0463	1
PETERSILIE HENRY	1LT	0-0483046	0343	1
PETERSON ALDEN E	LTC	0-0261698	0366	3
PETERSON ALFRED	CPT	0-0887562	1053	1
PETERSON ALICE E	CPT	N-0721454	0350	1
PETERSON ANDREW J	CPT	0-1302185	1051	1
PETERSON ARTHUR K	LTC	0-0258746	0667	3
PETERSON BERTHEL W	COL	0-0202729	1160	3
PETERSON BORDEN F	LTC	0-0336889	0662	1
PETERSON BRACY	CPT	0-2262395	0161	1
PETERSON BURTON C	1LT	0-1303774	0545	2
PETERSON CAPERS L	LTC	0-0261555	0167	3
PETERSON CARL A	CPT	0-0333178	1044	2
PETERSON CARL E	CW4	W-2115947	0355	1
PETERSON CARL H	LTC	0-0284479	0266	3
PETERSON CARL L	COL	0-0176731	0646	2
PETERSON CHARLES A	COL	0-0301533	1054	1
PETERSON CHARLES E	CPT	0-0392003	0346	2
PETERSON CHARLES R	LTC	0-0241007	1144	2
PETERSON CHESTER	COL	0-0226863	0564	3
PETERSON CHESTER A	MAJ	0-0575123	0266	2
PETERSON CHESTER T	MAJ	0-0954780	1064	1
PETERSON CHESTER W	LTC	0-1017498	0865	1
PETERSON CLARENCE	CPT	0-1689506	0845	2
PETERSON CLARENCE W	MAJ	0-0216301	0149	1
PETERSON CLEMENT	1LT	0-0168409	0156	3
PETERSON COLEMAN A	1LT	0-1051727	1062	1
PETERSON DERRELL F	COL	0-0386378	0964	3
PETERSON DON A	LTC	0-0341451	1167	3
PETERSON DONALD H	CPT	0-0412857	1045	2
PETERSON EARL J R	LTC	0-1549015	0764	1
PETERSON EDWARD J	CW3	W-2147858	0263	1
PETERSON EDWARD W	MAJ	0-1333116	0164	1
PETERSON EDWIN W	LTC	0-0198540	0862	3
PETERSON EMIL H	CW2	W-2143956	0656	1
PETERSON EVELYN S	MAJ	N-0772646	1063	1
PETERSON FRANCIS S	MAJ	0-0343979	0846	1
PETERSON GENE	MAJ	0-1299993	0164	1
PETERSON GEORGE E	MAJ	0-1055417	1156	2
PETERSON GEORGE G	CW3	W-2152194	0964	1
PETERSON GEORGE O	1LT	0-1797873	0146	2
PETERSON GILMAN P	CPT	0-1685250	1145	2
PETERSON GLENN O	2LT	0-1797347	1143	2
PETERSON GUSTAVE R	LTC	0-0244307	0164	3
PETERSON HAROLD	CPT	0-0106347	0648	3
PETERSON HAROLD	LTC	0-0364540	0460	1
PETERSON HAROLD W	COL	0-0355052	0667	3
PETERSON HAROLD W	CW3	W-2150782	1165	1
PETERSON HARRY L	MAJ	0-1285639	0162	1
PETERSON HARTWELL E	LTC	0-1593777	0863	1
PETERSON HARVEY L	2LT	0-1336252	0747	1
PETERSON HENRY L	MAJ	0-1018916	1055	1
PETERSON HENRY P	MAJ	0-0444900	0357	1
PETERSON HERBERT O	LTC	0-0408055	0961	1
PETERSON HOWARD G	LTC	0-1113390	0863	1
PETERSON I LILBOURN	COL	0-0210073	0154	3
PETERSON IRA R	CPT	0-0116725	0654	3
PETERSON IVAR E	LTC	0-1558810	0464	2
PETERSON JACK W	LTC	0-1307296	0264	1
PETERSON JAMES C	1LT	0-1325166	0850	1
PETERSON JAMES M	CW3	W-2005926	1266	1
PETERSON JAMES N	2LT	0-0436580	0345	2
PETERSON JAMES W	WO1	W-2119929	0464	1
PETERSON JOHN E	MAJ	0-4023236	0367	2
PETERSON JOHN F	MAJ	0-1179171	0661	1
PETERSON JOHN J	CPT	0-0967893	0960	1
PETERSON JOHN L	LTC	0-0187294	0955	3
PETERSON JOHN R	LTC	0-1012012	0961	1

NAME	GRADE	SVC NO	DATE RET MO YR	RET CODE
PETERSON JOSEPH L	COL	0-0235033	0259	3
PETERSON JOSEPH L	CW4	W-2111531	0261	1
PETERSON JR FRANK J	MAJ	0-2291540	1167	1
PETERSON JR JOSEPH H	1LT	0-1016203	1145	2
PETERSON JR LOUIS G	LTC	0-1293308	0263	1
PETERSON JR SOREN A	MAJ	0-0788080	0762	1
PETERSON JULIAN J	MAJ	0-0974128	0264	1
PETERSON KENDALL L	LTC	0-1048137	0463	1
PETERSON KENNETH F	2LT	0-1090753	0746	2
PETERSON LARS W	CPT	0-1921728	0456	2
PETERSON LEONARD O	LTC	0-0421473	0761	1
PETERSON LEROY R	MAJ	0-1695725	0859	1
PETERSON LLOYD F	LTC	0-0301614	1046	2
PETERSON LOUIS A	CPT	0-0527271	0667	1
PETERSON LYLE E	CPT	0-1182223	1146	2
PETERSON LYLE M	MAJ	0-0964598	0565	1
PETERSON LYMAN K	MAJ	0-0393309	1047	1
PETERSON MANFRED O	CW3	W-2144756	0564	1
PETERSON MARCEL G	CPT	0-0979945	1060	1
PETERSON MARLIN A	CPT	0-1013796	0756	1
PETERSON MARTIN B	1LT	0-1925832	0254	2
PETERSON MARTIN J	CPT	0-0452351	0944	1
PETERSON MARTIN W	MAJ	0-0452863	0657	1
PETERSON MILTON F	LTC	0-1294359	0859	1
PETERSON NATHANIEL	LTC	0-0151221	0149	3
PETERSON OSCAR G	LTC	0-1588805	0363	1
PETERSON PALMA L	1LT	N-0732403	0646	1
PETERSON PHILIP H	MAJ	0-1913224	0167	1
PETERSON QUENTIN E	CW2	W-2140252	0546	2
PETERSON RALPH M	LTC	0-0450102	0657	1
PETERSON RAY A	1LT	0-0387470	0144	2
PETERSON REBECCA E	2LT	N-0742621	0944	1
PETERSON RICHARD P	CW4	W-2110157	0365	3
PETERSON ROBERT A	LTC	0-1329277	1064	1
PETERSON ROBERT A	MAJ	0-4009104	1066	1
PETERSON ROBERT F	MAJ	0-1298121	0661	1
PETERSON ROBERT H	CPT	0-1314545	0561	2
PETERSON ROBERT W	2LT	0-1302186	0145	1
PETERSON RUSSELL C	CPT	0-1036333	0966	1
PETERSON RUSSELL W	CW2	W-2153048	0261	1
PETERSON SEVERIN O	CW2	W-2150134	0659	1
PETERSON STANLEY C	CPT	0-0307598	0145	2
PETERSON STANLEY J	LTC	0-0251340	0764	3
PETERSON THADDEUS E	MAJ	0-0141721	0152	3
PETERSON THEODORE H	MAJ	0-1692901	0863	1
PETERSON THEODORE W	COL	0-0249281	1264	3
PETERSON THOMAS J	MAJ	0-1018635	0461	1
PETERSON THOMAS O	LTC	0-1182441	0264	1
PETERSON TITUS T	WO1	W-2128828	0845	1
PETERSON VAUGHN	LTC	0-0265570	0259	1
PETERSON VERNON	COL	0-0120748	0953	1
PETERSON VERNON A	MAJ	0-1634211	0358	1
PETERSON VERNON W	LTC	0-0544631	0865	1
PETERSON VICTOR R	CW4	W-2128202	1066	1
PETERSON VICTOR W	2LT	0-1999958	0347	2
PETERSON VIRGIL J	LTC	0-1104339	1054	1
PETERSON WILBUR C	1LT	0-0103117	1045	2
PETERSON WILLIAM A	COL	0-0289225	0167	3
PETERSON WILLIAM H	MAJ	0-0250830	1057	3
PETERSON WILLIAM J	CPT	0-0252942	0153	3
PETERSON WILLIAM V	LTC	0-1796856	0464	3
PETERSON WYATT B	LTC	0-1650285	1065	1
PETH JOHN C	LTC	0-0149383	0-52	3
PETHICK JR FRANK I	B G	0-0248060	0467	3
PETICOLAS JOHN O	MAJ	0-0361241	1044	2
PETIGROW NORMAN B	1LT	0-1043460	1045	2
PETINGA SALVATORE	CPT	0-1297418	0655	1
PETIT ALEXANDER	CPT	0-0108349	0134	1
PETIT JOE F	MAJ	0-1558191	0358	1
PETIT WILFRED D	MAJ	0-1010174	0957	2
PETITBON LEO A	CPT	0-2055486	0456	1
PETITE FREDERICK	MAJ	0-0257877	0446	2
PETITO PETER A	COL	0-0369209	0661	1
PETOROCK JOHN J	MAJ	0-0964828	1162	1
PETRA RUDOLPH A	1LT	0-1110184	1044	2

NAME	GRADE	SVC NO	DATE RET MO YR	RET CODE
PETRABORG JARROLD A	COL	0-0102227	1153	2
PETRAKIS MANUEL M	LTC	0-0533338	1266	1
PETRANEK CHARLES W	MAJ	0-0228402	0557	3
PETRAS JOSEPH W	CPT	0-1283827	0345	1
PETRASEK ALBERT C	CPT	0-0487834	0346	2
PETRASH EDWARD B	MAJ	0-0467392	0364	1
PETRE JOSEPH K	CW4	W-2111037	0454	2
PETREE NOEL H	MAJ	0-0164569	0255	2
PETRESKY JOHN J	LTC	0-1044645	0461	1
PETRI JOHN	MAJ	0-0435927	1157	1
PETRICH ARTHUR C	LTC	0-0372655	0860	1
PETRICK JOSEPH L	LTC	0-0290075	0159	3
PETRICK LAWRENCE R	LTC	0-1291512	0960	1
PETRIE ANDREW H	MAJ	0-0186471	0356	3
PETRIE HAROLD J	MAJ	0-1010855	0546	1
PETRIE ROY A	1LT	0-0129614	1252	3
PETRIE WALTER E	LTC	0-0565406	1067	1
PETRILLI FRANK	CW3	W-2205685	0765	1
PETRING RALPH W	LTC	0-0913386	0862	2
PETRINI NEVIO	LTC	0-1101617	0261	1
PETRO VASIL W	CPT	0-1686049	0844	2
PETROCHKO WASIL R	CW2	W-2208504	0564	1
PETRONE FRANK R	CPT	0-1557061	0747	2
PETRONE JOHN C	MAJ	0-0325014	0146	2
PETRONE JOSEPH A	CPT	0-0508527	0345	2
PETROSKE LOUISE C	1LT	N-0721531	0546	1
PETROSKI STANLEY	1LT	0-1324647	0140	1
PETROVICH ENRIQUE	LTC	0-0373942	1160	1
PETROVICH JOHN J	2LT	0-1636467	0844	2
PETROVICH WALTER C	CW3	W-2150232	0659	1
PETROVSKY PAUL	LTC	0-1080738	0362	3
PETROWSKI JOSEPH P	1LT	0-0157571	0658	3
PETRU FRANK L	COL	0-0259436	0967	3
PETRY FRANCIS J	MAJ	0-0548538	0963	1
PETRY WILLIAM A	LTC	0-0490522	1145	2
PETSCH ALFRED P C	LTC	0-0103398	1153	3
PETSCH DOROTHY L	MAJ	N-0741491	0767	3
PETT MARLIN J	1LT	0-1300849	0246	2
PETTAWAY JOHN T	CPT	0-1559608	1161	1
PETTAY JOSEPH E	CW2	W-2116100	0553	1
PETTEE JOHN T	MAJ	0-0325109	1057	3
PETTENGELL ROBERT F	1LT	0-1182224	0461	1
PETTENGILL HENRY G	1LT	0-1797003	1143	2
PETTERSEN HERBERT C	COL	0-0198588	0463	3
PETTERSEN HERBERT F	LTC	0-0481234	0954	1
PETTERSEN PEDER G	COL	0-0300160	1057	3
PETTERSON MARCUS A	LTC	0-1576497	0660	1
PETTET JOSEPH W	LTC	0-0358201	0261	2
PETTI GEORGE H	CPT	0-0513680	0545	2
PETTIE FLOYD W	CW3	W-2152772	1160	1
PETTIE RICHARD C	CPT	0-4011155	1166	1
PETTIFORD ROBERT L	CW3	W-2144645	0363	2
PETTIFORD SAMUEL E	MAJ	0-1049605	0964	1
PETTIGREW GEORGE W	MAJ	0-1060922	0758	1
PETTIGREW JR ROBERT	MAJ	0-1948650	0165	1
PETTIGREW VERNEL W	2LT	0-1540694	1046	2
PETTIGREW WILLIAM B	MAJ	0-0678449	1062	1
PETTINE ULDRICH H	LTC	0-1168411	0165	1
PETTINGER JOHN L	LTC	0-0367610	0862	1
PETTINGER MARY E	CPT	N-0758038	0947	1
PETTINGER NEIL S	1LT	0-1700613	0443	2
PETTIS GEORGE S	CPT	0-0500064	0246	2
PETTIT ALFRED B	1LT	0-0351120	0145	2
PETTIT BILLY	MAJ	0-2262330	0263	1
PETTIT CHARLES A	LTC	0-0297868	0366	3
PETTIT EDWARD V	MAJ	0-0468407	0248	2
PETTIT LOYCE A	CPT	0-1649909	0954	1
PETTIT ROYCE E	MAJ	0-0210666	0555	3
PETTIT WILMER S	CPT	0-0911910	0545	2
PETTS FRANCES	1LT	N-0788871	1046	1
PETTUS BACON P	LTC	0-0156519	0253	3
PETTUS ELINOR S	2LT	N-0700167	0638	1
PETTUS FITZHUGH	CPT	0-0505224	1149	1
PETTWAY RICHARD W	LTC	0-0162562	0459	3
PETTY ADDISON E	LTC	0-0224594	0162	3

NAME	GRADE	SVC NO	DATE RET MO YR	RET CODE
PETTY ALBERT W	CW2	W-2147491	0961	1
PETTY BENNIE	CPT	0-4000208	1262	2
PETTY CHARLES D	LTC	0-1184130	0366	1
PETTY JEFFERSON	COL	0-0204557	0-53	1
PETTY JESSE M	CPT	0-0496523	0449	1
PETTY JOHN S	CPT	0-1167580	1045	2
PETTY MAUDE L O	2LT	N-0700831	1140	1
PETTY MILDRED L	MAJ	N-0755560	0767	3
PETTY PAUL L	CPT	0-0289983	0944	1
PETTY ROY C	CPT	0-1552356	0561	1
PETTY VERNON H	CW2	W-2212752	0865	1
PETTY VERNON L	CW3	W-2149799	0864	1
PETTY WILLIAM A	WO1	W-2130127	0445	2
PETTY WILLIE E	1LT	0-1648669	0852	1
PETTYJOHN H C	CW2	W-2209897	0664	1
PETTYJOHN WILLIAM J	CW3	W-2141410	1160	1
PETZOLD THEODORE A	CPT	0-0280005	1144	2
PETZOLDT ROBERT W	MAJ	0-0239005	1054	3
PEURA JAMES G	MAJ	0-2263610	0367	1
PEVERELL HAROLD O	CPT	0-1333698	1151	1
PEVERILL WILLIAM L	COL	0-0236437	0165	3
PEW FRANK W	MAJ	0-2009563	0663	1
PEYRONNIN CHESTER A	LTC	0-0286620	1163	3
PEYSER JULIAN I	2LT	0-1170522	1043	2
PEYTON CLIFFORD E	LTC	0-1648576	0463	1
PEYTON DONALD	MAJ	0-1897782	0563	1
PEYTON HAMILTON S	LTC	0-0284689	0164	3
PEYTON JR ALLEN T	LTC	0-1552956	0264	1
PEYTON PHILIP B	1LT	0-0317658	1042	2
PEZAKAT EDGAR T	MAJ	0-1824226	0765	3
PFAFF CHARLES W	MAJ	0-1542335	0548	2
PFAFF JULIAN F	COL	0-0328894	1165	1
PFAFF RICHARD H	1LT	0-1881404	0453	2
PFAFFMANN VALENTINE	1LT	0-1166811	0140	1
PFANNENSCHMIDT A R	LTC	0-0262855	0958	2
PFEFER ABRAHAM	LTC	0-0488229	0449	1
PFEFFER ALBERT J	LTC	0-0289377	0962	1
PFEFFER FRANCIS A	MAJ	0-0304105	0266	3
PFEIFER CHARLES R	LTC	0-1183392	0465	1
PFEIFER JOSEPH	1LT	0-1054363	1044	2
PFEIFFER ALEXIS V	LTC	0-0540948	0966	1
PFEIFFER BERNARD C	LTC	0-1945246	0967	1
PFEIFFER CARL F H	LTC	0-0247837	0465	3
PFEIFFER ERIC P	MAJ	0-0255730	0146	2
PFEIFFER FLOYD L	COL	0-0291257	0760	1
PFEIFFER HERBERT C	CPT	0-0259569	0144	1
PFEIFFER JOHN L	MAJ	0-1004660	0661	1
PFEIFFER THEODORE	LTC	0-0359068	0451	1
PFEIL WILLIAM A	LTC	0-1182681	0467	1
PFERSCH FRANK R	MAJ	0-1107040	0961	1
PFIEFER HAROLD E	LTC	0-1115063	1162	1
PFINGST ADOLPH	1LT	0-1319771	0246	2
PFIRRMANN KARL B	MAJ	0-1293469	0346	2
PFISTER EARL F	LTC	0-1593182	0661	1
PFISTER FRANCIS F	LTC	0-0295222	1067	3
PFISTER PAUL G	WO1	W-2132288	1150	1
PFISTER RALPH L	MAJ	0-1545554	0660	1
PFLEPSEN NICHOLAS M	2LT	0-1334741	0746	1
PFLIEGER JOHN A	LTC	0-0170096	0559	3
PFLUGER CLEMENS A	CPT	0-0241572	1061	3
PFLUGER WALTER L	LTC	0-0207686	1163	3
PFOHL RICHARD A	1LT	0-1166583	0444	2
PFROMMER FRED G	2LT	0-0540501	1045	2
PFUNKE WINSTON F	CPT	0-1318695	0 46	2
PHAGAN JULIUS G	CW2	W-2150609	0957	1
PHALEN THEODORE R	LTC	0-0181753	0855	3
PHANEUF VICTOR S	COL	0-0222296	0758	3
PHARAOH FRANK H	COL	0-0149398	1155	1
PHARR FRANK W	MAJ	0-1176763	0264	1
PHARR GEORGE T	MAJ	0-1105739	0465	1
PHARR STANLEY M	MAJ	0-1118104	0462	1
PHEASANT CLYDE O	CW3	W-2208550	0967	1
PHELAN JR JOHN A	CPT	0-0447254	1146	1
PHELAN MICHAEL V	MAJ	0-1559112	0962	1
PHELAN PAUL L	LTC	0-0257811	1047	2

NAME	GRADE	SVC NO	DATE RET MO YR	RET CODE
PHELPS ELBERT S	1LT	0-1108927	0945	2
PHELPS FOSTER C	LTC	0-0236472	0765	3
PHELPS FREDERICK	LTC	0-2047105	1262	1
PHELPS HAMILTON H	LTC	0-0293024	0860	1
PHELPS HARPER K	LTC	0-0104959	1151	3
PHELPS HAROLD B	LTC	0-0224525	1164	3
PHELPS HAROLD R	COL	0-0264456	0147	1
PHELPS HARRY F	LTC	0-0264624	0856	3
PHELPS HORACE F	MAJ	0-0165344	0758	3
PHELPS JEWELL O	CPT	0-1557657	0947	2
PHELPS MAX W	LTC	0-0321968	0757	2
PHELPS NEIL T	COL	0-0241643	0765	3
PHELPS RAYMOND A	COL	0-0219572	0853	3
PHELPS ROBERT J	MAJ	0-0452352	0848	1
PHELPS ROBERT J	2LT	0-1105103	1144	2
PHELPS ROSSWELL F	LTC	0-1167157	0258	1
PHELPS SR IRVIL D	CW3	W-2104373	0257	1
PHELPS STANLEY K	CW3	W-2149677	0866	1
PHELPS WILLIAM S	LTC	0-1293107	0766	1
PHERIGO JOHN B	2LT	0-1108237	1044	1
PHERO NORMAN F	LTC	0-1184921	0766	1
PHETTEPLACE RAY F	CW2	W-2152281	0861	1
PHIBBS ANDREW F	MAJ	0-0486072	0965	3
PHIFER OLLIE A	MAJ	0-1103862	0960	1
PHIFER PAUL H	CPT	0-1330218	1055	1
PHIFER WALTER L	1LT	0-1319227	0246	2
PHILBECK ROBERT H	CW3	W-2147291	1166	2
PHILBIN JOHN A	MAJ	0-0187193	0147	2
PHILBIN LEO P	2LT	0-2006468	1145	2
PHILBRICK ARNOLD D	CPT	0-0286888	1059	3
PHILBRICK JR LEON G	MAJ	0-0824713	0465	1
PHILBROOK MORTIMER	CW2	W-2116232	1146	1
PHILIP HERBERT A	MAJ	0-0447555	0246	2
PHILIP VAN N	COL	0-0204001	0756	3
PHILIPPS CARL J	2LT	0-1107631	0744	2
PHILIPS HOWARD E	LTC	0-0229094	0764	3
PHILIPS JULIAN H	LTC	0-1298919	0761	1
PHILIPS SR BILLY U	MAJ	0-2038853	1159	1
PHILIPS VINCENT O	LTC	0-0235186	1045	2
PHILIPSEN CLIFFORD A	MAJ	0-2019364	0865	1
PHILIPSEN GEORGE E	LTC	0-0268745	1063	3
PHILLABAUM C E	MAJ	0-1545596	0758	2
PHILLABAUM DONALD E	2LT	0-1309601	0444	2
PHILLABAUM JACK O	MAJ	0-4009456	0966	1
PHILLEBAUM LEONARD P	CW2	W-2205700	0663	1
PHILLEO ROLLAND A	LTC	0-0236164	0266	3
PHILLIPP JR JOSEPH J	CW3	W-2203496	0766	1
PHILLIPP LOUIS S N	COL	0-0100564	1053	3
PHILLIPPE CLAUDE C	1LT	0-1298753	1045	2
PHILLIPS ALBERT H	1LT	0-0376413	1044	2
PHILLIPS ALBERT S	CW3	W-2152832	0263	1
PHILLIPS ALBERT W	MAJ	0-1994554	0367	3
PHILLIPS ANTON A	CPT	0-0342944	0545	2
PHILLIPS ARTHUR W	CW3	W-2149371	0463	1
PHILLIPS BARRETT H	1LT	0-0452610	0352	1
PHILLIPS BASHAN B	CW4	W-2129116	0556	1
PHILLIPS BOBBY M	CW2	W-2210811	0767	1
PHILLIPS BUEL R	MAJ	0-0966635	0459	1
PHILLIPS CARL F	CPT	0-0120954	0456	3
PHILLIPS CARL E	MAJ	0-2262455	0662	1
PHILLIPS CARO E	1LT	0-0372678	0844	2
PHILLIPS CECIL F	MAJ	0-1309961	0965	1
PHILLIPS CHARLES B	MAJ	0-1173034	1162	1
PHILLIPS CHARLES E	LTC	0-0305856	0861	1
PHILLIPS CHARLES G	MAJ	0-1941900	0267	1
PHILLIPS CHARLES H	LTC	0-0200998	0545	2
PHILLIPS CHARLES I	LTC	0-1552770	1061	1
PHILLIPS CHARLES W	1LT	0-1170910	0546	1
PHILLIPS CLARENCE I	CW3	W-2145115	0561	1
PHILLIPS CLAURICE M	COL	0-0308484	0964	3
PHILLIPS CLYDE J	CW2	W-2145832	1155	1
PHILLIPS CYRIL J	MAJ	0-2023805	0762	1
PHILLIPS DOUGLAS H	CW4	W-2113946	0563	2
PHILLIPS EARL	1LT	0-0149160	0648	3
PHILLIPS EARL E	LTC	0-0209641	0450	3

NAME	GRADE	SVC NO	DATE RET MO YR	RET CODE
PHILLIPS EARL G	1LT	0-1177138	1045	2
PHILLIPS EARL G	CPT	0-1947163	1046	1
PHILLIPS EDWARD C	LTC	0-0165699	0552	3
PHILLIPS EDWARD J	CPT	0-1541036	0964	1
PHILLIPS EDWARD L	MAJ	0-2263111	C264	1
PHILLIPS EDWARD R	MAJ	C-1284758	C561	1
PHILLIPS EDWARD W	LTC	0-0503637	0657	1
PHILLIPS ELI K	1LT	0-1036680	0445	1
PHILLIPS FLETCHER	CW4	W-2124184	1153	1
PHILLIPS FRANCIS J	LTC	0-1553535	0760	1
PHILLIPS FRANKLIN A	2LT	0-1171718	C244	2
PHILLIPS FRED L	LTC	0-1284013	0564	1
PHILLIPS FREDERICK	LTC	0-0217885	C761	3
PHILLIPS FREDERICK	MAJ	0-2055164	0459	1
PHILLIPS GEORGE M	LTC	0-0550120	0565	1
PHILLIPS GILES T	LTC	0-0299638	0264	3
PHILLIPS GLENN J	CPT	0-0282762	0145	2
PHILLIPS HAL B	LTC	0-1051728	0862	1
PHILLIPS HAROLD	LTC	0-1302046	0263	1
PHILLIPS HAROLD W	CW2	W-2142187	1058	1
PHILLIPS HARRISON M	LTC	0-1321547	C764	1
PHILLIPS HARRY	CPT	0-0290609	0257	3
PHILLIPS HARRY	CPT	0-0498350	C549	2
PHILLIPS HARTSELL O	MAJ	0-0949714	1263	1
PHILLIPS HERBERT R	LTC	0-0473066	0865	3
PHILLIPS HERSCHEL A	1LT	0-0552047	0-48	1
PHILLIPS II HORACE B	MAJ	0-0461737	0347	2
PHILLIPS IVAN J	CW3	W-2147711	0766	1
PHILLIPS JACK R	MAJ	0-1338846	1164	1
PHILLIPS JAMES E	CPT	0-0980340	C662	1
PHILLIPS JAMES O	MAJ	C-1000170	0350	1
PHILLIPS JAMES O	CW3	W-2148880	0962	1
PHILLIPS JAMES R	LTC	0-1945038	0864	1
PHILLIPS JAMES T	COL	0-0246171	0461	3
PHILLIPS JAMES W	CPT	0-0505181	0546	2
PHILLIPS JAMES Y	MAJ	0-0515042	C146	2
PHILLIPS JESSE W	WO1	W-2113711	0558	1
PHILLIPS JOHN B	CPT	0-0420208	1144	2
PHILLIPS JOHN E	2LT	0-2005705	0646	2
PHILLIPS JOHN H	LTC	0-0439925	0954	1
PHILLIPS JOHN H	CW2	W-2208507	0463	1
PHILLIPS JOHN M	COL	0-0187445	1160	3
PHILLIPS JOHN M	LTC	0-0298606	0246	2
PHILLIPS JOHN P	MAJ	C-0103893	C850	3
PHILLIPS JOHN R	CPT	0-0558458	0946	2
PHILLIPS JOHN R	LTC	0-1596147	0764	1
PHILLIPS JOHN R	MAJ	C-2007797	1060	1
PHILLIPS JOHN R	MAJ	C-2097077	C565	1
PHILLIPS JOHN T	CW2	W-2206836	1064	1
PHILLIPS JOHNIE F	MAJ	C-1822904	1164	1
PHILLIPS JOHNNIE T	CPT	0-1108238	0245	2
PHILLIPS JOSEPH J	CPT	0-1060588	0947	2
PHILLIPS JOSEPH J	CW4	W-2003511	0267	3
PHILLIPS JOSEPH R	MAJ	C-0488809	C448	1
PHILLIPS JR CLAUDE R	MAJ	C-1307848	C862	1
PHILLIPS JR JOSEPH B	COL	0-0330996	0262	1
PHILLIPS JR PAUL E	CPT	0-1558520	C863	1
PHILLIPS JR ROBERT	CPT	0-1635206	0945	1
PHILLIPS JR WALTER	MAJ	C-1297419	1061	1
PHILLIPS KARL E	LTC	0-1055698	0465	1
PHILLIPS KENNETH L	1LT	0-1312960	1048	2
PHILLIPS KENNETH P	CPT	0-1920269	1162	1
PHILLIPS LAYMAN	CW2	W-2141823	0357	1
PHILLIPS LEE	WO1	W-2109487	1045	2
PHILLIPS LEE J	1LT	0-1845944	1045	2
PHILLIPS LELAND J	1LT	C-1293826	0146	2
PHILLIPS LESTER L	CW2	W-2152395	1055	1
PHILLIPS LOYD A	CPT	0-0499504	C855	1
PHILLIPS MARK H	CPT	0-0480013	0746	2
PHILLIPS MELVILLE	CPT	0-0465385	0747	1
PHILLIPS MERRILL F	MAJ	C-0222820	0656	3
PHILLIPS MORTON E	CW3	W-2152903	0764	1
PHILLIPS NOEL F	CPT	0-0262075	C866	3
PHILLIPS ORRIE E	CW2	W-2141882	1055	1
PHILLIPS PAUL	MAJ	C-1552957	0958	1

NAME	GRADE	SVC NO	DATE RET MO YR	RET CODE
PHILLIPS PURDY	LTC	0-1291690	0361	1
PHILLIPS RALPH E	MAJ	0-1878228	0967	1
PHILLIPS RALPH L	MAJ	0-0382171	0746	2
PHILLIPS RALPH L	MAJ	0-1173038	1162	1
PHILLIPS RAY C	MAJ	0-0510565	0855	1
PHILLIPS RAYMOND E	COL	0-0219287	0660	3
PHILLIPS RAYMOND L	CPT	0-0342312	0363	1
PHILLIPS RAYMOND M	2LT	0-1328840	1145	2
PHILLIPS RENDER T	2LT	0-2006867	0146	2
PHILLIPS RICHARD F	1LT	0-0409651	0644	2
PHILLIPS ROBERT C	CPT	0-1015494	0462	1
PHILLIPS ROBERT M	MAJ	0-0292892	0244	2
PHILLIPS ROBERT O	LTC	0-0402745	0765	1
PHILLIPS ROLAND J	MAJ	0-0885647	0457	1
PHILLIPS ROYAL G	CPT	0-0178231	0756	3
PHILLIPS RUPERT E	CW2	W-2214946	1066	1
PHILLIPS RUSSELL E	CPT	0-1325595	0246	2
PHILLIPS SAM B	MAJ	C-1179572	1058	1
PHILLIPS SAMUEL	LTC	0-1283501	1054	1
PHILLIPS SR HARRY L	CW4	W-2127847	0659	1
PHILLIPS SR MORGAN L	COL	0-0201552	0762	3
PHILLIPS STONEWALL	LTC	0-0288522	1145	2
PHILLIPS TALMAGE J	MAJ	0-1589441	0662	1
PHILLIPS THOMAS J	LTC	0-0420538	0152	1
PHILLIPS THOMAS R	CW2	W-2152506	1C57	1
PHILLIPS THOMAS W	MAJ	0-1030405	0960	1
PHILLIPS VIRGIL C	LTC	0-1643967	1060	1
PHILLIPS WADE H	LTC	0-0208417	0648	3
PHILLIPS WALLACE G	CPT	0-0309854	1145	2
PHILLIPS WALTER G	1LT	0-1181730	0646	2
PHILLIPS WALTER J	CW3	W-2151725	0564	1
PHILLIPS WAYNE G	MAJ	C-0100621	0928	1
PHILLIPS WENDELL B	CW2	W-2112672	1049	2
PHILLIPS WENDELL P	LTC	0-0452534	C764	1
PHILLIPS WILLIAM C	LTC	0-0321702	1060	3
PHILLIPS WILLIAM E	1LT	0-2262270	0358	1
PHILLIPS WILLIAM H	MAJ	0-0116969	0449	3
PHILLIPS WILLIAM H	MAJ	0-1020243	0161	1
PHILLIPS WILLIAM J	LTC	0-0362687	0766	3
PHILLIPS WILLIAM L	MAJ	0-1035047	0360	1
PHILLIPS WILLIAM T	LTC	0-1291513	0860	1
PHILLIPS WILLIAM T	WO1	W-2152683	0753	1
PHILLIPS WILLIAM W	1LT	0-1295426	1045	2
PHILLIPSEN EDWIN R	LTC	0-1302345	C762	1
PHILLPOTTS RONALD A	MAJ	0-0412497	0656	1
PHILMAN JACK M	1LT	0-0475318	0445	2
PHILMON LEE B	MAJ	0-2263578	0465	1
PHILP GEORGE B	LTC	0-1639495	0164	1
PHILPOT ERNEST W	LTC	0-0030627	1060	1
PHILPOT JAMES S	CW3	W-2149813	0166	1
PHILPOT MARION M	CW4	W-2146146	0966	2
PHILPOTT ROBERT J	COL	0-0256799	1066	3
PHILQUIST HARRIS F	MAJ	0-1578972	0865	1
PHINIZY JOHN A	CPT	0-0288633	1046	2
PHINNEY CARL L	M G	0-0244577	1164	3
PHINNEY EDWARD T	COL	0-0355187	0267	3
PHINNEY MABLE A	CPT	N-0787461	0346	1
PHINNEY WALLACE S	LTC	0-0300731	0667	3
PHIPPS ALTON T	LTC	0-1822051	0662	1
PHIPPS GEORGE E	1LT	0-0297705	0844	2
PHIPPS HARRY R	COL	0-0282815	0361	1
PHIPPS JAMES M	1LT	0-1692539	0447	2
PHIPPS WILBUR H	LTC	0-1646887	1067	1
PHLEEGER GUY O	MAJ	0-1172222	0261	1
PHOEBUS JOHN W	1LT	0-0452904	0245	2
PHOENIX MERRILL W	LTC	0-0432315	1054	1
PHYSIOC JOHN U	LTC	0-1101994	1061	1
PIASECKI EDMUND B	1LT	0-1297941	0845	2
PIASECKI STANLEY F	1LT	0-1289559	0945	2
PIASECZNY JOSEPH J	MAJ	0-1331220	0861	1
PIATT MALCOLM K	2LT	0-1108239	0145	2
PIAZZA EUGENE S	MAJ	0-1937583	0566	1
PICARD COLICE P	LTC	0-0397531	0757	1
PICARD HARRY L	1LT	0-1172225	0346	2
PICARD JOHN J	2LT	0-1316086	0644	2

NAME	GRADE	SVC NO	DATE RET MO YR	RET CODE
PICARD POLLY A F	1LT	L-0303818	0145	2
PICCIALLO BENJAMIN	2LT	0-1108929	0645	2
PICCININO JOSEPH	CW2	W-2206347	C863	1
PICCININO LEONARD J	CW3	W-2152396	0863	1
PICCIUOLO CHARLES	LTC	0-2042806	0461	1
PICCOLO SEBASTIAN	1LT	0-1921227	1052	2
PICHICHERO LARRY J	MAJ	0-0966610	0462	1
PICK CHARLES	WO1	W-2105821	1043	2
PICK CHARLES A	CW2	W-2204114	C862	1
PICK JOHN F	LTC	0-0513489	C646	2
PICKARD CHARLES M	LTC	0-0260288	0646	2
PICKARD HELEN E	1LT	N-0724432	0146	1
PICKARD JOSEPH A	CPT	0-1283828	0847	1
PICKEL JR FRNCIS M	1LT	0-0953769	0852	1
PICKEL JR ROBERT H	MAJ	C-0327827	0746	2
PICKELL HEYWARD M	LTC	0-0229071	C465	3
PICKENHEIM WALTER H	CW3	W-2147444	0566	1
PICKENS JAY W	LTC	0-0259568	1145	2
PICKENS JOE B	2LT	0-1823345	C944	2
PICKENS RALPH O	1LT	0-1102906	0546	2
PICKENS WILEY M	COL	C-0235829	0956	3
PICKERING FRANK I	MAJ	0-0165318	1047	1
PICKERING GEORGE F	LTC	0-1558521	0767	1
PICKERING GEORGE J	CPT	0-1167159	0547	1
PICKERING HILDEN D	MAJ	0-1060250	0762	1
PICKERING JAMES A	1LT	0-2037091	0745	2
PICKERING JOHN A	MAJ	C-1110186	0663	1
PICKERING JR S J	CW2	W-2148015	1058	1
PICKERING RAMON H	CPT	0-1305639	1060	1
PICKERING WALTER J G	LTC	0-0223143	0364	3
PICKETT CLYDE N	2LT	0-1177937	0245	2
PICKETT ELLIS H	LTC	0-1182226	0966	1
PICKETT EVAN S	LTC	0-1101167	0461	1
PICKETT FRED B	LTC	0-0324301	C265	3
PICKETT GEORGE H	CPT	0-4020972	1264	1
PICKETT HENRY F	CPT	0-0246325	1262	3
PICKETT HOWARD D	LTC	0-1994505	0764	1
PICKETT HOWARD L	CW3	W-2150761	0562	1
PICKETT JOHN L	COL	0-0245342	0658	3
PICKETT JOHN T	1LT	0-0423176	1047	2
PICKETT JR CHARLES M	LTC	C-0231917	C265	3
PICKETT JR WILLIAM	CW3	W-2205283	0766	1
PICKETT RICHARD P	2LT	0-1798509	0345	2
PICKETT SAMUEL P	COL	0-0232452	0261	3
PICKETT WALTER F	LTC	0-0206360	0446	2
PICKETT WILLIAM J	COL	0-0206366	0853	3
PICKETTE WILLIE B	CW4	W-2141411	0966	1
PICKHARDT ISAAC J	MAJ	0-1311358	C960	2
PICKHARDT OTTO C	LTC	0-0445678	0844	2
PICKING GLENN E	MAJ	0-1300526	0948	1
PICKINPAUGH THOMAS E	CPT	0-2023329	0761	1
PICKLE CHARLES E	MAJ	C-1316325	C859	1
PICKLE OLIVER W	CW3	W-2142889	1160	1
PICKLE OWEN B	MAJ	0-2204160	1263	1
PICKRELL ISAAC R	CW2	W-2147239	0260	1
PICKUP MICHAEL	LTC	0-0455106	0560	2
PICKWICK GEORGE B	COL	0-0241088	1060	1
PICO THOMAS M	LTC	0-1302513	0266	1
PICOTTE CARYL L	LTC	C-0131258	C947	2
PICOU ORA F	1LT	N-0734929	0746	1
PIOCOCK FINLEY S	MAJ	C-0223665	0458	3
PIDGEON DONALD F	CPT	0-1284933	0662	1
PIDGEON LARRY	CPT	0-0325594	0644	2
PIECUKONIS ALEXANDER	CW3	W-2145578	0164	1
PIEDRA CHARLES	LTC	0-1283665	0763	1
PIEKARSKI KASIMIR J	MAJ	C-0940741	0862	1
PIEKARSKI LEONARD J	LTC	0-1111835	0763	1
PIEKLIK WILLIAM	CW4	W-2103315	0267	1
PIEMME WALTER C	LTC	0-1171719	1264	1
PIENKOWSKI OLIVER E	LTC	0-0244145	0864	3
PIEPENBURG ARTHUR K	MAJ	0-0956864	0863	1
PIEPER CARL A	LTC	0-0512616	1065	1
PIEPER GEORGE R	CPT	0-0422267	1045	2
PIEPKORN ARTHUR C	COL	0-0340801	0767	3
PIER WALTER F	LTC	0-1289960	0861	1

NAME	GRADE	SVC NO	DATE RET MO YR	RET CODE
PIERCE ALONZO R	LTC	0-0374814	0859	1
PIERCE BOLTON S	LTC	0-0330045	1059	1
PIERCE BURTON	MAJ	0-1317338	1059	1
PIERCE CARL B	CPT	0-0959782	1061	1
PIERCE CHARLES H	CW3	W-2152773	0667	1
PIERCE CHESTER H	CPT	0-0168390	0850	3
PIERCE CLYDE W	MAJ	0-1313511	1057	1
PIERCE DAVID P	1LT	0-1015577	0146	2
PIERCE EARL S	LTC	0-1945675	0463	1
PIERCE EDMUND P	CPT	0-0978064	1058	2
PIERCE EMERSON J	CPT	0-0219184	0459	3
PIERCE ERIE F	LTC	0-0350148	0859	1
PIERCE FRANKLIN M	MAJ	C-1636474	0360	1
PIERCE GEORGE R	LTC	0-0338858	0660	1
PIERCE GEORGE J	1LT	0-1010644	0846	2
PIERCE HAROLD K	CPT	0-1045211	0248	1
PIERCE HARRY G	COL	0-0171807	0449	3
PIERCE HARRY W	MAJ	0-1297584	0462	1
PIERCE HORACE E	LTC	0-0334242	0865	1
PIERCE HORACE LEE	MAJ	0-0496140	0851	1
PIERCE IRA L	LTC	0-1686534	0166	1
PIERCE JACK B	MAJ	0-0312830	0654	1
PIERCE JACKSON A	MAJ	C-0966898	0263	1
PIERCE JAMES A	COL	0-0276201	1063	3
PIERCE JAMES F	CPT	0-0984364	0762	1
PIERCE JAMES L	CW2	W-3200290	0866	1
PIERCE JAMES T	LTC	0-0108366	0748	1
PIERCE JR LESTER W	LTC	0-1041275	0665	1
PIERCE LAWRENCE S	MAJ	0-0224514	0862	3
PIERCE LEON C	CPT	0-1180296	1046	2
PIERCE LESLIE W	MAJ	0-1950236	0966	3
PIERCE LLOYD G	CPT	0-2011962	0562	2
PIERCE LOUIS I	MAJ	0-2289503	0967	1
PIERCE MILLARD H	LTC	0-0287372	1058	2
PIERCE PAUL F	MAJ	0-2262764	0961	1
PIERCE RALPH W	COL	C-0163825	C548	2
PIERCE ROBERT E	LTC	0-0376628	0263	1
PIERCE ROBERT F	COL	0-0182125	0462	3
PIERCE ROBERT H	CW2	W-2144448	0559	1
PIERCE ROBERT L	LTC	0-1285116	0861	1
PIERCE ROBERT W	2LT	0-1327763	1045	2
PIERCE RUBY L	2LT	N-0737134	0545	1
PIERCE RUSSEL F	LTC	0-0341148	0463	3
PIERCE SUMNER W	COL	C-0241644	0363	3
PIERCE WILLIAM A	LTC	C-0358582	0663	1
PIERCE WILLIAM A	LTC	0-1300375	0764	1
PIERCE WILLIAM B	LTC	0-1289313	0261	1
PIERCE WILLIAM L	LTC	0-1551084	0462	1
PIERCE WILLIAM W	MAJ	0-0117674	0648	3
PIERCE WILLIAM W	LTC	0-0500250	1146	2
PIERCY EDITH T	MAJ	L-1010042	0466	1
PIERCY GAY V	LTC	0-0379785	0660	1
PIERCY KATHERINE	MAJ	N-0797446	0665	1
PIERCY WALTER W	MAJ	0-2014669	0163	1
PIERDOLLA EUGENIA	1LT	N-0702530	0243	1
PIERLUISI GUILLERMO	MAJ	C-0425132	1145	2
PIERNICK ROMAN T	LTC	0-0383287	0364	1
PIERPOINT OWEN W	CW3	W-2152714	0563	1
PIERPONT ROGER L	MAJ	0-0447904	104N	2
PIERPONT WILSON R	LTC	0-0376669	1262	1
PIERSALL RUSH C	WO1	W-2150357	0555	1
PIERSALL SHIRLEY L	LTC	0-1795965	0461	1
PIERSON BERT	MAJ	0-2014499	0666	1
PIERSON CLIFFORD G	2LT	0-1948808	0945	2
PIERSON DALTON T	MAJ	0-2052403	0866	3
PIERSON DON E	MAJ	0-0889244	1060	1
PIERSON EDWARD C	COL	0-0102155	0457	3
PIERSON FRANK M	LTC	0-0904895	0267	2
PIERSON GEORGE W	LTC	0-1001435	1161	2
PIERSON HAROLD R	CPT	0-0254364	1045	2
PIERSON JOSEPH R	LTC	0-0290500	0346	2
PIERSON JR HARRY T	MAJ	0-1333258	0267	1
PIERSON LEROY C	COL	0-0406556	0866	1
PIERSON RUSSELL H	LTC	0-1030920	C562	1
PIERSON STANLEY O	CPT	0-0948577	0860	1

NAME	GRADE	SVC NO	DATE RET MO YR	RET CODE
PIERSON VAL S	LTC	0-0418474	0262	1
PIERSON WARREN R	MAJ	0-0349733	C560	1
PIET JOHN F	MAJ	C-1944552	C763	1
PIETRANTONIC NICHOLA	MAJ	C-1924116	C566	1
PIETRI VICENTE	1LT	0-0180059	0352	3
PIETRO JOSEPH N	CPT	0-0510399	0747	1
PIETROVITO JEREMIAH	MAJ	C-1923601	1163	1
PIETRZYK JOSEPH A	2LT	0-1181408	1144	1
PIETTE HUBERT J	LTC	0-0235036	0662	3
PIETZ MARTAIN	MAJ	0-1015450	C759	1
PIFER JAMES R	LTC	0-0335133	1054	3
PIFER JR FERDINAND	MAJ	C-1298125	C861	1
PIGEAULT RENE J	MAJ	C-2262836	0267	1
PIGEON CARL R	MAJ	C-2020759	C963	1
PIGFORC CHARLES A	COL	0-0301607	0745	2
PIGG HERMAN E	CW2	W-2149315	C161	1
PIGG ROBERT W	MAJ	0-2029564	1263	1
PIGGOTT KENNETH S	LTC	0-0523915	1054	1
PIGHETTI JOHN C	LTC	0-C194021	0546	2
PIGMAN CHARLES E	MAJ	C-1342113	1162	1
PIGOTT THOMAS R	LTC	0-1041631	C866	1
PIKAITIS ANTHONY R	1LT	0-1302188	C456	1
PIKE CHARLES W	CW2	W-2116049	1154	1
PIKE ENIS H	MAJ	C-1165322	0765	1
PIKE JAMES T	CPT	0-1310342	0355	2
PIKE MILES N	LTC	0-0172307	1059	3
PIKE WAYNE S	MAJ	0-0522283	C947	1
PIKE WILLIS H	CPT	0-1294010	C447	1
PIKOR STANLEY W	CPT	0-1302515	C646	1
PIKULSKI JOSEPH A	MAJ	0-1308175	C662	1
PIKUS HARRY	COL	0-0212654	0261	1
PILACHOWSKI LEO B	CPT	C-0948050	0361	1
PILAT JOHN L	CW4	W-2107246	1053	1
PILAWSKI JOHN A	CPT	0-1178596	0851	2
PILCH IRVING	CW2	W-2112380	1055	1
PILCHER CHARLES D	CW2	W-2210206	0266	1
PILCHER LEWIS S	LTC	0-0468963	0646	2
PILE WENDELL J	CPT	0-1766608	1048	1
PILERT JR EDWARD	1LT	0-1586028	0647	2
PILEWSKI EDWARD J	LTC	0-1545716	1266	1
PILEWSKI JOSEPH M T	CW3	W-2127182	1054	1
PILGRIM CHARLES W	CW3	W-2141824	0762	1
PILGRIM OLLASTER C	MAJ	0-1951707	0762	1
PILGRIM VINCENT W	WO1	W-2141412	0259	1
PILKENTON WILLIAM H	2LT	0-0540598	1045	2
PILKINGTON GEORGE R	MAJ	0-1114263	1059	2
PILKINGTON JOSEPH	LTC	0-1184923	0966	2
PILLAR WILLIAM T	1LT	0-1305304	C445	1
PILLERICH JOHN A	CPT	0-0445050	0546	2
PILLIFANT THOMAS H	1LT	0-0439374	1045	2
PILLING EVERETT H	MAJ	C-1897754	0365	1
PILLON JAMES P	MAJ	C-1542248	1060	2
PILLSBURY MARJORIE A	1LT	N-0720169	C346	1
PILON OLIVER J	CPT	0-0507434	0253	2
PILON SR JOHN P	CPT	0-2014880	0861	1
PILSEN LOUIS	COL	0-1170915	1064	1
PILTZ GEORGE F	LTC	C-1692129	0345	2
PILUSO CARLO	COL	0-0248908	0764	3
PIMENTEL MERRILL A	COL	0-0236906	0466	3
PINALI FRANK	MAJ	C-1296421	0361	1
PINAUD GEORGE C	MAJ	C-1642470	0855	1
PINCKNEY FRANK D	M G	0-0246920	0464	3
PINCKNEY JR SAMUEL M	MAJ	C-2009680	0263	1
PINCKNEY MURRAY S	LTC	C-1183595	C461	1
PINCOMBE JOHN D	2LT	0-1822052	C645	2
PINCOSKE ANDREW M	CW3	W-2121280	0155	1
PINDER JR ROBERT F	MAJ	0-2028739	1166	1
PINE HELEN M	1LT	N-0763887	0745	1
PINE IRVING	CPT	0-0322114	1045	1
PINE PAUL W	CPT	0-0232693	C665	3
PINE SEYMOUR	CPT	0-1797522	C146	2
PINEDA MICHAEL V	CPT	0-0978132	0466	2
PINEIRO-RUIZ JOSE	CW4	W-2142260	0465	1
PINER RAYMOND E	MAJ	0-0319316	0666	3
PINET ALFRED J	MAJ	C-1845481	0860	3
PINETTE MATTIE A	LTC	L-0303523	0363	3
PINGREE JOHN	MAJ	0-1588228	0259	1
PINK HAROLD H	CW4	W-2144195	0466	1
PINKEL DONALD P	1LT	0-1874268	0355	2
PINKERTON CLIFFORD C	1LT	0-1055120	1145	2
PINKERTON JACKSON O	MAJ	0-0266821	0157	3
PINKERTON JAMES R	LTC	0-0252141	0465	3
PINKERTON JAY W	LTC	0-1641676	1266	1
PINKERTON JOHN E	MAJ	C-0997807	0964	1
PINKERTON JOHN G	LTC	0-0497000	1154	1
PINKERTON JOHN P	LTC	0-0295799	1145	2
PINKERTON WILLIAM R	MAJ	0-0274078	0358	3
PINKHAM ARTHUR G	MAJ	0-0492183	0857	1
PINKHAM FREDERICK	1LT	0-1048933	1145	2
PINKHAM VERNON C O	LTC	0-0162135	0460	3
PINKHAM WALTER R	LTC	0-1047730	0962	1
PINKLEY GEORGE R	LTC	0-0233065	0565	3
PINKLEY WILLIAM M	CPT	0-0308580	1045	2
PINKOWSKY FRANCIS T	MAJ	0-0344234	0662	1
PINKSTAFF WILLIAM D	CW2	W-2152303	0561	1
PINKSTON HUGH D	LTC	0-0271476	1263	3
PINKSTON LAMON H	LTC	0-1103359	1065	1
PINKSTON WILLIAM E	COL	0-0123345	C749	3
PINKUS PHIL F	2LT	0-1592515	0944	2
PINNELL WILLIAM H	CW4	W-2145654	0157	1
PINNEO JAMES A	CW4	W-2001597	0567	1
PINNEY THEODORE C	CPT	0-1081670	0547	1
PINNEY WARREN B	LTC	0-0259161	0864	3
PINNICK RALPH E	MAJ	0-0252024	0765	3
PINSKY DANIEL J	MAJ	0-0322713	0246	2
PINSON ANDREW J	CW4	W-2118026	0659	1
PINSON CHARLES A	MAJ	0-1106404	0563	2
PINSONEAULT RAYMOND	MAJ	0-1307745	0461	1
PINTEL JAMES J	COL	0-0167525	0352	3
PINTHER HAROLD O	COL	C-0190578	0656	3
PINZAK STEPHEN	CW3	W-2145195	0862	1
PINZINO DOMINICK J	MAJ	0-0494315	0962	1
PINZOLC JOHN R	MAJ	0-2055482	0460	1
PINZON FILIBERTO	CW3	W-2151625	0862	1
PIO MYRON R	CW2	W-2213475	0964	2
PIOMBINO NICHOLAS	CW3	W-2106470	1055	1
PIOMBO ANDREW T	2LT	0-1323964	0446	2
PIOS ANTHONY L	LTC	0-1322809	C267	1
PIOTROWSKI FRANK F	CPT	0-1015117	1047	2
PIOTROWSKI SIGMUND A	MAJ	0-0365787	0564	3
PIPALA JOSEPH S	MAJ	0-1636478	0861	1
PIPER BURGETT W	CPT	C-1683966	0158	2
PIPER DONALD W	LTC	0-1341235	0866	1
PIPER ELLIS G	COL	0-0228863	1157	1
PIPER FLOYD P	CW3	W-2153324	1263	1
PIPER HOMER S	COL	0-0288433	0860	1
PIPER LLOYD L	COL	0-0332585	0557	1
PIPER MARGARET B	CPT	N-0760117	0147	1
PIPER RALPH A	LTC	0-0188915	0246	2
PIPER SAM M	MAJ	0-1797004	0262	1
PIPER WILLIAM C	COL	0-0244113	0462	3
PIPKIN DEMPERE	1LT	0-0378976	1065	3
PIPOLO SANDY E	CW4	W-2152108	0860	1
PIPPEN AUBREY J	MAJ	0-0486607	0760	1
PIPPERT RAY E	1LT	0-1111305	0545	2
PIPPIN FRANK J	LTC	0-0300607	0866	3
PIPPIN WILLARD F	COL	0-0195444	1046	2
PIPPINS CALEB E	CW2	W-2150972	1262	1
PIPPITT LESLIE S	CW2	RW-2150512	1064	1
PIRIBEK JERRY	LTC	0-1049612	1167	1
PIRKLE JACK D	MAJ	C-1919988	0665	1
PIRKLE JR RUSSELL L	COL	0-0341790	0559	1
PIRKLE TYRUS J	CW2	W-2150989	1161	1
PIRNACK RICHARD D	LTC	0-0276515	0953	2
PIRNIE ALEXANDER	COL	0-0196965	0563	3
PIRONE ADELINA E	MAJ	M-0000513	1263	1
PIRSCH JOSEPH H	LTC	0-0159243	0648	3
PIRTLE LLOYD A	CW4	W-2113304	0659	1
PISANELLO ALFRED J	CW2	W-2110343	1060	1
PISANI GEORGE	CW4	W-2145292	0664	1
PISCOP JORDAN	LTC	0-0322705	1064	3
PISEGNA ANOSTA	LTC	0-1107046	1059	1
PITCHER GLEE J	CPT	0-1947440	1047	2
PITCHER HORACE E	1LT	0-0560229	0645	2
PITCHERALE JOSEPH	CW3	W-2122638	1055	1
PITCHFORD CARL R	CW4	W-2129520	0962	1
PITCHLYNN PETER P	CPT	0-0274790	C464	3
PITKETHLY DAVID A	LTC	0-0314472	0263	2
PITKIN HERBERT O	CW2	W-2211791	0766	1
PITLIK CLARENCE C	LTC	0-0250831	1263	3
PITMAN CLYDE F	CW2	W-2147098	0561	1
PITMAN IVY C	CPT	0-0379288	1145	2
PITMAN ROBERT B	2LT	0-1584742	C545	2
PITMAN ROBERT M	2LT	0-1314413	104N	2
PITMAN WILFORD G	1LT	0-1998452	0767	1
PITNEY GUY B	LTC	0-0188540	C-52	3
PITNEY MARVIN J	MAJ	0-0406632	0746	2
PITONIAK GREGORY M	CPT	0-2263698	1162	1
PITOSCIA GUSSIE D	MAJ	C-1304941	0263	1
PITPITAN GABINO	1LT	0-1896839	1049	1
PITRE CHARLES O	MAJ	C-2042897	C960	2
PITRE SR GEORGE L	COL	0-0194486	1262	3
PITT FRANK R	MAJ	0-0916217	0347	2
PITT HAMILTON	2LT	0-0411878	0442	2
PITT GRACE G	CW3	W-2008040	1066	3
PITT PERRY	CPT	0-1319541	0247	2
PITT STANTON	LTC	0-0473397	C862	1
PITTARD JOHN S	MAJ	0-0268470	0563	3
PITTENGER AUBREY C	COL	0-0298215	0955	1
PITTENGER JAMES S	LTC	0-0405349	0247	2
PITTENGER JR THAD H	1LT	0-1032038	1045	2
PITTENGER PAUL N	LTC	0-0103050	0648	3
PITTENGER RAY L	LTC	0-0328971	0559	3
PITTMAN CECIL	CW2	W-2146269	0659	1
PITTMAN CLAY M	CW3	W-2149346	0959	1
PITTMAN DUDLEY E	LTC	0-2047780	1262	1
PITTMAN FLOYD H	LTC	0-0447547	0247	1
PITTMAN HARRY R	LTC	0-0263150	C166	3
PITTMAN JIMMIE L	LTC	0-1047295	C563	1
PITTMAN JR JOHN C	LTC	0-0419075	0860	1
PITTMAN JR ROBERT T	LTC	0-1293110	C163	1
PITTMAN LEON E	LTC	0-1111836	1161	1
PITTMAN PAUL C	1LT	C-0417524	C745	2
PITTMAN ROY R	MAJ	0-2008161	C861	1
PITTMAN SAMUEL H	CW2	W-2120888	C946	1
PITTMAN WILLIAM A	CPT	0-1693001	C146	2
PITTS ALFRED H	CW3	W-2146778	1064	1
PITTS ATWOOD H	MAJ	0-0237664	0464	3
PITTS BAYNARD Y	CPT	0-1180002	0547	2
PITTS CHARLES A	CPT	0-1341819	C563	1
PITTS CHARLES L	MAJ	0-2262383	0966	1
PITTS FRANK R	LTC	0-0400527	0255	3
PITTS HARVEY C	LTC	0-0269965	1265	3
PITTS JOHN E	COL	0-0103336	1153	3
PITTS LEMUEL T	CPT	0-1303941	1045	2
PITTS NELSON A	CPT	0-1301032	0548	1
PITTS RALPH J	MAJ	0-1885927	C167	1
PITTS RICHARD G	1LT	0-1639501	C246	1
PITTS ROBERT L	COL	0-1301033	C965	1
PITTS ROY B	LTC	0-1634227	C865	1
PITTS RUFUS K	1LT	0-1582052	0745	2
PITTS THEODORE R	COL	0-0341150	0363	1
PITTS THOMAS V	CW3	W-2152304	C762	1
PITTS WALTER E	CPT	0-0499776	1046	1
PITTS WILLIAM	LTC	0-1330960	C866	1
PITZER GEORGE T	CW2	W-2209337	0864	1
PIURKOWSKY JOHN P	CPT	0-2033542	0257	1
PIVOVARNICK JOHN J	LTC	0-0268455	0657	3
PIXTON ROBERT C	COL	0-0236404	C746	2
PIZER VERNON	LTC	0-0406007	0763	1
PIZZILLO JOHN T	MAJ	0-1012339	0267	1
PLACE JR JOHN P	CPT	0-1590729	0945	2
PLACE KENNETH M	COL	0-0217699	1059	3
PLACE RICHARD C	CPT	0-0370893	0344	1
PLACE ROBERT H	CPT	C-0203646	1053	3
PLACHINSKI FLORIAN C	CPT	0-0385188	0147	1
PLACKO FRANK	LTC	0-0372230	0460	1
PLAENERT ALFRED B	LTC	0-0286615	1064	3
PLAGMANN REGINALD F	CW2	W-2144763	1155	1
PLAIN FERDINAND	LTC	0-0255295	0462	3
PLAIN IRVING H	1LT	0-0482554	0144	2
PLAINE ROBERT C	LTC	0-1285640	0954	1
PLAISANCE EDWARD B	COL	0-0366821	0766	1
PLAISANCE HARRY A	CW3	W-2146777	0664	1
PLAISTED MARK S	COL	0-0214424	1262	3
PLAKORUS MIKE G	MAJ	0-1643971	0263	1
PLAMBECK ERNEST	MAJ	0-0254031	0163	3
PLAMONDON WARREN A	MAJ	0-1686461	0363	1
PLANCE ROBERT E	CW2	W-2209077	0667	1
PLANDOR FRANCISCO	2LT	0-1896801	1047	1
PLANDOWSKI HENRY S	CPT	0-1176161	0862	1
PLANER JAMES E	LTC	0-1102426	0661	1
PLANITZ ARTHUR E	LTC	0-0456676	0261	1
PLANK ALLAN K	MAJ	0-0237423	1142	2
PLANK MAURICE O	CPT	0-0304048	0350	1
PLANK WILBUR L	COL	0-0227022	0963	3
PLANKENHORN CHARLES	LTC	0-0253299	0267	3
PLANKERS DEWEY A	MAJ	0-1296254	0259	1
PLANT EDWARD D	LTC	0-1542347	0461	1
PLANT PHILIP	LTC	0-1308540	0467	3
PLANT ROSS H	MAJ	C-0326118	1045	2
PLANT THOMAS G	COL	C-0500295	0150	3
PLANT WILLIS L	LTC	0-0314220	1060	1
PLANTAMURA JOSEPH A	LTC	0-0397767	0960	1
PLANTE MARGARET J	CW4	V-0204894	0266	1
PLANTS JAMES L	CPT	0-1944553	0846	1
PLANUTIS ALEX J	MAJ	0-1175535	0666	1
PLAPP ELMER B	MAJ	C-0167412	0554	3
PLARUS JOHN S	CW2	W-2210401	0361	1
PLARR ROBERT J	MAJ	0-1649580	1161	1
PLASKON ELI P	COL	0-0409855	0765	1
PLASKY JOHN	CPT	0-1111839	0450	1
PLASS JOHN B	CPT	0-0473152	0745	1
PLASTER ROY W	MAJ	0-1823769	1163	1
PLASTRIDGE ROBERT A	MAJ	0-0162974	0557	3
PLATANACK JOHN	MAJ	0-0502579	0852	1
PLATEK DANIEL A	CW3	W-2144689	0157	1
PLATH RICHARD I	1LT	0-1321812	1145	2
PLATKO MICHAEL A	MAJ	0-1575517	1164	1
PLATNER PAUL G	CW4	W-2101210	0257	1
PLATO ELKEN J	COL	0-0222560	0747	2
PLATSCH KENNETH F	LTC	0-1994678	0461	1
PLATT CHESTER L	MAJ	0-0443692	1053	2
PLATT DONALD L	MAJ	0-1173744	0162	1
PLATT DONALD W	MAJ	0-0255839	0967	3
PLATT DWIGHT H	CW2	W-2124074	1050	2
PLATT FREDERICK	CPT	0-0393283	0842	1
PLATT MATTHEW	CPT	0-0461610	1045	2
PLATT PHILLIP B	LTC	0-1041002	1065	3
PLATT ROBERT J	MAJ	0-1580170	0963	1
PLATT VINCENT J	WO1	W-2106728	0854	1
PLATT WILLIAM C	COL	0-0185924	0251	3
PLATUS LOUIS	CW2	W-2115879	0952	1
PLATZ JAMES L	LTC	0-1573511	0860	2
PLATZ JULIUS E	LTC	0-0270648	0467	3
PLAUTZ ARTHUR V	CW3	W-2205422	0266	1
PLAUTZ FREDERICK	MAJ	0-0968380	1065	2
PLAVNICKY CHARLES J	CW4	RW-2136733	0166	1
PLAZAK JAMES J	LTC	0-1648647	0363	1
PLEASANT MONROE	CPT	0-0479779	0347	1
PLEDGER LYLE J	LTC	0-0408804	0864	1
PLEFKA GEORGE	MAJ	0-2263009	0664	1
PLEMMONS ALTON H	MAJ	0-0491530	1047	1
PLEMMONS CLARENCE W	MAJ	0-1178292	0660	1
PLEMP FRANK W	1LT	0-0346503	0942	2
PLESS NICK G	CW3	W-2112911	0659	1
PLETSCHER HARVEY W	WO1	W-2120909	104N	2
PLETTA DAN H	MAJ	0-0229509	0164	3
PLETZER GOTTFRIED	MAJ	0-2020760	0563	1
PLEVINSKY RAYMOND	1LT	0-1296422	0245	2

NAME	GRADE	SVC NO	DATE RET MO YR	RET CODE
PLEXICO CLAUDE H	MAJ	C-0966764	0263	1
PLIER MILTON F	CW4	W-2126654	0961	1
PLINSKE VERNON H	MAJ	C-0975459	0966	1
PLISH STEVE	LTC	0-1552578	0464	1
PLISKIN REUBEN R	LTC	C-0319000	0746	1
PLOCICA JOSEPH E	MAJ	0-1796523	0263	1
PLOCK EDGAR F	CPT	0-0251969	0160	3
PLOGER VERNE R	MAJ	0-0575915	0957	1
PLONNINGS JR HERMAN	MAJ	C-1017233	C459	1
PLONSKE MARION E	CPT	N-0755473	1047	1
PLOSS ROY C	MAJ	0-0229246	0345	2
PLOTT PORTER I	LTC	0-1575518	C658	1
PLOUGH HAROLD H	MAJ	0-0127422	0452	3
PLOURDE THOMAS	LTC	0-1304942	1264	1
PLOUTZ DENNIS A	CW2	W-2145482	1055	2
PLOWDEN JR ALFRED J	COL	0-0340629	C547	1
PLOWMAN BLAIR E	CPT	0-0226271	1061	3
PLOWMAN STEPHEN W	MAJ	C-1297422	1161	1
PLUE RUSSELL J	LTC	0-0257693	1264	1
PLUIM WILLIS A	CW3	W-2144853	1060	1
PLUM HARRY E	MAJ	0-0481650	0348	1
PLUM RAYMOND J	CPT	0-1745091	1146	2
PLUMB HARRY A	CPT	0-0192232	C847	2
PLUMB RALPH E	LTC	0-0428174	C960	1
PLUMLEE BILLIE L	1LT	0-1913361	C754	2
PLUMLEY FRANCIS H	1LT	0-1294717	1146	1
PLUMLEY GUILFORD A	2LT	0-1288946	0445	2
PLUMLEY ROY R	LTC	0-1294718	0161	1
PLUMLEY WALTER P	LTC	0-0261530	1066	3
PLUMMER CHARLES E	MAJ	C-0126810	C356	3
PLUMMER HAROLD L	MAJ	C-0151444	C754	3
PLUMMER KENNETH C	LTC	0-0413498	C856	1
PLUMMER LEONARD B	LTC	0-0222397	C951	1
PLUMMER LOUIS F	MAJ	C-0382618	0646	2
PLUMMER MICHAEL J	LTC	0-1587541	0167	2
PLUMMER NATHAN S	CPT	0-2289282	C563	1
PLUMMER ROBERT J	CW2	W-2123367	1053	1
PLUMMER SR EDWARD W	CPT	0-1319542	1062	1
PLUMMER THOMAS H	COL	0-0211395	C654	1
PLUMMER WILLIAM	CPT	0-1299104	1047	2
PLUMMER WILLIAM E	COL	0-0261205	C166	3
PLUNKETT ELMER G	CPT	0-0399237	1144	2
PLUNKETT ELMER L	1LT	N-0734990	1046	1
PLUNKETT HENRY P	COL	0-0180254	0161	3
PLUNKETT ROBERT	CW3	W-2142261	0757	1
PLUNKETT ROBERT T	1LT	0-1102131	0345	2
PLUNKETT WOODROW C	CPT	0-1290999	C246	1
PLUTZ ANDREW	1LT	0-1112374	0345	2
PLYBON PAUL C	CPT	0-0419682	0145	2
PLYLER ORELL F	MAJ	0-0443424	1052	1
PLYLEY RAYMOND C	COL	0-0173944	0159	3
PLYMALE RAYMOND D	CW2	W-2215178	0767	1
PLYMATE ELEANOR A	MAJ	N-0732269	0262	1
PLYMEL ERNEST L	CPT	0-1590110	0761	1
PLYMIRE HAROLD N	1LT	0-1301034	0945	2
POAGE JAMES D	2LT	0-0384180	C142	2
POBLOCKI ROBERT J	MAJ	0-0453735	0446	2
POCHODOWICZ S J	CPT	0-0331064	0345	2
POCILUYKO NICHOLAS D	MAJ	C-2027772	C260	1
POCOCK CLIFFORD H	LTC	0-1338849	0766	1
POCZIK LESLIE J	MAJ	C-1105113	0164	1
PODCASY BERNARD J	CPT	0-1316326	1047	2
PODEYN EMIL M	LTC	0-0279934	C753	3
PODGORSKI ELIZABET	2LT	N-0744433	0944	1
PODLEWSKI NICK S	MAJ	0-0585185	0557	1
PODSCHUN WILLIAM A	CW3	W-2150253	0662	1
PODSIADLY EDWARD	LTC	0-1541111	0959	1
PODSOBINSKI MAURICE	CPT	0-1555460	C663	1
PODWORNY EDWARD C	LTC	0-0408485	C863	1
POE BRYCE	LTC	0-0274050	0447	2
POE CHARLES F	COL	0-0114486	1146	2
POE CHARLES T	1LT	0-0345121	0646	2
POE JAMES E	LTC	0-1533423	0757	1
POE JR LEWIS M	MAJ	0-0912574	1043	2
POE RALPH A	COL	0-0234977	C262	1
POE TEDDY	LTC	0-0285772	0266	3
POE VICTOR E	CPT	0-1823347	1158	1
POE WILLIAM A	COL	0-0185905	0358	1
POEHLMAN FRANK H	COL	0-0178980	0650	3
POEHLMANN GEORGE	CPT	0-0365733	0546	2
POEHLMANN JOHN L	1LT	0-1177583	0446	2
POEHLMANN THEODORE H	CW3	W-2148507	0566	1
POER MELVYN R	LTC	0-1109594	0762	1
POFF JOSEPH E	CW4	W-2112257	0659	1
POFFENBERG SCOTT B	LTC	0-0202068	1061	3
POFFENROTH JOHN F	1LT	0-1289794	1045	2
POGAR JOHN	MAJ	0-1181412	0358	1
POGGI JOHN J	1LT	0-2007035	0847	2
POGGIONE JOSEPH J	LTC	0-0361405	0963	3
POGUE EARL W	CPT	0-0331375	C562	3
POGUE FRANK L	MAJ	0-1291515	1159	1
POGUE HERBERT L	CPT	0-0977671	0161	1
POGUE JACK	CPT	0-0885620	0947	1
POGUE JAMES C	LTC	0-1166586	0164	1
POGUE JOSEPH G	MAJ	C-1591373	0959	1
POGUE ROGER R	CW2	W-2215045	0567	1
POH LAWRENCE C	MAJ	C-1177940	0560	1
POHL CHARLES M	MAJ	0-0336637	0346	2
POHL GLYN W	LTC	0-0365065	0161	1
POHL HARRY W	LTC	0-1580172	0761	1
POHLSON CARL I	LTC	0-0336289	0356	3
POHOWSKY JR ALEX	CPT	0-0441415	0146	1
POHZEHL LOUIS C	CPT	0-1319645	0246	2
POINDEXTER JAMES A	LTC	0-1171722	0457	1
POINSETT EDGAR H	LTC	0-1297247	0261	1
POINT ROBERT C	LTC	0-2206394	0867	1
POINTON HERBERT A	CW3	W-2151390	0866	1
POIRIER JOHN	CW4	W-2108001	0951	1
POIS JOHN	CPT	0-0213635	1045	2
POISSON JR PAUL H	CW3	W-2145294	0463	1
POKORNEY FRED M	LTC	0-0233070	1162	3
POKORNY ALBERT E	LTC	0-1102429	0262	1
POKORNY JERRY	MAJ	0-0417735	0848	1
POKORNY JOHN E	LTC	0-0189460	1046	1
POKORSKI MAX F	LTC	0-1823056	C866	1
POKUSA STANLEY M	1LT	0-1052127	1045	2
POLACEK JAMES V	MAJ	0-0133793	0948	3
POLAK BENJAMIN E	MAJ	0-2032276	0860	1
POLAND ARTHUR E	MAJ	0-2026038	0861	1
POLAND JR EUSTIS L	MAJ	0-0453085	C161	1
POLAND RAYMOND A	CW4	W-2104924	1059	1
POLAND ROBERT R	CPT	0-0217514	0656	3
POLASKE JOHN	2LT	0-0108262	1030	1
POLASKY LOIS I	CPT	N-0733648	0450	1
POLATIN ALVIN H	CPT	0-1938852	0654	2
POLCYN EDWARD W	MAJ	0-1926914	1264	1
POLERETCKI JOSEPH	MAJ	0-1115745	0256	1
POLHAMUS ALBERT A	1LT	0-4010815	1158	2
POLICANI GASPER V	MAJ	0-1542420	0857	1
POLICASTRO ARMONDO	1LT	0-1598350	0845	2
POLICH FRANK J	COL	0-0391844	0760	1
POLICOFF LOUIS	2LT	0-0967829	0453	1
POLING ANDREW W	1LT	0-2262948	0957	1
POLING CARL M	CPT	0-0298811	1045	2
POLING RICHARD R	2LT	0-1590732	1044	2
POLITZER FRANK	1LT	0-1285296	0546	2
POLK ARDITH T	CW3	W-2153034	1164	1
POLK ARTHUR B	MAJ	C-1638278	C356	1
POLK CHARLES K	MAJ	0-2033787	1265	1
POLK J L	CW2	W-2143166	0456	1
POLK JAMES K	COL	0-0448177	0166	3
POLK JAMES K	LTC	0-1103364	0161	1
POLK JOHN H	1LT	0-1315210	1052	1
POLK JR SAMUEL T	CPT	0-1307073	0646	2
POLK ROBERT L	CW2	W-2146156	0560	1
POLK SR HARVEY E	CW3	W-2143675	0965	1
POLK WILLIAM F	MAJ	0-0348195	C857	2
POLKA JAMES B	COL	0-0287125	0262	3
POLL DAVID J	1LT	0-2210426	1053	2
POLLACK IRVING S	CPT	0-0534155	1045	2
POLLACK JOSEPH A	LTC	0-1549024	1061	1
POLLACK JOSEPH J	CPT	0-1635211	0860	1
POLLAK LEO C	MAJ	C-2018215	0365	1
POLLARD ALBERT H	LTC	0-0347669	0161	3
POLLARD DONALD G	CPT	0-1642475	C457	1
POLLARD III ANDREW M	LTC	0-0254368	C867	3
POLLARD JACK	LTC	0-1103865	1161	1
POLLARD KENNETH B	CW3	W-2148219	0262	1
POLLARD RICHARD H	CPT	0-0171486	0854	3
POLLARD RICHARD R	CW3	W-2152566	C661	1
POLLARD ROBERT L	LTC	0-0162291	0348	2
POLLARD THOMAS D	LTC	0-0964554	C463	1
POLLARD VAN B	LTC	0-1576508	C760	1
POLLARD WILLIAM F	LTC	0-1055123	C164	1
POLLARO MARY T	CPT	N-0725439	1147	1
POLLET IRVING L	MAJ	C-0210134	C146	2
POLLEY GEORGE O	MAJ	0-1284572	C861	1
POLLICK ALBERT P	MAJ	C-1302876	C847	2
POLLINQUE EUGENE F	2LT	0-0519702	C845	2
POLLITT JAMES J	1LT	0-1822723	0551	1
POLLITZER HENRY H	CW3	W-2144247	0257	1
POLLOCK ALFRED L	LTC	0-0357460	1056	3
POLLOCK CARL A	LTC	C-0425238	C862	1
POLLOCK CLINTON A	CPT	0-1800114	0656	2
POLLOCK GEORGE M	MAJ	0-0275253	0457	1
POLLOCK JR OTTO G	1LT	0-0397338	0345	2
POLLOCK KATHERINE	MAJ	N-0724089	0561	1
POLLOCK KEITH A	CW3	W-2141865	1160	1
POLLOCK ROBERT W	LTC	0-0328962	C466	3
POLLOCK WILLIAM M	COL	0-0264656	0466	3
POLONSKI JOSEPH	CW3	W-2152336	0364	1
POLSE MAX L	MAJ	0-0492829	0146	2
POLSON EARL H	CPT	0-2212093	0556	1
POLSON JAMES L	LTC	0-0238310	C863	3
POLSTER ALVIN F	CW4	RW-0906955	C860	1
POLY ERNEST W	CPT	0-2014385	0357	1
POMEROY ERNEST T	CW2	W-2103322	1053	2
POMEROY FRANKLIN I	COL	0-0101351	0154	3
POMEROY JOHN W	LTC	0-0335004	0153	1
POMEROY JR PHILIP S	COL	0-0451035	1266	1
POMEROY MARGUERITE	MAJ	L-0603914	C463	1
POMEROY PLAYFORD R	LTC	0-0290886	0144	2
POMEROY ROLAND E	LTC	0-0389953	0846	2
POMEROY ROSCOE E	COL	0-0308718	1063	1
POMMETT SR FRANCIS A	MAJ	C-1821908	C761	1
POMO RALPH J	1LT	0-1011944	1045	2
POMPER WALTER C	CPT	0-1113397	0766	1
PONADER CARMAN W	1LT	0-1041223	1045	2
POND CLIFTON R	LTC	0-0196487	C256	3
POND HARRY S	LTC	0-0104334	C648	3
POND JR LESLIE L	CW4	W-2115846	1054	2
POND ROBERT C	CPT	0-0289929	0146	2
POND THOMAS B	CPT	0-1310760	0247	1
POND WOODY	1LT	0-1824504	C545	2
PONDELICEK MILES J	CPT	0-0965801	0859	1
PONDER CHARLES F	2LT	0-0504543	1048	1
PONDER HOYETT A	CPT	0-0328783	0645	2
PONDER MARY E	1LT	N-0737351	1152	2
PONDS WILLIAM J	1LT	C-1301679	0745	2
PONS FRANK J	MAJ	0-0944653	1061	1
PONT WALTER F	MAJ	C-1041880	C358	1
PONTIUS HERMAN W	LTC	0-0195011	0452	1
PONZAR WALTER F	LTC	0-0345128	0860	1
PONZIO HAROLD J	1LT	0-1308045	0945	2
POOL BERNARD E	CW3	W-2134685	C861	1
POOL FLOYD R	COL	0-0225269	C154	3
POOL FRANK M	MAJ	0-0394513	C146	2
POOL GEORGE F	MAJ	0-0911829	0246	2
POOL HANDFORD E	MAJ	0-0224674	0-52	3
POOL JOHN	LTC	0-0243580	1045	1
POOL JR SANFORD M	COL	0-0202292	0959	1
POOL LAFAYETTE	CW2	W-2149816	0960	2
POOL WALTER C	CW3	W-2121156	C857	1
POOLE ALBERT	CW3	W-2150160	0566	1
POOLE ARTHUR J	MAJ	C-2282586	1166	1
POOLE CHARLES E	CW3	W-2145483	1058	1
POOLE GEORGE D	COL	0-0255265	0655	3
POOLE GEORGE R	COL	0-0287053	0266	3
POOLE JESSE O	CW2	W-2145484	0462	1
POOLE JR JOHN M	WO1	W-2148499	0855	1
POOLE KENNETH W	1LT	0-1012290	1045	2
POOLE LAVERNE S	LTC	0-0520972	1064	3
POOLE LLOYD C	LTC	0-0258647	0947	2
POOLE LYNWOOD H	LTC	0-0320173	0464	1
POOLE MAURICE L	LTC	0-1284573	0666	3
POOLE REGINALD M	CW3	W-2144597	0264	1
POOLE RICHARD W	CPT	0-1545726	0157	1
POOLE ROBERT E	MAJ	0-0249803	0865	3
POOLE ROBERT H	LTC	0-0423576	0462	3
POOLE ROLAND J	MAJ	0-0171263	0648	3
POOLE SR WILLIAM L	LTC	0-0178913	0648	3
POOLE WILLIAM	MAJ	0-0266161	1060	1
POOLE WILLIAM B	MAJ	C-1111311	0266	1
POOLE WILLIAM C	LTC	0-0292403	1160	1
POOLER JAMES T	CPT	0-1924748	0763	1
POOLER PAUL L	LTC	0-0299087	0863	3
POOLEY RICHARD L	COL	0-0269386	1159	1
POORE ARCHIE P	COL	0-0247028	0747	2
POORE FREDERIC L	LTC	0-1583517	0267	1
POORE RAYMOND H	LTC	0-0379123	1062	1
POORE STUART H	LTC	0-0518007	1262	3
POORMAN DOROTHY E	1LT	N-0704040	0546	1
POORMAN FRED S	COL	0-0173458	1061	3
POORMAN JOHN A	LTC	0-0741622	0767	1
POPA RALPH	CW3	W-2152282	0963	1
POPE ALBERT H	CPT	C-0336437	1144	2
POPE BENJAMIN W	CPT	0-0469231	0650	1
POPE CHARLES A	MAJ	0-0354070	0367	3
POPE CHARLES F	LTC	0-0335733	0345	2
POPE CHARLES R	LTC	0-1054367	1166	3
POPE CHARLES S	LTC	0-0241190	0664	3
POPE CLAUDE F	MAJ	C-1550481	0157	1
POPE CLYDE F	MAJ	0-1695634	1153	1
POPE EDGAR A	CPT	0-0522415	1060	1
POPE EMIL S	MAJ	0-0980398	0264	1
POPE HARRIS M	LTC	0-1306466	0960	1
POPE HOWARD E	CW2	W-2150191	0760	1
POPE JOHN P	LTC	0-1113399	1263	1
POPE JOHN G	CPT	0-1110726	1047	1
POPE JR CHARLES F	1LT	0-0445745	1146	2
POPE JR EZRA T	COL	0-0151557	0457	3
POPE JR WILLIAM E	CW3	W-2149158	0465	1
POPE LAWRENCE F	1LT	0-2035018	1145	2
POPE MARY H	CW4	V-0609411	1263	1
POPE NORMAN L	1LT	0-1292585	1046	2
POPE RALPH P	LTC	0-0172693	0950	3
POPE RALPH W	CW4	W-2145087	1058	1
POPE RUFUS A	LTC	0-1300706	0161	1
POPE SIDNEY K	LTC	0-0268166	1065	3
POPE SOWELL G	LTC	0-1168036	0759	1
POPE WALTER C	LTC	0-0286400	0866	3
POPE WILLIAM J	CW2	W-2145695	0257	1
POPHAM JOHN S R	LTC	0-0484149	0763	3
POPOVICH ELLIOT G	CW3	W-2142263	0659	1
POPOVICH JAMES M	LTC	0-1797875	0961	1
POPOVICH MARCUS J	LTC	0-1945678	0861	2
POPOVICS JOHN	MAJ	0-2011617	0665	1
POPOVSKY NICHOLAS T	LTC	0-0275566	1065	3
POPP LEWIS	CW4	W-2114860	0559	1
POPPAS JR GEORGE	LTC	0-1173747	0466	1
POPPELL MASON L	MAJ	0-2262334	0763	1
POPPLE RICHARD W	CW3	W-2144714	0164	1
POPPLEWELL ARCHIE L	CW3	W-2144492	0659	1
POPPLEWELL ARVINE G	CPT	0-0936111	1148	1
POPWELL JOHNNIE C	CW3	W-2148935	0364	1
PORADA EDMUND S	LTC	0-2210138	0767	1
PORAT ALBERT	MAJ	0-0484074	0551	1
PORCARI STEPHEN	CPT	0-0332906	0962	1
PORCH JOSEPH W	MAJ	0-1329514	0764	1
PORCHE STANLEY E	LTC	0-1030406	0557	1

NAME	GRADE	SVC NO	DATE RET MO YR	RET CODE
PORCHER PHILIP G	CPT	0-0258715	1045	2
PORGES ARTHUR	1LT	0-1166356	0744	2
PORISCH ADOLPHE H	1LT	0-1312219	C446	2
PORR GEORGE L	LTC	0-0338428	1062	3
PORT AUGUST G	LTC	0-0151827	0648	3
PORT CHARLES S	CPT	0-0509356	0246	2
PORT HORACE W	MAJ	0-0342462	0645	2
PORT JOHN Y	MAJ	0-1047297	C465	1
PORT MURRAY	LTC	0-0314930	C266	3
PORT THOMAS D	1LT	0-1309823	1145	2
PORTE DAVID S	1LT	C-0331717	C664	1
PORTELROY JOHN C	COL	0-0278916	1065	3
PORTEOUS WILLIAM L	MAJ	C-0418833	0647	1
PORTER ALEXANDER	CPT	C-1168037	C153	1
PORTER ALLEN T	LTC	0-1170923	1163	1
PORTER BERNARD R	LTC	0-0268008	C666	3
PORTER BERNARD U	LTC	0-1291164	C465	1
PORTER CHARLES B	LTC	0-0382176	0854	1
PORTER CHARLES P	1LT	0-0885654	C744	2
PORTER CHARLES W	LTC	0-0244951	1048	2
PORTER CALLAS E	CPT	C-0248634	0865	3
PORTER EARNEST E	1LT	0-0497156	0452	1
PORTER FRANK H	2LT	0-1324648	C944	2
PORTER FRANK P	CW2	W-2144365	1157	1
PORTER GEORGE I	CPT	0-2262995	C461	1
PORTER GEORGE L	LTC	0-C170035	0755	3
PORTER HARLAN E	MAJ	C-0526800	C755	1
PORTER HAROLD A	LTC	0-1289361	C961	1
PORTER HAROLD E	LTC	0-0254419	0164	3
PORTER HOBART D	CW2	W-2210038	C664	1
PORTER HOMER A	CPT	0-1321580	1145	2
PORTER HOWARD O	LTC	0-C183055	0962	3
PORTER JAMES F	MAJ	0-2034803	0657	1
PORTER JAMES H	LTC	C-1305827	C461	1
PORTER JAMES M	1LT	0-1644675	1045	2
PORTER JAMES M	CW2	W-2146391	1059	1
PORTER JAMES W	MAJ	0-1174684	0563	1
PORTER JAMES W	LTC	0-1598249	C166	1
PORTER JOHN D	LTC	0-0404281	1060	1
PORTER JOHN D	LTC	0-0415053	0161	1
PORTER JOHN E	LTC	0-0372119	0246	2
PORTER JOHN M	MAJ	C-0209479	0345	2
PORTER JOHN R	CW4	W-2111975	0559	1
PORTER JOHN V	CPT	0-1309824	0346	2
PORTER JOSEPH H	1LT	C-1043464	1045	2
PORTER JR CANIEL B	COL	0-C295018	C966	1
PORTER JR HARRY	MAJ	C-2033070	0962	1
PORTER JR JOHN W	MAJ	0-1332412	C760	1
PORTER JR PHILIP H	LTC	0-0184342	C744	2
PORTER KENNETH A	WO1	W-2129446	0751	1
PORTER LANDON C	CPT	0-1059630	C567	3
PORTER LEON E	1LT	0-1172603	C846	2
PORTER LEONARD R	CPT	0-1599183	1058	1
PORTER PAUL B	COL	C-0241305	C849	3
PORTER PAUL E	MAJ	0-2017114	1265	1
PORTER PECK J	1LT	0-0220767	1046	1
PORTER PHILIP O	MAJ	C-1560379	C564	1
PORTER RICHARD L	1LT	0-1297943	0246	2
PORTER ROBERT F	MAJ	C-1015056	C361	1
PORTER ROBERT J	CPT	0-1533674	1062	1
PORTER ROBERT P	LTC	0-0277601	1057	3
PORTER ROBERT W	LTC	0-1646510	1163	1
PORTER ROBERT W	CPT	0-2202303	0466	1
PORTER THOMAS H	1LT	C-2207939	0553	2
PORTER THOMAS R	CW3	W-2000620	C159	1
PORTER THOMAS W	CPT	0-1289318	1146	2
PORTER WENDELL A	2LT	0-1309825	C545	1
PORTER WILBUR E	CW3	PW-2152613	0363	1
PORTER WILLIAM C	LTC	C-1286887	C561	1
PORTER WILLIAM E	MAJ	C-1291325	C558	1
PORTER WILLIAM L	LTC	0-1010008	1066	3
PORTERA JOHN J	LTC	0-0939691	0765	1
PORTERA JOHN O	MAJ	C-2263754	0565	1
PORTERFIELD ARTHUR R	1LT	0-1310876	1045	2
PORTERFIELD HARRY B	MAJ	C-0991254	0563	1

NAME	GRADE	SVC NO	DATE RET MO YR	RET CODE
PORTERFIELD JAMES W	CPT	0-0866520	1062	1
PORTERFIELD RICHARD	CW3	W-2152750	0867	1
PORTFOLIO DONALD N	MAJ	0-1635214	1064	1
PORTH RICHARD J	CPT	C-0331733	0664	3
PORTMAN ABRAHAM	1LT	0-0507805	1043	2
PORTMANN FREDERICK	CW2	W-2145485	0660	1
PORTNOFF BERT	1LT	0-0455585	0645	1
PORTNOY BRADFORD M	MAJ	0-1696212	0646	2
PORTO PEDRO	1LT	0-1311849	0356	1
PORTOR LAWRENCE W	WO1	W-2144401	0853	1
PORTWOOD VERA W	CPT	N-0784670	1047	1
PORTWOOD WESLEY C	1LT	0-0507384	1052	1
POSCHNER GEORGE W	CPT	0-0523320	1148	2
POSES ABRAHAM L	MAJ	0-0246134	0847	1
POSES MEYER	LTC	0-1948032	0767	3
POSEY ARBRADE J	CPT	0-0949126	0365	2
POSEY BARRON B	MAJ	0-1823057	C457	1
POSEY CARROLL L	CPT	0-1877815	1065	1
POSEY EVERETT C	LTC	0-0257650	0863	1
POSEY FARRIS J	LTC	0-1548287	0361	1
POSEY HERMAN C	CW3	W-2151989	0766	1
POSEY HORACE E	LTC	0-1323029	1262	1
POSEY JAMES C	1LT	0-1307746	0656	1
POSEY PAUL W	CW3	W-2144306	0261	1
POSEY ROBERT K	MAJ	0-0228681	0564	3
POSEY WALTER J	LTC	0-0508105	0865	3
POSHARD HERBERT M	CPT	0-0187864	0145	2
POSIK JOSEPH W	1LT	0-4010133	0757	2
POSLIK JOSEPH	MAJ	C-1313040	1048	1
POSNER CHARLES	CPT	0-1703244	0744	2
POSNER GEORGE E	MAJ	0-1185416	0258	1
POSNER SAUL	1LT	0-1043465	0447	1
POSPICHAL ARNOLD B	LTC	0-1577703	0258	1
POSS DAVID H	LTC	0-0378961	1066	1
POSS RUBY	1LT	N-0701935	0742	1
POSSIEL RAKENIUS J	COL	C-0218218	1061	3
POST BURNAP	1LT	0-1015067	0745	2
POST CHALMER F	LTC	0-1638290	0466	1
POST CHARLES G	CPT	0-0371104	0344	2
POST FRANK S	COL	0-0237338	0345	2
POST GEORGE R	LTC	0-1170142	0860	1
POST GERALD V	CPT	C-0315952	0844	2
POST HARRY W	LTC	0-0395845	0960	1
POST JOHN A	MAJ	0-0401848	1050	1
POST JR ARTHUR F	LTC	0-1280195	1163	1
POST JR CHARLES W	CPT	0-0518139	1147	1
POST MAURICE R	MAJ	0-1032385	0265	3
POST PAUL L	1LT	0-1018539	0846	2
POST RUTH E	MAJ	L-0125590	0563	1
POST SAMUEL S	COL	0-0352866	1266	1
POST WALTER H	1LT	0-1110727	1144	2
POST WESLEY V B	COL	0-0221425	1057	1
POST WILLIAM	CPT	0-1081715	0451	1
POSTEL MILO J	LTC	0-1640824	0861	2
POSTER RUSSELL E	CPT	0-1285493	1044	2
POSTICK FRED G	CPT	0-1342346	0159	1
POSTLETHWAIT VIRGIL	MAJ	0-1824909	0862	1
POSTLEWATE JAMES F	CPT	0-1997997	0863	1
POSTON JOHN W	LTC	0-1054091	0467	1
POSTON JR CHARLES B	MAJ	C-0954838	0463	1
POSVAR VLADIMIR L	LTC	0-0163100	0362	3
POSZ CHARLES H	MAJ	0-1285494	0859	3
POSZ JOSEPH A	LTC	0-0260253	0467	3
POTASZ THOMAS M	COL	0-0325967	0246	2
POTEET HOMER E	CPT	0-0427991	0552	1
POTEET HORACE E	LTC	0-1580180	1060	1
POTEET JR BRITTAIN	LTC	0-0210910	0262	3
POTEET JR JOHN W	LTC	0-0225684	0264	3
POTEET ROBERT W	MAJ	0-1645294	0859	1
POTEETE LEON	CW2	W-2144349	1164	1
POTENZA LOUIS F	CW3	W-2152397	1162	1
POTESKY ANTHONY	CPT	0-0164125	1026	1
POTHIER DOROTHY M	MAJ	N-0752421	0464	2
POTIER JOE F	CW2	W-2150732	0658	1
POTKONSKI LEOPOLD A	CPT	0-0357140	0446	2

NAME	GRADE	SVC NO	DATE RET MO YR	RET CODE
POTOCKI JOHNNIE A	LTC	0-0312075	C758	1
POTOLICCHIO GORDON G	MAJ	0-4009910	0466	1
POTRECZ JULIAN K	CW4	W-2118310	C157	1
POTSAID MAJIC S	CPT	0-1533653	C246	2
POTTEIGER ALFRED A	LTC	0-0410724	C658	1
POTTEIGER ROBERT W	CPT	C-1287056	0155	1
POTTER ALICE	2LT	N-0763538	1144	1
POTTER ALICE W	CPT	N-0787707	1047	1
POTTER ARTEMAS C	CW3	W-2152979	1063	1
POTTER BENJAMIN P	MAJ	0-1692078	0745	2
POTTER BRYAN W	LTC	0-0450344	C256	1
POTTER CECIL E	LTC	C-1004213	0966	3
POTTER CECIL V	MAJ	C-1881812	0266	1
POTTER CHARLES F	MAJ	C-1306316	1046	2
POTTER ELEANOR V	CPT	N-0744101	0549	2
POTTER EUGENE W	COL	0-0139969	C857	3
POTTER FRANK M	COL	0-0212683	0763	3
POTTER FRANKLIN J	MAJ	C-0220720	1058	3
POTTER GABE W	CPT	0-1920280	0262	1
POTTER GEORGE H	CPT	C-0285478	C747	2
POTTER HAROLD C	LTC	0-0453884	1260	1
POTTER HAROLD W	LTC	C-0212257	C245	2
POTTER HERBERT S	LTC	0-0125792	1150	3
POTTER IRA	LTC	0-0256040	0359	3
POTTER JAMES O	LTC	C-0972924	1166	1
POTTER JAMES W	WO1	W-2110027	1145	2
POTTER JOHN C	MAJ	C-1649334	C357	1
POTTER JR JOHN E	MAJ	C-0948978	C861	1
POTTER LELAND L	CW3	W-2141789	C864	1
POTTER LESLIE S	LTC	0-1319647	C665	1
POTTER MARSHALL O	COL	C-0219891	0161	3
POTTER MORELAND N	WO1	W-2105374	C364	1
POTTER RALPH A	CW2	W-2118731	1049	1
POTTER ROBERT B	LTC	0-1289484	0466	1
POTTER ROBERT C	LTC	0-1101999	C464	1
POTTER ROBERT H	CPT	0-1821765	C647	1
POTTER RUPERT W	CW2	W-2147726	0863	1
POTTER SR HENRY J	CPT	C-0308663	1154	3
POTTER STANLEY B	LTC	0-0493443	C566	3
POTTER THERESA C	2LT	N-0761736	1045	1
POTTER THOMAS F	1LT	0-1304944	C745	2
POTTER VERNON N	LTC	0-1044381	0166	1
POTTER WILLARD	MAJ	C-0147881	0557	3
POTTHOFF BERNARD B	LTC	0-1547748	C566	1
POTTLE CLARENCE E	CW2	W-2213524	C867	1
POTTORF HAROLD R	MAJ	0-1179579	1162	1
POTTRATZ WAYNE B	CW3	W-2146792	0562	1
POTTS ABEL	LTC	0-2035144	0760	1
POTTS BENNIE R	LTC	0-0498144	C159	3
POTTS C HARRIS	COL	C-0181094	1154	3
POTTS DAVID F	CPT	0-0500046	0647	1
POTTS EDITH W	CPT	N-0765400	0757	2
POTTS EDWARD J	CW4	W-2112025	C662	1
POTTS EDWIN L	CPT	0-1921727	0753	1
POTTS FRANCIS M	CW2	W-2150813	0961	1
POTTS GEORGE W	MAJ	C-0147757	1052	3
POTTS HORACE F	LTC	0-1167589	1160	1
POTTS JIMMIE N	CW2	W-2152148	C761	1
POTTS JOHN R	1LT	0-1284048	1045	2
POTTS JOHN W	2LT	0-1304440	C145	2
POTTS JR CHARLES T	MAJ	0-1635528	0459	1
POTTS JR WILLIAM C	MAJ	C-1001661	0855	1
POTTS MABEL	1LT	N-0726345	C348	1
POTTS RALPH F	MAJ	0-0121037	C254	3
POTTS RICHARD H	MAJ	C-1171724	C466	1
POTTS WILLIAM H	CW3	W-2148980	0163	1
POTTS 2ND ALFRED M	MAJ	0-0265075	0145	2
POTVIN ROLAND L	LTC	0-1554609	1063	1
POTWIN EARLE A	1LT	0-0453023	0757	1
POTWIN MAURICE L	CW3	W-2142775	C258	1
POTZ DAVID F	CPT	0-0973905	1265	2
POU CAYETANO R	LTC	0-0329569	C849	3
POU FRANK E S	LTC	0-0234496	1045	2
POUDRE LOUIS J	LTC	0-0405897	0954	1
POUJOL HARLEY K	MAJ	C-1559246	1263	2

NAME	GRADE	SVC NO	DATE RET MO YR	RET CODE
POULIN HOWARD C	COL	0-0386517	0967	1
POULIOT GERARD N	CW2	W-2111614	1046	2
POULIS BYRON	CPT	0-0213184	1262	3
POULNOT ROBERT J	1LT	0-2018051	0551	1
POULOS RICHARD L	MAJ	0-1177588	1060	1
POULSEN NIELS I	COL	0-0115069	0256	2
POULSEN OTTO L	2LT	0-0532152	0944	1
POULSON WILLIAM R	CPT	0-0212705	1060	3
POUND JOHN H	MAJ	C-0177221	0861	3
POUND JOHN M	COL	0-0358338	1062	3
POUND MARVIN E	LTC	0-0348995	0756	1
POUND MARVIN G	1LT	0-0115068	0352	3
POUND ROBERT L	MAJ	0-1999738	0561	1
POUNDS RUSSELL G	CW3	W-2142891	0163	1
POUNDS VEON C	CW2	W-2146901	0460	1
POUNDS WILLIAM M	MAJ	C-0481203	1048	1
POUNDSTONE ANSEL F	LTC	0-0151416	0153	1
POURROCK JOSEPH F	MAJ	0-0109280	0125	1
POUSARD ALFRED W	LTC	0-0419374	0661	1
POUSKA JR ALEXANDER	LTC	0-0411881	0966	1
POUSSON NICHOLAS	CPT	0-0510679	0847	1
POUST CASSIUS	COL	C-0178865	0-51	3
POUTTU THOMAS C	CPT	0-1300379	0847	1
POUTTU THOMAS E	MAJ	0-1688835	0264	1
POVERCHC PAUL	LTC	0-1010858	0963	1
POVERONO WILLIAM F	LTC	0-1115382	0464	1
POVEY PHILIP E	2LT	0-0511602	1244	1
POVSHA ROBERT J	CPT	0-2096562	0163	1
POW FREDERICK	LTC	0-0163052	0350	1
POWDERLY PATRICK J	CPT	0-4030937	0464	2
POWE HAROLD D	CPT	0-1293310	0347	2
POWELL ALFRED B	MAJ	C-0208362	0648	3
POWELL ARMOND V	CW2	W-2148681	0158	1
POWELL ARTHUR F	COL	C-1584844	0661	1
POWELL ARTHUR P	LTC	0-1102000	0166	3
POWELL BERRY F	MAJ	C-0364584	0262	1
POWELL BRADFORD G	LTC	0-2274882	0762	1
POWELL CHARLES A	LTC	0-1634515	0966	3
POWELL CHARLES F	MAJ	0-0107925	0648	3
POWELL CHARLES E	LTC	0-1305474	0762	1
POWELL CHARLES S	CPT	0-0310352	1145	2
POWELL CHARLES W	CPT	0-1333001	1060	1
POWELL CLARENCE J	LTC	0-0278749	0764	3
POWELL CLAUDE	LTC	0-1573517	0954	1
POWELL CLAUDE M	LTC	0-0139159	0249	3
POWELL CLEMENT J	LTC	0-0201485	0458	3
POWELL CLIFFORD R	M G	0-0102214	0753	3
POWELL CLIFFORD S	MAJ	0-1593785	0764	1
POWELL CLIFFORD W	CW2	W-2148096	0859	1
POWELL DAVID M	CPT	0-0328485	0249	2
POWELL DUPERT	CPT	0-0485477	0448	1
POWELL EDWARD	CW2	W-2147452	0462	1
POWELL EDWARD T	CW2	W-2149088	0761	2
POWELL ELDRED L	MAJ	0-1636495	1060	1
POWELL EVERETT A	MAJ	0-0491038	1046	1
POWELL FLOYD G	LTC	0-0237945	0645	2
POWELL FLOYD M	CW2	W-2103328	1046	2
POWELL FRANK M	CPT	0-0182507	0154	3
POWELL FRED A	MAJ	C-0942546	0865	1
POWELL FREDERICK	COL	0-0199777	0359	3
POWELL GEORGE M	LTC	0-0297045	1059	3
POWELL GEORGE W	MAJ	0-0183711	1045	2
POWELL GLENN A	LTC	0-0328933	0859	1
POWELL GRAYSON C	COL	0-0306403	0847	2
POWELL HAROLD B	CPT	0-0375507	1145	2
POWELL HAROLD N	LTC	0-0265365	0667	3
POWELL HAROLD R	CPT	0-0232583	1156	3
POWELL HERBERT G	CPT	0-0166125	0648	3
POWELL JOHN C	CPT	0-0103123	0854	3
POWELL JOHN M	MAJ	0-0245151	0352	3
POWELL JOHN P	MAJ	C-0300776	0358	1
POWELL JOHN R	LTC	0-1593786	0461	1
POWELL JOHN R	MAJ	0-1684424	0645	1
POWELL JOHN W	1LT	C-1113894	0246	2
POWELL JOSEE R	1LT	0-1645920	0246	2

NAME	GRADE	SVC NO	DATE RET MO YR	RET CODE
POWELL JOSEPH C	CPT	0-0189642	C644	2
POWELL JOSEPH C	CW4	W-2109425	0659	1
POWELL JOSEPH R	MAJ	C-1590111	0747	2
POWELL JOSEPH W	LTC	0-0332121	C359	1
POWELL JR CECIL P	1LT	C-0989206	0967	2
POWELL JR FRANK T	MAJ	0-2011964	0461	1
POWELL JR JOHN D	MAJ	0-2033987	C466	1
POWELL JR JOHN G	MAJ	0-1061821	0962	1
POWELL JR JOHN P	CPT	0-0984395	0162	2
POWELL JR THEO L	CW4	W-2111473	1158	1
POWELL LAMAR W	CW3	W-2150929	1062	1
POWELL LELAND T	MAJ	0-1172604	C258	1
POWELL LEO T	CPT	0-0384775	1047	2
POWELL LESTER	CW3	W-2150338	C657	1
POWELL LLOYC E	MAJ	0-1924573	0565	1
POWELL MARTIN F	LTC	0-0272626	0667	3
POWELL MCCLELLAN	CPT	0-1313125	C462	1
POWELL MILTON E	LTC	0-0217838	C662	3
POWELL NEVILLE A	LTC	0-0120707	C648	3
POWELL NORMAN F	LTC	0-1313012	0461	1
POWELL OWEN T	MAJ	0-1047737	1158	1
POWELL PAUL L	MAJ	C-1999954	0861	1
POWELL PHILLIP B	LTC	0-1582505	0163	1
POWELL RICHARD L	CW3	W-2152182	0764	1
POWELL RICHARC T	CW2	W-2215006	1166	1
POWELL ROBERT W	LTC	0-1291001	0263	1
POWELL ROBERT W	CPT	0-1549816	C746	2
POWELL STEPHEN B	1LT	0-1043466	0245	2
PCWELL THOMAS O	LTC	0-0485098	1155	2
POWELL VIRGIL O	CPT	0-0239343	0464	3
POWELL WALTER G	CPT	0-2003797	0667	1
POWELL WALTER H	MAJ	0-1686255	0765	1
POWELL WARREN C	MAJ	0-0270348	C363	3
POWELL WAYNE E	1LT	0-1925357	1053	2
POWELL WILLIAM B	LTC	0-0257287	C547	2
POWELL WILLIAM R	CPT	0-0963865	C761	1
POWELL WILLIAM S	MAJ	0-0389319	C861	1
POWELL WILLIAM T	LTC	0-0320749	0360	1
POWELL WILLIAM W	1LT	C-0444865	C844	2
POWELL WILLIE H	CW3	W-2145487	C659	1
POWELL WILLIS E	1LT	0-1174108	0647	2
POWELL WILLIS G	CPT	0-4006348	1065	1
POWELL WILSCN B	COL	0-0288169	0161	1
POWELL WILSON E	MAJ	C-1290126	0557	1
POWER ALICE F	2LT	N-0789718	0645	1
POWER ERNEST F	LTC	C-1643237	1262	1
POWER ERNEST J	MAJ	0-0476639	C446	1
POWER FRANK W	MAJ	C-0242793	1061	3
POWER CEORGE C	CPT	0-15346C1	0746	2
POWER HENRY F	CW2	W-2110768	0556	1
POWER JACK	MAJ	C-111292C	0464	1
POWER JOHN E	2LT	0-1183162	C844	2
POWER JCHN F	LTC	0-0248791	0461	1
POWER LAURENCE P	LTC	0-1894716	0662	2
POWER THOMAS F	LTC	0-0261700	0265	3
POWERS ALEXANCER	LTC	0-1573519	C251	1
POWERS ARTHUR B	COL	C-0384256	0460	1
POWERS CARLTON J	LTC	0-0234416	C245	2
POWERS CATHERINE	2LT	N-0703756	0942	1
POWERS CHARLES A	MAJ	C-1103867	1163	1
POWERS CHARLES L	2LT	0-1593787	0645	2
POWERS CAVIC B	COL	0-0229803	C863	3
POWERS CONALC M	MAJ	0-0286933	1063	3
POWERS CORIS J	1LT	N-0790353	C946	2
POWERS EDDIE J	CW2	W-2141415	C954	1
POWERS EDGAR N	LTC	0-1041420	0361	1
POWERS EDWARD L	CPT	0-2018567	0758	1
POWERS EUGENE A	1LT	0-1107636	C146	2
POWERS EUGENE E	LTC	0-0452342	C666	1
POWERS FRANCIS I	LTC	C-0322594	C447	2
POWERS FRANK E	MAJ	0-0232036	C954	3
POWERS GEORGE H	LTC	0-0302376	0167	3
POWERS GEORGE H	CPT	0-1055125	0963	2
POWERS HARLCW C	LTC	0-1280355	C761	1
POWERS JAMES G	MAJ	C-0301480	0959	3
POWERS JAMES J	LTC	0-0129924	0145	2
POWERS JAMES P	COL	0-0167517	0355	3
POWERS JAMES W	LTC	0-0415349	1161	1
POWERS JOHN E	COL	0-0261340	1064	3
POWERS JOHN J	LTC	0-0453281	1163	1
POWERS JCHN R	COL	0-0245243	0866	3
POWERS JOHN T H	MAJ	0-0110260	1050	3
POWERS JOSEPH A	CPT	0-1686058	0745	2
POWERS JOSEPH M	1LT	0-1057221	0546	2
POWERS JR JOHN A	LTC	0-1544239	0166	2
POWERS JR RAYMOND F	CW3	W-2206116	0466	1
POWERS JR WILLIAM J	1LT	0-1012137	0547	2
POWERS RALPH M	LTC	0-0331964	0563	1
POWERS RICHARD C	LTC	0-1305306	0765	1
POWERS RICHARC E	CPT	0-1558195	0347	2
POWERS ROBERT H	2LT	0-1182684	1045	2
POWERS ROBERT W	CPT	0-0466510	0245	2
POWERS ROGER F	1LT	0-0414764	0447	1
POWERS RONALC V	MAJ	0-0127451	1155	3
POWERS THOMAS B	1LT	0-0582261	0546	2
POWERS WILLIAM J	LTC	0-1112921	1062	1
POWERS WILLIAM J	LTC	0-1287057	0461	1
POWERS WILLIAM J	CW3	W-2146027	0860	1
POWERS WILLIE G	1LT	0-0169270	1146	1
POWERSCHEALD F	MAJ	0-1703237	0146	1
POWNALL ROGER F	COL	0-0261341	0867	3
POWNALL VIRGIL P	COL	0-0147842	0154	3
POYER JR CHARLES E	MAJ	C-1648991	0361	1
PCYNER THOMAS E	1LT	C-130C527	1043	2
PCYNER VERNON C	WO1	W-2109636	0245	2
POYNTER HAROLD E	MAJ	0-2035436	1062	1
PCYNTER VERNCN L	LTC	0-1030606	0260	1
POYNTER WILLIAM M	CPT	0-1301682	0145	2
POYTHRESS CLYDE L	CW2	W-2150510	0258	1
POZARD WILLIAM M	LTC	0-1000447	1055	1
PRACHER ALTHA M	MAJ	N-0785658	0565	1
PRACHT WILMER A	2LT	0-1059245	0745	2
PRACHYL LEWIS F	MAJ	0-1885813	1266	1
PRADO MIGUEL A	LTC	0-0943010	0864	1
PRAEL ROBERT F	LTC	0-1634236	1266	1
PRAETZ ECWARC F	LTC	0-0158657	0260	3
PRAGER ALEXANCER	COL	0-0308752	0166	3
PRAGER JCSEPH L	1LT	0-1173043	0449	2
PRAIL CHARLES F	CPT	0-1635915	0847	2
PRAISNAR ADAM	CW2	W-2116050	0155	1
PRANGE ERNEST S	MAJ	0-1683464	0960	1
PRANT CHARLES E	CW4	W-2145206	0267	3
PRATER GUY T	LTC	C-1287403	1060	1
PRATER JCHN P	LTC	0-1004216	0163	1
PRATER NEALEY	1LT	0-0176549	0648	3
PRATHER ARDEN	CW2	W-2148912	0763	1
PRATHER CARRCLL W	LTC	0-0222704	0950	3
PRATHER JAMES W	2LT	0-1118566	1145	2
PRATHER JOHN E	WO1	W-2105531	1150	2
PRATHER JOHN W	MAJ	0-098868C	0564	1
PRATHER RICHARD C	MAJ	C-1110731	0258	1
PRATHER THCMAS J	CPT	0-0544744	0647	1
PRATSCHER EDWARD J	CW3	W-214786C	0965	1
PRATT ARTHUR E	MAJ	C-0325574	0965	3
PRATT ARTHUR E	WO1	W-2126744	0545	2
PRATT CHARLES H	COL	C-043916C	1064	1
PRATT CHARLES L	MAJ	0-1923614	0865	1
PRATT CLARENCE C	CPT	0-0342954	1046	2
PRATT CONALD E	COL	0-1305962	0565	3
PRATT ECWARD B	COL	0-017123C	1052	3
PRATT ERNEST A	2LT	0-1286354	0944	2
PRATT EUGENE E	LTC	0-021356C	0552	3
PRATT FRANCIS W	COL	0-0100827	0454	3
PRATT GILBERT S	MAJ	0-018446C	0145	2
PRATT GORDON L	LTC	0-0505938	1062	3
PRATT JAMES H	CW3	W-2144362	0263	2
PRATT JR ALFRED S	MAJ	C-0466957	0245	2
PRATT JR LEMUEL F	COL	0-0352562	0665	1
PRATT LAWRENCE A	LTC	0-034894C	0246	2
PRATT LAWRENCE H	MAJ	0-2288312	1060	1
PRATT LYMAN M	LTC	C-0249728	0365	3
PRATT MARY F	1LT	N-0788298	C945	1
PRATT MERRITT C	LTC	0-0223693	C857	3
PRATT MILTON R	CW3	W-2205271	0364	1
PRATT REMUS S	LTC	C-1589637	0862	1
PRATT ROGER F	CPT	0-1013568	C447	1
PRATT RUPERT J	WO1	W-2007668	C565	3
PRATT SHERMAN W	LTC	0-2006846	1059	1
PRATT SR WILLIAM B	CW4	W-2144504	C462	1
PRATT STUART S	MAJ	0-0260720	0167	3
PRATT STUART W	CPT	0-13C3944	C649	2
PRATT THELMA A	MAJ	N-0752104	1063	1
PRATT WALTER M	LTC	0-0100821	1150	3
PRATT WESLEY F	MAJ	C-1949896	0758	1
PRATT WILLARD M	CPT	0-0128963	1055	3
PRAUGHT JCHN P	1LT	0-05C7210	0850	1
PRAY EUGENE W	1LT	0-2007499	1046	1
PRAZENKA STEPHEN	CPT	0-0958775	0264	1
PREAS HUGH L	LTC	0-0318105	0467	3
PREBLE CLARENCE E	MAJ	C-1177590	C758	1
PREBLE EUGENE W	COL	C-0237315	C665	3
PREBLE FRANK H	MAJ	C-1181735	1262	1
PREBLE ROBERT J	LTC	0-0347316	0864	1
PREBLE THEDCORE L	COL	C-01395C3	1153	3
PREBLE WELCON P	CPT	0-050235C	C251	1
PRECHEL EVERETT A	LTC	C-0254182	C767	3
PRECHTEL EARL O	MAJ	0-2008173	1160	1
PREDGO CHARLES J	CW3	W-2104385	1060	1
PREDMORE ARTHUR L	LTC	0-0347001	0861	3
PREDMORE CLAYTON L	MAJ	C-1039514	0267	1
PREDMORE LESTER C	LTC	0-0202695	C458	3
PREDOVICH MILAN E	CPT	0-0367660	C145	2
PREECE HARRY W	MAJ	C-117411C	0966	3
PREGER DANIEL A	1LT	0-0524356	0346	2
PREGGE CLIFFORD C	CPT	0-1298922	C-48	2
PREHEIM DICK H	WO1	W-2150749	0853	1
PREHLE JOHN	MAJ	C-0977607	0162	1
PREININGER LOUIS J	CPT	0-0496030	1045	1
PREISCH WILLIAM W	COL	0-0149529	0352	3
PREISCHE HENRY F	MAJ	C-1689551	0246	1
PREISS JOSEPH L	MAJ	0-1183947	C664	1
PREJEAN PAUL G	CW2	W-2149492	0461	1
PREM DONALD J	LTC	C-1182495	C467	1
PREMISLER HARRY	CPT	0-1690531	C545	2
PREMO HOWARD L	MAJ	C-2102983	0765	1
PREMPAS THOMAS G	COL	0-0277734	0558	3
PRENDERGAST JOHN F	1LT	0-1535613	1045	2
PRENDERGAST THOMAS A	2LT	0-4051896	0257	2
PRENN JAMES L	LTC	0-0352807	1147	2
PPENTICE ALLEN E	LTC	0-1046926	0365	1
PRENTICE CURTIS C	CPT	0-0976915	C264	2
PRENTICE JAMES M	LTC	0-0328973	C456	3
PRENTICE JOHN C	MAJ	C-1289672	0760	1
PRENTICE MAX G O	MAJ	0-C277758	1160	1
PRENTICE WILLIAM A	MAJ	C-1822054	1062	1
PRENTISS CHARLES H	MAJ	0-0325463	0546	2
PRENTISS HARRY A	MAJ	C-0172061	C653	3
PRENTISS HENRY M	MAJ	0-0209422	0853	3
PRENTISS JAMES A	MAJ	0-0303467	1060	3
PRENTISS NORVAL C	CW3	W-2143423	1160	1
PRENTISS ROBERT F	LTC	0-130205C	C967	1
PRENTISS ROBERT J	CPT	0-0346443	1041	2
PRENTISS STANTON H	LTC	0-0245212	C966	3
PRES WALTER P	CPT	0-1181415	0753	1
PRESBERG MOWEY	LTC	0-0320244	1164	3
PRESCOTT DONALD P	LTC	0-0350576	0466	3
PRESCOTT ELMO	LTC	0-1031912	1054	1
PRESCOTT FRANK L	CPT	0-0331276	0559	3
PRESCOTT GEORGE O	MAJ	0-0953862	1266	1
PRESCOTT HARRY W	LTC	0-0202194	0145	2
PRESCOTT JACK W	1LT	0-1296083	1043	2
PRESCOTT JOSEPH C	CPT	0-1919000	1263	1
PRESCOTT JULIAN P	LTC	C-0289116	1265	3
PRESCOTT KENNETH E	MAJ	0-0488422	0346	2
PRESCOTT LEONA B	MAJ	M-0000438	1262	1
PRESCOTT LUCAS M	LTC	0-0314011	0163	1
PRESCOTT MANFRED U	B G	0-0224176	1059	3
PRESCCTT REX K	2LT	0-1177941	1044	2
PRESCCTT RICHARD O	COL	0-0155888	0648	3
PRESCCTT THOMAS M	CPT	0-0409418	1045	2
PRESENT JULIAN O	CPT	0-0321285	0446	2
PRESLEY JAMES H	1LT	0-0401705	0444	2
PRESLEY JONES B	CW2	W-2205541	0262	1
PRESLEY ROBERT K	CPT	C-1167166	0561	1
PRESLEY THEODORE F	LTC	0-0348296	0354	1
PRESLEY VERDIE B	MAJ	0-1C5292C	0958	1
PRESNELL FRED P	CPT	0-0989015	0763	1
PRESNELL ROBERT R	COL	0-0107557	0454	3
PRESS CEORGE L	MAJ	0-0971184	1060	1
PRESS JOHN J	CW2	W-2149453	1057	1
PRESSER MEYER I	LTC	0-4003826	0856	2
PRESSEY HERBERT E	LTC	0-0328972	1156	3
PRESSLER JOHN I	MAJ	0-1109599	0447	2
PRESSLY JR CHARLES P	1LT	0-1542683	0246	2
PRESSMAN CLARENCE S	MAJ	0-0487853	0557	1
PRESSMAN ROBERT S	MAJ	C-0411540	0646	2
PRESSON JAMES H	CW4	W-2005158	0167	3
PRESSCN WILLIAM	1LT	0-116520C	0544	2
PRESTEL STANLEY V	CPT	0-047745C	0645	2
PRESTHCLT BENJAMIN H	LTC	0-0257917	0267	3
PRESTIEGE T J	CW2	W-2146138	1155	1
PRESTIN FRED J	1LT	C-1634238	0345	2
PRESTCN ARTHUR M	CPT	0-010C189	0152	3
PRESTON CHARLES M	1LT	0-1289135	0561	2
PRESTCN CLAUCE R	CPT	0-0921081	1152	1
PRESTON CLAY	MAJ	0-0279966	0653	3
PRESTON EDWIN P	COL	0-0468935	1062	3
PRESTON HAROLD D	CPT	0-0302601	1148	1
PRESTON HARRY H	MAJ	C-1054368	1060	1
PRESTON HENRY C	WO1	W-2147772	0755	1
PRESTON JACK I	MAJ	0-2017752	0765	1
PRESTON JAMES L	CW2	W-2148981	0757	1
PRESTON JAMES W	CW4	W-2146085	0767	1
PRESTON JESSE D	MAJ	C-0291973	0761	1
PRESTCN JOHN C	LTC	0-159252C	0262	1
PRESTCN JOHN W	CW2	W-214799C	0654	1
PRESTON JON F	CW2	W-2148549	0160	2
PRESTCN JR ALBERT G	MAJ	0-0333846	1047	2
PRESTON JR RCBERT B	1LT	0-1113896	0251	2
PRESTCN JR SAMUEL P	CPT	0-1165144	0945	2
PRESTCN LEONARD T	LTC	0-0251694	0963	3
PRESTCN LILLIAN T	1LT	N-0702958	0644	1
PRESTCN LLCYD R	MAJ	0-0196195	0562	3
PRESTON MALCCLM H	2LT	0-1173748	1043	2
PRESTON THOMAS R	LTC	0-0492105	0847	2
PRESTCN WALTER M	MAJ	0-040327C	0763	1
PRESTCN WILLIAM C	2LT	0-0296783	0564	3
PRESTCN WILLIAM G	CPT	0-1948034	C751	1
PRESTRIDGE ARTHUR	1LT	0-1633460	0545	2
PRESTRIDGE GEORGE N	LTC	0-1293471	1163	1
PRESTRUD CARL G	CPT	0-0173033	0648	3
PRESTWOOC GLADYS E	MAJ	N-0726184	0765	1
PRESTWOOD JR JAMES G	CPT	0-0352166	0446	2
PREUETT FRED O	MAJ	C-1293472	0461	1
PREUSKER WERNER C	LTC	0-1107642	0564	1
PREVATT ERNEST G	MAJ	0-2020761	0961	1
PREVATTE CHARLES C	CW3	W-2204995	1164	1
PREVICS MARTIN	LTC	0-0370946	0761	1
PREVILLE MARTIN R	MAJ	C-1638300	1066	2
PREVOST ALBERT F	MAJ	C-0959666	0263	1
PREVOST JOHN R	CW3	W-2144395	0663	1
PREVOST THURMAN E	1LT	0-1551931	1160	2
PREWETT JOHNNIE J	1LT	0-0415255	0843	2
PREWITT AUBREY R	MAJ	0-1317940	0159	1
PREWITT LOUIS L	MAJ	0-0502016	0461	1
PREWITT MALCCLM L	LTC	0-0272832	0367	3
PRIBYL JEROME W	2LT	0-1112382	0545	2
PRICE ALBERT A	LTC	0-0492787	1162	1
PRICE ALBERT E	1LT	0-0547691	1045	2
PRICE AMIT J	MAJ	0-2014675	1164	1

ARMY OF THE UNITED STATES RETIRED LIST

NAME	GRADE	SVC NO	DATE RET MO YR	RET CODE
PRICE ANDREW F	LTC	0-0218892	1144	2
PRICE ARCHIE A	MAJ	0-0207076	0853	3
PRICE ARCHIE N	CPT	0-0367454	0946	2
PRICE BLAIR W	MAJ	0-2262325	0765	1
PRICE BLISS A	LTC	0-1305640	0765	1
PRICE CALVIN W	MAJ	0-2016108	0660	1
PRICE CARLTON B	LTC	0-1319773	1061	1
PRICE CHARLES F	MAJ	0-0981040	0167	1
PRICE CHARLES W	LTC	0-0184453	0457	3
PRICE DANA H	CW2	W-2142985	0753	1
PRICE DONALD A	LTC	0-1635220	1162	2
PRICE DONALD L	MAJ	0-1648096	0557	1
PRICE EARL R	LTC	0-0297768	1046	2
PRICE EDWARD W	CPT	0-0109808	0244	1
PRICE ELBERT C	LTC	0-0176539	0656	3
PRICE ELLIS R	2LT	0-0947361	0251	1
PRICE ELMER C	MAJ	0-0510902	0153	1
PRICE ERNEST T	MAJ	0-1107055	1263	1
PRICE EVA N	MAJ	N-0754475	0665	1
PRICE FREDERICK	MAJ	0-1822823	0261	1
PRICE GEORGE P	LTC	0-0380798	0562	1
PRICE HAROLD C	COL	0-0314972	1166	1
PRICE HARRY	LTC	0-0182062	0862	3
PRICE HOLLIS A	MAJ	0-2026292	1165	1
PRICE HOMER I	MAJ	0-1285300	0759	1
PRICE HOWARD E	COL	0-0329365	0363	1
PRICE HOWARD P	CPT	0-0885722	0764	1
PRICE HOWARD T	1LT	0-0885642	1047	1
PRICE HUBERT O	MAJ	0-0245186	1149	3
PRICE IRNEY M	WO1	W-2123801	0547	2
PRICE JACK J	LTC	0-1176469	0466	1
PRICE JAMES I	CW3	W-2208491	0267	1
PRICE JAMES R	1LT	0-1314188	0547	2
PRICE JAMES T	MAJ	0-1053306	0364	1
PRICE JIMMIE R	CW2	W-2207717	0365	1
PRICE JOE P	COL	0-0236100	0965	3
PRICE JOHN C	CW2	W-2148907	1060	1
PRICE JOHN H	MAJ	0-0521640	1154	1
PRICE JOHN M	2LT	0-1644681	0944	2
PRICE JOHNNY C	LTC	0-2029844	0567	2
PRICE JR CHARLES L	1LT	0-0423070	0646	2
PRICE JR EDWARD F	COL	0-1588236	1264	1
PRICE JR ENOCH R	MAJ	0-0966340	1165	2
PRICE JR FRANCIS F	MAJ	0-0461039	0264	1
PRICE JR FRANK C	MAJ	0-2266283	0866	1
PRICE JR JOHN E	MAJ	0-0537444	0765	1
PRICE JR JOHN L	2LT	0-1951119	0947	2
PRICE JR THOMAS A	LTC	0-1042140	1262	1
PRICE JR WILLIAM S	CPT	0-1030510	0655	2
PRICE JULIAN R	COL	0-1573522	0261	1
PRICE KERMIT O	1LT	0-0889273	1057	1
PRICE KERMIT F	CW3	W-2143669	0961	1
PRICE LEE F	CW3	W-2205297	0767	1
PRICE LESLIE F	CPT	0-0401019	0346	2
PRICE LLOYD G	CPT	0-1013727	0748	2
PRICE LOTI W	CPT	0-1577709	0549	1
PRICE LOUIS	MAJ	0-0298551	0145	1
PRICE LOYD A	1LT	0-1167167	0145	1
PRICE MILTON I	CPT	0-1689693	0546	2
PRICE MILTON L	1LT	0-1046231	0545	2
PRICE MITCHELL R	1LT	0-1310151	1046	2
PRICE MOSES C	MAJ	0-0976152	0861	1
PRICE OSCAR O	LTC	0-0294911	1065	3
PRICE RALPH A	LTC	0-0297876	1163	3
PRICE RALPH C	COL	0-0270719	1266	3
PRICE RALPH L	CW2	W-2106650	0746	1
PRICE RAYMOND J	MAJ	0-0322825	0862	3
PRICE REYNOLD E	MAJ	0-1686755	0564	1
PRICE RICHARD M	LTC	0-0244219	0665	3
PRICE ROBERT J	LTC	0-0213544	0245	2
PRICE ROBERT K	MAJ	0-1554612	0163	1
PRICE ROBERT L	CW3	W-2104390	1059	1
PRICE ROBERT M	LTC	0-0185118	0958	3
PRICE ROBERT Y	MAJ	0-1648057	0160	1
PRICE RUPERT A	CPT	0-0976525	0960	1

NAME	GRADE	SVC NO	DATE RET MO YR	RET CODE
PRICE RUSSELL S	LTC	0-0246578	0857	2
PRICE SAMUEL H	MAJ	0-1686632	0762	1
PRICE SAMUEL J	COL	0-0145202	0353	3
PRICE SR PAUL T	2LT	0-2006230	1045	2
PRICE THEODORE R	1LT	0-0538382	0446	1
PRICE THOMAS	MAJ	0-1874878	0365	1
PRICE THOMAS A	LTC	0-0224586	1055	3
PRICE THOMAS M	MAJ	0-0320102	0153	2
PRICE VAL	LTC	0-0195648	0162	3
PRICE VAUGHN A	LTC	0-0176912	0260	3
PRICE VERNON C	CPT	0-0186034	0446	1
PRICE WALTER O	CW4	W-2128803	0856	1
PRICE WILBUR M	1LT	0-1325669	0646	1
PRICE WILLIAM A	CPT	0-2039152	0657	1
PRICE WILLIAM E	CW3	W-2143342	0665	1
PRICE WILLIAM G	CW4	W-2147422	0364	1
PRICE WILLIAM H	MAJ	0-1288118	1266	1
PRICE WILLIAM R	CPT	0-1284394	0359	1
PRICE WILLIAM T	MAJ	0-0137474	1151	1
PRICER JOHN C	MAJ	0-1822454	0758	1
PRICHARD ELBERT M	COL	0-0183990	0258	3
PRICHARD GEORGE W	LTC	0-0166914	0354	3
PRICHARD LESLIE A	COL	0-0246085	1161	3
PRICHARD MASON C	COL	0-0246804	0559	3
PRICHARD STANLEY N	LTC	0-1015320	1066	1
PRICHARD VERNON R	CPT	0-2212031	0960	1
PRICHARD WALDEMAR L	MAJ	0-0413167	0546	1
PRICKETT HENRY G	LTC	0-0196016	0650	3
PRIDDY CECIL T	LTC	0-0343680	0761	1
PRIDDY NEWTON O	LTC	0-0353921	0465	3
PRIDE ARCHIE C	CW3	W-2006728	0767	3
PRIDE HAROLD E	COL	0-0121493	0554	3
PRIDE RICHARD	MAJ	0-1061823	0561	1
PRIDE ROBERT S	LTC	0-0261451	0567	3
PRIDEAUX GEORGE E	1LT	0-2035371	0745	2
PRIDEMORE WILLIAM H	1LT	0-1573932	1051	2
PRIDGEN ROBERT H	2LT	0-1913881	0930	1
PRIDMORE GEORGE M	LTC	0-0354031	0561	1
PRIEBE ARTHUR H	CPT	0-0241810	1062	3
PRIEBE AUDREY W	LTC	0-1596190	0863	1
PRIEBE EGON A	1LT	0-1312591	1145	2
PRIEBE RUBY M	MAJ	N-0741810	0247	1
PRIEN CARROLL G	LTC	0-1798701	0358	1
PRIESS HAROLD E	LTC	0-0250427	1064	3
PRIESS JR CONRAD E	CPT	0-0394182	0544	2
PRIEST ARCHIE W	COL	0-0102803	0648	3
PRIEST CLARENCE L	LTC	0-0285917	1058	3
PRIEST CLIFTON W	1LT	0-1050427	0845	2
PRIEST NORMAN F	LTC	0-1031834	0164	1
PRIEST ROY R	MAJ	0-0181718	0455	3
PRIEST WILLIAM L	LTC	0-1305395	1163	1
PRIESTER PETER J	CW4	W-2001864	0354	3
PRIGAL ROBERT	WO1	W-2134238	1045	2
PRIGG LEIGH R	1LT	0-1302517	0945	2
PRIGGE HENRY T	MAJ	0-1641701	0158	2
PRILLER JAMES H	LTC	0-0925554	0765	3
PRIMAKOW MAX J	COL	0-0307493	1166	3
PRIME JESSE M	MAJ	0-0109948	1137	1
PRIME LOUIS J	LTC	0-0256030	0760	3
PRIME NICHOLAS P	COL	0-0313877	0657	1
PRIMEAUX ALEXANDER	MAJ	0-0968073	0561	1
PRIMER BENJAMIN M	COL	0-0368715	0460	3
PRIMER MABEL C	CPT	N-0700788	1146	2
PRIMM BENY J	1LT	0-2202681	0953	2
PRIMM CHARLES T	LTC	0-1644683	0762	1
PRIMM HUGH R	LTC	0-1031969	0564	1
PRIMM JOHN L	MAJ	0-0308581	1045	2
PRIMPAS CONSTANTIN	MAJ	0-0297463	1043	2
PRIMROSE FRANK	2LT	0-1872581	0453	2
PRIMROSE JAMES W	CPT	0-0219864	0955	3
PRIMROSE JOHN W	LTC	0-0246524	0346	1
PRINCE CHARLES C	LTC	0-0552228	0766	3
PRINCE DWIGHT E	LTC	0-1293312	0567	1
PRINCE EDWARD F	LTC	0-1323476	0661	2
PRINCE EUGENE	COL	0-0135384	0253	3

NAME	GRADE	SVC NO	DATE RET MO YR	RET CODE
PRINCE FORREST	CW2	W-2103330	0960	1
PRINCE FRANK C	LTC	0-0131364	0352	1
PRINCE HAROLD R	LTC	0-1703067	0962	1
PRINCE JAMES C	MAJ	0-1635518	0260	1
PRINCE JULIUS E	CW4	W-2109972	0863	1
PRINCE RAYMOND O	LTC	0-0386267	1060	1
PRINCE ROBERT C	LTC	0-0400547	0762	1
PRINCE WILLIAM	CW2	W-2152398	0862	1
PRINCE WILLIAM G	LTC	0-0281124	0867	3
PRINDEVILLE CHARLES	LTC	0-0168059	0157	3
PRINDLE ROBERT C	LTC	0-0339162	1166	1
PRINE GLYNN L	LTC	0-0358794	0562	1
PRINE WEBSTER C	1LT	0-0507989	1148	1
PRING NORVAL L	LTC	0-1173749	1060	1
PRINGLE JAMES L	MAJ	0-1049619	1059	2
PRINS JOHN M	MAJ	0-0163690	1061	3
PRINTUP ROY S	MAJ	0-0291617	0653	2
PRIOR IRVIE L	CW3	W-2136725	1162	1
PRIOR RAYMOND W	LTC	0-0346531	0655	1
PRIOR WILLIAM E	CW4	W-2146297	0265	2
PRISET GEORGE F	CW3	W-2148982	0566	1
PRISMON DONALD R	2LT	0-1295429	1143	1
PRITCHARD ARCHIE A	MAJ	0-1821909	0161	1
PRITCHARD CHARLES K	LTC	0-1582773	1066	1
PRITCHARD CHARLES N	1LT	0-1104348	0344	2
PRITCHARD EZRA L	CW3	W-2143636	1060	1
PRITCHARD FRANK R	LTC	0-0282598	0459	1
PRITCHARD FRANK S	COL	0-0139855	0659	3
PRITCHARD GEORGE P	LTC	0-0254314	0865	3
PRITCHARD GEORGE R	COL	0-0296032	0647	2
PRITCHARD GROVER E	2LT	0-1115987	0345	2
PRITCHARD HOWARD C	CW3	W-2003908	0667	1
PRITCHARD JACOB L	COL	0-0104146	0547	2
PRITCHARD JOHN M	2LT	0-0456203	0145	2
PRITCHARD ROWLAND	MAJ	0-0282600	0946	2
PRITCHARD THOMAS F	MAJ	0-1799659	0861	1
PRITCHETT BRUMLEY O	COL	0-0272215	0867	3
PRITCHETT CHARLES M	CPT	0-1596555	1052	1
PRITCHETT CLARK P	MAJ	0-0319001	0945	2
PRITCHETT DEAN	1LT	0-1048935	0856	1
PRITCHETT IRENE M	1LT	N-0728295	0945	1
PRITCHETT JAMES W	CW3	W-2152049	0563	1
PRITCHETT T H	LTC	0-2049687	1162	1
PRITIKIN ROLAND I	COL	0-0278803	0266	3
PRIVETT JOE H	1LT	0-0527853	0845	2
PRIVETTE WILLIAM P	COL	0-0264574	0367	3
PRIZZIA KATHARINE	2LT	N-0757241	0245	1
PROBASCO CYRIL F	MAJ	0-0990953	0366	1
PROBASCO JR MORGAN C	MAJ	0-1645297	0660	1
PROBECK ROBERT V	1LT	0-0486939	1045	2
PROBERT ALICE O	MAJ	N-0771374	0366	3
PROBES DONALD J	LTC	0-0294745	0658	1
PROBST ARNOLD M	COL	0-0131365	0648	3
PROBST JR WILLIAM	MAJ	0-0982947	0364	1
PROBST RUDOLPH O	COL	0-0163266	1149	3
PROCH RICHARD S	2LT	0-1294192	1144	2
PROCHASKA RALPH E	LTC	0-0328201	0563	1
PROCHAZKA JOSEPH	1LT	0-1303184	1144	2
PROCHKA JOHN S	1LT	0-1103369	0845	1
PROCISSI FREDERIC P	MAJ	0-1307998	0364	1
PROCK HARRY F	MAJ	0-2029826	0859	2
PROCTER CLAUDE M	LTC	0-0300705	0446	2
PROCTER JR HARRY L	CPT	0-0401500	0145	1
PROCTOR CARL E	CPT	0-1169694	0146	2
PROCTOR CARLTON S	COL	0-0173630	1043	2
PROCTOR EMMETT F	MAJ	0-1117711	1165	1
PROCTOR HARRY W	LTC	0-0379640	1166	3
PROCTOR JAMES H	LTC	0-0539945	0564	1
PROCTOR JOE K	LTC	0-1309605	0261	1
PROCTOR JOHN G	1LT	0-0499522	0661	1
PROCTOR ROBERT L	CW4	W-2003992	0765	1
PROCTOR ROBERT M	CPT	0-0278244	0846	1
PROCTOR ROLAND G	1LT	0-0291737	0645	2
PROCTOR SAMUEL E	LTC	0-0202435	0863	3
PROCTOR STEPHEN M	LTC	0-0481233	0555	2

NAME	GRADE	SVC NO	DATE RET MO YR	RET CODE
PROCTOR WALTER J	CW2	RW-2150221	0263	1
PROCTOR WARREN S	CPT	0-1102914	0755	2
PROCTOR WILLIAM A	1LT	0-2008544	0648	2
PROEHL WILLIAM H	LTC	0-1102915	0559	2
PROESCHEL ROBERT L	CW2	W-2129295	0949	2
PROETTO JOHN	WO1	W-2123426	1044	2
PROFFER CLEVEL C	CW3	W-2147362	0465	1
PROFFER ESTES E	LTC	0-0360087	0761	1
PROFFITT JOHN M	CW3	W-2146873	1263	1
PROFFITT JOSIAH C	COL	0-0295725	0861	3
PROFFITT SAMUEL L	MAJ	0-0885425	0347	1
PROFFITT SCOTT	MAJ	0-1306642	1156	1
PROFFITT WOODROW W	CW2	W-2148584	0859	1
PROHASKA ROBERT A	LTC	0-1105121	0561	1
PROKOP ALEXANDER	MAJ	0-0535555	0467	1
PROKOP VENNA V	MAJ	0-1303945	0158	1
PROMIN JOHN	CPT	0-0234964	0447	1
PRONCAVAGE WILLIAM F	MAJ	0-1181087	0863	1
PRONOZINSKI AARON G	LTC	0-0362079	0162	1
PROPER FRANCIS J	CPT	0-1294237	0658	2
PROPER THEODORE R	LTC	0-0491841	0646	2
PROPES WELDON D	LTC	0-0456102	0961	1
PROPST CLIFFORD H	MAJ	0-1310637	0561	1
PROPSTER HOWARD A	LTC	0-1291878	0961	1
PROSCENO HARRY A	CPT	0-0326665	0446	2
PROSE BOBBY B	CW3	W-2144423	1065	1
PROSERPI RAYMOND H	MAJ	0-1061221	0364	1
PROSKE DOROTHY L	2LT	N-0700690	0141	1
PROSNAK JOHN P	MAJ	0-1845090	0461	1
PROSNIT DANIEL R	1LT	0-1544548	0445	2
PROSS DALE E	CW2	W-2110775	1159	2
PROSSER BIRNEY E	MAJ	0-0408934	1060	1
PROSSER CORTLAND R	CPT	0-1650701	0959	1
PROSSER EVAN W	MAJ	0-1877869	0665	1
PROSSER HOLLIS P	CW2	W-2211132	0865	1
PROSSER LEWIS R	2LT	0-1587551	1045	2
PROTAS STANLEY J	1LT	0-1002504	0945	2
PROTEAU ROSE M	1LT	N-0720835	0946	1
PROTENIC JOSEPH A	CW4	W-2109090	0657	1
PROTHERO WALTER K	MAJ	0-1320859	1061	1
PROTHEROE LORANA R	2LT	L-0100333	0247	2
PROTHEROE MAURICE R	LTC	0-0224930	0165	3
PROTHRO RUFUS C	LTC	0-0451042	0156	1
PROUDE JAMES J A	COL	0-0264337	0655	2
PROULX ENNIS A	LTC	0-1102435	0162	1
PROULX THOMAS E	MAJ	0-1685514	0561	1
PROVAN RICHARD O	CPT	0-1294013	1146	2
PROVOST LOUIE	LTC	0-0946462	0667	1
PROVOST MURREL G	MAJ	0-0322538	1061	3
PROVOST RAYMOND J	LTC	0-1584761	1160	1
PROVOST ROLAND E	2LT	0-1334345	0146	2
PROVOW CHARLES O	MAJ	0-1291327	0862	1
PRUCE I JAMES	LTC	0-1636505	0865	1
PRUCNAL PETER G	MAJ	0-1011658	0954	1
PRUDDEN MORTON R	2LT	0-1557660	1144	2
PRUDEN JOSEPH O	MAJ	0-0527442	0665	1
PRUDEN KNOX P	COL	0-0273918	0950	1
PRUDHOMME LENANCE J	LTC	0-0289293	1060	1
PRUEGERT JOSEPH	CPT	0-0139856	0649	3
PRUEITT FELIX N	MAJ	0-0509636	1157	1
PRUEITT RAYMOND V	MAJ	0-0296433	0157	1
PRUET HENRY W	CW2	W-2205193	0262	1
PRUETT ALLEN K	MAJ	0-0575962	0660	1
PRUETT CARL A	CPT	0-2262984	0764	1
PRUETT ELDON A	LTC	0-0237901	1163	3
PRUETT FLOYD W	MAJ	0-1166357	1046	1
PRUETTE JAMES	2LT	0-2026334	1059	2
PRUITT GORDON A	CW4	W-2113623	0456	1
PRUITT JAMES D	MAJ	0-0231597	0665	3
PRUITT OSBIE T	CPT	0-1342115	1060	1
PRUITT ROBERT E	2LT	0-1290127	0644	2
PRUITT THOMAS W	1LT	0-0447926	0846	2
PRUITT VAN F	CPT	0-0135542	0949	3
PRUITT VESTER L	CW2	W-2148330	1055	1
PRUITT WILLIAM R	LTC	0-0249068	0367	3

NAME	GRADE	SVC NO	DATE RET MO YR	RET CODE
PRUNER CLINTON E	CPT	C-0279534	1044	2
PRUNER HAROLD M	1LT	0-1633463	0345	2
PRUNTY PAUL P	LTC	C-1822186	1161	1
PRUSIK CHARLES C	MAJ	C-0973153	1160	1
PRUSINOWSKI S J	2LT	0-1301875	C545	2
PRYCE LESLIE P	MAJ	C-1308375	C464	1
PRYDE THOMAS	LTC	0-0272499	1263	3
PRYOR PERNARD B	MAJ	C-1342347	C563	1
PRYOR HAROLC R	MAJ	C-1298756	1060	1
PRYOR III FRANCIS J	MAJ	C-0513055	C564	3
PRYOR JOHN R	LTC	C-0167494	C152	1
PRYOR JR WILLIAM I	1LT	0-0212577	0363	3
PRYOR MARY S	CPT	L-0502413	C455	2
PRYOR WILLIAM L	MAJ	C-1293474	C261	1
PRYPLESH STEPHEN	MAJ	0-1950241	C764	1
PSAKI CONSTANTIN	MAJ	C-0265888	0550	3
PSCHORR WILLIAM J	LTC	0-0276288	1057	3
PSILEKAS VASSIL L	MAJ	0-1117713	0765	1
PSURNY EDWARD S	LTC	0-1183949	1061	1
PSZEKAZA JOHN J	MAJ	C-2C147C0	0864	1
PTASZEK JOHN F	MAJ	C-1328930	1059	1
PUCHBAUER JOHN H	LTC	0-C335041	0351	1
PUCHER MIKE A	CPT	0-0484491	0256	1
PUCK EMERSON E	CW3	W-2147537	0564	1
PUCKETT ANDERSON H	MAJ	0-2096816	0165	2
PUCKETT JAMES A	LTC	C-0241895	1065	3
PUCKETT JAMES O	CPT	0-1576525	C255	2
PUCKETT JR THOMAS T	CW3	W-2148049	C963	1
PUCKETT JUDSON	MAJ	C-0959289	1061	1
PUCKETT LAWRENCE C	CW2	W-2116348	0146	2
PUCKETT LAWRENCE K	MAJ	C-1924654	C464	1
PUCKETT MERTON T	CW3	W-2203482	0765	1
PUCKETT ORVILLE	2LT	0-1288121	C657	1
PUCKETT SAMUEL R	WO1	W-2120046	0251	1
PUCKETT WILFRED R	MAJ	0-1650294	1063	2
PUDDY MARY M	2LT	N-0701662	1044	1
PUDIL HOWARD M	CW2	W-2142986	1054	1
PUDLINER WILLIAM G	1LT	0-1298757	1154	1
RUERNER LEO W	CPT	C-027958C	0958	3
PUETT JOSEPH F	COL	0-0288767	0559	1
PUFFER FRANCES B	1LT	N-0751441	104N	1
PUFFER NORMAN M	CW3	W-2147980	1264	1
PUGATCH MAX M	1LT	0-1578992	0346	1
PUGENS ERWIN R	CPT	0-1559841	0565	1
PUGH ALFRED E	CPT	0-0254316	0663	3
PUGH EDWARC E	2LT	0-1302152	0944	2
PUGH IRVING E	MAJ	C-0166598	C446	2
PUGH JOHN F	MAJ	C-0507748	0158	2
PUGH JR PETER J	CW3	W-2153335	C864	1
PUGH LAURENCE J	LTC	0-0329195	0547	2
PUGH LUSTER T	CW2	W-2147773	1060	1
PUGH MARY M	LTC	L-0909017	1162	1
PUGH THOMAS	LTC	0-1533655	C661	1
PUGH THOMAS F	MAJ	0-1696199	0646	1
PUGH WALTER S	COL	0-0209559	0556	3
PUGH WILLIAM C	COL	0-0911595	C564	1
PUGH WILLIAM V	CW3	W-2151128	1262	1
PUGIL WALTER F	CW3	W-2146392	0161	1
PUGLIA FRANK A	MAJ	C-0310859	C159	1
PUGLIESE JOHN	LTC	0-1643985	0862	1
PUGLIESE MARY J	CPT	N-0724169	1146	2
PUGZLES ANTHONY D	2LT	0-1287758	C844	1
PUIG JR PALCEMERO	CPT	0-0215501	1060	3
PUJOLS JAIME	1LT	0-0155889	1053	3
PUKL STEPHEN A	MAJ	0-0969642	0361	1
PULAKIS STRATO J	1LT	0-1300851	0746	2
PULASKI RAY C	LTC	0-1041004	1061	1
PULCIPHER KEELER D	COL	0-0121596	1056	3
PULHAM CHARLES T	COL	0-0102224	1054	3
PULLEN LARRY B	MAJ	C-1946135	1265	3
PULLEN MACK J	CW2	W-2149937	116C	2
PULLEN MARVIN C	CW3	W-2141420	1065	1
PULLEN ROYAL R	MAJ	0-0147551	0648	3
PULLEY BENJAMIN J	LTC	0-1299470	0261	1
PULLEY BOYD H	CPT	0-0305162	C945	2
PULLEY ECWIN E	CPT	0-4005843	0766	1
PULLEY JR LUBY C	MAJ	0-1170928	1059	1
PULLIAM HARVEY L V	1LT	0-1045293	0844	2
PULLIAM THOMAS P	LTC	0-1586051	0562	1
PULLIN WILLIAM M	LTC	0-1686761	1067	1
PULLINEN DIVA E	MAJ	0-1293644	1060	1
PULLIUM RAY C	CW4	W-2143607	0864	1
PULLIUM VENISCN G	LTC	0-0287198	0861	1
PULLMAN GEORGE J	CPT	0-1575085	0954	1
PULLUM WILLIAM C	LTC	0-2055C52	0566	1
PULLY ASHTCN H	COL	C-0327943	0461	1
PULLYBLANK WILLARD R	LTC	0-1576527	1066	3
PULMAN PETER B	LTC	0-022729C	0359	3
PULTZ RCBERT J	LTC	0-0494667	0963	1
PULVER MILTON B	LTC	0-0244405	C962	1
PUMP FREDDIE E	1LT	0-1013345	0345	2
PUMPHREY FREC H	LTC	0-0141492	0758	3
PUMPHREY JR ECWARD A	CPT	C-0377052	0144	2
PUMPHREY LEON P	CW3	W-2144301	0261	1
PUMPHREY LCIRA C	LTC	0-0253914	0162	3
PUMPHREY DTHC S	LTC	0-0297182	0262	1
PUNCH FRANK C	CW4	W-2006939	0667	3
PUNCOCHAR LEE B	2LT	0-1320558	C944	2
PUNLA BONIFACIO	1LT	0-1896448	1154	1
PUNLA MACARIC	1LT	0-1896776	1154	1
PUNTENNEY IRVING	CPT	0-0400081	1043	1
PURCELL BURGC	LTC	0-0114491	0648	3
PURCELL FRANCIS J	MAJ	C-0243992	1263	3
PURCELL FRANCIS R	COL	C-1324115	1265	1
PURCELL GEORGE W	MAJ	0-1923C29	C964	1
PURCELL ISMAEL A	CPT	0-0209892	0859	3
PURCELL JAMES B	1LT	0-1288947	0145	2
PURCELL JOHN J	COL	0-0308693	1067	3
PURCELL JR ARTHUR L	LTC	0-0364867	0760	1
PURCELL PHILIP J	MAJ	0-0239656	0361	3
PURCELL WILLIAM E	CW4	W-2152583	0161	1
PURCHASE RALPH K	1LT	0-0408987	1144	2
PURDIE KENNETH S	COL	0-0234586	0152	3
PURDON ROBERT L	CW3	W-2207598	0666	1
PURDUE CRREN L	COL	0-0255242	0663	3
PURDY ECWARD	COL	0-0221572	C859	1
PURDY ERNEST V	CPT	0-0412266	C845	2
RURDY JR TILDEN J	MAJ	C-1312795	0258	1
PURDY JULIAN M	CW4	W-2104398	0261	1
PURDY RALPH A	LTC	0-0530590	1063	1
PURFIELD EMMETT J	COL	0-C203083	0358	3
PURINGTCN GEORGE I	LTC	0-130CC81	0457	1
PURINGTON WILLIAM H	CW2	W-2110519	0853	1
PURINTCN JR JOHN A	MAJ	C-0443093	0346	2
PURINTCN ROSS F	LTC	0-0410895	0163	1
PURKHISER CHARLES W	1LT	0-1286181	1153	2
PURKHISER WILLIAM H	LTC	0-1647351	1067	1
PURLEE MENLO M	COL	0-0372205	0660	1
PURMAN RONALC R	CW3	W-2144073	0763	1
PURNELL FRANK J	CW2	W-2100026	0161	1
PURNELL LILLIE G	2LT	N-0745292	0945	2
PURNELL WILLIAM C	M G	0-0183312	1063	3
PURNHAGEN JR JOHN F	2LT	0-1301037	0444	2
PURPURA ANTHONY J	LTC	0-0237703	0663	1
PURRINGTON ALFRED L	COL	0-025331C	0562	3
PURSGLOVE PHILIP E	CPT	0-1294362	0860	1
PURSLEY JOHN O	MAJ	0-1576528	0462	1
PURSLEY JOSEPH R	MAJ	C-0322824	0745	2
PURSLEY LUTHER M	MAJ	0-1593198	0954	1
PURTELL WILLIAM E	1LT	0-055365C	0746	2
PURVES JAMES H	CPT	0-1293475	0257	1
PURVIANCE ROBERT E	CW3	W-2136744	0963	1
PURVIN LLOYD Z	LTC	0-1548289	0961	2
PURVINE HAROLD O	1LT	0-2000163	0453	1
RURVINE PAUL L	LTC	0-0291228	0558	1
PURVIS BURNETT A	CW3	W-2143429	0962	1
PURVIS DARVIN D	CPT	0-1998482	1155	1
PURVIS GEORGE B	CPT	0-0971825	C161	1
PURVIS JAMES C	MAJ	C-1549030	0257	1
PURVIS JOHN E	1LT	0-1315861	0645	2
PURVIS MILTON O	LTC	C-0338504	C964	3
PURVIS OTIS	COL	C-0211397	C251	1
PURVIS SIMON M	MAJ	C-0990340	0163	1
PURVIS TARANTULA	MAJ	C-0956451	0661	1
PURVIS WALTER M	LTC	0-0425341	0245	2
PUSATERI ANTHONY J	CW4	W-2129858	1060	1
PUSEL HENRY G	1LT	0-0508168	C653	1
PUSEY OSCAR L	1LT	0-2033854	C154	2
PUSEY RUSSELL A	CW4	W-2122141	C853	1
PUSITZ MANUEL E	MAJ	C-0487521	0146	2
PUSKAR JOHN	MAJ	0-2055829	1057	1
PUSKARICH JOHN	CPT	0-1549031	1044	1
PUSKARICH JOSEPH M	CW2	W-2214350	C566	1
PUSZYNSKI JOSEPH M	LTC	C-0288335	C363	1
PUTEGNAT GEORGE W	MAJ	0-0343380	C467	3
PUTIGNANO SAM	MAJ	0-1015452	0164	1
PUTMAN CLINT H	LTC	0-0452935	0657	1
PUTMAN FREDERICK	LTC	0-0365395	C261	1
PUTMAN JAMES H	MAJ	C-0312005	0246	2
PUTMAN RICHARC G	MAJ	C-0451168	C257	1
PUTMAN ROBERT L	COL	0-0284945	0758	3
PUTMAN ROSS D	1LT	0-1017634	0346	2
PUTNAM DARRELL J	MAJ	0-2016432	0563	1
PUTNAM EDWIN A	1LT	0-1045854	0845	2
PUTNAM FRANK L	COL	0-0178330	0755	3
PUTNAM GEORGE F	CW3	W-2143973	0563	1
PUTNAM MILES A	LTC	0-0253688	C557	3
PUTNAM PAUL M	LTC	0-0260456	1266	3
PUTNAM RUFUS W	COL	0-0900404	0651	3
PUTNAM THOMAS R	COL	0-0228257	1063	3
PUTNAN DOUGLAS G	LTC	0-0451415	C657	1
PUTNEY CHARLES A	MAJ	C-0949231	0262	1
PUTRYAE ECWARD J	LTC	0-0487624	0266	3
PUTT ALLEN A	COL	0-0139845	1157	3
PUTTERMAN SAMUEL	2LT	0-1014868	0844	2
PUTZ ARTHUR E	LTC	0-0257849	0261	1
PUTZIER RAYMOND E	MAJ	C-2036881	0962	1
PUYLARA JOHN A	CPT	0-0963856	0262	1
PYDESKI LEONARD B	LTC	0-0454096	0966	1
PYFRIN SHERMAN A	LTC	0-0210750	0658	3
PYLAND JOE M	CW3	W-2144196	0659	1
PYLAND VAN W	COL	0-0236089	0957	3
PYLE BELTON	CW2	W-2141421	0359	1
PYLE BEN E	CW2	W-2208775	C860	1
PYLE CLYDE B	LTC	0-0217136	C648	3
PYLE DONALD F	WO1	W-2209474	1058	1
PYLE EDWIN R	1LT	0-2049361	C246	2
PYLE GEORGE S	MAJ	0-0263092	1143	2
PYLE JR REA M	LTC	0-1325515	C765	1
PYLE NORMAN J	LTC	C-0143418	C145	2
PYLE ROBERT L	MAJ	C-1549032	1060	1
PYLE THEODORE H	LTC	0-0173397	C861	3
PYLE WILLIAM A	COL	0-0247500	0659	3
PYLE WILLIAM K	MAJ	0-2002520	0363	1
PYLES RAY S	CPT	0-0358168	0646	2
PYLYPETZ CATHERINE	MAJ	N-0721455	C864	1
PYNOUS MILTON H	CW2	W-2118904	C545	2
PYNE FREDERICK	LTC	0-0257045	1062	3
PYNE JAMES F	CW3	W-2145147	0162	2
PYNE WILLIAM E	CPT	0-1287237	0845	2
PYNN THOMAS E	LTC	0-0347530	0966	3
PYSIENSKI JOHN W	LTC	0-0450652	1163	1
PYTEL ALEK G	MAJ	C-1692975	C562	1
PYTLAK EDWARD E	LTC	0-0204650	C755	3
PYZIK STANLEY W	COL	0-0346382	0867	3
QUAAS MARION J	LTC	0-1166587	1055	1
QUACKENBOSS JOHN W	LTC	0-1542183	0267	3
QUACKENBUSH FRANK A	COL	0-0305180	1056	3
QUACKENBUSH ROGER W	LTC	0-2034573	C562	1
QUACKENBUSH RUSSELL	LTC	C-0269106	0461	1
QUAID WILLIAM H	LTC	0-0436872	0264	3
QUAINTANCE RICHARC E	LTC	0-0139055	C157	3
QUALLINS GEORGE A	MAJ	C-0276758	0161	3
QUALLS EVERETTE H	B G	0-0216229	0963	3
QUALLS GUY L	1LT	0-0415871	0646	1
QUALLS OPAL B	CW3	W-2151022	0666	1
QUALLS ROY J	CPT	0-0270334	C947	1
QUAMMEN CLARENCE	2LT	0-1686291	1166	3
QUAN THOMAS J	COL	0-0322885	1160	3
QUANTZ HERMAN C	MAJ	0-0368651	0643	2
QUANTZ WILLIAM	CPT	0-0191963	1039	1
QUARLES GEORGE P	LTC	0-0240984	0844	2
QUARLES JAMES T	MAJ	0-0153190	0648	3
QUARLES JR HUGH L	LTC	0-0918770	1066	3
QUARLES ROBERT W	MAJ	0-0382813	0856	1
QUARRY JOHN H	MAJ	0-0977324	1266	1
QUARTERMAN JR C H	CPT	0-0316268	1044	2
QUARTERMAN LEE S	MAJ	0-0340631	0661	1
QUATSOE ROSS J	LTC	0-0219106	0758	3
QUATTLEBAUM M G	LTC	0-1283836	1160	1
QUATTLEBAUM MANNING	MAJ	C-1047744	1161	1
QUEBBEMAN FORREST K	MAJ	0-164530C	0361	1
QUEBEDEAU ELIE P	MAJ	0-1544C79	0559	1
QUEEN CLARCN	CW4	W-2123193	0956	1
QUEEN CANIEL	CPT	0-0571793	0860	1
QUEEN DONALD R	MAJ	0-1047745	0158	1
QUEEN EDWARD O	COL	C-C166CC2	1153	3
QUEEN JAMES C	MAJ	0-1340929	0561	2
QUEEN RICHARD K	2LT	0-1017733	0644	2
QUEEN RICHARC R	1LT	0-0177817	0952	3
QUEISSER 3RD R L	1LT	0-0526958	1046	2
QUEL OTTO J	CPT	0-164810C	0657	1
QUENELLE OWEN G	CPT	0-0249181	0361	3
QUENTIN WILLIAM J	MAJ	0-0172611	0649	3
QUERRY CHARLES O	LTC	0-0318192	0767	3
QUERY ALDRICH	LTC	0-0213183	0862	3
QUESADA ANTONIO	MAJ	0-0443967	1160	1
QUESACA EUGENE	2LT	0-2264472	1147	1
QUESENBERRY GUY E	CPT	0-1937725	0165	1
QUESINBERRY POSEY B	LTC	0-0498125	C263	3
QUIAMBAC CORDULO P	1LT	0-1896747	0163	1
QUIAT GERALD M	1LT	0-0553278	1045	1
QUICK CLYDE K	CW2	W-2142189	1057	1
QUICK GERALD	1LT	0-0445525	0254	2
QUICK GUY H	LTC	0-1557770	0763	1
QUICK HOWARD C	CPT	0-0244318	0358	3
QUICK KARL E	MAJ	0-1334019	0864	1
QUICK LEROY	1LT	0-0501065	1146	1
QUICK MADELEINE	MAJ	L-1000103	0363	1
QUICK RILEY R	2LT	0-2054004	0645	2
QUICK ROY T	COL	0-0121165	0648	3
QUICK WALTER J	CW3	RW-2148081	0961	1
QUICK WAYNE E	MAJ	0-0421399	0464	1
QUIGEL ECWARD M	CW3	W-2143042	0462	1
QUIGG NORMAN L	CW4	W-2102239	0355	1
QUIGGIN RAYMOND H	CPT	0-1577716	0446	2
QUIGLEY CAVID W	2LT	0-1175548	0344	2
QUIGLEY FRANCIS C	LTC	0-1046615	C267	1
QUIGLEY HARVEY E	1LT	0-1297093	0645	2
QUIGLEY HARVEY P	CW4	W-2115358	1055	1
QUIGLEY JAMES F	MAJ	0-0976602	1164	1
QUIGLEY JAMES L	COL	0-0926042	0666	3
QUIGLEY JOHN A	LTC	0-1010985	0563	1
QUIGLEY Q A	COL	C-0181510	1052	3
QUIGLEY THOMAS A	MAJ	0-1577717	0262	1
QUIJANCE URBANO	CPT	0-1896485	1058	1
QUILICI LEO J	CW2	W-22C5100	0562	1
QUILLEN CLYDE H	COL	0-0311913	0957	1
QUILLEN EUGENE K	MAJ	0-1293645	0164	1
QUILLEN JOSEPH E	CPT	0-0376414	0248	2
QUILLEN MARVIN L	2LT	0-1031358	C445	2
QUILLIN EUGENE F	1LT	0-0161481	0155	3
QUILLIN FRANK V	LTC	0-0396882	0557	2
QUILLIN WALTER F	CPT	0-1165324	0548	2
QUILLINAN MAURICE W	CW3	W-2143112	0661	1
QUILTY LAWRENCE A	2LT	0-2006571	0246	2
QUILTY RALPH G	LTC	0-0286315	0661	3
QUIMBY CALVIN A	CPT	0-0269044	C756	3
QUIMBY RALPH W	LTC	0-0320613	0162	3
QUIMBY ROBERT C	LTC	0-0451169	0954	1

NAME	GRADE	SVC NO	DATE RET MO YR	RET CODE
QUINBY WILLIAM R	CW2	W-2142563	0761	1
QUINBY WILLIAM W	LTC	0-0407150	0862	1
QUINBY UPSHUR B	MAJ	0-1333872	0463	1
QUINET RAMON I	LTC	0-0299623	0960	3
QUINLAN JAMES P	CW4	W-2151796	1160	1
QUINLAN JOHN F	MAJ	0-0487366	0445	2
QUINLAN JOSEPH A	LTC	0-1590741	0962	1
QUINLIVAN ROBERT J	1LT	0-1010038	1044	2
QUINLIVAN WILLIAM O	CPT	0-1014306	0657	1
QUINN ARTHUR J	CPT	0-0493208	0446	1
QUINN ARVIL B	LTC	0-1016561	0963	1
QUINN CHARLES A	CPT	C-2042829	1162	2
QUINN CHARLES E	MAJ	0-1919205	0365	1
QUINN CLEMENT P	LTC	0-0139882	0954	3
QUINN DAVID E	COL	0-0272464	C561	3
QUINN DONALD T	1LT	0-1057570	0346	2
QUINN EDWARD	CW2	W-2145253	0960	1
QUINN EDWARD J	CW3	W-2205808	0365	1
QUINN FRANCIS J	CPT	0-1598990	0763	1
QUINN FRANCIS P	CPT	0-2014914	1263	1
QUINN FRANCIS S	MAJ	0-0377856	0961	1
QUINN FRANCIS W	LTC	0-1012317	0263	1
QUINN FRANK J	LTC	0-1290305	1062	1
QUINN FRANKLIN C	MAJ	D-0257303	0146	2
QUINN GUS G	CPT	0-0240202	1043	2
QUINN HAROLD P	CW3	W-2205398	0265	1
QUINN JAMES E	CW4	W-2145834	0865	1
QUINN JAMES K	MAJ	0-0963256	0865	1
QUINN JAMES N	COL	0-0114620	0745	2
QUINN JAY W	1LT	0-0460050	0247	2
QUINN JOHN E	COL	0-0235067	0765	3
QUINN JOHN F	CPT	0-1541505	C446	2
QUINN JOHN F	LTC	0-1949440	1167	1
QUINN JOHN R	CPT	0-1294014	0851	2
QUINN JOHN R	MAJ	C-0127369	C149	3
QUINN JOHN T	COL	0-0272170	0847	2
QUINN JOHN W	2LT	0-2023926	1045	2
QUINN JR AUGUSTINE	1LT	0-0439235	1043	2
QUINN JR EDWARD E	1LT	0-1546486	0545	2
QUINN JR FRANCES S	1LT	0-1175549	0246	2
QUINN JR LEONARD T	1LT	0-0985767	0757	2
QUINN JR RICHARD F	CW2	W-2214749	0767	1
QUINN MAURICE F	CPT	0-1797524	0446	2
QUINN ROBERT J	2LT	0-0440489	C445	2
QUINN THOMAS J	COL	0-0163890	1056	3
QUINN TIMOTHY P	CPT	0-1321949	0146	2
QUINN WILLIAM E	LTC	0-0108639	1147	1
QUINNETT JAMES G	MAJ	0-2263326	0967	1
QUINNEY AUSTIN F	MAJ	0-1325140	C264	1
QUINONES PEDRO J	CW3	W-2144980	0960	1
QUINSEY CARL L	MAJ	0-1919014	0865	1
QUINT HERBERT S	LTC	0-1035576	0361	1
QUINT JR ROY T	LTC	0-0340504	0762	1
QUINTANA PEDRO	LTC	0-0108225	0947	1
QUINTANA ROBERT	CW4	W-2004154	C767	1
QUINTAS JOSEPH C	MAJ	0-1948655	C464	1
QUINTO EMILIO F	MAJ	0-0888442	0558	1
QUINTON CARROLL D	MAJ	0-0421472	0957	1
QUINTON HOWARD E	CW2	W-2210489	0164	1
QUINTON JR MILTON T	LTC	0-1326662	C264	1
QUIRK EMMETT G	LTC	0-0394611	0760	1
QUIRK FRANCIS W	LTC	0-1310761	0662	1
QUIRK JOHN E	LTC	0-1695704	0761	1
QUIRK THOMAS C	2LT	0-0460451	0245	2
QUIRK WILLIAM J	LTC	0-1545262	0364	1
QUIROS EVAN B	LTC	0-0421393	0747	1
QUISENBERRY CURTIS O	MAJ	0-1542931	0363	1
QUIST ARVID F	CW3	W-2120897	C461	1
QUIST JASON N	MAJ	0-0368437	C547	1
QUIST LLOYD E	CW3	W-2109916	0856	1
QUIST NORMAN N	COL	0-0321226	0262	1
QUITTNER JOSEPH	LTC	0-0135386	0648	3
RA ZOR SR JAY F	LTC	0-1295317	0461	1
RAAB JR CARL H	MAJ	0-1685560	1264	1
RAAB MELVIN H	MAJ	0-1597896	0661	1

NAME	GRADE	SVC NO	DATE RET MO YR	RET CODE
RAAB RUSSEL R	LTC	0-0259861	0867	3
RAABE DONALD F	LTC	0-1000173	0756	1
RAABE DONALD M	2LT	0-2000813	0945	2
RAABE ERNEST W	LTC	0-0318172	0561	3
RAABE ORVAL J	MAJ	0-0280540	0347	1
RAABE WALLACE M	CW2	W-2210683	0965	1
RAABERG LEO C	CPT	0-0219230	0256	3
RAACK PAUL A	CPT	0-1104350	0253	1
RAASCH FRANK O	COL	0-0212985	0459	3
RAASCH URBAN C	CPT	0-1001443	0157	1
RABB EVERETT E	CW2	W-2115948	0466	1
RABB WILLIAM E	COL	0-0172393	0253	3
RABBITT FRANCES C	MAJ	N-0737263	1164	1
RABBITT ROBERT S	CW4	W-2141657	0862	1
RABBITT VERNON W	CW3	W-2146120	1263	1
RABBOTT DONALD F	LTC	0-1639522	0667	1
RABE LUCIO R	MAJ	0-1306752	0662	1
RABE ROBERT F	MAJ	0-2210060	0864	1
RABEDEAU MELBOURNE	LTC	0-0243354	0760	3
RABELL FORREST J	LTC	0-1329746	0165	1
RABER EDWARD B	CW4	W-2145490	0559	1
RABER HOWARD C	LTC	0-1552152	1166	1
RABIDEAU RAYMOND J	2LT	0-2048452	0345	2
RABINAK PETER P	1LT	0-1049621	1150	1
RABINER NATHAN M	1LT	0-0511998	1145	2
RABINOWITZ DAVID L	CPT	0-0470476	1046	1
RABINOWITZ HERMAN	COL	0-0253312	0262	3
RABOGLIATTI ALFRED J	MAJ	0-1110751	1063	2
RABOLD LEONARD J	MAJ	0-0419799	0646	2
RABON WILLIAM O	LTC	0-1548533	0960	1
RABUANC JOSEPH W	CW3	W-2144958	1065	1
RABUCHA WILLIAM M	CPT	0-2046791	0647	2
RABUN JOSEPH B	CPT	0-2262276	0456	1
RABURN MARY T	MAJ	N-0735615	0664	1
RACE GEORGE W	COL	0-0229168	C565	3
RACEK JOHN E	LTC	0-0366274	1060	1
RACEK WILLIAM O	MAJ	0-1334020	0766	1
RACH JR AUGUST J	LTC	0-1799368	0165	1
RACHAL JR WILLIE	CPT	0-1576533	0950	1
RACHEFF THEODORE N	LTC	0-0322323	0562	3
RACHEK JOHN W	LTC	0-1589452	1160	1
RACHEK WILLIAM O	LTC	0-0547742	0720	1
RACHELS COCK K	MAJ	0-1301878	1060	1
RACHELS JR THOMAS B	MAJ	0-0959656	0966	1
RACHKO JR JOHN	CW4	W-2101043	0357	1
RACHLIN IRVING	CPT	0-0344352	1145	2
RACHMEL LEO	LTC	0-1580193	1061	1
RACHUI WILLIAM T	MAJ	0-0974141	0866	1
RACICOT NAPOLEON A	COL	0-0169276	0559	3
RACICOT PHILEAS A	MAJ	0-0129417	0648	3
RACICOT ROBERT P	CW4	W-2110512	0958	1
RACINE NORMAN O	MAJ	C-2019785	0565	2
RACKLEY ANNETTE S	2LT	N-0764543	0547	1
RACKLEY PEYTON L	LTC	0-0414705	0562	1
RACKOW ELBERT J	CW3	W-2148660	0966	1
RACY FLOYD O	MAJ	0-1640838	1157	1
RACZKIEWICZ JOHN W	CPT	0-1050432	0847	2
RACZYNSKI JOHN F	CPT	0-1895894	0757	1
RACZYNSKI JOSEPH L	LTC	0-1313548	1265	1
RADAKOVICH NICHOLA	1LT	0-1329048	1047	1
RADCLIFFE CLIFFORD B	LTC	0-1292586	0561	1
RADCLIFFE DONALD E	1LT	0-0490511	1045	2
RADCLIFFE HAROLD L	2LT	0-0333829	0366	3
RADCLIFFE HERBERT E	COL	0-0230345	0663	3
RADCLIFFE MERBERT W	COL	0-0272478	1165	2
RADCLIFFE WILLIAM O	LTC	0-0257398	0767	3
RADDATZ NORMAN G	CW3	W-2126867	1060	1
RADDIN JESSE T	WOL	W-2144705	0860	1
RADDIN REGINALD F	COL	0-0276790	1058	3
RADDING IRVING H	CW3	W-2150715	0764	1
RADE JR JOSEPH J	1LT	0-1171320	0546	2
RADECKI JOSEPH A	CPT	0-0345721	0246	2
RADEK JOE F	LTC	0-0308719	1060	1
RADEMAKER CHARLES C	MAJ	0-1340493	0562	1
RADER COLUMBUS H	CPT	0-1640839	0656	1

NAME	GRADE	SVC NO	DATE RET MO YR	RET CODE
RADER JOSEPH A	1LT	0-0468838	1045	2
RADER JR LAURENCE G	LTC	0-1797877	1060	1
RADER MARK E	CW2	W-2210149	0663	1
RADEZ ERNEST	1LT	0-1591382	1145	2
RADFORD DUANE E	MAJ	C-1059041	0260	1
RADFORD EDGAR D	CPT	0-0510715	1050	1
RADFORD HAROLD G	LTC	0-1648654	0563	1
RADICK WILLIAM J	CPT	0-2042954	0746	2
RADIGAN JOHN T	LTC	0-0299798	0562	1
RADIKE MELVIN N	LTC	0-1108253	1262	1
RADKE WALTER L	LTC	0-0901115	C861	3
RADL ROBERT B	COL	0-0197958	C761	3
RADLAUER EDWARD	2LT	0-1946137	1144	2
RADLEY JR J M	1LT	0-1897798	1051	2
RADLEY PETE	1LT	0-1324787	C546	1
RADLOFF LAWRENCE J	LTC	0-0290910	1055	3
RADNEY WALTER S	MAJ	0-1329879	1063	1
RADNOR JESS C	COL	0-0303215	C264	3
RADO IRVING M	CPT	0-1060259	0561	2
RADOSZEWSKI B H	MAJ	C-1289622	0261	1
RADOW SAMMY E	LTC	0-0888438	1163	1
RADSCH REX W	COL	C-C251592	0761	1
RADTKE ALBERT H	MAJ	C-1877071	0666	1
RADTKE LAURENCE H	LTC	0-0559331	C759	1
RADTKE MERTON P	2LT	0-0543946	1144	2
RADTKE ROBERT E	CW3	W-2150959	1062	1
RADTKE WILLIAM D	MAJ	0-1699953	C163	1
RADULESCU GEORGE	1LT	0-0536C87	0747	1
RADZYMINSKI S F	LTC	0-0308768	0161	3
RAE DUDLEY O	LTC	0-0366573	C364	1
RAE JOHN T	MAJ	0-1284935	0947	2
RAEL SOL	1LT	0-1016926	114N	1
RAEZER LESTER N	MAJ	0-2046336	0364	1
RAFF JOSEPH S	COL	0-0310359	0462	3
RAFFA DOMENICK R	MAJ	0-1100291	0355	2
RAFFA LEO L	CPT	0-1284936	0547	2
RAFFENBEUL OTTO H	2LT	0-2006547	1045	2
RAFFENSBERGER E E	LTC	N-0700030	0246	1
RAFFENSPERGER HAROLD	LTC	0-0337917	0160	2
RAFFERTY DAVID H	MAJ	0-1017752	1262	1
RAFFERTY GEORGE W	COL	C-0542652	0364	1
RAFFERTY GLENN A	COL	0-0271906	0360	2
RAFFERTY JOHN C	1LT	0-0407841	0547	2
RAFFERTY JOHN J	MAJ	0-2023983	C161	1
RAFFERTY LOUIS L	LTC	0-0443006	0348	1
RAFFIELD ZENUS W	MAJ	0-1105127	0956	1
RAFTER EDWIN J	COL	0-0238993	C357	3
RAFTER PHILIP C	CPT	C-0298117	C966	3
RAFTER WILLIAM E	MAJ	0-0474842	0563	1
RAFTERY BERNARD G	LTC	0-1185783	1265	1
RAFTERY WILLIAM C	COL	0-0924046	1059	3
RAFY JAMES	MAJ	0-1798295	0560	1
RAGAN REX	LTC	0-0207223	0955	3
RAGAN ROBERT E	LTC	0-0332666	1054	1
RAGAN TILLMAN A	LTC	0-0300811	1063	3
RAGER RALPH E	MAJ	0-2020762	1063	1
RAGLAND ELBERT M	CW3	W-2142554	0164	1
RAGLAND JAMES C	MAJ	0-0345566	0557	1
RAGLAND JOHN J	MAJ	C-2000748	0463	1
RAGLAND MAURICE A	LTC	0-0964569	1067	1
RAGON FRANKLIN L	MAJ	0-1324870	C660	1
RAGSDALE BILLY E	MAJ	0-1042922	0263	1
RAGSDALE CHARLTON L	LTC	0-0232347	0347	2
RAGSDALE JOHN W	MAJ	C-0475319	1046	1
RAGSDALE JR JAMES W	CW4	W-2150661	1058	1
RAGSDALE ROBERT E	LTC	0-1580195	C960	1
RAGSDALE ROBERT G	LTC	0-0414152	1058	2
RAGUCKAS JR JOSEPH	1LT	0-1307166	1045	2
RAGULA JULYAN	CW3	W-2152980	1163	1
RAGUSA VINCENT J	MAJ	0-1556340	1059	1
RAGUSIN GEORGE A	LTC	0-0890116	0363	1
RAGUSKY FRANK	CW2	W-2118222	0257	1
RAHAIM MAZICK	LTC	0-1297094	0165	1
RAHAL DEROUN E	LTC	0-1288441	0165	1
RAHE JOSEPH Y	MAJ	0-0377446	0648	1

NAME	GRADE	SVC NO	DATE RET MO YR	RET CODE
RAHILLY FRANCIS H	LTC	0-1825055	1064	1
RAHLMANN DONALD F	2LT	0-0556948	0546	2
RAHM LAMBERT R	CPT	0-0504152	0445	2
RAHN JR CHARLES W	CW2	W-2210231	0465	1
RAHN LAWRENCE J	1LT	0-1881384	C556	2
RAHN LEON F	1LT	0-0438316	0744	1
RAHTE WALTER E	CPT	0-0372015	0959	2
RAIDER JACK H	MAJ	0-0313181	1045	2
RAIDER JOSEPH	LTC	0-0348105	0446	2
RAIGOZA JUAN	LTC	0-1059599	0761	1
RAILEY HILTON H	COL	0-0127454	0855	3
RAIN CHARLES R	COL	0-0255263	0859	1
RAINBOLT JR HENRY E	MAJ	0-1175836	0662	1
RAINBOLT NAPOLEON	COL	0-0153224	0950	1
RAINER LELAND L	1LT	0-1325321	0745	2
RAINES FRANK	CPT	0-0282294	0447	1
RAINES JAMES M	1LT	0-1103872	0146	2
RAINES JR WILLIAM P	LTC	0-1043759	1061	1
RAINES RAY T	LTC	0-0274679	1044	2
RAINES RAYMOND W	LTC	0-1011276	0866	1
RAINES ROBERT M	LTC	0-2038084	0865	1
RAINEY DAVID E	MAJ	0-0238291	0763	3
RAINEY DONALD	LTC	0-1289139	0165	1
RAINEY FRANCIS F	MAJ	0-1283837	0358	1
RAINEY HARRY T	1LT	0-1288791	0945	2
RAINEY HERBERT W	LTC	0-0535876	0764	1
RAINEY JR JAMES	1LT	0-1103873	0544	2
RAINEY LLOYD J	MAJ	0-0454116	0256	1
RAINEY MARION W	LTC	0-1545225	0967	1
RAINEY RAYMOND E	1LT	0-1298924	1045	2
RAINEY SAMUEL L	MAJ	0-2015594	0764	1
RAINEY WILLIAM	CW3	W-2151353	0263	1
RAINFORD CLIFFORD J	LTC	0-1311050	0162	1
RAINS ARTHUR O	LTC	0-0211114	0350	1
RAINS FLOYD A	COL	0-0440157	0446	1
RAINS FLOYD C	MAJ	0-0276890	0655	3
RAINS MYRTLE L	2LT	N-0700253	0836	1
RAINWATER CHARLES O	MAJ	0-1824364	0765	1
RAINWATER HAROLD G	CPT	0-0415896	1044	2
RAINWATER HOWARD L	MAJ	0-2206223	0866	1
RAINWATER LESTER F	CPT	0-1307572	0446	2
RAINWATER PAUL	MAJ	0-2033213	0362	2
RAINY CURTIS W	MAJ	0-0975817	0253	1
RAITCH SR THEODORE R	2LT	0-1996720	1052	1
RAITHEL ERNEST J	LTC	0-2006129	0263	1
RAJALA OLIVER M	LTC	0-0889598	1265	1
RAJCHEL THADDEUS P	MAJ	0-1330591	0565	1
RAJOTTE EDWIN J	MAJ	0-1998116	0261	1
RAJSKI ROMAN L	MAJ	0-1686311	0363	2
RAKOWSKI ANTHONY W	CPT	0-0962186	1160	2
RALEIGH JOHN M	COL	C-0383797	0764	1
RALEIGH WALTER O	CPT	0-0425946	104N	2
RALEY ROBERT L	LTC	0-1327282	0166	1
RALLS EUGENE O	1LT	0-1574507	0849	1
RALPH CARL C	CPT	0-0979362	1160	1
RALPH CLIFFORD W	MAJ	0-0358859	0464	1
RALPH JOHN S	LTC	0-1321061	0462	1
RALPH JR GEORGE F	CW2	W-2152057	0761	1
RALSTON EUGENE J	MAJ	0-0483201	0461	1
RALSTON JAMES G	LTC	0-0261748	0963	3
RALSTON JR FRANK G	CPT	0-0540876	0647	2
RALSTON JR THOMAS A	CW3	W-2151529	0766	1
RALSTON LLEWELLYN	LTC	0-0290099	0167	3
RALSTON RAY R	MAJ	0-0101223	1C56	3
RALSTON ROBERT C	CPT	0-0445131	0247	1
RALSTON WAYNE M	COL	0-0131445	C254	3
RALSTON WILLIAM A	CW2	W-2149152	1058	1
RALSTON WILLIAM C	LTC	0-0145253	0346	2
RAMAGE DANIEL O	CW3	W-2153267	0666	1
RAMAGE JR THOMAS W H	CW3	W-2149279	0162	1
RAMAGLIA ALFRED A	2LT	0-0885794	0444	2
RAMAGLIA JOSEPH	LTC	0-0482637	0163	2
RAMAY JAMES H	MAJ	0-1549037	0562	1
RAMRICUR ROBERT	MAJ	0-2016049	1264	1
RANBIN AGNES I	CPT	N-0737785	0855	2

NAME	GRADE	SVC NO	DATE RET MO YR	RET CODE
RAMBO CARLTON W	CW2	W-2208986	0862	1
RAMBO CHARLES R	LTC	0-1295769	0265	1
RAMBO DAVID A	LTC	0-0197507	0961	3
RAMBO LOUIS B	CPT	0-1061520	0747	1
RAMEE ROBERT E	CPT	0-1311329	1046	1
RAMEY JACK A	CPT	0-0972838	0561	1
RAMEY MEDFORD G	COL	0-0162866	0961	3
RAMEY SAMUEL M	CPT	0-1327462	1064	1
RAMEY VERNON F	CW4	W-2144363	1262	1
RAMICK GEORGE A	CW3	W-2150045	0163	2
RAMIL AMBROSIO	1LT	0-1896805	0657	1
RAMIRES CARLOS L	LTC	0-0337668	1066	3
RAMIREZ AGUSTIN A	LTC	0-0373943	1160	1
RAMIREZ ALBERTO	LTC	0-0362566	0248	2
RAMIREZ JOSE A	2LT	0-1319126	0545	2
RAMIREZ JOSEPH	LTC	0-0440035	1062	1
RAMIREZ LUIS R	LTC	0-1542607	0365	1
RAMIREZ PEDRO C	2LT	0-1896920	0348	1
RAMIREZ RAFAEL G	MAJ	0-1289365	0363	1
RAMIREZ RAMIRO R	LTC	0-1280753	0257	1
RAMIREZ VICTOR M	LTC	0-0369724	1160	1
RAMIREZ-ACEVEDO R H	MAJ	0-1339916	0965	1
RAMME PETER F	MAJ	0-0392694	0361	1
RAMNES OSCAR A	COL	0-0355065	0760	1
RAMO ARTHUR	1LT	0-1000846	0444	1
RAMON ADOLPH L	COL	0-0263857	0648	1
RAMONT GUSTAVE O	MAJ	0-0289125	0559	2
RAMOS EDILBERTO	CPT	0-1896288	0948	2
RAMOS EMILIO	CPT	0-1896436	0259	1
RAMOS FLORO R	MAJ	0-0888107	0962	1
RAMOS JOHN A	1LT	0-0890502	0750	1
RAMOS JOSE J	CW2	W-2214798	1167	1
RAMOS MAXIMIANO	1LT	0-1896764	0450	1
RAMOS PEDRO R	MAJ	0-1170150	0353	1
RAMOS ROBERT B	MAJ	0-0981423	1167	1
RAMOS SEGUNDO	1LT	0-0217526	0637	1
RAMOS-RODRIGUEZ CARL	MAJ	0-1329158	0763	1
RAMP JACK G	LTC	0-1286182	0262	1
RAMPTON WALTER E	MAJ	0-0778557	0565	1
RAMPULLA BENNIE	CPT	0-0410138	1143	2
RAMSAY ELLIOT	LTC	0-0192531	1159	3
RAMSAY GEORGE W	CPT	0-0980253	0561	2
RAMSAY JAMES M	CPT	0-0498457	0655	1
RAMSAY JAMES M	MAJ	0-1599061	0163	1
RAMSAY JOHN A	2LT	0-1048150	1043	1
RAMSAY JR MALCOLM	LTC	0-0452405	0363	1
RAMSAY ROBERT M	1LT	0-0472990	0246	1
RAMSAY SR GEORGE E	MAJ	0-1593793	0559	1
RAMSAY WALTER D	LTC	0-0506189	1060	1
RAMSAY WALTER G	COL	0-0319378	1262	3
RAMSDAN JR ROBERT H	CW2	W-2146393	0666	3
RAMSDELL EUGENE E	LTC	0-1578997	1058	1
RAMSDELL JACK A	2LT	0-0444735	0344	2
RAMSDEN JOHN C	COL	0-0299766	0167	3
RAMSDEN JOHN T	LTC	0-0396665	0157	1
RAMSEL CURTIS O	LTC	0-0465528	0962	1
RAMSEUR ARTHUR R	1LT	0-0270854	0345	2
RAMSEY CARL D	LTC	0-0885750	0556	1
RAMSEY CHARLES E	MAJ	0-1031208	0761	1
RAMSEY CHARLIE	CW4	RW-2119839	0762	1
RAMSEY CLYDE R	MAJ	0-0197008	1056	3
RAMSEY EARLE G	1LT	0-1103874	0446	1
RAMSEY EDWARD A	MAJ	0-0139440	1052	3
RAMSEY EDWARD W	MAJ	0-0349608	0246	2
RAMSEY FELIX	MAJ	0-0285016	0361	3
RAMSEY FRANK B	COL	0-0278183	0862	3
RAMSEY HAROLD L	MAJ	0-1304442	1158	1
RAMSEY HARVEY E	CPT	0-1176771	1055	2
RAMSEY HENRY H	CPT	0-0153125	0754	3
RAMSEY IRA C	CPT	0-0495405	0550	1
RAMSEY JACKIE B	CPT	0-1939372	0360	2
RAMSEY JAMES D	CPT	0-0301047	0746	2
RAMSEY JAMES O	CPT	0-1105128	0446	2
RAMSEY JOHN W	MAJ	0-1688456	1265	1
RAMSEY JOSEPH L	CPT	0-0450158	0545	1

NAME	GRADE	SVC NO	DATE RET MO YR	RET CODE
RAMSEY JR JAMES G	CW2	W-2151816	0760	1
RAMSEY KIRWIN R W	CPT	0-0199215	0351	3
RAMSEY LAWRENCE F	CW4	W-2120714	1165	1
RAMSEY RALPH J	MAJ	0-0231834	0646	2
RAMSEY RICHARD E	MAJ	0-0234582	1160	3
RAMSEY ROBERT A	CPT	0-0281805	1162	1
RAMSEY ROBERT E	LTC	0-0377304	0858	1
RAMSEY ROSS G	MAJ	0-0323400	0161	1
RAMSEY RUSSELL A	M G	0-0215598	0664	3
RAMSEY THEODORE V	LTC	0-0322833	0560	1
RAMSEY WILLIAM	MAJ	0-1950839	0564	1
RAMSEY WILLIAM H	CW3	W-2115783	0159	1
RAMSEY WILLIAM L	LTC	0-1586057	1162	1
RAMSEY WILLIAM T	CW2	W-2104404	1057	1
RAMSEY 3RD FRANCIS W	1LT	0-1647663	1145	2
RAMSLAND MAXWELL O	CPT	0-1107646	0248	2
RANAGER GAINES A	LTC	0-0360100	1262	3
RANCK WILLIAM A	COL	0-0179924	0452	3
RAND DEWEY	MAJ	0-0298648	0758	3
RAND GEORGE L	COL	0-0311927	1266	3
RAND JR HENRY O	1LT	0-1316087	1045	2
RAND JR WILLIAM T	1LT	0-2210059	0651	1
RAND PAUL	CPT	0-1726077	0247	2
RAND WARREN R	1LT	0-1231661	0452	1
RANDA SHERMAN O	LTC	0-1037247	0467	1
RANDACK MARGUERITE	MAJ	L-0705070	0667	1
RANDAL ZACK	MAJ	0-1922582	0865	1
RANDALL BEURELL V	CW2	W-2147193	0457	1
RANDALL CALVIN R	MAJ	0-2035971	0358	1
RANDALL CLARENCE K	CPT	0-0301518	0357	1
RANDALL CLYDE L	LTC	0-0220299	0358	3
RANDALL EDWIN H	CPT	0-1080742	0147	1
RANDALL FLETCHER S	CPT	0-0488714	0250	1
RANDALL GERALD C	LTC	0-1551498	1161	1
RANDALL GLEN L	LTC	0-1821910	0461	1
RANDALL GUY N	WO1	W-2104405	1055	1
RANDALL JIM F	CPT	0-0484382	1050	1
RANDALL JOHN E	LTC	0-0323135	1262	3
RANDALL JOHN J	LTC	0-0285887	0964	3
RANDALL JR CARL O	LTC	0-0388478	1146	2
RANDALL LAWRENCE E	LTC	0-1297589	1161	1
RANDALL MORTON H	MAJ	0-0481052	0346	2
RANDALL OSCAR	COL	0-0273022	1156	3
RANDALL PHILIP M	MAJ	0-0186771	0352	3
RANDALL RICHARD E	LTC	0-0422062	0960	1
RANDALL RUSSELL B	CPT	0-1100292	0354	1
RANDALL WILLIAM F	CPT	0-0204520	1044	2
RANDAZZISE ANTHONY	CPT	0-1312044	0446	2
RANDAZZO JOSEPH S	MAJ	0-1081303	0958	1
RANDEL CHARLES A	MAJ	0-0229641	0264	3
RANDELL ROLLAND P	LTC	0-1534119	0665	1
RANDELL RUSSELL R	LTC	0-0321940	0755	2
RANDER JOSEPH G	CW4	W-2117257	1154	1
RANDLE TOM	2LT	0-0179690	1150	3
RANDLES JOHN M	MAJ	0-0400400	0657	2
RANDOLPH BENJAMIN	WO1	W-2129817	0344	2
RANDOLPH DURWARD W	LTC	0-1305310	0364	1
RANDOLPH FREDERICK	MAJ	0-0271167	0667	3
RANDOLPH JAMES M	CW2	W-2114361	0659	1
RANDOLPH JAMES P	2LT	0-1306753	0544	2
RANDOLPH PHILIP S P	1LT	0-1030706	0645	1
RANDOLPH ROBERT A	MAJ	0-0236306	1162	3
RANDOLPH ROBERT F	LTC	0-1052924	0862	1
RANDOLPH SAMUEL O	LTC	0-1104352	1060	1
RANDOLPH WILLIAM J	CPT	0-0373882	1045	2
RANDOW JR THOMAS E	LTC	0-1004666	0763	1
RANER NORMAN G	2LT	0-2055880	0346	2
RANEY AIDAN A	MAJ	0-0331615	0646	2
RANEY ARTHUR	LTC	0-0315705	0754	1
RANEY BATES C	LTC	0-0195429	0559	3
RANEY BEN B	CPT	0-1684722	1045	2
RANEY JAMES G	MAJ	0-2005525	1160	1
RANEY JOHN K	MAJ	0-0139403	0550	3
RANEY MARGARET M	MAJ	N-0744458	1065	1
RANEY OLIVER C	2LT	0-1329159	0545	2

NAME	GRADE	SVC NO	DATE RET MO YR	RET CODE
RANFT ROBERT L	CW3	W-2103343	0356	1
RANG JOHN T	MAJ	0-1548535	0759	1
RANGE ARTHUR R	LTC	0-0709894	0763	1
RANGER ROBERT A	1LT	0-1309398	0446	2
RANGOON ELLEN M	1LT	N-0721693	0448	1
RANIERI BENJAMIN J	MAJ	0-2262628	0266	1
RANK EDWARD J	1LT	0-2035894	1045	2
RANK ROBERT O	LTC	0-1048542	1264	1
RANKE RUDOLPH F	CPT	0-0444122	0447	1
RANKIN CARL W	LTC	0-0969855	1167	1
RANKIN EDGAR R	MAJ	0-0139422	1151	3
RANKIN ELMO C	CPT	0-0238715	1165	3
RANKIN FRANK B	CPT	0-0450672	0346	2
RANKIN HARVEY R	CPT	0-0182769	1050	3
RANKIN HARVEY W	MAJ	0-0162406	104N	2
RANKIN HENRY H	LTC	0-1001031	0657	1
RANKIN HUGH F	1LT	0-1116969	0346	2
RANKIN JR JAMES L	LTC	0-0244986	0760	1
RANKIN JR JOHN H	LTC	0-2047121	1162	1
RANKIN JR LLOYD R	2LT	0-2263472	0453	1
RANKIN JR ROBERT C	1LT	0-1823058	0847	1
RANKIN LLOYD F	1LT	0-1012591	0646	2
RANKIN OTIS W	2LT	0-2007723	0960	1
RANKIN RALPH K	MAJ	0-0344604	0546	2
RANKIN RUSSELL L	LTC	0-0311405	0754	3
RANKIN VERNON H	MAJ	0-1294721	0547	2
RANKIN WALTER R	COL	0-0379860	0165	3
RANLET JR ROBERT	LTC	0-0400166	0964	3
RANNELLS WILLIAM P	LTC	0-0280915	0846	2
RANNEY LAWRENCE L	1LT	0-1895525	0446	2
RANNEY RALPH R	COL	0-0177460	0662	3
RANNEY RAYMOND F	1LT	0-1289140	0245	2
RANNEY WILLIS E	LTC	0-0237049	0364	3
RANSBOTTOM RICHARD N	1LT	0-1283672	0446	2
RANSDELL GEORGE W	MAJ	0-0399756	0245	2
RANSIER RONALD	COL	0-0414186	0466	1
RANSLER NICHOLAS	MAJ	0-0139430	0648	3
RANSOM HENRY C	COL	0-0166512	0648	3
RANSOM JR SETH J	1LT	0-2010541	0947	2
RANSOM PAUL W	LTC	0-0302420	0464	3
RANSOM RAYMOND A	LTC	0-0248584	0665	3
RANSOM WILLIAM B	LTC	0-0255790	1055	3
RANSOME JOSEPH T	CW2	W-2122512	0862	1
RANSON DOYLE M	LTC	0-0365361	0666	1
RANUS DON H	MAJ	0-0915454	0962	1
RANVIER GENE M	COL	0-0313834	0465	1
RAPACH ANNA B	MAJ	N-0756008	0663	1
RAPACH JOHN D	1LT	0-2053910	1052	1
RAPAPORT REUBEN	CPT	0-1689011	0646	2
RAPEE RUBY O A S	1LT	N-0733599	1046	1
RAPERTO RALPH B	LTC	0-1058103	0162	1
RAPHUN CHARLES H	LTC	0-1633470	0764	1
RAPKIN HAROLD	1LT	0-1718580	1048	2
RAPLEY LUCIA A	CPT	N-0725699	0348	2
RAPP ELIZABETH	MAJ	N-0760181	0264	1
RARR ERNEST F	1LT	0-0281555	1045	2
RAPP JAMES H	1LT	0-1322368	1145	2
RAPP OLIVER L	LTC	0-0277053	0161	3
RAPP RUPERT B	CW4	W-2103787	0955	1
RAPP VIVIAN	COL	0-0235306	0354	3
RAPPAPORT BERNARD	LTC	0-1542780	0765	1
RARPE LOGAN R	COL	0-0385255	0260	1
RAPPLEYEA JOHN C	COL	0-0230492	0461	5
RAPPOLT WILLIAM H	1LT	0-1042141	1144	2
RAPPORT HERMAN	CW4	W-2105045	0457	1
RAPPORT MILTON H	CPT	0-1794986	1045	2
RAPPORT VICTOR A	COL	0-0290340	0164	3
RAREY DONALD R	MAJ	0-0265721	0159	3
RAREY ERNEST G	COL	0-0141483	0644	2
RARICK WILMER E	CW3	W-2142058	0160	1
RASAY JOYCE W	MAJ	N-0758835	1264	1
RASBERRY HOWARD A	CW2	W-2208476	1159	1
RASBURY MANNING S	LTC	0-0410420	0661	1
RASBURY MURRAY P	CPT	0-1586061	0155	1
RASCH JR RICHARD F	MAJ	0-1331662	1266	1

NAME	GRADE	SVC NO	DATE RET MO YR	RET CODE
RASCHKE RUPERT T	LTC	0-0313435	0367	3
RASH CLARENCE F	MAJ	0-1300853	0158	1
RASH DILLMAN A	M G	0-0274004	0867	3
RASHLEIGH HELEN M	2LT	N-0772894	0345	1
RASIK FRANK A	CW4	W-2126156	1265	1
RASINEN EDWIN M	CPT	0-0364514	0144	2
RASMERS FRANZ E	MAJ	0-0107553	0648	3
RASMUS REX R	MAJ	0-0301770	0262	1
RASMUSSEN CLAIR H	LTC	0-0403634	0664	1
RASMUSSEN CLARENCE H	MAJ	0-0444443	0646	2
RASMUSSEN GARTH B	LTC	0-1104354	0963	1
RASMUSSEN HAROLD P	LTC	0-0347643	1066	3
RASMUSSEN HOWARD B	LTC	0-0242437	1164	3
RASMUSSEN JACK G	LTC	0-0373478	0461	1
RASMUSSEN JOHN D	COL	0-0176904	0957	3
RASMUSSEN JOHN P	MAJ	0-0502930	0645	2
RASMUSSEN RALPH W	LTC	0-1297779	0561	1
RASMUSSEN RAYMOND C	1LT	0-0408095	0544	2
RASMUSSEN RAYMOND R	MAJ	0-1583542	0962	2
RASMUSSEN ROGER J	MAJ	0-1105129	0163	1
RASMUSSEN TRACY A	MAJ	0-0417526	0358	1
RASMUSSEN VERNON F	2LT	0-1823931	1143	2
RASMUSSEN WILLIAM	MAJ	0-0525292	0354	2
RASOR LEE E	2LT	0-1316209	1145	2
RASPBURRY ALMA J	2LT	N-0763702	0645	1
RAST JAMES E	1LT	0-1881961	0953	2
RASZKOWSKI RAYMOND J	CW3	W-2141916	0159	1
RATACZAK ROBERT L	MAJ	0-0427345	0658	1
RATCLIFF ERMEL R	WO1	W-2150878	0356	1
RATCLIFF JAMES R	MAJ	0-1108255	0461	1
RATCLIFFE ELLIS C	MAJ	0-1326131	1159	1
RATCLIFFE FRED H	CPT	0-0496663	0356	1
RATCLIFFE GERALD R	CW2	W-2112264	0747	1
RATCLIFFE JAMES J	CPT	0-1170152	0761	1
RATCLIFFE ROBEY S	MAJ	0-0201172	0257	3
RATCLIFFE THOMAS E	MAJ	0-1168874	0646	2
RATH HAROLD G	CPT	0-0247112	1055	3
RATH HOWARD C	CPT	0-0104435	0648	3
RATH HOWARD W	MAJ	0-2006342	1159	1
RATH JR JAMES J	1LT	0-1323969	0346	2
RATHBUN DONALD	MAJ	0-1120082	1062	1
RATHBUN FRANK F	LTC	0-1303027	0463	1
RATHBUN GLENN E	LTC	0-0423833	0946	1
RATHBUN HAROLD V	LTC	0-0231255	0465	3
RATHBUN HOWARD JAM	MAJ	0-1320182	1265	1
RATHBUN WILLIAM A	LTC	0-0545449	1064	1
RATHERT RICHARD W	CW3	W-2147395	0663	1
RATHERT WILFRED E	1LT	0-1018974	0845	2
RATHIEWICZ WADISLAW	1LT	0-0510852	0447	1
RATHJEN GERALD A	LTC	0-1172238	0865	3
RATHKE HERBERT W	LTC	0-0153291	0851	3
RATHKE LOUIS H	MAJ	0-0153410	0648	3
RATHKE THEODORE O	CPT	0-0183348	0449	1
RATHMAN EDWARD	LTC	0-0507624	0154	1
RATHMANN ERNEST A	COL	0-0454530	0663	1
RATHMANN THOMAS H	1LT	0-1287406	0845	2
RATIGAN JOHN E	LTC	0-0170527	1058	3
RATLIFF ALVIN W	CW3	W-2153155	1065	1
RATLIFF JR JOHN H	MAJ	0-0450503	0657	1
RATLIFF LON	CPT	0-1555126	0446	2
RATLIFF MANFRED O	LTC	0-0311328	1155	1
RATLIFF THOMAS W	1LT	0-1181419	0346	2
RATNER CHARLES H	MAJ	0-0473844	0949	1
RATNER JULIUS B	1LT	0-0494927	0646	2
RATNER MILTON H	CPT	0-0508663	0444	2
RATTERMANN MARION F	LTC	0-0265600	0959	1
RATTRAY ALEXANDER	LTC	0-1301364	0664	1
RATTRAY CHARLES T	CPT	0-0168214	1155	3
RATY RAYMOND	LTC	0-0451046	0961	1
RAU JACOB F	LTC	0-0325766	0865	3
RAU JAMES J	WO1	W-2108336	0247	2
RAU JOHN F	LTC	0-0151573	0648	3
RAU JR WILLIAM C	CPT	0-1059250	0547	2
RAUCH ALFRED R	COL	0-0255684	1160	1
RAUCH GORDON L	CPT	0-0495204	0246	2

ARMY OF THE UNITED STATES RETIRED LIST

NAME	GRADE	SVC NO	DATE RET MO YR	RET CODE
RAUCH HAROLD D	2LT	0-1309879	C944	2
RAUCH KENNETH A	CW3	W-2203280	0165	1
RAUCH LAWRENCE J	CW2	W-3250216	0164	1
RAUCH ROBERT L	2LT	0-C495667	0545	2
RAUCH THOMAS R	MAJ	0-1107061	0647	2
RAUCK LINNAEUR B	CPT	0-0185238	C944	2
RAUGUST ARNOLD W	LTC	0-0475222	C662	2
RAUH JOSEPH C	LTC	0-0235092	C360	1
RAULERSON MAURICE J	CPT	0-1996484	1046	2
RAUSCH KENNETH E	2LT	0-C120391	0545	2
RAUSCHENBERG CHARLES	MAJ	0-2C11591	C862	1
RAUSCHKOLB FREDERI	2LT	C-1047307	0743	2
RAUTENSTRAUCH WALTER	LTC	0-0335779	1165	3
RAUTERBERG CARL R	LTC	0-0437685	C351	1
RAUZI FRANCIS A	LTC	0-1298288	0461	1
RAVELY MARVIN D	MAJ	0-1824683	0761	1
RAVEN CLARA	COL	K-052813C	C565	3
RAVEN WILBUR R	LTC	0-0494582	0557	1
RAVENSCRAFT DAIL F	CW3	W-2144C86	1060	1
RAVENSCROFT ESTILL P	LTC	0-1100738	0661	1
RAVERTY MARY J	1LT	N-0728648	C946	1
RAVITZ BENJAMIN R	1LT	0-1554619	1145	2
RAVITZ SAMUEL F	MAJ	C-0213636	0660	3
RAWCLIFFE WILLIAM F	LTC	0-C451751	0162	1
RAWDON FREDERICK	MAJ	C-0275259	C667	3
RAWDON ROBERT M	1LT	0-0420262	1043	1
RAWHOUSER DONALD W	MAJ	0-1686806	0166	1
RAWLEY PALMER B	COL	0-0145217	0152	3
RAWLEY STUART D	CPT	0-1315727	C946	2
RAWLINGS AUBREY J	MAJ	C-0167881	1054	3
RAWLINGS FREMONT G	LTC	0-1647665	1165	3
RAWLINGS HERBERT B	CW3	W-2150987	C862	1
RAWLINGS HERBERT L	LTC	0-1299472	0262	1
RAWLINGS JR JOHN A	LTC	0-0115990	1062	1
RAWLINGS MORRIS G	LTC	0-1165938	0564	1
RAWLINGS WILLIAM L	MAJ	C-0314995	C361	1
RAWLINS DANIEL H	MAJ	C-1923C56	C664	1
RAWLINS JR VICTOR E	MAJ	C-1559745	C963	1
RAWLINS WALTER A	1LT	0-0490924	C653	1
RAWLINS WILLIS H	LTC	0-0388353	1060	1
RAWLINSON HAVARD T	COL	0-0404980	0948	1
RAWLINSON HUBERT K	MAJ	0-1291006	1161	2
RAWLS BEN H	MAJ	C-0325959	C147	2
RAWLS ELIZABETH	1LT	N-0728514	C845	1
RAWLS JOE P	MAJ	0-2263279	0962	1
RAWLS JOHN M	LTC	0-1646893	1162	1
RAWLS LUCIAN R	MAJ	C-0176122	1153	2
RAWLS MARCELLUS	CPT	0-0510032	0549	1
RAWLS WALLACE G	MAJ	0-2102644	1165	1
RAWN ARNOLD F	CPT	C-0432156	C847	1
RAWSON GORDON H	LTC	0-1280975	C361	1
RAWSON HENRY P	LTC	0-0137346	0648	3
RAWSON JAMES S	CPT	0-1590937	1164	1
RAWSON JUSTIN L	CPT	0-0137347	1043	2
RAWSON VINTON R	LTC	C-023742C	0962	3
RAY ALBERT	CW2	W-2151028	0463	1
RAY ALFRED	CPT	0-1595114	C961	1
RAY ANDREW	CPT	0-2044403	C350	1
RAY CHARLIE C	MAJ	0-1177946	1060	1
RAY CLARK	CPT	0-2007518	0357	1
RAY DAVID W	MAJ	C-1018286	0855	1
RAY DUANE L	LTC	0-0219926	0259	3
RAY ERNEST A	LTC	0-0163503	C257	3
RAY FRANK S	LTC	0-0452862	1060	1
RAY FRANK W	COL	C-0322539	C166	3
RAY GARD W	CPT	0-0922774	1044	2
RAY GILBERT M	MAJ	C-1115390	0359	2
RAY GRANT L	1LT	C-05021C5	1047	1
RAY HOWARD K	CPT	0-0404140	0862	1
RAY HOWARD L	CW4	W-2127791	1060	1
RAY HUBERT L	CW3	W-2143548	0161	2
RAY JACK L	MAJ	0-1688752	0765	1
RAY JAMES A	LTC	0-1055705	1162	1
RAY JAMES E	CPT	0-1258591	0962	1
RAY JAMES M	MAJ	C-1311928	C960	1

NAME	GRADE	SVC NO	DATE RET MO YR	RET CODE
RAY JAMES P	CW3	W-2205516	0666	1
RAY JASPER L	MAJ	C-1555127	0361	1
RAY JOE A	MAJ	0-0967751	1061	1
RAY JOHNIE R L	CW2	W-2144146	0258	1
RAY JR FRANK E	CPT	0-163833C	0946	2
RAY JR GEORGE C	LTC	0-1010908	0763	1
RAY JR JOHN C	LTC	0-012736E	0957	3
RAY JR LUTHER G	MAJ	0-1168044	0657	1
RAY KEITH C	MAJ	C-027984C	0247	2
RAY KINLEY L	1LT	0-1323778	C546	2
RAY LOWELL R	1LT	0-0414086	0944	2
RAY LURA JC	MAJ	N-0726654	0764	1
RAY MARCUS H	COL	0-0267261	0158	2
RAY MARY E	1LT	N-07C0229	0644	1
RAY MICHAEL K	MAJ	C-0981027	0767	1
RAY PAUL J	LTC	0-0555974	0360	3
RAY RALPH R	LTC	0-028049C	0663	3
RAY REUBIN W	CPT	0-2263172	0857	1
RAY ROBERT L	CW3	W-2126318	0654	1
RAY SR HENRY G	1LT	0-0288512	0752	1
RAY WARNER C	CW4	W-2131586	1166	1
RAY WILLARD R	MAJ	C-1334623	0165	1
RAY WILLIAM	CW3	W-2109434	0558	1
RAY WILLIAM H	CPT	0-0386064	0644	2
RAYBOULD LOUIS C	MAJ	0-2210221	0761	1
RAYBOURN JESSE S	LTC	0-094959C	0967	1
RAYBUCK CLYDE W	LTC	0-1587561	0962	1
RAYBUCK VERNON J	LTC	0-15932C8	0965	1
RAYBURN FREDERICK	MAJ	0-0920489	0847	2
RAYBURN KENNETH W	LTC	0-0946973	0967	1
RAYCEVICH JR MIKE N	2LT	0-0442886	1144	2
RAYCRAFT MARJORIE E	1LT	N-0773581	0647	1
RAYFIELD BEVERLY F	1LT	0-1325777	C645	1
RAYFIELD GEORGE F	LTC	C-1051464	0166	1
RAYFIELD SR BENTON A	LTC	0-1551C89	1061	2
RAYKOWSKI HARLEY A	CPT	0-1700736	1143	1
RAYL JOHN F	MAJ	0-1575090	0162	1
RAYMAN MARTIN	2LT	0-1183954	0346	2
RAYMER JACK L	CPT	0-0368095	C846	2
RAYMOND ANAN	COL	C-0131596	1150	3
RAYMOND ARTHUR L	LTC	0-0282765	0167	3
RAYMOND BASIL J	1LT	0-1C12606	1145	2
RAYMOND CHARLES F	CPT	0-1295268	1046	2
RAYMOND EDWARD A	COL	0-0339955	0766	1
RAYMOND EDWARD A	MAJ	C-1634246	0656	1
RAYMOND FRANK	COL	C-0268672	0460	1
RAYMOND FREDERIC E	MAJ	C-1342001	0266	1
RAYMOND GEORGE E	MAJ	0-1311428	0960	1
RAYMOND JOHN W	COL	0-0124453	0854	3
RAYMOND LAUREN A	CPT	0-0386652	1045	1
RAYMOND NORMAN K	LTC	C-0260504	0667	3
RAYMOND RICHARD T	LTC	0-0248731	C865	3
RAYMOND ROY L	WO1	W-2115865	0261	1
RAYMOND VICTOR G	CPT	0-0424224	1066	3
RAYMOND VIRGINIA G	1LT	N-C771091	1045	1
RAYMOND WALTER A	CW2	W-2208142	1163	1
RAYMOND WILLIAM	MAJ	0-1924535	1265	1
RAYNER CHARLES E	CPT	0-1170932	0159	2
RAYNER JAY C	LTC	0-0376265	0661	1
RAYNOR JR J E	CPT	0-0358586	1064	2
RAZLER FRANK J	1LT	0-1944788	0446	2
RE VEAL IVAN	MAJ	0-01C1891	0655	3
REA HOWARD W	MAJ	0-1334624	0666	1
REA JAMES F	CPT	0-1299628	1045	2
REA JOHN P	LTC	C-1113901	0365	1
REA JR GEORGE S	LTC	0-1284763	1060	1
REA ROBERT G	MAJ	0-1688590	0567	1
REA WILLIAM N	CPT	0-047475C	0447	1
READ ALAN W	LTC	0-1341704	0567	1
READ CLARK R	LTC	0-1314328	0566	1
READ FLOYD R	CPT	C-0493638	0646	1
READ FRANK L	LTC	0-0253648	0560	1
READ HENRY C	LTC	0-0341395	0457	2
READ JOHN P	COL	0-0255741	1060	3
READ JOSEPH C	CPT	0-0471005	0963	3

NAME	GRADE	SVC NO	DATE RET MO YR	RET CODE
READ JR LATHROP R	LTC	0-0243340	0346	1
READ LESLIE A	LTC	0-1101630	0458	2
READ NORWOOD G	LTC	0-1011393	0161	1
READ ROBERT E	CPT	0-0370515	104N	2
READ WILLIAM H	MAJ	C-1915588	0367	1
READE ARTHUR C	LTC	0-0211398	0957	3
READE BRUCE M	MAJ	C-0311843	0546	2
READE JR VINCENT J	CPT	0-0370757	0445	2
READER CHARLES H	MAJ	0-0224754	1054	3
READMAN GEORGE B	MAJ	C-1301213	0762	1
READY DANIEL	LTC	0-0357794	C765	3
READY WILLIAM C	COL	0-0172282	C562	3
REAFSNYDER VICTOR J	COL	0-0333729	1162	1
REAGAN ARVIL R	CPT	0-1185808	0762	1
REAGAN CHARLES H	COL	0-0175178	0360	3
REAGAN EUGENE M	CPT	C-1292398	C448	2
REAGAN FRANK A	COL	0-0211502	0460	3
REAGAN HOMER L	1LT	0-1298926	104N	2
REAGAN JOHN F	COL	0-0400167	0760	1
REAGAN JOHN W	LTC	0-0533717	0864	1
REAGAN REGINALD	MAJ	0-0329891	0546	2
REAGIN CHARLES E	LTC	0-C239034	0658	3
REAKSECKER JOHN H	CPT	0-1052535	C157	1
REAL STEWART G	LTC	0-1698087	0765	1
REALS BERNARD B	CW4	W-2110538	C560	1
REALY JR FRED D	WO1	W-2122820	0147	2
REAM BERTRAND A	LTC	0-0410704	0964	3
REAM ELWOOD P	CPT	0-1182690	0254	2
REAM GEORGE G	COL	0-C292060	0365	2
REAM GRANVILLE	MAJ	C-1917912	C763	1
REAM JR EDWARD F	LTC	0-0272716	1067	3
REAMER GEORGE W	1LT	0-0407647	1044	2
REAMES CARL J	CW3	W-2144315	C860	1
REAMES EDWARD E	CPT	0-2010342	0157	1
REAMES JOHN P	LTC	0-0452054	1059	1
REAMES JULIAN T	MAJ	C-0352167	1145	2
REAMEY SANFORD	MAJ	C-1313447	1164	1
REAMS BERNARD O	MAJ	0-0702333	G662	1
REAMS CHARLES E	CPT	0-0498466	1047	2
REAMS EDWARD L	LTC	0-0381918	1165	2
REAMS JACK W	MAJ	C-13342C8	0464	1
REAMS LUTHER	CPT	0-1041424		2
REAMS PATRICK P	MAJ	C-0750842	0562	1
REAMS WILLIAM O	CPT	0-0441978	0-48	1
REARDON BERNARD A	LTC	0-1319249	1059	1
REARDON CURTIS R	CW2	W-2149714	0557	1
REARDON EUGENE L	MAJ	C-2200445	C366	1
REARDON EVELYN D	2LT	N-C753044	0846	1
REARDON JAMES H	COL	0-0338723	0857	1
REARDON JOHN W	MAJ	0-1913496	0166	1
REARDON MICHAEL A	LTC	0-0198945	C557	3
REARDON WILLIAM R	LTC	0-0277800	0-48	2
REARICK IRA P	MAJ	0-1555746	0760	1
REARICK PHILIP O	CPT	C-0307913	0943	2
REASENBERG MAX	1LT	0-1946839	0945	2
REASONOVER GEORGE C	MAJ	C-2206251	C264	1
REASONOVER JOHN R	LTC	0-0256718	1265	3
REAVELEY ROBERT O	LTC	0-0382821	1160	1
REAVES GEORGE W	CW2	W-2145857	0858	2
REAVES JOHN R	LTC	C-1284575	C461	1
REAVES ROBERT J	1LT	0-0491529	1146	2
REAVES THOMAS P	MAJ	0-0334279	C648	1
REAVES WALKER G	LTC	0-2047793	0261	1
REAVEY GEORGE J	2LT	0-1306782	C545	2
REAVIS EDNA M	2LT	N-0742253	0545	1
REAVIS ELIZABETHH	1LT	N-0757243	0646	1
REAVLEY JACK W	LTC	0-0309913	1165	3
REAVLEY JOE M	CPT	C-0494458	C245	2
REBER ROBERT J	CPT	0-1289805	C-48	2
REBHUN LESTER	2LT	0-0734602	0445	2
REBISZ CASIMIR	LTC	0-1050878	0962	2
REBMANN EDWARD O	MAJ	C-0224206	1264	3
REBO JOHN H	CW2	W-2145655	0659	1
RECH HAMEN	2LT	0-0192577	0527	1
RECHER FRED S	LTC	0-0463646	C854	1

NAME	GRADE	SVC NO	DATE RET MO YR	RET CODE
RECHTINE GLENN R	LTC	0-0400742	0360	2
RECK ALBERT P	CW3	W-2205662	0364	1
RECK FRANKIE E	1LT	N-0735223	0546	1
RECK WILLIAM R	MAJ	0-1800022	1160	1
RECKARD OSCAR J	LTC	0-0157766	0648	3
RECKLINGHAUSEN WILLI	MAJ	C-1304790	1264	1
RECKORD LELAND T	COL	0-0358311	0555	3
RECKORD MILTON A	M G	0-0102176	0546	2
RECKSIEK DANIEL M	LTC	0-1C60601	0862	1
RECORDS THOMAS H	LTC	0-0250545	1265	3
RECTOR CARROLL R	MAJ	0-0191326	0656	3
RECTOR CHARLES G	MAJ	C-1645305	0457	1
RECTOR CHARLES W	CPT	0-0546686	0846	2
RECTOR CHESTER H	CPT	0-1002101	0646	1
RECTOR GARRETT I	CW2	W-2115784	0647	1
RECTOR HENRY V	COL	0-0208908	0346	1
RECZEK WALTER A	1LT	0-0444324	C544	2
RED CARL L	WO1	W-2152056	1059	1
RED JAMES P	1LT	0-2001657	0396	2
REDD BENJAMIN D	MAJ	C-0399883	0257	1
REDD CHARLES F	MAJ	0-0197279	0662	3
REDD LOCK W	LTC	0-0164208	0147	2
REDD SAMUEL C	CPT	0-2025279	0956	1
REDDEN JR GEORGE D	CPT	0-1321128	0258	3
REDDEN LARRY O	CW3	W-214627C	0363	1
REDDEN LLOYD H	LTC	0-054828C	0664	1
REDDEN WALTER M	LTC	0-0373146	0260	1
REDDICK CLEVELAND	LTC	0-1824366	1263	1
REDDICK RICHARD O	LTC	0-1166359	0446	2
REDDICK WILLIS C	COL	0-0229527	0164	3
REDDIN GEORGE B	COL	0-0198329	1060	3
REDDIN RUBY C	MAJ	N-075945C	0967	1
REDDING EDWIN T	CW3	RW-2145835	0163	1
REDDING HERBERT J	CPT	0-0453282	0744	2
REDDING HOWARD R	CW3	W-214219C	0960	1
REDDING JOHN B	CW2	W-2150048	0860	1
REDDING JOHN O	LTC	0-1596948	1262	1
REDDING JOHN H	LTC	0-0215512	1157	3
REDDING JOSEPH A	M G	0-0126852	0754	3
REDDING JR CHARLES H	CW2	W-2112987	1043	2
REDDINGTON JOHN F	COL	0-1290130	0767	3
REDDY ALBERT J	LTC	0-0124659	0157	3
REDDY ANITA S	MAJ	N-0736969	0562	1
REDDY JOHN H	LTC	0-0300043	1065	3
REDDY JR BERNARD E	LTC	0-0498052	1057	1
REDELL ARCHIBALD	1LT	0-0335660	0559	1
REDELLA FRANCIS R	CPT	0-2049366	0746	2
REDELLA JOHN A	WO1	W-2109428	0845	2
REDENBAUGH CLETUS R	CW2	W-2205370	0562	1
REDENBO ROSS M	CPT	0-0160768	1155	3
REDFEARN PERCY R	LTC	0-0273756	1266	3
REDFEARN RUTH	MAJ	N-0765664	0565	1
REDFERN EDGAR F	LTC	0-0499711	0665	3
REDFIELD CHANDLER S	LTC	0-1291518	0662	1
REDFIELD ETHEL M	MAJ	N-0788499	0165	3
REDFIELD JOHN F	CPT	0-0341993	0558	1
REDFIELD RONALD L	MAJ	0-1694351	0146	2
REDHAIR GEORGE I	LTC	0-0236335	0863	3
REDICAN THOMAS F	CW3	W-2145240	0167	1
REDICK FLOYD C	LTC	0-0332140	0765	3
REDIFER RAYMOND O	MAJ	0-2212082	0465	1
REDIHAN BERNARD F	COL	0-027667C	0359	1
REDINGER JOSEPH C	MAJ	C-105174C	0260	1
REDINGTON DICK R	1LT	0-0527855	0967	2
REDKEY EARL C	CW3	W-2145656	0564	1
REDLINGSHAFER T A	LTC	0-0349973	0559	1
REDMAN CHARLES H	COL	0-0908443	0365	3
REDMAN ELMA W	LTC	0-0263545	1062	3
REDMAN HERBERT E	LTC	0-0123103	0644	2
REDMAN WILLIAM F	1LT	0-1581331	1045	2
REDMON JASON A	LTC	0-0104053	0849	3
REDMON JOHN C	LTC	0-155462C	0163	2
REDMON JR WILLIAM V	MAJ	0-1180679	0464	1
REDMON L GORDON	LTC	0-0509692	0456	2
REDMON WILLIAM F	MAJ	0-1945464	C762	1

NAME	GRADE	SVC NO	DATE RET MO YR	RET CODE
REDMOND DOYTT O	MAJ	0-1685525	0462	1
REDMOND GLINNIS	CPT	0-0499495	0854	1
REDMOND JOHN P	LTC	0-1636524	0967	1
REDMOND MARGARET Z	2LT	N-0760137	0445	1
REDMOND ROBERT F	MAJ	0-1876915	0365	1
REDMOND ROBERT J	LTC	0-1080066	0263	1
REDMOND ROBERT L	1LT	0-1994514	0951	1
REDMOND SPENCER W	MAJ	0-1885672	0466	1
REDMOND WILLIAM F	LTC	0-0399956	1161	2
REDNER FRANCIS B	COL	0-0139449	0554	3
REDUS JAMES L	MAJ	0-0290963	0364	3
REDUS JR ED P	LTC	0-1551296	1161	1
REDUS THELMA A	CPT	N-0734603	0445	1
REDWINE RUFFIN E	MAJ	0-0948893	0560	1
REDZICH JOHN	1LT	0-0497150	0860	1
REECE CLARENCE W	LTC	0-0320428	0754	1
REECE DAVID P	MAJ	0-1643490	0560	1
REECE FREDERICA	MAJ	N-0723132	0662	1
REECE GEORGE J	MAJ	0-0104570	0848	3
REECE HOWARD P	MAJ	0-0583489	0758	1
REECE JOHN W	MAJ	0-0322646	0262	2
REECE WALTER F	LTC	0-0289126	0247	2
REED ADOLPHUS O	CW4	W-2121393	0365	1
REED ALBERT J	CPT	0-1640850	0447	2
REED ALFRED G	CW3	W-2209340	0767	1
REED ARCHIE F	LTC	0-0145222	0452	3
REED ARTHUR N	CW2	W-2149800	0156	1
REED BENJAMIN M	COL	0-0194773	0663	3
REED BERNARD E	MAJ	0-1935718	1066	1
REED CARL D	LTC	0-1590938	0261	1
REED CARL E	LTC	0-1635242	1154	1
REED CHARLES H	MAJ	0-0207517	1150	3
REED CHARLES H	COL	0-0245471	0660	2
REED CHARLES L	LTC	0-0398196	0665	3
REED CHARLES O	LTC	0-0326709	0260	1
REED CHARLES S	CPT	0-0192982	0258	3
REED CHESTER A	CW2	RW-2153007	0363	1
REED CLAUDE H	LTC	0-1293317	0966	1
REED CLAUDE V	COL	0-0129338	0648	3
REED DAVID E	2LT	0-1015605	0844	2
REED DENTON H	COL	0-0478830	0261	3
REED DENZEL V	MAJ	0-1699988	0561	1
REED DICK B	LTC	0-0133696	0449	3
REED DONALD F	CW2	W-2151928	0762	1
REED EARCLE R	LTC	0-1288122	0261	1
REED EARNEST L	MAJ	0-1320964	0557	1
REED EDWARD M	MAJ	0-1922667	1265	1
REED EMILY J	2LT	N-0735661	0745	1
REED ERNEST J	CPT	0-0108205	0836	1
REED ERNEST V	COL	0-0114826	0648	3
REED FENWICK T	LTC	0-0263850	0757	3
REED FRANCIS B	CPT	0-2262613	1057	2
REED FRED R	LTC	0-1299109	0562	1
REED GAROLD E	LTC	0-1633476	0364	1
REED GEORGE A	LTC	0-2035493	0867	1
REED GEORGE C	CPT	0-1298927	0146	2
REED GEORGE H	MAJ	0-0264338	0166	3
REED GEORGE M	2LT	0-1059601	0545	2
REED GEORGE N	LTC	0-0171300	1061	3
REED GEORGE NOR	LTC	0-0149567	1050	2
REED GLEN G	CPT	0-0523871	0945	2
REED GUY A	LTC	0-0187539	1053	3
REED HEBER L	2LT	0-1306933	0244	2
REED HENLY E	LTC	0-1549361	1262	1
REED HENRY C	MAJ	0-0474819	0947	1
REED HENRY C	MAJ	0-0304040	0346	2
REED HOWARD B	CPT	0-0513222	0847	1
REED HOWARD E	COL	0-0200133	0655	3
REED HUBERT N	MAJ	0-2095894	0863	1
REED IRVIN T	COL	0-0311254	1164	1
REED JACK	2LT	0-1322712	0345	2
REED JACK C	1LT	0-1031017	0445	2
REED JAMES A	2LT	0-1576545	1044	2
REED JAMES D	CW2	W-2214652	0966	1
REED JAMES E	CW2	W-2150758	0360	1
REED JAMES F	MAJ	0-1114721	0557	1
REED JAMES L	LTC	0-0209107	1153	3
REED JAMES R	LTC	0-0269968	0259	1
REED JEAN R	LTC	0-0379866	0146	2
REED JOHN C	MAJ	0-0276890	0760	1
REED JOHN E	MAJ	0-0242458	0764	3
REED JOSEPH	CPT	0-1590748	1153	1
REED JOSEPH R	LTC	0-0477778	0651	1
REED JOSEPH V	CW2	W-2203315	1164	1
REED JR CHARLES A	MAJ	0-0999268	0562	1
REED JR CHARLES E	MAJ	0-1119241	0863	1
REED JR CHARLES E	WO1	W-2116259	0346	2
REED JR CHARLES L	COL	0-0220498	0262	3
REED JR CLYDE S	LTC	0-0489404	0767	1
REED JR FRANK H	COL	0-0261883	0161	1
REED JR GEORGE	CPT	0-0540499	1046	2
REED JR JAMES R	LTC	0-1291696	0361	1
REED JR ROY E	LTC	0-1342116	0767	1
REED JR WILLIAM P	CW3	W-2141425	0760	1
REED JR WILLIAM W	LTC	0-0417334	0767	1
REED LAUREN R	CPT	0-1321553	0146	1
REED LAURENCE F	CPT	0-0169935	0860	3
REED LELAND W	CW3	W-2206117	1066	1
REED LEO R	COL	0-0121483	0455	3
REED LOUIS B	COL	0-0153457	1151	3
REED LOUIS J	MAJ	0-0139678	0858	3
REED MARY L	2LT	N-0772602	0245	1
REED MAX E	LTC	0-0550107	0364	1
REED MYRON W	1LT	0-1294901	0645	2
REED OSCAR R	MAJ	0-0184417	0648	3
REED PAUL F	LTC	0-0275645	0665	3
REED PAUL W	MAJ	0-0218932	0357	3
REED PHILIP W	LTC	0-0468026	0851	1
REED RAYMOND J	CW4	W-2141424	1264	1
REED REXTON W	LTC	0-1311203	0861	1
REED ROBERT C	1LT	0-1115391	0646	2
REED ROBERT E	CW3	W-2147375	0761	2
REED ROBERT J	LTC	0-1167170	0161	1
REED ROBERT P	MAJ	0-2019932	0863	1
REED ROBERT R	COL	0-0355021	0859	1
REED RUFUS R	CPT	0-0261631	0952	3
REED RUSSELL H	LTC	0-0231402	0165	3
REED SHELTON	CPT	0-0355074	0548	1
REED SR DAVID R	MAJ	0-2262673	0962	1
REED TED E	MAJ	0-1015381	0149	2
REED THOMAS J	CW2	W-2150748	0258	1
REED THOMAS W	MAJ	0-0949452	1263	1
REED VIRGIL O	MAJ	0-0118886	1056	3
REED WALTER J	LTC	0-0313434	1059	3
REED WARREN C	LTC	0-0443155	0967	1
REED WILLARD W	CPT	0-1295269	0758	1
REED WILLIAM A	COL	0-0274513	0648	3
REED WILLIAM A	CPT	0-1293477	0750	1
REED WILLIAM C	COL	0-0203100	1154	3
REED WILLIAM C	CPT	0-0533901	0848	2
REED WILLIAM D	LTC	0-1037252	0957	3
REED WILLIAM D	CW3	W-2149372	0762	1
REED WILLIAM R	COL	0-0224667	0857	3
REED WILLIAM R	MAJ	0-1651169	1062	1
REED WILLIAM R	CW3	W-2148082	1062	1
REED WILLIE J	CPT	0-2012591	0765	2
REEDER CHARLES C	1LT	0-0319582	0945	2
REEDER FRANK	CW2	W-2116046	1151	1
REEDER GERALD W	CPT	0-0275985	0447	1
REEDER HENRY H	LTC	0-0265453	0850	3
REEDER HERMAN W	LTC	0-0228621	1264	3
REEDER JACK W	CPT	0-0423337	1146	2
REEDER JULIAN T	LTC	0-0323392	0860	1
REEDER JULIUS C	LTC	0-1300743	0662	1
REEDER TORRENCE W	CW3	W-2006655	0666	1
REEDER WILLIAM S	LTC	0-0248181	0166	3
REEDIE ARTHUR C	LTC	0-0502563	0964	3
REEDY MORRIS	MAJ	0-0201266	0763	3
REEDY PAUL W	1LT	0-1108260	1044	2
REEDY RAYMOND O	LTC	0-0445056	0155	1
REEDY WILLIAM H	MAJ	0-1176473	0565	1
REEGO JAMES H	LTC	0-1635243	0963	1
REEKS JR LLOYD D	CPT	0-1000455	0147	2
REEL JR LEROY R	LTC	0-1167171	0361	1
REEMS ALBERT B	WO1	W-2151079	1154	1
REENSTJERNA ROBERT L	LTC	0-0331918	0862	1
REENTS JOHN H	LTC	0-0415532	1161	3
REEP MURLEY A	LTC	0-0946869	0258	3
REES FREDERICK	MAJ	0-0420237	0246	2
REES GOMER S	LTC	0-0400670	0960	1
REES HENRY F	CPT	0-0110920	0749	3
REES JOHN L	LTC	0-1017048	0757	1
REES JOHN W	LTC	0-0172263	0951	3
REES JR JACK	1LT	0-0408335	0945	2
REES JR JOHN E	LTC	0-1544279	0267	1
REES JR MAHONE	COL	0-0255296	1165	3
REES JR THOMAS A	MAJ	0-0974616	0665	1
REES MAGDALENE	1LT	N-0733987	0546	1
REES MALCOLM C	COL	0-0124553	0455	3
REES MAX I	1LT	0-1113407	1045	2
REES WILLIAM D	2LT	0-1058362	1144	2
REESE ALICE L	CPT	N-0771655	0547	1
REESE ARVAN O	LTC	0-0281168	0761	1
REESE CHARLES O	MAJ	0-2033818	0465	1
REESE CHARLES T	LTC	0-1333535	0967	1
REESE CLYDE F	MAJ	0-0370567	0547	2
REESE EDGAR P	COL	0-0258772	1165	3
REESE FRANKLIN W	COL	0-0204229	0156	1
REESE GARLAND S	1LT	0-4025691	0162	2
REESE HAROLD B	CW2	W-2206551	0665	1
REESE HAROLD K	1LT	0-1172239	0546	2
REESE HARRY S	CW4	W-2101026	0855	1
REESE HOMER S	COL	0-0143110	1055	3
REESE JACK N	1LT	0-1313129	0745	2
REESE JAMES C	LTC	0-2037240	0866	1
REESE JEP H	1LT	0-0411620	1044	2
REESE JOHN D	MAJ	0-1822189	0861	1
REESE JOHN L	LTC	0-0357268	1151	1
REESE JR EDWARD J	MAJ	0-2029596	1264	1
REESE JR JOHN A	MAJ	0-1016986	0765	1
REESE KENNETH W	CW3	W-2152011	0958	1
REESE LAWRENCE W	LTC	0-0271042	1167	3
REESE OSCAR N	MAJ	0-0197227	1151	3
REESE ROBERT	LTC	0-1295937	1162	1
REESE ROBERT M	COL	0-0380691	0861	1
REESE TOMMY L	CW2	W-2118458	0945	2
REESE VICTOR C	MAJ	0-0162258	0648	3
REESE WILLIAM F	CW2	W-2144147	0160	1
REESE WILLIAM G	MAJ	0-0413211	0255	2
REESE WILLIAM N	LTC	0-0371143	0849	1
REESER JOHN A	1LT	0-0504159	0744	2
REESER ROBERT L	LTC	0-1043204	1265	1
REEVE CHESTER L	LTC	0-0507732	0556	1
REEVE EZEKIEL B	LTC	0-1542759	0557	1
REEVE HAROLD I	CW2	W-2146955	0466	1
REEVE THOMAS B	2LT	0-0446319	0645	2
REEVES ALLAN E	CW2	W-2150352	1164	1
REEVES ALLEN	LTC	0-0924305	1047	1
REEVES CHARLES	CW2	W-2142937	1155	1
REEVES CLARENCE E	CW4	W-2144898	0567	2
REEVES CURTIS C	1LT	0-0507352	0146	2
REEVES FOLK O	COL	0-0228242	1263	3
REEVES GEORGE R	MAJ	0-1294534	0447	2
REEVES JAMES E	LTC	0-1168046	1163	1
REEVES JOHN A	MAJ	0-0444674	0762	1
REEVES JOSEPH C	LTC	0-1169702	0361	1
REEVES JOSEPH S	LTC	0-1846513	1060	2
REEVES JR JULIUS R	2LT	0-1292588	0545	2
REEVES JR WALTER P	CPT	0-0926805	0646	2
REEVES JR WALTER T	1LT	0-0966991	0952	2
REEVES LEROY W	COL	0-0347583	0166	3
REEVES LOUIS P	COL	0-0190418	0462	3
REEVES LUNSFORD T	COL	0-0287966	1067	3
REEVES OSCAR E	MAJ	0-1878400	0667	1
REEVES PAUL W	LTC	0-0378981	0165	1
REEVES RAOUL B	LTC	0-0420077	0361	1
REEVES RAY C	COL	0-0208218	0842	2
REEVES ROBERT L	CPT	0-2036693	0547	2
REEVES ROBERT N	MAJ	0-0378625	0246	2
REEVES SR RALPH P	MAJ	0-1173046	1160	1
REEVES TED R	1LT	0-0312281	1061	3
REEVES THOMAS W	LTC	0-1342297	1266	1
REEVES WILLIAM A	MAJ	0-1110207	1062	1
REEVES WILLIAM C	CPT	0-0496193	1051	1
REFAKES ARISTIDES	MAJ	0-0236914	0265	3
REFFEL EDWARD W	CW2	W-2209859	0464	1
REFFETT LEROY R	LTC	0-1293649	0864	1
REFFNER HOWARD S	LTC	0-1332098	0967	1
REGA JOHN A	COL	0-0264334	1151	1
REGA JOHN J	CW4	W-2121195	0459	1
REGA MICHAEL	CW4	W-2145262	1059	1
REGALA ALFONSO M	2LT	0-1896503	0849	2
REGAN DAVID M	CPT	0-1697656	0845	2
REGAN EDWARD J	COL	0-0388223	0851	1
REGAN FRANK C	LTC	0-1588245	0966	3
REGAN HARRY C	CPT	0-0322672	0648	3
REGAN JAMES W	LTC	0-0493711	1062	1
REGAN JOHN J	1LT	0-1038093	0446	1
REGAN JR JOHN M	1LT	0-0509451	0246	2
REGAN LELAND S	CPT	0-0224088	1160	3
REGAN MICHAEL C	1LT	0-0108903	0626	1
REGAUER OTTO	WO1	W-2150340	0255	1
REGEHR CORNELIA	MAJ	N-0785271	0165	1
REGENS LOU	CPT	0-1294902	0147	2
REGENWETHER MARY E	1LT	N-0733890	0745	1
REGER CHRIS G	COL	0-0219877	0652	1
REGER HERMAN T	MAJ	0-1293117	0366	3
REGER 2ND WILLIAM H	CPT	0-0389167	0346	2
REGILIO JR FRANK	MAJ	0-0970685	0864	2
REGISTER BARNEY W	2LT	0-1104357	0644	2
REGLI WERNER E	LTC	0-0905579	0846	1
REGNIER JOSEPH C	CW3	W-2145492	0359	1
REGNIER WALTER O	MAJ	0-0239504	0560	3
REGUERA CESAREO	COL	0-0268662	1054	1
REH CHRISTIAN	LTC	0-0485393	0965	1
REHAK DONALD E	2LT	0-1289487	1043	2
REHANEK JAMES J	COL	0-0118061	0948	3
REHBACH WILLIAM E	CW3	W-2152305	0765	1
REHE AUGUST J	LTC	0-0438425	1152	1
REHKOP RUSSELL G	COL	0-0223467	0660	1
REHM CHARLES H	1LT	0-0378591	0745	2
REHM EVERETT R	LTC	0-0932867	0765	3
REHPOHL WILFRED L	CPT	0-1944790	0246	2
REIBER JR WILLIAM E	MAJ	0-1542488	0361	1
REIBER WILLIAM C	LTC	0-0294872	0155	1
REIBERG RUFUS	CPT	0-1038463	0246	2
REICH DANIEL J	LTC	0-1647667	0161	1
REICH EMIL J	2LT	0-1796526	0444	1
REICH MERRILL O	1LT	0-0443533	1144	2
REICH PAUL F	CPT	0-1691047	0545	2
REICH RALPH J	MAJ	0-1923578	1066	1
REICH ROBERT L	1LT	0-1796692	0146	2
REICH RUDOLPH M	LTC	0-1019324	0966	1
REICH RUDOLPH S	LTC	0-0193290	0254	3
REICH SAMUEL	CW2	W-2153139	0266	1
REICH WILLIAM	MAJ	0-2034695	0960	1
REICH WILLIAM F	LTC	0-0454137	0761	1
REICHE LAWRENCE E	CPT	0-1283839	1058	1
REICHEL ALBERT J	WO1	W-2002260	0267	3
REICHEL CHARLES P	MAJ	0-0295149	1043	2
REICHEL PAUL A	LTC	0-0222814	1049	3
REICHENAUER IRWIN E	MAJ	0-0265708	0358	3
REICHENBACH GLEN H	MAJ	0-0258311	0867	3
REICHENBACHER DAVI	MAJ	0-1799006	0757	1
REICHERS WILLIAM N	MAJ	0-0443400	0862	1
REICHERT DAVID L	LTC	0-1691474	0663	1
REICHERT FRED H	CPT	0-0298210	1044	1
REICHERT JOSEPH E	MAJ	0-1685710	0164	1
REICHERT MARION E	1LT	N-0777874	1046	1
REICHLE JR HENRY C	CPT	0-0977501	0762	1

NAME	GRADE	SVC NO	DATE RET MO YR	RET CODE
REICHLE SAMMY L	MAJ	0-1920046	0365	1
REICHLING FRANKLIN A	CW3	W-2153178	1163	1
REICHMAN DOROTHY S	1LT	N-0704026	0745	1
REICHMAN JULIAN F	1LT	0-1551938	0545	2
REICHMANN FRANCIS J	B G	0-0219282	0458	3
REICHMANN RICHARD S	MAJ	0-1101177	1146	1
REID ALEXANDER	LTC	0-0919378	0764	3
REID ALFRED J	MAJ	0-0256482	0753	3
REID AUBREY D	COL	0-0255099	0867	3
REID AUSTIN P	MAJ	0-0474367	0854	2
REID BEN C	CW2	W-2203348	0462	1
REID BOYD M	1LT	0-1593212	0145	2
REID CARN R	LTC	0-1107775	1062	1
REID CHARLES A	MAJ	0-1112932	1155	1
REID DAVID E	CPT	0-0961962	1161	1
REID EDWARD F	COL	0-0219648	0664	3
REID EDWIN M	LTC	0-1166163	0464	1
REID EDWIN P	CW3	W-2144142	1155	1
REID FRANCES E	MAJ	N-0732566	0165	3
REID GEORGE E	LTC	0-1553539	0766	3
REID GILMORE W	1LT	0-1102926	0345	2
REID GLENN R	MAJ	0-1327177	0566	2
REID HERBERT D	2LT	0-1047309	0344	2
REID HOWARD A	MAJ	0-0230443	0648	3
REID HYTHE A	1LT	0-0540042	0745	2
REID JACKSON B	CPT	0-0461729	0547	2
REID JAMES F	CPT	0-1314060	1154	2
REID JAMES J	MAJ	0-0334724	0862	1
REID JOHN C	CPT	0-0403229	1045	2
REID JOHN H	1LT	0-1166591	0148	2
REID JOHN M	LTC	0-1646898	0367	1
REID JOHN W	LTC	0-0281795	0261	1
REID JR DAVID T	CPT	0-2263093	0661	1
REID JR KINNEY E	1LT	0-1294723	0846	2
REID JR THOMAS J E	2LT	0-1311540	0744	2
REID JR WILLIAM S	LTC	0-0311239	0448	2
REID KENNETH R	MAJ	0-0948802	0165	1
REID LESLIE W	MAJ	0-1597804	0457	1
REID MARTIN T	CPT	0-0522351	1045	2
REID PATRICK M	MAJ	0-0505264	1052	1
REID ROBERT E	CPT	0-1013272	0760	2
REID ROBERT H	LTC	0-0180743	0952	3
REID ROBERT L	LTC	0-1554465	0863	1
REID ROBERT M	LTC	0-1551297	0457	1
REID ROBERT V	LTC	0-0241472	0366	3
REID ROGER C	COL	0-0287344	0865	3
REID SR DONALD R	MAJ	0-2263081	0165	1
REID STUART W	MAJ	0-1324850	0361	1
REID THOMAS G	CW3	W-2148588	0564	1
REID TRUMAN J	CPT	0-1168048	0746	2
REID VERNON	1LT	0-0216042	0260	3
REID WESLEY G	COL	0-0282855	0663	3
REID WILLIAM J	LTC	0-0434990	0464	3
REID WILLIAM T	LTC	0-0503233	0258	1
REIDELBACH FRANK	LTC	0-0382713	0761	1
REIDELBACH JAMES V	LTC	0-1638342	1265	1
REIDENBACH RICHARD C	1LT	0-0468425	0546	2
REIDPATH CHARLES C	COL	0-0178760	0949	3
REIDY DANIEL J	COL	0-0236915	0265	3
REIDY JOHN P	CPT	0-0505028	1046	1
REIDY PATRICK F	CPT	0-1107065	0855	1
REIDY RUDOLPH W	LTC	0-1951337	0967	1
REIDY WILLIAM F	1LT	0-1295270	0745	2
REIF LEONARD	1LT	0-1546126	0346	2
REIFEL BENJAMIN	LTC	0-0281241	1066	3
REIFENRATH HAROLD C	LTC	0-1003313	1160	1
REIGEL FRANK B	MAJ	0-0186417	0648	3
REIGHARD ROBERT H	MAJ	0-0316969	1048	1
REIHER ARNOLD F	LTC	0-0248833	0348	2
REIL HERMAN N	COL	0-1579003	0862	1
REILERT HAROLD	CPT	0-0481266	0246	2
REILEY RICHARD H	1LT	0-0497319	0845	2
REILING DANIEL L	MAJ	0-0955709	0262	1
REILLEY JOHN H	LTC	0-0131614	1146	2
REILLY DONALD E	LTC	0-1324952	0367	1

NAME	GRADE	SVC NO	DATE RET MO YR	RET CODE
REILLY EDWARD M	COL	0-0274391	0666	3
REILLY FRANCIS B	LTC	0-0513042	0463	2
REILLY FRANCIS J	LTC	0-0396871	0664	1
REILLY FRANK E	LTC	0-2005962	0766	1
REILLY GERTRUDE F	2LT	N-0723439	0944	1
REILLY GORDON G	LTC	0-0240586	0559	1
REILLY HOWARD E	MAJ	0-0452165	0346	2
REILLY JACK R	CW2	W-2110204	1053	1
REILLY JAMES E	COL	0-0339518	0660	1
REILLY JOHN A	LTC	0-0373790	0167	1
REILLY JOHN B	CPT	0-0410567	1046	2
REILLY JOHN F	MAJ	0-1596776	1061	1
REILLY JOHN M	COL	0-1635245	0767	2
REILLY JOHN R	COL	0-0187096	1046	2
REILLY JOHN R	COL	0-0198558	0758	3
REILLY JOSEPH A	LTC	0-0199108	0563	3
REILLY JOSEPH A	2LT	0-1799894	0949	1
REILLY JOSEPH F	COL	0-0453075	0963	1
REILLY JR JOHN A	LTC	0-1825437	0167	1
REILLY MICHAEL J	LTC	0-0205050	0961	3
REILLY PHILIP J	COL	0-0264597	0864	3
REILLY ROBERT J	MAJ	0-0520606	0447	2
REILLY STEPHEN J	CW2	W-2113454	0959	3
REILLY THOMAS F	CPT	0-1325141	0846	2
REILLY THOMAS J	CPT	0-1176474	0161	1
REILLY VINCENT E	1LT	0-1324788	0646	2
REILY PAUL A	CPT	0-1017870	0246	1
REIMAN LAWRENCE N	LTC	0-0319493	0461	1
REIMANN CURT A	LTC	0-1795819	0861	1
REIMER GEORGE L	LTC	0-1289624	1060	1
REIMERS C KENNETH	COL	0-0271586	0864	1
REIMLER GEORGE C	CW3	W-2150049	0464	1
REIN JR JOSEPH J	MAJ	0-1635247	0359	1
REINA DAVID J	COL	0-0319583	0661	1
REINA WILLIAM F	1LT	0-0477713	0144	2
REINBERG EINAR	LTC	0-0302686	0967	3
REINBERG MARTIN H	CPT	0-0542397	0346	2
REINBOTHE ALFRED H	LTC	0-0275497	1059	1
REINCKE FREDERICK	M G	0-0322850	1059	3
REINDERS HENRY A	LTC	0-1176475	0864	1
REINDL EDWARD W	CPT	0-2037092	1145	1
REINECK JOHN F	LTC	0-0288585	0559	1
REINECKE CALVIN C	CPT	0-0718020	0560	1
REINECKE CARL W	LTC	0-0225967	0364	3
REINECKE ERWIN P	LTC	0-0343794	0363	1
REINEKE ROY R	CW3	W-2143197	0762	1
REINEMEYER JOHN T	MAJ	0-1549584	0364	1
REINER ROBERT H	LTC	0-0258623	1160	1
REINER WALTER M	CPT	0-0442264	0144	2
REINERS CHARLES	1LT	0-2048459	1045	2
REINERS LILLIAN J	1LT	N-0703790	0146	1
REINERT GERVASE T	MAJ	0-0258271	0266	3
REINERT JOSEPH C	MAJ	0-0127562	0754	2
REINERT JR HOWARD O	MAJ	0-1291519	0859	1
REINERT PRICE D	MAJ	0-0428066	0462	1
REINES JOSE A	LTC	0-1284397	0266	1
REINFELD MARTIN H	MAJ	0-0549038	0564	1
REINFURT JOSEPH A	MAJ	0-0984327	0763	1
REINHARD WALTER F	CW3	W-2208929	0167	1
REINHARD WILLIAM S	MAJ	0-1017278	0264	1
REINHARDT BERT L	CPT	0-1302197	0662	1
REINHARDT CLARENCE W	LTC	0-0508448	0657	1
REINHARDT EDITH A	MAJ	N-0756360	0265	3
REINHARDT FRANK F	2LT	0-0440900	1144	2
REINHARDT GEORGE N	MAJ	0-1651875	0763	1
REINHART GEORGE P	CW3	W-2143445	1061	1
REINHART JAMES W	CPT	0-0510898	0141	1
REINHOLZ LEONARD J	LTC	0-0505429	1065	3
REININGER WILLIAM G	CW2	W-2205579	0760	2
REINKE HARRY A	COL	0-0275853	0166	3
REINKE RICHARD F	LTC	0-0341397	0467	3
REINKING HAROLD C	LTC	0-0360070	0761	1
REINOLD ARTHUR J	MAJ	0-1558609	1161	1
REINSMITH MARTIN C	CPT	0-1182232	0846	2
REIS FRANKLIN A	MAJ	0-1284576	0961	1

NAME	GRADE	SVC NO	DATE RET MO YR	RET CODE
REIS ROBERT	1LT	0-0347091	0945	2
REISCH HERMAN P	LTC	0-1580209	0461	1
REISEN WILLIAM E	CW4	W-2115263	0658	1
REISER CARLETON C	MAJ	0-0277060	1057	3
REISER JOSEPH	CPT	0-1308870	0446	2
REISER PAUL	MAJ	0-0323876	0746	2
REISIG CONRAD	1LT	0-0493959	0946	1
REISINE PHILIP	CW2	W-2210429	0662	1
REISING ANDREAS F	2LT	0-1575095	0743	2
REISING HENRY	MAJ	0-1173753	1057	1
REISING JOSEPH A	LTC	0-0219501	0664	3
REISINGER EDWARD A	CW2	W-2215284	0566	2
REISINGER EDWARD L	CW4	W-2148020	1067	1
REISINGER JOHN P VI	LTC	0-1796693	0461	1
REISLER BENNO J	CW3	W-2136728	0663	1
REISNER JR EDWARD H	CPT	0-0495055	1045	2
REISS FREDERICK	LTC	0-1181094	0467	1
REISS JACK	LTC	0-0322390	0866	3
REISS ROBERT S	CPT	0-0926070	0246	1
REISS SIDNEY A	COL	0-0321368	0766	3
REISTROFFER ROBERT J	LTC	0-1117195	0163	1
REISZ JR FRED C	MAJ	0-0450476	0557	1
REISZ LOUIS L	CPT	0-1576550	0948	1
REITEMEYER JOHN R	COL	0-0308796	0458	3
REITENBACH RUTH E	1LT	N-0728282	0346	1
REITER EDWARD	CPT	0-1306320	0347	2
REITH RICHARD T	MAJ	0-1924666	1264	1
REITHEL ROBERT J	LTC	0-0373115	0647	2
REITZ CHARLES B	LTC	0-0145088	0150	3
REITZ DELMAR A	2LT	0-2000752	0945	2
REITZ HENRY M	CPT	0-0466332	0745	1
REJMER STANLEY J	2LT	0-1323612	0145	2
RELAC PETER	LTC	0-1326169	0967	1
REMALEY CLARENCE A	COL	0-0295333	1052	2
REMALEY JOHN W C	COL	0-0237781	0566	3
REMALIA NEAL Z	1LT	0-0552584	0446	2
REMBIJAS MICHAEL F	MAJ	0-1041425	0660	1
REMEIN QUENTIN R	2LT	0-1288950	1044	2
REMER OSWALD M	LTC	0-1583553	0962	1
REMILY CONSTANCE	MAJ	N-0783231	0963	1
REMINGTON CECIL G	COL	0-0329403	1161	3
REMINGTON CHARLES E	COL	0-0329833	0365	3
REMINGTON KENNETH K	CW2	W-2149715	0565	1
REMINGTON LUCIUS D	1LT	0-0488722	1049	1
REMINGTON VYAN K	LTC	0-0510643	0563	3
REMLEY NORMAN W	LTC	0-0218024	0464	3
REMLEY ROBERT G	LTC	0-1797879	0658	1
REMMEL JOHN E	LTC	0-0354232	0767	3
REMMERS BERNHARD J	CPT	0-1586077	0154	1
REMMERS SR HERMAN R	CPT	0-0440589	0653	1
REMMIE JOHN A	LTC	0-1081717	0263	1
REMPE JAMES B	WO1	W-2147305	0866	2
REMSTER WALTER A	2LT	0-1341705	0349	2
REMUND DONALD E	LTC	0-0232275	0152	1
REMY JAMES G J	LTC	0-1576551	1163	1
REMY JOHN P	COL	0-0360539	1065	1
RENAK EDWARD T	CW4	W-2111903	1154	1
RENAKER CLINE R	CW2	W-2118135	1055	1
RENALD JOSEPH P	LTC	0-0250309	0857	3
RENARD LOUIS J	CW4	W-2003453	0765	3
RENAUD FRED E	CPT	0-2033868	0260	1
RENAUD ROGER J	MAJ	0-1298593	1060	1
RENBJOR CARL L	CW3	W-2152584	0765	1
RENCH CLIFFORD H	MAJ	0-2263466	1162	2
RENDEIRO CHRISTIAN	MAJ	0-1003151	0447	2
RENDEL ALLEN O	LTC	0-0225292	1159	3
RENDER ANDREW J	CW4	W-2142192	1265	1
RENDER HAROLD L	MAJ	0-1285642	0546	2
RENDINA RICHARD J	MAJ	0-1822626	0261	1
RENE JOSEPH L	CW2	W-2119603	0457	1
RENE VICTOR E	CW2	W-2211096	1263	1
RENEAU LONNIE M	CPT	0-0480752	1048	1
RENEAU THOMAS A	MAJ	0-0305285	1165	3
RENEGAR GERALD E	LTC	0-1045569	1058	1
RENFER RUDOLF A	CPT	0-0435028	0246	1

NAME	GRADE	SVC NO	DATE RET MO YR	RET CODE
RENFRO DONALD H	CPT	0-0162311	0160	3
RENFRO HENRY M	COL	0-0349066	1166	2
RENFRO IVOR P	CW2	W-2103355	0654	1
RENFROE DANIEL J	COL	0-0249999	0167	3
RENFROE EARL W	COL	0-0300463	0267	3
RENFROE GEORGE J	MAJ	0-1289806	1160	1
RENFROW DOUGLAS D	2LT	0-1318225	0445	2
RENFROW JR ARTHUR C	MAJ	0-1305951	0661	1
RENFROW LOUIS H	B G	0-0160948	0157	3
RENGER JULIUS J	MAJ	0-1703289	0446	2
RENICK FRED T	MAJ	0-0281613	0446	2
RENICK MAURICE D	CPT	0-0434159	0845	2
RENICK SAMUEL T	CPT	0-0444967	0349	1
RENIKER EVERETT T	COL	0-0418653	0662	1
RENK ROMAN J	CPT	0-1294903	1147	2
RENKEN GUSTAV H	CPT	0-1699903	0445	2
RENKEN HENRY E	COL	0-0223855	0857	3
RENN HAROLD J	CPT	0-0345916	1045	2
RENNA CARMEN J	1LT	0-1994981	0151	1
RENNARD ROBERT E	COL	0-0286163	0667	3
RENNEBAUM W C	1LT	0-1014279	0346	2
RENNER AUGUST N	CPT	0-0536913	1046	2
RENNER DONALD A	LTC	0-0395548	0960	1
RENNER HANS H	2LT	0-1644003	0944	2
RENNER JOSEPH	1LT	0-1102927	0944	2
RENNER JR GEORGE M	1LT	0-1299790	1045	2
RENNIE EDWARD F	CW2	W-2150600	1157	1
RENNIE JAMES F	LTC	0-0440901	0962	1
RENNIE SYLVESTER	MAJ	0-1683605	1044	2
RENO BILL E	CW3	W-2141661	1159	1
RENO RUSSELL R	LTC	0-0230250	1164	3
RENOFF GEORGE J	CPT	0-0359309	0146	2
RENSEMA ROBERT H	MAJ	0-1289965	0361	1
RENTMEESTERS WHILOME	MAJ	N-0773493	0661	2
RENTON BENJAMIN E	1LT	0-0447310	0646	2
RENTON JAMES M	1LT	0-0445189	0746	2
RENTON MAURICE F	CPT	0-0919604	0846	1
RENTZ ERIN E	LTC	0-0331427	1061	3
RENTZ NORMAN H	CW3	W-2114312	0860	1
RENZ ACEN D	LTC	0-0397814	0161	1
RENZI VERGINIO	LTC	0-1102586	0764	1
REODICA HERMOGINES	2LT	0-2032081	1047	1
REOH LYLE H	1LT	0-2040706	1144	2
REORDAN ROBERT E	LTC	0-1178303	1162	1
RERINE CLARENCE E	CW2	W-2207430	0263	1
REPKA ERIC J	CPT	0-2036929	0156	1
REPKE ALEXANDER	MAJ	0-0454401	0761	1
REPLOGLE NELSON R	MAJ	0-1576552	0961	1
REPLOGLE WILLIAM K	1LT	0-1018442	0446	1
REPPLINGER ELMER R	MAJ	0-2263063	0865	1
REPPOND CLYDE H	CW2	W-2149727	0467	1
REQUA EUGENE M	MAJ	0-0188371	0255	3
REQUEJO MARIANO P	1LT	0-1896712	0655	1
RESCHKE EDWARD E	1LT	0-1110758	0345	2
RESEK JR EPHRAIM F	COL	0-0198589	0762	3
RESEL FRANK L	CPT	0-1597259	0957	1
RESER JOHN W	LTC	0-1010715	0965	1
RESKEY BENJAMIN F	LTC	0-1533429	1057	1
RESNICOFF MURRA	LTC	0-0172906	0454	3
RESNICK JR WILLIAM V	MAJ	0-2008507	0161	1
RESNIKOFF ABRAHAM	1LT	0-1012581	1151	1
RESPESS BENJAMIN R	1LT	0-1305992	0445	1
RESSEGER JAMES L	1LT	0-1183600	0445	1
RESSL WILLIAM L	CW3	W-2003742	0666	1
RESSLER EDWIN A	MAJ	0-1013269	0561	1
RESSLER MARLIN A	CW2	W-2144969	1056	1
RESTEMAYER CLINTON E	CPT	0-1170159	0845	2
RESTERER ROBERT T	LTC	0-1012366	0161	1
RESTITUTO NICOLAS	1LT	0-1896791	0950	1
RESTO-VAZQUEZ JOSE A	CW3	W-2154864	0163	1
RESZCZYNSKI EUGENE	MAJ	0-1645942	0260	1
RETALLACK SHIRLEY W	CW2	W-2141896	1052	2
RETHEMEYER LLOYD O	MAJ	0-1105778	0262	1
RETTAGLIATA JOHN B	LTC	0-0402553	0661	1
RETTER EUGENE R	MAJ	0-1015947	0759	1

NAME	GRADE	SVC NO	DATE RET MO YR	RET CODE
RETTERER ALFRED C	LTC	0-1584784	C861	1
RETTIE WILLIAM	LTC	0-0371623	0757	1
RETZER EARL E	MAJ	C-0105135	0648	3
RETZKY CLARENCE	COL	0-0454052	0564	1
RETZLAFF ERNEST W	2LT	0-0397932	1041	2
REUBEN ARTHUR W	CPT	0-0451171	0149	1
REUBLIN KENNETH C	MAJ	0-1899407	1264	1
REUKEMA RUSSELL R	LTC	0-0193978	0860	3
REULET JEAN P	CW3	W-2149867	0865	1
REUM HARVEY E	MAJ	0-1648109	1056	1
REUPKE GORDON E	LTC	0-1170158	C462	1
REUS JR JOHN F	CW2	W-2208077	0559	1
REUSS GEORGE J	MAJ	C-1331868	C261	1
REUTER ALBERT J	LTC	0-1110760	0961	1
REUTER EUGENE A	LTC	0-1535266	0965	1
REUTER GEORCE J	CPT	C-0115754	0146	2
REUTER JR LOUIS	MAJ	0-1286706	1046	1
REUTER LESLIE S	CW4	W-2129190	0557	1
REUTER ORVILLE E	CW2	W-2116664	1143	2
REUTER ROBERT W	COL	0-0297767	1155	1
REUTERSHAN ALFRED O	COL	0-0167700	0558	3
REUTHER CHARLES R	CPT	0-0477955	C148	1
REUTTER DALLAS C	2LT	C-0524778	1044	2
REVELEY ROBERT W	LTC	0-0109429	0945	2
REVELL JAMES V	MAJ	C-1012979	0761	1
REVELL JOHN H	MAJ	0-0272872	0167	3
REVELLE RICHARD T	CW4	W-2144675	C360	1
REVERE DONALD J	LTC	0-1579009	0361	1
REVES NORMAN	CW3	W-2142265	C861	1
REVIER DONALD E	MAJ	0-0342229	C647	2
REVIS JOSEPH E	CPT	0-1290134	C446	2
REVIS JOSEPH H	CW2	W-2120833	0247	1
REVOIR RAY	2LT	0-1316091	1144	2
REW CLIFFORD R	CPT	0-1108262	0661	1
REW EDWARD A	COL	0-0245439	C759	1
REW HOWARD B	COL	0-0229420	C749	3
REWEY ORMOND E	COL	0-0179837	0756	3
REX SCOTT T	COL	0-0226748	C464	3
REXFORD CLARENCE F	COL	0-0129971	0648	3
REXFORD SIDNEY S	MAJ	0-1643268	0662	1
REXRODE HARRY M	LTC	C-0443979	0452	1
REY ANGEL	CPT	0-0203233	0563	3
REYBURN JOHN E	LTC	0-1055709	0366	2
REYER KARL O	COL	0-0167376	0959	3
REYES EVARISTO	1LT	0-0256855	0746	1
REYES JESUS	CPT	0-0260437	0744	2
REYES LOUIS F	LTC	0-1549045	0765	1
REYES OSMUNDO R	1LT	0-1896840	1162	1
REYES ROBERT L	MAJ	0-1913357	0564	1
REYES VIVIANO	CPT	0-1692559	0764	1
REYKALIN MARIE G	1LT	N-0784658	0546	1
REYNALDS GERALD H	LTC	0-0241521	0245	1
REYNARD LAWRENCE R	2LT	0-1020573	0348	2
REYNIERS ELMER E	MAJ	C-0504951	1056	1
REYNOLDS ALBERT G	CPT	0-0976814	1051	1
REYNOLDS BERNARD C	LTC	0-0312757	1065	3
REYNOLDS BERNARD E	LTC	0-2031828	0766	1
REYNOLDS BURNS	CPT	0-2262897	1264	2
REYNOLDS CHARLES L	LTC	0-0178451	0554	3
REYNOLDS CHARLES R	CPT	0-0942982	0357	1
REYNOLDS CHARLES W	LTC	C-0364128	0362	3
REYNOLDS CHARLES W	LTC	0-1030294	0961	1
REYNOLDS CYRIL H	LTC	0-1105758	0157	1
REYNOLDS DALE L	CPT	0-C539819	0747	2
REYNOLCS DAVID M	CPT	C-2262350	0958	1
REYNOLCS DONALD F	CW3	W-2150290	0265	1
REYNOLDS DONALD K	2LT	0-1303387	C344	2
REYNOLDS EARL E	LTC	0-1545021	1064	1
REYNOLDS EARL R	LTC	0-0376951	1060	1
REYNOLDS ERNEST W	1LT	0-1300219	0250	1
REYNOLDS EUGENE G	2LT	0-1047310	1051	1
REYNOLDS EUGENE J	MAJ	C-2020836	0660	1
REYNOLDS EUGENE P	MAJ	C-1015961	0760	1
REYNOLDS FLOYD H	WO1	W-2109024	0448	2
REYNOLDS FRANK J	CPT	0-1042147	C547	1

NAME	GRADE	SVC NO	DATE RET MO YR	RET CODE
REYNOLCS FREDERICK	1LT	0-1293308	0745	1
REYNOLDS GEAN H	MAJ	0-1288621	0161	1
REYNOLCS GEORGE W	1LT	0-0405903	0345	2
REYNOLDS GILBERT B	2LT	0-1112389	0144	2
REYNOLCS GRANT	CPT	0-0408560	0444	2
REYNOLCS GUY D	MAJ	C-2038879	0361	1
REYNOLCS HAROLD C	2LT	0-2055183	1044	2
REYNOLCS HELENE W	2LT	L-0402260	1044	2
REYNOLCS HENRY L	MAJ	0-0309458	0259	3
REYNOLCS HERSCHEL E	LTC	0-2038C27	0966	1
REYNOLCS HORACE L	COL	0-0243518	0864	3
REYNOLCS HORATIO N	LTC	0-0498511	0864	1
REYNOLCS HOWARD W	LTC	C-0299985	0667	3
REYNOLCS HUBER H	LTC	0-1577737	0760	1
REYNOLCS HUGH	LTC	0-1646902	0259	1
REYNOLDS JACK	LTC	0-2029763	0466	1
REYNOLCS JAMES A	LTC	0-0374485	0167	3
REYNOLCS JAMES E	LTC	0-0455553	0261	1
REYNOLCS JAMES E	CW3	W-2142658	0862	1
REYNOLCS JAMES H	LTC	0-0456568	0664	1
REYNOLCS JAMES H	2LT	0-1303546	0543	2
REYNOLCS JAMES M	LTC	0-0521016	0255	1
REYNOLCS JAY F	LTC	0-0230083	0756	3
REYNOLCS JESSE F	MAJ	0-0962188	0767	1
REYNOLCS JOHN	COL	C-0168122	0443	1
REYNOLCS JOHN F	CPT	0-1292760	1046	2
REYNOLDS JR JOHN L	LTC	0-1044932	0161	1
REYNOLCS JR WALTER A	MAJ	0-0959514	0166	1
REYNOLCS KENNETH P	MAJ	0-0334454	0847	2
REYNOLCS LEON K	MAJ	0-0151356	1055	3
REYNOLCS LEONARD E	MAJ	C-1291332	1062	1
REYNOLCS LLOYD A	LTC	0-0242551	0764	3
REYNOLCS MERLIN E	LTC	0-1004222	0962	1
REYNOLCS MICHAEL E	LTC	0-0535972	0264	1
REYNOLCS MILES H	CPT	0-0364947	0148	1
REYNOLDS NORMAN C	CPT	0-0357479	0645	2
REYNOLCS OLIVER W	2LT	0-0108254	0936	1
REYNOLCS OSCAR H	CW2	W-2151502	1060	1
REYNOLDS OSCAR L	CW4	W-2104412	0556	1
REYNOLCS PAUL L	CPT	0-0250404	0246	2
REYNOLDS PHILIP S	LTC	0-1320073	0367	1
REYNOLCS RAYMOND L	MAJ	0-2014571	0863	1
REYNOLCS RICHARD	LTC	0-1100299	1160	1
REYNOLCS RICHARD C	1LT	0-1103878	0246	2
REYNOLDS ROBERT C	MAJ	C-0982938	1262	1
REYNOLCS ROBERT H	LTC	0-0662826	0762	1
REYNOLCS ROBERT I	CPT	0-1685635	0857	2
REYNOLCS ROBERT J	MAJ	0-0958805	0163	1
REYNOLCS ROBERT V	MAJ	0-0977500	0164	1
REYNOLCS ROLAND W	CPT	0-0236165	1065	3
REYNOLCS ROY J	CPT	0-0969216	0860	1
REYNOLCS THOMAS J	CW4	W-2110682	1064	1
REYNOLCS ULRIC H	1LT	0-0372933	0846	2
REYNOLCS VIRGIL H	MAJ	0-1102010	0861	1
REYNOLCS WARREN C	CPT	0-2011127	0557	1
REYNOLCS WATSON J	CW3	W-2148222	0860	2
REYNOLCS WAYNE C	MAJ	0-1287411	1167	1
REYNOLCS WILLIAM D	LTC	0-1328402	1062	1
REYNOLCS WILLIAM G	CW3	W-2145496	0263	1
REYNOLDS WILLIAM J	1LT	0-1775506	0246	2
REYNOLCS WILLIAM M	COL	0-0274219	0453	3
REYNOLCS WILLIAM R	LTC	0-0175689	0157	3
REYNOLCS WILLIAM R	CW2	W-2146841	1060	1
REYNOLCS WILLIAM W	COL	0-0180526	0657	3
REZA BEULAH B	1LT	N-0801008	1047	1
REZABEK RICHARD A	2LT	0-1794989	0444	2
REZAC MARVIN J	MAJ	0-1341189	0166	1
REZARCH FRANK A	MAJ	0-1547536	1264	1
REZNICK IRWIN	CPT	0-1689543	1044	2
RHATIGAN BERNARD J	CPT	0-1286550	0265	1
RHEA GEORGE W	CW2	W-2209581	1164	1
RHEAUME FRANK O	CW2	W-2122494	1059	1
RHEAUME WALTER A	CW2	W-2151127	1163	1
RHEOMON DONALD T	MAJ	C-1304444	0157	1
RHEINGANS WILLIAM J	LTC	0-0151435	0858	3

NAME	GRADE	SVC NO	DATE RET MO YR	RET CODE
RHEUBY ELIZABETH	1LT	N-0763986	0846	1
RHEUPORT RICHARD W	MAJ	C-2028439	0866	1
RHINE DONALD C	MAJ	0-1636532	C847	2
RHINE RAYMOND D	LTC	0-0443100	0662	1
RHINEHART CLARENCE G	CW3	W-2207618	1066	1
RHINEHART FORREST H	MAJ	C-0280999	1161	3
RHOAD JR DANIEL L	LTC	0-C227699	0365	3
RHOADES CARL A	2LT	0-1305832	0545	2
RHOADES DONALD A	LTC	C-1101631	1061	1
RHOADES EARL A	LTC	0-1584785	1161	1
RHOADES FLETCHER D	MAJ	C-4006514	0267	1
RHOADS ALBERT W	LTC	0-0900284	0562	1
RHOADS EUGENE J	MAJ	0-1884210	0467	1
RHOADS GLENN W	LTC	0-0182961	0160	3
RHOADS HARLEY P	MAJ	0-0277841	0744	2
RHOADS JR WILLIAM F	LTC	C-1552585	1062	1
RHOADS RAYMOND O	1LT	0-1048547	C462	2
RHOADS WAYLAND	LTC	0-0199504	1152	3
RHODA WILLIAM O	MAJ	C-0889805	C863	1
RHODE RAYMOND H	MAJ	C-0400100	0760	1
RHODE RICHARD F	LTC	C-1112391	1062	1
RHODES CARL E	MAJ	0-0941040	C167	1
RHODES CHARLES M	CW2	W-2001744	C867	1
RHODES COOPER B	M G	0-0258656	1164	3
RHODES EARL D	CPT	0-0139818	1058	3
RHODES EDMOND A	MAJ	0-0972474	0865	1
RHODES EDNA F	2LT	N-0770019	C646	2
RHODES EDWARD J	CPT	0-0273344	C167	3
RHODES EDWARD P	MAJ	0-0442891	1044	2
RHODES FRED H	CPT	0-1057218	C747	1
RHODES GEORGE M	COL	0-0274369	1055	3
RHODES HENRY O	LTC	0-1002830	C961	1
RHODES HERMAN L	CPT	0-1683491	0647	2
RHODES JACK L	1LT	0-0543693	114N	2
RHODES JAMES A	CPT	0-0302295	C760	1
RHODES JOHN L	LTC	0-1302709	1263	1
RHODES JOHN M	CPT	C-0440586	0244	1
RHODES JOHN M	CPT	0-1308545	C847	2
RHODES JR CHARLES D	1LT	0-0557736	1045	2
RHODES JR CHARLTE E	CPT	0-0488308	0255	1
RHODES MARTIN C	COL	C-0191090	C146	2
RHODES PRENTICE B	MAJ	0-0494562	C347	1
RHODES RAY F	CPT	0-0345227	1045	2
RHODES RAYMOND E	MAJ	C-0998799	0965	1
RHODES RAYMOND K	2LT	0-2C09579	1046	2
RHODES RAYMOND R	WO1	W-2123284	C754	1
RHODES THOMAS D	CW3	W-2150844	C161	1
RHODES WILLIAM H	CW3	W-2148184	1059	1
RHODES WILLIAM J	LTC	0-1590753	1164	1
RHONE THOMAS B	LTC	0-0293624	0763	3
RHOTEN LOREN J	LTC	0-1172243	1262	1
RHU JR HERMAN S	MAJ	C-0518808	C646	2
RHUDY JAMES T	COL	0-0156189	1058	3
RHULE WALTER A	MAJ	C-1282392	1060	1
RHYNE LEE	CW2	W-2209342	1064	2
RHYNE LUADAN V	2LT	0-0109016	1152	1
RHYNE PLATO S	LTC	0-0288255	C267	3
RIALS THOMAS E	CW3	W-2154670	1164	1
RIANT IONEY A	CW3	W-2103359	C151	1
RIBA LEANDER W	LTC	0-0135397	C757	3
RIBAL RAYMOND R	COL	0-0243815	C761	3
RIBERDY BERNARD	MAJ	C-0959611	0865	1
RIBINSKY JOSEPH A	CW3	W-2142470	0261	1
RIBYAT MORRIS	2LT	0-0377897	0944	2
RICCARDI JOSEPH J	MAJ	G-2014543	C165	1
RICCARDI LOUIS B	CPT	0-0504590	C14C	2
RICCI ALFRED P	LTC	0-1301368	C958	1
RICCI ANTHONY J	MAJ	0-0260234	0364	3
RICCI FRANK G	CW2	W-3200715	1067	2
RICCI JR GABRIEL R	MAJ	C-1103880	C965	1
RICE ALFRED G	COL	0-0910429	0962	1
RICE ALLEN F	COL	0-0230223	C260	1
RICE CHARLES G	MAJ	0-1114274	C165	1
RICE CHARLES H	LTC	0-0391963	0860	1
RICE CHESTER	CPT	0-0989920	0561	1

NAME	GRADE	SVC NO	DATE RET MO YR	RET CODE
RICE CLARENCE C	MAJ	0-1015327	0564	1
RICE CLARK C	COL	0-0106255	0450	1
RICE DELAND C	LTC	0-0360308	0167	3
RICE DONALD C	LTC	0-1590220	0963	1
RICE DONOVAN J	COL	C-0257599	0665	1
RICE EARL J	LTC	0-0252434	0765	3
RICE EARL L	MAJ	C-0221546	C848	3
RICE ELDRIDGE N	1LT	0-1308706	0845	1
RICE ELLA M	MAJ	N-0743138	0165	1
RICE ELLSWORTH	MAJ	0-0118064	0256	3
RICE ERWIN M	LTC	0-1290542	0962	3
RICE EZEKIEL H	CPT	0-0476501	0348	1
RICE FREDERICK	MAJ	C-1107656	0363	1
RICE FREDERICK	CW2	W-2210211	0865	1
RICE FREEMAN D	CPT	0-0451733	0950	1
RICE G W	LTC	0-2018417	0766	1
RICE GEORGE	CPT	C-1290815	0857	1
RICE GLENN T	LTC	C-0371147	0861	1
RICE GUY V	LTC	C-0249317	0964	3
RICE HANS G	LTC	0-0355703	0346	2
RICE HARRISON S	CPT	0-0488967	1148	1
RICE HARVEY I	1LT	0-1167175	1045	2
RICE HELEN E	CPT	N-0742602	0647	1
RICE HENRY C	LTC	0-0189144	0846	1
RICE HORACE	CW2	W-2148985	0862	1
RICE HORACE G	LTC	0-0253152	1055	3
RICE HOWARD P	LTC	0-0304448	0864	3
RICE IRWIN G	MAJ	0-0546768	1264	1
RICE J MERRITT	CPT	0-0189958	0249	3
RICE JACK	CW3	RW-2150254	1265	1
RICE JOHN D	LTC	0-0435639	0863	1
RICE JOHN F	CPT	0-1577739	1265	3
RICE JOHN M	LTC	0-0414649	0564	1
RICE JOHN M	MAJ	0-1555610	0667	3
RICE JOSEPH	1LT	0-1913909	0235	1
RICE JOSEPH A	LTC	0-0407537	0762	1
RICE JOSEPH E	LTC	0-0102977	1044	2
RICE JOSEPH E	LTC	0-1014327	0167	3
RICE JOSEPH L	LTC	0-0260000	0762	1
RICE JOSEPH R	CW2	W-2102268	0649	1
RICE JR JAMES E	COL	0-0237316	0964	3
RICE JR JOHN L	1LT	0-1291883	0346	2
RICE JR JOSEPH C	LTC	0-1285499	0962	1
RICE JR LEE	CPT	0-0465790	0546	2
RICE JULEANNE J	MAJ	N-0756747	0165	1
RICE KEITH M	LTC	0-0329868	0858	1
RICE LELAND E	MAJ	0-0415919	1164	1
RICE LEONARD R	LTC	0-1294368	0657	1
RICE LEONARD W	CPT	0-1116570	0461	1
RICE LEROY	2LT	0-1045570	0844	2
RICE LESTER M	LTC	0-1011669	1064	1
RICE LOWELL C	LTC	0-0406827	1060	1
RICE LUIS F	MAJ	0-1288622	1160	1
RICE MARIAN K	CPT	L-0225400	0863	1
RICE MARWIN F	CW4	W-2110489	0659	1
RICE MELVIN W	MAJ	0-0324618	0961	1
RICE MERIDA	CPT	0-1286551	1052	1
RICE MILLARD F	MAJ	0-1882500	0365	1
RICE NEAL W	CPT	0-1184289	0962	2
RICE NOBLE R T	MAJ	0-0961199	0663	1
RICE NOLAND W	WO1	W-2128223	0756	1
RICE ORVILLE W	COL	0-0243847	1060	3
RICE PAUL W	MAJ	0-1557207	0455	1
RICE PETE L	MAJ	0-0493662	0557	1
RICE RALPH E	2LT	0-0258622	0266	3
RICE RAYMOND R	2LT	0-0378676	0442	1
RICE REGINALD M	CPT	0-0321216	1046	1
RICE RICHARD C	MAJ	0-2033632	0259	1
RICE RICHARD F	LTC	0-1109618	0962	1
RICE ROBERT C	COL	0-0247824	0255	3
RICE ROBERT J	LTC	0-1544768	0367	1
RICE ROBERT L	MAJ	0-1170937	0562	1
RICE SHEPHERD	MAJ	0-0270366	1167	3
RICE SIDNEY C	LTC	0-0174105	1263	3
RICE SUSAN K	2LT	N-0755339	0545	1

NAME	GRADE	SVC NO	DATE RET MO YR	RET CODE
RICE THOMAS A	COL	0-0342841	1060	1
RICE THOMAS R	LTC	0-1550690	0864	1
RICE TRUMAN A	LTC	0-0451384	C758	1
RICE WALTER A	MAJ	C-1318329	C861	1
RICE WALTER M	CPT	C-1297591	C247	1
RICE WALTER W	LTC	0-0274867	C963	3
RICE WILLIAM C	MAJ	C-1101632	C860	1
RICE WILLIAM G	CW4	W-2108850	1262	1
RICETTI JOHN	CW3	W-2205329	C264	1
RICH ARCHIE G	CPT	0-2007444	0857	1
RICH AUGUSTUS C	LTC	0-0195291	C454	3
RICH BRUCE A	MAJ	C-1844384	C757	1
RICH CHARLES	MAJ	C-1010472	C859	1
RICH EMORY E	1LT	0-1293118	C246	2
RICH GORDON	LTC	0-0918416	0864	3
RICH HAN H	MAJ	C-1055952	0261	1
RICH HENRY A	COL	0-0245146	0648	3
RICH LAWRENCE M	LTC	0-0313053	0863	3
RICH MAHLON S	LTC	0-1596475	C864	1
RICH MARGARET P	MAJ	N-0763304	C353	2
RICH ROBERT R	MAJ	0-1877102	1264	1
RICH SHERMAN G	2LT	0-1057219	0245	2
RICH THOMAS L	COL	0-0291118	C167	3
RICH THOMAS L	CPT	0-0965596	1057	1
RICH WALKER J	CPT	0-1281749	0846	2
RICH WILLIAM	COL	0-0188364	0455	2
RICH WILLIAM	CPT	0-0476383	1048	1
RICH WILLIAM L	LTC	0-0137038	0450	3
RICHARD ALLAN C	CPT	0-0411988	0844	2
RICHARD CHARLES A	1LT	0-2009737	0562	2
RICHARD ELI O	LTC	0-0310887	0559	3
RICHARD ERNEST C	LTC	C-0179963	0861	3
RICHARD GILBERT	2LT	0-2035973	0445	2
RICHARD HAROLD V	LTC	0-1289808	0960	1
RICHARD HENRY T	CPT	0-0248339	0444	2
RICHARD JOHN R	LTC	0-0276493	C862	3
RICHARD ROBERT E	MAJ	0-1285500	0446	2
RICHARD STANLEY G	LTC	C-1319338	0263	1
RICHARD W WAYNE	CW3	RW-2136741	1264	1
RICHARD WILTON J	LTC	0-0415804	C761	1
RICHARDE HENRY O	LTC	0-1185784	0163	1
RICHARDS ADDIE R	MAJ	N-0700464	0146	1
RICHARDS ANCIL D	CPT	0-0992539	0461	1
RICHARDS ARTHUR F	COL	0-0317506	0255	1
RICHARDS ARTHUR J	LTC	0-1039173	C961	1
RICHARDS BARBARA	CPT	L-0115605	C746	1
RICHARDS BURKE E	CPT	0-1058635	C855	2
RICHARDS CHARLES R	LTC	0-1556044	0366	1
RICHARDS CHARLES S	LTC	0-0170645	0254	3
RICHARDS CHARLES T	LTC	0-1102931	0562	1
RICHARDS CHARLES W	LTC	0-0471318	1167	3
RICHARDS CHARLES W	LTC	0-1053316	0763	3
RICHARDS CLAUDE	2LT	0-0157437	C940	1
RICHARDS DOROTHY M	MAJ	N-0799096	0765	1
RICHARDS EDWARD J	COL	0-0241036	0655	3
RICHARDS EDWARD R	1LT	0-1302350	1046	2
RICHARDS FRANK	[illegible]	0-0329568	1153	3
RICHARDS FRANK B	MAJ	C-0184676	1038	1
RICHARDS FRED J	1LT	0-1823750	1045	2
RICHARDS GEORGE E	LTC	0-0469768	0157	1
RICHARDS GEORGE H	1LT	0-0527535	1048	1
RICHARDS GEORGE H	CW2	W-2212985	1166	1
RICHARDS GEORGE S	1LT	0-0274065	0459	1
RICHARDS HAROLD T	LTC	0-1031753	C962	1
RICHARDS HARRY A	LTC	0-0231598	C264	3
RICHARDS HARTZEL E	LTC	0-0309310	C760	1
RICHARDS HERMAN	LTC	0-1534846	0561	1
RICHARDS HERMAN O	CPT	0-0303903	0544	1
RICHARDS HILTON	CPT	0-0491204	1147	1
RICHARDS HORACE S E	LTC	0-0313489	0863	1
RICHARDS JACK	LTC	0-0409654	1167	1
RICHARDS JAMES B	CW4	W-2001920	0467	3
RICHARDS JAMES H	CW3	W-2146739	0863	1
RICHARDS JAMES V	MAJ	0-1318930	1065	1
RICHARDS JESSE H	MAJ	C-1688376	0462	1
RICHARDS JOE G	COL	0-0405199	0946	2
RICHARDS JOHN P	LTC	0-1000458	0860	1
RICHARDS JOSEPH A	CW2	W-2144695	0663	1
RICHARDS JR ARTHUR F	CPT	0-1180313	0947	2
RICHARDS JR BURT L	CW4	W-2102269	0565	1
RICHARDS JR THOMAS E	COL	0-0343445	1066	3
RICHARDS JR WALTER L	1LT	0-0412840	0845	2
RICHARDS JR WILLIAM	CW2	W-2148265	0857	1
RICHARDS KENNETH E	CPT	0-0353884	1046	2
RICHARDS LEE C	CW2	W-2147120	0760	1
RICHARDS LEROY E	CW2	W-2205801	0863	2
RICHARDS MARCUS S	CPT	0-0482428	0145	2
RICHARDS MARY H K	2LT	N-0773740	1045	1
RICHARDS MAURICE E	MAJ	0-0888403	1056	2
RICHARDS NORMAN E	CW4	W-2143377	1166	1
RICHARDS PAUL H	MAJ	C-1172244	0264	1
RICHARDS REED H	COL	0-0272932	0464	3
RICHARDS ROBERT B	COL	0-0180646	0550	3
RICHARDS ROBERT E	MAJ	0-1171327	0862	1
RICHARDS ROBERT R	CPT	0-1693576	0345	2
RICHARDS ROBERT W	LTC	0-1547433	0263	1
RICHARDS STEPHEN L	CW4	W-2106144	0361	1
RICHARDS THOMAS O	MAJ	0-0961892	0263	1
RICHARDS THOMAS K	CPT	0-1634258	0748	2
RICHARDS WALTER W	LTC	0-1896005	0566	3
RICHARDS WILLIAM A	CPT	0-1113410	0846	2
RICHARDS WILLIAM S	COL	0-0290735	1261	1
RICHARDS WILLIAM S	CPT	0-0507899	0955	1
RICHARDS WILLIAM S	MAJ	0-1044654	0862	1
RICHARDSON ALAN	COL	0-0231005	0565	3
RICHARDSON ALBIN E	2LT	0-2033000	0448	2
RICHARDSON ALLEN	MAJ	0-0454046	0-53	1
RICHARDSON AMOS H	COL	0-0205661	0648	3
RICHARDSON ARTHUR K	2LT	0-1290660	1044	2
RICHARDSON ATLEE S	LTC	0-0884165	1264	3
RICHARDSON AUSTIN P	COL	C-0310165	0966	3
RICHARDSON BAXTER K	1LT	0-0180127	0450	3
RICHARDSON BRYANT F	LTC	0-1640866	0363	1
RICHARDSON CHARLES	LTC	0-0382112	1045	2
RICHARDSON CHARLES J	LTC	0-0113591	0747	2
RICHARDSON CHARLIE R	CPT	0-1998384	C455	1
RICHARDSON CHESLEY C	MAJ	0-0209648	0849	3
RICHARDSON CLAUDE	CPT	0-0245647	0648	3
RICHARDSON DALE N	CW3	W-2209409	0466	1
RICHARDSON DAVIS P	LTC	0-0253530	1162	3
RICHARDSON DEWEY F	CW2	W-2210343	1265	2
RICHARDSON DONALD V	LTC	0-0501015	1263	1
RICHARDSON DONALD W	1LT	0-1174690	1144	2
RICHARDSON EARL M	MAJ	0-1295273	0566	1
RICHARDSON EDWARD B	MAJ	0-0372778	0960	1
RICHARDSON EDWARD C	LTC	0-0209549	1059	3
RICHARDSON EDWARD R	LTC	0-0442234	0865	1
RICHARDSON ELMER M	LTC	0-02457CR	0161	3
RICHARDSON EMMETT V	COL	0-0269032	1066	3
RICHARDSON FRANCIS C	MAJ	0-1950617	0563	1
RICHARDSON FRANKLIN	LTC	0-1584789	0866	1
RICHARDSON GEORGE	CPT	0-0404921	0363	1
RICHARDSON GEORGE E	LTC	0-0374671	0962	1
RICHARDSON GEORGE H	LTC	0-0115944	0255	3
RICHARDSON GERALD A	CW2	W-2210450	0864	1
RICHARDSON GERALD E	LTC	0-1111330	1064	1
RICHARDSON HAMILTON	MAJ	0-1634255	0859	1
RICHARDSON HARLAN G	CW2	W-2116194	0347	2
RICHARDSON HAROLD W	CPT	0-1651990	0557	1
RICHARDSON HENRY B	CPT	0-1534367	1045	2
RICHARDSON HUGH F	LTC	0-1170164	0758	1
RICHARDSON IVAN O	MAJ	C-1644700	0157	1
RICHARDSON JAMES C	LTC	0-0329488	0365	1
RICHARDSON JAMES H	LTC	0-0384569	0564	3
RICHARDSON JEROME M	WO1	W-2116047	1051	1
RICHARDSON JESSE T	1LT	0-1914055	0247	1
RICHARDSON JIM W	LTC	0-0181277	0255	3
RICHARDSON JOHN O	MAJ	0-0206761	0749	3
RICHARDSON JR JOHN T	MAJ	C-0336419	0665	3
RICHARDSON LAWRENC	1LT	0-1286002	0145	1
RICHARDSON LOUIS K	CW3	W-2152981	1062	1
RICHARDSON LYMAN K	COL	0-0308070	0567	3
RICHARDSON MARION B	COL	0-0109403	C352	3
RICHARDSON MARVIN P	CPT	0-1165041	1150	1
RICHARDSON MARY S	MAJ	R-0002010	0266	1
RICHARDSON MELVIN O	CW2	W-2150951	0563	1
RICHARDSON NELSON R	LTC	0-0312503	0663	3
RICHARDSON NORWOOD G	LTC	0-1595782	0866	1
RICHARDSON ORRIE H	LTC	0-0372227	C862	1
RICHARDSON OVA K	MAJ	C-0534732	0950	1
RICHARDSON PAUL B	MAJ	0-2007278	1262	2
RICHARDSON PHILIP	CPT	0-1302351	C546	2
RICHARDSON RALPH W	LTC	0-0361978	C162	1
RICHARDSON ROBERT	MAJ	0-1644701	1159	1
RICHARDSON ROBERT A	MAJ	C-1115396	0259	1
RICHARDSON ROBERT B	2LT	0-1013488	1044	1
RICHARDSON ROBERT M	MAJ	C-1032041	0161	1
RICHARDSON ROONEY K	CW3	W-2205554	1266	1
RICHARDSON ROY L	2LT	0-1638359	C644	2
RICHARDSON RUPERT F	MAJ	0-1579014	1151	1
RICHARDSON WALTER F	LTC	0-0183087	1148	1
RICHARDSON WILLIAM	1LT	0-2036739	0556	1
RICHARDSON WILLIAM A	MAJ	0-2033619	0261	1
RICHARDSON WILLIAM K	MAJ	C-1041008	1059	2
RICHARDSON WILLIAM L	LTC	0-0553312	0166	1
RICHARDSON WILLIAM N	LTC	0-1108266	0564	1
RICHARDSON WILLIAM W	LTC	0-0175793	0961	3
RICHARDSON WILLOUG	LTC	0-0472669	1045	2
RICHARDSON WILSON O	CW2	W-2121062	C649	1
RICHARDSON WINNICK K	MAJ	C-1036353	0459	1
RICHBOURG ROBERT K	CPT	0-0271087	0146	2
RICHDORF MICHAEL L	CPT	0-0253942	C958	3
RICHE CHARLES H	CPT	0-0499814	0951	1
RICHERO ERNEST E	LTC	0-1577746	0267	1
RICHERSON JOHN L	LTC	0-0267039	0961	3
RICHERT ROBERT E A	COL	0-1583556	1166	2
RICHES HARRY L	LTC	0-0175155	C755	3
RICHESON EUGENE	CW2	W-2150050	C860	1
RICHESON LIONEL L	LTC	0-0229975	C963	3
RICHESON MARVIN G	COL	C-0185942	0348	2
RICHESON VOORHEIS	MAJ	0-0164834	1149	1
RICHEY CLAUDE G	MAJ	0-0282168	1058	3
RICHEY DWAIN W	2LT	C-1582075	0445	2
RICHEY ELBA L	MAJ	0-2097199	0767	1
RICHEY FRANK H	LTC	0-0277603	1162	3
RICHEY GEORGE H	2LT	0-1340808	1147	2
RICHEY GERALD L	MAJ	0-1641727	0463	1
RICHEY THURBER G	COL	0-0104977	1052	1
RICHEY TIM V	CPT	0-0368524	1045	2
RICHIE CHARLES W	CPT	0-0992463	0863	1
RICHIE ELLIS B	COL	0-0329574	0465	1
RICHIE JESSE T	LTC	0-1036695	0967	1
RICHIE JOHN L	LTC	0-1550904	0167	1
RICHIE OLLIE B	MAJ	0-1310372	0160	1
RICHIE RICHARD F	LTC	0-0239878	0766	3
RICHISTER WOODROW L	CW2	W-2141426	0958	1
RICHMAN ELMER	MAJ	0-0498207	C345	2
RICHMAN JOHN H	MAJ	0-1580222	0157	1
RICHMAN KENNETH	CPT	0-1014963	C854	1
RICHMAN MILTON H	COL	0-0361120	0758	3
RICHMAN MURRAY L	MAJ	0-1080141	0261	1
RICHMOND CHARLES B	COL	0-0266010	0166	3
RICHMOND CLARENCE	COL	0-0287025	C656	3
RICHMOND EDWARD A	MAJ	0-0127510	0648	3
RICHMOND FREDERICK	MAJ	0-1922648	0164	1
RICHMOND HARRY R	MAJ	0-0139164	0950	3
RICHMOND JOHN F	CPT	0-0461659	0347	1
RICHMOND JR ALLEN P	COL	C-0131011	0452	3
RICHMOND JR JOSEPH F	LTC	0-0454132	0267	1
RICHMOND LEROY M	MAJ	0-0959288	0163	1
RICHMOND LILLYN L	1LT	L-0700390	1045	2
RICHMOND MALCOLM F	CPT	0-1057573	0859	1
RICHMOND PAUL C	LTC	0-0329823	0267	3
RICHMOND RAYMOND E	CW4	W-2002900	0865	3
RICHMOND SIDNEY T	2LT	N-0726371	1145	1
RICHMOND WILLIAM E	MAJ	0-1894196	0564	2
RICHSTATTER ROBERT L	CPT	0-0949614	1060	1
RICHTER ARLINE F	CPT	N-0788035	0961	2
RICHTER EMANUEL J	MAJ	0-0272901	0246	2
RICHTER EUGENE A	LTC	0-0319441	0460	2
RICHTER EUGENE F	LTC	0-0342296	0346	2
RICHTER FORREST E	CPT	0-0456149	0645	2
RICHTER HIBBARD	COL	0-0127509	0546	2
RICHTER JOSEPH F	LTC	0-0264098	1145	2
RICHTER JR ALBERT E	LTC	0-1114725	1163	1
RICHTER JR STANLEY H	CW2	W-3430316	0967	1
RICHTER JULIUS J	CPT	0-0206975	0756	3
RICHTER ROBERT J	1LT	0-1304950	1145	2
RICHTER VIRGINIA O	2LT	N-0768100	0845	1
RICHWINE JR MARTIN W	COL	0-0291235	0463	3
RICK FRANK E	MAJ	0-0286487	0359	1
RICK LEO L	CPT	0-1319778	0446	1
RICKARD ERIC M	MAJ	0-0160718	0858	3
RICKARD HARRY C	LTC	0-0509682	0263	1
RICKARD WALLACE O	MAJ	0-1100741	0348	2
RICKARDS JOHN A	CPT	0-1583558	0362	2
RICKELL WILLIAM F	MAJ	C-1185379	0361	1
RICKER BERLE C	1LT	0-1016413	0446	2
RICKER CHESTER M	LTC	0-0124381	0846	2
RICKER ELMER J	LTC	0-0298518	0161	1
RICKER EUGENE K	MAJ	0-0133694	0945	2
RICKER RENARD	MAJ	0-1799185	0666	1
RICKER SHERWIN M	LTC	0-0244592	1064	3
RICKERT ALBERT A	LTC	0-2200539	1067	1
RICKES JOHN A	MAJ	0-1635255	0258	1
RICKETSON LEONARD W	COL	0-0233404	0355	2
RICKETSON MARION S	MAJ	0-0968508	0264	1
RICKETT NED	CPT	0-0410426	0245	2
RICKETT WILLIAM F	LTC	0-2055429	1262	2
RICKETTS WARREN E	CPT	0-0349514	0653	1
RICKETTS WILLIAM A	CPT	0-0997949	1157	1
RICKEY HARRY W	COL	0-0125073	0459	3
RICKEY VICTOR	MAJ	0-1597787	1060	1
RICKLE FRED M	CPT	0-0477704	1044	2
RICKLY FRANCIS A	COL	0-0133173	0156	3
RICKMOND CHARLES A	MAJ	0-0956274	0767	1
RICKS CECIL C	2LT	0-1286004	0157	1
RICKS GLENN W	CW3	W-2152109	0761	1
RICKSON RECY L	LTC	0-0451508	0255	1
RICOTTA SAMUEL J	2LT	0-1796153	0745	2
RIDDEL JAMES L	LTC	0-0526062	0446	2
RIDDELL HARRY M	1LT	0-1104365	0246	2
RIDDELL ROGER A	CPT	0-1110213	1059	1
RIDDER DON W	MAJ	0-1885369	0767	1
RIDDER PAUL A	1LT	0-1013223	0345	2
RIDDICK JOHN A	LTC	0-0242277	0164	3
RIDDICK JOHN F	MAJ	0-1031439	0360	1
RIDDICK WILBUR F	CW3	W-2145581	1060	2
RIDDINGER PHILIP H	COL	0-0288285	0961	1
RIDDLE AMOS J	CPT	0-0189691	0456	3
RIDDLE ARTHUR E	CPT	0-1579015	0762	2
RIDDLE BURGESS P	LTC	0-0460882	0763	3
RIDDLE GLENN N	MAJ	C-0145177	0648	3
RIDDLE LLOYD E	LTC	0-0322637	1164	3
RIDDLE PASKEL T	1LT	0-1016780	1154	1
RIDDLE RAYMOND L	MAJ	0-1641728	1160	1
RIDDLE ROBERT H	LTC	0-1684876	1266	3
RIDDLEBARGER G E	CPT	0-0958853	1060	1
RIDDLESWORTH A A	1LT	0-1582518	0347	2
RIDENOUR EMWOOD J	CW3	W-2152512	0964	1
RIDENOUR RUSSEL R	LTC	0-0107207	0450	3
RIDENOUR SAMUEL J	2LT	0-1845240	0245	1
RIDEOUT ERNEST W	1LT	0-1043208	0844	2
RIDEOUT EUGENE W	COL	0-0113245	0256	3
RIDER EUGENE F	MAJ	0-0205521	0642	1
RIDER IRVIN S	1LT	0-2012056	0358	1
RIDER JOHN F	LTC	0-0901793	0645	2
RIDER RALPH R	WO1	W-2126253	1047	1
RIDGAWAY BERT E	CW2	W-2147341	0264	1
RIDGE ALVIN	1LT	0-1302884	104N	2

NAME	GRADE	SVC NO	DATE RET MO YR	RET CODE
RIOGE BUPRELL B	CPT	0-1176780	1150	1
RIOGEWAY CLEM E	LTC	0-1176174	0967	1
RIOGEWAY OONALO F	LTC	0-0491156	0465	1
RIGGEWAY MARION E	CW2	W-2112989	C145	2
RIOGEWAY PAUL E	CPT	0-2263666	0663	1
RIOGLEY ARTHUR G	MAJ	0-0507301	0446	2
RIOGWAY OONALD O	MAJ	C-1016297	1061	1
RIDGWAY ROBERT J	CPT	0-0533718	1046	1
RIDING CECIL K	2LT	0-1048166	0244	2
RIOLEY JOHN H	CW3	W-2148302	1062	1
RIOLEY MARY JO	2LT	N-0703037	1041	1
RIOLON ERNEST S	CPT	0-0233903	1164	3
RIEBE JOHN	LTC	0-0495455	C758	1
RIEBE NORMAN J	COL	0-0298997	C463	3
RIEBER CHARLES W	CPT	0-0324232	1045	2
RIECK JR WILLIAM J	LTC	0-1171736	0864	1
RIECK WILLIAM E	CW3	RW-2135664	0862	1
RIECKEN JIMMIE F	LTC	C-1285305	C563	1
RIEDEBURG HERMAN W	LTC	0-0420529	0363	1
RIEOEL CHARLES A	MAJ	0-0177926	0462	3
RIEOEL ROBERT H	LTC	0-0251191	1045	2
RIEDINGER ALBERT A	LTC	0-0338954	C962	3
RIEDLEY EARLE C	LTC	C-0453647	0357	2
RIEOY OWEN L	CPT	0-1947812	0149	2
RIEF ROLAND W	1LT	0-0502919	0449	1
RIEFLING RICHARD C	LTC	0-0204397	0363	3
RIEGEL FRANK E	CPT	0-1039527	0364	1
RIEGEL LEO A	LTC	0-0322208	1059	3
RIEGELMAN HAROLD	COL	C-0211708	0852	3
RIEGER MORRIS J	CPT	0-1307077	C746	2
RIEGER WRAY M	COL	0-0223926	0662	3
RIEGERT JR LOUIS C	CPT	0-0480266	1045	2
RIEGLE ROY W	COL	0-0177389	0456	3
RIEGLER RICHARO O	MAJ	C-0375530	C560	1
RIEHM RICHARO W	LTC	0-155316C	0766	1
RIEKE BENNY A	CW3	W-2145497	1263	1
RIEKSE ROBERT J	MAJ	0-1165040	1047	2
RIEL DAVID H	MAJ	0-0304451	C954	1
RIEL JOSEPH L	CW2	W-2147411	0659	1
RIELANO GEORGE D	CPT	0-0397591	0944	2
RIELLY JAMES B	LTC	0-1544098	0465	1
RIELLY ROBERT W	CPT	0-0872093	1146	2
RIENDEAU NELSON N	CPT	0-0496689	C547	1
RIERSON GLENN O	LTC	0-0451050	0258	1
RIESENBERG MARGARET	1LT	N-0726896	C145	2
RIESINGER SIMON	MAJ	0-1300220	1166	1
RIESMEYER JOHN F	CPT	0-1107658	1050	1
RIESS ANDREW J	1LT	C-1593932	1147	2
RIESS WALTER G	CPT	0-1930335	C463	2
RIESSBECK JOHN	CPT	0-2103026	0462	1
RIEWERTS ERROLL S	MAJ	0-0974524	C563	1
RIFE BYRON	COL	0-0120862	0852	3
RIFE JOHN W	LTC	0-0337820	C660	1
RIFE STANLEY S	1LT	0-1312719	1045	2
RIFFEL EMERY J	CW3	W-2142892	C561	1
RIFFEL JOSEPH O	1LT	0-1648450	C159	2
RIFFENBURG WALTER V	CPT	0-0200328	0253	3
RIFFERT REYNOLOS H	1LT	0-1590135	1044	2
RIFKIN JULIAN S	CPT	0-0343983	1045	2
RIFLEMAN JAMES O	MAJ	0-18447C0	1162	1
RIGAL WALDO A	MAJ	C-0268380	0755	3
RIGBY OONALO N	COL	0-0178611	1160	3
RIGBY HENRY S	CPT	0-0438993	C446	2
RIGBY JACK B	LTC	0-1580225	1062	1
RIGBY JOUROAN	CPT	0-0443564	1045	2
RIGBY JR LOEHR M	LTC	0-1821913	0265	1
RIGBY LINOEN G	LTC	0-0410769	1045	1
RIGBY LUCY	MAJ	L-0807500	0663	1
RIGBY RAUL T	COL	0-0331137	C340	1
RIGBY ROBERT L	LTC	0-1579018	0261	2
RIGDON HAROLD E	LTC	0-1000656	1061	1
RIGDON RALPH E	LTC	0-1287062	0164	1
RIGG CLIFTON F	CW4	W-2147774	0866	1
RIGG JOHN P	LTC	0-0464205	1154	1
RIGGAN JOHN W	CRT	0-2263500	0162	1
RIGGIN BENJAMIN F	CPT	0-0278089	0855	3
RIGGIN GEORGE B	LTC	0-1000462	0657	1
RIGGIN JR BENJAMIN F	1LT	0-0420041	0146	2
RIGGINS EMMETT	MAJ	0-0487839	0946	1
RIGGINS JAMES L	LTC	0-2289189	0462	2
RIGGLE CLORAN O	LTC	0-0219947	0446	2
RIGGLE PAUL	MAJ	0-0271798	0442	1
RIGGLEMAN ESKER H	MAJ	C-1639548	0954	1
RIGGS CHARLES E	MAJ	0-0908662	0845	2
RIGGS CHARLES R	CPT	0-1644008	0746	2
RIGGS CLARENCE B	LTC	0-0267439	0240	2
RIGGS ECWARO C	MAJ	0-0971981	0163	2
RIGGS FRANK P	1LT	0-1327042	0746	1
RIGGS GLENN E	CPT	0-1289626	1045	2
RIGGS GRCVER C	LTC	C-0921986	1067	3
RIGGS LEO J	MAJ	0-1306471	1060	1
RIGGS ROBERT C	LTC	0-0239891	0559	3
RIGGS RUTH J	2LT	N-0701710	1040	1
RIGGS WILLIAM H	CW3	W-2110331	0158	1
RIGHTER HALL T	CW3	W-2143959	0163	1
RIGLER RALPH L	LTC	0-0383942	0764	1
RIGLER RAYMONO M	LTC	0-0382755	0766	1
RIGLEY ALBERT J	2LT	0-1318228	0344	2
RIGNEY HUBERT M	1LT	0-0185327	0151	3
RIGO CHARLES P	LTC	0-0339923	0862	2
RIGSBY CHARLES H	MAJ	0-0286367	1044	2
RIGSBY VERL W	MAJ	0-0407279	0646	2
RIHA JCHN O	MAJ	0-1C60609	0760	1
RIHELOAFFER WILLIAM	COL	0-0234376	1065	3
RIKARO WILLIAM E	MAJ	0-0336493	0467	3
RIKER CHARLES E	LTC	0-0520312	1165	3
RIKER CAVIC C	LTC	0-0405986	0155	1
RILEY AONREW R	LTC	0-1294371	0658	1
RILEY CHARLES H	LTC	0-0373448	0567	3
RILEY CCMNICK G	LTC	0-1590136	0464	1
RILEY FLCYD A	MAJ	0-1031835	0361	1
RILEY FRANK	MAJ	0-1686289	0155	1
RILEY FRANK E	CPT	0-0422826	C561	1
RILEY FRED A	CPT	0-1698848	0156	1
RILEY FREO T	CW4	W-2004524	0865	3
RILEY GALYE	1LT	0-0444112	0145	2
RILEY GECRGIA S	2LT	N-0742741	1044	1
RILEY HAROLO B	LTC	0-0173966	1057	1
RILEY HARRY T	LTC	0-117761C	0864	1
RILEY HERBERT E	2LT	0-1558076	0245	1
RILEY JAMES A	2LT	0-1321332	1045	2
RILEY JAMES F	CW3	W-2142266	1058	1
RILEY JAMES L	CPT	0-104963C	0460	2
RILEY JAMES L	CW3	W-2147918	0762	2
RILEY JAMES R	MAJ	C-0466568	0646	2
RILEY JCHN C	MAJ	C-0398950	0847	2
RILEY JCHN E	CW2	W-2151730	1062	1
RILEY JCHN W	MAJ	0-1030708	1060	1
RILEY JCHN W	LTC	0-1534610	0362	2
RILEY JR FRANCIS E	1LT	0-1594422	104N	2
RILEY JR HARRY A	CPT	0-1284399	0246	2
RILEY JR JOHN P	MAJ	0-0493859	0354	1
RILEY MARTIN G	COL	C-0888371	0862	1
RILEY MARVIN H	LTC	0-1166816	1059	1
RILEY MARY B	1LT	N-0735643	0447	1
RILEY MASON H	CPT	0-0129344	0354	3
RILEY MAX W	CPT	0-0260546	0949	1
RILEY PAGE M	CPT	0-1305112	0346	2
RILEY PERRY N	CPT	0-0450667	0757	1
RILEY PLEASANT O	CW2	W-2211906	0566	1
RILEY RENWICK N	LTC	0-1037904	0361	1
RILEY RICHARO C	1LT	0-2047799	0945	2
RILEY RCBERT R	MAJ	0-1015566	1162	1
RILEY ROY	1LT	0-04505C8	1043	2
RILEY SAMUEL W	LTC	0-1288446	0764	1
RILEY THCMAS E	1LT	0-1113913	0246	2
RILEY THOMAS M	2LT	0-0539800	1045	2
RILEY VIVIAN F	CPT	0-0261011	1045	2
RILEY WALTER F	CPT	0-1683473	1059	1
RILEY WARREN S	LTC	0-0226038	0964	3
RILEY WILLIAM C	1LT	0-1283841	0644	2
RILEY WILLIAM E	1LT	0-1015653	1045	2
RILEY WILLIAM J	CPT	0-0401637	0461	1
RILEY WILLIAM J	2LT	0-1797530	1043	2
RILEY WILLIAM L	CW3	W-2147027	0165	1
RILEY WILLIAM R	COL	0-1796859	0266	3
RILEY WILSON M	COL	0-0246769	0467	3
RILLONA CESAR C	1LT	0-1896932	C849	1
RIMBACK JOSEPH A	LTC	0-157413C	0561	1
RINER HOWARC W	MAJ	0-0278062	0466	3
RIMES WILLIAM G	CPT	0-1285501	C846	1
RIMMER JR BENNIE H	CPT	0-0579005	0746	2
RINALOUCCI RALPH J	LTC	0-0573117	1163	1
RINAMAN JAMES C	COL	0-0317293	0663	3
RINCK ROBERT E	LTC	0-0831804	0466	1
RINEBOLD WILLIAM C	CPT	C-1577750	C954	1
RINEHART BERNARD F	LTC	0-0280916	0467	3
RINEHART CLEO A	LTC	0-0175751	0162	3
RINEHART OEVDE A	1LT	0-0301575	0450	1
RINEHART ELWELL C	CPT	0-0295641	0645	1
RINEHART JOHN C	CW3	W-2208152	1067	1
RINEHART JOHN W	LTC	0-1013609	0261	1
RINEHART MIKE	LTC	0-0371635	C164	3
RINEHART ONRO W	CW3	W-2148699	0963	1
RINEHART ROBERT L	MAJ	0-1046624	1163	1
RINEHART STANLEY L	CW2	W-2103366	C447	1
RINER ROBERT D	CW2	W-2148083	0357	1
RING AOOLPHUS L	COL	0-0346915	0554	3
RING CARLYLE D	MAJ	0-2010344	1160	1
RING GUSTAVE A	COL	0-0282568	0263	3
RINGE JR CHARLES L	CPT	0-0332658	0146	2
RINGEL HAROLO L	1LT	0-1581338	C843	2
RINGEL WILLIAM E	LTC	0-0181161	0162	3
RINGENBACH RAYMOND F	2LT	0-1322125	1044	2
RINGER ECWARD L	CPT	0-0440755	1145	1
RINGER JOHN F	LTC	0-1041635	1165	1
RINGER MATTHEW J	LTC	0-1174121	1262	1
RINGER SMITH	1LT	0-0165777	0151	3
RINGEY LAWRENCE E	MAJ	0-1924536	1064	1
RINGGOLO GORDON B	COL	0-0205501	1163	3
RINGKVIST ROBERT C	LTC	0-0534666	0667	1
RINGLAND AUGUSTUS G	2LT	0-1012187	C944	2
RINGLAND EDWARD D	MAJ	0-1635258	C555	1
RINGLE LEO W	CW2	W-2143488	1054	1
RINGLER LEWIS J	1LT	0-0524161	1045	1
RINGLER MILTON E	CPT	0-0473320	0846	1
RINGLER WILLIAM F	MAJ	C-0909388	1044	2
RINGSRUO RONALD H	LTC	0-0355009	C467	1
RINGSTROM BERTIL L	CW3	W-2149737	0558	1
RINGWALO ROBERT K	1LT	0-1822056	0546	2
RINGWALT CHARLES C	LTC	0-0139999	0655	3
RINK TEC D	MAJ	C-1288958	0656	1
RINKAVAGE JOSEPH P	CW2	W-2440015	C566	1
RINKE JOSEPH G	CPT	0-0372822	C464	1
RINKER ALBERT E	MAJ	0-1031754	0360	1
RINKER CHARLES J	LTC	0-0912021	1164	3
RINKES EARL W	CW3	W-2144291	1062	2
RINKLE BILL	MAJ	C-1824370	C258	1
RINKS ZACK H	CPT	C-0483745	0248	1
RINN RALPH E	COL	0-0310109	0846	2
RINSLANO HENRY O	MAJ	0-0214922	0346	2
RINTLEMAN GLEN C	2LT	0-2023626	1045	2
RINTOUL WILLIAM	LTC	0-2051296	0266	1
RIOLLANO CARLOS	LTC	0-0359821	0960	1
RION GEORGE P	CW2	W-2118514	0553	1
RION HOWARO G	LTC	0-0349233	C447	2
RIORDAN DON F	LTC	0-1548133	1060	1
RIORDAN RALPH E	LTC	0-0247427	0457	2
RIORDAN THOMAS M	MAJ	C-1301881	1064	2
RIOS OAN J	2LT	0-1306789	0145	2
RIPALOA ANTONIO	1LT	0-1896889	1164	1
RIPICH JOHN W	CPT	0-0344742	1045	2
RIPLEY FRECERICK	1LT	0-1824371	C246	1
RIPLEY JR JOSEPH M	2LT	0-1699970	0848	1
RIPLEY RAUL H	CPT	0-1180687	0748	1
RIPP JACCB	MAJ	0-0356597	0446	2
RIPP JCHN P	LTC	0-1583563	0462	1
RIPPE HENRY A	LTC	0-0522179	C863	3
RIPPEE ROBERT L	MAJ	0-1542633	0661	1
RIPPER LLOYD E	CW2	W-2146578	0361	1
RIPPERTCN NACINE	2LT	N-0771458	0246	1
RIPPETCE DAVIO L	MAJ	0-2263424	0167	1
RIPPLINGER ORLEY K	LTC	0-0279855	0267	3
RIPPY BAYARD W	2LT	0-1309834	0451	1
RIPPY ELKIN L	LTC	0-0239890	0845	2
RIPPY PAUL	MAJ	0-1573541	1157	1
RIPSTRA EARL F	COL	0-0242610	1163	3
RIPSTRA HENRI I	LTC	0-1183172	0965	3
RIQUELME ALEXANDER	LTC	0-0476176	0-52	1
RISBURG RUBIN C	COL	0-0193640	0756	3
RISDEN MILFORD	CPT	0-0989046	1060	1
RISELEY JR JERRY B	1LT	0-0414699	0545	2
RISEN ROLLIN F	COL	C-0334411	1057	3
RISER GEORGE M	LTC	0-0228767	C664	3
RISH EARL B	CPT	0-2289641	0762	1
RISHE MARK N	LTC	0-1107076	0962	2
RISHEBARGER ECWARO S	LTC	0-1119536	0164	1
RISHEILL CLARENCE E	MAJ	0-1170939	0561	1
RISHELL CHESTER A	MAJ	C-0341497	0364	3
RISING CAROLL A	LTC	0-0273557	0765	3
RISING FREOERIC O	LTC	0-0168232	1157	3
RISING STANLEY A	LTC	0-1038805	1263	1
RISINGER ERNA E	2LT	N-0729401	1144	1
RISK ECWARO	CW2	W-2208337	0364	2
RISKE CHARLES W	LTC	0-1100304	0960	1
RISKIN SAMUEL	1LT	0-0157943	0355	3
RISKO EOWARO F	CW3	W-2141135	0959	1
RISLEY DANIEL L	LTC	0-0909704	0463	1
RISPOLI FRANK V	1LT	0-1229347	1045	2
RISSE EUGENE J	CPT	0-0255887	0141	1
RISSER ANDREW A	LTC	0-0242165	1163	3
RISSLER JOHN C	LTC	0-1534369	0661	1
RIST ALSTIN S	COL	0-1040061	0866	1
RIST CHARLES M	COL	0-0320384	0859	3
RISTAINO JCHN R	CW3	W-2141738	0860	1
RISTAU GUSTAV A	CPT	0-0245552	1047	2
RISTEOT ERNEST J	COL	0-0104062	0648	3
RISTINE LEONARD P	LTC	0-0354208	1146	1
RITCH ALLEN	LTC	0-0233845	1061	3
RITCHAROSON WALTER L	CPT	0-1341708	1160	1
RITCHEY HAROLO E	1LT	0-1176781	1046	2
RITCHEY JOHN A	MAJ	0-0318573	0243	1
RITCHEY ROY V	CW2	W-2209613	0363	1
RITCHIE CECIL C	LTC	0-1286362	0866	2
RITCHIE OAVIC K	CW3	W-2145233	0963	1
RITCHIF CAVIO D	CW3	W-2148148	1163	1
RITCHIE GUY G	MAJ	0-0970225	1264	1
RITCHIE III JCHN	COL	0-0911465	0464	3
RITCHIE JOHN G	MAJ	0-0967381	0965	1
RITCHIE KENNETH W	CPT	0-1824085	1056	2
RITCHIE LLOYC C	COL	C-0145365	0350	3
RITCHIE RALPH O	CPT	0-1878174	1265	1
RITCHIE RAY M	MAJ	0-0156782	0653	3
RITCHIE ROBERT B	LTC	0-0243946	0564	3
RITCHIE THOMAS N	COL	0-0280542	0460	1
RITCHIE VERL C	2LT	0-1589463	0743	2
RITCHIE WILLIAM B	CW2	W-2153188	0460	1
RITENOUR HARCLO R	CW3	W-2205537	0267	1
RITENOUR PAUL A	CW2	W-2150163	0659	1
RITHMAN CHARLES	1LT	0-2046705	0158	1
RITKO JOSEPH J	LTC	0-1645948	1063	1
RITNER JOHN A	MAJ	0-1634515	0260	1
RITTENBERG ECITH F	1LT	L-0116025	0446	1
RITTENER LOUIS G J	MAJ	C-0504311	0460	1
RITTENHCUSE WILLIAM	CRT	0-1285821	1265	1
RITTER ARTHUR E	CW4	W-2109013	0659	2
RITTER CLOVIS O	LTC	0-0316589	0266	1
RITTER OONALO L	LTC	0-0398471	0561	2
RITTER EUGENE S	CW4	W-2141664	0762	1
RITTER FREO J	LTC	0-0282898	0456	3

NAME	GRADE	SVC NO	DATE RET MO YR	RET CODE
RITTER GEORGE T	LTC	0-0347649	0558	3
RITTER HAROLD F	MAJ	0-1944571	0546	2
RITTER HAROLD K	CW3	W-2149965	C461	1
RITTER JOHN J	LTC	0-0267716	0140	2
RITTER JR CHARLES S	1LT	0-1795973	1144	1
RITTER LEONARD C	1LT	0-C885711	1055	1
RITTER LEROY A	LTC	0-0213535	0164	3
RITTER LESTER W	CPT	0-1596996	0566	1
RITTER RAYMOND N	CPT	C-1691736	1154	1
RITTER ROBERT J	CPT	0-1795974	0345	2
RITTER WARREN W	CPT	0-0976778	0657	1
RITTERHOLZ BERNARD J	CPT	0-0445821	1048	1
RITTERMAN HENRY	CPT	0-0485551	1045	2
RITTERSPACHER PHILLI	LTC	C-0297704	C867	3
RITZ ANTHONY A	LTC	0-1111331	0261	1
RITZ JR ROBERT S	LTC	0-1166818	1060	1
RITZ RALPH K	LTC	0-1335979	0766	1
RITZ SHERWOOD F	LTC	0-0909530	0657	2
RITZO EUGENE	LTC	0-1332420	0663	1
RIVARD REGINALD J	LTC	C-0451172	C658	1
RIVCHUN FREDERICK	MAJ	0-1010341	0446	2
RIVELLESE JULIUS C	CPT	0-0495949	0346	2
RIVELY JOSEPH C	LTC	0-0317309	1159	1
RIVENBARK GEORGE M	CW4	W-2125292	0758	1
RIVER HENRY L	CPT	0-1577756	0457	1
RIVERA ALFREDO	1LT	0-2263290	0460	1
RIVERA ANIBAL R	CPT	0-0417257	0261	1
RIVERA CESAR L	1LT	0-0504779	0847	2
RIVERA EDELMIRO	MAJ	0-1288447	0358	1
RIVERA EUGENIO M	LTC	0-0173227	0460	3
RIVERA GIL A	1LT	0-2027038	0951	1
RIVERA JACINTO	LTC	0-0405131	1060	1
RIVERA JAMES O	MAJ	0-0577095	1262	1
RIVERA JOSE	2LT	0-1583564	0247	1
RIVERA JOSE A	COL	0-0513618	C365	3
RIVERA JOSE A	MAJ	0-1288450	1060	1
RIVERA JOSE R	CW3	RW-2147670	0965	1
RIVERA JUAN J	MAJ	0-0200739	0352	3
RIVERA LUIS A	MAJ	C-1328748	1063	1
RIVERA MARIA G	MAJ	N-0779152	1065	3
RIVERA MIGUEL	1LT	0-0468066	C867	1
RIVERA PATRICIA M	1LT	N-0732092	0745	1
RIVERA RAFAEL M	CPT	0-0528185	1145	2
RIVERA RAMON	2LT	0-0275562	1051	1
RIVERA ROSLINA	1LT	N-0901539	1153	2
RIVERA VICTOR M	CPT	0-0420511	C645	1
RIVERA&NEGRON JORGE	2LT	0-C445051	0144	2
RIVERA-PEREZ SANTOS	CW3	W-2151665	C962	1
RIVERO HARRY	MAJ	0-4005259	0566	2
RIVERS FORREST E	1LT	0-0494271	0946	1
RIVERS III THOMAS N	CPT	C-1686684	0465	1
RIVERS LA VERNE L	LTC	C-0274547	0958	1
RIVERS LANGDON U	2LT	0-1311206	0944	2
RIVERS LEO A	CPT	0-1651658	0458	2
RIVERS SR JOHN L	CW2	W-3430449	1167	1
RIVERS THOMAS N	MAJ	0-0410870	0563	1
RIVES JOHN C	CPT	C-2262868	0461	1
RIVES POWELL F	1LT	0-0545693	0146	2
RIVES ROBERT C	LTC	C-0156785	1052	3
RIVIERE WILLIAM T	LTC	0-0151226	0347	2
RIVKIN NORMAN	2LT	0-0887699	0945	2
RIVKIN RAYMOND	CPT	0-0371893	0144	2
RIVOIRE EMMA C	LTC	N-C722502	0761	1
RIX THEODORE A	CW3	RW-2209602	0264	1
RIXEY GEORGE Y	COL	0-1583565	1266	1
RIZER ARTHUR L	1LT	0-1303547	C845	2
RIZNER ANDREW	MAJ	C-0262242	1058	3
RIZZARDI ALBERT J	2LT	0-2023754	0446	2
RIZZIO ANTHONY P	1LT	0-5013917	0865	2
RIZZO DOMINICK A	MAJ	C-1648114	C965	1
RIZZO FRANK A	CPT	0-2055149	C647	2
RIZZO FRANK P	COL	C-0252646	0963	3
RIZZO TORY	MAJ	0-2055165	0958	1
RIZZO VICTOR P	CPT	0-1175848	1060	1
ROACH AUSTIN S	MAJ	C-0977670	0961	1

NAME	GRADE	SVC NO	DATE RET MO YR	RET CODE
ROACH CHARLES A	2LT	0-1914343	1036	1
ROACH CURTIS C	MAJ	0-0220581	0861	3
ROACH HENRY B	COL	0-0276004	1266	3
ROACH IRA L	CW4	W-2115961	0957	1
ROACH JAMES E	CPT	0-1041887	0245	2
ROACH JOHN P	WO1	W-2123436	0744	2
ROACH JOHN W	LTC	0-0922381	0862	3
ROACH JR WILLIAM C	MAJ	0-1542134	1059	1
ROACH MARVIN E	MAJ	0-1053319	0760	1
ROACH PATRICK W	CPT	0-0509483	0945	2
ROACH REX O	B G	C-0337895	1165	3
ROACH RICHARD J	CPT	0-052109C	0145	2
ROACH SAMUEL P	COL	C-0910412	0263	1
ROACH WALTER J	MAJ	0-1053897	0158	1
ROACH WILLIAM L	COL	0-0141476	1057	3
ROACHE RUSSELL F	CPT	C-1011855	0945	2
ROADCAP ROBERT S	CPT	0-0302654	0753	3
ROADIFER HAROLD M	MAJ	0-1821770	0862	3
ROADMAN BERNICE M	MAJ	N-0732491	0264	3
ROAM JR WILLIAM E	CPT	0-1882390	0662	1
ROAN EARL H	2LT	0-1914052	0238	1
ROAN ROY R	CW3	W-2152246	0164	1
ROANE LAWRENCE H	MAJ	0-0214692	0345	2
ROANE WAYNE R	LTC	0-0257057	0967	3
ROARK BILL	LTC	0-1542036	0261	1
ROARK CHARLES V	MAJ	0-1588837	0462	1
ROARK FRANK E	CPT	0-0356993	0146	2
ROARK HAROLD E	CW2	W-2149089	1160	2
ROARK ROGER	CPT	0-2026991	0647	2
ROARK WILLIAM C	CW3	W-2206252	0966	2
ROARKE OWEN A	MAJ	0-0163186	0454	3
ROAT CHARLES E	CW3	W-2146271	0760	1
ROATEN SHELLEY P	1LT	0-1182693	0946	2
ROATH STEPHEN J	CW3	W-2153325	1066	1
ROBACK GEORGE S	CPT	0-1785728	0 47	2
ROBAK CHESTER L	MAJ	C-0160714	0852	3
ROBARDS WOODFORD L	CPT	0-0407376	0148	2
ROBAS FREDERICK	CW4	W-2103372	0153	2
ROBB DARYL G	LTC	0-0543212	0166	1
ROBB EDWIN P	1LT	0-0305196	1144	2
ROBB HARRY J	MAJ	0-0467142	0346	2
ROBB JAMES E	COL	C-0263191	1262	3
ROBB JOHN A	LTC	0-1633495	0163	1
ROBB JOHN R	LTC	0-0355393	1058	1
ROBB JR WILLIAM A	MAJ	0-1889767	0966	1
ROBB KENNETH R	LTC	0-1287762	1060	1
ROBB ROBERT H	MAJ	C-1889870	1067	1
ROBBEN GERHARD G	MAJ	0-0305807	0962	3
ROBBEN JR GEORGE M	MAJ	0-1634263	0757	1
ROBBERS JOSEPH C	LTC	0-0129637	0353	3
ROBBERSON ROY L	MAJ	0-1635260	0657	1
ROBBERT JR ALBERT A	MAJ	0-1013861	0747	2
ROBBIN HARRY N	CPT	0-0243220	0756	3
ROBBINS BERL	LTC	C-0330841	1059	1
ROBBINS BRAMBLE	CPT	0-1179592	0161	1
ROBBINS CHARLES F	LTC	0-1644705	1063	1
ROBBINS CHARLES H	LTC	0-0455913	0559	1
ROBBINS ELSIE	2LT	N-0700160	0733	1
ROBBINS ERNEST P	MAJ	0-098160C	0164	1
ROBBINS FLADGE	CPT	0-0495042	0250	1
ROBBINS FLOYD D	LTC	0-0288188	1045	2
ROBBINS FRED E	COL	0-0262702	0757	1
ROBBINS GERALD	LTC	0-0378694	0859	1
ROBBINS GERALD C	CPT	0-1318705	0646	2
ROBBINS HERBERT S	1LT	0-0334246	0444	2
ROBBINS HOMER O	MAJ	0-1172245	1065	1
ROBBINS HORACE M	COL	0-0235672	1052	3
ROBBINS JAMES A	LTC	0-1165552	0264	1
ROBBINS JAMES N	COL	0-0304939	0346	2
ROBBINS KENNETH R	CW3	W-2147103	1060	1
ROBBINS LEE O	LTC	0-0377750	0861	1
ROBBINS LEO C	CW3	W-2148625	1065	1
ROBBINS MAC	CPT	0-1636510	0845	2
ROBBINS MCINTYRE	CPT	0-0508635	0346	2
ROBBINS MORRISON B	COL	0-0326621	0367	1

NAME	GRADE	SVC NO	DATE RET MO YR	RET CODE
ROBBINS MORTON J	LTC	0-049348C	C646	2
ROBBINS RENNIE	MAJ	C-0266057	0250	3
ROBBINS RICHARD C	1LT	0-1292944	0245	2
ROBBINS RICHARD C	LTC	0-1597018	0667	1
ROBBINS ROBERT C	CPT	0-0411138	0747	1
ROBBINS ROBERT L	CW4	W-2109442	0960	1
ROBBINS SIDNEY	1LT	C-0438758	0844	2
ROBBINS STANLEY E	CW4	W-2117102	1157	1
ROBBINS STANTON O	CPT	0-0487023	0247	1
ROBBINS STEPHEN M	1LT	0-1317229	C147	2
ROBBINS TENNIS L	CW4	W-2149781	1067	1
ROBBINS THEODORE	MAJ	C-1297782	0161	1
ROBBINS WALTER C	MAJ	C-0303344	C266	3
ROBBINS WARREN E	WO1	W-2153052	1162	2
ROBBINS WILLIAM L	CW3	W-2209689	1067	1
ROBBLEE DONALD E	CPT	0-1288952	C849	1
ROBEL CHARLES A	1LT	0-2042867	0146	2
ROBERG ALFRED A	LTC	0-0139076	0853	3
ROBERSON BRUCE W	LTC	0-0885389	C860	1
ROBERSON CLARENCE W	LTC	0-0249529	1043	2
ROBERSON HOSMER M	LTC	0-0343385	C760	3
ROBERSON JR THEO P	CPT	0-2287555	0467	1
ROBERSON MARION J	CW4	W-2115458	1163	1
ROBERSON WILLIAM C	COL	C-0261812	1158	3
ROBERSON WILLIAM H	CW4	W-2142317	C463	1
ROBERSON WORSHAM B	MAJ	0-2050124	0663	1
ROBERTO FREDERICO	LTC	0-2016401	0663	1
ROBERTO PATRICK M	LTC	0-1036355	C962	1
ROBERTS ALBERT O	LTC	0-C255072	1155	3
ROBERTS ALEXANDER	LTC	0-0100022	C658	3
ROBERTS ALFRED R	CW2	W-2149868	0961	1
ROBERTS AMSTER	CPT	0-0490458	C944	2
ROBERTS ARCHIBALD	LTC	0-1542803	1065	1
ROBERTS ARTHUR H	LTC	C-0281644	1061	1
ROBERTS ARTHUR J	2LT	0-1307855	0145	1
ROBERTS ARTHUR W	MAJ	C-0979617	1162	1
ROBERTS BRAXTON L	MAJ	C-0135036	1145	2
ROBERTS BURCH J	COL	C-0347242	C346	2
ROBERTS CARL P	CW3	W-2207600	C666	1
ROBERTS CHARLES C	COL	0-0451387	1067	1
ROBERTS CHARLES D	MAJ	0-1116865	1058	1
ROBERTS CHARLES H	MAJ	0-0187377	0555	3
ROBERTS CHARLES H	CPT	0-2262268	1060	1
ROBERTS CHARLES R	MAJ	C-0260901	0367	3
ROBERTS CHARLES W	MAJ	C-0237748	C651	3
ROBERTS CLARENCE W	1LT	0-1338641	1047	2
ROBERTS CLAUDE	CW3	W-2147002	0981	1
ROBERTS CLAUDIUS H	COL	0-0173117	C954	3
ROBERTS CLIFFORD A	CW2	W-2146806	0758	1
ROBERTS CLINTON F	CPT	C-C496999	0845	2
ROBERTS DANIEL J	1LT	0-0395081	1045	1
ROBERTS DARRELL S	MAJ	C-0402785	C761	1
ROBERTS DEE F	MAJ	0-2019795	1262	1
ROBERTS DONALD A	CW2	W-2118453	0553	1
ROBERTS DONALD B	MAJ	C-0251973	0966	3
ROBERTS DONALD L	COL	C-0284112	0247	2
ROBERTS EDGAR W	1LT	C-2262627	C759	1
ROBERTS EDWIN T	1LT	0-1014909	1044	2
ROBERTS ELBERT M	LTC	0-0309204	0365	3
ROBERTS ELLIS M	2LT	0-1301690	0144	2
ROBERTS ELTON W	CPT	0-1576563	0454	1
ROBERTS EMITT	1LT	C-0496791	0953	1
ROBERTS ERNEST J	MAJ	C-1999915	1060	1
ROBERTS ERVIN L	CW2	W-2143864	C158	1
ROBERTS ESKELL F	1LT	0-1108273	0645	2
ROBERTS EUGENE	CPT	0-2263234	0957	1
ROBERTS EUGENE M	LTC	0-1109624	0965	3
ROBERTS EUGENE V	MAJ	C-02260C0	C864	3
ROBERTS EVAN R	MAJ	C-0244486	0664	3
ROBERTS FLOYD P	CPT	C-0105166	0454	3
ROBERTS FRED B	CW2	W-2206118	0266	1
ROBERTS FRED E	LTC	0-0224340	C260	3
ROBERTS GEORGE A	LTC	0-1583566	0261	1
ROBERTS GEORGE A	CPT	0-1718017	0651	1
ROBERTS GEORGE J	1LT	C-1320920	114N	2

NAME	GRADE	SVC NO	DATE RET MO YR	RET CODE
ROBERTS GEORGE W	LTC	0-2045221	0766	1
ROBERTS GORDON D	MAJ	0-0327257	0958	3
ROBERTS GORDON E	COL	0-0235801	0857	3
ROBERTS GORDON M	COL	0-0239665	0858	3
ROBERTS GRADY A	WO1	W-2107093	0155	1
ROBERTS HAROLD F	LTC	0-1118792	1065	1
ROBERTS HAROLD L	MAJ	0-0977203	0464	1
ROBERTS HARRY W	LTC	0-1894663	0760	1
ROBERTS HENRY G	MAJ	0-0133682	0654	3
ROBERTS HERBERT C	COL	0-0256363	1056	3
ROBERTS HERBERT J	LTC	0-0199886	0560	3
ROBERTS HERMAN H	CPT	0-1032596	0255	1
ROBERTS HERMAN M	MAJ	0-1947221	0961	2
ROBERTS HOLLIS V	CW3	RW-2147686	1064	1
ROBERTS HOWARD	MAJ	C-1913386	0966	1
ROBERTS HOWARD H	LTC	0-0201308	0555	3
ROBERTS HOYT K	MAJ	0-1590759	0561	1
ROBERTS JACK F	LTC	0-1544847	1055	1
ROBERTS JACK K	CPT	0-1002719	0257	1
ROBERTS JACK W	MAJ	0-1062930	1065	1
ROBERTS JACKSON R	CPT	0-1330755	0763	1
ROBERTS JAMES B	CW2	W-2141665	0865	1
ROBERTS JAMES C	CPT	0-1998063	0347	2
ROBERTS JAMES F	CPT	0-1928407	0264	2
ROBERTS JAMES O	MAJ	0-0435058	0446	1
ROBERTS JAMES R	CW3	W-2122047	0258	2
ROBERTS JAMES T	B G	0-0220864	1060	3
ROBERTS JESSE L	CW2	W-2142659	1054	1
ROBERTS JOHN C	CW4	W-2003256	1066	3
ROBERTS JOHN E	1LT	0-1856821	0154	2
ROBERTS JOHN G	1LT	0-1321249	0846	1
ROBERTS JOHN J	MAJ	0-0151821	0649	3
ROBERTS JOHN L	1LT	0-1004071	0952	1
ROBERTS JOHN O	MAJ	0-0514923	1054	1
ROBERTS JOHN W	1LT	0-0558237	114T	2
ROBERTS JR EARL O	LTC	0-2020345	1066	1
ROBERTS JR HENRY F	CW3	W-2152717	0563	1
ROBERTS JR SIDNEY E	LTC	0-1101636	0363	1
ROBERTS KEITH O	CW3	W-2148066	0161	1
ROBERTS KEITH M	COL	0-0340350	1066	1
ROBERTS KENNETH B	LTC	0-0264730	0965	3
ROBERTS LEE	CPT	0-1945258	1153	1
ROBERTS LEONARD F	CW2	W-2115595	0654	2
ROBERTS LEWIS S	MAJ	0-0962545	0764	1
ROBERTS LOUIS	1LT	0-1281473	1048	1
ROBERTS MALCOLM	LTC	0-1031441	0562	1
ROBERTS MARSHALL O	MAJ	C-1053326	0759	1
ROBERTS MARTIN W	CPT	0-0919248	0145	2
ROBERTS MARVIN F	2LT	0-1303777	0845	1
ROBERTS MARVIN L	CW3	W-2149901	0760	1
ROBERTS MILO A	CPT	0-0910596	0447	2
ROBERTS MOULTRIE O	LTC	0-0265210	0762	3
ROBERTS OLIVER M	CW3	W-2208678	0367	1
ROBERTS ORA F	COL	0-0167377	1045	2
ROBERTS PAUL E	1LT	0-1328186	0546	2
ROBERTS PAUL J	COL	0-0172671	0958	1
ROBERTS PAUL J	MAJ	0-0205083	0459	3
ROBERTS PAUL R	2LT	0-1319442	0945	2
ROBERTS PAUL R	LTC	0-1639555	0363	1
ROBERTS PERCY S	CPT	0-1002107	1157	1
ROBERTS QUENTIN R	CPT	0-1018495	1045	1
ROBERTS RAYMOND E	CW3	W-2141429	1057	1
ROBERTS REX E	MAJ	0-1014097	0959	1
ROBERTS RICHARD L	CPT	0-0174436	0654	3
ROBERTS RICHARD L	1LT	0-2035373	0146	2
ROBERTS ROBERT O	LTC	0-0941978	0266	1
ROBERTS ROLAND H	2LT	0-0538925	0845	2
ROBERTS ROSCOE L	LTC	0-0276073	1164	3
ROBERTS RUPERT J	MAJ	0-1995041	0855	2
ROBERTS SAMUEL L	MAJ	0-0451383	0860	1
ROBERTS SAMUEL N	CW2	W-2144927	0157	1
ROBERTS SIDNEY J	1LT	0-1994837	0745	2
ROBERTS SR JOHN O	MAJ	0-2033872	0265	1
ROBERTS STANLEY J	MAJ	0-0105757	0150	3
ROBERTS THEODORE J	LTC	0-0343363	1160	1

NAME	GRADE	SVC NO	DATE RET MO YR	RET CODE
ROBERTS THERON E	COL	0-0385537	C666	2
ROBERTS THOMAS C	CPT	0-0452475	1144	2
ROBERTS THOMAS H	LTC	0-1560059	0761	1
ROBERTS THOMAS J	MAJ	0-2028629	0265	1
ROBERTS THOMAS L	CPT	C-0331880	0346	2
ROBERTS THOMAS N	MAJ	C-0121846	C-53	3
ROBERTS THOMAS O	LTC	0-0909497	C762	1
ROBERTS WALTER C	COL	0-0156786	0959	1
ROBERTS WALTER J	WO1	W-2102287	0344	2
ROBERTS WALTER W	CW2	W-3150793	0865	1
ROBERTS WILEY L	CPT	C-2025254	0857	1
ROBERTS WILLIAM	MAJ	0-0325747	C153	1
ROBERTS WILLIAM A	1LT	0-1535268	1044	2
ROBERTS WILLIAM C	LTC	0-0274007	C467	3
ROBERTS WILLIAM E	B G	0-0233906	0258	3
ROBERTS WILLIAM G	MAJ	0-1924534	C563	1
ROBERTS WILLIAM J	CPT	0-0502706	1147	1
ROBERTS WILLIAM P	LTC	C-022246C	C358	3
ROBERTS WILLIAM R	LTC	0-0302926	C767	3
ROBERTS WILLIAM T	1LT	0-0531135	1045	2
ROBERTS WILLIAM W	CW3	RW-2206135	1065	1
ROBERTS WOODROW A	CW3	W-2148882	0363	1
ROBERTSON ALAN G	LTC	0-1998454	1162	1
ROBERTSON ALBERT W	LTC	0-0370706	0960	1
ROBERTSON ALFRED P	LTC	0-0247936	1058	1
ROBERTSON ANDREW C	CPT	0-1283491	1154	1
ROBERTSON ANDREW C	CPT	0-1296259	1146	1
ROBERTSON CHARLES A	LTC	0-0275816	0564	3
ROBERTSON CHARLES C	LTC	0-1316588	0166	1
ROBERTSON CHARLES M	MAJ	0-1312758	0447	2
ROBERTSON CHARLES W	CW3	W-2147482	1162	1
ROBERTSON CHESTER B	COL	0-0390788	0760	1
ROBERTSON CLARE F	WO1	W-2134507	1045	2
ROBERTSON DELLA M	2LT	N-0701723	0731	1
ROBERTSON DICKSON	1LT	0-0167734	0660	3
ROBERTSON DON	1LT	0-0402029	0344	2
ROBERTSON DON O C C	LTC	0-0239529	0446	2
ROBERTSON DONALD R	LTC	0-0217053	0958	3
ROBERTSON DOUGLAS A	COL	0-0169705	C161	3
ROBERTSON DURWOOD W	1LT	0-0405258	0746	2
ROBERTSON EARL A	MAJ	0-0299848	1064	1
ROBERTSON ELGAN C	B G	0-0100407	1149	3
ROBERTSON ELGIN G	MAJ	C-0471391	0356	1
ROBERTSON ERNEST C	MAJ	0-0949168	1262	1
ROBERTSON ERVIN E	MAJ	0-0887390	C561	1
ROBERTSON EVERETT L	LTC	0-1287065	C959	1
ROBERTSON F G	CPT	0-0377758	1147	1
ROBERTSON FRANCIS E	LTC	0-1051344	0264	1
ROBERTSON FRANCIS M	MAJ	0-1038273	0963	1
ROBERTSON FRANK O	MAJ	0-0355656	0345	2
ROBERTSON GARLAND R	1LT	0-2207643	0253	1
ROBERTSON GENE	MAJ	0-2283834	0463	1
ROBERTSON GEORGE C	MAJ	0-0450604	0658	1
ROBERTSON GEORGE H	COL	C-0450475	0560	1
ROBERTSON GEORGE J	CPT	0-0322947	C146	2
ROBERTSON GORDON L	LTC	0-0215580	1046	2
ROBERTSON HAROLD O	CPT	0-1685623	0165	1
ROBERTSON HARRY B	MAJ	0-0491159	0944	1
ROBERTSON HARRY H	LTC	0-0425484	0960	1
ROBERTSON HARRY L	WO1	W-2119561	0848	2
ROBERTSON HAYWOOD	CPT	0-0948327	0859	1
ROBERTSON IRWIN J	LTC	0-0175154	0462	3
ROBERTSON IVIE M	CW3	W-2146272	0366	1
ROBERTSON JAMES A	LTC	0-1640869	0866	1
ROBERTSON JAMES C	CPT	0-1700842	0446	2
ROBERTSON JAMES C	WO1	W-2119463	1146	1
ROBERTSON JAMES M	MAJ	0-2038875	0759	1
ROBERTSON JAMES R	CPT	0-1170538	C947	1
ROBERTSON JEROME R	CPT	0-0987291	1061	1
ROBERTSCN JOE V	MAJ	0-1018583	0157	1
ROBERTSON JCEL P	CW2	W-2152124	0158	2
ROBERTSON JOHN C	CPT	0-0466931	0744	2
ROBERTSON JOHN D	MAJ	C-1897721	0265	1
ROBERTSON JOHN G	LTC	0-0331849	C466	3
ROBERTSCN JOHN R	LTC	0-0371533	0561	1
ROBERTSCN JOHN R	MAJ	0-1172623	0662	1
ROBERTSCN JOSEPH L	CW3	W-2151776	1061	1
ROBERTSCN JR JAMES B	COL	0-0196886	0163	3
ROBERTSCN JR JAMES G	CPT	0-0482186	0546	1
ROBERTSCN JR JOHN O	LTC	0-1180317	0163	1
ROBERTSCN JR WILLIAM	MAJ	0-0135716	0959	3
ROBERTSCN KATHLEEN	1LT	L-0130275	0947	2
ROBERTSON LAWRENCE D	CW2	W-2145696	0960	1
ROBERTSCN LORRAINE G	MAJ	N-0761198	0967	1
ROBERTSCN LYLE J	COL	0-034136C	0161	1
ROBERTSCN MARSHALL J	CPT	0-0450509	0246	2
ROBERTSCN OLIVER W	MAJ	0-0956936	1062	1
ROBERTSON PHILLIP J	CPT	0-1552589	0562	1
ROBERTSON PORT G	CPT	0-0353886	1045	2
ROBERTSCN RALPH H	MAJ	0-2263401	0865	1
ROBERTSON RAYMOND	MAJ	0-1596783	1058	1
ROBERTSCN RICHARD T	MAJ	0-1102015	1061	1
ROBERTSCN ROBERT C	COL	0-0121896	0859	3
ROBERTSCN ROBERT L	COL	0-0452864	0457	1
ROBERTSCN RUSSEL A	LTC	C-0319789	1160	3
ROBERTSCN RUTH O	MAJ	N-0785118	1064	2
ROBERTSCN SAMUEL V	2LT	0-1290816	0344	2
ROBERTSCN STANLEY	CPT	0-1794858	0247	1
ROBERTSCN SYDENHAM B	CPT	0-1648115	1046	2
ROBERTSON THOMAS	CW3	W-214143C	0659	1
ROBERTSON THOMAS V	MAJ	0-1794859	0361	1
ROBERTSON TUCK M	CW3	W-2145838	0656	1
ROBERTSCN VICTOR M	LTC	0-0220939	0356	1
ROBERTSCN VIVIAN O	LTC	0-0286114	0661	3
ROBERTSON WILLIAM	CW3	W-214836C	0567	1
ROBERTSON WILLIAM B	1LT	0-0512869	0145	2
ROBERTSON WILLIAM R	1LT	0-2003618	0753	1
ROBERTSON WILLIAM J	LTC	0-0913087	0966	3
ROBERTSCN WILLIAM J	LTC	0-1325239	1061	1
ROBERTSCN WILLIAM M	CPT	0-0131132	0157	3
ROBERTUS JR HENRY	MAJ	0-0362463	0261	1
ROBEY JOHN M	CW2	W-2135177	0 55	2
ROBEY JR BENJAMIN F	CW3	W-2113941	0562	1
ROBEYSEK JAMES W	LTC	0-1101198	1160	1
ROBICHAUD ALBERT	LTC	0-2045268	1165	1
ROBICHAUD PHILIP A	CW3	W-2208842	0966	1
ROBICHAUD ROGER E	CPT	0-4010768	0266	1
ROBICHEAUX LAWRENC	MAJ	0-1180689	0562	1
ROBICHEAUX MABLE M	1LT	N-0745299	0949	1
RCBIDOLX EUGENE J	CPT	0-1107079	1047	1
ROBIE EVERTT M	LTC	0-0378308	1060	1
ROBIE THEODORE R	MAJ	0-0466530	1143	2
ROBIESCN FRANK W	MAJ	0-0194342	1054	3
ROBINET ALEX J	COL	0-0359288	0757	1
ROBINETT CLIFTON H	MAJ	0-0149292	1150	3
ROBINETTE CHARLES	1LT	0-1648116	0948	1
ROBINETTE CHARLES K	CW2	W-2146140	0855	1
ROBINETTE DELMAS O	LTC	0-0354301	0358	1
ROBINETTE GLENDON H	CW4	W-2145066	0665	2
ROBINETTE HAROLD L	CW3	W-2149023	1262	1
ROBINETTE MERRAL E	LTC	0-0477097	1051	1
ROBINETTE JAMES W	MAJ	0-134230C	0863	1
ROBINETTE JOE H	CPT	0-0511189	0346	1
ROBINS CLYDE A	1LT	0-1914058	0431	1
ROBINS FCYE C	MAJ	0-1336825	1164	1
ROBINS LEON D	CW2	W-2210812	0363	1
ROBINS WILLIAM F	LTC	0-0471314	1164	3
ROBINSCN ADRAIN M	LTC	0-0309386	0247	2
ROBINSCN ALBERT E	CPT	0-0109250	1131	1
ROBINSCN ALBERT F	MAJ	0-1881566	0167	1
ROBINSCN ALBERT L	CPT	0-1C59607	0447	2
ROBINSCN ALBERT R	CW3	W-214336C	0959	1
ROBINSCN ALBERT S	2LT	0-159443C	0944	2
ROBINSCN ALFRED A	COL	0-0298499	0862	1
ROBINSON ALFRED V	MAJ	0-0443702	0750	1
RGBINSCN ANNIE L	2LT	N-0727726	0246	1
ROBINSCN ANSON F	COL	0-0161708	0648	3
ROBINSCN ARTHUR C	MAJ	0-1549365	0161	1
ROBINSCN B C	LTC	0-0282871	0956	3
ROBINSON BEN B	COL	0-0210681	0155	3
ROBINSCN BESTOR	COL	0-0900111	0258	3
ROBINSON BEULAH P	1LT	N-C702707	1146	1
ROBINSON BILL A	MAJ	C-2265434	0767	1
ROBINSON BOGGS A	LTC	0-0313922	1065	1
ROBINSON CECIL W	LTC	0-0443156	C562	1
ROBINSON CHARLES M	LTC	0-0524330	C466	3
ROBINSON CHARLES C	LTC	0-0153526	0951	3
ROBINSON CHARLES S	LTC	0-0147047	0152	3
ROBINSON CHARLES W	CPT	0-1894817	0351	1
ROBINSON CHARLEY B	LTC	0-0360068	C259	3
ROBINSON CLIFFORD E	CPT	0-1104371	C852	1
ROBINSON DAVID	LTC	0-1583570	1160	1
RCBINSON DAVID S	CW2	W-2144625	0263	1
ROBINSON DOROTHY E	MAJ	N-0741289	1264	3
ROBINSON EDGAR L	LTC	0-2023594	0163	1
ROBINSON EDNA L	2LT	N-0777362	C846	1
ROBINSON EDWARD E	COL	0-0275267	0458	3
ROBINSON ELMER	LTC	0-1634266	0760	1
ROBINSON ELMER C	1LT	0-1171332	C645	2
ROBINSON ERNEST B	CPT	0-0383810	0346	2
ROBINSON ERNEST B	CPT	0-1173054	0447	1
ROBINSON EUGENE L	1LT	C-1185124	0845	2
ROBINSON EVERT A	CPT	C-1053321	C446	2
ROBINSON FRANK E	MAJ	0-0167006	0156	3
ROBINSON FRED	LTC	0-0359321	0764	3
ROBINSON FRED E	CW3	W-2141939	1159	1
ROBINSON FREDERICK	LTC	0-0282934	0467	3
ROBINSON GENE L	2LT	0-1999309	0945	2
ROBINSON GEORGE D	1LT	0-0425442	1043	2
ROBINSON GEORGE H	LTC	0-0913474	C266	3
ROBINSON GEROLD O	1LT	0-1031512	0346	1
ROBINSON HAROLD E	LTC	0-1102940	0658	1
ROBINSON HAROLD P	LTC	0-0364339	0854	1
ROBINSON HARRY H	MAJ	C-0133442	1159	3
ROBINSON HARRY W	MAJ	0-2203038	0766	1
ROBINSON HENRY A	COL	0-0186377	C547	2
ROBINSON HENSON L	COL	0-0178720	1056	3
ROBINSON HERBERT E	LTC	0-1554262	1055	1
ROBI ISON HERBERT C	COL	0-0184201	0555	3
ROBINSON HOWARD A	CW2	W-2146532	C967	1
ROBINSON HUBERT F	CW2	W-2152567	1160	1
ROBINSON HUBERT R	CW2	W-2117939	C753	1
ROBINSON HUGHES A	MAJ	0-0402437	0847	2
ROBINSON IVAN E	LTC	0-1894718	C863	1
ROBINSON IVAN E	MAJ	0-2020208	1060	1
ROBINSON JACK S	CPT	0-04866C4	0653	1
ROBINSON JAMES H	LTC	0-1062627	1166	2
ROBINSON JAMES L	MAJ	0-0480688	C246	2
ROBINSON JAMES W	MAJ	C-0323890	C546	2
ROBINSON JOEL W	CPT	0-1315547	0647	2
ROBINSON JOHN A	1LT	0-1015389	1144	2
ROBINSON JOHN C	LTC	0-0449468	0663	1
ROBINSON JOHN H	CPT	0-1011205	1047	1
ROBINSON JOHN J	MAJ	C-0888208	0647	2
ROBINSON JOHN M	CW4	W-2110416	0554	1
ROBINSCN JOHN T	LTC	0-1695675	0761	1
ROBINSON JOHNSTON	MAJ	0-0988327	0258	1
ROBINSON JOSEPH G	1LT	0-0499445	0553	1
ROBINSON JOSEPH N	LTC	0-0101402	1053	3
ROBINSON JR JAMES H	1LT	0-1017006	0646	2
ROBINSON JR SAMMIE L	LTC	0-05586C0	1264	1
ROBINSON JR SETH B	COL	0-0221530	0163	3
ROBINSON KENNETH A	COL	0-0231490	0963	3
ROBINSON KERNEY L	CW2	W-2148808	0358	1
ROBINSON LASTER E	CW2	W-2146573	1057	1
ROBINSON LAURENCE E	2LT	0-1045223	1045	2
ROBINSON LEON E	COL	0-0279414	1057	3
ROBINSON LEONARD R	LTC	0-0361770	0657	1
ROBINSON LESTER T	1LT	0-1308002	C745	2
ROBINSON LEWIS H	MAJ	0-2263286	0264	1
ROBINSON LIONEL E	COL	0-0248029	0855	3
ROBINSON LLOYD L	MAJ	0-0278861	1158	3
ROBINSON LUTHER E	CW3	W-2205778	1165	1
ROBINSON MACK L	CW2	W-2210515	C666	1
ROBINSON MARY B	CPT	N-0700291	1045	1
ROBINSCN MELVIN C	MAJ	C-118C692	1054	1
ROBINSCN MICHAEL T	CPT	0-1826174	0862	2
ROBINSCN MORDECAI L	LTC	0-0249279	0262	3
ROBINSCN NANCY	CPT	L-0115761	0263	1
ROBINSCN NORMAN A	LTC	0-0777023	0867	1
ROBINSCN NORMAN E	LTC	0-0253597	0259	3
ROBINSCN OLIVER K	CPT	0-0297975	1144	2
ROBINSCN OLIVER T	LTC	0-0514480	0164	1
ROBINSCN OTTC A	MAJ	0-0441103	0762	2
ROBINSCN PAUL V	LTC	0-0425556	0462	3
ROBINSON PHILIP E	LTC	0-1315619	0763	1
ROBINSCN RALPH E	CPT	0-0509477	0553	1
ROBINSCN RALPH R	MAJ	C-130712C	0857	2
ACBINSCN RALPH R	CW3	W-2144411	1264	1
ROBINSCN RANDOLPH	MAJ	0-0270325	1263	3
ROBINSCN RICHARD A	LTC	0-1103891	0861	1
ROBINSCN RICHARD C	MAJ	0-0119587	1057	3
ROBINSCN RICHARD W	COL	0-0214C75	0163	3
ROBINSCN ROBERT H	CPT	0-039021C	C845	2
RCRINSCN ROBERT H	CPT	0-2262980	0561	1
ROBINSCN ROLAND W	LTC	0-0363215	0957	2
ROBINSCN RONALD W	1LT	0-1167184	0645	2
ROBINSON SAMUEL J	LTC	0-0264346	0966	3
ROBINSCN SAMUEL J	LTC	0-1109625	1162	1
ROBINSCN SHERRILL E	MAJ	0-0185407	0953	3
ROBINSCN SPENCER J	LTC	0-0151225	0857	3
RCBINSCN THOMAS T	CPT	0-0268517	0566	3
ROBINSCN TIMOTHY E	COL	0-0299849	0661	1
ROBINSCN VINCENT H	1LT	0-1047746	C845	2
ROBINSON VIRGIL B	MAJ	0-1060614	C561	1
ROBINSCN VIRGIL E	MAJ	0-1051345	C366	1
ROBINSCN WALTER	WO1	W-2151063	1060	1
ROBINSCN WALTER B	2LT	0-1581344	C643	2
ROBINSON WALTER J	MAJ	0-1577765	1160	1
ROBINSCN WELO S	CPT	0-0498727	0262	2
ROBINSON WILFRED F	LTC	0-0260479	1166	3
ROBINSCN WILL G	COL	0-0276227	0553	3
ROBINSON WILLIAM A	MAJ	0-0279997	1054	1
ROBINSCN WILLIAM E	COL	0-0114873	0654	3
ROBINSCN WILLIAM F	CPT	0-0256829	1052	3
ROBINSON WILLIAM F	CW3	W-2147238	1056	1
ROBINSCN WILLIAM J	COL	0-0182744	0955	3
ROBINSON WILLIAM J	MAJ	0-0983953	0867	1
ROBINSCN WILLIAM R	MAJ	0-1169711	0261	1
ROBINSCN WILLIAM T	CW3	W-2149266	1264	1
ROBINSCN WILLIS J	1LT	0-0532285	0845	2
ROBIRTSCN WINFORD W	CW3	W-2143490	0157	1
ROBISON FRANK P	LTC	0-0125082	1050	3
ROBISON FRED J	CPT	0-0948994	0661	1
RCBISON HUSTON E	MAJ	0-1796698	0159	1
RCBISON JAMES K	LTC	0-0264548	0565	3
RCBISCN JESSE B	2LT	0-1305835	0544	2
ROBISON JOHN B	CW4	W-2142944	0561	1
ROBISON JR JOSEPH E	LTC	0-0303933	0559	1
ROBISON RAY C	MAJ	0-1335058	0165	1
ROBISON THOMAS J	LTC	0-024061C	0444	1
ROBLES JR JOSE	MAJ	0-0970430	1061	1
ROBLYER DELOS A	CPT	0-1288953	104N	2
ROBOHM JOHN F	COL	0-0127602	0154	3
ROBOHM JOHN F	LTC	0-1165443	0561	1
ROBOLO VIRGIL G	CW3	W-2146394	0959	1
ROBOTTI JOHN J	MAJ	0-1825643	0361	1
ROBSON ANDREW S	LTC	0-1823062	0462	1
ROBSON FRANK W	LTC	0-0915169	0766	1
ROBSON GCRDON E	CPT	0-0260235	0566	3
ROBSON JAMES E	LTC	0-0399087	0758	1
ROBSON JR GEORGE L	CPT	0-2300863	0765	1
ROBSON WALLACE W	MAJ	0-0402595	0647	2
ROBSON WARREN H	LTC	0-1636552	0763	1
ROBSON WILLIAM A	1LT	0-1309406	0246	2
ROBY DALE W	CPT	0-2023957	0458	2
ROBY JAMES F	LTC	0-1059256	0666	1
ROBY OLIVER C	MAJ	0-0980741	0464	1
ROCAP JR CHARLES E	LTC	0-1116741	0663	1
ROCCANCVA BERNARD	2LT	0-1645953	0445	1

NAME	GRADE	SVC NO	DATE RET MO YR	RET CODE
ROCCHIO LOIS C	CPT	N-0702237	0546	1
ROCHE ANDREW H	CPT	0-0475131	0546	1
ROCHE FRANCIS T	CW3	W-2142194	C662	1
ROCHE JOHN J	CW2	W-2152808	0960	1
ROCHE JOSEPH F	MAJ	C-1296261	CR65	1
ROCHE RICHARD B	MAJ	0-0393813	0966	1
ROCHE SIDNEY J	LTC	0-0569970	0966	1
ROCHEL EDWARD M	CW2	W-2207049	0461	1
ROCHEL HENRY J	MAJ	C-0274123	C744	2
ROCHELEAU WILFRED E	LTC	0-0287245	C456	2
ROCHFORD STEPHEN H	MAJ	0-2033033	C364	1
ROCHFORD THEODORE J	MAJ	0-1903372	0162	1
ROCHMAN GEORGE H	COL	0-0299825	0962	1
ROCHNOWSKI ARTHUR P	MAJ	C-1185953	1162	1
ROCHON HAROLD R	1LT	C-1180027	0245	2
ROCHOW HAROLD E	LTC	0-0318236	0963	3
ROCK ADA F	MAJ	N-0730233	1165	1
ROCK ALBERT H	LTC	0-1035585	C263	1
ROCK JOHN J	LTC	0-0453569	0961	1
ROCK JOHN W	LTC	0-0515707	0649	3
ROCK JOSEPH G	MAJ	C-1035995	1062	1
RCCK ROBERT F	LTC	0-1534372	C261	1
ROCK THOMAS F	1LT	0-1182949	C646	2
ROCKAFELLOW EDNA M	LTC	N-0700043	0245	1
ROCKE HERSCHEL M	1LT	0-0342452	0346	2
ROCKEFELLER CHESTER	1LT	0-1300085	0346	2
ROCKEFELLER EARL S	LTC	0-0100796	1053	3
ROCKER ROY H	CW2	W-2145501	0962	1
ROCKETT CARLTON A	CPT	0-1825257	C660	1
ROCKETT GRADY L	CW2	W-2113205	0144	2
ROCKETT RICHARD W	CW2	W-2147478	0261	1
ROCKETT THOMAS A	LTC	0-0245614	0648	3
ROCKEY CARLTON G	LTC	C-0263613	1052	1
ROCKEY FRANCIS C	LTC	0-0331239	0460	1
ROCKHILL ROBERT A	MAJ	0-0246118	1154	3
ROCKIS JOSEPH	COL	0-0331792	1159	1
ROCKNE LLOYD M	1LT	0-1183750	1045	2
ROCKWELL ALICE A	2LT	N-0772260	0845	1
ROCKWELL CHARLES F	2LT	0-0246314	0648	3
ROCKWELL DONALD L	MAJ	C-0885663	1160	1
ROCKWELL EDGAR A	CW3	W-2119223	C659	1
ROCKWELL LLOYD H	COL	0-0324566	0660	1
ROCKWELL MILTON R	LTC	0-1577766	0261	1
ROCKWELL NORMAN H	CW2	W-2148987	0859	1
ROCKWELL WILLARD F	LTC	0-0176711	0855	3
ROCKWELL WILLIAM O	MAJ	C-1951710	0466	1
ROCKWELL WILLIAM S	COL	C-0194679	0256	1
ROCKWERK LOUIS	MAJ	0-1308378	C863	1
ROCKWOOD JR BERT	CW3	W-2147218	1262	2
ROD HERBERT L	1LT	0-1015272	0947	1
RODAK STANLEY R	1LT	0-1308003	0446	2
RODAT WARREN K	CPT	0-1011738	1045	2
RODAWALT LEE R	MAJ	0-0959802	0466	1
RODDA BILL T	MAJ	C-0384617	1060	1
RODDEN LEO	CW3	W-2206626	1264	1
RODDEY OTHA C	LTC	0-0104408	0854	3
RODDICK WILLIAM C	1LT	0-1291887	CR52	1
RODDY FRANCIS G	COL	0-0211947	0648	3
RODDY FRANCIS J	LTC	C-0310345	C560	1
RODDY GUINDEL J	LTC	0-1634270	0460	1
RODDY THOMAS J	MAJ	C-1576560	0361	1
RODE JOHN A	MAJ	0-1313646	0957	1
RODECKER HAROLD H	COL	0-0311403	0365	3
RODEN CALVIN T	2LT	0-1287066	0744	2
RODEN CHARLES J	LTC	0-1103387	0164	1
RODEN HUGH F	MAJ	C-0135470	C-52	3
RODEN JOHN B	CW3	W-2114372	0461	2
RODENBERG ELMER J	COL	0-0309707	1063	3
RODENMAYER HAROLD W	LTC	0-0362989	1160	1
RODERICK ARTHUR R	LTC	0-1550490	0565	1
RODERICK EDWARD M	MAJ	0-0225994	0863	3
RODERICK EDWARD T	MAJ	C-1686654	0764	1
RODERICK JAMES W	MAJ	0-1010279	0658	1
RODERICK JOHN L	MAJ	0-0552588	1061	1
RODES ROBERT O	LTC	0-0277788	0760	3

NAME	GRADE	SVC NO	DATE RET MO YR	RET CODE
RODES THOMAS L	LTC	0-0197141	0547	2
RODES WILLIAM R	LTC	0-1042151	0767	1
RODEWALD ERIC E	MAJ	0-1312C48	0366	1
RODGERS ALBERT I	LTC	0-1167185	0261	3
RODGERS ALLAN	MAJ	0-1555274	1159	1
RODGERS ANNIE M	1LT	N-0726234	0748	2
RODGERS ARTHUR P	MAJ	0-1540875	0767	1
RODGERS DAVID E	MAJ	0-0243575	0957	3
RODGERS DENNIS D	CW3	W-2142004	0156	1
RODGERS EDWARD A	LTC	0-1289143	0657	1
RODGERS FORREST G	CPT	0-05229C4	1047	1
RODGERS GEORGE H	MAJ	0-1030827	C161	1
RODGERS GEORGE T	MAJ	0-1552976	1147	2
RODGERS GROVER	LTC	0-0186663	0844	2
RODGERS HARRY B	CW3	W-2145583	1165	1
RODGERS HONZIE L	LTC	0-0407750	1160	1
RODGERS JAMES	CPT	0-2035231	0250	1
RODGERS JESSE A	CW4	W-2145322	0159	1
RODGERS JOHN	CW2	W-2148334	0956	1
RODGERS JOHN E	LTC	0-1013897	0863	1
RODGERS JOSEPH W	CPT	0-1290481	0753	1
RODGERS JR JOHN B	MAJ	0-0270857	1266	3
RODGERS JR TOM	LTC	0-1635268	0760	1
RODGERS KENNETH W	MAJ	0-1110769	0661	2
RODGERS LOWELL D	CW3	W-2146354	1056	1
RODGERS MARTIN H	LTC	0-1590761	0662	1
RODGERS PATRICK G	LTC	0-2029640	1263	1
RODGERS PAUL C	MAJ	0-0957432	1065	1
RODGERS PAUL L	LTC	0-0175C42	0654	1
RODGERS RAYMOND A	MAJ	0-157903C	0954	1
RODGERS RICHARD M	LTC	0-5322171	1166	2
RODGERS ROBERT O	CW2	W-2210302	0765	1
RODGERS THOMAS E	LTC	0-0247278	0263	3
RODGERS VINCENT W	COL	0-0244372	0766	3
RODGERS WALTER F	LTC	0-1107664	0762	1
RODGERS WALTER H H	CW2	W-2152645	0460	1
RODGERS WAYNE	CW3	W-2152479	1262	1
RODGERS WILLIAM W	LTC	0-0957254	0267	1
RODIACK ROBERT E	2LT	0-0948275	0352	1
RODIER LOUIE B	COL	0-0440767	0659	2
RODISH ANDREW	CW2	W-2115785	0448	1
RODMAN BILLY R	2LT	N-0703066	0141	1
RODMAN HARRY A	1LT	0-1590140	0850	1
RODMAN JR GAGE B	CPT	0-1323482	1047	2
RODMAN JR WILEY C	LTC	0-0299970	1067	3
RODMAN OLIVER W	LTC	0-1172626	1066	1
RODNEY HARRY J	MAJ	0-0109188	0539	1
RODNEY JOSEPH A	MAJ	0-0361184	1044	2
RODOSEVICH KATHERINE	1LT	N-0775055	C946	1
RODRICK EUGENE L	LTC	0-024937C	0167	3
RODRIGC JOSEPH	COL	0-0247085	1065	3
RODRIGUES GEORGE	MAJ	0-1012818	1059	1
RODRIGUES VICTOR M	CW3	W-2146395	0562	1
RODRIGUEZ ALPHONSE	CW4	W-2144298	0966	1
RODRIGUEZ CARLOS F	1LT	0-0471844	0645	1
RODRIGUEZ CHARLES O	LTC	0-0275165	0158	3
RODRIGUEZ DAVID O	MAJ	0-1948817	0760	1
RODRIGUEZ EMILIO	CW3	W-2151644	0265	1
RODRIGUEZ FERNANDO E	1LT	0-0448044	1143	1
RODRIGUEZ FRANCISCO	CW3	W-215166C	1063	1
RODRIGUEZ JOSE	MAJ	0-0243628	0951	1
RODRIGUEZ JOSE M	LTC	0-0462235	0461	3
RODRIGUEZ JOSEFINA M	MAJ	N-0726861	0363	1
RODRIGUEZ JR JOSE	MAJ	0-0985363	0464	1
RODRIGUEZ JR OVIDIO	1LT	0-2028630	1053	2
RODRIGUEZ LUIS C	CW3	W-2147667	0265	1
RODRIGUEZ LUIS R	MAJ	0-1338514	0960	1
RODRIGUEZ MANUEL	CW3	W-2147469	0965	1
RODRIGUEZ RAYMOND T	CW2	W-2107098	0851	2
RODRIGUEZ RENATO A	MAJ	0-0272165	0867	3
RODRIGUEZ SAMUEL L	COL	0-0259902	1162	3
RODRIGUEZ-GARCI MAN	CW3	W-2147499	1061	1
RODRIGUEZ-MOLIN RAF	LTC	0-0231483	1061	3
RODRIGUEZ-SERRA TULI	CPT	0-0166891	0554	3
RODWELL JOSEPH J	CW4	W-2114861	0265	1

NAME	GRADE	SVC NO	DATE RET MO YR	RET CODE
ROE CHARLES H	COL	0-0137380	0649	3
ROE DENER A	CPT	0-1175292	0450	1
ROE EDWIN L	MAJ	0-0168850	0359	3
ROE JAMES B	LTC	0-0275517	1066	3
ROE JAMES V	LTC	0-1300222	0358	1
ROE JIMMIE	CW3	W-2205818	0367	1
ROE THEODORE J	CPT	C-0382415	C345	1
ROEAKE HARRISON L	LTC	0-1638384	0563	1
ROECKER RAYMOND H	MAJ	0-0971487	C962	1
ROEDEL ESTELLA	1LT	N-0728480	1046	1
ROEDEL LLOYD A	MAJ	0-1315367	C861	1
ROEDER HENRY W	CPT	0-0496583	C848	1
ROEDER JR CHESTER C	MAJ	C-0465392	0365	1
ROEDER JR GEORGE W	CW3	W-2150279	0760	1
ROEDER WALTER L	CW2	W-3200468	1167	1
ROEDER WILLIAM E	CW3	W-2151797	1262	1
ROEDLER GEORGE R	1LT	0-1294016	0345	1
ROEDTS GEORGE H	CW2	W-2143468	1057	1
ROEGNER FLOYD D	MAJ	C-1794992	0862	1
ROEGNER KENNETH A	MAJ	C-0156933	1055	3
ROEHLEN BURCHARD G	CW3	W-2150814	0662	1
ROEHM DONALD F	2LT	0-1114279	1044	2
ROEHRIG FREDERICK	LTC	0-0112812	1046	2
ROELING LOYOLA G	LTC	0-0297789	0865	3
ROEMER CHARLES T	LTC	0-0922456	0346	2
ROEMER HERBERT S	COL	0-0302756	0767	3
ROEMER JOHN P	LTC	0-0139769	C962	3
ROEMER MARGARET M	MAJ	L-0221000	0564	2
ROEMER ORLAND A	LTC	0-0259072	0261	1
ROENIGK JOHN A	CPT	0-0949167	0160	2
ROEPER EDWARD J	LTC	0-0353394	0766	3
ROES TONY	CPT	C-0276690	0248	1
ROESCH JULIUS A	LTC	0-0245563	0366	3
ROESCH ROBERT E	COL	0-0163191	0861	3
ROESCH WILBER H	CPT	0-1175560	0447	1
ROESSER MILLARD H	COL	0-0414188	0166	1
ROETTGER DON E	1LT	0-0885029	0744	2
ROETTGER WALTER H	CPT	0-0962492	1060	1
ROEWERT OTTO F	1LT	0-0536794	0250	1
ROFF EARL H	CPT	0-0968509	0261	1
ROFF STANLEY R	MAJ	0-0266636	0166	3
ROGACKI ALFRED G	MAJ	0-0497526	0457	1
ROGALA MARION A	MAJ	0-2011925	0963	1
ROGALESKIE JOHN H	MAJ	C-0481643	0747	1
ROGAN FRANCIS E	COL	0-0332098	1055	1
ROGAN JAMES L	MAJ	0-1923532	0565	1
ROGAN OWEN D	1LT	0-1305650	0745	2
ROGAN WILLIAM J	MAJ	0-1638385	0858	1
ROGASKI CHESTER A	LTC	0-1286553	0664	1
ROGELL HAROLD I	LTC	0-0226383	1061	3
ROGERS ALAN J	2LT	0-0556272	0646	2
ROGERS ALBERT J	LTC	0-2010879	1165	1
ROGERS ALBERT T	CW2	W-2149267	0758	1
ROGERS ALFRED W	CW2	W-2152558	1061	1
ROGERS ARTHUR G	COL	0-0286758	1263	3
ROGERS BEN C	MAJ	C-0122193	0756	3
ROGERS BETTY D	LTC	L-0500836	0865	2
ROGERS CARL L	CW2	W-2103377	C359	1
ROGERS CECIL B	LTC	0-0220619	1052	3
ROGERS CHARLES E	LTC	0-1648815	0662	1
ROGERS CLARENCE B	CPT	0-0135030	0857	3
ROGERS CLARENCE M	COL	0-0246371	1166	3
ROGERS CLIFFORD A	CW2	W-2150524	0859	1
ROGERS DON G	CW3	W-2203897	0467	1
ROGERS DONALD F	COL	0-0456346	0563	1
ROGERS DRAKE E	LTC	0-0386235	0962	1
ROGERS EDWARD C	LTC	0-1280002	0958	1
ROGERS EDWARD M	CW2	W-2114446	0154	1
ROGERS ELLERY R	LTC	0-1173932	0461	1
ROGERS EMORY S	LTC	0-0183051	0455	3
ROGERS ERLO L	1LT	0-1112399	0246	2
ROGERS EUGENE C	LTC	0-1166822	0258	1
ROGERS FAY R	CW2	W-2209343	1264	1
ROGERS FLORENTINE	2LT	N-0702521	0440	1
ROGERS GALEN A	LTC	0-0316131	0966	3

NAME	GRADE	SVC NO	DATE RET MO YR	RET CODE
ROGERS GEORGE A	MAJ	0-1330861	1163	1
ROGERS GEORGE N	1LT	0-0495581	0552	1
ROGERS GLENN W	LTC	0-1581345	1262	2
ROGERS GRACE B	CPT	N-0725318	0247	1
ROGERS GRANVILLE	MAJ	0-2C53504	1159	1
ROGERS HAROLD B	CPT	0-1824916	0667	1
ROGERS HASKEL R	1LT	0-0492380	1044	2
ROGERS HENRY	LTC	0-0112662	0648	3
ROGERS HENRY H	CPT	0-05297C4	1046	1
ROGERS HENRY H	LTC	0-1642515	0763	1
ROGERS HERMAN M	CW3	W-2135992	0662	1
ROGERS HOMER P	1LT	0-1015469	0446	2
ROGERS HORACE I	COL	0-0182487	0355	3
ROGERS HOWARD	MAJ	0-051630B	0448	2
ROGERS HOWARD A	WO1	W-2150074	0961	2
ROGERS HUGH R	LTC	0-0194075	0853	1
ROGERS HUNTER B	LTC	0-0246546	0264	3
ROGERS IRVIN W	CPT	0-1947069	1167	1
ROGERS JAMES A	MAJ	0-0508594	0947	2
ROGERS JAMES B	MAJ	0-1113417	0165	1
ROGERS JAMES C	MAJ	0-1321596	1060	1
ROGERS JAMES C	CW3	W-2152183	0665	1
ROGERS JAMES E	COL	0-0280049	0461	3
ROGERS JAMES E	CPT	0-0498955	1146	1
ROGERS JAMES H	MAJ	0-1285503	0450	1
ROGERS JAMES L	MAJ	0-0967662	1163	1
ROGERS JANSEN H	LTC	0-1636555	1066	1
ROGERS JOE O	CPT	0-1823064	0357	1
ROGERS JOHN	CPT	0-1030296	0650	1
ROGERS JOHN E	COL	0-0168967	0960	3
ROGERS JOHN L	LTC	0-0450099	0163	1
ROGERS JOHN W	MAJ	0-2034829	0167	1
ROGERS JOSEPH E	1LT	0-0416238	0245	2
ROGERS JOSEPH V	LTC	0-0467546	0254	1
ROGERS JR ALVIN L	1LT	0-1322267	0545	1
ROGERS JR EDGAR A	CPT	0-1533903	0147	1
ROGERS JR FRANK A	1LT	0-1307078	0345	1
ROGERS JR JAMES V	1LT	0-1735906	0647	1
ROGERS JR JOHN T	CPT	0-0532114	0447	1
ROGERS JR JONATHAN C	1LT	0-0519530	1145	2
ROGERS JR OTTO F	CPT	0-0309121	0145	2
ROGERS JR ROBERT E	LTC	0-0267360	1166	3
ROGERS JR ROY L	CW2	W-2154866	0263	1
ROGERS JR THOMAS E	LTC	0-1177164	1162	1
ROGERS JR WILLIAM F	LTC	0-1640873	0762	1
ROGERS JR WILLIAM S	CW3	W-2152306	0665	1
ROGERS KENT C	CPT	0-1825492	0346	1
ROGERS LANNES F	1LT	0-1042529	1044	2
ROGERS LAURENCE A	LTC	0-2044401	0761	1
ROGERS LEO K	LTC	0-1289627	0954	1
ROGERS LEON L	CW3	W-2203328	0167	1
ROGERS MARVIN C	LTC	0-0230617	0664	3
ROGERS MAX L	MAJ	0-1176176	0161	1
ROGERS MIKE	CW4	W-2114208	1052	1
ROGERS PAUL D	CPT	0-1639566	0146	2
ROGERS PAUL E	CPT	0-1919500	0662	1
ROGERS RALPH H	1LT	0-0206772	0251	3
ROGERS RAYMOND L	LTC	0-C35C019	0664	3
ROGERS RICHARD A	MAJ	0-0351653	0947	1
ROGERS RICHARD M	LTC	0-0949623	1067	1
ROGERS RICHARD S	MAJ	0-0228648	0752	3
ROGERS ROBERT A	MAJ	0-2021088	1264	1
ROGERS ROBERT E	MAJ	0-0972473	0661	1
ROGERS ROBERT E	MAJ	0-1881968	0367	1
ROGERS ROBERT F	MAJ	0-1941418	0267	1
ROGERS ROBERT L	LTC	0-0165346	0261	3
ROGERS ROBERT R	CPT	0-0414087	0761	1
ROGERS ROBERT W	LTC	0-0202893	0957	3
ROGERS ROBERT W	LTC	0-0225406	0564	3
ROGERS ROBERT W	WO1	W-2107494	0745	2
ROGERS ROLAND H	MAJ	0-1041888	1266	1
ROGERS ROSCOE O	MAJ	0-1876992	1163	1
ROGERS ROY E	LTC	0-0271998	0560	1
ROGERS ROYCE J	LTC	0-1586105	0762	1
ROGERS RUDOLF J	MAJ	0-1545538	0261	1

NAME	GRADE	SVC NO	DATE RET MO YR	RET CODE
ROGERS SAMUEL	1LT	0-1696810	0144	2
ROGERS SAMUEL L	MAJ	0-0238984	C957	3
ROGERS SHIRLEY N	CPT	0-0173964	0161	3
ROGERS THOMAS J	COL	0-0333474	0655	1
ROGERS THOMAS J	CPT	0-0914064	0146	2
ROGERS THOMAS O	LTC	0-1050442	0864	1
ROGERS THOMAS P	COL	0-0173616	1057	3
ROGERS THOMAS P	LTC	0-1322954	0267	3
ROGERS THOMAS S	MAJ	0-0193781	0454	3
ROGERS VELVIN O	MAJ	0-1049653	0357	1
ROGERS WALTER C	CPT	0-1167189	0857	1
ROGERS WALTER P	CPT	0-0492387	1049	1
ROGERS WALTER R	LTC	0-0336851	1055	1
ROGERS WAYNE S	2LT	0-0554879	0445	2
ROGERS WELOON A	CW2	W-2210030	1159	1
ROGERS WILLIAM C	COL	0-0256838	1162	1
ROGERS WILLIAM E	MAJ	C-1185774	1157	1
ROGERS WILLIAM J	MAJ	C-0205555	0352	3
ROGERS WILLIAM J	COL	0-0242898	0-53	1
ROGERS WILLIAM R	COL	0-0347861	0167	3
ROGERS WINTHROP H	COL	0-0266339	0957	2
ROGERSON DONALD J	MAJ	0-1101639	1262	1
ROGERSON GEORGE E	LTC	0-1292762	1263	1
ROGERSON WESLEY L	LTC	0-0322831	0266	3
ROGGE MYRON R	1LT	0-1170539	0445	2
ROGGE WILBUR E	CW3	W-2150795	0167	1
ROGGENKAMP JOSEPH M	LTC	0-0456232	0161	1
ROGGENSTEIN CHARLES	LTC	0-1297096	0765	1
ROGINSON DAVID S	CW2	W-2150617	0361	1
ROGNEY ROGER W	CW3	W-2146697	0962	1
ROGNLIEN DYVART G	MAJ	C-0254461	0664	3
ROGOISH DANIEL D	CPT	0-4030617	C667	1
ROGOWSKI JR ARTHUR A	LTC	0-0366502	0666	1
ROGOWSKI JULIAN J	WO1	W-2102297	0744	2
ROGOWSKI STANISLAUS	CW3	W-2118656	0760	1
ROHALY MICHAEL	CW4	W-2003008	1262	3
ROHAN WILLIAM R	LTC	0-0377269	0767	1
ROHOE GEORGE M	LTC	0-1579035	0960	1
ROHDE PAUL F	WO1	W-2124031	0661	2
ROHOE RAYMOND H	LTC	0-1115403	1064	1
ROHOE RUSSELL H	MAJ	0-2043228	0860	1
ROHLEDER GILBERT V	1LT	0-0441452	1145	2
ROHLF ECWARD L	MAJ	C-1700326	0246	2
ROHLFING ROBERT F	LTC	0-0299591	0854	1
ROHLING ARTHUR H	MAJ	0-0442669	0245	2
ROHNER EUGENE A	MAJ	0-1685561	1064	1
ROHNER PRESTON E	COL	0-0260506	0367	3
ROHNER ROBERT W	MAJ	C-1043216	0160	1
ROHR FRANK	COL	0-0145925	1152	3
ROHR IGNATIUS R	CPT	0-0442732	0749	2
ROHR JOHN M	1LT	0-1311254	0745	2
ROHR THEODORE E	MAJ	0-1583577	C860	1
ROHRBACH RICHARD R	MAJ	0-0184642	0848	1
ROHRBACHER CLARENCE	CPT	0-0887891	0548	2
ROHRBACHER HARRY W	MAJ	0-0331962	1046	2
ROHRE STUART M	LTC	0-0234806	1057	3
ROHRER JAMES R	LTC	0-0294883	1266	3
ROHRER JAY E	CPT	0-0195332	0362	3
ROHRER KENWOOD B	COL	0-0250526	0865	3
ROHRMAN FREDERICK	LTC	0-0226292	0264	3
ROHRMOSER ROBERT	MAJ	0-2208002	1265	1
ROHRS FLORENCE S	MAJ	N-0786520	0466	1
ROHRS FRANK A	COL	0-0133449	C351	3
ROHYANS KENNETH A	MAJ	0-1305836	1064	1
ROICKI STANLEY A	CPT	0-1040462	0767	1
ROIG FRANK N	LTC	0-1012223	1060	1
ROININEN EINO K	1LT	0-1051347	0546	2
ROISTACHER ALBERT S	LTC	0-0289029	0646	2
ROISUM JEROME O	LTC	0-1845618	1162	1
ROJAS WILLIAM D	CW2	W-2211753	1266	1
ROJO FERNANDO S	LTC	0-1543795	0556	1
ROLAN GEORGE T	LTC	0-0225158	0459	1
ROLAND CHARLES	1LT	0-1307468	1146	1
ROLAND EUGENE S	CW4	W-2121371	0459	1
ROLAND JEAN L	1LT	N-0000753	0946	1

NAME	GRADE	SVC NO	DATE RET MO YR	RET CODE
ROLAND VICTOR E	MAJ	0-1825062	0961	1
ROLANDER ARTHUR E	MAJ	0-0287755	0857	1
ROLF ECWARD C	CPT	0-1300386	0746	2
ROLF RAY H	MAJ	0-1291170	0954	1
ROLFE ARVIL E	LTC	0-1702987	0166	1
ROLFE RALPH E	CW2	W-2113701	0666	3
ROLFE HELEN M	CPT	N-0722124	1053	2
ROLFING HENRY W	MAJ	C-131484C	0164	1
ROLL BENJAMIN F	LTC	0-1115088	1167	1
ROLL CHARLES V	MAJ	0-0561936	1262	1
ROLL FRITA F	CPT	0-0377244	1145	2
ROLLASCH RICHARD N	LTC	0-0452074	0358	2
ROLLE JEROME C	MAJ	0-1574133	0560	1
ROLLER ARNOLD E	CPT	0-0466894	0550	1
ROLLER JOHN P	MAJ	0-0216389	1044	2
ROLLER ROBERT C	1LT	0-1316589	0646	2
ROLLINS EDWARD W	LTC	0-0918697	1065	3
ROLLINS FISKE	LTC	0-0262466	0766	3
ROLLINS FRED G	LTC	0-0173354	0955	3
ROLLINS GEORGE C J	MAJ	0-1107083	0856	1
ROLLINS HARRY W	LTC	0-1312334	0467	1
ROLLINS HELEN S	MAJ	N-0741083	0167	1
ROLLINS HERBERT R	1LT	0-0147939	0353	3
ROLLINS JACK P	1LT	0-1639568	0845	2
ROLLINS JOHN W	2LT	0-1048169	0944	2
ROLLINS JOSEPH	LTC	0-0482913	0954	1
ROLLINS JR CHARLES C	COL	0-0307324	0462	1
ROLLINS LOUIS B	CPT	0-1314192	0954	1
ROLLINS MAYNARD A	MAJ	0-050463C	0854	1
ROLLINS MELVIN L	2LT	0-1011820	0344	2
ROLLINS OLIVER E	LTC	0-0342373	1060	1
ROLLINS ORVAL W	MAJ	0-1174694	0562	1
ROLLINS PAUL C	LTC	0-1324363	C866	1
ROLLINS ROBERTA E	MAJ	N-0763059	1066	3
ROLLINS WILLIAM R	LTC	0-1111336	0163	1
ROLLMAN FREDERICK	CW3	W-2147101	1263	1
ROLLSTIN GILBERT C	LTC	0-0318068	0664	3
ROLLY DOROTHY L	1LT	L-0915323	0945	1
ROLLY JOHN W	CPT	0-0488483	0647	1
ROLPH ARTHUR B	LTC	0-0361584	0960	1
ROLPH CARL J	MAJ	0-0110790	0955	3
ROLSON CARL L	1LT	0-1944795	1044	2
ROLWES BERNARD A	CPT	0-0244388	0855	3
ROM GEMINIANC	1LT	0-0890482	1047	1
ROMAINE ALLIE H	LTC	0-0310108	0646	2
ROMAINE FRANK E	CPT	0-0505705	0745	2
ROMAN ALFRED J	LTC	0-0422778	0161	1
ROMAN CHARLES E	MAJ	0-0885747	0657	1
ROMAN FORTUNATO	COL	0-0167712	1053	3
ROMANCHEK JOSEPH J	MAJ	0-2047804	0258	1
ROMANCHEK LOUISE J	LTC	N-0702892	1060	1
ROMANI LOUIS A	1LT	0-0885726	0246	1
ROMANO FRANK E	1LT	0-1000280	1044	2
ROMANO FRANK J	LTC	0-1057221	0166	1
ROMANO GEORGE	CPT	0-1543723	0246	2
ROMANO MICHAEL J	CPT	0-0270102	0845	1
ROMANO PASQUALE A	LTC	0-1045904	0964	1
ROMANO PLACICO	1LT	0-1579037	0844	2
ROMANOFF ALEXANDER	1LT	0-2030998	1056	1
ROMANOV PAUL A	CPT	0-0507203	0845	1
ROMANOVICH SELMA R	MAJ	N-0734374	0961	2
ROMANOW DAVID	CPT	0-1685918	0346	1
ROMANOWSKI WILLIAM J	CPT	0-0888225	1047	1
ROMANSKI RAYMOND N	CPT	0-0976847	0851	2
ROMBACH PETER	MAJ	C-088860C	0753	1
ROME HOWARD J	CPT	0-0330383	1145	2
ROME MANUEL	1LT	0-0573161	0644	2
ROMER MAXIMILIAN	1LT	0-204652C	1044	2
ROMERO EDMUND J	MAJ	0-1031514	1157	1
ROMERO VICTOR M	CW3	W-214444C	0160	1
ROMERSBERGER RICHARD	1LT	0-0543332	0746	2
ROMEU LUIS A	LTC	0-1644713	1164	1
ROMICH NEIL G	MAJ	0-0228428	0544	2
ROMITI ALDO S	CPT	0-0304179	1046	1
ROMM BARNET I	CPT	0-0543542	1045	2

NAME	GRADE	SVC NO	DATE RET MO YR	RET CODE
ROMM MILTON	1LT	0-1325672	0146	2
ROMMEL SENTILE A	CPT	0-1000659	0252	1
ROMP THOMAS H	2LT	0-1542138	0466	2
ROMPOT EDWARD	LTC	0-1297593	0263	1
RONALD JR SIDNEY C	LTC	0-0302810	C467	3
RONAS JOHN S	MAJ	0-1540922	1262	1
RONCI FRANK A	1LT	0-0540242	0646	1
RONCONE EDWARD A	CW2	W-2000328	0147	2
RONDEAU EDMUND	MAJ	0-2008057	0563	1
RONDEAU JAMES C	CW4	W-2002831	0965	3
RONEY CALVIN R	CW2	W-2141432	0460	1
RONEY DONALD R	MAJ	0-1861667	C967	1
RONEY JOHN W	MAJ	0-1286896	0947	2
RONEY WALTER O	LTC	0-0288416	0463	3
RONEY WARD W	COL	0-0235727	0663	3
RONGAUS LEON F	2LT	0-1824917	1044	2
RONGEN JOHN A	1LT	0-0505265	1154	1
RONICKER FREDERICK	1LT	0-0396730	0646	2
RONING HARRY C	CW4	W-2001664	0364	3
RONINGER LOUIS E	LTC	0-0392113	C361	1
RONK RAPHAEL R	1LT	0-0445446	0245	2
RONKA ENSIO K F	COL	0-0303930	0158	3
RONN SIGFRED A	MAJ	C-2007279	0965	1
RONNE ROBERT R	LTC	0-0372893	0752	1
RONNEBERG CONRAD E	LTC	0-0135325	1153	3
RONNING LILY V	1LT	N-0727556	0446	1
RONNINGEN OTTO I	COL	0-0336200	0648	3
RONNOW DERRILL C	CPT	0-0453697	0245	1
RONQUILLO JOSE	CW2	W-2205697	0863	1
RONQUILLO MAXIMO C	1LT	0-1896646	0350	2
RONQUILLO TEODORO M	CPT	0-1896440	0357	2
RONSHAUSEN WILBER A	MAJ	0-0969843	0964	1
ROOD HAROLD	MAJ	0-1557779	0961	3
ROOD REGINALD S	LTC	0-0311198	0365	3
ROOF DONALD B	LTC	0-203490C	0962	1
ROOF EDWARD F	LTC	0-1109629	0862	1
ROOF JR ORA W	LTC	0-1577770	0961	1
ROOF JR WILLIAM J	MAJ	0-2007571	0960	1
ROOK ELMER D	CPT	0-0200991	1154	3
ROOKS ROBERT O	CPT	0-0348302	1165	3
ROOKS WILLIAM A	COL	0-0216137	1263	3
ROONEY ARTHUR E	LTC	0-0394471	0866	1
ROONEY CHARLES D	LTC	0-0419113	0460	1
ROONEY CHARLES H	CW3	W-2205231	0963	1
ROONEY DENNIS A	CPT	0-0961900	0163	1
ROONEY JOHN F	2LT	0-2047805	0745	1
ROONEY JOHN H	LTC	0-0397204	0563	2
ROONEY JR IRVING J	2LT	0-1298294	0345	2
ROONEY MARGARET A	2LT	N-0756533	C845	1
ROONEY RALPH F	MAJ	0-0404034	0163	1
ROONEY ROBERT F	LTC	0-1821916	0264	1
ROONEY ROBERT T	2LT	0-1639570	C445	2
ROONEY THOMAS C	LTC	0-2049701	1066	1
ROONEY VINCENT J	CW3	W-2102299	0557	1
ROOP DONALD R	LTC	0-0360318	C865	3
ROOP GERALD D	CW2	W-3430477	0267	1
ROOPE WILLIAM A	CW3	RW-2148070	1061	1
ROORDA HENRY M	CPT	0-0490212	0946	1
ROOS HAMPUS E	MAJ	0-0294914	0445	2
ROOS MAURICE I	2LT	0-1822907	0744	2
ROOSE CLARENCE N	MAJ	C-1054776	0265	3
ROOSEVELT ARICHIBA	LTC	0-0143128	0143	2
ROOT AMOS R	CW2	W-2110663	1149	1
ROOT CHARLES L	MAJ	0-0151045	0852	3
ROOT CHESTER L	MAJ	C-0465712	0452	1
ROOT DONALD S	MAJ	0-0137661	0252	3
ROOT ERNEST E	COL	0-0266181	0463	3
ROOT HOWARD S	CPT	0-0163728	C449	3
ROOT JAMES A	CPT	0-0417274	C744	2
ROOT JAMES H	MAJ	0-0404759	0464	1
ROOT JAMES W	CPT	0-0959546	0160	1
ROOT KARL E	MAJ	0-1639572	1058	1
ROOT LEWIS A	1LT	0-1949642	0846	2
ROOT MURPHY A	LTC	0-0257511	C867	3
ROOT NICHOLAS V	MAJ	0-4005500	0265	1

NAME	GRADE	SVC NO	DATE RET MO YR	RET CODE
ROOT PAUL F	CW2	W-2146192	0958	1
ROOT RICHARD M	CW3	W-2152559	0863	1
ROOT ROBERT L	LTC	0-0902819	0146	2
ROOT ROBERT R	LTC	0-0400844	0466	1
ROOT RODERICK M	MAJ	0-0261342	0367	3
ROOT ROY B	LTC	0-1302527	0867	1
ROOTE JESSE T	CPT	0-0365641	0447	2
ROOTS CLYDE C	1LT	0-1111875	0447	2
ROPER ARTHUR E	CPT	0-2018574	0156	1
ROPER BENJAMIN S	LTC	0-0310091	0347	2
ROPER ROBERT G	CPT	0-1311931	0547	2
ROPER WILLIS W	MAJ	0-1922536	0465	2
ROQUEMORE RICHARD O	COL	0-0282162	0954	3
ROQUETTE HENRY L	LTC	0-0174804	C454	3
RORBY EBBA C A	1LT	N-0700410	0443	1
RORICK ROLAND M	1LT	0-0515575	1148	1
RORICK SHIRLEY M	LTC	0-1177619	1067	1
RORK CATHERINE	MAJ	N-0800137	0865	2
RORK PHILIP J	LTC	0-1580244	0363	1
ROSA ANGEL	1LT	0-0371126	0945	2
ROSA CHARLES W	CW3	W-2112009	0760	1
ROSADO FRANCISCO	1LT	0-0162965	0456	3
ROSAL PAUL M	LTC	0-1101191	0365	1
ROSALER BENY	COL	0-0178150	1040	1
ROSALES JR JOSEPH A	CW3	W-2152984	1065	1
ROSAMOND PAUL H	1LT	0-0533468	0946	1
ROSARIC ABRAHAM	MAJ	0-0475822	0154	1
ROSARIC LUIS	MAJ	0-0423215	1057	1
ROSBACH JACK N	2LT	0-1592549	1043	2
ROSBOROUGH JAMES C	COL	0-0179173	0155	3
ROSCOE JOSEPH P	CW3	W-2203368	0965	1
ROSCOE JR ELI	2LT	0-1288954	0644	2
ROSCOE VROOM W	CW4	W-2003794	1061	3
ROSDAHL CONRAD E	CPT	0-0461519	0146	2
ROSE BOBBIE L	MAJ	0-2211468	0965	1
ROSE CHARLES E	MAJ	0-1938070	0466	1
ROSE CHARLES F	LTC	0-0338522	1066	3
ROSE CHARLES L	LTC	0-1798298	1166	1
ROSE CLIFFORD E	MAJ	0-1643294	0260	1
ROSE DAVID L	1LT	0-1285311	0944	2
ROSE DEWEY W	2LT	0-2011481	1145	2
ROSE DONALD C	CW3	W-2147665	0664	1
ROSE EARL A	LTC	0-0286619	0757	3
ROSE EDWARD C	M G	0-0102685	0954	3
ROSE EMYLE	LTC	0-0502021	0257	1
ROSE FRANCIS J	COL	0-0272741	1067	3
ROSE FRED C	CW2	W-2209536	0961	1
ROSE FREDERICK	MAJ	0-0410886	1047	2
ROSE GEORGE E	COL	0-0175750	0360	3
ROSE GEORGE W	LTC	0-0347276	0264	3
ROSE GLEN	CPT	0-0248387	0344	2
ROSE HANNIBAL C	CPT	0-0508064	0157	2
ROSE HAROLD E	LTC	0-0323516	0646	2
ROSE HORACE S	LTC	0-0423035	0765	1
ROSE HOWARD E	1LT	0-1059045	0846	1
ROSE IRVIN H	MAJ	0-0448582	0148	1
ROSE JACK W	LTC	0-1825493	0663	1
ROSE JC F	MAJ	0-1535819	0663	1
ROSE JOE W	LTC	0-1552978	1060	1
ROSE JOHN C	LTC	0-0500463	0-53	1
ROSE JOHN F	MAJ	0-1108278	0359	1
ROSE JOHN H	MAJ	0-0109500	1145	2
ROSE JOHN J	CPT	0-1635276	0156	1
ROSE JOHN M	MAJ	0-0167313	0653	3
ROSE JOSEPH	MAJ	0-0310144	0845	1
ROSE JOSEPH R	LTC	0-0403516	0761	1
ROSE JR JOHN D	LTC	0-0406024	0364	1
ROSE KEITH L	LTC	0-1845096	0761	1
ROSE KYLE L	LTC	0-0250229	0263	3
ROSE LANGTON F	WO1	W-2107649	0746	2
ROSE LENA M	CPT	N-0734736	0248	1
ROSE LEONARD J	LTC	0-0114604	0951	3
ROSE LLEWELLYN	LTC	0-0276840	0457	1
ROSE LUTHER I	MAJ	0-1914061	0725	1
ROSE LUTHER S	WO1	W-2102301	0243	2

NAME	GRADE	SVC NO	DATE RET MO YR	RET CODE
ROSE MILTON F	MAJ	0-0228559	0465	3
ROSE MURRELL S	CW4	W-2121006	0355	1
ROSE NORVAL R	MAJ	0-2262440	0267	1
ROSE OTIS R	MAJ	0-0494375	C954	1
ROSE PAUL A	COL	0-0922248	C967	3
ROSE PETER	LTC	0-1167193	0766	1
ROSE PHILIP	COL	0-0253309	0662	1
ROSE RALPH F	LTC	0-0920112	C865	3
ROSE RICHARD A	MAJ	C-0501428	1145	2
ROSE RICHARD L	CPT	0-0925467	1151	1
ROSE ROBERT A	LTC	0-0231180	C662	3
ROSE ROBERT R	COL	0-0103668	1150	3
ROSE ROBERT J	CPT	0-0538345	C747	1
ROSE ROBERT O	CW2	W-2148137	0856	1
ROSE ROGER J	LTC	0-1821632	0162	1
ROSE SAMUEL A	CPT	0-0468160	0745	2
ROSE SIDNEY	LTC	0-0279044	1056	3
ROSE STANLEY W	CW2	W-2147446	1059	1
ROSE SYDNEY A	1LT	0-1716582	1045	2
ROSE THOMAS O	LTC	0-1284402	0762	1
ROSE VIRGIL L	CPT	0-1300388	1047	1
ROSE WERNER J	COL	0-0229884	0962	3
ROSE WESLEY E	CW3	W-2203876	1064	1
ROSE WILLIAM B	COL	0-0353261	0267	1
ROSE WILLIAM R	CPT	0-1755913	0447	1
ROSE WILLIAM Y	MAJ	0-1165084	0862	1
ROSE WINSLOW A	CPT	0-0287496	0457	1
ROSEBERRY FLOYD M	1LT	0-1647675	C845	2
ROSEBERRY ROBERT C	MAJ	C-0503901	C954	1
ROSEBORROUGH JOSEPH	CW3	W-2209339	C866	1
ROSEBRAUGH STANLEY M	MAJ	0-0218891	C559	3
ROSEFIELD IRVING	LTC	0-0490436	1062	1
ROSEKRANS FREDERICK	CW4	W-2110544	0267	3
ROSELER HERBERT W	LTC	C-1543401	1163	1
ROSELL CHARLES T	LTC	0-1586112	0962	1
ROSELL HENRY	1LT	0-1039623	0346	1
ROSELL MARTIN B	LTC	0-0283922	1265	3
ROSELLE CLIFFORD H	CW3	W-2153133	0164	1
ROSEMAN LEO L	CPT	0-1821282	0646	2
ROSEMARK RICHARD I	MAJ	C-0358549	0567	3
ROSEMOND JAMES	1LT	0-2262765	1053	2
ROSEMONT BERNARD N	LTC	0-0254221	0763	3
ROSEN CHARLES	CPT	0-0514941	0545	2
ROSEN CLOYCE B	LTC	0-1295605	0462	1
ROSEN DAVID	LTC	0-0289340	0957	1
ROSEN HARRY E	LTC	0-1593812	1162	2
ROSEN HERMAN L	CPT	C-0318408	0945	2
ROSEN JACK	LTC	0-1651174	0667	1
ROSEN JEROME	CPT	0-0121913	C648	3
ROSEN JULIUS R	MAJ	0-1030929	0761	1
ROSEN MICHAEL M	MAJ	0-0253241	0945	2
ROSEN MURRAY	CW3	W-2152149	0357	1
ROSEN SAMUEL C	LTC	0-0337711	1063	3
ROSEN SYDNEY S	LTC	0-1183405	C467	3
ROSENBALM CARL	CW4	W-2126852	1054	1
ROSENBALM JAMES L	LTC	0-2035148	0866	1
ROSENBAUM ALEXANDER	LTC	0-0294102	1062	3
ROSENBAUM CHARLES R	COL	0-0303326	1160	1
ROSENBAUM FRANK W	CW2	W-2210432	C163	1
ROSENBAUM HAROLD C	CPT	0-0476074	C547	1
ROSENBAUM JOHN A	MAJ	0-0213760	C962	3
ROSENBAUM LEONARD	CPT	0-1284026	0645	2
ROSENBERG ERNEST R	COL	0-0184256	1152	3
ROSENBERG JOSEPH W	LTC	0-1592019	0167	3
ROSENBERG LOUIS	MAJ	C-0109441	1135	1
ROSENBERG NATHAN	LTC	0-0336315	C654	3
ROSENBERG ROBERT F	MAJ	0-1105147	C266	1
ROSENBERG VERNON L	CPT	0-1716129	C645	2
ROSENBERGER BRUCE N	2LT	0-0517610	0944	1
ROSENBERGER FIETTA K	LTC	N-0722523	0462	1
ROSENBERGER FINLEY O	1LT	0-1308709	1144	2
ROSENBERGER HARRY A	MAJ	C-1282089	C860	1
ROSENBERGER JOSEPH O	COL	0-0228187	0565	3
ROSENBERGER ROBERT E	MAJ	0-0959274	C563	1
ROSENBLATT JOSEPH K	CPT	0-1111876	0664	1

NAME	GRADE	SVC NO	DATE RET MO YR	RET CODE
ROSENBLATT WILLIAM H	CPT	0-1685108	0346	2
ROSENBLOOM PHILIP J	MAJ	0-0481677	0746	2
ROSENBLOOM SELIG	MAJ	0-1551301	0355	1
ROSENBLUM CHARLES	CPT	0-0256635	1065	3
ROSENBLUM HOWARD M	CPT	0-0447230	1045	2
ROSENBLUM HYMAN	LTC	0-0176959	0347	2
ROSENBLUM MEYER	MAJ	0-0352587	0446	2
ROSENCRANZ ARTHUR	1LT	0-1592552	0845	2
ROSENDAHL EDWARD F	COL	0-0358037	0766	3
ROSENER FREDERICK	CW3	W-2146681	0763	1
ROSENFELD ABRAM H	COL	0-0213685	1163	3
ROSENFELD LOUIS	2LT	0-1640881	0445	1
ROSENFELD ROBERT T	MAJ	0-0366847	0246	2
ROSENFIELD ABRAHAM B	MAJ	0-0197984	0246	2
ROSENGREN ROSWELL P	COL	0-0420484	0262	3
ROSENHEIM JR HARRY T	LTC	0-0324508	0865	3
ROSENSTOCK FRANCIS C	CW2	W-2145584	0462	1
ROSENTHAL ABNER H	CPT	0-1689371	0545	2
ROSENTHAL CARL J	CW2	W-2150680	0259	1
ROSENTHAL IRVING A	CPT	0-1683851	0544	2
ROSENTHAL JEROME B	2LT	0-1181437	0445	2
ROSENTHAL JOHN	LTC	0-0456304	0264	1
ROSENTHAL JR HARRY W	CPT	0-0969320	0859	2
ROSENTHAL LEONARD G	MAJ	C-0314204	1142	2
ROSENTHAL LIONEL H	LTC	0-0263508	0756	3
ROSENTHAL MAURICE	CW4	W-2101078	0953	1
ROSENTRATER ROBERT E	2LT	0-1293836	0845	2
ROSENWALD ARTHUR W	CW2	W-2112152	0361	2
ROSER ROBERT H	1LT	0-1292061	0646	2
ROSESCO ALFRED W	LTC	0-1014847	1161	1
ROSETO BENJAMIN J	LTC	0-1295943	0463	1
ROSEVEAR WILLIAM B	COL	0-0101987	0250	3
ROSFELD EMANUEL	CW3	W-2208478	0766	1
ROSHON JR CHARLES O	MAJ	0-0476935	0366	3
ROSIE LOUIS D	CW2	W-2152125	0559	1
ROSIER EUGENE R	CW2	W-2146315	1161	1
ROSINETTE THURMAN W	CW2	W-2144762	0957	1
ROSING WILLIS S	CPT	0-0129261	0156	3
ROSKAM CHARLES A	CW3	W-2144434	0263	1
ROSKAMP HUBERT A	MAJ	0-2033658	1262	1
ROSKOPP JOHN G	2LT	0-1323175	0344	2
ROSKOSKI JOHN	1LT	0-1825259	0157	2
ROSKUSZKA ROMAN S	CW2	W-2151062	0658	2
ROSLUND OLIVER S	CPT	0-0330423	0262	3
ROSNER ADOLPH G	MAJ	0-1288302	0152	1
ROSNER HAROLD	2LT	0-1056214	0944	2
ROSNER WILLIAM P	CPT	0-1799898	0858	1
ROSNICK MANNING J	CPT	0-1683922	0145	2
ROSOFF LEONARD	CPT	0-0400515	1045	1
ROSPOND ROBERT T	2LT	0-0557644	0347	2
ROSQUIST ARNE E	MAJ	0-1535957	0266	1
ROSS ALEX J	1LT	0-2017243	0852	1
ROSS CARLOS A	LTC	0-0168736	0358	3
ROSS CHARLES A	MAJ	0-0523752	0347	2
ROSS CHARLES E	LTC	0-0176127	0961	3
ROSS CHARLES E	MAJ	C-0968332	0967	1
ROSS CLARENCE F	LTC	0-0297676	0958	3
ROSS CLIFTON M	MAJ	0-0287859	1058	3
ROSS CONSTANCE	2LT	N-0778439	0348	1
ROSS COSBY F	CW2	W-2149090	0662	1
ROSS CYRIL C	CPT	0-0287214	1057	3
ROSS CYRIL M	CW3	W-2004449	1164	1
ROSS DAVID	COL	0-0355468	0960	1
ROSS DAVID C	1LT	0-2200832	0458	2
ROSS DAVID W	LTC	0-1579041	0266	3
ROSS DOMINIC R	CPT	0-1018205	0947	2
ROSS DONALD J	1LT	0-0393370	1148	2
ROSS DONALD R	CPT	0-0920518	0645	2
ROSS DONALD R	CW3	W-2145621	0363	1
ROSS DWIGHT H	CPT	0-0238067	0446	2
ROSS EARL R	COL	0-0205844	0754	3
ROSS EDITH M	2LT	N-0772394	0445	1
ROSS EDWARD H	MAJ	0-1330596	0666	3
ROSS EDWARD J	1LT	0-1055432	1045	2
ROSS EDWIN B	MAJ	0-0248880	0667	3

NAME	GRADE	SVC NO	DATE RET MO YR	RET CODE
ROSS EDWIN F	CPT	0-1544647	0647	2
ROSS ELLWOOD H	LTC	0-0250346	C566	3
ROSS ELTON S	COL	0-0313594	C147	1
ROSS EUGENE A	CPT	0-1826394	C547	1
ROSS EUGENE R	CW3	W-2146943	0563	1
ROSS FRANK A	CW4	W-2112139	1159	1
ROSS FRANK A	CW3	W-2152283	0765	1
ROSS FRANK E	COL	0-0300004	0165	3
ROSS FRANK P	LTC	C-1796157	1055	1
ROSS FRED E	LTC	0-0203820	C648	3
ROSS FRED J	1LT	0-1306152	1045	1
ROSS GEORGE H	COL	0-0212356	0262	3
ROSS GILBERT T	COL	0-0177289	C462	3
ROSS GORDON M	MAJ	C-1285120	0447	2
ROSS GORDON W	LTC	0-0900477	C563	1
ROSS HAROLD R	MAJ	0-2041372	0765	1
ROSS HARRY W	MAJ	0-1796357	0660	1
ROSS HENRY F	COL	0-0307704	0661	1
ROSS HERBERT F	CPT	0-0500154	0848	1
ROSS HERMAN	1LT	0-1289013	0545	2
ROSS HERMAN M	2LT	0-1825186	C645	2
ROSS HOWARD A	CPT	0-0461715	C646	2
ROSS HUBERT W	MAJ	0-1020185	C461	1
ROSS JACK	CW4	W-2145277	1167	1
ROSS JACK J	MAJ	0-0558616	0766	1
ROSS JAMES A	MAJ	C-1167195	C561	1
ROSS JAMES H	COL	C-0901972	0266	3
ROSS JAMES J	LTC	0-0403379	0163	1
ROSS JAMES W	COL	0-0100079	1149	1
ROSS JAMES W	CPT	0-4031259	0666	1
ROSS JAY H	LTC	0-0360840	0264	3
ROSS JOHN P	CW3	W-2142893	0958	1
ROSS JOSEPH L	LTC	0-0301827	1161	3
ROSS JOSEPH V M	CPT	0-1695284	1045	2
ROSS JR DANIEL	1LT	0-1878392	0355	2
ROSS JR JAMES A	CPT	0-1101192	1164	3
ROSS JR RUDOLPH R	MAJ	0-1579056	0455	1
ROSS KENNETH R	CPT	C-0143186	0858	3
ROSS LELAND G	CW3	W-2146488	0862	1
ROSS LEO	LTC	0-0384867	0967	3
ROSS LILLIAN R	2LT	N-0737610	C745	1
ROSS LIONEL E	CPT	0-0393559	0748	2
ROSS LUTHER J	COL	0-0288815	0760	1
ROSS MARTIN C	CW2	W-2153150	0459	1
ROSS MARVIN A	LTC	C-1170541	0258	1
ROSS MONETTE C	LTC	0-0310755	0558	1
ROSS OGDEN J	B G	0-0235302	0453	3
ROSS PAUL S	1LT	0-0524163	1147	2
ROSS PETER W	MAJ	0-0305886	0546	2
ROSS PHILIP R	COL	0-0245130	0967	3
ROSS RALEIGH R	LTC	C-0332186	1046	2
ROSS RICHARD A	WO1	W-2133161	1045	2
ROSS RICHARD S	2LT	C-1534850	0146	2
ROSS ROBERT	CPT	0-1166365	C446	2
ROSS ROBERT B	2LT	0-1111877	0645	2
ROSS ROBERT H P	LTC	0-0277927	1055	3
ROSS ROBERT R	CPT	0-1543796	0547	2
ROSS RODERICK O	CW2	W-2152736	0161	1
ROSS ROLLIN G	COL	0-0211735	1048	2
ROSS ROY W	COL	0-0331231	1066	3
ROSS SAMUEL	LTC	0-0310437	0246	2
ROSS SR DANIEL F	CPT	0-1686173	1053	2
ROSS THOMAS W	MAJ	0-0334206	1266	3
ROSS VICTOR G	2LT	0-1003156	0145	2
ROSS VIRGIL	CW2	W-2208930	0265	1
ROSS WADE H	CPT	0-2054003	1045	2
ROSS WALTER E	MAJ	0-1745229	0647	2
ROSS WEBSTER K	MAJ	0-0227329	0162	3
ROSS WILLARD C	LTC	0-0137299	0654	3
ROSS WILLIAM	1LT	0-1320185	1046	1
ROSS WILLIAM B	LTC	0-1324792	0761	3
ROSS WILLIAM E	LTC	0-0351952	0660	1
ROSS WILLIAM I	CW2	W-2122884	0762	1
ROSS WOODROW	CW4	W-2122576	0859	2
ROSSBERG RAYMOND A	COL	0-0209818	1153	3

NAME	GRADE	SVC NO	DATE RET MO YR	RET CODE
ROSSEN JOSEPH M	CPT	0-0498678	0545	2
ROSSER BERNADINE	1LT	N-0784646	0747	1
ROSSER BERNARD H	CPT	0-0372587	1145	2
ROSSER GLEN H	MAJ	0-1181745	1057	1
ROSSER LANDON C	COL	0-0236911	1054	3
ROSSETIE HENRY J	CPT	0-0201873	1145	1
ROSSETTER JAMES W	LTC	0-0259535	0865	3
ROSSETTI CHRISTOPHE	LTC	0-1638391	0164	1
ROSSI ALDO R	LTC	0-0448636	0755	1
ROSSI HAROLD F	CPT	0-1306321	0746	2
ROSSI MARY M	CPT	N-0720093	0546	1
ROSSI NEIL J	CW3	W-2147519	0862	1
ROSSI RALPH A	CPT	0-0497726	0446	2
ROSSIE WILLIAM L	LTC	0-0274802	0157	1
ROSSIO FRANK	CPT	0-0498102	0352	1
ROSSITER RUSSELL E	CPT	0-1312049	0848	2
ROSSITTO ANTHONY F	CPT	0-0369627	0343	2
ROSSKOFF JOHN K	LTC	0-1046251	1161	1
ROSSKOFF JOHN W	COL	0-0174206	0657	1
ROSSLOW ALWIN F	LTC	0-0206264	0263	3
ROSSLOW FRED S	1LT	0-1313134	0845	2
ROSSMAN BERNARD	CPT	0-0441415	0945	2
ROSSMAN FRANK E	LTC	0-0220685	C161	3
ROSSMAN JR HENRY C	MAJ	0-0370943	0945	2
ROSSNAGEL FREDERICK	LTC	0-1648463	0663	1
ROSSNAGEL JOHN M	COL	0-0364936	0765	1
ROSSON JR JULION C	CPT	0-1648464	1159	1
ROSSON SAMUEL I	LTC	0-0248388	0745	2
ROSSOW BENJAMIN O	COL	0-0239101	0166	3
ROSSOW DOMINIC	CPT	0-0571746	0961	2
ROST CECIL I	LTC	0-1326171	0366	1
ROSTEN HERBERT	LTC	0-1945930	0662	1
ROSTET WILHO W	LTC	0-0479053	1166	3
ROSTON MARK A	1LT	0-0536690	0246	2
ROSWELL KENNETH E	LTC	0-0302522	1167	3
ROSWOLD ROBERT E	CW2	W-2152775	0961	1
ROSZKOWSKI JOSEPH W	CW2	W-2141434	1054	1
ROTCHFORD FREDERICK	CW2	W-2149348	0561	1
ROTCHFORD HENRY M	LTC	0-1894983	0165	3
ROTELL RELLA T	1LT	N-0797575	0648	1
ROTEN CHARLES T	CPT	0-0397252	0245	2
ROTH ADOLPH J	WO1	W-2128423	0347	1
ROTH ADOLPH R	LTC	0-0513908	0865	3
ROTH ALFRED J	LTC	0-1169714	1163	1
ROTH ARTHUR I	LTC	0-0234893	0162	3
ROTH CARROLL W	LTC	0-0246347	1166	3
ROTH CHARLES H	MAJ	0-0127593	0649	3
ROTH DALE E	MAJ	0-0263014	0446	1
ROTH DANIEL P	MAJ	0-0356291	0745	2
ROTH DAVID A	1LT	0-1744894	1045	2
ROTH EDWARD	LTC	0-1310880	1062	1
ROTH ERGAN V	MAJ	0-1061842	0562	1
ROTH EUGENE	COL	0-0299374	1066	3
ROTH GEORGE H	1LT	0-1794862	0145	2
ROTH GEORGE R	LTC	0-0359809	0461	1
ROTH HAROLD F	LTC	0-1316513	1063	1
ROTH HAROLD W	CPT	0-1745543	0646	2
ROTH HENRY J	1LT	0-1546403	0346	2
ROTH HOWARD E	2LT	0-1293838	0145	2
ROTH IRWIN	LTC	0-1647247	0163	1
ROTH JAMES F	1LT	0-0426033	0744	2
ROTH JOSEPH P	2LT	0-1015859	0445	2
ROTH KENNETH L	MAJ	0-4006984	0466	1
ROTH LAWRENCE A	CW3	RW-2152423	0566	1
ROTH MAX	LTC	0-0315410	0449	1
ROTH MERALL	CPT	0-0422622	0648	1
ROTH MICHAEL M	LTC	0-0380690	0564	3
ROTH ROBERT E	LTC	0-1165668	0161	1
ROTH RUBEN	WO1	W-2123800	0850	2
ROTH SIGMUND	LTC	0-1999267	0562	2
ROTH VERNAL G L	LTC	0-0389443	0865	2
ROTH WAYNE W	CW2	W-2210074	0963	1
ROTH WILLIAM A	WO1	W-2130925	1045	2
ROTH WILLIAM E	CPT	0-0201823	0650	3
ROTHAUSER HARRY	MAJ	0-0488940	0157	2

NAME	GRADE	SVC NO	DATE RET MO YR	RET CODE
ROTHE CHARLES R	MAJ	0-1055960	0766	3
ROTHE MARSCHAL O	LTC	C-0147645	C456	3
ROTHE VINCENT L	MAJ	C-1182695	1058	1
ROTHERT PAUL P	LTC	0-0298774	1064	1
ROTHFEDER JOSEPH L	CPT	0-0471213	0546	2
ROTHGEB EDWIN E	CPT	0-0236938	0964	3
ROTHMAN ARTHUR F	CPT	0-1584826	0655	1
ROTHMAN BERNARD M	MAJ	C-0453024	C746	2
ROTHMAN DAVID	COL	0-0398936	0666	3
ROTHMAN HERMAN	CPT	0-1690473	0146	2
ROTHMAN HYMAN	1LT	0-0499226	0543	2
ROTHMAN MILTON M	LTC	0-2019509	1266	1
ROTHMAN SANFORD	CPT	0-0244180	1045	2
ROTHNER JACOBY T	MAJ	0-0232354	C962	3
ROTHNIE JAMES B	COL	0-0181896	1057	3
ROTHROCK HUBERT O	LTC	0-0252602	0960	3
ROTHROCK KENNETH M	MAJ	0-C277701	0864	3
ROTHROCK PHILIP W	CPT	C-0411231	0645	2
ROTHROCK ROBERT W	COL	0-0494576	0550	1
ROTHROCK WILLIAM C	LTC	0-1011891	C464	1
ROTHSCHILD BERNARD W	1LT	0-1535071	0146	2
ROTHSCHILD RICHARD	MAJ	0-0929749	1162	1
ROTHSEID MAURICE	CPT	0-1298600	0845	2
ROTHSTEIN ISADORE	MAJ	0-C336067	1045	2
ROTHWELL CLIFTON J	MAJ	C-0484395	0-53	1
ROTHWELL RALPH K	MAJ	0-1014155	C963	1
ROTHWELL STUART C	1LT	0-1173059	C444	2
ROTHWELL WALTER H	LTC	0-0957118	0667	1
ROTKOW MAURICE J	CPT	0-1700368	0446	2
ROTONI ROGER J	CPT	0-1290482	1047	1
ROTTENBERG MARVIN	LTC	0-1305319	0762	1
ROTTNER JOHN S G	COL	0-0345534	0467	3
ROTWEIN ABE A	1LT	0-1166824	1044	2
ROTZ SOLOMON G	CPT	0-0475847	0154	1
ROUDABUSH LESTER S	LTC	0-1304272	0363	1
ROUDEBUSH JR GEORGE	MAJ	0-1183608	0461	1
ROUFFY FERNAND E	MAJ	C-0184106	0445	2
ROUGAS JON N	1LT	0-1011118	C645	1
ROUGH JOSEPH M	MAJ	0-1649929	0664	1
ROUGHAN MARTIN P	CW2	W-2144761	0559	1
ROUGHSEDGE WALTER L	COL	0-2044395	0764	2
ROUILLE CHARLES V	CW4	W-2145503	0160	1
ROUND JAMES H	1LT	0-0444121	1046	2
ROUNDS ARVIN D	CPT	0-0102226	0752	3
ROUNDS DALE G	WO1	W-212612C	C444	2
ROUNDS DAVID E	LTC	0-1644026	0667	3
ROUNDS FRANCIS E	CPT	0-1308549	0762	1
ROUNDS GAIL S	1LT	0-1825260	0245	2
ROUNDS JACK S	MAJ	C-0175688	0861	3
ROUNDS PAUL H	CW3	W-2152614	0165	1
ROUNDY PAUL H	LTC	0-1185464	0966	1
ROUNDY WILLIAM D	CW3	PW-2207601	C966	1
ROUNER THOMAS J	COL	0-0240077	1158	3
ROUNSAVALL CLYDE M	MAJ	0-1176180	0561	1
ROUNSEVILLE HOWARD W	1LT	0-1169314	0446	2
ROUNTREE ELLERY L	LTC	C-0468629	0460	1
ROUNTREE JAMES R	CPT	0-0373676	0645	2
ROUNTREE LEWIS G	LTC	0-1309838	C562	1
ROUNTREE MCIVER	LTC	0-0305057	C263	1
ROUNTREE RALPH R	2LT	0-1299116	0145	2
ROUNTREE WALTER S	LTC	0-0234661	0161	3
ROURKE JAMES L	MAJ	C-037163C	0163	1
ROUSE CHARLES A	LTC	C-1306473	C263	1
ROUSE ELWOOD T	COL	0-0328791	0360	1
ROUSE HAROLD A	MAJ	0-1638395	0457	1
ROUSE HENRY F	LTC	0-0405512	0261	1
ROUSE HERMAN L	MAJ	0-1056215	0256	1
ROUSE HOWARD J	COL	C-0235030	0648	3
ROUSE JAMES W H	COL	0-0291502	0467	3
ROUSE JERRY E	COL	0-0339275	1061	1
ROUSE JOHN A	LTC	0-0200870	1056	3
ROUSE JOHN J	CPT	0-0270295	C445	2
ROUSE JR EDWARD B	LTC	0-0311342	0861	2
ROUSE MARY A	2LT	N-0756058	1044	1
ROUSE MILFORD E	CPT	0-0443411	0658	1

NAME	GRADE	SVC NO	DATE RET MO YR	RET CODE
ROUSE RALPH E	CW2	W-2214875	0267	1
ROUSE WALTER J	CPT	0-C503047	1046	1
ROUSE WAYNE W	MAJ	0-0455266	1060	1
ROUSE WILLIAM V	MAJ	C-1576586	0254	1
ROUSER RICHARD F	CW4	W-2150581	0764	1
ROUSER VELMA M C	1LT	N-0701920	0542	1
ROUSH CALVIN T	LTC	0-1291013	0761	1
ROUSH DEFOREST R	COL	0-0264430	0760	3
ROUSH DONALD E	MAJ	0-1111880	1264	1
ROUSH GARY W	LTC	0-044442C	0662	1
ROUSH GEORGE W	1LT	0-1292235	0845	2
ROUSH HOWARD W	LTC	0-1298762	1060	1
ROUSH JEAROLD S	CPT	0-0884927	1045	2
ROUSH JOHN W	MAJ	0-1320186	0262	1
ROUSH JR JOHN N	LTC	0-1822462	1163	1
ROUSH KENNETH W	MAJ	0-1549063	0161	1
ROUSH ROBERT W	CW4	W-2131797	0862	2
ROUSH SAMUEL F	CPT	0-0415711	0444	2
ROUSSEAU CECIL	LTC	0-1949644	0765	1
ROUSSEAU GENARO W	MAJ	0-0365018	0847	2
ROUSSEAU JACQUES M	CW3	W-2112558	0855	1
ROUSSEAU JR SAMUEL O	LTC	0-0337533	0760	1
ROUSSEAU WALTER S	LTC	0-0382412	1160	1
ROUTE HOWARD S	MAJ	0-1184580	0165	1
ROUTEN EUGENE V	LTC	0-1325706	1262	1
ROUTH ROSS H	B G	0-0287602	1065	1
ROUTSON CLARENCE E	CPT	0-1310765	0564	1
ROUTT RAYMOND J	CPT	0-2011219	0457	1
ROUTZAHN CHARLES O	LTC	0-1645535	0562	1
ROUTZOHN NORMAN E	COL	0-0299129	0862	3
ROUX ERNEST V	1LT	0-1896831	0861	1
ROUZIE THOMAS J	COL	0-0254145	0158	3
ROVANSEK JOSEPH S	LTC	0-0451390	0258	1
ROVIN MAURICE F	COL	0-0129244	0648	3
ROVNER EDWARD	2LT	0-117762C	0646	2
ROVNER MIAH H	1LT	0-0471301	1043	2
ROVZAR ROBERT R	CPT	0-0409861	1045	2
ROW JR ANDREW W	CPT	0-0408453	0846	1
ROWAN CLAUDE P	COL	0-0191087	0359	3
ROWAN DONALD W	CPT	0-0117336	0857	3
ROWAN FRANK E	CW3	W-2213910	0967	1
ROWAN JOHN E	LTC	0-0277789	1063	3
ROWAN JOHN L	LTC	0-0292740	0563	1
ROWAN JOHN P	CW4	W-2119574	0657	1
ROWAN JOSEPH E	CPT	0-0374349	0149	2
ROWAN LAWRENCE H	CPT	0-1325933	0261	1
ROWAN MELVIN B	LTC	0-0269767	0466	3
ROWAN RICHARD S	CPT	0-0181378	0557	3
ROWAN ROBERT W	CPT	0-2204401	1060	1
ROWAN WILLIAM K	CPT	0-1062743	0647	1
ROWAND JAMES C	1LT	0-0500062	0647	1
ROWE ELMER B	MAJ	0-1335585	0964	1
ROWE HERBERT O	1LT	0-1014254	0245	2
ROWE JOHN	CPT	0-0102540	0640	1
ROWE JOHN J	CPT	0-1324657	1047	1
ROWE MARION W	1LT	0-1306153	0846	2
ROWE PHILIP A	MAJ	0-0228151	0465	3
ROWE PRESTON B	MAJ	C-020174C	0854	3
ROWE RALPH L	CPT	0-1994987	1065	3
ROWE RAPHAEL P	1LT	0-0147641	0956	3
ROWE RICHARD J	CPT	0-1755519	0846	1
ROWE ROBERT P	LTC	0-0206511	0554	3
ROWE SAMUEL	LTC	0-0382543	0166	3
ROWE THOMAS W	MAJ	0-0315813	0263	1
ROWE WILLIAM H	1LT	0-0372025	1147	2
ROWE WILLIAM J	MAJ	0-1176181	0661	1
ROWE WILLIAM P	CPT	0-1884185	0965	1
ROWE WILLIAM T	1LT	0-1107092	0855	1
ROWELL IRVING H	LTC	0-0262960	0964	3
ROWEN BRYCE C	LTC	0-0446095	0563	1
ROWIN WILLARD C	CW2	W-215106C	0962	1
ROWLAND BILLY L	LTC	0-2010896	0566	1
ROWLAND CHARLES C	MAJ	0-2262654	1063	1
ROWLAND DWIGHT R	MAJ	0-1823350	0966	1
ROWLAND FYNES J	MAJ	0-2262462	0563	1

NAME	GRADE	SVC NO	DATE RET MO YR	RET CODE
ROWLAND GEORGE G	LTC	0-0372158	0460	1
ROWLAND JR HARRY W	2LT	0-1177170	0344	2
ROWLAND JR WILLIAM C	LTC	0-0225179	0657	1
ROWLAND LAWRENCE C	LTC	0-0324661	0266	3
ROWLAND NANCY T	1LT	N-0741773	0845	1
ROWLAND PRESTON B	1LT	0-0420964	C544	1
ROWLAND QUENTIN R	MAJ	0-1289146	0557	1
ROWLAND RALPH E	1LT	0-2006623	0147	1
ROWLAND ROGER W	1LT	0-0526388	1047	2
ROWLAND RUFUS S	2LT	0-1823777	0844	2
ROWLAND SIDNEY A	COL	C-0165030	0648	3
ROWLAND THOMAS H	MAJ	C-0109382	C224	1
ROWLAND THOMAS N	LTC	0-0197033	1155	3
ROWLAND WILL C	COL	0-0342971	0566	1
ROWLAND WILLIE W	CPT	0-2007445	0656	1
ROWLANDS ROBERT W	WO1	W-2132436	0246	2
ROWLETT CAIUS A	COL	C-0229668	0251	3
ROWLETT JOSEPH G	COL	C-0226715	C362	3
ROWLETTE AVERY P	COL	0-0258182	0166	3
ROWLEY ALBERT E G	MAJ	0-0382488	C446	2
ROWLEY JAMES S	1LT	0-1018284	1147	2
ROWLEY JAMES T	CPT	0-0962621	1065	2
ROWLEY MARIE	LTC	N-0722819	0262	1
ROWLEY NORMAN D	MAJ	C-1577777	C557	1
ROWLEY TONY W	CW4	W-2118119	0464	1
ROWORTH JOHN M	LTC	0-0347714	0560	1
ROWSE ROBERT J	COL	0-0127755	C147	1
ROWSELL LELAND R	LTC	0-0298028	0466	3
ROWSTON JOHN	CPT	C-0207665	C728	1
ROY EARL P	LTC	0-0171234	0752	3
ROY ERMIL L	LTC	0-1165943	C461	1
ROY HAROLD	MAJ	0-1166597	1059	1
ROY HAROLD C	LTC	0-1823213	C462	1
ROY JOSEPH FOL	1LT	0-0443157	0147	2
ROY JOSEPH H R	LTC	0-0961770	0163	1
ROY LAWRENCE R	LTC	0-1636570	0557	1
ROY LUTHER W	LTC	0-1307470	C361	1
ROY MICHAEL O	1LT	0-1311819	0846	2
ROY ROBERT G	CPT	0-0983498	0557	2
ROY THOMAS L	MAJ	C-1289628	0258	1
ROY WALLACE R	CPT	0-0243634	0845	2
ROY WENDELL P	MAJ	C-0255959	0867	3
ROYAL EDWARD E	MAJ	C-1798812	0165	1
ROYAL L J	CW4	W-2002839	0166	3
ROYAL RHEUTILIOU	MAJ	C-0216690	0363	3
ROYAL THAYER L	LTC	0-0221300	1061	3
ROYAL THOMAS E	LTC	0-1102022	0561	1
ROYALL LUBY F	MAJ	0-0296058	0255	3
ROYALL WALTER H	MAJ	C-1935684	0465	1
ROYALL WILLIAM A	LTC	0-0139085	C158	3
ROYCE FRANK F	CW2	W-2114624	0466	3
ROYCE JAMES D	LTC	0-0211089	0159	3
ROYCE JOHN E	LTC	0-0277445	0866	3
ROYCROFT FRANK E	CW3	W-2142507	0259	1
ROYE ROBERT L	MAJ	0-0423022	0960	1
ROYE WYATT E	CPT	C-0281614	0846	2
ROYER CLARENCE E	CPT	0-0966431	0161	1
ROYER CLARK W	CPT	0-0317845	1045	1
ROYER HERMAN L	MAJ	0-0248780	1165	3
ROYER MANSEL G	CPT	0-1305838	0160	1
ROYER WALTER J	COL	0-0500009	0463	3
ROYLE DONALD H	CW2	W-34C0C/C	0967	1
ROYONG SIMPLICIO	1LT	0-2027447	C349	1
ROYSE FRANCIS J	CPT	0-1018689	C263	1
ROYSTER JACK A	CPT	0-0375814	0946	2
ROYSTON CHARLIE A	COL	0-0221632	1061	3
ROYSTON WILLIAM R	MAJ	C-1031360	C557	1
ROZAK FRANK J	CW3	W-2142457	C761	1
ROZALSKY HERMAN	CPT	0-0392473	0346	2
ROZAR ROBERT L	CW2	W-2150731	C262	1
ROZEA CYRIL E	COL	0-0286006	0162	3
ROZECKI EDMUND O	LTC	0-2019227	0967	1
ROZER WILLIAM H	CW2	W-2205046	0960	1
ROZETT OSCAR	MAJ	0-05105C9	0546	1
ROZGA ANTHONY A	COL	0-0421653	0365	1

NAME	GRADE	SVC NO	DATE RET MO YR	RET CODE
ROZICH FRANCIS R	MAJ	0-1644724	C761	1
ROZIER HAROLD F	MAJ	0-0222352	0945	2
ROZMAN JOHN J	CW2	W-2146846	1066	1
ROZMAN MARIE R	1LT	N-0724874	0945	1
ROZMAN ROBERT W	LTC	0-2023703	1265	1
RUARK PARKE R	CPT	0-0209237	0943	2
RUBARD JAMES J	MAJ	0-0947482	0862	1
RUBAUM REUBEN S	CPT	0-0443354	0146	2
RUBBELKE LLOYD E	LTC	0-1291889	0962	1
RUBEL GEORGE K	COL	0-0193524	1061	3
RUBEL JR ERNEST M	LTC	0-0284510	1059	1
RUBELMAN LOUIS F	COL	0-0299417	0646	2
RUBEN JOSEPH E	CPT	0-0357105	C140	1
RUBEN LEAH M	2LT	N-0736892	0445	1
RUBENSON BERNARD	LTC	0-0368774	0460	1
RUBENSTEIN EDWIN V	LTC	0-0456622	1160	1
RUBENSTEIN JACOB F	LTC	0-1575123	0466	1
RUBENSTEIN ROBERT	1LT	0-0470809	0744	2
RUBIN DEAN L	LTC	0-0497161	0667	3
RUBIN HAROLD S	CPT	0-17C5950	0248	2
RUBIN IRVING	1LT	0-1697849	1144	2
RUBIN MANDEL	CPT	0-1012309	0247	1
RUBIN MARVIN H	1LT	0-1644726	0146	2
RUBIN NATHAN N	MAJ	0-1946151	0562	1
RUBIN RALPH R	1LT	0-0551326	0547	2
RUBIN SAMUEL	MAJ	0-0491389	0546	2
RUBIN WALTER E	LTC	0-0481013	0263	1
RUBINOFF JACOB	MAJ	0-0135765	1052	3
RUBINOWITZ STANLEY H	COL	0-1577778	1064	1
RUBINTON SAMUEL	LTC	0-0493982	1157	1
RUBIO BERNARDO	CPT	0-1896625	0359	1
RUBLE CLYDE R	CPT	0-0493962	0755	1
RUBLE ROY T	WO1	W-2107975	0757	1
RUBLE VIRGIL E	MAJ	0-0991264	1167	1
RUBLE WILLIS V	LTC	0-0441786	1154	1
RUBLEE EDMUND O	LTC	0-0231471	0364	3
RUBOTTOM ERNEST L	CPT	0-1031125	0257	1
RUBY JOHN L	LTC	0-0318744	0358	1
RUCH LAWRENCE W	CW3	W-2151682	0364	1
RUCH OMAR J	COL	0-0145323	0648	3
RUCINSKI JOHN	1LT	0-1549593	0646	2
RUCKER AARON E	LTC	0-0275001	0156	3
RUCKER CLYDE E	CW2	W-2144928	0459	1
RUCKER FRANK H	2LT	0-0538296	0145	2
RUCKER JAMES J	LTC	0-0451058	0357	1
RUCKER JOHN P	MAJ	0-1283143	0 48	2
RUCKER ROBERT H	CPT	0-0365364	0144	2
RUCKER ROY J	MAJ	0-2293194	0662	1
RUCKLE JAMES G	LTC	0-0239964	0665	3
RUCKMAN ALBERT	CW4	W-2141435	0666	2
RUCKMAN CHARLES W	MAJ	0-0226063	1262	3
RUCKMAN WILLIAM C	LTC	0-0292168	0755	2
RUDAT ROBERT L	LTC	0-1552782	0664	1
RUDBERG JEROME	LTC	0-1845098	1165	1
RUDD CHARLES	COL	0-0181205	0452	1
RUDD JOEL W	CPT	0-2048766	0448	1
RUDD JOHN H	CPT	0-2009672	1155	1
RUDD RAY V S	CPT	0-0241976	0648	3
RUDDELL DORIS N	1LT	N-0767888	0546	1
RUDDEN SARAH E	MAJ	L-1010038	0665	1
RUDDER FRED F	COL	0-0248000	0462	3
RUDDER MARSHALL C	CPT	0-2051537	0657	1
RUDDER PAUL L	LTC	0-1341583	1066	1
RUDDOCK WILLIAM M	LTC	0-0284926	0260	3
RUDDY JOHN G	2LT	0-1047321	1143	2
RUDDY JOSEPH C	MAJ	0-1688492	0765	2
RUDE HARRY E	1LT	0-1822194	0745	2
RUDE JAMES C	1LT	0-0544462	0646	2
RUDEEN SR PAUL E	CW3	W-2152776	0165	1
RUDELL ROBERT C	LTC	0-1307082	0862	1
RUDER JESSE H	LTC	0-0179094	0649	2
RUDERMAN JOSEPH O	1LT	0-0369381	0342	2
RUDERMAN MAURICE	CW3	W-2145586	0463	1
RUDICEL CHANDLER C	LTC	0-0253575	1160	2
RUDIN PHILIP G	LTC	0-0301204	0762	3

NAME	GRADE	SVC NO	DATE RET MO YR	RET CODE
RUDIN STUART	2LT	0-4037586	G256	2
RUDINE CLIFFORD	LTC	0-0153310	0-53	3
RUDINE FRANCIS B	1LT	0-1787142	1147	1
RUDIS ALGIRDAS M	LTC	0-1057588	1064	1
RUDISEL CARL V	2LT	0-1586121	0943	2
RUDISILL HENRY O	COL	0-0279096	0465	3
RUDISILL RICHARD F	COL	0-0174598	0254	3
RUDLEY EDWARD J	LTC	0-0255374	C458	3
RUDMAN NATHAN A	WO1	W-2122715	0645	2
RUDMAN PAUL	1LT	0-1048555	0345	2
RUDNICK EMILY M	CPT	N-0900066	1060	2
RUDNICKI FRANCIS	LTC	0-1287067	0258	1
RUDNICKY JAMES M	1LT	0-1317426	0350	1
RUDOLPH CHARLES W	CPT	0-0485455	0944	2
RUDOLPH DIXON	CPT	0-0300451	1144	2
RUDOLPH ELMER M	COL	0-0237556	0557	3
RUDOLPH FRANCIS F	CPT	0-0444871	114N	2
RUDOLPH JACK A	MAJ	0-0249857	0547	2
RUDOLPH JR SAMUEL F	MAJ	C-1885210	1067	1
RUDOLPH JULES E	CPT	0-4022165	C957	2
RUDOLPH KORRA F	MAJ	L-0704163	0467	1
RUDOLPH MARSHALL K	COL	0-0236354	1056	3
RUDOLPH PHILIP S	CPT	0-0305503	1044	2
RUDSER ORLANDO J	LTC	0-0291901	C967	3
RUDULPH ROBERT M	MAJ	0-0414482	0354	2
RUDY CHARLES A	LTC	0-0412098	1057	1
RUDY HAROLD A	MAJ	0-1686091	0546	2
RUDY THOMAS M	CPT	0-0490203	0646	1
RUDY WILBUR O	LTC	C-1697953	C557	1
RUF CHARLES H	COL	0-0394223	C958	1
RUF CLARENCE A	MAJ	C-0169206	1059	3
RUFF WERNER H	CPT	0-0192483	1160	3
RUFFF WILLIAM F	LTC	0-1113421	0464	1
RUEGSEGGER BOYD A	LTC	0-1001671	0859	1
RUEHE RICHARD W	MAJ	0-0973632	0867	1
RUEHLE CLARENCE C	CW3	W-2103386	C455	1
RUELAS BYRON H	MAJ	0-2018421	1162	1
RUESCH HAROLD R	LTC	0-1584833	0661	1
RUEST GILBERT J	LTC	0-0347050	1164	2
RUETH ANTON	CW2	W-2105963	0750	1
RUFF CARL N	MAJ	C-1294018	0347	2
RUFF DAVID J	CW2	W-2107847	C361	1
RUFF DONALD C	1LT	0-0446961	1044	2
RUFF HERMAN A	LTC	0-0393838	1060	1
RUFF RICHARD R	CPT	0-1557073	1062	1
RUFF WILLIE A	MAJ	0-0504006	0650	1
RUFF 3RD WILLIAM H	CPT	C-0362665	1045	2
RUFFEL EDWARD W	MAJ	0-1018364	1266	1
RUFFNER FREDERICK	LTC	0-0147654	C154	3
RUFFNER ROBERT B	LTC	0-1293123	1262	1
RUFKAHR CLOYDE B	CW2	W-2146804	0859	1
RUFLETH ELMER H	MAJ	0-0411635	1146	2
RUFO SANDY R	LTC	0-1598217	C367	1
RUFSVOLD OLAV M	LTC	C-0207516	0952	3
RUGG BENJAMIN	1LT	0-1294907	0645	2
RUGG JACK	CW2	W-2151393	0264	1
RUGGERI AUGUSTUS A	CPT	0-1690390	0745	2
RUGGIERI JOSEPH R	LTC	0-0524857	C366	1
RUGGIERO MICHAEL B	LTC	0-1012784	0467	1
RUGGIERO ORLANDO	MAJ	C-1015710	C661	1
RUGGLES GEORGE C	LTC	0-0312859	C967	3
RUGGLES WILLIAM B	COL	0-0151250	0351	3
RUGHEIMER EDGAR W	COL	0-0245727	0459	3
RUHAN KATHRYN I	LTC	N-0700189	1046	1
RUHL HARRY C	COL	0-0214353	0650	3
RUHL HOMER L	CW2	W-2117931	0649	1
RUHL JOSEPH R	LTC	0-1115095	C767	1
RUHL LEVI H	MAJ	0-0179851	1053	3
RUHL PAUL V	CPT	0-1016806	1053	1
RUHOFF JOHN R	COL	0-0264923	1046	2
RUIS RONALD H	2LT	0-1307083	1044	2
RUISH DUDLEY C	CW2	W-2149980	0764	1
RUIZ FRANCIS V	2LT	0-1896577	1159	1
RUIZ HERBERTO	CPT	0-0406949	C860	1
RUIZ JOSEPH T	1LT	C-1896661	1060	1

NAME	GRADE	SVC NO	DATE RET MO YR	RET CODE
RUIZ LUIS	CPT	0-0940758	1158	1
RUIZ RAFAEL T	1LT	0-1182241	0450	1
RULAND MARCLD C	CPT	0-1996561	1057	1
RULAND JR LEWIS O	1LT	0-1540884	1050	1
RULE MERTON R	2LT	0-15511C1	0145	2
RULE MILTON L	LTC	0-0288202	1047	2
RULE PERCY R	MAJ	0-0979123	0965	1
RULTSON VERNCN	COL	0-0450694	0766	1
RULLMAN EDWARDS F	1LT	0-1651318	1146	1
RULLMAN WILLIAM M	MAJ	0-1045233	0761	1
RULON BLANCHE S	CPT	N-0700004	1039	1
RUMANS EARL C	MAJ	0-1547765	0159	1
RUMANS WALTER D	MAJ	C-1019554	0564	1
RUMAZZA CARLC R	MAJ	0-03C8842	0947	2
RUMBAUCH EARL F	COL	0-0184349	1058	3
RUMBAUGH ROBERT H	LTC	0-1113422	0967	1
RUMBAUCH ROY M	CPT	0-0151271	1044	2
RUMBLE WILLIAM A	LTC	0-0293112	0761	1
RUMFLIEC CHARLES L	CPT	0-2025295	1060	1
RUMMAGE ROBERT E	1LT	0-1018671	0845	2
RUMMEL DAVID J	CPT	0-0266316	0760	3
RUMMEL JOSEPH L	CPT	0-1583598	0959	1
RUMMEL WILMER F	CPT	0-1686198	1147	1
RUMMIG JAMES A	CW3	RW-2209664	1166	1
RUMOLD WILLIAM F	LTC	0-1645962	1163	1
RUMP RCBERT L	MAJ	0-0995162	0265	1
RUMPF CARL H	COL	0-0275564	0157	3
RUMPF FRANK H	1LT	0-1327768	1046	2
RUMPFF ROY R	COL	0-0139787	0655	3
RUMPH ALBERT R	CW2	W-2109776	0354	2
RUMPLE PAUL V	1LT	0-0479643	1044	2
RUMPLEE JAMES J	MAJ	0-0347116	1060	1
RUMSE WILLIAM F	LTC	0-0176695	0-52	3
RUMSEY CLEC E	LTC	0-0217751	0363	3
RUMSEY HARRIS	CW3	W-2120707	0356	1
RUMSEY LEMUEL G	MAJ	0-1116353	0662	1
RUMSEY GRACE J	LTC	0-1312594	0567	3
RUNDALL JOHN R	MAJ	0-2019510	0361	1
RUNDE PAUL S	MAJ	0-1577781	0954	1
RUNDELL HUGH A	1LT	0-1319121	0446	2
RUNDLE JOSEPH T	MAJ	0-0362821	0356	1
RUNDLE PERCIVAL J	LTC	0-0206304	1157	3
RUNDLE THOMAS L	1LT	0-104494C	0945	2
RUNDQUIST CHARLES F	LTC	0-0354319	0546	2
RUNDQUIST WILLIAM A	MAJ	0-0286444	0266	3
RUNEWITSCH HERMAN A	CW3	W-2147895	0866	1
RUNG ADAM A	2LT	0-1305167	0744	2
RUNG JR PETER R	1LT	0-0502261	0344	2
RUNGE WILLIAM F	LTC	0-0306294	0259	3
RUNION ALLEN R	2LT	0-0363292	1165	3
RUNKLE ALBERT L	CPT	0-1174103	0761	1
RUNKLE DONALD R	CPT	0-1296430	1046	2
RUNKLE GEORGE A	MAJ	0-1016548	1061	1
RUNKLE SAMUEL C	CW2	W-2104436	1055	1
RUNNER WILLIAM R	CW3	W-2146157	0461	1
RUNNING FRED	MAJ	0-1030710	0256	1
RUNYAN FRANK	MAJ	0-0404665	C846	2
RUNYAN HUGH W	CPT	0-1321828	C346	2
RUNYAN PAUL H	COL	0-0191588	0657	3
RUNYON AGNES M	MAJ	N-0778091	0565	1
RUNYON CARROLL R	MAJ	0-0921533	1145	2
RUNYON GEORGE L	MAJ	0-1534851	1160	1
RUNYON HAROLD M	MAJ	0-0266349	1161	3
RUNYON JOHN K	LTC	0-0173446	0562	3
RUNYON ROLLIN A	CW3	W-2152004	0860	1
RUP CHESTER S	MAJ	0-1003028	0657	1
RUPE FRED D	COL	0-0498256	1050	1
RUPERT GEORGE S	CPT	0-0473925	0749	1
RUPERT HOWARD L	LTC	0-0141202	1149	3
RUPERT JAMES K	MAJ	0-1293839	0862	1
RUPERT MAXIE L	MAJ	0-0442954	1062	2
RUPERT CRAN H	LTC	0-0331356	0962	2
RUPERT PASCAL W	LTC	0-0205706	0845	2
RUPERT ROBERT P	MAJ	0-1919017	0464	1
RUPERT WILLIAM O	LTC	0-0800052	0366	1

NAME	GRADE	SVC NO	DATE RET MO YR	RET CODE
RUPERT WILLIAM P	CPT	0-2011879	0557	1
RUPP FREDERICK	MAJ	C-1120513	0663	1
RUPP HERMAN B	LTC	0-0307810	C962	1
RUPP KARL K	MAJ	C-0268651	1060	3
RUPP KENNETH J	LTC	0-0255975	0966	3
RUPPANNER JR PAUL W	2LT	0-0290341	1044	2
RUPPART HOWARD H	COL	0-0296102	0655	1
RUPPEL HENRY M	MAJ	C-0139784	C857	3
RUPPEL RAYMOND P	MAJ	C-1081672	0761	1
RUPPERSBERG JR ANTHO	COL	0-0306198	0767	3
RUPPERT HENRY	LTC	0-1331228	0764	1
RUPPLE HARRY F	LTC	0-0239721	0962	3
RUPY STANLEY B	1LT	0-1287068	1044	2
RUSBARSKY FRANK R	LTC	0-1948215	0164	1
RUSCH RODERIC F	CW3	W-2144663	0760	2
RUSCITTO PETER G	CPT	0-1281131	0646	2
RUSEK STEPHEN C	MAJ	0-0476732	1154	1
RUSH ELLIS F	LTC	0-0395348	1157	1
RUSH ERNEST J	COL	0-0165604	0647	2
RUSH GEORGE F	1LT	0-0553039	0847	1
RUSH JACK L	2LT	0-0887349	0645	2
RUSH JR HOWARD C	LTC	0-0213244	1262	3
RUSH JR RAYMOND J	LTC	0-1286897	1167	1
RUSH MERLE K	MAJ	C-0306754	0146	2
RUSH ORA W	LTC	0-0287242	1060	3
RUSH RALPH R	CW4	W-2106913	0955	1
RUSH ROBERT	LTC	C-0318541	0559	1
RUSH ROY C	1LT	0-1018316	C147	2
RUSH SAMUEL E	LTC	0-0402991	0163	1
RUSH THOMAS H	CPT	0-1825063	1047	1
RUSH WARD D	MAJ	0-1303195	1060	1
RUSHAKOFF OSCAR	CPT	0-1821508	1045	2
RUSHE BERNARD J	1LT	C-0885775	1145	2
RUSHER WILLIAM A	MAJ	C-1014592	0367	1
RUSHING EDGAR	COL	C-0130080	C956	3
RUSHING EDWARD C	CW2	W-2205118	0462	1
RUSHING REGINALD	LTC	0-0911140	0666	3
RUSHTON ALLEN	LTC	0-0234926	0764	3
RUSHTON BENJAMIN W	COL	0-0264404	0965	1
RUSHTON ELSMORE	MAJ	C-0220022	C549	1
RUSHTON MARION	COL	0-0208099	1053	3
RUSHTON PIERCE A	COL	0-0246481	1166	3
RUSHTON WILLIAM J	COL	0-0211867	0860	3
RUSINKO GEORGE	LTC	0-0475961	0255	1
RUSNOCK ANN R	MAJ	N-0725333	0166	1
RUSS ANTHONY	1LT	0-1081500	0745	2
RUSS JAMES R	1LT	0-1293484	C944	2
RUSS JOHN D	CPT	0-0200652	1054	1
RUSS KENNETH L	MAJ	0-2011708	0261	1
RUSS RICHARD W	CPT	0-1874863	0962	1
RUSSELL ALAN G	CW2	W-2105014	C145	2
RUSSELL ALLEN B	MAJ	C-1540935	C763	1
RUSSELL ANDREW G	COL	0-0278235	C957	2
RUSSELL BRUCE W	COL	0-0217631	C256	3
RUSSELL CARLOS L	LTC	0-0907094	0662	1
RUSSELL CHARLES L	MAJ	0-1549065	0461	2
RUSSELL CHARLES S	LTC	0-1591416	0162	2
RUSSELL CHESLEY B	LTC	C-0383357	0662	1
RUSSELL CHESTER A	CPT	0-0492980	0354	1
RUSSELL CLIFFORD A	CPT	0-1551728	0855	1
RUSSELL DEAN	CW3	W-2144609	0260	2
RUSSELL DONALD W	WO1	W-2118415	1052	2
RUSSELL DOUGLAS C	MAJ	0-1646915	0264	1
RUSSELL EDMOND F	COL	0-0195885	1162	3
RUSSELL EDWARD J	MAJ	C-0364011	0346	2
RUSSELL EDWARD J	LTC	0-1297257	0962	1
RUSSELL EUGENE	MAJ	0-0975886	0164	1
RUSSELL EZEKIEL B	LTC	0-1167607	0463	1
RUSSELL FRANCIS T	LTC	0-0884912	1160	1
RUSSELL FRANK	LTC	0-0889327	0765	1
RUSSELL GEORGE D	CW2	W-2118191	1047	2
RUSSELL GEORGE G	LTC	C-0294684	0367	3
RUSSELL GILBERT A	CW2	W-2104439	0444	2
RUSSELL HENRY	COL	0-0286872	0363	1
RUSSELL HENRY	CPT	0-C966085	1060	1

NAME	GRADE	SVC NO	DATE RET MO YR	RET CODE
RUSSELL HENRY D	M G	0-0212769	0251	3
RUSSELL HERBERT S	MAJ	0-1634279	1055	1
RUSSELL HOMER A	MAJ	0-0382704	0846	2
RUSSELL HOWARD C	MAJ	0-0163129	0648	3
RUSSELL HOWARD M	LTC	0-0309093	0660	1
RUSSELL JACK L	CPT	0-1031126	0847	2
RUSSELL JAMES A	LTC	0-0371280	0866	3
RUSSELL JAMES H	MAJ	0-1324953	0963	1
RUSSELL JAMES M	1LT	0-1105774	1147	2
RUSSELL JAMES M	MAJ	0-2103044	0467	1
RUSSELL JAMES R	MAJ	0-1298766	0861	1
RUSSELL JAMES S	CPT	0-0123965	0752	3
RUSSELL JEROME E	MAJ	0-0996685	0664	1
RUSSELL JIM	LTC	0-1641751	0464	1
RUSSELL JOHN A	LTC	0-2046458	0157	1
RUSSELL JOHN E	CW4	W-2147861	0861	1
RUSSELL JOHN F	MAJ	0-0395011	1045	2
RUSSELL JOHN F	CW4	W-2108393	0962	1
RUSSELL JOHN W	LTC	0-1032246	0261	1
RUSSELL JOSEPH J	LTC	0-1544731	0865	1
RUSSELL JOY A	MAJ	0-0229303	0263	3
RUSSELL JR GEORGE G	LTC	0-1047761	1163	1
RUSSELL JR LAWRENCE	LTC	0-0264382	0159	1
RUSSELL JR WALTER E	MAJ	0-2096492	0763	1
RUSSELL KENNETH W	CW2	W-2149755	0662	1
RUSSELL KENT R	MAJ	0-0994365	0466	1
RUSSELL L B	CPT	0-1297595	0546	2
RUSSELL LOUIS C	MAJ	0-1684013	0862	1
RUSSELL MARK W	MAJ	0-1173761	0661	1
RUSSELL MELVIN B	MAJ	0-1326172	0363	2
RUSSELL ORVILLE L	MAJ	0-1176497	0161	1
RUSSELL PAUL S	MAJ	0-1598373	0463	1
RUSSELL RICHARD T	MAJ	0-0966895	0164	1
RUSSELL RILEY J	CW2	W-2143365	0554	1
RUSSELL ROBERT	CPT	0-1292236	C246	2
RUSSELL ROBERT S	LTC	0-0274796	0965	3
RUSSELL ROY H	LTC	0-1102027	0463	1
RUSSELL RUBY H H	MAJ	N-0764034	0964	3
RUSSELL RUFUS R	LTC	0-0473394	0557	1
RUSSELL SAMUEL	COL	0-0137945	0560	3
RUSSELL SOLON F	COL	0-0163960	0655	3
RUSSELL STEPHEN B	CPT	0-0503040	0650	1
RUSSELL TED S	CPT	0-0497248	1053	1
RUSSELL THEODORE S	MAJ	0-0456617	0164	1
RUSSELL THOMAS R	CPT	0-1289631	0550	1
RUSSELL WALTER A	CPT	0-1179600	0163	2
RUSSELL WALTER B	LTC	0-0901598	0763	3
RUSSELL WILLIAM A	MAJ	0-0383844	0366	1
RUSSELL WILLIAM B	CPT	0-1297097	0146	2
RUSSELL WILLIAM E	MAJ	0-1335473	0363	1
RUSSELL WILLIAM E	MAJ	0-1797012	0161	1
RUSSELL WILLIAM G	LTC	0-0383319	0961	1
RUSSELL WILLIAM H	CW4	W-2110500	1056	1
RUSSELL WILLIAM K	CPT	0-2055151	0847	1
RUSSELL WILLIAM L	LTC	0-0423169	0765	1
RUSSERT LAWRENCE J	CPT	0-4005503	1264	1
RUSSIAN JOHN L	MAJ	0-1924824	0266	1
RUSSIE LESTER W	CW4	W-2114822	0565	1
RUSSO FRANK J	1LT	0-0389435	0645	2
RUSSO HAROLD J	COL	0-0903286	0763	3
RUSSO JOSEPH J	1LT	0-0445605	0844	2
RUSSO JOSEPH J	MAJ	0-1103900	0664	1
RUSSO JR JAMES A	1LT	0-0556562	0947	2
RUSSO JR VICTOR	CW2	W-3350355	0867	1
RUSSO CLGO A	1LT	0-1295277	0845	2
RUSSO PATRICK R	CW2	W-2147677	0262	1
RUSSO THOMAS J	LTC	0-1337452	1167	1
RUSSON RAYMOND S	CW3	W-2149902	0964	1
RUST CHARLES L	MAJ	0-0346332	0557	1
RUST JOSEPH H	CW2	W-2000517	0562	3
RUST MALCOLM B	LTC	0-0449651	0164	3
RUST VICTOR H	MAJ	0-0335838	0962	1
RUSTAD JOHN H	2LT	0-1316333	0944	2
RUSTARI EINO A	1LT	0-0507773	1157	1
RUSTICK JOSEPH S	CW3	W-2150621	1160	1

NAME	GRADE	SVC NO	DATE RET MO YR	RET CODE
RUSTIN ARTHUR L	MAJ	0-1543557	0960	1
RUSTIN SR NATHAN E	WO1	W-2145959	1163	2
RUSTON GEORGE M	CPT	0-0452978	0551	1
RUSZALA HENRY J	1LT	0-1640896	0445	2
RUT ADAM G	MAJ	0-0885147	0753	1
RUTA EDWARD J	MAJ	0-1821920	0457	1
RUTAN JAMES H	MAJ	0-0504198	0163	1
RUTAN WILTON L	COL	0-0105479	0155	3
RUTCAVAGE CHARLES J	CPT	0-1695226	1046	2
RUTH ALEX F	CPT	0-0299833	0749	1
RUTH BEVERLY P	MAJ	0-0205042	0352	1
RUTH FRANCIS D	LTC	0-1894773	0862	1
RUTH FRANCIS J	CW3	W-2003735	1266	1
RUTH WALTER H	COL	0-0298794	0963	3
RUTHE ALICE	MAJ	M-0002210	0963	2
RUTHERFORD ARTHUR B	MAJ	0-1108288	0961	1
RUTHERFORD ARTHUR L	CW3	W-2151187	0864	1
RUTHERFORD CARL R	1LT	0-1305652	1045	1
RUTHERFORD CHESTER A	1LT	0-1015639	1045	2
RUTHERFORD FLOYD A	COL	0-0102388	0554	1
RUTHERFORD FRANCIS H	LTC	0-0261506	1164	3
RUTHERFORD JAMES S	CW2	W-2208120	0962	1
RUTHERFORD JOE H	MAJ	0-1165329	0157	1
RUTHERFORD KENNETH M	MAJ	0-1544063	0259	2
RUTHERFORD RAYMOND E	LTC	0-0127799	0455	3
RUTHERFORD RICHARD E	CW2	W-2115786	0346	2
RUTHERFORD ROBERT B	COL	0-0317606	0346	2
RUTHERFORD SAMUEL A	LTC	0-1320288	0762	1
RUTHERFORD WILLIAM	CPT	0-2046542	0157	1
RUTHERFORD WILLIAM A	CPT	0-0487891	0446	2
RUTHERFORD WILLIAM C	COL	0-0247324	0962	3
RUTHERFORD WILLIAM G	LTC	0-2094932	0467	1
RUTHERFORD WILLIAM M	CPT	0-0505704	1047	2
RUTHERFORD WILSON R	MAJ	0-1112412	1163	1
RUTKA JOHN	1LT	0-0452100	0848	1
RUTKIN JOSEPH	LTC	0-1292592	0462	1
RUTKOSKI STANLEY	1LT	0-1825494	0862	1
RUTKOVSKY PAUL	MAJ	0-1080959	0259	1
RUTKOWSKI HENRY B	CPT	0-0940770	0557	1
RUTKOWSKI STEPHEN J	CPT	0-1307169	0646	2
RUTLAND ALSIE L	CPT	0-1333543	0158	1
RUTLAND LEROY E	LTC	0-0390627	0266	1
RUTLAND ROGER M	CW3	W-2149236	0662	1
RUTLEDGE ALBERT F	LTC	0-1284584	0764	1
RUTLEDGE ANGUS V	COL	0-0386987	0866	1
RUTLEDGE GLENN C	COL	0-0245264	0966	3
RUTLEDGE JAMES A	CW3	W-2150051	0665	1
RUTLEDGE JAMES H	COL	0-0243288	0757	3
RUTLEDGE JAMES R	MAJ	0-0673731	1058	1
RUTLEDGE JOHN M	LTC	0-0401827	0163	1
RUTLEDGE LLOYD A	CPT	0-1908748	0463	2
RUTLEDGE MELVIN M	MAJ	0-0169602	1048	3
RUTLEDGE ROBERT A	MAJ	0-1877846	1166	1
RUTLEDGE WAYNE M	MAJ	0-2025247	0359	1
RUTLEDGE WILLIAM M	LTC	0-1946154	0962	2
RUTLEDGE WILLIAM W	CPT	0-0502784	0358	1
RUTLEDGE WYATT A	MAJ	0-1296265	1157	1
RUTMAN HARRY	LTC	0-0496877	1166	3
RUTSTEIN RALPH	2LT	0-1321953	0445	2
RUTTAN FRANCIS M	MAJ	0-0287149	0562	3
RUTTAN MELVIN	CPT	0-1181108	0647	2
RUTTER ROBERT M	CW3	W-2150880	0765	1
RUTTER ROBERT R	CW3	W-2206056	0167	1
RUTTER THOMAS T	LTC	0-1045235	1162	1
RUTTLE JOSEPH F	CW4	W-2005358	1063	3
RUTZ CLARENCE A	CPT	0-0890302	1046	1
RUUD LOUIS A	LTC	0-0257785	0665	3
RUUD PHILLIP D	1LT	0-1824513	0947	2
RUVIO FRANK	CPT	0-0481053	0151	1
RUX JAMES P	2LT	0-2040759	1044	1
RUYLE EDWIN W	MAJ	0-1112951	1162	1
RYALL VERN B	MAJ	0-0232121	0162	3
RYALL WILLIAM J	MAJ	0-1896088	0153	1
RYALS JULIUS W	1LT	0-0984155	0753	2
RYAN ALICE L	1LT	N-0751118	1045	1

NAME	GRADE	SVC NO	DATE RET MO YR	RET CODE
RYAN AMBROSE A	LTC	0-0232404	0558	3
RYAN ARLAND D	CPT	0-0496287	0346	2
RYAN AUSTIN J	CPT	0-1112413	0253	1
RYAN BARRY A	COL	0-0453198	0862	1
RYAN BERNARD C	1LT	0-0390756	0245	2
RYAN BERNARD P	CW2	W-2146122	0861	1
RYAN CHARLES F	COL	0-0254037	0261	3
RYAN CHARLES J	LTC	0-1323487	0761	1
RYAN CHRISTOPHE	LTC	0-0215032	0160	3
RYAN CYRIL B	LTC	0-0400086	0960	1
RYAN DANIEL J	MAJ	0-0218285	0556	3
RYAN DANIEL P	CPT	0-1055962	1062	1
RYAN DON C	MAJ	0-0224497	1158	3
RYAN DONALD E	LTC	0-0209466	0164	3
RYAN DONALD E	LTC	0-1301546	0164	1
RYAN DONALD H	LTC	0-1057869	0867	1
RYAN DONALD H	CW3	W-2146882	0164	1
RYAN EDWARD F	2LT	0-1328525	0945	2
RYAN EVERETT W	COL	0-0335054	1164	3
RYAN FRANCIS A	MAJ	0-0250032	1060	3
RYAN FRANK S	MAJ	0-0361484	1060	1
RYAN FRANKLYN J	CPT	0-2017593	0756	1
RYAN FREDERICK	LTC	0-0191577	0646	2
RYAN GEORGE F	WO1	W-2145215	0853	1
RYAN GLENROY	LTC	0-1108289	1262	1
RYAN GOLDEN O	MAJ	0-0254467	0159	3
RYAN HAROLD F	CPT	0-1297597	0261	1
RYAN HAWARD V	CPT	0-0973288	1061	1
RYAN HELEN G	1LT	N-0754505	1047	1
RYAN HERBERT V	COL	0-0209801	0264	3
RYAN HUGH E	LTC	0-0420488	0947	1
RYAN JAMES F	LTC	0-0278410	0551	1
RYAN JAMES F	MAJ	0-0410346	0846	2
RYAN JAMES H	LTC	0-0365004	0463	3
RYAN JAMES J	CW2	W-3000411	0767	1
RYAN JAMES L	LTC	0-0403376	0761	1
RYAN JAMES L	CW2	W-2152646	0659	1
RYAN JOHN J	LTC	0-1797189	0163	1
RYAN JOHN L	MAJ	0-0981900	0765	1
RYAN JOHN M	LTC	0-0273389	0960	3
RYAN JOHN V	MAJ	0-0337831	0262	1
RYAN JOSEPH G	1LT	0-0504228	1049	1
RYAN JOSEPH G	LTC	0-1107673	1161	2
RYAN JOSEPH G	MAJ	0-1551304	0763	1
RYAN JOSEPH H	LTC	0-1106442	0366	1
RYAN JOSEPHINE	1LT	N-0751896	0645	1
RYAN JR ARCHIBALD	2LT	0-2204858	0852	1
RYAN JR JOHN A	CPT	0-1115058	0753	2
RYAN JR MARK F	LTC	0-1000852	0757	1
RYAN LAWRENCE E	LTC	0-0407276	0561	1
RYAN LAWRENCE F	LTC	0-0277835	0158	3
RYAN LEO F	LTC	0-0471793	0548	1
RYAN MARGARET A	MAJ	N-0798929	0865	1
RYAN MARGARET M	2LT	N-0732575	0145	1
RYAN MARTIN S	LTC	0-0247742	0456	1
RYAN MATTHIAS J	MAJ	0-0190640	0850	3
RYAN NEAL C	MAJ	0-2014077	1063	1
RYAN PETER J	LTC	0-0168942	0758	3
RYAN RAY E	LTC	0-0290532	0862	1
RYAN ROBERT W	CPT	0-1643305	0762	1
RYAN RUSSELL	LTC	0-0113483	0648	3
RYAN RUSSELL C	MAJ	0-0162219	0749	3
RYAN THOMAS A	CPT	0-0235617	0750	3
RYAN THOMAS E	2LT	0-1060907	0345	2
RYAN THOMAS J	MAJ	0-1582535	1060	1
RYAN THOMAS J	MAJ	0-1999959	0162	1
RYAN VERONICA L	MAJ	N-0786149	0665	1
RYAN VINCENT L	CW3	W-2150516	0163	1
RYAN WILLIAM	LTC	0-0335357	0464	3
RYAN WILLIAM A	MAJ	0-2034577	0460	1
RYAN WILLIAM C	COL	0-0167604	0755	3
RYAN WILLIAM E	COL	0-0162000	1056	3
RYAN WILLIAM E	1LT	0-1110225	0445	2
RYAN WILLIAM H	LTC	0-1048970	0662	1
RYAN WILLIAM J	2LT	0-1323617	0545	2

NAME	GRADE	SVC NO	DATE RET MO YR	RET CODE
RYAN WILLIAM V	MAJ	0-0270901	0865	3
RYBA HENRY H	LTC	0-0344041	0465	3
RYBA SYLVESTER	1LT	0-1041638	1044	2
RYBECK WILLIAM H	LTC	0-0111676	0354	3
RYBERG ROBERT W	CPT	0-2263147	0863	1
RYBKA WILLIAM J	LTC	0-1166825	0459	1
RYBOLT HENRY C	MAJ	0-1305840	1161	1
RYCRAFT CLARENCE A	COL	0-0200192	1047	2
RYDER EDWARD A	COL	0-0208454	1059	3
RYDER EDWIN W	MAJ	0-0366074	0765	1
RYDER EUGENE M	CPT	0-0281762	0458	2
RYDER FRANK A	MAJ	0-0323104	1044	2
RYDER HARRY L	LTC	0-1168449	0167	1
RYDER HOWARD G	LTC	0-0561965	1060	1
RYDER MYRON W	LTC	0-0261505	1265	3
RYDER OLIVER A	MAJ	0-1588268	1157	1
RYDZINSKI LAURENCE E	CW3	W-2209726	0866	1
RYE JR BURNIE W	MAJ	0-1296909	0960	1
RYKEN WILLIAM P	CPT	0-1325327	0946	1
RYKERT GEORGE L	LTC	0-0204168	0155	3
RYLAND HARRY H	MAJ	0-0247435	0466	3
RYLE JR JESSE T	MAJ	0-0198836	0658	3
RYMAN DEAN E	COL	0-0101073	1048	3
RYMER GRADY	CW3	W-2142309	0958	1
RYMILL ROBERT J	LTC	0-1894879	0767	1
RYNDERS GEORGE M	1LT	0-1317822	0845	2
RYNDERS THOMAS J	CW3	W-2209562	0967	1
RYNIEWICZ HILARY L	MAJ	0-0955708	0863	1
RYNN ROBERT A	MAJ	0-1599115	0963	1
RYON ALTON H	LTC	0-0264835	1164	3
RYON JOHN C	LTC	0-0415772	0866	1
RYSE ROY L	CPT	0-2009761	0258	1
RYSHKUS EUGENE J	MAJ	0-1636580	0160	1
SAAL WILBERT G	CPT	0-1823649	0662	1
SAALMAN OTIS E	MAJ	0-0348986	0751	1
SAAR WERNER R	LTC	0-0432772	0960	1
SAARI LEONARD V	COL	0-0250456	0266	3
SABATIER JOHN D	2LT	0-0528100	1044	2
SABATINI JOHN A	CW3	W-2203374	1161	1
SABATINO GERALD V	LTC	0-0438186	1264	1
SABATINO NATALE A	MAJ	0-0335957	0746	2
SABEL JAMES T	MAJ	0-0269686	0646	1
SABEL NORMAN A	MAJ	0-1885593	0567	1
SABERHAGEN HAROLD A	LTC	0-1040465	0355	1
SABEY WALTER D	CW3	W-2205864	0166	1
SABIA AGNES S	MAJ	N-0757538	0765	1
SABIA ANGELO J	1LT	0-1826103	0447	2
SABIA BERNARD J	1LT	0-1644732	0245	2
SABIK JOHN	CW2	W-2114807	1051	1
SABIN ANTHONY G	LTC	0-0249752	0961	3
SABIN CLAYTON C	CW2	W-2104443	0746	2
SABIN CORNELIUS	CPT	0-1302529	1147	2
SABIN HAROLD	MAJ	0-1108981	0254	1
SABIN WILLIAM A	MAJ	0-1594441	0556	1
SABIN WINFRED A	LTC	0-0149064	0354	3
SABINE FRANK A	LTC	0-0297077	1061	3
SABIO LIBERATO F	2LT	0-1897033	0358	1
SABISTON THOMAS J	LTC	0-1101646	1160	1
SABLE PHILIP R	2LT	0-1031515	0145	2
SABO JACK	MAJ	0-0109257	0647	1
SABOL JOSEPH S	CPT	0-1014760	0657	2
SABOM WILLIAM O	CPT	0-0325635	0147	2
SABOTNIK REX E	LTC	0-0273419	0861	1
SABRINSKY MICHAEL J	LTC	0-1797014	0863	1
SABRSULA WILLIE L	CW2	W-2149981	0761	2
SACCO GREGORY E	CPT	0-1688124	1143	2
SACCONE ERO	CW4	W-2152720	1060	1
SACHEROWITZ ALVIN	COL	0-0199907	0854	3
SACHAU DONALD F	1LT	0-1555759	0846	2
SACHLEBEN RAYMOND	CW3	W-2128011	1155	1
SACHS CARL W	LTC	0-1535414	0363	1
SACHS ELIHU M	LTC	0-0401299	0346	2
SACHS HENRY N	COL	0-0223120	0464	3
SACHS MANDEL J	MAJ	0-0348491	1046	2
SACHSE MARGARET E	MAJ	N-0799171	0665	1

NAME	GRADE	SVC NO	DATE RET MO YR	RET CODE
SACHSE WILLIAM D	LTC	0-1997765	1064	1
SACHT ALBERT R	MAJ	0-1798201	0159	1
SACK ERNEST A	MAJ	0-0187935	1259	3
SACK FRANK R	COL	0-0232218	0665	3
SACKETT CALVIN B	LTC	0-0233534	0459	1
SACKETT ROGER W	LTC	0-1541294	1262	1
SACKIN STANLEY	CPT	0-1688145	1145	2
SACKMAN HAROLD A	MAJ	0-0959287	0561	1
SACKMANN KARL C	LTC	0-0131578	1051	3
SACKRIDER GORDON	CW3	W-2146398	0463	1
SACKRIDER HAROLD A	MAJ	0-1876980	0965	1
SACKS EARL	CPT	0-1055438	0946	2
SACKS HAROLD J	CPT	0-0475259	0546	2
SACKSTEDER MARY E	MAJ	M-0002178	0165	1
SACRAMO NICHOLAS	CW2	W-2110255	0247	1
SADDLER GLENN W	LTC	0-0425618	0261	1
SADILEK JULIUS B	LTC	0-0396948	0960	1
SADJA ELLIOT D	1LT	0-1580261	0145	2
SADLER ALBERT A	LTC	0-0489401	0463	1
SADLER AUBREY E	COL	0-0250635	0964	3
SADLER BYRON P	MAJ	0-0371338	0248	2
SADLER CHARLES E	CW3	W-2145839	1262	1
SADLER CHARLES G	MAJ	0-1599136	0361	1
SADLER HARRY V	2LT	0-1118280	1045	2
SADLER PAUL W	LTC	0-0294851	1264	3
SADLER S ELOISE	1LT	N-0742900	1046	1
SADLER WARREN H	MAJ	0-0953592	1264	1
SADLER WOODSON A	MAJ	0-1168060	0960	1
SADOWSKI FRANCIS A	LTC	0-0456682	0261	1
SADOWSKI HENRY R	CPT	0-2262780	0358	1
SADUS MARY E	MAJ	N-0743492	1262	3
SAEFKE JOHN F	LTC	0-1167608	0162	1
SAEGER WILLIAM R	CW2	W-2109376	0154	2
SAEMENES PETER J	CW4	W-2003289	0967	3
SAEZ JOSE B	CW2	W-2147207	1060	1
SAFER JACOB V	CPT	0-0491787	0345	2
SAFFA LEONARD T	1LT	0-1175301	0750	1
SAFFER SIDNEY H	CPT	0-0496071	0745	1
SAFFOLD JESSE O	LTC	0-0179617	0154	3
SAFFORD EDWARD L	COL	0-0160722	0647	2
SAFFORD EMORY P	COL	0-0306053	0665	1
SAFFORD HARVEY D	CPT	0-0380120	0645	2
SAFFORD JAMES D	COL	0-0125633	0648	3
SAFFORD WINFIELD E	LTC	0-0438600	0355	1
SAFFRON MORRIS F	LTC	0-0288415	0246	2
SAFKO LEE C	MAJ	0-2046318	0761	1
SAFOUREK NORBERT J	LTC	0-0108307	0650	1
SAFSTROM ALLEN I	LTC	0-1304449	1163	2
SAGE ALFRED E	CPT	0-1081172	0859	1
SAGE ARTHUR L	MAJ	0-0476476	0962	1
SAGE CHARLES L	LTC	0-0463024	0954	1
SAGE JR GILBERT B	LTC	0-1043215	1262	1
SAGE JR ORA G	MAJ	0-1552161	0346	1
SAGE WINFIELD W	LTC	0-0141844	1058	3
SAGENDORF DOUGLAS	CW3	W-2210718	0764	1
SAGENDORF VINCENT W	CW2	W-2205298	0159	1
SAGER BERNARD	MAJ	0-0483363	0346	2
SAGER EMIL W	MAJ	0-0505523	0155	1
SAGER JAMES T	1LT	0-1292403	0644	2
SAGER WESLEY C	LTC	0-0359664	1060	1
SAGERT JAMES B	MAJ	0-1106443	0363	1
SAGIN GEORGE N	COL	0-0274399	0160	3
SAGMOEN CLARENCE M	COL	0-0196451	0663	3
SAGNERI JOSEPH	1LT	0-1551950	0647	2
SAGONA ROBERT G	MAJ	0-2265088	0667	1
SAHADI RAY	1LT	0-1591420	0347	1
SAHLI EDWARD A	COL	0-0372990	0564	3
SAHLIN BRUCE A	LTC	0-1551510	1061	1
SAHLIN ERNEST H	CPT	0-0927880	0549	2
SAHLIN WERNER G	2LT	0-2035732	1044	2
SAHM CLARENCE E	MAJ	0-1933726	0967	1
SAHM FRANCIS R	MAJ	0-1170959	0464	1
SAHM JOSEPH P	LTC	0-1639589	0258	1
SAIBER JACOB	MAJ	0-0313904	1146	2
SAIKI BARRY	LTC	0-1338279	1266	1

NAME	GRADE	SVC NO	DATE RET MO YR	RET CODE
SAIKI GEORGE	2LT	0-1331992	1045	1
SAIKLEY MITCHELL F	COL	0-0286019	0367	2
SAILER ADELINE J	CPT	N-0722477	0248	2
SAILER JAMES A	1LT	0-1055439	0651	1
SAILOR VANCE L	COL	0-0205088	1054	3
SAILORS JOHN J	COL	0-0265379	0246	2
SAILORS WILLIAM M	LTC	0-0442668	0265	3
SAIN JOSEPH R	LTC	0-1030828	0667	1
SAIN ROBERT L	CPT	0-0503651	0652	1
SAINIO PAUL H	MAJ	0-1947225	0962	1
SAITES LOUIS N	MAJ	0-0976223	0762	1
SAKAI KINICHI	CPT	0-0153837	0853	3
SAKAI TOSHIYUKI	MAJ	0-0961663	1263	1
SAKAMATO SAMUEL M	LTC	0-0349640	0666	1
SAKAMOTO KIYOSHI K	MAJ	0-1686540	0661	1
SAKANARI GEORGE R	LTC	0-1328405	1165	1
SAKELLARIOU EVANS N	LTC	0-0512713	1163	3
SAKER ANTHONY D	LTC	0-1286007	0364	1
SALADOW EDWARD C	1LT	0-1716674	1044	2
SALAMATA METRO	CPT	0-0494039	0550	1
SALAMEDA JOSEPH	1LT	0-1105853	0146	2
SALAMONE FRANK L	MAJ	0-0958899	0565	1
SALAS JR CHARLES F	WO1	W-2149177	0753	2
SALAS MERLA F	1LT	N-0731591	0246	1
SALAZAR ALBINO	1LT	0-2027442	0753	1
SALAZAR DAVID C	LTC	0-1045585	0161	1
SALAZAR JOSEPH L	2LT	0-0492768	0345	2
SALBERG ARTHUR K	1LT	0-0311215	1143	1
SALCEDO MARIANO	1LT	0-1896947	1150	1
SALCIDO AUGUSTINE	MAJ	0-1544761	0161	1
SALDANA-BLASCOE	LTC	0-1328850	0367	1
SALDIN ROBERT S	CPT	0-2007503	0148	1
SALDIVAR JULIAN T	LTC	0-0327257	1167	3
SALE POWELL O	MAJ	0-2262740	0663	1
SALEE HARTFORD F	COL	0-0359306	0960	1
SALEEBY CLAUDE	MAJ	0-1041013	0963	1
SALEN MODERWELL	LTC	0-0176998	0262	3
SALENSKY SELMA	CPT	N-0720877	0946	2
SALERNO SAM A	LTC	0-1287596	0461	1
SALES LAWRENCE N	CPT	0-1322811	0147	1
SALFEN AMBROSE G	CPT	0-0436682	0147	2
SALFINGERE FRANK W	LTC	0-0145635	0652	3
SALGET GEORGE R	CPT	0-1286899	0746	2
SALGUERO JR ARTHUR R	MAJ	0-0224608	1150	1
SALHANY EDWARD T	LTC	0-0410384	0860	1
SALHANY THEODORE T	CPT	0-1321665	0446	2
SALI VICTOR	CPT	0-0521496	0156	1
SALIC NICHOLAS F	2LT	0-2006290	0246	2
SALIN WARREN E	LTC	0-0248311	0266	3
SALINAS BASILLIO G	CPT	0-1688416	0760	1
SALISBURY ARTHUR J	COL	0-0331720	0256	1
SALISBURY CHARLES J	1LT	0-1327289	0346	2
SALISBURY EDWARD A	MAJ	0-0964442	0461	3
SALISBURY F W	MAJ	0-0328323	0647	1
SALISBURY GEORGE H	LTC	0-0247756	0164	3
SALISBURY JAMES E	MAJ	0-0354411	0348	2
SALISBURY LAURON F	LTC	0-0267859	0359	3
SALISBURY LUCIUS A	COL	0-0101747	0648	3
SALISBURY RALPH O	COL	0-0100643	0453	3
SALISBURY SAMUEL T	LTC	0-0116234	1145	1
SALISBURY THOMAS M	CW2	W-2153107	0764	1
SALITERMAN B I	MAJ	0-0288130	0347	2
SALIVAR THEODORE J	1LT	0-1257069	1064	1
SALLADA HOMER R	CW3	W-2145506	0157	1
SALLADAY ISAIAH R	MAJ	0-0120071	0947	2
SALLEY CLARENCE L	1LT	0-1043777	1045	2
SALLEY HARRY G	1LT	0-0377413	1144	2
SALLEY JR EDWARD M	COL	0-0231831	0665	3
SALLEY JR WILLIAM B	LTC	0-0390628	1160	1
SALLEY WILLIAM H	LTC	0-2033751	0967	1
SALLICK GEORGE	MAJ	0-1300533	0655	1
SALLING MINNIS H	CPT	0-2262563	1062	1
SALLINGER ELMER F	MAJ	0-1576600	0359	1
SALLIS HELEN N	MAJ	L-0130178	1163	1
SALLIS JESSIE I	CW4	W-2111078	0161	1
SALLMAN EDWIN L	COL	0-0264071	0555	1
SALLS KENNETH T	MAJ	0-0186834	0958	3
SALLY JOSEPH F	LTC	0-0324875	0645	2
SALMAN HARRY A	CPT	0-0393271	1052	1
SALMELA OLGA O R	CPT	N-0752613	0248	1
SALMON ARMAND J	COL	0-0230475	1061	3
SALMON EUGENE H	LTC	0-0305037	0860	1
SALMON I CHENERY	COL	0-0231944	0763	3
SALMON PHILIP A	LTC	0-0230561	0165	3
SALMON RICHARD	1LT	0-1293320	1045	2
SALMON STUART H	LTC	0-0299712	0264	3
SALMONS ELLIOTT O	MAJ	0-0256174	0967	3
SALMONS JR CLYDE R	MAJ	0-0961244	0263	1
SALMONS OREN R	MAJ	0-1037274	1160	1
SALO TOIVO E	CPT	0-1111345	1065	2
SALOME BEVERLEE M	MAJ	N-0728656	0462	1
SALON DAYTON D	MAJ	0-0468638	0846	2
SALOPEK THOMAS	CPT	0-0982514	0263	1
SALTER ABRAHAM	WO1	W-2140410	1146	2
SALTER ALYS L	LTC	N-0727063	1146	1
SALTER BILLY B	LTC	0-0378079	0857	1
SALTER BYRON M	MAJ	0-0299947	0356	3
SALTER CHARLES E	LTC	0-0456619	0861	1
SALTER GEORGE B	COL	0-0284797	0663	3
SALTER HIRAM P	CPT	0-0295496	0146	2
SALTER JAMES W	CPT	0-1309611	0446	2
SALTESS ALEX	1LT	0-2000816	1047	2
SALTZ NATHAN J	CPT	0-0381418	0745	2
SALTZMAN CHARLES F	M G	0-0275984	1063	3
SALUGA STEPHEN J	CW2	W-2003883	1167	1
SALVA CALVIN V	CPT	0-2027445	1058	2
SALVADOR ROBERT A	LTC	0-1323178	0163	2
SALVAS PAUL C	1LT	0-5320377	0666	2
SALVATO EDWARD T	LTC	0-0246813	0966	3
SALVICE LEWIS W	2LT	0-1081309	0944	2
SALVO CHARLES	CW2	W-2207330	1162	1
SALVO WALTER W	2LT	0-1291528	0243	2
SALYER GEORGE R	LTC	0-0347956	0658	1
SALYER HARRY T	MAJ	0-1573564	1158	1
SALYER RAMEY	LTC	0-2014724	0567	1
SALYERS JAMES G C	CPT	0-0108947	1044	2
SALZ LEO	1LT	0-1012630	0745	2
SALZ LOUIS C	COL	0-0139369	0155	3
SALZBERG LAWRENCE L	LTC	0-1105160	0961	1
SALZBERG THEODORE H	1LT	0-1112953	0446	1
SALZILLO WILLIAM H	LTC	0-1108291	0663	1
SALZMAN ALLE L	2LT	N-0700492	1034	1
SALZMAN BERNARD	LTC	0-1845101	0961	1
SALZMAN JAY K	CPT	0-0258153	0566	3
SAMANIEGO GEORGE	CPT	0-1318090	1053	2
SAMARAS GEORGE D	CPT	0-1303202	0346	2
SAMDAHL LEO R	LTC	0-0453676	0760	1
SAMMIS HERBERT F	MAJ	0-1001224	0860	1
SAMMON SR MARLAN C	MAJ	0-0970637	1163	1
SAMMONS WILLIAM A	1LT	0-0915282	0944	2
SAMMONS EUGENE	CPT	0-0450474	0762	1
SAMMONS FRED S	COL	0-0273787	0866	3
SAMMONS ROBERT L	CPT	0-1313177	0847	1
SAMMONS WILLIAM	1LT	0-0508705	0350	1
SAMONDS JR JOHN M	MAJ	0-1116183	0962	1
SAMONI WILLIAM F	MAJ	0-1338860	0564	1
SAMOTIN MAXWELL E	LTC	0-0920762	0665	3
SAMOUCE GEORGE A	MAJ	0-0200876	0259	3
SAMOURIAN HARRY A	CPT	0-0503102	0545	2
SAMPAGA CLEMENTE	1LT	0-0890545	0649	2
SAMPAGA DOMINADOR	1LT	0-1896915	0751	1
SAMPAYAN RUPERTO D	MAJ	0-1110783	0263	1
SAMPIER JOHN W	LTC	0-0250045	1065	3
SAMPIERI HORACE M	CW3	W-2207046	0967	1
SAMPLE ADIS E	MAJ	0-1115769	0966	2
SAMPLE CHARLES	CW3	W-2145657	0662	1
SAMPLE JOHN W	LTC	0-0282498	0747	2
SAMPLE KATHRYN F	1LT	N-0787760	0646	1
SAMPLES CECIL L	WO1	W-2148812	0160	2
SAMPLES GILBERT	2LT	0-1178962	1145	2
SAMPLES JACK L	LTC	0-2023864	0664	1
SAMPSELLE JACK S	CPT	0-0347165	0254	1
SAMPSON ARNOLD I	MAJ	0-2262363	0266	1
SAMPSON BERNARD L	MAJ	0-0346914	1045	2
SAMPSON CATHERINE	2LT	N-0721191	0844	1
SAMPSON CHARLES W	COL	0-0411864	1266	1
SAMPSON DAVID C	CW3	W-2141809	0757	1
SAMPSON EARL F	CW3	W-2150643	0764	1
SAMPSON FRANCIS A	LTC	0-1047326	1060	1
SAMPSON GEORGE L	LTC	0-0440000	0357	1
SAMPSON GEORGE V	COL	0-0344465	1165	3
SAMPSON JAMES B	LTC	0-0171684	0455	3
SAMPSON JOSEPH R	MAJ	0-1894496	0254	1
SAMPSON PAUL L	LTC	0-0887576	0466	1
SAMPSON PAULINE R	1LT	N-0751125	0746	1
SAMPSON PHILIP	LTC	0-0167113	0147	2
SAMPSON RAYMOND H	CPT	0-1633515	0246	2
SAMPSON RICHARD F	CPT	0-0980890	0163	1
SAMPSON ROBERT W	1LT	0-1557524	1044	1
SAMPSON SELVIN E	1LT	0-1309840	0945	1
SAMS FARRIS V	CW2	W-2129943	0159	1
SAMS UPSHAW H	MAJ	0-0541442	1163	1
SAMSON CLYDE D	MAJ	0-1638418	0961	1
SAMSON JOHN A	MAJ	0-1013888	0462	1
SAMTER MAXIMILLIA	CPT	0-0534486	0146	2
SAMUEL JAMES B	CPT	0-0490851	0962	1
SAMUELL JOHN H	LTC	0-0508771	0761	3
SAMUELS ANTHONY	LTC	0-1554082	0965	1
SAMUELS GEORGE	2LT	0-0556931	0146	2
SAMUELS GEORGE J	CPT	0-2103125	0266	1
SAMUELS JOHN P	MAJ	0-0359063	0762	1
SAMUELS JULIUS A	LTC	0-1041639	0162	1
SAMUELS NATHAN	COL	0-0499937	0866	3
SAMUELS WILLIAM S	COL	0-0220530	0452	3
SAMUELS WINFIELD H	CPT	0-1294020	1046	1
SAMUELSEN HERMAN W	CW2	W-2141773	0859	1
SAMUELSON ELWYN F	MAJ	0-0981992	0864	1
SAMUELSON ROLAND	CPT	0-1336551	0465	1
SAMUELSON ROMAIN N	WO1	W-2210820	0461	2
SAMULEVICH PETER J	MAJ	0-1923604	0567	1
SAN BORN ARTHUR C	CPT	0-0307999	0845	2
SAN MILLAN JR RAFAEL	MAJ	0-0703440	0963	3
SAN PABLO FELICIANO	1LT	0-1896535	0351	1
SAN VITO JAMES A	2LT	0-1309018	0744	2
SANABRIA RAFAEL	CPT	0-0163621	0159	3
SANANO ANDRES S	CPT	0-0395419	0157	1
SANANO JUSTINO	1LT	0-1896704	1163	1
SANAVITIS ANTHONY	1LT	0-0495501	0449	1
SANBORN EDWARD J	1LT	0-1303031	1150	2
SANBORN CERDA C	CPT	N-0778368	0655	2
SANBORN HARRY F	LTC	0-1181748	0266	1
SANBURG FRANK E	MAJ	0-0263982	0762	2
SANCHES DANIEL E	LTC	0-0442356	0756	1
SANCHEZ ARNOLD R	MAJ	0-2047481	1162	1
SANCHEZ ELIAS S	CW3	W-2141669	0659	1
SANCHEZ GERARDO	CW2	W-2142792	0357	1
SANCHEZ JOHN J	CPT	0-1014058	0664	1
SANCHEZ JR EUGENE M	MAJ	0-1946157	0466	1
SANCHEZ PHILIP P D	CPT	0-0477532	0844	1
SANCHEZ RAFAEL	CW4	W-2001092	1060	1
SANCHEZ RAYMOND	CPT	0-1333882	0960	1
SANCHEZ SALVADOR F	CW3	W-2143292	0263	1
SANCHEZ&CAMACHO A	1LT	0-1685783	1056	2
SANCHEZ-RIVERA GUILL	MAJ	0-1332744	0663	1
SANCHIS JOSEPH M	LTC	0-0524620	0941	3
SAND ALEXANDER	MAJ	0-0207397	1143	2
SAND DONNA M	1LT	N-0769753	1147	1
SAND RUSSELL A	COL	0-0263415	0967	3
SANDBERG CARL P	LTC	0-0240427	1165	3
SANDBERG DAVID W	CPT	0-0205999	1163	3
SANDBERG ELMER T	MAJ	0-0278066	0365	3
SANDBERG ERLAND L	COL	0-0213877	0163	3
SANDBERG FLOYD A	LTC	0-0217563	0863	3
SANDBERG RALPH L	MAJ	0-1549546	0361	1
SANDBERG TOIVO A	LTC	0-1645337	0367	1
SANDEN MILTON V	LTC	0-0232067	0361	3
SANDERCOCK WILLIAM J	LTC	0-1320364	1064	1
SANDERLIN JOE H	LTC	0-0192819	0253	3
SANDERS ADMIRAL D	LTC	0-0176414	0560	3
SANDERS ALERIE	MAJ	0-1644736	0156	1
SANDERS ARNOLD L	LTC	0-0362668	0647	2
SANDERS ARTHUR R	MAJ	0-0216252	0460	3
SANDERS BERLINE J	2LT	N-0702641	0235	1
SANDERS BERNARD	MAJ	0-0450662	1060	1
SANDERS BERNARD	MAJ	0-1923621	1165	1
SANDERS BERNARD A	CW2	W-2113175	0746	1
SANDERS BERNARD C	MAJ	0-1046255	0161	1
SANDERS BUCK	LTC	0-2054005	0754	1
SANDERS CARL W	2LT	0-0298253	0643	2
SANDERS CHARLES	1LT	0-1913916	0946	1
SANDERS CHARLES A	LTC	0-0346343	0856	1
SANDERS CHARLES C	CW2	W-2210590	0565	1
SANDERS CHARLES L	1LT	0-1018305	1047	2
SANDERS CHARLES R	CPT	0-1336966	0552	1
SANDERS CHRIS	MAJ	0-2030175	0363	2
SANDERS DALE	LTC	0-1310767	0866	1
SANDERS EARL C	1LT	0-0441380	1057	1
SANDERS EARL F	LTC	0-1290665	0267	1
SANDERS EDWARD	MAJ	0-0213431	1163	3
SANDERS ELBERT	CW2	W-2152324	1060	1
SANDERS ELIZABETH	1LT	L-0116993	1045	2
SANDERS ERIC A	MAJ	0-0979279	0365	1
SANDERS ERNEST C	COL	0-0267867	0964	3
SANDERS ERNEST L	CPT	0-1030829	0759	1
SANDERS ERVIN J	LTC	0-0888202	0266	1
SANDERS ERVIN L	LTC	0-1543305	0267	1
SANDERS EWING R	CW2	W-2149809	0961	1
SANDERS FATE	CW2	W-2142196	0662	2
SANDERS FRANK W	MAJ	0-1877929	0267	1
SANDERS GEORGE F	MAJ	0-1304164	0365	1
SANDERS GUY N	CW2	W-2149457	0357	1
SANDERS HERMAN	CW2	W-2121738	0845	2
SANDERS JACK C	CPT	0-1638864	0857	2
SANDERS JAMES F	MAJ	0-2020068	1160	1
SANDERS JOHN C	2LT	0-1913915	0143	1
SANDERS JOHN D	COL	0-0327130	0761	1
SANDERS JOHN H	1LT	0-0384914	0925	1
SANDERS JOHN T	LTC	0-1170548	1263	1
SANDERS JR FRED R	CW3	W-2205856	0567	1
SANDERS KEITH F	CPT	0-0250500	0266	3
SANDERS LESTER	1LT	0-1298136	1045	2
SANDERS LOUIS	CPT	0-1541160	0761	1
SANDERS LUCIEN S	LTC	0-0184380	0848	3
SANDERS MURRAY	LTC	0-0512356	0546	1
SANDERS NEIL H	CPT	0-0284165	0964	3
SANDERS PALMER W	LTC	0-0223484	0562	3
SANDERS PAUL L	LTC	0-0470828	0763	3
SANDERS QUINCY A	LTC	0-0202289	0864	3
SANDERS RICHARD D	LTC	0-0474117	1046	2
SANDERS ROBERT C	LTC	0-1055565	1066	1
SANDERS ROBERT E	2LT	0-2011726	0347	2
SANDERS ROBERT H	CW3	W-2206886	0566	1
SANDERS ROBERT J	CPT	0-1322087	0646	2
SANDERS ROBERT W	COL	0-0270860	1067	3
SANDERS ROBERT Y	LTC	0-0487905	0157	1
SANDERS ROSCOE E	CW2	W-2147510	1263	1
SANDERS SAMUEL M	COL	0-0100233	0360	3
SANDERS TROY H	LTC	0-1037702	0262	1
SANDERS WALTER E	LTC	0-1590963	0766	1
SANDERS WALTER F	CPT	0-0450487	0560	1
SANDERS WALTER W	MAJ	0-2030148	0160	1
SANDERS WILLIAM B	CW2	W-2151328	0563	2
SANDERS WOODROW W	1LT	0-1303032	0857	1
SANDERSON BURDETTE F	CPT	0-0259073	0765	3
SANDERSON CLINTON E	COL	0-0246484	1061	3
SANDERSON LLOYD R	LTC	0-0143030	0858	3
SANDERSON ROBERT B	1LT	0-0406758	0644	2
SANDERSON ROLAND D	MAJ	0-0782025	0267	1
SANDERSON VIRGIL	MAJ	0-1001225	0557	1
SANDERSON WILLIAM H	MAJ	0-1013104	0261	1

292-560 O - 68 - 20

ARMY OF THE UNITED STATES RETIRED LIST

NAME	GRADE	SVC NO	DATE RET MO YR	RET CODE
SANDFORD CHARLES B	1LT	0-0547263	0446	2
SANDICO MELANO	CPT	0-0324507	1053	1
SANDIDGE CHARLES R	COL	0-0294767	0565	1
SANDIFER JR FRED M	MAJ	0-0480302	1045	2
SANDLER WILLIAM	MAJ	0-1645338	1061	1
SANDLIN JACK L	MAJ	0-2048770	0560	1
SANDLIN JAMES L	LTC	0-0299856	0562	3
SANDMAN OTTO E	M G	0-0184611	0550	3
SANDOE JR CLAYTON	CPT	0-1176495	0567	1
SANDOVAL FILIBERTO	CW3	W-2147862	0959	1
SANDOZ THOMAS R	COL	0-0293213	0762	1
SANDRIDGE HENRY R	LTC	0-0287801	0659	3
SANDS CHARLES E	COL	0-0255387	0767	3
SANDS CLOYD D	MAJ	0-0277816	1060	3
SANDS JOSEPH E	LTC	0-0483735	0960	1
SANDS JR FRANK N	COL	0-0244062	0666	3
SANDS JR OLIVER J	COL	0-0243184	1165	3
SANDS JR THOMAS F	COL	0-0324311	0363	3
SANDS MAX	2LT	0-1011495	0545	2
SANDS ROBERT L	MAJ	0-0985926	0965	1
SANDS SPENCER C	LTC	0-0311835	0867	3
SANDS WILLIAM R	MAJ	0-1822463	0461	1
SANDS WILLIAM H	M G	0-0174202	0652	3
SANDSTROM CARL R	COL	0-0363207	0261	1
SANDSTROM CUTHBERT F	CPT	0-0249593	0157	3
SANDSTROM DONALD G	MAJ	0-0954247	1163	1
SANDUSKY PAUL	CW2	W-2151892	0461	1
SANDUSKY WILLIAM R	LTC	0-0295497	1166	3
SANDYGREN ELBERT W	MAJ	0-0492096	0347	1
SANFACON GEORGE A	2LT	0-1554631	1144	2
SANFILIPPO A A	2LT	0-1588865	1044	1
SANFILIPPO PAUL J	CPT	0-0466189	0246	2
SANFORD EMMONS M	LTC	0-0507670	0447	1
SANFORD GEORGE A	1LT	0-1108293	0645	1
SANFORD JOHN G	LTC	0-0201281	0957	3
SANFORD JOHN R	CPT	0-0306634	1146	1
SANFORD JOHN T	COL	0-0182976	0560	3
SANFORD LEONARD C	MAJ	0-1994518	0661	1
SANFORD MARVIN O	CW2	W-2150120	0959	1
SANFORD ROBERT H	MAJ	0-1316675	0864	1
SANFORD SLOAN M	MAJ	0-0213655	0544	2
SANFORD WALTER A	MAJ	0-1120165	1059	1
SANFORD WILBER F	CW4	RW-2141670	0867	1
SANGER EDWIN E	COL	0-0213816	0747	1
SANGER GORDON L	LTC	0-0494878	1062	1
SANGER ISADORE J	CW3	W-2145840	1162	1
SANGER NEO	LTC	0-0884114	1057	1
SANGER STEPHEN S	LTC	0-0232607	0263	3
SANGO GEORGE J	MAJ	0-1173444	1158	1
SANGSTON LAURENCE P	COL	0-0328942	1162	3
SANGUINET EDGAR Y	LTC	0-0298524	0161	1
SANGUINETTI JOHN F	LTC	0-0361561	1160	1
SANIGA ERWIN	LTC	0-1311688	0254	1
SANKEY GEORGE K	LTC	0-1686472	1067	1
SANKEY WILLIAM C	LTC	0-0314945	0461	3
SANLAND CLARK	MAJ	0-0203399	0453	3
SANNEBECK FRANK A	WO1	W-2114126	0345	2
SANNEMAN LAWRENCE F	WO1	W-2109786	0545	2
SANNER CHARLES G	COL	0-0182591	0554	3
SANNER ROBERT J	CW3	W-2153268	0959	1
SANSARONA SANY M	2LT	0-0890533	0358	1
SANSBURY SHELLEY S	CPT	0-0211957	1063	3
SANSKY MICHAEL J	MAJ	0-2018928	0165	2
SANSOM JAMES F	CPT	0-1058643	0763	1
SANSONE DOMINICK J	CW4	W-2143044	0264	1
SANSONE JAMES W	1LT	0-1112419	0546	2
SANTA ANA ERIBERTO	MAJ	0-1896787	0864	1
SANTAGNINI ERNEST	MAJ	0-0171392	1145	2
SANTAGO ANTHONY C	MAJ	0-1333883	1059	1
SANTARSIERO C J	CPT	0-1304275	1147	2
SANTELISES MARIANO D	1LT	0-2030389	0648	2
SANTERRE FRANK	MAJ	0-0108959	0945	2
SANTIAGO JOSE I	LTC	0-0489706	0954	1
SANTIAGO JUAN G	CW4	W-2113938	1163	1
SANTIAGO TOMAS	1LT	0-0274261	1040	1

NAME	GRADE	SVC NO	DATE RET MO YR	RET CODE
SANTIAGO-VAZQUE FRA	CW2	W-2208966	0861	1
SANTILLI ALCIDE	LTC	0-0500498	0965	1
SANTILLI JOSEPH F	COL	0-0262768	0559	3
SANTINI LUIS M	MAJ	0-0370993	0560	1
SANTINI RAMON	2LT	0-1318847	1044	2
SANTINO MATHEW	LTC	0-0293048	0656	1
SANTNER JOHN C	1LT	0-1320010	1145	2
SANTO CARL A	MAJ	0-0493963	0464	3
SANTO JOSEPH	LTC	0-0309425	0560	1
SANTONI GENEVIEVE	MAJ	N-0755665	0664	3
SANTOR WALTER	MAJ	0-0492155	0348	1
SANTORO ANGELO M	LTC	0-1822196	0862	1
SANTORO JOHN A	LTC	0-0358751	0364	1
SANTORO JOSEPH M	LTC	0-0261701	0967	3
SANTORO MARTIN P	MAJ	0-1895237	1160	2
SANTORO SAMUEL L	2LT	0-1292595	0144	2
SANTORO VINCENT H	LTC	0-0453477	0157	1
SANTOS AUGUSTIN L	MAJ	0-1305322	0264	1
SANTOS ROBERT A	1LT	0-4006830	0359	2
SANTOYAN RUTH	CPT	L-0201146	0263	1
SANTURBANE ERNEST F	LTC	0-1553548	0762	1
SANTY FRANK C	LTC	0-0421162	1156	1
SANVITO J VINCENT	CPT	0-0510277	1045	2
SANWALD FRED J	MAJ	0-0163753	1146	1
SANZONE JOSEPH	CW4	W-2122144	1059	1
SAPER NORMAN	CPT	0-0904212	0346	2
SAPHIR EDWARD	MAJ	0-0143082	0255	3
SAPIO ANGELO J	MAJ	0-2034578	0557	1
SAPORA GEORGE E	LTC	0-0302203	0858	1
SAPP DEWITT T	COL	0-0438344	1146	2
SAPP GEORGE F	LTC	0-1059623	1066	1
SAPP JOSEPH E	CW3	W-2121162	0552	1
SAPP JR WHITNEY P	1LT	0-1174194	1045	2
SAPP PAUL P	CW3	W-2144591	0765	1
SAPP WILLIE	CW2	W-2145984	0855	1
SAPPER CARL H	COL	0-0171132	1159	3
SAPPER FRED F	LTC	0-0171148	0858	3
SAPPER WILLIAM L	LTC	0-0250563	1166	3
SAPPINGTON HOMER A	COL	0-0209912	0357	3
SAPPINGTON JR JOHN W	LTC	0-1994690	0757	1
SAPUDAR JOSEPH J	CW3	W-2144774	1161	1
SARADARIAN ALBERT V	CPT	0-0421228	0546	1
SARAS VICENTE	MAJ	0-0430507	0755	1
SARASIN GEORGE F	CPT	0-0384306	0547	2
SARAZEN JAMES F	CW4	W-2110546	1266	3
SARCANDER WILLIAM A	COL	0-0112306	0356	3
SARCONE JOSEPH A	MAJ	0-2011035	0864	1
SARDY INA	1LT	N-0730575	1045	1
SARELAKOS T C	1LT	0-1059624	0452	1
SARGENT FRANCIS A	LTC	0-0249898	1263	3
SARGENT FRED M	CPT	0-0504430	0249	1
SARGENT GEOFFREY W	COL	0-0245784	0852	1
SARGENT GEORGE W	LTC	0-0153050	0745	2
SARGENT HAROLD A	LTC	0-1291706	0357	1
SARGENT HERBERT D	MAJ	0-0997862	1162	1
SARGENT HUGH H	COL	0-0272171	0557	1
SARGENT JOHN F	MAJ	0-1120609	0965	1
SARGENT JR CHARLES H	COL	0-0127021	0658	3
SARGENT JR JAMES H	MAJ	0-0961243	0167	1
SARGENT LESTER L	LTC	0-0505613	1059	3
SARGENT LLOYD G	LTC	0-0227775	1064	3
SARGENT MAURICE V	LTC	0-0323189	0665	3
SARGENT RONALD W	1LT	0-5320227	0767	2
SARGENT WARREN B	CPT	0-0374644	0345	2
SARGENT WARREN K	CPT	0-1290666	0346	2
SARGENT WILLIAM H	LTC	0-1176790	1167	1
SARGENT WINTHROP J	COL	0-0149026	0648	3
SARGIS JR GEORGE R	COL	0-1165559	0865	1
SARIK MICHAEL J	CPT	0-1640913	0661	1
SARINE WALTER G	CPT	0-0322144	1262	2
SARKA RUDOLPH A	MAJ	0-1534853	1060	1
SARKA STEPHEN	CPT	0-1319446	0446	1
SARKISIAN SARKIS G	MAJ	0-0251623	0367	3
SARKOVITZ LAWRENCE P	CW3	W-2149024	0266	1
SARLES DUANE Y	COL	0-0184900	0555	3

NAME	GRADE	SVC NO	DATE RET MO YR	RET CODE
SARLES EARLE R	COL	0-0149534	1055	3
SARLES ROBERT S	CW2	W-2150716	0561	1
SARLES THEODORE	LTC	0-0455100	0966	1
SARMAN ADOLPH F	CPT	0-0496949	0549	1
SARMIENTO IGNACIO M	CPT	0-1822465	1063	1
SARMIENTO PEDRO	CPT	0-0324272	0957	1
SARNER DAVID S	CPT	0-1323618	0947	1
SARNES OLIVER A	CPT	0-0255322	0148	1
SARNOFF DAVID	B G	0-0208338	0651	3
SARROW ALFRED F	CW4	W-2105864	1061	1
SARTELL ERVIN J	CW4	W-2000604	1054	2
SARTHOU PETER F	MAJ	0-0354896	0846	2
SARTOR JOLLY C	MAJ	0-1115773	0860	1
SARTOR RALPH H	COL	0-0137411	0648	3
SARTOR WARREN W	CPT	0-0428123	0643	2
SARTOR WILLIAM M	MAJ	0-1549370	0958	1
SARTORE ARTHUR J	1LT	0-1822827	0346	2
SARTWELL ROBERT E	CPT	0-1298767	0445	2
SARVER HOMER B	LTC	0-1283319	0164	1
SARWARK HENRY F	LTC	0-1549074	1167	1
SAS WALTER J	MAJ	0-1339664	0466	1
SASAKI JOSEPH Y	CW3	W-2144402	1064	1
SASAKI KAY K	CW3	W-2133596	0365	1
SASEEN CHARLES A	CPT	0-0399161	0944	2
SASTCH LOUIS	1LT	0-1037276	1045	1
SASKI WALTER H	CW3	W-2149886	0164	1
SASS ISIDORE	COL	0-0256882	0262	3
SASS RAYMOND W	MAJ	0-0210189	0264	3
SASSER JEFFERSON	CW2	W-2210405	1163	1
SASSER JR THADDEUS L	WO1	W-2109166	0854	1
SASSER LUTHER S	COL	0-0378215	0358	1
SASSER RALPH L	CW3	W-2205101	0866	1
SASSEVILLE EZRA M	LTC	0-0237064	0460	3
SASSO CHARLES A	LTC	0-0275872	1051	3
SASSO LOUIS A	1LT	0-4047417	0658	2
SATERWHITE R C	CW3	W-2205395	0667	1
SATHER DONALD E	1LT	0-1552785	0446	2
SATHER RICHARD N	CPT	0-0464814	0446	2
SATKOFF FRANK	MAJ	0-1587598	0163	1
SATO JAMES K	MAJ	0-1922579	1165	1
SATT CARL V	LTC	0-0275758	0347	2
SATTENSTEIN SIDNEY L	MAJ	0-0267400	0448	2
SATTERFIELD BARNEY C	CW4	W-2143337	0667	1
SATTERFIELD JAMES M	1LT	0-0449010	1044	2
SATTERFIELD MILMAN I	LTC	0-0366110	0267	3
SATTERFIELD SHELBY A	LTC	0-2055130	0960	1
SATTERLEE IRL G	MAJ	0-1544830	0160	2
SATTERLEE JR RUFUS B	MAJ	0-0967816	1162	1
SATTERLY ROBERT I	MAJ	0-0974960	0463	1
SATTERTHWAITE PHILIP	COL	0-0251974	1164	3
SATTERWHITE ALONZO V	LTC	0-0365545	0765	3
SATTERWHITE THURMAN	CW2	W-2209991	1265	1
SATURNINE JOHN F	CPT	0-1639592	1146	2
SAUCER ALVIN B	1LT	0-1321597	1149	1
SAUER ALVIN	COL	0-0244542	0363	3
SAUER BUDDY B	CPT	0-1326199	0846	2
SAUER JOHN	CW2	W-2000314	1156	3
SAUER JOHN A	MAJ	0-0220903	0664	3
SAUER WILLIAM A	CPT	0-0488545	0655	1
SAUERBIER SR JOHN O	CW3	W-2148988	1164	1
SAUERWEIN JAMES T	CW2	W-2147836	0859	1
SAUGSTAD RANDOLF C	MAJ	0-0235892	0956	3
SAUL BARTON A	LTC	0-1315972	0465	1
SAUL FREDRIC H	MAJ	0-1651495	0561	1
SAUL HAROLD L	MAJ	0-1281097	0862	2
SAULS JR MARCUS F	LTC	0-0329199	0257	1
SAULS NIRAM L	COL	0-1287415	0663	1
SAUM COURTNEY W	LTC	0-1113927	0163	1
SAUM OTIS O	LTC	0-1295609	0862	1
SAUNAR JOAQUIN	1LT	0-1896464	0564	1
SAUNDERS ALFRED M	LTC	0-1291018	0964	1
SAUNDERS BENJAMIN B	MAJ	0-1635298	0366	1
SAUNDERS CHANDLER W	MAJ	0-0513161	0452	1
SAUNDERS CHARLES H	CPT	0-0495054	0248	1
SAUNDERS DOUGLAS I	MAJ	0-1822197	0561	1

NAME	GRADE	SVC NO	DATE RET MO YR	RET CODE
SAUNDERS EARL F	CPT	0-1556347	0346	2
SAUNDERS EARL G	LTC	0-1292405	0563	1
SAUNDERS EDWARD H	MAJ	0-1302203	0763	1
SAUNDERS EVERETT L	CPT	0-0357253	0445	2
SAUNDERS FREDERICK	LTC	0-0254599	0267	3
SAUNDERS HOWARD C	MAJ	0-2042984	0857	1
SAUNDERS JAMES H	2LT	0-1822909	0545	2
SAUNDERS JAMES K	COL	0-0149850	0648	3
SAUNDERS JAMES R	CPT	0-1031589	0949	1
SAUNDERS JOSEPH W	LTC	0-0323422	0961	3
SAUNDERS JR HARRY W	2LT	0-0466709	0144	2
SAUNDERS JR IRVING F	LTC	0-0440578	0263	2
SAUNDERS JR RODNEY V	MAJ	0-1108987	0563	1
SAUNDERS LADDIE	CW4	W-2111363	0757	1
SAUNDERS LESLIE M	LTC	0-0291615	0947	1
SAUNDERS MILTON S	MAJ	0-2035559	0660	1
SAUNDERS MYRLE J	CW2	W-2119622	0654	1
SAUNDERS NORMAN H	COL	0-0171661	0659	3
SAUNDERS RAYMOND W	LTC	0-0297827	1058	1
SAUNDERS RAYMOND W	LTC	0-0382765	0761	2
SAUNDERS RICHARD C	MAJ	0-0225535	0964	3
SAUNDERS ROBERT S	MAJ	0-1586137	0959	2
SAUNDERS WALTER H	CW2	W-2147497	0860	1
SAUNDERS WILLIAM H	LTC	0-0295625	0858	2
SAUNDERS WILLIAM H	MAJ	0-0312078	0646	2
SAUNDERS WILLIAM H	CPT	0-0450548	0759	1
SAUNDERS WILLIAM L	LTC	0-0264694	0559	3
SAUNDERS WILLIAM R	CPT	0-0351062	0146	2
SAUNDERS WOODROW W	CPT	0-0686280	0561	1
SAUNDERSON DONALD H	MAJ	0-2020839	0862	1
SAURENMAN DONALD G	LTC	0-0250127	0366	3
SAURER HOWARD O	LTC	0-1316676	1065	3
SAURWEIN GEORGE K	MAJ	0-0163657	0649	3
SAUSSER EDWIN J	CPT	0-1795980	0148	2
SAUSSER WARREN E	LTC	0-1289817	0361	1
SAUSVILLE WILLIAM C	1LT	0-1301691	1045	2
SAUTER HENRY	1LT	0-1319789	0146	2
SAUTER JOSEPH L	1LT	0-1324660	0246	2
SAUTER JULIAN C	1LT	0-1994520	1045	2
SAUTER OTTO J	LTC	0-1845102	0662	1
SAUVE NATHANIEL	COL	0-0205029	1063	3
SAVACOOL KENNETH L	MAJ	0-0888309	0166	1
SAVAGE ARNO A	MAJ	0-1897718	0961	1
SAVAGE ARTHUR R	CPT	0-0211962	0744	2
SAVAGE FRANK L	LTC	0-1107105	1163	1
SAVAGE FRANKLIN W	CW2	W-2208298	0658	2
SAVAGE GEORGE S	MAJ	0-0104148	0648	3
SAVAGE GRADY H	CW4	W-2106072	0558	1
SAVAGE JAMES M	1LT	0-1579065	1146	2
SAVAGE JEREMIAH J	MAJ	0-0204476	0746	1
SAVAGE JOSEPH	1LT	0-0164216	0837	1
SAVAGE JOSEPH W	CPT	0-1017966	1047	2
SAVAGE JR JOHN H	COL	0-0266668	0465	3
SAVAGE JR LAWRENCE L	CPT	0-0959720	0967	1
SAVAGE JUDSON W	LTC	0-0183283	0252	3
SAVAGE LEDRU H	COL	0-0295534	1066	3
SAVAGE PAUL J	LTC	0-1559848	1062	1
SAVAGE ROBERT B	COL	0-1547443	1067	3
SAVAGE ROBERT O	MAJ	0-0256547	0557	1
SAVAGE THOMAS A	1LT	0-1320653	0545	2
SAVAGE WALTER O	1LT	0-0451392	0361	2
SAVARD ARTHUR M	LTC	0-0346292	0655	1
SAVARD CHARLES E	CPT	0-1923627	1065	1
SAVASTANO F	1LT	0-1295610	1148	2
SAVEDGE LEWIS B	CW3	W-2152355	0964	1
SAVEL DALE A	CPT	0-1319790	0846	2
SAVELL WILLIAM H	CPT	0-1311932	0646	2
SAVERY CHARLES R	MAJ	0-1331996	1059	1
SAVICH JOHN	WO1	W-2123637	1051	1
SAVICKAS BRUNO F	MAJ	0-1693112	0461	1
SAVICKAS MECISLAWAS	MAJ	0-1284404	1062	1
SAVIGNY HARRY A	COL	0-0249376	0466	3
SAVILLE RICHARD F	COL	0-0220917	0966	1
SAVILLE RALPH F	2LT	0-1013439	1043	2
SAVINAR NORMAN O	LTC	0-0377012	0246	2

NAME	GRADE	SVC NO	DATE RET MO YR	RET CODE
SAVINE HENRY J	1LT	0-1309680	0246	2
SAVINGTON HOWARD J	CW2	W-2207015	C762	1
SAVINI JOHN	CPT	0-0394474	0346	2
SAVIO WAYNE L	LTC	0-1107677	0465	1
SAVITSKY DAVID V	2LT	0-1056874	0644	2
SAVOIA BRUNO J	CPT	0-0446473	0845	2
SAVOIE JOSEPH A	CPT	0-1011077	0949	2
SAVOIE XAVIER	CW2	W-2145272	0355	1
SAVOY AUGUST T	MAJ	C-0373359	0963	1
SAVOY JOSEPH E	CW4	W-2109440	0158	1
SAVOY MICHAEL F	1LT	0-1165548	C645	2
SAWADA YUKIO K	MAJ	0-2030783	0165	1
SAWALLESH ERNEST F	COL	0-0298911	0859	1
SAWARYNSKI WILLIAM C	1LT	0-1018448	1045	2
SAWDON ROBERT J	CPT	0-1300862	0346	1
SAWEY HAROLD G	CPT	0-2055245	0859	1
SAWICKI HENRY N	CPT	0-0488096	1047	1
SAWIN HARRY C	LTC	0-0270992	C467	3
SAWIN JR ALTON	1LT	0-0521965	1145	2
SAWYER BENJAMIN F	MAJ	0-1303205	C662	1
SAWYER BERTRAM H	MAJ	0-0127350	C854	3
SAWYER BROOKE E	COL	0-0104580	0157	3
SAWYER CARROLL H	LTC	0-0184221	1062	3
SAWYER CHARLES F	LTC	0-0282300	C565	3
SAWYER FERDINAND	LTC	0-0395280	C163	1
SAWYER FRANK N	MAJ	0-0209012	0344	2
SAWYER GILBERT C	LTC	0-0888212	C862	1
SAWYER GRENVILLE	1LT	0-0331516	0743	2
SAWYER HUGH	COL	0-0958602	0765	2
SAWYER JAMES C	MAJ	C-0450113	0566	2
SAWYER JAMES H	CPT	0-0480689	0847	1
SAWYER JOHN H	LTC	0-1334754	0665	1
SAWYER JOHN J	MAJ	0-1055720	1160	1
SAWYER JOSEPH C E	LTC	0-1293321	0666	1
SAWYER JOSEPH O	LTC	0-0276484	0257	1
SAWYER LESLIE F	CPT	C-1171746	0145	1
SAWYER LESTER L	LTC	0-0178209	0853	3
SAWYER LYMAN E	MAJ	0-1636592	0761	1
SAWYER MABEL E	2LT	N-0757661	1044	1
SAWYER PRESTON W	1LT	0-0358086	1041	2
SAWYER SIMEAR F	MAJ	0-0916594	0246	2
SAWYER SPENCE F	CW3	W-2144495	C664	1
SAWYER THOMAS J	CW2	W-2142157	0765	1
SAWYER TOM J	LTC	0-0385499	0461	1
SAWYER WAYNE	CPT	0-0382725	C856	1
SAWYER WILLIAM F	MAJ	0-0278977	0257	3
SAWYER WILLIAM H	CPT	0-0419699	0346	2
SAX HAROLD W	COL	0-0218989	0761	1
SAXBY LEWIS W	MAJ	C-1309844	1062	1
SAXE EARLE B	CPT	0-3059498	1162	2
SAXER ELWOOD F	COL	0-0304926	0661	2
SAXON CLIFFORD T	LTC	0-0496715	0557	1
SAXON HERSCHEL A	LTC	0-0301181	0561	3
SAXON KEENE	LTC	C-0206497	0363	1
SAXON ROBERT D	LTC	0-0304755	C160	1
SAXTON ALTON J	LTC	C-0298709	1264	3
SAXTON ROBERT D	LTC	0-1326926	C866	1
SAXTON SR ELMER O	CW3	W-2147691	0165	1
SAXTON VINCENT L	CPT	0-2102944	1062	1
SAY JR GEORGE K	2LT	0-1340695	1265	2
SAYE HENRY W	MAJ	0-1638426	0757	1
SAYE MAYNARD	CW3	W-2142412	C161	1
SAYEN HARRISON H	COL	0-0147906	1058	3
SAYER EDWIN J	1LT	0-1183613	0646	2
SAYER JOHN M	WO1	W-2110702	0562	3
SAYERS ANDREW J	MAJ	0-0940780	0862	2
SAYERS CHARLES F	LTC	C-0445172	1064	3
SAYERS JOHN K	LTC	0-0403614	1165	2
SAYERS MILTON F	COL	C-0301652	0857	1
SAYFORD ALAN N	CPT	0-0371413	C445	1
SAYLE JACK	1LT	0-2262138	0856	1
SAYLES ARTHUR L	LTC	0-0245124	0867	3
SAYLES GRACE	2LT	N-0759114	0345	1
SAYLIN RALPH R	LTC	C-0401933	C166	1
SAYLOR HAROLD D	COL	0-0147905	0752	3

NAME	GRADE	SVC NO	DATE RET MO YR	RET CODE
SAYLOR JR ROBERT L	LTC	0-0506777	0967	3
SAYLOR LOUIS F	COL	0-0021733	1060	1
SAYLOR WILBERT O	CPT	0-0432416	0152	1
SAYNER WILLIAM V	COL	0-0238890	0963	3
SAYNISCH VICTOR L	MAJ	0-1559849	0563	1
SAYPOL GEORGE M	LTC	0-0332954	0947	2
SAYRE ALBERT L	LTC	0-0221323	0959	3
SAYRE CLIFFORD L	B G	0-0201040	1059	3
SAYRE GEORGE M	LTC	0-0903694	0264	3
SAYSON CONRADO S	CPT	0-1896649	0966	1
SAZAKI HARUO	MAJ	0-2262474	0364	1
SAZZMAN THEODORE	LTC	0-1116693	0662	1
SBARAGLIA GREGORY	2LT	0-2262749	1151	1
SBERTOLI LAWRENCE	LTC	0-0294823	0560	1
SBROLLA PHILIP A	CPT	0-1551106	0246	1
SCACE WILLIAM B	LTC	0-0251465	C665	3
SCAGLIONE GERALD A	1LT	0-1031268	0146	1
SCAGNELLI JOHN C	MAJ	0-1556656	1059	1
SCALA NICK A	2LT	0-0887509	0146	2
SCALBERG JAMES W	2LT	0-1998518	0146	2
SCALES JAMES M	LTC	0-0246798	1165	3
SCALES JAMES W	LTC	0-0260650	0767	3
SCALES LUCILLE L	1LT	N-0779199	0446	2
SCALES MARCELLUS	LTC	0-1556542	1161	2
SCALF HERBERT R	MAJ	0-1647434	0662	1
SCALION CHARLES	CPT	0-0494848	0953	1
SCALLIN CARLOS	LTC	0-0231280	1058	3
SCALLON HUBERT J	MAJ	0-0309731	0660	3
SCALLY PATRICK J	1LT	0-1011659	0545	2
SCANDELL JR ROY H	2LT	0-1318832	0846	2
SCANDIFFIO N J	2LT	0-1309020	1044	2
SCANLAN GEORGE C	CPT	0-0542642	0845	2
SCANLAN JAMES J	LTC	0-0313389	0359	1
SCANLAN JOSEPH A	LTC	0-1593242	1164	1
SCANLAN JR EDWARD F	LTC	0-1639967	1164	1
SCANLAN WILLIAM V	LTC	0-0513878	0365	3
SCANLON CECIL M	MAJ	0-0348374	0946	2
SCANLON FRANK C	CPT	0-1324740	0357	1
SCANLON JEROME A	2LT	0-1305958	0245	2
SCANLON MARY A	1LT	N-0700809	0943	1
SCANLON ROBERT J	MAJ	0-1638428	0264	1
SCANNELL JOHN W	CPT	0-0386942	0146	2
SCANNELL THOMAS P	CPT	0-0542176	0846	2
SCAPLEN FRANK W	LTC	C-1633656	0966	1
SCARANGELLA N A	MAJ	0-1651086	0957	1
SCARANI LOUIS P	1LT	0-1170179	0251	2
SCARBOROUGH CHAFFEE	MAJ	0-0215480	1262	3
SCARBOROUGH EARL W	MAJ	0-1797016	1059	1
SCARBOROUGH JAMES W	LTC	0-0363937	0661	2
SCARBOROUGH JOHN M	MAJ	C-0531224	0846	1
SCARBOROUGH JOSEPH C	MAJ	0-0989147	0964	1
SCARBOROUGH LELAND O	COL	0-1309845	0365	2
SCARBOROUGH OSCAR L	LTC	0-0259791	0967	3
SCARBOROUGH SIDNEY	LTC	0-0353033	0945	2
SCARBOROUGH ZACK T	CPT	0-0283931	0946	1
SCARBROUGH CROWELL W	CPT	0-0482447	1046	1
SCARBROUGH LEON T	LTC	0-1165945	0258	1
SCARBROUGH LOUIS R	LTC	0-1177965	0765	1
SCARBROUCH RAYMOND C	CW3	W-2147777	0364	1
SCARDINA ANTONIO	LTC	0-0322727	1164	3
SCARFF INA M	1LT	N-0776116	0745	1
SCARLE CHARLES F	CPT	0-0452575	0663	1
SCARNECCHIA JOHN L	CPT	0-1693543	0145	2
SCARPA JOSEPH	CPT	C-1590155	0648	1
SCARPONE PASQUALE W	LTC	0-1102588	0861	1
SCARRY MICHAEL M	2LT	0-1296095	0744	2
SCATES GEORGE L	MAJ	0-0488328	0249	1
SCATES SHELBY E	1LT	0-4027962	0357	2
SCATTERDAY JOHN R	LTC	0-0439404	0344	2
SCEARCE TROY W	MAJ	0-1917507	1266	1
SCEFONAS STANLEY A	1LT	0-1823067	0545	2
SCELLATO FRANCIS D	LTC	0-1638430	1162	1
SCHAAD EDWIN M	LTC	0-1638431	0962	1
SCHAAF JAMES C	LTC	0-0304364	1158	1
SCHAAF JAMES C	MAJ	0-0985750	1064	1

NAME	GRADE	SVC NO	DATE RET MO YR	RET CODE
SCHAAFSMA FRANK	CPT	0-1081173	0846	2
SCHAAL FRANK J	COL	0-0181800	1054	1
SCHAAR FREDERICK	CPT	0-1794994	C958	2
SCHABA GEORGE E	1LT	0-2027370	0749	1
SCHACHT WALTER G	1LT	0-1053342	0747	2
SCHACHTEL MAURICE	2LT	0-1048568	0145	2
SCHADE CALVIN H	CPT	0-4006911	0266	1
SCHADE FRANK F	COL	0-0269645	1166	3
SCHADE JR CHARLES E	MAJ	C-0300389	0762	1
SCHADE MELVIN A	1LT	0-1309846	1045	2
SCHADLF ALVA G	MAJ	0-1826104	1060	1
SCHADLER FREDERICK	MAJ	0-1534137	C958	1
SCHADO MICHAEL V	LTC	0-2011345	C263	1
SCHAEFER AMOS E	LTC	0-0313051	0361	3
SCHAEFER ARTHUR F	COL	0-0275495	0154	2
SCHAEFER DUFRED L	MAJ	0-1945479	0161	2
SCHAEFER FRANCIS H	LTC	0-0260077	C166	3
SCHAEFER HENRY J	CPT	0-1688838	C159	2
SCHAEFER HENRY W	MAJ	C-0958731	1064	1
SCHAEFER IRVING D	M G	0-0110672	0856	3
SCHAEFER JOHN H	COL	0-0104135	09 0	3
SCHAEFER JOHN L	1LT	0-0461377	0944	2
SCHAEFER LEO J	LTC	0-0135425	1055	3
SCHAEFER LEROY L	MAJ	C-1825888	C764	1
SCHAEFER LOUIS W	COL	0-0114939	1057	3
SCHAEFER ROBERT B	1LT	0-1645972	0147	2
SCHAEFER ROBERT G	LTC	0-0396341	0660	1
SCHAEFER ROBERT J	2LT	0-1012570	0144	2
SCHAEFER STEPHEN H	CW3	W-2208473	C766	1
SCHAEFER VINCENT W	CPT	0-0238122	0561	3
SCHAEFER WILLIAM H	CPT	0-1930839	1164	1
SCHAEFFER BERTRAM	CPT	0-1533439	1145	2
SCHAEFFER CHARLES O	MAJ	0-1039195	C462	1
SCHAEFFER CHARLES T	LTC	0-1062698	1165	1
SCHAEFLE JAMES M	CW4	W-2142268	0960	1
SCHAERTEL ELMER G	LTC	0-0346901	0167	3
SCHAETZEL NORMAN F	CW3	W-2150166	1165	1
SCHAEUFFLE JOHN G	CPT	0-0283643	0647	1
SCHAF LEONARD C	1LT	0-0253596	0244	2
SCHAFER ALBERT M	CPT	0-1945936	0246	1
SCHAFER AUGUST	MAJ	C-0974521	0961	1
SCHAFER CHARLES W	MAJ	0-0194703	0648	3
SCHAFER NORMAN H	MAJ	0-0271122	C245	2
SCHAFER PAUL J	CPT	C-1638433	C446	2
SCHAFER PHILIP R	LTC	0-0518292	0766	3
SCHAFER RAYMOND A	LTC	0-1289633	0358	1
SCHAFER ROBERT J	LTC	C-1293842	0765	1
SCHAFER ROBERT P	LTC	0-1640920	0367	1
SCHAFER VERNON L	LTC	0-1644048	C862	1
SCHAFER WILLIAM F	MAJ	C-2049923	0961	1
SCHAFFER ERWIN A	1LT	0-0360097	0249	2
SCHAFFER MARY C	2LT	N-0734002	1144	1
SCHAFFER ROBERT H	MAJ	0-2263157	0364	1
SCHAFFER WARREN F	CPT	0-0888855	C148	2
SCHAFFER WILLIAM	COL	0-0477533	1266	1
SCHAFFLER ALBERT J	LTC	0-1100319	0857	1
SCHAFISH CHARLES H	MAJ	0-1543436	0164	1
SCHAIBLY ROBERT L	1LT	0-1296912	0745	2
SCHAIN JAMES T	1LT	0-1845497	0844	2
SCHAIRER JR KARL C	MAJ	0-1041896	0666	1
SCHAKEL CORNELIUS	2LT	0-1300089	C844	2
SCHALK KURT W	LTC	0-0350364	CR61	3
SCHALL BASTIDA B	MAJ	N-0758097	0267	3
SCHALL JR ALBERT	2LT	0-1015581	0644	2
SCHALL MARTIN H	CPT	0-1634296	0647	1
SCHALL SAMUEL M	MAJ	0-0463739	1047	2
SCHALLER HARRY F	CPT	0-0334238	C545	2
SCHALLER KATHRYN C	CPT	N-0737243	0447	1
SCHALLER RALPH J	MAJ	0-1319021	0962	1
SCHALTEGGER OSCAR B	CW2	W-2148813	1160	1
SCHAM MANUEL J	COL	0-0322590	0267	3
SCHANCK JR GEORGE P	CPT	C-0478054	C346	2
SCHANEN MILTON W	1LT	0-1589484	0845	2
SCHANER LEONARD G	LTC	0-1796705	C266	1
SCHANHOFF SIR GEORGE	CW3	W-2145256	0762	1

NAME	GRADE	SVC NO	DATE RET MO YR	RET CODE
SCHANK ROBERT E	LTC	0-0441490	0767	1
SCHANNEN JOSEPH F	CW2	W-2141918	1166	2
SCHANNEN THEODORE R	LTC	0-0240326	1065	3
SCHANTZ RICHARD	CPT	0-1684581	0147	2
SCHANZENBACH EMIL E	CW3	W-2128092	0157	1
SCHAPER JACK F	1LT	0-1326173	1045	2
SCHAPIRO ISADORE S	CPT	0-0441327	0346	2
SCHAPIRO MORRIS	MAJ	0-0423064	0346	2
SCHAPLOW WILFRED H	MAJ	0-0381996	0257	2
SCHARDT HENRY P	MAJ	0-1595149	0157	1
SCHARF LEWIS E	CPT	0-0273278	0545	2
SCHARFENSTEIN LOUIS	CPT	0-4006406	0565	1
SCHARFF EDWARD G	1LT	0-1057592	1045	1
SCHARFF LYNTON L	MAJ	0-0182717	0457	3
SCHARFF RICHARD B	MAJ	0-0224964	C355	3
SCHARPF WILLIAM F	2LT	0-0539496	0745	1
SCHARR ALICE C	MAJ	N-0732333	0563	1
SCHARSCHMIDT LEWIS W	CPT	0-1012410	0546	2
SCHARTAU MELVIN I	CW3	W-2207651	0167	1
SCHARTLE RONALD N	LTC	0-0243468	0766	3
SCHATTE FREDERICK	1LT	0-1309848	0345	2
SCHATTENBERG GUS A	COL	0-0248285	0456	1
SCHATZ GEORGE	COL	0-0310805	0562	3
SCHATZMAN DONALD C	WO1	W-2152481	1053	2
SCHATZMAN EDWARD J	CPT	0-2035440	1063	1
SCHATZMAN THOMAS F	LTC	0-0279517	0264	1
SCHAU NILE C	MAJ	0-0493126	0-52	1
SCHAUB HAROLD W	COL	0-0114333	0251	3
SCHAUB LEWIS W	1LT	0-1058646	0346	2
SCHAUDT MAURICE H	1LT	0-0506178	0944	2
SCHAUER ERNEST J	LTC	0-1315103	0466	1
SCHAUER GORDON H	CPT	0-1577804	0955	1
SCHAUER ROBERT J	1LT	0-0158861	0650	3
SCHAUERMAN WILLIAM	2LT	0-1306892	0444	2
SCHAUFFELE WALTER H	1LT	0-2014892	0947	2
SCHAUFFLER ALLEN M	LTC	0-0143355	0951	3
SCHAUMBERG HENRY	MAJ	C-0176257	0945	2
SCHAUTZ ARTHUR G	MAJ	0-0183376	0356	3
SCHAYER ISADORE	LTC	0-0336205	0144	2
SCHEAFFER MILTON W	1LT	0-1331667	0546	2
SCHEARER JOSEPH L	LTC	0-1288128	0861	1
SCHECHER FRANCIS J	LTC	0-1638437	0965	1
SCHECHTMAN EMANUEL	1LT	0-1647256	0145	2
SCHECTER AARON F	CPT	0-0485764	1044	2
SCHECTER BEN	1LT	0-1299121	0545	2
SCHEEL EDWARD A	CPT	0-2036934	0547	2
SCHEEL IRMA C	1LT	N-0737960	0946	1
SCHEER ARTHUR A	LTC	0-0234528	0162	3
SCHEER CHARLES H	COL	0-0103051	0653	1
SCHEERER JOHN B	CPT	0-0277425	C660	3
SCHEERER RICHARD W	1LT	0-1297958	0145	2
SCHEETZ HARRY L	COL	0-0200727	1047	2
SCHEFFEL CHARLES	CPT	0-0446059	0145	2
SCHEFFLER EDMUND B	CW3	W-2206823	1066	1
SCHEFFLER HAROLD G	CPT	0-0515156	0846	2
SCHEFFLER LEWIS F	LTC	0-0524196	0965	3
SCHEFFNER WARREN H	LTC	0-0418787	0767	1
SCHEGOLIN JOHN E	MAJ	0-0451177	0260	1
SCHEIB JOHN E	CW2	W-2211890	0367	1
SCHEIBE CLARENCE E	CPT	0-0503501	0746	2
SCHEIBE EDMUND	LTC	0-0339013	0361	1
SCHEIBER EDWARD L	LTC	0-1644746	0257	1
SCHEIBNER CARL F	LTC	0-0236401	1053	3
SCHEID JR GEORGE T	CPT	0-1551306	1145	2
SCHEID LLOYD J	2LT	0-1324227	0545	2
SCHEIRER ELEANOR C	1LT	N-0734916	0346	1
SCHEIRER PAUL O	MAJ	0-1552164	1161	1
SCHEITERLE CHARLES	1LT	0-0241936	0554	3
SCHELIN CARL A	CPT	0-1014320	0846	1
SCHELL BERNARD J	LTC	0-1576613	1163	1
SCHELL CHARLES C	CPT	0-1320655	1146	1
SCHELL CHRISTIAN	MAJ	0-0237502	0851	3
SCHELL EMORY T	CPT	0-1317568	0760	1
SCHELL HENRY H	LTC	0-1633519	C561	1
SCHELL LOUIS C	CW2	W-2147617	0659	1

NAME	GRADE	SVC NO	DATE RET MO YR	RET CODE
SCHELL VALENTINE	MAJ	O-2200333	0466	1
SCHELL WILLIAM	MAJ	O-0455760	0757	1
SCHELL WILLIAM H	LTC	O-1102031	1262	1
SCHELLHAAS RICHARD B	MAJ	O-1113428	0263	1
SCHELLINGS WILLIAM	2LT	O-1331101	0140	2
SCHELPER LAWRENCE J	2LT	O-1324364	1145	2
SCHEMBER RAYMOND W	1LT	O-1325674	1046	1
SCHEMMEL HENRY F	2LT	O-0130074	1152	3
SCHEMMEL HERMAN H	1LT	O-1311211	0146	2
SCHEMMEL RUTH L	1LT	R-0000971	0346	2
SCHENA CHARLES J	MAJ	O-2032904	0364	1
SCHENCK HERSCHEL W	MAJ	O-0320991	0760	3
SCHENO JAMES F	CW3	W-2150518	1064	1
SCHENECK EDWIN B	1LT	O-0912613	0746	2
SCHENK CLINTON O	CPT	O-0164181	1126	1
SCHENKER BENJAMIN N	CPT	O-1692311	0145	2
SCHEPPACH MAXIMILIAN	MAJ	O-0151664	C-50	3
SCHEPPACH RAYMOND C	LTC	O-0302223	0265	3
SCHEPPLER FRED E	CPT	O-0117449	0550	3
SCHER LOUIS I	CW3	W-2145255	0656	1
SCHERBA JOHN M	WO1	W-2152325	0855	1
SCHERBA STEPHEN	MAJ	O-0345795	0446	2
SCHERECK WILLIAM J	2LT	O-1306955	0245	2
SCHERER ALFRED C	COL	O-0328340	0661	1
SCHERER EARL A	CPT	O-0182020	1154	3
SCHERER EDWARD A	CW2	W-2209997	1162	1
SCHERER LELAND H	1LT	O-0426658	0946	1
SCHERER WILLIAM R	LTC	O-1169320	0867	1
SCHEREF HARRY J	MAJ	O-0123246	0246	2
SCHERGER JOHN P	MAJ	O-0938025	0661	1
SCHERLEN EMIL O	LTC	O-0183977	0947	2
SCHERMER ALBERT B	CPT	O-0301154	1043	2
SCHERMERHORN A E	MAJ	O-1644748	0960	1
SCHERMERHORN H A	CPT	O-1013978	0846	2
SCHERMERHORN JOHN W	COL	O-0193213	0461	3
SCHEROTTER HOWARD	2LT	O-2207975	1151	2
SCHERTZ JEAN E	2LT	N-0795245	0846	1
SCHERWAT WILLIAM C	CPT	O-0120089	0453	3
SCHERWERTS DANIEL	CPT	O-0226382	1040	1
SCHETTLER HAYDN A	LTC	O-0236212	0665	3
SCHEUER GEORGE R	MAJ	O-1573571	0854	1
SCHEUFLER ROBERT C	MAJ	O-0870670	0163	1
SCHEUMACK JOHN T	COL	O-0253907	0351	3
SCHEUPLEIN JOHN W	CW3	W-2147366	0757	1
SCHEVIS JR JOHN	MAJ	O-0966636	1262	1
SCHEWE CLIFFORD H	CPT	O-1540646	1046	1
SCHEYD JR WILLIAM F	COL	O-0300787	0767	1
SCHIAVELLI GEORGE F	LTC	O-0249625	0367	3
SCHIBLER JOHN M	LTC	O-1636605	1060	1
SCHICK CHARLES F	LTC	O-1169722	0860	1
SCHICK GEORGE A	LTC	O-0451549	0258	1
SCHICK HERBERT M	CPT	O-0105183	0455	3
SCHICK LOUIS T	1LT	O-1316219	0146	2
SCHICK WALTER R	CPT	O-0554058	0947	1
SCHICKEL JOSEPH	CPT	O-1685237	0347	2
SCHICKER ROBERT O	MAJ	O-0955800	0566	1
SCHIDZIG ANDREW J	MAJ	O-1293322	1047	1
SCHIEBER HERMAN A	CW2	W-2143340	0461	1
SCHIEFFER GEORGE R	CPT	O-0977262	0462	1
SCHIEFERSTEIN CARL J	COL	O-0290258	0962	1
SCHIEK JR IRVING E	CPT	O-0532406	0246	2
SCHIELD EMMETT L	LTC	O-0129410	0459	3
SCHIELDCE JR W C	1LT	O-1306476	0945	2
SCHIELE GEORGE C	COL	O-0281767	0866	3
SCHIENDELMAN LEON M	MAJ	O-2000776	1060	1
SCHIERHORST EDWIN C	CPT	O-1100321	0944	2
SCHIERS ROBERT A	2LT	O-2055120	0645	2
SCHIERZ PEARLE I	1LT	N-0784460	0348	1
SCHIFF ABE L	MAJ	O-0499353	0247	2
SCHIFF ISADORE J	CPT	O-0382052	1142	2
SCHIFFBAUER JOHN E	2LT	O-1698159	0944	2
SCHIFFMAN WILLIAM L	MAJ	O-0498571	0646	2
SCHILDKNECHT OTTO C	CW3	W-2146614	0561	1
SCHILOT JAMES F	MAJ	O-1183409	0860	1
SCHILL JOHN S	1LT	O-1110790	0146	2

NAME	GRADE	SVC NO	DATE RET MO YR	RET CODE
SCHILLER DANIEL	CW3	RW-2145362	0663	1
SCHILLER HERBERT A	CPT	O-0420203	1044	1
SCHILLER HORACE G	LTC	O-0238459	0666	3
SCHILLER MAX	CPT	O-0885811	0646	2
SCHILLER MELVIN D	2LT	O-1173769	0444	2
SCHILLETTER W A	COL	O-0149003	0354	2
SCHILLING CHARLES A	CW3	W-2151207	1164	1
SCHILLING GEORGE W	COL	O-0350170	0265	1
SCHILLING JOSEPH F	MAJ	O-1330969	0962	1
SCHILLING RUSSELL R	1LT	O-1105795	0847	2
SCHILLINGER EDWARD N	COL	O-0234012	0550	3
SCHIMENTI MATTHEW L	CPT	O-0406232	0445	2
SCHIMMACK AUGUST F	MAJ	O-0192969	0-51	3
SCHIMMEL CARL L	MAJ	O-0266948	0163	3
SCHIMMEL III JOHN	LTC	O-0196173	0363	3
SCHINAZI LEON R	COL	O-0214429	0954	3
SCHINDELHEIM SAMUE	MAJ	O-0497224	0246	2
SCHINDLER EDWARD C	MAJ	O-1560071	1062	1
SCHINDLER WARREN H	CW3	W-2144760	0464	1
SCHIPPERS RICHARD J	1LT	O-1823495	0550	1
SCHIPPCREIT GEORGE P	LTC	O-0300132	0658	1
SCHIRA PEDRO G	CPT	O-0263957	0259	3
SCHIRMACHER THEODORE	COL	O-0918017	0366	1
SCHIRMER FREDERICK	LTC	O-1118281	0866	1
SCHIRMER ROY E	CPT	O-0337290	1045	2
SCHIRRU SPARTACO R	CW4	RW-2144930	0767	1
SCHISGALL LEC	LTC	O-0205262	0460	3
SCHISKA MARTIN T	MAJ	O-0129356	0958	3
SCHLABAUGH DONALD	CPT	O-1015836	1146	2
SCHLACHTA FRANK J	CPT	O-1882393	0463	2
SCHLAFLI JR ALFRED	COL	O-0380570	0861	1
SCHLAFLY JOHN P	CW3	W-2142607	1057	1
SCHLAGER EDWARD O	CPT	O-0548193	0846	1
SCHLAGER ROLAND G	LTC	O-0453214	1066	3
SCHLAIRET CHARLES V	CPT	O-0486448	0546	2
SCHLAPPER LLOYD H	1LT	O-0132457	0547	2
SCHLAUERSBACH ADAM	CW4	W-2136534	1263	1
SCHLECHTE ARNOLD W	CW2	W-2115352	1048	1
SCHLECHTWEG CHARLES	WO1	W-2215168	0764	2
SCHLEDER JR GEORGE	CW2	W-2209996	0264	1
SCHLEGEL CHARLES E	CW4	W-2102327	0657	1
SCHLEGEL FRANCIS J	CW2	W-2119653	0852	2
SCHLEGEL LESLIE H	1LT	O-1305485	1045	2
SCHLEGELMILCH EARL G	CPT	O-1182700	0562	3
SCHLEI ELMO W	LTC	O-0308483	0256	3
SCHLEIDER EMLIE J	MAJ	N-0734288	0154	2
SCHLEIFFER THEODORE	MAJ	O-4006620	1167	1
SCHLEICH ROSS O	MAJ	O-0153249	0744	2
SCHLEMMER NORMAN C	1LT	O-0545994	0745	2
SCHLENKER C F	1LT	O-1056877	0146	1
SCHLENKER IRVIN	MAJ	O-4011514	0265	1
SCHLENKER JAMES A	CW3	W-2143113	1059	1
SCHLENKER ROBERT O	1LT	O-1013172	0446	2
SCHLESINGER LEE H	COL	O-0284361	0665	3
SCHLESINGER MELVIN H	COL	O-0129714	1155	3
SCHLESINGER MEYER	LTC	O-1544036	1166	3
SCHLESINGER MORTON	2LT	O-1101303	0844	1
SCHLESINGER NOLAN R	1LT	O-1324955	0146	2
SCHLESINGER THOMAS O	MAJ	O-0949274	1064	1
SCHLEUDER ERNEST A	LTC	O-0205571	0857	2
SCHLEY ERVIN L	MAJ	O-1168901	0561	2
SCHLICHER ROYCE E	CPT	O-1015530	0561	1
SCHLICHTMAN JOHN O	CW2	W-2152660	0463	1
SCHLICKER EDWARD H	CPT	O-1554473	0164	2
SCHLIEPER ARTHUR W	CPT	O-1058647	0547	2
SCHLIETER WILLARD R	CW3	W-2141439	0561	1
SCHLIEVE RUTH T	2LT	N-0777256	0548	1
SCHLITZKUS GUS W	LTC	O-0337620	0958	1
SCHLORCHM WILLIAM A	MAJ	O-1633522	1160	1
SCHLOESSER DOROTHY M	2LT	R-0001151	0945	1
SCHLOSSBERG MAX	MAJ	O-1182701	1263	1
SCHLOSSER RICHARD W	1LT	O-1796707	0448	2
SCHLOTH WILLIAM J	MAJ	O-0339137	0246	2
SCHLUEDER THOMAS O	1LT	O-1824234	0763	1
SCHLUETER DEAN A	MAJ	O-1342302	0860	1

NAME	GRADE	SVC NO	DATE RET MO YR	RET CODE
SCHLUETER JOHN E	WO1	W-2150363	0756	2
SCHLUETER KENNETH W	COL	O-0453324	1061	1
SCHLUETER THEODORE L	MAJ	O-0264641	1059	1
SCHLUNTZ JOACHIM M	LTC	O-0262416	0166	3
SCHLUSSEL MAURICE J	LTC	O-0313050	0867	3
SCHMADER WILBUR P	LTC	O-0372984	0160	1
SCHMAHLENBERGER CARL	MAJ	O-2208020	0564	1
SCHMAL ROBERT E	LTC	O-0306795	0162	1
SCHMALHOFER GEORGE F	MAJ	O-2005693	0263	1
SCHMALL ALEXANDER	WO1	W-2123740	0253	2
SCHMALZIGAN JACK B	CPT	O-0969260	0167	1
SCHMANSKA KATHERIN	1LT	N-0751021	1145	1
SCHMECKERT RAYMOND H	WO1	W-2109812	0864	3
SCHMEDEMAN ALBERT G	LTC	O-0279442	1161	3
SCHMEDEMANN ALBERT J	MAJ	O-0170840	0153	3
SCHMEICHEL JULIUS	LTC	O-0166550	0156	3
SCHMELA WOODROW W	MAJ	O-0356237	0346	2
SCHMELING ALFRED	CPT	O-0491080	0348	1
SCHMELTZER C B	MAJ	O-0166461	0956	3
SCHMELTZER ROBERT M	LTC	O-1030930	0962	1
SCHMELZER JOHN H	LTC	O-0223971	0157	3
SCHMENK CATHERINE	MAJ	N-0769562	0467	1
SCHMERBAUCH HUBERT B	CPT	O-1295091	1049	1
SCHMICKLE ROBERT O	LTC	O-0250785	0966	3
SCHMICKLEY PAULINE	MAJ	N-0784400	0164	1
SCHMID EARL W	MAJ	O-1289819	0856	1
SCHMID ELLS P	MAJ	O-1341908	1060	2
SCHMID HAROLD W	LTC	O-0216959	0164	3
SCHMID HELMUT K	COL	O-0372521	0260	1
SCHMID KARL A	LTC	O-0405239	0547	2
SCHMIDGALL FRANK W	CPT	O-1881262	0863	1
SCHMIDT CHARLES A	CPT	O-1316677	0657	1
SCHMIDT DAVID G	COL	O-0311206	1166	3
SCHMIDT DELMER A	MAJ	O-1169725	1161	1
SCHMIDT EDWARD J	COL	O-0159420	0753	3
SCHMIDT EDWIN A	CPT	O-1580281	0546	2
SCHMIDT ELDON M	CW4	W-2114259	0359	1
SCHMIDT ELVIRA C	2LT	N-0737038	0943	1
SCHMIDT ERNEST A	CW3	W-2151686	0864	1
SCHMIDT EUGENE A	LTC	O-0403751	1163	1
SCHMIDT FRED J	LTC	O-1101206	0761	1
SCHMIDT FREDERICK	COL	O-0256280	1058	3
SCHMIDT FREDERICK	LTC	O-0323579	0963	3
SCHMIDT FREDERICK	LTC	O-1300396	0657	1
SCHMIDT GEORGE F	CW2	W-2210356	1063	1
SCHMIDT GEORGE P	CPT	O-0253298	0142	2
SCHMIDT GEORGE W	CW2	W-2148266	0163	1
SCHMIDT HANS W	COL	O-0312696	0765	3
SCHMIDT HARRY	CPT	O-0244523	0445	1
SCHMIDT HARRY E	MAJ	O-0502554	1045	2
SCHMIDT HUGO A	CPT	O-0415069	0345	2
SCHMIDT JAMES R	MAJ	O-0356908	0846	2
SCHMIDT JOHN B	LTC	O-0329186	0864	1
SCHMIDT JOHN H	CPT	O-0427910	0644	1
SCHMIDT JR EDWARD L	LTC	O-0251825	0660	1
SCHMIDT JR HILTON A	1LT	O-0396183	0443	2
SCHMIDT JR JOSEPH I	CPT	O-1171749	0862	1
SCHMIDT KENNETH G	MAJ	O-0273447	0366	3
SCHMIDT LELAH M	1LT	N-0743837	0845	1
SCHMIDT LEONARD B	1LT	O-1297259	104N	2
SCHMIDT LEROY A	MAJ	O-1185347	0361	1
SCHMIDT LINDLEY G	COL	O-0177834	0547	2
SCHMIDT LORRIMER M	MAJ	O-0505658	1146	2
SCHMIDT LOUVERA B	LTC	O-0230718	0460	3
SCHMIDT MARVIN T	MAJ	O-0964471	0662	1
SCHMIDT MAURICE S	LTC	O-1534138	0863	1
SCHMIDT OTTO H	LTC	O-0332063	0152	3
SCHMIDT PAUL W	COL	O-0123534	0556	3
SCHMIDT PHILIPP E	MAJ	O-0257330	0157	3
SCHMIDT RICHARD P	2LT	O-0552401	0845	2
SCHMIDT ROBERT A	COL	O-0332201	0665	3
SCHMIDT ROBERT D	COL	O-0332392	1145	2
SCHMIDT ROBERT F	CW2	W-2144429	1060	1
SCHMIDT WALTER	CW3	W-2129412	1154	1
SCHMIDT WALTER G	LTC	O-1639606	0162	1

NAME	GRADE	SVC NO	DATE RET MO YR	RET CODE
SCHMIDT WALTER J	MAJ	O-0481638	0845	2
SCHMIDT WARREN R	CPT	O-1340405	1064	1
SCHMIDT WILLIAM C	LTC	O-0220704	0553	3
SCHMIDT WILLIAM G	CPT	O-1295438	0747	1
SCHMIDT WOODROW C	MAJ	O-2007691	1058	1
SCHMIED WILLIAM C	MAJ	O-0378730	0747	1
SCHMIEDEKE JOHN A	LTC	O-1319023	0466	1
SCHMIER ADOLPH A	MAJ	O-0508573	0646	2
SCHMILSKI RHINEHARD	MAJ	O-1541681	1159	1
SCHMINKE GEORGE C	LTC	O-0240733	1264	3
SCHMITCKE RALPH B	CW4	W-2127514	0659	1
SCHMITS LOUIS H	CW3	W-2143961	0363	1
SCHMITT BENEDICT C	CW2	W-2205809	0164	1
SCHMITT CHARLES J	MAJ	O-0239995	1164	3
SCHMITT CHRIST G	LTC	O-0302168	0167	3
SCHMITT EDWARD	COL	O-0127926	0956	3
SCHMITT MARTIN J	CPT	O-0996075	0158	2
SCHMITT ROBERT J	LTC	O-0451065	0762	1
SCHMITTDIEL HENRY A	1LT	O-1580284	0545	2
SCHMITZ ARTHUR H	LTC	O-0290618	0860	2
SCHMITZ ENGELBERT	MAJ	O-0330445	0657	3
SCHMITZ FLORA D	MAJ	N-0767013	0563	1
SCHMITZ JOHN T	COL	O-0319265	0861	1
SCHMOLL JR EDWARD A	LTC	O-1533910	0461	1
SCHMOOCK WALDEMAR C	LTC	O-0910100	0866	3
SCHMOYER ARTHUR R	1LT	O-0508304	0845	2
SCHMUCK EDWARD J	LTC	O-0349795	0546	2
SCHMUHL LORENZ C	LTC	O-0121598	0358	3
SCHMUS JACK C	MAJ	O-0524502	0954	1
SCHNABEL HERMAN J	MAJ	O-0445787	0962	1
SCHNABEL IRVING D	2LT	O-1110792	0145	2
SCHNABEL JAMES F	LTC	O-1176795	0964	1
SCHNABEL LOUIS F	COL	O-0374673	0764	1
SCHNACKENBERG FREDER	LTC	O-1326587	0763	1
SCHNAP ISIDORE	COL	O-0467348	0866	3
SCHNATHORST WILLIA	MAJ	O-0504491	1044	2
SCHNECK JACOB O	LTC	O-0451432	0957	1
SCHNECK ROSE B	1LT	N-0730517	0546	1
SCHNEDLER WILFRED J	LTC	O-0316443	0664	3
SCHNEE CHARLES W	LTC	O-0371229	1167	3
SCHNEIDER ALBERT C	MAJ	O-0468050	0247	1
SCHNEIDER ALBERT L	MAJ	O-1054111	1064	1
SCHNEIDER ARLON B	1LT	O-0370982	1044	2
SCHNEIDER CATHEREN M	LTC	N-0733277	1162	1
SCHNEIDER CHARLES L	MAJ	O-1545259	1067	3
SCHNEIDER CHARLES P	CPT	O-0446271	0845	2
SCHNEIDER CHRISTIAN	CW2	W-2209730	0863	1
SCHNEIDER CLAUDE R	MAJ	O-0212496	1054	3
SCHNEIDER CLEMMENS	LTC	O-0333525	1159	3
SCHNEIDER EARL A	CPT	O-1011763	0557	1
SCHNEIDER EDWARD H	LTC	O-0312191	1264	3
SCHNEIDER EMMA F	1LT	N-0772790	0746	1
SCHNEIDER EUGENIE H	1LT	N-0743964	0645	1
SCHNEIDER FREDDIE J	WO1	W-2148937	0656	1
SCHNEIDER FREDERICK	MAJ	O-0286816	0260	3
SCHNEIDER GEORGE H	MAJ	O-2026412	1162	1
SCHNEIDER GLENN W	LTC	O-1317685	0664	1
SCHNEIDER HAROLD B	1LT	O-1581359	0756	1
SCHNEIDER HARRY	LTC	O-1299315	1055	1
SCHNEIDER HENRY J	COL	O-0451570	1166	2
SCHNEIDER HERBERT A	1LT	O-1302206	114N	1
SCHNEIDER JOHN	2LT	O-1051773	1043	2
SCHNEIDER JOHN M	CPT	O-0452061	0156	1
SCHNEIDER JOHN T	COL	O-0290102	0655	3
SCHNEIDER JOSEPH H	LTC	O-1307942	1162	1
SCHNEIDER KENNETH E	LTC	O-1295780	0765	1
SCHNEIDER LOUIS	LTC	O-0250394	0164	3
SCHNEIDER MAURICE H	MAJ	O-2262364	0462	1
SCHNEIDER MORRIS D	LTC	O-0344521	0262	1
SCHNEIDER ORVILLE N	CPT	O-0348493	0767	3
SCHNEIDER OTTO B	LTC	O-0397929	0860	1
SCHNEIDER PHILIP	CW3	RW-2147923	1163	1
SCHNEIDER RALPH W	LTC	O-0903531	0865	3
SCHNEIDER RAYMOND F	LTC	O-0237550	1065	3
SCHNEIDER ROBERT	2LT	O-0420310	0545	2

NAME	GRADE	SVC NO	DATE RET MO YR	RET CODE
SCHNEIDER ROLLANC E	LTC	0-1059272	C867	1
SCHNEIDER WILLIAM N	MAJ	C-1597917	1063	1
SCHNEIDER WILLIAM R	MAJ	C-0989014	1165	1
SCHNEIDEWIND A R	COL	0-0184070	1058	3
SCHNELL HERMAN F	CPT	C-0322691	1153	2
SCHNELL JACK C	MAJ	C-1583632	0565	2
SCHNELL JOHN H	LTC	0-0301325	1054	2
SCHNELL MICHAEL W	MAJ	0-1549599	1158	2
SCHNELLENBACH KURT	COL	0-0475887	0255	1
SCHNELLER RAYMOND J	MAJ	0-0370406	0746	1
SCHNETZLER ROBERT H	CW4	W-2141440	1167	1
SCHNIERING JOHN	LTC	0-130378C	0966	1
SCHNITTMAN JOSEPH L	CW2	W-2153153	0364	1
SCHNOOR HENRY L	COL	0-0229240	0465	3
SCHNUR JAMES F	LTC	0-1041645	0352	1
SCHNURR FREDERICK	MAJ	C-1826248	1165	1
SCHOCH FRANCIS J	CW3	W-2149951	0764	1
SCHOCH JAMES B	MAJ	C-0167344	0455	3
SCHOCH LEO M	CPT	0-0479593	0955	1
SCHOCHET SYCNEY S	MAJ	0-0114730	0347	2
SCHOEBEN BERNARD W	WO1	W-2129906	0144	2
SCHOEBERL GEORGE M	LTC	0-1574136	0556	1
SCHOEBERL ROBERT H	MAJ	C-0971964	1063	1
SCHOECH OSCAR W	LTC	C-0376641	0860	1
SCHOELLER JULIUS E	LTC	0-1042425	1062	1
SCHOEN JOSEPH F	COL	0-0916551	0763	3
SCHOEN LEON W	LTC	0-0272021	0964	3
SCHOENBAECHLER GILBE	MAJ	0-2033995	C566	1
SCHOENBAUM GEORGE H	MAJ	C-0290871	0745	2
SCHOENBECK EDWIN H	CPT	0-1030714	1046	2
SCHOENBERG T E	1LT	C-1823219	C346	2
SCHOENBERGER LAURENC	MAJ	0-0302901	0962	1
SCHOENBORN FREDERICK	LTC	0-0239840	0864	3
SCHOENENBERGER A P	CPT	0-1697773	0645	2
SCHOENKOPFF EDWARC E	LTC	0-0200387	0552	3
SCHOENMAN JR HARRY P	LTC	C-1052152	0764	1
SCHOENTAG CAVID C	CPT	0-1312232	0849	2
SCHOENWETHER KENNETH	LTC	0-0295753	1165	1
SCHOENY RICHARD L	LTC	0-1011963	0763	1
SCHOETTLE JR JACOB F	2LT	0-1335700	0446	1
SCHOFFSTALL WAYNE	CPT	0-0219692	0347	1
SCHOFFSTOLL LOUIS E	LTC	0-1824924	1162	1
SCHOFIELD EVERETT H	CW4	W-2116195	0359	2
SCHOFIELD FLOYD O	CPT	0-0114942	0156	3
SCHOFIELD HERBERT M	COL	0-0210660	0648	3
SCHOFIELD JOHNC	MAJ	C-0293375	1048	1
SCHOFIELD LAWRENCE E	MAJ	0-0300439	1145	2
SCHOFIELD MORGAN G	LTC	0-1587605	0156	1
SCHOFIELD OSCAR	CPT	C-0331367	0745	2
SCHOFIELD THEODORE H	MAJ	0-0978170	0962	1
SCHOLEY THEODORE R	LTC	0-0238692	0462	3
SCHOLL CLYDE L	LTC	0-1944587	0562	1
SCHOLL DONALD F	CPT	0-1919170	1264	1
SCHOLL EARL S	2LT	0-1014860	1045	2
SCHOLL GEORGE A	LTC	0-1294540	1060	1
SCHOLL HAROLD I	WO1	W-2146274	C558	1
SCHOLL HENRY	2LT	0-0217219	1024	1
SCHOLL JAMES N	1LT	0-1014395	C846	2
SCHOLL JOHN A	CPT	0-0358382	0145	2
SCHOLL STANLEY F	LTC	0-0347738	0354	2
SCHOLLARD JOHN	1LT	0-0404981	0745	2
SCHOLLE JESS L	LTC	0-0315820	0564	1
SCHOLLER JOSEPH P	CPT	0-0322308	C645	2
SCHOLLIAN HAROLD F	MAJ	0-1316678	0864	3
SCHOLLMEYER KURT	1LT	0-1289149	1045	2
SCHOLLY WILLIAM C	MAJ	0-1336429	1164	1
SCHOLOM JACOB	CPT	0-1171750	0646	2
SCHOLTZ ERWIN V	LTC	0-1575694	1055	1
SCHOLTZ FRANK C	MAJ	C-0297317	C545	1
SCHOLTZ JULIUS R	LTC	0-0463600	1145	2
SCHOLZ HARVEY A	LTC	0-1994848	1060	1
SCHOLZ JOSEPH W	2LT	0-1312803	0346	2
SCHOLZ RUDOLPH J	COL	0-0167879	0656	3
SCHOLZE JACK J	CPT	0-1305486	0248	1
SCHOMBURG CARL F	MAJ	0-1582889	0760	1
SCHOMISCH RORERT C	MAJ	C-0464000	0347	1
SCHON HUBERT A	COL	0-0276627	0367	3
SCHCN RUTH	1LT	N-0775197	0945	1
SCHONE CARL G	COL	0-1573573	0963	1
SCHONFELD PAUL O	2LT	0-1003160	0445	2
SCHONFELD SEYMOUR A	CW2	RW-2108332	0560	1
SCHONFELD WILLIAM A	MAJ	0-169060C	0946	1
SCHONGAR GEORGE P	1LT	0-0423021	0545	2
SCHOOK ROBERT N	CW2	W-3250218	0466	1
SCHOOLER JR ERNEST	MAJ	0-2019655	0263	1
SCHOOLEY JESSE B	LTC	0-0422581	0261	1
SCHOOLFIELD HUGH M	LTC	0-1107106	0862	1
SCHOOLING JAMES F	LTC	0-0220325	1053	3
SCHOONCYKE RCRERT E	2LT	0-1328537	C845	2
SCHOONMAKER FRED T	1LT	0-0345538	0347	2
SCHOONOVER FRED E	CPT	0-130C864	0147	1
SCHOONOVER KENNETH E	MAJ	0-1112425	0361	1
SCHOPP ALVIN C	MAJ	0-0356511	0746	2
SCHOPPER WALTER P	COL	0-0508664	0863	2
SCHOR EDWARD P	LTC	0-0310416	1061	3
SCHORK CHRISTIAN	MAJ	C-0482545	0849	1
SCHORR HYMAN J	CPT	0-0517041	1145	2
SCHORSTEN EDWARD S	MAJ	0-2016036	0363	1
SCHOTT FRANK L	1LT	0-1040063	1144	2
SCHOTT NAOMI R	2LT	N-0723945	1044	1
SCHOTT ROYAL M	CW4	W-2202629	0867	3
SCHOTT STUART	CPT	0-0490716	0146	2
SCHOTTLAND STANLEY A	1LT	0-1315624	C745	2
SCHOUVALOFF PETER	LTC	0-0922661	1065	3
SCHOWALTER HERBERT P	COL	0-021C991	0953	3
SCHOWENGERDT WILLIAM	COL	C-0314849	0864	3
SCHRADE RALPH F	CW3	W-2150122	0463	1
SCHRADER CHARLES H	COL	0-0348211	0863	1
SCHRADER JOHN P	MAJ	0-0248635	1044	2
SCHRADER JULIUS J	MAJ	0-2208417	0466	1
SCHRADER LOWELL G	MAJ	0-0239567	1146	2
SCHRAEDER EDNA	CPT	N-0726899	1045	1
SCHRAGER ARTHUR U	LTC	0-0368623	0166	3
SCHRAM CHARLES R	COL	C-0349508	0558	3
SCHRAM JR CHARLES	1LT	0-1323034	0745	2
SCHRAMAR JOHN	1LT	0-1913578	0336	1
SCHRAMM ERIC	MAJ	C-1850063	1061	1
SCHRAMM MARVIN L	MAJ	0-1108992	0959	1
SCHRANCT CHARLES C	MAJ	0-0346437	0855	3
SCHRANK JOHN W	LTC	0-0354186	0867	3
SCHRANTZ GEORGE N	COL	C-0287238	0961	2
SCHRANZ FRANCIS M	1LT	0-1298604	0745	2
SCHRAVESANDE JOHN B	COL	0-0916433	0364	3
SCHRECK FRANCIS C	1LT	0-1308551	104N	2
SCHRECK ROBERT W	MAJ	0-1554CR5	0366	1
SCHREIBER RICHARD C	CW3	W-2141867	0861	1
SCHREIBER ROBERT E	2LT	0-0513548	0145	2
SCHREIBER WALTER R	CPT	0-0515152	1144	2
SCHREIBER WILLIAM A	COL	0-0358623	0864	1
SCHREIBSTEIN ROBERT	LTC	0-1644754	0964	1
SCHREINER CARL E	MAJ	0-1045591	1160	1
SCHREINER FRANK	MAJ	0-2016118	0467	1
SCHREINER GEORGE W	MAJ	0-2014716	0167	1
SCHREINER ORA C	LTC	0-0294281	1066	3
SCHREINER ROGER W	LTC	0-1598394	0667	1
SCHREINER WILLIAM J	LTC	0-0202351	0163	3
SCHREMF WILLIAM R	CPT	0-1173C67	1264	1
SCHREY JACK W	CPT	0-0351805	1045	2
SCHREYER MILTON M	MAJ	0-1297785	0361	1
SCHRICKER ROBERT L	1LT	0-1928819	1156	2
SCHRIPPF KENNETH A	MAJ	0-1050069	1162	1
SCHRODER CARLTON J	MAJ	0-0548194	0966	2
SCHRODER CHARLES	2LT	0-0328981	1041	2
SCHROEDER ALFRED J	LTC	0-0504313	0457	1
SCHROEDER CARL J	LTC	0-0225311	0360	3
SCHROEDER CLARENCE H	MAJ	C-1892458	0967	1
SCHROEDER CLEMONS C	2LT	0-1642556	0944	2
SCHROEDER CLCYDE P	LTC	0-0182898	0850	1
SCHROEDER DIETRICH	LTC	0-1591433	1063	3
SCHROEDER EARLE W	LTC	0-0303914	0562	1
SCHROEDER EDGAR A	CPT	0-1172645	C149	2
SCHROEDER EDGAR E	COL	0-0183128	1160	3
SCHROEDER EDWARD P	1LT	0-1326666	C346	1
SCHROEDER EDWIN E	MAJ	C-0102023	0156	3
SCHROEDER ERNEST J	MAJ	C-0423272	0246	2
SCHROEDER FREDERIC W	COL	0-0219333	0159	3
SCHROEDER GEORGE R	LTC	0-1046259	1064	1
SCHROEDER JAMES M	LTC	0-1338863	0766	1
SCHROEDER JULIUS T	MAJ	C-1930961	1066	1
SCHROEDER LESLIE L G	CPT	0-0221812	0764	3
SCHROEDER NORMAN C	LTC	0-0494871	C645	2
SCHROEDER RAYMOND H	COL	0-0231897	C356	3
SCHROEDER RICHARD J	2LT	0-0783635	C361	2
SCHROEDER ROBERT F	CW2	W-2142721	0157	1
SCHROEDER RUTH E	CPT	N-0773620	0449	1
SCHROEDER WALTER	LTC	0-025368C	1055	3
SCHROEDER WILFRED G	CPT	C-1319664	0647	1
SCHROEDER WILLIAM K	MAJ	C-0242674	1051	1
SCHROEER LORRAINE	1LT	N-0703097	C143	1
SCHROETER HERBERT F	CPT	0-1305487	0767	1
SCHROETER THOMAS I	LTC	0-0456194	0456	1
SCHROLL GERALD C	MAJ	C-1640929	0567	1
SCHROTH EDWARD W	MAJ	C-1922723	1167	1
SCHROYER GEORGE W	CW2	W-2131443	C348	1
SCHRYER LAWRENCE M	LTC	0-1580289	1162	1
SCHRYVER LEWIS A	CPT	0-0165526	0350	1
SCHUBERT CHARLES A	LTC	0-0270991	0858	1
SCHUBERT GEORGE E	LTC	0-0364531	0459	1
SCHUBERT HAROLD J	COL	C-0375822	0658	1
SCHUBERT JAMES A	LTC	0-0907498	0463	1
SCHUBERT JOSEPH R	2LT	0-1588871	0944	2
SCHUBERT PAUL W	COL	C-0314331	1062	2
SCHUBERT URIEL	CPT	0-1048573	1045	2
SCHUBERT WARREN F	COL	C-0387733	0963	1
SCHUBERT WOODROW H	LTC	C-1101209	0461	1
SCHUBKEGEL PAULINE	1LT	N-0783817	1046	2
SCHUBMEHL WILLIAM J	LTC	0-0299762	0960	2
SCHUCH ADAM F	LTC	0-0269293	0667	3
SCHUCHAT VICTOR E	2LT	0-1588273	0744	2
SCHUCK GEORGE E	LTC	0-0494987	0854	1
SCHUCK LAWRENCE A	1LT	0-1289326	1045	2
SCHUCK RALPH T	MAJ	C-2042840	1054	1
SCHUCKER HARRY R	MAJ	0-0109183	C744	1
SCHUE CHARLES S	CW3	W-2113744	C659	1
SCHUE EDWARD B	MAJ	0-1335065	C762	1
SCHUE LLOYD	CPT	0-0264316	0846	1
SCHUELLER JOHN P	2LT	0-1310507	0645	2
SCHUENEMAN HELEN L	1LT	N-0703852	0646	1
SCHUERMEYER CARLYLE	LTC	C-0281127	C365	3
SCHUETTE EARL R	LTC	0-1556943	C863	1
SCHUETTE ROBERT F	LTC	0-0178323	0660	3
SCHUETTNER RICHARD C	LTC	0-0290776	0467	3
SCHUETZ GORDON R	CW3	W-2147597	0863	1
SCHUETZ LILLIAN M	MAJ	N-0737416	C665	3
SCHUFF JR EUGENE J	COL	0-0276659	0466	3
SCHUGAR EMANUEL	LTC	0-0320854	C746	2
SCHUGG CARL V	1LT	0-0264120	0256	3
SCHUH MARION G	MAJ	N-0703828	1263	1
SCHUH WILLIAM P	MAJ	C-1321338	C957	2
SCHUHERT WILLIAM A	CPT	C-0977604	0261	1
SCHUL JOSEPH	MAJ	0-2012085	0263	1
SCHULD WALTER O	2LT	0-1177627	C744	2
SCHULENBERG DONALD F	LTC	0-0479286	0965	1
SCHULER LESTER W	MAJ	C-0235834	0861	3
SCHULER PAUL H	LTC	C-0378828	0660	1
SCHULHOFF JOSEPH	1LT	0-1175857	1145	2
SCHULKIN LESLIE M	2LT	0-1300433	C245	2
SCHULLER JOHN C	LTC	0-0291856	0467	3
SCHULMAN DANIEL R	1LT	0-1584865	C345	2
SCHULSTAD LAWRENCE M	LTC	0-0309339	C866	3
SCHULTE ARDEN C	CPT	0-0991592	0961	1
SCHULTE JESSE J	CW4	W-2142777	1264	1
SCHULTE JOHN H	CPT	0-1644756	0357	1
SCHULTE LOUIS C	COL	C-0100913	1053	3
SCHULTZ ALBERT V	CW3	W-2151860	0960	1
SCHULTZ ARCHIE D	1LT	0-1322088	C945	2
SCHULTZ CHRISTIAN	LTC	0-2042770	0757	1
SCHULTZ DALE L	MAJ	0-1798C68	1060	1
SCHULTZ DELBERT E	B G	0-0309296	0666	3
SCHULTZ EDWARD G	LTC	0-0221581	0755	3
SCHULTZ EDWARD J	LTC	0-0327619	1045	2
SCHULTZ FRANK B	LTC	0-0333503	0958	3
SCHULTZ FRANK R	MAJ	0-1055725	0460	1
SCHULTZ HARRY H	COL	0-0343384	0962	3
SCHULTZ HERMAN C	LTC	0-2262779	0867	2
SCHULTZ JAMES F	1LT	0-1288454	0445	2
SCHULTZ JAMES H	CPT	0-1924979	1063	1
SCHULTZ JOHN H	MAJ	0-1052558	0764	1
SCHULTZ JOHN M	LTC	0-0333189	0547	2
SCHULTZ JOHN M	CPT	0-1104390	0947	1
SCHULTZ JOSEPH F	LTC	0-2037C18	0762	1
SCHULTZ JR JOHN H	MAJ	0-0997293	0667	1
SCHULTZ LEONHARDT	CPT	0-1010057	0646	2
SCHULTZ LORRAINE A	MAJ	L-C704059	0765	2
SCHULTZ NATHAN	CW2	W-2152535	1C63	1
SCHULTZ ORVILLE W	1LT	0-1113430	0645	2
SCHULTZ OSCAR E	MAJ	0-0238072	1155	3
SCHULTZ PAUL F	2LT	0-1315376	1043	2
SCHULTZ PAUL H	LTC	0-1794996	1162	1
SCHULTZ ROBERT R	CPT	0-1293323	0147	2
SCHULTZ THOMAS P	CW3	W-2146275	1C63	1
SCHULTZ WALTER A	COL	0-0216955	0563	3
SCHULTZ WILLIAM C	CW2	W-2148684	1055	2
SCHULTZ WILLIAM F	CW3	W-2153361	0760	1
SCHULTZE BENJAMIN R	MAJ	0-1059631	0361	1
SCHULTZE MAX O	COL	0-0437754	0666	3
SCHULZ ARTHUR W	LTC	0-0153609	0452	3
SCHULZ CHARLES T	MAJ	0-0247015	1056	3
SCHULZ ELDER J	LTC	0-0438416	0767	1
SCHULZ GEORGE J	COL	0-0294340	0155	3
SCHULZ JAMES G	1LT	0-1598226	0147	1
SCHULZ JR WILLIAM J	CPT	0-1320658	1146	1
SCHULZ LYNN W	2LT	0-1290485	1144	2
SCHULZ MILTON J	LTC	0-0219527	0361	3
SCHULZ ROBERT P	M G	0-0330078	1065	3
SCHULZ VERNIE A	MAJ	0-2037768	0567	3
SCHULZE KENNETH C	WO1	W-3100719	0667	1
SCHULZE LUTHER W	LTC	0-0329613	0866	3
SCHULZE THEODORE L	CW2	W-2144557	1163	1
SCHUMACHER ADOLPH G	LTC	0-1590789	0366	3
SCHUMACHER ARTHUR B	LTC	0-0292510	1165	3
SCHUMACHER ARTHUR F	COL	C-0247786	0852	3
SCHUMACHER ARTHUR L	LTC	0-1289493	0762	1
SCHUMACHER B F	CPT	0-0169812	0159	3
SCHUMACHER CHARLES A	LTC	0-0256143	0363	3
SCHUMACHER CLAIR F	COL	0-0176631	0455	2
SCHUMACHER ERNST F	LTC	0-1317946	0962	1
SCHUMACHER FRED W	CW3	W-2146168	1160	1
SCHUMACHER HEARY A	MAJ	0-0170945	0757	3
SCHUMACHER IRWIN C	COL	0-0184311	1153	3
SCHUMACHER JOHN H	LTC	0-1105758	C165	1
SCHUMACHER LELAND L	LTC	0-1550048	0561	2
SCHUMACHER MELVIN M	MAJ	0-2024239	1160	1
SCHUMACHER WALTER L	LTC	0-0919998	0867	3
SCHUMACHER WILLIAM F	MAJ	0-1315455	0463	1
SCHUMACHER WILLIAM G	CW4	W-2002197	1163	3
SCHUMAKER FREDERICK	CPT	0-1917927	1264	2
SCHUMAN IRVING	COL	C-0329842	0567	3
SCHUMAN STANLEY	2LT	0-1294913	0344	2
SCHUMANN HARVEY H	LTC	0-0924273	0367	3
SCHUMANN ROLF A P	MAJ	0-1885626	1166	1
SCHUMANN WILLIAM F	1LT	0-1017625	0845	2
SCHUMMERS WILLIAM M	LTC	0-1001674	0566	1
SCHUNIOR GEORGE E	COL	0-0294918	0463	1
SCHUPP DONALD L	MAJ	0-1168070	1061	1
SCHUPPNER HARRY R	COL	0-0125468	1047	2
SCHURIG OTTO R	COL	0-0246936	0550	3
SCHURMAN ERICH P	1LT	0-0499493	0557	1
SCHURR EMILE H	CW4	W-2000434	0961	3
SCHURTZ JACK C	CPT	0-1044546	0662	1

NAME	GRADE	SVC NO	DATE RET MO YR	RET CODE
SCHUSSLER ECWARD	2LT	0-1595814	1044	2
SCHUSSLER EOWARD W	LTC	0-0419627	C760	2
SCHUSTER ARTHUR A	1LT	0-1325837	1045	2
SCHUSTER JAMES D	LTC	0-0131128	1048	3
SCHUSTER JOHN C	MAJ	0-0107997	1054	3
SCHUSTER JOSEPH A	1LT	0-0918794	0551	2
SCHUSTER MAYNARD B	1LT	0-1825191	1145	2
SCHUTT JR ERNEST C	MAJ	0-1052156	0361	1
SCHUTT LESTER F	LTC	0-1895255	0562	1
SCHUTTLER WALTER H	CPT	0-0973582	1060	1
SCHUTZ CHARLES O	MAJ	0-0389669	C446	1
SCHUTZE WALTER	LTC	0-0260899	0367	3
SCHUYLER GEORGE B	LTC	0-0193012	0458	3
SCHUYLER JAMES T	MAJ	0-0123248	C648	3
SCHUYLER JOHN J	COL	0-0377465	C265	1
SCHUYLER PHILIP	CPT	0-0290768	1044	2
SCHUYLER PHILIP G	CPT	0-1308768	C146	2
SCHWAB ARTHUR J	1LT	0-1307857	C945	2
SCHWAB DONALD K	1LT	0-1290315	1045	2
SCHWAB ERWIN N	MAJ	0-1052559	C962	1
SCHWAB FLORENCE C	CPT	N-0725836	0947	1
SCHWAB GEORGE P	CPT	C-0400720	C450	1
SCHWAB JR JOHN S	MAJ	0-1319344	0264	1
SCHWAB LOUIS	CPT	0-1745651	0947	1
SCHWABE ADOLPH R	1LT	0-0890411	0252	1
SCHWABE OTTC	2LT	0-1174136	0351	2
SCHWAEBLE ELSIE	MAJ	N-070022C	0946	1
SCHWAGER VINCENT V	1LT	0-1032600	0945	2
SCHWAGER WILLIAM P	CPT	0-1638462	C157	1
SCHWAIGER LUDWIG A	CW4	W-2108306	1154	1
SCHWALBACH PARK J	CPT	0-0534949	C848	1
SCHWALL ALFRED J	2LT	0-1060964	1044	2
SCHWALL REEDE L	MAJ	C-0453927	0758	1
SCHWALM ARTHUR W	1LT	0-0451178	0246	2
SCHWALM VIRGIE M	MAJ	N-0797765	C765	1
SCHWAMBERGER RALPH F	CPT	0-1295946	C546	2
SCHWANECK JOHN T	LTC	0-0325066	0246	2
SCHWANKE JAMES W	LTC	0-0258066	0465	3
SCHWARCZ GILBERT G	LTC	0-0284884	0162	3
SCHWARM ERNEST R	MAJ	C-0272766	0367	3
SCHWARTZ AARON	1LT	0-1574524	0944	2
SCHWARTZ ABNER B	CPT	0-1011661	1044	2
SCHWARTZ ALBERT F	2LT	0-1594458	1045	2
SCHWARTZ ANDREW J	LTC	0-0189682	0956	3
SCHWARTZ BENJAMIN	LTC	0-09C687C	0765	3
SCHWARTZ BYRON W	COL	0-0183844	1055	1
SCHWARTZ DAVID	2LT	C-1177628	C244	2
SCHWARTZ EDWARD	CPT	0-0316805	C845	2
SCHWARTZ EDWARD A	CW3	W-2148188	0262	1
SCHWARTZ ELMER L	CW3	W-2152519	C862	1
SCHWARTZ ELWOOD G	LTC	0-1042163	0157	1
SCHWARTZ EMANUEL	CPT	0-0540606	0446	2
SCHWARTZ FLOYD K	MAJ	C-1011473	1167	1
SCHWARTZ FRANCIS R	CW4	W-2136043	0661	1
SCHWARTZ GEORGE E	CW3	W-2150719	0267	1
SCHWARTZ GEORGE I	LTC	0-1303209	1262	1
SCHWARTZ GERALD D	1LT	0-1715610	0545	2
SCHWARTZ HARRY L	MAJ	C-1697685	0646	2
SCHWARTZ HERMAN J	LTC	0-1555132	0463	1
SCHWARTZ ISADORE R	LTC	0-0274499	0164	3
SCHWARTZ JEROME	1LT	0-1062287	0747	1
SCHWARTZ JOHN F	COL	0-0296471	1064	1
SCHWARTZ KENNETH C	COL	0-0239778	0465	3
SCHWARTZ LEO A	MAJ	0-0503778	1045	2
SCHWARTZ LOUIS	LTC	0-0344456	0363	3
SCHWARTZ MARCUS	COL	0-0240038	0663	3
SCHWARTZ MELVIN B	CPT	0-0390674	0246	2
SCHWARTZ MORRIS L	COL	0-0167009	1156	3
SCHWARTZ MORRIS S	COL	0-0185522	0358	3
SCHWARTZ NATHAN F	CPT	0-0503972	1145	2
SCHWARTZ ROBERT J	2LT	0-1294731	1044	2
SCHWARTZ ROBERT L	LTC	0-1308233	C666	1
SCHWARTZ ROBERT M	LTC	0-0401669	1160	1
SCHWARTZ SAMUEL Z	CPT	0-0381978	0663	1
SCHWARTZ SEYMOUR M	1LT	0-1303036	0745	2

NAME	GRADE	SVC NO	DATE RET MO YR	RET CODE
SCHWARTZ SR JOSEPH	MAJ	0-1113431	0959	1
SCHWARTZ STANLEY L	CPT	0-0484258	1147	2
SCHWARTZ THEODORE	CPT	0-0503443	0845	2
SCHWARTZ WILLAIM A	CPT	0-0474489	1045	2
SCHWARTZ WILLIAM A	CW3	W-2149459	1162	2
SCHWARTZ WILLIAM F	CW4	W-2115268	0359	1
SCHWARTZ WILLIAM W	MAJ	0-0988416	0965	1
SCHWARZ CHARLES E	CW3	W-2145508	0959	1
SCHWARZ HENRY F	LTC	0-1040810	1060	1
SCHWARZ JANOCN	CPT	0-0341343	0144	2
SCHWARZ JOHN H	COL	0-0319969	1059	3
SCHWARZE FREDERICK	LTC	0-0832254	C666	1
SCHWARZKOPF CONALD F	MAJ	0-0364181	1163	1
SCHWARZKOPF LEROY C	LTC	0-1337096	0966	1
SCHWARZMILLER R E	1LT	0-1312385	0246	1
SCHWECKE HUGH R	COL	0-0274636	1153	1
SCHWEDE WALTER A	CPT	0-0342966	0444	2
SCHWEDERSKY GEORGE H	COL	0-0285051	0457	3
SCHWEERS ROBERT J	CPT	0-1649604	0267	2
SCHWEICKART LOWELL G	COL	0-0264979	0267	3
SCHWEIKERT ALBERT C	MAJ	0-0404609	1163	1
SCHWEIKHARD FRED H	MAJ	0-0450796	0858	1
SCHWEINHART HARRY C	CPT	0-1290143	0746	1
SCHWEINLER FRANCIS F	B G	0-0279772	0966	3
SCHWEITZER CHARLES N	2LT	0-1032391	0345	2
SCHWEITZER ELMER	MAJ	0-1174703	0358	2
SCHWEITZER GEORGE C	CPT	0-1053348	0764	1
SCHWEITZER GEORGE M	CPT	0-1110799	0656	2
SCHWEITZER WILLIAM H	CW4	W-2111335	0255	1
SCHWEIZER ALEXANDRIA	MAJ	N-0725754	0862	1
SCHWEIZER HERMAN W	LTC	0-0311683	0765	3
SCHWENC GEORGE E	1LT	0-1174704	0246	2
SCHWENCINGER ROYAL O	MAJ	0-0386377	1046	2
SCHWENCEL FRANK R	B G	0-0175046	0653	3
SCHWENK HERMAN P O	MAJ	0-0179283	0650	3
SCHWENKA MEDRIC C	CW2	W-2150614	0660	1
SCHWENN GAYHART M	MAJ	C-1015862	0261	1
SCHWEPPE HENRY I	COL	0-0202666	0359	3
SCHWERIN WILLIAM E	LTC	0-0994929	0360	1
SCHWERIN WILLIAM F	MAJ	0-0233509	0454	3
SCHWIDCE JESSE T	CPT	0-0407253	0546	2
SCHWIEBERT EDWARD H	CPT	0-0332675	C446	2
SCHWIEC WILLIAM E	CPT	0-0471158	0548	1
SCHWIEGER DEKOVEN L	LTC	0-0307657	0665	3
SCHWIEKER PAUL B	COL	0-0324147	0861	1
SCHWING DORIS L	1LT	N-0770144	0847	1
SCHWINHART THOMAS J	LTC	0-0259946	0965	3
SCHWITZ FRED	2LT	0-1315625	0844	2
SCHWOERKE ORVILLE L	COL	0-0242205	0964	3
SCHWOLSKY HARRY	COL	0-0322770	0954	3
SCHWOYER ARTHUR J	1LT	0-1996442	0646	2
SCHWULST ROLAND C	MAJ	0-0509417	0260	2
SCIALLA DOMINIC A	1LT	0-1018894	0346	1
SCIALLY JOHN	LTC	0-0137887	0854	3
SCILLIAN OSCAR T	1LT	0-1590791	0162	2
SCIOTTI FRED	LTC	0-0257452	0246	2
SCIRE JAMES	CPT	0-2262996	0561	1
SCIULLE VINCENT F	CPT	0-0490810	0646	2
SCOBEE ELMER C	CW3	W-2148267	0457	1
SCOBEY JOSEPH W	COL	0-0203095	0255	2
SCOBIE JR FRANK G	CW3	W-2150327	1062	1
SCOBY CCNALD L	LTC	0-1293128	0561	1
SCOFIELD JOSEPHINE	2LT	N-0785530	0546	1
SCOFIELD KENDALL C	CPT	0-1697983	0246	1
SCOFIELD MARGARET M	1LT	N-073058C	1045	1
SCOFIELD RALPH G	MAJ	0-0923127	0946	2
SCOFIELD TIMOTHY C	CPT	0-0253638	0853	1
SCOFIELC VERNON	1LT	0-1557084	1045	2
SCOGGIN BERT L	MAJ	0-1590164	1263	1
SCOGGIN JAMES F	COL	0-0161315	0954	3
SCOGGIN JR WILLIAM G	CPT	0-1297961	0547	1
SCOGGIN WILLIAM C	COL	0-0241938	1159	1
SCOGGINS JR JAMES E	LTC	0-0426651	0557	1
SCOGGINS JR WILLIS L	MAJ	0-2295413	1066	1
SCOGGINS WALTER P	COL	0-027764C	0557	1

NAME	GRADE	SVC NO	DATE RET MO YR	RET CODE
SCOLES EARL E	MAJ	C-0957154	1165	1
SCOLES JR PAUL B	2LT	0-1304125	C853	1
SCOLLARD LLOYD T	CW4	W-2145658	1161	1
SCOLLARD PAUL T	LTC	0-0246873	0962	3
SCOLLON ROBERT B	CW2	W-2209183	0667	1
SCOLNIK AVERN B	LTC	0-0180658	1155	3
SCONYERS JOSEPH M	LTC	0-1290669	0863	1
SCOPEL FRANCIS E	LTC	0-0960035	1067	1
SCOPELLETI FRANK R	CW2	W-2145296	0557	1
SCOPELLITI PATSY J	CW3	W-2152809	1163	1
SCOPOLI MARIANO	CPT	0-2212007	0860	1
SCORDO LEO	MAJ	0-0404679	1046	2
SCOTHORNE WILFRED H	CPT	0-0255430	0854	3
SCOTT ALBA L	LTC	0-1313804	C562	1
SCOTT ALBERT E	1LT	0-1043490	C145	2
SCOTT ALBERT L	CPT	0-4058584	1063	2
SCOTT ALFRED E	1LT	0-1579087	0546	2
SCOTT ALLISON F	COL	0-0167998	0955	3
SCOTT ALVESTER	LTC	0-1301221	0166	1
SCOTT ARNOLD W	CW4	W-2000419	0260	1
SCOTT ARTHUR B	LTC	0-0226970	C360	3
SCOTT ARTHUR G	LTC	0-1597266	0763	1
SCOTT BEVERLY R	MAJ	0-1001229	1059	1
SCOTT BILLIE L	LTC	0-1059941	0266	1
SCOTT BIRDIE	CPT	0-0966758	0761	1
SCOTT BLANCHE L	MAJ	L-0303576	1265	1
SCOTT BRUCE F	CPT	0-2008083	0556	1
SCOTT BURT A	LTC	0-0346193	C866	3
SCOTT CARROLL E	LTC	0-0244661	0454	3
SCOTT CARSON R	CPT	0-1286715	1059	1
SCOTT CECIL H	LTC	0-1030715	0858	1
SCOTT CHARLES H	COL	0-0268200	0747	2
SCOTT CHARLES H	CW3	RW-2152985	C663	1
SCOTT CHARLES W	LTC	0-179807C	0667	1
SCOTT CHARLEY B	LTC	0-1287764	1054	1
SCOTT CHESTER F	CPT	0-1288630	0766	3
SCOTT CHRIS S	LTC	0-0265473	1061	1
SCOTT CLAIR	CPT	0-0246856	0745	1
SCOTT CLARENCE F	CPT	0-0492665	0847	1
SCOTT CLYDE O	LTC	0-0200921	0959	3
SCOTT CORNELIUS	CPT	0-1296100	0945	2
SCOTT DANIEL J	CW3	W-2117027	C261	1
SCOTT DAVID A	MAJ	0-0286175	C553	3
SCOTT DELMONT H	CW3	W-2152520	1065	1
SCOTT DONALD A	MAJ	C-132412C	C365	1
SCOTT EDWARD J	1LT	0-1043515	C545	2
SCOTT EDWARD M	CPT	0-0481243	C345	2
SCOTT ENOS P	COL	C-0188435	0353	3
SCOTT EUGENE W	CW2	W-2210153	0464	1
SCOTT EWING B	2LT	0-0501434	0144	2
SCOTT FRANK E	COL	C-0295626	0967	3
SCOTT FRANK W	LTC	0-0512311	0463	1
SCOTT GENEVIEVE	1LT	N-0744479	C446	1
SCOTT GEORGE C	2LT	0-0251326	C354	3
SCOTT GEORGE D	LTC	0-0306010	0663	3
SCOTT GEORGE J	COL	0-0320024	1062	3
SCOTT GEORGE J	CW2	W-2110174	0347	2
SCOTT GEORGE R	LTC	0-1286371	1062	1
SCOTT GEORGE W	MAJ	0-0226022	0564	3
SCOTT GEORGE W	LTC	0-0323424	C864	3
SCOTT GEORGE W	COL	0-1821922	0667	1
SCOTT GLENN W	MAJ	0-2000810	0263	1
SCOTT GORDON W	COL	0-0303546	0961	1
SCOTT HAL L	CW2	W-3430208	1265	2
SCOTT HARRY E	WO1	W-2127663	0450	1
SCOTT HARRY L	CW2	W-2151196	0859	2
SCOTT HARRY R	1LT	0-0491407	0651	1
SCOTT HELEN	1LT	N-C722972	C646	2
SCOTT HENRY B	LTC	0-0213984	0646	2
SCOTT HOWARD O	CPT	0-0887345	0147	1
SCOTT INMAN O	MAJ	C-1286372	0857	1
SCOTT IRA G	MAJ	0-1897716	0563	1
SCOTT IRVING J	MAJ	0-0508734	1153	2
SCOTT JAMES	CW3	W-2147903	0659	1
SCOTT JAMES A	COL	0-0301794	0460	1

NAME	GRADE	SVC NO	DATE RET MO YR	RET CODE
SCOTT JAMES P	MAJ	0-1686825	0566	1
SCOTT JESSE C	CW2	W-2150931	0161	1
SCOTT JESSE O	1LT	0-1288796	0545	2
SCOTT JOE H	CPT	0-0990610	1161	1
SCOTT JOHN B	1LT	0-0500400	0545	2
SCOTT JOHN E	COL	0-0247175	0854	3
SCOTT JOHN H	COL	0-0242287	1059	2
SCOTT JOHN W	LTC	0-0451416	1054	2
SCOTT JOHN W	LTC	0-1040085	1264	1
SCOTT JOHN W	MAJ	0-1844748	1164	1
SCOTT JOSEPH S	CPT	0-1320970	0264	2
SCOTT JR DANIEL J	CPT	0-1304957	1146	2
SCOTT JR DANIEL W	CPT	0-0472673	0145	2
SCOTT JR HARVEY J	CPT	0-0970512	1060	1
SCOTT JR JAMES P	CPT	0-0981441	1262	1
SCOTT JR JCE	CW3	W-2142413	0862	1
SCOTT JR JOHN T	MAJ	C-0251791	0146	2
SCOTT JR JOHN T	LTC	0-0384678	0164	1
SCOTT JR RICHARD P	CW3	W-2146048	0861	1
SCOTT JR THOMAS P	CPT	0-1036721	0147	2
SCOTT JUDSON R	COL	0-0301173	1160	1
SCOTT KELTON M	LTC	0-2037512	0964	1
SCOTT LANE T	MAJ	0-2041297	0863	1
SCOTT LAWRENCE R	MAJ	0-0956931	1166	2
SCOTT LEON	1LT	0-1019121	1045	2
SCOTT LEONARD E	MAJ	0-1294542	0961	1
SCOTT LESLIE B	MAJ	0-2262691	0961	1
SCOTT LEVERNE W	MAJ	0-1588278	0856	2
SCOTT LEWIS C	MAJ	0-0182184	0644	2
SCOTT MALCOLM F	CPT	0-1301041	0845	2
SCOTT MARION H	LTC	0-0522200	0464	1
SCOTT MILTON R	LTC	0-0222164	1062	3
SCOTT MINOT E	COL	0-0287087	0267	3
SCOTT MONROE A	MAJ	0-1894790	1157	1
SCOTT NORMAN	LTC	0-1105804	0862	1
SCOTT OKEY H	MAJ	0-1328938	C565	2
SCOTT OLIVER F	LTC	0-0230378	0751	3
SCOTT OLIVER J	1LT	0-1534139	0351	1
SCOTT ORVEL M	1LT	0-0235935	0944	1
SCOTT OTIS	CW2	W-2150255	0662	2
SCOTT OTIS T	COL	0-0179687	0346	1
SCOTT PATRICIA C	MAJ	N-0757856	0464	1
SCOTT PAUL A	MAJ	0-0953910	1262	1
SCOTT PAUL M	MAJ	0-1182248	0666	1
SCOTT PETER W	COL	0-0291958	0260	1
SCOTT PHALAS W	CW2	W-2110296	0348	1
SCOTT RALPH	2LT	0-1038837	0844	2
SCOTT RAY J	1LT	0-0929715	C844	2
SCOTT RAYMONC	MAJ	0-0977200	0363	1
SCOTT RAYMOND M	CPT	0-0218274	1057	3
SCOTT RAYMOND O	LTC	0-0284362	0364	3
SCOTT RAYMONC P	MAJ	0-2035980	0665	1
SCOTT RAYMONC R	MAJ	0-0981136	0563	1
SCOTT REID K	MAJ	0-0962241	0265	1
SCOTT REYNOLDS G	CPT	0-0903872	0545	2
SCOTT RICHARD L	1LT	0-0453891	0144	2
SCOTT RICHARD P	LTC	0-040865C	0761	1
SCOTT ROBBIE L	MAJ	N-0734993	1066	1
SCOTT ROBERT C	MAJ	0-0298923	0467	3
SCOTT ROBERT C	LTC	0-0296127	0759	1
SCOTT ROBERT C	CW3	W-2151685	0464	1
SCOTT ROBERT F	LTC	0-1292633	0766	1
SCOTT ROBERT L	2LT	0-1326667	0545	2
SCOTT ROBERT P	CPT	0-0420442	0745	2
SCOTT ROBERT R	WO1	W-2116300	0657	1
SCOTT ROBERT S	LTC	0-0432792	1167	1
SCOTT ROBERT W	COL	0-0313706	0263	1
SCOTT ROLLAND G	LTC	0-0228937	1057	1
SCOTT ROSS W	MAJ	0-0442711	1165	1
SCOTT ROY J	LTC	0-0440772	1049	1
SCOTT RUPERT W	MAJ	0-1300092	1057	1
SCOTT SR WILLIAM H	2LT	0-1557579	0645	2
SCOTT STANLEY L	CW4	W-2118525	0953	2
SCOTT STONEWALL	CW3	W-2148285	0163	1
SCOTT STUART W	CW2	W-2141675	0961	1

ARMY OF THE UNITED STATES RETIRED LIST

NAME	GRADE	SVC NO	DATE RET MO YR	RET CODE
SCOTT THOMAS J	LTC	0-0241235	0964	3
SCOTT VELDON M	CPT	0-0451179	0657	1
SCOTT VERNON M	LTC	0-0407156	0760	1
SCOTT VICTOR	LTC	0-1643316	0365	1
SCOTT VIVIAN N	COL	0-0178724	0958	3
SCOTT WALTER J	MAJ	0-1534858	0257	1
SCOTT WALTER L	CW3	W-2148764	0963	1
SCOTT WALTER M	COL	0-0170870	1152	3
SCOTT WALTER M	1LT	0-0222781	0256	3
SCOTT WESLEY W	LTC	0-1557085	0163	1
SCOTT WILBUR W	CW4	W-2143425	1065	1
SCOTT WILLIAM H	2LT	0-1597267	0445	2
SCOTT WILLIAM L	1LT	0-1297791	0945	2
SCOTT WILLIAM L	LTC	0-1338520	0267	1
SCOTT WILLIAM M	MAJ	0-0972311	0667	1
SCOTT WILLIAM R	CPT	0-2008366	0657	2
SCOTT WINFORD T	CW2	W-2206622	0763	1
SCOTT WOODSON D	COL	0-0227543	0859	3
SCOTT-SMITH QUENTIN	MAJ	0-1330230	0464	1
SCOTTI ELIO	LTC	0-1295282	0564	2
SCOTTI STEPHEN G	MAJ	0-1938655	0267	1
SCOVEL CHARLES E	MAJ	0-1324058	0355	1
SCOVILLE CHAUNCEY W	LTC	0-0196603	0262	3
SCOVILLE CLARENCE E	1LT	0-0408117	0345	1
SCOVILLE CURTISS W	LTC	0-0175940	0662	3
SCOVILLE DUANE J	MAJ	0-0966649	1061	1
SCRACHTEL MAURICE W	CPT	0-0537631	0246	2
SCRANAGE ROBERT R	CPT	0-0361070	0744	2
SCRANTON JOHN A	LTC	0-1317200	0467	1
SCRANTON WALTER A	CPT	0-1291178	0846	2
SCRIBNER ROBERT W	MAJ	0-0977682	1062	1
SCRINOPSKIE ROBERT M	2LT	0-1822637	0944	2
SCRIPTER DONALD L	CW2	W-2206375	1262	1
SCRIVNER JAMES	LTC	0-0141328	1055	3
SCROGHAM JOSEPH P	CPT	0-2019938	1059	1
SCROGHEM ALPHEUS M	LTC	0-0224449	0956	3
SCRUBY DELBERT K	COL	0-0164939	0249	3
SCRUGGS BAXTER S	LTC	0-0204182	0354	3
SCRUGGS CLINTON W	LTC	0-0390057	0660	1
SCRUGGS EDWARD P	LTC	0-0180169	0553	3
SCRUGGS ERNEST N	1LT	0-1045592	1045	2
SCRUGGS JAKE C	CW3	W-2148702	0261	1
SCRUGGS JOHN H	1LT	0-0219453	0164	3
SCRUGGS JR WILLIAM R	LTC	0-0376335	0765	1
SCRUGGS KATHRYN	MAJ	N-0732928	1062	1
SCRUGGS MALCOLM F	MAJ	0-1935891	1165	1
SCRUGHAM ETHELBERT	MAJ	0-0302644	0162	3
SCRUTON ROBERT A	LTC	0-1319142	0455	1
SCUDDER CHARLES P	MAJ	0-0253743	1045	2
SCUDDER ELMER F	COL	0-0330191	0264	3
SCUDDER HUGH G	CPT	0-0369781	0746	2
SCULL JR JOHN L	LTC	0-1165564	0266	1
SCULL ORVILLE E	LTC	0-0493543	1049	1
SCULL THOMAS R	CPT	0-1576626	1044	2
SCULLEY HAROLD F	MAJ	0-1302365	0361	1
SCULLY ERNEST W S	CPT	0-0496404	0246	2
SCULLY GRANT H	MAJ	0-0349696	1051	1
SCULLY HAROLD P	CW3	W-2144267	0960	1
SCULLY III JAMES W	LTC	0-0919320	1063	3
SCULLY JOHN J	2LT	0-2029320	1147	2
SCULLY JR EDWARD F	CW2	W-2148814	0567	1
SCULLY LEO L	1LT	0-1181119	0945	2
SCULLY RAYMOND E	LTC	0-1595820	0464	1
SCULLY RICHARD F	LTC	0-0418297	0361	1
SCULLY THOMAS G	1LT	0-1013819	0846	2
SCULLY WILLIAM A	LTC	0-0309909	0765	3
SCURR KENNETH R	COL	0-0179563	0156	3
SEABORN WALTER J	1LT	0-1314963	1046	2
SEABOURNE JOSIAH C	COL	0-0137662	0846	2
SEABRIDGE FREDERICK	LTC	0-0288406	0362	3
SEABRIGHT GLENN W	MAJ	0-0407532	1147	1
SEABROOK STERLING W	1LT	0-0533895	0346	2
SEABURG GENE H	MAJ	0-0957271	1065	1
SEABURY GORDON H	MAJ	0-0277882	0345	2
SEABURY JOHN C	LTC	0-1285648	0762	1
SEABURY ROLAND T	MAJ	0-0218216	0963	3
SEACORD CHARLES L	CPT	0-0445073	0645	2
SEAGER CHARLES W	MAJ	0-0218391	0564	3
SEAGER NORMAN	1LT	0-1107111	0646	2
SEAGLE GLADYS T	2LT	L-0302151	0644	2
SEAGO ERNEST W	CPT	0-0341010	0944	2
SEAGO WILNA J	LTC	0-0320268	0262	1
SEAGRAVE DANIEL W	LTC	0-1555285	0962	1
SEAGRAVE DAVID C	COL	0-0105046	0351	3
SEAGRAVE GERALD K	LTC	0-0453584	0860	1
SEAGRAVE RODMAN G	LTC	0-1554476	0662	1
SEAGRAVES WALTER R	MAJ	0-2035545	0261	1
SEAGROVES MAE	MAJ	N-0724554	0365	3
SEAHA BRUNO J	1LT	0-1292598	1045	1
SEAL S L	CW3	W-2146093	0864	1
SEALANDER MELVIN W	MAJ	0-1056544	0661	1
SEALE BRYAN P	MAJ	0-0576222	1058	1
SEALE ERNEST F	1LT	0-2017907	0651	1
SEALE JOHN C	LTC	0-1108999	0962	1
SEALE MAXWELL L	MAJ	0-2055523	0358	1
SEALE SR EDWIN L	CW3	RW-2148051	0762	1
SEALE SR THOMAS F	2LT	0-2052558	0246	2
SEALE WILLIAM A	1LT	0-1322593	0646	2
SEALES LOYT C	WO1	W-2149268	0953	1
SEALS JAMES D	2LT	0-1323358	0745	2
SEALS JAMES F	MAJ	0-0451393	0657	1
SEALS RAY D	MAJ	0-0927996	0965	1
SEALS RAY E	CPT	0-4074425	0965	2
SEAMAN CHARLES H	MAJ	0-1308715	1161	1
SEAMAN CLIFTON F	MAJ	0-2010507	0164	2
SEAMAN EDWARD W	1LT	0-0320915	1157	1
SEAMAN GEORGE A	LTC	0-1945485	0361	1
SEAMAN HENRY	LTC	0-0205962	0546	2
SEAMAN JOHN T	LTC	0-0194025	0662	3
SEAMAN PAUL M	CW2	W-2209220	1263	1
SEAMAN SR VICTOR B	WO1	W-2150135	0556	2
SEAMAN WAYNE R	1LT	0-0522632	0146	2
SEAMANDS GEORGE A	LTC	0-2044314	0557	1
SEAMANS JOHN F	MAJ	0-0354164	1045	2
SEARNO RAMON Y	1LT	0-2032115	0853	1
SEARCH WILLIAM C	CPT	0-1321957	0346	2
SEARCY DONALD M	1LT	0-1102590	0944	2
SEARCY JOSEPH W	LTC	0-1535524	0766	1
SEARCY JR RALFE C	COL	0-0359141	0163	1
SEARCY KENNETH F	LTC	0-0385633	1160	1
SEARCY LEE R	MAJ	0-2050634	0263	1
SEARIGHT GEORGE T	MAJ	0-2047818	1057	1
SEARIGHT WILLIAM H	2LT	0-1045913	1044	2
SEARL SHERBURN C	1LT	0-0447472	0746	1
SEARLE GERALD F	MAJ	0-2055175	0761	1
SEARLE HOWARD S	B G	0-0123165	0-51	3
SEARLE JOHN G	MAJ	0-1012390	0261	1
SEARLES DONALD E	LTC	0-1307471	0866	1
SEARLES JOHN W	LTC	0-0231609	0764	3
SEARLES SR STANLEY N	MAJ	0-2033324	0865	1
SEARLS CHESTER R	LTC	0-1300866	0866	1
SEARLS WELLINGTON	COL	0-0234322	0753	3
SEARS ARTHUR M	MAJ	0-1287074	0358	1
SEARS CECIL W	LTC	0-1174567	0263	1
SEARS DAVID M	2LT	0-1540765	0246	2
SEARS DEMAS L	COL	0-0160472	0254	3
SEARS DONALD R	LTC	0-1553355	0164	1
SEARS EDWARD W	COL	0-0171330	0551	3
SEARS EUGENE F	CW3	W-2150112	0165	2
SEARS GEORGE W	LTC	0-0278300	1160	2
SEARS JAMES E	CW3	W-2208374	0867	1
SEARS JR JOSEPH H	LTC	0-1181122	0762	1
SEARS JR THOMAS P	MAJ	0-1172646	0561	1
SEARS JULIAN A	MAJ	0-1332320	0463	1
SEARS MILLICENT	MAJ	L-1010498	0866	1
SEARS RICHARD E	MAJ	0-0991239	0364	1
SEARS RICHARD L	1LT	0-2262110	0359	1
SEARS RICHARD M	CPT	0-1554633	0261	1
SEARS ROY C	1LT	0-0257759	1166	3
SEARS SAMUEL	LTC	0-0264330	1055	3
SEARS THURMAN E	CPT	0-0399854	1045	2
SEARS WILLIAM B	LTC	0-0423173	0763	1
SEARS WILLIAM G	MAJ	0-0331227	1046	1
SEARS WILLIAM H	1LT	0-1320782	0447	2
SEARSON REX L	MAJ	0-1341588	0666	1
SEASE ELBERTA W	MAJ	N-0726895	0864	1
SEASE GEORGE A	LTC	0-0312289	0361	1
SEASHOLES HENRY C	LTC	0-0203462	1060	3
SEASTRAND CONRAD M	1LT	0-1015554	0161	2
SEATON JOHN A	1LT	0-0918762	0844	2
SEATON THOMAS W	CW2	W-2154671	0657	2
SEATON VICTOR T	LTC	0-1796163	0461	1
SEATVET JOHN	LTC	0-0437665	0554	1
SEAVER ROBERT S	COL	0-0330966	0765	1
SEAVEY CALVIN C	COL	0-0129701	0458	3
SEAVEY EDGAR S	MAJ	0-1030612	0559	1
SEAVEY HAROLD V	CPT	0-1314066	0859	1
SEAVEY POWELL J	CW2	W-2148335	1059	1
SEAVEY REX W	LTC	0-1289152	0454	1
SEAVY LOUIS M	LTC	0-0903944	1167	3
SEAWELL COLUMBUS J	MAJ	0-1055454	0747	2
SEAWELL VERGIL L	LTC	0-1549088	0663	1
SEAWELL WALTER	LTC	0-0471714	0366	3
SEAWELL WILLIAM A	MAJ	0-0259331	0345	2
SEAWELL WILLIAM A	2LT	0-1324442	0145	2
SEAWRIGHT PATRICK E	M G	0-0277902	0957	3
SEAY ALBERT E	1LT	0-1303392	0346	2
SEAY DANIEL F	1LT	0-1169329	0444	2
SEAY EMBREY W	LTC	0-1166176	0761	1
SEAY FURMAN R	CW3	W-2151349	1063	1
SEAY RICHARD R	1LT	0-0765108	0945	2
SEAY ROGER	CW3	W-2152839	0966	1
SEBASTIAN EDDIE G	1LT	0-1897003	1157	1
SEBASTIAN HARRY M	LTC	0-0481709	0854	1
SEBOLD GEORGE	CW4	W-2136623	1064	1
SEBOURN ALBERT C	MAJ	0-1181123	0555	1
SEBOURN JAMES	CPT	0-0492204	0945	2
SEBRING HARRY D	2LT	0-2000139	1050	1
SEBRING HARVEY D	1LT	0-2018226	0647	2
SECHREST THOMAS P	CPT	0-2037513	0956	2
SECHRIST DAVID C	CPT	0-2001686	1051	1
SECHRIST LEROY E	CPT	0-0283613	0452	1
SECHRIST WILLIAM R	MAJ	0-2021416	1161	1
SECK HARRY F	LTC	0-1636627	0956	1
SECKINGER GEORGE M	LTC	0-0308541	1060	1
SECOR ERNEST R	CPT	0-4031110	0167	1
SECOR RICHARD W	LTC	0-0408926	0361	1
SECOR WILLIAM H	LTC	0-1795982	0557	1
SECREST HORACE G	MAJ	0-0226846	0748	3
SECREST JR HORACE G	MAJ	0-0974679	0464	1
SECRIST ESTHER D	1LT	N-0704000	0745	2
SEDA DELYLE L	LTC	0-1031678	0966	1
SEDDON FRANK	MAJ	0-0370432	0246	2
SEDDON JR ARTHUR J	CPT	0-1597074	0159	1
SEDDON WILLIAM A	LTC	0-0230623	0663	3
SEDGWICK ALEXANDER	COL	0-0188448	0259	1
SEDGWICK HARRY K	CPT	0-0408106	1046	2
SEDGWICK WALTER E	LTC	0-0476037	0457	1
SEDILLO JUAN A A	COL	0-0224107	0362	3
SEDILLO RUFINO R	COL	0-0334777	1053	1
SEDLACEK LEO B	COL	0-0257063	0756	3
SEDLAK ANTHONY T	LTC	0-0348342	0157	1
SEDLAK MARY R	MAJ	L-0506791	1163	1
SEDMAK MICHAEL P	CPT	0-1306156	0947	2
SEDOLA PHYLLIS W	2LT	N-0723117	0444	1
SEDWICK JACK O	MAJ	0-0356304	0346	2
SEE DANIEL M	2LT	0-1182249	0345	2
SEE HENRY S	LTC	0-0244311	0245	2
SEE LEROY	CW3	W-2142778	0859	1
SEE MACK	CW2	W-2148443	0757	1
SEE MAXWELL W	LTC	0-1645354	1163	1
SEE WILLIAM T	LTC	0-0323531	0260	1
SEEBER JOHN A	MAJ	0-1043491	0258	1
SEEDORF HERBERT G	1LT	0-1314400	1045	1
SEEFOS ERNEST E	CW3	W-2153269	0762	1
SEEFELD WILLIAM F	1LT	0-1307579	0146	2
SEEGAR EARLIE B	MAJ	0-0981483	0663	1
SEEGER GEORGE H	LTC	0-1542236	0167	1
SEEGERT NEAL	CPT	0-0423517	1045	2
SEEKER MAX D	MAJ	0-1165788	0860	1
SEEKINS WINFIELD T	LTC	0-1018059	0867	1
SEELAND ELIAS	LTC	0-0285842	0566	3
SEELER JR ALFRED J	CW2	RW-2147276	0762	1
SEELEY DOUGLAS C	MAJ	0-0311488	1067	3
SEELEY ELWOOD W	MAJ	0-0350327	0246	2
SEELEY GEORGE E	MAJ	0-0379356	0444	2
SEELEY HARLAN A	2LT	0-2010584	0957	1
SEELEY JR ALLAN H	1LT	0-1641779	0149	2
SEELEY THOMAS C	MAJ	0-0239965	1263	3
SEELY DAVID F	MAJ	0-2037861	0562	1
SEELY GEORGE M	CW3	W-2152865	0862	1
SEELY LAWRENCE R	COL	0-0385051	0561	1
SEELY MITT	MAJ	0-0502154	1048	1
SEELY ROGER G	LTC	0-0281842	0867	3
SEELYE RICHARD M	MAJ	0-4009979	0667	1
SEELYE WALTER B	CPT	0-1702431	0645	2
SEEM DONALD L	LTC	0-1342304	0966	1
SEEMAN MARVIN P	CW2	RW-2150897	0464	1
SEEMANN JULIUS A	MAJ	0-0486819	0347	2
SEEMEYER ROGER F	MAJ	0-2038032	0264	1
SEENEY CALTON E	CW3	W-2203660	0165	1
SEERY JAMES L	LTC	0-1315734	0261	1
SEES JOHN C	LTC	0-1579090	1263	1
SEESHOLTZ RAMON C	MAJ	0-1590168	0461	1
SEEWER RAY H	CPT	0-1118285	0957	1
SEEWER TRUMAN A	CW2	W-2144128	0559	1
SEFCAK EDWARD J	MAJ	0-1555895	0760	1
SEFCIK DEL F	1LT	N-0737854	0346	1
SEFCIK EDWARD F	CPT	0-0386763	1045	2
SEFCIK STEPHEN P	1LT	0-1284586	0744	1
SEFF BERNARD	CPT	0-0488876	1044	2
SEFTON BINGER H	MAJ	0-0268121	0656	3
SEFTON HARRY B	LTC	0-0282149	0264	3
SEGAL JEROME M	1LT	0-1299799	0146	2
SEGAL MOREY M	MAJ	0-0509525	0746	1
SEGALL LOUIS	LTC	0-0120101	0747	1
SEGARS JAMES J	1LT	0-0294464	0146	1
SEGEL PAUL	LTC	0-0319668	0167	3
SEGERSTROM HAROLD A	MAJ	0-0378325	0245	2
SEGERSTROM HENRY T	CPT	0-0547000	0647	1
SEGESKY MIKE	CPT	0-1181819	0660	1
SEGNA FRANCIS R	CPT	0-0515779	0450	1
SEGUIN MARCEL G	CW3	W-2205232	0666	1
SEGUIRANT REGINALD M	MAJ	0-0965454	0762	1
SEGUR GERALD H	MAJ	0-0114951	1058	1
SEHRING GEORGE H	CPT	0-0510156	0346	2
SEHRT VERNON R	MAJ	0-1289574	0446	1
SEIB VINCENT J	COL	0-0277038	0963	3
SEIBEL JOHN J	LTC	0-0439477	1150	1
SEIBEL ROBERT H	MAJ	0-1877046	1065	1
SEIBERT EUGENE R	LTC	0-0400621	0367	1
SEIBERT JR WALTER E	1LT	0-1318252	1045	2
SEIBOLD CHARLES A	LTC	0-1002122	1162	1
SEIBT ALVIN H	LTC	0-0444628	0256	1
SEIDEL CARL L	LTC	0-1045248	0962	1
SEIDEL OTTO K	COL	0-0133756	0353	3
SEIDEL RICHARD H	MAJ	0-1825933	1164	1
SEIDEL ROBERT D	CW3	W-2150147	0461	1
SEIDEL RUSSELL Z	LTC	0-1534621	1167	1
SEIDELMANN HERBERT W	CPT	0-1111359	0347	2
SEIDENER ROBERT S	COL	0-0303407	0467	3
SEIDENFELD BERNICE D	1LT	N-0772155	1045	1
SEIDENFELD MORTON A	COL	0-0246681	1066	3
SEIDENGLANZ CHARLES	LTC	0-0238416	1265	3
SEIDENGLANZ LEONARD	COL	0-0919082	1065	3
SEIDENZAHL AUGUST T	COL	0-0330561	1262	3
SEIDL AUGUSTINE	CW4	W-2002716	0567	1
SEIDL PETER J	1LT	0-1053804	1045	2
SEIDLER FRANK B	MAJ	0-0971802	0563	1
SEIDMAN JACOB S	WO1	W-2149802	1154	1

NAME	GRADE	SVC NO	DATE RET MO YR	RET CODE
SEIDMAN JOSHUA I	CPT	0-0503977	1045	2
SEIDNER NORBERT W	LTC	0-0463020	0954	1
SEIFARTH CHARLES K	LTC	0-1692622	0861	2
SEIFARTH VIRGINIA M	1LT	N-0767128	1045	1
SEIFERLEIN A L	CPT	0-0301352	C845	2
SEIFERT ANN P	1LT	N-0722844	0546	2
SEIFERTH SOLIS	MAJ	0-0123254	0255	3
SEIFFERLEIN HILMER F	CPT	0-1554478	0446	2
SEIFFERT FRANK H	MAJ	C-1683432	0255	1
SEIFRIED JOHN D	CPT	0-1015097	0346	2
SEIFRIED WALTER G	CPT	0-1284032	1146	2
SEIGEL BURTON H	WO1	W-2120030	1047	1
SEIGNEUR WILLIAM R	MAJ	0-0976998	0264	2
SEIL NOLAND B	CPT	0-0117362	1054	3
SEILER DONALD J	LTC	0-1323359	1163	1
SEILER FRANK B	LTC	0-0321972	C667	1
SEILER GEORGE B	COL	0-0276853	C358	3
SEILING JOHN M	1LT	0-1301695	C545	2
SEILLER EDWARD F	LTC	0-0183886	0857	3
SEINO JAMES W	MAJ	0-1922652	C465	1
SEIP WILLIAM H	CPT	0-0981817	0960	1
SEIPEL ALOYSIUS	LTC	C-0465577	1049	1
SEIPT DEWEY F	MAJ	0-0480852	1148	1
SEITELBACH LEO	CW3	W-2150865	1165	1
SEITNER ROBERT L	COL	0-0127486	0255	3
SEITZ ALFRED G	COL	0-0324662	C665	3
SEITZ CHARLES R	MAJ	C-0253745	0153	3
SEITZ FRANK C	COL	0-0214945	0957	1
SEITZ JOE	1LT	0-1644068	0556	1
SEITZ JR GEORGE H	COL	C-0236275	C266	3
SEITZ JR WILLIAM H	LTC	0-0358442	C160	1
SEITZ LEONARD F	LTC	0-1175307	C462	1
SEITZER PAUL W	MAJ	C-1549091	C861	1
SEITZINGER EDWARD F	2LT	0-0507660	0944	2
SEITZINGER JOHN R	MAJ	C-1686714	0767	1
SEIX ERNEST J	CW3	W-2143553	0161	1
SEKAN EDWARD J	LTC	0-0423876	1057	1
SEKOWSKI BENJAMIN J	LTC	0-0480018	0162	1
SEKULIC PHIL M	CPT	0-1553358	0358	1
SEKULOVICH MILO	1LT	0-1327187	C546	2
SELANDER GEORGE W	CW2	W-2143963	0361	2
SELBY CHARLES A	COL	C-0332854	1067	3
SELBY EDWIN D	COL	0-0430193	0163	1
SELBY ORVAL C	LTC	0-0127887	C848	3
SELDEN JOSEPH H	LTC	0-0420230	0763	1
SELDEN METELLUS D	LTC	C-0341647	0765	3
SELDEN WILLARD W	MAJ	C-0280161	1065	3
SELDNER MAC E	LTC	0-1181124	C866	1
SELENSKI LEONARD S	2LT	C-1640934	1144	2
SELF CHARLES B	LTC	0-0378987	C853	1
SELF CHARLES M	MAJ	C-2021183	0764	1
SELF CHARLIE E	CW2	W-2108565	0758	1
SELF COYE R	LTC	0-2005480	0766	1
SELF DAN J	CW3	W-2144855	0460	1
SELF ELBERT E	LTC	0-1305846	0361	1
SELF JAY D	CW3	W-2144502	1162	1
SELF JOSIE	1LT	N-0702546	0444	1
SELF RICHARD B	LTC	0-1012363	0760	1
SELF ROY M	CW2	W-2143403	0755	1
SELFE HILBERT A	CPT	0-0218838	1058	3
SELIG SETH J	CW2	W-2214940	0766	1
SELISKAR CARL E	1LT	0-1059634	1145	2
SELK HAROLD F	MAJ	0-1542851	1157	1
SELKIRK WYATT D	COL	0-0149168	0648	3
SELL ALLEN M	CPT	0-0288460	0454	3
SELL ESTHER G	1LT	N-0775833	0746	1
SELL FREDERICK	1LT	0-0476886	1144	2
SELL GUY S	CPT	0-0261647	0667	3
SELL HOWARD L	CPT	0-1553905	1146	2
SELL RAY H	1LT	0-2007360	0350	1
SELLAND GLENNIS P	MAJ	C-1326931	0366	1
SELLAROS H CRADY	MAJ	0-0217355	0257	3
SELLAROS JR DAVID F	COL	0-0171206	1061	3
SELLARS JR RICHARD C	1LT	0-1040468	C643	2
SELLARS RALPH N	MAJ	0-1937977	0267	1

NAME	GRADE	SVC NO	DATE RET MO YR	RET CODE
SELLE FRED A	LTC	0-0740569	0763	1
SELLECK CLYDE F	LTC	0-1015896	0367	3
SELLECK HAROLD B	1LT	0-1309419	0745	2
SELLEK LEROY W	LTC	0-1641782	0662	1
SELLER PAUL J	MAJ	0-0105299	0650	3
SELLERS ALBERT R	LTC	0-1100326	0266	3
SELLERS CLYDE C	LTC	0-0378889	0757	1
SELLERS EMMETT L	MAJ	0-1917735	1163	1
SELLERS FREDERICK	MAJ	0-0211716	1163	3
SELLERS GEORGE J	CPT	0-1917893	0254	2
SELLERS HERBERT P	LTC	0-0239230	0363	3
SELLERS JOHN M	MAJ	0-0207868	0453	1
SELLERS JR WILLIAM L	CPT	0-1683024	1144	2
SELLERS NORMAN G	MAJ	0-0964102	1265	1
SELLERS PHILIP A	CW2	W-2150210	0259	1
SELLERS ROBERT L	MAJ	0-1304126	1160	1
SELLERS ROSCOE A	MAJ	0-0890316	0757	1
SELLERS THOMAS E	MAJ	0-1599065	1063	1
SELLERS WILBUR R	MAJ	0-2212017	0564	1
SELLERS WILFRED J	LTC	0-0404285	0464	1
SELLERS WILLIAM Z	MAJ	0-0321878	0661	1
SELLETT LEONARD V	CPT	0-0496290	1145	2
SELLEW ROLAND W	COL	0-0186566	1055	3
SELLIN JACK C	MAJ	C-1825778	C464	1
SELLING HOLGER C	MAJ	0-0184084	0557	3
SELLINGER CECIL T	COL	0-0447596	1262	3
SELLS JACK O	CPT	0-1013747	0361	1
SELMAN JOSEPH R	LTC	0-1642570	0565	1
SELNAU FREDERICK	CW2	W-2153187	1162	1
SELOGIE LOUIS A	CPT	0-1995336	0347	2
SELSEMEYER JOHN	LTC	0-0200089	0849	3
SELTZ ROLAND L	1LT	0-1105809	0345	2
SELTZER EUGENE P	COL	0-0143927	1056	3
SELTZER MAURICE	MAJ	0-0231307	0661	3
SELTZER RAYMOND E	MAJ	0-0394646	0247	2
SELVIDCE KENNETH W	CPT	0-0360190	0145	2
SELVIG KERMIT H	MAJ	0-1296270	0361	1
SELWYN GEORGE V	COL	0-0350926	1263	3
SEMANCIK MICHAEL A	MAJ	0-1016989	0963	1
SEMANS WILLIAM O	LTC	0-0169277	0652	3
SEMBRA NICK	CW3	W-2141791	1157	1
SEMEGA BERNARD P	MAJ	0-1303041	0457	1
SEMEL MAX	1LT	0-1307087	0645	2
SEMELMAKER MORTON	LTC	0-1019109	0163	1
SEMENOFF PETER	LTC	0-1285321	0957	1
SEMENOGG WALTER	LTC	0-1285834	1057	1
SEMKEN GEVERT	1LT	0-0277855	0860	3
SEMKEN HOMER L	MAJ	0-2029424	0662	1
SEMLEK ROBERT	MAJ	0-0452571	0163	1
SEMLER ADOLPH	CPT	0-0178633	0239	1
SEMLER ALBERT E	LTC	0-0302245	C261	1
SEMLER ROBERT K	2LT	0-0982559	1051	1
SEMMENS RICHARD T	LTC	0-1581363	0762	1
SEMMES BUFORD R A	LTC	0-1038283	0167	1
SEMMES GEORGE W	COL	0-0210229	0249	3
SEMMES JR HARRY H	1LT	0-1013698	0945	2
SEMOFF MILTON C F	1LT	0-0357688	1142	2
SEMON JOHN A	CPT	0-1036019	0662	1
SEMON NORMAN N	MAJ	0-2208463	0167	1
SEMPLE WILLIAM R	COL	0-0266649	0461	3
SEMROW RUSSELL P	WO1	W-2128195	0950	1
SEMSKER ALBERT	LTC	0-0906573	0862	3
SEMSTEAD ALLAN R	MAJ	0-1181125	0855	1
SEMUTA MICHAEL	CW3	W-2129953	1154	1
SEN JOHN J	LTC	0-1331598	1266	1
SENCY LOUIS F	CPT	0-1284947	0862	1
SENDERS JOHN A	MAJ	0-0447131	0657	1
SENDROFF DAVID	1LT	0-0537138	1146	1
SENECAL FRANCIS G	1LT	0-1945274	104N	2
SENERCTE LEONARD A	CPT	0-1306157	1158	1
SENEY RCOGER E	2LT	0-1315868	1144	2
SENFF HENRY W	MAJ	0-0308377	0145	2
SENFT CRAIG T	CPT	0-1326114	1146	2
SENG OLA H	2LT	N-0729120	0944	1
SENGER JOSEPH W	LTC	0-1312054	1060	1

NAME	GRADE	SVC NO	DATE RET MO YR	RET CODE
SENCPIEHL ARTHUR P	LTC	0-0311825	0160	3
SENIC GEORGE	1LT	0-1288310	0744	1
SENIK JOSEPH	2LT	0-1550499	C145	2
SENIOR LEO V	CW3	W-2147934	1061	1
SENIOR SOLOMON E	COL	0-0266079	1063	3
SENKER RICHARD E	CW4	W-2152616	0866	1
SENKEWICH WILLIAM	CW2	W-2147209	0457	1
SENKO JOSEPH M	LTC	0-1306481	0461	1
SENN HANS	1LT	0-1174706	0549	1
SENN JACQUES L	2LT	0-1303393	1144	2
SENN JR EDWARD L	1LT	0-0194754	1056	3
SENN NORMAN H	CPT	0-0478510	0360	1
SENNE ARTHUR M	LTC	0-0312823	1046	2
SENNE WALTER W	MAJ	C-1593259	1160	1
SENOWSKI JOHN R	1LT	0-0922357	1143	2
SENSE GEORGE A	LTC	0-0323095	0661	1
SENSENBACH ELMER E	LTC	0-0682398	0966	1
SENSOR EARL C	CPT	0-0251591	0257	3
SENTELL JOHN E	LTC	0-0151026	0145	2
SENTGERATH GEORGE J	CW3	W-2147981	0464	1
SENTI GENE C	MAJ	0-2055187	0161	1
SENZ FRANCIS J	MAJ	0-0934557	C361	1
SEPULVEDA EUGENIO E	CW3	W-2147649	C963	1
SEPULVEDA JR JOSE	CW2	W-2209226	1060	1
SERAFIN THADDEUS P	2LT	0-1307758	0762	1
SERAFINI FRANCIS H	LTC	0-1825192	C661	1
SERAFINI LOUIS	CPT	0-1060290	0448	2
SERAFINI LOUIS J	2LT	0-1061857	1145	2
SERBENSKI JOSEPH J	CPT	0-4009200	0366	1
SERBOUSEK EMIL E	LTC	0-0495424	0554	1
SERBY JESSE L	CPT	0-0487298	0345	1
SERDA JOSEPH E	1LT	0-1321958	1045	2
SERENA JOSEPH R	LTC	C-0314540	0761	1
SERETAN MORRIS A	1LT	0-1302714	C446	2
SERFAS LELAND E	CW3	W-2141741	1057	1
SERFASS HARRY A	LTC	0-0246755	1046	2
SERFIN ADOLPH T	LTC	0-0435618	0164	1
SERGIO JAMES J	LTC	0-0407562	1060	1
SERGIO LOUIS S	CPT	0-1302208	1046	1
SERLES ROBERT T	LTC	0-1648487	0263	1
SEROKA GEORGE	MAJ	0-1919498	1265	1
SEROLA MICHAEL M	CW2	W-2141940	0161	1
SERPA JAMES O	WO1	W-2144531	0353	2
SERTICH JOHN	1LT	0-2044297	0553	1
SERVICE ALBERT	1LT	0-1822063	1044	2
SERVIN DONALD K	CPT	0-1321555	0646	2
SERVIS CLYDE E	MAJ	0-0337954	0954	1
SERYAK FRANK W	LTC	0-0382830	0665	3
SESE GERVASIO G	MAJ	0-1324812	1162	1
SESINGER ESTHER A	MAJ	N-0752517	0164	1
SESINGER HAROLD B	MAJ	C-1014716	0761	1
SESIT MYRON F	LTC	0-0348352	0965	3
SESLOWE HYMAN	LTC	0-0329938	C766	3
SESNA GERALD T	2LT	0-1080148	0643	2
SESSA CARL L	CPT	0-0429547	0245	2
SESSION ALBERT S	1LT	0-4034363	0259	2
SESSIONS ALVIN	COL	0-0165560	0250	3
SESSIONS EDGAR H	MAJ	C-1321341	1157	1
SESSIONS JAMES L	CPT	0-0239311	1265	3
SESSIONS JAMES R	LTC	0-1309852	0366	1
SESSIONS JR WILL A	LTC	0-0323727	C865	3
SESSIONS LEWIS B	CPT	0-2033992	0263	1
SESSIONS THADDEUS J	CPT	0-0419104	0945	2
SESSIONS THOMAS M	COL	C-0291592	1059	2
SESSOMS JAMES C	CPT	0-0490902	0350	1
SESTRIC MICHAEL S	LTC	0-1824089	C866	1
SETARO JOHN G	LTC	0-1590797	0964	1
SETH GEORGE L	COL	0-0205971	0846	2
SETH RICHARD G	CPT	0-1826335	0455	2
SETHER HOWARD B	CPT	0-1059635	0646	2
SETSER HORACE L	CW2	W-2149716	1057	1
SETTANNI MICHAEL O	1LT	0-1306158	1044	1
SETTLE HERBERT B	LTC	0-2038088	1266	3
SETTLE LYLE L	MAJ	0-0382812	0762	1
SETTLE WALTER R	MAJ	0-1692528	0862	1

NAME	GRADE	SVC NO	DATE RET MO YR	RET CODE
SETTLES HENRY D	LTC	0-0382480	0757	1
SETTLES RALPH H	CPT	0-0910148	0945	2
SETZE TOM B	LTC	0-1577826	1161	1
SETZER JAMES L	1LT	0-2204975	0453	1
SETZER SHELTON R	2LT	0-1795824	0544	2
SETZER WORTH A	LTC	0-0289846	1158	3
SETZKE MAX A	MAJ	0-0409310	0959	1
SEUFERT JAMES R	MAJ	0-1114744	0566	1
SEVALL JR JOSEPH R	LTC	0-1016469	0962	1
SEVCHUK WILLIAM	1LT	0-1289975	0254	1
SEVENER BERNARD C	LTC	0-1107113	0366	3
SEVENER CLINTON J	CPT	0-0300764	0943	1
SEVER JOSEPHINE	LTC	N-0759618	0463	1
SEVERANCE GUY C	MAJ	0-1639625	0657	1
SEVERANCE MYRTLE	MAJ	L-0117418	0963	1
SEVERE LILLIAN M	MAJ	N-0724077	C361	1
SEVERINI CAMILLO G	CW3	W-2148618	0763	1
SEVERSON GERTRUDE B	2LT	N-0761364	1044	1
SEVERSON HARVEY H	LTC	0-0306054	0163	1
SEVERSON STANLEY B	2LT	0-1114745	0844	2
SEVERSON THOMAS B	MAJ	0-1019490	0960	1
SEVIER GEORGE B	CW2	W-2209734	0263	1
SEVIER JAMES H	LTC	0-0287516	0260	3
SEVIER JOHN C	WO1	W-2125150	1046	2
SEVY VERNON K	COL	0-0155883	0954	1
SEWALL THOMAS K	CPT	0-0350742	0545	2
SEWARD JR ROYAL H	LTC	0-1173073	1265	1
SEWART GEORGE F	WO1	W-2122639	0151	1
SEWELL GAINES E	MAJ	0-0186723	0648	3
SEWELL GILBERT H	2LT	0-1320187	1044	2
SEWELL HOKE S	CW2	W-2145908	0358	1
SEWELL JACK H	CPT	0-1302715	1051	1
SEWELL JONATHAN E	CW4	W-2103425	0756	1
SEWELL JR BENNIE R	LTC	0-2036446	0962	1
SEWELL MILTON A	LTC	0-0510765	0353	1
SEWELL ORAL L	MAJ	0-0572042	0461	1
SEWELL PRESTON O	MAJ	0-1589005	0656	1
SEWELL RALPH E	MAJ	0-1112432	0264	1
SEWELL ROBERT E	MAJ	0-1560244	0163	1
SEWELL ROBERT M	MAJ	0-1031839	1066	2
SEWELL VIRGIL T	CPT	0-1166602	0645	2
SEXSMITH WILFRED H	LTC	0-1646575	0766	1
SEXSON JACK	MAJ	0-1004830	0957	1
SEXSON JOSEPH H	CW3	W-2150804	0963	1
SEXTON BARBARA H	2LT	N-0731024	0944	1
SEXTON CHARLES R	LTC	0-0209790	1057	3
SEXTON CHARLES V	CPT	0-0335064	0648	3
SEXTON JAMES N	COL	0-0252712	1047	2
SEXTON LAURENCE R	COL	0-0201307	0-48	3
SEXTON LOUIS A	MAJ	0-1045923	0261	1
SEXTON MARGARET E	1LT	N-0760264	104N	1
SEXTON WILLIAM N	LTC	0-1948394	0463	1
SEYB DILLON W	LTC	0-1845645	0967	3
SEYBERT GEORGE I	LTC	0-0274482	0454	3
SEYFRIED CARL L	MAJ	0-0250289	0965	3
SEYFRIED RUDOLPH J	COL	0-0163771	0749	3
SEYKOSKI MICHAEL	1LT	0-1303555	0266	2
SEYLE DOUGALD B	CPT	0-0317536	0863	3
SEYMOUR CLARENCE W	LTC	0-0115468	0648	3
SEYMOUR ERNEST H	MAJ	0-0196438	0661	3
SEYMOUR FREDERICK	MAJ	0-0516290	C953	2
SEYMOUR FREDERICK	LTC	0-1107114	0264	1
SEYMOUR JOHN H	MAJ	0-0427389	0954	1
SEYMOUR JR HUBERT E	1LT	0-0538502	0845	2
SEYMOUR KENNETH W	LTC	0-0392123	0957	2
SEYMOUR MARMADUKE	MAJ	C-0110831	0648	3
SEYMOUR PERSHING K	MAJ	0-1646931	1062	1
SEYMOUR ROBERT A	2LT	0-1311216	0344	2
SEYMOUR STUART L	LTC	0-0297758	0964	3
SEYSTER MICHAEL E	LTC	0-0243752	0162	1
SGARRO MICHAEL J	LTC	0-1796165	0567	3
SHAAD ROBERT B	1LT	0-0554934	0747	2
SHACHTMAN JOSEPH M	MAJ	0-0403056	0745	1
SHACKEL EDWARD G	LTC	0-1636633	0158	1
SHACKELFORD B W	CPT	0-0905337	0-48	2

NAME	GRADE	SVC NO	DATE RET MO YR	RET CODE
SHACKELFORD GORDON E	CPT	0-0407966	C646	2
SHACKELFORD HOWARD F	CW2	W-2145871	1058	2
SHACKELFORD JAMES A	LTC	0-2054033	C862	1
SHACKELFORD JAMES E	CW2	W-2107537	1045	2
SHACKELFORD JAMES F	MAJ	0-0258542	1066	3
SHACKELFORD RICHARD	COL	0-0215595	C862	3
SHACKELFORD ROBERT O	MAJ	C-1535076	1061	1
SHACKELFORD TOM G	LTC	0-0304890	1059	1
SHACKLEFORD EARL C	LTC	0-1016172	0962	1
SHACKLFFORD PAUL A	CPT	0-0390762	0546	2
SHACKLEFORD R H	CW2	W-2147672	1155	1
SHACKLETTE ELMER C	CPT	0-2009973	0255	1
SHACKLETTE JOSEPH W	CW2	W-2144220	1059	2
SHACKMAN ALEXANDER	WO1	W-2128397	0146	2
SHACKTON ROBERT W	1LT	0-1309971	C845	2
SHADDEAU WILLIAM A	LTC	0-1015181	1060	1
SHADDOCK HENRY	CPT	0-2055116	0647	1
SHADE ADELAIDE E	CPT	N-0724721	0649	2
SHADE ERVIN H	LTC	0-0232165	1047	2
SHADE KENNETH N	1LT	0-0311768	C144	2
SHADE RAYMOND A	CPT	0-0246241	1145	2
SHADE RICHARD E	LTC	0-1341590	0666	1
SHADE VERONICA R	MAJ	N-0799206	0665	1
SHADFORD EUGENE S	CPT	0-0184591	C851	3
SHADIS ARTHUR	MAJ	C-1794998	0157	1
SHADLE FRECERICK	LTC	0-1297793	0166	1
SHADRICK JAMES B	CPT	0-1296919	1063	1
SHAEFER HENRY C	MAJ	0-1641786	C564	1
SHAEFFER CLAYTON C	CW3	W-2144961	0159	1
SHAEFFER CRAWFORD C	CPT	0-0483410	0347	1
SHAEFFER FRANCES Z	2LT	N-0785488	C946	1
SHAFE LOWELL F	CPT	0-1110247	1163	1
SHAFER ALBERT H	LTC	0-0213022	0446	2
SHAFER DELPHA E	MAJ	N-0732023	1165	1
SHAFER DONALD M	MAJ	C-0345171	0346	2
SHAFER ERNEST A	MAJ	0-0133784	0349	3
SHAFER HENRY A	CPT	0-0967815	1060	1
SHAFER HERBERT J	2LT	0-1102954	C545	2
SHAFER QUINTON R	CW3	W-2144345	1164	1
SHAFFER BENJAMIN E	LTC	0-0190185	1151	3
SHAFFER CARLETON R	COL	0-0145143	0648	3
SHAFFER CHARLES N	MAJ	0-0414948	1145	2
SHAFFER CLYDE G	CW4	W-2122622	C266	1
SHAFFER DONALD Y	COL	0-0296906	0566	3
SHAFFER FREC W	LTC	0-0285731	C163	3
SHAFFER FRECERICK	LTC	0-0212550	0249	3
SHAFFER GEORGE O	LTC	0-1636635	C463	1
SHAFFER HARRY T	CW2	W-2145622	0957	1
SHAFFER HOWARD P	COL	0-0256375	0958	3
SHAFFER J O	MAJ	C-2017767	0560	1
SHAFFER JACK G	MAJ	C-0885757	0261	1
SHAFFER JAY O	CW4	W-2142898	0367	2
SHAFFER JOHN W	WO1	W-2141826	0854	1
SHAFFER JR ALBERT	1LT	0-0357677	0145	2
SHAFFER JR LYLE R	1LT	0-1182959	1048	2
SHAFFER LEE J	COL	0-0237094	1064	3
SHAFFER MORRIS	CW3	W-2104451	1054	1
SHAFFER ORRIN G	LTC	0-1165952	C765	1
SHAFFER PAUL R	LTC	0-0213300	C462	3
SHAFFER SUSAN	1LT	N-0761078	C847	1
SHAFFER WALTER G	LTC	0-0916527	1062	1
SHAFFER WAYNE C	MAJ	C-0513034	0265	1
SHAFFER WILLIAM O	COL	0-0186287	0848	3
SHAFFER WILLIE L	MAJ	0-0205610	1059	1
SHAFFER XENOPHON B	LTC	0-0196913	C857	3
SHAFFRAN JOHN	CW2	W-2104463	C753	2
SHAHAN WILLIAM H	LTC	0-0900536	1062	3
SHAMON HENRY I	MAJ	0-0492592	0346	1
SHAIA FONAO T	CW2	W-2110438	1052	1
SHAKARIAN CHARLES G	MAJ	0-0998771	1165	1
SHAKE JULIAN R	MAJ	C-0962436	0363	1
SHAKULA JOHN H	MAJ	C-2000792	0562	1
SHALALA JOHN S	LTC	0-1100762	0966	1
SHALE JOHN H	1LT	0-128333C	0245	1
SHALL MORRIS J	CPT	0-0263054	1065	3

NAME	GRADE	SVC NO	DATE RET MO YR	RET CODE
SHALLCROSS DONALD C	CPT	0-0444623	0646	2
SHALLCRCSS FRANK A	LTC	0-0179946	0253	3
SHALLER DOROTHY E	2LT	N-0761526	1044	1
SHALLER SIDNEY B	CPT	0-1309421	0246	2
SHALLINGTON THOMAS W	COL	0-0394475	0263	1
SHALVEY JOSEPH P	MAJ	0-1184296	0962	1
SHAMBAUGH GORDON I	LTC	0-0368062	1265	3
SHAMBAUGH HOWARD T	LTC	0-1549094	0662	2
SHAMBAUGH WILSON R	MAJ	0-1286017	0760	2
SHAMBLIN HOWARD C	MAJ	0-1013256	0760	1
SHAMBURGER SAMUEL L	CPT	0-2263647	0864	1
SHAMEL WILLIAM L	LTC	0-0203675	1154	3
SHAMLIN ED M	LTC	0-1324583	0865	1
SHAMPER CLIVIA K	2LT	N-0730209	0943	1
SHANABARGER ROBERT G	CPT	0-0970660	1060	1
SHANAFELT JOHN L	1LT	0-1010864	0446	2
SHANAHAN CHARLES M	MAJ	0-1998440	1163	1
SHANAHAN CORNELIUS	MAJ	0-1297794	0661	1
SHANAHAN JOHN R	MAJ	0-1300536	0147	2
SHANAHAN ROBERT E	LTC	0-1577830	0660	1
SHANOS OSCE H	CPT	0-0473719	0460	3
SHANE HENRY K	LTC	0-017574C	0562	3
SHANE SEYMOUR L	MAJ	0-1182960	0165	1
SHANER ELMER E	LTC	0-1112433	0765	1
SHANGRAW CLAYTON C	MAJ	0-0172697	0556	3
SHANK JR OLIVER O	LTC	0-1052958	1165	1
SHANKEY ANASTATIA	CPT	R-0001309	1246	1
SHANKMAN ROBERT A	MAJ	0-1031444	1160	1
SHANKS JOHN N	LTC	0-0219050	0947	1
SHANLEY JOHN M	MAJ	0-022985C	0665	3
SHANLEY PATRICK J	LTC	0-0451548	0962	1
SHANLEY WILLIAM T	CPT	0-1113438	0846	2
SHANNON ALBERT L	COL	0-0415427	0264	1
SHANNON BURDETTE A	LTC	0-1102956	0856	1
SHANNON CHARLES H	CW3	W-2107943	1060	1
SHANNON DALLAS L	MAJ	0-1334362	0662	1
SHANNCN DONALD C	LTC	0-0361301	0363	1
SHANNON EDMUND W	LTC	0-1327387	1067	1
SHANNCN FRANK W	CW3	W-2147899	1161	1
SHANNON CEORGE I	LTC	0-0141147	0946	2
SHANNON HARRY J	CPT	0-0885883	0848	1
SHANNCN HARRY L	LTC	0-1108314	1060	1
SHANNCN JACK T	COL	0-0361736	1160	1
SHANNCN JACKSCN G	1LT	0-1286906	0943	2
SHANNON JOE A	CPT	0-1638490	0456	1
SHANNCN JOHN A	CPT	0-0486570	0843	2
SHANNCN JOSEPH J	CW2	W-2114755	0962	1
SHANNCN JOSEPH X	LTC	0-1649939	0366	1
SHANNON JR JAMES	CW3	W-2153326	0766	1
SHANNON MILORED C	MAJ	N-0744644	0163	1
SHANNON RALPH T	LTC	0-0312190	0846	1
SHANNCN ROGER R	MAJ	0-0321597	0345	2
SHANNON ROSCCE W	MAJ	0-0141146	0657	3
SHANNON ROY A	LTC	0-1823073	0561	1
SHANNCN STANLEY E	MAJ	0-0289745	0861	1
SHANNON THOMAS J	MAJ	0-1639632	0863	1
SHANNCN WILLIAM H	COL	0-0158250	0648	3
SHANNON WILLIAM V	MAJ	0-017275C	0162	3
SHANOR CEORGE B	COL	0-0172546	0564	2
SHAPBELL EDITH M	CPT	N-0760775	0153	1
SHAPIRA JAKE	MAJ	0-0430282	0246	2
SHAPIRC ALBERT	CPT	0-0449521	0745	2
SHAPIRC CEORGE W	CPT	0-1690020	0246	2
SHAPIRC HERMAN H	COL	0-0409140	1264	3
SHAPIRC HERMAN L	COL	0-0530972	1064	3
SHAPIRC HYMAN D	LTC	0-0482271	0446	2
SHAPIRC JACOB	LTC	0-0341427	0146	2
SHAPIRC JOHN L	CPT	0-0419805	0945	2
SHAPIRC JOSEPH	MAJ	0-1689607	0646	2
SHAPIRC MAX	1LT	0-0399281	0444	2
SHAPIRC MORRIS	CW3	W-2109212	0159	1
SHAPIRC SOLOMON S	LTC	0-0233755	0546	2
SHAPIRC SYDNEY H	1LT	0-1544484	1045	2
SHAPIRC THEODCRE	CPT	0-1173455	0446	2
SHAPLAND LESTER B	COL	0-0133811	1151	3

NAME	GRADE	SVC NO	DATE RET MO YR	RET CODE
SHAPLEY BENJAMIN S	LTC	0-0317612	C561	3
SHAPO DALTON J	COL	0-0243516	0766	3
SHAPPELL EARL R	LTC	0-1039913	0364	1
SHAPPY FOSTER F	1LT	0-1299802	0348	1
SHAPRO FRANK	COL	0-0222150	1047	2
SHAPTER PETER L	MAJ	C-1289976	C657	1
SHARBAUGH JOHN J	CPT	0-0422619	0145	2
SHARBONDA VIVIAN P	1LT	N-0783852	1045	1
SHARER DONALD V	CPT	0-1300402	1146	1
SHARIN BERNARD	2LT	0-1997339	C945	2
SHARKEY ECWARD M	1LT	0-1310158	C845	2
SHARKEY JOSEPH J	MAJ	0-1324195	0359	1
SHARKEY MARY E	2LT	N-0768346	C845	1
SHARO SAMUEL M	COL	0-0220678	1161	3
SHARON JOSEPH L	2LT	0-1895655	C944	2
SHARON MAY	MAJ	N-0727866	0762	2
SHARP ALVA C	CPT	0-1649610	0657	1
SHARP BENJAMIN C	CPT	0-0400953	0345	2
SHARP BOYD F	LTC	0-0253131	0960	1
SHARP CHARLTON D	CW2	W-2103796	0652	2
SHARP CLARENCE L	CPT	0-0102933	0250	3
SHARP DALLAS A	LTC	0-0412071	0463	1
SHARP DAVID M	CPT	0-1876047	0966	2
SHARP EVERETT W	LTC	C-0249907	C165	3
SHARP FRANK L	1LT	0-0221432	C353	3
SHARP HAROLC K	LTC	0-1593264	1062	1
SHARP HIRAM F	LTC	0-0269531	0467	3
SHARP JOHN H	COL	0-0194054	0-48	2
SHARP JOHN H	COL	0-0219789	0557	1
SHARP JOHN H	CPT	0-1287420	1045	2
SHARP JOSEPH C	MAJ	C-0276252	0458	3
SHARP PAUL W	COL	0-0218792	0758	3
SHARP RALPH T	1LT	0-2055198	C951	1
SHARP RALPH V	MAJ	C-0544630	0264	1
SHARP ROBERT E	LTC	0-0470969	0750	1
SHARP ROLLINS H	MAJ	C-0966759	1062	1
SHARP SR WILLIAM R	MAJ	C-1185497	C858	1
SHARP THEODORE L	LTC	0-0306298	1166	3
SHARP WILLIAM R	CW2	W-2215380	C867	1
SHARPE CLIFFORD M	LTC	0-0396845	1045	2
SHARPE CEORGE A	CW2	W-2145587	1056	1
SHARPE JOHN H	LTC	0-0300514	0860	1
SHARPE JOHN R	CPT	0-1080149	0347	1
SHARPE JR LUTHER E	COL	0-0450765	C166	1
SHARPE PHILIP J	LTC	0-1322479	0164	1
SHARPE THEODORE G	MAJ	0-0966771	0164	1
SHARPES KENNETH	1LT	0-1544105	0551	2
SHARPNACK GEORGE L	CPT	0-1180043	0648	2
SHARPS FRANK	1LT	0-0381805	0145	2
SHARRETT VICTOR A	MAJ	0-0235488	1265	3
SHARTEL PAUL W	MAJ	0-1015167	0357	1
SHARY 2ND JOHN H	CPT	0-0533475	1047	2
SHASTEEN JOHN L	CW4	W-2118339	0560	1
SHATTAN BOAZ	1LT	0-1716661	0245	2
SHATTUCK LEE C	CPT	0-4005511	1063	1
SHATTUCK WILLIAM R	LTC	0-0225808	C762	3
SHAUB BENJAMIN M	MAJ	0-0215960	0153	3
SHAUB CAVID R	1LT	0-0490769	0146	2
SHAUB ROBERT C	1LT	0-0512913	1043	2
SHAUCK CHARLES W	LTC	0-0360912	0760	1
SHAUGHNESSEY PETER G	CPT	0-1595827	0953	1
SHAUGHNESSY MICHAEL	LTC	0-2011055	1163	1
SHAUGHNESSY ROBERT C	MAJ	0-2017768	0763	1
SHAUKLAS VICTOR F	MAJ	C-0940786	C162	2
SHAUL REX K	COL	0-0313126	0464	1
SHAULIS CALVIN F	LTC	0-0151323	0955	3
SHAULIS MILCRED A	2LT	N-C789066	0844	1
SHAULIS MITCHELL	CW2	W-2142899	0453	2
SHAVE HENRY A	MAJ	0-2262454	0267	2
SHAVER CHARLES O	CPT	0-1180044	C747	2
SHAVER DANIEL M	CPT	0-0177187	1058	3
SHAVER CARNETT M	WO1	W-2151323	1054	1
SHAVER CEORGE E	MAJ	0-1165954	0960	1
SHAVER GLENN A	WO1	W-2118483	0750	1
SHAVERS IVERSON E	LTC	0-1593266	1062	1

NAME	GRADE	SVC NO	DATE RET MO YR	RET CODE
SHAW ALLAN G	2LT	0-1311823	0545	2
SHAW ALTON D	COL	0-0453215	0261	1
SHAW ARTHUR F	COL	0-0143824	1044	2
SHAW ARTHUR R	COL	0-1165334	0662	1
SHAW ARTHUR W	MAJ	0-0492417	0758	1
SHAW BERNARD G	MAJ	0-0454162	0850	2
SHAW CHARLES B	COL	0-0444074	1054	2
SHAW CLARKE M	COL	0-0202190	0758	1
SHAW DAVID S	LTC	0-0291055	0761	1
SHAW DELCYD C	MAJ	0-0220053	1059	3
SHAW DENNIS J	LTC	0-1032602	0961	2
SHAW DONALD B	MAJ	0-0200574	0258	3
SHAW DONALD E	LTC	0-1018546	0463	2
SHAW DOROTHY J	1LT	N-0788136	0546	1
SHAW DWIGHT B	COL	0-0284882	0658	3
SHAW EARL W	LTC	0-0258199	0746	2
SHAW EARL W	MAJ	0-1584885	0655	1
SHAW EDWIN O	COL	0-0124037	0756	1
SHAW EMMON R	COL	0-0360495	0960	1
SHAW EUGENE C	MAJ	0-1304451	0962	1
SHAW FRANK H	LTC	0-1633538	1262	1
SHAW GLEN E	COL	0-0296573	0766	1
SHAW HALBERT C	MAJ	0-0266976	1145	2
SHAW HAROLD R	COL	0-0243589	0364	3
SHAW HARRY O	MAJ	0-2017289	0463	1
SHAW HELEN L	1LT	N-0728145	0744	1
SHAW HOWARD K	LTC	0-0184547	0459	3
SHAW HOWARD W	CPT	0-1549095	0854	1
SHAW HUGH P	MAJ	0-1289154	0660	1
SHAW JAMES A	MAJ	0-0291515	0365	1
SHAW JAMES E	COL	0-0281282	0761	2
SHAW JAMES H	LTC	0-1299803	1057	1
SHAW JEWEL M	1LT	N-0783682	0447	1
SHAW JOHN B	MAJ	0-0145123	0457	3
SHAW JOHN C	COL	0-1694200	0267	1
SHAW JOHN D M	MAJ	0-0282000	0862	1
SHAW JOHN E	CPT	0-1111907	0559	1
SHAW JOHN E	CPT	0-1318713	0646	2
SHAW JOHN T	CPT	0-1925128	0959	2
SHAW JOSEPH	LTC	0-1594472	0766	3
SHAW JOSEPH C	CPT	0-0503679	0246	2
SHAW JOSEPH E	COL	0-0147367	0256	3
SHAW JR ALEXANDER	CPT	0-1291753	0844	2
SHAW JR CHARELS E	MAJ	0-1186367	1265	1
SHAW JR FRANK W	CPT	0-0339456	0645	2
SHAW JR JOHN C	LTC	0-0379739	0160	2
SHAW JR LELANC H	1LT	0-1032652	104N	2
SHAW JR QUINCY A	COL	0-0127600	0457	3
SHAW JR WARD M	1LT	0-1315528	0547	2
SHAW JUNE M	1LT	N-0784377	0546	1
SHAW KENNETH E	MAJ	0-1108316	0167	1
SHAW LAUREN L	LTC	0-0278587	0756	3
SHAW LESLIE A	MAJ	0-0236784	0266	3
SHAW LLEWELLYN	LTC	0-0224322	0559	1
SHAW LOUISE A	MAJ	N-0754266	0565	3
SHAW LUTHER D	COL	0-0464434	1064	3
SHAW LYMAN A	COL	0-0141123	0250	3
SHAW MARJORIE A	1LT	N-0751178	0146	1
SHAW MARVIN H	MAJ	0-1645529	0461	1
SHAW MARVIN W	LTC	0-2009039	0767	1
SHAW MAURICE A	CPT	0-1173456	0557	1
SHAW MELVIN	1LT	0-1178332	0744	2
SHAW MILTON	LTC	0-0182370	0749	3
SHAW MILTON S	MAJ	0-1103399	0662	1
SHAW MINARD P	LTC	0-1583661	0558	1
SHAW MURRAY L	MAJ	0-1546771	0857	1
SHAW OREN V	COL	0-0221230	0858	3
SHAW ORVILLE T	MAJ	0-1326521	0559	1
SHAW PAUL A	MAJ	0-1306324	0861	1
SHAW RALPH W	CPT	0-1540778	0659	1
SHAW RANDOLPH C	COL	0-0111116	1052	1
SHAW RAYMOND C	MAJ	0-0449990	1061	3
SHAW RCBERT E	CW2	W-2129945	0261	1
SHAW RCBERT H	LTC	0-0360547	0757	2
SHAW RCBERT H	LTC	0-0915768	0867	3

NAME	GRADE	SVC NO	DATE RET MO YR	RET CODE
SHAW ROBERT R	2LT	0-1031445	0643	2
SHAW ROLIN W	LTC	0-C198002	0648	3
SHAW ROY L	MAJ	C-0222187	C249	1
SHAW SIDNEY E	CPT	0-1117077	0854	1
SHAW THOMAS M	1LT	0-1295443	0645	2
SHAW VAUGHAN A	MAJ	0-0357108	0146	1
SHAW WALTER F	MAJ	C-1946378	1060	1
SHAW WARREN C	2LT	0-C540043	0945	2
SHAW WILLIAM A	MAJ	0-0300720	0344	2
SHAW WILLIAM F	MAJ	C-1286019	1060	1
SHAW WILLIAM J	COL	0-0235610	1052	3
SHAW WILLIAM J	LTC	0-1042428	0365	1
SHAW WILLIAM R	LTC	0-0342833	1160	2
SHAW WILLIS F	2LT	0-1309973	0644	2
SHAW WILLOUGHBY	1LT	0-1292071	1043	2
SHAWHAN OLEN B	COL	0-0180370	1057	3
SHAWVER DORIS A	1LT	N-0737205	C846	1
SHAWVER WILLIAM C	LTC	0-1111361	C257	1
SHAY CLARENCE R	MAJ	0-1690918	0960	1
SHAY DAN B	LTC	0-1016762	0766	1
SHAY HARRY	LTC	0-0484089	1054	1
SHAY NEIL E	CPT	0-0903212	0344	2
SHAYDAK JOHN C	MAJ	0-0888226	0960	1
SHEA CHARLES R	CW4	W-2111636	0660	1
SHEA CLARENCE J	CW4	W-2141677	1062	2
SHEA CLIFFORD H	LTC	0-1324705	1062	1
SHEA DAVID S	CPT	0-0383832	0146	2
SHEA DONALD W	CPT	0-1C47345	0965	2
SHEA ELEANOR F	1LT	N-0720358	0946	1
SHEA ELISABETH	1LT	N-0752519	0146	1
SHEA FRANCIS B	CPT	0-1593840	0346	2
SHEA FRANK H	1LT	0-2034700	1045	2
SHEA FRANK S	MAJ	0-0220865	1158	3
SHEA GEORGE S	LTC	0-2035896	0767	1
SHEA HENRY B	LTC	0-0288693	0164	3
SHEA IRVING R	LTC	0-0913070	0962	1
SHEA JAMES B	LTC	0-0147454	0455	3
SHEA JOSEPH C	LTC	0-0475725	0753	1
SHEA JR CHARLES A	2LT	0-0917666	0445	2
SHEA JR JAMES M	LTC	0-0908939	0264	3
SHEA JR WILLIAM J	1LT	0-1017652	0446	2
SHEA LANGAN E	CW4	W-2102355	0958	1
SHEA LAWRENCE	MAJ	0-0475012	0946	1
SHEA RAYMOND E	MAJ	0-1167214	0356	1
SHEA ROBERT S	CW3	W-2148190	0963	1
SHEA STANLEY O	COL	0-1280393	1060	1
SHEA THOMAS E	MAJ	C-0445255	0346	1
SHEAC WALTER J	CW3	W-2144414	1059	1
SHEAFE EARLE V	COL	0-0103743	0648	3
SHEAFFER CHARLES G	CW2	W-2151689	0760	1
SHEAFFER WALTER A	1LT	0-0476676	1145	2
SHEAHAN FRANCIS R	CW4	W-2151040	0867	1
SHEAHAN JOHN J	CPT	0-0280368	1145	2
SHEAHAN WILLIAM H	LTC	0-1640938	0661	1
SHEAKS ELBERT F	CPT	0-1168458	C153	1
SHEALY JESSE A	LTC	0-0476261	0446	1
SHEALY JOHN R	LTC	0-2014737	0666	1
SHEAR ALEX E	1LT	0-1030711	0945	2
SHEAR SIDNEY P	CPT	0-0386241	0246	2
SHEARD WILDER H	COL	C-0301496	0560	1
SHEARER BARRY E	MAJ	0-2033599	C965	1
SHEARER CYRUS N	MAJ	0-0201419	1046	2
SHEARER FRANCIS B	COL	0-0211630	0658	1
SHEARER GEORGE M	LTC	0-0218770	1058	3
SHEARER JAMES L	COL	0-0248843	0852	3
SHEARER JR FRED C	1LT	0-0537485	1147	2
SHEARER LEE	W01	W-2110133	0350	2
SHEARER MARK O	LTC	0-1103403	0764	1
SHEARER MARY E	MAJ	N-0760095	C165	1
SHEARER OSCC	MAJ	0-0449671	0550	1
SHEARER ROBERT L	CPT	0-0361206	1145	2
SHEARIN GEORGE S	CW4	W-2143667	0164	1
SHEARIN WILLIAM F	MAJ	0-0332338	0660	1
SHEARROW CHARLES W	CW2	W-2150017	1262	1
SHEARS CLARA B	2LT	N-0763804	0245	1

NAME	GRADE	SVC NO	DATE RET MO YR	RET CODE
SHECKELS JOHN C	CW3	W-2105031	1151	1
SHECKLER CHARLES L	LTC	0-1183969	0565	1
SHEDD GEORGE C	W01	W-2130241	0653	1
SHEDOUDY EMIL J	CPT	0-0300020	0750	1
SHEEDY JOHN	LTC	0-0463643	1054	1
SHEEHAN BERNARD J	LTC	0-1591558	0967	1
SHEEHAN CHARLES J	2LT	0-0975236	0152	1
SHEEHAN DANIEL F	LTC	0-0220216	1046	1
SHEEHAN EARL J	MAJ	0-1036373	0665	3
SHEEHAN EDWARD L	LTC	0-0166809	0246	2
SHEEHAN EVELYN M	2LT	L-0601837	0245	2
SHEEHAN GEORGE T	MAJ	0-0123212	0648	3
SHEEHAN JAMES G	LTC	0-0407152	0351	1
SHEEHAN JOHN G	COL	0-0224570	1156	3
SHEEHAN JOHN P	LTC	0-0232039	0666	3
SHEEHAN JOHN C	1LT	0-0432962	1045	2
SHEEHAN KATHERINE	2LT	N-0759755	0944	1
SHEEHAN RICHARD O	CPT	0-0370930	1046	1
SHEEHAN THOMAS F	LTC	0-2018586	1164	1
SHEEHE NORMAN L	LTC	0-0195769	0853	3
SHEEHY JOHN J	LTC	0-1294733	0266	1
SHEEHY JOSEPH S	CPT	0-1825829	0454	2
SHEEHY JULIAN R	MAJ	0-1996412	1158	1
SHEEHY OLIVER J	CPT	0-0100095	0953	3
SHEEHY ROBERT J	1LT	0-1325067	C265	1
SHEEHY THORNTON E	MAJ	0-1635323	1060	1
SHEELY ARTHUR C	COL	0-0207217	1058	3
SHEELY CHARLES W	LTC	0-0179203	1060	3
SHEELY EARL O	1LT	0-0498851	0547	1
SHEELY GILBERT H	CPT	0-1030532	0747	2
SHEEN CHARLES E	LTC	0-012327C	0157	3
SHEER HERBERT	LTC	0-1013579	1061	1
SHEERAN JAMES H	CPT	0-0199310	0546	1
SHEERAN LAWRENCE W	LTC	0-1291182	0565	1
SHEERIN JOSEPH G	2LT	0-0425389	1043	2
SHEETINGER ERNEST J	MAJ	0-0220075	0760	3
SHEETS ALBERT E	LTC	0-0191271	0-53	3
SHEETS HARRY D	COL	0-0260645	0857	1
SHEETS JACK C	COL	0-0242069	0566	3
SHEETS ROBERT V	CPT	0-0444947	0748	1
SHEETS WILLIAM M	MAJ	0-0199193	0862	2
SHEETZ GEORGE E	LTC	0-0265C23	0158	3
SHEFFER WILLIAM B	LTC	0-0335786	1057	1
SHEFFIELD AZOR O	1LT	0-0383428	1045	2
SHEFFIELD HAROLD C	LTC	0-0370204	0361	1
SHEFFIELD LOUIS MC C	W01	W-2123551	1044	2
SHEFFIELD RICHARD E	LTC	0-1169736	0761	2
SHEFFLER JR ABBOTT H	1LT	0-0514656	0945	1
SHEFFY CARY L	CPT	0-1322090	1162	1
SHEFRIN NORMAN	CPT	0-0543884	1145	1
SHEFT THADDEUS J	CPT	0-0410919	1047	2
SHEHAB ALFRED H M	LTC	0-1012319	0363	1
SHEHAN CHARLES E	MAJ	0-1923593	1063	1
SHEHAN MILLARD P	CW2	W-2148815	1166	1
SHEHANE BARNEY A	COL	0-0263758	0863	3
SHEIL JOHN J	CPT	0-0510291	1047	1
SHEIL NICHOLAS F	LTC	0-1306225	0762	1
SHEIMAN SAMUEL C	CPT	0-1690196	0346	2
SHELBAER ROSS	CW4	W-2102359	0557	1
SHELBERT MICHAEL R	CW2	W-2152617	0858	1
SHELBY CECIL R	MAJ	0-1881825	0166	1
SHELBY CHARLES T	1LT	0-1558977	0346	2
SHELBY CHARLES T	MAJ	0-1592047	0667	1
SHELBY HERMAN J	MAJ	0-1821777	1060	1
SHELBY HOWARD J	MAJ	0-0248682	0164	3
SHELBY JOHN O	MAJ	0-0885777	0259	2
SHELBY ROBERT W	MAJ	0-0450153	0952	2
SHELBY TROY H	COL	0-0314663	0764	1
SHELDEN HOWARD W	LTC	0-019377C	0951	3
SHELDON ARVIC K	MAJ	0-2292024	0866	1
SHELDON EDGAR E	1LT	0-0213973	0347	2
SHELDON HARRY B	CPT	0-1715057	1047	2
SHELDON HOLLIS F	MAJ	0-1580314	0264	1
SHELDON HOYNE S	COL	0-0300C39	1065	2
SHELDON JOSEPH V	COL	0-0401466	0157	1

NAME	GRADE	SVC NO	DATE RET MO YR	RET CODE
SHELDON NINUS W	MAJ	C-0497428	0762	3
SHELDON RAYMOND W	CW4	W-2000126	1051	2
SHELDON ROBERT B	LTC	0-0371964	C657	1
SHELDON ROSS A	CPT	0-2017909	C662	1
SHELDON WILLIAM H	MAJ	0-0133605	C944	2
SHELEY MAURICE C	LTC	0-1844705	C362	2
SHELHORN JR ROBERT H	LTC	0-0523405	C963	1
SHELINE WILLIAM H	CPT	0-0234655	0544	1
SHELL HERBERT	1LT	0-1283856	0246	2
SHELLER EUGENE W	1LT	0-1309102	C146	2
SHELLER SAMUEL M	MAJ	0-2015502	0562	1
SHELLEY AUBREY E	LTC	0-0408491	1263	1
SHELLEY FRANCIS R	2LT	0-1080816	0744	2
SHELLEY HARRY S	COL	0-0291116	0761	3
SHELLEY HULLIOUS R	1LT	0-1995168	0347	2
SHELLEY JOHN E	MAJ	0-1699971	1061	1
SHELLEY MACK C	LTC	0-1286195	C157	1
SHELLEY OTTO S	MAJ	C-1308191	0357	1
SHELLEY SR ROBERT G	CW3	W-2146881	0760	1
SHELLEY THOMAS L	LTC	0-0271957	C960	3
SHELLEY WILSON E	MAJ	0-1306326	0257	1
SHELLMAN ERNEST J	MAJ	C-0196575	C356	3
SHELLOW HAROLD	MAJ	0-0496516	0946	2
SHELMAN PHILLIP T	CW3	W-2144719	1264	1
SHELNUTT HOMER H	CW3	W-2144628	0966	2
SHELTON A L	CW3	W-2152866	0962	2
SHELTON ALBERT E	1LT	0-1303211	0346	2
SHELTON ALJEAN L	MAJ	C-0419956	0361	1
SHELTON AUBREY J	LTC	0-1328531	C363	1
SHELTON CHARLES L	LTC	0-0364075	0267	3
SHELTON CLARENCE B	LTC	0-1044376	0366	3
SHELTON COY R	CW2	W-2148191	0756	1
SHELTON DAVID S	MAJ	C-1298449	1047	2
SHELTON EDWARD E	LTC	0-1996368	0665	1
SHELTON FAY S	2LT	0-117471C	0445	2
SHELTON FRED T	LTC	0-1168912	1060	1
SHELTON GEORGE L	LTC	0-2053835	0764	1
SHELTON GERALDINE	CW2	W-2119863	0545	2
SHELTON IRWIN O	MAJ	C-1119245	0962	1
SHELTON JAMES E	MAJ	C-1319587	0357	1
SHELTON JAMES R	MAJ	0-1823949	C760	1
SHELTON JOHN B	CPT	0-0497878	0548	1
SHELTON JOHN W	CPT	0-0988085	0162	1
SHELTON JR BAKER C	LTC	0-1584889	0666	3
SHELTON LEONARD A	2LT	0-2008775	0552	2
SHELTON LLOYD W	2LT	C-2006236	0864	2
SHELTON LOUIS E	CPT	0-1540786	0557	1
SHELTON LYNN C	MAJ	0-1335189	0864	1
SHELTON MILLER F	CPT	0-0402300	0144	2
SHELTON MILTON	MAJ	0-0211315	0450	3
SHELTON ORVILLE E	1LT	0-1031446	0945	2
SHELTON PRESTON K	CW2	W-2007227	0767	1
SHELTON RAYMOND P	LTC	C-1322273	0166	1
SHELTON ROLAND H	MAJ	0-0959181	0865	1
SHELTON RUFUS B	MAJ	C-0968430	C961	1
SHELTON WILLIAM A	LTC	0-1291712	0760	1
SHELTON WILLIAM A	CW2	W-2211049	1165	1
SHELTON WILLIAM B	1LT	0-0323744	1146	2
SHELY REX	CW2	W-2120937	C853	1
SHEMELYNEC STEPHEN	CW3	W-2152439	C564	1
SHEMIOT ANTHONY R	CPT	0-0444103	0944	2
SHENBERGER JACK W	MAJ	C-1930905	0967	1
SHENK DAVID H	1LT	0-1032177	0447	2
SHENK EDGAR L	LTC	0-1636641	0461	2
SHENK HAROLD H	1LT	0-1303784	C347	2
SHENK MERRITT M	CW2	W-2119548	C147	1
SHENKEL—JOHN H	LTC	0-0145280	1153	3
SHENKYR BONITA H	1LT	N-0776445	C446	1
SHENOSKY PETER S	1LT	0-1174436	0545	2
SHEPARD ALAN B	LTC	0-0131392	0951	3
SHEPARD ARTHUR C	CPT	0-2206106	0265	1
SHEPARD BURLEIGH W	1LT	0-111394C	0446	1
SHEPARD CHAUNCEY B	MAJ	0-1996501	1159	1
SHEPARD COREY R	1LT	0-1284225	C246	2
SHEPARD EARL W	CW3	W-2144213	0161	1

NAME	GRADE	SVC NO	DATE RET MO YR	RET CODE
SHEPARD EDMOND C	W01	W-2115843	1048	1
SHEPARD FRED E	MAJ	0-0173319	0460	3
SHEPARD FREDERICK	COL	0-0252889	1155	3
SHEPARD GEORGE M	LTC	0-0127840	0748	3
SHEPARD GEORGE W	MAJ	C-1168915	0258	1
SHEPARD HAROLD P	CPT	0-0297C89	1043	2
SHEPARD HARRY D	CPT	0-0211185	0354	3
SHEPARD IRVIN G	LTC	0-0386076	1056	2
SHEPARD JOHN B	COL	0-0169298	0860	3
SHEPARD JULIUS T	COL	0-0380688	0867	1
SHEPARD KENNETH T	1LT	0-1701703	1044	2
SHEPARD MERRILL L	LTC	0-1184147	0767	1
SHEPARD RICHARD A	MAJ	0-0474187	1047	2
SHEPARD ROBERT B	MAJ	C-0360931	0846	2
SHEPARD ROY C	CPT	0-0505580	0356	1
SHEPARD VINCENT N	MAJ	0-1291183	0261	1
SHEPARDSON PEARL H	MAJ	N-0744517	0962	1
SHEPEK JOE H	CPT	0-0279904	0744	2
SHEPHARD WILLIAM G	1LT	0-0959676	1154	2
SHEPHERD ALTA R	CPT	L-0115797	0847	2
SHEPHERD CARLETON H	LTC	0-1646582	0663	1
SHEPHERD CHARLES H	COL	0-0209157	0556	3
SHEPHERD CLARENCE E	MAJ	0-0223131	C351	3
SHEPHERD EARL L	COL	0-0355057	0566	3
SHEPHERD EDWIN M	MAJ	0-0489671	0746	2
SHEPHERD ELMORE	W01	W-2110969	1148	1
SHEPHERD GEORGE S	1LT	0-1313652	0845	2
SHEPHERD GLENN L	COL	0-0232608	0365	3
SHEPHERD HAROLD K	LTC	0-1291055	0161	1
SHEPHERD HENRY B	CPT	0-0482203	0845	1
SHEPHERD JOHN T	MAJ	0-0948901	0162	1
SHEPHERD JR WALTON S	MAJ	0-0261261	1065	3
SHEPHERD REGINALD	CW2	W-2102364	1047	1
SHEPHERD REGINALD W	1LT	0-0386566	0445	2
SHEPHERD ROY O	1LT	0-1113441	1145	2
SHEPHERD RUFUS W	COL	0-0269899	1067	3
SHEPHERD WILLIAM E	COL	0-0108833	0151	3
SHEPLER MYRON E	COL	0-0340566	1264	1
SHEPPARD ALBERT D	LTC	0-0190904	0845	2
SHEPPARD BAZEL B	MAJ	0-0203951	1063	3
SHEPPARD DON A	COL	0-0225568	1163	3
SHEPPARD FORREST N	LTC	0-0225567	1262	3
SHEPPARD HILLIARD G	CW2	W-2144358	0361	1
SHEPPARD III W J	MAJ	0-2055166	1152	2
SHEPPARD JAMES D	LTC	0-1167216	0961	1
SHEPPARD JESSE J	MAJ	0-1797024	1266	3
SHEPPARD JR HARLD J	LTC	0-1013013	1060	1
SHEPPARD LOUIS B	MAJ	0-0494595	0645	2
SHEPPARD LOVIC P	1LT	0-0496582	0446	1
SHEPPARD REGINALD R	MAJ	0-0452027	0457	1
SHEPPARD ROBERT B	MAJ	0-1004685	0857	1
SHEPPARD ROBERT W	2LT	0-1326115	0745	2
SHEPPARD STANLEY R	MAJ	0-0261813	0959	1
SHEPPARD SYLVESTER	LTC	0-0451180	0663	1
SHEPPF ARTHUR T	COL	0-0256119	1164	3
SHEPPERD ALSTON L	COL	0-0267602	0362	3
SHER ABC S	COL	0-0285247	0666	3
SHER JOSEPH	CPT	0-1543639	1045	2
SHERARD ROY L	MAJ	0-0955272	0166	1
SHERBERT JR HENRY G	MAJ	0-2204411	0367	1
SHERBURN MERL L	COL	0-0246356	0959	1
SHERER ELLIS H	MAJ	0-2001700	0161	1
SHERER JOHN C	LTC	0-0199769	0159	3
SHERFY KAY L	CW4	W-2113305	0764	1
SHERIDAN EDWIN H	MAJ	0-0263734	0461	1
SHERIDAN FRANCIS E	MAJ	0-0570218	0755	1
SHERIDAN HARRY H	LTC	0-179719C	0562	2
SHERIDAN JAMES D	LTC	0-0358084	0948	1
SHERIDAN JOHN J	1LT	0-1312345	1045	2
SHERIDAN LAWRENCE V	COL	0-0186728	0649	3
SHERIDAN MARTIN J	CW2	W-2117C89	0957	1
SHERIDAN PHILIP J	W01	W-2127795	0646	2
SHERIDAN ROBERT J	MAJ	0-1551115	1054	1
SHERIDAN SR HENRY A	CW2	W-2206572	0562	2
SHERIDAN VICTOR A	MAJ	0-0908060	0347	2

NAME	GRADE	SVC NO	DATE RET MO YR	RET CODE
SHERIDAN WILLIAM C	CPT	0-0495311	1048	1
SHERIDAN WILLIAM F	LTC	0-1584890	0562	1
SHERIDAN WILLIAM J	LTC	0-1645363	C565	1
SHERIDAN 2ND HARRY C	2LT	0-2017600	0546	2
SHERIFF ELMER E	CPT	0-1004394	0261	1
SHERK JOHN T	MAJ	0-0248358	C462	3
SHERLING JAMES E	CPT	0-0274765	1266	3
SHERLOCK FRANCIS J	CW4	W-2102366	C165	1
SHERLOCK JR JOHN F	CPT	0-1107122	0750	1
SHERLOCK JR THOMAS J	LTC	0-0443405	C663	1
SHERMAN ARTHUR	LTC	C-0359661	0864	3
SHERMAN ARTHUR W	CW4	W-2115156	0559	1
SHERMAN CARLETON W	COL	C-0297094	0464	3
SHERMAN CHARLES E	MAJ	C-1049343	1163	1
SHERMAN CORNELIUS	MAJ	0-1335071	C763	1
SHERMAN DANA	1LT	0-1170192	1046	2
SHERMAN DONALD E	CPT	0-1575156	0246	1
SHERMAN DORA J	2LT	N-C743644	CA45	1
SHERMAN EARL F	CPT	0-0290360	0247	1
SHERMAN EARLE D	MAJ	0-0302359	0852	3
SHERMAN EARNEST G	CW3	W-2205419	C966	1
SHERMAN ELLIOTT W	LTC	0-0231036	0349	1
SHERMAN ELMER R	COL	0-0255745	C658	3
SHERMAN FOREST A	CPT	0-0509890	0346	1
SHERMAN FRANK S	COL	0-0495219	0756	1
SHERMAN GEORGE C	COL	0-0253377	0954	3
SHERMAN HAROLD F	LTC	0-1118491	1167	1
SHERMAN HENRY T	CPT	0-0314968	0546	2
SHERMAN HERBERT J	CPT	0-1106463	1053	2
SHERMAN JAMES B	CPT	0-1115106	C862	1
SHERMAN JESS M	CPT	0-1297601	0759	1
SHERMAN JOHN T	2LT	0-0449999	0945	2
SHERMAN JR FRANK J	COL	C-019215C	0662	3
SHERMAN JR THOMAS M	LTC	0-0298939	0760	1
SHERMAN KATHLEEN E	1LT	N-0754709	0947	1
SHERMAN LEO F	MAJ	C-0235268	C861	3
SHERMAN LESLIE K	LTC	0-0490387	0567	3
SHERMAN MAURICE	COL	C-0266870	1055	3
SHERMAN RALPH E	CPT	0-0389410	0445	2
SHERMAN ROY	CPT	0-1845245	C346	1
SHERMAN SAMUEL R	CPT	0-0444942	0746	2
SHERMAN SR JAMES A	MAJ	0-0546145	0265	1
SHERMAN WILLIAM A	LTC	0-021509C	0963	3
SHERMAN WILLIAM H	LTC	0-1106464	0767	1
SHERMAN WILLIAM M	CPT	0-0422279	0961	1
SHERMAN WINCHESTER	1LT	0-0447452	1044	2
SHERMER ROBERT E	WO1	W-2148514	0254	2
SHERMETTA MICHAEL	CW3	W-2147959	0960	2
SHERON RAYMOND H	WO1	W-2121066	0145	2
SHERR EARLE J	LTC	0-1584894	0565	1
SHERRARD HERMAN H	MAJ	C-0113511	0251	3
SHERRARD JACK G	MAJ	0-0391028	0646	2
SHERRATT LLOYD C	MAJ	0-2262967	1263	1
SHERREN JOSEPH E	MAJ	0-0406848	1060	1
SHERRER JOHN D	LTC	0-0272314	C765	3
SHERRICK PAUL H	COL	0-0217535	0259	3
SHERRILL DON D	CPT	0-02C3195	0357	3
SHERRILL ELWOOD E	CPT	0-1294546	1047	2
SHERRILL FRANKLIN C	MAJ	C-0454420	0958	1
SHERRILL FRED G	COL	0-0236194	1054	3
SHERRILL PARKS R	CW2	W-2151926	0460	1
SHERRILL RALPH E	CPT	0-0889800	1058	1
SHERRIS SAMUEL	LTC	0-1555901	0567	1
SHERROD JULIAN A	CPT	0-0498231	015C	1
SHERROD VINCENT A	1LT	0-0475652	0744	2
SHERRON ALBERT E	LTC	0-0493531	0657	1
SHERRY DEAN	COL	0-0151719	0550	3
SHERRY FRANCIS J	MAJ	0-1573579	0461	1
SHERRY JOSEPH E	LTC	0-0370118	0357	1
SHERRY PAUL J	MAJ	0-1922583	0164	1
SHERRY ROY J	COL	0-0357432	C165	1
SHERTZER ROBERT S	LTC	0-0167183	0953	3
SHERVA CHESTER D	1LT	0-0345555	1143	2
SHERVANICK THOMAS S	MAJ	0-0509639	0857	1
SHERVEN EDWARD R	CPT	0-0340723	1059	3

NAME	GRADE	SVC NO	DATE RET MO YR	RET CODE
SHERWIN EDWARD P	LTC	0-0392879	0361	1
SHERWIN GRAMMAR C	2LT	N-0724557	C844	1
SHERWIN HERBERT	LTC	0-0263292	0863	3
SHERWIN MITCHELL J	1LT	0-1589498	0140	2
SHERWOOD CALVIN L	WO1	W-2107401	1052	1
SHERWOOD DAVID J	CPT	0-1038840	C648	2
SHERWOOD DORA M	CPT	L-0500013	0945	2
SHERWOOD ELMER W	MAJ	0-0257335	0356	3
SHERWOOD GRANT M	CW4	W-2111676	0756	1
SHERWOOD HERBERT A	CPT	0-0199743	0352	3
SHERWOOD JACK C	MAJ	0-1337389	1162	1
SHERWOOD JOHN A	MAJ	0-1040812	0661	1
SHERWOOD REX E	LTC	0-1101212	0260	1
SHERWOOD ROGER R	MAJ	0-0488644	0752	1
SHERWOOD WALTER L	CPT	0-0509499	0547	1
SHERWOOD WARREN F	LTC	0-0982616	1163	3
SHERWOOD WILLIAM F	COL	0-0237052	0865	3
SHEVALIER WATSON R	MAJ	0-1579105	0263	1
SHEVCHIK WALTER V	MAJ	0-0450117	0256	1
SHEVICK JOSEPH	CPT	0-1311334	0958	1
SHEVIN SELIG A	1LT	0-0498208	0843	2
SHEW OPAL E	WO1	W-2132154	0960	2
SHEWAN JR WILLIAM H	2LT	0-0516875	0445	2
SHIBER JOHN S	MAJ	0-0371804	1045	2
SHICK DANIEL E	MAJ	0-1165448	0646	2
SHICK JOHN R	LTC	0-1293134	0261	1
SHICK WAYNE L	1LT	0-0396736	1043	2
SHIDEL JR FREDERIC C	LTC	0-0297555	C466	3
SHIELD ELGEAN	MAJ	0-0262524	0945	2
SHIELDS BILLY F	CW3	W-2149460	0864	1
SHIELDS CECIL C	MAJ	0-2038117	0564	1
SHIELDS CHARLES J	CPT	0-1306002	1047	2
SHIELDS DORIS I P	1LT	N-0774637	0547	1
SHIELDS DAYLE	CPT	C-1178338	0361	1
SHIELDS GEORGE H	CW2	W-2211519	0765	1
SHIELDS HAROLD A	CPT	0-1822065	0163	1
SHIELDS HOMER E	COL	0-0393280	0165	1
SHIELDS JAMES R	MAJ	0-1017091	0747	1
SHIELDS JOHN E	CW3	W-2150811	0563	1
SHIELDS JOHN W	MAJ	0-1109006	0663	1
SHIELDS JOHN R	COL	C-0137582	0753	3
SHIELDS JR F W	2LT	0-2049099	0146	2
SHIELDS JR GEORGE C	LTC	0-0451181	0854	2
SHIELDS JR JAMES H	CPT	0-1822322	0246	1
SHIELDS JR R T	MAJ	0-0441859	0945	1
SHIELDS LEE G	CPT	0-0437756	0346	1
SHIELDS LEM W	COL	0-0330839	0462	1
SHIELDS LIN	LTC	0-0224242	0154	1
SHIELDS LUKE S	LTC	0-0379818	0764	3
SHIELDS PAUL R	MAJ	0-042623C	0764	1
SHIELDS ROBERT R	2LT	0-2017136	0851	1
SHIELDS WILLIAM I	CPT	0-1172653	0161	1
SHIELDS WILLIAM M	2LT	0-0553677	0246	2
SHIELDS ZOLLIE H	LTC	0-1591441	0761	2
SHIELS THOMAS D	COL	C-0174845	0361	3
SHIER CYRIL W	LTC	0-0297341	0559	3
SHIER SIGMUND	LTC	0-1583668	0361	1
SHIERMAN HAROLD D	LTC	0-0239148	1061	3
SHIFFMAN ROBERT	CPT	0-1715169	0846	2
SHIFLETT ELBERT O	MAJ	C-2262265	0764	1
SHIGLEY FRED M	MAJ	0-0282462	0656	3
SHIKANY SAMUEL E	CPT	0-1702370	1145	2
SHIKOSKI LEO F	MAJ	0-1334763	0864	1
SHILOT HARRY R	CW2	W-2104468	1049	1
SHILLCOCK JOHN G	CW4	W-2114643	0860	1
SHILLER EDWIN S	CPT	0-1635513	0262	2
SHILLING MARVIN F	LTC	0-0141648	0354	3
SHILLING RUSSELL T	MAJ	0-0207134	1263	3
SHILLING WILLIAM K	LTC	0-0364070	1265	3
SHIMAMOTO FRANK M	CW3	W-2136039	0465	1
SHIMBERG HARRY W	CPT	0-2033119	0658	1
SHIMEL ROY E	LTC	0-1649944	1163	1
SHIMER RALPH W	1LT	0-1826345	0747	2
SHIMMEL FRANK W	MAJ	0-0479058	0254	1
SHIMMEL JOHN B	CPT	0-1649220	0957	1

NAME	GRADE	SVC NO	DATE RET MO YR	RET CODE
SHIMODA SATORU C	CW4	W-2136383	1266	2
SHIMUNEK FRANK J	2LT	0-1540603	0645	2
SHINABERGER HOWARD L	LTC	0-0199136	0962	3
SHINDELAR EDWARD	LTC	0-1168462	1263	1
SHINE BERNICE C	CPT	L-0312381	0158	2
SHINE III DUDLEY S	MAJ	C-0370665	1160	1
SHINE JOHN C	CPT	0-1325600	1047	2
SHINE ROBERT H	1LT	0-0557360	C446	2
SHINER JR WILLIAM F	1LT	0-1824517	C146	2
SHINKLE JOHN E	2LT	0-0988138	0152	1
SHINN FLOYD C	LTC	0-C258965	0567	3
SHINN JR FRANK R	COL	0-0244619	0960	2
SHINN KENNETH E	1LT	0-0537887	1045	2
SHINN ROBERT V	COL	0-0323157	1060	1
SHINN WILLIAM E	MAJ	0-0192941	0760	3
SHIPE CHARLES F	LTC	0-0225966	0265	3
SHIPE WESLEY Z	MAJ	0-1116697	0657	1
SHIRES WILLIE O	CW2	W-2149153	0757	1
SHIPFERLING GEORGE E	COL	0-0397006	0267	3
SHIPLETT DAVID A	LTC	0-0904185	C947	2
SHIRLEY ALEX B	COL	0-033235C	C965	3
SHIPLEY ALVIN J	MAJ	C-0965793	0965	1
SHIPLEY DOUGLAS B	CW3	W-2147960	1063	2
SHIRLEY ERVIN W	CW3	W-2150659	0566	1
SHIRLEY JOHN S	CPT	0-0257697	1265	3
SHIRLEY JR R H	2LT	0-0532117	C945	2
SHIRLEY MICHAEL	MAJ	0-0198491	1045	2
SHIRLEY NORMAN M	COL	0-0351412	C846	1
SHIPMAN GERALD A	CW3	W-2150292	1163	1
SHIPMAN WALTER H	CW2	W-2118369	1047	1
SHIRMAN WILLIAM F	MAJ	C-0159543	1043	2
SHIPREE GARELD A	2LT	0-1320189	1143	2
SHIPPEY PAUL M	CPT	0-1844429	C446	2
SHIPPEY THOMAS L	LTC	0-0292653	C546	2
SHIPPEY WEBSTER B	MAJ	0-0120185	1156	3
SHIPPEY WILLIAM L	CPT	0-0292336	0744	2
SHIRTON FRANCIS F	LTC	C-0358371	0555	1
SHIPTON WAYNE F	CW3	W-2146802	0760	1
SHIPWAY JOHN N	MAJ	0-2037175	0658	1
SHIRE HERBERT	2LT	0-0544387	C345	2
SHIRES HARRY F	MAJ	0-117531C	0366	1
SHIRES HENRY G	MAJ	0-0149980	0855	3
SHIRES SARA D	1LT	N-0722232	0146	1
SHIREY MERLE M	MAJ	C-0179844	0347	1
SHIREY ROBERT E	CPT	0-1922553	C162	1
SHIREY WILLIAM B	LTC	0-0153723	0159	3
SHIRK AMOS C	CW2	W-2114474	0846	2
SHIRK DAVILLA C	COL	0-0239768	1065	3
SHIRK HAROLD G	MAJ	C-0275392	1155	3
SHIRK JOSEPH D	CW2	W-2152737	0661	1
SHIRLAW HELEN A	LTC	L-0903697	C867	1
SHIRLEY BARKER L	1LT	0-0336986	0263	1
SHIRLEY CARL R	MAJ	0-2017466	0158	1
SHIRLEY CYRUS	CW3	W-21C2370	C953	1
SHIRLEY HARVEY G	LTC	0-0169686	0949	3
SHIRLEY HARVEY J	LTC	0-0509361	1046	2
SHIRLEY HERMAN M	1LT	0-2046554	C846	2
SHIRLEY JAMES C	LTC	0-0166146	0852	3
SHIRLEY JOE H	CW2	W-2208379	0461	1
SHIRLEY JOSEPH W	LTC	0-1289156	0762	1
SHIRLEY JR CHARLES L	MAJ	0-095933C	0162	1
SHIRLEY JR RILEY P	1LT	0-1306761	0946	2
SHIRLEY LEWIS H	WO1	W-2149350	1052	2
SHIRLEY OTHO A	MAJ	C-1319350	0557	1
SHIRLEY ROBERT H	MAJ	0-0256754	0966	3
SHIRLEY WARREN B	CW3	W-2203370	0965	1
SHIRLEY WILLIAM K	CPT	0-0460001	0647	2
SHIRLEY WILLIAM N	MAJ	C-0151725	C555	3
SHIRLING SR MILO R	CW3	W-2145909	C562	1
SHIROMA HARRY I	1LT	0-1998658	0251	2
SHIRREFF JOHN A	CW2	W-2215010	0167	1
SHIRVANIAN LEVON H	CPT	0-0139389	0944	2
SHIVEL HUBERT L	CW2	W-2111331	1153	1
SHIVELEY HARRY T	LTC	0-0452569	1060	1
SHIVELY DONALD L	MAJ	C-1338865	C367	1

NAME	GRADE	SVC NO	DATE RET MO YR	RET CODE
SHIVELY JOWARREN B	MAJ	0-1340585	0965	1
SHIVELY VERNON H	LTC	0-1173457	1160	1
SHIVELY WILLARD R	LTC	0-0230776	0153	3
SHIVER NOBLE C	CPT	0-0168635	0560	3
SHIVERS GERALD W	LTC	0-0401127	0761	1
SHIVES JAMES D	1LT	0-0383015	C845	2
SHIVLEY VIRGIL W	1LT	0-0509753	0846	1
SHLEVIN IDA M	2LT	N-0700402	0839	1
SHOAF JR CHARLES	CPT	0-12942C5	0245	2
SHOAF RICHARD R	CPT	0-0291001	1044	2
SHOAFF ROSS L	CPT	0-1593272	0162	1
SHOAFF WALTER R	COL	0-0143930	1056	3
SHOBERT CHARLES O	CPT	0-051032C	0750	1
SHOCHET HARRY	CW3	W-2147805	0765	1
SHOCKEY FLOYD E	CPT	0-0269551	0645	2
SHOCKEY JOHN E	LTC	0-0507368	0567	3
SHOCKEY JOHN W	COL	0-0366998	0266	1
SHOCKEY JR WILLIAM M	MAJ	0-0997239	1164	1
SHOCKLEY LEVERT E	CPT	0-0460826	0547	1
SHOCKLEY ORIEN C	CPT	0-1291582	1045	2
SHOCKLEY ROBERT E	1LT	0-04363C6	0545	2
SHOCKRO HARRY W	LTC	0-1319450	0962	1
SHOEMAKER ALBERT M	LTC	0-0481876	0962	1
SHOEMAKER CHARLES M	CW3	W-2200672	0165	1
SHOEMAKER ELMER F	LTC	0-0227376	0952	3
SHOEMAKER FORREST M	MAJ	0-1298481	0561	1
SHOEMAKER GEORGE O	LTC	0-0284214	1061	1
SHOEMAKER HARVEY J	COL	0-0183091	0745	1
SHOEMAKER JOSEPH J	COL	0-0186879	0649	3
SHOEMAKER JR J L	MAJ	0-0242055	C645	2
SHOEMAKER LEO V	MAJ	0-1596511	0266	1
SHOEMAKER M F	MAJ	N-0727115	0348	1
SHOEMAKER ORVILLE E	COL	C-0329860	C866	3
SHOEMAKER PHILIP C	COL	0-0309114	0964	3
SHOEMAKER ROBERT E	MAJ	0-2051712	0461	1
SHOEMAKER VERNON K	MAJ	0-132659C	0961	1
SHOEMAN GORDON C	CW4	W-2130702	0854	1
SHOENBERGER F P	MAJ	0-1C37300	0557	1
SHOFFSTALL ELVIN H	CPT	0-C287812	0844	1
SHOGREN PHILIP E	LTC	0-1171353	0361	1
SHOLAR CLARENCE W	MAJ	0-0965895	0662	2
SHOLAR JAMES R	MAJ	0-4002294	0463	2
SHOLARS BRUNSWIG	CPT	0-1170978	0654	2
SHOLL HERBERT A	1LT	0-1292243	0345	2
SHOLL PAUL E	CPT	0-0184533	0557	3
SHOLLENBERGER JOSEPH	LTC	C-1304803	1262	1
SHOLLENBURG RAYMOND	2LT	0-2020766	1051	2
SHOLTIS JOSEPH H	MAJ	0-0482201	1052	1
SHOMER VERN F	CPT	0-1290826	0649	2
SHONERD GEORGE D	CPT	0-1691852	0258	1
SHONKWILER VIRGIL G	MAJ	0-0400626	0246	2
SHONS CHARLES H	LTC	0-0164547	1049	3
SHOOK CALE C	2LT	0-1540687	0754	1
SHOOK EDWIN H	MAJ	0-2262739	1264	1
SHOOK EUGENE F	COL	0-1557669	0165	1
SHOOK GARNETT W	CPT	0-0323859	0367	3
SHOOK MARGARET M	MAJ	N-0700157	0444	1
SHOOK THEODORE	LTC	0-104379C	0361	1
SHOOP CLYDE C	CPT	0-1174971	0967	3
SHOOSHAN MARTIN D	LTC	0-0298417	C663	3
SHOOSTER MARGARET L	MAJ	N-0767532	1164	1
SHOPE CHARLES D	CPT	0-0345071	0446	2
SHOPE WILLARD M	LTC	0-0236925	1060	1
SHOPNITZ JOSEPH W	2LT	0-2012462	0346	1
SHOR ELAINE E	1LT	N-C795056	0847	1
SHOR ROBERT L	CPT	0-5218684	0866	2
SHORE AARON	1LT	0-1297264	0246	1
SHORE ALLEN W	CW4	W-2110727	0555	1
SHORE JOHN M	CW4	W-2144484	0866	1
SHORE LEON F	MAJ	0-2008766	0763	1
SHORE PAUL D	CPT	0-0483285	0446	1
SHORE SCHILLER F	LTC	0-033C854	0560	1
SHORE VENETA L	MAJ	N-0788718	1063	1
SHORES JAMES A	CW2	W-2208551	0264	1
SHORES JR CHARLES V	MAJ	0-2028750	0167	1

NAME	GRADE	SVC NO	DATE RET MO YR	RET CODE
SHOREY HENRY A	1LT	0-1170979	C945	2
SHOREY JR MILES C	LTC	0-0335625	0546	2
SHORT ALBERT W	CPT	0-1300405	0951	1
SHORT CLAUO	MAJ	C-1175575	0557	1
SHORT ELVEN H	MAJ	C-0485043	1059	2
SHORT FRANK E	MAJ	0-0532211	C246	2
SHORT FREELAN J	CPT	0-0474580	0745	2
SHORT GEORGE C	CW2	W-2116171	0245	2
SHORT HAROLC A	LTC	0-1000185	0555	1
SHORT J D	MAJ	C-2262473	C464	1
SHORT JAMES C	COL	0-0474877	0847	2
SHORT JAMES K	CPT	0-0480151	1045	1
SHORT JOHN G	LTC	0-0428540	C763	1
SHORT JR CLAIR A	MAJ	0-0320513	1143	2
SHORT JR EDWARD L	CW2	W-2211513	0266	1
SHORT JR ROLAND	LTC	0-0499611	0655	1
SHORT KENNETH L	CPT	0-1317202	C562	1
SHORT LEONARO V	MAJ	0-0503981	0646	2
SHORT MELVIN M	MAJ	0-1002340	1052	1
SHORT NORMAN V	CPT	0-1049645	1059	1
SHORT OLIVER T	CPT	0-1541240	0450	1
SHORT RAYMOND W	COL	C-0125028	C848	2
SHORT WELDON M	MAJ	C-0535574	0556	2
SHORT WILLIAM E	CW3	W-2141894	1060	1
SHORTER CHARLES R	LTC	0-1170194	C764	1
SHORTER JR WILLIE C	CW2	W-2106752	0445	2
SHORTER WALTER C	COL	0-0183049	0962	3
SHORTER WOODSON S	1LT	0-1325028	1045	2
SHORTESS JULIAN F	CW4	W-2104471	0859	2
SHORTLIDGE JAMES L	CW2	W-2105484	C857	1
SHORTRIDGE NORMAN H	LTC	0-0244908	0654	1
SHORTSLEEVES W L	1LT	0-0497275	C646	1
SHORTT BILLY H	MAJ	0-1102591	1060	1
SHORTT PETER J	LTC	0-0917059	0847	2
SHOSTAK MAX R	LTC	0-0225353	0165	3
SHOSTROM EVERETT L	1LT	0-0551206	C746	2
SHOTSMAN HARRY	LTC	0-0912558	C545	2
SHOTT DONALD C	CW2	W-2152400	0961	2
SHOTT JOSEPH W	MAJ	0-1116976	0760	1
SHOTTS JAMES E	COL	0-0216976	1052	3
SHOTWELL JACK B	MAJ	C-1634322	1064	1
SHOUCAIR EDWARD T	CPT	0-0349890	C865	3
SHOUDY CHARLES F	CPT	0-0989406	0366	2
SHOUP MARION L	MAJ	0-0248781	1266	3
SHOUSF JOHN E	MAJ	C-1333722	0661	1
SHOVAR MARK	LTC	0-0290392	0551	1
SHOVER FRANK E	CPT	0-1101657	C861	1
SHOWALTER DANIEL E	LTC	0-1016446	1266	1
SHOWALTER JACKSON H	MAJ	C-2014451	1165	1
SHOWALTER JAMES A	MAJ	C-0526917	C756	1
SHOWALTER JAMES F	COL	0-0442030	0466	1
SHOWALTER JCHN E	LTC	0-0109404	0844	1
SHOWALTER MARIE J	MAJ	N-0761329	1164	3
SHOWELL CARTER S	LTC	0-0271572	0865	3
SHOWERS JAMES R	LTC	0-128532C	C760	1
SHOWS JOHN H	CW2	W-2206909	C867	1
SHOWS NORMAN R	CW2	W-2145045	C156	2
SHOWS ROSCOE J	CPT	0-1877852	0562	1
SHRADER BRYANT E W	MAJ	C-2263123	1162	1
SHRADER EARL A	COL	C-0182215	C854	3
SHRAKE ROBERT E	CPT	0-1103406	0964	1
SHRECK GEORGE W	CPT	0-0910055	C146	2
SHRECK HORACE W	COL	C-0332055	C867	3
SHREDER RAYMOND J	LTC	0-1105818	C861	1
SHREEVE CALEB A	COL	0-0279366	1161	3
SHREEVE ORVILLE W	CW2	W-2141827	0656	1
SHREVE CHARLES U	COL	0-0158193	0358	3
SHREVE HAROLD E	MAJ	C-0982148	0863	1
SHREVE JOHN C	LTC	0-1044676	C966	1
SHREVE PAUL E	2LT	0-1554088	0246	2
SHREVE ROY J	CPT	0-0495779	1157	1
SHREVES JR JOHN P	2LT	0-0354253	1142	2
SHREVES MELVILLE N	MAJ	C-0218399	0648	3
SHREWSBURY ARCHIE K	1LT	0-0956521	CR67	2
SHREWSBURY CHARLES E	CPT	0-0472121	C746	1

NAME	GRADE	SVC NO	DATE RET MO YR	RET CODE
SHREWSBURY GECRGE W	CW3	W-2150223	0959	1
SHRIGLEY OTTC E	CPT	0-0108434	0840	1
SHRINER EDWARD C	MAJ	C-0209C81	0948	3
SHRINER MARQUIS A	LTC	0-0963442	1162	1
SHRIVER ANN	MAJ	N-0767249	0766	3
SHRIVER GLENA G	MAJ	0-0969894	0163	1
SHRIVER JAY W	CPT	0-1700477	0745	2
SHRIVER JOSEPH G	CW3	W-2144261	0461	1
SHRIVER KARL H	COL	0-0108278	0648	3
SHROCK WAYNE T	MAJ	0-0274335	0159	3
SHROPSHIRE JAMES S	LTC	0-0257698	0966	3
SHROUT AMBROS	CPT	0-0479407	0846	1
SHROUT CARL C	CW3	W-2148765	0661	1
SHROY RICHARC E	COL	0-0357372	1162	1
SHROYER FRED N	MAJ	0-1685735	1065	1
SHRUM PAUL L	COL	0-0176857	0758	3
SHUBART STANLEY C	COL	0-0232692	0766	3
SHUDER RUSSELL M	COL	0-0348543	0861	1
SHUE HAROLD I	LTC	0-1018485	0263	1
SHUER JAY J	1LT	0-1283506	0845	2
SHUEY EDWARD W	CW3	W-2146443	0463	1
SHUFELT CECRGE H	COL	0-0266028	0359	3
SHUFF KING W	CW2	W-2149154	0760	1
SHUFFIELD JR JAMES W	1LT	0-1048572	0144	2
SHUFFLEBARGER JOHN H	MAJ	0-1116256	0561	1
SHUFLATA JR GEORGE J	LTC	0-1081097	0861	1
SHUFORC NORMAN C	MAJ	0-0139427	1048	3
SHUGART CLARENCE M	LTC	0-0887425	0463	1
SHUGART GLENN W	MAJ	0-2016145	0359	1
SHUGART MARIEN L	LTC	0-0244698	0766	3
SHUGART R T	LTC	0-0287005	1060	1
SHUGERT JAMES M H	LTC	0-1050C86	0863	1
SHUH JUDSON	1LT	0-0409145	0543	2
SHUKERS CARRCLL F	COL	0-0319981	1065	3
SHUKIS ROMANUS	CW4	W-2136652	1167	1
SHULAR JR WILLIAM A	MAJ	0-1295283	0265	1
SHULENBERG LEROY E	MAJ	0-097023C	0365	1
SHULER JOHN H	LTC	0-0252818	1066	3
SHULKCUM EDWARD	MAJ	C-0260648	0864	3
SHULL EDWIN L	B G	0-0335061	0764	3
SHULL HOMER	2LT	0-1913936	1031	1
SHULL LESTER A	LTC	0-0260033	0264	3
SHULL RALPH G	MAJ	0-0947426	1159	1
SHULMAN HERBERT	CPT	0-0368272	1045	2
SHULMAN MAURICE	MAJ	0-0141240	1052	3
SHULMAN MAX L	MAJ	C-0281833	0346	2
SHULT BRUCE E	LTC	0-0399248	0657	1
SHULTICE ROBERT W	CPT	0-1593275	0363	1
SHULTS CAMERCN	LTC	0-0401656	0860	1
SHULTS THOMAS N	1LT	0-0358722	0345	2
SHULTZ EARL F	LTC	0-0947052	0767	1
SHULTZ HAROLD M	CPT	0-1283858	0448	2
SHULTZ HERMAN N	CW2	W-2145358	0160	1
SHULTZ JAMES O	CPT	0-1589502	0347	2
SHULTZ NANCY S	2LT	N-0760276	1144	1
SHULTZ RALPH	COL	0-0149231	1046	2
SHUMAKER CLARENCE A	LTC	0-0104468	0159	3
SHUMAKER GEORGE L	COL	0-0379230	1067	1
SHUMAKER HENRY	COL	0-0373045	1058	1
SHUMAKER JR WARREN B	LTC	0-0674807	0266	1
SHUMAKER MEREDITH L	COL	0-0377823	0765	1
SHUMAN HAROLC	LTC	0-0306961	0560	1
SHUMAN JAMES R	LTC	0-0404764	0762	1
SHUMAN ROBERT L	CPT	0-0367139	0645	2
SHUMATE BAYARD S	COL	0-0234770	1156	3
SHUMATE BRUCE E	COL	0-0316506	0866	3
SHUMATE CARL T	1LT	0-1683492	0346	2
SHUMATE EDWARD M	CW3	W-2152401	0764	1
SHUMOCK EARL F	CW3	W-2152326	0263	1
SHUMPERT FLOYD A	MAJ	0-1303358	0247	2
SHUMWAY HYRUM S	1LT	0-0524584	1046	2
SHUPE ARTHUR R	LTC	0-1296756	0854	1
SHUPERT VERNCN C	2LT	0-1304129	0644	2
SHUPING ALEXANDER	CPT	0-0208768	0658	3
SHUPP LEO B	LTC	0-1340502	0667	1

NAME	GRADE	SVC NO	DATE RET MO YR	RET CODE
SHUPUT MICHAEL M	CW4	W-2142722	1262	2
SHUR HENRY	MAJ	0-0390779	0647	2
SHURBET WILLIAM E	CPT	0-0342786	0144	2
SHURE ABRAHAM L	MAJ	0-1683222	0446	2
SHURLEY HOMER C	2LT	0-1597088	0653	1
SHURLEY JR WILLIAM R	LTC	0-0418527	0261	2
SHURTLEFF CLINTON D	MAJ	0-0279127	0745	2
SHURTLEFF HORACE W	COL	0-0287321	0658	3
SHURTLEFF JR W H	COL	C-0195689	1054	1
SHURTLEFF L J	COL	C-0193666	0-53	1
SHURTLIFF WESLEY O	LTC	0-0320433	1063	1
SHURTS NORMAN	LTC	0-1113443	0267	1
SHURTZ EUGENE F	LTC	0-1576644	0764	1
SHURTZ JOHN R	1LT	0-1822202	C546	2
SHUSTER PHILIP L	CW3	W-2116030	0155	2
SHUTE DONALD M	COL	0-0275817	0161	3
SHUTE EMIL	LTC	0-0397040	1057	1
SHUTE JEAN P	LTC	0-0311170	0859	1
SHUTES HOWARD A	LTC	0-1596496	0166	1
SHUTT GEORGE B	LTC	0-1010066	0360	1
SHYTLE CARL D	COL	0-0267536	0958	1
SIAS HAROLD E	LTC	0-1690828	0962	1
SIAS RUSSELL O	CPT	0-0285647	C644	2
SIBAL CEZAR	MAJ	C-1896748	C161	1
SIBALA HILARIO	CPT	0-1896676	1060	1
SIBBETT WILLIAM A	1LT	0-1055975	1147	2
SIBERT DENNIS W	MAJ	C-1798522	1058	1
SIBERT HAROLD W	LTC	C-0443528	1054	1
SIBERT JR JOHN W	COL	0-0190000	0962	3
SIBERT LOTHER B	COL	C-0352905	C964	1
SIBERT RALPH E	CPT	0-1018589	1156	1
SIBERT RAY S	LTC	0-0399886	0161	1
SIBERT ROBERT L	WO1	W-2128124	1046	1
SIBERZ LLOYD W	LTC	0-1545011	1062	1
SIBLEY KENNETH L	MAJ	C-0488898	0555	1
SIBLEY KENNETH R	MAJ	0-1541583	0457	1
SIBLEY LINWOOD I	LTC	0-1551517	1164	1
SIBLEY WALTER C	1LT	0-1043498	0545	2
SIBRAY DONALD L	LTC	0-0174237	0258	3
SIBRAY JR WILLIS S	1LT	0-1542538	0845	2
SIBSON WALTER W	2LT	0-1535620	0245	2
SICA ALPHONSO J	CPT	0-0257111	0347	1
SICA FRANK A	CPT	0-0486517	0646	2
SICAY TEOFILO C	MAJ	0-1896962	0461	1
SICHER MAX F	MAJ	0-4013551	0567	1
SICILIA FRANK	LTC	0-2007891	0365	3
SICILIANO JOSEPH M	CPT	0-0339263	0946	1
SICILIANO PHYLLIS V	1LT	N-0730162	C546	2
SICKELS GLENN	2LT	0-1550918	1043	2
SICKENGA JACK H	LTC	0-0388906	1060	1
SICKEROTT CARL O	CPT	0-0462360	1146	2
SICKING ROBERT C	1LT	C-1054411	0946	2
SICKLER JESSE O	COL	C-0317551	1055	3
SICKMAN JONATHAN V	MAJ	0-1105819	1067	3
SICURANZA JACK L	LTC	0-1576857	0557	1
SIDARIS NICKOLAS J	1LT	0-0769964	1147	2
SIDDALL MARY I	1LT	N-0775583	1046	1
SIDDALL WILLIAM S	LTC	0-1102047	0266	1
SIDDONS ARTHUR W	CPT	0-1102466	0954	1
SIDEBOTTOM RUSSELL L	CW2	W-2207499	0565	1
SIDERIS CHRIS Z	1LT	0-2050133	0847	2
SIDERS WALTER F	LTC	0-0497167	C767	3
SIDLE CHARLES L	COL	0-0266681	0546	2
SIDLER II EARL R	LTC	0-0402191	0566	3
SIDLEY WILLIAM F	MAJ	C-1899423	0165	1
SIDMORE PHILIP R	LTC	0-0327848	0163	1
SIDOTI JOSEPH T	CW3	W-2150973	0763	1
SIDWELL JOSEPH H	CPT	0-0293866	0246	2
SIEBE JR CHARLES C	1LT	0-1050465	1047	2
SIEBEN CERALD M	CPT	0-0481787	0445	2
SIEBER LOUIS M	MAJ	C-0997948	0264	1
SIEBERT WALTER A	LTC	0-0283060	0459	1
SIEBRECHT JAMES K	CPT	0-0417352	0144	2
SIEDER EVERETT N	LTC	0-0220803	0663	3
SIEDSCHLAG EVERETT W	1LT	0-0530182	0851	1

NAME	GRADE	SVC NO	DATE RET MO YR	RET CODE
SIEFERT CLARENCE L	LTC	0-1546313	0167	1
SIEGAL EDWARD I	COL	0-0349942	0567	3
SIEGEL ALVIN	LTC	0-1341714	0467	1
SIEGEL ANNE A	MAJ	N-0760650	1167	3
SIEGEL ERWIN A	CPT	0-0666096	0262	1
SIEGEL KENNETH I	MAJ	0-1306327	1058	1
SIEGEL LEO	MAJ	0-0139483	0146	2
SIEGEL MARTIN	MAJ	0-1182255	1062	1
SIEGEL MICHAEL	MAJ	0-0503356	0954	1
SIEGEL NATHAN	LTC	0-0523185	0855	1
SIEGEL OSCAR A	2LT	0-1045929	0944	2
SIEGEL PETER	COL	0-0298637	0463	3
SIEGEL SHEPPARD M	CPT	0-2264474	1155	2
SIEGENTHALER S K	1LT	0-1061859	1145	2
SIEGER GILBERT G	CW2	W-2209727	1061	1
SIEGERT SHELOCN R	CPT	0-1549839	0947	1
SIEGFRIEC CHARLES W	MAJ	0-1294377	0861	1
SIEGFRIED JR JOHN	CPT	0-1786193	0146	2
SIEGLER MARETTA D	1LT	N-0775836	0146	1
SIEGLING EDMOND M	MAJ	0-1109666	0663	3
SIEGMONC CLEC F	1LT	N-0731739	1146	1
SIEGMUND RUDOLPH A	CPT	0-1100765	0947	2
SIEGRIST ADOLPH W	1LT	0-0342241	1144	2
SIEGRIST JR C J	CPT	0-0348463	0744	2
SIEGRIST KENNETH J	1LT	0-0493712	1045	2
SIEKER JCHN H	CPT	0-0196172	0263	3
SIEKIERSKI ALCISIUS	CW3	W-2143513	0561	1
SIEMASKO ALPHONSE W	1LT	0-1998108	0248	2
SIEMINSKI LEON	MAJ	0-0450358	0854	1
SIEMON ADOLPH V	1LT	0-1288795	0844	2
SIEMON ROSA L	1LT	N-0703026	0646	1
SIEMONSMA CLARENCE E	LTC	0-0921466	0564	3
SIENES DEMETRIO	2LT	0-0890503	C654	1
SIENKIEWICZ SOPHIE T	2LT	N-0792256	0749	2
SIER ROBERT M	CW3	W-2146997	0559	1
SIEROCKI CHESTER R	CPT	0-1535302	0364	2
SIERRA GEORGE	CW2	W-2214785	1066	1
SIERZEGA EMIL M	1LT	0-1183192	0248	2
SIEVERS BERNARD M	MAJ	0-2021191	0166	1
SIEVERS EDWARD L	LTC	0-179500C	0766	1
SIEVERS EDWIN R	MAJ	0-0338852	0461	3
SIEVERT EDGAR W	CPT	0-0289384	0649	2
SIEVWRIGHT ELMER B	CPT	0-1042705	0863	1
SIEVWRIGHT RICHARD H	MAJ	0-1338867	0567	1
SIEWERS CEORGE M	LTC	0-1823224	0864	1
SIEWERT ORVILLE R	MAJ	0-2014776	0264	1
SIFOOL RAYMOND S	MAJ	0-0175443	0344	2
SIGAUD LOUIS A	LTC	0-0133719	0953	3
SIGEL DAVE	COL	0-0151781	0446	2
SIGELO PATRICK J	LTC	0-1295094	1264	1
SIGETY DAVID R	CW3	W-2152647	0966	1
SIGLER LYNN E	1LT	0-1327671	C646	2
SIGLER MAHLON O	MAJ	0-0268261	1049	1
SIGLER PHARES O	COL	0-0319652	0659	3
SIGLER RUSSELL K	1LT	0-1324564	1045	2
SIGLER THOMAS V	COL	0-0406899	1062	1
SIGLEY ALLEN L	CPT	0-1582129	0347	2
SIGMANN WILLIAM J	MAJ	0-1018431	0963	1
SIGMON ERNEST E	MAJ	0-0585800	0856	1
SIGMONC HENRY I	LTC	0-0253267	0962	3
SIGNORELLI PATRICK L	CW2	W-2143237	0960	1
SIGOUIN ROLANC G	CW3	W-2153355	0663	2
SIGOURNEY DAVID R	LTC	0-0159339	0953	3
SIGSBEE HAROLD J	LTC	0-1167221	0967	3
SIGSWORTH ALLYN B	MAJ	0-2017912	0664	1
SIGWALC JOHN J	LTC	0-0231793	0360	1
SIGWELL RUSSELL E	LTC	0-203608C	0860	1
SIHTO JR THOMAS	CPT	0-0285176	1050	1
SIKES DANIEL O	MAJ	0-0249233	0164	3
SIKES DERRILL F	MAJ	0-1947084	0764	1
SIKES JAMES I	LTC	0-044199C	0365	1
SIKES JAMES S	CPT	0-1289157	1057	1
SIKES ROBERT L	CPT	0-0499876	0463	1
SIKORA ALFONS	CPT	0-2010659	0359	1
SIKORSKI JOSEPH C	MAJ	C-1050089	0561	1

NAME	GRADE	SVC NO	DATE RET MO YR	RET CODE
SIKORSKI WILLIAM	LTC	0-1177183	0658	1
SIKORSKY JR ANDREW J	LTC	0-1294207	0663	1
SILAN STEVE	MAJ	0-1118809	0959	1
SILATA FRANK	1LT	0-1996347	0546	2
SILBAUGH JACK	MAJ	0-2032324	0665	1
SILBER JR PAUL G	1LT	0-1327891	0247	2
SILBER WILLIAM H	LTC	0-1320783	0866	1
SILBERBERG JULES W	MAJ	0-2208409	0666	1
SILBERT ARVID E	CPT	0-1041913	0146	2
SILBERT DAVID	LTC	0-1002128	0766	3
SILCOX ISAAC	CPT	0-2018229	0358	1
SILCOX RAY W	LTC	0-0376231	1146	2
SILENCE JOSEPH F	1LT	0-1822640	1067	2
SILER ARNOLD	MAJ	0-0421254	1060	1
SILER ELMER W	MAJ	0-0307777	0944	2
SILER JAMES G	MAJ	0-0267383	0363	3
SILFEN CHARLES	CPT	0-1325936	0556	1
SILL MORTON H	LTC	0-1011315	0358	1
SILL ROBERT F	LTC	0-1556219	0166	1
SILLER RALPH E	CPT	0-1584906	0246	2
SILLIMAN BENJAMIN O	LTC	0-0122803	0955	3
SILLIMAN CHARLES A	1LT	0-0407478	0346	2
SILLIMAN CHESTER W	MAJ	0-0278582	0667	3
SILLIMAN 3RD FRANK	COL	0-0179174	0157	3
SILLMAN CHESTER W	1LT	0-1311694	0545	2
SILLONA GAUDENCIO	MAJ	0-0267129	0554	1
SILLS JOHN F	LTC	0-0349630	1160	1
SILO BENJAMIN	1LT	0-1897023	0164	1
SILSBEE 2ND HENRY O	COL	0-0124188	0749	3
SILSBY DON J	LTC	0-0294813	0865	3
SILVA ALVIN K	COL	0-0175152	0660	3
SILVA ANTONIO R	LTC	0-0182910	0657	3
SILVA ERNEST P	LTC	0-1012493	0764	1
SILVA EURIPIDES	COL	0-0245105	0555	3
SILVA JOHN B	2LT	0-1112973	1044	2
SILVA JOHN J	MAJ	0-1110804	0562	1
SILVA JULIO N	CPT	0-4010748	1165	1
SILVA SATURNINO	LTC	0-1300095	0848	2
SILVA TORIVIO	MAJ	0-1533675	1060	1
SILVA WALTER G	LTC	0-0453882	1060	1
SILVER CHARLES H	1LT	0-0438331	0646	1
SILVER DAVID	LTC	0-1332749	0766	1
SILVER FRANCIS F	MAJ	0-0369549	0247	2
SILVER GEORGE A	MAJ	0-0475110	0546	2
SILVER HARRY R	MAJ	0-0476397	0945	2
SILVER HORACE S	CW3	W-2208057	0566	1
SILVER IRVING	CPT	0-1283682	0546	2
SILVER JONAS	CPT	0-1690052	0344	1
SILVER MICHAEL W	1LT	0-0368967	0146	2
SILVER RAYMOND R	CW3	W-2147060	0465	1
SILVER RICHARD F	LTC	0-0285340	1264	3
SILVERA TOM B	CPT	0-0491302	0845	2
SILVERBERG EDWARD M	COL	0-0113728	0754	3
SILVERBERG ISRAEL	LTC	0-1796715	0965	3
SILVERIO BONIFACIO	2LT	0-1896891	1251	2
SILVERMAN ABRAHAM G	COL	0-0170178	0657	1
SILVERMAN MARTIN H	CW3	W-2145297	0464	2
SILVERMAN MAX H	COL	0-0539332	1167	1
SILVERMAN MEYER	1LT	0-0107995	1037	1
SILVERMAN PHILIP	CPT	0-0265770	0855	3
SILVERNAIL EDMUND M	LTC	0-1016169	0864	1
SILVERSTEIN BERNARD	LTC	0-0262629	1163	3
SILVERSTEIN STUART H	1LT	0-1185312	0146	2
SILVERTHORN CHARLES	MAJ	0-1951635	0665	1
SILVESTRO THOMAS	CW3	W-2147288	1165	1
SILVEY FREDERICK	LTC	0-0356134	0349	2
SILVEY SR CHARLES O	CW3	W-2152168	0465	1
SILVEY WILLIAM R	COL	0-0208512	0258	3
SILVIA WILLIAM J	WO1	W-2105382	1049	1
SIM ALEX T	1LT	0-0112455	1054	3
SIMANK ARTHUR	CPT	0-1796716	1258	2
SIMARO JOSEPH G E	1LT	0-1577850	0245	2
SIMARO STANLEY B	1LT	0-0339958	1044	2
SIMCHICK JOSEPH L	1LT	0-1317599	0944	2
SIMCOX CLARENCE H	MAJ	0-1301044	0557	1
SIMENSON RAYMOND S	CPT	0-0356719	1045	2
SIMES GARDNER M	LTC	0-0251821	0467	3
SIMICH ALEXANDER	CW4	W-2116025	0157	1
SIMIELE FRANK	COL	0-0456666	0665	1
SIMKIN THEODORE T	CPT	0-1015946	0846	1
SIMKINS HOMER A	MAJ	0-0246992	0349	3
SIMKINS JR WILLIAM B	MAJ	0-1844394	0762	2
SIMKINS LESLIE C	COL	0-0236954	0464	3
SIMKINS MURRAY K	1LT	0-1179709	1144	2
SIMKINS ROY G	MAJ	0-0217147	0145	1
SIMMERMAN WALTER H	CW2	W-2210922	0166	1
SIMMERS RICHARD C	CPT	0-1289977	1045	1
SIMMERT ROBERT H	B G	0-0271897	0467	3
SIMMIE ALBERT F	CPT	0-0890373	0847	2
SIMMINGTON JR T	MAJ	0-0417591	0553	1
SIMMONDS GEORGE H	MAJ	0-1306897	0462	1
SIMMONDS HAROLD W	LTC	0-0329913	0158	3
SIMMONDS JOE G	CPT	0-1291024	0847	1
SIMMONDS MAURICE R	LTC	0-0275306	0457	1
SIMMONITE HENRY G	COL	0-0257292	0465	3
SIMMONS A J LOWE	MAJ	0-1172657	0155	1
SIMMONS ALFRED J	CW3	W-2209917	1060	1
SIMMONS AMOS F	MAJ	0-0966292	0163	1
SIMMONS BESSIE O	1LT	N-0797678	0647	1
SIMMONS CARL A	LTC	0-1685020	0166	1
SIMMONS CARL G	MAJ	0-0341477	0146	2
SIMMONS CHARLES F	CPT	0-0509076	0147	1
SIMMONS CHESTER B	LTC	0-0277853	0466	3
SIMMONS CLARENCE C	LTC	0-0466241	0560	3
SIMMONS CLIFFORD H	1LT	0-0382607	0245	2
SIMMONS DANIEL H	LTC	0-1049647	0164	1
SIMMONS EDWARD E	CPT	0-1038289	1154	2
SIMMONS EDWIN R	LTC	0-1175577	0764	1
SIMMONS ELMER M	LTC	0-0164221	0753	1
SIMMONS ELMER N	MAJ	0-0501192	0854	1
SIMMONS ELMORE P	MAJ	0-0514544	0457	1
SIMMONS ELVIS A	1LT	0-0519423	0447	2
SIMMONS EMIL	LTC	0-0493416	0257	1
SIMMONS FARRIS C	MAJ	0-1305328	0761	1
SIMMONS FLAVIUS K	MAJ	0-0936090	0762	1
SIMMONS FLOYD L	COL	0-0100037	0748	3
SIMMONS FRANK G	CPT	0-0353351	0346	2
SIMMONS FRED H	LTC	0-0254748	1163	3
SIMMONS FREMONT	CPT	0-0157514	0238	1
SIMMONS GEORGE E	COL	0-0276427	1164	3
SIMMONS GEORGE E	CPT	0-1306159	0745	2
SIMMONS GEORGE F	MAJ	0-1324795	0163	1
SIMMONS GEORGE L	CW2	W-2000725	0644	2
SIMMONS GERALD W	CW4	W-2103437	0759	2
SIMMONS GORDON H	LTC	0-0522634	0967	1
SIMMONS GRANT A	MAJ	0-0976461	1263	1
SIMMONS HARRIMAN N	LTC	0-0272277	0464	3
SIMMONS HARRY E	MAJ	0-0101999	0258	3
SIMMONS HERBERT W	CW2	W-2109057	0453	1
SIMMONS J W	CPT	0-1184725	1060	1
SIMMONS JAMES L	1LT	0-0393073	0445	2
SIMMONS JAMES W	MAJ	0-1292074	0747	2
SIMMONS JAMES W	LTC	0-1594481	1262	2
SIMMONS JOHN D	LTC	0-1315487	1164	1
SIMMONS JOHN W	LTC	0-0386896	0961	1
SIMMONS JOSEPH F	MAJ	0-2015749	1165	1
SIMMONS JR ABRAM F	CW3	W-2152153	1063	1
SIMMONS JR ARTHUR B	1LT	0-0341869	1043	1
SIMMONS JR GEORGE H	2LT	0-0540601	1144	2
SIMMONS LEON G	LTC	0-2055896	0765	1
SIMMONS LLOYD B	MAJ	0-0452175	0762	1
SIMMONS MARVIN H	MAJ	0-1591445	0964	3
SIMMONS MELVIN C	MAJ	0-1639648	1063	1
SIMMONS MELVIN L	CPT	0-0984721	1161	1
SIMMONS NOLA	1LT	N-0744732	0548	1
SIMMONS PHILIP F	MAJ	0-0402258	0649	2
SIMMONS R B	MAJ	0-0967139	0462	1
SIMMONS ROBERT W	1LT	0-1296272	1145	2
SIMMONS ROSS Y	CPT	0-1291025	0657	1
SIMMONS SAMUEL O	CW4	W-2002083	1164	3
SIMMONS SR ROY P	MAJ	0-1015102	0559	1
SIMMONS THOMAS C	MAJ	0-0335235	1044	2
SIMMONS THOMAS S	MAJ	0-1634326	1057	1
SIMMONS TOM R	MAJ	0-0176221	0462	1
SIMMONS VICTOR C	LTC	0-0305785	1047	2
SIMMONS VICTOR H	MAJ	0-1580325	0762	1
SIMMONS WALTER L	MAJ	0-1323622	0257	1
SIMMONS WILLARD C	LTC	0-1000473	0862	1
SIMMONS WILLIAM	MAJ	0-0488544	0953	2
SIMMONS WILLIAM E	LTC	0-0169008	0360	3
SIMMONS WILLIAM H	1LT	0-1824927	0449	2
SIMMONS WILLIAM H	CW2	W-2142051	1061	1
SIMMONS WILLIAM J	MAJ	0-2032866	0463	1
SIMMONS WILLIAM K	MAJ	0-0444345	0150	1
SIMMONS WILTON L	COL	0-0372208	0361	1
SIMMS BERNARD G	LTC	0-0414862	0763	1
SIMMS CHARLES H	LTC	0-0321522	0258	1
SIMMS CLARENCE J	LTC	0-0294922	0866	3
SIMMS EDWARD A	CW3	W-2145510	0264	1
SIMMS GEORGE C	LTC	0-0202217	0757	1
SIMMS HAROLD A	CPT	0-0131561	0648	3
SIMMS HARWELL	MAJ	0-1296923	0761	1
SIMMS JR EDWARD W	LTC	0-1582132	0962	1
SIMMS WILLIAM H	LTC	0-1320258	1167	1
SIMMS WILLIAM P	1LT	0-1324957	0246	2
SIMON ANNE MARIE	CPT	N-0759050	1147	1
SIMON CHARLES	CPT	0-0372136	0745	2
SIMON CHARLES J	MAJ	0-0206254	1163	3
SIMON FRANCIS E	CPT	0-1319129	0746	2
SIMON FRANCIS M	CW2	W-3200319	1266	1
SIMON HARRY R	1LT	0-5504381	0860	2
SIMON HENRY	MAJ	0-0501534	1045	2
SIMON JOHN D	MAJ	0-0270465	0246	2
SIMON JR FELIX M	CPT	0-0987099	1062	1
SIMON JR JOHN M	MAJ	0-2025898	0363	1
SIMON KONA	MAJ	0-0371956	0346	2
SIMON LESTER E	MAJ	0-0252535	0647	2
SIMON MAX R	LTC	0-0139439	0648	3
SIMON MICHAEL R	MAJ	0-0558854	1145	2
SIMON MORTON L	1LT	0-1574527	0444	2
SIMON NORMAN	CPT	0-0379670	1045	2
SIMON SAMUEL S	CW2	W-2151870	0361	1
SIMON SIDNEY	2LT	0-1298771	0245	2
SIMON STANLEY J	LTC	0-0291027	0151	2
SIMONDS EDWARD P	LTC	0-1322722	0764	1
SIMONDS JACK L	MAJ	0-1913374	0265	1
SIMONELLI MARIO	CPT	0-0501735	0245	2
SIMONEN LAURA L	1LT	N-0703604	0546	1
SIMONETTI LOUIS J	LTC	0-0520018	0466	3
SIMONIDES HOWARD A	LTC	0-1047781	0264	1
SIMONS BERNARD C	CPT	0-0947033	0557	2
SIMONS CHARLES H	CPT	0-2029673	1059	1
SIMONS EDWARD H	CPT	0-1291187	0560	2
SIMONS KENNETH L	LTC	0-0225809	0265	3
SIMONS LYLE E	LTC	0-1319030	0757	2
SIMONS MILTON N	LTC	0-0294873	0863	1
SIMONS WEBSTER L	COL	0-0221680	0557	1
SIMONSEN JR EDWARD G	1LT	0-1337767	0751	1
SIMONSON ARNOLD L	MAJ	0-0535175	0759	2
SIMONSON CHARLES H	1LT	0-0115084	0555	3
SIMONSON DONALD B	CPT	0-1700686	0246	2
SIMONSON JOE A	LTC	0-0245595	0860	2
SIMONSON RAE L	1LT	0-1293845	0346	2
SIMONTON RAY M	1LT	0-1322961	1045	2
SIMOWITZ BERNARD	MAJ	0-0241588	0466	3
SIMPKINS SILAS C	MAJ	0-0192813	0655	3
SIMPSON ARTHUR T	MAJ	0-0166463	0648	3
SIMPSON BAILEY L	LTC	0-0206514	1054	1
SIMPSON CARL C	LTC	0-1178625	0164	1
SIMPSON CHARLES H	WO1	W-2122577	1045	2
SIMPSON CHARLES J	LTC	0-2024342	0461	1
SIMPSON CHARLES W	LTC	0-1686296	0765	2
SIMPSON CHARLIE F	1LT	0-0495768	0951	1
SIMPSON CLAUDE F	CW3	W-2145753	0262	1
SIMPSON CLAUDE S	LTC	0-0401080	0260	1
SIMPSON CLAYTON R	MAJ	0-2263017	0663	1
SIMPSON CLINTON F	LTC	0-0135594	0653	3
SIMPSON DAN C	LTC	0-0214576	0164	3
SIMPSON DAVID R	LTC	0-0172623	0648	3
SIMPSON DAVID V	MAJ	0-0347971	1163	3
SIMPSON DONALD M	1LT	0-0200164	0762	3
SIMPSON EARLE A	CPT	0-2006366	0458	2
SIMPSON EDGAR F	LTC	0-0265622	0759	3
SIMPSON EDWIN H	1LT	0-1592058	0761	1
SIMPSON EUGENE L	MAJ	0-1552384	0760	1
SIMPSON EUGENE R	1LT	0-0971325	0857	1
SIMPSON EVERETT W	LTC	0-0114382	0755	3
SIMPSON FELIX T	LTC	0-0184516	0-52	3
SIMPSON GEORGE E	LTC	0-1002528	0166	3
SIMPSON GERALD M	CW3	W-2206305	0867	1
SIMPSON GLENN C	LTC	0-1686537	1166	1
SIMPSON GLYNN W	MAJ	0-1635333	0358	1
SIMPSON GRAYSON	CPT	0-0386271	0254	2
SIMPSON HARRY B	LTC	0-0280646	0260	3
SIMPSON HARVEY A	1LT	0-1302367	0745	2
SIMPSON HOMER D	CPT	0-2262185	0257	2
SIMPSON IRA C	CW3	W-2116011	1154	1
SIMPSON JACK B	MAJ	0-0976050	0466	1
SIMPSON JACK L	1LT	0-1301379	0853	1
SIMPSON JAMES	LTC	0-0275607	0754	3
SIMPSON JAMES B	1LT	0-2042773	1045	2
SIMPSON JOHN A	1LT	0-1038843	0945	2
SIMPSON JOHN E	LTC	0-0373268	1164	1
SIMPSON JOHN M	CW3	W-2147546	0764	1
SIMPSON JOSEPH M	COL	0-0222086	0560	3
SIMPSON JOSEPH T	MAJ	0-0450904	0459	1
SIMPSON JR ANDREW	CW3	W-2206371	1265	1
SIMPSON JR BEN R	CPT	0-0392474	0546	1
SIMPSON JR JOHN P	COL	0-0251664	0966	3
SIMPSON JR R B	CW2	W-3100520	1167	1
SIMPSON JUBE A	MAJ	0-1550919	0662	2
SIMPSON LAVAUGHAN	CPT	0-1582894	0856	1
SIMPSON MARK H	2LT	0-1633550	0343	1
SIMPSON MARTHA I	MAJ	N-0724090	0361	1
SIMPSON MAURICE M	MAJ	0-1549840	0962	1
SIMPSON NELL A	2LT	N-0786747	1046	1
SIMPSON RAY M	LTC	0-0395771	0960	1
SIMPSON RAYMOND	LTC	0-0525864	0463	1
SIMPSON REUBEN J	CW2	W-2209044	0565	1
SIMPSON RICHARD S	1LT	0-0403167	1045	2
SIMPSON ROBERT A	CW4	W-2148985	0958	1
SIMPSON ROBERT B	COL	0-0291975	1061	1
SIMPSON ROBERT S	MAJ	0-0475601	0446	2
SIMPSON SYDNEY E	CPT	0-1307862	0246	2
SIMPSON THOMAS C	LTC	0-0255211	1262	2
SIMPSON THOMAS D	2LT	0-1183414	0245	2
SIMPSON VERNON R	MAJ	0-0959187	0267	1
SIMPSON VERNON W	CPT	0-0515867	0159	1
SIMPSON VICTOR C	LTC	0-1180337	0467	1
SIMPSON WALTER L	LTC	0-0127921	0648	3
SIMPSON WILLIAM A	1LT	0-1048191	0845	1
SIMPSON WILLIAM A	MAJ	0-1306486	0764	1
SIMPSON WILLIAM E	CPT	0-0153900	0748	3
SIMPSON WILLIAM E	COL	0-0339393	0660	1
SIMPSON WILLIAM R	1LT	0-0462475	0246	2
SIMS BILL H	MAJ	0-1535691	1061	1
SIMS CARL C	MAJ	0-1796718	0560	1
SIMS CHARLES E	MAJ	0-0276480	0356	3
SIMS CLAIR W	LTC	0-0253716	0567	3
SIMS CLAUDE E	CPT	0-2026856	0859	2
SIMS CLAYTON C	COL	0-1302537	1263	1
SIMS DEWARD W	MAJ	0-1169739	0361	1
SIMS DURWARD M	MAJ	0-0947791	0865	1
SIMS ELBURN T	COL	0-0184133	0246	2
SIMS FRED A	CW3	W-2141829	1262	1
SIMS FRED E	LTC	0-0249732	0457	1
SIMS HAROLD S	CPT	0-2011137	0853	1
SIMS HOWARD C	2LT	0-4076205	1158	2
SIMS HUBERT M	CW3	W-2148192	0761	1
SIMS JAMES S	CW4	W-2143236	0466	1

ARMY OF THE UNITED STATES RETIRED LIST

NAME	GRADE	SVC NO	DATE RET MO YR	RET CODE
SIMS JR MATT B H	MAJ	0-1340702	0765	1
SIMS JR WILLIAM H	CPT	0-1290672	0146	2
SIMS KENNETH P	LTC	0-1559258	0263	1
SIMS LEONARD F	CPT	0-0477368	C148	1
SIMS MURPHY M	LTC	0-0388153	0955	2
SIMS ORLEY J	LTC	0-1318717	0964	1
SIMS RALEIGH N	LTC	0-1300724	1060	1
SIMS ROBERT J	MAJ	0-1692935	C559	1
SIMS SAMUEL	CPT	0-1699866	0745	2
SIMS SAMUEL E	CPT	0-1111362	0446	2
SIMS STANLEY R	1LT	0-0404358	0167	3
SIMS THOMAS J	CW3	W-2142199	C756	1
SIMS VIRGIL	WO1	W-2126108	C145	2
SIMS VIVIAN H	MAJ	L-1010027	1164	1
SIMS WALTER K	LTC	0-0338996	0760	1
SIMS WILLIAM F	LTC	0-0294061	0967	3
SIMS WILLIAM L	CW2	W-2146957	0358	1
SIMURO BERNARD F	1LT	0-1318230	1045	2
SINAIKO RUSSELL P	CPT	C-0361553	C346	2
SINCAVAGE JOSEPH J	MAJ	0-0456596	0658	1
SINCIC EDWARD B	1LT	0-1291715	0546	2
SINCLAIR DONALD	CW2	W-2152152	0860	1
SINCLAIR DONALD R	1LT	0-1100766	1044	2
SINCLAIR HARRY	CW3	W-2119411	0157	1
SINCLAIR JOHN M	CPT	0-1598237	C364	1
SINCLAIR JR HARRY B	LTC	0-0273640	1046	2
SINCLAIR LILLIAN H	CPT	N-0760707	1148	2
SINCLAIR THEODORE R	LTC	0-0155556	0556	3
SINDELL BERNARD I	2LT	0-1053811	C644	2
SINDERMAN MARVIN L	MAJ	C-1312598	1059	1
SINE HIRAM K	COL	0-0174486	0955	1
SINEATH LEROY F	CPT	0-0127959	C544	2
SINEATH WALTON A	LTC	0-1053812	0767	1
SINEX JAMES M	CPT	0-0519424	1046	2
SINEX WILLIAM E	LTC	0-0384616	0562	1
SINGER ALFRED L	LTC	0-1041917	1061	2
SINGER BENJAMIN L	CPT	0-0298542	1166	3
SINGER ELEANOR R	2LT	N-0783366	0646	1
SINGER FRANK S	LTC	0-0415652	0647	1
SINGER FRED J	MAJ	0-0151785	0559	3
SINGER IRVING G	CPT	0-0145200	0953	1
SINGER JACK L	CPT	0-0455371	0445	2
SINGER MAX	CPT	0-0529572	0246	2
SINGER THEODORE B	CW2	W-2152630	1262	1
SINGER WILLIAM I	MAJ	C-0240726	1045	2
SINGEWALD GEORGE L	MAJ	0-0275819	0947	2
SINGLE HERMAN J	MAJ	C-1175314	1060	1
SINGLER JOHN M	CPT	0-1684863	C146	2
SINGLETARY CONRAD F	CPT	0-1918988	0463	1
SINGLETARY DAVE M	2LT	0-1913709	0547	1
SINGLETARY NED	MAJ	0-0352885	1154	1
SINGLETON BURT N	LTC	0-0243927	0961	3
SINGLETON CLIFTON E	COL	0-0192580	0360	1
SINGLETON ELHANON	1LT	0-0497374	0147	1
SINGLETON FRANK P	MAJ	C-0443625	0657	2
SINGLETON HOWARD W	2LT	0-1922815	1156	2
SINGLETON NELSON W	MAJ	0-0337092	0261	1
SINGLETON ROBERT R	1LT	0-C482526	1145	2
SINGLETON WALTER T	CPT	0-0402846	0146	2
SINGLETON WILBERT F	LTC	0-1316496	0862	1
SINGLETON WILLIAM O	LTC	0-0263682	0246	2
SINGLETON WILLIAM O	CPT	C-1690844	0258	1
SINGMASTER LAWRENCE	CPT	0-0461445	0745	2
SINGSON AMBROSIO P	1LT	0-0255496	1048	1
SINKLER CECIL I	MAJ	0-0398235	0759	1
SINKOV ABRAHAM	COL	0-0300669	0967	3
SINKOVIC WILLIAM V	MAJ	C-1055978	0160	1
SINNARD HERBERT R	LTC	C-0217278	1263	3
SINNOCK ALBERT J	1LT	0-0243559	0-50	3
SINNOTT JOSEPH J	LTC	0-1823950	C962	1
SINNOTT PHILIP J	LTC	0-0282849	0453	3
SINOR CLAUDE F	CW2	W-2152251	0765	1
SIPES ROBERT H	LTC	0-0252008	0566	3
SIPLE JOHN J	MAJ	C-1552176	0961	1
SIPOLE ALBERT G	MAJ	C-2042841	0356	1

NAME	GRADE	SVC NO	DATE RET MO YR	RET CODE
SIPOLSKI JAMES	LTC	0-0108991	1040	1
SIPOS ANDREW J	MAJ	0-0182519	0851	3
SIPOS ANDREW J	MAJ	0-1997476	0863	1
SIPPEL WALTER A	LTC	0-1044954	0762	1
SIPPLE ERVIN E	CW2	W-214738C	0461	1
SIPPY MALCOLM B	LTC	0-1C03843	0461	1
SIRACUSS FRANCES R	2LT	N-0796678	0346	1
SIRAN MATTHEW F	LTC	0-1826062	0865	1
SIRAN WALTER J	1LT	0-1581374	0959	1
SIRDEVAN JAMES F	CPT	0-0920172	0147	2
SIREN SYLVESTER	MAJ	0-0156855	0955	3
SIRES JR JOSEPH T	CPT	0-1036025	0652	1
SIRI EUGENE W	MAJ	0-1C35601	0951	1
SIRIANNE RAYMOND A	LTC	0-15568CC	1163	1
SIRK WILLIAM S	CPT	0-0451185	0250	1
SIRKIN LOUIS J	MAJ	0-129913C	0463	1
SIRLES CLYDE P	COL	0-0408214	0962	1
SIROIS EDWARD D	M G	0-0174246	1058	3
SIROIS SAMUEL F	CPT	0-1323781	0547	2
SIROTA JONAS H	CPT	0-0478457	0545	1
SISCO BOBBY J	CW3	W-2209329	0767	1
SISCO ROBERT E L	CPT	0-1795984	0352	1
SISCOE FRED F	MAJ	0-1593280	0865	1
SISEMORE ROBERT L	MAJ	0-094906C	0563	1
SISK HORACE L	MAJ	0-0997097	0866	1
SISK JOHN L	MAJ	0-0346577	0745	2
SISKEL MAURICE	MAJ	C-0275361	1153	2
SISLER BRUCE H	COL	0-0277717	0761	3
SISON JOSE S	CPT	0-1914200	1140	1
SISSON DORIS J	MAJ	L-1010596	0163	1
SISSON GEORGE E	CPT	0-0352662	1044	2
SISSON JAMES A	MAJ	0-0182108	1047	1
SISTAD ARDEN W	LTC	0-1043794	0655	1
SISTEK CHARLES M	MAJ	0-1036741	0755	1
SISTEK EDITH W	2LT	N-0720583	1043	1
SISTI FRANCIS E	MAJ	0-117444C	0361	1
SISTRUNK JOEL B	MAJ	0-2018778	0657	1
SISTRUNK LOUIE W	2LT	0-1053814	0744	2
SITAR STEPHEN B	MAJ	0-1324706	0157	1
SITARIK JOHN P	MAJ	0-2016026	0161	1
SITES CLAUDE W	MAJ	0-1919107	0665	1
SITES HARRY	MAJ	0-1001243	0557	1
SITES LAWRENCE D	LTC	0-2011004	0762	1
SITES MARY E	MAJ	N-0752315	C667	1
SITLER HERBERT G	COL	0-0289444	1164	1
SITNEY JULIAN J	CPT	0-1821410	0446	2
SITNIK BRONISLAW	MAJ	0-1047784	C757	1
SITTON FRANKLIN G	LTC	0-1542137	0960	1
SITTS RALPH J	MAJ	0-0187838	0553	1
SITZMAN SR PHILIP E	LTC	0-1797730	1160	1
SIVAK ANDREW	CW3	W-2147875	0365	1
SIVERSON ADOLPH G	COL	0-0121526	1155	3
SIVERTSON GAYLORD O	LTC	0-1335072	0663	1
SIVETS JOHN W	MAJ	0-1303047	0162	1
SIVIL CLIFFORD L	LTC	0-1300539	0662	1
SIWINSKI ARTHUR G	COL	0-0240051	0166	3
SIWY WALTER J	1LT	0-0419079	0245	2
SIZEMORE DENVER	MAJ	0-0955782	0262	1
SIZEMORE LAMAR T	LTC	0-2019664	1266	1
SIZER EDMUND A	LTC	0-1573589	1154	1
SJODING HAROLD N E	LTC	0-1644092	0556	1
SJORUP CHRISTOPHE	MAJ	0-0959331	0165	1
SKABLA JAMES C	CW3	W-2151780	0363	1
SKABO TORGER	MAJ	C-0258888	0764	3
SKADDEN JAMES O	LTC	0-1103929	0664	1
SKAER JR ARTHUR W	1LT	0-1846067	0746	2
SKAFF DAVID J	MAJ	0-0287688	1144	2
SKAGGS CLINT H	CPT	0-0123472	1054	3
SKAGGS ELMER M	LTC	0-0265660	0459	2
SKAGGS HORACE G	CPT	0-0402355	1045	2
SKAGGS JAMES S	MAJ	0-0156872	0749	3
SKAGGS LOREN O	COL	0-0479095	1152	1
SKAILES THOMAS J	CPT	0-0924174	0244	2
SKAITH LEROY J	LTC	0-1314558	0763	1
SKALICKY EMIL	LTC	0-0375312	0563	1

NAME	GRADE	SVC NO	DATE RET MO YR	RET CODE
SKANSE GEORGE W	MAJ	C-1109013	C463	1
SKARI LUTHER C	CW4	W-2141681	0757	1
SKARRY ARTHUR	COL	0-0234780	0460	3
SKEAHAN THOMAS J	COL	0-0237777	0556	1
SKEEN HENRY C	CPT	0-0164239	0438	1
SKEEN ROBERT P	MAJ	C-1598238	C863	1
SKEEN VICTOR L	1LT	0-1999175	1045	2
SKELLEY LILLIAN L	MAJ	N-0742368	1264	2
SKELLY EDWARD K	LTC	0-0475026	1158	2
SKELLY EDWARD W	COL	C-0299202	0362	3
SKELLY JOSEPH T	MAJ	0-1081031	1160	1
SKELLY MILTON	COL	C-0266873	0665	3
SKELLY WALTER J	COL	0-0199519	0160	1
SKELTON BERYL O	MAJ	N-0756922	0663	3
SKELTON BUSTER L	MAJ	0-0969418	0565	1
SKELTON CLARENCE C	COL	0-0277839	0959	3
SKELTON DOYLE C	COL	C-0277852	1066	3
SKELTON EUGENE	MAJ	0-0984800	1263	1
SKELTON HERBERT J	MAJ	0-0249534	1265	3
SKELTON JR JAMES H	COL	0-0115975	C157	3
SKELTON LAWRENCE R	LTC	0-1302539	0460	1
SKELTON SEWELL G	LTC	C-0327801	1045	2
SKELTON WINIFRED	1LT	N-0721385	C645	1
SKEMP CHARLES P	MAJ	0-0104067	C254	3
SKEMP HAL P	COL	0-0260285	C166	3
SKENDER MILDRED M	2LT	N-0790055	C845	1
SKENDROVIC NORMAN A	LTC	0-1049648	1067	1
SKEOCH RALPH M	CW2	W-2203269	1060	1
SKERKOWSKI FREDERICK	MAJ	0-1686798	1266	1
SKERSTON ISABELLE O	CPT	N-0783768	1146	1
SKERYANC ANTHONY R	MAJ	0-2047831	0358	1
SKEWES CRAIG C	CPT	0-4009064	1162	2
SKIDMORE COOPER	2LT	0-2016963	0161	1
SKIDMORE FRANCIS J	COL	0-0309004	0163	3
SKIDMORE LYDIA G	MAJ	L-1010108	0964	1
SKIDMORE WILLIAM F	LTC	0-0936707	C866	1
SKIELVIG WALTER H	COL	0-0364891	0460	1
SKIFF KENNETH H	LTC	0-1549603	0163	1
SKILLEN JAMES R	COL	0-0236520	1262	3
SKILLEN ROBERT W	LTC	0-0311738	0267	3
SKILLING HAROLD C	MAJ	0-0205233	0550	3
SKILLINGER ROBERT C	LTC	0-1551116	0661	1
SKILLMAN HAROLD R	COL	0-0203796	0457	3
SKILLMAN JR F C	COL	0-0319783	1058	1
SKIMIN ROBERT E	MAJ	0-1686586	0867	1
SKINNER ARTHUR L	MAJ	0-1651325	0863	1
SKINNER BAILEY	MAJ	0-0457846	0449	1
SKINNER CHARLES A	CPT	0-0966942	C560	1
SKINNER EARL D	MAJ	0-0135501	C954	3
SKINNER EARL M	CPT	0-1183971	1146	2
SKINNER EUGENE D	1LT	0-0473512	0744	2
SKINNER EUGENE L	COL	0-0219850	0763	3
SKINNER HARRY J	MAJ	C-0890440	1160	1
SKINNER JAMES C	MAJ	0-2019515	C863	1
SKINNER JAMES D	MAJ	C-2289184	1060	1
SKINNER JAMES M	MAJ	0-1587631	1062	1
SKINNER JOHN T	MAJ	0-0981567	C865	1
SKINNER JR CHARLES E	CPT	0-0137920	0159	3
SKINNER JR LOUIS C	CPT	0-0472036	0445	2
SKINNER JR OTIS R	CPT	C-1339575	C259	2
SKINNER KENYON R	LTC	0-0384628	1064	2
SKINNER LEO	CW3	W-2148399	0767	1
SKINNER MILLARD E	CPT	0-0343812	1044	2
SKINNER RAPHAEL S	MAJ	0-0205757	C460	3
SKINNER RICHMOND H	LTC	0-0123155	0651	1
SKINNER ROBERT M	CW2	W-2131519	0747	1
SKINNER ROGER C	MAJ	0-1306676	C364	1
SKINNER THOMAS E	LTC	0-1110805	C663	1
SKINNER WILLIAM F	MAJ	0-0250677	1165	3
SKINNER WILLIAM J	MAJ	0-2042723	0749	2
SKIPPER JR JOHN T	CW3	W-2145910	0263	1
SKIPTON GERALD F	1LT	0-1593282	0761	1
SKIPTON ROY K	CPT	0-0463943	1046	1
SKIRVING CHARLES O	LTC	0-1582137	C167	1
SKITSKO GEORGE	MAJ	0-1051783	0259	1

NAME	GRADE	SVC NO	DATE RET MO YR	RET CODE
SKLAR MURRAY A	WO1	W-2130597	0647	2
SKLAR SOL H	MAJ	0-0507767	0446	2
SKOBBA JOSEPH S	COL	0-0313015	1164	3
SKOLD BERNARD H	LTC	0-0052013	1060	1
SKOLNICK MAX H	CPT	0-0486015	0645	1
SKOLNICK SOLOMON H	LTC	0-0442166	0747	2
SKOLUDA ERIC R	COL	0-0359453	0665	3
SKOMSKI ANTHONY J	2LT	0-0974934	0352	1
SKOOG ALMA T	LTC	N-0700207	1045	1
SKOOG CLINTON L	CW3	W-2147555	0767	1
SKOPANSKI MARTIN	CW2	W-2121177	0949	1
SKORHEIM FRANCIS	1LT	0-105573C	0246	2
SKOVIRA ANNA V	MAJ	N-0720863	0263	1
SKOVRON JOSEPH W	MAJ	0-2015684	1057	1
SKOW HAROLD C	CPT	0-1036742	0446	2
SKOWRON JOHN J	CPT	0-0469460	0246	2
SKOWRONEK ANTON J	CPT	0-1697958	0346	2
SKOWRONSKI CASMIR A	CPT	0-0477027	0446	2
SKRAMSTAD GAYLE L	1LT	0-1311656	0347	2
SKRIPSKY STANLEY J	CPT	0-1796165	0261	2
SKUTAS BERNICE C	LTC	L-0610745	1167	1
SKUTTLE IRVING M	MAJ	0-0224896	0145	2
SKVARNA JR JOHN J	MAJ	0-1336704	1263	1
SKVORAK MICHAEL J	LTC	0-0886865	0366	1
SLACK EARL V	LTC	0-1549095	0964	1
SLACK HERBERT L	CW3	W-2151893	0764	1
SLACK JOHN K	CPT	0-1646593	0462	1
SLACK JOHN M	CPT	0-0190138	0151	3
SLACK ROBERT C	CPT	0-0403314	C549	2
SLADE DONALD S	LTC	0-0220273	0558	3
SLADE EDWARD J	LTC	0-1108328	0761	1
SLADE JR MELBOURNE	LTC	0-1183972	0265	1
SLADE RAY O	LTC	0-0270599	1156	1
SLADE RICHARD S	1LT	0-0403552	0346	1
SLADE WORDIE B	MAJ	0-1551962	0557	1
SLADECK MARIE J	1LT	N-0730532	0946	1
SLADER DANIEL A	CPT	0-1824954	0548	2
SLAGER JACOB J	LTC	0-1115418	1266	1
SLAGLE MARION A	CPT	0-0489783	0450	1
SLAHTOVSKY ANNA C	MAJ	N-0759471	0763	1
SLAKER RAYMOND H	1LT	0-130690C	0146	2
SLAMAN ALBERT	CPT	0-1821641	0747	1
SLAMIN ARTHUR	1LT	0-1313808	0546	2
SLANK CONSTANCE	MAJ	N-0793662	0365	1
SLANKARD RICHARD G	CW3	W-2143967	0567	1
SLATE CLYDE R	CW3	W-2205315	0867	1
SLATE ROBERT D	1LT	0-1321343	0646	2
SLATER ALFRED T	CPT	0-1307863	1065	1
SLATER EDWIN E	LTC	0-1295953	1066	1
SLATER ELMER S	1LT	0-1308717	0146	2
SLATER FRANK J	1LT	0-1016360	0747	2
SLATER GEORGE F	MAJ	0-0349732	0156	3
SLATER GERALD A	2LT	0-1320568	C744	2
SLATER HAROLD K	LTC	0-0412904	0363	1
SLATER JAMES M	LTC	0-134240C	0966	1
SLATER JAMES R	MAJ	0-0151895	0256	3
SLATER JOEL H	COL	C-0245843	0957	3
SLATER JOHN E	LTC	0-0129375	C551	2
SLATER JOHN E	CW3	W-2146095	0360	1
SLATER JOHN W	MAJ	0-1897764	0561	1
SLATER MABEL B F	1LT	N-C737768	1045	1
SLATER MARION R	MAJ	0-201C627	0763	1
SLATER NORMAN S	LTC	0-0320124	0561	1
SLATER ROLAND A	COL	0-0214885	0660	3
SLATER WALTER J	MAJ	0-1638527	0661	1
SLATER WILLIAM K	MAJ	0-1938511	0367	1
SLATES BURL Y	MAJ	0-0248355	1065	3
SLATOR WILLIAM J	LTC	0-0187866	0-53	3
SLATORE LEE R	MAJ	0-0112723	1155	3
SLATTERY ARTHUR R	LTC	0-0232818	0260	1
SLATTERY BYRON P	CPT	0-1039568	1052	2
SLATTERY EUGENE V	COL	0-0311536	0665	3
SLATTERY JOHN J	1LT	0-1287957	0346	1
SLATTERY ROBERT F	LTC	0-1293329	0964	1
SLATTERY RUTLEDGE	LTC	0-0245210	0766	3

NAME	GRADE	SVC NO	DATE RET MO YR	RET CODE
SLATTUM HAWKINS L	LTC	0-1100339	0456	1
SLAUGHTER CHARLES T	LTC	0-1290673	0557	1
SLAUGHTER CLARE E	LTC	0-0196271	0962	3
SLAUGHTER GEORGE R	1LT	0-0304891	1043	2
SLAUGHTER GLEN A	LTC	0-0403928	C467	3
SLAUGHTER HARRY	LTC	0-0185693	1149	3
SLAUGHTER HERBERT C	CPT	0-0342803	1045	1
SLAUGHTER JAMES O	1LT	C-0387266	0845	2
SLAUGHTER JAMES H	LTC	0-0263683	0964	3
SLAUGHTER JOHN C	MAJ	C-0306407	1147	1
SLAUGHTER MARION W	1LT	0-0532740	1146	2
SLAUGHTER ROBERT J	CPT	0-0507733	0849	1
SLAUGHTER ROBERT N	CPT	0-0230159	0948	3
SLAUGHTER SOLOMON W	LTC	0-1081376	0764	2
SLAUGHTER STEPHEN F	LTC	0-0529409	0763	1
SLAUGHTER TALMADGE C	CW2	W-2214865	C966	1
SLAUSON IRVIN O	MAJ	0-2208229	0965	1
SLAVEN ROBERT K	MAJ	0-1633553	0758	1
SLAVENS DWIGHT E	CPT	0-0286136	0348	1
SLAVING ARNOLD W	COL	0-0289077	0959	3
SLAVIS ANTHONY	1LT	0-2024167	0347	2
SLAWSON FRED H	CPT	0-1684946	1061	1
SLAWSON JOHN E	LTC	0-0423263	C660	1
SLAY MAURICE S	MAJ	0-1823787	C564	1
SLAY NOEL G	CW2	W-2142430	0655	1
SLAYDEN WALTER S	CPT	0-1285510	0253	1
SLAYMAKER WILLIAM H	CPT	0-1290674	0346	1
SLAYMAN WILLIAM J	LTC	C-1167633	1164	2
SLAYSMAN CLARENCE L	LTC	0-0361381	C163	1
SLAYTER VERNIE	LTC	0-0372343	0858	1
SLAYTON BARNEY W	MAJ	C-1031025	0359	1
SLEATOP RALPH W	LTC	0-0240335	1060	3
SLEE HAROLD M	CW2	W-215136C	0563	1
SLEETER LEROY H	CPT	0-1635342	1047	2
SLEETH JR ROBERT S	1LT	0-1012354	1145	2
SLEIGHT ROBERT G	1LT	0-0888234	0945	2
SLEMMER WILLIAM W	MAJ	0-1317048	0264	1
SLEPIAN ROBERT	LTC	0-1309617	0862	2
SLESINGER BENJAMIN	MAJ	0-1638447	1156	1
SLETTEN NORMAN O	MAJ	C-1054818	1162	1
SLEVIN JOHN G	COL	0-0257857	0263	3
SLEVIN RICHARD A	CW4	W-2126261	1059	1
SLEZAK CLYDE L	MAJ	0-0264830	1164	3
SLEZAK JOHN	COL	0-0203778	0556	3
SLEZAK WILLIAM E	LTC	0-1285511	1060	1
SLICK JOSEPH D	1LT	0-2284025	0455	3
SLIDER AUSTIN K	MAJ	0-1533447	C662	1
SLIGER JR GLEN T	MAJ	0-1031130	1160	1
SLIGER THOMAS F	CPT	0-1311936	0748	2
SLIGH WILLIAM O	LTC	0-0193109	1060	3
SLIGH WILLIAM L	CW2	W-2145165	0257	1
SLIKER ROBERT B	MAJ	0-1102052	0564	1
SLINGO HERBERT J	COL	C-0183965	1055	2
SLINZAK JOHN E	MAJ	0-0423380	0358	1
SLIPAKOFF SAMUEL A	LTC	0-0287778	1059	3
SLITER JR ELMER H	COL	0-0180858	0462	3
SLOAN DWIGHT H	LTC	0-0363599	0261	1
SLOAN EDWIN	CW4	W-2147779	1163	1
SLOAN FRANK S	LTC	0-0184163	0656	3
SLOAN GEORGE H	LTC	0-0242549	C564	3
SLOAN JAMES J	CPT	0-0508806	0159	2
SLOAN JR ARTHUR H	CW4	W-2152252	0867	1
SLOAN JR HAROLD R	MAJ	0-1305658	0764	1
SLOAN LAVERN O	1LT	0-1052969	0564	1
SLOAN PAUL G	LTC	0-0436615	1147	2
SLOAN RICHARD G	MAJ	0-1994531	0758	1
SLOAN RICHARD V	LTC	0-0258026	1064	3
SLOAN SAMUEL J	1LT	0-1298610	0247	2
SLOAN SHELTON S	MAJ	0-2032833	0863	1
SLOANE GEORGE A	MAJ	0-2017294	0260	1
SLOANE JOSEPH	MAJ	C-1549369	0361	1
SLOANE JR MEDWYN O	COL	0-0302433	0966	1
SLOANE THELMA L	MAJ	N-0724804	0961	1
SLOAT CHARLES A	MAJ	0-0176491	1058	3
SLOAT ERNEST H	1LT	0-1179619	0546	2

NAME	GRADE	SVC NO	DATE RET MO YR	RET CODE
SLOBODIAN DANIEL	1LT	0-1295096	1145	2
SLOBODKIN MORRIS	COL	0-0313133	0766	3
SLOCOMB DON B	1LT	0-0283271	0645	2
SLOCUM CHARLES R	LTC	0-0277851	0646	1
SLOCUM EUGENE F	CPT	0-1309315	1046	2
SLOCUM HARRIET M	2LT	N-0744939	0545	1
SLOCUM RAYMOND A	MAJ	0-2263615	C662	2
SLOCUM WINFIELD S	COL	0-0179151	0151	3
SLOCUM YUDELL K	LTC	0-0320385	0764	3
SLOCUMB PARKER V	CW4	W-2104823	0559	1
SLOMA FRANCIS M	1LT	0-1038485	C845	2
SLONAKER EDWARD G L	CPT	0-1218837	0547	2
SLONE AUGUSTUS D	CPT	0-0482511	1046	2
SLONE CHARLES R	1LT	0-1939908	1055	2
SLONE CULLEN B	CW3	W-2145513	0161	1
SLONE WILLIAM R	LTC	0-0360494	0760	1
SLOTE ARTHUR O	CPT	0-1015815	0446	2
SLOTERBECK JOHN B	CW4	W-2106816	0464	2
SLOTKOWSKI EUGENE L	1LT	0-0475257	1045	2
SLOTT NORMAN	MAJ	0-0245465	0966	3
SLOUGH ROY	LTC	0-0121523	0851	3
SLOVER GORDON F	LTC	0-0301936	0866	3
SLOVISCZEK RICHARD P	CPT	0-2C34702	0247	2
SLOWIK JOSEPH	CPT	0-130566C	0646	1
SLUSS DAVID H	COL	0-0181893	1057	3
SLUSSER ELWOOD K	LTC	0-0359889	1266	3
SLUSSER WILBUR F	CW2	W-2142376	0255	1
SLUTTER JEROME S	MAJ	0-0277850	0544	2
SLUTTS EDWARD J	LTC	0-1591452	0361	1
SLUYTER HARLAN L	LTC	0-1031679	C261	1
SLY ROBERT E	MAJ	0-038682C	0146	2
SLYE DEAN J	MAJ	0-1105826	1060	1
SLYE JR ERNEST R	MAJ	0-0509922	0258	1
SMACHLO WALTER	1LT	0-0542939	0547	2
SMALL ALLEN L	1LT	0-0924478	1144	2
SMALL ALVIN L	LTC	0-1301225	0363	1
SMALL ARNOLD E	LTC	0-1101218	0361	1
SMALL ARTHUR L	CW4	W-2103443	0955	1
SMALL CALVERT P	COL	0-0329898	1163	3
SMALL CARLTON F	COL	0-0111595	0154	3
SMALL CHARLES W	1LT	0-0185436	0446	1
SMALL CEE	CPT	0-0121522	1055	3
SMALL EDWARD	LTC	0-0301608	0459	3
SMALL ERNEST L	LTC	0-0123686	1C51	3
SMALL FREDERICK	LTC	0-0208769	0959	3
SMALL GEORGE	COL	0-0210049	0958	3
SMALL GEORGE W	COL	0-0125531	0650	3
SMALL HIRAM F	CPT	0-0326566	0146	2
SMALL IRVING C	LTC	0-0290706	0466	3
SMALL JAMES G	CPT	0-0384921	0844	2
SMALL JR MARTIN A	LTC	0-1635346	1061	1
SMALL RALPH R	LTC	0-0346419	0265	3
SMALL STEPHEN W	MAJ	0-1312235	C856	1
SMALLEY ARZA G	2LT	0-2C12432	0546	2
SMALLEY FREDERICK	MAJ	C-1174441	0356	1
SMALLEY JACK R	LTC	0-1822832	C466	1
SMALLEY JAMES F	MAJ	0-0445272	0854	1
SMALLEY RICHARD M	1LT	0-1017194	1045	2
SMALLEY ROBERT B	CPT	0-0487231	0346	2
SMALLFELT CECIL L	MAJ	0-0211857	0961	3
SMALLING JR JOHN F	CW3	W-2147732	0463	1
SMALLWOOD HENRY W	2LT	0-1010699	1144	2
SMALLWOOD HERBERT C	LTC	0-1293491	0466	1
SMALLWOOD THOMAS W	1LT	0-0547395	0446	2
SMALLWOOD WILLIAM	LTC	0-0451290	0258	1
SMARDAK FRANK R	MAJ	0-2037177	1263	1
SMARR KENNETH M	1LT	0-1545100	0345	2
SMARR WYATT C	MAJ	C-2011235	0560	1
SMARSH LEO F	MAJ	0-1573947	0247	2
SMART ALBERT G	CW3	W-2142029	0556	1
SMART DANIEL J	LTC	0-0232212	1057	1
SMART FRED E	MAJ	0-0983707	0259	2
SMART HARRY V	MAJ	C-0181647	0960	3
SMART HELEN G	1LT	N-0760156	104N	1
SMART HENRY C	MAJ	0-1922632	0965	1

NAME	GRADE	SVC NO	DATE RET MO YR	RET CODE
SMART OSCAR J	1LT	C-0185466	1048	1
SMART THEODORE T	MAJ	C-0215990	1060	3
SMART WILLARD F	1LT	0-1309432	1045	2
SMATHERS BARBARA S	MAJ	N-0720677	C564	1
SMATHERS CARROLL L	CW3	W-2206330	1265	1
SMATHERS DON L	LTC	0-1311574	0364	1
SMATHERS JAMES L	COL	C-0237648	0459	3
SMATHERS RAY K	COL	C-0106163	C857	2
SMATHERS VAN C	MAJ	C-0507491	C852	1
SMAWLEY JACK O	MAJ	0-1060978	C866	1
SMAY JOSEPH E	CPT	0-0221223	0658	3
SMEAL GLENN W	CW3	W-2206067	0465	1
SMEDES EARLE R	1LT	0-1313656	0651	1
SMEDLEY FRANK H	LTC	0-0253359	1055	3
SMEDS ERLING T	LTC	0-0441258	C467	1
SMEE FREDERICK	LTC	0-1103934	1163	1
SMEED DALLAS B	CW3	W-2148817	1062	1
SMEJKAL JAMES	MAJ	C-1111916	1160	1
SMELLEY EVAN J	CPT	0-1303402	0947	1
SMELLEY HOWARD M	LTC	0-1283154	0163	1
SMELLIE HERBERT H	LTC	0-0354076	C560	1
SMELTER JOSEPH J	CPT	0-2055534	C851	1
SMELTZER GERALD M	CPT	0-05763C9	C546	2
SMELTZER PAUL T	COL	0-0420710	0262	1
SMELTZER SAMUEL M	LTC	0-0221368	C562	3
SMERAK EUGENE F	MAJ	C-10202C4	0265	1
SMETANA JOHN	MAJ	C-17C3937	0657	1
SMETANA LOUIS V	LTC	C-025C198	C763	3
SMETANA PAUL E	2LT	0-1643343	0745	2
SMETHERS SADIE M	1LT	N-0794074	1047	1
SMICK DONALD C	MAJ	C-1287424	1060	1
SMIOT JOHN	MAJ	0-0494989	0145	1
SMIETANOWSKI JOSEPH	CPT	C-1324667	1145	2
SMIGA JOSEPH	MAJ	C-1650748	C663	1
SMIGEN GEORGE A	MAJ	0-1020259	C463	1
SMIGIELSKI LEONARD S	CPT	0-1923580	C664	1
SMILEY ALBERT B	CW2	W-2214840	0767	1
SMILEY FRANK H	LTC	0-0168601	0660	3
SMILEY HOWARD C	LTC	0-0272974	1156	3
SMILEY JAMES A	LTC	0-1107691	0963	1
SMILEY JAMES V	LTC	0-1107133	C463	1
SMILEY JOHN H	LTC	0-0242826	0364	3
SMILEY JOHN W	COL	0-0240989	0766	3
SMILEY JR JAMES J	MAJ	C-0261885	C765	3
SMILEY LLOYD E	MAJ	C-1176512	1160	1
SMILEY ROBERT M	MAJ	C-0507631	C361	1
SMILIE CHARLES R	MAJ	0-1172287	0361	1
SMINK CHARLES E	MAJ	C-2263650	0463	1
SMIRES CLIFFORD L	COL	0-0405792	0760	2
SMIRES MARY L	MAJ	L-1010090	0965	1
SMIRES RALPH C	MAJ	C-0405178	0760	1
SMIT MORTON J	CPT	C-1291716	1046	1
SMITH AARON	CPT	0-0496803	0853	1
SMITH ADAIR M	1LT	0-1301699	1061	1
SMITH ADELBERT P	1LT	0-1544167	C147	2
SMITH ADLEY O	MAJ	C-1302368	0859	1
SMITH ALBERT A	MAJ	0-0319766	0658	1
SMITH ALBERT C	LTC	0-0347984	1057	1
SMITH ALBERT E	1LT	0-1638866	0145	1
SMITH ALBERT L	LTC	0-0420976	C861	1
SMITH ALBERT W	MAJ	C-1320193	0662	1
SMITH ALDEN H	LTC	0-0383324	0962	1
SMITH ALEX C	LTC	0-1588297	0860	1
SMITH ALFRED E	WO1	W-2210809	1060	2
SMITH ALFRED H	WO1	W-2115253	0950	1
SMITH ALFRED W	MAJ	C-0137611	C648	3
SMITH ALICE E	1LT	N-0721211	0646	1
SMITH ALLEN	CPT	0-1308718	0547	2
SMITH ALTON K	LTC	0-1036033	0160	1
SMITH ALVA R	LTC	0-0324739	0460	1
SMITH ALVIN L	MAJ	C-1648832	0563	1
SMITH ALVIN P	MAJ	0-1015520	1263	1
SMITH AMIEL	CW2	W-2143639	0257	1
SMITH ANNA F	MAJ	N-0793551	1263	2
SMITH ANTHONY A	LTC	0-0149525	C552	3

NAME	GRADE	SVC NO	DATE RET MO YR	RET CODE
SMITH ARDEN C	LTC	0-1172288	0262	1
SMITH ARGUS F	MAJ	0-1319232	0862	1
SMITH ARTHUR A	LTC	0-0238691	0463	3
SMITH ARTHUR B	LTC	0-0285826	0360	1
SMITH ARTHUR C	LTC	0-0237720	1159	1
SMITH ARTHUR C	CW2	W-2102388	1146	1
SMITH ARTHUR H	MAJ	0-0151794	0649	3
SMITH ARTHUR H	1LT	0-0324593	0261	3
SMITH ARTHUR M	MAJ	0-0238767	0466	3
SMITH ARTHUR N	MAJ	C-2014090	0164	1
SMITH ARTHUR W	COL	0-0174241	0-53	3
SMITH AUSTIN B	LTC	0-0296248	0865	3
SMITH AUSTIN D	COL	0-0209772	0854	3
SMITH AUSTIN W	CPT	0-0280087	1165	3
SMITH AUSTIN W	MAJ	0-1289329	1159	1
SMITH BAILEY B	LTC	0-0196272	0361	1
SMITH BASIL	MAJ	0-0497955	1046	1
SMITH BEECHER L	COL	0-0292482	0862	3
SMITH BEN W	CW2	W-2147090	0159	1
SMITH BENJAMIN F	MAJ	0-2206425	0162	1
SMITH BENJAMIN H	CPT	0-0445496	0247	1
SMITH BENJAMIN N	MAJ	0-0962546	0663	1
SMITH BERNARD H	CPT	0-0110989	0-50	3
SMITH BERNARD J	2LT	0-1181462	0844	2
SMITH BERNARD L	CPT	C-0370606	0847	2
SMITH BERNARD L	MAJ	0-1020301	0165	1
SMITH BERT I	LTC	0-0764738	0167	1
SMITH BERTRAM B	LTC	0-1001244	0860	1
SMITH BERTRAM L	COL	C-0300204	1051	3
SMITH BISHOP B	MAJ	C-0451417	1053	1
SMITH BONNIE	MAJ	C-0468570	1048	1
SMITH BOYD L	2LT	0-0409703	1142	2
SMITH CARL A	LTC	0-128964C	0764	1
SMITH CARL B	COL	0-0175502	0258	3
SMITH CARL W	LTC	0-1165572	0661	1
SMITH CARLESS R	LTC	0-0468515	0-53	1
SMITH CARLETON R	MAJ	0-0229546	0264	3
SMITH CARLOS C	COL	0-0277917	1065	3
SMITH CARLTON H	2LT	0-2035155	0345	2
SMITH CARLTON J	MAJ	0-2267613	0964	2
SMITH CARLTON K	B G	0-0231996	1061	3
SMITH CARLTON P	COL	C-0186359	0847	1
SMITH CARROL B	CPT	0-164962C	0555	2
SMITH CARSON E	CW2	W-2149717	0955	1
SMITH CECELIA	2LT	N-0737684	0644	1
SMITH CECIL C	MAJ	0-0118869	0253	3
SMITH CHANDLER C	1LT	0-1640961	0645	2
SMITH CHARLES A	LTC	C-028513C	0966	3
SMITH CHARLES A	2LT	0-0302726	0363	3
SMITH CHARLES A	2LT	0-1650334	1045	2
SMITH CHARLES A	CW4	W-2001665	0363	3
SMITH CHARLES C	COL	0-0225519	0564	3
SMITH CHARLES C	COL	0-0288176	0664	3
SMITH CHARLES C	MAJ	C-0972055	0364	1
SMITH CHARLES D	MAJ	C-0343683	0945	1
SMITH CHARLES O	LTC	0-1175316	0267	1
SMITH CHARLES O	1LT	0-1295287	0345	1
SMITH CHARLES E	MAJ	0-044290C	0649	1
SMITH CHARLES E	LTC	0-C4950C7	0448	2
SMITH CHARLES E	CPT	0-1294378	0257	2
SMITH CHARLES E	MAJ	C-1884175	0866	1
SMITH CHARLES F	LTC	0-0248182	0766	3
SMITH CHARLES H	CPT	0-0137766	0857	3
SMITH CHARLES H	MAJ	0-1032047	C759	1
SMITH CHARLES L	1LT	0-0379482	0446	2
SMITH CHARLES P	COL	0-0252843	0665	3
SMITH CHARLES R	COL	0-0171852	1060	3
SMITH CHARLES R	LTC	C-0247301	0165	3
SMITH CHARLES R	MAJ	0-032C218	1047	1
SMITH CHARLES R	LTC	0-1550055	0157	1
SMITH CHARLES S	MAJ	0-0245553	0858	3
SMITH CHARLES S	LTC	0-0295905	0867	3
SMITH CHARLES T	CW2	W-3C00219	1163	1
SMITH CHARLES W	LTC	0-0177553	1159	3
SMITH CHARLES W	CPT	0-1307475	C847	1

NAME	GRADE	SVC NO	DATE RET MO YR	RET CODE
SMITH CHESTER A	CPT	0-0145609	1055	3
SMITH CHESTER A	LTC	0-0354059	0862	1
SMITH CHESTER A	MAJ	0-1284953	0759	1
SMITH CHESTER A	2LT	0-1299807	0944	2
SMITH CHESTER D	CPT	0-1700935	0646	2
SMITH CLAIR B	MAJ	0-1881274	1065	1
SMITH CLAIRE D	MAJ	0-1644097	0264	1
SMITH CLARENCE C	1LT	0-0542331	0445	2
SMITH CLARENCE E	1LT	0-1303554	0753	1
SMITH CLARENCE E	CW3	W-2147394	0958	1
SMITH CLARENCE F	COL	0-0300205	1060	3
SMITH CLARENCE J	LTC	0-0298155	0356	1
SMITH CLARENCE W	MAJ	0-0479933	0859	1
SMITH CLARK B	CPT	0-0259733	0667	3
SMITH CLAUD	LTC	0-1011956	0954	1
SMITH CLAUDE A	CW2	W-2213557	0167	1
SMITH CLAUDE J	MAJ	0-0889095	0864	1
SMITH CLIFF	MAJ	0-0509241	0348	1
SMITH CLIFFORD H	CPT	0-1010248	0860	1
SMITH CLIFFORD W	LTC	0-1647278	0259	1
SMITH CLINE C	1LT	0-1574146	1044	2
SMITH CLINT G	CPT	0-0255541	1064	3
SMITH CLYDE D	COL	0-0242435	0462	3
SMITH CLYDE K	MAJ	0-1283091	0962	1
SMITH CLYDE M	COL	0-0335588	0867	3
SMITH CLYDE W	LTC	0-0279071	1162	1
SMITH CONOVER C	MAJ	0-0234735	1163	3
SMITH CONRAD A	CPT	0-1102470	0453	1
SMITH COURTLAND	LTC	0-0256065	0358	3
SMITH COURTNEY	MAJ	0-0357808	0554	1
SMITH CRAWFORD J	COL	0-0496878	0857	2
SMITH CURTIS H	LTC	0-0313417	1054	1
SMITH CURTIS N	CW3	W-2151006	0563	1
SMITH CURTIS O	MAJ	0-1325791	0561	1
SMITH DALE E	LTC	0-1335485	0766	1
SMITH DAN L	CW3	W-2206942	0167	1
SMITH DARREL	LTC	0-1634333	0457	1
SMITH DAVID H	LTC	0-1294030	0862	1
SMITH DAVID L	MAJ	0-0271391	1264	3
SMITH DAVID P	LTC	0-0396827	0262	1
SMITH DAVID R	MAJ	0-0177051	0162	3
SMITH DAVID W	MAJ	0-1799797	1162	1
SMITH DAVIS M	LTC	0-1292951	0663	1
SMITH DEAN E	MAJ	0-0960345	0363	1
SMITH DENNIS F	1LT	0-0557141	1046	1
SMITH DICK C	MAJ	0-1114752	1059	1
SMITH DONALD B	LTC	0-1041027	0762	1
SMITH DONALD D	LTC	0-0299355	1061	1
SMITH DONALD F	CW3	W-2148268	0863	1
SMITH DONALD H	MAJ	0-1048193	1263	1
SMITH DONALD H	LTC	0-1321256	0464	1
SMITH DONALD L	CW2	W-2211430	0164	1
SMITH DONALD M	MAJ	0-1686731	0363	1
SMITH DONALD R	LTC	0-0185018	0958	3
SMITH DONALD V	2LT	0-1014074	0744	2
SMITH DONALD W	LTC	0-0234815	0659	3
SMITH DONALD W	CPT	0-1331884	0360	1
SMITH DONET C	CPT	0-0490178	0747	1
SMITH DOTT E	COL	0-0171077	0648	2
SMITH DOUGLAS E	MAJ	0-0967219	0663	1
SMITH DOUGLAS R	MAJ	0-0868411	1163	1
SMITH DUDLEY L	CPT	0-0369849	0943	2
SMITH DURWOOD J	CPT	0-0413358	0646	1
SMITH E RAY	CW3	W-2114347	0856	1
SMITH EARL C	2LT	0-1325055	0645	2
SMITH EARL D	1LT	0-1946859	0546	2
SMITH EARL E	MAJ	0-0326286	0358	1
SMITH EARL E	CW3	W-2149142	1262	1
SMITH EARL F	LTC	0-0364238	1064	3
SMITH EARL W	MAJ	0-0477974	0150	1
SMITH EDGAR E	LTC	0-0885434	1055	1
SMITH EDGAR W	LTC	0-0486186	0157	1
SMITH EDMOND J	CW4	W-2117929	0457	1
SMITH EDWARD	1LT	0-1017735	0845	2
SMITH EDWARD	CPT	0-2042002	1262	1

NAME	GRADE	SVC NO	DATE RET MO YR	RET CODE
SMITH EDWARD B	LTC	0-1946171	0964	2
SMITH EDWARD E	1LT	0-1168083	1046	2
SMITH EDWARD F	LTC	0-1178630	0864	1
SMITH EDWARD J	MAJ	0-1693111	1061	1
SMITH EDWARD L	COL	0-0137621	1049	3
SMITH EDWARD S	MAJ	0-0190167	0648	3
SMITH EDWARD T	LTC	0-0206142	0860	3
SMITH EDWARD V	MAJ	0-1110262	0964	1
SMITH EDWIN E	LTC	0-0125495	0652	3
SMITH EDWIN H	CW4	W-2105275	0966	1
SMITH EDWIN M	LTC	0-0335127	0560	1
SMITH EDWIN S	CW2	W-2141446	1158	1
SMITH EDWIN T	CPT	0-0391163	0244	2
SMITH EDWIN W	CPT	0-0364258	1045	2
SMITH EDWIN W	CW2	W-2209431	0764	1
SMITH ELDON E	CPT	0-0419635	1145	2
SMITH ELGIN	MAJ	0-0163486	0648	3
SMITH ELIJAH M	LTC	0-0338863	0461	3
SMITH ELIZABETH	MAJ	N-0729893	0563	2
SMITH ELIZABETH	2LT	N-0735109	1044	1
SMITH ELLA J	2LT	N-0700140	0336	1
SMITH ELLIOTT V	LTC	0-0220960	0563	3
SMITH ELLIS I	LTC	0-0281425	1166	3
SMITH ELMER C	1LT	0-0441082	0944	2
SMITH ELTON R	MAJ	0-0313751	0465	3
SMITH ELWYN W	MAJ	0-1103936	0547	2
SMITH EMBUR V	LTC	0-0313492	1158	3
SMITH EMERSON W	LTC	0-0361176	0367	3
SMITH EMERY V	CPT	0-0497933	0845	2
SMITH EMMETT A	MAJ	0-1056237	1162	1
SMITH ERNEST A	LTC	0-0375114	0666	3
SMITH ERNEST A	1LT	0-1285324	0146	2
SMITH ERNEST C	CPT	0-0967238	1159	1
SMITH ERNEST C	CPT	0-0920218	0245	2
SMITH ERNEST L	CPT	0-0966615	0862	2
SMITH ERNEST M	COL	0-0251007	0161	3
SMITH ERNEST W	LTC	0-1011144	0165	1
SMITH ERSKINE O	CW3	W-2141898	1054	1
SMITH EUGENE B	MAJ	0-1913349	1265	2
SMITH EUGENE H	1LT	0-1284411	0245	2
SMITH EUGENE P	CW2	W-2143438	0261	1
SMITH EVERETT C	LTC	0-0465754	0552	1
SMITH EVERT E	MAJ	0-1184726	0364	1
SMITH EZEKIEL C	MAJ	0-1298611	0347	1
SMITH EZRA L	CPT	0-4003709	1166	2
SMITH FATIMA O	2LT	N-0727474	0744	1
SMITH FELIX J	MAJ	0-0339268	0545	2
SMITH FELIX R	MAJ	0-0953879	1161	1
SMITH FENELON O	LTC	0-0284858	0566	3
SMITH FINIS M	CPT	0-1012315	0446	1
SMITH FISHER J	LTC	0-0320360	0667	3
SMITH FLORIE P	LTC	0-1590190	1062	1
SMITH FLOYD E	MAJ	0-0332883	0161	3
SMITH FOREST R	MAJ	0-1300873	0263	1
SMITH FORREST G	COL	0-0288366	1155	3
SMITH FORREST H	CW2	W-2141941	0655	1
SMITH FORREST W	COL	0-0268636	0661	3
SMITH FRANCIS B	LTC	0-1293875	1060	1
SMITH FRANCIS J	MAJ	0-2018829	1265	2
SMITH FRANCIS M	COL	0-0100088	0648	3
SMITH FRANCIS T	MAJ	0-1013513	1062	2
SMITH FRANCIS V	LTC	0-0283550	0860	1
SMITH FRANK	LTC	0-1080581	0461	1
SMITH FRANK A	LTC	0-0450360	0355	1
SMITH FRANK A	1LT	0-1286723	0745	2
SMITH FRANK B	LTC	0-1324796	1061	1
SMITH FRANK B	CW4	W-2127161	1155	1
SMITH FRANK C	COL	0-0103254	1058	1
SMITH FRANK C	COL	0-0272930	1061	1
SMITH FRANK E	LTC	0-0471606	0762	1
SMITH FRANK H	CPT	0-0500477	0554	1
SMITH FRANK H	MAJ	0-1641807	0161	1
SMITH FRANK J	CPT	0-0491955	0847	1
SMITH FRANK L	LTC	0-0326245	0154	1
SMITH FRANK M	CW2	W-2149718	1058	1

NAME	GRADE	SVC NO	DATE RET MO YR	RET CODE
SMITH FRANK P	CPT	0-1691077	0146	2
SMITH FRANK W	MAJ	0-2032829	1059	1
SMITH FRANKLIN A	MAJ	0-0174702	1049	3
SMITH FRANKLIN H	CPT	0-0411279	1045	1
SMITH FRED A	LTC	0-0504120	0156	1
SMITH FRED A	LTC	0-1639662	0658	1
SMITH FRED A	CPT	0-2262400	0160	1
SMITH FRED C	1LT	0-1031520	1045	1
SMITH FRED D	MAJ	0-2000434	1262	1
SMITH FRED O	CW2	W-2105252	0649	2
SMITH FRED L	COL	0-0403597	1060	1
SMITH FRED L	MAJ	0-2102973	0565	1
SMITH FREDERICK	MAJ	0-0237926	0262	3
SMITH FREDERICK	LTC	0-0314283	1058	1
SMITH FREDERICK	MAJ	0-0412246	1045	2
SMITH GENE W	MAJ	0-1338753	1164	1
SMITH GEORGE A	MAJ	0-1052971	0961	2
SMITH GEORGE A	LTC	0-1332649	1166	1
SMITH GEORGE A	1LT	0-2043269	0151	2
SMITH GEORGE A	2LT	0-4032436	1055	2
SMITH GEORGE B	COL	0-0263356	0267	3
SMITH GEORGE B	MAJ	0-2263600	1163	1
SMITH GEORGE C	1LT	0-0582425	0645	2
SMITH GEORGE D	LTC	0-1581376	0861	1
SMITH GEORGE E	MAJ	0-1120410	0962	1
SMITH GEORGE E	CPT	0-1173783	0258	1
SMITH GEORGE F	MAJ	0-0476884	1046	2
SMITH GEORGE G	LTC	0-0506685	1265	3
SMITH GEORGE H	LTC	0-0464988	0854	1
SMITH GEORGE H	2LT	0-1018450	0844	2
SMITH GEORGE J	MAJ	0-1045256	1163	1
SMITH GEORGE L	MAJ	0-0119511	0855	3
SMITH GEORGE P	MAJ	0-1037722	0557	1
SMITH GEORGE R	CW2	W-2148990	0760	2
SMITH GEORGE W	CPT	0-0227268	0165	3
SMITH GEORGE Y	CPT	0-0400985	0346	2
SMITH GEORGIA H	MAJ	L-0603303	0363	1
SMITH GERALD L	LTC	0-1167227	0961	1
SMITH GERALD W	LTC	0-0470151	1262	2
SMITH GILBERT	WO1	W-2123132	0445	2
SMITH GLEN E	CPT	0-2006263	0261	1
SMITH GLENN A	LTC	0-0386948	0361	1
SMITH GLENN A	LTC	0-0902721	1157	2
SMITH GLENN E	MAJ	0-0222875	0754	3
SMITH GLENN H	COL	0-0293587	1065	3
SMITH GLENN M	LTC	0-0256057	0558	3
SMITH GORDON	COL	0-0187398	0947	2
SMITH GORDON L	MAJ	0-1102058	0158	1
SMITH GORDON W	LTC	0-0378126	0765	3
SMITH GRANVILLE	LTC	0-0206840	0154	2
SMITH GROVER C	MAJ	0-1032654	1060	1
SMITH GROVER C	2LT	0-1290322	1044	2
SMITH GUY R	CW3	W-2150552	1265	2
SMITH HARDY	MAJ	0-0218985	0244	2
SMITH HAROLD A	2LT	0-0468433	0344	2
SMITH HAROLD A	2LT	0-1176806	0545	2
SMITH HAROLD C	LTC	0-0322848	0954	1
SMITH HAROLD C	LTC	0-0919336	0164	3
SMITH HAROLD C	2LT	0-1308281	0345	2
SMITH HAROLD F	MAJ	0-1117744	0966	3
SMITH HAROLD F	1LT	0-1328086	1046	2
SMITH HAROLD J	MAJ	0-1544544	0561	2
SMITH HAROLD L	1LT	0-2003139	0954	2
SMITH HAROLD T	MAJ	0-1173080	1163	1
SMITH HAROLD V	1LT	0-0498604	0752	1
SMITH HAROLD V	CW2	W-2209892	0763	1
SMITH HAROLD W	MAJ	0-0127402	1055	3
SMITH HAROLD W	LTC	0-0361814	0467	1
SMITH HARRIS C	LTC	0-1638538	0762	1
SMITH HARRIS L	LTC	0-1044404	1165	1
SMITH HARRY	CPT	0-2046704	1046	1
SMITH HARRY B	CPT	0-0231469	0164	3
SMITH HARRY C	MAJ	0-0948737	0263	1
SMITH HARRY E	COL	0-0171203	1047	2
SMITH HARRY E	CPT	0-0488559	0248	1

NAME	GRADE	SVC NO	DATE RET MO YR	RET CODE
SMITH HARRY E	CW2	W-2143015	1059	1
SMITH HARRY F	LTC	0-1056556	1166	1
SMITH HARRY F	CW2	W-2118029	0454	1
SMITH HARRY F	CW3	W-2205185	0267	1
SMITH HARRY G	MAJ	0-1309168	1060	1
SMITH HARRY K	MAJ	0-0248782	0665	3
SMITH HARRY P	COL	0-0345224	0555	1
SMITH HARRY R	COL	0-0423294	1054	1
SMITH HARRY W	COL	0-0172357	0353	3
SMITH HARRY W	LTC	0-0552312	0764	1
SMITH HARVEY A	LTC	0-0230533	0163	3
SMITH HARVEY J	CW2	W-2111322	0154	1
SMITH HARVEY L	CW3	W-2121079	0755	1
SMITH HARVEY W	LTC	0-1635664	0967	3
SMITH HAZEL F	MAJ	N-0726722	0962	1
SMITH HELEN C	MAJ	N-0737763	1262	1
SMITH HELEN S	CPT	N-0787429	1148	2
SMITH HENRY B	1LT	0-1171772	0245	2
SMITH HENRY C	MAJ	0-0306637	0567	3
SMITH HENRY C	LTC	0-0329857	1162	1
SMITH HENRY E	CPT	0-0234609	0757	3
SMITH HENRY G	LTC	0-0343373	0960	1
SMITH HENRY L	MAJ	0-1112984	0964	1
SMITH HENRY M	COL	0-0233408	1156	3
SMITH HENRY M	MAJ	0-1316965	0457	2
SMITH HENRY T	COL	0-0196001	0951	3
SMITH HENRY T	2LT	0-1913932	0142	1
SMITH HENRY V	MAJ	0-1298972	1162	1
SMITH HERBERT A	M G	0-0189961	0761	3
SMITH HERBERT B	LTC	0-1280034	0148	2
SMITH HERBERT E	CPT	0-1299131	0347	1
SMITH HERBERT H	COL	0-0280596	0353	1
SMITH HERBERT J	MAJ	0-1646602	1066	1
SMITH HERBERT K	1LT	0-0371716	0146	2
SMITH HERBERT M	LTC	0-0241957	0444	2
SMITH HERBERT T	1LT	0-1103411	1045	2
SMITH HERBERT W	MAJ	0-0213999	1153	3
SMITH HERMAN	CPT	0-0975643	0154	2
SMITH HERMAN E	LTC	0-0141907	0652	3
SMITH HERMAN T	MAJ	0-1688524	0965	1
SMITH HEYBURN O	LTC	0-0228867	0863	3
SMITH HIRAM N	COL	0-0360645	0154	1
SMITH HOBART V	COL	0-1548145	1185	1
SMITH HOKE	CW3	W-2143532	1059	1
SMITH HOMER	CW2	W-2148193	1061	2
SMITH HOMER A	WO1	W-2107635	0648	1
SMITH HOMER L	LTC	0-0169120	0758	3
SMITH HOMER L	LTC	0-0500331	0157	1
SMITH HOMER W	CW3	W-2147919	1060	1
SMITH HORACE R	LTC	0-1651191	1263	1
SMITH HOWARD A	LTC	0-0410504	1160	1
SMITH HOWARD A	LTC	0-1333555	0965	1
SMITH HOWARD B	MAJ	0-0407561	0960	1
SMITH HOWARD C	CPT	0-1326116	0448	2
SMITH HOWARD C	MAJ	0-1295954	0747	2
SMITH HOWARD D	MAJ	0-1878144	0166	1
SMITH HOWARD H	LTC	0-0158580	0562	3
SMITH HOWARD K	2LT	0-1299809	0445	2
SMITH HOWLAND C	LTC	0-0242098	1164	3
SMITH HOYT P	MAJ	0-0349510	0952	1
SMITH HUBERT F	CPT	0-0207413	0547	1
SMITH HUBERT M	LTC	0-2053970	0657	1
SMITH HUGH P	LTC	0-0473796	0745	2
SMITH II JOSHUA C	LTC	0-1946172	1166	1
SMITH IRA W	MAJ	0-0478548	0642	1
SMITH IRVIN T	LTC	0-1181764	0960	1
SMITH ISAAC R	CPT	0-1695101	1043	2
SMITH ISAAC V	MAJ	0-1875476	1166	1
SMITH IVAN C	LTC	0-0234333	0346	2
SMITH IVAN J	MAJ	0-0344638	0750	2
SMITH J B	2LT	0-0557374	0750	2
SMITH J W	LTC	0-0451769	0160	1
SMITH J WINTER	CPT	0-0132525	0648	3
SMITH JACK	CPT	0-0970058	1060	1
SMITH JACK C	CW4	W-2146163	0666	1

NAME	GRADE	SVC NO	DATE RET MO YR	RET CODE
SMITH JACK E	LTC	0-2040912	0960	1
SMITH JACK R	1LT	0-0441156	0750	2
SMITH JACKSON A	COL	0-0173781	0557	3
SMITH JAMES B	LTC	0-0399187	0367	1
SMITH JAMES B	CPT	0-2202342	0866	1
SMITH JAMES C	LTC	0-0195976	0161	3
SMITH JAMES C	COL	0-0248289	0655	3
SMITH JAMES E	LTC	0-0198969	0955	3
SMITH JAMES F	CW2	W-2209813	1060	1
SMITH JAMES F	COL	0-0299183	0961	1
SMITH JAMES F	CPT	0-0501587	0450	1
SMITH JAMES F	LTC	0-1010687	0464	1
SMITH JAMES F	2LT	0-1115795	0244	2
SMITH JAMES G	LTC	0-1106480	0766	1
SMITH JAMES G	LTC	0-1577861	0462	1
SMITH JAMES H	2LT	0-0445211	0545	2
SMITH JAMES H	CPT	0-1015218	0556	1
SMITH JAMES H	CPT	0-1299488	0446	2
SMITH JAMES H	MAJ	0-1554617	0161	1
SMITH JAMES H	LTC	0-1822472	0658	1
SMITH JAMES J	MAJ	0-2295218	0866	1
SMITH JAMES L	CPT	0-1320346	0547	1
SMITH JAMES L	CW3	W-2103453	1157	1
SMITH JAMES L	CW3	W-2146489	0765	1
SMITH JAMES L	CW3	W-2149129	0464	1
SMITH JAMES N	LTC	0-0248546	0566	3
SMITH JAMES P	COL	0-0176961	0956	3
SMITH JAMES O	MAJ	0-0504419	0850	1
SMITH JAMES S	CW3	W-2152127	0262	1
SMITH JAMES T	1LT	0-0417856	1046	2
SMITH JAMES W	1LT	0-1177983	0646	2
SMITH JASPER K	CPT	0-0337098	0263	3
SMITH JASPER K	LTC	0-1169744	0161	1
SMITH JAY C	LTC	0-1112449	0765	1
SMITH JAY O	LTC	0-0484980	1145	2
SMITH JENNINGS B	MAJ	0-1004523	0255	1
SMITH JESSE	CW2	W-2109630	0347	1
SMITH JESSE H	MAJ	0-1558905	0364	1
SMITH JESSE J	MAJ	0-1293330	0562	1
SMITH JESSE R	MAJ	0-1796538	0657	1
SMITH JOE W	LTC	0-1080241	0366	1
SMITH JOHN	LTC	0-0184905	0550	3
SMITH JOHN A	LTC	0-0284672	0366	3
SMITH JOHN A	1LT	0-1014076	0149	1
SMITH JOHN A	MAJ	0-1796171	0961	1
SMITH JOHN B	COL	0-0253622	0154	3
SMITH JOHN C	MAJ	0-0377213	0446	2
SMITH JOHN C	CPT	0-2017771	1161	1
SMITH JOHN C	CPT	0-0525460	0846	2
SMITH JOHN C	LTC	0-1306330	0163	1
SMITH JOHN D	CW3	W-2151709	0664	1
SMITH JOHN F	CPT	0-1323493	0547	2
SMITH JOHN F	COL	0-0289443	0660	1
SMITH JOHN F	2LT	0-5501512	0862	2
SMITH JOHN F	WO1	W-2148666	1162	1
SMITH JOHN H	COL	0-0298701	0264	1
SMITH JOHN H	CPT	0-1294737	0747	2
SMITH JOHN J	LTC	0-0501439	0954	1
SMITH JOHN J	MAJ	0-1923561	0865	1
SMITH JOHN L	LTC	0-0451514	0457	1
SMITH JOHN L	LTC	0-1325032	0462	1
SMITH JOHN M	COL	0-0225480	0550	3
SMITH JOHN P	MAJ	0-1297441	0562	1
SMITH JOHN P	CW3	W-2149308	0665	1
SMITH JOHN R	MAJ	0-0971689	0565	1
SMITH JOHN R	LTC	0-1824522	0765	1
SMITH JOHN R	MAJ	0-1882115	0764	1
SMITH JOHN S	CPT	0-1798622	1162	1
SMITH JOHN S	CW2	W-2153010	0962	1
SMITH JOHN T	LTC	0-0343987	0247	2
SMITH JOHN T	CPT	0-1995530	0359	1
SMITH JOHN V	CW2	W-2129859	0447	1
SMITH JOHN W	CPT	0-1001464	0764	1
SMITH JOHN W	MAJ	0-1030518	0166	1
SMITH JOHN W	1LT	0-2000947	0554	1
SMITH JOHN W	CW3	W-2142900	0659	1
SMITH JOHNNIE T	MAJ	0-0963717	0764	2
SMITH JOSEPH	COL	0-0320251	0256	3
SMITH JOSEPH	2LT	0-1016638	0445	2
SMITH JOSEPH A	LTC	0-0233196	0255	3
SMITH JOSEPH C	MAJ	0-1555138	0457	1
SMITH JOSEPH C	MAJ	0-2010517	1060	1
SMITH JOSEPH F	1LT	0-1298145	0845	2
SMITH JOSEPH H	LTC	0-0172519	0648	3
SMITH JOSEPH R	WO1	W-2106051	0256	1
SMITH JOSEPH S	LTC	0-1329998	0863	1
SMITH JOSEPH W	1LT	0-0164574	0157	3
SMITH JOSEPH W	MAJ	0-0483748	0946	2
SMITH JOSEPH W	MAJ	0-1030093	1046	2
SMITH JOSEPH W	1LT	0-1050492	0845	2
SMITH JOSHUA W	CPT	0-1548555	0351	1
SMITH JR ALAN P	COL	0-0261395	0855	3
SMITH JR ALEXANDER	LTC	0-1845832	0762	1
SMITH JR ALTON	CPT	0-1293137	0646	2
SMITH JR ALVA B	CPT	0-1101219	1043	2
SMITH JR BEN H	CPT	0-1328760	1160	2
SMITH JR CHARLES	COL	0-0112724	0953	3
SMITH JR CHAUNCEY	MAJ	0-1011297	0861	1
SMITH JR CLARENCE M	LTC	0-1555903	1064	1
SMITH JR DANIEL L	MAJ	0-0239310	1065	3
SMITH JR EDGAR K	1LT	0-1042958	0246	2
SMITH JR ELLIS E	CPT	0-1103935	0545	2
SMITH JR ERNEST G	1LT	0-1706236	0346	1
SMITH JR EUGENE A	LTC	0-0342354	0163	1
SMITH JR FREDERICK	1LT	0-0181464	1051	1
SMITH JR GEORGE A	CPT	0-1284037	0845	2
SMITH JR GEORGE F	1LT	0-1317551	0867	1
SMITH JR GRANT H	LTC	0-0370657	0949	1
SMITH JR HERBERT A	2LT	0-1798210	0844	2
SMITH JR HERBERT E	LTC	0-0399732	0646	2
SMITH JR HOWARD R	CPT	0-1318585	0859	1
SMITH JR JAMES A	2LT	0-1825585	0750	2
SMITH JR JAMES H	1LT	0-0450840	1044	2
SMITH JR JAMES R	LTC	0-0570300	0867	1
SMITH JR JAMES T	MAJ	0-2263084	0665	1
SMITH JR JERRY M	LTC	0-1314337	1062	1
SMITH JR JOHN	MAJ	0-1552389	0357	1
SMITH JR JOHN L	LTC	0-1172289	0167	1
SMITH JR JOHN P	LTC	0-0235292	1162	3
SMITH JR JOSEPH D	1LT	0-0281860	0543	2
SMITH JR JOSEPH O	MAJ	0-1299132	0462	1
SMITH JR JOSEPH M	CPT	0-1116257	1148	2
SMITH JR JOSEPH W	CPT	0-0301436	0547	2
SMITH JR LEE R	MAJ	0-1688745	0666	1
SMITH JR LEONARD H	COL	0-0253683	0556	1
SMITH JR LEWIS A	MAJ	0-0254866	1054	3
SMITH JR LOUIS M	CPT	0-0385222	0745	1
SMITH JR LUCIEN L	CPT	0-1012487	1045	2
SMITH JR OSCAR L	MAJ	0-1825069	0662	1
SMITH JR REUBEN W	COL	0-0184836	0545	2
SMITH JR RICHARD E	1LT	0-1299810	0845	2
SMITH JR ROBERT C	1LT	0-0521838	1145	2
SMITH JR ROBERT O	CPT	0-0401658	0245	1
SMITH JR ROBERT W	COL	0-0287036	1066	3
SMITH JR REDMAN	1LT	0-1316706	0345	2
SMITH JR ROY H	CPT	0-1878042	0165	1
SMITH JR SIDNEY C	MAJ	0-0559547	0663	1
SMITH JR THOMAS D	MAJ	0-0329533	0561	1
SMITH JR WILLIAM F	MAJ	0-0965187	0961	1
SMITH JR WILLIAM F	CPT	0-1110263	0350	2
SMITH JR WILLIAM H	LTC	0-0300725	0665	3
SMITH JR WILLIAM H	LTC	0-0378776	0860	1
SMITH JR WILLIAM H	LTC	0-1579144	1162	1
SMITH JULE R	COL	0-0159158	1054	3
SMITH JULIAN B	LTC	0-0352469	0662	1
SMITH JUNIUS R	MAJ	0-0226485	1044	2
SMITH KARL J	WO1	W-2113448	0745	2
SMITH KARL W	LTC	0-1174146	0861	1
SMITH KATE M	MAJ	N-0734339	0354	2
SMITH KEMP H	COL	0-0221531	1061	3
SMITH KENNETH E	MAJ	0-1799669	0662	1
SMITH KENNETH H	CPT	0-2262107	1060	1
SMITH KENNETH M	CPT	0-0495919	1052	1
SMITH KENNETH M	CW3	W-2143582	1158	1
SMITH KENNETH T	LTC	0-0358132	0266	1
SMITH KENNETH W	CPT	0-0310476	0147	2
SMITH KIRK B	CW2	W-2150875	0461	1
SMITH LAROY A	MAJ	0-2102945	0464	1
SMITH LARUE W	LTC	0-1010851	0761	1
SMITH LAURENCE A	LTC	0-1062432	0962	1
SMITH LAURENCE A	WO1	W-2105975	0153	2
SMITH LAURENCE H	COL	0-0112011	0850	3
SMITH LAVELLE	CPT	0-1634340	0162	2
SMITH LAVERNE E	CW3	W-2147124	0663	1
SMITH LAVON F	MAJ	0-1166376	0960	1
SMITH LAWRENCE E	MAJ	0-1294738	0662	1
SMITH LAWRENCE E	MAJ	0-1877147	1165	1
SMITH LAWRENCE T	MAJ	0-0179019	0644	2
SMITH LEE A	LTC	0-0168587	0958	3
SMITH LEE O	MAJ	0-1185253	0562	1
SMITH LEE R	CW3	W-2149760	0163	1
SMITH LELAND	LTC	0-1307093	0456	2
SMITH LENDALL A	1LT	0-1049354	0845	2
SMITH LENWOOD	CPT	0-0965046	0660	1
SMITH LEO J	MAJ	0-0475772	0846	1
SMITH LEO M	1LT	0-0579279	0362	2
SMITH LEON C	LTC	0-0244011	0560	1
SMITH LEON E	CW2	W-2149160	0661	1
SMITH LEON F	MAJ	0-0239570	0163	3
SMITH LEONARD	CPT	0-0246726	1063	3
SMITH LEONARD A	MAJ	0-0256484	1053	3
SMITH LEONARD C	MAJ	0-0249535	0364	3
SMITH LEONARD J	2LT	0-2263068	1151	2
SMITH LEONIDAS H	LTC	0-1554484	1165	3
SMITH LEROY C	WO1	W-2147535	0957	1
SMITH LEROY J	1LT	0-0967068	0861	2
SMITH LEROY J	1LT	0-1175583	0745	2
SMITH LEROY N	CW3	W-2152327	0665	1
SMITH LEROY W	MAJ	0-1592071	0765	1
SMITH LESLIE A	MAJ	0-0120275	0350	3
SMITH LESLIE A	CPT	0-0488676	0861	1
SMITH LESLIE E	MAJ	0-0977260	0665	1
SMITH LESSLIE W	LTC	0-0226546	0463	3
SMITH LESTER B	1LT	0-1798304	1045	2
SMITH LESTER O	MAJ	0-1334365	0962	1
SMITH LEVI B	MAJ	0-2036030	1165	1
SMITH LEWIS A	CPT	0-0143432	1155	3
SMITH LEWIS C	LTC	0-1039221	0865	3
SMITH LEWIS E	LTC	0-1316457	1062	1
SMITH LEWIS V	LTC	0-0260521	0159	1
SMITH LINTON B	MAJ	0-1184586	0462	1
SMITH LLOYD A	LTC	0-1584933	0662	1
SMITH LLOYD N	LTC	0-1102060	0265	1
SMITH LOUIS A	CPT	0-0116538	0349	3
SMITH LOUIS D	LTC	0-0250170	0364	3
SMITH LOUIS G	COL	0-0105917	1057	3
SMITH LUKE D	LTC	0-0236955	0960	3
SMITH LUTHER B	LTC	0-1646604	0467	1
SMITH LYLE E	2LT	0-1030802	0645	2
SMITH LYNN C	1LT	0-0499955	0847	1
SMITH M JANE	1LT	N-0756215	0546	1
SMITH MALCOLM J	MAJ	0-0247024	1060	1
SMITH MARINER T	COL	0-0408907	1165	3
SMITH MARION P	LTC	0-0394601	0262	1
SMITH MARION R	MAJ	0-0253229	0464	3
SMITH MARK A	MAJ	0-2008797	0762	1
SMITH MARLO F	1LT	0-1299954	0846	2
SMITH MARVIN C	MAJ	0-0299250	0667	3
SMITH MARVIN C	MAJ	0-0445320	0146	2
SMITH MARVIN C	MAJ	0-1796369	0157	1
SMITH MARVIN D	LTC	0-1173463	0960	1
SMITH MARY T	1LT	N-0723079	0246	1
SMITH MAURICE	CW3	W-2153122	0463	1
SMITH MAURICE L	LTC	0-1573594	1064	1
SMITH MAX C	CW2	W-2111178	0348	1
SMITH MAXINE V	LTC	L-0302038	0663	1
SMITH MELVIN G	CW2	W-2208116	1266	1
SMITH MERLIN F	MAJ	0-0974120	0966	1
SMITH MERLYN H	LTC	0-0409934	0665	1
SMITH MILTON B	1LT	0-0525722	1045	2
SMITH MILTON C	CW2	W-2106317	0762	3
SMITH MILTON T	CPT	0-0249236	0766	3
SMITH MORSE E	LTC	0-0230886	0964	3
SMITH MORTON	COL	0-0242311	1165	3
SMITH MYRIAM M	LTC	L-0401685	0465	3
SMITH MYRON R	LTC	0-0364042	0859	1
SMITH NEAL D	MAJ	0-0242675	1059	3
SMITH NEORA L	1LT	N-0729646	0348	1
SMITH NELAND E	LTC	0-1341481	0967	1
SMITH NEWMANN B	MAJ	0-0214347	0763	3
SMITH NEWTON D	CPT	0-0225280	0950	3
SMITH NORMAN L	CPT	0-0965731	0764	1
SMITH NORMAN W	COL	0-0213878	0147	2
SMITH OCTAVE M	COL	0-0214414	0356	3
SMITH OLIVER M	LTC	0-1295786	0766	1
SMITH ORVILLE A	1LT	0-1016592	1145	2
SMITH OSCAR E	1LT	0-0197778	1048	1
SMITH OSCAR T	MAJ	0-0113654	1054	3
SMITH OSCAR W	WO1	W-2102395	0744	2
SMITH OTIS	CW2	W-2144526	0658	1
SMITH OTIS L	LTC	0-1293492	1160	1
SMITH OTIS M	LTC	0-0451473	1065	1
SMITH OTTO F	CPT	0-1030418	0447	1
SMITH PATRICK M	CW3	W-2145588	1264	1
SMITH PAUL	CW3	W-2143105	0960	1
SMITH PAUL H	CW2	W-2120463	0550	1
SMITH PAUL I	MAJ	0-1937060	0267	1
SMITH PAUL M	LTC	0-0885426	1166	1
SMITH PAUL P	LTC	0-0374801	0461	1
SMITH PAUL R	MAJ	0-1108330	0846	2
SMITH PAUL W	MAJ	0-0404876	0546	2
SMITH PAUL W	MAJ	0-1103943	0460	1
SMITH PAULINE E	1LT	N-0767052	0246	1
SMITH PEARL M	CW2	W-2104825	0553	1
SMITH PERCIVAL W	MAJ	0-0231120	0964	3
SMITH PETER	COL	0-0267426	0150	3
SMITH PHILIP	CPT	0-0453749	0945	2
SMITH PHILIP C	2LT	0-2010629	1045	2
SMITH PHILIP E	COL	0-0278533	0160	1
SMITH PHILIP E	LTC	0-1102061	1060	1
SMITH PHILIP G	CPT	0-1286561	1044	2
SMITH PROSPER O	COL	0-0183939	1146	1
SMITH R ESTON	LTC	0-1288639	0961	1
SMITH RAE M	LTC	0-0888419	1160	1
SMITH RALPH E	LTC	0-0205489	0967	3
SMITH RALPH O	1LT	0-1825376	0246	2
SMITH RALPH T	MAJ	0-0181642	0561	3
SMITH RALPH V	CW2	W-2144542	0163	1
SMITH RALPH W	MAJ	0-2012694	1060	1
SMITH RANDOLPH M	COL	0-0296246	0546	2
SMITH RAYMOND F	LTC	0-1638541	0361	1
SMITH RAYMOND E	CW3	W-2207448	0967	1
SMITH RAYMOND G	MAJ	0-1341128	0167	1
SMITH RAYMOND H	LTC	0-0369037	0763	3
SMITH RAYMOND M	1LT	0-1018641	0846	2
SMITH RAYMOND O	COL	0-0212926	0554	2
SMITH RAYMOND T	LTC	0-0450361	0759	1
SMITH REX A	LTC	0-1797549	0862	1
SMITH REX L	COL	0-0275070	1264	3
SMITH RHEA M	COL	0-0508608	0567	3
SMITH RICHARD A	LTC	0-0556801	0464	1
SMITH RICHARD C	1LT	0-0388454	0945	2
SMITH RICHARD E	CPT	0-1287960	0446	1
SMITH RICHARD F	MAJ	0-1596810	1159	1
SMITH RICHARD H	LTC	0-1100341	1162	1
SMITH RICHARD H	LTC	0-1640966	0266	1
SMITH RICHARD J	LTC	0-1039222	1167	1
SMITH RICHARD M	2LT	0-1177189	0444	2
SMITH RICHARD P	CW4	W-2127142	0656	1
SMITH RICHARD R	MAJ	0-1913265	1263	1

292-560 O - 68 - 21

NAME	GRADE	SVC NO	DATE RET MO YR	RET CODE	NAME	GRADE	SVC NO	DATE RET MO YR	RET CODE	NAME	GRADE	SVC NO	DATE RET MO YR	RET CODE	NAME	GRADE	SVC NO	DATE RET MO YR	RET CODE
SMITH RICHARD W	2LT	O-1926933	0358	2	SMITH SIDNEY E	CW4	W-2122568	0359	1	SMITH WAYNE B	LTC	O-1167639	0967	2	SMITHLING JOHN F	CW4	W-2133218	1160	1
SMITH ROBERT	CPT	O-1290830	0647	2	SMITH SIDNEY F	LTC	O-1555297	1164	1	SMITH WAYNE D	LTC	O-0399711	0761	1	SMITHSON CHARLES E	LTC	O-0185767	0-49	3
SMITH ROBERT A	LTC	O-0405509	0667	1	SMITH SILAS	MAJ	O-1032783	0261	1	SMITH WAYNE H	CPT	O-1108332	0847	2	SMITHSON ERNEST	CW3	W-2209627	1067	1
SMITH ROBERT A	2LT	O-1180341	0144	2	SMITH SILAS R	LTC	O-0168156	0957	3	SMITH WAYNE W	LTC	O-0191999	0462	3	SMITHSON JR ALBERT L	LTC	O-0403367	0960	1
SMITH ROBERT A	MAJ	O-1644107	0759	1	SMITH SOMERS S	LTC	O-0348594	0463	3	SMITH WELDON A	CPT	O-0971967	0361	1	SMITHWICK VINCENT J	MAJ	O-1549846	0257	1
SMITH ROBERT B	CPT	O-0493922	1044	2	SMITH SPENCER O	MAJ	O-1101221	0255	1	SMITH WELDON D	MAJ	O-0133662	0648	3	SMITHYMAN WILLIAM F	LTC	O-1322845	1067	1
SMITH ROBERT B	2LT	O-1014741	0443	2	SMITH SR HAROLD B	MAJ	O-2262180	0761	1	SMITH WENFRED W	CPT	O-1683438	0858	1	SMITZES GEORGE S	CPT	O-0189822	0852	3
SMITH ROBERT C	LTC	O-0113066	0755	3	SMITH SR JAMES S	CW2	W-2212406	1066	1	SMITH WESLEY C	1LT	O-0240432	0545	2	SMOAK ALVA G	MAJ	O-0969415	0966	1
SMITH ROBERT C	LTC	O-1057289	0166	1	SMITH SR WILLIAM J	MAJ	O-0179344	0648	3	SMITH WILBERT E	MAJ	O-2036703	0764	1	SMOAK JR LAURIE C	CPT	O-0534223	0947	1
SMITH ROBERT C	MAJ	O-1168924	1057	2	SMITH STANDFORD	1LT	O-1924609	0155	2	SMITH WILBUR L	CW2	W-2152867	0360	1	SMOAK LILLIAN	MAJ	N-0764476	0567	1
SMITH ROBERT C	CPT	O-1591123	0552	1	SMITH STANHOPE C	COL	O-0211351	0155	3	SMITH WILLARD A	1LT	O-1112454	0346	2	SMOCK LYMAN	MAJ	O-0166645	0647	1
SMITH ROBERT D	MAJ	O-0757095	0863	1	SMITH STANLEY	LTC	O-0145681	0851	1	SMITH WILLARD F	COL	O-0338465	0854	1	SMOCK WALTER W	CPT	O-0538582	0946	2
SMITH ROBERT E	CW3	W-2143456	0564	1	SMITH STEVE S	WO1	W-2105309	0744	2	SMITH WILLIAM	2LT	O-1583883	1044	2	SMOKLER JACK	CPT	O-0521522	0845	2
SMITH ROBERT G	CPT	O-1055692	0162	1	SMITH STEWARD H	CPT	O-1686013	0645	2	SMITH WILLIAM A	MAJ	O-0330509	0150	3	SMOLARK JOHN A	LTC	O-0333360	0167	3
SMITH ROBERT H	CPT	O-0463944	0747	2	SMITH STUART E	LTC	O-0266397	0263	3	SMITH WILLIAM A	CPT	O-0450912	1145	2	SMOLCZYNSKI STEPHEN	LTC	O-0309194	0963	3
SMITH ROBERT H	MAJ	O-1062438	0365	1	SMITH STUART J	CW3	W-2106983	1165	3	SMITH WILLIAM A	1LT	O-0476478	0445	2	SMOLEN GEORGE	1LT	O-1557673	0146	1
SMITH ROBERT H	CPT	O-2019385	1159	1	SMITH STUART W	LTC	O-0207122	0457	1	SMITH WILLIAM B	CPT	O-0193085	0463	3	SMOLEN JOHN	CPT	O-0490668	0146	1
SMITH ROBERT I	LTC	O-1040331	0762	1	SMITH SUMNER E	COL	O-0206735	0161	3	SMITH WILLIAM B	LTC	O-0287188	0755	2	SMOLEN JOSEPH	MAJ	O-1300546	0464	1
SMITH ROBERT I	LTC	O-1287961	0264	1	SMITH SYDNEY	MAJ	O-1108331	1163	1	SMITH WILLIAM C	COL	O-0244543	1160	3	SMOLEN SEYMOUR S	1LT	O-1012407	0645	2
SMITH ROBERT I	CW3	W-2151124	0563	1	SMITH TANIS	MAJ	O-1634344	0263	2	SMITH WILLIAM C	LTC	O-1012121	0466	1	SMOLENS NATHAN M	COL	O-0314274	0265	3
SMITH ROBERT L	LTC	O-0320625	0866	3	SMITH TAYLOR	LTC	O-0163734	0753	1	SMITH WILLIAM D	1LT	O-1287426	1044	1	SMOLIK VINCENT W	CPT	O-1685692	1058	2
SMITH ROBERT L	LTC	O-0421852	0266	1	SMITH TED J	LTC	O-1826304	0565	1	SMITH WILLIAM D	CW3	W-2146279	1059	1	SMOLIN EDWIN M	2LT	O-0554880	0346	2
SMITH ROBERT L	CPT	O-0448148	1147	1	SMITH TEMPLE C	LTC	O-1584939	0961	1	SMITH WILLIAM E	CPT	O-0245508	0150	3	SMOLKA CLARENCE	MAJ	O-0315467	0943	2
SMITH ROBERT L	MAJ	O-0985653	1163	1	SMITH THEODORE T	LTC	O-1945713	0565	3	SMITH WILLIAM E	MAJ	O-1112989	0462	1	SMOLLAN DAVID	CPT	O-0263192	1265	3
SMITH ROBERT L	LTC	O-1322278	1166	1	SMITH THEODORE W	MAJ	O-0495573	1051	1	SMITH WILLIAM E	LTC	O-1303963	1060	1	SMOLLEN JOHN P	LTC	O-1176198	0667	2
SMITH ROBERT L	2LT	O-4017333	0355	2	SMITH THOMAS A	LTC	O-0475684	0255	1	SMITH WILLIAM F	LTC	O-0107303	0648	3	SMOLLON JOHN E	1LT	O-1052972	0848	2
SMITH ROBERT M	MAJ	O-0418980	0247	2	SMITH THOMAS B	CPT	O-1321258	0347	2	SMITH WILLIAM F	LTC	O-0240965	0266	3	SMOOT ARTHUR E	LTC	O-1306010	0665	1
SMITH ROBERT M	MAJ	O-0477542	0453	1	SMITH THOMAS C	MAJ	O-0524318	0565	3	SMITH WILLIAM F	CPT	O-0954749	0859	1	SMOOT CHARLES H	LTC	O-1636665	0766	1
SMITH ROBERT P	CPT	O-1061265	0546	2	SMITH THOMAS C	MAJ	O-4007079	0267	1	SMITH WILLIAM G	CPT	O-0331585	0849	3	SMOOT GEORGE W	COL	O-0292123	0667	1
SMITH ROBERT R	MAJ	O-1876401	0164	1	SMITH THOMAS E	MAJ	O-1550057	1055	1	SMITH WILLIAM H	1LT	O-0113350	0455	3	SMOOT JAMES C	COL	O-0102166	0960	3
SMITH ROBERT S	MAJ	O-1310946	1046	1	SMITH THOMAS E	MAJ	O-2033053	0461	1	SMITH WILLIAM H	COL	O-0250274	1264	3	SMOOT JR WENDELL M	CPT	O-0465272	1145	1
SMITH ROBERT S	MAJ	O-2018782	0964	1	SMITH THOMAS J	MAJ	O-0964435	1060	1	SMITH WILLIAM H	CPT	O-0404292	0346	2	SMOOT MARVIN L	LTC	O-0346462	1060	1
SMITH ROBERT V	CPT	O-1319144	0346	2	SMITH THOMAS J	CW3	W-2149027	0365	1	SMITH WILLIAM H	MAJ	O-0490862	0155	1	SMOOT RICHARD H	LTC	O-0294268	1062	1
SMITH ROBERT W	COL	O-0202616	0262	3	SMITH THOMAS P	CPT	O-0453030	0845	1	SMITH WILLIAM H	1LT	O-1043228	0744	2	SMOOT WESLEY A	CW2	W-2112561	0461	2
SMITH ROBERT W	MAJ	O-1018151	0461	1	SMITH THOMAS T	COL	O-0277897	0955	1	SMITH WILLIAM H	CPT	O-2055870	0453	1	SMOTHERS JOHN W	LTC	O-0371583	0760	1
SMITH ROBERT W	CPT	O-1285651	0546	2	SMITH THOMAS W E	MAJ	O-2262204	0263	1	SMITH WILLIAM J	COL	O-0264377	1163	1	SMOTHERS ODELL W	LTC	O-0407418	0363	1
SMITH ROBERT W	LTC	O-1638543	1061	1	SMITH THURMOND S	MAJ	O-0174112	0960	3	SMITH WILLIAM J	1LT	O-0423766	0944	2	SMOUSE JOHN R	LTC	O-0279153	0966	3
SMITH RODERICK K	CPT	O-0451418	0648	2	SMITH TREMAINE F	LTC	O-1185000	1262	1	SMITH WILLIAM J	1LT	O-1286198	0345	2	SMOUT ETHAN P	1LT	O-1296925	104N	2
SMITH ROGER F	LTC	O-0492519	0455	1	SMITH TRUEITT B	LTC	O-1060299	1167	1	SMITH WILLIAM J	1LT	O-1308877	0545	2	SMRCEK MARY	CPT	N-0775905	0959	2
SMITH ROGER N	MAJ	O-1313737	0861	1	SMITH TUTTLE F	COL	O-0238707	0360	1	SMITH WILLIAM J	LTC	O-1544249	0466	1	SMRSTIK GEORGE E	CPT	O-1319145	0547	2
SMITH ROGER W	CPT	O-1311697	0559	1	SMITH U S	2LT	O-1015846	1043	2	SMITH WILLIAM J	CW2	W-2144776	0555	1	SMUCK JOHN C	COL	O-0141251	0257	3
SMITH ROLAND L	LTC	O-0177966	1160	3	SMITH UEL	CW2	W-2143826	0559	1	SMITH WILLIAM L	1LT	O-1297443	0265	1	SMUIN JOHN W	CPT	O-0444485	0245	2
SMITH ROLLIN H	LTC	O-0462700	1262	3	SMITH ULYSSES G	MAJ	O-1176515	1162	1	SMITH WILLIAM L	1LT	O-1342214	0749	2	SMULLEN WILLARD C	MAJ	O-0461536	0246	2
SMITH RONALD D	MAJ	O-2210467	0665	1	SMITH VANNAS C	MAJ	O-1597782	0561	1	SMITH WILLIAM M	LTC	O-0105400	0745	2	SMULLIN JR THOMAS E	MAJ	O-2021113	0964	1
SMITH RONALD E	LTC	O-0257177	0244	2	SMITH VAUGHN T	CPT	O-1109674	0453	2	SMITH WILLIAM M	CPT	O-0336553	1045	2	SMULLIN THOMAS E	LTC	O-0133611	0760	3
SMITH RONALD E	MAJ	O-0477209	0857	1	SMITH VERNON C	CW2	W-2149655	1261	1	SMITH WILLIAM M	1LT	O-0528929	0146	2	SMYERS JR BERTRAND H	LTC	O-0172008	0759	3
SMITH RONALD D	LTC	O-0223217	0656	3	SMITH VICTOR H	LTC	O-0129711	0353	3	SMITH WILLIAM M	MAJ	O-2283918	0863	1	SMYLE RUSSELL C	LTC	O-1796410	0667	1
SMITH RONALD V	CW2	W-2147961	0457	1	SMITH VINSON S	LTC	O-2035982	0461	1	SMITH WILLIAM O	CW2	W-2147408	0261	1	SMYRE JR CARTER	CW3	W-2205576	0366	1
SMITH ROSWALD F	MAJ	O-0103661	1144	2	SMITH VIRGIL E	CPT	O-1300100	1145	2	SMITH WILLIAM O	LTC	O-1044107	0961	1	SMYRE WELFORD A	CPT	O-0453226	1045	2
SMITH ROY A	COL	O-0321441	0766	3	SMITH VIRGINIA M	CPT	N-0751185	0746	1	SMITH WILLIAM R	MAJ	O-0402334	1044	2	SMYTH HARRY	COL	O-0205091	0154	3
SMITH ROY B	LTC	O-0297093	0265	3	SMITH VIVIAN C	COL	O-0254644	0867	3	SMITH WILLIAM R	MAJ	O-1296312	0661	1	SMYTH JOSEPH J	2LT	O-2015705	0655	1
SMITH ROY B	CPT	O-1540841	0758	1	SMITH W EUGENE	COL	O-0328433	0450	1	SMITH WILLIAM T	1LT	O-1292773	0645	2	SMYTH LEON L	1LT	O-0180414	0158	3
SMITH ROY J	LTC	O-1288805	0859	1	SMITH WADDELL F	COL	O-0397209	1146	2	SMITH WILLIAM T	MAJ	O-1576671	1264	1	SMYTHE DANNY H	LTC	O-1825831	1063	1
SMITH ROY L	LTC	O-0120308	0345	2	SMITH WALDON B	1LT	O-1318339	0446	2	SMITH WILLIAM V	MAJ	O-0175663	1161	1	SMYTHE FRANCIS	LTC	O-1117532	1167	1
SMITH ROY W	LTC	O-0539541	1067	2	SMITH WALLACE J	CW4	W-2113461	0564	1	SMITH WILLIAM W	MAJ	O-0222850	1052	3	SMYTHE JR MARCUS H	CPT	O-0454166	0645	2
SMITH RUFUS S	WO1	W-2149143	0453	2	SMITH WALLACE P	LTC	O-0234790	0265	3	SMITH WILLIAM W	COL	O-0235789	1065	3	SMYTHE LESTER A	MAJ	O-0474365	1047	1
SMITH RULON E	COL	O-0329929	0860	3	SMITH WALTER B	COL	O-0907732	0762	3	SMITH WILLIAM W	MAJ	O-0502405	1150	1	SMYTHE SAMUEL S	CW3	W-2116328	0159	1
SMITH RUSSELL	MAJ	O-0450362	1045	2	SMITH WALTER E	MAJ	O-0210636	0457	3	SMITH WILLIE E	MAJ	O-2040992	0363	1	SNAJCZUK STEPHEN R	1LT	O-1283509	1043	2
SMITH RUSSELL C	LTC	O-0360577	0346	2	SMITH WALTER F	MAJ	O-1996345	0261	1	SMITH WILMOT O	LTC	O-0264496	0364	3	SNAPP HERBERT L	LTC	O-0265684	0162	3
SMITH RUTH F	1LT	N-0787010	0246	1	SMITH WALTER G	MAJ	O-0364340	1045	2	SMITH WILSON G	MAJ	O-1032603	0559	1	SNAPP LLOYD E	LTC	O-0450478	1157	1
SMITH SAM C	MAJ	O-1179713	0760	1	SMITH WALTER H	MAJ	O-0281926	1066	3	SMITH WINFIELD W	COL	O-0113527	0744	2	SNAPP REGINALD E	2LT	O-0552595	0346	2
SMITH SAMUEL A	COL	O-0145789	0450	1	SMITH WALTER H	MAJ	O-1315981	0764	1	SMITH WINT	B G	O-0123028	1152	3	SNAVELY EARL S R	CPT	O-0510878	0147	1
SMITH SAMUEL F	1LT	O-0439236	0246	2	SMITH WALTER H	LTC	O-1825575	0764	1	SMITH WOODROW H	CW2	W-2142201	0459	1	SNAVELY HARRY L	LTC	O-0341095	0663	1
SMITH SAMUEL G	LTC	O-0475846	0555	1	SMITH WALTER K	MAJ	O-0178008	0362	1	SMITH WORTHINGTO	COL	O-0231135	0356	3	SNAVELY JR GUY E	LTC	O-0246267	0766	3
SMITH SAMUEL H	MAJ	O-1300099	0955	1	SMITH WALTER S	CW2	W-2146679	0554	1	SMITH WORTHINGTO	LTC	O-1292411	0567	3	SNEAD BENJAMIN F	CPT	O-0221908	0954	3
SMITH SAMUEL H	LTC	O-1536289	0464	1	SMITH WALTER W	MAJ	O-0493960	0447	1	SMITH YEVE L	CW3	W-2152402	1264	1	SNEAD GORDON P	CW3	W-2148382	0359	1
SMITH SAMUEL L	CPT	O-0197758	0960	3	SMITH WALTER W	LTC	O-0498493	0355	1	SMITHER GERALD S	MAJ	O-1107139	0961	1	SNEAD JR SAM	CPT	O-0441083	0947	2
SMITH SAMUEL L	MAJ	O-0249077	0965	3	SMITH WALTER W	MAJ	O-1646605	0161	1	SMITHERMAN BOB	MAJ	O-1182964	0161	1	SNEAD YOUNGER F	LTC	O-0274680	1266	3
SMITH SAMUEL L	COL	O-0328065	0247	1	SMITH WALTON	COL	O-0230101	0646	2	SMITHERMAN JOHN L	MAJ	O-1823226	0962	1	SNEATH VERYL L	MAJ	O-1540870	0865	1
SMITH SAMUEL P	LTC	O-1550703	0957	1	SMITH WARREN D	CW3	W-2152358	0666	1	SMITHERS CHARLES C	CPT	O-0201486	1153	3	SNECINSKI JOSEPH F	1LT	O-0369178	0345	2
SMITH SCHUYLER	1LT	O-1913927	0539	1	SMITH WARREN E	1LT	O-1014954	1047	2	SMITHERS LOUIS F	MAJ	O-0165034	0551	3	SNEDDON JAMES W	CPT	O-1582153	0657	1
SMITH SCOTT C	MAJ	O-0209685	0355	3	SMITH WARREN F	CW3	W-2145012	1059	1	SMITHERS WILLIAM B	COL	O-0266462	0657	3	SNEDEKER GEORGE	LTC	O-1031760	0663	1
SMITH SHERMAN W	MAJ	O-1173085	1060	1	SMITH WARREN H	CW2	W-2148008	1060	1	SMITHEY CECIL C	1LT	O-1298775	0245	1	SNEDEKER RUSSELL S	MAJ	O-1641813	0261	1
SMITH SHERROD S	1LT	O-1543575	0146	2	SMITH WARREN C	LTC	O-1170200	0162	1	SMITHEY THADDEUS R	LTC	O-1104400	0258	1	SNEE THOMAS J	LTC	O-0253257	0567	3
SMITH SHERWOOD B	COL	O-0439997	0560	3	SMITH WARREN W	1LT	O-1799670	1161	2	SMITHGALL HARRY M	LTC	O-0236019	1160	3	SNEE THOMAS R	COL	O-0316172	1164	1

NAME	GRADE	SVC NO	DATE RET MO YR	RET CODE
SNEED ARTHUR E	CPT	C-1284778	0657	1
SNEED HENRY P	MAJ	C-0108253	0545	1
SNEED REPSIE J	CW3	W-2148361	C961	1
SNEED RICHARD H	MAJ	C-0364076	0558	1
SNEED THEO W	LTC	0-0235197	1265	3
SNEIDER MILTON J	CPT	0-0521717	C845	2
SNELL ARTHUR T	LTC	C-1100343	0656	1
SNELL FRANK L	COL	C-0208972	1059	1
SNELL GILBERT P	LTC	0-0293940	0959	3
SNELL IVAN B	LTC	0-0439212	C853	1
SNELL JAY P	2LT	0-2007428	0156	2
SNELL JOHN R	CPT	0-0222229	C363	3
SNELL LLOYD L	CW2	W-2141449	0760	1
SNELL MAYNARD J	LTC	C-1535297	C462	1
SNELL WALTER M	MAJ	C-1544711	1058	1
SNELLING DAVID B	MAJ	C-0263294	0246	1
SNELLING SIDNEY B	CPT	0-2033980	0262	1
SNELLINGS WILLIAM R	MAJ	C-0415355	0247	2
SNELSON SYDNEY E	MAJ	C-1641814	0857	1
SNEPENGER JOE	CPT	0-1307867	1045	2
SNIDER BYRON R	1LT	C-1047335	C745	2
SNIDER EDWIN T	1LT	0-2046516	0350	1
SNIDER ELLWOOD H	COL	C-0207225	C358	3
SNIDER JOHN F	COL	0-0188468	C454	1
SNIDER JOHN W	1LT	0-1168086	1145	2
SNIDER JOSEPH D	CW3	W-2150224	0963	1
SNIDER RAYMOND L	MAJ	0-0888923	0157	1
SNIDER RICHARD	CPT	0-1305332	C746	2
SNIDER ROBERT E	LTC	0-1109020	C367	1
SNIDER ROBERT E	MAJ	C-2017606	0164	1
SNIDER ROSS F	MAJ	C-0475300	0853	1
SNIDER SR EMORY A	MAJ	C-2017138	0462	1
SNIDER WILLIAM A	LTC	C-0544447	1266	1
SNIDER WILLIAM A	CPT	0-1015500	0148	1
SNIDOW LEE C	MAJ	0-2263385	1262	1
SNIFFIN EDWARD H	1LT	0-1298146	C546	2
SNIPES CHARLIE L	CW3	W-2147109	1163	1
SNITJEN WAYNE J	1LT	0-1053817	0745	2
SNIZER RICHARD G	1LT	0-1648658	C847	2
SNODDY WILLIAM H	MAJ	0-0157000	1054	3
SNODGRASS ANSEL N	MAJ	C-0911800	C246	2
SNODGRASS EDWARD E	LTC	0-0277950	0853	1
SNODGRASS FRANCIS F	MAJ	0-1308195	C966	3
SNODGRASS GEORGE F	COL	0-0273537	C266	3
SNODGRASS HARVEY A	CW3	W-2149904	0165	1
SNODGRASS JOHN M	CW3	W-2151345	1165	1
SNODGRASS LEROY A	CW4	W-2114471	0559	1
SNODGRASS ORIS R	LTC	0-0545771	C364	1
SNODGRASS REA L	LTC	0-1577868	C167	3
SNODGRASS RICHARD G	LTC	0-1257975	1060	1
SNODGRASS ROBERT B	LTC	C-1111367	1163	1
SNODGRASS ROGER G	MAJ	C-1584945	1162	1
SNODGRASS WALTER F	MAJ	C-0239769	C760	3
SNODGRASS WALTER M	WO1	W-2121187	C944	2
SNODGRASS WARREN M	LTC	0-1016328	C264	1
SNOOK GLENN D	LTC	0-1316344	0266	1
SNOOK HOWARD P	LTC	C-1546596	0867	1
SNOOK JESSE	CPT	0-0520958	1041	1
SNOOK ORRIE V	LTC	0-0278193	0357	2
SNOOK RUSSELL A	COL	C-0267119	C960	3
SNOPKOWSKI STEPHEN M	MAJ	C-1048194	0854	1
SNOVER JAMES A	CW3	W-2145213	0963	1
SNOW ABNER L	1LT	C-1290679	0559	1
SNOW AETHRA C	MAJ	C-1038850	1059	1
SNOW ARTHUR W	COL	0-0173907	0751	3
SNOW ASBURY O	COL	C-C291008	C163	1
SNOW BERNARD D	CPT	0-0291156	0147	2
SNOW CHESTER R	CW2	W-2146030	0859	1
SNOW EDITH E	LTC	N-0798927	0765	1
SNOW EDWARD C	COL	0-0214151	0260	3
SNOW FRANCIS H	CW4	RW-2115964	C861	1
SNOW FRANK	CPT	0-2046339	0355	1
SNOW FRED F	1LT	0-1322814	0745	2
SNOW GALEN	LTC	0-0127070	0755	3
SNOW GEORGE N	CPT	0-C481268	C346	1
SNOW GEORGE W	MAJ	0-0173297	0-51	3
SNOW JACK R	LTC	0-0217896	0246	2
SNOW JAMES W	CPT	0-2020768	1160	2
SNOW JOHN R	LTC	0-0452722	0956	1
SNOW JR ROGER W	LTC	0-0380703	0859	1
SNOW JR THOMAS R	LTC	0-1175321	0962	1
SNOW MICHAEL	MAJ	0-1295955	1159	1
SNOW PARKER D	LTC	0-0376194	0363	1
SNOW R E	CPT	0-1691775	0558	1
SNOW RAYMOND	CW2	W-2147921	1157	1
SNOW ROBERT A	LTC	0-0265237	0364	3
SNOWDEN CHARLES R	MAJ	0-0113351	0952	3
SNOWDEN FRANK M	COL	0-0210148	0648	3
SNOWDEN GLADYS B	MAJ	N-0724295	0763	1
SNOWDEN JAMES C	CW3	W-2113264	0760	1
SNOWDEN JOSEPHINE	MAJ	N-2298647	0467	1
SNOWDER HAROLD W	MAJ	0-1318099	0163	1
SNOZEK JOHN E	MAJ	0-1117026	0557	1
SNURKOWSKI CHARLES V	LTC	0-0268055	C256	3
SNYDER A J	CW2	W-2142117	1056	1
SNYDER ALBERT E	MAJ	0-0345942	1150	1
SNYDER ARTHUR B	1LT	0-0149595	1049	3
SNYDER ARTHUR G	LTC	0-0445953	1047	2
SNYDER ARTHUR J	CW3	W-2148991	0664	1
SNYDER BERNARD A	CW3	W-2151205	0863	1
SNYDER BURR W	LTC	0-0435723	1048	1
SNYDER CATHERINE	1LT	N-0737851	1151	1
SNYDER CEDRICK V	1LT	0-1295099	0145	2
SNYDER CHARLES H	CPT	0-0278122	1256	3
SNYDER CHARLES T	MAJ	0-0256584	1044	2
SNYDER CHESTER O	CW2	W-2144994	0660	1
SNYDER CLAUDE F	LTC	0-0490839	0356	1
SNYDER DONALD J	CW3	RW-2209974	0966	1
SNYDER DONALD L	1LT	0-0371097	1044	2
SNYDER DRENNEN	1LT	0-2048784	0945	2
SNYDER EARLE C	COL	0-0174503	0349	3
SNYDER EDGAR M	MAJ	0-2049401	0157	1
SNYDER EDWARD E	CW4	W-2001843	1065	1
SNYDER EDWARD N	LTC	0-1294380	0657	1
SNYDER EDWIN H	MAJ	0-1113453	0855	2
SNYDER ERNEST C	MAJ	0-1001245	0759	1
SNYDER EUGENE B	CW3	W-2145659	0566	1
SNYDER EUGENE H	MAJ	0-1825278	C161	1
SNYDER FLOYD T	MAJ	0-0912415	0346	2
SNYDER FRANK J	LTC	0-1168925	0664	1
SNYDER FREDERICK	MAJ	0-1542026	0658	1
SNYDER GARREL O	LTC	0-0282825	0662	3
SNYDER GEORGE G	CPT	0-1575568	0246	2
SNYDER GLEN E	MAJ	0-0229723	0458	3
SNYDER HAROLD H	COL	0-0508449	0865	3
SNYDER HAROLD R	LTC	0-1171777	1262	1
SNYDER HERBERT	COL	0-0127580	1055	3
SNYDER HERBERT L	MAJ	0-0982858	1060	1
SNYDER HOLLIS F	MAJ	0-1340706	1161	2
SNYDER HUBERT E	COL	0-0193810	0648	3
SNYDER III NELSON T	CPT	0-2028636	0366	1
SNYDER INEZ V	LTC	L-0115629	0147	2
SNYDER JACK A	LTC	0-1303789	0761	1
SNYDER JAMES B	LTC	0-0240966	0265	3
SNYDER JAMES E	COL	0-0196604	0463	3
SNYDER JAMES L	CPT	0-1894986	0745	2
SNYDER JESS W	MAJ	0-0167936	0446	1
SNYDER JOHN P	CW3	W-2150192	0263	1
SNYDER JOHN W	COL	0-0103058	0655	3
SNYDER JOHN W	MAJ	0-0974109	1263	1
SNYDER JOSEPH L	1LT	0-0482252	0157	1
SNYDER JOSEPH V	MAJ	0-1296107	0657	1
SNYDER JOSEPH W	1LT	0-0451930	0945	2
SNYDER JR ALLEN L	LTC	0-2012535	0266	1
SNYDER JR CHESTER A	CPT	0-1584946	0645	2
SNYDER JR CLARENCE J	MAJ	0-1057903	0865	1
SNYDER JR JOHN T	CW3	W-2148886	0663	1
SNYDER JR WILLIAM O	LTC	0-1113454	0664	1
SNYDER KATHRYNE R	MAJ	N-0774655	0567	1
SNYDER LAWRENCE	MAJ	0-1797551	0258	1
SNYDER LAWRENCE M	CW3	W-3150542	1266	1
SNYDER LEROY T	LTC	0-0477828	0865	1
SNYDER LLWYC C	LTC	0-0237124	0262	3
SNYDER LYLE O	LTC	0-0493998	0166	3
SNYDER MAXWELL C	M G	0-0242582	0860	3
SNYDER MELVIN C	COL	C-0253968	1058	3
SNYDER MELVIN L	1LT	0-1167642	C347	1
SNYDER MERLE B	LTC	0-0239597	1263	3
SNYDER MERVIN E	CW2	W-2147733	1056	2
SNYDER MILDRED L	CPT	N-0733816	0946	1
SNYDER MILO O	LTC	0-0100041	C648	3
SNYDER MILTON A	COL	C-0147436	C647	2
SNYDER NATHAN C	COL	0-0229534	1063	3
SNYDER NEIL N	LTC	0-0171204	1049	3
SNYDER PAUL C	LTC	0-0472597	C259	1
SNYDER PHILIP E	COL	0-0374216	0667	1
SNYDER RAYMOND K	LTC	0-0210368	0360	3
SNYDER RICHARD F	LTC	0-0184241	0656	3
SNYDER ROBERT G	MAJ	C-0257558	1165	3
SNYDER ROBERT L	LTC	0-0303549	0647	2
SNYDER ROBERT V	COL	0-0409985	1266	1
SNYDER ROBERT W	LTC	0-1553909	0662	1
SNYDER ROSS M	MAJ	C-1640973	0862	1
SNYDER RUFUS A	LTC	C-0402949	0146	2
SNYDER SAMUEL F	MAJ	C-0449522	0749	1
SNYDER SIDNEY A	CPT	C-0358561	C346	2
SNYDER SIDNEY W	MAJ	C-0110987	0656	3
SNYDER SIEGFRIED	CPT	0-1798082	0661	1
SNYDER SR JAMES C	1LT	0-1951547	0549	2
SNYDER STANLEY	CPT	0-1112457	1162	2
SNYDER THURMAN F	LTC	0-0922018	C867	3
SNYDER VICTORY A	CPT	0-0498508	0347	2
SNYDER WARREN	MAJ	0-2055167	1161	1
SNYDER WESLEY E	LTC	0-0900029	0746	1
SNYDER WILLIAM J	MAJ	C-0329161	0546	2
SNYDER WILLIAM P	MAJ	0-2067899	0763	1
SNYDER WILTON R	LTC	C-0214477	0655	3
SOBCZAK JOHN J	CPT	0-1877853	0963	1
SOBCZYK NICHOLAS V	2LT	0-1336275	C646	2
SOBECK CYRIL C	LTC	0-0352191	0646	2
SOBEK ADAM J	1LT	0-1844933	C547	1
SOBEL LOUIS	LTC	0-0905797	0467	3
SOBEL MIN	LTC	L-0220162	0363	1
SOBELL JACK	CPT	C-0310103	C445	2
SOBELMAN JACK S	MAJ	0-0966740	1160	1
SOBEY ARTHUR W	LTC	C-1575179	0965	1
SOBEY WILFRED M	MAJ	0-2032849	1262	1
SOBIN JULIUS	COL	0-0135456	1053	3
SOBLEN WALTER J	1LT	0-1636667	1144	2
SOBOLESKI STEVEN A	2LT	0-1300726	0244	2
SOBOLESKY HELEN T	1LT	N-0725923	1045	1
SOBOLEWSKI WILLIAM C	MAJ	C-1327896	C261	1
SOBOTTA CORNELIUS	MAJ	0-2009409	0860	1
SOBUT VINCENT T	MAJ	C-1059645	C562	1
SOCHA EDMUND J	MAJ	C-1102474	0261	1
SOCHA JOSEPH V	CW3	W-2148223	0362	2
SOCHON STANLEY J	CW2	W-2111367	C864	1
SOCIA MARVIN H	CW2	W-2104491	1045	2
SODA WILLIAM E	CPT	0-0343913	1143	2
SODDY THOMAS B	1LT	0-0403636	0444	2
SODEN JAMES R	LTC	0-0906587	1265	3
SODERBERG EDWARD R	CW3	W-2001523	0762	3
SODERBERG JOHN W	2LT	0-1004038	C845	2
SODERBERG KERMIT J	MAJ	C-0312878	C146	2
SODERBERG ROBERT E	MAJ	C-0446265	0550	1
SODERGREN CARL I	COL	0-1175865	C861	1
SODERLUND KENNETH G	MAJ	C-2211319	1262	1
SODERQUIST RICHARD W	MAJ	C-0381626	0745	2
SODERSTROM GLEN A	LTC	C-0350574	C462	1
SODORFF RICHARD L	1LT	0-0550595	C146	2
SOEDER ROBERT G	MAJ	C-2047503	0962	1
SOELLNER FRED W	CPT	C-1304135	C659	2
SOERHOFF ROBERT A	CPT	0-1322096	0347	1
SOETERS EUGENE L	MAJ	0-0973877	1162	1
SOEURT WILLIAM J	COL	C-0255836	0964	3
SOFER HERMAN	CPT	0-1690616	1044	2
SOFFE CLYDE C	MAJ	C-0358912	0566	3
SOFFEL QUINTIN I	MAJ	C-0244776	0146	2
SOGARD THEODORE L	COL	0-0127673	1053	3
SOHN HYMAN	1LT	0-1317695	1145	1
SOHN JR LOUIS S	MAJ	0-0394282	0146	2
SOHNGEN WILLIAM F	CPT	0-1693604	0146	2
SOIFER IRVIN T	CPT	0-0490808	0646	2
SOINE ARTHUR W	LTC	0-0925597	C564	3
SOISSON JOHN L	2LT	0-0360360	0966	3
SOISSON WILLIAM H	LTC	0-0294492	0945	2
SOISSONS ALFRED E	COL	0-0483746	0747	2
SOJKA PATRICK J	MAJ	0-1081033	0860	1
SOKEN EDWARD B	LTC	0-0247205	0966	3
SOKOL ANTHONY J	LTC	0-0545244	C564	1
SOKOL ARNOLD	LTC	0-0451245	1162	1
SOKOLOWSKA ANNA	2LT	N-0722695	C744	1
SOKOLOWSKI JOSEPH J	MAJ	0-1184728	1161	1
SOKOLSKY SAMUEL	1LT	0-1315226	0146	2
SOLA MARCELO	CW2	W-2147641	1060	1
SOLA SR GERALD C	LTC	0-0133755	0253	3
SOLANDER JOHN O	CW3	W-2146555	0161	1
SOLANICK WILLIAM C	MAJ	0-1309105	0965	1
SOLAR LESLIE S	LTC	0-0126211	0855	3
SOLARI LOUIS S	LTC	0-0266062	0362	3
SOLBAKKEN IVAR A	CPT	0-0453158	0945	2
SOLBERG CHRIS	LTC	0-0287639	0754	1
SOLBERG JOHN C	COL	0-0243102	0251	3
SOLBERG NELS G	MAJ	0-0129253	0255	3
SOLGANY WILLIAM J	MAJ	0-0500004	0950	1
SOLDATE JOSEPH A	1LT	0-1824242	1059	1
SOLODOVNICK JACOB S	CPT	0-0532565	0746	2
SOLOZ LESTER C	CPT	0-1291344	C347	1
SOLEN ALBERT W	CPT	0-0381872	0444	2
SOLINSKY NORMAN T	LTC	0-1635259	C560	1
SOLIS JOSEPH	MAJ	0-1642598	0661	1
SOLIS LOUIS R	CW2	W-2208300	0565	2
SOLIS PAUL J	LTC	0-0271560	1066	3
SOLKOT ROY	MAJ	0-0518169	0965	1
SOLL ANDREW M	1LT	0-1001606	0346	2
SOLLENBERGER WILLIAM	CPT	0-0523257	0746	2
SOLLEY LOUIE W	MAJ	0-1298613	1057	1
SOLO ALEXANDER	2LT	0-0158788	0456	3
SOLOMKIN MARK	CPT	0-0467940	1045	2
SOLOMON ADOLPH F	COL	0-0281510	0561	1
SOLOMON BRUCE L	LTC	0-0774338	1167	1
SOLOMON BURTON	1LT	0-0514651	0446	2
SOLOMON ELKAN F	LTC	0-0247855	C361	1
SOLOMON HUBERT L	MAJ	0-2204331	0863	1
SOLOMON IRA T	CW3	W-2152403	1263	1
SOLOMON JACOB M	LTC	0-0235402	1165	3
SOLOMON JEROME J	COL	0-0244876	0866	3
SOLOMON JOSEPH C	LTC	0-0536197	0164	1
SOLOMON JR JAMES E	LTC	0-1102963	1160	1
SOLOMON JR LOUIS E	1LT	0-0485931	1044	2
SOLOMON MEYER	CPT	0-0484610	0845	2
SOLOMON NELSON	CPT	0-1895300	1155	1
SOLOMON PAUL A	1LT	0-0497189	0848	1
SOLOMON PAUL E	CPT	0-0890311	0556	1
SOLOMON SAUL	COL	0-0348806	1165	3
SOLOMON TOUFIC J	CW3	W-2203488	1266	1
SOLOMONOW EDWARD J	LTC	0-0312332	0646	2
SOLON THOMAS F	CPT	0-0470270	0246	2
SOLOT MORTON A	CPT	0-1290832	0447	1
SOLOVE SAMUEL	CPT	0-1544865	0546	2
SOLOVEN BOLIESLAU	CW2	W-2143249	0162	1
SOLOVSKOY GEORGE R	LTC	0-1297801	0261	1
SOLTOW EDWARD A	LTC	0-1059287	0262	1
SOLTYS ANDREW T	LTC	0-1045259	0461	1
SOLTYS STANLEY	LTC	0-0860577	0962	1
SOLYOM RICHARD L	MAJ	0-0310763	0146	2
SOMBAR MICHAEL J	MAJ	0-2035388	0564	1
SOMERALL JAMES R	1LT	0-1323753	1145	2
SOMERS DANIEL A	MAJ	0-0335990	0464	3
SOMERS GAYLE H	CPT	0-0189064	0453	3

NAME	GRADE	SVC NO	DATE RET MO YR	RET CODE
SOMERS JAMES F	1LT	0-1586932	C446	1
SOMERS LEE W	CPT	0-2008640	0157	1
SOMERS LOWELL M	CPT	0-1040154	0245	2
SOMERS PETER	MAJ	C-1101669	0860	1
SOMERS VERNON H	MAJ	C-0228809	1163	3
SOMERVILLE GEORGE W	MAJ	0-2210441	0566	1
SOMERVILLE JAMES	CPT	0-1319673	1146	2
SOMERVILLE ROBERT L	CW3	W-2143180	0660	1
SOMES ALFRED H	CPT	0-0468150	0344	1
SOMMER JAMES E	LTC	0-0395721	0464	1
SOMMERMEYER W C	LTC	0-0395329	1060	1
SCMMERS JR ALBERT P	CPT	0-1291719	1046	1
SOMMERVOLD WILLIAM A	MAJ	0-2035500	1060	1
SONDEREGGER R P	2LT	0-1181465	C145	2
SONENFELD HOWARD	CPT	0-0508661	0946	2
SONEY RALPH C	LTC	0-0469183	0447	2
SONGY STANLEY R	1LT	0-0421413	0546	2
SONIAT SIDNEY L	LTC	0-0282242	1060	3
SONIVILLE FRED T	LTC	0-1322097	C765	1
SONKIN JESSE	LTC	0-0302132	1166	3
SONLEY JOSEPH L	MAJ	0-0969853	0263	1
SONNE IRVIN M	LTC	0-0119609	0147	2
SONNEBORN JAMES E	MAJ	C-0949659	0365	1
SONNELAND SIDNEY C	MAJ	C-0206933	C245	2
SONNET HARRY M	MAJ	0-1579154	0951	1
SONNHEIM EDWARD B	LTC	0-0230816	0664	3
SONNIE JAMES E	MAJ	0-2006873	0165	1
SONNIER JOHN J	MAJ	0-0264216	0966	3
SONNIER WILLIAM	MAJ	0-0216373	0748	2
SONNTAG EUGENE W	MAJ	C-1284780	0161	1
SONNTAG JOSEPH H	LTC	0-0903544	C467	3
SONNTAG RICHARD W	1LT	0-1702708	1044	1
SONOWSKI JOSEPH F	CW3	W-2142054	0959	1
SONSTEIN JACK	MAJ	0-1586933	0965	1
SOOBY JOHN T	CW4	W-2146842	1265	1
SOOLPOVAR DAVID	LTC	0-1172667	0461	2
SOPER ANN W	MAJ	N-0797057	0767	1
SOPER ARTHUR D	LTC	0-0133535	1054	3
SOPER CLARENCE E	MAJ	0-0282532	0245	2
SOPER DONALD	CPT	0-1649911	0949	1
SOPHER PHILIP	MAJ	C-1556662	0361	2
SOPKA JOHN	MAJ	C-0494701	1053	1
SOPRE ANTHONY J	CW2	W-2146400	0155	2
SORADY FRED E	LTC	0-1100791	0760	1
SORAHAN FRANK R	LTC	0-1298777	0155	2
SORBELLO MICHAEL	MAJ	0-1044108	0861	1
SORBER MILDRED R	1LT	N-0722768	0745	1
SOROEN JR EDWARD H	CW2	W-2211477	C167	1
SORENSEN BETTE M	2LT	N-0785579	0546	1
SORENSEN CARLYLE A	CPT	0-0313599	0245	2
SORENSEN CLARENCE N	MAJ	C-0462073	C546	2
SORENSEN EUGENE E	MAJ	0-1170564	0158	1
SORENSEN FRED F	CPT	0-1336559	0662	1
SORENSEN HARRY L	LTC	0-1302375	0759	1
SORENSEN HARRY S	CW3	W-2147865	C664	1
SORENSEN JR JOHN	MAJ	C-0982656	0865	1
SORENSEN KEITH A	CW3	W-2140938	1262	1
SORENSEN ORVEL B	LTC	0-1592079	0962	2
SORENSEN PETER	MAJ	0-0109894	1044	2
SORENSEN REUBEN S	CPT	0-0948926	0960	1
SORENSEN VALDEMAR M	CW3	W-2203393	0765	1
SORENSEN VERNAL T	LTC	0-0293944	1051	1
SORENSEN WESTON C	MAJ	C-1825832	C264	1
SORENSON ELMER C	LTC	0-0448734	0662	1
SORENSON HAROLD J	1LT	0-1543625	C646	2
SORENSON JR JEROME W	MAJ	0-0328672	0346	2
SORG ROBERT F	LTC	0-1580353	1061	1
SORGI JR CHARLES F	2LT	0-1294212	C745	2
SORIANO FRED D	MAJ	0-1896563	0561	2
SORIERO WILLIAM A	CPT	0-0386024	0944	2
SORILLA ROSEN S	MAJ	0-1896781	0861	1
SORLEY MILFORD S	MAJ	0-0118143	1044	2
SOROKA ALEXANDER	LTC	0-1041445	C264	1
SORRELL HERBERT E	MAJ	0-1926202	C266	1
SORRELL HERBERT S	1LT	0-0482394	0742	2
SORRELL JAMES D	LTC	0-0211936	1057	2
SORRELS JR AARON I	CPT	0-1058658	0556	1
SORRENTINO FELIX G	CW4	W-2105741	0258	1
SORRICK DAVID C	CW3	P W-3150572	0767	1
SORROUGH JAMES E	CPT	0-1688300	0457	1
SORSDAHL DOUGLAS	1LT	0-1324669	0246	2
SOS JOSEPH P	LTC	0-1060648	0664	1
SOSEBEE HERMAN H	CW2	W-2152027	0961	1
SOSKIN HERSHEL A	LTC	0-0259546	0657	1
SOSKY JOSEPH W	CW2	W-2141451	0557	1
SOSNA MAX E	MAJ	0-0500160	0658	1
SOSNAY THEODORE	LTC	0-1316791	0765	1
SOSNOVE WILLIAM	LTC	0-1057606	0667	1
SOSNOWSKI PETER P	CPT	0-1109676	0163	1
SOTO III CHARLES T	LTC	0-1577874	0262	1
SOTO LOUIS H	LTC	0-0337463	0459	1
SOTO-REMOS JULIO	CPT	0-0222444	0563	3
SOTOMAYOR BONIFACIO	MAJ	0-0108069	0144	1
SOTTONG GEORGE V	COL	0-0288253	0857	1
SOUCHON CLIFFORD P	LTC	0-1031273	0162	1
SOUCIER LOUIS R	CPT	0-0289962	0458	3
SOUCY RAYMOND L	CPT	0-0988380	1061	2
SOUDER ROBERT H	LTC	0-0358306	0161	1
SOUHRADA ALBERT H	MAJ	0-0311415	0944	2
SOUKARAS KOMNENUS M	MAJ	0-0251575	1165	3
SOUKUP WILLIAM L	MAJ	0-0971812	0266	1
SOULOS EDWARD H	LTC	0-1308196	0363	1
SOULE FRANK A	MAJ	0-0218292	1160	3
SOURLY RAY A	LTC	0-1179623	0165	1
SOUSA JAMES J	MAJ	0-2018594	0664	1
SOUSA LEO	MAJ	0-0939669	1262	1
SOUSA MANUEL B	CW2	W-2144837	0155	1
SOUSA ROBERT J	MAJ	0-1308014	1162	1
SOUTH KEITH H	COL	0-0127880	0657	3
SOUTH ROBERT L	MAJ	0-1930844	0266	1
SOUTH SAMUEL L	COL	0-0240611	0-52	3
SOUTHALL COPELAND S	MAJ	0-0151988	0255	3
SOUTHALL SAM R	CW3	W-2145842	0163	1
SOUTHARD FRANK L	LTC	0-0921941	0465	3
SOUTHARD JAMES W F	COL	0-0287441	0559	3
SOUTHER CLIFFORD J	LTC	0-1326138	0765	1
SOUTHER JAMES R	MAJ	0-0341944	0145	2
SOUTHER JOHN K	LTC	0-0290132	0260	1
SOUTHERLAND C C	CW2	W-2147697	1059	1
SOUTHERLAND JOHN A	CPT	0-1031211	1156	1
SOUTHERLAND LEE V	MAJ	0-0404291	0962	1
SOUTHERN BOB N	CPT	0-1337497	0664	1
SOUTHERN DONALD E	MAJ	0-1885262	0866	1
SOUTHERN DONALD L	1LT	0-0417056	0345	2
SOUTHERN FREDERICK	MAJ	C-0452611	0162	1
SOUTHERN HAROLD K	MAJ	0-0361465	0263	3
SOUTHERN HUBERT A	MAJ	0-1577876	0653	1
SOUTHERN JOHN A	LTC	0-0360774	C165	3
SOUTHERN JOHN W	1LT	0-1169749	1051	1
SOUTHERN ROY	MAJ	0-1555904	0960	1
SOUTHWARD WILBUR R	COL	0-0267137	0863	3
SOUTHWELL EDWIN T	1LT	0-1177990	0945	2
SOUTHWELL JOSEPH A	CW2	W-2210150	0964	1
SOUTHWICK THOMAS S	LTC	0-0236169	0765	3
SOUTHWICK WILLIAM B	CPT	0-0447821	0556	2
SOUTHWORTH CHARLES G	MAJ	0-1634349	0557	1
SOUTHWORTH GILBERT E	MAJ	0-1636674	0457	1
SOUTHWORTH HAVEN E	LTC	0-0242547	0366	3
SOUTHWORTH JOHN A	MAJ	C-0244596	0863	3
SOUTHWORTH JOSEPH E	CPT	0-0334996	0545	2
SOUTHWORTH JR JAMES	CPT	0-0388047	0446	2
SOUTHWORTH MAYNARD N	CPT	0-0291444	0446	2
SOUTHWORTH ROBERT B	COL	0-0253035	1166	3
SOUTHWORTH WILLIAM E	2LT	0-2012600	0646	2
SOUWEINE LEON E	CW3	W-2104493	0862	1
SOUZA LAWRENCE P	MAJ	0-1301896	1160	1
SOVA EDWIN M	1LT	0-1292413	0453	1
SOVA STANLEY J	CPT	0-0978203	0164	1
SOVERNS JAMES W	LTC	0-1550056	0462	1
SOVINSKY WILLIAM P	CPT	0-1551522	0348	1
SOVITSKI CHARLES	MAJ	0-1053371	C863	1
SOWA JOSEPH E	LTC	0-1307582	0663	1
SOWA WALTER D	LTC	C-1309106	0762	1
SOWASH CARL O	CPT	0-1081861	C247	2
SOWASH CLARE R	LTC	0-0183951	0159	3
SOWDER SAMUEL R	CW4	W-2113662	0263	1
SOWELL KAVY V	CW3	W-2150036	1055	1
SOWELL LEWIS C	LTC	0-0272267	0767	3
SOWELL ROBERT A	LTC	0-1549604	0962	1
SOWER DONALD L	LTC	C-1107701	0863	1
SOWER WARREN O	MAJ	0-0425487	0361	1
SOWERS HAROLD E	1LT	0-1822326	C746	1
SOWERS JESSE E	CPT	0-1288134	0345	2
SOWERS LOYD G	1LT	0-1291027	104N	2
SOWKA SAMUEL H	LTC	0-1109024	0862	1
SOWL WILLIAM F	CPT	0-1586936	1058	1
SOWLE CHARLES H	CPT	0-1580356	0263	1
SOXMAN R C	COL	0-0231753	0264	3
SOYKE JOHN R	1LT	0-1307583	0745	2
SPACKEEN PAUL J	CW3	W-2203355	0963	1
SPADAFORD JOSEPH F	1LT	0-1314686	1145	2
SPADE JOHN S	LTC	0-1573599	0860	1
SPADEY FRANCIS X	CPT	0-1581381	0446	2
SPADOLA RENATO F	MAJ	0-0389390	C246	2
SPAE WILLIAM M	LTC	0-1317742	0366	1
SPAHN OTTO J	LTC	0-0184303	0959	3
SPAHR ERNEST K	LTC	0-0277741	0159	3
SPAHR KIMBALL	MAJ	C-0413110	0747	2
SPAHT CARLOS G	COL	0-0264652	0966	3
SPAIN JOSEPH C	LTC	0-0450767	0858	1
SPAIN VERNIE B	1LT	N-0742078	1045	1
SPAINHOWER EARL E	LTC	0-0167245	0954	3
SPAINHOWER JOHN W	LTC	0-0276384	0361	1
SPAKE WILLIAM T	LTC	0-1640976	0261	1
SPALDING MALCOLM C	LTC	C-1287428	0265	1
SPALDING PHILIP C	1LT	0-1304626	1045	2
SPALDING THOMAS J	MAJ	C-0317560	0945	2
SPALDING WESLEY F	CPT	0-1693816	0656	1
SPALONE ALFRED L	MAJ	0-0478239	0446	2
SPANGE HELGE W	LTC	0-0276655	0254	3
SPANGENBERG WARREN E	CPT	0-1796723	0446	2
SPANGLER GEORGE R	CPT	0-0272216	1143	2
SPANGLER HENRY A	MAJ	C-0222955	1064	3
SPANGLER MATTHEW J	1LT	0-1310891	1047	2
SPANGLER THOMAS M	LTC	0-0227484	1046	1
SPANIER HAROLD B	LTC	0-0135295	0451	3
SPANIER SEYMOUR E	LTC	0-0504296	1061	1
SPANN CHARLES A	MAJ	C-0483747	1043	2
SPANNARE KARL L	LTC	0-1634351	0364	1
SPANNRAFT FRANK D	CW4	W-2111386	0561	1
SPANSKI EDWARD J	LTC	0-0525209	0266	3
SPANUTIUS EDWARD R	MAJ	0-0959286	1064	1
SPARER PHINEAS J	MAJ	C-0525991	0946	2
SPARGER WILBUR L	CW2	W-2147373	0559	2
SPARKMAN GUY A	2LT	0-0940737	C656	1
SPARKMAN LEWIS A	MAJ	C-1798893	1165	1
SPARKMAN MAURICE K	MAJ	0-0931326	1062	1
SPARKMAN THOMAS B	COL	G-0207231	0648	3
SPARKS CARL A	LTC	0-0187246	0255	3
SPARKS COURTLEIGH	LTC	C-1640978	0162	1
SPARKS DELILAH M	LTC	N-0700341	0347	1
SPARKS DONALD L .	CPT	0-1599092	0365	1
SPARKS ENOCH P	LTC	0-1549105	0658	1
SPARKS GEORGE T	MAJ	C-0975202	0365	1
SPARKS JAMES M	CPT	0-1004039	1046	2
SPARKS JAMES V	MAJ	C-0118239	0943	2
SPARKS JR BENJAMIN F	CPT	0-1109677	0446	2
SPARKS JR CLIFFORD C	MAJ	C-2021138	C364	1
SPARKS LARRY E	CW3	W-2143114	1067	1
SPARKS LAWRENCE E	LTC	0-1080584	0766	1
SPARKS LLOYD	CPT	0-1574532	0550	1
SPARKS MERLE A	COL	0-0246627	0966	3
SPARKS RAYMOND W	MAJ	0-0287451	C358	3
SPARKS WALTER D	MAJ	0-0968218	0566	1
SPARKS WAYNE J	1LT	0-1303965	C446	2
SPARKS 4TH ROBERT W	CPT	0-0412234	0346	2
SPARLING HAROLD J	LTC	0-0286332	0756	3
SPARROW HOWARD M	2LT	0-0246046	0356	3
SPARROW RICHARD S	1LT	0-0528410	0246	2
SPARROW WILBUR O	1LT	0-2030155	0747	1
SPARTI JOSEPH F	WO1	W-2144164	0459	2
SPASARE FRANK	MAJ	0-1541011	0563	1
SPASEFF MARY M	1LT	N-0760537	0746	1
SPATCHER FRANCIS	MAJ	0-1341829	1162	1
SPATZ AGNES L	MAJ	L-0702252	0363	1
SPATZ CHARLES G	CPT	0-1011870	0147	2
SPAUGH WILLIAM W	CW3	W-2132070	0254	2
SPAULDING HORACE M	MAJ	0-0326238	0846	2
SPAULDING JAMES A	1LT	0-1319451	0246	2
SPAULDING JAMES B	COL	0-0160788	0151	3
SPAULDING JAMES F	MAJ	0-0751475	C465	1
SPAULDING MERTON D	MAJ	0-1332004	0863	1
SPAULDING THOMAS E	LTC	0-0225514	C557	3
SPAUR GEORGE	COL	0-0214067	0463	3
SPAW CARL S	MAJ	0-0370367	0446	1
SPAYD GEORGE F	MAJ	0-1285652	1060	1
SPEAK WILLIAM B	CPT	0-2000864	0358	1
SPEAKER HARRY A	LTC	0-0345364	1047	2
SPEAKER HARRY H	LTC	0-0371965	0765	3
SPEAKS DONALD W	1LT	0-0526962	0845	2
SPEAKS STANFORD S	COL	0-0176665	1046	2
SPEAR CARTER H	MAJ	0-0495741	0654	1
SPEAR FRANK A	LTC	0-0286811	0361	3
SPEAR HUNTER J	MAJ	0-1339403	0162	1
SPEAR JR CHARLES O	LTC	0-0242625	0844	1
SPEAR JR RAYMOND L	MAJ	0-0323362	0462	1
SPEAR RHEA C	MAJ	N-0756179	0364	3
SPEARMAN FRANCIS W	LTC	0-0360366	0564	2
SPEARMAN JR JAMES P	CW3	W-2205487	0263	1
SPEARS AUGUSTUS C	LTC	0-0476882	0464	3
SPEARS CHARLIE R	1LT	0-1547461	0145	2
SPEARS DORMAN A	MAJ	0-0246692	0165	3
SPEARS ELSWORTH W	MAJ	0-1597819	0761	2
SPEARS FRED M	CPT	0-1286386	0264	1
SPEARS HOMER R	2LT	0-2001824	0657	1
SPEARS JOHN E	CW3	W-2143579	0259	1
SPEARS JOHN R	MAJ	0-0410752	0561	1
SPEARS LEROY C	LTC	0-0790730	0964	1
SPEARS RALPH W	MAJ	0-1010361	0357	1
SPEARS WILLIAM K	CPT	0-0579105	0161	1
SPEARY JOHN A	LTC	0-1107144	0461	1
SPEAS KENNETH R	LTC	0-1166615	0761	1
SPECHT FRANCIS K	CW3	W-2150351	1065	1
SPECHT MALCOLM A	COL	C-0250898	1266	3
SPECHT ORVILLE A	LTC	0-1595835	0964	1
SPECHT VELMA M	CPT	N-0771340	0648	1
SPECK DONALD W	LTC	0-1327189	0464	1
SPECK DUNBAR V	CW4	W-2105933	1154	1
SPECK JEFFERSON	MAJ	0-0377670	0947	1
SPECK WILLIAM R	MAJ	0-1544028	1165	3
SPECKER JOHN C	COL	0-0273225	0367	3
SPECKERT MARIE	1LT	N-0700112	0742	1
SPECTOR DANIEL H	COL	0-0425654	0963	1
SPECTOR HENRY	LTC	0-0447351	0852	1
SPECTOR MELVIN M	CPT	0-1551119	0857	1
SPECTOR WILLIAM S	2LT	0-1533451	0745	2
SPEECE HAROLD E	LTC	0-0385140	1060	1
SPEED ALONZO C	CPT	0-0258546	0265	3
SPEED EARL	MAJ	0-2005528	0656	1
SPEEGLE CLEN H	1LT	0-0109845	1028	2
SPEELMAN ROONEY A	MAJ	0-0545773	0464	1
SPEENBURGH GLEASON B	CPT	0-2052075	1045	2
SPEER FRED L	LTC	0-1172293	0263	1
SPEER JAMES R	COL	0-0183695	0648	3
SPEER JOHN F H	LTC	0-0302525	0459	3
SPEER JOSEPH R	MAJ	0-2262924	1062	1
SPEER RENWICK W	CPT	0-2263409	0162	1
SPEER RICHARD D	LTC	0-1634352	0264	1
SPEER THOMAS J	LTC	0-1634353	0755	1
SPEER WILLIAM C	1LT	0-1575183	0644	2

NAME	GRADE	SVC NO	DATE RET MO YR	RET CODE
SPEERS CHESTER C	MAJ	C-0451247	0561	1
SPEERS ROBERT W	CPT	0-2021133	1162	1
SPEES HAROLC L	1LT	C-1548441	C161	1
SPEES MILTON H	1LT	0-1884163	0754	2
SPEEVACK MAHER	CPT	0-1685231	C646	2
SPEHR PETER E	LTC	0-0230689	0964	3
SPEIGHT BILLY B	CPT	0-2029847	C366	1
SPEIGHTS PAUL E	2LT	C-1110818	1045	2
SPEIR ROSS C	COL	0-0102458	0648	3
SPELCE CARL C	MAJ	0-0356181	0547	2
SPELICH MATTHEW P	MAJ	C-1017045	0760	1
SPELL JOSEPH D	CW2	W-2146993	0857	1
SPELLMAN CLARENCE F	CW2	W-2151720	1060	1
SPELLMAN JAMES L	COL	C-0324821	0161	1
SPELLMAN JAMES W	LTC	0-0904329	0263	1
SPELLMAN JOSEPH L	LTC	0-0276794	C766	3
SPELLMAN VERNON C	1LT	0-1017600	0546	2
SPELLMEYER EDWARD L	MAJ	0-0357880	1147	1
SPELTA VICTOR F	LTC	0-1845796	0167	1
SPELTZ REINHARD L	COL	C-0406278	0158	1
SPENCE ADELINE	MAJ	N-0756134	C463	1
SPENCE CURTIS T	LTC	0-0407824	C665	2
SPENCE DAVIC A	LTC	0-0171313	C756	3
SPENCE HOMER M	MAJ	0-0363926	0946	1
SPENCE JAMES T	MAJ	C-0108974	1054	3
SPENCE JOHN F	LTC	C-0489854	1057	1
SPENCE JOSEPH W	CPT	0-2025333	0760	1
SPENCE JR THOMAS R	CW3	W-2143778	C161	1
SPENCE NAVEN D	MAJ	0-5301713	1067	1
SPENCE RALPH K	CPT	0-0172483	0452	3
SPENCE ROBERT J	1LT	0-1316227	0645	1
SPENCE THOMAS E	CPT	0-2262698	0261	1
SPENCE WILLIAM L	CPT	C-1341593	0+60	1
SPENCER ADAM C	CPT	0-0164258	C340	1
SPENCER ALLEN W	LTC	0-0295389	0160	1
SPENCER BURFORD A	CPT	0-0167929	1158	3
SPENCER CLAUDE W	MAJ	0-2262217	0966	1
SPENCER DEANE F	2LT	0-1303218	1144	2
SPENCER EDWARD A	CPT	C-2287136	0867	1
SPENCER EUGENE A	CPT	0-1543876	1154	2
SPENCER EUGENE M	MAJ	C-0333440	0363	1
SPENCER FLOYD B	COL	0-0358373	0961	1
SPENCER FOREST H	COL	0-0246593	1054	3
SPENCER FRANK W	CPT	0-1013933	0960	1
SPENCER FRANKLIN H	LTC	0-0179181	0557	3
SPENCER GAYLE H	1LT	C-1016843	0945	2
SPENCER GEORGE B	MAJ	0-1320893	1047	1
SPENCER GEORGE W	LTC	0-1109027	0764	1
SPENCER HAL P	MAJ	0-0275350	C258	3
SPENCER HARVEY H	LTC	0-0967240	0363	3
SPENCER HENRY A	CW3	W-2146629	0966	1
SPENCER HENRY R	MAJ	C-1923581	1065	1
SPENCER HERBERT	COL	C-0176785	1054	3
SPENCER HERBERT M	1LT	0-1111926	0246	2
SPENCER JAMES B	LTC	0-0309464	0462	1
SPENCER JAMES D	MAJ	0-0312946	1047	2
SPENCER JIM L	MAJ	C-2024306	0764	1
SPENCER JIMMIE O	MAJ	C-2103079	0265	1
SPENCER JOHN A	COL	0-0314668	C164	1
SPENCER JOHN R	LTC	0-0268224	C462	1
SPENCER JOHNNY H	MAJ	C-0888884	C860	1
SPENCER JOSEPH L	COL	0-0219500	0664	3
SPENCER JOSEPH O	LTC	0-0337530	0658	1
SPENCER JR ALFRED J	LTC	0-0958256	0767	1
SPENCER JR CURTIS	MAJ	0-1284412	C757	2
SPENCER JR JOHN B	MAJ	0-1913227	0767	1
SPENCER JR SEAVER B	LTC	0-1289333	1065	1
SPENCER JULIUS F	MAJ	0-0385236	0546	2
SPENCER KENNETH A	CPT	0-1882121	1065	1
SPENCER LAILA	CPT	N-0722471	0846	1
SPENCER LAWRENCE D	LTC	0-1297108	C363	1
SPENCER LEWIS R	CW3	W-2144998	1160	2
SPENCER LINCOLN R	1LT	0-1107145	0461	1
SPENCER LOUIS C	MAJ	C-0162304	0160	3
SPENCER MARSHALL E	1LT	0-0539828	0546	2

NAME	GRADE	SVC NO	DATE RET MO YR	RET CODE
SPENCER MELVIN	LTC	0-0499642	0446	2
SPENCER MYRON O	WO1	W-2126782	0949	1
SPENCER NEIL	CPT	0-2011168	1066	3
SPENCER OLLIE	CPT	0-0495854	0549	1
SPENCER OTTO F	MAJ	C-0372792	1C61	1
SPENCER PAUL A	CPT	0-0577053	0961	1
SPENCER RALPH P	CPT	0-2002366	0757	1
SPENCER RALPH V	CW3	W-2142415	0562	1
SPENCER RICHARD R	LTC	0-0420018	0547	1
SPENCER ROBERT A	LTC	0-1012314	0456	1
SPENCER ROBERT O	LTC	0-0327426	1061	1
SPENCER ROBERT P	LTC	0-0321771	0661	3
SPENCER SAMUEL M	MAJ	0-1553366	0765	1
SPENCER THOMAS B	CPT	0-1689103	1045	2
SPENCER THOMAS H	LTC	0-0332447	0161	2
SPENCER THOMAS N	LTC	0-0301828	1064	3
SPENCER VERNON H	MAJ	0-0490326	0254	2
SPENCER WALTER E	1LT	0-2055834	1048	2
SPENCER WILLIAM L	MAJ	0-0450602	1146	2
SPENCER WILLIAM M	LTC	0-0145395	0856	3
SPENCER WILLIAM O	LTC	0-0168715	0860	3
SPENDLOVE KATHERINE	MAJ	N-0752113	0965	1
SPENGEMAN CARL G	CPT	0-1307868	1146	2
SPENIK JOHN	1LT	0-1897765	0555	1
SPER MARTIN T	MAJ	0-0983269	1263	1
SPEREAU HARRY R	1LT	0-1324121	0846	2
SPERLING GEORGE R	LTC	0-1553911	0363	1
SPERLING JOSEPH	CPT	0-0492816	0146	2
SPERLING RUTH E	MAJ	N-0735482	1265	3
SPERLING SIDNEY S	LTC	0-1042950	1C65	1
SPERRY CLARENCE E	COL	0-0243269	0661	1
SPERRY GEORGE A	MAJ	0-0885120	0666	1
SPERRY HIRAM	COL	0-0263799	1060	3
SPERRY JOHN W	CW3	W-2144965	0559	1
SPERRY LEONARD	2LT	0-1643471	1044	2
SPERRY WILLIAM O	LTC	0-0287014	0557	1
SPERSEN HENRY G	CW4	W-2002257	0864	3
SPEZZACATENA DANIEL	MAJ	0-2033130	0561	1
SPICE CHARLES E	WO1	W-2142779	0264	1
SPICER CLAUDE H	MAJ	0-0241964	1055	3
SPICER GEORGE H	MAJ	0-0239571	1063	3
SPICER HENRY D	LTC	0-1000865	0359	1
SPICER HOWARD E	LTC	0-016979C	0460	3
SPICER MALCOLM F	LTC	0-1331567	0467	2
SPICER ROBERT J	COL	0-0288434	0767	3
SPICER WILLIAM L	CW2	W-2141453	0557	1
SPICKARD HAROLD E	COL	0-0271421	0655	3
SPICKELMIER JOHN P	LTC	0-0344827	0457	1
SPICKELMIRE VERNON L	CPT	0-0100835	0648	3
SPICUZZA JOHN H	CW3	W-2142270	0661	1
SPIDLE HARRY W	WO1	W-2152359	1061	2
SPIEGEL DAVID	COL	0-1797034	1065	2
SPIEGEL GEORGE F	COL	0-0359055	0461	1
SPIEGEL LEWIS H	CPT	0-0345215	0144	2
SPIEGEL SIDNEY S	WO1	W-2111528	0145	2
SPIEGELBERG GEORGE R	COL	0-0900951	1045	1
SPIELMAN SOL	1LT	0-1717366	0545	1
SPIER JAMES E	COL	0-0190832	0357	3
SPIERING DONALD P	1LT	0-1299955	1045	1
SPIERS REED A	MAJ	0-2033171	0562	1
SPIERS ROBERT H	CPT	0-014365C	0155	3
SPIES JR GEORGE R	1LT	0-0486038	1043	2
SPIESS FRANK G	COL	0-0266094	0467	3
SPIESS GEORGE G	LTC	0-0243495	1052	2
SPIESS JEROME J	CW3	W-2147419	0962	1
SPIKES JR RICHARD W	LTC	0-1595840	1162	1
SPILLANE JOHN J	LTC	0-045015C	0157	1
SPILLANE ROBERT F	CPT	0-1059649	0746	2
SPILLE FREDERICK	CW3	W-2208538	0367	1
SPILLER DAVID H	1LT	0-1642602	0447	2
SPILLER ERNEST M	CPT	0-0208465	0648	3
SPILLER GEORGE M	LTC	0-1168927	1160	1
SPILLER JR THOMAS B	COL	0-0315078	0466	1
SPILLER ROLAND L	CW3	W-2146125	0863	1
SPILLER WILLIAM F	LTC	0-0149675	0948	3

NAME	GRADE	SVC NO	DATE RET MO YR	RET CODE
SPILLERS ARTHUR R	COL	C-0902022	C967	3
SPILLERS CURTIS W	LTC	0-1541242	0661	1
SPILLMAN AMIEL F	CPT	0-1297272	1046	1
SPILLMAN HARVEY M	CW2	W-2145514	0162	1
SPILLMAN KENNETH R	COL	0-0330158	0962	3
SPILLMAN RUSSELL L	CPT	C-1556357	C561	1
SPILLUM WESLEY T	1LT	C-1697841	0145	2
SPILMAN CHARLES M	COL	0-0194719	1058	3
SPILMAN JAMES A	1LT	0-1861988	1153	2
SPINDLER ALFRED C	MAJ	0-0225323	C444	1
SPINDLER CLARENCE F	LTC	0-0313658	0965	3
SPINDLER ELWIN J	1LT	0-1925682	0454	2
SPINELLI GEORGE L	1LT	0-1547159	0147	2
SPINK JOHN E	MAJ	C-1326779	C962	1
SPIOTTO ANTHONY	LTC	0-1290325	C954	1
SPIRA JACOB I	LTC	0-4055482	0857	2
SPIRES EZRA T	CPT	0-1044110	1162	2
SPIRES L E	CPT	0-0390643	0245	2
SPISHAKOFF NATHAN N	CPT	0-0344257	C145	1
SPITAL JACK	MAJ	C-0544694	0663	1
SPITLER JR WILLIAM H	2LT	C-0504000	1144	2
SPITZ ALLAN G	COL	0-0109603	0652	1
SPITZ JOHN R	1LT	0-1053374	1265	1
SPITZ RUTH L	MAJ	N-0762618	1164	1
SPITZER HAROLD S	LTC	0-0335426	0960	1
SPITZER JACK R	CW2	W-2153168	C464	1
SPITZER LAWRENCE L	CPT	0-0400978	C145	2
SPITZER LOUIS	MAJ	C-1310919	C765	1
SPIVACK ISAAC D	COL	0-0268562	0962	3
SPIVAK JACK	CPT	0-0487682	0546	2
SPIVEK SOLLY A	LTC	0-1013838	0366	3
SPIVEY ALLEN T	CW2	W-2208751	0860	1
SPIVEY ARTHUR W	MAJ	C-0345279	0246	2
SPIVEY DAVID W	LTC	0-1770994	0860	1
SPIVEY EDWARD P	1LT	0-1011045	0545	2
SPIVEY JR JOSEPH H	1LT	0-1317726	0845	1
SPIVEY MARY L	2LT	N-0760087	0545	1
SPIVEY OSCAR M	MAJ	0-1178631	1160	1
SPIVEY THOMAS H	CW3	W-2143695	0560	1
SPIVEY WILLIAM D	MAJ	0-1284594	0346	2
SPLEEN STEPHEN E	LTC	0-0183205	0351	3
SPOEDE HERMAN H	COL	0-0151951	0952	1
SPOFFORD BOSWORTH E	MAJ	0-0223133	1145	2
SPOHR CHARLES O	CPT	0-0363424	0947	2
SPONAMORE BENJAMIN F	LTC	0-0507003	0466	3
SPONENBURGH ELSTON S	LTC	0-0352827	0960	1
SPONENBURGH JOHN	LTC	0-0383198	0265	1
SPONTAK CHARLES	CW4	W-2120823	0659	1
SPOO CHARLES E	1LT	0-1648706	0652	1
SPOO GEORGE L	1LT	C-2055406	1045	2
SPOON DONALD O	B G	0-0401940	0667	3
SPOONER CHARLES E	MAJ	C-0300382	C253	2
SPOONER TRUMAN R	COL	0-0206107	C346	2
SPOOR FERRIS G	MAJ	C-0347171	0147	1
SPOOR JOHN A	CW3	W-2152751	0165	1
SPOOR JR WILLIAM J	CW2	W-22C6813	0963	2
SPOOR MARIE A	CPT	N-0758367	C447	1
SPORBERT WILLIAM O	1LT	0-1292414	C944	2
SPORCIC STEPHEN	MAJ	C-1037919	0166	3
SPORE HELEN L	CPT	L-0601353	0964	1
SPORER JR HENRY	2LT	0-1861607	1053	2
SPORING GEORGE C	CW3	W-2141455	0163	1
SPORL JONAS C	COL	0-0309171	0966	3
SPORT FRANK S	MAJ	C-2033231	C561	2
SPOTWOOD SR W R	CW2	W-2149719	0758	2
SPRACLIN RANDALL T	CW3	W-2152798	1165	1
SPRADLING QUENTIN M	COL	0-0335126	1062	3
SPRAGGINS GEORGE V	MAJ	C-1923589	0667	1
SPRAGGINS HENRY G	CPT	0-0508765	1147	2
SPRAGUE CARL T	MAJ	C-0169463	0555	3
SPRAGUE DONALD A	CPT	0-0331944	C767	3
SPRAGUE ERNEST L	LTC	0-1013714	0765	1
SPRAGUE FLOYD L	CPT	0-1319058	0247	2
SPRAGUE FRANK W	LTC	0-0406263	0667	3
SPRAGUE RAYMOND S	CPT	C-0264669	0545	2

NAME	GRADE	SVC NO	DATE RET MO YR	RET CODE
SPRAGUE ROBERT C	MAJ	0-1797377	0754	2
SPRAGUE ROBERT M	LTC	0-0306295	1164	1
SPRAGUE WILBUR E	CW3	W-2209328	0767	1
SPRAGUE WINFIELD A	MAJ	0-1650753	0164	1
SPRANDEL MARTIN E	1LT	0-1290326	0645	1
SPRATLEY DOLORES R	MAJ	L-1010041	0163	1
SPRAUER EDWARD J	MAJ	0-0334503	0446	2
SPRAWLS RICHARD O	CPT	0-0545833	0450	1
SPRAYBERRY WILLIE R	MAJ	0-1923502	1064	1
SPRECHER WILLIAM J	CW2	W-2107573	0246	2
SPREEMANN FREDERIC	CPT	0-1307869	0847	1
SPREEN ELGIN W	1LT	0-0430189	0346	1
SPREITZER ERNEST R	CPT	0-1293668	0649	2
SPRENG FREE C	LTC	0-0250046	0464	3
SPRENG GEORGE W	CW2	RW-221C435	0863	1
SPRENKEL SAMUEL L	MAJ	0-0237594	0158	3
SPRIGGS JOHN A	MAJ	0-1559985	0164	1
SPRIGGS JR WALTER E	MAJ	C-0977498	0662	1
SPRINDIS STEPHEN W	LTC	0-1289671	0948	1
SPRING ARLINGTON	MAJ	0-C168016	0453	3
SPRING CARL C	MAJ	0-02447C2	0659	3
SPRING JOHN P	1LT	0-1924727	C254	2
SPRING JR ELBERT B	MAJ	C-1114303	0862	1
SPRING ROBERT B	MAJ	0-0456133	0647	1
SPRINGER ALBERT G	LTC	0-0199263	0754	3
SPRINGER ARTHUR G	2LT	0-1328763	1045	1
SPRINGER AVIS J H	2LT	N-075834C	0546	1
SPRINGER EDWARD F	CPT	0-0181442	0643	1
SPRINGER HARRY B	LTC	0-0302455	0665	3
SPRINGER HENRY C	COL	0-0207770	0257	3
SPRINGER JAMES H	CPT	0-0481692	0448	1
SPRINGER JR GEORGE W	MAJ	0-0123047	1052	3
SPRINGER KEITH	MAJ	0-1180348	0163	1
SPRINGER PERCY A	WO1	W-2143471	0853	1
SPRINGER ROBERT C	MAJ	0-1301702	0663	2
SPRINGER ROBERT G	COL	0-0206399	1162	3
SPRINGER ROBERT W	COL	0-0192015	1053	2
SPRINGFIELD EDWARD L	CW3	W-2142399	1157	1
SPRINGFIELD THOMAS	CPT	0-1823227	0446	1
SPRINGFORD ELBRIDGE	COL	0-0241646	0864	3
SPRINGMEYER CHARLES	2LT	0-0392542	0643	2
SPRINKEL HAROLD H	CW4	W-2114246	C755	1
SPRINKLE DAVID G	LTC	0-0502398	0962	1
SPRINKLE ERNEST H	MAJ	0-0258496	1059	3
SPRINKLE HARMON G	CW3	W-2144321	0962	1
SPROAT CLARENCE O	WO1	W-2129389	0364	3
SPROAT JOHN R	CPT	0-0177168	0957	3
SPROULL CHARLES B	LTC	0-0251237	0966	3
SPROULL TOM	CW3	W-215206C	0860	1
SPROUSE GEORGE C	CPT	0-0321155	0463	3
SPROUSE ROBERT F	MAJ	0-1302897	0160	2
SPROUT DEANE C	CPT	0-0386197	1045	2
SPROW GUY	CPT	0-029641C	0545	1
SPROWLS GEORGE M	MAJ	C-0139282	1048	3
SPRUCK DONALD C	MAJ	0-0969885	0562	1
SPRUILL MARION C	1LT	N-0725929	0745	1
SPRUILL WILLIAM R	LTC	0-1558205	0563	1
SPRUNG CLIFFORD C	LTC	0-0231495	0762	3
SPRY BYRON P	LTC	0-020888C	0850	3
SPRY CLIFFORD	CW2	W-2147806	0661	1
SPRY FRANCIS N	LTC	0-0257578	0162	3
SPUNT EDWARD T	COL	0-0291152	0351	1
SPURGEON GLEN H	CPT	0-0337329	0854	3
SPURGIN EARNEST M	LTC	0-1107147	0565	1
SPURGIN HAROLD S	LTC	0-0324655	0665	3
SPURLIN RUSSELL M	CPT	0-1292415	0845	2
SPURLIN WILLIAM H	MAJ	0-1599189	1161	1
SPURLOCK BEN E	LTC	0-0531497	0465	1
SPURLOCK FRANCIS M	CPT	0-1640033	0346	2
SPURLOCK RALPH C	LTC	0-0220786	0558	1
SPURLOCK WILLIAM W	LTC	0-0211076	0747	2
SPURR GENEVA M	2LT	N-0742804	1144	1
SPURRIER JAMES O	MAJ	0-1101226	0847	2
SPURRIER MERRILL D	MAJ	0-0137978	1157	3
SPURRIER RICHARD R	CPT	0-0455131	0146	2

ARMY OF THE UNITED STATES RETIRED LIST

NAME	GRADE	SVC NO	DATE RET MO YR	RET CODE
SPURRIER ROBERT F	LTC	0-1290682	0162	1
SPYKER WILLIAM D	LTC	0-1060650	0662	1
SQUALLS CORNELIUS	CPT	0-1876912	0262	1
SQUIER BASIL C	MAJ	0-0164225	0534	1
SQUIER EDWARD M	LTC	0-0143701	0857	3
SQUIER ROGER W	LTC	0-0242556	0863	3
SQUIER WILLARD A	CPT	0-0500307	0158	1
SQUIRE DONALD A	MAJ	0-2048494	1162	1
SQUIRE GEORGE R	CPT	0-1899367	0261	1
SQUIRE JAMES L	CPT	0-0228053	0344	2
SQUIRE MAX E	MAJ	0-1081251	0361	1
SQUIRES BLANNIE	CPT	N-0751028	0955	2
SQUIRES CHARLES O	LTC	0-0490594	0546	2
SQUIRES DALE C	CPT	0-1056559	1059	1
SQUIRES HAROLD O	COL	0-0119291	0648	3
SQUIRES LAURICE F	LTC	0-1321673	0167	1
SQUIRES LYNDON H	MAJ	0-0411852	0162	1
SQUITTIERI GILBERT D	1LT	0-1114304	0445	2
SQUYERS HORACE M	MAJ	0-1950286	1160	1
SROICH LOUIS R	MAJ	0-0555837	0763	1
SROKA JOHN C	MAJ	0-0451188	0154	1
SROMOVSKY JOHN A	CW3	W-2145254	0367	1
SRUBAR JOE F	CW3	W-2145149	0859	1
ST AMAND ALBERT R	CW2	W-2110178	0361	1
ST AMANT PHILEMON A	LTC	0-0378772	0859	1
ST ANGELO NICHOLAS	LTC	0-2048159	0762	1
ST CLAIR CROMWELL D	MAJ	0-0426910	0266	1
ST CLAIR FORREST W	LTC	0-1292238	0762	1
ST CLAIR MARVIN W	CW3	W-2150777	1057	1
ST CLAIR MATTHEW	MAJ	0-1168479	0358	1
ST CLAIR NORMAN E	COL	0-0269105	0366	3
ST CLAIR WALLACE C	CW3	W-2148373	0565	1
ST CLAIRE FELIX L	LTC	0-0280406	0260	2
ST GEORGE EARL W	LTC	0-0253808	0167	3
ST GEORGE WILFRED C	LTC	0-1651044	0465	1
ST JAMES ROBERT H	CPT	0-0358822	1045	2
ST JEAN WILLIAM J	MAJ	0-1178637	1063	1
ST JOHN CLARENCE C	CW3	W-2141461	0556	1
ST JOHN ELMER G	MAJ	0-0302475	0745	2
ST JOHN HELEN M	MAJ	N-0799295	0665	1
ST JOHN ILA N	MAJ	L-1010054	0263	1
ST JOHN JOHN	MAJ	0-0403557	0546	2
ST JOHN JOSEPH A	1LT	0-1286205	0945	2
ST JOHN JOSEPH W	CPT	0-1018128	0757	1
ST JOHN JR ALFRED	MAJ	0-1118478	0865	1
ST LOUIS DONALD W	MAJ	0-2019388	0363	1
ST LOUIS HAROLD	CPT	0-1634373	0147	1
ST MARTIN WILFRED A	COL	0-0265790	1161	3
ST MARY JR ERNEST F	1LT	0-0548596	0347	2
ST ONGE ARTHUR P	LTC	0-0451480	1263	1
ST ONGE HUBERT L	LTC	0-1285134	1166	1
ST ONGE NORMAN E	CW4	W-2103395	0658	1
ST ONGE VICTOR A	COL	0-0212245	0945	2
STAAB CARLYLE H	LTC	0-0303110	0267	3
STAAB RUDOLPH L	CPT	0-0481051	1045	2
STAAR WILLIAM F	COL	0-0387319	0760	1
STAAK WILLIAM R	MAJ	0-1648838	0364	1
STAAKE HUGH E	1LT	0-1015552	0346	2
STABINGAS ELEANOR C	MAJ	N-0724962	0467	1
STACEY HOWARD A	MAJ	0-1543281	0859	1
STACEY THOMAS R	LTC	0-0474210	0954	2
STACEY WILLIAM T	MAJ	0-2046830	0261	1
STACH JAMES A	LTC	0-0268869	0165	3
STACHELSKI ALEXANDER	LTC	0-1051393	0364	2
STACHWICK ROY A	LTC	0-1055162	0163	1
STACK BERNARD O	MAJ	0-0367667	0445	1
STACK JOHN H	CPT	0-0398410	1045	1
STACK LOUIS T	LTC	0-0186301	1057	3
STACK RICHARD J	LTC	0-1062706	1266	1
STACK WILLIAM	LTC	0-1330001	0365	1
STACKHOUSE EARL A	CPT	0-1822477	0646	2
STACKHOUSE GEORGE L	CW2	W-2122574	0754	2
STACKHOUSE HOWARD J	CW4	W-2142271	0360	1
STACKHOUSE WILLIAM M	MAJ	0-0980954	0962	1
STACKLIN ROBERT J	CW2	W-2211655	0766	1

NAME	GRADE	SVC NO	DATE RET MO YR	RET CODE
STACKPOLE ALBERT H	M G	0-0107158	0657	3
STACKPOLE LESLIE B	CPT	0-0426771	0546	2
STACKS ROLAND R	LTC	0-1336445	1166	1
STACY ALBERT J	1LT	0-1287777	1045	2
STACY HAROLD M	CW3	W-2144479	0559	1
STACY HENRY D	MAJ	0-2055952	0160	1
STACY JOHN F	LTC	0-1049355	0562	1
STACY JOHN T	CPT	0-0406435	1049	1
STACY JR ADAM	MAJ	0-0494295	0346	2
STACY ROBERT E	2LT	0-0424544	0343	2
STACY SHERWOOD J	COL	0-0372154	1063	3
STACY THEODORE E	CPT	0-0534437	1045	2
STACY WALTER S	LTC	0-0543975	0964	3
STACY WINTON T	COL	0-0214883	0456	3
STADECK ALOIS J	CPT	0-0473612	0946	1
STADIE HERMAN E	CPT	0-0166106	0330	1
STADLER RUTH R	2LT	N-0700193	0838	1
STADNICK THEODORE	MAJ	0-1895426	0457	1
STADTLER JR GEORGE J	COL	0-0242961	1060	3
STADTLER JULIAN P	LTC	0-1315502	0464	1
STAEFFLER RICHARD P	COL	0-0285249	0146	2
STAEHLE WILLIAM C	1LT	0-1695702	0346	2
STAELENS IRMA M	MAJ	N-0726442	0761	1
STAELENS JOSEPH C	MAJ	0-1595841	0762	1
STAFF EDGAR J	LTC	0-0185452	0352	3
STAFF HENRY	LTC	0-0345524	0561	3
STAFFIER ANTHONY R	CPT	0-0497050	0845	2
STAFFIERI LEONARD	MAJ	0-0290053	0459	1
STAFFORD ARVEL C	LTC	0-0357949	0758	1
STAFFORD CHARLES E	CW3	W-2150567	0465	2
STAFFORD CLINE	1LT	0-1312351	1051	1
STAFFORD DAVID F	1LT	0-0446062	1045	1
STAFFORD EMMA M	CPT	N-0726212	0857	2
STAFFORD EUGENE	1LT	0-2046831	0850	1
STAFFORD FREDERICK	CPT	0-0208501	0546	2
STAFFORD GEORGE H	MAJ	0-1693124	0164	2
STAFFORD GEORGE W	1LT	0-2015538	0647	2
STAFFORD GEROME H	1LT	0-1293669	1045	2
STAFFORD HALBERT H	LTC	0-0217216	1160	3
STAFFORD JOHN C	CW3	W-2145515	0661	1
STAFFORD JOHN H	LTC	0-1109683	1163	1
STAFFORD JOSEPH	WO1	W-2115088	1051	2
STAFFORD JOSEPH W	CW3	W-2145873	0357	1
STAFFORD JR GEORGE T	CPT	0-0438709	0846	1
STAFFORD MASON L	1LT	0-1920271	1057	2
STAFFORD MIAL O	LTC	0-1317435	0467	1
STAFFORD NICHOLAS T	LTC	0-1167647	0866	1
STAFFORD PHILIP M	COL	0-0127018	0652	3
STAFFORD RAYMOND R	MAJ	0-2212011	1264	1
STAFFORD RUTH V	1LT	N-0721200	1145	1
STAFFORD THOMAS	CPT	0-0192333	0350	1
STAFFORD THOMAS L	MAJ	0-2025475	0663	1
STAFFORD WILLIS L	CPT	0-0475510	0645	1
STAGE KENNETH M	CW3	W-2148766	0162	1
STAGE WILLIAM F	CPT	0-0940759	1058	1
STAGER LORANZA C	CW4	W-2142202	0264	1
STAGG GRANVILLE	LTC	0-2029556	0766	1
STAGG GROSJEAN M	MAJ	0-1579165	0161	1
STAGG WILLIAM F	LTC	0-2019944	0266	1
STAGG 3RD HOWARD J	MAJ	0-0351754	1045	2
STAGGS DOUGLAS E	LTC	0-1294382	0359	1
STAGGS JOSEPH B	CW3	W-2114910	0856	1
STAGGS LOWELL C	1LT	0-1109684	0553	1
STAGGS MILLIE L	2LT	N-0734234	0345	1
STAGGS ORVILLE L	MAJ	0-1283511	0155	2
STAHL ADOLPH F	LTC	0-0453754	0763	1
STAHL CHOUTEAU P	LTC	0-0203337	0963	3
STAHL HAROLD J	LTC	0-0283456	0467	3
STAHL HERBERT G	1LT	0-0513906	0246	2
STAHL JR BENJAMIN F	COL	0-0256539	0660	1
STAHL JUDSON H	CW3	W-2144026	0763	1
STAHL LEWIS F	CPT	0-1315873	1047	2
STAHLER CHRISTOPHE	MAJ	0-0285969	1045	2
STAHLMAN HAROLD F	MAJ	0-2033936	1165	1
STAHLY LEONARD L	CW3	W-2145317	0467	1

NAME	GRADE	SVC NO	DATE RET MO YR	RET CODE
STAIGER FRANKLIN H	COL	0-0147983	0152	3
STAIGER LEA R	COL	0-0319931	0963	3
STAINES WILLIAM L	LTC	0-0166537	0945	2
STAINS JR WATSON A	LTC	0-0364155	0960	1
STAINTON WILLIAM F	LTC	0-0226772	0660	3
STAIRS CARROLL A	LTC	0-1558096	0367	1
STAKER GORDON L	LTC	0-0334985	0767	3
STALBAUM MAX R	MAJ	0-1686809	0765	1
STALCUP GENE S	MAJ	0-1317207	0361	1
STALCUP JOHN W	CPT	0-1018252	1146	1
STALEY BAILEY B	LTC	N-0734170	1264	1
STALEY CHARLES N	LTC	0-0210726	0245	2
STALEY DONALD V	LTC	0-0325007	0358	3
STALEY FRANCIS S	CPT	0-0385622	0762	1
STALEY GEORGE E	MAJ	0-2006401	0157	1
STALEY HARRY H	MAJ	0-1106501	0962	1
STALEY JACK A	CPT	0-0372679	1045	2
STALEY JAMES E	LTC	0-2036081	1067	1
STALEY JR JOHN H	1LT	0-0535336	0945	2
STALEY JR RAYMON M	MAJ	0-1947949	0761	1
STALEY KENNETH V	MAJ	0-1330002	0959	1
STALEY LEO C	MAJ	0-2028367	1066	1
STALEY MARCUS R	LTC	0-0226644	0959	3
STALEY MARTIN E	MAJ	0-0167338	1157	3
STALGAITIS JOSEPH G	CW3	W-2151298	1167	1
STALIN GUSTAF S	MAJ	0-1050473	0562	1
STALIONS KENNETH W	CW2	W-2144431	0559	1
STALKER RICHARD W	1LT	0-1558207	1047	2
STALL JOSEPH W	MAJ	0-1581384	0558	1
STALLARD ALTON V	COL	0-0195039	1161	3
STALLINGS GEORGE W	COL	0-0253637	1156	1
STALLINGS HARTWELL F	MAJ	0-0238315	0264	3
STALLINGS JESSE O	CPT	0-0371389	1047	2
STALLINGS RICHARD E	CPT	0-1583710	0863	1
STALLINGS TOLBERT L	LTC	0-0175354	0561	1
STALLINGS WILLIAM H	CPT	0-0263058	0245	1
STALLINGS WILLIAM T	LTC	0-0407696	0959	1
STALLWITZ GEORGE	COL	0-0275078	0764	3
STALLWORTH EDWARD	CW3	W-2151731	0764	1
STALLWORTH WILLIAM E	CPT	0-0406255	0447	2
STALTER ROBERT A	MAJ	0-0445498	0562	1
STALZER MILDERD A	1LT	N-0786049	1046	1
STAMAN LILBURN R	LTC	0-0252320	0167	3
STAMAS STANLEY	LTC	0-1301226	1167	1
STAMATE EVA H	2LT	N-0730678	1044	1
STAMBACH ALBERT R	MAJ	0-0135920	0355	3
STAMBACH GERALD M	1LT	0-0885701	0346	2
STAMBACH MAX E	CPT	0-2006548	0461	1
STAMBAUGH CLYDE	CPT	0-1330871	0354	2
STAMBAUGH JACOB L	MAJ	0-0159294	0749	3
STAMBERG STANLEY A	MAJ	0-0230098	0658	3
STAMEY HENRY C	MAJ	0-0488619	1151	1
STAMM JOHN J	LTC	0-1309859	0862	1
STAMM LUTHER A	1LT	0-1995032	0753	2
STAMMER HELEN	2LT	N-0736877	1045	1
STAMMREICH IRVING H	MAJ	0-1640036	0157	1
STAMP EMILY C F	CPT	N-0787375	0946	1
STAMP FRANK T	CPT	0-0375554	0244	2
STAMPA ALLAN J	COL	0-0171139	0762	3
STAMPER CHARLES E	MAJ	0-1284782	0546	2
STAMPER LUCIAN A	CPT	0-1684564	1045	2
STAMPER ROBERT M	MAJ	0-1285653	0461	1
STAMPS MARGARET H	1LT	N-0771821	0945	1
STAMPS MARTIN E	CW2	W-2145247	0563	1
STAMS NICK R	LTC	0-1551753	1162	1
STAN LEONARD J	MAJ	0-2033570	0763	1
STANBACK JEFFREY F	LTC	0-0137644	0154	3
STANBERRY ALLAN W	MAJ	0-1048600	0161	1
STANCARI LOUIS F	LTC	0-1542258	0862	1
STANCATO ANTHONY L	1LT	0-1306332	0451	1
STANCHOS ALVIN A E	MAJ	0-0295686	0662	1
STANCIL WILLIAM C	2LT	0-1303790	0544	2
STANCKIEWITZ WALTER	LTC	0-1555300	0961	1
STANDAFER EZRA E	CW2	W-2147866	1061	2
STANDAL HJALMAR L	MAJ	0-1041655	0862	1

NAME	GRADE	SVC NO	DATE RET MO YR	RET CODE
STANDER THOMAS R	COL	0-0287251	0857	3
STANDISH ALBERT	MAJ	0-1297976	0662	1
STANDISH HENRY H	MAJ	0-0984396	0766	1
STANDISH THEODORE C	CPT	0-1113460	1045	2
STANDISH WALTER R	MAJ	0-1317827	0757	1
STANDLEY IRVIN L	MAJ	0-0358547	1045	2
STANDOCK STEPHEN D	CPT	0-1166620	0657	1
STANDRIDGE HAROLD S	CW3	W-2142450	0859	1
STANEK MILLARD A	CW3	W-2150670	0263	1
STANEK ROBERT T	MAJ	0-1182010	0260	1
STANFIELD ELMO L	LTC	0-0110885	0955	3
STANFIELD MERLYN L	CPT	0-5305724	1065	2
STANFIELD ROBERT R	MAJ	0-1174151	0361	1
STANFIELD RUFUS A	MAJ	0-0439634	0946	1
STANFIELD THOMAS J	LTC	0-0573462	0455	1
STANFILL JOHN L	MAJ	0-2262981	0266	1
STANFILL KERMIT J	MAJ	0-1999167	0859	1
STANFORD HENRY J	MAJ	0-0273845	1045	2
STANFORD MARY R R	1LT	N-0772474	1046	1
STANFORD ROBERT F	CW3	W-2110521	0859	1
STANFORD WILLIAM	CPT	0-0496245	0844	2
STANG HENRY J	LTC	0-0170936	0757	3
STANGEL VICTOR	CPT	0-0493356	0646	2
STANGER THOMAS A	MAJ	0-1545637	1164	1
STANGL FREDERICK	LTC	0-2031902	0765	1
STANGL TONY E	LTC	0-1283688	0461	1
STANICH MICHAEL A	2LT	0-1288641	1045	2
STANICK BERNARD L	LTC	0-1289988	1055	1
STANIEC STEPHEN	CPT	0-0971744	1060	1
STANIFER ROM D	LTC	0-0245088	0364	3
STANION WARREN F	LTC	0-0285181	0665	3
STANIS JOHN E	LTC	0-0534136	0864	1
STANISH THEODORE J	LTC	0-1286563	1266	1
STANISLO NICK K	LTC	0-0352904	0366	1
STANK ALBERT F	CW2	W-2146280	0657	1
STANKO GEORGE	CPT	0-1998373	0254	2
STANKO WILLIAM M	1LT	0-1185315	0647	1
STANKUS SR ANTHONY A	LTC	0-0496660	0455	1
STANLEY ARTHUR L	CPT	0-0369260	0644	1
STANLEY BEN W	1LT	0-1596511	1045	2
STANLEY CALVIN E	CW3	W-2149270	1162	1
STANLEY CHARLES A	LTC	0-0186381	0648	3
STANLEY CHARLES M	CW4	W-2113272	0555	1
STANLEY CHESTER H	MAJ	0-0983754	0865	1
STANLEY CLEON E	LTC	0-0163285	0761	3
STANLEY CLIFFORD	MAJ	0-1338409	1264	1
STANLEY EDWARD T	MAJ	0-1638626	1061	1
STANLEY EMERY R	LTC	0-0323651	0160	3
STANLEY ERNEST K	CPT	0-2055303	0561	1
STANLEY FOSTER L	COL	0-0118912	1055	3
STANLEY FRANK A	LTC	0-1100349	0161	1
STANLEY FREMONT B	LTC	0-1167649	1160	1
STANLEY GEORGE R	CPT	0-1593309	0350	1
STANLEY GLEN R	1LT	0-1288642	0744	2
STANLEY JOHN G	COL	0-2042895	1160	1
STANLEY JOSEPH	CW3	W-2148651	0963	1
STANLEY JR ARTHUR J	LTC	0-0234148	0463	3
STANLEY JR ERNEST P	MAJ	0-0949083	0366	1
STANLEY JR FELIX W	MAJ	0-0036428	1060	1
STANLEY JR FRANK C	1LT	0-1320349	1045	2
STANLEY LISBETH M	CPT	N-0720348	1054	2
STANLEY MILFORD W	MAJ	0-0410674	0662	1
STANLEY NORMAN D	MAJ	0-0976911	1263	2
STANLEY RAYMOND L	MAJ	0-0360879	0563	1
STANLEY ROBERT	CPT	0-0525215	0347	1
STANLEY ROME	CPT	0-0493534	0447	1
STANLEY RUDOLPH S	LTC	0-0287432	0966	3
STANLEY SAMUEL F	MAJ	0-1182969	1060	1
STANLEY WILFRED R	LTC	0-0268240	0560	1
STANLEY WILLIAM C	LTC	0-0348149	0361	1
STANLY GEORGE P	CPT	0-0173776	1061	3
STANN STANLEY J	MAJ	0-0394649	0861	1
STANN STANLEY S	LTC	0-0387560	0561	1
STANN WALTER A	MAJ	0-1110270	0958	1
STANNACK GUY	LTC	0-1559126	0564	1

NAME	GRADE	SVC NO	DATE RET MO YR	RET CODE
STANO FERDINAND	LTC	C-0372168	0358	1
STANPHILL DELMAR R	MAJ	C-0969257	C764	1
STANPHILL OCELL	CPT	C-0804245	C461	1
STANSBURY ALFRED B	MAJ	0-0349895	0156	1
STANSBURY HARRY R	LTC	0-1115805	C966	1
STANSBURY JR JAMES E	LTC	0-0300368	1161	1
STANSBURY MARCELLU	CPT	0-0551878	0846	2
STANSBURY PAUL	COL	C-0384570	1262	1
STANSELL JOHN W	CPT	0-1297110	0747	1
STANSELL JR ROBERT B	1LT	0-1312727	C746	2
STANSIFER JOHN O	2LT	0-1930037	1054	2
STANTON CHARLES W	LTC	0-1041921	0564	1
STANTON CHARLOTTE	1LT	N-0722667	0945	1
STANTON CLARENCE H	MAJ	0-0320800	0164	3
STANTON EDWARD V	MAJ	0-1695920	0246	2
STANTON FARRIS C	1LT	0-0420770	1045	2
STANTON FORD B	LTC	0-0282508	0267	3
STANTON GEORGE M	LTC	0-1594645	0466	3
STANTON HOMER E	CW4	W-2104498	0664	1
STANTON JAMES C	LTC	0-0147997	0250	3
STANTON JOSEPH A	MAJ	0-1306333	1164	1
STANTON JR DOUGLAS W	LTC	0-1822072	C865	1
STANTON JR ROSS H	1LT	0-1316102	C645	2
STANTON KENNETH A	MAJ	C-1101672	1159	1
STANTON KENNETH J	LTC	0-0234914	C965	3
STANTON LEE B	LTC	0-0245303	0966	3
STANTON LEGETTE	CW2	W-2205562	0164	1
STANTON LOUIS E	LTC	C-0217309	0346	2
STANTON LUCIE	2LT	N-C744274	C744	1
STANTON MARK A	MAJ	C-0692520	C759	1
STANTON PAUL M	2LT	0-1322963	C345	2
STANTON THOMAS F	CPT	0-1181467	C354	2
STANTON WILLIAM F	LTC	0-0450914	0658	1
STANTON WYLLYS G	LTC	C-0232800	0346	2
STANULIS EDWARD A	MAJ	0-1303567	C85C	1
STANULONIS STANLEY F	MAJ	C-0962235	1161	2
STAPLES ELTON E	LTC	0-0226865	1163	3
STAPLES FRANK	CPT	0-0108439	0326	1
STAPLES JAMES L	2LT	C-1165959	1044	2
STAPLES JEREMIAH G	LTC	0-0257889	0965	3
STAPLES JR ERNEST A	MAJ	0-1186759	1164	1
STAPLES JR RALPH	MAJ	0-1556663	1160	1
STAPLES MARGARET F	1LT	N-0700861	C143	1
STAPLES ROBERT R	LTC	0-0283662	0365	3
STAPLES WILLIAM O	1LT	0-0283165	C842	2
STAPLETON CLAUDE F	CW2	W-2208126	1061	1
STAPLETON EUGENE C	CW2	W-2210862	0766	1
STAPLETON JAMES A	CPT	0-0369905	C445	2
STAPLETON JOHN L	LTC	0-0288564	1164	3
STAPLETON JOSEPH I	MAJ	0-1032395	0263	1
STAPLETON JR C A	MAJ	0-1949222	1060	1
STAPLETON ROBERT G	CPT	0-1044959	0966	1
STAPLETON SAMUEL J	MAJ	C-0976357	0963	1
STAPOWICH JOSEPH R	LTC	0-0366479	1060	1
STARR J D	CW4	W-2106984	1058	1
STARR JOHN W	MAJ	0-1931343	0866	1
STARR ROBERT R	LTC	0-0395419	1164	1
STARR ROY D	CPT	0-0481520	1050	1
STARR WILLIAM J	LTC	0-0917085	C966	3
STARRLER FRIEDRICH	LTC	0-1080327	1266	1
STARULA JAMES E	LTC	0-1114760	1062	1
STARBIRD CHESTER E	CPT	0-0165054	0648	3
STARBIRD JAMES C	MAJ	0-0360905	1051	1
STARBOARD EARL D	CPT	0-0159784	C755	3
STARBUCK CHARLES O	LTC	0-0377271	0862	1
STARBUCK JACK C	1LT	0-1534869	C444	2
STARBUCK JAMES L	WO1	W-2211565	0367	1
STARCEVICH PAUL J	CPT	0-0500585	0643	1
STARCHER EVERETT H	LTC	0-0244772	0857	3
STARCHER LEROY	LTC	0-0468719	1163	1
STARCK CARL D	CPT	C-0456841	1046	2
STARE ANDREW	MAJ	C-1050099	0866	1
STARICHA LOUIS	CW4	W-2108628	0351	1
STARK ABRAM L	WO1	W-2133269	1047	1
STARK ALFRED B	CPT	0-0232421	0646	2

NAME	GRADE	SVC NO	DATE RET MO YR	RET CODE
STARK ALONZO F	LTC	0-0278402	0463	3
STARK BETTY	1LT	N-0736328	1046	1
STARK CLARENCE A	LTC	0-0238110	1062	3
STARK ELOFF R	LTC	0-0274375	1264	3
STARK GEORGE O	CPT	0-0493125	C447	1
STARK HOWARD H	LTC	0-0913285	C264	2
STARK HUGH G	LTC	0-0403790	0954	1
STARK HUGO J	COL	0-0228521	0465	3
STARK JESSE O	COL	0-0291207	0160	3
STARK JOSEPH V	CW3	W-2144206	0562	1
STARK JULIAN H	LTC	0-0177851	1061	3
STARK JULIUS A	B G	0-0143760	1C54	3
STARK MARY E	MAJ	L-1010213	0565	1
STARK MELVILLE I	LTC	0-0334783	1145	2
STARK MERRILL L	2LT	0-1177646	0344	2
STARK MORRIS	CPT	0-0501052	1045	2
STARK ROBERT B	2LT	0-2006126	0446	2
STARK ROBERT E	LTC	0-0487815	0166	3
STARK ROY W	2LT	0-1109698	0644	2
STARK THOMAS H	MAJ	0-C498072	0947	1
STARKE JR HORACE M	LTC	0-0241481	0259	3
STARKE MILTON B	CW3	W-2152135	C864	2
STARKE ROBERT J	CPT	0-0259186	0666	3
STARKEY CHARLES G	COL	0-0166837	0656	3
STARKEY ERNEST	CPT	0-0143848	0656	3
STARKEY JOHN A K	1LT	0-0337772	0542	1
STARKEY JOHN E	MAJ	0-1535970	0463	1
STARKEY JOHN H	LTC	0-1289829	1060	1
STARKEY JOHNNY W	MAJ	0-2027369	C961	1
STARKEY JR BERNARD C	CPT	0-1012113	0646	1
STARKEY RALPH W	MAJ	0-0262821	1265	3
STARKEY RAYMOND F	2LT	0-2005581	1146	1
STARKMAN MICHAEL C	1LT	0-1576688	0844	2
STARKOWICZ STANLEY P	LTC	0-1317828	1062	1
STARKS CHARLES W	LTC	0-0444668	0346	2
STARKS FREDERICK	CW3	W-2152184	0865	1
STARKS WALTER	CW2	W-3430475	0167	1
STARKWEATHER WILLIAM	MAJ	0-0283508	0346	1
STARLING HERMAN W	MAJ	0-1171376	0756	1
STARLING HUIE D	CPT	0-2007881	0454	2
STARLING JOHN C	CPT	0-0438817	1149	2
STARLING RALPH F	CPT	0-1328088	0661	1
STARLING RICHARD G	MAJ	0-0409974	0261	1
STARMAN RAPHAEL F	CPT	0-1318233	0747	1
STARMER JOHN W	1LT	0-0495220	0761	1
STARNES GILBERT D	LTC	0-0420278	0957	1
STARNES HAROLD F	CW2	W-2149367	0261	1
STARNES JAMES M	MAJ	0-0199042	0347	1
STARNES JAMES V	COL	0-0341524	1060	1
STARNES JR CAMERON S	MAJ	0-0291283	0648	2
STARNES JR JOE	1LT	0-0520866	0945	2
STARNES WILLIAM G	COL	0-0901246	0946	1
STARNS CLYDE	CPT	0-0966531	0960	1
STARNS JOE F	LTC	0-1288643	0259	1
STARON FRANK J	1LT	0-1647252	0445	2
STARON JOHN W	MAJ	0-0497960	0445	2
STARR AMBROSE M	1LT	0-1663364	0146	1
STARR DAVID J	MAJ	0-1030304	0563	1
STARR DONALD F	COL	0-0455512	1264	1
STARR ERASMUS F	LTC	0-1322381	1262	1
STARR FRANK C	COL	0-0143057	0648	3
STARR FRANK H	MAJ	0-0248356	0848	3
STARR GEORGE	MAJ	0-1059295	0965	1
STARR GEORGE J	LTC	0-0200327	0650	3
STARR HERBERT L	CPT	0-0308920	0345	2
STARR JAMES W	LTC	0-0382822	0361	1
STARR JOHN F	LTC	0-0179342	0555	3
STARR JOSEPH L	LTC	0-0401616	0954	1
STARR LORIS P	LTC	0-0358490	0761	1
STARR PETER J	MAJ	0-2016458	1061	2
STARR ROBERT A	LTC	0-0451532	0864	2
STARR ROGERS F	LTC	0-0362308	0460	1
STARR ROSE M	MAJ	N-0724543	0766	1
STARR WILLIAM T	COL	0-0251467	0365	3
STARRET HOWARD A	MAJ	0-0158384	0842	2

NAME	GRADE	SVC NO	DATE RET MO YR	RET CODE
STARRETT HENRY A	COL	C-0127519	0156	3
STARRETT JOSEPH C	MAJ	0-1685580	1264	1
STARRETT SAMUEL P	MAJ	C-1167234	0859	1
STARRY DON A	COL	0-0330433	0157	3
STARTT JOHN W	CPT	0-0385183	0550	1
STARTUP ALBERT A	CW3	W-2150303	1263	1
STARZYK WILLIAM J	MAJ	0-1947455	0555	1
STASI EMILIO	MAJ	0-2262653	0264	1
STASKIEWICZ LEO J	LTC	0-0288580	C762	3
STASSI VICTOR B	MAJ	0-0263865	1144	2
STATEN VIRGINIA C	1LT	N-0741459	0846	1
STATESIR VERNON A	CPT	0-0191498	0860	3
STATHIS H ROBERT	LTC	0-2044377	0267	3
STATHOS VRASIDA D	CW4	W-2003455	1165	1
STATON LORY G	MAJ	0-0495301	1053	1
STATON SAMUEL D	CPT	0-0454786	0847	1
STATON WOODS W	1LT	0-0554509	0546	2
STAUB ROBERT E	LTC	0-1685673	0667	1
STAUBACH WILLIAM S	CW2	W-2215336	0467	1
STAUDENMAIER W G	CPT	0-0185631	1154	3
STAUDIGL HENRY J	CPT	0-0464796	0545	2
STAUDINGER JOSEPH F	LTC	0-0885382	0255	1
STAUDT CHARLES P	CW2	W-2150928	0657	1
STAUDT GEORGE L	LTC	0-0334807	1045	2
STAUFF JOHN H	CPT	0-1183628	0247	2
STAUFFACHER CHARLES	CPT	0-1699937	0646	2
STAUFFER CARRYL F	MAJ	0-0218373	0564	3
STAUFFER IVERY C	LTC	0-1053377	C464	1
STAUFFER LILA L	1LT	N-0804848	0453	1
STAUFFER PAUL W	WO1	W-2122633	C852	1
STAUFFER ROYCE A	MAJ	C-1920032	C865	1
STAUFFER WILLARD F	CPT	0-1306164	0949	1
STAUNCH STEPHEN	WO1	W-2104829	0345	2
STAUSS ELMER A	MAJ	C-0257557	0945	2
STAUSS SELMA I	CPT	L-0912498	C348	1
STAVINOHA HENRY F	MAJ	0-0257947	0765	3
STAVISH JEROME W	CPT	0-0920752	1044	2
STAWINSKY JOANN	MAJ	C-1181149	1060	1
STAYNER FLOYD L	COL	0-0258153	C861	1
STAYTON FLOYD F	COL	0-0225339	1264	3
STAYTON SAMUEL A	CPT	0-1599191	0258	1
STEACY HUBERT M	CW3	W-2122113	0655	1
STEAD EARLE C	COL	0-0147004	1055	3
STEAD OLIN W	MAJ	C-0242415	0665	3
STEADLER CLARENCE M	COL	0-0172016	0356	3
STEARNES HARDIN	MAJ	0-0234519	0959	3
STEARNES WILLIE B	CW2	W-2119878	0651	1
STEARNS ALBERT C	MAJ	0-0156210	0555	3
STEARNS CLYDE C	CPT	0-0139245	0955	3
STEARNS FRED S	MAJ	C-0479633	0555	2
STEARNS HARRY A	LTC	0-0193738	0648	3
STEARNS MARGARET F	1LT	N-0769454	0647	1
STEARNS MORRIS L	1LT	0-1062641	0460	1
STEARNS PARLEY M	1LT	0-1554826	1045	2
STEARNS ROBERT J	MAJ	0-0963846	0366	2
STEARNS RUSSEL M	COL	0-0347356	1161	3
STEARNS STEVEN H	1LT	0-0939683	1150	1
STEATES EDWARD C	1LT	0-1292444	0446	2
STEBBINS PHILIP A	COL	0-0270230	0363	3
STEBBINS CHESTER F	MAJ	C-0304703	0165	3
STEBBINS GEORGE B	COL	0-0127146	0648	3
STEBBINS JUNE H	LTC	0-0936305	0866	1
STEBBINS LAWRENCE C	CW2	W-2150243	1060	1
STEBBINS ROY W	2LT	0-1638578	0666	3
STECH RICHARD J	CW2	W-2207678	1163	1
STECHER ADOLPH	CW4	W-2141457	0266	1
STECHER ANTHONY F	COL	0-0117768	0855	3
STECHER HAROLD I	LTC	0-0203116	1061	3
STECHER PETER J	LTC	C-1996566	0761	1
STECK HAROLD P	1LT	C-1323496	1145	2
STECK III CHARLES F	LTC	0-1645401	0763	1
STECK JOHN E	CW2	W-2150759	0864	1
STECKBAUER WILLIAM J	CW4	W-2002676	0761	1
STECKBECK HENRY J	MAJ	0-1575573	0249	1
STECKEL EVERETT I	MAJ	C-0404849	1160	1

NAME	GRADE	SVC NO	DATE RET MO YR	RET CODE
STECKLER EDMUND J	MAJ	0-0977594	1265	1
STECKLER PHILIP P	MAJ	0-0504785	0851	1
STEDGE ERNEST J	2LT	0-0464712	0843	1
STEDMAN HARRY E	COL	0-0170516	0654	3
STEDMAN W THACHER	COL	C-0177941	1050	1
STEEBER WILLIAM L	CPT	0-2039639	0256	1
STEED BASIL G	2LT	0-1587650	0157	1
STEED HAROLD E	1LT	0-1302064	0546	2
STEED JR ALBERT M	2LT	0-1326064	1045	2
STEED ROBERT	CPT	0-0302971	1047	1
STEED WILLIAM C	LTC	0-1635368	0561	1
STEEL ERNEST W	COL	0-0190874	0853	3
STEEL JOHN A	CPT	0-0403609	0146	1
STEELE ALFRED M	MAJ	0-0340535	1158	1
STEELE ARTHUR F S	1LT	0-1315231	0146	2
STEELE ASA G	WO1	W-2110964	0766	3
STEELE CELIA G	2LT	N-0721172	1144	1
STEELE CHARLES W	COL	0-0469173	0166	3
STEELE CHESTER O	LTC	0-1030095	0664	1
STEELE CLARENCE R	LTC	0-0209669	0648	3
STEELE CLIFTON R	1LT	0-1314846	0747	2
STEELE CORNELIUS	CPT	0-1634364	0346	2
STEELE DONALD P	1LT	C-1169349	0145	2
STEELE FRANK R	MAJ	0-0965172	0765	1
STEELE GARLAND F	LTC	0-0902116	0947	2
STEELE GEORGE T	CPT	0-2033293	0863	1
STEELE GERALD H	LTC	0-0239732	0765	3
STEELE GORDON K	MAJ	0-0354705	0359	1
STEELE HENRY M	LTC	0-0186177	0750	3
STEELE HOWARD C	CPT	0-1326472	0248	2
STEELE HOWARD J	MAJ	0-1549848	0457	1
STEELE JAMES C	LTC	0-2005287	0666	1
STEELE JAMES H	MAJ	0-0239254	0345	2
STEELE JESSE I	COL	0-0264786	0265	3
STEELE JOHN G	MAJ	0-0338795	0755	1
STEELE JOHN H	MAJ	0-1554095	0364	1
STEELE JOHN N	CPT	0-0369112	1044	2
STEELE JOHN P	MAJ	0-2262181	0163	1
STEELE JOHN W	CPT	0-0528699	0352	1
STEELE JOSEPH C	CPT	0-0331566	0862	1
STEELE JOSEPH R	COL	C-0268938	0465	1
STEELE JR CLYDE F	MAJ	0-1307320	0664	1
STEELE MARVIN J	LTC	0-0761338	0467	1
STEELE MARY F	2LT	N-0796012	0346	1
STEELE MERRILL L	COL	0-0199717	0353	3
STEELE MILAN G	MAJ	0-0165347	1159	3
STEELE MYRON T	MAJ	C-1582568	0962	1
STEELE PAUL L	LTC	0-0451421	1055	1
STEELE PAUL C	MAJ	0-0426656	0857	1
STEELE RALPH C	COL	0-0210592	0856	3
STEELE ROBERT V	MAJ	0-1101673	0859	1
STEELE ROBERT W	MAJ	0-1282347	0962	1
STEELE ROY R	MAJ	0-1999045	0460	1
STEELE VIRGIL S	MAJ	C-0250001	1045	2
STEELE WARREN B	COL	0-0169296	0960	1
STEELE WILLIAM	MAJ	0-0419676	0746	2
STEELE WILLIS G	1LT	0-2262832	0357	1
STEELMAN JAMES F	MAJ	0-1102970	0361	1
STEELSMITH ERNEST W	MAJ	C-0400846	0146	2
STEELY STEWART L	2LT	0-1556664	1043	2
STEEN JAMES P	1LT	0-1295957	1044	2
STEEN JOHN M	MAJ	0-1640990	0562	1
STEEN JULIAN P	LTC	0-0237904	0265	3
STEEN MARVIN D	COL	0-0159284	0847	2
STEEN PHILIP M	MAJ	0-1170208	0361	1
STEENBARGER CHARLES	LTC	0-0416914	0364	1
STEENSGAARD RAYMON	CPT	0-1032247	C856	1
STEENSLAND THOMAS T	1LT	0-0540930	1145	2
STEERE MANSON F	MAJ	0-1046961	1060	1
STEERS WALTER A	MAJ	0-0423620	1060	1
STEES ERNEST W	LTC	0-1636690	0766	1
STEFANCIN JOSEPH F	2LT	0-1595980	0546	2
STEFANIAK LEO	MAJ	0-0151952	0648	3
STEFANICH FRANK A	1LT	0-1168970	0646	2
STEFANKIEWICZ VICTOR A	LTC	0-0382664	0462	1

ARMY OF THE UNITED STATES RETIRED LIST

NAME	GRADE	SVC NO	DATE RET MO YR	RET CODE
STEFEN WILLIAM	LTC	C-1328194	C566	1
STEFFEN BERTRAM L	CW4	W-2142468	0158	1
STEFFEN FRECERICK	COL	0-0118940	1149	3
STEFFEN GERALD B	MAJ	0-1295451	1061	1
STEFFEN MARTIN H	COL	C-0309853	1159	1
STEFFENHAGEN DEWEY H	MAJ	0-0490010	1045	2
STEFFENS LINCOLN F	COL	0-0297571	0266	3
STEFFENSEN WALLACE H	MAJ	C-0483055	C945	2
STEFFENSON ALBERT P	MAJ	C-1177196	0563	1
STEFFER ORVILLE R	MAJ	0-1011195	0157	1
STEFFER SOPHIE S	MAJ	N-0758698	1064	1
STEFFEY HOWARD L	LTC	C-0311381	0659	2
STEGALL CELBERT L	CPT	0-1550509	0654	1
STEGALL DORSEY F	LTC	0-1118504	1163	1
STEGALL HARRY E	MAJ	0-1688388	1160	1
STEGALL JAMES R	MAJ	0-0926603	1061	1
STEGALL OLIVER N	MAJ	C-0355665	0346	2
STEGALL VERCIE T	CW3	W-2116175	1060	1
STEGALL WHITNEY	MAJ	C-1644813	0747	2
STEGEMAN LEROY C	LTC	0-0253010	0459	3
STEGENGA MINER	MAJ	C-0171953	0251	3
STEGER LAWRENCE P	CW3	W-21452C5	0564	1
STEGER PAUL J	MAJ	0-0285786	0347	2
STEGMAN HAZEL M	2LT	N-0742647	C847	1
STEGMANN DONALD F	LTC	0-1309621	0962	1
STEGMANN HENRY R	CPT	0-1309109	C246	2
STEGMEIER HERBERT O	MAJ	C-1340824	C365	1
STEGNER ALBERT L	COL	0-0240196	0765	3
STEGNER DEWAYNE O	MAJ	C-0131174	0648	3
STEGNER LLOYD F	COL	0-0122093	0556	3
STEHLIN EARL K	MAJ	0-4074753	1167	1
STEIBEL LOUIS R	COL	C-0199618	C149	3
STEIBLER ROBERT L	1LT	0-0223742	C549	3
STEIG LESTER R	MAJ	C-0311256	1046	2
STEIG MILAN R	COL	0-0239279	0864	3
STEIGERWALT WILLIAM	LTC	0-15507C0	0862	1
STEIMER RALPH N	COL	C-0147006	0955	3
STEIMLE MARTHA L	MAJ	N-0773831	1167	1
STEIN ALFRED E	CPT	0-0283274	C645	2
STEIN ARTHUR D	MAJ	C-0961566	0464	2
STEIN FRANK P	MAJ	0-0265376	0860	3
STEIN FREDRICK A	1LT	0-0400421	0344	2
STEIN HARRY C	LTC	0-0185570	0648	3
STEIN HENRY G	COL	C-0333626	0254	3
STEIN HENRY J	MAJ	C-1951562	0764	1
STEIN JR JEROME O	CPT	C-1298948	1047	2
STEIN KARL E	LTC	0-1037733	0666	1
STEIN LEONARD J	LTC	0-1169756	1160	1
STEIN LOUIS	MAJ	C-0230404	1263	3
STEIN LOUIS H	1LT	0-0167153	0959	3
STEIN MORRIS B	CPT	0-1715558	C346	2
STEIN MORTON P	1LT	0-1586234	1045	2
STEIN RAYMOND S	MAJ	0-1548315	0361	1
STEIN STANLEY S	CPT	0-1C39578	0946	2
STEINBACH GEORGE C	LTC	0-1633025	0457	1
STEINBAUGH HUBERT D	MAJ	0-0221118	C358	1
STEINBECK PAUL W	COL	0-0017670	0859	2
STEINBERG CHARLES	1LT	0-0885792	1045	2
STEINBERG HARRY	LTC	0-0497593	1065	3
STEINBERG JOE	1LT	0-0417448	0845	2
STEINBERG MARTIN R	LTC	0-0484973	0745	2
STEINBERG SAM	1LT	C-1576694	0246	2
STEINBERG SAMUEL J	LTC	0-0246827	1266	3
STEINBERG SAUL	MAJ	0-0483911	C846	1
STEINBRUEGGE GERTRUD	CPT	N-0787736	0946	1
STEINECK SHIRLEY S	2LT	N-0731351	0345	1
STEINEGEWEG CHARLE	2LT	0-2000823	1045	2
STEINEKER ALFRED W	1LT	0-1018465	C446	2
STEINER ELLIS A	MAJ	C-189463C	C154	1
STEINER HELEN E	CPT	N-0787466	0846	1
STEINER HOWARD A	CPT	0-0493557	1145	2
STEINER JOHN H	MAJ	0-1596195	1264	1
STEINER JOHN J F	COL	0-0206815	C553	3
STEINER LEO E	LTC	0-0179914	0851	3
STEINER NICHOLAS W	CPT	0-0492676	1043	2
STEINER RANALC E	MAJ	0-1100783	1059	1
STEINER RAYMOND P	LTC	0-0325865	0161	1
STEINER SAMUEL	CPT	0-1551122	0858	2
STEINERT BEVERLY A	1LT	N-0743326	0446	1
STEINES LEO J	CW2	W-2149679	1163	1
STEINFELD HOWARD F	MAJ	0-1294742	0258	1
STEINFIELD THCMAS G	LTC	0-0320760	1059	3
STEINHARCT ALBERT J	LTC	0-0108164	0940	1
STEINHART ARDEN C	LTC	0-0262967	1266	3
STEINHAUER ROBERT A	CPT	0-1317831	0862	1
STEINHAUSEN RICHARD	LTC	0-1292777	0864	1
STEINHILPER JACK H	LTC	0-0450661	0657	1
STEINHCFF CARL F	B G	0-0245045	1054	3
STEINHCUR RUSSELL B	LTC	0-0502106	0657	1
STEINKRUGER ANTHON	LTC	0-0276952	0359	1
STEINMAN DONALD E	CW2	W-2144385	0463	1
STEINMAN ROBERT E	LTC	0-0279975	0466	3
STEINMAN RUDCLPH	1LT	0-2000795	0756	1
STEINMANN WILLIAM E	MAJ	0-1C16042	0761	1
STEINMETZ GEORGE P	LTC	0-0210057	0456	3
STEINMETZ JOHN R	MAJ	0-2002545	0461	2
STEINMETZ THCMAS J	MAJ	0-1118814	0160	1
STEINMEYER HARRY A	MAJ	0-0967145	0861	1
STEINMEYER WILMER H	1LT	0-0233854	0965	3
STEINREICH OTTO S	CPT	0-0369169	0746	2
STEINSIEK CLYDE W	LTC	0-1040311	0561	1
STEINWACHS DCN P	LTC	0-0347483	1153	1
STEINWAND DONALD A	CPT	0-0998886	0462	1
STEIRNAGLE WENDELL F	CPT	0-1043235	1058	2
STEIS WILLIAM B	MAJ	0-1291192	0447	2
STEJBACK WILLIAM J	CW3	W-2203874	0967	1
STEJSKAL JULIUS	MAJ	0-0300410	0663	3
STEKERT FRANKLIN	MAJ	0-0233367	0448	2
STELFCX LEONARD F	1LT	0-1109656	0146	2
STELL JR OTIS A	CPT	0-1584976	0147	1
STELL SR JAMES L	COL	0-0255362	1062	3
STELLA ABEL	CPT	0-1289990	1054	1
STELLA MANUEL	MAJ	0-1284595	0763	3
STELLA MICHAEL J	2LT	0-1302409	0144	2
STELLER HOWARD M	CPT	0-0325056	0167	3
STELLINGER CALVIN W	LTC	0-0452983	1163	1
STELLMANN EDWARD B	COL	0-0169358	0960	3
STELLRECHT TROY P	CPT	0-2035391	0547	1
STELMAN HENRY H	LTC	0-0302597	0767	3
STELTZNER ROGER L	LTC	0-0423268	0863	1
STEM RICHARD C	MAJ	0-0690268	0661	2
STEMBER ABRAHAM	MAJ	0-1634365	1067	3
STEMEN RICHARD J	MAJ	0-1031843	1263	1
STEMLER CAVIC R	2LT	0-0495354	0145	2
STEMNCCK LEONARD V	CW3	W-2139657	0559	1
STEMPEL FRANKLIN H	LTC	0-0303482	0647	2
STEMPLE CLYDE F	CPT	0-1324201	1064	1
STEMPLE EARL C	LTC	0-0520970	0464	1
STENBERG FRANCIS R	2LT	0-1303569	0344	2
STENDER LECN E	2LT	0-1590828	0545	1
STENDER WILBUR P	MAJ	0-1545079	0962	1
STENE CORDON S	LTC	0-1312062	0766	1
STENERSCN RAYMOND H	LTC	0-1286201	0157	1
STENGEL HENRY J	CPT	0-1821144	0443	2
STENGEL JAMES D	CW2	W-2150514	0656	1
STENGEL WILLIAM M	1LT	0-1178351	0745	2
STENGER FRED C	LTC	0-0237724	0559	3
STENGER ROBERT	LTC	0-1314687	0966	1
STENGLE WILLIAM T	2LT	0-0348314	0555	3
STENHCUSE JOE L	LTC	0-1288136	0959	1
STENINGER HOWARC W	MAJ	0-1542423	0157	1
STENINGER MILO C	1LT	0-0356420	1144	1
STENJEM ELDON M	COL	0-0159397	1054	3
STENMOE CLARENCE S	MAJ	0-1318248	0862	1
STENN ARTHUR	CPT	0-1821195	0843	2
STENNER JOHN	2LT	0-2027513	0549	1
STENQUIST GECRGE W	COL	0-0268219	0162	3
STENSBY JOHN L	CW3	W-2143139	0560	1
STENSLAND ARTHUR O	CPT	0-0266981	0853	3
STENSLAND ROY E	CPT	0-0386242	0550	1
STENSLIE ARNE	LTC	0-0203696	0557	1
STENSON RUSSELL C	LTC	0-0406140	0960	1
STENSON VIRGINIA M	1LT	N-C756714	0246	1
STENSTROM ETHEL C	CPT	L-0400546	0549	2
STEPANOVICH NICK	COL	0-0259434	0967	3
STEPHAN CARL	LTC	0-05190C6	0954	1
STEPHAN EDWARD W	1LT	0-1052587	C846	2
STEPHAN EMMA E	CW3	V-0217521	0564	1
STEPHAN PAUL J	CW2	W-22C5330	0463	2
STEPHAN ROBERT S	CPT	0-2288975	0565	1
STEPHANI PAUL W	LTC	0-1165960	0965	1
STEPHANS FRED L	LTC	C-0254606	0364	3
STEPHANY CARL R	MAJ	0-0137675	C744	2
STEPHEN ANNA E B P	CPT	N-0797749	1059	2
STEPHEN JAMES E	CW3	W-2148269	0863	1
STEPHEN JOHN M	CW4	W-2002569	0264	3
STEPHENS ALBERT K	CW2	W-2115888	1054	1
STEPHENS ALEXANDER	LTC	0-0263992	0664	3
STEPHENS ALZIE L	CPT	0-1944602	0958	1
STEPHENS BEN T	LTC	0-1010742	0763	1
STEPHENS CHARLES E	CPT	0-0504404	0157	1
STEPHENS CHARLES H	COL	0-1576695	0665	1
STEPHENS CLARENCE E	CW4	W-2126125	1058	1
STEPHENS EDWARD H	CW4	W-2143449	C466	1
STEPHENS ELMER	LTC	0-0453016	1057	1
STEPHENS FOSTER L	LTC	0-0254822	0764	3
STEPHENS FRANKLIN L	MAJ	C-1575196	0166	1
STEPHENS FRANKLIN T	CW3	W-2150164	0465	2
STEPHENS GEORGE H	LTC	0-1018550	0967	1
STEPHENS GEORGE J	LTC	0-0149068	C449	3
STEPHENS GILES O	LTC	0-0348879	0954	1
STEPHENS HARRY H	CW2	W-3200119	0265	1
STEPHENS HENRY M	LTC	0-1558906	0763	1
STEPHENS HOMER E	CPT	0-0235411	0753	3
STEPHENS HOWARD A	LTC	0-1288969	1159	1
STEPHENS IRA A	LTC	0-0296854	0866	3
STEPHENS JAMES E	LTC	0-1166845	C261	1
STEPHENS JAMES F	CPT	0-0463049	1047	1
STEPHENS JAMES H	MAJ	C-0485270	0747	1
STEPHENS JAMES H	CW3	W-2152688	1265	1
STEPHENS JAMES P	MAJ	0-1638585	0561	1
STEPHENS JAMES R	MAJ	C-0400881	1066	3
STEPHENS JAMES R	MAJ	C-0964860	0765	1
STEPHENS JAMES R	WO1	W-2109366	1044	2
STEPHENS JOE B	1LT	0-2263769	0657	2
STEPHENS JOHN B	MAJ	0-0452936	0856	1
STEPHENS JOHN G	LTC	0-0323763	0451	1
STEPHENS JOSEPH	CW2	W-2111324	0251	2
STEPHENS JOSEPH P	CPT	0-1640041	0657	1
STEPHENS JR CARL C	MAJ	0-1186619	0663	1
STEPHENS JR JCHN P	1LT	0-1101676	0546	2
STEPHENS LAWRENCE W	LTC	0-0332191	1160	1
STEPHENS LLOYD E	MAJ	0-1295958	0161	1
STEPHENS LOUIS B	COL	0-0325866	0864	1
STEPHENS LOUIS P	MAJ	C-1036393	0657	1
STEPHENS LYNN C	1LT	0-1011991	1045	2
STEPHENS MANUEL W	CW4	W-2147650	1161	2
STEPHENS MARION A	MAJ	0-0228442	1150	3
STEPHENS OLEN	CW3	W-2142610	0256	1
STEPHENS OLIVER J	MAJ	C-1110273	0263	1
STEPHENS PAUL W	MAJ	C-0360152	0448	2
STEPHENS RANDALL P	MAJ	0-1303406	0164	1
STEPHENS RAY E	MAJ	0-2055168	0261	1
STEPHENS RICHARD A	CW2	W-2205510	0663	1
STEPHENS RICHARD F	LTC	0-0238590	1060	3
STEPHENS RICHARD T	LTC	0-0247115	0457	3
STEPHENS RUSSELL R	CPT	0-0503351	0447	1
STEPHENS THELMA M	CPT	N-0787467	C448	1
STEPHENS VINCENT R	1LT	0-0366656	0145	2
STEPHENS WALTER M	1LT	C-0238512	0865	3
STEPHENS WILFRED R	CPT	0-0375038	1044	2
STEPHENS WILLIAM A	LTC	0-0325796	0761	1
STEPHENS WILLIAM A	MAJ	C-2019813	0263	1
STEPHENS WILLIAM O	CW2	W-2209811	0364	1
STEPHENS WILLIAM H	1LT	0-2042975	0854	1
STEPHENS WILLIAM L	LTC	0-0329164	0559	3
STEPHENS WILLIS E	LTC	0-1634367	0967	1
STEPHENSCN ALBAN J	1LT	0-1169350	0248	2
STEPHENSCN ALVIN B	CW3	W-2147963	0863	1
STEPHENSON CHARLES H	MAJ	0-0425821	C746	2
STEPHENSON CHARLES L	COL	0-0194111	1046	2
STEPHENSON CLARK B	COL	0-0354728	1162	1
STEPHENSCN DALE J	LTC	0-0399392	0554	2
STEPHENSCN DONALD B	2LT	0-1302378	0445	2
STEPHENSCN ECGAR H	CPT	0-0501C29	0253	1
STEPHENSON EDWARD F	COL	0-0333736	0755	3
STEPHENSON ECWARD R	LTC	0-1642610	1058	1
STEPHENSCN EDWIN A	COL	0-0170012	0261	3
STEPHENSON ELLIOTT O	CPT	0-0412434	1144	2
STEPHENSCN FRANCIS R	MAJ	0-1177997	0664	1
STEPHENSCN GENE R	MAJ	0-0453070	0856	1
STEPHENSON GECRGE W	2LT	0-2C49731	0645	2
STEPHENSON HARRY H	CPT	0-2008447	0253	1
STEPHENSON JAMES G	1LT	0-204816C	0746	2
STEPHENSCN JCE	LTC	0-1286916	1055	1
STEPHENSCN JOSEPH L	CPT	0-1298311	0662	1
STEPHENSCN JF L F	LTC	0-1824243	1060	1
STEPHENSCN JR OWEN T	MAJ	0-1917934	0164	1
STEPHENSCN LOUIS B	LTC	0-0311387	0664	3
STEPHENSON MACK C	CPT	0-1184955	0357	1
STEPHENSON PAUL H	LTC	0-1013995	0963	1
STEPHENSON RAYMOND P	MAJ	0-1030522	0861	1
STEPHENSON RCY E	1LT	0-1059072	1046	2
STEPHENSON STANLEY W	LTC	0-0374755	0666	1
STEPHENSON WALLACE L	CPT	0-1825321	0755	1
STEPHENSON WARD C	LTC	0-1596514	0263	1
STEPHENSON WILBUR F	COL	0-0270178	0257	1
STEPHENSON WILLIAM A	COL	0-0506836	1064	3
STEPHENSON WINNIE M	MAJ	N-0744142	1062	1
STEPHSEN ANN L	MAJ	N-0799717	C865	1
STEPP JR JCSEPH J	LTC	0-2204022	0767	1
STEPPING HENRY	1LT	0-1823666	0246	2
STEPT RAYMONC	CPT	0-0348565	0744	2
STEPTCE ROBERT P	MAJ	0-1165576	0349	2
STERETT JACK L	CW3	W-2147547	0564	1
STERGAR FRANK E	MAJ	0-0956470	0164	1
STERGIADES THEODORE	LTC	0-1544680	1165	1
STERKEN JR ECWARD J	LTC	0-1044399	0561	1
STERLE JCHN H	MAJ	0-1307477	0557	1
STERLING BOBBY G	CW2	W-2212278	1266	1
STERLING CECIL L	1LT	0-0539870	0646	1
STERLING EDWARD A	COL	0-0153579	1154	3
STERLING GERALD B	LTC	0-1634368	0557	1
STERLING HERMAN S	LTC	0-0317482	0762	2
STERLING JACK V	MAJ	0-0967496	0464	1
STERLING JAMES K	LTC	0-1173795	0962	1
STERLING JOSEPH R	LTC	0-0425503	0167	3
STERLING JULIUS H	CPT	0-0917039	1145	2
STERLING MICHAEL J	CPT	0-1303407	0647	2
STERLING MILDRED A	2LT	N-0731502	0445	1
STERLING RAYMOND C	CW2	W-2117988	0650	1
STERLING THOMAS A	CPT	0-0506841	0350	1
STERMER JOSEPH E	LTC	0-0274190	1060	1
STERMER LEE R	CW3	W-2152880	1263	1
STERN ALBERT R	LTC	0-0277716	1066	3
STERN ARTHUR L	1LT	0-1312813	1145	2
STERN ELMER V	1LT	0-0512365	1043	2
STERN EUGENE C	1LT	0-0489739	0446	2
STERN FRED	CPT	0-188417C	0363	1
STERN GECRGE J	WO1	W-2003850	0567	3
STERN HENRY W	1LT	0-1294745	1044	2
STERN I HENRY	COL	0-0219407	0364	3
STERN JEROME	1LT	0-1541325	1044	2
STERN JOSEPH	2LT	0-1824244	1044	2
STERN JOSEPH F	COL	0-0323607	0966	3
STERN JOSEPH J	COL	0-0298027	0865	3
STERN CTTO	CPT	0-1586237	1146	2
STERN SAMUEL Z	LTC	0-0294854	0346	2
STERN SIDNEY	COL	0-0288036	0861	1
STERN WALTER F	MAJ	0-1551123	0161	1

NAME	GRADE	SVC NO	DATE RET MO YR	RET CODE
STERN WILLIAM A	MAJ	0-2018597	0364	1
STERNBECK LAWTON L	LTC	0-0693572	0962	1
STERNBERG CHARLES	CPT	0-0450454	0865	1
STERNBERG RANDOLPH W	2LT	0-0281133	C343	2
STERNE JR MORTIMER C	LTC	C-0455659	0962	1
STERNER JOHN H	CW3	W-2145591	0964	1
STERNER THOMAS R	CW2	W-2152721	1163	1
STERNHAGEN JOSEPH P	LTC	0-0137167	0648	3
STERNIG MARTIN	CPT	0-1690002	1145	2
STERNS FRANK W	CPT	C-0242626	C752	3
STERRETT JR ANDREW G	LTC	0-1821646	C761	1
STERRETT PARIS V	1LT	0-0480121	1143	2
STESS IRA Z	CPT	0-1636696	1047	2
STETLER DONALD A	LTC	0-0403574	0164	1
STETLER ELMER	CPT	0-0185129	0648	3
STETSON CHARLES G	CPT	0-0282384	0 43	2
STETTER RAY N	LTC	0-0470763	C750	1
STETTLER LILLIAN C	MAJ	N-0760461	1264	3
STETZ ALBERT W	LTC	0-1796541	1065	1
STETZER JOHN W	LTC	0-0492624	0954	1
STEUART DELL K	COL	0-0336855	1053	2
STEUART GERARD J	CPT	0-0210306	0862	1
STEUDING ERNEST A	LTC	0-0252711	C167	3
STEUERWALD ROBERT C	LTC	0-0291590	0857	3
STEVEN ROBERT A	LTC	0-0226966	0642	2
STEVENS ALBERT A	MAJ	0-1949667	0960	1
STEVENS ALBERT B	LTC	0-0236530	1264	3
STEVENS ALBIN C	COL	C-0336010	0865	1
STEVENS ALLEN J	COL	0-0174054	C757	3
STEVENS ALTUS A	CW3	W-2205464	C366	1
STEVENS ARMENIOUS	CW4	W-2143530	0667	1
STEVENS ARTHUR B	CW3	W-2143056	1264	1
STEVENS ARTHUR E	MAJ	C-0496765	0148	1
STEVENS ARTHUR G	COL	0-0111474	0153	3
STEVENS ARTHUR G	MAJ	C-0347066	0766	2
STEVENS ARTHUR H	LTC	0-1030614	0763	1
STEVENS ARTHUR H	CW2	W-2000121	056C	3
STEVENS ARTHUR L	MAJ	0-1824816	0762	1
STEVENS BOYD	MAJ	C-0233800	0664	3
STEVENS BYRON L	MAJ	0-0966308	0762	1
STEVENS CALVIN E	1LT	0-1318249	0553	2
STEVENS CARLETON H	1LT	0-1303966	0246	2
STEVENS CARROLL H	MAJ	0-0268001	0448	1
STEVENS CHARLES D	LTC	0-1322964	0763	1
STEVENS CHARLES E	LTC	0-0309884	0162	1
STEVENS CHARLES F	MAJ	C-2036449	0557	1
STEVENS CHARLES R	LTC	0-0361648	0446	1
STEVENS CLAUDE M	LTC	0-1102592	C265	3
STEVENS CLINTON V	MAJ	0-0184715	0459	3
STEVENS DANIEL	1LT	0-1030721	0346	2
STEVENS DANIEL W	COL	0-0291288	1055	3
STEVENS DAVID A	COL	0-0184023	1153	3
STEVENS DONALD L	MAJ	0-0297065	0367	3
STEVENS DONALD O	CW3	W-2146801	0763	1
STEVENS EDGAR C	WO1	W-2146457	1056	2
STEVENS EDWARD A	LTC	0-0334387	C862	1
STEVENS EDWARD H	LTC	0-0515083	0657	1
STEVENS EDWARD R	LTC	0-1683449	C864	1
STEVENS EDWARD S	LTC	0-1796877	1062	2
STEVENS ELSON H	MAJ	0-1885584	1065	1
STEVENS EMMETT	LTC	0-0261397	0854	1
STEVENS FLORENCE R	MAJ	N-0721017	C362	2
STEVENS FRANCIS J	MAJ	0-1168481	0461	1
STEVENS FRANK O	LTC	0-0248476	0557	1
STEVENS GEORGE B	MAJ	C-0956830	1158	1
STEVENS GEORGE H	1LT	C-1116541	0146	2
STEVENS GORDON L	CW2	W-3430032	C167	1
STEVENS HAROLD F	MAJ	0-0104032	0949	3
STEVENS HAROLD P	1LT	0-0920261	C944	2
STEVENS HARRY A	LTC	0-1180352	0867	1
STEVENS HARRY F	MAJ	C-0966014	0361	1
STEVENS HARRY L	WO1	W-2110420	0347	2
STEVENS HENRY S	LTC	0-0254655	C367	3
STEVENS HERBERT C	1LT	0-0209913	0944	2
STEVENS HERBERT K	1LT	0-1822329	C845	2

NAME	GRADE	SVC NO	DATE RET MO YR	RET CODE
STEVENS HERMAN W	LTC	0-1171377	1054	1
STEVENS HOYT C	LTC	0-0131328	0455	3
STEVENS IOWD W	CPT	0-0486569	0649	2
STEVENS JAMES C	MAJ	0-0984266	0365	1
STEVENS JOHN A	LTC	0-0349615	1146	2
STEVENS JOHN H	LTC	0-0451466	0657	1
STEVENS JOHN J	CPT	0-0519475	0961	2
STEVENS JOSEPH L	2LT	0-20C0930	0246	2
STEVENS JR HENRY L	LTC	0-0237057	0156	3
STEVENS JR RALPH A	COL	0-0124322	0755	1
STEVENS JR SAMUEL C	CW2	W-2147451	0965	1
STEVENS JR WALTER D	LTC	0-1291720	0462	1
STEVENS JULIAN B	LTC	0-0323578	0361	3
STEVENS LEWIS	MAJ	0-1555911	0158	1
STEVENS LILBURN H	M G	0-0275376	1062	3
STEVENS LOWELL G	CPT	0-1044114	0662	1
STEVENS LOYD	CPT	0-0279588	0144	2
STEVENS LUTHER R	COL	0-0232434	0848	2
STEVENS LYLE V	CW2	W-2151732	1060	1
STEVENS MELDEN L	MAJ	0-0888913	0954	2
STEVENS MERL B	1LT	0-1014845	0948	2
STEVENS MICHAEL S	2LT	0-1580438	0644	2
STEVENS MILES G	COL	0-0271858	0158	3
STEVENS MORRIS W	LTC	0-0172574	0754	3
STEVENS PAUL	MAJ	0-1062449	0861	1
STEVENS PHILIP L	2LT	0-0286241	0659	3
STEVENS ROBERT C	CW3	W-2144794	0763	1
STEVENS ROBERT G	LTC	0-1284229	0766	2
STEVENS ROBERT J	1LT	0-0526769	0146	2
STEVENS ROBERT L	CPT	0-0268265	0948	1
STEVENS ROBERT L	CPT	0-0977C52	0361	1
STEVENS ROBERT R	2LT	0-2014969	0446	2
STEVENS ROBERTIE	NAJ	N-0742853	0665	1
STEVENS ROY	CPT	0-2016969	0556	1
STEVENS THOMAS F	MAJ	0-0300571	0667	3
STEVENS WARREN B	MAJ	0-0547522	0563	1
STEVENS WAYNE R	LTC	0-1105841	1265	1
STEVENS WILLIAM V	CW3	W-2148768	0762	2
STEVENS WINFRED G	MAJ	0-2006202	0860	1
STEVENSON ALFRED S	MAJ	0-0317199	1145	2
STEVENSON BETTY L	2LT	N-0700607	1140	1
STEVENSON CARL A	2LT	0-2009337	0846	1
STEVENSON CHARLES G	B G	0-0233309	0663	3
STEVENSON DEWITT A	CPT	0-0395391	0446	2
STEVENSON EDDIE	1LT	0-2025845	0447	1
STEVENSON EDWARD H	MAJ	0-0277128	1047	1
STEVENSON FRANK M	MAJ	0-0129309	0657	3
STEVENSON GEORGE S	COL	0-025247C	0264	3
STEVENSON GILBERT M	LTC	0-0246838	0861	3
STEVENSON HAROLD F	MAJ	0-0453757	0848	2
STEVENSON HOWARD G	LTC	0-0539398	0963	1
STEVENSON JAMES N	LTC	0-1845248	0364	1
STEVENSON JOHN	CW4	W-2122617	0461	1
STEVENSON JOSEPH W	LTC	0-1302901	0361	1
STEVENSON JR OLEN J	MAJ	0-1595190	1162	1
STEVENSON KURL	CPT	0-1579176	1045	1
STEVENSON MARION W	LTC	0-1290837	0563	1
STEVENSON MARJORIE G	1LT	N-0757616	0745	1
STEVENSON PAUL J	WO1	W-2149417	0753	2
STEVENSON PETER J	COL	0-0143185	0758	3
STEVENSON RICHARD H	LTC	0-0113311	0648	3
STEVENSON RICHARD H	CPT	0-0123939	C648	3
STEVENSON ROBERT H	MAJ	0-014701C	0954	3
STEVENSON ROBERT L	COL	0-0120958	1154	1
STEVENSON ROBERT L	MAJ	0-1291031	1061	1
STEVENSON ROGER H	MAJ	0-0438060	0146	2
STEVENSON RUSH W	CPT	0-0391628	0861	1
STEVENSON SARA I	LTC	N-0700608	0445	1
STEVENSON THOMAS T	COL	0-0197539	0659	3
STEVENSON WILBUR O	CPT	0-0498497	0853	1
STEVENSON WILLIAM R	LTC	0-1165453	0457	1
STEVER ORVAL B	MAJ	0-1913377	0365	1
STEVESKEY JOSEPH M	1LT	0-0380728	0157	1
STEWARC HAROLD O	LTC	0-C452C25	0261	1
STEWARC JOHN J	LTC	0-0341456	1164	3

NAME	GRADE	SVC NO	DATE RET MO YR	RET CODE
STEWARD WILLIAM E	CW2	W-22C9539	0765	1
STEWARDSON DON J	LTC	0-1290152	1061	1
STEWART ALEXANDER	COL	C-0203758	1062	3
STEWART ALFRED E	CW2	W-2126551	0365	1
STEWART ARCHIE M	LTC	0-0291991	1167	3
STEWART ARTEMAS J	LTC	0-0262465	0667	3
STEWART CHANDIS L	CW3	W-2203351	0564	1
STEWART CHARLES	1LT	C-1015392	0745	2
STEWART CHARLES L	MAJ	0-0953702	0667	1
STEWART CHARLES M	MAJ	C-0404732	C146	2
STEWART CHARLES R	CW4	W-2110717	0559	1
STEWART CLARENCE O	LTC	0-1586949	0561	1
STEWART CLARENCE J	COL	0-0260552	1264	3
STEWART DON L	MAJ	C-1305496	1163	1
STEWART DONALD L	LTC	0-0272779	C862	3
STEWART DOROTHY L	MAJ	N-0732361	C964	3
STEWART EARL C	COL	0-0175687	1061	3
STEWART EDNA M	1LT	N-0779418	0749	2
STEWART EDWARD J	LTC	0-0422612	0965	1
STEWART ELDON C	MAJ	C-1110829	0657	1
STEWART EMRY V	COL	C-0262120	1046	2
STEWART ERNEST D	LTC	0-0450593	0758	1
STEWART EVERETT S	LTC	0-0374152	C657	1
STEWART FAYE H	COL	0-0358024	0346	2
STEWART FERGUSON C	LTC	0-0366287	0361	1
STEWART FLOYD W	B G	C-0113310	0553	3
STEWART FRANCIS X	MAJ	0-1325068	1060	1
STEWART FRANK B	LTC	C-0491221	0651	1
STEWART GARNET D	LTC	0-1549118	1066	1
STEWART GENE V	MAJ	C-1799907	1263	1
STEWART GEORGE B	CPT	0-0889059	0662	1
STEWART GEORGE F	MAJ	C-4010390	0767	1
STEWART GEORGE G	LTC	0-1645404	0265	1
STEWART GEORGE L	MAJ	C-2008461	0960	1
STEWART GEORGE T	MAJ	0-0310617	C747	2
STEWART GLENN D	CPT	0-0269487	1158	1
STEWART HAROLD A	COL	0-0201897	0457	3
STEWART HAROLD L	LTC	0-0227077	1046	2
STEWART HAROLD O	CPT	0-05285C8	1145	2
STEWART HARRY G	MAJ	0-0450366	0657	1
STEWART HERMAN E	CPT	0-1308558	C549	2
STEWART HOLLIS P	MAJ	C-1032657	0863	1
STEWART HOMER T	MAJ	0-1596516	0857	1
STEWART HORACE H	COL	0-0350299	0946	2
STEWART HUGH J	LTC	0-0304186	0861	1
STEWART IRWIN M	LTC	C-0239842	1047	2
STEWART JACK K	CW2	W-2149406	1163	1
STEWART JACK L	LTC	0-1291350	1061	1
STEWART JACKSON W	LTC	0-1639694	1262	1
STEWART JACOB M	MAJ	0-04489C1	0745	1
STEWART JAMES	WO1	W-21C6784	1051	2
STEWART JAMES A	COL	0-0258234	1162	1
STEWART JAMES A	MAJ	C-0977081	0463	1
STEWART JAMES D	LTC	0-0237881	0265	3
STEWART JAMES E	COL	0-0357549	1154	1
STEWART JAMES E	CPT	0-0968206	0562	1
STEWART JAMES F	CPT	0-1797036	104N	1
STEWART JAMES M	1LT	0-0411855	0245	1
STEWART JAMES O	LTC	0-1108346	0161	1
STEWART JAMES O	MAJ	0-2023559	0762	1
STEWART JAMES P	MAJ	0-1108347	0961	1
STEWART JAMES R	2LT	0-1309320	0945	2
STEWART JAMES T	COL	0-0353818	0963	1
STEWART JASPER D	CPT	C-1058388	1146	2
STEWART JOHN A	LTC	0-0357553	0161	1
STEWART JOHN A	CPT	0-0528895	C448	2
STEWART JOHN B	2LT	0-1329174	C560	2
STEWART JOHN C	LTC	0-1635375	0761	1
STEWART JOHN D	1LT	0-0536741	0946	2
STEWART JOHN L	1LT	0-2035739	0745	2
STEWART JOHN R	MAJ	C-0340382	1143	2
STEWART JOHN R	2LT	0-1310166	1045	2
STEWART JOHN W	MAJ	C-0149146	0955	3
STEWART JOHN W	COL	0-0325908	1161	1
STEWART JR ALBERT R	MAJ	C-1175872	0167	2

NAME	GRADE	SVC NO	DATE RET MO YR	RET CODE
STEWART JR ARCHIE W	CPT	0-1296442	1045	2
STEWART JR HARRY L	LTC	0-1695939	0346	2
STEWART JR RAY E	LTC	0-1319C37	1162	1
STEWART JR ROBERT C	LTC	0-1281053	0862	1
STEWART JR ULYSSES G	MAJ	0-155093C	0862	1
STEWART KATHRYN R	1LT	N-0789231	0946	1
STEWART KENNETH N	LTC	0-1058389	0167	1
STEWART KERMIT D	COL	0-0239239	0165	3
STEWART KERMIT G	LTC	0-1319452	1062	1
STEWART LLOYD R	LTC	0-0335458	1058	1
STEWART LOUIS G	MAJ	C-0252817	0666	3
STEWART MARLIN M	LTC	0-0376784	C467	1
STEWART MARVIN R	CPT	0-1106510	1046	2
STEWART MARY V	2LT	N-0742847	0345	1
STEWART MERVILLE E	CPT	0-2016970	1048	1
STEWART MILLER J	MAJ	0-C306005	0966	3
STEWART MURRAY C	LTC	0-0412956	0263	2
STEWART NORMAN R	MAJ	0-0494609	0157	1
STEWART OLIVER W	MAJ	0-0256969	0866	3
STEWART OSWALD B	LTC	0-0223664	0557	1
STEWART OTHEL W	COL	0-0257653	0859	1
STEWART PAUL B	MAJ	0-0209832	0645	2
STEWART PERCY M	1LT	0-0521897	0856	3
STEWART PHILOMENA	1LT	N-0795335	1147	1
STEWART PRICE C	MAJ	0-1535085	0159	1
STEWART RAY S	CW3	W-2145592	0361	1
STEWART RAYMOND H	CPT	0-1286565	1045	2
STEWART RICHARD G	COL	0-0231975	0463	3
STEWART RICHARD W	1LT	0-1016711	0247	1
STEWART ROBERT	2LT	0-1305129	0745	2
STEWART ROBERT	2LT	0-1823C83	1044	1
STEWART ROBERT A	MAJ	0-1295102	0254	1
STEWART ROBERT B	CPT	0-0303906	1045	2
STEWART ROBERT G	LTC	0-0249628	0765	3
STEWART ROBERT L	COL	0-028663C	0856	3
STEWART ROBERT S	LTC	0-0251067	0267	3
STEWART ROBERT W	1LT	0-0295419	1043	2
STEWART ROBERT W	2LT	0-0407584	0442	2
STEWART ROY C	CPT	0-0490143	0646	2
STEWART ROY F	CW3	W-2141792	0659	1
STEWART ROY P	LTC	0-0905350	1165	3
STEWART SADIE E	1LT	N-0764773	0247	1
STEWART SAMLEN S	LTC	0-0532118	1164	1
STEWART SELDON C	MAJ	0-0496758	1152	1
STEWART STANLEY D	MAJ	0-1549386	0766	1
STEWART SYDNEY D	LTC	0-0265850	0247	2
STEWART WILLIAM R	MAJ	C-0283969	1146	2
STEWART WILLIAM H	1LT	0-0305467	0242	2
STEWART WILLIAM H	CPT	0-0890237	1057	2
STEWART WISDOM H	LTC	0-0405378	1158	1
STEYAART CHARLES L	COL	0-0252446	0762	3
STIBR JOSEPH R	CPT	0-0326188	0253	3
STICE MARC A	MAJ	0-0237403	0648	3
STICE MILTON A	LTC	0-05644C8	0555	1
STICE SILAS P	CW3	W-214295C	1057	1
STICKEL VINCENT J	MAJ	0-1947604	1059	1
STICKELS M JEANNE	1LT	N-0774028	0148	1
STICKLE JOHN R	LTC	0-0305961	1060	1
STICKLER LEE R	MAJ	0-0383209	0461	1
STICKLER MERTON H	CPT	0-0169121	0957	3
STICKLES JOSEPH M	MAJ	0-164881C	0961	1
STICKLEY JOSEPH W	1LT	0-1584983	0745	2
STICKNEY EDWIN F	CPT	0-0300095	0757	3
STICKNEY GERALD R	LTC	0-1308016	0465	1
STICKNEY JR JOSEPH E	1LT	0-0514613	0846	1
STICKNEY RICHARD W	CPT	0-1181473	0447	1
STIDHAM JAMES C	CPT	0-1165048	0146	2
STIDHAM TAYLOR	LTC	0-2029462	0667	1
STIEBER GEORGE L	CPT	0-0488907	0649	1
STIEFF RAY A	MAJ	0-1012367	0858	1
STIEGLER ERNEST G	1LT	0-1335709	1047	2
STIEGLER HAROLD W	LTC	0-0217901	0455	3
STIEGLITZ ALLEN	1LT	0-1042955	0945	2
STIEGMAN FRED M	MAJ	0-0186105	0750	3
STIELOW EMIL F	CPT	0-0204672	0455	3

NAME	GRADE	SVC NO	DATE RET MO YR	RET CODE
STIENECKER H M	CPT	0-0447765	C647	2
STIER HERBERT E	LTC	0-0321175	C466	3
STIERLE WILLIAM R	1LT	0-2035867	0154	1
STIERS WALTER E	CW2	W-2104507	0854	1
STIFF ELBERT H	COL	0-0272722	0566	1
STIFFLER PRESTON F	WO1	W-2121825	C645	2
STIGGINS LILLIAN D	MAJ	N-0726333	1264	2
STIGLIANO JAYNE J	2LT	N-0755403	C945	1
STILE LOUIS	CPT	0-0516487	0247	2
STILES AARON K	COL	0-0174798	0760	3
STILES AUSTIN C	LTC	0-0190565	0554	3
STILES EDWARD G	CPT	0-0994765	1061	1
STILES FREDERIC C	CPT	0-0184807	0555	3
STILES GEORGE F	CW4	W-2143115	C964	1
STILES GEORGE M	MAJ	0-1644127	1062	1
STILES HERMAN R	CPT	0-1301556	1146	2
STILES JR WILLIAM L	MAJ	0-0235052	0345	2
STILES LEO T	MAJ	0-1845798	0757	1
STILES LOUISE L	MAJ	R-0002330	0765	1
STILES MARY K	2LT	R-0000883	1144	1
STILES MELVIN C	CPT	0-1107158	0549	2
STILES WENDEL A	LTC	0-0175276	1059	3
STILEY JR JOSEPH F	CPT	0-0513476	0563	1
STILL EDWARD H	MAJ	0-1553181	0466	2
STILL GEORGE R	LTC	0-0109906	0436	1
STILL JOHN	MAJ	0-0370268	0154	1
STILL NORMAN J	CW2	W-2147675	1059	1
STILL WRIGHT P	CPT	0-1165961	0547	2
STILLE WALTER H	CW3	W-2141458	0659	1
STILLGER RAYMOND E	LTC	0-1304580	0664	2
STILLINGS WILLIAM A	CW4	W-2111966	0760	1
STILLMAN FREEMAN L	MAJ	C-0330529	1043	2
STILLMAN ISADORE W	MAJ	0-0507905	1046	2
STILLMAN ROBERT C	MAJ	C-2019247	0465	1
STILLMAN RUFUS C	1LT	0-1014233	0845	2
STILLMUNKS HARMON L	CW2	W-2211634	0566	1
STILLSON CLAUDE E	MAJ	0-1536226	0463	1
STILLWAGON ARTHUR N	CW2	W-2119688	1163	2
STILLWAGON THOMAS	MAJ	C-1326267	1262	2
STILLWELL CLYDE	CPT	0-0172432	1051	3
STILLWELL HAROLD V	CPT	0-1920292	0663	2
STILSON ALDEN E	B G	0-0320041	0261	3
STILWELL CHARLES A	CW2	W-2213705	1167	1
STILWELL JAMES L	MAJ	0-1111934	1061	1
STILWELL LELAND E	COL	0-0256707	C454	3
STILWELL MELVYN S	LTC	0-0326986	1160	1
STILWELL ROBERT L	COL	0-0119180	0-53	3
STILWELL RONALD L	CPT	0-1796179	0248	1
STIMMELL LEE	LTC	0-1558907	1165	1
STIMPSON JR DONALD	LTC	0-1284961	0361	1
STIMPSON NABOTH G	CPT	0-1557914	C351	1
STIMSON GORDON	LTC	0-0236613	0665	3
STIMSON ROLLAND H	LTC	0-0285288	1060	1
STINCHCOMB JUDD T	LTC	0-0169529	0852	3
STINCHCOMB PAUL A	MAJ	0-1341831	0765	1
STINE GORDON T	1LT	0-1291351	0446	2
STINE JOSEPH	LTC	0-0455297	1063	1
STINEBAUGH DANIEL L	CPT	0-2035393	C850	1
STINNETT EARL W	CPT	0-0373582	0244	2
STINNETT WILLIAM C	MAJ	0-0384287	0763	1
STINSON FORREST A	CPT	0-0298855	0645	2
STINSON HOWARD E	MAJ	C-2211416	1066	2
STINSON JOHN	1LT	0-1109038	0546	2
STINSON LEONARD E	CPT	0-1926566	C366	1
STINSON MARION J	1LT	0-1011167	0945	2
STINSON MAURICE J	CW3	W-2152812	1059	1
STINSON WADE R	1LT	0-1338148	C947	2
STINSON WILLIAM B	COL	0-0265143	0460	1
STIO ROCCO L	CPT	0-0322702	0145	1
STIPE SR JOHN W M	MAJ	0-0526344	C664	3
STIPP GEORGE M	COL	0-0251977	0165	3
STIRES FREDERICK	LTC	0-0432841	1059	1
STIRLING JAMES R	MAJ	0-1298616	1160	1
STIRLING SHELDON L	LTC	0-0205349	1163	3
STITELER CHESTER G	LTC	0-0330991	0866	3
STITES HENRY J	COL	0-0183202	0949	3
STITH CHARLES R	LTC	0-1300229	1167	1
STITH DON J	LTC	0-0464561	0145	2
STITH JR BENJAMIN F	MAJ	0-1304631	0961	1
STITH STEPHEN W	CPT	0-C488095	0251	1
STITHEM DALE D	LTC	0-1031031	0260	1
STITT ALBERT A	CPT	0-0400006	1146	2
STITT GEORGE S	LTC	0-0288379	0958	1
STITT JOHN B	MAJ	0-1821648	C463	1
STITT LYNN B	CPT	0-0361185	C745	2
STITZENBERGER WILBER	LTC	0-0912583	0764	3
STIVERS ROBERT T	2LT	0-1636703	0245	2
STIVES JOHN H	MAJ	0-0412554	0546	2
STOBAUGH WILLARD L	LTC	0-0357196	0747	2
STOCK BERNARD A	MAJ	C-0570407	0464	1
STOCK HARRY J	WO1	W-2119336	0747	1
STOCK HOWARD R	1LT	0-0409833	0145	2
STOCK JAMES E	2LT	0-1312456	1144	2
STOCK JOSEPH J	LTC	0-1314235	0361	1
STOCKARD JR HENRY J	1LT	0-0541495	1045	1
STOCKARD JR THOMAS J	1LT	0-1298949	0345	2
STOCKDALE GEORGE R	LTC	0-0407775	C766	2
STOCKDALE PAUL H	1LT	0-2009710	1052	1
STOCKDER HANS J	COL	0-0199905	0951	3
STOCKDEN WALLACE I	LTC	0-0171571	0444	2
STOCKELL ALBERT W	MAJ	0-0416474	0661	1
STOCKER STEWART J	1LT	0-1299491	1047	2
STOCKETT JOHN H	MAJ	0-0306540	0360	1
STOCKHAMMER S F	LTC	0-0255913	0560	3
STOCKLAND CLARENCE O	LTC	0-0288324	0764	3
STOCKMAN GILBERT	MAJ	0-1186298	0967	1
STOCKMAN PERRY J	1LT	0-128846C	0465	1
STOCKMAN WILLIAM A	CPT	0-0220239	0945	1
STOCKNER LESTER W	CPT	0-028278C	0843	2
STOCKS ERNEST J	LTC	0-0281515	C867	3
STOCKS JESSE T	MAJ	0-0270380	0767	3
STOCKSON MATHEW	LTC	0-0487978	0357	1
STOCKTON ARTHUR E	MAJ	0-0491303	1044	2
STOCKTON CHRISTOPHE	MAJ	0-0349535	0943	2
STOCKTON JACK P	LTC	0-1291352	1060	1
STOCKTON JOHN L	1LT	0-1177199	0466	1
STOCKTON JR PURL A	MAJ	0-0537243	0563	1
STOCKTON ROBERT A	MAJ	0-1294926	0865	2
STOCKTON SHERMAN E	WO1	W-2111128	0456	2
STOCKTON WILLIAM H	1LT	0-1046288	0246	2
STOCKTON WILLIAM W	LTC	0-1168095	0860	1
STOCKTON WILLIE R	MAJ	0-1305863	0765	1
STOCKUNAS JOSEPH W	CW2	W-2210713	1262	1
STOCKWELL HARVEY L	LTC	0-1113002	0566	1
STOCKWELL RICHARD V	LTC	0-1177998	0266	1
STOCKWELL ROY	LTC	0-0153336	0648	3
STODART WILLIAM E	MAJ	0-1922644	0567	1
STODDARD ARTHUR E	M G	0-0371507	0558	3
STODDARD CARROLL S	COL	0-0230693	0148	2
STODDARD ELLIOTTE A	LTC	0-0241821	0159	3
STODDARD GLENN G	MAJ	0-0245513	0855	3
STODDARD HENRY R	COL	0-0240838	0363	3
STODDARD JACK C	MAJ	0-1823513	0462	1
STODDARD JAMES K	MAJ	C-0494835	0645	2
STODDARD JR LEONARD	2LT	0-1286391	0945	2
STODDART MARJORIE	1LT	N-0793554	1046	1
STOECKEL JR JOSEPH F	MAJ	0-0175064	0352	3
STOECKLEY CLARENCE F	LTC	0-1304139	1262	1
STOEFEN HARLAN J	LTC	0-1542001	1262	1
STOEHR ERWIN A	CW3	W-2143971	0161	1
STOEHR HENRY G	CPT	0-2263021	0661	2
STOELTZING ERNST R	MAJ	0-2049113	0365	1
STOETZER CHARLES E	LTC	0-0376201	0960	1
STOFFEL JOSEPH F	MAJ	0-1554830	0761	1
STOFFT FREDERICK	B G	0-0273771	0665	3
STOFT JOSEF C	MAJ	0-0346102	0747	2
STOGSDILL JAMES E	COL	0-0212615	1060	3
STOHLER MAURICE H	CPT	0-0545998	0647	2
STOHLMAN ROBERT F	MAJ	0-1577905	0666	1
STOK DANIEL D	LTC	0-0327641	0263	1
STOKAN DONALD A	MAJ	0-2021189	1264	1
STOKE HERSCHEL R	LTC	0-0119778	0754	3
STOKELY CLAYTON E	MAJ	0-0281692	0746	2
STOKER EMORY D	COL	0-0163926	0863	1
STOKER HENRY C	WO1	W-2147084	0457	1
STOKES ARTHUR	1LT	0-0250104	0164	3
STOKES BENJAMIN F	MAJ	C-0131351	0155	3
STOKES FRED O	MAJ	0-1306203	C861	1
STOKES JAMES D	1LT	0-1321675	1045	2
STOKES JAMES G	CPT	0-0163509	1155	3
STOKES JAMES H	CPT	0-0529511	0452	1
STOKES JR MELMOTH Y	COL	0-0179148	C454	3
STOKES JR PAUL L	MAJ	0-2033233	0161	1
STOKES JR WILLIAM M	M G	0-0166391	0658	2
STOKES KENNETH E	COL	0-0213443	0564	3
STOKES REDMOND F	1LT	0-1300727	0846	2
STOKES ROBERT N	MAJ	C-1295620	0561	1
STOKES WILLIAM J	COL	0-0332517	0960	1
STOKES WILLIAM R	CPT	0-1301705	1057	2
STOKINGER WILLIAM A	LTC	0-0468231	0865	1
STOKKE HENRY C	CPT	0-0410840	0147	2
STOKLEY LAWTON W	LTC	0-0245007	0966	3
STOKLOSA OTTO J	MAJ	0-1648840	1057	1
STOKOE JAMES S	1LT	0-0285544	1044	2
STOLARSKI MACK G	MAJ	0-1172682	C858	1
STOLBERG JOHN C	MAJ	0-0212590	0948	3
STOLEN ERNEST G	CPT	0-0521599	0346	2
STOLL CHARLES G	MAJ	0-1684252	0246	2
STOLL FRANK J	CW2	W-2118251	0548	1
STOLL FRED H	COL	C-0171275	1157	1
STOLL FREDERICK	LTC	0-0492939	0455	1
STOLL HERBERT M	MAJ	C-0177471	C361	3
STOLL JOHN E	LTC	0-0235661	0560	3
STOLL JOSEPH W	CPT	0-1323042	C248	2
STOLLAK JULES S	CPT	0-0949181	0861	1
STOLLE CARL M	LTC	0-0156168	1045	2
STOLLE EDWARD J	MAJ	C-0237129	1144	1
STOLLER LOUIS W	MAJ	0-0488325	1045	2
STOLOFF ALFRED H	1LT	0-1113003	0945	2
STOLPESTAD C T	CPT	0-0501030	1044	1
STOLTZ FLEETWOOD	LTC	0-0255744	0767	3
STOLTZ JOSEPH H	LTC	0-1168091	1265	1
STOLZ ALFRED A	LTC	C-0379850	0960	1
STOLZ FRED C	LTC	0-0280202	C867	3
STOLZ FREDERICK	LTC	0-1548563	1265	1
STONAKER MARGARET R	MAJ	N-0760800	0964	1
STONBRAKER KENNETH O	CPT	0-2262302	0261	1
STONE ALFRED W	MAJ	C-0979499	0963	1
STONE AMOS E	1LT	0-1179744	0146	2
STONE BARTOL F	MAJ	C-1641831	1163	1
STONE BERNARD W	CPT	0-0317140	0244	2
STONE BOYD W	MAJ	C-0518895	0345	2
STONE CARRINGTON	COL	0-0114853	0246	2
STONE CHARLES A	LTC	0-0300081	0464	3
STONE CHARLES R	LTC	0-1310343	0465	3
STONE DAVID B	COL	0-0019976	1060	1
STONE DEE W	COL	0-0165561	0252	3
STONE DONALD O	LTC	0-0257065	0659	3
STONE DUDLEY J	LTC	0-0320039	0565	3
STONE EARL F	WO1	W-2120927	0447	2
STONE ELRY	COL	0-0207696	0454	3
STONE ERIC P	LTC	C-0173655	C352	3
STONE FRANK L	MAJ	0-1313140	0757	1
STONE FRANKLIN W	1LT	C-0347223	0443	2
STONE GEORGE F	MAJ	0-0903897	0746	2
STONE GEORGE R	2LT	0-2010988	1152	1
STONE GLENN A	MAJ	0-1643371	0764	1
STONE HARVEY L	2LT	0-1595193	1044	2
STONE HENRY C	LTC	0-0411897	0264	1
STONE HUBERT L	CW3	W-2128214	1056	1
STONE IVAN J	MAJ	0-1320665	0347	2
STONE JAMES H	1LT	0-0520369	0947	2
STONE JAMES M	LTC	0-0323989	0867	3
STONE JEFF O	CW3	W-2142432	0559	1
STONE JEFFREY A	COL	0-0410143	C446	2
STONE JOHN E	LTC	0-0292257	0760	2
STONE JOHN F	LTC	0-1058130	1263	1
STONE JOHN J	MAJ	0-1039234	0562	1
STONE JOSEPH H	CPT	0-1031032	0157	1
STONE JOSEPH P	MAJ	0-1559626	0864	1
STONE JR CALEB S	LTC	0-0473273	0746	2
STONE JR MEAD W	1LT	0-0527281	0346	2
STONE JUNIUS F	CPT	0-0502108	0260	1
STONE LEVERETT C	LTC	0-0232405	1051	3
STONE LOUIS	CPT	0-0109861	0339	1
STONE MALCOLM C	1LT	0-0980000	0854	2
STONE MATTYE L	MAJ	N-0765173	0565	1
STONE OTIS L	CW2	W-2207501	0359	1
STONE PAUL M	LTC	0-0451566	0557	1
STONE RAYMOND D	MAJ	0-0218339	1054	3
STONE RAYMOND W	LTC	0-1035605	0164	1
STONE RICHARD H	1LT	0-1042962	0443	2
STONE ROBERT H	CPT	0-1169355	1045	2
STONE ROBERT O	LTC	0-1533455	0563	1
STONE ROY	LTC	0-0172249	0553	3
STONE ROY E	LTC	0-0274364	1062	3
STONE RUFUS B	CPT	0-0254829	0763	3
STONE SANFORD J	MAJ	0-1334924	0863	1
STONE THEODORE J	MAJ	0-1692573	0666	1
STONE WALTER C	MAJ	0-0959235	1062	1
STONE WALTER E	CPT	0-0890076	1046	1
STONE WILBUR H	MAJ	0-0919191	0845	2
STONE WILLIAM C	MAJ	0-0251086	0345	2
STONE WILLIAM H	LTC	0-1573706	1157	2
STONE WILLIAM P	COL	0-0482739	0962	3
STONEBACK DONALD F	1LT	0-1293144	1044	2
STONEBERG NORMAN E	MAJ	0-1540865	0364	1
STONEBERGER WARREN H	CW3	W-2141460	0661	1
STONEBRAKER ERNEST M	CPT	0-0222268	0460	3
STONEBRAKER FRANK J	MAJ	0-1285842	0860	1
STONEBRAKER JOHN H O	MAJ	0-1333898	0362	2
STONEBRIDGE W E	MAJ	0-0244804	1054	3
STONEBRUNER JOHN G	CW2	W-2122735	0645	2
STONECIPHER BABARA	1LT	L-0502047	1044	2
STONEHOCKER CLARENCE	LTC	0-0265215	0358	1
STONEKING LEO T	CPT	0-0975981	0162	1
STONEMAN HARRY	MAJ	0-0175871	1058	3
STONER DORWIN E	1LT	0-1320873	1145	2
STONER FRANK C	COL	0-0110962	0955	3
STONER JOHN W	LTC	0-1318483	0163	1
STONER JR EDGAR B	MAJ	0-1579184	1060	1
STONER MAURICE E	CPT	0-0436673	1045	2
STONIER LYNN C	MAJ	0-0347807	0660	1
STONIK ANDREW R	LTC	0-1107160	1158	1
STOODLEY GERALD F	CPT	0-0104253	0853	3
STOOL WILLIAM M	CPT	0-0331586	1043	2
STOPFEL MARLIN E	1LT	0-1184954	0647	1
STOPPELLI DANIEL O	COL	0-0308983	0654	1
STORBRAATEN SIDNEY N	COL	0-0253820	0954	1
STORCH ALFRED W	COL	0-0914106	1165	3
STORER JOHN A	LTC	0-1641832	1162	1
STOREY CARL L	1LT	0-2053873	0546	1
STOREY J S	CPT	0-1584964	0754	1
STOREY JACK A	LTC	0-2263367	0767	1
STOREY JAMES E	LTC	0-1185317	0262	1
STOREY LEONARD W	LTC	0-0418735	0762	1
STOREY LUTHER R	COL	0-0178454	1154	1
STOREY MELVIN H	MAJ	0-0987078	0466	1
STOREY PRINT E	LTC	0-1825719	1262	1
STOREY ROBERT L	CPT	0-1338149	0757	1
STORIE JAMES C	LTC	0-1639700	0860	1
STORLIE CLIFFORD J	CPT	0-1001251	0951	1
STORM CECIL V	COL	0-1101681	0660	1
STORM EDGAR A	CW2	W-2104509	1044	2
STORM ERIC F	COL	0-0188432	0256	3
STORM HARVEY W	COL	0-0245808	0955	2
STORM HOWARD T	MAJ	0-2208412	0266	1
STORM JOSEPH L	CW2	W-2146283	0358	2
STORM JOSEPH P	LTC	0-2012011	0564	1
STORM RUSSELL F	CW2	W-2150296	1058	1

NAME	GRADE	SVC NO	DATE RET MO YR	RET CODE
STORM SYLVESTER	1LT	0-0323963	0147	2
STORMES ROBERT G	1LT	0-0342762	0146	2
STORMINGER GEORGE M	LTC	0-0506875	1059	1
STORMS ARNOLD J	2LT	0-1591466	0445	2
STORMS ISAAC D	LTC	0-0485850	1054	1
STORRS BARRIE E	MAJ	0-1017896	0862	1
STORRS JOHN N	MAJ	0-0221663	1061	3
STORTZ FRANK J	LTC	0-0110912	0756	3
STORUP ELTON T	1LT	0-1185467	1051	2
STORY CHARLES G	CW3	W-2152689	0265	1
STORY CHESTER L	CW3	W-2147409	0167	1
STORY DONALD H	CPT	0-1320197	0847	2
STORY DOUGLAS E	CW2	W-2205049	1161	1
STORY EMIL R	CPT	0-0358707	1045	2
STORY FRIEDA P	1LT	N-0731063	0445	2
STORY HARRY R	CPT	0-1298317	0862	1
STORY JOSEPH H	CPT	0-0220629	1046	1
STORY MELVIN E	1LT	0-0473828	0744	2
STORY WILLIAM J	MAJ	0-1685559	0963	1
STOSE JOHN	MAJ	0-4055933	0767	1
STOSHITCH IVAN	MAJ	0-0446937	0263	1
STOSS HELMUT G W	CW3	W-2142991	1163	1
STOTLER HARRY E	WO1	W-2117976	0953	1
STOTT GERTRUDE A	1LT	N-0757258	0946	1
STOTT JR GEORGE S	2LT	0-1340509	1054	2
STOTT KENHELM W	COL	0-0191716	0552	3
STOTT LAWRENCE J	MAJ	0-0333087	1058	3
STOTTS EARL E	LTC	0-1106512	0562	1
STOTTS WILCHER C	MAJ	0-1169760	1160	1
STOTZ JOHN K	COL	0-0145965	[illegible]	3
STOUCH JOHN R	CW3	W-2148867	0462	1
STOUDT KENNETH M	LTC	0-0934278	0767	1
STOUDT LOGAN H	2LT	0-2000213	0346	2
STOUFFER JAY E	MAJ	0-1542159	0962	1
STOUFFER NELSON W	MAJ	0-0980114	0266	1
STOUFFER THOMAS M	LTC	0-0204386	1157	1
STOUGH WILLIAM P	LTC	0-1080153	0761	1
STOUGHTON CECIL W	MAJ	0-2288315	0567	1
STOUGHTON JOSEPH B	1LT	0-1797553	0452	1
STOUGHTON WILLIAM L	MAJ	0-0285611	1061	3
STOUT BERNARD N	MAJ	0-1181474	0662	1
STOUT CHARLES J	CPT	0-4013585	0655	2
STOUT DONALD G	CPT	0-0523412	1053	2
STOUT DONALD T	MAJ	0-0405309	0164	1
STOUT GEORGE S	1LT	0-1030525	0645	1
STOUT GROVER C	1LT	0-0176933	0740	1
STOUT HARRY R	2LT	0-1031450	0944	2
STOUT HORACE F	COL	0-0231846	0954	3
STOUT HOWARD M	1LT	0-0443820	1143	2
STOUT JAMES M	CW3	W-2205789	1062	2
STOUT JAY N	LTC	0-1554643	0365	3
STOUT JOSEPH W	MAJ	0-0225553	0150	1
STOUT LEROY	LTC	0-0255363	0159	2
STOUT MARION R	CW4	W-2111955	0554	1
STOUT RICHARD R	MAJ	0-0231373	0945	2
STOUT ROBERT P	COL	0-0137295	0455	3
STOUT STEWART G	CPT	0-0485720	1046	2
STOUT VICTOR H	LTC	0-1644826	0566	1
STOUT WALTER C	CPT	0-0312473	1045	2
STOUTENBURGH ELIOT G	COL	0-0256608	1167	3
STOVALL ANDREW J	CW2	W-2146284	0862	1
STOVALL CARTIER H	LTC	0-0179629	0657	2
STOVALL CLYDE D	CW4	W-2142611	0863	1
STOVALL DAVID P	MAJ	0-0326084	0761	3
STOVALL JAMES J	LTC	0-0362509	1057	2
STOVALL JOE	MAJ	0-0464158	0654	2
STOVALL JONATHAN R	1LT	0-1063051	0346	1
STOVALL ORAN C	COL	0-0348288	0853	1
STOVALL RALPH M	COL	0-0276010	0467	3
STOVALL SID	LTC	0-1546526	0962	1
STOVALL WILLIAM S	CPT	0-2262941	0461	1
STOVALL WILLIAM T	MAJ	0-0453357	1054	1
STOVEN JAMES H	CW3	W-2151706	0262	1
STOVER CHARLES V	CPT	0-0496993	0754	1
STOVER GEORGE M	LTC	0-0323557	0966	3
STOVER GLEN W	MAJ	0-2027265	1262	1
STOVER HAROLD F	LTC	0-0248183	0165	3
STOVER HENRY A	CW3	W-2147310	0265	1
STOVER JACOB P	LTC	0-1175873	0966	1
STOVER JAMES A	CPT	0-1102074	0547	2
STOVER JR EDWARD C	LTC	0-0135632	0353	3
STOVER KENNETH F	LTC	0-0384902	0863	1
STOVER ORVILLE H	MAJ	0-0450659	0259	1
STOVER ROBERT F	WO1	W-2210152	0160	1
STOVER WALTER O	MAJ	0-0453260	0954	1
STOVER WILLIAM H	MAJ	0-0278985	1053	3
STOVER WILLIAM H	MAJ	0-1597141	0363	1
STOVIN PHILIP R	LTC	0-0197247	0862	3
STOWE JAMES J	MAJ	0-1013741	1059	1
STOWE NORMAN L	MAJ	0-1923510	0664	1
STOWELL ALVIN C	LTC	0-1895515	0765	3
STOWELL CHARLES W	LTC	0-2046701	0966	1
STOWELL FRED M	LTC	0-1540545	0362	2
STOWELL JAMES F	CW2	W-2211947	0567	1
STOWELL SAMUEL	MAJ	0-0192315	0762	3
STOWER IRVING C	CPT	0-0481515	0245	2
STOWERS DEWEY M	LTC	0-0349256	0862	3
STOWERS JAMES C	COL	0-0245145	0966	3
STOWERS JAMES L	WO1	W-2122763	0845	2
STOWERS JOHN H	M G	0-0176135	0861	3
STOY HAROLD T	CPT	0-0189044	0157	3
STOY HENRY F	MAJ	0-0229699	0245	2
STOYNOFF KARL J	LTC	0-1845354	1065	1
STOZIC NICHOLAS	WO1	W-2106050	0247	2
STRACHAN JOHN W	LTC	0-1282330	0866	1
STRACHAN JR HARRY L	MAJ	0-0490574	1145	1
STRADER BENNIE J	MAJ	0-0488493	0854	1
STRADER RODMAN W	MAJ	0-0371762	0363	1
STRADLEY JOSEPH L	LTC	0-1002843	0966	3
STRAHL JOHN A	1LT	0-1574154	1143	2
STRAIN EARL E	MAJ	0-1950461	0863	1
STRAIN JEROME C	LTC	0-0252702	0146	2
STRAIN PAUL W	LTC	0-1294036	0461	1
STRAIN ROBERT A	LTC	0-1800084	0466	1
STRAIN WILLIAM J	CPT	0-0254974	0867	3
STRAIT ELWIN A	1LT	0-1181475	1145	2
STRALLY MICHAEL J	MAJ	0-1644131	0859	1
STRAMAT THOMAS E	CPT	0-0961425	0361	1
STRAMM WILLIAM	CW4	W-2112232	0166	1
STRANATHAN WILLIAM	MAJ	0-0145839	0557	3
STRAND CHARLES D	1LT	0-1535540	0845	2
STRAND HILMA C	CPT	N-0736939	0147	1
STRAND JR WALTER	1LT	0-1044967	1046	2
STRAND KENNETH E	MAJ	0-0961412	0467	1
STRAND ORVILLE W	MAJ	0-0947034	0965	1
STRAND WESLEY M	LTC	0-2035858	0363	1
STRANDE ORIN E	LTC	0-0445232	0455	1
STRANG ARTHUR L	LTC	0-1165151	0267	3
STRANG JOSEPH W	COL	0-0456347	0566	1
STRANG TOM R	LTC	0-0377874	0746	2
STRANG WARREN C	MAJ	0-1644132	0158	1
STRANGE BILL M	CW2	W-2115840	0446	2
STRANGE FRANCIS O	1LT	0-2019946	1052	1
STRANGE FRANK L	COL	0-0924330	1063	3
STRANGE FRED A	CPT	0-0496665	0652	1
STRANGE GLEN L	MAJ	0-1011156	0547	2
STRANGE JOHN G	LTC	0-1103956	1167	1
STRANGE JR JOSEPH L	LTC	0-0949454	0667	2
STRANGE LOUIS P	1LT	0-1017424	0845	2
STRANGE ROY C	LTC	0-0251578	1057	1
STRANGE WESLEY R	CW4	W-2112077	0565	1
STRANGE WILLIAM C	CPT	0-1846225	0354	1
STRANLEY OTTO R	LTC	0-0901750	0363	3
STRANO JOHN S	2LT	0-1699960	0657	2
STRANSKY JAMES F	1LT	0-1543846	0445	1
STRASBURGER ALFRED	1LT	0-1577916	1044	2
STRASH VICTOR C	1LT	0-0253950	0753	3
STRASSBERGER ARUNAH	LTC	0-1002346	0964	1
STRASSBURG HARRY E	MAJ	0-0250836	0864	3
STRASSBURGER HELLMUT	MAJ	0-0969100	0465	1
STRASSBURGER RICHARD	CW3	W-2147185	0664	2
STRASSER EDWARD J	CW3	W-2205416	0767	1
STRASSER FRANCIS C	MAJ	0-0388940	0959	2
STRASSER JOHN W	LTC	0-1175874	1164	1
STRATER EDWARD H	CPT	0-1555632	0665	1
STRATMOEN RALPH O	LTC	0-1703029	0364	1
STRATTE ALF K	LTC	0-0266098	0256	3
STRATTOM CLELL T	CPT	0-1645410	1159	1
STRATTON ALBERT G	MAJ	0-1877886	1166	1
STRATTON ARTHUR L	CW3	W-2149947	0364	1
STRATTON DOUGLAS R	1LT	0-0408772	0945	2
STRATTON EDWARD J	1LT	0-0513485	0146	2
STRATTON JOEL B	COL	0-0174751	0761	3
STRATTON JOHN N	LTC	0-0480850	0766	1
STRATTON JR ROBERT H	MAJ	0-0276171	0467	3
STRATTON LAWRENCE	MAJ	0-0406139	0548	1
STRATTON LLOYD W	MAJ	0-0973527	1061	1
STRATTON MARSHALL J	CW2	W-3250493	0467	1
STRATTON REGINALD H	COL	0-0232789	1063	3
STRATTON THOMAS H	LTC	0-0307939	0962	1
STRAUB DELBERT T	CW2	W-2142077	0256	1
STRAUB ELMER F	COL	0-0267270	1054	3
STRAUCH IRVING M	2LT	0-1638604	0644	2
STRAUGHAN MILLETT A	1LT	0-0412164	0747	2
STRAUGHN CHARLES E	MAJ	0-2019451	0763	2
STRAUS FRANCIS H	MAJ	0-0445483	0645	2
STRAUS MAURICE L	CPT	0-0319290	0146	2
STRAUSER PEARL B	CW3	V-0700055	0764	1
STRAUSS CHARLES	MAJ	0-1951448	0665	1
STRAUSS DANIEL J	MAJ	0-0478822	1147	1
STRAUSS EMANUEL M	LTC	0-0460005	1062	1
STRAUSS HARRY H	MAJ	0-1321676	0761	1
STRAUSS LEROY J	1LT	0-1341196	0553	2
STRAUSS MACK	LTC	0-1598516	1165	1
STRAUSS ROBERT W	CPT	0-0389216	1146	1
STRAUSS ROGER F	LTC	0-0921189	0164	3
STRAUSSER ELWOOD L	1LT	0-1296285	0544	2
STRAW JR RAYMOND K	MAJ	0-1183199	0263	1
STRAW LEO S	LTC	0-0321591	0863	3
STRAW RALSTON	CW4	W-2147676	1167	1
STRAW RICHARD S	LTC	0-0274889	0866	3
STRAW RUTH B	1LT	N-0731780	0246	1
STRAWBRIDGE GEORGE T	LTC	0-1305667	0763	1
STRAWHORN JOHN C	MAJ	0-1686508	1164	2
STRAWN ARTHUR H	CPT	0-0918402	0844	2
STRAWN BUFORD T	LTC	0-0264684	0466	3
STRAWN GEORGE M	LTC	0-0451249	0258	1
STRAWN LEO S	COL	0-0182233	1155	3
STRAWN THOMAS F	LTC	0-0475338	1067	3
STRAWN WILLIS G	MAJ	0-0541236	1063	1
STRAWTHER WILLIAM H	CPT	0-1342129	0561	1
STRAZICICH EMILE J	LTC	0-1165344	1158	1
STREAM CHARLES T	MAJ	0-1684929	0862	1
STREB ROBERT C	MAJ	0-0291099	1066	3
STREBEL FRANK R	CPT	0-1310895	0546	2
STREBIG GLENN K	CW3	W-2141729	1060	1
STRECK EDWIN P	COL	0-0325104	1154	3
STRECKER EDWARD H	MAJ	0-1037325	0267	1
STRECKER JOHN M	2LT	0-1116425	0245	2
STRECKER WERNER C	COL	0-0211961	0755	3
STREET GLENN M	LTC	0-0330171	0657	3
STREET IRL H	MAJ	0-1299815	0157	1
STREET JOHN E	MAJ	0-0501251	0958	1
STREET LAWRENCE W	LTC	0-0350065	0849	1
STREET PAUL J	CPT	0-2263176	0661	1
STREET PHILIP F	LTC	0-0278552	1063	3
STREET SAMUEL S	LTC	0-0143281	0457	3
STREET WILLIAM A	LTC	0-1001059	0962	1
STREET WILLIAM G	CPT	0-1290361	0646	2
STREETER DANIEL D	LTC	0-0135631	0648	3
STREETER GEORGE A	CPT	0-1577919	1053	1
STREETER MARVIN L	1LT	0-0322801	0861	1
STREETER THEODORE	MAJ	0-0286269	0361	1
STREETMAN WILLIAM J	LTC	0-0450855	0459	2
STREETT ANNE F	MAJ	N-0761593	0246	1
STREETT WILLIAM L	LTC	0-1951563	1166	1
STREHL ROBERT M	1LT	0-1017791	1045	2
STREHLE MALCOLM L	CPT	0-0314598	0162	1
STREHLE WILBUR J	CW3	W-2145084	1057	1
STREHLOW JR HERMAN F	LTC	0-0258884	0964	3
STREHLOW LOUIS H	COL	0-0454819	0163	1
STREIBIG JR FRANK J	COL	0-0206158	0653	1
STREICHER HERMAN J	COL	0-0297955	0147	2
STREICHER WILHELM G	CPT	0-0380653	0746	1
STREIDL WALTER R	MAJ	0-1545418	0958	1
STRENNER JR STEVEN	LTC	0-1294555	0560	1
STRETCH GEORGE L	1LT	0-0123972	0253	3
STRETCH JAMES J	LTC	0-1795004	0863	1
STRETCHER JOHN P	MAJ	0-0401426	0447	2
STREUBER DOUGLAS W	CPT	0-1545210	0567	1
STREYCKMANS FELIX B	COL	0-0194449	0663	3
STRIBLING ANDREW C	MAJ	0-0201298	0849	3
STRIBLING FRED D	COL	0-0151654	1154	3
STRIBLING JR C R	LTC	0-0156524	0157	3
STRIBLING ROSS M	LTC	0-0260406	0767	3
STRIBLING SAM G	LTC	0-0918050	0864	3
STRICK JACOB	CPT	0-1690336	0146	2
STRICKER FRANK W	CW2	W-2143550	0158	1
STRICKER JOSEPH H	CPT	0-0502107	0447	1
STRICKLAND CADE	MAJ	0-1919855	0367	2
STRICKLAND CHARLES S	MAJ	0-1014031	0661	2
STRICKLAND EMMA P	1LT	N-0744851	1045	1
STRICKLAND ERNEST H	CW3	W-2142612	0465	1
STRICKLAND FRANK Z	LTC	0-0491595	0555	1
STRICKLAND HARRY G	LTC	0-1821926	1060	1
STRICKLAND HENRY H	MAJ	0-0205544	0248	2
STRICKLAND HUNTER A	MAJ	0-0238591	0466	3
STRICKLAND JAMES M	CW3	W-2207389	0462	1
STRICKLAND JESSE C	LTC	0-0395661	0764	1
STRICKLAND JOE R	1LT	0-0200607	0257	3
STRICKLAND JOHN H	WO1	W-2121001	0445	2
STRICKLAND JR OLIE A	MAJ	0-1055471	0161	1
STRICKLAND MARVIN A	CW2	W-2142905	1057	1
STRICKLAND ROBERT L	COL	0-0105842	0849	3
STRICKLAND ROBERT T	CPT	0-2017922	1160	1
STRICKLAND ROY W	COL	0-0322401	0152	1
STRICKLAND RUFUS K	LTC	0-1113005	0766	1
STRICKLAND SAMUEL C	CPT	0-0491178	0748	1
STRICKLAND SAMUEL H	COL	0-0274652	0561	3
STRICKLAND SHELLEY T	1LT	0-1304316	0547	2
STRICKLAND TOM E	MAJ	0-0887492	0860	1
STRICKLAND WEYMAN L	MAJ	0-0258694	1063	3
STRICKLER DANIEL B	M G	0-0101518	0557	3
STRICKLER HUGH	MAJ	0-1688830	1163	1
STRICKLER PHILIP A	LTC	0-1292246	0460	1
STRICKLER STAUFFER J	MAJ	0-0348887	1161	1
STRICKLIN HENRY C	1LT	0-1702754	1152	1
STRICKLIN L T	MAJ	0-0531896	0856	1
STRICKLIN SOLOMON F	CW3	W-2146618	0964	1
STRIDER FRANK E	MAJ	0-2026047	0763	1
STRIEBY JAMES N	LTC	0-1552998	0862	1
STRIEGEL JOHN L	LTC	0-1319676	1162	1
STRIEPLING JOHN A	2LT	0-1644828	0245	2
STRIGHT ROBERT M	MAJ	0-1054831	0766	1
STRIKE CLARENCE E	MAJ	0-1693106	0762	1
STRIKE WILLIAM J	LTC	0-1798817	0265	1
STRILEY WAYNE A	LTC	0-1646041	0762	1
STRIMPLE GEORGE R	MAJ	0-1643375	0357	1
STRINE CHARLES W	LTC	0-0273702	1066	3
STRINGER HENRY H	WO1	W-2146285	1056	1
STRINGER JOHN L	LTC	0-0439327	0262	1
STRINGER RALPH E	LTC	0-0120357	1055	3
STRINGFELLOW BERTIE	MAJ	0-0368222	0960	1
STRINGFIELD WILLIAM	MAJ	0-1699972	0461	1
STRINGHAM DONALD R	LTC	0-0232555	1156	3
STRIPLING JOHN L	LTC	0-1042179	0564	1
STRIPLING LEWIS	WO1	W-2108970	0165	1
STRITZLER CONRAD	MAJ	0-1689856	0147	2
STROBEL ALICE C	2LT	N-0725744	1044	1
STROBEL LAWRENCE A	COL	0-0253033	0566	3

NAME	GRADE	SVC NO	DATE RET MO YR	RET CODE
STROBEL RUDOLPH W	LTC	0-0322053	0566	3
STROBEL WILLIAM J	CW3	W-2204982	0167	1
STROBL CATHERINE	LTC	L-0711954	0566	1
STROBL WALTER M	MAJ	0-1322658	0960	1
STROBLE CHARLES R	MAJ	0-1926332	1064	1
STROBLE JR CHARLES P	CPT	0-0390702	0146	2
STROCK ALEX	1LT	0-0963304	0354	2
STROCK MOSES S	COL	0-0423087	1161	3
STRODE EDWARD M	COL	0-0294610	1157	2
STRODERO WILBERT J	CW3	W-2153011	0463	1
STROEBEL GEORGE J	MAJ	0-0957652	0962	2
STROEBELE HERMAN A	LTC	0-0518513	0763	1
STROHBEHM DOUGLAS W	1LT	0-1030424	0246	2
STROHECKER SAMUEL	COL	0-0238936	1060	3
STROHM JOHN G	COL	0-0141335	0648	3
STROHN ALBERT L	LTC	0-0355077	1060	1
STROHSCHEIN CARL	1LT	0-1686511	1046	2
STROLLO MARIO G	1LT	0-1174159	0153	2
STROM CARL J	1LT	0-1317576	0645	2
STROM CHARLES H	1LT	0-1315235	0346	2
STROM EDWARD T	CPT	0-0921605	0945	2
STROM ELMER A	COL	0-0232150	0463	3
STROM HJALMER R	LTC	0-0279773	0151	1
STROM VICTOR E	LTC	0-1283163	0461	2
STROMBERG DONALD C	MAJ	0-1105212	0347	1
STROME GRANT U	CPT	0-0119786	0648	3
STROMGREN LLOYD W	LTC	0-1106516	0461	1
STROMME ADOLPH K	LTC	0-1304814	0867	3
STROMMEN ARTHUR K	LTC	0-0278690	0664	3
STROMMEN THEODORE A	CPT	0-0265745	0146	2
STROMSTED ARTHUR R	CW2	W-2108729	0553	1
STROMWALL EDGAR A	CPT	0-0127722	0648	3
STRONG BILLY G	MAJ	0-1296603	0661	1
STRONG CHESTER A	CW4	W-2102437	0755	1
STRONG CHESTER E	CW2	W-2142283	1155	1
STRONG CLARA C	1LT	N-0726501	0146	1
STRONG CLAUDE W	LTC	0-0401996	0560	1
STRONG DAVID A	MAJ	0-2017143	0465	1
STRONG EARLE R	CPT	0-0113776	0558	3
STRONG GILES H	MAJ	0-0218309	1152	3
STRONG JAMES D	COL	0-0275668	0459	1
STRONG JOY B	LTC	0-0258314	0557	1
STRONG JR HENRY	WO1	W-2148232	1055	1
STRONG RALPH M	CPT	0-1042720	0561	1
STRONG ROBERT B	COL	0-0230343	1162	3
STRONG WARD R	COL	0-0257217	0763	3
STRONG WILLIAM G	CW3	W-2147529	0664	1
STROOBAND CHARLES E	LTC	0-1169356	0363	1
STROOTMAN RALPH E	LTC	0-0460586	0865	1
STROSNIDER GEORGE U	LTC	0-0494669	1162	1
STROSS WALTER C	2LT	0-0482722	1144	2
STROTHER RALPH D	CW2	W-2106598	0860	2
STROUBE ESTHEL E	WO1	W-2139766	1050	2
STROUD DAVID V	MAJ	0-0993062	0164	1
STROUD GEORGE H	LTC	0-0147074	0358	3
STROUD JOSEPH D	MAJ	0-1886140	0866	1
STROUD MARVIN F	CW2	W-2147116	0956	2
STROUD ROBERT F	LTC	0-1302226	0962	1
STROUD ROBERT L	MAJ	0-0333587	1059	3
STROUD ROGER C	MAJ	0-0305402	0567	3
STROUD ROLAND R	LTC	0-1169357	0861	2
STROUDE GILBERT M	MAJ	0-0989384	0266	1
STROUP CECIL H	LTC	0-0239210	0564	3
STROUP CLARENCE S	LTC	0-0188524	0455	3
STROUP DONALD G	CPT	0-1534873	1047	2
STROUPE HOWARD E	1LT	0-0544148	1045	2
STROUSE CARL H	LTC	0-1171383	0962	1
STROUSE ROBERT L	MAJ	0-1062084	0864	1
STRUB DANIEL E	MAJ	0-1924099	0964	1
STRUB HARRY	CW2	W-2152840	0961	1
STRUBEL CLARENCE	2LT	0-1877302	0359	2
STRUBEL WAYNE A	2LT	0-2049407	0545	2
STRUBEL WILLIAM E	LTC	0-1316794	0764	1
STRUBILLA VICTOR S	CW2	W-2149373	1059	2
STRUBLE CLARENCE E	CPT	0-1636713	0158	1

NAME	GRADE	SVC NO	DATE RET MO YR	RET CODE
STRUBLE GILBERT C	COL	0-0275359	1266	3
STRUCEL BERT J	LTC	0-1328766	0167	1
STRUCK CAROLINE K	2LT	N-0700182	0239	1
STRUCK FREDERICK	CPT	0-1165045	0446	2
STRUCKMEYER JR F C	1LT	0-1298952	0945	2
STRUEWING WILFRED H	MAJ	0-1342402	0763	1
STRUM WILLIE C	COL	0-0275531	0859	3
STRUNESKI JOSEPH F	MAJ	0-1636714	0859	1
STRUSINSKI NICHOLA	LTC	0-0491240	1045	2
STRUTH JOSEPH F	CW4	W-2143057	0361	1
STRUYK ARIE R	2LT	0-1311939	1044	2
STRUZENSKI JOHN F	CPT	0-0201773	1156	3
STRYJEWSKI JOSEPH S	MAJ	0-1550276	0549	1
STRYKER HARRY R	LTC	0-0266440	0861	3
STUART BROOKS S	LTC	0-0227704	0664	3
STUART BURTON W	LTC	0-0479280	0754	1
STUART CHARLES C	MAJ	0-1549385	1160	2
STUART CHARLES P	MAJ	0-1183426	1158	1
STUART DONALD C	COL	0-0167636	1046	2
STUART DOROTHY A	2LT	N-0783290	0445	1
STUART FREDRIC W	MAJ	0-0283353	0361	3
STUART GEORGE D	MAJ	0-0170751	0956	3
STUART GILBERT K	MAJ	0-0955275	0366	1
STUART HARRY A	LTC	0-1638618	0667	1
STUART HARRY M	WO1	W-2129948	0753	1
STUART HUGH L	MAJ	0-2008253	0865	1
STUART JACK F	CW3	W-2152937	1163	1
STUART JOE V	MAJ	0-0475960	0348	1
STUART JOHN A	CPT	0-0277925	0161	3
STUART JOHN B	MAJ	0-0751573	1064	1
STUART NORMAN C	CW3	W-2206385	1064	1
STUART OMAR G	LTC	0-0294904	0967	3
STUART PAUL W	LTC	0-0350105	0661	1
STUART PERCY E	LTC	0-1824530	0463	2
STUART ROBERT F	CPT	0-0552796	1047	2
STUART ROBERT I	LTC	0-0261959	0167	3
STUART ROBERT M	LTC	0-1289006	0363	1
STUART ROBERT T	MAJ	0-0384243	1061	1
STUART RUSSELL W	MAJ	0-0323952	0165	3
STUART THOMAS E	MAJ	0-1824935	0962	1
STUART WENDELL A	CPT	0-1057281	0960	1
STUART WILBERT E	1LT	0-0394859	1143	2
STUART WILLIAM P	LTC	0-1598873	1167	1
STUART WILLOUGHBY	COL	0-0266233	0466	3
STUART-DUBERG J C	1LT	0-0495707	0944	2
STUBBLEBINE BEULAH	MAJ	N-0901994	0566	2
STUBBLEFIELD H I	COL	0-0216105	0757	3
STUBBLEFIELD JAMES P	CPT	0-0924879	0844	2
STUBBS ARCHIE F	LTC	0-0351605	0467	1
STUBBS BEVERLY W	MAJ	0-2206008	0466	1
STUBBS CHARLES A	LTC	0-0263207	1163	3
STUBBS CHARLES F	CW2	RW-2150620	0763	1
STUBBS DANIEL W	MAJ	0-0370544	0661	1
STUBBS DONALD W A	MAJ	0-1636715	1057	1
STUBBS JAMES R	MAJ	0-0355933	1044	1
STUBBS JOHN H	LTC	0-1003050	0662	1
STUBBS JOSEPH J	LTC	0-0177270	0560	3
STUBBS ROBERT E	MAJ	0-0385721	1156	1
STUBBS WILLIAM E	LTC	0-0198057	0456	3
STUBE CHARLES K	CPT	0-1301707	0946	2
STUBENRCD WILLIAM G	MAJ	0-2010482	1062	1
STUBER JUNIOR W	MAJ	0-1014934	1264	1
STUBERT CLARENCE E	1LT	0-1998470	1046	2
STUBLER JOHN N	LTC	0-0205383	0858	3
STUCK VERNON M	MAJ	0-1950935	0963	1
STUCKART JOAN M	2LT	N-0759949	0545	1
STUCKART PAUL G	MAJ	0-1638619	0561	1
STUCKEY AL H	LTC	0-0350057	0462	1
STUCKEY ALEXANDER	CW2	RW-2141088	0565	1
STUCKEY IRA H	MAJ	0-0304749	1167	3
STUCKEY LYLE E	LTC	0-0235372	0760	3
STUCKMEYER WILLIAM	LTC	0-1030192	0361	1
STUCKWISCH LEONHARDT	MAJ	0-0524246	0466	3
STUDDARD WOODROW	CW3	W-2144318	1159	1
STUDEBAKER GEORGE W	COL	0-0198737	0154	1

NAME	GRADE	SVC NO	DATE RET MO YR	RET CODE
STUDER BERTRAM J	1LT	0-2263491	0554	2
STUDER JOHN F	LTC	0-0153010	1156	3
STUDER MAGNUS P	MAJ	0-1897744	0360	1
STUDER WESLEY P	1LT	0-0452476	1043	2
STUDLEY FRED M	LTC	0-0508462	0766	1
STUDWELL JOHN R	COL	0-0180413	0756	3
STUDY EARL H	COL	0-0444897	0865	3
STUEBE LOUIS F	B G	0-0170245	1059	3
STUEBEN EDMUND B	CPT	0-0408627	1045	2
STUELKE THERON R	LTC	0-0280520	0446	2
STUESSY EUGENE F	CPT	0-1038497	0846	2
STUFFLEBEAM WILBUR H	LTC	0-0291744	0161	1
STUFFLEBEAN JOHN H	1LT	0-0445866	1143	2
STUHRMAN JERRY	LTC	0-1313320	0865	1
STUKEY RAYMOND G	CPT	0-1824246	0347	1
STULL AINSLEE J	CW2	W-2207294	0759	2
STULL CHARLES W	LTC	0-1550064	0561	1
STULL HAROLD C	LTC	0-0199102	0648	3
STULL RAYMOND L	MAJ	0-1039938	1160	1
STULL ROBERT A	CPT	0-0176744	0355	3
STULL ROBERT K	LTC	0-0388769	0966	1
STULTS ROBERT L	CW4	W-2146286	0967	1
STULTS ROY	CW2	W-2106164	0464	1
STULTZ JOSEPH B	CW2	W-2148819	0557	1
STULTZ JR BAILEY G	MAJ	0-1583734	0660	1
STULTZ OLIVER V	WO1	W-2123036	0152	1
STUMBAUGH LEO A	MAJ	0-1016316	0762	1
STUMBAUGH LYLE H	1LT	0-1178357	1145	2
STUMP CLAUD W	MAJ	0-0222502	1047	2
STUMP EDWARD B	CW2	W-2147520	0263	1
STUMP LEROY C	MAJ	0-0370117	0761	1
STUMP ROBERT M	COL	0-0263852	0662	3
STUMP WILLIAM B	LTC	0-1598703	0166	1
STUMPF ANDREW	CW3	W-2143649	0364	1
STUMPO GAETANO J	CW3	W-2144633	0562	1
STUPPLE ALFRED E	1LT	0-1923564	1057	2
STURDIVANT C W	LTC	0-0376912	0246	2
STURDIVANT WILLIS P	CPT	0-0497751	1046	1
STURGEON JR JAMES H	CPT	0-1322505	0746	1
STURGEON ROBERT C	LTC	0-0266650	0861	3
STURGES EDWARD E	2LT	0-1586251	0544	2
STURGES GEORGE R	COL	0-0174892	0648	3
STURGILL DORAN R	CW2	W-2139636	0455	1
STURGIS FLORENCE M	1LT	N-0726821	0546	1
STURGIS JOHN E	LTC	0-0283841	0165	3
STURGIS JR DUDLEY C	MAJ	0-0341292	0647	2
STURGIS JR JAMES F	LTC	0-0974119	0766	2
STURGIS JR NORMAN R	CPT	0-1182270	0947	1
STURKEN FRANK	MAJ	0-0464830	0246	1
STURM CHARLES F	LTC	0-0424989	0966	1
STURM EMET L	1LT	0-0252880	0356	3
STURM JOSEPH M	MAJ	0-1556810	1154	1
STURM LOUIS P	CPT	0-0505665	0154	1
STURMAN HARRY H	1LT	0-0522792	0445	2
STURMAN OLIVE M H	1LT	N-0735890	0648	1
STURMAN ROLAND B	COL	0-0378886	0762	1
STURROCK ALAN L	1LT	0-1583735	0444	2
STURTEVANT JR LEVI W	MAJ	0-1648720	0461	1
STURTEVANT ROSS H	CPT	0-2042956	0762	2
STURZL BUDD F	LTC	0-1167243	0760	1
STUTEVILLE CLYDE D	CPT	0-0519426	1146	2
STUTEVOSS JAMES F	LTC	0-0141878	1053	2
STUTMAN LOUIS E	LTC	0-1311549	0562	1
STUTMAN MARTIN H	1LT	0-1294929	0852	1
STUTSMAN WILLIAM O	1LT	0-1582180	0247	1
STUTTS JOHN R	LTC	0-0346386	0960	1
STUTTS ROBERT T	MAJ	0-0249082	0167	3
STUTZ RUDOLPH R	CPT	0-1555478	0859	1
STUTZ SHERWOOD S	MAJ	0-1685521	0961	1
STUTZMAN JR FLETCHER	MAJ	0-0998140	0667	1
STUURMANS ANNA	CPT	L-0902781	1263	1
STYLE KENNETH S	MAJ	0-1643378	0862	1
STYLER MICHAEL	MAJ	0-2055481	0367	3
STYLES ALBERT W	1LT	0-1319678	0446	2
STYRON DAVID F	2LT	0-1595856	0545	2

NAME	GRADE	SVC NO	DATE RET MO YR	RET CODE
STYRON JAMES C	M G	0-0177742	0658	3
SUAREZ JOHN H	CW2	W-2122038	1046	1
SUAREZ JOHN M	CW2	W-2205379	1262	1
SUBERS SPENCER C	LTC	0-0269981	0667	3
SUCH JOSEPH F	CPT	0-0498447	0744	1
SUCHANEK JOHN A	MAJ	0-0913300	0363	1
SUCHARA THADDEUS W	LTC	0-1309434	0660	1
SUCHIER OSCAR A	LTC	0-1287617	0261	1
SUCHMINSKI JOHN C	MAJ	0-0139877	0257	3
SUCHY RAYMOND W	2LT	0-0503716	1045	2
SUDDATH PAUL R	MAJ	0-1300103	0962	1
SUDDERTH JAMES A	LTC	0-1310947	0766	1
SUDDETH VERNON T	MAJ	0-0194279	0956	3
SUDERMAN BERYL D	CPT	0-1102075	0549	1
SUDMAN EMIL W	CPT	0-0252637	1059	3
SUDMAN GLENN F	LTC	0-0916308	0546	2
SUDNICK NORMAN E	CPT	0-1536512	0365	2
SUE JULIAN D	LTC	0-0394831	0860	1
SUENKEL WILLIAM J	LTC	0-1019292	0765	1
SUESS HERBERT R	LTC	0-1580391	0662	1
SUESZ ROBERT W	CW3	W-2146493	0863	1
SUFFECOOL WILSON L	LTC	0-1641002	0361	1
SUFFIELD VANCE P	1LT	0-0431747	0244	1
SUFKA ANDREW P	LTC	0-1326783	0264	1
SUGARMAN JOSEPH R	LTC	0-0336633	0545	2
SUGARS RICHARD H	LTC	0-1288325	0367	1
SUGARS WILLIAM J	CPT	0-2033812	0656	2
SUGEL WILLIAM J	MAJ	0-1324256	0756	1
SUGG ANDREW I	CPT	0-0232579	0-51	3
SUGGS JOHN P	CPT	0-0548810	0264	1
SUGGS ROBERT E	MAJ	0-1293146	0561	1
SUGIYAMA YONE J	MAJ	0 1338151	0261	1
SUHAR JOHN	MAJ	0-1286029	1047	2
SUHR ARNOLD W	CPT	0-0344700	1045	2
SUHR JEROME W	LTC	0-0327158	0460	1
SUHRE MAURICE E	LTC	0-0280057	0764	3
SUHUSKE JOHN J	MAJ	0-1298150	0758	1
SUIT PAUL C	MAJ	0-0975806	0961	1
SUITER LEO F	MAJ	0-2097014	0964	1
SUITER LUTHER	CPT	0-0333936	1046	2
SUITS WINFORD	MAJ	0-0236919	0252	3
SUITT THOMAS N	MAJ	0-1015302	1263	1
SUKIENNIK STAZY J	LTC	0-0354479	0160	2
SULAK STANLEY A	CPT	0-1171003	1264	1
SULEK ARTHUR E	LTC	0-0345073	0448	2
SULKOWSKI MARY A	2LT	N-0764576	1145	1
SULLENGER WILBUR C	1LT	0-1296931	0845	2
SULLEY WILLIAM F	CW2	W-2149720	0359	1
SULLINGER CARL O	LTC	0-1044690	1262	1
SULLIVAN ADAM	LTC	0-0326750	0754	1
SULLIVAN AGNES P	1LT	N-0731417	0445	1
SULLIVAN AMBROSE J	MAJ	0-0359647	0145	2
SULLIVAN ANN M	2LT	N-0754360	0946	1
SULLIVAN ANNE KITEC	2LT	N-0721059	1144	1
SULLIVAN AUGUSTINE	CW2	W-2101104	0146	2
SULLIVAN BARRY A	CPT	0-1010241	0561	2
SULLIVAN BENJAMIN E	COL	0-0357950	0963	3
SULLIVAN CAMILLUS C	LTC	0-0206688	0661	3
SULLIVAN CARL O	MAJ	0-1798083	1060	1
SULLIVAN CHARLES M	MAJ	0-0253694	0157	3
SULLIVAN CORNELIUS	MAJ	0-1922502	0862	1
SULLIVAN DANIEL M	LTC	0-0202343	0862	3
SULLIVAN DANIEL P	MAJ	0-1014129	0662	1
SULLIVAN DANIEL P	MAJ	0-2262100	0864	1
SULLIVAN DAVID H	MAJ	0-1924899	0166	1
SULLIVAN DAZZEL E	MAJ	0-1555916	1160	1
SULLIVAN DEMPSEY D	MAJ	0-1581406	0665	1
SULLIVAN DENNIS P	LTC	0-0184004	0453	3
SULLIVAN DONALD T	CPT	0-1177202	0248	2
SULLIVAN DORIS M	2LT	N-0733881	0345	1
SULLIVAN DOUGLAS E	2LT	0-1011360	0844	2
SULLIVAN EDMUND C	LTC	0-0422338	1263	1
SULLIVAN EDSON T	CPT	0-0512091	0153	1
SULLIVAN EDWARD P	MAJ	0-0426252	0546	2
SULLIVAN EDWIN J	1LT	0-1297116	0760	2

NAME	GRADE	SVC NO	DATE RET MO YR	RET CODE
SULLIVAN EDWIN W	LTC	0-0413913	0161	1
SULLIVAN ELIZABETH	2LT	N-0768948	0946	2
SULLIVAN ELMER	LTC	0-0267591	0565	3
SULLIVAN EUGENE F	1LT	0-2036256	114N	2
SULLIVAN FORREST K	CPT	0-1014123	0547	2
SULLIVAN FRANCIS C	MAJ	0-0194813	0862	3
SULLIVAN FRANCIS D	CPT	0-0468089	0747	1
SULLIVAN FRANCIS J	MAJ	0-0421441	0863	1
SULLIVAN FRANCIS X	1LT	0-0925572	0745	2
SULLIVAN FRANK T	MAJ	0-0198927	1054	3
SULLIVAN FREDERICK	LTC	0-0312389	1065	3
SULLIVAN FREDERICK	MAJ	0-1794879	0161	1
SULLIVAN GEORGE C	COL	0-0112334	1056	3
SULLIVAN GEORGE H	1LT	0-1040158	0544	2
SULLIVAN GERALD P	COL	0-0267260	1164	3
SULLIVAN GOODRICH M	COL	0-0342431	0864	3
SULLIVAN HARRY F	CW3	W-2153271	0965	1
SULLIVAN HARRY L	CPT	0-1037328	0745	2
SULLIVAN HARVEY G	LTC	0-0341698	0550	1
SULLIVAN HENRY	LTC	0-1549125	0361	2
SULLIVAN HENRY C	LTC	0-0547203	1165	1
SULLIVAN HENRY C	LTC	0-1687371	1266	3
SULLIVAN HENRY M	MAJ	0-1280073	0460	1
SULLIVAN HOBERT G	CW2	W-2213623	0767	1
SULLIVAN JAMES A	LTC	0-0283842	1060	1
SULLIVAN JAMES E	CPT	0-0422558	1046	2
SULLIVAN JAMES F	LTC	0-1172304	0561	1
SULLIVAN JAMES H	MAJ	0-0526406	0856	1
SULLIVAN JAMES J	LTC	0-0240639	0562	3
SULLIVAN JAMES W	CPT	0-1996518	0147	2
SULLIVAN JESSE A	LTC	0-0505100	1152	1
SULLIVAN JOHN C	LTC	0-0356656	0546	2
SULLIVAN JOHN D	LTC	0-0402933	0161	1
SULLIVAN JOHN E	MAJ	0-1103960	0561	1
SULLIVAN JOHN F	MAJ	0-2262830	0563	1
SULLIVAN JOHN H A	MAJ	0-0344301	1046	2
SULLIVAN JOHN J	2LT	0-0447819	0944	2
SULLIVAN JOHN J	2LT	0-1876116	0454	2
SULLIVAN JOHN J	LTC	0-2030585	0165	1
SULLIVAN JOHN J M C	CPT	0-0498516	1045	2
SULLIVAN JOHN J S	LTC	0-0502920	1060	1
SULLIVAN JOHN L	LTC	0-0343949	0560	1
SULLIVAN JOHN L	2LT	0-1324228	0545	2
SULLIVAN JOHN M	CW4	W-2111151	0858	1
SULLIVAN JOHN P	2LT	0-1000077	0743	2
SULLIVAN JOHN T	MAJ	0-2210050	1166	1
SULLIVAN JOSEPH C	MAJ	0-0429551	0347	1
SULLIVAN JOSEPH D	2LT	0-1310320	0445	2
SULLIVAN JOSEPH F	2LT	0-1999078	1045	2
SULLIVAN JOSEPH J	LTC	0-0388793	0546	2
SULLIVAN JOSEPH J	2LT	0-1111383	0145	2
SULLIVAN JOSEPH L	LTC	0-0299839	0865	3
SULLIVAN JR CLARKE	MAJ	0-1283868	0954	2
SULLIVAN JR DANIEL E	LTC	0-1055168	0763	1
SULLIVAN JR DANIEL L	LTC	0-1051404	0261	1
SULLIVAN JR JOHN F	MAJ	0-0324388	0148	1
SULLIVAN JR WILSON T	CW3	W-2119883	1263	1
SULLIVAN KENNETH H	MAJ	0-1110913	1055	1
SULLIVAN LAVERN E	WO1	W-2108000	0757	2
SULLIVAN LEO B	MAJ	0-0472357	0662	1
SULLIVAN LEONARD P	LTC	0-1296287	0865	1
SULLIVAN LOFTON D	CPT	0-0397275	0843	2
SULLIVAN LOREN W	LTC	0-0411447	0960	1
SULLIVAN MARTIN W	COL	0-0280424	1059	1
SULLIVAN MARY O V	1LT	N-0722781	0548	1
SULLIVAN MELVIN T	LTC	0-0330089	0567	3
SULLIVAN MICHAEL F	LTC	0-1575208	0462	1
SULLIVAN MICHAEL J	1LT	0-1914092	1135	1
SULLIVAN OLIVER J L	CW3	W-2151342	0163	1
SULLIVAN PATRICK D	MAJ	0-1638625	1060	1
SULLIVAN PATRICK R	LTC	0-0439165	1147	2
SULLIVAN PHILIP V	LTC	0-0931873	0665	1
SULLIVAN RALPH R	COL	0-0463035	1265	3
SULLIVAN RAYMOND J	1LT	0-0517030	0745	2
SULLIVAN RICHARD J	MAJ	0-0518527	0557	1
SULLIVAN RICHARD M	2LT	0-1575209	0145	2
SULLIVAN RICHARD P	LTC	0-0399856	0546	2
SULLIVAN ROBERT H	CPT	0-0493530	0647	1
SULLIVAN ROBERT J	1LT	0-0278450	0348	2
SULLIVAN ROBERT M	LTC	0-1100786	0962	1
SULLIVAN ROBERT W	LTC	0-1550933	0363	1
SULLIVAN SAMUEL T	LTC	0-1081181	0665	1
SULLIVAN STANLEY L	LTC	0-0212137	0450	1
SULLIVAN THOMAS D	CW3	W-2141793	0158	1
SULLIVAN THOMAS E	CW3	W-2207110	0767	1
SULLIVAN THOMAS F	LTC	0-1011898	0966	1
SULLIVAN VINCENT J	MAJ	0-1044119	1060	1
SULLIVAN WALTER A	MAJ	0-1948835	0261	2
SULLIVAN WALTER M E	COL	0-0233344	0553	2
SULLIVAN WILBER H	MAJ	0-0300728	0245	1
SULLIVAN WILLIAM B	MAJ	0-1635391	0361	1
SULLIVAN WILLIAM E	CW2	W-2151733	0264	1
SULLIVAN WILLIAM F	LTC	0-0243365	0566	3
SULLIVAN WILLIAM F	MAJ	0-1183203	1164	1
SULLIVAN WILLIAM H	CPT	0-0963659	0759	1
SULLIVAN WILLIAM J	LTC	0-1012504	1262	1
SULLIVAN WILLIAM M	LTC	0-1103430	0767	1
SULLIVAN WILLIAM P	1LT	0-1310648	1145	2
SULLIVAN WILLIAM T	MAJ	0-0311998	1144	2
SULLIVAN WILLIAM W	LTC	0-0384485	0966	3
SULOFF SIDNEY E	LTC	0-0168868	0444	2
SULT EDWARD T	CW4	W-2114212	1154	1
SULTAN ERNEST H	CPT	0-0464071	0744	2
SULTZER MORTON	COL	0-0135636	0749	3
SULZBACH WILBUR H	MAJ	0-0240433	0165	3
SUMAN HERBERT A	LTC	0-0276178	0950	3
SUMARAGA ERNESTO	1LT	0-1896913	1161	2
SUMBRY 3RD AUSTIN	WO1	W-2142433	0952	2
SUMEK EDWARD J	MAJ	0-0837220	1266	1
SUMM ALVIN L	MAJ	0-1589644	1160	1
SUMMARELL RUFUS R	LTC	0-1580393	0967	1
SUMMER DAVID	MAJ	0-0339072	104N	1
SUMMER ELBY H	CW2	W-2147300	0755	2
SUMMER ROGER W	CW3	W-2141919	1057	1
SUMMER WILLIAM C	COL	0-0251775	0762	3
SUMMERFIELD MAX H	LTC	0-0127231	0754	3
SUMMERHAYS JOHN W	LTC	0-0290468	0750	3
SUMMERHILL ROBERT J	CW3	W-2145518	0859	1
SUMMERILL C W L	MAJ	0-0298740	1144	2
SUMMERLOT ROBERT L	MAJ	0-1317352	0663	1
SUMMERS BYRON P	MAJ	0-1513208	0157	1
SUMMERS CHARLES A	LTC	0-0247454	0664	3
SUMMERS CHARLES F	MAJ	0-2263085	0767	1
SUMMERS CHARLES F	CW3	W-2152690	0665	1
SUMMERS FRANKLIN L	COL	0-0118096	0652	1
SUMMERS GEORGE	CW3	W-2145782	0161	1
SUMMERS GEORGE C	LTC	0-0369800	1165	3
SUMMERS HARRISON C	2LT	0-0887964	1045	2
SUMMERS JOHN R	1LT	0-1304286	0646	2
SUMMERS JR GEORGE E	MAJ	0-1643379	1060	1
SUMMERS JR LEONARD	CPT	0-0527866	0846	2
SUMMERS LILLIE C	MAJ	N-0758727	0465	2
SUMMERS NELLIE G	1LT	N-0780393	0148	1
SUMMERS ROBERT E	MAJ	0-2019389	0765	1
SUMMEY JAMES C	LTC	0-0450658	0255	1
SUMMITT BUREN L	2LT	0-0496797	0645	1
SUMMITT KENNETH A	1LT	0-1032053	0645	2
SUMNER HANSFORD A	CW2	W-2152329	0161	1
SUMNER HARRIS C	COL	0-0382490	1060	1
SUMNER JOSEPH G	LTC	0-2037102	1165	1
SUMNER JR F S	MAJ	0-1586257	0547	2
SUMNER MARK	COL	0-0228995	0464	3
SUMNER RAYMOND A	CW2	W-2205304	1063	1
SUMNERS RAY H	1LT	0-1031979	0459	1
SUMPTER JR LEE R	LTC	0-0364477	0660	1
SUMRALL EDDIE F	CPT	0-2289191	0862	1
SUMRALL HENDRI A	MAJ	0-1876967	0265	1
SUNDAHL ALBERT H	CPT	0-0156191	0744	2
SUNDAL EDNA M	1LT	N-0730094	1147	1
SUNDAY HENRY V	MAJ	0-1179641	0361	1
SUNDAY IRA E	LTC	0-0451343	0757	1
SUNDAY JANE W	2LT	N-0769735	1046	1
SUNDBERG LYNDON A	LTC	0-0380787	0757	1
SUNDE ELVEN	MAJ	0-0981442	0662	1
SUNDELL ROYAL D	MAJ	0-0117761	0452	3
SUNDERLAGE WILLIAM E	MAJ	0-0958662	0764	1
SUNDERLAND JOSEPH L	2LT	0-1325531	1044	2
SUNDERMAN GEORGE H	COL	0-0221825	0648	3
SUNDERMAN JACK J	LTC	0-1100359	1163	1
SUNDET LYLE J	LTC	0-0342301	0858	2
SUNDHEIMER THOMAS A	1LT	0-1318588	1045	1
SUNDSTROM VINCENT B	LTC	0-0446130	0466	3
SUNDT MARTIN C	CPT	0-0170419	0555	3
SUNDWALL EDWARD N	2LT	0-1320978	0945	2
SUNDY ROBERT C	LTC	0-0505177	0357	1
SUNNER CURTIS L	CW2	W-2136720	0963	1
SUNSERI ANTHONY J	1LT	0-1302227	0450	1
SUOJANEN ANNE A	2LT	N-0759430	0345	1
SUPENSKY JOHN A	COL	0-0173637	0859	1
SUPERNAW NOEL R	1LT	0-0485269	0453	1
SUPLEMENTO JEROME O	1LT	0-2032109	0450	1
SUPONCIC JOSEPH P	CW4	W-2127888	0658	1
SUPPLE BERNARD P	MAJ	0-2097024	0766	1
SUPPLE LEO E	MAJ	0-0190662	0154	3
SUPPLEE CHARLES L	COL	0-0101241	0855	3
SURACI ALFRED J	LTC	0-0346092	1046	2
SURDYNSKI JOSEPH S	CPT	0-0978475	0262	1
SURGNER STANLEY G	LTC	0-0277543	0858	3
SURINE CLYDE J	CW4	W-2119650	1054	1
SURINGTON CYRIL T	COL	0-0319011	0167	3
SURKEIN ROBERT J	MAJ	0-1951261	0161	1
SURKIN NORMAN	LTC	0-2050370	0166	1
SURLES SR RICHARD H	MAJ	0-2202206	1265	1
SURLS JOSEPH K	COL	0-0199524	0546	2
SURMAIN ANDRE	1LT	0-1320158	0545	2
SURPRISE CHESTER P	1LT	0-1634383	0146	2
SURRATT CLELON M	LTC	0-1534396	0558	1
SURRATT ETHAN R	MAJ	0-0290095	1146	1
SUSBILLA FRANCISCO	1LT	0-1896706	0662	1
SUSKIN SAMUEL	CPT	0-0349158	0344	2
SUSKO MICHAEL J	MAJ	0-0474785	0647	1
SUSS IRVING D	CPT	0-1018896	0347	2
SUSSE JOHN E	COL	0-0264343	0957	3
SUSSELL SANFORD P	COL	0-0452364	1163	2
SUSSKIND GILBERT O	COL	0-0344533	0565	1
SUSSKY JOSEPH J	CW2	W-2148534	0558	1
SUSSMEIER RICHARD	CW2	W-2214630	0767	1
SUTER HORACE R	2LT	0-1309436	0744	2
SUTER JAMES E	CW2	RW-3430020	0466	1
SUTER WILLIAM R	CPT	0-1321072	0649	2
SUTERA SALVATORE	LTC	0-0302856	0264	1
SUTFIN HARRY E	WO1	W-2106811	0650	2
SUTFIN JUANITA G	MAJ	L-0401076	0467	1
SUTHERLAND ARTHUR E	COL	0-0237530	0362	3
SUTHERLAND CARL T	M G	0-0258676	0265	3
SUTHERLAND CHARLIE T	MAJ	0-0943863	1262	1
SUTHERLAND FRANK E	LTC	0-1323757	1062	1
SUTHERLAND GERTRUD	CPT	N-0755582	0348	1
SUTHERLAND HAROLD M	COL	0-0162545	0654	3
SUTHERLAND HAROLD M	CW2	W-2144320	1154	1
SUTHERLAND HENRY A	LTC	0-0265641	0466	3
SUTHERLAND JAMES D	MAJ	0-0241437	0265	3
SUTHERLAND JOHN A	LTC	0-0291264	0960	3
SUTHERLAND JOHN G	MAJ	0-1315529	1161	1
SUTHERLAND JOHN H	CPT	0-1289162	0661	1
SUTHERLAND JOSEPH E	CW4	W-2115850	0355	1
SUTHERLAND KENNETH R	LTC	0-1030842	1065	1
SUTHERLAND PAUL E	COL	0-0187350	0256	3
SUTHERLAND ROLAND W	1LT	0-0543146	0646	2
SUTHERLAND RUSSELL E	CPT	0-1030527	1153	2
SUTHERLAND WILLIAM B	LTC	0-1039237	1266	1
SUTHERLAND WILLIAM M	2LT	0-1109048	0544	2
SUTHERLIN LEE	COL	0-0119686	0749	3
SUTLEY ALFRED W	LTC	0-2208445	1067	1
SUTLIFF DONALD A	CW2	W-2108239	1052	2
SUTLIFF EDWARD H	MAJ	0-0137435	0250	3
SUTOR FRANK J	MAJ	0-1329410	0164	1
SUTORIK GEORGE J	LTC	0-1645417	0666	1
SUTPHIN HERMAN T	LTC	0-0498642	0954	1
SUTPHIN LEONA G	CPT	N-0703010	0545	1
SUTTER ERNEST M	1LT	0-0416968	0145	1
SUTTER MARTHA M	2LT	N-0700599	0637	1
SUTTER ROBERT L	1LT	0-0524362	1045	2
SUTTERFIELD W R	CPT	0-1294038	0556	1
SUTTERLIN FRANK W	MAJ	0-0530732	0846	2
SUTTLE JOHN F	CPT	0-0485162	0646	2
SUTTLE REID D	CW4	W-2136648	0865	1
SUTTLES JAMES C	LTC	0-1573610	0557	1
SUTTON ARTHUR M	CPT	0-0483986	0144	2
SUTTON CECILE A	1LT	N-0752632	0248	1
SUTTON EDWARD L	CPT	0-0362970	0746	2
SUTTON EVERETT G	LTC	0-1182469	1066	1
SUTTON FRANCIS O	CPT	0-1998036	0756	1
SUTTON FRANK W	LTC	0-0123037	0756	3
SUTTON GEORGE J	MAJ	0-1102974	0360	1
SUTTON GRANGER G	LTC	0-0185405	1162	3
SUTTON HAZEL D	CPT	N-0703319	0945	1
SUTTON JACK D	CPT	0-0383561	1145	1
SUTTON JAMES C	LTC	0-0188699	0657	3
SUTTON JAMES H	MAJ	0-1291194	0161	1
SUTTON JAMES H	MAJ	0-1308019	1159	1
SUTTON JEFF W	CPT	0-0499114	0954	1
SUTTON JOHN W	CPT	0-1944610	0947	2
SUTTON JOSEPH A	COL	0-0147980	1152	3
SUTTON JR ALBERT T	MAJ	0-0492766	0465	1
SUTTON JR RICHARD L	MAJ	0-0511361	0146	2
SUTTON JR WILLIAM B	MAJ	0-1341922	1266	1
SUTTON KENNETH L	1LT	0-0444961	0445	2
SUTTON LEONARD	CPT	0-1309437	0646	2
SUTTON LEVI W	1LT	0-1701921	0145	1
SUTTON OLIVER W	CW3	W-2152857	0763	1
SUTTON ROBERT F	MAJ	0-1925986	0966	1
SUTTON ROBERT H	MAJ	0-1599071	0262	1
SUTTON SEARS G	MAJ	0-1303411	0159	1
SUTTON SHERMAN L	CW3	W-2141794	1061	1
SUTTON SHERWOOD A	MAJ	0-0467828	0446	1
SUTTON WILLIAM	CPT	0-0505631	0145	1
SUYDAM JAMES H	COL	0-0304856	0947	2
SUYDAM JOHN H	LTC	0-1056568	1262	1
SUZUKAWA FRED F	MAJ	0-2030605	0464	1
SUZUKI TARO	MAJ	0-0242011	1146	2
SUZUKI TOSHIE T	MAJ	0-0942999	0264	1
SVEC JOSEPH R	LTC	0-0486224	0754	1
SVELA JACOB	1LT	0-0381763	0952	1
SVENDSEN GUSTAV	COL	0-0319319	0764	3
SVENSON HULDA	2LT	N-0700197	0737	1
SVEROLIK ABE A	LTC	0-0335194	0646	2
SVERDRUP LEIF J	M G	0-0129029	0358	3
SVEUN LYNN M	1LT	0-1181479	0846	2
SVIEN MYRON R	LTC	0-1081103	0467	1
SVIGALS FRED	LTC	0-0335535	1160	3
SVIRSKY HERMAN H	1LT	0-2102932	0664	2
SVITAK WILLIAM J	CW2	W-2205162	0461	2
SVITAVSKY LEO E	1LT	0-1288139	1144	2
SVITZER DOROTHY W	2LT	N-0798897	0847	1
SVOBODA ALBERT A	COL	0-0103865	0746	2
SVOBODA CHARLES V	CW4	W-2148417	0556	1
SVOBODA GEORGE W	COL	0-0313625	0167	1
SVOBODA HENRY	CW3	W-2146287	0157	1
SVOBODA LLOYD J	1LT	0-0550514	0146	2
SWABB FRED C	MAJ	0-1647747	0258	1
SWABEY WILLIAM A	CPT	0-0147979	1157	3
SWABON JR JOHN J	MAJ	0-1917941	0965	1
SWACK HARRY J	LTC	0-0289080	1153	1
SWAD CHARLES E	MAJ	0-1917820	0865	1
SWADELL ERIC E	LTC	0-0514896	1059	2
SWAFFORD EDWIN G	LTC	0-0207279	0862	3
SWAFFORD FRED G	LTC	0-0271962	0260	3
SWAFFORD PAUL C	COL	0-0229966	0660	1
SWAGERTY F CEDONIA	1LT	N-0779101	0845	1

NAME	GRADE	SVC NO	DATE RET MO YR	RET CODE
SWAGGERT REX J	CW2	W-2112140	0447	1
SWAGLER RUDYARD M	CPT	0-0428614	0746	1
SWAILS ARMSTRONG	CPT	0-0327127	C845	2
SWAILS FLOYD P	COL	0-0383550	0162	1
SWAIM JAMES C	1LT	0-1110279	0346	2
SWAIM LEBERT E	CPT	0-C359593	0745	2
SWAIM RALPH	2LT	C-1933558	0254	2
SWAIM WAYLAND A	1LT	0-0887611	0348	2
SWAIN EARL R	1LT	0-1579193	1058	1
SWAIN FRANK	CPT	0-1037329	C761	1
SWAIN GEORGE F	CPT	0-0986501	1060	1
SWAIN JAMES W	LTC	0-1051795	1063	1
SWAIN JR FRANK R	LTC	0-C234068	1263	3
SWAIN JR MILES	CW3	W-2144932	0462	1
SWAIN NELLIS C	MAJ	0-1648514	C755	1
SWAIN WILLIAM H	1LT	C-1559265	C847	2
SWALLOW JAMES F	CPT	0-1049364	1060	1
SWALLWELL JAMES	CW2	W-2152405	0760	1
SWAN EDWARD H	LTC	0-1013047	0467	1
SWAN FORREST	LTC	C-1110838	1262	2
SWAN GARTH V	2LT	0-0393943	1043	2
SWAN GEORGE E	CPT	0-1577925	1065	1
SWAN GEORGE F	LTC	0-1313817	1062	1
SWAN HARRY E	2LT	0-1314740	0744	2
SWAN HENRY T	COL	0-0241428	0159	3
SWAN JR ERVIN D	MAJ	0-0185109	0446	1
SWAN JR JAMES E	LTC	0-0239290	0665	3
SWAN PARK P	MAJ	0-1185694	0361	1
SWAN ULMONT	COL	0-0207388	1055	3
SWAN VERNER M	CPT	0-1756922	0849	1
SWAN VICTOR B	MAJ	0-1555638	1263	1
SWAN WILLIAM H	MAJ	0-0364014	1047	2
SWANBERG CHARLES M	CW3	W-2143694	1163	1
SWANBERG F C	MAJ	0-035089C	0446	1
SWANBOM ELMER E	MAJ	0-012977C	0553	3
SWANCARA ARNOLD L	CPT	0-0482507	0647	1
SWANEY ACY L	CPT	0-1684949	0161	1
SWANGO JOHN V	COL	0-1307326	1067	1
SWANK CHARLES W	LTC	C-0308472	0358	1
SWANK CHESTER L	MAJ	0-0503954	1047	2
SWANK CLARENCE E	1LT	0-1592642	0553	1
SWANKE CHRIST A	LTC	0-0493545	0657	1
SWANN EDGAR A	1LT	0-1287433	C344	2
SWANN EDMOND J	MAJ	C-0179166	0850	3
SWANN ERWIN L	CW4	W-2018795	1154	1
SWANN JEFFERSON	LTC	0-1179221	1062	1
SWANN JR LEONARD V	CPT	0-1081788	0361	1
SWANNER ORBY	MAJ	0-2206135	1266	1
SWANO ANTHONY G	CPT	0-0524467	0767	3
SWANSON ARTHUR	CPT	0-0504806	0845	2
SWANSON AUSTIN L	LTC	0-0347429	0860	1
SWANSON CARL E	LTC	0-0252185	0266	3
SWANSON CECIL V	MAJ	0-1646045	1263	1
SWANSON CHARLES E	LTC	0-0406354	C861	1
SWANSON DALE V	COL	0-0240321	1164	3
SWANSON EARL H	LTC	0-0133521	0656	3
SWANSON EDWIN E	CPT	0-0212880	0352	3
SWANSON EDWIN E	MAJ	0-0230013	0744	2
SWANSON EVERETT A	LTC	0-0213087	0761	3
SWANSON EVERETT M	MAJ	0-0224155	C345	2
SWANSON FRANK J C	MAJ	0-0276571	0156	3
SWANSON FREDERICK	COL	0-0119685	0648	3
SWANSON FREDERICK	LTC	0-0238356	0961	3
SWANSON GEORGE S	COL	0-0301519	0355	1
SWANSON GEORGE W E	CPT	0-1185833	C860	1
SWANSON GREGORY H	MAJ	0-1557098	0962	1
SWANSON HAROLD A	LTC	0-1105218	0767	3
SWANSON HARRY W	CW4	W-2124077	1154	1
SWANSON HENRY J	MAJ	0-2053964	0855	1
SWANSON HERBERT S	LTC	0-0279134	0855	3
SWANSON JOHN L	MAJ	0-1794880	1060	1
SWANSON KARL J	CW2	W-2146401	0158	1
SWANSON LEONARD E	CPT	0-0188659	0458	3
SWANSON LEONARD E	LTC	0-0240885	C858	3
SWANSON PAUL H	LTC	C-0174273	1160	3

NAME	GRADE	SVC NO	DATE RET MO YR	RET CODE
SWANSON RAYMOND J	CPT	0-028127C	0663	3
SWANSON RAYMOND J	1LT	0-2262579	0654	2
SWANSON RICHARD	COL	0-0255972	0156	3
SWANSON RUDOLPH	LTC	0-0309009	0954	1
SWANSON STEWART	CPT	0-2046470	0955	1
SWANSON THEODORE R	1LT	0-1173103	1059	1
SWANSON WILFRED O	LTC	0-1576714	0561	1
SWANSON WILLIAM T	COL	0-0275162	0648	3
SWANTEK MARJORIE A	2LT	N-0773032	0345	1
SWANWICK EVA R M	MAJ	N-0759190	1262	1
SWANWICK WILLIAM J	CW3	W-2103505	0963	1
SWANZ GEORGE J	CW2	W-2150763	0456	1
SWARBERG JOHN F	MAJ	0-1535542	0966	1
SWARNER JOHN L	LTC	0-0296843	0167	3
SWARRINGIM HOWARD W	1LT	0-2005316	1055	1
SWART MALCOLM R	CPT	0-0521097	1153	2
SWART MURL F	LTC	0-0284026	0957	3
SWARTHOUT JOSEPHINE	MAJ	N-0793982	0466	1
SWARTHOUT ROBERT E	MAJ	0-1688441	0665	1
SWARTHOUT SR GERARD	LTC	0-0267451	0556	3
SWARTHOUT WALTER E	LTC	0-0298624	0462	3
SWARTS CHARLES A	1LT	0-023346C	0648	3
SWARTSEL CHARLES V	MAJ	0-1165578	0954	1
SWARTZ CARLYLE O	LTC	0-1103562	0261	1
SWARTZ GEORGE J	MAJ	0-2032134	0263	1
SWARTZ GLENN E	LTC	0-0165651	0245	2
SWARTZ HARRY C	LTC	0-0333986	0265	3
SWARTZ JOHN L	CW3	W-2152631	0164	1
SWARTZ JOSEPH W	CPT	0-1643381	0746	2
SWARTZ MORRIS	LTC	0-0526299	0657	1
SWARTZ OLIVER H	LTC	0-0258497	1062	3
SWARTZ PETER W	CPT	0-0194302	0648	3
SWARTZ RALPH A	MAJ	0-1110839	0466	3
SWARTZ RALPH R	MAJ	0-0290046	0343	2
SWARTZ RICHARD H	1LT	0-1C56906	1145	2
SWARTZ RONALD R	MAJ	0-0408235	0957	1
SWARTZ SPENCER D	MAJ	0-0211881	0648	3
SWARTZ THOMAS S	MAJ	0-1118512	0960	1
SWARTZ WILEY R	1LT	0-1288326	1045	2
SWARTZELL CHARLES A	CPT	0-0957598	1160	1
SWASICK MAX E	LTC	0-1100789	0766	1
SWAST JOHN J	MAJ	0-1294218	0446	2
SWATEK MATHEW J	MAJ	0-0235227	0454	3
SWATKO MICHAEL R	LTC	0-1171789	1061	1
SWATOSH ROBERT B	LTC	0-0363057	0860	1
SWATTS ROBERT W	COL	0-0108006	0256	3
SWAVELY CHARLES A	MAJ	0-1107170	1160	1
SWAVELY STANLEY L	CW3	W-2143572	0464	1
SWAYZE KENNETH W	LTC	0-1175596	0763	1
SWAZEY VAUGHN R	MAJ	0-0452982	0758	1
SWEARENGIN HENRY F	WO1	W-2121018	1046	1
SWEARINGEN LLOYD E	COL	0-0192378	0857	3
SWEARINGEN ROBERT W	LTC	0-0492998	0665	2
SWEARINGEN WARREN W	MAJ	C-1593328	0557	1
SWEARINGEN WILLARD P	COL	0-0311312	1061	2
SWEARINGER HARRY P	CW3	W-2147459	0167	1
SWEASEY ARCHIE W	LTC	0-0166786	0157	3
SWEAT ERNEST L	LTC	0-0400004	0960	1
SWECKER EDWIN E	2LT	0-0929093	0645	2
SWEDBERG ARTHUR V	COL	0-0123924	0454	3
SWEDBERG CLARENCE H	LTC	0-0453154	0261	1
SWEDBERG WILLIAM A	CPT	0-042585C	0443	2
SWEDE ALLEN G	COL	0-0139385	0757	3
SWEELEY WILLIAM J	LTC	0-0309558	0760	3
SWEELY JOE W	LTC	0-1109053	0365	1
SWEEN ALFRED M	LTC	0-0359307	1152	3
SWEENEY ALAN F	CPT	0-1859672	0861	2
SWEENEY BERNARD J	MAJ	0-1638631	1150	1
SWEENEY CLAIR R	CPT	0-1797745	0164	2
SWEENEY DANIEL C	CPT	0-0243023	0458	3
SWEENEY EDWARD A	LTC	0-1101683	1061	1
SWEENEY FRANCIS C	COL	0-0261448	0467	3
SWEENEY FRANCIS E	COL	0-0252682	0860	3
SWEENEY FRANCIS R	COL	0-0203012	0846	2
SWEENEY FRANK E	1LT	0-118116C	0745	2

NAME	GRADE	SVC NO	DATE RET MO YR	RET CODE
SWEENEY FRANK J	LTC	C-0118090	0658	3
SWEENEY HARRY D	1LT	0-1313819	0945	2
SWEENEY HUGH A	1LT	0-1321842	C647	2
SWEENEY JAMES R	COL	0-0368456	1263	1
SWEENEY JAMES S	COL	0-0484302	1045	1
SWEENEY JEROME K	LTC	0-1647298	1165	1
SWEENEY JOHN J	MAJ	C-0359286	0745	2
SWEENEY JOHN P	LTC	0-0396821	0546	2
SWEENEY JOHN S	2LT	0-1039240	0944	2
SWEENEY JOSEPH T	CW3	W-2147005	1158	1
SWEENEY JR JAMES A	MAJ	C-0371828	0963	3
SWEENEY LEO P A	COL	0-0243503	1159	3
SWEENEY MERCER W	LTC	0-0239744	0262	3
SWEENEY MICHAEL K	2LT	0-1950652	C346	2
SWEENEY MICHAEL M	CPT	0-1285661	C660	1
SWEENEY RALPH C	COL	0-0108393	0156	3
SWEENEY ROBERT J	MAJ	0-0346931	0546	2
SWEENEY ROBERT L	LTC	0-1285137	0361	1
SWEENEY RUSSELL W	MAJ	C-1307878	0861	1
SWEENEY SAMUEL P	MAJ	0-1796728	0459	1
SWEENEY WILLIAM A	MAJ	C-2002551	1061	1
SWEENEY WILLIAM H	CW2	W-2215069	1266	1
SWEENEY WILLIAM R	CPT	0-0415385	0750	1
SWEET ARTHUR J	COL	C-0287442	0162	3
SWEET CHARLES T	MAJ	0-0962543	1263	1
SWEET FRANCIS R	MAJ	0-0939681	C762	1
SWEET FREDERICK	LTC	0-2018241	1067	2
SWEET GUSTAF	LTC	0-0380913	0145	2
SWEET HOWARD J	CW3	W-2205340	0166	1
SWEET JR ALVAN A	CW4	W-2129118	0656	1
SWEET JR JOHN J	MAJ	C-1300571	0653	1
SWEET LEROY W	MAJ	C-0506512	0357	1
SWEET ROBERT D	LTC	0-0467529	1264	1
SWEET ROSS B	CPT	0-1541588	0245	2
SWEET STUART G	LTC	0-1011970	0166	3
SWEET WILLIAM B	LTC	0-1313934	0762	1
SWEETEN GLEN D	CPT	0-1822482	0446	2
SWEETEN GOMER A	COL	0-0370036	0766	1
SWEETEN WILBUR A	COL	C-0460366	0654	1
SWEETEN WILLIAM L	CPT	0-2056116	0856	1
SWEETING ESTELLA W	1LT	N-0797751	1147	1
SWEETING GEORGE D	MAJ	C-2262791	1265	1
SWEETLAND RUSSELL A	MAJ	0-2034617	0661	1
SWEETMAN HAROLD W	LTC	0-1039941	1062	1
SWEEZEY JR RAYMON J	MAJ	0-0677316	0561	1
SWEGER SR ARTHUR S	1LT	0-1165300	C446	1
SWEIER JR GEORGE O	CPT	0-0493180	0145	2
SWEIGART BERT A	MAJ	0-0205821	0553	3
SWEIGART EARL S	LTC	0-1292085	0961	1
SWEM GILBERT S	MAJ	C-1030193	1051	1
SWENDA STEVE	WO1	W-2123326	0349	1
SWENEY LOWRY M	LTC	0-0147168	0157	3
SWENIE DENIS J	LTC	0-1030194	0866	3
SWENSEN GEORGE M	COL	0-0323975	0561	1
SWENSON ARNOLD	LTC	0-1548320	1055	1
SWENSON DONALD D	MAJ	0-1317701	C259	1
SWENSON EARL W	COL	0-0327344	1060	3
SWENSON GEORGE K	1LT	0-2035984	1045	1
SWENSON GUSTAVE P	MAJ	C-2202213	1163	1
SWENSON JOHN W	CPT	0-0387201	0343	2
SWENSON OLIVER L	CW2	W-2149056	0865	1
SWENSON PAUL A	1LT	0-1542164	1145	2
SWENSON WILTON G	CPT	0-1333021	0959	1
SWENTY JOHN D	CPT	0-1292086	0261	1
SWERDLIN GEORGE D	MAJ	0-2020482	0263	1
SWERDLOFF GEORGE	LTC	0-0425118	1065	1
SWERYDA JOHN	MAJ	0-0423014	0358	1
SWESNIK ROBERT M	CPT	0-0353894	0144	2
SWETNAM JOHN M	CPT	0-1304289	0545	1
SWETNAM MICHAEL N	CW2	W-2208212	0361	1
SWETT ARTHUR J	LTC	0-0217038	0844	2
SWETT STANTON L	LTC	0-0192420	0661	3
SWETZ CHARLES	1LT	0-1557799	0746	2
SWEZEY CHARLES M	COL	0-0101701	0948	3
SWEZEY ROBERT H	CW3	W-2136530	0965	1

NAME	GRADE	SVC NO	DATE RET MO YR	RET CODE
SWIATEK STANLEY E	LTC	0-1299961	1064	2
SWIBEL MORRIS	2LT	0-1320608	0544	1
SWICEGOOD HARRY L	COL	0-0232806	0862	3
SWICK GREGORY H	LTC	0-2030155	1158	2
SWICK LOYAL P	LTC	0-0305015	1262	1
SWICK WILLIARD R	LTC	0-0278514	1059	1
SWICKERATH CARL HE	CPT	0-1287265	0145	2
SWIDELSKY JOHN E	MAJ	0-1641006	1166	1
SWIDERSKI FRED J	MAJ	0-1333022	C361	1
SWIECA BRUNO J	CPT	0-1303571	0848	2
SWIECKOWSKI S A	MAJ	0-1016223	0258	1
SWIEKATOWSKI S J	MAJ	0-0164755	1146	1
SWIETZER HUGH A	CPT	0-0491208	0857	1
SWIFT ALLAN M	MAJ	0-0367720	0745	1
SWIFT CLARENCE E	CW2	W-2105857	1044	2
SWIFT COE T	CPT	0-0506644	0246	1
SWIFT DAVID H	LTC	0-0310523	0456	1
SWIFT FRANCIS L	2LT	0-0557699	0146	2
SWIFT GEORGE T	LTC	0-1176211	0261	1
SWIFT GEORGE W	LTC	0-1306764	0162	1
SWIFT HARLEY L	COL	0-0147172	0154	3
SWIFT HARRY R	LTC	0-2017299	0563	1
SWIFT HERBERT R	CPT	0-0359749	0966	3
SWIFT HOWELL A	CW3	W-2147026	1163	1
SWIFT IVAN H	MAJ	0-0418101	1149	1
SWIFT JAMES P	MAJ	0-0522364	0954	1
SWIFT JOHN O	WO1	W-2120979	C865	3
SWIFT NEIL K	CPT	0-0416198	104N	2
SWIFT ROBERT G	COL	0-0239858	0946	2
SWIFT VAUGHN F	LTC	0-1212068	1164	1
SWIFT WILLIAM R	LTC	0-1179223	0767	1
SWIGART KENNETH E	LTC	0-1533925	0662	1
SWIGERT CAMILLE B	LTC	L-0500193	1162	1
SWIGERT VERNE W	MAJ	0-1821214	C146	2
SWIHART DONALD W	COL	0-0240322	0265	3
SWIM BRUCE E	CPT	0-0553908	1161	1
SWIM CHARLES H	MAJ	0-2014588	0164	1
SWIMM FRANKLIN A	WO1	W-2111632	114N	2
SWINDALL VERNON	LTC	0-0408431	0661	1
SWINDELL JR GEORGE R	LTC	0-0324955	0962	1
SWINDELL MYRTLE N	MAJ	N-0727309	C762	1
SWINDELLS JOEL W	LTC	0-0338083	0465	3
SWINDEN ANNA M	2LT	N-0722118	0443	1
SWINDLE DUANE R	1LT	0-1113470	1045	2
SWINDLE JAMES T	MAJ	0-0417870	1146	2
SWINDLER THOMAS H	CPT	0-1642634	1C64	2
SWINDOA CLIFFORD W	MAJ	0-1309438	1060	1
SWINEHART BILLY J	2LT	0-0519427	0745	2
SWINGLE ERNEST A	LTC	0-0257406	0648	3
SWINHOE WALTER A	COL	0-0494594	0656	1
SWINK DONALD D	1LT	0-1638639	1050	1
SWINK JR PAUL C	MAJ	0-2001124	0960	1
SWINK LLOYD J	LTC	0-1170217	1C60	1
SWINNY BOEN	COL	0-0245221	0959	3
SWIONTKOWSKI S D	CPT	0-0317981	1044	2
SWISHER EDWIN S	2LT	0-1321848	C244	2
SWISHER FLOYD E	CW2	W-2210845	0263	1
SWISHER KEATH M	LTC	0-0258481	1059	3
SWISHER ROBERT M	MAJ	0-0451423	1C47	2
SWITKES HERMAN I	COL	0-0485445	0866	3
SWITZER FRANK C	LTC	0-0255370	0359	3
SWITZER HENRY C	COL	0-0109587	0955	3
SWITZER HUGH E	LTC	0-2033583	0866	1
SWITZER LEE P	LTC	0-0455834	0263	1
SWITZER MARION A	1LT	N-0743117	0846	1
SWITZER MARK E	COL	0-1107711	0764	1
SWITZER ROBERT L	1LT	0-1307589	0644	2
SWITZER W HOMER	COL	0-0343821	0162	1
SWOBODA LEO A	COL	0-0193542	0558	3
SWOBODA ROBERT C	LTC	0-1315636	1064	1
SWOFFORD JOSEPH A	MAJ	0-0919552	1163	2
SWOFFORD JR ROBERT T	CPT	0-0257040	1155	3
SWOISH WILLIAM G	CPT	0-1318585	0647	2
SWOISKIN BERNARD L	CPT	0-0399452	1044	2
SWOKLA STANLEY	MAJ	0-1287084	0855	1

NAME	GRADE	SVC NO	DATE RET MO YR	RET CODE
SWCNGER HARRY G	CPT	0-0338609	C548	1
SWOPE CHARLES L	LTC	0-1298153	0763	1
SWOPE IANTHE	MAJ	N-0744248	0567	1
SWOPE JR JOHN H	MAJ	0-0910167	0446	2
SWOPE LAWRENCE E	COL	C-0387457	1147	2
SWOPE ROBERT S	MAJ	C-1550934	1160	1
SWOPF WALTER F	CW2	W-2149964	0357	1
SWOPE WILLIAM F	MAJ	0-0402870	0960	1
SWORD CATHERINE	1LT	N-0787264	0945	2
SWORD JOHN W	CPT	0-0108496	1037	2
SWOROS JR LARRY G	CW2	W-2151031	0161	1
SWOYER GROVER F	CPT	C-0141361	C849	3
SWYGERT LUTHER L	LTC	0-0417218	0965	3
SWYHART CARL A	MAJ	0-0331635	1154	1
SWYTAK WALTER	CPT	0-1081761	0462	2
SYDORKO MICHAEL	MAJ	0-0452639	1057	1
SYKES ARTHUR G	1LT	0-0419409	0345	2
SYKES FLOYD L	MAJ	C-1598534	0164	1
SYKES JOY V	CPT	0-1693038	C145	2
SYKES JR ALFRED	LTC	0-1306493	1266	1
SYKES MAURICE C	CPT	0-1877865	0865	1
SYKES WALTER E	MAJ	0-1183981	1262	1
SYKES WILLIAM E	MAJ	0-1289831	0365	1
SYLCE HARRY R	LTC	0-1286206	0161	1
SYLVAN DAVIC L	2LT	0-0109381	0337	1
SYLVANOWICZ S F	2LT	0-1081254	0845	1
SYLVEST TRUMAN W	1LT	0-1010905	1045	2
SYLVESTER CAL R	CPT	0-0431738	1046	2
SYLVESTER CHARLES M	2LT	0-1327902	0446	2
SYLVFSTER FLLIS P	COL	C-0238293	1165	3
SYLVESTER ELMER	LTC	0-0296693	0667	3
SYLVESTER GEORGE E	LTC	0-0364687	1060	1
SYLVESTER JR ATHOL R	CPT	0-0376982	0942	1
SYLVESTER RORERT E	1LT	0-1874892	1062	2
SYLVIA ALBERT K	1LT	0-0925266	0645	2
SYMANSKI THEODORE V	LTC	0-0240723	0858	3
SYMC7YK WALTER J	MAJ	0-1305498	0460	1
SYME WILLIAM M	1LT	0-0391350	C945	2
SYMMES FREDERICK	LTC	0-0359490	1165	1
SYMNS ROBERT V	LTC	0-0924538	C863	1
SYMON ROBERT	1LT	0-1169362	1045	2
SYMONCS GEORGE C	LTC	0-0275939	1049	3
SYMONDS JR N W	2LT	0-1311448	0845	2
SYMONDS MARY K	1LT	N-0762171	1045	1
SYMONS JOHN H	CPT	0-1046663	0646	2
SYMS ZELLA F	1LT	N-0735884	0945	1
SYNHORST STANLEY H	CPT	0-0356419	0645	2
SYNOWSKI ALEXANDER	LTC	0-04515C7	0158	1
SYNOWSKY JOHN	MAJ	0-1310172	0561	1
SYRAN ARTHUR G	COL	C-0223286	0764	3
SYRCLE FLOYD T	MAJ	0-0251755	1047	1
SYROID MICHAEL	MAJ	0-2263185	0762	1
SZABO ALEXANDER	MAJ	0-1690907	1059	1
SZARES JOHN W	LTC	0-1306169	0363	1
SZCZECH EDWARD T	CW3	W-2146865	1061	1
SZCZEPANIK STANLEY J	CW2	W-2145520	0860	1
SZCZEPANSKI JOHN J	MAJ	C-2033173	0762	1
SZCZOTKA LEC A	CPT	0-1302229	1045	2
SZCZUDLIK JOSEPH A	CPT	0-0414505	1145	2
SZEFLINSKI CHESTER C	CPT	0-2262630	0364	1
SZEMCSAK STEPHEN T	MAJ	C-0980091	0763	1
SZILVASY GEORGE A	MAJ	0-1308878	0361	1
SZLICHTA STANLEY K	MAJ	C-1296288	1061	2
SZMARA WALTER	1LT	0-1016162	0146	2
SZOROTA STEVE	CPT	0-2025563	0557	1
SZOKE CHARLES V	CW3	W-2126215	1154	1
SZORADY ANTHONY E	LTC	0-110079C	0266	1
SZPEINSKI WENCEL	CPT	0-0467338	0452	1
SZUBA CHARLES H	CPT	0-0540837	0752	2
SZUKALSKI JOSEPH P	LTC	0-0226106	C760	3
SZUMACHOWSKI VICTCR	CW2	W-2145029	0260	1
SZUSZITZKY VELOON P	CPT	0-0232720	1161	3
SZWABO EARL M	CW2	W-2150367	1060	1
SZWAJER THADDEUS X	MAJ	C-1643384	0461	1
SZWALEK STANLEY J	1LT	0-0504831	0448	2

NAME	GRADE	SVC NO	DATE RET MO YR	RET CODE
SZYMANSKI JAMES	CPT	0-1895258	0958	3
SZYMANSKI JOHN V	MAJ	0-2262341	1161	2
SZYMANSKI MARCELL	1LT	0-1319680	0847	2
SZYMCZAK EMIL T	MAJ	0-1997176	0959	1
SZYMCZAK NCRBERT S	CW3	W-2143527	0161	1
SZYMKIEWICZ JOSEPH	LTC	0-0484353	0156	1
SZYMKOWICZ FRANK J	MAJ	0-1288463	0857	2
TAAFEL FRANK C	LTC	0-0243168	0758	3
TABB THCMAS R	MAJ	0-1540861	0263	1
TABELCN EMILIANO	1LT	0-2032089	0655	1
TABER BEACH E	MAJ	0-0206867	0648	3
TABER CLARENCE R	CW3	W-2150757	1064	1
TABER CAVID T	LTC	0-0396771	0160	1
TABER ECNALD E	CPT	0-2287218	0767	1
TABER CERALD F	CW2	W-2208484	0761	1
TABER HARRY A	2LT	0-1913953	0631	1
TABER IRVING J	LTC	0-0214555	1046	2
TABER JR AUGUSTUS K	MAJ	0-0933917	1165	1
TABINO SANTIAGO	1LT	0-1896456	0558	1
TABOCK JACK	1LT	0-1039943	1147	2
TABOR CARL P	MAJ	0-0367281	1153	1
TABOR CLIFFORD C	LTC	0-0279164	0667	3
TABOR EDWARD F	CPT	0-0956707	0960	1
TABOR JOSEPH H	1LT	0-0422063	1043	2
TABOR LYLIA H	2LT	L-0611361	0845	2
TABOR RALPH A	1LT	0-0325966	0245	2
TACEY RCBERT F	MAJ	C-2039490	1161	1
TACHOIR ROBERT E	LTC	0-1634388	0561	1
TACKER JR HUSTON J	CW4	W-2143235	1265	1
TACKER LOYAL W	LTC	0-1934708	0356	2
TACKETT CHARLES L	LTC	0-1703757	0257	1
TACKETT DONALD H	MAJ	C-1825282	0265	1
TACKETT JR LCUIS L	CW2	W-2210085	0465	1
TACKETT LITTLE O	CPT	0-1540902	1159	1
TACKLIND FLOYD O	COL	0-0301735	0360	1
TADINI FRED A	LTC	0-1551316	0861	1
TADLOCK AUD L	MAJ	0-1325174	0959	1
TADLOCK MARICN C	COL	0-0194384	0358	1
TADTMAN EMERSON L	MAJ	0-0961192	1061	1
TAFFEN JACK H	1LT	0-1177205	1045	2
TAFF ANTHONY	CPT	0-0505989	0347	1
TAFFE RICHARD P	LTC	0-1283654	0366	1
TAFS WILLIAM D	LTC	0-1543384	0760	1
TAFT FORREST D	LTC	0-1289648	0563	1
TAFT JCHN L	MAJ	C-1336837	0763	1
TAFT MARSHALL F	1LT	0-1036052	1045	2
TAFT THCMAS G	LTC	0-1046293	0764	1
TAFT WILLARD C	CPT	0-0346927	0264	1
TAGAMI KAN	MAJ	0-2010011	0361	1
TAGER BENJAMIN N	MAJ	0-0507999	0146	2
TAGER ROBERT F	MAJ	0-187689C	0365	1
TAGGART GORDCN F	LTC	0-0966378	0763	1
TAGGART RICHARD L	LTC	0-0451424	0953	1
TAGGART ROBERT M	MAJ	0-0956935	0865	1
TAGGART ROBERT M	LTC	0-131469C	0562	1
TAGGART SAMUEL R	COL	0-0253156	0563	3
TAGLIAFERRO JAMES J	1LT	C-2012579	1046	2
TAGLIARINO V A	CPT	0-1685141	1144	2
TAGUE HARRY R	CPT	0-1931286	0765	1
TAGUE JACK L	1LT	0-0439144	0346	2
TAIMI THCMAS T	CPT	0-1114774	1047	2
TAINTER WILLIS K	CPT	0-0274252	0863	3
TAIPALE TAUNC A	MAJ	C-1291724	0748	2
TAIT ARTHUR F	MAJ	0-0294671	0760	1
TAIT ECWARD J	MAJ	C-1043807	1159	1
TAIT HAROLD G	MAJ	0-1647751	0462	1
TAIT LAWRENCE	MAJ	0-2035395	1060	1
TAITTE NEIL	LTC	0-0463019	1152	1
TAKACS WILLIAM J	LTC	0-1172689	1060	1
TAKAHASHI SACAO	MAJ	0-2030787	0461	1
TAKAHASHI TERRY Y	LTC	C-2038042	0364	1
TAKAI RCY T	LTC	0-2010035	0466	1
TAKANO SEIJI	MAJ	0-1337103	0661	1
TALAMBAS SPIRC A	1LT	0-1317117	0646	2
TALAMINI ANTHCNY G	LTC	0-0964118	1066	1

NAME	GRADE	SVC NO	DATE RET MO YR	RET CODE
TALAN CHARLES J	2LT	0-0455164	0643	2
TALBERT CHARLES F	MAJ	0-1580398	1060	1
TALBERT JOHN N	MAJ	0-0377429	0747	2
TALBERT JOHNNIE B	COL	0-0193337	0160	1
TALBERT WILLIAM R	LTC	0-1945068	1162	1
TALBOT CHARLES H	LTC	0-0442884	1162	2
TALBOT CHARLIE F	COL	0-0302361	C966	3
TALBOT DANIEL G	COL	0-0233595	0965	3
TALBOT GEOFFREY W	MAJ	0-0179877	0648	3
TALBOT GEORGE K	COL	0-018973C	0753	3
TALBOT LYMAN R	COL	0-0268085	1049	3
TALBOT MANNY J	1LT	0-1946398	C658	1
TALBOT RAYMOND S	CW4	W-2144654	0167	1
TALBOT VINCENT A	MAJ	0-1596822	0363	1
TALBOTT DONALD C	LTC	0-0888418	0866	1
TALBOTT HOWARD H	2LT	0-0515629	0845	2
TALBOTT JR JOHN R	CPT	0-0389365	C545	2
TALBOTT WALLACE T	LTC	0-1011704	1163	1
TALBOTT WILLIAM A	CW3	W-2150781	0358	1
TALCOTT JAMES B	2LT	0-2034959	0845	2
TALCOTT LEONARD O	1LT	0-1305854	0146	2
TALCOTT ROBERT V	MAJ	C-0342564	0846	2
TALIAFERRO HENRY C	CPT	0-1018445	C646	2
TALIAFERRO LAUREL M	MAJ	0-0133266	0656	3
TALIAFERRO WILLIAM C	LTC	0-1577933	0364	1
TALL LUTHER S	CPT	0-0168790	0560	3
TALLAU HOWARD G	1LT	0-1030844	0145	2
TALLENT JAMES E	LTC	C-1301053	0761	1
TALLENT LOYD	LTC	0-1288813	1060	1
TALLEY CARTHAL M	MAJ	0-1289504	1060	1
TALLEY CLIFTON P	COL	0-0335970	0854	1
TALLEY CLURON O	CW3	W-2144882	0662	1
TALLEY DAVID	LTC	0-0234052	1163	3
TALLEY DWIGHT M	LTC	0-0253675	0665	3
TALLEY ELDRED J	COL	0-1592647	0467	1
TALLEY EVANS E	MAJ	0-0468118	C246	2
TALLEY FRANK T	LTC	0-0358587	0861	1
TALLEY HAROLD H	CPT	C-2018944	0456	1
TALLEY HELEN BELK	2LT	N-0727852	1145	1
TALLEY JAMES W	LTC	0-0557193	0565	1
TALLEY JAMES W	LTC	0-1036053	0463	1
TALLEY JR BOLIVER E	MAJ	0-1920052	1166	1
TALLEY LOUIS	MAJ	C-1111943	C858	2
TALLEY WILLIAM H	LTC	0-0450495	1046	1
TALLICHET RENE L	LTC	0-0328071	C861	2
TALLMAN FRANK L	LTC	0-1010415	1063	1
TALLMAN HAROLD L	1LT	0-1287266	0246	2
TALLMAN JOHN O	LTC	C-2048795	1064	1
TALLMAN MAMIE B	MAJ	N-0778075	0665	1
TALLMAN RAYMOND L	MAJ	0-1181483	0759	1
TALLON CHARLES F	1LT	0-1945503	0756	1
TALMADGE DANIEL W	CPT	0-0516130	0147	2
TALMADGE JACK A	LTC	0-0451250	1060	1
TALMAGE RALPH H	COL	0-0234452	0460	3
TALMAGE WILLIAM G	MAJ	0-0281618	0246	2
TALPIS STANLEY I	2LT	0-0524422	0444	2
TALSEY WILLIAM C	MAJ	0-0163661	1056	3
TALUBAN REDORO M	CW2	W-2149848	0862	1
TAM HUNG E	MAJ	C-030936R	1063	3
TAMAMIAN LEO	COL	0-03344C8	0464	1
TAMANINI FRANK O	CW2	W-2206692	0664	1
TAMASI JOSEPH J	MAJ	0-0384811	0545	1
TAMAYO FREDERIC	MAJ	0-2027371	0657	1
TAMBLYN GORDON O	LTC	0-1950290	0566	1
TAMER ABRAHAM F	1LT	0-1554982	0256	2
TAMMARO ALFONSO	LTC	C-0261431	0962	3
TAMMARO MILLIE M	2LT	N-0763367	0146	1
TAMMARO RALPH F	CW2	W-2109833	1044	2
TAMPKE HOMER A	CW4	W-2100006	0966	1
TAMPLIN JACK O	MAJ	0-2023845	0760	1
TAMRAZ JOHN P	MAJ	0-1341131	0865	1
TAMSE SIDNEY	MAJ	C-0467579	0246	2
TANAKA PAUL A	CW2	W-2209804	1165	1
TANAKA WALTER	MAJ	0-2030569	0661	1
TANBERG LUCILLE A	2LT	N-0737079	C944	1

NAME	GRADE	SVC NO	DATE RET MO YR	RET CODE
TANBERG MONROE N	MAJ	0-1948063	0862	1
TANCREDI LOUIS	WO1	W-2141093	0259	2
TANDY FRANK C	COL	0-0266303	0758	1
TANGHE ALBERT L F	MAJ	0-1C81C38	0961	1
TANI MATT A	CW3	W-2152253	0462	1
TANIMURA JOHN M	CPT	0-021463C	0362	3
TANK JR HAROLD J	CPT	0-1919233	0263	1
TANKERSLEY JCHN H	CPT	0-0949620	0760	1
TANKERSLEY RICHARD E	LTC	0-0450922	0962	1
TANKERSLEY WILLIAM C	LTC	0-0312636	0967	3
TANKSLEY CARL B	2LT	0-1328854	0246	2
TANN LEO	CPT	0-0500856	0646	2
TANNASCCLI RCCCO P	LTC	0-1175336	0960	1
TANNEHILL F H	CPT	0-054363C	0546	2
TANNEHILL GECRGE L	CPT	0-0358776	1044	2
TANNER ALVIN L	CPT	0-0267877	0463	1
TANNER AVON W	CPT	0-0230464	C747	1
TANNER CECIL	MAJ	0-2263018	1061	1
TANNER DELBERT M	COL	0-0371337	0960	1
TANNER GLENN A	LTC	0-1633590	1264	1
TANNER HERBERT E	MAJ	0-0946625	0664	1
TANNER HCMER W	CPT	0-0496909	0449	1
TANNER JANE M	MAJ	L-0302573	1046	1
TANNER JOSEPH J	LTC	0-1168942	0763	1
TANNER JR CLAUDE E	1LT	0-1306658	0645	1
TANNER MALCOLM Z	LTC	0-1306765	0766	1
TANNER MERTON W	LTC	0-0419645	1065	3
TANNER PAUL	LTC	0-0171808	0652	3
TANNER WILKINS E	2LT	0-0401400	0443	2
TANNER WILLIAM F	LTC	0-1288464	0367	1
TANNERY FRED M	LTC	0-0410280	0761	1
TANNEY WILLIAM W	CPT	0-0129040	C156	3
TANNHEIMER J A R	1LT	0-0439475	0945	2
TANNO AL	MAJ	0-1332434	0365	1
TANSIL GEORGE O	MAJ	0-1317998	0266	1
TANSKI SR WILLIAM V	LTC	0-1595860	0467	1
TANSLEY MAYNARD S	LTC	0-2042952	0963	1
TANTCA L M	MAJ	0-1288814	1156	1
TANZER VELMA M	2LT	N-0737096	0745	1
TAPIA JCHN R	MAJ	0-0947809	1065	1
TAPIE ANTHONY M	LTC	0-1166393	0765	1
TAPLEY HOWARD A	MAJ	0-0920169	0547	2
TAPLIN RICHARD O	CPT	0-1894601	0846	2
TAPLIN SABIN C	LTC	0-0400438	0561	2
TAPOVATZ WEB W	1LT	0-1897797	0649	1
TAPP ERNEST M	COL	0-027239C	0664	3
TAPP FELIX C	LTC	0-0276592	1264	3
TAPP GUS M	CPT	0-1822483	0760	1
TAPPA ALBERT	CW4	W-2142906	0266	1
TAPPAN JR WILLIAM R	MAJ	0-1171796	1066	1
TAPPEN DOROTHY R	1LT	N-079736C	0847	1
TAPSCCT JO J	COL	0-0248035	0855	3
TARA JR CAVID M	MAJ	0-0383251	0960	2
TARA MARGARET W	1LT	N-0703599	0945	1
TARACKC ADAM [	MAJ	0-2026233	0764	1
TARALLC FRANK J	LTC	0-0365992	0463	1
TARALLC GUERRINO J	LTC	0-1104416	0163	1
TARANTC MORRIS B	1LT	0-0548352	1145	2
TARBETT LEWIS N	CPT	0-0379361	0964	1
TARBI SUE R	2LT	N-C738009	1043	1
TARBOX GEORGE O	CPT	0-0365912	1043	2
TARBOX HENRY A	COL	0-0454142	0567	2
TARBOX II CHARLES M	1LT	0-0297914	0165	3
TARBUTTON EDMUND H	LTC	0-1329179	C466	1
TARCY RAUL	LTC	0-0438711	1166	3
TARDIF LEO J	CW2	W-2206277	0363	1
TARDIFF ROLAND A	MAJ	0-0266473	0960	3
TARDY JAMES N	MAJ	0-0153087	1157	3
TARKINCTON CHARTER F	CPT	0-1318486	0667	3
TARKINGTON KENNETH E	1LT	0-1165052	0544	2
TARLAU MILTON	MAJ	0-1690161	0446	2
TARLOW CHARLES M	MAJ	0-0276875	1057	3
TARNO WARREN E	LTC	0-101656C	0267	1
TARPAY CHARLES M	MAJ	0-0506741	0157	1
TARPENING JOHN O	MAJ	0-0393604	1145	1

NAME	GRADE	SVC NO	DATE RET MO YR	RET CODE
TARPENNING ROBERT A	MAJ	0-0999672	0167	1
TARPLEY CHARLES O	LTC	0-1548569	0363	1
TARPLEY MELVIN	CW2	W-2210484	C364	1
TARPLEY SELDEN A	CPT	0-0184000	1056	3
TARPLEY TROY E	CW2	W-2123066	0556	1
TARR CLARENCE W	CPT	0-0990629	0761	2
TARR FLOYD H	LTC	0-1579198	1055	1
TARR ROBERT M	LTC	0-0363699	0257	1
TARR WILLIAM M	LTC	0-1552809	0867	1
TARRALL ELMER	CPT	0-1594523	C746	2
TARRANCE WILLIAM N	LTC	0-0358963	0466	3
TARRANT ALBERT E	COL	0-0308405	C765	3
TARRANT HOWARD G	MAJ	0-0961239	0361	1
TARRANT JR MARION B	MAJ	C-2262971	0961	1
TART EARL F	CW2	W-2146288	0559	1
TART GUY A	LTC	0-1055746	0165	1
TARTER CLYDE S	LTC	0-0174768	C845	2
TARTER MARVIN N	MAJ	0-2023966	0764	2
TARTER ORAL	2LT	0-0497796	0346	1
TARTY ROY L	MAJ	0-1031766	0859	1
TARVER ROBERT L	LTC	0-0490516	1162	1
TARVER WILLIAM S	LTC	0-0240124	0466	3
TARVES HARRY J	MAJ	0-0371065	C463	1
TARVIN EARL W	CW2	W-2208143	0763	1
TARZON FRANCIS D	MAJ	0-2023560	0656	1
TASCHNER LESLIE E	MAJ	0-0462069	0165	3
TASK LEON	1LT	0-0234512	0345	2
TASKE MEYER	CPT	0-0228361	1056	3
TASKER LEIGHTON E	LTC	C-0410374	1059	1
TASLOV HELEN M	2LT	N-0772432	C745	1
TASSI LAWRENCE A	LTC	0-1558347	0166	3
TATE ANDREW L	CPT	0-2012703	0657	1
TATE CURVIN E	CPT	0-1556812	1047	2
TATE EUGENE R	LTC	0-1320199	1062	1
TATE HAROLD S	LTC	0-0213446	0164	3
TATE JACOB E	CW3	W-2148132	0261	1
TATE JOHN B	WO1	W-2152781	1164	1
TATE JOHN C	LTC	0-0477022	1046	2
TATE JOHN H	2LT	0-1301054	0745	2
TATE JR SIDNEY F	COL	0-0357746	1060	1
TATE LINWOOD C	2LT	0-1824817	1045	2
TATE PERRY L	LTC	0-0554581	0763	1
TATE ROBERT C	1LT	0-0980309	0762	1
TATE ROBERT L	CPT	0-0495784	0648	1
TATE SOLON H	MAJ	0-2001438	0763	1
TATE SR HARRY A	CPT	C-0180839	1055	3
TATE WILLIS O	MAJ	0-0289021	0353	1
TATEM EARL W	1LT	0-1306172	C147	1
TATES EDWARD W	CPT	0-4013553	0464	1
TATOM HENRY G	LTC	0-0204383	0862	3
TATUM DAVE H	MAJ	0-0414504	0161	1
TATUM ED	CW3	W-21457C1	0860	1
TATUM FRANK J	MAJ	0-0279335	1167	3
TATUM HERBERT M	LTC	0-0215677	0364	3
TATUM HORACE B	1LT	0-1181777	1045	2
TATUM JAMES B	MAJ	C-1298953	0163	1
TATUM JOHN M	COL	0-0255534	0655	3
TATUM JOSEPH C	COL	C-0309262	0465	3
TATUM JR GROVER C	CPT	C-0390724	C546	2
TATUM REUBEN L	COL	0-0267233	0952	2
TATUM VICTOR E	COL	0-0102140	0954	3
TAUBE HARRY J	1LT	0-1579202	0745	2
TAUBER MAX	CPT	0-0350330	0346	2
TAUBER RAYMOND L	2LT	0-1178360	0744	2
TAULBEE CHARLES P	LTC	0-1047407	0264	1
TAUS MAURICE R	LTC	0-0309220	0859	1
TAUSCH NORMAN F	MAJ	0-0452055	C561	1
TAUSCHER WALTER E	MAJ	0-0967873	0661	1
TAUSEK THEODORE S	MAJ	0-1797385	C563	1
TAUSEND STANLEIGH	CPT	0-0242252	0346	2
TAUSER LOUIS G	LTC	0-0470980	0357	1
TAUTFEST BENJAMIN M	CW2	W-2119081	0645	2
TAVENNER JOHN L	CPT	0-1821210	1045	2
TAVERNER WILLIAM G	LTC	0-0232696	0147	1
TAVES TAPP S	CPT	0-0478759	1045	2
TAVILLE WILBERT L	MAJ	0-0969604	0263	1
TAVIS VICTOR L	CW4	W-2136693	1164	2
TAVOIAN LAMAR A	MAJ	0-0402054	C459	1
TAVORMINA IGNATIUS J	MAJ	C-0292427	0162	1
TAW RICHARD L	CPT	0-0448626	1145	2
TAWES ROBERT L	CPT	0-1290334	0546	2
TAXSAR MEYER J	1LT	0-1291195	0444	2
TAYE ARNOLD C	CPT	0-0297539	0145	1
TAYLOE JR HENRY G	LTC	0-0339543	0467	1
TAYLOR ABNER U	COL	0-0300457	1057	3
TAYLOR ALBERT L	MAJ	0-0354571	1050	1
TAYLOR ALFRED L	LTC	0-0235059	0961	3
TAYLOR ALLEN L	LTC	0-1547177	1166	1
TAYLOR ALVIN C	LTC	0-2034862	0861	1
TAYLOR ALVIS M	MAJ	0-1945292	1059	1
TAYLOR AMYTH H	CW4	W-2003641	0265	1
TAYLOR ANDREW J	CPT	0-1640060	0465	1
TAYLOR ARCH K	CPT	0-1598883	0459	1
TAYLOR ARNOLD D	CW3	W-2153328	0965	1
TAYLOR AUBREY A	1LT	0-0501607	0644	2
TAYLOR BAILEY E	1LT	0-0507131	0745	2
TAYLOR BARNEY B	CPT	0-1323045	0346	2
TAYLOR BENJAMIN F	MAJ	0-0250326	1164	3
TAYLOR BENJAMIN G	CPT	0-2262685	0461	1
TAYLOR BERNICE A	CPT	0-1298462	0148	1
TAYLOR BILLY R	MAJ	0-2266171	0767	1
TAYLOR BORDEN E	LTC	0-1296935	1265	3
TAYLOR BRUCE S	1LT	0-1795994	0546	2
TAYLOR BUFORD C	2LT	0-1826177	1145	2
TAYLOR BURNLEY W	MAJ	0-0995219	0863	1
TAYLOR BYRL O	LTC	0-0438831	0867	1
TAYLOR CARL L	MAJ	0-1013529	0466	1
TAYLOR CAROLYN F	1LT	N-0763825	0646	1
TAYLOR CHARLES	LTC	0-0344545	1166	3
TAYLOR CHARLES C	LTC	0-1951548	0766	1
TAYLOR CHARLES E	CPT	0-0239015	0862	3
TAYLOR CHARLES E	LTC	0-1183775	C260	1
TAYLOR CHARLES L	CW2	W-2116967	0554	1
TAYLOR CHARLES S	CPT	0-1576726	0345	2
TAYLOR CHARLES W	1LT	0-2047518	0147	1
TAYLOR CHARLEY S	2LT	0-0451425	1043	2
TAYLOR CHESTER A	LTC	0-0260611	0253	3
TAYLOR CLARA R	2LT	N-0763471	0344	1
TAYLOR CLARENCE W	COL	0-0248331	1063	3
TAYLOR CLARENCE W	CW2	W-2205496	0560	1
TAYLOR CLARK L	MAJ	0-0347962	0847	1
TAYLOR CLAYTON M	MAJ	0-1823371	1060	1
TAYLOR CLIFFORD C	LTC	0-0268335	1162	3
TAYLOR CLYDE A	CPT	0-1178361	1158	1
TAYLOR CLYDE E	CW3	W-2149035	1262	1
TAYLOR DANIEL H	LTC	0-1036054	1166	2
TAYLOR DELOS C	LTC	0-0212849	1059	3
TAYLOR DEWEY	CPT	0-0349041	0750	1
TAYLOR DEWEY	CPT	0-0492203	0749	1
TAYLOR DONALD	MAJ	C-1825322	C261	1
TAYLOR DONALD A	MAJ	0-0373924	C663	1
TAYLOR DUARD E	MAJ	0-2262767	1266	1
TAYLOR EARL A	COL	0-0171126	0256	3
TAYLOR EDGAR L	CPT	0-1591474	0847	1
TAYLOR EDITH C	MAJ	M-0002404	0867	2
TAYLOR EDWARD A	1LT	0-0954527	1053	2
TAYLOR ELIZABETH	MAJ	N-0741047	1067	1
TAYLOR ELLSWORTH	CW3	W-2152834	0662	1
TAYLOR ETHEL E	2LT	N-0700672	0539	1
TAYLOR EUGENE E	MAJ	0-0480691	1045	2
TAYLOR EVAN J	MAJ	0-0961375	0766	1
TAYLOR FLOYD A	CPT	0-0107835	0648	3
TAYLOR FLOYD W	CW3	W-2146631	0263	1
TAYLOR FRANK	CW2	W-2152225	1060	1
TAYLOR FRANK A	MAJ	0-0245067	0463	3
TAYLOR FRANK C	MAJ	0-0364647	0147	1
TAYLOR FRANK R	MAJ	0-1577936	1157	2
TAYLOR FRED	CPT	0-1598111	0353	2
TAYLOR FREDERICK	MAJ	0-0125064	0544	2
TAYLOR GEORGE A	CPT	0-0707416	1060	1
TAYLOR GEORGE D	MAJ	0-1042965	0457	1
TAYLOR GEORGE F	LTC	0-0386157	0657	1
TAYLOR GEORGE E	CPT	0-2262201	1060	1
TAYLOR GEORGE F	LTC	0-0237117	0262	3
TAYLOR GEORGE G	MAJ	0-1296113	0447	2
TAYLOR GEORGE H	COL	0-0173617	0361	3
TAYLOR GEORGE L	LTC	0-0382663	1164	1
TAYLOR GEORGE M	MAJ	0-1338413	1264	1
TAYLOR GEORGE R	LTC	C-0346790	C859	3
TAYLOR GERALD W	LTC	0-0919549	1266	3
TAYLOR GILBERT H	CW3	W-2108018	0655	1
TAYLOR GLENN S	1LT	0-0925589	0145	2
TAYLOR GUY	CPT	0-0487857	0548	1
TAYLOR HAFFRED N	1LT	C-0450456	1044	2
TAYLOR HAROLD A	COL	0-0100236	0454	3
TAYLOR HAROLD A	COL	0-0228432	0556	3
TAYLOR HAROLD E	MAJ	C-1302067	0761	1
TAYLOR HAROLD G	CPT	0-1845253	C359	1
TAYLOR HARRY A	2LT	C-1303414	C644	2
TAYLOR HARRY E	LTC	0-0179254	0151	3
TAYLOR HARRY F	CPT	0-0499653	0754	1
TAYLOR HARRY F	CPT	0-1105856	0147	2
TAYLOR HARRY M	CPT	0-0315700	0966	3
TAYLOR HARVEY D	COL	0-0187459	0347	2
TAYLOR HENRY B	2LT	0-1323989	0745	2
TAYLOR HENRY H	CPT	0-0101714	C851	3
TAYLOR HENRY L	COL	0-0153581	1056	3
TAYLOR HENRY L	LTC	0-0278432	1160	3
TAYLOR HENRY M	COL	0-0156284	0255	3
TAYLOR HERBERT C	COL	0-0190078	0556	3
TAYLOR HERBERT J	MAJ	C-1684969	1262	1
TAYLOR HOWARD M	1LT	C-0511013	0352	1
TAYLOR HOWARD W	LTC	0-0450923	0563	2
TAYLOR HOWELL	CW2	W-2120776	0354	1
TAYLOR HUGH	CPT	0-0313450	C866	3
TAYLOR HUGH B	CPT	0-0282324	0845	2
TAYLOR INGRAM C	LTC	0-0484881	1164	3
TAYLOR JACOB W	CPT	0-2007257	0857	1
TAYLOR JAMES A	MAJ	C-0511776	1044	2
TAYLOR JAMES B	COL	0-0463474	0456	1
TAYLOR JAMES B	MAJ	0-2263487	C763	1
TAYLOR JAMES D	COL	0-0330155	0846	2
TAYLOR JAMES D	MAJ	0-1947101	0163	1
TAYLOR JAMES E	LTC	0-0278146	0561	3
TAYLOR JAMES E	M G	C-0376731	0766	3
TAYLOR JAMES F	MAJ	0-2021229	1066	1
TAYLOR JAMES L	COL	0-0211915	0258	3
TAYLOR JAMES L	MAJ	0-0486646	0954	1
TAYLOR JAMES L	MAJ	0-1547475	1161	1
TAYLOR JAMES W	1LT	0-0923832	0145	2
TAYLOR JAMES W	CW3	W-2146289	1058	1
TAYLOR JEROME E	MAJ	0-1037930	1164	1
TAYLOR JESSE W	MAJ	0-0424192	0665	1
TAYLOR JIM	CPT	0-0496902	0153	1
TAYLOR JOE G	WO1	W-2127719	1051	1
TAYLOR JOHN A	MAJ	0-1579204	0257	1
TAYLOR JOHN B	COL	0-0197248	0463	3
TAYLOR JOHN B	LTC	0-0377276	1066	3
TAYLOR JOHN B	1LT	0-1639721	0746	2
TAYLOR JOHN C	LTC	0-0437659	0155	2
TAYLOR JOHN E	LTC	0-0297779	0565	3
TAYLOR JOHN F	COL	0-0477260	0754	1
TAYLOR JOHN G	LTC	0-0164265	C549	3
TAYLOR JOHN G	LTC	0-1294040	1057	1
TAYLOR JOHN L	MAJ	0-1004047	1154	1
TAYLOR JOHN M	1LT	0-0962886	0163	2
TAYLOR JOHN P	CPT	0-0508869	1046	1
TAYLOR JOHN R	MAJ	0-1046981	0466	1
TAYLOR JOHN W	CPT	0-0368766	0745	2
TAYLOR JOHN W	CPT	0-0451251	0960	1
TAYLOR JOHN W	1LT	0-0511455	0760	1
TAYLOR JOHN W	MAJ	0-1685019	1165	1
TAYLOR JOHNNY H	CW3	W-2150331	1062	1
TAYLOR JOSEPH K	MAJ	0-0997956	0364	1
TAYLOR JOSEPH W	CW4	W-2127155	0555	1
TAYLOR JR ALBERT W	2LT	0-1060666	0445	2
TAYLOR JR CHARLES F	1LT	0-2049118	0945	2
TAYLOR JR CHARLES O	MAJ	0-2018435	0962	1
TAYLOR JR CLYDE H	LTC	0-1168489	1062	1
TAYLOR JR DAVID F	COL	0-0192115	0163	3
TAYLOR JR HENRY W	1LT	0-1174984	0145	2
TAYLOR JR JAMES L	LTC	0-0141342	0648	3
TAYLOR JR JAMES O	CW2	W-2146843	1162	1
TAYLOR JR JAMES R	MAJ	0-1917671	0666	1
TAYLOR JR JOHN G	LTC	0-0886401	0764	1
TAYLOR JR LYMAN J	LTC	0-1636728	1062	1
TAYLOR JR ORCIE P	LTC	0-1030616	1061	2
TAYLOR JR RALPH L	CW3	W-2144025	0862	1
TAYLOR JR ROBERT I	CPT	0-0538302	0646	2
TAYLOR JR ROBERT L	2LT	0-1054137	0444	2
TAYLOR JR ROBERT R	MAJ	0-1550937	0660	1
TAYLOR JR RONALD V	2LT	0-1297983	1044	2
TAYLOR JR ROYCE R	LTC	0-0449421	0662	1
TAYLOR JR TALBERT L	CPT	0-1553741	0961	1
TAYLOR JR THOMAS R	LTC	0-1173484	C364	1
TAYLOR KATHRYN O	1LT	N-0755407	0746	1
TAYLOR KENNETH K	MAJ	0-095955C	0366	1
TAYLOR LAMAR W	LTC	0-0453151	1264	1
TAYLOR LANE F	LTC	0-1556225	1266	3
TAYLOR LEE E	LTC	0-0386654	0760	1
TAYLOR LEON W	CPT	0-0526191	0147	1
TAYLOR LEWIS	MAJ	0-0334879	1057	3
TAYLOR LLOYD K	CPT	0-0987842	0361	1
TAYLOR LONNIE R	2LT	0-2010992	0646	2
TAYLOR LORENZO J	LTC	0-1534166	0461	1
TAYLOR LOUIS	1LT	0-1010291	0845	1
TAYLOR LOUIS J	MAJ	0-1949948	0367	1
TAYLOR LYNN C	MAJ	0-0277330	0362	3
TAYLOR MALCOLM I	CPT	0-1004525	1157	1
TAYLOR MANUEL J	MAJ	0-1685507	0263	1
TAYLOR MARSHALL E	CPT	0-2026841	1057	1
TAYLOR MARY L	MAJ	N-0754267	0665	1
TAYLOR MATHILDA W	CPT	N-0783058	0546	1
TAYLOR MAURICE E	CPT	0-0541784	0448	2
TAYLOR MELVIN B	MAJ	0-1996406	1060	1
TAYLOR MERLE V	MAJ	0-1056944	1262	1
TAYLOR MINOR T	CW4	W-2143567	0266	1
TAYLOR MORRIS B	LTC	0-2005979	0562	1
TAYLOR MORRIS N	1LT	0-0367897	0944	2
TAYLOR MYRON O	1LT	0-1030939	0146	2
TAYLOR NUEL L	CW2	W-2145875	0562	1
TAYLOR OLIN A	2LT	0-117766C	1144	2
TAYLOR OZIER C	1LT	0-1297117	0453	1
TAYLOR PAUL W	LTC	0-0171003	0648	3
TAYLOR PHILIP H	COL	0-0192419	0462	3
TAYLOR PHILLIP E	LTC	0-0272916	1263	3
TAYLOR POWELL P	1LT	0-0485730	1146	1
TAYLOR RALPH	CPT	0-1583755	0658	1
TAYLOR RALPH L	LTC	0-0227332	0560	3
TAYLOR RAY C	MAJ	0-1043822	0660	1
TAYLOR RAYMOND A	LTC	0-0283782	0146	2
TAYLOR RAYMOND T	CW3	W-2113884	0461	1
TAYLOR REX A	CPT	0-1291725	1046	1
TAYLOR RICHARD E	COL	0-0336C58	0366	1
TAYLOR RICHARD F	LTC	0-040868C	0161	1
TAYLOR RICHARD S	CPT	0-2030456	0861	1
TAYLOR ROBERT	CW3	W-2148993	0962	1
TAYLOR ROBERT B	1LT	0-1583757	0546	2
TAYLOR ROBERT B	CPT	0-1874947	0262	1
TAYLOR ROBERT G	LTC	0-1574162	0361	1
TAYLOR ROBERT J	MAJ	0-1337654	0962	1
TAYLOR ROBERT L	COL	0-0321031	0767	3
TAYLOR ROBERT L	COL	0-0346564	0467	3
TAYLOR ROBERT M	LTC	0-0263872	0446	2
TAYLOR ROBERT M	CW4	W-2142664	0563	1
TAYLOR ROSS G	MAJ	0-0466852	1262	1
TAYLOR ROSS H	MAJ	0-1651316	0162	1
TAYLOR ROY O	CPT	0-0989977	1060	1
TAYLOR RUSSELL B	CPT	0-1308075	1046	2
TAYLOR RUSSELL P	MAJ	0-0921993	1162	1

ARMY OF THE UNITED STATES RETIRED LIST

NAME	GRADE	SVC NO	DATE RET MO YR	RET CODE
TAYLOR SAM H	LTC	0-0375817	C963	1
TAYLOR SAMUEL C	WO1	W-2152484	0464	2
TAYLOR SETH	CW2	W-2143627	1055	1
TAYLOR SIGISMUND	MAJ	O-1109707	0363	2
TAYLOR SR EARNEST E	MAJ	C-0251272	0549	1
TAYLOR THEODORE	LTC	0-028007C	0648	3
TAYLOR THERON J	LTC	0-0171235	C952	3
TAYLOR THOMAS H	1LT	0-0386545	0944	2
TAYLOR THOMAS L	MAJ	0-2020980	C765	1
TAYLOR THURMAN M	CPT	0-1997976	0258	1
TAYLOR TOM L	LTC	0-0243988	0554	3
TAYLOR UTRHA U	1LT	N-0721538	104N	1
TAYLOR V O	WO1	W-2146523	C659	1
TAYLOR VICTOR R	LTC	0-0279266	0561	1
TAYLOR VIRGIL E	CW2	W-2113569	1053	1
TAYLOR WAIGHTS M	LTC	0-0316954	0765	1
TAYLOR WALTER L	CW4	W-2142907	0167	1
TAYLOR WARREN E	CPT	O-1012521	1047	2
TAYLOR WESLEY B	LTC	0-0318763	0764	1
TAYLOR WILLIAM A	CW3	W-2147345	C863	1
TAYLOR WILLIAM B	CPT	0-0137065	C648	3
TAYLOR WILLIAM B	LTC	0-1039242	0966	1
TAYLOR WILLIAM D	COL	0-0396127	0966	1
TAYLOR WILLIAM E	LTC	0-1042724	C161	1
TAYLOR WILLIAM H	MAJ	C-0177339	1045	2
TAYLOR WILLIAM H	LTC	0-0422833	C663	1
TAYLOR WILLIAM L	LTC	C-0542590	0163	1
TAYLOR WILLIAM L	CW3	W-2145709	0363	1
TAYLOR WILLIAM N	MAJ	C-1557802	1064	1
TAYLOR WILLIAM W	LTC	0-0123190	C648	3
TAYLOR WOFFORD L	CW3	W-2147328	1264	1
TAYLOR WYMAN C	LTC	0-0251286	0358	3
TAYS EUGENE	LTC	0-0111971	0549	3
TAYS JAMES H	MAJ	0-0181624	1145	1
TCHAKIRIDES HARRY	LTC	0-1172309	1264	2
TEAGUE CHARLES M	MAJ	C-2046404	0258	1
TEAGUE CHARLES D	MAJ	0-1310526	0764	1
TEAGUE JR NORRIS M	MAJ	0-1294219	C760	1
TEAGUE JR WALTER D	MAJ	C-1587673	C961	1
TEAGUE OLIN E	COL	0-0294931	1146	2
TEAGUE SEMON L	CW3	W-2142742	0766	1
TEAGUE TERRELL A	MAJ	0-1920172	0965	1
TEAGUE WALTER E	MAJ	C-1533692	0959	1
TEAGUE WILLIAM A	2LT	0-1914328	C422	2
TEAL HORACE D	MAJ	C-1298621	C954	1
TEALEY EARL H	LTC	0-0298009	C266	3
TEANEY DARREL F	1LT	0-1825285	0646	2
TEANEY ROBERT J	CW2	W-2151734	1164	1
TEAS HOWARD J	MAJ	C-0208872	0754	3
TEASLEY JR RICHARD	CW4	W-2124106	C660	1
TEATER MARGARET E	2LT	N-0786297	0346	1
TEBBETTS HENRY M	CW2	W-2209542	1161	1
TEBBY ERNEST H	2LT	0-1108361	1143	2
TEBERG ERNEST J	COL	0-0176783	0553	3
TEBO BEN C	MAJ	C-0336679	0953	2
TEBO FRANK A	LTC	C-0252229	0365	3
TEBOREK JAMES J	LTC	0-0211242	C258	3
TEBOW ERIC T	COL	C-0225794	C363	3
TECLER WILLIAM	LTC	0-0294332	C246	2
TEDD ROBERT N	MAJ	0-1182471	1262	2
TEDESCHI JOSEPH E	LTC	C-1104418	0966	1
TEDESCO JAMES	MAJ	C-1288645	0648	1
TEDFORD CHARLES H	LTC	0-0441373	C663	3
TEDROWE JR JOHN P	MAJ	C-1032252	C461	1
TEEBKEN GEORGE D	CPT	0-0498136	1051	1
TEECE JOSEPH A	M G	0-0242853	0459	3
TEEL CHARLES O	MAJ	C-0261702	0665	3
TEEFEY FRANCIS J	CPT	0-1306661	0147	1
TEEHAN RICHARD J	LTC	0-1339488	C866	1
TEEHEE ROBERT	1LT	0-0403677	1045	2
TEEL EDWARD M	LTC	0-0888590	0657	1
TEEM MARTIN V B	CPT	0-0309710	1044	1
TEEMS THOMAS B	CPT	0-0499652	0247	1
TEEPE SUZANNA F	1LT	N-0729375	1045	1
TEER JAMES B	MAJ	C-1292421	0757	1
TEESE HARRY F	COL	0-022C292	0455	3
TEETER EARL R	MAJ	0-1582195	0854	1
TEETER RUSSELL V	LTC	0-1000482	0462	1
TEETERS CHARLES A	MAJ	0-0348992	1262	3
TEETERS HIRAM L	WO1	W-2104523	0645	2
TEETSEL WILLIAM J	CPT	0-0289212	114N	2
TEFFT ROGER F	LTC	0-1342015	0867	1
TEFT DONALD E	LTC	0-2053581	0166	1
TEICH DAVID E	MAJ	C-2014574	0963	1
TEICHART ALVIN E	LTC	0-0280047	1044	2
TEICHERT JOHN	MAJ	0-1590849	0662	1
TEICHMAN JAMES A	CPT	0-13C567C	0457	1
TEICHMAN LAWRENCE I	CPT	0-2025797	0750	1
TEIEN ROBERT E	MAJ	0-0744517	0365	1
TEIKA ERNEST	CW3	RW-2209723	0566	1
TEINERT JOHN G	LTC	0-1581415	1163	1
TEITELBAUM JACK	1LT	0-1288646	0145	2
TEITLER MAX H	CPT	0-0498147	1043	1
TEIXEIRA FRANK L	MAJ	0-1287086	0154	1
TEJA RAY	CPT	0-1293675	0862	1
TEKULVE ELMER R	1LT	0-1319681	0546	2
TELCHIK LEO	MAJ	0-1688755	0763	1
TELESE ALPHONSE R	LTC	0-1013345	0765	2
TELFER WALDO B	CPT	0-0242812	0858	3
TELFORD DONALD M	LTC	0-1036767	C361	1
TELFORD EDWARD T	COL	0-0241594	0359	3
TELFORD ELDRIDGE W	LTC	0-0236753	1062	3
TELFORD JOHN C	MAJ	0-1534168	0164	1
TELFORD WILLIAM E	1LT	0-2032859	0852	1
TELL JOHN A	LTC	0-1555918	0863	1
TELLEJOHN BENJAMIN H	MAJ	0-0471952	1041	1
TELLER HAROLD R	CW2	W-2148820	1061	1
TELLMAN RALPH L	MAJ	0-0243615	0666	3
TELMAN HARRY	MAJ	C-0570496	0463	1
TEMBRINA PASCUAL C	1LT	0-1896806	1052	1
TEMPERTON LEON E	CPT	0-1951194	0358	1
TEMPINSKI JULIA M	MAJ	N-075434C	0565	1
TEMPLE EDGAR W	1LT	0-1684922	0944	2
TEMPLE EDISON M	LTC	0-1185903	0667	1
TEMPLE ELWOOD L	LTC	0-0469167	0165	1
TEMPLE HARRY G	CPT	0-0288899	0467	3
TEMPLE HENRY E	1LT	0-1017292	0152	1
TEMPLE JOHN W	MAJ	0-0387836	1047	1
TEMPLE LANNIS W	MAJ	0-1002138	0656	1
TEMPLE LONNIE C	LTC	0-1636725	1060	1
TEMPLE RALPH R	COL	0-0523284	0966	3
TEMPLE ROBERT C	WO1	W-2142502	0352	2
TEMPLE RUSSEL E	CW2	W-2141466	1154	1
TEMPLE THOMAS F	CPT	0-1796884	0246	2
TEMPLER ROBERT C	LTC	0-1053839	0165	1
TEMPLETON CECIL C	LTC	0-0504009	0167	3
TEMPLETON CONRAD C	LTC	0-0332997	C566	3
TEMPLETON DICK C	CW3	W-2152562	0462	1
TEMPLETON DONALD E	1LT	0-1323187	0646	1
TEMPLETON HALL R	2LT	0-1045278	0745	2
TEMPLETON JACK C	MAJ	0-0958531	0467	1
TEMPLETON JOHN J	LTC	0-1799396	0866	1
TEMPLETON RAY M	LTC	0-0921051	0263	1
TEMPLETON ROBERT L	LTC	0-0372632	0759	1
TEMPLETON STOKES S	2LT	0-1018478	0547	2
TEMPLETON WILLIAM E	MAJ	0-0240969	1065	3
TEMPLIN FRED M	CW4	W-2132789	0366	1
TEMPLIN PAUL W	LTC	0-0488188	0966	3
TEMPLIN WALLACE W	CW4	W-2104522	1058	1
TEN EYCK JOHN J	2LT	0-1302386	0245	2
TENANT CLARK H	MAJ	0-1017371	1163	1
TENBORG HARRY R	MAJ	0-0332150	0144	2
TENCH FREDERICK	MAJ	0-0421425	0164	1
TENEROWICZ STANLEY A	2LT	0-1549618	1044	2
TENNANT DON L	1LT	0-17950C8	0345	2
TENNANT JR ROY I	LTC	0-1542672	1061	1
TENNANT ROBERT O	CW4	W-2008576	0665	3
TENNANT WALTER F	MAJ	0-1303796	0561	2
TENNER ROBERT J	LTC	0-0356768	0246	2
TENNERY RICHARD F	LTC	0-1316867	0267	3
TENNEY EDWARD S	LTC	0-0310699	0360	1
TENNEY PHILLIP H	MAJ	0-1757087	0758	2
TENNEY ROBERT I	CPT	0-1316238	0446	2
TENNEY ROCKWELL C	COL	0-0170846	0554	3
TENNIS CHARLES H	LTC	C-1297451	0461	1
TENNIS MILTON C	CW4	W-2004892	C866	3
TENNISON CLARA H	MAJ	L-0800284	0766	1
TENNISON GUY	CW4	W-2148386	0456	1
TENORE FRANCIS A	LTC	0-1796183	1060	1
TENWINKEL HERBERT F	LTC	0-1040315	1057	1
TEPE PAUL L	LTC	0-0338342	0160	1
TEPERSON HYMAN I	COL	0-0162713	C253	3
TEPLE LAWRENCE S	CPT	0-0367835	1045	2
TEPP LOUIS E	MAJ	0-0244241	0251	3
TEPPER SOL H	1LT	0-1291930	0546	2
TERAKAWA ROBERT H	MAJ	C-1924807	1166	1
TERAZAWA TOKIO G	MAJ	0-2030812	C562	1
TERBORG NORMAN R	2LT	0-1643391	C744	2
TERCERO ISMAEL A	CW3	W-2144143	C466	1
TERCY FRANK J	LTC	0-1584994	1161	1
TERESHINSKI THOMAS J	CPT	0-0557231	1047	1
TERESHKO HELEN M	1LT	N-0725406	0946	1
TERESHUK LOUIS	MAJ	C-1111946	0859	1
TERGERSON ALLOY	MAJ	0-0329930	1045	2
TERHUNE ALMA W	2LT	L-0811704	C744	2
TERHUNE JOHN W	MAJ	C-2012354	0262	1
TERKOSKI SYLVESTER	MAJ	0-1545442	0262	2
TERLAP MARTIN W	MAJ	0-0497038	1053	1
TERLECKI WILLIAM J	LTC	C-1178363	1062	2
TERLIZZI BRUNO C	LTC	0-1299954	0862	1
TERNEY GEORGE E	1LT	0-1112474	C145	2
TERNOSKY MICHAEL A	MAJ	0-0401473	1047	2
TERPENING ROBERT J	LTC	0-0353819	0661	1
TERRA FRANCIS J	MAJ	0-0150243	0-51	3
TERRALL THOMAS A	1LT	0-1288142	1145	2
TERRAZAS PAUL A	CW4	W-2142665	0765	1
TERRELL HERMAN B	CW2	W-2144148	1060	1
TERRELL HERSCHEL H	1LT	0-1294220	0344	2
TERRELL HOMER	COL	0-0481134	0154	1
TERRELL JOHN E	COL	0-0280081	0167	3
TERRELL JR RALPH P	LTC	0-2204085	0767	1
TERRELL KENNETH O	CPT	0-0422871	0246	2
TERRELL RUFLS H	MAJ	C-0251489	C645	2
TERRELL SAMMIE	CPT	0-1293495	C762	1
TERRELL WILLIAM S	LTC	0-0351549	1159	1
TERRILL DUDLEY R	LTC	0-0906173	0765	3
TERRY AGNES G	2LT	N-0788507	0445	1
TERRY ALLEN L	LTC	0-0293677	1058	1
TERRY CHARLES H	MAJ	0-0202712	C648	3
TERRY CHESTER W	COL	0-0216763	C961	3
TERRY CLARENCE	MAJ	0-2043111	0361	1
TERRY EDMUND F	MAJ	0-0502103	1155	1
TERRY EDWARD A	LTC	0-0100425	0660	3
TERRY ELMER E	CW3	W-2114186	0255	1
TERRY EVERETT C	MAJ	C-1109059	1061	1
TERRY FOCH P	MAJ	0-1016280	1262	1
TERRY FORD M	LTC	0-0203948	C553	3
TERRY FRANK E	LTC	0-0388747	0358	1
TERRY FREDERICK	LTC	0-0427394	0660	1
TERRY GEORGE R	COL	0-0232804	0164	3
TERRY GLENN E	1LT	C-1998069	0347	2
TERRY HARRY W	COL	0-0159765	C648	3
TERRY I C HAROLD	MAJ	0-1297807	1062	1
TERRY JAMES H	LTC	0-0417592	0261	1
TERRY JOHN F	MAJ	0-0384627	0546	1
TERRY JOSEPHINE	2LT	N-0753228	1045	2
TERRY JR ARCHIE	CW2	W-2209282	1262	1
TERRY JR LESLIE C	MAJ	C-1290842	C960	1
TERRY JR ROY H	CPT	0-0405712	0448	2
TERRY LAWRENCE D	LTC	0-0453069	1060	1
TERRY LEON E	CW3	RW-2150685	0463	1
TERRY LEROY B	CW3	W-2147964	0863	1
TERRY MARJORIE O	CPT	N-0763462	C547	1
TERRY PAUL L	MAJ	0-0451917	0657	1
TERRY RAY	CW3	W-2148769	0761	1
TERRY RICHARD R	1LT	0-1314074	1144	2
TERRY ROBERT T	MAJ	0-0308075	0946	2
TERRY ROSE VENA	1LT	N-0756803	0446	1
TERRY ROY K	COL	0-0141266	0949	3
TERRY SHIRL L	MAJ	0-1558213	0659	2
TERRY THOMAS E	COL	0-0239153	1053	3
TERRY WALLACE C	MAJ	0-1542675	0855	1
TERRY WILLIAM E	LTC	0-0555841	0765	1
TERRY WILLIAM H	MAJ	0-1041459	0464	1
TERRY WOODROW	LTC	0-1633655	1057	1
TERRYLL GRANT V	CW3	W-2147838	0964	1
TERSCHUREN ALLAN R	CPT	0-1541955	0646	2
TERSTEEGE JOHN F	LTC	0-0369510	0550	1
TERWELP JR ROME A	LTC	0-1545844	0767	1
TERWILLEGAR ROBERT E	LTC	0-0273626	0667	3
TERWILLIGER CHARLES	MAJ	0-0957110	0865	1
TERWILLIGER F WELLS	CPT	0-0358627	0846	2
TERWILLIGER LELAND H	LTC	0-1080076	0361	1
TERWILLIGER RICHARD	LTC	0-227543C	0264	1
TERZELLA JOHN C	MAJ	0-0324501	1047	2
TESALLA ERNESTO	1LT	0-1896482	0849	1
TESCHAN ERHARD G	COL	0-0151773	1049	3
TESCHE WALTER C	MAJ	0-1055476	0662	1
TESCHEL WILLIAM R	MAJ	0-1304291	0747	2
TESDALE THOR L	CW4	W-2143137	0766	1
TESENEER CHARLES W	2LT	0-2003411	0554	2
TESKE BERNARD A	CPT	0-0234710	0357	3
TESKE CLYDE L	MAJ	0-0890450	1057	1
TESLAR MICHAEL J	WO1	W-2120947	1058	1
TESSIER ADRIAN J	CPT	0-0887599	0346	2
TESSIER ALBERT E	CPT	0-0501235	0645	2
TESSIER JR AMOS E	1LT	0-129645C	0445	2
TESSLER ARTHUR D	CPT	0-0484807	0345	2
TESSLER ERNEST W	MAJ	0-2055118	0160	1
TESSMER LLOYD M	CPT	0-2011102	1158	1
TESTA JOHN F	MAJ	0-0336303	0561	1
TESTER JAMES L	LTC	0-1551318	1061	1
TESTER JOSEPH J	CW3	W-2136729	0655	1
TESTERMAN ROBERT H	CW3	W-2148064	0263	1
TESTI EOLO	MAJ	0-1036406	0560	2
TETA ANTHONY R	2LT	0-0111114	0254	3
TETER ELMER P	2LT	0-1551531	0943	2
TETER HOWARD G	CW2	W-2114147	0350	2
TETLEY OWEN P	LTC	0-1291355	0761	1
TETOR PAUL S	MAJ	0-1339776	0265	1
TETRAULT EDWARD J	CPT	0-1545504	0454	1
TETRAULT LEONARD R	LTC	0-1326942	0862	1
TETRUD WILLIAM H	LTC	0-0320989	0467	3
TEUKE GILBERT A	CPT	0-1287087	0946	2
TEVAULT RONALD E	MAJ	0-0579011	0966	1
TEWALT JAMES A	1LT	0-1174726	0244	2
TEWMEY BRUCE F	MAJ	0-1340715	0665	1
TEWSON RONALD E	LTC	0-0268327	1266	3
TEXTER KENNETH G	1LT	0-0405158	0743	2
TEYSSIER ROGER J	LTC	0-0398234	0562	1
TEZAK JOHN	LTC	0-0464941	0762	1
THACH HENRY C	LTC	0-1295794	0267	3
THACHER CHARLES S	MAJ	0-1576736	0661	1
THACHER JAMES S	1LT	0-2292648	0654	3
THACKAPERRY SAMUEL J	LTC	0-0471574	C966	3
THACKER COKE C	LTC	0-0250081	0866	3
THACKER ROWENA R	2LT	N-0726292	0844	1
THACKER WILLIAM A	LTC	0-035560C	0646	2
THACKERY ROGER L	CPT	0-0582495	C361	1
THACKREY SAMUEL I	COL	0-0107681	0547	2
THACKSTON JOHN A	MAJ	0-1285138	0147	2
THADEN HERBERT V	MAJ	0-0127296	0258	3
THALER CLARK M	LTC	0-0363693	0859	1
THAMES HENRY S	CW2	W-2207C58	0464	1
THAMES JAMES P	MAJ	C-1289339	1060	1
THAMES JAMES R	CPT	0-1874281	0762	1
THANE JR GEORGE	1LT	W-2200186	0666	3
THARP CHARLES M	LTC	0-0910783	0463	3
THARP KATHLEEN N	1LT	N-0795071	0847	1
THARP MARVEL M	MAJ	L-0701925	1063	1

292-560 O - 68 - 22

NAME	GRADE	SVC NO	DATE RET MO YR	RET CODE
THARPE LUTHER	2LT	0-0496805	C453	1
THATCHER CARL V	CW2	W-2132064	C450	2
THATCHER DONALD D	1LT	C-1546190	C646	2
THATCHER JR MOSES	COL	0-0306149	0766	3
THATCHER ROBERT L	CPT	0-0678976	1147	2
THAU AUGUST O	LTC	0-0262421	1266	3
THAXTON EMMETT	CPT	0-0219674	1150	3
THAXTON HUGH B	1LT	0-0357485	0144	2
THAXTON MARVIN L	LTC	0-2275045	0462	1
THAXTON WILLIAM D	CPT	0-0966359	0657	1
THAYER ALBERT M	MAJ	0-2033543	0163	1
THAYER EDWIN B	CPT	0-0396974	1045	2
THAYER GEORGE E	CPT	0-0252155	0367	3
THAYER JOHN E	LTC	0-1285518	1061	1
THAYER JOHN M	LTC	0-0239240	0359	2
THAYER JR EDWARD A	CPT	0-0538140	C846	2
THAYER LEROY F	MAJ	0-0321506	0455	1
THAYER PHILLIPS D	MAJ	C-0200817	C458	3
THAYER PHILLIPS L	LTC	0-0420196	0963	3
THEBERT FREDERICK	CPT	0-1105862	C347	2
THEBERT LEO W	CPT	0-0507852	0450	1
THEDOS JACK V	MAJ	C-0455098	0161	1
THEIL LEON S	CPT	0-1995014	C246	2
THEIS ETHEL J	CPT	R-0000627	1163	1
THEIS JOHN F	LTC	0-0272311	0167	3
THEISEN EUGENE C	2LT	0-1327302	C146	2
THEISS HENRY D	MAJ	C-0312435	0363	3
THEISS JOHN S	MAJ	0-0244139	1165	3
THELEN JR LEO A	1LT	0-1044401	1145	2
THEN JOHN V	LTC	0-0358290	0957	1
THEO ERNEST	MAJ	C-0270405	C865	3
THEOBALD HERBERT P	LTC	0-1166632	0163	1
THEOBALD JOHN W	LTC	0-0557567	1163	1
THEODORE NORBERT A	COL	0-0358294	0762	3
THERIAULT GERALD F	LTC	0-1306173	C861	2
THEROUX JR LEO B	MAJ	0-1913413	C967	1
THEROUX KENNETH J	CW3	W-2205588	0666	1
THEUS JAMES T	LTC	0-0439237	0862	1
THEUS JR FRANK P	MAJ	0-1020130	C461	1
THEWLIS LEONARD L	MAJ	0-1057910	0163	1
THIBAUDEAU PHILIP A	MAJ	C-0255809	1259	3
THIBAULT GILBERT A	LTC	0-0549035	0965	1
THIBEAU ROY S	LTC	0-0331229	1059	1
THIBEAULT RAYMOND E	LTC	0-1174985	C865	1
THIBEAUX SR LOUIS A	2LT	0-1950807	1046	1
THIBODEAU FRANK W	CW3	W-2143143	1061	1
THIBODEAU GEORGE F	MAJ	C-1314349	1263	1
THIBODEAU WILLIAM J	COL	0-0286837	C853	3
THIBODEAUX JASON J	MAJ	0-0966629	1066	1
THIBODEAUX SIDNEY J	CPT	0-1319358	0358	1
THIERAUTH CHARLES K	LTC	0-1052997	0567	1
THIEL CLIFFORD R	CW3	W-2142069	0662	1
THIEL LESLIE D	MAJ	0-0236957	C165	3
THIEL NORMAN E	MAJ	C-1691226	0346	2
THIEL RAYMOND M	2LT	0-1310785	0545	2
THIEL ROBERT A	CPT	0-1107175	C747	2
THIEL ROBERT L	LTC	0-1182977	1162	1
THIEL WILFRED E	CW3	W-2205114	0364	1
THIELE WALTHER H	COL	C-0333816	1165	3
THIELEN RAYMOND J	MAJ	0-0564462	C162	1
THIELER GEORGE	LTC	0-0220328	1156	3
THIEMAN LIONEL O	CW3	W-2147186	0967	1
THIEMANN VINCENT A	MAJ	0-0212369	0464	3
THIEME EARL L	MAJ	0-1882412	1147	1
THIEME HOWARD T	1LT	0-1109061	0345	2
THIEROLF DWIGHT R	CPT	0-2262907	0661	1
THIEROLF LEROY F	CW4	W-2143547	0165	1
THIERRY JOHN H	1LT	0-1316240	0347	2
THIERS WENDELL H	CW3	W-2144197	0261	1
THIES FLOYD L	MAJ	0-1824098	0757	1
THIES LAWRENCE H	CPT	0-1042966	0757	1
THIESS WILLIAM J	2LT	0-1285139	0244	2
THIGPEN OSWALD C	MAJ	0-0249206	C965	3
THILL LEONARD C	MAJ	C-0245030	1061	3
THISLER JOHN O	LTC	0-1302550	0662	1

NAME	GRADE	SVC NO	DATE RET MO YR	RET CODE
THISTEL MOSES N	LTC	0-0108277	0856	3
THISTLE THOMAS L	LTC	0-0214990	0354	3
THIXTON JAMES O	CPT	0-1287088	0161	1
THODE EVERETT W	CPT	0-0542985	0947	2
THODE HARRY W	COL	0-1055994	0966	1
THOE REUBEN S	1LT	0-1315638	0346	2
THOEMKE GEORGE W	MAJ	0-1322486	0763	1
THOENEN CLARENCE A	CW3	RW-2147327	1265	1
THOIN PHILIP P	COL	0-0301605	0266	3
THOLEN HARRY J	LTC	0-1045954	1161	1
THOLL JR ERWIN F	MAJ	0-2033789	1265	1
THOM ERNEST P	MAJ	0-0145231	0952	3
THOM GEORGE E	CW3	W-2123283	0661	1
THOM HAROLD H	MAJ	0-0132069	0648	3
THOM JR CHARLES H	CPT	0-0484340	0240	1
THOM SR VICTOR L	LTC	0-0334635	0760	1
THOMA DANIEL R	LTC	0-0315001	1159	1
THOMA HARRY C	LTC	0-0250444	0965	3
THOMA JOSEPH L	CPT	0-1535093	1046	2
THOMAN KENNETH R	LTC	0-0231494	0561	3
THOMAN ROBERT J	COL	0-0194669	0761	3
THOMAS ALBERT I	MAJ	0-1540612	0558	1
THOMAS ALLEN B	LTC	0-1595864	0967	3
THOMAS AMBROSE R	2LT	0-1031615	1045	2
THOMAS ANNA N	CPT	N-0727624	0846	1
THOMAS ANTHONY	MAJ	0-1648187	0457	1
THOMAS ARLENE M	MAJ	N-0797351	0665	1
THOMAS ARTHUR B	COL	0-0263895	0258	3
THOMAS ARTHUR H	COL	0-0326452	0966	3
THOMAS ARTHUR S	CW3	W-2145594	0466	2
THOMAS AUSTIN M	CPT	0-1950808	1064	1
THOMAS BENJAMIN F	MAJ	0-0172248	0254	3
THOMAS BERT S	COL	0-0222926	1054	3
THOMAS BRENNAN S	LTC	0-0252575	1044	2
THOMAS BROWER B	LTC	0-0518293	0666	3
THOMAS CARL L	CPT	0-0545587	0158	1
THOMAS CASSIUS L	MAJ	0-1287434	0860	1
THOMAS CHARLES H	CW4	W-2103522	0260	2
THOMAS CHARLES L	1LT	0-1102501	0146	2
THOMAS CHARLES L	MAJ	0-1824391	0847	1
THOMAS CHARLES M	LTC	0-0275604	0246	2
THOMAS CHESTER A	MAJ	0-1593884	0761	1
THOMAS CHESTER B	LTC	0-1948235	0663	1
THOMAS CLARENCE F	CPT	0-1315237	1058	1
THOMAS CLARENCE H	CW2	W-2148422	1060	1
THOMAS CLIFFORD A	CW3	W-2205550	0766	1
THOMAS COYL B	LTC	0-0257950	0666	3
THOMAS CALF E	LTC	0-0289757	0557	1
THOMAS DALLAS O	MAJ	0-1289650	1058	1
THOMAS DANIEL C	MAJ	0-0359418	0963	1
THOMAS DANIEL C	LTC	0-1179719	0962	1
THOMAS DANIEL L	MAJ	0-0422582	1059	1
THOMAS DELMUS D	MAJ	0-1306910	0857	1
THOMAS DONALD J	MAJ	0-1285847	0563	1
THOMAS DOUGLAS S	LTC	0-2047523	0762	1
THOMAS DWIGHT H	MAJ	0-0190160	0744	2
THOMAS EARLE L	LTC	0-0124160	0754	3
THOMAS EDGAR L	CW2	W-2148384	1060	1
THOMAS EDWARD C O	COL	0-0107795	0152	3
THOMAS EDWARD H	CPT	0-0122363	0152	3
THOMAS EDWARD W	2LT	0-1334777	C863	2
THOMAS EDWIN	MAJ	0-0425750	1161	1
THOMAS EDWIN M	COL	0-0368710	0964	3
THOMAS ELMER S	MAJ	0-0475091	0148	1
THOMAS ELZY A	CW3	W-2152254	0666	1
THOMAS ERNEST R	CPT	0-0314915	C259	3
THOMAS EUGENE	MAJ	0-1182281	0657	1
THOMAS EVERETT A	LTC	0-0260439	0567	3
THOMAS FRANCES	MAJ	N-0742828	0365	1
THOMAS FRANCIS L	MAJ	0-2034074	0963	1
THOMAS FRANK	CW4	W-2101061	0155	1
THOMAS FRANK H	CW3	W-2152752	0466	1
THOMAS FRANK J	LTC	0-1035382	1263	1
THOMAS FRANK N	LTC	0-0264525	0266	3
THOMAS FRANK P	1LT	0-1291543	0745	2

NAME	GRADE	SVC NO	DATE RET MO YR	RET CODE
THOMAS FRED C	CPT	0-0498999	0448	1
THOMAS FRED E	LTC	0-0450909	0762	1
THOMAS FRED J	MAJ	0-1797905	C857	1
THOMAS FREDERICK	MAJ	0-0113762	0449	3
THOMAS FREDERICK	LTC	0-0229855	0755	3
THOMAS G CLARE	MAJ	0-0402885	0546	2
THOMAS GARRY C	CW2	W-2117530	0957	1
THOMAS GEORGE H	LTC	0-0260523	1060	3
THOMAS GEORGE J	MAJ	0-1338657	C163	2
THOMAS GEORGE R	LTC	0-1325533	C163	1
THOMAS GEORGE S	CPT	0-0542329	0548	2
THOMAS GILBERT L	MAJ	0-1339408	1264	1
THOMAS GORDON C	LTC	0-0343988	0146	2
THOMAS GORDON E	COL	C-0241198	0466	3
THOMAS GORDON W	CPT	0-0428586	0946	2
THOMAS GROVER F	MAJ	0-0456679	0258	1
THOMAS HAROLD B	MAJ	0-1653568	0245	2
THOMAS HAROLD C	COL	0-0167043	0547	2
THOMAS HAROLD E	LTC	0-0243748	0766	3
THOMAS HAROLD F	MAJ	C-2036893	0459	1
THOMAS HAROLD H	LTC	0-1286354	1060	1
THOMAS HAROLD P	COL	0-0160353	0156	3
THOMAS HAROLD W	COL	0-0237795	0562	3
THOMAS HARRY A	1LT	0-0497824	0646	2
THOMAS HARVEY R	CPT	0-1641854	0357	1
THOMAS HENRY A	CW2	W-2147316	0361	1
THOMAS HENRY E	MAJ	C-1329254	C161	1
THOMAS HIRAM	CPT	0-0497212	C546	2
THOMAS J T	LTC	0-0353895	1060	1
THOMAS JACK N	CW2	W-2148889	0760	1
THOMAS JACKSON C	CPT	0-0888920	1054	1
THOMAS JAMES A	2LT	0-C108993	0234	2
THOMAS JAMES E	COL	0-0246179	0353	1
THOMAS JAMES E	CPT	C-0450576	C952	1
THOMAS JAMES H	CPT	0-1295642	0446	2
THOMAS JAMES M	CW4	W-2113571	0260	1
THOMAS JAMES R	1LT	0-1998039	1047	2
THOMAS JAMES T	CPT	0-0920228	0346	2
THOMAS JAMES T	LTC	0-1651662	0966	1
THOMAS JAMES W	LTC	0-0370278	0763	3
THOMAS JANIE	CPT	N-0789316	0747	1
THOMAS JERRY	MAJ	0-0455947	0457	1
THOMAS JESSE D	MAJ	0-1951637	0561	1
THOMAS JEWELL A	MAJ	N-0720397	C761	1
THOMAS JOE	COL	0-0165098	0859	3
THOMAS JOHN A	LTC	0-0393561	1262	1
THOMAS JOHN B	MAJ	0-0956559	0463	1
THOMAS JOHN H	LTC	0-0261707	0464	3
THOMAS JOHN H J	CPT	0-0243383	0545	2
THOMAS JOHN P	MAJ	C-0456411	0746	1
THOMAS JOHN R	LTC	0-0234615	1065	3
THOMAS JOHN W	COL	0-0286097	C562	1
THOMAS JOHN W	1LT	0-0373044	1149	1
THOMAS JOHN W	2LT	0-1336285	C247	2
THOMAS JOSEPH C	MAJ	C-0973461	0163	1
THOMAS JOSEPH M	LTC	0-0259875	C466	3
THOMAS JOSEPH R	MAJ	C-1172693	0660	1
THOMAS JR ALBERT S	CPT	0-0315668	1045	2
THOMAS JR CHARLES A	2LT	0-1081183	C844	2
THOMAS JR HUBERT M	LTC	0-1181782	0565	1
THOMAS JR JOHN P	LTC	0-1058136	0864	1
THOMAS JR PETER B	MAJ	0-1688656	0166	1
THOMAS JR TOM E	LTC	C-1177663	1161	1
THOMAS JR WALTER	COL	C-0344189	C853	1
THOMAS JR WILLIAM	CPT	0-1052639	C161	1
THOMAS JR WILLIAM J	CW2	W-2148941	0162	1
THOMAS KARL W	MAJ	C-2055860	1060	1
THOMAS KENNETH E	LTC	0-0414481	0556	2
THOMAS KENNETH L	MAJ	0-1293676	0157	1
THOMAS KENNETH R	1LT	0-1286395	C346	2
THOMAS KENNETH W	LTC	0-1644848	C161	1
THOMAS LAWRENCE W	MAJ	0-1746294	0261	2
THOMAS LEANDER K	CW4	W-2110469	1154	1
THOMAS LEO F	MAJ	0-1306768	0864	1
THOMAS LEON A	MAJ	0-1540926	0663	1

NAME	GRADE	SVC NO	DATE RET MO YR	RET CODE
THOMAS LEONARD M	1LT	0-0496C48	0447	1
THOMAS LEROY	LTC	0-0347893	0560	1
THOMAS LEROY	MAJ	0-2008523	0763	1
THOMAS LESTER C	MAJ	0-2009388	0158	1
THOMAS LESTER H	2LT	0-2033234	1055	1
THOMAS LLOYD I	CW3	W-2204970	0167	1
THOMAS LUTHER M	LTC	0-1314972	0862	1
THOMAS MANLY J	CW4	W-2142526	0667	1
THOMAS MARK E	LTC	0-0230045	0765	3
THOMAS MARTIN A	LTC	0-0360664	1056	1
THOMAS MARVIN J	CW3	W-2150365	0863	1
THOMAS MICHAEL R	MAJ	0-1949026	0766	1
THOMAS MORRIS C	COL	0-0278489	1065	3
THOMAS MORTIMER B	2LT	0-1324675	1144	2
THOMAS NEIL C	COL	0-0229753	0261	3
THOMAS NELSON A	LTC	0-0511194	0565	3
THOMAS OCTAVE F V	LTC	0-0406207	0465	1
THOMAS OTAWAY M	LTC	0-1042728	1158	2
THOMAS PAUL B	1LT	0-1315639	0346	2
THOMAS PETER	CPT	0-1796378	0762	1
THOMAS PHILIP B	LTC	0-0198922	0461	3
THOMAS PHILIP E	1LT	0-1181165	0945	2
THOMAS RALPH L	MAJ	0-0902876	1045	2
THOMAS RAMON	LTC	0-0331923	C560	1
THOMAS RAY C	COL	0-0168157	1058	3
THOMAS RAY C	MAJ	0-1166849	0157	2
THOMAS RAY S	LTC	0-1590851	0863	1
THOMAS RAYMOND B	CPT	0-1725977	C154	2
THOMAS RAYMOND M	CW4	W-2136753	0862	1
THOMAS REBECCA	1LT	N-0727687	C149	2
THOMAS RICHARD C	2LT	0-1594526	0744	2
THOMAS RICHARD H	MAJ	0-1056588	C761	1
THOMAS RICHARD S	MAJ	0-0966015	C866	1
THOMAS ROBERT C	CPT	0-1043812	C359	1
THOMAS ROBERT C	CPT	0-2210220	C166	1
THOMAS ROBERT D	MAJ	0-0221390	0763	3
THOMAS ROBERT E	1LT	0-0475908	0747	2
THOMAS ROBERT J	LTC	0-0564468	0661	1
THOMAS ROBERT C	LTC	0-1044127	0563	1
THOMAS ROBERT R	LTC	0-0175415	0359	3
THOMAS ROBERT R	LTC	0-1305698	0556	1
THOMAS ROBERT S	LTC	0-0228623	0462	1
THOMAS ROBERT T	CPT	0-2019673	0461	1
THOMAS RODGER L	MAJ	0-0249955	0544	1
THOMAS ROGER W	2LT	0-1181485	0145	2
THOMAS ROLEN E	CW4	W-2113691	0657	1
THOMAS ROLLIN R	MAJ	0-2096903	0666	1
THOMAS RONALD F	LTC	0-0256720	0960	1
THOMAS ROSCOE	1LT	0-1305133	0246	2
THOMAS ROY C	LTC	0-1765231	0864	1
THOMAS ROY G	2LT	0-1300885	0845	2
THOMAS RUFUS R	CW3	RW-2142908	0562	1
THOMAS SAMUEL M	B G	0-0230963	0164	3
THOMAS SAMUEL M	1LT	0-0372941	0745	2
THOMAS SARAH F	1LT	N-0725211	1146	1
THOMAS SHIPLEY	COL	0-0103241	1052	3
THOMAS SHIRLEY J	MAJ	0-1013588	0662	1
THOMAS SR GEORGE H	MAJ	0-1947274	0761	1
THOMAS TATUM L	LTC	0-0282919	0267	3
THOMAS THOMAS J	LTC	0-0312154	0562	2
THOMAS VESSIE H	MAJ	0-0472659	1045	2
THOMAS VICTOR G	MAJ	0-1173810	0657	1
THOMAS VIRGINIA E	2LT	N-0773396	0346	1
THOMAS WALTER D	COL	0-0151724	0655	1
THOMAS WALTER E	LTC	0-1797906	0261	1
THOMAS WALTER J	MAJ	0-0398265	0856	1
THOMAS WALTER M	LTC	0-0309216	0964	3
THOMAS WESLEY F	LTC	0-1114310	0463	1
THOMAS WILLARD J	1LT	0-0387815	0946	2
THOMAS WILLIAM C	CW3	W-2141468	0161	1
THOMAS WILLIAM E	MAJ	0-0924653	0451	1
THOMAS WILLIAM E	LTC	0-1300551	0261	1
THOMAS WILLIAM G	LTC	0-0110422	0150	3
THOMAS WILLIAM H	LTC	0-0814842	0265	1
THOMAS WILLIAM H	CW2	W-2211868	0164	1

NAME	GRADE	SVC NO	DATE RET MO YR	RET CODE
THOMAS WILLIAM J	MAJ	C-0266080	0956	3
THOMAS WILLIAM J	CW3	W-2141469	0161	1
THOMAS WILLIAM L	LTC	0-1166398	1160	1
THOMAS WILLIAM L	CPT	0-1923529	0764	1
THOMAS WILLIAM L	MAJ	0-1923565	0267	1
THOMAS WILLIAM P	LTC	0-0316931	0146	2
THOMAS WILSON	LTC	0-0234021	0657	3
THOMAS WINTHROP A	LTC	0-0191050	0163	3
THOMASON EDWARD A	LTC	0-0236362	1263	3
THOMASON HENRY I	MAJ	0-0222927	0356	3
THOMASON JOHN R	CW2	W-3200474	0867	1
THOMASON LEO B	1LT	0-1301560	1045	2
THOMASON WILLIAM J	1LT	0-5323654	0567	2
THOMASSEN THOMAS T	MAJ	0-1549391	1164	1
THOMASSON HAROLD	MAJ	0-0226166	0164	3
THOMASSON JAMES F	MAJ	0-1642647	0461	1
THOMASSON JOHN D	CW2	W-2147342	0764	1
THOMASSON SR EARL L	CW3	W-2120845	0760	1
THOMBS WILLIAM H	1LT	0-1573626	0662	1
THOME LEONARD J	LTC	0-0285626	0552	1
THOMLEY VESTER G	LTC	0-1313324	0360	1
THOMPSON ALBERT	MAJ	C-0243643	0558	3
THOMPSON ALBERT A	CW2	W-2131808	0653	2
THOMPSON ALBERT C	CW3	W-2146771	1064	1
THOMPSON ALFRED W	CW3	W-2205361	0367	1
THOMPSON ALLEN T	CPT	0-1899402	1059	1
THOMPSON ARTHUR B	CPT	0-0425561	0247	1
THOMPSON ARTHUR L	WO1	W-2123093	0946	2
THOMPSON AYLMER S N	CPT	0-0139598	0251	3
THOMPSON BEAUFORD A	CPT	0-0493966	1047	2
THOMPSON BENJAMIN H	LTC	0-2027053	0366	1
THOMPSON BERNICE G	1LT	N-0763272	0246	1
THOMPSON CARL R	1LT	0-1635406	1046	2
THOMPSON CARLETON K	CW4	W-2113624	0659	1
THOMPSON CARROLL B	LTC	0-1320375	0962	1
THOMPSON CARROLL I	LTC	0-1555641	0462	1
THOMPSON CHARLES	CPT	0-1014884	0147	2
THOMPSON CHARLES A	2LT	0-0438044	0545	2
THOMPSON CHARLES P	LTC	0-0390046	0147	2
THOMPSON CHARLES F	LTC	0-0275880	1160	3
THOMPSON CHARLES F	CPT	0-0465758	0447	2
THOMPSON CHARLES H	CPT	0-0499491	0356	3
THOMPSON CHARLES J	LTC	0-1289165	0761	1
THOMPSON CHARLES R	LTC	0-0153270	0956	3
THOMPSON CHARLES R	LTC	0-1641016	1061	1
THOMPSON CLARENCE H	MAJ	0-0346977	0955	1
THOMPSON CLAUD W	LTC	0-1178008	1160	1
THOMPSON CLAUDE S	LTC	0-0215950	0962	3
THOMPSON CLAUDE V	COL	0-0200713	0255	3
THOMPSON CLAYTON F	LTC	0-1646655	0163	1
THOMPSON CLAYTON R	CW2	W-2210099	0666	1
THOMPSON CLYDE F	CPT	0-1546750	0546	2
THOMPSON CLYDE R	MAJ	0-0970620	0747	2
THOMPSON CLYDE R	CW4	W-2119298	0865	1
THOMPSON CORNELIUS	MAJ	C-1280713	1160	1
THOMPSON COURTENAY	CPT	0-0918446	1045	2
THOMPSON DALCOURTE	CPT	C-0890124	0454	2
THOMPSON DAVID L	MAJ	C-1846078	1157	1
THOMPSON DAVID O	MAJ	C-1684073	0546	2
THOMPSON DEWITT	COL	0-0441693	0954	1
THOMPSON DONALD C	MAJ	C-1017737	0758	1
THOMPSON DONALD H	WO1	W-3430001	0261	1
THOMPSON DONALD O	CPT	0-1325680	0559	1
THOMPSON DONALD O	CPT	0-2017302	0958	1
THOMPSON EARL G	MAJ	C-0279615	0565	3
THOMPSON EARL R	CPT	0-0271609	0458	3
THOMPSON EARLE A	CPT	0-0213447	0462	3
THOMPSON EDMUND G	MAJ	C-1063054	1263	1
THOMPSON EDWARD A	LTC	0-0423237	0161	2
THOMPSON EDWARD J	COL	0-0272780	1264	3
THOMPSON EDWARD K	CPT	0-0288995	0561	3
THOMPSON EDWARD L	CW3	W-2148771	0955	1
THOMPSON ELBERT J	1LT	0-1041661	0145	2
THOMPSON ELDON A	LTC	0-1280608	0165	3
THOMPSON ELI A	CPT	0-0496773	0657	1
THOMPSON ELMER B	CPT	0-1103438	0246	2
THOMPSON ELMYRA	2LT	N-0763794	0446	1
THOMPSON EMMETT W	LTC	0-0414557	0161	1
THOMPSON ERIC D	CPT	0-1717465	0446	2
THOMPSON ERNEST F	MAJ	0-1550514	0449	2
THOMPSON EUGENE E	CPT	0-0252703	1054	3
THOMPSON FLOYD A	LTC	0-0300088	1066	3
THOMPSON FRANCIS A	MAJ	0-0175635	0959	3
THOMPSON FRANCIS G	LTC	0-0454496	0758	1
THOMPSON FRANCIS J	1LT	0-1797042	0845	2
THOMPSON FRANK B	COL	0-0180801	0755	3
THOMPSON FRANK G	MAJ	0-0397747	0660	1
THOMPSON FRANK L	1LT	0-0456255	0946	2
THOMPSON FRANKLIN B	LTC	0-0147502	0854	3
THOMPSON FRED F	MAJ	C-0182453	1057	3
THOMPSON FREDERICK	CPT	0-0388924	1045	2
THOMPSON GEORGE H	MAJ	0-0212990	0860	3
THOMPSON GEORGE D	LTC	0-0261681	0761	3
THOMPSON GEORGE V	LTC	0-0922530	0363	3
THOMPSON GEORGE W	MAJ	0-0212992	0363	3
THOMPSON GEORGE W	CPT	0-1173486	0158	1
THOMPSON GERALD W	LTC	0-1168491	0962	1
THOMPSON GILBERT	LTC	0-0443923	0453	1
THOMPSON GILBERT	CPT	0-2275904	0857	2
THOMPSON GILBERT T	MAJ	0-1166196	0847	2
THOMPSON GLEN D	MAJ	0-0216009	0655	3
THOMPSON HAROLD C	COL	0-0114272	0457	3
THOMPSON HAROLD H	CW3	W-2145522	0461	1
THOMPSON HAROLD W	LTC	0-0161500	0955	3
THOMPSON HARRY G	CPT	0-1937564	0466	1
THOMPSON HARRY W	LTC	0-0234514	0757	3
THOMPSON HARVEY R	CW4	W-2147615	0657	1
THOMPSON HASKELL L	LTC	0-0530315	1265	1
THOMPSON HENRY C	CPT	0-0969252	1161	1
THOMPSON HENRY C	MAJ	0-0573495	0464	1
THOMPSON HERBERT W	MAJ	0-1316241	0649	2
THOMPSON HOMER E	LTC	0-0283157	1167	3
THOMPSON HOMER W	LTC	0-0460273	1064	3
THOMPSON HOWARD E	LTC	0-0406120	0764	1
THOMPSON HOWARD W	LTC	0-0509183	0257	1
THOMPSON HUGH J	MAJ	0-0993164	0963	1
THOMPSON IRA B	LTC	0-0169496	0649	3
THOMPSON JACK	MAJ	0-0296254	1047	2
THOMPSON JACK	CPT	0-1648518	0348	2
THOMPSON JACK H	MAJ	0-1648733	1162	1
THOMPSON JAMES B	CPT	0-0971747	0761	1
THOMPSON JAMES C	CPT	0-0437655	0855	1
THOMPSON JAMES D	MAJ	0-0574081	1061	1
THOMPSON JAMES E	1LT	0-0413515	0644	2
THOMPSON JAMES F	WO1	W-2145913	1053	1
THOMPSON JAMES H	LTC	0-0272412	1062	1
THOMPSON JAMES H	CPT	0-0553878	0361	1
THOMPSON JAMES L	MAJ	0-0478783	0650	2
THOMPSON JAMES O	LTC	0-0406157	0664	1
THOMPSON JAMES R	MAJ	C-0272221	1165	3
THOMPSON JAMES R	CPT	0-1924065	1165	1
THOMPSON JAY E	MAJ	0-0208729	0-48	3
THOMPSON JEROME F	COL	0-0113633	1155	3
THOMPSON JERRY J	2LT	0-0536044	0845	2
THOMPSON JERRY N	2LT	0-1638658	0344	2
THOMPSON JESSE C	CW2	W-2206316	0963	1
THOMPSON JESSIE C	2LT	N-0700557	1040	2
THOMPSON JOE A	CW3	W-2208308	0866	1
THOMPSON JOHN B	CPT	0-1684084	1143	1
THOMPSON JOHN C	COL	0-0273883	0661	3
THOMPSON JOHN C	MAJ	0-1589543	1162	1
THOMPSON JOHN H	2LT	0-1185202	0145	2
THOMPSON JOHN J	MAJ	0-2036588	0461	1
THOMPSON JOHN R	COL	0-0111140	0648	3
THOMPSON JOHN R	1LT	0-0532287	0447	2
THOMPSON JOHN R	CPT	0-1302388	0546	2
THOMPSON JOHN R	CW3	W-2148362	1262	1
THOMPSON JOHN W	1LT	0-0268581	0653	1
THOMPSON JOHN W	LTC	0-0460008	0762	1
THOMPSON JOSEPH G	MAJ	0-0922926	0946	2
THOMPSON JOSEPH H	CPT	0-1587681	0157	1
THOMPSON JOSEPH M	LTC	0-0298343	0845	2
THOMPSON JOSEPH P	LTC	0-0262883	0567	3
THOMPSON JR F L	MAJ	C-0399648	0448	2
THOMPSON JR HUBERT A	MAJ	C-1306175	0161	1
THOMPSON JR LLOYD L	CPT	0-1685148	1045	1
THOMPSON JR LOUIS G	MAJ	C-1822652	0867	1
THOMPSON JR N B	MAJ	C-0167846	0950	3
THOMPSON KARL B	LTC	0-0452951	0756	1
THOMPSON KENNETH F	1LT	0-1303575	0845	2
THOMPSON KENNETH F	CW3	W-2144161	0667	1
THOMPSON KENNETH W	MAJ	0-0112315	1053	3
THOMPSON LARGENT C	MAJ	C-0497491	0154	1
THOMPSON LARRY D	1LT	0-0425628	0445	2
THOMPSON LAVERNE F	CPT	0-1947369	0259	1
THOMPSON LAWRENCE L	CPT	0-0974118	0662	1
THOMPSON LEE B	COL	0-0213541	0546	2
THOMPSON LEIGH	LTC	0-0451500	0860	1
THOMPSON LELAND W	CW4	W-2105725	0662	1
THOMPSON LEON G	1LT	0-0109838	1034	1
THOMPSON LEONARD A	1LT	0-1822212	0246	1
THOMPSON LEONARD R	CPT	0-1589017	0860	1
THOMPSON LESLIE B	LTC	0-0450654	0657	1
THOMPSON LESTER E	LTC	0-0188229	0349	3
THOMPSON LLEWELLYN	LTC	0-1928261	0262	2
THOMPSON LLOYD J	1LT	0-0483656	0645	2
THOMPSON LOUIS R	LTC	0-0216585	0364	3
THOMPSON LOYD	MAJ	0-0259045	0867	3
THOMPSON LOYD B	MAJ	0-0432909	1158	1
THOMPSON MARSHALL F	LTC	0-2053894	0357	1
THOMPSON MCDUFFIE	CW2	W-2209108	0261	1
THOMPSON MERON J	1LT	0-2008403	0547	2
THOMPSON MERRILL R	CPT	0-0177404	1059	3
THOMPSON MIKE	CPT	0-1013661	0550	1
THOMPSON MILTON E	CW4	W-2144482	0167	1
THOMPSON MYRON M	MAJ	C-1575226	0263	1
THOMPSON NATHAN P	LTC	0-0350077	0660	1
THOMPSON NORMAN E	1LT	0-1018463	0857	1
THOMPSON NORMAN F	CPT	0-0486010	1046	1
THOMPSON NORMAN L	COL	0-0189013	0857	1
THOMPSON NORMAN R	MAJ	0-1011964	0860	1
THOMPSON NORMAN R S	LTC	0-0125089	0154	3
THOMPSON OLE E	LTC	0-0251771	0545	2
THOMPSON ORAL H	2LT	N-0736546	0845	1
THOMPSON ORVILLE H	MAJ	0-0196842	0256	1
THOMPSON ORVILLE J	CW4	W-2000608	0461	2
THOMPSON PATRICK H	1LT	0-1018618	0845	2
THOMPSON PAUL M	LTC	0-0489923	1054	1
THOMPSON PAUL M	MAJ	C-1285519	1065	1
THOMPSON PAUL W	2LT	0-2000984	1045	2
THOMPSON RALPH S	MAJ	0-1019356	0261	1
THOMPSON RAYMOND C	MAJ	0-1591479	1162	1
THOMPSON RICHARD G	MAJ	C-1291196	1165	1
THOMPSON RICHARD J	CPT	0-0549316	0548	1
THOMPSON ROBERT A	1LT	0-1924691	0555	2
THOMPSON ROBERT C	LTC	0-1320981	0167	1
THOMPSON ROBERT E	COL	0-0298882	1061	3
THOMPSON ROBERT H	COL	0-0247431	0263	3
THOMPSON ROBERT H	LTC	0-1323875	0361	1
THOMPSON ROBERT J	CW2	W-2214056	0667	1
THOMPSON ROBERT W	LTC	C-1946624	1066	1
THOMPSON ROGER M	MAJ	0-1287786	1055	1
THOMPSON ROSCOE R	CPT	0-1120786	1060	1
THOMPSON ROY B	CW3	W-2142666	0359	1
THOMPSON ROY E	1LT	0-0448405	0145	2
THOMPSON ROY H	COL	0-0297221	0167	3
THOMPSON RUSSELL F	COL	C-0260292	0766	3
THOMPSON RUSSELL J	LTC	C-1031767	0766	1
THOMPSON RUTH E	1LT	N-0730929	1045	1
THOMPSON TAYLOR F	LTC	0-0403231	0354	2
THOMPSON THEARON F	CW4	W-2203281	0556	1
THOMPSON THEODORE A	MAJ	C-1292255	0261	2
THOMPSON THOMAS F	1LT	0-1845801	1045	2
THOMPSON THOMAS M	LTC	0-0371985	0561	1
THOMPSON TOMMY	MAJ	0-0222068	1046	1
THOMPSON TRACY L	MAJ	0-2262146	1164	1
THOMPSON VELORIS O	CPT	0-1017788	0261	1
THOMPSON VERNON C	MAJ	0-1639730	0863	1
THOMPSON VICTOR L	LTC	0-0213361	0962	3
THOMPSON VIRGIL G	CW2	W-2150699	1056	1
THOMPSON WALTER	LTC	0-0232161	0560	1
THOMPSON WALTER B	CPT	0-0499651	1053	1
THOMPSON WALTER R	LTC	0-2055487	0261	1
THOMPSON WARREN	CW2	W-3150191	1062	1
THOMPSON WAYNE W	MAJ	0-0958665	0563	1
THOMPSON WILLARD D	CPT	0-2029565	1057	1
THOMPSON WILLARD N	LTC	0-1582579	1062	1
THOMPSON WILLARD O	1LT	0-0574697	0457	1
THOMPSON WILLIAM A	LTC	0-1166401	0566	1
THOMPSON WILLIAM E	COL	0-0240636	1163	3
THOMPSON WILLIAM E	COL	0-0308509	0257	1
THOMPSON WILLIAM G	LTC	0-0400848	0760	1
THOMPSON WILLIAM H	LTC	0-0421680	0663	1
THOMPSON WILLIAM N	MAJ	0-0251804	0467	3
THOMPSON WILLIAM P	CW3	W-2150790	0165	1
THOMPSON WILLIAM R	LTC	0-1100364	0763	1
THOMPSON WILLIAM R	CPT	0-1796546	0564	1
THOMPSON WILLIAM T	CPT	0-0505212	0356	1
THOMPSON WILLIE E	1LT	0-2042855	0451	1
THOMPSON WINSTON C	CW3	W-2151721	0562	1
THOMPSON WOODBERRY	MAJ	C-0885769	1054	1
THOMPSON-BOWERS IAN	MAJ	C-0321865	0253	1
THOMS FORREST	MAJ	0-1046668	0562	1
THOMSON CLINTON	MAJ	0-1302069	0656	1
THOMSON DONALD R	LTC	0-1041250	0562	1
THOMSON EARL W	COL	0-0124147	1053	3
THOMSON HENRY S	LTC	0-0263530	0749	3
THOMSON ISAAC L	LTC	0-0147508	1154	3
THOMSON JAMES L	CPT	0-1300732	0846	1
THOMSON JAMES R	CW2	W-3150896	0267	1
THOMSON JOHN W	MAJ	0-1575227	0859	2
THOMSON JR ROBERT	COL	0-0253717	0860	1
THOMSON LEONARD S	CPT	0-1182473	0347	1
THOMSON RANDOLPH M	1LT	0-1176010	0646	2
THOMSON ROBERT B	MAJ	0-0939689	0262	1
THOMSON ROBERT L	1LT	0-1286736	0146	2
THOMSON WILLIAM H	MAJ	0-0253423	0152	3
THOMY GEORGE A	1LT	0-1315389	0445	2
THOR ROSE M	MAJ	N-0731335	0863	3
THORARINSON GERALD O	MAJ	0-1822653	0461	1
THORESEN LESLIE B	LTC	0-1551571	0765	1
THORESEN TRYGVE	2LT	0-1536816	0754	2
THORESON CARL H	MAJ	0-2097404	0467	1
THORESON WILBUR A	1LT	0-1322732	0845	2
THORLEY JR IRA D	COL	0-0248948	1064	3
THORLIN REGINALD	LTC	0-0468834	0760	2
THORMAN BENJAMIN W	MAJ	C-0221647	1056	3
THORMAN JAMES G	CW3	W-2203481	0967	1
THORN EILAND H	CW2	W-2147839	0961	2
THORN EDWARD W	CPT	0-2000649	0954	2
THORN MARVIN D	MAJ	0-1795751	0165	3
THORN WILLIAM T	MAJ	0-1798315	0657	1
THORNAL REUBEN B	LTC	0-0286804	1058	1
THORNBER MERRILL S	CPT	0-0377505	0245	1
THORNBERRY HALBERT H	CPT	0-0215769	0163	3
THORNBERRY JOHN H	LTC	0-0500921	0463	3
THORNBOROUGH WILLIAM	MAJ	0-0232967	0563	3
THORNBRUE CARL N	CPT	0-0496119	0754	1
THORNBURG CYRIL F	LTC	0-1310174	1062	1
THORNBURG HAROLD C	CPT	0-0286334	0259	3
THORNBURG MARGARET S	1LT	N-0760985	0746	1
THORNBURG THOMAS H	2LT	0-1932520	0753	2
THORNBURGH CONWAY D	1LT	0-1032317	0347	1
THORNBURGH MARY G	1LT	N-0784673	0548	1
THORNDIKE AUGUSTUS	COL	0-0226573	0356	3
THORNE ALBERT J	LTC	0-1646656	0866	1
THORNE BAILEY M	CW4	W-2102469	0564	3
THORNE ENNIS P	LTC	0-0429549	1261	3
THORNE JAMES H	CPT	0-0969679	1060	1
THORNE JOE F	CW2	W-2141871	0659	1

NAME	GRADE	SVC NO	DATE RET MO YR	RET CODE
THORNE JOHN C	COL	0-0366083	0960	1
THORNE LEWIS W	MAJ	C-0539313	0965	1
THORNE RONALD B	CW3	W-2151004	0764	1
THORNE VIRGIL A	CW2	W-2104530	0246	2
THORNE WILLIAM A	WO1	W-2124227	1146	1
THORNE WILLIAM D	LTC	0-1030617	0361	2
THORNE WILLIAM E	LTC	0-0276407	1057	1
THORNHILL CLYDE M	LTC	0-0321627	0457	1
THORNHILL JOHN B	COL	C-0172900	0546	1
THORNLEY CLARENCE E	CPT	0-0527869	1047	2
THORNLEY JOHN D	CPT	0-0941959	1059	1
THORNLEY JR BERT L	2LT	0-1559405	C646	2
THORNSVARD HARRY C	LTC	0-1582208	1167	1
THORNTON BARRIE M	MAJ	C-0407198	0860	1
THORNTON CHARLES S	CW2	W-2104531	0565	1
THORNTON DELMAR D	MAJ	C-1103973	0548	2
THORNTON EARL L	COL	0-0117632	0648	3
THORNTON EUGENE A	MAJ	C-194507C	0759	1
THORNTON EVANS C	MAJ	0-1283168	0446	2
THORNTON FRANK B	CPT	0-1315238	0246	1
THORNTON FRANK S	CPT	0-0221945	0751	3
THORNTON HORACE E	1LT	0-1544459	0757	3
THORNTON HOWARD L	CW2	W-2210724	1065	1
THORNTON JAMES M	LTC	0-0382983	0363	1
THORNTCN JOHN R	CW3	W-2209718	C867	1
THORNTCN JOHN S	LTC	0-0369600	0367	3
THORNTON JR EARLE O	COL	0-0307494	0960	1
THORNTON LESLIE B	1LT	0-1299651	1145	2
THORNTON LOUIS M	CW2	W-2147170	1065	2
THORNTON LOUISE G	2LT	N-0763903	1044	1
THORNTON OSCEOLA T	LTC	0-0331267	1166	1
THORNTON RALPH E	LTC	0-0210081	0563	3
THORNTON RAYMOND A	CPT	0-2262709	0361	1
THORNTON ROBERT F	COL	0-0483573	0862	1
THORNTON ROBERT F	1LT	0-1311994	0844	2
THORNTON ROZIER L	MAJ	C-1042968	C460	1
THORNTON THOMAS F	LTC	0-0388354	0358	1
THORNTON WALTER J	CW2	W-2152407	C861	1
THORNTON WILLIAM O	MAJ	C-0160619	0151	3
THORNTON WILLIAM M	MAJ	C-2204075	0366	1
THORNTON WILLIAM S	CW2	W-2145523	0559	1
THORP EDWARD G	LTC	0-0125952	0164	3
THORP ELLIS H	LTC	0-1013236	0767	1
THORP PAUL J	MAJ	C-0270232	0151	1
THORPE CHARLES E	CPT	0-1047808	0657	2
THORPE EDITH	MAJ	N-0721886	1262	1
THORPE JR THOMAS W	LTC	0-0452360	0966	1
THORPE KENNETH M	1LT	0-1586973	1045	2
THORPE THOMAS O	CPT	0-2032883	0956	1
THORSEN ARNOLD M	1LT	0-0545050	0445	2
THORSEN THEODORE R	WO1	W-2151177	0463	2
THORSEN THORWALD	MAJ	0-0178950	1144	2
THORSEN WILLIAM L	2LT	0-1824536	0844	2
THORSTAD JOHN E	MAJ	0-1822337	C261	1
THORSTED EDWARD L	LTC	0-1294563	C566	1
THORSTENSEN ROY F	MAJ	C-118298C	0561	1
THORWALD WALTER E	1LT	0-1323047	0745	2
THRAILKILL FRED W	CW4	W-2127512	0461	1
THRALL C BURTON	COL	C-0277965	0351	3
THRALL GENTRY H	CW2	W-2152255	1157	1
THRALL WILMA E	MAJ	N-0737298	C962	2
THRALLS HAROLD L	MAJ	0-0966088	0663	1
THRAN CLAIRE N	MAJ	0-1342018	0561	1
THRAP RALPH E	CPT	0-1168108	0753	1
THRASH KENNETH M	COL	0-0252051	1166	3
THRASH MAURICE C	CW2	W-2149952	0857	1
THRASH THOMAS A	COL	0-0118072	0755	3
THRASHER BELIAS L	MAJ	0-1018303	1263	1
THRASHER JAMES W	2LT	0-1113017	0345	2
THRASHER LAWRENCE E	LTC	0-0256004	0967	3
THRASHER LEONARD R	LTC	0-0369844	0762	1
THRASHER WILLARD D	CW2	W-2149469	0761	1
THREADER WILFRED G	LTC	0-0111873	C950	3
THREET WEBB	LTC	0-1169766	0965	3
THRESHER WILLIAM A	CW3	W-2143144	0361	1
THRIFT CHESTER B	LTC	0-0259159	0367	3
THRIFT CEORGE N	LTC	0-0237323	0965	3
THRIFT HENRY S	LTC	0-0407688	1060	1
THRISTINC FRANK L	2LT	0-1294564	0944	2
THROCKMORTON C C	CPT	0-0201031	0155	3
THROCKMORTON JAMES F	MAJ	C-0216929	0760	3
THROGMORTON JAMES H	CPT	0-1877232	0165	1
THRONE LAWRENCE D	LTC	0-1166197	0263	1
THRONE THOMAS	MAJ	0-2027352	0761	1
THRONEBERRY MARVIN L	CW3	W-2152256	1163	1
THRONTVEIT CARL R	MAJ	0-1998342	0662	1
THROOP J C	CW4	W-2141685	0962	1
THROOP JR WILLARD L	1LT	0-1287435	0145	2
THROWER CLELLAN C	MAJ	0-1328651	C866	1
THROWER EARL C	COL	0-0246C88	1054	1
THROWER JOHN H	CPT	0-0246272	0342	2
THROWER MAXWELL O	COL	0-0240504	0753	1
THRUN FRED M	COL	0-0171721	0756	3
THRUSH WILLIAM C	CPT	0-1549140	1057	1
THUES RAYMOND L	LTC	0-094757C	0567	1
THULIEN HAROLD R	CPT	0-1038869	1059	1
THUM OTTO F	LTC	0-0469021	0762	1
THUN JACK K	MAJ	0-2263164	0563	1
THURBER CHARLES R	CPT	0-0975982	0356	1
THURBER CEORGE H	COL	0-0309626	0664	3
THURBER CEORGE L	1LT	0-1324962	0346	2
THURBER RAYMOND O	LTC	0-0299861	0565	3
THURESCN JOHN D	LTC	0-1581424	0561	1
THURLOW HENRY P	MAJ	0-0153272	0549	3
THURLOW JERRY J	CW3	RW-2145756	0763	1
THURLOW MADALINE V	MAJ	N-0760761	0663	1
THURMAN ARTHUR R	2LT	0-1549853	0743	2
THURMAN DAVID O	LTC	0-1586279	0761	1
THURMAN CEORGE C	MAJ	0-0269742	0645	2
THURMAN RUFUS S	LTC	0-0310885	0656	1
THURMAN SOLOMON	CW4	W-2108641	0358	1
THURMAN WILLIAM R	CPT	0-1288973	0559	1
THURMOND JAMES S	M G	0-0191221	0163	3
THURMONC WILLIAM L	MAJ	0-2035077	0467	2
THURSTCN IRA L	MAJ	0-0195239	0861	3
THURSTCN IRVING	LTC	0-0176535	1055	3
THURSTCN JOSEPH O	CW4	W-2103531	1058	1
THURSTON KATHERINE	2LT	N-073C391	0845	1
THURSTCN VERNON L	MAJ	0-1286737	0261	1
THURSTCN WILLIAM A	LTC	0-0545785	0365	1
THURTLE GEORGE S	MAJ	0-0391113	0547	2
THUSS ELMER E	MAJ	0-0286627	0362	3
THWAITS PRIOR	MAJ	0-0890154	1060	2
THWEATT CARROLL P	MAJ	0-0127863	0349	3
THYSELL PHILIP W	CPT	0-1017918	1054	1
TIBBE WILLIAM	MAJ	0-0450147	0755	1
TIBBETS ROY R	CPT	0-1540653	1147	1
TIBBETT RALPH W	MAJ	0-1113018	0666	2
TIBBETTS GEORGE E	MAJ	0-1550939	1158	1
TIBBETTS JAMES O	LTC	0-1309442	1162	1
TIBBETTS JOSEPH W	CW2	W-2106419	0847	2
TIBBETTS LESTER K	LTC	0-1113019	0664	2
TIBBETTS STANLEY B	LTC	0-0280046	0364	3
TIBBITS JOHN M	2LT	0-1823086	0645	2
TIBBITT JOHN M	CW3	W-2144251	0363	1
TIBBITTS GORDON C	LTC	0-0203452	0350	1
TIBBS LUTHER W	CW3	W-2149987	0465	1
TIBERI JOHN V	1LT	0-1294752	0745	2
TICARIC NICHOLAS	CPT	0-1014345	0562	1
TICE ALBERT K	MAJ	0-0324939	0546	2
TICE CARL E	MAJ	0-0948740	1062	1
TICE FLETCHER F	MAJ	0-026041C	0166	3
TICE GORDON M	1LT	0-1590856	0844	2
TICE JOHN L	LTC	0-0360265	C863	3
TICHELI LEO P	LTC	0-1044129	0860	2
TICHENOR HILTON R	MAJ	0-0415890	0665	1
TICK JEAN D	2LT	0-0406605	1144	2
TIDBALL PAUL B	CPT	0-0286117	0562	3
TIDD CHARLES A	CW2	W-2144035	0459	1
TIDD LUZERNE M	COL	0-0122873	0756	3
TIDERMAN ROBERT R	LTC	0-0888198	0164	1
TIDMORE WILLIAM E	LTC	0-0276311	0560	3
TIDWELL DON	MAJ	0-1688827	1264	1
TIDWELL EDGAR L	COL	0-0399970	0764	1
TIDWELL JR JESSE M	MAJ	C-1295625	C760	1
TIEDE JOSEPH W	COL	0-0231315	C159	3
TIEDEMAN LEROY E	CPT	0-0253304	1155	3
TIEDEMANN ELEANORE H	CPT	L-0204388	1046	1
TIEDGEN ARNO R	CW4	W-2121959	C860	1
TIEGS GEORGE E	MAJ	0-0450498	0747	1
TIEMAN MILTON C	MAJ	0-0943626	0666	1
TIEMANN NORBERT T	2LT	0-0955879	0252	1
TIEMANN PHILIP W	COL	0-0173656	0760	3
TIEMEYER CHARLOTTE	1LT	N-0728894	0446	1
TIENKEN II WILLIAM	LTC	0-1177213	0763	2
TIERNAN CHARLES M	MAJ	0-1167671	C861	1
TIERNAN JAMES T	CW3	W-2132953	0461	1
TIERNAN SR ROBERT W	MAJ	0-1168493	0661	1
TIERNAN WILFRED H	MAJ	0-0178972	0-52	3
TIERNEY JAMES E	MAJ	0-0954978	0767	1
TIERNEY RICHARD J	CPT	0-027794C	0863	3
TIERNEY ROBERT J	CW3	W-2151629	1265	1
TIESING BERTHOLD U	CPT	0-0367480	C460	1
TIETJEN EDWARD H	CPT	0-1305674	0553	2
TIETJEN OTTOMAR H	COL	0-0514981	0767	1
TIFFANY CHARLES A	1LT	0-0468095	1145	2
TIFFANY FREEMAN R	MAJ	C-2020596	0763	2
TIFFANY HOWARD H	LTC	0-0371699	0756	1
TIFFANY JOHN L	MAJ	0-1313935	C866	1
TIFFANY WILLIAM A	LTC	0-1030428	0557	1
TIGER DAVID	LTC	0-0109159	1046	2
TIGER KENNETH R	LTC	0-2036033	1067	1
TIGERT JR CLAUDE A	CPT	0-0557265	1047	2
TIGH LOUIS M	MAJ	C-0888270	1046	1
TIGHE EDWARD J	MAJ	0-1307479	1160	1
TIGHE JAMES J	MAJ	0-1052999	0762	1
TIGHE JOHN G	LTC	0-0507589	0167	3
TIGHE JOHN J	LTC	0-1638666	0161	1
TIGHE OWEN E	CPT	0-0494822	0649	1
TIGHE ROGER J	COL	0-0218320	0547	2
TIGNER ARMON R	CW2	W-2151908	CR63	1
TIGNER OSCAR C	LTC	0-0235775	0166	3
TIGNER VERNON M	CW3	W-2150309	1061	1
TIGNO BENNETT S	2LT	0-1896568	0364	1
TILDEN JOHN	LTC	C-0183115	C552	3
TILEY PAUL L	CPT	0-2262131	1060	1
TILFORD ATLAS B	1LT	0-1301714	1144	2
TILGHMAN ELWAYNE E	MAJ	0-1174727	C562	1
TILKE EDWARD T	MAJ	0-1317054	0159	1
TILKER GEORGE J	LTC	0-0353062	0460	1
TILL FRED N	MAJ	0-2028898	0962	1
TILL JR SHELTON C	LTC	0-0441637	0257	2
TILL WOODROW J	LTC	0-1548324	0563	1
TILLACK RAYMOND L	LTC	0-0505540	0667	1
TILLEMANS DONALD L	MAJ	C-1010530	0959	1
TILLER HOWARD B	MAJ	0-1683948	0446	2
TILLERY JAMES P	MAJ	0-1288974	0259	1
TILLERY JOHN L	COL	0-0281792	0847	1
TILLERY SAMUEL H	MAJ	C-0298092	0864	3
TILLES ALBERT	1LT	0-2049744	0847	1
TILLETT SCOTT E	MAJ	C-1684940	1262	1
TILLEY HARRY F	MAJ	0-1825082	0960	1
TILLEY RALPH C	LTC	0-0202145	0756	3
TILLEY WILLIAM H	CPT	0-0286183	0357	3
TILLI OLIVER E	LTC	0-0661897	0165	1
TILLINGHAST LEWIS G	LTC	0-1555143	0461	1
TILLINGHAST THEOSE E	MAJ	0-0266423	0553	3
TILLMAN CLARENCE C	LTC	0-0329205	0860	1
TILLMAN JAMES C	CW2	W-2206085	1160	1
TILLMAN JEAN P	CPT	0-0389077	0263	1
TILLMAN JOHN	LTC	0-0282625	0247	2
TILLMAN JOHN G	MAJ	0-0410989	0361	1
TILLMAN OLIVER C	CW2	W-2146402	1159	1
TILLMAN RICHARD G	LTC	0-2204110	0767	1
TILLMAN ROBERT	CW2	W-2205782	1159	1
TILLMAN ROBERT L	MAJ	0-0540635	0863	1
TILLMAN SAMUEL C	WO1	W-2120008	1045	2
TILLMAN STEPHEN F	COL	0-0171470	1060	3
TILLMAN THOMAS B	LTC	0-0363320	0265	3
TILLOTSCN ROY	LTC	0-1285520	1060	1
TILLOTSON WILLIAM B	MAJ	0-1170582	0157	1
TILLQUIST DAVID E	1LT	0-0266967	0461	3
TILLSON ROGER K	1LT	0-1016152	0246	2
TILSON GEORGE H	COL	0-0205300	1163	3
TILSON JR CHARLES V	1LT	0-1297616	0145	2
TILSON LEMUEL G	MAJ	0-2000059	0862	1
TILTON JOHN E	LTC	0-0406839	0161	1
TILTON NORMAN L	1LT	0-1062088	1045	2
TIMBERLAKE JR R E	LTC	0-0351990	0161	1
TIMBERLAKE TEDSAN S	MAJ	0-0573588	0861	1
TIMBOE ARTHUR C	COL	0-0262939	0160	1
TIMBRELL JOHN O	LTC	0-0266463	0766	3
TIMEWELL SHIRLEY R	LTC	N-078316C	0665	2
TIMMERMAN FRED	COL	0-0238688	0954	2
TIMMERMAN WILFRED R	MAJ	0-0995961	0765	1
TIMMERMAN WILLIAM H	1LT	0-1306176	0745	2
TIMMINS RICHARD H	CPT	0-0954854	0954	2
TIMMINS WESLEY O	LTC	0-2047861	0866	1
TIMMONS JOHN C	MAJ	0-029363C	0560	3
TIMMONS MARION	CW2	W-2145846	1057	1
TIMMONS PAUL E	MAJ	0-1340594	0665	1
TIMMONS THADDEUS A	LTC	0-0250105	0946	2
TIMNEY CHARLES J	LTC	0-1641863	0766	1
TIMPANC ANGELO J	CPT	0-0938015	0959	1
TIMSON HORACE W	MAJ	0-1168495	0854	1
TINDALL ALBERT W	1LT	0-1999831	0748	1
TINDALL JOHN R	LTC	0-0188045	1060	3
TINDALL MORRIS H	MAJ	0-0337893	0945	2
TINDER FLOYD S	LTC	0-0902818	0664	3
TINER EDGAR A	MAJ	0-0311812	1047	1
TINETTI ERNEST F	CPT	0-1687271	1145	2
TINGLE EDGAR J	LTC	0-0368374	1160	1
TINGLE JACK K	LTC	0-0100429	1145	2
TINGLEY OSCAR N	CPT	0-1305675	1145	2
TINKER ALLAN M	COL	0-0206542	0259	3
TINKER HAROLD E	CW4	W-2144198	1066	1
TINKER JOHN G	LTC	0-0268328	1064	1
TINKER LEE E	MAJ	0-1326435	C261	1
TINKHAM CHARLES J	COL	0-0291115	1159	1
TINKHAM ERNEST R	LTC	0-0509796	1064	3
TINKHAM LEROY B	MAJ	0-1297810	0246	2
TINNEL OLEN L	MAJ	0-1178011	1160	1
TINNEN HASKELL L	CW3	W-2145524	0761	1
TINNEY JOE R	MAJ	0-1920255	0365	1
TINNIN ALVIS L	2LT	0-1334231	0246	2
TINNIN JOHN V	LTC	0-0482926	1054	2
TINSLEY EVELYN H	1LT	N-0763513	0546	1
TINSLEY JAMES H	MAJ	0-0493215	0352	1
TINSLEY JOHN N	MAJ	0-0974674	0862	1
TINSLEY K C	LTC	0-0316077	1066	3
TINSLEY LEE F	CPT	0-0332322	1059	3
TINT HERMAN	CPT	0-0297502	0343	1
TINTARY PERLEE W	MAJ	0-2028640	0167	1
TIPA MICHAEL	LTC	0-1323876	0764	1
TIPP VICTOR L	MAJ	0-1311450	0563	1
TIPPETS CARRELL R	CPT	0-0928679	0859	1
TIPPETT JR ROBERT G	LTC	0-1050116	0261	1
TIPPINS EUGENE A	CW3	W-2142684	0163	1
TIPPINS WILLIAM C	COL	0-0196759	0962	3
TIPPIT JAMES H	CW2	W-2147671	0860	1
TIPPIT MATTHEW L	LTC	0-1555481	0562	1
TIPPIT WILSON C	WO1	W-2144735	0657	1
TIPPIT WYLIE A	CPT	0-0179939	0746	2
TIPPLE ALBERT M	MAJ	0-0318073	0646	2
TIPS CHARLES R	COL	0-0157014	0652	3
TIPTON CARL M	MAJ	0-1588922	1157	1
TIPTON JOHN B	COL	0-0119037	0757	3
TIPTON JOHN H	COL	0-0335118	0757	3
TIPTON JR ROY E	MAJ	0-1317577	1059	1
TIPTON JR WILLIAM L	MAJ	0-2288849	0962	1

NAME	GRADE	SVC NO	DATE RET MO YR	RET CODE
TIPTON LLOYD R	LTC	0-1647304	1262	1
TIPTON MARY E	CPT	N-2310456	C166	2
TIPTON ROYAL N	MAJ	0-1646967	C363	1
TIPTON WILLIAM W	MAJ	C-0450190	0358	1
TIRADO PEDRO W	MAJ	C-0953913	0161	1
TIRRELL LORING V	LTC	0-0127009	0956	3
TISCHBIN ROBERT M	1LT	C-1102089	1045	2
TISCHER PHILIP A	MAJ	0-1299963	C861	2
TISCHLER CHARLES	LTC	0-1556815	C761	1
TISCHLER LOUIS N	LTC	0-0300051	0667	3
TISDALE ALBERT A	LTC	0-0357976	0167	3
TISDALE DONALD A	MAJ	C-1C44408	0359	1
TISDALE GLENN W	LTC	0-0137974	0753	3
TISDALE JAMES R	MAJ	C-0379488	1045	2
TISDALE JR JOHN F	MAJ	0-2034926	0164	1
TISDALE LEONARD I	MAJ	C-0978555	1163	1
TISDALE WILLIAM G	MAJ	C-0410786	0746	1
TISDALE WILLIAM J	LTC	0-1C38502	0467	1
TISDELL NORMAN A	LTC	0-0369231	0667	3
TISHMAN PETER	1LT	0-1597298	C346	2
TISON GERALD J	COL	0-0328107	C358	1
TISSUE JOHN W	CPT	0-1799398	0356	1
TITCHENER FREDERICK	LTC	0-0169245	0646	2
TITEL FRED C	LTC	0-0151232	0253	3
TITERA LADIMIR V	LTC	0-0242282	0962	3
TITKO ANDREW	MAJ	C-04555C2	C558	1
TITLEMAN MYER R	CPT	0-1703232	C545	1
TITTLE JAMES T	MAJ	0-2204078	C267	1
TITTLE MORGAN L	MAJ	C-1593887	0563	1
TITUS CLIFF K	COL	0-0331312	0750	3
TITUS EDGAR F	MAJ	0-C884936	0163	1
TITUS ELROY W	CW3	W-2148772	0666	1
TITUS FRANK G	CW2	W-2152101	0762	1
TITUS FRANK L	LTC	0-0425885	C966	3
TITUS JAMES C	LTC	0-0405663	1165	1
TITUS JOHN B	MAJ	0-0208033	1145	2
TITUS JR ANDREW P	LTC	0-0339335	1161	1
TITUS JR ROBERT L	1LT	0-0354668	0545	2
TIVENAN JOHN J	MAJ	C-0324972	C959	3
TJADER CALLEN	LTC	0-0167654	C746	2
TKACIK JOHN	CPT	0-0109207	C535	1
TOBEY JAMES A	COL	0-0235426	0754	3
TOBEY MILTON K	LTC	C-0489216	0257	1
TOBIAS CARL A	CPT	C-0511156	1145	2
TOBIAS EDWIN R	MAJ	C-1105868	1266	1
TOBIAS HARRY C	CW3	W-2152408	C461	1
TOBIAS HENRY H	CPT	0-1320914	C548	1
TOBIAS HERBERT J	MAJ	0-1055996	0567	3
TOBIAS RICHARD F	CW3	W-2150869	0963	1
TOBIAS WALTER A	MAJ	C-1945071	0157	1
TOBIASON PERA Z	1LT	N-0734426	0452	2
TOBIE LOUIS J	CW2	W-2114240	1066	3
TOBIN CHARLEY B	CPT	0-2053960	0449	1
TOBIN CLEMENT J	MAJ	C-0110734	1054	3
TOBIN DAVID I	CW2	W-2148942	0364	1
TOBIN DAVID P	LTC	0-1000293	0858	2
TOBIN EDWARD G	LTC	0-1175604	0862	2
TOBIN EDWARD H	LTC	0-1182284	1262	1
TOBIN FRANK L	MAJ	0-1947536	0966	1
TOBIN JAMES M	CPT	0-2000902	1060	2
TOBIN JERRY P	MAJ	0-0231046	0565	3
TOBIN MARY W	1LT	N-0701263	0732	1
TOBIN ROBERT P	LTC	C-0294151	1047	2
TOBIN THOMAS B	2LT	0-1322164	C245	2
TOBIN WALTER E	CW3	W-2207469	C167	1
TOCCI JOSEPH A	MAJ	C-1917545	1164	1
TOCCO JOSEPH J	MAJ	0-1030198	0351	1
TOD CARREL I	LTC	0-1001919	0265	3
TODARO PAUL	CPT	0-0901678	0345	2
TODD BRUCE J	1LT	C-1018304	1045	2
TODD CHARLES E	MAJ	0-1340595	1060	1
TODD CHARLES M	MAJ	0-1321587	1161	1
TODD CHARLES W	1LT	C-128514C	0944	2
TODD CLYDE C	CPT	0-1031277	0455	1
TODD COLEMAN B	COL	C-0185486	0551	3
TODD DANA L	MAJ	0-0191769	0655	3
TODD DIMITRI W	LTC	0-1824393	1262	1
TODD DONALD A	1LT	0-1100365	0544	2
TODD EUGENE E	MAJ	0-1013758	0661	1
TODD FREDERICK	COL	0-0264384	C563	3
TODD GEORGE	CW2	W-2120647	1046	1
TODD HARRISON T	COL	0-0236134	0665	3
TODD HARRY F	MAJ	0-0553070	1163	1
TODD HOWARD R	CW4	W-2145C13	0766	1
TODD IVAN C	CW3	W-2104535	1057	1
TODD JACK R	COL	0-0405963	0461	1
TODD JAMES C	LTC	0-0182564	0854	1
TODD JAMES O	LTC	0-0178421	0753	3
TODD JESS D	CW2	W-2214790	0667	1
TODD JOHN A	LTC	0-0315923	0146	2
TODD JOHN F	CPT	0-1926572	0264	1
TODD JR DAVID B	LTC	0-0114810	1154	3
TODD JR EDWARD F	LTC	0-0222032	1062	3
TODD JR GROVER C	LTC	0-1558217	0865	1
TODD JR JOSEPH W	LTC	0-0957243	0667	1
TODD MARTILLUS	COL	0-0205534	0251	3
TODD MYRON G	MAJ	0-1535097	C461	1
TODD RALPH L	LTC	0-0327459	0757	1
TODD ROBERT E	1LT	0-0416007	C644	2
TODD ROLAND H	COL	0-0117203	0648	3
TODD RONALD E	MAJ	0-2021197	0767	1
TODD SAMUEL R	COL	0-0168693	0648	3
TODD SR WILLIAM M	MAJ	C-1300416	0957	2
TODD WILLIAM P	CPT	0-0387816	1045	2
TODD WILLIAM J	LTC	0-1336452	1266	1
TODD WILLIAM S	MAJ	0-0981612	1064	1
TODISH FRANK C	CW2	W-2114629	0948	2
TODCROFF ALEXANDER	LTC	0-0450601	1058	1
TOEPFER ELVERA L	CPT	N-0758292	1048	2
TOEWE CLINTON H	CPT	C-1695816	1145	2
TOEWS HELENA	1LT	N-0743929	0548	1
TOFFT LEROY E	MAJ	0-0476898	0954	1
TOGERSEN ROBERT F	COL	0-0451427	0763	1
TOHER PAUL V	MAJ	0-0507243	0754	1
TOHILL DON O	MAJ	C-1822339	1059	2
TOIA MATTHEW J	COL	0-0323C34	0163	1
TOIVANEN WAYNE T	LTC	0-1945968	0167	3
TOKER JOHN R	MAJ	0-1314853	0461	1
TOKLE ALF S	LTC	0-1011438	0164	1
TOKUDA SEIKO	MAJ	0-1923048	1166	1
TOKUSHIGE WILLIAM T	MAJ	0-2262213	0865	1
TOLAN HAROLD J	LTC	0-0488616	0865	3
TOLAR DOUGLAS S	1LT	0-0407751	0644	2
TOLAR FREDERICK	CPT	0-0242331	0346	2
TOLAR GRAY W	LTC	0-1575600	1055	1
TOLAR JAMES W	MAJ	0-1291727	0760	1
TOLAR WILLIAM F	COL	0-0264286	0160	3
TOLBERT CHARLES C	LTC	0-1043243	0461	1
TOLBERT MARTHA S	LTC	L-0402344	0967	1
TOLBERT SANTFORD C	CW2	W-2206301	1160	1
TOLBERT THOMAS N	CW3	W-3150546	1067	1
TOLCES FRANCIS T	LTC	0-1797748	0367	3
TOLCH WIENAND A	CW2	W-2210940	0864	1
TOLEDO HENRY A	CW2	W-2209092	1165	1
TOLENTINO LUCIO	2LT	0-1896728	1048	2
TOLER CARLYN G	MAJ	0-1797909	0260	1
TOLER JR JAMES P	LTC	0-0143315	0957	3
TOLER MELVYN C	CPT	0-1312055	1165	2
TOLER WILLIAM A	1LT	0-1318723	0345	1
TOLIN HAROLD C	CW2	W-221043C	0366	1
TOLIN ROY W	LTC	0-0240325	0465	3
TOLIN WILLIAM G	CW3	W-2147992	1264	2
TOLINE CLARENCE A	MAJ	0-0192917	0356	3
TOLINS RICHARD R	1LT	0-1176526	0945	2
TOLIVER CHARLES A	COL	0-0411630	1060	1
TOLIVER EMERY H	CPT	0-2262296	1159	1
TOLIVER JAMES T	LTC	0-0363225	0261	1
TOLL ROBERT M	COL	0-0367858	0764	1
TOLLE BONNIE E	MAJ	N-0727745	1163	3
TOLLE CECIL F	LTC	0-0335688	0648	3
TOLLE JOHN F	MAJ	0-022547C	C363	3
TOLLE ROBERT F	LTC	0-1290500	0561	1
TOLLEFSON ALVIN G	2LT	0-1825083	0745	2
TOLLEFSON CHARLES I	LTC	0-1169768	C561	1
TOLLEFSON GEORGE E	1LT	0-1291356	0445	2
TOLLEFSON JOHN L	1LT	0-5700277	0362	2
TOLLEFSON MAYNARD	CPT	0-0295757	C945	2
TOLLEFSON WILLIAM G	COL	0-0455427	0960	1
TOLLER VIRGIL C	COL	0-0267887	C364	3
TOLLETT JR H T EARL	MAJ	0-2014686	0465	1
TOLLIS DAVID P	LTC	0-1117336	0764	1
TOLLISON CHARLES H	CPT	C-2006514	0558	1
TOLLISON FRANK J	LTC	0-1541004	0157	1
TOLMAN HUGH H	COL	0-0137477	1048	3
TOLMAN KENNETH W	CPT	0-0510486	0557	1
TOLMAN WILLIAM J	MAJ	C-1330985	1263	1
TOLNAS OLAF J	LTC	0-0106233	0450	3
TOLOCKA FRANK J	LTC	C-1303431	0367	1
TOLSON CARL L	1LT	0-1325607	C959	1
TOLSON CHARLES G	LTC	0-0272040	1164	3
TOLTZIEN FRITZ J	MAJ	C-1181168	1162	1
TOM CLYDE F	MAJ	C-0247828	1155	3
TOM HENRY K	COL	0-0256386	0567	3
TOM KIONG F	LTC	0-0383866	0964	3
TOMA JOHN J	LTC	0-0349907	0146	2
TOMADA ALFREDO	1LT	0-0935647	1148	1
TOMAN GEORGE J	LTC	0-0326240	0146	2
TOMAN JOHN J	COL	0-0359426	0560	1
TOMAN WILLIE A	CW2	W-2149680	0957	1
TOMANENG MAGDALENO	LTC	0-1302234	0461	1
TOMARCHIO JOHN A	1LT	0-1318236	0146	2
TOMASEK CHARLES A	CPT	0-0161260	C648	3
TOMASELLO THERON R	1LT	0-1304819	1145	1
TOMASIK EDMUND J	COL	0-0373015	1162	1
TOMASINI SILVIO R	CW3	W-2148613	0763	1
TOMASKO JOHN M	CW2	W-2146533	0562	1
TOMASKY STANLEY	CPT	0-1041039	1064	1
TOMASULO MICHAEL A	MAJ	0-1041251	0960	1
TOMAW DELLIE W	LTC	0-1055173	0462	2
TOMBERG JOSEPH J	CPT	0-1167673	0147	2
TOMBERLIN KNAPP A	MAJ	0-1588923	0361	1
TOMBERLIN WILLIAM P	MAJ	0-2204453	0366	1
TOMEI VINCENT C	LTC	C-1796186	1059	1
TOMER ABRAHAM	CW3	W-2149310	0161	1
TOMES GEORGE J	CW2	W-2119294	C857	1
TOMES JR ROBERT L	1LT	0-0442619	0945	2
TOMEY JACK P	CW4	W-2146556	0467	1
TOMICH JOHN J	CPT	0-1593890	0246	2
TOMKIES DOUGLAS C	LTC	C-0157263	1056	3
TOMKINSON ROBERT L	LTC	C-0375590	0263	1
TOMLIN JACK L	MAJ	C-1292256	0856	1
TOMLIN MERRILL	CW4	W-2003327	1065	3
TOMLINSON CHARLES H	LTC	0-1038871	1164	1
TOMLINSON FLEET	1LT	0-0214013	0842	2
TOMLINSON FLOYD L	MAJ	0-1050957	1164	1
TOMLINSON GILBERT E	CPT	0-1177462	C162	3
TOMLINSON GORDON L	CPT	0-1535545	C947	2
TOMLINSON HOWARD J	LTC	0-0326706	C961	3
TOMLINSON LYNN C	MAJ	0-1295796	1157	1
TOMLINSON SAMUEL A J	LTC	0-0916145	C464	3
TOMLINSON WALDO R	CW3	W-2205993	0566	1
TOMLINSON WALTER G	MAJ	0-017866C	0949	1
TOMPKINS ARTHUR F	CPT	0-0347969	C754	2
TOMPKINS CHARLES E	COL	0-0423211	1053	1
TOMPKINS CLARK W	2LT	0-1013733	0344	2
TOMPKINS GEORGE H	LTC	0-0239096	1264	3
TOMPKINS HARVEY J	COL	0-0312806	0766	3
TOMPKINS L C	CPT	C-0971328	0261	1
TOMPKINS LELAND V	MAJ	C-1549854	C266	1
TOMPKINS MAURICE F	MAJ	0-1333564	0363	1
TOMPKINS ROBERT D	1LT	0-1312731	1045	2
TOMPKINS SMITH H	LTC	0-0260103	1045	2
TOMPLAIT BENNET J	WO1	W-2116977	0245	2
TOMS RAYMOND W	LTC	C-0284870	0960	3
TOMS ROBERT W C	CPT	0-1544898	C954	1
TOMS ROYCE T	CPT	0-2C34767	0464	1
TOMSU EDWARD M	MAJ	0-0570552	0861	2
TONDERYS WILLIAM F	MAJ	0-1994862	0361	1
TONORD LYMAN W	LTC	0-0353134	0846	1
TONER JAMES I	LTC	0-1639736	0558	1
TONER JOSEPH P	1LT	0-1688626	0854	2
TONETTI SERGE	LTC	0-1C35059	0262	1
TONEY AUDY E	MAJ	C-0238353	1063	3
TONEY ROBERT M	COL	0-0263101	0967	3
TONG WONG K	1LT	0-1596833	1045	2
TONGE MANEF L	MAJ	0-0218315	0446	2
TONGE RAPHAEL F	CPT	0-0341699	0544	2
TONJES FREDERICK	MAJ	0-1042572	0258	1
TONKIN WARREN G	CPT	0-1012499	0947	2
TONKS PAUL R	COL	0-0393770	1060	1
TOOHEY JAMES W	CW3	W-2147139	1C63	1
TOOHEY JOHN T	CW3	W-2132954	0762	1
TOOHY JOHN P	1LT	0-0464428	1142	1
TOOKE AUTHER D	CW3	W-2146718	0160	1
TOOLE DON P	MAJ	0-0168350	0145	1
TOOLE MACK	LTC	0-1633598	1263	1
TOOLE THOMAS F	CPT	0-0307086	1044	2
TOOLE WILLIAM F	COL	0-0181823	1152	3
TOOLEY JR FRANCIS L	1LT	0-1032771	C146	1
TOOLEY ROY	CW4	W-2107879	1157	1
TOOLIN EDWARD V	MAJ	0-0598395	0363	1
TOOLIN PAUL V	COL	C-0249900	0864	3
TOOMER FRANK	CPT	0-0421454	0447	1
TOOMEY HENRY J	COL	0-0102043	0553	3
TOOMEY JR SAMUEL K	COL	0-0306071	0264	1
TOOMEY WILLIAM F	CPT	0-0384007	0644	2
TOOMOTH FREDRIC B	CPT	0-157523C	C859	1
TOON JAMES A	COL	C-0139744	1154	3
TOONE FERD E	LTC	0-0201371	0763	3
TOOTHAKER GILBERT E	MAJ	0-1636743	0960	1
TOOZE LAMAR	M G	0-0107927	0257	3
TOOZE VICTOR A	MAJ	0-0264902	0547	2
TOPACIC CONRADO S	LTC	0-0500448	1262	1
TOPCHIK ALFRED	MAJ	0-1545295	0762	1
TOPCIK HARRY A	LTC	0-0296635	0963	3
TOPE BILLY J	LTC	0-1055482	0567	1
TOPE GEORGE W	WO1	W-2110012	0561	2
TOPE HENRY P	CPT	0-0502406	0349	1
TOPFER KIMMETT	MAJ	0-2002553	1060	1
TOPHAM VERNON C	1LT	0-1323759	1159	1
TOPIC GEORGE L	MAJ	0-134160C	0566	1
TOPLEY EARL J	CPT	0-1103976	0663	3
TOPOLCSKY HARRY W	1LT	0-0494804	1043	2
TOPP JR JOHN S	1LT	0-1285665	0146	2
TOPP WILLIAM F	CPT	0-1894968	0240	2
TOPPEN ROBERT P	1LT	0-1288819	0245	2
TOPPER ARTHUR O	1LT	0-0496776	0357	1
TOPPER FREDRICK R	LTC	0-1294935	C661	1
TOPPER GEORGE E	CW2	W-2102747	1055	1
TOPPING JR FRANCIS F	1LT	0-1314693	0945	2
TOPPING WALTER A	COL	0-0168191	0859	3
TOPPING WALTER S	MAJ	0-1297278	1047	1
TORBERSON CHRISTIAN	MAJ	C-0221317	C648	3
TORBERT ALFRED S	CW4	W-2136651	0865	1
TORBERT MAX H	LTC	0-0266002	0449	1
TORBETT DAVID S	2LT	0-4005383	0254	2
TORCELLINI L J	CPT	0-1311099	0-48	1
TOREN OSCAR F	2LT	0-1635414	0944	2
TORGAN EMERSON A	CPT	0-0336416	1044	2
TORGERSON BLAIR H	1LT	0-0350853	0545	2
TORGERSON ELIZABET	1LT	N-0790753	0947	1
TORGERSON JAMES E	LTC	0-1018782	0163	1
TORGERSON JEROME H	LTC	0-1823521	0361	1
TORGERSON WALLACE O	MAJ	0-1633599	0963	1
TORIA JOSEPH	LTC	0-204851C	0263	1
TORIE ALEX D	LTC	0-0185423	1157	3
TORKELSON GLEN R	MAJ	0-1315240	0165	1
TORMEY JACK C	2LT	0-0413807	0343	2
TORMEY THOMAS J	2LT	0-1997637	0246	2
TORN ELMORE R	LTC	0-0249441	0766	3

NAME	GRADE	SVC NO	DATE RET MO YR	RET CODE
TORNELL CLAUS A	COL	0-0279012	1055	2
TORO-PEREZ JR JUAN F	CW2	W-2213447	1067	1
TOROIAN EDWARD	MAJ	0-0886439	1158	1
TORQUATI ROBERT	CW3	W-2206885	0766	1
TORR ALBERT F	CPT	0-1309444	0447	2
TORRANCE CHARLES C	MAJ	C-0222521	C444	2
TORRANCE HUGH F	LTC	0-0454432	1063	1
TORRE FRANCIS V	LTC	0-1554651	1262	1
TORRES ARCADIO	MAJ	0-0276773	0567	3
TORRES ERASMO	1LT	0-2263228	0657	1
TORRES JOSE M	1LT	0-0217523	0841	1
TORRES MANUEL	1LT	0-1293677	C350	1
TORRES MIGUEL A	CW4	W-2102475	0656	1
TORRES PABLO P	MAJ	C-1115133	0660	1
TORRES SIFREDO	LTC	0-0183916	0260	3
TORRES WALTER	COL	C-0414841	0664	3
TORRES-RODRIGUE CON	MAJ	C-1328773	1063	1
TORRES-RODRIGUE WEN	CW2	W-2007831	1166	1
TORREY MELVIN L	MAJ	C-0961819	0265	1
TORRUELLA JR JUAN N	MAJ	0-0240635	0444	2
TORTORELLA SALVATORE	MAJ	0-1585013	0565	1
TORWICK OLIVER E	2LT	0-1577964	0444	2
TOSCANO GLADYCE A	CPT	N-0783207	0546	1
TOSCO WILLIAM	MAJ	0-1312361	0662	1
TOSH VERNIE O	MAJ	0-1332887	1062	2
TOSONOTTI EDWARD H	2LT	0-1695619	0146	2
TOSSY PAUL G	LTC	0-0219070	0462	3
TOSTON WILLIAM L	CPT	0-0484082	0749	1
TOTH JR DAVID	LTC	0-1053895	1162	1
TOTH JULIUS J	COL	0-0450328	0761	1
TOTH LOUIS L	LTC	0-1288468	0960	1
TOTH VICTOR N	MAJ	0-1112480	0964	1
TOTH WILLIAM A	MAJ	0-0139684	0450	1
TOTHACER AUSTIN J	COL	C-0395453	0864	1
TOTMAN OTTO L	COL	C-0123891	1054	3
TOTOLO CHRISTOPHE	MAJ	C-1107724	0662	1
TOTTEN HAROLD K	1LT	0-1109715	0146	2
TOTTEN HENRY P	LTC	0-0170883	1152	3
TOTTEN LAWRENCE E	LTC	0-0262046	0965	3
TOTTEN SAMUEL A	1LT	0-0291456	0945	2
TOTZ BEVERLY	CPT	N-0767816	0947	1
TOUCHET ALBERT W	MAJ	C-0481930	0154	1
TOUCHETTE ALCIDE A	CPT	0-0341173	0144	1
TOUEY JAMES A	LTC	0-1011485	0758	1
TOUGH TRACY N	LTC	0-0278171	0663	3
TOUKATLIAN VICTORIA	CPT	N-0724441	0961	2
TOUNGE HARRY G	CPT	0-1685358	1045	1
TOUPS ARTHUR L	LTC	0-0473235	0350	1
TOUPS JOSEPH C	LTC	0-1045615	C263	1
TOURTLOTT OERLESS J	CW2	W-2149242	1162	2
TOURVILLE BERNARD J	LTC	0-1000189	0658	1
TOURVILLE CLARENCE W	LTC	0-0287013	0166	3
TOURVILLE HENRY W	COL	0-0260613	0166	3
TOURVILLE KENNETH H	CPT	0-0291566	1052	1
TOURVILLE LESLIE W	1LT	0-1324856	C546	2
TOUSEY THOMAS E	1LT	0-1914365	1022	2
TOUSSAINT ROBERT C	1LT	0-1591483	1148	2
TOW ANNABELLE	CPT	N-0737625	0947	1
TOWARD PERCY	COL	0-0278175	1056	3
TOWBER PAUL Z	MAJ	C-1822341	1058	1
TOWE LONNIE F	CW2	W-2152632	0461	1
TOWELL ANNE M	1LT	L-0125010	C845	2
TOWER HERBERT E	1LT	0-1325949	0146	2
TOWER MARCUS R	1LT	0-1686183	0446	2
TOWER MERLE J	MAJ	0-0347476	0662	3
TOWERS EDWARD J	COL	0-0102160	0648	3
TOWERS JOSEPH A	CPT	0-1167674	C546	2
TOWERS WILBUR E	CW2	W-2122314	1045	2
TOWERY JR EUGENE S	CPT	0-0420107	C545	1
TOWERY LUTHER F	LTC	0-1168952	C560	1
TOWEY ANN E	MAJ	N-0775834	0449	2
TOWEY REX W	1LT	0-1110299	0146	2
TOWLE GEORGE	MAJ	0-0402882	1046	2
TOWLE RICHARD B	CW3	W-2105804	0560	1
TOWLE VICTOR M	MAJ	0-0511537	C446	2

NAME	GRADE	SVC NO	DATE RET MO YR	RET CODE
TOWLER BERTHA E	2LT	N-0702665	C539	1
TOWLES ALTON M	MAJ	0-0215479	0863	3
TOWLES FREDDIE B	CPT	0-1300233	1048	1
TOWN CARLES H	MAJ	0-1179652	0161	1
TOWN EDWARD A	MAJ	0-0197900	0261	3
TOWN LEE E	CPT	0-1013859	1058	1
TOWNE CEDRIC C	MAJ	0-1040628	0760	1
TOWNE CHARLES E	COL	0-0371706	0766	3
TOWNE EUGENE M	LTC	0-0556742	0766	1
TOWNE JR MAURICE H	LTC	0-0938197	0866	1
TOWNE VERL F	MAJ	0-1181171	0959	1
TOWNLEY CLYDE W	1LT	0-1285141	0947	2
TOWNLEY GEOFFREY J	CPT	0-0363239	1143	2
TOWNLEY PAUL	2LT	0-1996625	0757	1
TOWNS EDWARD B	COL	0-0161739	0855	3
TOWNSAN NICHOLAS R	LTC	0-1557382	0866	1
TOWNSEND AARON E	CW3	W-2154672	1159	1
TOWNSEND ALAN C	CW4	W-2145759	0857	1
TOWNSEND ALBERT S	COL	0-0162425	0951	3
TOWNSEND ARTHUR M	CPT	0-2263798	0762	1
TOWNSEND CLIFFORD	LTC	0-1000190	0157	1
TOWNSEND CLIFFORD O	CW2	W-2123330	1054	1
TOWNSEND DARRELL J	MAJ	0-1641018	1160	1
TOWNSEND DAVID W	MAJ	0-0121732	0-49	3
TOWNSEND FRANCIS M	CPT	0-0449253	0447	1
TOWNSEND FRANK C	CPT	0-0201155	0844	1
TOWNSEND HAROLD L	LTC	0-0168943	1056	2
TOWNSEND HENRY J	LTC	0-0331846	0166	3
TOWNSEND JACK H	1LT	0-0423531	1044	2
TOWNSEND JAMES H	LTC	0-0401418	0346	2
TOWNSEND JAMES L	LTC	0-1180369	0360	1
TOWNSEND JAMES N	CW3	W-2206048	1166	1
TOWNSEND JAMES R	CW3	W-2203545	0765	1
TOWNSEND JAMES S	LTC	0-1030847	1162	1
TOWNSEND JAMES S	1LT	0-1302235	0546	2
TOWNSEND JAMES V	MAJ	0-2288313	1160	1
TOWNSEND JAY G	COL	0-0175043	0254	3
TOWNSEND JOHN L	MAJ	0-1946628	0255	1
TOWNSEND JOHN O	1LT	0-0914712	0546	2
TOWNSEND JR C A	MAJ	0-0374692	0460	1
TOWNSEND JR GEORGE F	LTC	0-1036411	0864	1
TOWNSEND KEITH E	1LT	0-1634408	0246	2
TOWNSEND LINCOLN H	LTC	0-1550940	0164	1
TOWNSEND LLOYD W	WO1	W-2003833	0252	2
TOWNSEND MAURICE L	COL	0-0163280	0648	3
TOWNSEND RAYMOND B	MAJ	0-0270661	0861	3
TOWNSEND ROBERT	MAJ	0-0225498	0644	2
TOWNSEND SHERWOOD M	2LT	0-1081039	0344	2
TOWNSEND THOMAS H	LTC	0-1583776	0563	2
TOWNSEND WAYNE W	LTC	0-0279605	0457	3
TOWNSEND WILSON L	COL	0-0201238	1150	3
TOWNSON KENNETH C	B G	0-0163716	0949	3
TOWSON FRANCES A	MAJ	L-0600259	0567	1
TOWSON JAMES R	MAJ	0-0966081	0163	1
TOY JOSEPH C	COL	0-0300023	0560	1
TOY WILLIAM K	LTC	0-1298587	1160	1
TOYAMA KCRUYCSHI	MAJ	0-2263462	0666	1
TOYE JOSEPH J	MAJ	0-0468543	0446	1
TOYN WILSON C	CW3	W-2120536	0754	1
TOYNBEE CHARLES M	COL	0-0240002	1157	3
TOYODA SUSUMU	MAJ	0-2023656	1262	1
TOZIER ALLAN W	LTC	0-1309629	1166	1
TOZIER GEORGE D	MAJ	0-1592664	0761	1
TOZZI GEORGE A	MAJ	0-1107726	0562	1
TRABER OSCAR W	COL	0-0171224	1058	3
TRACEY DAVID J	MAJ	0-1305136	1058	2
TRACEY JOHN C	COL	0-0206883	1057	3
TRACEY THOMAS H	COL	0-0121871	0254	3
TRACEY WILLIAM F	CPT	0-1688767	0564	2
TRACH BENEDICT	CPT	0-1700855	1044	2
TRACHSEL DAVID	CW2	W-2150628	0359	1
TRACHTENBERG ISRAEL	CPT	0-1690398	0546	2
TRACHTENBERG L	1LT	0-1046671	0744	2
TRACY ALFRED H	LTC	0-0263208	0263	3
TRACY DONALD E	CPT	0-1053849	0546	2

NAME	GRADE	SVC NO	DATE RET MO YR	RET CODE
TRACY ELMER F	CW3	W-2005857	0266	1
TRACY EUGENE R	MAJ	C-0943386	0665	1
TRACY FRANK L	LTC	0-0331874	0864	3
TRACY GEORGE T	MAJ	0-4010777	1167	1
TRACY JAMES K	1LT	0-1323632	1045	2
TRACY JIM F	LTC	0-1013293	0563	1
TRACY JOHN	CPT	0-0428253	0754	1
TRACY JOHN F	LTC	0-1050119	0667	1
TRACY JOHN F	MAJ	C-1303798	1165	1
TRACY JOSEPH P	LTC	0-0252209	0467	3
TRACY JULIA R	MAJ	N-0755045	0365	3
TRACY NATHAN B	CPT	0-0450600	0556	1
TRACY NEAL H	1LT	0-1184318	0147	2
TRACY NORMAN S	LTC	0-1319683	0663	1
TRACY RICHARD L	CW3	W-2147575	1264	1
TRACY ROBERT W	LTC	C-1286035	0860	1
TRACY WARREN	CPT	0-1116322	0346	1
TRACY WINTON G	LTC	0-0332318	0363	3
TRADER PAUL F	MAJ	0-1999973	1060	1
TRAEGER CARL F	LTC	0-1577967	0961	1
TRAFFORD GEORGE H	LTC	0-1285142	0658	2
TRAFTON STANLEY M	CW3	W-2208655	C867	1
TRAGER LAWRENCE	2LT	0-2008445	C246	2
TRAGESER PAUL J	1LT	0-2040915	1045	2
TRAGLE HENRY I	LTC	0-1012511	0264	1
TRAHAN JOSEPH E R	CPT	0-1575233	1156	1
TRAIL CORAN F	CW3	W-2142909	1059	2
TRAIN J LEWIS	COL	0-0301080	1064	3
TRAINA PHILIP	COL	0-0499622	1066	1
TRAINER TREVLYN	LTC	0-0285730	0459	1
TRAINOR CHARLES F	LTC	0-0259537	1167	3
TRAINOR CHARLES F	CW2	W-2152409	0661	1
TRAINOR JAMES F	LTC	0-0207741	1153	3
TRAINOR JOHN T	CW3	W-2147592	0567	1
TRAINOR JR CHARLES E	1LT	0-1302552	0246	2
TRAINOR KATHLEEN M	MAJ	L-0116546	0565	3
TRAINOR PAUL W	MAJ	C-1917722	1163	1
TRAINOR PETER J	CW3	W-2148539	0765	1
TRAMELL JOE R	MAJ	0-1330986	0763	1
TRAMMELL CLAUDE W	2LT	0-1586977	0645	2
TRAMMELL JACK R	1LT	C-2268000	0556	2
TRAMMELL JOHN M	MAJ	0-2016567	0562	1
TRAMMELL JOSEPH F	CW4	W-2003371	1265	1
TRAMMELL WILLIAM H	COL	0-0311646	0546	2
TRAMONTI ALBERT	1LT	0-0298377	0561	3
TRANBERGER CARL	CPT	0-0161742	0648	3
TRANK DAVID	CPT	0-0491227	0449	1
TRANTER CHARLES J	LTC	0-1041462	C861	1
TRAPANI ALPHONSO M	CW2	W-2119733	0946	2
TRAPMAN MIKE A	COL	0-0255282	1765	3
TRAPNELL ERNEST L	LTC	0-1062748	1163	1
TRAPP FRITZ C	1LT	0-0551222	0945	1
TRAPP VERN F	2LT	0-1308023	0744	2
TRAPP WALTER S	LTC	C-1550714	C764	1
TRASHER JOSEPH F	CW2	W-2142207	0756	1
TRASK BURTON W	LTC	0-0307510	0564	3
TRASK CARLTON E	LTC	0-1553744	0562	1
TRASK EVERETT R	CPT	0-0981985	0261	1
TRASK FLORENCE	MAJ	N-0000663	0263	3
TRASK ROBERT W	1LT	0-1018157	1148	2
TRASK SAMUEL G	LTC	0-0307542	0360	1
TRASK VICTOR M	LTC	0-0218152	0163	3
TRASTER HARRY B	CPT	0-0523244	1046	2
TRATHEN ROBERT O	LTC	0-1035385	1057	1
TRATZ ROBERT F	MAJ	C-1551973	0561	1
TRAUB JOHN L	MAJ	0-0256225	1066	3
TRAUBE JR LIONEL	2LT	0-1821653	0843	2
TRAUBE MARTIN H	CW4	W-2110599	0364	3
TRAUCHT FRANK J	MAJ	0-0336191	0166	3
TRAUGOTT EDGAR H	LTC	0-1324301	C767	1
TRAUPANE PHILIP E	MAJ	C-0970834	0866	1
TRAURIG MAX R	COL	0-0309452	0558	3
TRAUSNECK WILLIAM M	CPT	0-1046971	0446	2
TRAUTMAN FRANK J	MAJ	0-0287539	0260	3
TRAUTMAN FRANK W	CW3	W-2101103	1054	1

NAME	GRADE	SVC NO	DATE RET MO YR	RET CODE
TRAUTMAN JEAN E	MAJ	0-1638681	1057	2
TRAUTMANN PHYLLIS F	MAJ	N-0730049	0367	3
TRAVELSTEAD CLYDE	LTC	0-0238627	1061	3
TRAVER GEORGE C	COL	0-0209945	0849	3
TRAVER HAROLD E	CW3	W-2152185	0663	2
TRAVER JR WALLACE H	LTC	0-0750892	0967	1
TRAVER PERRY C	COL	0-0121873	1045	2
TRAVERS HAROLD C	LTC	0-0188986	0359	3
TRAVERS JOSEPH H	COL	0-0181934	0360	3
TRAVERS JR JOHN H	COL	0-0258655	0747	2
TRAVERS MILTON P	MAJ	0-0485782	0746	2
TRAVERS WILLIAM J	MAJ	0-2048177	0461	1
TRAVINSKI ROBERT W	1LT	0-5219654	0665	2
TRAVIS ARTHUR L	LTC	0-1168953	0761	1
TRAVIS DONALD A	MAJ	0-2053939	1054	1
TRAVIS ELDRED G	2LT	0-1312363	1144	2
TRAVIS ELROY W	1LT	0-1325340	0246	2
TRAVIS GEORGE M	2LT	0-1317057	0245	2
TRAVIS HARRY F	LTC	0-0145807	0648	3
TRAVIS JAMES E	LTC	0-0257604	0560	3
TRAVIS JOHN W	CPT	0-1641868	0146	2
TRAVIS MARY H	1LT	N-0773273	0146	2
TRAVIS PAUL W	CPT	0-0360820	0746	2
TRAVIS ROBERT H	CPT	0-0186633	0555	3
TRAVIS SAMUEL H	CW3	W-2144679	1262	1
TRAVIS SIDNEY E	LTC	0-1574549	0558	1
TRAVIS STANLEY E	LTC	0-0281855	0964	3
TRAWEEK WALTER W	1LT	0-1017049	0446	2
TRAWICK HENRY E	CPT	0-0959336	0161	1
TRAXLER CEAVER W	COL	0-0220427	0262	3
TRAXLER ROBERT M	LTC	0-0343767	0955	1
TRAYLOR BORRIE D	CW3	W-2208414	0267	1
TRAYLOR FRED R	1LT	0-1297617	0645	1
TRAYLOR PASCHAL E	CW3	W-2141472	1059	1
TRAYNOR ANDREW F	MAJ	0-2050984	0557	1
TRAYNOR ARTHUR R	CPT	0-1015904	0953	2
TRAYNOR BOYD K	CW3	W-2118411	1154	1
TRAYNOR CLIFFORD J	LTC	0-1100802	0663	1
TRAYNOR JAMES A	LTC	0-0481239	0946	2
TRAYNOR OWEN J	CPT	0-0501746	0947	1
TRAYNOR PATRICK E	MAJ	0-1549146	0952	1
TRAYNOR SR ARCHIE R	LTC	0-0359878	0157	1
TRCALEK BENNIE F	2LT	0-1184319	0945	2
TREACY ANDREW J	CPT	0-0377306	1065	3
TREADAWAY STEPHEN T	MAJ	0-0962236	0861	1
TREADC BEN	LTC	0-0212071	0852	3
TREADO CLARENCE F	CPT	0-1951720	0260	2
TREADWAY CHARLES L	MAJ	0-1310788	0258	1
TREADWAY RAYMOND R	MAJ	C-1036773	0459	1
TREADWAY WILLIAM E	COL	0-0286528	0162	3
TREADWELL BILL V	1LT	0-2212040	0852	1
TREADWELL CLEC A	LTC	0-0352823	0362	3
TREADWELL EDWIN H	2LT	0-1101693	1143	2
TREADWELL FRANCIS A	MAJ	0-2201439	0562	1
TREADWELL JAMES H W	LTC	0-0377467	0461	1
TREANOR JAMES J	MAJ	0-0910260	0246	2
TREANOR ROBERT A	2LT	0-2297638	0958	3
TREANOR ROBERT L	1LT	0-1336843	0148	1
TREAS EARL W	CPT	0-0172537	0852	3
TREASH RICHARD R	LTC	0-0453106	1165	1
TREAT DONALD E	MAJ	0-2014520	1066	1
TREBBE JR CHARLES F	LTC	0-0967524	0967	1
TREBILCOCK GEORGE R	LTC	0-1316246	0863	1
TRECARTIN CYRUS S	MAJ	0-0496924	0948	2
TRECK ANTHONY S	CW4	W-2120921	0157	1
TREDWAY WILLIAM H	CW3	W-2148774	0165	1
TREECE FRANCIS O	1LT	0-0370545	1046	2
TREECE LAWRENCE G	B G	0-0291041	1265	3
TREES EDWARD J	COL	0-0242717	0265	3
TREFETHEN HAROLD P	COL	0-0347385	0264	3
TREFFIACER GLENN R	LTC	0-0336469	0562	3
TREFFRY HARRY R	LTC	0-1289652	0463	1
TREGO LAWRENCE O	2LT	0-1597150	0851	2
TREIBLE JOHN E	MAJ	0-0980410	0166	1
TREIER ALBERT J	CPT	0-0448858	0851	1

ARMY OF THE UNITED STATES RETIRED LIST

NAME	GRADE	SVC NO	DATE RET MO YR	RET CODE
TREITLER PAUL	CPT	0-1002845	1047	1
TRELOGGEN CLYDE H	MAJ	C-0475013	0748	1
TRELSTAD BERTRAM L	MAJ	C-0326050	C146	2
TREMAINE MYRON J	B G	0-0336516	1066	3
TREMARELLO JOSEPH	MAJ	C-0266472	0757	1
TREMAYNE RUTH L	1LT	N-0785599	1048	1
TREMBATH WILLIAM R	CW4	W-2000509	1059	3
TREMBLAY DONALD A	MAJ	0-2200006	0766	1
TREMBLAY HENRY C	MAJ	C-0227002	C245	2
TREMBLAY JR JOHN F	MAJ	0-1080249	0551	1
TREMBLAY LEO A	CW3	W-2144278	0660	1
TREMBLAY TELESPHOR	1LT	0-2005942	0857	1
TREMOLACA SERGIO J	LTC	0-1590226	1162	1
TREMPER CHARLES E	MAJ	C-0476265	0761	1
TRENAM ARTHUR L	MAJ	C-0885512	1158	1
TRENAM MILTON E	CPT	0-0258028	1065	3
TRENARY HORACE I	MAJ	0-0196121	0163	3
TRENT RACHEL H	1LT	N-0757715	0546	1
TRENT RALPH W	LTC	0-0276420	0465	3
TRENT ROBERT L	MAJ	C-0352656	1160	1
TRENT ROBERT L	MAJ	0-0969627	1262	1
TRENT SR GALE	MAJ	0-2033235	C161	1
TRENT THEODORE R	MAJ	0-1120224	0167	1
TRENTINE ARTHUR J	CW2	W-2145259	1061	1
TREPPARD CHARLES E	WO1	W-2125442	1044	2
TRESCA WILLIAM H	CPT	0-0420492	C546	1
TRESENTE JOHN J	1LT	0-1046673	0545	2
TREU WILLIAM L	LTC	0-0180997	1060	3
TREUTEL ALFRED A	MAJ	0-0155713	1153	3
TREVERTON WILLIAM M	MAJ	0-0250497	0367	3
TREVINO VICTOR O	CPT	0-1105872	0965	2
TREVOR EDWIN F	LTC	0-0246358	0365	3
TREVOR GLENN A	CPT	0-C198022	1044	2
TREVOR JR THOMAS W	1LT	0-1293678	1146	2
TREXLER CHARLES D	COL	0-0245135	C648	3
TREZISE EVERETT A	CPT	0-1341601	0860	1
TRIBBETT WILLIAM A	CW3	W-2203275	0261	1
TRIBBEY BURL P	MAJ	0-0291178	1145	2
TRIBBLE EDWIN	LTC	0-0917569	1046	2
TRIBBLE JAMES M	COL	C-0114844	C850	3
TRIBBLE WALTER W	2LT	0-0510149	0152	1
TRIBBY CHARLES H	LTC	0-1016438	0762	1
TRIBOU SHERWOOD G	LTC	0-0350613	0965	3
TRICE HERMAN M	LTC	0-1640084	0567	1
TRICE JAMES C	MAJ	C-2212094	0763	1
TRICE JR PETER A	CPT	0-1735706	C848	2
TRICE JR WILLIAM A	LTC	0-0408363	0363	1
TRICKETT CHARLES P	MAJ	0-2017306	0263	1
TRICKEY JOHN C	CPT	0-1913483	0462	1
TRICKLE LENOX E	COL	0-0181467	0556	3
TRICOMI JOSEPH N	MAJ	C-1553922	0761	1
TRIER LESTER A	CPT	0-1041252	0146	2
TRIER OTIS M	LTC	0-1037936	0867	1
TRIESCH GUSTAVE M	COL	0-0252640	1153	3
TRIFILO SANTO S	1LT	0-0890305	0448	1
TRIGG WILLIAM G	LTC	0-1047811	1161	1
TRIGGER NORMAN	CPT	0-0478164	1048	1
TRIGGS WAYNE I	MAJ	0-2088138	0665	1
TRIGILIO RICHARD C	MAJ	0-2002555	C167	1
TRILLANCES BERNARDIN	CPT	0-1896513	0859	1
TRIM LEONARD H	CW2	W-2115203	0246	2
TRIM LOUIE F	MAJ	0-2018952	0760	1
TRIMBLE CARL E	LTC	0-0378628	0447	1
TRIMBLE DONALD F	MAJ	0-0404408	0764	1
TRIMBLE FLOYD	LTC	0-0280521	0167	3
TRIMBLE GEORGE C	CW3	W-2206250	0966	1
TRIMBLE HARRY H	MAJ	C-1110302	0562	1
TRIMBLE HENRY W	LTC	0-0468146	0457	1
TRIMBLE JR HENRY J	CPT	0-0312127	0448	2
TRIMBLE JR HENRY W	1LT	C-0443921	0145	2
TRIMBLE KIRK E	1LT	0-1325175	0746	2
TRIMBLE MADISON E	LTC	0-0289567	1057	3
TRIMBLE WALTER E	CPT	0-0450928	0244	2
TRIMBLE WEBB W	LTC	0-0286228	0466	3
TRIMBY JAMES E	MAJ	C-1951721	1263	1
TRIMMER ROY J	MAJ	0-1555145	0461	1
TRIMPI ALLAN W	CPT	0-0527290	0854	2
TRINDAL GLEN W	LTC	0-0155591	0155	1
TRINDLE JOSEPH W	1LT	0-0426060	0346	1
TRINER JOSEPH	COL	0-0185724	1054	3
TRINGHESE DOMINECK C	CW2	W-2143975	0454	2
TRINIDAD JOSE M	CPT	0-0959393	0162	2
TRINKNER HENRY G	MAJ	0-2035899	1163	1
TRIPLETT HARRY J	1LT	0-0964094	0453	2
TRIPLETT JR SAMUEL O	MAJ	0-0239639	0264	3
TRIPLETT VERLON D	MAJ	0-2262636	0262	1
TRIPLETT WILLIAM H	COL	0-0180128	0445	2
TRIPLETT WILLIAM J	LTC	0-0311841	1066	3
TRIPLETT WILLIAM J	MAJ	0-1876992	0565	1
TRIPLETT WILLOUGHBY	LTC	0-1169371	0962	1
TRIPLIT FRANK C	1LT	0-0885859	0553	1
TRIPODI ANTONIO	COL	0-0117927	0948	3
TRIPP BEVERLY H	LTC	0-1795996	1160	1
TRIPP CHARLIE C	1LT	0-1553766	0945	1
TRIPP EVERETT G	CPT	0-0121991	0653	3
TRIPP GEORGE W	COL	0-0299996	0157	3
TRIPP LOWELL O	LTC	0-1102508	0966	1
TRIPP MORTON M	MAJ	0-1799400	0564	1
TRIPP WILLIAM E	LTC	0-0252751	0365	3
TRIPP WILLIAM R	LTC	0-1651334	0963	1
TRIPPE JAMES E	LTC	0-0295918	0357	3
TRISKET ROBERT G	MAJ	0-1559859	1266	1
TRITLE ROBERT C	MAJ	0-0268154	1161	3
TRITSCH JR ARTHUR A	MAJ	0-1030528	1166	1
TRITTEN JOHN S	LTC	0-0228624	0564	3
TRITTENBACH EDWARD V	CW3	W-2145314	C166	1
TRITTICO FRANK	LTC	0-1994542	0259	3
TRIVELLA MARIANO L	CW4	W-2120637	1265	1
TRODERMAN FRANK F	LTC	0-0465036	0463	3
TRODICK HARRY C	MAJ	0-2035446	0860	1
TROEGER FERDINAND	CPT	0-0278204	0355	3
TROESTER JOSEPH	CW3	W-2152919	0562	1
TROGDON DOROTHY L	MAJ	N-0765284	0565	1
TROHMAN JACOB R	CPT	0-1172698	0746	2
TROLAN JR WILLIAM A	COL	0-C282959	0658	3
TROLAND THOMAS E	B G	0-0115989	0153	3
TROLINGER JR W P	2LT	0-0485048	0545	2
TROLINGER RALPH M	LTC	0-0918664	0565	3
TROLLMAN JR JOHN	LTC	0-0304139	0667	3
TROMBLE ANDREW R	CW4	W-2117940	1054	1
TROMINSKI WALTER	COL	0-0320813	0763	3
TROMLEY CHESTER O	CW3	W-2118294	1054	1
TROMMETTER CHARLES F	1LT	0-1304820	1051	2
TRONIK JOSEPH	CW2	W-2110611	0353	1
TRONSETH CLIFFORD A	1LT	0-1577968	1044	2
TRONSON WILLIAM R	CPT	0-0410879	1145	2
TROOLIN WALTER	LTC	0-1280035	0854	1
TROP WILLIAM	LTC	0-0198539	1160	3
TROSETH PAUL E	CW4	W-2118132	0967	1
TROSKA ADAM	LTC	0-1057285	1266	1
TROSKE THEODORE R	CW3	W-2147465	0865	1
TROSSEN KENNETH F	MAJ	0-0420558	0361	1
TROST LAWRENCE J	1LT	0-2046644	1147	2
TROST LOUIS F	LTC	0-0324807	0265	3
TROSTER OLIVER J	COL	0-0133628	0854	3
TROSTLE CHARLES H	CPT	0-1284429	0445	2
TROSTLE KENNETH L	CPT	0-1041040	0746	2
TROTT EMMETT O	MAJ	0-0225117	0648	3
TROTT HAROLD W	CPT	0-0526987	0148	2
TROTT JR MAYNARD J	LTC	0-1170229	0861	2
TROTT LEROY F	LTC	0-1634411	1060	1
TROTT WILLIAM D	LTC	0-0281136	0465	3
TROTTER CLARENCE E	LTC	0-0280690	0450	3
TROTTER CLARENCE R	LTC	0-0246233	0162	3
TROTTER DORSET B	MAJ	0-0968262	0563	1
TROTTER ISHAM E	CW4	W-2141687	0167	1
TROTTER JO	1LT	0-2018607	0165	1
TROTTER MENCIE B	2LT	N-0755108	0445	1
TROTTER WILLIAM O	CW2	W-2210076	0160	1
TROTTIER EDMUND J	CPT	0-0218709	0547	1
TROUP ARTHUR B	LTC	0-0333156	0662	1
TROUP KENNETH F	CW2	W-2153014	1157	1
TROUPE HAROLD F	LTC	0-1560084	0967	1
TROUSDALE GEORGE W	M G	0-0189048	0361	3
TROUT GEORGE H	CW3	W-2144373	0161	1
TROUT GEORGE W	LTC	0-0210732	0258	3
TROUT LESTER	LTC	0-0194345	1055	3
TROUT STEWARD R	MAJ	C-0508139	0746	2
TROUTMAN FRANK H	MAJ	0-1179233	1059	1
TROUTMAN WILLIAM J	CPT	0-1049374	0745	2
TROW MARION	MAJ	L-1010062	1263	1
TROWBRIDGE HARVEY M	1LT	0-0432463	0744	2
TROWBRIDGE IRVIN	COL	0-0208450	1055	3
TROWBRIDGE LEON E	CPT	0-1558352	C859	1
TROWBRIDGE ROBERT L	CW2	W-2207041	0164	1
TROXELL ALEXANDER	LTC	0-0239794	0653	1
TROXELL NOLAN	COL	0-0302498	C855	1
TROY CAJETAN J	LTC	0-0498555	0167	1
TROY THOMAS J	MAJ	C-1638650	1163	1
TROY WILLIAM	COL	C-0319818	0655	1
TROY WILLIAM G	2LT	0-1012552	0445	1
TROY WILLIAM G	CW4	W-2101320	0163	1
TROYER ORVE J	2LT	0-2055083	0251	2
TRUAX ALFRED F	LTC	0-0108806	0137	1
TRUAX CHARLES M	MAJ	C-1030199	0657	1
TRUAX DOROTHY B	1LT	N-0741728	1045	1
TRUAX IRENE G	2LT	N-0700876	0741	1
TRUAX NOAH F	LTC	0-0224064	0462	3
TRUB MATHIAS C	COL	0-0326725	C860	1
TRUBEY RAYMOND C	LTC	0-1176527	0463	1
TRUBEY ROBERT N	1LT	0-0558590	0252	1
TRUBY GEORGE E	1LT	0-0221122	C543	2
TRUDE ORVIS J	MAJ	0-0980709	1163	1
TRUDEAU DONALD D	CW2	W-2210087	0666	1
TRUDEAU FLOYD H	MAJ	0-0720618	0267	1
TRUDEAU FRANCIS H	MAJ	0-1166199	1059	1
TRUDEAU HUBERT F	CPT	C-0502299	1046	2
TRUDELL HERBERT A	MAJ	C-0200315	C256	3
TRUDELL JOHN N	MAJ	0-1648740	C661	1
TRUE CLYDE I	MAJ	C-0326879	1166	3
TRUE HOWARD R	COL	0-0292246	0965	3
TRUE WILBUR N	CPT	0-1922694	1262	1
TRUE WILLIAM H	CPT	0-0228156	0664	3
TRUEBGER HAROLD M	MAJ	0-0462511	1146	2
TRUEBLOOD LAUREL E	CPT	0-0258619	C766	3
TRUEBLOOD NORMAN N	MAJ	0-0507439	0547	2
TRUEBLOOD ROGER L	LTC	0-0279984	1161	3
TRUEMAN KENNETH F	CW2	W-2214671	0867	1
TRUESDALE MORTEN H	MAJ	C-0976877	0962	1
TRUESDELL ARTHUR J	WO1	W-2146524	0167	3
TRUETT RANDLE B	LTC	0-0225934	C463	3
TRUETT SAM W	CPT	0-0488803	C856	1
TRUEX CUTHBERT M	MAJ	0-2207028	0965	1
TRUEX LESTER S	MAJ	C-2035903	C862	1
TRUFANT ROBERT H	CW4	W-2142008	0659	1
TRUHON ANDREW R	CW3	W-2110128	1054	1
TRUITT AVERY O	LTC	0-1113487	0662	1
TRUITT CECIL A	LTC	0-1636745	C166	1
TRUITT JAMES G	COL	0-0157022	1155	3
TRUITT JOHN	LTC	0-0141597	0648	3
TRUITT RAY A	LTC	0-0519818	0765	3
TRUJILLO GENE B	MAJ	0-0959355	C764	1
TRUJILLO JESSE	CPT	0-1053400	C261	1
TRUJILLO MARIE D	2LT	N-0777876	0348	1
TRUJILLO WILLIAM A	MAJ	0-1287965	0758	1
TRULOVE DENNIS K	CW2	W-2142015	1154	1
TRULUCK JOHN G	CW2	W-2209776	0966	1
TRUMAN GEORGE C	MAJ	0-0292439	0842	2
TRUMAN HARRY S	COL	0-0129869	0153	3
TRUMBLE JOHN W	LTC	0-0408655	C962	1
TRUMBLE LORAN R B	1LT	0-2262657	0164	2
TRUMBLE MANLEY H	MAJ	0-1047814	0557	1
TRUMBO GEORGE H	CPT	0-0452042	0144	2
TRUMBORE JACOB S	MAJ	C-1062793	0264	1
TRUMBULL ALBERT F	COL	0-0240871	0366	3
TRUHM BRUCE F	1LT	0-C455910	1044	1
TRUMP VIRGINIA E	2LT	N-0728943	1043	1
TRUMPF FREDERICK	MAJ	0-0415745	1060	1
TRUNCELLITO EDWARD	LTC	0-1588331	0866	1
TRUNDLE GEORGE H	LTC	0-0123996	0455	3
TRUNK DONALD E	CPT	0-1111952	0663	1
TRUOG CLARENCE R	MAJ	0-0497065	1143	2
TRUPP GARRISON G	CPT	0-1685478	0646	1
TRUSCOTT JAMES	COL	0-0263802	0962	3
TRUSCOTT JOHN P	MAJ	0-0178806	0361	3
TRUSDELL WARREN N	LTC	0-0308688	0965	3
TRUSH JOHN	LTC	0-0167119	1038	1
TRUSKO JOSEPH R	MAJ	0-1546867	0559	1
TRUSSELL ALBERT R	MAJ	0-1043244	1060	1
TRUSSELL ERNEST H	LTC	0-1046674	0667	1
TRUSSELL GEORGE O	CW2	W-2106026	0547	1
TRUTOR JOHN	LTC	0-1036064	0457	1
TRUX WILLIAM N	MAJ	0-098628C	0667	1
TRYBALSKI THADDEUS J	CPT	0-1165092	0856	1
TRYGGVI CARL B	LTC	0-0338094	0862	3
TRYTTEN GINA	MAJ	N-0743799	0365	3
TRZECIAK JOSEPH J	CPT	0-1332109	0455	1
TSCHIRHART PETE L	1LT	0-0153236	0156	3
TSCHUDIN HANS W	COL	0-0233928	0956	3
TSHUDY ROBERT E	MAJ	0-2263109	0764	1
TSIMPDES ANDREW G	2LT	0-1030850	0545	2
TSUBOTA SHIGERU	LTC	0-0386483	0264	1
TSUKUNE HARUNOBU	1LT	0-1998666	0647	1
TUBBS HAZEL L	2LT	N-0775679	1045	1
TUBBS JOE S	MAJ	0-0401703	1060	1
TUBBS JR WARREN	CPT	0-0334564	0147	2
TUBBS LAWRENCE D	LTC	0-1575233	0455	1
TUBBS MARJORIE M	2LT	N-C736050	0345	1
TUBBS MARSHALL A	CW4	W-2115730	0959	1
TUBBS WALTER E	MAJ	0-0402973	C960	1
TUBBS WILLIAM C	MAJ	0-1109719	0164	1
TUBRIDY FRANK J	LTC	0-0235910	0166	3
TUCCINARDI THOMAS E	1LT	0-1639745	1144	2
TUCHMAN JOSEPH N	1LT	0-1323501	0845	2
TUCK ALBERT C	CPT	0-0506662	0545	2
TUCK JOSEPH R	CPT	0-0403454	0246	2
TUCK LELAND M	2LT	0-1324592	0445	2
TUCK THADDEUS	CPT	0-0382820	0546	2
TUCKER ALLEN L	LTC	0-0350617	0555	1
TUCKER ANDREW L	LTC	0-0151059	0555	3
TUCKER BETTY E	MAJ	L-1C10304	0365	1
TUCKER BILL L	1LT	0-1111398	0945	2
TUCKER BROWN C	CW2	W-2114698	0444	2
TUCKER CARL L	CPT	0-1553373	0263	1
TUCKER CLEO W	CW2	W-2143621	0363	1
TUCKER COLIN B	CPT	0-1582223	0546	1
TUCKER CORA L	MAJ	N-0793263	0365	1
TUCKER DAVID J	MAJ	0-1323633	0161	1
TUCKER DELMAR E	CW4	W-2114830	1154	1
TUCKER DWIGHT W	CW4	W-2141473	0467	1
TUCKER EDWARD W	WO1	W-2126351	1051	1
TUCKER EDWIN L	COL	0-0229779	0157	1
TUCKER ERNEST R	MAJ	0-0970661	0165	1
TUCKER FLOYD J	CPT	0-0231913	0558	3
TUCKER FRANCIS M	CPT	0-0264063	0745	2
TUCKER GEORGE E	2LT	0-1308732	0644	2
TUCKER GEORGE T	LTC	0-0179716	0956	3
TUCKER GORDON E	CPT	0-2033236	0364	1
TUCKER GROVER G	COL	0-0250679	0764	3
TUCKER GUY L	LTC	0-1284964	0261	1
TUCKER HELEN F	MAJ	N-0720212	1047	1
TUCKER HERBERT L	LTC	0-1109069	0661	1
TUCKER HYMAN	LTC	0-0219779	0756	3
TUCKER JACK C	MAJ	0-1534404	0562	2
TUCKER JACK W	CPT	0-0365370	0845	2
TUCKER JAMES R	1LT	0-0515590	0545	2
TUCKER JOHN C	LTC	0-1045617	1063	1
TUCKER JOHN M	LTC	0-1109070	0862	1
TUCKER JOHN S	CW2	W-2142454	0757	1
TUCKER JOSEPH F	2LT	0-1540716	1050	1

NAME	GRADE	SVC NO	DATE RET MO YR	RET CODE
TUCKER JOSEPH S	MAJ	C-2000521	0859	1
TUCKER JR JOHN H	COL	0-0123913	0251	3
TUCKER JR RCLLIN S	LTC	0-1114786	0955	2
TUCKER JULIAN P	LTC	0-0452145	0161	1
TUCKER LEE H	COL	0-0167645	0555	3
TUCKER LEE W	CPT	0-1113489	0247	1
TUCKER LESLIE E	1LT	0-1318591	1045	2
TUCKER LESTER M	MAJ	0-2023336	0265	1
TUCKER LLOYD H	1LT	0-0372379	0861	1
TUCKER MATTHEW	CPT	0-0387934	0845	2
TUCKER ROBERT C	CPT	0-0414194	C545	2
TUCKER ROBERT C	1LT	0-1325243	C945	2
TUCKER ROBERT E	CW2	W-2144100	0762	1
TUCKER ROY J	CPT	0-0481340	1146	1
TUCKER ROYAL K	LTC	0-0107440	0648	3
TUCKER SAM H	1LT	0-2005270	1047	2
TUCKER SR BILLY J	CPT	0-2017616	0961	1
TUCKER WILLIAM B	CPT	C-1931990	0264	1
TUCKER WILLIAM G	LTC	0-1591489	0864	1
TUCKER WILLIAM H	CPT	0-0514173	C257	1
TUCKER WILLIS D	MAJ	0-1796733	0257	1
TUCKERMAN ALFRED G	M G	0-0181648	1061	3
TUCKERMAN CHESTER W	LTC	0-1825992	0966	1
TUCKETT ROBERT L	MAJ	0-0254485	C665	3
TUCKEY ROBERT L	COL	0-0523849	C766	3
TUCKMAN FLORENCE	2LT	N-0758513	0945	1
TUOHOPE ARTHUR K	LTC	0-0231616	0859	1
TUDOR ARTHUR J	1LT	0-1286925	0746	2
TUDOR JOHN S	LTC	0-0206011	0949	1
TUDOR ROY	CPT	0-0503657	0747	1
TUEGEL WILLIAM C	CPT	0-1341602	1060	1
TUELL CHARLES H	CW3	W-2102483	0356	1
TUERFFS ALBERT M	1LT	0-1549148	0545	2
TUFAROLO LIBERINO	1LT	0-0397052	0144	2
TUFFNER MICHAEL	CW3	W-2141475	0760	1
TUFTE CHESTER O	LTC	0-1044978	0662	1
TUFTE EDWARD E	CPT	0-0382253	0146	2
TUFTE OLIVIA C	2LT	N-0733992	0345	1
TUFTS BEN L	LTC	0-1011126	0963	1
TUFTS JOSEPH E	MAJ	0-0165942	0857	3
TUFTS MELVIN J	MAJ	0-1924590	0863	1
TUGGLE ALFRED A	CPT	0-0511300	0750	1
TUGGLE CLARENCE A	MAJ	C-1017707	0662	1
TUGGLE HAROLD D	LTC	0-1318489	1061	1
TUHUS MELVIL O	LTC	0-0156246	0954	3
TUIN HERMAN	CW3	W-2148994	0963	1
TUINSMA FRIEDA Z	2LT	N-0702202	1031	1
TULISZEWSKI VICTOR J	LTC	0-1080158	0961	1
TULL ELVON L	LTC	0-0291047	0648	3
TULL FISHER A	MAJ	0-0240345	1044	2
TULLBANE JOHN E	MAJ	0-1323877	C359	1
TULLER ALFRED J	CPT	0-1321560	0146	2
TULLER DALE K	COL	0-0181698	0456	3
TULLEY JOHN N	MAJ	C-0336083	1166	3
TULLEY METHOD T	MAJ	0-0965505	0961	1
TULLIS ELONZO A	CW2	W-2110134	1150	2
TULLIS JOHN H	CPT	0-1996421	C761	1
TULLOCH JOHN C	MAJ	0-0139772	0560	3
TULLOCH JR JAMES L	LTC	0-1303612	1161	2
TULLY CHARLEY W	CW3	W-2144933	1060	1
TULLY GORDON R	LTC	0-0274147	0660	1
TULLY JAMES J	CW2	W-2107997	1146	2
TULLY MARTIN J	2LT	0-1182287	1044	2
TULLY THOMAS H	MAJ	0-0169390	0460	3
TULLY THOMAS N	CPT	0-0384176	1065	3
TUMA HARRY L	LTC	0-2016977	0565	1
TUMAN GEORGE O	MAJ	0-1117765	1066	3
TUMAN JAMES F	MAJ	0-0953852	0865	1
TUMAN WILLIAM G	MAJ	0-0238641	0364	3
TUMINELLA SAMUEL	MAJ	0-0533110	0457	1
TUNING DALLAS D	MAJ	0-1647307	0261	1
TUNISON MERLE E	MAJ	0-1557103	0258	1
TUNNELL JR BEN F	LTC	0-1556671	1066	1
TUNSTALL JAMES F	CPT	0-0487489	1145	2
TUNSTALL WILLIAM C	1LT	0-1319457	C746	2
TUNTLAND JOHN O	WO1	W-2123424	0844	2
TUNTLAND MARTELL F	1LT	0-0504935	0945	2
TUCHY EDWARD L	LTC	0-0273471	0460	2
TUPPER BETTY L	1LT	N-0742222	0146	1
TUPPER EARNEST H	LTC	0-1119002	0564	1
TUPPER NORMAN C	MAJ	0-1297812	1165	1
TUPPER WILLIAM R	CPT	0-0315151	0346	2
TURACEK RACHEL B	MAJ	N-0723707	0266	3
TURBEVILLE WILLIE B	CPT	0-0478163	1046	1
TURBYFILL EARL L	LTC	0-0237646	0161	3
TURCEK JOSEPH	MAJ	0-1320202	0757	1
TURCK HENRY C	MAJ	0-1059087	0260	2
TURCOTTE EVARISTE	CPT	0-1635747	0954	1
TURCOTTE RICHARD L	LTC	0-0570578	0366	1
TUREK ANNA A	MAJ	N-0792264	0667	1
TUREK EDWIN V	COL	0-0242456	0862	3
TUREMAN JR GARNET R	1LT	0-1725992	0745	2
TURGEON ROY W	MAJ	0-1309445	1060	1
TURINA JOSEPH F	CPT	0-0578474	1060	1
TURISH ANDREW J	LTC	0-1036413	0167	3
TURK EDWARD M	LTC	0-1287792	0663	1
TURK FRED	MAJ	0-118202C	0162	1
TURK JOHN H	CPT	0-0170073	0959	3
TURK LESTER	2LT	0-1176218	0545	2
TURK MERVYN R	LTC	0-0199257	1152	3
TURKEL HENRY M	CPT	0-1786028	0647	2
TURKISH WILLIAM A	CPT	0-1540925	0663	2
TURKLA BERNARD	LTC	0-1107731	1062	1
TURLEY JOSEPH G	MAJ	0-1183635	1262	1
TURLEY LOUIS C	CPT	0-0354914	0245	2
TURLEY ROBERT S	1LT	0-0497412	0350	1
TURLEY ROSCOE W	LTC	0-1292964	1166	1
TURLEY THOMAS H	MAJ	0-0386352	0557	1
TURLINGTON RICHARD C	CPT	0-0210524	0264	3
TURMAN HUBERT M	LTC	0-1638697	0366	1
TURMAN JAMES A	1LT	0-1556817	0147	2
TURNBULL CHARLES R	MAJ	0-0978320	0762	1
TURNBULL DAVID L	MAJ	0-0267159	0947	1
TURNBULL FRANKLIN M	LTC	0-0497528	0962	1
TURNBULL GEORGE C	COL	0-0256783	0956	3
TURNBULL JAMES L	LTC	0-0226550	0264	3
TURNBULL NORMAN A	LTC	0-0289343	0962	1
TURNBULL RICHARD G	1LT	0-1316607	0146	2
TURNBULL RODERIC F	LTC	0-2041065	1164	1
TURNBULL WILLIAM G	LTC	0-0255102	1055	1
TURNBULL WILLIAM L	LTC	0-1289998	0264	1
TURNELL LLOYD Y	MAJ	0-0173587	0950	3
TURNER ADLAI S	COL	0-0162939	0350	3
TURNER ALICE J	1LT	N-0783311	0446	1
TURNER AMOS	CW3	W-2141476	1163	1
TURNER ARCH	1LT	0-0331108	0561	1
TURNER ARCHIBALD	LTC	0-0109538	1053	1
TURNER ART	COL	0-0253009	0665	3
TURNER ARTHUR E	CW3	W-2145876	0267	1
TURNER BENNIE A	MAJ	0-0493621	0657	1
TURNER CARL M	MAJ	0-0332207	0367	3
TURNER CARL R	LTC	0-0252001	0965	3
TURNER CARLOS L	CPT	0-0381400	0445	2
TURNER CARRELL O	LTC	0-0262974	0465	3
TURNER CECIL R	2LT	0-1332551	0247	2
TURNER CHARLES E	LTC	0-0229780	0463	3
TURNER CHARLES G	LTC	0-0385856	0765	2
TURNER CHARLES N	MAJ	0-1647764	1063	2
TURNER CHARLES T	1LT	0-0540848	1044	2
TURNER CLARENCE	CW4	W-2109361	0857	1
TURNER CLEVELAND	MAJ	0-1173112	1061	1
TURNER CLIFFORD H	CPT	0-1552409	0551	1
TURNER CLYDE M	MAJ	0-1303231	1059	1
TURNER DAVID E	1LT	0-0313029	0844	2
TURNER DAVID H	WO1	W-2145760	0458	2
TURNER DEAN W	CW2	W-2152989	0559	1
TURNER DONALD W	MAJ	0-1053855	0463	1
TURNER EARL A	2LT	0-1002846	0544	2
TURNER EARL A	LTC	0-1175888	0865	1
TURNER EARL A	LTC	0-2012751	0464	1
TURNER EDWARD F	MAJ	0-0973554	C167	1
TURNER EDWIN R	CPT	0-0988208	0561	1
TURNER EOYTHE	COL	N-0726939	1062	1
TURNER ELBERT P	MAJ	C-1013713	0761	1
TURNER EMMETT L	MAJ	0-0426229	C657	1
TURNER FORREST O	LTC	0-0267834	1266	3
TURNER FRANCIS J	LTC	0-1636748	1065	1
TURNER FRANK H	CPT	0-128443C	0356	1
TURNER FRED A	LTC	0-1280398	0462	1
TURNER FREDERIC P	MAJ	0-1633606	0755	1
TURNER GEORGE F	CW2	W-2107978	C645	2
TURNER GEORGE H	COL	0-C258031	0962	3
TURNER GLENN E	COL	0-0266841	0855	1
TURNER GLYN M	1LT	0-1307329	0645	2
TURNER GRADY T	MAJ	0-0175832	1054	3
TURNER HARMON M	MAJ	0-0267825	0256	3
TURNER HENRY D	CPT	0-0245285	C553	3
TURNER HENRY E	LTC	0-0365164	C662	1
TURNER HOWARD L	CPT	0-2037808	0456	1
TURNER HOWARD V	CPT	0-0445558	0147	2
TURNER JACK H	MAJ	0-1298788	0359	1
TURNER JACKSON A	CW3	W-2147008	1063	2
TURNER JAMES C	MAJ	0-2266239	0466	1
TURNER JAMES E	CW3	W-2152362	1265	1
TURNER JAMES F	MAJ	0-4009931	0966	1
TURNER JAMES J	MAJ	0-2262113	0164	1
TURNER JESSE H	COL	C-0251259	0666	3
TURNER JOE F	MAJ	C-1823958	C762	1
TURNER JOEL L	CPT	0-2262205	1060	1
TURNER JOHN E	1LT	0-1294566	0845	1
TURNER JOHN F	MAJ	0-4000070	0367	1
TURNER JOHN G	LTC	0-0245492	0764	3
TURNER JOHN H C	CW3	W-2152061	0964	1
TURNER JOHN J	CW3	W-2209911	0466	2
TURNER JOHN L	MAJ	0-0184791	1056	3
TURNER JOHN P	CPT	0-0908981	C449	1
TURNER JOHN S	MAJ	0-1688392	0563	2
TURNER JOSEPH R	CPT	0-1177529	0354	2
TURNER JR EDWARD F	1LT	0-1319907	1145	2
TURNER JR EMMONS H	MAJ	0-0408678	0246	1
TURNER JR HENRY E	LTC	0-1293680	C661	1
TURNER JR HERBERT A	MAJ	0-0927194	1164	1
TURNER JR JAMES A	MAJ	0-0407004	C348	1
TURNER JR JESSE R	LTC	0-0366523	0166	1
TURNER JR LINTON L	MAJ	0-1593350	0759	1
TURNER JR SHERMAN F	LTC	0-1825512	0163	1
TURNER JR THOMAS D	COL	0-0233648	0454	2
TURNER JR THOMAS K	MAJ	0-1996400	C562	1
TURNER JR WILLIAM B	2LT	0-1012260	C544	2
TURNER JULIAN J	LTC	0-0237557	0364	3
TURNER LEON B	LTC	0-0197643	1061	3
TURNER MARGARET C	1LT	N-0742053	0346	1
TURNER MARGARET E	2LT	N-0760397	0545	1
TURNER MARY F	1LT	N-0728581	0846	1
TURNER MAX H	COL	0-0399490	0662	1
TURNER MELVIN L	CW2	W-2210383	0262	1
TURNER MILO M	1LT	0-0407556	0144	2
TURNER NELSON T	LTC	0-0379986	1065	3
TURNER NICHOLAS F	1LT	0-1642667	0246	2
TURNER NORMAN	CW3	W-2205512	C366	1
TURNER ODILLION C	CPT	0-0263808	C855	3
TURNER PHILIP M	LTC	0-0370241	0860	1
TURNER RALPH S	MAJ	0-024688C	0248	2
TURNER RALPH S	MAJ	0-1037345	0561	1
TURNER RAY	LTC	0-0196337	1160	3
TURNER RAY E	CW3	W-2142333	0760	1
TURNER RICHARD	CW2	W-3151355	C967	1
TURNER RICHARD C	MAJ	0-1295628	C947	2
TURNER ROBERT A	CW2	W-2115793	0556	1
TURNER ROBERT B	MAJ	0-4006939	0167	1
TURNER SR HENRY P	CW4	W-2004748	1062	3
TURNER THOMAS F	CW3	W-2121095	C561	1
TURNER THOMAS R	CW2	W-3430189	0966	1
TURNER TOM W	LTC	0-1323366	C962	1
TURNER VIRGINIA H	1LT	N-0731650	0445	1
TURNER VIVIAN C	MAJ	C-0955314	C567	1
TURNER WALKER M	CPT	0-0478676	0346	2
TURNER WEAVER A	MAJ	0-2036895	1060	1
TURNER WESLEY S	MAJ	0-2033875	1165	1
TURNER WILBUR D	LTC	0-1057287	1162	1
TURNER WILLIAM H	MAJ	0-2043315	0162	1
TURNER WILLIAM J	COL	0-0100202	0954	3
TURNER WILLIAM L	CPT	0-0416096	1050	1
TURNER WILLIAM L	LTC	0-1105875	1061	1
TURNER WILLIAM M	LTC	0-0304053	0265	1
TURNER WYLIE C	COL	0-0333737	0654	3
TURNEY ALFRED W	LTC	0-1102513	0663	1
TURNEY EARL P	WO1	W-2127649	0753	1
TURNEY EVERETT C	MAJ	0-1341924	0862	1
TURNEY FORREST N	LTC	0-0356843	0465	3
TURNEY ROBERT C	MAJ	0-0548754	1163	1
TURNEY VALE P	CW4	W-2141901	0566	1
TURNEY WILFRED R	MAJ	0-1542572	0646	2
TURNEYGHIGH HARRY H	COL	0-0264748	0259	3
TURNIPSEED JESSE D	LTC	0-1299146	0363	1
TURPIN CHARLES U	MAJ	0-0141645	0755	3
TURPIN CLAYTON P	MAJ	0-0555435	0864	1
TURPIN HERMAN R	CW2	W-2209187	1263	1
TURPIN LEONARD J	CW2	W-2150005	0760	1
TURQUEZA ARSENIC A	MAJ	0-2262264	1164	1
TURRELL DONALD B	LTC	0-1822748	1066	1
TURSI MARTIN C	CPT	0-2262860	0361	1
TURUNEN LUCIA E	LTC	N-0772028	0566	1
TURVENE HORACE V	COL	0-0141259	1054	1
TUSA JOSEPHINE	1LT	N-0726064	0648	1
TUSING WILLIAM C	CW2	W-2147716	0854	1
TUSTISON ALBERT P	LTC	0-0279315	C764	3
TUTAK JR LAWRENCE A	LTC	0-1596836	0163	1
TUTEN CHARLES	CW2	W-2118071	0853	1
TUTEN JR JAMES M	2LT	0-1341726	0949	2
TUTHILL FRANK S	2LT	0-1056582	1044	1
TUTHILL HOWARD E	MAJ	0-2038903	0463	1
TUTLIS STANLEY J	LTC	0-0376490	0655	1
TUTRONE DAVIC A	MAJ	0-0367955	0746	2
TUTTERROW EDWIN B	WO1	W-2120712	0544	2
TUTTLE ARTHUR W	CPT	0-1633608	0345	2
TUTTLE BLAINE E	CPT	0-0334473	0743	2
TUTTLE ELBERT P	B G	0-0135785	0757	3
TUTTLE HARRY W	CPT	0-0252597	0648	3
TUTTLE JACOB A	MAJ	0-1596837	0856	1
TUTTLE JAMES H	CPT	0-0141633	0358	3
TUTTLE JR CHARLES F	LTC	0-1080590	0663	1
TUTTLE JR WILLIAM D	CW2	W-2212188	0267	1
TUTTLE LAWRENCE W	MAJ	0-0349434	0545	2
TUTTLE LEO F	CPT	0-0496120	0147	1
TUTTLE LESLIE E	LTC	0-1293336	0861	1
TUTTLE LOWELL K	LTC	0-0370952	1059	1
TUTTLE PAUL R	LTC	0-0377144	0161	1
TUTTLE RICHARD F	LTC	0-0946477	0867	1
TUTTLE RICHARD P	MAJ	0-1300552	0161	1
TUTTLE WILDAN R	LTC	0-0338614	0467	3
TUTTON ROBERT L	CW2	W-2144515	0957	2
TUXBURY CLARENCE W	LTC	0-2283836	1264	2
TUXBURY GEORGE P	LTC	0-0907594	0762	1
TUXWORTH JR FRANK E	LTC	0-0257904	C467	3
TVEDT CHESTER G	MAJ	0-0214004	0853	3
TWARDZIAK ANTHONY J	MAJ	0-1558353	0759	1
TWAY THOMAS C	COL	0-0145374	0154	1
TWEDDELL RICHARD	1LT	0-0443954	0745	2
TWEED JENNIE M	1LT	N-0729705	1145	1
TWEEDIE CLAF H	CW3	W-2139999	0367	2
TWEEDY ROBERT W	LTC	0-0385453	0560	1
TWEEDY WALTER K	COL	0-0220575	0862	3
TWEEDY WILLIAM H	COL	0-0291378	0460	1
TWEET IRENE J	2LT	N-0775832	0345	1
TWEIT PHYLLIS E	MAJ	N-0772724	1264	1
TWELMEYER THEODORE A	LTC	0-0355058	0958	1
TWENTIER MAX E	1LT	0-1312459	0145	2
TWENTYMAN CHESTER H	LTC	0-0403751	0558	1
TWICHELL ALAN F	MAJ	0-1060316	0461	1

NAME	GRADE	SVC NO	DATE RET MO YR	RET CODE
TWIFORD JOHN B	MAJ	0-0117665	0155	3
TWIGG RICHARD B	2LT	0-1551327	0744	2
TWILLA ROBERT E	CW3	W-2153108	0466	1
TWILLEAGER JOHN W	CW2	W-2214857	0866	1
TWINEM LINN K	LTC	0-0262103	0767	3
TWINING ELIZABETH	MAJ	N-0758012	0764	1
TWINING HAROLD C	LTC	0-0334085	0267	3
TWISS RAYMOND L	CW3	W-2151044	1057	1
TWIST FRANK R	LTC	0-0265653	0751	3
TWIST JACK B	CPT	0-0312680	0844	2
TWIST WILLIAM J	LTC	0-1575608	1062	1
TWITCHELL RICHARD M	LTC	0-0355026	0460	1
TWITTY 3RD WILLIAM C	1LT	0-0523321	1045	1
TWOHY JR DANIEL W	COL	0-0289744	0965	3
TWOMBLY EDWARD B	LTC	0-0145045	C251	3
TWOMBLY JOSEPH G	MAJ	0-1015533	0962	1
TWOMBLY MAYNARD C	CW2	W-2152587	0562	1
TWOMEY CHARLES F	COL	0-0263984	C563	3
TWOMEY JAMES C	MAJ	0-0255342	1066	3
TWOREK GEORGE J	MAJ	C-2262461	1064	1
TWYMAN FREDERICK	CPT	0-1030851	1160	1
TYACK WILLIAM R	MAJ	0-1182730	0564	1
TYBROSKI MAX M	1LT	0-2263006	0366	1
TYE JR RENNIE V	CPT	0-0414095	0246	2
TYE THOMAS H	LTC	0-0199616	0648	3
TYE WILLIAM H	2LT	0-1998329	0446	2
TYER JR DONALD H	MAJ	C-1646076	0258	1
TYER LLOYD	CW2	W-2151097	1057	1
TYER ROBERT H	MAJ	C-1595232	0357	1
TYERYAR JOSEPHINE	MAJ	N-0724816	0662	1
TYERYAR THOMAS L	MAJ	0-2033074	0361	1
TYLENDA JOSEPH	CW2	W-2150745	1059	1
TYLER ALFRED R	MAJ	C-2007169	0461	1
TYLER CARL H	MAJ	0-0332297	0146	2
TYLER CLEMENT	1LT	0-1642668	0745	2
TYLER DAVID G	LTC	0-0207398	C459	3
TYLER DEROY	CW3	W-2142275	0659	1
TYLER EDWARD J	CPT	0-0453520	0147	2
TYLER FRANKLIN A	LTC	0-0155613	0854	3
TYLER GEORGE A	LTC	0-0212325	0162	3
TYLER GERALD R	COL	0-0170550	C755	1
TYLER HARRY W	LTC	0-0499487	0954	1
TYLER HERMAN H	MAJ	0-0992001	1063	1
TYLER JACK A	MAJ	0-2019743	1060	1
TYLER JOE C	LTC	0-0245562	0259	1
TYLER JOHN A	1LT	0-1010741	0746	2
TYLER JOHN N	MAJ	0-0189214	C662	3
TYLER JR HUNTER W	LTC	0-1946401	0163	1
TYLER JR JOHN	MAJ	0-0339502	0446	2
TYLER JR MARK V	LTC	0-1636751	1264	1
TYLER KEITH W	1LT	0-0507603	0844	2
TYLER KENNETH A	MAJ	C-1179658	0762	1
TYLER LUCIUS C	CW4	W-2118085	0157	1
TYLER NATHAN I	MAJ	0-0240850	0566	3
TYLER OLIN C	LTC	0-0323021	0967	3
TYLER PETER C	CPT	0-1914329	1040	1
TYLER RALPH A	MAJ	0-0213532	0862	3
TYLER RICHARD O	1LT	0-0536742	0146	2
TYLER ROBERT E	2LT	0-1320674	1044	2
TYMNIAK WALTER	MAJ	0-0398497	C861	1
TYNDALL ANDREW	MAJ	0-1703894	0859	1
TYNDALL JOSEPH V	LTC	0-0408225	0563	1
TYNDALL LYNWOOD H	CW3	W-2143779	0963	1
TYNDALL PAUL E	COL	0-0203432	1046	2
TYNDALL PLATO	WO1	W-2124701	0747	1
TYNDALL ROBERT O	LTC	0-1337511	C966	1
TYNER ERNEST C	WO1	W-2109430	0545	2
TYNER FURMAN H	COL	0-0221676	0559	3
TYNER JR CLARENCE E	MAJ	0-1120567	C865	1
TYNER JR LEE R	MAJ	C-1897722	0463	2
TYNER ROBERT R	MAJ	0-0687168	0765	1
TYNER ROY H	CW2	W-2145068	0457	1
TYNER TED H	CPT	0-1824708	0261	1
TYNES ROBERT M	CW3	W-2205116	0365	1
TYNES SEOGIE B	LTC	0-1302669	0657	1
TYREE CLARENCE	1LT	0-0486565	0949	1
TYREE HERMAN E	LTC	0-1541057	0761	1
TYREE JAMES H	MAJ	0-1053404	1063	1
TYREE JR FRANK L	COL	0-0149688	0-52	3
TYREE LAWRENCE H	LTC	0-0418526	1060	1
TYREE PAUL W	CW2	RW-2149462	1262	1
TYRONE MARCUS L	LTC	0-0469753	0666	3
TYRRELL STANLEY C	MAJ	0-1304296	0960	1
TYRRELL WILLIAM L	LTC	0-0201330	0758	3
TYSKOWSKI THEODORE E	MAJ	0-1597659	0762	1
TYSON ARTHUR W	CW4	W-2122867	C161	1
TYSON DANA R	COL	0-0286279	1262	3
TYSON EDWARD B	MAJ	0-1688058	0946	1
TYSON FREDERICK	MAJ	0-1795036	0455	1
TYSON HARRY D	COL	0-0216107	0950	1
TYSON JOHN W	LTC	0-0200183	0648	3
TYTUS JOHN R	CPT	0-1017C82	0246	2
TYUS WELMON T	1LT	0-0535653	0645	2
TYVAND RAYMOND E	LTC	0-0278405	1263	3
UBARRC PATRICIO	CPT	0-0359964	0260	1
UBL JOSEPH L	COL	0-0186997	1053	2
UCHIC NELLIE M	MAJ	N-0770149	0965	1
UCHMAN EDWARD	2LT	0-1550077	1143	2
UDALL JESSE A	LTC	0-0237228	0653	3
UDBYE PAUL	LTC	0-0231146	0657	3
UDELL GEORGE	LTC	0-0393254	0466	3
UDELL GERALD S	MAJ	0-0286045	0362	2
UDOUJ HENRY J	1LT	0-1314975	0446	2
UFFNER RAPHAEL L	CPT	0-037582C	0545	2
UGLAND NILS F	LTC	0-1315292	0962	1
UGLICK GEORGE V	1LT	0-1318346	0463	1
UGLUM HELMER J	LTC	0-0450146	0454	1
UGRO JOSEPH V	MAJ	0-1639752	0658	1
UHAZI GEORGE	MAJ	0-2014777	1164	1
UHER JERMONE M	CW2	W-2150366	0858	1
UHL AUGUST F	MAJ	0-0191635	0640	1
UHLAND CATHERINE	1LT	N-0724247	104N	1
UHLAND RAY G	MAJ	0-0547792	0264	1
UHLENBERG JOSEPH A	1LT	0-1313472	0246	2
UHLER DAVID M	LTC	0-1646665	1057	1
UHLER EARL D	LTC	0-0220076	0-53	3
UHLER ROMAYNE T	COL	0-0176496	0653	2
UHLER WALTER V	LTC	0-0246381	0461	3
UHLFELDER ALVIN R	1LT	0-1169375	1145	2
UHLICH WILFRED O	LTC	0-0329470	1167	3
UHLS WILLIAM C	CPT	0-1179659	1064	2
UHRICH CARL M	2LT	0-1823798	C845	2
UHRICH GERARD I	COL	0-0355936	1167	3
UIBERALL ERNEST R	LTC	0-1334781	0366	1
UITZ JACOB M	CPT	0-1111401	0447	2
ULAN ALFRED A	CPT	0-1037347	0858	1
ULAN LEWIS A	CPT	0-0526089	0446	2
ULAND IVAN C	LTC	0-0386218	0465	3
ULANDER JR ROLAND J	MAJ	0-0966120	0866	1
ULEKOWSKI WALTER J	CW3	W-2208807	0667	1
ULERICH WILLIAM W	CPT	0-117140C	0746	2
ULERY CLARENCE	COL	0-0166831	0746	2
ULERY JOHN W	LTC	0-0281810	0360	3
ULIASZ JOHN T	MAJ	0-1690721	0260	1
ULICNY FRANK S	1LT	0-1944612	0245	2
ULLENBRUCH WILLIAM J	MAJ	0-017975C	0759	3
ULLERY WILLIAM G	LTC	0-1295964	0367	1
ULLESTAD ROLF J	LTC	0-0200925	0159	3
ULLMAN BERNARD F	LTC	0-1641883	0463	1
ULLMANN KARL H	CPT	0-2053822	0757	3
ULM GERALD K	CPT	0-0411899	0845	2
ULMER JOSEPH J	CW4	W-2101321	0261	1
ULMER JR BOSWELL R	COL	0-0339119	0463	1
ULMER WALTER F	COL	0-0264359	0363	3
ULRICH FREDERICK	MAJ	0-1641884	0666	1
ULRICH GEORGE M	CPT	0-2265176	0359	2
ULRICH GEORGE R	CW2	W-3430246	0867	1
ULRICH JOHN L	1LT	0-1C49678	1145	2
ULRICH KARL A	1LT	0-2035399	0246	2
ULRICH RICHARD W	LTC	0-0416041	0366	1
ULRICH RODGER K	MAJ	C-0410618	1046	2
ULRICH SAMUEL C	MAJ	C-1013772	0654	1
ULSAKER LAWRENCE T	COL	0-0267556	0557	1
ULSAMER ANDREW G	2LT	0-117683C	0245	2
ULVENES HOWARD K	MAJ	0-0383293	0966	3
UMAN GEORGE L	CPT	0-0909965	0546	2
UMANOFF LEONARD	LTC	0-0320283	1159	1
UMBARGER JOHN N	LTC	0-0269004	1167	3
UMIKER HENRY G	CW2	W-2215782	0967	1
UMLAND LESLIE W	CW2	W-3200347	0766	1
UMLANG EMIL E	LTC	0-0238521	0266	3
UMPLEBY CLIFFORD R	CPT	0-0119026	0948	3
UMPREY JOHN W	LTC	0-0420854	0453	1
UNCIANO ISAAC F	CPT	0-1102098	C661	1
UNDEN RAGNAR	CPT	0-0260293	0659	3
UNDERDONK ROBERT J	CW3	W-2142208	0660	1
UNDERDUE BRUCE	CW2	W-2105425	1060	1
UNDERHILL MARION H	COL	0-0382295	0467	1
UNDERWOOD CLARENCE L	LTC	0-0156954	C745	2
UNDERWOOD CLARENCE L	MAJ	C-0189788	C748	2
UNDERWOOD CLYDE G	MAJ	0-1635430	1060	1
UNDERWOOD EARL F	MAJ	0-0953880	1062	1
UNDERWOOD EARL G	MAJ	0-2204154	0663	1
UNDERWOOD EDWARD B	COL	0-0325112	C364	3
UNDERWOOD ERVIN E	MAJ	C-1165683	1146	1
UNDERWOOD EUGENE T	LTC	0-0178233	0648	3
UNDERWOOD IRENE L	1LT	N-0752131	0845	1
UNDERWOOD JOHN C	COL	0-0192676	0963	3
UNDERWOOD JOHN D	LTC	0-1639754	0458	2
UNDERWOOD JOSEPH L	MAJ	0-0489845	0257	1
UNDERWOOD JR JAMES A	MAJ	C-0559420	0457	1
UNDERWOOD LAURENCE E	MAJ	0-0195757	1046	2
UNDERWOOD MURRIE	CPT	0-0497502	1057	1
UNDERWOOD ORIAN A	MAJ	0-1030942	C956	1
UNDERWOOD RALPH	LTC	0-1168960	C664	1
UNDERWOOD RICHARD M	LTC	0-1113492	0463	1
UNDERWOOD ROBERT F	CPT	0-0527393	0645	2
UNDERWOOD VERNON L	MAJ	C-1080972	C563	1
UNDERWOOD W T W	LTC	0-0127122	C648	3
UNDERWOOD WILLIAM D	MAJ	0-1015285	0861	1
UNDERWOOD WILLIAM H	MAJ	0-129832C	0261	1
UNDERWOOD WILLIAM W	COL	0-0417675	0767	1
UNGAR HENRY P	CW3	W-2152724	0563	1
UNGER ARTHUR F	2LT	0-1823091	0144	2
UNGER ARTHUR W	LTC	C-1307105	C157	1
UNGER CHARLES J	CPT	0-1594539	0148	1
UNGER EARL R	COL	0-0399142	1063	1
UNGER GEORGE N	LTC	0-0100454	0255	3
UNGER JEROME F	CW3	W-2153186	1265	1
UNGER JOHN F	1LT	0-1016032	0353	2
UNGER JOSEPH	LTC	0-0450931	0152	1
UNGER JOSEPH M	LTC	0-0227737	C665	3
UNGER LOUIS	LTC	0-1291548	C455	1
UNGER OSCAR W	CW3	W-2203841	1265	1
UNGER RALPH G	COL	0-0276280	0165	3
UNGER SAMUEL	LTC	0-0910782	0466	3
UNGER THOMAS H	LTC	0-0184382	0462	3
UNGVARY ROBERT L	1LT	0-0509337	C945	2
UNLEY WALTER W	COL	0-0305286	0167	3
UNO HOWARD Y	CW3	W-2144266	0163	1
UNRATH WALTER J	MAJ	0-1052188	0658	1
UNREIN GERARD A	LTC	0-0441663	0762	1
UNRUH CHARLES L	LTC	0-0301048	0257	3
UNTALAN PEDRO	MAJ	0-1896917	0762	2
UNTHANK EDGAR	LTC	0-1323188	C867	1
UNTIET CHARLES J	1LT	0-1304462	0847	2
UNVERDORBEN MARY E	MAJ	N-0725158	C967	1
UNVERSAW WALTER H	COL	0-0171574	0648	3
UNWIN JR JOSEPH O	COL	0-0380028	0165	1
UP&DEGGRAFF JOHN R	CW4	W-2134061	0559	1
UPCHURCH BARBEE F	CW3	W-3150214	C767	1
UPCHURCH FRED	MAJ	0-0377145	1047	2
UPCHURCH JR C W	1LT	0-0554170	0847	1
UPDEGRAFT KENNETH E	MAJ	0-2015722	0259	2
UPDYKE HARLEY W	CW2	W-3150715	0566	1
UPDYKE RANDALL E	1LT	0-0544029	0546	2
UPHAM FRANCIS B	COL	0-0180207	0553	3
UPHAM JACK W	MAJ	C-0463452	0757	2
UPHAM WILLIAM E	CPT	0-0257249	0865	3
UPHOFF MILTON M	CW3	W-2142910	1061	1
UPHOUSE WILLIAM R	LTC	0-0544642	0966	2
UPP WALDEEN	LTC	0-1047819	0565	1
UPPERCO MARTIN T	2LT	0-1306772	0451	1
UPSHAW ELBERT R	1LT	0-1306685	0845	2
UPSHAW JACKSON E	CPT	0-0522959	0346	2
UPSHUR JAMES M	MAJ	0-0949265	1162	1
UPSON EDITH M	1LT	N-0734994	0945	1
UPSON NEVILLE U	MAJ	0-0396968	0860	1
UPTON CALVIN W	COL	0-0450932	0656	1
UPTON GEORGE E	LTC	0-1585022	1163	1
UPTON JOHN F	MAJ	0-129512C	0563	1
UPTON JR BADGER V	CPT	0-0959103	0759	2
UPTON JR WILLIAM F	LTC	0-0124014	1055	3
UPTON RAYMOND V	LTC	0-1318593	0862	1
UPTON THOMAS H	COL	0-0299867	0861	3
URATSU MASAJI G	MAJ	0-2030815	0562	1
URBACH RUDOLF	LTC	0-1845529	0960	1
URBAITIS JOHN C	LTC	0-0271801	1066	3
URBAN ALBERT O	LTC	0-0285548	1263	3
URBAN CLARENCE W	1LT	0-C157958	0949	3
URBAN GEORGE H	MAJ	0-0964802	0963	2
URBAN MATTY	LTC	0-0416199	0246	2
URBAN ROSS O	WO1	W-2126024	1145	2
URBAN RUSSELL L	COL	0-0147941	1056	3
URBAN SR CHARLES H	LTC	0-0421005	0254	2
URBAN STANLEY J	LTC	0-1165352	0148	1
URBAN WILLARD F	MAJ	0-0279848	1062	1
URBANEK ANN R	2LT	N-0723872	0545	1
URBANICK CHESLAR	LTC	0-1534885	0759	1
URBANSKI EDWARD	MAJ	0-1638704	0361	1
URBANSKI JULIA M	CPT	N-0732058	1047	1
URBANSKI STEVEN M	LTC	0-1642670	1163	1
URBANTKE IRWIN A	LTC	0-1823373	C357	2
URBINA GEORGE S	CPT	0-1686276	1060	1
URBOM OSCAR W	LTC	0-0149713	0648	3
URE WILLIAM G	CPT	0-0417071	0346	1
URECH FRED M	1LT	0-0497845	1153	1
URENSON BERTHA	1LT	N-0755714	1146	1
URETTE SAMUEL S	LTC	0-0278859	1158	1
URIAN RICHARD H	MAJ	0-1800086	0761	1
URICH RUSSELL	1LT	0-0509849	0144	1
URIE EDWIN A	CPT	0-0300812	0465	3
URIU TACASHI	CW3	W-2135972	0762	1
URLING WENDELL P	1LT	0-0518427	1045	1
URQUHART HUGH G	MAJ	0-0914414	0762	2
URSERY JESSE	MAJ	0-0450933	1150	1
URSICH CHARLES C	CPT	0-0319451	1046	2
URSPRUNG ALLEN J	LTC	0-0451458	0259	1
URSPRUNG RUDOLPH S	COL	0-0162588	0851	3
URSTEIN HARRY	CPT	0-0507117	0246	2
URTES JOHN N	LTC	0-1054146	0863	1
URWILLER CLIFFORD S	COL	0-0180676	1054	1
URY JOSEPH	CW2	W-2149969	0361	1
USHAKOFF MICHAEL M	MAJ	0-0253933	0447	1
USHER JOHN W	MAJ	0-1041667	0966	1
USHER THOMAS J	LTC	0-1315744	1160	1
USI EUGENIC B	1LT	0-1896615	0750	1
USINGER EDWARD M	LTC	0-1558447	0166	1
USSERY JOHN E	LTC	0-1546459	0667	1
USSERY WILLIAM T	LTC	0-0509332	0457	1
USTACH STANLEY F	MAJ	0-0346351	0651	1
USTRUCK MICHAEL F	CPT	0-0295777	0345	2
UTKE RAYMOND R	CPT	0-1307481	0248	2
UTLEY EUGENE F	COL	0-0445223	0364	1
UTLEY HAROLD C	LTC	0-1048625	0466	1
UTLEY JOHN H	LTC	0-0227420	0265	3
UTLEY KENNETH O	CW2	W-2203821	0260	1
UTLEY THOMAS E	CW4	W-2142C68	0462	1
UTTER FLOYD J	COL	0-0284382	0266	3
UTTER JOSEPH W	COL	0-0167798	0959	3

NAME	GRADE	SVC NO	DATE RET MO YR	RET CODE
UTTERBACK GENE I	LTC	0-0277104	0361	1
UTTERBACK JR ALVIN P	LTC	0-0380479	1046	1
UTTERBACK ORVAL N	1LT	0-0499650	0655	1
UTTERBACK ROBERT L	CW3	W-2129156	0760	1
UYEDA MASAO H	MAJ	C-0956827	1264	2
UYEYAMA KAHN	LTC	C-0317636	0347	2
UZARAVITZ EDWARD T	MAJ	0-0479699	0953	1
UZZEL NORRIS H	MAJ	0-0963524	0661	1
UZZELL THOMAS M	LTC	0-0402796	0163	3
VACCA JOHN V	LTC	0-0332094	1060	2
VACCA PETER	LTC	C-0289334	1160	3
VACCARO FRANK T	MAJ	C-1543884	0563	1
VACCARO WILLIAM	LTC	0-0427386	C461	1
VACEK JOHN E	LTC	0-0198053	0558	3
VACHA HELEN E	MAJ	N-0726329	C847	1
VACHER EUGENE D	CW3	W-2146734	0765	1
VACINEK ROBERT O	CW3	W-2146942	0665	1
VACURA HAROLD J	MAJ	C-0418417	C960	1
VADA ALBERT J	LTC	0-1016107	1262	1
VADEN ANDREW C	1LT	0-0378885	C446	2
VADEN DAVID J	CPT	0-0506935	C649	1
VADEN FLOYD L	LTC	0-1293681	1163	1
VADEN JR FRANK S	COL	0-0254623	0566	3
VADEN SAMUEL A	MAJ	C-1060673	0467	1
VADEN THOMAS H	LTC	0-0174869	0760	3
VADNAIS ARTHUR A	CW2	W-2109482	0946	1
VADNER LAWRENCE S	MAJ	0-0102330	C158	3
VADNEY EVELYN E	1LT	N-0720746	0945	1
VAESSEN CORNELIUS	LTC	0-1105879	0166	1
VAGUSKI JOSEPH	CW4	W-2148344	1157	1
VAIL DAVID B	LTC	0-1638707	0165	1
VAIL RALPH	MAJ	0-0922657	C745	2
VAILATI LOUIS T	CPT	C-2012320	0657	1
VAILLANCOURT MARY M	1LT	N-0720299	0546	1
VAILLANCOURT OLIVER	MAJ	0-1824101	0762	1
VAILLANCOURT SIDNEY	CW2	W-2151833	0260	1
VAILLANCOURT VINCENT	CW3	W-2153272	0762	1
VAIRA JACK A	LTC	0-1111402	1062	1
VAITONIS ANTON F	CPT	0-1323189	0251	1
VAITONIS MARJORIE P	CPT	N-0773789	1052	1
VALDERENAS NUMERIA	2LT	0-0888116	0850	1
VALDEZ JR ISIDRO S	LTC	0-1997748	1262	1
VALDEZ LIBRADO P	MAJ	C-1924997	C965	1
VALDEZ RETRONILO	1LT	0-0890552	1054	1
VALDEZ WALTER E	2LT	0-1329536	1145	2
VALE CHARLES F	MAJ	C-1644861	0758	1
VALE RAMON	LTC	0-0423251	0162	1
VALENCIA LUIS	MAJ	C-0982273	0762	2
VALENTA MARCUS A	LTC	C-0305250	0865	3
VALENTI CHARLES N	MAJ	G-0976921	1062	1
VALENTI JOHN S	LTC	0-1638709	1265	1
VALENTIC JOHN A	MAJ	0-1875552	0765	1
VALENTINE ALICE	MAJ	M-0000975	C364	1
VALENTINE ARLIE J	COL	C-0444966	0663	3
VALENTINE EDWARD A	MAJ	C-0158984	0853	3
VALENTINE EDWARD R	MAJ	0-0191904	C854	3
VALENTINE HENRY D	CPT	0-0189431	0648	3
VALENTINE JOHN J	LTC	0-1322385	C462	1
VALENTINE JOHN W	MAJ	0-2051729	0359	1
VALENTINE KENNETH R	CPT	0-0123106	0855	3
VALENTINE MAURICE L	LTC	0-1639756	0865	1
VALENTINE PAUL F	COL	0-0917238	1163	3
VALENTINE WILLIAM F	2LT	0-1638710	1143	2
VALENTINI EVELYN E	LTC	0-0100530	0648	3
VALENTINO FILOMENA A	MAJ	N-0722170	1161	1
VALENZUELA CECIL R	CPT	0-1896382	1063	2
VALENZUELA EDWARD J	MAJ	0-2028756	0964	1
VALENZUELA RAOUL P	LTC	0-1549153	0661	1
VALERA MARIANO	1LT	0-0890504	0849	2
VALERIC CHARLES F	CW3	W-2146682	0363	1
VALES JAMES P	LTC	0-0330754	0367	3
VALESKA DONALD G	MAJ	0-1018862	C761	1
VALIGORSKY N M	CW2	W-2146291	0360	1
VALIMAKI TAUNO E	MAJ	C-1339828	0566	1
VALKO ANDREW A	CPT	0-1559131	0156	1

NAME	GRADE	SVC NO	DATE RET MO YR	RET CODE
VALLACHER THEODORE L	CPT	0-0905872	0945	2
VALLANCINGHAM CLINTO	CW2	W-2211082	0164	1
VALLANCINGHAM JOHN T	MAJ	0-0122973	0649	3
VALLARIC RUDOLPH A	LTC	0-1047821	0765	1
VALLAZZA WILLIAM J	LTC	0-1550079	0260	2
VALLE PETER M	LTC	0-0408693	0860	1
VALLEDOR SID C	2LT	0-1896873	0459	1
VALLEEN MARY F	2LT	N-0771755	0544	1
VALLEJO ROY J	MAJ	0-1543280	0366	1
VALLERY JERRY	LTC	0-1113030	0263	1
VALLESE MARIO J	MAJ	0-1293682	0864	1
VALLEY GEORGE A	MAJ	0-2019676	1160	2
VALLIERE JOSEPH H	LTC	0-0451256	0955	1
VALLO JULIA M	2LT	N-0730626	0743	1
VALLO SEBASTIAN	MAJ	0-0345842	0646	2
VALLOR JOHN C	LTC	0-027346C	0661	1
VALLOW HERBERT P	MAJ	0-1796551	0852	1
VALOIS DOUGLAS J	1LT	0-1647767	0646	2
VALTER EDWARD T	CPT	0-1796189	0557	2
VALVERDE MARIO F	MAJ	0-0350115	0146	2
VAN ACKER EMIL A	CW2	W-2148133	0657	1
VAN AKEN CHETWOOD G	CPT	0-1311950	0461	1
VAN ALLEN ALFRED	LTC	0-1004711	0263	1
VAN ANBURGH PAUL F	MAJ	0-0265948	0943	2
VAN ANCEL ALBERT E	CPT	0-0501748	0750	1
VAN ANCEL SHERMAN L	CW2	W-2214858	0966	1
VAN ANROY OSCAR J	CW4	W-2004563	0164	3
VAN ANTWERP ELMER C	CPT	0-0282298	0662	3
VAN ANTWERP MAURICE	LTC	0-0223481	0964	3
VAN ANTWERP WILLIAM	COL	0-0197205	1159	1
VAN ARNAM WILLIAM D	MAJ	0-0189138	0858	1
VAN ARSDALE FRANK W	CW2	W-2141688	0463	1
VAN ARSDALE WILLIA	LTC	0-0204940	0359	3
VAN ATTA FREDERICK	COL	0-0267544	0960	3
VAN AUKEN KENNETH R	CW2	W-2148306	0564	1
VAN BERKUM FRED	2LT	0-1032606	0946	1
VAN BESIAN GEORGE J	MAJ	0-0372367	0846	2
VAN BORKUM ARNOLD J	COL	0-0337438	0662	2
VAN BUREN GEORGE B	MAJ	C-1548330	1061	1
VAN BUREN HENRY T	CPT	0-0465158	0546	2
VAN BUREN MARTIN E	CPT	0-0514431	0547	2
VAN BUSKIRK ADELBE	CPT	0-0276504	0146	2
VAN BUSKIRK WILLIAM	LTC	0-1798819	1064	1
VAN CAMPEN JIM A	CW2	W-2208325	0164	1
VAN CAMPEN RICHARD J	LTC	0-1101249	1160	1
VAN CISE PHILIP S	COL	0-0703825	0648	3
VAN CLEAVE DANIEL R	MAJ	0-1297620	0356	1
VAN COCK ARTHUR F	LTC	0-1172702	0664	1
VAN COURTLAND W R	2LT	0-1633613	0944	2
VAN DAM DON H	LTC	0-0306074	0167	3
VAN DAM JOHN H	MAJ	0-1633028	0253	1
VAN DE CARR FRANCIS	LTC	0-0282208	1161	2
VAN DE GRAAFF WILL	LTC	0-0245236	0354	2
VAN DE MARK DANIEL	1LT	0-0383793	0346	2
VAN DELLEN CLARENC	MAJ	0-1299148	0554	2
VAN DER WALL HAROLD	1LT	0-0977402	1055	1
VAN DERHOEF FLOYD C	LTC	0-1300108	1060	1
VAN DERLICK EARLE V	MAJ	C-1949560	0767	3
VAN DERRIPE W S	LTC	0-0910330	1060	3
VAN DEUSEN GEORGE W	LTC	0-0290051	0762	3
VAN DEVENTER ROY W	COL	0-0199582	0946	2
VAN DEVENTER WILLIAM	COL	0-0330757	0265	3
VAN DOERN FREDERIC A	LTC	0-0925105	0963	1
VAN DORN LLOYD S	MAJ	0-0195979	0458	3
VAN DORPE JOHN H	1LT	0-1315453	0446	2
VAN DUSEN CHARLES R	CW4	W-2110390	0660	1
VAN DUSEN DANIEL	LTC	0-0232318	1060	3
VAN DUSER DAMON E	CPT	0-2012262	0258	1
VAN DUYN JACK H	CPT	0-0355104	0246	2
VAN DUYN ROGER C	COL	0-0387179	1262	1
VAN DUYNE GARDNER	CPT	0-0915646	1046	2
VAN DUYNE RICHARD	CPT	0-1169753	1147	2
VAN DYCK JOHN F	LTC	0-1183212	0162	1
VAN DYKE GEORGE S	LTC	0-1543868	1164	1
VAN DYKE SETH H	LTC	0-0275530	1054	3

NAME	GRADE	SVC NO	DATE RET MO YR	RET CODE
VAN DYNE JOSEPH R	MAJ	0-0439064	C746	2
VAN EGEREN ROBERT J	CPT	0-0445447	0146	2
VAN ELZAKKER JOHN S	2LT	0-1314205	0445	2
VAN EMST JAMES H	LTC	C-1592676	0263	1
VAN EPPS JOHN A	LTC	0-0451723	0361	1
VAN ES ERNST A	COL	0-0913166	1161	3
VAN ESSO ANDREW E	COL	0-0241739	0965	3
VAN ETTEN GLEN G	CPT	0-1108383	C646	2
VAN FLEET GEORGE L	LTC	C-1325682	C865	1
VAN FLEET JAMES K	LTC	0-1307107	0366	1
VAN GOETHEM CYRIL C	CW4	W-2141932	C966	1
VAN GORDEN CLINTON	CPT	0-1341728	0757	1
VAN GORDON ARCHIE H	CPT	0-0393255	C144	2
VAN HAAFTEN EDWARD C	LTC	0-0274122	0754	3
VAN HALF LAURENCE A	MAJ	C-0319403	0246	1
VAN HARDEVELD JACC	COL	0-027458C	0558	1
VAN HAUSEN WILLIS H	CPT	0-1555312	0463	1
VAN HEUCKEROTH ARTHU	LTC	0-0321874	1264	3
VAN HISE EDWARD P	MAJ	0-0110496	0856	3
VAN HOLLEN RUSSELL L	COL	0-0274096	0661	3
VAN HOLSBAKE LEON A	MAJ	0-1031983	0952	1
VAN HOOGEN ANDRE A	1LT	0-0994432	0655	2
VAN HOOK ELMER E	LTC	0-0442611	0846	2
VAN HOOK GEORGE J	CW3	W-2152288	C764	1
VAN HOOK SAMUEL M	MAJ	0-1110858	0458	2
VAN HOOK WARREN B	LTC	C-0372263	1060	1
VAN HOOK WILLIAM Y	LTC	0-0394260	0666	1
VAN HOOMISSEN F H	2LT	N-0736371	1043	1
VAN HOOREBEKE O H	CPT	0-0976430	0261	1
VAN HOOSER HOMER L	MAJ	0-0953765	C862	1
VAN HOOZER FRED O	LTC	C-0422760	C563	1
VAN HORN EUGENE G	MAJ	C-2007089	0264	1
VAN HORN HAROLD	CPT	0-4011089	0963	1
VAN HORN JOSEPH B	MAJ	0-1030620	0261	1
VAN HORN MAURICE W	LTC	0-0338944	1059	1
VAN HORN WILBUR B	CW3	W-2148271	0463	1
VAN HOUSEN CHARLES	CPT	0-2021883	C464	1
VAN HOUTEN LOUIS M	LTC	0-0378991	1067	3
VAN HOUTEN ROBERT A	LTC	0-0317116	0760	1
VAN HOY LOUIE R	LTC	0-1301227	0461	1
VAN HOY WILLIAM L	LTC	0-0292283	0361	1
VAN HUSS CARL W	MAJ	C-1923509	C765	1
VAN HUSS LYLE J	CW3	W-2150226	0264	1
VAN KAN HUBERT J	LTC	0-1633614	0366	1
VAN KEUREN GERALD M	LTC	0-1548577	C865	1
VAN KIRK JAY K	CPT	0-2028356	0857	2
VAN KIRK JOHN C	CPT	0-0335578	0845	2
VAN KRIEKEN JOHN	CPT	0-1284434	0957	1
VAN KUREN HARRY D	LTC	C-1551136	0367	3
VAN LEEUWEN CHARLES	MAJ	0-0410371	C762	1
VAN LENTEN WILBUR	MAJ	C-0513038	0763	1
VAN LOO MILTON F	MAJ	0-2020597	0865	1
VAN LUVENDER WESLEY	CW3	W-2145212	0364	1
VAN MAASTRICHT PETER	MAJ	C-1175605	1160	1
VAN MAMEREN JOHN A	LTC	0-1042975	C164	1
VAN METER ALBERT R	LTC	0-0445059	0457	1
VAN METER DONALD S	LTC	0-0501011	1163	1
VAN METER JEROME R	1LT	0-1052189	1045	2
VAN METER WHITAM K	COL	0-0233248	0959	1
VAN NATTA MILES C	CPT	0-0385589	0757	1
VAN NESS NOBLE	LTC	0-0294303	C357	3
VAN NESS SHERMAN H	CW2	RW-2209782	0961	1
VAN NEST ARDEN L	MAJ	0-0249545	1266	3
VAN NORMAN GARNETT L	MAJ	0-0208762	1047	1
VAN NOSDALE FREDERIC	MAJ	0-1686597	0664	1
VAN NOSTRAND MANNI	1LT	0-0483697	0943	2
VAN NOTE JR HARRY T	LTC	0-0385205	1161	1
VAN NOTE LEROY J	LTC	0-0281590	0459	3
VAN NOY LESLIE N	LTC	0-0328043	0546	2
VAN OOSBREE FRANK	MAJ	0-0368457	0861	1
VAN OOSTEN JOHN	LTC	0-1287090	0860	1
VAN ORDEN MAZEL W	LTC	C-0300154	1263	3
VAN ORMAN CHESTER W	MAJ	0-2212096	0862	1
VAN ORMAN GEORGE A	MAJ	C-0450114	0357	1
VAN OS SEYMOUR	COL	0-0123018	0-53	3

NAME	GRADE	SVC NO	DATE RET MO YR	RET CODE
VAN OSDEL RICHARD L	CW2	W-2150590	0363	1
VAN PATTEN MAX M	1LT	0-1012801	0245	2
VAN PELT CLARENCE D	CW2	W-2102494	0956	1
VAN PELT CLIFFORD A	CW4	W-2132094	1060	1
VAN PELT ERNEST A	CW2	W-2146946	0855	1
VAN PELT JOHN C	CW4	W-2001933	0466	3
VAN PELT THEODORE L	CW2	W-2206304	0661	1
VAN POPERING ALDEN	MAJ	0-1634424	1062	1
VAN POYCK WALTER S	MAJ	0-1283345	1046	2
VAN PRAAG DAVID B	1LT	0-4063766	0161	2
VAN PRAAG SAUL	2LT	0-1298622	C845	2
VAN RAALTE ARNOLD R	MAJ	0-0171093	0648	3
VAN RAALTE DERK B K	CPT	0-1313000	0547	2
VAN RAVENSWAAY D P	2LT	N-0759602	0545	1
VAN REED JOHN C	MAJ	0-1290849	0361	1
VAN REET LEO	CW3	W-2147427	1064	1
VAN RIPER ROBERT F	1LT	0-1304593	0447	2
VAN RIPER WENDELL J	LTC	0-2036453	0960	1
VAN RODEN EDWARD L	COL	0-0139956	0652	3
VAN SACERS LEONARD R	MAJ	0-1552611	0866	1
VAN SANT DANIEL M	1LT	0-0551032	1045	2
VAN SANT ELEANOR B	MAJ	N-0721201	0967	1
VAN SANT ELWOOD W	CW3	W-2149132	0559	1
VAN SANT GEORGE A	CPT	0-1645452	0556	1
VAN SANT JOHN E	LTC	0-0386321	0860	1
VAN SANT JOHN W	CPT	0-0494336	0747	1
VAN SANTEN JR JOHN H	LTC	0-2033014	1266	1
VAN SAUN ARTHUR C	MAJ	0-0191121	0644	2
VAN SCHOICK RICHAR	CPT	0-0346295	0648	1
VAN SCIVER HARRY B	COL	0-0321824	0648	3
VAN SCOYOC MELWOOD W	CPT	0-0233201	0763	3
VAN SICKLE ALBERT K	1LT	0-0497771	0845	2
VAN SICKLE MERRILL F	LTC	0-0375354	C562	1
VAN SICKLE ROGER E	MAJ	0-1597846	0867	3
VAN SICKLE VERNON L	CW2	W-2144624	1060	1
VAN SISE FREDERICK	2LT	0-1050495	1050	1
VAN SLYKE GORDON E	1LT	0-1638718	0648	2
VAN SLYKE HELEN L	2LT	N-0721035	C345	2
VAN SLYKE LELAND P	CPT	0-1280177	0144	2
VAN SLYKE STUART O	LTC	0-0392195	0765	1
VAN SLYKE VACER H	LTC	0-0225153	1264	3
VAN SMITH HERBERT C	LTC	0-0131370	1154	3
VAN STECKUM ANTON W	LTC	0-0253935	0650	3
VAN STORY JR JOE	CW2	W-2212695	1167	1
VAN STUCK W	COL	0-0903193	1165	3
VAN SWARINGEN R L	LTC	0-0411448	0960	1
VAN SWEARINGEN JOS	CPT	0-0923953	0647	2
VAN TASSEL GERALD K	COL	0-0374248	0862	2
VAN TASSEL GORDON E	2LT	0-0451631	0444	2
VAN TASSEL REX	CW2	W-2147983	0261	1
VAN TILL JOHN H	CPT	0-0486654	C451	1
VAN TREESE CHARLES O	1LT	0-1166855	C545	2
VAN TUYL PAUL	COL	0-0253641	0159	3
VAN VALKENBURG GUY A	1LT	0-1287969	1045	2
VAN VALKENBURG KENNE	CPT	0-0370540	0867	3
VAN VALKENBURGH DALE	CPT	0-1825204	1263	1
VAN VELZOR JAMES D	CPT	0-1306204	1047	2
VAN VLECK MARVIN F	2LT	0-1055178	0944	1
VAN VLIET SYLVESTE	MAJ	0-1167684	0155	2
VAN VOAST JR H S	LTC	0-0234941	0361	3
VAN VOORHIES ROBERT	CPT	0-0342514	0146	2
VAN VOSSEN NORMAN	2LT	0-1317707	1144	2
VAN VRANKEN RALPH	MAJ	0-0190329	0955	3
VAN WAGENEN JAMES H	LTC	0-0265568	0164	3
VAN WART ROBERT J	1LT	0-1031280	0746	2
VAN WERT HAROLD J	MAJ	0-1286929	0747	2
VAN WERT WAYNE W	LTC	0-1575240	0561	1
VAN WEY CARL C	CPT	0-0488375	0648	1
VAN WICKLE CHARLES D	CPT	0-0262795	0467	3
VAN WINKLE SPENCER	WO1	W-2135062	1045	2
VAN WINKLE THOMAS	1LT	0-1583789	1047	2
VAN WINKLE WILSON W	LTC	0-0392715	1058	1
VAN WOERKOM JOHN W	LTC	0-1100809	0767	1
VAN WYCK WILLIAM O	2LT	0-0390649	0544	2
VAN WYCKHOUSE ROBERT	CW4	W-2143436	0766	1

NAME	GRADE	SVC NO	DATE RET MO YR	RET CODE
VAN WYK FRANK J	COL	O-0267019	0163	3
VAN YSSELDYK JACOB L	CPT	O-1011261	0553	1
VAN ZANDT ARNOLD C	COL	O-0164959	0948	3
VAN ZANDT GILBERT F	CPT	O-1184964	0159	1
VAN ZANDT JOHN P	CPT	O-0228415	0554	3
VAN ZANT ELMER L	MAJ	O-0496559	1156	1
VAN ZANT HERBERT	LTC	O-0366661	0160	1
VANDEEBOGART A A	2LT	O-1010837	0745	1
VANDEEKAMP ARTHUR H	1LT	O-1168961	0745	1
VANDEEVENTER DALE	WO1	W-2144548	1053	1
VANDEEWALKER LYLE E	1LT	O-1168499	0646	2
VANDERSLUGT PETER	COL	O-0194414	0452	3
VAN-DEN-HEUVEL STAN	2LT	O-0388038	1043	2
VANAKER BERNARD S	MAJ	O-1540753	0561	1
VANAMAN ROBERT B	MAJ	O-1643405	0258	1
VANASKY JOHN	1LT	O-1579248	0445	2
VANASSE BEATRICE M	1LT	N-0754204	0850	1
VANATTA HARRY W	LTC	O-1580442	1264	1
VANCE ARLINGTON	CW4	W-2141478	0965	1
VANCE BRUCE B	COL	O-0335432	0361	3
VANCE CHARLES S	COL	O-0118125	0155	1
VANCE HAROLD R	MAJ	O-0315469	1047	2
VANCE HARVEY C	MAJ	O-1031279	0854	1
VANCE HEBER G	CPT	O-0343451	1046	2
VANCE HOMER P	MAJ	O-1593354	0361	1
VANCE JAMES D	COL	O-0304390	0861	1
VANCE JAMES W	MAJ	O-1541135	1055	1
VANCE JOHN E	B G	O-0229832	0665	3
VANCE LUTHER J	1LT	O-2018440	0161	1
VANCE ROBERT C C	1LT	O-1001922	0945	2
VANCE STEWART H	LTC	O-1846373	1062	1
VANCE WENDEL E	CPT	O-0450202	0746	2
VANCE WILLIAM M	COL	O-0141733	0357	2
VANCE WILLIAM T	MAJ	O-2030997	1167	1
VANCIL FRANCE E	MAJ	O-0425241	0565	1
VANDAHL HENRY C	MAJ	O-0485078	0945	2
VANDE VEGT JOSEP	MAJ	O-1287624	1160	1
VANDE-WATER CLAREN	CPT	O-1787794	0353	1
VANDEBRAKE CLARENCE	1LT	O-2034709	0946	1
VANDECAVEYE GEORGE R	CW2	W-2214460	0667	1
VANDEGRIFT GEORGE E	MAJ	O-1081679	0265	1
VANDENBERG GERALD	MAJ	O-0241586	1264	3
VANDENBERG MILTON H	CPT	O-0516128	0346	2
VANDENBERG ROBERT L	2LT	O-1320675	0644	2
VANDENBERG ROBERT W	CPT	O-1302236	0645	2
VANDER HEIDE IRWI	LTC	O-0486305	0266	3
VANDER HEYDEN DON	MAJ	O-0948741	0363	1
VANDER HEYDEN RAL	MAJ	O-0976045	1064	1
VANDER VEER FRANC	LTC	O-0281681	1263	3
VANDER VLIET A	CPT	O-0262174	0957	1
VANDER VLIET ANTH	CPT	O-2262174	0957	1
VANDER ZWIEP P J	COL	O-0287932	0161	1
VANDERSVOORT DALE G	1LT	O-0552206	0346	2
VANDER-LINDEN WILLIA	1LT	O-0485920	0248	1
VANDER-STOLP WILLA	1LT	O-1303439	0845	2
VANDERBERG JOHN H	2LT	O-1014816	0645	2
VANDERBURG ALBERT L	MAJ	O-0455752	0159	1
VANDERBURG JACK R	LTC	O-1643406	0667	1
VANDERBURGH ARNOTT K	LTC	O-0382493	0154	1
VANDERBURGH LESTER R	MAJ	O-0487636	0553	1
VANDERBURGH WARREN M	MAJ	O-0385163	0762	1
VANDERFORD HAROLD J	MAJ	O-0267072	0966	3
VANDERFORD JOHN H	1LT	O-1320877	0752	2
VANDERGOOT WILBUR	WO1	W-2105949	0947	2
VANDERGRIFF RAYMOND	CW3	W-2147399	0462	1
VANDERHOFF JAMES R	MAJ	O-2038830	0460	1
VANDERHOFF JESS W	LTC	O-0276491	0966	3
VANDERHOFF MALCOLM J	MAJ	O-1688415	1164	1
VANDERKAMP BERNARD J	1LT	O-1012543	0445	2
VANDERLIP ARTHUR N	LTC	O-0250931	0861	3
VANDERPOOL JOSEPH G	1LT	O-0887588	0762	1
VANDERPOOL LEROY J	CPT	O-1951671	1263	1
VANDERPOOL WILLIAM F	MAJ	O-1582229	0161	1
VANDERVOORT WILLIAM	LTC	O-0297358	0663	1
VANDERVORT CHARLES E	LTC	O-1048627	0361	1
VANDERWILT BERT	COL	O-0139961	0953	3
VANDERZALM THEODORE	COL	O-0324515	0853	3
VANDEVENTER JEROME J	MAJ	O-0278043	1059	3
VANDEWATER REGINAL	COL	O-0238948	0648	3
VANDISH ARTHUR J	LTC	O-0255590	1146	1
VANDIVER COMER L	COL	O-0250020	1264	3
VANDIVER DAN C	CW2	W-2208430	1064	1
VANDREUIL RAYMOND L	LTC	O-1032124	0962	1
VANEK VACLAV H	COL	O-0358545	1064	1
VANGE SIMON C	1LT	O-1040632	1148	1
VANGEN TERRANCE A	LTC	O-1283873	0259	1
VANGENE KERMIT E	LTC	O-0415058	1160	1
VANHOLME FLORIMOND	COL	O-0393321	0161	1
VANHOOK JOHNIE L	CW3	W-2141479	0460	1
VANKIRK TRAVIS L	CW3	W-2150603	0559	1
VANN JAMES R	LTC	O-0504344	1154	1
VANN LUTHER R	LTC	O-0345112	0362	3
VANN WILLIAM F	LTC	O-1180077	0563	1
VANNEY JOSEPH J	1LT	O-1283874	1145	2
VANNI LOUIS J	1LT	O-1643408	0345	2
VANNIER EDWARD S	MAJ	O-0212533	0949	3
VANNONI VASILLI P	CW2	W-2214892	0866	1
VANNORDSTRAND PAUL A	LTC	O-0408635	0960	1
VANNOY GARNETT R	CW2	W-2145170	0956	1
VANNOY THOMAS H	CPT	O-0335661	0756	1
VANNUCCI ALBERT O	1LT	O-1555645	1045	2
VANOSDOL PERRY H	1LT	O-0468055	0845	2
VANSANT ALLEN S	LTC	O-0277962	0565	3
VANSTICKLE JAMES A	MAJ	O-1882257	0967	1
VANSTON AUGUST R	LTC	O-1115442	1064	3
VANSTON PAUL J	1LT	O-1296297	1145	2
VANUCCI FRANK	CPT	O-0308447	1045	2
VANZANDT BILLY J	CW3	RW-2145598	0665	1
VANZANT CHARLES V	MAJ	O-1014996	0961	1
VARA JR JOSEPH J	MAJ	O-2204111	0466	1
VARDEN HARRY J	LTC	O-1573649	0556	1
VARELA OSMUND L	LTC	O-0175462	0348	2
VARELLI FRANCIS P	CPT	O-0959337	0562	1
VARETONI RAYMOND	MAJ	O-1635437	0358	1
VARGA ANTHONY A	CW2	W-2149271	1262	2
VARGA WILLIAM	CW3	W-2118536	1157	1
VARGO JOHN C	MAJ	O-2055492	0854	1
VARGO JOSEPH R	MAJ	O-0472126	0854	1
VARGO MARGARET M	LTC	N-0728070	0361	1
VARGO WILLIAM J	MAJ	O-1823374	0859	1
VARIAN JESSE W	LTC	O-0206858	0556	1
VARLAND JR ARTHUR T	CPT	O-0380130	0143	2
VARLEY JOHN W	CPT	O-0340363	1147	2
VARLEY ROLAND	LTC	O-0238522	0965	3
VARNADO JR HUGH R	CPT	O-1046306	0547	2
VARNADO NORMAN L	2LT	O-0557747	1045	2
VARNER DWIGHT S	MAJ	O-0402879	0245	2
VARNER LAURENCE W	COL	O-0198797	0954	1
VARNEY AUSTIN A	LTC	O-1169376	0261	1
VARNEY EARLE L	CW2	W-2145273	0561	1
VARNEY FRED W	MAJ	O-0953161	0547	1
VARNEY GEORGE C	CPT	O-0532796	1145	2
VARNEY HARLEY R	MAJ	O-1821112	1045	2
VARNEY IRVIN J	LTC	O-0309832	0764	1
VARNEY JR LINWOOD L	MAJ	O-1550287	0358	1
VARNEY KENNETH A	LTC	O-0251218	0764	3
VARNEY LYMAN D	COL	O-0209137	0254	3
VARNEY RODERIC A	LTC	O-1080975	1164	1
VARNEY THEODORE R	LTC	O-0248162	0466	3
VARNEY WILLIAM F	MAJ	O-1636765	0859	1
VARNI JOSEPH C	CPT	O-2027804	0456	1
VARNUM HARVEY C	1LT	O-1306664	0844	2
VARRAVETO MILDRED F	MAJ	N-0785444	0365	1
VARRELMANN GALE L	1LT	O-0540547	0346	2
VARZALY EUGENE	MAJ	O-1582812	0161	1
VASEY JOHNNIE F	CPT	O-2014849	0460	1
VASIL LEON N	MAJ	O-1044415	0756	1
VASILAKE JOHN G	CPT	O-1289169	0562	2
VASILOL GEORGE	CW3	W-2143058	0861	1
VASKO JOHN R	COL	O-0235205	1061	3
VASS GEORGE T	1LT	O-0462665	0146	2
VASS JR ERNEST A	MAJ	O-1043823	1159	1
VASSALLO ANTHONY L	LTC	O-0453357	0856	1
VASSAR CHARLES T	1LT	O-0504035	0645	2
VASSAR WILLIAM F	LTC	O-0389152	0766	1
VASSEL WILLIAM D	LTC	O-1325843	1264	2
VASSER ROY	LTC	O-1102100	0557	1
VASTINE JOHN R	CPT	O-0490688	0944	2
VASU CLAUDE F	1LT	O-1323207	1045	2
VATER FREDERICK	LTC	O-0183774	0648	3
VATH CHARLES H	LTC	O-0267627	0861	3
VAUDRY JAMES W	MAJ	O-0381305	0246	2
VAUGHAN ALVIN A	CPT	O-0502462	0546	1
VAUGHAN CARL F	WO1	W-2110578	1044	2
VAUGHAN CHARLES C	LTC	O-0906227	0266	3
VAUGHAN DANIEL V	CPT	O-1823241	0761	1
VAUGHAN DONALD G	LTC	O-0222573	1061	3
VAUGHAN EUGENE L	2LT	O-1032608	0744	2
VAUGHAN FREDERICK	MAJ	O-0308140	0262	3
VAUGHAN GEORGE	1LT	O-1036776	0246	2
VAUGHAN HARRY H	M G	O-0205101	0153	1
VAUGHAN HENRY S	1LT	O-1328425	0746	2
VAUGHAN HERMAN A	CW2	W-2118257	1048	1
VAUGHAN JAMES F	MAJ	O-0508945	0756	1
VAUGHAN JR CONAN W	COL	O-0237325	0566	3
VAUGHAN JR JAMES H	COL	O-0412094	0267	1
VAUGHAN JR TURNER J	CW3	W-2144199	0861	1
VAUGHAN LEWIS C	LTC	O-1283093	1062	1
VAUGHAN MARY S	2LT	N-0794356	1046	1
VAUGHAN MYRON C	MAJ	O-1557386	0863	1
VAUGHAN PERRY A	CPT	O-1043247	0745	2
VAUGHAN ROBERT	LTC	O-0453290	1265	1
VAUGHAN ROBERT B	MAJ	O-1283699	1158	1
VAUGHAN ROBERT W	MAJ	O-0969526	0663	1
VAUGHAN RUFUS E	COL	O-0246417	0954	3
VAUGHAN SAMUEL E	COL	O-0177348	0461	3
VAUGHAN WALES	MAJ	O-0418813	0366	1
VAUGHAN WILLIAM H	MAJ	O-1182985	0861	1
VAUGHN CHARLES E	CPT	O-1108386	1051	2
VAUGHN CHARLES H	1LT	O-1543620	1153	1
VAUGHN ERNEST A	MAJ	O-1542667	0555	1
VAUGHN FRED H	COL	O-0122925	0648	3
VAUGHN GUY V	CPT	O-2001663	1057	1
VAUGHN JAMES A	CPT	O-1586307	0559	1
VAUGHN JAMES F	MAJ	O-1874889	1266	1
VAUGHN JIMMIE D	MAJ	O-0889717	0860	1
VAUGHN JOE D	MAJ	O-0239474	0666	3
VAUGHN JOHN H	LTC	O-2011631	0567	1
VAUGHN JOHN L	CPT	O-0501747	0347	1
VAUGHN JR GEORGE A	LTC	O-0139465	0557	3
VAUGHN MAURICE B	MAJ	O-1010196	1060	1
VAUGHN MILTON S	LTC	O-1048629	0662	1
VAUGHN RALPH W	COL	O-0237884	0865	3
VAUGHN VIRGIL E	LTC	O-1014362	0656	1
VAUGHN WALTER R	2LT	O-2010677	0446	2
VAUGHN WILBERT F	CPT	O-2036086	0257	2
VAUGHN WILLIS C	LTC	O-1558357	0958	1
VAUGHN WINFRED F	CPT	O-0389767	1045	2
VAUGHT LESLIE L	CPT	O-0282785	0945	2
VAUPEL ROBERT V	MAJ	O-0302942	0350	1
VAUTRAIN PAUL A	CPT	O-0488169	0853	2
VAUX JR JOSEPH	CW2	W-3411014	1166	1
VAZQUEZ ANGELICO	MAJ	O-1302420	1053	1
VAZQUEZ GENEROSO	COL	O-0331489	0756	3
VAZQUEZ JUAN	CPT	O-0190387	0146	1
VAZQUEZ RICARDO V	MAJ	O-1285342	1060	1
VAZQUEZ ROBERTO	CW3	W-2005790	0965	1
VAZQUEZ SAMUEL C	MAJ	O-1340597	0866	1
VAZQUEZ WILLIAM	CW3	W-2005312	1266	1
VAZQUEZEMILAN HIRAM	1LT	O-1727087	0345	2
VAZQUEZ-GARCIA V	MAJ	O-2014803	0566	1
VAZZANA WILLIAM F	LTC	O-1295967	0661	1
VEACH ROBERT T	CPT	O-2000646	0657	1
VEADER JOHN F	CW3	W-2152330	0764	1
VEAHMAN PHILLIP H	CW2	W-2211429	0567	1
VEAL CURTIS	MAJ	O-0293588	0846	2
VEAL HORACE	CPT	O-1299821	0954	1
VEAL WILLIE O	COL	O-0246815	0658	1
VEATCH CHARLES K	LTC	O-0297075	0561	1
VEATCH ROBERT W	CPT	O-0296963	1046	2
VEAZEY HAROLD A	COL	O-0236615	0260	1
VEAZEY MYRTLE E	1LT	L-0408607	0149	1
VECCHIO ALEXANDER	MAJ	O-2036284	0258	1
VECCHIOLA CHARLES	1LT	O-1995017	0845	2
VECCHIOLLA FRANK L	LTC	O-0347524	0564	3
VECQUERAY EDWARD F	MAJ	O-4009657	0367	1
VEDELER RICHARDS G	LTC	O-0120969	0360	3
VEDELL HOWARD L	LTC	O-1328654	1167	1
VEECH JAMES F	CPT	O-1550082	0250	1
VEEDER ARTHUR K	1LT	O-0444670	1043	2
VEENSTRA ROBERT J	LTC	O-0337632	1162	2
VEESER LEO W	MAJ	O-0219010	1154	3
VEGA PEDRO A	LTC	O-0368718	0560	1
VEGA VICTOR J	MAJ	O-1101252	1046	2
VEGH MARGARET A	1LT	N-0729005	0546	1
VEGIARD ELSWORTH N	CPT	O-0311786	0743	2
VEGO JOSEPH V	MAJ	O-1322106	0765	1
VEHRS HERMAN F	MAJ	O-0471565	0947	2
VEITCH ALBERT H	LTC	O-0222735	0964	3
VELASQUEZ PERFECTO J	1LT	O-2027805	0854	1
VELAZQUEZ JUSTO P	CW2	W-2005791	0858	2
VELEZ JOBINO	2LT	O-0277618	1050	1
VELISANO GABRIEL	1LT	O-2030126	0149	1
VELONIS STAMATIS G	COL	O-0357366	0966	3
VELTRI SANTO	MAJ	O-0501346	0453	1
VELTRO FRANK E	MAJ	O-0230065	0761	3
VENABLE CLARENCE H	MAJ	O-1917915	0164	1
VENABLE JR HORACE J	MAJ	O-2262492	0365	1
VENABLE MARVIN C	LTC	O-1533698	0662	1
VENABLE ROY P	MAJ	O-1317846	0462	1
VENARD THOMAS W	CW2	W-3350144	0763	1
VENCELIK ROSEMARY	CPT	N-0785062	1156	2
VENDITTI EDO G	CPT	O-1046977	0755	1
VENDLEY CLARENCE E	COL	O-0216482	1162	3
VENDOLA LOUIS A	MAJ	O-0969269	1162	1
VENEGAS FRED C	MAJ	O-0195767	0546	1
VENEZIA JOSEPH P	LTC	O-0363814	0462	1
VENN CHARLES F	MAJ	O-0158274	1148	3
VENN EUGENE C	1LT	O-1319237	0745	2
VENN ROLLO E	COL	O-0225772	1162	3
VENNE RICHARD J	1LT	O-1108387	0350	1
VENOR DANIEL A	CPT	O-1917604	0363	1
VENSEL HARRY R	COL	O-0137225	0651	3
VENSKUS ISADORE E	CPT	O-1282393	0557	1
VENTERS ANDREW L	LTC	O-1047823	0764	1
VENTIMIGLIA VITO	CW3	W-2145238	0761	1
VENTRESCO THERESA A	1LT	N-0805433	0153	2
VENTURA JAMES P	MAJ	O-1594542	0960	1
VENTURO RALPH C	MAJ	O-0462068	0646	1
VER BEEK JOHN	CW3	W-2149833	0766	1
VER MEULEN PET	MAJ	O-0127653	0649	3
VERA JR JOSE	CPT	O-1684927	1060	1
VERACRUZ JUAN N	2LT	O-1896948	1148	1
VERAGE FAYE C	MAJ	N-0731579	0966	1
VERBOSH GEORGE	MAJ	O-1924559	0866	1
VERBOSH MICHAEL	LTC	O-0451257	1157	1
VERBURG KEITH B	MAJ	O-2038049	0361	1
VERBURG MITCHELL R	LTC	O-1284965	1264	1
VERCOE SAM G	LTC	O-0257602	0162	1
VERDERBER FRANK J	LTC	O-1011426	0861	1
VEREEN HELEN L	MAJ	N-0727584	0565	1
VERGA FRANK A	COL	O-0376552	0965	3
VERGA SALVATORE	LTC	O-1040162	1060	1
VERGAGNI ROLAND E	MAJ	O-0993810	1163	1
VERGEER SHIRLEY	MAJ	N-0789739	0164	1
VERGHIS GEORGE W	LTC	O-1287970	0167	1
VERHAECHE GEORGE M	1LT	O-1322456	1045	2
VERHAGE MARTIN O	CPT	O-1686882	0945	2
VERHEYEN KATHRYN J	1LT	N-0772537	0248	1
VERHULST GEORGE J	CPT	O-0972470	1062	1

NAME	GRADE	SVC NO	DATE RET MO YR	RET CODE
VERIS HOWARD E	CW3	W-2148821	0767	1
VERITY FRED V L	CPT	0-0184674	0150	3
VERMES EDWARD D	LTC	0-1111407	0865	1
VERMETTE ALBERT L	CW4	W-2142209	0659	1
VERMETTE LAFAYETTE	2LT	0-1900120	0256	1
VERMETTE MARCEL P	LTC	0-0408652	0361	1
VERMEUL JACK E	MAJ	0-1047378	C867	1
VERMILLION PAUL E	MAJ	0-0303249	0146	2
VERMILYEA HARVEY C	MAJ	C-018121C	0453	3
VERMONT ROLAND	2LT	0-0301065	C557	3
VERMUELLEN EMMA F	1LT	N-0789078	0846	1
VERNA FRANK P	LTC	0-1795014	0266	1
VERNARELLI ARNOLD F	LTC	0-1288331	0561	1
VERNER PAUL E	CW3	W-2142667	1160	1
VERNER THOMAS	CPT	0-2037753	1156	1
VERNEY ADOLPH A	LTC	0-1111957	0463	1
VERNEY BERNARD	LTC	0-0913165	0967	3
VERNIEL JACOB	CPT	C-1050456	0358	1
VERNON CLINTON M	LTC	0-0215931	0163	3
VERNON DODD	MAJ	C-1311236	0447	2
VERNON EDWARD C	MAJ	0-1634428	C857	1
VERNON GORDON L	MAJ	0-0991506	0667	1
VERNON HENRY L	2LT	0-1894577	0344	2
VERNON JR ALBERT E	LTC	0-1035390	0867	2
VERNON RALPH R	LTC	0-0263893	0656	2
VERNON RALPH W	LTC	C-1306025	C166	1
VERNON RICHARD P	MAJ	0-1051424	096C	1
VERNON THOMAS D	2LT	C-1914005	C837	1
VERNOSKY HYMAN LTCD	LTC	0-0451546	0258	1
VERRALL JR RALPH W	CW3	W-2152170	1060	1
VERRAN ALMA R	2LT	N-0700289	0338	1
VERREY JOHN P	MAJ	0-0971795	1060	1
VERRILL HERBERT S	1LT	0-0552113	0946	1
VERSCHOOR BASTIAN C	MAJ	C-0512346	0346	2
VERSCHOYLE HUBERT H	2LT	0-0533510	0745	2
VERSEN HARLIS L	1LT	0-1296947	1045	2
VERSTEEG MARSAILLES	LTC	0-0283563	1263	3
VERTNER WALTER E	CW2	W-2112565	C446	2
VERTREES ALVIN M	MAJ	C-0961905	0164	1
VERVAET ARTHUR W	1LT	0-1326785	0746	2
VERZI MARTIN A	LTC	0-1544147	0862	2
VESCE LEILA P	2LT	N-0752341	0345	1
VESCIO PHILLIP L	CW3	W-2147118	0865	1
VESELOVEC STEPHEN	MAJ	C-2046691	0356	1
VESS JAMES A	2LT	0-2019532	0858	1
VESSELL CLETUS R	CW4	W-2119943	0355	1
VESSER WILLIAM	CW2	W-2141691	1060	1
VEST MAURICE O	COL	0-17C1060	0267	3
VEST WILLIAM M	CPT	0-1700464	0545	2
VESTAL HERMAN H	LTC	0-0250881	0364	3
VESTER HERMAN K	LTC	0-2036087	0565	1
VESTERBY VORIS P	CPT	0-1312733	1046	2
VESTNER ELIOT N	LTC	0-0219677	0256	1
VETRANO VICTOR J	2LT	0-1038881	1144	2
VETTER ANDREW G	LTC	0-0299137	0146	2
VETTER ERICH F	CPT	C-1306212	1152	1
VETTER FRANCIS J	CW3	W-2148827	0958	1
VETTERLING HERMAN M	CPT	0-0504420	1048	1
VEXLER CLARENCE J	COL	0-0137137	C354	3
VEZINA CLARA A	MAJ	N-0742451	0562	1
VEZINA LEO O	CW3	W-2142668	0659	1
VEZIS WILFORD J	MAJ	C-0976920	0365	1
VEZZA VINCENT	LTC	0-1944613	0462	1
VEZZETTI HAROLD B	MAJ	0-1634430	0557	1
VEZZOLI DANTE	LTC	0-1548582	0961	1
VIA GEORGE T	WO1	W-2148060	1153	2
VIAJAR CESAR	2LT	0-C395499	0959	1
VIAL LESTER J	2LT	0-1798682	1144	2
VIALL OTIS O	LTC	0-0447303	1162	1
VIANI BRUNO R	CPT	0-1307482	1145	2
VIARENGO LIVIO	CW3	W-2145528	0366	1
VICENTE ELISIO F	LTC	0-0373140	0164	3
VICK ARTHUR P	CPT	0-1181176	0460	1
VICK DONALD N	MAJ	0-1885224	1266	1
VICK GILBERT M	MAJ	C-0260885	0365	3

NAME	GRADE	SVC NO	DATE RET MO YR	RET CODE
VICK JR J E	COL	0-1101253	0261	1
VICK JR WILLIAM J	MAJ	0-0983474	0664	1
VICK KENNETH S	CW3	W-2102496	0852	2
VICK MAYNARD U	CPT	0-0347725	0161	1
VICK PHARES G	MAJ	0-1113034	0467	1
VICK WARREN A	LTC	0-0465227	0863	1
VICKER WILLIAM L	WO1	W-2116726	0445	2
VICKERMAN CHARLES E	LTC	0-0251042	0966	3
VICKERS ELVIN C	CW4	W-2144777	1160	1
VICKERS LAWRENCE H	1LT	0-0436248	1045	2
VICKERS MARION W	LTC	0-1292965	1161	1
VICKERS RAUL A	LTC	0-1102519	0760	1
VICKERS RICHARD H	CPT	0-0378781	0244	2
VICKERS WILBUR N	CPT	0-2029123	0158	1
VICKERS WILLIAM O	LTC	0-1593896	0263	1
VICKERY CHARLES R	MAJ	0-1948537	0764	1
VICKERY CHESTER B	COL	0-1032254	1167	1
VICKERY GRADY M	CPT	0-1999810	0960	1
VICKERY HIRAM K	CW4	W-2146621	0464	1
VICKERY JOE B	1LT	0-0414430	0346	2
VICKERY JOE E	CPT	0-1583796	1154	2
VICKERY PHILIP M	1LT	0-0453779	1143	2
VICKNAIR ROBERT E	CW2	W-2210034	0965	1
VICKREY WILLIAM W	COL	0-0100299	0949	3
VICKSELL ROBERT	CW2	W-2000623	0854	3
VICTOR BERT A	CPT	0-0486879	0747	2
VICTOR CHARLES L	MAJ	0-1284437	0360	1
VICTOR THOMAS M	CPT	0-1324068	1145	2
VICTORY ARMEL T	MAJ	0-0137135	0251	3
VIDA GEORGE	LTC	0-0542465	1061	2
VIDA JOSEPH J	CW3	W-2144873	0955	1
VIDAL LAWRENCE E	LTC	0-0166163	0755	3
VIDALLON WILLIAM A	1LT	0-1896569	0557	1
VIDAURRI ROBERTO E	MAJ	0-2050155	C866	1
VIDLOCK WILFORD E	LTC	0-0498537	0363	1
VIDRA JOHN J	MAJ	0-0499458	1149	1
VIEAU VINCENT K	CPT	0-1295300	0546	2
VIELE HOWARD J	CPT	0-0395487	1143	2
VIERGUTZ GEORGE J	1LT	0-2029187	1151	1
VIERLING RAYMOND A	CW3	W-2206125	0567	1
VIERS RAYMOND L	MAJ	0-4030860	0867	1
VIERS WESLEY L	LTC	0-0397745	0860	1
VIERTEL GEORGE F	MAJ	0-1633029	0456	1
VIESTENZ RALPH J	MAJ	0-0972665	0465	1
VIETS LLOYD C	CPT	0-1548584	0867	1
VIEWEG HERMANN F	COL	0-0100439	1060	3
VIEWEGER ARTHUR L	LTC	0-0237950	0664	3
VIGEANT BERTRUM A	LTC	0-1312366	0265	1
VIGEL CARL V	MAJ	0-1641033	0357	1
VIGIL FRED	LTC	0-1798629	0461	1
VIGLIERO JOHN A	MAJ	0-0183319	0648	3
VIGNEAU ROBERT A	2LT	0-1105447	0145	2
VIGNERON EUGENE M	LTC	0-0168042	0754	3
VIGNOVICH DEMETRE	LTC	0-1011247	0662	1
VIGOR WILLIAM N	MAJ	0-0281585	0146	2
VIGORITO JOSEPH P	1LT	0-0449490	0845	2
VIGUS VICTOR E	LTC	0-1323049	0267	3
VIK CHESTER E	1LT	0-1317959	0546	2
VILAR CARLOS M	CPT	0-0395492	0844	2
VILDA WILLIAM S	1LT	0-1011561	0745	2
VILE LEARNARD A	CW2	W-2115831	0456	1
VILLA FRANK R	LTC	0-1945970	0960	1
VILLA HAZELETT V	1LT	0-2262912	1154	1
VILLA ROMULO S	1LT	0-189657C	0762	1
VILLADEMOROS JOSEP	CPT	0-0452041	0345	2
VILLADER EDMUND	1LT	0-1897005	0565	1
VILLADER RAYMOND	1LT	0-1896411	1058	1
VILLAESCUSA FRANK A	LTC	0-0516280	0956	1
VILLAFANE JUAN A	LTC	0-0934492	0667	1
VILLAFLOR GREGORY P	LTC	0-0357357	0958	2
VILLANDRE JAMES F	CPT	0-1540593	0258	1
VILLANO RALPH	MAJ	0-1644180	0664	1
VILLANTI MARIO T	COL	0-0427369	0767	1
VILLAPANDO PRIMITI	1LT	0-1896898	0353	1
VILLARCMAN ISABELO R	1LT	0-0515107	0845	2

NAME	GRADE	SVC NO	DATE RET MO YR	RET CODE
VILLEGAS PAUL	2LT	0-2055188	1044	2
VILLEMEZ CLARENCE L	LTC	0-1104429	0860	1
VILLEMEZ CLYDE J	LTC	0-1101255	0960	1
VILLENEUVE ALFRED J	LTC	0-0309278	1067	3
VILLEPIGUE WILLIAM J	CPT	0-0179531	0849	1
VILLEY STEVE	2LT	0-189653C	0149	1
VILLINES AUBREY T	LTC	0-1596843	0766	1
VILLOTT LOUIS P	MAJ	C-1299497	0761	1
VILMUR WALTER M	CW2	W-2108577	1148	1
VILNES MAGNUS	CW4	W-2134449	1154	1
VINAL VICTOR E	CW4	W-2110986	1054	1
VINCE JULIUS	CW3	W-2142539	0659	1
VINCENT ARTHUR T	1LT	0-1691490	1045	2
VINCENT CLYDE O	MAJ	0-2016493	0464	1
VINCENT DOYLE C	MAJ	C-1010309	0658	1
VINCENT DWIGHT W	LTC	0-1010591	1160	1
VINCENT EDWARD	MAJ	C-1547817	1262	1
VINCENT FLORENCE	2LT	N-0700486	0640	1
VINCENT HENRY	MAJ	0-0155901	0850	3
VINCENT JOHN L	MAJ	C-0278674	0863	3
VINCENT JOSEPH E	MAJ	0-0319855	0954	2
VINCENT LEE P	LTC	0-1017876	0363	1
VINCENT RUSSELL	LTC	0-0241014	0348	2
VINCENT RUSSIE H	MAJ	0-0263515	C160	3
VINCENT STANLEY J	MAJ	0-1334653	0662	1
VINCENT VARD V	MAJ	C-1543629	0955	1
VINCENT VICTOR K	LTC	0-1639775	0861	1
VINCENT WALTER N	1LT	0-0477578	0643	2
VINCENT WILLIAM G	LTC	0-0449561	0863	1
VINCENT WILLIS E	COL	0-0145364	1054	3
VINCENTI WILFREDO	MAJ	0-1044139	C463	1
VINCETT ERNEST M	MAJ	0-1919315	1165	1
VINCIGUERRA ARMANDO	LTC	0-0505618	0358	3
VINCIGUERRA L	CPT	0-1302393	0157	1
VINCIUS SAMUEL A	CPT	0-0164958	0-49	3
VINCOLI VINCENT	CW2	W-2144517	0656	1
VINDING RANDOLPH H	COL	0-0474952	0361	1
VINER RICHARD A	MAJ	0-0509679	0445	2
VINES HERBERT M	MAJ	C-0394173	0647	1
VINES THELBERT D	CW2	W-2142782	0655	1
VINEYARD DOLMAN W	LTC	0-1175345	0366	1
VINEYARD JR HENRY C	MAJ	C-1182026	0358	1
VINIER CHARLES C	LTC	0-0145357	C648	3
VINING CHARLIE B	CPT	0-2046434	0947	1
VINING WILLIAM F	CW3	W-2148822	1065	2
VINK DONALD R	1LT	0-1298156	1145	2
VINSON BILLY E	MAJ	0-1100378	0857	2
VINSON GEORGE M	CW3	W-2205000	0267	2
VINSON KERMIT J	2LT	0-2005484	1050	1
VINSON MERRILL R	LTC	0-0920791	0260	3
VINSON WILBUR J	MAJ	0-1289347	1057	1
VINTON HAROLD W	CW2	W-2205382	0959	1
VIOLA PETER L	MAJ	C-0171599	0547	1
VIOLETTE ADRIAN J	LTC	0-1298623	0467	1
VIOLYN ROMAN R	CPT	0-0499947	1145	2
VIOX FRANCIS J	LTC	C-0372942	0667	1
VIRAG ALFRED	COL	0-0244080	0866	3
VIRANT LEO B	LTC	0-0202182	0965	1
VIRDEN EMERSON H	LTC	0-0141086	0557	3
VIRDIN JOSEPH D	LTC	0-0176469	0262	3
VIRGIL MAX P	LTC	0-0954773	0766	1
VIRGILIO JOSEPH C	LTC	0-0460868	1061	3
VIROK ARTHUR S	MAJ	C-0975010	0266	1
VIRTS NELLIE M	MAJ	N-0724633	0264	1
VIRTUE JAMES R	LTC	0-0275927	0960	3
VISCO RALPH A	COL	0-0258361	0457	1
VISCONTI CHARLES E	LTC	0-0373094	1163	3
VISCONTI SAMUEL	CW2	W-2214859	0866	1
VISCONTI VINCENT P	WO1	W-2103566	0952	1
VISEL GEORGE V	LTC	0-0501510	0657	1
VISPERAS JUAN	1LT	0-2030579	0250	1
VISTI INA M	2LT	N-0728494	0246	2
VITACCO ALFRED G	LTC	0-2034592	1165	1
VITEK JR JOHN R	LTC	0-0450143	0658	1
VITIKAS HELEN L	1LT	N-0786892	0750	1

NAME	GRADE	SVC NO	DATE RET MO YR	RET CODE
VITRIKAS HAROLD L	CW3	W-2110319	0358	1
VITT EDWARD A	LTC	0-0223282	0351	3
VITT GUSTAVE E	LTC	0-0451451	0455	1
VITULLO GEORGE V	1LT	0-1322288	0945	2
VITULLO ORLANDO E	MAJ	0-1014609	0361	1
VITULLO THEODORE L	LTC	0-1042197	0261	1
VIVIANO CLEO L	LTC	0-1312367	1163	2
VIVONA WILLIAM	CPT	0-1289999	0856	1
VLACK JOSEPH B	COL	0-0173569	0561	3
VLAHOS PETER	MAJ	0-0129485	0453	3
VLAMING JOSEPH H	LTC	0-2012086	1065	1
VLASAK FRANK S	LTC	0-2011099	0166	1
VLASICH WILLIAM P	COL	0-0505218	0764	3
VLAZNY ADALBERT L	CPT	0-1684361	0645	2
VLIET RICHARD S	LTC	0-1644185	0763	1
VOBEYDA LUMIR F	CPT	0-0290701	0246	2
VOCKERY WILLIAM	MAJ	0-0450500	1054	2
VODREY JR JAMES R	CPT	0-1115139	1161	2
VOEGELE WILLIAM C	MAJ	0-1102101	0862	1
VOEHL CHARLES A	LTC	0-1041043	1266	3
VOELKER EDWARD C	COL	0-0239208	0157	3
VOELKER JOACHIM F	LTC	0-0255214	1163	3
VOELKLE PAUL H	CPT	0-2025238	0756	1
VOELKLI HUGO H	CW4	W-2114636	0367	3
VOELTER THEODORE F	COL	0-0171503	1053	3
VOGAL JACK L	LTC	0-1312071	0863	1
VOGEL ALVIN T	1LT	0-179600C	0945	2
VOGEL CLARENCE F	COL	0-0133508	1047	2
VOGEL EDWARD F	1LT	0-1184746	0546	2
VOGEL EDWARD J	MAJ	0-0185146	0648	3
VOGEL FRANCIS O	MAJ	0-0298269	0964	3
VOGEL GEORGE F	1LT	0-1100810	1145	2
VOGEL JOHN H	MAJ	0-1634435	C362	2
VOGEL JR ALBERT T	CPT	0-1326143	1146	2
VOGEL JR CARLOS E	MAJ	0-0949668	1265	1
VOGEL NELSON W	MAJ	0-0979107	0665	1
VOGEL PHILIP J	MAJ	0-0400522	0146	2
VOGEL ROBERT H	2LT	0-1171405	1044	2
VOGEL VICTOR H	LTC	0-0309564	0755	1
VOGEL WALTER	CPT	0-0518801	0245	2
VOGELSANG LEWIS O	COL	0-0240140	0262	3
VOGELSTEIN HENRY	2LT	0-1577999	0845	2
VOGL OSCAR J	LTC	0-0351971	0759	1
VOGLE VERNON V	CW3	W-2147982	0162	1
VOGLER GEORGE L	MAJ	0-1170234	0865	1
VOGLER HENRY J	MAJ	0-0395088	0760	1
VOGT ERIC A	LTC	0-1313001	0965	3
VOGT FRED K	COL	0-0352870	0267	1
VOGT GEORGE R	LTC	0-1583800	0563	1
VOGT HAROLD M	1LT	0-0970173	0557	1
VOGT HERBERT G	MAJ	0-1011559	1165	1
VOGT JEROME E	LTC	0-025941C	0566	3
VOGT JOHN E	CW2	W-2111167	0645	2
VOGT JR MAX C	LTC	0-1796553	1062	2
VOGT LLOYD W	LTC	0-0297359	0161	1
VOGT ROBERT G	CPT	0-0411336	0645	2
VOGT WILLIAM	2LT	0-2009263	0146	2
VOGT WILLIAM N	2LT	0-1913993	0240	1
VOHL WILLIAM H	LTC	0-0201493	0251	1
VOIGHT MICHAEL E	LTC	0-0338060	0850	1
VOIGT HERMAN O	LTC	0-0363065	0657	1
VOIGT JR ADOLPH E	LTC	0-2007133	1067	1
VOIGT LORENZO G	LTC	0-0211082	1163	3
VOIT JR OTTO W	LTC	0-1186782	0766	1
VOL JAAIN DANI	LTC	0-0408482	0960	1
VOLCHCK ROBERT J	1LT	0-1039606	0845	2
VOLD CARL H	1LT	0-0369634	0842	1
VOLD STERLING R	MAJ	0-1312652	0363	2
VOLIN MELDEN E	MAJ	0-0304638	0566	3
VOLK FLOYD F	COL	0-0156396	0953	3
VOLK ROBERT	1LT	0-1307892	0658	1
VOLKER FLORENCE E	1LT	N-0771623	0146	1
VOLKL LESTER E	1LT	0-1293337	1044	2
VOLKOBER JOHN A	CPT	0-1304975	1146	1
VOLKRIAGER JOSEPH A	LTC	0-1282069	1263	1

NAME	GRADE	SVC NO	DATE RET MO YR	RET CODE
VOLLBRACHT ROY J	1LT	O-0957504	0853	1
VOLLENTINE JOHN T	LTC	O-0411157	0961	1
VOLLMAN NICK W	MAJ	O-4006647	0267	1
VOLLRATH BERNARD F	COL	O-0242168	0662	3
VOLPE ALBERT J	CW2	W-2143192	0460	1
VOLPE PETER A	MAJ	O-0282079	1146	1
VOLPE WILLIAM H	MAJ	O-1703918	0754	2
VOLSEN ARTHUR J	1LT	O-1288332	0346	2
VOLTZ HENRY E	1LT	O-1290000	0745	2
VOLUNGIS LOUIS V	CPT	O-0977459	0959	2
VOLZ FRED E	CW3	W-2103567	0859	1
VOLZ JOHN G	LTC	O-0320232	0962	3
VOLZ LEONARD F	CPT	O-1950476	0464	1
VON BARGEN GERALD C	LTC	O-1640097	0867	1
VON BERGEN EDWARD F	LTC	O-0336763	0662	1
VON BREMEN DANIEL W	MAJ	O-0910142	0446	2
VON DAACKE FRED J	COL	O-0175836	0660	3
VON DEESTEN ARTHUR P	LTC	O-0219238	0952	3
VON DETTE ALLEN E	LTC	O-2042737	0756	1
VON DOLTEREN CHARLES	MAJ	O-1638729	0761	1
VON ELM HENRY W	CPT	O-1549157	114N	2
VON ESCH JR ROBERT A	1LT	O-2016980	1051	2
VON ESSEN THEODOR	CW2	W-2146940	1055	1
VON HAAM EMMERICH	COL	O-0400460	0963	3
VON HALBAN GEORGE R	COL	O-1031529	0462	1
VON HOFE GODFREY	CPT	O-0206181	0757	3
VON KELLER NIKOLAI A	MAJ	O-0385613	1046	1
VON LEHR FREDERIC	MAJ	O-2049423	1160	1
VON MILLER CORWIN C	LTC	O-155806	0766	1
VON NESSEN HAROLD W	LTC	O-1799806	0762	1
VON NUNES CHARLES S	LTC	O-0492690	0854	1
VON NUNES JESSIE M	2LT	N-0787751	0345	1
VON SABO THEODORE J	COL	O-0270674	0867	3
VON SCHILLING LEOPOLD	LTC	O-0234470	1065	3
VON SEETH EDWARD H	COL	O-0239674	0366	3
VON SETH WILLIAM J	CPT	O-2033527	0457	1
VON TOM GEORGE E	LTC	O-1319686	0265	1
VON VOIGTLANDER KARL	COL	O-0289547	0163	1
VON WEIEN BERYL B	2LT	N-0731447	1144	1
VONDRACEK FELIX J	LTC	O-0175597	1061	3
VONLAND GEORGE O	COL	O-0185776	0157	3
VONTAGEN WILLIAM E	1LT	O-1172703	1044	2
VOORHEES DONALD L	MAJ	O-1551768	0561	1
VOORHEES MALCOLM D	COL	O-0183441	0559	3
VOORHEES NELSON A	LTC	O-0141081	1055	3
VOORHEES WILLIAM D	CPT	O-1725305	0748	2
VOORHIS CHARLES C	LTC	O-0415569	0646	2
VOORHIS THOMAS K	MAJ	O-1049005	0261	1
VOORTMEYER WILLIAM B	LTC	O-0888540	0563	1
VORHIES JAMES H	COL	O-1000685	1167	1
VORICK ALBERT P	MAJ	O-2200116	0764	1
VORISEK ELMER A	COL	O-0304941	1060	3
VORLANDER CARL C	LTC	O-0319304	0563	1
VORPAHL ADOLPH F	LTC	O-0258364	0846	1
VORTRIEDE HARRY M	MAJ	O-1178023	0261	1
VOS OSBORNE R	1LT	O-0888237	1045	2
VOSBURGH STEPHEN E	LTC	O-2049135	0767	1
VOSE CHARLES S	CPT	O-1290507	0345	2
VOSE HAROLD L	MAJ	O-2023454	0362	2
VOSMEIER LEONARD H	MAJ	O-0122696	0444	2
VOSS CLINTON E	MAJ	O-2033091	0865	1
VOSS EDDIE P	CPT	O-0370142	0944	2
VOSS ERNEST E	COL	O-0165135	0755	2
VOSS HAROLD J	CW3	W-2143019	0361	1
VOSS JOHN R	CPT	O-1302086	0447	1
VOSS JOHN C	LTC	O-0383530	0561	1
VOSS LOUIS A	MAJ	O-0179335	0652	3
VOSS LYLE G	CW3	W-2147558	0762	1
VOSS ROBERT F	1LT	O-1057923	0946	2
VOSS VERNON V	MAJ	O-0980143	0761	1
VOSS WARREN H	MAJ	O-1103987	0561	1
VOSSBRINCK KARL R	2LT	O-1048631	1044	2
VOTAW FLOYD C	LTC	O-0508443	0862	1
VOTAW GEORGE J	MAJ	O-0339609	0246	2
VOTE CLARENCE E	CPT	O-1295632	1147	2

NAME	GRADE	SVC NO	DATE RET MO YR	RET CODE
VOTRUBA FRANCIS J	MAJ	O-0330481	0347	2
VOTYPKA JOSEPH A	MAJ	O-0388534	0346	2
VOUTE REINIER F	CPT	O-5403088	0663	2
VOWELL EDITH	MAJ	N-0726307	1263	1
VOWELL FLETCHER W	CPT	O-0281159	0645	2
VOWELL ROBERT E	MAJ	O-1552200	0959	1
VOYCE VERONICA B	MAJ	N-0796242	0267	1
VOYER ALFRED J	LTC	O-1167261	1163	1
VRABEL VICTOR T	MAJ	O-0354794	0163	1
VRABLIK JR SAMUEL	LTC	O-1001925	1061	1
VRACARICH LAZARETH	MAJ	O-1109726	1161	1
VRADENBURG BRADY J	LTC	O-1945732	0662	1
VREDENBURGH FLETCHER	LTC	O-0414980	0761	1
VREELAND ALBERT L	COL	O-0298640	0861	3
VREELAND ANDREW B	CW4	W-2122828	1163	1
VRNAK FRANK L	CPT	O-1295633	0646	2
VROMAN ALBERT H	2LT	O-1181177	0644	2
VROMAN VERDON	LTC	O-0266176	0256	3
VROOM LAWRENCE M	LTC	O-1045294	0265	1
VROOMAN ROSEMARY A	2LT	N-0779066	0146	1
VUCINOVICH THOMAS H	1LT	O-1547837	0145	2
VUKASIN MILOS N	LTC	O-1340139	0767	1
VYN KENNETH L	MAJ	O-1307628	0262	1
WAARA LEROY J	CW3	W-2152869	0866	1
WACH EDWIN F	CW3	W-2113122	0959	1
WACHHOLZ PAUL F	LTC	O-0451259	0561	1
WACHS ADAM R	MAJ	O-0122754	0648	3
WACHSMITH JOHN W	1LT	O-0985651	1153	2
WACHSMUTH JOHN E	LTC	O-0517680	0463	1
WACHTELL CHARLES W	CPT	O-0581312	0863	1
WACHTER FREDERICK	1LT	O-1319102	1045	2
WACHTLER PETER J	CPT	O-1170236	1046	2
WACHTMAN JACOB C	LTC	O-0297911	0962	3
WACKER CHARLES P	CW2	W-2116376	0847	2
WACKER GEORGE P	CPT	O-0504421	0945	2
WACKOWICZ HELEN	MAJ	N-0901269	0866	2
WACKYM MITCHELL A	MAJ	O-0260415	0265	3
WADDEL KENNETH L	LTC	O-0257763	0567	3
WADDELL ALEX W	1LT	O-1317060	0145	2
WADDELL DONALD H	CW2	W-2214945	0567	1
WADDELL HAROLD G	MAJ	O-1691915	0762	1
WADDELL HENRY G	COL	O-0102456	0545	2
WADDELL HUBERT E	CPT	O-2289239	1263	1
WADDELL JOHN C	1LT	O-1822343	1045	2
WADDELL ROBERT G	MAJ	O-1318725	0962	1
WADDELL THOMAS J	1LT	O-1116818	0446	2
WADDEN VINCENT R	COL	O-0178039	1050	3
WADDING ELEANOR M	1LT	N-0794445	0747	1
WADDINGHAM FRANCIS	MAJ	O-0358854	0962	3
WADDLE SAMUEL H	COL	O-0226273	0963	3
WADDY EDWARD P	MAJ	O-0387721	0461	1
WADDY WILLIAM H	CPT	O-1003063	0766	3
WADE BATTAILLE	LTC	O-0221288	0363	3
WADE CECIL C	LTC	O-0205244	0763	3
WADE DELMER T	CW3	W-2152570	0666	1
WADE DONALD W	LTC	O-0517978	0867	3
WADE ELLIS M	MAJ	O-0329920	0846	2
WADE FRANCIS M	1LT	O-1317212	0547	2
WADE FREDERICK	CW2	W-2122112	0948	1
WADE HOBERT B	CPT	O-1290852	1050	1
WADE JAMES L	1LT	O-1105243	1059	1
WADE JOSEPH W	COL	O-0251984	0467	3
WADE JR JOHN C	1LT	O-1115141	0746	1
WADE JR WALTER H	1LT	O-0447908	1044	2
WADE LEROY E	LTC	O-0296587	0759	1
WADE MARGARET	CPT	L-0115876	1053	2
WADE MARGARET C	1LT	M-0000575	0145	1
WADE NOBLE E	MAJ	O-0163349	1054	3
WADE PIERCE H	1LT	O-2031912	0945	2
WADE RALPH E	MAJ	O-0173147	0352	3
WADE RALPH M	COL	O-0173499	1059	3
WADE RALPH M	CPT	O-0540979	0750	2
WADE RICHARD H	CPT	O-1554991	0749	1
WADE ROBERT	MAJ	O-0109857	0238	1
WADE ROBERT L	CW2	W-2205665	0862	1

NAME	GRADE	SVC NO	DATE RET MO YR	RET CODE
WADE ROBERT M	CPT	O-2262524	1062	1
WADE SR ARTHUR W	MAJ	O-1288978	0862	1
WADE SYDNEY L	CPT	O-0308373	1145	2
WADE WALTER O	LTC	O-1010834	0757	1
WADE WALTER R	MAJ	O-0416102	0651	1
WADE WARREN C	MAJ	O-0127589	0648	3
WADE WILLIAM I	MAJ	O-0287293	0245	2
WADE WILLIAM I	MAJ	O-2036285	0259	1
WADELL PAUL M	CPT	O-0274278	0645	2
WADELL VERNA M	MAJ	N-0787440	0665	3
WADELTON EDWIN F	LTC	O-0336831	0267	3
WADHAM LESTER B	LTC	O-0346652	0662	3
WADIAK JOSEPH	MAJ	O-1704140	0563	1
WADLEY BURR P	MAJ	O-0486703	0448	1
WADLINGTON JR W J	COL	O-0343255	1058	3
WADLOW REGINALD C	2LT	O-1698084	0145	2
WADSWORTH AGNES C	2LT	N-0726426	0744	1
WADSWORTH CORWIN G	LTC	O-0401999	0361	1
WADSWORTH DURANT	CW4	W-2005494	1264	1
WADSWORTH GEORGE E	CW2	W-2104554	1059	1
WADSWORTH JULIUS	LTC	O-0217986	0662	3
WADSWORTH LOUIS C	B G	O-0260016	0666	3
WAELDE DEWITT C	LTC	O-1633620	0461	1
WAFFLE ROBERT L	COL	O-0331110	0767	3
WAFUL GLENN H	1LT	O-1108394	0545	2
WAGAMAN RAY D	MAJ	O-0998800	0765	1
WAGEMAN JAY J	LTC	O-0347922	0255	1
WAGENBRETH PETER P	LTC	O-1586314	0163	1
WAGENER ALBERT H	MAJ	O-1050978	0461	1
WAGENHALS RUPERT S	CPT	O-0368158	0946	1
WAGER LEONARD F	CPT	O-1294941	0561	1
WAGERS ISAAC S	MAJ	O-0504607	0157	1
WAGES COLEMAN	MAJ	O-154576	0157	1
WAGES J P	CW3	RW-2151129	1066	1
WAGGAMAN ROY D	MAJ	O-0488921	0153	1
WAGGONER CECIL C	MAJ	O-2017479	0361	1
WAGGONER CLARA L	CW4	V-0708181	0465	1
WAGGONER HARRY N	COL	O-0372603	0566	3
WAGGONER JR EDWIN P	COL	O-0231928	0566	3
WAGGONER PARKE H	COL	O-0201111	0157	3
WAGNER ARTHUR H	LTC	O-0284463	0864	3
WAGNER CHARLES B	CPT	O-1342315	0957	1
WAGNER CHARLES H	LTC	O-0448437	1164	3
WAGNER CHARLES M	CW3	W-2145190	1262	1
WAGNER CHARLES S	LTC	O-1109727	1167	1
WAGNER CHESTER S	COL	O-0236321	0163	3
WAGNER CHESTER T	LTC	O-0285803	0657	2
WAGNER DAVID H	1LT	O-0311909	0160	1
WAGNER DONALD J	MAJ	O-4005531	0665	1
WAGNER DONALD L	MAJ	O-1174464	1060	1
WAGNER DONN H	LTC	O-1107202	0463	1
WAGNER EDWARD W	1LT	O-1298625	0446	2
WAGNER EDWARD W	1LT	O-1794887	0244	2
WAGNER FLOYD E	1LT	O-1111410	0753	1
WAGNER FLOYD H	LTC	O-1553747	0863	1
WAGNER FRANCIS E	MAJ	O-0237932	0744	2
WAGNER FRANK W	CW4	W-2131517	0257	1
WAGNER GEORGE E	MAJ	O-179908	1263	2
WAGNER GEORGE E	CW2	W-2208167	0567	1
WAGNER GERALD A	LTC	O-1634438	0566	1
WAGNER HAROLD C	MAJ	O-1081257	0359	1
WAGNER HAROLD M	MAJ	O-0383685	1145	2
WAGNER HAROLD S	LTC	O-0248792	0565	3
WAGNER HENRY T	LTC	O-1044986	0765	1
WAGNER HENRY W	LTC	O-0261847	0662	1
WAGNER HERMAN H	COL	O-0226947	0365	3
WAGNER HOWARD	MAJ	O-1001268	0559	1
WAGNER HOWARD	CW2	W-2115589	0547	2
WAGNER JACK W	CW2	W-2148998	0261	1
WAGNER JOHN C	CW4	W-2145244	0267	1
WAGNER JOHN G	2LT	O-1014446	0644	2
WAGNER JOHN J	LTC	O-2000195	0965	1
WAGNER JR ERNEST W	MAJ	O-1552201	0459	1
WAGNER JR HUNTER T	1LT	O-1056591	0146	2
WAGNER JR IRA G	COL	O-0283786	0866	3

NAME	GRADE	SVC NO	DATE RET MO YR	RET CODE
WAGNER JR STANLEY A	1LT	O-1310020	0146	2
WAGNER JULIUS	LTC	O-0335742	1160	3
WAGNER JULIUS W	COL	O-0231047	0962	3
WAGNER LADDIE S	COL	O-0272587	0366	3
WAGNER LARKIN L	MAJ	O-0488227	0157	1
WAGNER LEONARD A	LTC	O-0338636	1062	1
WAGNER MARGUARITE	1LT	N-0736816	0846	1
WAGNER OSCAR S	MAJ	O-1684008	1058	1
WAGNER RALPH P	MAJ	O-0191104	0853	3
WAGNER RAY H	LTC	O-1307894	0863	1
WAGNER RAYMOND N	MAJ	O-0965644	0566	1
WAGNER RICHARD P	LTC	O-0248100	0865	3
WAGNER ROBERT A	LTC	O-1309992	0766	1
WAGNER ROBERT A	MAJ	O-1311452	1158	1
WAGNER ROBERT H	LTC	O-1001269	0167	1
WAGNER ROBERT S	LTC	O-0750899	0167	1
WAGNER ROBERT W	CPT	O-1116024	1166	2
WAGNER ROY A	2LT	O-1299498	0745	2
WAGNER ROY J	COL	O-0139622	0456	3
WAGNER RUDOLPH R	LTC	O-0108177	0133	1
WAGNER STUART M	CPT	O-1797566	0462	1
WAGNER THEODORE S	CPT	O-1056592	0247	2
WAGNER VERNON L	MAJ	O-0557396	0761	1
WAGNER WILLIAM J	MAJ	O-1575247	1263	1
WAGNITZ MILTON F	LTC	O-0200269	0854	3
WAGONER ALBERT E	CW2	W-2141483	0457	1
WAGONER EDGAR W	MAJ	O-1879107	0266	1
WAGONER GEORGE E	MAJ	O-1824541	0462	1
WAGSTAFF GLADYS I	MAJ	N-0736796	0365	3
WAGUESPACK FENWICK E	MAJ	O-1285172	0554	1
WAHL CARL G	COL	O-0267785	0758	2
WAHL CORNELIUS	CW4	W-2110488	0264	1
WAHL EDWARD R	COL	O-0310430	0258	1
WAHL SR JAMES F	COL	O-0173054	0861	3
WAHLBERG ELMER R	LTC	O-1535104	0862	1
WAHLBOM ERNEST T	LTC	O-0223491	0547	2
WAHLBOM PHILIP C	COL	O-0246763	0646	2
WAHLE CLARENCE W	LTC	O-0160812	0258	3
WAHLE JR GEORGE F	1LT	O-1011925	0845	2
WAHLE LEROY L	LTC	O-0178377	0662	3
WAHLGREN NELSON C	LTC	O-0314861	0660	1
WAHLQUIST JOHN A	CPT	O-0408631	0146	2
WAID FRANCES T	MAJ	R-0001346	0265	1
WAID SAMUEL T	LTC	O-0521878	0165	1
WAIDLICH WILLIAM G	LTC	O-1040838	1055	1
WAIKSNIS JOHN P	CPT	O-1645463	1166	2
WAIN JACK C	WO1	W-2120058	0344	2
WAINER ALEX M	MAJ	O-0910452	1046	2
WAINHOUSE EDWARD R	LTC	O-1044717	1262	1
WAINRIGHT CHARLES R	COL	O-0355591	1060	1
WAINWRIGHT CLINTON	MAJ	O-1174185	1159	1
WAINWRIGHT MAX V	LTC	O-1686535	1065	1
WAINWRIGHT WILLIAM H	CPT	O-1292426	0863	2
WAIT RUE S	CPT	O-0482709	0146	2
WAITE ALPHONSE A	LTC	O-0296694	1266	3
WAITE BURREL V	LTC	O-0503599	0658	1
WAITE CLEMENT F	COL	O-0139656	0649	3
WAITE DAN J	CPT	O-0343796	0544	2
WAITE EMMETT P	LTC	O-0252069	0866	3
WAITE FRANK I	1LT	O-0927573	0549	1
WAITE GILBERT A	LTC	O-0319565	0260	1
WAITE HERALD P	CW3	W-2143168	0659	1
WAITE LOREN A	LTC	O-1012163	0457	1
WAITE MORRISON R	CW2	W-2211991	0267	1
WAITSMAN NATHAN	MAJ	O-0335206	1054	1
WAITT CLAUDE R	LTC	O-1011528	0565	1
WAKEFIELD HAROLD F	LTC	O-0156322	0351	3
WAKEFIELD LESTER E	CPT	O-1946882	1057	1
WAKEFIELD PAUL W	MAJ	O-0979153	1160	1
WAKEFIELD ROBERT C	COL	O-0238525	0865	3
WAKEHAM ALBERT R	CPT	O-0301937	0548	2
WAKELY GLEN	LTC	O-0293101	0266	3
WAKEMAN MAURICE M	LTC	O-0165805	0660	3
WAKEN DOROTHY L	CPT	J-2291665	1066	2
WALAS THOMAS S	1LT	O-2005651	0747	2

NAME	GRADE	SVC NO	DATE RET MO YR	RET CODE
WALBERT JOHN S	CPT	0-0173570	1162	3
WALBORN CHARLES F	MAJ	0-0240872	1165	3
WALBCRN ROBERT A	CPT	0-0309177	1145	2
WALCH JAMES W	MAJ	0-1032125	0366	1
WALCH JR ROBERT L	1LT	0-0524629	0346	1
WALCH RUSSELL	1LT	0-0507304	0450	1
WALCHAK GEORGE A	1LT	0-0886893	0147	2
WALCHER EVERETT E	LTC	0-0248229	0364	3
WALCOTT THEODORE E	CW3	W-2008267	0167	3
WALCZAK CHARLES J	MAJ	C-1042199	1163	1
WALD HORACE A	1LT	0-0495376	0144	2
WALDBART RICHARD H	CPT	0-1323369	0549	2
WALDEN BETTY J	CPT	N-2289582	0162	2
WALDEN CHANEY F	CW3	W-2203254	1265	1
WALDEN FARRIS D	CPT	0-0441383	0650	1
WALDEN HENRY E	COL	0-0256674	0751	3
WALDEN LEONARD L	CW3	W-2149093	0764	1
WALDEN LOUIS H	COL	0-0285552	1053	2
WALDEN MARK C	CW2	W-2210068	0264	1
WALDEN PHILIP S	1LT	0-1015350	0846	2
WALDEN RALPH C	MAJ	0-2263709	0867	1
WALDEN REUBEN L	MAJ	0-0401487	0947	2
WALDEN TALMAGE	CPT	0-1319364	0654	2
WALDER HARRY L	LTC	0-1184600	0662	1
WALDER J O	CPT	0-2262947	0461	1
WALDER JOHN A	MAJ	C-0530298	0853	1
WALDIKE STEPHEN M	LTC	0-0484583	1155	1
WALDING MALCOLM M	COL	0-0232550	0861	3
WALDMAN CHARLES V	MAJ	0-1303802	0760	1
WALDMAN MURRY R	WO1	W-2127048	0947	2
WALDMAN ROBERT G	CW3	W-2146729	0566	1
WALDO GREGG L	LTC	0-1107204	0664	1
WALDO JESS W	CW3	W-2150666	0463	1
WALDO LYNN L	MAJ	0-0309103	1166	3
WALDOCK JAMES L	MAJ	0-0347358	1044	2
WALDORF FRANCIS E	LTC	0-1648538	0866	1
WALDREP DEUWARD S	LTC	C-0296191	0566	3
WALDRIP MONTGOMERY	CW3	W-2152412	0659	1
WALDRON DALE W	1LT	0-0885768	0347	1
WALDRON ELDRIGE L	CW2	W-2152258	0861	1
WALDRON HAZEL M	LTC	0-0520585	0465	3
WALDRON JACK F	CPT	0-1703919	0855	1
WALDRON JOSEPH H	CPT	0-1639780	1055	2
WALDRON NELLO B	LTC	0-0368703	0967	3
WALDROP HENRY O	CW4	W-2146164	0266	1
WALDROP JOHN J	CW2	W-2119317	0150	1
WALDROP LOUIS G	CW4	W-2141693	0860	1
WALDROP MELVIN T	CW2	W-2208521	1061	1
WALDROP WILFRED E	MAJ	0-0237885	0561	1
WALEA ALFRED S	MAJ	0-0490899	1047	1
WALEN JOHN	MAJ	C-1554298	0855	1
WALENGA RICHARD A	1LT	0-0531216	0646	2
WALES HOMER L	CPT	0-0243224	0556	3
WALES ROBERT F	LTC	0-0249736	0662	1
WALGREN SYLVAN P	MAJ	0-1181179	0761	1
WALINSKI ERWIN F	LTC	0-1551141	0964	1
WALK GENEVIEVE	LTC	N-0741869	0862	1
WALKE JOHN T	LTC	0-0387981	0346	2
WALKENEYER WILLIAM	LTC	0-0109271	1047	1
WALKER AB D	LTC	0-0305764	0148	2
WALKER ALBERT E	CPT	0-1103990	0346	2
WALKER ALFRED P	COL	0-0162611	1160	3
WALKER ALLEN	CPT	0-1182735	0146	1
WALKER ALLEN J	CW3	W-2152102	0861	1
WALKER ANSIL L	MAJ	0-1303971	0259	1
WALKER ARGYLL E	MAJ	0-1580465	0657	1
WALKER ARTHUR H	LTC	0-0240756	1264	3
WALKER AUSTIN E	COL	0-1010661	1047	1
WALKER BAILEY T	CW4	W-2121153	0858	1
WALKER BARTON F	LTC	0-0122147	C655	3
WALKER BRUCE	LTC	0-1109082	0667	1
WALKER CALVIT L	MAJ	0-1642689	0363	1
WALKER CARL F	1LT	0-0558063	0246	2
WALKER CECIL P	MAJ	0-1937876	0566	1
WALKER CHARLES D	MAJ	0-1035140	0662	1
WALKER CHARLES F	CW2	W-2213853	0266	1
WALKER CHARLES M	MAJ	0-1012401	0158	2
WALKER CHARLES R	MAJ	C-1303417	0661	1
WALKER CHARLES W	LTC	0-0442455	0367	1
WALKER CHARLES W	CW3	W-2148823	0663	1
WALKER CLAUDIUS J	MAJ	0-0306281	1167	3
WALKER DARWYN E	LTC	0-1307895	0666	1
WALKER DAVID M	MAJ	0-1298322	0757	1
WALKER DEAN C	CPT	0-0480218	0347	1
WALKER DEAN H	1LT	0-1015837	0446	2
WALKER DONALD O	LTC	0-1697942	0961	1
WALKER DOYLE T	CW3	W-2144265	0263	1
WALKER EARL	LTC	0-033393C	0155	1
WALKER EARL E	MAJ	0-1309188	1160	1
WALKER EARL J	MAJ	0-1105247	0461	2
WALKER EDGAR T	1LT	0-1047375	0444	2
WALKER EDWARD	CPT	0-1307483	0845	2
WALKER EDWARD L	COL	0-0241473	0254	3
WALKER EDWARD T	MAJ	0-0264378	0463	3
WALKER EDWIN M	LTC	0-0481180	0266	3
WALKER ELLEN H	CPT	N-0733164	0547	1
WALKER ELMER	CW3	W-2150877	1063	1
WALKER ENOS G	COL	0-0263429	0159	3
WALKER ERNEST L	CPT	0-1575616	0546	2
WALKER ERSAL O	MAJ	0-0887630	1160	1
WALKER FORREST A	LTC	0-1825515	0163	1
WALKER FRANK H	CPT	0-1319687	1157	1
WALKER FRANK N	CPT	0-1311550	1060	1
WALKER GARLAND R	1LT	0-0518133	0346	2
WALKER GEORGE	1LT	0-2000621	1049	1
WALKER GERALD B	LTC	0-1058146	0267	1
WALKER GILBERT P	LTC	0-0122144	0155	3
WALKER GLEN	LTC	0-1549155	0764	1
WALKER HAMILTON T	COL	0-014582C	0657	3
WALKER HARRY E	MAJ	C-0294865	0444	2
WALKER HARRY L	MAJ	0-1948675	0357	1
WALKER HARVEY	LTC	0-0267242	0360	3
WALKER HENRY P	LTC	0-0307984	0560	1
WALKER HERBERT C	MAJ	0-1586995	0961	1
WALKER HOMER O	MAJ	0-0228974	0365	3
WALKER HORACE L	CPT	0-1166635	0348	1
WALKER HOWARD T	CPT	0-1338534	0159	1
WALKER IRA H	CW4	W-2112237	0659	1
WALKER IVAN W	MAJ	0-2000080	0565	1
WALKER J P	MAJ	0-2050993	1059	1
WALKER JAMES	MAJ	C-129549C	0855	1
WALKER JAMES A	LTC	0-0259138	0466	3
WALKER JAMES C	LTC	0-1001070	0658	1
WALKER JAMES L	LTC	0-1287442	1060	1
WALKER JAMES M	LTC	0-0171632	0756	3
WALKER JAMES P	CW3	W-2147896	0864	2
WALKER JAMES S	MAJ	0-0352211	0546	2
WALKER JESSE S	MAJ	0-0289651	0956	3
WALKER JOHN A	LTC	0-0921183	0166	3
WALKER JOHN C	1LT	0-105098C	0944	2
WALKER JOHN E	CPT	0-1056935	1055	1
WALKER JOHN E	CPT	0-1596536	0548	2
WALKER JOHN H	LTC	0-0268569	0960	1
WALKER JOHN J	CW3	W-2152441	0464	1
WALKER JOHN L	CW2	W-2146985	0860	1
WALKER JOHN M	1LT	0-1102107	0345	2
WALKER JOHN C	CPT	0-0502658	0859	1
WALKER JOHN S	MAJ	0-0240184	0861	3
WALKER JOHN T	LTC	0-0278849	0753	3
WALKER JOHN W	LTC	0-0462167	1262	2
WALKER JOSEPH A	LTC	0-0450331	0455	1
WALKER JOSEPH J	COL	0-0217502	0751	3
WALKER JR CHARLES W	CW4	W-2118212	0161	1
WALKER JR EMORY C	1LT	0-1882526	1055	2
WALKER JR ERWIN R	LTC	0-0321632	0753	2
WALKER JR FRED A	LTC	0-0531614	0567	1
WALKER JR HOWARD O	CW2	W-2144133	0659	1
WALKER JR JOHN F	MAJ	0-1825291	0663	1
WALKER JR JOHN R	MAJ	0-0407583	0563	1
WALKER JR JOHN R	LTC	0-0915148	0663	1
WALKER JR NEAL G	2LT	0-1594320	1044	2
WALKER KATHLEEN W	1LT	N-0756891	0546	1
WALKER LOUIS C	1LT	0-0224034	0145	2
WALKER MARCELLUS	COL	C-0264537	0867	3
WALKER MARK C	CPT	0-0329645	0344	2
WALKER NEWPORT H	LTC	0-0216870	1161	3
WALKER NORMAN R	COL	0-0438053	0154	1
WALKER OPAL	MAJ	N-0723496	1164	1
WALKER RANSOM D	WO1	W-2125690	0647	2
WALKER RAYMOND	LTC	0-1647002	0663	1
WALKER RAYMOND A	LTC	0-0222132	0964	3
WALKER RAYMOND F	LTC	0-0274835	C860	3
WALKER RAYMOND E	WO1	W-21205C4	0547	2
WALKER RAYMOND G	CW3	W-2102509	1154	1
WALKER RAYMOND W	LTC	0-0510815	1066	3
WALKER RENO R	LTC	0-0230528	0365	3
WALKER RICHARD C	MAJ	0-2026539	0163	1
WALKER RICHARD O	1LT	0-13117C8	0246	2
WALKER RICHARD H	CPT	0-0389441	0254	1
WALKER RICHARD S	LTC	0-1165216	1165	1
WALKER ROBERT B	MAJ	0-0359181	0749	1
WALKER ROBERT H	CPT	0-0346480	0558	3
WALKER ROBERT J	MAJ	0-1012383	0764	1
WALKER ROBERT L	2LT	C-0858025	0750	2
WALKER ROBERT W	LTC	0-1292619	C457	1
WALKER ROBERT W	WO1	W-2148667	0155	1
WALKER ROBERT W	CW2	W-2207094	0363	1
WALKER ROY F	LTC	0-0100110	1054	3
WALKER ROY S	MAJ	0-0906458	0546	1
WALKER RUBYE E	MAJ	N-0763730	1063	1
WALKER RUSSELL	CPT	0-1599116	1058	1
WALKER RUSSELL A	CPT	0-0294612	0345	2
WALKER SAMUEL E	1LT	0-1292263	0845	2
WALKER SIDNEY R	MAJ	0-0268723	1167	3
WALKER SIMS H	LTC	0-1105889	0463	1
WALKER SR JOHN F	LTC	0-0167479	0648	3
WALKER SR PAUL P	MAJ	0-0949010	1160	1
WALKER STANLEY M	LTC	0-0336913	0461	1
WALKER STERLING A	CPT	0-0359094	1043	2
WALKER STEVE F	COL	0-0265202	0367	3
WALKER STEWART J	1LT	0-0388455	0245	2
WALKER THEODORE J	LTC	0-0274770	1064	3
WALKER THOMAS E	1LT	0-1016792	0446	2
WALKER THOMAS H	MAJ	0-0248861	0145	2
WALKER TROY A	CPT	0-0498519	1051	1
WALKER TROY O	LTC	0-0285890	1159	1
WALKER VERNON G	CW3	W-2144874	0457	1
WALKER VICTOR L	LTC	0-1332761	1062	1
WALKER VIRGIL R	LTC	0-0254723	0766	3
WALKER WALDO L	CPT	0-1287627	0647	1
WALKER WILFORD A	COL	0-0127094	C455	3
WALKER WILLIAM B	CW2	W-2150000	0960	1
WALKER WILLIAM H	COL	0-0292802	1158	3
WALKER WILLIAM J	CW2	W-2150894	0460	1
WALKER WILLIAM P	LTC	0-0275402	0863	3
WALKER WILLIAM R	LTC	C-0118185	0257	3
WALKER WILLIAM S	LTC	0-0364548	0461	1
WALKER WILLIAM S	2LT	0-2036972	1144	2
WALKER ZACK T	CW3	W-2150755	0763	1
WALKUP JR SAM H	CPT	0-0557108	0847	2
WALKUP KENNETH	1LT	0-1308567	1045	2
WALKUP RICHARD W	LTC	0-1550289	1060	1
WALKUW STANLEY L	LTC	0-1177226	0761	1
WALL ARCHIE C	LTC	0-0220337	C545	1
WALL ARNOLD R	LTC	0-0299942	0647	2
WALL CARL H	LTC	0-0374366	0859	1
WALL CHARLEY K	MAJ	0-0114756	0252	3
WALL EDWARD A	1LT	0-1321355	C349	1
WALL EDWARD C	MAJ	0-0357792	0346	2
WALL FRANCIS T	MAJ	0-0987987	0265	1
WALL HAROLD C	COL	0-0246907	0966	1
WALL HERMAN V	MAJ	0-0475985	0146	1
WALL JAMES L	CPT	0-0221960	0949	3
WALL JAMES T	CW3	W-2149684	1265	2
WALL JAMES W	MAJ	0-1645465	0963	1
WALL JEFF C	CPT	0-1168508	0858	1
WALL JOHN C	COL	0-0249775	0962	1
WALL JOHN C	MAJ	0-0991825	1063	1
WALL JOHN E	LTC	0-1011607	1061	1
WALL JOHN R	MAJ	0-1295801	0866	1
WALL JR IRA E	CW2	W-221095C	C266	1
WALL JR JAMES R	CPT	0-0324335	1046	2
WALL JR RUSSELL V	CW3	W-2143415	0659	1
WALL LARRY D	MAJ	0-1335866	1062	1
WALL LECLUS L	LTC	0-0414117	1060	1
WALL PERCY L	COL	0-0180746	0258	2
WALL RAYMOND O	MAJ	0-1305683	0161	1
WALL ROBERT B	CPT	0-1313937	0246	2
WALL ROBERT R	MAJ	0-2263297	1166	1
WALL SAMUEL H	CPT	0-0967806	1160	1
WALL SR JACK C	CPT	0-1826116	0862	1
WALL THOMAS W	CW4	W-2005004	1263	3
WALL W L	1LT	0-1292264	1044	2
WALL WILFRED W	WO1	W-2146403	0956	1
WALL WILLIAM E	LTC	0-0922610	0267	3
WALL WILLIAM F	CPT	0-1316610	1046	2
WALL WILLIAM S	LTC	0-0416008	0761	1
WALLA WILLIAM M	LTC	0-0357399	0265	3
WALLACE BRENTON G	B G	0-0185391	0651	3
WALLACE CHARLES A	MAJ	0-1110867	1160	1
WALLACE CHARLES H	MAJ	0-1553574	0561	1
WALLACE CRISBY D	LTC	0-0450937	0256	1
WALLACE DARREL R	CW2	W-2120106	0653	1
WALLACE DONALD L	MAJ	0-1925857	1167	1
WALLACE EARLE	1LT	0-1013883	0546	2
WALLACE EDWIN F	CPT	0-0499745	0645	1
WALLACE EDWIN R	CPT	0-0265858	0-53	3
WALLACE ELBERT C	LTC	0-0450651	0954	1
WALLACE ELENSWORTH	LTC	0-0270062	1161	3
WALLACE ELSIE H	2LT	N-0726446	0345	1
WALLACE FRANCES E	2LT	N-0734575	1042	1
WALLACE FRANK M	LTC	0-0274085	0961	3
WALLACE GEORGE F	MAJ	0-0486213	0954	1
WALLACE GEORGE S	LTC	0-C280031	0253	3
WALLACE GLEN P	MAJ	0-0166080	0455	3
WALLACE GUY O	1LT	0-1292966	0645	2
WALLACE HARRY E E	CW3	W-2208263	0667	1
WALLACE J P TOLBER	LTC	0-1581438	1262	1
WALLACE JAMES G	MAJ	0-1643422	0161	1
WALLACE JAMES J	MAJ	0-2028454	0264	1
WALLACE JOHN S	1LT	0-1312254	1045	2
WALLACE JOSEPH E	LTC	0-1648858	0867	1
WALLACE JR JACK	LTC	0-0392477	0562	2
WALLACE JR JAMES M	LTC	0-0262803	0264	3
WALLACE JR JOHN J	LTC	0-1049379	0565	1
WALLACE KARL E	COL	0-0149824	0856	3
WALLACE LAWRENCE	CPT	0-0371467	0559	1
WALLACE LENORE S	1LT	N-0723987	1145	1
WALLACE LEE A	1LT	0-1996602	1046	2
WALLACE LEONARD A	LTC	0-0450483	0656	1
WALLACE LYNN D	COL	0-1938498	0665	3
WALLACE MARGARET G	1LT	N-0702989	0646	1
WALLACE MARION S	CPT	0-0227547	0463	3
WALLACE MARK V	2LT	0-1310655	0844	2
WALLACE MARY C	1LT	N-0720525	0646	1
WALLACE MORGAN M	M G	0-0275387	0260	3
WALLACE NEWELL G	CPT	0-0346423	0845	2
WALLACE NORMAN A	MAJ	0-1977934	0962	1
WALLACE ORVAL D	MAJ	0-1554494	0662	1
WALLACE PERC A	2LT	0-1017341	0247	1
WALLACE RALPH	LTC	0-1041672	0566	3
WALLACE RICARDO F	LTC	0-0232184	1058	3
WALLACE RICHARD H	CW3	W-2208965	0567	1
WALLACE RICHARD T	MAJ	0-1996658	0663	1
WALLACE ROBERT E	COL	0-0318767	0567	1
WALLACE ROBERT E	COL	0-0358519	1158	1
WALLACE ROBERT E	LTC	0-19457?4	0966	1
WALLACE ROBERT F	LTC	0-0455507	0264	1
WALLACE RUSSELL G	LTC	0-0249883	0666	3
WALLACE SAMUEL O	LTC	0-0232725	0261	3

NAME	GRADE	SVC NO	DATE RET MO YR	RET CODE
WALLACE SAMUEL T	B G	C-0331327	0565	3
WALLACE TEO	MAJ	O-1046679	1157	1
WALLACE THEODORE I	2LT	O-1304466	1146	2
WALLACE THEODORE R	1LT	O-1552819	0446	2
WALLACE VERNON R	CW2	W-2148196	1159	1
WALLACE VINCENT E	CPT	O-0362499	1046	2
WALLACE WALTER W	MAJ	O-1553748	0459	1
WALLACE WASHINGTON	LTC	O-1003064	0755	1
WALLACE WILEY B	CW2	W-2142117	0357	1
WALLACE WILLIAM A	COL	O-0227456	0160	3
WALLACE WILLIAM A	CW4	W-2125212	0461	1
WALLACE WILLIAM C	LTC	O-1309632	0763	1
WALLACE WILLIAM C	CW3	W-2208416	0166	1
WALLACE WILLIAM J	LTC	O-1056265	1062	1
WALLACE WILLIAM O	MAJ	O-0522449	1154	1
WALLACE WOODROW W	LTC	O-0382175	0656	1
WALLACH EUGENE	WO1	W-2122801	0745	2
WALLACH GEORGE L	CPT	O-0482307	0145	2
WALLACH JR DONALD M	MAJ	O-1342407	1162	1
WALLACH MARTIN A	CW2	W-2212259	1164	1
WALLAR BETTY J	1LT	N-0798121	0747	1
WALLAT EDWIN M	WO1	W-2122812	1052	1
WALLEN ELMER G	MAJ	O-0289689	1158	3
WALLENBERG ALICE C	MAJ	N-0723298	0867	1
WALLENBORN LESLIE T	MAJ	O-1309994	1158	1
WALLENSTEIN WALTER	MAJ	O-0529476	0548	1
WALLER ALVIN L	CPT	O-0493457	0347	2
WALLER EDWARD C	MAJ	O-1824943	0760	2
WALLER LOUIS O	CW2	W-2150872	0361	1
WALLER MACK P	CPT	O-1287093	0450	1
WALLER NATHANIEL	MAJ	O-0294072	0944	2
WALLER ROBERT B 3	CPT	O-0345618	0947	2
WALLER ROBERT O	COL	O-0259450	0666	3
WALLESCH HUBERT G	CPT	O-2023696	0856	1
WALLEY ROMAN J	LTC	O-1756149	0867	2
WALLIN FRANK A	CW3	W-2148686	0757	1
WALLIN JAMES W	CW4	W-2105768	0859	1
WALLIN RICHARD A	1LT	O-1552414	0145	2
WALLING PERCY L	1LT	O-0166663	0554	3
WALLING RAYMOND V	LTC	O-1946199	0867	3
WALLINGFORD MAC I	LTC	O-0279505	0767	3
WALLINGFORD MELVIN O	2LT	O-1014820	0845	1
WALLINGFORD WILBERT	LTC	O-1110319	1265	1
WALLIS CECIL W	CW3	W-2110992	0157	1
WALLIS GALE A	CPT	O-1294575	0564	1
WALLIS GLENN D	CW2	W-2143100	0965	1
WALLIS JOHN P	LTC	O-0289482	0864	3
WALLIS LYNN R	LTC	O-0234560	0850	1
WALLIS MARTIN J	CW3	W-2103575	1155	1
WALLIS RICHARD L	LTC	O-2036034	0562	1
WALLIS WILLIAM R	MAJ	O-0280408	0367	3
WALLK SILAS	1LT	O-0936992	0449	2
WALLNER JOSEPH J	MAJ	O-1100380	0157	1
WALLRATH MAURICE	LTC	O-0221268	1062	3
WALLS CECIL V	CPT	O-1822495	0157	1
WALLS FRANKLYN H	MAJ	O-0297267	1045	2
WALLS JESS W	COL	O-0450332	0666	1
WALLS JOHNNIE B	CPT	O-2263065	0265	1
WALLS RAYMOND G	MAJ	O-0231372	1058	3
WALLS WALTER S	COL	O-0284829	0865	3
WALLS WILLIAM R	1LT	O-1590875	0460	1
WALMER BERMUD K	MAJ	O-1685555	0164	1
WALMER HILLARD W	LTC	O-0170864	1043	2
WALMER RICHARD	LTC	O-0334773	0656	1
WALMER ROBERT F	MAJ	O-1556517	0764	1
WALMSLEY PHILIP M	CPT	O-1296772	0347	1
WALNES ROBERT U	LTC	O-2009725	0467	1
WALPER WILLIAM	LTC	O-0441446	0847	2
WALQUIST RAYMOND C	CPT	O-0208660	0755	3
WALRATH CLIFFORD B	LTC	O-2047879	0163	1
WALRATH RICHARD M	LTC	O-0297785	0763	3
WALSER BOBBY J	CPT	O-1932436	0565	1
WALSER HAROLD W	LTC	O-0312451	0762	1
WALSH ALEXANDER	LTC	O-0245113	0464	3
WALSH ALICE V	2LT	N-0722978	0545	1
WALSH ALOYSIUS J	MAJ	O-0172031	0-53	3
WALSH BERNARD W	2LT	O-0421919	0545	2
WALSH CHARLES C	MAJ	O-1285343	0461	1
WALSH CHARLES J	1LT	O-1290510	0446	2
WALSH CHARLES J	CW2	W-2111847	0246	2
WALSH CHARLOTTE	2LT	N-0724244	0543	1
WALSH CLARENCE H	COL	O-0198803	1056	3
WALSH DAVID J	LTC	O-0420892	0346	2
WALSH DENA G	CPT	N-0702020	0845	1
WALSH EARL F	COL	O-0172523	0752	3
WALSH EDWARD F	MAJ	O-1061016	0561	1
WALSH EDWARD G	CPT	O-1325610	0662	1
WALSH EDWARD J	LTC	O-0281502	0558	3
WALSH EDWARD T	LTC	O-0451544	0465	1
WALSH ELLARD A	M G	O-0158385	0648	3
WALSH FRANK J	COL	O-0347710	1059	2
WALSH GEORGE C	MAJ	O-1185206	0566	1
WALSH GEORGE T	CW3	W-2146186	0663	1
WALSH GILBERT C	CPT	O-0448189	0944	2
WALSH GLENN F	1LT	O-0465121	0745	2
WALSH JAMES J	CPT	O-1313043	0963	1
WALSH JAMES F	COL	O-0115438	0556	1
WALSH JAMES T	COL	O-0211659	0962	3
WALSH JOACHIM F	1LT	O-0529316	0344	2
WALSH JOHN A	CW3	W-2142914	0559	1
WALSH JOHN F	M G	O-0256059	0758	3
WALSH JOHN P	1LT	O-1308053	0945	2
WALSH JOHN R	CPT	O-0242958	0656	3
WALSH JOHN R	1LT	O-1174466	0745	2
WALSH JOSEPH D	CPT	O-1108400	0257	1
WALSH JOSEPH G	MAJ	O-0515817	0356	1
WALSH JOSEPH L	1LT	O-0430067	0345	2
WALSH JOSEPH T	LTC	O-1543186	1060	1
WALSH JR CHARLES E	COL	O-0263555	0264	3
WALSH JR CLARENCE H	MAJ	O-1635458	0560	1
WALSH JR DAVID J	LTC	O-1556966	0463	1
WALSH JR EDMUND C	LTC	O-0302105	0762	1
WALSH JR FRANCIS C	CW3	RW-2206455	0965	1
WALSH JR FRANK O	LTC	O-0195336	0363	3
WALSH JR FRED H	LTC	O-0401747	0347	2
WALSH JR JOHN J	LTC	O-2047880	1066	1
WALSH JR MARTIN T	CPT	O-1300421	0248	2
WALSH JR RICHARD M	CPT	O-0353797	1143	1
WALSH JR ROBERT J	LTC	O-0236276	0166	3
WALSH JR ROBERT J	MAJ	O-0982675	0365	1
WALSH JR THOMAS P	LTC	O-1585041	0264	1
WALSH KENNETH M	MAJ	O-1558222	0862	1
WALSH MARY F	1LT	N-0751302	0946	1
WALSH PAUL R	MAJ	O-1917783	1064	1
WALSH RAYMOND J	LTC	O-1590877	0167	3
WALSH RICHARD J	MAJ	O-2262895	0763	1
WALSH RITA H	CPT	N-0756393	1047	1
WALSH THOMAS J	LTC	O-0230797	0261	3
WALSH THOMAS J	COL	O-0266012	1061	3
WALSH THOMAS J	CW4	W-2004860	1165	1
WALSH THOMAS R	1LT	O-1314236	0746	2
WALSH WILLIAM F	COL	O-1169380	0966	1
WALSH WILLIAM J	COL	O-0189957	0758	3
WALSH WILLIAM J	1LT	O-1169784	0845	1
WALSKI FRANCIS L	LTC	O-0364190	0446	2
WALSTON CECIL O	LTC	O-1017342	1063	1
WALSTON KINDLE	MAJ	O-1703755	1053	2
WALTEMATH CLARENCE	CPT	O-1308736	0746	1
WALTER ARTHUR C	LTC	O-0506570	1265	3
WALTER BERNARD W	LTC	O-0683357	1166	1
WALTER BILLY H	MAJ	O-1800087	0161	1
WALTER CHARLES K	MAJ	O-0196335	0762	3
WALTER CHARLES S	LTC	O-1535106	0662	1
WALTER EDWIN A	CPT	O-2018797	0356	1
WALTER EDWIN J	MAJ	O-0232546	0363	3
WALTER ELMER J	2LT	O-1913999	0734	1
WALTER FLORENCE A	MAJ	N-0723361	0763	1
WALTER FRANK M	LTC	O-0499317	1166	3
WALTER FREDERICK	LTC	O-1650382	1066	1
WALTER FREDERICK	CW3	RW-2142738	0661	1
WALTER HENRY M	LTC	O-0194950	0263	3
WALTER IAN	CPT	O-1289348	0465	1
WALTER JOSEPH R	MAJ	O-0227548	0761	3
WALTER JR GEORGE H	LTC	O-0918262	0263	1
WALTER LLOYD O	LTC	O-0171799	0648	3
WALTER MORLEY C	LTC	O-0127742	0-51	3
WALTER ROBERT H	LTC	O-0973563	0867	1
WALTER ROY F	CW3	W-2143287	0262	1
WALTER RUDOLPH L	CPT	O-1290689	0546	2
WALTER WILLIAM F	MAJ	O-1824256	0557	1
WALTER WILLIAM J	MAJ	O-1688394	0961	1
WALTERS AGNES T	MAJ	N-0760452	1266	3
WALTERS ARTHUR M	LTC	O-1110870	0862	1
WALTERS CARL C	2LT	O-1882528	0753	2
WALTERS DALE F	1LT	O-2051574	0647	2
WALTERS DOLF W	LTC	O-1288147	0962	1
WALTERS DOUGLAS W	CW3	W-2145191	0263	1
WALTERS ELMER	LTC	O-1576769	0461	1
WALTERS ERNEST G	1LT	O-1288827	1045	2
WALTERS EUGENE P	COL	O-0145895	0355	3
WALTERS GENE H	CW3	W-2208396	1266	1
WALTERS GERALD A	1LT	O-1316250	0764	2
WALTERS GORDON G	LTC	O-0343297	0854	1
WALTERS HARRIS E	MAJ	O-1589647	1159	1
WALTERS HARRY F	CW2	W-2152726	0558	1
WALTERS HENRY O	MAJ	O-0109303	0247	1
WALTERS HOWARD C	COL	O-0338343	0364	3
WALTERS HURLIE A	CPT	O-0208697	0554	3
WALTERS JAMES E	CW4	W-2201593	1167	1
WALTERS JAMES H	1LT	O-1302558	0745	2
WALTERS JAMES H	MAJ	O-2262867	0961	1
WALTERS JAMES R	MAJ	O-0481079	0958	1
WALTERS JOHN B	CPT	O-0240482	0265	3
WALTERS JR ROBERT O	MAJ	O-1996856	0462	1
WALTERS LEONARD C	CW4	W-2115967	1163	1
WALTERS LOUIS V	LTC	O-0514064	1164	3
WALTERS MARCUS R	MAJ	O-2263231	1061	1
WALTERS MURRAY M	CPT	O-0501328	0446	2
WALTERS NORMAN P	CPT	O-1825723	0947	2
WALTERS PAUL W	MAJ	O-0965040	0963	1
WALTERS PETER	CW3	W-2150722	0864	1
WALTERS RAIMON G	COL	O-0122813	0454	3
WALTERS RALPH	MAJ	O-2030957	1060	1
WALTERS ROBERT E	MAJ	O-1330611	0463	1
WALTERS ROBERT L	1LT	O-1302099	1047	2
WALTERS ROY W	LTC	O-0145893	1153	3
WALTERS THURMOND L	COL	O-0352241	1160	1
WALTERS TYRE G	1LT	O-0423463	0965	3
WALTERS WAYNE D	LTC	O-1290339	1060	1
WALTERS WAYNE W	LTC	O-1101263	0756	1
WALTERS WILLIAM F	LTC	O-0450650	0657	1
WALTERS WILLIAM F	CW3	W-2149685	0865	1
WALTERS WILLIAM G	LTC	O-0403453	1165	1
WALTERS WILLIAM J	CW4	W-2146712	0767	1
WALTERS WILLIAM J	CW2	W-2148999	1157	1
WALTERS WINTRHOP F	CPT	O-1184437	0847	2
WALTHALL JAMES W	CPT	O-1296301	0347	1
WALTHALL MELVIN C	MAJ	O-0972979	0963	1
WALTHER RICHARD L	LTC	O-1032562	0763	1
WALTHER WILLIAM C	LTC	O-0237517	0761	1
WALTHERS GEORGE F	LTC	O-1640102	0163	1
WALTHERS HARRY V	1LT	O-0264278	0254	3
WALTMAN JAMES R	LTC	O-0123813	0850	3
WALTMAN KENNETH D	CW2	W-2208216	0864	1
WALTMAN LEE R	CW3	W-2146480	0561	2
WALTMAN RICHARD	CPT	O-1689590	0845	1
WALTON ABBOTT B	COL	O-0361106	0466	2
WALTON CHARLES F	LTC	O-2042979	0962	1
WALTON CHARLES J	CW3	W-2147808	0562	1
WALTON CHARLES W	MAJ	O-1576771	0861	1
WALTON CLARENCE M	LTC	O-0511529	1266	1
WALTON CORWIN T	LTC	O-1555316	0666	1
WALTON DELBERT P	MAJ	O-0359688	0744	2
WALTON EUGENE R	MAJ	O-1648280	0961	1
WALTON FRANK W	CW4	W-2005946	0762	3
WALTON FRANKLIN E	COL	O-0238874	0446	2
WALTON HAROLD C	LTC	O-0394033	0760	1
WALTON JAMES PHIL	2LT	O-1644198	0351	2
WALTON JOHN E	CPT	O-1697679	0345	2
WALTON JOHN W	COL	O-0232842	0765	3
WALTON JOSEPH F	1LT	O-0529686	0246	2
WALTON JOSEPH P	MAJ	O-1019082	0361	1
WALTON JR CURTIS R	LTC	O-1180374	0461	1
WALTON JR SAMUEL E	LTC	O-1288653	0363	2
WALTON LAWRENCE E	1LT	O-1879232	1054	2
WALTON MARION M	LTC	O-0271297	1066	3
WALTON NORMAN L	MAJ	O-0491184	0747	1
WALTON PETER W	MAJ	O-1546249	0766	3
WALTON RALPH F	MAJ	O-1315877	1060	1
WALTON RICHARD T	MAJ	O-0283709	0258	3
WALTON ROLAND L	1LT	O-1821941	1044	2
WALTON RUFUS R	CPT	O-0283721	1047	1
WALTON VERA N	MAJ	O-0145361	0-50	3
WALTON WAYNE A	1LT	O-0412492	1143	1
WALTON WILLIAM A	1LT	O-0496529	0256	1
WALTON WILLIAM S	MAJ	O-1110871	0760	1
WALTON WILLIAM W	CPT	O-0957506	0560	1
WALTRIP JESSE R	MAJ	O-0330526	0545	2
WALTRIP TERRY D	CPT	O-0339121	0145	2
WALTZ DAVID C	CPT	O-1822925	0960	1
WALTZ IRA D	LTC	O-0507964	0659	3
WALTZ JACK L	LTC	O-1184438	0567	1
WALTZ STANLEY G	COL	O-0286747	0359	3
WALTZ WILLIAM E	MAJ	O-1313538	0862	1
WALTZINGER AUGUST F	MAJ	O-1165382	0962	1
WALUSH FRANCIS J	LTC	O-1639788	0262	1
WALWORTH ALLEN C	LTC	O-1591509	0262	1
WALWORTH THOMAS K	CW4	W-2136501	0865	1
WALZ AUGUST F	LTC	O-0251425	0264	3
WAMMACK ROBERT F	1LT	O-1294046	0145	2
WAMPLER JOHN J	CPT	O-2262453	1060	1
WAMPLER RAY W	LTC	O-0329564	0666	3
WAMPLER ROBERT L	1LT	O-1861925	0553	2
WAMPOLE JOHN H	LTC	O-1046680	0363	1
WAMSLEY JAMES G	LTC	O-1176839	1061	1
WANAT JOHN T	LTC	O-0471610	0753	1
WANCHECK JOSEPH N	CW3	W-2142788	0460	1
WANCIO JOSEPH	CPT	O-1289841	1262	1
WANDELL WILBUR H	LTC	O-0223747	1054	1
WANDREY ALFRED F	1LT	O-1313044	0745	2
WANEK HAROLD E	MAJ	O-0318605	0961	1
WANG MALVIN P	COL	O-0226855	0665	3
WANGDAHL ERLAND J	MAJ	O-0502713	1263	3
WANGEMAN CLAYTON P	LTC	O-0302566	0346	2
WANGERIEN WILLIAM F	LTC	O-1041939	0663	1
WANGLER AMBROSE J	CPT	O-0890040	1045	1
WANITSHKA CHARLES F	CPT	O-1555151	0858	1
WANKEN LELAND G	MAJ	O-1886431	0267	1
WANN HENRY S	LTC	O-0488520	0164	1
WANN ROBERT A	MAJ	O-1303235	0761	1
WANNAMAKER A J M	COL	O-0202346	0252	1
WANNAMAKER GEORGE W	COL	O-0145360	0446	2
WANNAN JR CHARLES W	1LT	O-0418355	0145	2
WANNEBO JOSEPH T	CW2	W-2149721	0963	1
WANTUCK LOUIS B	LTC	O-0305273	0361	1
WANTZ RAYMOND E	LTC	O-1032183	0861	1
WAPENSKY VLADIMIR A	CW3	W-2153148	0465	1
WAPINSKI STANLEY W	LTC	O-1324685	0163	1
WAPLE GEORGE H	CPT	O-0963868	0662	1
WAPNER JOSEPH A	1LT	O-1306667	0146	2
WARACK JOHN L	LTC	O-0301513	0660	1
WARAKSA PETER J	CW2	W-2107263	1047	2
WARBURG FREDERICK	COL	O-0161510	1057	3
WARBURTON JOHN H	LTC	O-1059093	0563	1
WARCHOLIK VICTOR	LTC	O-0393793	0357	1
WARD AARON C	LTC	O-0311528	0761	3
WARD ALBERT	1LT	O-1596396	0347	1
WARD ARTHUR J	LTC	O-0365879	0765	2
WARD ARTHUR T	MAJ	O-0887631	1059	1
WARD ARTHUR W	2LT	O-1825454	0851	2

NAME	GRADE	SVC NO	DATE RET MO YR	RET CODE
WARD BEVERLY M	LTC	0-0525113	1064	1
WARD BILLY E	MAJ	C-2265545	C766	2
WARD BYRON G	LTC	0-1309451	0762	1
WARD CHARLES A	CW3	W-2136393	0563	1
WARD CHARLES C	CW2	W-2147687	0563	1
WARD CHARLES D	LTC	0-0394876	0965	3
WARD CHARLES E	COL	0-C354064	0747	1
WARD CHARLES E	MAJ	0-1924659	0966	1
WARD CHARLES R	CPT	0-0275031	1145	2
WARD CHARLES S	COL	0-0444518	0954	1
WARD CHARLOTTE	2LT	N-C736099	1145	1
WARD CHESTER J	MAJ	0-0279298	0765	3
WARD CLETUS O	MAJ	C-2036455	0954	1
WARD CLIFFORD F	MAJ	C-1C49011	1161	2
WARD DELLA A	CPT	N-0702101	0246	1
WARD DELMAR E	MAJ	0-1011343	0951	1
WARD DENNIS R	LTC	0-0346653	1059	1
WARD DOYLE P	LTC	0-0231542	0255	3
WARD EARL E	MAJ	C-0488296	0350	1
WARD EDWARD J	LTC	0-0301833	0847	2
WARD EUGENE A	LTC	0-0271442	0367	3
WARD FLOYD R	CPT	0-1999124	0864	1
WARD FRANK T	CW3	W-2151935	0965	1
WARD GENE G	CW3	W-2142434	1059	1
WARD GEORGE E	CPT	0-0292362	0266	3
WARD GEROGE A	1LT	0-0402520	1144	2
WARD GILBERT J	2LT	0-2012589	0946	2
WARD GLEN F	CPT	0-2262783	0557	1
WARD HAROLD M	MAJ	0-1119007	0461	1
WARD HAROLD T	LTC	0-0333763	0556	1
WARD HARRISON F	LTC	0-0242676	0752	3
WARD HARRY H	1LT	0-1648220	0845	2
WARD HELEN G	MAJ	N-0720304	C964	3
WARD HENRY P	COL	0-0266401	1262	1
WARD J B	MAJ	C-0302266	1144	2
WARD JAMES H	CPT	0-0286682	0365	3
WARD JAMES W	MAJ	0-2205311	0667	1
WARD JESSE R	LTC	C-1166203	0361	1
WARD JOHN A	CW4	W-2109613	0360	1
WARD JOHN J	MAJ	C-1044417	1062	1
WARD JOHN T	MAJ	0-1926337	C266	1
WARD JOSEPH L	CPT	0-2006327	0361	1
WARD JR JAMES A	LTC	0-0360407	0460	1
WARD JR LEWIS J	1LT	C-0540225	0646	2
WARD JR PHILIP J	COL	C-0291955	1061	3
WARD JR ROBERT B	MAJ	C-2032123	0866	1
WARD JR VIRGIL J	CW3	W-2152307	C163	1
WARD JR WILLIAM R	CPT	0-0541196	0446	2
WARD JULIAN H	CPT	0-1030946	0656	1
WARD KENNEDY G	MAJ	0-2C07202	0461	1
WARD KENNETH D	MAJ	C-0300288	0262	3
WARD KENNETH L	1LT	0-1101703	C645	2
WARD KENNON J	CPT	0-0256428	1161	2
WARD LEE R	WO1	W-2114187	0145	2
WARD LEE R G	LTC	0-0107976	1047	1
WARD LEROY J	1LT	0-1634442	0445	2
WARD LYCURGOS B	CPT	0-0366C86	0947	1
WARD MARSHALL M	CPT	C-0164056	1045	2
WARD MARY R	MAJ	N-0756508	1063	2
WARD NORMAN J	LTC	0-0748287	0365	1
WARD PARMELEE	LTC	0-0286916	1265	3
WARD PAUL C	LTC	0-1558827	0466	2
WARD RALPH B	LTC	0-0165883	1156	3
WARD RALPH B	CW4	W-2113652	0553	1
WARD RALPH C	1LT	0-0518732	1144	2
WARD RALPH L	LTC	0-0492351	0863	3
WARD RICHARD C	LTC	0-0918569	0664	3
WARD RICHARD C	LTC	0-1574175	0266	1
WARD ROBERT O	1LT	C-0921332	C245	2
WARD ROBERT L	1LT	0-1103994	1045	2
WARD ROBERT L	LTC	0-1583814	C562	1
WARD ROBERT S	MAJ	0-0968127	C563	1
WARD ROBERT W	LTC	C-0301051	0260	1
WARD ROY M	1LT	0-0903812	0644	2
WARD SR JACK	1LT	0-1575620	0157	1

NAME	GRADE	SVC NO	DATE RET MO YR	RET CODE
WARD SR JAMES A	CW2	W-2107952	0857	1
WARD SR WILLIAM L	CPT	0-0476718	0862	1
WARD STANLEY A	LTC	0-0243825	C266	3
WARD STEPHEN A	CPT	0-0340775	1046	2
WARD STEWART H	LTC	0-0281708	0667	3
WARD THEODORE B	LTC	0-0492960	0959	1
WARD THOMAS A	COL	0-0267345	1161	1
WARD THOMAS C	LTC	0-0474575	0257	1
WARD THOMAS P	COL	0-0249982	0557	3
WARD THOMAS R	MAJ	0-1553011	0561	1
WARD THOMAS W	CPT	0-1168969	0647	2
WARD THURMAN L	LTC	0-0355203	0762	1
WARD VERNON	CW4	W-2007068	0567	1
WARD VIRGIL L	MAJ	0-2262102	0765	1
WARD WALTER J	MAJ	0-1173498	0367	1
WARD WALTER R	CPT	0-0302842	1057	1
WARD WILLIAM B	LTC	0-0235871	0166	3
WARD WILLIAM E	LTC	0-1549163	0661	1
WARD WILLIAM W	COL	0-0257323	0761	3
WARD WILMA B	2LT	N-0736047	1143	1
WARDELL CECIL J	LTC	0-1165583	1061	1
WARDELL LLOYD L	LTC	0-0108800	0247	1
WARDEN EDWARD A	LTC	0-132337C	0764	1
WARDEN JOHN B	COL	0-0147395	0656	3
WARDEN LEO W	MAJ	0-1179669	0864	1
WARDEN LEON N	LTC	0-1043533	1066	3
WARDER JR FREDERIC B	LTC	0-0516127	0767	1
WARDIN HERBERT B	CPT	0-0133400	0454	3
WARDLAW JOSEPH G	LTC	0-017C949	1161	3
WARDLE CLARENCE J	LTC	0-0278984	1055	1
WARDLOW HILDA A	1LT	N-0760491	1045	1
WARDLOW LOUIS M	CW3	W-2144364	1064	1
WARDLOW THEODORE G	LTC	0-1166642	0258	1
WARDNER WALTER C	LTC	0-0196191	0961	3
WARDROP HARVEY R	MAJ	0-1103453	0658	1
WARDROP ROBERT W	LTC	0-0331851	0862	1
WARDWELL HILLIARE P	MAJ	0-0291100	1045	2
WARE CHARLES W	LTC	0-0355495	1058	1
WARE DEWEY F	2LT	0-1308028	0744	2
WARE EDWARD R	COL	0-0219533	0452	3
WARE EDWARD V	1LT	0-0445216	0746	1
WARE GEORGE L	CPT	0-044676C	0445	2
WARE GEORGE W	MAJ	0-0196290	0163	3
WARE HERBERT M	CPT	0-0373C97	1148	2
WARE IVAN H	MAJ	0-0162349	0258	3
WARE JAMES M	1LT	0-1293500	1045	2
WARE JR WILLETT	LTC	0-0278722	0663	1
WARE JUSTIN J	CPT	0-1286933	0446	2
WARE MARVIN K	CW4	W-2144450	1166	1
WARE MAURICE L	1LT	0-1295303	0645	2
WARE MAX E	COL	0-0380743	0360	1
WARE ROBERT B	CPT	0-0494143	0450	1
WARE ROBERT E	COL	0-0214782	0663	3
WARE ROBERT L	LTC	0-0226569	0264	3
WARE ROSWELL C	MAJ	C-2026176	1265	1
WARE RUFUS L	1LT	0-1296949	0745	2
WARE RUSSELL H	CPT	0-0149470	0756	3
WARE SAMUEL J	1LT	0-0125463	1051	3
WARE STEPHEN C	COL	0-0270302	0266	3
WARE WILLIAM L	CPT	0-2033241	0460	1
WARE WILSON P	CPT	0-1317847	0546	2
WARFEL CHARLES O	COL	0-0118903	0648	3
WARFIELD HARRY R	COL	0-0252363	0964	3
WARFIELD JR DAVID K	LTC	0-1330014	0964	1
WARFIELD PAUL E	B G	0-0246401	1162	3
WARFIELD WILLIAM K	CW2	W-2205155	1262	1
WARFORD GEORGE F	MAJ	0-1635789	0662	1
WARG ELLEN B	1LT	N-0743802	0346	1
WARGA ANNA H	CPT	N-0751980	1048	1
WARGA CHARLES J	CPT	0-1307899	0246	2
WARGACKI RICHARD T	CPT	0-1573976	1051	1
WARHEIT HARRY G	CPT	0-2C11C05	0556	1
WARHURST WILBUR L	CW3	W-2147046	0461	1
WARING CLARK D	MAJ	0-0151079	0657	3
WARING FRANK S	COL	0-0200996	0260	1

NAME	GRADE	SVC NO	DATE RET MO YR	RET CODE
WARING THOMAS L	COL	C-0248758	0564	3
WARK GEORGE H	B G	0-0183827	C648	3
WARK JOHN T	1LT	C-1310535	0151	2
WARKER PETER F	MAJ	0-0172314	0156	3
WARLEY EKLEY H	MAJ	C-0512378	0147	1
WARLICK G W	1LT	C-0449256	0347	2
WARLICK GEORGE C	CPT	0-0208462	C954	3
WARLICK JOHN L	WO1	W-2118165	C666	1
WARLICK WILLIAM A	LTC	0-1167265	0262	1
WARMAN CLARENCE S	MAJ	0-1102110	1060	1
WARMOUTH LOUIS A	MAJ	0-1308438	0263	1
WARMUTH IVAN J	CPT	0-1180375	0862	1
WARNDOF CHARLES R	COL	C-0153058	1159	3
WARNECKE ADOLPH F	LTC	0-0887976	0564	1
WARNEK OLEG V	MAJ	0-2210266	0664	1
WARNER ARTHUR H	COL	0-C198052	0953	3
WARNER CARL J	MAJ	0-2046391	1057	1
WARNER CHARLES J	MAJ	C-0389839	0457	1
WARNER DANIEL E	1LT	0-1105594	1045	1
WARNER DAVID J	1LT	0-1895622	0745	2
WARNER ETHEL C	MAJ	L-1010116	0564	1
WARNER FLOYD N	COL	0-0273409	0356	2
WARNER FRANCIS L	MAJ	0-1293502	0267	1
WARNER FRANK T	LTC	0-0184390	0154	3
WARNER GEORGE B	MAJ	0-0321293	C767	3
WARNER HAROLD C	COL	0-0333870	0861	3
WARNER HAROLD J	MAJ	0-0145890	1043	2
WARNER HAROLD P	1LT	0-0394483	C643	2
WARNER JARED	1LT	0-0450517	0345	2
WARNER JOHN E	1LT	0-0314549	0544	2
WARNER JOHN H	CPT	C-1284061	0745	2
WARNER JOHN W	MAJ	0-0276046	0865	3
WARNER JR VICTOR E	LTC	0-0326147	C957	1
WARNER LAURENCE P	MAJ	0-0159404	0860	3
WARNER LEWIS W	COL	0-0122136	0951	3
WARNER LORING K	LTC	0-0143898	0648	3
WARNER LYNN J	CPT	0-1183644	0646	2
WARNER MARK T	COL	0-0237614	0249	3
WARNER MORRIS T	COL	0-0156562	1059	3
WARNER OLIVER M	LTC	0-0492369	1055	3
WARNER RAYMOND	CW3	W-2149000	0163	1
WARNER ROBERT E L	CPT	0-0487184	0351	1
WARNER ROY C	CPT	0-2046854	0157	1
WARNER ROY C	MAJ	C-0996924	0863	1
WARNER ROY F	COL	0-0297605	1066	3
WARNER WALTER H	CPT	C-1296773	0547	1
WARNER WILLIAM M	CPT	0-0206934	0647	1
WARNER WOODREW W	MAJ	0-1580476	0959	1
WARNKE CLIFFORD	CW2	W-2144208	0358	1
WARNKEN MICHAEL P	CPT	0-0395388	0444	2
WARNOCK BRUCE B	1LT	0-1054167	1046	1
WARNOCK NORMAN M	LTC	0-1585050	0865	1
WARREN ALBERT F	MAJ	0-0156563	0-52	3
WARREN ARBER J	CPT	0-0234128	0747	1
WARREN ARCHIE A	CW3	W-2146767	0465	1
WARREN ARTHUR	MAJ	C-1956734	0960	1
WARREN CHARLES H	LTC	0-0175366	1055	3
WARREN CLYDE B	MAJ	0-0925374	0859	3
WARREN CLYDE R	MAJ	C-1895023	0560	1
WARREN CULLEN	CW3	W-2146557	0365	1
WARREN DONALD H	LTC	0-1544343	0464	1
WARREN EDWIN H	CPT	0-2036717	0746	2
WARREN FRANCES A	MAJ	N-0727422	0862	1
WARREN FREDERICK	M G	0-0266247	0963	3
WARREN GEORGE O	CW3	W-2143976	0862	1
WARREN GEORGE M	CPT	0-2046519	0952	1
WARREN GORDON R	MAJ	C-1341837	0164	1
WARREN HAROLD C	CW3	W-2142277	0463	1
WARREN HAROLD F	LTC	0-0450941	0859	1
WARREN HARRIS B	1LT	0-1321971	C845	2
WARREN HOWARD J	CW2	W-2104569	0746	2
WARREN JACK A	1LT	0-1291552	0644	2
WARREN JAMES W	WO1	T-0066402	0563	2
WARREN JOHN	COL	0-0307693	1167	3
WARREN JOHN B	WO1	W-2117531	1152	1

NAME	GRADE	SVC NO	DATE RET MO YR	RET CODE
WARREN JOHN R	LTC	0-1699942	0665	1
WARREN JR GEORGE B	LTC	0-1C38509	0365	2
WARREN JR GEORGE C	LTC	0-0352162	0161	1
WARREN JR JAMES A	COL	0-0227551	0366	3
WARREN KEITH L	LTC	0-2039165	0766	1
WARREN KENNETH O	LTC	0-0885755	C655	1
WARREN LAWRENCE	CPT	0-0272697	0466	3
WARREN LEONARD P	LTC	0-0225695	0165	3
WARREN LYNN R	1LT	0-0515657	1145	1
WARREN MALCOLM S	1LT	0-0271417	1142	2
WARREN MAX A	MAJ	0-2210333	0866	1
WARREN MERL R	COL	0-0189660	0256	3
WARREN MORRILL T	1LT	0-1012396	0750	1
WARREN PAT R	LTC	0-0258108	1058	3
WARREN PAUL N	LTC	0-0478103	0255	1
WARREN RALPH F	MAJ	0-1110326	0857	1
WARREN RALPH M	CW2	W-2150932	0461	1
WARREN RICHARD	CW2	W-2112909	1053	1
WARREN RICHARD A	CPT	0-0461107	0647	2
WARREN RICHARD K	CW2	W-34302C1	1167	1
WARREN ROBERT C	LTC	0-0298125	0158	2
WARREN ROBERT F	MAJ	0-0496567	0945	2
WARREN ROBERT K	MAJ	0-1019848	0962	1
WARREN ROBERT L	MAJ	0-1341926	0266	1
WARREN RUFUS C	LTC	0-0277111	1060	3
WARREN SAMUEL H	LTC	0-1285344	0263	1
WARREN STANLEY D	MAJ	0-0288761	0267	3
WARREN THOMAS L	CPT	0-0245526	0454	3
WARREN VIRGINIA L	1LT	N-0727205	1047	1
WARREN WILLIAM H	MAJ	0-0299230	0364	3
WARREN WILLIAM H	NAJ	0-1289176	0161	1
WARREN WILLIAM J	LTC	0-0392492	0356	2
WARREN WILLIS R	1LT	0-1319803	0247	2
WARREN WOODROW	COL	0-0423367	C767	1
WARREN WOODROW W	CW3	W-2204957	1065	1
WARRENBURG CLARENCE	LTC	0-0280986	0765	3
WARRICK HAROLD L	1LT	0-1945308	0146	1
WARRICK JAMES W	LTC	0-1102992	0557	1
WARRICK JOHN L	MAJ	0-0174021	0760	3
WARRICK JR JAMES R	LTC	0-1289516	1161	1
WARRING WILLARD B	COL	0-0251461	0562	3
WARROW LEWIS H	MAJ	0-1111419	0261	1
WARSAW EUGENE	CPT	0-0494379	1145	2
WARSHALL ALEXANDER	LTC	0-1324471	C866	1
WARSHAW ISADORE	1LT	0-1326952	1146	2
WARSHAWSKY EUGENE	CW2	W-215135C	0661	1
WARTERS CHARLES J	MAJ	0-1170912	1166	1
WARTNER JR ALOYS	COL	0-0258881	1166	3
WARTSKY MUNDELL	1LT	0-1044720	0546	2
WARWICK CECIL T	MAJ	0-0521205	1047	2
WARWICK CLARENCE E	MAJ	0-0299470	1043	2
WARWICK HENRY	CW4	W-2103580	1057	1
WASCAK ANDREW	CPT	0-1306778	0546	2
WASECKA STEPHEN	LTC	0-1295466	0166	1
WASELEWSKY STANLEY	MAJ	0-1582248	1057	2
WASER JR WILLIAM B	CW3	W-2148776	0762	1
WASH GEORGE M	MAJ	0-2040845	0261	1
WASHBOURNE KYLE V	LTC	0-1044143	1163	1
WASHBURN ARTHUR M	COL	0-0209127	0450	3
WASHBURN CARLYLE	1LT	0-1103996	1045	2
WASHBURN CHARLES E	CPT	0-0181359	0648	3
WASHBURN DULAN R	1LT	0-0886910	1047	1
WASHBURN FRANK E	LTC	0-0182767	1149	3
WASHBURN GERALD M	2LT	0-1048233	0245	2
WASHBURN GORDON G	LTC	0-1182298	0865	1
WASHBURN JR ARTHUR S	COL	0-0341430	0163	1
WASHBURN JR GEORGE T	CW2	W-2145163	1056	2
WASHBURN JR GEORGE W	MAJ	0-1301728	0660	1
WASHBURN LESTER L	LTC	0-0253063	1166	3
WASHBURN PERLEY A	LTC	0-0151946	0157	1
WASHBURN RICHARD P	MAJ	0-2265548	0566	1
WASHBURN SHERMAN S	LTC	0-1043252	0266	1
WASHBURN WILLIAM E	CPT	0-0212487	0648	3
WASHBURN WILLIAM H	MAJ	0-0252546	0964	3
WASHBURN WILLIAM H	MAJ	0-1646094	0161	1

NAME	GRADE	SVC NO	DATE RET MO YR	RET CODE
WASHBURNE CLAUDE R	COL	0-0145461	0752	3
WASHER PHINEAS	LTC	0-0232611	0162	3
WASHINGTON ALBERT F	LTC	0-1895064	0961	1
WASHINGTON CHARLES A	CPT	0-0976924	0361	1
WASHINGTON CHARLES W	MAJ	C-1917631	0163	1
WASHINGTON CLARA E	LTC	N-0700232	0146	1
WASHINGTON JOHN H	LTC	0-1575255	0561	1
WASHINGTON JOHN R	CW3	W-2143068	0765	1
WASHINGTON RICHARD R	LTC	0-0394906	0262	1
WASHINGTON ROBBIN E	LTC	0-1165261	0861	1
WASHINGTON WILLIAM D	CPT	0-0232672	1062	3
WASHINGTON WILLIAM H	MAJ	0-0122961	0753	3
WASHLICK MATTHEW E	LTC	0-1557924	0463	1
WASHNOK ROBERT L	LTC	C-0291829	1265	1
WASILEWSKI ADAM J	CPT	0-1331350	0755	1
WASKE LEONARD	CW2	W-2109621	0647	2
WASKO THEODORE E	MAJ	C-1649975	0767	1
WASKOM GEORGE F	CW2	W-2150013	0461	1
WASKOW HARRY N	MAJ	0-1300422	0360	1
WASNETSKY JOHN	CW3	W-2152259	1062	1
WASON ALEXANDER	1LT	0-1595884	0746	2
WASON ALFRED B	LTC	0-0127100	0757	3
WASON GEORGE F	LTC	C-0174209	0958	3
WASON THOMAS H	LTC	0-0314343	C646	2
WASS JR JOHN R	LTC	0-0419534	0657	1
WASSER ALFRED	MAJ	C-0250895	1265	3
WASSERMAN ISIDORE	1LT	0-0526210	0245	2
WASSERMAN JULIAN	1LT	0-1342023	0852	1
WASSERMAN NATHAN	LTC	C-0341700	0266	3
WASSERSTEIN JACK J	LTC	0-0204043	1056	3
WASSON CLARENCE C	CPT	0-1844773	C159	2
WASSON EARL D	MAJ	0-1042735	0162	2
WASSON LAWRENCE	CW3	W-2203263	0564	1
WASSON LELAND H	MAJ	0-0180078	0351	3
WASSON ROY C	LTC	0-1179670	1166	1
WASSON WILLIAM A	COL	0-0370156	0157	1
WASSON WILLIAM O	MAJ	C-1825206	0962	1
WASSUM ROBERT A	MAJ	C-1685223	C446	2
WATANABE LLOYD K	CW3	W-2152753	0265	1
WATCKE HENRY S	MAJ	0-0556411	0863	1
WATERHOUSE EDWARD J	MAJ	0-0169886	0259	3
WATERHOUSE GEORGE T	CPT	C-1043534	0944	2
WATERHOUSE ROBERT L	MAJ	C-1304977	C859	1
WATERHOUSE WILLIAM H	CPT	0-1798630	0554	2
WATERMAN ERNEST A	LTC	0-0336896	C261	3
WATERMAN JEROME A	LTC	0-0171660	0648	3
WATERMAN JOSEPH M	MAJ	C-0406963	0747	2
WATERMAN LEONARD E	MAJ	C-0502548	1147	2
WATERMAN MARCUS M	1LT	0-0922118	1046	2
WATERMAN MEREDITH T	CPT	0-0224576	0144	2
WATERS ARCHIE C	LTC	0-0206833	1263	3
WATERS ARTHUR C	LTC	0-0173813	0256	3
WATERS BRUCE C	2LT	0-1822752	C344	2
WATERS FRANK H	LTC	C-0240085	1161	1
WATERS FRED D	LTC	C-0414882	1160	1
WATERS GEORGE L	COL	0-0385817	0566	1
WATERS GEORGE M	LTC	0-0435933	0447	2
WATERS HARGET D	MAJ	0-0982453	0764	1
WATERS HARRY O	MAJ	C-0321947	C860	1
WATERS JACK T	MAJ	C-4011094	0967	1
WATERS JAMES F	COL	0-0248463	0766	3
WATERS JAMES M	MAJ	C-2200444	C666	1
WATERS JAMES T	LTC	0-1995019	0766	1
WATERS JOHN T	2LT	C-1014242	0744	2
WATERS JOSEPH B	2LT	0-1585055	0245	2
WATERS JULIAN H	CW3	W-2149865	0863	1
WATERS LAUGHLIN F	CPT	0-0363553	1145	2
WATERS LEE E	MAJ	C-0383149	0945	2
WATERS LEE T	LTC	C-1588948	0463	1
WATERS MARTIN H	LTC	0-0331609	C461	3
WATERS MARY T	CPT	N-0731549	0447	1
WATERS MELVIN C	LTC	C-1001490	0548	1
WATERS PATTISON A	COL	0-0189546	0453	3
WATERS PHILEMON R	LTC	0-0168702	1060	3
WATERS RICHARD W	LTC	0-0330745	0960	1

NAME	GRADE	SVC NO	DATE RET MO YR	RET CODE
WATERS ROBERT L	MAJ	C-0977371	1164	1
WATERS ROBERT P	LTC	0-0142404	0648	3
WATERS ROBERT W	MAJ	0-0888217	0963	1
WATERS VERLON E	2LT	0-0987691	1051	1
WATERS WILLIAM A	CPT	0-0172885	0848	2
WATERS WILLIAM P	CPT	0-1597319	0747	1
WATERS 3RD JOHN S	CPT	0-0456055	0746	2
WATERSTREET KENNET	1LT	0-0924395	1044	2
WATFORD SR RAYMOND E	CW3	W-2147314	0765	1
WATHEN BUELL S	2LT	0-0206409	0640	1
WATKINS ANNABEL	MAJ	R-0010033	0366	1
WATKINS AVIS M	MAJ	L-0115648	0963	1
WATKINS BAZZ	WO1	W-2118351	0550	1
WATKINS CHARLES B	COL	0-0264198	0151	3
WATKINS CLARENCE C	LTC	0-0332454	0658	3
WATKINS CLIFFORD W	MAJ	0-0207184	0154	3
WATKINS CRAIG C	COL	0-1640106	1066	3
WATKINS DACY P	LTC	0-0268246	0660	3
WATKINS DAVIS	LTC	0-0271143	0267	3
WATKINS EDWARD W	LTC	0-0243252	0964	3
WATKINS ELLIS H	2LT	0-2035170	0845	2
WATKINS ELLIS S	LTC	0-1296886	0561	1
WATKINS EUNICE R	MAJ	N-0741719	1165	3
WATKINS EVERETT C	WO1	W-2106280	0548	1
WATKINS EVERETT W	LTC	0-0227495	0963	3
WATKINS FLOYD R	2LT	C-2053914	0645	2
WATKINS GEORGE E	MAJ	0-0122834	0353	3
WATKINS GLENN D	1LT	0-1311240	0745	2
WATKINS HARRY	1LT	0-0205531	0953	3
WATKINS HARRY G	CPT	0-2002564	0457	1
WATKINS HENRY F	1LT	0-0308015	0343	2
WATKINS JAMES C	MAJ	C-2024284	0961	1
WATKINS JOHN B	COL	C-0233324	C659	3
WATKINS JOHN H	MAJ	C-0199643	0746	1
WATKINS JOHN R	MAJ	0-1552822	0859	1
WATKINS JR HERRICK C	MAJ	0-0192481	1060	3
WATKINS JR JOHN D	LTC	0-0476121	0646	2
WATKINS JR MARTIN D	CPT	0-0460013	0747	2
WATKINS JR PERRY R	MAJ	C-2266061	0267	1
WATKINS JR ROBERT A	1LT	0-1289177	1056	1
WATKINS PERSHING V	LTC	0-1303581	0365	1
WATKINS PETER F	LTC	0-0408687	1060	1
WATKINS RAYMOND	COL	0-0243351	0662	3
WATKINS REGINALD G	LTC	C-0410785	0161	1
WATKINS ROBERT B	1LT	0-0467830	0545	1
WATKINS ROBERT H	LTC	C-0213552	0956	3
WATKINS ROBERT L	B G	0-0244532	0866	3
WATKINS ROBERT M	CPT	0-0492788	0246	2
WATKINS THELMA C	1LT	N-0764036	0146	1
WATKINS THOMAS H	COL	C-0233013	1061	1
WATKINS THOMAS J	MAJ	C-1051444	0157	1
WATKINS THOMAS R	LTC	0-0432755	0962	1
WATKINS VERNON L	COL	C-0220134	0359	2
WATKINS VICTOR	CW2	W-2148526	1161	2
WATKINS WALLACE	CW4	W-2109484	0456	1
WATKINS WATT	WO1	W-2131465	0344	2
WATLAND LLOYD A	MAJ	0-0541517	0765	1
WATROUS CHARLES A	LTC	0-0105814	0445	2
WATROUS WILLIAM L	MAJ	C-2008074	C462	1
WATSON ALAN M	COL	0-0163882	0160	3
WATSON ALBERT P	MAJ	0-2028761	0864	1
WATSON ALFRED E	CPT	0-1308223	1147	2
WATSON ALFRED W	MAJ	0-1108405	0561	1
WATSON ALLEN J	MAJ	C-0283678	0846	1
WATSON ALMYRA M	MAJ	N-0726087	0963	1
WATSON ARCHIE A	CPT	0-0248454	0945	1
WATSON ARTHUR R	LTC	0-0115393	0750	2
WATSON BARTON H	LTC	0-1822088	0164	1
WATSON BEN O	1LT	0-1030431	0455	1
WATSON BILLY R	2LT	0-2006220	0264	2
WATSON BURTON L	CPT	0-0192143	1054	2
WATSON CHARLES D	WO1	W-2115689	0644	2
WATSON CHARLES G	LTC	0-0545523	0664	1
WATSON CHARLES L	1LT	0-0804007	0865	1
WATSON CHARLES P	LTC	0-0122425	0549	3

NAME	GRADE	SVC NO	DATE RET MO YR	RET CODE
WATSON CLARENCE R	CPT	0-1321092	C555	1
WATSON CLIFFORD A	1LT	0-4048864	0959	2
WATSON COMER D	1LT	0-1648546	0456	1
WATSON COVINGTON	MAJ	C-2019256	0260	1
WATSON CULLUM B	COL	0-0422204	C561	1
WATSON DALE I	MAJ	C-2262554	0765	1
WATSON DANIEL G	LTC	0-0332123	1046	1
WATSON DEANE C	1LT	0-0537623	1145	2
WATSON DEWARD H	MAJ	C-1120699	C161	1
WATSON DON R	MAJ	C-1056008	0866	1
WATSON DONALD M	MAJ	0-2006962	1063	1
WATSON DORSEY J	CPT	0-0471802	0448	1
WATSON DURWARD L	CW4	W-2143623	0657	1
WATSON EDWARD L	LTC	0-0443787	0347	2
WATSON ELMER S	COL	0-0264495	0945	2
WATSON FELTON L	LTC	0-0250530	0664	3
WATSON FRANCIS M	LTC	0-0297702	C246	2
WATSON FRANK	CPT	0-0479054	1053	1
WATSON FRANK J	CPT	0-1304830	0254	2
WATSON FRANK P	MAJ	0-15409C9	1061	1
WATSON GALE A	LTC	0-1050986	0962	1
WATSON GEORGE	LTC	C-1015601	0363	2
WATSON GEORGE D	MAJ	0-2017154	0461	1
WATSON GEORGE R	LTC	0-0252211	1265	3
WATSON GEORGE S	COL	0-0272590	0863	1
WATSON GEORGIA B	MAJ	L-0402018	0146	2
WATSON GUY M	MAJ	0-0970140	0962	1
WATSON HARRY B	CPT	0-1052613	0963	1
WATSON HARRY H	LTC	C-0157479	C833	1
WATSON HENRY B	LTC	0-0288336	0557	1
WATSON HENRY L	LTC	0-0953869	0466	1
WATSON HENRY P	MAJ	0-1535326	0751	1
WATSON HERBERT R	COL	0-0212179	0754	3
WATSON HUGH R	MAJ	C-1319367	0261	1
WATSON ISABEL M	1LT	N-0734024	1045	1
WATSON JAMES D	MAJ	0-0438873	C246	1
WATSON JAMES R	1LT	0-1301062	0945	2
WATSON JOHN L	LTC	0-0220478	0144	2
WATSON JOHN L	CPT	0-1284249	0945	2
WATSON JOHN M	CW2	W-2149723	0764	1
WATSON JOHN W	COL	0-0278228	0663	3
WATSON JOHNNY J	LTC	0-1040481	1160	1
WATSON JOSEPH	LTC	0-1304624	0666	1
WATSON JOSEPH D	MAJ	0-2204344	0367	1
WATSON JOSEPH L	CW2	W-2208446	0962	1
WATSON JOSEPH W	COL	0-0255847	0647	2
WATSON JR HARRY T	1LT	C-0300729	0145	2
WATSON JR JAMES E	COL	0-0333577	1067	3
WATSON JR JOSEPH M	LTC	0-0280685	1067	3
WATSON JR LESLIE L	1LT	0-1575250	1045	2
WATSON JR WHITE C	CPT	0-1946202	0551	2
WATSON JR WILLIAM F	COL	0-0143102	1057	3
WATSON JR WILLIAM W	CPT	C-0523236	0946	1
WATSON LEASON K	LTC	0-1101707	1060	1
WATSON LEWIS T	CW2	W-2118188	C149	1
WATSON MARION T	COL	0-0143872	0857	3
WATSON MELVIN L	CW4	W-2149887	0965	1
WATSON MILLARD F	2LT	0-0887708	0253	1
WATSON OLIVER P	MAJ	0-1316799	C360	1
WATSON PARDON O	COL	C-0218727	1047	2
WATSON PAUL R	CPT	0-0362996	C645	2
WATSON RANDOLPH C	CPT	0-1297627	C745	2
WATSON RAY E	COL	0-0323388	C-51	3
WATSON RAYMOND C	CPT	0-0232934	0165	3
WATSON ROBERT F	CW2	W-2209544	1263	1
WATSON ROBERT G	1LT	0-0493778	0549	1
WATSON ROBERT J	MAJ	C-1319368	C663	1
WATSON ROBERT R	CW2	W-2152882	1161	1
WATSON ROE O	MAJ	0-1285345	0346	2
WATSON ROGER L	CW3	W-2149401	0464	1
WATSON ROYAL A	CPT	0-0525310	0347	1
WATSON RUSSELL C	CW3	W-2115996	0559	1
WATSON SHIRLEY R	2LT	N-0743419	C845	1
WATSON STEPHEN B	MAJ	0-1328858	C666	1
WATSON SYLVIA A	MAJ	N-0773802	0167	1

NAME	GRADE	SVC NO	DATE RET MO YR	RET CODE
WATSON THOMAS E	COL	C-0398329	1160	1
WATSON THOMAS V	1LT	0-1324711	C846	2
WATSON WALTER L	CW2	W-2119573	0648	1
WATSON WILFRED H	2LT	0-1052221	1044	2
WATSON WILLIAM C	MAJ	C-1336983	0867	1
WATSON WILLIAM E	MAJ	C-1555317	1062	1
WATSON WILLIAM F	MAJ	0-1588950	1060	2
WATSON WILLIAM J	LTC	0-0321427	0646	2
WATSON WILLIAM J	LTC	0-1573657	0757	1
WATSON WILLIAM L	MAJ	0-0969072	0866	1
WATSON WILLIAM L	CPT	0-1309998	1046	2
WATT ALEX S	LTC	C-0213349	0963	3
WATT ALEXIS	MAJ	0-0359869	0357	1
WATT HUGH C	CPT	0-0889475	0455	1
WATT JAMES F	COL	0-0300555	0157	1
WATT JEWELL K	COL	0-0191406	1059	1
WATT JOHN R	CPT	0-0488396	0149	1
WATT RAYMOND	B G	0-0209364	1262	3
WATTERBERG JOHN P	1LT	0-0494776	1145	1
WATTERS CURTISS W	MAJ	0-0415060	0261	1
WATTERS GEORGE W	1LT	0-0466501	0345	1
WATTERS JAMES J	WO1	W-2109173	0651	2
WATTERS JOHN	LTC	0-0298364	0462	3
WATTERS KEIRAN J	CW3	W-2205727	0265	1
WATTERS SR WALTER P	MAJ	0-1592688	0855	2
WATTERSON EULA R	MAJ	N-0759865	0563	1
WATTERSON ROBERT S	LTC	0-0265288	0865	3
WATTIE ARNOLD H	1LT	0-2055143	C848	1
WATTIGNY CHARLES C	MAJ	0-1293157	0561	1
WATTS ARTHUR P	COL	C-0300016	C565	3
WATTS AUGUSTUS A	LTC	C-0293157	0260	1
WATTS CECIL E	LTC	0-0129028	C446	2
WATTS CHARLES W	MAJ	0-1642699	C357	2
WATTS CLARENCE B	MAJ	0-0358911	C661	1
WATTS EDGAR L	CPT	0-2262159	C461	1
WATTS FLOYD J	1LT	0-0427223	1043	2
WATTS HOLWAY O	COL	0-0292772	1161	3
WATTS HOWARD E	LTC	0-0297653	0958	3
WATTS JACK E	WO1	W-2114353	0158	1
WATTS JACK J	LTC	0-0375604	0867	1
WATTS JAMES A	LTC	0-0291213	0759	1
WATTS JAMES L	LTC	0-0294535	0858	1
WATTS JOHN A	CW3	W-2145602	0358	1
WATTS JOHN H	MAJ	0-0726525	0664	1
WATTS JOSEPH C	LTC	0-0242432	1064	3
WATTS JOSEPH W	LTC	0-1111422	0762	1
WATTS JR JAMES P	MAJ	0-0961421	1163	1
WATTS JR JOSEPH C	MAJ	0-2263315	C564	1
WATTS JR JOSEPH R	LTC	0-0504140	0559	2
WATTS JR SEWELL S	MAJ	C-0241735	0564	3
WATTS KENNETH B	MAJ	0-1061577	0758	1
WATTS LAVAUGHN F	MAJ	0-1004057	0561	1
WATTS MONROE H	MAJ	0-2010714	0662	1
WATTS NATHAN E	CPT	0-0398324	1066	2
WATTS OWEN J	COL	C-0103652	0455	3
WATTS RAY A	CPT	0-2026558	1157	1
WATTS ROBERT C	MAJ	0-2018615	0164	1
WATTS RUSSELL G	MAJ	0-1643427	0760	1
WATTS STANLEY F	MAJ	0-1328953	0763	1
WATTS THEODORE F	LTC	0-0101829	1048	3
WATTS ULYSSES V	LTC	0-0450141	0652	1
WATTS WALTER C	MAJ	0-1315985	0457	1
WATTS WILLIAM L	LTC	0-1552205	C863	1
WATZ EARL P	CPT	0-0304004	0646	2
WAUGH ALBERT A	MAJ	0-0420040	1067	3
WAUGH KENNETH B	LTC	0-1551142	0762	1
WAVREK GORDON J	LTC	0-1549165	0166	1
WAWREJKO THAD J	LTC	C-1293857	0561	1
WAXMUTH WILLIAM	MAJ	0-0169803	1058	3
WAY JR JACOB E	2LT	0-1328428	0846	2
WAY JR POWELL E	MAJ	0-1056938	0463	1
WAY LLOYD G	MAJ	0-0972021	0861	1
WAY PAUL P	1LT	0-1297628	0647	2
WAYBURN GATES J	1LT	0-0475483	0750	2
WAYCOTT WILFRED H	LTC	0-1646158	0666	3

292-560 O - 68 - 23

ARMY OF THE UNITED STATES RETIRED LIST

NAME	GRADE	SVC NO	DATE RET MO YR	RET CODE
WAYLAN ZULETTA M	MAJ	N-0736778	0665	3
WAYMAN LEON H	LTC	0-0135240	C156	3
WAYMAN LUCIUS A	COL	0-0244745	0565	3
WAYMAN LYNFORD A	CW4	W-2117220	1262	1
WAYMENT HAROLD S	MAJ	0-2262726	0664	1
WAYMOTH HARRY K	CPT	0-3398847	0857	1
WAYNE BESSE M	1LT	N-0760446	0346	1
WAYNE FRANK P	MAJ	C-2040904	C561	1
WAYNE FREDERICK	CPT	0-0298972	0860	3
WAYNE WILFORD	CW2	W-2205726	0358	2
WAYT MURL R	CW2	W-2142118	1154	1
WEADER RICHARD J	LTC	0-0356456	0858	1
WEADOCK LEO V	LTC	0-1105256	1064	1
WEAKLAND PAUL A	MAJ	C-1822843	0962	1
WEAKLEY CHARLES L	LTC	0-0174655	C361	3
WEAKLEY KENNETH C	MAJ	0-0254749	0666	3
WEAPPA RUEBEN A	MAJ	C-1544280	1059	1
WEAR JOHN E	2LT	0-1042202	1144	2
WEAR JR THEODORE G	LTC	0-0219206	1062	3
WEARE BUEL F	COL	0-0321667	C163	3
WEARE HAROLD G	LTC	0-0294864	1167	3
WEARLEY DAVID A	LTC	0-1304469	C967	1
WEARS HENRY J	MAJ	0-0330525	0157	1
WEASE ARMON E	MAJ	C-0347233	0746	2
WEASNER NELSON	2LT	0-1317711	1044	2
WEATHERBEE CLIFFORD	CW2	W-2151522	0764	1
WEATHERFORD EDWARD E	COL	C-1575251	0464	1
WEATHERFORD VENUS L	MAJ	0-0380149	C346	1
WEATHERFORD WILLIA	CPT	0-1687879	1145	2
WEATHERLEY JOSHUA W	CPT	0-0402450	1043	2
WEATHERLY CARROLL O	MAJ	0-0498143	0645	1
WEATHERLY ROBERT L	MAJ	0-2000143	0267	1
WEATHERRED PRESTON A	B G	C-0170749	0648	3
WEATHERS DON R	1LT	0-0378211	0244	2
WEATHERS JR ARTHUR F	MAJ	0-0958797	0264	1
WEATHERS NED S	MAJ	0-0914257	0155	2
WEATHERS ROBERT M	LTC	0-1001272	0161	1
WEATHERS ROY L	CW2	W-2210033	0164	1
WEATHERS UDELL H	2LT	C-0977238	0251	1
WEAVER ALVIN C	CW2	W-3100499	1067	1
WEAVER ARTHUR F	LTC	0-0179380	0652	1
WEAVER ARTHUR T	LTC	0-1650796	0866	1
WEAVER BARRETT M	MAJ	C-1286574	0557	1
WEAVER BURR S	MAJ	0-0127585	0949	3
WEAVER CARL H	MAJ	0-0483541	0650	1
WEAVER CECIL H	2LT	0-1823805	C145	2
WEAVER DAVID E	MAJ	0-0513306	0163	1
WEAVER DAVID K	CW4	W-2141696	0756	1
WEAVER DIXON N	CW3	W-2147568	1162	1
WEAVER EDWARD K	1LT	0-0576630	0746	2
WEAVER EDWIN M	MAJ	0-0984973	0164	1
WEAVER ELLSWORTH	LTC	0-0275446	C863	3
WEAVER FLOYD A	MAJ	0-1686525	1060	1
WEAVER FLOYD E	MAJ	0-1172705	1054	1
WEAVER FOREST K	MAJ	0-2033075	1062	1
WEAVER FRANK M	COL	0-0236358	0266	3
WEAVER GENE A	CPT	0-1309633	0647	2
WEAVER GEORGE E	LTC	0-0922371	C862	3
WEAVER HARRY L	LTC	0-0419958	1060	1
WEAVER HEBRON T	MAJ	0-1167270	0557	1
WEAVER HENRY P	CPT	0-0520853	0844	1
WEAVER HOWARD E	MAJ	0-2001793	1064	1
WEAVER JAMES H	COL	0-0302379	0267	3
WEAVER JAMES H	CW3	W-2144863	0661	1
WEAVER JAMES L	CPT	0-1544268	0860	1
WEAVER JAMES P	1LT	0-0919447	1045	2
WEAVER JEROME M	1LT	0-1876619	1057	2
WEAVER JOHN H	MAJ	0-0249200	1057	2
WEAVER JOHN H	LTC	0-1105258	0559	1
WEAVER JOHN M	LTC	0-1648903	1266	1
WEAVER JOHN N	1LT	0-0455174	0847	1
WEAVER JOHN W	CPT	0-1597189	C862	2
WEAVER JR WILLIAM G	CPT	0-C547051	0763	1
WEAVER KENNETH R	2LT	0-1013182	1044	2
WEAVER LUTHER T	WO1	W-2123124	1050	2

NAME	GRADE	SVC NO	DATE RET MO YR	RET CODE
WEAVER MALCOLM	1LT	0-1109735	1045	2
WEAVER MARY A	CPT	N-0757887	0247	1
WEAVER RALPH E	LTC	0-1165262	1061	1
WEAVER RAYMOND J	1LT	0-1323882	C845	2
WEAVER REX W	MAJ	C-0427632	1045	2
WEAVER RICHARD W	LTC	0-0423877	0256	2
WEAVER ROBERT J	CPT	0-1302356	0448	2
WEAVER RUSSELL W	CW3	W-2143731	0163	1
WEAVER STANLEY C	1LT	0-1030432	0445	2
WEAVER THOMAS D	LTC	0-0221667	C950	3
WEAVER WALTER L	MAJ	C-0452559	0361	1
WEAVER WILLIAM G	COL	C-0156430	0560	3
WEAVER WILLIAM L	CPT	0-1109736	0352	2
WEAVER WILLIAM N	LTC	0-0423308	C767	3
WEAVER WILLIAM T	LTC	0-0271300	0467	3
WEAVER WILLIAM W	MAJ	C-1050130	0361	1
WEAVER WILLIAM W	CW3	W-2150031	0964	1
WEAVERLING M ELIZA	2LT	N-0700105	0141	1
WEBB ALBERT E	1LT	0-0374609	1043	2
WEBB ARCHIBALD	LTC	0-0368668	0967	3
WEBB CARL F	CPT	0-1046984	0346	2
WEBB CHARLES B	CW2	W-2211074	0867	1
WEBB CHARLES H	LTC	0-0288797	0167	3
WEBB CHARLES J	MAJ	C-1011990	0761	1
WEBB CHARLES W	MAJ	0-0979361	0663	1
WEBB CLIFFORD G	1LT	0-1821659	0964	1
WEBB DENNIS	LTC	0-1288981	0861	1
WEBB EARL M	CPT	0-0524470	0750	1
WEBB FAIN E	1LT	0-0302063	0643	2
WEBB FRANK M	LTC	0-1553196	0762	1
WEBB HAROLD C	MAJ	0-1003069	0557	1
WEBB HARRY J	COL	0-0253525	0365	3
WEBB HENRY L	LTC	0-0334211	0262	1
WEBB HERBERT E	1LT	0-1578017	0845	2
WEBB IRA V	MAJ	0-0164232	0944	2
WEBB JACKSON S	CPT	0-1320081	0146	2
WEBB JAMES A	COL	C-0185637	1152	3
WEBB JAMES B	COL	0-0243564	1265	3
WEBB JAMES F	2LT	0-1012635	0451	2
WEBB JAMES H	CW2	RW-2205402	1263	1
WEBB JOHN B	B G	0-0244400	0264	3
WEBB JOHN B	LTC	0-0374127	0165	1
WEBB JOHN F C	CPT	0-0505021	0161	1
WEBB JR CHARLES M	COL	0-0195539	0762	3
WEBB JR HOMER C	MAJ	0-1016442	1064	1
WEBB JR ROY	CPT	0-1317061	0552	1
WEBB JR THOMAS W	LTC	0-0379233	0867	1
WEBB JR WILLIAM C	MAJ	C-0334571	0160	1
WEBB JYLES L	1LT	0-0591291	0954	2
WEBB LAWRENCE G	CW3	W-2105433	1057	1
WEBB LESTER F	COL	0-0336719	1166	3
WEBB LLOYD E	MAJ	0-1947850	0457	1
WEBB MILBURNE	COL	0-0917129	0564	3
WEBB NANCY S	2LT	N-0734968	0945	1
WEBB OSWALD W	LTC	0-1548590	0162	1
WEBB PAUL L	COL	0-0234849	0859	1
WEBB RALPH L	COL	0-0287714	1059	2
WEBB RAYMOND E	CPT	0-0385322	1155	1
WEBB ROBERT O	2LT	0-2035171	0445	2
WEBB ROBERT E	CPT	0-1999386	0948	1
WEBB ROBERT H	MAJ	0-0963222	0566	1
WEBB THOMAS M	2LT	0-1168512	0745	2
WEBB WALTER J	1LT	0-0109253	0542	1
WEBB WARREN H	CPT	0-4031022	1067	1
WEBB WAYNE S	1LT	0-0514049	0445	2
WEBB WILLARD	B G	0-0341298	1163	3
WEBB WILLIAM M	LTC	0-0415782	0766	1
WEBB WILLIAM M	MAJ	0-1289842	1060	1
WEBB WILLIAM V	MAJ	0-0503635	0954	1
WEBBEN JAMES H	1LT	0-1016173	0745	2
WEBBER BERT W	LTC	0-1339680	1167	1
WEBBER CHARLES C	COL	0-0245223	1059	3
WEBBER FRANK R	MAJ	C-0464230	1148	1
WEBBER GEORGE L	LTC	0-0235375	0646	2
WEBBER HAROLD W	CW4	W-2102522	0659	1

NAME	GRADE	SVC NO	DATE RET MO YR	RET CODE
WEBBER JAMES E	MAJ	C-1579277	C557	1
WEBBER JAMES M	CW3	W-2107069	0359	1
WEBBER JOHN B	2LT	0-1308412	1144	2
WEBBER PAUL L	CPT	0-0969256	1057	1
WEBBER ROBERT M	CPT	0-0343087	1045	2
WEBBERE GEORGE A	LTC	0-1045965	C962	1
WEBBLEY FREDERICK	COL	C-0202624	0658	3
WEBER ALBERT	MAJ	0-1299501	0457	1
WEBER ALBERT F 3	MAJ	0-1057303	0164	1
WEBER ALVAN J	LTC	0-1183444	1265	1
WEBER ALVIN E	LTC	0-1575253	0563	1
WEBER ARTHUR J	LTC	C-1844498	1162	1
WEBER CHARLES H	1LT	C-1015172	0846	2
WEBER CORNELIUS	CPT	0-1319044	0547	2
WEBER DAVID E	LTC	0-0262492	0661	3
WEBER EDMUND	MAJ	C-1000297	0756	1
WEBER EDMUND W	LTC	0-0312161	0659	3
WEBER EDWARD T	LTC	0-1011916	0864	1
WEBER EMILE D	CW3	W-2146748	0565	1
WEBER ETHEL H	CPT	N-0736721	0356	2
WEBER GEORGE E	CPT	0-2263690	0862	1
WEBER GORDON P	LTC	0-0289996	0967	3
WEBER HAROLD T	B G	0-0171181	1153	3
WEBER HENRY P	LTC	0-1821794	0666	1
WEBER HERMAN J	LTC	0-0135688	0648	3
WEBER JACOB B	CPT	0-0521494	0950	1
WEBER JAMES L	CPT	0-2055475	C647	2
WEBER JOHN	LTC	0-1543549	0364	1
WEBER JOSEPH J	CW2	W-2151826	0356	1
WEBER JR HARRY R	LTC	0-0309428	0965	3
WEBER KALMAN E	CPT	0-1284795	C947	2
WEBER KARL T	MAJ	0-1560395	0761	1
WEBER KENNETH A	LTC	0-1894720	1165	1
WEBER KENNETH J	LTC	0-1588354	1066	1
WEBER LEONARD J	MAJ	0-1119780	1162	1
WEBER LEROY E	COL	0-0266441	0255	2
WEBER LOUIS S	LTC	0-0370821	0166	3
WEBER LYNN C	LTC	C-1558224	0662	1
WEBER REGINALD T	COL	0-0346214	C557	1
WEBER RICHARD H	LTC	0-1105673	0661	1
WEBER RICHARD M	CPT	0-0215630	0342	2
WEBER STANLEY P	MAJ	0-1642703	C659	1
WEBER WALTER C	LTC	0-0168194	0660	3
WEBER WAYNE V	CW3	W-2153661	1265	1
WEBER WILFRED H	COL	0-0205528	1058	3
WEBER WILLIAM H	CW2	W-2000912	0444	2
WEBERT ALTON J	2LT	0-5704553	C761	2
WEBSTER ALBERT A	MAJ	0-1533467	C953	1
WEBSTER ALFRED D	LTC	0-0374495	0960	1
WEBSTER ARTHUR C	MAJ	0-0215309	0461	3
WEBSTER BELTON O	CW3	W-2119407	C762	1
WEBSTER DONALD M	LTC	0-0315405	C662	3
WEBSTER EDWARD S	MAJ	0-0203954	C257	3
WEBSTER ELBERT M	LTC	0-0156291	0150	3
WEBSTER FORREST U	LTC	0-0174536	0356	3
WEBSTER FREDERICK	MAJ	C-0370294	0946	2
WEBSTER GEORGE M	LTC	0-0512238	0463	3
WEBSTER GLEN M	COL	0-0104557	C459	3
WEBSTER GLENN R	MAJ	0-2008085	0461	1
WEBSTER HAROLD G	1LT	0-1305140	0547	2
WEBSTER HENRY W	CW3	W-2203064	0166	1
WEBSTER HERSHELL F	CW2	W-3350125	1060	1
WEBSTER JACK M	CPT	0-1285153	0246	2
WEBSTER JACKSON D	CPT	0-0519984	C147	2
WEBSTER JR ASBURY	CW2	W-3200341	0666	1
WEBSTER JR CARLOS G	COL	0-0246882	1158	3
WEBSTER JR DORSEY L	CPT	0-0315091	0845	2
WEBSTER JR JOSEPH A	1LT	0-1284616	0745	2
WEBSTER LAURENCE A	MAJ	C-1014153	1264	1
WEBSTER LAWRENCE B	LTC	0-0450518	1155	1
WEBSTER LEONARD E	COL	0-0256186	0560	3
WEBSTER MAURICE W	LTC	0-1311833	0862	1
WEBSTER NOEL E	MAJ	0-1101266	0358	1
WEBSTER NORMAN A	MAJ	0-0263319	0845	2
WEBSTER REMINGTON	LTC	0-1101711	1162	1

NAME	GRADE	SVC NO	DATE RET MO YR	RET CODE
WEBSTER ROBERT B	CPT	0-1307112	0147	2
WEBSTER ROBERT W	LTC	0-0387216	0860	1
WEBSTER THEODORE J	CPT	0-1294398	0559	2
WEBSTER WILLIAM B	LTC	0-1111425	0664	1
WEBSTER WILLIAM H	LTC	0-0403992	0546	2
WEBSTER WILLIAM R	LTC	0-0418835	0767	1
WEBSTER WILLIAM V	LTC	0-0260528	0456	3
WECHSLER GEORGE J	1LT	0-1321563	1044	2
WECHSLER LOUIS J	CPT	0-0109044	0127	1
WECKER JOHN F	MAJ	C-0962160	0163	1
WEDDLE CHARLES D	CPT	0-0487820	C845	2
WEDDLE LEROY R	CPT	0-0409304	1045	2
WEDDUM FOLMER	1LT	0-2055850	1044	2
WEDGE CHARLES D	CPT	0-2C19537	0761	1
WEDMORE ARTHUR R	1LT	0-0500912	1053	2
WEEBER RICHARD P	LTC	0-0338555	0662	3
WEED CHARLES A	MAJ	0-1285524	1047	2
WEED JOHN H	MAJ	0-1848621	0863	1
WEED MAHLON S	B G	0-0231252	1159	3
WEEDEN JACK W	MAJ	0-1290691	0261	1
WEEDMAN GEORGE C	MAJ	C-2262701	0463	1
WEEDON HUGH H	LTC	0-0918574	0255	2
WEEKES LEROY R	MAJ	0-0331270	0447	2
WEEKES WILLIAM F	CPT	0-0480553	0755	1
WEEKLEY CHARLES E	WO1	W-2125238	0246	2
WEEKLEY ROBERT O	2LT	0-0136455	0646	2
WEEKLY III HERBERT S	CPT	0-1307336	0547	1
WEEKS ARTHUR E	LTC	0-0966105	C766	1
WEEKS BENJAMIN J	1LT	0-1586997	0262	1
WEEKS BILLY J	CW3	W-2206514	0666	1
WEEKS CARL A	LTC	0-1054860	0964	1
WEEKS CARL G	CPT	0-0384879	0348	2
WEEKS CLYDE E	MAJ	0-0212904	1043	2
WEEKS GEORGE W	COL	0-0345668	1264	3
WEEKS HOWARD L	LTC	0-0371516	0361	1
WEEKS HUBERT	LTC	0-0215475	0564	3
WEEKS JAMES F	CPT	0-0961057	0564	2
WEEKS JOHN S	COL	0-0268074	0864	3
WEEKS JOSEPH W	CPT	0-2263133	0367	1
WEEKS JR ELBERT W	LTC	0-0110712	1043	2
WEEKS JR FRANK D	MAJ	C-1650387	0463	1
WEEKS JR MALVIN H	CPT	0-0923749	C147	2
WEEKS JR THEODORE W	CPT	0-0435181	0246	2
WEEKS LEE R	CPT	0-1331580	0154	2
WEEKS MARVIN E	CPT	0-1574362	0749	1
WEEKS MARVIN L	CPT	0-1014595	0946	2
WEEKS PAUL A	1LT	0-1299329	0146	2
WEEKS RICHARD B	COL	0-0247C99	0962	3
WEEKS ROBERT P	MAJ	0-1548591	1060	1
WEEKS ROLAND L	LTC	0-1058685	C263	1
WEEKS WALLACE W	CPT	0-0339408	0944	2
WEEKS WILL O	2LT	0-1056941	0545	2
WEEKS WILLIAM W	LTC	0-1557392	0463	1
WEELDREYER CARL J	LTC	0-0452153	0358	1
WEEMS DAVID A	1LT	0-0476883	1044	2
WEEMS MALLORY P	CPT	0-1685103	1046	2
WEEMS TROY E	LTC	0-0280552	0747	1
WEEMS WARREN R	CW2	W-2149134	0863	1
WEES DALE R	LTC	0-077788C	0966	1
WEESE CHARLES H	CPT	0-0405846	0749	1
WEESE JACK	MAJ	0-0256706	0353	3
WEESE LAWRENCE L	CPT	0-1938079	1264	1
WEESE MABEL C	1LT	N-0730889	0645	1
WEEST HARRY W	COL	0-0171630	1154	3
WEETMAN HAROLD R	COL	0-0300344	0761	1
WEFEL ROBERT L	CW3	W-2148943	0665	1
WEFLER JOHN C	MAJ	0-1920252	0165	1
WEGE HANS F	LTC	0-0275181	1060	1
WEGERSKI MYRON A	CPT	0-1306500	1058	2
WEGHORST RICHARD H	CPT	0-0914985	0647	2
WEGLOSKI ADAM F	LTC	0-1642706	0163	1
WEGNER ELMER L C	LTC	0-0243811	0645	2
WEGNER ELMER R	LTC	0-1040636	1161	1
WEGNER FRANKLIN J	LTC	0-1646693	0466	1
WEGNER WILLIAM A	MAJ	0-0274704	0354	3

NAME	GRADE	SVC NO	DATE RET MO YR	RET CODE
WEHLING MARTIN P	COL	0-0242785	0-53	1
WEHRER FRANK E	CPT	0-1300558	1046	1
WEHRHEIM JAMES A	1LT	0-0422202	0446	2
WEIBELT JR AUBREY J	CW3	W-2206515	1165	1
WEIBY EDWIN O	1LT	0-1113044	0454	2
WEICHEL FREDERICK	LTC	0-1288334	1060	1
WEICHSELDORFER W H	CPT	0-2008532	0257	1
WEICKERT HAROLD N	LTC	0-0169153	1060	3
WEIDEMAN FRANK A	CPT	0-1579280	0845	2
WEIDENHAMER JOHN P	CPT	0-0506834	0544	1
WEIDERHOLC FRED E	LTC	0-2036718	0867	1
WEIDMAN HARVEY O	MAJ	0-0890422	0846	1
WEIDMAN JAY G	CPT	0-0550041	0946	2
WEIDNER JOHN J	CPT	0-2097003	0667	1
WEIDNER JOHN M	LTC	0-0309356	0861	3
WEIDNER WARREN W	LTC	0-0277385	0857	3
WEIDNER WILLIAM J	1LT	0-0491462	0344	1
WEIDT GEORGE W	LTC	0-1015590	1064	1
WEIGEL HENRY S	MAJ	0-0194492	0662	3
WEIGEL WILMER F	CPT	0-1647324	0846	1
WEIGELE HAROLD A	LTC	0-0423567	0866	3
WEIGHTMAN LLOYD E	LTC	0-0289917	1060	3
WEIGHTMAN RICHARD H	LTC	0-0363409	0866	1
WEIGHTMAN WILLIAM R	COL	0-0188217	0858	3
WEIGLE GERALD V	COL	0-0364468	1047	2
WEIGLEY WAYNE M	CW4	W-2119276	0655	1
WEIH HANS	CPT	0-1891188	0463	1
WEIHE MARVIN A	MAJ	0-0317762	0445	2
WEIHING GEORGE J	1LT	0-0515800	0645	1
WEIHRAUCH OTHMAR H	LTC	0-1291202	1064	1
WEIKEL IVAN W	MAJ	0-0304190	1146	2
WEIKEL THOMAS E	CPT	0-2262411	0161	1
WEIKEL WALTER D	COL	0-0253296	0663	3
WEIKER CARL	CW4	W-2006659	0862	3
WEIL ALBERT H	LTC	0-0244859	0866	3
WEIL ANDRE F	2LT	0-1031985	0245	2
WEIL CHARLES F	LTC	0-0230998	0665	3
WEIL CHARLES F	CW3	W-2147925	0363	1
WEIL JAMES M	MAJ	0-0486214	0353	1
WEIL JR SOL B	CPT	0-0463209	1143	2
WEIL LEONARD L	CPT	0-0480187	0845	2
WEIL LESTER H	CPT	0-0507076	0257	3
WEIL LUDWIG J	CW4	W-2127588	0461	1
WEIL MONROE J	1LT	0-1580484	0645	1
WEILAND HERMAN G	CPT	0-1634451	0345	2
WEILAND THOMAS	MAJ	0-1922706	1166	1
WEILAND THOMAS J	MAJ	0-0450942	0363	1
WEILENMANN CHARLES	CPT	0-0510068	0846	1
WEILER GEORGE W	1LT	0-1319045	0844	2
WEILER NORBERT E	CPT	0-1288148	0545	2
WEILER RICHARD P	CPT	0-1015104	0446	2
WEILER ROBERT J	LTC	0-1548160	0561	1
WEILER WILLIAM F	B G	0-0237255	0256	3
WEIMAN JOHN R	CW3	W-2209399	1266	1
WEIMANN GUSTAVE H	COL	0-0387741	1160	1
WEIMAR EARL E	LTC	0-0191894	1045	2
WEIMAR WILLIAM C	MAJ	0-1644205	0243	1
WEIMER ROBERT G	CW2	W-2210581	0366	1
WEIN ARTHUR B	CPT	0-0416532	0246	2
WEIN JOHN A	CW3	RW-2145119	0763	1
WEINARD EARL R	MAJ	0-1181499	0265	1
WEINBERG JEROME	MAJ	0-2035183	0455	1
WEINBERG JOSEPH A	MAJ	0-0206467	1145	2
WEINBERG MORRIS L	1LT	0-1308738	0246	2
WEINBERG SYDNEY G	LTC	0-0354790	0865	3
WEINBERG WILLIAM J	CPT	0-0350842	0545	2
WEINBERGER HOWARD J	MAJ	0-0416505	0146	2
WEINBERGER MARTIN I	1LT	0-0538970	0546	2
WEINBERGER SIDNEY	2LT	0-1998345	1045	2
WEINBRENNER BILLIE M	MAJ	L-0800255	0864	1
WEINER BERTRAM T	LTC	0-1698119	0966	1
WEINER ELI	1LT	0-1105261	0945	2
WEINER HARRY H	MAJ	0-0247325	0544	1
WEINER JACOB	1LT	0-0497566	0644	2
WEINER JOSHUA H	CPT	0-0419458	0346	2
WEINER LEON	1LT	0-0529190	0745	1
WEINER SAM F	CPT	0-0418464	1145	2
WEINER SAMUEL D	1LT	0-1325611	0246	2
WEINER STANLEY	LTC	0-0416200	1046	2
WEINER WELFORD H	1LT	0-1575627	0745	2
WEINFELD JOSEPH S	LTC	0-0391647	0167	3
WEINFIELD ALLAN	LTC	0-1012022	1061	1
WEINGAR WILLIAM H	LTC	0-0234327	0648	3
WEINGART ROBERT A	CPT	0-1825517	0664	2
WEINGARTEN F W	MAJ	0-0345764	1144	2
WEINGARTNER VICTOR J	CPT	0-1307901	0249	2
WEINGAST HARRY	1LT	0-1321006	0245	2
WEINHEIMER HOWARD F	LTC	0-1166646	0667	1
WEINMEISTER OSCAR K	CW4	W-2142540	0265	1
WEINRICH ARTHUR J	MAJ	0-2016981	1061	1
WEINRICH ROBERT J	1LT	0-0308206	0144	2
WEINSCHEL GEORGE	CPT	0-1557234	1045	2
WEINSHELBAUM SAMUEL	MAJ	0-0966692	1161	1
WEINSTEIN BARNETT	COL	0-0265620	1166	3
WEINSTEIN EDWARD A	1LT	0-1052207	1157	1
WEINSTEIN HYMAN W	CPT	0-0503424	1045	2
WEINSTEIN ISRAEL	LTC	0-0218277	0546	2
WEINSTEIN LEO	1LT	0-1307902	0645	2
WEINSTEIN LEO S	CPT	0-1691146	0845	2
WEINSTEIN LEWIS H	COL	0-0507972	0565	3
WEINSTEIN LOUIS J	COL	0-0324753	0767	3
WEINSTEIN MAX V	1LT	0-0545360	0545	2
WEINSTEIN MAXWELL	CPT	0-0508044	1049	1
WEINSTEIN MORRIS J	1LT	0-1579281	0545	2
WEINSTEIN ROBERT	2LT	0-1118675	0245	2
WEINSTEIN SAMUEL H	CPT	0-1301731	0546	2
WEINSTEIN STANLEY	CPT	0-1697039	0545	2
WEINSTOCK CHESTER E	LTC	0-1557108	1264	1
WEINTRAUB ARTHUR	MAJ	0-0494195	0947	2
WEINTRAUB HENRY J	MAJ	0-0368312	0750	2
WEINTRAUB I IRVING	MAJ	0-0421436	0950	2
WEINTRAUB SOLOMON	COL	0-0249911	0459	3
WEINTROB JOSEPH	LTC	0-0907032	0163	3
WEIR BROCK M	1LT	0-1300735	0145	2
WEIR DICK R	MAJ	0-0307290	1048	1
WEIR EDWARD R	LTC	0-1596849	0665	3
WEIR JAMES A	LTC	0-1586340	0862	1
WEIR NORMAN L	MAJ	0-0371589	0760	1
WEIR ROBERT L	MAJ	0-0351444	0646	2
WEIR RUSSELL R	MAJ	0-0242124	0964	3
WEIR THOMAS L	CW4	W-2127000	0665	3
WEIR THOMAS C	LTC	0-0476854	0756	1
WEIR TRUETT	LTC	0-1551986	1165	1
WEIR WILLIAM H	COL	0-0192948	0561	3
WEIRICH ALFRED F	COL	0-0261534	0358	1
WEIRICH JR COLIN R	WO1	W-2149001	1059	1
WEIS JOSEPH F	CPT	0-1184440	0248	1
WEISBERG HERBERT	LTC	0-0454551	0465	2
WEISBLUM JOSEPH	LTC	0-0338149	0767	3
WEISENBERG JOSEPH	MAJ	0-0281144	0148	1
WEISENHORN PAUL G	COL	0-0122063	0452	3
WEISER CONRAD W	CPT	0-0466558	0245	1
WEISER JOSEPH	LTC	0-0331492	1162	2
WEISER LEMOINE O	MAJ	0-0334671	0945	2
WEISERT WILSON G	1LT	0-0447308	0745	2
WEISFELD JOSEPH J	1LT	0-0541378	0745	2
WEISGERBER ADOLPH F	1LT	0-0233737	1148	3
WEISHAUPT ROSEMARY E	1LT	N-0743020	0546	1
WEISHEIT ARTHUR J	LTC	0-1109740	0854	1
WEISHEIT LENAS G	MAJ	0-2023757	0661	1
WEISKIRCHER ERNEST H	MAJ	0-0218153	0461	3
WEISLER HERMAN L	COL	0-0482613	0367	3
WEISLER JOHN C	LTC	0-0502723	0256	1
WEISLO EDMUND	2LT	0-1298467	1043	2
WEISMAN EDWIN	MAJ	0-1102995	0248	1
WEISMAN IRVING	2LT	0-1595254	0544	2
WEISMAN JACOB I	CPT	0-0382637	0143	2
WEISMAN PAUL G	LTC	0-0235318	0750	3
WEISMAN SAMUEL A	MAJ	0-0169539	0544	2
WEISS ALBERT E	1LT	0-1316265	0851	1
WEISS ANGELA D	CPT	N-0756113	0746	1
WEISS ARTHUR M	LTC	0-0234465	0759	3
WEISS BARRY L	2LT	0-4038648	0157	2
WEISS BERNARD	LTC	0-0399746	1061	2
WEISS DAVID	MAJ	0-0319528	0546	2
WEISS GEORGE A	LTC	0-0481080	0365	3
WEISS GEORGE H	LTC	0-0454620	0364	1
WEISS HAROLD W	COL	0-0288394	0161	1
WEISS HARRY	MAJ	0-1690493	0246	2
WEISS HERMAN S	MAJ	0-1312368	0261	1
WEISS HORTON C	MAJ	0-1053010	0859	1
WEISS JAMES E	MAJ	0-0355663	0346	1
WEISS JOHN F	1LT	0-1597957	0352	1
WEISS JULIUS E	2LT	0-1310905	1045	2
WEISS LOUIS R	COL	0-0309633	0566	3
WEISS MALCOLM P	CPT	0-0467258	0447	2
WEISS MARY I P	2LT	N-0736784	0845	1
WEISS PEARL	LTC	L-0200176	1162	1
WEISS PHILIP H	2LT	0-1169820	0144	2
WEISS RICHARD J	LTC	0-0291748	0861	1
WEISS SAMUEL	LTC	0-0463023	0450	1
WEISS SHELDON	1LT	0-0542204	0946	2
WEISS THOMAS G	LTC	0-0920384	1265	3
WEISS THOMAS W	LTC	0-1280036	1057	1
WEISS VICTOR R	LTC	0-0317137	0851	1
WEISS WILLIAM D	MAJ	0-0495046	1146	2
WEISSELBERGER DAVID	1LT	0-0543770	0945	2
WEISSENBURGER LAWREN	LTC	0-1822222	0866	1
WEISSER LILLIAN	2LT	N-0723868	0346	1
WEISSHAUS STANLEY Z	LTC	0-0333750	0562	3
WEISSKOPF RAYMOND	LTC	0-1541513	0361	1
WEISSMAN JOSEPH I	LTC	0-0167200	0656	2
WEISSMAN PAUL	1LT	0-1945075	0345	2
WEISSMAN PHILIP	1LT	0-1648229	0346	2
WEISSMANN HARRY M	CW4	W-2106717	0660	1
WEISZ WALTER S	CPT	0-0446228	0344	2
WEITFLE PAUL L	COL	0-0236527	0760	3
WEITZ MARTIN L	MAJ	0-0238991	0447	1
WEITZEL BERNARD J	CPT	0-1690891	1055	1
WEITZEL GLADYS T	1LT	N-0736497	1046	1
WEITZEL THEODORE R	MAJ	0-0492213	1154	1
WEITZEL WILLIAM A	LTC	0-0215457	1060	3
WEITZMAN LEONARD	1LT	0-0541746	0547	2
WEITZMANN ALBERT M	CPT	0-1579288	0745	2
WEIX JEROME J	MAJ	0-0991361	0163	1
WEKALL OLIVER C	COL	0-0350326	0867	3
WEKER MEYER	LTC	0-1798631	0866	3
WELBORN DOROTHY	2LT	N-0755239	0744	1
WELBORN JAMES H	1LT	0-1324378	1045	2
WELBORN ROBERT T	MAJ	0-0156633	0254	3
WELBOURN ROY E	CPT	0-1821795	0960	2
WELCH BRENT A	MAJ	0-0300645	0545	2
WELCH CARROLL	LTC	0-1546709	0857	1
WELCH CHARLES E	MAJ	0-0913710	0164	3
WELCH CHARLES E	MAJ	0-1053868	0265	1
WELCH CLARENCE W	LTC	0-0445749	0763	1
WELCH CLAUDE L	MAJ	0-0306217	0945	2
WELCH DAVID J	LTC	0-0222288	1156	3
WELCH EDWARD W	CPT	0-1284254	1051	1
WELCH EMMETT J	LTC	0-0404522	0162	1
WELCH ERNEST R	COL	0-0223425	1164	3
WELCH FELIX P	MAJ	0-0259583	0966	3
WELCH FREDERICK	MAJ	0-0964063	0464	1
WELCH FREDERICK	1LT	0-1331582	0152	1
WELCH GARY R	CPT	0-4062023	0467	2
WELCH HAROLD A	CW3	W-2149850	0161	1
WELCH HAROLD E	LTC	0-0453937	0562	1
WELCH ISABELLE E	MAJ	L-0603794	1065	1
WELCH JAMES L	CPT	0-1319690	0647	1
WELCH JAMES W	CW2	W-2213792	0966	1
WELCH JOHN	LTC	0-1011887	0465	1
WELCH JOHN G	MAJ	0-0954066	0264	1
WELCH JOHN J	MAJ	0-0390211	0456	1
WELCH JOHN M	COL	0-0220140	0664	3
WELCH JOHN W	MAJ	0-0269329	0367	3
WELCH JR FRANCIS W	MAJ	0-1081540	0759	1
WELCH JR HARRY F	2LT	0-1996372	0745	2
WELCH JR WILFORD W	MAJ	0-1696774	0964	1
WELCH JR WILLIAM H	MAJ	0-0411642	1147	2
WELCH LEO J	LTC	0-0807371	1067	1
WELCH LEROY L	MAJ	0-1305356	0556	2
WELCH LESTER C	LTC	0-0491158	0457	1
WELCH MARY A	2LT	N-0773545	0645	1
WELCH MARY L	MAJ	N-0756005	0566	1
WELCH NED W	MAJ	0-1110335	0861	1
WELCH NORBERT F	LTC	0-1590255	1167	3
WELCH PARRIS C	MAJ	0-1171296	0361	1
WELCH RAYMOND	LTC	0-1301393	0158	1
WELCH REX M	CPT	0-1686610	0560	1
WELCH RICHARD D	LTC	0-0273052	0155	2
WELCH RICHARD F	COL	0-0225556	1056	3
WELCH ROBERT Z	MAJ	0-1180089	1159	1
WELCH ROGER M	LTC	0-1585068	0162	1
WELCH THOMAS C	MAJ	0-0321915	1064	1
WELCH WALLACE C	MAJ	0-0450140	1160	1
WELCH WILLIAM E	COL	0-0246762	0760	1
WELCH WILLIAM I	COL	0-0321778	0755	1
WELCHER ALEXANDER	LTC	0-0355496	1063	1
WELCHER CLARENCE G	MAJ	0-1634455	0457	1
WELCHER ROBERT E	MAJ	0-0966684	0967	1
WELCHMAN PHILIP J	LTC	0-1588955	0962	1
WELCOME EARL H	COL	0-0176655	0648	3
WELD GEORGE S	MAJ	0-0125880	0159	3
WELD STEPHEN M	MAJ	0-0178368	0162	3
WELDEN JAMES W	MAJ	0-1181186	1061	1
WELDON CHARLES N	CPT	0-0492162	0260	3
WELDON GEROLD W	CW2	W-2144712	1159	1
WELDON JOSEPH O	CW2	W-3430091	1066	1
WELDON MARCUS D	LTC	0-0228649	1060	3
WELOY MAX W	1LT	0-0359495	1042	1
WELGE LOUIS A	1LT	0-0914329	0946	2
WELGEHAUSEN KURT A	LTC	0-0260882	1266	3
WELK EDWARD	1LT	0-0509497	0646	1
WELKER HAROLD L	1LT	0-1305507	0246	2
WELKER JOHN H	WO1	W-2105321	0645	2
WELKER RUSSELL J	2LT	0-2030204	1046	2
WELKER WINIFRED S	2LT	N-0703317	1144	1
WELL JULIUS W	MAJ	0-0518752	0346	2
WELLEN CLYDE W	LTC	0-0153627	1052	3
WELLENS ALBERT G	1LT	0-0395641	0446	2
WELLER GEORGE M	CPT	0-0211192	0855	3
WELLER MALCOLM R	MAJ	0-0330579	1266	3
WELLER MILFORD F	1LT	0-1320677	0845	2
WELLER NELLE B	2LT	N-0728541	0244	1
WELLER VICTOR C	1LT	0-1057305	0446	2
WELLES CHARLES B	COL	0-0197204	0961	3
WELLES EDWARD M	1LT	0-1534657	1144	2
WELLES GUY B	LTC	0-0250490	1052	3
WELLHAUSEN FRED C	LTC	0-1110336	0462	1
WELLHOUSE WILLIAM T	2LT	0-0461274	1043	2
WELLING ARTHUR L	MAJ	0-0195154	1047	1
WELLING ARTHUR W	CPT	0-0355195	1144	2
WELLING GRANT M	LTC	0-1648868	0367	1
WELLING HOWARD C	COL	0-0286765	1159	1
WELLINGTON L C	CPT	0-0517304	1144	2
WELLIVER DELBERT C	CPT	0-1795829	1060	1
WELLMAN CLARA J	2LT	N-0703219	1042	1
WELLMAN JOHN M	COL	0-0240354	0466	3
WELLMAN ROY W	MAJ	0-0286457	0454	2
WELLMAN WALTER J	COL	0-0321450	0960	1
WELLS ARLAND R	MAJ	0-0294256	1145	2
WELLS AUSTIN L	COL	0-0505505	0866	3
WELLS BILLY G	MAJ	0-1882262	0867	1
WELLS CARL O	COL	0-0371591	0765	1
WELLS CATHERINE	CPT	N-0751715	0547	1
WELLS CECIL A	1LT	0-2042849	0357	1
WELLS CECIL E	CW2	W-2120774	0244	2
WELLS CHARLES	MAJ	0-0479113	0748	1
WELLS CHARLES A	MAJ	0-1306781	1063	1
WELLS CHARLES G	CPT	0-0233803	0860	3

NAME	GRADE	SVC NO	DATE RET MO YR	RET CODE
WELLS CLARENCE R	MAJ	0-0454181	1145	2
WELLS CLYDE E	CW2	W-2207382	0661	1
WELLS COYE L	1LT	0-1315991	1145	2
WELLS DAMON	CW2	W-2148136	0361	1
WELLS DANIEL W	2LT	0-1550087	0945	2
WELLS DON L	COL	0-0113702	0650	3
WELLS EBEN A	COL	0-0261502	0166	3
WELLS EDMOND J	CPT	0-0986721	0761	1
WELLS EDWARD S	LTC	0-1030435	1164	1
WELLS ELBERT E	LTC	0-0360730	0655	1
WELLS EUGENE O	COL	0-0116586	0348	2
WELLS FLOYD J	LTC	0-0486875	0657	1
WELLS GAREY M	LTC	0-0494525	0159	1
WELLS GEORGE	MAJ	0-0279450	0359	3
WELLS GEORGE H	COL	0-0310267	0367	3
WELLS GEORGE T	CPT	0-0489925	0855	1
WELLS HANSEL P	1LT	0-0359470	0149	2
WELLS HARVEY F	MAJ	0-1013975	0761	1
WELLS HARVIE L	1LT	0-0490202	1054	1
WELLS HERBERT A	LTC	0-0270704	0866	3
WELLS II ADDISON E	COL	0-0268175	1161	3
WELLS III GEORGE I	CW2	W-2210956	0567	1
WELLS JACKSON H	2LT	0-1686335	0745	1
WELLS JAMES A	COL	0-0264061	0766	3
WELLS JAMES C	CPT	0-0220753	0751	3
WELLS JAMES C	CPT	0-1795018	0953	2
WELLS JAMES E	MAJ	0-0956787	0867	1
WELLS JAMES F	MAJ	0-1107226	1147	2
WELLS JAMES H	CPT	0-0212794	0646	2
WELLS JAMES P	LTC	0-1284439	1061	1
WELLS JAMES R	COL	0-0190401	1050	3
WELLS JAMES R	CPT	0-0890028	0846	1
WELLS JAMES T	CPT	0-1301732	0747	2
WELLS JEANNE A	1LT	N-0730791	0845	1
WELLS JOSEPH L	COL	0-0224442	0360	3
WELLS JR ALBERT W	CPT	0-1285154	0861	1
WELLS JR JOHN W	LTC	0-1010863	0661	1
WELLS LEONARD A	MAJ	0-1797398	0657	1
WELLS LESLIE S	COL	0-0272769	1266	3
WELLS LOUIS R	MAJ	0-1824828	0260	1
WELLS LOUISE F	LTC	N-0724264	0963	1
WELLS PAUL D	MAJ	0-1824543	0265	1
WELLS PAUL I	LTC	0-0415386	1060	1
WELLS PAUL K	LTC	0-0558290	0867	1
WELLS RALPH H	LTC	0-0250504	0546	2
WELLS RAY A	MAJ	0-2024268	0959	1
WELLS RICHARD C	COL	0-0355119	1063	3
WELLS RICHARD L	1LT	0-1284617	0144	2
WELLS ROBERT A	CPT	0-0402762	0145	2
WELLS ROBERT S	CW2	W-2152990	1064	1
WELLS ROYCE V	CPT	0-1012154	0663	1
WELLS RUDOLPH G	CPT	0-1922556	0365	1
WELLS RUSSELL L	LTC	0-1055499	0564	1
WELLS SHELDON R	LTC	0-1013185	1166	1
WELLS SIDNEY J	MAJ	0-0900452	0845	2
WELLS SOPHIA G	1LT	N-0799575	0949	1
WELLS THEODORE H	MAJ	0-1704141	0962	1
WELLS THOMAS H	CW2	W-2141489	0955	1
WELLS THORNLEY F	LTC	0-0243829	0861	3
WELLS WELDON R	LTC	0-0349739	0854	1
WELLS WILLIAM H	CW2	W-2144727	0457	1
WELMS LOUIS C	CW3	W-2151817	0665	1
WELSBY ALBERT	1LT	0-1295804	0946	2
WELSCH CATHERINE	1LT	N-0767247	0845	1
WELSCH CHARLES C	LTC	0-0215389	0562	3
WELSCH GLENN A	MAJ	0-0450943	0446	2
WELSCH HAROLD T	COL	0-0302603	0964	3
WELSCH HENRY	CW3	W-2114809	1053	1
WELSCH JULIAN	LTC	0-0324764	0463	3
WELSH ALBERT C	COL	0-0256622	1058	3
WELSH CHARLES H	MAJ	0-1312612	0761	1
WELSH DON M	MAJ	0-0102502	0844	2
WELSH FRANCIS E	CW3	W-2208788	0467	1
WELSH GEORGE B	LTC	0-0333512	0863	3
WELSH JOHN H	MAJ	0-0100852	1053	3

NAME	GRADE	SVC NO	DATE RET MO YR	RET CODE
WELSH LOIS C	MAJ	L-0900048	0962	1
WELSH MAYME P	MAJ	N-0756904	0465	1
WELSH ROBERT F	1LT	0-1313704	0247	2
WELSH SPURGEON F	COL	0-0269623	1166	3
WELSH STEPHEN S	MAJ	0-0451199	1057	1
WELSH WALTER	LTC	0-0495216	1054	1
WELSH WILLIAM W	LTC	0-0214175	1162	3
WELSHANS ALBERT H	CW3	W-2149002	0566	1
WELSON MORRIS L	1LT	0-0166367	0255	3
WELTE EUGENE J	COL	0-0206300	0661	3
WELTER VALERIAN	CW3	W-2006753	0967	3
WELTMER WILLIAM E	CPT	0-0109839	0735	1
WELTON THEODORE M	1LT	0-0391171	0246	2
WELTSCH LEO D	MAJ	0-0970536	1166	1
WELTY ELMER E	COL	0-0246986	1066	3
WELTY JOHN A	CPT	0-0540844	0347	2
WELTY KENNETH D	CPT	0-0506753	0145	2
WELTZIN CLARENCE W	MAJ	0-0133156	0-51	3
WELZBACHER DAMPTHA N	1LT	N-0772422	1045	1
WEMPA ROBERT F	1LT	0-4045022	065	2
WEMPLE JOHN F	COL	0-0177564	1061	3
WENBORNE ARTHUR S	LTC	0-0386037	0566	1
WENDEL ALFRED W	MAJ	0-1301394	0461	1
WENDEL DAVID D	COL	0-0167763	0859	3
WENDELIN CARL G	LTC	0-0267329	1065	3
WENDELKEN HERBERT	COL	0-0324420	0767	3
WENDELL ARNOLD H	CPT	0-1574178	0946	2
WENDELL CHARLES A	COL	0-0288189	0859	3
WENDELL JR LEWIS C	MAJ	0-2020092	0162	1
WENDLAND RICHARD H	LTC	0-1291363	0766	1
WENDLE CORNELIUS	MAJ	0-0331601	1145	2
WENDLING EDGAR C	CW3	W-2143538	0860	1
WENDLING ROBERT L	CPT	0-1284066	1045	2
WENDLINGER HAROLD M	LTC	0-2208505	0667	1
WENDORF JR DENVER F	1LT	0-1327064	0447	2
WENDT CHARLES F	1LT	0-1579291	0346	2
WENGER EDWARD J	LTC	0-0920483	0466	3
WENGER RENE L	LTC	0-0285555	0960	3
WENGERT ROBERT R	MAJ	0-1544612	0863	1
WENIG BERNARD	2LT	0-1894486	1144	2
WENK FREDERICK	CPT	0-0141368	0358	3
WENNER ARTHUR M	1LT	0-1291204	0145	2
WENNER CHARLES	MAJ	0-1545172	0157	1
WENNERGREN VIRGIL J	LTC	0-1017396	0664	1
WENNERHOLM NORMAN J	1LT	0-1596542	0250	1
WENNINGER GEORGE L	LTC	0-0918510	0866	3
WENRICH JAMES R	LTC	0-0902044	0663	3
WENRICH JOHN W	LTC	0-1950667	0564	1
WENT JAMES T	1LT	0-1013061	0450	1
WENTHOLD RALPH J	MAJ	0-1691932	0860	1
WENTWORTH EDWARD T	COL	0-0190620	0648	3
WENTWORTH HARRY R	MAJ	0-0385169	0561	1
WENTWORTH JR N N	CPT	0-0361487	0745	2
WENTWORTH RICHARD O	MAJ	0-1886591	0766	1
WENTWORTH-ROHR R J	MAJ	0-0472305	0146	2
WENTZ ARTHUR E	1LT	0-1794890	0145	2
WENTZ CHARLES J	LTC	0-1018922	1262	1
WENTZ ISABEL M	1LT	N-0725629	0945	1
WENTZ LUTHER A	WO1	W-2134018	0645	2
WENTZ RALPH C	1LT	0-1031600	0947	1
WENTZ RAYMOND D	MAJ	0-0887544	1063	1
WENTZ WILLIAM G	LTC	0-0444404	0556	1
WENZEL CARL L	CPT	0-4005865	1066	2
WENZEL ROBERT J	1LT	0-1014456	0556	1
WENZEL RUSSELL A	LTC	0-0368786	0254	2
WENZEL VICTOR	CW2	W-2001980	0662	3
WENZEL WALTER J	LTC	0-0278743	0457	3
WENZLER RAYMOND E	MAJ	0-2262407	1163	1
WERBA DANIEL R	LTC	0-0233870	0159	3
WERBLOW SOL C	CPT	0-1683858	1145	1
WERDER ROBERT F	1LT	0-1324076	0146	2
WERES JAMES	CPT	0-1696119	0146	2
WERLINGER LOUIS J	MAJ	0-0422588	0854	1
WERLY EMIL F	LTC	0-0258156	1064	3
WERMINE CARL F H	CPT	0-0382174	1055	2

NAME	GRADE	SVC NO	DATE RET MO YR	RET CODE
WERMUTH FLOYD	CPT	0-0938000	1156	2
WERNDLE FRANK G	MAJ	0-2033276	0464	2
WERNE JOHN L	MAJ	0-1686275	0261	1
WERNENTIN EDWIN G	LTC	0-0202129	0962	3
WERNER ADRIAN F	COL	0-0127786	0255	3
WERNER ARNOLD B	CW3	W-2150034	0762	1
WERNER DONALD E	CPT	0-1049693	0656	1
WERNER EDWARD A	LTC	0-1638770	0663	1
WERNER EMILE W	CPT	0-1324307	0248	2
WERNER ERNEST J	CW4	W-2002451	0965	3
WERNER FRANCIS J	MAJ	0-1580493	0247	2
WERNER FRED A	LTC	0-0340185	0562	1
WERNER HAROLD C	LTC	0-1336461	0665	1
WERNER HAROLD W	MAJ	0-1885663	0567	1
WERNER HARRY	CW3	W-2104578	0161	1
WERNER HARRY E	COL	0-0407582	0660	1
WERNER JOHN	MAJ	0-0510888	0954	1
WERNER JOHN A	MAJ	0-1049017	0361	1
WERNER LAWRENCE C	CPT	0-1557596	0446	2
WERNER MAX	CPT	0-0496424	1045	2
WERNER RICHARD J	COL	0-0219225	0246	2
WERNER ROBERT M	LTC	0-0990809	0266	1
WERNER WILLIAM M	MAJ	0-0978450	0867	1
WERNER WILLIAM P	LTC	0-1320575	0962	1
WERNSMAN LAWRENCE J	MAJ	0-1297816	0263	1
WERONECKI STANLEY A	1LT	0-1301065	0745	2
WERP JOSEPH	LTC	0-0404351	0960	1
WERRELL ANGUS J	COL	0-0201549	0754	3
WERRLEIN WILLIAM J	1LT	0-1823734	0747	2
WERSCHLER WALTER F	CPT	0-0942970	0658	1
WERSICK WILLIAM K	CPT	0-0504834	1048	1
WERSING RICHARD F	LTC	0-0538484	0567	1
WERSKEY PAUL F	MAJ	0-1686551	0160	1
WERTH CLARA J	CPT	N-0730200	0746	1
WERTHEIMER PHILIP	LTC	0-0261535	0567	3
WERTS MERRILL H	1LT	0-0552126	0346	2
WERTZ CLYDE E	LTC	0-1045968	0361	1
WERTZ WILLIAM J	COL	0-0338413	1056	3
WERTZBERGER JAMES C	CPT	0-1311716	0465	1
WESELEY LOUIS J	CPT	0-1689399	0650	2
WESLEY EARLIN	CPT	0-4005166	0563	1
WESLEY JOSEPH G	2LT	0-1012450	0650	2
WESNER CHARLES T	MAJ	0-0276309	0267	3
WESNER DEAN C	MAJ	0-1886498	0967	1
WESNER IRENE R	1LT	N-0724437	0646	1
WESNER JAMES E	CW2	W-2214867	0866	1
WESNOUSKY WILLIAM	MAJ	0-2262770	0262	1
WESOLOWSKI JOSEPH A	LTC	0-0367458	1057	1
WESSA EDWIN L	CPT	0-0203451	0159	3
WESSLING ALFRED L	MAJ	0-0131345	0648	3
WESSLING JR ANDREW L	LTC	0-1032664	0562	1
WESSMAN PHILIP H	MAJ	0-2210216	0964	1
WESSMANN MARGARET Y	1LT	N-0724764	0146	2
WESSON BILLY H	MAJ	0-1998394	1160	1
WESSON HAROLD L	CW2	W-2215368	1266	1
WESSON NATHANIEL	CW2	W-2144084	1159	1
WESSON ROY A	LTC	0-0281887	1265	3
WESSON RUFUS	COL	0-0341835	1146	1
WESSON WILLIAM T	CPT	0-0394485	0447	1
WEST ALFRED C	MAJ	0-0921511	1145	2
WEST ALTHEA L	2LT	N-0736202	0245	1
WEST BAIRD F	LTC	0-0239916	0165	3
WEST CLARENCE	CPT	0-1046686	0863	2
WEST CLYDE G	MAJ	0-1030947	0161	1
WEST DON L	1LT	0-1010866	0645	1
WEST DOROTHY A	LTC	L-0304599	0163	1
WEST EARL W	CW3	W-2146798	1064	1
WEST ELMER J	LTC	0-0290082	0959	3
WEST EUGENE N	CPT	0-0440798	0445	2
WEST FLOYD H	MAJ	0-2046523	0254	1
WEST FRANCIS C	LTC	0-0486722	1054	1
WEST FRANK H	MAJ	0-0257572	0155	3
WEST FRANK J	LTC	0-1289179	0954	1
WEST GEORGE B	COL	0-0239114	1047	2
WEST GEORGE G	COL	0-0125872	1059	3

NAME	GRADE	SVC NO	DATE RET MO YR	RET CODE
WEST GERALD V	CPT	0-2289279	0462	1
WEST GILBERT E	MAJ	0-0252452	0166	3
WEST GORDON H	1LT	0-1011715	0545	1
WEST HARLEY B	M G	0-0268317	0463	3
WEST HAROLD R	CW4	W-2115175	0756	1
WEST HENRY E	MAJ	0-2019826	1262	1
WEST HORACE W	MAJ	0-2005251	1160	1
WEST HUGH S	LTC	0-0264197	0145	2
WEST JAMES R	CW2	W-2141920	0561	1
WEST JAMES F	LTC	0-0909618	1264	3
WEST JAMES F	LTC	0-1166207	0164	1
WEST JESSE W	LTC	0-0430960	0756	1
WEST JOHN L	MAJ	0-1044147	0959	1
WEST JOHN P	LTC	0-0186415	0352	3
WEST JOHN V	CPT	0-1011517	0650	2
WEST JOHN W	CPT	0-0373964	0646	2
WEST JOHN W	MAJ	0-1895516	0156	1
WEST JOSEPH W	B G	0-0235499	0853	3
WEST JR EDWARD	CPT	0-1015537	0546	2
WEST JR GEORGE J	CPT	0-1573662	0945	2
WEST JR HENRY D	1LT	0-0460016	0545	2
WEST JR HERBERT	CW3	W-2143980	1262	1
WEST JR JAMES B	1LT	0-1303065	0745	2
WEST JR MELVIN E	CW2	W-2206948	1062	1
WEST JR PERRY	LTC	0-1177694	0762	1
WEST JR ROLAND D	LTC	0-1327909	1166	1
WEST KEITH L	MAJ	0-0974117	0266	1
WEST KENNETH	CPT	0-2033039	0958	1
WEST KENNETH B	MAJ	0-0956698	0261	1
WEST KENNETH L	LTC	0-0372363	1164	1
WEST KENNETH C	MAJ	0-1032406	0462	1
WEST KENT W	MAJ	0-1107228	0863	1
WEST LAWRENCE F	MAJ	0-1951565	0762	1
WEST LEO E	LTC	0-1310356	0762	1
WEST LEO K	CW4	RW-2122647	0163	1
WEST LIONEL M	LTC	0-0262765	0560	3
WEST LISLE C	MAJ	0-2023951	1064	1
WEST LUKE H	LTC	0-1038319	1061	1
WEST MADELINE L	1LT	N-0744516	0646	2
WEST MARGARET N	2LT	N-0760155	0944	1
WEST MITCHELL	CW4	W-2142557	1262	1
WEST NELLIE R	CW3	V-0400063	1162	1
WEST NORMAN E	CW2	W-2151653	0662	1
WEST ORLY F	CPT	0-0500133	0157	1
WEST PAUL O	WO1	W-2104579	1043	2
WEST PERCY L	LTC	0-0342829	0263	3
WEST RALEIGH B	1LT	0-1017462	0246	1
WEST RAYMOND T	COL	0-0335450	0465	3
WEST ROBERT	MAJ	0-2055793	0951	1
WEST THEODORE M	LTC	0-1283885	0667	1
WEST THOMAS R	LTC	0-0488555	0947	1
WEST WARREN K	CW3	W-2152754	1164	1
WEST WAYNE G	COL	0-0281804	0858	1
WEST WILBUR M	2LT	0-1173828	0545	2
WEST WILLIAM J	CW2	W-2210469	0865	1
WEST WILLIAM R	CW2	W-2145848	0959	1
WEST WILLIAM S	CPT	0-0381589	0246	2
WEST WILLIE B	CW3	W-2143546	0859	1
WEST WILLIE P	2LT	0-1047386	0746	2
WESTALL THAD E	CW3	W-2150258	0664	1
WESTALL WALTER S	LTC	0-0278818	1157	3
WESTBERG ALVIN L	CW2	W-2147057	0363	1
WESTBERRY JR K F	1LT	0-0315253	0346	2
WESTBERRY MCCLOHON	WO1	W-2139975	0745	2
WESTBROCK CHARLES C	CPT	0-0314260	1145	2
WESTBROOK BERTELLA C	2LT	N-0723335	0844	1
WESTBROOK CHARLES W	MAJ	0-1114802	0862	1
WESTBROOK JAMES A	MAJ	0-0271488	0246	2
WESTBROOK JOSEPH W	LTC	0-0295056	0667	3
WESTBROOK MILDRED O	1LT	L-0405057	0650	1
WESTBROOK WILLIAM G	LTC	0-1051440	0762	1
WESTBROOKE WILLIAM E	LTC	0-0510106	0557	1
WESTBURY JOSEPH E	COL	0-0292227	0562	1
WESTBY GEORGE R	CPT	0-1281433	0246	2
WESTCOTT EDWIN T	MAJ	0-2262766	0465	1

ARMY OF THE UNITED STATES RETIRED LIST

NAME	GRADE	SVC NO	DATE RET MO YR	RET CODE
WESTCOTT GARDNER W	CW3	W-2151933	1162	1
WESTCOTT MARVIN C	CW2	W-2143979	0855	1
WESTENBERGER RALPH G	CW3	W-2142784	C761	1
WESTENBROEK ABEL B	CW4	W-2151085	0556	1
WESTER BILLY I	CW3	W-2152522	0565	1
WESTER JOHN A	COL	C-0336806	0762	1
WESTER JOHN D	MAJ	0-0924929	0146	2
WESTER JOHN W	LTC	0-0147805	C852	3
WESTERDAHL ANDREW W	LTC	0-1015065	1262	2
WESTERFIELD CHARLES	MAJ	0-2014525	0367	1
WESTERFIELD JAMES R	LTC	0-0214002	0155	3
WESTERFIELD ROY A	MAJ	C-0163350	0648	3
WESTERGARD PAUL J	CPT	0-0245185	C656	3
WESTERHOLM HAROLD S	MAJ	C-1685533	C963	1
WESTERMAN ACES M	CPT	0-1293686	0647	2
WESTERMAN EDWARD J	LTC	0-0267607	0751	1
WESTERMAN FRANCIS H	COL	0-0246765	1162	3
WESTERMAN FRANK C	MAJ	C-1917987	1264	1
WESTERMAN GEORGE F	1LT	0-0334302	0245	2
WESTERMAN MYRON P	LTC	0-2206200	C766	1
WESTFALL LACY R	COL	0-0369908	1065	3
WESTFALL RUDOLPH E	LTC	0-0317566	0564	3
WESTFALL THEODORE R	MAJ	0-0223504	0348	2
WESTFALL WILLIAM M	LTC	0-0205588	1163	3
WESTHALL HAROLD G	LTC	0-1102997	0464	1
WESTHEIMER SAMUEL	LTC	C-1313004	1166	3
WESTHOLM ROBERT L	LTC	0-1559997	0466	1
WESTMAN GEORGE E	LTC	0-0225940	1156	3
WESTMORE HAL G	1LT	0-1307596	1163	1
WESTMORELAND GRADY W	MAJ	C-0145740	0356	3
WESTMORELAND JAMES B	LTC	0-0315677	0660	1
WESTMORELAND JAMES B	CPT	0-0540403	1147	2
WESTMORELAND JOHN C	MAJ	0-2018962	1063	1
WESTMORELAND JOHN F	LTC	0-1294227	C861	1
WESTNEDGE JOSEPH S	2LT	0-0425942	1043	2
WESTON CLARENCE F	2LT	0-1574553	0643	2
WESTON FRED S	LTC	0-1039259	0763	1
WESTON GIFFORD L	COL	0-0242563	1160	1
WESTON GILBERT B	1LT	0-1286217	C944	2
WESTON HARRY B	CPT	0-0204446	0251	3
WESTON JAMES F	1LT	0-2012602	1157	1
WESTON JEROME C	CW3	W-2143981	0562	1
WESTON JOHNSTON W	1LT	C-1287096	0747	2
WESTON JULIAN R	COL	0-0197888	C263	3
WESTON LEON G	LTC	0-2036348	0463	1
WESTON MARION F	1LT	0-0945876	0351	1
WESTON MICHAEL E	LTC	0-0307690	0667	3
WESTON ROBERT T	1LT	0-0286027	C647	1
WESTON STANLEY A	CW3	W-2148272	0660	1
WESTON STANLEY J	CPT	0-0325530	0146	2
WESTON WILLIAM A	MAJ	C-0975494	C764	1
WESTON WILLIAM J	LTC	0-0256198	0962	3
WESTPHAL RICHARD C	MAJ	0-1103461	1166	1
WESTPHAL WILLIAM A	1LT	0-1017141	0546	2
WESTRICK ALFRED A	COL	0-0266467	C964	3
WESTWOOD RAYMOND S	LTC	0-1293687	1165	1
WETHERBEE LOWELL A	MAJ	C-0959340	C165	1
WETHERED THEODORE J	MAJ	C-1304154	0264	1
WETHERELL WINTON W	LTC	0-0183677	C360	3
WETHERHOLT JOHN P	COL	0-0199828	1056	3
WETHERINGTON C J	CPT	0-1280391	1053	2
WETHERINGTON LONNIE	LTC	0-1798053	C463	1
WETHINGTON RAYMOND L	LTC	0-1176847	1264	1
WETHINGTON THOMAS H	CW3	W-2142669	0659	1
WETTERAU JOHN A	CPT	0-0505633	C946	1
WETTERAUER DONALD G	LTC	0-0240928	1264	3
WETTIG PAUL R	LTC	0-0129699	0648	3
WETTLAUFER JULES L	COL	C-0427825	C853	1
WETZEL EDWARD G	LTC	C-0262426	C167	3
WETZEL GEORGE L	CPT	0-0314064	0747	2
WETZEL HAROLD B	MAJ	C-1553753	0361	1
WETZEL HAROLD F	LTC	0-0337882	1045	2
WETZEL JAMES J	CW3	W-2205725	1166	1
WETZEL JAMES W	LTC	0-0475484	0564	3
WETZSTEIN ARNOLD L	CPT	0-0975471	1058	1
WEXLER CHARLES	LTC	0-0923008	0866	3
WEXLER MONROE L	LTC	0-0384343	1064	3
WEYAND FOSTER H	COL	C-0274177	0259	1
WEYAND JAMES C	LTC	0-0504569	0367	3
WEYAND MELVIN J	2LT	C-1288476	0445	2
WEYENETH NORRIS E	1LT	0-1175359	1046	2
WEYER JR GEORGE S	LTC	0-1105910	1059	1
WEYHE WILLIAM L	CPT	0-0257619	0357	3
WEYMANN COVERT	LTC	C-0204363	0253	3
WEYRICK JOSEPH B	1LT	0-1288477	0664	1
WEYRICK LEROY	COL	0-0165766	0851	3
WHAITE GILBERT G	WO1	W-2148512	1059	1
WHALEN CHANDLER M	CW3	W-2142729	0161	1
WHALEN CHARLES J	CPT	0-1292098	0358	1
WHALEN DONALD H	LTC	0-2055212	0863	1
WHALEN EMMETT M	CPT	0-1052626	0448	1
WHALEN HERBERT W	CPT	0-0249548	0465	3
WHALEN JAMES J	1LT	0-1300425	C646	2
WHALEN JOHN A	CW3	W-2144795	0164	1
WHALEN JOHN J	MAJ	0-0396617	1147	2
WHALEN PAUL	MAJ	C-1120523	0163	1
WHALEN ROBERT J	CPT	0-1549632	1044	2
WHALEN THOMAS F	LTC	0-1294947	0165	1
WHALEN THOMAS J	LTC	0-0242224	0255	3
WHALEN WILLIAM L	COL	0-2052273	1166	1
WHALEY HARRY F	LTC	0-0156740	0452	3
WHALEY JAMES L	COL	0-0223887	C859	3
WHALEY ROBERT S	CPT	0-0977461	1060	1
WHALEY THOMAS F	MAJ	0-1955189	1057	1
WHALEY WILLIAM B	CPT	0-0491438	0156	2
WHANG JAMES H S	CPT	0-1640118	0562	1
WHARTON JAMES H	CPT	0-0463950	0245	2
WHARTON JUDSON K	MAJ	C-2008336	0662	1
WHARTON RAEBURN J	COL	C-0137202	0952	3
WHARTON THOMAS	MAJ	0-0319324	1047	1
WHARTON THOMAS J	CPT	0-0313114	0447	1
WHARTON WALTER W	CW4	W-2105882	0459	1
WHARTON WILLIAM G	COL	0-0918375	0158	3
WHATES JOHN	CPT	0-1692585	0455	1
WHATLEY JACK W	CPT	0-2204435	0664	1
WHATLEY JOHN C	MAJ	C-0281161	1166	3
WHATLEY MARGARET I	CPT	L-0403211	1048	1
WHATLEY THOMAS B	LTC	0-0481137	0953	2
WHATLEY WILLIAM W	LTC	0-1108414	0961	2
WHATTON RICHARD T	MAJ	0-1321574	0261	1
WHEAT ELLIS F	1LT	0-1318730	0845	1
WHEAT GEORGE F R	CPT	0-0143206	1154	3
WHEAT JAMES D	CPT	0-5408586	0763	2
WHEAT JOHN O	CPT	0-1544441	0346	1
WHEAT JOHN R	LTC	0-1013066	1163	1
WHEAT LLOYD F	2LT	0-0531147	0844	2
WHEAT OSCAR G	LTC	0-0213350	1262	3
WHEAT RALPH M	CPT	0-1324966	C746	2
WHEAT ROBERT L	MAJ	0-1634460	0258	1
WHEAT WILLIAM T	2LT	0-0921451	0144	2
WHEATCROFT JOHN A	MAJ	0-1303973	0567	3
WHEATLAND FERN R	CPT	0-0289007	0462	1
WHEATLEY CHARLES W	MAJ	0-4030563	0367	1
WHEATLEY JEFFERSON	WO1	W-2115442	0254	1
WHEATLEY JOHN H	MAJ	0-0239212	0466	3
WHEATLEY TERRENCE R	CW3	W-2136682	1059	1
WHEATLY LEONARD S	MAJ	0-1313836	0664	1
WHEATON JR HARRY M	2LT	0-1002150	1043	2
WHEATON RODRICK K	COL	0-0370694	0861	1
WHEATON SIDNEY L	COL	0-0182548	0656	3
WHEELOCK JR ROBERT H	LTC	0-0372526	0857	1
WHEELOCK MILO	MAJ	0-0259685	C158	3
WHEELER ARTHUR L	MAJ	0-0378602	1046	2
WHEELER BURDETTE J	LTC	0-1002749	1062	1
WHEELER CALVIN W	CPT	0-0528927	1046	2
WHEELER CARL C	CW3	W-2145535	0163	1
WHEELER CARLTON L	MAJ	0-0122895	0648	3
WHEELER CHARLES R	CPT	0-0401742	0144	2
WHEELER CHESTER L	2LT	0-0448776	0445	2
WHEELER DONALD O	CW2	W-2125210	0148	1
WHEELER DUANE E	CPT	0-2263033	0464	1
WHEELER EDGAR W	LTC	0-0309112	0659	3
WHEELER ELDEN L	LTC	0-0228626	C265	3
WHEELER EWELL N	LTC	0-0420855	0666	1
WHEELER FRANCIS R	MAJ	C-1055505	0865	1
WHEELER FRED K	CPT	0-1551776	1055	2
WHEELER HAROLD E	CW3	W-2141490	0761	1
WHEELER HARRY M	COL	0-0245838	0563	3
WHEELER HOWARD J	LTC	0-0922438	C967	3
WHEELER ISHAM C	1LT	0-0198723	0657	3
WHEELER JACK J	CW3	W-2205623	0464	1
WHEELER JAMES E	1LT	0-1300426	114N	2
WHEELER JAMES H	LTC	0-0421404	1060	1
WHEELER JAMES H	1LT	0-1785551	0545	2
WHEELER JAMES M	CW4	W-2121028	1154	1
WHEELER JOHN	LTC	0-1644898	1163	1
WHEELER JOHN F	CPT	0-1015325	C546	1
WHEELER JOHN P	CPT	0-1285861	C347	2
WHEELER JOHN R	MAJ	C-1031695	C564	1
WHEELER JOHN S	COL	0-0296955	0264	3
WHEELER JOHN W	COL	0-0118291	0553	3
WHEELER JOSEPH	2LT	0-1913998	0615	1
WHEELER JOSEPH J	MAJ	0-1588363	C262	1
WHEELER JR EDWARD W	MAJ	C-0395322	C158	1
WHEELER JR FRANK T	MAJ	0-0133050	0750	3
WHEELER JR JOHN P	CW3	W-2143679	0862	1
WHEELER JR RUFUS H	MAJ	C-1946636	0460	1
WHEELER JR WILLIAM C	LTC	0-1107230	1060	1
WHEELER JUSTUS B	CPT	0-0389153	1145	1
WHEELER LELAND E	LTC	0-0184471	0755	3
WHEELER LEO G	CPT	0-0473185	C245	2
WHEELER LUTHER C	MAJ	C-0333922	0756	1
WHEELER MYRON F	MAJ	0-1580497	C465	1
WHEELER NICHOLAS A	MAJ	0-0468175	C246	2
WHEELER OLIVER R	CW2	W-3200274	0167	1
WHEELER ORVILLE R	1LT	0-1328778	C248	2
WHEELER PAUL A	MAJ	C-0756767	C862	1
WHEELER RAYMOND R	CPT	0-0492984	0847	1
WHEELER RICHARD E	CW3	W-2144205	1058	1
WHEELER ROBERT M	MAJ	0-0408739	1061	1
WHEELER THOMAS R	COL	C-1284067	0966	1
WHEELER WALTER L	MAJ	C-1338766	1164	1
WHEELER WILBUR A	CW3	W-2153282	0665	1
WHEELER WILLIAM E	MAJ	0-0143845	C447	2
WHEELER WILLIAM F	1LT	0-1313359	C854	1
WHEELER WILLIAM R	MAJ	0-1169390	1160	1
WHEELER WILLIAM W	LTC	0-0104054	0850	1
WHEELOCK WILLIAM N	CPT	0-0261242	1059	3
WHEELWRIGHT EDMUND M	MAJ	0-1053870	1060	1
WHEELWRIGHT MARTHA	1LT	N-0727443	0745	2
WHEETING LAWRENCE C	LTC	0-0180842	0356	3
WHEIR IONE M	CW3	V-0912088	0763	1
WHELAN JAMES R	LTC	0-0200631	0546	2
WHELAN JOHN F	LTC	0-1823808	0766	1
WHELAN JOSEPH A	LTC	C-0210479	0560	3
WHELAN JOSEPH A	COL	0-0309072	C766	3
WHELAN THOMAS A	LTC	0-0247577	0366	3
WHELAN THOMAS J	1LT	0-1003652	C246	2
WHELDON MAURICE A	LTC	0-0281788	0954	2
WHELESS JAMES A	LTC	0-0326732	C461	3
WHELESS JOHN R	CPT	0-0488659	1049	1
WHERLEY CHARLES W	1LT	C-1014625	1045	2
WHERLEY RICHARD D	2LT	0-2006312	1145	2
WHERRETT WILLIAM V	MAJ	C-0165208	0649	1
WHERRY BYRON T	MAJ	C-0115679	0648	3
WHERRY RALPH A	1LT	0-1289521	0345	1
WHETHAM MAURICE F	1LT	C-1288831	1045	2
WHETSEL ROBERT C	MAJ	C-1796390	1060	1
WHETSELL JACOB W	CW4	W-2146099	0159	1
WHETSTINE CHARLES F	MAJ	C-1877802	1163	1
WHETZEL JOSHUA C	MAJ	0-0151674	0653	3
WHICHARD WILLIS K	LTC	0-0475267	0955	1
WHICHER AGNES S	2LT	N-0700117	0337	1
WHIDDEN JAMES J	MAJ	0-2263160	1061	1
WHIDDEN JR RALEIGH J	CW3	W-2206013	0764	1
WHIDDON ERNEST C	1LT	0-1043833	0645	2
WHIDDON FRANK M	LTC	0-0189750	0253	3
WHILDEN ALBERT F	LTC	C-1111979	1062	1
WHILDEN JR HARRIS	CW2	W-2152663	0967	1
WHIPP LEE A	2LT	0-1317713	0944	2
WHIPPEN LEONARD S	CPT	0-0133053	0850	3
WHIPPLE FLOYD M	MAJ	C-1550088	0461	1
WHIPPLE FREDERICK	LTC	0-1183216	0564	1
WHIPPLE IVAN C	COL	0-0412327	0857	2
WHIPPLE JAMES F	WO1	W-2107187	1048	1
WHIPPLE JAMES G	LTC	0-0402076	0263	1
WHIPPLE KENNETH E	CW2	W-3150185	1165	1
WHIPPLE LESTER S	LTC	0-0156606	0256	3
WHIPPLE ROBERT A	LTC	0-2018805	0566	1
WHIPPLE ROBERT S	LTC	0-0241811	0560	3
WHIPPLE THEODORE W	CW3	W-2152571	0263	1
WHIPPS GILBERT F	CPT	0-0415202	0546	2
WHISENANT JAMES H	LTC	0-1056943	1165	1
WHISENANT WILLIAM L	LTC	0-1596224	0967	1
WHISENHUNT HOWELL O	1LT	0-1292969	0345	2
WHISENHUNT JOHN M	LTC	0-1548595	0261	1
WHISLER NELO T	1LT	0-0495920	0249	1
WHISONANT FRANK	1LT	0-1540697	0346	2
WHISTLER JOHN K	MAJ	0-0312973	0859	1
WHITACRE ESTON J	LTC	0-0398326	0760	1
WHITAKER CHARLES C	1LT	C-0423296	0946	2
WHITAKER CLIFFORD W	COL	C-0222761	0159	3
WHITAKER DONALD O	LTC	0-1173116	0255	1
WHITAKER EUGENE G	CPT	0-0512038	0844	1
WHITAKER FRANK	MAJ	0-1320208	0759	1
WHITAKER HERBERT E	MAJ	C-0178479	1057	3
WHITAKER JOSEPH M	COL	C-0243178	0263	3
WHITAKER JR JOHN W	1LT	0-1291733	0545	2
WHITAKER JR LLOYD O	CPT	0-0386870	0460	1
WHITAKER LLOYD R	MAJ	0-1693136	0864	1
WHITAKER LYNN C	COL	0-0208925	0155	3
WHITAKER MILLARD H	WO1	W-2128829	1147	1
WHITAKER PAUL R	LTC	0-0348163	1165	1
WHITAKER WALTER L	LTC	0-1583831	0957	1
WHITAKER WARREN E	CW4	W-2145307	0559	1
WHITAKER WARREN S	MAJ	C-1590258	0265	1
WHITAKER WILLIAM	WO1	W-2124585	0745	2
WHITAKER WILLIS F	LTC	0-0141548	0757	3
WHITBECK PHILIP F	CPT	C-0292536	0945	2
WHITBREAD WALTER W	MAJ	0-1059681	0365	1
WHITBURN FANCHER K	COL	0-0280204	0961	1
WHITBY JR GERTHA L	CW4	W-2143780	0865	1
WHITCANACK JAMES A	MAJ	0-1318241	0359	1
WHITCHURCH ROY B	CPT	0-0488394	1047	1
WHITCHURCH THOMAS W	LTC	0-1104446	1164	1
WHITCOMB CECIL B	B G	0-0190131	0359	3
WHITCOMB CHARLES A	COL	C-0348387	1162	1
WHITCOMB CHARLES K	LTC	0-0303556	0662	1
WHITCOMB FRANCIS C	MAJ	0-1171831	0263	1
WHITCOMB HERBERT L	LTC	0-0121988	C250	3
WHITCOMB JR ARTHUR	2LT	0-2007752	1145	2
WHITCOMB LAURA M	CPT	N-0754671	0459	2
WHITCOMB RICHARD S	B G	0-0164276	1054	3
WHITCOMB ROBERT J	MAJ	0-1042463	1160	1
WHITCOMB RUTH	MAJ	N-0751626	1164	1
WHITCOMB WILMER R	CW3	W-2206396	0866	1
WHITE ADAMS R	CPT	0-0197907	0544	2
WHITE AILEEN D	1LT	N-0723853	1046	1
WHITE ALFRED C	LTC	0-1105701	1262	1
WHITE ALFRED C	CPT	0-1299321	1046	2
WHITE ALVIN A	CW2	W-2147840	1061	1
WHITE AMA M	1LT	0-1333912	0467	1
WHITE ARCHIE B	CPT	0-0509893	0460	1
WHITE ARCHIE M	LTC	0-0386506	0954	1
WHITE ARTHUR J	MAJ	C-1685638	1060	1
WHITE BERTRAM H	LTC	0-0366004	0546	2
WHITE BEVERLY G	CPT	0-1292621	0246	2
WHITE BOYCE J	CW4	W-2109448	1059	1
WHITE BURL V	LTC	0-2035024	1263	1
WHITE CARL D	2LT	0-2263210	0354	2

NAME	GRADE	SVC NO	DATE RET MO YR	RET CODE
WHITE CATHERINE	2LT	N-0760169	1045	1
WHITE CECIL R	2LT	0-0323745	0265	3
WHITE CECIL B	LTC	0-0450127	1057	1
WHITE CHARLES C	MAJ	0-1053016	0761	1
WHITE CHARLES E	MAJ	0-0967550	1062	1
WHITE CHARLES E	LTC	0-1302243	0264	2
WHITE CHARLES F	B G	0-0285841	1059	3
WHITE CHARLES F	1LT	0-0374028	0246	2
WHITE CHARLES J	CPT	0-0243309	1262	3
WHITE CHARLES J	LTC	0-1541270	0461	1
WHITE CHARLES L	CPT	0-0505486	0547	2
WHITE CHARLES R	LTC	0-1796391	0262	1
WHITE CHARLES R	CW3	W-2143078	1162	1
WHITE CLARENCE H	LTC	0-0119370	0655	2
WHITE CLARENCE L	MAJ	0-1105704	0662	1
WHITE CLAUDE H	LTC	0-0044029	1060	1
WHITE CLAUDE W	LTC	0-1038896	0963	2
WHITE CLEMMENSE	COL	0-0190079	0853	3
WHITE CLIFTON L	1LT	0-1595260	0647	2
WHITE CLYDE H	LTC	0-0384103	0760	1
WHITE DAVID A	1LT	0-1301734	0645	2
WHITE DEE M	COL	0-0271312	0155	3
WHITE DELMAS L	LTC	0-0425861	1058	1
WHITE DONALD D	1LT	0-0515283	0645	1
WHITE DONALD J	MAJ	0-4032693	0966	1
WHITE DOROTHY C	1LT	N-0720593	1045	1
WHITE DOUGLAS A	COL	0-0298955	0953	3
WHITE DOYLE	CW2	W-2150245	1057	1
WHITE EARL L	MAJ	0-0383244	0346	2
WHITE EDWARD A	MAJ	0-0524540	1054	1
WHITE EDWARD C	LTC	0-0962631	0667	1
WHITE EDWARD J	MAJ	0-0224173	0257	3
WHITE EDWIN D	1LT	0-1925141	0554	2
WHITE ENNIS L	COL	0-1001275	0767	1
WHITE EVERETT B	CPT	0-0942965	0859	1
WHITE FRANK A	LTC	0-0904039	1064	1
WHITE FRANK C	CW3	W-2150627	0957	1
WHITE FRANK E	MAJ	0-1575205	0261	1
WHITE FRANK G	LTC	0-0257636	0262	3
WHITE FRED R	CPT	0-1302399	0159	1
WHITE FREDERICK	LTC	0-0297497	0954	2
WHITE FREDERICK	MAJ	0-1312854	0365	1
WHITE GARVASE N	MAJ	0-0973190	0263	1
WHITE GEORGE C	1LT	0-1045324	1044	2
WHITE GEORGE L	1LT	0-0113681	1055	3
WHITE GEORGE L	LTC	0-1574365	0955	1
WHITE GEORGE S	1LT	0-0393540	0944	2
WHITE GILBERT L	CPT	0-0168730	0861	2
WHITE GRADY O	LTC	0-2274560	1065	1
WHITE HARRY B	MAJ	0-1287811	0257	1
WHITE HARRY C	LTC	0-0363614	0762	1
WHITE HARRY C	CW2	W-2147612	0964	1
WHITE HARRY H	CPT	0-0194186	1045	2
WHITE HARRY J	LTC	0-1797401	1062	1
WHITE HARRY L	COL	0-0133576	1148	2
WHITE HARRY V	CPT	0-0538862	1051	1
WHITE HARVEY E	MAJ	0-0345260	0246	2
WHITE HARVEY L	COL	0-0216796	0256	3
WHITE HENRY E	LTC	0-1533230	1057	3
WHITE HENRY G	LTC	0-0143462	0552	3
WHITE HENRY L	MAJ	0-0131657	0864	1
WHITE HENRY L	MAJ	0-1557238	1266	2
WHITE HENRY M	CW2	W-2141491	0561	1
WHITE HERBERT E	WO1	W-2109485	0547	2
WHITE HOMER	CW3	W-2143151	0263	1
WHITE HOMER H	MAJ	0-1185351	0258	1
WHITE HOWELL S	MAJ	0-0102372	1057	3
WHITE IRVIN	MAJ	0-1295970	0261	1
WHITE ISAAC E	CW3	W-2152938	0563	1
WHITE IVAN M	CW3	W-2205811	0766	1
WHITE J O	LTC	0-1296130	0761	1
WHITE JACK	LTC	0-0450944	1054	1
WHITE JACK	MAJ	0-1119732	1060	2
WHITE JACK E	MAJ	0-1636817	0961	1
WHITE JACK H	1LT	0-0375327	0246	2

NAME	GRADE	SVC NO	DATE RET MO YR	RET CODE
WHITE JAMES A	MAJ	0-0252999	0447	1
WHITE JAMES A	LTC	0-0302034	0959	1
WHITE JAMES A	MAJ	0-1340044	0663	1
WHITE JAMES E	1LT	0-0378461	0546	2
WHITE JAMES E	CPT	0-0492007	0746	2
WHITE JAMES L	CPT	0-1878591	0665	2
WHITE JAMES M	COL	0-0251611	1065	3
WHITE JAMES O	CPT	0-1994721	0157	1
WHITE JAMES P	CW4	W-2107128	0859	1
WHITE JAMES R	MAJ	0-0450337	0357	1
WHITE JAMES V	MAJ	0-1825725	0455	1
WHITE JAMES W	CW2	W-2150145	0662	1
WHITE JESSE E	CPT	0-1824947	0957	1
WHITE JESSE H	LTC	0-0168539	0648	3
WHITE JEWEL C	LTC	0-0292540	0560	1
WHITE JOE L	LTC	0-0291292	0859	1
WHITE JOHN	COL	0-0480770	0962	1
WHITE JOHN	CW4	W-2105058	1060	3
WHITE JOHN A	COL	0-0296590	0958	1
WHITE JOHN B	COL	0-0236676	1158	2
WHITE JOHN B	CW2	W-2142123	0156	1
WHITE JOHN C	LTC	0-1042464	0563	1
WHITE JOHN C	CPT	0-2036458	0367	3
WHITE JOHN E	LTC	0-0227708	0165	3
WHITE JOHN E	CPT	0-0488612	0249	1
WHITE JOHN E	MAJ	0-0504521	0446	1
WHITE JOHN G	1LT	0-1056270	1145	2
WHITE JOHN L	COL	0-0204144	0-51	3
WHITE JOHN M	CPT	0-0189422	1043	2
WHITE JOHN M	COL	0-0331102	0561	1
WHITE JOHN N	MAJ	0-0278137	0658	3
WHITE JOHN P	2LT	0-1590259	1044	2
WHITE JOHN O	CW3	W-2151059	0164	1
WHITE JOHN R	COL	0-0238771	0763	1
WHITE JOHN W	LTC	0-1047841	0166	1
WHITE JOSEPH A	MAJ	0-0135225	0248	1
WHITE JOSEPH A	MAJ	0-1289660	0660	1
WHITE JOSEPH C	CW3	RW-2151807	0563	1
WHITE JOSEPH G	CW3	W-2136734	0255	1
WHITE JOSEPH L	CW4	W-2123427	1053	1
WHITE JOSEPH S	LTC	0-0182546	1156	3
WHITE JR ALVIN O	LTC	0-1054867	0665	1
WHITE JR BENJAMIN F	1LT	0-1173830	0551	2
WHITE JR DONALD M	COL	0-0271082	0267	3
WHITE JR HUGH L	LTC	0-1184755	0867	1
WHITE JR IVAN	LTC	0-0314865	0847	1
WHITE JR JOHN B	LTC	0-0386289	0864	1
WHITE JR JOHN J	LTC	0-1310537	0467	3
WHITE JR PAUL	LTC	0-1286049	0661	1
WHITE JR RICHARD J	MAJ	0-0124017	0450	3
WHITE JR SHELBY L	CPT	0-0422490	0945	2
WHITE JR SILAS H	WO1	W-2126877	0851	2
WHITE JR WALTER	LTC	0-1284441	0859	1
WHITE KATHERINE	MAJ	L-0117476	0666	3
WHITE KENNETH E	MAJ	0-0567899	0861	1
WHITE KENNETH J	LTC	0-0490846	0457	1
WHITE KENNETH S	COL	0-0181287	0157	3
WHITE KENNETH S	LTC	0-0275639	0257	1
WHITE LAWRENCE M	CW3	W-2147949	0263	1
WHITE LEO A	MAJ	0-1304157	0960	1
WHITE LEONARD R	CW3	W-2151081	0264	1
WHITE LEROY M	1LT	0-2017786	0167	2
WHITE LLOYD A	CPT	0-2049757	0757	1
WHITE LOUIS A	LTC	0-0439257	0764	1
WHITE LOUIS A	CW4	W-2145099	0466	1
WHITE LOUIS J	LTC	0-0493006	1062	3
WHITE LOUIS L	MAJ	0-0490807	0447	1
WHITE LOUIS R	MAJ	0-0533085	0846	2
WHITE LYLE B	LTC	0-1995021	0461	1
WHITE LYLE E	2LT	0-0157266	0847	1
WHITE LYMAN G	LTC	0-0337690	0557	2
WHITE MAC P	CPT	0-1055509	1046	2
WHITE MALCOLM B	1LT	0-0395176	1042	1
WHITE MARY R	CW4	V-0609154	0964	1
WHITE MASTIN C	COL	0-0334078	0261	3

NAME	GRADE	SVC NO	DATE RET MO YR	RET CODE
WHITE MERRILL M	WO1	W-2146472	0854	1
WHITE MILLER G	M G	0-0286638	0155	2
WHITE MORTON	LTC	0-0290479	1165	3
WHITE NEWELL D	MAJ	0-0314949	0545	2
WHITE NEWMAN W	LTC	0-0306523	0345	1
WHITE ORVAL V	1LT	0-1307598	0246	2
WHITE OWEN M	CW3	W-2149272	0762	1
WHITE PAUL A	MAJ	0-1284968	0654	1
WHITE PAUL E	MAJ	0-2014736	1167	1
WHITE PAUL H	LTC	0-0123670	0158	3
WHITE PAUL H	MAJ	0-0124016	0458	3
WHITE PAUL L	COL	0-0268447	0663	3
WHITE PAUL R	COL	0-0248827	0962	1
WHITE PAUL R	LTC	0-1040858	0964	1
WHITE RAY C	CPT	0-2289278	0867	1
WHITE RAYMOND E	1LT	0-2006589	1049	2
WHITE RAYMOND F	CW4	RW-2113883	0363	1
WHITE RAYMOND L	MAJ	0-0399018	0944	1
WHITE REX O	LTC	0-0923787	0265	1
WHITE RICHARD J	WO1	W-2118246	0352	1
WHITE RICHARD K	LTC	0-0463533	1265	3
WHITE ROBERT	CW2	W-2112178	0645	2
WHITE ROBERT A	CPT	0-1050513	0363	1
WHITE ROBERT F	LTC	0-1101273	0963	1
WHITE ROBERT G	B G	0-0171250	0360	3
WHITE ROBERT G	CW2	W-2150618	1166	1
WHITE ROBERT H	LTC	0-1702671	0763	2
WHITE ROBERT L	CW2	W-2105000	1048	2
WHITE RONALD B	CW3	W-3150692	0467	2
WHITE ROSS	1LT	0-1318947	0246	2
WHITE RUBEN G	CPT	0-1825584	1055	1
WHITE RUSSELL E	CPT	0-1107231	0545	2
WHITE RUSSELL E	CW3	W-2147484	0966	1
WHITE RUSSELL G	COL	0-0231817	1263	3
WHITE SAMUEL E	LTC	0-1036084	0767	1
WHITE SHIRLEY L	2LT	N-0788971	0245	1
WHITE SIDNEY C	COL	0-0204868	0359	3
WHITE SR CHARLES	CW3	W-2144686	0263	1
WHITE SR WILLIAM B	CW2	W-2146923	1061	1
WHITE STANLEY E	CPT	0-1315454	0251	1
WHITE SYLVIA E	MAJ	N-2297656	0867	2
WHITE TED L	LTC	0-1304159	0264	1
WHITE TED L	MAJ	0-1797402	0661	1
WHITE THADDEUS H	CPT	0-0472440	0646	2
WHITE THEO L	LTC	0-0224632	0460	2
WHITE THOMAS A	MAJ	0-0193384	0654	3
WHITE THOMAS C	1LT	0-1315884	1045	2
WHITE THOMAS J	LTC	0-0225011	0956	3
WHITE THOMAS J	COL	0-0317498	0446	2
WHITE THOMAS J	1LT	0-1288150	0346	2
WHITE THOMAS M	LTC	0-0451263	0258	1
WHITE TURNER D	MAJ	0-0264083	0263	1
WHITE URVEN V	COL	0-0361890	0361	3
WHITE VAN R	COL	0-0230557	0457	1
WHITE WALTER O	CW2	W-2210085	0361	1
WHITE WALTER J	CW3	W-2149724	0366	1
WHITE WALTER R	MAJ	0-0540952	1166	2
WHITE WALTER R	CPT	0-2288467	0562	1
WHITE WALTER R	CW3	W-2148825	0862	1
WHITE WARREN N	2LT	0-0528108	0545	2
WHITE WILLARD S	MAJ	0-2036722	0563	1
WHITE WILLIAM A	LTC	0-0226499	0945	2
WHITE WILLIAM A	MAJ	0-0301874	0144	2
WHITE WILLIAM A	MAJ	0-0978088	0765	1
WHITE WILLIAM B	CPT	0-0492546	1147	1
WHITE WILLIAM G	LTC	0-1284255	0557	2
WHITE WILLIAM J	LTC	0-0276291	0966	3
WHITE WILLIAM P	1LT	0-1116433	0546	2
WHITE WORTH O	LTC	0-1286939	0960	1
WHITEAKER ATHA B	CPT	0-1031688	1060	1
WHITEBROOK MAXWELL M	CPT	0-0288448	0850	1
WHITECAR ROBERT W	MAJ	0-0974719	1162	1
WHITED BOWMAN T	COL	0-0304395	0465	1
WHITED NORMAN W	LTC	0-0207138	0848	3
WHITEFIELD LYTLE B J	LTC	0-0396606	0965	1

NAME	GRADE	SVC NO	DATE RET MO YR	RET CODE
WHITEFOOT HILDA R	1LT	N-0771693	0346	1
WHITEFORD ROGER S	COL	0-0244043	0664	3
WHITEHAIR RAYMOND F	1LT	0-1533944	0945	2
WHITEHEAD ARTHUR V	COL	0-0408662	1060	1
WHITEHEAD CLAUDE E	COL	0-0315305	0661	3
WHITEHEAD DEWIE	CW3	W-2117987	0259	1
WHITEHEAD DONALD F	CW2	W-2104586	0845	2
WHITEHEAD EDWARD L	LTC	0-1292970	0966	1
WHITEHEAD EDWARD Z	CW2	W-3430513	0867	1
WHITEHEAD IRA L	1LT	0-0438830	0246	2
WHITEHEAD JACK	CW3	W-2136705	0261	1
WHITEHEAD JOSEPH A	MAJ	0-0428616	1146	2
WHITEHEAD ORAN R	LTC	0-1313481	0365	1
WHITEHEAD RICHARD S	LTC	0-0273280	0867	3
WHITEHEAD SR FRED R	LTC	0-0381253	1161	1
WHITEHEAD THOMAS H	COL	0-0223410	1064	3
WHITEHEAD VEARL G	1LT	0-1318109	1045	1
WHITEHEAD WALTER J	CW3	W-2142417	0861	1
WHITEHEAD WILLIAM G	COL	0-0190636	0757	3
WHITEHEAD WILLIAM S	COL	0-0920532	0667	3
WHITEHILL HARVEY H	LTC	0-1045627	0762	1
WHITEHOUSE FRANK H	LTC	0-0234643	0465	3
WHITEHOUSE HARVEY J	LTC	0-1103001	0161	1
WHITEHOUSE RICHARD K	LTC	0-0726532	0166	1
WHITEHURST EDWARD R	COL	0-0278131	0755	1
WHITEKNACT JOHN E	LTC	0-1576808	0662	1
WHITELEGG RUDOLPH F	COL	0-0185722	0654	3
WHITELEY BRAINARD A	MAJ	0-1553014	1263	1
WHITELEY ELI L	CPT	0-1310907	0546	2
WHITELEY JAMES E	CW4	W-2113358	0166	1
WHITELEY PHILIP W	COL	0-0223947	0955	3
WHITEMAN VERN O	LTC	0-0267868	0966	3
WHITEMAN WAYNE W	CPT	0-2009620	0261	1
WHITEMORE ARTHUR C	LTC	0-0268852	0657	1
WHITENER PAUL R	CPT	0-0248849	0545	2
WHITESIDE JAMES E	MAJ	0-1336579	1064	1
WHITESIDE PAUL W	1LT	0-0948171	0853	2
WHITESIDE WILLIAM H	MAJ	0-2212057	1064	1
WHITESIDES LAWSON E	LTC	0-0299531	0446	2
WHITETREE MAX R	CPT	0-1305145	0246	2
WHITETURKEY RAY L	MAJ	0-1115153	1162	1
WHITFIELD AUBRY J	CPT	0-1877310	1162	1
WHITFIELD CLAUDE	MAJ	0-1635475	0457	1
WHITFIELD HARVEY J	MAJ	0-0353919	0745	2
WHITFIELD ROBERT W	CW2	W-2149814	0857	1
WHITFIELD WILLIAM A	CPT	0-0485891	1155	1
WHITFORD ANITA B C	2LT	N-0785706	0746	1
WHITFORD MATTHEW C	MAJ	0-1113055	1061	1
WHITFORD ORRIS C	MAJ	0-1290860	0954	1
WHITMAN KEITH W	LTC	0-1342223	0767	1
WHITIN GEORGE W	1LT	0-1050134	0446	2
WHITING CHESTER F	LTC	0-0936552	1060	1
WHITING DAVID D	MAJ	0-1825388	1060	1
WHITING DONALD J	2LT	0-1030627	0545	2
WHITING EBEN S	MAJ	0-0359969	0945	2
WHITING FRANCIS S	MAJ	0-0954034	0166	1
WHITING FRED N	COL	0-0233075	0464	3
WHITING HARVEY A	CW3	W-2146710	0761	1
WHITING HERBERT S	LTC	0-0327170	0266	3
WHITING JR ROYAL G	1LT	0-1169829	104N	1
WHITING MURRAY D	MAJ	0-1314237	1058	1
WHITING NORMAN O	LTC	0-0236965	1045	2
WHITING WILLARD W	LTC	0-1170438	0966	1
WHITKER RICHARD P	COL	0-0921199	0267	3
WHITLAW NATHANIEL	COL	0-0292663	0857	1
WHITLEDGE ALVAH O	MAJ	0-0967094	0962	1
WHITLEDGE OSCAR L	CW2	W-2147428	0861	1
WHITLEY CLIFTON M	CPT	0-1649104	0856	1
WHITLEY EDWARD D	LTC	0-0450129	0557	1
WHITLEY FREDERIC N	LTC	0-0240062	0466	3
WHITLEY GEORGE D	CPT	0-0309870	1144	2
WHITLEY GEORGE H	CW2	W-2118674	0453	1
WHITLEY JAMES V	MAJ	0-0302434	1144	2
WHITLEY PHILIP R	LTC	0-0232981	0865	3
WHITLEY ROBERT D	CW3	W-2205153	0565	1

NAME	GRADE	SVC NO	DATE RET MO YR	RET CODE
WHITLOCK ARTHUR	CPT	0-0461185	C347	1
WHITLOCK DEAN R	MAJ	0-1638784	1060	1
WHITLOCK FRED W	LTC	0-0251171	0264	3
WHITLOCK HOMER N	CPT	0-0995735	1057	2
WHITLOCK JAMES R	CPT	0-1546284	0156	1
WHITLOCK JOHN A	LTC	0-0261061	C867	3
WHITLOCK JOHN L	1LT	0-1105915	0346	2
WHITLOCK MAURICE B	WO1	W-2139778	C946	2
WHITLOCK ROBERT S	MAJ	0-1049392	1263	1
WHITLOCK WILLIAM A	1LT	0-1038517	1045	2
WHITLOCK WILLIAM H	CW3	W-2150014	0364	1
WHITLOW FLOYD C	LTC	0-1280114	0657	1
WHITMAN CHARLES B	LTC	0-0461077	0365	3
WHITMAN HAROLD W	CPT	0-0461772	1146	1
WHITMAN HENRY G	LTC	0-1587725	C462	2
WHITMAN JOHN H	MAJ	C-1554112	1063	1
WHITMAN JOHN R	CPT	0-1109746	0952	1
WHITMAN JOSEPH J	MAJ	0-0262277	0765	3
WHITMAN LESTER J	CW3	W-2149312	1061	1
WHITMAN ORLANDO O	LTC	0-1170248	C357	1
WHITMAN ROBERT F	CPT	0-1002152	0857	1
WHITMAN RUSSELL S	WO1	W-2152755	1054	1
WHITMAN STANLEY J	CPT	0-1295805	0158	1
WHITMAN WILLIAM H	LTC	0-0384325	C858	1
WHITMARSH CARYL L	MAJ	C-0262131	0757	3
WHITMER GERALD L	MAJ	C-0959663	1167	1
WHITMER HOBERT E	MAJ	0-1937456	0966	1
WHITMEYER GEORGE L	LTC	0-1315747	1265	1
WHITMIRE HANKINS N	MAJ	C-0494339	0855	1
WHITMIRE JR ELBERT N	MAJ	0-0348581	0446	2
WHITMIRE ROBERT A	MAJ	C-1080457	C258	1
WHITMIRE THOMAS O	LTC	0-0542427	C264	1
WHITMORE EARL B	LTC	0-0299815	C657	1
WHITMORE GARLAND W	MAJ	C-2002571	0262	1
WHITMORE GEORGE I	LTC	0-1015930	0865	1
WHITMORE JAMES M	CW4	W-2139559	1060	1
WHITMORE LUCIAN R	CPT	0-0668170	0159	1
WHITMORE MORRIS T	COL	0-0162929	0455	3
WHITMORE RALPH L	LTC	0-0422201	0960	1
WHITMORE RUSSELL E	LTC	0-1018712	1066	1
WHITMORE SHIRLEY H	CW3	W-2122916	1162	2
WHITMORE WAYNE E	MAJ	0-0450946	1154	1
WHITMORE WILLIAM B	CPT	0-2262209	0261	1
WHITMORE YOTT E	MAJ	C-2016C87	0762	1
WHITNEY ALDEN J	MAJ	0-1280261	1162	1
WHITNEY CLARENCE A	LTC	0-0123737	C850	3
WHITNEY CLARENCE E	LTC	0-0129717	1053	3
WHITNEY COURTNEY	M G	0-0398227	0551	1
WHITNEY EDWIN F	COL	0-0347225	0660	1
WHITNEY ERNEST L	MAJ	C-2262475	0365	1
WHITNEY FRANCES S	1LT	L-0302504	C545	2
WHITNEY GEORGE H	CPT	0-0501505	C854	1
WHITNEY HARRY P	1LT	0-2055205	1047	1
WHITNEY HERBERT W	LTC	0-0260840	0466	3
WHITNEY HUGH L	1LT	0-0494047	1148	1
WHITNEY JAMES H	CPT	0-0480122	0346	2
WHITNEY JOHN C	1LT	0-2007055	C147	2
WHITNEY JR CARL E	LTC	0-0398275	C661	1
WHITNEY JR FRANK A	1LT	0-1014393	0345	2
WHITNEY LELAND A	LTC	0-1598724	0367	1
WHITNEY MAURICE	COL	0-0214963	0852	3
WHITNEY NORMAN E	COL	0-0185440	0753	3
WHITNEY WILLIAM B	LTC	0-128918C	0558	1
WHITNEY WILLIAM J	CW3	W-2151007	1060	1
WHITPAN HOWARD G	COL	0-0278067	0448	2
WHITSELL FAY M	MAJ	0-0501563	0445	2
WHITSIT ROBERT J	COL	0-0418880	0761	1
WHITSON JAMES F	MAJ	0-2026839	1060	1
WHITSTON LAVAUGHN V	CW3	W-2151799	0562	1
WHITT BUFORD M	LTC	0-0330070	0264	3
WHITT HOWARD O	CPT	0-0509830	0346	1
WHITT JOHN H	CPT	0-0534572	0146	2
WHITT OLLIE B	CPT	0-0123768	C553	3
WHITT WILLIAM W	CW2	W-2149244	1060	1
WHITTAKER CHARLES E	CW3	W-2205154	0165	1

NAME	GRADE	SVC NO	DATE RET MO YR	RET CODE
WHITTAKER EDGAR P	CW3	W-2150886	1164	1
WHITTAKER HENRY F	LTC	0-0196453	0454	3
WHITTAKER JAMES A	1LT	0-0454834	0844	1
WHITTAKER LEE	MAJ	0-1931677	0366	1
WHITTAKER ROBERT L	CW3	W-2148893	0766	1
WHITTAKER WOODROW M	CPT	0-204915C	0348	1
WHITTED HAROLD H	CPT	0-0279783	0145	2
WHITTED LLOYD M	MAJ	0-1593515	1060	1
WHITTEMORE FORREST J	LTC	0-0127331	0351	3
WHITTEMORE HERBERT	MAJ	C-0208168	1044	2
WHITTEMORE IRVING C	COL	0-0125862	1155	3
WHITTEMORE JOHN G	LTC	0-0935343	0867	1
WHITTEN BEN H	MAJ	0-1576858	0756	1
WHITTEN ELLWOOD T	CPT	0-1920263	0962	1
WHITTEN GEORGE E	1LT	0-2007C39	1048	1
WHITTEN HAROLD F	1LT	0-1553199	0146	2
WHITTEN JAMES F	CPT	0-1685989	0245	2
WHITTEN JOE W	LTC	0-0228115	0364	3
WHITTEN JR CARSON O	MAJ	0-2289718	0763	1
WHITTEN RICHARD C	LTC	0-1046319	0662	1
WHITTEN WILLIAM J	CW3	W-2151679	0766	1
WHITTIER FLORENCE E	MAJ	N-078580C	0565	1
WHITTIER GEORGE E	LTC	0-0450525	0859	1
WHITTIER LEON W	1LT	0-2049429	1055	1
WHITTINGHAM EDWARD R	COL	0-0166332	0951	3
WHITTINGHILL C L	CPT	0-0353073	0945	2
WHITTINGSTALL CHARLE	MAJ	0-0983813	0263	1
WHITTINGTON JACK E	LTC	0-1314700	0161	1
WHITTINGTON JOHN P	MAJ	C-1302423	1263	1
WHITTINGTON JOHN R	MAJ	0-1582912	0667	3
WHITTINGTON JOSEPH M	MAJ	0-1300242	0261	1
WHITTINGTON PAUL E	MAJ	0-0275498	1067	3
WHITTLE ALBERT O	MAJ	0-0504317	0653	1
WHITTLE CHARLES B	COL	C-0347667	0358	1
WHITTLE CHARLES E	2LT	0-1003349	1044	2
WHITTLE VERNON L	CW3	W-2147536	0767	1
WHITTLE WILLIAM O	MAJ	C-0973924	0963	1
WHITTLESEY FRED L	COL	0-0257789	1265	3
WHITTLESEY SR MAX M	MAJ	C-2014538	0363	1
WHITTON CHARLIE M	CW2	W-2205225	0364	1
WHITTON JAMES R	LTC	0-0349771	0357	1
WHITTON MARGARET J	MAJ	N-0731768	0661	2
WHITTON TEEL O	LTC	0-0327227	1048	1
WHITTON TRUMAN W	CW2	W-2106924	0650	1
WHITTY PAUL X	CW3	W-2153137	1165	1
WHITWELL OMER D	1LT	0-0550527	0447	1
WHOLLEY SALLY J	CPT	N-0720382	0446	1
WHORTON BLAINE H	1LT	0-1107757	1045	2
WHORTON HAROLD	MAJ	0-1060683	0761	1
WHORTON ROBERT J	1LT	0-0487001	1144	2
WHYBREW ROBERT E	LTC	0-1102544	1164	1
WHYTENA JOHN E	CW2	W-2151883	1057	2
WIACEK JOSEPH J	MAJ	C-1040163	0159	1
WIARD DEHART C	LTC	0-0372541	0157	1
WIARD JR LAURENCE E	CW2	W-2147143	1060	1
WIARD SETH	COL	0-0163906	0754	3
WIBERG MORRIS C	1LT	0-1294948	0845	1
WIBLE JOHN	MAJ	0-010826C	0848	2
WICHAS JOHN J	CPT	C-1298472	0860	1
WICHERT HOWARD C	MAJ	0-1650441	0464	1
WICHMAN THEODORE O	MAJ	0-1311458	0562	1
WICHMANN JR CARL B	CW2	W-2152782	1264	1
WICHROWSKI BOL	LTC	0-0382173	1166	3
WICHTERMAN ROY F	CPT	0-0263062	0765	3
WICK CATHERINE	2LT	N-0700587	0538	1
WICK ELMER L	MAJ	0-1799491	0662	1
WICK ROBERT L	LTC	0-0238661	0765	3
WICKA ANTHONY J	CPT	0-0885738	0546	2
WICKE DICK	1LT	0-0400850	0146	2
WICKE MARGARET K	1LT	N-0729649	0346	1
WICKER EDMOND L	MAJ	C-1113058	0859	1
WICKER GLENES E	LTC	C-0412414	0661	1
WICKER HOMER F	COL	0-0156655	0957	3
WICKER JAMES C	CW3	W-2143732	0663	1
WICKER WORTH	LTC	0-0336096	0246	2

NAME	GRADE	SVC NO	DATE RET MO YR	RET CODE
WICKERSHAM C W	B G	0-0147303	C648	3
WICKERSHAM GEORGE L	MAJ	0-0363060	0462	1
WICKESSER ROBERT A	MAJ	0-1549177	C847	2
WICKHAM JOHN A	LTC	0-0147307	0452	1
WICKHAM ROBERT E	CW2	RW-2209379	0862	1
WICKLAND DONALD J	MAJ	0-1000494	C457	1
WICKLAND LYNN R	LTC	0-1107235	1066	3
WICKLANDER GRANT H	CW4	W-2110307	0360	1
WICKLIFFE KEITH V	LTC	0-C411088	1160	1
WICKLINE HARRY F	LTC	0-1641062	1164	3
WICKLUND DAGNE O	MAJ	N-073659C	0365	3
WICKMAN IRVING G	LTC	C-0216975	0455	3
WICKMAN ROBERT E	CPT	0-1688834	C959	2
WICKORD THEODORE F	COL	C-0345291	1146	2
WICKOREN CLARENCE M	MAJ	0-2008801	1062	1
WICKS ARTHUR J	LTC	0-0131669	0648	3
WICKS EARL N	LTC	0-1053017	1062	1
WICKS HERBERT N	MAJ	C-0392499	0146	2
WIDDIFIELD GLENN P	CW3	W-2151827	C164	1
WIDDOWSON LYLE E	LTC	0-0368657	1061	1
WIDDOWSON WILLIAM W	COL	0-0363117	0966	3
WIDINCAMP JOHN S	CW4	W-21036C2	1160	1
WIDING HARRY E	MAJ	C-2036724	0961	1
WIDING JR WILLIAM E	MAJ	C-1296955	1161	1
WIDMAN DAVID E	CPT	0-0396976	0847	2
WIDMANN ERWIN	COL	0-0319808	1165	3
WIDMAYER LAWRENCE A	CPT	0-0516380	0948	1
WIDMER ALBERT J	LTC	0-1287632	0161	1
WIDMER ERHARDT E	1LT	0-0923312	C744	2
WIDMOYER FRED B	LTC	0-0147311	0655	3
WIDMYER EARL G	LTC	0-0328516	1153	2
WIDMYER IRVING C	MAJ	C-0918338	0747	1
WIDRICH JACK	CPT	0-1693462	1145	2
WIEBE ALVIN F	CPT	0-1045632	0845	2
WIEBEN CLARENCE P	CPT	0-1557239	0962	1
WIEBER PAUL A	1LT	0-1331689	0746	1
WIEBKING WALTER R	MAJ	C-1547366	1160	1
WIEBUSCH ROBERT G	LTC	0-1845125	C161	1
WIECHMAN FRED H	COL	0-0252240	0562	3
WIECK ARTHUR M	COL	0-0324824	0760	1
WIEDELMAN LAWRENCE W	COL	0-0299575	C965	3
WIEDMAN CLARENCE J	COL	C-0287799	1059	1
WIEDRICK WALTER W	CW2	W-21C1110	0246	2
WIEGAND FREDERICK	COL	0-0184142	C158	3
WIEGAND VINCENT A	CPT	0-0949230	0659	1
WIEGANDT MARVIN R	2LT	0-0555199	0745	2
WIEGERS ROBERT M	CPT	0-1291364	1047	2
WIEHENKAMP PAUL H	LTC	0-0415643	1060	1
WIEK NORMAN E	1LT	0-1016252	0845	2
WIELAND CHARLES C	MAJ	0-1175011	1165	1
WIELAND HERMAN	LTC	0-0266940	0354	3
WIEMEYER BURGE A	MAJ	C-0492969	0864	3
WIENAND JR JOHN H	LTC	0-0263552	0865	3
WIENCEK VINCENT	CPT	0-0451455	0559	1
WIENEKE CARTER H	1LT	0-0548664	0245	2
WIENER FREDERICK	COL	0-0338743	0766	3
WIENER JEAN	LTC	L-0304087	C855	2
WIENER MORRIS F	LTC	0-0264174	0465	3
WIENERT RAYMEN C	LTC	0-0259012	0566	3
WIENTJES CHARLES N	MAJ	0-1317456	0459	1
WIEPKING HERBERT B	CW2	W-2118975	0745	2
WIER CHESTER	1LT	C-1014361	0745	1
WIER DONALD G	CPT	0-1296459	0261	1
WIER HERBERT I	CPT	0-1290862	0745	2
WIER JOHN B	2LT	0-1333150	1046	2
WIER JOHN S	COL	0-0238876	1061	3
WIER ROBERT W	CPT	C-1534187	C154	1
WIERMAN JOHN R	CPT	0-1554113	0946	2
WIERSEMA HENRY	LTC	0-0119336	0556	3
WIERSEMA MATTHEW J	CPT	0-1171834	0847	2
WIERTS PAUL H	1LT	0-1558625	1046	1
WIESE FRED W	COL	0-0167351	1053	1
WIESE GLENN L	MAJ	C-1546248	0766	3
WIESE JOHN H	LTC	0-1635480	1166	1
WIESEL LEON L	CPT	0-0476773	C246	2

NAME	GRADE	SVC NO	DATE RET MO YR	RET CODE
WIESEN JOHN R	2LT	0-1303974	0844	2
WIESEN SEYMOUR A	MAJ	0-0455147	0157	1
WIESENBERG HERBERT	CPT	0-1944430	0546	2
WIESENBURGER WALTER	CW2	W-2149917	0258	1
WIESENTHAL SAM	MAJ	0-0487743	0247	2
WIESNER JEROME J	1LT	0-1775767	0247	1
WIESS II CHARLES R	LTC	0-1317457	1162	2
WIESSNER WALTER H	LTC	0-110527C	0263	1
WIEST ALBERT F	COL	0-0401874	1064	1
WIESTER HARRY R	LTC	0-0207537	0954	1
WIETHORN GUS D	MAJ	0-0289301	0460	1
WIETZ GENEVIEVE	2LT	N-C789C82	0944	1
WIGEN DONALD M	CW3	W-2144140	0563	1
WIGGANS CLARENCE E	LTC	0-0249273	0366	3
WIGGER ELMER C	MAJ	C-2262365	0465	1
WIGGER GEORGE F	COL	0-0299724	1157	1
WIGGERS GERALD J	1LT	0-1C12582	0347	2
WIGGIN ARNOLD T	MAJ	0-0260239	0567	3
WIGGIN FRANKLIN W	CPT	0-1649005	1166	3
WIGGIN MORRILL	COL	0-0547185	0646	2
WIGGIN WILLIAM B	CPT	0-0202652	0644	2
WIGGINS ARTHUR E	CPT	0-1316353	0557	1
WIGGINS EARL L	1LT	0-0527876	1145	2
WIGGINS EDGAR C	COL	0-0174125	0361	3
WIGGINS FREDERIC G	LTC	0-0392350	0262	1
WIGGINS FREDERICK	LTC	0-0188657	0750	3
WIGGINS GILBERT N	COL	C-0204034	0858	3
WIGGINS HENRY	MAJ	0-1913491	0963	1
WIGGINS HOYT A	LTC	0-0249201	1265	3
WIGGINS IRIS E R	1LT	N-0774105	0247	1
WIGGINS JOSEPH H	MAJ	0-04801C4	0549	2
WIGGINS JR JOHN L	1LT	0-1C16431	1145	2
WIGGINS ROSALIE H	MAJ	N-0733432	1163	1
WIGGINS STANLEY R	COL	0-014150C	0648	3
WIGGINS THOMAS A	MAJ	0-1288834	0258	1
WIGGINS THOMAS H	1LT	0-1104008	0446	2
WIGGS JOHN H	COL	0-0380512	1162	1
WIGGS NORMAN S	COL	0-0184590	0152	3
WIGGS W N	WO1	W-2126207	0647	2
WIGHT ANNA O	2LT	N-0700566	0336	1
WIGHT ARTHUR E	CPT	0-0240549	0862	3
WIGHT HEWITT G	CPT	0-0534142	0847	2
WIGHTMAN WILFRED V	COL	0-0218565	0464	3
WIGHTMAN WILLIAM W	MAJ	0-0251855	0346	2
WIGIM TRUEMAN H	LTC	0-2035509	0562	1
WIGINGTON JR LETCHER	MAJ	C-0407808	0546	2
WIGLEY JEREMIAH J	MAJ	C-1103005	0658	1
WIGLEY LAWRENCE J	CW3	W-2142011	1060	1
WIGMORE CHARLES D	CPT	0-1822844	0564	1
WIHR NORMAN L	COL	0-0287931	0266	3
WIHTOL KARL F	LTC	0-0284959	0959	3
WIIG PAUL O	1LT	C-0273250	1042	2
WIKE RALPH A	CPT	0-0217115	1045	2
WIKE SR DAVID W	CPT	0-1636822	0256	1
WIKER BERNARD	CPT	0-2049152	1047	2
WIKLE JR ROBERT M	MAJ	0-1293507	0261	1
WIKNER ERIC E	LTC	0-0337240	0757	1
WIKOFF LOWELL C	MAJ	0-201601C	0562	1
WIKSTROM HOLGAR A	MAJ	C-0423901	0845	1
WILBANKS REX A	LTC	0-0340635	C365	1
WILBANKS SCURLOCK W	CW2	W-2145762	1060	1
WILBANKS THOMAS O	LTC	0-0255309	0162	3
WILBER CHARLES O	CW2	W-2150280	0862	1
WILBER GEORGE E B	1LT	0-1012794	0445	2
WILBER JR HAROLD A	2LT	0-1284798	0844	2
WILBER MARLIN A	CPT	0-1702796	1044	2
WILBER MORTIMER D	LTC	0-1318845	0264	1
WILBERGER CALVIN L	LTC	0-1331898	0863	1
WILBERGER EVERETT D	MAJ	0-0233603	C857	3
WILBORN EARL A	CW3	W-215164C	0862	1
WILBORN MESSER	1LT	0-0109205	1037	1
WILBUR EDWARD L	COL	0-0129740	1156	3
WILBUR JOHN F	LTC	0-1300736	0865	1
WILBURN CLYDE A	LTC	0-0358196	0560	1
WILBURN JOSHUA M	CPT	0-1587019	0761	1

NAME	GRADE	SVC NO	DATE RET MO YR	RET CODE
WILBURN LEON	MAJ	0-1540851	0563	1
WILBURN LUKE J	MAJ	0-0115139	0356	3
WILBURN MURREL D	LTC	C-0276299	1063	3
WILCE JOSEPH M	1LT	0-1545745	C154	1
WILCH CLETUS F	LTC	C-0484828	1165	1
WILCKE HAROLD L	LTC	0-0244972	0966	3
WILCOX BERNARD A	LTC	0-0262239	0464	3
WILCOX BERNHARD B	LTC	0-0204054	0249	3
WILCOX CHARLES L	CW3	W-2148038	0361	1
WILCOX ELEANOR D	2LT	N-0756223	C245	1
WILCOX ELLIS J	MAJ	0-0248314	0167	3
WILCOX G NEIL	COL	C-0472010	1065	1
WILCOX HARVEY L	CPT	0-1302400	1264	2
WILCOX HOWARD J	CW2	W-2110303	0648	2
WILCOX JERRA	LTC	0-C259021	0564	3
WILCOX JR ALBERT M	LTC	0-0341998	1062	2
WILCOX LAWRENCE G	2LT	0-1112519	0545	1
WILCOX LELAND F	MAJ	C-0281725	0446	2
WILCOX PAUL K	CPT	0-1032665	C947	2
WILCOX PAUL V	LTC	0-0183707	0260	3
WILCOX PERRY D	MAJ	C-2300992	0765	1
WILCOX ROBERT D	LTC	0-0555557	1167	1
WILCOX ROBERT T	CW2	W-3440011	0667	1
WILCOX THEODORE R	LTC	0-0359663	C363	3
WILCOX WALTER	MAJ	0-0418944	0346	2
WILCOX WALTER J	MAJ	C-0980527	0662	1
WILCOX WILFRED H	COL	0-0282692	0563	3
WILCOX WILLARD S	2LT	0-0256439	0258	3
WILCOXSON CHARLES L	CW3	W-2102547	0354	1
WILCOXSON THOMAS R	CPT	0-1001707	C754	1
WILCUTTS HELEN D	1LT	L-0304117	C946	2
WILD HAROLD A	MAJ	0-1053432	C865	3
WILD JAMES M	COL	0-0312935	0246	2
WILDAY CEDRIC A	CW3	W-2109039	0653	1
WILDE JOHN J	WO1	W-2111750	0646	2
WILDE JR CHARLES E	1LT	0-0512557	C345	2
WILDEBUSH JOSEPH F	MAJ	C-0301706	1143	2
WILDEN SAMUEL J	MAJ	C-0319367	1045	2
WILDER ALLEN S	COL	0-0281051	0665	1
WILDER CHARLES	1LT	0-1311075	1045	2
WILDER DELORES AL	1LT	N-0726091	1045	1
WILDER EUGENE H	LTC	0-0372766	0567	3
WILDER FRANK A	LTC	0-0298301	1045	2
WILDER GEORGE E	MAJ	C-1636825	0748	1
WILDER GUY B	LTC	0-0267259	1061	3
WILDER HARLIS T	MAJ	0-1319460	1160	1
WILDER HARRY	MAJ	0-2018622	0166	1
WILDER JILES C	CPT	0-0499757	1049	1
WILDER JR OSCAR	LTC	0-0450947	0656	1
WILDER LUTHER V	CW2	W-2150697	1157	1
WILDER OMER O	LTC	0-0401343	0860	1
WILDER THOMAS P	MAJ	0-0375231	1047	2
WILDER WILLIAM H	COL	0-0118147	0648	3
WILDER WILLIAM S	MAJ	0-0318069	1166	3
WILDERCM MORRIS	MAJ	C-1693566	0146	2
WILDEY RUSSELL J	LTC	0-0359452	0465	1
WILDHABER FERDINAND	CPT	0-0153587	0144	1
WILDMAN ALBERT C	COL	0-0196638	1260	1
WILDMAN HARRY J	2LT	0-1321723	0245	2
WILDMAN ROBBINS L	CPT	0-2208730	0859	1
WILDMAN STANLEY F	LTC	0-0205860	0545	2
WILDMAN VERNON	LTC	0-0475024	0249	1
WILDS WILLIAM	LTC	0-0106459	0648	3
WILEMAN RICHARD D	MAJ	0-1019644	0661	2
WILES ELMER J	LTC	0-0232831	0647	2
WILES FRED F	CW4	W-2143642	0556	1
WILES HAROLD J	CW3	W-2150562	0763	1
WILES RONALD P	CW4	W-2117938	0960	1
WILES WILLIAM G	COL	0-0305383	0362	3
WILEY ALBERT	LTC	0-0253245	0565	3
WILEY AUDREY M	1LT	N-0744141	0146	1
WILEY BELL I	COL	0-0922753	0266	3
WILEY BERT C	CPT	0-4002020	1154	2
WILEY CHARLES A	CW3	W-2144375	0461	1
WILEY CHARLES O	1LT	0-1103006	0644	2

NAME	GRADE	SVC NO	DATE RET MO YR	RET CODE
WILEY CHARLES D	WO1	W-2006587	0763	3
WILEY CLARENCE R	MAJ	0-1039618	0557	1
WILEY CORNELIUS	LTC	0-0450338	0652	1
WILEY GARETH W	MAJ	C-1826117	1059	1
WILEY HAROLD	CW2	W-2150553	0757	1
WILEY HARRY M	CPT	0-1315136	0546	2
WILEY JOHN O	COL	0-0188177	0852	3
WILEY PAUL C	LTC	0-1306922	0561	2
WILEY ROBERT L	CW3	W-2120027	0456	1
WILEY STEPHEN J	MAJ	0-1320703	C157	1
WILEY THEODORE	1LT	0-1011162	1045	2
WILFLEY JOHN S	COL	0-0252578	0562	3
WILFONG ALBERT E	B G	0-0147726	0545	2
WILFONG WILLIAM T	MAJ	0-0174698	1147	1
WILFORE WILLIAM C	LTC	0-1000495	0858	1
WILGEN CHARLES H	LTC	0-0327332	0161	1
WILHELM CECELIA W	MAJ	N-0796863	0267	3
WILHELM CHARLES P	MAJ	C-0123952	0642	2
WILHELM DAVID W	LTC	0-0281645	1167	3
WILHELM ROBERT H	LTC	0-0358409	0564	3
WILHELM WARREN	CPT	0-1172337	1146	2
WILHELMI ROY A	CW3	W-2151201	0165	1
WILHELMSON BERNARD W	1LT	0-1299970	0146	2
WILHITE CARL M	MAJ	0-1922594	0367	1
WILHITE RICHARD O	LTC	0-0247490	0466	3
WILHOUR RICHARD D	MAJ	0-1114004	1059	1
WILIE JIM B	MAJ	0-2200004	0762	1
WILJANEN MARTIN V	2LT	0-1826404	0854	1
WILK JOHN S	1LT	0-2037110	0446	2
WILKE CHARLES H	CPT	0-1823529	1163	1
WILKE GILBERT C	CW2	W-2114652	0965	3
WILKE HARLAN A	CW3	W-2152063	0564	1
WILKEN HAROLD W	MAJ	0-1649667	0357	1
WILKER RICHARD T	LTC	0-1287108	0264	1
WILKERSON CARL F	MAJ	0-1175360	0760	1
WILKERSON CHARLES E	LTC	0-0381164	C846	2
WILKERSON ENOCH H	LTC	0-0178135	1058	3
WILKERSON JAMES R	COL	0-0345940	1053	1
WILKERSON JAMES R	2LT	0-1825456	0745	2
WILKERSON JOHN C	COL	0-0284077	1060	1
WILKERSON JOHN W	MAJ	0-0509838	0158	2
WILKERSON LYNDAL E	LTC	0-0210221	0664	1
WILKERSON RALPH L	CPT	0-0160465	C459	3
WILKERSON ROY D	CPT	0-0993710	0361	1
WILKERSON WALTER E	MAJ	0-0985121	0864	1
WILKERSON WILLIAM H	1LT	0-1293158	0346	2
WILKES EARL C	CPT	0-1303420	0447	1
WILKES JAMES G	CW3	W-2152633	0360	1
WILKES JOHN V	MAJ	0-2032983	0563	1
WILKES KENNETH G	COL	0-0306296	0547	2
WILKES THOMAS M	LTC	0-0280816	0545	2
WILKES WILLIAM C	LTC	0-0114899	0358	3
WILKIE JAMES R	MAJ	0-1320494	0862	1
WILKIE JR EDWARD H	COL	0-0334862	0363	1
WILKIN FREDERICK	MAJ	0-1013551	0549	2
WILKINS AUGUSTUS R	CPT	0-0481240	0844	2
WILKINS AUSTIN M	LTC	0-1303599	0263	1
WILKINS CHARLIE S	COL	0-0288599	0465	3
WILKINS EDWIN A	MAJ	0-2018082	0761	1
WILKINS ELMER L	CPT	0-1051828	1054	1
WILKINS FRANK M	COL	0-0319184	0163	1
WILKINS GEORGE E	MAJ	0-2271228	0866	1
WILKINS JAMES F	COL	0-0175634	0958	1
WILKINS JAMES P	COL	0-0382964	0557	1
WILKINS JESSIE T	COL	0-0200095	0253	1
WILKINS JOSEPH P	1LT	0-1320576	0146	2
WILKINS JR HARRY L	CPT	0-1293159	1057	2
WILKINS JR JOHN E	CPT	0-1642724	0745	2
WILKINS MARION K	LTC	0-0249240	0466	3
WILKINS PAUL E	MAJ	0-0180935	0261	3
WILKINS RAYMOND A	MAJ	0-0195234	0761	3
WILKINS WILLIAM A	MAJ	0-0354538	0163	1
WILKINSON ALTON P	COL	0-0266599	0246	2
WILKINSON CARL C	LTC	0-0330804	0960	3
WILKINSON CECIL	CW2	W-2214923	1266	1

NAME	GRADE	SVC NO	DATE RET MO YR	RET CODE
WILKINSON CHARLES E	MAJ	C-1307904	0564	1
WILKINSON CHARLES T	COL	0-0327487	C159	3
WILKINSON EARL H	MAJ	C-0386367	C246	2
WILKINSON EDWARD W	MAJ	0-0253214	C356	3
WILKINSON GEORGE G	2LT	0-1046321	0544	2
WILKINSON GORDON J	CPT	0-1059978	0747	2
WILKINSON HAROLD B	2LT	0-0928580	0451	2
WILKINSON HARRY J	MAJ	C-0294766	0550	1
WILKINSON HENRY E	CPT	0-0408452	0240	2
WILKINSON HORACE A	CPT	C-0321751	C551	3
WILKINSON JACK W	LTC	0-1326959	0265	1
WILKINSON JAMES G	CPT	0-0186898	0753	3
WILKINSON JOHN J	LTC	0-2012330	0562	1
WILKINSON JOSEPH B	COL	0-0261672	0262	3
WILKINSON JR HARRY R	CW2	W-2207350	0161	1
WILKINSON NED A	CW3	W-2149870	0962	1
WILKINSON PAUL R	1LT	0-1554998	0163	3
WILKINSON ROBERT E	1LT	0-2021031	1163	2
WILKINSON ROBERT W	CPT	0-0295420	0744	2
WILKINSON STANLEY S	1LT	0-0399960	0846	2
WILKINSON THOMAS C	COL	C-0332142	1059	3
WILKINSON THOMAS E	LTC	0-1300562	0163	1
WILKINSON VERNON R	CW3	W-2142993	0561	1
WILKINSON WALTER R	CPT	0-0482281	0545	2
WILKINSON WILLIAM	1LT	0-0554175	0946	2
WILKINSON WILLIAM S	COL	0-0184689	0255	3
WILKIRSON EUGENE P	MAJ	0-0168058	0654	3
WILKOF ERVIN	1LT	C-1295309	1045	2
WILKOWSKI VICTOR	LTC	0-0550622	0667	1
WILKS BEN	CPT	0-1177248	1047	2
WILKS LESTER W	MAJ	C-0450339	0662	1
WILKS PAUL A	COL	0-0127625	1155	3
WILL CAMERON G	CPT	0-0153598	0648	3
WILL CLARENCE A	LTC	0-0143499	0648	3
WILL GEORGE	1LT	0-1895314	C350	1
WILLAR MARY C	2LT	N-0777559	0146	1
WILLARD CHARLES W	LTC	0-1182742	1067	1
WILLARD EUGENE L	MAJ	0-0522249	0246	1
WILLARD FRANK A	LTC	0-0187812	1053	3
WILLARD GEORGE W	CPT	0-0462807	0246	2
WILLARD GORDON W	MAJ	C-2014444	0663	1
WILLARD JOHN H	LTC	0-0316551	1063	1
WILLARD JOSEPH P	CW2	W-2147512	1157	1
WILLARD PIERCE M	LTC	0-0168840	0958	3
WILLARD ROBERT A	CPT	0-0491447	C955	1
WILLARD ROBERT S	CPT	0-1081261	C454	2
WILLARD WILLIAM W	CW2	W-2104848	0260	1
WILLCOX HUGH L	LTC	0-0335926	0965	3
WILLCOX JAMES E	MAJ	0-1290694	0460	1
WILLCUT CLARE F	CW3	W-2146528	0464	2
WILLECKE EDWARD C	LTC	0-0467859	0962	1
WILLEMS JR FRANCIS M	MAJ	C-0959283	0164	1
WILLENS ANTHONY T	MAJ	C-1649239	0557	1
WILLESS HERSEL F	CPT	0-0372042	C843	2
WILLET BYRON C	MAJ	C-0322864	1046	2
WILLETS DAVID B	COL	0-0245460	0866	3
WILLETT HUBERT T	1LT	0-1301078	0850	1
WILLETT JAMES F	LTC	0-0240069	0146	2
WILLETT MARION L	CPT	0-1011255	0745	2
WILLETT PRENTICE A	LTC	0-0257703	1263	3
WILLETTE HENRY J	WO1	W-2139596	0148	1
WILLEY EVERETT W	LTC	0-1558626	0864	3
WILLEY JAMES B	MAJ	0-0246254	1264	3
WILLEY JOSEPH G	MAJ	0-2005304	0664	1
WILLEY JR EDWARD P	CPT	0-0273789	1045	2
WILLEY NORMAN O	COL	0-0324432	1262	1
WILLEY RALPH E	COL	0-0213781	0460	3
WILLEY SEAVER A	CW4	W-2108695	0161	1
WILLEY WILLIAM W	LTC	0-0290347	0367	3
WILLEY WINSTON E	LTC	0-0295134	0462	1
WILLHOIT THOMAS O	LTC	C-1115848	0663	1
WILLIAMS ADRIAN H	COL	0-0233204	0365	3
WILLIAMS ALAMANCA L	LTC	0-1288984	0861	1
WILLIAMS ALBERT C	CW2	RW-2151858	0961	1
WILLIAMS ALFRED A	MAJ	0-0220900	0660	3

NAME	GRADE	SVC NO	DATE RET MO YR	RET CODE
WILLIAMS ALFRED L	LTC	0-0313377	1047	1
WILLIAMS ALLEN H	COL	0-0501099	1057	3
WILLIAMS ALLEN H	1LT	0-1541344	0651	1
WILLIAMS ALTON P	LTC	0-1101278	0661	1
WILLIAMS ANCEL F	CW2	W-2150259	0561	1
WILLIAMS ANDREW A	CW2	W-2150756	0263	1
WILLIAMS ANDREW J	CPT	0-0494538	0653	1
WILLIAMS ARBERY R	LTC	0-0325045	0759	1
WILLIAMS ARCHIBALD	MAJ	0-0180481	0644	1
WILLIAMS ARTHUR M	CPT	0-1167282	0645	2
WILLIAMS ARTHUR V	COL	0-0250035	0160	2
WILLIAMS ARTIS O	2LT	C-2009747	0257	1
WILLIAMS AUBREY L	LTC	0-1031040	1164	1
WILLIAMS AVERY D	1LT	0-2014995	0152	2
WILLIAMS BEN	CW3	W-2115796	0804	1
WILLIAMS BENJAMIN H	CPT	0-0277957	0861	3
WILLIAMS BENJAMIN S	CW2	W-2152085	0559	1
WILLIAMS BENNIE M	MAJ	C-1341737	0266	1
WILLIAMS BERNARD E	MAJ	0-1639816	0160	1
WILLIAMS BERNARD O	MAJ	0-0576596	1061	1
WILLIAMS BERT C	MAJ	0-1182304	1060	1
WILLIAMS BEULAH O	2LT	N-0744421	0645	1
WILLIAMS BRISTOL W	MAJ	C-1549179	1157	1
WILLIAMS CADINE W	CPT	N-0735039	1148	2
WILLIAMS CARL	CPT	C-1324213	1146	2
WILLIAMS CARL E	LTC	0-2040985	1263	1
WILLIAMS CARL M	2LT	0-0516682	0943	2
WILLIAMS CARLYLE R	LTC	0-0382454	0560	1
WILLIAMS CATHERINE	2LT	N-0772398	0945	1
WILLIAMS CECIL R	CW3	W-2150348	0465	1
WILLIAMS CHARLES A	LTC	0-0363613	0759	1
WILLIAMS CHARLES A	CPT	0-0419076	0944	2
WILLIAMS CHARLES C	CW2	W-2145608	0755	1
WILLIAMS CHARLES E	1LT	0-1594558	0945	2
WILLIAMS CHARLES E	MAJ	0-2096705	0764	1
WILLIAMS CHARLES H	LTC	0-0245552	0966	3
WILLIAMS CHARLES H	CW2	W-2146986	0359	1
WILLIAMS CHARLES L	MAJ	0-1684999	0464	1
WILLIAMS CHARLES R	COL	0-0255895	0261	3
WILLIAMS CHARLES R	LTC	0-0452537	1056	1
WILLIAMS CHARLES T	1LT	0-1317458	1046	1
WILLIAMS CHESTER A	LTC	0-0454184	0857	1
WILLIAMS CHESTER A	CW2	W-2104594	0845	2
WILLIAMS CLARENCE V	MAJ	0-0165331	0648	3
WILLIAMS CLARK E	CPT	0-1109753	1047	1
WILLIAMS CLAUDE A	MAJ	0-2262611	0765	1
WILLIAMS CLIFFORD J	CPT	0-1286220	1051	1
WILLIAMS CLYDE J	CPT	0-0108580	0540	1
WILLIAMS CURTIS F	MAJ	0-2035745	0456	1
WILLIAMS DALE E	LTC	0-1289661	0960	1
WILLIAMS DALE V	CW2	W-2151403	0556	1
WILLIAMS DAN	MAJ	0-1017251	0757	1
WILLIAMS DAN W	MAJ	0-1690915	0361	1
WILLIAMS DANIEL C	MAJ	0-2018451	0563	1
WILLIAMS DAVIC	CPT	0-1323376	0848	1
WILLIAMS DAVID C	MAJ	0-2263691	1165	1
WILLIAMS DAVID E	MAJ	0-0318838	0446	2
WILLIAMS DAVID E	CW4	W-2143345	1266	1
WILLIAMS DAVID T	CPT	0-1311459	0266	1
WILLIAMS DENNIS S	WO1	W-2109767	1046	1
WILLIAMS DEXTER B	LTC	0-0506689	0863	3
WILLIAMS DON L	MAJ	0-0269693	1067	3
WILLIAMS DONALD B	CPT	0-0227935	0862	3
WILLIAMS DONALD D	CPT	0-1694391	1045	2
WILLIAMS DONALD W	COL	0-0302100	0761	1
WILLIAMS DORIS H	1LT	N-0720391	0244	1
WILLIAMS DUDLEY	LTC	0-0127865	0158	1
WILLIAMS DUDLEY M	COL	C-2047541	0865	3
WILLIAMS DWIGHT L	LTC	0-0130732	0753	3
WILLIAMS EARL E	MAJ	0-1107759	0946	2
WILLIAMS EARL J	CW3	W-2203307	0965	1
WILLIAMS EARL R	LTC	0-0388356	0461	1
WILLIAMS EARL T	LTC	0-1541339	0461	1
WILLIAMS EARLE B	COL	0-0244570	0962	3
WILLIAMS EDWARD	CPT	0-0110937	0454	3

NAME	GRADE	SVC NO	DATE RET MO YR	RET CODE
WILLIAMS EDWARD B	1LT	0-1012182	0846	2
WILLIAMS EDWARD E	LTC	0-0206932	0157	3
WILLIAMS EDWARD W	MAJ	0-2263394	0263	1
WILLIAMS EDWIN E	MAJ	0-0968265	1062	1
WILLIAMS EDWIN L	CW3	W-2203336	1167	1
WILLIAMS EDWIN M	CPT	0-0942979	0457	2
WILLIAMS EFFIE F	CPT	N-0764109	1047	1
WILLIAMS ELTON V	1LT	0-1647332	1061	1
WILLIAMS ELWOOD E	CPT	0-1003350	0660	1
WILLIAMS EMORY L	MAJ	0-0330802	1056	1
WILLIAMS ERNEST E	CW2	W-2150107	0164	1
WILLIAMS ERNEST E	CW2	W-2205549	0161	1
WILLIAMS EUGENE H	2LT	0-1999120	0763	2
WILLIAMS EUGENE V	MAJ	0-1331124	1064	1
WILLIAMS EZRA M	LTC	0-0375357	0761	1
WILLIAMS FRANCIS R	LTC	0-1646705	0566	1
WILLIAMS FRANK E	2LT	0-1297630	1144	2
WILLIAMS FRANK F	MAJ	0-2017319	0665	1
WILLIAMS FRANK M	MAJ	0-0114505	0152	3
WILLIAMS FRANK M	LTC	0-0265083	0364	3
WILLIAMS FRANK M	MAJ	0-0276754	0258	3
WILLIAMS FRANK M	CPT	0-1305360	0947	1
WILLIAMS FRED E	2LT	0-1286750	0145	2
WILLIAMS FREDDIE M	CPT	0-1540898	0259	1
WILLIAMS FREDERICK	MAJ	0-0465613	0645	2
WILLIAMS FREDERICK	MAJ	0-1646111	1154	1
WILLIAMS FREDERICK	CW3	W-2142619	0363	1
WILLIAMS GARLAND H	COL	0-0197966	0264	3
WILLIAMS GARNET C	LTC	0-0289398	1040	2
WILLIAMS GARVIN D	LTC	0-0222596	0149	3
WILLIAMS GEORGE C	MAJ	0-2263283	1061	1
WILLIAMS GEORGE E	CPT	0-0487416	0447	2
WILLIAMS GEORGE F	CPT	0-1186963	0657	1
WILLIAMS GEORGE F	1LT	0-1298327	0347	2
WILLIAMS GEORGE H	LTC	0-1580505	0761	1
WILLIAMS GEORGE J	COL	0-0261070	0462	1
WILLIAMS GEORGE K	CPT	0-2035997	0460	1
WILLIAMS GEORGE L	MAJ	0-1590265	1064	1
WILLIAMS GEORGE T	MAJ	0-0488365	0156	1
WILLIAMS GEORGE W	CPT	0-0538231	0646	2
WILLIAMS GEORGE W	MAJ	0-0974553	0962	1
WILLIAMS GERALD O	MAJ	0-1165054	1046	1
WILLIAMS GIBSON	MAJ	0-2265111	0366	1
WILLIAMS GILBERT W	2LT	0-1587732	0345	2
WILLIAMS GILBERT W	MAJ	0-0232790	0546	2
WILLIAMS GLENN B	MAJ	0-0259487	0964	3
WILLIAMS GLENN C	COL	0-0100386	0552	3
WILLIAMS GLYNN W	CPT	0-1304299	0263	2
WILLIAMS GOVIE L	1LT	0-0460021	0845	2
WILLIAMS GRANT J	LTC	0-0365852	0156	2
WILLIAMS GUS	1LT	0-1913981	0327	1
WILLIAMS GUSS E	LTC	0-1172338	1167	1
WILLIAMS GUY M	COL	0-0145910	0857	3
WILLIAMS HAROLD B	LTC	0-1294401	0857	1
WILLIAMS HAROLD D	1LT	0-0381847	1044	2
WILLIAMS HAROLD E	LTC	0-1031852	0166	1
WILLIAMS HAROLD E	2LT	0-2006852	0846	2
WILLIAMS HAROLD F	CPT	0-1555156	0965	1
WILLIAMS HAROLD F	CW3	W-2148670	1065	1
WILLIAMS HAROLD H	MAJ	0-0501708	0349	1
WILLIAMS HAROLD L	CPT	0-0500660	1145	2
WILLIAMS HAROLD L	MAJ	0-0967658	0664	2
WILLIAMS HAROLD O	LTC	0-0257497	0262	3
WILLIAMS HAROLD T	LTC	0-0261979	0866	3
WILLIAMS HARRY G	COL	0-0253746	0153	3
WILLIAMS HARRY K	CPT	0-0548872	1046	1
WILLIAMS HARRY L	CPT	0-0500284	0550	1
WILLIAMS HARRY L	1LT	0-1053877	1045	2
WILLIAMS HARRY M	CPT	0-1341611	0456	1
WILLIAMS HARRY N	CW3	W-2144864	0961	1
WILLIAMS HARRY S	MAJ	0-0946721	0166	1
WILLIAMS HARVEY J	MAJ	0-0283208	1067	3
WILLIAMS HARVEY V	LTC	0-0137291	1051	3
WILLIAMS HASKELL G	MAJ	0-2014554	1263	1
WILLIAMS HENRY C	CW2	W-2149357	0459	1
WILLIAMS HENRY D	COL	0-0362695	0861	1
WILLIAMS HENRY E E	CW3	W-2151937	1064	1
WILLIAMS HENRY W	COL	0-0232072	1163	3
WILLIAMS HERBERT A	CW2	W-2143487	0360	1
WILLIAMS HERBERT L	MAJ	0-1105724	0266	1
WILLIAMS HERBERT M	MAJ	0-1636831	0364	1
WILLIAMS HIRAM W	CW4	W-2119760	0261	1
WILLIAMS HOMER A	CPT	0-0301573	0450	1
WILLIAMS HOMER D	CW3	W-2146622	0263	1
WILLIAMS HOMER P	CW4	W-2145858	1061	1
WILLIAMS HORACE S	CPT	0-1999764	1053	1
WILLIAMS HOWARD	COL	0-0275383	0764	3
WILLIAMS HOWARD B	CW4	W-2108980	1154	1
WILLIAMS HOWARD F	LTC	0-0286065	1061	3
WILLIAMS HOWARD K	MAJ	0-2035844	0363	1
WILLIAMS HOWARD W	CW2	W-2148423	1060	1
WILLIAMS HUBERT H	CPT	0-1796892	0755	1
WILLIAMS HUBERT M	CPT	0-1541956	0349	2
WILLIAMS HUGH R	CPT	0-0218997	0347	1
WILLIAMS IRA	CW4	W-2123198	0363	1
WILLIAMS IRENE R	MAJ	N-0702342	0560	1
WILLIAMS IRWIN T	CW2	W-2205952	0363	1
WILLIAMS J C S	CW3	W-2147593	0965	1
WILLIAMS J D	CW2	W-2148401	0559	1
WILLIAMS J STEWART	MAJ	0-0456046	0546	2
WILLIAMS JACK	LTC	0-0452725	1058	1
WILLIAMS JACK A	1LT	0-1030538	0745	2
WILLIAMS JACK C	LTC	0-0450521	0657	1
WILLIAMS JACK G	CPT	0-1574555	1045	2
WILLIAMS JACK L	LTC	0-1050140	0865	1
WILLIAMS JAMES	CPT	0-1824261	0658	2
WILLIAMS JAMES B	2LT	0-1319696	0244	2
WILLIAMS JAMES B	MAJ	0-2024438	1059	1
WILLIAMS JAMES C	LTC	0-0301105	0665	3
WILLIAMS JAMES C	MAJ	0-0886899	1159	1
WILLIAMS JAMES C	MAJ	0-1329654	0157	1
WILLIAMS JAMES D	LTC	0-0366830	0263	1
WILLIAMS JAMES D	LTC	0-1324215	1062	1
WILLIAMS JAMES E	CPT	0-0250083	0865	3
WILLIAMS JAMES H	MAJ	0-1799925	1262	1
WILLIAMS JAMES H	LTC	0-1548249	0164	1
WILLIAMS JAMES H	MAJ	0-2047543	1162	1
WILLIAMS JAMES J	MAJ	0-1640125	0257	1
WILLIAMS JAMES M	2LT	0-1873678	0966	2
WILLIAMS JAMES R	MAJ	0-1703924	1054	1
WILLIAMS JAMES R	MAJ	0-1920289	1165	1
WILLIAMS JAMES S	COL	0-0163259	0256	3
WILLIAMS JAMES T	LTC	0-0491045	0361	2
WILLIAMS JAMES T	MAJ	0-0970837	1161	1
WILLIAMS JAMES T	CPT	0-1287801	0950	1
WILLIAMS JEFFERSON	CPT	0-1288986	1045	2
WILLIAMS JESSIE E	LTC	0-1115156	0762	1
WILLIAMS JOEL L	CPT	0-1945975	0448	2
WILLIAMS JOHN	CPT	0-0502355	1045	2
WILLIAMS JOHN	MAJ	0-1926821	0567	1
WILLIAMS JOHN B	CW2	W-2122222	0647	1
WILLIAMS JOHN C	COL	0-0239922	0263	3
WILLIAMS JOHN C	MAJ	0-0283591	0350	1
WILLIAMS JOHN C	1LT	0-1596856	1045	2
WILLIAMS JOHN E	COL	0-0172422	1060	3
WILLIAMS JOHN F	COL	0-0143669	0154	3
WILLIAMS JOHN F	LTC	0-1165263	0566	2
WILLIAMS JOHN F	LTC	0-1946639	0264	1
WILLIAMS JOHN J	COL	0-0201995	1146	2
WILLIAMS JOHN M	MAJ	0-1575638	0-48	1
WILLIAMS JOHN R	1LT	0-1292435	0445	2
WILLIAMS JOHN T	WO1	W-2115679	0547	1
WILLIAMS JOHN W	CPT	0-0355041	0945	2
WILLIAMS JOSEPH B	MAJ	0-1578047	0953	1
WILLIAMS JOSEPH H	MAJ	0-2055206	0358	1
WILLIAMS JOSEPH J	2LT	0-1328547	0446	2
WILLIAMS JR ALFRED H	CPT	0-1016166	0146	2
WILLIAMS JR BERT A	1LT	0-0414884	0545	2
WILLIAMS JR CORAN L	MAJ	0-1116488	0760	1
WILLIAMS JR DAVID J	LTC	0-0174178	0944	2
WILLIAMS JR EDWARD F	CPT	0-1917790	0764	1
WILLIAMS JR ERNEST F	MAJ	0-1874753	0466	1
WILLIAMS JR EVAN A	CPT	0-1040066	0661	1
WILLIAMS JR GEORGE	MAJ	0-0502387	0954	1
WILLIAMS JR GEORGE	LTC	0-1548164	0561	1
WILLIAMS JR GEORGE H	LTC	0-0450566	0758	1
WILLIAMS JR JOSLYN J	1LT	0-1884102	0154	2
WILLIAMS JR L D	LTC	0-1541184	0161	1
WILLIAMS JR MASON L	LTC	0-1045640	1065	1
WILLIAMS JR OSCAR A	CPT	0-0520144	0147	2
WILLIAMS JR ROBERT C	MAJ	0-1540895	1264	1
WILLIAMS JR THOMAS C	LTC	0-1296461	1163	2
WILLIAMS JR W R	CPT	0-0354069	1059	1
WILLIAMS JR WILEY W	CW2	W-2211694	0867	1
WILLIAMS JR ZACK R	MAJ	0-1294053	0464	1
WILLIAMS KATHRYN L	1LT	N-0770044	0747	1
WILLIAMS KENNETH	MAJ	0-1313334	0962	1
WILLIAMS KENNETH L	MAJ	0-1534190	1057	1
WILLIAMS KERMIT C	CPT	0-1595271	0457	1
WILLIAMS KRESS R	COL	0-0254833	1166	3
WILLIAMS L J	2LT	0-1914121	0548	1
WILLIAMS L KEMPER	B G	0-0125140	0648	3
WILLIAMS LELAND H	LTC	0-0397205	0960	1
WILLIAMS LEO C	WO1	W-2119341	0349	1
WILLIAMS LEONARD E	CPT	0-1031284	0546	1
WILLIAMS LEONARD L	CPT	0-1305149	0747	2
WILLIAMS LEROY	1LT	0-1001276	0145	2
WILLIAMS LESLIE E	COL	0-0245097	0164	3
WILLIAMS LESTER B	LTC	0-0343425	0461	1
WILLIAMS LEWIS H	LTC	0-1949979	0166	1
WILLIAMS LEWIS O	LTC	0-0905629	1061	3
WILLIAMS LEWIS S	LTC	0-0139946	0-53	3
WILLIAMS LLOYD A	MAJ	0-0493070	1062	1
WILLIAMS LLOYD J	CPT	0-2262558	0762	2
WILLIAMS LONNIE B	LTC	0-0430190	1149	1
WILLIAMS LOREN L	MAJ	0-0231519	0159	3
WILLIAMS LOUGENE	CW2	W-2209371	1263	1
WILLIAMS LOUIE L	LTC	0-1635483	0358	1
WILLIAMS LOUIS E	LTC	0-0453832	0761	1
WILLIAMS LOWELL C	CW4	W-2006362	0365	3
WILLIAMS LOWELL E	MAJ	0-1053884	0761	1
WILLIAMS MARK F	MAJ	0-0309986	0446	2
WILLIAMS MARTIN J	LTC	0-1946640	0161	1
WILLIAMS MARY F	1LT	N-0751174	0945	1
WILLIAMS MAURICE M	LTC	0-1080760	0763	1
WILLIAMS MAX O	CW2	W-3100524	0967	1
WILLIAMS MAXWELL L	MAJ	0-1552420	0858	1
WILLIAMS MILLARD J	LTC	0-0242209	0766	3
WILLIAMS MORRIS C	MAJ	0-1016854	0566	1
WILLIAMS MORRIS F	MAJ	0-2026340	1061	1
WILLIAMS MYRON F	MAJ	0-0336046	0661	1
WILLIAMS NELLIE K	MAJ	L-0904015	1063	3
WILLIAMS NELSON B	CPT	0-1290169	1045	2
WILLIAMS NEWTON A	MAJ	0-0369335	0555	1
WILLIAMS NORMAN W	1LT	0-1324607	0248	2
WILLIAMS ODELL D	COL	0-1100395	0761	1
WILLIAMS OK G	MAJ	0-1169793	1160	1
WILLIAMS OLIVER O	COL	0-0258258	0258	1
WILLIAMS OMER F	LTC	0-1798429	0966	1
WILLIAMS ONIE O	MAJ	0-0284702	0645	1
WILLIAMS PALMER C	LTC	0-0171836	1054	3
WILLIAMS PAUL L	CPT	0-0530455	0546	2
WILLIAMS PAUL S	CW3	W-2148894	1162	1
WILLIAMS PHILLIP E	COL	0-0235418	0465	3
WILLIAMS PHYLLIS J	2LT	N-0771595	0944	1
WILLIAMS PRESTON A	1LT	0-0509881	1050	1
WILLIAMS PRICE W	MAJ	0-0149605	0950	3
WILLIAMS QUINTON A	1LT	0-2007366	0353	1
WILLIAMS RALPH C	1LT	0-1311953	0350	1
WILLIAMS RALPH D	MAJ	0-0988683	1162	1
WILLIAMS RALPH T	CPT	0-1039799	0446	2
WILLIAMS RAY E	LTC	0-0238228	0161	3
WILLIAMS RAYMOND E	LTC	0-0241369	0756	3
WILLIAMS RAYMOND J	1LT	0-1798537	0655	1
WILLIAMS RAYMOND L	1LT	0-2025187	0247	1
WILLIAMS REIMAN K	MAJ	0-1594427	0767	1
WILLIAMS RICHARD H	CPT	0-0233212	1159	3
WILLIAMS RICHARD O	1LT	0-1913956	0738	1
WILLIAMS ROBERT	LTC	0-2008363	0767	1
WILLIAMS ROBERT C	LTC	0-0259678	1064	3
WILLIAMS ROBERT C	LTC	0-0947674	0867	1
WILLIAMS ROBERT C	CPT	0-1798538	0353	1
WILLIAMS ROBERT C	CW2	W-2145006	1159	1
WILLIAMS ROBERT D	MAJ	0-0987374	0565	1
WILLIAMS ROBERT D	CPT	0-1313006	0146	2
WILLIAMS ROBERT D	CW2	W-2210746	0766	1
WILLIAMS ROBERT F	COL	0-0157739	0357	3
WILLIAMS ROBERT H	LTC	0-0362706	1164	1
WILLIAMS ROBERT H	MAJ	0-1301738	0562	1
WILLIAMS ROBERT J	MAJ	0-1014096	1163	1
WILLIAMS ROBERT K	LTC	0-1101719	1162	1
WILLIAMS ROBERT L	1LT	0-1042743	0144	2
WILLIAMS ROBERT L	CW3	W-3150363	0767	1
WILLIAMS ROBERT M	2LT	0-1016082	0145	2
WILLIAMS ROBERT M	CPT	0-1110347	0645	2
WILLIAMS ROBERT W	LTC	0-0388417	0660	1
WILLIAMS ROBERT W	CPT	0-1700202	0845	2
WILLIAMS ROGER B	LTC	0-0157861	0857	3
WILLIAMS ROGER C	COL	0-0216449	1163	3
WILLIAMS ROY F	CPT	0-0450522	0358	1
WILLIAMS RUFUS E	CW4	W-2115085	0153	1
WILLIAMS RUPERT E	LTC	0-0129457	0450	3
WILLIAMS SAMUEL E	LTC	0-0291835	1164	3
WILLIAMS SAMUEL H	LTC	0-0219982	0645	1
WILLIAMS SHEDRICK M	WO1	W-2144460	0856	1
WILLIAMS SHRABLE O	LTC	0-0445033	0663	1
WILLIAMS SIDNEY A	COL	0-0354313	1263	3
WILLIAMS SIDNEY J	MAJ	0-2208466	0965	1
WILLIAMS SR ELBERT B	CW4	W-2142213	0462	1
WILLIAMS STANLEY E	MAJ	0-1821947	0261	1
WILLIAMS STANLEY M	CW2	W-2149144	0762	1
WILLIAMS STARLIN I	1LT	0-1995539	1147	2
WILLIAMS STELLA E	2LT	N-0700804	1038	1
WILLIAMS THADDEUS E	CPT	0-0486429	1045	2
WILLIAMS THELMA B	MAJ	N-0762460	0864	1
WILLIAMS THOMAS A	CPT	0-2050695	0856	1
WILLIAMS THOMAS C	MAJ	0-1100396	0853	1
WILLIAMS THOMAS C	CW2	W-2147202	0755	1
WILLIAMS THOMAS D	CW4	W-2109193	1057	1
WILLIAMS THOMAS E	MAJ	0-1587023	0459	1
WILLIAMS THOMAS J	CPT	0-0387003	0845	2
WILLIAMS THOMAS M	LTC	0-0235053	0457	3
WILLIAMS THOMAS M	LTC	0-0252153	0166	3
WILLIAMS THOMAS M	LTC	0-0289485	0361	2
WILLIAMS TRACY	MAJ	0-0506976	0457	1
WILLIAMS TROY	WO1	W-2144513	0760	1
WILLIAMS TROY	CW2	W-2149145	0459	2
WILLIAMS TURNER N	1LT	0-0428111	0546	2
WILLIAMS VERNARD E	CW3	W-2114473	0457	2
WILLIAMS VERNON S	MAJ	0-1105273	0264	1
WILLIAMS VIRGIL B	COL	0-0194139	0-51	3
WILLIAMS VIRGIL C	LTC	0-0394262	0660	1
WILLIAMS VIRGIL E	CW2	W-2145046	0762	1
WILLIAMS VIRGIL H	COL	0-0244104	0458	1
WILLIAMS WALTER	LTC	0-0351052	0759	1
WILLIAMS WALTER A	LTC	0-0235693	0358	3
WILLIAMS WALTER B	LTC	0-0288682	1158	3
WILLIAMS WALTER D	LTC	0-2036846	0566	1
WILLIAMS WALTER H	CPT	0-1314356	0747	2
WILLIAMS WALTER M	COL	0-0286775	0247	2
WILLIAMS WALTER W	CW2	W-3200275	1165	1
WILLIAMS WENTWORTH	COL	0-0124936	0955	3
WILLIAMS WESLEY E	LTC	0-0452313	0461	1
WILLIAMS WILBURN	CW3	W-2152363	1262	1
WILLIAMS WILL J	MAJ	0-0493389	0-53	1
WILLIAMS WILLARD C	1LT	0-1031216	0445	2
WILLIAMS WILLIAM A	LTC	0-0403292	0962	1
WILLIAMS WILLIAM B	CPT	0-0379493	0446	2
WILLIAMS WILLIAM E	COL	0-0266046	1054	3
WILLIAMS WILLIAM E	2LT	0-1593396	0545	2

NAME	GRADE	SVC NO	DATE RET MO YR	RET CODE
WILLIAMS WILLIAM F	LTC	0-0342517	0359	1
WILLIAMS WILLIAM F	LTC	0-0480721	0262	1
WILLIAMS WILLIAM G	CPT	0-0547402		2
WILLIAMS WILLIAM H	COL	0-0335927	0556	3
WILLIAMS WILLIAM H	MAJ	C-1179247	C462	1
WILLIAMS WILLIAM J	MAJ	0-187487C	C963	1
WILLIAMS WILLIAM J	CW3	W-2207637	0966	1
WILLIAMS WILLIAM L	LTC	0-0259448	1264	3
WILLIAMS WILLIAM D	LTC	0-1001277	0658	1
WILLIAMS WILLIAM T	CW4	W-214262C	0267	1
WILLIAMS WILLIF	1LT	0-117867C	0546	2
WILLIAMS WILLIE C	CW2	W-2145263	1154	1
WILLIAMS WILLIE F	2LT	0-1651256	0552	1
WILLIAMS WILLIE L	CW3	W-2148630	0863	1
WILLIAMS WILSON C	COL	0-0213651	1058	3
WILLIAMS WINTFORD N	CW2	W-3151383	1067	1
WILLIAMS WINTHROP W	LTC	C-0119434	C560	3
WILLIAMSON ADRIAN	COL	C-0103062	C554	3
WILLIAMSON ADRIAN P	CPT	0-2102784	0862	2
WILLIAMSON ALFRED S	LTC	C-0145840	0655	3
WILLIAMSON ALFRED S	1LT	0-1695661	0560	1
WILLIAMSON ARTHUR M	MAJ	0-1116194	0763	2
WILLIAMSON CARMEN A	LTC	0-0406592	0662	1
WILLIAMSON CHESTER B	2LT	0-0494652	0145	2
WILLIAMSON CLARENCE	LTC	0-0337883	0346	2
WILLIAMSON CLARENCE	CW3	W-2149803	0963	1
WILLIAMSON CYRUS M	1LT	0-0547403	1045	2
WILLIAMSON DALE F	CW4	W-2151755	0863	1
WILLIAMSON DON E	2LT	0-1294585	0544	2
WILLIAMSON EARL	CW2	W-2141874	C559	1
WILLIAMSON EDWARD J	LTC	0-0384916	0864	1
WILLIAMSON EDWIN A	MAJ	C-0378213	0848	1
WILLIAMSON ELVIN G	LTC	0-0487590	0858	1
WILLIAMSON EUGENE R	LTC	0-1049024	0662	1
WILLIAMSON FORREST R	CW3	W-2151032	C559	1
WILLIAMSON GEORGE R	MAJ	C-1305362	0165	1
WILLIAMSON GEORGE W	CW2	W-2148424	C766	1
WILLIAMSON GLYNN E	LTC	0-0281189	1067	3
WILLIAMSON HARRY H	MAJ	0-0504477	0350	1
WILLIAMSON HAZEL R	1LT	N-0763532	0546	1
WILLIAMSON HENRY B	WO1	W-21086C6	0646	1
WILLIAMSON HOWELL E	LTC	0-2000966	0766	1
WILLIAMSON J C	1LT	0-1703055	C245	2
WILLIAMSON J C	WO1	W-2129525	1157	2
WILLIAMSON JAMES C	MAJ	C-1588373	0363	1
WILLIAMSON JOE E	CW4	W-2144577	0364	1
WILLIAMSON JOHN	COL	0-0137446	0648	3
WILLIAMSON JOHN F	MAJ	C-1332555	C865	1
WILLIAMSON JOHN L	LTC	0-0483117	C252	1
WILLIAMSON JOSEPH F	LTC	0-0188164	0953	3
WILLIAMSON JULIAN S	MAJ	0-0371233	C267	3
WILLIAMSON LINDSAY	LTC	0-1845845	0766	3
WILLIAMSON MARION	B G	0-0196761	0762	3
WILLIAMSON MARION A	MAJ	N-0751313	0563	2
WILLIAMSON MAURICE	CPT	0-0274597	1144	2
WILLIAMSON MELVIN J	1LT	0-1030539	1045	2
WILLIAMSON MORTON T	MAJ	0-0359514	0545	2
WILLIAMSON NORMAN J	MAJ	0-0454936	0862	1
WILLIAMSON ROBERT C	LTC	0-1548339	0757	1
WILLIAMSON ROBERT C	MAJ	C-2040717	0756	1
WILLIAMSON ROBERT E	1LT	0-0386223	1144	2
WILLIAMSON ROBERT E	LTC	0-0445061	1053	2
WILLIAMSON ROBERT N	MAJ	C-1049032	1160	1
WILLIAMSON ROLAND F	MAJ	C-0275328	0965	3
WILLIAMSON ROSCOE E	LTC	0-0283698	1266	3
WILLIAMSON RUFUS S	LTC	C-0151735	0757	3
WILLIAMSON S E	CW2	W-2152086	0555	1
WILLIAMSON SAMUEL D	CW3	W-2205437	C861	1
WILLIAMSON SHIRLEY E	2LT	0-1010723	C544	2
WILLIAMSON SR BUEL A	LTC	C-0268458	0555	2
WILLIAMSON STEPHEN A	LTC	0-0102077	0656	1
WILLIAMSON STEPHEN E	2LT	0-1327C67	1145	2
WILLIAMSON SYLVESTER	MAJ	C-0425738	1262	1
WILLIAMSON THOMAS	CPT	0-0449019	0347	1
WILLIAMSON THOMAS L	LTC	0-0202612	0153	3

NAME	GRADE	SVC NO	DATE RET MO YR	RET CODE
WILLIAMSON THOMAS S	LTC	0-100089C	0862	1
WILLIAMSON WARD W	MAJ	0-2036455	0260	1
WILLIAMSON WAYNE C	LTC	0-0331120	0261	1
WILLIAMSON WILLIAM B	LTC	0-1308743	0466	3
WILLIAMSON WILLIAM E	1LT	0-1554116	0850	1
WILLIAMSON WILLIAM G	LTC	0-0402560	0760	1
WILLIAMSON WILLIAM P	CW2	W-2210136	0365	1
WILLIAMSTON HOMER	CW3	W-2141494	0461	1
WILLIARD WILLIAM C	LTC	0-1175010	0561	1
WILLIBY IVOR J	LTC	0-0336371	0948	2
WILLIE LEON A	MAJ	0-1287635	1160	1
WILLIE WALTER G	CPT	0-092208C	0845	2
WILLIFORD HENRY N	LTC	0-0450523	1056	1
WILLIFORD ROBERT B	COL	0-0354302	1264	3
WILLIG SAMUEL	LTC	0-1945980	1063	3
WILLIMON JR WALTER F	1LT	0-1306248	0545	1
WILLING CARL H C	MAJ	0-1302579	0361	1
WILLINGHAM ALBERT J	CW3	W-2141495	0960	1
WILLINGHAM BURTON A	CW3	W-2149138	0567	1
WILLINGHAM OSCAR B	CPT	0-0378834	0246	2
WILLINGHAM T R	CW3	W-2109073	0556	1
WILLIS ALLEN H	CPT	0-1040328	0647	2
WILLIS ALVIE P	CPT	0-0479704	1048	1
WILLIS AUBREY D	CW2	W-221C995	0765	1
WILLIS BILLY R	CW3	W-2149687	0964	1
WILLIS BURTON D	COL	0-0256871	1057	3
WILLIS CARL P	MAJ	0-2024432	0759	2
WILLIS CHARLES A	B G	0-0357988	0766	3
WILLIS CHARLES O	CPT	0-1310007	0948	2
WILLIS CHARLES E	MAJ	0-1303978	1062	1
WILLIS CHARLES G	1LT	0-0478881	0946	1
WILLIS CHARLES R	MAJ	C-2033243	0564	1
WILLIS DEWEY J	LTC	0-0250729	0659	3
WILLIS DILLARD L	CPT	0-1289844	0846	1
WILLIS DELMAN W	1LT	0-010C725	0257	3
WILLIS EUGENE	LTC	0-0313225	1162	1
WILLIS FRED L	LTC	0-0468913	1167	3
WILLIS GEORGE	CPT	0-1C01708	0457	1
WILLIS GEORGE W	CW2	W-2210422	0262	1
WILLIS HARRY R	1LT	0-0108408	0137	1
WILLIS HENRY J	LTC	0-0375009	1160	1
WILLIS HOMER A	CW2	W-2104600	0554	1
WILLIS HOUSTON P	MAJ	0-1551338	0760	1
WILLIS HOWARD L	CW3	W-2206475	1065	1
WILLIS JACK H	CW2	W-2151884	0563	1
WILLIS JAMES B	CPT	0-0386214	0844	2
WILLIS JAMES E	MAJ	0-1050518	0766	1
WILLIS JAMES E	MAJ	0-1114807	0959	1
WILLIS JESSE M	CPT	0-0289097	0145	2
WILLIS JOE C	CPT	0-2262663	0562	1
WILLIS JOHN A	LTC	0-0665484	0567	1
WILLIS JR GEORGE C	MAJ	C-1054453	0660	1
WILLIS JR JOHN C	LTC	0-165123C	0866	1
WILLIS JR THOMAS L	CW2	W-2210123	0864	2
WILLIS MERRITT M	1LT	0-0381135	0845	2
WILLIS PAUL W	CPT	0-1036800	0648	2
WILLIS RALPH M	CPT	0-1542125	C446	2
WILLIS RAY R	2LT	0-0545831	0545	2
WILLIS RAYMOND F	MAJ	0-1174744	0159	1
WILLIS ROBERT	WO1	W-2120621	0944	2
WILLIS ROBERT E	MAJ	0-0483842	0253	1
WILLIS WALDO	COL	0-0179333	0852	3
WILLIS WESTON H	M G	0-0289949	0367	3
WILLIS WILLIAM E	COL	0-0291451	0366	1
WILLIS WILLIAM H	COL	0-0238355	0565	3
WILLIS WOODROW	CW2	W-2149974	1158	2
WILLISTON EDWARD M	2LT	0-0396090	1144	2
WILLISTON JOHN O	LTC	0-0410792	0762	1
WILLITT VICTOR C	LTC	0-1638801	0667	3
WILLKIE ROBERT T	COL	0-0361092	0649	1
WILLMAN WALTER K	LTC	0-0127861	0556	3
WILLMORE CARL	LTC	0-0362685	1264	3
WILLMS HENRY C	1LT	0-0448106	0646	2
WILLOUGHBY CHARLES W	LTC	0-0348906	0260	1
WILLOUGHBY CLEO M	LTC	0-1C39803	0763	1

NAME	GRADE	SVC NO	DATE RET MO YR	RET CODE
WILLOUGHBY FRANCIS A	CPT	0-1296778	0447	2
WILLOUGHBY FREDERICK	LTC	0-1314861	0662	1
WILLOUGHBY GERALD E	CW3	W-2148225	0764	1
WILLOUGHBY HAROLD J	1LT	0-1290863	1045	1
WILLOUGHBY KENNETH D	COL	C-0252722	0663	3
WILLOUGHBY ROSCOE R	CPT	0-0188302	C454	3
WILLOUGHBY WILLIAM G	MAJ	0-1936380	C966	1
WILLS ALEXANDER	LTC	0-C338090	1265	3
WILLS DAVID H	CPT	0-0937349	0757	1
WILLS DAVID H	MAJ	C-0959282	0965	1
WILLS HARLAN J	LTC	0-0451195	1160	1
WILLS HAROLD P	LTC	0-0225865	0659	1
WILLS HAROLD P	LTC	0-0269626	0767	3
WILLS HOWARD	LTC	0-1542635	0963	1
WILLS HOWARD D	1LT	0-0297968	0945	1
WILLS MARGARET	1LT	L-0220183	C146	2
WILLS MERLIN V	LTC	0-0237780	0165	3
WILLS OLIVER T	MAJ	0-1686739	0765	1
WILLS WILLIAM H	MAJ	0-0888243	0463	1
WILLS WILLIAM L	CPT	0-2263045	0662	1
WILLSON FOY T	CPT	C-1047844	0258	1
WILLSON HARRY S	COL	0-0125434	C556	3
WILLSON JR ALLEN F	MAJ	0-2202030	0866	1
WILLSON STANLEY G	CW3	W-2150228	1161	1
WILLSON VIRGIL A	LTC	0-0173594	0959	3
WILLSON WESLEY W	LTC	0-0282038	1056	3
WILMARTH CARL B	CPT	0-0336755	1045	2
WILMER FREDERIC P	LTC	C-0163200	0961	3
WILMER RICHARD H	COL	0-0114573	1152	3
WILMETH ELWOOD E	LTC	0-1045637	0663	1
WILMORE ALLEN E	LTC	0-1947615	0163	1
WILMORE CHARLES W	COL	0-0288746	0367	3
WILMORE RALPH C	1LT	0-0487829	1144	2
WILMOT BASIL A	1LT	0-2C55173	0446	2
WILMOTH EDWARD M	LTC	0-0182225	1055	3
WILMOTH LUTHER H	COL	0-0287765	0660	3
WILMUTH GLEN E	2LT	0-0420932	0544	2
WILNER JULIAN P	2LT	0-1543358	0844	2
WILSEY LEONARD L	MAJ	0-1996644	1062	1
WILSON ADA E	1LT	N-0764582	0746	1
WILSON AGNES G	1LT	N-0775183	1045	1
WILSON ALBERT A	COL	0-0411572	1164	2
WILSON ALBERT VIN	COL	C-0103700	C952	3
WILSON ALBERT W	LTC	0-0530759	1166	2
WILSON ALEXANDER	1LT	0-1032256	0148	2
WILSON ALEXANDER	1LT	0-1895024	1045	2
WILSON ALFRED J P	COL	C-0255186	0661	3
WILSON ALLAN C	LTC	0-1050995	1067	1
WILSON ALPHUS	LTC	0-0239227	1163	3
WILSON ALVA H	COL	0-0236076	0266	3
WILSON AMOS P	CPT	0-1765122	0746	2
WILSON ANDREW J	LTC	0-0499710	0556	1
WILSON ARCHIE T	CPT	C-1003351	C946	1
WILSON ARDEN R	MAJ	0-1105274	0656	1
WILSON ARNOLD W	CPT	0-1785266	C754	2
WILSON ARTHUR J	CPT	0-0475278	0749	1
WILSON ARTHUR K	LTC	0-1303979	0962	1
WILSON ARTHUR L	CPT	0-0974419	1060	1
WILSON ARTHUR N	MAJ	C-1292624	1057	1
WILSON ARTHUR S	1LT	0-1178984	0345	2
WILSON AUBREY A	COL	0-0298288	0159	3
WILSON BARLE O	1LT	0-1287099	0256	1
WILSON BENJAMIN F	MAJ	C-1179250	1060	1
WILSON BERT E	LTC	0-1554999	1262	1
WILSON BRYANT	MAJ	C-0113103	0648	3
WILSON BRYON C	WO1	W-2101013	C551	1
WILSON BURGESS R	LTC	0-1303980	C862	1
WILSON CARL A	MAJ	0-0222944	1061	3
WILSON CARL J	MAJ	C-1017940	0561	1
WILSON CARNOT H	CW2	W-2142671	1163	1
WILSON CATO	COL	0-0229150	1164	3
WILSON CHANCLER W	MAJ	0-0990943	1163	2
WILSON CHARLES A	1LT	0-1543992	0445	2
WILSON CHARLES E	MAJ	0-2018083	C861	1
WILSON CHARLES H	MAJ	0-0275110	0145	2

NAME	GRADE	SVC NO	DATE RET MO YR	RET CODE
WILSON CHARLES H	1LT	0-1298474	0462	1
WILSON CHARLES J	MAJ	0-0328474	1052	1
WILSON CHARLES L	LTC	0-0414440	0166	1
WILSON CHARLES M	MAJ	0-0982314	0365	1
WILSON CHARLES M	1LT	0-1014948	0346	2
WILSON CHARLES W	CPT	0-1336581	0365	1
WILSON CHARLES T	CPT	0-2262923	1063	1
WILSON CHARLEY E	MAJ	0-0485079	0949	1
WILSON CHESTER S	MAJ	0-0127619	0648	3
WILSON CHRIS	LTC	0-0317485	0263	3
WILSON CLARENCE C	1LT	0-1823098	0546	2
WILSON CLAUDE	MAJ	C-0969106	0165	1
WILSON CLETUS L	CW3	W-2150125	0562	1
WILSON CLYDE E	CPT	0-0407987	0945	2
WILSON CLYDE R	CW2	W-2210338	0564	1
WILSON CLYDE S	COL	0-0115861	0-51	3
WILSON CLYDE W	LTC	0-1690901	1161	1
WILSON COLWELL P	1LT	0-1549494	0852	1
WILSON CONSON C	COL	0-0147583	0754	3
WILSON COYE M	CPT	0-1002754	0947	1
WILSON DAVID A	MAJ	0-1535434	0863	1
WILSON DAVID G	LTC	0-0227271	0157	1
WILSON DEAN E	MAJ	0-1931598	0666	1
WILSON DEANEL B	MAJ	C-1996514	1059	1
WILSON DELMAR G	LTC	0-0342809	0155	2
WILSON DENVER W	COL	0-0278007	0158	2
WILSON DEWEY M	1LT	0-0500071	0548	1
WILSON DONALD E	CW2	W-2208648	0864	1
WILSON DONALD J	COL	0-0235827	0259	3
WILSON DONNELL L	MAJ	0-0559341	0665	1
WILSON DOROTHY J	1LT	N-0776763	0549	1
WILSON DOUGLAS	CW3	W-2152076	0763	1
WILSON DUANE C	COL	0-0304046	0860	1
WILSON EARL F	LTC	0-0404551	0761	1
WILSON EARL J	LTC	0-1180772	1061	1
WILSON EARL R	CW3	W-2209432	1067	1
WILSON EARL S	MAJ	C-0197593	0961	3
WILSON EARL S	MAJ	C-1111988	0859	1
WILSON EDGAR H	CW2	W-2142743	0856	1
WILSON EDWARD F	CPT	0-0450950	0146	2
WILSON EDWARD S	CPT	0-0251495	0866	3
WILSON EDWARD T	LTC	0-0263707	1166	3
WILSON EDWIN D	CPT	C-0242955	0857	3
WILSON EDWIN W	1LT	0-2018967	0859	1
WILSON EDYTHE E	MAJ	N-0733438	1262	1
WILSON ELEANOR B	MAJ	L-060029C	0163	1
WILSON ELMER L	1LT	0-0493573	0451	1
WILSON ELYMO	LTC	0-1951723	0766	1
WILSON EMBREY E	2LT	0-1895931	0945	2
WILSON ERLING E	LTC	0-0444172	1154	2
WILSON ERNEST P	LTC	0-1080335	1153	1
WILSON EUGENE	LTC	0-1575280	0860	1
WILSON EUGENE A	LTC	0-2045156	0963	1
WILSON EUGENE V	CPT	0-1917747	0563	1
WILSON FLAVIUS K	CPT	0-0264090	0464	3
WILSON FORREST R	MAJ	0-1513394	1065	1
WILSON FOSTER M	MAJ	0-1685111	1044	2
WILSON FRANCIS C	MAJ	0-1103469	1061	1
WILSON FRANCIS K	LTC	0-0180948	0162	3
WILSON FRANK	CW2	W-2112259	0345	2
WILSON FRANK A	LTC	0-0496633	1262	1
WILSON FRANK B	CPT	0-018266C	0255	3
WILSON FRANKLIN B	LTC	0-0505822	1054	1
WILSON FRANKLIN E	1LT	0-1585088	1167	1
WILSON FRED E	CPT	0-0125432	0358	3
WILSON FRED E	COL	0-0253991	0460	1
WILSON FRED E	CW2	W-2115989	0859	2
WILSON FRED T	MAJ	C-0450485	C854	1
WILSON FREDERICK	WO1	W-2109936	0749	1
WILSON GEORGE D	LTC	0-15545CC	0662	2
WILSON GEORGE F	MAJ	0-0323897	0246	2
WILSON GEORGE H	COL	0-0311484	0965	3
WILSON GEORGE H	LTC	0-1579309	1266	1
WILSON GEORGE L	COL	0-0302338	0364	1
WILSON GEORGE L	LTC	0-1182489	0467	3

NAME	GRADE	SVC NO	DATE RET MO YR	RET CODE
WILSON GEORGE M	CW4	W-2114269	1154	1
WILSON GEORGE T	MAJ	0-0354233	0960	1
WILSON GEORGE W	MAJ	C-0133593	C650	3
WILSON GEORGE W	1LT	0-1012780	0146	2
WILSON GERARD E	LTC	0-1646710	0967	1
WILSON GLEASON W	LTC	0-1101287	1263	1
WILSON GLENN H	LTC	0-1048646	1265	1
WILSON GLENN O	1LT	C-1320211	0645	2
WILSCN GLYN	CPT	0-1307172	C347	2
WILSCN GRANT P	CW3	W-2153304	1066	1
WILSON HARDY O	CW2	W-2211686	0167	1
WILSON HAROLD A	CPT	0-0503280	0447	1
WILSON HAROLD G	LTC	0-0286681	0260	1
WILSON HAROLD L	LTC	C-0289841	1160	1
WILSON HAROLD P	CPT	0-1845126	C656	1
WILSON HARRY B	CW3	W-2153040	0664	1
WILSON HARRY M	COL	0-1685355	C765	3
WILSON HARRY W	CW2	W-2144225	C557	1
WILSON HARTWELL T	1LT	0-1324382	C546	1
WILSON HARVEY E	COL	0-0223362	C756	2
WILSON HARVEY W	CW3	W-2149997	C659	1
WILSON HENRY	MAJ	0-1283707	C257	1
WILSON HENRY	LTC	0-1543256	0161	1
WILSON HENRY R	LTC	0-0358139	0765	1
WILSON HERBERT R	CPT	0-0428959	0944	2
WILSON HERBERT T	LTC	0-0349994	0762	3
WILSON HILLEARD	MAJ	0-0494633	0550	1
WILSON HORACE H	LTC	0-0226529	C365	3
WILSCN HOWARD C	1LT	0-1288728	C945	2
WILSCN HOWARD E	MAJ	C-1335870	C866	1
WILSON HOWARD W	MAJ	C-1547503	1161	1
WILSON HOYT G	MAJ	0-1639822	0359	1
WILSON HUGH R	MAJ	0-0169070	0460	3
WILSON III ARTHUR M	LTC	0-0222844	1065	3
WILSCN JACK P	CW3	W-2145011	1060	1
WILSON JACK R	CPT	0-2033016	C960	1
WILSON JACQUES H	CPT	0-2034069	0464	1
WILSON JAMES	1LT	0-0503681	0747	1
WILSON JAMES	MAJ	C-1688511	1165	1
WILSON JAMES A	COL	0-0119351	C449	3
WILSON JAMES A	COL	0-0355091	0960	1
WILSON JAMES A	MAJ	C-0359427	1168	3
WILSON JAMES C	MAJ	0-1040250	0759	1
WILSON JAMES E	COL	0-0190100	1157	3
WILSON JAMES E	MAJ	C-1553387	0265	1
WILSON JAMES F	CW2	W-2145926	066C	1
WILSON JAMES F	LTL	0-0494172	0666	3
WILSON JAMES H	CW2	W-2203367	C461	1
WILSON JAMES L	CW3	W-2142918	C757	1
WILSON JAMES M	CPT	0-0494509	0448	1
WILSON JAMES P	LTC	0-0382479	C457	1
WILSON JAMES S	MAJ	C-0251084	C466	3
WILSON JAMES W	LTC	0-1102120	C363	1
WILSON JAMES W	MAJ	C-1919091	0164	1
WILSON JAMES W	MAJ	0-2019113	0162	2
WILSON JAMES W	CW4	W-2112143	1057	1
WILSON JANE E	2LT	N-0700547	0537	1
WILSON JEAN T	2LT	0-0537924	0645	2
WILSON JIM L	2LT	0-0545607	0945	2
WILSON JOHN	CW2	W-2150544	1162	1
WILSCN JOHN A	CPT	0-0445375	0246	2
WILSON JOHN A	MAJ	0-1327596	C364	1
WILSON JOHN C	M G	0-0291915	0365	3
WILSON JOHN D	LTC	0-0239633	C356	3
WILSON JOHN D	MAJ	0-0967342	0563	1
WILSCN JOHN E	CPT	0-0173273	0648	3
WILSCN JOHN E	1LT	0-0450951	0443	1
WILSON JOHN F	MAJ	0-1541983	1060	1
WILSON JOHN H	CW3	W-2146931	1263	1
WILSON JOHN M	LTC	0-1534662	1265	1
WILSON JOHN R	LTC	0-0233360	C865	3
WILSON JOHN T	LTC	0-0504428	0157	1
WILSCN JOHN T	1LT	0-1169835	1144	2
WILSON JOSEPH C	1LT	0-0445100	0450	2
WILSON JOSEPH E	MAJ	0-0480334	0954	1

NAME	GRADE	SVC NO	DATE RET MO YR	RET CODE
WILSON JOSEPH P	2LT	0-1044428	0244	2
WILSON JOSEPH W	COL	0-1100829	0261	1
WILSON JOSEPH W	CW2	W-2143984	0961	1
WILSON JR C P	LTC	0-0372123	1262	2
WILSON JR CHALMERS R	COL	0-027065C	0165	3
WILSON JR CHARLES	1LT	0-1292806	0845	2
WILSON JR CHARLES W	CPT	0-2016210	1056	1
WILSON JR DANIEL D	LTC	0-1101285	0155	1
WILSON JR EDWARD L	MAJ	0-1897786	1262	1
WILSON JR FLOYD C	LTC	0-118497C	0263	1
WILSON JR GEORGE O	CPT	0-0351485	0145	2
WILSON JR ISAAC R	MAJ	0-0294575	1165	3
WILSON JR JOHN	COL	0-0333868	0865	3
WILSCN JR JOHN A	LTC	0-0163756	0245	2
WILSON JR JOHN K	LTC	0-0263632	0859	3
WILSON JR JOHN S	LTC	0-1646712	0561	1
WILSON JR NEIL S	CW2	W-2206394	0661	1
WILSON JR OMER B	MAJ	0-1313844	0857	1
WILSCN JR PERRY B	1LT	0-1175906	0845	2
WILSON JR RAY M	CPT	0-1549637	0755	2
WILSON JR ROBERT L	COL	0-0181327	0762	3
WILSON JR THOMAS H	LTC	0-1333290	1266	1
WILSON JR WILLIAM H	CW2	W-2208886	0965	1
WILSON JR WILLIAM L	1LT	0-0384035	C544	2
WILSON JR WILLIAM M	CPT	0-0259943	0967	3
WILSON JR WILLIAM P	LTC	0-1167698	0246	2
WILSON JULIAN C	CW2	W-2209090	0860	1
WILSON KENNETH A	CPT	0-0180202	0757	3
WILSON KENNETH W	1LT	0-1294054	0346	2
WILSON KENT R	MAJ	C-0177543	0455	3
WILSON LAURENCE E	LTC	0-0192480	0559	3
WILSON LAWRENCE E	2LT	0-1325050	0357	1
WILSON LAWRENCE L	CW4	W-2142732	0666	1
WILSON LAWRENCE O	MAJ	0-1314702	0966	1
WILSON LAWRENCE R	LTC	0-0422641	0161	1
WILSON LESTER R	COL	C-0249109	0959	3
WILSON LEWIS B	CPT	0-0415364	0846	1
WILSON LEWIS D	LTC	0-0406772	0860	1
WILSCN LEWIS G	LTC	0-0234752	0665	3
WILSON LLOYD A	MAJ	0-0323988	0347	1
WILSON LLOYD A	MAJ	0-0390060	1163	1
WILSON LOGAN E	MAJ	0-1552828	1057	1
WILSON LOUIS C	CPT	0-2018807	0862	1
WILSON MADRILE R	LTC	0-1043841	0161	1
WILSON MARGARET M	1LT	N-0786682	0348	2
WILSON MARION J	MAJ	0-0221689	0860	3
WILSON MARK L	LTC	0-1555324	0967	1
WILSON MARK S	COL	C-1580509	1167	1
WILSON MARLYN C	MAJ	C-1590896	0760	1
WILSON MASSEY F	COL	C-0298295	0260	2
WILSON MCCULLOCH	MAJ	0-0162945	0648	3
WILSON MCCULLOCH	MAJ	0-0990227	0663	1
WILSON MELVIN T	LTC	0-0470923	0767	3
WILSON MERLE E	CPT	0-0232230	0950	3
WILSON MERLE E	LTC	0-0307252	1164	3
WILSON MILLARD H	1LT	0-1300427	0857	1
WILSCN MYLDRED R	CPT	N-0787566	0347	1
WILSON MYRON R	MAJ	0-2021134	1066	1
WILSON NAT J	LTC	0-0315099	0264	3
WILSON OLIVER E	1LT	0-1080428	0555	1
WILSON OLIVER W	1LT	0-0245752	0363	3
WILSON OLLIE J	COL	0-0359154	1045	2
WILSON OWEN D	LTC	0-1543631	0560	1
WILSON OZZIE L	CPT	0-0503847	0849	1
WILSON PERRY J	CW2	W-2148619	0160	2
WILSON PHILIP	COL	0-0127939	0357	3
WILSON PHILIP	COL	0-0266106	1161	3
WILSON PHILIP M	COL	0-1056947	0464	1
WILSON PRINCESS L	LTC	N-0729172	0365	3
WILSON RAMEY E	LTC	0-1179682	0962	1
WILSON RANDALL R	LTC	0-0300476	0144	2
WILSON RAYMOND C	MAJ	C-0455146	1058	1
WILSON RAYMOND E	1LT	0-1013633	0846	1
WILSON RAYMOND H	CW3	W-2121928	0157	1
WILSON RAYMOND R	MAJ	0-1685621	0761	1

NAME	GRADE	SVC NO	DATE RET MO YR	RET CODE
WILSON REGINALD S	MAJ	C-1111990	C361	1
WILSON ROBERT	MAJ	C-1329303	C265	1
WILSCN ROBERT B	MAJ	C-0106049	0250	3
WILSON ROBERT D	LTC	0-1111445	C864	1
WILSON ROBERT E	MAJ	C-099443C	0367	1
WILSON ROBERT F	1LT	0-0463430	C447	1
WILSCN ROBERT F	CW3	W-2144856	0363	1
WILSCN ROBERT J	COL	0-0445449	C755	2
WILSCN ROBERT L	CW2	W-2205599	0264	1
WILSON ROBERT M	1LT	0-1297822	1045	1
WILSON ROBERT P	COL	0-0304025	0959	1
WILSON ROBERT R	COL	0-0189532	0961	3
WILSON ROBERT T	MAJ	C-1178985	1161	1
WILSON ROBERT W	M G	0-0233644	0-53	3
WILSON ROBERT W	COL	0-0925319	C250	3
WILSON ROSS E	LTC	0-0181303	0955	3
WILSON ROYAL C	LTC	0-0246510	1159	1
WILSON SAM T	LTC	0-0356845	0156	2
WILSON SAM T	LTC	C-1281547	1064	1
WILSON SEWARD S	MAJ	0-1301069	0660	1
WILSON SHORIA G	1LT	0-0521876	C246	1
WILSON SIDNEY A	CW2	W-2102563	0247	1
WILSON SR BOYD T	COL	0-1321977	0967	1
WILSON SR DENNIS R	CW2	W-2147576	0861	1
WILSON STANFORD R	MAJ	C-1925472	0866	1
WILSON STEPHEN F	2LT	C-1941632	1055	2
WILSON SUMNER S	MAJ	C-1038521	0265	1
WILSON THEODORE	MAJ	C-4006226	0967	1
WILSON THERON O	MAJ	0-0289685	1057	3
WILSON THOMAS C	1LT	0-0154229	1045	2
WILSON THOMAS E	CPT	0-0910099	0745	2
WILSON THOMAS F	CPT	C-1995540	C352	2
WILSON THOMAS G	CW3	W 2206958	C167	1
WILSON THOMAS I	LTC	0-0384501	1066	3
WILSON THOMAS S	MAJ	0-0370990	0660	1
WILSON THOMAS W	LTC	0-0347684	1266	1
WILSON THOMAS W	LTC	0-155199C	0167	1
WILSON THOMAS W	LTC	0-1796197	1058	1
WILSON TILDEN O	CPT	0-0482715	C746	2
WILSON VERNON A	MAJ	0-0370516	0965	3
WILSON VERNON A	MAJ	C-1111991	0765	1
WILSON VERNON C	LTC	0-0913795	1166	3
WILSON WALLACE E	COL	0-0145536	0655	3
WILSON WALLACE P	MAJ	C-0398743	0657	1
WILSON WALTER W	MAJ	0-0141015	0753	3
WILSON WARREN A	1LT	0-0527881	0346	2
WILSON WARREN H	CPT	0-1301070	1059	1
WILSON WENDELL R	LTC	0-0177336	1061	3
WILSON WENDELL W	CW2	W-2152332	0157	1
WILSON WILBUR C	MAJ	C-0247942	1264	3
WILSON WILLIAM A	MAJ	0-2048523	0765	2
WILSON WILLIAM C	CPT	0-2015822	0652	1
WILSON WILLIAM C	MAJ	0-0452814	0546	2
WILSON WILLIAM E	MAJ	0-0321794	0847	2
WILSON WILLIAM E	CW3	W-2150533	0666	1
WILSON WILLIAM F	WO1	W-2126910	C749	1
WILSON WILLIAM H	MAJ	C-2005939	0561	1
WILSON WILLIAM H	MAJ	0-2010875	C862	1
WILSON WILLIAM J	WO1	W-2105249	1047	1
WILSON WILLIAM L	MAJ	0-0414601	0865	1
WILSON WILLIAM O	1LT	0-0383445	0447	2
WILSON WILLIAM P	COL	C-0324307	C247	1
WILSON WILLIAM R	MAJ	0-0340445	0966	1
WILSON WILLIAM W	LTC	0-1325615	1265	3
WILSON WILLIE M	LTC	0-0450131	0556	1
WILSCN WOODROW L	CW2	W-2208378	0764	1
WILSON WOODROW P	MAJ	0-0326125	1147	2
WILSON WOODROW T	LTC	0-0332213	0562	1
WILSON ZELMER C	CW4	W-2146295	0559	1
WILSON 3RD ROBERT C	CPT	0-0464766	1147	1
WILT CHARLES H	CW2	W-2148570	1060	1
WILT ROBERT H	LTC	0-0119506	0-53	3
WILTON DONALD C	LTC	0-1635486	0960	1
WILTON ELLA A	LTC	L-0220109	1164	1
WILTON JR OTIS N	MAJ	C-2028765	C667	1

NAME	GRADE	SVC NO	DATE RET MO YR	RET CODE
WILTRAKIS GEORGE A	COL	0-0278953	0465	3
WILTSE JR HARRY W	MAJ	0-2045017	0562	1
WILTSEE DONALD L	MAJ	C-0214750	0664	3
WILTSHIRE MALCOLM	CPT	0-1315653	1047	2
WILVERT MURLEY T	LTC	0-1111446	0963	1
WIMBERLY FRED N	COL	0-022966C	0657	1
WIMBERLY JAMES R	LTC	0-0271304	0448	2
WIMBERLY LUCILLE H	CPT	L-0903074	1151	1
WIMBERLY VERNON L	LTC	0-0289543	0446	2
WIMBERLY VERNON M	MAJ	0-0206543	0645	2
WIMER FRANK C	MAJ	0-0157268	0255	3
WIMMER VERNON C	LTC	0-1556825	0766	1
WIMMER WILLIAM K	LTC	0-1317856	0465	1
WIMPLEBERG AUGUST	LTC	0-0263804	0152	3
WINAND KATHRYN E	2LT	N-0703653	1044	1
WINANS CHARLES E	1LT	0-0256646	1263	3
WINANS DOUGLAS K	MAJ	0-1597857	0464	1
WINANS HERMAN L	MAJ	0-2262883	0266	1
WINBORN CLAUDE O	COL	0-0280989	1064	3
WINBORN JR THOMAS A	1LT	0-0476713	0445	2
WINBURN DON C	CW2	W-2147273	0259	1
WINBURN HARRY W	LTC	0-0313152	0660	2
WINBURN HERBERT L	1LT	0-1301739	0845	2
WINCH AL R	CPT	0-2034597	0867	3
WINCH NORMAN M	LTC	0-0461488	1166	3
WINCH STANTON G	LTC	0-0249947	0365	3
WINCHESTER LEROY A	CW4	W-2005136	1066	1
WINCHESTER WILLARD P	MAJ	0-0286037	0661	3
WINDAUGH CARL E	MAJ	0-1017277	0557	1
WINDEBANK EDWARD A	LTC	0-1822135	C264	1
WINDHAM ALFORD R	CW4	W-2103617	0955	1
WINDHAM JAMES B	LTC	0-0450952	0857	2
WINDHAM JOSEPH P	COL	0-0248431	0862	2
WINDHAM RAY K	LTC	0-0252840	0364	3
WINDHAM WILLIAM R	MAJ	0-1314862	0960	1
WINDISCH HERMAN G	CPT	0-1165467	0659	1
WINDISCH ROBERT F	MAJ	0-1579315	0459	1
WINDISH JR JOHN J	1LT	0-1031691	0645	2
WINDLE WILLIAM B	COL	0-0157976	0648	3
WINDMOELLER HENRY F	LTC	0-1581465	0461	1
WINDOM LOREN G	M G	0-0275591	0965	3
WINDOM RALPH	CPT	0-1877906	1062	2
WINDOM RUTH C	2LT	N-0726117	1146	1
WINDORFER JOHN H	1LT	0-1765892	1145	2
WINDSOR BUFORD L	CW2	W-2147295	0960	1
WINDSOR JR ALTON S	1LT	0-1861926	0554	2
WINDSOR JR JACK	MAJ	0-1595273	0461	1
WINDSOR KENNETH H	MAJ	0-1588966	1060	1
WINDSOR MERRILL C	LTC	0-0166027	0260	1
WINE WILLIAM C	COL	0-0312019	1263	2
WINEBERG CHARLES T	WO1	W-2150688	0361	2
WINEBRENNER VICTOR M	LTC	C-1334940	0864	1
WINEBURGH JACOB J	CPT	0-0486881	0245	2
WINEGARD CHARLES I	COL	0-0449520	0954	1
WINEGARDNER JAY H	1LT	0-1168981	0545	2
WINER HAROLD	MAJ	C-0294229	1046	2
WINER JULIUS H	CPT	0-0338856	1146	2
WINER MEYER	MAJ	C-0158246	0150	3
WINES CARROLL F	MAJ	C-2016986	0762	1
WINFREE ROBERT N	LTC	0-0153408	0959	3
WINFREY WILL R	COL	0-1574369	0861	2
WING DUNCAN	CPT	0-0109431	0934	1
WING HAROLD M	CW3	W-2206185	0965	1
WING KENNETH A	LTC	0-0254821	0165	3
WING LEONARD A	LTC	0-0272471	0766	3
WING LLBERT	MAJ	C-1919398	0965	1
WING ROBERT B	COL	0-0275785	0767	3
WING WALLACE C	CW2	W-2152728	0261	1
WINGARD BARRINGER	COL	0-024910C	0666	3
WINGARD JOSEPH E	MAJ	0-1825296	0258	1
WINGATE HARVEY P	LTC	0-0167382	1057	3
WINGATE WILLIAM L	CW2	W-2147200	0961	1
WINGEBACH CHARLES F	CPT	0-0203754	0462	3
WINGERT DONALD G	MAJ	0-0287797	0166	3
WINGFIELD CONRAD B	LTC	0-1583851	0765	1

NAME	GRADE	SVC NO	DATE RET MO YR	RET CODE
WINGFIELD DONALD W	CW3	W-2145088	0361	1
WINGFIELD HENRY R	1LT	0-0365442	0146	2
WINGFIELD SAM A	CPT	0-0980887	1166	1
WINGO BURLEY M	CPT	0-2001822	1055	1
WINGO BURREL W	MAJ	C-2024337	C264	1
WINGO GEORGE N	CW2	W-2153197	1160	1
WINGO GERALD C	LTC	0-1291367	C765	1
WINGO JESSE M	MAJ	0-1284620	C846	1
WINGO JR CHARLES M	MAJ	0-0344421	0945	2
WINGROVE JOSEPH F	CPT	0-0149419	0556	3
WINGROVE MARVIN V	CW3	W-2142012	0660	1
WINGROVE WILLIAM H	1LT	0-0511521	0648	1
WINIKER DICK B	CPT	0-0890218	1045	1
WININGER ALBERT J	CW2	W-2110120	0648	1
WINK EUGENE A	LTC	0-0247027	0854	3
WINK PETER	1LT	0-1946892	0557	1
WINK ROBERT J	CPT	0-1877698	0565	1
WINK SR JOSEPH C	LTC	0-0330576	0165	1
WINKEL ROBERT C	LTC	0-1291555	C966	1
WINKENWERDER R H	LTC	0-0412127	0760	1
WINKING CYRIL H	MAJ	0-1533474	0946	2
WINKLER EARL C	LTC	0-0385218	0960	1
WINKLER FRANK C	LTC	0-0109002	0846	2
WINKLER HERBERT W	MAJ	0-0924804	1163	1
WINKLER IRVEN G	MAJ	C-1037782	C760	1
WINKLER PATRICK J	LTC	0-0918868	0165	3
WINKLER PROVINCE M	MAJ	0-0338281	0246	2
WINKLER ROBERT B	CPT	0-1015623	1054	2
WINLAW JOHN P	2LT	0-0393612	0142	2
WINN ARVEY S	MAJ	C-1844568	C457	1
WINN CHARLES	MAJ	0-2018626	0166	1
WINN CHARLES E	LTC	0-0276483	0761	1
WINN DALE	WO1	W-2003776	0564	3
WINN FREDERICKS	LTC	0-0236574	0365	3
WINN HERBERT P	COL	0-0353361	0966	3
WINN III RICHARD J	MAJ	C-1333291	1263	1
WINN JR HENRY	CPT	0-2040918	C160	1
WINN JR JOHN J	LTC	0-0498400	1045	2
WINN JR PERCY E	LTC	0-1179251	0363	1
WINN LOUIS E	CPT	0-0464281	0949	1
WINN MARK	LTC	0-1042746	C961	1
WINN MONROE G	CPT	0-1030318	1054	2
WINN ROY H	1LT	0-1056603	0654	1
WINN WARREN R	COL	0-0265305	C845	1
WINN WILLIAM B	2LT	0-2027752	C246	2
WINNER EDWARD C	1LT	0-1032496	C546	2
WINNER THOMAS A	CPT	0-1320683	1047	1
WINNIE CHARLES O	CW2	W-2150267	0859	2
WINNING WALTER B	1LT	0-1580518	C961	3
WINNINGHAM RICHARD B	LTC	0-1293342	C661	1
WINOGRAD ALVIN M	CPT	0-1684283	0546	2
WINSAUER LESLIE R	CPT	0-0285584	1044	2
WINSHIP WILLIAM H	MAJ	0-1795026	1161	1
WINSKOWSKI SIGMUND J	MAJ	C-2035599	1061	1
WINSKY STANLEY G	MAJ	C-1997648	0163	1
WINSLAGE HAZEL L	1LT	N-0703289	1144	1
WINSLETT EDMUND J	LTC	0-0103458	C657	3
WINSLETT JIM H	CW4	W-2144796	0666	1
WINSLOW BERRY O	LTC	0-0503062	0657	1
WINSLOW CECIL M	MAJ	C-0153537	0858	3
WINSLOW HUGH W	COL	C-0414909	1053	1
WINSLOW JOHN W	CPT	0-0319666	0746	1
WINSLOW JR FRANK	1LT	0-1325428	C853	1
WINSLOW LYNWOOD A	LTC	0-0491944	0755	1
WINSLOW MARTIN L	CPT	0-1012138	0648	1
WINSOR CARLTON W	MAJ	0-0320924	0944	1
WINSOR EDWARD F	MAJ	0-1297461	0261	1
WINSOR MILTON G	LTC	0-0359848	0157	1
WINSOR PAUL B	CPT	0-0272042	1167	3
WINSOR RICHARD R	MAJ	C-1633644	0358	1
WINSTEAD AMBLER W	MAJ	0-0971829	1061	1
WINSTEAD ELTON O	LTC	0-0354444	1057	1
WINSTEAD FREDERICK	MAJ	C-1759412	1264	1
WINSTEAD RICHARD B	CW4	W-2005311	0665	1
WINSTON BURMAN L	MAJ	C-1107764	1265	2

NAME	GRADE	SVC NO	DATE RET MO YR	RET CODE
WINSTON CARL A	CW3	W-2207750	0466	1
WINSTON CLARENCE N	COL	C-0176512	1054	3
WINSTON DALE L	CPT	0-1336852	C657	1
WINSTON EDWARD J	CW4	W-2002017	0863	3
WINSTON GEORGE E	CW3	W-2126390	0562	1
WINSTON WALDEN C	COL	0-0259814	1157	1
WINTER ALAN W	MAJ	C-0352016	0646	2
WINTER CECIL L	MAJ	C-0116057	0654	3
WINTER EARL C	LTC	0-1691798	0862	1
WINTER ELBERT R	MAJ	0-1542234	0561	1
WINTER FRANKLIN I	MAJ	0-0111255	C648	3
WINTER HAL F	LTC	0-0317888	0349	2
WINTER HERBERT A	MAJ	C-1115459	0861	1
WINTER JOHN H	1LT	0-1590900	1045	1
WINTER JOHN W	COL	0-0280160	0546	2
WINTER MARVIN M	MAJ	C-0137127	0853	1
WINTER ROBERT G	LTC	0-1109117	0467	1
WINTER ROBERT H	MAJ	0-0965105	1265	1
WINTER ROBERT L	MAJ	0-2263016	0464	1
WINTER STANLEY T	LTC	0-C250C47	0365	3
WINTER WALDO J W	COL	0-0270460	0248	1
WINTER WILLIAM A	WO1	W-2132642	0546	2
WINTER WILLIS G	LTC	0-0277838	0755	1
WINTERBOTTOM JAMES E	LTC	0-1585095	1059	2
WINTERBURG DON E	LTC	0-0193809	0364	3
WINTERHALTER ARTHUR	2LT	0-1011807	1043	2
WINTERHOFF WALTER J	LTC	0-0346948	0247	2
WINTERMUTE EARL C	COL	0-0464875	0765	1
WINTERROTH EDWARD G	1LT	0-1691764	C745	2
WINTERS EARL R	MAJ	0-0965329	0964	1
WINTERS GEORGE J	CPT	0-0447986	1146	1
WINTERS HENRY S	MAJ	0-4011100	0767	1
WINTERS JAMES E	CPT	0-0170861	0844	2
WINTERS JOHN P	CW4	W-2111987	1160	1
WINTERS JOHN R	MAJ	0-0739159	0365	1
WINTERS LESLIE C	LTC	0-0240731	0366	3
WINTERS RAYMOND E	2LT	0-1547210	1044	1
WINTERS RICHARD O	CW2	W-2150762	0561	1
WINTERS THOMAS H	LTC	0-0265271	1044	1
WINTERS WALTER F	COL	0-0245132	0860	3
WINTERS WILLIAM P	LTC	0-1587027	0656	1
WINTERS WILLIAM R	1LT	0-1182746	0845	2
WINTERS WILLIAM W	LTC	0-1043838	0764	1
WINTERS WILLIS H	2LT	0-1314989	0246	2
WINTERSTEIN WILLIAM	LTC	0-1553756	0157	1
WINTRISS GEORGE	MAJ	0-0349770	0445	2
WINTRODE ROLLIN V	CW3	W-2151861	0265	1
WINZENREAD WILLIAM H	LTC	0-1646116	1163	1
WIPF WILLIAM	LTC	0-0250732	1154	1
WIPPERMAN RUDOLPH P	LTC	0-0944760	0267	3
WIRE DAVID B	1LT	0-0491275	0646	2
WIREBAUGH FRED W	MAJ	C-0166384	0-52	3
WIREY CARL O	CPT	0-0464108	1045	2
WIRRICK ROY E	CW3	W-2145852	1066	2
WIRSCHING THOMAS M	2LT	0-0427347	0544	2
WIRTH DAVID K	1LT	0-1312031	1145	2
WIRTH EARL A	LTC	C-0967142	0762	1
WIRTH HAROLD C	CPT	0-2026492	0257	1
WISAKOWSKY EMIL E	MAJ	C-0442277	1060	1
WISBY HERMAN B	MAJ	0-0510519	0246	1
WISCH LEONA M M	CPT	N-0729898	0847	1
WISCHER FRANCIS M	CW4	W-2127501	0658	1
WISCOWITCH GUSTAVO	2LT	0-2050699	0246	2
WISDOM CHARLES L	MAJ	0-0386584	1144	2
WISDOM GEORGE B	WO1	W-2131826	1051	2
WISDOM WILLIAM E	CPT	0-1824262	C659	1
WISE ALBERT J	1LT	0-1825900	0146	1
WISE BERNARD C	LTC	0-0505783	1046	2
WISE CHARLES S	1LT	0-1690300	0245	2
WISE ERNEST F	MAJ	C-0130125	C546	2
WISE EUGENE W	LTC	0-0278C03	0461	3
WISE FRANCIS J	CPT	0-0504908	1148	1
WISE FRANK J	CPT	0-0247166	0455	3
WISE GEORGE E	COL	0-0361407	0561	1
WISE HAROLD L	CPT	0-2265694	0665	1

NAME	GRADE	SVC NO	DATE RET MO YR	RET CODE
WISE HARRIET M	MAJ	L-0504451	0363	1
WISE JACK N	CPT	0-1690998	0765	1
WISE JAMES I	1LT	C-0229262	1262	3
WISE JAY N	CW2	W-2141812	0666	1
WISE JEFF	CPT	C-0445224	1046	1
WISE JOHN E	LTC	0-1032666	0561	1
WISE JOHN H	MAJ	0-0979268	1164	1
WISE JOHN K	LTC	0-1590269	0163	1
WISE JOHN W	CW4	W-2148778	1263	1
WISE JR WHITRY F	2LT	C-0395966	0543	1
WISE LESLIE J	1LT	0-1014543	0348	1
WISE LOUIS J	COL	0-0100671	0352	3
WISE PAUL F	CPT	0-0518545	0453	1
WISE PRENTICE L	COL	0-0359340	1060	2
WISE RICHARD K	MAJ	0-1534192	0953	1
WISE RICHARD P	1LT	0-1882645	0856	2
WISE ROBERT H	LTC	0-1319372	1062	1
WISE ROBERT M	LTC	0-0394958	1265	1
WISE STANLEY C	CPT	0-1322112	C249	1
WISE WALTER A	1LT	0-1327792	0147	2
WISE WARREN R	1LT	0-1844538	1044	2
WISE WILLARD W	MAJ	C-1316355	C862	1
WISEHEART JOHN W	LTC	C-0202138	066C	2
WISEMAN JAMES A	MAJ	0-1688785	C267	1
WISEMAN JOHN T	CW4	W-2142672	1158	1
WISEMAN RICHARD A	MAJ	C-0971694	0266	1
WISEMAN T J	CW4	W-2136024	C863	1
WISEMAN WILLIAM R	LTC	C-1037369	1061	1
WISER MERLE E	CPT	0-1289526	0246	2
WISHART ANDREW J	MAJ	C-0971297	C960	1
WISHART FRANCIS E	COL	0-0326749	0355	3
WISHART JOHN C	LTC	0-1105786	0462	1
WISHNEFSKY PHILIP	2LT	0-1328207	C546	2
WISHNICK SEYMOUR O	CPT	0-0534234	0846	2
WISLER ROY A	COL	0-0153549	0-53	1
WISMAN CALVIN S	COL	0-0390304	C564	1
WISMANN JOHN A	CW3	W-2145171	0862	1
WISMER RAYMOND J	COL	0-0250400	1062	3
WISNEFSKI JOSEPH W	1LT	0-1690486	0943	2
WISNER CLIFFORD W	CW3	W-2141921	0756	1
WISNER JOHN C	MAJ	C-0410149	0961	2
WISNER JOHN H	2LT	0-1560173	C146	2
WISNESKI EDWARD V	MAJ	C-0963604	1163	1
WISNESKI EMILIA	CPT	N-0735715	C547	1
WISNIEWSKI BERNARD	WO1	W-2114989	0744	2
WISNIEWSKI STANLEY A	MAJ	C-1019842	1265	1
WISOR ROBERT L	LTC	0-1314380	C861	1
WISSE WILLIAM	CPT	C-1299342	1047	2
WISSENBURGER C E	LTC	0-1636803	1160	1
WISSINGER HELEN G	1LT	N-0759182	1145	1
WISSLER ALFRED E	COL	0-0301746	0157	3
WISTAIN LINCOLN O	LTC	0-0196536	1261	3
WISTERMAN JESSE H	CPT	0-0503641	0757	2
WITCOSKY JOHN W	CPT	0-1288991	1046	1
WITEK JOHN J	MAJ	0-1705330	C848	2
WITHAM FRANK R	MAJ	0-0173128	0961	3
WITHEREL MURVEN J	1LT	0-1305152	1045	2
WITHERELL LEONARD O	MAJ	0-0262878	1046	2
WITHEROW ELMER	CW3	W-2147112	0264	2
WITHERS ARNOLD M	LTC	0-1592718	0163	1
WITHERS ROBERT L	MAJ	0-0137281	C654	3
WITHERS WILLIAM B	LTC	0-0238594	C963	3
WITHERS WINSTON R	MAJ	C-0102693	0555	3
WITHERSPOON JOHN F	COL	0-0354514	0861	1
WITHERSPOON SHIRLEY	LTC	0-0256863	1266	3
WITHERSTINE EDWARD J	1LT	C-0116646	0851	3
WITHERUP EMMA C	2LT	N-0700526	0738	1
WITHINGTON ALBERT F	MAJ	C-1314864	0863	1
WITHINGTON HARRY O	COL	0-0237837	0648	3
WITHINGTON JOSEPH S	COL	0-0219047	1157	1
WITHINGTON WILLIAM J	CW3	W-2147787	0863	1
WITHINGTON WILLIAM M	2LT	0-1184336	0744	2
WITHROW BERNARD O	LTC	C-1171846	C967	1
WITHROW FRED	MAJ	0-1931437	C567	1
WITHROW JOHN W	1LT	0-1306034	0952	2

NAME	GRADE	SVC NO	DATE RET MO YR	RET CODE
WITKOSKIE JAMES A	CPT	0-0544470	0353	1
WITKOWSKI HENRY J	MAJ	0-1822932	0665	1
WITKOWSKI THOMAS F	LTC	0-1305687	1162	1
WITMAN JOSEPH W	1LT	0-1799495	0546	2
WITMER CHARLES R	2LT	0-1295469	1043	2
WITMER JOHN H	LTC	0-0488273	0755	1
WITMER MAX O	LTC	0-0334428	0955	3
WITMER RICHARD L	CPT	0-1040307	0845	2
WITSCH JOHN E	MAJ	0-0972831	0765	1
WITT CHARLES R	LTC	0-1013278	1061	1
WITT DUANE M	COL	0-1283181	1066	1
WITT EDWARD R	MAJ	C-0493183	0457	1
WITT EUGENE M	LTC	0-0389188	0760	1
WITT FRITZ	CPT	0-0278605	0364	3
WITT HARLEY A	MAJ	0-1177698	0362	2
WITT HARRY	1LT	0-0399297	0744	2
WITT JAMES N	CPT	0-2048198	0347	2
WITT JAMES W	MAJ	C-1648248	0859	1
WITT JAMES W	MAJ	0-2009705	0461	1
WITT JR JAMES O	MAJ	C-0448107	0747	2
WITT JR WALTER H	2LT	0-0435048	0445	2
WITT KENNETH G	MAJ	0-1794892	0461	1
WITT LESLIE L	MAJ	0-1294055	0658	1
WITT MILTON W	COL	0-0279314	0659	1
WITT PLEASANT B	CW4	W-2107063	0859	1
WITT RAE B	2LT	N-0779593	1046	1
WITT SCOTT J	1LT	0-0554362	0446	2
WITT VINCENT E	MAJ	0-2000980	0959	1
WITTA JR FRED	LTC	0-0404280	0365	1
WITTE ALFRED F	LTC	0-0235990	0754	3
WITTE ARTHUR M	1LT	0-1012534	1045	2
WITTE GRANT L	1LT	0-0386374	C445	1
WITTE HERBERT J	COL	0-0258996	0954	1
WITTE JAMES O	LTC	0-0349178	0367	3
WITTEKIND EUGENE C	MAJ	0-1183220	1063	1
WITTEKIND HAROLD H	LTC	0-0415612	0165	1
WITTEN GEORGE W B	LTC	0-0220068	0745	1
WITTEN JR WILLIAM W	LTC	0-1557998	0762	1
WITTEN NASH A	CPT	0-0121201	0949	3
WITTENBERG SHELDON E	CPT	0-1644920	0457	1
WITTER JOSEPH A	MAJ	0-1686873	1045	2
WITTIG DONALD A	MAJ	0-0390075	0546	2
WITTKE ROBERT E	MAJ	0-1651259	1265	1
WITTKOP GEORGE F	CPT	0-1534415	0656	1
WITTKOFF PHILIP W	CPT	0-1313007	0546	2
WITTKOPP LELAND A	1LT	0-0555983	0646	2
WITTKOWER JR LOUIS O	LTC	0-0398417	0161	1
WITTLAKE OSCAR D	LTC	0-0253943	0763	3
WITTLER JACOB F	LTC	0-0292814	1057	1
WITTMAACK CHARLES C	CW2	W-2152883	1163	1
WITTMANN JR JOHN G	LTC	0-0234644	1062	3
WITTMUS WALDEMAR A	LTC	0-0343633	0859	1
WITTROCK JACK E	LTC	0-0353758	0264	1
WITTSTROM MARTIN O	MAJ	0-1059347	1060	1
WITTWER GLADE S	LTC	0-1101289	0361	1
WITTY STUART E	MAJ	0-1166415	0261	1
WITWICKE JOHN	CW3	W-2142275	1059	2
WITZEL EWALD L	CPT	0-0137273	1054	3
WITZEL VERNA G	2LT	N-0769717	0546	1
WITZIGMAN FREDERICK	MAJ	0-0344984	0866	3
WITZLEBEN EUGENE A	CW3	W-2141109	0563	1
WIWI PAUL J	CPT	0-1297462	1046	2
WIXCEY EARL R	COL	C-0147921	0258	3
WLADKOWSKI JOSEPH A	CW2	W-3350148	0266	1
WNEK HENRY A	CPT	0-1307606	0348	1
WNEK RUSSELL J	LTC	0-1292104	1061	1
WOCHNER LISLE C	COL	0-0264890	0663	3
WOCKENFUSS ROLAND C	1LT	0-0384573	1144	2
WODARCZAK HUBERT T	CW3	W-2143986	1060	1
WOODRCF WILLIAM H	CPT	0-2032877	1157	1
WOERLEIN THOMAS J	MAJ	0-1173510	0461	1
WOERPEL CHARLES W	MAJ	0-0451702	1160	2
WOFFORD MONTIE W	MAJ	0-0450467	0658	1
WOGAN MAURICE	MAJ	0-0478786	0147	2
WOGSLAND WALTER	CPT	0-0490324	0145	2

NAME	GRADE	SVC NO	DATE RET MO YR	RET CODE
WOHLFERD LEO A	MAJ	0-1895966	0467	3
WOHLFORD EARL G	LTC	0-1036810	0867	1
WOHLGEMUTH GEORGE F	LTC	0-0245922	0259	3
WOHLGEMUTH STEPHEN H	CW4	W-2004201	1056	3
WOHLTMAN ROBERT M	MAJ	0-0274682	0763	3
WOICK FRED H	LTC	0-0506556	0262	3
WOIDA LOUIS D	CW4	W-2146620	0560	1
WOITH MELVIN P	CW2	W-2209809	0863	1
WOITY SOLOMON F	MAJ	0-1581467	1060	1
WOJACK WALTER L	2LT	0-2034712	0845	2
WOJAHN HAROLD F	MAJ	0-1924541	1167	1
WOJCIECHOWICZ J C	CW2	W-2206854	0760	1
WOJTAL JR EDWARD S	1LT	0-1289846	1045	2
WOJTANOWSKI HENRY P	MAJ	0-2008762	0365	1
WOJTASZEK JOSEPH H	MAJ	0-0256309	0665	3
WOKULICH JOHN	CW3	W-2143987	1162	1
WOLBERT ROBERT E	LTC	0-1183453	0864	1
WOLCHICK MICHAEL T	1LT	0-1050521	1154	1
WOLCOTT LORENE M	MAJ	L-0400509	0845	2
WOLCZYK STANLEY J	1LT	0-0413315	0444	2
WOLD HAROLD	1LT	0-1311257	0845	2
WOLD ROBERT M	COL	0-0230400	0462	3
WOLDER MURRAY P	1LT	0-1301742	0345	2
WOLENBERG HOWARD C	LTC	0-1592723	0862	1
WOLEVER STANLEY E	LTC	0-1169404	0861	1
WOLF ALFRED H	1LT	0-0478976	0847	2
WOLF DEWITT G	LTC	0-1017467	0766	1
WOLF EARL E	COL	0-0425188	1061	2
WOLF EDWARD D	M G	0-0298530	1064	3
WOLF EDWARD T	LTC	0-0177363	0845	2
WOLF EDWIN J	COL	0-0910396	0667	3
WOLF EUGENE F	LTC	0-0380688	0160	1
WOLF GEORGE R	MAJ	0-0222438	0865	3
WOLF GORDON J	COL	0-0225015	0265	3
WOLF HENRY A	CPT	0-0242223	C64A	3
WOLF IRVING	2LT	0-1004263	0245	1
WOLF JOHN S	LTC	0-0386692	0645	1
WOLF JR RICHARD D	MAJ	0-1336013	0765	1
WOLF KARL R	LTC	0-0251043	1265	3
WOLF MAURICE A	COL	0-0165989	0751	3
WOLF MELVIN E	MAJ	0-1688473	0665	1
WOLF PAUL V	CPT	0-1044429	0855	1
WOLF RALPH L	LTC	0-0256288	0359	3
WOLF ROBERT H	CPT	0-1062457	0947	2
WOLF SHELDON L	CPT	0-0488395	0745	2
WOLF VINCENT E	2LT	0-1308284	0644	2
WOLF WALTER C	CPT	0-0446121	0849	1
WOLFBERG EDGAR H	MAJ	0-0133603	1053	3
WOLFBERG JOHN M	1LT	0-1015865	0945	2
WOLFE ALBERT	CW4	W-2112432	0162	2
WOLFE ALBERT E	CW2	W-2152634	0662	1
WOLFE BURTON A	LTC	0-0451564	0860	1
WOLFE CARL L	LTC	0-0356280	0461	1
WOLFE CHARLES H	CPT	0-1582278	0546	2
WOLFE CHESTER W	COL	0-0277596	1047	2
WOLFE CLAY W	1LT	0-0494342	0947	1
WOLFE CLEMENT V	CPT	0-0213381	1045	2
WOLFE CURTIS M	LTC	0-1642737	0162	1
WOLFE DALE H	CW3	W-2209875	1066	1
WOLFE ESTILL	CPT	0-0488558	0545	2
WOLFE EUGENE	LTC	0-0210932	0-53	1
WOLFE FRANK E	CW2	W-2151171	1058	2
WOLFE FREDERIC S	1LT	0-0320396	0743	2
WOLFE GARLAND H	COL	0-0248759	0560	3
WOLFE GEORGE W	1LT	0-0357700	0646	2
WOLFE HAROLD	1LT	0-1320704	0446	2
WOLFE HENRY M	LTC	0-0135654	0549	3
WOLFE HILREY W	CPT	0-0969412	0861	2
WOLFE HOWARD D	MAJ	0-0114173	0832	1
WOLFE IRA C	MAJ	0-0268770	0255	3
WOLFE JAMES W	2LT	0-1824719	0344	2
WOLFE JOHN H	LTC	0-1588383	0462	1
WOLFE JOSEPH	MAJ	0-0225944	0246	2
WOLFE JOSEPH D	1LT	0-0381830	0443	2
WOLFE JOSEPH H	MAJ	0-1947123	0463	1
WOLFE JR GEORGE A	CPT	0-0359649	1065	3
WOLFE MARTIN D	LTC	0-0193796	1263	3
WOLFE MARTIN R	1LT	0-0312854	0345	2
WOLFE MIRIAM D	2LT	N-0735227	0545	1
WOLFE NEC P	1LT	0-1547507	0745	2
WOLFE NORMAN B	1LT	0-1062658	0750	1
WOLFE ORIN K	CW4	W-2104609	0659	1
WOLFE PETER F	MAJ	0-1103474	0555	1
WOLFE RANALD M	LTC	0-0505943	0267	3
WOLFE RAYMOND D	LTC	0-1286404	0661	1
WOLFE RUSSELL S	COL	0-0147600	0751	3
WOLFE STANLEY	COL	0-0167395	0853	3
WOLFE THOMAS J	LTC	0-0454186	0364	1
WOLFE THOMAS L	COL	0-0242177	1054	3
WOLFE THOMAS P	LTC	0-0255759	0561	3
WOLFE VICTOR	MAJ	0-1633648	0348	2
WOLFEL C STONEY S	LTC	0-1646124	1062	1
WOLFER FREDERIC F	COL	0-0275670	0159	1
WOLFF BERNARD P	LTC	0-0397967	1145	1
WOLFF CHARLES R	1LT	0-1649671	0347	2
WOLFF EDWARD L	COL	0-0357616	0466	1
WOLFF HAROLD J	MAJ	0-1286052	0266	1
WOLFF HEINZ C L	CPT	0-0538414	0646	2
WOLFF JAMES A	MAJ	0-0551079	1065	1
WOLFF JOHN	LTC	0-2052086	0566	3
WOLFF JOHN P	LTC	0-0291219	1058	3
WOLFF LUTHER H	LTC	0-0296324	1167	3
WOLFF MAXWELL J	MAJ	0-0493762	0645	1
WOLFF MILDRED M	CPT	M-0783853	0148	1
WOLFF MORTIMER	LTC	0-0395916	0966	3
WOLFF RAYMOND R	CW3	W-2143138	0962	1
WOLFF ROBERT B	MAJ	0-1330244	0665	1
WOLFF WALTER L	MAJ	0-1333578	0762	1
WOLFF 3RD CHARLES	COL	0-0287042	0856	3
WOLFINGER WILLIAM F	LTC	0-1590314	0763	2
WOLFMAN AVE	1LT	N-0758465	0846	1
WOLFMAN MILTON	MAJ	0-1182042	0763	1
WOLFORD JOHN P	CW2	W-2208951	0862	1
WOLFORD ROY A	COL	0-0233446	0854	3
WOLFORD SAMUEL H	MAJ	0-0488317	0854	1
WOLFORTH WILLIAM A	LTC	0-1314865	1162	1
WOLFRAM KENNETH G	MAJ	0-1300111	0758	1
WOLFSKILL CLIFFORD L	LTC	0-1824549	1062	1
WOLFSON HENRY	MAJ	0-0137148	0949	3
WOLFSON IRVING	LTC	0-0272187	0866	3
WOLFSON MELVIN L	CPT	0-1041062	1044	2
WOLFSON SARAH A	MAJ	N-0725641	0663	1
WOLFSON SIDNEY H	MAJ	0-1585099	0261	1
WOLGAMOTT MURRAY W	1LT	0-2055324	0556	1
WOLICKI MARCELLI A	CW2	W-2143815	0859	1
WOLICKI WALTER J	CW3	W-2150329	0762	1
WOLK GEORGE	2LT	0-1589014	0744	2
WOLK HAROLD	1LT	0-1043258	1045	2
WOLKEN LEO B	MAJ	0-0948742	0763	1
WOLKOW SAM J	MAJ	0-0494088	0654	1
WOLKOWSKY MELVIN	1LT	0-1736448	0104	2
WOLLAK THEODORE	CPT	0-0252625	1043	2
WOLLENBERG C H	LTC	0-0238747	0559	3
WOLLENMAN MAX J	LTC	0-0245740	0661	3
WOLLMER CHARLES A	CPT	0-1011429	0546	2
WOLLNER FRANK E	CW3	W-2148895	0864	1
WOLOTIRA ROBERT J	CPT	0-1283182	0845	1
WOLPE LEONARD	CPT	0-1012559	0446	2
WOLPERS JOHN A	1LT	0-1288154	0344	2
WOLPERT HOWARD A	MAJ	0-0971722	0562	1
WOLPIN ALVIN W	2LT	0-1177701	0644	2
WOLTER FRED W	COL	0-0208721	1156	3
WOLTER FRED W	1LT	0-0695397	1043	2
WOLTER JR HERBERT H	MAJ	0-2046638	1060	1
WOMAC JAMES C	LTC	0-1290170	0860	1
WOMACK DAVID C	MAJ	0-2041141	0964	1
WOMACK HORACE D	MAJ	0-1914031	0636	1
WOMACK JR CHARLES T	CPT	0-1293164	0946	2
WOMACK LAWRENCE F	CW3	W-2146731	0962	1
WOMACK LEHMAN E	CW3	W-2144636	0461	1
WOMACK LEONARD D	CPT	0-2040765	0858	1
WOMACK WILLIAM J	COL	0-1102553	0763	1
WOMBLE LYNDELL E	CW3	W-2207502	1166	1
WOMBLE WALTER F	COL	0-0270467	0460	1
WOMELDORFF VIRGIL L	COL	0-0222880	0964	3
WONDER GORDON F	1LT	0-0267723	1042	2
WONDERS GLENN D	LTC	0-1546853	0966	1
WONDRACK ARTHUR J	CPT	0-0261538	0367	3
WONDRASEK STEPHEN M	MAJ	0-1039270	0657	1
WONG GILBERT L	LTC	0-0277929	1060	1
WONG JAMES S F	LTC	0-0259392	0965	3
WONG ROBERT W Y	CW4	W-2135991	0466	1
WONNENBERG RAYMOND H	LTC	0-0132880	0150	3
WOOD ALBERT W	CPT	0-0383965	0446	2
WOOD ALONZO E	COL	0-0171619	1058	1
WOOD ALVIN	CPT	0-0388285	0344	2
WOOD ALVYN P	LTC	0-2006903	1163	1
WOOD ANDREW L	CW3	W-2150041	0862	2
WOOD ARCHIE N	LTC	0-0262141	0357	3
WOOD ARTHUR C	LTC	0-0199792	0254	2
WOOD AUGUST R	LTC	0-0269763	0363	1
WOOD BARLOW L	1LT	0-1310658	0345	2
WOOD BASIL A	COL	0-0212522	0857	2
WOOD BENNETT R	CPT	0-0226110	1059	3
WOOD BERNARD P	LTC	0-0267124	0366	3
WOOD BILLY	LTC	0-0552589	0663	1
WOOD BILLY A	CW2	W-2150682	0961	1
WOOD BILLY B	CPT	0-1643469	1147	2
WOOD BILLY J	CW2	W-3000415	1067	1
WOOD BRENNAN C	CPT	0-1285683	0945	1
WOOD CECIL H	COL	0-0288922	0662	1
WOOD CHARLES C	CPT	0-0147226	1055	3
WOOD CHARLES G	MAJ	0-2028460	0465	1
WOOD CHARLES J	LTC	0-0396204	0861	1
WOOD CHARLES R	MAJ	0-1640139	0961	1
WOOD CHARLES T	MAJ	0-0218679	0646	2
WOOD CHARLES W	MAJ	0-1598882	0166	1
WOOD CLARENCE A	MAJ	0-0163816	1151	3
WOOD CLYDE C	CPT	0-0224757	0447	1
WOOD CLYNER M	CW3	W-2149167	1060	1
WOOD CONNIE C	CW2	W-2102569	0949	1
WOOD CORDELLE A	LTC	0-0236842	0858	3
WOOD DAVID B	1LT	0-0970839	0454	2
WOOD DAVID L	COL	0-0276956	1062	1
WOOD CEAN K	CPT	0-0336712	0549	1
WOOD DON P	CW3	W-2122834	0167	1
WOOD DONALD F	MAJ	0-2014473	0765	1
WOOD DONALD K	CW2	W-2206985	1163	1
WOOD DONALD L	LTC	0-0122157	0144	1
WOOD DONALD M	2LT	0-1311724	0344	2
WOOD EARL L	COL	0-0174912	1054	3
WOOD EARL S	MAJ	0-1923672	0367	1
WOOD EDWARD J	CW4	W-2142673	0758	1
WOOD EDWARD L	1LT	0-0304223	0742	2
WOOD EDWARD M	CW3	W-2142919	0157	1
WOOD EDWARD S	LTC	0-0390059	0660	2
WOOD EDWARD W	LTC	0-0230431	0259	3
WOOD EDWIN C	1LT	0-1183797	0946	2
WOOD ELDON B	MAJ	0-0276422	1060	1
WOOD ELMER D	MAJ	0-0229198	0546	2
WOOD ERNEST	CPT	0-0109628	0931	1
WOOD ERNEST L	LTC	0-1635492	0259	1
WOOD FENTON M	COL	0-0166365	0955	2
WOOD FRANK B	LTC	0-0228190	1163	3
WOOD FRANK D	LTC	0-0182911	1060	2
WOOD GASTON M	COL	0-0216671	1263	3
WOOD GEORGE F	LTC	0-1175364	0563	1
WOOD GEORGE W	MAJ	0-0207267	0554	3
WOOD GEORGE W	COL	0-0257822	0565	3
WOOD GILBERT F	COL	0-0451533	1060	1
WOOD GLEN P	COL	0-0256692	0159	3
WOOD HAROLD N	COL	0-0392351	0467	1
WOOD HAROLD S	CW4	W-2119645	0959	1
WOOD HARRY C	MAJ	0-1181806	0457	1
WOOD HEREFORD M	COL	0-0323741	0546	2
WOOD HERMAN A	LTC	0-0412077	0162	1
WOOD HOLLIS D	CW3	W-2141500	0159	1
WOOD HOMER C	MAJ	0-1796592	1266	3
WOOD HORACE	CW4	W-2118293	1154	1
WOOD HORACE M	COL	0-0259447	0963	1
WOOD HOWARD C	LTC	0-1796895	1061	1
WOOD HOWARD S	1LT	0-2049768	0846	2
WOOD JACK H	CPT	0-0520437	0546	1
WOOD JACK N	CW2	W-2152664	0361	1
WOOD JAMES A	COL	0-0111565	0648	3
WOOD JAMES C	CPT	0-0991588	0757	2
WOOD JAMES E	COL	0-0203813	0954	1
WOOD JAMES E	LTC	0-0471423	0955	1
WOOD JAMES E	CW3	W-2144202	0961	1
WOOD JAMES I	CW2	W-3250454	0567	1
WOOD JASON G	CPT	0-1701733	1044	2
WOOD JOE T	LTC	0-0509574	1054	1
WOOD JOEL B	LTC	0-0341756	0459	1
WOOD JOHN B	1LT	0-1322389	0846	2
WOOD JOHN H	MAJ	0-0965804	1162	1
WOOD JOHN H	1LT	0-1551993	0451	1
WOOD JOHN H	MAJ	0-2263051	1164	1
WOOD JOHN M	1LT	0-1311461	0846	1
WOOD JOHN O	LTC	0-1172344	1160	1
WOOD JOHN P	CPT	0-1016397	1262	1
WOOD JOHN V	CW3	W-2149032	0557	1
WOOD JOSEPH	LTC	0-1543746	0361	1
WOOD JOSEPH C	MAJ	0-0975532	0267	1
WOOD JOSEPH E	LTC	0-0248315	1163	3
WOOD JR BURTON M	1LT	0-1294760	0245	1
WOOD JR CHARLES A	COL	0-0241851	0865	2
WOOD JR CHARLES O	1LT	0-1300885	1045	1
WOOD JR CHARLES S	LTC	0-0316216	0862	1
WOOD JR FRANK C	LTC	0-0105418	1051	3
WOOD JR HARRY A	1LT	0-5513350	0264	2
WOOD JR MORTON	1LT	0-0549684	0952	1
WOOD JR ROLAND M	LTC	0-0451518	0960	1
WOOD JR WILLIAM E	MAJ	0-1042747	0159	1
WOOD JUSTIN A	LTC	0-0185060	0855	3
WOOD KENNETH A	MAJ	0-0204550	0154	3
WOOD LAWRENCE E	CPT	0-0346206	0544	2
WOOD LEONARD B	MAJ	0-1342144	0866	1
WOOD LEONARD E	LTC	0-1185325	1163	1
WOOD LESLIE C	LTC	0-0294452	1061	1
WOOD LESLIE F	CW4	W-2118342	0559	1
WOOD LOUIS F	1LT	0-1796198	0551	1
WOOD MARK A	MAJ	0-1585594	0264	3
WOOD MASON H	1LT	0-1030733	0245	2
WOOD MORRIS B	CPT	0-0505524	1146	1
WOOD NEWELL C	1LT	0-0432524	0444	2
WOOD PAUL W	CPT	0-0122443	0656	3
WOOD PENMAN J	CPT	0-0145901	0853	3
WOOD PHILIP A	CPT	0-0392493	0944	2
WOOD RALPH H	CPT	0-0968635	1157	1
WOOD RAYMOND E	CPT	0-1288476	0346	2
WOOD REED O	CPT	0-1826044	0647	2
WOOD REGINALD H	COL	0-0173485	0550	3
WOOD RHYS C	LTC	0-1081044	0767	1
WOOD RICHARD A	LTC	0-1640140	0561	1
WOOD RICHARD H	COL	0-0397972	1045	2
WOOD RICHARD S	MAJ	0-1895674	1262	1
WOOD ROBERT B	COL	0-0345737	0161	1
WOOD ROBERT F	2LT	0-0234038	0255	3
WOOD ROBERT J	CPT	0-1878634	0264	2
WOOD ROBERT L	MAJ	0-1037952	0464	1
WOOD ROY S	LTC	0-0115564	0756	3
WOOD RUSSELL H	MAJ	0-0233487	0264	3
WOOD RYAN L	LTC	0-0180607	0361	3
WOOD SAMUEL S	LTC	0-0339123	0659	1
WOOD THOMAS C	1LT	0-0335056	0264	3
WOOD THOMAS L	LTC	0-0284118	0264	3
WOOD THOMAS S	MAJ	0-0221314	1059	3
WOOD THOMAS W	LTC	0-0302898	0859	2
WOOD THORNTON H	LTC	0-0243587	0757	3
WOOD VIBERT E	LTC	0-0923735	1157	1

NAME	GRADE	SVC NO	DATE RET MO YR	RET CODE
WOOD VICTOR H	LTC	0-1556827	1167	1
WOOD WALTER A	LTC	0-0236618	1263	3
WOOD WALTER J	LTC	0-0525578	1165	3
WOOD WARREN W	CW2	W-2004756	0760	2
WOOD WEBSTER D	1LT	0-0443966	0146	2
WOOD WILLARD W	MAJ	0-0279113	0857	3
WOOD WILLIAM A	LTC	0-0202134	0252	3
WOOD WILLIAM A	COL	0-0361652	0147	2
WOOD WILLIAM A	MAJ	0-0397852	1060	1
WOOD WILLIAM A	LTC	0-0499027	0763	3
WOOD WILLIAM B	2LT	0-0920370	1043	2
WOOD WILLIAM E	LTC	0-0304557	0662	1
WOOD WILLIAM F	MAJ	0-1948855	1065	1
WOOD WILLIAM J	LTC	0-1166872	0858	1
WOOD WILLIAM K	COL	0-0287119	0357	1
WOOD WILLIAM L	CW3	W-2125856	0457	2
WOOD WILLIAM N	LTC	0-0483155	0655	1
WOOD WILLIAM O	CPT	0-1651075	0557	1
WOOD WILLIAM S	B G	0-0273707	0658	3
WOOD WILSON B	COL	0-0185638	0158	3
WOOD WOODROW W	2LT	0-1315250	0845	2
WOOD WYATT B	MAJ	0-1013202	0361	1
WOODALL CHARLES W	LTC	0-0171501	0648	3
WOODALL EMERY L	1LT	0-0919068	0943	2
WOODALL JOHN B	MAJ	0-1328208	0762	1
WOODALL JOHN F	MAJ	0-1688624	0563	1
WOODALL PAUL F	CPT	0-0995951	0861	1
WOODALL RALPH G	CPT	0-0281139	0146	2
WOODALL RAY T	LTC	0-0298793	0962	2
WOODARD ALVIN H	CW4	W-2106066	0555	1
WOODARD CARLETON R	CW2	W-3430172	1166	1
WOODARD CHARLES C	1LT	0-0552060	0346	2
WOODARD DONALD S	1LT	0-1011636	0445	2
WOODARD JOHN C	CPT	0-0314815	0845	2
WOODARD LYLE E	WO1	W-2126094	1046	1
WOODARD RANDLE	CW2	W-2146147	0659	1
WOODARD ROBERT C	CPT	0-1045003	0446	2
WOODARD WILFRID H	CW3	W-2111435	0255	1
WOODARD WILLIAM O	MAJ	0-1015063	0757	1
WOODARD WILLIAM R	MAJ	0-0400062	0646	1
WOODBECK CAROL E	CW2	RW-2210186	0965	1
WOODBERRY JAMES W	LTC	0-0373443	0260	2
WOODBRIDGE MULFORD	MAJ	0-1560466	0666	1
WOODBRIDGE WILLIAM W	LTC	0-0297893	0246	2
WOODBURN JOHN C	LTC	0-0317889	0263	1
WOODBURN ROBERT L	MAJ	0-1289848	0750	2
WOODBURNE ARTHUR R	COL	0-0263888	1261	3
WOODBURY CLARENCE C	MAJ	0-0157577	1047	1
WOODBURY CORYTON M	B G	0-0252344	0766	3
WOODBURY EDWARD L	LTC	0-1105935	1161	1
WOODBURY JOSEPH L	CPT	0-0273400	0154	1
WOODBURY LYNN W	CW2	W-2206049	0163	1
WOODBURY ROLISTON S	1LT	0-0178109	0755	3
WOODBURY WILLIAM W	1LT	0-1283183	0545	2
WOODCOCK DON B	1LT	0-1108429	1144	1
WOODDELL JOSEPH S	LTC	0-1845128	0665	3
WOODELL CARLTON D	LTC	0-1015847	0364	1
WOODEN LEVY K	CPT	0-1053023	0662	1
WOODEND ELMER E	COL	0-0284210	0662	3
WOODFIELD JAMES E	CW3	W-2147812	0465	1
WOODFIN HOWEL W	CPT	0-1545549	0447	2
WOODFORD MARION J	CPT	0-0245441	1064	3
WOODFORD WILLIAM H	COL	0-0326586	0962	1
WOODFORD WILLIAM I	LTC	0-0406587	0364	3
WOODHAM GRADY H	CPT	0-1081262	0157	1
WOODHOUSE HANS C	CPT	0-0446576	0245	2
WOODHOUSE MILTON E	LTC	0-0332916	0661	3
WOODHOUSE THOMAS J	CW2	W-2149314	1060	1
WOODILLA JOHN E	MAJ	0-0244571	1048	2
WOODIN KNOWLTON M	LTC	0-0174413	0259	3
WOODIN WILLIS E	MAJ	0-0290047	0853	3
WOODLAND PAUL S	MAJ	0-0980218	1056	1
WOODLEY FORREST L	CPT	0-0265681	0464	3
WOODLEY GERALD A B	COL	0-0254770	1266	3
WOODLEY JR TOLLEY D	LTC	0-1018005	0566	1

NAME	GRADE	SVC NO	DATE RET MO YR	RET CODE
WOODLEY LOREN G	1LT	0-1585104	1047	2
WOODMAN ARNOLD J	LTC	0-0196069	1158	3
WOODMAN ARTHUR P	LTC	0-0274662	0354	3
WOODMAN DONALD H	CPT	0-0302943	0246	2
WOODMAN KARL W	LTC	0-0482976	0659	1
WOODRING JR JOSEPH H	MAJ	0-0955914	0364	1
WOODRING ORVILLE W	CW2	W-2151116	1059	1
WOODRING RAYMOND B	1LT	0-1180097	0546	2
WOODROME MITCHELL	CPT	0-0475383	0654	1
WOODROW CHARLES W	COL	0-0168444	1060	3
WOODROW FITZ W M	COL	0-0113801	0551	3
WOODROW JACK H	2LT	0-1051838	0745	2
WOODROW JAMES Y	MAJ	0-0910781	0964	3
WOODRUFF BERTRAM F	MAJ	0-0490572	1052	1
WOODRUFF BYRON E	1LT	0-1293868	1144	2
WOODRUFF CHARLES W	COL	0-0193767	0856	3
WOODRUFF DEMA F	MAJ	N-0734115	0265	1
WOODRUFF EDITH M	CPT	L-0521506	0447	2
WOODRUFF FRANCIS R	MAJ	0-0180580	1155	3
WOODRUFF GERALD G	COL	0-0247769	1154	3
WOODRUFF HALBERT E	LTC	0-0238295	0745	2
WOODRUFF HIRAM G	1LT	0-0236702	1165	3
WOODRUFF JAMES M	WO1	W-2124534	0257	1
WOODRUFF MARION W	LTC	0-0262446	0165	3
WOODRUFF NORBERT A	CW3	W-2205589	0167	1
WOODRUFF RED J	CW3	W-2207139	0666	1
WOODRUFF WARREN V	COL	0-0302501	0662	1
WOODRUFF WILLIAM H	CW3	W-2151769	0959	1
WOODRUFF WILLIAM L	COL	0-0260203	0446	2
WOODRUFF WILLIAM L	LTC	0-0447622	0657	1
WOODRUM RICHARD B	2LT	0-2025688	0153	1
WOODS BEN H	MAJ	0-1341612	0861	1
WOODS CHESTER A	CPT	0-0464231	0855	1
WOODS CLAIR L	CW4	W-2141963	0766	1
WOODS CLELL L	1LT	0-1294057	0346	2
WOODS DON E	LTC	0-0216140	1060	3
WOODS EDWIN R	MAJ	0-0978087	1164	1
WOODS ERNEST J	MAJ	0-0267177	1057	3
WOODS FOLEY C	CPT	0-0503864	0755	1
WOODS FORREST M	1LT	0-1995483	1049	1
WOODS FRANCIS J	MAJ	0-1302912	1065	1
WOODS FRANCIS L	LTC	0-0290753	0765	3
WOODS FRANK N	MAJ	0-0196537	0260	3
WOODS GEORGE E	CW2	W-2151055	0658	1
WOODS HARRY L	CW2	W-2148896	0760	1
WOODS IVAN F	1LT	0-0455327	0445	2
WOODS JACOB C	LTC	0-1548598	0661	1
WOODS JAMES J	LTC	0-0180590	0649	3
WOODS JAMES R	LTC	0-1110898	0163	1
WOODS JAMES S	1LT	0-1062752	0346	2
WOODS JOE W	CW2	W-2114070	1159	1
WOODS JOE W	CW2	W-2144857	0755	1
WOODS JOHN I	MAJ	0-1799497	0562	1
WOODS JOHN L	MAJ	0-1016860	0457	1
WOODS JOHN T	CW2	W-2210692	0364	1
WOODS JOSEPH M	CPT	0-0176226	1057	3
WOODS JR CHARLES A	MAJ	0-0215583	0763	3
WOODS JR CHARLES H	LTC	0-0201336	0857	3
WOODS JR EDWARD M	LTC	0-0208344	0263	3
WOODS KENNETH M	LTC	0-1551344	0263	1
WOODS LEE I	CPT	0-2262871	0361	1
WOODS LELAND L	MAJ	0-1683469	1060	1
WOODS LESTER K	LTC	0-0251235	0265	3
WOODS LIZZIE O	MAJ	N-0734366	0661	1
WOODS MARJORIE F	CPT	N-0767256	1146	1
WOODS NOEL A	CPT	0-0435830	1045	2
WOODS NORMAN T	LTC	0-0422278	0162	1
WOODS ONEIL	CW3	W-2146104	0959	1
WOODS OREN L	WO1	W-2146913	0161	1
WOODS PATRICK	MAJ	0-1314216	0657	1
WOODS PERRY L	LTC	0-0234095	0654	3
WOODS RALPH E	CW4	W-2152015	1266	1
WOODS ROBERT E	LTC	0-1168983	0764	1
WOODS ROBERT F	LTC	0-0347957	0660	1
WOODS SAMUEL H	MAJ	0-1575645	0446	2

NAME	GRADE	SVC NO	DATE RET MO YR	RET CODE
WOODS THOMAS	CW4	W-2102574	0955	1
WOODS WILLIAM J	CPT	0-1825390	0946	1
WOODS WILLIAM M	CW4	W-2117251	1154	1
WOODS WOODROW F	CPT	0-2263555	0463	2
WOODSIDE ALBERT	CW4	W-2142418	0865	1
WOODSIDE ARTHUR L	LTC	0-0309050	1045	2
WOODSIDE CHARLES L	1LT	0-0232866	0665	3
WOODSIDE JAMES P	CPT	0-0327139	0651	2
WOODSIDE ROBERT B	MAJ	0-1639833	0957	1
WOODSON BOB M	CPT	0-1045316	0860	1
WOODSON LEWIS E	CPT	0-0954782	1058	1
WOODSON ROBERT S	LTC	0-0246805	1054	3
WOODSON WALTON W	CPT	0-1550732	0946	2
WOODWARD CALVIN L	CW3	W-2206100	0464	1
WOODWARD EARL B	CPT	0-1173130	0655	1
WOODWARD EDWIN O	LTC	0-0145903	0256	3
WOODWARD FRANCES L	1LT	N-0732030	0746	1
WOODWARD FRANK A	MAJ	0-0188525	0648	3
WOODWARD FRANK L	COL	0-0364937	0963	3
WOODWARD FRED H	CW3	W-2143306	0265	1
WOODWARD FRED W	CPT	0-0309942	1061	3
WOODWARD GETTA	CPT	0-0176541	0932	1
WOODWARD HAROLD S	LTC	0-0196711	0961	3
WOODWARD HERBERT E	CW3	W-2144033	0661	2
WOODWARD JOHN W	MAJ	0-1824951	0961	1
WOODWARD JR JABISH H	MAJ	0-0118972	0849	3
WOODWARD JR JESSE A	CW3	W-2142920	0659	1
WOODWARD LEWIS M	LTC	0-0265559	0665	3
WOODWARD RAY O	MAJ	0-1105937	0553	1
WOODWARD ROBERT E	COL	0-0175949	1056	3
WOODWARD ROBERT H	COL	0-0266777	1158	3
WOODWARD STANLEY	CPT	0-0279596	0351	1
WOODWARD THEODORE E	LTC	0-0368004	1046	1
WOODWARD WALLACE W	MAJ	0-0333009	0246	2
WOODWARD WALTER H	LTC	0-0488840	0457	1
WOODWARD WILLIAM S	CW3	W-2003752	0767	1
WOODWORTH HAROLD A	1LT	0-1303244	0645	2
WOODWORTH MARION C	COL	0-0334887	0557	3
WOODWORTH PHILIP S	CPT	0-1946895	1050	1
WOODWORTH VALORUS C	LTC	0-1646130	0864	1
WOODWORTH WALTER R	LTC	0-1947124	0867	1
WOODWORTH WAYNE D	CPT	0-2262944	0866	2
WOODY CLARENCE W	1LT	0-0197846	0648	3
WOODY JR RONAL E	MAJ	0-1309642	0446	2
WOODY MONTFORD H	MAJ	0-0193719	0843	2
WOODY THOMAS W	MAJ	0-0304279	0446	2
WOODYARD ELMER A	CPT	0-0493948	0946	1
WOODYARD WILLARD A	COL	0-0351013	0860	1
WOOFTER CLARENCE J	CPT	0-0473121	1046	1
WOOG AUDREY J	2LT	N-0772367	0845	1
WOOLARD BERL L	1LT	0-1030438	0645	2
WOOLAVER CECIL G	CPT	0-1080593	1044	2
WOOLDRIDGE GLEN E	CPT	0-0491453	0953	1
WOOLDRIDGE JOHN R	LTC	0-0410067	0960	1
WOOLDRIDGE KERMIT O	LTC	0-0451748	0258	1
WOOLDRIDGE TROY T	CW3	W-2146789	0763	1
WOOLDRIDGE WARD	MAJ	0-0924784	0648	2
WOOLDRIDGE WILLIAM F	COL	0-0189631	1053	1
WOOLERY BRUCE A	1LT	0-1825582	1045	2
WOOLEVER NEIL F	LTC	0-1177252	0663	1
WOOLEY MYRTIS N	LTC	N-0743351	1062	1
WOOLF DONALD O	CPT	0-0105903	0258	3
WOOLF EMERSON C	CPT	0-0143265	0648	3
WOOLF HAROLD E	LTC	0-0904984	0562	1
WOOLF MARTIN P	CPT	0-0512972	1045	2
WOOLFORD FRANK B	LTC	0-0195368	0961	3
WOOLFORD JR LEON M	CW3	W-2143384	0762	1
WOOLFSON ALBERT	MAJ	0-0528207	0546	2
WOOLHEATER ELWOOD J	CW2	W-2146466	0766	2
WOOLHEATER RAYMOND H	CW3	W-2207057	0665	1
WOOLLETT JR WILLIAM	1LT	0-1882271	0254	2
WOOLLEY ARTHUR H	LTC	0-1283708	0860	1
WOOLLEY EARL K	MAJ	0-2014809	0663	1
WOOLLEY FRED K	LTC	0-0271568	0867	3
WOOLLEY GEORGE R	LTC	0-0257307	0663	3

NAME	GRADE	SVC NO	DATE RET MO YR	RET CODE
WOOLLEY MAURICE W	MAJ	0-0485536	0247	1
WOOLPERT WALTER R	COL	0-0906790	1053	2
WOOLRIDGE LUKE C	CPT	0-0314926	0366	3
WOOLRIDGE REGINALD H	MAJ	0-1173514	0265	1
WOOLSEY ERNEST L	MAJ	0-0278634	0560	3
WOOLSEY GEORGE C	COL	0-0385954	0661	1
WOOLSEY ROBERT J	MAJ	0-0260158	0267	3
WOOLSEY WILLIAM P	CPT	0-1180098	0746	1
WOOLSTENCROFT W B	1LT	0-1101722	0843	2
WOOLUMS ALBERT B	COL	0-0108586	0753	3
WOOLUMS CHARLES N	CPT	0-0402189	0763	1
WOOLVERTON WILLIAM H	MAJ	0-0182261	0553	3
WOOSLEY FRANK P	1LT	0-0438365	0245	1
WOOSTER CHARLES L	CPT	0-0341072	0967	3
WOOSTER JAMES F	LTC	0-0253883	0562	3
WOOSTER MALLERY D	LTC	0-0236441	0165	3
WOOTAN EDWARD C	CPT	0-1102124	0562	1
WOOTEN BOYD W	CW2	W-2148911	0464	1
WOOTEN JAMES A	LTC	0-1297464	0565	1
WOOTEN LEWELL C	MAJ	0-0981844	1264	1
WOOTEN WOOTEN	MAJ	0-0351014	0760	2
WOOTERS PERCIVAL C	COL	0-0304428	1158	1
WOOTON JAMES E	CPT	0-1312831	0965	1
WORCOTT ARTHUR J	COL	0-0166470	0151	3
WORD FRED L	MAJ	0-1100402	0959	1
WORD KARL H	MAJ	0-0245792	0966	3
WORDEN BRUCE L	1LT	0-2017322	0747	2
WORDEN GEORGE F	MAJ	0-0961537	0163	1
WORDEN ROBERT P	MAJ	0-0407816	0446	2
WORDEN WILLIAM G	LTC	0-0492786	1262	1
WORDLEY CARL E	LTC	0-1288838	0954	1
WORDLEY STANLEY C	COL	0-1534422	1263	1
WORF GEORGE H	LTC	0-1307608	0763	1
WORHUCK GEORGE W	CW4	W-2120910	0155	1
WORK ARTHUR L	CW4	W-2119872	1154	1
WORK EDGAR A	COL	0-0251985	1066	3
WORK HERMAN	COL	0-0145782	0848	3
WORK JAMES E	LTC	0-0433317	0665	1
WORK RALPH H	LTC	0-0501738	0158	1
WORKING JESSE O	MAJ	0-0133434	1050	3
WORKMAN JOHN H	1LT	0-1041266	0345	1
WORKMAN WARNER G	LTC	0-0127873	0648	3
WORKMAN WILLIAM V	CPT	0-0419528	0545	2
WORKS ROY C	CPT	0-2033323	1058	1
WORLAND WILFRID V	COL	0-0270095	0667	3
WORLEIN FRANCIS L	CW2	W-2151819	0262	1
WORLEY BERNICE	LTC	N-0728217	0661	1
WORLEY DELMA A	MAJ	N-0760611	0663	1
WORLEY HORACE O	LTC	0-1533552	0656	1
WORLEY JESSIE E	1LT	N-0759688	0546	1
WORLEY JR OLIVER N	LTC	0-1580528	0562	1
WORLEY STEWART E	LTC	0-0248550	1165	3
WORLUND CARL R	CPT	0-0987298	1161	1
WORMAN BENJAMIN	1LT	0-1303985	0246	1
WORMSER YESNER M	LTC	0-1287641	1164	1
WORMSLEY CLAUDE U	CW2	W-2149852	0361	1
WORONIECKI JOHN	MAJ	0-0999017	0165	1
WORRALL C L	CPT	0-0417768	1145	2
WORRALL JR JAY W	LTC	0-1633652	0766	1
WORRALL KENNETH R	LTC	0-1583863	1164	1
WORRALL WILLIAM E	LTC	0-0455111	1160	1
WORRELL DENVER	WO1	W-2118088	0149	1
WORRELL EDGAR V	COL	0-0461071	0954	1
WORRELL JAMES B	LTC	0-0482670	1054	1
WORRELL THOMAS A	LTC	0-1044732	0162	1
WORSHAM WALLACE V	CW4	W-2106098	0960	1
WORSLEY JOSEPH E	1LT	0-0439385	0444	2
WORST HAROLD J	LTC	0-0286161	1059	3
WORTH AMOS R	LTC	0-1045005	0966	1
WORTH ARLINE E	1LT	N-0761844	1145	1
WORTH GEORGE A	MAJ	0-1114815	1159	1
WORTH JACK L	MAJ	0-0787224	0865	1
WORTH LEWIS B	LTC	0-0485510	0450	1
WORTH SR RAYMOND J	CPT	0-0535210	1165	1
WORTHAM HOWARD F	COL	0-0133815	0152	3

NAME	GRADE	SVC NO	DATE RET MO YR	RET CODE
WORTHAM JR SAMUEL S	CPT	0-0450135	0146	2
WORTHEM CAIL R	CW2	W-2152756	0163	1
WORTHEN FRANK P	LTC	C-1168984	C960	1
WORTHEN LFE V	LTC	0-0945676	0667	1
WORTHING KENNETH F	COL	0-0250447	C265	3
WORTHINGTON CHARLE	COL	C-0418259	1154	1
WORTHINGTON CHARLIE	MAJ	0-0475362	0753	1
WORTHINGTON ELIZARET	MAJ	N-0759585	C866	3
WORTHINGTON FREO	LTC	C-0471418	0853	1
WORTHINGTON FREO H	MAJ	C-0290731	1045	2
WORTHINGTON GEORGE E	CPT	0-0135525	C648	3
WORTHINGTON NEAL	MAJ	C-1638827	0760	1
WORTHINGTON SETH	CPT	0-1285163	C146	2
WORTHLEY PAUL L	LTC	0-1823680	0163	1
WORTHY LYNWOOO N	CPT	0-1878180	0867	2
WORTMAN HUGH M	CPT	C-0204358	C856	3
WOTHERSPOON GEORGE N	LTC	0-0451795	C965	1
WOTHERSPOON HUGH	MAJ	0-1824164	C666	1
WOTHERSPOON MATTHEW	MAJ	0-0993770	0664	1
WOTRING OONALO R	CW3	W-2153274	0161	1
WOTRING MARGARETN	2LT	N-C729636	1144	1
WOTT ALFREO	1LT	0-0289052	C843	2
WOTTLIN WILLIAM O	CPT	C-0404295	1044	2
WOYTON HENRY T	MAJ	0-0224574	1161	3
WOZENCRAFT JAMES P	MAJ	0-1885920	1166	1
WOZENSKI JOSEPH P	LTC	0-0407474	0464	1
WOZNEY MICHAEL J	COL	0-0308754	0362	2
WOZNIAK JOHN	MAJ	C-2005690	0366	1
WOZNIAK JOSEPH J	CW4	W-2111356	1165	2
WRANG ARVIE L	MAJ	0-2006844	C166	1
WRATCHFORO CORCEY H	LTC	C-1284621	0456	1
WRAY ANOREW F	MAJ	0-0174129	0462	3
WRAY CHARLES V	CPT	0-0390664	0245	2
WRAY FRANCIS M	LTC	C-0174992	0651	1
WRAY GEORGE W	COL	C-0214701	C863	3
WRAY JOHN J	MAJ	0-0113002	0648	3
WRAY JR SAMUEL S	LTC	0-0511082	C564	1
WRAY LINCOLN A	LTC	0-1017937	0563	1
WRAY WALTER N	CPT	0-0160290	1145	2
WREN CLOVIS B	1LT	0-2025853	C949	1
WREN J T	LTC	0-1100839	C359	1
WREN JAMES T	LTC	0-2274783	1265	1
WREN JR WILLIAM F	LTC	0-0196854	0958	1
WRENN LAWRENCE W	LTC	0-1586380	1165	1
WRENN OSCAR I	B G	0-0221793	0364	3
WREVER JACK	1LT	0-0886898	C550	1
WRIGHT ALBERT H	COL	0-1307609	1263	3
WRIGHT ALBERT J	LTC	C-2046304	C657	1
WRIGHT ALFREO C	CW3	W-2129247	1058	1
WRIGHT ALONZO W	CPT	0-1695214	0545	2
WRIGHT ANITA W	MAJ	N-0753077	0964	1
WRIGHT ARTHUR	CW3	W-2143758	0365	2
WRIGHT AUBREY B	2LT	0-0210775	C245	1
WRIGHT BEN	WO1	W-2113834	0862	2
WRIGHT BERTRAM C	LTC	0-0282988	C860	1
WRIGHT BRUTUS L	CW2	W-2213000	0567	1
WRIGHT BYRON C	MAJ	0-0278572	0752	3
WRIGHT CARROLL	COL	0-0284216	1163	3
WRIGHT CHARLES A	LTC	C-0247581	C466	3
WRIGHT CHARLES F	COL	0-0245375	C966	3
WRIGHT CHARLES H	WO1	W-2122484	C247	1
WRIGHT CHAUNCEY J	1LT	0-0506641	1263	1
WRIGHT CHESTER F	COL	0-C106003	0752	3
WRIGHT CLARENCE J	CPT	0-1042990	0755	1
WRIGHT CLEO J	1LT	0-0378499	1045	2
WRIGHT CLIFTON A	LTC	C-1303586	1262	1
WRIGHT OANA M	LTC	0-0165588	1051	3
WRIGHT OANIEL P	1LT	0-0405379	0960	1
WRIGHT CAVIO E	MAJ	0-2024320	C662	1
WRIGHT CAVIO J	MAJ	0-2001068	1060	1
WRIGHT CESSIE E	1LT	C-0309137	C745	2
WRIGHT OEWITT	LTC	0-1288155	C457	1
WRIGHT OONALO G	CPT	0-2033613	C657	1
WRIGHT OOUGLAS O	CPT	0-1282388	C157	1
WRIGHT OUWARO O	COL	0-0372751	0546	2
WRIGHT EARL R	CPT	0-0526401	0653	1
WRIGHT ECWARC E	LTC	0-0266172	1044	2
WRIGHT ECWARC S	CW3	W-2205647	1064	1
WRIGHT ECWIN C	CW2	W-2146105	0559	1
WRIGHT ELBERT J	CW2	W-2206574	1059	1
WRIGHT ELIZABETH	1LT	N-0751726	0346	1
WRIGHT ELWOOC J	LTC	0-1573690	1053	1
WRIGHT EMORY L	1LT	0-1296959	1045	2
WRIGHT ERNEST C	1LT	0-1320213	1045	2
WRIGHT EUGENE O	2LT	0-1330956	0346	2
WRIGHT EUGENE J	CW3	W-2145611	0863	2
WRIGHT EUGENE L	LTC	0-1597222	0166	3
WRIGHT FRANCIS L	CW2	W-2209222	0861	1
WRIGHT FRANK H	COL	0-0113001	0860	1
WRIGHT FRANKLIN B	CPT	0-1114336	0261	1
WRIGHT FRED A	MAJ	C-0103871	1151	3
WRIGHT FREO A	LTC	0-0122535	1050	3
WRIGHT FREC L	1LT	0-0490676	0452	1
WRIGHT FREOERICK	MAJ	C-0371119	0751	2
WRIGHT FREOERICK	CW2	W-2151399	0660	1
WRIGHT GARVIN O	2LT	0-1596549	0145	2
WRIGHT CEORGE E	MAJ	0-1179257	0765	1
WRIGHT CEORGE E	COL	0-1284259	0962	1
WRIGHT CEORGE H	MAJ	C-2018624	0661	1
WRIGHT CEORGE R	LTC	C-0332975	0447	2
WRIGHT CEORGE T	COL	0-0919957	0764	3
WRIGHT CEORGE W	LTC	0-0273935	0462	3
WRIGHT GEORGE W	MAJ	0-1102557	1160	1
WRIGHT GROVER L	MAJ	0-1646719	0556	1
WRIGHT HAL O	LTC	C-0310212	0666	3
WRIGHT HARCLC C	LTC	0-1003656	0962	1
WRIGHT HAROLO E	CPT	0-1328862	0161	1
WRIGHT HARCLC O	CW2	W-2119565	0252	2
WRIGHT HARRY J	LTC	0-1310330	0962	1
WRIGHT HAZELLE L	2LT	N-0743443	0944	1
WRIGHT HENRY J	LTC	0-0903820	1065	3
WRIGHT HERBERT M	CPT	0-1316116	0646	2
WRIGHT HERSEY L	LTC	C-0321520	0954	1
WRIGHT HOMER A	MAJ	0-0553223	0664	1
WRIGHT HCMER O	COL	0-0180725	0656	3
WRIGHT HOMER E	LTC	0-0402666	0762	1
WRIGHT HCRACE E	LTC	0-1166218	0157	1
WRIGHT HCWARC	COL	C-0172676	0648	3
WRIGHT HOWARC E	CPT	0-2041857	1062	1
WRIGHT HCWARC H	CPT	0-0471025	1044	2
WRIGHT IRA L	MAJ	0-0122534	0150	3
WRIGHT IRVIN W	MAJ	0-1296140	0864	1
WRIGHT JACK H	WO1	W-2129684	0245	2
WRIGHT JACK R	2LT	0-1325347	C845	2
WRIGHT JACK W	LTC	C-1050149	0864	1
WRIGHT JAMES A	MAJ	0-1576831	1061	1
WRIGHT JAMES B	MAJ	0-1996341	0861	1
WRIGHT JAMES C	COL	0-0250021	0346	1
WRIGHT JAMES F	1LT	0-C447055	0352	1
WRIGHT JAMES H	COL	0-0285378	0964	3
WRIGHT JAMES P	1LT	C-2035511	1045	2
WRIGHT JAMES T	MAJ	0-1558991	0961	1
WRIGHT JASPER K	COL	0-0125046	1054	3
WRIGHT JEFF C	CPT	0-0411089	0761	1
WRIGHT JESSE	CPT	0-0493442	0145	1
WRIGHT JESSE J	MAJ	0-2102955	0765	1
WRIGHT JOE O	1LT	0-1724521	0246	2
WRIGHT JCHN A	CW3	W-2149273	1062	1
WRIGHT JCHN H	2LT	0-0550528	0146	2
WRIGHT JCHN L	LTC	0-0228687	0344	2
WRIGHT JCHN S	MAJ	0-0299726	1164	3
WRIGHT JCHN T	2LT	0-1598733	0446	2
WRIGHT JCHN W	CPT	0-0464212	0547	1
WRIGHT JCHN W	MAJ	C-1309682	0863	1
WRIGHT JCNES T	1LT	0-1554121	0245	2
WRIGHT JCSEPH	LTC	0-0453661	0356	1
WRIGHT JCSEPH F	MAJ	C-0122044	0457	3
WRIGHT JOSEPH H	COL	0-0267842	1265	3
WRIGHT JR CARL J	MAJ	C-1040640	1160	1
WRIGHT JR CHARLES E	LTC	0-0543492	1063	1
WRIGHT JR FRANK R	MAJ	C-0818082	0867	1
WRIGHT JR GABRIEL N	LTC	0-1101296	1066	3
WRIGHT JR HARLAN P	LTC	C-0216348	C760	3
WRIGHT JR JCSEPH H	LTC	0-0450132	0357	1
WRIGHT JR MEREDITH S	CW3	W-2149496	0664	1
WRIGHT JR RCBERT A	COL	0-C295059	1057	1
WRIGHT JR ROBERT F	CPT	C-1826038	0567	1
WRIGHT JR ROBERT R	LTC	0-0397060	0862	1
WRIGHT JR WILLIAM E	LTC	C-1290171	1066	1
WRIGHT KATHLEEN O	CPT	N-0722885	C348	1
WRIGHT KENNETH A	MAJ	C-1594575	0357	1
WRIGHT KENNETH A	MAJ	0-1890595	0667	2
WRIGHT LAWRENCE H	LTC	0-0430370	1262	1
WRIGHT LEE W	LTC	0-1549186	0262	1
WRIGHT LEIGH O	LTC	0-0274816	0354	3
WRIGHT LENN	LTC	C-1588387	0167	1
WRIGHT MARTHA G	MAJ	N-0770124	1065	2
WRIGHT MAURICE K	COL	0-0273897	0860	1
WRIGHT MORGAN J	MAJ	0-0451576	0163	1
WRIGHT OLIVER A	MAJ	C-1540297	1162	1
WRIGHT OWEN O	MAJ	C-1032130	0562	1
WRIGHT PAUL	LTC	0-0922516	1163	3
WRIGHT PAUL G	COL	0-0275419	0146	2
WRIGHT QUENTIN E	CPT	0-1017993	0746	2
WRIGHT RAPHAEL G	MAJ	0-0292823	1162	3
WRIGHT RAYMONO H	MAJ	C-0122005	1055	3
WRIGHT RAYMOND L	MAJ	C-1876433	0367	2
WRIGHT RICHARC A	MAJ	0-1886372	C465	1
WRIGHT RICHARO H	CW3	W-2205187	1164	1
WRIGHT RICHARO P	LTC	0-1176859	1163	1
WRIGHT ROBERT A	LTC	0-0903811	0762	1
WRIGHT ROBERT C	LTC	0-1579324	0946	2
WRIGHT ROBERT H	MAJ	0-1639835	0757	1
WRIGHT ROBERT J	MAJ	C-1639836	C460	1
WRIGHT ROBERT J	MAJ	0-1686627	0162	1
WRIGHT ROGER E	LTC	0-0365314	C263	1
WRIGHT ROSE B	2LT	N-0725469	C944	1
WRIGHT RUSSEL A	1LT	0-1545252	0346	2
WRIGHT SAMUEL P	LTC	C-0510276	C657	1
WRIGHT THERESA A	1LT	N-0774033	0449	1
WRIGHT THOMAS E	MAJ	C-1549190	0461	1
WRIGHT THOMAS H	LTC	0-0339060	0463	1
WRIGHT THOMAS H	LTC	0-0921557	C263	3
WRIGHT THOMAS H	2LT	0-1258329	1043	2
WRIGHT TIOY F	WO1	W-2105906	0146	2
WRIGHT VERL A	CW2	W-0219149	0445	2
WRIGHT WALLACE O	LTC	0-0250022	C367	3
WRIGHT WALTER B	CPT	0-0447724	1145	2
WRIGHT WALTER W	CW2	W-2146139	0658	1
WRIGHT WARREN K	2LT	0-1003078	0844	2
WRIGHT WAYNE W	CPT	0-1012954	1047	2
WRIGHT WILBUR T	MAJ	C-0101331	0555	3
WRIGHT WILBUR W	LTC	0-1635495	C961	1
WRIGHT WILLIAM A	CW2	W-2152693	0659	1
WRIGHT WILLIAM B	1LT	0-0325753	0345	2
WRIGHT WILLIAM C	COL	C-0106356	0956	3
WRIGHT WILLIAM E	CPT	0-1703006	0246	2
WRIGHT WILLIAM F	MAJ	0-0272177	0157	3
WRIGHT WILLIAM G	LTC	C-0902127	C347	2
WRIGHT WILLIAM H	CW2	W-2206974	1262	1
WRIGHT WILLIAM P	CW3	W-2145880	0167	1
WRIGHT WILMER R	LTC	0-0249389	0865	3
WRIGHTMAN ERNEST R	MAJ	C-2041220	0765	1
WRIGLEY HAROLO J	CPT	0-0241005	1060	3
WRIGLEY SR EOMUNO J	LTC	0-0904334	0954	3
WRIGLEY WILLIAM S	1LT	0-1314218	0747	1
WROBEL THEOCORE	CW3	W-2141501	0656	1
WROBLESKI ALBERT L	MAJ	0-1043541	0462	1
WROBLEWSKI FREO J	2LT	0-1639837	0844	1
WROBLEWSKI RAYMONO J	CW3	W-2152729	1165	1
WROE DUGGINS M	MAJ	C-1540885	C766	1
WRONA THEOOORE W	2LT	0-1305515	C545	2
WRONKOSKI JCHN F	2LT	0-1299972	0445	2
WROTEN CECIL H	MAJ	C-0417215	1066	3
WROTEN CHARLES W	1LT	0-1796398	0356	1
WROTEN JENNINGS W	LTC	0-0278619	0957	3
WROTNOWSKI WANDA B	MAJ	N-0900417	0962	2
WUBKER ROBERT F	MAJ	0-0285581	0467	3
WUCHER JR ROBERT	COL	C-0336351	0861	1
WUCHTER OONALC H	LTC	0-1597971	0463	1
WUDARSKI EOWARO	LTC	0-1290006	0163	1
WUEPPER ROBERT C	LTC	0-1183003	1162	1
WUERMLI JOSEPH C	LTC	0-1316117	0967	1
WUETHRICH EMMETT H	CW2	W-2147256	0560	1
WULF HCRACE F	COL	0-0234413	0156	3
WULF WILLIAM F	COL	C-0245000	0863	3
WULFF EOWIN T	MAJ	0-0447377	0845	2
WULFF MARCUS W	1LT	0-0389011	0444	2
WULFTANGE JOHN A.	1LT	0-1014150	0546	2
WULK WALTER H	LTC	0-0169527	0948	1
WULSIN LUCIEN	1LT	0-1113531	1045	2
WUNDER BERNARC J	CPT	0-1303636	0366	2
WUNOERLICH ALBERT M	LTC	0-0256296	0260	1
WUNDERLICH EDWARO H	CPT	0-0529318	0745	2
WUNOERLICH ERNEST G	MAJ	0-0137222	0453	3
WUNDERLICH FREO J	MAJ	0-1534194	0346	2
WUNOERLICH JR EOWARO	1LT	0-1324450	1045	2
WUNSCH CHARLES L	COL	0-0345088	0166	3
WUNSCH VALENTINE	WO1	W-2118541	0146	2
WUROEMAN RCBERT M	MAJ	0-1293345	0361	1
WURDEMANN WILLIAM	LTC	0-0425930	0359	1
WURM JAMES F	2LT	0-0513846	0145	1
WURMSTICH ARTHUR P J	1LT	0-1287805	0546	2
WURTH CHARLES	LTC	C-0402971	0760	1
WURTZ JR JOHN G	CPT	0-0352702	0844	2
WURTZ RCBERT H	LTC	0-1311078	0363	1
WURZBACH FREDERICK	CPT	0-0502711	1057	1
WURZBACH WILLIAM A	LTC	0-0216792	0464	3
WUSTERBAPTH JR H J	1LT	0-1327915	0347	2
WUTZKE ALVIN C	MAJ	C-1646722	1060	1
WYANDT LOREN H	LTC	0-0274115	0355	3
WYANT PEARL F	CPT	0-0973207	C758	2
WYANT VICTCR R	MAJ	0-1821677	0161	1
WYANT WALTER M	1LT	0-1582286	0346	2
WYATT ANNIE L	1LT	N-0727093	0446	1
WYATT CARL F	LTC	C-0346527	1067	3
WYATT CECILLE B	1LT	N-0734913	0646	2
WYATT CHARLES N	COL	C-0249117	0264	3
WYATT CLIFFCRD C	CW2	W-2143276	1155	1
WYATT CCROTHY M	MAJ	N-0733894	0747	1
WYATT FINIS C	CPT	0-0490068	0343	2
WYATT CLENN E	MAJ	C-1821800	C557	1
WYATT JOSEPH A	LTC	0-0492357	0764	3
WYATT JOSEPH R	1LT	C-0543427	1145	1
WYATT JR LEONARO N	CW2	W-2208884	0264	1
WYATT JR MCRTCN G	MAJ	0-0413538	0546	2
WYATT LEONARC C	CPT	0-0274844	1047	1
WYATT MASON L	CW2	W-2141875	0556	1
WYATT RCBERT T	CW3	W-2142505	0959	1
WYATT RCBERT W	MAJ	0-0974514	0764	1
WYATT WILLIAM J	CW3	W-2144765	0960	1
WYBENGA SIMCN H	LTC	0-1058156	1063	1
WYBORSKI ALOYSIUS S	1LT	0-1292974	0445	2
WYCHE ALBERTA M	2LT	N-0797416	0246	1
WYCHE MURRAY F	LTC	0-0227573	0664	3
WYCKOFF CEORCE C	CPT	C-0491411	0745	2
WYCKOFF GEORCE F	LTC	0-1641084	0662	1
WYCKOFF JOHN H	LTC	0-1109127	0364	1
WYCKOFF JOHN W	LTC	0-0265127	0957	3
WYCKOFF LOWELL A	CPT	0-1291207	0361	1
WYCOFF SAMUEL N	CPT	0-0282922	1059	2
WYERS RALPH L	CW2	W-2152489	1059	1
WYGAL WILLIAM T	MAJ	C-1684971	0964	1
WYGLE JACK M	LTC	0-1169802	1057	1
WYKERT CEORGE C	CW4	W-2122282	0456	1
WYKES THOMAS V	1LT	0-1322611	0346	2
WYKOFF NCRMAN F	LTC	0-0212180	0648	3
WYLIE PALDWIN	LTC	0-0249204	0548	2
WYLIE OCNALO P	COL	0-0243898	0766	3
WYLIE JEROME T	1LT	0-4023943	0656	2

NAME	GRADE	SVC NO	DATE RET MO YR	RET CODE
WYLIE JOHN P	LTC	0-1179259	C462	1
WYLIE JR FRANK B	MAJ	0-0357323	C547	1
WYLIE ROSS	LTC	0-0906607	C566	3
WYLIE WILLIAM A	2LT	0-1057943	1044	2
WYLIE WILLIAM B	1LT	0-1043543	1045	2
WYLIE WILLIAM J	2LT	0-1110355	0644	2
WYLLIE JAMES J	CPT	0-046142C	0348	2
WYLLIE JOHN S	MAJ	0-0946715	C166	1
WYLLIE ROBERT	LTC	0-1062105	C962	1
WYMAN JEAN M	1LT	N-0757498	1045	1
WYMAN JOHN F	CPT	0-0275225	0661	3
WYMAN JOHN H	LTC	0-0179495	0848	3
WYMAN MARION H	COL	0-0211631	0648	3
WYMAN OLIVER C	COL	C-0113100	0648	3
WYMAN RALPH J	LTC	0-0335971	0556	2
WYMAN VAUGHN L	MAJ	C-1047001	0863	1
WYMAN WILLARD F	CW4	W-2115876	0660	1
WYMER OTTO U	CPT	0-0105714	1043	2
WYMER ROBERT W	CW3	W-2147051	1163	2
WYMORE DONALD H	1LT	C-0355805	C840	2
WYMORE PERDUE A	CPT	0-0482476	0653	1
WYNALDA MARTIN	CPT	0-1309644	0646	2
WYNANT RALPH E	MAJ	0-0518327	1048	2
WYNDHAM JOHN H	CW2	W-2151676	0659	1
WYNER ALEXANDER	1LT	C-0218795	1161	3
WYNN ELLISON C	MAJ	0-1303423	1163	1
WYNN KAY W	LTC	0-1825458	0962	1
WYNN NORMAN	CPT	0-0277898	1044	1
WYNN VERNON	CW2	W-2102583	0250	1
WYNN WILLIAM R	MAJ	0-1112537	1062	1
WYNNE HAHN	LTC	0-1048259	0562	1
WYNNE JAMES F	MAJ	C-1185564	1266	1
WYNNE JOHN T	COL	0-04145C6	0865	1
WYNNE MICHAEL A	LTC	0-0205967	0961	3
WYNNE THOMAS E	LTC	0-0483425	1265	3
WYON REGINALD F	LTC	0-0915369	0967	3
WYRE HARRY W	LTC	C-1114337	C561	1
WYRICK GEORGE P	CPT	0-C103095	0452	1
WYRUCHOWSKI EDWARD P	LTC	C-0202691	0648	2
WYSE RALPH M	LTC	0-0451866	0657	1
WYSOCKI BARBARA K	2LT	N-0720961	1144	1
WYSOCKI JOSEPH J	1LT	0-0508520	0260	1
WYSOCKI JR LOUIS C	CW3	W-2205453	0265	1
WYSOCKI PETER W	MAJ	0-1012904	C847	2
WYSOCKY LAWRENCE C	MAJ	C-1010607	C348	2
WYSONG KENNETH W	LTC	0-0265141	0565	3
WYSZYNSKI JOHN	CPT	0-1923568	1262	1
WYSZYNSKI WALTER P	1LT	0-0482848	0744	2
WYTON ROBERT O	1LT	0-1303245	0146	2
WYTTENBACH JOHN E	COL	C-027833C	0561	3
WYVELL HARVEY R	1LT	0-0301867	C744	2
WYZGA MICHAEL A	LTC	C-0451428	1046	2
WZIONTKA STANLEY	CPT	0-0960916	1060	1
XANTHOPOULOS JOHN S	1LT	0-1183004	1046	1
YABE DONALD T	CPT	0-1899436	0865	1
YABLON ABRAHAM	1LT	0-1688073	1044	2
YACHELSON SAMUEL	LTC	C-1894941	0665	3
YACHNIN SAMUEL C	COL	0-0337002	1264	3
YADEN LYNN B	LTC	0-0297729	0448	2
YADRICH JOHN B	1LT	0-1310957	0546	2
YAEGER PHILIP E	MAJ	0-1549187	0661	1
YAFFE SOL	CPT	0-1590278	0346	2
YAGER GEORGE E	MAJ	0-1319810	0461	1
YAGER IRVIN I	CPT	0-0352727	C246	2
YAGER JESSE A	1LT	0-1299165	1145	2
YAGER JR LESLIE	MAJ	C-0207431	0452	3
YAGGI HARRY G	LTC	0-0516237	0864	3
YAISLE KARL B	2LT	C-0233738	1158	3
YAKELY HAROLD E	LTC	0-0167419	0258	3
YAKERSON ROBERT	MAJ	C-0411056	106C	1
YALOVITZ MARVIN S	CPT	0-1735222	1045	2
YAMADA SUSUMU	MAJ	C-1998659	0261	1
YAMAKI BILL S	LTC	0-2037914	0965	1
YAMAMOTO STEVE S	LTC	0-0888916	C861	1
YAMAT FEDERICO N	2LT	C-1896876	0957	2
YAMAUCHI JOHN K	MAJ	0-1899404	0364	1
YAMAZAKI ALFRED A	LTC	0-1339499	0267	1
YAMBAO FORTUNATO	1LT	0-1896718	0952	1
YAMBAO FRANCISCO	1LT	0-1896675	0349	1
YAMBOR STEVE P	CPT	0-2055843	0461	1
YANAUSCH ALBERT J	CPT	0-0241261	0662	3
YANCEY ERNEST V	1LT	0-401019C	0358	2
YANCEY JR DANIEL L	COL	0-0268567	0863	3
YANCEY ROBERT C	LTC	0-1588385	0363	2
YANCEY ROBERT C	WO1	W-2113187	0244	2
YANCEY STEPHEN	CPT	0-0492954	0353	1
YANCEY THEODORE F	LTC	0-0233502	0865	3
YANCEY WILLIAM H	CPT	0-0259082	1066	3
YANCOFSKI LEONARD	CW3	W-2143090	1160	1
YANCY EARL B	CW4	W-2119895	0251	1
YANG SUNG CHAI	CW3	W-2149465	0865	1
YANKOFF BORIS F	CPT	0-0934445	0554	1
YANKOSKY JAMES G	MAJ	0-1179691	0363	1
YANKOVICH MATTHEW J	MAJ	C-0454441	0358	1
YANT JOHN F	MAJ	0-1318242	0565	1
YANT JOHN T	MAJ	C-2289697	1165	1
YANTZ THOMAS J	MAJ	C-1317261	0263	1
YANZ HERMAN H	MAJ	0-0502098	0247	2
YAPIT FELIX	1LT	0-1896868	0653	1
YAPP JAMES R	CW2	W-2113722	0948	1
YARBER JR CHARLES H	MAJ	0-2055948	0457	1
YARBER RUTH M	2LT	N-0767165	1044	1
YARBOROUGH ARTHUR P	MAJ	C-1924653	0864	1
YARBOROUGH JOHN M	CPT	0-0264518	0444	2
YARBOROUGH MARVIN D	LTC	0-1041268	0962	2
YARBOROUGH NEILL A	COL	0-0410004	0863	1
YARBOROUGH OWEN H	1LT	0-1300112	0347	2
YARBOROUGH RICHARD L	MAJ	0-2016990	0263	1
YARBROUGH CHARLES L	MAJ	C-1312616	1060	1
YARBROUGH CHARLIE F	CPT	0-0451646	0745	2
YARBROUGH DONALD R	MAJ	0-0972251	0667	1
YARBROUCH HERMAN E	1LT	0-1556828	1045	2
YARBROUGH JACK B	CW4	W-214669C	0666	1
YARBROUGH JAMES A	MAJ	0-1918956	1166	1
YARBROUGH JOHN M	LTC	0-2007907	0565	1
YARBROUGH LUCIEN B	LTC	0-0269535	0964	3
YARBROUGH RICHARD T	MAJ	0-0974500	0163	1
YARBROUGH RUPERT H	LTC	0-0371450	0760	1
YARD ARTHUR J	MAJ	0-0928224	0767	1
YARDLEY FRANK	LTC	0-0509662	1051	1
YARDLEY RALPH B	CPT	0-038F045	1045	1
YARFITZ LEO J	CPT	0-1636853	0845	2
YARIAN LESTER O	MAJ	0-0118995	0757	3
YARMAN CLIFFORD L	MAJ	0-2C50706	1059	1
YARNALL DANIEL E	WO1	W-2125219	0450	1
YARNELL RAY A	MAJ	0-0327775	0347	2
YAROSH WASEL	LTC	0-1580533	1061	1
YARTER MAURICE A	CPT	0-1824218	1047	2
YASINOW AARON R	CPT	0-0147043	1145	2
YASKONISH JACOB	CW3	W-2129927	0361	2
YASVIN RUTH L	MAJ	N-0799489	0765	1
YATES ANDY O	COL	0-0190310	0855	3
YATES ARTHUR T	CPT	0-0450134	0457	1
YATES CLAUD F	CPT	C-0482910	1147	2
YATES EARL J	COL	C-0110662	0955	1
YATES EDWARD W	1LT	0-1015086	0945	2
YATES FRANK I	CW2	W-2102585	0953	1
YATES FRANKLIN W	CW2	W-2110000	0245	2
YATES HARRY	CPT	0-0172515	1156	3
YATES HIAWATHA	CPT	C-0502918	1047	1
YATES HUISH F	LTC	0-0373748	0963	1
YATES JOHN A	LTC	0-0885894	0155	1
YATES JR CORNELIUS	MAJ	0-0252698	1162	3
YATES JUSTIN J	LTC	0-0298488	0566	3
YATES KENNETH	CPT	0-1081115	1147	2
YATES ONA P	LTC	N-0757609	0367	3
YATES RALPH J	MAJ	C-1300431	1146	1
YATES ROBERT B	LTC	0-0285173	0746	2
YATES VINCENT A	COL	0-0265680	0163	3
YATES WILLIAM E	LTC	0-0352560	0358	1
YATES WILLIAM H	LTC	0-1102559	1067	1
YAUGER AARON J	MAJ	0-0177735	C361	3
YAUKEY JAMES V	CPT	0-0212610	0546	2
YAVELAK WILLIAM	LTC	0-1291557	C657	1
YAVELOW ISSACHER	MAJ	C-0519131	1046	2
YAVNER MAX	MAJ	0-0127266	1052	3
YAWORSKY JOHN	MAJ	C-1824181	C157	1
YDEEN BROOKS C	LTC	0-1640146	0863	1
YEAGER ABE H	CPT	0-0156230	0648	3
YEAGER CHARLES	CW3	W-2142291	0261	1
YEAGER CHARLES C	MAJ	C-1549419	0765	1
YEAGER GEORGE F	CW2	W-342002C	0467	1
YEAGER KENNETH G	LTC	0-1575646	1061	1
YEAGER LAWRY H	MAJ	C-0969276	0263	2
YEAGER MARY R	MAJ	N-0755864	0667	1
YEAGER ULYSSES B	LTC	0-0229965	0762	3
YEAGLE LAWRENCE C	MAJ	C-0450526	1058	1
YEAKEL HAROLD J	CW2	W-2211656	1265	1
YEAKEY LEON L	LTC	0-0192365	C453	3
YEAKLEY HARRY C	CPT	0-2035998	0646	2
YEAROUS GLENN	LTC	0-0182566	1045	2
YEARWOOD IRVING D	LTC	0-1591548	1163	1
YEARY MICHAEL	1LT	0-1053444	0147	1
YEASLEY ROBERT J	LTC	0-0520171	1166	2
YEATES HARRIS S	CW2	W-2104618	C361	1
YEATS ROBERT R	MAJ	0-0542501	1163	1
YEISER WILLIAM C	LTC	0-0338025	0258	1
YELDELL THOMAS J	LTC	0-1045985	0767	1
YELDERMAN ROBERT L	1LT	0-0441435	C844	1
YELLEN HIRAM S	COL	C-0137335	C146	2
YELLEN MILTON	CPT	C-0482612	1044	2
YELVERTON IRA A	CPT	0-1295973	C746	2
YELVERTON JOHN A	2LT	0-1298477	0444	2
YELVERTON JOHN V	MAJ	0-1995025	0662	1
YENCHAR JOHN G	LTC	0-0135639	0155	3
YENCHO JOHN K	MAJ	C-1081045	0658	1
YENNE WALTER D	MAJ	0-2080592	0666	1
YENS OTTO C	COL	0-0194582	0661	2
YENSAN ALBERT F	CPT	0-1313151	0158	1
YENSUS VINCENT T	MAJ	0-1295313	1055	1
YENTER RAYMOND A	B G	0-0120313	C648	3
YEO CHARLES R	COL	0-1180389	1166	1
YEOKUM GEORGE H	1LT	0-0160264	C953	3
YEOMAN DALE A	MAJ	0-0318775	C446	2
YERBY MARION L	MAJ	0-1643474	0159	1
YEREANCE ALEXANDER	MAJ	0-0189608	0250	3
YEREGA WILLIAM	1LT	0-1184340	1145	1
YERKA JAY H	CPT	0-1304477	0661	1
YERKES PAUL E	LTC	0-0395896	0157	2
YERKS RAYMOND A	LTC	0-1894881	1067	3
YERMAN JESSE	CW4	W-2142785	0563	1
YESKAWICH MICHAEL J	CW2	W-2211922	0967	1
YETSCHKE CLARENCE	MAJ	C-0237415	0956	3
YETTER JR CHARLES W	CW2	W-2152783	0357	2
YETTER JR JOSEPH F	LTC	C-1549743	0162	1
YETTER RUSSELL J	LTC	0-0218585	0254	2
YINGST PARKE O	MAJ	C-0270553	0146	2
YLINEN JOHN S	LTC	0-1051846	0662	1
YOAST JR SAMUEL H	MAJ	0-1114338	0761	1
YOCIS JEROME C	CPT	0-1101725	0646	2
YOCKEY CONWAY E	LTC	0-0172882	0159	3
YOCOM GEORGE F	MAJ	C-0504061	C447	2
YOCUM ALVIN L	MAJ	0-2262887	1163	1
YOCUM DOROTHY E	MAJ	N-0769762	0765	1
YOCUM HORACE C	LTC	0-0135570	1054	3
YOCUM HOWARD R	COL	0-0287082	0265	3
YOCUM MAUDE M	2LT	N-0731030	1044	1
YODER ALVIN B	LTC	0-0296369	1047	2
YODER RUSSELL E	LTC	0-0924901	0667	3
YODER THOMAS W	MAJ	0-1701656	0564	1
YOE WILLIAM S	LTC	0-1324601	0263	1
YOES RALPH	1LT	0-1288665	0345	2
YOFFA ALLAN M	1LT	0-0384261	0745	2
YOHALEM MORTON	CPT	0-1689231	0843	2
YOHANNAN JOHN D	CPT	0-0475856	0451	1
YOHE CLAIR F	LTC	0-0478282	0464	3
YOHE JR CARL J	LTC	0-0316150	0759	2
YOHE PERCE P	COL	0-0104439	0153	3
YOHMAN JOSEPH A	1LT	0-0529540	0945	2
YOHN ROBERT A	CW4	W-2108359	0957	1
YOHO ARNOLD J	LTC	0-1012157	0764	1
YOKE NORRIS H	WO1	W-2184564	0155	1
YOKELEY GILBERT W	LTC	0-0461744	0265	3
YOKLEY WILLIAM R	MAJ	0-0137461	0648	3
YOKSAS ALBERT C	LTC	0-1573696	0461	1
YONAN NORMAN J	1LT	0-1321079	0646	2
YONKER JR GEORGE H	1LT	0-1318504	0557	2
YONKERS ARTHUR J E	CPT	0-1172349	1164	2
YONKERS DURWARD W	LTC	0-0291521	0664	3
YONKERS LEO E	CPT	0-1321981	0946	1
YONTS ROBERT W	MAJ	0-0517491	0863	1
YONTZ WELDON J	LTC	0-1012964	0761	1
YOQUELET RAY A	MAJ	0-1323644	1057	1
YORDAN JOAQUIN	MAJ	0-1337258	0863	1
YORDE JOHN J	MAJ	C-2212092	0863	1
YORICHI ALEX N	MAJ	0-2033620	0263	1
YORK BEN H	MAJ	0-2016620	0960	1
YORK BROWER V	LTC	0-0163916	0258	3
YORK CHARLES A	LTC	0-0124075	0551	3
YORK EDWARD	CPT	0-0109453	1137	1
YORK FRANCIS L	CPT	0-1018796	0951	1
YORK FRANK E	MAJ	C-2005305	0961	1
YORK GUSTER R	CPT	0-0491454	0953	1
YORK JAMES	LTC	0-0503626	0457	1
YORK JAMES A	CPT	0-0395894	0246	2
YORK JAMES H	MAJ	0-1108436	0158	1
YORK JAMES H	LTC	0-1306190	0857	1
YORK JAMES L	CW2	W-3200389	1167	1
YORK JAMES O	CW3	W-215226C	0159	1
YORK JOHN S	MAJ	0-2212021	0661	1
YORK NORMAN J	CW4	W-2110388	0659	2
YORK OTIS E	CPT	0-0450502	1044	2
YORK SAMUEL W	CW3	W-2141723	0858	1
YORK THOMAS C	LTC	0-0196416	0459	3
YORK VINCENT H	MAJ	C-2000086	1060	1
YORK WALTER R	COL	0-0901981	0762	3
YORKE ELEANOR E	MAJ	N-0793254	0465	1
YOSHIMURA NOBORU	MAJ	0-2030581	0562	1
YOSKIT HARRY	MAJ	0-0162061	0152	3
YOST CHARLES L	LTC	C-0145638	1055	3
YOST CLIFFORD W	MAJ	0-0498456	0856	1
YOST DENZEL M	WO1	W-2116785	0644	2
YOST JAMES F	LTC	0-1688339	0966	1
YOST JORIER H	CPT	0-1284445	0448	2
YOST LELAND J	1LT	0-0113806	0258	3
YOST LIGHT B	COL	0-0288323	0867	3
YOST RICHARD W	CPT	0-0921284	1044	2
YOSTE FLORIAN H	CPT	0-1290699	1045	2
YOTIVE SIMON R	CPT	0-1794860	0346	2
YOTT GEORGE F	MAJ	0-0217095	0461	3
YOUMAN GEORGE L	LTC	0-0429548	C562	1
YOUMANS CORREN P	COL	C-0234659	1052	3
YOUMANS ROSS C	MAJ	C-0289687	0558	3
YOUNOT ALBERT J	COL	0-0287672	0160	1
YOUNG ALBERT	CPT	0-1297466	0251	2
YOUNG ALEXANDER	COL	0-0212480	0663	3
YOUNG ALFRED A	2LT	0-1081499	1144	2
YOUNG ALFRED G	CW3	W-2146925	0160	1
YOUNG ALFRED H	LTC	0-0193997	0860	3
YOUNG ALGERNON G	1LT	0-0398273	0146	2
YOUNG ALPHE B	LTC	0-0181100	1156	3
YOUNG ARNOLD R	LTC	0-1295814	1167	1
YOUNG ARTHUR F	COL	0-0335928	0658	3
YOUNG BENJAMIN W	CW2	W-2104853	0664	1
YOUNG BLAINE E	MAJ	C-1080981	0258	1
YOUNG C K BOB	CPT	0-0583017	0450	1
YOUNG CALVIN	CW3	W-2145031	0758	1
YOUNG CAREY M	LTC	0-0528163	1156	2
YOUNG CARLETON S	LTC	0-0570890	1165	3
YOUNG CECIL L	CW3	W-2144757	0960	1

NAME	GRADE	SVC NO	DATE RET MO YR	RET CODE
YOUNG CHARLES A	COL	0-0183595	C862	3
YOUNG CHARLES C	MAJ	0-0110878	0648	3
YOUNG CHARLES E	LTC	0-0166206	0361	3
YOUNG CHARLES L	MAJ	0-0189140	1055	1
YOUNG CHARLES M	MAJ	C-1103021	1060	1
YOUNG CHARLES R	CW2	W-2150182	1158	2
YOUNG CHESTER R	LTC	0-1289184	0767	1
YOUNG CLAIR F	2LT	0-1320495	0145	2
YOUNG CLARK	COL	0-0224486	0855	2
YOUNG CLAUDE E	LTC	0-1583871	0467	3
YOUNG CLIFFORD L	MAJ	C-0330099	C567	3
YOUNG CLIFTON H	LTC	0-0339053	C660	1
YOUNG CLYDE B	CPT	0-0462133	C245	2
YOUNG DEEL E	MAJ	0-0491991	0154	1
YOUNG DEWITT C	LTC	0-0118996	0146	2
YOUNG DONALD C	LTC	C-1588391	1162	1
YOUNG EDDIE M	LTC	0-0250992	0164	3
YOUNG EDWARD C	1LT	0-1181516	1145	2
YOUNG EDWARD S	CPT	0-1053025	C166	1
YOUNG EDWIN L	LTC	0-1582288	0762	1
YOUNG EDWIN S	CPT	0-0450321	1063	3
YOUNG EMERSON J	MAJ	C-0503739	0657	1
YOUNG EMITTE E	MAJ	C-1300902	C959	1
YOUNG EVERETT L	LTC	0-0177450	0261	3
YOUNG FLOYD L	1LT	0-1175454	1045	2
YOUNG FOSTER J	LTC	0-0213323	C660	3
YOUNG FRANCIS H	LTC	0-0131223	0653	3
YOUNG FRANCIS J	2LT	0-0888228	0145	2
YOUNG FRANCIS T	LTC	0-1186527	0667	1
YOUNG FRANK G	MAJ	0-0251356	0744	2
YOUNG FRANK H	LTC	0-0888453	0263	1
YOUNG FRANK R	1LT	0-0519986	0945	2
YOUNG FRANKLIN R	MAJ	0-2002382	0355	1
YOUNG FRED I	CPT	0-1914157	0933	1
YOUNG FREDERICK	LTC	0-1284622	0167	1
YOUNG GAIL K H	1LT	N-0789694	1045	1
YOUNG GUILFORD E	CPT	0-0258615	C945	2
YOUNG HAROLD E	CPT	0-1103484	0146	2
YOUNG HAROLD E	LTC	0-1167704	0263	1
YOUNG HAROLD L	2LT	0-1062554	0544	2
YOUNG HARRISON E	CPT	C-1702513	C945	2
YOUNG HARRY C	LTC	0-1010306	1060	1
YOUNG HENRY E	MAJ	C-1646725	0655	1
YOUNG HERBERT	CPT	0-0501624	0747	1
YOUNG HIRAM O	MAJ	0-0319334	1153	1
YOUNG HOMER O	CW4	W-2111120	0454	1
YOUNG HORACE A	WO1	W-2135685	0659	1
YOUNG IVA C	MAJ	L-0900064	0862	1
YOUNG JACK	1LT	0-1301744	0745	2
YOUNG JACK G	1LT	0-2096994	0259	2
YOUNG JAKE K	1LT	0-2055192	0246	1
YOUNG JAMES C	MAJ	0-1315655	0263	1
YOUNG JAMES D	MAJ	C-0263353	0665	3
YOUNG JAMES O	1LT	0-1296310	C544	2
YOUNG JAMES E	LTC	0-0164200	1136	1
YOUNG JAMES F	LTC	0-0282902	0959	1
YOUNG JAMES J	2LT	0-1306352	0145	2
YOUNG JAMES K	1LT	0-1322500	0746	2
YOUNG JAMES L	MAJ	0-0450955	0356	1
YOUNG JAMES V	LTC	0-2206414	1067	1
YOUNG JAN B	1LT	0-1053445	C744	2
YOUNG JOHN L	CW2	W-2206302	C862	1
YOUNG JOHN L H	COL	0-0239396	0965	3
YOUNG JOHN R	CW2	W-2152172	0761	1
YOUNG JOHN T	MAJ	0-1533714	0657	1
YOUNG JOHN T	2LT	C-2025614	1045	2
YOUNG JOHN W	LTC	0-0214134	1060	3
YOUNG JOHN W	1LT	0-1294059	0646	1
YOUNG JOSEPH E	MAJ	C-0183071	1044	2
YOUNG JOSEPH E	CW2	W-2142621	1159	1
YOUNG JOSEPH L	LTC	0-0228783	0565	3
YOUNG JR ALLEN B	2LT	0-1647345	0645	2
YOUNG JR CHAPMAN	CPT	0-1296961	0146	2
YOUNG JR EDWARD M	1LT	0-1578073	0453	1
YOUNG JR FRANCIS A	CW3	W-2147993	1062	1
YOUNG JR FRANK E	COL	0-0271577	0567	3
YOUNG JR FREDERICK	MAJ	0-1926004	0666	1
YOUNG JR LOUIS D	MAJ	0-1919072	1063	1
YOUNG JR RAYMOND B	2LT	0-1648568	0146	2
YOUNG JR ROBERT S	CW2	W-2211917	0367	1
YOUNG JR WILLIAM A	CW3	W-2204999	0266	1
YOUNG JR WILLIAM T	CW3	W-2141705	0159	2
YOUNG JULIUS D	MAJ	0-0386489	0562	1
YOUNG KATHERINE	2LT	N-0702799	1041	1
YOUNG KENNETH E	COL	0-023640C	0159	1
YOUNG KENNETH E	MAJ	0-1695639	1061	1
YOUNG LENWOOD W	MAJ	C-0537671	0758	1
YOUNG LEO A	MAJ	C-0286772	0458	3
YOUNG LEROY J	LTC	0-0243363	0666	3
YOUNG LEWIS A	WO1	W-2128045	0563	1
YOUNG LUCIUS E	LTC	0-0303909	0261	1
YOUNG MALCOLM E	1LT	0-1180783	0952	1
YOUNG MARVIN	COL	0-0178541	0661	3
YOUNG MAURICE	CPT	0-1585113	0844	2
YOUNG MAX E	1LT	0-0532758	0546	2
YOUNG MAX F	LTC	0-0887816	0466	1
YOUNG MAX P	LTC	0-0416047	1061	2
YOUNG MILDRED J	2LT	N-0727586	1044	1
YOUNG NATHANIEL	LTC	0-0393611	0646	2
YOUNG OLIVER F	CPT	0-2013942	0754	2
YOUNG RALPH A	LTC	0-1011572	0557	1
YOUNG RALPH M	MAJ	0-0291063	0346	2
YOUNG RALPH W	1LT	0-2000081	0547	2
YOUNG RANDOLPH M	CW2	W-2209093	0964	1
YOUNG RAY C	MAJ	0-0143775	0455	3
YOUNG RICHARD A	LTC	0-0178734	0534	1
YOUNG RICHARD D	LTC	0-0918723	0467	3
YOUNG RICHARD E	LTC	0-1557401	1163	1
YOUNG ROBERT A	1LT	0-1549420	1144	2
YOUNG ROBERT A	CW3	W-2111642	1263	2
YOUNG ROBERT C	CPT	0-0693540	1051	1
YOUNG ROBERT E	LTC	0-0422516	0462	1
YOUNG ROBERT G	MAJ	C-1100845	1046	1
YOUNG ROBERT H	CPT	0-0885770	0946	1
YOUNG ROBERT L	CW3	W-2149155	0662	1
YOUNG ROBERT N	1LT	0-1315750	0846	2
YOUNG ROBERT S	2LT	0-1031043	0445	2
YOUNG ROGER L	COL	0-0344975	0265	1
YOUNG RONALD L	LTC	0-0397854	C261	1
YOUNG RUBYE P	MAJ	N-0764460	0764	1
YOUNG RUTH A	1LT	N-0720990	1050	2
YOUNG RUTH V	1LT	N-0752064	1145	1
YOUNG SAMUEL G	LTC	0-0165444	1149	3
YOUNG STEWART	1LT	0-1914025	0527	1
YOUNG THOMAS E	LTC	0-1169409	0561	1
YOUNG THOMAS H	WO1	W-2125093	0356	2
YOUNG VERNON C	1LT	0-1102140	1045	2
YOUNG VIRGIL A D	CW4	W-2127968	1155	1
YOUNG VIRGIL J	MAJ	0-1582828	1062	1
YOUNG WARREN H	MAJ	0-1545991	0960	1
YOUNG WARREN J	2LT	0-1112000	0444	2
YOUNG WAYNE B	COL	0-0345021	0561	1
YOUNG WHITNEY L	CPT	0-0248482	0662	1
YOUNG WILBUR P	LTC	0-0292069	0761	1
YOUNG WILEY R	1LT	0-0452120	0346	2
YOUNG WILL	CW3	W-2141502	1058	1
YOUNG WILLIAM A	CPT	0-1166655	0767	1
YOUNG WILLIAM A	CW3	W-2148150	0762	1
YOUNG WILLIAM E	LTC	0-1542443	0865	1
YOUNG WILLIAM F	MAJ	0-201637C	0363	1
YOUNG WILLIAM M	COL	0-0201144	0858	3
YOUNG WILLIAM M	CPT	0-0319839	0549	1
YOUNG WILLIAM N	LTC	0-0308657	0660	3
YOUNG WILLIAM P	LTC	0-1167252	1066	1
YOUNG WILLIAM W	COL	0-0258557	0860	1
YOUNGBLOOD CLOVIS H	1LT	0-1323642	0146	2
YOUNGBLOOD JACK A	LTC	0-0934750	1166	1
YOUNGBLOOD JAMES C	2LT	0-1597335	1045	2
YOUNGDAHL ELLIS U	LTC	0-0275217	1046	2
YOUNGDAHL HERBERT M	CPT	0-0978108	1061	1
YOUNGER EVERETT W	CPT	0-1107249	C647	1
YOUNGER JAMES L	CPT	C-1298798	0147	2
YOUNGER JR GEORGE A	CW3	W-215249C	C264	1
YOUNGER WILLIAM C	2LT	0-0985435	C451	1
YOUNGFLESH STANLEY F	LTC	C-0204505	C963	3
YOUNGKAMP JOSEPH G	COL	0-0358557	1264	3
YOUNGQUIST REUBEN C	LTC	0-0251343	0366	3
YOUNGREEN DONALD R	MAJ	0-0273004	0666	3
YOUNGREN HARRISON	LTC	0-0341322	0762	1
YOUNGREN RALPH L	MAJ	0-0179606	C644	2
YOUNGS CALVIN J	LTC	0-1017324	0661	1
YOUNGS JOHN B	LTC	0-0401607	0960	1
YOUNGS JR MARCUS L	1LT	0-0512159	0645	2
YOUNGS JR WALTER C	LTC	0-0246495	C764	3
YOUNGS THURSTON B	CW3	W-2152364	C566	1
YOUNGSON WILLIAM F	MAJ	C-2006127	C165	1
YOUNK WALTER A	MAJ	0-0979913	1062	1
YOUNKMAN ESTHER G	1LT	N-0776267	0645	1
YOUNT BURTON T	CPT	0-2033134	0960	1
YOUNT HAROLD J	CPT	0-0920122	C245	2
YOUNT JOHN B	MAJ	C-1286223	0161	1
YOUNT JR CLARENCE E	LTC	0-0252931	0166	3
YOUNT LEWIS L	2LT	0-1314867	C444	2
YOUNT MARCUS D	LTC	0-0133418	1052	3
YOUNT RICHARD H	MAJ	0-1648875	1162	1
YOUNTS PAUL R	COL	0-0185367	C159	3
YOUTS CLAUDE D	CPT	0-1549192	0945	1
YOVAN JR GEORGE	2LT	0-1309143	C444	2
YOWELL BENJAMIN W	COL	0-0285861	0159	1
YRI KENNETH E	2LT	0-1309470	C644	2
YRI WILLIAM	LTC	0-1032410	0662	1
YSMAEL ARTHUR R	1LT	C-0890322	0754	1
YSMAEL BARTOLOME	2LT	0-2027372	1047	1
YU HICO DELFI	CPT	0-0888175	C648	2
YUCKMAN WILLIAM	COL	0-0324747	C163	3
YUEN ALEXANDER	LTC	0-0365845	C863	3
YUEN DUAN H	MAJ	0-0253189	0746	2
YUHAS JOHN	CPT	0-0361950	0159	1
YUHAS JOHN J	CW4	W-2132981	0361	3
YUHOSS JR JOSEPH	CW3	W-2144685	1263	1
YUILL RALPH W	MAJ	0-0227512	C858	3
YUILLE NINIAN L	B G	0-0270933	0666	3
YUKE BENJAMIN J	MAJ	0-0479832	0746	1
YUKNIS LEONARD B	LTC	0-1698134	0566	1
YUNG GEORGE P	LTC	0-0450322	0657	1
YUNKER LEO D	1LT	0-0463010	0144	2
YUNKER ROBERT J	LTC	0-1946895	C664	1
YUNQUE MARCIAL	MAJ	0-1301745	C560	1
YURASEK CECELIA A	MAJ	N-0755457	0165	1
YURCHEK FRANK S	MAJ	0-1545203	1162	1
YURCHISIN MICHAEL	CPT	0-1283353	0245	2
YURICK EDWARD A	LTC	0-0252778	C265	3
YURICK GEORGE	CPT	0-0509346	0650	1
YUSKANICH ANDREW E	1LT	0-0466776	1143	2
YUSKIS ANTHONY J	MAJ	0-1947280	0457	1
YUTUC RICARDO R	1LT	0-1896716	0166	1
YUTZY SCOTT G	CW2	W-2143990	0464	1
ZABALDANO FRANK C	LTC	0-1171854	C167	1
ZABEL HERMAN J	LTC	0-0235039	C654	3
ZABELLE VICTOR F	MAJ	0-2263628	0966	1
ZABIN ALEXANDER	COL	0-0302467	0567	3
ZABLACKAS KASTON R	MAJ	0-1120641	0364	1
ZABLOCKI STANLEY	LTC	0-1592741	0363	1
ZABOVNIK RICHARD J	MAJ	C-2026543	1161	1
ZABUSKI ZIGMOND A	CPT	0-1306927	0463	1
ZACH JOHN M	MAJ	0-0375380	C161	1
ZACHARIAS WILLMAN O	LTC	0-0184436	0952	3
ZACHARY OTIS O	MAJ	C-1293695	0656	1
ZACHARY ZENO N	1LT	0-1031145	0944	2
ZACHOW LAWRENCE E	LTC	0-0324006	0461	1
ZACHRY ABNER T	2LT	0-2006533	0146	2
ZACK LEO R	LTC	0-0342034	C865	3
ZACKEO NICHOLAS T	MAJ	0-1328866	1161	1
ZACKEY JR SAMUEL A	CW2	W-2208804	0863	1
ZACOUR JAMES N	WO1	W-2005802	0651	2
ZACUR MAURICE M	1LT	0-1302745	0945	2
ZADNIK ANTON F	1LT	0-1285870	1145	2
ZADRA ROBERT E	LTC	0-1110907	0663	1
ZADROZNY ALICE C	MAJ	N-0752243	0659	2
ZADYLAK FRANK V	1LT	0-1316477	0245	2
ZAFFY JOSEPH P	CPT	0-1598735	0647	2
ZAGAMI NATALE R	LTC	0-0349502	0860	1
ZAGATA CHARLES A	MAJ	0-1312370	0760	1
ZAGORSKI WALTER E	CPT	0-0489206	0544	2
ZAGRAPAN CYRIL M	1LT	0-1290868	1056	1
ZAGRODZKY WILLIAM D	MAJ	C-1019600	1061	1
ZAHARA MIKE E	CPT	0-0447238	1048	2
ZAHARKO JOSEPH	MAJ	0-1306928	0358	1
ZAHAROFF STEVEN	CW3	W-2149274	0760	1
ZAHL JOHN A	LTC	0-1045988	1167	1
ZAHLER JAMES W	MAJ	C-1996328	0266	1
ZAHN CARL J	1LT	0-0929539	1147	2
ZAHORIAN ELMER	CW3	W-214878C	0966	1
ZAHRN GILBERT E	CPT	0-1287982	0154	1
ZAINO COSTANTINO	COL	C-0324036	0666	3
ZAIS CARL G	LTC	0-1042468	0357	1
ZAJ EDWARD A	LTC	0-0340500	0858	1
ZAJAC WALTER L	2LT	0-1797408	0144	2
ZAJICEK JAMES C	CW4	W-211436C	0960	1
ZAK FELIX	MAJ	0-1586677	0757	1
ZAK FREDERICK	COL	0-0238463	0765	3
ZAKBY ABDALLAH K	LTC	0-0305513	0959	1
ZAKOTA JR JOHN J	LTC	0-0354649	0163	1
ZAKULA MICHAEL	1LT	0-1766382	0446	2
ZALAZNIK EDWARD G	CW3	W-2141933	0659	1
ZALOD JR WILLIAM T	LTC	0-0290588	0960	1
ZALEGOWSKI FRANK S	MAJ	0-1796835	1057	1
ZALESKI OLEG Z	MAJ	0-0450780	0358	1
ZALESKI THADDEUS J	MAJ	0-1318603	1061	1
ZALESKY LEWIS E	LTC	0-0292088	0462	1
ZALESKY RICHARD C	COL	C-0038682	1060	1
ZALFA NORMAN G	CW2	W-2211916	0766	1
ZALLES REGINALD G	1LT	0-1303988	0746	2
ZALUSKI EDWARD L	1LT	0-1289187	0844	2
ZAMBA PETER	LTC	0-0298383	0761	3
ZAMBRANA EFRAIN	MAJ	0-0972347	0463	2
ZAMECNIK CHARLES	MAJ	C-1308578	0360	1
ZAMMARELLA LOUIS J	MAJ	C-0948932	0765	1
ZAMMNER EARL R	CW3	W-2144236	0863	1
ZAMORA JR UBALDO	CW3	W-2209345	0767	1
ZAMORA LAMBERTINI	MAJ	N-0736C15	1062	1
ZAMORA PEDRO J	CPT	0-0156628	1152	3
ZAMPELLA ALBERT A	LTC	0-0330813	0267	3
ZANDER ALBERT A	CPT	0-1102563	0944	2
ZANECCHIA ARMANDO L	LTC	0-1994872	0361	1
ZANETTE ALFRED A	CPT	0-0502910	0445	2
ZANETTI JOAQUIN E	COL	0-0177195	C648	3
ZANG JOHN L	LTC	0-1011091	0557	1
ZANOLINI ALBERT S	MAJ	C-1112002	0261	1
ZANON LENA M	2LT	N-0743937	0844	1
ZANS JAMES E	CW3	W-2208377	0367	1
ZANT ROYCE D	LTC	0-1556376	0664	1
ZAPALSKI DANIEL J	MAJ	0-1999268	1063	1
ZAPF MICHAEL	MAJ	0-0971958	0364	1
ZAPOTOCKY FRANK E	CPT	0-0503919	0348	1
ZAREMBA EDWARD J	CW3	W-2150230	0765	1
ZAREMSKI ANTHONY J	MAJ	0-2011934	C564	1
ZARIK HARRY	1LT	0-1555498	0846	2
ZARIT JOHN I	MAJ	0-0498354	C745	2
ZARLENGO ERNEST P	CPT	0-0468575	0744	2
ZARLING KENNETH A	MAJ	0-1081838	0955	1
ZARTARIAN SARKIS M	COL	0-0171485	C445	2
ZATKOWSKI STANLEY E	2LT	0-1325144	0345	2
ZAUGG FELIX R	1LT	0-0157099	1153	3
ZAVALICK JOSEPH J	CW4	W-2115922	0659	1
ZAVELOFF ABRAHAM	MAJ	0-0202238	0955	3
ZAVITZ BURDETT N	1LT	0-2040771	0246	2
ZAVOD WILLIAM A	MAJ	0-0501527	0346	2
ZAVOYIANIS SAVAS	MAJ	0-0496150	1046	2
ZAWADSKI ALFONSO S	LTC	0-1012233	0757	1

292-560 O - 68 - 24

NAME	GRADE	SVC NO	DATE RET MO YR	RET CODE
ZAWALSKI VIOLET	1LT	N-0755841	1045	1
ZAWATSON PAUL J	MAJ	0-1823248	0163	1
ZAWDRA EDWARD A	LTC	0-1061914	0466	1
ZAYAS ANGEL R	CW2	W-2141706	1159	1
ZAZZI MELVIN A	COL	0-0289481	0665	3
ZBIKOWSKI EUGENE F	CW2	W-3150186	0666	1
ZBORALSKE FLORIAN F	CPT	0-0553685	0245	2
ZBUDOWSKI ALEXANDE	CPT	0-1687148	0745	2
ZBYLUT ALEXANDER	1LT	0-0885735	1046	2
ZDEB THOMAS J	CW3	W-2151074	1165	2
ZDRAVECKY STEPHEN F	LTC	0-0454198	0757	1
ZDUNCZYK SR HARRY J	CPT	0-1169806	0862	2
ZDUNEK MARCELL J	WO1	W-2141143	1048	1
ZEABLE VICTOR C	LTC	0-0489332	0363	2
ZEBAL FRANCIS T	MAJ	0-1117561	0960	1
ZEBELEAN THEODORE	MAJ	0-2262994	0363	1
ZEBLEY JOSEPH T	LTC	0-1324084	0166	1
ZEBLEY JR JOSEPH W	MAJ	0-1573700	0763	1
ZEBLEY JR ROBERT F	CPT	0-0282655	0258	1
ZEBROSKI CHESTER C	MAJ	0-1593929	0565	1
ZEBROWSKI JULIAN J	MAJ	0-1649993	0657	1
ZEBROWSKI VICTOR J	CPT	0-1045646	1160	1
ZECCHIN MALACHI A	CPT	0-1061596	0750	2
ZEEFF BERT	LTC	0-0274291	1057	1
ZEGOLIS GEORGE M D	COL	0-0287619	1161	1
ZEHALA MICHAEL A	LTC	0-0530314	0761	1
ZEHLER CHARLES R	CW3	W-2203812	0267	1
ZEHNER JOHN M	LTC	0-2048203	0466	1
ZEHNER WILLIAM B	2LT	0-1588979	1043	2
ZEIDMAN SIDNEY E	MAJ	0-0977297	1064	1
ZEIEN HENRY	COL	0-0321828	0457	1
ZEIER FRANCIS G	MAJ	0-0370783	0646	2
ZEIGER ARTHUR	1LT	0-1081730	0646	2
ZEIGER MICHAEL R	MAJ	0-0310386	0945	2
ZEIGLER MARTIN L	1LT	0-0536051	1045	2
ZEIGLER ROLAND L	LTC	0-1175370	0962	1
ZEIS DONALD M	LTC	0-0226914	0863	1
ZEISZLER ERNEST E	LTC	0-0455634	0157	1
ZEITLER EDGAR A	MAJ	0-1014566	1059	1
ZEITLER PHYLLIS S	MAJ	N-0756441	0167	3
ZEITLER WOODROW W	1LT	0-1286410	0750	1
ZEITZ AUGUST B	MAJ	0-1542452	0761	1
ZEITZ SIDNEY J	LTC	0-0274472	0863	3
ZEKAN PAUL R	LTC	0-1340730	0967	1
ZELAZNY JR JOSEPH J	LTC	0-1109774	0263	1
ZELEK STANLEY M	2LT	0-1018656	0645	2
ZELENKA LOUIS G	MAJ	0-0260564	0966	3
ZELENKO TONY	MAJ	0-1052642	1065	1
ZELEPSKY STANLEY D	1LT	0-1294235	0647	2
ZELEZNIK LAWRENCE E	1LT	0-1298157	1045	2
ZELINSKAS HELEN	2LT	N-0728354	0845	1
ZELINSKY ROBERT L	MAJ	0-1080680	0464	1
ZELL NORMAN H	CW2	W-2142994	0358	1
ZELL WILLIAM B	CPT	0-1309144	0246	2
ZELLER DONALD F	MAJ	0-0573865	1156	1
ZELLER GEORGE W	LTC	0-1013428	0364	1
ZELLER STANLEY A	CPT	0-2006837	0255	1
ZELLER WILLIAM B	COL	0-0220215	0162	3
ZELLERMAYER JACOB	MAJ	0-0341345	1046	2
ZELLERS WOODROW W	CW2	W-2208696	0365	1
ZELLNER NORMAN O	1LT	0-0555596	0646	2
ZELNICK BERNARD	1LT	0-0471718	0245	1
ZELNICKER EDWIN A	MAJ	0-0193304	0857	3
ZELTMAN CHARLES F	LTC	0-0910301	0364	1
ZEMAN ALOIS	CW2	W-2142995	0155	1
ZEMBAS PHILIP	CW3	W-2147058	0363	1
ZEMKE ERHART E	CPT	0-0263435	0145	2
ZEMLA STEPHEN G	CPT	0-1894776	0461	1
ZEMO HARRY	CW4	W-2147927	1266	1
ZEMOTEL JOHN	1LT	0-1554672	1046	2
ZEMSKY DAVID H	CPT	0-0524934	0647	2
ZENDT JAMES E	LTC	0-0213935	0564	3
ZENER FRANCIS B	LTC	0-0214878	0346	2
ZENI ANGELO M	MAJ	0-0961920	1067	1
ZENIZO GERALD H	1LT	0-1031286	1045	2

NAME	GRADE	SVC NO	DATE RET MO YR	RET CODE
ZENKER CHARLES W	1LT	0-0129080	0653	3
ZENO TULIO N	LTC	0-0264560	0663	3
ZENSEN GILBERT O	MAJ	0-0508024	0954	1
ZENTNER MILTON C	LTC	0-1934701	0658	2
ZEPER PHILIP	LTC	0-0512039	0765	1
ZERANSKI HENRY E	MAJ	0-1533716	1058	1
ZERBACH EARL F	LTC	0-0487174	0561	1
ZERBI LOUIS	CPT	0-1303246	1047	1
ZERBY RAYMOND D	CW2	W-2144581	0357	1
ZERDA VINCENT M	MAJ	0-1299573	0665	3
ZERDY ALFONCE W	CPT	0-1695229	0245	2
ZERGER CARL R	2LT	0-1313941	1044	2
ZERMUEHLEN HERMAN W	COL	0-0250459	0466	3
ZERNIA MYRON A	MAJ	0-0317986	0764	3
ZETLAU WALTER S	MAJ	0-1699961	1061	1
ZETTERHOLM MAURICE E	COL	0-0180767	0353	3
ZETTERMAN FRED V	CPT	0-1295315	0446	2
ZEVITAS ERNEST J	LTC	0-2038891	0367	1
ZIAYA JOSEPH J	CPT	0-1171020	0346	2
ZICK LILLIAN E	2LT	N-0794873	0846	1
ZICKEFOOSE MARBLE L	LTC	0-0331428	0967	3
ZID FRANK A	LTC	0-1574186	0461	1
ZIDJUNAS FRANK E	CPT	0-1322503	0347	1
ZIEBARTH CHARLES F	LTC	0-0299773	0359	3
ZIEBE OTTO E	LTC	0-0237399	1065	3
ZIEBELL MILTON F	COL	0-0246219	0562	3
ZIEBER FRED H	LTC	0-0320416	0465	3
ZIEG DONALD E	MAJ	0-0405240	0662	1
ZIEGFELD JACOB J	2LT	0-1016330	1044	2
ZIEGLER EDWARD F	1LT	0-1112003	0747	2
ZIEGLER EDWIN A	COL	0-0141223	0648	3
ZIEGLER EDWIN G	MAJ	0-0174720	0648	3
ZIEGLER FRANCIS A	COL	0-0206925	0863	3
ZIEGLER GERALD F	1LT	0-0263817	0653	1
ZIEGLER HARRY E	MAJ	0-1175019	1065	1
ZIEGLER JAMES D	CW4	W-2141444	1166	1
ZIEGLER LEO F	LTC	0-1294236	0261	1
ZIEGLER MAURICE S	CPT	0-1168535	0546	1
ZIEGLER RAY A	MAJ	0-1894399	0357	1
ZIEGLER THEODORE F	MAJ	0-1319996	0263	1
ZIEGLER WILFRED O	CPT	0-1103487	0645	2
ZIEHM RUDOLPH H	LTC	0-0184391	0159	1
ZIEHNERT JULIAN F	MAJ	0-1048263	0561	1
ZIEL MAX G	MAJ	0-0139609	0352	3
ZIELINSKI ANTHONY F	MAJ	0-1019286	0860	1
ZIELINSKI JOSEPH A	LTC	0-0163681	0149	3
ZIELINSKI JOSEPH T	MAJ	0-1557113	0162	1
ZIELSDORF ARTHUR H	CW3	W-2119358	1057	1
ZIEMBA THOMAS P	MAJ	0-1053446	0162	2
ZIEMSKI FRANK J	LTC	0-1057945	1263	1
ZIENK ANTHONY E	CW2	W-2143296	0658	1
ZIERDT JR WILLIAM H	LTC	0-0346173	0161	1
ZIERDT WILLIAM H	COL	0-0167999	0648	3
ZIES FREDERICK	COL	0-0219955	1063	3
ZIESING BENEDICT V	LTC	0-1578079	1058	1
ZIEV BENJAMIN	CW2	W-2116388	0644	2
ZIFCAK MICHAEL G	MAJ	0-0983402	0165	1
ZIFCAK MICHAEL J	COL	0-0436569	1266	1
ZIGLAR HORACE W	LTC	0-1167711	1054	1
ZIGLINSKI JOSEPH H	LTC	0-1635504	0962	1
ZIKE FERMA L	CW2	W-3350164	0864	1
ZIKOWITZ ROBERT F	MAJ	0-0955407	0762	1
ZILE GLEN E	LTC	0-1175570	0966	1
ZILINSKAS ANTHONY F	MAJ	0-1894722	0261	1
ZILKIE JR AUGUST A	LTC	0-1320685	0961	1
ZILSKE KARL L	LTC	0-1550305	0364	1
ZIMET JOHN J	COL	0-0474609	1065	1
ZIMMEK HENRY C	CPT	0-0477541	1148	1
ZIMMER JOHN	CPT	0-0496181	0665	3
ZIMMER JOHN W	LTC	0-2035513	0761	1
ZIMMER JOSEPH E	LTC	0-0244846	0763	3
ZIMMER JR GEORGE E	CPT	0-2014418	1059	1
ZIMMER RALPH W	LTC	0-1105949	0462	1
ZIMMER ROBERT A	CW3	W-2205813	1067	1
ZIMMER WILLIAM K	MAJ	0-2016197	0663	1

NAME	GRADE	SVC NO	DATE RET MO YR	RET CODE
ZIMMERMAN AUGUST A	MAJ	0-1583879	0549	2
ZIMMERMAN AUGUST J	MAJ	0-0199402	0351	3
ZIMMERMAN BARBARA M	2LT	N-0722872	0445	1
ZIMMERMAN CARL C	2LT	0-2007184	1145	2
ZIMMERMAN CARLE C	MAJ	0-0267572	0557	3
ZIMMERMAN CECIL J	LTC	0-0315982	0259	3
ZIMMERMAN COLER	CPT	0-0283788	0446	2
ZIMMERMAN EDGAR	LTC	0-0359876	0757	1
ZIMMERMAN EDWARD F	LTC	0-1104463	0560	1
ZIMMERMAN FRED R	LTC	0-0202798	0944	2
ZIMMERMAN GEORGE C	1LT	0-1012483	0645	2
ZIMMERMAN GRACE I	1LT	N-0760903	0646	1
ZIMMERMAN HENRY G	1LT	0-1052644	0245	2
ZIMMERMAN HENRY H	LTC	0-1304303	0164	1
ZIMMERMAN HORACE S	LTC	0-0336705	1162	1
ZIMMERMAN IRVING M	CPT	0-1590913	0665	2
ZIMMERMAN JAMES A	COL	0-0352534	0766	1
ZIMMERMAN JEAN R	CPT	N-0732805	0347	1
ZIMMERMAN JOHN M	LTC	0-1576849	0461	1
ZIMMERMAN JOSEPH	1LT	0-1327998	0546	2
ZIMMERMAN JUAN M	MAJ	0-2021041	0164	1
ZIMMERMAN KARL	LTC	0-0251857	1163	3
ZIMMERMAN LEO W	MAJ	0-0474245	0745	2
ZIMMERMAN MORRIS L	LTC	0-0204275	0157	2
ZIMMERMAN PAUL J	LTC	0-0258216	1067	3
ZIMMERMAN ROBERT F	LTC	0-1185511	0967	1
ZIMMERMAN RUBIN	LTC	0-0512542	0965	3
ZIMMERMAN STANLEY G	LTC	0-1015360	1265	1
ZIMMERMAN WILLARD P	1LT	0-0516687	0645	2
ZIMMERMAN WILLIAM C	CPT	0-1291210	0561	1
ZIMMERMAN WOODROW	LTC	0-1822464	0664	1
ZIMNOSKI JOSEPH F	CPT	0-1596981	0954	1
ZIMNOWSKI ANTHONY F	1LT	0-1115438	0745	1
ZIMOAT LEONARD J	2LT	0-1109778	0345	2
ZIMRIN HENRY L	CPT	0-1312073	0546	2
ZIMRING ALLAN J	MAJ	0-1821142	0246	2
ZIMRING ROBERT H	2LT	0-1294953	0744	2
ZIMRING WILLIAM J	CPT	0-1821159	0546	2
ZINGA ANDREW S	1LT	0-1014423	0146	2
ZINGERELLA PETER A	1LT	0-1559644	1147	1
ZINGLER CLIFFORD F	MAJ	0-0333660	0846	2
ZINK DONALD C	MAJ	0-1595289	0163	1
ZINK HAROLD L	MAJ	0-1686616	0162	1
ZINK HARRY G	CPT	0-0510331	1044	1
ZINK JACK O	1LT	0-1013026	1046	2
ZINK JR OTTO A	CPT	0-1181812	0546	2
ZINK WILLIAM S	LTC	0-0263256	0262	3
ZINN JOHNNIE P	LTC	0-1587747	0966	1
ZINN LUCILLE E	MAJ	N-0799201	0965	1
ZINN ROBERT W	LTC	0-1061598	0966	1
ZINNAMON DAVID R	COL	0-0251294	1057	1
ZINSKI ALEX A	1LT	0-1308405	1147	2
ZINTEK SYLVESTER	COL	0-0211723	1058	3
ZINTER REINHOLD H	LTC	0-0502075	0565	3
ZINZ FLORENCE	1LT	N-0759813	0346	1
ZIOMEK EDWARD S	MAJ	0-1062839	0462	1
ZION JACOB J	MAJ	0-1003597	1167	3
ZION WALTER S	MAJ	0-0259737	0949	2
ZIPEN JOSEPH L	CPT	0-0497277	1145	1
ZIPF JAMES L	MAJ	0-0327553	1058	1
ZIPP CHARLES C	MAJ	0-1334802	1163	1
ZIPPLE KARL G	1LT	0-0381004	0245	2
ZIRBEL JOSEPH	CW2	W-2211081	0765	1
ZIRJACKS HAMILTON	LTC	0-0450958	0660	1
ZIRKLE PAUL J	LTC	0-1633169	0361	1
ZISCHKAU WILLIAM C	CPT	0-0268989	0857	3
ZISKA CLARENCE W	COL	0-0263459	0657	3
ZISKIND JOSEPH	COL	0-0488926	0467	3
ZITELLI THOMAS S	MAJ	0-1285167	0262	1
ZITKOVICH ROSE P	2LT	N-0731810	1045	1
ZITKUS JOSEPH E	CW3	W-2149999	0166	1
ZITO ANTHONY J	CPT	0-1003871	0256	1
ZITO JOHN	MAJ	0-1559926	0359	1
ZITO JOSEPH	CW4	W-2148363	1264	1
ZITO MICHAEL R	CPT	0-0267240	0158	3

NAME	GRADE	SVC NO	DATE RET MO YR	RET CODE
ZITTEL HAROLD E	COL	0-0215855	0859	3
ZITTEL JR GEORGE H	MAJ	0-2033094	0561	1
ZITTELMAN ROY G	LTC	0-1165694	0464	1
ZITTRALER SIMON D	CPT	0-0887330	0357	1
ZIVICH GEORGE J	COL	0-0377903	0867	1
ZLOTNIK MEYER	WO1	W-2127609	0945	2
ZOBEL RUDOLPH O	COL	0-0245610	0847	2
ZOBEL SIDNEY	COL	0-0112816	0352	3
ZOBERSKI RAY	MAJ	0-1305364	0961	1
ZOBKIW BOHDAN	1LT	0-1100407	0264	2
ZOBROSKY CLARENCE F	CW3	W-2152499	0163	1
ZODER WALLACE L	LTC	0-0240193	0964	3
ZOELLIG PAUL H	1LT	0-1947544	0546	1
ZOELLNER MAX N	CW2	W-2154673	0256	1
ZOELLNER WALTER J	LTC	0-0337265	0760	1
ZOLLINGER DON R	MAJ	0-1544733	0664	1
ZOLLO CHARLES A	COL	0-0190218	1148	1
ZOLNINGER LAMAR	CW2	W-2212499	1066	1
ZOLTY JOHN S	CPT	0-0941983	0261	1
ZOOK HERBERT O	MAJ	0-1690745	0962	1
ZOOK JOHN C	LTC	0-0348903	1059	2
ZOOLE ASHER	LTC	0-0332570	0267	3
ZOPFI JOHN C	MAJ	0-0949047	0763	1
ZOPPI ANTHONY G	2LT	0-1588394	0445	2
ZORN HARVEY A	COL	0-0264983	0765	3
ZORN JR JOSEPH F	LTC	0-0324706	1060	1
ZORNEK JOSEPH F	LTC	0-1106549	0164	1
ZOSCHAK MARY	MAJ	N-0755823	0363	1
ZRALKA ALBERT J	1LT	0-1325145	0845	2
ZSCHACH KARL G	LTC	0-1576850	0765	1
ZSCHAU ERNEST	LTC	0-0173620	0161	3
ZSCHOKKE WALTER J	CW4	W-2146535	1060	1
ZSIPAY GEORGE	CW3	W-2200596	1067	3
ZUBER ANTONE C	CPT	0-2262431	0755	1
ZUBER MARION	LTC	0-1541075	0761	1
ZUBROD JOSEPH R	CW3	W-2152738	0263	1
ZUCCA ANTHONY C	MAJ	0-0983029	0667	1
ZUCCO CAETAN W	COL	0-0924268	1065	3
ZUCK ANTHONY B	CPT	0-1574567	0444	2
ZUCKER MARTIN M	1LT	0-1895180	0545	2
ZUCKER MILTON D	MAJ	0-0475491	0946	2
ZUCKERBROD MORRIS	MAJ	0-0471215	0746	2
ZUCKERMAN HERMAN	LTC	0-0242704	0665	3
ZUCKERMAN LOUIS	LTC	0-0250936	0150	1
ZUCKERMAN SARA	CPT	N-0728593	0547	1
ZUCKERMAN WILLIAM	LTC	0-0273415	1052	3
ZUCKERNICK SAUL	2LT	0-1913547	0838	1
ZUERLEIN EDWARD G	CPT	0-1590915	0857	1
ZUFELT FRED	CW2	W-2205359	0358	1
ZUG RICHARD V	LTC	0-0919059	0967	3
ZUGSCHWERDT WERNER H	COL	0-0265828	0865	3
ZUIDEMA HENRY B	LTC	0-0454611	1262	1
ZUK CHARLES R	MAJ	0-1303588	0962	1
ZUKOSKI JOSEPH J	CPT	0-1695140	0545	2
ZUKOWSKI EDWARD	1LT	0-1304986	0845	2
ZUMALT ROBERT E	CW2	W-2150149	0860	1
ZUMBRUNN NORMAN J	LTC	0-0195229	0762	3
ZUMWALT DERYL B	CPT	0-0888324	1045	2
ZUMWALT ELMO R	COL	0-0238616	1053	3
ZUMWALT RALPH H	LTC	0-0492907	1162	1
ZUND JOSEPH K	MAJ	0-0260190	0160	3
ZUNDEL PAUL BAUH	MAJ	0-1296143	0447	2
ZUNICH MICHAEL	CW4	W-2153329	0662	1
ZUNIS GEORGE P	LTC	0-0456662	1065	1
ZUPAN JOSEPH J	CPT	0-2263139	0761	1
ZUPI LOUIS M	MAJ	0-2043300	0765	1
ZUPKO MICHAEL E	COL	0-0262998	0666	3
ZURBRUGG MARY E	1LT	N-0730380	0746	1
ZURETTI ERNEST V	LTC	0-1058708	0867	1
ZURFLUH MILTON G	CPT	0-0310467	1263	1
ZURIAN GEORGE	CW2	W-2205441	0957	1
ZURLO PASCHAL L	CW2	W-2214851	0467	1
ZURN HAROLD W	LTC	0-0382138	0760	1
ZURTH FREDERICK	CPT	0-0065290	1060	1
ZUSSMAN IRVING W	LTC	0-1587045	0462	1

NAME	GRADE	SVC NO	DATE RET MO YR	RET CODE
ZUTAVERN NORMAN E	CW3	W-2106809	0761	1
ZUVER PAUL E	COL	O-0017373	0157	2
ZUZULO FRANCIS X	CPT	O-0353189	0644	2
ZWART CORNELIUS	LTC	O-1642756	1062	1
ZWART EDWARD A	CPT	O-0414546	0151	1
ZWART JOE G	LTC	O-0330468	0566	3
ZWECKER ROBERT G	MAJ	O-4009309	0366	1
ZWELLING HERBERT W	2LT	O-1579337	0245	2
ZWERDLING JOSEPH	1LT	O-2052517	0146	2
ZWERLING SAMUEL	LTC	O-0137242	1054	3
ZWICK WALTER H	LTC	O-0295287	1264	3
ZWICKER LEON	LTC	O-0461682	0754	1
ZWIRBLE EDWARD A	MAJ	O-1338770	0661	1
ZWIRNBAUM ABRAHAM M	MAJ	O-0452585	0456	1
ZWIRNER JR ARTHUR P	MAJ	O-0983327	0765	1
ZWITZER MARTIN N	COL	O-1000303	0855	1
ZYCH LLOYD C	MAJ	O-2002112	0962	1
ZYMBOLY JOHN	CW2	W-2113661	0853	1
ZYSK JOHN W	MAJ	O-0988708	0766	1
ZYSKOWSKI ZIGMUND	CPT	O-1323643	0855	1
ZYVITH EDWARD J	MAJ	O-1543590	1160	1
ZYWASKI CHARLES M	COL	O-0280241	0751	1

SECTION 3

TEMPORARY DISABILITY RETIRED LIST

The Temporary Disability Retired List is composed of officers and warrant officers placed on the Temporary Disability Retired List under Title 10, USC, Sections 1202 and 1205 (formerly Section 402, Career Compensation Act of 1949) for physical disability which may be of a permanent nature.

NAME	GRADE	SVC NO	DATE RET MO YR	RET CODE
ACCIARDI ALBERT F	LTC	0-1636949	0663	4
ADAMS STANLEY F	LTC	0-1312449	0667	4
ADDINGTON ALLISON R	MAJ	0-0964938	0165	4
ALLEN DONIVAN D	CW3	W-2205874	1067	4
ALLINSON CELIA	MAJ	N-0721800	0363	4
AMES WARWICK M	CPT	0-1824422	0959	4
ANGLEY JAMES A	MAJ	0-2212044	0264	4
ANTONIELLO KATE G	MAJ	N-0051121	0466	4
ARCHER RUBYE W	LTC	N-0001634	0567	4
ARNETT EDWIN W	CPT	0-1596252	0463	4
ARNOLD WARREN C	CW2	W-2210044	0462	4
ARSENA NINO	1LT	0-5419195	0567	4
ASCHENBACH JULIUS O	CPT	0-0957777	0267	4
ATROCHIN PAUL A	MAJ	0-1634961	0466	4
AULTMAN JOHN L	CPT	0-2204082	0163	4
AYERS EDITH A	MAJ	L-0000099	0159	4
BABBITT PAUL E	MAJ	0-4031337	0567	4
BABOVEC BENJAMIN S	LTC	0-1115174	1263	4
BACON RICHARD H	LTC	0-0028656	0867	4
BALES JR ARTHUR W	CW4	W-2118074	1166	4
BALLENTINE GEORGE D	LTC	0-1172366	0666	4
BARBER JR ANDREW C	MAJ	0-2263456	0567	4
BARDENHAGEN CHRISTOP	MAJ	0-1004444	1158	4
BARKER GEORGE E	MAJ	0-0245636	0360	4
BARNES GLENN G	CPT	0-1938748	0467	4
BARNES LAWRENCE G	WO1	W-3152383	0866	4
BARRINGER MICHEL L	MAJ	0-0097882	0967	4
BARWICK JR ALBERT F	MAJ	0-1878085	0967	4
BAST ADELBERT C	CW4	W-2142686	0261	4
BAUCOM DONALD C	CPT	0-5304293	0467	4
BAUR CHARLES K	CW2	W-3440050	0567	4
BAZEMORE ROBERT E	CPT	0-2262397	0767	4
BEAM KEITH J	CPT	0-5301020	0764	4
BECHTOLD KENNETH I	LTC	0-1038165	0767	4
BEHANNON HOLLIS R	CPT	0-0086994	1064	4
BENNETT EDWARD A	MAJ	0-2263170	1062	4
BENNETT REBECCA L	MAJ	L-0302612	0667	4
BENSON ANDREW S	1LT	0-5710817	0767	4
BENSON JR WALTER R	LTC	0-0039180	0167	4
BERGMAN PHILIP A	COL	0-0022772	1066	4
BERGSTROM WAYNE A	CPT	0-5525537	1066	4
BERRY ALICE F	MAJ	N-0001882	0460	4
BERRY EVA I	CW4	V-0414874	0765	4
BERRY JR HENRY N	CPT	0-1885159	0463	4
BETTINGER RONALD G	CPT	0-5217638	0267	4
BEVEL BOB B	1LT	0-0890182	0463	4
BICKFORD ROSS P	MAJ	0-1893078	0867	4
BILLINGS EUGENE O	LTC	0-0030816	1264	4
BILLINGSLEA CHARLES	M G	0-0020367	0766	4
BLACKMORE ROBERT P	CPT	0-0059473	1060	4
BLIZZARD JOHN G	CW4	W-2123113	0667	4
BLUM ANDREW J	MAJ	RW-2148273	0862	4
BODEEN JERRIE W	CPT	0-5517520	0367	4
BOND LEROY	MAJ	0-2000026	0963	4
BOND VAN H	M G	0-0018601	0966	4
BONIFAY ISAAC F	COL	0-0040061	1166	4
BOYCE FRANCIS J	LTC	0-1588128	0567	4
BOYD BOBBY	CW2	W-2206478	0663	4
BOYD CHARLES A	MAJ	0-2206264	0267	4
BOYETT JR JAMES C	CW3	W-2206660	1065	4
BOYLE JOHN J	CW3	W-2152087	0565	4
BRACK JOSEPH L	COL	0-0051746	0566	4
BRACKEN GLENN A	MAJ	0-0084956	0767	4
BRADLEY SUE T	LTC	L-0000188	0565	4
BRADY RAYMOND E	CPT	0-1933690	1166	4
BRANDT ROBERT I	CPT	0-5706179	0767	4
BRANIGAN JR GEORGE H	LTC	0-1650019	1166	4
BRICE EMMETT T	LTC	0-0088589	0367	4
BRIDWELL ARTHUR W	MAJ	0-0066730	0467	4
BRIGMAN JR LANEAU M	MAJ	0-0082147	0465	4
BROWN ARCHIE J	CPT	0-0401101	0367	4
BROWN CHARLES W	CPT	0-1030124	0767	4
BROWN HARLEY D	COL	0-0029911	0164	4
BROWN HARVEY L	CPT	0-0093589	0965	4
BROWN JR STANLEY W	1LT	0-5007631	0965	4

NAME	GRADE	SVC NO	DATE RET MO YR	RET CODE
BRUHNS LOWELL	MAJ	0-0692475	0963	4
BRULEY HENRY L	LTC	0-0035457	0564	4
BUNDREN ELMO L	LTC	0-1825586	0266	4
BURKE CRANE D	1LT	0-5405651	0663	4
BURKE JR EDMUND J	1LT	0-5327171	0267	4
BUTLER BILLIE D	CPT	0-1999465	1057	4
BYRD DAVID R	WO1	W-3200669	0866	4
CALLAWAY CHARLES V	LTC	0-1018067	1167	4
CALLAWAY ROBERT L	WO1	W-2150586	0765	4
CAMPBELL BRADLEY S	1LT	0-5323679	0167	4
CANNON JOHN C	LTC	0-1997676	0766	4
CARR FREDERIC C	CW3	W-2143230	1263	4
CARROLL ROBERT E	LTC	0-1798647	0667	4
CASSIDY BERNARD J	CPT	0-1037552	0266	4
CAVANAUGH DOROTHY W	LTC	N-0002384	0964	4
CEHRS BERNICE J	COL	0-0029220	0961	4
CHAPA MANUEL O	MAJ	0-4024749	0267	4
CHARONIS ANASTASIA	MAJ	N-0001805	0764	4
CHILDERS CALVIN C	CW3	W-2205814	0764	4
CHRISTENSEN DONALD P	COL	0-0020257	0161	4
CHRISTIANSON J MILTO	LTC	0-0065965	0966	4
CHURCH CHARLES T	LTC	0-0414559	0463	4
CIARAVINO JAMES R	1LT	0-5214911	0964	4
CIVELLO ADOLPH J	CW3	W-2209610	0967	4
CLARK CHARLES E	MAJ	0-1633755	0267	4
CLARK JR FELIX G	MAJ	0-2203403	0465	4
CLARK MILDRED I	COL	N-0000608	1067	4
CLARK ROBERT S	CW3	W-2147705	0267	4
CLARK SAM J	COL	0-0040064	1166	4
CLARK WARREN M	LTC	0-0065294	0967	4
CLARK WILLIS H	LTC	0-0050686	1264	4
CLAY ANTHONY H	2LT	OF-0104674	0566	4
CLIFTON JOSEPH M	CPT	0-1289392	0564	4
COLBY JOHN R	CPT	0-4074460	0366	4
COMBS MARY L	CPT	M-2313256	0467	4
COMITO SALVATORE	1LT	0-5013743	1265	4
COMM EDWARD C	COL	0-0031484	0567	4
CONRAD MARY C	MAJ	L-1000105	0963	4
CONROY GEORGE L	LTC	0-1050607	0966	4
COOCH JOSEPH W	COL	0-0063707	0867	4
COOK JONATHAN L	1LT	0-5321759	0466	4
COOK ROBERT L	CW3	W-2208234	1066	4
COPELAND KENNETH W	COL	0-0040177	0867	4
COULD KENNETH	MAJ	0-1556587	0456	4
CRAIG ROLLIN B	MAJ	0-1556404	1163	4
CRONIN DANIEL W	MAJ	0-0071333	0765	4
CRUZ GLORIA J P	CPT	N-5315804	0966	4
CURRAN KENTON W	CPT	0-0088640	0364	4
CZELUSNIAK JOHN L	1LT	0-5015982	0965	4
DARLEY GEORGE L	COL	0-0029693	0362	4
DAVANZO LOUIS T	LTC	0-1323668	1167	4
DAVIS JULIA A	MAJ	N-0761082	0465	4
DAWSON JR EMMETT C	LTC	0-1895009	0567	4
DAY NORMAN C	CPT	0-2014509	0264	4
DE FRANCESCO FRED L	CPT	0-0096896	1263	4
DE LA GARZA CARL	CPT	0-2263552	0363	4
DE MOSS EDWARD L	CW4	W-2003605	0767	4
DE SPAIN LA MAR A	LTC	0-0032587	0966	4
DEAL JR WILLIAM H	2LT	0-5413878	0364	4
DEAN GERALD M	MAJ	0-2014441	0465	4
DECK PATRICK A	1LT	0-5017756	0166	4
DECKER JAMES W	LTC	0-0078791	1265	4
DEUTSCHER EDWIN J	1LT	0-5005159	0364	4
DIAL EVELYN E	MAJ	N-0002444	0564	4
DIAZ GEORGE F	LTC	0-0078798	1166	4
DICKENS RANDOLPH C	B G	0-0020290	0866	4
DICKSON DONALD J	1LT	0-5018852	0767	4
DILLARD MONDELL	MAJ	0-2206054	0467	4
DIRCK FLOYD C	CW3	W-2149694	0166	4
DODD JOHN C	CW3	W-2205410	0366	4
DOWSETT PETER J	CPT	0-5712891	0467	4
DREHER MELVIN M	CPT	0-1637326	0764	4
DRESBACK WILLIAM W	1LT	0-5213052	0663	4
DROSS ALLEN E	CPT	0-0089677	1163	4
DUGAN DONALD C	LTC	0-1305025	0466	4

NAME	GRADE	SVC NO	DATE RET MO YR	RET CODE
DUKE WILLIAM G	COL	0-0366484	0166	4
DULEY CLARA M	LTC	N-0001637	0660	4
DUNCAN MILDRED	MAJ	N-0002621	0167	4
DUNGAN JAMES A	CW3	W-0904108	0863	4
DUNN JAMES S	COL	0-0040173	0867	4
ECKSTEIN PHILIP L	CPT	0-5508488	1263	4
EFFENGHAM ESTHER M	LTC	L-0000324	1167	4
EGGSTAFF CHARLES M	LTC	0-1995247	0764	4
ELLIS HAROLD J	CPT	OF-0102323	1067	4
EMERSON JAMES W	MAJ	0-0997324	0366	4
EMERY JOHN E	MAJ	0-1311750	0267	4
EMERY JR WALTER T	MAJ	0-1103153	1064	4
ENGEL TIBOR	CPT	0-5219989	0967	4
ENGLER JEAN H	CPT	0-0087101	1265	4
ENGLISH WILLIAM W	CW2	W-2001825	0867	4
ERLANDSON KENNETH W	CW3	W-2205523	0566	4
EVANS JR GILBERT P	CW2	W-3100413	0267	4
EZELL JOSEPH J	MAJ	0-1884172	0767	4
FAGG JR WILLIAM L	1LT	0-0083218	1059	4
FAHEY NICHOLAS F	LTC	0-1032584	0464	4
FALCHETTA STEPHEN L	CPT	OF-0101812	0567	4
FALK DONALD G	CW2	W-3400117	0867	4
FANNIN CLYDE	WO1	W-2119951	0366	4
FARRELL JOSEPH E	LTC	0-1307387	0167	4
FEIN JACOB M	CW4	W-2144489	0467	4
FERRIS CHARLES J	CPT	0-2308323	0967	4
FINESINGER JOSEPH	CPT	0-5224005	0765	4
FINNERTY WILLIAM J	2LT	0-1999398	0965	4
FISHER MARSHALL U	MAJ	0-1327828	0764	4
FITZGERALD FRANCIS X	1LT	0-1598372	0367	4
FIVES PAUL E	COL	0-0032170	0467	4
FLANAGAN ANDREW P	COL	0-0030609	0466	4
FLANAGAN JAMES A	MAJ	0-0953542	0365	4
FLANAGAN JAMES M	CPT	0-5317362	1067	4
FLATT FRANCIS L	COL	0-0051180	0763	4
FLETCHER AARON J	CPT	0-5209176	0466	4
FOLEY LAWRENCE E	MAJ	0-1822788	1063	4
FOSTER JAY W	LTC	0-0084316	1262	4
FOUKE JOSEPH E	CPT	0-2103089	0667	4
FOWLER STEPHEN A	1LT	0-2279323	1163	4
FOX RICHARD J	CPT	0-0338123	0264	4
FRANK ARTHUR L	CW2	W-2212526	0365	4
FRANKLIN OLIVER W	CPT	0-0408234	0365	4
FRANKS WILLIAM A	COL	0-0043301	0365	4
FRAZIER WALTER K	MAJ	0-4010496	0167	4
FREEMAN RAYMOND R	1LT	0-5000499	0360	4
FREYTAG ROBERT J	MAJ	0-2262786	0463	4
FRYE JR RAYMOND E	CPT	0-5210933	0967	4
FUERST LOUIS R	LTC	0-2034967	0766	4
GAFNER SR RICHARD L	CPT	0-0073331	0365	4
GAGNON WILFRED E	CPT	0-1589211	1166	4
GALLOWAY HENRY T	CW3	W-3350267	0667	4
GAMBLE ROBERT O	LTC	0-1994604	0266	4
GANNS RALPH R	COL	0-0020184	0762	4
GARDNER RAY	LTC	0-1112727	0467	4
GAUDREAU LAWRENCE J	1LT	0-5322081	0867	4
GENTRY ROY C	MAJ	0-0074989	1066	4
GERHARDT HARRISON A	M G	0-0018697	0567	4
GETCHELL JOHN S	LTC	0-0339149	0563	4
GIBSON JOHN R	COL	0-0063454	0667	4
GIBSON JOYCE W	1LT	N-0902131	0356	4
GIGLIERANO ALFRED	MAJ	0-1999380	0667	4
GILHART CHARLES C	2LT	0-2312157	0164	4
GILLMAN WILLIAM D	2LT	0-1929498	0255	4
GILSON CLAIRE E	MAJ	N-0002874	1067	4
GITTES HYMAN R	LTC	0-1037002	0663	4
GLEASON JOSEPH L	MAJ	0-1172463	0965	4
GOODHAND O GLENN	B G	0-0051511	0664	4
GORDON DONALD B	COL	0-0032573	0367	4
GORDON MATTHEW E	CPT	0-2203405	0766	4
GRAHAM ALEXANDER	COL	0-0018688	0862	4
GRAHAM JACKIE C	CPT	0-1936662	0766	4
GRAHAM JACKSON	M G	0-0020553	0367	4
GRANT EDWARD R	2LT	0-2318709	0766	4
GRANTHAM DOUGLAS O	2LT	0-5318502	1164	4

NAME	GRADE	SVC NO	DATE RET MO YR	RET CODE
GREENE QUENTIN R	CPT	0-2017838	0567	4
GRIVERS STANLEY J	CPT	0-2271708	0863	4
GUERDRUM THORVALD J	LTC	0-0043825	0861	4
GUSTAFSON PAULINE	MAJ	N-0002148	0162	4
GUTHRIE SIDNEY C	MAJ	0-0057451	0765	4
HALE JAMES L	CPT	0-5530736	0867	4
HALL ROBERT E	COL	0-0031747	0862	4
HAMILTON LAURENCE G	2LT	0-5013885	0964	4
HAMLETT BARKSDALE	GEN	0-0018143	0964	4
HAMMOND JAMES R	LTC	0-1582359	0565	4
HAMNER SHIRLEY O	CW2	W-3430580	0867	4
HARD ILC B	LTC	0-0397703	0763	4
HARDEN ANN R	CPT	N-2298815	0863	4
HARRIGAN WILLIAM F	COL	0-0036438	0667	4
HARRINGTON JOHN W	MAJ	0-0974548	0567	4
HARRIS BRADY R	LTC	0-0061563	0167	4
HARRIS GIDEON J	MAJ	0-0964149	1265	4
HARRIS JR ARTHUR C	LTC	0-0020874	0665	4
HARRISON BRUCE E	1LT	0-5517230	1265	4
HARRISON JR WALTER R	LTC	0-0057433	0666	4
HATFIELD ROGER L	1LT	0-5320167	0965	4
HEALEY JR JAMES R	COL	0-0042906	0267	4
HEANEY MICHAEL K	1LT	0-5019463	0267	4
HEARD CHARLES C	CPT	0-5325748	0967	4
HEATON LEONARD D	LTG	0-0016960	1166	4
HELLEN JOHN H	MAJ	0-1922597	0663	4
HENDERSON TONY S	LTC	0-0039279	0767	4
HENNESSEY RAYMOND F	MAJ	0-1795901	1067	4
HENNIGAN PATRICK C	LTC	0-1295878	0863	4
HERBERT SELMA A	MAJ	L-0000047	0264	4
HICKS WILFRED R	1LT	0-1584357	0467	4
HIGHTOWER LOUIS V	M G	0-0018502	1063	4
HILL GARRETT L	COL	0-0033941	0666	4
HILL MAURICE H	CW4	W-2113881	0864	4
HILL RONALD E	1LT	0-5417975	0767	4
HODSON EDMUND R	COL	0-0349568	0765	4
HOENSCHEID MILO J	2LT	0-2297227	0362	4
HOFFMAN ALAN C	MAJ	0-0088101	0564	4
HOFFMAN MICHAEL F	1LT	0-5019219	0367	4
HOLLINGSWORTH LINDY	CPT	0-4076117	0966	4
HOLMES ROBERT R	LTC	0-1311774	0167	4
HOLZENTHALER M L	MAJ	L-0220092	0267	4
HOOKS WALTER A	LTC	0-0080877	0665	4
HORAN JOHN J	CPT	0-1302926	0463	4
HOWDESHELL HARMON M	COL	0-0039973	0765	4
HOWES RICHARD H	MAJ	0-0075623	1166	4
HUFF DUANE F	CPT	0-5405247	1265	4
HUTHOEFER GERALD E	1LT	0-5023828	0767	4
HUTSON THOMAS M	MAJ	0-1922902	1166	4
IMWALLE FRANK E	CW3	W-2148077	1167	4
INGRAM SAMUEL T	CPT	0-0085578	0666	4
INNES WILLIAM H	COL	0-0043867	0866	4
IRVINE II FREDERIC H	MAJ	0-0981776	1066	4
IVY MARION R	MAJ	0-2265861	0367	4
JACKSON MARSHALL O	LTC	0-0037625	0466	4
JACKSON WALLACE L	CPT	0-0092669	0365	4
JACOBSON BERNARD	COL	0-4022544	0866	4
JEANETTE ROBERT J	1LT	0-5016225	1166	4
JEFFERSON HARRY F	MAJ	0-0451642	0567	4
JENSEN EMILIE K	COL	N-0000060	1164	4
JESS JAMES R	LTC	0-1061143	0763	4
JOHNAKIN EVANDER L	1LT	OF-0104138	0567	4
JOHNSON JR JOSEPH A	CPT	0-5402483	0966	4
JOHNSON LEWIS C	LTC	0-1597692	1166	4
JOHNSON RICHARD C	CPT	0-5303641	0366	4
JONES JAMES W	MAJ	0-2204417	1266	4
JORDAN ARTHUR C	LTC	0-1573314	0467	4
JORDAN IVA M	CPT	N-0763519	0360	4
JORDAN RALPH E	COL	0-0021911	0863	4
JULICH ARNOLD C	LTC	0-1184858	0763	4
KAMINSKY NEAL S	1LT	0-5710429	0866	4
KAUFMANN MICHAEL M	1LT	0-5012052	1264	4
KEATING GEOFFREY J	CPT	0-5006677	0567	4
KELLER PERCY A	CW3	W-2207292	1166	4
KELLER STANISLAUS	CPT	0-2276566	0964	4

TEMPORARY DISABILITY RETIRED LIST

NAME	GRADE	SVC NO	DATE RET MO YR	RET CODE
KELLY JESSE J	LTC	0-0400658	0963	4
KENYON GILBERT A	1LT	0-1823458	1164	4
KEOUGH THOMAS F	MAJ	0-2203039	0667	4
KERCHEVAL BENJAMIN B	COL	0-0023933	0667	4
KINDER DONALD L	MAJ	C-2014159	1063	4
KING EVERETT G	COL	C-0061170	0467	4
KING ILENE O	MAJ	N-0765496	C765	4
KING JAMES A	CPT	0-2308565	0964	4
KINTER KENNETH E	MAJ	C-2005940	0365	4
KNOBLAUCH FREDERICK	COL	0-0021672	0667	4
KNOX RAYMOND A	LTC	0-0051921	0765	4
KOLSTER JIM H	LTC	0-0065265	C867	4
KOMOLL RICHARD A	CW2	W-2207081	C265	4
KONITZER KENNETH R	CW2	W-3430406	C467	4
KRAMER ELDON L	MAJ	0-2029632	0165	4
KUBALAK RAYMOND R	1LT	0-5222033	1265	4
LA FLAMME ERNEST H	COL	0-0020781	0163	4
LA PLANTE FREDERICK	CPT	0-0993251	C763	4
LAETARE ARLA R	1LT	N-5417401	C567	4
LAMMERS MARVIN E	CPT	0-2266731	0465	4
LANE JR GEORGE H	MAJ	C-0089240	0967	4
LANGHAM HARAULD O	LTC	0-0032518	1167	4
LANGSTON JOE V	COL	0-0024182	C367	4
LAVIGNE JACK E	MAJ	C-0397837	C566	4
LAYCOCK JEANNE G	MAJ	N-5003312	0265	4
LEONARD LAWRENCE M	LTC	0-0076335	C767	4
LEWIS IVA D	MAJ	N-0001083	1163	4
LIGHT ERNEST H	2LT	0-1032368	1063	4
LILLY CYRIL R	CPT	0-1048874	0264	4
LINDAU MARJORIE J	LTC	N-0002154	0564	4
LINDEMAN PHILIP F	M G	0-0272444	C367	4
LINDLEY ROGER M	COL	0-0410141	C266	4
LINROTHE ROBERT N	LTC	0-0080976	0767	4
LITTLETON EARL P	1LT	0-1176410	0966	4
LITWAK PHILIP	1LT	0-5519931	0366	4
LOMBARDO RICCARDO J	CW3	W-3150498	0467	4
LONG JAMES E	MAJ	C-0097150	1166	4
LONG LUTHER F	COL	0-0355271	C366	4
LONSDALE WILLIAM L	MAJ	C-2050550	0567	4
LOUIE LOUISE	CPT	N-2302310	0667	4
LOVELL BUDDY	MAJ	C-4006957	1166	4
LYTTLE RICHARD N	MAJ	0-2013861	0967	4
MAC HOTT HYMAN E	MAJ	C-1054316	0264	4
MADIGAN FRANCIS L	LTC	C-2010028	C866	4
MAGUIRE RALPH E	LTC	0-1115684	C965	4
MAHER JOHN R	MAJ	C-0084832	0763	4
MANHART ASHTON H	LTG	0-0018773	0867	4
MANZO FRANK A	1LT	0-5020268	0167	4
MARANGER GEORGE J	LTC	C-0069525	C667	4
MARDICK CLINTON H	LTC	0-1031108	C365	4
MARQUEZ HERNAN G	CPT	0-5015141	C766	4
MARR JOHN E	CPT	0-5211616	0467	4
MARVIN SIDNEY L	COL	0-0057063	C867	4
MASSEY BASTON C	MAJ	C-1541020	0554	4
MASSINGILL GERALDINE	MAJ	N-0001158	C565	4
MATSUZAKI MASAKO	CPT	N-0901484	1065	4
MC BRIDE DOROTHY	MAJ	N-0002004	C665	4
MC CLELLAND ELLIS F	MAJ	0-0094772	1066	4
MC CLURE RICHARD B	1LT	0-5009386	0964	4
MC CONNELL WAYNE C	COL	0-0043457	1066	4
MC CORMICK OTTO L	CPT	0-0066049	0460	4
MC COY JOHN T	LTC	C-2021022	C567	4
MC DERMOTT ARTHUR R	LTC	0-0399306	C367	4
MC FEE HAROLD F	LTC	0-1280615	C867	4
MC INTYRE MICHAEL J	1LT	0-0098833	0565	4
MC LEOD WALTER G	LTC	0-0060748	1055	4
MC MAHON JR JOSEPH M	CPT	0-0064848	0466	4
MC MAHON RICHARD J	MAJ	C-1874291	0165	4
MC NANUS MYLES M	LTC	0-1292383	C666	4
MC NUTT JAMES N	MAJ	0-0385784	0866	4
MC SHEA ROYAL E	COL	0-0051881	0667	4
MEAD CHARLES E	LTC	0-0036314	0265	4
MEAD DAVID	CPT	0-1924826	0264	4
MEADOR MAURICE A	COL	C-0030835	1164	4
MEIS RAYMOND C	LTC	0-1290975	0967	4
MELLNIK STEPHEN M	B G	0-0018754	1163	4
MELODY PHILIP B	COL	0-0038782	0964	4
MERRITTS ARLINGTON	CPT	0-0966388	0767	4
METZKER JEFF J	MAJ	0-1924856	0864	4
MEYERS IRA R	LTC	0-1796669	1166	4
MEYERS JAY M	LTC	0-1337462	0467	4
MICHEL NORA W	CPT	N-2297702	0165	4
MIEZIO DONALD S	CPT	0-5525857	1166	4
MILLER BLAINE L	MAJ	0-1924981	0764	4
MILLER DAVID A	CW2	W-3250215	1064	4
MILLER FRANK L	COL	0-0057564	0866	4
MILLER IVA R	MAJ	N-0001177	0863	4
MILLER JR WALTER L	LTC	0-0024495	C161	4
MILLER SAMUEL D	MAJ	C-1019274	0267	4
MINCKLER REX C	LTC	0-0025581	1065	4
MISSIK BERNARD	MAJ	0-1575472	0864	4
MIZE EDWARD M	COL	0-0461638	1265	4
MOBLEY WILLIAM A	MAJ	0-2283755	0667	4
MONTESI STEVEN G	1LT	0-5419388	0767	4
MOON JR HOWARD H	1LT	0-5516745	0665	4
MOORE ROY N	CPT	0-5405083	0265	4
MORGAN JAMES S	1LT	0-5326444	0667	4
MORROW JACK C	LTC	0-0067730	0866	4
MORT KENNETH H	CPT	0-5320201	1067	4
MUELLER EDMUND L	B G	0-0034292	1167	4
MUELLER ROBERT A	CPT	0-5525811	0966	4
MULE WALTER	LTC	0-1047655	0663	4
MULLER RALPH P	1LT	0-5218663	0764	4
MULLINS DEMPSEY F	MAJ	0-2046353	1158	4
MURRAY BILL M	CPT	0-5410269	0567	4
MYERS HAROLD	MAJ	0-1686718	0463	4
NAUS LEO	CW4	W-2150604	0564	4
NELSON ORVILLE W	CPT	0-2279614	0165	4
NEWARK HENRY G	CW3	W-2149021	0166	4
NEWBOLD WILLIAM G	MAJ	0-2037084	0667	4
NEWMAN JR SAMUEL H	CPT	0-5405029	0565	4
NEWSOM SAMUEL J	COL	0-0057042	1064	4
NICK HENRY J	CW4	W-2149135	0667	4
NICODEMUS ROBERT E	LTC	0-1011046	0865	4
NIDA GLENN F	COL	0-0030140	0764	4
NIEHOFF JR JOHN	LTC	0-1055926	1165	4
NIERLING DON C	1LT	0-5013715	0765	4
NORTH ROBERT L	1LT	OF-0101634	0766	4
NORTHROP CHARLES R	MAJ	0-1051708	0164	4
NORTON HENRY C	CW3	W-3150336	1166	4
OAKES JAMES L	LTC	0-0051643	0264	4
OBRYAN JAMES M	CPT	OF-0100998	0367	4
OHARA JR JOHN J	LTC	0-2048734	0767	4
OLIVER REX G	MAJ	0-1877824	0264	4
OLSEN EARL R	CPT	0-0093483	0564	4
OLSON LESTER K	COL	0-0030640	0166	4
ORSINO GUY A	COL	0-0030168	0364	4
OSBORNE PATRICIA J	CPT	N-2313636	0966	4
OSZCZAKIEWICZ WALTER	CW4	W-0903644	0767	4
OTTO THOMAS W	COL	0-0030799	0866	4
OWEN ETHEL	MAJ	N-0752149	0266	4
OWENS FLOYD E	LTC	0-1177125	0166	4
OWENS WARREN R	CPT	0-0069259	0864	4
OXX LAWRENCE M	LTC	0-0548340	0664	4
PALIN CALIXTE A	CW4	W-0903653	0364	4
PAPPAS ALLEN	COL	0-0031056	0763	4
PARADIS CLARENCE E	1LT	0-4011062	0767	4
PARKER DAVID B	M G	0-0020571	1167	4
PARSONS DON R	LTC	0-1588218	0767	4
PASSARELLI EUGENE	LTC	0-1638225	0666	4
PATE CONLEY O	LTC	0-0958251	0764	4
PEACOCK DAVID R	MAJ	0-1020161	0164	4
PEARSON MILTON H	CW3	W-2205869	0665	4
PEENE AVA L	LTC	N-0000663	0966	4
PELHAM JR ALFRED M	1LT	0-5532692	0967	4
PERCIACCANTO PETER P	LTC	0-1324738	1064	4
PETRIK VERNON F	MAJ	0-0092113	0567	4
PETRY JR FRANK	CW4	W-2144570	0967	4
PETTET JOSEPH D	CPT	0-0072196	0664	4
PHILLIPS SR EUGENE F	1LT	0-1057566	0566	4
PIASECKI DONALD F	1LT	0-5706534	0963	4
PIERCE WILLIAM H	CPT	0-0984583	0861	4
PIERSOL WILBER S	MAJ	C-1012424	0664	4
PISINSKI LUCY I	MAJ	N-0751424	0863	4
PLEMONS HARRY F	MAJ	C-0967241	0163	4
POE CUPID R	CPT	0-5540188	0967	4
POLANCIC JOSEPH C	1LT	0-1173745	1064	4
PONIKISKI MITCHELL S	LTC	0-2048116	1065	4
PORTER JR DONALD A	CPT	0-5415498	0567	4
POTEET HARRY H	COL	0-0305532	0161	4
POTTS EDWIN H	LTC	0-0031009	0563	4
POWELL FREDERICK	1LT	0-1315481	1166	4
POWELL GEORGE M	M G	0-0019340	0266	4
POWELL HARRY C	LTC	0-0039336	0264	4
POWELL ROBERT E	CPT	0-4011931	0966	4
POWELL ROSS F	LTC	0-0033980	0565	4
POWELL VELMA L	MAJ	N-0002495	C864	4
POWERS NORMAN W	CPT	0-5525088	1066	4
PRICE JR GEORGE W	MAJ	0-0087588	1166	4
PROUTY DWIGHT W	2LT	0-5323479	0465	4
QUINN GENE	COL	0-0030839	0365	4
QUINN JOHN T	CPT	C-0099961	0866	4
RAKE CLIFFORD D	WO1	W-2127006	0564	4
RAY JR ERNEST E	LTC	C-1554074	C366	4
RAY JR WILLIAM K	LTC	0-0980104	C867	4
REECE WILLIAM F	CW3	W-2209993	0667	4
REED OLIF B	MAJ	N-0001723	0964	4
REES KENNETH R	CPT	0-0059875	0963	4
REID WILLIAM M	CPT	0-5314872	0566	4
REID WILLIAM S	MAJ	C-1054843	C865	4
REILAND NICHOLAS J	CW2	W-2212839	C166	4
REINHART BERNARD J	CPT	0-1556341	C267	4
RICCITELLI MARY A	CPT	N-2318306	0867	4
RIDER JR ROBINSON B	2LT	0-5233879	0667	4
RIORDAN JR MICHAEL W	CPT	0-0083442	0463	4
RIOS ALBERT J	MAJ	0-0084508	C267	4
ROACH JR ARMAND O	CPT	0-0089281	C865	4
ROBERTS JAMES J 3D	CPT	0-0093913	0667	4
ROBERTSON MARY M	MAJ	N-0002432	0865	4
ROBIDEAUX ROBERT J	LTC	0-0032066	0566	4
ROBINS ROBERT E	1LT	0-2017590	0763	4
ROBINSON BILLY L	LTC	C-0539095	1265	4
RODERMUND KARL A	LTC	0-1582088	0666	4
ROGERS LEE F	MAJ	0-0091368	0967	4
ROLLE RUFUS M	CPT	0-5306013	1166	4
ROMEO PHILIP J	2LT	0-5019142	1264	4
ROSCOE RICHARD D	1LT	0-5534804	1166	4
ROSEN STEPHEN G	CPT	0-5315916	0765	4
ROW JR HENRY C	LTC	0-0060433	C866	4
RUBENSTEIN BARRY L	CPT	0-5012683	0963	4
RUDNICK JAMES J	1LT	0-0052849	0264	4
RULONG BERNARD C	LTC	0-2288107	0767	4
RYSER ROBERT L	WO1	W-2146090	1166	4
SALANCE CHARLES	CPT	0-1634284	0766	4
SALOPEK MARY A	MAJ	N-0760121	1065	4
SAMPLES JAMES C	MAJ	0-1919354	1165	4
SATTLER WALTER W	1LT	0-2043295	C564	4
SAURER HAROLD D	WO1	W-3155363	0567	4
SCHARN EDWARD O	LTC	0-1642545	0665	4
SCHNEIDER ELEANOR T	MAJ	N-0792322	0367	4
SCHOENBERG HARRY I	CPT	0-1305469	0567	4
SCOTT FRANKLIN E	COL	0-0051898	C863	4
SCOTT RAYMOND L	CPT	0-4049262	0464	4
SEITZ JOHN A	B G	0-0030137	1067	4
SEXTON HERBERT M	1LT	0-1342125	0566	4
SHANKLIN WILLIAM S	1LT	0-5800365	1065	4
SHELNUTT HENRY F	MAJ	0-1639637	C563	4
SHERLOCK JOHN V	LTC	0-0080366	0664	4
SHIPMAN FRANKLIN D	CPT	0-2315662	1067	4
SHIRLEY ALFRED S	CPT	0-0974546	0466	4
SIMMONS SIDNEY L	MAJ	C-1112974	0963	4
SIMONE VINCENT A	CPT	0-5525171	1066	4
SMITH EARL L	MAJ	C-1019464	0966	4
SMITH ELBRIDGE A	LTC	0-0080188	1166	4
SMITH LINDA G	2LT	N-5520492	0267	4
SMITH MARLO E	LTC	0-0056924	1060	4
SMITH MICHAEL A	LTC	0-2208594	1167	4
SMITH VONNIE C	CPT	0-0452589	0566	4
SNYDER ERNEST C	MAJ	0-0574596	1163	4
SPARKS AARON C	1LT	0-5315153	0865	4
SPAULDING DONALD S	COL	0-1280359	0965	4
SPAULDING NORBERT V	MAJ	0-1100776	0364	4
SPRAGUE GEORGE R	CPT	MN-3125318	0967	4
SPURLOCK ROBERT N	LTC	0-0346460	0266	4
STARKEY JAMES H	MAJ	0-2016211	0666	4
STARR LEONARD B	MAJ	0-0088498	0766	4
STEADMAN DONALD J	CPT	0-0959677	0866	4
STEELE CARL W	CW3	W-2151598	0364	4
STEWART ROBY F	MAJ	0-2073424	0765	4
STIDHAM ROBERT J	CPT	0-0098968	0667	4
STOKES JAMES R	MAJ	0-0566089	0564	4
STONE WILLIAM B	LTC	0-1174722	1164	4
STOUGHTON TOM R	M G	0-0018156	0667	4
STRANG TOM H	LTC	0-1115118	0565	4
STRECK ROYALLE A	MAJ	0-1923562	1263	4
STREET JR HAROLD L	LTC	0-0081263	0467	4
STRICKLEN WILLIAM A	COL	0-0031473	0866	4
STRUNCK JACK	MAJ	0-0997715	0964	4
STRUNK STANLEY W	CPT	0-5708414	0766	4
STUART CLARK C	CPT	0-2295848	1065	4
STUART DAVID M	CPT	0-4315841	1265	4
SUMNER GEORGE	LTC	0-1045270	0866	4
SWALM OLIVER E	CPT	0-4055949	0565	4
SWEENEY PATRICK C	1LT	0-5017536	0766	4
SZYMKOWICZ RAYMOND T	CPT	0-1528202	0264	4
TASHJIAN LEVON D	CPT	0-5217675	0763	4
TAYLOR H B	CW2	W-3350258	0467	4
TEGGE GLENN A	LTC	0-1317443	0667	4
TENNYSON WILLIAM W	COL	0-0301437	1266	4
TERRELL CHAILLE H	MAJ	0-1167250	0965	4
TERRY MILTON C	MAJ	0-1045279	0964	4
THOMAS CURTIS R	LTC	0-1184312	1065	4
THOMAS JACK W	MAJ	0-1540862	1063	4
THOMAS JR EMMETT N	MAJ	0-0967149	1064	4
TIPPINS JR BEDELL A	LTC	0-0065479	0665	4
TKACIK JOHN J	LTC	0-0026590	0665	4
TOM RAYMOND	CPT	0-5708988	0266	4
TOUCHETTE NORBERT E	LTC	0-0081873	0767	4
TOWNROE FREDERICK	MAJ	0-0063395	0866	4
TOWNSEND THEODORE H	MAJ	0-4030848	1166	4
TRAUL JAMES H	COL	0-1110853	0565	4
TRUAX HARRY D	WO1	W-2146984	0866	4
TRUJILLO MARY A	1LT	N-5417316	1166	4
TRUSSELL ARTHUR S	CW2	W-2213114	0467	4
VALLANDINGHAM MARGAR	MAJ	N-0725155	0667	4
VAN FLEET RAYMOND	COL	0-0051801	0866	4
VETTER GERHARDT R	LTC	0-1595235	1163	4
VICKERS ROBERT F	MAJ	0-1685625	0465	4
VIEHMANN FRANCIS L	CPT	0-5322030	0767	4
WAKEFORD MARY W	MAJ	L-0402047	0555	4
WALKER ADA M	MAJ	N-0002480	0564	4
WALL J V	LTC	0-1316249	1066	4
WALLACE MILTON I	LTC	0-0021467	1066	4
WALLS DAVID L	CPT	0-5712794	0867	4
WALSH NORBERT W	LTC	0-1169783	0766	4
WALSH PAUL J	LTC	0-1035616	0567	4
WALTER MERCER C	M G	0-0017151	0764	4
WARD ROBERT J	LTC	0-0035689	1063	4
WARD STEPHEN R	1LT	0-5018077	0965	4
WARDINSKI WALTER I	MAJ	0-1926813	0966	4
WARNER CARL L	1LT	0-0089635	0863	4
WARNER GEORGE P	B G	0-0032462	1166	4
WATSON ANN M	MAJ	N-0771777	1065	4
WEAVER CHARLES D	CPT	0-2315038	1266	4
WEBER ROBERT D	1LT	0-5531185	0166	4
WELCH CHARLES R	WO1	T-0005935	0664	4
WERTZ MILTON E	COL	0-0313535	0667	4
WEST JR ARTHUR L	M G	0-0025269	0867	4
WHEELER JARVIS A	CW2	W-3430231	0266	4
WHITE CHARLES	LTC	0-1183791	1166	4

TEMPORARY DISABILITY RETIRED LIST

NAME	GRADE	SVC NO	DATE RET MO YR	RET CODE
WHITE JOSEPH A	CPT	0-1313839	0965	4
WHITE ROBERT T	2LT	0-1996655	1066	4
WHITEHAIR ELMER V	LTC	C-1641058	C366	4
WHITEHURST WILLIAM W	CPT	0-4032531	0264	4
WHITESIDES ALAN B	LTC	0-2210067	0467	4
WHITTINGTON HULON B	MAJ	0-0954831	0363	4
WIEDEMER JR GEORGE J	LTC	0-1019576	0367	4
WIESE WALTER C	CW3	W-2144603	0965	4
WILCOX ALVIN J	CPT	C-1285676	0467	4
WILKINSON PAUL	LTC	0-1994722	C665	4
WILLIAMS EDWARD O	CPT	0-0997090	0467	4
WILLIAMS ERNEST E	MAJ	C-1931517	C967	4
WILLIAMS JACK L	COL	0-0042800	0265	4
WILLIAMS JR LOUIS F	CPT	0-0071428	0365	4
WILLIAMS JUANITA M	MAJ	N-0761223	0467	4
WILLIAMS KENDALL F	CW3	W-2153273	0464	4
WILLIAMS WILLIAM R	MAJ	0-0068176	0266	4
WILLIAMSON SR IVAN E	MAJ	C-2034015	C567	4
WILLIS HETTIE E	MAJ	N-0727793	0164	4
WITT WANDAL D	LTC	0-0505498	0863	4
WODA CHESTER J	CW3	W-2205735	0966	4
WOERNER GARY C	CPT	C-2313065	C367	4
WOLANGE NELLIE M	MAJ	N-0721273	C264	4
WOLCZIK WALTER	CPT	0-1646716	0664	4
WOODBURY JR LEROY B	COL	0-0030598	C266	4
WOODWARD JOSEPH G	LTC	0-0039101	0867	4
WOODWARD MARIE F	MAJ	N-0722363	0367	4
WOODWARC TIMOTHY F	LTC	C-1041689	C264	4
WREIOT NIEL M	LTC	0-0034753	C667	4
WRIGHT WILLIAM P	COL	0-0083574	0567	4
YEAST DENTON W	1LT	0-1176232	1264	4
YORMAN WILLIAM H	LTC	0-1995026	0767	4
ZALDUONDO FERNANDO	2LT	0-5826439	1064	4
ZEIGLER CLYDE C	COL	C-0019720	0265	4
ZIELKIEWICZ ANTHONY	MAJ	C-1823249	C366	4

SECTION 4

EMERGENCY OFFICERS RETIRED LIST

The Emergency Officers Retired List is composed of officers, other than Regular Army officers, who incurred physical disability in line of duty while in the service of the United States during World War I.

NAME	GRADE	SVC NO	DATE RET MO YR	RET CODE
ABERNATHY CHARLES	2LT		1028	5
ACKLEY JOHN F	CPT		0528	5
ADAMS DANIEL W	LTC		0628	5
ADAMS JOHN J	1LT		0528	5
ADAMSON DOVA W	1LT		0628	5
ADDISON JOHN D	1LT		0628	5
ADKINS EUGENE M	1LT		0728	5
AFFHOLDER IRVIN E	2LT		0429	5
AFFOLTER GEORGE R	1LT		0529	5
ALE JOHN H	1LT		0528	5
ALLEN CHARLES B	2LT		0628	5
ALLEN GROVER C	2LT		0628	5
ALLEY WILLIAM L	1LT		0728	5
AMET HERBERT P	1LT		0628	5
ANDERSON CECIL H	CPT		0628	5
ANDERSON CLIFTON R	2LT		0628	5
ANDERSON HANSON H	1LT		0329	5
ANDERSON JAMES W	2LT		0628	5
ANDREWS BENJAMIN T	2LT		0628	5
ANDREWS LAWRENCE G	2LT		0628	5
ANGOVE CLARENCE V	2LT		1128	5
APGAR GEORGE L	1LT		0528	5
APPERSON JOHN W	2LT		0628	5
ASHMUN LOUIS H	1LT		0928	5
BACHELDER FRANK E	MAJ		0828	5
BAGALEY EDWARD T	1LT		0828	5
BAIL FRANK W	1LT		0628	5
BAILEY GEORGE T	2LT		0628	5
BAILEY PAUL E	2LT		0628	5
BAILEY SAMUEL T	1LT		0628	5
BAISDEN JR ROY T	2LT		0928	5
BAKER HORACE	CPT		0628	5
BAKER JR RICHARD R	2LT		0828	5
BALL LOGAN M	2LT		0228	5
BANKS THOMAS G	CPT		0628	5
BARCAS VICTOR	CPT		1028	5
BARLOW ALFRED M	1LT		0628	5
BARNES GERALD C	1LT		0728	5
BARNES HARRY D	2LT		0429	5
BARR JESSE W	1LT		0728	5
BARTON CHARLES W	2LT		0628	5
BARTRAM ALFRED J	1LT		0628	5
BASH HENRY E	1LT		0628	5
BATES VERNON E	1LT		0528	5
BEAN HERBERT S	2LT		0528	5
BECK THEODORE	1LT		0628	5
BENNERS ALLEN C	1LT		0728	5
BENNETT CLARENCE W	2LT		1028	5
BERG ELMER W	1LT		0628	5
BERGLUND CLYDE V	CPT		0628	5
BERNARD MARCUS A	2LT		0628	5
BIDDLE JUSTICE M	2LT		0628	5
BILL ROSWELL H	2LT		0129	5
BILLINGS EARL K	2LT		0529	5
BIRKMAN FREDERICK	2LT		0828	5
BITTNER EARL R	2LT		0528	5
BLAIN WEST E	CPT		0528	5
BLAIR GEORGE A	CPT		0528	5
BLANCHARD HOWARD E	CPT		0628	5
BLAND ARTHUR V	1LT		0628	5
BLATHERWICK EDWIN	1LT		1028	5
BLECKAZ JOHN W	1LT		0429	5
BLOCK EDGAR N	CPT		0828	5
BOBST FRANK T	1LT		0628	5
BOCHER LAWRENCE C	2LT		0528	5
BOCOY ELIAS M	2LT		0728	5
BOERKE EDISON M	1LT		0628	5
BOLDRIDGE CHAUNCEY	CPT		0229	5
BOLIN FRANK E	CPT		0429	5
BORST FENTON F	1LT		0728	5
BOSTER HAROLD A	1LT		0828	5
BOTJER HENRY G	1LT		0628	5
BOYD CLARENCE E	1LT		0628	5
BOYD LEONARD C	1LT		0628	5
BOYD ROBERT S	1LT		0528	5

NAME	GRADE	SVC NO	DATE RET MO YR	RET CODE
BOYD THEODORE E	2LT		0628	5
BOYD WILLIS M	1LT		0728	5
BOYES ANDREW M C	1LT		0628	5
BRADBURY WILLIAM E	2LT		0628	5
BRADFORD LEONARD G	2LT		0740	5
BRADLEY GLADE T	CPT		1128	5
BRADLEY THOMAS R	1LT		0429	5
BREEN FREDERICK	1LT		0928	5
BREEN VINCENT C	CPT		0628	5
BRENNAN LENNOX C	CPT		0529	5
BROCHE ARTHUR T	1LT		0429	5
BROCK RAYMOND O	2LT		0628	5
BROCKMEYER EDWIN J	2LT		0329	5
BROOKS JR LOUIS J	CPT		0628	5
BROUGHTON AVERELL	1LT		0528	5
BROWN CLARENCE S	MAJ		0628	5
BROWN EMMETT W	CPT		0728	5
BROWN HARRY O	CPT		0529	5
BROWN JOHN D	1LT		0628	5
BROWN JR WILLIAM H	1LT		0628	5
BROWN MORROW O	CPT		0628	5
BROWN VAN LEONAR	1LT		0728	5
BROWNING HERBERT E	2LT		0840	5
BROWNING JOHN W	CPT		0528	5
BROYLES WATKINS A	2LT		0928	5
BRUCE WALTER H	LTC		1028	5
BRUENN JOHN J	2LT		1028	5
BRYANT DONALD R	2LT		0229	5
BRYANT FRED S	CPT		0828	5
BRYANT JOHN L	2LT		0529	5
BUCKLES WALTER A	CPT		0928	5
BUGGY FRANK R	CPT		0528	5
BUIE RODERICK M	CPT		0728	5
BUNGE ROBERT C	CPT		0528	5
BURNLEY EDWIN R	2LT		0129	5
BURNS ELLIS P	CPT		0429	5
BURNS JAMES F	CPT		0529	5
BURNS WILLIAM F	1LT		0628	5
BURR BENJAMIN E	1LT		0628	5
BUSH MARTIN M	1LT		0740	5
BUSH WALTER L	1LT		0528	5
BUTLER STANLEY C	1LT		0628	5
BUTT KIRK	2LT		0628	5
BYERS JAMES E	1LT		0628	5
BYRD JOHN H	1LT		0828	5
CAFFERTY EDMUND J	1LT		0628	5
CALLAHAN FRANCIS X	2LT		0329	5
CAMMER CLAUDE R	1LT		0628	5
CAMP EARL F	2LT		0528	5
CANN WILLIAM G	1LT		0529	5
CARDWELL FOWLER H	2LT		0940	5
CARLISLE JOHN G	1LT		0628	5
CARLSON GEORGE N	CPT		0628	5
CARLSON JOHN R	1LT		0628	5
CARNEY JAMES J	2LT		0628	5
CARPENTER CLARK B	1LT		0728	5
CARROLL DANIEL B	1LT		0628	5
CASEY JR WILLIAM F	2LT		0628	5
CATALA ARTURO	2LT		0828	5
CAVANAGH JOHN	CPT		0528	5
CHAFFEE CHARLES L	CPT		0840	5
CHAPMAN RALPH O C	1LT		0628	5
CHASE CLIFFORD E	MAJ		0528	5
CHAUDREN PERCY D	LTC		0628	5
CHEATHAM CLEMENT A	1LT		0828	5
CHEEK OVID H	1LT		0529	5
CHESHIRE JAMES W	1LT		0628	5
CHRISTENSEN WALTER	CPT		0329	5
CLARKE CECIL A	1LT		0628	5
CLEARY JOHN J	2LT		1028	5
CLEWORTH CLARENCE	2LT		1029	5
CLIFFORD JOHN J	CPT		0529	5
CLOWER CLIFFORD	1LT		0628	5
COATES ARTHUR F	2LT		0928	5
COFFMAN FRANK	2LT		0628	5

NAME	GRADE	SVC NO	DATE RET MO YR	RET CODE
COGHLAN CHARLES C	2LT		1028	5
COLBERT JOHN W	MAJ		0828	5
COLE ARTHUR C	1LT		0840	5
COLLINS LAWRENCE D	CPT		1128	5
COMERFORD JOHN T	CPT		0628	5
CONEY MASON C	1LT		0928	5
CONLIN ALAN B	2LT		0628	5
COOK MORTIMER P	1LT		0329	5
COOLEY BEAMON S	1LT		0828	5
COOVER MERLE E	1LT		0628	5
COPSEY FAY M	2LT		1028	5
CORCORAN WILLIAM W	1LT		0528	5
CORMIER JOSEPH A	2LT		0528	5
CORT THOMAS L	CPT		0928	5
COSGROVE LOUIS C	CPT		0928	5
COSTELLO JOHN T	CPT		0528	5
COSTLOW GLENN C	1LT		0628	5
COTCHER EDWARD H	CPT		0740	5
COURTWRIGHT BENJAM	MAJ		0828	5
COX HARVEY B	1LT		0628	5
COX WILLIAM M	CPT		0728	5
CRADDOCK ABRAM P J	CPT		0329	5
CRAIG HENRY H	CPT		0929	5
CRANDELL HERBERT R	2LT		0840	5
CRAWFORD HILARY H	1LT		0828	5
CRAWFORD LEWIS C	1LT		0628	5
CROCHERON HAL H	2LT		0728	5
CROSBY GASTON F	2LT		0628	5
CROSBY JAMES H	1LT		0628	5
CROSS JAMES	2LT		0628	5
CROW FLOYD A	2LT		0828	5
CULLEN FREDERICK	MAJ		0828	5
CUMMINS ROSCOE D	1LT		0740	5
CUNNINGHAM PETER P	2LT		0628	5
CURLEY HARRY O	CPT		0628	5
CUSHING JOHN B	1LT		1028	5
CZASKOS EDMUND T	CPT		0529	5
DABBS CHARLES H	CPT		0828	5
DALE PHILIP M	CPT		0828	5
DANIELS CHARLES L	CPT		0628	5
DARBY EARL M	1LT		0628	5
DASHIELL WILLIAM A	1LT		0528	5
DAVIS ARTHUR M	2LT		1028	5
DAVIS FREDERIC W	1LT		0728	5
DAVIS HARWELL G	MAJ		1028	5
DAVIS JOHN P	2LT		0628	5
DAVIS JOSEPH A	2LT		0628	5
DAVY JESSE J	CPT		0728	5
DAY WALLACE C	1LT		0828	5
DEAN WILLIAM K	1LT		0628	5
DECKER JOSEPH S	2LT		0828	5
DEERING PRENTISS C	1LT		0728	5
DEGRUMMOND HENRY C	1LT		0728	5
DELANCEY CLINTON C	CPT		0728	5
DEMALIGNON FRANCIS	2LT		0728	5
DEVINE JOSEPH J	2LT		0628	5
DILLARD ROBERT B	CPT		0628	5
DIXON FRANK M	2LT		0229	5
DODD WILLIAM A	1LT		0728	5
DODGE JR WILLIAM W	2LT		0628	5
DOEN RALPH W	CPT		0628	5
DOLAN JAMES H	1LT		1028	5
DORRIS BENJAMIN F	1LT		0628	5
DOUGLAS RICHARD	CPT		0528	5
DOW JULIAN N	CPT		0329	5
DOWNES JOSEPH W	2LT		0129	5
DOZLER JAMES C	1LT		0529	5
DRAYTON FREDERICK	CPT		0628	5
DRUGG WALTER C	2LT		0628	5
DRUMMOND FRANK C P	2LT		0628	5
DUNAGIN GEORGE A	1LT		0528	5
DYSON HENRY B	1LT		0628	5
EASTHAM GRANVILLE	1LT		0628	5
EBY ALLEN O	2LT		0529	5
ECK GUSTAVE E	CPT		0728	5

NAME	GRADE	SVC NO	DATE RET MO YR	RET CODE
EDDY EMMETT W	CPT		0529	5
EDENS NELSON W	1LT		0940	5
EDISON SAMUEL M	CPT		0628	5
EDMISTEN JR ANDREW	2LT		0329	5
EDWARDS BRYANT B	1LT		0628	5
EDWARDS HARRY O	1LT		0528	5
EDWARDS RICHARD	2LT		0728	5
EDWARDS WILL E	1LT		0728	5
EGGLETON WILLIAM J	CPT		0628	5
ELLIOTT WELLWOOD C	1LT		1028	5
ELLIS EDWARD K	CPT		0628	5
EMBRY TALTON H	2LT		0528	5
EMERSON JOHN E	2LT		0728	5
EMISON JAMES W	1LT		0740	5
ENSIGN CHESTER O	1LT		0628	5
EPPERSON CARRICK M	2LT		0628	5
ERICSSON RALPH B	1LT		0628	5
EUBANK ALBIA L	2LT		0529	5
EVERETT LEROY	1LT		0129	5
EWELL NATHANIEL	CPT		0628	5
FAIRCHILD HOXIE N	2LT		0529	5
FARRAR BENJAMIN O	2LT		0628	5
FAUGSTED GEORGE E	CPT		0628	5
FELDENHEIMER ROY	2LT		0628	5
FELFOLDY EDMOND	2LT		0129	5
FENNER FRED A	2LT		0628	5
FERGUSON DAVID MCG	2LT		0628	5
FERRIER WILLIAM H	CPT		0628	5
FESSELMEYER W T	2LT		0429	5
FICKLE MELVIN E	2LT		0628	5
FIECHTER WALTER	1LT		0928	5
FIREY FRANK P	1LT		0628	5
FISHER TUNIS H	2LT		0628	5
FITTS BURON R	2LT		0828	5
FITZHUGH EDWARD J	2LT		0529	5
FLEMING JOHN A	1LT		0828	5
FLICK FRED S	2LT		0529	5
FLOOD JOHN V	2LT		0628	5
FLOOD PETER H A	CPT		0840	5
FLYNN BERNARD A	1LT		0628	5
FLYNN FRANK S	CPT		0628	5
FOGERTY CLEMENT A	COL		0129	5
FOLEY THOMAS F	MAJ		0628	5
FOLKEDAHL JOSEPH B	2LT		0628	5
FOOTE ALFRED F	LTC		0828	5
FOREMAN EVAN H	CPT		0329	5
FOREMAN HERBERT S	1LT		0828	5
FOX ROBERT M	CPT		0728	5
FOX WILLIAM S	1LT		0628	5
FRANKLIN RICHARD	2LT		0840	5
FRARY LEWIS S	2LT		0628	5
FRASER CHARLES E	CPT		0528	5
FRASER DONALD W	2LT		0628	5
FRAZIER WILLIAM	CPT		0628	5
FREDEN GUSTAF E N	2LT		0628	5
FREEMAN JOHN I	CPT		0129	5
FREY NEWT	1LT		0628	5
FULLER HENRY C	2LT		0628	5
FULMER ROLAND H	CPT		0628	5
FUSS JOHN C	CPT		0728	5
GALLISHAW JOHN	2LT		0529	5
GAMBLE CLARK R	1LT		0840	5
GANFIELD ROY W	1LT		0628	5
GARDNER GEORGE W	1LT		0628	5
GARDNER WILLIAM J	CPT		1028	5
GARRETTE EDWIN C	2LT		0628	5
GARRISON DAVID M	1LT		0628	5
GARRY JAMES J	2LT		0728	5
GARVEY PHIL F	2LT		0628	5
GATTERCAM EUGENE A	1LT		0928	5
GEER CLARENCE W	CPT		0728	5
GEIS CARL E	CPT		0841	5
GELLERSTEDT ROBERT	1LT		0429	5
GENTNER JOHN M	CPT		0529	5
GERARD FRED L	1LT		0129	5

NAME	GRADE	SVC NO	DATE RET MO YR	RET CODE
GERSTENKORN ROY E	1LT		0628	5
GESELL WALTER R	2LT		0928	5
GETTINGS JAMES A	CPT		0628	5
GIFT LYLE H	CPT		0628	5
GILBERT ROY O	2LT		0628	5
GILLICK OWEN P	1LT		0628	5
GILLIS FREDERICK	1LT		0128	5
GILLIS JOHN A	2LT		0628	5
GILMOUR FREDERICK	CPT		0628	5
GIVENS FRED G	CPT		0529	5
GJELLUM ARTHUR B	CPT		0628	5
GLIDDEN BURT R	2LT		0628	5
GOLDMAN ABRAHAM S	2LT		0628	5
GOODMAN ALLEN L	1LT		0628	5
GOODSPEED EARL L	1LT		0628	5
GORE VERNON	2LT		0628	5
GOSSETT ECKLEY G	CPT		0728	5
GOULD JR JAMES R	1LT		1028	5
GRAHAM STUART D	2LT		0628	5
GRANT JAMES L	2LT		0628	5
GRAUPNER ADOLPHUS	CPT		0528	5
GRAVES HAROLD F	2LT		0529	5
GRAY GEORGE E	CPT		0728	5
GRAY JESSY F	1LT		0628	5
GRAY LOWELL H	2LT		0529	5
GRAYSON THOMAS J	COL		1028	5
GREEMAN NELSON W L	1LT		0129	5
GREENE ALBERT V N	2LT		0528	5
GREENE PAUL C	1LT		0728	5
GRIESEMER ZADOC L	MAJ		0628	5
GRIMES EUSTIS B	2LT		0728	5
GROAH EDWARD H	1LT		0628	5
GUICE JOHN I	1LT		0429	5
GUNDERSON SOPHUS C	2LT		1028	5
GUY THOMAS J	2LT		0628	5
HAAN ALBERT E	CPT		0528	5
HAIGHT WALTER L	CPT		0628	5
HAIR ARTHUR J	1LT		0828	5
HALL EDWARD F	2LT		0529	5
HALL KENNETH C	2LT		0628	5
HALL WILLIAM O	1LT		0628	5
HALLEY JAMES M	2LT		0628	5
HALVERSON HENRY F	CPT		0429	5
HAMILL ROBERT M	2LT		0628	5
HAMPSHIRE CLAUDE C	1LT		0628	5
HANABERGH FRANK J	MAJ		0628	5
HANDLY LUCIUS L	1LT		0728	5
HANSEN JOHN C	CPT		0329	5
HARNED POMEROY	1LT		0628	5
HARRIS ARTHUR C	1LT		0628	5
HARRIS EMORY L	CPT		0928	5
HARRIS RUFUS C	1LT		0828	5
HART GEORGE C	CPT		0628	5
HARTNETT CORNELIUS	2LT		0728	5
HARWOOD MANTON F	1LT		0628	5
HATCH CARL T	2LT		0529	5
HATCH ROSCOE C	1LT		0229	5
HATCHER WILLIAM R	1LT		0628	5
HAUBOLD EGON G	CPT		0728	5
HAUSER SIMEON F	2LT		0528	5
HAVERSTICK FRANK W	CPT		0229	5
HAYS HARLAND R	2LT		1128	5
HAYS VERNE	1LT		0628	5
HEALEY PATRICK F	1LT		0728	5
HEARN GUILFORD C	1LT		0528	5
HECK MAURICE E	CPT		0828	5
HELMER PHIL F	2LT		0628	5
HEMPSTONE FRANK W	1LT		0529	5
HENDERSON JAMES A	2LT		0628	5
HENDLER ULLMANN C	CPT		0429	5
HENNESSEY CARLETON	1LT		0429	5
HENRY JR THOMAS J	1LT		0628	5
HENRY ROBERT H	2LT		0628	5
HENSKE GODFREY W	1LT		0728	5
HERRICK MYRON C	2LT		0728	5

NAME	GRADE	SVC NO	DATE RET MO YR	RET CODE
HEWITT JOHN E	MAJ		0628	5
HEYMAN FRED G	2LT		1028	5
HICKS JACOB L	CPT		0628	5
HICKS SAMUEL C	1LT		0840	5
HILL CHARLES A	CPT		0740	5
HILL EDWARD C	CPT		0620	5
HILLIARD CLAUDE P	2LT		0529	5
HINCHMAN EDWARD M	1LT		0529	5
HITZ ALEX M	1LT		0628	5
HOCKRIDGE RICHARD	1LT		0628	5
HODGSON HAROLD B	2LT		1040	5
HOENSTINE FLOYD G	2LT		0628	5
HOFFMAN ARTHUR R	1LT		0628	5
HOGAN CICERO F	CPT		0628	5
HOLMAN WILLIAM S	MAJ		0628	5
HOOK JAMES P	1LT		0628	5
HOPKINS WAYNE L	2LT		0628	5
HOUCHIN ERVIN W	2LT		0628	5
HOUSTON CLARENCE P	CPT		0628	5
HOWARD WILLIAM H	1LT		0628	5
HOYT FRANK W	2LT		0429	5
HOYT HOWARD C	1LT		0229	5
HUDGENS ROBERT W	CPT		0628	5
HUEBNER ALBERT F	CPT		0628	5
HUGHEY GEORGE H	1LT		0628	5
HUGHSTON JAMES B	2LT		0628	5
HULL RICHARD M	1LT		0628	5
HULTZEN LEE S	1LT		0528	5
HUNT HERBERT P	1LT		0628	5
HUNT WILLIAM C	2LT		0628	5
HUNTER GILBERT M	1LT		0628	5
HUNTER JR DAVID	CPT		0529	5
HUNTER WILLIAM G	CPT		0628	5
HUTCHESON ROBERT S	2LT		0529	5
HUTCHINSON ALVA R	2LT		0628	5
HUTCHISON FRANCIS	CPT		0628	5
HYNDS ARTHUR A	2LT		0628	5
INCE EDWARD G	CPT		0528	5
INMAN GILBERT P	1LT		0728	5
IRELAND WALTER M	1LT		0229	5
IRION EDWIN C	1LT		0447	5
JACOB CLYDE H	1LT		0628	5
JACOBS JOHN M	2LT		0628	5
JACOBUS JESSE J	1LT		0429	5
JAMES ALLEN M	2LT		0628	5
JEFFERS GEORGE L	2LT		0628	5
JELLUM KRISTEN	1LT		0129	5
JERVEY FRANK J	CPT		0528	5
JOHNSON CORTLAND A	2LT		0429	5
JOHNSON WILLIAM B	1LT		0728	5
JONES ALBERT E B	2LT		0429	5
JONES CASEY M	1LT		0628	5
JONES CHARLES H	1LT		0628	5
JONES FRED A	2LT		0628	5
JONES HENRY B	1LT		0628	5
JONES HUBERT B	CPT		0628	5
JONES JAMES W	CPT		1028	5
JONES RAY W	2LT		0628	5
JONES WILLIAM W	1LT		1028	5
JOSEPHSON MAURICE	1LT		0629	5
JULIEN CARL T	2LT		0628	5
KAMINSKI THEOPHILE	2LT		1028	5
KAMPMEIER ARTHUR J	1LT		1028	5
KANE JACK F	2LT		0740	5
KEARNS THOMAS W	1LT		0928	5
KEATH HOWARD R	2LT		0628	5
KEENAN BARRY	1LT		0429	5
KEIM THURMAN E	CPT		0429	5
KELLEY HENRY E	1LT		0429	5
KELLEY JAMES	2LT		0628	5
KELLEY JAMES R	2LT		0628	5
KELLEY RALPH A	1LT		0329	5
KELLIS JOHN H	1LT		0628	5
KELLY HARRY F	2LT		0628	5
KELLY JR RICHARD B	CPT		0528	5

NAME	GRADE	SVC NO	DATE RET MO YR	RET CODE
KEMMAN HUGO A	2LT		0628	5
KENNEDY HARVEY J	2LT		0628	5
KERNS SAMUEL M	MAJ		0828	5
KERR JAMES	2LT		0928	5
KESKEY CHARLES A	1LT		0628	5
KESTNBAUM MEYER	2LT		0429	5
KEYSER GEORGE A	1LT		0840	5
KIBBE GORDON M	1LT		0628	5
KILLIKELLY C	CPT		0528	5
KIMBALL GEORGE P	1LT		0628	5
KING EDWARD	1LT		1028	5
KING JR SAMUEL L	2LT		0528	5
KIRBY THOMAS	CPT		0429	5
KIRK GEORGE B	1LT		0828	5
KIRKPATRICK LESTER	1LT		0628	5
KIVLIN ALFRED P	2LT		0628	5
KNAUTH FELIX W	1LT		0628	5
KNEEBONE JOHN H	2LT		0529	5
KNIGHT CHANDLER S	1LT		0728	5
KNIGHT LAURENCE E	1LT		0628	5
KNOBLOCK CECIL C	2LT		0529	5
KNOX LEROY J	2LT		0828	5
KOENNE EDWARD A	2LT		0429	5
KOLPIEN KENNETH H	2LT		0628	5
KRAUSE ROBERT S	1LT		0628	5
KRICHEL JOSEPH H	1LT		0329	5
KRIECHBAUM ROY R	CPT		0628	5
KUEHNE ALBERT W	1LT		1028	5
KVETON PATRICK H	CPT		0628	5
LA PAZE PERCY W	2LT		0628	5
LACEWELL ALEXANDER	2LT		0628	5
LAING DEWITT B	1LT		0628	5
LAMB ORIN R	1LT		0129	5
LANDRUM MARVIN M	1LT		0828	5
LANSDALE GEORGE L	CPT		0628	5
LANSDEN DAVID S	2LT		0628	5
LASSITER JOHN H	CPT		0828	5
LAUER KURVIN W	2LT		1028	5
LAUX THOMAS C	2LT		0628	5
LAWSON EDWIN L	1LT		0528	5
LAWSON HENRY G	CPT		0740	5
LEDFORD JOHN	1LT		0228	5
LEE HENRY D	2LT		0629	5
LEE THOMAS H	1LT		0528	5
LEFELER ROBERT W	1LT		0628	5
LEFTWICH SNOWDEN M	CPT		0629	5
LEGG HENRY F	1LT		0129	5
LEHARDY FRANK M	2LT		0229	5
LEISNER PAUL W	2LT		0528	5
LEMBKE CHARLES H	1LT		0728	5
LEMON ANDREW M	2LT		0528	5
LEOPOLD ELMER E	2LT		0628	5
LERSCH JOSEPH F	2LT		0728	5
LEWIS RAYMOND P	2LT		0429	5
LIGGETT HARRY R	2LT		0728	5
LITTLE LOWELL	CPT		0628	5
LITTY JOHN C	2LT		0628	5
LIVELY CARLOS J	2LT		0928	5
LONGFELLOW HAROLD	2LT		0841	5
LOOMIS WALTER O	2LT		0528	5
LOPEZ ENRIQUE	2LT		0328	5
LOTZ TRUMAN L	2LT		0628	5
LOW HAROLD W	1LT		0629	5
LOYE HARRY A	2LT		0628	5
LUCK EVERETT J	1LT		0628	5
LUNDBLAD WALTER E	CPT		0429	5
LUNSTEAD EUGENE L	2LT		0728	5
LUTZ JR JAMES A	1LT		0628	5
LYKSETT ALBERT J	1LT		0928	5
MAC DOUGALL DANIEL	2LT		0728	5
MAC MURPHY ALLEN B	2LT		1028	5
MAC NUTT CECIL C	2LT		0628	5
MAGUIRE EDWARD B	1LT		0728	5
MALONE BENJAMIN F	2LT		0329	5
MANARD HARDIN B	1LT		0253	5

NAME	GRADE	SVC NO	DATE RET MO YR	RET CODE
MANLY JETHRO	CPT		0728	5
MANN CHARLES H	MAJ		0628	5
MANN EARL W	1LT		0628	5
MARCUS SAMUEL M	CPT		0429	5
MARINE JAMES S	1LT		1164	5
MARKUS NORBERT W	2LT		0628	5
MARQUISS CHARLES R	1LT		0628	5
MARSHALL CLYDE M	2LT		0528	5
MARSHALL FOSTER	2LT		0528	5
MARSHALL THOMAS B	1LT		0628	5
MARTIN WILLIAM G	2LT		0728	5
MARX ROBERTS S	CPT		0628	5
MARXMILLER HARRY G	MAJ		0628	5
MASON CLINTON C	CPT		0628	5
MASON JAMES R D	1LT		0628	5
MATHIS ALLEN W	1LT		0628	5
MAYVILLE EDWARD M	CPT		0728	5
MC BRAUN JAMES B	2LT		0728	5
MC CALL GEORGE T	1LT		0628	5
MC CANN JAMES S	1LT		0529	5
MC CARTY WILLIAM H	2LT		0628	5
MC CAWLEY HARRISON R	1LT		0946	5
MC CLELLAND FRANK A	1LT		0628	5
MC CLUER EDWIN A	1LT		0628	5
MC COLLOM FRANCIS B	CPT		0840	5
MC CUE EARL N	MAJ		0628	5
MC CUNE MURRAY M	2LT		0628	5
MC DANIEL WINFRED P	CPT		0628	5
MC DONALD F H	1LT		0728	5
MC DONALD GEORGE T	1LT		0329	5
MC DONOUGH HUBERT B	2LT		0529	5
MC DONOUGH JAMES P	1LT		1029	5
MC DOWELL STEWART A	2LT		1140	5
MC ELROY JOSEPH E	CPT		0628	5
MC GUIRE JAMES A	1LT		0628	5
MC INTYRE HARRY J	2LT		1028	5
MC KAY ARTHUR J	2LT		0628	5
MC KAY JAMES O	1LT		0628	5
MC KENNEY HARRY	2LT		0428	5
MC KENZIE GEORGE S	2LT		0628	5
MC KILLIPS C F	1LT		0741	5
MC LEAN CHARLES E	1LT		0129	5
MC LEOD HOWARD L	1LT		0628	5
MC MANIGAL JOHN W	1LT		0628	5
MC NEIL HARRY D	1LT		1128	5
MC NERNEY JOSEPH O	1LT		0628	5
MC QUEEN JOE W	CPT		0628	5
MC TAGGART ERNEST	1LT		0728	5
MC VEY ERIC A	CPT		0628	5
MEADE RAY	1LT		0828	5
MEEHAN EDWARD J	LTC		1128	5
MELLEN JR CHASE	2LT		0129	5
MENEFEE MARVIN J	1LT		0329	5
MERRILL GEORGE R	1LT		1028	5
MERRILL HENRY M	2LT		1128	5
MERRILL ROBERT A	MAJ		0828	5
MESS GEORGE R	2LT		0429	5
METZROTH CARL F	1LT		0628	5
MEYERING WILLIAM D	CPT		0628	5
MEYERS WILLIAM H	LTC		0129	5
MIDDLETON ULYSSES G	1LT		0528	5
MILLBERRY MARK A	CPT		0429	5
MILLER BENJAMIN W	1LT		0728	5
MILLER BOYCE E	CPT		0728	5
MILLER CLARENCE L	1LT		0928	5
MILLER DAVID B	1LT		0528	5
MILLER EARL G	CPT		0628	5
MILLER EDWIN E	CPT		0628	5
MILLER FRANCIS L	2LT		0628	5
MILLER FRANKLIN L	MAJ		0528	5
MILLER GEORGE H	2LT		1028	5
MILLER HAYCOCK H	1LT		0628	5
MILLER JESSE C	2LT		0628	5
MILLER LOUIS L	1LT		0229	5
MILLER WALTER J	1LT		0628	5

EMERGENCY OFFICERS RETIRED LIST

NAME	GRADE	SVC NO	DATE RET MO YR	RET CODE
MILLER WARREN J	2LT		1028	5
MILLIS JOHN M	2LT		0329	5
MILLSAP CHARLES H	1LT		1040	5
MILUM VERN G	2LT		0628	5
MITCHELL FRANK M	1LT		0528	5
MOLONEY HERBERT W	1LT		0628	5
MOORE JOHN R	2LT		0628	5
MOORE WILLIAM A	2LT		0829	5
MOORE WILLIAM B	2LT		0928	5
MORGAN GEORGE H	2LT		0529	5
MORGAN LEWIS R	CPT		0628	5
MORGENSTERN A H	1LT		0229	5
MORRIS GRAYDON L	2LT		0840	5
MORRIS HAROLD R	2LT		0728	5
MORRISON LEWIS R	2LT		0728	5
MOSER ELMER R	1LT		0728	5
MOSES ANDREW	1LT		0628	5
MOSES ROBERT L	1LT		0628	5
MOUSER MERRILL K	1LT		0628	5
MULLER JULIUS	1LT		1028	5
MURDOCK JAMES D	CPT		0129	5
MURPHY EWELL E	2LT		0728	5
MURREY JOSEPH H	1LT		0728	5
MURTHA WILLIAM H	2LT		0628	5
MYERS JAY H	1LT		0528	5
MYRLAND EIEL H	1LT		0529	5
NANCE ALEXANDER	1LT		0628	5
NASH JOSEPH E	2LT		0828	5
NEWELL JAMES K	1LT		0928	5
NEWHALL RICHARD A	2LT		0628	5
NEWSOM ERLE T	CPT		0728	5
NEWTON ROY C	2LT		0129	5
NICHOLLS MELVIN H	2LT		0628	5
NICOL ALEXANDER	1LT		0628	5
NIMS JR FREDERICK	2LT		0429	5
NOBLE GEORGE B	1LT		0229	5
NOWLIN JR JOSEPH C	1LT		0628	5
NOYES EDWIN M	2LT		0740	5
OBERSCHMIDT LEON P	2LT		0529	5
OBRIEN JAMES F	2LT		0628	5
OBRIEN MARTIN A	1LT		0429	5
OBRIEN PATRICK F	1LT		0628	5
OBRIEN RAYMOND J	1LT		0628	5
OHMART WALTER A	1LT		0628	5
OKELLEY LAWRENCE L	2LT		0429	5
OLDHAM RALPH W	2LT		0628	5
OLEARY EDWIN D	2LT		1128	5
OLIVER FRED N	MAJ		0528	5
ONEIL FRANK P	CPT		0628	5
ONEILL EDWARD G	2LT		0329	5
ORRELL EUGENE D	1LT		0628	5
OSBORN MORSE F	CPT		0728	5
OWENS FRANK M	2LT		0628	5
OWENS JOHN J	CPT		0528	5
PAGE MARION W	CPT		0628	5
PARK DURWARD B	CPT		0529	5
PARKER EMERSON F	2LT		0129	5
PARKS PAUL B	2LT		0728	5
PARRISH EARL T	1LT		0628	5
PATTEN MORGAN H	1LT		0828	5
PAUL CHARLES H	1LT		0840	5
PAUL EDWARD R	1LT		0628	5
PEACOCK JR ELI J	MAJ		0628	5
PEARSALL FRANCIS S	2LT		0628	5
PECKHAM HOWARD D	CPT		0628	5
PEEL JR DAVID W	1LT		0629	5
PEISTRUP EDWARD C	1LT		0329	5
PELTON HAROLD P	CPT		0628	5
PENNINGTON EDGAR J	2LT		0628	5
PERRY HAROLD C	2LT		0828	5
PERRY OWEN H	1LT		0728	5
PERRY RUFUS A	2LT		0542	5
PETTY WALLACE S	CPT		0628	5
PHELPS FRANCIS M	1LT		0629	5
PHELPS JOSEPH S	1LT		0328	5
PHILLIPS GEORGE W	2LT		0628	5
PHILLIPS WENDEL J	1LT		0628	5
PIERZYNSKI T S	1LT		0728	5
PINNEY NORMAN W	2LT		0728	5
PINTO RENE W	2LT		0628	5
PLANT GEORGE F	CPT		0329	5
PORTMANN MILTON C	MAJ		0529	5
POST FREDERICK	CPT		0129	5
POTTER WILLIAM J	MAJ		0628	5
POWELL ALFRED T	CPT		0628	5
POWELL HERBERT J	1LT		0728	5
POWELL MATHEW J	2LT		0928	5
POWER HERMAN	1LT		0628	5
PRICE EDWARD H	1LT		0628	5
PRITCHARD GEORGE L	1LT		0728	5
PROSISE ALAN B	1LT		0728	5
PRUETT EUGENE F	2LT		0628	5
PULLIS STEPHEN E	CPT		0628	5
PYLES HARRY H	2LT		0629	5
RADEMACHER FRED M	CPT		0840	5
RAEDER WILLIAM J	1LT		0628	5
RALPH KENDRICK J	1LT		0628	5
RANLETT LOUIS F	2LT		0628	5
RAY LECIL S	2LT		0528	5
READ WILLIAM S	2LT		1128	5
REARDON TIMOTHY J	2LT		1128	5
REBUCK WALTER E	2LT		0628	5
REED CHARLES S	2LT		0329	5
REEVES FRANK H	1LT		1028	5
REILLY JOSEPH J	CPT		0628	5
RENSHAWE CLARENCE W	1LT		0828	5
REPASS MERLE M	2LT		0728	5
RICE HAROLD E	2LT		0628	5
RICE MAX	2LT		0628	5
RICHARDSON HARRY F	CPT		0628	5
RICKETTS JOSEPH W	CPT		1128	5
RIDER CARROLL A	2LT		0628	5
RIECKE HENRY A	CPT		0628	5
RIEHL LOUIS A	2LT		0429	5
RILEY FRANKLIN G	CPT		0628	5
RITCHIE JR WILLIAM	CPT		0728	5
ROBB GEORGE S	1LT		0141	5
ROBERT JAMES J	MAJ		1028	5
ROBERTS WILLIAM J	CPT		0628	5
ROBINSON ARTHUR	2LT		0628	5
ROBINSON FRANK C	MAJ		0628	5
ROBINSON GUY T	1LT		0928	5
ROBISON EDWARD M	CPT		0528	5
ROEMER LEON F	2LT		0529	5
ROGERS ALAN	2LT		0828	5
ROGERS GEORGE B	1LT		0628	5
ROGERS JOHN A	2LT		0528	5
ROLLER FRANCIS O	2LT		1028	5
ROSBOROUGH WILLIAM M	1LT		0429	5
ROSENFIELD MILTON S	2LT		0628	5
ROSS JOHN J W	CPT		0229	5
ROWAN WALTER F	2LT		0329	5
ROWELL JAMES T	1LT		0628	5
RUFF HORACE E	MAJ		0528	5
RUHNKA ROY	CPT		0628	5
RYALL ERNEST V	2LT		0529	5
RYAN CHARLES C	1LT		1040	5
RYAN EDWARD L	1LT		0329	5
RYAN THOMAS A	CPT		1028	5
RYLANDER WILBER E	2LT		0628	5
SABOL STEPHEN A	1LT		1028	5
SALADINE JOHN W	1LT		0840	5
SAMS FERROL A	CPT		0129	5
SANCHEZ GILBERT J	2LT		1128	5
SANDERS JAMES L	2LT		0529	5
SAUNDERS WILLIAM H	2LT		0628	5
SAVAGE JAMES A	2LT		0728	5
SAWHILL DONALD V	2LT		0229	5
SAYRES ARTHUR R	1LT		0628	5
SCARBOROUGH C C	1LT		0628	5
SCARLES HERBERT L	1LT		0229	5
SCHAEFFER JOHN A	1LT		0429	5
SCHARDT ARLIE A	LTC		0352	5
SCHAUFELBERGER H S	2LT		0529	5
SCHELLER LOUIS	1LT		0628	5
SCHELTER LOUIS J	CPT		0828	5
SCHIDE CLARENCE C	2LT		0628	5
SCHLESINGER ALBERT L	2LT		1128	5
SCHNECK MAXIMILIAN	2LT		0628	5
SCHOENBERG LOUIS	2LT		0529	5
SCHUH CARL A	1LT		0728	5
SCHULTZ WILLIAM J	1LT		0628	5
SCHUMACHER CLARK P	1LT		0628	5
SCHUMACHER JOHN F	1LT		0628	5
SCHUSTER GEORGE A R	2LT		1028	5
SCOTT BYRON R	2LT		1128	5
SCOTT JOHN W	2LT		0628	5
SCOTT SAMUEL H	1LT		0728	5
SCOTT THOMAS W	1LT		0529	5
SCOTT WILLIAM R	CPT		0628	5
SCRAFTON WALLACE T	1LT		0628	5
SEAGRAVES CHARLES	1LT		0628	5
SEE MART	MAJ		0728	5
SERGEANT FLOYD A	2LT		0628	5
SEVIER HENRY C	2LT		0828	5
SHAMBURGER LACY L	1LT		0429	5
SHARKEY RALPH L	1LT		0628	5
SHARP ROY F	2LT		0628	5
SHARTLE ALBERT J	1LT		0628	5
SHAUGHNESSY PAUL F	CPT		0528	5
SHEA MARTIN C	2LT		0828	5
SHEEHAN EDWARD B	CPT		0628	5
SHEEHAN WALTER B	1LT		0628	5
SHERIDAN LEO D	2LT		0628	5
SHERIDAN WALTER D	2LT		0628	5
SHERWOOD GEORGE W	2LT		0728	5
SHEWALTER GEORGE H	1LT		0529	5
SHINKEL JACOB M	1LT		0628	5
SHISLER GEORGE	2LT		0628	5
SHOEMAKER GEORGE J	2LT		0728	5
SHOEMAKER PHILIP C	1LT		0628	5
SHOLES EBER C	2LT		0628	5
SHRIVER ALFRED W	1LT		0329	5
SHRIVER RAY D	1LT		0429	5
SHUSTER JR WILLIAM H	1LT		0229	5
SIMMONS BENJAMIN F	2LT		0529	5
SIMPKINS WILLARD S	1LT		0728	5
SIMPSON CHARLES P	2LT		0841	5
SLYH DONALD M	1LT		0629	5
SMEAD BURTON A	LTC		0628	5
SMEALLIE JAMES D	1LT		0628	5
SMITH BERT L	CPT		0229	5
SMITH CLARENCE R	1LT		0628	5
SMITH EDWARD P	2LT		0628	5
SMITH EMMETT P	CPT		0528	5
SMITH ERNEST D	1LT		0529	5
SMITH HAROLD F	1LT		1028	5
SMITH HOWARD G	1LT		0628	5
SMITH IRVING D	1LT		0528	5
SMITH JOHN H	1LT		1140	5
SMITH JR DANIEL T	2LT		0429	5
SMITH ROBERT L	CPT		0528	5
SMITH SAMUEL T	1LT		0529	5
SMITH SHIRLEY S	1LT		0628	5
SMITH TAYLOR B	1LT		0628	5
SMITH WILLIAM D	CPT		0329	5
SMITH WINGATE	2LT		0728	5
SNIDER ROBERT J	CPT		0629	5
SNOWDEN FRANK B	1LT		0729	5
SOUTHARD EARL	1LT		0628	5
SOUTHARD WILLIAM F	LTC		1028	5
SPALDING OLIVER R	1LT		0429	5
SPARKS DENTON H	2LT		0829	5
SPENCER JR C R	2LT		0628	5
SPILLYARDS HENRY H	1LT		0628	5
SPONY ALBERT	1LT		0628	5
SPRINGER MARK O	CPT		1029	5
SQUIER LOWELL W	2LT		0628	5
ST JOHN FRANK L	CPT		0529	5
STAGGERS WILLIAM L	1LT		0528	5
STEARNS CAREY S	2LT		0628	5
STEFFY JOHN L	1LT		0628	5
STEIDLE EDWARD	CPT		0528	5
STEINBERGER OTTO C	CPT		0628	5
STELLING SIDNEY J	1LT		0628	5
STEPHENS CLARENCE C	1LT		0628	5
STEUART EDWARD P	2LT		0329	5
STEVENS JR GEORGE R	1LT		0628	5
STEVENSON MAURICE S	1LT		0528	5
STEWART HOWARD B	2LT		0628	5
STEWART JOHN A	CPT		0628	5
STICKNEY GEORGE L	CPT		0740	5
STILLWELL RICHARD C	2LT		0528	5
STOUT FRANCIS R	2LT		0628	5
STOUT WILLIAM	CPT		0528	5
STOWBRIDGE JR R W	1LT		0628	5
STRATTON JOHN M	1LT		0528	5
STRAYER ELMER C	1LT		0628	5
STROLE GLENN F	2LT		0141	5
STRONG ELBERT	1LT		0728	5
STROTHER CARL R	1LT		1128	5
STRYKER WILLIAM L	CPT		0229	5
SULLIVAN DANIEL J	CPT		0740	5
SULLIVAN LESTER E	2LT		0928	5
SULLIVAN WALTER J	CPT		0628	5
SUMNER CHARLES F	CPT		1040	5
SUTTON DANIEL F	1LT		0728	5
SWEENEY JAMES L	2LT		1028	5
SWOPE JOHN D	2LT		0329	5
SYMES CLARENCE D	CPT		0528	5
TALLMADGE F A	CPT		0828	5
TAYLOR BEN B	2LT		0728	5
TAYLOR BRADLEY	2LT		0822	5
TAYLOR NORMAN B	CPT		1028	5
TENNEY GERALD E	CPT		0728	5
TERRALL RALPH E	1LT		0928	5
THAANUM DEAN C	2LT		0728	5
THACKER EDWARD C	2LT		0728	5
THAYER WAYNE	1LT		0628	5
THETFORD ALPHONSO	1LT		0528	5
THICKSTUN DORSEY W	LTC		0628	5
THOMAS JOHN W M	2LT		0628	5
THOMAS LAWRENCE G	1LT		0429	5
THOMPSON DAYTON R	2LT		0840	5
THOMPSON DONALD R	1LT		0728	5
THOMPSON GEORGE	2LT		0828	5
THOMPSON HERBERT L	CPT		0628	5
THOMPSON HERMAN W	CPT		0628	5
THOMPSON JOHN B	2LT		0728	5
THOMPSON JOHN H	1LT		0728	5
THOMPSON JOSIAH D	CPT		0529	5
THORNBURG ZEBULON B	1LT		0528	5
TILDEN JOHN A	1LT		0628	5
TILGHMAN GEORGE D	1LT		0528	5
TITTMANN EUGENE C	1LT		0728	5
TOLLEY JR CHARLES S	1LT		0628	5
TONGATE JAMES M	2LT		1128	5
TRAUT FRED G	1LT		0628	5
TRAVERS WILLIAM A	2LT		0728	5
TUCKER CLAUDE C	1LT		0628	5
TURCK RAYMOND C	COL		0329	5
TURNER JR WALTER L	2LT		0629	5
TWITCHELL F M	2LT		0628	5
TWOMEY THOMAS A	1LT		0529	5
TYLER CLYDE L	1LT		0529	5
TYSON ALFRED	1LT		0728	5
TYSON JOHN T	CPT		0628	5
UPTON FORD J	1LT		0628	5
VINCENT JAMES A	CPT		0628	5
VOGES JOHN C	2LT		0628	5

EMERGENCY OFFICERS RETIRED LIST

NAME	GRADE	SVC NO	DATE RET MO YR	RET CODE
VOLL BERNARD J	1LT		0628	5
VOLLENWEIDER W F	2LT		C628	5
VOLLMER WILLIAM S	2LT		C928	5
WALE GARLAND B	1LT		C628	5
WALKER JOHN H	2LT		0628	5
WALKER NEWTON W	2LT		0628	5
WALLACE GEORGE L	1LT		0628	5
WALLER LUTHER H	1LT		0329	5
WALSH FRANCIS W	1LT		C728	5
WALSH MALCOLM	1LT		C429	5
WALTMIRE JR C A	2LT		1040	5
WALTON JAMES O	1LT		1128	5
WARE THOMAS G	2LT		0628	5
WARNER RUSSELL A	1LT		0528	5
WARREN EDWARD R	1LT		0528	5
WASSON CLYDE H	1LT		0529	5
WAYBUR ROBERT R	1LT		C529	5
WEATHERFORD ZADOC L	1LT		0628	5
WEAVER ROBERT H	2LT		0628	5
WEBB BYFORD H	1LT		0429	5
WEBSTER GEORGE D	CPT		0628	5
WEED LEE H	2LT		0728	5
WELLS LEROY T	2LT		C628	5
WENDE JOHN A	1LT		0628	5
WERTZ HAROLD B	1LT		0828	5
WESTPHAL FREDERICK	2LT		0828	5
WESTRATE WILLIAM	1LT		0628	5
WHALEY HARRY R	2LT		0628	5
WHEELER EDGAR L	2LT		0928	5
WHITAKER LEE W	1LT		C628	5
WHITE DAVID L	1LT		0628	5
WHITE EDMOND G	2LT		0529	5
WHITE JOHN R	LTC		0728	5
WHITE RICHARD G	1LT		0628	5
WHITEHEAD JOSEPH L	2LT		C628	5
WHITTHORNE HARRY S	CPT		C628	5
WIDMANN JESSE E	1LT		0728	5
WIGGINS WILLIAM F	1LT		0528	5
WILD CHARLES A	CPT		0628	5
WILLIAMS EDWARD J	CPT		0628	5
WILLIAMS ROBERTS	1LT		C628	5
WILLIAMS THOMAS C	2LT		0928	5
WILLIAMSON PHILIP H	1LT		0828	5
WILSON CHAUNCEY G	2LT		0828	5
WILSON HARVEY W	2LT		0628	5
WILSON JAMES H	CPT		0429	5
WILSON RICHARD T	1LT		0828	5
WILSON ROSKO J	1LT		C628	5
WILSON WILBE R	1LT		0528	5
WILSON WILLIAM V	1LT		0628	5
WILTSHIRE TURNER H	MAJ		0928	5
WINSLOW CHARLES S	2LT		0529	5
WINSLOW GUY H	1LT		0728	5
WIRTHS CARL W	1LT		0628	5
WISE EARL G	1LT		C628	5
WISE JOHN B	1LT		0429	5
WISE JR CHARLES F	CPT		0329	5
WITTHACK HENRY F	2LT		0628	5
WOLCOTT LESTER D	1LT		0528	5
WOOD EVANS B	1LT		C628	5
WOOD RAIFORD J	2LT		0529	5
WOODLEY SAMUEL S	2LT		0728	5
WOODRUFF ERNEST W	1LT		0628	5
WOODS PHILIP H	CPT		0528	5
WOODSON HYLAN H	1LT		0628	5
WOOLFORD AUSTIN W	2LT		C628	5
WORNALL FRANCIS	2LT		0628	5
WORTHINGTON LELAND G	1LT		0129	5
WRIGHT JOHN E	2LT		0628	5
YAEGER ROBERT E	2LT		0628	5
YOUNG CHARLES F	1LT		0628	5
YOUNG HARRY R	2LT		C628	5
YOUNG JESSE E	1LT		C329	5
ZACHARIAS JOHN A	CPT		0529	5
ZACHER VERNON B A	1LT		0329	5

SECTION 5

LOSSES TO THE RETIRED LISTS

This section is composed of officer and warrant officer losses to all of the retired lists.

NAME	GRADE	SVC NO	DATE LOSS MO YR
ABBEY WALTER W	COL	0-0246670	0567
ABBOTT RICHARD W	LTC	0-0291265	0867
ABRAMOWITZ REUBEN	LTC	0-0443624	0367
ACKERMAN JOSEPH V	CPT	0-0167543	
ADAMS EUGENE F	CPT	0-0499148	
ADAMS JAMES J	COL	0-0031044	0567
ADAMS JR EDWARD A	CPT	0-0183617	
ADAMS THOMAS C	LTC	0-0258030	
ADAMS WALTERRE	COL	0-0004628	
ADCOCK CLARENCE L	M G	0-0009310	0167
ADELMAN MAX	MAJ	0-0503114	
AHLEFELD CHARLES R	MAJ	0-0504695	1266
AINLEY RICHARD H	CPT	0-0927256	0567
AKELEY ALICE I	CPT	N-0700380	0367
ALDENHOVEN CARL J	MAJ	0-0265020	0267
ALKIRE HOYT M	CW2	W-2118053	1166
ALLEN LAUCIE C	LTC	0-0213551	0267
ALLISON JOSEPH L	LTC	0-1168152	1166
ALMAN SAMUEL	MAJ	0-0181749	0966
ALSEN MORRIS B	2LT	0-1580570	1066
ALSUP E HERSCHEL	COL	0-0080275	1266
AMES ALLEN	MAJ	0-0246277	0367
AMOS ALAN J	1LT	0-1000657	0867
ANDERSON EDWARD B	MAJ	0-0507814	
ANDERSON HAROLD M	LTC	0-1315892	0667
ANDERSON LELAND H	LTC	0-0276664	1166
ANDERSON NORMAN W	COL	0-0018635	
ANDERSON ORLEY K	2LT	0-1011506	0467
ANDREWS EDWARD L	LTC	0-0015676	
ANDREWS PAUL S	COL	0-0165179	0467
ANGSTADT WALTER E	1LT	0-1010022	0767
ANUSKEWICZ P T	LTC	0-0181301	0667
APPLIN FRANK C	COL	0-0002663	0667
ARAUJO LERED S	CPT	0-1013191	0367
ARBUCKLE GEORGE R	LTC	0-1595351	0667
ARMSTRONG JOHN E	COL	0-0012392	0667
ARMSTRONG WESLEY F	COL	0-0267646	0167
ARNESEN SIGURD J	COL	0-0146321	1066
ARNOLD CHARLES H	LTC	0-0200931	1066
ARNOLE SAMUEL R	MAJ	0-0032664	0267
ARNOTT JOHN D	MAJ	0-1583896	0167
ASHLEY SPRAGUE W	CPT	0-0140038	0567
ASHWILL RAYMOND M	CW2	W-0901129	0667
ASPIRAS MARIANO	1LT	0-2032074	
ATKINSON ALBERT K	LTC	0-0115058	1266
AUSPITZ JR HARRY	COL	0-0030081	
AUSTIN GENE W	CW3	W-2148591	0767
AUSTIN JOHN J	CPT	0-0194929	0667
AYLESWORTH ISAAC R	COL	0-0114144	1266
AZBELL CLAUDE W	COL	0-0271883	0567
BABCOCK CHARLES S	LTC	0-0030668	1166
BABIN ERNEST R	MAJ	0-1338175	
BACON REGINALD R	LTC	0-0007455	1166
BAER CARL T	COL	0-0219155	1266
BAILEY GEORGE W	LTC	0-0426287	1266
BAILEY HARVEY P	CPT	0-0280909	1166
BAIRD ANNIE D	1LT	N-0700502	0667
BAKKEN CLARENCE J	COL	0-0238099	
BALDWIN KARL F	COL	0-0002472	0467
BALIUS JOHN	CPT	0-0481453	0567
BANAHAN JOHN J JR	2LT	0-1032034	0767
BANTA GEORGE JR	MAJ	0-0267218	1166
BAREFOOT FORREST F	LTC	0-0321853	0467
BARHYDT ROY W	LTC	0-0195833	0667
BARKAN JULIUS Y	CPT	0-0480508	0667
BARKER AUGUSTUS L	LTC	0-0214962	0667
BARKES LEWIS C	COL	0-0015735	1266
BARKLEY JAMES R	CW2	W-2144296	0667
BARNWELL EDWARD H	COL	0-0216978	0167
BARNWELL RANDALL J	CW3	W-2125059	0667
BAROFF MOE C	COL	0-0233358	0767
BARR HERBERT	MAJ	0-0115219	0267
BARRET ROBERT C	CPT	0-0300153	
BARRETT AUSTIN F	CW4	W-2122889	0767
BARRETT EARL S	WO1	W-2117978	
BARRETT RAYMOND H	MAJ	0-0310057	0167
BARRY ALFRED R	CW4	W-2002844	0767
BARRY MICHAEL J	LTC	0-1284810	0467
BARRY RAYMOND A	1LT	0-0335122	0667
BARTH PAUL M	CPT	0-0120440	0767
BARTON THOMAS M	COL	0-0166664	0267
BASSITT ROYCE D	CW2	W-2205521	0467
BASTINE WILFRID S	COL	0-0189874	0767
BATCHELOR JAMES H	COL	0-0172754	
BATES HERVEY L	LTC	0-0151069	
BAUER CHARLES T	LTC	0-0241373	1166
BAUER JOHN	CPT	0-0236370	1166
BAUMGARTNER ROYD G	MAJ	0-0180410	0767
BEALL WILSON W	LTC	0-0284315	
BEANE MARY S	MAJ	N-0737450	0567
BEARD ARCHIE	LTC	0-0515081	
BEAVERS MARTIN E	CPT	0-0228878	1066
BECHTOLD JACOB E	COL	0-0005694	0267
BEECHER GLEN	CPT	0-0498725	1166
BELCHER WILLIAM W	COL	0-0005899	
BELL WALTER F	LTC	0-1553398	0167
BENDER CHARLES R JR	LTC	0-0452824	0467
BENDLER FRED D JR	COL	0-0030691	0267
BENEDICT MARION H	LTC	0-0447675	1166
BENEDICT RAY W	COL	0-0110062	0767
BENJAMIN ADRIAN T	COL	0-0162710	0567
BENNER RALPH C	COL	0-0010275	0667
BENNETT JAMES R	CPT	0-0283731	0567
BENNETT JR JOHN J	LTC	0-0101393	
BENOIT EDWARD G	LTC	0-0273360	0467
BENTON MITCHELL M JR	CPT	0-2004373	0467
BERGEN HANSEN	LTC	0-0187774	
BERGERON DAVID C	MAJ	0-1081725	0567
BERGERON THEODORE H	LTC	0-1313953	0667
BERGFIELD GEORGE A	COL	0-0166711	1166
BERMAN JOSEPH E	COL	0-0221356	0767
BERRY JAMES E	MAJ	0-0164907	1166
BERTHOLD JOHN H	COL	0-0243566	0667
BERWICK DUDLEY R	LTC	0-0051546	
BESSE ARTHUR H	CPT	0-0006992	0367
BESSETTE RAYMOND C	CPT	0-0333283	0467
BETHEL ARLAND H	1LT	0-1580951	0367
BETTISON WILLIAM R	COL	0-0013930	0667
BEVER CLARENCE L	LTC	0-0246545	1166
BICKEL JOHN W	2LT	0-0212547	1166
BICKNELL GEORGE W	COL	0-0162814	
BIEDENHARN HERMAN H	1LT	0-1051875	0567
BIGELOW ARLAND E	LTC	0-0051687	0267
BILLING ALBERT F	COL	0-0008354	0767
BIRD WILLIAM T	COL	0-0347734	0267
BIRDSONG BAILEY S	COL	0-0238421	0666
BISHOP CHARLES F	1LT	0-0436611	0567
BISHOP PERCY P	M G	0-0000655	0467
BISHOP WALTER J	LTC	0-0324385	0667
BLACK CHARLES H JR	LTC	0-1283713	0567
BLACKACAR CLARENCE W	CPT	0-1081389	0467
BLACKMON HEYWARD J	LTC	0-0271025	0267
BLACKWELL IRA W	MAJ	0-1168174	
BLADES RUSSELL F	LTC	0-0251111	
BLAIR DONALD S	COL	0-0289457	0467
BLAIR GEORGE R	LTC	0-1016625	0167
BLAKELY GEORGE	B G	0-0000232	1165
BLALOCK WALTER W	WO1	W-2126813	0867
BLOCK ALBERT F	1LT	0-0495305	0167
BLOOM RUDOLPH	COL	0-0166802	
BLOUNT HARRY G	MAJ	0-0167019	1266
BLUMERT WALTER	CPT	0-0113010	0767
BLUNT PAUL B	LTC	0-0368357	0967
BLUNT WILFRID M	COL	0-0002106	0567
BOATRIGHT WILLIAM E	LTC	0-0300129	0767
BODNAR MICHAEL T	LTC	0-0353377	0467
BOGAN PATRICK W	LTC	0-1550750	
BOGGS HELEN M	MAJ	L-0000209	0467
BOGGS JAMES A	CPT	0-0349490	0367
BOLL MILFORD W	CW2	W-2108777	0367
BOLTON CLIFFORD T	CPT	0-0417734	0467
BOLTON WILLIAM B	COL	0-0100556	0467
BOMAN CECIL R	CPT	0-0118836	1266
BOOKER LEONARD R	LTC	0-0213469	
BORDEN WILLIAM A	B G	0-0003443	
BORGEN CLIFFORD F	MAJ	0-1592176	
BORROR JAMES C	CPT	0-0425558	1266
BOSSON JAMES	MAJ	0-0471888	0167
BOUCHARD LIONEL P	CW2	W-2014645	0367
BOULE LEROY L	CPT	0-0181291	
BOUNDS RALPH M	CPT	0-1282218	0867
BOURNE GEORGE S	MAJ	0-0482009	0167
BOWEN ALBERT S	COL	0-0002768	0467
BOWERS KARL B	COL	0-0164568	0667
BOYEA RAGEL H	1LT	0-1304852	0567
BRADLEY WARREN F	LTC	0-1058449	1266
BRADY JAMES L	1LT	0-1946917	0367
BRADY JOSEPH F	MAJ	0-1011488	0367
BRACY WILLIAM S	LTC	0-0234114	0667
BRANCHE HAROLD S	MAJ	0-0140099	0767
BRANN WILLIAM	CPT	0-1644396	0767
BRANTINGHAM GEORGE L	MAJ	0-0286526	0167
BRASWELL NICHOLAS T	CPT	0-0270642	
BRAVENDER PAUL R	MAJ	0-0274772	0367
BREELAND LEONARD R	CW2	W-2141205	0567
BRENT IRL D SR	COL	0-0126890	1166
BRES EDWARD S	M G	0-0121208	
BRESLIN FRANCIS J	WO1	W-2153224	0267
BREWER PAUL M	LTC	0-0113683	1266
BRICKER EDWIN D	B G	0-0000599	0467
BRIDGES EARL B	LTC	0-0505653	0467
BRIGGS RUSSELL A	CW2	W-2114630	0667
BRILLANTE JOSE R	CPT	0-1896736	0467
BRINDLEY ARTHUR F	MAJ	0-0036504	0167
BRINEY LLOYD G	LTC	0-1586458	0167
BRISTOL FRANKLIN F	LTC	0-1307364	1266
BROCK HOBART M	LTC	0-0251076	0267
BROCKUS JAMES R	MAJ	0-0164531	1166
BROOKS JAMES D	LTC	0-1637089	0167
BROWN CHARLES L	1LT	0-2043291	0767
BROWN HAROLD A	LTC	0-0012433	1266
BROWN HAROLD E	CW2	W-2143612	1166
BROWN JOHN E	COL	0-0008903	1266
BROWN JOSEPH	2LT	0-0108672	0367
BROWN JR DANIEL B	LTC	0-1295659	
BROWN PAUL J	LTC	0-0038959	
BROWN REX D	MAJ	0-0477949	0467
BROWN THOMAS C	LTC	0-0005829	0567
BRUNENI LOUIS P	MAJ	0-0211115	1166
BRYAN THOMAS R	MAJ	0-0252967	0767
BRYANS WILLIAM B	COL	0-0344785	0767
BRYANT LAWRENCE J	MAJ	0-0311640	0167
BUCHANAN ARTHUR J	CPT	0-0199895	0767
BUCHANAN KENNETH	B G	0-0208343	0467
BUCK HARRY F	CPT	0-0264031	
BUCKLEW LESLIE G	CPT	0-0488707	
BUCKNUM CORNELIUS L	LTC	0-0200374	0267
BUEGLER ELMER F	MAJ	0-1304457	0567
BUELL EARL	2LT	0-1914167	0367
BULLENE LATHROP R	COL	0-0012665	0767
BULLMAN STEPHEN J	CPT	0-1549673	
BULLOCK HERMAN C	CW3	W-2142061	1167
BUNDY LEO W	CPT	0-0522140	0367
BUONOPANE CARLO	CPT	0-1302450	0966
BURCH MORTON W	LTC	0-0920793	1166
BURCHELL JOHN A	CPT	0-0146771	0567
BURFEINDT ANNA F	CPT	N-0730197	1266
BURGER ELVIN H	COL	0-0015444	1166
BURGIN HOWARD N	COL	0-0018932	0467
BURK HENRY R	1LT	0-0494840	1166
BURKE GEORGE C	CW2	W-2110773	0467
BURKE ROBERT W	COL	0-0011042	1266
BURNHAM KENNETH B	MAJ	0-0287283	
BURNSIDE HERMAN L	MAJ	0-0344977	0667
BURPO GEORGE	2LT	0-1913570	0467
BURRELL FRANK C	2LT	0-2305008	
BURT JESSE F	LTC	0-0232613	1266
BUSH RALPH R	COL	0-0177443	1266
BUTLER ERNEST G	MAJ	0-0445538	0767
BUTLER JOHN C	LTC	0-0155253	
BUTTON ROBERT L	1LT	0-1292126	0467
BUYVID PETER P	1LT	0-1945771	0667
CAMERON JOSEPH M	COL	0-0029180	0667
CAMPBELL CHARLES A	1LT	0-0165543	
CAMPBELL FRANK J	LTC	0-1845708	
CAMPBELL JOHN C	MAJ	0-0167140	1166
CAMPBELL JOSEPH H	1LT	0-0526737	0367
CAMPBELL MYRON M	MAJ	0-0227442	
CAMPBELL THOMAS E	CPT	0-0504014	0267
CANFIELD JOSEPH V	MAJ	0-0247263	
CANN WILLIAM R	CW2	W-2147065	1266
CANNING AUSTIN J	COL	0-0003654	0567
CANNON CORNELIUS V	LTC	0-0134975	0467
CAPONERA NELLO F	2LT	0-1318386	0767
CARD LEE W	COL	0-0007713	
CARDFICLIO LOUIS E	LTC	0-0246477	0667
CARON BRUCE W	COL	0-0030475	0667
CARROLL JOHN W	COL	0-0006811	0167
CARROLL ROBERT J	CPT	0-1177321	0367
CARROLL WILLIAM F	LTC	0-0104493	0367
CARTER CLIFTON C	COL	0-0016501	0167
CARTER THEODORE P	MAJ	0-0331947	0567
CARTLIDGE MARION C	1LT	0-1176744	0267
CASE DAVID V	1LT	0-0291067	0667
CASEY CLAY	MAJ	0-0487908	
CASHIN WILLIAM J	COL	0-0245117	0667
CASNER MAURICE L	1LT	0-2039670	0667
CAUGHEY FRANK M	LTC	0-0186998	0167
CAVANAUGH RICHARD	1LT	0-1913574	0467
CHAMBERLIN FRANK T	COL	0-0011745	1266
CHAMBERS STUART H	CW4	W-2111640	1266
CHAMLESS BUIL	1LT	0-0232278	0167
CHANDLER JOE P	LTC	0-0480087	0667
CHAPMAN ALVIN L	MAJ	0-0217540	0767
CHAPMAN LYLE B	MAJ	0-0192862	1166
CHASE THORNTON	COL	0-0008007	0367
CHEATHAM WILLIAM L	COL	0-0352101	0267
CHENAULT WILLIAM P	MAJ	0-0237116	0267
CHERRY JAMES M	COL	0-0172273	1166
CHERRY WILLIAM W	CW4	W-2118262	0667
CHILDERS GUY S	1LT	0-0200029	
CHILDRESS THEODORE J	MAJ	0-0278434	0667
CHRISTIE ALONZO B	LTC	0-0021723	
CHRISTIE CHARLES A	CPT	0-0100217	1066
CHURCH HENRY C	LTC	0-0208982	
CLAIR JR HARRY E	COL	0-0146867	
CLANEY KENNETH MC C	2LT	0-0538580	0267
CLARK HENRY C	COL	0-0009281	0567
CLARK JEROME W	LTC	0-0280771	
CLARK JOHN H JR	LTC	0-0146492	0267
CLARK JOSEPH C	MAJ	0-0119128	0367
CLARK ROBERT A	COL	0-0335369	1166
CLARK VICTOR	CPT	0-0321707	
CLARK WALTER V	MAJ	0-0510383	0267
CLARK WILSON S	CPT	0-1586454	0667
CLAUSEN EVALD V	MAJ	0-0204494	
CLAXTON IRA C	LTC	0-0464199	1166
CLAYTON MARCUS M	COL	0-0118634	1266
CLAYTON ROBERT V	CPT	0-0444044	0767
CLINE CLIFF R	CPT	0-0260251	0267
CLOSSON LESLIE V	MAJ	0-0341493	0267
CLOUGH CLARENCE W	MAJ	0-0188113	0567
COATES EDMUND F	MAJ	0-1013797	
COBB GEORGE A	MAJ	0-1307372	0567
COBEL PAUL S	LTC	0-0332223	0367
COCHRANE WARREN O	COL	0-0286571	0367
COENNEN GEORGE A	CPT	0-0890278	
COHEN MICHAEL	LTC	0-0265454	0767
COHEN ROBERT	LTC	0-0252172	0267
COLE DONALD M	MAJ	0-0004643	0167

292-560 O - 68 - 25

NAME	GRADE	SVC NO	DATE LOSS MO YR
COLE JOSEPH J JR	CPT	0-0916644	0367
COLE THOMAS E	CPT	0-0266458	0467
COLEMAN JAMES C	LTC	0-0300907	1166
COLES HAROLD L	1LT	0-1285198	0567
COLLINS HOMER B	1LT	0-1775403	
COLLINS ROBERT W	COL	0-0001230	0267
COLLINS SOOLS A	MAJ	0-0256786	0367
COLRIN EMMETT R	LTC	0-0007800	0267
COMSTOCK GLENN E	LTC	0-0214482	0367
COMSTOCK HILLIARD	LTC	0-0113158	
CONDREN EDWARD J	COL	0-0243384	0667
CONINE MARVIN H	MAJ	0-0273388	0367
CONLEY EDWARD J	MAJ	0-1948721	0367
CONNAUGHTON F J	MAJ	0-0198914	1167
CONNAUGHTON OWEN N	MAJ	0-0961992	0367
CONNELL WILLIAM F	LTC	0-0104299	
CONNOLLY MARY L	CPT	L-0501126	
CONROY JAMES G	LTC	0-0197535	1266
CONROY THOMAS J	COL	0-0301182	0167
CONWELL JOHN D	MAJ	0-0376460	0966
COODY WILSON R	1LT	0-1297600	0567
COOK DANIEL M	MAJ	0-0152540	0667
COOK FREDERICK M	CPT	0-1291079	0567
COOK WALTER I	CW4	W-2105170	0467
COOK WILLIAM B	LTC	0-0247857	0167
COOKE ROLAND W	CW2	W-0900306	1166
COOKE THOMAS W	COL	0-0020307	0867
COONS DANIEL C	LTC	0-0010789	0667
COOPER GUSTAVAS A	CW2	W-2122007	
COOPER MARY F	CPT	N-0000552	0567
COOPER RUSSELL R	COL	0-0289339	0767
CORE ARCH	CPT	0-0200454	
COPELAND KERN H	LTC	0-0110760	0367
COPENHAVER JOHN K	LTC	0-0155323	
CORR LEROY S	COL	0-0265679	1266
CORKE HUBERT L	MAJ	0-0182378	0767
CORLE EIRVIN D	MAJ	0-1688461	0367
CORNISH GEORGE H	LTC	0-0040038	0367
CORPENING MAXWELL M	COL	0-0209542	0467
CORST VINCENT	LTC	0-1695652	0167
CORTHAY HELEN M	LTC	L-0000098	1266
COSBY JAMES W	CW3	RW-2145406	0467
COSGROVE JAMES H	LTC	0-1104102	1066
COTTRELL CHESTER H	CW2	W-2146903	0667
COWHEY JOSEPH L	COL	0-0019091	
COX RICHARD F	LTC	0-0222385	0567
CRAIG GILBERT	CW3	W-2143146	0767
CRAIG MELVIN L	COL	0-0007575	0867
CRANE ROSCOE T	COL	0-0505413	0866
CRANMER GORDON S	COL	0-0216461	0667
CRAWFORD STUART F	COL	0-0018078	0567
CRAWFORD WILLIAM S	MAJ	0-0270779	1166
CREARY GEORGE H	1LT	0-0921335	1266
CRELLIN HAROLD	LTC	0-0331416	0767
CREPEAU EDWARD L	CPT	0-0972671	1266
CRONANDER GERSUM	COL	0-0006341	0267
CRONIN EDWARD T	LTC	0-1257502	0867
CROSMAN RALPH	MAJ	0-0182200	0767
CROSSON WILLIAM L	1LT	0-0444083	1266
CROW EDWARD W	CPT	0-0926848	
CROWE FRANCIS E	COL	0-0189782	0367
CROWELL WILLIAM C	LTC	0-0506355	
CROWLEY MERL F	MAJ	0-0255525	1166
CROYLE ELLSWORTH JR	CW3	W-2151188	1166
CRUM REGINALD W	1LT	0-0200751	
CRYSLER ARTHUR C	MAJ	0-0490896	
CUMMINS CARL E	MAJ	0-1541527	0467
CUNNEEN ODELL R	MAJ	0-0144209	0267
CUNNINGHAM RENICK C	CW4	W-2110170	0767
CURRAN EDGAR A C	LTC	0-0010639	0667
CURRAN EDWARD A	LTC	0-0509834	
CUSHMAN GEORGE H	COL	0-0008051	0567
CAILEY FRANK JR	COL	0-0362923	0867
CALTON JOHN H	1LT	0-0332144	0267
DAMORE TONY	LTC	0-0307525	0567

NAME	GRADE	SVC NO	DATE LOSS MO YR
DANADICH FRANK J	1LT	0-2053961	
DANFORD EVA	MAJ	N-0767261	
DANIEL LARK C JR	LTC	0-0189011	1266
DANIELS VICTOR E	MAJ	0-1541039	0167
DANSKIN WILLIAM F	COL	0-0189027	1066
DARLING WILLIAM D	MAJ	0-0221353	
DARROCH WILLIAM	CPT	0-0108146	0267
DAUPHINEE URIEL V	CW2	W-2148461	0367
DAVID WILLIAM R	LTC	0-0297703	0467
DAVIES GEORGE G	COL	0-0903695	
DAVIES WALTER N	COL	0-0264473	0667
DAVIS CHARLES A	CPT	0-0323046	0567
DAVIS CLARENCE S	LTC	0-0347745	0867
DAVIS FRANK E	COL	0-0001618	0567
DAVIS FRANK C	COL	0-0012380	0367
DAVIS JOHN C	CPT	0-0187053	1266
DAVIS MARY F	1LT	N-0728750	0567
DAVIS RALPH H	CPT	0-0378437	0167
DAVIS THOMAS A	COL	0-0184247	0367
DAVIS WALTER B	1LT	0-0014416	1266
DAWN JAMES E	LTC	0-0166153	0367
DAWSON GEORGE R	COL	0-0171478	1166
DAWSON LEO	CPT	0-0479044	0767
DAY LEE P	CW3	W-2147951	0367
DAYTON JULIAN	COL	0-0010425	0367
DE CARRE OCTAVE	COL	0-0003206	
DE LISLE JOSEPH F	1LT	0-0870558	0567
DE PREZ DANIEL W	B G	0-0171585	0267
DE WEESE JAMES M	LTC	0-0007679	0767
DEGLAPERCIX HUGO J	1LT	0-1301269	0567
DEATON JAMES A	LTC	0-0446002	0167
DECKER LAVERNE	CPT	0-0505296	
DEES EUGENE A	LTC	0-0022641	0167
DEKEUSTER VERNON N	1LT	0-2006666	1266
DENITHORNE GEORGE S	MAJ	0-0146842	0467
DENNIS DONALD E	1LT	0-0297898	0666
DENNIS GEORGE F	LTC	0-0306153	0366
DESROCHERS REAL H	LTC	0-0278933	
DEUTCH HARRY S	1LT	0-1580859	0467
DEVINE JAMES	LTC	0-0100453	
DEVINE JAMES W	COL	0-0231274	
DICKERSON OLIVER M	LTC	0-0128426	1166
DICKINSON GORDON A	CPT	0-0322580	0667
DILL EDWARD E	CW2	W-2145155	1266
DISNEY PAUL A	M G	0-0017004	0965
DITTRICH LLOYD H	LTC	0-0218887	1166
DIXON ERNEST R	MAJ	0-0500376	0267
DOANE ETHRIDGE F	LTC	0-0291864	
DOANE JOHN H	COL	0-0183736	0267
DOBSON WILLIAM V	1LT	0-2040897	0567
DOCHERTY MARGARET	1LT	N-0700240	1166
DODGE JAMES P	LTC	0-0208518	0567
DODRILL MORTON	LTC	0-0261671	0567
DODSON CLAUDE C	COL	0-0020495	0567
DODSON WILLIAM F	LTC	0-0444330	1266
DOKA JULIUS G	MAJ	0-1551195	1266
DOLD OPAL B	LTC	0-0116092	0167
DONAGHY JAMES K	COL	0-0483935	1166
DONALD JOHN A	1LT	0-1109901	
DONNELLY TERENCE	LTC	0-1302120	
DONNER CLAY M	COL	0-0220473	0167
DONNOCKER CHARLES J	LTC	0-0179119	
DORAN PATRICK H	CPT	0-0510076	1066
DORMINY HERBERT N	CPT	0-2263797	0866
DORRIEN HUGH C	COL	0-0011154	
DOSCHER RALPH S	LTC	0-0245080	1066
DOTEN LEONARD S	MAJ	0-0005437	0567
DOUGAN WILLIAM K	LTC	0-1286804	0867
DOUGLAS HENRY G	COL	0-0016742	
DOWELL ROBERT L	CPT	0-0370446	
DOWNEY ARTHUR J	COL	0-0031914	0367
DOWNS CHARLES P	LTC	0-0266717	0567
DRAYSON EDGAR T	MAJ	0-0247047	0567
DRESSLER JOSEPH	CW2	W-0901294	0467
DRUMMOND GARRETT B	LTC	0-0223200	0267

NAME	GRADE	SVC NO	DATE LOSS MO YR
DRURY RALPH W	LTC	0-0001732	0567
DU BOIS IVAN C	MAJ	0-0227364	1266
DUNLAP JOSEPH H	COL	0-0189709	0767
DURA WILLIAM M	CPT	0-0988059	0667
DURBIN JAMES L	CW3	W-2147165	1266
DURBIN MARION E	CW4	W-2105235	
DURST WALLACE E	COL	0-0007747	0267
DUSINBERRE ANNA J	1LT	N-0729102	0567
DWINELLE JOSEPH H	LTC	0-0296598	0366
DWYER MARGARET	MAJ	N-0700569	0467
DYCHE LEONARD T	COL	0-0200748	0467
EARLE MARSDEN P	LTC	0-0208819	
EARLY CLIFFORD C	COL	0-0002067	0467
EARP CLAUDE C	COL	0-0161006	0767
EASTON LESLIE O	MAJ	0-0201996	0367
EDDY HOWARD C	COL	0-0262287	0167
EDES SAMUEL H	MAJ	0-0326098	0367
EDWARDS FRANK B	COL	0-0001148	0567
EDWARDS HARLEY A	CPT	0-0479441	0167
EDWARDS HOWARD W JR	MAJ	0-2018320	0767
EDWARDS ROBERT B	2LT	0-0335276	0767
EHINGER VINCENT K	CPT	0-0337006	0467
EKLUND WILLIAM J	LTC	0-0224974	0567
ELDERS BERNARD C	CPT	0-0558204	0267
ELIAS MAX A	CPT	0-1917486	0467
ELLERS KENNETH W	CPT	0-0384480	
ELLIS WILLIAM B	2LT	0-1016170	0667
ELMORE LLOYD V SR	LTC	0-0921154	0567
ELY CLYDE E	COL	0-0170747	0567
EMBURY GILBERT W	M G	0-0233743	0667
ENGEL EMIL	LTC	0-0001859	
ENGLISH CHARLES R	1LT	0-1297340	0167
ENSMINGER GEORGE P	COL	0-0225039	0567
ERB WILLIAM	CPT	0-0132676	0167
ERICKSON CONRAD E	1LT	0-0108886	
ERLENBORN FRANZ J	CPT	0-0262969	0267
ERWIN VINCENT R	MAJ	0-0003134	0367
EVANS MILFORD H	LTC	0-0483644	0567
EVANS SYLVESTER M	LTC	0-0186069	0167
EVANS THOMAS H	MAJ	0-0468246	0867
EVERALL JAMES R	1LT	0-0140306	0963
EVERS ALBERT L	LTC	0-0296142	1166
EVERS RAYMOND R	COL	0-0080749	0567
EVERTS PALMER W	LTC	0-0136362	0367
EXLEY DAVID W	MAJ	0-0389409	
FAHRINGER FREDERICK	LTC	0-0255561	
FALK ERWIN H	LTC	0-0168558	0467
FALL ARCHIBALD	COL	0-0007521	
FALLS CLYDE L	MAJ	0-0109922	
FARNHAM GEORGE W	LTC	0-0163963	
FARRELL THOMAS F	M G	0-0227201	0467
FAULKNER GEORGE G	CPT	0-0967060	1166
FAUST MAX H	CPT	0-0164354	0867
FEAGIN RALPH B JR	1LT	0-1326237	1266
FEBIGER GEORGE L	COL	0-0004546	0367
FELICELLI NELLO M	LTC	0-0359246	1066
FELLMAN JOHN	COL	0-0227902	0567
FERNANDEZ ANGEL W	LTC	0-0155768	
FIELD E LEWIS	LTC	0-0009958	1266
FIELDS JESSE E	CPT	0-1913676	1166
FIGLEAR GEORGE J	CPT	0-0483358	0167
FILIPEK BOLESLAW S	MAJ	0-0505033	
FILLINGER RALPH W	1LT	0-1318658	
FINCHAM JACK M	1LT	0-0904294	0367
FINE SAMUEL F	MAJ	0-0256931	1266
FINLEY JOHN G SR	CPT	0-2262681	1166
FINN KENNETH G	CPT	0-0979380	
FINNEY ROBERT V	CPT	0-0006682	0366
FISCHER FRED C	1LT	0-0488859	0167
FISCHER WALTER F	CPT	0-0243645	0267
FISHER LEWIS B	CPT	0-0499594	0667
FISHER NEAL H	2LT	0-0326329	1266
FISKE MARY F	MAJ	N-0723547	
FITZGERALD JOSEPH E	CPT	0-1689356	0267
FITZGERALD THEODORE	MAJ	0-0252826	

NAME	GRADE	SVC NO	DATE LOSS MO YR
FLEMING FLO F JR	MAJ	0-1997077	0767
FLINT WALTER F JR	1LT	0-0517364	1066
FOLEY JAMES J V	CW4	W-0903103	0167
FOLEY JAMES M	2LT	0-2007613	0367
FOLSOM CHARLES O	LTC	0-0045951	
FOOTE WILLIAM C	COL	0-0003570	0167
FORAN ARTHUR F JR	LTC	0-0402828	0167
FORAN HENRY T	CPT	0-1945132	0767
FORBES DONALD B	1LT	0-0512160	
FORBES PAULINE C	1LT	N-0751384	
FORD WILLIAM W	MAJ	0-1049174	0267
FORGETT JOSEPH A	LTC	0-0136211	1066
FORREST HERBERT O	COL	0-0132143	
FORT ALFRED M	LTC	0-0472629	
FOULTZ WALTER H	MAJ	0-1575218	0667
FOWLER GODFREY A	CPT	0-0020355	0567
FOX JOHN R	COL	0-0042024	0467
FRANCISCO RAY J	LTC	0-1032799	
FRANK JAMES C	M G	0-0289883	0867
FRANSEN ARTHUR M	LTC	0-0430352	1266
FRASER HARRY C	COL	0-0009540	1266
FRAZIER BEECHER M	1LT	0-0498476	0467
FRAZIER RAY A	WO1	W-2111124	0267
FREDERICK LELAND M	COL	0-0235774	0367
FREDRICH ALAN G	CW3	W-2151973	
FREEMAN JAMES E	CW3	W-2141280	
FREEMON JOSEPH A	1LT	0-1035153	0567
FRENIERE JOHN J	CPT	0-0516540	
FREY PAUL A	LTC	0-0131806	0167
FRICK ROBERT B	WO1	W-0800093	1266
FRIEDMAN LEWIS S	COL	0-0192041	0467
FRIEND ROYDON L	1LT	0-0120379	1066
FRIES ROSS R JR	CW3	W-2150946	1266
FRINK CLIFFORD A	LTC	0-0492663	0667
FRITZ ANTHONY E	1LT	0-0372461	0167
FROMMELT CLIFFORD C	CPT	0-1010382	0367
FULLAM EDWIN W	COL	0-0110538	0167
FULTON JEFFERSON H	COL	0-0154058	1266
FURLONG CHARLES W	COL	0-0124413	
FURQUERON JAMES M	MAJ	0-1593563	0167
FURY THOMAS G	CPT	0-0288923	
GAFFNEY LEO F	COL	0-0080780	1266
GAHR JOHN A	LTC	0-0051947	
GALLAHER CHARLES W	COL	0-0004909	0867
GALLANT FERDINAND J	MAJ	0-0189012	0367
GALLOWAY GORDON C	MAJ	0-1043636	1066
GALLUP FRED H	LTC	0-0015029	0167
GALPERN EDWARD H	CW3	W-2153177	0567
GANNON WILLIAM J	COL	0-0304925	
GARDE GEORGE H	COL	0-0336854	0267
GARDINER GEORGE H	LTC	0-0003434	0567
GARDNER ALEXANDER	WO1	W-2147945	1166
GARDNER JOSEPH H	MAJ	0-0229086	0167
GARLAND JR CLAUDE	CPT	0-1010131	
GARRISON GLEN H	LTC	0-0019260	1266
GARVIN EDWARD M	1LT	0-1308810	0767
GASKYN STANLEY K	MAJ	0-0466666	0267
GATCHELL OSCAR J	B G	0-0003357	0966
GATTON JAMES W	CPT	0-0257580	0267
GAUMNITZ PERCY I	LTC	0-0346777	0267
GAUVREAU CHARLES A	CW4	W-0901796	0367
GEARY DONALD	MAJ	0-0110725	0966
GEDDINGS LADSON I	LTC	0-1285572	0567
GEE CLEVELAND	COL	0-0002576	
GEGG CHAUNCY H	1LT	0-1946496	
GEIB GEORGE A	LTC	0-0186144	1266
GEORGE RUSSELL T	COL	0-0005849	0167
GERLACH LEONARD J	MAJ	0-0194245	0567
GERRITY JOHN F	CW2	W-0901529	0567
GERVAIS ROYAL L	COL	0-0010307	0767
GIBNEY JOHN T	LTC	0-0232503	
GIBSON KENNETH L	CW4	W-0903145	
GIFFIN GLENN C	CPT	0-0492263	1166
GILBERT HAROLD L	LTC	0-0280229	1266
GILLESPIE JAMES B	LTC	0-0003593	0167

NAME	GRADE	SVC NO	DATE LOSS MO YR
GILLIS DONALD F	LTC	0-1106759	0867
GILMORE WILLIAM W	COL	0-0230811	0167
GILREATH SAM B	MAJ	0-0517629	0966
GIORDANE JOSEPH B	COL	0-0030381	
GLADSTONE WILLIAM C	CPT	0-0138129	0167
GLANZ ROBERT E	1LT	0-2001013	0367
GLASGOW WILLIAM J	B G	0-0000381	0867
GLATTLY HAROLD W	B G	0-0016967	
GLEASON WILLIAM E	LTC	0-0239688	
GLEIM ROBERT F	COL	0-0100355	1266
GLICK IRWIN	CPT	0-0512422	0567
GLYNN MARY M	2LT	N-0797772	
GOERGER JAMES N	CPT	0-0450733	0367
GOLDBLATT LOUIS J	CPT	0-0144933	1166
GOODLOE MASON F	COL	0-0030161	0767
GOODMAN MORRIS	1LT	0-1169535	0467
GOODRIDGE RAYMOND E	COL	0-0173904	1266
GORMAN JOHN F	MAJ	0-0140267	
GORMAN ROBERT B	MAJ	0-0022784	1266
GOSNELL WILFRED C	LTC	0-0921310	
GOSSER WALTER G	LTC	0-0247107	0667
GOZA PASCHAL C	CPT	0-0932588	0667
GRAHAM LAROY S	COL	0-0015053	0167
GRANDY LLOYD H	COL	0-0208481	1266
GRASSMYER ANNA M	MAJ	N-0000017	0667
GRAYBILL WALTER R	MAJ	0-1183299	0567
GREEN THOMAS A	CW2	W-2118019	
GREENBERG ABRAHAM	CPT	0-0311802	0567
GREENE CARROLL L III	MAJ	0-1647051	0467
GREENFIELD HORACE C	LTC	0-0136715	
GREGORY THOMAS O	CPT	0-1924562	1266
GRICE CLARENCE F	CW2	W-0901500	0367
GRIFFIN ROY	MAJ	0-1103665	0567
GRIFFITH LUCIAN S	MAJ	0-0493318	0367
GRIFFITH ROBERT C	MAJ	0-0240147	
GRIFFITHS DAVID W	COL	0-0012040	0267
GRIMES JOHN J	MAJ	0-0509634	0567
GRINDLE WADE L	COL	0-0123762	0267
GRINDOL JAMES W	MAJ	0-0257157	0567
GRINNELL CARROLL J	COL	0-0171802	0467
GRITTON WESLEY J	COL	0-0225542	0867
GROTH BERNHARD J	MAJ	0-0188027	0267
GROVER CHESTER A	LTC	0-0172565	0667
GUBSCH CHARLES	CW2	W-0901406	0767
GUILD WILLIAM P JR	CPT	0-1062373	0467
GUILLEMET ERNEST A	LTC	0-0007965	
GULLEY JOHN B	LTC	0-1796268	0367
GUNBY THOMAS S	COL	0-0011395	0167
GUNN WILLIAM D	CW3	W-2141766	0367
GURNEY AUGUSTUS M	B G	0-0005239	0467
GUTENSOHN ALVIN C	LTC	0-0002269	0467
GUYETTE RAYMOND A	MAJ	0-1924129	
GWILLIM THEADORE R	LTC	0-0042546	0667
GWIN WILLIAM T	MAJ	0-1574248	
HACKER JOHN E	1LT	0-1914412	
HADDOCK JOHN P	CPT	0-1180926	0567
HAFER JOSEPH B	COL	0-0009810	
HAGAN RALPH G	LTC	0-0344519	0867
HAGEMANN H J SR	CW2	W-2147317	0267
HAGOOD LEE	1LT	0-0014321	0867
HAJJAR SOLOMON G	CPT	0-0328865	1266
HALEY JAMES H	COL	0-0011433	0867
HALEYARD RICHARD M	1LT	0-4027747	0667
HALL JOHN A	COL	0-0016173	0467
HALL VIRGIL T	CPT	0-1585548	0367
HALL WENDELL F	MAJ	0-0503112	0467
HAMILTON C R JR	MAJ	0-0178187	0267
HAMMOND THOMAS H	COL	0-0163784	0966
HAMMOND WILLIAM H	COL	0-0005211	
HAMPTON VERNON W	LTC	0-0223046	0367
HANDLEY WILLIAM	1LT	0-1914305	0467
HANDWERK MORRIS C	B G	0-0007335	0867
HANKINS HARRIET P	LTC	N-0701297	
HANKINS STANLEY H	COL	0-0051100	0367
HANNA WILLIAM C	MAJ	0-0004864	0267
HANNEY THOMAS F	CPT	0-0244826	1266
HANNON PATRICK J	MAJ	0-0484327	0467
HARDIGG CARL A	M G	0-0003460	0167
HARDIN WILLIAM C	WO1	W-2128521	1266
HARDING JOHN E	LTC	0-0031627	0267
HARKINS THOMAS A JR	CPT	0-0535401	0667
HARMON JAMES D	1LT	0-0329968	
HARMON KENNETH R	COL	0-0002842	0667
HARMON MERLE S	LTC	0-0189797	0567
HARPER GROVER L	CPT	0-1013469	
HARRINGTON FRANCIS W	MAJ	0-0114586	0667
HARRINGTON JUDSON M	1LT	0-0505897	0267
HARRIS HINMAN A	CPT	0-0337717	1166
HARRIS JOHN J	COL	0-0142100	0267
HARRIS JR TOLBERT	CPT	0-0488452	
HARROD LILLIAN W	2LT	N-0763143	1266
HARSHA JOHN A	CW4	W-2133869	1266
HART HOWARD H	COL	0-0274812	0367
HARTER GILBERT S	LTC	0-0014284	0767
HARTLEY JAMES D	LTC	0-0298848	0167
HARVEY JAMES S	LTC	0-0126767	1166
HASTEE JAMES F	1LT	0-1914424	0767
HASTINGS HARRY R	CW3	W-2101271	0166
HASTINGS WALLACE H	COL	0-0015498	0667
HATFIELD JOSEPH	1LT	0-0505759	0767
HATHAWAY GEORGE J	COL	0-0246308	0167
HAVENS ROBERT A	LTC	0-1573266	0667
HAWTHORNE HERBERT	CPT	0-0484545	0167
HAY ALEXANDER B	LTC	0-0193402	1066
HAY JAMES	LTC	0-0308568	0867
HAYCOCK GEORGE A	MAJ	0-0418252	0367
HAYES CASEY H	COL	0-0003627	
HAYES THOMAS J	M G	0-0003360	0367
HAYNEY JOHN J	2LT	0-1051172	0467
HAYS HERBERT R	LTC	0-0302267	
HAYS JOHN G	CW3	W-2208518	0667
HAYS MILES M	MAJ	0-1047158	
HAYS THOMAS L	CW2	W-2209106	0167
HAZEN VOYLE H	MAJ	0-0334011	
HEADLEY JOSEPH C	COL	0-0217084	1166
HEATH GEORGE P	CPT	0-0508758	
HEATH JOHN M	COL	0-0010490	0767
HEBERTSON THORIT C	LTC	0-0244936	1066
HEDSTROM PAUL G	LTC	0-0290732	
HEIDER EDWARD G	MAJ	0-0452742	0667
HEIM LEON V	COL	0-0247765	0667
HELSER CHARLES W JR	COL	0-0917570	1066
HEMPERGER ARTHUR J	COL	0-0020485	0267
HENDERSHOT DONALD L	CPT	0-1176666	0667
HENDRICK EDWARD W	COL	0-0186601	1266
HENDRICKS AXEL	2LT	0-1913726	0767
HENDRIX MILTON L	1LT	0-1290600	
HERNANDEZ FRANCISCO	2LT	0-0182549	0567
HEROLD HERBERT E	LTC	0-0256440	0367
HERRMANN CARL R	COL	0-0116888	
HERRMANN CHARLES S	COL	0-0332255	1266
HEWETT HOBART	M G	0-0012328	0367
HEWETT OSCAR K JR	CW4	W-2126238	0667
HEYMAN LAURENCE J	COL	0-0191420	1266
HICKEY FRANCIS X	CPT	0-0376276	
HICKS WILLIAM W	COL	0-0002407	0767
HIDY ROY D	LTC	0-0513875	0867
HILDEBRAND RICHARD D	MAJ	0-0142155	1266
HILL ARTHUR W	LTC	0-0321897	0267
HILL HOWARD R	CPT	0-0492973	0267
HILLIARD ALBERT L	2LT	0-1913737	0567
HILLS AVERY S	COL	0-0167684	
HILTON ELVIE H	LTC	0-1080377	0667
HINTON JOHN	COL	0-0012113	0667
HINZE RICHARD C	LTC	0-0246841	
HITCHCOCK WADE	CPT	0-0485718	0167
HOFFMAN IVAN G	CW4	W-2142239	1166
HOIDAHL HAROLD I	COL	0-0165108	0167
HOLBECK ELMER S	LTC	0-0105823	0367
HOLIHAN JOSEPH R	CPT	0-0499482	0667
HOLLOWELL THOMAS P	LTC	0-0256283	0567
HOLMER HANS W	COL	0-0016734	0167
HOLMES ERLE R	LTC	0-0185610	0267
HOLMES GUY H	MAJ	0-0100907	0567
HOLMES WILLIAM H	COL	0-0006713	
HOOKER WILLIAM I	MAJ	0-0969389	0867
HOOPER CHARLES J	MAJ	0-1559929	0367
HOOPER CHAUNCEY M	COL	0-0241942	1266
HOOPER EDWARD L	COL	0-0001920	0667
HOPPING HAROLD E	COL	0-0183266	0466
HOPPOUGH CLAY I	COL	0-0005653	0867
HORD OLIVER A	LTC	0-0424449	
HORNBECK STANLEY K	COL	0-0110330	1266
HORNUNG HERBERT K	LTC	0-0286271	0167
HORSFALL ELMER R	COL	0-0332211	1266
HOUBERG SIMON E	CW4	W-2107020	0367
HOUGH MILES E	LTC	0-1314638	0167
HOUGHTON WASHINGTON	CW3	W-2151906	0267
HOWARD WILLIAM H B	COL	0-0039613	0467
HOWE DAN D	LTC	0-0004774	1166
HOWELL REESE M	B G	0-0003862	0367
HOWELL WILLIS A	MAJ	0-0515832	
HUDDELL HOWARD E	LTC	0-0493345	0467
HUFFMAN DOMER J	MAJ	0-0397754	0667
HUGHES DONALD K	LTC	0-0038708	0467
HUGHES JR MARTIN	MAJ	0-0079335	
HUGHES LAWRENCE F	MAJ	0-0941962	
HUGHES SHELLY G	COL	0-0165757	
HULSLANDER CLAIR A	LTC	0-0274703	1266
HUNDLEY JOHN R	MAJ	0-0163581	
HUNT JAMES A	2LT	0-2006028	
HUNTER WILLIAM B	LTC	0-0165826	0567
HUNTSBERRY WALTER A	B G	0-0019200	
HURD LESTER W	COL	0-0104232	0567
HUSKE JOSEPH S	LTC	0-0137818	0767
HUTCHINS ALBERT G	LTC	0-1307246	0567
HUTCHINSON WILLIAM P	CPT	0-0977603	
HUTHSTEINER GEORGE E	COL	0-0005592	0667
HYDE ALONZO C	COL	0-0299134	0567
IHDE WILLIAM C	MAJ	0-0167032	1166
IKUND FRANK M	LTC	0-0296823	0267
INGALLS RAYMOND E	COL	0-0001503	1266
IRISH CULLEN W	COL	0-0210158	0767
IRVIN CLARENCE G	LTC	0-0885690	0267
IRVIN JOSEPH A	LTC	0-1637733	0467
ISEMAN JOSEPH W	COL	0-0039651	0467
JACKSON WILLIAM F	COL	0-0168996	0267
JACOBS GEORGE E	COL	0-0008114	
JACOBS HAROLD H	LTC	0-0110440	
JACOBS JESSE E	COL	0-0140684	
JACOBS MARK L	MAJ	0-0102429	0167
JACOBY FRED C	MAJ	0-1594915	
JACQUES WILLIAM H	MAJ	0-0166532	0966
JAEGER FRED H	LTC	0-0345310	1166
JAEGER GARFIELD C	CPT	0-0361172	0267
JAFFARIAN JOHN R	MAJ	0-1691373	0167
JAMES HENRY C	2LT	0-0164865	0767
JAMES RICHARD K	LTC	0-0305849	0267
JEFFERSON ROBERT M	MAJ	0-0924680	
JEFFERY VOGEL J	CPT	0-0261375	
JENIGEN WALTER A	MAJ	0-1295377	1066
JENKINS GRANT V	LTC	0-0169980	0667
JENNER JOHN F	MAJ	0-1577373	
JENSEN JENS P	COL	0-0154353	0767
JEZEK JAMES J	2LT	0-1319955	0767
JOHNS THOMAS M	CPT	0-0107570	1066
JOHNSON CHARLES R	MAJ	0-1913746	0267
JOHNSON CLARENCE T	LTC	0-0113531	
JOHNSON GUY H	MAJ	0-1548863	
JOHNSON HENRY C	LTC	0-0101129	
JOHNSON HERBERT L	LTC	0-0100701	0667
JOHNSON JAMES E	LTC	0-0238601	0866
JOHNSON KARL G	MAJ	0-0224251	
JOHNSON MINNIE O	2LT	N-0731667	1066
JOHNSON VICTOR E	MAJ	0-0383984	0167
JOHNSON WILLIAM H	LTC	0-0008477	0767
JOHNSON WILLIAM T	CPT	0-0493201	1166
JOHNSTON HOWARD M	COL	0-0104320	
JOHNSTONE FREDERIC S	CPT	0-1011585	0767
JONES ALBERT M	M G	0-0003186	0567
JONES EARL W	1LT	0-1823164	
JONES EDWARD M	LTC	0-0030197	0667
JONES HARRY F JR	MAJ	0-1951693	0167
JONES HOWARD B	LTC	0-0299098	0467
JONES JOHN W	MAJ	0-1322037	0267
JONES JOSEPH W	MAJ	0-1633217	0267
JONES MARCELLUS E	LTC	0-0325851	0367
JONES MARTIN W	COL	0-0166908	0567
JONES MYRL F	CPT	0-1913741	
JONES PAUL H	COL	0-0252776	
JONES RICHARD H	CPT	0-0925318	0867
JONES WILLIAM M	LTC	0-0171979	0167
JORDAN MARVIN A	COL	0-0451129	
JORDAN RUSSELL A	LTC	0-0144763	1266
JORGENSEN ALBERT J	1LT	0-1166751	0467
JOSEPHSON FRED	COL	0-0368477	
JOSSELSON FRANK I	COL	0-0199175	1266
JUDKINS FRANCIS E	LTC	0-0230001	0667
KABEISEMAN OTTO C	MAJ	0-0268674	
KANE FRANCIS B	COL	0-0014922	0367
KANE PAUL J	CPT	0-0533345	
KARESH IRVIN R	1LT	0-1554571	0561
KARKOFF HARRY B	MAJ	0-0108817	1166
KASH EARL C	1LT	0-1053666	1166
KEELER FREDERICK	LTC	0-0015787	
KEIPER FRANK	LTC	0-0280206	
KELLER DWIGHT W	LTC	0-0905980	0367
KELLEY WILLIAM R	LTC	0-0114066	0167
KELLOGG JOHN F JR	COL	0-0063703	0467
KELLY LEW F	2LT	0-0108056	1066
KELLY MARY P	1LT	N-0700153	1266
KELLY PATRICK H	CW2	W-2205980	
KEMP EARNEST	COL	0-0041469	0467
KEMP HARRY	CPT	0-0192855	
KEMPER WILMER G	COL	0-0344299	0567
KEMPSTER GEORGE L	CW3	W-2146817	
KENNEDY EDWIN M	COL	0-0197632	0167
KENNEDY JOHN E	LTC	0-0240215	0167
KENNEDY JOHN J	WO1	W-2006707	0667
KENNEDY JOHN P JR	COL	0-0015008	0267
KERTZMAN JACOB	MAJ	0-1689568	0667
KEYES GEOFFREY	LTG	0-0003561	
KIECHEL DOANE F	COL	0-0028810	
KIELBASINSKI S J	CPT	0-0535303	0167
KIMBALL EDWARD A	COL	0-0010377	0167
KIMM KATHRYN B	1LT	N-0777605	0467
KING BEN E	LTC	0-0275671	1266
KING GEORGE L JR	COL	0-0230771	0467
KING GEORGE R	MAJ	0-0229755	0367
KING HARRY L	LTC	0-0131530	1266
KING REUBEN R JR	CPT	0-1645718	0367
KING ROBERT F	CW4	W-2101931	0367
KIRKELIE RAYMOND C	WO1	W-2106041	0567
KIRKLAND JOSEPH B	CPT	0-0179875	0667
KIRLEY ARTHUR T	LTC	0-0028975	0767
KLEINSCHMIDT W M	WO1	W-2104734	0367
KLEMME CARL J	CPT	0-0167660	
KLINGLER ALBERT G	WO1	W-0901510	0167
KNIGHT ALFRED S	COL	0-0006111	0267
KNIGHT HARRY	COL	0-0010104	0667
KOBY EMIL J	CW2	W-2124488	0667
KOCHLI FRED E	CPT		
KOENIG GEORGE A	COL	0-0134953	0467
KOENIG GLENN L	LTC	0-1312019	1266
KOERKE JAMES C	LTC	0-2169797	0667
KOHL HARVEY R	CPT	0-1553117	0567
KONIETZKO F W 2ND	CPT	0-0140398	0367
KOZLOWSKI STANLEY F	MAJ	0-1032809	0767
KRAFT JAMES R	COL	0-0015800	0267
KRATZKE ATREUS H	LTC	0-0147463	0367

LOSSES TO THE RETIRED LIST

NAME	GRADE	SVC NO	DATE LOSS MO YR
KRCHNAUT ELSIE	MAJ	N-0002188	
KREINER RICHARD E	MAJ	0-0078925	0667
KRINER FREDERICK	LTC	0-1011537	
KRUEGER WALTER	GEN	0-0001531	0867
KRUPP CAVID D	MAJ	0-0137014	0867
KUBISTAL LYDIA H T	MAJ	N-0730670	0667
KUCHER PAUL C	COL	0-0191407	1166
KUHLMAN HOWARD J	2LT	0-0887620	0467
KULAKOWSKI EDWARD W	2LT	0-2009625	0767
KUPFER ALBIN K	MAJ	0-0004931	
LA FLEUR LEILAN G	LTC	0-0267093	
LA GARDE RICHARD C	COL	0-0013858	0267
LADD ROLLA V	COL	0-0006326	0167
LADENSOHN SAMUEL H	COL	0-0131692	0367
LAFAY WILLIAM J	1LT	0-1583246	1266
LAIL WILLIAM F	LTC	0-0335832	
LAMBERT CLARENCE J	LTC	0-0119623	
LAMBIE JOHNS JR	COL	0-0179420	0667
LAMMONS FRANK R	COL	0-0007870	0267
LANCE OLES E	MAJ	0-1100633	1166
LANDRETH EARL	COL	0-0003754	0167
LANDRUM EUGENE M	M G	0-0004570	0767
LANDRY JOHN H	COL	0-0219689	0667
LANDY LESTER	1LT	0-1319063	1166
LANG JOHN W	B G	0-0002253	
LAPAN HAROLD H	MAJ	0-1548904	0167
LARNED PAUL A	MAJ	0-0013928	0167
LARSON MARVEN L	1LT	0-2000794	0567
LARSON MARVIN O	LTC	0-0283472	1066
LARSON ROAL C	CPT	0-0323170	0466
LATER ATHOL E	LTC	0-0117642	
LATTIMORE WALTER C	COL	0-0005772	0867
LAVINE JOSEPH	CW3	W-0906854	0466
LAWRENCE WALTER T	LTC	0-0371597	0567
LAWSON HAGAR L	LTC	0-0559517	
LEACH FRANCIS W	COL	0-0264145	
LEARMAN BIRDSEY L	COL	0-0021324	0667
LEE ALLEN W	MAJ	0-1798745	0267
LEE HELLEN R	1LT	N-0755575	0267
LEE VERNON E	CW3	W-2147010	
LEHMAN DORRANCE R	MAJ	0-1913767	0467
LEICHLITER JOHN W	COL	0-0313516	
LELAND RICHARD M JR	LTC	0-0222826	0767
LEONARD WARREN H	LTC	0-0189585	0866
LESSARD WILFRED E JR	COL	0-0232542	0567
LEVESQUE PIERRE H	MAJ	0-0009845	0667
LEVINE MAX	COL	0-0119570	0767
LEWENSTEIN HOWARD	MAJ	0-1939135	0667
LEWIS CHARLES A	COL	0-0002134	
LEWIS GEORGE K	COL	0-0253703	0167
LEWIS RUEL H	LTC	0-1691457	0267
LIBSTAFF ELMER W	MAJ	0-0925524	1066
LIGON JAMES E	COL	0-0339407	0667
LILLIESTROM GEORGE H	CPT	0-0164152	0567
LINDGREN OSCAR S	MAJ	0-0162877	0467
LINDSEY ROBERT L	CPT	0-0503658	0667
LINFOOT BENJAMIN	LTC	0-0255724	0167
LINTHICUM WILLIAM H	MAJ	0-2103118	0467
LIPINSKY JOHN	1LT	0-1541003	0867
LIPTON LOUIS	LTC	0-0233159	1166
LIVENGOOD JOHN A	LTC	0-0169792	
LLOYD HIRAM D	COL	0-0197811	
LOCKIE DAVID S	COL	0-1280849	0367
LOGAN EDWARD C	CW3	W-2120672	0667
LOGSDON FRANK D	MAJ	0-0171800	0767
LOMBARD BLAKE	LTC	0-0204941	
LONGFELLOW EBEN S	LTC	0-0232032	1266
LOONEY JR ROBERT H	COL	0-0021726	
LOUGHRAN CYRIL J	LTC	0-0268572	1266
LOVELAND RALPH A	M G	0-0186778	1266
LOWRY HOWARD J	COL	0-0193797	
LUCAS CLINTON M	COL	0-0005693	0367
LUDWIG EDWARD W	LTC	0-0302107	
LYON EDWARD C	COL	0-0135714	0466
MABY ROBERT L	COL	0-0136400	0567
MAC ARTHUR ROGER A	COL	0-0241163	
MAC DONALD JOHN K	COL	0-0265687	0267
MAC GARRIGLE GEORG	CPT	0-0265016	1166
MAC KECHNIE A R	COL	0-0006566	0867
MAC KIE ROBB S	COL	0-0005784	1266
MAC PHERSON JOHN D	CW2	W-2142174	
MACHESNEY HAINES A	LTC	0-0178975	0767
MACHUTA STEPHEN J	CW4	W-0903469	1266
MACK STANLEY L	COL	0-0128453	0867
MADEIRA CRAWFORD C	LTC	0-0178592	0167
MADIGAN FRANK T	LTC	0-0010128	0967
MAEBERT F WALTER	2LT	0-1596410	1266
MAHNKE FRED J	CPT	0-0234565	0167
MAHONY MICHAEL J	LTC	0-0261064	
MALONEY EDWARD J	COL	0-0007637	
MANGER MAX	CPT	0-1289933	
MANGOLD LAURENCE B	MAJ	0-0188287	
MANSHIP ELLIS A	MAJ	0-0196817	0567
MAPLE GUY F	COL	0-0447555	0167
MARAIST CLARENCE O	1LT	0-0385281	0167
MARBLE WILEY H	MAJ	0-0168536	0767
MARCH FRANCIS A	B G	0-0012138	
MARLOWE LEONARD E	LTC	0-0489007	0867
MARSH HADLEIGH	MAJ	0-0133229	
MARSH JOHN R	COL	0-0100495	0367
MARSHALL ROBERT P	COL	0-0138555	0667
MARTENS CLARENCE H	1LT	0-1015592	
MARTIN CARL	MAJ	0-2262904	0767
MARTIN EDWARD	M G	0-0147122	0367
MARTIN FRANCIS F	LTC	0-0411628	
MARTIN FRED H	LTC	0-0304986	0767
MARTIN LARKIN D	LTC	0-1284174	0167
MARTIN ROBERT J	COL	0-0029412	0467
MARTIN WILLIAM F	LTC	0-0428085	0167
MARTYN CHARLES JR	CPT	0-0364727	1166
MASON HENRY R	CPT	0-0497843	0467
MATHESCA ELLMORE H	CW4	W-2112010	0167
MAXWELL HUSTON E	LTC	0-0322468	
MAXWELL WILLIAM J	MAJ	0-0238077	0667
MAY CHARLES C JR	LTC	0-0391283	0767
MAYS SAMUEL E	COL	0-0017783	0267
MC ARTHUR ROBERT	CPT	0-0887888	
MC CAIN JOSEPH C	COL	0-0277719	0267
MC CALLUM DWIGHT M	COL	0-0243306	1266
MC CAMPBELL CHARLES	MAJ	0-0235127	0467
MC CARNES HENRY W	MAJ	0-1291858	
MC CARTHY JOHN R	LTC	0-1585848	0667
MC CARTY JAMES H	CW4	W-2107144	0667
MC CASKEY DONALD O	COL	0-0011824	
MC CLAIN RUSSELL	LTC	0-0518593	0667
MC CLELLAN CATHERINE	LTC	L-0403009	0567
MC COLLOM GEORGE E	1LT	0-0262949	0766
MC CONNELL WILLIAM B	CPT	0-0334023	
MC CORMACK ALPHONSUS	MAJ	0-0130536	
MC CORMICK JOHN P	1LT	0-0374356	
MC CREARY FRANK O	LTC	0-0058747	0267
MC CULLOUGH HUBERT L	COL	0-0255650	0667
MC CUTCHEN GEORGE T	LTC	0-0481673	
MC DANIEL BRUCE W	LTC	0-0113518	1166
MC DONALD FLORIN L	COL	0-0249722	0367
MC DONALD FLOYD H	MAJ	0-0144029	0167
MC DONOUGH JAMES E	CW2	W-2102069	0867
MC DOWELL GEORGE E	CW4	W-0903507	0367
MC GARRY DONALD E	CPT	0-1301342	0267
MC GINLEY JAMES M	LTC	0-0152406	1166
MC GOWAN DONALD W	M G	0-0179512	
MC GRATH JAMES A	LTC	0-0002685	0667
MC GUIRE MAURICE J	LTC	0-0005148	0567
MC ILWAINE FRED W	1LT	0-1309294	1266
MC INTOSH LAURENCE O	COL	0-0175880	0967
MC KAMY JAMES K	1LT	0-0490059	0966
MC KEE SAMUEL JR	COL	0-0136159	0667
MC KEE WILLIAM M	COL	0-0145615	0267
MC KIE ALVA P	COL	0-0004066	
MC KIM W ROY	LTC	0-1544042	
MC KINLEY WILLIAM G	MAJ	0-0167558	0467
MC KINNEY JAMES M	1LT	0-0335816	0267
MC KNIGHT HAROLD C	MAJ	0-0500704	0767
MC LAUGHLIN JOHN C	M G	0-0221264	0467
MC MAHON EDWARD O	LTC	0-0237208	0267
MC MAHON FRANCIS M	CW3	W-2148659	
MC MILLEN JUNE C	COL	0-0114164	0567
MC MONIGLE CARBY	CPT	0-0494489	1266
MC MURRER JAMES F	COL	0-0158573	1166
MC MURRY JESSE N	CW3	W-2143565	0767
MC NAMEE JOSEPH	MAJ	0-0131716	0966
MC NEILL DANIEL A	CPT	0-0122505	0966
MC OWEN WILLIAM C	LTC	0-0166883	0267
MC SWEEN JOHN C	LTC	0-0116329	0667
MC WHORTER FONVILLE	COL	0-0118774	0767
MEAD JOHN W	COL	0-0169485	
MEDECKE CHARLES A	1LT	0-1177526	0467
MEHLDAW HENRY A	CPT	0-1690226	1166
MELVILLE ALBERT C	CPT	0-0121667	
MENDONSA ARTHUR A	MAJ	0-0129936	0567
MENKENS LAWRENCE M	MAJ	0-1333994	
MERCHANT ROBERT S	LTC	0-0195253	1266
MEROTH JOHN A	LTC	0-1590042	0767
MERRICK JOSEPH B	CPT	0-1310286	0566
MERRITT HERBERT L	LTC	0-0010538	0467
MERVIN JOHN J	1LT	0-0492445	0167
MEYER AUGUST H	LTC	0-0195827	
MIKKELSEN WILLIAM H	COL	0-0018844	
MILAN EDWARD F	MAJ	0-0534239	0367
MILES DAVID B	MAJ	0-0221856	1166
MILES HOPE C	LTC	0-0266533	0167
MILES LOUIS S	LTC	0-0281141	
MILLER CHARLES S	COL	0-0009100	0867
MILLER CLIFFORD A	LTC	0-0163719	1166
MILLER CLIFFORD L	COL	0-0004376	0667
MILLER DONALD B	LTC	0-0996294	0267
MILLER ESTON D	CPT	0-1796130	
MILLER GEORGE H	LTC	0-0183872	0667
MILLER HARRY R	2LT	0-1013341	1166
MILLER HORACE M	LTC	0-0208818	0167
MILLER HUBERT V	1LT	0-1292735	
MILLER OLIVER C	2LT	0-1914206	0367
MILLER WILBUR A	MAJ	0-0335616	0267
MILLETT FRANK A	LTC	0-0163332	1066
MILSTEAD EARL L	LTC	0-0411345	
MINICK JOHN H	2LT	0-0254352	0467
MINKLER EDWARD	CPT	0-0257526	1166
MITCHELL CHESTER R	MAJ	0-0117973	0867
MITCHELL EDWIN F	CPT	0-0181781	0667
MITCHELL GEORGE W	CPT	0-0190817	0367
MITCHELL JOHN E JR	COL	0-0052328	1266
MITZLAFF WILLIAM R	MAJ	0-0224901	
MOE GUILFORD	LTC	0-0212061	0167
MOINEAU HECTOR A	MAJ	0-0241249	1266
MONAHAN PHILIP A	CPT	0-0265787	0267
MOODY WILLIAM R	CPT	0-0520019	
MOORE CHARLES A	CW3	W-2145158	
MOORE JAMES C	CW2	W-0901361	
MOORE JOHN T	COL	0-0103513	
MOORE MERLE G	CPT	0-1945648	0167
MOORE NORMAN A	COL	0-0029370	
MOORE SAMUEL G	2LT	0-1296463	
MOREY FRANCIS W	CW2	W-2110542	
MORGAN ALAN S	COL	0-0237534	
MORGAN DAVID T	MAJ	0-1040401	0667
MORGAN JACK A	LTC	0-0254932	0767
MORIARTY MURL M	CW4	W-0904169	0267
MORIS ALFRED	CPT	0-0510672	
MORLEY HOWARD P	LTC	0-0143658	0367
MORNINGSTAR ALAN M	COL	0-1575479	0667
MORONEY THOMAS J	COL	0-0101864	
MORONEY WILLIAM J	COL	0-0012473	0567
MORRILL GEORGE W	COL	0-0202642	0567
MORRIS ALFRED A	MAJ	0-0167040	0167
MORRIS GEORGE L	COL	0-0230047	
MORRIS SAMUEL B	LTC	0-1037641	0267
MORRISON GEORGE R	1LT	0-1183732	0567
MORRISON WILLIAM L	LTC	0-0005910	0567
MOSELEY LASSE O	MAJ	0-0328159	0262
MOSHER ELMER R	CPT	0-1642412	0667
MOTHNER JULIUS R	LTC	0-1945218	
MOUSSET ARTHUR	CPT	0-1060221	0567
MUELLER EDGAR C	LTC	0-1101573	0267
MULL EMERSON E	MAJ	0-0108440	0167
MULLER ELLSWORTH W	MAJ	0-0198345	0167
MULLINS WALTER R	CPT	0-0129720	
MUNCIE JAMES F	MAJ	0-0472651	1166
MUNDAY CHARLES V	CPT	0-0109862	0567
MUNGOVAN WALTER R	COL	0-0206753	0267
MUNSON EDWARD L JR	B G	0-0016503	0667
MUNSON F GRANVILLE	COL	0-0003324	0267
MURPHY EDWARD J	LTC	0-1845477	1166
MURPHY JESSE J	2LT	Z-0000633	0766
MURPHY JOHN L	MAJ	0-0007131	0567
MURPHY JOSEPH A	CW3	W-2143590	0567
MURRAY JAMES F	CPT	0-0241503	0167
MYER WILLIAM M	1LT	0-1105055	0467
MYERS ELMER W	COL	0-0343545	1066
MYERS HAROLD J	LTC	0-0192043	0567
MYERS LESTER J	COL	0-0208433	1167
MYERS SMITH L	LTC	0-0197568	0167
NEF PATRICK J	COL	0-0114954	0167
NEFF GILES J	CW2	W-2150251	0367
NELSEN NORMAN M	COL	0-0007616	0367
NELSON ELZIE R	CW4	W-0907115	0667
NELSON HOWARD M	LTC	0-0182610	1166
NELSON JOHN R	MAJ	0-0104496	1266
NELSON OTIS E	MAJ	0-0143401	
NELSON SVEND A	1LT	0-1301193	
NEMETH JULIUS R	1LT	0-0558297	1266
NESTOR JAMES F	COL	0-0135552	0267
NESVIG LARS C	CPT	0-1301522	0667
NETTLETON HERBERT S	1LT	0-0011785	
NEWCOMER FRANCIS K	B G	0-0003529	0867
NEWMAN CARL T F	MAJ	0-0171834	
NEWTON CHERUBUSCO JR	COL	0-0003133	0867
NEWTON JOHN C	COL	0-0008319	0867
NICHOL WALTER F	LTC	0-0255594	
NICHOLAS WILBUR E	MAJ	0-1292928	
NICHOLS ALBERT C	CW2	W-2121389	1266
NICHOLSON SAMUEL E	COL	0-0338313	0567
NICKEL WALTER H	COL	0-0163564	0967
NIERLICH FRANZ G	CW2	W-0901010	0167
NILSON KAROLINE F	2LT	N-0700511	0267
NORRIS JOHNNIE J	1LT	0-1288943	
NORRIS MELVIN C	LTC	0-0475959	0367
NORTHCUTT MURL C	CPT	0-1548990	0367
NOVAK JOSEPH F	CPT	0-1589411	
NOYER FREDERICK K	MAJ	0-0373929	1266
NULL RUTH H	MAJ	N-0799583	0567
OAKLEY PARKER L	LTC	0-0364783	0267
OBRIEN WALTER P	COL	0-0006413	1166
OBROWSKY FREDRICK W	MAJ	0-0271501	0167
OCONNELL EDWARD P	CPT	0-0004408	1266
ODELL SANTFORD C	1LT	0-0497524	0367
OHEARN JOHN J	1LT	0-1513893	0167
OLDAKER LYNN E	CPT	0-0209298	0167
OLIN JOHN F	MAJ	0-0358424	0667
OLIVER NEIL	CPT	0-1328736	1166
OLNESS BERNHARD	LTC	0-0340800	
OLTON WILLIAM H	CW3	W-2146577	0267
ONEAL CARL F	MAJ	0-1946826	0167
ONEAL CHARLES O	COL	0-0175063	0467
ONEAL THOMAS G	MAJ	0-0261564	0467
ONOSHKE GEORGE P	MAJ	0-1287051	0767
ORDWAY GODWIN JR	COL	0-0016208	1166
OREHEK FRANK T	COL	0-1533163	0467
OREILLY JOHN J	COL	0-0189564	0467
ORR ROBERT L	MAJ	0-0504359	0567
OSBORNE THOMAS O	COL	0-0002035	0467

NAME	GRADE	SVC NO	DATE LOSS MO YR
OSGOOD WARREN L	CPT	0-0179956	0767
OSTROW IRVING	CPT	0-0482264	0567
OSULLIVAN CURTIS D	M G	0-0113537	0667
OTTERBEIN FRED F	CPT	0-1317814	
OTTIS JOHN C	1LT	0-1322076	1165
OWEN ALVIN W	LTC	0-0102325	0567
OWEN WILLIAM M	CPT	0-1171305	0567
OWNBEY JOHN B	CPT	0-0425664	
PACANO ALFRED J	1LT	0-1544802	0966
PAGE JOHN R	CPT	0-0475781	1166
PAGE JOSEPH H	LTC	0-0215233	0667
PAGE LEWIS A	COL	0-0007209	0367
PAGE THOMAS M	LTC	0-0008715	0567
PAIGHT CATHERINE E	1LT	N-0798920	1066
PAINE WILLIAM H	COL	0-0013479	
PALMER PRESCOTT W	CPT	0-0478116	1166
PALMER ROBERT E	LTC	0-1040056	0567
PAOLOZZI THOMAS	LTC	0-0441123	0267
PAPE WESLEY F	COL	0-0200907	0867
PARHAM KENNON W	LTC	0-0120223	0567
PARKER EDWARD	MAJ	0-0255947	0367
PARKER JASPER R	LTC	0-0260381	0267
PARKER WILLIAM H	LTC	0-0962184	0667
PARMENTIER MARCEAU R	LTC	0-0525593	1266
PATCH JOSEPH D	M G	0-0003126	1166
PATERAS PANAGOSE F	WO1	W-2131103	0767
PATRICK JR GLENN A	CPT	0-1285289	
PATRICK MELTON H	CPT	0-0486918	1266
PATTERSON BAYARD R	CPT	0-0162297	1266
PATTERSON RICHARD C	COL	0-0106489	0966
PATTERSON WILLIAM	CPT	0-1313789	1266
PATTON OMAR P	CPT	0-0121927	0667
PAULEY PETER	CPT	0-0127955	0667
PAULSEN WARREN E	1LT	0-1317664	1166
PAULSON ROY L	LTC	0-1596805	1266
PEARCE JESSE S	COL	0-0171053	0267
PEARCE WILLIAM C	CPT	0-0487833	0867
PEASE CHARLES W	LTC	0-0124300	
PEED CHARLES T	2LT	0-0231447	0167
PEELE EDWARD W	1LT	0-1582037	0667
PELTON CHARLES H	CPT	0-0105176	0567
PEMBERTON RICHARD L	CPT	0-1913891	0367
PENNIMAN GLENN G	LTC	0-0260100	0767
PERKINS EDGAR Y	CPT	0-0165761	0167
PERLEY REUBEN N	COL	0-0003142	1266
PERLMAN SAMUEL	MAJ	0-0246740	1066
PERRY CHARLES F JR	COL	0-0242292	0267
PERSON JAMES A	COL	0-0175479	0867
PETERS RONALD H	LTC	0-0174235	0267
PETERSEN FRED C	MAJ	0-0198822	0467
PETERSON FRITZ A	B G	0-0123014	0167
PETERSON WILLIAM F	CPT	0-0496975	0367
PETRIE CLEE H	LTC	0-0338925	0267
PEVEY JAMES E	LTC	0-0336507	0167
PEYTON PAUL P	CPT	0-0497745	
PFEIFER FRANCIS F	LTC	0-2044967	
PHELPS PHYLLIS A	1LT	N-0743473	0167
PHILLIPS MATTHEW D	LTC	0-0177472	0167
PIASECKI PETER F	COL	0-0181551	0767
PIERCE RAYMOND C	MAJ	0-0200815	
PIGNATARO JOSEPH A	MAJ	0-1636476	0167
PINNEY JAMES F	LTC	0-0042506	0467
PIRTLE JAMES J	COL	0-0007624	0767
POLAND EUSTIS L	COL	0-0004565	0467
POLLOCK CHARLES A	MAJ	0-0953893	0267
POND LEON D	COL	0-0042412	0467
POOS EDGAR F	LTC	0-0115552	
PORTER LESLIE S	LTC	0-0171523	0567
PORTER OTIS	COL	0-0004868	0167
PORTER ROGERS	WO1	W-2123429	0767
PORTS ROBERT A	COL	0-0018175	0467
POST THEODORE J	COL	0-0056787	1266
POTTER HAROLD F	COL	0-0008043	
POVALL ALLIE S	LTC	0-0325206	0667
POWER GEORGE W	COL	0-0260206	0567

NAME	GRADE	SVC NO	DATE LOSS MO YR
POWERS JOSHUA D	LTC	0-0005345	1166
PRATT BERTRAM P	1LT	0-1894764	
PRATT FRANK C	LTC	0-0246874	1266
PRICE ERNEST E	MAJ	0-0201280	0367
PRICE HENKEL H	CPT	0-0365166	1166
PRICE REESE L	CW4	W-2104803	0467
PRITCHARD WILLIAM S	COL	0-0102782	0267
PRITCHETT ROBERT G	CPT	0-0074816	0467
PRODIGO EUSEBIO	2LT	0-1896598	0567
PROFETA NICHOLAS J	CW3	W-2141419	0667
PROFFITT WILLIAM F	COL	0-0171394	0567
PRZEWLOCKI BERNARD S	MAJ	0-1171315	0667
PURCELL JOHN C	LTC	0-0924069	
PUSHKIN FRANK S	CW2	W-2113950	
PUTTER BENJAMIN B	MAJ	0-0189843	
PYLES WILLIAM H	LTC	0-0323703	0467
QUICKE JUANITA C	MAJ	L-1010105	1266
RAMIREZ LISANDRO	COL	0-0153802	
RAMSEY EDWARD L	COL	0-0183259	
RAMSEY THEODORE C	CW2	W-2120055	0167
RANDALL JOHN N	1LT	0-0109875	0867
RANDALL WILLIAM V	MAJ	0-0009167	0567
RANSOM GUY C	MAJ	0-0910606	1066
RAUCH HAROLD E	WO1	W-2129920	0267
RAY CHARLES C	LTC	0-0365421	
RAY HARLEN C	LTC	0-0253037	0567
READING CHARLES M	COL	0-0208282	1266
READLE HOWARD J	CPT	0-0910557	0267
REED FRANK E	B G	0-0234982	0267
REES CHESTER A	LTC	0-0302437	0367
REEVE ORSON L	MAJ	0-0557063	0567
REEVES LEWIS A	COL	0-0244583	1166
REID DALTON L	MAJ	0-0216757	0367
REID HOWARD S	LTC	0-0289869	0167
REILLY HARVARD J	CPT	0-0110347	0467
REILLY THOMAS F	CW2	W-2147359	0867
REINERS JOHN T	LTC	0-0180098	1266
REISS JACK	LTC	0-0322350	1266
REITER FRANKLIN F	WO1	W-2139829	
REMINGTON HAROLD	COL	0-0137997	0767
RENN JR WALTER L	COL	0-0251696	
RENWICK AVERY W	COL	0-0443663	0367
REYNOLDS FRANCOIS	COL	0-0011848	
REYNOLDS GROVER C	LTC	0-0109722	0267
RHOADS OWEN R	COL	0-0006702	
RICE JAMES E	LTC	0-0030983	0267
RICE LEDA F	1LT	N-0727770	0167
RICHARDS EARL J	LTC	0-0486537	1066
RICHARDSON ELMER P	WO1	W-0800282	1266
RIDDLE RICHARD H	CW2	W-2148333	0866
RINGLAND FRANK G	COL	0-0004572	1266
RISCH WILLIAM V	MAJ	0-1300282	
RISTINE BEN F	COL	0-0001834	0167
RITCHIE WILLIAM M	MAJ	0-1994949	0567
RITTENBERRY CLARENCE	MAJ	0-0447376	
RIVERS RUBIN T	1LT	0-0282028	
RIVERS WILLIAM L	CPT	0-0214934	
ROACH CLOVIS J	CW2	W-2205937	0467
ROACH JOHN H	1LT	0-0103099	0267
ROBBINS ROGER S	CPT	0-0127670	0167
ROBERTS CAESAR R	COL	0-0007892	0367
ROBERTS HERBERT R	COL	0-0008035	
ROBERTSON DAN F	LTC	0-0449462	0167
ROBERTSON DONALD L	CPT	0-0498255	1066
ROBINS RAYMOND R	COL	0-0015864	0367
ROBINSON DONALD R	B G	0-0161276	0167
ROBINSON NICHOLAS J	COL	0-0016175	0367
ROCHE MARTIN A	LTC	0-0549369	0667
ROCKEL JR MICHAEL F	COL	0-0137382	
RODRIGUEZ ERNESTO	CPT	0-0452012	
ROE JOSEPH H	CPT	0-0157196	0567
ROGAN HENRY A	LTC	0-0318341	0766
ROGERS GORDON B	LTC	0-0015620	0767
ROGERS GRACE D	CPT	N-0788875	
ROGERS WILLIAM K	LTC	0-0255247	0267

NAME	GRADE	SVC NO	DATE LOSS MO YR
ROLF EMIL G	MAJ	0-0109864	1266
ROLLER MANUEL	CW4	W-2118223	0467
ROMBERGER JOSEPH A	CW3	W-2143459	
RONAY STEPHEN H	LTC	0-0915893	1166
ROPER HENRY E	COL	0-0235138	
RORICK MELVIN W	LTC	0-1018313	0167
ROSBACK LEE H	MAJ	0-0251012	0667
ROSE ARTHUR F	1LT	0-0498724	0167
ROSE EDWARD L	LTC	0-0408468	0367
ROSELAND HAROLD T	1LT	0-0462156	0267
ROSEN JACK	CW2	W-2134483	0567
ROSENBERGER ANDREW T	COL	0-0166603	1266
ROSENFELD JOHN D	LTC	0-0224184	0567
ROSNER SAMUEL	CPT	0-0493276	0267
ROSS THOMAS W	1LT	0-0014753	0667
ROTH JOHN P	LTC	0-1846350	
ROTH SYLVESTER W	LTC	0-0360983	1266
ROTHENHOEFER BYRON R	WO1	W-2103380	0567
ROZWOOD STANLEY	CW2	W-2144830	0367
RUBIN PHILIP C	1LT	0-0189421	0767
RUDSER KARL L	LTC	0-0029110	0467
RULNEY MAX	LTC	0-0309415	0367
RUMSEY HOWARD B	LTC	0-0441073	1266
RUNDELL JAMES R	COL	0-0399127	0267
RUSSELL SAM C	M G	0-0018678	1266
RUSSELL WARNER F	CPT	0-0473917	0367
RUSSOM HOLLIS E	1LT	0-1300714	0167
RYAN WILLIAM	CPT	0-0461506	0667
RYAN WILLIAM M	MAJ	0-0445468	1067
RYLES WILLIAM F	MAJ	0-0489175	0367
SACHERS GUSTAVE E	1LT	0-0163793	0767
SAGE CHARLES G	M G	0-0171863	0267
SAMREY JOHN R	COL	0-0123621	
SAMUSSON ERNEST	LTC	0-0006110	
SANDERS LEWIS	COL	0-0100024	0367
SANTIAGO CONRADO	2LT	0-0109920	0367
SATTERFIELD W P	1LT	0-1634291	
SAUNDERS CHANDLER	LTC	0-0884904	
SAUNDERS ORA E	CPT	0-0222477	
SAUVIGNE EMIL E	MAJ	0-0279702	1166
SAYLES JOHN T	LTC	0-0001333	0467
SAYRE HAROLD O	CPT	0-0443514	0467
SCANLAN HERBERT V	COL	0-0006951	0367
SCANNELL CARL O	CPT	0-0322570	0267
SCARBOROUGH HARRY M	LTC	0-0135699	
SCHAFER REMOND	COL	0-0347531	1266
SCHARFF MAURICE R	COL	0-0145141	0467
SCHELL WALTER F	CPT	0-0503041	0467
SCHELLBERG KENNETH D	COL	0-0039743	0367
SCHERER CHRISTIAN D	1LT	0-1913923	0867
SCHICK LAWRENCE E	B G	0-0012736	
SCHMIDT ROBERT	MAJ	0-0209390	0167
SCHMITT PAUL J	1LT	0-1031514	0167
SCHNEIDER FRANK V	COL	0-0003419	0367
SCHOLL TERESA E	CPT	N-0751310	0167
SCHOLTENS HENDRICK	WO1	W-0901026	1266
SCHRENK JOHN G	1LT	0-0108568	
SCHROEDER AUGUST F	COL	0-0137514	1166
SCHULTZ JUNE B	MAJ	N-0002351	0267
SCHUMACHER HAROLD	CPT	0-0471957	1266
SCHUMAKE LAWRENCE P	LTC	0-0418625	
SCHWARTZ LOUIS B	1LT	0-0411546	1066
SCHWARTZ SEYMOUR C	COL	0-0004161	0367
SCHWARZENBACH EDGAR	MAJ	0-0473550	0367
SCHWENCH JAMES C R	COL	0-0003113	0167
SCHWIND ROBERT J	LTC	0-0033900	0167
SCOTT ALLEN L	1LT	0-2044505	0167
SCOTT ARTHUR R	LTC	0-0256015	
SCOTT FRANCIS W	1LT	0-0885646	0667
SCOTT LESLIE O	COL	0-0261227	1166
SCOTT REESE V	COL	0-0321928	0567
SCOTT RICHARD F	CW3	W-2146864	0567
SCOTT ROY L	MAJ	0-0253336	0166
SCULLY EUGENE	MAJ	0-2014824	
SEELEY GEORGE W	LTC	0-0209096	

NAME	GRADE	SVC NO	DATE LOSS MO YR
SEEWALD NORMAN C	LTC	0-0242689	
SEGARD EDWIN S	LTC	0-0016368	0167
SEIDEL RICHARD H	MAJ	0-1341371	0867
SEIKEL JOHN R	1LT	0-1575149	0367
SELBY EVERETT V	LTC	0-0153770	0167
SELLAR WILLIAM C	COL	0-0346199	
SELLERS FRED M	CPT	0-0165618	0766
SEMPLE WESLEY A	MAJ	0-0444432	1266
SERREM MARK M	COL	0-0006598	0267
SERVIN OSCAR	CW2	W-2117914	0167
SEVERANCE CHESTER J	CPT	0-0295116	
SEVERIN EUGENE T	COL	0-0204200	0567
SEVERIN VIRGIL L	CPT	0-1821776	
SHACKELFORD W A	CW4	W-0903795	0567
SHANNON J VERNON	LTC	0-0198228	0167
SHAW CLIFFORD D	CPT	0-0996192	
SHEELOR KENNETH H	MAJ	0-0114734	0567
SHEPARD KENNETH J	CPT	0-0281812	0367
SHERMAN DONALD P	CPT	0-0238697	0167
SHERMAN FRANKLIN III	MAJ	0-0226481	1166
SHERMAN JAMES F	LTC	0-0202790	0567
SHERRY BERTRAM J	COL	0-0008944	
SHEVLIN JOHN T	2LT	0-1013962	
SHIER ISAAC G	MAJ	0-0299035	0467
SHIPLEY WALTER V	LTC	0-0111260	1266
SHIRA JR CLANTON C	CPT	0-0476056	
SHIRLEY CLIFTON M	MAJ	0-0480653	0567
SHIRLEY ROBERT A	LTC	0-0922045	0267
SHOBER FRED W	COL	0-0245025	0667
SHODER BARNEY	2LT	0-1579108	0167
SHOOK CHARLES F	COL	0-0009507	1166
SHOR GEORGE G	LTC	0-0137113	0667
SHORT HAROLD L	CPT	0-5301560	1166
SHORT THOMAS J	CPT	0-0322241	0267
SHORTEN DAVID B	1LT	0-1949464	0567
SHOWALTER WILBER H	1LT	0-0143894	0667
SHUGART CLEO Z	COL	0-0016618	
SHURE PAUL	CPT	0-0398846	0467
SHUTE MARTYN H	COL	0-0002145	0667
SIDLE CARL P JR	MAJ	0-1310889	0767
SIEBENHAUSEN C H	1LT	0-0158058	1266
SILKMAN JOHN M	COL	0-0007037	
SILSBY DON H	COL	0-0127530	1166
SIMONSON SIGWERT W	CPT	0-0383973	1166
SIMPSON FRANCIS P	LTC	0-0008644	0167
SIMPSON LAWRENCE L	COL	0-0008169	
SIMPSON THOMAS M JR	LTC	0-1576652	0367
SISK JOSEPH B	MAJ	0-2204030	0567
SKAGGS LELAND W	COL	0-0006049	0767
SKINNER MYRON L	COL	0-0127966	0767
SKINNER RANSOM P	1LT	0-0279274	0367
SKOGEN RALPH I	MAJ	0-1173461	
SLADE GEORGE E	COL	0-0368791	
SLATER IRVING	MAJ	0-0525266	0467
SLATER PAUL R	COL	0-0258185	
SLOAN PRESTON F	LTC	0-0123153	0766
SMALLEY HOWARD R	COL	0-0001611	0167
SMELSER RAYMOND B	CPT	0-2000058	0567
SMITH CLARENCE T	CPT	0-0915567	0667
SMITH DARWIN E	CPT	0-0229416	0667
SMITH EDWARD J	CPT	0-0125853	0367
SMITH EDWARD J	MAJ	0-1055522	0667
SMITH EDWARD M	M G	0-0129155	0554
SMITH FRANCIS F	CPT	0-0917024	
SMITH GEORGE F	LTC	0-0196110	0267
SMITH GEORGE L	COL	0-0003643	0467
SMITH JAMES R	CPT	0-0904317	0467
SMITH JOHN G	CW3	W-2115894	0667
SMITH JOSEPH S W	MAJ	0-0165897	0667
SMITH JOSEPH V	COL	0-0030030	0767
SMITH JR OWEN W	2LT	0-1313658	
SMITH MARVIN A	2LT	0-1307581	0267
SMITH PETER J	CPT	0-0502031	0167
SMITH PRESLEY A L JR	LTC	0-0113742	0567
SMITH ROBERT L	MAJ	0-1015583	

NAME	GRADE	SVC NO	DATE LOSS MO YR
SMITH TED J	CW3	W-2141448	0367
SMITH WALTER	WO1	W-0800735	1266
SMITH WILLIAM B	COL	0-0260678	1066
SMITH WILLIAM J	LTC	0-0035320	
SNOW EARL W	1LT	0-1182965	0567
SNYDER CHARLES H	LTC	0-0361223	1266
SOHN MILTON G	COL	0-0266628	
SOLON LORIN	COL	0-0190917	0367
SORLEY LEWIS S JR	COL	0-0012483	0866
SOUDER CHARLES G	COL	0-0004265	0767
SOUTER STERLING	CW3	W-2147962	
SOWERS CLAUDE F	LTC	0-0163438	
SPAHR RICHARD R	COL	0-0110985	0467
SPEARMAN WALTER D	COL	0-0030848	0567
SPERRY LANGLEY	CPT	0-0117688	1166
SPIELMAN ALAN V	CPT	0-0479052	
SPOONER LLOYD S	COL	0-0007796	1266
SPOOR WILLIAM J	CPT	0-0204530	0467
SQUIRE JOHN W	B G	0-0155858	0167
STACK HARRY G	LTC	0-0274587	0167
STACKPOLE EDWARD J	M G	0-0171837	
STACY ELINOR C	MAJ	N-0002260	0467
STAHL LOUIS J	LTC	0-0174810	
STAKES BENJAMIN F	MAJ	0-0226600	0767
STALSBURG CHARLES	COL	0-0008506	0467
STAMPER WILLIAM H	1LT	0-0109930	0167
STANFORD JOHN C	MAJ	0-0170620	0167
STANLEY WILLIAM J	CW2	W-2205482	0467
STANRIDGE JESSE J	LTC	0-0916275	0267
STARKER HENRERT H	LTC	0-0214204	0667
STECKER PAULINE L	MAJ	N-0724966	0667
STEIGER HOWARD A	LTC	0-0179207	1266
STEINLE CARL H	MAJ	0-1166189	0467
STEPHENS RICHARD L J	CPT	0-1171782	1166
STERLING WILBUR F	COL	0-0406669	1266
STEVENS CHARLES N	COL	0-0004788	0567
STEWARD MARTIN W	LTC	0-0267725	1266
STEWART ELAM L	COL	0-0011121	1266
STEWART GEORGE W	COL	0-0197928	0767
STEWART JOHN A	COL	0-0015728	1266
STEWART JR RUSSELL W	COL	0-0252048	
STEWART MAGNUS J	LTC	0-0221011	
STEWART NORMAN W	LTC	0-1100353	1266
STEWART ROBERT B	CPT	0-1308723	0467
STIGERS JAMES W	LTC	0-0023767	0267
STILES CECIL F	LTC	0-0171906	0367
STIMMEL CLARENCE C	CPT	0-0008702	1066
STINSON BATES R	1LT	0-0449742	
STINSON GLADYS C	1LT	N-0775703	0467
STOCKSTILL DALE P	LTC	0-0570410	0467
STOCKWELL FRED E	LTC	0-0141163	0767
STONER JOHN I	CPT	0-1294035	0367
STORMONT MARION F	MAJ	0-0509744	0167
STRAHL MILTON I	COL	0-0209938	0267
STRAUSPAUGH DONN P	LTC	0-0045681	0467
STRICKLAND FRANK H	CPT	0-0010003	0567
STUART JOHN T	COL	0-1002537	
STUBBS MAURICE G	COL	0-0007520	0667
STUEMPFLE JOHN G	MAJ	0-1824936	0167
STURGES CONRAD B	COL	0-0282307	
STURGES FRED W	CPT	0-1557917	0867
STURTEVANT GILBERT R	1LT	0-1173102	0667
STURTEVANT WARNER B	CPT	0-0127433	0667
STUTLER WARREN H	COL	0-0036148	
SUCKOW FRANKLIN D	CPT	0-0983129	
SUGGS NELL	MAJ	N-0700149	0767
SULLIVAN AUBREY J	CW4	W-2102442	0467
SULLIVAN KENNETH A	CW3	W-2143149	0567
SULLIVAN OWEN J	LTC	0-0510473	0767
SUMMER HARRIS N	MAJ	0-0143113	0567
SUMMERS CHARLES F	WO1	W-2115461	0467
SUND VIRGIL T	CPT	0-0489050	1066
SUNDERLAND JETT D	MAJ	0-0573522	0967
SUPP LEONARD J	CPT	0-1100787	1266
SUTHERLAND EDWIN W	COL	0-0012359	

NAME	GRADE	SVC NO	DATE LOSS MO YR
SUTHERS WILLIAM D	CPT	0-0477647	0667
SUTTON JESSE A	1LT	0-0109368	
SWANSON GEORGE F	COL	0-0235563	0367
SWARD ERICK W P	COL	0-0004537	1266
SWEDBERG EDWIN W	LTC	0-0246247	0966
SYDENHAM HAROLD G	COL	0-0012601	0167
TALCOTT HARRISON W	LTC	0-0117742	1166
TANNER SHELDON C	MAJ	0-0520685	1066
TARPEY FRANCIS J	MAJ	0-0228828	0567
TARTT JR ELNATHAN	MAJ	0-0744464	
TAYLOR IRA D L	MAJ	0-0887415	1266
TAYLOR LARUE	CPT	0-0141344	0267
TAYLOR NERRIS D	CPT	0-0123151	0667
TEEKELL MILAN J	CPT	0-1311273	1266
TEMPLETON ROBERT J	LTC	0-0161962	0467
TERRELL REED E	1LT	0-1312357	1166
TERRY GEORGE M	MAJ	0-1796377	1266
TERRY THEODORE M	MAJ	0-0186111	0467
THAYER ARTHUR P	COL	0-0004561	
THAYER JOHN F	LTC	0-0198751	0267
THAYER RALPH E	MAJ	0-0256258	0767
THIBAUT DALE V	LTC	0-0267846	1066
THIGPEN WILLIAM F	CPT	0-0247774	1266
THOMAS FREDERIC C	MAJ	0-0241803	
THOMAS HOWARD F	1LT	0-1913958	0267
THOMAS ROBERT J	CPT	0-0508799	0567
THOMPSON ASA W	CPT	0-0256789	
THOMPSON CHARLIE E	CPT	0-0492517	0567
THOMPSON DANA L	LTC	0-1111949	1166
THOMPSON JAMES S	CPT	0-0105812	
THOMPSON WILLIAM C	COL	0-0041374	1266
THORNTON HARVEY J	COL	0-0010272	
THORSON TRUMAN C	M G	0-0010264	1266
THROWELL DOUGLAS S	LTC	0-0286073	0567
THURSTON ROBERT E	MAJ	0-0341428	
TICHY VLADIMIR L	LTC	0-0281566	0467
TIEMANN EDWARD F	LTC	0-1036409	
TIERNEY JAMES H	LTC	0-0002689	1266
TILLOTSON HAROLD E	MAJ	0-1327587	0267
TIMBERLAKE TOMMY H	CW2	W-2123835	
TIMMERMAN FREDERIC H	LTC	0-0007068	1166
TISCHER THEODORE W	LTC	0-0504266	0467
TOFTOY HOLGER N	M G	0-0016422	0467
TOMLINSON RAYMOND O	2LT	0-1015692	0367
TOMPKINS ARTHUR H	CPT	0-0172398	1166
TOOMEY JOSEPH M	CPT	0-0193273	0367
TOOMEY THOMAS N	MAJ	0-0160928	0267
TORMA ANTHONY	MAJ	0-0286099	0767
TORNABENE FRANK	MAJ	0-0218898	
TOTTEN JAMES W	M G	0-0019834	0367
TOWERY JACK	CPT	0-1048597	1166
TRAMMELL CHARLES M	COL	0-0111644	0767
TRAVIS RALPH L	MAJ	0-0450771	0367
TREMAINE EDWARD G	LTC	0-0254329	
TREMAN LEONARD C	MAJ	0-0172033	
TRIBBLE DILLON O	MAJ	0-0119035	0367
TRINZ JAMES K	1LT	0-1309630	
TROWER WENDELL P	COL	0-0012061	0267
TURNER HIRAM B	COL	0-0010166	0167
TURNER JOHN J	COL	0-0011065	0467
TURNER MILDRED	LTC	N-0000174	0167
TURNLEY PERCY R	LTC	0-0384030	
TURNQUIST HERBERT E	MAJ	0-0232265	1266
TUTHILL EMMOR G	MAJ	0-0100714	0167
TWEIT ARCHIE C	LTC	0-0329859	
TWOHIG JOSEPH F	MAJ	0-0474126	0867
TYE HIRAM S	LTC	0-0060602	0267
UHRIG JACOB E	COL	0-0009001	1166
UNDERWOOD ARCHIE C	MAJ	0-0504486	0767
UPCHURCH STANLEY B	MAJ	0-1648207	0367
UPDEGRAFF RALPH K JR	CPT	0-1693534	0466
UPDIKE FURMAN H	MAJ	0-1032182	0167
VALENTINE ROBERT G	LTC	0-0037585	0267
VAN ALLER ALGERNON R	CPT	0-0108973	0667
VAN BIBBER EDWIN M	COL	0-0017789	0167

NAME	GRADE	SVC NO	DATE LOSS MO YR
VAN VLIET JOHN H	COL	0-0003559	0667
VAN VOORST MARION	B G	0-0012141	
VAUGHAN RUFUS G	CPT	0-0006472	0667
VAUGHN DALE O	CW2	W-2154870	0267
VETTER RICHARD G	MAJ	0-0235519	
VIA JAMES B	LTC	0-0025121	0167
VICKREY HENRY H	COL	0-0111038	0567
VICKROY WILLIAM F	LTC	0-1110862	0267
VINCENT STEWART T	COL	0-0015021	0867
VOGEL IRVING A	MAJ	0-0135108	0467
VONDRASEK CHARLES A	1LT	0-1797750	
VREELAND HERBERT H	B G	0-0115042	0367
WACHTELL JOSEPH B	LTC	0-0105411	1166
WADE ERNEST	LTC	0-1894953	1266
WADE HARRY H	LTC	0-0156321	
WAGENSELLEE SAMUEL M	MAJ	0-1821292	0367
WAGENSELLER SAMUEL M	MAJ	0-1821292	0367
WAGER GORDON C	1LT	0-1108355	0567
WAGGONER CLINTON A	LTC	0-0042552	
WAGNER FRANK M JR	CPT	0-1300418	0467
WAGNER HAROLD N	CPT	0-1643418	
WAGNER HAYDEN W	COL	0-0135401	0367
WAGNER SEISS E	COL	0-0018569	0667
WAINER CHARLES G	LTC	0-0468284	0467
WAINGER CHARLES K	CPT	0-0326722	0866
WALDECK VINCENT D	CPT	0-0276800	0567
WALDRON JOSEPH G JR	CW3	W-2144738	0467
WALDRON NORMAN E	B G	0-0007321	1266
WALECKA JOSEPH L	CPT	0-0011527	0367
WALENSKY EUGENE	CPT	0-1287972	1166
WALKER DEAN M	COL	0-0016712	
WALKER DONALD L	CW2	W-2148457	1266
WALKUP WILLIAM E	COL	0-0284774	
WALL JOSEPH J	MAJ	0-0225617	0467
WALLACE JACK D	CW2	W-2121019	0767
WALLACE JOHN	COL	0-0004309	0567
WALSER ERVIN A	LTC	0-0218528	1166
WALSH HARRY D SR	WO1	W-0907041	0367
WALSH JAMES J	CW2	W-2114182	
WALSH JOHN E	MAJ	0-1175349	
WALSH THOMAS P	COL	0-0008457	1266
WALTER ALFRED	MAJ	0-0167644	
WANSTREET WILLIAM J	CPT	0-0335011	
WANTLAND JOHN C	MAJ	0-1287276	0866
WARD JACOB L	LTC	0-1638745	0367
WARD RUSSELL R	COL	0-0135873	
WARD WILLIAM R	MAJ	0-1588946	
WARDINSKI GEORGE A	COL	0-0266894	
WARNER STONEWALL	LTC	0-0272217	
WARREN JAMES A	MAJ	0-0165312	1166
WARREN JAMES F	CPT	0-0516816	0267
WATSON VIRGIL V	LTC	0-0204222	1166
WATTS LAURENCE	COL	0-0002893	
WEATHERLY MARION K	CPT	0-1300557	0767
WEAVER CHARLES A	MAJ	0-0271938	
WEAVER CHARLES A	COL	0-0281589	
WEAVER JAMES R N	B G	0-0003100	0867
WEAVER RALPH P A	CW3	W-2150519	0367
WEBBER HARRY E	CPT	0-0014393	
WEBSTER GLEN A	COL	0-0041383	0167
WEINSTEIN BERNARD M	CPT	0-0295499	
WEISBROD BENJAMIN H	COL	0-0122062	1066
WEISEL GEORGE F	COL	0-0133045	
WEISHAAR HENRY T J	COL	0-0005500	1266
WELCH GEORGE M	LTC	0-0305399	0567
WELLS HARRY R	MAJ	0-0145431	1166
WELLS LUCIEN F JR	COL	0-0015832	0267
WELSCH HARRY A	COL	0-0151461	
WELTMAN WILLIAM C	LTC	0-0234943	0267
WERKMEISTER EDWIN L	MAJ	0-0153624	
WERNER LOUIS	MAJ	0-0141365	
WESNER CHARLIE	COL	0-0016842	0867
WESTLUND CARL W	LTC	0-0016302	0367
WETMORE DON O	MAJ	0-0499952	0567
WHARTON RICHARD H	CPT	0-0303050	0767

NAME	GRADE	SVC NO	DATE LOSS MO YR
WHEELER ARTHUR B	1LT	0-1587012	1166
WHEELER JOHN A	COL	0-0008741	0767
WHEELER MERRITT I	2LT	0-0155551	1266
WHINNERY KARL E	LTC	0-0139492	1166
WHITAKER REGINALD	COL	0-0009328	1166
WHITE ARCH W	CPT	0-2036721	
WHITE CALOWAY C	LTC	0-0337987	
WHITE LEROY C	1LT	0-1030625	0667
WHITE ROBERT W M	MAJ	0-0162810	0966
WHITE ROY M	CPT	0-0273138	
WHITE SAMUEL	COL	0-0007380	0667
WHITE THURMAN J	MAJ	0-1186688	
WHITENER JOSEPH B	COL	0-0180043	0767
WHITESIDES S E JR	COL	0-0012482	1266
WHITLOW JOSEPH E	LTC	0-0219386	0467
WHITMAN EDWARD B	MAJ	0-0189735	0167
WHITNEY CLIFFORD C	COL	0-0009272	0367
WHITNEY HARRIET M	LTC	N-0700406	0567
WHITTAKER LEROY A	COL	0-0009672	0367
WHITTEN HAROLD E	COL	0-0174244	0567
WHITWORTH JOHN F JR	MAJ	0-0205609	0167
WILDE GRANVILLE M	MAJ	0-1307465	0567
WILDER CECIL N	LTC	0-0173544	0367
WILDMAN RUSSELL C	1LT	0-0947676	1166
WILEY CHARLES F	LTC	0-0305388	0567
WILKE ARTHUR M	CW2	W-2210324	
WILKES HAROLD K	LTC	0-1825839	
WILLEMS NORMAN D	LTC	0-1049397	0167
WILLEY ANDREW R	LTC	0-0287784	
WILLIAMS ALSON E	LTC	0-1280037	
WILLIAMS ALVIN	1LT	0-0194006	0167
WILLIAMS CHARLES L	MAJ	0-0002306	1266
WILLIAMS GWILYM T	MAJ	0-0212686	1166
WILLIAMS HORACE G JR	MAJ	0-0451820	0267
WILLIAMS JOHN B	COL	0-0485081	0467
WILLIAMS JOSEPH B	MAJ	0-1018221	0267
WILLIAMS ROBERT K	MAJ	0-0264246	
WILLIAMS VERN D	CPT	0-0184965	0367
WILLIS HAROLD A	COL	0-0010065	0767
WILLNER ABRAHAM J	MAJ	0-0256780	
WILSKE CARL A	MAJ	0-0254940	0867
WILSON CARLISLE B	COL	0-0008663	1266
WILSON CHARLES M	COL	0-0008288	0567
WILSON EARL C	LTC	0-0510097	0767
WILSON GEORGE H	LTC	0-0268274	0467
WILSON HARRY R	MAJ	0-0105982	0667
WILSON JOHN C	LTC	0-0235061	0167
WINANT FREDERICK	CPT	0-0014399	0267
WINDREM EDWARD W	CW4	W-2006123	0167
WINN DEAN F	B G	0-0004065	0167
WINTER WILLIAM M	LTC	0-0335676	
WINTERS ROY H	LTC	0-0039580	0867
WISE ROBERT C	MAJ	0-0122160	0667
WISEMAN MERRILL R	LTC	0-0253232	0467
WITCHER CARL	COL	0-0109687	0667
WOLFE ROY L	1LT	0-2055325	0767
WOLFF ADOLPH T	2LT	0-0234717	
WOLL PAUL D	LTC	0-1340149	0467
WOOD FRANK A	LTC	0-0238943	0367
WOOD LAWRENCE G	MAJ	0-0217444	1266
WOODBURY JOHN C C	MAJ	0-0484822	0667
WOODLOCK GEORGE T	2LT	0-0207572	
WOODRUFF FRANK H	COL	0-0009472	0867
WOODRUFF WILLIAM S	COL	0-0016363	0966
WOODS HARLAND C	LTC	0-0192510	1166
WOODS HAROLD	LTC	0-0214078	1266
WORTHINGTON JACK F	MAJ	0-2012371	0567
WRIGHT CHARLES L	COL	0-0300036	1166
WRIGHT FORREST D	MAJ	0-0190637	0767
WRIGHT HAROLD R	CW2	W-2152692	0167
WRIGHT WILLARD C	LTC	0-1114016	
WROCKLOFF LAURENCE E	COL	0-0229361	0767
WYATT CLARON	MAJ	0-0476259	0767
WYERS ROBERT E	LTC	0-0244833	0467
WYLIE PAUL K	CW4	W-0907068	1266

NAME	GRADE	SVC NO	DATE LOSS MO YR
YANDELL CHARLES W	1LT	O-1909521	
YANISCH OTTO F	MAJ	O-0300923	0267
YEAKEL ROY J	CPT	O-2016204	
YEATS JOSEPH J	LTC	O-0010915	0667
YEILDING RICHARD P	MAJ	O-0024903	0367
YEC LEO G	1LT	O-1302565	1266
YORK WILLIAM J	LTC	O-0292754	0767
YOST HOWARD MC C	COL	O-0006299	1166
YOUNG FRANK A	LTC	O-0216086	0467
YOUNG FRED C	CPT	O-0471667	
YOUNG HAGBEN D	LTC	O-2055430	
YOUNG JAMES M	CPT	O-2010467	
YOUNG LAWRENCE W	B G	O-0002962	1266
YOUNG WILLIAM C	COL	O-0214294	0867
ZAFONTE CHARLES F	1LT	O-0495588	
ZANKEL MAX C	1LT	O-0351129	
ZEHRER FREDERICK A	COL	O-0041774	0667
ZIENTEK FLOYD J	1LT	O-0988508	0567
ZIVELL WILLIAM L	CPT	O-1659842	

NAME	GRADE	SVC NO	DATE LOSS MO YR

NAME	GRADE	SVC NO	DATE LOSS MO YR

NAME	GRADE	SVC NO	DATE LOSS MO YR

U. S. GOVERNMENT PRINTING OFFICE : 1968 O - 292-569